W9-CIK-200

TOTALBaseball

The Ultimate Baseball Encyclopedia

www.sportclassicbooks.com

NYACK LIBRARY
59 South Broadway
Nyack, NY 10960

Copyright © 2004 SPORT Media Publishing, Inc.

All rights reserved.
No part of this book may be reproduced or transmitted in any form or by
any means, electronic or mechanical, including photocopying, recording, or
by any information storage and retrieval system, without permission in
writing from the publisher.

Published in the United States of America by Sport Media Publishing Inc.,
Wilmington, Delaware, and simultaneously in Canada.

For information about permission to reproduce selections from this book,
please write to:

Permissions
Sport Media Publishing, Inc.,
21 Carlaw Ave.,
Toronto, Ontario, Canada, M4M 2R6
www.sportclassicbooks.com

Cover design: Paul Hodgson / pHd

Front cover photo of Barry Bonds: AP Photo/Eric Risberg
Back flap photo of Honus Wagner: The National Baseball Hall of Fame Library
Back cover photos of (clockwise from top left): Alex Rodriguez, AP/Mary Altaffer; Jackie Robinson, Ozzie Sweet;
  Nap Lajoie, The National Baseball Hall of Fame Library; Mickey Mantle, Ozzie Sweet;
  Bob Feller, The SPORT Collection

Interior design and layout: Paul Hodgson / pHd, Greg Oliver and John Pasternak

Several John Thorn essays within this volume were previously published elsewhere and are copyrighted by him as
  follows: "Our Game," 1988; "The True Father of Baseball," 1991; "The First Great Pitcher" and "Rube Waddell:
  The Peter Pan of Baseball," both 1992; and "Why Baseball," 1994.

ISBN: 1-894963-27-X

   Library of Congress Control Number: 2004101773

Printed in United States of America

Acknowledgements

The success of *Total Baseball* has always hinged on the contributions, often unheralded, of a small army of editors, researchers, fact checkers, writers, designers, production people, marketers, and administrators. This eighth edition is no different. The book you now hold would not have been possible without the colossal efforts of our dedicated colleagues.

The principal editors and contributors are credited on the front cover and in the table of contents; others may be acknowledged within the text or in the contributors section at the back of the book. The publishers wish to acknowledge the invaluable input of all these people, plus many others whose diligence behind the scenes made this book happen.

First among these is Greg Oliver, whose many and varied contributions involved everything from page layout, fact checking and photo selection to content and design strategist. He was our Lou Gehrig. No one toiled harder or with more passion, unless it was Peter Grucza. Peter worked hand in hand with statistical editor Phil Birnbaum to organize the millions of bytes of data that comprise the Player and Pitcher Registers, as well as many other statistical components of *Total Baseball*. Hundreds of hours of programming, updating, fact checking, and massaging were required before the raw numbers could be transformed into the intricate statistical registers that comprise more than 1,400 pages of this book. Peter did much of the dirty work, while Phil's detailed knowledge of baseball statistics proved invaluable and earned him our rookie-of-the year nomination.

Designer Paul Hodgson wins kudos for his outstanding dust jacket, as well as for designing the Total Baseball Gallery of color photos. Typographer John Pasternak, whose work has graced *Total Hockey*, *Total Basketball* and *Total Tennis*, expertly designed the expanded Player and Pitcher Registers, as well as the Postseason Registers. Joe O'Leary spent countless hours scanning and color correcting photographs and also assisted with data management and statistical compilation.

John Thorn, a co-founder of *Total Baseball*, is the chief editor of this volume, but that hardly does justice to his contribution. He was a principal author and strategist whose countless ideas, suggestions and quality-control initiatives guaranteed not only the editorial success of the project but also opened doors for our sales and marketing efforts. Bill Deane's editing skills and broad knowledge of baseball are evident throughout these pages. Deane, the principal liaison with *Total Baseball's* army of writers from past editions, also polished and updated several chapters himself when not helping track down an obscure fact or lending his expertise to varied editorial matters.

A tip of the hat goes to the writers, photographers and editors of the former *SPORT* magazine. *SPORT* was among the preeminent chroniclers of baseball in the quarter century after World War II, and we are delighted to reprise some of the magazine's best work in this edition.

We are also indebted to the Society for American Baseball Research. Executive Director John Zajc graciously consented to grant us access to SABR's biographical player data, while Bill Carle, chair of the Biographical Research Committee, and David Vincent ably facilitated the exchange of information. SABR member Charlie Bevis pointed us toward the late-breaking William Edward White story in the Providence Journal; we thank him, the newspaper, and the author, W. Zachary Malinowski. Many other SABR members who lent a hand are listed in the contributors section.

We wish to acknowledge a platoon of baseball statistical experts. First among these are David Smith and Tom Ruane of Retrosheet, whose contributions were varied and invaluable. Thanks also go out to David Vincent and Lyle Spatz for offering valued advise. Our gratitude is also extended to sabermetric genius Bill James for allowing us to incorporate his Win Shares into *Total Baseball*, and to Stats Inc. for facilitating the process, and to Kevin Johnson and Baseball Primer's "tangotiger," (who wishes to remain anonymous but is known to answer to Tom) who assisted in double-checking the statistical calculations in the Player Register, and to Charlie Pavitt and John Matthew IV, whose input improved the "Sabermetrics" chapter. The umpires and coaches rosters are more complete due to the efforts of Larry Gerlach and Mike Crain, while Maxwell Kates improved the executives roster. A tip of the cap to Will Lingo, Meredith Renwick, Alex Ristic, Jon Waldman, Karthik Thiagarajan and Kevin O'Leary for some vital last-minute help, and a special thanks, also to Harold Dellinger and Richard Malatzky, who helped clarify the register entries of Thomas Gorman and Ed Carfrey respectively.

For photographs we relied on multiple sources, but particular thanks to Bill Burdick of the National Baseball Hall of Fame, as well as to John Thorn, who made his own private collection available, and to Donna Habersaat who scanned the photos, as well as SPORT Media Enterprises, Inc., the proprietors of the *SPORT* collection.

For marketing and promotional advice we are grateful for the wise counsel of Wes Seeley. The office administration of Julie Leahey is also appreciated.

Total Baseball will always reflect the contributions of five individuals who were critical to its founding and development. First among these is Pete Palmer, whose statistical database, sabermetric wisdom, and genial brilliance informed every edition from the first through the seventh. David Reuther's efforts were vital to the first and second editions and those of David Pietrusza and Matt Silverman to the ones that followed. Mike Gershman was a principal editor of editions three through six.

Since 1989 an army of readers has accepted our invitation to send in corrections and suggestions. We thank them all. Given the scope of *Total Baseball* we acknowledge the inevitability of error and omission. For these, the publisher accepts full responsibility, and welcomes your emails at stats@sportmediagroup.com.

—Wayne Parrish & Jim O'Leary,
SPORTClassic Books

Table of Contents

Table of Contents

Section Five:
The Modern Game 1969-2003

Section Six: The Postseason

Section Seven: Features

Section Eight: Other Leagues

Roy Campanella and Duke Snider
The Dodger sluggers show off some of the lumber that carried them to a combined 83 home runs in 1953.

Introduction

In the 15 years since the inaugural edition of *Total Baseball*, the world has undergone an information explosion. For baseball fans the result has been not only more coverage, but a deluge of detailed information delivered through cable television, all-talk radio, wireless communication, newspapers, books, magazines and, of course, the Internet. The challenge for new editions of *Total Baseball* has been to continue to provide an experience that is deep and wide, and beyond that offered anywhere else.

Total Baseball has always been a dynamic product, with each new edition building on the previous volumes by adding new features, revising and expanding existing ones, and sometimes retiring old favorites to make way for new ones. This eighth edition is no different.

To our Player and Pitcher Registers we have added Win Shares, the revolutionary statistic developed by baseball's sabermetric genius Bill James, plus many other stats not seen in previous editions. New essays examine Barry Bonds and the "Moneyball" phenomenon, as well as assess the greatest teams and the most influential people in baseball history. We take a look at the startling discovery early this year that a former slave, William Edward White, was the first African-American to play in the major leagues, suiting up for Providence in 1879. In addition, long-time readers will be delighted that we have revived and updated several memorable essays from past editions, including: "The True Father of Baseball," "The First Great Pitcher," "The Business of Baseball," "Jackie Robinson's Signing," "Baseball and the Law," and a dramatically enhanced "Ballparks Past and Present."

What has always separated *Total Baseball* from other baseball encyclopedias is that we have endeavored to tell the history of America's pastime in stories as well as statistics. For this eighth edition, we have taken an additional giant step forward and included more than 200 classic photographs, including the *Total Baseball* Gallery, a 24-page color insert that pays tribute to the game's glorious past. Although assembled from several sources, the bulk of the photos came from the outstanding archives of the old *SPORT* magazine and the National Baseball Hall of Fame.

And speaking of *SPORT*, another exciting addition to this edition is the inclusion of 18 essays by some of America's most noted baseball writers that appeared in *SPORT* magazine during the 1940s, '50s and '60s. In addition to seven essays that examine some of the great teams in baseball history, the *SPORT* contribution includes profiles of eight Hall of Fame players from the first half of the 20th century, a piece on Chicago's famous early-century infield of Joe Tinker, Johnny Evers and Frank Chance, as well as a look at Curt Flood and Hank Aaron in the tumultuous 1970s. These 18 time capsules from *SPORT* transport the reader to earlier times with a sense of immediacy that even the best historical retrospective can't equal.

The final new element is year-by-year reviews of every season in major-league history, from 1871 through 2003. This was a mammoth undertaking that amounted to producing enough copy to fill an entire book unto itself, plus statistical overviews that comprise standings, award winners, postseason and All Star Game results, and league batting and pitching leaders across several categories.

When it first appeared, in 1989, *Total Baseball* was the most complete, most authoritative, and most informative—not to mention the biggest—baseball book ever published. It came into being because its creators saw there was nothing else like it and because its publishers had faith that fans would want such a book—a virtual baseball library in one volume. Today, despite the advent of so many alternate sources of information, that faith remains unshaken.

As usual, the book is divided into two parts. The first consists of prose features on subjects of interest to all baseball fans that were written by experts in their fields, as befits an encyclopedic reference work. The same holds true for the second part, which contains the playing and pitching registers, a year-by-year statistical summary of major league play since 1871, season and career statistical leaders, and more. The cornucopia of stats old and new of baseball's 16,003 players—for everyone from all-time leaders to cup-of-coffee nonentities—will provide days, months, and years of archaeological delight for baseball fans of all stripes.

Benefiting from the painstaking research of hundreds of friends and colleagues in the Society for American Baseball Research (SABR), we have corrected many errors and omissions in the historical record, relying not upon the numbers enshrined by tradition or official edict but upon the evidence. This book is as good as we know how to make it, but we do want to hear from you about our blunders (we know there will be some) or about your research (which may be important to subsequent editions of *Total Baseball*). We believe that history is process, not product, and our aim continues to be to attract the top minds in baseball to ensure that each new edition will be even better than the last.

The Florida Marlins, 2003
Marlins pitcher Josh Beckett is carried off the Yankee Stadium field after beating the New York Yankees 2-0 in Game 6 to win the World Series. Beckett was named Series MVP.

FAMOUS FIRSTS

2000: In the first regular season game ever played outside North America, the Chicago Cubs defeat the New York Mets 5-3 to open the season in Tokyo.

2001: Ichiro Suzuki becomes the first Japanese-born player and the first rookie to receive the most votes, 3,373,035, in fan balloting for the All-Star Game.

2002: In a 5-3 win over Texas, Shigetoshi Hasegawa and Kazuhiro Sasaki of Seattle to become the first Japanese-born tandem to earn a win and save in the same game.

2002: Al Leiter, 36, defeats the Arizona Diamondbacks to become the first pitcher in major league history to defeat all 30 teams.

2002: For the first time in history, a major league game is streamed live over the Internet when Texas plays at New York.

2003: Arturo Moreno completes his purchase of the Anaheim Angels from The Walt Disney Company to become the first member of an ethnic minority with a controlling interest in a major league team.

2003: Barry Bonds becomes the first major leaguer with 500 home runs and 500 stolen bases.

Chapter 1

Why Baseball

By John Thorn

Fundamentally, baseball is what America is not, but has longed or imagined itself to be. It is the missing piece of the puzzle, the part that makes us whole ... a fit for a fractured society. Baseball is about connecting; America is about breaking apart. America, independent and separate, is a lonely nation in which culture, class, ideology, and creed fail to unite us; baseball is the tie that binds. While the imperative for Americans has always been to forge ahead, in search of the new, baseball has always been about the past. In this land of opportunity, a man must venture forth to make his own way. Baseball is about coming home.

Yet more than anything else, America is about hope and renewal. And gloriously, so is baseball, pulsing with the mystery of the seasons and of life itself.

This great game opens a portal onto our past, both real and imagined, comforting us with intimations of immortality and primordial bliss. But it also holds up a mirror, showing us as we are. And sometimes baseball even serves as a beacon, revealing a path through the wilderness.

It is true enough that baseball is a sort of Rosetta Stone for deciphering our still revolutionary experiment in nationhood. It is no less true that baseball has realized—through individual brilliance or teamwork or racial harmony—the highest of our country's ideals. But the game's greatest gift to America has been to provide a haven *from* it—a Providential antidote to our raging, tearing, relentless progress, an evergreen field that provides rest and recreation, myths and memories, heroes and history.

"It's our game," wrote Walt Whitman, "*America's* game ... it belongs as much to our institutions, fits into them as significantly, as our Constitution's laws; is just as important in the sum total of our historic life." Baseball fits us today, and will tomorrow, in the same ways it always has, for the place of baseball in our nation's life is not different from its role in our own lives. It is a hard thing to be resolutely independent, despite all the fierce pride it permits. Baseball meets our occasional need for dependency. It is what Mother England was to us once, what our own mothers were to us before we found it necessary to fly from their embrace: the repository of sustaining legend and the wellspring of our beliefs about ourselves. Baseball is our home base, replenishing our spirits, restoring our hopes, repairing our losses and blessing us to journey anew.

Our continuing failure to form a more perfect union, to live up to our forefathers' plan, is a key to this game's enduring appeal. Healing deep rifts, or in the course of a contest papering them over, baseball has shaped and been shaped by the national character since the 1840s. It was then that advancing industry and urban migration first imbued rural life with a utopian, and by definition false, nostalgia. Idyllic America had not disappeared, for in fact it had never existed. Young bachelors who now streamed into the cities forgot the endless monotony and grinding physical labor of backwoods and farm; in their hearts they ached for their Paradise Lost,

and regained it on the Elysian Fields. In the park within the city, they could go home again.

Bat-and-ball games are not unique to America; they are depicted in Egyptian hieroglyphs and find their origins in fertility rituals, blood renewals of the earth. It may be argued that baseball itself is not uniquely American, because some English forerunners—rounders, cricket, feeder, cat ball, trap ball, prisoners' base, town ball—had been played in New England since the latter half of the seventeenth century. A game called baseball, though differing markedly from any we would recognize by that name, had been played in America as early as the Battle of Valley Forge. But the game that these United States embraced as their national pastime was none of the ones mentioned above. What rendered unique the version of baseball pioneered by the Knickerbocker Base Ball Club of New York was the state of the nation at the time of its origin.

Sport indulged in by grown men in the 1820s and 1830s—

indeed, any physical exercise taken for its own sake—brought scorn from puritanical souls and derision from men of business, who had long ago given over boyish things. Ralph Waldo Emerson wrote despairingly of the "invalid habits of this country."

Americans were blind to the virtues of play, much to the contempt of visiting Englishmen like W. E. Baxter, who wrote in *America and the Americans* that "to roll balls in a ten pin alley by gas-light or to drive a fast trotting horse in a light wagon along a very bad and dusty road, seems the Alpha and Omega of sport in the United States."

But as the lure of employment and relative leisure herded country boys into crowded cities, an outdoor movement was born. "Who in this community really takes exercise?" wrote Thomas Wentworth Higginson. "Even the mechanic confines himself to one set of muscles, the blacksmith acquires strength in his right arm, and the dancing teacher in his left leg. But the professional or business man, what muscles has he at all?" (Higginson's crusade for exercise lifted ice skating into such prominence that in the 1850s it became known as Higginson's Revival. Grassy fields were enclosed and flooded, to become skating rinks; subsequently, shrewd promoters took advantage of the spring thaw to create baseball fields for paid admission.)

The Knickerbockers were comprised of flaccid professional and business men when they began to gather for exercise at New York City's Madison Square Park in 1842. They were exhilarated by the crack of the bat and the sting of the ball and, to use Whitman's description, the "snap, go, fling" of their new American game, no less manly than its English counterpart but lightning-fast compared to cricket's languor. By 1845 the Knickerbockers had shifted their play ground across the Hudson River to the Elysian Fields of Hoboken, a landscaped retreat of picnic grounds and scenic vistas that was designed by its proprietors to relieve New Yorkers of city air and city care, and to give the urban populace a place reminiscent of the idealized farms that presumably had sent all these lads to the metropolis.

The Knickerbockers adopted fourteen playing rules in response to their new constraints of space (such as the concept of foul territory) and their quest for dignity (runners to be thrown out at base, not *at* on their way to base). On September 23, 1845, the Knickerbocker Base Ball Club was formally organized and its rules were recorded. The statistics of their games were noted in a scorebook that survives to this day. Baseball was not a game for boys anymore.

So, if one had been asked the question, "Why Baseball?" in the 1840s and 1850s, the answer would have been this: first, the novelty and excitement of play, a rebellion against Puritanism; second, the opportunity for sallow city clerks to expend surplus energy—the sort that impedes hard work at a desk—in a sylvan setting, communing with an American Eden of the mind; and third, the assertion of a binding national identity, independent of John Bull.

The era of Anglo-American amity had not yet dawned; our country's spiritual separation from the Mother Country, begun in 1776, was still in process. And nominating baseball to rival and replace cricket—for cricket was, after horse racing, the most popular sport in America—became an important step in that process. Moreover when England, seeking to maintain its supply of cotton from the American South during the Civil War, appeared overly cordial to the Confederate cause, anti-British feeling swept the North. By 1865 cricket in this country had been reduced to a diversion for a shrinking band of Anglophiles, while the New York

Game of Baseball was spreading across the landscape like dandelions, courtesy of returning veterans whose first exposure to the game might have come in a prisoner-of-war camp.

Actually, cricket was doomed in this country regardless of England's actions in the Civil War. The pace was too slow and, more importantly, the requirements for field maintenance were too fastidious for it to be played by soldiers forever on the move. What America did to cricket was what it does to all exogenous innovation—repackage it to suit its own tastes. Baseball borrowed much of cricket's nomenclature, its copious recordkeeping, its style of play and, most significantly, its emblematic relation to its nation of origin.

Many other clubs had sprung up after the Knickerbockers in 1845—the Gothams, Eagles, Mutuals, Excelsiors, Atlantics, Eckfords, and scores more. The class struggle of white collar and blue collar was played out on the field, and not surprisingly the working man won out; after the Knickerbockers' initial attempts at limiting baseball competition to men of genteel stock, it was playing ability, not social standing, that counted in baseball. The gentlemanly players of baseball's first team retreated from the field, shaking their heads in dismay at how common riffraff had perverted the "grand old game"—not even a generation old—and probably ruined it forever.

For patriotic Americans, bred to honor individualism and democracy, this was yet another reason to embrace baseball as the national game. Industrialism had already begun to create vast inequities of personal wealth and political influence unrelated to voting power. Yet Americans were slow to turn cynical; most still believed in the promise of the new world, and were gratified to find that in baseball it didn't matter whom you knew—victory went to the team that scored more runs. Just as the game had drawn a new urban America back to its pseudo-Edenic past, it now helped to carry forward, into a new and increasingly corrupt body politic, the hypothetical democratic values of a bygone age.

One of the ways in which baseball and America manifest hope for the future is to lie about the reality of the present, or at the least to engage in self-delusion. There is nothing terribly evil in this, for the lie is sometimes all that sustains the dream. Undelivered promise is, when viewed one way, the tragedy of both the nation and its pastime; viewed another, it is the measure of their souls—an uncaring nation or game would feel no compulsion to rationalize its failures.

The great exception to any equivocal view of baseball's hypocrisy must be in the matter of race, where clubs (which by their very nature include some and exclude others) systematically barred African-Americans for no reason besides plain prejudice. Black baseball teams had been formed in the early 1860s and had played against white teams just a few years later. Integrated teams were fairly common in the North in the late 1870s, and by the middle of the next decade, blacks were playing with whites at the highest levels of Organized Baseball—the minor leagues and the majors. And then there were none, for sixty years. It is baseball's shame, and the nation's.

The Knickerbockers' vaunted purity was not long for this world. Again following the trail blazed in cricket, gambling led inevitably in baseball to paid admissions, which led with equal inevitability to covert professionalism; enclosed ball fields led in turn to percentage-of-gate arrangements with leading clubs, and hence open professionalism. Game-fixing ("hippodroming") became known in the 1860s and commonplace by the '70s. Where had it all begun? With that primal organization of amateurs, the

Knickerbockers. Bowing to the reality that baseball could no longer be reserved for the upper crust, and that they would slide from the top rank of competition, the Knicks recruited Harry Wright to join them in 1858. This signaled their abandonment of gentlemanly pretense and their dedication to winning, for young Harry was a professional cricket bowler and a budding baseball genius. This was baseball's first hint of the professionalism soon to come.

The age of baseball heroes dawned in 1860 with the Brooklyn Excelsiors' peerless pitcher, Jim Creighton, a remarkable embodiment of baseball's transecting trends just prior to the Civil War. A declared amateur, he nonetheless accepted money to switch teams and thus became the game's first true professional; henceforth skilled players would never again be satisfied to contemplate a game of ball as merely a jolly field exercise to be followed by noble toasts and cornucopian banquets.

Creighton was a high-principled, unassuming youth whose gentlemanly manner and temperate habits were exemplary attributes for the promotion of baseball as a "hygienic" pastime. ("Baseball Fever—Catch It!" would never have done in the 1860s.) All the same, he changed the game forevermore not by his prowess but by cheating and getting away with it: pitching a spinning, rising ball with a then illegal snap of the wrist, masked so skillfully that no umpire could detect it. By playing within the strictures of the intricate game of baseball, Creighton gratified those Americans who revered the rule of law, and by evading those strictures he gained the esteem of that even greater number of Americans who despise lawmakers.

How did this simple game come to resonate so deeply all of America's ideals and idealized visions of itself? How did it come to be *our* game? Like other American institutions, baseball proceeded from the spark of individual genius to the dynamism of group effort and, in a paradoxical flourish, was simultaneously corrupted and enriched by the entrance of capital. Money came into the game first in the form of gambling; next, as payments to "revolvers," players who would switch clubs; and finally, as entrepreneurial investment. Money was not the snake in the Garden, spoiling a pastoral, amateur idyll, but instead the stimulus to creativity and excellence.

Indeed, the same could be said for corruption. If gamblers had not found amateur baseball of interest—as professional footraces and prizefighting had been before it—there would have been no ascendancy within a score of years to a level of skill that would command the interest of an adult spectatorship. In the years before the Civil War, the very term "professional" was for baseball players an epithet; by the end of the decade it had become synonymous, as it is today, with precise execution and peak achievement.

The National Association, baseball's first professional league, was brought down by crooked play, on-field drunkenness and, most of all, by the birth of a bigger idea. That great notion was the National League, a capitalist consortium of stock companies dreamed up by William Hulbert, the game's least celebrated hero. If baseball players go to bed at night with prayers of thanks for John Ward and Curt Flood (they don't but they ought to), the owners should hit their pillows with hosannas to Hulbert. Among his accomplishments—besides the reserve clause, which in the Owners' Secret Hall of Fame is enough to earn him the gaudiest plaque—was to clean up the league after the Louisville Four, particularly pathetic Jim Devlin, conspired to toss away the 1877 pennant.

Gambling did not return to the game in a big way until the twentieth century: attempts were made to "fix" both the 1903 and 1905 World Series, and in the 1914 Series the Philadelphia Athletics, according to losing owner Connie Mack, played to the gamblers' tune. Hal Chase was tossing away ball games throughout his big-league career, which lasted from 1905 through 1919. The Black Sox Scandal of 1919 did not arise *ex nihilo*. Joe Jackson, Eddie Cicotte, and Hap Felsch were guilty, sure, but they were dimwitted victims, too, just as Jim Devlin had been.

In our beginnings are our ends. How can you tell where you're going if you don't know where you've been? Why baseball? Whence baseball? To ask the latter is to answer the former. And in that answer lies yet another question, the one that now weighs on the minds of all who love the game: *Whither baseball?*

In the 1980s baseball was touched by the drug problem endemic in our society. Baseball's victims were highly publicized and their fall from grace was judged more reprehensible for all the advantages that players enjoy. But the game is an American institution reflecting what is wrong with our people as well as what is right. Baseball punished those players who used illegal drugs but ultimately welcomed them back into the fold, even the most incorrigible recidivists. In this most difficult area, baseball was humane and wise and, in recognizing that drug addiction was not a matter of personal election, *led* America—as it did with integration—rather than follow it.

Even if our current understanding of addiction ultimately proves to be more charitable than scientific, baseball has done right to acknowledge human frailty and help those who have fallen. Why not now, when baseball's own house is in such transparent disarray, proclaim an amnesty for all its blacklisted players? America, a nation of immigrants, is about second chances. America is about hope and renewal. We love comeback stories and prodigal sons; we extend rehabilitation and parole and pardons to the most dubious prospects for reform. Isn't it time for baseball to be as generous as America? Come home, Joe Jackson. Come home, Jim Devlin. You've been out in the cold long enough. Come home, Denny McLain. Come home, Pete Rose.

As Monte Irvin said in the context of integration, "Baseball has done more to move America in the right direction than all the professional patriots with their billions of cheap words." Baseball can do it again.

The gyrations of the past few years seem positively frenetic for fans accustomed to the game's unhurried rhythms and resistance to change. Yet for all its shifts and reversals, baseball has not strayed far from its origins. What sustains baseball in the hearts of Americans, finally, is not its responsiveness to trends in society nor its propensity for novelty, but the promise that it will be the same as it ever was. And oddly, despite the scheduling carousel of three divisions and wild-card entrants into the playoffs, baseball is still our game.

"This is the age of contrivance," wrote Daniel Boorstin. "The artificial has become so commonplace that the natural begins to seem contrived." In baseball, domed stadiums with artificial turf had been the norm for new construction for two decades. When the Baltimore Orioles opened their new stadium at Camden Yards the effect was dazzling. Open air? Real grass? Ornamental ironwork? It was the shock of the old. And fans loved it, instantly. They sensed that here was, in Boorstin's phrase, "an oasis of the uncontrived."

That same phrase applies to baseball itself. It is a game that reminds us of an America that was—and, even more distantly, of a land of wonders to which we can never return. It is the game of our past, our nation's and our own; it is the game of our future, in which our sons and daughters take their places alongside us, and replace us. It reflects who we have been, who we are, and whom we might, with the grace of God, become.

Chapter 2

Barry Bonds: Is He the Greatest Ever?

By John Thorn

Barry Bonds has surpassed long-held records, changed the way his opponents play the game, and distanced himself from the performance level of his peers to a degree not thought possible, let alone made real, since the days of Babe Ruth. Over the course of half a century of paying serious attention to baseball, I have never seen anyone like him.

Through 2003, the man won six MVPs. He holds the single-season record in batting's most significant categories: home runs, slugging percentage, on-base average, and on-base plus slugging (OPS), that now ubiquitous measure of total batting excellence. He might have topped other important columns too, if he didn't also hold the record for bases on balls in a season (198). And while the all-time home-run record may prove to be his monument, the intentional base on balls is his enduring tribute.

Convinced that Bonds is the greatest? I didn't think so.

In fact, it is only once we put

Barry and Bobby Bonds
Bobby Bonds offers his son Barry of the Giants a good-luck kiss before a home game against the Pirates on August 9, 2002. The younger Bonds would hit his 600th career home run in the game.

forward a reasonable answer that the question posed by the title begins to reverberate down the canyons of baseball history. Other gods of the past, not only Ruth but also Honus Wagner and Ty Cobb, rise up in protest. King Kelly and Buck Ewing wonder how they could have been forgotten when once they had been immortals. Until the day before yesterday, it seems, there was general agreement that in the "modern era"—the years after baseball integration—Ted Williams was the best pure hitter and Willie Mays the most complete player, while Hank Aaron was left to puzzle what he had to do to get a nod. Today's fans may support Alex Rodriguez as the greatest player in the game and perhaps one day the greatest ever, as Bonds will have turned 40 before A-Rod hits 30. And then there is Albert Pujols, who has accomplished so much in so short a time…

If one required proof that fame is fleeting and fortune fickle, consider that only three years ago this essay might have been titled, "Ken Griffey: The Greatest Ever?" At the All-Star Game in 1999, when Major League Baseball announced the fan balloting for the 25 spots on its All-Century Team, Griffey was the only active posi-

tion player elected, with 645,389 votes; Bonds, who did not make the cut despite three MVPs in the decade, had 173,279.

In baseball the question "Who is the greatest ever?" is answered by a hero with a hundred faces, depending upon: (a) what we are measuring, (b) how we are measuring it, (c) when the measurement is made, (d) whom the plausible contenders may be, and (e) what recent development occasions the exercise.

Defining Greatness

There's no getting around it. We are going to have to agree what we mean when we talk about greatness. Are we naming the greatest hitter, pitcher, fielder, or all-around player? What factors constitute greatness—Branch Rickey's "five tools" (run, throw, catch, hit, and hit with power), or should we throw in some additional points for timely performance, especially in the World Series? Do we consider a man's present value only, or do we extrapolate his future proficiency as well as longevity? Do we care about what previous generations thought and why they thought it? Does character count? Are statistics the true-north guide to greatness?

When we say "great," do we really mean to say "best"? This is not merely a semantic quibble but the yawning gap between celebrity and skill. Achilles will always be a greater warrior than Patton, in no small measure because he had Homer as his advance man.

To assess skill it is invaluable to possess a sophisticated understanding of statistics, including the use of adjustments for era and home ballpark; we may look at the player panels in this volume and count up the "black ink" entries that indicate league leadership in a category; we may tote up World Series and All-Star Game appearances; or we may look for a hidden code in arcane sabermetric figures as a key to greatness. To assess celebrity, on the other hand, it is necessary to learn how a player was viewed in his day, not merely how he may be regarded at present. Yet to identify fame—an enduring place in the game's lore that is informed by the facts but stands outside and above them, like legend and myth—no metric is sufficient and no explanation fully satisfies.

Over the past two decades baseball sophisticates have derided the voting patterns and special selections of the Baseball Hall of Fame as a measure of nothing except sentimentality, foolishness and cronyism. How did Rabbit Maranville get a plaque? Or Joe Tinker? Or Roger Bresnahan? Yet the Hall's purpose in honoring worthies of a bygone age, no longer famous but once so, has been to secure for them a sure pedestal in the pantheon, beyond challenge from future savants or the mere forgetfulness of a later generation. Examining the concept of a baseball pantheon, where renown may endure beyond records, provides a valuable context for understanding just where Barry Bonds fits in the grand scheme of things.

A Brief History of Fame

The phrase "Baseball Hall of Fame" made its first appearance in the December 15, 1907 *Washington Post,* in a story about the top managers of the day, "the greatest galaxy of baseball brains." Barely three years later, *Baseball Magazine* announced its intention to form (in print, anyway) "The Hall of Fame for the Immortals of Baseball; Comprising the Greatest Players in the History of the Game." Inspiring the magazine's editors, no doubt, was the Hall of Fame for Great Americans, founded in New York City in 1900 (many mistakenly think that the Baseball Hall of Fame in Cooperstown was the nation's first such institution).

In the previous century Henry Chadwick had often rambled about the best players he had seen in his long exposure to the game, and he had done much to espouse statistics as the superior way to judge a player: "Many a dashing general player, who carries off a great deal of éclat in prominent matches, has all 'the gilt taken off the gingerbread,' as the saying is, by these matter-of-fact figures," he wrote in 1864. "And we are frequently surprised to find that the modest but efficient worker, who has played earnestly and steadily through the season, apparently unnoticed, has come in, at the close of the race, the real victor."

Chadwick's statistics, rudimentary as they were, were a necessary corrective to the flowery praise that came to so many early players for their pluck, their headiness, their dash and daring. As the number of statistics exploded in the 1870s, it became increasingly difficult to credit such intangibles; who was the greatest player of the age might still be left to those of a poetic bent, but identifying the best batter or fielder at a position was now a matter of record, in the *New York Clipper* and elsewhere. Not until the

1890s did newspapers begin to conduct surveys among veteran players as to who had been the top player of all, and the answers were most often Kelly, Ewing, and Cap Anson. The *Reach Guide* of 1894 featured a section entitled "Who Is the King Player?" that contained the opinions of such stalwarts as George Wright, Al Spalding, Fred Pfeffer, and Frank Selee, supporting the claims on fame of, respectively: Cal McVey; Wright and Ross Barnes; Kelly; and Ewing and Kelly.

Baseball Magazine's editors, notably Jacob C. Morse, took a new tack by moving beyond naming all-star teams of the season just past or soliciting old-timers to wrap themselves in nostalgic reverie. They sought to create a pantheon of heroes that would make Olympians of the best exponents of the national pastime, securing their places for all time, and they would take suggestions from their readers rather than flog statistics or the opinions of one-time teammates.

"It is a universal trait of humanity," they wrote in the January 1911 issue, "to wish to know who are the leaders, the tiptop men, in all kinds of human activity. We have ourselves felt a keen interest in selecting the All-America nine for the past season; and we know by the large degree of enthusiasm displayed in the public press, as well as in our own correspondence, that the general public was interested too.

"But the problem of selecting an All-America nine is a slight one compared with the task of picking out the greatest players in history. Here it would seem that the most ardent fan has the haziest kind of a notion, and the conflict among such opinions as are expressed, is very great.

"The older generation of fans is pretty much of the opinion that the old-time ball players were in a class by themselves, while the younger generation can see nothing but the brilliant feats of some of our present-day stars. The real unprejudiced truth, we imagine, lies somewhere between these two extremes. ...

"We can think of nothing more interesting in all baseball than a discussion of the greatest players which the game ever knew. ..."

Over the next six months, *Baseball Magazine* named 18 men to its Hall of Fame, beginning with "three names of famous ball players who, we feel sure, would be entitled to almost universal consent, to a place in our list." These three were Cap Anson, Ed Delahanty and King Kelly. The last three named were the first whose careers were principally if not entirely in the new century: Nap Lajoie, Honus Wagner and Ty Cobb. Of the twelve in between, six may come as a surprise to modern fans: pitcher Charlie Ferguson and outstanding fielders Ed Williamson, Charlie Bennett, Fred Pfeffer, Jerry Denny, and James Fogarty. Although these six were all well known to fans of 1911, only 25 years later, when Cooperstown began its election process, they were consigned to the dustbin of history, their reputations never to revive (as those of, for example, Roger Connor, Mickey Welch and Sam Thompson would in the 1970s, thanks to *The Baseball Encyclopedia*'s unearthing of their statistical records).

As *Baseball Magazine* froze its Hall of Fame at 18 immortals with the July issue, sportswriters for the daily newspapers began a series on the greatest players. Most notable of these was former player Sam Crane's "Fifty Greatest Ball Players in History," for the *New York Evening Journal,* commencing in November 1911. Crane stopped the series at 30, and included a few choices that may have stumped even his contemporaries (Archie Bush, Dupee Shaw) but by and large his subjects may have had more lasting influence with the public than the *Baseball Magazine* picks, as evi-

denced by their eventual elevation to Cooperstown: Harry Wright, Jim O'Rourke, Dickey Pearce, Candy Cummings, Hughie Jennings, Cy Young, John McGraw, and Connor. Crane also named his 20 best of all time, including some players who weren't among the first 30 stories (such as Bill Lange and Willie Keeler) perhaps because he had arranged his 50 chronologically and had stopped at 30.

In 1936 the Baseball Hall of Fame conducted its first elections, one polling 226 members of the Baseball Writers Association, the other an old-timers' committee of 78. The writers elected the "founding five" of Ruth, Wagner, Cobb, Christy Mathewson and Walter Johnson; failing to get the required 170 votes were Lajoie, Tris Speaker and Cy Young, all of whom were elected the following year. Grover Cleveland Alexander made the cut in 1938 and George Sisler, Eddie Collins, Willie Keeler, and Lou Gehrig entered in 1939. (Keeler thus became the only 19th-century player to be elected to the Hall; all the others were selected by committee.) In the veterans' election of 1936, no one garnered the necessary 75 percent. The two top vote-getters (tied at 40) were Anson and Ewing. By the time the Hall opened its doors on June 12, 1939, they were joined by old-timers Morgan Bulkeley, George Wright, Connie Mack, John McGraw, Henry Chadwick, Charles Comiskey, Candy Cummings, Al Spalding, Ban Johnson, and Alexander Cartwright.

Where *Baseball Magazine* had tabbed 18 men in 1911, Cooperstown welcomed 25 … but only eight were honored in common. The early candidates for baseball's greatest player appeared to have been placed on not marble pedestals but greased poles.

When the Associated Press conducted a poll in 1950 to select the "Ten Most Outstanding in Sports," four were baseball players, if you count Jim Thorpe, the leading vote-getter; the three fulltime players were Ruth (second), Cobb (fourth) and Gehrig (ninth). When the AP conducted its Athlete of the Century poll in 1999, Ruth stood atop the heap, with Thorpe dropping to third. No other baseball player made it into the top 10. Of the 100 athletes named, the only baseball players who commenced their careers after 1965 were Cal Ripken (82) and Mark McGwire (84). The message was clear: baseball is your father's game.

ESPN's Sports Century poll of that same year seconded the sentiment. Of the top 100 athletes, 20 were selected for their baseball accomplishments alone, while three were multi-sport stars whose baseball exploits would not have been enough to place them on the list. Although 20 is a very respectable number, more than that for any other sport, this was a list topped by Michael Jordan and including many athletes only recently retired; ESPN's baseball players *all* had commenced their careers before 1965.

But 1999 also produced another poll, one unconcerned with other sports and designed to display the diamond of the present amid the glories of the past: Major League Baseball's All-Century Team. In a dry run in 1969, the centennial of professional baseball, the Baseball Writers Association had named Ruth the game's all-time outstanding player, outdistancing Cobb, Wagner and DiMaggio, who was named the greatest living player. Thirty years later Joe was gone from the scene and, at a memorable All-Star Game at Boston's Fenway Park, an ailing Ted Williams, surrounded by the giants of the game, was its heartwarming embodiment of greatness.

A "blue-ribbon panel" (of which I was one) had selected the 100 all-time greats from whom the fans, in a nationwide poll, would choose 25. Then, because the popular vote had predictably given short shrift to some indisputable luminaries, the panel added five more (Warren Spahn, Lefty Grove, Stan Musial, Mathewson, and Wagner), plus four stars to honor the Negro Leagues (Oscar Charleston, Cool Papa Bell, Josh Gibson, and Buck Leonard; the absence of Satchel Paige was impossible to explain, unless he somehow integrated himself into oblivion by pitching in the "big leagues" after the age of 42).

The outcome was fascinating, as much for who was out as who was in, and for the disparities in vote totals among players who were statistically quite comparable. Ruth pulled in the most votes, with 1,158,044, but Aaron trailed him by less than 1,300. Williams, Mays, DiMaggio, Mantle, Cobb, Griffey, and Rose rounded out the outfield allotment. Where was Barry Bonds? Nowhere—18th place in the vote totals, behind the no less snubbed Rickey Henderson.

At first base Lou Gehrig more than doubled Mark McGwire's vote but both made the team. George Sisler and Bill Terry brought up the rear with puny totals. Going around the horn, Jackie Robinson and Rogers Hornsby filled out second base, leaving no room for Collins or Lajoie. Shortstop went to Cal Ripken and, in an upset, Ernie Banks over not only Wagner but also Ozzie Smith. Third base went to Mike Schmidt and Brooks Robinson, far outdistancing Eddie Mathews.

As to the battery, catcher went to Johnny Bench and Yogi Berra by wide margins, with Gabby Hartnett, a sabermetric star, registering on only 24,196 ballots. Nolan Ryan topped all pitchers with 992,040 votes, with Sandy Koufax coming in second. Cy Young polled a very healthy 867,523 to come in third, proving that it is good have an award named after you.

The Hall of Fame's founding five all made the team (though Wagner and Mathewson required a boost from the panel). One active player made it (Griffey) and six others who had commenced their careers after 1965. Of the original pool of 100 players, six were active and 18 others had commenced their careers after 1965. The undertow of baseball's past was strong but the modern generation held its own.

Think of the All-Century 100 this way: if the Baseball Hall of Fame had not started up when it did, but instead at the end of the 20th century, these are the men whose plaques would be on the wall. Sure, we would name some token representatives of the 19th century—maybe Anson, Ewing, Kelly, and Cartwright—and we could name Mack and McGraw as managers and maybe Ban Johnson and Bill Klem, and then look to the future for fresh nominees. But something irreplaceable would be lost.

With mammoth statistical compendia available to us, we may be better equipped than our forefathers to assess achievement, but in perception of greatness they may have had an edge on us, because theirs was a more romantic age and they loved stories more than stats.

Is Bonds the greatest ever?

Let's look at those who were once honored, as part of such a question. Every one of the men in the chart below was once hailed as the greatest in his decade. Some, highlighted in **bold**, were called the greatest ever, regardless of position or era, and were still held high long after their playing days ended. Remember, this chart portrays not necessarily the men who were *the best*, as might be indicated by their statistics (which may be found elsewhere in this volume), but who won acclaim as *great* players—men of character, vigor, magnetism.

THE EVOLUTION OF FAME

1850s	1880s	1910s	1940s	1970s	2000s
Joe Leggett	**King Kelly**	Eddie Collins	**Ted Williams**	Pete Rose	Sammy Sosa
Charles DeBost	**Buck Ewing**	Tris Speaker	**Joe DiMaggio**	Joe Morgan	**Alex Rodriguez**
Pete O'Brien	Ed Williamson	**Ty Cobb**	Stan Musial	Johnny Bench	**Barry Bonds**
Louis Wadsworth	**Cap Anson**	Grover Alexander	Ralph Kiner	Reggie Jackson	Albert Pujols
Frank Pidgeon	John Clarkson	**Walter Johnson**	Bob Feller	Tom Seaver	Vladimir Guerrero
1860s	**1890s**	**1920s**	**1950s**	**1980s**	
Charley Smith	Ed Delahanty	**Babe Ruth**	**Ted Williams**	Mike Schmidt	
Joe Start	Hugh Duffy	Tris Speaker	Mickey Mantle	George Brett	
George Wright	Willie Keeler	Rogers Hornsby	**Willie Mays**	Cal Ripken	
Dickey Pearce	Bill Lange	George Sisler	Ernie Banks	Rickey Henderson	
Jim Creighton	Amos Rusie	Frankie Frisch	Eddie Mathews	Nolan Ryan	
1870s	**1900s**	**1930s**	**1960s**	**1990s**	
Ross Barnes	Nap Lajoie	Jimmie Foxx	Frank Robinson	Frank Thomas	
Deacon White	Honus Wagner	**Joe DiMaggio**	**Hank Aaron**	Tony Gwynn	
George Wright	**Ty Cobb**	Lou Gehrig	**Willie Mays**	**Barry Bonds**	
Cap Anson	Rube Waddell	Carl Hubbell	Roberto Clemente	**Ken Griffey, Jr.**	
Al Spalding	**Christy Mathewson**	Lefty Grove	**Sandy Koufax**	Greg Maddux	

Studying what people believe to be true is often far more interesting than ascertaining what may actually be true, for even generally accepted falsehoods (the Abner Doubleday concoction, for example) reveal much about the hopes of an age. Legends are not mere falsehoods, but the end product of a process that begins in fact, extends to story, ascends to history, and ultimately transcends all of these to approach the realm of myth. From those heights, legend binds and nourishes a culture worn down and bored by humdrum fact ... and thus becomes socially useful, as history used to be, and as embellished story captivated our forebears around the campfire. Barry Bonds may retain hold of his records for generations, but will stories attach to him the way they do to Kelly, Ruth, Cobb, Williams, and Mays? Or will his statistics have to speak for him, as they do for Rogers Hornsby or Jeff Bagwell?

Evaluating the Contenders

Looking to the chart above, we may narrow the field. Kelly, Ewing, and Anson were the greats of their century. Creighton and Wright were the game's first heroes, and Creighton's role rapidly transformed to legend because he died in his prime; however, neither man was selected to the *Baseball Magazine* pantheon in 1911, so we may reasonably remove them from consideration now. Anson and Ewing made their mark in a game with very different rules, including in Anson's case a pitching distance that increased twice over the course of his career. For me, Kelly is the greatest player of the century: his on-field heroics were burnished by a folkloric combination of jester, knave and fool, capped by a picturesque if premature demise (falling off a stretcher as he was taken to hospital with a fatal case of pneumonia, he is said to have remarked, "Boys, I've made me last slide"). Like Yogi Berra, not half the things he said or did were so, but it doesn't matter.

When the game's rules stabilized in the first decade of the new century, two stars emerged who must still be considered today when we assess the greatest player ever: Wagner and Cobb. John McGraw, who had seen all the stars including Ruth, went to his grave in 1934 still favoring Wagner, in large part because he was not only a great hitter and baserunner but also splendid at the most difficult position in the field, excluding catcher. (That view—a good-hitting shortstop must be more valuable than a good-hitting outfielder or first baseman—has come around again, in support of Alex Rodriguez's candidacy.) All the same, in the Hall of Fame writers' ballot of 1936, Cobb's vote total was higher than that of either Wagner or Ruth, and it's impossible to ignore his all-time-high batting average and 12 batting titles in 13 years. The greatest

pitcher of the years before World War II was surely Walter Johnson, but he and his most excellent kin (Grove, Feller, Mathewson, Koufax) are excluded from consideration because their contribution to team success isn't as great as that of the top position players.

This brings us to Ruth, DiMaggio and Williams as all-time greats who began or, in Ruth's case, completed their careers before racial integration, night ball, air travel, relief pitchers, or the proliferation of the slider. DiMaggio was esteemed for his style, his grace, his pinstripes, his World Series rings, his singular batting streak, and his silence, which was taken for grandeur. But he's not the batting equal of Williams, who maintained excellence over a much longer career, and the New York media that celebrated his ethereal charm is long gone. While DiMaggio's reputation dwindled over the last twenty years that of Williams soared: statisticians were awed by his on-base average and younger fans embraced him as The Last American Hero; the gruff style that had irked the knights of the keyboard, as Ted derisively labeled them, was now colorfully authentic. The fans had changed, but in truth so had Ted; mellowing with each passing year, he was becoming beloved, like the Babe.

What's left to say about Ruth? He revolutionized the game, making even Cobb's lofty batting averages seem a wasted effort, and he was voted the top American athlete in 1999 and the top player of all time in that year's All-Century Team election. He no longer has his home-run records, nor his formerly unassailable slugging percentage marks of 1920 and 1921 (.847 and .846), nor his walks record of 1923 (170). But he retains this unique trump card: before he became the game's greatest slugger he was the American League's best left-handed pitcher, winning 94 games and twice—1916 and 1917—throwing over 300 innings while winning 23 and 24 games, respectively. And until Bonds no one dominated the game the way Ruth did: he hit 60 homers in 1927 when no other team in the American League hit that many; he led the league in slugging percentage 13 years out of 14, and more.

Yet I maintain that Williams is the superior hitter, Aaron the better home-run slugger and Mays the best all-around player. Reflect that Ruth faced pitchers who threw complete games about half the time (today it is about 5 percent), and thus faced the same delivery through four to six plate appearances (not to mention that he faced no relievers as we understand them today). Reflect that Ruth never had to hit at night. Reflect that African-Americans never graced the same field as Ruth; had they done so, many white players would have lost their positions and the overall level of competition would have risen. One could add that Ruth never faced a

slider or a split-fingered fastball; rarely faced a pitcher who would throw a breaking ball when behind in the count, and on. Ruth may have been better than any baseball player ever was or will be; however, it defies reason to claim that Ruth's opposition was likewise better.

Ruth's dominance was not only the measure of Ruth; *it was also the measure of the competition he faced.* To the extent that the league performs at an average level that from a later perspective seems easily attained, a colossus may so far outdistance his peers as to create records that are unapproachable for all time. When Williams retired, it was beyond imagining that we could reasonably compare batters of one era against batters of another simply by measuring the extent to which they surpassed the league average; now it is commonplace. But the large question that remains unanswered, and is perhaps not perfectly answerable, is: how to compare one era's average level of play to that of another. In swimming, track, basketball, football, hockey, golf—any sport you can name—the presumption is that today's athletes are bigger, stronger, better trained, and, on average, more proficient. World athletic records— in such competitions as the 100-meter dash, the 1500-meter run, the shot put, discus, javelin, high jump, 100-meter freestyle in swimming—have all been bettered by at least 15 percent and in some events far, far more.

Only baseball, with its Punch and Judy battle between pitcher and batter to entertain the public while rules makers and ballpark architects invisibly pull strings from above, labors to maintain the illusion that nothing changes in the grand old game. A dollar in 1904 may not bear much resemblance to a dollar in 2004, but a .300 batting average remains the mark of a good hitter. Only in baseball do fans bemoan expansion, deride talent dilution and deteriorating fundamentals, and imagine that a 1927 team such as the New York Yankees would defeat all comers if they could be teleported to the American League East. (Strangely, no one thinks that about the 1906 Chicago Cubs.)

Barry Bonds: Best or Greatest?

Baseball was better in Williams' day than it was in Ruth's; it is better yet today. If you could transport Cobb, Wagner, Ruth, or Williams to the 21st century, they would benefit from improved training and nutrition, and because they would be smart enough to adjust to present conditions, they would be stars. But they wouldn't perform the way they did in their own day, and thus they would no longer be the Cobb, Wagner, Ruth, and Williams of the record books. Maybe they would be as good as Hank Aaron and Willie Mays; my guess is they would not.

Bonds, especially in 2001 through 2003, has exceeded the average batting performance in the National League to an extent greater than Ruth managed in his best years … while playing in a pitchers' park where home runs other than his are scarce. This is an astounding accomplishment, for with the average skill level increasing, it is mathematically ever more difficult to exceed it by a large margin. As Stephen Jay Gould memorably demonstrated, it is harder to post high rates of success in an era with a high level of average performance. Once .400 hitters were plentiful because it was relatively common to exceed the norm by 40 percent or more when many less-skilled players competed with a few exceptional ones. In baseball's pre-WWII period, when the league batting average was .260, there was a slim chance that someone would hit .400; as the league average ascended to .280 or .300, someone

could reasonably be expected to surpass that by 40 percent. When Ruth slugged .847 in 1920, the American League slugged .388. When Bonds slugged .863 in 2001, the National League slugged .425, a comparable level of dominance, but in an era marked by greater average proficiency.

Yet for a number of reasons—aloof personality, whispered steroid use, no World Series ring, age-reduced effectiveness in the field, an armored right elbow that permits him to peer over the plate with little fear of harm—neither media nor fans seem willing to call Barry Bonds the greatest player ever, only "one of the greats." The steroid issue swirling around Bonds, in particular, has risen to a higher volume with less substance than Mark McGwire's use of the legal strength supplement androstenedione or such wink-nudge cheating as Gaylord Perry's spitball or Whitey Ford's scuffball, which carried them to the Hall of Fame; or the near-universal use of greenies (amphetamines) in the clubhouses of the 1970s.

That title of "Game's Greatest Player" seemed easier to affix to Alex Rodriguez, the shortstop who signed the biggest contract in history, $252 million over ten years, and then proceeded to live up to it, hitting 52, 57 and 47 home runs in his three years with the Texas Rangers. But when Rodriguez joined the New York Yankees for the 2004 season, he prepared to shift to third base, where power bats have been more common over the past half-century than at shortstop. He will be great at any position he elects to play, but the shift to third makes his historical competitors Mike Schmidt and Eddie Mathews, not Honus Wagner and Cal Ripken, and his batting record does not yet compare to that of Bonds.

Albert Pujols is a dark-horse candidate, only because of his youth, to become the greatest player ever. Certainly no one has ever done what he has in his first three years. But for now the proper comparisons for Pujols are to Hal Trosky and Cesar Cedeno, not Ruth, Williams, Aaron, and Mays.

No, the competition for Bonds is not from his contemporaries. It's the fat guy, the one who changed the way batters approach their task and thus changed the whole game of baseball. Bonds has not yet done that, but he may. In 2001 his batting stroke was so grooved that he hit 73 home runs against only 49 singles. In 2002, at the age of 38, he batted .370 to win his first batting crown and walked a record 198 times. In 2003 he took 65.9 percent of the pitches thrown to him yet still managed to hit 45 homers in only 390 at-bats. He has learned plate discipline, as Ted Williams did, and he cannot be induced to widen his strike zone. When Bonds gets a pitch to hit, he does … and, choking up for greater bat control, he not only has a compact swing but also, with his maple mace, a larger sweet spot. Also like Williams, he is a consummate guess hitter, smacking home runs off pitches so high and so tight that they could not have been hit into fair territory unless he had begun to turn his hips and hands in advance. Truly, Bonds is not a slugger with a big swing like Ruth or Mantle or Jackson, but a technician like Williams, with the fastest swing and most powerful torque ever seen in the game. He is the perfect hero for a cold analytical age that prizes excellence over legend.

In previous times, people liked their heroes to be larger than life, to surround their prodigious feats with story; the feats were never enough. Folks preferred Ruth to Gehrig, Cobb to Heilmann, Kelly to Ewing, Waddell to Mathewson, even Doubleday to Cartwright. Bonds' accomplishments outstrip everyone's, including Ruth's, but the Babe lives in memory and we will tell his stories, or our ancestors' stories about him, as if they were our own.

Chapter 3

Moneyball: Does the Strategy Work?

By Peter Wayner

Now statistics are supposed to be a scientific remedy for making decisions based on anecdotes, but I would like to start and end this essay with two anecdotes that capture our endless tussle with baseball statistics. The first happened on a beautiful spring afternoon when the Orioles were playing a day game. I don't remember the other team, but it doesn't matter. We had seats on the third-base side, only several dozen rows from the field. The sun was shining and we weren't at work.

A guy sitting next to me was also skipping out of the office. We talked a bit about the game and it became clear that he was a big fan of Rafael Palmeiro. While I'm a bit of a fair-weather fan, this guy loved Palmeiro. He was a devotee who had found some magic bond with the ballplayer and, unfortunately, the ballplayer's ability to get on base. There are probably some psychologists out there who might look at his devotion as unhealthy, but I enjoyed the company. He told me how Palmeiro was a great hitter; Palmeiro made plays that others couldn't; Palmeiro was a leader just like Cal. He went on.

Billy Beane and Ken Macha
The star of *Moneyball*, Beane has been winning converts to a radical, budget-conscious approach to using computer analysis to build a successful baseball team.

Unfortunately, on that particular day, Palmeiro was not living up to this reputation. He went to the plate and the pitcher sent him back to the dugout. I don't remember whether he struck out, popped out, or grounded out, but he did nothing in the least bit impressive the entire game. This began to bother my neighbor, who got very angry, muttered about the cost of the tickets, cursed the price of the beer, and then said something like, "What are the odds that I would pay so much to see him and he wouldn't get on base?"

Lacking common sense, I decided to compute this for him. A .300 hitter fails 70 percent of the time, an approximation that made the math easier. Such a hitter will fail in two consecutive trips about (.7 x .7) or about 49 percent of the time. (I was ignoring walks, hit by a pitch and other details.)

I told him the 49 percent number and he smoldered. Then I realized that 49 percent was almost 50 percent and I could square this again in my head to conclude that a .300 hitter would fail to get on base about every four days or about 25 percent of the time, assuming that the player got four at bats during a game.

When I told him this, he stopped talking to me. Palmeiro, though, had five trips on that particular day and he did nothing with any of them. Just to be certain, I approximated one more time

and told my neighbor that about 18 percent of the time, call it one of five days, a mighty .300 hitter will go home a goat. Didn't he feel a bit better? It happens, as they say, to everyone. Not just some of the time, but one out of five days!

None of these numbers helped my neighbor get over his grief. I think he hated me for reducing mighty Rafael Palmeiro to some back-of-the-head numbers. Baseball for him was a quest for triumph, a chance to commune with some saints, an opportunity to crush those Red Sox, Yankees or whomever it was that day. One out of five days? Garbage men come by the house on one of the five days of the week.

None of this would matter but baseball, and indeed much of modern society, is struggling with the ultimate meaning of numbers like these. Are the stats a real tool for divining the measure of the game, or are they just a diversion for geeks and weenies? Is baseball just a big pachinko game where the balls bounce into the glove in one instance and the right hole in another?

The pachinko game is the right metaphor. A pinball game takes skill. It's conceivable that a deaf, dumb and blind man could run a pinball table all night because it takes skill to run the flippers. The balls in the pachinko games largely fall where they will, following the path determined by the laws of chance and guided by the

unseen hand of physics.

This question is not just for baseball fans. The very popular science-fiction movie *The Matrix,* and its two sequels, explored the philosophical question of whether we're just big cogs in some artificial intelligence whirring along in a big computer. Neo, the protagonist, breaks out of this machine, the so-called Matrix, and battles for the future of humanity.

Casting the game of baseball into this mechanistic, life-is-a-crapshoot view is terribly depressing to some, myself included. What about character? And drive? And devotion to America? And clean living? And, let's be inclusive, not-so-clean living? What about Mom? Is she going to be proud of her son because he came to bat with the bases loaded and then did just what some big set of dice decided? Albert Einstein knew a few things about statistical mechanics and random models of the universe and he decided that God doesn't roll dice.

Alas, there are those in the field of baseball today who may think that while Einstein deserves some respect for the great things he did with the atomic bomb, the big guy doesn't know anything about baseball. A number of managers are hiring computer guys, modern-day non-Einsteins, to crunch numbers, analyze statistics, and make decisions about who has the right talents to make it to the major leagues. Being nice to Mom, displaying the right character, and working hard doesn't mean anything if you don't have the right numbers.

This wouldn't be a problem for the romantics if the computer guys weren't doing so well. The biggest story in baseball after the turn of the new millennium is the success of little teams with small budgets. The Yankees may spend a fortune, but all that does is make them look a bit stupider when teams like the Florida Marlins and the Oakland Athletics do just as well on about a third of the Yankee budget. Why? Smart guys with good computer programs and a healthy disrespect for the views of Dr. Einstein.

The story of the Oakland A's is now well-known because a talented former bond salesman from Salomon Brothers named Michael Lewis wrote a great book telling their story. The author of *Moneyball* grew up using sophisticated computer programs to haggle over what some bonds are worth and he found, as they say in corporate-speak, great synergy with the number-crunching, stats-loving guys running the A's. In his memoirs of his days at Salomon Brothers, Lewis noted that some of his colleagues even spent some time trying to write software to predict when people would die so they could place the right bets by buying up the right mortgages that would be cashed in when the relatives would sell the real estate of the deceased.

After spending his formative years with colleagues like that, it's no wonder that Michael Lewis wouldn't see much terribly wrong with looking at baseball like a big pachinko machine. If you do the right research, buy the right players, put them in the right spots, the balls will bounce into the right places as the season grinds on. There may be a few bad days, but wins will outnumber the losses according to the computer.

Moneyball does a great job of capturing the life of Billy Beane, the GM of the Oakland A's, who many feel is largely responsible for their great success in 2001, 2002 and 2003. Beane did not act alone. He was encouraged by Sandy Alderson, a former lawyer and Marine Corps officer, who saw the power of numerical thinking, and Paul DePodesta, who did the math. They, in turn, relied on famous works of statistical insight such as Bill James's *Baseball Abstracts,* John Thorn and Pete Palmer's *The Hidden Game of Baseball,* and many of the papers published by statistical researchers. The book makes it clear that Beane's success is a vindication for the stat-heads and number junkies who were so long ignored by the cool jocks in control.

Oakland's success, at least according to the book, came from strict application of rules like these:

- Choose players with a high on-base percentage. Wins come when smart players balance the advantages and the costs of swinging at each pitch.
- Choose players who can hit home runs, if only because pitchers are more careful when the sluggers come to the plate.
- Choose pitchers who give up few walks and home runs, statistics that are directly related to the final score. Avoid concentrating on the speed of their fastball, a statistic that is only weakly related to whether the hitter will get on base.
- Don't attempt to steal bases or move a player along with a sacrifice bunt. The computers make it clear that these are losing bets.
- Outs, not hits, are the true measure of the game. Every out from your batters is a step toward a loss. Every out dealt by your defense is another step toward a win.

These are all well-tested ideas from the baseball research community that, at least according to Lewis, never found enough respect in the offices of major league baseball teams. Beane and his computer-driven stats machines got it. The old-school scouts were too swayed by their eyes and their image of what a ballplayer should look like. Beane repeatedly picks the overweight, fudgeball players over the sculpted pretty boys and chides his scouts for trying to "sell jeans" instead of win ballgames.

The insights are, for the most part, successful. The A's made the playoffs in 2002 and then again in 2003. The wins did not come every day and they did not come often enough in the playoffs themselves, but they were still impressive. The team may have been as pretty as others, the women did not swoon in the stands, but the computers helped the A's find hidden gems that had been overlooked by baseball's scouting machine.

Beane even explicitly notes that this pachinko theory of baseball won't work in the playoffs or the World Series. Just as a .300 hitter will go 0 for 5 some of the time, a great ball club can lose to a not-so-great club in a best-of-seven series. You can calculate the odds. The pachinko balls only bounce into the right holes if you watch them over 162 games.

The A's, however, succeed where others fail. Despite their having one of the lowest salaries, Beane's devotion to more important numbers like the on-base percentage produces a very good team.

Unfortunately, stories this good always have weaknesses. To be truly great, books need to follow one strong path to a satisfying conclusion. A writer might dawdle a bit around an interesting point, but the reader wants a resolution. If this stats-driven machine had any significant weakness, it would be impossible for Lewis to dwell upon it. A book can only tell half of the story.

Baseball games are not books. They can't be edited, sculpted or formed. A manager can't simply forget that there's a runner on first base, no matter that it may ruin the plot. A book may build to a great conclusion, but no one knows whether a baseball game will end with a dramatic ninth inning or just six quick outs. Great games like baseball survive and endure precisely because every strategy has a counterstrategy. They may not always be equal and opposite each other, but the strategies are out there, pushing and pulling at each

other in some eternal, fantasy baseball space. As Yogi Berra said it more simply, "Good pitching beats good hitting and vice versa."

The holes in the pachinko theory are apparent from the beginning of the book. Billy Beane was a major league prospect with impeccable numbers. He was fast, sharp and nearly invincible in high school. His sophomore and junior year, he hit over .500. The scouts loved him, the jean-ad creators drooled over him, *and* he delivered a very convincing set of numbers.

Alas, success spoiled him and he never developed the psychological tools to deal with adversity. Although he rose through the minor leagues and eventually played for Minnesota, Detroit and Oakland, he never delivered the big-league numbers that his high school figures foretold. Lewis suggests he was haunted by demons and frozen by his fear of failure.

One quote stands out in the book. Harvey Dorfman, the baseball psychologist, said, "The guy believes in his talent. What he doesn't believe in is himself. He sees himself exclusively in his statistics. If his stats are bad, he has zero self-worth." The result is a bad feedback loop. When Beane missed a few pitches, had a few bad days, he spiraled down into a lengthy depression.

The result was an odd paradox: believing in the stats produced results that weren't predicted by the stats. If the numbers from the last few days say you stink, well it must be true and you tended to stink even more. Just because a .300 hitter goes 0 for 5, it doesn't mean he's not a .300 hitter. But if someone looks at the .000 batting average for the day and believes in it, well, then he goes from a .300 hitter to a .000 hitter for good. (Palmerio sure lost the unwavering devotion of one fan that day.)

Beane learned from this failure. Today, he feels that the best players are the ones who go out there day in and day out and try to beat every pitcher. Every trip to the plate is a new one. The stats have nothing to do with it.

Beane now understands the law of large numbers and the fact that random pachinko games eventually deliver the performance dictated by the odds. In the book, Beane congratulates one player, Scott Hatteberg, who went 0 for 3. Why? Because Hatteberg took his time, worked his way through the count and forced the pitcher to throw dozens of times. Hatteberg may not have gone anywhere, but his approach would eventually deliver, at least according to the stats.

This is a nice, heartwarming story for a book, but it masks the reality. Hatteberg can work his way through the count as much as he wants, but eventually he's going to have to get on base. He's going to have to hit the ball. No computer stat machine is going to help him with that.

The deepest problem with the stats-driven, pachinko view of baseball is the disconnection between what stats measure and what must be accomplished in a game. Statistics are a great tool for summarizing what happened before. They distill the past and offer us a quick way to talk about what happened before. Winning games, however, lies off in the inchoate future. Casey, mighty Casey, struck out despite all of his wonderful stats.

Billy Beane seems to realize this, even though he doesn't profess it. A true pachinko man will stick by a slumping ballplayer and continue to play him even if he just stands there while the strikes come whizzing by. The rule of statistics guarantees that eventually there will be a big payoff. The slumps must be balanced out by stunning feats of hitting—if you wait long enough.

Beane also seems to realize, and I'm guessing here, that the economist John Maynard Keynes was right when he said, "In the long run, we're dead." The pachinko theory suggests that we could prop up Babe Ruth's corpse at the plate and he would hit 50 to 60 home runs. After all, he's got great stats. Beane obviously realizes that numbers often fail. He trades his players often, in part because he must realize that things don't always work out, even if the numbers suggest that they are.

Consider another Oriole, Brady Anderson, who hit 50 home runs in 1996, after hitting a total of 72 in his first seven years in the major leagues. Which years provide a true measure of Anderson, the first seven years or 1996? And what did the 50 home runs in 1996 predict about the future? The most he ever hit after that was 24 in 1999. What decision would you, the manager, make about Anderson? Which numbers would you use?

Players change and Beane knows this. He, perhaps more than any other general manager, likes to change his team. He's constantly trading players and trading up. The A's have become known for playing significantly better in the second half of the season. The jokers always note that it's literally true that they're playing like a whole new team because they *are* a new team. The starting lineup for the A's that begins the season in April is usually significantly different by July.

Part of this may be because, as Lewis claims, many other teams just give up halfway through the year. When their playoff hopes fade, they sell off their highest quality players for a song. Beane sees this as a buying opportunity and nabs it. Their second-half record certainly backs this up.

Lewis also suggests that Beane trades often because he doesn't have a budget. The A's computers discover diamonds hidden, if you believe Lewis, behind layers of blubber and then sell them off when their talent is proven to the world. The Athletics can't afford to keep the talent around so Beane must do the best with his short-term rentals.

These are all very persuasive theories that must have some basis in fact but if you look a bit closer, things begin to blur. In one chapter on trading, Beane tries to trade away Mike Venafro, a pitcher who had just been sent back to the minor leagues. "Venafro's fine," Beane tells the other team. Sure.

Or consider Jeremy Giambi, a player Lewis calls, "Exhibit A in Billy Beane's lecture on The New and Better Way to Think About Building a Baseball Team." Halfway through the 2002 season, a newspaper reported Giambi visited a strip club. Beane traded him away soon afterwards.

Anyone who was truly running the A's with a computer would not care about visits to a strip club. The computers don't measure things like paternity suits, drug arrests, drinking binges, steroid use, or, for that matter, trips to the local cancer ward, flowers sent to the Mrs., or large donations to charity. The machines just count the hits and walks. These are ballclubs, not Rotary Clubs.

But somehow, character seems to count for something in Beane's book and Giambi went packing soon after he displayed some bit of character that didn't seem to fit Beane's model.

It could be computers and numbers aren't really the secret sauce behind Beane's success. Perhaps Beane's real No. 1 rule for running the ballclub is that "change is always good." Sure, the stats suggest that a club configured a certain way will eventually win 90-some games. The computers practically guarantee it. But Beane never seems to stick with the team defined by those numbers. He just keeps jiggering and rejiggering the team until the season ends. Perhaps this change keeps the team unbalanced enough to stay hungry and focused enough to work hard to keep their job?

There are other, deeper problems with this pachinko view of

baseball. Beane, for instance, discourages stealing bases. To him, the cost of an out is much greater than any gain that may come from moving from first to second. He has solid research behind him on this one. In *The Hidden Game of Baseball*, Pete Palmer and John Thorn calculated that "a runner on first with no outs is worth .478 runs; a steal of second increases this to .699; a failure leaves no one on base and two out, worth .095."

How did they determine this? They looked into the past and averaged the number of runs produced from these situations. An average of .478 runs came out of having someone on first. Palmer and Thorn figured that it would only make sense to steal if the base runner had greater than about a 2 out of 3 chance of succeeding. Anything less was a bad gamble.

This is certainly a good insight, but it only tells us about the past, a time when stealing bases was venerated as a way of "manufacturing runs." In those days, the pitchers watched the runners closely, the second baseman did not wander far from the bag, the catchers had to have a strong arm, and the runners had to be fast. There are probably a thousand different subtle effects that come from the threat of a stolen base.

A manager playing Beane's teams, however, doesn't need to worry about those things. Why start the catcher with a great arm if you've got one who is a better hitter? Why bother with a left-handed pitcher if the pitcher won't need to be watching first base? Why not let the second baseman drift into a better place to stop a hit? Life is a bit easier for the opposing team when they don't need to worry about stolen bases.

When someone is as open and honest about not stealing, the numbers like .478 or .699 don't apply. They came from a different era when managers would order players to steal. What are the right numbers for today? I don't know and I doubt that Billy Beane knows. The game changes in subtle ways. All of the statistical analysis of the past can't predict how it will change the future.

Perhaps these details are of little consequence. Beane's teams succeeded despite giving away these advantages to the opponents. But maybe they would have done even a bit better if they had a Rickey Henderson on the team. Maybe they would have done better with a steal at a defining moment of a game? Just a few attempts can change the defense dramatically. But we'll never know.

Given these holes in the argument for the success of numbers-driven pachinko baseball, I would propose these rules for statistics:

- The numbers are excellent tools for measuring the past. If you want to know the dominant hitter of 1996, well, the statistics will give us the tools to figure out who contributed the most.
- Statistics help identify hidden gems. Some people may not look good to the eye, but statistics can help us find ballplayers with the talent for getting on base.
- Statistics can't predict the future. No matter how much faith the Oakland A's place in the computer, winning is still just a matter of getting on base.
- Statistics can't measure chemistry or cohesion. Beane often replaces one player with a statistically equivalent one. Why bother, unless something else is part of the equation?
- Statistics can't substitute for drive or ability. If the ballgame were truly just a pachinko game with the odds defined by the stats, Billy Beane himself would have been a dominant player.

This brings me to my final anecdote, one that is hard to swallow and difficult to believe. One of my neighbors has a friend known as the Swami. Why? The Swami has an uncanny ability to predict the outcome of ballgames. His talent is far from perfect. He must watch the first several innings before he gets a feeling for what will happen. This feeling doesn't come to him every game. It isn't always strong. But when it arrives, he can make some amazing predictions.

I witnessed this power on August 27, 1997 when the Kansas City Royals came to Baltimore. The score was tied at zero and Scott Erickson was still pitching a perfect game for the Orioles. The Swami called in, we pressed him for a prediction, and he told us, "The Orioles will win and Palmeiro will win the game with a home run."

This was, at the time, a bold move. Palmeiro hit only .253 in 1997, his worst year aside from his rookie season. Despite these low numbers, he played 158 games and batted in 110 runs while striking out more than ever in his career, 109 times.

In the fifth inning, none of the numbers mattered. Palmeiro delivered a solid home run off Kevin Appier with no one on base. It was a good start, because Erickson continued to hold off the Royals. After the Orioles scored two more insurance runs in the sixth, the Swami looked very good.

But it's not over until it's over. The Royals' Chili Davis came to bat in the seventh with two on base and tied the score. Baltimore could still win the game, but it would be hard for the Swami to argue that Palmeiro's home run had done it.

Luckily, good stories have a way of getting better or else we would just forget them. Palmeiro came to bat in the eighth with the bases loaded and delivered all of the heroism that his fans had come to love and expect. A few minutes later, the ball was gone and the Orioles took the lead for good. The Swami's deep clairvoyance had locked onto Palmeiro's second home run, not his first.

There are moments like this in baseball. I suppose it is possible that the Swami was just lucky. The pachinko ball just happened to bump into Palmeiro's bat at the right time before it bounced out of the park. The numbers certainly suggested it was likely to happen eventually. Palmeiro did bat .319 in 1994 and .310 in 1995. The Swami gambled and won.

But I think it's entirely possible that some unseen force was sweeping through the park that night. The Swami tied into it and used it to see the future of the game. Perhaps it was the Swami's clean living, perhaps it was his devotion to his family, perhaps it was some odd thing that we'll never comprehend. But this force is out there and he had his hooks into it.

Napolean once said that the quality he most admired in his generals was luck. The Swami has done this often enough that it isn't just luck. Good managers and good generals have a way of tying into this force that's out there. Billy Beane may claim that he's just playing by the numbers and approaching everything with a statistical purity, but I think he's also got a bit of the Swami in him. He may not know it, he may not admit it, but it's there. That's why he trades .300 hitters for .300 hitters and makes numerically inexplicable changes.

So what does this mean about statistics? Should we abandon the probabilistic view of baseball just because some Swami can predict what will happen to the Orioles? Should we rejoice because some unseen force means that we're not guided by some hidden set of dice? I'm tempted to say it's true about four out of five times a week. That fifth time, even a .300 hitter will go 0 for 5.

It may be better for me to say, "I just don't know." Only you can test this by trying to channel your inner Swami, tie into your own hidden telegraph system, and make up your own mind. I can't be certain, but I suspect that a warm spring day, a good seat, a day away from the office and a glass or two of beer can help focus the mind and enhance the connection.

Chapter 4

Why the '39 Yankees Are the Greatest Team in Baseball History

By Rob Neyer

For three-quarters of a century, the default setting for "Greatest Team" has been '27 Yankees. And for good reason. After all, the 1927 Yanks won 110 games, then swept the Pirates in the World Series. Babe Ruth was their best player, and he's the greatest player who ever lived. Lou Gehrig was their second-best player, and he's the greatest first baseman who ever lived. With Tony Lazzeri and Earle Combs, the Yankees' lineup featured two more future Hall of Famers. Add power-hitting left fielder Bob Meusel, and you've got "Murderers Row," the most famous lineup in major league history.

People tend to forget, though, that once you got past the first five hitters in the lineup, the Yankees weren't particularly strong. Third baseman Jumping Joe Dugan, shortstop Mark Koenig, and catcher Pat Collins weren't patsies, but they did give the enemy hurler something of a breather. What's more, if these Yankees were really so awesome, then why did they finish 18 games out of first place in 1929, just two years later?

Do these things mean the '27 Yankees were *not* the greatest ever? Not necessarily. But they do help us realize just how complicated the question actually is. For every team that you throw out for consideration as the greatest ever, I can come up with at least a couple of *yabbits*, as in "Yeah, but ..."

Yeah, even the '27 Yankees. In fact, in his book *Baseball Between the Lines*, Bob Carroll rates the '27 Yankees as *the* most overrated team in major league history. Why? Carroll mentions a pitching staff without a superstar and a soft bench, but his biggest problem is that the Yankees, playing in the still lily-white American League, didn't have to face some of the best players in America. As Carroll concludes, "In my book ... there can't be a pre-Jackie Robinson 'best ever.' Anything monochrome is overrated."

That's one big *yabbit*. But it's also something of a red herring. After all, we're not directly comparing teams of one era to those of another. If we did that, our list of greatest teams would be dominated by those we've seen on color TV, because the '27 Yankees, if we could resurrect them today, would likely get swept by the '04 Devil Rays in a best-of-seven series. (Skin color will come into play as a *yabbit* later in this essay, but in a different way.) What I think we want to know is, which were the greatest teams *within the contexts of their times*. That said, we do have to realize that during some

Joe DiMaggio
With DiMaggio leading the offense, the 1939 New York Yankees outscored the opposition by a major league record 411 runs en route to a fourth consecutive World Series championship.

eras, it's simply been easier to dominate the competition and post gaudy records. Simply put, it was easier to win 70 percent of your games in 1906 than it was in 1936 (or any year since). And that counts, too.

What I've tried to do, in what you'll read below, is discuss virtually every team that anyone has *suggested* might be the greatest team ever. To be sure, there will be "missing" teams here; you'll say, "Why are the 1984 Tigers here, but not the 1967 Cardinals?" It's a fair question. My answer is, "I had to draw the line somewhere." There are undoubtedly at least a few teams missing that are better than a few teams included. But I honestly don't think anybody can construct a rational argument that the *greatest* team isn't mentioned somewhere in these pages. And that's what this article is about: coming up with a list of candidates, and then ranking some of them in admittedly idiosyncratic order. Yes, we could come up with a set of strict statistical formulae, and rank the teams accordingly. But as William H. Macy said in an episode of *Sports Night*, "Life's a lot more interesting than that, Dana."

I should also mention that you're not going to read much about the positives that compelled me to include the teams under consideration. Why? Because the positives tend to be the same: win a

lot of games, then win the World Series. And also because if you're interested in specifics—who drove in 175 runs, who won 20 games—you've got many sources for that information, including but not limited to the wonderful book you're looking at right now.

Rather, I'm going to focus on the negatives, because it's actually the negatives—the *yabbits*—that separate these great teams. And also because it's the negatives that underline the difficulty of the endeavor.

Speaking of difficulties, it's not easy to get a handle on the teams of the 19th century, because things were changing all the time: the cities, the leagues, the schedules, the rules ... you name it. For that reason—and also, I suppose, because most fans just don't care about years that start with "18"—most books about the greatest teams don't even bother with the 19th century. There are, however, at least a couple of teams that deserve real consideration.

The best team of the 19th century? Hard to say, but the most *legendary* team of the 19th century was Ned Hanlon's Baltimore Orioles, later mythologized by ex-Orioles like John McGraw, Wilbert Robinson and Hughie Jennings. In this case, the legend very nearly was matched by the reality. My choices for the best of those teams was the **1895 Orioles**, but one could just as reasonably choose the '94 or '96 squads, as all three won National League pennants while posting winning percentages ranging from .669 to .698 (in those days, the difference between .669 and .698 was roughly three wins). If there's a knock against this team, it's that they were postseason flops; in three Temple Cup series—pitting the top two National League finishers against one another—the Orioles were twice decisively beaten (though they did, in 1896, sweep the Cleveland Spiders).

The **1886 St. Louis Browns**, in the midst of winning four straight American Association pennants, were statistically even more impressive than the Orioles. However, the American Association was, by most accounts, not as strong as the rival National League during this period, which somewhat lessens the Browns' claim to greatness (granted, the Browns did do fairly well in three early versions of the World Series, and in '86 they beat the National League champion Chicago White Stockings).

Just in terms of one 19th-century season, we should mention two early professional teams: the **1875 Boston Red Stockings**, who went 71-8 in the last season of the National Association, and **1876 Chicago Whites**, who went 52-14 in the first season of the National League.

The **1902 Pittsburgh Pirates** are one of the great (mostly) forgotten teams, and they're forgotten because they went 103-36 in the last season before the National and American Leagues began their annual postseason face-offs. It's well known that many baseball fans, even devotees of baseball history (including this one) tend to ignore the 19th century, but it might be more accurate to say we ignore baseball before 1903, the year of the first "modern" World Series. But 103-36 is 103-36, Series or no Series.

However, we might reasonably question the quality of Pittsburgh's competition that season, what with the youthful American League raiding National League rosters ... except the Pirates' roster. At least one writer has suggested that AL President Ban Johnson purposefully avoided raiding the Pirates, in hopes of making a mockery of the National League's pennant race. And while I'm skeptical about that theory, the fact is that the Pirates were the only NL team that managed to win more than 75 games that season.

If only the **1906 Chicago Cubs** had managed to beat the White

Sox—the so-called "Hitless Wonders"—in the World Series, they would rank very high on most lists of the greatest teams. But they lost to the White Sox, and so people forget their 116-36 record—which still ranks as the best winning percentage by a major league team since 1885—and they also forget that the Cubs played brilliantly and *did* win the World Series in both 1907 and 1908 (from 1906 through '08, the Cubs won 70.3 percent of their regular-season games, the best percentage of the century).

Nobody talks about the **1912 New York Giants** for a very simple reason: they didn't win the World Series. Not that year, or the year before, or the year after. They did, over the course of those three seasons, win two-thirds of their games and three straight National League pennants. It was an awesome club that just couldn't come into a little October luck (and of course, it didn't help that their American League opponents in all three of those World Series were powerful teams in their own right).

I understand the public infatuation with Shoeless Joe Jackson, who was a great player and had a very cool nickname besides. What I don't understand is the affection—now mostly expired, I'm pleased to report—once held by many for Jackson's *team*, the **1917 Chicago White Sox**. Hey, they were a good club, but there are plenty of teams that posted a .650 (or thereabouts) winning percentage and won the World Series. And the 1919 Black Sox were even worse, with a lower winning percentage *and* a bunch of crooked players. The notion that Jackson's Sox should even be considered among the greatest 20 teams ever is preposterous.

We've already discussed the **1927 New York Yankees**, but it's worth noting that the Yankees came back in 1928 and went 101-53, then swept the Cardinals in the World Series. No, the Yankees didn't have any truly great pitchers (especially in '28), but they had plenty of good ones. And of course they had a lot of great *hitters*.

It's also worth noting that, Bob Carroll notwithstanding, almost everybody winds up picking the '27 Yankees as the greatest.

Still, another thing that makes me wonder about the '27 Yankees is just how quickly the **1929 Philadelphia Athletics** knocked the Yankees off their perch. From '29 through '31, the Yankees didn't once finish within 13 games of the pennant-winning Athletics. Granted, the A's were legitimately a great team, thanks largely to Hall of Famers Lefty Grove, Mickey Cochrane, Jimmie Foxx, and Al Simmons. They piled up triple-digit victories in all three of those seasons, also winning the World Series in 1929 and '30 (and just missing in '31).

Weaknesses? There's only one: the Athletics' run differential over these three seasons wasn't nearly as good as their record, which suggests that luck played something of a role in those outstanding records. It's often said that luck evens out over the course of a whole season, but that's simply not true. Sometimes teams get lucky for a whole season, and sometimes they even get (at least a little) lucky over the course of two or three seasons.

Purely in terms of wire-to-wire dominance, nobody can match the late-'30s Yankees, and my pick for the best of those teams is the **1939 New York Yankees**. Consider that 1) from 1936 through 1939, the Yankees won four straight pennants without being seriously challenged, and 2) they capped each of those seasons with World Series victories, winning 16 games and losing only 3. Why the '39 edition rather than one of the others? With 106 wins, these were the winningest Yankees of the era, and they outscored their opponents by 411 runs, the best run differential in major league history. In fact, I would argue that if Lou Gehrig hadn't taken ill early in the season—he was replaced by weak-hitting Babe

Dahlgren—the '39 Yankees would have surpassed the '27 Yankees in the popular imagination, because they would have won more than 110 games rather than 106.

Negatives? Well, Dahlgren was a hole in the lineup. More seriously, one can certainly question the quality of the Yankees' competition. The Tigers, and later the Red Sox, were both solid franchises in that stretch, but the Browns and Athletics were so horrible that they made everybody else in the league look a bit better than they were. That's picking nits, though. In terms of quality *and* consistency, it's hard to match the Yankees of the late 1930s.

Rick Van Blair has written that the **1942 St. Louis Cardinals** "were, and to this day still are, the most underrated great team in major league baseball history." I don't know if that's precisely true, but Van Blair certainly isn't far off.

There's no doubt about the Cardinals' greatness. After winning 97 games in 1941 but finishing in second place, they came back in 1942 and won 106 games, then beat the vaunted Yankees in the World Series. And next? The Cardinals won 105 games in 1943 *and* 1944, losing the Series in '43 but winning again in '44.

So assuming the Cardinals were and are underrated, why? Because of the war. In 1942, nobody was really thinking about baseball any more, and except for Pete Gray, most of what happened from 1942 through '45 has been either forgotten or ignored. Also, wartime achievements have been discounted because so many of the best players were building bridges or flying airplanes or (let's be honest) playing baseball in faraway places. But that doesn't really apply to the '42 Cardinals, because in '42 most of the players still hadn't been called into service. It wasn't until '43 that the draft made a real difference, and it didn't completely decimate the rosters until '44 and '45.

That said, we do have to discount the Cardinals' post-1942 success—or at least consider the difference in the rosters—and we should also note that their run differentials in these years was not wildly impressive.

When a franchise wins five straight World Series, it's not easy to pick just one year and say, "You're the best." And that's especially true when each of the five teams wins roughly the same number of games. Nevertheless, I've chosen the **1953 New York Yankees** to represent the longest-lasting dynasty in World Series history. Beginning in 1949, the Yankees not only won five straight Series, but in each of those years they won more than 94 games and fewer than 100. What's more, in 1954, when they did *not* win the pennant, the Yankees won 103 games, their highest total between 1942 and 1961. All of which is to say, the dynastic Yankees of the early '50s were no fluke.

That said, winning five straight pennants without once winning 100 games probably says something about the quality of the competition. Too, the '53 club was the only one of the five that led the American League in runs scored and allowed.

The **1954 Cleveland Indians** won 111 games, which broke the American League record set by the '27 Yankees and stood as the record for the rest of the 20th century. Were they really that good, in a fundamental sort of way? Well, the Tribe won 92 games in '53 and 93 in '55, which gives us a pretty good read on their true quality, especially considering that rosters in those days weren't turned over as they are now. Still, if the Indians hadn't been soundly beaten by the Giants in the '54 World Series, they would be remembered much more fondly than they have been.

The **1955 Brooklyn Dodgers** are particularly notable for one thing: they finally, in their sixth try, beat the Yankees in a World Series (it was also the first Series the Dodgers won at all, after previously playing in seven of them). The Dodgers won "only" 98 games in '55, and some might prefer the '53 team that won 105 games. But the '53 Bums didn't boast particularly impressive pitching, while the '55 squad 1) led the league in runs scored *and* allowed and 2) beat the Yankees.

Negatives? Well, again, the '55 Dodgers won only 98 games, and that's the cream filling. The chocolate cookies on the outside were 92 wins (1954) and 93 (in '56). Don't get me wrong, the Boys of Summer were an extraordinary collection of talent. But they—like a team from the 1990s we'll meet later—didn't completely dominate their regular-season competition *and* they had their problems in October.

There were, at least until 1998, a fair number of people who argued that the **1961 New York Yankees**, and not the '27 edition, should be considered the greatest team ever. Why? In large part, because of Mickey Mantle and Roger Maris, but also because between 1927 and 1961 the (so-called) major leagues had finally been integrated. However, this leaves aside the fact that in 1961 the American League had still not been *well* integrated. That season, the major leagues were home to 10 future Hall of Famers who, prior to 1947, wouldn't have been allowed to play because of the color of their skin ... and all 10 of them were National Leaguers. Quite simply, there's very good evidence that in the 1960s the National League was better than the American League, and for that reason I believe we must discount—to what degree, we can argue—the accomplishments of American League teams in that era.

The '61 Yanks do have some things going for them. They won 109 games. They won their second of what would be five straight American League pennants. They swamped the Reds in the World Series. But they didn't lead the league in runs scored *or* runs allowed. And they didn't have to worry about many of the greatest players, because all of the great black players were in the other league.

In terms of regular-season wins, no team in recent memory can touch the **1970 Baltimore Orioles**; or rather, the 1969-1971 Orioles. The O's won 108 games—and the World Series—in 1970, between winning 109 games in '69 and 101 games in '71. So why are the Orioles rarely mentioned when people talk about the greatest teams? Because they lost two World Series, and in '69 they lost to the Miracle Mets, who are remembered *far* more often than the Orioles are. Oddly, though, people forget that those Mets were 1) a damn good team that won 100 regular-season games, and 2) exceptionally lucky in the World Series.

A couple of negatives ... Major League Baseball added four teams in 1969, and while I generally don't buy the argument that expansion significantly waters down the competition, four teams at once is a lot, and it might not be a coincidence that the Orioles won 217 games in '69 and 70. Also, at that point the National League clubs were still, on the whole, doing a better job of fielding the greatest black players (think of Joe Morgan, Jimmy Wynn, Fergie Jenkins, Cleon Jones, Bobby Bonds, Cesar Cedeno, and Dick Allen; now try to think of a similar list of great black players in the American League).

But the Orioles had a great manager, great pitching, great defense, and future Hall of Famers at third base (Brooks Robinson) and in right field (Frank Robinson). You can find fault with them, but you have to be real creative.

If this article were specifically about dynasties rather than particular teams—and I know I've blurred the distinction, but please bear with me—then we would have to seriously consider the **1974**

Oakland A's and their earlier manifestations, because beginning in 1972 the A's won three straight World Series, which makes them one of only four teams—and the only non-Yankees—to accomplish that feat. But leaving aside how those three seasons ended, the A's just didn't play all that brilliantly. Much like the 1949-1953 Yankees, the A's played just well enough to win, both in the regular and post seasons. But the A's were slightly *less* impressive than the Yankees in both the regular and post seasons, *and* they didn't do it for quite so many years.

They weren't part of a three-year World Series dynasty, but there's little doubt that the **1975 Cincinnati Reds** were the greatest team of the decade. They won 108 games in 1975, 102 more in '76, and they won the World Series in both seasons. They had four Hall of Famers in the lineup (yes, for the sake of argument I'm including Pete Rose), and the other four everyday players were all pretty good, too. And this was a lineup that could do it all; in '76, the Reds led the National League in virtually every offensive statistic, including batting average, home runs, walks, and steals.

If there's a knock on this club, it's against their pitching, as no Reds pitcher won more than 15 games in either season. But this was partly just bad luck (there were a few starters who pitched well enough and often enough to win 20) and partly by design (Sparky Anderson didn't get the nickname "Captain Hook" for nothing). Bottom line, the Reds played in a hitter's park, and yet Cincinnati's pitching staff finished third in the league in ERA in '75 (and fifth in '76). No, it wasn't a great staff. But it certainly was a great team.

Thirty years after the Indians won 111 games, the **1984 Detroit Tigers** similarly lapped the American League field, but of course the Tigers did something the Indians didn't: they won the World Series (and in convincing fashion, first sweeping the Royals in the ALCS and then besting the Padres in five games). However, people often forget that the Tigers won 104 regular-season games, which isn't particularly noteworthy by historical standards. Granted, after opening the season 35-5, the Tigers might be excused for coasting a bit down the stretch. But the Tigers had won 92 games in 1983 and would win only 84 games in '85. This was a very good team that played brilliantly for seven months, thanks in part to a squad of bench players that collectively played over its head.

Nobody really talks about the **1986 New York Mets**, and it's not real hard to understand why. After all, the Mets didn't even reach the postseason in '85 or '87 (and were one round and done in '88), and of course they wouldn't have won the '86 World Series without a *highly* improbable ninth-inning rally in Game 6. But this was one hell of a team. The Mets won 98 games in 1985 (but finished second), 108 games in '86, then 92 and 100 in 1987 and '88, respectively.

I'll throw the **1998 Atlanta Braves** into the discussion because 1) they won 106 games, and 2) anybody who was around in the 1990s is well aware that the Braves dominated their division as no team has since divisions were invented in 1969. But the Braves didn't even reach the World Series in 1998, and in all the other years they managed to win just one World Series. That was in 1995 ... when they won only 90 games (granted, that was a strike-shortened season, and their .625 winning percentage was truly excellent, if not historical). What the Braves did in the 1990s and the first few years of the 21st century was awfully impressive. But the naked

truth is that the Braves were not, over any period of more than six months or thereabouts, an awfully *great* team.

On the other hand, there is very, very little about the **1998 New York Yankees** not to like. They won 114 games—at the time, an American League record—and they led the league in both runs scored (965) and runs allowed (656) by healthy margins. The Yankees fairly romped through the postseason, sweeping the Rangers in the Division Series, beating the Indians in a six-game ALCS, and then sweeping the Padres in the World Series. And of course the Yankees were far from a fluke, winning the World Series again in 1999 and 2000.

All that said, there are a few chinks in the Yankees' pinstriped armor. For one thing, 1998 was an expansion season, and the Yankees took advantage with an 11-1 mark against the upstart Devil Rays. For another, by 1998 there was a clear stratification between the teams that could compete financially and the teams that couldn't.

As impressive as the '98 Yankees' 114 wins were, just three years later the **2001 Seattle Mariners** made them look somewhat less impressive by winning 116 games (and arguably against tougher competition, as two of the other three teams in their division finished better than .500). But the M's barely escaped their Division Series against the Indians, and they did *not* escape their ALCS match-up against the Yankees. What's more, the Mariners bookended those 116 wins in '01 with 91 wins in 2000 and 93 in '02. The M's in 2001 were a very good team that happened to enjoy a truly great season.

So how does one make sense of it all? The Perfect Baseball Team—which is to say, the *obvious* choice for "the greatest team what ever was" (in Bill James' phraseology)—would be ... well, perfect: tough competition, superstars dotting the roster, historic run differential, impressive postseason performance, great seasons before and/or after (to "prove" that it wasn't a fluke), and of course a great number of wins.

But you know what? The absolutely, positively Perfect Baseball Team doesn't exist. If your goal is to poke a hole in the reputation of even the very greatest teams, you can do it (and I have). There are some teams, though, that were very nearly perfect, and here are the ten that I think came the closest:

1. 1939 Yankees	6. 1927 Yankees
2. 1970 Orioles	7. 1929 Athletics
3. 1998 Yankees	8. 1986 Mets
4. 1975 Reds	9. 1942 Cardinals
5. 1906 Cubs	10. 1974 A's

This list is almost identical to what I presented in my book (*Baseball Dynasties*), except I've replaced the '61 Yankees with the 1974 A's in the No. 10 slot. Why the change? Because since the book was published in 2000, I've come to believe that the level of competition in the early-'60s American League simply wasn't quite what I'd thought it was.

The author wishes to thank Eddie Epstein for developing the statistical measures that informed the choices for the great teams under consideration in this article.

Chapter 5

Our Game

By John Thorn

Baseball has been, most often for better but occasionally for worse, the American game. It has given our people rest and recreation, myths and memories, heroes and history, and hope. It has mirrored our society, sometimes propelling it with models for democracy, community, commerce, and common humanity, sometimes lagging behind with equally instructive models of futility and resistance to change. And as our national game, baseball in no small measure defines us as Americans, connecting us with our countrymen across all barriers of generation, class, race, and creed.

Baseball in the Americas is more than a game, an observation to which the scope of this book is testimony and tribute. But it is first and foremost about *play,* a fact obscured amid today's ferment of free agency, salary caps, and sky boxes. Some 150 years ago, an overly solemn America was first indebted to baseball for the freedom it gave to play. As overture to this volume's chronicle of baseball's history, let's look at how child's play came to be our national pastime.

America Learns to Play

Even when baseball was in its infancy in the 1850s—having just broken away from the boyhood game of rounders and its more formalized derivative, town ball—the sport was already shaping the life of the country. Americans of the previous generation had been blind to the virtue of play, much perplexing our European cousins. We permitted ourselves few amusements that could not be justified in terms of social or business utility, or "seriousness." Nonconformists like the Olympic Town Ball Club of Philadelphia in the 1830s had to put up with a lot of guff, as this contemporary account details:

The first day that the Philadelphia men took the field … only four men were found to play, so they started in by playing a game called cat ball. All the players were over twenty-five years of age,

Senator Robert Kennedy, Mickey Mantle
Ever since President Andrew Johnson attended a professional game in 1867, politicians have maintained a close association with the American game.

and to see them playing a game like this caused much merriment among the friends of the players. It required "sand" in those days to go out on the field and play, as the prejudice against the game was very great. It took nearly a whole season to get men enough together to make a team, owing to the ridicule heaped upon the players for taking part in such childish sports.

What brought scorn upon the heads of these staunch devotees of town ball (also known as "Boston Ball" or the "Massachusetts

Game") was that although the features of the game included regularly positioned fielders and a modicum of strategic play, it still bore the childish essence of rounders: the retirement of a baserunner by throwing the ball at him, which necessitated a softer, less resilient ball than that used in the manly sport of cricket.

Who was the genius who came up with the idea of retiring a runner by touching him with the ball or securing it "in the hands of an adversary on the base"? Perhaps it was Alexander Cartwright, who is known to many as "the man who invented baseball," though baseball was not invented; it evolved. But it may have been Daniel Lucius Adams or William Wheaton or Lewis F. Wadsworth.

No matter—this was the first step toward making an American game that could challenge boys and men alike, and that could take its place in the life of our nation as cricket had done in England. Henry Chadwick, the English-born cricket reporter who popularized the term "national pastime" and became known as the "Father of Baseball," wrote that early on he

> ... was struck with the idea that base ball was just the game for a national sport for Americans and ... that from this game of ball a powerful lever might be made by which our people could be lifted into a position of more devotion to physical exercise and healthful out-door recreation than they had, hitherto, been noted for. ... In fact, as is well-known, we were the regular target for the shafts of raillery and even abuse from our outdoor-sport-loving cousins of England, in consequence of our national neglect of sports and pastimes, and our too great devotion to business and the "Almighty Dollar." But thanks to Base Ball ... we have been transformed into quite another people.

The transformation was from a hard-working but grim citizenry to a nation devoted to fresh air and exercise, not unlike the recent rage for jogging, aerobics, and body building. Amateur baseball clubs proliferated in the years immediately before the Civil War, but these were formed more for camaraderie and calisthenics than the pursuit of victory or the honing of skills. The demands of the new game on athleticism were few, as the one-bound rule remained in effect (an out was recorded if a ball was caught on a bounce), and a bit of practice was all it took to become a serviceable player.

Men viewed baseball as a mild pastime, or relief from the mental strains of work; as a tonic, restorative of the physical energies needed for work; or as a release of the surplus nervous energy that impedes young men in their pursuit of purposeful work. America in the mid-1850s was learning how to play, but still viewed sport in terms of its salutary effects on commerce; not until the close of the War Between the States would the focus shift to learning how to play well, for its own sake.

The Charm of the Game

Today we think of baseball as an anachronism, a last vestige of America's agrarian paradise—an idyllic game that takes us back to a more innocent time. But baseball originated in New York City, not rural Cooperstown, and in truth it was an exercise in nostalgia from the beginning. Alexander Cartwright and his Knickerbockers began play in Madison Square in 1842, and the city's northward progress soon compelled them to move uptown to Murray Hill.

When the grounds there were also threatened by the march of industry, the Knicks ferried across the Hudson River to the Elysian Fields of Hoboken, a landscaped retreat of picnic grounds and scenic vistas that was designed by its proprietors to relieve New Yorkers of city air, city care, and a dollar or two. In other words, the purpose of baseball's primal park was the same as Boston's Fenway Park.

Thus the attraction of the game in its earliest days was first the novelty and exhilaration of play; second the opportunity for deskbound city clerks to expend surplus energy in a sylvan setting, freed from the tyranny of the clock; and third, to harmonize with an American golden age that was almost entirely legendary.

Simple charms, simple pleasures. In the late 1860s, advancing skills led to heightened appetites for victory, which led to hot pursuit of the game's gifted players, which inevitably led to sub rosa payments and, by 1870, rampant professionalism. (Doesn't that chain reaction put one in mind of college football or basketball?) The gentlemanly players of baseball's first generation retreated from the field, shaking their heads in dismay at how greed had perverted the "grand old game."

Sound familiar? It should—the same dire and premature announcements of the demise of the game have been issued ever since, spurred by free-agent signings, long-term contracts, no-trade provisions, strikes and lockouts, integration, night ball, rival leagues, ad infinitum. The only conclusions a calm head might draw from this recurring cycle of disdain for the present and glorification of the past are that (a) things aren't what they used to be and never were; (b) accurate assessment of a present predicament is impossible, for it requires perspective; and (c) no matter what the owners or players or rules-makers or fans do, they can't kill baseball.

All three conclusions are correct. In baseball, the distinction between amateur and professional is not clear-cut: an amateur may play for devotion to the game (*amat* being the Latin for "he loves"), but a professional does not play for pursuit of gain alone; he plays for love, too.

> *Oh, don't you remember the game of base-ball we saw twenty years ago played,*
> *When contests were true, and the sight free to all, and home-runs in plenty were made?*
> *When we lay on the grass, and with thrills of delight, watched the ball squarely pitched at the bat,*
> *And easily hit, and then mount out of sight along with our cheers and our hat?*
> *And then, while the fielders raced after the ball, the men on the bases flew round,*
> *And came in together—four batters in all. Ah! That was the old game renowned.*
> *Now salaried pitchers, who throw the ball curved at padded and masked catchers lame*
> *And gate-money music and seats all reserved is all that is left of the game.*
> *Oh, give us the glorious matches of old, when love of true sport made them great,*
> *And not this new-fashioned affair always sold for the boodle they take at the gate.*
>
> H. C. Dodge

That doomsday ditty was published in 1886.

The National Pastime

America before the Civil War was still populated by a handful of veterans of the Revolutionary War and many who remembered

vividly the War of 1812. The era of Anglo-American amity had not yet dawned; our country's spiritual separation from the Mother Country, though effected by treaty in 1783, was still in process. And having baseball to rival and replace cricket was an important step in that process. When England, seeking to maintain its supply of cotton during the Civil War, appeared to favor the Confederacy, antipathy toward John Bull swept the North. An America long suffering from an inferiority complex toward England now turned against cricket and embraced baseball with increased fervor.

From 1856 on, Henry Chadwick had been eager for baseball to rise to the status in America that cricket held in his native England. He championed the game tirelessly, helping to refine its rules and practices to make it the equal of cricket as a "manly" and "scientific" game. And baseball soon became, in his words, like cricket "a game requiring the mental powers of judgment, calculation and quick perception to excel in it—while in its demands upon the vigor, endurance and courage of manhood, its requirements excel those requisite to become equally expert as a cricketer."

Chadwick invented a method of scorekeeping and statistical compilation patterned on those of cricket. Baseball was an elemental game—pitch, hit, catch, throw—like other games of ball; but keeping records of the contests and later printing box scores and individual averages elevated it from rounders and placed it on an equal footing with its transatlantic counterpart. (As important, the records served to legitimize men's concern with what had been merely a boys' exercise by making it more systematic, like the numerically annotated world of business.) Today a baseball without records is inconceivable: They are what keep Babe Ruth and Ty Cobb and Walter Johnson alive in our minds in a way that President James K. Polk, Walter Reed, or Admiral Dewey—arguably greater men—are not.

By the end of the Civil War, cricket in this country remained a pastime for a shrinking band of Anglophiles, while the New York Game of Baseball (as it was then called to differentiate it from the nearly vanished Massachusetts Game) was spreading across the country, courtesy of returning veterans whose first exposure to baseball might have come in a prisoner-of-war camp. In the press, baseball was typically proclaimed The National Game— the same term Britons used for cricket.

Play for Pay

From its creation in 1871 to its crash five years later, the National Association had a rocky time as America's first professional league. Franchises came and went with dizzying speed, often folding in midseason. Schedules were not played out if a club that was slated to go on the road saw little prospect of gain. Drinking and gambling and game-fixing were rife. And the Boston Red Stockings of Al Spalding and the Wright brothers dominated play, going 71–8 in the last of their four straight championship seasons; their predictable and one-sided victories crushed the competition and, at last, interest in the entire circuit.

But from the ashes of the National Association emerged the Red Stockings' model of success and the entrepreneurial genius of Chicago's William Hulbert. After raiding Boston to obtain four of the biggest stars in the game—Spalding, Ross Barnes, Deacon White, and Cal McVey—and lining up the services of the Philadelphia Athletics' Adrian "Cap" Anson, the White Stockings were ready to roll in the National League of Professional Base Ball Clubs, founded on February 2, 1876 in New York's Grand Central Hotel.

The first five years of the NL were nearly as unsettled as the final years of the NA, with franchises appearing and then disappearing in such cities as Syracuse, Indianapolis, and Hartford while major cities like New York and Philadelphia were, after the league's inaugural year, unrepresented. In 1878 the fledgling circuit was forced to cut back to six teams: Milwaukee, Indianapolis, Chicago, Providence, Cincinnati, and Boston. National League? National Game? It seemed Americans had plenty of appetite for playing the game, but not much for watching it.

Yet as the National League suffered with growing pains, it was introducing some elements that were critical to the explosion of interest that was to come with the 1880s. It created a professional (paid) umpiring crew; insisted that the league schedule be honored; banned pool-selling and hard-liquor consumption in the stands; and created a system of management-owned teams as opposed to the player-run cooperatives that had largely characterized the NA. As the public's renewed faith in the integrity of the game coincided with an upswing in the national economy, not only did the National League flourish—along came an interloper, the rival American Association, to offer patrons 25-cent baseball (NL admissions were 50 cents), Sunday games, and beer. With the public's new appetite for the game seeming insatiable, a group of investors led by St. Louis' Henry Lucas launched a third major league, the Union Association, for 1884.

As brash stars like Cap Anson, Tim Keefe, Dan Brouthers, and the larger-than-life King Kelly captured the newspaper headlines and the nation's imagination, the age of the baseball idol arrived. Before this decade, men like Jim Creighton, Joe Start, and George Wright had been admired in New York and New England, but now a baseball hero's image could be mass-produced for nationwide sale, or licensed for advertising, or inspire odes and songs. Kelly inspired "Slide, Kelly, Slide," its arcane references now largely forgotten but once the most popular song in the land:

Slide, Kelly, slide!
Your running's a disgrace!
Slide, Kelly, slide!
Stay there, hold your base!
If someone doesn't steal ya,
And your batting doesn't fail ya,
They'll take you to Australia! Slide, Kelly, slide!

And although Ernest Lawrence Thayer always denied it, Kelly could well have been the model for "Casey at the Bat," the immortal lyric ballad Thayer penned in 1888. ("Casey" was sometimes reprinted in the newspapers of the 1880s as "Kelly at the Bat," changing the locale from Mudville to Beantown.)

Baseball was ascendant in the 1880s, and like the budding nation whose pastime it was, pretty cocksure of itself. In the same year that "Casey" made his debut, Albert Spalding led a contingent of baseball players on a round the world tour, spreading the gospel of bat and ball to such places as Egypt, Italy, England, Hawaii, and the above-mentioned Australia. Baseball, America thought, was too grand a game to be merely a national pastime; it ought to be the international pastime.

At a New York banquet for Spalding's returning "world tourists" in 1889, speaker Mark Twain declared, "Baseball is the very symbol, the outward and visible expression of the drive and push and rush and struggle of the raging, tearing, booming nineteenth century." Spalding himself later wrote:

I claim that Base Ball owes its prestige as our National Game to the fact that as no other form of sport it is the exponent of American Courage, Confidence, Combativeness; American Dash, Discipline, Determination; American Energy, Eagerness, Enthusiasm; American Pluck, Persistency, Performance; American Spirit, Sagacity, Success; American Vim, Vigor, Virility.

In fact baseball had become more than the mere reflection of our rising industrial and political power and its propensity for bluster and hokum: the national game was beginning to supply emblems for democracy, industry, and community that would change America and the world—not in the ways that Spalding's Tourists may have envisioned, but indisputably for the better.

A Model Institution

Father Henry Chadwick had been typically prescient when he wrote in 1876, the inaugural year of the National League and the centenary of America's birth:

What Cricket is to an Englishman, Base-Ball has become to an American. ... On the Cricket-field—and there only—the Peer and the Peasant meet on equal terms; the possession of courage, nerve, judgment, skill, endurance and activity alone giving the palm of superiority. In fact, a more democratic institution does not exist in Europe than this self-same Cricket; and as regards its popularity, the records of the thousands of Commoners, Divines and Lawyers, Legislators and Artisans, and Literateurs as well as Mechanics and Laborers, show how great a hold it has on the people. If this is the characteristic of Cricket in aristocratic and monarchical England, how much more will the same characteristics mark Base-Ball in democratic and republican America.

Chadwick's vision of baseball as a model democratic institution would have to wait for the turn of the century to be fully articulated, and for Jackie Robinson and Branch Rickey to be fully realized. But his belief that baseball could be more than a game, could become a model of and for American life, presaged baseball's golden age of 1903 to 1930.

The tumultuous 1890s witnessed a player revolt against high-handed and monopolistic management, epitomized by a cap on salaries, followed by a nearly ruinous contraction from three major leagues to one 12-team circuit. The national economy suffered a panic in 1893 and a sluggish recovery thereafter; baseball attendance dwindled; and the lack of postseason interleague competition after 1890 (as there had been since 1884) was sorely felt. The game was in a period of consolidation, or hibernation, or stagnation; one's perspective depended upon whether one was an owner, fan, or player.

But then Ban Johnson came along, fired by the same vision of a rival league that had inflamed the Players League and the American and Union Associations before him, and that would beckon to the Federal and Continental Leagues later on. With the declaration by the American League that it would conduct business as a major league in 1901, and the signing of a peace treaty with the Nationals two years later, the World Series was resumed, prosperity returned, and the popularity and influence of the game exploded.

Baseball mania seized America as new heroes like Christy Mathewson, Honus Wagner, Ty Cobb, Walter Johnson, and Nap Lajoie found a public hungry for knowledge of their every action, their every thought. A fan's affiliation with his team could exceed

in vigor his attachment to his church, his trade, his political party—all but family and country, and even these were wrapped up in baseball. The national pastime became the great repository of national ideals, the symbol of all that was good in American life: fair play (sportsmanship); the rule of law (objective arbitration of disputes); equal opportunity (each side has its innings); the brotherhood of man (bleacher harmony); and more.

The baseball boom of the early 20th century built on the game's simple charms of exercise and communal celebration, adding the psychological and social complexities of vicarious play: civic pride, role models, and hero worship. It became routine for the President to throw out the first ball of the season. Supreme Court Justices had inning-by-inning scores from the World Series relayed to their chambers. Business leaders, perhaps disingenuously, praised baseball as a model of competition and fair play. "Baseball," opined a writer for *American Magazine* in 1913, "has given our public a fine lesson in commercial morals. ... Some day all business will be reorganized and conducted by baseball standards."

Leaders of recent immigrant groups advised their peoples to learn the national game if they wanted to become Americans, and foreign-language newspapers devoted space to educating their readers about America's strange and wonderful game. (New York's *Staats-Zeitung,* for example, applauded *Kräftiges Schlagen*—hard hitting—and cautioned German fans not to kill the *Unparteiischer.*) As historian Harold Seymour wrote, "The argot of baseball supplied a common means of communication and strengthened the bond which the game helped to establish among those sorely in need of it—the mass of urban dwellers and immigrants living in the anonymity and impersonal vortex of large industrial cities. ... With the loss of the traditional ties known in a rural society, baseball gave to many the feeling of belonging." And rooting for a baseball team permitted city folk, newcomers and native-born, the sense of pride in community that was in former times—when they may have lived in small towns—commonplace.

Thus baseball offered a model of how to be an American, to be part of the team: Baseball was "second only to death as a leveler," wrote essayist Allen Sangree. Even in those horrifically leveling years of 1941 to 1945, when so many of our bravest and best gave their lives to defend American ideals, baseball's role as a vital enterprise was confirmed by President Franklin Delano Roosevelt's "green light" for continued play. Many of baseball's finest players—Ted Williams, Joe DiMaggio, Hank Greenberg, Bob Feller, to name a few—swapped their baseball gear for Uncle Sam's, and served with military distinction or helped to boost the nation's morale. Even old-timers like Babe Ruth, Walter Johnson, and Ty Cobb donned uniforms in service of their country—baseball uniforms, as they staged exhibitions on behalf of war bonds. Servicemen overseas looked to letters from home and the box scores in *The Sporting News* to keep them in touch with what they had left behind, and what they were fighting for—an American way of life that was a beacon to a world in which the light of freedom had been nearly extinguished.

I was one of the countless immigrants who from the 1860s on saw baseball as the "open sesame" to the door of their adopted land. A Polish Jew born in occupied Germany to Holocaust survivors, I arrived on these shores at age 2. After checking in at Ellis Island, I happened by chance to spend the first night in my new land in the no longer-elegant hotel where in 1876 the National League had been founded. I learned to read by studying the backs of Topps baseball cards, and to be an American by attaching myself passion-

ately to the Brooklyn Dodgers (who also taught me about the fickleness of love).

Those Dodgers, in the persons particularly of Rickey and Robinson, also taught America a lesson: that baseball's integrative and democratic models, by the 1940s long held to be verities, were hollow at the core. David Halberstam has written:

> ... it was part of our folklore, basic to our national democratic myth, that sports was the great American equalizer, that money and social status did not matter upon the playing fields. Elsewhere life was assumed to be unfair: those who had privilege passed it on to their children, who in turn had easier, softer lives. Those without privilege were doomed to accept the essential injustices of daily life. But according to the American myth, in sports the poor but honest kid from across the tracks could gain (often in competition with richer, snottier kids) recognition and acclaim for his talents.

Until October 23, 1945, when Robinson signed a contract to play for the Montreal Royals, Brooklyn's top farm club, the myth as far as African-Americans were concerned was not a sustaining legend but a mere falsehood.

Rickey's rectitude and Robinson's courage have become central parables of baseball and America, exemplars of decency and strength that inspire all of us. Their "great experiment" came too late for such heroes of black ball as Josh Gibson, Oscar Charleston and Ray Dandridge, but its success has been complete. Once the integrative or leveling model of baseball—all America playing and working in harmony—was extended to African-Americans, the effect on the nation was profound. Eighty years after the Civil War, America had proved itself unable to practice the values for which it was fought; baseball showed the way. This is what Commissioner Ford Frick said to the St. Louis Cardinals, rumored to be planning a strike in May 1947:

> If you do this you will be suspended from the league. You will find that the friends you think you have in the press box will not support you, that you will be outcasts. I do not care if half the league strikes. Those who do it will encounter quick retribution. They will be suspended and I don't care if it wrecks the National League for five years. This is the United States of America, and one citizen has as much right to play as any other. The National League will go down the line with Robinson whatever the consequence.

As Monte Irvin said, "Baseball has done more to move America in the right direction than all the professional patriots with their billions of cheap words." The Supreme Court decision of *Brown v. Topeka Board of Education*; civil rights heroes like Martin Luther King Jr., James Meredith, Thurgood Marshall, and others; the freedom marches and the voting rights act—all were vital to America's progress toward unity, but the title of one of Jackie Robinson's books may not overstate the case: *Baseball Has Done It*.

A final way in which baseball supplies models for America is one that has been present from the game's beginning: a model for children wishing to be grownups, wrestling with their insecurities and wondering, What does it mean to be a man? What does a man do? (Most of us old boys occasionally wonder this as well.) The answers in baseball, at least, are unequivocal; as Satchel Paige said in his later years, "I loved baseball. There wasn't no 'maybe so' about it."

Baseball gives children a sense of how wide the world is, not only in its possibilities but also in its geography. Reading the summations of minor league ball in *The Sporting News* each week piqued the curiosity of baseball-mad boys like me: where were Kokomo and Mattoon and Thibodeaux and Nogales? How did people behave in Salinas or Rocky Mount? What did they eat in Artesia? How many exciting, exotic places this enormous country contained! But a note of comfort—they couldn't be all that strange if baseball was played there.

And to that other vast terra incognita—the world of adults—baseball also offered a road map. How many boys and girls learned to talk with adults, principally their fathers, by nodding wisely at an assessment of a shortstop's range or a pitcher's heart, and mockconfidently venturing an opinion about the hometown team's chances? Our dads are our first heroes (and, decades later, our last); but in between, baseball players are what we want to be. For heroes are larger than life, and when as adults we have taken the measure of ourselves and found we are no more than life-size, and on our bad days seemingly less than that, baseball can puff us up a bit.

Douglass Wallop put it nicely:

> ... only yesterday the fan was a kid of nine or ten bolting his breakfast on Saturday morning and hurtling from the house with a glove buttoned over his belt and a bat over his shoulder, rushing to the nearest vacant lot, perhaps the nearest alley, where the other guys were gathering, a place where it would always be spring. For him, baseball would always have the sound and look and smell of that morning and of other mornings just like it. Only by an accident of chance would he find himself, in the years to come, up in the grandstand, looking on. But for a quirk of fate, he himself would be down on that field; it would be his likeness on the television screen and his name in the newspaper high on the list of .300 hitters. He was a fan, but a fan only incidentally. He was, first and always, himself a baseball player.

The Fifties

If the America that was survives anywhere as more than a memory, it is in baseball, that strangely pastoral game in no matter what setting—domed stadium or Little League field. As hindsight improves upon foresight, memory improves upon reality, so that the endless monotony and grinding physical labor of small-town life before the Civil War are now thought quite romantic. For all our justifiable complaints today, it may likewise be argued that America is better than it ever was.

Today's players are better than those in the game's golden age; the strategy of the game and even its execution are more adept (forget all that moaning about how nobody knows the "fundamentals" any more ... the average player of 50 years ago didn't know them either); and the opportunities to watch baseball, if not to play it, far exceed those of say, the 1950s, today broadly regarded as the game's halcyon era. (A golden age may be defined flexibly, it seems, so as to coincide with the period of one's youth.) For all its pull toward the good old days, for all its statistical illusions of an Olympian era when titans strode the basepaths, for all its seeming permanence in a world aswirl with change, baseball has in fact moved with America, and improved with it.

The period after World War II was a heady time for the nation and its pastime, both of them buoyed by returning veterans and removed restrictions. But in 1946 the major leagues still represented only the 16 cities that had participated in the National Agreement of 1903, none west of St. Louis; a handful of African-Americans were just entering the minor leagues after a half-cen-

tury's exclusion; and because television was not yet a staple of the American home, most baseball fans had never seen even a single big-league game.

Women had been courted as patrons (even nonpaying patrons) ever since the game's dawn. Baseball management hoped that their presence would lend "tone" to the proceedings and keep a lid on the rowdies, in the stands and on the field. But women's participation in the game's labor force and management was even more limited than their role in the nation's business and industry—Rosie the Riveter and Eleanor Roosevelt as yet had no counterparts in Organized Baseball. The All-American Girls Baseball League made its debut in 1943, the brainchild of Chicago Cubs' owner Philip K. Wrigley. The women's "league of their own" won many admirers over the next decade, but the majors always regarded it as separate and unequal.

On the amateur level, while American Legion Junior Baseball had begun as early as 1928, and Little League in 1939, neither attained their heights until after the War ended. Naysayers will point out that baseball has lost ground as more kids today play football, basketball, soccer, and tennis than fifty years ago—but far more play baseball, too, and not only in America. The annual pursuit of the Little League championship in Williamsport, Pennsylvania (like the Pan-American Games), has become an international affair, an instrument of diplomacy that State Department officials envy. Indeed, baseball may yet hold the key to neighborly relations with all nations in the hemisphere.

Baseball in the colleges, now so vibrant and so fertile with major league talent, was on the path to extinction by the end of the War, only to be brought back from the brink by the G.I. Bill: the explosive growth in enrollment that the returning veterans produced also created a sudden need for expanded athletic programs, and baseball was the prime beneficiary. The NCAA's introduction of the College World Series in 1947 affirmed the game's recovery on campus; since locating in Omaha three years later it has grown steadily.

In 1951 Major League Baseball, as dated from the inception of the National League in 1876, reached the august age of 75 and proclaimed its "diamond jubilee." Celebratory banquets were held, a plaque was erected at the old hotel where the league was founded, and all NL players wore a commemorative patch on their sleeves. (Coincidentally but less flashily the American League marked its 50th birthday as a major circuit.) Let's take a moment to look at where baseball stood at that point.

There was no question it was booming. On the professional level, a whopping 59 leagues contained 448 teams employing about 8,000 players—or about 20 minor leaguers competing for each of the then 400 spots in the big show. Little League would soon send its first alumnus to the majors, which had already accepted hundreds of graduates from Legion and other programs. Commissioner Happy Chandler secured from television a then mind-boggling but now quaint $6 million for broadcast rights to the next six World Series. And with the game's most powerful teams bunched in New York City—the Yankees, the Dodgers, and the Giants—the publicity mills and the turnstiles were spinning as they had never spun before.

But the excitement of the first five postwar years was not confined to New York: even such perennial tailenders as the Boston Braves, the Philadelphia Phillies, and the Cleveland Indians fought their way into the World Series; and staid old Cleveland, under Bill Veeck's carnival-barker aegis, set staggering new attendance records. Many of the newly admitted African-American players had become

stars and—satisfyingly, though few but Branch Rickey had predicted it—box-office attractions: Jackie Robinson, Roy Campanella, and Don Newcombe of the Dodgers; Monte Irvin and rookie Willie Mays of the Giants; Sam Jethroe of the Braves; Larry Doby and Satchel Paige of the Indians. Many pre-War stars continued to shine, like Bob Feller, Stan Musial, and Ted Williams (though with the Korean War he answered Uncle Sam's call yet again), and new ones like Gotham's center field trio of Duke Snider, Mickey Mantle, and Mays replenished the stock as heroes like Joe DiMaggio hung up their spikes.

But most of these blessings had their downside. Opening the game to African-Americans was indubitably right, but it killed the Negro Leagues, ruining owners and abruptly ending many playing careers. The increasing organization of youth baseball, particularly the rise of Little League, heightened the stress of the game at its formative levels and drained much of the fun, as driven parents began to see their Junior as tomorrow's big leaguer, not as just a boy having fun while learning a thing or two. The game on the field was dominated by the home run, making for a brand of ball that some might term dull. League champs registered such puny stolen-base totals as Dom DiMaggio's 15 or Jackie Jensen's 22; Early Wynn led the AL in ERA one year with a mark of 3.20; and the three-base hit, despite the big old parks still prevalent, went the way of the dodo. And the pennant domination by the three New York teams—principally the Yankees, of course—made the national pastime a rather parochial pleasure; it was hard for fans in Pittsburgh or Detroit to wax rhapsodic over a Subway Series. No, the blessings of the 1950s were not unmitigated, any more than on the national scene the tranquility of the Eisenhower years was without cost.

Take television, for instance: the revenues were great, and so was the publicity value of electronically extending major league play to people in Southern and Western areas. But the novelty of big-time heroes on the small screen kept those folks at home when formerly they had gone to the local ballpark. The minors began their long decline, one that didn't bottom out until 1964; by then the 59 leagues of 1951 had become 19, and the 8,000-odd professional players had dwindled to fewer than 2,500.

Moreover, television whetted the baseball appetites of Californians and Texans (and Georgians and Washingtonians and more). That demand plus the development of faster passenger planes gave ideas to owners of two of baseball's decaying franchises. Walter O'Malley, owner of the Brooklyn Dodgers, and Giants' owner Horace Stoneham had seen the solidarity of the original 16-city composition broken in 1953, when the venerable Boston Braves (a franchise established in the first year of the National Association, 1871) became the darlings of Milwaukee; then they saw it further weakened by the defections in 1954 and 1955, respectively, of the St. Louis Browns to Baltimore and the Philadelphia Athletics to Kansas City. Amid weeping and gnashing of teeth that continue to this day, the Dodgers and Giants left for the Golden West in 1958.

In a strange twist, the architect of the move, Walter O'Malley, was (and in the East, still is) widely reviled as the man responsible for ending the grand old game's paradisical age. Yet the placement of franchises in California, as distressing as it was for Brooklyn and Manhattan and as roundly condemned as it was by traditionalists, may now be seen as the best thing to happen to baseball in the decade. And Walter O'Malley, if you will permit your mind a considerable stretch, may be viewed not as the snake offering baseball

the mortal apple but as a latter-day Johnny Appleseed (in the footsteps of Alexander Cartwright, who in 1849 also headed for California in pursuit of gold, yet who is remembered not for his venality but for bringing the New York Game to the West).

It was imperative that baseball should take the game to where the people were, precisely as it had in 1903. America's population had already begun the westward and southward shift that was to become so pronounced in the 1960s and 1970s. The move to Los Angeles and San Francisco, rather than confirming those cities' stature as "big league," as is so often written, brought baseball into step with America, which had long recognized them as such. Baseball could now call itself the national pastime without apology.

The Sixties

A chaotic decade for our country, the 1960s were worrisome, stormy years for baseball as well, with dramatic changes in league composition, playing styles, competitive balance and, most distressingly, the game's appeal to the American people. Baseball endured its ordeal by fire, and came through not unscathed but strengthened.

The departure of the Dodgers and Giants in 1958 created a vacuum in New York and an increased hunger for baseball in boomtowns like Houston, Atlanta, and Minneapolis. Enter Branch Rickey, nearly 80 but still possessed of a keen nose for new opportunity. The great innovator who had already brought baseball the farm system and integration now created the Continental League, a paper league with paper franchises. Nonetheless, Rickey's mirage worried Organized Baseball into expansion.

Two of the Continental "franchises"—the future New York Mets and Houston Colt .45s—were admitted for 1962. The American League was authorized to commence its western foray one year earlier with the expansion-draft Los Angeles Angels and the relocated Minnesota Twins (the latter being the transplanted Washington Senators, who were replaced in the nation's capital by an ill-fated expansion team).

Other franchise shifts and startups in the decade saw baseball's original vagabonds, the Milwaukee Braves by way of Boston, move to Atlanta in 1966. Two years later the erstwhile Athletics of Philadelphia, having failed in Kansas City, directed their caravan toward Oakland.

The A's were quickly replaced in KC by the Royals, one of two new teams introduced in each league with the expansion of 1969. This in turn precipitated divisional play and the League Championship Series, both inventions much decried at the time but now generally applauded. And in one of baseball's more forgettable debacles, the expansion Pilots of 1969 lost their course in Seattle after only one year and ran aground in Milwaukee, where they were rechristened as the Brewers. The National League's expansion into San Diego and Montreal proceeded more smoothly, although Padres' attendance lagged expectations and the Expos' Olympic Stadium (replacing the stopgap Jarry Park) took longer to open its dome than Michelangelo took to paint St. Peter's.

On the field, the big-bang game of the 1950s was giving way to a pitching-and-defense formula, at least in the National League, which began to outstrip its long-time tormentor at the box office and in World Series and All-Star confrontations. Speed returned to the equation, too, as personified by first Maury Wills and then Lou Brock (though both were preceded, in the AL, by Luis Aparicio). And a revolution in baseball strategy was brewing, as the 1959 suc-

cess of such relievers as Larry Sherry, Lindy McDaniel, and Roy Face paved the way for the universal adoption of the bullpen stopper in the 1960s.

In the American League expansion year of 1961, the first played to a 162-game schedule, the Bronx Bombers hit a prodigious 240 homers. Sluggers Harmon Killebrew, Norm Cash, Jim Gentile, and Rocky Colavito all hit more than 40 homers; Mickey Mantle hit more than 50. These totals were troubling to Commissioner Ford Frick, but nowhere near as consternating as the 61 homers struck by Roger Maris to top the game's most famous record, the 60 that Babe Ruth had walloped in 1927. After seeing the National League's scoring increase in 1962, its first year of expansion, Frick became concerned that pitchers were becoming an endangered species. He said:

I would even like the spitball to come back. Take a look at the batting, home run, and slugging record for recent seasons, and you become convinced that the pitchers need help urgently.

Disastrously, Frick convinced the owners to widen the strike zone for 1963 to its pre-1950 dimensions: top of the armpit to bottom of the knee. The result was to increase strikeouts, reduce walks, and shrink batting averages within five years to levels unseen since 1908, the nadir of the Dead Ball Era. The once-proud Yankees, who had continued their long domination of the American League to mid-decade, saw their team batting average sink to an incredible .214 in 1968. That year produced an overall AL mark of .230 and a batting champion, Carl Yastrzemski, with an average of .301.

As pitchers vanquished batters, seemingly for all eternity, the bottom line was that the fans stayed away in droves. Attendance in the National League, which in 1966 reached 15 million, fell by 1968 to only 11.7 million. In fact, despite the addition of four new clubs in 1961 and 1962, attendance in 1968 was only 3 million more than it had been in 1960. Critics charged that baseball was a geriatric vestige of an America that had vanished, a game too slow for a nation that was rushing toward the moon; its decline would only steepen, they claimed, as that more with-it national pastime, pro football, extended its mastery of the airwaves.

But the sky was not falling, despite the alarms. The owners acted quickly to redress the game's balance between offense and defense, reducing the strike zone and lowering the pitcher's mound. But the most important change may have been one that was introduced in 1965 and was only beginning to take effect: the amateur free-agent draft. Typically successful teams like the Yankees, Dodgers, Braves, and Cardinals had stayed successful because of their attention to scouting. Consistently they were able to garner more top prospects for their farm systems than clubs with less deep pockets or more volatile management. Now, teams that had fallen on hard times need not look toward a generation of famine before returning to the feast. Now, dynasties—awe-inspiring but not healthy for the game—were suddenly rendered implausible. Now, baseball had a competitive balance that could produce a rotation of electrifying successes among the leagues' cities, like the ascension of the Boston Red Sox from ninth place in 1966 to the pennant the next, and the amazing rise of the New York Mets from the netherworld they had known to World Champions in 1969. The game would still have some hard rows to hoe in the 1970s, but there was no mistaking the reversal of its downturn: in the new age of "relevance," baseball was back.

The Seventies

The 1970s saw a continuation of the trend toward new stadium construction that had marked the 1960s and may well have triggered that decade's batting drought, as hitter's havens like Ebbets Field, the Polo Grounds and Sportsman's Park fell to the wrecker's ball. The 1960s had brought new ballparks to 11 cities—San Francisco, Los Angeles, Washington, Bloomington, New York (NL), Houston, Atlanta, Anaheim, St. Louis, Oakland, and San Diego. In 1970 and 1971, baseball bade farewell to old friends Crosley Field, Forbes Field and Shibe Park as new stadiums—artificial-turf clones of each other—sprang up in Cincinnati, Pittsburgh, and Philadelphia. Other new parks were built in Arlington, Kansas City, Montreal, Seattle, and Toronto (the latter two, expansion franchises added to the American League in 1977), and Yankee Stadium underwent a massive facelift.

All this construction activity seemed to bespeak the game's profitability. Indeed, attendance was climbing in almost all major league cities, as heroes like Henry Aaron, Johnny Bench, Reggie Jackson, and Pete Rose, to name but a few, gave the fans plenty to cheer about. And the controversial adoption of the designated hitter innovation by the American League in 1973 gave a further boost to hitting while giving fans much to argue about, which after all is one of the game's great pleasures.

But the game's financial health was imperiled by rising unrest over labor issues, centered on the reserve clause, which bound a player to his team in perpetuity while denying him the opportunity to gauge his worth in the free market. The reformulation of the relationship between players and management became the hallmark of the decade and sorely tested fans' devotion to the game.

It began with the momentous case brought against Organized Baseball by veteran outfielder Curt Flood in 1970, challenging the legality of the reserve clause. The Supreme Court ruled against Flood the following year, but the tenor for the 1970s had been set. A 13-day player strike delayed the opening of the 1972 season, and arbitrator Peter Seitz ruled in 1975 (in what has come to be known as the Messersmith-McNally case) that a player could establish his right of free agency by playing out his option year without a signed contract. The writing on the wall was clear: free agency was the wave of the future.

Big-name players like Jim Hunter, Reggie Jackson, and Rich Gossage migrated to New York, and lesser lights like Wayne Garland and Oscar Gamble signed elsewhere for figures that seemed incredible. In the race to sign available talent some owners spun out of control while others like Minnesota's Cal Griffith, without corporate coffers behind them, had no choice but to sit on the sidelines. Player movement among stars jeopardized fan allegiances, pundits alleged, as Gossage and Jackson played for three teams in three years and championship teams like the Oakland A's and Boston Red Sox were broken up through trades that were forced by the specter of impending—and uncompensated—free-agent departures.

(Comfortingly to the historian, all this hubbub had occurred in very much the same way in 1869 and 1870, before the advent of the reserve clause, when Henry Chadwick was fulminating about the perniciousness of players "revolving" from one team to another simply to advance their fortunes. Also, baseball's first avowedly professional team, Harry Wright's Cincinnati Red Stockings of those years, were roundly abused for constructing their powerhouse team with "mercenaries" from other states—thus scorning baseball's core appeal to civic pride.)

What truly compromised fan loyalties in the 1970s was not player movement—it took Yankee fans, oh, maybe, ten minutes to regard Reggie as a born pinstriper—but player salaries. When the major league minimum was under $5,000 or so and only a Mantle, Williams, Musial, and DiMaggio made $100,000 a year, fans saw with their heroes as, by and large, working colleagues who had the supreme good fortune to play ball for a living. If a star made a splendiferous salary, that was socially useful as a proof that any worker could make it big if only he had sufficient ability to emerge from the pack. But when stars began routinely to command seven-figure salaries, and, more importantly, the annual wage of the *average* major leaguer rose to six-figure levels, and eventually seven figures, many adult breadwinners struggled to remain fans.

That they succeeded is testament to their love of the game, for fans have had a difficult assignment in reshaping their views of baseball players along the lines of media stars. The princely compensations of actors and pop musicians have long been accepted as the verdict of the marketplace. If the movie *The Terminator* makes hundreds of millions of dollars for its studio and distributor, then Arnold Schwarzenegger's multimillion-dollar fee for the film seems not out of line. Analogously, if the Dodgers were fabulously lucrative for ownership, then a lofty salary for Steve Garvey ought not to have given rise in the 1970s to resentment among the fans. This sort of reeducation is by no means complete, but barroom banter about baseball in the ensuing decades was not as bitterly one-note about "greedy players" as it had been.

And one didn't hear a peep about pro football replacing baseball as the national game.

The Eighties, Nineties and Beyond

The game on the field in the 1970s had been marked by an unprecedented co-mingling of power and speed; the great teams of Cincinnati, Baltimore and Oakland; the return to prominence of the Yankees; and the historic exploits of Henry Aaron and Pete Rose. The game in the 1980s would begin with the Philadelphia Phillies, led by free-agent Rose and future Hall of Famers Mike Schmidt and Steve Carlton, ridding the franchise of a historic stain. Until their victory over the Kansas City Royals, the Phils were the only one of the original 16 major league franchises never to have won a World Series (the St. Louis Browns had to accept the help of their modern incarnation, the Baltimore Orioles).

The next year brought baseball's darkest moment since the Brotherhood revolt and ensuing Players League of 1890, as major league players walked off their jobs at the height of the season and didn't return for 50 days. By that time even diehard fans were thoroughly fed up with baseball's seeming inability to resolve its problems fairly and with dispatch. Talk of a fan boycott never amounted to much, but as players and management looked toward their Basic Agreement negotiation in 1989—the centenary of the Brotherhood's break with Organized Baseball—both reflected back on the damage wrought in 1981.

The 1980s brought unprecedented parity on the playing field and misery off it. The drug problem endemic in our society struck baseball, and Pete Rose's itch for gambling disgraced him and the game. Baseball's victims are highly publicized and their fall from grace is judged more reprehensible for all the advantages that today's players enjoy—but the game is an American institution reflecting what is wrong with our people as well as what is right with them. In this most difficult area of addictive behavior baseball led America—as it did with integration—rather than follow it.

The year of 1989 became a nightmare, with Commissioner Bart Giamatti's expulsion of Rose followed by his own sudden and shocking death days later, a second finding of collusion by owners to undermine the free-agent market, and a Bay Area World Series rudely interrupted by an earthquake. But baseball recovered even from these calamities, as well as a spring training lockout in 1990, to embark upon an era that gave promise of unprecedented prosperity.

And then came 1994, a year of wonderment on the playing fields, as Ken Griffey Jr., Matt Williams, Frank Thomas, Jeff Bagwell, Tony Gwynn, Greg Maddux, and a host of others appeared to be initiating a new golden age of baseball . . . until play stopped on August 12 and did not resume.

As fans, we were presented with a dilemma: to side with the players, who went on strike hoping to extend their gains of the previous two decades? Or to side with the owners, who stood fast in insisting upon a balance between costs and revenues? As fans, we tried to side with the game of baseball, and to wish that its most intense contests would soon reconvene to the field of play.

Baseball is not a conventional industry. It belongs neither to the players nor management, but to all of us. It is our national pastime, our national symbol, and our national treasure.

The monumental 1998 season enriched that treasure in so many ways, from the excitement of the home run race between Mark McGwire and Sammy Sosa to the unprecedented victory total of the New York Yankees. Gloriously, baseball's ghosts came back to life, in the daily press and in dinner-table conversations everywhere. Roger Maris, Babe Ruth, Hack Wilson, even Tinker and Evers and Chance, cavorted invisibly alongside our heroes of today.

Yankee heroics in succeeding Octobers included an eerily nostalgic Subway Series victory and a spectacular comeback spirit in 2001, even though the resilient Diamondbacks came back, too, capturing the crown. Barry Bonds performed jaw-dropping feats, creating new seasonal marks for home runs, slugging percentage, and on base average. Ichiro Suzuki's remarkable "rookie" season made us rethink all our assumptions about the quality of play in the Japanese major leagues.

All this from a game that had been "spoiled" back in 1870. Ever changing in ways that are so small as to preserve the illusion that "nothing changes in baseball," the game has introduced, in the lifetime of many of us: night ball, plane travel, television, integration, bullpen stoppers, expansion, the amateur draft, competitive parity, indoor stadiums, artificial turf, free agency, the designated hitter, wild-card contestants, interleague contests, international play, and expansion to 30 teams in 1998.

The Weather of Our Lives

For fans accustomed to the game's languorous rhythms and conservative resistance to innovation, the changes of the past two decades in particular seem positively frenetic. Yet for all its changes, baseball has not strayed far from its origins, and in fact has changed far less than other American institutions of equivalent antiquity. What sustains baseball in the hearts of Americans, finally, is not its responsiveness to changes in society nor its propensity for novelty, but its myths, its lore, its records, and its essential stability. As historian Bruce Catton noted in 1959:

> A gaffer from the era of William McKinley, abruptly brought back to the second half of the twentieth century, would find very little in modern life that would not seem new, strange, and rather bewildering, but put in a good grandstand seat back of first base he would see nothing that was not completely familiar.

It's still a game of bat and ball, played without regard for the clock; a game of ninety-foot basepaths, nine innings, nine men in the field; three outs, all out; and three strikes still send you to the bench, no matter whom you know in city hall. It's the national anthem before every game; it's playing catch with your son or daughter; it's learning how to win and how to deal with loss, and how to connect with something larger than our selves.

"Baseball," wrote Thomas Wolfe, "has been not merely 'the great national game' but really a part of the whole weather of our lives, of the thing that is our own, of the whole fabric, the million memories of America." Spring comes in America not on the vernal equinox but on Opening Day; summer sets in with a Memorial Day doubleheader and does not truly end until the last out of the regular season. Winter begins the day after the World Series.

Where were you when Bobby Thomson hit the shot heard 'round the world? Or the night Carlton Fisk hit his homer in the 12th? Or when the Mets, with batter after batter one strike away from their loss in the World Series, staged their famous rally? These are milestones in the lives of America and Americans.

We grow up with baseball; we mark—and, for a moment, stop—the passage of time with it; and we grow old with it. It is our game, for all our days.

BASEBALL HISTORY GOES BACK ... BACK ... BACK ...

. . . to 1791, and maybe its future. In a dramatic development just as this book was going to press, the author, with Mayor James Ruberto of Pittsfield, Massachusetts and former major-league pitcher Jim Bouton, revealed the existence of a Pittsfield town ordinance recorded on September 5, 1791 that represented the first recorded mention of baseball by that name on the North American continent. The modest prohibition stated that "... for the Preservation of the Windows in the New Meeting House ... no Person or Inhabitant of said Town, shall be permitted to play at any game Called Wicket, Cricket, Baseball, Batball, Football, Cat, Fives or any other Game or Games with Balls, within the Distance of Eighty Yards from said Meeting House."

Since 1990 researchers had pushed back the earliest American citations for baseball from 1845 to 1823, and references to the problematic games of "base" and "baste" (were they running games? batting games? two equal teams?) had been located for the mid-1780s.

The discovery of the "Pittsfield Prohibition" was a big news story, presented as something of a curiosity as well as an opportunity for Cooperstown, New York City, Hoboken, and Pittsfield to engage in a food fight over who was *really* first. Lost amid the hoopla and the intercity and interstate rivalries was the charm of baseball's Garden of Eden magically being located in the backyard of historic Wahconah Park, a dowager ballpark in a city whose best days seemed, even to many of its most proud and loyal citizens, behind it.

And therein lies the tale, the true meaning of the find. That for Old America—New England—and its grand old game, the one that grew up alongside the nation, the future might lie in the past. Who would know to look there, anymore than to find Eden? The only way to find some things is not to look for them; they find you. Celebrate, honor, revivify what made our game and our people great, and they might indeed be great once again.

—*John Thorn*

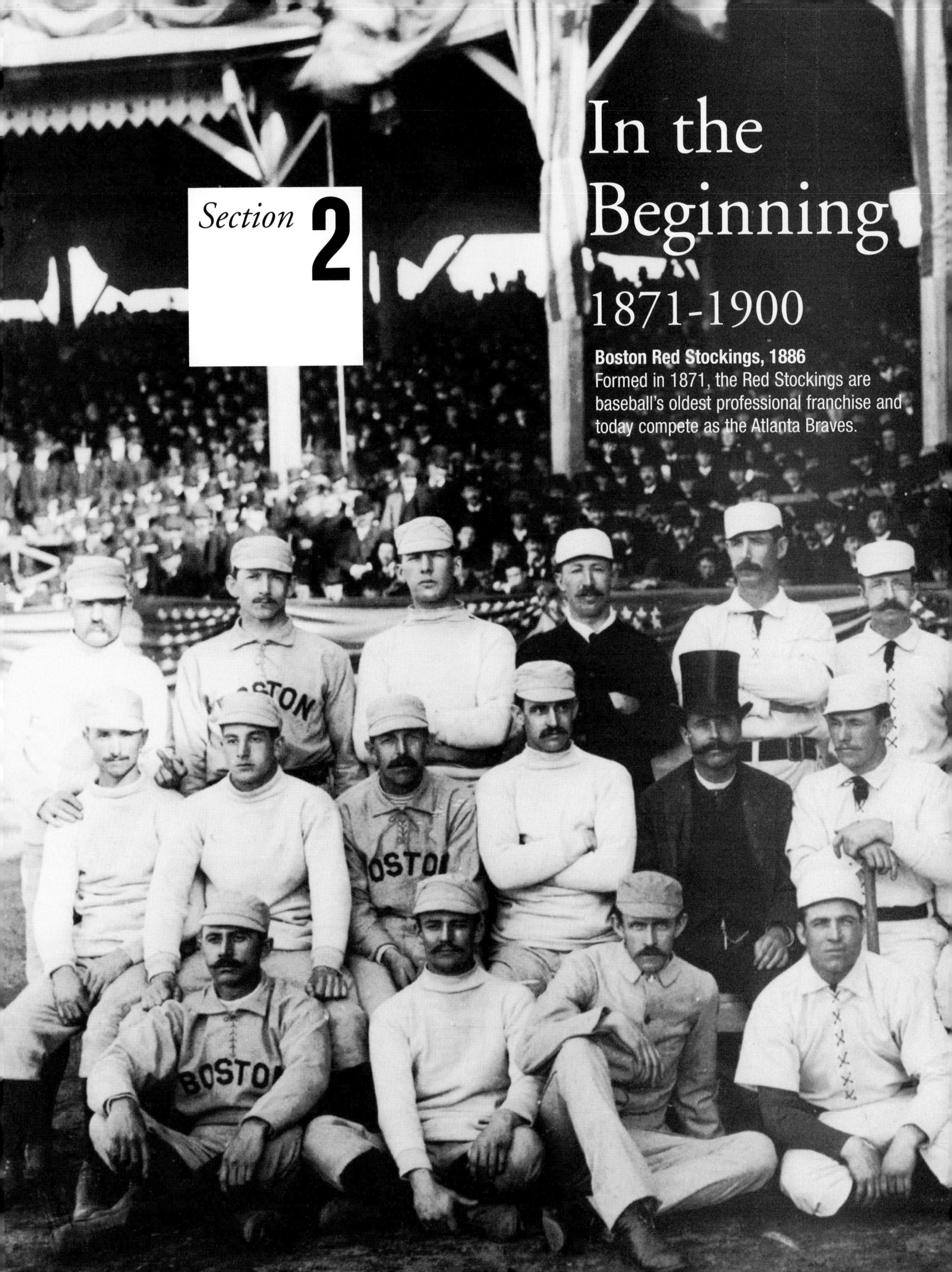

In the Beginning

1871-1900

Boston Red Stockings, 1886
Formed in 1871, the Red Stockings are baseball's oldest professional franchise and today compete as the Atlanta Braves.

FAMOUS FIRSTS

1871: The first professional league, the National Association, is formed and in the first game, played May 4, Cleveland Forest Citys lose, 2-0, at Fort Wayne.

1875: Philadelphia's Joe Borden hurls professional baseball's first no-hitter.

1876: The National League is formed and its first game, Boston at Philadelphia, is played on April 22.

1876: Baseball gloves are introduced to professional baseball in Chicago by Al Spalding.

1878: Paul Hines of Providence wins the first Triple Crown and executes the first unassisted triple play.

1880: Worcester's Lee Richmond hurls the major leagues' first perfect game, against Cleveland on June 12.

1882: The American Association introduces the first salaried umpiring staff.

1886: Major league players organize their first union and call it "The Brotherhood of Ball Players."

1894: Boston's Bobby Lowe is first major league player to smash four homers in one game.

Chapter 6

America Falls in Love With This New Game Called Baseball

The formative years of major league baseball were rife with upheaval, rivalry, bickering and, on occasion, tragedy, but they were also a time of incredible energy and innovation from which emerged the game as we know it today.

The game had seen remarkable growth since 1845, the year the Knickerbocker Base Ball Club of New York devised a set of rules that, over the next 12 years, came to include: a diamond-shaped infield with bases 90 feet apart; a pitcher's box 45 feet from home plate; nine-man sides; three outs per team per inning; nine innings; and methods to make an out that included three strikes, catching a hit ball in the air (or on the first bounce), and throwing a fielded ball to the first baseman before the runner arrived. By 1860, as the prospect of gate receipts became real, clubs were starting to recruit and pay good players.

Baseball's popularity was high when the Civil War broke out, and rose even higher when returning soldiers, who'd played the game in camps and in prison compounds, ignited a boom in post-Civil War America. Soon, some entrepreneurial owners began charging admission to games, and some baseball clubs were sowing the seed of professionalism by dividing receipts among the players.

Before 1869 the professional movement was mainly covert, but then the Cincinnati Red Stockings fielded a fully salaried team, becoming the first club to acknowledge their professionalism. Led by player-manager Harry Wright (the "Father of Professional Baseball") the Reds toured the country that summer, winning some 60 games without a loss. The Red Stockings inspired imitators and, in March 1871, there emerged baseball's first professional baseball organization, which quickly led to the creation of the first major league—the National Association of Professional Base Ball Players. The National Association had a short life (only five seasons), but the National League arose to take its place, creating a new model for professional baseball.

Barely surviving the rocky 1870s, the National League entered a golden age in the 1880s and its success gave rise to imitators—three new leagues between 1882 and 1890: the American Association, the Union Association and the Players League. By 1900 those rivals were gone and the warring National and American Leagues led baseball into the 20th century.

Change came rapidly in the first 30 years of major league baseball. Rules of play were increasingly standardized and modified. By 1893, the pitcher's distance was set at 60 feet, 6 inches and, after decades of experimentation, it was finally agreed that three strikes constituted an out and four balls a walk. Other rule changes allowed player substitutions, established the infield-fly rule, treated foul bunts as strikes, and introduced the pentagon-shaped home plate.

On the playing fields, players wore stylized uniforms (with such exotic variations as calf-exposing stockings in colors that often gave an enduring nickname to the club). Most players sported gloves by the mid-1880s, with catchers employing the big "Decker" mitt and wearing masks and chest protectors. In terms of strategy, signals became common to trigger offensive and defensive movements,

John McGraw
His schoolboy looks masked a fiery disposition that made McGraw, Baltimore's star third baseman, one of the bad boys of the 1890s.

infielders aligned themselves to turn double plays, outfielders employed cutoffs and relays, batters perfected bunting, sacrificing, sliding, stealing, and hit-and-run plays, and pitchers perfected curve balls and changeups.

The game itself became more respectable because of the National League's clampdown on drinking, gambling and Sunday baseball. But the early major leagues suffered because of ongoing disputes between players and owners, primarily related to the reserve clause, and because of such issues as competitive imbalance and syndicate ownership.

That major league baseball survived is in large part due to the emergence of the game's first star players. The exploits of such luminaries as Cap Anson, King Kelly, Hugh Jennings, Kid Nichols, Wee Willie Keeler, Cy Young and many others attracted significant newspaper attention and enticed ticket buyers by the thousands into old wooden stadiums. By the turn of the century, major league baseball was cemented in American sports culture and set to grow at a pace undreamed of even by its founders.

1871

By 1871 there were nearly two dozen professional clubs and fans were clamoring for a champion to be declared based on regular play. Thus, on March 17, 1871, representatives of 10 of the best clubs met to organize America's first professional baseball league, the National Association of Professional Base Ball Players. The league, with James N. Kerns from Philadelphia as the first president, comprised the strongest teams and best players and is regarded as the first major league. The players controlled the league and enjoyed full freedom of contract and movement. That resulted in frequent roster changes as teams tried to outbid each other for talent.

Admission required the payment of a ten-dollar franchise fee. Each team was expected to play each rival five times, but there was no fixed schedule and, to save travel costs, teams ended up playing an uneven number of games. The championship pennant was awarded to the team with the most victories, and a championship committee was empowered to rule on disputes.

The first season featured an exciting three-way battle between the Chicago White Stockings, Philadelphia Athletics, and Harry Wright's Boston Red Stockings. (The Boston and Chicago clubs still exist today as the Atlanta Braves and Chicago Cubs, respectively.) The White Stockings had a fast start to the season but, after their new, 7,000-seat wooden park was destroyed in the Great Chicago Fire that October, they were forced to play out their schedule on the road in motley, borrowed uniforms. They finished in third place, and subsequently dropped out of the league until 1874.

At season's end, the Athletics and Red Stockings each had won 22 games, but the championship committee awarded the pennant to the Athletics, who had fewer losses. Harry Wright's plea that his Boston Reds had come closer to meeting their scheduled obligations was disallowed. (In subsequent years, the official standings were adjusted to exclude games played against Fort Wayne, which did not finish the season. The amended standings still had Philadelphia on top with 21 wins, one more than Boston.)

In spite of the season-ending controversy, the National Association enjoyed an auspicious debut. Total attendance was 266,500 as most clubs profited, and only one team, the Kekionga of Fort Wayne, folded during the season

1872

Although the National Association's inaugural season was a modest success, the league's structural defects began to take a toll in 1872. The player-run association wielded little control over players or teams, resulting in contract jumping, drunkenness and game fixing. The inexpensive admission fee—which remained at $10—made for a chronic dropout problem as disenchanted teams found it easy to turn their backs on such a small payment. The absence of a fixed playing schedule meant few contending teams played their required quota of games, while a reliance on volunteer umpires caused never-ending disputes. Clubs also quarreled over ticket pricing and the division of gate receipts. Add it all up and several teams lost money, resulting in tension between players and league investors.

Eleven clubs began the season but six weren't around at the end—Cleveland Forest City, Brooklyn Eckfords, Middletown Mansfields, Washington Nationals, Washington Olympics, and Troy Haymakers. Overall attendance declined by 11 percent to 237,000.

On the field, hopes for a wide-open race were crushed by Harry Wright's powerful Boston team, which rolled to the championship on a 39-8 record, well ahead of the Baltimore Lord Baltimores, who had four fewer wins despite playing nine more games. Stocked with stars like pitcher Al Spalding (who led the league with 38 wins), infielder Ross Barnes (whose league-best .432 batting average was aided by his bunting prowess in an era of the 'fair-foul' hitting rule), and shortstop George Wright, the Red Stockings won the first of four consecutive pennants.

But perhaps the season will be best remembered as the year the curveball gained acceptance in baseball. Although first thrown in the late 1860s, the pitch remained somewhat of an oddity until curveball specialist William "Candy" Cummings (who is widely regarded as the inventor of the curveball) baffled hitters to win 33 games in 1872.

1873

Among the National Association's first stars was Boston pitcher Al Spalding—and he may never have been better than in 1873. He led the league in wins (41), innings pitched (497) and games (60), while batting .317. Along the way, he accounted for all but two of Boston's wins that season (and took all but two of Boston's 16 losses).

Despite Spalding's superb play, the Red Stockings needed a late-season rally to defend their pennant. The season had seen the addition of four new teams but only one, the Philadelphia White Stockings, played a full schedule. The newcomers, behind 36-game winner George Zettlein, led the league for much of the season, but were passed down the stretch by a Red Stockings team that, in addition to Spalding, boasted the league's top offense, outscoring Philadelphia over the season by an average of 1.27 runs per game.

Boston's Ross Barnes had a dominant year, leading the league in just about every offensive category, including runs, hits, doubles, total bases, average, on-base percentage and slugging percentage. He was second in RBIs to teammate Deacon White, a catcher.

Overall league attendance was again down, and the Washington Washingtons, Elizabeth Resolutes and Maryland of Baltimore didn't make it through the season.

The league continued to be plagued by unruly behavior, which reached a peak in midseason when substitute umpire Bob Ferguson, who also served as president of the National Association and played for the Brooklyn Atlantics, broke the arm of the

1871–1900 STANDINGS

1871 National Association

TEAM	G	W	L	PCT	GB
Philadelphia Athletics	28	21	7	.750	—
Boston Red Stockings	31	20	10	.667	2
Chicago White Stockings	28	19	9	.679	2
New York Mutuals	33	16	17	.485	7.5
Washington, D.C., Olympics	32	15	15	.500	7
Troy Haymakers	29	13	15	.464	8
Cleveland Forest City	29	10	19	.345	11.5
Fort Wayne Kekiongas	19	7	12	.368	9.5
Rockford (Ill.) Forest City	25	4	21	.160	15.5

1872 National Association

TEAM	G	W	L	PCT	GB
Boston Red Stockings	48	39	8	.830	—
Baltimore Lord Baltimores	58	35	19	.648	7.5
New York Mutuals	56	34	20	.630	8.5
Philadelphia Athletics	47	30	14	.682	7.5
Troy Haymakers	25	15	10	.600	13
Brooklyn Atlantics	37	9	28	.243	25
Cleveland Forest City	22	6	16	.273	20.5
Middletown (CT) Mansfields	24	5	19	.208	22.5
Brooklyn Eckfords	29	3	26	.103	27
Washington, D.C., Olympics	9	2	7	.222	18
Washington, D.C., Nationals	11	0	11	.0	21

1873 National Association

TEAM	G	W	L	PCT	GB
Boston Red Stockings	60	43	16	.729	—
Philadelphia White Stockings	53	36	17	.679	4
Baltimore Lord Baltimores	57	34	22	.607	7.5
New York Mutuals	53	29	24	.547	11
Philadelphia Athletics	52	28	23	.549	11
Brooklyn Atlantics	55	17	37	.315	23.5
Washington Washingtons	39	8	31	.205	25
Elizabeth (N.J.) Resolutes	23	2	21	.87	23
Baltimore Marylands	6	0	6	.0	16.5

Mutuals' Nat Hicks with a baseball bat during an argument. There were two notable rule changes: Fan interference was prohibited, and using clothing, including the cap, to catch the ball was banned.

1874

The comparatively new American game of baseball presented itself to the world stage during the summer of 1874. Two entire teams from the National Association—the Boston and Philadelphia clubs—traveled to England in midseason for exhibitions arranged by the game's three leading names, pitcher Albert Spalding, manager Harry Wright and baseball writer Henry Chadwick.

The British weren't exactly overwhelmed, although they agreed to stage the exhibitions after Spalding allowed as how the Association stars might engage in a few cricket matches on the side. The tour had stops in Liverpool, Manchester and London, after which a British reporter offered this assessment: "The verdict of the spectators is almost universally against base ball as a competitor with our national game ... it has so many inherent defects."

Back home, defects of another kind continued to plague the National Association. Clubs continued to struggle to turn a profit amid accusations of gambling and game-fixing. After the season, Philadelphia's John Radcliff was expelled for attempting to bribe an umpire. On the positive side, the Chicago White Stockings, forced to close shop following the Great Chicago Fire, returned to the league and only one team, the Lord Baltimores, disbanded during the season. Attendance was also up slightly.

On the field, Wright's Boston Red Stockings earned their third consecutive pennant, winning 52 games, 10 more than the second-place New York Mutuals. Wright's team was the only one to play its full schedule of games. Al Spalding won all 52 of Boston's games and led the league in several other pitching categories. Catcher Cal McVey emerged as Boston's new batting star, leading the league in runs, hits, total bases, RBIs, and finishing second in average (.359) behind Levi Meyerle of Chicago (.394).

1875

The National Association's final year was also the season of major league baseball's first no-hitter. It was thrown by the Philadelphia Whites' Joe Borden, a first-year pro who began his career under the pseudonym "Nedrob" (and later as "Josephs") because his well-to-do family disapproved of baseball. In only his eighth major league appearance, Borden no-hit the Chicago White Stockings in a 4-0 Philadelphia victory.

Thirteen teams opened the season, but only six remained at the finish. The league finally succumbed to the problems of competitive imbalance, financial losses, gambling, and excessive player freedom. But, for all its weaknesses, the National Association succeeded in advancing the popularity of professional baseball.

Supporters like Henry Chadwick, the innovative sportswriter who became known as the "Father of Base Ball," publicized the league by his coverage of games and by his statistics-laden guidebooks, which he had commenced in 1860 Chadwick's reports, which provided detailed accounts that included box scores, encouraged expanding coverage by leading newspapers.

The Association's most respected innovator was Harry Wright, who set high standards for professional promotion. His envious colleagues sometimes referred to the association as "Harry Wright's League." As Boston's manager, he presided over a $35,000 annual budget—baseball's highest until the early 1880s—and dealt creatively with such problems as groundskeeping, equipment design and procurement, advertising, and the recruiting and training of players. Wright's mastery paid off in his team becoming baseball's first dynasty, winning four consecutive pennants.

In 1875 the Boston juggernaut, headed by Al Spalding, Ross Barnes, Jim O'Rourke, Deacon White, Cal McVey, and George Wright, buried all rivals. With a Boston player topping just about every batting category, the Reds posted a 71-8 record to finish 15 games up on their nearest pursuers. In the National Association's five seasons, the Red Stockings placed second in 1871 and then won four consecutive pennants.

But by the end of the National Association's fifth season, its structural defects seemed no closer to repair. Gambling was rife and raised questions about the product's integrity. "Revolving," the practice of players jumping teams in midseason, destroyed any prospect of club stability and ensured that the richest clubs had the best talent. And most clubs continued to lose money.

1876

With the National Association teetering in 1875, the time was ripe for a reformist movement that would build a league to better serve the financial backers. A new breed of club directors, headed by William A. Hulbert of the Chicago White Stockings, decided to form a rival league. Hulbert moved decisively at the end of the 1875 season to poach the heart of the Boston Red Stockings lineup, signing Al Spalding, Ross Barnes, Jim White, and Cal McVey. Hulbert also signed Cap Anson of the Philadelphia Athletics, who later became Chicago's longtime player-manager and the first major leaguer to reach 3,000 hits. The signing gave Hulbert instant credibility.

He then followed up by meeting with several other club directors and investors, and in February announced the formation of the National League of Professional Base Ball Clubs. The new league placed the interests of owners ahead of the players. Admitted as members were well-financed, joint-stock company clubs, each

1871–1900 STANDINGS

1874 National Association

TEAM	G	W	L	PCT	GB
Boston Red Stockings	71	52	18	.743	—
New York Mutuals	65	42	23	.646	7.5
Philadelphia Athletics	55	33	22	.600	11.5
Philadelphia White Stockings	58	29	29	.500	17
Chicago White Stockings	59	28	31	.475	18.5
Brooklyn Atlantics	56	22	33	.400	22.5
Hartford Dark Blues	53	16	37	.302	27.5
Baltimore Lord Baltimores	47	9	38	.191	31.5

1875 National Association

TEAM	G	W	L	PCT	GB
Boston Red Stockings	82	71	8	.899	—
Hartford Dark Blues	86	54	28	.659	18.5
Philadelphia Athletics	77	53	20	.726	15
St. Louis Brown Stockings	70	39	29	.574	26.5
Philadelphia White Stockings	70	37	31	.544	28.5
New York Mutuals	71	30	38	.441	35.5
Chicago White Stockings	69	30	37	.448	35
New Haven Elm City	47	7	40	.149	48
Washington Washingtons	28	5	23	.179	40.5
St. Louis Red Stockings	19	4	15	.211	37
Philadelphia Centennials	14	2	12	.143	36.5
Brooklyn Atlantics	44	2	42	.45	51.5
Keokuk (Iowa) Westerns	13	1	12	.77	37

1876 National League

TEAM	G	W	L	PCT	GB
Chicago White Stockings	66	52	14	.788	—
St. Louis Brown Stockings	64	45	19	.703	6
Hartford Dark Blues	69	47	21	.691	6
Boston Red Caps	70	39	31	.557	15
Louisville Grays	69	30	36	.455	22
New York Mutuals	57	21	35	.375	26
Philadelphia Athletics	60	14	45	.237	34.5
Cincinnati Reds	65	9	56	.138	42.5

paying annual dues of $100 to finance the league administration, which included the hiring of umpires who would be paid $5 a game.

The eight charter clubs were aligned on an east-west basis, and each was granted a monopoly over its territory. Each team was required to play each rival ten times, with expulsion the penalty for failing to do so. A uniform 50-cent admission fee was set. Adopting a high moral stance, the new league banned gambling, liquor sales and Sunday games, and required players to sign contracts to prevent "revolving."

For the players this was tough medicine, but with the strongest teams from the National Association now enrolled in the new league, there was little option but to submit.

In the first game in NL history, April 22, 1876, Boston defeated Philadelphia 6-5, with Jim O'Rourke recording the first hit, a single to left in the first inning. The league's first home run was not hit until May 22, when Chicago's Ross Barnes, who would win the league's first batting title, connected off Cincinnati's Cherokee Fisher.

The White Stockings were the class of the league. Spalding, in his final season as a player, pitched and managed the Chicago club to a 52-14 record, topping St. Louis and Hartford by six games. With Chicago so far ahead in the late-season standings, the Philadelphia Athletics and New York Mutuals decided to forego their final games in the west, figuring the trips were certain to lose money. Hulbert expelled the pair, confirming that his league would adhere to its principles even at the cost of a vacancy in the nation's two largest cities. New York and Philadelphia would remain on the outside until 1883.

1877

The ballfield of the 1870s may have been a place for sporting men, but it was not yet wholly a place for gentlemen. It was still possible, for instance, to find someone willing to take a wager on the outcome of a game. And that meant it was still possible to find someone willing to fix the outcome of a game.

The Louisville Grays, fifth place finishers the season before, had bolstered their lineup through the addition of players like first baseman Juice Latham, shortstop Bill Craver, and outfielders George Hall and Orator Shaffer. This revitalized team won 27 of its first 40 games, taking a comfortable hold on first place and, it seemed, becoming a certainty to win the pennant. Late in the season, though, Louisville began to lose games consistently, and under mysterious circumstances. The team lost 12 of its final 20 games, surrendered the league lead to Boston, and finished a distant second, seven games back.

A probe by team management implicated Hall and pitcher Jim Devlin of crookedness in those final 20 games. Hall confessed—as later did Devlin—and implicated substitute Al Nichols as the go-between with gamblers. All three were permanently expelled from the league, as was Craver, the one player who refused to cooperate with the investigation.

That season marked the adoption of baseball's first set schedule, as well as the introduction of the mask by St. Louis catcher Mike Dorgan. But the expulsion of New York and Philadelphia left the league with only six teams. Following the betting scandal, the Louisville franchise was forced out of business. The clubs in Hartford and St. Louis also went under.

Meanwhile the NL was facing competition from the newly formed International Association. A loose league of mostly cooperative (gate-receipt-sharing) teams, the IA threat prompted NL leaders to form a "League Alliance" of independent teams. By paying fees of ten dollars a year, League Alliance teams won the right to play exhibitions with NL teams, and the NL also pledged to honor their territorial rights and player contracts. In the League Alliance one may identify the seed of minor-league baseball.

1878

Of the eight founding franchises that opened the 1876 season, only three—Boston, Chicago and Cincinnati—remained intact after two seasons. The new league was foundering at the gate and was trying to fend off a challenge from the upstart International Association. To replace the three clubs that collapsed in 1877, the NL awarded franchises to Milwaukee, Indianapolis and Providence. To counter the IA, it raided the rivals' rosters.

As in the old National Association, Boston emerged as the new league's top club. Its advantage started on the bench, with Harry Wright's leadership. The unquestioned genius of baseball strategy since his organization of the Cincinnati Red Stockings in 1869, Wright had led Boston to four Association pennants, and followed with pennants in the NL's second and third seasons.

Wright had a knack for spotting talent. After losing four of his stars to Chicago in 1876, he rebuilt the team around his brother George, Jim O'Rourke and Tommy Bond. In 1878, George Wright led all shortstops in putouts, double plays and fielding average, while O'Rourke was a rock in center field and batted .278, tops on a team most noted for its fielding. But Perhaps Boston's most valuable player that year was Bond, a workhouse from the old National Association who joined the Boston club in 1877, winning 40 games.

Bond, who learned the art of throwing a curveball from Candy Cummings, was outstanding in 1878, too, leading the league in wins (40), innings (532), strikeouts (182) and shutouts (9). His 40 wins were 10 more than the second-best record, by Cincinnati's Will White.

Behind Bond, the Red Stockings cruised to a record of 41-19 to finish four games ahead of Cincinnati, and eight up on Providence.

1879

Boston baseball fans received a shock prior to the 1979 season when star shortstop George Wright parted ways with his brother Harry's Red Stockings, jumping to the Providence Grays following a dispute with ownership. The Wright Brothers had combined to

---

1871–1900 STANDINGS

1877 National League

TEAM	G	W	L	PCT	GB
Boston Red Caps	61	42	18	.700	—
Louisville Grays	61	35	25	.583	7
Hartford Dark Blues	60	31	27	.534	10
St. Louis Brown Stockings	60	28	32	.467	14
Chicago White Stockings	60	26	33	.441	15.5
Cincinnati Reds	58	15	42	.263	25.5

1878 National League

TEAM	G	W	L	PCT	GB
Boston Red Caps	60	41	19	.683	—
Cincinnati Reds	61	37	23	.617	4
Providence Grays	62	33	27	.550	8
Chicago White Stockings	61	30	30	.500	11
Indianapolis Blues	63	24	36	.400	17
Milwaukee Grays	61	15	45	.250	26

1879 National League

TEAM	G	W	L	PCT	GB
Providence Grays	85	59	25	.702	—
Boston Red Caps	84	54	30	.643	5
Buffalo Bisons	79	46	32	.590	10
Chicago White Stockings	83	46	33	.582	10.5
Cincinnati Reds	81	43	37	.538	14
Cleveland Blues	82	27	55	.329	31
Syracuse Stars	71	22	48	.314	30
Troy Trojans	77	19	56	.253	35.5

win six pennants in Boston, four in the National Association and two in the National League, with Harry regarded as the brightest manager in the game and George the slickest fielder.

George became player-manager with the Grays, a team that was a major force in the early years of the National League. The 1879 club was particularly memorable, boasting a roster that included three future Hall of Famers: right fielder Jim O'Rourke, who batted .348, pitcher John Ward, who won 47 games, and Wright, the player-manager who not only led his club to a 59-25 record, but finished five games ahead of brother Harry's Red Stockings to win the pennant.

For the struggling league, it was another year of flux. After finishing at the bottom in both league standings and attendance in 1878, Milwaukee and Indianapolis were disbanded. But the league added four teams—Syracuse, Buffalo, Troy, and Cleveland—to bring the number of clubs back to its original eight.

To stem persistent losses, the league imposed rigid austerity measures. Salaries were slashed and players were compelled to buy their own uniforms and share the costs of meals. Moreover, to restrict player mobility, a reserve clause was inserted into some player contracts. (By 1883 the reserve system was applied to most contracts and would become a major bone of contention between owners and players.) But the measures could not save the Syracuse club, which folded before the end of the season.

On the field, Cincinnati's Will White pitched 75 complete games and 680 innings, both still major league records, while his 43 wins were second best to the 47 by Providence's John Ward.

1880

Worcester pitcher John Lee Richmond enjoyed a career replete with noteworthy "firsts." As a rookie, he was the first left-hander in the National League to lead his team in victories, winning 32 games for Worcester in 1880. (He had made his professional debut while still a student in 1879 by throwing a no-hitter in an exhibition against the Chicago White Stockings). He was the first medical doctor to play in the major leagues and he was the first pitcher to give up a grand-slam home run.

But it was on June 12, 1880, that Richmond recorded his most famous "first." In a 1-0 victory over Cleveland in Worcester, Richmond pitched pro baseball's first perfect game.

News accounts of the time downplayed the achievement. The local paper recounted that "the most wonderful game on record, and one of the shortest, was played this afternoon.... The Worcesters played without an error and, for nine straight innings, retired their opponents in one, two, three order, not a man getting a base hit or reaching first base." Just five days later, John Ward pitched a perfect game for Providence, defeating Buffalo 5-0.

As the decade of the 1880s dawned, major league baseball was still only a pale reflection of the popular spectacle that it would become. The NL's financial performance was dismal: no NL club

had yet to match the profits of Wright's 1875 Boston Reds, player salaries barely exceeded those of the 1869 Cincinnati Reds, numerous franchise failures underscored the league's instability, and the NL had no team in the populous New York and Philadelphia areas. At this point, however, the game received a powerful stimulus from America's booming economic and urban growth, sparking vigorous expansion through the 1880s.

The NL's changing fortunes coincided with the emergence of a dynasty in Chicago. Led by Cap Anson, among the top players of the century, the Chicago team won five pennants in seven years, beginning in 1880, when the White Stockings finished 15 games ahead of Providence. Chicago's offense led the league by 119 runs, and White Stockings players placed first in several batting categories, including runs, hits and total bases by Abner Dalrymple; RBIs by Anson; and batting average, on-base percentage and slugging percentage by George Gore. Pitcher Larry Corcoran had a no-hitter and led the league with 45 wins.

Significant changes to the game included the number of balls constituting a walk being reduced to seven and balls caught on the first bounce were no longer considered an out.

1881

A feature of the young NL was the emergence of a central authority to regulate several aspects of the game. The league was determined to take baseball to a higher moral ground and, in particular, quash such 1870s practices as gambling and drunkenness at the ballpark. To that end, a rule was passed prior to the 1881 season that abolished liquor sales and Sunday baseball. When the Cincinnati Red Stockings refused to accept the changes their league membership was revoked, and a new franchise was awarded to the Detroit Wolverines.

So the 1881 season proceeded with eight franchises and, in many respects, it was a very successful year, with league attendance growing to more than 300,000. The rules continued to mature, with the most significant change in 1881 being that the pitcher's box was moved from 45 to 50 feet from home plate.

On the field, Chicago was once again the class of the league, taking the pennant by nine games over Providence, but the league, for the first time, started to see a semblance of competitive balance. Worcester placed last but won 32 games, so that the difference between second and last place was just 14 games. The expansion Wolverines placed fourth with a 41-43 record.

The White Stockings' powerful offense, which again was the best in the NL by more than 100 runs, propelled Chicago to a 56-28 record. Cap Anson had a stellar season, leading the league in hits (137), RBIs (82), batting average (.399) and on-base average (.442), and was second in doubles (29) to teammate King Kelly (37). Elsewhere, a notable first occurred when Troy first baseman Roger Connor hit the NL's first grand-slam home run, off Worcester's John Richmond.

1871-1900 STANDINGS

1880 National League TEAM	G	W	L	PCT	GB
Chicago White Stockings	86	67	17	.798	—
Providence Grays	87	52	32	.619	15
Cleveland Blues	85	47	37	.560	20
Troy Trojans	83	41	42	.494	25.5
Worcester Ruby Legs	85	40	43	.482	26.5
Boston Red Caps	86	40	44	.476	27
Buffalo Bisons	85	24	58	.293	42
Cincinnati Reds	83	21	59	.263	44

1881 National League TEAM	G	W	L	PCT	GB
Chicago White Stockings	84	56	28	.667	—
Providence Grays	85	47	37	.560	9
Buffalo Bisons	83	45	38	.542	10.5
Detroit Wolverines	84	41	43	.488	15
Troy Trojans	85	39	45	.464	17
Boston Red Caps	83	38	45	.458	17.5
Cleveland Blues	85	36	48	.429	20
Worcester Ruby Legs	83	32	50	.390	23

1882 National League TEAM	G	W	L	PCT	GB
Chicago White Stockings	84	55	29	.655	—
Providence Grays	84	52	32	.619	3
Buffalo Bisons	84	45	39	.536	10
Boston Red Caps	85	45	39	.536	10
Cleveland Blues	84	42	40	.512	12
Detroit Wolverines	86	42	41	.506	12.5
Troy Trojans	85	35	48	.422	19.5
Worcester Ruby Legs	84	18	66	.214	37

Although hardly noticed at the time, on June 20 the Cincinnati Red Stockings, fresh from their NL expulsion, reformed as an independent club, and would subsequently lead efforts to launch a rival league, the American Association.

1882

By 1882 the National League had become sufficiently established that competition was inevitable. It came in the form of the American Association.

The AA launched in the spring of 1882, moving into some prime markets with six teams, in Philadelphia, Baltimore, Cincinnati, Louisville, Pittsburgh and St. Louis. Three of the original six (Pittsburgh, Cincinnati and St. Louis) still represent their cities in the majors today.

The Cincinnati Red Stockings, expelled in 1881 from the NL in a dispute over liquor sales at the ballpark, were primary proponents of the new league, so it was unsurprising that the AA adopted more liberal standards. Sunday ball was allowed, as was the sale of alcohol in the ballpark. The AA offered 25-cent admission, half the price of the standard NL ticket. To entice good players, the AA rejected the NL's reserve clause, and to ensure orderly play, hired salaried umpires—an innovation soon imitated by the NL.

The maiden season was a resounding success. Total attendance for the six franchises was 400,000, compared to 404,388 for the eight-team NL (on average, total attendance for each AA club was 66,666, compared to 50,548 for each NL club). The AA's St. Louis entry led all clubs with total attendance of 135,000, a professional baseball record.

Cincinnati, led by pitcher Will White, won the inaugural AA pennant by 11-1/2 games over Philadelphia. White led the league in wins (40), complete games (52), shutouts (8) and innings pitched (480) as Cincinnati racked up a 55-25 record. Pete Browning of Louisville hit .378 to win the circuit's first batting crown.

Meanwhile in the NL, Chicago, again powered by a spectacular offense, won its third consecutive pennant, finishing three games ahead of Providence in the closest race in the NL's brief history. The league also welcomed a 54 percent surge in overall attendance that was fueled by baseball's growing popularity and a booming national economy.

In an unofficial postseason encounter between the champions of the rival leagues, Cincinnati and Chicago split a pair of games before AA officials canceled this harbinger of the World Series.

1883

In response to the rise of the AA, particularly its incursion into New York and other large cities, the NL responded by replacing league doormats Troy and Worcester—the clubs with the lowest attendance in 1881—with teams in New York and Philadelphia. Both cities had been expelled from the NL in 1876 for refusing to play road games to close out the season schedule. But the AA had

been shrewd to target large cities and the NL had no choice but to regain a foothold in the two largest eastern baseball markets.

The AA, which had included Philadelphia in its inaugural season, went head-to-head with the NL in 1883 by placing a team in New York. It also awarded a franchise to Columbus, bringing the total number of AA teams to eight, equaling the NL. By rejecting the NL's reserve clause, the AA had lured a number of disgruntled NL players into its ranks. Thus strengthened, the AA staged another profitable campaign. In the battle for spectators, the AA was a clear winner. Total attendance in the AA topped 1 million, compared to slightly more than 600,000 for the NL. In Philadelphia, the Athletics of the AA had a total attendance of 305,000—a baseball record—compared to just 56,000 for the NL's Phillies.

On the field in the AA, power-hitting first baseman Harry Stovey led the Athletics to the pennant, one game ahead of the St. Louis Browns. Stovey led the league in home runs (14), doubles (31) and slugging average (.506). In an expanded 98-game NL schedule, Boston got 37 wins from Jim Whitney to finish four games ahead of Chicago, ending the White Stockings' three-year reign.

The AA's impressive second season prompted the NL to seek a truce with its rival at the end of the season. That fall, executives of the two leagues negotiated the National Agreement of 1883 (to take affect in 1884), which recognized the AA as a major league in return for the AA adopting the reserve clause and stopping its raids of NL players. The agreement also instituted World Series play between the two leagues and provided for major league control over lower levels of professional baseball by recognizing the territorial rights of minor-league signatories.

1884

The agreement between the NL and AA was barely concluded when a new league made a bid for major league recognition. The Union Association of Base Ball Clubs was organized in Pittsburgh in the fall of 1883. To entice players from the established majors, the UA rejected the reserve clause. But only a few players jumped to the new league from the NL or the AA.

With mostly unknown players, the eight-team UA commenced playing a 128-game schedule, but, plagued by financial losses, only five charter teams made it through the season and the league folded that fall. Nevertheless, the UA drained attendance from the established majors—especially the AA, which unwisely expanded to counter the threat and suffered heavy financial losses.

The collapse of the UA left the dual major league system intact, but relations between the NL and AA were strained. AA leaders accused the NL of duplicity for persuading the AA to expand to 12 teams to counter the UA's incursion.

Despite these hard feelings, the first "World Series" was played between the AA's New York Mets, 6-1/2 game pennant winners over Columbus, and the NL's Providence Grays, 10-1/2 -game winners over Boston. It was no contest. With Charlie "Old Hoss" Radbourn

---

1871–1900 STANDINGS

1882 American Association

TEAM	G	W	L	PCT	GB
Cincinnati Red Stockings	80	55	25	.688	—
Philadelphia Athletics	75	41	34	.547	11.5
Louisville Eclipse	80	42	38	.525	13
Pittsburgh Alleghenys	79	39	39	.500	15
St. Louis Brown Stockings	80	37	43	.463	18
Baltimore Orioles	74	19	54	.260	32.5

1883 National League

TEAM	G	W	L	PCT	GB
Boston Beaneaters	98	63	35	.643	—
Chicago White Stockings	98	59	39	.602	4
Providence Grays	98	58	40	.592	5
Cleveland Blues	100	55	42	.567	7.5
Buffalo Bisons	98	52	45	.536	10.5
New York Gothams	98	46	50	.479	16
Detroit Wolverines	101	40	58	.408	23
Philadelphia Quakers	99	17	81	.173	46

1883 American Association

TEAM	G	W	L	PCT	GB
Philadelphia Athletics	98	66	32	.673	—
St. Louis Browns	98	65	33	.663	1
Cincinnati Red Stockings	98	61	37	.622	5
New York Metropolitans	97	54	42	.563	11
Louisville Eclipse	98	52	45	.536	13.5
Columbus Buckeyes	97	32	65	.330	33.5
Pittsburgh Alleghenys	98	31	67	.316	35
Baltimore Orioles	96	28	68	.292	37

picking up all three wins, Providence won the series, 3-0, outscoring New York 21-3. At the conclusion, the influential weekly *Sporting Life* proclaimed Providence the "Champions of the World," sowing the seed for the championship to be called the World Series.

The AA also suffered setbacks in the boardroom. First, following the collapse of the UA, the St. Louis Maroons were brought into the NL to compete directly with the AA's St. Louis Browns. Then the New York Mets were "raided" of some of their best players by the NL New York Giants, though it was an "inside job" as the teams had the same owner. It was a difficult season for the AA, but the NL emerged from the turmoil in relatively good shape.

The older league continued to boast most of the star players. In 1884, none was a bigger star than Radbourn, a notoriously surly but effective pitcher. A new rule legalized overhand pitching, but Radbourn continued to throw underhand or sidearm and started 73 games, hurling 629 innings, and compiling an ERA of 0.99. He won 59 games, a record unlikely ever to be broken. Meanwhile, Chicago's Ed Williamson hit 27 home runs—25 of them at his home field, Lakefront Park, where the fence was a mere 180 feet from home plate—which remained the single-season record until broken by Babe Ruth.

The 1884 season also saw major league baseball flirt with integration. Moses "Fleet" Walker, an African-American, caught 42 games that season for Toledo of the AA. But when Toledo folded that fall, Walker ran into an invisible "color barrier" that would not be lowered until 1947.

1885

After slipping to fifth place in 1884, the Chicago White Stockings rediscovered their championship form to win their fourth pennant—but not before overcoming a bit of skullduggery by the New York Giants.

By purchasing a stake in the AA New York Mets the previous season, the Giants were able to pluck ace pitcher Tim Keefe from the Mets roster. Keefe was teamed with Mickey Welch to give the Giants the most potent one-two pitching punch in the majors. Together they accounted for 76 of New York's 85 wins (44 for Welch, 32 for Keefe), but the Giants still fell two games short of the pennant.

The White Stockings set an NL record by winning 87 games and, as it was early in the decade, they were powered by the most explosive offense in baseball. Chicago, led again by Cap Anson, King Kelly and Abner Dalrymple, outscored New York by 143 runs. The White Stockings also got a workhorse year from John Clarkson, who led the majors in wins (53), complete games (68), shutouts (10), and innings pitched (623).

In the AA, the St. Louis Cardinals got 40 wins from Bob Caruthers and a solid season from Charles Comiskey to romp to

the pennant, finishing 16 games ahead of Cincinnati.

Chicago and St. Louis then squared off in a controversial World Series that would be declared a tie, although the struggling AA could claim a moral victory. The first game was called for darkness with the score 5-5 after eight innings. In the second game, with Chicago leading 5-4 in the sixth inning, the game was forfeited to the White Sox when the Browns, upset at the umpire, left the field.

Heading into Game 7, Chicago led the series 3-2-1 but, prior to the game, the two teams agreed to throw out the Game 2 forfeit, leaving the series tied going into the final game. But when St. Louis won the game 13-4 and, it seemed, the World Series, Anson declared that Chicago would keep its forfeit win after all. The dispute went to a select committee, which upheld the forfeit, resulting in a World Series tie, 3-3-1.

1886

At 5-foot-7, 140 pounds, Bob Caruthers didn't look particularly formidable. But the St. Louis Browns star had few equals as a dual pitching and hitting threat. And Caruthers was at the top of his game in 1886 as the Browns dominated the AA, winning 93 games and the pennant by 12 games over Pittsburgh.

That season, Caruthers became the first pitcher to record four extra-base hits in a game, smashing two home runs, a double and a triple. He finished the season second in slugging percentage (.527) and fourth in batting average (.334). On the mound, he teamed with Dave Foutz to give the Browns the stingiest pitching in the league. Foutz had a league-best 41 wins; Caruthers had 30. Foutz also led the league in ERA (2.11), with Caruthers second (2.32).

When that pitching was coupled with the hitting of such stalwarts as Arlie Latham, Tip O'Neill and Charlie Comiskey, the Browns became a sure bet to win the World Series. At least, that was the view of the team's colorful owner, Chris Von der Ahe. After St. Louis clinched the pennant, Von der Ahe challenged the National League champion Chicago White Stockings to a winner-take-all $15,000 World Series.

It was a brave move. The White Stockings were baseball's best team of the 1880s, winners of four pennants in six seasons, with a roster loaded with some of the best players in the game. They were coming off another outstanding season. Led by batting champion King Kelly and RBI leader Cap Anson, Chicago won 90 games, beating a rebuilt Detroit club by 2-1/2 games.

The World Series went seven games and could not have been closer. With the scored tied 3-3 in the bottom of the 10th inning of Game 7, Browns outfielder Curt Welch stole home with the winning run, a daring bit of thievery that came to be called "Welch's $15,000 slide."

1871–1900 STANDINGS

1884 National League

TEAM	G	W	L	PCT	GB
Providence Grays	114	84	28	.750	—
Boston Beaneaters	116	73	38	.658	10.5
Buffalo Bisons	115	64	47	.577	19.5
New York Gothams	116	62	50	.554	22
Chicago White-Stockings	113	62	50	.554	22
Philadelphia Quakers	113	39	73	.348	45
Cleveland Blues	113	35	77	.313	49
Detroit Wolverines	114	28	84	.250	56

1884 American Association

TEAM	G	W	L	PCT	GB
New York Metropolitans	112	75	32	.701	—
Columbus Buckeyes	110	69	39	.639	6.5
Louisville Eclipse	110	68	40	.630	7.5
St. Louis Browns	110	67	40	.626	8
Cincinnati Red Stockings	112	68	41	.624	8
Baltimore Orioles	108	63	43	.594	11.5
Philadelphia Athletics	108	61	46	.570	14
Toledo Blue Stockings	110	46	58	.442	27.5
Brooklyn Atlantics	109	40	64	.385	33.5
Richmond Virginians	46	12	30	.286	30.5
Pittsburgh Alleghenys	110	30	78	.278	45.5
Indianapolis Hoosiers	110	29	78	.271	46
Washington Nationals	63	12	51	.190	41

1884 Union Assocation

TEAM	G	W	L	PCT	GB
St. Louis Maroons	114	94	19	.832	—
Milwaukee Grays	12	8	4	.667	35.5
Cincinnati Outlaw Reds	105	69	36	.657	21
Baltimore Monuments	106	58	47	.552	32
Boston Unions	111	58	51	.532	34
Chicago Browns/ Pittsburgh Stogies	93	41	50	.451	42
Washington Nationals	114	47	65	.420	46.5
Philadelphia Keystones	67	21	46	.313	50
St. Paul White Caps	9	2	6	.250	39.5
Altoona Unions	25	6	19	.240	44
Kansas City Unions	82	16	63	.203	61
Wilmington Quicksteps	18	2	16	.111	44.5

Although both leagues were becoming more stable, the NL added two teams in 1886—the Kansas City Cowboys and Washington Senators. They replaced the Providence Grays, winners of the first World Series in 1884, and the Buffalo Bisons. Kansas City folded at the end of its first season and was replaced by the Indianapolis Browns. But, despite these setbacks, attendance in both leagues was still growing and combined ticket sales surpassed two million for the first time.

1887

The storyline for 1887 was established in February when the Chicago White Stockings sold their most popular player, King Kelly, to Boston for the then-unheard-of sum of $10,000. A player of Kelly's stature had never before been sold. He had led the league in runs scored from 1884 to 1886, led the league in doubles three times and won the batting crown in 1886 with a .388 average.

Kelly was an exceptional ballplayer and a genuine character beloved by the fans. When he returned to Chicago for Boston's first visit of 1887, a throng of 10,000 fans greeted him. The King did not disappoint his loyalists, whacking a triple and two singles. Kelly had been a key contributor to the White Stockings dynasty of the 1880s; without him Chicago ceased to be a pennant contender.

Chicago's decline opened the door for the Detroit Wolverines. They had rebuilt their club a year earlier by laying out $7,500 to obtain Buffalo's "Big Four"—Dan Brouthers, Hardy Richardson, Deacon White, and Jack Rowe. That deal ultimately killed the Buffalo franchise, but it allowed Detroit to contend in 1886 before winning the 1887 pennant by 3-1/2 games over the Philadelphia Phillies.

It was a season of wildly inflated batting averages due to rule changes that modified the ball-strike balance (it took four strikes to fan, and eight balls to work out a walk) and scored bases on balls as hits. Detroit feasted under the new rules as Sam Thompson and the "Big Four" led the Wolverines to a league-best team batting average of .348 (.299 when adjusted for base on balls).

It was even wilder in the AA where the St. Louis Browns batted .363, led by Tip O'Neill's .485 average. But even after accounting for walks, O'Neill still batted .435 in one of the most amazing batting seasons in baseball history. He led the AA in every significant batting category—runs, hits, doubles, triples, total bases, home runs, RBI, on-base percentage and slugging average. He was the main reason the Browns won a record 95 games and took the pennant by 14 games over Cincinnati.

The World Series between St. Louis and Detroit was a 15-game marathon played in 10 cities. Lady Baldwin and Charlie Getzien each won four games and Thompson batted .393 as Detroit won 10 games and their first World Series.

After the season, the rules committee scuttled the average-inflating scoring practice and the NL increased its playing schedule to 132 games.

1888

Tim Keefe was regarded among the most consistent and successful pitchers of his era. In his first five seasons in New York, two with the AA Mets and three with the NL Giants, the right-hander had never failed to win fewer than 32 games. But it wasn't until 1888 that Keefe was able to lead the Giants to their first World Series.

Keefe, the first pitcher since Al Spalding to use the changeup as his principal weapon, won 35 games to lead the NL. He also led the league in shutouts (8), strikeouts (335) and ERA (1.74) that season as the Giants won 84 games to win the pennant, 9 games ahead of Chicago. At one point in the season, Keefe reeled off 19 consecutive wins, a streak that to this day has been matched (by Rube Marquard in 1912) but never beaten.

It was a season in which rules makers confirmed, once and for all, the three-strikes rule, and established four balls as the number required for a free base. It was also the year that Ernest L. Thayer was paid $5 for authoring the most famous baseball poem ever written, "Casey at the Bat."

In New York, the AA Mets had folded leaving the Giants as the only pro team in Manhattan. They responded by setting a major league attendance record of 305,455 and, with veteran Roger Connor providing the spark to the offense, they prepared for a World Series encounter with the powerful St. Louis Browns.

The Browns had a typical season, winning 92 games to finish 6-1/2 games ahead of Brooklyn. Tip O'Neill again led the league in batting and Silver King was the dominant pitcher, winning 45 games with an ERA of 1.63.

But the Browns, making their fourth consecutive World Series appearance, were no match for the Giants. With Keefe winning four games with a combined ERA of 0.51, the Giants took six of ten games, clinching the Series with an 11-3 win in Game 8.

1889

Relations between owners and players were strained for much of the latter half of the 1880s and in 1889 there was open talk of baseball's first players' strike. At issue was a salary classification plan ratified by the owners after the 1888 season. The plan, which fixed pay according to a player's perceived "skill," infuriated John M. Ward, president of the Brotherhood of Professional Base Ball Players, because it had the effect of lowering and then freezing salaries between $1,500 and $2,500.

The Brotherhood had been formed in 1885 by nine members of the New York Giants. Ostensibly founded to promote professionalism, the organization also served as an outlet for player complaints about such devices as the reserve clause. Ward openly criticized the buying and selling of players, and the reserve clause, using terms like "slavery" and "serfdom."

Since its formation, the Brotherhood had lived in an uneasy peace with ownership, and as Ward tried without success

---

1871–1900 STANDINGS

1885 National League

TEAM	G	W	L	PCT	GB
Chicago White Stockings	113	87	25	.777	—
New York Giants	112	85	27	.759	2
Philadelphia Quakers	111	56	54	.509	30
Providence Grays	110	53	57	.482	33
Boston Beaneaters	113	46	66	.411	41
Detroit Wolverines	108	41	67	.380	44
Buffalo Bisons	112	38	74	.339	49
St. Louis Maroons	111	36	72	.333	49

1885 American Association

TEAM	G	W	L	PCT	GB
St. Louis Browns	112	79	33	.705	—
Cincinnati Red Stockings	112	63	49	.563	16
Pittsburgh Alleghenys	111	56	55	.505	22.5
Philadelphia Athletics	113	55	57	.491	24
Louisville Colonels	112	53	59	.473	26
Brooklyn Grays	112	53	59	.473	26
New York Metropolitans	108	44	64	.407	33
Baltimore Orioles	110	41	68	.376	36.5

1886 National League

TEAM	G	W	L	PCT	GB
Chicago White Stockings	126	90	34	.726	—
Detroit Wolverines	126	87	36	.707	2.5
New York Giants	124	75	44	.630	12.5
Philadelphia Quakers	119	71	43	.623	14
Boston Beaneaters	118	56	61	.479	30.5
St. Louis Maroons	126	43	79	.352	46
Kansas City Cowboys	126	30	91	.248	58.5
Washington Nationals	125	28	92	.233	60

throughout 1889 to reach a negotiated settlement of the new salary-classification scheme, relations became further strained. Yet Ward counseled the players against striking.

Meanwhile, the NL and AA were each experiencing the tightest pennant races in their histories. In the NL, Boston, led by John Clarkson's 49 wins, waged a furious challenge to the defending champion New York Giants. But the Giants held on to take their second pennant, by a single game. In the AA, the Browns four-year reign ended by finishing two games back of the Brooklyn Bridegrooms.

It was a difficult pill for Browns' fans to swallow. After losing the 1888 World Series, Cardinals ownership had sold their ace pitcher Bob Caruthers to Brooklyn for $8,250. The Bridegrooms promptly made Caruthers the highest paid player in baseball with a $5,000 contract and watched him lead the league with 40 wins and 7 shutouts.

So it was a New York vs. Brooklyn World Series, and the start of what would become a great rivalry. Game 2 drew a record crowd of 16,000 in Brooklyn. But after Brooklyn took a 3-games-to-1 lead, the Giants won four straight to take the Series 6-3.

1890

Strained relations between the players and owners, which dated as far back as the NL seizure of power in 1876 and reached boiling point in 1889, culminated in the formation of a new league controlled by the Brotherhood of Professional Base Ball Players. The Players League sprang out of the refusal of NL owners to budge on the issue of salary classification, or, as the players viewed it, a salary ceiling.

The upstart league succeeded in enticing many of the game's biggest stars and attracted financial backers who accepted John M. Ward's plan of sharing profits and power with the players and competing head-on with the NL. Gate receipts were shared evenly between the home and visiting clubs, the reserve clause was discarded and players were invited to purchase stock in their clubs. The eight-team PL opened play with well-stocked teams in every NL city except Cincinnati.

Faced with a battle for survival, the NL, under a "war committee" headed by Al Spalding, met the PL head-on by scheduling games on the same dates as PL teams, bribing PL players to jump ranks, initiating costly lawsuits over the reserve clause, lowering ticket prices, cajoling press support by threats to withdraw advertising, and raiding the AA and minor-league rosters for players. Several good players were persuaded to stay with the NL, while raids on AA teams lured stars like Billy Hamilton and Tommy Tucker; and promising rookies like pitchers Kid Nichols and Cy Young, infielder Bobby Lowe and outfielder Jess Burkett.

The Players League War was a disaster for baseball. The PL won the battle at the turnstiles, but its teams lost $340,000. In the NL, losses were as much as a half million dollars for each franchise as gate receipts plummeted in such key markets as New York, Philadelphia and Chicago. Within a few weeks of Mike Kelly's Boston team winning the PL pennant by 6-1/2 games over Brooklyn, the PL went out of business. Its financial backers pulled out and its franchises were purchased by their NL counterparts.

Magnanimous in victory, Spalding imposed no reprisals on PL players, but he gave no ground on the key issues.

Meanwhile, the AA struggled through a difficult season. In addition to losing many of its best players to PL and NL raids, prior to the season the Brooklyn and Cincinnati franchises joined the NL. Thus depleted, the AA ran a poor third to the NL and the PL. Louisville, which had lost 111 games and placed dead last in 1889, won the AA's dismal race by 10 games.

The Brooklyn Bridegrooms, losers of the 1889 World Series as the AA representative, won the NL pennant by six games over the Chicago Colts and met Louisville in the Series. But the event seemed meaningless to many who believed the best team in baseball was Boston of the PL. The seven-game series ended tied, 3-3-1, and although there was talk of a tie-breaking eighth game, the idea was abandoned due to cold weather and waning interest. Just 300 tickets had been sold for Game 7.

1891

The clear winner of the Players League War of 1890 was the National League. Not only did it vanquish the PL in its head-to-head battle but it watched the financially drained American Association enter its death throes following a costly year-long competition for players and fans.

In a shrewd move, the NL delayed re-implementation of the salary ceiling, which had been put in abeyance during the free-spending war with the PL. The NL's insistence on a salary ceiling in 1889 had led directly to the formation of the PL, but now its removal would enable the wealthier NL clubs to crush the AA and create a monopoly in major league baseball in which the players' position would be weaker than ever.

The collapse of the PL should have been a boon for the AA, but instead all-out war erupted with the NL over the return of players and the relocation of franchises. The most newsworthy battle involved King Kelly, the game's most popular player.

When the AA's weak Cincinnati club folded in midseason, Kelly, its popular manager, joined the AA Boston Reds, but after just four games he jumped to the NL's Boston Beaneaters. Both Boston teams had emerged from the PL wars with strong teams and were locked in a fierce battle for fans. The Reds were led by sluggers Dan Brouthers and Duke Farrell; the Beaneaters countered with Harry Stovey and veteran pitcher John Clarkson. The Reds won the AA pennant by 8-1/2 games; the Beaneaters won the NL by 3-1/2.

But in the all-important battle for fans, the Beaneaters scored a coup by luring Kelly to their lineup. Among the most charismatic players of the 19th century, Kelly had led Boston to the PL

1871–1900 STANDINGS

1886 American Association

TEAM	G	W	L	PCT	GB
St. Louis Browns	139	93	46	.669	—
Pittsburgh Alleghenys	140	80	57	.584	12
Brooklyn Grays	141	76	61	.555	16
Louisville Colonels	138	66	70	.485	25.5
Cincinnati Red Stockings	141	65	73	.471	27.5
Philadelphia Athletics	139	63	72	.467	28
New York Metropolitans	137	53	82	.393	38
Baltimore Orioles	139	48	83	.366	41

1887 National League

TEAM	G	W	L	PCT	GB
Detroit Wolverines	127	79	45	.637	—
Philadelphia Quakers	128	75	48	.610	3.5
Chicago White Stockings	127	71	50	.587	6.5
New York Giants	129	68	55	.553	10.5
Boston Beaneaters	127	61	60	.504	16.5
Pittsburgh Alleghenys	125	55	69	.444	24
Washington Nationals	126	46	76	.377	32
Indianapolis Hoosiers	127	37	89	.294	43

1887 American Association

TEAM	G	W	L	PCT	GB
St. Louis Browns	138	95	40	.704	—
Cincinnati Red Stockings	136	81	54	.600	14
Baltimore Orioles	141	77	58	.570	18
Louisville Colonels	139	76	60	.559	19.5
Philadelphia Athletics	137	64	69	.481	30
Brooklyn Grays	138	60	74	.448	34.5
New York Metropolitans	138	44	89	.331	50
Cleveland Blues	133	39	92	.298	54

pennant in 1890. His return to Boston excited the fans. They flocked to see him play, first with the Reds and then in droves after he bolted to captain the Beaneaters to the pennant. But, with the AA foundering, and interleague squabbling at its height, there was no World Series between the two Boston clubs.

At the end of the season, the NL bought and closed four AA franchises, including Boston, and added four others—St. Louis, Louisville, Baltimore, and Washington—to their league. The AA, after 10 seasons, ceased to exist, leaving the NL as baseball's sole major league.

1892

As the 1892 season dawned, the National League once again reigned supreme over major league baseball. But victory was costly: buying out four AA clubs saddled the NL with a $130,000 debt. It was a price the NL was willing to pay to create a 12-team monopoly that would endure for the rest of the decade.

Boston emerged as the class of the refurbished league. Paced by pitcher Kid Nichols, who won 35 games in 1892 (and 297 that decade), Boston won the pennant played under a split-season format in which the winners of the first and second half met in a championship series.

Easy winners in the first half, Boston finished the second half three games behind manager Pat Tebeau's Cleveland Spiders. The Spiders were led by the great Cy Young who, in just his second full season, led the league with 36 wins, 9 shutouts and a 1.93 ERA.

The championship series opened with Young and Jack Stivetts, a 35-game winner for Boston, pitching an 11-inning scoreless gem that was halted by darkness. Boston then took over the series, winning the final five games, with Nichols and Stivetts each recording two wins and outfielder Hugh Duffy batting .462.

Compared to the upheaval of recent past seasons, 1892 was tranquil—but for the issue of Sunday baseball. The NL had banned Sunday ball in 1877, a move that contributed to the creation of the AA. By absorbing four AA teams, where Sunday ball was popular, the NL now faced a clamor for games on the Sabbath; for many working fans, Sunday was the only day they could attend games. Thus NL owners finally agreed to drop the Sunday ban and allow play where law and custom dictated. (Sunday ball was illegal in many Eastern states, including New York, Pennsylvania and Massachusetts, for decades to come.)

Clubs had the option of playing on Sunday, and those that did occasionally faced righteous indignation. On one occasion, Cleveland's Ministerial Association and Liquor League filed complaints, resulting in the arrest of the entire Cleveland and Washington teams.

Of note on the field, on June 10 Baltimore catcher Wilbert Robinson hits safely seven times in seven trips to the plate against St. Louis, a feat that went unduplicated in a nine-inning game for more than seven decades.

1893

Baseball fans—especially statistical mavens—love to debate the date from which baseball's "modern era" begins. But perhaps the most logical case for a "modern era," a point beyond which records ought to be considered as fairly and evenly achieved, is 1893. That was the season of one of the last fundamental changes in the game's rules, the relocation of the pitcher (implementation of the foul strike awaited the turn of the century).

Many baseball historians believe Amos Rusie was the impetus for this change. The game had never seen a pitcher who could throw as hard as Rusie. A perennial strikeout leader (and walks leader), "The Hoosier Thunderbolt" was an imposing 6-foot-1, 200-pounder whose renowned wildness terrified hitters.

With that in mind, and with overall offensive numbers lagging, league owners decided to move the pitcher's position back by five feet. It had been set at 50 feet from home plate—as measured from the front of a five-and-a-half-foot pitcher's box—but in 1893 the position for the pitcher's back foot was moved to created a pitching distance of 60 feet, 6 inches that has been constant in all the years since. Indeed, the pitching box was removed altogether, replaced by a rectangular block of rubber. Pitchers were required to anchor one foot on the rubber, rather than select a comfortable place in a box and throw from an angle. (The box has been gone from baseball for over a century, yet in every game, someone observes that a pitcher has been "knocked out of the box.")

The immediate effect of the change was to send batting averages soaring. Philadelphia outfielder Billy Hamilton batted .380 and the overall league average rose from .245 to .280, although pitchers occasionally shined. On August 16 Bill Hawke of the Baltimore Orioles became the first pitcher to toss a no-hitter (over the Washington Senators) from the new distance. Yet, for the rest of the decade, individual batting averages above .400 were commonplace.

Fans responded positively to a game with more offense. Despite a stock-market crash that triggered a four-year recession, league attendance continued to climb. Fans also endorsed a change that saw the unpopular split-season format dropped.

Managed by Frank Selee, and led by Hugh Duffy's hitting and 34 wins by Kid Nichols, the powerful Boston Beaneaters won their second straight pennant, finishing five games ahead of Pittsburgh.

1894

If the first season of the new pitching distance was a challenge for pitchers, the second season was a nightmare. The league batting average rose 30 points to .310 while total runs, compared to 1892, were up by 2,408, a 25 percent increase. The league ERA was 5.32. And nowhere was a pitcher's misery more acute than when facing the Philadelphia Phillies.

As a team, the Phillies batted .350 and their four-man outfield of Ed Delahanty, Sam Thompson, Billy Hamilton, and Tuck Turner, each topped .400. But the batting crown went to the

---

1871–1900 STANDINGS

1888 National League

TEAM	G	W	L	PCT	GB
New York Giants	138	84	47	.641	—
Chicago White Stockings	136	77	58	.570	9
Philadelphia Quakers	132	69	61	.531	14.5
Boston Beaneaters	137	70	64	.522	15.5
Detroit Wolverines	134	68	63	.519	16
Pittsburgh Alleghenys	139	66	68	.493	19.5
Indianapolis Hoosiers	136	50	85	.370	36
Washington Nationals	136	48	86	.358	37.5

1888 American Association

TEAM	G	W	L	PCT	GB
St. Louis Browns	137	92	43	.681	—
Brooklyn Bridegrooms	143	88	52	.629	6.5
Philadelphia Athletics	136	81	52	.609	10
Cincinnati Red Stockings	137	80	54	.597	11.5
Baltimore Orioles	137	57	80	.416	36
Cleveland Blues	135	50	82	.379	40.5
Louisville Colonels	139	48	87	.356	44
Kansas City Cowboys	132	43	89	.326	47.5

1889 National League

TEAM	G	W	L	PCT	GB
New York Giants	131	83	43	.659	—
Boston Beaneaters	133	83	45	.648	1
Chicago White Stockings	136	67	65	.508	19
Philadelphia Quakers	130	63	64	.496	20.5
Pittsburgh Alleghenys	134	61	71	.462	25
Cleveland Spiders	136	61	72	.459	25.5
Indianapolis Hoosiers	135	59	75	.440	28
Washington Nationals	127	41	83	.331	41

Beaneaters' Hugh Duffy, whose .440 mark is the highest in major league history (excluding 1887, when bases on balls were counted as hits). Duffy also led the league with 18 home runs, but his bat was not enough to carry Boston to a third consecutive pennant.

That honor went to the Baltimore Orioles, who catapulted from eighth place in 1893 to finish three games ahead of the New York Giants (Boston was eight back) and win their first pennant. Every Orioles regular on a star-studded team topped the .302 mark and the team batted a remarkable .343, led by such future Hall of Famers as Dan Brouthers, Hugh Jennings, John McGraw, Joe Kelley, Willie Keeler, and Wilbert Robinson.

In a season that saw the adoption of the infield fly rule and Bobby Lowe of the Beaneaters become the first player to hit four home runs in a game, the NL owners established a new postseason contest for a best-of-seven playoff series known as the Temple Cup. It was named after Pittsburgh Pirates president William Chase Temple, who donated a two-foot tall silver cup valued at $800. The Orioles-Giants matchup was a classic case of prolific hitting against stingy pitching and, as so often is the case, pitching triumphed.

The Giants, led by Amos Rusie's 36 wins and Jouett Meekin's 33, had a team ERA of 3.81 in a season when the second-best club was more than a full run higher at 4.98. Against the Orioles, Rusie and Meekin earned two wins each, allowing just four earned runs as the Giants swept the series in four games.

1895

They may have been the dirtiest team in the history of baseball. They may also have been the most inventive. Beyond question, in taking their second of three consecutive pennants, the Baltimore Orioles solidified their place as one of the most important teams that ever took the field. It isn't just that the Orioles won, taking the pennant with an 87-43 mark, three games ahead of the Cleveland Spiders. More than anything, it was the methods the Orioles invented in order to win. Under combative manager Ned Hanlon, the Orioles perfected the hit-and-run play, the double steal, and the bunt single. They also refined the art of cheating.

The Orioles knew that the single umpire employed in those days could not possibly see everything. Accordingly, they stored spare balls in the outfield for use in emergencies, they cut corners when running the bases, and their catcher was known to drop pebbles in the shoes of batters so as to slow them down. A base running excursion in Baltimore could resemble a rugby scrum; runners expected to be jostled at first, second and third.

But the Orioles could also play. Led by rookie ace Bill Hoffer's 31 wins, they allowed the fewest runs in the league while scoring the second most, and compiled a brilliant 54-14 record at home. Once again, however, the Orioles failed in the Temple Cup after running into outstanding pitching.

This time, their nemesis was Cy Young. Coming off a season in which he led the league with 35 wins, Young was superb against the Orioles. He had three wins in three starts, allowing just seven earned runs, as the Spiders won the series four games to one. In the deciding fifth game, Young battled Hoffer into a scoreless sixth inning before he doubled to spark the game-winning three-run rally in a 5-2 win. The winners pocketed $528.33; the losers $316.

1896

The Baltimore Orioles had a lineup of future Hall of Famers, including John McGraw, Joe Kelley and Willie Keeler, but the team captain and leader was their irascible shortstop, Hugh Jennings. He was the Orioles' best player through the mid-1890s and the main cog in the wheel that, in 1896, won its third consecutive pennant.

Orioles manager Ned Hanlon prized players who could combine skill with a win-at-any-cost mentality. McGraw and Jennings epitomized those qualities. Close friends, they ranked among the most detested players in the league, forever screaming obscenities at umpires, taunting opponents and bending the rules at their pleasure. They were the poster boys for the ugly, dirty, dishonest— but wildly successful—baseball played by the Orioles.

But in 1896 Jennings was deprived of his running mate as McGraw was limited to just 23 games. Jennings responded by batting .401 with 121 RBIs (second-best league numbers in both categories), and for the fourth straight season led all shortstops in fielding. He also led the league that season by being plunked 49 times by opposing pitchers, a record that stood until 1971. The Orioles also got the standard stellar seasons from Willie Keeler and Joe Kelly en route to a franchise-best, 90-38 record and their third consecutive pennant, finishing 9-1/2 games ahead of Cleveland.

The Orioles had been upset in the Temple Cups of 1894 and '95, but made amends this time by sweeping the Spiders, 4-0. However, only 1,500 fans attended the final game in Cleveland.

Elsewhere, Philadelphia's Ed Delahanty, one of five brothers to play in the majors and among the greatest hitters of his era, led the league in several batting categories that season and slugged four home runs in a single game one July afternoon. On the flip side, fireballer Amos Rusie had his most forgettable season. Incensed that a $200 fine levied at the end of the 1895 season was not rescinded, Rusie sat out the entire 1896 campaign.

1897

The 1897 season began in splendid fashion for the defending champion Baltimore Orioles as Wee Willie Keeler reeled off a record-setting 44-game hit streak that began on opening day and lasted until June 19. The streak, matched in 1978 by Pete Rose, still stands as the National League record (although the 56-game streak by New York Yankees star Joe DiMaggio in 1941 is the major league record). Keeler went on to bat .424 to win his first of two consecutive batting crowns, but the season was less kind to his Orioles.

1871-1900 STANDINGS

1889 American Association

TEAM	G	W	L	PCT	GB
Brooklyn Bridegrooms	140	93	44	.679	—
St. Louis Browns	141	90	45	.667	2
Philadelphia Athletics	138	75	58	.564	16
Cincinnati Red Stockings	141	76	63	.547	18
Baltimore Orioles	139	70	65	.519	22
Columbus Solons	140	60	78	.435	33.5
Kansas City Cowboys	139	55	82	.401	38
Louisville Colonels	140	27	111	.196	66.5

1890 National League

TEAM	G	W	L	PCT	GB
Brooklyn Bridegrooms	129	86	43	.667	—
Chicago Colts	139	84	53	.613	6
Philadelphia Phillies	133	78	54	.591	9.5
Cincinnati Reds	134	77	55	.583	10.5
Boston Beaneaters	134	76	57	.571	12
New York Giants	135	63	68	.481	24
Cleveland Spiders	136	44	88	.333	43.5
Pittsburgh Alleghenys	138	23	113	.169	66.5

1890 American Association

TEAM	G	W	L	PCT	GB
Louisville Colonels	136	88	44	.667	—
Columbus Solons	140	79	55	.590	10
St. Louis Browns	139	78	58	.574	12
Toledo Maumees	134	68	64	.515	20
Rochester Broncos	133	63	63	.500	22
Baltimore Orioles	38	15	19	.441	24
Syracuse Stars	128	55	72	.433	30.5
Philadelphia Athletics	132	54	78	.409	34
Brooklyn Gladiators	100	26	73	.263	45.5

The three-time defending champions matched their 90 wins of the 1896, but placed two games back of a refurbished Boston Beaneaters club that went 93-39 to reclaim the pennant it had relinquished to the Orioles in 1894. The resurgence of the Beaneaters was the result of trades that brought Billy Hamilton and Jimmy Collins to Boston, bolstering a lineup already featuring future Hall of Famers Hugh Duffy and Kid Nichols.

Collins was the key. Although Boston property in 1895, Collins could not dislodge veteran Billy Nash from third base and was sold to Louisville. There, he quickly established himself as the slickest third baseman in the league. He revolutionized the position by being the first major leaguer to execute the barehanded pickup-and-throw to first base. He also was the first to position himself off the bag, standing a few steps toward shortstop or, in bunting situations, moving in toward home.

The Beaneaters, regretting the 1895 deal, reacquired Collins in 1897 and, to make room, traded the veteran Nash to Philadelphia for Billy Hamilton, a former batting champion and the top base stealer of this era. The 198 runs Hamilton scored in 1894 remains a major league record.

The impact of Hamilton and Collins was immediate. Hamilton led the league with 152 runs and 105 bases on balls, and added 68 stolen bases; Collins was second with 132 RBIs. Adding them to Hugh Duffy's power hitting and 97 RBIs from rookie Chick Stahl gave Boston the league's top offense. Throw in Kid Nichols' league-leading 31 wins and the Beaneaters became dominant.

But in the final Temple Cup ever played, Baltimore turned the tables on Boston, winning the series 4-1. Attendance for the final game in Baltimore was only 700. The Temple Cup had proved to be a money loser that, one observer said, no more resembled the old World Series than a "crabapple does ... a pippin." The league returned the Cup to William Chase Temple, and there was no post-season series until 1900.

1898

After several years of stability and growth, baseball took a backward step in 1898. Not all of the problems were of baseball's own doing. The outbreak of the Spanish-American War cast a degree of uncertainty across all facets of the nation, but baseball's problems were compounded by several factors that contributed to a 20 percent drop in overall attendance.

The issues varied from city to city. For example, in Cleveland, a strike at the team owner's streetcar company resulted in calls for a boycott of Spiders games and forced them to play 114 of 156 games on the road. In St. Louis, the left-field stands and bleachers were destroyed by a fire that injured 100 people and resulted in a 30 percent decrease in attendance.

Despite increasing the schedule to 154 games, huge declines in ticket sales were also experienced in Baltimore, Boston, Brooklyn,

New York, and Washington. In Brooklyn, Charles Ebbets took over the running of the team, moved the Bridegrooms into a new stadium and fired the manager. When the new manager quit after three games, Ebbets assumed managerial duties. The team finished in 10th place and saw ticket sales nosedive from 220,831 in 1897 to 122,514.

But the league's biggest ongoing problem might have been its competitive imbalance. In the decade of the 1890s, Boston, Baltimore and Brooklyn were the only teams to win pennants, and in 1898 Washington and St. Louis each lost more than 100 games.

The pennant race was a repeat of the previous season, a two-team battle between Boston and Baltimore. Willie Keeler repeated as batting champion and John McGraw led the league in runs and walks to pace the Orioles to 96 wins. But the Beaneaters, led once again by the bats of Billy Hamilton and Jimmy Collins and the pitching arm of Kid Nichols, rolled to 102 wins, their second consecutive pennant and fifth in eight years.

Elsewhere, it was a season of firsts: Philadelphia pitcher Bill Duggleby hit a grand slam home run in his first major league at-bat, a feat that has gone unmatched to this day; Ted Breitenstein and Jay Hughes tossed no-hitters on the same day, a major league first; and for the first time, official scorers were instructed to award hits, not errors, on hard-hit balls that were bobbled.

1899

The monopoly created when the Players League and American Association folded in the early part of the decade enabled National League owners to run baseball without regard for fan interests. Several, for example, purchased control of more than one team and moved players between those clubs to suit their personal profits, rather than the best interests of the club.

The culmination of this "syndicate" approach to baseball occurred in 1899, when such shenanigans distorted both the top and bottom tiers of the pennant race.

While retaining their ownership of the Baltimore team, Harry Van Der Horst and Ned Hanlon also purchased control of Brooklyn and sold the best Orioles to the Dodgers. Infused by such talent as Willie Keeler, Joe Kelley, Hugh Jennings, Dan McGann, Doc McJames, and Jim Hughes, Brooklyn improved by a remarkable 47 games in the standings, leaping from 10th place to the pennant, 7-1/2 games ahead of Boston. The once-vaunted Orioles, meanwhile, who had become a money loser despite finishing no lower than second in the previous five years, fell to fourth.

It would have been worse in Baltimore if John McGraw, who had business interests in Baltimore, had not refused to go to Brooklyn. McGraw became the Orioles manager and, through some shrewd trades, kept his team in the race until late in the season, when his wife died, sending him into seclusion and his team into a free fall.

1871–1900 STANDINGS

1890 Players League

TEAM	G	W	L	PCT	GB
Boston Reds	130	81	48	.628	—
Brooklyn Ward's Wonders	133	76	56	.576	6.5
New York Giants	132	74	57	.565	8
Chicago Pirates	138	75	62	.547	10
Philadelphia Athletics	132	68	63	.519	14
Pittsburgh Burghers	128	60	68	.469	20.5
Cleveland Infants	131	55	75	.423	26.5
Buffalo Bisons	134	36	96	.273	46.5

1891 National League

TEAM	G	W	L	PCT	GB
Boston Beaneaters	140	87	51	.630	—
Chicago Colts	137	82	53	.607	3.5
New York Giants	136	71	61	.538	13
Philadelphia Phillies	138	68	69	.496	18.5
Cleveland Spiders	141	65	74	.468	22.5
Brooklyn Grooms	137	61	76	.445	25.5
Cincinnati Reds	138	56	81	.409	30.5
Pittsburgh Pirates	137	55	80	.407	30.5

1891 American Association

TEAM	G	W	L	PCT	GB
Boston Reds	139	93	42	.689	—
St. Louis Browns	141	86	52	.623	8.5
Milwaukee Brewers	36	21	15	.583	22.5
Baltimore Orioles	139	71	64	.526	22
Philadelphia Athletics	143	73	66	.525	22
Columbus Solons	138	61	76	.445	33
Cincinnati Kelly's Killers	102	43	57	.430	32.5
Louisville Colonels	141	55	84	.396	40
Washington Statesmen	139	44	91	.326	49

It was a similar story in Cleveland, where owners Frank De Haas and Matthew Robison invested in the St. Louis team as well. The heart of the Spiders—Cy Young, Jesse Burkett, Patsy Tebeau, Bobby Wallace, Cupid Childs, Jack Powell, and "Peach Pie" Jack O'Connor—were packed off to St. Louis. The rebuilt St. Louis team climbed from the cellar to claim fifth place, while the ravaged Spiders lost 134 games (which remains the all-time record), finishing an incredible 83-1/2 games out of first place.

In the aftermath of this farcical campaign, the twelve-club big league was reduced to eight teams. Baltimore, Cleveland, Washington, and Louisville were folded at a cost of $100,000, a buyout shared by the eight surviving teams.

1900

When baseball owners created the major league monopoly early in the decade they styled themselves as magnates presiding over a million-dollar entertainment industry. The magnates fully expected their monopoly league to produce unprecedented cash and glory. But their dreams were dashed by a combination of external economic factors and internal ones, including greed and, at times, stupidity.

The 12-team National League was doomed because the owners consistently failed to address the issue of competitive imbalance and, in fact, exacerbated the problem by "syndicate" ownership, which decimated such clubs as Baltimore and Cleveland. By reducing the league to eight teams, the owners left many unemployed players and created a vacuum in some attractive markets—all at a time when the national economy was about to boom.

Into this vacuum stepped Byron "Ban" Johnson, who had long held the ambition of elevating his Western League, founded in 1894, into a major league. With the backing of lieutenants like Charles Comiskey and Connie Mack, Johnson renamed his circuit the American League and unilaterally declared it a major league. His clubs snapped up surplus NL players, and Comiskey moved his team to Chicago where, taking the NL entry's discarded name of White Stockings, he boldly confronted the Cubs. With solid financial backing and a new ballpark, Comiskey's major league castoffs and promising youngsters captured the first AL pennant in a profitable campaign, while inflicting upon the Cubs a 30 percent decline in attendance. The seed was sown for another baseball war.

First, though, the stacked Brooklyn team, led this time by 28-game winner Joe McGinnity, successfully defended the NL pennant, finishing 4-1/2 games ahead of a young Pittsburgh team that was headed for greatness. When the Louisville franchise was shut down after the 1899 campaign, its owner, Barney Dreyfuss, acquired the Pittsburgh Pirates and took many of his players with him, including a gangly youngster who could play almost any position. His name was Honus Wagner, and he hit .381 to win the 1900 batting crown. Wagner was joined by outfielder Fred Clarke and together they would form the heart of a Pirate order that would win three consecutive pennants starting in 1901.

1871–1900 STANDINGS

1892 National League

TEAM	G	W	L	PCT	GB
Boston Beaneaters	152	102	48	.680	—
Cleveland Spiders	153	93	56	.624	8.5
Brooklyn Grooms	158	95	59	.617	9
Philadelphia Phillies	155	87	66	.569	16.5
Cincinnati Reds	155	82	68	.547	20
Pittsburgh Pirates	155	80	73	.523	23.5
Chicago Colts	147	70	76	.479	30
New York Giants	153	71	80	.470	31.5
Louisville Colonels	154	63	89	.414	40
Washington Senators	153	58	93	.384	44.5
St. Louis Browns	155	56	94	.373	46
Baltimore Orioles	152	46	101	.313	54.5

1893 National League

TEAM	G	W	L	PCT	GB
Boston Beaneaters	131	86	43	.667	—
Pittsburgh Pirates	131	81	48	.628	5
Cleveland Spiders	129	73	55	.570	12.5
Philadelphia Phillies	133	72	57	.558	14
New York Giants	136	68	64	.515	19.5
Cincinnati Reds	131	65	63	.508	20.5
Brooklyn Grooms	130	65	63	.508	20.5
Baltimore Orioles	130	60	70	.462	26.5
Chicago Colts	128	56	71	.441	29
St. Louis Browns	135	57	75	.432	30.5
Louisville Colonels	126	50	75	.400	34
Washington Senators	130	40	89	.310	46

1894 National League

TEAM	G	W	L	PCT	GB
Baltimore Orioles	129	89	39	.695	—
New York Giants	137	88	44	.667	3
Boston Beaneaters	133	83	49	.629	8
Philadelphia Phillies	129	71	57	.555	18
Brooklyn Grooms	134	70	61	.534	20.5
Cleveland Spiders	130	68	61	.527	21.5
Pittsburgh Pirates	132	65	65	.500	25
Chicago Colts	135	57	75	.432	34
St. Louis Browns	133	56	76	.424	35
Cincinnati Reds	132	55	75	.423	35
Washington Senators	132	45	87	.341	46
Louisville Colonels	130	36	94	.277	54

1895 National League

TEAM	G	W	L	PCT	GB
Baltimore Orioles	132	87	43	.669	—
Cleveland Spiders	131	84	46	.646	3
Philadelphia Phillies	133	78	53	.595	9.5
Chicago Colts	133	72	58	.554	15
Brooklyn Grooms	133	71	60	.542	16.5
Boston Beaneaters	132	71	60	.542	16.5
Pittsburgh Pirates	134	71	61	.538	17
Cincinnati Reds	132	66	64	.508	21
New York Giants	132	66	65	.504	21.5
Washington Senators	132	43	85	.336	43
St. Louis Browns	135	39	92	.298	48.5
Louisville Colonels	133	35	96	.267	52.5

1896 National League

TEAM	G	W	L	PCT	GB
Baltimore Orioles	132	90	39	.698	—
Cleveland Spiders	135	80	48	.625	9.5
Cincinnati Reds	128	77	50	.606	12
Boston Beaneaters	132	74	57	.565	17
Chicago Colts	132	71	57	.555	18.5
Pittsburgh Pirates	131	66	63	.512	24
New York Giants	133	64	67	.489	27
Philadelphia Phillies	130	62	68	.477	28.5
Washington Senators	133	58	73	.443	33
Brooklyn Bridegrooms	133	58	73	.443	33
St. Louis Browns	131	40	90	.308	50.5
Louisville Colonels	134	38	93	.290	53

1897 National League

TEAM	G	W	L	PCT	GB
Boston Beaneaters	135	93	39	.705	—
Baltimore Orioles	136	90	40	.692	2
New York Giants	137	83	48	.634	9.5
Cincinnati Reds	134	76	56	.576	17
Cleveland Spiders	132	69	62	.527	23.5
Washington Senators	135	61	71	.462	32
Brooklyn Bridegrooms	136	61	71	.462	32
Pittsburgh Pirates	135	60	71	.458	32.5
Chicago Colts	138	59	73	.447	34
Philadelphia Phillies	134	55	77	.417	38
Louisville Colonels	134	52	78	.400	40
St. Louis Browns	132	29	102	.221	63.5

1898 National League

TEAM	G	W	L	PCT	GB
Boston Beaneaters	152	102	47	.685	—
Baltimore Orioles	154	96	53	.644	6
Cincinnati Reds	157	92	60	.605	11.5
Chicago Orphans	152	85	65	.567	17.5
Cleveland Spiders	156	81	68	.544	21
Philadelphia Phillies	150	78	71	.523	24
New York Giants	157	77	73	.513	25.5
Pittsburgh Pirates	152	72	76	.486	29.5
Louisville Colonels	154	70	81	.464	33
Brooklyn Bridegrooms	149	54	91	.372	46
Washington Senators	155	51	101	.336	52.5
St. Louis Browns	154	39	111	.260	63.5

1899 National League

TEAM	G	W	L	PCT	GB
Brooklyn Superbas	150	100	47	.680	—
Boston Beaneaters	153	95	57	.625	7.5
Philadelphia Phillies	154	94	58	.618	8.5
Baltimore Orioles	152	86	62	.581	14.5
St. Louis Perfectos	155	84	67	.556	18
Cincinnati Reds	157	83	67	.553	18.5
Pittsburgh Pirates	155	76	73	.510	25
Chicago Orphans	152	75	73	.507	25.5
Louisville Colonels	156	75	76	.497	27
New York Giants	153	60	90	.400	41.5
Washington Senators	155	54	98	.355	48.5
Cleveland Spiders	154	20	134	.130	83.5

1900 National League

TEAM	G	W	L	PCT	GB
Brooklyn Superbas	142	82	54	.603	—
Pittsburgh Pirates	140	79	60	.568	4.5
Philadelphia Phillies	141	75	63	.543	8
Boston Beaneaters	142	66	72	.478	17
St. Louis Cardinals	142	65	75	.464	19
Chicago Orphans	146	65	75	.464	19
Cincinnati Reds	144	62	77	.446	21.5
New York Giants	141	60	78	.435	23

Chapter 7

The True Father of Baseball

By John Thorn

The history of baseball is a lie from beginning to end, from its creation myth to its rosy models of commerce, community and fair play. The game's epic feats and revered figures, its pieties about racial harmony and bleacher democracy, its artful blurring of sport and business—all of it is bunk, tossed up with a wink and a nudge. Yet Abner Doubleday, for example, will not be consigned to the dustbin of baseball history no matter how convincingly one argues that he did not invent baseball.

But if the history of baseball is a lie, it is a glorious, vibrant and, in the grand scheme of life, harmless lie, gripping us in a way that good, gray fact seldom can. The bearer of fact cannot hope to annihilate the legends in baseball's Elysian Fields, but simply to play alongside them, occasionally getting a turn at bat.

I believe that the conventional tale of the game's birth is substantially incorrect. By this I refer not to the Doubleday fable, pointless to attack, but to the scarcely less legendary development of the Knickerbocker game, ostensibly sired by Alexander Cartwright.

Let's look at the delicate condition of baseball's paternity. There would have been no need to establish Alexander Cartwright as a baseball deity had the Mills Commission report of 1907—created by Albert Spalding not to explore the origins of the game but to confirm its American roots—not named Abner Doubleday the father of the game; however, the absurdity of the Doubleday claim agitated Cartwright's son Bruce so much that he protested to Spalding, and to *Collier's* writer Will Irwin, that baseball did not exist before the advent of Cartwright and the Knickerbocker Base Ball Club of New York City. This claim came at a time when men were still alive who had seen some rural variant of baseball in the 1820s or 1830s or who had even played baseball in an urban setting with one of the several ballclubs that had preceded the formation of the Knicks in 1845, such as the New York Base Ball Club, the Brooklyn Ball Club, the Eagles of New York, or the Olympics of Philadelphia.

Earlier histories of baseball—from those published annually by Henry Chadwick in the Beadle, DeWitt and Spalding Guides to book-length histories such as Charles Peverelly's *Book of American Pastimes* (1866) and Jacob Morse's *Sphere and Ash* (1888)—gave credit to the Knickerbockers for the eventual ascendance of the New York Game of baseball over the competing Massachusetts Game; however, they did not single out Cartwright as the sole creator. In 1860, in the premier edition of the *Beadle Dime Base Ball Player,* Chadwick acknowledged the existence of the New York Base Ball Club prior to the organization of the Knicks, but stated "we shall not be far wrong if we award to the Knickerbocker the honor of being the pioneers of the present game of base ball." Still, he never swerved from his assertion in that same essay that it was

rounders, the English childhood game, "from which base ball is derived." Only in the next century did Cartwright become, no less than Doubleday, a tool of those who wished to establish baseball as the product of an identifiable spark of American ingenuity, without foreign or Darwinian taint.

What did Cartwright do? He suggested that the Knickerbockers, who had been playing informally since at least 1842, be organized as a club, with a constitution and playing rules that he did much to formulate (although not alone—three other Knickerbockers were equally involved in drafting the original fourteen playing rules). Notable among these rules—which simply codified the game that the Knicks were already playing—were the laying out of baseball on a "diamond" rather than a square, the concept of foul territory and the elimination of the rounders and town-ball practice of retiring a runner by throwing the ball at him.

These are critical differences from earlier games, sufficient in and of themselves to term the Knickerbocker game a landmark in the evolution of baseball. But what Cartwright assuredly did not do was any of the three central things credited to him on his plaque in the Baseball Hall of Fame:

"Set bases 90 feet apart. Established 9 innings as a game and 9 players as a team." (More on this in a moment.) He also did not create the 45-foot pitching distance, nor the requirement that a ball be caught on the fly to register an out, nor a system for calling balls and strikes.

The truth of the paternity question? Eighty-year-old Henry Chadwick had it right when he said in 1904, only one year before the formation of the Mills Commission, "Like Topsy, baseball never had no 'fadder'; it jest growed." In fact, until Papa Doubleday was pulled out of the hat, it was Chadwick himself who had most frequently been honored with the sobriquet "Father of Baseball," not for any powers of invention but for his role in popularizing and shaping the game. Others to have been accorded patriarchal honors were Harry Wright, who organized the first openly professional team; Albert Spalding, the tireless player, magnate and tour promoter; William Hulbert, founder of the National League in 1876; and Daniel L. Adams, whose name today is scarcely known.

Daniel Lucius Adams was born on November 1, 1814, in Mt. Vernon, New Hampshire, the younger of two sons and at least three daughters of Dr. Daniel Adams (born in 1773; graduated from Dartmouth College, 1797, and received his medical degree from the school in 1799) and Nancy Mulliken Adams. In addition to being a doctor of medicine, the father was a noted orator and author, whose mathematics textbook *The Scholar's Arithmetic, Or, Federal Accountant* was in constant use under varying titles and editions from 1806 to the Civil War. The younger Adams received his early education at the Mt. Pleasant Classical Institution in Amherst, Massachusetts, going on to spend his first two years of

Daniel Lucius Adams

college at Amherst after entering in 1831. He graduated from Yale in 1835, progressing to a medical degree from Harvard in 1838 and then a general practice in New York City, coupled with an active involvement with treating the poor at the New York Dispensaries. He first resided and practiced at 511 Broadway, moving to 45 White Street in 1843; ultimately he settled in at 14 Bond Street in the 1850s.

"Doc" Adams, as he was known to all, began to play baseball in 1839. "I was always interested in athletics while in college and afterward," he told an interviewer at the age of 81, "and soon after going to New York I began to play base ball just for exercise, with a number of other young medical men. Before that there had been a club called the New York Base Ball Club, but it had no very definite organization and did not last long. Some of the younger members of that club got together and formed the Knickerbocker Base Ball Club, September 24, 1845 [actually September 23]. The players included merchants, lawyers, Union Bank clerks [like Cartwright], insurance clerks and others who were at liberty after 3 o'clock in the afternoon. They went into it just for exercise and enjoyment, and I think they used to get a good deal more solid fun out of it than the players in the big games do nowadays.

"About a month after the organization of this club, several of us medical fellows joined it, myself among the number. The following year I was made president and served as long as I was willing to retain the office."

What's new here? Plenty. According to Adams, the New York Base Ball Club not only preceded the Knickerbocker, but formed it; for example, such early New York Base Ball Club members as James Lee, Abraham Tucker and William Wheaton all became Knickerbockers in 1845-1846. As early as 1840, Adams played a game in New York that he understood to be baseball. It was the same game as that played by the men who would become the Knickerbockers, played on a square, at first with eleven men on a side, as in cricket and perhaps the Massachusetts Game.

This game—called base ball and not rounders or town ball—was played in New York City as early as 1832 by two clubs, one composed of residents of the first ward (the lower part of the city), the other in the upper part of the city (ninth and 15th wards). By 1843, when the Knicks were still playing at their original site in Madison Square, the teams had been reduced to eight—which included a "pitch," a "behind," three basemen and three in the field—and the playing field had been changed from a square to a diamond, as in rounders. According to Alphonse Martin, a prominent pitcher in the 1860s who left an unpublished manuscript "History of Base Ball," it was Cartwright who prompted this move. In later years, when asked how the game of baseball originated, Doc Adams declined to identify a distinct starting point; he believed it grew from rounders.

Actually, baseball as played by the Knicks in the years 1845-1849 (Cartwright left for California in the gold-rush spring of 1849) was almost never a nine-man game; eight, ten, and eleven were all more frequently employed numbers to the side. (As late as 1855, an unsigned columnist for the New York *Clipper* wrote: "Base Ball can be played by any number from five upwards; nine, however, being the usual number of each side.") Play was conducted in accord with Cartwright's model of only three basemen, and on the rare occasions when nine or more fielding positions

Abner Doubleday

were created by a surfeit of players, the "extras" were put into the outfield. In a game in late May 1847, for example, when eleven men were available to each side, the Knickerbockers' response was to play with nine, including four outfielders, and hold two men out as substitutes.

The advent of the short fielder, or shortstop, was a crucial break with rounders, and this position was created in 1849 or 1850 by Adams. "I used to play shortstop," he reminisced, "and I believe I was the first one to occupy that place, as it had formerly been left uncovered." But when Adams first went out to short, it was not to bolster the infield but to assist in relays from the outfield. The early Knickerbocker ball was so light that it could not be thrown even 200 feet; thus the need for a short fielder to send the ball in to the pitcher's point.

"We had a great deal of trouble in getting balls made," Adams recalled, "and for six or seven years I made all the balls myself, not only for our club but also for other clubs when they were organized. [He also supervised the turning of the bats during this period.] I went all over New York to find someone who would undertake this work, but no one could be induced to try it for love or money. Finally I found a Scotch saddler who was able to show me a good way to cover the balls with horsehide, such as was used for whip lashes. I used to make the stuffing out of three or four ounces of rubber cuttings, wound with yarn and then covered with the leather. Those balls were, of course, a great deal softer than the balls now [i.e. 1896] in use."

When the ball was wound tighter, gaining more hardness and resilience, it could be hit farther and, crucially, thrown farther. This permitted the shortstop to come into the infield, which Adams did.

Even more important, the introduction of the hard ball permitted a change in the dimensions of the playing field. The Knickerbocker rules of 1845 had specified no pitching distance, and no baseline length; all that was indicated was: "from 'home' to second base, 42 paces; from first to third base, 42 paces, equidistant." It has been presumed by scholars that when a three-foot pace is plugged in, the resulting baselines of eighty-nine feet are close enough to the present ninety so that we can proclaim Cartwright's genius. In fact, the pace in 1845 was either an imprecise and variable measure—to gauge distances by "stepping off"—or precisely two and a half feet, in which case the distance from home to second would have been 105 feet and the Cartwright basepaths would have been 74.25 feet.

The pace of 1845 could not have been interpreted as the precise equivalent of three feet, although a three-foot pace was sometimes employed for itinerary distances. This alternate definition of a pace was not listed among dictionary definitions until much later in the century. Here is the definition of a pace from *An American Dictionary of the English Language,* by Noah Webster, 1828: "1. A step. 2. The space between the two feet in walking, estimated at two feet and a half. But the geometrical pace is five feet, or the whole space passed over by the same foot from one step to another." This definition was not changed for Webster's 1853 revised edition.

Personal research indicates that 75-foot basepaths were the norm well into the mid-1850s—when the basepaths were first prescribed as "42 paces or yards"—and were the standard for youth play well into the next decade.

In 1848 Adams, as Knickerbocker president, headed the Committee to Revise the Constitution and By-Laws; Alexander Cartwright served under him. Adams' interest in refining the rules of the game, already evident, was further piqued by the formation of additional clubs, beginning with the Washington Base Ball Club in 1850, which was constructed around several former New York Base Ball Club members. In 1852 the Washingtons were renamed the Gothams and took in additional players, and the Eagle Club, which had been organized to play town ball in 1840, reconstituted itself to become the Eagle Base Ball Club.

"The playing rules remained very crude up to this time," Adams said, "but in 1853 the three clubs united in a revision of the rules and regulations. At the close of 1856 there were 12 clubs in existence, and it was decided to hold a convention of delegates from all of these for the purpose of establishing a permanent code of rules by which all should be governed.

"A call was therefore issued, signed by the officers of the Knickerbocker Club as the senior organization, and the result was the assembling of the first convention of base ball players in May, 1857. I was elected presiding officer."

It was at this meeting, eight years after Cartwright's western expedition, that the winner of a game was defined as the team that was ahead at the conclusion of nine innings rather than the first team to score 21 runs (originally the convention had favored a seven-inning game but, persuaded by Knickerbocker first baseman Lewis F. Wadsworth, finally settled at nine innings). "In March of the next year the second convention was held, and at this meeting the annual convention was declared a permanent organization, and with the requisite constitution and by-laws became the 'National Association of Ball Players.'

"I was chairman of the Committee on Rules and Regulations from the start and so long as I retained membership. I presented the first draft of rules, prepared after much careful study of the matter, and it was in the main adopted. The distance between bases I fixed at 30 yards—the only previous determination of distance being 'the bases shall be from home to second base 42 paces, from first to third base 42 paces equidistant'—which was rather vague. In every meeting of the National Association while a member, I advocated the fly-game—that is, not to allow first-bound catches—but I was always defeated on the vote. The change was made, however, soon after I left, as I predicted in my last speech on the subject before the convention.

"The distance from home to pitcher's base I made 45 feet. Many of the old rules, such as those defining a foul, remain substantially the same today," he concluded in 1896, "while others are changed and, of course, many new ones added. I resigned in 1862, but not before thousands were present to witness matches, and any number of outside players standing ready to take a hand on regular playing days."

In the 1840s players could not be relied upon to show up for practice. Adams recalled that the Knickerbockers frequently went to Hoboken to find only two or three members present, and were often obliged to take their exercise "in the form of 'old cat,' 'one,' or 'two' as the case might be." (Bat-and-ball games of cat, or catapult or trap ball, could be played by as many players as were on hand, with the number of bases or holes expanding with the cast of characters—the game was really one ol' (hole) cat, and had nothing to do with superannuated felines.) But, he summed up in 1896, "we pioneers never expected to see the game so universal as it has now become."

On May 7, 1861, Adams married Cornelia A. Cook. Less than a year later he resigned from the Knickerbocker Base Ball Club, and in 1865 he retired from his practice in New York and moved to Ridgefield, Connecticut. There he lived on Main Street in the former home of Revolutionary War hero Colonel Philip Burr Bradley. Soon becoming a prominent citizen of his new hometown, Adams served in the State House of Representatives for the legislative session of 1870 and, in the following year, was elected the first president of the Ridgefield Savings Bank. Adams remained in that position for eight years and then, after a five-year hiatus, resumed the post for another two, serving until July 1, 1886. Between terms as president of the bank, he was elected the first treasurer of the Ridgefield Library.

Although he played his last formal game of baseball on Sept. 27, 1875, in an oldtimers' contest arranged by longtime Knickerbocker comrade James Whyte Davis, Adams continued to play backyard ball with his sons even into his eighth decade, when he moved his family to New Haven, where the boys attended Sheffield Scientific School. After suffering five days from influenza that developed into pneumonia, on January 3, 1899, Daniel Lucius Adams died in his home at 146 Edwards Street.

Success has many fathers, failure none. For his role in making baseball the success it is, Doc Adams may be counted as first among the Fathers of Baseball.

| Chapter 8 | Baseball and the Civil War |

Union Army soldiers
Baseball had taken hold in many northern states in the 1850s and was a popular pastime among troops during the Civil War.

By Patricia Millen

Many writers and historians have argued that baseball's rise in popularity during the late 19th century was the result of the spread of the game by thousands of young men from all over the country during the American Civil War. Robert Weaver's thesis is typical of early baseball writers. In 1939 he extolled: "During this conflict ... the game became nationalized ... When the soldiers were not fighting they played baseball; teams from different regiments frequently played games; soldiers from the North carried the game into Confederate prison camps." Sporting goods tycoon and former ballplayer Albert Spalding wrote in 1911, "For, during those years of unhappy conflict, on both sides of the line 'Yankees' and 'Johnnies' were playing ball and laying the foundation for the game which, when war's alarms cease, would be national in its spirit and national in its perpetuity."

Contemporary writers—even grammar and high-school textbooks—continue to credit the Civil War for the dissemination of the game on the battlefield and in Southern prison camps. The singular print of Union prisoners playing baseball at the Confederate prison at Salisbury, North Carolina, is often used as evidence to exaggerate the progression of the game during the Civil War years.

Long before the first shot was fired at Fort Sumter, however, the game of baseball had already entrenched itself into American society and was well on its way to becoming "America's National Game." By examining available sources on the leisure-time activities of Civil War soldiers in the Union and Confederate armies, it is clear that baseball was indeed played with great enthusiasm by Northern and Southern troops, though with far less regularity than other recreational pursuits. Baseball would have advanced throughout the 19th century as America's favorite sport even without the four-year interruption of the American Civil War. The game was not dramatically advanced by Northern soldiers moving south during the War, nor by the sometime exchanges between Union and Confederate soldiers.

From colonization to the start of the American Civil War in

1861, primitive stick-and-ball games—such as one old cat, two old cat, stool ball, rounders, base, feeder, and town ball—were played in early America. Base (a running game played both with and without a ball) or goal ball had been played in England in the early 18th century. By the late 18th and early 19th century, base and "base ball" were well known in the United States. Forms of these ball and bat games were often documented as being played in Colonial America in English and Dutch settlements. As one diarist recorded in his journal in 1753 while traveling through New York state, "Even at the celebration of the Lord's-supper, [the Dutch boys] have been playing bat and ball the whole term around the house of God."

One of the earliest cited references to baseball in the colonies during a military campaign was at Valley Forge, Pennsylvania, during the American Revolution. On April 7, 1778, George Ewing, a Continental soldier, wrote in his diary of exercising in the afternoon and in the intervals he "playd at base." In the antebellum South many diaries, reminiscences and travel accounts also mention ball as being played in the 17th, 18th, and early 19th centuries. According to a study done by Ruth Fink on the recreational activities in the "Old South," the author concluded that recreational pursuits of people living in the South were not even far removed from most Americans of the present century. Residents in the states of Virginia, Alabama, Louisiana, Georgia, and the Carolinas, for example, enjoyed dancing, hunting, fishing, barbecues, and playing games of bowling, tag, and games that were not unlike modern baseball.

Prior to the Civil War, baseball was played in the Southern states in both the aristocratic setting of the plantation and in the areas reserved for people held as slaves. In *Baseball: The Early Years*, author Harold Seymour describes a Deep South scene of tents spread under the branches of giant oak trees for the protection of the ladies while "polite stewards of the clubs" waited on the delicate fans watching a game played in 1859. Ball play was also a source of entertainment among slave children living on small farms and on large plantations south of the Mason-Dixon Line during the 18th and 19th centuries.

Slave children used sticks to get a ball in a hole or a goal during games of "rolly hole" or shinny—a game that resembled hockey. And baseball was played, recalled a former slave in Kentucky, using a ball made out of yarn with a sock used as a cover. Most likely such ball games were variations of the games played by Southern whites. Henry Baker, a former slave from Alabama, recalled that players ran from one base to the other and were called out if they were hit with the ball.

According to one account, laws were even on the books as early as 1797 in the city of Fayetteville, North Carolina, to prohibit the organized play of baseball on Sundays by African-Americans. Organized athletic competition began in the 1820s with the increase of inter-collegiate sports and amateur and professional competition as the United States grew into an industrialized nation. By the 1840s the game of baseball had evolved into a game that any modern-day observer would have recognized. In 1856 *Porter's Spirit of the Times* reported: "This fine American game seems to be progressing in all parts of the United States with new spirit, while in New York and its neighborhood its revival seems to have been taken up almost as a matter of national pride. Matches are being made all around us, and games are being played on every available green plot within a 10-mile circuit of the city."

Foul lines, bleachers, stands, dressing rooms, gate receipts, and refreshment sales attracted more and more spectators to an organized-sports arena. The game of baseball had developed from a simple children's game to a commercial sporting venture with newspapers carrying full-column descriptions of games. In 1859, two years before the start of the Civil War, *Harper's Weekly* ran an article debating whether football or baseball was America's national pastime.

Baseball games were played all along the eastern seaboard, in western territories, and in the South, hastened by strides in 19th-century communication and transportation. The expanding railroad system promoted interstate rivalries and baseball tours. Ballclubs were formed in California before the start of the Civil War, where the "New York" game was the "only style of ball playing" at all encouraged in the Golden State as reported in December of 1860 by *Wilkes' Spirit of the Times*.

Throughout the 19th century, the South was still very much an agrarian region with dispersed populations and therefore lagged behind the North in the organization of formal teams and baseball clubs. By 1860, however, at least seven teams were organized in New Orleans; cities such as Baltimore, Washington and Louisville also had burgeoning baseball clubs. According to an 1859 news clipping, young men in Augusta, Georgia were encouraged to play the "noble and manly game of base ball ... to toughen the muscles ... and to stir the sluggish blood." Henry Chadwick, who came to be known as the "Father of Baseball" for his commentary on the game, even attempted to form a baseball team in Richmond, Virginia, but his efforts were interrupted by the start of the Civil War. Still, town ball and baseball were routinely played in the states that would later become the Confederacy. When the call was made for troop enlistments by presidents Abraham Lincoln and Jefferson Davis at the start of the Civil War, many of the soon to be combatants knew how to play baseball.

Veteran Ballplayers as Army Veterans

Members of social clubs and sporting societies, farmers, professional men, journeymen, college men, and young boys in the North and South, caught up in the excitement of the war, hurried into military service. Fear and anxiety gripped the country, as can be seen in the actions of leisure-time participants. The New York Yacht Club canceled its regatta at the start of the war in fear of Confederate raiders; colleges with intercollegiate baseball teams postponed matches; and the National Association of Base Ball Players cut short its season in 1861. By the second year of the war, "The great game of iron and lead ball, between the loyal and rebellious States," wrote the *New York Clipper*, was engrossing all attention. "We hope that the last innings will soon be played," and "the Union will be quickly and indissolubly restored—and that our fields may soon echo with shouts, 'How's that umpire?' and 'Foul!' as in the days that once were."

When the Civil War began, most people concluded that the conflict would be over quickly following a singular decisive battle. The war raged, however, until 1865 and cost America over half a million men. Many of these soldiers, whose median age was 24, first left for battle as if for a holiday. If the testimony of A.G. Mills (later president of the National League in 1882) and Albert Spalding is to be believed, many of these young men from the North and South went off to war with a baseball and bat tucked into their haversacks.

By the onset of the Civil War men living in the Union and Confederate states had grown up with a sporting heritage. The

erratic demands of army life afforded both armies "down" time to engage in sport in between confrontations with the enemy and during long months spent in winter quarters. Both armies usually stood idle during the months of late November or early December until the spring thaw in April or May—waiting for passable roads and hospitable conditions for fighting. It was during these times that the monotony of drilling, drilling, and more drilling was broken by an occasional game of football or baseball.

There was certainly time available to play baseball. In *A War to Petrify the Heart,* Virginia Hughes Kaminsky describes a typical day in 1862 for Private Richard Van Wyck of the 150th New York Infantry: "At half-past five, the drums beat for us to get up." Van Wyck's company ate breakfast, drilled, had most of the day off with "exception of two hours between three and five, drill, we have leasure. Leasure is meant meal time or anything we choose to do."

There appears to be no substantial difference in how the two armies spent this leisure time. Letters and accounts from Union and Confederate soldiers mention a wide variety of activities that occupied a soldier's down time in camp. Many waited anxiously for news from home or spent their spare time writing to family and friends. Soldiers in both armies also spent their quiet hours reading, playing cards, chuck-a-luck (a dice game), chess, checkers, quoits, tenpins, and dominoes. Often bivouacked near a water source, soldiers reported fishing and swimming as a frequent pastime. A Confederate soldier wrote that his regiment looked "like so many puddle ducks in a barnyard stock pond" while he watched dozens of his comrades swim in a river during June of 1861.

Civil War doctors acknowledged the importance of physical exercise such as swimming to the health of their men. Doctor Julian Chisolm, a published surgeon in the Confederate Army, wrote that while in camp, "Temporary gymnasia might be established, and gymnastic exercise should be encouraged as conductive to health, strength, agility and address." The Southern doctor was also familiar with and recommended the "manly play of ball" as an important addition to a soldier's daily exercise regime. Such recommendations were made but soldiers, often lacking equipment and organization, made do with sport of a spontaneous nature by challenging each other to foot races, wheelbarrow races, wrestling or boxing contests.

Athletic games, including baseball, became a way for soldiers in both armies to prove their manhood and to receive recognition in army circles. Team sports such as baseball and football played during the war demanded "physical courage and prowess" and oftentimes guaranteed fame for a soldier that might not be found on the battlefield. Soldiers won accolades for their ability to run, swim, hunt, shoot, box, "snowball," or play baseball even though their soldiering might have been less than admirable. John Adams, a soldier in the Union 19th Massachusetts Regiment, even came to view Confederate soldiers in a more favorable light after he witnessed their skill as baseball players.

Baseball games were played during camp and in between hostilities by both armies on many occasions. Confederate Corporal William Harding wrote while stationed in Georgia in 1863 that he "had a fine game of Town ball which gave me good exercise." James Hall of the 24th Alabama Regiment observed his men playing baseball "just like school boys" while waiting for the advance of Union General William T. Sherman. The 13th Massachusetts played amongst themselves daily during April and May of 1862, while members of the 51st Pennsylvania played every evening on their drill field. The extensive documentation of such games in both armies strongly suggests that baseball was the most popular of sports engaged in by troops of both armies during the war. But many embellished accounts of great ball games include snowball battles, which reveal them as the most "pervasive" of activities in Union and Confederate camps during the winter months.

These ball games were played, however, not as a result of the war spreading the game, but because men in both armies went into the army with a history of playing baseball. Baseball may have been the most popular active pastime for Union and Confederate soldiers, but for men exhausted by drilling, forced marches, lack of proper nutrition and rest, documentation shows leisure hours were more often spent playing cards than any other activity. Soldiers who had the energy to play baseball more often than not played impromptu games with men in their own regiments and played by "home" regulations. One soldier remembered in his diary that he and the boys from his company played baseball with the 26th Regiment from Pennsylvania in a "new way" but he had already forgotten the different rules.

Although the times when Confederate and Union soldiers fraternized was not as common as Civil War myth would indicate, there are a few known instances when the meeting, or confrontation, did involve baseball. A game was played near Alexandria, Louisiana, for example, and was recounted in the writings of George Putnam. The men of the 114th New York were playing a game when Rebel skirmishers shot the right fielder, captured the center fielder, and ran off with Putnam's only ball!

In Albert Spalding's 1911 book, *America's National Game,* he wrote "at periods when active hostilities were in abeyance, a series of games was played between picked nines from Federal and Confederate forces." This scenario, which he indicated as occurring during the long campaign outside Richmond, is possible but would have been a novelty. Even Spalding admittedly remarked, "I have heard rumors of this series repeatedly, but have not been able to trace them to any authoritative source."

Tyler's Farm in Virginia in May of 1862 became a playground for the Irish Brigade, which was attached to Union General George McClellan's army. Football and baseball were played, and one Union soldier insinuated that all the ruckus being made "must have aroused no small amount of curiosity in the rebels waiting across the Chickahominy." One Sunday morning a baseball game was played by members of the 57th New York and the 69th New York on the Tyler farm. As with many calm moments during the War, reality often interrupted. The blast of a Confederate cannon ended the game abruptly.

It was often on holidays that soldiers, Union and Confederate alike, had opportunities to relax and they indulged in sport as an alternative to their customary holiday celebrations. A wheelbarrow race and a contest to catch two greased pigs rounded out the Christmas Day festivities for a soldier from Maryland, for example, after he witnessed the officers of his company play three innings of baseball. Soldiers held footraces, boxing and wrestling matches, and marksmanship contests, or challenged other regimental units to games of football or baseball to fill the day when most soldiers were especially homesick and lonely for family. Like all leisure activities, baseball helped soldiers forget their troubles and endure terrible hardships. Most soldiers, however, because of the realities of life in the army, never played baseball with any regularity for any length of time, and only a handful actually ever played in prison camps.

Little Time for Play in Prison

A print "drawn from nature" by Otto Boetticher, an artist from New York City, depicts a bucolic scene with a baseball game taking place on the grounds of the Confederate prison camp in Salisbury, North Carolina. This popular image, published in 1863, is often used by modern-day historians to underscore how baseball was frequently played in prison camps during the Civil War. Boetticher was a prisoner at Salisbury; he was Captain of Company G of the 68th New York Volunteers and was captured and sent to the camp during the summer of 1862. But the diaries and letters of several Union prisoners and writings of a Confederate chaplain who resided in the city of Salisbury give us a more accurate picture of the conditions of the camp and the baseball games played there.

Before the great influx of prisoners who were shipped to Salisbury in October of 1864, the prison population remained relatively low. The Confederate government renovated an old cotton factory and intended the prison to house about 2,500 men. Salisbury's buildings and grounds were relatively spacious and prisoners were allowed "liberty of the yard," according to a 1989 article by Jim Sumner. Some of the men enjoyed afternoon and evening games of baseball.

"Took a little walk in the evening and watched some of the officers play ball," wrote 23-year-old Charles Gray, who was captured and sent to the prison in May of 1862. Gray was a Union doctor who remained a spectator of the games at Salisbury and mentioned them frequently in his diary. "A good state of cheerfulness, thanks to the open space is fairly prevailing," he wrote in a journal entry. "Ball play for those who like it and are able, walking, card playing as keep us in employment; but reading matter is about used up."

Josephus Clarkson, a ship chandler's apprentice from Boston before the war, recalled baseball games played at Salisbury with the prison guards. "Since many of the men were in a weakened condition, it was agreed," wrote Clarkson in his diary, "to play the faster but less harsh New York rules. ... The game of baseball had been played much in the South, but many of them (the guards) had never seen the sport devised by Mr. Cartwright."

One pitcher, a Confederate from Texas, was expelled from playing the game by widespread agreement for "badly laming" too many of the prisoner players. The Southerners kept forgetting that "plugging" the runner, or hitting the runner with the ball, was not allowed under the New York rules. Such fond memories of baseball games, for the majority of men imprisoned at Salisbury, are very few. As the population of prisoners soared in the fall of 1864, the conditions became unbearable. Baseball games would have been impossible as survival became paramount in a soldier's mind.

"For months Salisbury was the most endurable prison I had seen; there were 600 inmates," former prisoner Willard W. Glazier recalled in 1866. "They were exercised in the open air, comparatively well fed, and kindly treated. Early in October, 10,000 regular prisoners of war arrived. It immediately changed into a scene of cruelty and horror; it was densely crowded, rations were cut down and issued very irregularly." The prison, Glazier remembered, "became so notorious during the War as one of the most loathsome dungeons in rebeldom."

Rations at the Salisbury prison, toward the end of its existence, were intolerable and meager. They were not substantial enough to support most soldiers for very long, especially when the lack of food was compounded by the scarcity of shelter, heat and medical attention. In Louis Brown's *The Salisbury Prison, A Case Study of Confederate Military Prisons,* one soldier described the not always daily fare at the prison in 1864 as consisting of "coarse meal, cob, and all ground together, and so musty that a decent hog would not eat it." Starving soldiers ate anything they could get their hands on to stay alive, including roaming dogs, cats and rats. The Confederate Army hadn't the means to feed its own men, let alone its prisoners of war.

When the Union Army marched into Salisbury on April 12, 1865, three days after Robert E. Lee surrendered at Appomattox Courthouse, Union General George Stoneman ordered the prison burned to the ground. The best estimate of the dead at Salisbury would tally almost 4,000 men, most of whom died during the last year of the prison's operation.

It is easy for historians to surmise that the game of baseball spread as a result of the Civil War due to the many references to the game being played in the army, and because of its growth in popularity in America during the decades following the war. But, as research proves, the popularity of the game was well on its way before the start of the Civil War, when all leisure-time activities were blossoming in the developing urbanized American society.

As author Harold Seymour confirmed, "by the time of the Civil War the rapid spread of the Knickerbockers style of baseball manifested itself in both the Union and Confederate armies." These rules, devised by the Knickerbocker Base Ball Club of New York in 1845, were no doubt taught to many soldiers during the course of the war, but whether it was town ball, baseball, or rounders, men from the North and the South had already learned to play ball *before* they became soldiers. Regardless of the Civil War, baseball was already on its way to becoming the "National Game."

Chapter 9

The First Great Pitcher

By John Thorn

James Creighton (1841-1862) was the greatest pitcher of his day. Famous principally for his exploits on behalf of the champion Excelsiors of Brooklyn in the years 1860 to 1862, he possessed an unprecedented combination of speed, spin and command that virtually defined the position for all those who followed. Prior to Creighton, pitchers had been constrained by the rule that "the ball must be pitched, not thrown, for the bat." This meant that (a) the ball had to be delivered underhand, in the stiff-armed, stiff-wristed manner borrowed from cricket's early days and (b), in the absence of called strikes, an innovation of 1858, or called balls, which came into the game six years later, the ball had to be placed at the batter's pleasure: the infant game of baseball was designed to display and reward its most difficult skill, which was neither pitching nor batting, but fielding.

The 1850s did produce some pitchers who tried to deceive batters with "headwork"—which meant changing arcs and speeds, and sometimes bowling wide ones until the frustrated batter lunged at a pitch. (The latter tactic produced such incredible, documented pitch totals as that in the second Atlantic-Excelsior game of 1860, when the Atlantics' Matty O'Brien threw 325 pitches in nine innings, Creighton 280 in seven.) On balance, however, the pioneer pitcher and batter were collaborators in putting the ball in play rather than the mortal adversaries they have been ever since Creighton added an illegal but imperceptible wrist snap to his swooping low release.

Known to few fans today and an unlikely, if deserving, candidate for the Baseball Hall of Fame, Jim Creighton was a remarkable embodiment of transecting trends in America and in baseball: cricket vs. baseball, amateur vs. professional, North vs. South, playing by the rules or playing with them. The legion of baseball players followed along the path that Creighton blazed. In life he was a star performer, but it was his startling death that transformed his life into legend.

Born to James and Jane Creighton on April 15, 1841, in Manhattan, Jim grew up in Brooklyn. By the age of sixteen, his abilities in cricket and baseball were evident, particularly with the bat. He and some neighborhood youths started a junior baseball club which they called Young America. It played a handful of games in 1857, then disbanded. Jim then joined the fledgling Niagaras of Brooklyn, for whom he claimed second base. At shortstop was George Flanley, another accomplished young player.

In 1859 the Niagaras challenged the Star Club, then the crack junior team. In the fifth inning of the game, with the Niagaras trailing badly, their regular pitcher, Shields, was replaced by Creighton. Peter O'Brien, captain of the Atlantics, witnessed this game, and "when Creighton got to work," he observed, "something new was seen in base ball—a low, swift delivery, the ball rising from the ground past the shoulder to the catcher. The Stars soon saw that they would not be able to cope with such pitching. Their cap-

James Creighton
One of the sport's early stars, Creighton threw baseball's first recorded shutout, but died at age 21 after being injured during a game.

tain, after consulting other base ball players present, sent in his wildest pitcher. They, by these tactics, were enabled to win the game, which resulted in the breaking up of the Niagara Club, and Creighton and Flanley at once joined the Stars. The next year he with Flanley joined the Excelsior Club."

How to explain all this movement? That old snake in the garden, money. In the 1860s such restlessness came to be termed revolving; today it would be called free agency. According to the sporting press, Creighton was a high-principled, unassuming youth whose gentlemanly manner and temperate habits were ideal attributes for the amateur age of baseball; all the same, he became (at the same time as Flanley) baseball's first professional, through under-the-table "emoluments" from the Excelsiors, who were hungry to surpass the rival Atlantics. Just as he changed the game forever more by breaking the rule against the wrist snap, so did he assure that skilled baseball players could never again be content with field exercise followed by groaning banquets.

In 1860 the Excelsiors embarked on the first tour by any baseball club, with stops in Albany, Buffalo, Canada, Philadelphia, Washington, and Baltimore, among others. That year, in 20 match games, Creighton scored 47 runs while being retired only 56 times. Not once did he strike out. He also threw baseball's first recorded shutout, on November 8.

But the best was to be saved for last. After another championship campaign in 1861, Creighton went through the 1862 season as not only the game's peerless pitcher but also its top batsman, being retired only four times, either in plate appearances or on the basepaths.

At the same time that Creighton was extending the frontier in baseball he was also a prominent member of the cricketing fraternity. The national sport of England and its boyish variants like wicket had been played on these shores since the Colonial period, and the first formal American cricket club had taken shape in Boston in 1809 (the Union Club of Philadelphia followed in 1832, and the St. George of New York in 1838.) When the all-England team crossed the Atlantic to play against (and drub) selected American clubs at the Elysian Fields and elsewhere, Creighton took part in the contests. In a match of 11 Englishmen against 16 Americans, Creighton clean bowled 5 wickets out of 6 successive balls. English Cricketer John Lillywhite, on seeing Creighton pitch a baseball, instantly saw the dilemma that overmatched American batsmen faced: "Why, that man is not bowling, he is throwing underhand. It is the best disguised underhand throwing I ever saw, and might readily be taken for a fair delivery."

Cricket continued to be source of pleasure and profit for Creighton through the next two years, during which he and the Excelsiors were proving themselves to be the top baseball team in the land. Coincidentally, several other Excelsiors were good enough at cricket to play for established clubs—John Whiting, A. T. Pearsall, John Holder, and Asa Brainard, later to become famous as Creighton's successor with the Excelsiors and as the pitcher for the undefeated Cincinnati Red Stockings of 1869. Creighton performed for the American Cricket Club in both 1861 and 1862, joined by Brainard in both years but with John "Death to Flying Things" Chapman of the Atlantics taking the place of the Virginian Pearsall in 1862; he had returned to Richmond when hostilities broke out to enlist in the Confederacy.

In 1861 Brainard and Creighton had jumped the gentlemanly Excelsiors for the working-class Atlantics, no doubt lured once again by covert lucre. After three weeks, without having played a game in the hated rivals' uniforms, the pair sheepishly returned to the fold.

On October 14, 1862, in a match against the tough Unions of Morrisania, Creighton played the field while Brainard pitched the first five innings. In four trips to the plate, he hit four doubles. In the sixth Creighton came in to pitch, and then in the next inning something happened. John Chapman later wrote: "I was present at the game between the Excelsiors and the Unions of Morrisania at which Jim Creighton injured himself. He did it in hitting out a home run. When he had crossed the [plate] he turned to George Flanley and said, 'I must have snapped my belt,' and George said, 'I guess not.' It turned out that he had suffered a fatal injury. Nothing could be done for him, and baseball met with a severe loss. He had wonderful speed, and, with it, splendid command. He was fairly unhittable."

Creighton had swung so mighty a blow—in the manner of the day, with hands separated on the bat, little or no turn of the wrists,

and incredible torque applied by the twisting motion of the upper body—that it was reported he ruptured his bladder. (Later review of the circumstances, aided by modern medical understanding, pointed to a ruptured inguinal hernia.) After four days of hemorrhaging and agony at his home at 307 Henry Street, Jim Creighton passed away on October 18, at the age of 21 years and 6 months, having given his all to baseball in a final epic blast that Roy Hobbs (the cinematic one, that is) might have envied.

But is that the way it really happened? Creighton's last run home instantly ascended to the realm of myth, giving baseball its martyred saint. Obsequies included such syrupy statements as "He was very modest, and never severe in his criticisms of the play of others. He did not care to talk about his own playing, was gentlemanly in his deportment, and very correct in his habits, and to sum up all, was a model player in our National Games [understood here not as a typo, but signifying baseball *and* cricket]. His death was a loss not only to his club but to the whole base ball community, which needed such as he as a standard of honorable play and ability." Rule-breaking, revolving, *sub rosa* professionalism, all were now to be dismissed. Icon-making was in full production.

Creighton's Excelsior teammates mourned his loss at their black-draped clubhouse at 133 Clinton Street and subscribed toward a fine monument over his remains, in Brooklyn's Greenwood Cemetery. (Both the clubhouse and the monument are still standing, and represent two of baseball's oldest and greatest shrines; if you go to Greenwood to pay homage to Creighton, as I did, stop at Henry Chadwick's gravesite, too. I signed baseballs to each and placed them on top of their tombs; you'll know what to do.) But the Excelsiors were not at all sure that it was a good thing for baseball to take the blame for Creighton's death; this might not promote the healthful properties of the new game. What if his injury had been sustained a day or two earlier, say, at a cricket match?

According to a contemporary account, at the National Association convention of 1862, the Excelsior president, Dr. Jones, "briefly made allusion to the death of Creighton, and paid high tribute to his memory; in doing which he availed himself of the opportunity to correct a mis-statement that has found its way into print in reference to his death being caused by injuries sustained in a baseball match. This, he said, was not so; the injury he received in a cricket match."

The battle for the nation's sporting allegiance was at a crucial point. Cricket had been the favored sport until only recently, when the Excelsior tour and Creighton's exploits had created a mania for baseball and had elevated it into parity. Now, with Creighton gone and the Excelsiors falling back into the pack, might the British import be restored to primacy? These fears may have been running through the minds of some in the baseball community, already concerned with the new game's incipient professionalism, and thus may have moved them to propagandize for baseball's spotlessness, as well as Creighton's. Jim had carried the game to new heights; in death he would prove even more useful.

> *Smart lad, to slip betimes away*
> *From fields where glory does not stay*
> *And early though the laurel grows*
> *It withers quicker than the rose.*
> — A. E. Housman

Creighton preserved, even enhanced, his purity by dying young.

Celebrated though he was, at the time of his demise he was not the game's greatest player—by general acclamation the laurels went to his catcher, Joseph B. Leggett. Who hears of him today? (I know, who hears of Creighton—well, at least a thousand for every one that recognizes Leggett's name.) Creighton died when he was all potential—no possibility of loss through aging, change, even growth. He became a plaster saint onto whom one could project whatever social or moral values one wished to promote in the population at large. Cut off in his prime, he joined other such deified national figures—mostly martial ones like Nathan Hale or Davy Crockett. Those golden boys who die young, from Arthur Rimbaud to Harry Agganis, from Charlie Ferguson to Buddy Holly, from Ernie Davis to Lyman Bostock, are forever young in the land of might have been, safe.

A Johnny Appleseed of baseball through his role in the grand tour of 1860, Creighton won far-flung fame. His death, coming as it did "in action" and at a time when the nation was preoccupied with the destruction of a generation, became emblematic of the losses of the Civil War. At the end of all the carnage, the lamented pitcher even became a symbol of national reconciliation.

On July 5, 1866, the Nationals of Washington visited the Excelsiors, reciprocating the favor of their visit six years earlier. The Brooklyn team gave them a warm reception, capped by a visit to Creighton's monument. According to the *New York Times* report the next day, "a silent tear was dropped to the memory of the lamented James Creighton, whose beautiful monument is a prominent feature of the city of the dead," while the *Brooklyn Eagle* called the gravesite "the Mecca of baseball players, the sole relic of the noblest and manliest exponent that the national game has ever had." Two years later, a team in Norfolk, Virginia took the name "Creightons." And in 1872 a Creighton club was formed in Washington, D.C. Oddly, on this team named in homage to the fallen hero—whose appetite for money had given rise to professionalism and, even in his lifetime, gambling—was a young player named Albert Nichols who in 1877 would be one of the four Louisville players expelled from baseball for game-fixing.

In death Creighton's real accomplishments rapidly took on an accretion of myth, much as his death itself may have. Baseball, today universally recognized as a vibrant anachronism, was not always a backward-looking game in which the plays and players of yore set unsurpassable standards of excellence. In the 1850s and '60s, baseball was new, and strictly a "go ahead" business, in the watchword of the day. Creighton's death implanted the game with nostalgia. More than 20 years after his passing, veteran observers might say without fear of challenge that Keefe and Radbourn were fine pitchers, sure, but they *warn't no Creighton.*

Chapter 10

The 1869 Red Stockings

Baseball's first professional team introduced knickers and the bed-check to the game, and compiled the longest winning streak in history

By Jack Zanger
SPORT Magazine, May 1969

*We are a band of baseball players
From Cincinnati City.
We come to toss the ball around
And sing to you our ditty;
And if you listen to the song
We are about to sing,
We'll tell you all about baseball
And make the welkin ring.
The ladies want to know,
Who are those gallant men in
Stockings red, they'd like to know.*

— from the original song of the
old Red Stockings,
written by a member

The 1869 Cincinnati Red Stockings
Sitting (L to R): Charles Sweasy, Fred Waterman, Harry Wright, Asa Brainard, Charles Gould.
Standing (L to R) Dick Hurley, George Wright, Doug Allison, Cal McVey, Andy Leonard.

Those gallant men in stockings red banded together in 1869 to play baseball, got paid for their services and thus became the game's first openly professional team. By so doing, they opened the way for others, in an era when playing for pay was considered seamy, if not downright immoral.

Years before the birth of the pro Red Stockings, baseball was a booming amateur sport. The National Association of Baseball Players was formed in 1857, and by the mid-'60s there were over a thousand organized teams. Supposedly, everyone played for the sheer joy of the game, but in major cities where there were rivalries among two or more clubs, it was common practice to hire some outstanding ballplayers. The Red Stockings themselves, in fact, had at least four members under salary the year before they officially turned pro.

To end the hypocrisy—and to field the best team possible in 1869—the Red Stockings' leaders agreed to go professional all the way. They recruited vigorously, offering salaries ranging between $600 and $1,400 for the season. And they named their 34-year-old pitcher-outfielder, Harry Wright, as manager. Wright had come to Cincinnati in 1865 to coach cricket and inevitably became involved in baseball. By his wedding day in 1868 he had emerged as so much a baseball idol that Cincinnati fans gave him a gold watch wrapped in a $100 government bond and his teammates gave him an inscribed gold medal. The bride, we must presume, came in a separate deal.

When the Red Stockings took the field in '69, they were the first team ever to be dressed in knickers. They looked sharp for the times, and played even sharper. In their first games of the season, they beat teams from Cincinnati and Fort Wayne, by one-sided scores like 24-15, 50-7, 45-9 and 86-8.

Those were the preludes to an extensive Eastern tour. The night before the tour, the Red Stockings were given a farewell party at the Gibson House, a Cincinnati hotel. The players were to stay there overnight. Fearing that some of his athletes might stray off the reservation and not be in proper condition to launch the trip, club president A. B. Champion made a personal inspection of their rooms that night, thereby enacting what was probably baseball's first ritual bed check.

Playing 13 games over the next three weeks, the Red Stockings scored overwhelming victories in Cleveland, Buffalo, Rochester, Troy, Albany, Springfield and Boston. Reports of their conquests were telegraphed back to Cincinnati by *Commercial* correspondent Harry M. Millar. On June 14 they arrived in New York, where they were scheduled to play the Mutuals the following day. The Mutuals had just defeated the Brooklyn Atlantics and the Philadelphia Athletics and were now regarded as the most powerful team in the

East. Whenever the Red Stockings were recognized in restaurants and bars that night they were greeted with the same taunts. "Wait till you meet the Mutuals," they were told. "They'll show you how to play baseball."

Despite threatening weather, a crowd estimated at 10,000 turned up at the Union grounds in Brooklyn the next day. Surrounding streets were clogged with traffic and more than 1,000 people flocked to the rooftops of nearby buildings to get a glimpse of the game. In those days, both teams tossed a coin for the option of either hitting first or taking the field. The Red Stockings won the toss and elected to hit last. It was a wise choice, for they broke a tie in the bottom of the ninth to win, 4-2. Millar's story called it a game of rare defensive brilliance. Certainly the score was a low one considering that fielders weren't yet wearing gloves.

News of the Red Stockings' win set off a citywide celebration in Cincinnati. More than 2,000 people had gathered at the Gibson House, waiting far into the night for word on the game; now they spilled into the streets, cheering wildly. Bands all over town struck up rich, martial music and parades began spontaneously. A group wired the club at its hotel in New York: "On behalf of the citizens of Cincinnati, we send you greeting. The streets are full of people, who give cheer after cheer for their pet club. Go on with the noble work. Our expectations have been met."

Now the Red Stockings began working their way back to Cincinnati. They beat the Atlantics in Brooklyn, moved on to Philadelphia, where they topped the Athletics and Keystones, then went into Washington for a series of games against the Nationals and Olympics. A Washington newspaper reported that the club drew the most aristocratic crowds ever seen at a baseball match and even President Ulysses S. Grant came out to see them win one of their games; later, he gave them a private interview. Before departing Washington, the team was taken on a tour of the capital city. As their fame spread, the Red Stockings were becoming good-will ambassadors for all of baseball.

By the time they returned to a heroes' reception on June 30, the Red Stockings had won 24 consecutive games away from home, probably the most successful road trip in baseball history. The following day, they played a game against a select team and won, 53-11. Immediately after the game, a wagon was wheeled onto the field hauling a 27-foot bat with the words "Champion Bat" and all of the players' names inscribed on it. It was presented by the Cincinnati Lumber Company, whose spokesman told them that since they were the heaviest hitters in all of baseball, he was certain they wouldn't find this bat too heavy to handle. That night, at a banquet honoring the team, president Champion stood up and said, "Someone asked me today whom I would rather be, President Grant, or President Champion of the Cincinnati Baseball Club. I immediately answered him that I would by far rather be president of the baseball club." Everyone cheered appropriately.

The most spectacular game the Red Stockings played that season was their 17-17 tie with the Troy Haymakers, which was halted after five innings. It was played in Cincinnati in late August during a western tour by the Haymakers. By now, every team in the country was out to snap the Reds' unbeaten string, and every Cincinnati game received national attention.

The crowd for this one began building up more than two hours before game-time and swelled to over 10,000 when play began at 3 p.m. People came in excursion groups from as far away as Columbus and Cleveland. The umpire, M.R. Brockway of Cincinnati's Buckeyes team, was one of the most highly respected umpires in the country. The Haymakers won the coin toss and took the field.

In the opening inning, the Red Stockings were held to a single and a stolen base by shortstop George Wright, Harry's kid brother, but the Haymakers exploded against Asa Brainard for six runs in their half. The Reds looked terrible in the field, fumbling grounders and misjudging fly balls, and the partisan crowd began getting on them. But they came back with ten runs in the top of the second, knocking starter Charley Bearman out of the box. The inning was marked by bobbled grounders, a couple of passed balls, three stolen bases and a pair of bases-clearing doubles by Cal McVey and Doug Allison. The Haymakers now led, 13-10, but by the sixth inning the score was tied, 17-17.

Then trouble suddenly erupted. McVey, leading off for the Reds in the sixth, tipped a two-strike pitch. Bill Craver, the Haymakers' catcher, appeared to scoop the ball out of the dust, and umpire Brockway ruled it a foul tip instead of a third strike. Craver immediately waved his teammates off the field, and Cherokee Fisher, the Haymaker captain who was now pitching, stormed off the mound protesting vehemently.

After the Haymakers repeatedly refused to go back on the field, Brockway awarded the game to the Red Stockings.

The Red Stockings won their remaining games, giving them 64 in all. The fact is, they didn't lose until the following June, by which time they had extended their streak to 92 games. They were beaten by the Atlantics in extra innings, 8-7. But the Red Stockings had made their point for professional baseball and succeeded in changing the scope of the game. In 1871, the National Association of Professional Baseball Players was formed, supplanting the amateur body, and professional baseball was on its way.

The 1870 season, however, spelled the last hurrah for the Red Stockings. After their loss to the Atlantics, interest in the Red Stockings declined sharply, and before the year was out the club broke up. All of the original '69 Red Stocking regulars caught on with clubs in the new professional association.

Harry Wright went to Boston to start and manage a new club, which became known as the Boston Red Stockings. They took their name from the famed Red Stocking insignia which Wright had brought along with him. Thus, in another historic first, Wright had given baseball its first franchise shift. But Cincinnati did not field another team for five long years, not until baseball took another giant step forward. It was called expansion.

Early Days
1901-1945

Monte Pearson and Lou Gehrig
After picking up a win for the Yankees in 1936, Pearson relaxes in the Yankee clubhouse by taking a seat on Gehrig's lap.

FAMOUS FIRSTS

1901: In the first American League game ever played, Cleveland loses at Chicago on April 24.

1909: Shibe Park, North America's first concrete-and-steel-stadium, is opened in Philadelphia.

1909: Baseball's first game-related death occurs when Doc Powers succumbs to injuries incurred when he collided with the outfield wall while making a catch.

1911: The first cork-and-rubber baseball is used in a major league game.

1921: For the first time in major league play, umpires are instructed to rub balls with clay to remove their shine.

1921: The first radio broadcast of a game, by Harold Arlin of KDKA, is transmitted from Forbes Field.

1925: The first resin bags appear on major league pitchers' mounds.

1929: The Cleveland Indians are the first team to experiment with numbers on the back of their jerseys, and the Yankees become the first team to permanently adopt numbers.

1935: The first night game in major league history is played in Cincinnati.

1939: Brooklyn plays in Cincinnati in the first televised major league game.

Chapter 11

A New Century, A New Game

As the century turned, the decade-long National League monopoly on top-flight professional baseball met a challenge from Ban Johnson's Western League, renamed in 1900 as the American League and proclaimed, one year later, as a major league rival.

The AL raided not only NL talent but also franchises abandoned in the senior circuit's consolidation from twelve teams to eight. The war between the leagues was fought in the courts and on the playing fields.

By the end of the 1903 campaign peace reigned, a three-man National Commission was created to govern the game, and the World Series had been revived. New stars, thrilling pennant races (1908 was particularly memorable in both leagues), and fresh capital combined to create explosive fan interest. Baseball embarked upon a thrilling period of low-scoring strategic play that came to be known as the Dead Ball Era (1901-1920). Ty Cobb and Honus Wagner were the batting stars of their leagues, but the era was dominated by such pitchers as Christy Mathewson, Rube Waddell, Grover Cleveland Alexander, and Walter Johnson.

As attendance skyrocketed, the men who owned the clubs felt encouraged to build new concrete-and-steel edifices as monuments to themselves and their burgeoning businesses. Forbes Field, Shibe Park, Ebbets Field, Comiskey Park, and Fenway Park were all built between 1909 and 1913, and the venerable Polo Grounds was extensively renovated following a fire in 1911. A rival Federal League was emboldened to competed for the fans' allegiance in 1914 and 1915. Its rise boosted player salaries across the board but these soon feel again; its collapse left a more enduring monument, the Chicago Whales ballpark that we know today as Wrigley Field.

Up to 1918, the Boston Red Sox were the game's greatest team, winning all five of the World Series in which they appeared. After the 1919 season, however, the landscape changed as their star pitcher and rising slugger, Babe Ruth, was shipped to the bedraggled New York Yankees. Even more distressingly, eight members of the pennant-winning Chicago White Sox of that year conspired with gamblers to throw the World Series to the Cincinnati Reds. In the wake of these two events, Judge Kenesaw Mountain Landis became the game's first commissioner, the Red Sox began a long trek into baseball's wilderness, and the Yankees, led by Ruth, became the game's premier franchise. Ruth shattered home-run records and, as part of the legendary Murderers Row (abetted principally by first baseman Lou Gehrig) dominated the game.

Less celebrated than the Yankees but equally important to the future course of the game was the St. Louis Cardinals. Like the Yankees they had won no pennants in the first two decades of the century but then, led by Branch Rickey's nose for talent and genius for organization, the Cardinals built a farm system that took them to the World Series eight times from 1926 to 1944.

The Depression threw most of the 16 major league clubs into receivership at some time in the 1930s, but somehow they all survived. Innovations such as the All-Star Game and night baseball,

Babe Ruth
After being traded from Boston to New York in 1919, Ruth's home-run production helped salvage baseball after the Black Sox scandal.

born of desperation, proved to be enduring institutions.

As war engulfed Europe in 1941, baseball commenced perhaps its finest season, featuring the revived Brooklyn Dodgers in their first of many postseason battles with the Yankees. Joe DiMaggio captured the hearts of the nation as he hit safely in 56 consecutive games, and Ted Williams collected six hits on the season's final day to finish with a batting average of .406. On October 23, 1945, baseball changed. Branch Rickey, now heading the Dodgers, signed Jackie Robinson to play for Brooklyn's farm club in Montreal.

1901

American League born amid newspaper cries to clean up the game

The National League staggered to its 25th anniversary through gambling scandals, regular rowdyism in the stands and on the field, and gimcrack parks far too vulnerable to fires and collapses. That it had outlasted three major challenges to its primacy—the American Association (1882-1891), the Union Association (1884) and the Players League (1890)—owed more to the disorganization, undercapitalization and impatient venality of its rivals than to its own structural stability. The formation of Ban Johnson's American League in 1901 (Boston, Philadelphia, Baltimore, Washington, Cleveland, Milwaukee, Chicago, Detroit) promised none of those escape hatches, and the newspapers of the day embraced his vow to clean up the sport by banning gambling and putting a stop to abusive incidents involving players, fans and umpires. While the NL went to court to try to head off its new competitor, the AL proceeded to play its first game on April 24, an 8-2 victory by Chicago over Cleveland.

Johnson's chief resource was coal magnate Charles Somers, who not only ran the Cleveland franchise but also propped up other money-short teams when they were about to go under. Five future Hall of Famers were likewise critical to the survival of the league and to the shape hostilities with the NL would take. Two of them, former NL stars Charles Comiskey and Clark Griffith, used their considerable influence to draw players away from the older circuit with offers of higher salaries. Jimmy Collins, who jumped from the NL to the AL in Boston, took with him crowds that outdrew the older club almost two-to-one and that established the Red Sox as a Massachusetts institution. John McGraw, the playing manager of Baltimore, conducted himself so raucously that he was at war constantly with Johnson; he finally fled to the Giants with some of his best players, giving the league boss the last excuse he needed to shift the Orioles to New York, where they would eventually be known as the Yankees. Finally, there was Nap Lajoie, who jumped from the Phillies to the Athletics, where he proceeded to lead the new league in every important offensive category (including a .426 batting average). The second baseman's defection sparked a Phillies-solicited court injunction preventing him from playing in Pennsylvania, but also gave the AL the kind of major box-office attraction that left the NL apoplectic.

The AL pennant race came down to pitching, and despite the presence of 33-game winner Cy Young on its staff, Boston didn't have quite as much as Chicago. The White Sox ace was Griffith, who won 24. Next to Lajoie, the league's most impressive hitter was

Nap Lajoie
A career .338 hitter, Lajoie won three AL batting titles and seven fielding crowns, and ranks among the top players of his era.

Boston first baseman Buck Freeman, the only other player to knock in more than 100 runs.

The Pirates were the class of the NL, with Honus Wagner playing all over the diamond while batting .353 and leading the league in doubles, steals and RBIs. The batting titlist was Cardinals outfielder Jesse Burkett (.382). Six of the eight NL clubs boasted at least two pitchers with 18 wins or more, with Brooklyn's Wild Bill Donovan leading with 25. The loudest ticking bomb, though, was to be found at the Polo Grounds, where Christy Mathewson recorded the first of his 13 seasons with at least 20 victories.

1901 SEASON HIGHLIGHTS

NATIONAL LEAGUE

	W	L	Pct.	GB
Pittsburgh	90	49	.647	—
Philadelphia	83	57	.593	7.5
Brooklyn	79	57	.581	9.5
St. Louis	76	64	.543	14.5
Boston	69	69	.500	20.5
Chicago	53	86	.381	37
New York	52	85	.380	37
Cincinnati	52	87	.374	38

AMERICAN LEAGUE

	W	L	Pct.	GB
Chicago	83	53	.610	—
Boston	79	57	.581	4
Detroit	74	61	.548	8.5
Philadelphia	74	62	.544	9
Baltimore	68	65	.511	13.5
Washington	61	72	.459	20.5
Cleveland	54	82	.397	29
Milwaukee	48	89	.350	35.5

NO AWARDS
NO POSTSEASON

"A pitcher's got to be good and he's got to be lucky to get a no-hit game."

— Cy Young

NATIONAL LEAGUE LEADERS

Home Runs
Crawford-Cin	16
Sheckard-Bro	11
Burkett-StL	10

Runs Batted In
Wagner-Pit	126
Delahanty-Phi	108
Sheckard-Bro	104
Crawford-Cin	104

Batting Average
Burkett-StL	.376
Delahanty-Phi	.354
Sheckard-Bro	.354
Wagner-Pit	.353
Keeler-Bro	.339

On Base Percentage
Burkett-StL	.440
Thomas-Phi	.437
Delahanty-Phi	.427
Wagner-Pit	.416
Hartsel-Chi	.414

Slugging Average
Sheckard-Bro	.534
Delahanty-Phi	.528
Crawford-Cin	.524
Burkett-StL	.509
Flick-Phi	.500

Stolen Bases
Wagner-Pit	49
Hartsel-Chi	41
Strang-NY	40
Harley-Cin	37
Beaumont-Pit	36

Wins
Donovan-Bro	25
Harper-StL	23
Phillippe-Pit	22
Hahn-Cin	22

Innings Pitched
Hahn-Cin	375.1
Taylor-NY	353.1
Donovan-Bro	351.0
Powell-StL	338.1
Mathewson-NY	336.0

Saves
Powell-StL	3
Donovan-Bro	3
Sudhoff-StL	2

Strikeouts
Hahn-Cin	239
Donovan-Bro	226
Hughes-Chi	225
Mathewson-NY	221
Waddell-Pit-Chi	172

Earned Run Average
Tannehill-Pit	2.18
Phillippe-Pit	2.22
Orth-Phi	2.27
Willis-Bos	2.36
Chesbro-Pit	2.38

Complete Games
Hahn-Cin	41
Taylor-NY	37
Mathewson-NY	36
Donovan-Bro	36
Donahue-Phi	34

AMERICAN LEAGUE LEADERS

Home Runs
Lajoie-Phi	14
Freeman-Bos	12
Grady-Was	9

Runs Batted In
Lajoie-Phi	125
Freeman-Bos	114
Anderson-Mil	99
Mertes-Chi	98
Williams-Bal	96

Batting Average
Lajoie-Phi	.426
Donlin-Bal	.340
Freeman-Bos	.339
Seybold-Phi	.334
Collins-Bos	.332

On Base Percentage
Lajoie-Phi	.463
Jones-Chi	.412
Donlin-Bal	.409
Hoy-Chi	.407
Freeman-Bos	.400

Slugging Average
Lajoie-Phi	.643
Freeman-Bos	.520
Seybold-Phi	.503
Williams-Bal	.495
Collins-Bos	.495

Stolen Bases
Isbell-Chi	52
Mertes-Chi	46
Seymour-Bal	38
Jones-Chi	38

Wins
Young-Bos	33
McGinnity-Bal	26
Griffith-Chi	24
Miller-Det	23
Fraser-Phi	22

Innings Pitched
McGinnity-Bal	382.0
Young-Bos	371.1
Miller-Det	332.0
Fraser-Phi	331.0
Carrick-Was	324.0

Saves
Hoffer-Cle	3
Garvin-Mil	2

Strikeouts
Young-Bos	158
Patterson-Chi	127
Dowling-Mil-Cle	124
Garvin-Mil	122
Fraser-Phi	110

Earned Run Average
Young-Bos	1.62
Callahan-Chi	2.42
Yeager-Det	2.61
Griffith-Chi	2.67
Winter-Bos	2.80

Complete Games
McGinnity-Bal	39
Young-Bos	38
Miller-Det	35
Fraser-Phi	35
Carrick-Was	34

THE YEAR IN BASEBALL

February 8: The news leaks out that Phillies' second baseman Nap Lajoie, the NL's leading hitter, has jumped to the new Philadelphia AL club.

February 27: The NL rules committee decrees that all fouls are to count as strikes, except after two strikes.

March 2: Jimmy Collins leaves the Boston NL club to manage the AL's new Boston Somersets.

April 8: After a two-year layoff, Amos Rusie makes his first start for Cincinnati and loses 14-3. He makes two more appearances before retiring.

April 18: Jimmy Sheckard of the Superbas is hissed by Philadelphia fans every time he bats because he had jumped from the American to the National League. In spite of the hostile crowd, Sheckard whacks the Phillie pitchers for three triples. Sheckard's leap earned him the appellation of "Grasshopper Jim."

April 25: George Stallings' Detroit Tigers make their AL debut by scoring 10 runs in the last inning to beat Milwaukee, 14-13.

April 28: The White Sox are unable to make anything except singles off Bock Baker of Cleveland—but they gather 23 of them.

April 28: The Tigers, the original cardiac kids, for the fourth time in succession since their debut, get runs necessary to defeat Hugh Duffy's Milwaukee team in the last inning.

May 9: Earl Moore of Cleveland holds the White Sox without a hit for nine innings, but in the 10th the Chicagoans get two hits and win, 4-2.

May 22: Frank "Noodles" Hahn, Cincinnati left-hander, fans 16 Boston batters in nine innings, whiffing everybody in the lineup.

June 26: The Red Sox show up unexpectedly in Philadelphia to play a game when they were scheduled to play in Baltimore.

July 15: Christy Mathewson pitches a no-hit game against St. Louis.

September 3: Baltimore pitcher Joe McGinnity hurls two complete games against Milwaukee, winning 10-0 and 6-1.

September 19: All games are cancelled due to the funeral of President William McKinley, who died from gunshot wounds on Sept. 14.

1902

National Agreement brings peace at last to major leagues

The juggling Ban Johnson continued spinning his eight plates, this time moving one from Milwaukee to St. Louis, where it was dubbed the Browns. St. Louis became the fourth market for head-to-head competition with the NL—and, as in Boston, Philadelphia and Chicago, quickly began outdrawing the older club.

Among those who made the Browns appealing at the ticket window was 1901 NL batting champion Jesse Burkett, one of several jumpers from the Cardinals. Johnson also had an answer to the court injunction preventing Nap Lajoie from playing in Pennsylvania: He simply arranged for the infielder to be traded to Cleveland and to skip road games against the Athletics.

The John McGraw bolt to take over the Giants as manager set off a more elaborate tit-for-tat. First, there was the connivance of McGraw, the Reds, and the Giants, ending with every major Baltimore player wearing a Cincinnati or New York uniform. Then there was Johnson taking over the skeletal remains of the Orioles franchise and (after one forfeit because Baltimore had only five players in uniform) keeping it playing until the end of the season, when it was transferred to New York. Finally, the transferred club, originally dubbed the Highlanders, stocked its roster with more jumpers from the NL, including Wee Willie Keeler from the Dodgers and pitchers Jack Chesbro and Jesse Tannehill, who had won a total of 48 games for the 1902 Pirates.

As battered as the NL was from all the battling, Johnson's Mister Clean image also took some hits, so both sides had reason to sit down to work out a peace accord after the season. The resultant National Agreement recognized both leagues as major, ratified the reserve clause and existing contracts, and allowed the AL to keep most of the players pirated away from the NL. The tradeoff for accepting the Highlanders in New York was a commitment by Johnson not to go through with a plan to transfer the Tigers from Detroit to Pittsburgh. The agreement also established a ruling administrative body known as the National Commission that consisted of Johnson, NL president Harry Pulliam and Cincinnati owner Garry Herrmann. Despite the ostensible 2-1 NL majority, Johnson exercised stern control over the triumvirate thanks to his influence over Herrmann.

On the field, Connie Mack's Athletics overcame the loss of Lajoie to win the pennant, largely on the strength of six everyday .300 hitters in the lineup and 20-win seasons from Rube Waddell and Eddie Plank. The gutted Orioles kept the hopes of St. Louis and Boston alive well into September, but neither team could play the Baltimore wreck often enough to make up the Philadelphia lead. The batting titlist was Washington's Ed Delehanty (.376), with Boston's Buck Freeman driving in the most runs (121).

Pittsburgh made a joke of the NL race, finishing 27-1/2 games ahead of Brooklyn. While batting champion Ginger

Honus Wagner
Pittsburgh's versatile star led the NL in runs, doubles, RBIs, slugging percentage, and stolen bases as the Pirates romped to the pennant.

Beaumont (.357) teamed with Honus Wagner and Fred Clarke to hammer the league's pitchers, the soon-to-be-gone Chesbro and Tannehill combined with Deacon Phillippe to deliver 68 wins. McGraw inherited a last-place team when he arrived at the Polo Grounds and could do nothing about it over his two months on the job. What he did accomplish in the nick of time, however, was to put an end to his predecessor Heinie Smith's intention of converting Christy Mathewson into an infielder.

1902 SEASON HIGHLIGHTS

NATIONAL LEAGUE

	W	L	Pct.	GB
Pittsburgh	103	36	.741	—
Brooklyn	75	63	.543	27.5
Boston	73	64	.533	29.0
Cincinnati	70	70	.500	33.5
Chicago	68	69	.496	34.0
St. Louis	56	78	.418	44.5
Philadelphia	56	81	.409	46.0
New York	48	88	.353	53.5

AMERICAN LEAGUE

	W	L	Pct.	GB
Philadelphia	83	53	.610	—
St. Louis	78	58	.574	5
Boston	77	60	.562	6.5
Chicago	74	60	.552	8
Cleveland	69	67	.507	14
Washington	61	75	.449	22
Detroit	52	83	.385	30.5
Baltimore	50	88	.362	34

NO AWARDS
NO POSTSEASON

"McGraw was one of the hardest men in the league to control and now that he has left I cannot see how the American League has lost anything."

— Ban Johnson after suspending John McGraw indefinitely

NATIONAL LEAGUE LEADERS

Home Runs
Leach-Pit	6
Beckley-Cin	5
Sheckard-Bro	4
McCreery-Bro	4

Runs Batted In
Wagner-Pit	91
Leach-Pit	85
Crawford-Cin	78
Dahlen-Bro	74

Batting Average
Beaumont-Pit	.357
Crawford-Cin	.333
Keeler-Bro	.333
Wagner-Pit	.330
Beckley-Cin	.330

On Base Percentage
R.Thomas-Phi	.414
Tenney-Bos	.409
Beaumont-Pit	.404
Clarke-Pit	.400
Wagner-Pit	.394

Slugging Average
Wagner-Pit	.463
Crawford-Cin	.461
Clarke-Pit	.449
Beckley-Cin	.427
Leach-Pit	.426

Stolen Bases
Wagner-Pit	42
Slagle-Chi	40
Donovan-StL	34
Beaumont-Pit	33
Smith-NY	32

Wins
Chesbro-Pit	28
Willis-Bos	27
Pittinger-Bos	27
Taylor-Chi	23
Hahn-Cin	23

Innings Pitched
Willis-Bos	410.0
Pittinger-Bos	389.1
Taylor-Chi	324.2
Hahn-Cin	321.0
White-Phi	306.0

Saves
Willis-Bos	3
M.O'Neill-StL	2
Newton-Bro	2
Leever-Pit	2

Strikeouts
Willis-Bos	225
White-Phi	185
Pittinger-Bos	174
Donovan-Bro	170
Mathewson-NY	159

Earned Run Average
Taylor-Chi	1.33
Hahn-Cin	1.77
Tannehill-Pit	1.95
Lundgren-Chi	1.97
Phillippe-Pit	2.05

Complete Games
Willis-Bos	45
Pittinger-Bos	36
Hahn-Cin	35
White-Phi	34
Taylor-Chi	33

AMERICAN LEAGUE LEADERS

Home Runs
Seybold-Phi	16
Hickman-Bos-Cle	11
Freeman-Bos	11
Bradley-Cle	11
Delahanty-Was	10

Runs Batted In
Freeman-Bos	121
Hickman-Bos-Cle	110
L.Cross-Phi	108
Seybold-Phi	97

Batting Average
Delahanty-Was	.376
Hickman-Bos-Cle	.361
Dougherty-Bos	.342
L.Cross-Phi	.342
Bradley-Cle	.340

On Base Percentage
Delahanty-Was	.453
Dougherty-Bos	.407
Barrett-Det	.397
Selbach-Bal	.393
Jones-Chi	.390

Slugging Average
Delahanty-Was	.590
Hickman-Bos-Cle	.539
Bradley-Cle	.515
Seybold-Phi	.506
Freeman-Bos	.502

Stolen Bases
Hartsel-Phi	47
Mertes-Chi	46
Fultz-Phi	44

Wins
Young-Bos	32
Waddell-Phi	24
Powell-StL	22
R.Donahue-StL	22
Dinneen-Bos	21

Innings Pitched
Young-Bos	384.2
Dinneen-Bos	371.1
Powell-StL	328.1
Orth-Was	324.0
R.Donahue-StL	316.1

Saves
| Powell-StL | 2 |

Strikeouts
Waddell-Phi	210
Young-Bos	160
Powell-StL	137
Dinneen-Bos	136
Plank-Phi	107

Earned Run Average
Siever-Det	1.91
Waddell-Phi	2.05
Bernhard-Phi-Cle	2.15
Young-Bos	2.15
Garvin-Chi	2.21

Complete Games
Young-Bos	41
Dinneen-Bos	39
Powell-StL	36
Orth-Was	36

THE YEAR IN BASEBALL

March 27: The name "Cubs" is coined by the Chicago *Daily News*.

April 21: The Pennsylvania Supreme Court, reversing a lower-court decision, bars Nap Lajoie, Chick Fraser and Bill Bernhard from playing for the A's, or any team but the Phillies.

May 7: When the distance from the pitcher's mound to the plate is found to be 15 inches short after a Giants-Cubs game, the Giants protest and two games are ordered to be replayed.

May 24: Cleveland's Bill Bradley becomes the first AL player to hit a home run in each of four consecutive games.

June 11: Connie Mack signs Rube Waddell, who was pitching in the Pacific Coast League, and Waddell goes 24-7 for the Phillies.

June 15: Corsicana defeats Texarkana 51-3 in a Texas League game. Nig Clarke of Corsicana hits eight home runs.

July 1: Rube Waddell, pitching his first game in Philadelphia for Connie Mack, manages a peculiar feat. In three innings—the third, sixth, and ninth—he retires the same three batsmen on strikes, these being Billy Gilbert, Harry Howell, and Jack Cronin. The Rube whiffed 13 Orioles and faced only 27 batters.

July 8: How's this for a debut? Danny Murphy, due to play his first game with the Athletics, does not arrive at the park in Boston until after the game has started and so only receives the opportunity to bat six times. He makes six hits, including a home run off Cy Young with the bases full.

July 16: After pitching 41 consecutive runless innings, Jack Chesbro of the Pirates is scored on by Boston in the seventh inning—a new record for the National League.

July 19: John McGraw assumes management of the Giants and is beaten by Philadelphia, 4-3.

September 15: The first double play is recorded by the historic combination of Tinker-to-Evers-to-Chance.

December 9: The AL announces the purchase of grounds in New York for a ballpark, prompting the NL to sue for peace with the rival league.

1903

Baseball welcomes a new beginning— and World Series

The first year of peaceful coexistence between the leagues didn't produce much suspense in the pennant races. In the NL, the Pirates went into first place to stay in mid-June, capturing their third straight pennant. Honus Wagner, settling down as a full-time shortstop, won the batting crown at .355, four points ahead of teammate Fred Clarke. Wagner and Giants outfielder Sam Mertes were the only players to drive in 100 runs. The pitching was led by Deacon Phillippe and Sam Leever, who shook off the defections of Jack Chesbro and Jesse Tannehill to combine for 49 wins.

For Pittsburgh, however, there was also an ominous sign of things to come when John McGraw turned the Giants around by 36 games to finish in second place. There was little mystery about the biggest motors in the New York rise: Aside from Mertes' RBI bat and a .350 mark from catcher Roger Bresnahan, Joe McGinnity and Christy Mathewson stood above the league with 31 and 30 victories, respectively. If they had bothered to look carefully at Chicago, the Pirates would have found another source of future trouble in the first full-season positioning of first baseman Frank Chance, second baseman Johnny Evers and shortstop Joe Tinker in the Cubs infield. Not until 1914 would a team other than these three win the NL pennant.

In the AL, Boston cruised to a flag behind big years—again—from Buck Freeman and Cy Young. While Freeman provided the circuit's only 100-RBI bat, Young's 28 wins were good enough to lead in that category for the third year in a row. The New Englanders also got 21 victories from Bill Dinneen and 20 from Tom Hughes. For all its success on the field, however, Boston was beset all season by clubhouse tensions among the players and between player-manager Jimmy Collins and the front office. That the club nevertheless finished 14-1/2 games ahead of pitching-laden Philadelphia (a third future Hall of Famer, Chief Bender, joined Rube Waddell and Eddie Plank in the rotation) was attributed in no small part to Collins' dugout smarts. The batting champion was again Nap Lajoie, who hit .355 for Cleveland.

The most significant development of the year came in mid-September, when Pittsburgh's Barney Dreyfuss and Boston's Henry Killilea agreed to meet in a postseason best-of-nine series between the league champions for determining a "world" champion. National Agreement or not, the idea was attacked by the Giants and other NL teams as according far too much recognition to the AL's supposed equality. Killilea also had problems selling the postseason series to his own players, since their contracts officially ran out on September 30 (Dreyfuss had the Pirates under contract until mid-October). With the players demanding the full gate receipts as their price for taking the field, the Boston owner entered into days of tense negotiations, finally emerging with a compromise to pay everyone an extra two weeks salary plus a bonus.

The first World Series game was played before 16,242 fans at the Huntington Avenue Baseball Grounds on October 1, with the visiting Pirates belting Young around for a 7-3 victory. Pittsburgh took two of the next three as well, but then the ALers came roaring

Christy Mathewson
Shown here in his final minor-league season with Norfolk, Mathewson emerged as a 30-game winner and anchor of the Giants pitching staff.

back to win the last four and the first world championship. Dinneen won three for Boston, while Phillippe won all three games taken by Pittsburgh. Although the owner of the losing team, Dreyfuss handed out bonuses to the Pirates players that amounted to more than the winning shares.

1903 SEASON HIGHLIGHTS

NATIONAL LEAGUE

	W	L	Pct.	GB
Pittsburgh	91	49	.650	—
New York	84	55	.604	6.5
Chicago	82	56	.594	8
Cincinnati	74	65	.532	16.5
Brooklyn	70	66	.515	19
Boston	58	80	.420	32
Philadelphia	49	86	.363	39.5
St. Louis	43	94	.314	46.5

AMERICAN LEAGUE

	W	L	Pct.	GB
Boston	91	47	.659	—
Philadelphia	75	60	.556	14.5
Cleveland	77	63	.550	15
New York	72	62	.537	17
Detroit	65	71	.478	25
St. Louis	65	74	.468	26.5
Chicago	60	77	.438	30.5
Washington	43	94	.314	47.5

NO AWARDS

POSTSEASON
WORLD SERIES
Boston Pilgrims 5, Pittsburgh Pirates 3

Oct. 1: Pittsburgh 7, BOSTON 3
Oct. 2: BOSTON 3, Pittsburgh 0
Oct. 3: Pittsburgh 4, BOSTON 2
Oct. 6: PITTSBURGH 5, Boston 4
Oct. 7: Boston 11, PITTSBURGH 2
Oct. 8: Boston 6, PITTSBURGH 3
Oct. 10: Boston 7, PITTSBURGH 3
Oct. 13: BOSTON 3, Pittsburgh 0

Home team in CAPS

> "All us Youngs could throw. I used to
> kill squirrels with a stone when I was a
> kid, and my granddad once killed a
> turkey buzzard on the fly with a rock."
>
> — Cy Young

NATIONAL LEAGUE LEADERS

Home Runs

Sheckard-Bro	9
Seymour-Cin	267
Wagner-Pit	265

Runs Batted In

Mertes-NY	104
Wagner-Pit	101
Doyle-Bro	91
Leach-Pit	87
Steinfeldt-Cin	83

Batting Average

Wagner-Pit	.355
Clarke-Pit	.351
Donlin-Cin	.351
Bresnahan-NY	.350
Seymour-Cin	.342

On Base Percentage

Thomas-Phi	.453
Bresnahan-NY	.443
Chance-Chi	.439
Sheckard-Bro	.423
Donlin-Cin	.420

Slugging Average

Clarke-Pit	.532
Wagner-Pit	.518
Donlin-Cin	.516
Bresnahan-NY	.493
Steinfeldt-Cin	.481

Stolen Bases

Sheckard-Bro	67
Chance-Chi	67
Wagner-Pit	46
Strang-Bro	46
Mertes-NY	45

Wins

McGinnity-NY	31
Mathewson-NY	30
Phillippe-Pit	25
Leever-Pit	25

Innings Pitched

McGinnity-NY	434.0
Mathewson-NY	366.1
Pittinger-Bos	351.2
Jones-Bro	324.1
Taylor-Chi	312.1

Saves

Miller-NY	3
Lundgren-Chi	3

Strikeouts

Mathewson-NY	267
McGinnity-NY	171
Garvin-Bro	154
Pittinger-Bos	140
Weimer-Chi	128

Earned Run Average

Leever-Pit	2.06
Mathewson-NY	2.26
Weimer-Chi	2.30
Phillippe-Pit	2.43
McGinnity-NY	2.43

Complete Games

McGinnity-NY	44
Mathewson-NY	37
Pittinger-Bos	35
Hahn-Cin	34
Taylor-Chi	33

AMERICAN LEAGUE LEADERS

Home Runs

Freeman-Bos	13
Hickman-Cle	12
Ferris-Bos	9
Seybold-Phi	8

Runs Batted In

Freeman-Bos	104
Hickman-Cle	97
Lajoie-Cle	93
L.Cross-Phi	90
Crawford-Det	89

Batting Average

Lajoie-Cle	.344
Crawford-Det	.335
Dougherty-Bos	.331
Barrett-Det	.315
Bradley-Cle	.313

On Base Percentage

Barrett-Det	.407
Hartsel-Phi	.391
Lajoie-Cle	.379
Lush-Det	.379
Green-Chi	.375

Slugging Average

Lajoie-Cle	.518
Bradley-Cle	.496
Freeman-Bos	.496
Crawford-Det	.489
Hartsel-Phi	.477

Stolen Bases

Bay-Cle	45
Pickering-Phi	40
Holmes-Was-Chi	35
Dougherty-Bos	35
Conroy-NY	33

Wins

Young-Bos	28
Plank-Phi	23

Innings Pitched

Young-Bos	341.2
Plank-Phi	336.0
Chesbro-NY	324.2
Waddell-Phi	324.0
Mullin-Det	320.2

Saves

Young-Bos	2
Powell-StL	2
Orth-Was	2
Mullin-Det	2
Dinneen-Bos	2

Strikeouts

Waddell-Phi	302
Donovan-Det	187
Young-Bos	176
Plank-Phi	176
Mullin-Det	170

Earned Run Average

Moore-Cle	1.74
Young-Bos	2.08
Bernhard-Cle	2.12
White-Chi	2.13
Joss-Cle	2.19

Complete Games

Young-Bos	34
Waddell-Phi	34
Donovan-Det	34

THE YEAR IN BASEBALL

January 9: Frank Farrell and Bill Devery buy an AL franchise for New York, picking up abandoned Baltimore; this team would be called the Highlanders, and later the Yankees.

January 9: After the AL rejects an NL proposal for a consolidated 12-team league, an agreement is reached for the two leagues to co-exist peacefully.

January 12: Detroit pitcher Win Mercer, winner of 15 games in 1902, commits suicide in San Francisco.

February 28: A syndicate headed by Pittsburgh owner Barney Dreyfuss and James Potter buys the Philadelphia Phillies for $170,000.

March 7: In the first inter-league trade since the peace agreement, the Giants trade Heinnie Smith to Detroit for Kid Gleason, who is immediately moved to the Phils.

April 20: The Highlanders, playing their first game in the American League, are beaten by Washington 3-1, as Jack Chesbro loses to Al "The Curveless Wonder" Orth.

June 9: The Pirates, after having blanked their opponents in 57 successive innings, are scored on in the fourth by the Phillies. Kaiser Wilhelm was the pitcher yielding the run.

July 2: Ed Delahanty falls off a railway bridge and his body is recovered a week later after being washed over Niagara Falls.

August 1: Only one New York Highlander—Kid Elberfeld—is able to get hits off Rube Waddell of the Athletics. He raps four hits while the rest of his teammates are fanning 13 times. New York wins, 3-2.

August 8: For the second time in eight days, Joe McGinnity pitches two games for the Giants. He defeats Brooklyn twice, by scores of 6-1 and 4-3, and allows 13 hits.

August 31: For the third time inside of a month, Joe McGinnity pitches and wins two games for New York. Philadelphia is beaten by scores of 4-1 and 9-2.

September 14: John McGraw tries a young pitcher named Leon Ames against the Cardinals and in his debut he allows neither a hit nor a run—the game, however, lasts only five innings.

October 1: In the first modern World Series game, played at Boston's Huntington Avenue Grounds, Pittsburgh defeat's Boston 7-3.

December 12: In a deal with the Cards, the Cubs get Three-Finger Brown and Jack O'Neill for Jack Taylor and Larry McLean.

1904

Giants dominate with one-two pitching punch

I f there was an epicenter to the 1904 season, it was in the pitching mounds to be found in Upper Manhattan, in both the Polo Grounds and Hilltop Park. In the NL, John McGraw finished his quick franchise-revival work by leading the Giants to a 13-game romp over runner-up Chicago. The club's 106 victories were the most it would record in either New York or San Francisco for the next 100 years.

The dominance of the Giants was particularly evident whenever Joe McGinnity (35 wins) or Christy Mathewson (33) took the hill, but Dummy Taylor also notched 21 and the staff as a whole contributed a 2.18 ERA. Offensively, McGraw's ability to get the most out of walks, steals and hit-and-run plays was never so much in evidence: although the club batted only .262, that was good enough to create 744 runs—team highs not only in the NL, but in both leagues. In a Year of the Pitcher, New York shortstop Bill Dahlen's 80 RBIs paced NL batters. Pittsburgh, which slipped to fourth with the help of injuries to Fred Clarke and Deacon Phillippe, had the sole consolation of another batting title for Honus Wagner (.349).

The pitching wasn't so bad on New York's AL club, either. To Ban Johnson's enormous gratification, the Highlanders more than doubled their attendance from their inaugural 1903 season, proving that New Yorkers weren't committed solely to the Giants or Dodgers. The biggest reason for the Hilltop Park mob scenes was Pirates defector Jack Chesbro, who set the modern big-league record with 41 wins, completing 48 of his 51 starts. Mainly thanks to the spitballing right-hander and a .343 mark from another NL jumper, the ex-Dodger Willie Keeler, the Highlanders found themselves in a pennant race in the second year of their removal from Baltimore. The final act was the first in what would become a century of showdowns between the Yankees and Red Sox. On the final weekend of the season, with only a half-game separating the clubs, the Highlanders won, then dropped a doubleheader, forcing them to sweep another twin bill on the very last day of the campaign if they wanted the flag. With the score knotted at 2-2 in the ninth of the opener, however, Chesbro uncorked a wild pitch that scored Lou Criger with the pennant-deciding tally.

As dominant as Chesbro was, he wasn't the only pitcher in the league. On May 5, 26-game-winner Cy Young pitched the league's first perfect game, against the Athletics; the performance was the centerpiece of an amazing 24-1/3 consecutive innings and 76 batters during which the right-hander didn't yield a hit. In addition to Young, Boston got 20-win seasons from Bill Dinneen and Jesse Tannehill. For their part, the Athletics accomplished the improbable by having two 26-game winners (Eddie Plank and Rube Waddell) but still finishing only fourth. Nap Lajoie won another batting crown (.381); he was only one of six batters in the league to average .300.

Boston's triumph didn't open the door to another World Series.

Jack Chesbro
The Highlanders ace won 41 games but a wild pitch on the last day of the season cost New York the AL pennant.

Fearful he might end up having to play the Highlanders, with far too much municipal prestige at risk, Giants owner John T. Brush decreed long before the end of the campaign that his team would be making no postseason appearances if it won the flag. When even the Giants players protested the lost opportunity to take on Boston, McGraw stepped forward to shift the issue to the supposed unworthiness of any AL team. Ninety years would elapse before another World Series wasn't played.

1904 SEASON HIGHLIGHTS

NATIONAL LEAGUE

	W	L	Pct.	GB
New York	106	47	.693	—
Chicago	93	60	.608	13
Cincinnati	88	65	.575	18
Pittsburgh	87	66	.569	19
St. Louis	75	79	.487	31.5
Brooklyn	56	97	.366	50
Boston	55	98	.359	51
Philadelphia	52	100	.342	53.5

AMERICAN LEAGUE

	W	L	Pct.	GB
Boston	95	59	.617	—
New York	92	59	.609	1.5
Chicago	89	65	.578	6
Cleveland	86	65	.570	7.5
Philadelphia	81	70	.536	12.5
St. Louis	65	87	.428	29
Detroit	62	90	.408	32
Washington	38	113	.252	55.5

NO AWARDS
NO WORLD SERIES

"Christy Mathewson was the greatest pitcher who ever lived. It was wonderful to watch him pitch ... when he wasn't pitching against you."

— Connie Mack

NATIONAL LEAGUE LEADERS

Home Runs
Lumley-Bro 9
Brain-StL 7

Runs Batted In
Dahlen-NY 80
Mertes-NY 78
Lumley-Bro 78
Wagner-Pit 75
Corcoran-Cin 74

Batting Average
Wagner-Pit .349
Beckley-StL .325
Seymour-Cin .313
Chance-Chi .310
Beaumont-Pit .301

On Base Percentage
Wagner-Pit .423
Thomas-Phi .416
Chance-Chi .382
Huggins-Cin .376
Beckley-StL .374

Slugging Average
Wagner-Pit .520
Seymour-Cin .439
Chance-Chi .430
Lumley-Bro .428
Brain-StL .408

Stolen Bases
Wagner-Pit 53
Mertes-NY 47
Dahlen-NY 47
McGann-NY 42
Chance-Chi 42

Wins
McGinnity-NY 35
Mathewson-NY 33
Harper-Cin 23
Taylor-NY 21
Nichols-StL 21

Innings Pitched
McGinnity-NY 408.0
Jones-Bro 377.0
Mathewson-NY 367.2
Taylor-StL 352.0
Willis-Bos 350.0

Saves
McGinnity-NY 5
Wiltse-NY 3

Strikeouts
Mathewson-NY 212
Willis-Bos 196
Weimer-Chi 177
Pittinger-Bos 146
McGinnity-NY 144

Earned Run Average
McGinnity-NY 1.61
Garvin-Bro 1.68
Brown-Chi 1.86
Weimer-Chi 1.91
Nichols-StL 2.02

Complete Games
Willis-Bos 39
Taylor-StL 39
McGinnity-NY 38
Jones-Bro 38

AMERICAN LEAGUE LEADERS

Home Runs
Davis-Phi 10
Murphy-Phi 7
Freeman-Bos 7

Runs Batted In
Lajoie-Cle 102
Freeman-Bos 84
Bradley-Cle 83
Anderson-NY 82

Batting Average
Lajoie-Cle .376
Keeler-NY .343
Flick-Cle .306
Bradley-Cle .300
Seybold-Phi .292

On Base Percentage
Lajoie-Cle .413
Keeler-NY .390
Flick-Cle .371
Stahl-Bos .366
Burkett-StL .363

Slugging Average
Lajoie-Cle .552
Flick-Cle .449
Murphy-Phi .440
Hickman-Cle-Det .437
Stahl-Bos .416

Stolen Bases
Flick-Cle 38
Bay-Cle 38
Heidrick-StL 35
Davis-Chi 32
Conroy-NY 30

Wins
Chesbro-NY 41
Young-Bos 26
Plank-Phi 26
Waddell-Phi 25

Innings Pitched
Chesbro-NY 454.2
Powell-NY 390.1
Waddell-Phi 383.0
Mullin-Det 382.1
Young-Bos 380.0

Saves
Patten-Was 3

Strikeouts
Waddell-Phi 349
Chesbro-NY 239
Powell-NY 202
Plank-Phi 201
Young-Bos 200

Earned Run Average
Joss-Cle 1.59
Waddell-Phi 1.62
White-Chi 1.78
Chesbro-NY 1.82
Owen-Chi 1.94

Complete Games
Chesbro-NY 48
Mullin-Det 42
Young-Bos 40
Waddell-Phi 39
Powell-NY 38

THE YEAR IN BASEBALL

January 22: William H. Yawkey buys the Detroit Tigers for $50,000.

April 26: Tyrus Raymond Cobb plays his first game in Organized Baseball with the Augusta, Ga., club of the South Atlantic League against Columbia, S.C., at Augusta. Batting seventh he made a double and a home run in four at bats.

May 5: Cy Young, in the midst of a 24-inning hitless streak, hurls a perfect game against the A's.

May 11: Cy Young leads the Red Sox to a 1-0 victory over Detroit in 15 innings, his pitching rival being Ed Killian.

May 14: After Cubs outfielder Jack McCarthy sprains an ankle by stepping on an umpire's broom at home plate, the NL orders that umps use pocket-sized brooms from now on.

May 27: The Giants Dan McGann steals five bases, a feat not duplicated until 1974 by Davey Lopes.

June 11: Bob Wicker leads the Cubs to a 1-0 victory over the Giants in 12 innings, thus branding Joe McGinnity with his first defeat of the year, following 12 victories in a row.

July 7: Jack Chesbro of the Yankees, after winning 14 games in a row, is beaten by Norwood Gibson of the Red Sox, 4-1.

August 6: Bill Dinneen, Norwood Gibson, Freddy Parent and Hobe Ferris of the Boston Pilgrims are heralded as heroes after they extinguish a hotel blaze.

September 22: Jim O'Rourke, although 52 years old, catches a full game for the Giants and goes 1 for 4 at bat.

October 3: Chrtisty Mathewson strikes out a record 16 Cards in a 3-1 Giants victory that is over in one hour, 15 minutes.

October 10: After winning 41 games, spitballer Jack Chesbro unleashes a ninth-inning wild pitch on the last day to cost New York the AL pennant.

October 28: Nap Lajoie is named manager of the Cleveland Blues.

1905

Mathewson's mastery carries NY Giants to Series triumph

Pitching continued to be the diamond story in 1905, with 17 pitchers in both leagues winning at least 20 and another 10 a minimum of 18. On the other hand, only three regulars in the AL—Elmer Flick (.308), Willie Keeler (.302) and Harry Bay (.301)—topped the .300 mark, while Harry Davis' 83 RBIs for the Athletics was tops in that department. The NL had only slightly more pop, much of it due to a breakout year by Reds outfielder Cy Seymour (a league-best .377 and 121 RBIs) and the reliable Honus Wagner (.363 with 101 RBIs). One of the anomalous byproducts of the tame offense was the emergence of Cincinnati outfielder Fred Odwell as the NL home run leader with nine; Oddwell, who couldn't have been better named, hit only one other home run in his four-year big league career.

The ubiquity of good pitching made for a particularly hot race in the AL. Through most of the first half of the season, the White Sox, anchored by pitchers Frank Owen and Nick Altrock, went back and forth with Cleveland, the only squad in the circuit tilted toward offense. But as soon as Nap Lajoie was forced to the sidelines with blood poisoning, Chicago's chief nemesis became Philadelphia, with a staff on its way to having three 20-game winners (Rube Waddell, Eddie Plank and Andy Coakley). Bolstered by the spot contributions of rookie Ed Walsh, the punchless White Sox hung in until the final week of the season, when they lost two out of three to the A's and then blew a subsequent series to the last-place Browns.

In the NL, the Giants maintained a comfortable lead over the Pirates practically wire-to-wire. Christy Mathewson won 32, Joe McGinnity and Red Ames more than 20, and Mike Donlin's .356 and 56 walks got him on base often enough to enable him to lead the league in runs scored (124). John McGraw injected more interest in the pennant race than it might have otherwise had by deliberately insulting Pirates owner Barney Dreyfuss in public, then ridiculing NL president Harry Pulliam as a creature of the Pittsburgh executive. The press dragged out the melodrama for weeks, reporting fines that were never paid and suspensions that were never enforced.

Another famous feud saw Cubs teammates Joe Tinker and Johnny Evers brawl over Evers' taking a taxi to an exhibition game. Although the most famous double play combination in the game, Tinker and Evers would not speak to each other for years.

As a counterpoint to the NL's masterful pitching, the Braves produced four 20-game losers—Irv Young, Vic Willis, Chick Fraser, and Kaiser Wilhelm.

Largely because Connie Mack's Athletics were involved, McGraw agreed to a World Series. What ensued was the greatest postseason pitching series in history. In the opening game, Mathewson pitched a four-hit shutout with no walks in a 3-0 Giants win; in Game Two, it was the turn of Chief Bender to blank the Giants; in the third game, Mathewson pitched another four-hit shutout, walking one, in a 9-0 victory; Game Four saw McGinnity twirl a five-hit whitewash; then, finally, it was Mathewson again, and he allowed just six hits and no walks in a 2-0 win—

Rube Waddell
The Athletics' colorful lefthander topped the AL in wins, strikeouts and ERA and led Philadelphia into the World Series.

Mathewson's third shutout in five games—as the Giants became world champions. In three games against Mathewson, the A's advanced a total of one runner to third base.

Walsh wasn't the only major figure to make his debut during the season. On August 30, Ty Cobb played his first game for the Tigers, managing a double off the Highlanders' Jack Chesbro. The Detroit outfielder would get 723 more doubles and 4,188 more hits before he was through.

1905 SEASON HIGHLIGHTS

NATIONAL LEAGUE

	W	L	Pct.	GB
New York	105	48	.686	—
Pittsburgh	96	57	.627	9
Chicago	92	61	.601	13
Philadelphia	83	69	.546	21.5
Cincinnati	79	74	.516	26
St. Louis	58	96	.377	47.5
Boston	51	103	.331	54.5
Brooklyn	48	104	.316	56.5

AMERICAN LEAGUE

	W	L	Pct.	GB
Philadelphia	92	56	.622	—
Chicago	92	60	.605	2
Detroit	79	74	.516	15.5
Boston	78	74	.513	16
Cleveland	76	78	.494	19
New York	71	78	.477	21.5
Washington	64	87	.424	29.5
St. Louis	54	99	.353	40.5

NO AWARDS

POSTSEASON

WORLD SERIES
New York Giants 4, Philadelphia Athletics 1
Oct. 9: New York 3, PHILADELPHIA 0
Oct. 10: Philadelphia 3, NEW YORK 0
Oct. 12: New York 9, PHILADELPHIA 0
Oct. 13: NEW YORK 1, Philadelphia 0
Oct. 14: NEW YORK 2, Philadelphia 0

Home team in CAPS

> "Many fans look upon an umpire as a sort of necessary evil to the luxury of baseball, like the odor that follows an automobile."
>
> — Christy Mathewson

NATIONAL LEAGUE LEADERS

Home Runs

Odwell-Cin	9
Seymour-Cin	8
Lumley-Bro	7
Donlin-NY	7
Dahlen-NY	7

Runs Batted In

Seymour-Cin	121
Mertes-NY	108
Wagner-Pit	101
Magee-Phi	98
Titus-Phi	89

Batting Average

Seymour-Cin	.377
Wagner-Pit	.363
Donlin-NY	.356
Thomas-Phi	.317
Chance-Chi	.316

On Base Percentage

Chance-Chi	.449
Seymour-Cin	.428
Wagner-Pit	.425
Thomas-Phi	.417
Donlin-NY	.413

Slugging Average

Seymour-Cin	.559
Wagner-Pit	.505
Donlin-NY	.495
Titus-Phi	.436
McGann-NY	.434

Stolen Bases

Maloney-Chi	59
Devlin-NY	59
Wagner-Pit	57
Mertes-NY	52
Magee-Phi	48

Wins

Mathewson-NY	31
Pittinger-Phi	23
Ames-NY	22
McGinnity-NY	21

Innings Pitched

Young-Bos	378.0
Willis-Bos	342.0
Mathewson-NY	338.2
Pittinger-Phi	337.1
Fraser-Bos	334.1

Saves

Elliott-NY	6
Wiltse-NY	4
McGinnity-NY	3

Strikeouts

Mathewson-NY	206
Ames-NY	198
Overall-Cin	173
Ewing-Cin	164
Young-Bos	156

Earned Run Average

Mathewson-NY	1.28
Reulbach-Chi	1.42
Wicker-Chi	2.02
Briggs-Chi	2.14
Brown-Chi	2.17

Complete Games

Young-Bos	41
Willis-Bos	36
Fraser-Bos	35
Taylor-StL	34

AMERICAN LEAGUE LEADERS

Home Runs

Davis-Phi	8
Stone-StL	7

Runs Batted In

Davis-Phi	83
L.Cross-Phi	77
Donahue-Chi	76
Crawford-Det	75
Turner-Cle	72

Batting Average

Flick-Cle	.308
Keeler-NY	.302
Bay-Cle	.301
Crawford-Det	.297
Stone-StL	.296

On Base Percentage

Hartsel-Phi	.409
Flick-Cle	.383
Keeler-NY	.357
Crawford-Det	.357
Selbach-Bos	.355

Slugging Average

Flick-Cle	.462
Crawford-Det	.430
Davis-Phi	.422
Stone-StL	.410
Hickman-Det-Was	.405

Stolen Bases

Hoffman-Phi	46
Fultz-NY	44
Stahl-Was	41
Hartsel-Phi	37

Wins

Waddell-Phi	27
Plank-Phi	24
Killian-Det	23
Altrock-Chi	23
Tannehill-Bos	22

Innings Pitched

Mullin-Det	347.2
Plank-Phi	346.2
Owen-Chi	334.0
Waddell-Phi	328.2
Howell-StL	323.0

Saves

Buchanan-StL	2

Strikeouts

Waddell-Phi	287
Young-Bos	210
Plank-Phi	210
Howell-StL	198
Smith-Chi	171

Earned Run Average

Waddell-Phi	1.48
White-Chi	1.76
Young-Bos	1.82
Coakley-Phi	1.84
Altrock-Chi	1.88

Complete Games

Plank-Phi	35
Mullin-Det	35
Howell-StL	35
Killian-Det	33
Owen-Chi	32

THE YEAR IN BASEBALL

April 18: George Winter of the Red Sox holds Washington to one hit, made by infielder Mullin, but is beaten, 1-0.

April 22: A free game for 30,000 Highlanders (Yankee) fans results from the club's failure to issue rainchecks the previous day, when a storm broke early.

April 26: Jack McCarthy, Cub center fielder, figures in three double plays in a game with Pirates, nailing three men who tried to score. No other major league outfielder ever had started three double plays in the same game.

April 30: Future major league umpire Cy Rigler begins the practice of raising his right arm to indicate strikes during a minor league game at Evansville, Ind.

May 16: The Cubs sustain their third straight shutout at the hands of the Giants, Red Ames winning over them, 4-0. Dummy Taylor beat them on May 13, 1-0, and Joe McGinnity conquered them the next day, 4-0.

July 1: Frank Owen of the White Sox pulls an Iron Man stunt on the Browns, beating them twice, 3-2 and 2-0.

July 4: The Athletics win over the Red Sox, 4-2, in 20 innings, Rube Waddell besting Cy Young.

July 31: Charles P. Taft, brother of a future U.S. president, finances Charles W. Murphy's purchase of the Chicago Cubs for $125,000.

August 30: Ty Cobb plays his first game with Detroit, hitting a double off Jack Chesbro of the Yankees.

September 14: Teammates Joe Tinker and Johnny Evers engage in a fistfight on the field during an exhibition game after Evers took a taxi to the ballpark, leaving Tinker behind in the hotel lobby.

October 7: Beaneaters first baseman Fred Tenney records his 152nd assist of the season to set an NL record.

October 14: Christy Mathewson blanks the Athletics 2-0 to give the Giants the championship four games to one. All games ended in shutouts, with Matty getting three, Joe McGinnity one, and Chief Bender one.

1906

Cubs, White Sox give Windy City year to remember

By any measure, 1906 was the greatest year in Chicago baseball history. Most obviously, the Cubs trampled the NL with a record 116 victories, finishing 20 games ahead of the second-place New York Giants, while the White Sox won 93 games to take the AL pennant by three games over the New York Highlanders.

The Cubs produced slaughterhouse numbers that included a never-approached 60-15 road mark. They led the National League in batting average, runs scored, fewest runs allowed, slugging, earned run average, fewest hits per game, shutouts, fielding average, and fewest errors. In August and September, with the race already decided, they won 50 of their final 57 games.

The Cubs also had a significant piece of the game's most invulnerable individual performance record, when Jack Taylor was knocked out of the box on August 13. Taylor's departure ended a phenomenal 188 consecutive complete games that, together with relief appearances, covered 1,727 innings. The right-hander's streak covered stints with the Cubs, the Cardinals, then back with the Cubs again as of July 1.

By the time Taylor returned to the Windy City, however, Mordecai Brown (26 wins, 1.04 ERA), Jack Pfiester (20, 1.56), and Ed Reulbach (19, 1.65) had pretty much tamed the NL. Considering the team's victory total, the offense was modest, with only Frank Chance, third baseman Harry Steinfeldt and catcher Johnny Kling averaging .300; Steinfeldt's 83 RBIs tied with Pittsburgh's Jim Nealon for the league best. The batting crown once again went to Honus Wagner (.339).

The NL also had its rocky moments, both on and off the field. In Boston, the Braves defied the odds by producing still another quartet of 20-game losers—the same Irv ("Young Cy") Young who'd done it in 1905, plus Vive Lindaman, Gus Dorner, and Jeff Pfeffer. In Philadelphia, an April brawl between Giants manager John McGraw and local third baseman Paul Sentell spilled out into the street after the game, causing a general riot. New York catcher Roger Bresnahan locked himself into a grocery store for safety; rescued a half-hour later, he was served a summons for disturbing the peace.

In the AL, the White Sox did their part for municipal pride by finishing ahead of the Highlanders by three games. The turning point of their season came with a 19-game winning streak in August. The "Hitless Wonders" produced a team batting average of .230 and a slugging average of .286; home runs for the season totaled six. The pitching was another story, with Frank Owen and Nick Altrock once again reaching the 20-win plateau, Doc White setting the league pace with his 1.52 ERA, and Ed Walsh coming into his own with 10 shutouts and a 1.88 mark. White aside, most of the year's league leaders were to be found on the also-rans—outfielder George Stone batting .358 for the Browns, Harry Davis producing 94 RBIs for the Athletics and Al Orth winning 27 for the Highlanders.

Two expectations led into the World Series: that there wouldn't be much hitting and that the Cubs would make short work of their

Frank Chance
The veteran first baseman batted .319 and led the NL in runs scored as the Cubs romped to 116 wins and the pennant.

South Side rivals. The first forecast proved accurate when the ALers batted .198 and the NLers two points below even that. The second prediction cost everyone who gambled on it, when the White Sox emerged with the championship in six games, thanks largely to two wins by Walsh and a couple of critical triples by last-minute third-base substitute George Rohe. Because of the citywide fever for the games, an armory and a theater were opened for the mass reception of instant telegraph reports on the play-by-play; in the widest sense of the term, this represented the first "broadcasting" of ballgames.

1906 SEASON HIGHLIGHTS

NATIONAL LEAGUE

	W	L	Pct.	GB
Chicago	116	36	.763	—
New York	96	56	.632	20
Pittsburgh	93	60	.608	23.5
Philadelphia	71	82	.464	45.5
Brooklyn	66	86	.434	50
Cincinnati	64	87	.424	51.5
St. Louis	52	98	.347	63
Boston	49	102	.325	66.5

AMERICAN LEAGUE

	W	L	Pct.	GB
Chicago	93	58	.616	—
New York	90	61	.596	3
Cleveland	89	64	.582	5
Philadelphia	78	67	.538	12
St. Louis	76	73	.510	16
Detroit	71	78	.477	21
Washington	55	95	.367	37.5
Boston	49	105	.318	45.5

NO AWARDS

POSTSEASON
WORLD SERIES
Chicago White Sox 4, Chicago Cubs 2
Oct. 9: White Sox 2, CUBS 1
Oct. 10: Cubs 7, WHITE SOX 1
Oct. 11: White Sox 3, CUBS 0
Oct. 12: Cubs 1, WHITE SOX 0
Oct. 13: White Sox 8, CUBS 6
Oct. 14: WHITE SOX 8, Cubs 3

Home team in CAPS

"One percent of ballplayers are leaders of men. The other ninety-nine percent are followers of women."

— John McGraw

NATIONAL LEAGUE LEADERS

Home Runs
Jordan-Bro	12
Lumley-Bro	9
Seymour-Cin-NY	8
Schulte-Chi	7

Runs Batted In
Steinfeldt-Chi	83
Nealon-Pit	83
Seymour-Cin-NY	80
Jordan-Bro	78

Batting Average
Wagner-Pit	.339
Steinfeldt-Chi	.327
Lumley-Bro	.324
Chance-Chi	.319
Clarke-Pit	.309

On Base Percentage
Chance-Chi	.418
Bresnahan-NY	.418
Wagner-Pit	.415
Devlin-NY	.396
Steinfeldt-Chi	.395

Slugging Average
Lumley-Bro	.477
Wagner-Pit	.459
Steinfeldt-Chi	.430
Chance-Chi	.430
Jordan-Bro	.422

Stolen Bases
Chance-Chi	57
Magee-Phi	55
Devlin-NY	54
Wagner-Pit	53
Evers-Chi	49

Wins
McGinnity-NY	27
Brown-Chi	26
Willis-Pit	23
Mathewson-NY	22
Leever-Pit	22

Innings Pitched
Young-Bos	358.1
McGinnity-NY	339.2
Willis-Pit	322.0
Sparks-Phi	316.2
Lindaman-Bos	307.1

Saves
Ferguson-NY	7
Wiltse-NY	6

Strikeouts
Beebe-Chi-StL	171
Pfeffer-Bos	158
Ames-NY	156
Pfiester-Chi	153

Earned Run Average
Brown-Chi	1.04
Pfiester-Chi	1.51
Reulbach-Chi	1.65
Willis-Pit	1.73
Leifield-Pit	1.87

Complete Games
Young-Bos	37
Pfeffer-Bos	33

AMERICAN LEAGUE LEADERS

Home Runs
Davis-Phi	12
Hickman-Was	9
Stone-StL	6
Seybold-Phi	5

Runs Batted In
Davis-Phi	96
Lajoie-Cle	91
Davis-Chi	80
Williams-NY	77
Chase-NY	76

Batting Average
Stone-StL	.358
Lajoie-Cle	.355
Chase-NY	.323
Flick-Cle	.311
Keeler-NY	.304

On Base Percentage
Stone-StL	.417
Lajoie-Cle	.392
Flick-Cle	.372
Hartsel-Phi	.362
Davis-Phi	.355

Slugging Average
Stone-StL	.501
Lajoie-Cle	.465
Davis-Phi	.459
Flick-Cle	.441
Hickman-Was	.421

Stolen Bases
Flick-Cle	39
Anderson-Was	39
Isbell-Chi	37
Altizer-Was	37
Donahue-Chi	36

Wins
Orth-NY	27
Chesbro-NY	23
Rhoads-Cle	22
Owen-Chi	22

Innings Pitched
Orth-NY	338.2
Hess-Cle	333.2
Mullin-Det	330.0
Chesbro-NY	325.0
Rhoads-Cle	315.0

Saves
Hess-Cle	3
Bender-Phi	3

Strikeouts
Waddell-Phi	196
Falkenberg-Was	178
Walsh-Chi	171
Hess-Cle	167
Bender-Phi	159

Earned Run Average
White-Chi	1.52
Pelty-StL	1.59
Joss-Cle	1.72
Powell-StL	1.77
Rhoads-Cle	1.80

Complete Games
Orth-NY	36
Mullin-Det	35
Hess-Cle	33
Rhoads-Cle	31

THE YEAR IN BASEBALL

March 16: Lloyd Waner is born; "Little Poison" starred in the Pittsburgh outfield alongside brother Paul ("Big Poison") from 1927 through 1940.

March 27: Toad Ramsey dies; erratic lefty fanned 499 in 1886.

April 16: John Lush of the Phillies pitches a freak game against New York, passing and fanning 10 men. He won 4-2.

April 29: New York sees its first Sunday major league game as the Yanks and A's play a benefit for victims of the San Francisco earthquake.

May 7: Bill Donovan, Detroit pitcher, steals his way around the bases in one inning on catcher Fritz Buelow of Cleveland.

May 8: The Athletics have to play a pitcher in left against the Red Sox. That pitcher—Chief Bender—hits two home runs.

June 1: Women are allowed at the Polo Grounds ticket windows for the first time.

June 7: The Cubs beat up the Giants, scoring 11 runs in the first inning off Christy Mathewson, Joe McGinnity, and George Ferguson and winning, 19-0.

June 17: Brooky Superbas president Charles Ebbets is arrested along with his manager Ned Hanlon, visiting manager Joe Kelley and starting pitcher Mal Eason for playing baseball on Sunday. They are subsequently cleared because no admission was charged for the game.

July 4: The tightest game to that time (topped by Sandy Koufax and Bob Hendley in 1965) is played by the Pirates and Cubs, each team making only one hit. Lefty Leifeld of the Bucs loses to Mordecai Brown, 1-0.

July 7: Satchel Paige is born; 42 years later to the day, he would sign a major league contract with Cleveland.

August 7: Umpire James E. Johnstone is barred from the Polo Grounds by New York management and the game is forfeited to the Cubs.

August 13: Jack Taylor is knocked out of the box by Brooklyn in the third frame, bringing a close to his streak of 1,727 consecutive innings without requiring relief that began in 1901.

August 25: The White Sox, after winning 19 in a row, are stopped by Washington.

October 4: The Cubs record their 116th win of the season, setting a major league record that would not be equalled until 2001.

October 10: The Cubs' Ed Reulbach pitches the first World Series one-hitter beating the White Sox.

November 25: Arthur Soden, owner of the Boston team in the NL since 1877, sells out to the Dovey brothers, and the team's nickname became the Doves.

1907

Cubs again sublime while Cobb shines and Mack whines

Nobody expected the Cubs to be as good in 1907 as they had been the year before, and they weren't; they won merely 107 times, nosing out the second-place team (Pittsburgh) by the slimmer margin of 17 games. Pitching once again carried the day, with Orvie Overall winning 23 and Mordecai Brown 20. More striking, the five Chicago pitchers with at least 20 starts on the season registered ERAs near invisibility—Overall at 1.68, Brown at 1.39, Carl Lundgren at 1.17, Ed Reulbach at 1.69, and the league-leading Jack Pfiester at 1.15.

With the entire league pitching at 2.47, it was hardly surprising that only four regulars reached .300—Honus Wagner with another batting title (.350), Philadelphia's Sherry Magee (.328), Ginger Beaumont of the Braves (.322), and Tommy Leach of Pittsburgh (.303). Magee's 85 RBIs were the most in that department, while Christy Mathewson racked up another 24 wins.

In the AL, the center of attention was Detroit, where Hughie Jennings took over as manager, Ty Cobb took over as the league's dominant offensive player, and fellow Tigers took over from one another in trying to drive their unpopular Georgia teammate out of the league. One of Jennings' first moves was moving Cobb from center to right field so he would be separated from left fielder Marty McIntyre; A charter member of the Hate Cobb Club, McIntyre had resorted to such gambits as feinting after balls hit to left-center so Cobb would pull up, the ball would fall, and pitchers would go after the center fielder following the game. Cobb, who had taken to carrying a gun as protection, also spiced the season by choking the wife of a black groundskeeper during a spring-training argument—the first of several racist incidents of the kind.

On the field, though, the lefty swinger won the first of his batting titles with a .350 mark, throwing in other league-leading efforts with his 212 hits, 116 RBIs and 49 steals. Wild Bill Donovan, Ed Killian and George Mullin took care of the pitching, with 70 wins among them. The turning point of the campaign came in a late September game against contending Philadelphia, when Cobb clouted a ninth-inning homer to tie the contest and an interference call in the 14th inning nullified an extra-base hit that would have put the winning run in easy scoring position for the Athletics. The interference call sparked a melee involving players and fans, delaying matters long enough to allow only three more innings of play before darkness left everything deadlocked. Connie Mack, for one, always insisted the interference call had cost Philadelphia the pennant.

The World Series with the Cubs, on the other hand, proved to be an embarrassment for Detroit. After a 12-inning tie in the opener, the ALers scored only three runs over the next four games, making for an asterisked Chicago sweep.

For sheer embarrassment, however, nothing compared with

Ty Cobb
By leading the league in batting and RBIs, Cobb emerged as the AL's top offensive star—and the Tigers' most disliked player.

Branch Rickey's experience on June 28, when the Highlanders catcher watched 13 Senators steal off him. The game effectively marked Rickey's departure from the field as a receiver—merely the first chapter of the baseball book he would write over the next 60 years.

Of note, future Hall of Famer Walter Johnson won his first major league game Aug. 7, beating Cleveland 7-2. After one August game against Washington, Cobb wrote that he had "encountered the most threatening sight I ever saw on the ball field," a pitcher whose throws "hissed with danger." The pitcher was Johnson.

1907 SEASON HIGHLIGHTS

NATIONAL LEAGUE

	W	L	Pct.	GB
Chicago	107	45	.704	—
Pittsburgh	91	63	.591	17
Philadelphia	83	64	.565	21.5
New York	82	71	.536	25.5
Brooklyn	65	83	.439	40
Cincinnati	66	87	.431	41.5
Boston	58	90	.392	47
St. Louis	52	101	.340	55.5

AMERICAN LEAGUE

	W	L	Pct.	GB
Detroit	92	58	.613	—
Philadelphia	88	57	.607	1.5
Chicago	87	64	.576	5.5
Cleveland	85	67	.559	8
New York	70	78	.473	21
St. Louis	69	83	.454	24
Boston	59	90	.396	32.5
Washington	49	102	.325	43.5

NO AWARDS

POSTSEASON
WORLD SERIES
Chicago Cubs 4, Detroit Tigers 0, 1 tie
- Oct. 8: CHICAGO 3, Detroit 3
- Oct. 9: CHICAGO 3, Detroit 1
- Oct. 10: CHICAGO 5, Detroit 1
- Oct. 11: Chicago 6, DETROIT 1
- Oct. 12: Chicago 2, DETROIT 0

Home team in CAPS

> "When I began playing the game, baseball was about as gentlemanly as a kick in the crotch."
>
> — Ty Cobb

NATIONAL LEAGUE LEADERS

Home Runs	
Brain-Bos	10
Lumley-Bro	9
Murray-StL	7
Wagner-Pit	6
Browne-NY	5

Runs Batted In	
Magee-Phi	85
Wagner-Pit	82
Abbaticchio-Pit	82
Seymour-NY	75
Steinfeldt-Chi	70

Batting Average	
Wagner-Pit	.350
Magee-Phi	.328
Beaumont-Bos	.322
Leach-Pit	.303
Seymour-NY	.294

On Base Percentage	
Wagner-Pit	.408
Magee-Phi	.396
Clarke-Pit	.382
Thomas-Phi	.375
Devlin-NY	.374

Slugging Average	
Wagner-Pit	.513
Magee-Phi	.455
Lumley-Bro	.425
Beaumont-Bos	.424
Brain-Bos	.420

Stolen Bases	
Wagner-Pit	61
Magee-Phi	46
Evers-Chi	46
Leach-Pit	43
Devlin-NY	38

Wins	
Mathewson-NY	24
Overall-Chi	23
Sparks-Phi	22
Willis-Pit	21

Innings Pitched	
McGlynn-StL	352.1
Ewing-Cin	332.2
Mathewson-NY	315.0
Karger-StL	314.0
McGinnity-NY	310.1

Saves	
McGinnity-NY	4
Overall-Chi	3
Brown-Chi	3

Strikeouts	
Mathewson-NY	178
Ewing-Cin	147
Ames-NY	146
Overall-Chi	141
Beebe-StL	141

Earned Run Average	
Pfiester-Chi	1.15
Lundgren-Chi	1.17
Brown-Chi	1.39
Leever-Pit	1.66
Overall-Chi	1.68

Complete Games	
McGlynn-StL	33
Ewing-Cin	32
Mathewson-NY	31
Karger-StL	29
Willis-Pit	27

AMERICAN LEAGUE LEADERS

Home Runs	
Davis-Phi	8
Seybold-Phi	5
Hoffman-NY	5
Cobb-Det	5

Runs Batted In	
Cobb-Det	119
Seybold-Phi	92
Davis-Phi	87
Crawford-Det	81
Wallace-StL	70

Batting Average	
Cobb-Det	.350
Crawford-Det	.323
Stone-StL	.320
Flick-Cle	.302
Nicholls-Phi	.302

On Base Percentage	
Hartsel-Phi	.405
Stone-StL	.387
Flick-Cle	.386
Cobb-Det	.380
Crawford-Det	.366

Slugging Average	
Cobb-Det	.468
Crawford-Det	.460
Flick-Cle	.412
Stone-StL	.399
Davis-Phi	.399

Stolen Bases	
Cobb-Det	49
Flick-Cle	41
Conroy-NY	41
Ganley-Was	40
Altizer-Was	38

Wins	
White-Chi	27
Joss-Cle	27
Killian-Det	25
Donovan-Det	25

Innings Pitched	
Walsh-Chi	422.1
Mullin-Det	357.1
Plank-Phi	343.2
Young-Bos	343.1
Joss-Cle	338.2

Saves	
Dinneen-Bos-StL	4
Walsh-Chi	4
Hughes-Was	4

Strikeouts	
Waddell-Phi	232
Walsh-Chi	206
Plank-Phi	183
Dygert-Phi	151
Young-Bos	147

Earned Run Average	
Walsh-Chi	1.60
Killian-Det	1.78
Joss-Cle	1.83
Howell-StL	1.93
Young-Bos	1.99

Complete Games	
Walsh-Chi	37
Mullin-Det	35
Joss-Cle	34
Young-Bos	33
Plank-Phi	33

THE YEAR IN BASEBALL

January 10: John McGraw stops a runaway team of horses in Los Angeles and is credited with saving two young women from injury.

March 28: Red Sox manager Chick Stahl commits suicide at spring training, leaving a note that said: "Boys, I just couldn't help it. You drove me to it."

April 11: The Giants forfeit their home opener to the Phils after New York fans, who had been pelting the visitors with snowballs, invade the field.

April 11: New York catcher Roger Bresnahan appears wearing shin guards for the first time in a major league game.

June 18: Andy Coakley, Cincinnati pitcher, cripples two Giants with successive pitches, beaning Roger Bresnahan (who was given last rites as he lay unconscious) and then breaking Dan McGann's right wrist.

June 28: Branch Rickey, behind the plate for the Yankees, lets the Senators steal 13 bases.

July 8: Bombarded by pop bottles in Brooklyn, irate Cubs manager Frank Chance throws one back and injures a boy. He requires a police escort to leave the park.

July 30: Cincinnati manager Ned Hanlon, whose managing career began in 1889, announces that this will be his last season.

August 2: Pitcher Walter Johnson, 19, makes his debut with Washington and loses, 3-2, to Detroit.

August 11: In the second game of a twin bill, shortened by agreement, Ed Karger of the Cardinals pitches a seven-inning perfect game against Boston.

October 2: Ty Cobb earns a $500 bonus for recording his 200th hit of the season.

1908

One Giants misstep allows sly Cubs to claim pennant

A lot of what happened in 1908 shouldn't have happened. Then there were the claims about what hadn't happened, but were submitted for belief anyway. In the latter category went the "findings" of a so-called panel of experts that Abner Doubleday, an officer in the Civil War, had invented baseball out of whole cloth in the late 1830s. The Doubleday myth was largely the work of Albert Spalding, the sporting-goods entrepreneur and one-time diamond star who had decided the United States needed a creation tale free of any European influences.

As for the merely unlikely, that began with Honus Wagner's solemn spring training announcement that he intended retiring after the season, at the age of 34. The Pittsburgh shortstop then proceeded to play more games than he had in 10 years, to win his sixth batting title (.354) and third RBI crown (109), and to pace the NL in hits, doubles, triples, total bases, and stolen bases. He would end up sticking around for another nine years (and two more batting titles).

Closer to science-fiction was the outcome of the NL pennant race, ultimately turning on what became known as Merkle's Boner. At the Polo Grounds on September 23, with the Giants and Cubs tied for first place, New York appeared to break a tie in the ninth inning when Al Bridwell singled in Moose McCormick. But when Fred Merkle, the runner at first, veered off the basepaths before touching second so he could join an on-field celebration (or avoid the fans streaming onto the turf), the Cubs called for the ball to touch second to record a simple force-out. Umpires, confronted with the prospect of a riot, left without saying anything, but recommended to NL president Harry Pulliam that the Chicago argument be accepted. Pulliam ruled that a makeup game would be necessary if the teams ended up tied at the end of the year. They did, the Cubs won, and John McGraw and the New York press stepped up a campaign that had been underway for years to hound Pulliam from office.

The Chicago effort was led by Mordecai Brown (29 wins) and Ed Reulbach (24) on the mound. The offense was even flatter than usual, with only Johnny Evers getting to .300 and nobody topping Joe Tinker's 68 RBIs. The most stalwart of the losing Giants was again Christy Mathewson, with his league-leading 37 wins, 11 shutouts, and 1.43 ERA. Pittsburgh, which also stayed in the race until the final day of the regular season, had a pair of 23-game winners in Nick Maddox and Vic Willis.

The AL race also came down to the final day, with the Tigers edging out the Indians by a mere half-game and the White Sox by a game-and-a-half. The fraction was due to a Detroit rainout the team didn't have to make up; it was only after the season that regulations were passed covering postponements with a bearing on the pennant race. Individually, Ty Cobb was once again the headliner

Joe Tinker
The slickest fielder of his era, shortstop Joe Tinker, left, led the Cubs in RBIs and anchored Chicago to a World Series triumph.

offensively with another batting title (.324) and RBI crown (108). The single most impressive performance of the year, however, came from Chicago's Walsh, who kept the White Sox in the race despite the team's .224 average and merely three home runs. Compiling an awesome 464 innings, the right-hander went 40-15 with a 1.42 ERA; he would turn out to be baseball's last 40-game winner. One of his losses was an October 2 classic in which he fanned 15 Indians while allowing only four hits and an unearned run but lost to a perfect game by Addie Joss.

The World Series was another fairly easy run for the Cubs, though this time the Tigers stretched it to five games. Brown and Orvie Overall hurled back-to-back shutouts to conclude matters.

1908 SEASON HIGHLIGHTS

NATIONAL LEAGUE

	W	L	Pct.	GB
Chicago	99	55	.643	—
New York	98	56	.636	1
Pittsburgh	98	56	.636	1
Philadelphia	83	71	.539	16
Cincinnati	73	81	.474	26
Boston	63	91	.409	36
Brooklyn	53	101	.344	46
St. Louis	49	105	.318	50

AMERICAN LEAGUE

	W	L	Pct.	GB
Detroit	90	63	.588	—
Cleveland	90	64	.584	0.5
Chicago	88	64	.579	1.5
St. Louis	83	69	.546	6.5
Boston	75	79	.487	12.5
Philadelphia	68	85	.444	22
Washington	67	85	.441	22.5
New York	51	103	.331	39.5

NO AWARDS

POSTSEASON
WORLD SERIES
Chicago Cubs 4, Detroit Tigers 1
Oct. 10: Chicago 10, DETROIT 6
Oct. 11: CHICAGO 6, Detroit 1
Oct. 12: Detroit 8, CHICAGO 3
Oct. 13: Chicago 3, DETROIT 0
Oct. 14: Chicago 2, DETROIT 0

Home team in CAPS

"Anybody's best pitch is the one batters aren't hitting that day."

— Christy Mathewson

NATIONAL LEAGUE LEADERS

Home Runs
Jordan-Bro	12
Wagner-Pit	10
Murray-StL	7
Tinker-Chi	6

Runs Batted In
Wagner-Pit	109
Donlin-NY	106
Seymour-NY	92
Bransfield-Phi	71
Tinker-Chi	68

Batting Average
Wagner-Pit	.354
Donlin-NY	.334
Bransfield-Phi	.304
Evers-Chi	.300
Lobert-Cin	.293

On Base Percentage
Wagner-Pit	.415
Evers-Chi	.402
Bresnahan-NY	.401
Donlin-NY	.364
Bridwell-NY	.364

Slugging Average
Wagner-Pit	.542
Donlin-NY	.452
Magee-Phi	.417
Lobert-Cin	.407
Murray-StL	.400

Stolen Bases
Wagner-Pit	53
Murray-StL	48
Lobert-Cin	47
Magee-Phi	40
Evers-Chi	36

Wins
Mathewson-NY	37
Brown-Chi	29
Reulbach-Chi	24

Innings Pitched
Mathewson-NY	390.2
McQuillan-Phi	359.2
Rucker-Bro	333.1
Wilhelm-Bro	332.0
Wiltse-NY	330.0

Saves
McGinnity-NY	5
Mathewson-NY	5

Strikeouts
Mathewson-NY	259
Rucker-Bro	199
Overall-Chi	167
Raymond-StL	145
Reulbach-Chi	133

Earned Run Average
Mathewson-NY	1.43
Brown-Chi	1.47
McQuillan-Phi	1.53
Camnitz-Pit	1.56
Coakley-Cin-Chi	1.78

Complete Games
Mathewson-NY	34
Wilhelm-Bro	33
McQuillan-Phi	32
Wiltse-NY	30
Rucker-Bro	30

AMERICAN LEAGUE LEADERS

Home Runs
Crawford-Det	7
Hinchman-Cle	6
Niles-NY-Bos	5
Stone-StL	5
Davis-Phi	5

Runs Batted In
Cobb-Det	108
Crawford-Det	80
Lajoie-Cle	74
Ferris-StL	74
Rossman-Det	71

Batting Average
Cobb-Det	.324
Crawford-Det	.311
Gessler-Bos	.308
Hemphill-NY	.297
McIntyre-Det	.295

On Base Percentage
Gessler-Bos	.394
McIntyre-Det	.392
Hemphill-NY	.374
Hartsel-Phi	.371
Dougherty-Chi	.367

Slugging Average
Cobb-Det	.475
Crawford-Det	.457
Gessler-Bos	.423
Rossman-Det	.418
McIntyre-Det	.383

Stolen Bases
Dougherty-Chi	47
Hemphill-NY	42
Schaefer-Det	40
Cobb-Det	39
J.Clarke-Cle	37

Wins
Walsh-Chi	40
Summers-Det	24
Joss-Cle	24
Young-Bos	21
Waddell-StL	19

Innings Pitched
Walsh-Chi	464.0
Joss-Cle	325.0
Howell-StL	324.1
Vickers-Phi	317.0
Summers-Det	301.0

Saves
Walsh-Chi	6
Hughes-Was	4
Waddell-StL	3

Strikeouts
Walsh-Chi	269
Waddell-StL	232
Hughes-Was	165
Dygert-Phi	164
Johnson-Was	160

Earned Run Average
Joss-Cle	1.16
Young-Bos	1.26
Walsh-Chi	1.42
Summers-Det	1.64
Johnson-Was	1.65

Complete Games
Walsh-Chi	42
Young-Bos	30
Joss-Cle	29
Howell-StL	27
Mullin-Det	26

THE YEAR IN BASEBALL

February 27: The sacrifice fly rule is adopted.

March 16: Honus Wagner announces his retirement, but has a change of heart and ends up leading the NL in several batting categories after playing in 151 games.

April 2: After a two-year investigatoin the Mills Commission declares that baseball, despite overwhelming evidence to the contrary, was invented by Abner Doubleday in Cooperstown, New York, in 1839.

April 6: Of only 14 catchers in the Hall of Fame, two were born on this day—Mickey Cochrane in 1903 and Ernie Lombardi in 1908.

April 17: The White Sox almost live up to their names of Hitless Wonders. Rube Waddell of the Browns gives them just one blow, this being the product of Jake Atz.

July 4: George "Hooks" Wiltse pitches a 10-inning no-hit game for the Giants against the Phillies, winning over George McQuillan, 1-0. Hooks blew his perfect game when, on an 0-2 count, he hit the Phillie pitcher, 27th man to face him, on the arm.

July 17: Every National League game is a shutout. Boston beat Pittsburgh, 4-0; Philadelphia beat St. Louis, 3-0; Cincinnati beat Brooklyn, 2-0; and Chicago beat New York, 1-0.

August 20: Rube Waddell strikes out 17 Washington Nationals in 10 innings.

September 5: Nap Rucker, Brooklyn left-hander, pitches a no-hit game against Boston, striking out 14 men.

September 23: When Fred Merkle does not touch second in the ninth inning of a game with the Cubs, the game ends in a tie, 1-1, instead of a New York victory, 2-1. This oversight costs the Giants the pennant, for the season ends in a tie and the Cubs win the one-game playoff.

September 26: Ed Reulbach of the Cubs performs the greatest iron-man stunt on record in the majors by twice blanking Brooklyn. Scores were 5-0 and 3-0. Superbas got five singles in the first game, three in the second, and never got nearer the plate than second base.

October 2: Addie Joss of Cleveland pitches a perfect game, winning 1-0 over the White Sox. Ed Walsh gives up only four hits and fans 15 in a dazzling encounter.

October 6: On the final day of the AL season, with the pennant at stake for the winner and third place awaiting the loser, Bill Donovan's two-hitter gives Detroit the decision over Chicago.

1909

Ugly racial incident, Wagner heroics taint Cobb's Triple Crown

There was good news, better news and familiar news for the Tigers in 1909. The good news was that the Cubs didn't win the NL pennant. The better news was that Detroit won its third in a row in the AL. The familiar news was that the Ty Cobb club still lost the World Series.

The AL season proceeded much as the last two years had, with Cobb demonstrating his superiority at the plate. Not only did he set the pace in batting (.377) and RBIs (107), but he completed the Triple Crown with a league-best nine home runs; strikingly, all nine homers were inside-the-park jobs. The Detroit offense was so protean that Frank Baker of the Athletics was the only non-Tiger to lead in any hitting category, in triples. The club's pitching wasn't bad, either, with George Mullin setting the pace with 29 wins and Ed Willett contributing another 22.

Again, though, the Detroit season was tarnished by a racial incident involving Cobb. This time, the so-called Georgia Peach slapped a black elevator operator in Cleveland for being "insolent," precipitating a brawl with knives and an assault charge from the city's district attorney. Cobb avoided arrest only by being excluded from the team's visits to Cleveland.

The Athletics didn't win the pennant, but they unveiled the first steel-and-concrete stadium at Shibe Park on April 12. Built at a then-staggering cost of $300,000, it featured a double-decked grandstand and bleachers and could seat more than 20,000 people. Other teams quickly followed, and the era of wooden stadiums was over. Unfortunately, the opening in Philadelphia was marred when catcher Doc Powers crashed into a wall in pursuit of a pop-up; two weeks later, Powers died after internal injuries had brought on gangrene and other complications. On a brighter note, the same Athletics produced the only perfect player in baseball history. In his only big league appearance, John Kull gained a victory in relief, singled in his one turn at bat, and earned an assist in his lone fielding chance—giving him career marks of 1.000 in pitching, hitting, and fielding.

Much of the NL season was Pittsburgh. Like the Athletics, the Pirates moved into a steel-and-concrete stadium, Forbes Field, on June 30. The very first batter, Chicago's Johnny Evers, singled, therein launching the facility's 61-year history of never hosting a no-hit game. Meanwhile, Honus Wagner continued his "post-retirement" production by winning another batting title (.339) and driving in a league-best 100 runs, in the process leading Pittsburgh to the flag. On May 2 and 3 against the Cubs, the Pirates shortstop also showed he had some life left in his legs by stealing his way around the bases in consecutive games. Other big years came from Chicago's Mordecai Brown with 27 victories and New York's Christy Mathewson with a miniscule 1.14 ERA.

The World Series was billed as a personal duel between base-

Mordecai Brown
Cubs ace Three Finger Brown had six consecutive 20-win seasons, including his league-leading 27 (with 32 complete games) in 1909.

ball's two best hitters—a faceoff won by Wagner, when he batted .333 against Cobb's .231. More important, the infielder's timely hitting contributed to a Pittsburgh victory in seven games. The star of the series was Pirates right-hander Babe Adams, who pitched three complete-game wins, including a shutout in the finale. Detroit's third straight loss to the NL infuriated Ban Johnson, who put the blame on the team's manager Hughie Jennings. Noting the pilot's playing background, the AL president steamed: "We do all right in the World Series except when that damn National Leaguer Jennings gets into it."

1909 SEASON HIGHLIGHTS

NATIONAL LEAGUE

	W	L	Pct.	GB
Pittsburgh	110	42	.724	—
Chicago	104	49	.680	6.5
New York	92	61	.601	18.5
Cincinnati	77	76	.503	33.5
Philadelphia	74	79	.484	36.5
Brooklyn	55	98	.359	55.5
St. Louis	54	98	.355	56
Boston	45	108	.294	65.5

AMERICAN LEAGUE

	W	L	Pct.	GB
Detroit	98	54	.645	—
Philadelphia	95	58	.621	3.5
Boston	88	63	.583	9.5
Chicago	78	74	.513	20
New York	74	77	.490	23.5
Cleveland	71	82	.464	27.5
St. Louis	61	89	.407	36
Washington	42	110	.276	56

NO AWARDS

POSTSEASON
WORLD SERIES
Pittsburgh Pirates 4, Detroit Tigers 3
Oct. 8: PITTSBURGH 4, Detroit 1
Oct. 9: Detroit 7, PITTSBURGH 2
Oct. 11: Pittsburgh 8, DETROIT 6
Oct. 12: DETROIT 5, Pittsburgh 0
Oct. 13: PITTSBURGH 8, Detroit 4
Oct. 14: DETROIT 5, Pittsburgh 4
Oct. 16: Pittsburgh 8, DETROIT 0

Home team in CAPS

"Guys who can field you can shake out of any old tree. Find me guys who can hit."

— Rogers Hornsby

NATIONAL LEAGUE LEADERS

Home Runs
Murray-NY	7
Leach-Pit	6
Doyle-NY	6
Becker-Bos	6

Runs Batted In
Wagner-Pit	100
Murray-NY	91
D.Miller-Pit	87
Mitchell-Cin	86
Konetchy-StL	80

Batting Average
Wagner-Pit	.339
Mitchell-Cin	.310
Hoblitzell-Cin	.308
Doyle-NY	.302
Bridwell-NY	.294

On Base Percentage
Wagner-Pit	.420
Bridwell-NY	.386
Clarke-Pit	.384
Mitchell-Cin	.378
Evers-Chi	.369

Slugging Average
Wagner-Pit	.489
Mitchell-Cin	.430
Doyle-NY	.419
Hoblitzell-Cin	.418
Magee-Phi	.398

Stolen Bases
Bescher-Cin	54
Murray-NY	48
Egan-Cin	39
Magee-Phi	38
Burch-Bro	38

Wins
M.Brown-Chi	27
Mathewson-NY	25
H.Camnitz-Pit	25
Willis-Pit	22

Innings Pitched
M.Brown-Chi	342.2
Mattern-Bos	316.1
Rucker-Bro	309.1
Moore-Phi	299.2
Willis-Pit	289.2

Saves
M.Brown-Chi	7
Crandall-NY	6

Strikeouts
Overall-Chi	205
Rucker-Bro	201
Moore-Phi	173
M.Brown-Chi	172
Ames-NY	156

Earned Run Average
Mathewson-NY	1.14
M.Brown-Chi	1.31
Overall-Chi	1.42
H.Camnitz-Pit	1.62
Reulbach-Chi	1.78

Complete Games
M.Brown-Chi	32
Bell-Bro	29
Rucker-Bro	28
Mathewson-NY	26

AMERICAN LEAGUE LEADERS

Home Runs
Cobb-Det	9
Speaker-Bos	7
Stahl-Bos	6
Crawford-Det	6
Murphy-Phi	5

Runs Batted In
Cobb-Det	107
Crawford-Det	97
Baker-Phi	85
Speaker-Bos	77
Davis-Phi	75

Batting Average
Cobb-Det	.377
Collins-Phi	.346
Lajoie-Cle	.324
Crawford-Det	.314
Lord-Bos	.311

On Base Percentage
Cobb-Det	.431
Collins-Phi	.416
Bush-Det	.380
Lajoie-Cle	.378
Stahl-Bos	.377

Slugging Average
Cobb-Det	.517
Crawford-Det	.452
Collins-Phi	.449
Baker-Phi	.447
Speaker-Bos	.443

Stolen Bases
Cobb-Det	76
Collins-Phi	67
Bush-Det	53
Lord-Bos	36
Dougherty-Chi	36

Wins
Mullin-Det	29
Smith-Chi	25
Willett-Det	21

Innings Pitched
Smith-Chi	365.0
Mullin-Det	303.2
Johnson-Was	296.1
Young-Cle	295.0
Morgan-Bos-Phi	293.1

Saves
Arellanes-Bos	8
Powell-StL	3

Strikeouts
Smith-Chi	177
Johnson-Was	164
Berger-Cle	162
Bender-Phi	161
Waddell-StL	141

Earned Run Average
Krause-Phi	1.39
Walsh-Chi	1.41
Bender-Phi	1.66
Joss-Cle	1.71
Killian-Det	1.71

Complete Games
Smith-Chi	37
Young-Cle	30
Mullin-Det	29
Johnson-Was	27
Morgan-Bos-Phi	26

THE YEAR IN BASEBALL

February 4: John Clarkson dies; he won 53 games to lead Chicago to the 1885 NL flag, and won 208 in a five-year span.

February 18: The Boston Red Sox trade Cy Young to the Cleveland Naps for pitchers Charlie Chech and Jack Ryan, plus $12,500.

February 27: Joe "Iron Man" McGinnity is released by the Giants.

March 2: Mel Ott born; only 5-foot-9 and 165 pounds, he used an unorthodox swing to launch 511 homers, then an NL record.

April 12: The first game is played in Shibe Park, which came to be known as Connie Mack Stadium.

April 15: Fans discover that the "K" in Leon Ames' name stands for Kalamity. The Giant pitcher retires the Superbas for nine innings without a hit, but New York cannot make a run for him and the game lasts four more innings. Brooklyn, with Kaiser Wilhelm pitching, wins 3-0.

April 24: Walter Johnson, who the year before had pitched three shutouts in four days against the Highlanders, loses to them by a score of 17-0.

May 2: Honus Wagner steals his way from first to the plate in the first inning of a game with the Cubs.

May 29: Frank Baker smacks the first of his many home runs over the right-field wall at Philadephia's Shibe Park.

June 19: Washington's Walter Johnson, in a game against the Yankees, turns loose four wild pitches, passes seven men and hits a man, yet wins nevertheless, 7-4.

June 30: Pittsburgh's Forbes Field opens, with the Cubs winning over the Pirates, 3-2, as Ed Reulbach nipped Vic Willis.

July 16: The Tigers and Senators, in Detroit, play 18 innings to a runless draw. Ed "Kickapoo" Summers goes the entire route for Detroit.

July 19: Neal Ball, Indians shortstop, makes the century's first unassisted triple play in a game against Boston. With Charley Wagner running from second and Jake Stahl from first, he takes a liner hit by Amby McConnell, touches second, and then tags Stahl.

July 29: NL president Harry Pulliam, despondent over his inability to handle the problems and controversies of the league, dies of a self-inflicted gunshot wound.

August 28: In the oddest one-hit game on record in the majors, Washington's William Denton "Dolly" Gray is beaten, 6-4, by the White Sox. He gives eight bases on balls in the second, of which seven come in succession to force in five runs.

November 26: The Phils are sold for $350,000 to a group headed by sportswriter Horace Fogel.

1910

Cubs romp to pennant as Cobb targeted in batting conspiracy

The season got off to a ceremonious start when William Howard Taft inaugurated the tradition of U.S. presidents throwing out the first ball on Opening Day in Washington. Senators right-hander Walter Johnson then framed the event by hurling a one-hit shutout against the Athletics. It turned out to be one of the few bad days in the season for Philadelphia, which romped home with 102 wins, 14-1/2 games ahead of New York. The Philadelphia effort was keyed offensively by second baseman Eddie Collins (.322, 81 RBIs, and a league-leading 81 steals), while Jack Coombs led the pitchers with 31 victories, a 1.30 ERA, and a record 13 shutouts.

With the Athletics in cruise control most of the year, more than usual attention was paid to a couple of charades played out by also-rans. In New York, the Highlanders surprised by rising to second place with a new star hurler in Russ Ford (26 wins) and entertained with a melodrama over first baseman Hal Chase's various maneuvers to replace George Stallings as manager. With the help of long-time Stallings antagonist Ban Johnson, Chase ultimately got the job.

In St. Louis, Browns manager Jack O'Connor, a member in good standing of the Hate Cobb Club, sought to foil another batting title for the Tigers outfielder by ordering his third baseman to play back on the outfield grass against Cleveland's Nap Lajoie during a doubleheader on the final day of the season; the result was six bunt singles by Lajoie that instigated 70 years of controversy over the AL batting leader. Most immediately, Johnson threw O'Connor out of the league and claimed that his office's statisticians had found Cobb the winner anyway. There the matter lay uneasily until 1981, when *Sporting News* researcher Paul McFarlane and Pete Palmer came across a duplicate two-hit game attributed to Cobb that, when subtracted, returned the title to Lajoie. But then Commissioner Bowie Kuhn stepped in to reject the finding and keep Lajoie out in the cold. The Kuhn ruling gave Cobb the title at (the researched) .383—a point less than Lajoie's final .384.

In the NL, the Cubs had their fourth 100-plus-victory season in five years, keeping ahead of the Giants and Pirates by double figures for most of the campaign. Mordecai Brown notched another 25 wins to pace the pitchers, while outfielder Solly Hofman (.325, 86 RBIs) did the most conspicuous hitting. The biggest bat in the league belonged to Philadelphia's Sherry Magee, who set the pace in batting average (.331), RBIs (123), and runs scored (110). A Magee teammate, George McQuillan, had the lowest ERA at 1.60, while Christy Mathewson was in his familiar place with the most victories (27).

Jack Coombs
After winning 12 games in 1909, Coombs exploded to a major league high 31 in 1910 as the A's won the AL pennant by 14-1/2 games.

Despite finishing 13 games ahead of the Giants, the Cubs went into the World Series as underdogs because of the superior Athletics pitching, a broken leg at the end of the season that sidelined Johnny Evers, and the obvious aging of the second baseman's fabled infield partners Frank Chance and Joe Tinker. The oddsmakers were proven right when 12 Chicago errors, three complete-game Coombs wins, and a Philadelphia team batting average of .316—spearheaded by Collins' .429—gave the A's the championship in five games. Overall, the A's outscored the Cubs 35-15, and the .316 average stood as a World Series record for 50 years.

1910 SEASON HIGHLIGHTS

NATIONAL LEAGUE

	W	L	Pct.	GB
Chicago	104	50	.675	—
New York	91	63	.591	13
Pittsburgh	86	67	.562	17.5
Philadelphia	78	75	.510	25.5
Cincinnati	75	79	.487	29
Brooklyn	64	90	.416	40
St. Louis	63	90	.412	40.5
Boston	53	100	.346	50.5

AMERICAN LEAGUE

	W	L	Pct.	GB
Philadelphia	102	48	.680	—
New York	88	63	.583	14.5
Detroit	86	68	.558	18
Boston	81	72	.529	22.5
Cleveland	71	81	.467	32
Chicago	68	85	.444	35.5
Washington	66	85	.437	36.5
St. Louis	47	107	.305	57

NO AWARDS

POSTSEASON
WORLD SERIES
Philadelphia Athletics 4, Chicago Cubs 1
Oct. 17: PHILADELPHIA 4, Chicago 1
Oct. 18: PHILADELPHIA 9, Chicago 3
Oct. 20: Philadelphia 12, CHICAGO 5
Oct. 22: CHICAGO 4, Philadelphia 3
Oct. 23: Philadelphia 7, CHICAGO 2
Home team in CAPS

"I have observed that baseball is not unlike a war, and when you come right down to it, we batters are the heavy artillery."
— Ty Cobb

NATIONAL LEAGUE LEADERS

Home Runs
Schulte-Chi	10
Beck-Bos	10
Doyle-NY	8
Daubert-Bro	8

Runs Batted In
Magee-Phi	123
Mitchell-Cin	88
Murray-NY	87
Hofman-Chi	86
Wagner-Pit	81

Batting Average
Magee-Phi	.331
Hofman-Chi	.325
Snodgrass-NY	.321
Wagner-Pit	.320
Bates-Phi	.305

On Base Percentage
Magee-Phi	.445
Snodgrass-NY	.440
Evers-Chi	.413
Hofman-Chi	.406
Huggins-StL	.399

Slugging Average
Magee-Phi	.507
Hofman-Chi	.461
Schulte-Chi	.460
Merkle-NY	.441
Snodgrass-NY	.432

Stolen Bases
Bescher-Cin	70
Murray-NY	57
Paskert-Cin	51
Magee-Phi	49
Devore-NY	43

Wins
Mathewson-NY	27
Brown-Chi	25
Moore-Phi	22
Suggs-Cin	20
Cole-Chi	20

Innings Pitched
Rucker-Bro	320.1
Mathewson-NY	318.1
Bell-Bro	310.0
Mattern-Bos	305.0
Brown-Chi	295.1

Saves
Gaspar-Cin	7
Brown-Chi	7
Crandall-NY	5
Richie-Bos-Chi	4

Strikeouts
Moore-Phi	185
Mathewson-NY	184
Frock-Pit-Bos	171
Drucke-NY	151
Rucker-Bro	147

Earned Run Average
Cole-Chi	1.80
Brown-Chi	1.86
Mathewson-NY	1.89
Ames-NY	2.22
Adams-Pit	2.24

Complete Games
Rucker-Bro	27
Mathewson-NY	27
Brown-Chi	27
Bell-Bro	25
Barger-Bro	25

AMERICAN LEAGUE LEADERS

Home Runs
Stahl-Bos	10
Lewis-Bos	8
Cobb-Det	8
Speaker-Bos	7
Crawford-Det	5

Runs Batted In
Crawford-Det	120
Cobb-Det	91
Collins-Phi	81
Stahl-Bos	77
Lajoie-Cle	76

Batting Average
Lajoie-Cle	.384
Cobb-Det	.383
Speaker-Bos	.340
Collins-Phi	.322
Oldring-Phi	.308

On Base Percentage
Cobb-Det	.456
Lajoie-Cle	.445
Speaker-Bos	.404
Collins-Phi	.381
Milan-Was	.379

Slugging Average
Cobb-Det	.551
Lajoie-Cle	.514
Speaker-Bos	.468
Murphy-Phi	.436
Oldring-Phi	.430

Stolen Bases
Collins-Phi	81
Cobb-Det	65
Zeider-Chi	49
Bush-Det	49
Milan-Was	44

Wins
Coombs-Phi	31
Ford-NY	26
Johnson-Was	25
Bender-Phi	23
Mullin-Det	21

Innings Pitched
Johnson-Was	370.0
Walsh-Chi	369.2
Coombs-Phi	353.0
Ford-NY	299.2
Morgan-Phi	290.2

Saves
Walsh-Chi	5
Browning-Det	3

Strikeouts
Johnson-Was	313
Walsh-Chi	258
Coombs-Phi	224
Ford-NY	209
Bender-Phi	155

Earned Run Average
Walsh-Chi	1.27
Coombs-Phi	1.30
Johnson-Was	1.36
Morgan-Phi	1.55
Bender-Phi	1.58

Complete Games
Johnson-Was	38
Coombs-Phi	35
Walsh-Chi	33
Ford-NY	29
Mullin-Det	27

THE YEAR IN BASEBALL

April 14: Two one-hit games are pitched in the American League, Walter Johnson accomplishing the feat for Washington and Frank Smith for Chicago. Frank Baker of the Athletics and Ray Demmitt of the Browns, respectively, got the only hits

April 20: Addie "The Human Slat" Joss of the Indians retires the White Sox without a hit, winning over Doc White, 1-0. He passed two men and one error, a fumble by Bradley, was made behind him. Joss had 10 assists.

April 21: Emery ball is introduced to the American League by Russ Ford of the Yankees. With it he beats the Athletics, 1-0 and fans nine men, striking out "Home Run" Harry Davis all four times he appears.

May 10: Heinie Zimmerman of the Cubs, in a game with the Giants, has as many errors at short as hits—four.

May 12: Chief Bender almost pitches a perfect game for the Athletics against Cleveland. He slips up by passing Terry Turner in the sixth. Ira Thomas nailed Turner when he tried to steal, so only 27 men faced the Chippewa Chieftain.

May 26: The Pirates' Honus Wagner and John Miller narrowly escape death when their car crashes into the safety gates of a railroad crossing.

June 1: Miller Huggins of the Cardinals does not have a time at bat charged against him in six trips to the plate in a game with Philadelphia, walking four times and sacrificing twice.

July 19: Cy Young registers his 500th victory in the major leagues when he leads Cleveland to a 5-2 win over Washington in 11 innings. No pitcher before Young had won 500 games and no pitcher after him is likely to.

July 31: The Cubs have to stop play in their game with the Cardinals at the end of the seventh to catch a train, possibly costing King Cole a no-hit contest. He didn't allow any hits in seven innings that were played and no men were left on base, four who walked being erased either on double plays or trying to steal.

August 4: Jack Coombs, of the Athletics, and Ed Walsh, of the White Sox, wage a 16-inning battle in which no runs are scored. Philadelphia's star allowed three hits and fanned 18 men; the Chicagoan permitted six blows and whiffed 10.

October 21: The Giants defeat the Yankees, four games to two, in the first New York City Series; Christy Mathewson wins all four Giant victories.

1911

Cobb has career year but Coombs leads Athletics to Series

The season couldn't have begun any worse for the Giants, when an April 14 fire destroyed a substantial part of the Polo Grounds and forced the team to play most of its home games at Hilltop Park. Once ensconced in the AL facility a few blocks away, however, John McGraw's club ran opponents ragged with an attack centered around a never-equaled 347 stolen bases. The principal thieves were outfielders Josh Devore and Fred Snodgrass, who combined for 112 thefts. The pitching was captained by Christy Mathewson and southpaw Rube Marquard, who put together 50 wins between them and were stymied only by Philadelphia's Grover Cleveland Alexander (28 wins) in claiming all the league's mound bests. Together with a Cubs decline owing to age and injuries, New York crossed the finish line first, 7-1/2 strides ahead of Chicago. Giants players themselves attributed some of their success to the enigmatic Charlie Faust, a would-be player who couldn't hit, pitch or field but who traveled with the team anyway because he was regarded as a good-luck charm.

In the AL, Ty Cobb had the single best year of his career, topping the league in batting (.420), hits (248), doubles (47), triples (24), runs (147), RBIs (144), and steals (83). But with little sustained help from anyone except outfielder Sam Crawford (.378 and 115 RBIs), he ended up going home at season's end while the Athletics went on to meet the Giants in the World Series. Philadelphia's dominance was keyed by the completion of the "$100,000 infield" with the nifty-fielding Stuffy McInnis going to first base to join second baseman Eddie Collins, third baseman Frank Baker and shortstop Jack Barry. With five regulars batting well over .300, the team turned in a season average of .296. As usual, the pitching was formidable, with Jack Coombs winning a league-leading 28, Eddie Plank 22 and Chief Bender 17.

Aside from the Athletics, the most talked-about AL franchise was Cleveland. Stunned by the sudden death of their long-time ace Addie Joss in April, Indians players announced they were going to forego their scheduled opener in Detroit in order to be at funeral ceremonies in Toledo. When both Cleveland and Detroit managements nixed that idea, the players said they were going anyway, prompting AL president Ban Johnson to threaten retaliations. With the press questioning their cold hearts, the executives finally had to agree to push back the opener a day— what the players had been proposing all along. On the diamond, the team also attracted notice for two new lights—outfielder Joe

Grover Cleveland Alexander
As a rookie, Alexander led the NL with 28 wins to launch a career that would span 20 seasons and bring 373 victories.

Jackson, who batted .408 in his first full season, and southpaw Vean Gregg, who won 20 games for the first of three straight years and led the league in ERA at 1.81.

In contrast to their previous meeting in 1905, the Giants and Athletics didn't manage a single shutout in the 1911 World Series. But Coombs, Plank and Bender did team up for an ERA of 1.29 in defeating New York in six games. Two clutch clouts by Baker, following his league-leading 11 blasts during the regular season, fixed him with the nickname Home Run for the rest of his 13-year career, although he never hit more than 12 in any single season.

1911 SEASON HIGHLIGHTS

NATIONAL LEAGUE

	W	L	Pct.	GB
New York	99	54	.647	—
Chicago	92	62	.597	7.5
Pittsburgh	85	69	.552	14.5
Philadelphia	79	73	.520	19.5
St. Louis	75	74	.503	22
Cincinnati	70	83	.458	29
Brooklyn	64	86	.427	33.5
Boston	44	107	.291	54

AMERICAN LEAGUE

	W	L	Pct.	GB
Philadelphia	101	50	.669	—
Detroit	89	65	.578	13.5
Cleveland	80	73	.523	22
Chicago	77	74	.510	24
Boston	78	75	.510	24
New York	76	76	.500	25.5
Washington	64	90	.416	38.5
St. Louis	45	107	.296	56.5

AWARDS

NL MVP: Frank Schulte, CHI
AL MVP: Ty Cobb, DET

POSTSEASON
WORLD SERIES
Philadelphia Athletics 4, New York Giants 2
Oct. 14: NEW YORK 2, Philadelphia 1
Oct. 16: PHILADELPHIA 3, New York 1
Oct. 17: Philadelphia 3, NEW YORK 2
Oct. 24: PHILADELPHIA 4, New York 2
Oct. 25: NEW YORK 4, Philadelphia 2
Oct. 26: PHILADELPHIA 13, New York 2

Home team in CAPS

"The only way to get a ball past Honus Wagner is to hit it eight feet over his head."

— John McGraw

NATIONAL LEAGUE LEADERS

Home Runs
Schulte-Chi	21
Luderus-Phi	16
Magee-Phi	15
Doyle-NY	13

Runs Batted In
Wilson-Pit	107
Schulte-Chi	107
Luderus-Phi	99
Magee-Phi	94

Batting Average
Wagner-Pit	.334
Miller-Bos	.333
Sweeney-Bos	.314
Doyle-NY	.310
Daubert-Bro	.307

On Base Percentage
Sheckard-Chi	.434
Wagner-Pit	.423
Bates-Cin	.415
Sweeney-Bos	.404
Doyle-NY	.397

Slugging Average
Schulte-Chi	.534
Doyle-NY	.527
Wagner-Pit	.507
Magee-Phi	.483
Wilson-Pit	.472

Stolen Bases
Bescher-Cin	80
Devore-NY	61
Snodgrass-NY	51
Merkle-NY	49

Wins
Alexander-Phi	28
Mathewson-NY	26
Marquard-NY	24
Harmon-StL	23

Innings Pitched
Alexander-Phi	367.0
Harmon-StL	348.0
Leifield-Pit	318.0
Rucker-Bro	315.2
Moore-Phi	308.1

Saves
Brown-Chi	13
Crandall-NY	5

Strikeouts
Marquard-NY	237
Alexander-Phi	227
Rucker-Bro	190
Moore-Phi	174
Harmon-StL	144

Earned Run Average
Mathewson-NY	1.99
Richie-Chi	2.31
Adams-Pit	2.33
Marquard-NY	2.50
Alexander-Phi	2.57

Complete Games
Alexander-Phi	31
Mathewson-NY	29
Harmon-StL	28
Leifield-Pit	26
Adams-Pit	24

AMERICAN LEAGUE LEADERS

Home Runs
Baker-Phi	11
Speaker-Bos	8
Cobb-Det	8

Runs Batted In
Cobb-Det	127
Crawford-Det	115
Baker-Phi	115
Bodie-Chi	97
Delahanty-Det	94

Batting Average
Cobb-Det	.420
Jackson-Cle	.408
Crawford-Det	.378
Collins-Phi	.365
Cree-NY	.348

On Base Percentage
Jackson-Cle	.468
Cobb-Det	.467
Collins-Phi	.451
Crawford-Det	.438
Speaker-Bos	.418

Slugging Average
Cobb-Det	.621
Jackson-Cle	.590
Crawford-Det	.526
Cree-NY	.513
Baker-Phi	.508

Stolen Bases
Cobb-Det	83
Milan-Was	58
Cree-NY	48
Callahan-Chi	45
Lord-Chi	43

Wins
Coombs-Phi	28
Walsh-Chi	27
Johnson-Was	25

Innings Pitched
Walsh-Chi	368.2
Coombs-Phi	336.2
Johnson-Was	322.1
Ford-NY	281.1
Wood-Bos	275.2

Saves
Walsh-Chi	4
Plank-Phi	4
Hall-Bos	4
Wood-Bos	3

Strikeouts
Walsh-Chi	255
Wood-Bos	231
Johnson-Was	207
Coombs-Phi	185
Ford-NY	158

Earned Run Average
Gregg-Cle	1.80
Johnson-Was	1.90
Wood-Bos	2.02
Plank-Phi	2.10
Bender-Phi	2.16

Complete Games
Johnson-Was	36
Walsh-Chi	33
Ford-NY	26
Coombs-Phi	26

THE YEAR IN BASEBALL

April 14: Pitcher Adrian "Addie" Joss dies in Toledo, Ohio of a rare form of tubercular meningitis. He was 31.

April 29: Yankee pitchers Jim Vaughn and Jack Quinn pitch seven balls to Stuffy McInnis of the Athletics. Off these he made five singles, hitting the first pitch three times and the second twice.

May 13: Grover Cleveland Alexander, relieving George Chalmers in the ninth inning of a game against Cincinnati, pitches eight hitless rounds. The Phillies win in the 16th, 5-4.

June 5: In a Boston-Chicago game, reliever Smokey Joe Wood strikes out three pinch hitters in the ninth to secure the win, 5-4.

July 7: Joe Wood, pitching for the Red Sox, holds the Browns to one hit and fans 15 men, losing a no-hitter when Burt Shotton cracks a hit in the ninth.

July 12: Ty Cobb scores a hitless run in the first inning of a game with the Athletics. After getting a pass from Harry Krause, he steals second, third and the plate.

July 24: A group of American League All-Stars play the Indians in a benefit game for the late Addie Joss.

July 24: Owen Wilson of the Pirates, who next year would hit a record 36 triples, hits three in one game against Brooklyn.

August 19: After having won 22 straight games from Cincinnati, Christy Mathewson is beaten by them, 7-4. His conqueror is Art Fromme.

August 22: Josh Devore of the Giants raps five hits—each on the first pitch.

August 27: Ed Walsh pitches a no-hit game for the White Sox against the Red Sox; Clyde Engle, who walked, is the one man to reach first.

September 7: Rookie Grover Cleveland Alexander of the Phils takes a 1-0 thriller from 44-year-old Cy Young, of the Boston Braves.

September 18: Larry Doyle of the Giants steals home twice in the same game.

September 22: Cy Young of Boston records the 511th and final win of his career, beating Pittsburgh 1-0.

December 21: Josh Gibson is born; from his debut with the Homestead Grays in 1930 to his death in 1947, he was the home-run king of black baseball.

1912

Cy Young calls it quits as baseball ushers in pinstripes and Fenway

More than one tradition was born and more than one familiar face faded from the scene in 1912. On Opening Day, the AL club in New York wore pinstripes for the first time. The season also marked the opening of Fenway Park, destined to become the longest-surviving stadium in the major leagues. On the other hand, Cy Young formally announced in the spring that he was retiring after 22 years and a never-approached 511 victories. April 12 also turned out to be the last time Frank Chance, Johnny Evers and Joe Tinker took the field together for the Cubs.

In the NL, the Giants broke out of the gate with a 43-11 record and, until slumping in August, appeared primed to top Chicago's 116 victories in 1906. The most dazzling performance of the year came from Rube Marquard, who won 19 consecutive games. The offense was spearheaded by second baseman Larry Doyle, who knocked in 90 runs with his .330 average. Marquard's 26 victories tied him with Chicago's Larry Cheney for the most in the league. Honus Wagner again set the pace with 102 RBIs, but his .324 fell far short of the .372 registered by Heinie Zimmerman of the Cubs for the batting crown.

In the AL, Boston put together 105 victories, the most in franchise history, for a runaway pennant. The biggest performances came from outfielder Tris Speaker and pitcher Joe Wood. While Speaker batted .383 with 98 RBIs and a league-leading 10 homers, right-hander Wood swept to a mark of 34-5 (1.91 ERA) that included one run of 16 consecutive victories. Hugh Bedient and Buck O'Brien also had 20-win seasons for the Red Sox. Category leaders from the rest of the league included Philadelphia's Frank Baker for his 130 RBIs, Washington's Walter Johnson for a 1.39 ERA, and Detroit's Ty Cobb for his .409 batting average.

Cobb's sixth straight hitting title was overshadowed by another violent incident. On May 15, during a game at Hilltop Park, he climbed into the stands and began punching and kicking heckler Claude Luecker. He said afterwards he had been driven to his attack by Luecker's shouts that he was a "half-nigger." Informed the fan had lost four fingers in a printing-press accident, Cobb said he didn't care "if he has no feet." When Ban Johnson suspended the outfielder for using what he called "vicious language," the rest of the team warned it would strike if the penalty weren't rescinded. Johnson held firm, the players did too, and Tigers owner Frank Navin had to put together a squad from among manager Hughie Jennings, his coaches, and Philadelphia sandlotters to go through with a May 18 game against the Athletics or face his own fines, and perhaps even the loss of his franchise. The improvised Tigers were shellacked 24-2, after which Cobb himself ended the follies by appealing to his teammates to resume playing.

Johnny Evers
An era ended in 1912 when Cubs' infielders Evers, Joe Tinker and Frank Chance lined up together for the last time.

The Boston-New York World Series was a tense affair that ended up going eight games because of an extra-inning tie in Game Two. The Red Sox prevailed on Wood's three victories and the all-around ill-fated play of Giants outfielder Fred Snodgrass. In the 11th inning of the second game, Snodgrass had his potentially leading run thrown out on the basepaths. In the bottom of the 10th inning of the finale, he muffed an easy fly that allowed Boston to rally for the championship. His overall batting mark for the eight games was .212.

1912 SEASON HIGHLIGHTS

NATIONAL LEAGUE

	W	L	Pct.	GB
New York	103	48	.682	—
Pittsburgh	93	58	.616	10
Chicago	91	59	.607	11.5
Cincinnati	75	78	.490	29
Philadelphia	73	79	.480	30.5
St. Louis	63	90	.412	41
Brooklyn	58	95	.379	46
Boston	52	101	.340	52

AMERICAN LEAGUE

	W	L	Pct.	GB
Boston	105	47	.691	—
Washington	91	61	.599	14
Philadelphia	90	62	.592	15
Chicago	78	76	.506	28
Cleveland	75	78	.490	30.5
Detroit	69	84	.451	36.5
St. Louis	53	101	.344	53
New York	50	102	.329	55

AWARDS

NL MVP: Larry Doyle, NY
AL MVP: Tris Speaker, BOS

POSTSEASON
WORLD SERIES
Boston Red Sox 4, New York Giants 3, 1 tie

Oct. 8: Boston 4, NEW YORK 3
Oct. 9: BOSTON 6, New York 6
Oct. 10: New York 2, BOSTON 1
Oct. 11: Boston 3, NEW YORK 1
Oct. 12: BOSTON 2, New York 1
Oct. 14: NEW YORK 5, Boston 2
Oct. 15: New York 11, BOSTON 4
Oct. 16: BOSTON 3, New York 2

Home team in CAPS

"He would climb a mountain
to take a punch at an echo."

— Bugs Baer, on Ty Cobb

NATIONAL LEAGUE LEADERS

Home Runs
Zimmerman-Chi	14
Schulte-Chi	12
Wilson-Pit	11
Merkle-NY	11

Runs Batted In
Wagner-Pit	102
Sweeney-Bos	100
Zimmerman-Chi	99
Wilson-Pit	95
Murray-NY	92

Batting Average
Zimmerman-Chi	.372
Sweeney-Bos	.344
Evers-Chi	.341
Doyle-NY	.330
Wagner-Pit	.324

On Base Percentage
Evers-Chi	.431
Huggins-StL	.422
Paskert-Phi	.420
Zimmerman-Chi	.418
Sweeney-Bos	.416

Slugging Average
Zimmerman-Chi	.571
Wilson-Pit	.513
Wagner-Pit	.496
Doyle-NY	.471
Cravath-Phi	.470

Stolen Bases
Bescher-Cin	67
Carey-Pit	45
Snodgrass-NY	43
Murray-NY	38

Wins
Marquard-NY	26
Cheney-Chi	26
Hendrix-Pit	24
Mathewson-NY	23
Camnitz-Pit	22

Innings Pitched
Alexander-Phi	310.1
Mathewson-NY	310.0
Cheney-Chi	303.1
Suggs-Cin	303.0
Benton-Cin	302.0

Saves
Sallee-StL	6
Rucker-Bro	4
Reulbach-Chi	4

Strikeouts
Alexander-Phi	195
Hendrix-Pit	176
Marquard-NY	175
Benton-Cin	162
Rucker-Bro	151

Earned Run Average
Tesreau-NY	1.96
Mathewson-NY	2.12
Rucker-Bro	2.21
Robinson-Pit	2.26
Ames-NY	2.46

Complete Games
Cheney-Chi	28
Mathewson-NY	27
Suggs-Cin	25
Hendrix-Pit	25
Alexander-Phi	25

AMERICAN LEAGUE LEADERS

Home Runs
Speaker-Bos	10
Baker-Phi	10
Cobb-Det	7

Runs Batted In
Baker-Phi	130
Lewis-Bos	109
Crawford-Det	109
McInnis-Phi	101

Batting Average
Cobb-Det	.409
Jackson-Cle	.395
Speaker-Bos	.383
Lajoie-Cle	.368
Collins-Phi	.348

On Base Percentage
Speaker-Bos	.464
Jackson-Cle	.458
Cobb-Det	.456
Collins-Phi	.450
Lajoie-Cle	.414

Slugging Average
Cobb-Det	.584
Jackson-Cle	.579
Speaker-Bos	.567
Baker-Phi	.541
Crawford-Det	.470

Stolen Bases
Milan-Was	88
Collins-Phi	63
Cobb-Det	61
Speaker-Bos	52
Zeider-Chi	47

Wins
Wood-Bos	34
Johnson-Was	33
Walsh-Chi	27
Plank-Phi	26
Groom-Was	24

Innings Pitched
Walsh-Chi	393.0
Johnson-Was	369.0
Wood-Bos	344.0
Groom-Was	316.0
Ford-NY	291.2

Saves
Walsh-Chi	10
Warhop-NY	3
Mogridge-Chi	3
Lange-Chi	3
Dubuc-Det	3

Strikeouts
Johnson-Was	303
Wood-Bos	258
Walsh-Chi	254
Gregg-Cle	184
Groom-Was	179

Earned Run Average
Johnson-Was	1.39
Wood-Bos	1.91
Walsh-Chi	2.15
Plank-Phi	2.22
Collins-Bos	2.53

Complete Games
Wood-Bos	35
Johnson-Was	34
Walsh-Chi	32
Ford-NY	30

THE YEAR IN BASEBALL

January 3: Frenchy Bordagaray is born; fined $500 for spitting at an umpire, he protested, "Maybe I did wrong, but the penalty was a little more than I expectorated."

April 11: Rube Marquard begins a 19-game win streak with 18-3 win vs. Brooklyn.

April 20: Boston's Fenway Field opens, with the Red Sox beating the Yankees in 11 innings, 7-6.

April 20: The White Sox and Browns play 15 innings to a scoreless draw, Jim Scott pitching against George Baumgardner.

April 27: The Pirates get 27 hits off three Cincinnati pitchers and win, 23-4.

May 18: Rallying behind the suspended Ty Cobb, Detroit players refuse to play, resulting in a makeshift team being assembled to avoid a forfeit of the franchise. They lose to the A's, 24-2.

June 14: Washington's Clyde "Deerfoot" Milan steals five bases in a game with Cleveland.

June 20: Josh Devore, of the Giants, in ninth inning of game with Braves, steals four bases. New York wins, 21-12, but Boston gets 10 runs in the last inning off Ernie Shore, then making his big-time debut.

July 4: Ty Cobb steals second, third, and home in the fifth inning of the opener of a twin bill with St. Louis Browns; Tiger teammate George Mullin throws a no-hitter in the nightcap to celebrate his birthday.

July 8: Rube Marquard, after winning 19 games in a row for the Giants, is stopped by Jimmy Lavender of the Cubs, 7-3.

September 1: Smokey Joe Wood of the Red Sox beats Walter Johnson of the Senators, 1-0, in a specially arranged pitching duel at Boston. This was the 14th straight win for Wood; Johnson had won 16 straight earlier in the season. When the season ended, Wood had 34 wins, Johnson 32.

September 6: Jeff Tesreau of the Giants, slightly assisted by some New York correspondents who use their persuasive powers on an official scorer, pitches a no-hitter against the Phillies, winning over Eppa Rixey, 3-0. A ball hit to Fred Merkle was recorded as a hit and later changed to an error.

September 11: The Athletics' Eddie Collins steals six bases in a game with Detroit, an AL record; eleven days later, he would do it again.

September 17: Casey Stengel, purchased conditionally from Montgomery, breaks in with Brooklyn by blasting Pittsburgh pitching for four hits and a walk in five tries, also stealing a base in 7-3 victory.

September 26: The Cubs have the Reds shut out 9-0 up to the ninth when Cincinnati scores 10 runs off Jimmy Lavender, Fred Toney and Larry Cheney. But the Cubs rebound for two runs against Ralph Works and Rube Benton to win, 11-10.

October 16: Fred Snodgrass drops an easy fly ball in the 10th inning that permits the Red Sox Sox to go on to score twice and win the Series from the Giants.

1913

Johnson wins 36, Dodgers open Ebbets as Athletics romp

The Giants won the NL pennant in another cakewalk, but they didn't dominate all of the circuit's summer headlines. In terms of lore, the biggest event of the year was the opening of Ebbets Field in Brooklyn on April 9. Although finishing sixth, the Dodgers also produced the league's leading hitter in first baseman Jake Daubert (.350). The Phillies had other talking points, not least a franchise sale that left the club in the control of a former New York City police commissioner, William Baker. Generally regarded as a middle-of-the-pack team, Philadelphia surprised everyone by holding on to first place as late as mid-July and not tumbling below second. The unexpected showing was largely thanks to a league-leading 27 victories from Tom Seaton and the slugging of outfielder Gavvy Cravath, who paced the NL with his 179 hits, 19 home runs and 128 RBIs.

John McGraw's main problem during the season was trying to persuade his players they could win without the presence of their good luck charm Charlie Faust. As in 1912, however, Faust's absences inevitably brought losing streaks, resigning the manager to reserve another train berth on the team's travels. (The problem would ultimately resolve itself with Faust's commitment to a mental institution.) Offensively, the club was solid without setting off fireworks. The pitching was something else, with Christy Mathewson winning 25 (and leading the league with his 2.06 ERA), Rube Marquard 23 and Jeff Tesreau 22.

The Cubs completed their breakup with Frank Chance going off to manage the Yankees, Joe Tinker taking over as pilot of the Reds, and Mordecai Brown pitching in Cincinnati. All three ended up wearing the uniforms of a seventh-place team. In taking over the Cubs as dugout boss, Johnny Evers spent the season fighting with his own players. On one occasion, Chicago shortstop Al Bridwell took a swing at him on the field; on another, outfielder Tommy Leach ran from his position to the mound after interpreting an Evers gesture as criticism of his fielding.

In the AL, Philadelphia returned to the World Series on the strength of familiar elements: Eddie Collins batted .345, Frank Baker topped the league in both home runs (12) and RBIs (117), and Chief Bender won 21. Much of runner-up Washington's hopes lay with two A's pitchers—the aging (37) Eddie Plank and the injured Jack Coombs. Plank disappointed the Senators by throwing the most complete games on the Athletics staff, appearing more often as a reliever, and winning 18. To replace Coombs, manager Connie Mack found Boardwalk Brown, who

Walter Johnson
The Big Train had 10 consecutive 20-win seasons, including a major league high 36 in 1913, en route to 417 lifetime victories.

won 17. Not even Walter Johnson's AL-leading 36 victories and 1.14 ERA could make up the difference. The year's other category leaders included another batting title for Ty Cobb (.390).

The Athletics carried their dominance into the World Series, defeating the Giants in five games. The highlights were two tense duels between Mathewson and Plank, split by the future Hall of Famers. Otherwise, the Series turned on Baker's seven RBIs and Bender's two victories.

1913 SEASON HIGHLIGHTS

NATIONAL LEAGUE

	W	L	Pct.	GB
New York	101	51	.664	—
Philadelphia	88	63	.583	12.5
Chicago	88	65	.575	13.5
Pittsburgh	78	71	.523	21.5
Boston	69	82	.457	31.5
Brooklyn	65	84	.436	34.5
Cincinnati	64	89	.418	37.5
St. Louis	51	99	.340	49

AMERICAN LEAGUE

	W	L	Pct.	GB
Philadelphia	96	57	.627	—
Washington	90	64	.584	6.5
Cleveland	86	66	.566	9.5
Boston	79	71	.527	15.5
Chicago	78	74	.513	17.5
Detroit	66	87	.431	30
New York	57	94	.377	38
St. Louis	57	96	.373	39

AWARDS

NL MVP: Jake Daubert, BRO
AL MVP: Walter Johnson, WAS

POSTSEASON
WORLD SERIES
Philadelphia Athletics 4, New York Giants 1
Oct. 7: Philadelphia 6, NEW YORK 4
Oct. 8: New York 3, PHILADELPHIA 0
Oct. 9: Philadelphia 8, NEW YORK 2
Oct.10: PHILADELPHIA 6, New York 5
Oct. 11: Philadelphia 3, NEW YORK 1

Home team in CAPS

> "People ask me what I do in winter when there's no baseball. I'll tell you what I do: I stare out the window and wait for spring."
>
> — Rogers Hornsby

NATIONAL LEAGUE LEADERS

Home Runs		Runs Batted In		Batting Average	
Cravath-Phi	19	Cravath-Phi	128	Daubert-Bro	.350
Luderus-Phi	18	Zimmerman-Chi	95	Cravath-Phi	.341
Saier-Chi	14	Saier-Chi	92	Viox-Pit	.317
Magee-Phi	11	Miller-Pit	90	Zimmerman-Chi	.313
Wilson-Pit	10	Luderus-Phi	86	Magee-Phi	.306

On Base Percentage		Slugging Average		Stolen Bases	
Huggins-StL	.432	Cravath-Phi	.568	Carey-Pit	61
Cravath-Phi	.407	Zimmerman-Chi	.490	Myers-Bos	57
Daubert-Bro	.405	Saier-Chi	.480	Lobert-Phi	41
Viox-Pit	.399	Magee-Phi	.479	Burns-NY	40
Leach-Chi	.391	Smith-Bro	.441	Cutshaw-Bro	39

Wins		Innings Pitched		Saves	
Seaton-Phi	27	Seaton-Phi	322.1	Cheney-Chi	11
Mathewson-NY	25	Adams-Pit	313.2	Crandall-NY	6
Marquard-NY	23	Alexander-Phi	306.1	Brown-Cin	6
Tesreau-NY	22	Mathewson-NY	306.0	Sallee-StL	5
Alexander-Phi	22	Cheney-Chi	305.0		

Strikeouts		Earned Run Average		Complete Games	
Seaton-Phi	168	Mathewson-NY	2.06	Tyler-Bos	28
Tesreau-NY	167	Adams-Pit	2.15	Mathewson-NY	25
Alexander-Phi	159	Tesreau-NY	2.17	Cheney-Chi	25
Marquard-NY	151	Demaree-NY	2.21	Adams-Pit	24
Adams-Pit	144	Pearce-Chi	2.31	Alexander-Phi	23

AMERICAN LEAGUE LEADERS

Home Runs		Runs Batted In		Batting Average	
Baker-Phi	12	Baker-Phi	117	Cobb-Det	.390
Crawford-Det	9	McInnis-Phi	90	Jackson-Cle	.373
Bodie-Chi	8	Lewis-Bos	90	Speaker-Bos	.363
Jackson-Cle	7	Pratt-StL	87	Collins-Phi	.345
		Barry-Phi	85	Baker-Phi	.337

On Base Percentage		Slugging Average		Stolen Bases	
Cobb-Det	.467	Jackson-Cle	.551	Milan-Was	75
Jackson-Cle	.460	Cobb-Det	.535	Moeller-Was	62
Collins-Phi	.441	Speaker-Bos	.533	Collins-Phi	55
Speaker-Bos	.441	Baker-Phi	.493	Cobb-Det	51
Baker-Phi	.413	Crawford-Det	.489	Speaker-Bos	46

Wins		Innings Pitched		Saves	
Johnson-Was	36	Johnson-Was	346.0	Bender-Phi	13
Falkenberg-Cle	23	Russell-Chi	316.2	Hughes-Was	6
Russell-Chi	22	Scott-Chi	312.1	Bedient-Bos	5
Bender-Phi	21	V.Gregg-Cle	285.2		
		Falkenberg-Cle	276.0		

Strikeouts		Earned Run Average		Complete Games	
Johnson-Was	243	Johnson-Was	1.14	Johnson-Was	29
V.Gregg-Cle	166	Cicotte-Chi	1.58	Russell-Chi	26
Falkenberg-Cle	166	Scott-Chi	1.90	Scott-Chi	25
Scott-Chi	158	Russell-Chi	1.90		
Groom-Was	156	Mitchell-Cle	1.91		

THE YEAR IN BASEBALL

January 8: Frank Chance agrees to manage the New York Yankees.

January 22: The Yankees reach a one-year agreement with the Giants to use the Polo Grounds for home games—but stay there until 1922.

February 1: Olympian Jim Thorpe signs with the New York Giants but he is more of a gate attraction than a threat at the plate.

March 8: The Federal League is organized as a six-team "outlaw" circuit to play 120 games in 1913.

April 9: In the first regular-season game at Ebbets Field, the Dodgers lose to the Phillies, 1-0, before a crowd of 12,000.

April 10: The Washington Senators defeat the Yankees, 2-1, in their home opener. Walter Johnson allows a run in the first inning, but will not give up another run for 56 consecutive innings.

May 6: The Federal League begins play with seven teams.

May 14: Walter Johnson, after keeping his opponents runless for 56 innings, is scored on by the Browns, who had beaten him the year before after he had won 16 straight.

May 26: Walter Johnson retires the Athletics in the sixth inning on three pitched balls.

May 30: John McGraw wins his 1,000th game as a manager.

July 18: Christy Mathewson yields a base on balls to snap a string of 68 consecutive innings without issuing a walk.

July 25: Relieving Tom Hughes in the fourth inning, Walter Johnson keeps the Browns to one run and seven hits in 11-1/3 innings and fans 16 of them.

September 29: Walter Johnson wins his 36th game of the season as the Senators beat the A's, 1-0.

October 7: Living up to his nickname, John Franklin "Home Run" Baker connects with a homer that enables the A's to beat the Giants in the World Series opener, 6-4.

November 2: St. Louis Browns manager George Stovall is the first major leaguer to jump to the Federal League, signing to manage Kansas City.

December 24: Louis Sockalexis dies; the Penobscot Indian who hit .338 as a Cleveland rookie gave that team its nickname.

1914

New Federal League overshadows year of Miracle Braves

The rise of the Federal League as a third, self-proclaimed major league brought back all of the drama of the turn of the century: players jumping teams, owners marching into courtrooms and fans going where the action was. Spearheaded by millionaire Chicago coal dealer James Gilmore, the Feds set up for business in four NL-AL markets (Brooklyn, Pittsburgh, Chicago, St. Louis) and in four big minor-league cities (Buffalo, Baltimore, Indianapolis, Kansas City). Among the biggest names defecting were Joe Tinker, Mordecai Brown, Hal Chase, George Mullin, and Tom Seaton. The FL's banner franchise turned out to be Indianapolis, which eked out a pennant on the final day of the season ahead of Chicago. The latter's consolation was that it drew seven times more fans for the climactic game than the Cubs and White Sox, also both home for the day, did together. The circuit's biggest find was Indianapolis outfielder Benny Kauff, who led the way in batting (.370), runs (120), and doubles (44). Teammate Frank LaPorte had the most RBIs (107) and Chicago's Claude Hendrix the most wins (29).

The biggest story in the NL was Boston, which started the season by losing 18 of its first 22 and which remained mired in last place, 15 games behind the Giants, as late as early July. But then the Miracle Braves of George Stallings won 52 of their last 66 games, passing all seven other clubs between July 19 and September 8. Enthusiasm for the team ran so rampant in Boston that the Red Sox even offered the NLers use of Fenway Park for key games. Pitching was the key to the Boston surge, with Dick Rudolph and Bill James combining for 53 wins. For the second year in a row, Brooklyn's Jake Daubert won the batting crown (329) and Philadelphia's Gavvy Gravath hit the most home runs (19). Two other Phillies also headed categories—Sherry Magee with 103 RBIs and Grover Cleveland Alexander with 27 wins. On June 9, Pittsburgh's Honus Wagner got his 3,000th hit, a double off Philadelphia's Erskine Mayer.

Tris Speaker
The Grey Eagle led the AL in hits, runs and total bases while batting .338—a typical season for Speaker, who batted .345 over a 22-year career.

There was less drama in the AL, where the heavily favored Athletics trumped second-place Boston by 8-1/2 games. The A's pennant owed to some of the usual suspects, including 85-plus RBIs from Eddie Collins, Frank Baker and Stuffy McInnis. But the pitching strength was more spread out, with Chief Bender (17-3) leading seven hurlers who won in double figures. The league's most untouchable pitchers were Boston's Dutch Leonard, whose 0.96 ERA would never be topped, and Washington's Walter Johnson with 28 wins. Ty Cobb (.368) and Detroit teammate Sam Crawford (104 RBIs) led the hitters.

Boston's four-game sweep of the .172-hitting Athletics concluded what Connie Mack always called the unhappiest year of his career. Variously accusing the team of not having played hard enough, the fans of becoming too smug with the club's winning, and the Feds of pressuring his payroll, he sold Collins to the White Sox and released both Bender and Eddie Plank after the World Series.

There was one footnote to the season: On July 11, Babe Ruth made his debut for the Red Sox with a 4-3 win over Cleveland. The southpaw pitcher struck out in his first at-bat.

1914 SEASON HIGHLIGHTS

NATIONAL LEAGUE

	W	L	Pct.	GB
Boston	94	59	.614	—
New York	84	70	.545	10.5
St. Louis	81	72	.529	13
Chicago	78	76	.506	16.5
Brooklyn	75	79	.487	19.5
Philadelphia	74	80	.481	20.5
Pittsburgh	69	85	.448	25.5
Cincinnati	60	94	.390	34.5

AMERICAN LEAGUE

	W	L	Pct.	GB
Philadelphia	99	53	.651	—
Boston	91	62	.595	8.5
Washington	81	73	.526	19
Detroit	80	73	.523	19.5
St. Louis	71	82	.464	28.5
New York	70	84	.455	30
Chicago	70	84	.455	30
Cleveland	51	102	.333	48.5

FEDERAL LEAGUE

	W	L	Pct.	GB
Indianapolis	88	65	.575	—
Chicago	87	67	.565	1.5
Baltimore	84	70	.545	4.5
Buffalo	80	71	.530	7
Brooklyn	77	77	.500	11.5
Kansas City	67	84	.444	20
Pittsburgh	64	86	.427	22.5
St. Louis	62	89	.411	25

POSTSEASON
WORLD SERIES
Boston Braves 4, Philadelphia Athletics 0
Oct. 9: Boston 7, PHILADELPHIA 1
Oct. 10: Boston 1, PHILADELPHIA 0
Oct. 12: BOSTON 5, Philadelphia 4
Oct. 13: BOSTON 3, Philadelphia 1

Home team in CAPS

> "What was usually an innocent enough wisecrack became cause for a fist fight if Ty Cobb was invovled."
> — Davy Jones, a Cobb teammate

AWARDS
NL MVP: Johnny Evers, BOS
AL MVP: Eddie Collins, PHI

NATIONAL LEAGUE LEADERS

Home Runs
Cravath-Phi	19
Saier-Chi	18
Magee-Phi	15
Luderus-Phi	12

Runs Batted In
Magee-Phi	103
Cravath-Phi	100
Wheat-Bro	89
D.Miller-StL	88
Zimmerman-Chi	87

Batting Average
Daubert-Bro	.329
Becker-Phi	.325
Dalton-Bro	.319
Wheat-Bro	.319
Stengel-Bro	.316

On Base Percentage
Stengel-Bro	.404
Burns-NY	.403
Cravath-Phi	.402
Huggins-StL	.396
Dalton-Bro	.396

Slugging Average
Magee-Phi	.509
Cravath-Phi	.499
Wheat-Bro	.452
Becker-Phi	.446
Daubert-Bro	.432

Stolen Bases
Burns-NY	62
Herzog-Cin	46
Dolan-StL	42
Carey-Pit	38

Wins
Alexander-Phi	27
Tesreau-NY	26
Rudolph-Bos	26
James-Bos	26
Mathewson-NY	24

Innings Pitched
Alexander-Phi	355.0
Rudolph-Bos	336.1
James-Bos	332.1
Tesreau-NY	322.1
Mayer-Phi	321.0

Saves
Sallee-StL	6
Ames-Cin	6
Cheney-Chi	5
Pfeffer-Bro	4
McQuillan-Pit	4

Strikeouts
Alexander-Phi	214
Tesreau-NY	189
Vaughn-Chi	165
Cheney-Chi	157
James-Bos	156

Earned Run Average
Doak-StL	1.72
James-Bos	1.90
Pfeffer-Bro	1.97
Vaughn-Chi	2.05
Sallee-StL	2.10

Complete Games
Alexander-Phi	32
Rudolph-Bos	31
James-Bos	30
Mathewson-NY	29
Pfeffer-Bro	27

AMERICAN LEAGUE LEADERS

Home Runs
Baker-Phi	9
Crawford-Det	8
T.Walker-StL	6
Fournier-Chi	6

Runs Batted In
Crawford-Det	104
McInnis-Phi	95
Speaker-Bos	90
Baker-Phi	89
Collins-Phi	85

Batting Average
Collins-Phi	.344
Speaker-Bos	.338
Jackson-Cle	.338
Baker-Phi	.319
Crawford-Det	.314

On Base Percentage
Collins-Phi	.452
Speaker-Bos	.423
Jackson-Cle	.399
Crawford-Det	.388
Baker-Phi	.380

Slugging Average
Speaker-Bos	.503
Crawford-Det	.483
Jackson-Cle	.464
Collins-Phi	.452
Baker-Phi	.442

Stolen Bases
Maisel-NY	74
Collins-Phi	58
Speaker-Bos	42
Shotton-StL	40

Wins
Johnson-Was	28
Coveleski-Det	22
Collins-Bos	20
Leonard-Bos	19

Innings Pitched
Johnson-Was	371.2
Coveleski-Det	303.1
Hamilton-StL	302.1
Dauss-Det	302.0
Weilman-StL	299.0

Saves
Shaw-Was	4
Mitchell-StL	4
Faber-Chi	4
Dauss-Det	4
Bentley-Was	4

Strikeouts
Johnson-Was	225
Mitchell-Cle	179
Leonard-Bos	176
Shaw-Was	164
Dauss-Det	150

Earned Run Average
Leonard-Bos	0.96
Foster-Bos	1.70
Johnson-Was	1.72
Caldwell-NY	1.94
Cicotte-Chi	2.04

Complete Games
Johnson-Was	33
Coveleski-Det	23
Dauss-Det	22
Caldwell-NY	22

FEDERAL LEAGUE LEADERS

Home Runs
Zwilling-Chi	16
Kenworthy-KC	15
Hanford-Buf	13
Evans-Bro	12

On Base Percentage
Kauff-Ind	.447
Evans-Bro	.416
Lennox-Pit	.414
Meyer-Bal	.395
Wilson-Chi	.394

Wins
Hendrix-Chi	29
Quinn-Bal	26
Seaton-Bro	25
Falkenberg-Ind	25
Suggs-Bal	24

Strikeouts
Falkenberg-Ind	236
Moseley-Ind	205
Hendrix-Chi	189
Seaton-Bro	172
Groom-StL	167

Runs Batted In
LaPorte-Ind	107
Evans-Bro	96
Zwilling-Chi	95
Kauff-Ind	95
Kenworthy-KC	91

Slugging Average
Evans-Bro	.556
Kauff-Ind	.534
Kenworthy-KC	.525
Lennox-Pit	.493
Zwilling-Chi	.485

Innings Pitched
Falkenberg-Ind	377.1
Hendrix-Chi	362.0
Quinn-Bal	342.2
Suggs-Bal	319.1
Moseley-Ind	316.2

Earned Run Average
Hendrix-Chi	1.69
Ford-Buf	1.82
Watson-Chi-StL	2.01
Falkenberg-Ind	2.22
Lange-Chi	2.23

Batting Average
Kauff-Ind	.370
Evans-Bro	.348
Campbell-Ind	.318
Kenworthy-KC	.317
Louden-Buf	.313

Stolen Bases
Kauff-Ind	75
McKechnie-Ind	47
Myers-Bro	43
Chadbourne-KC	42

Saves
Ford-Buf	6
Wilhelm-Bal	5
Packard-KC	5
Hendrix-Chi	5

Complete Games
Hendrix-Chi	34
Falkenberg-Ind	33
Moseley-Ind	29
Quinn-Bal	27

THE YEAR IN BASEBALL

April 1: At the age of 37, Rube Waddell dies of tuberculosis; the eccentric lefthander fanned 349 batters in 1904, a record that stood for over 60 years.

April 13: After declaring itself a major league, the Federal League debuts in Baltimore as the home team defeats the Buffalo entry 3-2.

April 22: Babe Ruth debuts in the International League at age 19. He throws a six-hit, 6-0 win for Baltimore over Buffalo.

May 6: Ed Lennox of the FL's Pittsburgh Rebels hits for the cycle during a 10-4 victory over the Kansas City Packers.

May 28: Harry Hooper, Duffy Lewis and Tris Speaker of the Red Sox make a triple steal on Rip Hagerman and Fred Carisch of the Indians. The triple steal led to a triple squeal and Umpire Oliver Chill banished Indians' Joe Birmingham, Carisch, and Ivy Olson from game.

June 9: Honus Wagner gets his 3,000th hit.

July 11: Babe Ruth plays his first game in the American League. He pitches seven innings for the Red Sox and gets the win over Cleveland.

September 27: Cleveland second baseman Nap Lajoie gets his 300th hit.

November 25: Joe DiMaggio is born.

December 27: A postseason All-Star tour—AL led by Connie Mack, NL by Frank Bancroft—disbands at San Diego after 44 games across U.S. and Hawaii.

1915

Federal League runs out of money; Ruth wins 18

The Federal League's second and last year of existence featured the closest pennant race in big-league history. On the final day of the season, a single game separated Chicago, St. Louis and Pittsburgh. By evening, St. Louis had one more victory than Chicago—but also one more loss and merely second place, .001 out of the lead. Third-place Pittsburgh finished .004 away from the title. The two Chicago rainouts accounting for the miniscule percentage difference were not made up, as they would have been in the AL or NL. The league's big sticks once again included Benny Kauff, who recorded his pace-setting .342 average for Brooklyn. But Kauff was also emblematic of the league's shaky financial footing in that he had been dealt to Brooklyn by 1914 champion Indianapolis as the latter, a bust at the gate, was being transferred to Newark for the 1915 campaign. George McConnell's 25 wins for Chicago led the pitchers.

In the AL, the gutted Athletics fulfilled predictions by plunging to last place. For most of the season, the Tigers and Red Sox seesawed for the top spot, until finally Boston's pitching proved superior to Detroit's hitting. Five Boston pitchers won in double figures, including Rube Foster with 20, Babe Ruth with 18 for his first full season, and Joe Wood with 14 and a league-leading 1.49 ERA. Detroit took the hitting honors, with Ty Cobb collecting another batting title with his .369 and outfield teammates Sam Crawford and Bobby Veach tying at 112 RBIs. Washington's Walter Johnson paced hurlers with another 27 victories.

In the NL, the Braves started off as though ready to repeat their 1914 miracle, but were gradually overtaken by a Phillies club led by Grover Cleveland Alexander on the mound (a league-best 31 wins and 1.22 ERA) and outfielder Gavvy Cravath at the bat (tops in the NL for his 24 homers and 115 RBIs). Aided by Baker Bowl's short fences, it was the third of six times Cravath would lead the circuit in homers in the pre-Ruth slugging era. Larry Doyle of the Giants took the batting crown (.320).

Boston's World Series victory in five games was much closer than it appeared. Alexander's 3-1 win in the opener was the only game settled by more than one run and Foster's 5-4 victory in the finale followed three straight 2-1 Red Sox decisions.

A growing series of administrative and financial crises forced the Federal League to fold its tent after the season. Accord stipulations among the three leagues permitted Phil Ball, owner of the FL franchise in St. Louis, to buy the AL Browns, and Charles Weeghman,

Eddie Collins
A year after winning the 1914 MVP award, second baseman Collins, a lifetime .333 hitter, was sold by the Athletics to the White Sox.

his Chicago counterpart, to take over the NL Cubs. Baltimore, the one franchise left out in the cold by the agreement, pursued a lawsuit that would go on for years all the way up to the Supreme Court. The judicial trail would finally end on May 29, 1922, with Chief Justice Oliver Wendell Holmes declaring that Organized Baseball was immune to antitrust statutes because it did not engage in interstate commerce.

1915 SEASON HIGHLIGHTS

NATIONAL LEAGUE

	W	L	Pct.	GB
Philadelphia	90	62	.592	—
Boston	83	69	.546	7
Brooklyn	80	72	.526	10
Chicago	73	80	.477	17.5
Pittsburgh	73	81	.474	18
St. Louis	72	81	.471	18.5
Cincinnati	71	83	.461	20
New York	69	83	.454	21

AMERICAN LEAGUE

	W	L	Pct.	GB
Boston	101	50	.669	—
Detroit	100	54	.649	2.5
Chicago	93	61	.604	9.5
Washington	85	68	.556	17
New York	69	83	.454	32.5
St. Louis	63	91	.409	39.5
Cleveland	57	95	.375	44.5
Philadelphia	43	109	.283	58.5

FEDERAL LEAGUE

	W	L	Pct.	GB
Chicago	86	66	.566	—
St. Louis	87	67	.565	—
Pittsburgh	86	67	.562	0.5
Kansas City	81	72	.529	5.5
Newark	80	72	.526	6
Buffalo	74	78	.487	12
Brooklyn	70	82	.461	16
Baltimore	47	107	.305	40

POSTSEASON
WORLD SERIES
Boston Red Sox 4, Philadelphia Phillies 1
Oct. 8: PHILADELPHIA 3, Boston 1
Oct. 9: Boston 2, PHILADELPHIA 1
Oct. 11: BOSTON 2, Philadelphia 1
Oct. 12: BOSTON 2, Philadelphia 1
Oct. 13: Boston 5, PHILADELPHIA 4
Home team in CAPS

> "He's got a gun concealed on his person. They can't tell me he throws them balls with his arm."
> — Ring Lardner, on Walter Johnson

NO AWARDS

NATIONAL LEAGUE LEADERS

Home Runs
Cravath-Phi	24
Williams-Chi	13
Schulte-Chi	12
Saier-Chi	11
Becker-Phi	11

Runs Batted In
Cravath-Phi	115
Magee-Bos	87
Griffith-Cin	85
H.Wagner-Pit	78
Hinchman-Pit	77

Batting Average
Doyle-NY	.320
Luderus-Phi	.315
Griffith-Cin	.307
Hinchman-Pit	.307
Daubert-Bro	.301

On Base Percentage
Cravath-Phi	.393
Luderus-Phi	.376
Daubert-Bro	.369
Hinchman-Pit	.368
Doyle-NY	.358

Slugging Average
Cravath-Phi	.510
Luderus-Phi	.457
Long-StL	.446
Saier-Chi	.445
Doyle-NY	.442

Stolen Bases
Carey-Pit	36
Herzog-Cin	35
Saier-Chi	29
Baird-Pit	29
Cutshaw-Bro	28

Wins
Alexander-Phi	31
Rudolph-Bos	22
Mayer-Phi	21
Mamaux-Pit	21
Vaughn-Chi	20

Innings Pitched
Alexander-Phi	376.1
Rudolph-Bos	341.1
Tesreau-NY	306.0
Dale-Cin	296.2
Pfeffer-Bro	291.2

Saves
Hughes-Bos	9
Benton-Cin-NY	5
Lavender-Chi	4
Cooper-Pit	4

Strikeouts
Alexander-Phi	241
Tesreau-NY	176
Hughes-Bos	171
Mamaux-Pit	152
Vaughn-Chi	148

Earned Run Average
Alexander-Phi	1.22
Toney-Cin	1.58
Mamaux-Pit	2.04
Pfeffer-Bro	2.10
Hughes-Bos	2.12

Complete Games
Alexander-Phi	36
Rudolph-Bos	30
Pfeffer-Bro	26
Harmon-Pit	25
Tesreau-NY	24

AMERICAN LEAGUE LEADERS

Home Runs
Roth-Chi-Cle	7
Oldring-Phi	6

Runs Batted In
Veach-Det	112
Crawford-Det	112
Cobb-Det	99
S.Collins-Chi	85
J.Jackson-Cle-Chi	81

Batting Average
Cobb-Det	.369
E.Collins-Chi	.332
Fournier-Chi	.322
Speaker-Bos	.322
McInnis-Phi	.314

On Base Percentage
Cobb-Det	.486
E.Collins-Chi	.460
Fournier-Chi	.429
Speaker-Bos	.416
Shotton-StL	.409

Slugging Average
Fournier-Chi	.491
Cobb-Det	.487
J.Jackson-Cle-Chi	.445
E.Collins-Chi	.436
Veach-Det	.434

Stolen Bases
Cobb-Det	96
Maisel-NY	51
E.Collins-Chi	46
Shotton-StL	43
C.Milan-Was	40

Wins
Johnson-Was	27
Scott-Chi	24
Faber-Chi	24
Dauss-Det	24
Coveleski-Det	22

Innings Pitched
Johnson-Was	336.2
Coveleski-Det	312.2
Dauss-Det	309.2
Caldwell-NY	305.0
Faber-Chi	299.2

Saves
Mays-Bos	7

Strikeouts
Johnson-Was	203
Faber-Chi	182
Wyckoff-Phi	157
Coveleski-Det	150
Mitchell-Cle	149

Earned Run Average
Wood-Bos	1.49
Johnson-Was	1.55
Shore-Bos	1.64
Scott-Chi	2.03
Fisher-NY	2.11

Complete Games
Johnson-Was	35
Caldwell-NY	31
Dauss-Det	27
Scott-Chi	23
Dubuc-Det	22

FEDERAL LEAGUE LEADERS

Home Runs
Chase-Buf	17
Zwilling-Chi	13
Kauff-Bro	12
Konetchy-Pit	10

Wins
McConnell-Chi	25
Allen-Chi	23
Davenport-StL	22
Cullop-KC	22

Runs Batted In
Zwilling-Chi	94
Konetchy-Pit	93
Chase-Buf	89
Kauff-Bro	83
Borton-StL	83

Innings Pitched
Davenport-StL	392.2
Crandall-StL	312.2
Schulz-Buf	309.2
McConnell-Chi	303.0
Cullop-KC	302.1

Batting Average
Kauff-Bro	.342
Magee-Bro	.323
Konetchy-Pit	.314
Flack-Chi	.314
Campbell-New	.310

Saves
Bedient-Buf	10
Barger-Pit	6
Wiltse-Bro	5
Upham-Bro	5

On Base Percentage
Kauff-Bro	.446
W.Miller-StL	.400
Borton-StL	.395
Evans-Bro-Bal	.392
Cooper-Bro	.388

Strikeouts
Davenport-StL	229
Schulz-Buf	160
McConnell-Chi	151
Plank-StL	147

Slugging Average
Kauff-Bro	.509
Konetchy-Pit	.483
Chase-Buf	.471
Zwilling-Chi	.442
Mann-Chi	.438

Earned Run Average
Moseley-New	1.91
Plank-StL	2.08
Brown-Chi	2.09
McConnell-Chi	2.20
Davenport-StL	2.20

Stolen Bases
Kauff-Bro	55
Mowrey-Pit	40
Kelly-Pit	38
Flack-Chi	37
Magee-Bro	34

Complete Games
Davenport-StL	30
Hendrix-Chi	26
Schulz-Buf	25
Allen-Pit	24

THE YEAR IN BASEBALL

January 5: Thirteen years after leaving the Athletics, Nap Lajoie returns to the Philadelphia team.

April 17: Fritz Maisel of the Yankees steals his way from first to the plate in the ninth inning of a game with the Athletics.

April 22: Nap Lajoie, at second base for the Athletics against Boston, has five errors, managing to make one putout and three assists cleanly.

April 22: Pinstripes appear on Yankee uniforms for the first time.

April 24: Pitcher Babe Ruth is withdrawn from the game with Philadelphia by manager Bill Carrigan so that Hick Cady—lifetime, one home run—could pinch hit for him.

May 6: Babe Ruth starts on his home-run career in the AL, hitting for the circuit in a game with the Yankees against Jack Warhop.

June 20: St. Louis Browns show up in Detroit without any uniforms. The Tigers lend them their spare uniforms, then whip them, 1-0.

June 23: Bruno Phillip Haas, pitching his first major league game for the Athletics, passes 16 Yankees, makes three wild pitches, and is beaten, 15-7.

September 14: The Giants, despite making 14 hits off Larry Cheney of the Cubs, can't score a run and are beaten, 7-0.

December 22: For two years a rival to the American and National Leagues, the Federal League disbands.

1916

Speaker, Mathewson among several stars involved in trades

The collapse of the Federal League brought trouble when AL and NL owners sought to cut back on the salaries they had felt pressured to raise when the third circuit had been a lure for contract jumping. A representative clash came in Boston, where Tris Speaker's balking before a pay slash prompted his trade to Cleveland. The deal didn't affect the outfielder's offensive prowess; he went on to win the batting title (.386). The Red Sox had little to regret, however, edging out the White Sox for the pennant. Babe Ruth shone on the mound with 23 wins and a league-best 1.75 ERA; only Washington's Walter Johnson (25) and New York's Bob Shawkey (24) won more. Del Pratt of St. Louis had the most RBIs (103).

In the NL, Brooklyn, New York, Boston, and Philadelphia waged the only all-Eastern Division pennant battle into September during the eight-team league era. Adding extra spice to the competition was the fact that the Dodgers were managed by Wilbert Robinson, long-time crony and coach for John McGraw who was fired by the Giants pilot in a snit after the 1913 World Series. The relationship came to the fore in late September when the Giants, on the edge of elimination, lost some key games to the Dodgers. When McGraw walked off the field in visible disgust before the end of one of the defeats, the Phillies interpreted the body language ominously, charging (vainly) that New York players had thrown the games for their old coach Robinson. New York's tumble to fourth place by the end of the campaign came despite a 17-game winning streak in May and an even more astonishing, record 26-game skein down the stretch.

The NL's individual honors went to Cincinnati's Hal Chase for batting (.339), Heimie Zimmerman of the Cubs and Giants for RBIs (83), and Philadelphia's perennial Grover Cleveland Alexander for both wins (33) and ERA (1.55). Zimmerman wasn't the only player who spent just a part of the season in a Giants uniform. A month before the August 28 exchange that brought him to the Polo Grounds for Larry Doyle, McGraw pulled off the so-called Hall of Fame Trade with Cincinnati. In return for second baseman Buck Herzog and outfielder Red Killefer, the Giants surrendered pitcher Christy Mathewson, outfielder Edd Roush, and catcher Bill McKechnie (all three players going to the Reds ended up in Cooperstown). Mathewson also took over immediately as their manager. Also notable was the Cubs home opener on April 20, an extra-inning 7-6 win over Cincinnati. The game was the first to be played by the NL in what was then called Weeghman Park—the facility inherited with the purchase of the franchise by the Federal League's Charles Weeghman; within 10 years, the park would be known as Wrigley Field.

Babe Ruth
In just his second full season, Ruth (still a pitcher) won 23 games and led the AL with nine shutouts as the Red Sox won the World Series.

The Boston-Brooklyn World Series provided Ruth with his biggest stage to that date. In Game 2, he tangled with Sherry Smith of the Dodgers for 14 innings before finally emerging with a 2-1 victory. The triumph in five games by the Red Sox also included two wins by Ernie Shore.

1916 SEASON HIGHLIGHTS

NATIONAL LEAGUE

	W	L	Pct.	GB
Brooklyn	94	60	.610	—
Philadelphia	91	62	.595	2.5
Boston	89	63	.586	4
New York	86	66	.566	7
Chicago	67	86	.438	26.5
Pittsburgh	65	89	.422	29
St. Louis	60	93	.392	33.5
Cincinnati	60	93	.392	33.5

AMERICAN LEAGUE

	W	L	Pct.	GB
Boston	91	63	.591	—
Chicago	89	65	.578	2
Detroit	87	67	.565	4
New York	80	74	.519	11
St. Louis	79	75	.513	12
Cleveland	77	77	.500	14
Washington	76	77	.497	14.5
Philadelphia	36	117	.235	54.5

NO AWARDS

POSTSEASON
WORLD SERIES
Boston Red Sox 4, Brooklyn Dodgers 1
Oct. 7: BOSTON 6, Brooklyn 5
Oct. 9: BOSTON 2, Brooklyn 1
Oct. 10: BROOKLYN 4, Boston 3
Oct. 11: Boston 6, BROOKLYN 2
Oct. 12: BOSTON 4, Brooklyn 1

Home team in CAPS

"What do you want me to do? Let them sons of bitches stand up there and think on my time?"

— Grover Cleveland Alexander,
explaining why he pitched so quickly

NATIONAL LEAGUE LEADERS

Home Runs		Runs Batted In		Batting Average	
Williams-Chi	12	Zimmerman-Chi-NY	83	Chase-Cin	.339
Robertson-NY	12	Chase-Cin	82	Daubert-Bro	.316
Cravath-Phi	11	Hinchman-Pit	76	Hinchman-Pit	.315
Z.Wheat-Bro	9	Kauff-NY	74	Hornsby-StL	.313
Kauff-NY	9	Z.Wheat-Bro	73	Z.Wheat-Bro	.312

On Base Percentage		Slugging Average		Stolen Bases	
Cravath-Phi	.379	Z.Wheat-Bro	.461	Carey-Pit	63
Hinchman-Pit	.378	Chase-Cin	.459	Kauff-NY	40
Williams-Chi	.372	Williams-Chi	.459	Bescher-StL	39
Daubert-Bro	.371	Hornsby-StL	.444	Burns-NY	37
Groh-Cin	.370	Cravath-Phi	.440	Herzog-Cin-NY	34

Wins		Innings Pitched		Saves	
Alexander-Phi	33	Alexander-Phi	389.0	Ames-StL	8
Pfeffer-Bro	25	Pfeffer-Bro	328.2	Packard-Chi	5
Rixey-Phi	22	Rudolph-Bos	312.0	Marquard-Bro	5
Mamaux-Pit	21	Mamaux-Pit	310.0	Hughes-Bos	5
		Toney-Cin	300.0		

Strikeouts		Earned Run Average		Complete Games	
Alexander-Phi	167	Alexander-Phi	1.55	Alexander-Phi	38
Cheney-Bro	166	Marquard-Bro	1.58	Pfeffer-Bro	30
Mamaux-Pit	163	Rixey-Phi	1.85	Rudolph-Bos	27
Toney-Cin	146	Cooper-Pit	1.87	Mamaux-Pit	26
Vaughn-Chi	144	Pfeffer-Bro	1.92	Demaree-Phi	25

AMERICAN LEAGUE LEADERS

Home Runs		Runs Batted In		Batting Average	
Pipp-NY	12	Pratt-StL	103	Speaker-Cle	.386
Baker-NY	10	Pipp-NY	93	Cobb-Det	.371
Schang-Phi	7	Veach-Det	91	Jackson-Chi	.341
Felsch-Chi	7	Speaker-Cle	79	Strunk-Phi	.316
		Jackson-Chi	78	Gardner-Bos	.308

On Base Percentage		Slugging Average		Stolen Bases	
Speaker-Cle	.470	Speaker-Cle	.502	Cobb-Det	68
Cobb-Det	.452	Jackson-Chi	.495	Marsans-StL	46
E.Collins-Chi	.405	Cobb-Det	.493	Shotton-StL	41
Jackson-Chi	.393	Veach-Det	.433	E.Collins-Chi	40
Strunk-Phi	.393	Felsch-Chi	.427	Speaker-Cle	35

Wins		Innings Pitched		Saves	
Johnson-Was	25	Johnson-Was	369.2	Shawkey-NY	8
Shawkey-NY	24	Coveleski-Det	324.1	Russell-NY	6
Ruth-Bos	23	Ruth-Bos	323.2	Leonard-Bos	6
Coveleski-Det	21	Myers-Phi	315.0	Cicotte-Chi	5
Dauss-Det	19	Davenport-StL	290.2	Bagby-Cle	5

Strikeouts		Earned Run Average		Complete Games	
Johnson-Was	228	Ruth-Bos	1.75	Johnson-Was	36
Myers-Phi	182	Cicotte-Chi	1.78	Myers-Phi	31
Ruth-Bos	170	Johnson-Was	1.90	Bush-Phi	25
Bush-Phi	157	Coveleski-Det	1.97	Ruth-Bos	23
Harper-Was	149	Faber-Chi	2.02	Coveleski-Det	22

THE YEAR IN BASEBALL

January 5: Charles H. Weeghman buys the Cubs for $500,000 and moves them to the stadium he built for his Federal League Chicago Whales. The field will become known as Wrigley Field.

January 8: The Boston Braves are sold for $500,000 to Harvard's famous football coach Percy Haughton and a banking associate.

February 15: After sitting out all of 1915, "Home Run" Baker is sold by the decimated Philadelphia A's to New York for $35,000.

April 12: Tris Speaker is traded from Boston to Cleveland for Sam Jones, Fred Thomas, and $50,000.

April 13: Babe Adams, Pittsburgh veteran, pitches a one-hitter against the Cardinals.

April 29: The Cubs new owner, Charles H. Weeghman, announces that, for the first time, fans will be allowed to keep balls hit into the stands.

May 14: Cardinals' rookie Rogers Hornsby gets his first major league home run, an inside-the-park hit against the Dodgers.

May 29: The Giants set an all-time record by winning their 17th consecutive road game.

July 1: Honus Wagner, at age 42 years, four months, becomes the oldest player to hit an inside-the-park home run.

August 15: Babe Ruth wins a 13-inning pitching battle with Walter Johnson, 1-0, Jack Barry's third hit of the day sending in the only run.

August 26: Joe Bush of the Athletics pitches a hitless and runless game against Cleveland, with Jack Graney, the first batter, who walked, being the only man to reach base.

September 4: In a sentimental hurling duel that marks the final appearance for both, Christy Mathewson of the Reds outlasts Three-Finger Brown of the Cubs, 10-8.

September 30: The Giants, after winning 26 straight games and creating a new major league record, are beaten by the Braves, 8-3. George Tyler stops the McGrawites and makes Brooklyn the champion of the National League.

October 9: Babe Ruth wins Game 2 of the World Series 2-1 and begins a streak of 29-2/3 scoreless World Series innings.

October 16: Brooklyn owner Charles Ebbets causes a stir by raising the price of World Series tickets from $3 to $5.

November 1: Harry H. Frazee, a New York theater owner, buys the Red Sox for $675,000.

1917

War and bookies spread dark cloud over unusual season

A disconcerting odor hung over the 1917 season, much of it emanating from gamblers clustered around the White Sox and Reds, the same two teams that would figure in the 1919 Black Sox scandal. In the AL, Chicago's every victory seemed to elate bookmakers, its every loss put them in a funk. The worst public incident took place in Boston in June, when gamblers sought to abort a Red Sox victory by charging onto the field with hopes of causing a forfeit against the local team. In September, the Tigers were accused of taking payoffs to drop consecutive doubleheaders to the White Sox. The whispering in the NL was focused around Cincinnati first baseman Hal Chase, who developed a suspicious penchant for wild throws to the pitcher covering the bag.

America's entry into World War I also cast a pall on the season. Over the course of the war, 227 major leaguers joined one of the services. Club owners also faced concerns regarding attendance. Given the sobering temperament of the times, crowds slackened during most of 1917. (Overall, attendance fell by more than 1.25 million from 1916 levels.)

On the field, the White Sox star was right-hander Ed Cicotte, who paced the AL with his 28 wins and 1.53 ERA. Lefty Williams and Red Faber teamed up for another 33 victories, while outfielder Hap Felsch drove in 102 runs. As usual, the Tigers were prominent offensively, with Ty Cobb taking another batting crown (.383) and Bobby Veach another RBI title (103).

The NL season got off to a turgid start when April rains forced the postponement of 48 games. On May 2, Chicago's Hippo Vaughn and Cincinnati's Fred Toney hooked up in a duel for the ages—a double no-hitter through nine innings. Then, on June 23, Red Sox pitcher Babe Ruth walked the leadoff batter, slugged umpire Brick Owen, and was ejected. His replacement, Ernie Shore, watched as the runner was thrown out trying to steal, then retired the next 26 hitters to complete the strangest "perfect game" in major league history.

The Reds finally scratched out two singles in the 10th frame for a victory. The pennant race wasn't all that suspenseful, with the Giants going into first place to stay in June and coming home 10 games in front of the Phillies. The chief contributors to the New York flag were 21-game winner Ferdie Schupp and league RBI leader Heinie Zimmerman (102). Philadelphia's Grover Cleveland Alexander won 30 games for the third year in a row, and also led pitchers with his 1.83 ERA. Cincinnati's Edd Roush had the highest average at .341. It took the better part of two seasons, but on May 26, Cardinals outfielder Walton Cruise hit the first home run out of Braves Field. (The lefty swinger also hit the second one into the right-field seats of the cavernous park—four years later as a

Rogers Hornsby
Hornsby led the NL in triples and slugging percentage at 21 and offered a prelude of six consecutive batting titles to come.

member of the home team.)

Chicago's six-game World Series victory over the Giants left John McGraw a loser in four straight postseason appearances. The difference was Faber, who won three times. The right-hander also added to the sport's legendary boners when, in the second game, he completed what might have been a successful steal of third, except for the fact that teammate Buck Weaver was already standing on the bag.

1917 SEASON HIGHLIGHTS

NATIONAL LEAGUE

	W	L	Pct.	GB
New York	98	56	.636	—
Philadelphia	87	65	.572	10
St. Louis	82	70	.539	15
Cincinnati	78	76	.506	20
Chicago	74	80	.481	24
Boston	72	81	.471	25.5
Brooklyn	70	81	.464	26.5
Pittsburgh	51	103	.331	47

AMERICAN LEAGUE

	W	L	Pct.	GB
Chicago	100	54	.649	—
Boston	90	62	.592	9
Cleveland	88	66	.571	12
Detroit	78	75	.510	21.5
Washington	74	79	.484	25.5
New York	71	82	.464	28.5
St. Louis	57	97	.370	43
Philadelphia	55	98	.359	44.5

NO AWARDS

POSTSEASON
WORLD SERIES
Chicago White Sox 4, New York Giants 2
Oct. 6: CHICAGO 2, New York 1
Oct. 7: CHICAGO 7, New York 2
Oct. 10: NEW YORK 2, Chicago 0
Oct. 11: NEW YORK 5, Chicago 0
Oct. 13: CHICAGO 8, New York 5
Oct. 15: Chicago 4, NEW YORK 2

Home team in CAPS

"I didn't expect to make it all the way to the big leagues, but I just had to get away from them damn cows."
— Edd Roush, son of a dairy farmer

NATIONAL LEAGUE LEADERS

Home Runs
Robertson-NY	12
Cravath-Phi	12
Hornsby-StL	8

Runs Batted In
Zimmerman-NY	102
Chase-Cin	86
Cravath-Phi	83
Stengel-Bro	73
Luderus-Phi	72

Batting Average
Roush-Cin	.341
Hornsby-StL	.327
Kauff-NY	.308
Groh-Cin	.304
Burns-NY	.302

On Base Percentage
Groh-Cin	.385
Hornsby-StL	.385
Burns-NY	.380
Roush-Cin	.379
Kauff-NY	.379

Slugging Average
Hornsby-StL	.484
Cravath-Phi	.473
Roush-Cin	.454
Burns-NY	.412
Groh-Cin	.411

Stolen Bases
Carey-Pit	46
Burns-NY	40
Kauff-NY	30
Maranville-Bos	27
Baird-Pit-StL	26

Wins
Alexander-Phi	30
Toney-Cin	24
Vaughn-Chi	23
Schupp-NY	21
Schneider-Cin	20

Innings Pitched
Alexander-Phi	388.0
Toney-Cin	339.2
Schneider-Cin	333.2
Cooper-Pit	297.2
Vaughn-Chi	295.2

Saves
Sallee-NY	4

Strikeouts
Alexander-Phi	200
Vaughn-Chi	195
Douglas-Chi	151
Schupp-NY	147
Schneider-Cin	138

Earned Run Average
Anderson-NY	1.44
Alexander-Phi	1.83
Perritt-NY	1.88
Schupp-NY	1.95
Vaughn-Chi	2.01

Complete Games
Alexander-Phi	34
Toney-Cin	31
Vaughn-Chi	27
Barnes-Bos	27
Schupp-NY	25

AMERICAN LEAGUE LEADERS

Home Runs
Pipp-NY	9
Veach-Det	8
Bodie-Phi	7

Runs Batted In
Veach-Det	103
Felsch-Chi	102
Cobb-Det	102
Heilmann-Det	86
Jackson-Chi	75

Batting Average
Cobb-Det	.383
Sisler-StL	.353
Speaker-Cle	.352
Veach-Det	.319
Felsch-Chi	.308

On Base Percentage
Cobb-Det	.444
Speaker-Cle	.432
Veach-Det	.393
Sisler-StL	.390
E.Collins-Chi	.389

Slugging Average
Cobb-Det	.570
Speaker-Cle	.486
Veach-Det	.457
Sisler-StL	.453
Jackson-Chi	.429

Stolen Bases
Cobb-Det	55
E.Collins-Chi	53
Chapman-Cle	52
Roth-Cle	51
Sisler-StL	37

Wins
Cicotte-Chi	28
Ruth-Bos	24
Johnson-Was	23
Bagby-Cle	23
Mays-Bos	22

Innings Pitched
Cicotte-Chi	346.2
Ruth-Bos	326.1
Johnson-Was	326.0
Bagby-Cle	320.2
Coveleski-Cle	298.1

Saves
Danforth-Chi	9
Bagby-Cle	7
Boland-Det	6
Coumbe-Cle	5

Strikeouts
Johnson-Was	188
Cicotte-Chi	150
Leonard-Bos	144
Coveleski-Cle	133
Ruth-Bos	128

Earned Run Average
Cicotte-Chi	1.53
Mays-Bos	1.74
Coveleski-Cle	1.81
Faber-Chi	1.92
Russell-Chi	1.95

Complete Games
Ruth-Bos	35
Johnson-Was	30
Cicotte-Chi	29
Mays-Bos	27

THE YEAR IN BASEBALL

April 14: Eddie Cicotte pitches a no-hit, no-run game for the White Sox against St. Louis, passing three men and having one error behind him.

April 14: Ray Bates of the Athletics, batting twice in the seventh inning against Charley Jamieson and Yancey Ayers of Washington, drives in three runs with a triple and two more with a double—five RBIs in one inning.

May 2: In a unique double no-hit game, Fred Toney keeps the Cubs hitless for nine innings and Jim Vaughn does the same thing to the Reds. In the tenth, Vaughn is reached for hits by Larry Kopf and Jim Thorpe and Cincinnati wins, 1-0.

May 5: Ernie Koob of the Browns pitches a hitless game against the White Sox and wins, 1-0 over Eddie Cicotte, who three weeks previously had prevented St. Louis from getting a hit.

May 6: Bob Groom of the St. Louis Browns imitates moundmate Ernie Koob and pitches a no-hit game against the Chicago White Sox—the second day in succession against this team and a major league record.

June 1: With war raging in Europe, Hank Gowdy of the Braves becomes the first major league player to enlist.

June 8: Giants manager John McGraw takes a swing at umpire Bill "Lord" Byron, splitting Byron's lip. McGraw is fined $500 and suspended for 16 days. He is subsequently fined an additional $1,000 for bad-mouthing the penalty.

June 23: Babe Ruth, peeved because umpire Brick Owens called a ball that gave Ray Morgan, the first Washington batter, his base, tries to slug Brick and is put out of the game. Ernie Shore then becomes Boston's pitcher and retires in order the 26 men who face him, plus getting credit for the 27th out when catcher Sam Agnew threw out Morgan trying to steal.

June 28: Lee Magee of the Yankees has four assists from center field in a game with the Athletics.

October 11: Grover Cleveland Alexander is traded to the Cubs with Bill Killefer for Mike Prendergast, Pickles Dillhoefer and $60,000.

October 26: Miller Huggins signs a two-year contract to manage the Yankees.

December 13: Needing cash, the A's Connie Mack sends pitcher Joe Bush, catcher Wally Schang and outfielder Amos Strunk to the Red Sox for three players plus $60,000.

1918

Shutout streak ends but Ruth leads Sox to Series victory

The most important baseball figure in 1918 was Washington owner Clark Griffith, who spent months cultivating his federal government contacts to keep the sport going despite the U.S. entry into World War I. The sport was ultimately ruled a "nonessential" industry, but also allowed to continue through to Labor Day. By then, numerous players had already received draft notices or gone off to war-industry jobs. The fact that so many of the civilian jobs turned out to be fronts for playing with shipyard or factory baseball teams turned the grandstands against the major leaguers, bringing widely heard charges of "slacker" against such stars as Shoeless Joe Jackson. The games played over the abbreviated big-league schedule included Sunday ball in Washington, where relaxation for war workers took precedence over the strictures of Sabbatarians and doomed the cause of the militant religious movement.

On the field, the Cubs went into the season as NL pennant favorites because of their trade for Grover Cleveland Alexander from the Phillies. Chicago did win, and handily, but not because of Alexander, who was drafted. The crucial acquisition turned out to be that of Lefty Tyler from the Braves; the southpaw's 19 wins and 2.00 ERA complemented Hippo Vaughn's league-leading 22 victories and 1.74 ERA and another 19 from Claude Hendrix to make the club's poor hitting academic. Brooklyn's Zack Wheat won the batting title (.335) and Cincinnati's Sherry Magee knocked in the most runs (76). But Magee's effort couldn't prevent the scandal that consumed his team in August, when manager Christy Mathewson announced the suspension of Hal Chase for suspicious play. Chase denied the charges, Mathewson volunteered for the Armed Forces before he had to provide too many particulars personally, and the NL put off a hearing on everything until the following January.

In the AL, the Red Sox, hit hard by the draft, surprised prognosticators by finishing 2-1/2 games ahead of the Indians. As decisive as 21 wins from Carl Mays and Babe Ruth's all-around effort (13 wins, a league-leading 11 homers, a team-leading .300) was the one-week suspension of Cleveland star Tris Speaker at the peak of the pennant race for a blistering argument with an umpire. Ty Cobb took another batting title (.382), fellow Tiger Bobby Veach another RBI crown (78), and Washington's Walter Johnson led the way again in both victories (23) and ERA (1.27).

The World Series came close to being suspended before the fifth game when players from the Red Sox and Cubs ganged up to demand more money. A threatened walkout was averted only when

George Sisler
A speedy first baseman, Sisler not only won two batting titles, but led the AL four times in stolen bases, including 1918, when he stole 45.

an inebriated Ban Johnson persuaded Boston player representative Harry Hooper that the players were hardly going to gain sympathy from fans by striking in the middle of a war. The Red Sox won the Series in six games, with Mays and Ruth both winning twice. In the eighth inning of the fourth game, the Cubs scored a run against Ruth that broke his streak of 29-2/3 innings of shutout ball in the postseason; he would always cite that as his most satisfying diamond achievement. The 1918 Series was the last in which neither team hit a home run, as well as the last won by a team from Massachusetts.

1918 SEASON HIGHLIGHTS

NATIONAL LEAGUE

	W	L	Pct.	GB
Chicago	84	45	.651	—
New York	71	53	.573	10.5
Cincinnati	68	60	.531	15.5
Pittsburgh	65	60	.520	17
Brooklyn	57	69	.452	25.5
Philadelphia	55	68	.447	26
Boston	53	71	.427	28.5
St. Louis	51	78	.395	33

AMERICAN LEAGUE

	W	L	Pct.	GB
Boston	75	51	.595	—
Cleveland	73	54	.575	2.5
Washington	72	56	.563	4
New York	60	63	.488	13.5
St. Louis	58	64	.475	15
Chicago	57	67	.460	17
Detroit	55	71	.437	20
Philadelphia	52	76	.406	24

NO AWARDS

POSTSEASON
WORLD SERIES
Boston Red Sox 4, Chicago Cubs 2

Sep. 5: Boston 1, CHICAGO 0
Sep. 6: CHICAGO 3, Boston 1
Sep. 7: Boston 2, CHICAGO 1
Sep. 9: Boston 3, Chicago 2
Sep. 10: Chicago 3, Boston 0
Sep. 11: BOSTON 2, Chicago 1

Home team in CAPS

"You can't hit what you can't see."

— Walter Johnson on his fastball

NATIONAL LEAGUE LEADERS

Home Runs

Cravath-Phi	8
Williams-Phi	6
Cruise-StL	6

Runs Batted In

S.Magee-Cin	76
Cutshaw-Pit	68
Luderus-Phi	67
R.Smith-Bos	65
Merkle-Chi	65

Batting Average

Z.Wheat-Bro	.335
Roush-Cin	.333
Groh-Cin	.320
Hollocher-Chi	.316
Daubert-Bro	.308

On Base Percentage

Groh-Cin	.395
Hollocher-Chi	.379
R.Smith-Bos	.373
S.Magee-Cin	.370
Z.Wheat-Bro	.369

Slugging Average

Roush-Cin	.455
Daubert-Bro	.429
Hornsby-StL	.416
S.Magee-Cin	.415
Wickland-Bos	.398

Stolen Bases

Carey-Pit	58
Burns-NY	40
Hollocher-Chi	26
Cutshaw-Pit	25
Baird-StL	25

Wins

Vaughn-Chi	22
Hendrix-Chi	20
Tyler-Chi	19
Grimes-Bro	19
Cooper-Pit	19

Innings Pitched

Vaughn-Chi	290.1
Nehf-Bos	284.1
Cooper-Pit	273.1
Grimes-Bro	269.2
Tyler-Chi	269.1

Saves

Toney-Cin-NY	3
Oeschger-Phi	3
Cooper-Pit	3
Anderson-NY	3

Strikeouts

Vaughn-Chi	148
Cooper-Pit	117
Grimes-Bro	113
Tyler-Chi	102
Nehf-Bos	96

Earned Run Average

Vaughn-Chi	1.74
Tyler-Chi	2.00
Cooper-Pit	2.11
Douglas-Chi	2.13
Grimes-Bro	2.14

Complete Games

Nehf-Bos	28
Vaughn-Chi	27
Cooper-Pit	26
Tyler-Chi	22
Hendrix-Chi	21

AMERICAN LEAGUE LEADERS

Home Runs

Walker-Phi	11
Ruth-Bos	11
Burns-Phi	6
Baker-NY	6

Runs Batted In

Veach-Det	78
Burns-Phi	70
Wood-Cle	66
Ruth-Bos	66
T.Cobb-Det	64

Batting Average

T.Cobb-Det	.382
Burns-Phi	.352
Sisler-StL	.341
Speaker-Cle	.318
Baker-NY	.306

On Base Percentage

T.Cobb-Det	.440
E.Collins-Chi	.407
Speaker-Cle	.403
Sisler-StL	.400
Hooper-Bos	.391

Slugging Average

T.Cobb-Det	.515
Burns-Phi	.467
Sisler-StL	.440
Speaker-Cle	.435
Walker-Phi	.423

Stolen Bases

Sisler-StL	45
Roth-Cle	35
T.Cobb-Det	34
Chapman-Cle	30
Speaker-Cle	27

Wins

Johnson-Was	23
Coveleski-Cle	22
Mays-Bos	21
Perry-Phi	20
Bagby-Cle	17

Innings Pitched

Perry-Phi	332.1
Johnson-Was	326.0
Coveleski-Cle	311.0
Mays-Bos	293.1
Bush-Bos	272.2

Saves

Mogridge-NY	7
Bagby-Cle	6
Russell-NY	4
Geary-Phi	4

Strikeouts

Johnson-Was	162
Shaw-Was	129
Bush-Bos	125
Morton-Cle	123
Mays-Bos	114

Earned Run Average

Johnson-Was	1.27
Coveleski-Cle	1.82
Sothoron-StL	1.94
Perry-Phi	1.98
Bush-Bos	2.11

Complete Games

Perry-Phi	30
Mays-Bos	30
Johnson-Was	29
Bush-Bos	26
Coveleski-Cle	25

THE YEAR IN BASEBALL

January 9: Brooklyn trades Casey Stengel to Pittsburgh in a multi-player deal that brings them Burleigh Grimes.

February 23: Barney Dreyfuss of the Rules Committee launches a campaign to ban the spitter. He will succeed in 1920.

April 16: The Pittsburgh Pirates, in their first game of the year, are held to one hit—a double by Casey Stengel in the fourth inning. Pete Schneider pitched for the Reds.

May 14: Sunday baseball is made legal in Washington, D.C.

May 24: The third 19-inning game is played in the American League, Cleveland winning from New York, 3-2 on Joe Wood's second home run.

July 20: Despite concern that the season would shut down because of the war, both leagues vote to continue playing, but cut the season short by ending on September 2.

July 25: Walter Johnson wins over St. Louis, 1-0, in 15 innings, with Allan Sothoron pitching against him.

July 27: After Harry Heitman debuts with the Dodgers by yielding hits to the first four men to face him, he enlists in the Navy and never pitches in the majors again.

August 9: Reds manager Christy Mathewson suspects Hal Chase of accepting bribes to fix games and suspends him for indifferent play.

August 27: Christy Mathewson resigns from the Reds to accept a commision as a captain in the chemical warfare branch of the army.

August 30: Ted Williams is born.

September 5: Because of the war in Europe, the World Series starts a month early and Babe Ruth of the Red Sox outpitches Jim Vaughn of the Cubs to win the opener, 1-0. During the seventh-inning stretch a military band plays "The Star Spangled Banner" to begin a tradition of playing it at every World Series game and, beginning during WWII, at all games.

December 10: National League secretary John Heydler is elected president of the league.

1919

Black Sox scandal gives shocking end to scandalous season

The charade that was the 1919 season began in January with NL president John Heydler tossing out game-throwing charges against Cincinnati's Hal Chase and it ended with Charles Comiskey raising concerns about the honesty of his own team in the World Series

Heydler's decision to clear Chase was an inevitable outcome of merely hearsay testimony, critical contradictions by a key accuser (pitcher Jimmy Ring), enigmatic pronouncements by another witness (Giants manager John McGraw), and the continued absence in Europe by the chief finger-pointer, former Reds manager Christy Mathewson. Making the proceedings all the more wondrous was that McGraw had barely finished contributing to Chase's acquittal when he obtained the first baseman in a trade with Cincinnati. A few days after that, Mathewson returned to the U.S. from military duty to take a job as a Giants coach.

The regular NL season turned out to be about the same two teams, with only the Giants entertaining (brief) hopes of braking a Cincinnati runaway. Edd Roush won his second batting title for the Reds (.321) in support of Slim Sallee (21 wins), Hod Eller (20) and Dutch Ruether (19). New York remained in it as long as it did mainly thanks to Jesse Barnes's emergence as the staff (and league) leader with 25 wins. Back from the Army for the Cubs, Grover Cleveland Alexander paced hurlers with his 1.72 ERA.

In the AL, the White Sox tussled most of the year with the Indians. As in 1918, Cleveland fell short because of its star Tris Speaker, this time because the outfielder lost his focus at bat after being forced to take over the club as manager during the season. Belying its former Hitless Wonders tag, Chicago led the league in batting (.287), with Joe Jackson most prominent with his .351 and 96 RBIs. On the mound, Ed Cicotte and Lefty Williams combined for 52 wins. Detroit's Ty Cobb won yet another batting title (.384) and Washington's Walter Johnson yet another ERA crown (1.49). The loudest numbers of all, though, came from Babe Ruth in Boston, with his AL-leading 29 homers and 114 RBIs.

In sheer boxscore terms, Cincinnati won the World Series five games to three (in the first of three straight best-of-nine postseason duels). The mound star was Eller, with two complete-game victories and 15 strikeouts in 18 innings. The Reds offense was led by its outfield: Greasy Neale, who had 10 hits and a .357 average; Pat Duncan, who drove in eight runs; and Roush, who made the most of a mere six hits by scoring six runs and driving in seven. But suspicions that something was amiss arose immediately with the first game, when Cincinnati pounded Cicotte 9-1. As bad as Cicotte was in the opener, Williams was worse, losing all three of his deci-

Joe Jackson
A marvelous hitter and smooth fielder, Jackson was expelled from baseball for his role in the Black Sox scandal at the 1919 World Series.

sions. Chicago had been a heavy favorite but after losing the series under suspicious circumstances rumors of a fix ran rampant.

When White Sox owner Charles Comiskey voiced doubts about the honesty of his team's play, both NL president Heydler and his AL counterpart Ban Johnson mocked him as a sore loser. But the following September Cicotte and Williams were implicated in a fix, along with Jackson, first baseman Chick Gandil, shortstop Swede Risberg, third baseman Buck Weaver, outfielder Hap Felsch, and pinch-hitter Fred McMullin. Cicotte and Jackson would admit to accepting bribes of $10,000 and $5,000 respectively. It also emerged that Cincinnati players, including pitchers Eller and Sallee, were also approached by gamblers during the Series.

1919 SEASON HIGHLIGHTS

NATIONAL LEAGUE

	W	L	Pct.	GB
Cincinnati	96	44	.686	—
New York	87	53	.621	9
Chicago	75	65	.536	21
Pittsburgh	71	68	.511	24.5
Brooklyn	69	71	.493	27
Boston	57	82	.410	38.5
St. Louis	54	83	.394	40.5
Philadelphia	47	90	.343	47.5

AMERICAN LEAGUE

	W	L	Pct.	GB
Chicago	88	52	.629	—
Cleveland	84	55	.604	3.5
New York	80	59	.576	7.5
Detroit	80	60	.571	8
St. Louis	67	72	.482	20.5
Boston	66	71	.482	20.5
Washington	56	84	.400	32
Philadelphia	36	104	.257	52

NO AWARDS

POSTSEASON
WORLD SERIES
Cincinnati Reds 5, Chicago White Sox 3
Oct. 1: CINCINNATI 9, Chicago 1
Oct. 2: CINCINNATI 4, Chicago 2
Oct. 3: CHICAGO 3, Cincinnati 0
Oct. 4: Cincinnati 2, CHICAGO 0
Oct. 6: Cincinnati 5, CHICAGO 0
Oct. 7: Chicago 5, CINCINNATI 4
Oct. 8: Chicago 4, CINCINNATI 1
Oct. 9: Cincinnati 10, CHICAGO 5

Home team in CAPS

"The man who thinks he is keeping his mistakes under wraps will never advance a single step until he sees the light."

— John McGraw

NATIONAL LEAGUE LEADERS

Home Runs
Cravath-Phi	12
Kauff-NY	10
Williams-Phi	9
Hornsby-StL	8
Doyle-NY	7

Runs Batted In
Myers-Bro	73
Roush-Cin	71
Hornsby-StL	71
Kauff-NY	67
Groh-Cin	63

Batting Average
Roush-Cin	.321
Hornsby-StL	.318
Youngs-NY	.311
Groh-Cin	.310
Stock-StL	.307

On Base Percentage
Burns-NY	.396
Groh-Cin	.392
Hornsby-StL	.384
Youngs-NY	.384
Roush-Cin	.380

Slugging Average
Myers-Bro	.436
Groh-Cin	.431
Roush-Cin	.431
Hornsby-StL	.430
Kauff-NY	.422

Stolen Bases
Burns-NY	40
Cutshaw-Pit	36
Bigbee-Pit	31
Smith-StL	30

Wins
J.Barnes-NY	25
Vaughn-Chi	21
Sallee-Cin	21

Innings Pitched
Vaughn-Chi	306.2
J.Barnes-NY	295.2
Cooper-Pit	286.2
Rudolph-Bos	273.2
Nehf-Bos-NY	270.2

Saves
Tuero-StL	4

Strikeouts
Vaughn-Chi	141
Eller-Cin	137
Alexander-Chi	121
Meadows-StL-Phi	116
Cooper-Pit	106

Earned Run Average
Alexander-Chi	1.72
Vaughn-Chi	1.79
Ruether-Cin	1.82
Toney-NY	1.84
Adams-Pit	1.98

Complete Games
Cooper-Pit	27
Pfeffer-Bro	26
Vaughn-Chi	25
Rudolph-Bos	24

AMERICAN LEAGUE LEADERS

Home Runs
Ruth-Bos	29
T.Walker-Phi	10
Sisler-StL	10
Baker-NY	10
Smith-Cle	9

Runs Batted In
Ruth-Bos	114
Veach-Det	101
Jackson-Chi	96
Heilmann-Det	93
Lewis-NY	89

Batting Average
Cobb-Det	.384
Veach-Det	.355
Sisler-StL	.352
Jackson-Chi	.351
Tobin-StL	.327

On Base Percentage
Ruth-Bos	.456
Cobb-Det	.429
Jackson-Chi	.422
Leibold-Chi	.404
E.Collins-Chi	.400

Slugging Average
Ruth-Bos	.657
Sisler-StL	.530
Veach-Det	.519
Cobb-Det	.515
Jackson-Chi	.506

Stolen Bases
E.Collins-Chi	33
Sisler-StL	28
Cobb-Det	28
Rice-Was	26

Wins
Cicotte-Chi	29
Coveleski-Cle	24
Williams-Chi	23
Dauss-Det	21

Innings Pitched
Shaw-Was	306.2
Cicotte-Chi	306.2
Williams-Chi	297.0
Johnson-Was	290.1
Coveleski-Cle	286.0

Saves
Russell-NY-Bos	5
Shawkey-NY	5
Shaw-Was	5
Coveleski-Cle	4

Strikeouts
Johnson-Was	147
Shaw-Was	128
Williams-Chi	125
Shawkey-NY	122
Coveleski-Cle	118

Earned Run Average
Johnson-Was	1.49
Cicotte-Chi	1.82
Weilman-StL	2.07
Mays-Bos-NY	2.10
Sothoron-StL	2.20

Complete Games
Cicotte-Chi	30
Williams-Chi	27
Johnson-Was	27
Mays-Bos-NY	26
Coveleski-Cle	24

THE YEAR IN BASEBALL

January 14: Charles Hempstead sells the New York Giants to Charles Stoneham, John McGraw and Francis X. McQuade; the Stonehams controlled the Giants for the next 56 years.

January 30: The Reds hire Pat Moran as manager when it appears Christy Mathewson will not return from the war in time for the season.

January 31: Jackie Robinson is born.

February 5: Charges that Hal Chase fixed games are dismissed by NL president John Heydler, who rules Chase's so-called "indifferent" play was just carelessness.

March 1: Connie Mack makes one of the poorest trades of his career when he sends Larry Gardner, Charlie Jamieson and Elmer Myers to Cleveland for Robert "Braggo" Roth.

April 23: For the fifth time, Walter Johnson starts the season by pitching a shutout. He wins over Scott Perry of the Athletics in 13 innings, 1-0.

May 4: The Giants play their first legal Sunday game before 35,000 fans.

June 8: The Phillies run wild on the Giants, setting a record for most stolen bases in one inning, the ninth, as four runners reach first base, and each steals second and third.

June 23: Red Sox first baseman Stuffy McInnis makes his first fielding error after 526 chances.

August 14: White Sox outfielder Oscar Felsch ties the major league record with four outfield assists in one game.

September 27: Babe Ruth hits his record setting 29th and final home run of the season, having hit one or more at every American League park.

October 1: On the eve of the World Series, the highly favored White Sox become betting underdogs, but it will take another year before the Black Sox scandal is publicly unearthed, leading to eight players receiving life bans.

December 26: Although it will not be announced until the new year, the Yankees buy Babe Ruth from the Red Sox, paying financially strapped Boston owner Harry Frazee $100,000 and guaranteeing a $300,000 loan.

1920

Dirty players banned; Ray Chapman killed as Red Sox sell Ruth

What 1918 and 1919 had wrought, 1920 publicized, to the point that games often seemed like an afterthought. Admissions by former Cincinnati second baseman Lee Magee that he and Hal Chase had connived to fix games during the 1918 season persuaded the first baseman to retire from the major leagues. Numerous other players, including three-time 20-game winner Claude Hendrix, found themselves playing their final innings before being barred by owners for involvement with gamblers. The Black Sox names came out during the final stretch of the season, prompting the immediate suspension of the suspects. After years of bridling under Ban Johnson's dicta, the Yankees, Red Sox and White Sox put their various resentments in one pot with the NL in a scheme that would have gutted the AL and left just one super-circuit; the plot turned out to be the first step toward neutralizing Johnson's power through the dismantling of the National Commission and the appointment of Kenesaw Mountain Landis as the first commissioner. And even all that wasn't the half of it.

On January 3, Boston officially announced its December 1919 sale of Babe Ruth to the Yankees for $125,000 and a $300,000 loan (with Fenway Park as collateral). Before the calendar year was out, Red Sox owner Harry Frazee would also ship another future Hall of Famer, hurler Waite Hoyt, to the Bronx. On August 16, another pitcher dispatched by Boston to New York the previous year, five-time 20-game winner Carl Mays, beaned Cleveland shortstop Ray Chapman, killing him. Baseball's only such fatality produced an avalanche of threats from Indians fans against Mays, necessitating extra security when the teams met again.

Between the white lines, the pre-suspension White Sox appeared on the verge of a second straight pennant before losing critical games down the stretch to the Indians. At least one of the Black Sox scandal witnesses, one-time outfielder Bill Maharg, charged that the defeats were deliberate dumps. Despite finishing second to Cleveland, Chicago delivered the game's first quartet of 20-game winners—the indicted Ed Cicotte and Lefty Williams and the unindicted Dickie Kerr and Red Faber. Cleveland's path to the pennant was smoothed by the league's biggest winner Jim Bagby (31), while New York's Bob Shawkey posted the lowest ERA at 2.45. The batting crown went to St. Louis' George Sisler (.407). Ruth not only drove in a league-best 137 runs, but his 54 home runs were more than every *team* except his own and the Phillies.

The Dodgers earned the NL flag mainly on the hitting of outfielders Zack Wheat and Hy Myers and 23 wins from Burleigh Grimes. But it was another Dodger right-hander, Leon Cadore, who appeared in the season's most memorable game on May 1,

Hal Chase
Long associated with gamblers and game-fixing, Chase was finally forced out of the game in the wake of the Black Sox scandal.

when he hooked up with Boston's Joe Oeschger in the longest contest in baseball history, a 26-inning 1-1 tie. Both pitchers went the distance. Rogers Hornsby of the Cardinals won the batting title (.370), Grover Cleveland Alexander of the Cubs had the most wins (27) and lowest ERA (1.91).

Cleveland took the best-of-nine World Series in seven games, with Stan Coveleski hurling three complete-game wins. The Indians also supplied three firsts for postseason competition—a home run by a pitcher (Bagby), a grand-slam homer (Elmer Smith) and an unassisted triple play (Bill Wambsganss).

1920 SEASON HIGHLIGHTS

NATIONAL LEAGUE

	W	L	Pct.	GB
Brooklyn	93	61	.604	—
New York	86	68	.558	7
Cincinnati	82	71	.536	10.5
Pittsburgh	79	75	.513	14
St. Louis	75	79	.487	18
Chicago	75	79	.487	18
Boston	62	90	.408	30
Philadelphia	62	91	.405	30.5

AMERICAN LEAGUE

	W	L	Pct.	GB
Cleveland	98	56	.636	—
Chicago	96	58	.623	2
New York	95	59	.617	3
St. Louis	76	77	.497	21.5
Boston	72	81	.471	25.5
Washington	68	84	.447	29
Detroit	61	93	.396	37
Philadelphia	48	106	.312	50

NO AWARDS

POSTSEASON
WORLD SERIES
Cleveland Indians 5, Brooklyn Dodgers 2
Oct. 5: Cleveland 3, BROOKLYN 1
Oct. 6: BROOKLYN 3, Cleveland 0
Oct. 7: BROOKLYN 2, Cleveland 1
Oct. 9: CLEVELAND 5, Brooklyn 1
Oct. 10: CLEVELAND 8, Brooklyn 1
Oct. 11: CLEVELAND 1, Brooklyn 0
Oct. 12: CLEVELAND 3, Brooklyn 0

Home team in CAPS

"Say it ain't so, Joe."
— A young boy after Jackson confessed to
participating in the 1919 World Series fix

NATIONAL LEAGUE LEADERS

Home Runs
Williams-Phi	15
Meusel-Phi	14
Kelly-NY	11
Robertson-Chi	10
McHenry-StL	10

Runs Batted In
Kelly-NY	94
Hornsby-StL	94
Roush-Cin	90
Duncan-Cin	83
Myers-Bro	80

Batting Average
Hornsby-StL	.370
Youngs-NY	.351
Roush-Cin	.339
Wheat-Bro	.328
Williams-Phi	.325

On Base Percentage
Hornsby-StL	.431
Youngs-NY	.427
Roush-Cin	.386
Wheat-Bro	.385
Groh-Cin	.375

Slugging Average
Hornsby-StL	.559
Williams-Phi	.497
Youngs-NY	.477
Meusel-Phi	.473
Wheat-Bro	.463

Stolen Bases
Carey-Pit	52
Roush-Cin	36
Frisch-NY	34
Bigbee-Pit	31
Neale-Cin	29

Wins
Alexander-Chi	27
Cooper-Pit	24
Grimes-Bro	23
Toney-NY	21
Nehf-NY	21

Innings Pitched
Alexander-Chi	363.1
Cooper-Pit	327.0
Grimes-Bro	303.2
Haines-StL	301.2
Vaughn-Chi	301.0

Saves
Sherdel-StL	6
McQuillan-Bos	5
Alexander-Chi	5
Hubbell-NY-Phi	4
Mamaux-Bro	4

Strikeouts
Alexander-Chi	173
Vaughn-Chi	131
Grimes-Bro	131
Haines-StL	120
Schupp-StL	119

Earned Run Average
Alexander-Chi	1.91
Adams-Pit	2.16
Grimes-Bro	2.22
Cooper-Pit	2.39
Ruether-Cin	2.47

Complete Games
Alexander-Chi	33
Cooper-Pit	28
Rixey-Phi	25
Grimes-Bro	25
Vaughn-Chi	24

AMERICAN LEAGUE LEADERS

Home Runs
Ruth-NY	54
Sisler-StL	19
T.Walker-Phi	17
Felsch-Chi	14

Runs Batted In
Ruth-NY	137
Sisler-StL	122
Jacobson-StL	122
Jackson-Chi	121
Gardner-Cle	118

Batting Average
Sisler-StL	.407
Speaker-Cle	.388
Jackson-Chi	.382
Ruth-NY	.376
E.Collins-Chi	.372

On Base Percentage
Ruth-NY	.530
Speaker-Cle	.483
Sisler-StL	.449
Jackson-Chi	.444
E.Collins-Chi	.438

Slugging Average
Ruth-NY	.847
Sisler-StL	.632
Jackson-Chi	.589
Speaker-Cle	.562
Felsch-Chi	.540

Stolen Bases
Rice-Was	63
Sisler-StL	42
Roth-Was	24
Menosky-Bos	23
Tobin-StL	21

Wins
Bagby-Cle	31
Mays-NY	26
Coveleski-Cle	24
Faber-Chi	23
Williams-Chi	22

Innings Pitched
Bagby-Cle	339.2
Faber-Chi	319.0
Coveleski-Cle	315.0
Mays-NY	312.0
Cicotte-Chi	303.1

Saves
Shocker-StL	5
Kerr-Chi	5
Burwell-StL	4

Strikeouts
Coveleski-Cle	133
Williams-Chi	128
Shawkey-NY	126
Faber-Chi	108
Shocker-StL	107

Earned Run Average
Shawkey-NY	2.45
Coveleski-Cle	2.49
Shocker-StL	2.71
Rommel-Phi	2.85
Bagby-Cle	2.89

Complete Games
Bagby-Cle	30
Faber-Chi	28
Cicotte-Chi	28
Mays-NY	26
Coveleski-Cle	26

THE YEAR IN BASEBALL

January 5: The Yankees announce they have bought Babe Ruth from the Red Sox after a season in which he hit a record 29 homers.

January 6: Early Wynn is born; he pitched 23 seasons, more than any American Leaguer, and won the Cy Young Award at age 39, going 22-10 for the 1959 White Sox.

April 14: Babe Ruth plays his first game with the Yankees. He gets two singles off Scott Perry of the Athletics and muffs a fly in the eighth that gave the Mackmen two runs and the decision, 3-1.

April 20: Manager Gavvy Cravath of the Phils inserts himself as a pinch hitter and beats New York with a three-run homer, his last in the majors.

May 1: Brooklyn Superbas (today's Dodgers) and Boston Braves, playing in Boston, go 26 innings before quitting with the score tied, 1-1. Leon Cadore and Joe Oeschger go the full distance for contesting teams. Also on this day, Babe Ruth made his first home run as a Yankee, hitting it off Herb Pennock of Boston.

May 3: The Superbas become the undisputed long-distance champions of the world by figuring in their third extra-inning game in three successive days. This time they lose to Boston in 19 innings, bringing their three-day total to 58. In each game Brooklyn used only one pitcher and so did the opposition, Leon Cadore and Joe Oeschger being paired in the first, Burleigh Grimes and George Smith in the second and Sherrod Smith and Dana Fillingim in the third.

May 29: John Lavan of the Cardinals "pulls a John Anderson" in the game with Chicago, stealing third with Jacques Fournier there. Because of this mental lapse the Cubs win, 8-5.

July 1: Walter Johnson pitches a no-hit game against Boston, with a Bucky Harris fumble on Harry Hooper in the seventh being the only thing that stood between Johnson and a perfect game.

July 19: For the fifth time during the year, Babe Ruth hits two home runs in a game. Dickie Kerr of the White Sox yields both, one in the fourth and one in the ninth.

August 17: Ray Chapman, Cleveland shortstop, becomes the lone casualty in major league history, dying from an accidental beaning by Carl Mays the previous day.

September 22: Bob Lemon is born; after coming to the Indians as a third baseman in 1941, he found his true vocation on the mound, winning 20 games seven times.

September 28: George Sisler equals and breaks the American League record of hits for a season (made by Ty Cobb in 1911) in a game with the Indians, getting his 248th, a homer, and 249th, a triple.

November 12: Judge Kenesaw Mountain Landis is named to the newly created position of Commissioner of Baseball.

November 15: Waite Hoyt and Wally Schang are traded to the Yankees by Boston's Harry Frazee, the man who sold the Yanks Babe Ruth.

November 21: Stan Musial is born; he played 22 years and retired as the major league leader in total bases.

1921

Landis takes control as Ruth swats 59 to save game's image

The 1921 campaign saw postseason play become an intramural New York affair. More than from the same city, the Giants and Yankees dominated their leagues from within the same stadium, the Polo Grounds of Upper Manhattan. Chicago played under the shadow of Commissioner Kenesaw Landis' decision to ban eight White Sox players (along with St. Louis Browns infielder Joe Gedeon) for their roles in the 1919 World Series fix. Ignoring the August acquittal of the players by a Cook County jury, Landis decreed that "no player who throws a ballgame, no player that undertakes to throw a ballgame, no player that sits in conference with a bunch of crooked players and gamblers where the ways and means of throwing a ballgame are discussed and does not promptly tell his club about it, will ever play baseball."

In the NL, St. Louis' Rogers Hornsby won the second of six consecutive batting titles (.387), inheriting Honus Wagner's mantle as the league's star of stars. The second baseman was also tops in RBIs, with 126. Bill Doak of the Cardinals (2.59 ERA) and Burleigh Grimes of the Dodgers (22 wins) were the leading pitchers. The pennant race was largely a two-team duel between the Giants and Pirates. The difference was New York's hitting, with five regulars batting .300. First baseman George Kelly paced the league with his 23 homers, while infielder Frankie Frisch averaged .341 and stole a league-best 49 bases. In addition to Kelly and Frisch, the lineup included two other future Hall of Famers—shortstop Dave Bancroft and outfielder Ross Youngs.

The AL was mostly Babe Ruth and the Yankees. The right fielder's 59 homers, 171 RBIs, .378 batting average, and .846 slugging percentage devastated pitchers, overwhelming even teammate Bob Meusel's 24 homers and 135 RBIs. The only player taking a nick out of

Frankie Frisch
The Fordham Flash, pictured here as a member of the Cardinals, helped take the Giants to the NL pennant with a league leading 49 stolen bases.

his season was Detroit's Harry Heilmann, who won the batting crown at .394, denying Ruth the Triple Crown (something he would never achieve). Carl Mays of the Yankees and Urban Shocker of the Browns tied for the most victories at 27, while Chicago's Red Faber was the stingiest mound presence with his 2.48 ERA.

The World Series, the last played to a best-of-nine format, drew 270,000 for a Giants triumph in eight games. Chest-thumping was as prevalent on the field as among fans of the two teams in the stands. After infielder Mike McNally stole home against the Giants

in the opener, Meusel not only did the same in the second game, but shouted to Yankees pitcher Waite Hoyt that he was about to do so as he took a lead off third base. As far as Miller Huggins was concerned, however, Mays didn't enter into the spirit of the competition, to the point that the Yankee manager suspected the staff ace of throwing both the fourth and seventh games. Although no evidence was ever found against Mays, Huggins would renew the charges during the 1922 World Series. For their part, the Giants preferred to attribute the championship to Meusel's seven RBIs and two victories apiece by Jesse Barnes and Phil Douglas.

1921 SEASON HIGHLIGHTS

NATIONAL LEAGUE

	W	L	Pct.	GB
New York	94	59	.614	—
Pittsburgh	90	63	.588	4
St. Louis	87	66	.569	7
Boston	79	74	.516	15
Brooklyn	77	75	.507	16.5
Cincinnati	70	83	.458	24
Chicago	64	89	.418	30
Philadelphia	51	103	.331	43.5

AMERICAN LEAGUE

	W	L	Pct.	GB
New York	98	55	.641	—
Cleveland	94	60	.610	4.5
St. Louis	81	73	.526	17.5
Washington	80	73	.523	18
Boston	75	79	.487	23.5
Detroit	71	82	.464	27
Chicago	62	92	.403	36.5
Philadelphia	53	100	.346	45

NO AWARDS

POSTSEASON
WORLD SERIES
New York Giants 5, New York Yankees 3
- Oct. 5: Yankees 3, GIANTS 0
- Oct. 6: YANKEES 3, Giants 0
- Oct. 7: GIANTS 13, Yankees 5
- Oct. 9: Giants 4, YANKEES 2
- Oct. 10: Yankees 3, GIANTS 1
- Oct. 11: Giants 8, YANKEES 5
- Oct. 12: GIANTS 2, Yankees 1
- Oct. 13: Giants 1, YANKEES 0

Home team in CAPS

> "Regardless of the verdict of juries, no player that throws a ballgame will ever play professional baseball."
>
> — Commissioner Kenesaw Mountain Landis

NATIONAL LEAGUE LEADERS

Home Runs
Kelly-NY	23
Hornsby-StL	21
Williams-Phi	18
McHenry-StL	17
Fournier-StL	16

Runs Batted In
Hornsby-StL	126
Kelly-NY	122
Youngs-NY	102
McHenry-StL	102
Frisch-NY	100

Batting Average
Hornsby-StL	.397
McHenry-StL	.350
Fournier-StL	.343
Meusel-Phi-NY	.343
Frisch-NY	.341

On Base Percentage
Hornsby-StL	.458
Youngs-NY	.411
Fournier-StL	.409
Grimes-Chi	.406
Carey-Pit	.395

Slugging Average
Hornsby-StL	.639
McHenry-StL	.531
Kelly-NY	.528
Meusel-Phi-NY	.515
Fournier-StL	.505

Stolen Bases
Frisch-NY	49
Carey-Pit	37
Johnston-Bro	28
Bohne-Cin	26
Maranville-Pit	25

Wins
Grimes-Bro	22
Cooper-Pit	22
Oeschger-Bos	20
Nehf-NY	20
Rixey-Cin	19

Innings Pitched
Cooper-Pit	327
Luque-Cin	304
Grimes-Bro	302.1
Rixey-Cin	301
Oeschger-Bos	299

Saves
North-StL	7
Barnes-NY	6
McQuillan-Bos	5

Strikeouts
Grimes-Bro	136
Cooper-Pit	134
Luque-Cin	102
McQuillan-Bos	94

Earned Run Average
Doak-StL	2.59
Adams-Pit	2.64
Glazner-Pit	2.77
Rixey-Cin	2.78
Grimes-Bro	2.83

Complete Games
Grimes-Bro	30
Cooper-Pit	29
Luque-Cin	25

AMERICAN LEAGUE LEADERS

Home Runs
Ruth-NY	59
Williams-StL	24
Meusel-NY	24
T.Walker-Phi	23
Heilmann-Det	19

Runs Batted In
Ruth-NY	171
Heilmann-Det	139
Meusel-NY	135
Veach-Det	128
Gardner-Cle	120

Batting Average
Heilmann-Det	.394
Cobb-Det	.389
Ruth-NY	.378
Sisler-StL	.371
Speaker-Cle	.362

On Base Percentage
Ruth-NY	.512
Cobb-Det	.452
Heilmann-Det	.444
Speaker-Cle	.439
Williams-StL	.429

Slugging Average
Ruth-NY	.846
Heilmann-Det	.606
Cobb-Det	.596
Williams-StL	.561
Sisler-StL	.560

Stolen Bases
Sisler-StL	35
Harris-Was	29
Rice-Was	25
Johnson-Chi	22
Cobb-Det	22

Wins
Shocker-StL	27
Mays-NY	27
Faber-Chi	25
Jones-Bos	23
Coveleski-Cle	23

Innings Pitched
Mays-NY	336.2
Faber-Chi	330.2
Shocker-StL	326.2
Coveleski-Cle	315.0
Kerr-Chi	308.2

Saves
Middleton-Det	7
Mays-NY	7

Strikeouts
Johnson-Was	143
Shocker-StL	132
Shawkey-NY	126
Faber-Chi	124
Leonard-Det	120

Earned Run Average
Faber-Chi	2.48
Mogridge-Was	3.00
Mays-NY	3.05
Hoyt-NY	3.09
Jones-Bos	3.22

Complete Games
Faber-Chi	32
Shocker-StL	30
Mays-NY	30
Coveleski-Cle	28

THE YEAR IN BASEBALL

January 21: Judge Kenesaw Mountain Landis officially takes over as baseball's commissioner.

February 5: The Yankees buy a 20-acre plot of land in the Bronx which will become the site of the new Yankee Stadium.

March 4: Boston's long-time right fielder Harry Hooper switches the color of his sox from red to white as he is traded for Shano Collins and Nemo Leibold.

April 23: Warren Spahn is born.

May 20: Hal Newhouser born; he led the AL in wins in 1944-46 with 29, 25, and 26

June 6: The Detroit Stars' Bill Gatewood pitches the first no-hitter in Negro League history, defeating the Cuban Stars 4-0.

June 13: Umpires in both leagues begin the practice of rubbing mud into the balls before each game using a special clay from a New Jersey farm.

July 12: Babe Ruth becomes the all-time home run leader when he passes Roger Connor.

August 2: A jury brings in a verdict of not guilty against eight Chicago "Black" Sox, but commissioner Kenesaw Landis bans all eight from baseball for life.

August 5: The first radio broadcast of a major league game, the Pirates vs the Phillies, is heard over KDKA in Pittsburgh.

August 19: At age 34, Ty Cobb becomes the youngest player ever to reach the 3,000-hit plateau.

September 5: Walter Johnson gets strikeout No. 2,287 to break Cy Young's career record.

September 30: Rogers Hornsby's consecutive hitting streak is stopped at 33 games.

October 1: Babe Ruth makes a rare pitching appearance, blowing a 6-0 Yankee lead before his Yankees beat the A's 7-6.

October 4: It is announced that, for the first time, every game of the World Series will be broadcast on the radio.

October 16: Babe Ruth, Bob Meusel and Bill Piercy defy commissioner Kenesaw Landis and embark on a postseason barnstorming tour, prompting fines of $3,326.26 and suspensions until May 20, 1922.

November 19: Roy Campanella is born; a superb receiver and power hitter, he was MVP in 1951, 1953, and 1955.

1922

New rules, live ball make home run totals take dramatic rise

Babe Ruth missed the first month of the season serving out a suspension levied by Commissioner Landis, but his spirit permeated the 1,055 home runs clouted by the two leagues. Only two years after a mere 16 batters had reached double figures in round-trippers, the intervening outlawing of the spitball and introduction of a livelier (and cleaner) ball all but doubled that number to 31. The biggest clouters were Ken Williams in the AL and Rogers Hornsby in the NL. The Browns outfielder Williams not only led the circuit with his 39 homers and 155 RBIs, but his 37 steals also made him baseball's first 30-30 player—a feat not duplicated until 1956. As for Hornsby, his 42 blasts went with 152 RBIs and a .401 average—good for the first of his two Triple Crowns.

Ruth drew his suspension for violating a Landis rule prohibiting World Series participants from barnstorming after the season. It turned out to be the first of four suspensions he served during the year, the others meted out for on-field brawls and arguments. Mainly because of his absences, the Browns stayed even with New York until a violence-marred September series set back St. Louis. Ruth ended up leading the team anyway with his 35 homers and 99 RBIs, while Joe Bush (26), Bob Shawkey (20) and Waite Hoyt (19) paced the pitching. In addition to Williams, the Browns received major production from first baseman George Sisler, who won the batting crown with a .420 mark. Philadelphia's Eddie Rommel overcame a seventh-place club to register the most wins (27) and Chicago's Red Faber had the lowest ERA at 2.81.

Ruth's absences from the lineup had another consequence when the Yankees sought to make up for them in late July by purchasing third baseman Joe Dugan and outfielder Elmer Smith from the Red Sox for $40,000. The outcry from the Browns and White Sox that New York was buying its pennants forced a new rule imposing a June 15 trading deadline.

In the NL, the Giants offense was again the story. With the exception of third baseman Heinie Groh, every regular batted at least .320. Although the team didn't have a 20-game winner, it placed first and second in the ERA department, with Phil Douglas (2.63) and Rosy Ryan (3.01). But Douglas also had his problems. After being criticized by manager John McGraw in late August, the right-hander got drunk and wrote an incriminating letter suggesting he was open to throwing games to get back at the pilot. The letter ultimately cost Douglas his career.

On the field, the NL's biggest winner was Eppa Rixey of Cincinnati, with 25 victories. But St. Louis general manager Branch Rickey had even more to crow about with the arrival of first

Ken Williams
The Browns star outfielder became baseball's first 30-30 player when he led the AL in 1922 with 39 home runs and added 37 steals.

baseman Jim Bottomley. He played only a handful of games for the Cardinals, but Bottomley was the first product of the farm system established by Rickey and St. Louis owner Sam Breadon to gain a spot on the big-league roster.

The Giants made short work of the Yankees in the World Series, but not as short as Landis would have liked. When the second game ended in an extra-inning tie, reports circulated that the teams had played to the draw to recover some of the money lost by reducing to the Series to a best-of-seven. Landis ended the controversy by giving that day's gate to charity, then watched the Giants sweep.

1922 SEASON HIGHLIGHTS

NATIONAL LEAGUE

	W	L	Pct.	GB
New York	93	61	.604	—
Cincinnati	86	68	.558	7
St. Louis	85	69	.552	8
Pittsburgh	85	69	.552	8
Chicago	80	74	.519	13
Brooklyn	76	78	.494	17
Philadelphia	57	96	.373	35.5
Boston	53	100	.346	39.5

AMERICAN LEAGUE

	W	L	Pct.	GB
New York	94	60	.610	—
St. Louis	93	61	.604	1
Detroit	79	75	.513	15
Cleveland	78	76	.506	16
Chicago	77	77	.500	17
Washington	69	85	.448	25
Philadelphia	65	89	.422	29
Boston	61	93	.396	33

AWARDS
AL MVP: George Sisler, STL

POSTSEASON
WORLD SERIES
New York Giants 4, New York Yankees 0, 1 tie
Oct. 4: GIANTS 3, Yankees 2
Oct. 5: Giants 3, YANKEES 3
Oct. 6: GIANTS 3, Yankees 0
Oct. 7: Giants 4, YANKEES 3
Oct. 8: GIANTS 5, Yankees 3

Home team in CAPS

> "George (Sisler) was a great first baseman and a great hitter, but he was too quiet and clean-living to win headlines."
>
> — Eddie Collins

NATIONAL LEAGUE LEADERS

Home Runs
Hornsby-StL	42
Williams-Phi	26
Lee-Phi	17
Kelly-NY	17

Runs Batted In
Hornsby-StL	152
Meusel-NY	132
Wheat-Bro	112
Kelly-NY	107

Batting Average
Hornsby-StL	.401
Grimes-Chi	.354
Miller-Chi	.352
Bigbee-Pit	.350
Tierney-Pit	.345

On Base Percentage
Hornsby-StL	.459
Grimes-Chi	.442
O'Farrell-Chi	.439
Carey-Pit	.408
Bigbee-Pit	.405

Slugging Average
Hornsby-StL	.722
Grimes-Chi	.572
Tierney-Pit	.515
Williams-Phi	.514
Miller-Chi	.511

Stolen Bases
Carey-Pit	51
Frisch-NY	31
Burns-Cin	30
Maranville-Pit	24
Bigbee-Pit	24

Wins
Rixey-Cin	25
Cooper-Pit	23
Ruether-Bro	21
Pfeffer-StL	19
Nehf-NY	19

Innings Pitched
Rixey-Cin	313.1
Cooper-Pit	294.2
Morrison-Pit	286.1
Nehf-NY	268.1
Ruether-Bro	267.1

Saves
Jonnard-NY	5
North-StL	4

Strikeouts
Vance-Bro	134
Cooper-Pit	129
Ring-Phi	116
Morrison-Pit	104
Grimes-Bro	99

Earned Run Average
Douglas-NY	2.63
Ryan-NY	3.01
Donohue-Cin	3.12
Cooper-Pit	3.18
Nehf-NY	3.29

Complete Games
Cooper-Pit	27
Ruether-Bro	26
Rixey-Cin	26

AMERICAN LEAGUE LEADERS

Home Runs
Williams-StL	39
Walker-Phi	37
Ruth-NY	35
Miller-Phi	21
Heilmann-Det	21

Runs Batted In
Williams-StL	155
Veach-Det	126
McManus-StL	109
Sisler-StL	105
Jacobson-StL	102

Batting Average
Sisler-StL	.420
Cobb-Det	.401
Speaker-Cle	.378
Heilmann-Det	.356
Miller-Phi	.335

On Base Percentage
Speaker-Cle	.474
Sisler-StL	.467
Cobb-Det	.462
Ruth-NY	.434
Heilmann-Det	.432

Slugging Average
Ruth-NY	.672
Williams-StL	.627
Speaker-Cle	.606
Heilmann-Det	.598
Sisler-StL	.594

Stolen Bases
Sisler-StL	51
Williams-StL	37
Harris-Was	25
Johnson-Chi	21
Rigney-Det	68

Wins
Rommel-Phi	27
Bush-NY	26
Shocker-StL	24
Uhle-Cle	22
Faber-Chi	21

Innings Pitched
Faber-Chi	352.0
Shocker-StL	348.0
Shawkey-NY	299.2
Rommel-Phi	294.0
Uhle-Cle	287.1

Saves
Jones-NY	8
Pruett-StL	7
Wright-StL	5

Strikeouts
Shocker-StL	149
Faber-Chi	148
Shawkey-NY	130
Ehmke-Det	108
Johnson-Was	105

Earned Run Average
Faber-Chi	2.81
Pillette-Det	2.85
Shawkey-NY	2.91
Wright-StL	2.92
Shocker-StL	2.97

Complete Games
Faber-Chi	31
Shocker-StL	29
Uhle-Cle	23
Johnson-Was	23

THE YEAR IN BASEBALL

April 29: The New York Giants hit four inside-the-park home runs in Braves Field.

April 30: Charlie Robertson of the White Sox pitches the last perfect game in the majors until Don Larsen's masterpiece in the 1956 World Series.

May 5: After being told by the Giants they will be evicted from the Polo Grounds at the end of the season, the Yankees decide to build their own $2.5 million stadium.

May 30: Max Flack of the Cubs and Cliff Heathcote of the Cards trade uniforms between a.m. and p.m. games, with both outfielders seeing action in both games of a doubleheader.

July 17: Ty Cobb gets five hits in a game for the fourth time in his career.

July 22: Both St. Louis teams win to move into first place in the AL and NL, marking the first time both clubs have been on top of the standings at the same time.

July 23: Ray Grimes drives in a run in his 17th straight game (27 total).

July 31: Hank Bauer is born.

August 14: Lizzie Murphy becomes the first female to play for a major-league club when she plays first base for an AL All-Star team against the Boston Red Sox.

August 23: George Kell is born.

August 25: A total of 49 runs are scored as the Cubs edge the Phillies 26-23 in a game featuring 51 hits, 23 walks and 10 errors.

September 18: George Sisler's 41-game hit streak is stopped by New York's Joe Bush.

September 21: The AL reinstates the MVP Award, which had been dormant since 1914.

September 30: Rogers Hornsby's 33-game hitting streak is snapped by Brooklyn pitcher Burleigh Grimes.

October 1: Rogers Hornsby goes 3-for-5 to set an NL record of 250 hits in a season, while raising his average to .401 and becoming the first NL player since 1899 to bat .400.

October 27: Ralph Kiner is born.

1923

Giants left behind as Yankees move to House that Ruth Built

Two straight World Series wins weren't enough for the Giants when it came to the Yankees. Growing fury by John McGraw at the popularity of the home-run game epitomized by Babe Ruth, plus three years of being outdrawn in their own park, led the NLers to end their rental arrangement with Jacob Ruppert's team after the 1922 campaign. Ruppert's response was to build a triple-decked facility on the other side of the Harlem River within sight of the Polo Grounds. Yankee Stadium had its official opening on April 18, 1923, with Bob Shawkey defeating the Red Sox, 4-1; the margin of victory was a three-run homer by Ruth. The Yankees claimed a gate of 74,217, though that was probably exaggerated by about 10,000. It didn't take long for the Bronx facility to become known as the House That Ruth Built.

The rest of the season went about the same way for the Yankees; only the Tigers and Indians finished within 20 games of them. Ruth batted a career-high .393 and paced the league in both homers (41) and RBIs (131). Once again, though, he was stymied in capturing a Triple Crown by Detroit's Harry Heilmann, who batted .403. Other important Yankee offense came from first baseman Wally Pipp (.304 and 108 RBIs) and outfielder Bob Meusel (.313 and 91 RBIs). The best New York pitching came from Sad Sam Jones (21), Herb Pennock (19) and Joe Bush (19). For the league as a whole, Cleveland boasted both the biggest winner in George Uhle (26) and hardest to hit in Stan Coveleski (2.76). Walter Johnson of the Senators reached two milestones: On May 2, he became the first (and only) pitcher to record 100 shutouts; on July 22, he became the first to register 3,000 strikeouts.

In the NL, the Giants sought to make up for their lost rental income from the Yankees by enlarging the Polo Grounds, but they still ended up trailing their erstwhile tenants in attendance by 180,000. Those who did show up saw another offense-oriented club propping up erratic pitching. The most potent bats belonged to NL RBI leader Irish Meusel (125) and second baseman Frankie Frisch (.348 with 111 RBIs). Rosy Ryan and Jack Scott led the pitchers with 16 wins, and only the bottom-of-the-league Braves and Phillies had staff ERAs higher than the pennant winners. The league's individual honors were spread around among Cincinnati's Dolf Luque (27 wins and a 1.93 ERA), Philadelphia's Cy Williams (41 homers) and St. Louis' Rogers Hornsby (.384).

The ouster of the Yankees from the Polo Grounds provided yet more tension for the all-New York World Series. Over the first three games, Giants outfielder Casey Stengel contributed two clutch homers to put the NLers up 2-1. But then the Yankees,

Pie Traynor
Pittsburgh's slick-fielding third baseman led the NL with 19 triples and was third with 208 hits while batting .338 with 101 RBIs.

riding a second victory from Pennock and eight RBIs from Bob Meusel, stormed back to take the next three and the championship. Ruth, who had been held relatively at bay by the Giants in 1921 and 1922, walloped three homers—a symbol to many that the Ruth Era had officially displaced the McGraw Age.

1923 SEASON HIGHLIGHTS

NATIONAL LEAGUE

	W	L	Pct.	GB
New York	95	58	.621	—
Cincinnati	91	63	.591	4.5
Pittsburgh	87	67	.565	8.5
Chicago	83	71	.539	12.5
St. Louis	79	74	.516	16
Brooklyn	76	78	.494	19.5
Boston	54	100	.351	41.5
Philadelphia	50	104	.325	45.5

AMERICAN LEAGUE

	W	L	Pct.	GB
New York	98	54	.645	—
Detroit	83	71	.539	16
Cleveland	82	71	.536	16.5
Washington	75	78	.490	23.5
St. Louis	74	78	.487	24
Philadelphia	69	83	.454	29
Chicago	69	85	.448	30
Boston	61	91	.401	37

AWARDS
AL MVP: Babe Ruth, NY

POSTSEASON
WORLD SERIES
New York Yankees 4, New York Giants 2
Oct. 10: Giants 5, YANKEES 4
Oct. 11: Yankees 4, GIANTS 2
Oct. 12: Giants 1, YANKEES 0
Oct. 13: Yankees 8, GIANTS 4
Oct. 14: YANKEES 8, Giants 1
Oct. 15: Yankees 6, GIANTS 4

Home team in CAPS

> "I have only one superstition. I make sure to touch all the bases when I hit a home run."
>
> — Babe Ruth

NATIONAL LEAGUE LEADERS

Home Runs
Williams-Phi	41
Fournier-Bro	22
Miller-Chi	20
Meusel-NY	19
Hornsby-StL	17

Runs Batted In
Meusel-NY	125
Williams-Phi	114
Frisch-NY	111
Kelly-NY	103
Fournier-Bro	102

Batting Average
Hornsby-StL	.384
Bottomley-StL	.371
Fournier-Bro	.351
Roush-Cin	.351
Frisch-NY	.348

On Base Percentage
Hornsby-StL	.459
Bottomley-StL	.425
Youngs-NY	.412
Fournier-Bro	.411
O'Farrell-Chi	.408

Slugging Average
Hornsby-StL	.627
Fournier-Bro	.588
Williams-Phi	.576
Bottomley-StL	.535
Roush-Cin	.531

Stolen Bases
Carey-Pit	51
Grantham-Chi	43
Smith-StL	32
Heathcote-Chi	32

Wins
Luque-Cin	27
Morrison-Pit	25
Alexander-Chi	22
Grimes-Bro	21
Donohue-Cin	21

Innings Pitched
Grimes-Bro	327.0
Luque-Cin	322.0
Rixey-Cin	309.0
Alexander-Chi	305.0
Ring-Phi	304.1

Saves
Jonnard-NY	5
Ryan-NY	4

Strikeouts
Vance-Bro	197
Luque-Cin	151
Grimes-Bro	119
Morrison-Pit	114
Ring-Phi	112

Earned Run Average
Luque-Cin	1.93
Rixey-Cin	2.80
Keen-Chi	3.00
Kaufmann-Chi	3.10
Haines-StL	3.11

Complete Games
Grimes-Bro	33
Luque-Cin	28
Morrison-Pit	27
Cooper-Pit	26
Alexander-Chi	26

AMERICAN LEAGUE LEADERS

Home Runs
Ruth-NY	41
Williams-StL	29
Heilmann-Det	18
Speaker-Cle	17
Hauser-Phi	17

Runs Batted In
Ruth-NY	131
Speaker-Cle	130
Heilmann-Det	115
J.Sewell-Cle	109
Pipp-NY	108

Batting Average
Heilmann-Det	.403
Ruth-NY	.393
Speaker-Cle	.380
Collins-Chi	.360
Williams-StL	.357

On Base Percentage
Ruth-NY	.545
Heilmann-Det	.481
Speaker-Cle	.469
J.Sewell-Cle	.456
Collins-Chi	.455

Slugging Average
Ruth-NY	.764
Heilmann-Det	.632
Williams-StL	.623
Speaker-Cle	.610
Harris-Bos	.520

Stolen Bases
Collins-Chi	49
Mostil-Chi	41
Harris-Was	23
Rice-Was	20
Jamieson-Cle	19

Wins
Uhle-Cle	26
Jones-NY	21
Dauss-Det	21
Shocker-StL	20
Ehmke-Bos	20

Innings Pitched
Uhle-Cle	357.2
Ehmke-Bos	316.2
Dauss-Det	316.0
Rommel-Phi	297.2
Vangilder-StL	282.1

Saves
Russell-Was	9
Quinn-Bos	7
Harriss-Phi	6

Strikeouts
Johnson-Was	130
Shawkey-NY	125
Bush-NY	125
Ehmke-Bos	121

Earned Run Average
Coveleski-Cle	2.76
Hoyt-NY	3.02
Russell-Was	3.03
Vangilder-StL	3.06
Mogridge-Was	3.11

Complete Games
Uhle-Cle	29
Ehmke-Bos	28
Shocker-StL	24
Dauss-Det	22
Bush-NY	22

THE YEAR IN BASEBALL

January 30: The Red Sox trade Herb Pennock, future Hall of Famer, to the Yanks, for three nondescript players and cash; over the next six years, he wins 115 games.

February 22: Christy Mathewson is named president of the Braves after joining with two partners to buy the club for $300,000.

April 18: Yankee Stadium opens, with Babe Ruth dedicating it by clouting three-run homer for 4-1 victory over Boston.

May 21: Jake Ruppert completes his purchase of the Yankees for $1.5 milion, buying out his partner.

July 11: Harry Frazee, owner of the Red Sox since 1916, sells out to a group of Ohio businessmen for more than $1 million.

July 26: Hoyt Wilhelm is born.

August 11: AL president Ban Johnson decrees that only one-piece bats will be permitted, forcing Babe Ruth, among others, to stop using a bat made from four pieces of wood glued together.

August 24: Carl Mays of the Yanks beats the A's for the 23rd consecutive time, a streak that began on August 30, 1918, when he was with the Red Sox.

October 2: Harry Heilmann goes 2-for-2 to raise his average above .400 and then doesn't start the final two games and wins the batting championship with a .403 average.

October 19: Citing the unsavory people associated with boxing, AL president Ban Johnson persuades both AL and NL owners to prohibit boxing matches in their parks.

October 26: Frank Chance is signed to manage the White Sox, replacing Kid Gleason, but Chase resigns four months later dut to illness.

December 10: Former Yankees and Phillies manager Will Bill Donovan is killed in a train wreck.

1924

Riots, bribery scandal take some luster off Senators' big season

All three New York clubs took loud shots at the postseason in 1924, with more than one riot scene spicing up their games. Only the Giants made it to the World Series, and even they would have been disqualified if executives outside New York had had their say. Amid all the tumult, Walter Johnson finally succeeded in translating his routinely formidable numbers into a championship for Washington.

In the NL, the Giants and Dodgers waged a battle befitting the intense rivalry between managers (and ex-friends) John McGraw and Wilbert Robinson. The climax came in a September duel at Ebbets Field when descending crowds numbered thousands more than the park's capacity. Not only did fans storm through the rotunda and jump over walls to get in, but some of them uprooted a telephone pole to batter down the centerfield gate. Brooklyn owner Charlie Ebbets finally had to agree to stretching ropes across the outfield to accommodate everyone. The subsequent 8-7 win by the Giants included 11 ground-rule doubles hit into the overflow crowd.

In October, Giants outfielder Jimmy O'Connell accosted Phillies shortstop Heinie Sand with a proposition to take it easy against New York. The approach was reported to Commissioner Landis; O'Connell and New York coach Cozy Dolan were thrown out of baseball; and executives in both leagues demanded the Giants be excluded from the World Series. Landis rejected the demands despite indications more players than the dispensable O'Connell had been involved in the would-be bribery.

On the field, the New York effort was spearheaded by a lineup in which the biggest bat belonged to first baseman George Kelly (.324 with 21 homers and a league-leading 136 RBIs). Brooklyn stayed in contention chiefly because of first baseman Jack Fournier (an NL-best 27 homers with 116 RBIs and a .334 average) and right-hander Dazzy Vance (tops for both his 28 wins and 2.16 ERA). Rogers Hornsby of St. Louis again won the batting title (with a 20th-century record .424).

Johnson led the Senators to their first pennant with his AL-best 23 wins and 2.72 ERA. Washington's biggest offense came from outfielder Goose Goslin (.344 and a league-tops 129 RBIs). Babe Ruth again snatched two-thirds of a Triple Crown—this time with homers (46) and batting (.378). The New York outfielder was also at the center of the season's rowdiest scene in June, when he tackled Ty Cobb in Detroit for the latter's relentless jeering of him as a "nigger." More than 1,000 Detroit fans eventually joined the fray, others smashed up the grandstand, and the game was forfeited to the Yankees.

George Kelly
The New York Giants were led to the World Series by their first baseman, Kelly, who batted .324 with 21 homers and a league-leading 136 RBIs.

The World Series started off as a disaster for Johnson, when he dropped his two starts, giving the Giants a 3-2 edge after five games. But following Tom Zachary's second Series win in Game 6, the Senators, with the help of a grounder that hit a pebble and bounced over third baseman Freddie Lindstrom's head to drive in the tying runs, called on their ace again for four innings of spotless relief into overtime in the finale. The championship was finally decided in the bottom of the 12th inning when a second bouncer to Lindstrom, this one hit by outfielder Earl McNeely, also caromed over his head after hitting something in the dirt.

1925 SEASON HIGHLIGHTS

NATIONAL LEAGUE

	W	L	Pct.	GB
Pittsburgh	95	58	.621	—
New York	86	66	.566	8.5
Cincinnati	80	73	.523	15
St. Louis	77	76	.503	18
Boston	70	83	.458	25
Philadelphia	68	85	.444	27
Brooklyn	68	85	.444	27
Chicago	68	86	.442	27.5

AMERICAN LEAGUE

	W	L	Pct.	GB
Washington	96	55	.636	—
Philadelphia	88	64	.579	8.5
St. Louis	82	71	.536	15
Detroit	81	73	.526	16.5
Chicago	79	75	.513	18.5
Cleveland	70	84	.455	27.5
New York	69	85	.448	28.5
Boston	47	105	.309	49.5

AWARDS

NL MVP: Rogers Hornsby, STL
AL MVP: Roger Peckinpaugh, WAS

POSTSEASON
WORLD SERIES
Pittsburgh Pirates 4, Washington Senators 3
- Oct. 7: Washington 4, PITTSBURGH 1
- Oct. 8: PITTSBURGH 3, Washington 2
- Oct. 10: WASHINGTON 4, Pittsburgh 3
- Oct. 11: WASHINGTON 4, Pittsburgh 0
- Oct. 12: Pittsburgh 6, WASHINGTON 3
- Oct. 13: PITTSBURGH 3, Washington 2
- Oct. 15: PITTSBURGH 9, Washington 7

Home team in CAPS

> "Confidentially—and you can print this—Miller Huggins is dumb."
>
> — Babe Ruth after being suspended by the Yankees manager

NATIONAL LEAGUE LEADERS

Home Runs
Hornsby-StL	39
Hartnett-Chi	24
Fournier-Bro	22
Meusel-NY	21
Bottomley-StL	21

Runs Batted In
Hornsby-StL	143
Fournier-Bro	130
Bottomley-StL	128
Wright-Pit	121
Barnhart-Pit	114

Batting Average
Hornsby-StL	.403
Bottomley-StL	.367
Wheat-Bro	.359
Cuyler-Pit	.357
Fournier-Bro	.350

On Base Percentage
Hornsby-StL	.489
Fournier-Bro	.446
Blades-StL	.423
Cuyler-Pit	.423
Carey-Pit	.418

Slugging Average
Hornsby-StL	.756
Cuyler-Pit	.598
Bottomley-StL	.578
Fournier-Bro	.569
Harper-Phi	.558

Stolen Bases
Carey-Pit	46
Cuyler-Pit	41
Adams-Chi	26
Roush-Cin	22
Frisch-NY	21

Wins
Vance-Bro	22
Rixey-Cin	21
Donohue-Cin	21
Meadows-Pit	19

Innings Pitched
Donohue-Cin	301.0
Luque-Cin	291.0
Rixey-Cin	287.1
Ring-Phi	270.0
Vance-Bro	265.1

Saves
Morrison-Pit	4
Bush-Chi	4

Strikeouts
Vance-Bro	221
Luque-Cin	140
Ring-Phi	93
Blake-Chi	93
Aldridge-Pit	88

Earned Run Average
Luque-Cin	2.63
Rixey-Cin	2.88
Donohue-Cin	3.08
Benton-Bos	3.09
Sherdel-StL	3.11

Complete Games
Donohue-Cin	27
Vance-Bro	26
Rixey-Cin	22
Luque-Cin	22
Ring-Phi	21

AMERICAN LEAGUE LEADERS

Home Runs
Meusel-NY	33
Williams-StL	25
Ruth-NY	25
Simmons-Phi	24
Gehrig-NY	20

Runs Batted In
Meusel-NY	138
Heilmann-Det	134
Simmons-Phi	129
Goslin-Was	113
Sheely-Chi	111

Batting Average
Heilmann-Det	.393
Speaker-Cle	.389
Simmons-Phi	.387
Cobb-Det	.378
Wingo-Det	.370

On Base Percentage
Speaker-Cle	.479
Cobb-Det	.468
Collins-Chi	.461
Heilmann-Det	.457
Wingo-Det	.456

Slugging Average
Simmons-Phi	.599
Cobb-Det	.598
Speaker-Cle	.578
Heilmann-Det	.569
Goslin-Was	.547

Stolen Bases
Mostil-Chi	43
Rice-Was	26
Goslin-Was	26

Wins
Rommel-Phi	21
Lyons-Chi	21
Johnson-Was	20
Coveleski-Was	20
Harriss-Phi	19

Innings Pitched
Pennock-NY	277.0
Lyons-Chi	262.2
Rommel-Phi	261.0
Ehmke-Bos	260.2
Wingfield-Bos	254.1

Saves
Marberry-Was	15
Doyle-Det	8
Connally-Chi	8
Walberg-Phi	7

Strikeouts
Grove-Phi	116
Johnson-Was	108
Harriss-Phi	95
Ehmke-Bos	95
Jones-NY	92

Earned Run Average
Coveleski-Was	2.84
Pennock-NY	2.96
Blankenship-Chi	3.03
Johnson-Was	3.07
Dauss-Det	3.16

Complete Games
Smith-Cle	22
Ehmke-Bos	22
Pennock-NY	21
Lyons-Chi	19
Wingfield-Bos	18

THE YEAR IN BASEBALL

April 14: Two future Hall of Famers, Left Grove and Mickey Cochrane, make their major league debuts with the A's.

April 18: Charles Ebbets, Dodger president, dies on the morning of the opening of Ebbets Field.

May 1: The A's introduce their third future Hall of Famer of the season when Jimmie Fox, 17, debuts as a pinch-hitter.

May 5: Ty Cobb goes 6-for-6 with three home runs, in Detroit's 14-8 win over the Browns

May 7: Pittsburgh shortstop Glenn Wright makes an unassisted triple play in the ninth inning to end the game.

May 30: Rogers Hornsby is named manager of the Cardinals, replacing Branch Rickey, who remains as GM.

June 1: Lou Gehrig pinch hits for Pee Wee Wanninger and starts his 2,130-game playing streak.

June 3: White Sox playing-manager Eddie Collins gets career hit No. 3,000

August 29: After a night on the town, Babe Ruth is late for batting practice and is suspended and fined $5,000 by manager Miller Huggins.

October 7: Christy Mathewson dies of tuberculosis at Saranac Lake, NY at the age of 45.

December 3: Harry Simpson born; traded in midseason five times in five years, he was given one of the game's great nicknames, "Suitcase."

1926

Speaker, Cobb retire amid fixing charges as Cards take Series

Under player-manager Rogers Hornsby, the Cardinals stunned the rest of the league by capturing their first pennant. Among the major contributors to the win were first baseman Jim Bottomley with a league-best 120 RBIs, catcher Bob O'Farrell with his timely hitting and masterful command of the pitching staff, and right-hander Flint Rhem, one of four hurlers in the league to win 20. Hornsby himself had a decidedly mild year at .317, but still drove in 93 runs and never let anybody forget he regarded the flag as his chief priority. During the stretch drive in September, he begged off attending his own mother's funeral in Texas, saying he couldn't be away from the club.

St. Louis' chief competition came from Cincinnati, whose catcher Bubbles Hargrave was the first at his position to win a batting title (.353). The Reds also had one of the other 20-game winners in Pete Donohue; the others were Pittsburgh right-handers Lee Meadows and Ray Kremer. Kremer had the league's best ERA at 2.61. Chicago unveiled a bona-fide slugger in Hack Wilson, whose 21 homers led the circuit; the right-hand-hitting outfielder had ended up on the Cubs only because John McGraw had no room for him on the Giants roster.

In the AL, a healthy Babe Ruth came back to power the Yankees past the Indians with 47 home runs and 146 RBIs. Lou Gehrig also had the first of his 100-plus RBI seasons, a plateau reached as well by second baseman Tony Lazzeri. The most reliable New York pitching came from Herb Pennock (23), Urban Shocker (19), and Waite Hoyt (16). Runner-up Cleveland had the single biggest winner in George Uhle (27), while Philadelphia's Lefty Grove marked his sophomore year with a league-best 2.51 ERA. Detroit's Heinie Manush had the highest average at .378.

Cleveland's chase of the Yankees played out before behind-the-scenes scurrying by Commissioner Landis to ascertain the truth of charges by retired pitcher Dutch Leonard that the hurler, Indians manager Tris Speaker, Tigers pilot Ty Cobb, and retired right-hander Joe Wood had been involved in a fix dating back to 1919. Although Landis ultimately exonerated Speaker, Cobb, and Wood, it was only after the two playing managers had been forced to resign from their posts, after AL president Ban Johnson had sought to use the scandal for his own political ends, and after the fingered players had threatened lawsuits against one and all.

The Yankees-Cardinals World Series was a seven-game pitched battle that came down to a duel between Ruth's speed and O'Farrell's throwing arm. In the fourth game, the New York slugger became the first to wallop three homers in a postseason contest. In the fifth game, Pennock went the distance the second time for a win. In Game 6, it was Grover Cleveland Alexander's turn to post his second victory. Then, in Game 7, with the Cardinals up 3-2 in the seventh inning, Alexander came in again to strike out Lazzeri with the bases loaded. The score remained the same until two out in the ninth, when Ruth drew a walk. But he was then promptly thrown out trying to steal by O'Farrell to end the tension-packed Series.

Bubbles Hargrave
By hitting .353 Hargrave became the first catcher to win a batting title, but his bat wasn't enough to carry Cincinnati to the NL pennant.

1926 SEASON HIGHLIGHTS

NATIONAL LEAGUE

	W	L	Pct.	GB
St. Louis	89	65	.578	—
Cincinnati	87	67	.565	2
Pittsburgh	84	69	.549	4.5
Chicago	82	72	.532	7
New York	74	77	.490	13.5
Brooklyn	71	82	.464	17.5
Boston	66	86	.434	22
Philadelphia	58	93	.384	29.5

AMERICAN LEAGUE

	W	L	Pct.	GB
New York	91	63	.591	—
Cleveland	88	66	.571	3
Philadelphia	83	67	.553	6
Washington	81	69	.540	8
Chicago	81	72	.529	9.5
Detroit	79	75	.513	12
St. Louis	62	92	.403	29
Boston	46	107	.301	44.5

AWARDS

NL MVP: Bob O'Farrell, STL
AL MVP: George Burns, CLE

POSTSEASON
WORLD SERIES
St. Louis Cardinals 4, New York Yankees 3

Oct. 2: NEW YORK 2, St. Louis 1
Oct. 3: St. Louis 6, NEW YORK 2
Oct. 5: ST. LOUIS 4, New York 0
Oct. 7: New York 10, ST. LOUIS 5
Oct. 7: New York 3, ST. LOUIS 2
Oct. 9: St. Louis 10, NEW YORK 2
Oct. 10: St. Louis 3, NEW YORK 2

Home team in CAPS

> "The great trouble with baseball today is that most of the players are in the game for the money and that's it—not for the love of it, the excitement of it, the thrill of it."
> — Ty Cobb

NATIONAL LEAGUE LEADERS

Home Runs

Wilson-Chi	21
Bottomley-StL	19
Williams-Phi	18
L.Bell-StL	17
Southworth-NY-StL	16

Runs Batted In

Bottomley-StL	120
Wilson-Chi	109
L.Bell-StL	100
Southworth-NY-StL	99
Pipp-Cin	99

Batting Average

Waner-Pit	.336
Leach-Phi	.329
Brown-Bos	.328
L.Bell-StL	.325
Roush-Cin	.323

On Base Percentage

Waner-Pit	.413
Blades-StL	.409
Wilson-Chi	.406
Grantham-Pit	.400
Bancroft-Bos	.399

Slugging Average

Wilson-Chi	.539
Waner-Pit	.528
L.Bell-StL	.518
Bottomley-StL	.506
Herman-Bro	.500

Stolen Bases

Cuyler-Pit	35
Adams-Chi	27
Frisch-NY	23
Douthit-StL	23
Youngs-NY	21

Wins

Rhem-StL	20
Meadows-Pit	20
Kremer-Pit	20
Donohue-Cin	20
Mays-Cin	19

Innings Pitched

Donohue-Cin	285.2
Mays-Cin	281.0
Petty-Bro	275.2
Root-Chi	271.1
Carlson-Phi	267.1

Saves

Davies-NY	6
Scott-NY	5
Kremer-Pit	5
Ehrhardt-Bro	4

Strikeouts

Vance-Bro	140
Root-Chi	127
May-Cin	103
Benton-Bos	103
Petty-Bro	101

Earned Run Average

Kremer-Pit	2.61
Root-Chi	2.82
Petty-Bro	2.84
Bush-Chi	2.86
Barnes-NY	2.87

Complete Games

Mays-Cin	24
Petty-Bro	23
Root-Chi	21
Rhem-StL	20
Carlson-Phi	20

AMERICAN LEAGUE LEADERS

Home Runs

Ruth-NY	47
Simmons-Phi	19
Lazzeri-NY	18
Williams-StL	17
Goslin-Was	17

Runs Batted In

Ruth-NY	146
Lazzeri-NY	114
Burns-Cle	114
Gehrig-NY	112
Simmons-Phi	109

Batting Average

Manush-Det	.378
Ruth-NY	.372
Heilmann-Det	.367
Burns-Cle	.358
Goslin-Was	.354

On Base Percentage

Ruth-NY	.516
Heilmann-Det	.445
Bishop-Phi	.431
Goslin-Was	.425
Manush-Det	.421

Slugging Average

Ruth-NY	.737
Simmons-Phi	.564
Manush-Det	.564
Gehrig-NY	.549
Goslin-Was	.542

Stolen Bases

Mostil-Chi	35
Rice-Was	25
Hunnefield-Chi	24
McNeely-Was	18
J.Sewell-Cle	17

Wins

Uhle-Cle	27
Pennock-NY	23
Shocker-NY	19
Lyons-Chi	18

Innings Pitched

Uhle-Cle	318.1
Lyons-Chi	283.2
Pennock-NY	266.1
Johnson-Was	260.2
Shocker-NY	258.1

Saves

Marberry-Was	22
Dauss-Det	9
Pate-Phi	6
Grove-Phi	6
Jones-NY	5

Strikeouts

Grove-Phi	194
Uhle-Cle	159
Thomas-Chi	127
Johnson-Was	125
Whitehill-Det	109

Earned Run Average

Grove-Phi	2.51
Uhle-Cle	2.83
Lyons-Chi	3.01
Rommel-Phi	3.08
Buckeye-Cle	3.10

Complete Games

Uhle-Cle	32
Lyons-Chi	24
Johnson-Was	22
Grove-Phi	20
Pennock-NY	19

THE YEAR IN BASEBALL

January 30: The rules committee decides to give pitchers access to a resin bag while on the mound.

May 1: Satchel Paige, 19, debuts for Chattanooga in the Negro Southern League.

May 23: Hack Wilson becomes the first player to hit a ball off the Wrigely Field scoreboard.

June 8: Babe Ruth launches what may be the longest home run ever—over 600 feet—and homers again in the 11th for 11-9 win at Navin Field.

June 22: The Cardinals pick up 39-year-old Grover Cleveland Alexander on waivers from the Cubs, and he goes 9-7 down the stretch.

August 15: Babe Herman doubles into a double play, and though three Dodgers wind up at third on the play, Herman gets credit for driving in the game's winning run against Braves.

August 21: Ted Lyons of the White Sox pitches a 6-0 no-hitter over the Red Sox in one hour and seven minutes.

August 28: Emil Levsen of the Indians pitches two complete game wins over the Red Sox, 6-1 and 5-1. He did not fan a batter in either game.

September 19: Edwin "Duke" Snider is born; the Dodger center fielder hit 40 or more home runs in five straight years.

September 30: Robin Roberts is born; the 28 games he won for the Phils in 1952 are the NL's high-water mark of the last half-century.

October 10: Grover Alexander leaves the bullpen in seventh inning of seventh World Series game to strike out Tony Lazzeri with bases loaded and two out, then holds Yanks scoreless the next two innings to win.

December 20: In a shocking trade of baseball's best second sackers, the Cards send Rogers Hornsby to the Giants and receive Frankie Frisch.

1927

Ruth whacks 60, Cobb gets 4,000th as Cubs top 1 million

The 1927 season became synonymous with the Murderers Row Yankees, who coasted to a second straight pennant, 19 games ahead of runner-up Philadelphia. But curiously, about the only team or individual record set during the year that was not eventually eclipsed was one of simple manpower: From April to October, New York didn't make a single change in its 25-man roster. Outside the Bronx, the season was notable for stellar players doing big things in strange uniforms. On July 18, Ty Cobb recorded his 4,000th hit—not as a member of the Tigers, but against them, following his move to the Athletics after the fix charges that Dutch Leonard had leveled in 1926. In the NL, second basemen Rogers Hornsby and Frankie Frisch continued to pummel pitchers, but with the former as a Giant and the latter as a Cardinal in the wake of a winter trade.

With the Yankees outscoring the opposition by some 400 runs, the only suspense in the AL was over how high players could build their individual statistics. The gaudy numbers included league-leading figures by Babe Ruth in home runs (60), Lou Gehrig in RBIs (175), Waite Hoyt in wins (22, tied with Chicago's Ted Lyons), and Wilcy Moore in ERA (2.28). Ruth, Gehrig and outfielders Earle Combs and Bob Meusel all batted between .337 and .373, while Ruth, Meusel and Tony Lazzeri joined Gehrig in batting in more than 100 runs. Despite all the Yankee Stadium offense, however, the batting champion once again came from Detroit, with Harry Heilmann's .398. Philadelphia also had an historical consolation prize for its distant second-place finish in actually having more future Hall of Famers on its squad than the Yankees (7-5).

In the NL, the Pirates and Cardinals went down to the final day of the season before settling the tussle in Pittsburgh's favor. The Giants and Cubs also had moments in the first-place sun along the way but the Pirates went in front to stay with a 22-9 September. Pittsburgh's biggest bat belonged to outfielder Paul Waner, who paced the league in both hitting (.380) and RBIs (131). Ray Kremer pitched in with 19 wins and a league-low 2.47 ERA. If there was a People's Choice team in the league, though, it was the Cubs. Chicago became the first club in the league to draw more than a million fans—in part because of outfielder Hack Wilson's league-leading 30 homers, in part because owner William Wrigley had successfully calculated that radio broadcasts of games could sell more tickets. Aside from Wilson, the Cubs boasted the presence of outfielder Riggs Stephenson (whose .336 career average is the highest for any ten-year position player not elected to the Hall of Fame) and Charlie Root, whose 26 wins paced the league.

Paul and Lloyd Waner
Pittsburgh's brother act was led by Paul, who topped the NL with a .380 average and 131 RBIs.

The World Series was over almost before it started. Although clouting around NL pitching at a .305 rate during the season, the Pirates managed to score more than one run in an inning only once over a four-game New York sweep. They also chose the wrong time to fall down defensively. In addition to several key errors along the way, they blew the finale on a bases-loaded, ninth-inning wild pitch by reliever Johnny Miljus.

1927 SEASON HIGHLIGHTS

NATIONAL LEAGUE

	W	L	Pct.	GB
Pittsburgh	94	60	.610	—
St. Louis	92	61	.601	1.5
New York	92	62	.597	2
Chicago	85	68	.556	8.5
Cincinnati	75	78	.490	18.5
Brooklyn	65	88	.425	28.5
Boston	60	94	.390	34
Philadelphia	51	103	.331	43

AMERICAN LEAGUE

	W	L	Pct.	GB
New York	110	44	.714	—
Philadelphia	91	63	.591	19
Washington	85	69	.552	25
Detroit	82	71	.536	27.5
Chicago	70	83	.458	39.5
Cleveland	66	87	.431	43.5
St. Louis	59	94	.386	50.5
Boston	51	103	.331	59

AWARDS
NL MVP: Paul Waner, PIT
AL MVP: Lou Gehrig, NY

POSTSEASON
WORLD SERIES
New York Yankees 4, Pittsburgh Pirates 0
Oct. 5: New York 5, PITTSBURGH 4
Oct. 6: New York 6, PITTSBURGH 2
Oct. 7: NEW YORK 8, Pittsburgh 1
Oct. 8: NEW YORK 4, Pittsburgh 3

Home team in CAPS

"The way a team plays as a whole determines its success. You may have the greatest bunch of individual stars in the world, but if they don't play together, the club won't be worth a dime."

— Babe Ruth

NATIONAL LEAGUE LEADERS

Home Runs
Wilson-Chi 30
Williams-Phi 30
Hornsby-NY 26
Terry-NY 20
Bottomley-StL 19

Runs Batted In
P.Waner-Pit 131
Wilson-Chi 129
Hornsby-NY 125
Bottomley-StL 124
Terry-NY 121

Batting Average
P.Waner-Pit .380
Hornsby-NY .361
L.Waner-Pit .355
Stephenson-Chi .344
Traynor-Pit .342

On Base Percentage
Hornsby-NY .448
P.Waner-Pit .437
Harper-NY .435
Stephenson-Chi .415
Harris-Pit .402

Slugging Average
Hornsby-NY .586
Wilson-Chi .579
P.Waner-Pit .549
Terry-NY .529
Bottomley-StL .509

Stolen Bases
Frisch-StL 48
Carey-Bro 32
Hendrick-Bro 29
Adams-Chi 26
Richbourg-Bos 24

Wins
Root-Chi 26
Haines-StL 24
Hill-Pit 22
Alexander-StL 21

Innings Pitched
Root-Chi 309.0
Haines-StL 300.2
Meadows-Pit 299.1
Hill-Pit 277.2
Vance-Bro 273.1

Saves
Sherdel-StL 6
Nehf-Cin-Chi 5
Mogridge-Bos 5
Henry-NY 4

Strikeouts
Vance-Bro 184
Root-Chi 145
May-Cin 121
Grimes-NY 102
Petty-Bro 101

Earned Run Average
Kremer-Pit 2.47
Alexander-StL 2.52
Vance-Bro 2.70
Haines-StL 2.72
Petty-Bro 2.98

Complete Games
Vance-Bro 25
Meadows-Pit 25
Haines-StL 25
Hill-Pit 22
Alexander-StL 22

AMERICAN LEAGUE LEADERS

Home Runs
Ruth-NY 60
Gehrig-NY 47
Lazzeri-NY 18
Williams-StL 17
Simmons-Phi 15

Runs Batted In
Gehrig-NY 175
Ruth-NY 164
Heilmann-Det 120
Goslin-Was 120
Fothergill-Det 114

Batting Average
Heilmann-Det .398
Gehrig-NY .373
Fothergill-Det .359
Cobb-Phi .357
Combs-NY .356

On Base Percentage
Ruth-NY .487
Heilmann-Det .475
Gehrig-NY .474
Bishop-Phi .442
Cobb-Phi .440

Slugging Average
Ruth-NY .772
Gehrig-NY .765
Heilmann-Det .616
Williams-StL .525
Goslin-Was .516

Stolen Bases
Sisler-StL 27
Meusel-NY 24
Neun-Det 22
Lazzeri-NY 22
Cobb-Phi 22

Wins
Lyons-Chi 22
Hoyt-NY 22
Grove-Phi 20

Innings Pitched
Thomas-Chi 307.2
Lyons-Chi 307.2
Hudlin-Cle 264.2
Grove-Phi 262.1
Hoyt-NY 256.1

Saves
Moore-NY 13
Braxton-Was 13
Marberry-Was 9
Grove-Phi 9

Strikeouts
Grove-Phi 174
Walberg-Phi 136
Thomas-Chi 107
Lisenbee-Was 105
Braxton-Was 96

Earned Run Average
Moore-NY 2.28
Hoyt-NY 2.63
Shocker-NY 2.84
Lyons-Chi 2.84
Hadley-Was 2.85

Complete Games
Lyons-Chi 30
Thomas-Chi 24
Hoyt-NY 23
Gaston-StL 21

THE YEAR IN BASEBALL

January 8: After 22 years with the Detroit Tigers, Ty Cobb signs with the Philadelphia A's.

January 9: In a three-way deal, pitcher Burleigh Grimes goes from Brooklyn to the Giants.

January 12: Zack Wheat, released on Jan. 1 by Dodgers, signs with Athletics—rest home for Eddie Collins, Ty Cobb, and in 1928, Tris Speaker.

January 31: NL president John Heydler rules that Rogers Hornsby can not continue to hold stock in the Cardinals and play for the Giants.

February 9: In trade of Hall of Famers, Giants send George Kelly to Cincy for Edd Roush.

March 27: Joe Start dies; "Old Reliable" first baseman played first base at the top grade of competition from 1860 through 1886 spanning the amateur and professional eras.

April 2: Billy Pierce born; a top AL pitcher in the 1950s who was traded to the Giants in 1962, he took to his new home by going 12-0 at Candlestick Park.

April 28: Charlie Maxwell is born; Tiger outfielder specialized in hitting homers on Sunday.

May 14: A fan is killed in a stampede that occurs after a section of stands collapses at Philadelphia's Baker Bowl.

July 27: Mel Ott, 18, hits his first major league home run.

September 30: Babe Ruth hits 60th homer, surpassing his own record by one. The victim is Tom Zachary of the Senators.

October 22: Future Hall of Famer Ross Youngs dies of Brights disease at age 30.

November 2: Ban Johnson, founder of AL, resigns as league president.

December 13: Detroit trades outfielder Heinie Manush to the Browns, for whom he would hit .378.

December 26: Stu Miller is born; the changeup artist was said to throw pitches at three speeds—slow, slower and slowest.

1928

Ruth, Gehrig, Gomez carry Yankees to World Series repeat

The 1928 Yankees came close to being as infamous as the club's 1927 edition became famous. After what appeared to be another saunter toward an AL flag, the team squandered a formidable 13-1/2-game lead over the Athletics, to the point that Philadelphia even occupied first place for a few hours in early September. The A's weren't the only team that had exasperation as a reward for the season. In the NL, the Giants wound up two games behind the Cardinals despite recording 25 victories in September.

New York blamed much of its August troubles on injuries to such key players as Bob Meusel, Joe Dugan and Herb Pennock, but the fact was that the Athletics, reinvigorated by such young players as Mule Haas and Bing Miller, rarely lost after a slow start. The turning point of the season came on September 9, when a record 85,264 jammed Yankee Stadium to see the home team get back on track with a doubleheader sweep of the A's. Ultimately, the bashing of Al Simmons (.351, 107 RBIs) was no match for that of Babe Ruth (a league-leading 54 homers and 142 RBIs) and Lou Gehrig (.374 and tying Ruth's 142 RBIs). Where staff aces were concerned, it was a wash between New York's George Pipgras and Philadelphia's Lefty Grove, both 24-game winners, but the Yankees also got 23 victories from Waite Hoyt.

Fourth-place Washington took home some of the year's consolation prizes. Outfielder Goose Goslin won the hitting crown at .379 and southpaw Garland Braxton, who would end up with sub-.500 career numbers, had his best year in leading the league with a 2.51 ERA. One of the circuit's most embarrassing days came on September 25, when the once-colorful Tigers could draw merely 404 fans to a game against the Red Sox.

In the NL, the Cardinals edged out the Giants for the pennant, in large part because John McGraw and Rogers Hornsby had proved one ego too many for the Polo Grounds dugout and the New York manager had peddled the second baseman to Boston before the season. While Hornsby went on to win his seventh batting title (.387) in a Braves uniform, the Giants gave up too many outs with his successor Andy Cohen. Another Hornsby successor, Frankie Frisch, was at the heart of the Cardinal drive to the pennant, but not even he proved as valuable as Jim Bottomley. The lefty-swinging first baseman batted .325, tied Chicago's Hack Wilson for the most homers with 31, and drove in the most runs in the league (136). Bill Sherdel (21) and Jesse Haines (20) led the St. Louis drive from the mound. The league's most successful pitchers were all from New York City—Larry Benton of the Giants and Burleigh Grimes of the Dodgers each winning 25, and Brooklyn's Dazzy Vance playing Scrooge at 2.09.

In the World Series, the Yankees more than avenged their 1926 loss to the Cardinals. In their four-game sweep, New York got complete games from Hoyt (twice), Pipgras and Tom Zachary—the only pitchers it used. Gehrig and Ruth combined for seven homers, and the team's nine home runs (like Gehrig's nine RBIs) were only one less than the 10 runs scored by the NLers. Ruth put the finishing touches to the massacre by clouting three homers in the fourth game.

Goose Goslin
The Senators outfielder rapped a single on his last at-bat of the season to raise his average to .379, narrowly taking the AL batting title.

1928 SEASON HIGHLIGHTS

NATIONAL LEAGUE

	W	L	Pct.	GB
St. Louis	95	59	.617	—
New York	93	61	.604	2
Chicago	91	63	.591	4
Pittsburgh	85	67	.559	9
Cincinnati	78	74	.513	16
Brooklyn	77	76	.503	17.5
Boston	50	103	.327	44.5
Philadelphia	43	109	.283	51

AMERICAN LEAGUE

	W	L	Pct.	GB
New York	101	53	.656	—
Philadelphia	98	55	.641	2.5
St. Louis	82	72	.532	19
Washington	75	79	.487	26
Chicago	72	82	.468	29
Detroit	68	86	.442	33
Cleveland	62	92	.403	39
Boston	57	96	.373	43.5

AWARDS
NL MVP: Jim Bottomley, STL
AL MVP: Mickey Cochrane, PHI

POSTSEASON
WORLD SERIES
New York Yankees 4, St. Louis Cardinals 0
Oct. 4: NEW YORK 4, St. Louis 1
Oct. 5: NEW YORK 9, St. Louis 3
Oct. 7: New York 7, ST. LOUIS 3
Oct. 9: New York 7, ST. LOUIS 3

Home team in CAPS

"He was built along the lines of a beer keg and not unfamiliar with its contents."
— Shirley Povich, on Hack Wilson

NATIONAL LEAGUE LEADERS

Home Runs
Wilson-Chi	31
Bottomley-StL	31
Hafey-StL	27
Bissonette-Bro	25
Hornsby-Bos	21

Runs Batted In
Bottomley-StL	136
Traynor-Pit	124
Wilson-Chi	120
Hafey-StL	111
Lindstrom-NY	107

Batting Average
Hornsby-Bos	.387
P.Waner-Pit	.370
Lindstrom-NY	.358
Sisler-Bos	.340
Herman-Bro	.340

On Base Percentage
Hornsby-Bos	.498
P.Waner-Pit	.446
Grantham-Pit	.408
Stephenson-Chi	.407
Wilson-Chi	.404

Slugging Average
Hornsby-Bos	.632
Bottomley-StL	.628
Hafey-StL	.604
Wilson-Chi	.588
P.Waner-Pit	.547

Stolen Bases
Cuyler-Chi	37
Frisch-StL	29
Walker-Cin	19
Thompson-Phi	19

Wins
Grimes-Pit	25
Benton-NY	25
Vance-Bro	22
Sherdel-StL	21

Innings Pitched
Grimes-Pit	330.2
Benton-NY	310.1
Rixey-Cin	291.1
Vance-Bro	280.1
Fitzsimmons-NY	261.1

Saves
Sherdel-StL	5
Haid-StL	5
Carlson-Chi	4
Benton-NY	4

Strikeouts
Vance-Bro	200
Malone-Chi	155
Root-Chi	122
Grimes-Pit	97
Benton-NY	90

Earned Run Average
Vance-Bro	2.09
Blake-Chi	2.47
Nehf-Chi	2.65
Clark-Bro	2.68
Benton-NY	2.73

Complete Games
Grimes-Pit	28
Benton-NY	28
Vance-Bro	24
Sherdel-StL	20
Haines-StL	20

AMERICAN LEAGUE LEADERS

Home Runs
Ruth-NY	54
Gehrig-NY	27
Goslin-Was	17
Hauser-Phi	16
Simmons-Phi	15

Runs Batted In
Ruth-NY	142
Gehrig-NY	142
Meusel-NY	113
Manush-StL	108

Batting Average
Goslin-Was	.379
Manush-StL	.378
Gehrig-NY	.374
Simmons-Phi	.351
Miller-Phi	.329

On Base Percentage
Gehrig-NY	.467
Ruth-NY	.461
Goslin-Was	.442
Bishop-Phi	.435
Manush-StL	.414

Slugging Average
Ruth-NY	.709
Gehrig-NY	.648
Goslin-Was	.614
Manush-StL	.575
Simmons-Phi	.558

Stolen Bases
Myer-Bos	30
Mostil-Chi	23
Rice-Det	20
Cissell-Chi	18
Bluege-Was	18

Wins
Pipgras-NY	24
Grove-Phi	24
Hoyt-NY	23
Crowder-StL	21
Gray-StL	20

Innings Pitched
Pipgras-NY	300.2
Ruffing-Bos	289.1
Thomas-Chi	283.0
Hoyt-NY	273.0
Gray-StL	262.2

Saves
Hoyt-NY	8
Hudlin-Cle	7
Lyons-Chi	6
Braxton-Was	6

Strikeouts
Grove-Phi	183
Pipgras-NY	139
Thomas-Chi	129
Ruffing-Bos	118
Earnshaw-Phi	117

Earned Run Average
Braxton-Was	2.51
Pennock-NY	2.56
Grove-Phi	2.58
Jones-Was	2.84
Quinn-Phi	2.90

Complete Games
Ruffing-Bos	25
Thomas-Chi	24
Grove-Phi	24
Pipgras-NY	22

THE YEAR IN BASEBALL

January 25: Baseball immortal Tris Speaker is given his unconditional release by Washington.

February 1: Hugh Jennings dies.

April 18: The Cubs set an opening day NL attendance record when 46,000 fans jam into Wrigley Field to see a 9-8 Cincinnati win.

June 15: Ty Cobb steals home for the 50th, and final, time of his career.

July 26: Bob Meusel hits for the cycle for the third time in his career, a record tied only by Babe Herman, who did it three times in 1931.

August 11: Future Hall of Famer Carl Hubbell's first major league victory is a 4-0 shutout over Philadelphia.

September 3: Ty Cobb, 41, records the last hit of his career, No. 4,189.

September 27: Lefty Grove of the A's fans the White Sox in the seventh inning with nine pitched balls, the second time he turned trick this season (also August 23 vs. Cleveland).

October 21: Whitey Ford is born; the Yankees' "Chairman of the Board" won 236 games plus an all-time high of 10 more in World Series competition.

November 3: Massachusetts voters approve Sunday baseball for Boston, provided that the ballpark is more than 1,000 feet from the church.

November 7: Manager—and less replaceably, .387 hitter—Rogers Hornsby is traded from Boston to the Cubs for $200,000 and five players.

December 11: NL president John Heydler's proposal that baseball introduce a designated hitter to bat in place of the pitcher is rejected.

December 17: The major leagues pass a rule banning the signing of players under the age of 17.

1929

Hornsby paces Cubs but Mack's Athletics get all the breaks

Rogers Hornsby was again at the center of NL events when he persuaded the Braves they were better off trading him than paying him one of the largest salaries in the game as a player-manager. A resultant deal with the Cubs, making four teams in four years for the fractious superstar, was the last piece Chicago needed to win the pennant. On the other hand, Boston assured itself of another two decades of misery by acquiring three pitchers whose ERA was closer to five than four, a catcher who batted .160, and a second baseman who never appeared in the majors.

Hornsby's .380 average, 39 home runs and 149 RBIs slid seamlessly into a lineup in which all three outfielders—Hack Wilson, Kiki Cuyler and Riggs Stephenson—also drove in at least 100 runs and batted a minimum of .345. Wilson's 159 RBIs were the most in the league, as were Chicago right-hander Pat Malone's 22 victories. The circuit's other big offensive numbers came from the comfortable confines of Philadelphia's Baker Bowl, where Chuck Klein belted the majority of his 43 homers and Lefty O'Doul fell just two points short of .400. With the league as a whole batting .295, the 3.09 ERA posted by Bill Walker of the Giants was the lowest. The Hornsby-less Braves, meanwhile, hit their nadir between September 4 and 15, when they were forced to play nine straight double-headers; in one five-day stretch, they lost 10 con-secutive games.

In the AL, the Athletics forewent their slow 1928 start to take pennant matters in hand almost immediately, ending up 18 games over the Yankees. The Philadelphia attack was led by outfielder Al Simmons and first baseman Jimmie Foxx, who combined for 67 homers and 274 RBIs, while bat-ting .365 and .354, respectively. Simmons also paced the league individually with his 157 RBIs. The strong A's pitching included the league's biggest winner, George Earnshaw (24), and hardest to hit, Lefty Grove (2.81), as well as 18-game winner Rube Walberg. Despite big years from Babe Ruth (an AL-best 46 homers with 154 RBIs), Lou Gehrig (35 and 126) and Tony Lazzeri (.354 and 106 RBIs), the Yankees couldn't overcome sharp declines by Bob Meusel, Herb Pennock and Waite Hoyt. The melancholy season turned even darker when manager Miller Huggins, ailing for some time, died of erysipelas 11 games short of the end of the season. Cleveland first baseman Lew Fonseca won the batting title at .369.

The Athletics did nothing in orthodox ways in the World Series. In Game 1, Connie Mack gave the ball to journeyman sidearmer Howard Ehmke instead of to proven winners Earnshaw, Grove or Walberg. Ehmke, who had pitched only 55 innings during the season, struck out 13 Cubs for a then-postseason record on his way to a complete-game victory. In Game 4, Mack was on the verge of resting his regulars with Chicago ahead 8-0 in the seventh inning but, with the crucial help of a misjudged fly ball by Wilson, Philadelphia staged a 10-run rally. In Game 5, the A's went into the bottom of the ninth shut out by Malone, but then got a two-run homer from Mule Haas and an RBI-double from Bing Miller to become the first club to rally from behind in the ninth inning for a world championship.

Tony Lazzeri
A combination of power hitting and sound defense made Lazzeri an outstanding second basemen, and his .354 average and 18 home runs of 1929 were career highs.

1929 SEASON HIGHLIGHTS

NATIONAL LEAGUE

	W	L	Pct.	GB
Chicago	98	54	.645	—
Pittsburgh	88	65	.575	10.5
New York	84	67	.556	13.5
St. Louis	78	74	.513	20
Philadelphia	71	82	.464	27.5
Brooklyn	70	83	.458	28.5
Cincinnati	66	88	.429	33
Boston	56	98	.364	43

AMERICAN LEAGUE

	W	L	Pct.	GB
Philadelphia	104	46	.693	—
New York	88	66	.571	18
Cleveland	81	71	.533	24
St. Louis	79	73	.520	26
Washington	71	81	.467	34
Detroit	70	84	.455	36
Chicago	59	93	.388	46
Boston	58	96	.377	48

AWARDS

NL MVP: Rogers Hornsby, CHI

POSTSEASON

WORLD SERIES
Philadelphia Athletics 4, Chicago Cubs 1
Oct. 8: Philadelphia 3, CHICAGO 1
Oct. 9: Philadelphia 9, CHICAGO 3
Oct. 11: Chicago 3, PHILADELPHIA 1
Oct. 12: PHILADELPHIA 10, Chicago 8
Oct. 14: PHILADELPHIA 3, Chicago 2
Home team in CAPS

"He was a tantrum thrower... but when he punched a locker he always did it with his right hand. He was a careful tantrum thrower."

— Ted Williams on Lefty Grove

NATIONAL LEAGUE LEADERS

Home Runs
Klein-Phi	43
Ott-NY	42
Wilson-Chi	39
Hornsby-Chi	39
O'Doul-Phi	32

Runs Batted In
Wilson-Chi	159
Ott-NY	151
Hornsby-Chi	149
Klein-Phi	145
Bottomley-StL	137

Batting Average
O'Doul-Phi	.398
Herman-Bro	.381
Hornsby-Chi	.380
Terry-NY	.372
Stephenson-Chi	.362

On Base Percentage
O'Doul-Phi	.465
Hornsby-Chi	.459
Ott-NY	.449
Stephenson-Chi	.445
Cuyler-Chi	.438

Slugging Average
Hornsby-Chi	.679
Klein-Phi	.657
Ott-NY	.635
Hafey-StL	.632
O'Doul-Phi	.622

Stolen Bases
Cuyler-Chi	43
Swanson-Cin	33
Frisch-StL	24
Herman-Bro	21
Allen-Cin	21

Wins
Malone-Chi	22
Root-Chi	19
Lucas-Cin	19

Innings Pitched
Clark-Bro	279.0
Root-Chi	272.0
Bush-Chi	270.2
Lucas-Cin	270.0
Hubbell-NY	268.0

Saves
Morrison-Bro	8
Bush-Chi	8
Koupal-Bro-Phi	6

Strikeouts
Malone-Chi	166
Clark-Bro	140
Vance-Bro	126
Root-Chi	124
Hubbell-NY	106

Earned Run Average
Walker-NY	3.09
Grimes-Pit	3.13
Root-Chi	3.47
Malone-Chi	3.57
Lucas-Cin	3.60

Complete Games
Lucas-Cin	28

AMERICAN LEAGUE LEADERS

Home Runs
Ruth-NY	46
Gehrig-NY	35
Simmons-Phi	34
Foxx-Phi	33
Alexander-Det	25

Runs Batted In
Simmons-Phi	157
Ruth-NY	154
Alexander-Det	137
Gehrig-NY	126
Heilmann-Det	120

Batting Average
Fonseca-Cle	.369
Simmons-Phi	.365
Manush-StL	.355
Lazzeri-NY	.354
Foxx-Phi	.354

On Base Percentage
Foxx-Phi	.463
Gehrig-NY	.431
Ruth-NY	.430
Lazzeri-NY	.429
Fonseca-Cle	.427

Slugging Average
Ruth-NY	.697
Simmons-Phi	.642
Foxx-Phi	.625
Gehrig-NY	.584
Alexander-Det	.580

Stolen Bases
Gehringer-Det	27
Cissell-Chi	25
B.Miller-Phi	24
Rothrock-Bos	23
Johnson-Det	20

Wins
Earnshaw-Phi	24
Ferrell-Cle	21
Grove-Phi	20
Marberry-Was	19

Innings Pitched
Gray-StL	305.0
Hudlin-Cle	280.1
Grove-Phi	275.1
Walberg-Phi	267.2
Crowder-StL	266.2

Saves
Marberry-Was	11
Moore-NY	8
Shores-Phi	7
Ferrell-Cle	5

Strikeouts
Grove-Phi	170
Earnshaw-Phi	149
Pipgras-NY	125
Marberry-Was	121

Earned Run Average
Grove-Phi	2.81
Marberry-Was	3.06
Thomas-Chi	3.19
Earnshaw-Phi	3.29
Hudlin-Cle	3.34

Complete Games
Thomas-Chi	24
Uhle-Det	23
Gray-StL	23
Hudlin-Cle	22
Lyons-Chi	21

THE YEAR IN BASEBALL

January 22: The Yankees announce they will put numbers on the back of their uniforms, becoming the first baseball team to do so.

February 20: The Red Sox announce that they will play Sunday games for the first time, but they'll be played at Braves Field because Fenway is too near to a church.

April 16: Cleveland outfielder Earl Averill becomes the first AL player to hit a home run in his first major league at-bat.

April 17: Babe Ruth marries actress Claire Hodgson in a 5 a.m. ceremony to avoid crowds.

May 8: The Giants Carl Hubbell pitches an 11-0 no-hitter against the Pirates, the first no-hitter by a lefthander since 1918.

May 18: Brooklyn and Philadelpia score a major league record 50 runs in a doubleheader at the Baker Bowl.

July 5: The New York Giants become the first team to use a public address system in a big-league park.

July 18: To curb hitters, NL president John Heydler orders umpires to rub up new balls before games to remove gloss.

August 10: Grover Cleveland Alexander, pitching in relief, beats the Phils 7-1 for his 373rd and last NL victory

September 25: Yankees manager Miller Huggins, 49, dies of blood poisoning three days after turning the team over to coach Art Fletcher.

October 5: Chuck Klein hits his 43rd home run of the season, breaking the NL record of 42 shared by Mel Ott and Rogers Hornsby.

October 12: A's rally for 10 runs in the eighth inning to win over Cubs, 10-8, on Mule Haas' lost-in-the-sun three-run homer that eluded Hack Wilson.

November 14: Joe McGinnity dies.

1930

Sluggers go on spree until bats silenced in World Series

The offensive onslaught that had been building up for the better part of a decade exploded in 1930. With some critical help from the Baker Bowl Factor in the NL, the senior league hit a robust .304 with 892 home runs. Only the Braves and Reds failed to reach .300, while the Giants rose to a dizzying .319. The home-run level would not be topped until 1949. Symptomatic of NL events, the last-place Phillies boasted two hitters (Chuck Klein and Lefty O'Doul) who averaged better than .380, registered a team percentage of .315—and gave it all away again with a team ERA of 6.72! The league's ERA as a whole was 4.98, with the Dodgers coming in best at 4.03. The AL was much the same story, though with less offense from the truly bad clubs. The Yankees batted .309 even without Baker Bowl on their itinerary. Washington's 3.97 was the only ERA in either circuit below four.

The main beneficiary of the offense in the NL was St. Louis, where all eight regulars hit .300 to bail out a staff anchored by the untried Bill Hallahan (15) and the aging Burleigh Grimes and Jesse Haines (13 each). Second baseman Frankie Frisch and outfielder Chick Hafey each drove in more than 100 runs. Chicago kept close largely because of a big year from Hack Wilson, who made a run at Babe Ruth's home run record by clouting 56 and established the RBI standard with 191. Pat Malone also topped NL pitchers again, tying Pittsburgh's Ray Kremer with 20, but neither he nor Wilson could overcome a foot injury that reduced Rogers Hornsby to 104 at bats. The batting crown was taken by Bill Terry, whose .401 marked the last time an NLer reached that mark. Brooklyn's Dazzy Vance was the only pitcher in the league to yield less than three runs a game (2.61).

In the AL, the Athletics had little competition outside the Senators in putting together a second straight 100-win season. The bulwarks of the pennant drive were the familiar Al Simmons (a .381 batting crown to go with 36 homers and 165 RBIs), Jimmie Foxx (.335, 37, 156), Lefty Grove (league-best for his 28 wins and 2.54 ERA), and George Earnshaw (22 wins). From April to October, Philadelphia made it clear it was never out of a game, even when it came to its leaden feet on the bases. Although stealing fewer bases than any club in the league except the last-place Red Sox, the A's pulled off two triple steals against the Indians in a July 25 game. As had become customary, New York's Babe Ruth (49) and Lou Gehrig (174) took AL honors in home runs and RBIs, respectively. Midway through the year, Washington and Detroit pulled off the

Hack Wilson
A power-hitting outfielder, Wilson took a run at Babe Ruth's record by clubbing 56 home runs while adding a record 191 RBIs for the 1930 Cubs.

first trade of former batting champions in exchanging Goose Goslin for Heinie Manush.

The World Series was a matter of the Athletics making as much as possible out of little. Despite all the offense in both leagues during the season, Philadelphia ended up hitting only .197 and St. Louis merely .200 in a six-game postseason duel. But 18 of the 35 hits managed by the Athletics were for extra bases and were seldom wasted. The timely hitting complemented sterling efforts from Grove and Earnshaw, who combined for a 1.02 ERA while winning two games apiece.

1930 SEASON HIGHLIGHTS

NATIONAL LEAGUE

	W	L	Pct.	GB
St. Louis	92	62	.597	—
Chicago	90	64	.584	2
New York	87	67	.565	5
Brooklyn	86	68	.558	6
Pittsburgh	80	74	.519	12
Boston	70	84	.455	22
Cincinnati	59	95	.383	33
Philadelphia	52	102	.338	40

AMERICAN LEAGUE

	W	L	Pct.	GB
Philadelphia	102	52	.662	—
Washington	94	60	.610	8
New York	86	68	.558	16
Cleveland	81	73	.526	21
Detroit	75	79	.487	27
St. Louis	64	90	.416	38
Chicago	62	92	.403	40
Boston	52	102	.338	50

NO AWARDS

POSTSEASON
WORLD SERIES
Philadelphia Athletics 4, St. Louis Cardinals 2
Oct. 1: PHILADELPHIA 5, St. Louis 2
Oct. 2: PHILADELPHIA 6, St. Louis 1
Oct. 4: ST. LOUIS 5, Philadelphia 0
Oct. 5: ST. LOUIS 3, Philadelphia 1
Oct. 6: Philadelphia 2, ST. LOUIS 0
Oct. 8: PHILADELPHIA 7, St. Louis 1
Home team in CAPS

"The boy's got talent and desire, but
he ain't got no neck."

— John McGraw, on Hack Wilson

NATIONAL LEAGUE LEADERS

Home Runs
Wilson-Chi	56
Klein-Phi	40
Berger-Bos	38
Hartnett-Chi	37
Herman-Bro	35

Runs Batted In
Wilson-Chi	190
Klein-Phi	170
Cuyler-Chi	134
Herman-Bro	130
Terry-NY	129

Batting Average
Terry-NY	.401
Herman-Bro	.393
Klein-Phi	.386
O'Doul-Phi	.383
Lindstrom-NY	.379

On Base Percentage
Ott-NY	.458
Herman-Bro	.455
Wilson-Chi	.454
O'Doul-Phi	.453
Terry-NY	.452

Slugging Average
Wilson-Chi	.723
Klein-Phi	.687
Herman-Bro	.678
Hafey-StL	.652
Hartnett-Chi	.630

Stolen Bases
Cuyler-Chi	37
P.Waner-Pit	18
Herman-Bro	18

Wins
Malone-Chi	20
Kremer-Pit	20
Fitzsimmons-NY	19

Innings Pitched
Kremer-Pit	276.0
French-Pit	274.2
Malone-Chi	271.2
Vance-Bro	258.2
Seibold-Bos	251.0

Saves
Bell-StL	8
Heving-NY	6
Clark-Bro	6

Strikeouts
Hallahan-StL	177
Vance-Bro	173
Malone-Chi	142
Root-Chi	124
Hubbell-NY	117

Earned Run Average
Vance-Bro	2.61
Hubbell-NY	3.87
Walker-NY	3.93
Malone-Chi	3.94
Elliott-Bro	3.95

Complete Games
Malone-Chi	22
Brame-Pit	22
French-Pit	21
Vance-Bro	20
Seibold-Bos	20

AMERICAN LEAGUE LEADERS

Home Runs
Ruth-NY	49
Gehrig-NY	41
Goslin-Was-StL	37
Foxx-Phi	37
Simmons-Phi	36

Runs Batted In
Gehrig-NY	174
Simmons-Phi	165
Foxx-Phi	156
Ruth-NY	153
Goslin-Was-StL	138

Batting Average
Simmons-Phi	.381
Gehrig-NY	.379
Ruth-NY	.359
Reynolds-Chi	.359
Cochrane-Phi	.357

On Base Percentage
Ruth-NY	.493
Gehrig-NY	.473
Foxx-Phi	.429
Bishop-Phi	.426
Combs-NY	.424

Slugging Average
Ruth-NY	.732
Gehrig-NY	.721
Simmons-Phi	.708
Foxx-Phi	.637

Stolen Bases
McManus-Det	23
Gehringer-Det	19
Goslin-Was-StL	17
Johnson-Det	17
Cronin-Was	17

Wins
Grove-Phi	28
Ferrell-Cle	25
Lyons-Chi	22
Earnshaw-Phi	22
Stewart-StL	20

Innings Pitched
Lyons-Chi	297.2
Ferrell-Cle	296.2
Earnshaw-Phi	296.0
Grove-Phi	291.0
Crowder-StL-Was	279.2

Saves
Grove-Phi	9
Braxton-Was-Chi	6
Quinn-Phi	6
Sullivan-Det	5
McKain-Chi	5

Strikeouts
Grove-Phi	209
Earnshaw-Phi	193
Hadley-Was	162
Ferrell-Cle	143
Ruffing-Bos-NY	131

Earned Run Average
Grove-Phi	2.54
Ferrell-Cle	3.31
Stewart-StL	3.45
Uhle-Det	3.65
Hadley-Was	3.73

Complete Games
Lyons-Chi	29
Crowder-StL-Was	25
Ferrell-Cle	25
Stewart-StL	23
Grove-Phi	22

THE YEAR IN BASEBALL

January 10: Art "The Great" Shires, first baseman for the White Sox, TKO's Boston Braves' catcher Al Spohrer in a boxing match at Boston Garden.

January 20: Commissioner Kensaw Mountain Landis bans boxing for all players in the major leagues.

March 8: Babe Ruth ends a holdout and becomes the highest paid player ever by signing for $80,000; asked why he should earn more than President Hoover, he replied, "Why not? I had a better year."

March 12: Vern "Deacon" Law born; he took Cy Young Award honors in 1960.

May 12: Giants pitcher Larry Benson sets a major league record by giving up six home runs in a single game, but he gets the win, 14-12.

June 3: Grover Cleveland Alexander is released by the Phillies, ending his career with 373 wins.

July 25: The A's come up with a triple steal in the first inning and again in the fourth against Cleveland. This is the only time two triple steals are achieved in one game.

August 3: Smokey Joe Williams of the Homestead Grays beats Chet Brewer of the Kansas City Monarchs, 1-0 in 12 innings. Williams gave up only one hit and fanned 27.

August 26: Hack Wilson hits hits his 44th home run to break Chuck Klein's year-old record.

September 12: Brooklyn catcher Al Lopez hits the last "bounce" home run in the major leagues when he whacks a one-hopper into the bleachers at Ebbets Field. From 1931, such hits are ruled doubles.

September 27: The Cubs' Hack Wilson, who one week earlier set a major league record with his 176th RBI, hits his final two homers of the season, giving him 56 for a NL record, which stood until the Mark McGwire-Sammy Sosa home run race of 1998.

September 27: Babe Ruth hurls a 9-3 complete game win in Boston, and Lou Gehrig plays left field to end a streak of 885 consecutive games at first base.

1931

A Triple Crown for Lefty Grove, but Cards take Series

Baseball's only suspenseful pennant races in 1931 were to be found in the minor leagues. Both the AL Athletics and NL Cardinals stormed through their seasons with token competition. Their biggest distraction—as it was for the major leagues in general—was the economic depression taking tighter hold of the country. Only the Cubs drew a million fans, and they would be the last NL club to reach that level until 1941. In the AL, the million-customer plateau would prove elusive for the rest of the decade for all but the 1935 and 1937 Tigers.

The Athletics just about clinched matters with a 17-game winning streak in May; lingering skeptics were converted with another 12-game skein in July. As had become habit, Philadelphia's offense relied mainly on Jimmie Foxx (30 homers, 120 RBIs) and Al Simmons (22 homers, 128 RBIs, and a league-leading .390). But the biggest story in Shibe Park and around the rest of the league was Lefty Grove, who won his second straight pitching Triple Crown with 31 victories, a 2.06 ERA, and 175 strikeouts. At one point in the season, the southpaw fired off 16 straight wins. His final numbers represented the third of four times he compiled the most wins, the fourth of nine times he had the lowest ERA, and the seventh consecutive season of leading the circuit in strikeouts. The only thing equal to Grove's abilities was his temper. On one occasion, backup outfielder Jim Moore, who had misjudged a fly ball, hid in the clubhouse to protect life and limb as the pitcher tore up lockers because the miscue had cost him a win. Only when Grove had calmed down did he admit his cursing of "that &*!!$** outfielder" had been directed against Simmons, whose bad stomach had necessitated the insertion of Moore into the lineup in the first place.

The Yankees finished a distant 13-1/2 games from the top spot despite scoring a record 1,067 runs. Much of that was produced by Babe Ruth and Lou Gehrig, who shared the league home run lead (46), and by the latter's AL-record 184 RBIs. With its contest of August 3, New York would also launch a 308-game streak extending into 1933 without being shut out. In another offensive note, Boston's Earl Webb set the record for doubles in a season with 67.

In the NL, the batting race provided some of the tension the flag chase couldn't. When all the numbers were in, the Cardinals' Chick Hafey edged the Giants' Bill Terry by the margin of .3489 to .3486; Hafey teammate Jim Bottomley closed out at .348. St. Louis pitcher Bill Hallahan also emerged in the victory category by the thinnest of whiskers, his 19 wins tying him with Heinie Meine of Pittsburgh and Jumbo Jim Elliott of Philadelphia. Bill Walker of the Giants posted the best ERA at 2.26, while Philadelphia's Chuck Klein had the most homers (31) and RBIs (121).

The World Series was close to being the Pepper Martin Show. As in 1930, Grove and George Earnshaw did most of the Philadelphia pitching, ending up with three wins between them. But that gave them one less than the St. Louis tandem of Hallahan and Burleigh Grimes. As the difference, Martin went 12-24, with five RBIs, five runs scored, and five stolen bases.

Lefty Grove
The Athletics amazing southpaw had 16 straight wins, and 31 victories overall, to lead Philadelphia into the World Series.

1931 SEASON HIGHLIGHTS

NATIONAL LEAGUE

	W	L	Pct.	GB
St. Louis	101	53	.656	—
New York	87	65	.572	13
Chicago	84	70	.545	17
Brooklyn	79	73	.520	21
Pittsburgh	75	79	.487	26
Philadelphia	66	88	.429	35
Boston	64	90	.416	37
Cincinnati	58	96	.377	43

AMERICAN LEAGUE

	W	L	Pct.	GB
Philadelphia	107	45	.704	—
New York	94	59	.614	13.5
Washington	92	62	.597	16
Cleveland	78	76	.506	30
St. Louis	63	91	.409	45
Boston	62	90	.408	45
Detroit	61	93	.396	47
Chicago	56	97	.366	51.5

AWARDS

NL MVP: Frankie Frisch, STL
AL MVP: Lefty Grove, PHI

POSTSEASON
WORLD SERIES
St. Louis Cardinals 4, Philadelphia Athletics 3

Oct. 1: Philadelphia 6, ST. LOUIS 2
Oct. 2: ST. LOUIS 2, Philadelphia 0
Oct. 5: St. Louis 5, PHILADELPHIA 2
Oct. 6: PHILADELPHIA 3, St Louis 0
Oct. 7: St. Louis 5, PHILADELPHIA 1
Oct. 9: Philadelphia 8, ST. LOUIS 1
Oct. 10: ST. LOUIS 4, Philadelphia 2

Home team in CAPS

> "He could throw a lamb chop past a wolf."
>
> — Bugs Baer, on Lefty Grove

NATIONAL LEAGUE LEADERS

Home Runs		Runs Batted In		Batting Average	
Klein-Phi	31	Klein-Phi	121	Hafey-StL	.349
Ott-NY	29	Ott-NY	115	Terry-NY	.349
Berger-Bos	19	Terry-NY	112	Klein-Phi	.337
Herman-Bro	18	Traynor-Pit	103	O'Doul-Bro	.336
Arlett-Phi	18	Herman-Bro	97	Grimm-Chi	.331

On Base Percentage		Slugging Average		Stolen Bases	
Hafey-StL	.404	Klein-Phi	.584	Frisch-StL	28
Cuyler-Chi	.404	Hafey-StL	.569	Herman-Bro	17
P.Waner-Pit	.404	Ott-NY	.545	Martin-StL	16
Grantham-Pit	.400	Terry-NY	.529	Adams-StL	16
Klein-Phi	.398	Herman-Bro	.525	Watkins-StL	15

Wins		Innings Pitched		Saves	
Meine-Pit	19	Meine-Pit	284.0	Quinn-Bro	15
Hallahan-StL	19	French-Pit	275.2	Lindsey-StL	7
J.Elliott-Phi	19	Johnson-Cin	262.1	J.Elliott-Phi	5
		Fitzsimmons-NY	253.2	Hallahan-StL	4
		Root-Chi	251.0	Collins-Phi	4

Strikeouts		Earned Run Average		Complete Games	
Hallahan-StL	159	Walker-NY	2.26	Lucas-Cin	24
Hubbell-NY	155	Hubbell-NY	2.65	Brandt-Bos	23
Vance-Bro	150	Brandt-Bos	2.92	Meine-Pit	22
Derringer-StL	134	Meine-Pit	2.98	Hubbell-NY	21
Root-Chi	131	Johnson-StL	3.00	French-Pit	20

AMERICAN LEAGUE LEADERS

Home Runs		Runs Batted In		Batting Average	
Ruth-NY	46	Gehrig-NY	184	Simmons-Phi	.390
Gehrig-NY	46	Ruth-NY	163	Ruth-NY	.373
Averill-Cle	32	Averill-Cle	143	Morgan-Cle	.351
Foxx-Phi	30	Simmons-Phi	128	Cochrane-Phi	.349
Goslin-StL	24	Cronin-Was	126	Gehrig-NY	.341

On Base Percentage		Slugging Average		Stolen Bases	
Ruth-NY	.495	Ruth-NY	.700	Chapman-NY	61
Morgan-Cle	.451	Gehrig-NY	.662	Johnson-Det	33
Gehrig-NY	.446	Simmons-Phi	.641	Burns-StL	19
Simmons-Phi	.444	Averill-Cle	.576	Lazzeri-NY	18
Blue-Chi	.430	Foxx-Phi	.567	Cissell-Chi	18

Wins		Innings Pitched		Saves	
Grove-Phi	31	Walberg-Phi	291.0	Moore-Bos	10
Ferrell-Cle	22	Grove-Phi	288.2	Hadley-Was	8
Gomez-NY	21	Earnshaw-Phi	281.2	Marberry-Was	7
Earnshaw-Phi	21	Ferrell-Cle	276.1	Kimsey-StL	7
Walberg-Phi	20	Whitehill-Det	271.1	Earnshaw-Phi	6

Strikeouts		Earned Run Average		Complete Games	
Grove-Phi	175	Grove-Phi	2.06	Grove-Phi	27
Earnshaw-Phi	152	Gomez-NY	2.67	Ferrell-Cle	27
Gomez-NY	150	Hadley-Was	3.06	Earnshaw-Phi	23
Ruffing-NY	132	Brown-Was	3.20	Whitehill-Det	22
Hadley-Was	124	Marberry-Was	3.45	Stewart-StL	20

THE YEAR IN BASEBALL

January 4: Roger Connor dies; his 138 career homers stood as the record until Ruth topped it in 1921.

January 31: Ernie Banks is born.

February 21: The White Sox and Giants become the first two major league teams to play a night game when they meet in Houston's Buffs Stadium.

February 28: Ban Johnson, founder of the American League, dies after a long illness.

May 6: Willie Mays is born.

August 5: Tommy Bridges of the Tigers retires the first 26 Senators before pinch hitter Dave Harris gets a bloop single. Bridges wins, 13-0.

August 21: Babe Ruth hits his 600th home run, off George Blaeholder of the Browns.

August 23: Lefty Grove, attempting to win a record 17th consecutive games, loses 1-0 to the Browns after a routine fly ball is misplayed.

September 1: Lou Gehrig hits third grand slam in four days.

September 17: Earl Webb of the Red Sox sets a major league record with his 65th double of the season.

September 19: Lefty Grove becomes the first pitcher to win 30 games in a season since 1920.

September 20: Lou Gehrig drives in four runs to break his record of 175 in a season. He finishes with 184.

September 30: Babe Herman sets a record by hitting for the cycle for the third time in one season.

October 23: Brooklyn announces that Wilbert Robinson is through as manager and that the team will no longer be known as the Robins.

October 20: Mickey Mantle is born.

December 9: In response to the Depression, owners vote to reduce rosters from 25 to 23 players.

December 11: Two future Hall of Famers switch teams when Burleigh Grimes is traded by the Cards to the Cubs for Hack Wilson.

1932

A season of change ends with fabled Ruth 'called' homer

Before, during and after the season, 1932 was a year of major transitions. Prior to the campaign, Barney Dreyfuss died of complications from surgery after 31 years as Pirates owner. On June 4, the Giants announced that Dreyfuss' chief nemesis, John McGraw, was stepping down as manager after three decades. In August, Rogers Hornsby, reduced to a backup playing role for the first time in his career, also lost his managership of the Cubs after one conflict too many with players and team president William Veeck, Sr.; he would make only token appearances in the batter's box from then on. And following the season, Connie Mack would start breaking up the Athletics so definitively he would never again manage a postseason game.

Mack's decision to sell Al Simmons, Mule Haas and Jimmy Dykes to the White Sox came after the Yankees had turned the tables on Philadelphia from the previous year by streaking to their own pennant by the margin of 13 games. The reversal was hardly the fault of the key players on the A's: Jimmie Foxx paced the league in both homers (58) and RBIs (169) while averaging .364, Simmons turned in a typical .322-35-151 performance, and Lefty Grove won another 25 and another ERA title (2.84). But the 37-year-old Babe Ruth still had enough left in him for .341-41-137, Lou Gehrig was right there with him at .349-34-151, and both second baseman Tony Lazzeri and outfielder Ben Chapman also had 100 RBIs. On June 3, in Philadelphia, Gehrig became the first ALer to hit four home runs in a game. The ace of the New York pitching staff was Lefty Gomez (24 wins). The AL's biggest winner was Alvin Crowder of the Senators (26). The batting title went to first baseman Dale Alexander (.367), the first to capture it despite being traded during the season (from Detroit to Boston).

In the NL, Chicago took the flag by having the best replacements in the league. Although Hornsby already had the Cubs in first, his successor, first baseman Charlie Grimm, led them to twice as many victories over .500. The new second baseman, Billy Herman, restored range to the infield while batting .314. And after regular shortstop Billy Jurges was shot by a woman in a hotel, Mark Koenig came over from the Yankees to bat .353. Chicago's Lon Warneke led the league in both wins (22) and ERA (2.37). The other bests were New York's Mel Ott and Philadelphia's Chuck Klein for homers (38), Don Hurst of the Phillies for RBIs (143), and Lefty O'Doul of the Dodgers for batting (.368).

Koenig's contribution to the Chicago flag became a *casus belli* in

Lefty Gomez
With 24 wins, 176 strikeouts and a .774 win percentage, Gomez emerged as the ace of the Yankees staff.

the World Series against the Yankees. When the New Yorkers began mocking the Cubs for voting their ex-teammate only a half-share of the postseason pool, tensions built between the clubs. It was against this background that, in Game 3, Ruth walloped a homer off Charlie Root that, according to legend, he had predicted with great bravado by pointing to the center-field stands before swinging. The Cubs denied any such gesture. The controversy over the call was the highlight of the four-game Yankee sweep. Ruth and Gehrig combined for five homers and 14 RBIs as New York swatted the Chicago pitching staff at a .313 pace.

1932 SEASON HIGHLIGHTS

NATIONAL LEAGUE

	W	L	Pct.	GB
Chicago	90	64	.584	—
Pittsburgh	86	68	.558	4
Brooklyn	81	73	.526	9
Philadelphia	78	76	.506	12
Boston	77	77	.500	13
New York	72	82	.468	18
St. Louis	72	82	.468	18
Cincinnati	60	94	.390	30

AMERICAN LEAGUE

	W	L	Pct.	GB
New York	107	47	.695	—
Philadelphia	94	60	.610	13
Washington	93	61	.604	14
Cleveland	87	65	.572	19
Detroit	76	75	.503	29.5
St. Louis	63	91	.409	44
Chicago	49	102	.325	56.5
Boston	43	111	.279	64

AWARDS

NL MVP: Chuck Klein, PHI
AL MVP: Jimmie Foxx, PHI

POSTSEASON
WORLD SERIES
New York Yankees 4, Chicago Cubs 0
Sep. 28: NEW YORK 12, Chicago 6
Sep. 29: NEW YORK 5, Chicago 2
Oct. 1: New York 7, CHICAGO 5
Oct. 2: New York 13, CHICAGO 6

Home team in CAPS

> "The Good Lord was good to me. He gave me a strong body, a good right arm and a weak mind."
>
> — Dizzy Dean

NATIONAL LEAGUE LEADERS

Home Runs
Ott-NY	38
Klein-Phi	38
Terry-NY	28
Hurst-Phi	24
Wilson-Bro	23

Runs Batted In
Hurst-Phi	143
Klein-Phi	137
Whitney-Phi	124
Wilson-Bro	123
Ott-NY	123

Batting Average
O'Doul-Bro	.368
Terry-NY	.350
Klein-Phi	.348
P.Waner-Pit	.341
Hurst-Phi	.339

On Base Percentage
Ott-NY	.424
O'Doul-Bro	.423
Hurst-Phi	.412
Klein-Phi	.404
P.Waner-Pit	.397

Slugging Average
Klein-Phi	.646
Ott-NY	.601
Terry-NY	.580
O'Doul-Bro	.555
Hurst-Phi	.547

Stolen Bases
Klein-Phi	20
Piet-Pit	19
Watkins-StL	18
Frisch-StL	18
K.Davis-Phi	16

Wins
Warneke-Chi	22
Clark-Bro	20
Bush-Chi	19

Innings Pitched
Dean-StL	286.0
Hubbell-NY	284.0
Warneke-Chi	277.0
French-Pit	274.1
Clark-Bro	273.0

Saves
Quinn-Bro	8
Benge-Phi	6
Luque-NY	5
Cantwell-Bos	5

Strikeouts
Dean-StL	191
Hubbell-NY	137
Malone-Chi	120
Carleton-StL	113
Brown-Bos	110

Earned Run Average
Warneke-Chi	2.37
Hubbell-NY	2.50
Betts-Bos	2.80
Swetonic-Pit	2.82
Lucas-Cin	2.94

Complete Games
Lucas-Cin	28
Warneke-Chi	25
Hubbell-NY	22

AMERICAN LEAGUE LEADERS

Home Runs
Foxx-Phi	58
Ruth-NY	41
Simmons-Phi	35
Gehrig-NY	34
Averill-Cle	32

Runs Batted In
Foxx-Phi	169
Simmons-Phi	151
Gehrig-NY	151
Ruth-NY	137
Averill-Cle	124

Batting Average
Foxx-Phi	.364
Gehrig-NY	.349
Manush-Was	.342
Ruth-NY	.341
Walker-Det	.323

On Base Percentage
Ruth-NY	.489
Foxx-Phi	.469
Gehrig-NY	.451
Bishop-Phi	.412
Cochrane-Phi	.412

Slugging Average
Foxx-Phi	.749
Ruth-NY	.661
Gehrig-NY	.621
Averill-Cle	.569
Simmons-Phi	.548

Stolen Bases
Chapman-NY	38
Walker-Det	30
Johnson-Det-Bos	20
Cissell-Chi-Cle	18

Wins
Crowder-Was	26
Grove-Phi	25
Gomez-NY	24
Ferrell-Cle	23
Weaver-Was	22

Innings Pitched
Crowder-Was	327.0
Grove-Phi	291.2
Ferrell-Cle	287.2
Walberg-Phi	272.0
Gomez-NY	265.1

Saves
Marberry-Was	13
Moore-Bos-NY	8
Hogsett-Det	7
Grove-Phi	7
Faber-Chi	6

Strikeouts
Ruffing-NY	190
Grove-Phi	188
Gomez-NY	176
Hadley-Chi-StL	145
Pipgras-NY	111

Earned Run Average
Grove-Phi	2.84
Ruffing-NY	3.09
Lyons-Chi	3.28
Crowder-Was	3.33
Bridges-Det	3.36

Complete Games
Grove-Phi	27
Ferrell-Cle	26
Ruffing-NY	22

THE YEAR IN BASEBALL

January 12: Cincinnati's Edd Roush, the premier center fielder of his day, retires from baseball.

January 26: William K. Wrigley, owner of the Cubs since 1919, dies and is succeeded by his son, Philip K. Wrigley.

February 5: Barney Dreyfuss, owner of the Pirates, dies. National League President John Heydler says "I cannot tell how deeply I feel the loss of Barney Dreyfuss. He discovered more great players than any man in the history of Baseball."

March 14: The Dodgers trade Ernie Lombardi, Babe Herman, Wally Gilbert to the Reds for Tony Cuccinello, Joe Stripp, Clyde Sukeforth.

May 11: Cardinals pitcher "Wild" Bill Hallahan throws three wild pitches in one inning to tie the record set in 1903 by Jake Weimer.

June 4: Lou Gehrig becomes the first player in the century to hit four homers in a game, but the headlines go to John McGraw's resignation as Giant manager.

July 10: Philadelphia's Athletics defeat the Indians, 18-17, in 18 frames even though winning pitcher Ed Rommel allows 29 hits in 17 innings of relief. Cleveland's Johnny Burnett gets nine hits.

July 31: Cleveland opens the new Municipal Stadium before a crowd in excess of 80,000.

August 21: Cleveland's Wes Ferrell becomes the first pitcher to win at least 20 games in each of his first four seasons.

September 3: Jimmie Fox joins joins Babe Ruth and Hack Wilson as the only players to hit 50 home runs in a season when he whacks Nos. 50 and 51.

September 7: Pirates catcher Earl Grace makes a wild throw to end a streak of 110 errorless games, an NL record.

December 14: The Browns trade Goose Goslin to Senators, whom he will lead to the 1933 pennant.

1933

All-Star Game debuts as Philly witnesses double Triple Crown

The biggest show of the year took place on July 6, when the National and American leagues met at Comiskey Park in the first All-Star game. The exhibition was promoted by the *Chicago Tribune* and its sports editor Arch Ward in conjunction with the city's Century of Progress Exposition. With the retired John McGraw managing the NL and Connie Mack the AL, the junior circuit managed a 4-2 victory, largely (and appropriately) on the strength of a two-run homer by Babe Ruth.

In regular-season competition, Philadelphia had the best players of the year, but New York and Washington ended up with the entries to the World Series. In a never-duplicated feat for one city, both Chuck Klein of the Phillies and Jimmie Foxx of the Athletics won the Triple Crown. Klein did it with .368-28-120, Foxx with .356-48-163. Another Philadelphian, Lefty Grove, tied with Washington's Alvin Crowder for the most AL wins (24), while Cleveland's Monte Pearson recorded the lowest ERA (2.33). In the NL, Carl Hubbell of the Giants had both the most wins (23) and lowest ERA (1.66).

New York's NL flag was a big surprise, not only because of the club's sixth-place finish in 1932, but also because of manager Bill Terry's problems with personnel. Over the winter, Terry had lobbied successfully for the trading of Freddie Lindstrom because of the third baseman's resentment he hadn't been chosen as McGraw's successor; hardly had spring training begun than the dugout boss got into a fistfight with coach Billy Southworth, who had his own managerial ambitions (and even experience at the major league level). Terry himself led the team with his .322 average, while Mel Ott clouted 23 homers and drove home 103. Aside from Hubbell, the team got 19 wins from Hal Schumacher and 16 from Freddie Fitzsimmons.

As with Terry and the Giants, the Senators were driven to their pennant by a playing manager—shortstop Joe Cronin. Also like Terry, Cronin represented a good part of his team's offense—batting .309 with 118 RBIs. In addition to Crowder, the team got 22 wins from Earl Whitehill—one of three pitchers Cronin had urged owner Clark Griffith to get during the off-season behind a promise they would bring Washington a pennant. The other two—Lefty Stewart and Jack Russell—did their share, as well, combining for 27 wins. The bottom line was 99 victories, the most ever recorded by the Senators. In toppling the Yankees, the club also engaged in a series of nasty brawls with the reigning champions. One April melee at Griffith Stadium led to fines and suspensions of players and arrests of fans.

Washington's only real moment in the World Series came with a Game 3 shutout by Whitehill. Otherwise, the story was Hubbell,

Mickey Cochrane
Athletics manager Connie Mack sold Cochrane, one of the greatest catchers in major league history, to Detroit following the 1933 season.

who pitched two complete-game victories spanning 20 innings and yielding no earned runs.

After the season, Mack continued his breakup of the Athletics by dealing Grove and Rube Walberg to the Red Sox, Mickey Cochrane to the Tigers and George Earnshaw to the White Sox.

1933 SEASON HIGHLIGHTS

NATIONAL LEAGUE

	W	L	Pct.	GB
New York	91	61	.599	—
Pittsburgh	87	67	.565	5
Chicago	86	68	.558	6
Boston	83	71	.539	9
St. Louis	82	71	.536	9.5
Brooklyn	65	88	.425	26.5
Philadelphia	60	92	.395	31
Cincinnati	58	94	.382	33

AMERICAN LEAGUE

	W	L	Pct.	GB
Washington	99	53	.651	—
New York	91	59	.607	7
Philadelphia	79	72	.523	19.5
Cleveland	75	76	.497	23.5
Detroit	75	79	.487	25
Chicago	67	83	.447	31
Boston	63	86	.423	34.5
St. Louis	55	96	.364	43.5

AWARDS

NL MVP: Carl Hubbell, NY
AL MVP: Jimmie Foxx, PHI

ALL-STAR GAME

Comiskey Park, Chicago
July 6: AL 4, NL 2

POSTSEASON
WORLD SERIES
New York Giants 4, Washington Senators 1
Oct. 3: NEW YORK 4, Washington 2
Oct. 4: NEW YORK 6, Washington 1
Oct. 5: WASHINGTON 4, New York 0
Oct. 6: New York 2, WASHINGTON 1
Oct. 7: New York 4, WASHINGTON 3

Home team in CAPS

"He has muscles in his hair."

— Lefty Gomez, on the strength
of Jimmie Foxx

NATIONAL LEAGUE LEADERS

Home Runs
Klein-Phi	28
Berger-Bos	27
Ott-NY	23
Medwick-StL	18

Runs Batted In
Klein-Phi	120
Berger-Bos	106
Ott-NY	103
Medwick-StL	98
Vaughan-Pit	97

Batting Average
Klein-Phi	.368
Davis-Phi	.349
Terry-NY	.322
Schulmerich-Bs-Phi	.318
Martin-StL	.316

On Base Percentage
Klein-Phi	.422
Davis-Phi	.395
Vaughan-Pit	.388
Martin-StL	.387
Terry-NY	.375

Slugging Average
Klein-Phi	.602
Berger-Bos	.566
B.Herman-Chi	.502
Medwick-StL	.497
Vaughan-Pit	.478

Stolen Bases
Martin-StL	26
Fullis-Phi	18
Frisch-StL	18
Klein-Phi	15
Orsatti-StL	14

Wins
Hubbell-NY	23
Dean-StL	20
Cantwell-Bos	20
Bush-Chi	20
Schumacher-NY	19

Innings Pitched
Hubbell-NY	308.2
Dean-StL	293.0
French-Pit	291.1
Brandt-Bos	287.2
Warneke-Chi	287.1

Saves
Collins-Phi	6
Hubbell-NY	5
Harris-Pit	5
Bell-NY	5

Strikeouts
Dean-StL	199
Hubbell-NY	156
Carleton-StL	147
Warneke-Chi	133
Parmelee-NY	132

Earned Run Average
Hubbell-NY	1.66
Warneke-Chi	2.00
Schumacher-NY	2.16
Brandt-Bos	2.60
Root-Chi	2.60

Complete Games
Warneke-Chi	26
Dean-StL	26
Brandt-Bos	23
Hubbell-NY	22

AMERICAN LEAGUE LEADERS

Home Runs
Foxx-Phi	48
Ruth-NY	34
Gehrig-NY	32
Johnson-Phi	21
Lazzeri-NY	18

Runs Batted In
Foxx-Phi	163
Gehrig-NY	139
Simmons-Chi	119
Cronin-Was	118
Kuhel-Was	107

Batting Average
Foxx-Phi	.356
Manush-Was	.336
Gehrig-NY	.334
Simmons-Chi	.331
Gehringer-Det	.325

On Base Percentage
Cochrane-Phi	.459
Foxx-Phi	.449
Bishop-Phi	.446
Ruth-NY	.442
Gehrig-NY	.424

Slugging Average
Foxx-Phi	.703
Gehrig-NY	.605
Ruth-NY	.582
Cochrane-Phi	.515
Johnson-Phi	.505

Stolen Bases
Chapman-NY	27
Walker-Det	26
Swanson-Chi	19
Kuhel-Was	17

Wins
Grove-Phi	24
Crowder-Was	24
Whitehill-Was	22

Innings Pitched
Hadley-StL	316.2
Crowder-Was	299.1
Grove-Phi	275.1
Whitehill-Was	270.0
Blaeholder-StL	255.2

Saves
Russell-Was	13
Hogsett-Det	9
Moore-NY	8
Heving-Chi	6
Grove-Phi	6

Strikeouts
Gomez-NY	163
Hadley-StL	149
Ruffing-NY	122
Bridges-Det	120
Allen-NY	119

Earned Run Average
Harder-Cle	2.95
Bridges-Det	3.09
Gomez-NY	3.18
Grove-Phi	3.20
Weaver-Was	3.25

Complete Games
Grove-Phi	21
Whitehill-Was	19
Hadley-StL	19
Ruffing-NY	18

THE YEAR IN BASEBALL

January 2: Kid Gleason dies.

January 7: Commissioner Kenesaw Mountain Landis cuts his salary 40% as a signal that salaries must be trimmed because of the Depression.

February 25: Tom Yawkey and former star player Eddie Collins by the Boston Red Sox from Robert Quinn.

April 29: Luke Sewell of the Washington Senators tags out two Yankees at home on the same play.

June 9: Walter Johnson takes over as Cleveland manager.

July 2: Carl Hubbell of the Giants hurls an 18-inning shutout, allowing Cardinals six hits and no walks, to tie a record for the longest 1-0 game.

July 6: The first All-Star Game is played at Comiskey Park, with the AL defeating the NL, 4-2, on Babe Ruth's two-run homer.

July 26: Fired as the Cardinals' manager the previous day, Rogers Hornsby signs to manage the Browns, so he doesn't even have to move out of his apartment in St. Louis.

July 30: Dizzy Dean becomes the first pitcher in the 20th century to record 17 strikeouts in a game.

August 1: Carl Hubbell breaks Ed Reulbach's 1908 NL record for consecutive scoreless innings when his streak reaches 45-1/3.

August 14: Jimmie Foxx hits for the cycle and sets an AL record by driving in nine runs.

October 1: Nick Altrock pinch hits for Washington at age of 57; like Minnie Minoso, he played in five decades.

November 21: After winning the Triple Crown, Chuck Klein is sent to the Cubs in exchange for $125,000 and three players: Mark Koenig, Harvey Hendrick and Ted Kleinhans.

1934

Tigers G-Men romp as Gas House Gang delights St. Louis

With the help of some shrewd publicizing by general manager Branch Rickey, St. Louis' scruffy Gashouse Gang became the emblematic team of one of the worst Depression years. The popularity and success of the Cardinals came despite some individual performances that should have made New York the game's epicenter.

For folklore purposes, the season got under way during the February winter meetings when Giants manager Bill Terry's rhetorical question of "Is Brooklyn still in the league?" was taken out of context by Dodgers officials and exploited to full headline and ticket-window effect. For 127 of the season's 138 days, this didn't deter New York from occupying first place, in good part because of Mel Ott's league-leading numbers in homers (35) and RBIs (135) and Carl Hubbell's pace-setting 2.30 ERA. But the 11 days the team wasn't on the top rung included the final hours of the campaign, when the lowly Dodgers came back to bite Terry while Dizzy and Paul Dean were defeating the Reds for St. Louis. The Cardinals comeback, driven by Dizzy Dean's 30 victories, climaxed a year begun with Rickey inventing nicknames ("The Wild Horse of the Osage" for Pepper Martin, "Ducky" for Joe Medwick, etc.) and habits (all-night carousing, especially) for his players that they took on only through exposure to their own press clippings. The biggest bat in the Cardinals lineup was first baseman Rip Collins, who tied Ott's 35 homers and drove in 128 runs to go with his .333 average. Pittsburgh's Paul Waner won the batting title at .362.

In the AL, the Yankees accounted for the most impressive individual heroics, but still ended up seven games behind Detroit's G-Men, Hank Greenberg, Charlie Gehringer and Goose Goslin. Not only did Lou Gehrig win the hitting Triple Crown at .363-49-165, but teammate Lefty Gomez took its pitching equivalent with 26 victories, a 2.33 ERA, and 158 strikeouts. For their part, the .300-hitting G-Men trio combined for 366 RBIs; shortstop Billy Rogell also reached the century mark. The Tiger pitching was led by Schoolboy Rowe (24) and Tommy Bridges (22). For its part, Washington tried to attract attention to its dreary seventh-place club with promotions and stunts, one of which was the signing of the streamer-bearded Allen Benson from the semi-pro House of David team; the right-hander quit after two games and an ERA over 12.

The World Series story should have been the Dean brothers. After winning seven times over the last eleven days of the regular season, the Deans combined for four more victories in a seven-game tussle against the Tigers. But even their efforts were eclipsed

Dizzy Dean
The colorful pitcher won 30 games and combined with his brother, Paul, to win four more as the Cardinals won the World Series.

by Game 7 ugliness precipitated when, with St. Louis already up 8-0, Medwick crashed into Detroit third baseman Marv Owen. After the players exchanged a few blows, Tiger fans began unleashing their frustration on the Cardinal left fielder. Commissioner Kenesaw Landis, in attendance, finally had to ask manager Frankie Frisch to remove Medwick from the game to head off rioting, a forfeit, or both.

The year's melancholy note came after the season, when the Yankees sent 39-year-old Babe Ruth on his way; he later signed with the Braves.

1934 SEASON HIGHLIGHTS

NATIONAL LEAGUE

	W	L	Pct.	GB
St. Louis	95	58	.621	—
New York	93	60	.608	2
Chicago	86	65	.570	8
Boston	78	73	.517	16
Pittsburgh	74	76	.493	19.5
Brooklyn	71	81	.467	23.5
Philadelphia	56	93	.376	37
Cincinnati	52	99	.344	42

AMERICAN LEAGUE

	W	L	Pct.	GB
Detroit	101	53	.656	—
New York	94	60	.610	7
Cleveland	85	69	.552	16
Boston	76	76	.500	24
Philadelphia	68	82	.453	31
St. Louis	67	85	.441	33
Washington	66	86	.434	34
Chicago	53	99	.349	47

AWARDS

NL MVP: Dizzy Dean, STL
AL MVP: Mickey Cochrane, DET

ALL-STAR GAME
Polo Grounds, New York
July 10: AL 9, NL 7

POSTSEASON
WORLD SERIES
St. Louis Cardinals 4, Detroit Tigers 3
Oct. 3: St. Louis 8, DETROIT 3
Oct. 4: DETROIT 3, St. Louis 2
Oct. 5: ST. LOUIS 4, Detroit 1
Oct. 6: Detroit 10, ST. LOUIS 4
Oct. 7: Detroit 3, ST. LOUIS 1
Oct. 8: St. Louis 4, DETROIT 3
Oct. 9: St. Louis 11, DETROIT 0

Home team in CAPS

"If I'd known what Paul was gonna
do, I would have pitched one, too."
— Dizzy Dean, after Paul Dean pitched
a no-hitter in the second half of a
Dean brothers double-header.

NATIONAL LEAGUE LEADERS

Home Runs
Ott-NY	35
Collins-StL	35
Berger-Bos	34
Hartnett-Chi	22
Klein-Chi	20

Runs Batted In
Ott-NY	135
Collins-StL	128
Berger-Bos	121
Medwick-StL	106
Suhr-Pit	103

Batting Average
P.Waner-Pit	.362
Terry-NY	.354
Cuyler-Chi	.338
Vaughan-Pit	.333
Collins-StL	.333

On Base Percentage
Vaughan-Pit	.431
P.Waner-Pit	.429
Ott-NY	.415
Terry-NY	.414
Koenecke-Bro	.411

Slugging Average
Collins-StL	.615
Ott-NY	.591
Berger-Bos	.546
P.Waner-Pit	.539
Medwick-StL	.529

Stolen Bases
Martin-StL	23
Cuyler-Chi	15
Bartell-Phi	13
Taylor-Bro	12

Wins
D.Dean-StL	30
Schumacher-NY	23
Warneke-Chi	22
Hubbell-NY	21

Innings Pitched
Mungo-Bro	315.1
Hubbell-NY	313.0
D.Dean-StL	311.2
Schumacher-NY	297.0
Warneke-Chi	291.1

Saves
Hubbell-NY	8
Luque-NY	7
D.Dean-StL	7
Bell-NY	6

Strikeouts
D.Dean-StL	195
Mungo-Bro	184
P.Dean-StL	150
Warneke-Chi	143
Derringer-Cin	122

Earned Run Average
Hubbell-NY	2.30
D.Dean-StL	2.66
Hoyt-Pit	2.93
C.Davis-Phi	2.95
Fitzsimmons-NY	3.04

Complete Games
Hubbell-NY	25
D.Dean-StL	24
Warneke-Chi	23
Mungo-Bro	22
Brandt-Bos	20

AMERICAN LEAGUE LEADERS

Home Runs
Gehrig-NY	49
Foxx-Phi	44
Trosky-Cle	35
Johnson-Phi	34
Averill-Cle	31

Runs Batted In
Gehrig-NY	165
Trosky-Cle	142
Greenberg-Det	139
Foxx-Phi	130
Gehringer-Det	127

Batting Average
Gehrig-NY	.363
Gehringer-Det	.356
Manush-Was	.349
Simmons-Chi	.344
Greenberg-Det	.339

On Base Percentage
Gehrig-NY	.465
Gehringer-Det	.450
Foxx-Phi	.449
Cochrane-Det	.428
Myer-Was	.419

Slugging Average
Gehrig-NY	.706
Foxx-Phi	.653
Greenberg-Det	.600
Trosky-Cle	.598
Averill-Cle	.569

Stolen Bases
Werber-Bos	40
White-Det	28
Chapman-NY	26
Fox-Det	25
Walker-Det	20

Wins
Gomez-NY	26
Rowe-Det	24
Bridges-Det	22
Harder-Cle	20
Ruffing-NY	19

Innings Pitched
Gomez-NY	281.2
Bridges-Det	275.0
Rowe-Det	266.0
Newsom-StL	262.1
Ruffing-NY	256.1

Saves
Russell-Was	7
L.Brown-Cle	6
Newsom-StL	5

Strikeouts
Gomez-NY	158
Bridges-Det	151
Ruffing-NY	149
Rowe-Det	149
Pearson-Cle	140

Earned Run Average
Gomez-NY	2.33
Harder-Cle	2.61
Murphy-NY	3.12
Burke-Was	3.21
Auker-Det	3.42

Complete Games
Gomez-NY	25
Bridges-Det	23
Lyons-Chi	21
Rowe-Det	20

THE YEAR IN BASEBALL

January 5: The Yankees release two Hall of Famers on the same day—Joe Sewell and Herb Pennock.

February 5: Henry Aaron is born.

February 25: John McGraw dies of uremia at his home in New Rochelle, NY, at age 60. His turn as the NL manager at the 1933 All-Star Game turned out to be his last public appearance.

April 17: Casey Stengel makes his managerial debut in an 8-7 Dodgers loss to the Braves.

April 28: Goose Goslin of the Tigers grounds into four double plays in one game.

April 29: Luis Aparicio is born.

July 13: Babe Ruth hits home run number 700.

August 18: Roberto Clemente is born.

September 13: In the first time a fee is collected, the World Series broadcast rights are sold to the Ford Motor Company for $100,000

September 21: Dizzy Dean and brother Paul each shut out the Dodgers in a twin bill. Diz throws a three-hitter in then opener, and then Paul outdoes him by hurling a no-hitter in the nightcap.

October 9: Dizzy Dean blanks the Tigers, 11-0, in Game 7, and the Cardinals take the World Series, 4-3.

October 26: The Bosox get Joe Cronin from Washington for $250,000 and Lyn Lary in a deal in which the Senators' owner Clark Griffith dealt his own son-in-law.

November 8: Ford Frick is named NL president.

November 21: The Yankees buy Joe DiMaggio from the San Francisco Seals for $25,000 and four players—he had hit in 61 straight games in 1933.

December 11: The NL votes to permit night baseball, authorizing a maximum of seven games for any team that installs lights. The AL does not follow suit until 1937.

1935

Ruth has last hurrah, Tigers take Series without Greenberg

With the exception of one game, Babe Ruth's return to Boston was a disaster. Only he took seriously a title as "second vice-president" and only the reigning Braves pilot, the threatened Bill McKechnie, took seriously his other supposed post as "assistant manager" of the last-place team. Amid all the resultant disgruntlement, Ruth worked himself up to one final star performance—three homers and a single against the Pirates on May 25. After another hitless contest and a final at bat against the Phillies, he announced his retirement on June 2.

At the other end of the NL, the Cubs wrestled most of the year with the Cardinals and Giants before taking the pennant. The issue was resolved mathematically when Chicago went on a 21-game winning tear down the stretch, but manager Charlie Grimm's most decisive move came much earlier, when he benched himself in favor of 19-year-old Phil Cavaretta; the teenage first baseman teamed with second baseman Billy Herman (.341) to give the Cubs a defensive fortress on the right side of the infield while also driving home 82 runs. Both Bill Lee and Lon Warneke contributed 20 wins. St. Louis finished four back despite Dizzy Dean's 28 victories. The year's other top achievers were Boston's Wally Berger (34 homers and 130 RBIs) and Pittsburgh's Arky Vaughan (.385) and Cy Blanton (2.58 ERA). Although hardly evident at the time, the league's signal event of the season was at Crosley Field on May 24, when Cincinnati's Larry MacPhail presided over the first big-league night game. Before 20,422 fans, the lighting system was activated via a remote-control button operated in Washington by President Franklin Delano Roosevelt. The only reason NL owners had permitted what they called an "experiment" was they had been losing money for years going to Crosley to play the drab Reds.

In the AL, the Tigers overcame an early-season residence in the cellar to win their second-straight flag. The Detroit attack was led by first baseman Hank Greenberg's league-leading 36 homers and 170 RBIs. The other two charter members of the G-Men—second baseman Charlie Gehringer and outfielder Goose Goslin—also racked up more than 100 RBIs. The final three-game edge over the Yankees owed no little to a rotation of Tommy Bridges (21), Schoolboy Rowe (19), Elden Auker (18), and Alvin Crowder (16). It was the Red Sox, however, who flashed the most imposing one-two punch from the mound, with Wes Ferrell winning 25 and Lefty Grove posting a 2.70 ERA. Washington second baseman Buddy Myer took the batting title (.349). A former Senator, Walter Johnson,

Gabby Harnett
A perennial all-star, the Cubs power-hitting catcher batted .344 and was named the NL's MVP after leading Chicago into the World Series.

spent the first half of the year as Cleveland manager dodging the brickbats of his players and the pop bottles of angry fans before he was fired.

An opening game shutout by Warneke and Greenberg's broken wrist in the second game appeared to give the Cubs a huge edge in the World Series. But with Bridges winning twice and unheralded outfielder Pete Fox collecting 10 hits and key RBIs, Detroit rebounded for a championship win in six games.

After the season, Connie Mack completed his dismemberment of the Athletics by dealing slugger Jimmie Foxx to the Red Sox.

1935 SEASON HIGHLIGHTS

NATIONAL LEAGUE

	W	L	Pct.	GB
Chicago	100	54	.649	—
St. Louis	96	58	.623	4
New York	91	62	.595	8.5
Pittsburgh	86	67	.562	13.5
Brooklyn	70	83	.458	29.5
Cincinnati	68	85	.444	31.5
Philadelphia	64	89	.418	35.5
Boston	38	115	.248	61.5

AMERICAN LEAGUE

	W	L	Pct.	GB
Detroit	93	58	.616	—
New York	89	60	.597	3
Cleveland	82	71	.536	12
Boston	78	75	.510	16
Chicago	74	78	.487	19.5
Washington	67	86	.438	27
St. Louis	65	87	.428	28.5
Philadelphia	58	91	.389	34

AWARDS

NL MVP: Gabby Hartnett, CHI
AL MVP: Hank Greenberg, DET

ALL-STAR GAME

Municipal Stadium, Cleveland
July 8: AL 4, NL 1

POSTSEASON
WORLD SERIES
Detroit Tigers 4, Chicago Cubs 2
Oct. 2: Chicago 3, DETROIT 0
Oct. 3: DETROIT 8, Chicago 3
Oct. 4: Detroit 6, CHICAGO 5
Oct. 5: Detroit 2, CHICAGO 1
Oct. 6: CHICAGO 3, Detroit 1
Oct. 7: DETROIT 4, Chicago 3

Home team in CAPS

"There's a big difference between knowing what's coming and hitting it."
— Hank Greenberg

NATIONAL LEAGUE LEADERS

Home Runs
Berger-Bos	34
Ott-NY	31
Camilli-Phi	25
Medwick-StL	23
R.Collins-StL	23

Runs Batted In
Berger-Bos	130
Medwick-StL	126
R.Collins-StL	122
Ott-NY	114
Leiber-NY	107

Batting Average
Vaughan-Pit	.385
Medwick-StL	.353
Herman-Chi	.341
Terry-NY	.341
Leiber-NY	.331

On Base Percentage
Vaughan-Pit	.491
Ott-NY	.407
Hack-Chi	.406
Galan-Chi	.399
P.Waner-Pit	.392

Slugging Average
Vaughan-Pit	.607
Medwick-StL	.576
Ott-NY	.555
Berger-Bos	.548
R.Collins-StL	.529

Stolen Bases
Galan-Chi	22
Martin-StL	20
Bordagaray-Bro	18
Hack-Chi	14
Goodman-Cin	14

Wins
D.Dean-StL	28
Hubbell-NY	23
Derringer-Cin	22
Warneke-Chi	20
Lee-Chi	20

Innings Pitched
D.Dean-StL	325.1
Hubbell-NY	302.2
Derringer-Cin	276.2
P.Dean-StL	269.2

Saves
Leonard-Bro	8
Johnson-Phi	6
Hoyt-Pit	6

Strikeouts
D.Dean-StL	190
Hubbell-NY	150
Mungo-Bro	143
P.Dean-StL	143
Blanton-Pit	142

Earned Run Average
Blanton-Pit	2.58
Swift-Pit	2.70
Schumacher-NY	2.89
French-Chi	2.96
Lee-Chi	2.96

Complete Games
D.Dean-StL	29
Hubbell-NY	24
Blanton-Pit	23
Warneke-Chi	20
Derringer-Cin	20

AMERICAN LEAGUE LEADERS

Home Runs
Greenberg-Det	36
Foxx-Phi	36
Gehrig-NY	30
Johnson-Phi	28
Trosky-Cle	26

Runs Batted In
Greenberg-Det	170
Gehrig-NY	119
Foxx-Phi	115
Trosky-Cle	113
Solters-Bos-StL	112

Batting Average
Myer-Was	.349
Vosmik-Cle	.348
Foxx-Phi	.346
Cramer-Phi	.332
Gehringer-Det	.330

On Base Percentage
Gehrig-NY	.466
Foxx-Phi	.461
Cochrane-Det	.452
Myer-Was	.440
Appling-Chi	.437

Slugging Average
Foxx-Phi	.636
Greenberg-Det	.628
Gehrig-NY	.583
Vosmik-Cle	.537
Fox-Det	.513

Stolen Bases
Werber-Bos	29
Lary-Was-StL	28
Almada-Bos	20
White-Det	19
Chapman-NY	17

Wins
W.Ferrell-Bos	25
Harder-Cle	22
Bridges-Det	21
Grove-Bos	20
Rowe-Det	19

Innings Pitched
W.Ferrell-Bos	322.1
Harder-Cle	287.1
Whitehill-Was	279.1
Rowe-Det	275.2
Bridges-Det	274.1

Saves
Knott-StL	7

Strikeouts
Bridges-Det	163
Rowe-Det	140
Gomez-NY	138
Grove-Bos	121
Allen-NY	113

Earned Run Average
Grove-Bos	2.70
Lyons-Chi	3.02
Ruffing-NY	3.12
Gomez-NY	3.18
Harder-Cle	3.29

Complete Games
W.Ferrell-Bos	31
Grove-Bos	23
Bridges-Det	23
Rowe-Det	21

THE YEAR IN BASEBALL

February 26: Babe Ruth, released by the Yankees, signs a three-year contract with the Braves.

April 16: Babe Ruth makes his National League debut with a single and home run for the Braves in front of a record opening day crowd in Boston of 25,000.

May 9: After breaking his ankle in spring training, the Braves Rabbit Maranville sets a record for NL service by appearing in his 23rd season.

May 24: In the first major league night game, the Reds beat the Phillies 2-1 at Crosley Field, Cincinnati.

May 25: Babe Ruth hits his last major league homer, off Guy Bush in Pittsburgh, clearing the right-field roof after having hit two homers earlier in the same game.

July 10: Paul Hines dies. He played from 1872-91 in Washington and Providence. In 1878, he was the first to achieve the Triple Crown in the National League.

August 4: Walter Johnson resigns as Cleveland manager and is replaced by Steve O'Neill.

August 26: Zeke Bonura, of all people, steals home in the 15th frame to give the White Sox a 9-8 win over the Yankees.

August 31: Vern Kennedy pitches the first AL no hitter since 1931, and the first ever at Comiskey Park, blanking Cleveland 5-0.

September 27: The Cubs win their 21st consecutive game without a loss or tie (the 1916 New York Giants won 26 with one tie) and clinch the pennant.

November 9: Bob Gibson is born.

December 10: Jimmie Foxx, with Johnny Marcum, is sold by the A's to the Red Sox for $150,000.

1936

Year of the rookie: DiMaggio bats .325, Feller fans 15 in debut

Injuries, streaks and very special rookies vied for attention in 1936. On the injury front, Detroit slugger Hank Greenberg, who had missed most of the 1935 World Series with a broken wrist, suffered a similar setback a mere 12 games into the season and was lost for the year. The pressure of trying to catch the Yankees without his best hitter proved too much for Tigers playing manager Mickey Cochrane, who had to be sent home in midseason on the verge of a nervous breakdown. In the National League, the Cardinals couldn't overcome the Giants in good part because of arm miseries that sidelined Paul Dean. Even pennant-winning New York had to get along most of the year without playing manager Bill Terry, whose knee problems persuaded him to retire at the end of the campaign.

Without the Tigers to worry about, the Yankees rolled easily to the AL pennant. Lou Gehrig once again posed the biggest offensive threat with a league-leading 49 homers to go along with a .354 average and 152 RBIs. But right behind him was New York rookie Joe DiMaggio at .323-29-125. The fact that DiMaggio was in pinstripes also owed somewhat to an injury: After the outfielder had banged up his knee in the Pacific Coast League in 1934, original enthusiasm by other teams for his services waned significantly, leaving only New York executive George Weiss ardent to sign him. DiMaggio wasn't the only first-year player to make an instant impression. On August 23, 17-year-old Bob Feller debuted for the Indians with a 15-strikeout performance against the Browns; three weeks later, he struck out 17 Athletics. The season honors were spread around among Cleveland's Hal Trosky (162 RBIs), Chicago's Luke Appling (.388), Detroit's Tommy Bridges (23 wins), and Boston's Lefty Grove (2.81 ERA).

For a good part of the year, the Giants, Cubs and Cardinals went back and forth at the top of the NL. In June, Chicago won 15 in a row, only to have New York match that streak in July. Even more decisive, however, was a 16-game winning streak by Carl Hubbell, which steadied the Giants pitching staff down the stretch. Hubbell led the league in both wins (26) and ERA (2.31). Mel Ott led the offense at the Polo Grounds with a league-leading 33 homers to go along with 135 RBIs. No other member of the team homered in double figures or drove in more than 67 runs; among the pitchers, the biggest winner after Hubbell was Al Smith with a shruggable record of 14-13. The league's other offensive leaders for the year were Joe Medwick of the Cardinals (138 RBIs) and Paul Waner of the Pirates (.373).

The return to an all-New York World Series disappointed dramatically. After Hubbell's opening-game victory, the Yankees ran roughshod over Giants pitching, even clouting the NL ace for four quick runs in Game 4. Gehrig and second baseman Tony Lazzeri

Carl Hubbell
A 16-game winning streak led Hubbell to a league-best 26 wins and 2.31 ERA as he carried the Giants into a World Series showdown against the Yankees.

ended up with seven RBIs each, Jake Powell and Red Rolfe with 10 hits apiece, and Lefty Gomez with two victories.

Prior to the 1936 season, the results of the first Hall of Fame election balloting were announced. Named as the pioneer members were Ty Cobb, Babe Ruth, Honus Wagner, Christy Mathewson, and Walter Johnson. The quintet was not actually inducted until the formal opening of the Cooperstown museum on June 12, 1939.

1936 SEASON HIGHLIGHTS

NATIONAL LEAGUE

	W	L	Pct.	GB
New York	92	62	.597	—
St. Louis	87	67	.565	5
Chicago	87	67	.565	5
Pittsburgh	84	70	.545	8
Cincinnati	74	80	.481	18
Boston	71	83	.461	21
Brooklyn	67	87	.435	25
Philadelphia	54	100	.351	38

AMERICAN LEAGUE

	W	L	Pct.	GB
New York	102	51	.667	—
Detroit	83	71	.539	19.5
Chicago	81	70	.536	20
Washington	82	71	.536	20
Cleveland	80	74	.519	22.5
Boston	74	80	.481	28.5
St. Louis	57	95	.375	44.5
Philadelphia	53	100	.346	49

AWARDS

NL MVP: Carl Hubbell, NY
AL MVP: Lou Gehrig, NY

ALL-STAR GAME

Braves Field, Boston
July 7: NL 4, AL 3

POSTSEASON
WORLD SERIES
New York Yankees 4, New York Giants 2
Sept. 30: GIANTS 6, Yankees 1
Oct. 2: Yankees 18, GIANTS 4
Oct. 3: YANKEES 2, Giants 1
Oct. 4: YANKEES 5, Giants 2
Oct. 5: Giants 5, YANKEES 4
Oct. 6: Yankees 13, GIANTS 5

Home team in CAPS

"We could finish first or in an asylum."

— Frankie Frisch, manager of the
1936 Cardinals "Gas House Gang"

NATIONAL LEAGUE LEADERS

Home Runs
Ott-NY	33
Camilli-Phi	28
Klein-Chi-Phi	25
Berger-Bos	25
Mize-StL	19

Runs Batted In
Medwick-StL	138
Ott-NY	135
Suhr-Pit	118
Klein-Chi-Phi	104

Batting Average
P.Waner-Pit	.373
Medwick-StL	.351
Demaree-Chi	.350
Vaughan-Pit	.335
Herman-Chi	.334

On Base Percentage
Vaughan-Pit	.453
Ott-NY	.448
P.Waner-Pit	.446
Camilli-Phi	.441
Suhr-Pit	.410

Slugging Average
Ott-NY	.588
Camilli-Phi	.577
Medwick-StL	.577
P.Waner-Pit	.520
Klein-Chi-Phi	.512

Stolen Bases
P.Martin-StL	23
S.Martin-StL	17
Hack-Chi	17
Chiozza-Phi	17

Wins
Hubbell-NY	26
D.Dean-StL	24
Derringer-Cin	19

Innings Pitched
D.Dean-StL	315.0
Mungo-Bro	311.2
Hubbell-NY	304.0
Derringer-Cin	282.1
MacFayden-Bos	266.2

Saves
D.Dean-StL	11
Brennan-Cin	9
Smith-Bos	8
Johnson-Phi	7
Coffman-NY	7

Strikeouts
Mungo-Bro	238
D.Dean-StL	195
Blanton-Pit	127
Hubbell-NY	123
Derringer-Cin	121

Earned Run Average
Hubbell-NY	2.31
MacFayden-Bos	2.87
Gabler-NY	3.12
D.Dean-StL	3.17
Lucas-Pit	3.18

Complete Games
D.Dean-StL	28
Hubbell-NY	25
Mungo-Bro	22
MacFayden-Bos	21
Lee-Chi	20

AMERICAN LEAGUE LEADERS

Home Runs
Gehrig-NY	49
Trosky-Cle	42
Foxx-Bos	41
DiMaggio-NY	29
Averill-Cle	28

Runs Batted In
Trosky-Cle	162
Gehrig-NY	152
Foxx-Bos	143
Bonura-Chi	138
Solters-StL	134

Batting Average
Appling-Chi	.388
Averill-Cle	.378
Gehringer-Det	.354
Gehrig-NY	.354
Walker-Det	.353

On Base Percentage
Gehrig-NY	.478
Appling-Chi	.474
Foxx-Bos	.440
Averill-Cle	.438
Gehringer-Det	.431

Slugging Average
Gehrig-NY	.696
Trosky-Cle	.644
Foxx-Bos	.631
Averill-Cle	.627
DiMaggio-NY	.576

Stolen Bases
Lary-StL	37
Powell-Was-NY	26
Werber-Bos	23
Chapman-NY-Was	20
Hughes-Cle	20

Wins
Bridges-Det	23
Kennedy-Chi	21
Ruffing-NY	20
W.Ferrell-Bos	20
Allen-Cle	20

Innings Pitched
W.Ferrell-Bos	301.0
Bridges-Det	294.2
Newsom-Was	285.2
Kennedy-Chi	274.1
Ruffing-NY	271.0

Saves
Malone-NY	9
Knott-StL	6
Murphy-NY	5
Brown-Chi	5
Hildebrand-Cle	4

Strikeouts
Bridges-Det	175
Allen-Cle	165
Newsom-Was	156
Grove-Bos	130
Pearson-NY	118

Earned Run Average
Grove-Bos	2.81
Allen-Cle	3.44
Appleton-Was	3.53
Bridges-Det	3.60
Pearson-NY	3.71

Complete Games
W.Ferrell-Bos	28
Bridges-Det	26
Ruffing-NY	25
Newsom-Was	24
Grove-Bos	22

THE YEAR IN BASEBALL

February 2: Ty Cobb leads the balloting in the first election for the Hall of Fame; he is joined by Babe Ruth, Honus Wagner, Christy Mathewson and Walter Johnson.

May 3: Joe DiMaggio collects three hits in his major league debut with the Yankees.

May 24: Tony Lazzeri, batting eighth for the Yankees, drives in 11 runs with a triple and three home runs—two of them grand slams—in a 25-2 rout of the A's.

June 29: Harmon Killebrew is born.

July 7: After three consecutive losses, the NL finally beats the AL in the All Star Game, 4-3.

July 21: Cardinals slugger Joe Medwick connects with his 10th consecutive hit to equal the NL record.

July 23: Don Drysdale is born.

August 12: The largest crowd ever to see a baseball game, estimated at between 90,000 and 125,000, sees a demonstration game as an event at the Summer Olympics in Berlin.

August 23: Seventeen-year-old pitcher Bob Feller strikes out 15 Browns in his first major league start.

September 14: Pittsburgh's Paul Waner ties Rogers Hornsby's modern NL record by reaching 200 hits for the seventh time.

September 23: Carl Hubbell notches his 16th consecutive win and 26th of the season. He pushes the streak to 24 consecutive wins in 1937.

September 25: Joe Medwich breaks an NL record by collecting his 64th double of the season.

October 2: The Yankees score a World Series record 18 runs in beating the Giants 18-2 in Game 2.

1937

All New York Series outshines Medwick Triple Crown

In many respects 1937 was a replay of 1936. Once again the Giants ended up squaring off against the Yankees in the World Series, the Tigers and Cardinals were devastated by injuries, and familiar names appeared at the top of offensive and pitching categories.

If ever pitching earned its reputation as 75 percent of the game, it was in the 1937 AL race. Despite matching the Yankees offensively all season, even out-hitting them by nine points, Detroit's loss of Schoolboy Rowe to a bad arm and its failure to find another big winner left the club a distant 13 behind New York. The loudest swatting in the Bronx came from Joe DiMaggio, who led the league with his 46 homers, while batting .346 and driving home 167. In what amounted to his last super-season, Lou Gehrig wasn't far behind at .351-37-139. Catcher Bill Dickey also drove in 133 runs with his .332 mark. New York's ace was Lefty Gomez, who topped the league in wins (21) and ERA (2.33); Red Ruffing won 20 and Johnny Murphy racked up 13 victories and 10 saves. Detroit's Roxie Lawson won 18, but the nature of most of those was indicated by his 5.27 ERA. Hank Greenberg paced the circuit in RBIs with 183 and Charlie Gehringer in average (.371). The Tigers also got 100-plus RBIs from outfielder Gee Walker and catcher Rudy York. York was pressed into service after playing manager Mickey Cochrane was beaned by Bump Hadley of the Yankees in May. After hovering between life and death for several days, Cochrane recovered enough to resume his managerial duties later in the year, but was through as a player.

The secret to the success of the Giants in the NL was all-around hitting and defense, Carl Hubbell, and Dizzy Dean. Any hopes the Cardinals nurtured to topple New York ended at the July All-Star game when Cleveland's Earl Averill lined a ball off Dean's toe. In an effort to compensate for the broken digit, the right-hander changed his pitching motion, bringing on arm problems that prevented him from ever again winning in double figures. Hubbell, meanwhile, went on to lead the league again with his 22 victories. Offensively, the club did the little things, and usually in the clutch; only Mel Ott (a league-leading 31 homers) posed a significant power threat, and even he couldn't reach the 100-RBI mark. The most powerful bat of the year belonged to St. Louis' Joe Medwick, who won the Triple Crown by tying Ott's 31 homers, driving in 154 runs, and batting .374; it would be the last NL Triple Crown of the century. Boston's Jim Turner took the ERA title at 2.38. Aside from Hubbell, only three NL pitchers won 20—Turner and Lou Fette of the Braves and Cliff Melton of the Giants. All three of them notched their 20th victory within five days of each other against the lowly Phillies.

The World Series rematch between the two New York teams went as widely forecast—a five-game romp for the Yankees with only Hubbell sneaking in a win for the NLers. The Yankee effort was spread around, with four players getting six hits, outfielder George Selkirk knocking in six, and Gomez winning twice.

Charlie Gehringer
One of the Tigers' famed G-Men (along with Hank Greenberg and Goose Goslin), Gehringer batted .371 in 1937 to win his only batting title.

1937 SEASON HIGHLIGHTS

NATIONAL LEAGUE

	W	L	Pct.	GB
New York	95	57	.625	—
Chicago	93	61	.604	3
Pittsburgh	86	68	.558	10
St. Louis	81	73	.526	15
Boston	79	73	.520	16
Brooklyn	62	91	.405	33.5
Philadelphia	61	92	.399	34.5
Cincinnati	56	98	.364	40

AMERICAN LEAGUE

	W	L	Pct.	GB
New York	102	52	.662	—
Detroit	89	65	.578	13
Chicago	86	68	.558	16
Cleveland	83	71	.539	19
Boston	80	72	.526	21
Washington	73	80	.477	28.5
Philadelphia	54	97	.358	46.5
St. Louis	46	108	.299	56

AWARDS

NL MVP: Joe Medwick, STL
AL MVP: Charlie Gehringer, DET

ALL-STAR GAME

Griffith Stadium, Washington
July 7: AL 8, NL 3

POSTSEASON
WORLD SERIES
New York Yankees 4, New York Giants 1
Oct. 6: YANKEES 8, Giants 1
Oct. 7: YANKEES 8, Giants 1
Oct. 8: Yankees 5, GIANTS 1
Oct. 9: GIANTS 7, Yankees 3
Oct. 10: Yankees 4, GIANTS 2

Home team in CAPS

"I have two good friends in the world—the buckerinos and the base hits. If I get the base hits I will get the buckerinos."

— Joe Medwick

NATIONAL LEAGUE LEADERS

Home Runs
Ott-NY	31
Medwick-StL	31
Camilli-Phi	27
Mize-StL	25
Galan-Chi	18

Runs Batted In
Medwick-StL	154
Demaree-Chi	115
Mize-StL	113
Suhr-Pit	97
Ott-NY	95

Batting Average
Medwick-StL	.374
Mize-StL	.364
P.Waner-Pit	.354
Whitney-Phi	.341
Camilli-Phi	.339

On Base Percentage
Camilli-Phi	.446
Mize-StL	.427
Medwick-StL	.414
P.Waner-Pit	.413
Ott-NY	.408

Slugging Average
Medwick-StL	.641
Mize-StL	.595
Camilli-Phi	.587
Ott-NY	.523
Demaree-Chi	.485

Stolen Bases
Galan-Chi	23
Hack-Chi	16

Wins
Hubbell-NY	22
Turner-Bos	20
Melton-NY	20
Fette-Bos	20
Warneke-StL	18

Innings Pitched
Passeau-Phi	292.1
Lee-Chi	272.1
Weiland-StL	264.1
Hubbell-NY	261.2
Fette-Bos	259.0

Saves
Melton-NY	7
Brown-Pit	7
Grissom-Cin	6
Root-Chi	5
Hollingsworth-Cin	5

Strikeouts
Hubbell-NY	159
Grissom-Cin	149
Blanton-Pit	143
Melton-NY	142

Earned Run Average
Turner-Bos	2.38
Melton-NY	2.61
D.Dean-StL	2.69
Bauers-Pit	2.88
Fette-Bos	2.88

Complete Games
Turner-Bos	24
Fette-Bos	23
Weiland-StL	21

AMERICAN LEAGUE LEADERS

Home Runs
DiMaggio-NY	46
Greenberg-Det	40
Gehrig-NY	37
Foxx-Bos	36
York-Det	35

Runs Batted In
Greenberg-Det	183
DiMaggio-NY	167
Gehrig-NY	159
Dickey-NY	133
Trosky-Cle	128

Batting Average
Gehringer-Det	.371
Gehrig-NY	.351
DiMaggio-NY	.346
Bonura-Chi	.345
Travis-Was	.344

On Base Percentage
Gehrig-NY	.473
Gehringer-Det	.458
Greenberg-Det	.436
Johnson-Phi	.425
Dickey-NY	.417

Slugging Average
DiMaggio-NY	.673
Greenberg-Det	.668
Gehrig-NY	.643
Bonura-Chi	.573
Dickey-NY	.570

Stolen Bases
Chapman-Was-Bos	35
Werber-Phi	35
Walker-Det	23

Wins
Gomez-NY	21
Ruffing-NY	20
Lawson-Det	18
Grove-Bos	17
Auker-Det	17

Innings Pitched
W.Ferrell-Bos-Was	281.0
Gomez-NY	278.1
Newsom-Was-Bos	275.1
DeShong-Was	264.1
Grove-Bos	262.0

Saves
Brown-Chi	18
Murphy-NY	10
Wilson-Bos	7
Malone-NY	6

Strikeouts
Gomez-NY	194
Newsom-Was-Bos	166
Grove-Bos	153
Feller-Cle	150
Bridges-Det	138

Earned Run Average
Gomez-NY	2.33
Stratton-Chi	2.40
Allen-Cle	2.55
Ruffing-NY	2.98
Grove-Bos	3.02

Complete Games
W.Ferrell-Bos-Was	26
Gomez-NY	25
Ruffing-NY	22
Grove-Bos	21
DeShong-Was	20

THE YEAR IN BASEBALL

January 19: Nap Lajoie, Tris Speaker and Cy Young are voted into the Baseball Hall of Fame.

January 27: Flood waters of Ohio River inundate Crosley Field.

May 18: Brooks Robinson born.

May 27: Carl Hubbell wins his 24th straight game over two seasons, a record, as he comes out of the bullpen to vanquish the Reds, 3-2.

May 25: Mickey Cochrane's career is ended when his skull is fractured by a Bump Hadley pitch.

June 5: Gus Suhr's NL record of 822 consecutive games, begun on September 11, 1931, ends when he attends his mother's funeral.

July 7: Dizzy Dean suffers a broken toe at the All-Star Game, causing him to change his pitching motion which results in an arm injury that ultimately ends his career.

August 29: The A's set a NL record against the White Sox by scoring 12 runs in the first inning, six of which are driven in by Bob Johnson.

August 31: Detroit rookie Rudy York hits his 18th home run in August breaking Babe Ruth's record for most homers in a month; Detroit beats the Washington Senators, 12-3.

September 19: Hank Greenberg hits the first ever home run into the center field stands at Yankee Stadium.

October 25: Boston Bees sign Casey Stengel as manager.

1938

Lights out for Pirates after Hartnett homer; Yanks keep rolling

Two of the most noted events in pitching history took place in the NL in 1938. On June 11 and June 15, Cincinnati southpaw Johnny Vander Meer pitched back-to-back no-hitters against the Braves and Dodgers, respectively; the second game was also the first ever played under the lights in Brooklyn. On September 28, Pittsburgh's Mace Brown, pitching with two outs in the ninth inning at Wrigley Field in a tied game, grooved a pitch to Chicago's Gabby Hartnett that the player-manager deposited for the "homer in the gloamin'." If Brown had even rolled the delivery to home plate to waste another minute or two, the contest would have been called for darkness and ordered replayed; instead, the Hartnett blast gave the Cubs a half-game lead over the Pirates and a giant step to the flag three days later.

Chicago was an unlikely pennant winner. After getting off to a slow start, manager Charlie Grimm himself suggested a switch to Hartnett, who did indeed bring new life to the team. But even then, the squad was unable to boast of a bigger run-producer than outfielder Augie Galan, who knocked in 69, evoking the early-century days of the Tinker-Evers-Chance clubs. The team's biggest star was Bill Lee, who topped the league in both victories (22) and ERA (2.66). The most conspicuous performers around the rest of the league were New York's Mel Ott (36 homers), St. Louis' Joe Medwick (122 RBIs), and Cincinnati's Ernie Lombardi (.342).

In the AL, the Yankees rolled to their third consecutive pennant in the face of an awakened Boston franchise. Joe DiMaggio moved more firmly into the field leadership of the club with his .324, 32 homers and 140 RBIs. Catcher Bill Dickey also knocked in 115. On the other hand, the slowing Lou Gehrig, while still turning in numbers the envy of most hitters (.295-29-114), produced his lowest average since 1925, his fewest RBIs since 1926 and his fewest homers since 1928. Red Ruffing contributed 21 wins to the flag, and was one of only two 20-game winners in the league (the other was Bobo Newsom of the Browns). Boston's rise to second after 19 years of finishing no higher than fourth was fueled by two former Athletics—first baseman Jimmie Foxx, who paced the league in RBIs (175) and batting (.349), and pitcher Lefty Grove, with a 3.08 ERA. On June 16, the Browns had seen enough of Foxx's prowess to walk him six straight times. The home-run title went to Detroit's Hank Greenberg (58). In the course of the season, two notable records were set. In June, Red Sox third baseman Pinky Higgins collected hits in 12 straight official at-bats; in October, Cleveland right-hander Bob Feller struck out 18 Tigers in a 4-1 loss.

As in 1932, the Yankees made quick work of the Cubs in the World Series, sweeping them in four. Ruffing won twice and New York's double-play combination of Joe Gordon and Frankie Crosetti drove in 12 runs between them.

The biggest boardroom development of the year was Commissioner Kenesaw M. Landis' decision to declare 74 Cardinal farmhands free agents on the grounds that Branch Rickey's minor-league system survived on monopolistic practices. Among those lost to St. Louis was future Dodger star Pete Reiser.

Jimmie Foxx
Boston made a leap in the standings due largely to Foxx, the standout first baseman, leading the league in batting (.349) and RBIs (175).

1938 SEASON HIGHLIGHTS

NATIONAL LEAGUE

	W	L	Pct.	GB
Chicago	89	63	.586	—
Pittsburgh	86	64	.573	2
New York	83	67	.553	5
Cincinnati	82	68	.547	6
Boston	77	75	.507	12
St. Louis	71	80	.470	17.5
Brooklyn	69	80	.463	18.5
Philadelphia	45	105	.300	43

AMERICAN LEAGUE

	W	L	Pct.	GB
New York	99	53	.651	—
Boston	88	61	.591	9.5
Cleveland	86	66	.566	13
Detroit	84	70	.545	16
Washington	75	76	.497	23.5
Chicago	65	83	.439	32
St. Louis	55	97	.362	44
Philadelphia	53	99	.349	46

AWARDS

NL MVP: Ernie Lombardi, CIN
AL MVP: Jimmie Foxx, BOS

ALL-STAR GAME
Crosley Field, Cincinnati
July 6: NL 4, AL 1

POSTSEASON
WORLD SERIES
New York Yankees 4, Chicago Cubs 0
Oct. 5: New York 3, CHICAGO 1
Oct. 6: New York 6, CHICAGO 3
Oct. 8: NEW YORK 5, Chicago 2
Oct. 9: NEW YORK 8, Chicago 3

Home team in CAPS

"Man may penetrate the outer reaches of the universe. He may solve the very secret of eternity itself. But for me, the ultimate human experience is to witness the flawless execution of the hit-and-run."

— Branch Rickey

NATIONAL LEAGUE LEADERS

Home Runs
Ott-NY	36
Goodman-Cin	30
Mize-StL	27
Camilli-Bro	24
Rizzo-Pit	23

Runs Batted In
Medwick-StL	122
Ott-NY	116
Rizzo-Pit	111
McCormick-Cin	106
Mize-StL	102

Batting Average
Lombardi-Cin	.342
Mize-StL	.337
McCormick-Cin	.327
Medwick-StL	.322
Vaughan-Pit	.322

On Base Percentage
Ott-NY	.442
Vaughan-Pit	.433
Mize-StL	.422
Hack-Chi	.411
Suhr-Pit	.394

Slugging Average
Mize-StL	.614
Ott-NY	.583
Medwick-StL	.536
Goodman-Cin	.533
Lombardi-Cin	.524

Stolen Bases
Hack-Chi	16
Lavagetto-Bro	15
Koy-Bro	15
Vaughan-Pit	14
Gutteridge-StL	14

Wins
Lee-Chi	22
Derringer-Cin	21
Bryant-Chi	19
Weiland-StL	16

Innings Pitched
Derringer-Cin	307.0
Lee-Chi	291.0
Bryant-Chi	270.1
Turner-Bos	268.0
Mulcahy-Phi	267.1

Saves
Coffman-NY	12
Root-Chi	8
Hamlin-Bro	6
Errickson-Bos	6

Strikeouts
Bryant-Chi	135
Derringer-Cin	132
VanderMeer-Cin	125
Lee-Chi	121

Earned Run Average
Lee-Chi	2.66
Root-Chi	2.86
Derringer-Cin	2.93
MacFayden-Bos	2.95
Klinger-Pit	2.99

Complete Games
Derringer-Cin	26
Turner-Bos	22
Walters-Phi-Cin	20
MacFayden-Bos	19
Lee-Chi	19

AMERICAN LEAGUE LEADERS

Home Runs
Greenberg-Det	58
Foxx-Bos	50
Clift-StL	34
York-Det	33
DiMaggio-NY	32

Runs Batted In
Foxx-Bos	175
Greenberg-Det	146
DiMaggio-NY	140
York-Det	127
Clift-StL	118

Batting Average
Foxx-Bos	.349
Heath-Cle	.343
Chapman-Bos	.340
Myer-Was	.336
Travis-Was	.335

On Base Percentage
Foxx-Bos	.462
Myer-Was	.454
Greenberg-Det	.438
Averill-Cle	.429
Cronin-Bos	.428

Slugging Average
Foxx-Bos	.704
Greenberg-Det	.683
Heath-Cle	.602
DiMaggio-NY	.581
York-Det	.579

Stolen Bases
Crosetti-NY	27
Lary-Cle	23
Werber-Phi	19
Lewis-Was	17
Fox-Det	16

Wins
Ruffing-NY	21
Newsom-StL	20
Gomez-NY	18
Harder-Cle	17
Feller-Cle	17

Innings Pitched
Newsom-StL	329.2
Caster-Phi	281.1
Feller-Cle	277.2
Ruffing-NY	247.1
Lee-Chi	245.1

Saves
Murphy-NY	11
McKain-Bos	6
Humphries-Cle	6
Potter-Phi	5
Appleton-Was	5

Strikeouts
Feller-Cle	240
Newsom-StL	226
L.Mills-StL	134
Gomez-NY	129
Ruffing-NY	127

Earned Run Average
Grove-Bos	3.08
Ruffing-NY	3.31
Gomez-NY	3.35
Leonard-Was	3.43
Lee-Chi	3.49

Complete Games
Newsom-StL	31
Ruffing-NY	22
Gomez-NY	20
Feller-Cle	20
Caster-Phi	20

THE YEAR IN BASEBALL

January 10: Willie McCovey is born.

January 18: Curt Flood is born; his 1970 suit against Organized Baseball, though defeated in the U.S. Supreme Court, ushered in the free-agency revolution.

January 24: Jim Mutrie dies; proud manager of the New York Gothams, he called them his "Giants," and so they became; he led them and the rival-league Mets to pennants.

February 18: Manny Mota born; he held the record for most career pinch hits, 150.

March 6: The Phillies trade Dolf Camilli to the Dodgers for Eddie Morgan and $45,000.

March 27: Luke Appling breaks his leg in an exhibition game with the Cubs, forcing him to miss half the season.

May 30: The largest crowd in Yankee history, 83,533, see the Yankees beat the Red Sox 10-0 in a game that featured a famous fight between Yankee outfielder Jake Powell and Boston player-manager Joe Cronin.

June 15: Johnny Vander Meer of the Reds pitches his second straight no-hit, no-run game, spoiling Dodgers' arc-light opener at Ebbets Field.

June 16: Slugger Jimmie Foxx does not get much chance to hit as the Browns walk him six times in succession. The Red Sox win anyway, 12-8.

June 21: In two successive doubleheaders (four games), Pinky Higgins of the Red Sox bangs out 12 consecutive hits (with two walks interspersed).

August 20: Lou Gehrig hits the 23rd and last grand slam of his career to extend his AL record.

September 28: Gabby Hartnett's homer in gathering darkness breaks a 5-5 tie with the Pirates and puts the Cubs into first place to stay.

October 2: Bob Feller sets a major league record by striking out 18 Tigers, yet loses 4-1.

October 9: The Yankees become the first team to win three successive World Series championships by sweeping the Cubs.

1939

Williams' grand debut is overshadowed by Gehrig's sad farewell

Working from the fable that Abner Doubleday had created the sport out of whole cloth in Cooperstown, New York in 1839, Organized Baseball marked the year as a centennial celebration, providing extra pomp for the opening of the Baseball Hall of Fame. In the same vein of accenting "history" amid Depression-depressed gates, Cincinnati was authorized to begin its season a day before other clubs in recognition of the impact of the 1869 Red Stockings. What not even Reds fans expected was that the club would also still be playing after other NL teams had gone home for the year.

Cincinnati's first appearance in the postseason since the benighted 1919 World Series owed most to first baseman Frank McCormick and right-handers Bucky Walters and Paul Derringer. While McCormick led the league with his 209 hits and 128 RBIs, Walters and Derringer finished one-two in wins at 27-25. Walters, converted to the mound after some years as a third baseman, also had the circuit's lowest ERA (2.29). Derringer's mastery, which included key victories in late September against a final charge from the Cardinals, came six years after he had lost an astonishing 27 games. St. Louis remained in the race thanks largely to the hitting of first baseman Johnny Mize, who led in home runs (28) and batting average (.349).

The AL witnessed another dramatic changing of the guard with the departure of Lou Gehrig and the arrival of Ted Williams. On May 2, the New York first baseman, enervated by what was soon diagnosed as amyotrophic lateral sclerosis, asked out of the lineup to end his consecutive game streak at 2,130; two months later, on July 4, he made his "luckiest man on the face of the earth" speech at Yankee Stadium ceremonies to close his 17-year career. In Boston, Williams fulfilled predictions (including his own) by leading the league with 145 RBIs. But neither that explosion nor prime efforts by teammates Jimmie Foxx (most homers, 35) and Lefty Grove (lowest ERA, 2.54) got the Red Sox any closer than 17 games to the runaway Yankees. The only hope for a meaningful race came in early July, when Boston swept five straight from the

Lou Gehrig and Joe McCarthy
Manager Joe McCarthy presented Gehrig with a trophy on "Lou Gehrig Day," July 4, 1939, in recognition of the contribution of the Yankees' Iron Man.

Yankees, but that accomplishment was quickly swamped by a 4.56 pitching staff that would have yielded well over five runs a game without the presence of Grove. The New York drive was spearheaded by batting champion Joe DiMaggio, who averaged .381 while clouting 30 homers and driving in 126. Joe Gordon, George Selkirk and Bill Dickey also attained the 100-RBI level, and Red Ruffing paced the pitchers with 21 wins. The league's biggest winner was Cleveland's Bob Feller (24). On May 16, Feller's Indians were the triumphant visitors (8-3 in 10 innings) in the league's first night game, held at Philadelphia's Shibe Park before some 15,000 fans.

The World Series was once again a Yankee cakewalk. The star of the four-game sweep was outfielder Charlie Keller, who led both clubs in batting (.438), homers (3), RBIs (6), and hits (7). Keller's 8 runs scored also equaled the output of the Reds for the entire Series. In Game 2, Yankees right-hander Monte Pearson carried a no-hitter into the eighth inning before having to settle for a two-hit shutout.

1939 SEASON HIGHLIGHTS

NATIONAL LEAGUE

	W	L	Pct.	GB
Cincinnati	97	57	.630	—
St. Louis	92	61	.601	4.5
Brooklyn	84	69	.549	12.5
Chicago	84	70	.545	13
New York	77	74	.510	18.5
Pittsburgh	68	85	.444	28.5
Boston	63	88	.417	32.5
Philadelphia	45	106	.298	50.5

AMERICAN LEAGUE

	W	L	Pct.	GB
New York	106	45	.702	—
Boston	89	62	.589	17
Cleveland	87	67	.565	20.5
Chicago	85	69	.552	22.5
Detroit	81	73	.526	26.5
Washington	65	87	.428	41.5
Philadelphia	55	97	.362	51.5
St. Louis	43	111	.279	64.5

AWARDS

NL MVP: Bucky Walters, CIN
AL MVP: Joe DiMaggio, NY

ALL-STAR GAME
Yankee Stadium, New York
July 11: AL 3, NL 1

POSTSEASON
WORLD SERIES
New York Yankees 4, Cincinnati Reds 0
Oct. 5: NEW YORK 2, Cincinnati 1
Oct. 6: NEW YORK 4, Cincinnati 0
Oct. 8: New York 7, CINCINNATI 3
Oct. 9: New York 7, CINCINNATI 4

Home team in CAPS

> "You always get a special kick on opening day, no matter how many you go through. You look forward to it like a birthday party when you're a kid. You think something wonderful is going to happen."
>
> — Joe DiMaggio

NATIONAL LEAGUE LEADERS

Home Runs
Mize-StL	28
Ott-NY	27
Camilli-Bro	26
Leiber-Chi	24
Lombardi-Cin	20

Runs Batted In
McCormick-Cin	128
Medwick-StL	117
Mize-StL	108
Camilli-Bro	104
Leiber-Chi	88

Batting Average
Mize-StL	.349
McCormick-Cin	.332
Medwick-StL	.332
P.Waner-Pit	.328
Arnovich-Phi	.324

On Base Percentage
Ott-NY	.449
Mize-StL	.444
Camilli-Bro	.409
Goodman-Cin	.401
Arnovich-Phi	.397

Slugging Average
Mize-StL	.626
Ott-NY	.581
Camilli-Bro	.524
Goodman-Cin	.515
Medwick-StL	.507

Stolen Bases
Handley-Pit	17
Hack-Chi	17
Werber-Cin	15
Lavagetto-Bro	14
Hassett-Bos	13

Wins
Walters-Cin	27
Derringer-Cin	25
Davis-StL	22
Hamlin-Bro	20
Lee-Chi	19

Innings Pitched
Walters-Cin	319.0
Derringer-Cin	301.0
Lee-Chi	282.1
Passeau-Phi-Chi	274.1
Hamlin-Bro	269.2

Saves
Shoun-StL	9
Bowman-StL	9
Davis-StL	7
Brown-NY	7
Brown-Pit	7

Strikeouts
Passeau-Phi-Chi	137
Walters-Cin	137
Cooper-StL	130
Derringer-Cin	128
Lee-Chi	105

Earned Run Average
Walters-Cin	2.29
Bowman-StL	2.60
Hubbell-NY	2.75
Casey-Bro	2.93
Derringer-Cin	2.93

Complete Games
Walters-Cin	31
Derringer-Cin	28
Lee-Chi	20
Hamlin-Bro	19
Posedel-Bos	18

AMERICAN LEAGUE LEADERS

Home Runs
Foxx-Bos	35
Greenberg-Det	33
Williams-Bos	31
DiMaggio-NY	30
Gordon-NY	28

Runs Batted In
Williams-Bos	145
DiMaggio-NY	126
Johnson-Phi	114
Greenberg-Det	112

Batting Average
DiMaggio-NY	.381
Foxx-Bos	.360
Johnson-Phi	.338
Trosky-Cle	.335
Keller-NY	.334

On Base Percentage
Foxx-Bos	.464
Selkirk-NY	.452
DiMaggio-NY	.448
Keller-NY	.447
Johnson-Phi	.440

Slugging Average
Foxx-Bos	.694
DiMaggio-NY	.671
Greenberg-Det	.622
Williams-Bos	.609
Trosky-Cle	.589

Stolen Bases
Case-Was	51
Kreevich-Chi	23
Fox-Det	23
McCosky-Det	20

Wins
Feller-Cle	24
Ruffing-NY	21
Newsom-StL-Det	20
Leonard-Was	20
Bridges-Det	17

Innings Pitched
Feller-Cle	296.2
Newsom-StL-Det	291.2
Leonard-Was	269.1
Lee-Chi	235.0
Ruffing-NY	233.1

Saves
Murphy-NY	19
Brown-Chi	18
Heving-Bos	7
Dean-Phi	7
Appleton-Was	6

Strikeouts
Feller-Cle	246
Newsom-StL-Det	192
Bridges-Det	129
Rigney-Chi	119
Chase-Was	118

Earned Run Average
Grove-Bos	2.54
Lyons-Chi	2.76
Feller-Cle	2.85
Ruffing-NY	2.93
Hadley-NY	2.98

Complete Games
Newsom-StL-Det	24
Feller-Cle	24
Ruffing-NY	22
Leonard-Was	21
Grove-Bos	17

THE YEAR IN BASEBALL

January 3: Yankees owner Colonel Jacob Ruppert dies.

May 2: Lou Gehrig benches himself after playing 2,130 consecutive games.

May 16: The first AL night game is played at Shibe Park between Philadelphia and Cleveland.

May 17: In the first baseball game ever televised Princeton beats Columbia 2-1 in 10 innings at Baker Field.

June 12: The National Baseball Museum and Hall of Fame is dedicated at Cooperstown, N.Y., on baseball's proclaimed centennial.

June 21: The Yankees announce the retirement of Lou Gehrig, who is suffering from amyotrophic lateral sclerosis.

July 4: A tearful Lou Gehrig tells 61,808 fans at Yankee Stadium, "I consider myself the luckiest man on the face of the earth." His uniform number 4 is retired, making Gehrig the first player so honored.

August 26: The first major league baseball game is telecast from Ebbets Field as the Dodgers and Reds split a doubleheader.

September 24: Eighteen years after his major league debut, Johnny Cooney of the Braves hits his first homer, a wrong-field slice in the Polo Grounds; the next day, he adds another.

December 8: Mindful of Lou Gehrig's illness, the writers waive the five-year rule and vote him into the Hall of Fame by acclamation.

1940

Tigers juggle lineup to dethrone Yankees but Reds take Series

Cleveland's Bob Feller got the season off to an unprecedented start on April 16, when he pitched the only Opening Day no-hitter (against the White Sox). The right-hander's achievement set up two things: a hoary baseball riddle (What team had its entire lineup batting the same after a game as before it?) and the first tight pennant race in the AL in five years. By the finish line, merely two games would be separating the Indians, Yankees and Tigers.

There were three keys to the race in the junior circuit. The first was New York's abysmal start and the adamant refusal of the front office to call up Ernie Bonham from the minors until mid-August; the right-hander won nine times over the final weeks. The second was a revolt by Cleveland players against manager Ossie Vitt that earned the club the tag of "Crybaby Indians"; by the end of the season, players not dispirited by ownership's refusal to bring in a new pilot were using their own in-game signals in defiance of whatever Vitt's tactics dictated. The third was a spring-training decision by Tigers manager Del Baker to move Hank Greenberg from first base to the outfield, Rudy York from catcher to first base, and Birdie Tebbetts to full-time duty behind the plate. The result was a final standings showing Detroit a game ahead of Cleveland and two ahead of New York.

The Tiger victory was spearheaded by Greenberg's league-leading numbers in homers (41) and RBIs (150). York wasn't too far behind at 33-134. The pitching staff was anchored by 21-game winner Bobo Newsom, already pitching for his sixth club; in a 20-year career, the right-hander would change uniforms 17 times, including repeated return trips to some clubs. Feller didn't let up after Opening Day, going on to a Triple Crown coup in wins (27), ERA (2.61) and strikeouts (261). Joe DiMaggio of the Yankees took his second straight batting title, at .352.

In the NL, it was all about Reds and ex-Reds. In May, Larry MacPhail, the former Cincinnati executive transplanted to Brooklyn, organized the first airplane flight of a full baseball team; during the season, he also introduced a cap band that represented the first step toward a batting helmet. MacPhail's Dodgers posed the only substantial threat to a Cincinnati runaway—at least until shortstop Pee Wee Reese and third baseman Cookie Lavagetto were sidelined in August. The Reds' drive to a second straight pennant was again led by right-handers Bucky Walters (a league-leading 22

Hank Greenberg
The Tigers slugger swatted a league-best 41 homers and 150 RBIs to power Detroit past the three-time defending AL champion New York Yankees.

victories and 2.48 ERA) and Paul Derringer (20) and by Frank McCormick (127 RBIs). Also as in 1939, Johnny Mize of the Cardinals had no peers in homers (43) and RBIs (137). Debs Garms of the Pirates took the batting honors (.355).

Cincinnati went into the World Series with 39-year-old Jimmie Wilson behind the plate. Wilson had been taken off the coaching lines after backup catcher Willard Hershberger had committed suicide in August and regular receiver Ernie Lombardi had sprained an ankle in September. The veteran ended up going 6-17, preventing the Tigers from stealing a single base, and stealing one of his own. Walters and Derringer shared the four wins in the seven-game series.

1940 SEASON HIGHLIGHTS

NATIONAL LEAGUE

	W	L	Pct.	GB
Cincinnati	100	53	.654	—
Brooklyn	88	65	.575	12
St. Louis	84	69	.549	16
Pittsburgh	78	76	.506	22.5
Chicago	75	79	.487	25.5
New York	72	80	.474	27.5
Boston	65	87	.428	34.5
Philadelphia	50	103	.327	50

AMERICAN LEAGUE

	W	L	Pct.	GB
Detroit	90	64	.584	—
Cleveland	89	65	.578	1
New York	88	66	.571	2
Chicago	82	72	.532	8
Boston	82	72	.532	8
St. Louis	67	87	.435	23
Washington	64	90	.416	26
Philadelphia	54	100	.351	36

AWARDS

NL MVP: Frank McCormick, CIN
AL MVP: Hank Greenberg, DET

ALL-STAR GAME

Sportsman's Park, St. Louis
July 9: NL 4, AL 0

POSTSEASON
WORLD SERIES
Cincinnati Reds 4, Detroit Tigers 3
Oct. 2: Detroit 7, CINCINNATI 2
Oct. 3: CINCINNATI 5, Detroit 3
Oct. 4: DETROIT 7, Cincinnati 4
Oct. 5: Cincinnati 5, DETROIT 2
Oct. 6: DETROIT 8, Cincinnati 0
Oct. 7: CINCINNATI 4, Detroit 0
Oct. 8: CINCINNATI 2, Detroit 1

Home team in CAPS

"I ain't what I used to be, but who the hell is?"

— Dizzy Dean

NATIONAL LEAGUE LEADERS

Home Runs
Mize-StL	43
Nicholson-Chi	25
Rizzo-Pit-Cin-Phi	24
Camilli-Bro	23

Runs Batted In
Mize-StL	137
F.McCormick-Cin	127
VanRobays-Pit	116
Fletcher-Pit	104
Young-NY	101

Batting Average
Hack-Chi	.317
Mize-StL	.314
Gleeson-Chi	.313
F.McCormick-Cin	.309
Walker-Bro	.308

On Base Percentage
Fletcher-Pit	.418
Ott-NY	.407
Mize-StL	.404
Camilli-Bro	.397
Hack-Chi	.395

Slugging Average
Mize-StL	.636
Nicholson-Chi	.534
Camilli-Bro	.529
Slaughter-StL	.504
F.McCormick-Cin	.482

Stolen Bases
Frey-Cin	22
Hack-Chi	21
Moore-StL	18
Werber-Cin	16
Reese-Bro	15

Wins
Walters-Cin	22
Passeau-Chi	20
Derringer-Cin	20

Innings Pitched
Walters-Cin	305.0
Derringer-Cin	296.2
Higbe-Phi	283.0
Passeau-Chi	280.2
Mulcahy-Phi	280.0

Saves
Brown-NY	7
Brown-Pit	7
Beggs-Cin	7
Shoun-StL	5
Passeau-Chi	5

Strikeouts
Higbe-Phi	137
Wyatt-Bro	124
Passeau-Chi	124
Schumacher-NY	123

Earned Run Average
Walters-Cin	2.48
Passeau-Chi	2.50
Sewell-Pit	2.80
Turner-Cin	2.89
Olsen-Chi	2.97

Complete Games
Walters-Cin	29
Derringer-Cin	26
Mulcahy-Phi	21
Passeau-Chi	20
Higbe-Phi	20

AMERICAN LEAGUE LEADERS

Home Runs
Greenberg-Det	41
Foxx-Bos	36
York-Det	33
Johnson-Phi	31
DiMaggio-NY	31

Runs Batted In
Greenberg-Det	150
York-Det	134
DiMaggio-NY	133
Foxx-Bos	119
Williams-Bos	113

Batting Average
DiMaggio-NY	.352
Appling-Chi	.348
Williams-Bos	.344
Radcliff-StL	.342
Greenberg-Det	.340

On Base Percentage
Williams-Bos	.442
Greenberg-Det	.433
Gehringer-Det	.428
DiMaggio-NY	.425
Appling-Chi	.420

Slugging Average
Greenberg-Det	.670
DiMaggio-NY	.626
Williams-Bos	.594
York-Det	.583
Foxx-Bos	.581

Stolen Bases
Case-Was	35
Walker-Was	21
Gordon-NY	18
Lewis-Was	15
Kreevich-Chi	15

Wins
Feller-Cle	27
Newsom-Det	21
Milnar-Cle	18
Hudson-Was	17

Innings Pitched
Feller-Cle	320.1
Leonard-Was	289.0
Rigney-Chi	280.2
Newsom-Det	264.0
Auker-StL	263.2

Saves
Benton-Det	17
Brown-Chi	10
Murphy-NY	9

Strikeouts
Feller-Cle	261
Newsom-Det	164
Rigney-Chi	141
Bridges-Det	133
Chase-Was	129

Earned Run Average
Feller-Cle	2.61
Newsom-Det	2.83
Rigney-Chi	3.11
Smith-Chi	3.21
Chase-Was	3.23

Complete Games
Feller-Cle	31
Lee-Chi	24
Leonard-Was	23

THE YEAR IN BASEBALL

January 14: Commissioner Kenesaw Landis, citing coverups of the movement of players within the Tigers organization, awards free agency to 91 Detroit players and farmhands.

April 16: Cleveland's Bob Feller throws major league baseball's first opening-day no-hitter.

May 8: After the Pirates acquire Dom DiMaggio, the Waner brothers, Paul and Lloyd, lose their places in Pittsburgh's outfield.

May 14: Boston's Jimmie Foxx hits what is considered the longest home run in the history of the original Comisekly Park when his 10th-inning blast clears the left-field roof.

May 24: In the first night game at the Polo Grounds the Giants rip the Boston Bees 8-1 before 22,260.

July 14: After a spate of beanballs, Spalding begins to advertise a batting helmet with ear flaps in *The Sporting News*.

August 3: Reds catcher Willard Hershberger, in a fit of depression, commits suicide in Boston's Copley Plaza Hotel.

August 24: Boston's Ted Williams pitches the last two innings in a 12-1 loss to Detroit, allowing one run on three hits.

September 16: Leo Durocher is suspended for "inciting a riot" at Ebbets Field that resulted in umpire George Magerkurth being pummeled by a fan.

September 24: Jimmie Foxx hits the 500th home run of his career.

November 5: Walter Johnson, who won 417 games for the Senators, goes down in defeat as a Republican candidate for the U.S. House of Representatives from Maryland.

December 20: Connie Mack acquires controlling interest in the Athletics for $42,000.

1941

Williams, DiMaggio earn a special place in baseball history

In the last pre-World War II season, Joe DiMaggio and Ted Williams put their imprint on baseball for good—the former with a 56-game hitting streak, the latter by risking (and building on) his .400 average on the final day of the campaign. The suspense generated by the two sluggers made New York's rout of the AL almost an afterthought.

DiMaggio began his streak with a first-inning single off Chicago's Ed Smith on May 15. He was finally stopped by Jim Bagby, Jr. and another Smith, Al Smith of Cleveland, on July 17—but only thanks to third baseman Ken Keltner's grabs of two smashes behind third base. Over the span, the Yankees center fielder batted .408.

During the same 56 games, Williams hit .412. On the final day of the season, the Red Sox slugger dismissed suggestions he sit out a meaningless double-header against the Athletics so that his .39955 average could be rounded off to .400; instead, he played both games, collecting six hits and finishing at .406. He also paced the league in home runs with 37, while DiMaggio took the RBI title with 125. New York's walk to a flag also featured big years from Charlie Keller (33-142), Tommy Henrich (31-85), and Joe Gordon (24-87). The league's best pitcher was Cleveland's Bob Feller for his 25 wins and 260 strikeouts. Thornton Lee of the White Sox posted the lowest ERA (2.37). Detroit's fall from first in 1940 to fifth was aided by the Selective Service, which drafted Hank Greenberg into the Army 19 games into the season.

In the NL, the Dodgers ended 21 years in the wilderness by edging out the Cardinals. The Brooklyn victory reflected general manager Larry MacPhail's trading ability and manager Leo Durocher's field and clubhouse leadership. Among the players obtained by MacPhail in deals or as free agents over the previous couple of years were first baseman Dolf Camilli (NL leader in homers with 43 and RBIs with 120), outfielder Pete Reiser (batting champion at .343), and right-handers Kirby Higbe and Whitlow Wyatt (tied at a league-best 22 wins). Elmer Riddle of Cincinnati was the hardest to score against, at 2.24.

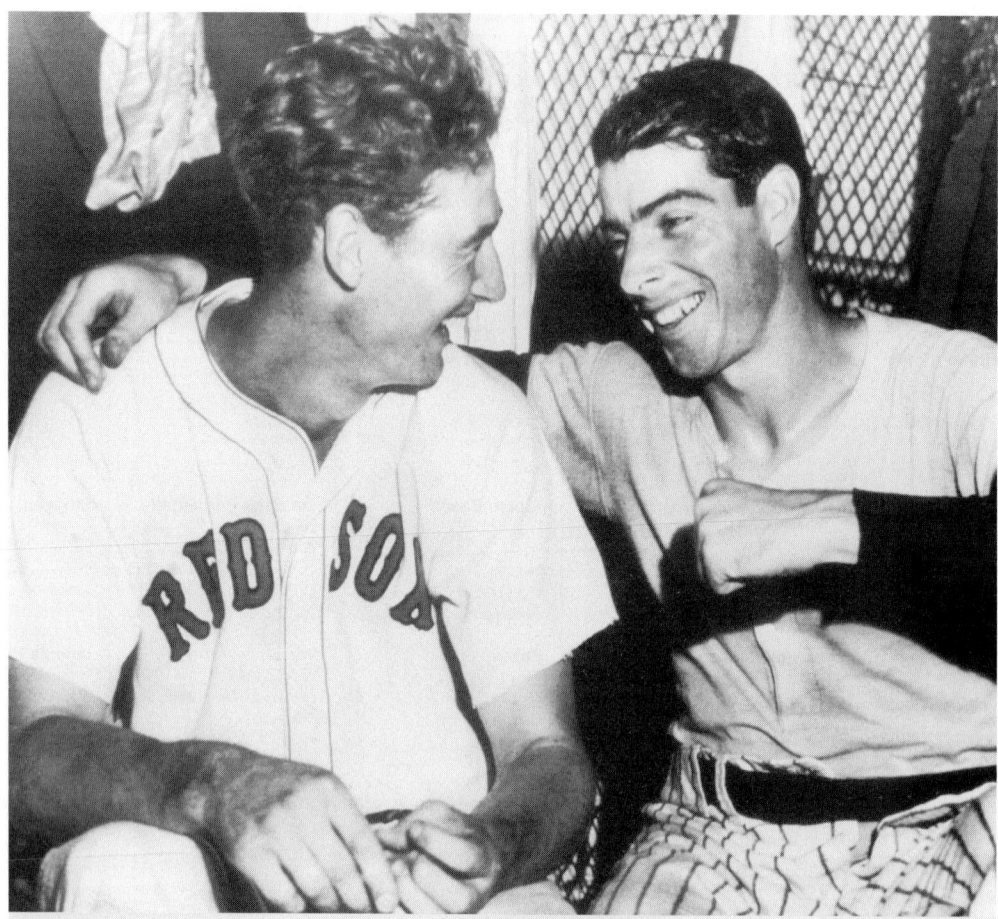

Ted Williams and Joe DiMaggio
Photographed at the 1941 All-Star Game, Williams, left, and DiMaggio assembled two of baseball's most enduring accomplishments—batting .406 and hitting in 56 straight games.

The first of seven Brooklyn-Bronx World Series over the next fifteen years delivered its most memorable moment with two out in the ninth inning of the fourth game, when Dodger catcher Mickey Owen couldn't hold on to Hugh Casey's third strike to Henrich. The Yankees took advantage of the miscue to produce a single, two doubles and two walks, turning a certain 4-3 Brooklyn win into a 7-4 defeat. Although that was the only contest in the five-game series not decided by more than two runs, the Dodgers were outclassed by New York's pitching, hitting merely .182. The offensive stars were Gordon and Keller, who combined for 14 hits and 10 runs batted in.

Following the December 7 attack on Pearl Harbor, Washington owner Clark Griffith had the task of lobbying the White House to make sure the sport could continue through the war. He won that consent from President Franklin Delano Roosevelt, but not an exemption of players from the draft. The start of World War II also aborted plans by the Browns to move to Los Angeles for the 1942 season.

1941 SEASON HIGHLIGHTS

NATIONAL LEAGUE

	W	L	Pct.	GB
Brooklyn	100	54	.649	—
St. Louis	97	56	.634	2.5
Cincinnati	88	66	.571	12
Pittsburgh	81	73	.526	19
New York	74	79	.484	25.5
Chicago	70	84	.455	30
Boston	62	92	.403	38
Philadelphia	43	111	.279	57

AMERICAN LEAGUE

	W	L	Pct.	GB
New York	101	53	.656	—
Boston	84	70	.545	17
Chicago	77	77	.500	24
Cleveland	75	79	.487	26
Detroit	75	79	.487	26
Washington	70	84	.455	31
St. Louis	70	84	.455	31
Philadelphia	64	90	.416	37

AWARDS

NL MVP: Dolph Camilli, BRO
AL MVP: Joe DiMaggio, NY

ALL-STAR GAME

Briggs Stadium, Detroit
July 8: AL 7, NL 5

POSTSEASON

WORLD SERIES
New York Yankees 4, Brooklyn Dodgers 1
Oct. 1: NEW YORK 3, Brooklyn 2
Oct. 2: Brooklyn 3, NEW YORK 2
Oct. 4: New York 2, BROOKLYN 1
Oct. 5: New York 7, BROOKLYN 4
Oct. 6: New York 3, BROOKLYN 1

Home team in CAPS

"There is always some kid who may be seeing me for the first or last time. I owe him my best."

— Joe DiMaggio

NATIONAL LEAGUE LEADERS

Home Runs			Runs Batted In			Batting Average		
Camilli-Bro	34		Camilli-Bro	120		Reiser-Bro	.343	
Ott-NY	27		Young-NY	104		Medwick-Bro	.318	
Nicholson-Chi	26		Mize-StL	100		Hack-Chi	.317	
Young-NY	25		DiMaggio-Pit	100		Mize-StL	.317	
Dahlgren-Bos-Chi	23		Nicholson-Chi	98		Etten-Phi	.311	

On Base Percentage			Slugging Average			Stolen Bases		
Fletcher-Pit	.421		Reiser-Bro	.558		Murtaugh-Phi	18	
Hack-Chi	.417		Camilli-Bro	.556		Benjamin-Phi	17	
Camilli-Bro	.407		Mize-StL	.535		Handley-Pit	16	
Reiser-Bro	.406		Medwick-Bro	.517		Frey-Cin	16	
Mize-StL	.406		Slaughter-StL	.496		Hopp-StL	15	

Wins			Innings Pitched			Saves		
Wyatt-Bro	22		Walters-Cin	302.0		Brown-NY	8	
Higbe-Bro	22		Higbe-Bro	298.0		Crouch-Phi-StL	7	
Walters-Cin	19		Wyatt-Bro	288.1		Casey-Bro	7	
E.Riddle-Cin	19		Sewell-Pit	249.0		Pearson-Phi	6	
			Warneke-StL	246.0				

Strikeouts			Earned Run Average			Complete Games		
VanderMeer-Cin	202		E.Riddle-Cin	2.24		Walters-Cin	27	
Wyatt-Bro	176		Wyatt-Bro	2.34		Wyatt-Bro	23	
Walters-Cin	129		White-StL	2.40		Tobin-Bos	20	
Higbe-Bro	121		VanderMeer-Cin	2.82		Passeau-Chi	20	
M.Cooper-StL	118		Walters-Cin	2.83				

AMERICAN LEAGUE LEADERS

Home Runs			Runs Batted In			Batting Average		
Williams-Bos	37		DiMaggio-NY	125		Williams-Bos	.406	
Keller-NY	33		Heath-Cle	123		Travis-Was	.359	
Henrich-NY	31		Keller-NY	122		DiMaggio-NY	.357	
DiMaggio-NY	30		Williams-Bos	120		Heath-Cle	.340	
York-Det	27		York-Det	111		Siebert-Phi	.334	

On Base Percentage			Slugging Average			Stolen Bases		
Williams-Bos	.551		Williams-Bos	.735		Case-Was	33	
Cullenbine-StL	.452		DiMaggio-NY	.643		Kuhel-Chi	20	
DiMaggio-NY	.440		Heath-Cle	.586		Heath-Cle	18	
Keller-NY	.416		Keller-NY	.580		Tabor-Bos	17	
Foxx-Bos	.412		S.Chapman-Phi	.543		Kreevich-Chi	17	

Wins			Innings Pitched			Saves		
Feller-Cle	25		Feller-Cle	343.0		Murphy-NY	15	
Lee-Chi	22		Lee-Chi	300.1		Ferrick-Phi	7	
D.Newsome-Bos	19		Smith-Chi	263.1		Benton-Det	7	
Leonard-Was	18		Leonard-Was	256.0		Ryba-Bos	6	
			Newsom-Det	250.1				

Strikeouts			Earned Run Average			Complete Games		
Feller-Cle	260		Lee-Chi	2.37		Lee-Chi	30	
Newsom-Det	175		Benton-Det	2.97		Feller-Cle	28	
Lee-Chi	130		Wagner-Bos	3.07		Smith-Chi	21	
Rigney-Chi	119		Russo-NY	3.09		Lyons-Chi	19	
			Feller-Cle	3.15		Leonard-Was	19	

THE YEAR IN BASEBALL

January 24: The last surviving National Leaguer from the circuit's original year of 1876, Tommy Bond, dies. He debuted in 1876 as an 18-year-old with the Hartford Dark Blues and played 8 seasons with five teams, ending his career in 1884. He later coached at Harvard.

April 20: The Dodgers start to wear protective liners in their caps as a cautious response to the numerous beanball wars of 1940 that sent Joe Medwick and Billy Jurges to hospital.

April 26: Wrigley Field becomes the first major league ballpark to install an organ.

May 6: In his last game before induction into the army Hank Greenberg has two homers to lead Detroit to a 7-4 win over the Yankees.

May 15: Joe DiMaggion begins his 56-game hit streak with a single off Ed Smith of Chicago.

June 1: Mel Ott of the Giants collects the 400th home run and 1500th RBI of his career in a 3-2 win over the Reds.

June 2: Lou Gehrig dies at age 37.

July 3: The Yankees' Joe DiMaggio hits in his 45th straight game, breaking the record set by Willie Keeler in 1897.

July 8: In the most dramatic finish to an All-Star Game, Ted Williams connects off Claude Passeau for a three-run homer with two outs in the ninth to give the AL a 7-5 win.

July 17: Joe DiMaggio's 56-game hitting streak is stopped by Al Smith and Jim Bagby in a Cleveland night game, with third baseman Ken Keltner making two great plays against the Yankee Clipper.

July 25: Lefty Grove, 41, wins his 300th game.

August 3: Joe DiMaggio's streak of reaching base in 74 consecutive games is ended by the Browns.

September 17: Stan Musial makes his major league debut and goes 2-for-4. He plays 12 games in September and hits .426.

September 28: Ted Williams goes 6-for-8 in a season-ending double header to close the season with a batting average of .406.

October 5: Brooklyn catcher Mickey Owen drops the third strike of what would have been the last out of a Dodger victory over the Yankees in Game 4 of the World Series. Given a second chance, the Yankees score four runs to win the game, and eventually the Series.

1942

Cards year-end rally humbles cocky Dodgers and powerful Yankees

Nine years before the Dodgers would become synonymous with blowing leads, they warmed up for the dubious distinction by giving away a mid-August 10-1/2-game edge over St. Louis. If there was any difference from the 1951 collapse, it was that the 1942 club's decline coincided with the loss of its best player, outfielder Pete Reiser, to an injury. Outside of Ebbets Field, there were few tears shed around the league for the Dodger breakdown. The swaggering of Leo Durocher's team had become so notorious that in one game Cubs pitchers knocked down 15 consecutive Brooklyn batters. For their part, the Cardinals won 43 of their last 51 games, and still had to beat off a last-gasp Brooklyn drive to regain the lead.

The St. Louis victory represented another vindication of general manager Branch Rickey's farm system. Mort Cooper's league-leading 22 wins and 1.78 ERA and Johnny Beazley's 21 victories paced the pitchers, while the home-grown outfield of Enos Slaughter (.318), Terry Moore (.288) and Stan Musial (.315) helped produce the most runs in the circuit. The most potent sluggers were to be found on the Giants, where playing manager Mel Ott won his sixth (and last) home run crown and first baseman Johnny Mize drove in an NL-best 110 runs. Cincinnati's Ernie Lombardi won his second batting title, at .330.

In the AL, it was once again the Yankees against Ted Williams. A year after hitting .406, the Red Sox left fielder won the Triple Crown by averaging .356 with 36 homers and 137 RBIs. With only second baseman Bobby Doerr (102) and right-hander Tex Hughson (a league-tops 22 wins) offering prominent support, however, the Williams effort was spent for another second-place club. The standings also cost the outfielder an MVP trophy, which went instead to New York second baseman Joe Gordon for his .322 with 18 homers and 103 RBIs. Joe DiMaggio (114) and Charlie Keller (108) also had big RBI years, while Ernie Bonham emerged as the staff ace with 21 wins. Chicago's Ted Lyons recorded the lowest ERA (2.10).

Red Ruffing's first-game win seemed to augur a quick New York World Series championship, but the Cardinals came back for a stunning four straight victories. The Series turning point was Game 3, when Ernie White, who had won only seven games against the NL, blanked the Yankees on six hits. Beazley did most of the rest, throwing two complete-game wins.

The St. Louis championship did not prevent the year's biggest off-field development shortly after the World Series. Following growing tensions with owner Sam Breadon, Rickey ended his quarter-century association with the franchise to move on to the Dodgers. There was a position waiting for him in Brooklyn only because Larry MacPhail resigned his post to join the Army. Although MacPhail would always say patriotism alone had dictated his decision, he had also come to the end of the line with Dodger stockholders who wanted to know why the team's success was rarely translated into dividend payments rather than into more development money and higher salaries for front-office executives.

Mel Ott
The veteran slugger won the last of his six home-run crowns, swatting 30, while a player-manager with the New York Giants.

1942 SEASON HIGHLIGHTS

NATIONAL LEAGUE

	W	L	Pct.	GB
St. Louis	106	48	.688	—
Brooklyn	104	50	.675	2
New York	85	67	.559	20
Cincinnati	76	76	.500	29
Pittsburgh	66	81	.449	36.5
Chicago	68	86	.442	38
Boston	59	89	.399	44
Philadelphia	42	109	.278	62.5

AMERICAN LEAGUE

	W	L	Pct.	GB
New York	103	51	.669	—
Boston	93	59	.612	9
St. Louis	82	69	.543	19.5
Cleveland	75	79	.487	28
Detroit	73	81	.474	30
Chicago	66	82	.446	34
Washington	62	89	.411	39.5
Philadelphia	55	99	.357	48

AWARDS

NL MVP: Mort Cooper, STL
AL MVP: Joe Gordon, NY

ALL-STAR GAME

Polo Grounds, New York
July 6: AL 3, NL 1

POSTSEASON
WORLD SERIES
St. Louis Cardinals 4, New York Yankees 1
Sep. 30: New York 7, ST. LOUIS 4
Oct. 1: ST. LOUIS 4, New York 3
Oct. 3: St. Louis 2, NEW YORK 0
Oct. 4: St. Louis 9, NEW YORK 6
Oct. 5: St. Louis 4, NEW YORK 2

Home team in CAPS

"You don't save a pitcher for tomorrow. Tomorrow it may rain."

— Leo Durocher

NATIONAL LEAGUE LEADERS

Home Runs
Ott-NY	30
Mize-NY	26
Camilli-Bro	26
Nicholson-Chi	21
West-Bos	16

Runs Batted In
Mize-NY	110
Camilli-Bro	109
Slaughter-StL	98
Medwick-Bro	96
Ott-NY	93

Batting Average
Slaughter-StL	.318
Musial-StL	.315
Reiser-StL	.310
Mize-NY	.305
Novikoff-Chi	.300

On Base Percentage
Fletcher-Pit	.417
Ott-NY	.415
Slaughter-StL	.412
Hack-Chi	.402
Musial-StL	.397

Slugging Average
Mize-NY	.521
Ott-NY	.497
Slaughter-StL	.494
Musial-StL	.490
Nicholson-Chi	.476

Stolen Bases
Reiser-Bro	20
Reese-Bro	15
Fernandez-Bos	15
Merullo-Chi	14
Hopp-StL	14

Wins
M.Cooper-StL	22
Beazley-StL	21
Wyatt-Bro	19
Passeau-Chi	19
VanderMeer-Cin	18

Innings Pitched
Tobin-Bos	287.2
M.Cooper-StL	278.2
Passeau-Chi	278.1
Starr-Cin	276.2
Javery-Bos	261.0

Saves
Casey-Bro	13
Adams-NY	11
Beggs-Cin	8
Sain-Bos	6
Gumbert-StL	5

Strikeouts
VanderMeer-Cin	186
M.Cooper-StL	152
Higbe-Bro	115
Walters-Cin	109
Melton-Phi	107

Earned Run Average
M.Cooper-StL	1.78
Beazley-StL	2.13
Davis-Bro	2.36
VanderMeer-Cin	2.43
Lohrman-StL-NY	2.48

Complete Games
Tobin-Bos	28
Passeau-Chi	24
M.Cooper-StL	22
Walters-Cin	21
VanderMeer-Cin	21

AMERICAN LEAGUE LEADERS

Home Runs
Williams-Bos	36
Laabs-StL	27
Keller-NY	26
York-Det	21
DiMaggio-NY	21

Runs Batted In
Williams-Bos	137
DiMaggio-NY	114
Keller-NY	108
Gordon-NY	103
Doerr-Bos	102

Batting Average
Williams-Bos	.356
Pesky-Bos	.331
Spence-Was	.323
Gordon-NY	.322
Case-Was	.320

On Base Percentage
Williams-Bos	.499
Keller-NY	.417
Judnich-StL	.413
Fleming-Cle	.412
Gordon-NY	.409

Slugging Average
Williams-Bos	.648
Keller-NY	.513
Judnich-StL	.499
DiMaggio-NY	.498
Laabs-StL	.498

Stolen Bases
Case-Was	44
Vernon-Was	25
Rizzuto-NY	22
Kuhel-Chi	22

Wins
Hughson-Bos	22
Bonham-NY	21
Marchildon-Phi	17
Bagby-Cle	17
Chandler-NY	16

Innings Pitched
Hughson-Bos	281.0
Bagby-Cle	270.2
Auker-StL	249.0
Marchildon-Phi	244.0
Hudson-Was	239.1

Saves
Murphy-NY	11
Haynes-Chi	6
Brown-Bos	6
Newhouser-Det	5
Caster-StL	5

Strikeouts
Newsom-Was	113
Hughson-Bos	113
Marchildon-Phi	110
Benton-Det	110
Niggeling-StL	107

Earned Run Average
Lyons-Chi	2.10
Bonham-NY	2.27
Chandler-NY	2.38
Newhouser-Det	2.45
Borowy-NY	2.52

Complete Games
Hughson-Bos	22
Bonham-NY	22
Lyons-Chi	20
Hudson-Was	19

THE YEAR IN BASEBALL

January 6: Cleveland pitcher Bob Feller, proclaiming "I've always wanted to be on the winning side," enlists in the navy.

January 15: President Roosevelt gives the green light to baseball to continue during the war and encourages more night games so workers may attend.

February 7: The Reds trade Ernie Lombardi to the Braves; in his only year in Boston, he took the NL batting championship with a mark of .330.

May 19: Paul Waner of the Boston Braves joins Cap Anson and Honus Wagner as the only NL players to collect 3,000 hits.

May 31: A crowd of 22,000 sees Satchel Paige pitch five innings to defeat the Dizzy Dean All-Stars.

June 2: Ted Williams enlists as a navy aviator but will finish out the season, winning a Triple Crown.

August 23: In a pre-game attraction that raised $80,000 for the Army-Navy relief, Babe Ruth hits a pitch from Walter Johnson into the stands.

September 13: Chicago Cubs shortstop Lenny Merullo ties a major league record with four errors in one inning and then names his new-born son Boots.

November 1: After two decades in St. Louis, Branch Rickey splits with owner Sam Breadon and signs to become general manager of Brooklyn.

November 15: Joe Gunson dies in Philadelphia. He debuted with the Washington Nationals in 1884 and played 4 seasons on 5 teams.

December 23: Southpaw Jerry Koosman born; as a rookie with the Mets in 1968, he tied an NL rookie record with seven shutouts.

1943

Players go off to war as managers bicker and Yanks win again

There were lots of reminders in 1943 that baseball was just a tolerated activity on the sidelines of the war. Because of travel restrictions, teams were prohibited from setting up spring-training bases south of the Mason-Dixon line, leading to improvised camps in the crisp weather of places like New Jersey and upstate New York. Rosters also began mirroring the steady exodus of players into the military. Clark Griffith's solution for the Senators was to start bringing in Cubans and other Hispanics; not only were they cheap, they weren't obligated to register for the draft until 1944.

But perhaps the most-discussed change to the game was the introduction of a new baseball. Due to limitations in the supply of imported horsehide and cork, the major leagues were forced to introduce a ball that featured a domestic horsehide cover and a core of granulated cork encased in balata, the hard-rubber covering familiarly used on golf balls. This "balata ball," as it came to be known, represented the first major change in the baseball's construction in a quarter century, and it was roundly cursed. Players insisted it was deader than the usual ball. Statistical evidence was contradictory and, although there was a decline in some offensive totals, it had to be noted that several batting stars, including Joe DiMaggio, had entered the service.

The pennant races were that in name only, with the Cardinals and Yankees running away from their rivals. It was anything but a coincidence that the two clubs had the most developed farm systems in baseball, allowing for better-honed replacements when Uncle Sam came calling. Typical was the case of southpaw Howie Pollet, who stuck around long enough to win eight games and post an NL-leading 1.75 ERA for St. Louis; when he went off to military service, Pollet was replaced by another left-hander, Harry Brecheen, who picked up nine wins. Mort Cooper won 21 for the Cardinals (tying him with Pittsburgh's Rip Sewell and Cincinnati's Elmer Riddle for the league best), while Stan Musial burst out with a batting title (.357) and the most doubles (48) and triples (20). The slugger of the year was Chicago's Bill Nicholson, who recorded the most homers (29) and most RBIs (128).

Off the field, Brooklyn and Philadelphia provided the NL entertainment. With the Dodgers, it was a circus of general manager Branch Rickey suspending coaches for winning money from players at poker games, manager Leo Durocher getting into fights and near-fights with his veterans, and one and all threatening to retire from baseball. The only one to make good on such a threat was first baseman Dolf Camilli, who endeared himself to Dodger fans by refusing a July trade to the Giants, saying he would rather stay home than play for the local enemy.

With the Phillies, it was owner William Cox insisting on taking the field with his club during spring training, changing the team's nickname from the Phillies to the Blue Jays, and admitting to Commissioner Kenesaw Landis that he was in the habit of placing "sentimental bets" on his club. Cox was forced to sell out, and was banned for life.

In the AL, the Yankees got unexpected production from first

Stan Musial
The popular Musial led St. Louis to the World Series by leading the league in batting (.357), doubles (48) and triples (20).

baseman Nick Etten (a team-leading 107 RBIs) and 31 homers from outfielder Charlie Keller to back the pitching of a staff headed by Spud Chandler (20) and Ernie Bonham (15). Chandler's victories tied him with Detroit's Dizzy Trout for the most in the league and his 1.64 ERA was the best. Chicago's Luke Appling won the batting crown (.328), Detroit's Rudy York both the home run (34) and RBI (118) honors. Outfielder George Case's 61 steals for Washington represented his fifth year in a row at the top of that category.

In the World Series, the Yankees exacted symmetrical revenge for their defeat in five games by St. Louis the previous year. Chandler hurled two complete-game victories, including an odd 10-hit shutout in the finale.

1943 SEASON HIGHLIGHTS

NATIONAL LEAGUE

	W	L	Pct.	GB
St. Louis	105	49	.682	—
Cincinnati	87	67	.565	18
Brooklyn	81	72	.529	23.5
Pittsburgh	80	74	.519	25
Chicago	74	79	.484	30.5
Boston	68	85	.444	36.5
Philadelphia	64	90	.416	41
New York	55	98	.359	49.5

AMERICAN LEAGUE

	W	L	Pct.	GB
New York	98	56	.636	—
Washington	84	69	.549	13.5
Cleveland	82	71	.536	15.5
Chicago	82	72	.532	16
Detroit	78	76	.506	20
St. Louis	72	80	.474	25
Boston	68	84	.447	29
Philadelphia	49	105	.318	49

AWARDS
NL MVP: Stan Musial, STL
AL MVP: Spud Chandler, NY

ALL-STAR GAME
Shibe Park, Philadelphia
July 13: AL 5, NL 3

POSTSEASON
WORLD SERIES
New York Yankees 4, St. Louis Cardinals 1
Oct. 5: NEW YORK 4, St. Louis 2
Oct. 6: St. Louis 4, NEW YORK 3
Oct. 7: NEW YORK 6, St. Louis 2
Oct. 10: New York 2, ST. LOUIS 1
Oct. 11: New York 2, ST. LOUIS 0
Home team in CAPS

"I got a million dollars worth of free advice and a very small raise."
— Eddie Stanky, after negotiating a contract with Dodgers' executive Branch Rickey

NATIONAL LEAGUE LEADERS

Home Runs
Nicholson-Chi	29
Ott-NY	18
Northey-Phi	16
Triplett-StL-Phi	15
DiMaggio-Pit	15

Runs Batted In
Nicholson-Chi	128
Elliott-Pit	101
Herman-Bro	100
DiMaggio-Pit	88

Batting Average
Musial-StL	.357
Herman-Bro	.330
Elliott-Pit	.315
Witek-NY	.314
Nicholson-Chi	.309

On Base Percentage
Musial-StL	.425
Galan-Bro	.412
Herman-Bro	.398
Fletcher-Pit	.395
Tipton-Cin	.395

Slugging Average
Musial-StL	.562
Nicholson-Chi	.531
Elliott-Pit	.444
Kurowski-StL	.439
Northey-Phi	.430

Stolen Bases
Vaughan-Bro	20
Lowrey-Chi	13
Workman-Bos	12
Russell-Pit	12
Gustine-Pit	12

Wins
Sewell-Pit	21
Riddle-Cin	21
M.Cooper-StL	21
Bithorn-Chi	18
Javery-Bos	17

Innings Pitched
Javery-Bos	303.0
VanderMeer-Cin	289.0
Andrews-Bos	283.2
M.Cooper-StL	274.0
Sewell-Pit	265.1

Saves
Webber-Bro	10
Adams-NY	9
Shoun-Cin	7
Head-Bro	6
Beggs-Cin	6

Strikeouts
VanderMeer-Cin	174
M.Cooper-StL	141
Javery-Bos	134
Lanier-StL	123
Higbe-Bro	108

Earned Run Average
Lanier-StL	1.90
M.Cooper-StL	2.30
Wyatt-Bro	2.49
Sewell-Pit	2.54
Andrews-Bos	2.57

Complete Games
Sewell-Pit	25
Tobin-Bos	24
M.Cooper-StL	24
Andrews-Bos	23

AMERICAN LEAGUE LEADERS

Home Runs
York-Det	34
Keller-NY	31
Stephens-StL	22
Heath-Cle	18

Runs Batted In
York-Det	118
Etten-NY	107
Johnson-NY	94
Stephens-StL	91
Spence-Was	88

Batting Average
Appling-Chi	.328
Wakefield-Det	.316
Cramer-Det	.300
Case-Was	.294
Curtright-Chi	.291

On Base Percentage
Appling-Chi	.419
Cullenbine-Cle	.407
Keller-NY	.396
Boudreau-Cle	.388
Curtright-Chi	.382

Slugging Average
York-Det	.527
Keller-NY	.525
Stephens-StL	.482
Heath-Cle	.481
Wakefield-Det	.434

Stolen Bases
Case-Was	61
Moses-Chi	56
Tucker-Chi	29
Appling-Chi	27
Vernon-Was	24

Wins
Trout-Det	20
Chandler-NY	20
Wynn-Was	18
Smith-Cle	17
Bagby-Cle	17

Innings Pitched
Bagby-Cle	273.0
Hughson-Bos	266.0
Wynn-Was	256.2
Chandler-NY	253.0
Trout-Det	246.2

Saves
Maltzberger-Chi	14
Heving-Cle	9
Brown-Bos	9
Murphy-NY	8
Caster-StL	8

Strikeouts
Reynolds-Cle	151
Newhouser-Det	144
Chandler-NY	134
Bridges-Det	124
Trucks-Det	118

Earned Run Average
Chandler-NY	1.64
Bonham-NY	2.27
Haefner-Was	2.29
Bridges-Det	2.39
Trout-Det	2.48

Complete Games
Hughson-Bos	20
Chandler-NY	20
Wensloff-NY	18
Trout-Det	18
Grove-Chi	18

THE YEAR IN BASEBALL

January 5: Big league clubs decide to train in the North due to World War II.

February 20: Phil Wrigley and Branch Rickey charter the All-American Girls Softball League to operate in the Chicago area.

March 13: As a war measure, the major leagues approve an official ball made from reclaimed cork and balata in the interior, but the new ball is unpopular with players.

August 18: Braves manager Casey Stengel is hit by a taxi, suffering a fractured leg that causes him to miss much of the season.

June 1: Rip Sewell of the Pirates, on his way to 20 wins, throws his "dew-drop" ball in a game. It arcs 18 to 20 feet in the air on its way to the plate.

July 13: In the first All-Star Game played under lights, the AL edges the NL 5-3 at Shibe Park.

July 18: The Giants and Phillies combine to strand 30 baserunners, a major league record.

August 18: Carl Hubbell wins his 253rd, and final, game in the majors.

August 24: The Phillies tie a league record by suffering their 20th consecutive loss.

September 6: Philadelphia pitcher Carl Scheib, 16 years, 248 days, becomes the youngest player in the century.

November 23: Commissioner Kenesaw Landis imposes a lifetime ban on Phils owner William D. Cox for having bet on his own team.

1944

Browns meet Cards in an unexpected all-St. Louis Series

If ever there was an omen for a baseball campaign, it was in the Browns winning their first nine games in 1944. In its 42-year AL existence up to then, St. Louis had never won a pennant and had finished second only twice. But in a season dominated by the too young, too old, and too unskilled taking the field, the Browns made the bizarre and unusual work for them in one of the circuit's most melodramatic finishes.

Expectations that St. Louis would fold before the finish line were still alive in the final hours of the season, when Detroit took a one-game lead, then fell back again into a flat-footed tie. On the final day of the schedule, the Browns completed an improbable four-game sweep of the third-place Yankees on the strength of two homers by outfielder Chet Laabs while the Tigers were losing 4-1 to the last-place Senators. The victory over New York was witnessed by 34,625—the largest crowd ever to see the team at home and an astonishing contrast to the mere 894 that had been at Sportsman's Park for the club's ninth straight win at the start of the year. The principal agents of the St. Louis pennant were right-handers Nelson Potter and Jack Kramer, who won 36 games between them, and shortstop Vern Stephens, who led the league with his 109 RBIs. The team's overall .252 average was the lowest for a pennant winner in either league since the Red Sox in another war year, 1918.

The AL's biggest winner on the year was Detroit's Hal Newhouser, with 29 victories. Teammate Dizzy Trout, himself a 27-game winner, posted the best ERA at 2.12. Nick Etten of the Yankees hit the most home runs (22); Cleveland's playing manager Lou Boudreau had the highest average (.327). Among those seeing service in the league because of the depleted talent pool were Athletics pitcher Carl Scheib, at 17 the youngest ALer ever; Washington third baseman Eddie Yost, only a couple of months older; and Cleveland reliever Joe Heving, who at the age of 43 led the circuit in appearances (63).

Lou Boudreau
As Cleveland's 27-year-old player-manager, Boudreau won the AL batting crown (.327) and set records for fielding percentage and double plays by a shortstop.

In the NL, the Cardinals got through another year without losing such key players as Stan Musial, Marty Marion, Whitey Kurowski, and Mort Cooper, so ended up with a 14-1/2-game bulge over Pittsburgh. First baseman Ray Sanders complemented Musial's .336 and Cooper's 22 wins with 102 RBIs. For the second year in a row, Chicago's Bill Nicholson had the most homers (33) and RBIs (122). The batting title went to Brooklyn's Dixie Walker (.357); Cincinnati's Bucky Walters registered the most victories (23); and Ed Heusser of the Reds was the hardest to score against, at 2.38. A third Cincinnati pitcher, Joe Nuxhall, became the youngest player in 20th-century major league history when, on June 10 at the age of 15 years, 10 months, and 11 days, he worked two-thirds of an inning. The southpaw surrendered two hits and five walks, making for an ERA of 67.50.

Pro-Browns sentiment in the first and only all-St. Louis World Series got a lift when the ALers won two of the first three games. But then, largely because of Browns errors (they made 10 in the Series), the Cardinals came ripping back for three straight victories. Cooper's 2-0 shutout in Game 5 proved to be the turning point.

1944 SEASON HIGHLIGHTS

NATIONAL LEAGUE

	W	L	Pct.	GB
St. Louis	105	49	.682	—
Pittsburgh	90	63	.588	14.5
Cincinnati	89	65	.578	16
Chicago	75	79	.487	30
New York	67	87	.435	38
Boston	65	89	.422	40
Brooklyn	63	91	.409	42
Philadelphia	61	92	.399	43.5

AMERICAN LEAGUE

	W	L	Pct.	GB
St. Louis	89	65	.578	—
Detroit	88	66	.571	1
New York	83	71	.539	6
Boston	77	77	.500	12
Philadelphia	72	82	.468	17
Cleveland	72	82	.468	17
Chicago	71	83	.461	18
Washington	64	90	.416	25

AWARDS

NL MVP: Marty Marion, STL
AL MVP: Hal Newhouser, DET

ALL-STAR GAME

Forbes Field, Pittsburgh
July 11: NL 7, AL 1

POSTSEASON
WORLD SERIES
St. Louis Cardinals 4, St. Louis Browns 2
Oct. 4: Browns 2, CARDINALS 1
Oct. 5: CARDINALS 3, Browns 2
Oct. 6: BROWNS 6, Cardinals 2
Oct. 7: Cardinals 5, BROWNS 1
Oct. 8: Cardinals 2, BROWNS 0
Oct. 9: CARDINALS 3, Browns 1

Home team in CAPS

> "He is easily the slowest ballplayer since Ernie Lombardi was thrown out at first base trying to stretch a double into a single."
>
> — Stanley Frank, on Lou Boudreau

NATIONAL LEAGUE LEADERS

Home Runs
Nicholson-Chi	33
Ott-NY	26
Northey-Phi	22
McCormick-Cin	20
Kurowski-StL	20

Runs Batted In
Nicholson-Chi	122
Elliott-Pit	108
Northey-Phi	104
Sanders-StL	102
McCormick-Cin	102

Batting Average
Walker-Bro	.357
Musial-StL	.347
Medwick-NY	.337
Hopp-StL	.336
Cavarretta-Chi	.321

On Base Percentage
Musial-StL	.440
Walker-Bro	.434
Galan-Bro	.426
Ott-NY	.423
Hopp-StL	.404

Slugging Average
Musial-StL	.549
Nicholson-Chi	.545
Ott-NY	.544
Walker-Bro	.529
Hopp-StL	.499

Stolen Bases
Barrett-Pit	28
Lupien-Phi	18
Hughes-Chi	16
Hopp-StL	15
Kerr-NY	14

Wins
Walters-Cin	23
M.Cooper-StL	22
Voiselle-NY	21
Sewell-Pit	21
Tobin-Bos	18

Innings Pitched
Voiselle-NY	312.2
Tobin-Bos	299.1
Sewell-Pit	286.0
Walters-Cin	285.0
Raffensberger-Phi	258.2

Saves
Adams-NY	13
Schmidt-StL	5
Rescigno-Pit	5
Davis-Bro	4
Cuccurullo-Pit	4

Strikeouts
Voiselle-NY	161
Lanier-StL	141
Javery-Bos	137
Raffensberger-Phi	136

Earned Run Average
Heusser-Cin	2.38
Walters-Cin	2.40
M.Cooper-StL	2.46
Wilks-StL	2.64
Lanier-StL	2.65

Complete Games
Tobin-Bos	28
Walters-Cin	27
Voiselle-NY	25
Sewell-Pit	24
M.Cooper-StL	22

AMERICAN LEAGUE LEADERS

Home Runs
Etten-NY	22
Stephens-StL	20
York-Det	18
Spence-Was	18
Lindell-NY	18

Runs Batted In
Stephens-StL	109
B.Johnson-Bos	106
Lindell-NY	103
Spence-Was	100
York-Det	98

Batting Average
Boudreau-Cle	.327
Doerr-Bos	.325
B.Johnson-Bos	.324
Stirnweiss-NY	.319
Spence-Was	.316

On Base Percentage
B.Johnson-Bos	.431
Boudreau-Cle	.406
Doerr-Bos	.399
Etten-NY	.399
Byrnes-StL	.396

Slugging Average
Doerr-Bos	.528
B.Johnson-Bos	.528
Lindell-NY	.500
Spence-Was	.486

Stolen Bases
Stirnweiss-NY	55
Case-Was	49
Myatt-Was	26
Moses-Chi	21
Gutteridge-StL	20

Wins
Newhouser-Det	29
Trout-Det	27
Potter-StL	19
Hughson-Bos	18

Innings Pitched
Trout-Det	352.1
Newhouser-Det	312.1
Newsom-Phi	265.0
Kramer-StL	257.0
Borowy-NY	252.2

Saves
Maltzberger-Chi	12
Caster-StL	12
Berry-Phi	12
Heving-Cle	10
Barrett-StL	8

Strikeouts
Newhouser-Det	187
Trout-Det	144
Newsom-Phi	142
Kramer-StL	124
Niggeling-Was	121

Earned Run Average
Trout-Det	2.12
Newhouser-Det	2.22
Hughson-Bos	2.26
Niggeling-Was	2.32
Kramer-StL	2.49

Complete Games
Trout-Det	33
Newhouser-Det	25

THE YEAR IN BASEBALL

January 27: Lou Perini, Guido Rugo and Joseph Maney buy the Braves and oust Casey Stengel as manager.

April 27: Jim Tobin of the Braves pitches a no-hitter over the Dodgers at Boston, winning 2-0. He also hits a homer.

May 23: War-time restrictions are eased an night ball returns to the Polo Grounds for the first time since 1941.

June 6: All major league games are cancelled when it is announced that Allied Forces had invaded occupied France on D-Day.

June 10: Fifteen-year-old southpaw Joe Nuxhall becomes the youngest to play in the majors in this century.

July 11: Phil Cavarretta of the Cubs sets an All Star Game record by reaching base five consecutive times in a 7-1 NL win.

July 23: Bill Nicholson of the Chicago Cubs is ordered intentionally passed with the bases filled by New York Giants manager Mel Ott in the eighth inning, after he had rocked them with four consecutive homers in two days; though Cubs rally to tie game at 10-all, Giants win, 12-10.

August 3: Tommy Brown, just 16 years, eight months old, plays shortstop for Brooklyn in both games of a doubleheader.

August 10: Red Barrett of the Boston Braves throws only 58 pitches in a complete-game shutout of the Reds.

November 25: Active as baseball's commissioner until the last, Judge Kenesaw Mountain Landis dies in Chicago. His contract had just been extended to January 1953, at which point he would have been 86 years old.

December 28: Former Washington third baseman John "Buddy" Lewis wins the Distinguished Flying Cross.

December 30: The White Sox buy Browns' infielder Floyd Baker, who would set a record of sorts by hitting only one home run in 13 years' play.

1945

Greenberg returns to power Tigers to Series victory

The death of Kenesaw Landis in November 1944 put Happy Chandler in the commissioner's office at the start of play in 1945. With all but a handful of all-star players wearing Army or Navy uniforms, there was no heavy betting on such traditional favorites as the Cardinals, Yankees, and Tigers making it to World Series. In fact, Detroit did make it—but only on the final day of the season.

The AL race was one of the most bizarre in league history, thanks especially to the Senators. For openers, the Washington rotation consisted of four knuckleballers—Roger Wolff, Dutch Leonard, Mickey Haefner, and Johnny Niggeling. Its offense was so mild that first baseman Joe Kuhel hit the only home team homer at Griffith Stadium all year—and that was an inside-the-park job. Then there was owner Clark Griffith, who thought so little of his club's pennant chances that he jammed doubleheaders into the beginning of September so the NFL Redskins could have Sunday dates at Griffith Stadium later in the month. The upshot was that the Senators had completed their schedule as the Tigers, merely a game ahead of Washington, stumbled through a final week of losses and rain postponements trying to apply the clincher in a series against the Browns. They finally made it on the last day of the year thanks to a grand-slam home run from Hank Greenberg, recently returned from four years of military service. The Detroit effort was led by southpaw Hal Newhouser's league-leading 25 wins and 1.81 ERA.

Vern Stephens of St. Louis had the most AL homers (24) and Nick Etten of the Yankees the most RBIs (111). The batting champion was second baseman George Stirnweiss of the Yankees (.309), but with a big hand from the tactlessness of the White Sox. Two days before the end of the year, Chicago announced shortstop Tony Cuccinello would not be returning in 1946 because of the expected discharge of younger players from the armed forces. The 37-year-old Cuccinello ended up losing the title to Stirnweiss by the margin of .00009. Among the others to be seen on AL diamonds because of those younger players still in the wings were one-armed outfielder Pete Gray on the Browns and one-legged pitcher Bert Shepard on the Senators.

The NL race turned on a July deal in which the Cubs paid the Yankees $97,000 for hurler Hank Borowy, who ended up going 11-2, with a league-best 2.13 ERA. The other major factors in Chicago's win over St. Louis were first baseman Phil Cavaretta's batting title (.355), outfielder Andy Pafko's 110 RBIs and a 21-1

Hal Newhouser
The Tigers ace southpaw led the AL with 25 wins and 1.81 ERA, anchoring a Detroit staff that downed the Cubs in the World Series.

record against the seventh-place Reds. It didn't hurt, either, that the Cardinals lost slugger Stan Musial to the military for the year. One reason St. Louis stayed as close as it did was another midseason transaction in which it obtained Red Barrett from the Braves; the right-hander led NL pitchers with his 21 victories. Boston's Tommy Holmes hit the most homers (28) and Brooklyn's Dixie Walker drove in the most runs (124).

The Tigers took the World Series in seven games, mainly because Cubs manager Charlie Grimm couldn't stay away from Borowy, starting him three times and using him in relief once. Greenberg drove in seven runs in what would be Chicago's last World Series appearance into the 21st century.

1945 SEASON HIGHLIGHTS

NATIONAL LEAGUE

	W	L	Pct.	GB
Chicago	98	56	.636	—
St. Louis	95	59	.617	3
Brooklyn	87	67	.565	11
Pittsburgh	82	72	.532	16
New York	78	74	.513	19
Boston	67	85	.441	30
Cincinnati	61	93	.396	37
Philadelphia	46	108	.299	52

AMERICAN LEAGUE

	W	L	Pct.	GB
Detroit	88	65	.575	—
Washington	87	67	.565	1.5
St. Louis	81	70	.536	6
New York	81	71	.533	6.5
Cleveland	73	72	.503	11
Chicago	71	78	.477	15
Boston	71	83	.461	17.5
Philadelphia	52	98	.347	34.5

AWARDS

NL MVP: Phil Cavarretta, CHI
AL MVP: Hal Newhouser, DET

ALL-STAR GAME CANCELLED

POSTSEASON
WORLD SERIES
Detroit Tigers 4, Chicago Cubs 3
Oct. 3: Chicago 9, DETROIT 0
Oct. 4: DETROIT 4, Chicago 1
Oct. 5: Chicago 3, DETROIT 0
Oct. 6: Detroit 4, CHICAGO 1
Oct. 7: Detroit 8, CHICAGO 4
Oct. 8: CHICAGO 8, Detroit 7
Oct. 10: Detroit 9, CHICAGO 3

Home team in CAPS

> **"I've found that you don't need to wear a necktie if you can hit."**
> — Ted Williams

NATIONAL LEAGUE LEADERS

Home Runs
Holmes-Bos	28
Workman-Bos	25
Adams-Phi-StL	22
Ott-NY	21
Kurowski-StL	21

Runs Batted In
Walker-Bro	124
Holmes-Bos	117
Pafko-Chi	110
Olmo-Bro	110
Adams-Phi-StL	109

Batting Average
Cavarretta-Chi	.355
Holmes-Bos	.352
Rosen-Bro	.325
Hack-Chi	.323
Kurowski-StL	.323

On Base Percentage
Cavarretta-Chi	.449
Galan-Bro	.423
Hack-Chi	.420
Holmes-Bos	.420
Stanky-Bro	.417

Slugging Average
Holmes-Bos	.577
Kurowski-StL	.511
Cavarretta-Chi	.500
Ott-NY	.499
Olmo-Bro	.462

Stolen Bases
Schoendienst-StL	26
Barrett-Pit	25
Clay-Cin	19

Wins
Barrett-Bos-StL	23
Wyse-Chi	22
Gregg-Bro	18
Burkhart-StL	18
Passeau-Chi	17

Innings Pitched
Barrett-Bos-StL	284.2
Wyse-Chi	278.1
Gregg-Bro	254.1
Roe-Pit	235.0
Voiselle-NY	232.1

Saves
Karl-Phi	15
Adams-NY	15
Rescigno-Pit	9

Strikeouts
Roe-Pit	148
Gregg-Bro	139
Voiselle-NY	115
Mungo-NY	101
Hutchings-Bos	99

Earned Run Average
Prim-Chi	2.40
Passeau-Chi	2.46
Brecheen-StL	2.52
Walters-Cin	2.68
Wyse-Chi	2.68

Complete Games
Barrett-Bos-StL	24
Wyse-Chi	23
Passeau-Chi	19
Strincevich-Pit	18
Heusser-Cin	18

AMERICAN LEAGUE LEADERS

Home Runs
Stephens-StL	24
Cullenbine-Cle-Det	18
York-Det	18
Etten-NY	18
Heath-Cle	15

Runs Batted In
Etten-NY	111
Cullenbine-Cle-Det	93
Stephens-StL	89
York-Det	87
Binks-Was	81

Batting Average
Stirnweiss-NY	.309
Dickshot-Chi	.302
Estalella-Phi	.299
Myatt-Was	.296
Moses-Chi	.295

On Base Percentage
Lake-Bos	.412
Cullenbine-Cle-Det	.402
Estalella-Phi	.399
Grimes-NY	.395
Etten-NY	.387

Slugging Average
Stirnweiss-NY	.476
Stephens-StL	.473
Cullenbine-Cle-Det	.444
Etten-NY	.437
Estalella-Phi	.435

Stolen Bases
Stirnweiss-NY	33
Myatt-Was	30
Case-Was	30
Metkovich-Bos	19
Dickshot-Chi	18

Wins
Newhouser-Det	25
Ferriss-Bos	21
Wolff-Was	20
Gromek-Cle	19

Innings Pitched
Newhouser-Det	313.1
Ferriss-Bos	264.2
Newsom-Phi	257.1
Potter-StL	255.1
Gromek-Cle	251.0

Saves
Turner-NY	10
Berry-Phi	5

Strikeouts
Newhouser-Det	212
Potter-StL	129
Newsom-Phi	127
Reynolds-Cle	112

Earned Run Average
Newhouser-Det	1.81
Benton-Det	2.02
Wolff-Was	2.12
Leonard-Was	2.13
Lee-Chi	2.44

Complete Games
Newhouser-Det	29
Ferriss-Bos	26
Wolff-Was	21
Potter-StL	21
Gromek-Cle	21

THE YEAR IN BASEBALL

January 19: Stan Musial enlists in the U.S. Navy; coming back to the Cards in 1946, he didn't skip a beat, hitting .365 to lead the league.

January 25: Larry MacPhail, Dan Topping and Del Webb purchase the New York Yankees for $2.8 million.

May 20: The Browns' one-armed outfielder Pete Gray stars as St. Louis sweeps a doubleheader from the Yankees.

July 1: In his first game back after returning from the war, Hank Greenberg hits a home run.

July 10: The All Star Game at Fenway Park is cancelled due to war-time travel restrictions.

August 1: Mel Ott hits the 500th home run of his career.

August 13: Branch Rickey becomes a principal stockholder of the Dodgers by joining with Walter O'Malley and John Smith to acquire a 50% interest for $750,000.

August 15: World Series radio rights are sold for $150,000.

August 19: Phillies' 37-year-old slugger Jimmie Foxx pitches seven innings, allowing one run, to earn a victory in the second half of a doubleheader.

August 20: Tommy Brown, 17-year-old shortstop of the Dodgers, becomes the youngest major league player to hit a home run, smacking one off Preacher Roe of the Pirates.

August 24: A crowd of 46,477 is on hand for the return of Bob Feller from the navy, and they see him strike out 12 in a 4-2 Cleveland win.

September 7: Joe Kuhel hits an inside-the-park home run that is the only home run of the season in Washington's spacious Griffith Stadium.

September 9: Philadelphia pitcher Dick Fowler returns from a three-year stint with the Canadian Army and, in his first game, no-hits the Browns.

October 23: Branch Rickey announces the signing of Jackie Robinson by the Dodger organization.

Chapter 12

Rube Waddell: Peter Pan of Baseball

By John Thorn

George Edward "Rube" Waddell was baseball's most kaleidoscopic character. In 1903 he began the year sleeping in a firehouse at Camden, New Jersey, and ended it tending bar in Wheeling, West Virginia. "In between those events," wrote Lee Allen, "he won twenty-two games for the Philadelphia Athletics, played left end for the Business Men's Rugby Football Club of Grand Rapids, Michigan, toured the nation in a melodrama called The Stain of Guilt, courted, married, and separated from May Wynne Skinner of Lynn, Massachusetts, saved a woman from drowning, accidentally shot a friend through the hand, and was bitten by a lion."

The stories go on and on about this wild and crazy guy and, remarkably, most of them are true. Playing marbles under the stands at game time while his teammates searched for their starting pitcher; being paid his year's salary of $2,200 in one-dollar bills because he was so impulsive a spender; hurling both ends of a doubleheader just so that he could get a few days off to go fishing; calling his outfielders to the sidelines, then striking out the batter.

The Rube was not merely an oddball, like Germany Schaefer, or an entertaining tippler like Bugs Raymond, or a braggart like Art Shires, though he was all of these things and more. The eccentric "sousepaw" was an original, a boy who never grew up yet was a giant among men on the ball field.

A quick look at Waddell's career record reveals seven strikeout crowns, six of them in succession in 1902-07; a lifetime ERA of 2.16 with a single-season best of 1.48; and four straight 20-win seasons. But a closer examination shows just how awesome he was at his peak. In 1902 he won a commendable 24 games for the Philadelphia Athletics—but he didn't pitch for them until June 26, by which time he had already won 12 games with Los Angeles of the Pacific Coast League. He won 10 games for the A's in the month of July, a feat unmatched by any hurler since. His 24 wins for them came over a period of only 87 games played by the club, a percentage of team wins also unmatched since. In 1904 Waddell fanned 349 batters, a total not surpassed until Sandy Koufax came along in 1965; nearly one hundred years later, Waddell's mark is still the best by an American League lefthander. In 1955, at age 93, Connie Mack called Rube the greatest pitcher, in terms of pure talent, he had ever seen—and Connie had seen them all, from Hoss Radbourne and Amos Rusie through Cy Young and Walter Johnson, on up to Lefty Grove and Bob Feller.

In his six years in Philadelphia, Rube married four times. Although the aforementioned Miss Skinner, the second of his wives, left him after only three weeks of marriage, and he did spend some time in jail for throwing flatirons at each of his in-laws (an impulse with which some of us may empathize), this man-child had a good heart. On more than one occasion his penchant for running after fire engines led him to rush into a burning building to effect a rescue. And his premature death, at age 37 in 1914 (on

Rube Waddell
One of baseball's true original characters, Waddell was also one of its most accomplished pitchers.

April Fool's Day) resulted from a severe cold he contracted after standing for hours in icy waters up to his armpits, placing sandbags in advance of rising waters from a broken dam.

No one Waddellian tale conveys the heroic quality of the man; Rube's whole life had the quality of legend, the kind that sustained our nation in the years before The Great War. Before the frontier closed, before radio and rural electrification truly united our states into a homogeneous national culture, America gave rise to such icons as Paul Bunyan, the all-powerful lumberjack landscaper; Mose the Bowery B'hoy, the common rough, comic boor, and guardian angel of the underprivileged (and, like Waddell, pride of the volunteer fire laddies); and Sam Patch, the foolhardy millhand who won fame by jumping off bridges and immortality in his

failed leap over Niagara Falls. (Nathaniel Hawthorne wrote of him, though the words might as easily have been applied to Waddell: "How stern a moral may be drawn from the story of poor Sam Patch! ... Was the leaper of cataracts more mad or foolish than other men who throw away life, or misspend it in pursuit of empty fame, and seldom so triumphantly as he?") These three, along with other folkloric figures of America's formative years, culminate in the form of Rube Waddell.

In baseball, he descended from a line of hell-raising, hard-drinking heroes like King Kelly, Arlie Latham, and Radbourne. When college man Christy Mathewson came along to contend with Waddell for favor in the first decade of the century, the moralists at last had a suitable role model in baseball; but the conformist Matty never captured the hearts of boys as the Rube did. While adults clucked their disapproval, Rube's sense of mischief and disregard for adult ways endeared him to youth. He was them, figured large, with the power not only to move about in the adult world but also to transform it, to make it uniquely his.

The arrival of Babe Ruth marked a restoration of the rebellious spirit in sport, as did Dizzy Dean. But while both were "naturals" like the semi-demented Waddell, the Babe was neither a clown nor a yokel, and Ol' Diz played the rube act with self-promotional cunning.

Why do we glorify natural athletes when hard workers, conscientious practitioners of their craft, are so much more admirable as men? Because in their untutored excellence these fortunate few seem to be touched with the divine, the mysterious gift of the gods—a spirit of play akin to the inexplicable animating force of art.

Waddell was a legend while he was alive; that he has ceased to be one in death is testament to how our country has changed. Why are heroes today so colorless, so pale? Even great talents like Michael Jordan or Nolan Ryan are personally boring. Why do we still gravitate toward the bad boys, the rebels, even when their abilities are beneath those of the goody-two-shoes of the sports world? Conformists may be admired, but nonconformists are adored and/or feared.

Man's attraction to fame is like that of moth to flame. The moralists among us—like Hawthorne in his dispatch of Sam Patch—delight in the failure of heroes, affirming that man should not be so filled with hubris as to presume to deity. Thus is played the inevitable cycle of fame, paralleling that of life itself: hero to celebrity to commodity to trash. Rube Waddell sidestepped that descent by dying young, but perhaps more importantly, by never really enlisting as a functional adult. Like a messenger of God, or one who has struck a pact with the devil, in the cadences of conventional life Rube was always an outsider. He stood outside civilization, culture, rationalism, team play, the work ethic—all Western, Christian values. He was an individualist, nonconformist, rebel, hero—honored and scorned at the same time, for he was also a rube: a bumpkin, rustic, hayseed, farmer, yokel, hoosier, backwoodsman, fool.

The term "rube" derived from Reuben, a hinterlands name that provoked mirth among the city swells and traveling gents and those rural types who fancied themselves "in the know." Waddell began pitching for his town team of Butler, Pennsylvania, at age 18, in 1895, later moving on to pitch for the Prospect nine. When he showed up at Franklin in 1896, green as any farmboy ever was but hoping for an audition, one of the Franklin men called out, "Hey, Rube!"—the circus/carny term used as a cry for help, or rallying charge, against outsiders, like those who would cut the canvas to gain free admission. (Often as not, the call "Hey, Rube!" would lead to a heyrube—a fracas or hubbub, what Red Barber and other Southerners came to call a rhubarb. The Franklin players were not only mocking the farmboy Waddell ("Reuben") but also rallying the clan against an outside intrusion.*

Rube the farmboy was an outsider when he stepped onto the rural ballfield of Franklin, but perhaps less so when he went on to pitch for big cities like Philadelphia and St. Louis. The enclosed ballparks there were designed to give an increasingly urban populace a park within the city, a place reminiscent of the idealized farms that had sent all those rubes to the metropolis in the first place. After all, baseball itself is inextricably tied to the land, deriving as it does from a pagan rite of fertility.

And George Edward Waddell was also an outsider in that he was lefthanded (sinister, evil, endowed with sorcery) and dimwitted. The age of magic in baseball was in full flower during Waddell's career. Society at large feared the misshapen as manifestations of God's wrath, regarded the feebleminded as signs of God's humor, and imbued the lame and the halt with heightened goodness, like Tiny Tim in Charles Dickens' *Christmas Carol*. Major league teams employed mascots like Louis Van Zelst, a hunchbacked cripple, who drew luck to the A's until he died in 1915; dwarf Eddie Bennett, who brought pennants to the White Sox in 1917 and 1919, then to the Dodgers and Yankees; and the aptly named Victory Faust, a hayseed mental defective who "helped" the Giants to pennants in 1911-13. All of these mascots sat in uniform on the bench or, in the case of Faust, entertained the crowd before the game.

In baseball's version of the Faust legend, Douglass Wallop's *The Year the Yankees Lost the Pennant* and the ensuing musical version, *Damn Yankees*, the devil stops time so that the aging process of a fiftyish salesman can be reversed, transforming him into the heroic Joe Hardy, savior of the downtrodden Washington Senators. For Rube Waddell, the aging process was simply halted—as it was for Peter Pan and the lost boys who died before reaching manhood. Waddell was the ultimate man-child, with the body of a man and the brain of a child, an emblem of what baseball is all about—to play, to play past when your mother calls you in for supper, to play and play and play until mortality itself is cheated.

Sam Crawford, who faced Rube Waddell many times in his years with the Detroit Tigers and went on to join Rube in the Hall of Fame, said in his later years: "Rube was one of a kind—just a big kid, you know. He'd pitch one day and we wouldn't see him for three or four days after. He'd just disappear, go fishing or something, or be off playing ball with a bunch of twelve-year-olds in an empty lot somewhere. You couldn't control him 'cause he was just a big kid himself. Baseball was just a game to Rube."

It was never just a game to him, of course; he was paid to play, and so he was termed a professional. But he was at heart an amateur, playing the game because he loved it. That was part of what made him a hero, and it is the same essential condition of heroics on the playing fields today: we admire proficiency, but we cherish the men who have retained their zest for play.

Green kids breaking into professional ball today are no longer called Rube. Maybe this is a good thing; it is a divisive name, a mean one. But it would be fine if baseball were again to be visited by an outsider who conveyed the Rube's message: honor your childhood, cherish a sense of play, and show a healthy disrespect for convention and order.

---

* According to Eric Partridge's *Dictionary of Slang and Unconventional English*, "Rhubarb, rhubarb, rhubarb" was "the muttering of actors when simulating the sound of a crowd." Rube Waddell may thus be viewed as a man of the people or a demotic demigod.

Chapter 13

Tinker to Evers to Chance: Chicago's Double-Play Masters

They battled with opponents and they battled with each other, but when it came time to winning Joe Tinker, Johnny Evers and Frank Chance were always on the same side.

By Frank Graham
SPORT Magazine, June 1949

Joe Tinker   **Johnny Evers**   **Frank Chance**

On September 15, 1902, at the old West Side Park in Chicago, where the Cubs were playing the Cincinnati Reds, a forgotten scorer set down on the sheet before him:

"Double play: Tinker to Evers to Chance."

He didn't know it, but he was writing one for the book. He was linking on paper for the first time in that fashion the names of a double-play combination which, if not the greatest of all time, certainly was the most colorful—Joe Tinker, Johnny Evers and Frank Chance. They never set any record for knocking off two enemy baserunners at once. But they were hard men in a clutch and by slowing down or shutting off traffic on the paths when it looked as though a ballgame might get away from them, they helped to win four pennants for the Cubs from 1906 through 1910.

They were three rugged individuals at the core of the Cub striking force that wrecked the Giants, the Pirates, and the other contenders, ruled the National League and won two World Series. They were—and remain—symbols of ferocity. They fought with John McGraw and his Giants, with Fred Clarke and his Pirates, with all the rivals with whom they tangled. But, most often, they fought with each other.

"It's a wonder Chance didn't kill me," Evers once said. "Like the time Orvie Overall was pitching for us. He had won 10 games in a row and was trying for the 11th and he was doing all right until they got two hits off him in succession. I yelled at Chance:

"'Are you going to keep him in there?'

"He said: 'Sure.'

"And I said: 'If he wasn't a Native Son, he'd be out of there. But I guess you Native Sons have to stick together!'

"Chance called time and walked down to me. Nobody could talk to him like I could and I could make him madder than anybody but I never saw him as mad as he was this time.

"'You little blankety-blank!!!' he said. 'I'm going to pull you apart!'

"I thought he was, too, but Overall and Tinker and some of the others got between us. That was one nice thing about being a little guy. Somebody always was sure to hold the big guys when they wanted to hit me."

They fought with each other—Chance, the manager and first baseman ("The Peerless Leader," Charlie Dryden, famous Chicago baseball writer called him); Evers, whom Dryden had tagged "The Crab," at second base; and dark, glowering Tinker at shortstop. But they fought with the other players, too—with Overall and Mordecai (Three Fingered) Brown and Johnny Kling and Harry Steinfeldt and the others. Steinfeldt, the third baseman, raging under Tinker's rough tongue-lashing in the clubhouse after a game one day, seized a pair of the trainer's shears, and tried to kill him.

The big blow came one day when Evers and Tinker got on each other and hurled insults that could not be borne by either and for which, at the time, there could be no forgiveness.

"That was in 1908," Evers said, "and although we won two pennants after that, playing side by side, we never spoke to each other again except in anger. Every time something went wrong on the field, we would be at each other and there would be a fight in the clubhouse after the game. Joe weighed 175 pounds and I weighed about 135, but that didn't make any difference. He'd rush at me and get me by the throat and I'd punch him in the belly and try to cut him with my spikes and then Chance or one of the other big guys would come to my rescue. But let anybody on another club pick on one of us, and the two of us would jump him.

"We didn't speak to each other—friendly, that is—until we had been out of baseball for years. We were invited to a baseball broadcast in Chicago when we were there to see the Braddock-Louis fight in 1937. Neither of us knew the other would be in the studio and when we met it looked as though we were going to start all over again and then all of a sudden Joe threw his arms around me and I threw mine around him and we hugged each other and cried like a couple of babies."

Chance was the first of the three to reach Chicago. That was in 1898. Out of Fresno, California, six feet tall and weighing 190 pounds, he was called Husk and had caught for the University of California team. Tough-fibered, fearless, and a terrific fighter—he once had to be dragged away from James J. Corbett in a brawl that

started in Corbett's Broadway cafe when Chance accused Jim of fixing a fight with Kid McCoy—many of his friends had urged him to enter the ring. But he preferred to be a ballplayer and he joined the Cubs as a catcher when he was 25 years old. For a time, he was used behind the plate and as an outfielder, but his final move was to first base. That was in 1902, the year Tinker and Evers joined the club. Tinker, from Muscotah, Kansas, had played minor-league ball for two years before he was brought up by the Cubs and assigned to third base. Evers, a scrawny kid weighing only 95 pounds, lantern-jawed, hard-eyed, and driven by a ceaseless, burning urge to win, reached the major leagues in the course of a single season.

Born in Troy, New York, as he grew up he worked in a collar factory and played sandlot ball on Saturday afternoons and Sundays. Then the plant in which he worked was struck and, with nothing to do on weekdays, he haunted the grounds of the local club in the old New York State League. Ultimately granted a trial, in which the odds seemed terribly against him because of his spindly frame and his utter lack of professional experience, he so impressed Lou Bacon, the owner of the club, that he was signed at a salary of $60 a month. That was in May of 1902, and after he had played 84 games for Troy, he was sold to the Cubs. Reporting to manager Frank Selee in Philadelphia, he immediately was posted at shortstop, with Tinker at third and the veteran Bobby Lowe at second. Chance still was alternating between the catcher's spot and the outfield, but very soon thereafter was moved to first base.

The swift use of the bushers, Tinker and Evers, the switch of Chance to first base—these were details of the rebuilding program by Selee. Subsequently, he got Steinfeldt from Cincinnati and moved Tinker to shortstop and Evers to second. The Cubs began to roll. They were third in 1903 and second to the Giants in 1904.

Now Selee had the team he wanted and he almost surely would have won a pennant with it. But in 1905, halfway through the campaign, his health, which had been poor for a long time, compelled him to retire. Chance was appointed as his successor, and that year the Cubs finished third ... but they were on their way.

The Giants had won the pennant and the World Series with the Athletics in 1905. McGraw thought to the day he died that this was the greatest team he ever managed—Mathewson and McGinnity and Bresnahan and Devlin and all that crew—and for the only time in his life, he predicted another pennant.

In that one yielding in all his life to the importunities of overconfidence, McGraw reckoned without the Cubs—without Tinker and Evers and Chance. One day in Chicago, the Cubs beat the Giants, 19-0, and the world champions rode back to their hotel through a shower of abuse and brickbats. A feud which was to roar through the league in years to come had been launched in earnest.

The Cubs won the pennant in 1906 but lost in the World Series to the White Sox in one of baseball's greatest upsets. They won again in 1907 and beat the Tigers in the Series. In 1908, they achieved one of their greatest triumphs. They won the pennant for the third time in a row by taking a playoff game from the Giants at the Polo Grounds. Their victory over the Tigers in the second World Series meeting of these teams was an anticlimax.

The playoff was necessitated by a tie resulting from a Giant-Cub game, also at the Polo Grounds, on September 23, when Evers called the attention of the umpires to the fact that Fred Merkle, who had been on first base, had not touched second in the final play, but had cut straight to the clubhouse when he saw that Moose McCormick had scored from third base on a single by Al Bridwell with what apparently was the winning run. Merkle was called out

on a force play much to the chagrin of the Giants. And so, when the Cubs and the Giants finished the season in a tie, they were ordered to replay the game of September 23.

"I'll never forget that day," Evers said, long years after. "My telephone rang all morning and the message always was the same: If I played, they would kill me, cut my ears off and send them to my mother. Some thoughtful tramp even called my mother in Troy and repeated the warning to her. She called me and begged me not to play, and I promised her I wouldn't. After all, there was no radio in those days and she wouldn't know until she got the papers that night or the next morning whether I had played or not."

Of course, he played, and so did Tinker and Chance, and the Cubs won and the hit that beat the Giants and all but broke McGraw's heart was a triple by Tinker off Mathewson.

"After the game," John said, "a mob waited for us outside the clubhouse. While they waited, they threw rocks at the windows. They were still throwing rocks and calling us names and telling us what they would do to us when the police smuggled us out of a gate on the Speedway side and escorted us to the High Bridge station, where we caught a train for Chicago."

That was roughly the time in which Franklin P. Adams, who has written many better verses, wrote these with which, whether he likes it or not, his name will be joined forever.

These are the saddest of possible words:
"Tinker to Evers to Chance."
Trio of bear cubs, and fleeter than birds,
Tinker and Evers and Chance.
Ruthlessly pricking our gonfalon bubble,
Making a Giant hit into a double—
Words that are heavy with nothing but trouble:
"Tinker to Evers to Chance."

They had another good year, these three, leading the Cubs to the pennant in 1910, then losing to the Athletics in the World Series. But they were slowing now.

Near the end of the 1912 season, Chance, who constantly suffered severe headaches as a result of having been hit on the head so many times by pitched balls, so that his playing was affected, was relieved as manager and sent to the Reds on waivers. He never played for Cincinnati, but was released so that he might sign as a manager of the Yankees. Tinker went to Cincinnati as manager, then after a year jumped to the Federal League to manage the "outlaw" Chicago club. Evers, having rejected a bonus of $30,000 and a five-year contract of $15,000 a year to join the Chicago Feds—partly out of loyalty to Organized Baseball and partly to an unwillingness to play for his still-hated friend, Tinker—was traded to the Braves. There he hooked up with Rabbit Maranville and helped "Miracle Man" George Stallings win the pennant and beat the Athletics in the 1914 World Series.

Thus within the space of two years, the three were toiling in different leagues.

As recently as 1940, Evers said, "Every once in a while somebody asks me how many of the old trio are dead. I tell them we're all dead, but Chance is the only one who's buried."

Now they're all dead ... and buried. First Chance, then Evers, then Tinker. They didn't need the Hall of Fame at Cooperstown to keep the memory of them alive, but they're all in there. It was in 1946 that they were voted in. Tinker ... and Evers ... and Chance ... all moved in together. And how else should they have moved ... these three who had been together through the brightest years of their lives?

Chapter 14

Fiery John McGraw and His Talented–but Hated–'05 Giants

They boozed and brawled; in their own city they were called "The Hoodlums."
The surprise wasn't that they won, but that they survived the wild '05 season

By John Devaney
SPORT Magazine, October 1963

It was a team of its time, made in the image of its creator, raging and hissing in defeat, swaggering and blustering in victory. It was the kind of team that can never be built again.

The time was 1905 and the team was John McGraw's New York Giants, the one he later would call "the greatest I ever managed."

Few teams have been more despised. In Pittsburgh and Chicago, Cincinnati, St. Louis, and Philadelphia, howling mobs surged around the horse-drawn carriages transporting the Giants to the ballpark and showered them with stones and rotten fruit. Even in New York, sportswriters called them "The Hoodlums." In the clubhouse, the players snarled among themselves; during one game at the Polo Grounds, two of them had a fist-fight in the dugout. From their bench came a stream of obscenities aimed at umpires and opposing pitchers. "They use names," wrote New York newspaperman Joe Vila, "that not even a moral degenerate could invent."

Leading the abuse was the lean, jut-jawed McGraw, five feet, six inches and 156 pounds of black-Irish fury. In this 1905 season, he would publicly call a club owner a welcher and humiliate the president of the league, sending that tragic man on a lonely road that ended in suicide. Almost psychotic in his need to win, he would shout to baseball: John McGraw is the law!

The names of the men he led come out of the lyrics for an Irish reel: There was Roger Bresnahan, called the Duke of Tralee. There were smiling Dan McGann, Turkey Mike Donlin and little Billy Gilbert. There were Bad Bill Dahlen, Artie Devlin, Christy Mathewson and Iron Man Joe McGinnity. There were others who did not wear the green, but this was a team that had the map of Ireland as its symbolic insignia.

They drank. Ah! and how they drank. Turkey Mike Donlin had boozed himself right off the Cincinnati team. McGraw, after a defeat, would walk into a saloon, quickly down four or five shots of whisky, then hurl bottles against the wall (after which he would hand the bartender a $50 bill and walk out). They had the ethics of Fagins. They cheated each other at cards, they made secret World Series deals with the Philadelphia Athletics, putting the winning and losing shares in a common pool, to be split 50-50 no matter who won the Series.

Yet there were worse men in baseball of that day. "If you tried to run a league with teetotalers alone," said Brooklyn manager Ned Hanlon, "the boozers would start another league and outplay you and outsell you." During road trips, players in an alcoholic haze wandered off, sometimes never came back.

The power symbol of baseball was the clenched fist. Mobs swept

John McGraw
The Giants' player-manager was 156 pounds of Irish fury, a hard-drinking, merciless competitor who made the 1905 Giants winners.

out of stands to bloody umpires or visiting players. Players punched umpires, and umpires punched back. The day John McGraw joined the Orioles in 1891, he was dumped on the floor by a burly outfielder. McGraw, who weighed 120 pounds then, leaped on the man, clawing, scratching, kneeing. Only then was rookie McGraw a member of the team.

Baseball was not a game for the genteel spectator. Shouting and swearing in the old wooden Polo Grounds were the loudly dressed

actors, vaudevillians and race-track touts from Broadway; burly German and Irish immigrants swilling glasses of beer; and the men in derbies and mustaches who were the city's streetcar conductors, laborers, bartenders, clerks and subway groundhogs. This was their game. The wife and kids stayed home.

Yet these were changing times. In Washington, President Theodore Roosevelt was drawing up new trustbusting legislation against the meat-packing industry. In Chicago union teamsters were fighting bloody battles in the streets against imported strikebreakers. On the streets of Manhattan's Hell's Kitchen, muck-raking writers were discovering the shame of our cities: sweatshops; cockroaches on the walls of tenements; sour-smelling flophouses where women immigrants huddled with their babies on sawdust-covered floors for two cents a night. Out of the fighting and muckraking would come the social legislation of Roosevelt, Wilson and F.D.R.

The winds of change had already shaken baseball. In 1903, after a bitter war in which players had jumped between leagues, the American and National Leagues made peace. President and founder of the American was Ban Johnson, a gutty ex-newspaperman who backed his umpires against rowdyism—some called it McGrawism—with stiff fines and suspensions. President of the National League was Harry Pulliam, a slim, intense young man from an aristocratic Kentucky family, who didn't relish rough-and-tumble infighting.

Both Pulliam and Johnson pleaded for "clean baseball." With attendance at critical levels in many cities, they pointed out, baseball would not survive if rioting made men afraid to go to games, and if obscene language made them unwilling to take their wives and children. Opposing them as the leader of the Rowdy Wing was John Joseph McGraw.

With the Orioles, McGraw had refined the hit-and-run, the cutoff play, the double steal, tactics that he liked to call "scientific baseball." Other McGraw tactics were scientific the way street fighting is. With a runner on third and a fly hit to the outfield, third-baseman McGraw would hook his fingers around the back of a runner's belt while the lone umpire was watching the ball. When the runner started for home, McGraw's grip held him for an important second.

Arguing with umpires, McGraw pushed, shoved and cursed. Some umpires were scared off by these explosions. Others, who battled back, found themselves out of jobs; owners were learning that Muggsy (a name McGraw hated) was a box-office draw.

In July, 1902, McGraw jumped to the Giants, becoming manager for $11,000 a year, a fantastic salary at the time. He persuaded the nucleus of the Baltimore club to jump with him: Bresnahan, then a pitcher and outfielder; pitcher McGinnity, and first-baseman Dan McGann. Arriving in New York with the Giants in last place, he took one look at the team's roster and fired nine of the 23 men on it. Of the 14 left, only three would remain: pitchers Mathewson and Luther (Dummy) Taylor, and catcher Frank Bowerman.

After finishing last in 1902, McGraw signed second-baseman Billy Gilbert, released by Baltimore. He bought outfielder George Browne from Philadelphia and picked up from the minors a kid third-baseman, Art Devlin. From Chicago he bought Samuel (Sandow) Mertes, a 30-year-old utilityman, and tried him in left field.

The Giants jumped to second in 1903. Mathewson was 30-13, McGinnity was 31-20. Before the 1904 season, McGraw brought up from the minors a young righthander, Leon (Red) Ames, and a lefthander, George (Hooks) Wiltse. In a trade with Brooklyn, he

obtained shortshop Bad Bill Dahlen, a troublemaker no other manager wanted. Midway through the 1904 season, he picked up Donlin.

The Giants won the pennant in 1904, with Mathewson (33-12), McGinnity (35-8), and Taylor (21-15) doing nearly all the pitching. Devlin, Bresnahan and Browne were the best hitters, though no regular batted over .300.

At the start of the 1905 season. McGraw switched Bresnahan from the outfield to catcher, where he would become a Hall of Famer. His team was set and his team was wild. In spring training at Savannah, Georgia, they ritually rolled up to the home of a physician and called for the doctor. The doctor would come out and ask what they wanted.

"What we wanna know, doc," one would yell, "is where the hell do you bury your patients?"

On the road McGraw maintained a 10:30 p.m. curfew, but in New York the players had only to dodge McGraw at *his* favorite places, mostly the restaurants frequented by actors and race-track habitues. The most artful dodger of McGraw was the team's best hitter, Donlin, nicknamed Turkey Mike because of the strutting way he carried his stocky figure. Twenty-seven years old and handsome, Turkey Mike was a favorite of Broadway chorus girls, and he kept them content. Once, when he heard of night games being played in the minors, he said in honest wonder: "Gee, imagine taking a ballplayer's *nights* away from him."

Donlin ran with the hotbloods of the town. Late in 1905, on a train with some wild ones, he pulled out a gun when the steward refused to serve any more drinks. "George," growled Donlin, "get me a drink."

"My name ain't George," said the waiter. "And you had enough."

"If you don't get me a drink," said Donlin, grinning drunkenly at his friends, "Mr. Gun's going to introduce himself to George. And Mr. Gun barks loud."

The steward walked out and called a conductor, who had Donlin and his pals thrown into jail at the next stop.

First-baseman McGann, 33, a strapping six-footer, was the captain. Nearly always with a big lazy grin on his face, he talked with a soft Kentucky drawl and drank hard and he would be dead just five years later. Second-baseman Gilbert, 29, was 5-6 and 150 pounds, but he had a heavyweight's measure of obscenities. He let them loose at opposing pitchers, and even at his teammate Mathewson when he once suspected the big man of dogging it.

Third-baseman Devlin, 26, had come out of Georgetown University with an education and quick temper. During a game at the Polo Grounds early in the 1905 season, Bresnahan turned to him in the dugout and grunted, "You're playing rotten." Within seconds Devlin threw two quick punches, closing one of Bresnahan's eyes, while the crowds in the Polo Grounds looked on in astonishment.

It was a dark defeat for the proud, stocky Bresnahan, then 25, who as a teenager had fought and played with the Orioles. Called the Duke of Tralee after his birthplace in Ireland, Bresnahan had the booming brogue and the heavy magisterial air of an Irish country squire. Later he would manage the Cardinal and Cubs, and in 1945, a year after his death, he would be selected to the Hall of Fame.

Shortstop Dahlen, the old man of the regulars at 34, was a heavy-set, moody, surly man, seemingly lazy and indifferent, who kept mostly to himself, glowering into space like a sick cat. But the seeming indifference, said McGraw years later, "made him an iceberg on the field, keeping the others cool in the tightest situations."

Rightfielder Browne, 29, had the reputation for being the fastest man on a team considered then to be the fastest ever assembled. Browne lived well. He was popular with ballplayers around the league, a guy who went where the laughs were. But 16 years later he would be destitute, coughing out his life in a tubercular ward, while his friend, Artie Devlin, was organizing benefit games on Bronx sandlots to raise money for Browne's wife and two children. Mertes, 33, played left field as this was usually the sunfield. In a game late in 1905, he ran back for a drive and, looking straight into the sun, made a leaping bare-handed catch that McGraw later called the greatest he had seen in 30 years of baseball.

Reserve catcher Frank Bowerman, 37, a hulking six-footer, was a sour-natured man. Once he raced a woman for a seat on the ferry and beat her to it. Annoyed when Bowerman laughed at her, the woman slapped him. Bowerman called a cop and had her arrested for assault.

Idol of the fans was Mathewson, 24, handsome, well-tailored and gentlemanly, with a high voice that got him the nickname "Sis" on the Giants. Once a student at Bucknell and with an intelligence that won the respect of McGraw (Matty was the only player McGraw, as a manager, ever roomed with), he possessed an incredible memory. One of his favorite pastimes was playing checkers blindfolded against seven or eight opponents at the same time. He rarely lost.

His best pitch was his famous fadeaway, which he developed himself. As a rookie he had noticed how batters timed themselves to hit curves breaking away from them. He developed a reverse spin on his curve, making it fall in across the batter's shoetops. "Batters near broke their necks trying to hit it," recalled McGraw years later. The winner of 373 games, Matty later would manage Cincinnati and later still would catch a lungful of German gas on a French battlefield and die in 1925 at 45, the once handsome face a pinched, grey victim of tuberculosis.

McGinnity, 34, earned his nickname, Iron Man, during the off-seasons by bending iron over a red-hot blast furnace in McAlester, now Oklahoma but then Indian Territory. He lived up to the nickname summers by pitching doubleheaders. In 1903, on August 1, 8 and 31, he had pitched both games of doubleheaders and won all six games. Two decades later, at 54, he was still pitching in the minor leagues.

A deaf-mute, Dummy Taylor, 29, had a moon face and flat nose that gave him a comic look to match a comic spirit. During an argument with umpire Hank O'Day, Taylor, using sign language, cursed the ump. The Giant players understood the signs and roared. Suddenly, O'Day turned to Taylor and said, "You're fined twenty-five dollars."

"Why?" asked McGraw, grinning. "What did he say?"

"He called me a ..." and O'Day rattled off precisely what Taylor had "said." Later, Taylor, $25 poorer, learned that O'Day had a deaf-mute relative.

McGraw ran the team from the bench with a bewildering variety of signals. "Do what I tell you," he told the players, "and I'll take the blame if it goes wrong."

But in defeat, he lashed out in the clubhouse so fiercely that these men, tough by any standard, would shiver for an hour under icy showers rather than face his rages.

The 1905 Giants opened at home against Boston on Friday, April 16. McGinnity won, 10-1, and Donlin hit a home run. The overflow crowd, standing 20 deep in the open center field, was delighted. During the next seven days, a pattern of pitching emerged that would dominate 1905 baseball. Matty beat Boston,

15-0, Red Ames beat Philadelphia, 6-5, Hooks Wiltse lost in relief to the Phils, 4-3, but then it was the Iron Man's turn again, 10-2 over Philadelphia, then Matty 5-4, then Taylor 8-1, and the Giants were in first place by three games.

Swinging a thick bat that looked like a tall Coca-Cola bottle, Donlin was leading the league in hitting, Bresnahan. McGann and Mertes were all hitting over .300. On the bases the Giants were the nightmares of catchers. Said Hughie Duffy, then manager of the Phils: "This is the fastest team ever assembled."

The first rumble of trouble came in mid-May. This was how *The Sporting News* reported it: "In Philadelphia, Hoodlum McGann lost his temper because Magee threw him out at the plate in trying to score from second on a hit and punched catcher Abbott. The latter threw the ball at the big tough and hit him in the back. Both squared off to fight, but were ejected from the game.

"Mathewson, just to show that his association with the old Baltimore crowd had also made a hoodlum out of him, hit and knocked down a lemonade boy passing in front of the players' bench, splitting the boy's lip and loosening his teeth. [Such an attack seems out of character for Mathewson; the writers of the day, in their anger at McGraw, perhaps got back at him by insulting his favorite player, Matty.]

"After the game, several thousand mobbed the players in their carriages, throwing stones and missiles. A team of one hundred officers was needed to rescue McGraw and his men.

"When will the baseball public of New York get onto these hoodlum tactics? Indeed they are intolerable to all decent, self-respecting people."

A week later, McGraw set off another riot—and angry mumbling around the league—by shoving an umpire. "It is a matter of common talk," wrote Joe Vila, "that the umpires have been afraid to decide against McGraw ... Could the so-called Giants win the pennant if they were compelled to leave the umpires alone?"

In early June the Giants arrived in Pittsburgh. The Pirates, led by Honus Wagner, were in second place. After putting on their uniforms at the hotel, as was the custom, the Giants set off for the park in their carriages, emblazoned with the sign: "World Champions." Perhaps infuriated by the sign or by the Giants' recent activities, hundreds of Pittsburgh fans surrounded the carriages near the park, howling threats and hurling rotten fruit. When McGinnity stood up to defend himself against an attacker armed with a club, he was socked in the rear of his pants by four well-ripened tomatoes. Sammy Strang was hit by an avocado.

When Pittsburgh came to New York the next month, McGraw sought revenge. His players cursed so loudly at the Pittsburgh pitcher that women and even men scurried from box seats, hands over ears. McGraw's insults enraged Pittsburgh manager Fred Clarke. Warned by umpire Bill Klem, McGraw insinuated that Klem was on the Pittsburgh payroll. Finally thrown out of the game, McGraw met Pittsburgh owner Barney Dreyfuss near the clubhouse and called him a liar and a welsher on bets (both Dreyfuss and McGraw were avid horse players).

When league president Pulliam received Klem's report of McGraw's behavior on the field, he astounded baseball by fining McGraw $150 and suspending him for 15 days. Baseball faced a "crisis," said Pulliam, that would determine whether it or McGraw was stronger.

Immediately Dreyfuss asked Pulliam to hold a hearing on McGraw's outburst off the field against him. Pulliam agreed, ordering a special board to convene in Boston. McGraw rushed to

Boston with a dozen pals, who all testified (they were not under oath) that McGraw had been a perfect gentleman with Dreyfuss. Dreyfuss, thinking his word would be enough, had brought no witnesses. The board cleared McGraw and censured Dreyfuss for making the charges.

McGraw went to Boston Superior Court and asked for an injunction against his 15-day suspension on the grounds that Pulliam had not given him a chance to present his side of the Klem incident. The judge granted the injunction, and McGraw, his team cheering outside the courtroom, swaggered off to the Boston ballpark for the game that afternoon.

Pulliam could not go into court to fight the injunction, since the league's owners were already horrified by the bad publicity. McGraw's suspension was never enforced, Dreyfuss was the joke of the league, and Pulliam's power to back up his umpires was riddled. McGraw, wrote sportswriters angrily, was now baseball's "King Muggsy." Snarled the king at Pulliam: "I ... have done more for baseball than you could do in a hundred years."

Pulliam remained league president for three more years, but his authority was gone. Always high-strung, he grew more and more melancholy. In 1909, alone in a hotel room, he put a bullet into his brain.

After McGraw's court victory ("What has baseball come to?" said Dreyfuss), the Giants went west, where angry crowds mobbed their carriages in Cincinnati, St. Louis and Chicago. McGraw, it was reported, had to hire private detectives as guards. Back home, obviously shaken, he said to his team, "We're lucky to get back alive."

But though the team came back eight games in front, writer Joe Vila still sneered, "If the so-called Giants ever run up against a high-class team for a world championship," Vila wrote, "they will get a dressing down long to be remembered. When McGraw and his four-flushers were invited to meet Boston [in 1904], we all know of their disgraceful backdown. ..."

The Giants had refused to meet the American League winners in 1904 mainly because of the growing hatred between McGraw and Ban Johnson, the American League president. But in the late summer of 1905, McGraw agreed to play in a best-of-seven Series, the first ever held.

By mid-September it was clear the Giants would face Connie Mack's Philadelphia Athletics in the World Series. Analyzing the teams, experts agreed that pitching would be decisive, with the A's Rube Waddell (a 26-game winner by September 1st) and Eddie Plank (26-12) matched against Matty and McGinnity. "If Waddell can beat them in the first game," wrote Vila, "it will be all over."

There was just one hitch, Vila admitted: Waddell would have to be kept sober. In a game of boozers, the Rube was a champion. Waddell was not kept sober, however. Falling drunkenly on a train, he hurt his shoulder and was out of the Series.

Amid rumors that Waddell had been bribed not to pitch, the Series opened in Philadelphia's tiny Columbia Park. Mathewson opposed Plank.

The Giants played as they had played all year, combining excellent pitching, alert defense, clutch hitting and smart base running. With the score 0-0 in the fifth, Matty led off with a single. Bresnahan forced him at second, but when the ball was thrown wild on a double-play attempt, Bresnahan ran past first and into second. He scored on Donlin's single, and when the A's threw home, Turkey Mike trotted into second, from where he scored on Mertes' double.

In the sixth the A's put men on first and third with one out.

Outfielder Topsy Hartzel hit a dribbler up the line. Matty scrambled off the mound, grabbed the ball and threw to Bresnahan, who tagged out the sliding runner. Never again in the Series would the A's come as close to scoring off Matty.

The Giants got another run in the ninth on Gilbert's single, Matty's sacrifice, and Bresnahan's single to win, 3-0.

In the second game, played at New York, the A's Chief Bender shut out the Giants, 3-0. McGinnity was the loser, beaten, really, by two infield errors. Mathewson won the third game, 9-0, and McGinnity won the fourth, 1-0, outpitching Plank.

With the Giants ahead, three games to one, Bender opposed Matty in the fifth game. In the fifth inning, Mertes and Devlin walked. Dahlen moved them up with a sacrifice and Gilbert's fly scored Mertes, In the eighth, Mathewson walked and scored on Bresnahan's double. Ahead 2-0, he walked to the mound in the ninth and pitched his 27th scoreless inning to close a Series in which each game had ended in a shutout.

The winning share was $1142, the losing one $370, but the news leaked out that the players—with the exceptions of Mathewson, Bresnahan, McGraw, and Connie Mack—had secretly agreed to put the two shares together and divide 50-50. In 1923 McGraw wrote that he had been "disgusted with their unwillingness to take a chance." But he added that while the best team he ever saw was the Orioles of 1894, '95 and '96, "the best team I ever managed was the Giants of 1905."

Many people have wondered why. The team did have four men who would be elected to the Hall of Fame—Bresnahan, Matty, McGinnity and McGraw. It did win 105 games to win by nine, but in a league weakened by loss of stars to the American League. It could only beat second-place Pittsburgh and third-place Chicago 12 times each in 22 tries. It had won the Series, but against a team missing its best pitcher. It led the league in hitting, but only two Giants (Donlin at .351 and Bresnahan at .302) were among the 12 men in the league who hit over .300.

The pitching, of course, had been tremendous: Matty (31-9), McGinnity (21-15), Ames (22-8), Taylor (16-9), and Wiltse (15-6). But Ames never won 20 again, and McGinnity and Taylor were in the minors three years later. In fact, by 1908—after finishing second, fourth and second—McGraw broke up the team, trading away all but Matty, Wiltse, Ames, Devlin, and Donlin.

Why did McGraw call this team his greatest? "There was its indomitable team spirit," he said. All could have hit for higher averages, he once claimed, but instead were willing to give themselves up by hitting behind a runner to move him along.

There was its smartness. "The 1912 team was faster," McGraw said. "But the 1905 team was the smartest on the bases." Donlin led the league in stolen bases with 59, Mertes had 52, Dahlen 37, Devlin 33, Browne 26, Strang 23, McGann 22, and Bresnahan 11.

And there was its cocky, spit-in-your-eye arrogance before howling mobs. "A team that will fight back on an enemy diamond and before an enemy crowd," said McGraw, "is pretty well able to take care of itself."

Cockiness. Arrogance. Brains. Team spirit. These were the qualities of the 1905 team that made it McGraw's favorite. And why not? They were his own qualities. He would have eight more pennant winners, but in the changing climate of baseball in which umpires like Bill Klem and Hank O'Day would rise to gag the obscenity and stop the rowdyism, none of his teams would ever be so much like Muggsy McGraw.

Chapter 15

Murderers' Row: The Saga of the '27 New York Yankees

They had class, color, stars and superstars. And, driving them through the long season, the men of Murderers' Row had the memory of a humiliation they had to avenge.

1927 New York Yankees
Led by Lou Gehrig (standing, far left) and Babe Ruth (standing, fifth from left) the Murderers' Row Yankees won 110 games and the World Series.

By Josh Greenfeld
SPORT Magazine, October 1962

"Nothing to it. Those '27 Yankees were the best team ever. Figure it out. After we got going we won all those World Series games in a row. It was murder. We had the greatest push baseball ever knew. We never even worried five or six runs behind. Ruth—Gehrig—Lazzeri—Combs—Meusel: Wham! Wham! Wham! Wham! And wham! —no matter who was pitching."
—Babe Ruth

"The secret of success as a pitcher lies in getting a job with the Yankees."
—Waite Hoyt

If the Twenties were the Golden Age of Sport, then the 1927 New York Yankees were the Golden Team. A few years ago The Sporting News conducted a poll among the members of the Baseball Writers Association to determine baseball's greatest team. The '27 Yankees won with 71 votes. The 1919 Chicago White Sox were second with 15 votes. It was a victory margin characteristic of the '27 Yankees, who dominated baseball as no team has, before or since.

The '27 Yankees won the American League pennant by 19 games. They won 110 games, lost only 44. The club batting average was .307, four points higher than the next club. Five regu-

lars hit over .300: Lou Gehrig .373, Babe Ruth .356, Earle Combs .356, Bob Meusel .337, Tony Lazzeri .309. Ruth led the league with an unasterisked 60 home runs, Gehrig was second with 47, Lazzeri third with 18. Only five other men in the league hit more than ten. Ruth's personal total was greater than that of any other club as a whole.

But the.'27 Yankees weren't merely fence busters. Their infield—Gehrig, Lazzeri, Mark Koenig, and Joe Dugan—was a smoothly functioning fielding unit. Their outfield—Ruth, Combs and Meusel—had as much all-round skill as any ever put together. Their pitching was the best in the league. Three starters won 18 or more games each: Waite Hoyt, 22, Herb Pennock, 19, Urban Shocker, 18. Wilcy Moore, the first of the great modern relief pitchers, won 19 games and led the league with a 2.28 earned-run average.

The '27 Yankees were a team of overbearing pride, contemptuous of any foe; they did not have to rise to an occasion, they merely had to meet it. In the showcase of sport, the World Series, the Yankees beat the Pittsburgh Pirates in four straight games. They won that Series, really, by simply showing up for it.

It had not been that way the season before. The '26 Yankees, not yet jelled as an overpowering unit, won the pennant mostly because the Cleveland Indians folded in the stretch. In the World Series against the St. Louis Cardinals, the Yankees were defeated

and demoralized. They made sandlot mistakes in the field and they failed to hit in the clutch. Symbolically, the final out they made in the Series came when hefty slugger Ruth, hearkening to some strange drum, was thrown out on an attempted steal, of all things. There was no hint in that 1926 World Series that the Yankees, with but a few changes, would go on in 1927 to become the greatest in baseball history.

But while the Yankees who reported to the St. Petersburg training camp in the spring of 1927 were essentially the same, their spirit was different. They came—as a weak-hitting, fancy-fielding, utility infielder in their camp that spring, later said—to play. They were stung by their sad showing in the Series the previous fall and were determined to redeem themselves. They hustled, they talked it up, and they responded to manager Miller Huggins' orders with a fierce loyalty. No longer was the little (five-foot-three) manager presented with disciplinary problems. (The Babe had once dangled him, holding him by his ankles, off the rear end of a moving train.)

Huggins was both a brainy and fiery leader. In an era when many major-league ballplayers bordered close to illiteracy, Huggins possessed a degree from the University of Cincinnati and was qualified to practice law. However, he chose to play baseball and was a big-league second-baseman for 11 years and, since 1919, a big-league manager with the Yankees.

In 1921 Huggins had brought the Yankees their first American League pennant and in 1923, their first world championship. He and general manager Ed Barrow had begun building a Yankee dynasty, threatened now after the weak showing in the '26 World Series. So it was an alert and a vengeful Huggins who carefully studied the personnel before him in St. Petersburg while puffing on his ever-present pipe.

At first base Huggins had Gehrig, who had been signed off the Columbia University campus by scout Paul Krichell. Entering his third year as a Yankee, Lou seemed on the edge of greatness. The quiet, dignified Gehrig had always been a skilled natural slugger and an awkward, clumsy fielder. Now Lou was applying himself diligently to a program of mastering the mysteries of fielding. His natural fielding skills were slight, but his dedication was massive, and he was in the process of remaking himself as few athletes ever have. Wally Pipp, the man Gehrig replaced at first base in 1925— a position Gehrig did not relinquish until a record consecutive 2130 games later—said: "Lou wasn't learning quickly, but he was learning thoroughly, sweating out each detail, step by step." Lou Gehrig was working hard.

At second base the Yankees had Lazzeri, in his second big-league season. Like Gehrig, Tony was quiet, but his silence seemed more like a repressed rage. He resembled in appearance a figure in a Renaissance painting: tall, lean and supple, and his black eyes burning above his high, olive-skinned cheekbones. At the plate he would jut his chin out menacingly; and any pitcher facing him felt he was the object of some deep and ancient blood vendetta. Every aspect of Lazzeri was fierce and bold; his slightest gesture seemed to hint of violence; and his voice projected an angry sullenness. "Interviewing that guy," said one writer, "is like trying to mine coal with a nail file and a pair of scissors." Yet on the field, he was all calmness and poise, turning his taut body into the graceful instrument required for the execution of the double play. On any other ballclub he would have batted in the cleanup position; on this ballclub Huggins had him penciled in for sixth.

At the most crucial moment of the '26 World Series, Lazzeri, with the bases loaded, had struck out against Grover Cleveland Alexander. Through the winter Tony had been billed as the flop of the year. Huggins lashed out at such talk as spring training began in 1927. "Lazzeri was the man who really made my club last season," Huggins said. "He was a tower of strength to Gehrig and Koenig when they were unsure of themselves. Anybody can strike out, but ballplayers like Lazzeri come along once in a generation."

Koenig, the shortstop, was also dark-haired, dark-eyed and hot blooded. Inclined to be jittery and temperamental, he was unpredictable at the plate. He could be relied on, however, in the clutch. But on the field, with the steadying Lazzeri alongside of him, he was smooth and stylish. Huggins liked him, mostly for his fight and spirit, and so did his teammates.

Third base belonged to the old pro, Jumping Joe Dugan, so named for his ability to leap into the air and pull down line drives. Dugan, who had started as a shortstop for Connie Mack's Athletics in 1917, couldn't jump as high as he once could, but he was still the best-fielding third-baseman in the league. He was a clever batter, someone who knew how to look them over, and always dangerous in the pinch. Like Koenig, he was not a .300 hitter, but his long experience made him indeed a very handy man to have around.

Huggins' outfield was set. And what an outfield! There may have been better fielding outfields, such as the Red Sox's unit of Tris Speaker, Duffy Lewis and Harry Hooper; but there had never been one to match this Yankee trio for sheer power. In right field was the incomparable Big Fellow, Babe Ruth, starting his eighth season as a Yankee. The Babe, if not the greatest ballplayer of all time—only Ty Cobb's name can be mentioned in the same sentence—was certainly the most dramatic. He singlehandedly changed the history of the game as he revolutionized the basic concept of baseball, from that of obtaining a run through the niggardly pursuit of a base at a time, to that of collecting runs through one fell swoop: the Home Run. In 1921 he set a record that seemed destined to last forever— 59 home runs in a single season. He had created a new type of fan, the fan who came out to the ball park to see the Babe hit the long ball. Although Huggins, himself a product of the earlier "base at a time" day, may have disliked the kind of baseball Ruth represented, he never resented the Babe's talents. And now, with a matured Gehrig following Ruth in the batting order, Huggins knew he had matchless one-two power punch.

Combs, the lanky Kentuckian with prematurely graying hair, was a classy center fielder and an ideal leadoff man. If he had a batting weakness, the pitchers of his era had yet to discover it. A free-swinger, he showered his base hits to all fields. It was a constant shower. Getting 200 hits a season was par for Combs. With his long legs he was fast, both in covering ground in center field and in racing around the bases. If an infield played back for him, he had the speed and skill to bunt and beat it out; if infielders played in, he had the batting talent to slash line drives over their heads. Furthermore, once on base, he was always a source of distraction to an opposing pitcher.

Left fielder Meusel was a superb all-round ballplayer. His throwing arm may have been the best of all time. He was a fine hitter (a .309 lifetime), especially productive in the clutch because he was a cool customer to the point of downright surliness. He was a "loner" by preference and the common modes of communication seemed difficult for him, but he always bore the professional respect of his teammates.

With the acquisition of Johnny Grabowski, a good workman-like catcher, from the White Sox to go along with the capable

Benny Bengough and Pat Collins, manager Huggins had no worries at that position. He had the pitchers of potential, too. Hoyt, the Brooklyn high school graduate (Erasmus Hall) who once took a course in undertaking, appeared to be at the top of his form. Pennock, a wild-man in his youth, had discovered the secret of control and had become the best left-handed pitcher in baseball. Veteran Urban Shocker, with both his spitter and his wisdom, was still consistently effective. And as a fourth starter, Huggins had the fast-developing George Pipgras up from St. Paul. For relief and doubleheader work there were Dutch Ruether and Bob Shawkey, both past their prime, but both men who could come up with a key game when needed, and Lefty Garland Braxton, Myles Thomas and Joe Giard.

There was also a newcomer at the camp, a lumbering, good-natured Oklahoma dirt farmer, who had never pitched in the major leagues. Huggins, at first, disparaged him: "Your curve ball wouldn't go around the button on my vest." But gradually Huggins was impressed by his perfect control, his nerves of steel—nothing seemed to faze this new man—and his sinker, which was deceptively difficult to hit. And finally Huggins signed the big fellow to a contract. Little did even the astute Huggins realize that with Wilcy Moore he had acquired pennant insurance.

But Huggins did realize the team had the makings of greatness. It had always had the natural abilities, but now it had the proper espirit de corps—forged in the humiliation of the previous World Series defeat. Nervously, almost anxiously, Huggins awaited the start of the 1927 season.

Once the season began there was never a moment's doubt. Starting with a rush, slowing down to a burst, and finishing with a rampage, the Yankees welded into a cohesive unit, daily destroyed their opponents. It was "Wham. Wham. Wham. Wham. And wham!" as Ruth so picturesquely put it. People began to call the lineup "Murderers' Row." Every man in the lineup could and did break up ball games. Koenig, the weakest hitting regular, batted .285; the catching slot was good for .275. The pitching staff kept pace with the hitters. Hoyt, unplagued by arm trouble, was unbeatable; Pennock was as strong as ever; Shocker was always reliable; Pipgras won regularly. And whenever a starter weakened, the 28-year-old rookie, Wilcy Moore, shuffled in from the bullpen to put out the brush fire.

The race was over by July 4th. The Washington Senators, with a June streak behind them, were charging after the Yankees. But in the holiday doubleheader at Yankee Stadium, Huggins' mob declared its independence from the rest of the league. The winning scores: 12-1 and 21-1. After that, the Senators were finished as contenders.

The team came from behind so powerfully in the late innings that Combs described it with a phrase that would live in legend: "Five o'clock lightning." And the rest of the league feared these five o'clock uprisings as much as the man in the ad fears the shadow of the same time. Ruth was having his greatest year and Gehrig was right behind him, both in the batting order and in home-run totals.

The club enjoyed itself, too. It had to. Not only was it winning, but it had the Big Fellow on it: "Jidge," as his teammates called Babe Ruth. The Babe was as rollicking off the field as he was Olympian on it. "Like W. C. Fields," as Roger Kahn has noted, "Babe Ruth never tasted liquor before he was six." In his suite at the Hotel Ansonia on Broadway, Babe always stocked a few cases of bootleg liquor and had a keg of beer in the bath tub. He was always prepared to play host to any stray lady callers. And when the lady callers didn't come around, his teammates did. The Babe was a generous host: he poured as much for the visitor as for himself and that says it all. The Babe, of course, could afford to be free with his money; he was earning $70,000 that season and he knew his talents were in no way diminishing. Still he was awfully haphazard about money matters. Once he loaned Joe Dugan $500 on the road. When back in New York Dugan repaid him, the Babe just looked at the money and said: "How do you like that, I thought I blew it."

The Babe was also a joker, and an irreverent one, whether to prisoner or to president. In those days the Yankees played an annual exhibition at Sing Sing with the prison team. When one of the convicts, acting as umpire, called a close one against the Yankees, the Babe, to the delight of the prisoner spectators, boomed, "Robber!"

When President Calvin Coolidge came out to a ballgame in Washington, the Yankees lined up for formal introductions. The President walked down the row, shaking hands with each ballplayer. And the players responded respectfully.

"How do you do, Mr. President," said Waite Hoyt.

"Good day, sir," said Herb Pennock.

Coolidge proceeded slowly, nodding his head and shaking hands as he went along. Meanwhile, the Babe waiting, took off his cap and wiped his forehead.

"Mr. Ruth," Coolidge said approaching him.

"Hot as hell, ain't it, prez?" said Mr. Ruth.

But the Babe was singular. And so were his exploits, even though he and Gehrig were matching homer for homer, 40, 41, 42, going into September. Both paused in their private home-run derby to help the team clinch the pennant in Boston on Labor Day. With the pennant in hand, the hit-happy team proceeded to celebrate on the pullman back from Boston. One bright athlete began to kick the shoes, waiting for the porters' shines outside of each compartment, through the length of the train to the first car. Others joined in. And the result was a kind of mayhem that was not soccer.

Still the season was not over, there were ballgames to play, and home runs for Babe Ruth to hit. By the last day of the season he tied his 1921 record of 59 homers. The finale was against Washington at the Stadium. In his first three times up, the Babe drew a walk and hit two singles. In the eighth inning, with the score tied at two and Tom Zachary, a lefty, pitching, Koenig led off with a triple to left. Zachary got Gehrig and now Ruth was up—his last chance at the record unless the game went into extra innings. The first pitch to him was a slow screwball that broke in. Ruth let it go by for a called strike. Zachary came back with another screwball. Ruth hit on the line. Umpire Bill Dinneen crouched on the foul line. The ball sailed 15 rows back into the bleachers. For a moment the fans held their breath—there was a question of whether it was fair or foul. Dinneen signaled fair. By about six inches. They were enough.

The Yankees rushed out of the dugout to greet Ruth as he crossed home plate. The fans cheered. Ruth tipped his cap. He trotted into the dugout. He had home run No. 60. He had set the most famous record in sports history.

Five minutes later the season was over.

The Yankees had won their pennant with a .714 percentage. The closest contenders were Connie Mack's Philadelphia

Athletics with a .591 percentage.

Their Series opponents, the Pirates, were a strange ball club. (They won their league championship after a close race with the defending Cardinals.) Three future Hall of Famers—Harold (Pie) Traynor, Paul Waner and Joe Cronin—were on the Pirates, but Cronin could then only make the team as a second-string short-stop. Two of the pitchers, Lee Meadows and Carmen Hill, wore spectacles—unusual in that day and age. The right side of their infield was never set throughout the season. The team's best power hitter, Kiki Cuyler, did not play regularly. It was a crazy-quilt team.

But it was a good one. The left side of the Pittsburgh infield was perfect. Traynor protected the foul line better than any other third baseman in baseball; Glenn Wright was like a steamshovel at short. The outfielders could hit. Clyde Barnhart was always dangerous; Paul (Big Poison) Waner had led the National League in batting with a .380 average; and Lloyd (Little Poison) Waner had poked out 223 hits. And they had such pitchers as Ray Kremer, Vic Aldridge and Johnny Miljus.

They were also an impressionable ball club—and that proved their undoing. Huggins, aching for World Series victory, played his psychological cards like a bearded Viennese. The day before the Series opened, both clubs were scheduled to work out at Forbes Field; first the home team and then the visiting Yankees. Huggins knew the Pirates had heard tales of his Murderers' Row, but they had never seen them. Now he was determined to show them. He waited until the Pirates had dressed and were in the stands before starting the Yankee workout. Then he called over Hoyt, who was scheduled to pitch the Series opener: "Go out there and pitch batting practice. And I want you to loosen up, by laying them all in there."

Hoyt stepped to the mound and threw the pitches to each hitter's power. Combs, Koenig, Ruth, Gehrig, Meusel, Lazzeri, Dugan, Collins, Grabowski stepped up to the plate in turn, and walloped the baseballs into the stands. Over the stands. Ruth hit one out of the ball park in center. Gehrig shot one over the seats in right. Meusel cleared the left-field fence. Lazzeri hit it even farther. "The residents in the area," Paul Gallico has recalled, "must have thought it was raining baseballs."

The awesome show was not lost on the Pirate players. They noted it sadly.

Little Poison Waner, 5-foot-7 and 145 pounds, turned to Big Poison Waner, 5-8, 155 pounds, and gasped, "Gee, they're big. And powerful." Paul shook his head slowly and walked out. The other Pirates followed. They had seen enough. Too much.

The Series itself was anticlimactic. It was the first World Series broadcast over nationwide radio and most oldtimers recall it chiefly for the "We want Cuyler" chants the Pirate fans repeated regularly and hoarsely. Cuyler didn't get off the bench in the Series—not even to pinch hit—but it's doubtful if he would have made any difference. It was the Yankees all the way. Hoyt, with the help of Moore, won the first game, 5-4; the Yanks won behind Pipgras, 6-2, in the second; Pennock pitched a no-hitter for the first seven innings of the third game and in the Yankee part of the seventh, the five o'clock lightning exploded for six runs (one a homer by the Babe) as the Yankees won, 8-1.

The Yankees, with three straight wins, decided to let Moore start the fourth as a reward for his relief duties throughout the season. The Babe drove in a run in the first inning and got two more runs for Wilcy in the fifth by hitting a home run with Combs on base. Meanwhile, the Pirates had matched the run in the first and made two tie-making runs in the seventh.

The score was 3-3 going into the bottom of the ninth inning. Johnny Miljus was on the mound for Pittsburgh. Combs led off with a walk; Koenig, laying down a sacrifice bunt, beat it out. Now the Big Fellow was up and Miljus, pressing hard, unleashed a wild pitch. Both runners advanced a base. Pittsburgh then walked Ruth intentionally, loading the bases.

With none out, Gehrig was up. Miljus struck him out. Now Meusel stepped in. A fly ball could still win the game. But Miljus, bearing down, also struck him out. Next came Lazzeri—and it seemed as if history was repeating itself. In almost the similar situation in the '26 World Series, Tony had struck out. If Miljus could get by him, perhaps even strike him out the way Alexander had, the back of the Yankee spirit could be shattered.

But Miljus was eager, too eager. He put too much stuff on the ball and it sailed over catcher Johnny Gooch's head. Combs streaked in from third with the winning run. The Series was over. The Yankees had taken four straight. The humiliation of the previous fall was forgotten. They were the champions of the world.

They were also, according to experts, the best team baseball had ever seen. So said the conservative fox, Clark Griffith. So, too, echoed one of the original Orioles, Dodger manager Uncle Wilbert Robinson: "This Yankee team would have murdered the old Orioles. We never saw the day we could make runs like Huggins' Mob."

But perhaps the greatest tribute came from the witty Waite Hoyt. One day in the spring of 1930, as the New York players moved slip-shod during training, Hoyt studied them. Finally he looked to the sportswriters gathered about him. "Know what's the matter with this club?" said Hoyt. "There are too many fellows on it who are not Yankees."

The sportswriters nodded. They knew what he meant. They had all seen the proud, powerful, spirited, Yankee team of 1927. Murderers' Row and more.

George (Whitey) Kurowski
The rookie third baseman was hoisted by teammates after hitting a two-run, ninth-inning homer that clinched the World Series over the Yankees.

Chapter 16

Down but Not Out: The Amazing Story of the '42 Cardinals

The names of their stars became well known—Musial, Marion, Slaughter among them. But in 1942 they were not yet proven, and, trailing the Dodgers by ten games in August, they seemed to have no chance of winning the pennant.

By Bob Broeg
SPORT Magazine, July 1963

The iced beer cooled Casey Stengel's throat, but not his temper. As he drank he spoke strongly about the baseball game that had ended hours earlier. His Boston team, down low in National League standings this August 1942 day, had been involved in a vicious beanball battle with the league-leading Brooklyn Dodgers. Casey thought the Dodgers' manager, Leo Durocher, had made a big mistake.

"If I had a ballclub as good as Durocher's," Stengel said, "I wouldn't throw at a ballclub as bad as mine. We're going to battle these guys all the harder from now on, and I've talked to Frisch, Wilson and other managers who feel the same.

"Sure, they've got a big lead"—and the raspy voice rose in belligerence—"but they're not in yet. In case you guys didn't notice it, St. Louis is winning steadily."

Stengel's audience, mostly New York and Boston baseball writers, laughed. A droll fellow, Ol' Casey. Why, the Dodgers held a 10-game lead over the Cardinals. The close race between Brooklyn and St. Louis simply hadn't materialized. The Dodgers, pennant winners in 1941, seemed certain to repeat even though the "experts" had predicted a pennant for St. Louis. Why had the Cardinals, second in 1941, been the preseason favorites in 1942?

Because, for one thing, St. Louis in 1941 had lost the pennant by just two games despite an incredible string of injuries. Right fielder Enos Slaughter had suffered a fractured collarbone, catcher Walker Cooper a broken shoulder blade and third baseman Jimmy Brown a broken nose. Pitcher Mort Cooper had undergone surgery for elbow chips, first baseman Johnny Mize had nursed a bad shoulder and, finally, center fielder Terry Moore had suffered a severe brain concussion.

Baseball experts figured that, physically sound, the Cardinals in 1942 would accomplish what they narrowly had missed the year before. Besides, the previous September, just too late to help win the pennant but early enough to make a tremendous impression, the Cardinals had brought up a converted pitcher who, playing the outfield, batted .426 in 12 games.

The young St. Louis Swifties, as New York cartoonist Willard Mullin named them, were an incredibly fast ballclub, defensively spectacular, particularly at shortstop, Marty Marion's position, and in the outfield, where Moore was flanked by Slaughter and the converted pitcher, Stan Musial, a young man from Pennsylvania.

The strength of the ballclub, though, lay in a pitching staff that, as Grantland Rice wrote that spring, had "exceptional depth." Leading the staff were Cooper, Lon Warneke, Max Lanier, Ernie

White, Harry Gumbert, Howard Krist, and Howard Pollet.

"Pollet," the Cardinal owner Sam Breadon told Rice, "isn't yet 21, but he's the smartest young pitcher I ever saw, and his control is so good he can pitch into a tin cup."

Another New York writer, Harry Grayson, pointed out that manager Billy Southworth's biggest problem was to choose from among the most promising minor-league pitching prospects, a dazzling list that included Murry Dickson, Harry Brecheen, George Munger, Max Surkont, Al Jurisich, Henry Nowak and a dark, handsome young righthander Grayson said looked like "another Dizzy Dean"—Johnny Beazley.

Aside from pitchers and Musial, who since has called himself "the lemon on the Grapefruit League in '42," St. Louis' rookies included outfielders Harry Walker and Erv Dusak, infielders George Kurowski and Bud Blattner and a stoop-shouldered first baseman, Ray Sanders, thrust into the spotlight by a winter deal.

In the winter Breadon and his shrewd general manager, Branch Rickey, had sent their slugging first baseman, Johnny Mize, to the New York Giants for catcher Ken O'Dea, pitcher Bill Lohrman and cash. Bluntly, both the St. Louis front office and the field management felt that Mize had pampered himself the previous season by refusing to play with what they considered minor injuries. Frank Frisch, then the Pittsburgh manager, predicted that Mize's loss could cost St. Louis the pennant, particularly since Brooklyn had added All-Star infielder Arky Vaughan to its strong roster, which already included Pete Reiser, Joe Medwick, Dixie Walker, Dolph Camilli, and Billy Herman.

On opening day at Sportsman's Park, St. Louis, the 1942 Cardinals lined up with Frank Crespi, second base; Stan Musial, left field; Terry Moore, center field; Enos Slaughter, right field; Ray Sanders, first base; Jimmy Brown, third base; Ken O'Dea, catcher; Marty Marion, shortstop, and Mort Cooper, pitcher. The lineup, though formidable, wasn't good enough to win. St. Louis lost to Chicago, 5-4, and was stifled without a run for three innings by left-handed relief pitcher Johnny Schmitz.

Left-handers continued to trouble St. Louis, and so did little things. Southworth felt the team lacked the proper mental attitude. He was angry at a sloppy pre-game infield workout in Boston. He was angry at a pitcher who had taken a 15-minute workout and then retired to the clubhouse for a rubdown without asking permission. He refused to confirm a report that he had fined one regular $200, but as the Cardinals, 15-15 on the season, prepared to play Brooklyn for the first time, he said:

"I'm cracking down on everybody, myself included. We're not going all-out, but we will from now on, I assure you. You'll see a change in this ballclub."

That day Mort Cooper beat the Dodgers, 1-0. The run was scored by his brother, Walker, who came home on a fly ball after tripling. From then on the Cardinals picked up, in spirit if not in the standings. Their speed and exuberance on the bases caused Jimmy Wilson, managing the Cubs, to moan:

"Too much energy, entirely too much. No team can keep charging around a park the way they do and stay in one piece. The Cardinals knock you out of the way just for fun."

Not for fun. To win—with their sharp pitching, tight defense, bunt-and-run offense. And especially not for fun when they played the Dodgers, with whom their relations had been rowdy since 1940. The bad feelings began shortly after St. Louis traded Joe Medwick to the Dodgers. Medwick had argued in a New York elevator with Cardinal pitcher Bob Bowman, and in a game that night one of Bowman's pitches hit Medwick in the head, forcing Joe to the hospital. Although Bowman was not a Cardinal in 1942, the feud he had triggered remained.

In Brooklyn's first visit to St. Louis in 1942, Medwick stepped on Sanders' left ankle on a play at first base. Players ran to the field from both benches ready for battle. Another time, after the Dodgers' Les Webber twice had thrown pitches behind him, rookie Musial started out toward the mound and had to be hauled back.

Rhubarb really sprouted in a June series at Brooklyn when Medwick, attempting to advance on a short passed ball, slid hard into Marion, knocking down the skinny shortstop. They argued and prepared to fight. Before they could swing, however, Crespi, rushing over from second base, knocked down Medwick.

In the ensuing scramble, Dixie Walker tackled Jimmy Brown, Medwick and Crespi continued fighting. Medwick and Crespi were thrown out of the game and fined $25 each by National League president Ford Frick.

Despite the bitterness of the feud, Southworth spoke with admiration of the Dodgers. At mid-season, with St. Louis eight games behind Brooklyn, Billy said, "They've got a fine ballclub. In fact they have two fine ballclubs. That's what makes them so tough to beat. When one man goes out of the lineup, another comes in who is just as strong. They remind me of Notre Dame when Knute Rockne had two teams—shock troops who softened you up and then a first team to polish you off."

The Dodgers reminded the rest of the National League of something else—bullies. Lording it over the league, they began to push around the non-contenders. More specifically, they—the Dodger pitchers—began to knock down the batters on non-contending clubs. In turn, Pittsburgh's Frisch, Chicago's Wilson and then Boston's Stengel spoke bitterly against the terror tactics of Leo Durocher's team.

The day Stengel suggested, outlandishly, that the Dodgers weren't "in" turned out to be the turning point in one of the most incredible pennant races in major-league history. On August 8, the Braves beat Brooklyn's ace pitcher, Whitlow Wyatt, for the first time in four years and the Cardinals overcame a five-run Pittsburgh lead to tie the Pirates in 16 innings. They tied the score when young Musial tripled, then faked a steal of home so cleverly that Luke Hamlin balked the run across.

The Cardinals went to St. Louis to begin a 22-game home stand with a revised lineup. Brown, the regular third-baseman, had been out for ten days with a chip fracture of the big toe on the right foot and his replacement, rookie Whitey Kurowski, had shown so much batting potential at third base that Brown returned to the lineup at second base, in place of Crespi. Johnny Hopp had taken Sanders'

job at first base so Marion was the only infield regular at his opening-day position.

There was another change in August, too, made by Mort Cooper. Twice, in 1941, Mort had lost games trying for his 14th victory of the season. Now, with 13 1942 victories, the big pitcher, who'd flouted superstition by wearing uniform No. 13, discarded his shirt and put on the No. 14 shirt worn by catcher Gus Mancuso.

The shirt switch worked. Coop beat Cincinnati, 4-0, allowing only two hits. After the game the Swifties serenaded him. The Cardinals' colorful trainer, Harrison J. (Doc) Weaver, twanged his mandolin. Stan Musial played a slide whistle. Harry Walker kept time with coat hangers on a clubhouse chair, and Johnny Beazley raised his voice in an off-key tenor.

"Put on another record," someone yelled, and Weaver, custodian of the clubhouse phonograph, substituted one Spike Jones novelty number for another. In place of *Jingle, Jangle, Jingle,* he put on one he'd just bought: *Pass The Biscuits, Mirandy.*

Daily, down the stretch, Mirandy passed the biscuits as the young lineup, in which Terry Moore was the only regular over 30 years old, began to put on the pressure.

Borrowing brother Walker's No. 15 shirt, Mort won his 15th game. When the Dodgers came to town for the last time in late August, Cooper borrowed Ken O'Dea's No. 16 shirt. Pitching against Wyatt, Mort seemed to have tripped over 13 again. Brooklyn broke a scoreless tie in the 13th inning, but in the bottom of the 13th, brother Walker singled home a run for St. Louis. The Cardinals won in the 14th, 2-1. The Cardinals were now 5-1/2 games behind. Beazley beat the Dodgers the next night, again 2-1. It was the rookie right-hander's 16th win in 21 decisions and brought to mind reaction early in July when the Cardinals had sold Warneke to Chicago for the waiver price.

A cynical suggestion had been offered then. The sale of Warneke appeared to be a desire to save salary and also, in effect, a surrender to the Dodgers. Warneke's estimated $15,000 salary had been the highest on the '42 Cardinals.

Breadon had angrily answered the charges, saying, "We've sold this veteran to make room for young blood—like Beazley."

Beazley made Breadon a prophet and a rich profit. Warneke helped, too. The Dodgers won the last game of that late-August series, Curt Davis beating Lanier, 4-1, and left town with a 5-1/2-game lead. Their next stop was Chicago, where Warneke, now a Cub, beat them, 4-3.

Other teams began beating Brooklyn, and the Cardinals continued to win. On September 11, when the Cards came to Brooklyn for the final two games between the teams, the Dodgers' lead had been pared to two games. Tense, almost glassy-eyed, the red-hot Redbirds seemed finally to have felt the pennant pressure.

But they didn't show it on the field. Mort Cooper, still trading uniform shirts, drove in a run and beat Wyatt, 3-0 in the September 11 game. It was Mort's 20th victory and eighth shutout. The big man with the flaming fastball and dipping forkball had beaten Brooklyn five times.

The next day another reliable Brooklyn-beater, left-hander Lanier, won, 2-1. The Cards scored their runs in the second inning on Walker Cooper's single, presently followed by Kurowski's home run. As happened so frequently that season Dodger manager Durocher and coach Charley Dressen were thrown out of the game for protesting an umpire's decision too violently. Dressen was not giving orders at third base, therefore, when Vaughan tried to score the tying run in the seventh inning. Arky attempted to come home

from second base on a wild pitch and was thrown out.

The victory was St. Louis' 29th in 34 games. The Cardinals had defeated the Dodgers 13 out of 22 games for the season and were now tied for first place with 14 games remaining on their schedule.

The Cardinals traveled happily by train that evening to Philadelphia for a Sunday doubleheader. If they had known how often they would have to win to remain in pennant contention—or what was ahead of them at Broad Street station—they wouldn't have been so happy.

As the players stepped off the train, Beazley refused to let a Red Cap carry his suitcase. The Red Cap cursed him and Beazley threw his bag at the man. Then the Red Cap pulled a knife and, as Beazley defended himself, slashed the pitcher on the right thumb. Beazley chased the Red Cap down the platform, but couldn't catch him. There, dripping blood from his pitching hand, stood the young star scheduled to pitch the next day.

With the deep cut bandaged, Beazley pitched (he had a superstar's guts and ability and probably would have been one if arm trouble suffered in World War II hadn't ended his career) against the Phillies and lost, 2-1.

In the second game, Moore hit a tie-breaking home run and Bill Beckman, just called up from Rochester, pitched six scoreless relief innings as St. Louis won, 2-1. By contrast, Bobo Newsom, just acquired by Brooklyn from Washington, failed as the Dodgers lost a doubleheader to Cincinnati.

The Cardinals, for the first time, were in first place. They had 12 games remaining and though they didn't know it then, they could afford to lose only one of those games.

They didn't lose a game in their next four. Brooklyn played two games in that span and lost one. The Cardinals, with 34 victories in their last 40 games, led the league by three games, and Sam Breadon cheerfully announced that World Series ticket reservations would be accepted. The players, though, studiously avoided using the word "pennant."

"Look," team captain Moore said. "I've been trying to win one of these things since 1935—finished second four times—and I'm not saying anything. You know, that 21-game winning streak the Cubs reeled off in September, '35, taught me something. We didn't fold, but they went right past us."

The 1942 Dodgers didn't fold, either. They won nine of their last ten games. But St. Louis, after losing a game in Chicago, swept seven straight. The Cards won one game by breaking up a scoreless battle between Cooper and Warneke with a play called "Kansas City Lou," a variation of the double steal. Hopp walked and ran to third on Kurowski's short single. With two out, Whitey made a delayed break for second, then stopped halfway. Catcher Eddie Hernandez's throw was cut off by the shortstop, Bob Sturgeon, who took a step or two toward Kurowski, then whirled and threw to Stan Hack at third, trapping Hopp. Johnny ran toward the plate the instant Sturgeon threw to third and beat Hack's throw home to score the game's one run. They won another when Musial came to bat against Pittsburgh's Rip Sewell and, with St. Louis losing, 3-0, hit a grand-slam home run, the first of Stan's big-league career. They clinched the pennant on the final day of the season when Ernie White, finally recovered from a sore arm that had sidelined him much of the season, beat the Cubs, 9-2.

The Cardinals had won 43 of their last 52 games. The Dodgers won 104 games in the 154-game season, the most ever won by a second-place team. But St. Louis had 106 victories, the most by a

National League team since 1909.

How did the Cardinals do it?

Not by knocking the ball over or against fences. They hit only 60 homers—the Giants led the league with 109 that year—and their only .300 hitters were Slaughter, .318, and Musial, .315. But they had speed—on offense where they went from first to third on any hit, where they stretched singles into doubles, where they pressured eager fielders into making errors; on defense where they made outstanding catches, where they chased down baseballs fast enough to prevent extra bases. And they had pitchers so outstanding they held the opposition to only 482 runs for the year, an average of 3.1 runs a game.

Mort Cooper and Beazley were 1-2 in the league in victories and earned-run average. Cooper, 22-7 with ten shutouts and a 1.77 ERA, won the Most Valuable Player award. Beazley, 21-6 with a 2.13 ERA, beat out Musial for rookie-of-the-year recognition.

Pitchers Lloyd Moore and Harry Gumbert were the only '42 Cardinals not developed in the St. Louis farm system. The farm system, designed and operated by Branch Rickey, had produced a team that, beginning in 1942, would win three straight pennants and four pennants in five years. But in the 1942 World Series, as he was feeling the full flush of his latest success, Rickey was told his 25-year association with the Cardinals was over. The psalm-singing, teetotaling Rickey had formed an effective baseball partnership with Breadon, the barber shop baritone who liked to raise the cup that cheers. Rickey had provided the baseball imagination, Breadon the business sense. But suddenly, Singing Sam notified Rickey that the contract which returned Branch $80,000 in salary and bonuses would not be renewed.

Still, Rickey remained loyal to his team which went into the Series a 9-20 betting underdog against the Yankees.

"Usually with a team so young, both in years and baseball experience, you see three or four men go to pot under stress," Branch said. "That has not happened with Southworth's team, which is a great tribute to him. If the Cardinals keep their feet on the ground and play the kind of ball they have been playing, they can win."

The Cardinals didn't play that kind of ball in the first game of the World Series. They committed four errors behind Mort Cooper and couldn't work up an assault against Red Ruffing, the Yankee pitcher. They were hitless until the eighth inning, in fact, when Terry Moore singled. But then they knocked out Ruffing, and before Spud Chandler stopped them they scored four runs. Musial, batting with the bases loaded, grounded out to end the game. New York won, 7-4, but the ninth-inning rally, it was obvious in the quiet but not downcast losers' clubhouse, had proved to the young St. Louis players that the famous Yankees could be beaten.

In the second game Beazley shut out the Yankees until the eighth, 3-0. Then they struck with typical Yankee savagery, tying the score with two out when Roy Cullenbine beat out an infield hit, Joe DiMaggio singled and Charley Keller homered over the right-field pavilion in St. Louis.

The 1942 Cardinals had been coming back since August, though. In their eighth-inning batting turn, they regained the lead on a double by Slaughter and single by Musial. They led, 4-3, in the ninth.

In the ninth Bill Dickey beat out an infield hit and Tuck Stainback ran for him. Buddy Hassett singled to right, where Slaughter ran to his left, grabbed the ball, pivoted and fired perfectly to Kurowski at third. Stainback was tagged out. The next

batter, Ruffing, pinch-hitting for Ernie Bonham, belted a long fly ball, which could have scored a runner from third. All it was, though, was an out and St. Louis won for Beazley, 4-3.

When the Series shifted to New York for a third game played before a record 69,123, the country kids—and most of the Cardinals were as rural as a sickle and silo—didn't let the size of the audience or amphitheatre awe them. In fact, they calmly backed White with magnificent defense and Ernie became the first pitcher to shut out the Yankees in a World Series since 1926. The Cardinals won, 2-0, in a game highlighted by acrobatic catches made by Moore, Musial and Slaughter.

In the fourth game the Cardinals knocked out Hank Borowy in a six-run fourth inning which Musial began with a bunt single and capped with a double. In between, they challenged DiMaggio's throwing arm and took extra bases with dash and daring. The Yankees knocked out Cooper in the sixth and tied the score at six. But the young Cardinals weren't flustered. Facing Atley Donald, Slaughter walked and, on a 3-2 pitch to Musial, ran to second. The pitch was ball four and when Dickey threw into center field, Slaughter raced to third. He scored on Walker Cooper's single. Bonham replaced Donald, and the Cardinals scored two more runs to win, 9-6.

Puffed up with success, the Cardinals had enjoyed themselves that day, chiding the Yankees about beefing at the umpires. The Cardinals' trainer, Doc Weaver, led the cheers and jeers, too, as the Redbirds merrily ran the bases, and he got assistance from the St. Louis equipment manager, little Morris (Butch) Yatkeman.

The next day as Moore brought up the Cardinals' lineup to the home plate, he was told by umpire Bill Summers that the Yankees objected to the equipment manager's presence in the dugout.

"To little Butch?" Moore said. "Why, Bill, he's always on our bench."

"I know, Terry," Summers said, "but, under the rules, they're within their rights."

Moore's strawberry complexion deepened into an angry red. "Okay," he said and, staring at Yankee coach Art Fletcher, said coldly:

"There's not going to be any 'tomorrow' in this Series."

There wasn't. Completing their astonishing upset of the Yankees, the Cardinals swept to a fourth straight victory. Beazley and Ruffing battled into the ninth, 2-2. Then Walker Cooper singled, Hopp sacrificed and Kurowski, who had struck out three straight times, hit a two-run homer into the left-field stands.

One moment of drama remained. In the Yankees' ninth, Joe Gordon singled to left and Brown fumbled Dickey's grounder. On the Cardinals' bench, Frank Crespi leaned over to Weaver. "Quick, Doc," the utility infielder said, "the whammy."

The trainer nodded. He moved into the mouth of the dugout. With index and little finger protruding from an otherwise clenched fist, Weaver pointed at the batter, Jerry Priddy, obviously up to sacrifice.

"Better make it a double whammy, Doc," Crespi said.

"A splendid idea," said the dignified-looking Doc. "I have had especially good fortune with my double whammy on Gordon. I think I will concentrate on him."

So with the right hand above the left, each fist clenched except for the pointing, horn-like index and little fingers, Doc Weaver cast his "spell" on the runner on second base.

Beazley pushed Priddy back from the plate with an inside pitch and his catcher, Walker Cooper, fired the ball to Marion, who had slipped in behind the runner. Gordon, though taking only a modest lead, was picked off.

Priddy then popped up to Brown. The Series ended on the next play when Brown fielded George Selkirk's grounder and threw him out.

The Cardinals went wild in a manner befitting hungry young men, many of whom—Musial, Kurowski, Beazley, among others—had earned more in only five World Series games, $6192.50 apiece, than they had all season.

In the visitors' clubhouse at Yankee Stadium, the players grabbed Commissioner Kenesaw Mountain Landis and hoisted him toward the ceiling. They ripped National League president Ford Frick's hat to pieces and boosted him to their shoulders. They hugged Beazley and pounded Kurowski, screaming and pulling hair like wild women at a bargain-basement rummage sale. Kurowski was lifted overhead and when his cleated shoes hit the concrete again, teammates grabbed him by the seat of his uniform pants and ripped them into shreds for souvenirs.

Kurowski still clutched the game-winning bat—the only bat he had taken to New York—as he finally worked his way into the shower, where amid great clouds of billowing steam tenors, baritones and bassos sang one hillbilly tune, "Good Old Mountain Music," then broke into their good-luck number of the sensational stretch run.

Yes, Mirandy had passed the biscuits for guys who had grown up on short rations during the Depression. None had known more hardships, though, than Kurowski, the thick-legged, crooked-arm second-generation Pole from Reading, Pennsylvania.

At nine, after falling off a fence, he had suffered osteomyelitis in his right arm, forcing the removal of the ulna bone of the forearm. Dr. Robert F. Hyland, famed surgeon-general of baseball, always marveled that Whitey could have overcome that physical disability to play big-league baseball. At 18, the year Whitey decided to challenge professional ball, his older brother, Frank, was killed in a cave-in at a coal mine. And in the spring of '42, when Whitey was trying to make the big-league ballclub, his father fell dead of a heart attack.

Somehow, Whitey Kurowski symbolized the spirit of the 1942 Cardinals, an unforgettable ballclub that just didn't know when it was beat.

The Golden Era
1946-1968

Willie Mays and Mickey Mantle
After entering the major leagues together in 1951, Mays and Mantle established themselves as the top center fielders in the game.

FAMOUS FIRSTS

1947: Jackie Robinson becomes the first African-American player in
modern major league history.

1956: Don Larsen of the Yankees becomes the first pitcher to throw a
perfect game in the World Series.

1957: The first Gold Glove Awards are presented.

1958: American League players are required for the first time to wear
batting helmets.

1959: Joe Cronin becomes first former player to become league president
when he assumes leadership of the American League.

1960: Jerome Holtzman proposes the "save" as a measure of relief-
pitching skill.

1961: Major League baseball expands for the first time.

1965: The first enclosed stadium, the Astrodome, opens in Houston.

Chapter 17

Go West, Young Man!

With the return from valorous service of such stars as Ted Williams, Hank Greenberg, Bob Feller, Joe DiMaggio and hundreds more, the game was back to prewar standards of play and the fans flocked to the ballparks in unprecedented numbers. The 1946 World Series pitted the Red Sox of Ted Williams against the Cardinals of Stan Musial in a marquee matchup of the two men who would symbolize their leagues even into their ballplaying dotage.

But the big action was in Brooklyn and the Bronx, where in 1947, as Red Barber put it, "all hell broke loose." The Dodgers featured an African-American first baseman named Jackie Robinson, but the man who was supposed to run interference for him as manager of the Brooklyn club, Leo Durocher, was banned from baseball for a year because of the unsavory nature of his off-field associates. The Yankees, meanwhile, had a messy management shakeup in which Larry MacPhail, booted out as co-owner as well as general manager, was replaced in the latter role by George Weiss, who in turn paved the way for the return of Casey Stengel.

In the ensuing years pennants flew in such uncharacteristic locales as Boston's Braves Field, Philadelphia's Shibe Park, and Cleveland's Municipal Stadium before settling into a decade of Gotham hegemony, with one or more New York teams in the Series every year but two from 1949 to 1964. The watershed year of 1951 saw the advent of rookies Mickey Mantle and Willie Mays, the retirement of Joe DiMaggio, and the most famous moment in the game's history: the "shot heard 'round the world," Bobby Thomson's blast that capped an improbable run to the pennant by the Giants, who had trailed the Dodgers by 13-1/2 games with six weeks left in the season.

For New York City fans the 1950s seemed a golden age, but after five postwar boom years attendance began to sag everywhere, including Brooklyn, Manhattan and the Bronx. Ubiquitous television and radio broadcasts began to corrode the minor-league fan base, and big-league attendance declined for other reasons. Shifting population patterns, aided by improved air travel, interstate highways, and air conditioning made the layout of the major leagues— 16 teams in 11 cities, none west of St. Louis—seem out of touch with an America on the move.

In 1953, following 50 years of franchise stability, the Braves moved from Boston to Milwaukee, the Browns from St. Louis to Baltimore (where they revived the old Oriole name), and even Connie Mack's Athletics packed up and shipped off to Kansas City. But none of these moves gave rise to the wailing, keening, and gnashing of teeth that came after the 1957 season when both the Giants and the Dodgers went west to, respectively, San Francisco and Los Angeles.

Also as the '50s drew to a close, Branch Rickey stepped forward for one last hurrah—the Continental League, a feigned rival threat designed to scare the major leagues into expansion. Suing for peace, the majors agreed to an AL expansion with new teams in Washington and Los Angeles in 1961. In this expansion year, Mantle and teammate Roger Maris assaulted Babe Ruth's single-

Jackie Robinson, Don Newcombe
The face of baseball was changed forever in 1947 when Robinson, left, joined the Brooklyn Dodgers, soon to be followed by Newcombe.

season home-run record, with Maris breaking it on the final day of the expanded 162-game season. The NL expanded to New York and Houston the following year.

Fearful that pitchers were becoming an endangered species, commissioner Ford Frick overreacted to Maris' new mark by expanding the strike zone and ushering in nuclear winter for batters. In 1968, the "Year of the Pitcher"—in which Denny McLain won 31 games and Bob Gibson posted an ERA of 1.12—batting averages plummeted to levels not seen since the Dead Ball Era. The AL batted .231 as a whole and the Yankees, the team that gave us Murderers Row, batted .214.

With the spectacular rise to prominence of pro football in the 1960s and the increasing attention devoted to pro basketball, baseball—with its endless stream of 1-0 and 2-1 games—seemed to be drifting into irrelevance.

1946

Boston Slaughtered as post-war boom revitalizes baseball

The end of World War II brought more than 18.5 million fans into ballparks, including a first-ever $2-million-plus gate (at Yankee Stadium). But there was little time to gloat.

Before the start of the season, Mexican millionaire Jorge Pasquel lured a score of players south of the border with inflated contracts. Although many of them made a U-turn when Pasquel's promises of launching a new major league turned out to be little more than posturing for local political ends, they remained barred from the NL and AL for years because of a ban imposed by Commissioner Happy Chandler. North of the border with the Dodger farm club in Montreal, the presence of Jackie Robinson as the first black in Organized Baseball since the 19th century sent shivers through the anti-integration establishment. And in Pittsburgh, a serious effort to unionize players created rancor within the Pirates clubhouse while setting the bases for more vocal player-contract demands.

The NL race was a two-team struggle between the Dodgers and Cardinals. Although the return of

Enos Slaughter
In one of the most dramatic finishes in World Series history, Slaughter slid safely home with the winning run, scoring from first on a base hit, as St. Louis beat Boston in seven games.

such stars as Stan Musial, Enos Slaughter, and Howie Pollet favored St. Louis on paper, the clubs ended the season with identical records of 96-58, necessitating the first best-of-three pennant playoff. As in 1942, Brooklyn's efforts down the stretch were hampered by a sidelining injury to Pete Reiser, the one-time St. Louis farmhand released by Commissioner Kenesaw Landis in 1938. Without the outfielder in the lineup, the Dodgers were outgunned, and went down in two games. Most of the individual honors also went to the Cards—Musial for batting average (.365), Slaughter for RBIs (130), and Pollet for wins (21) and ERA (2.10). The home-run king was Pittsburgh's Ralph Kiner (23).

In the AL, Ted Williams traded his previous Triple Crown accomplishments for second place in all three hitting categories as the price for the Red Sox rising from second to first in the standings. The slugger belted 38 homers (behind the 44 of Detroit's Hank Greenberg), drove in 123 runs (behind Greenberg's 127), and averaged .342 (behind the .353 of Washington's Mickey Vernon). The other major contributors to the Boston pennant were first baseman Rudy York (119 RBIs), second baseman Bobby Doerr (116 RBIs), and right-handers Boo Ferriss (25 wins) and Tex

Hughson (20). Detroit's Hal Newhouser and Cleveland's Bob Feller both won 26 times, with Newhouser also posting the league's best ERA (1.94).

Boston's better hitting made it the favorite in the World Series, but the seven-game struggle went back and forth over the first six games. In the finale, the Cardinals took a 3-1 lead into the eighth, only to see it disappear on a tying double by Dom DiMaggio. In the bottom of the frame, Slaughter opened with a single, stayed put for two outs, but then was off and running when Harry Walker drove a shot into left-center. When shortstop Johnny Pesky hesitated a fraction of a second on the relay, Slaughter had the room he needed to score the championship run. Cardinals southpaw Harry Brecheen was the other hero, winning three decisions. Musial and Williams both had tepid series, the former going 6-for-27, the latter 5-for-25.

Meanwhile, in the International League, Jackie Robinson faced taunts from fans and threatened protests from opposing players in his rookie pro season with the Montreal Royals. By the end of the summer he was a nervous wreck, but he was also league batting champion (.349) and clearly ready for the major leagues.

1946 SEASON HIGHLIGHTS

NATIONAL LEAGUE

	W	L	Pct.	GB
St. Louis	98	58	.628	—
Brooklyn	96	60	.615	2
Chicago	82	71	.536	14.5
Boston	81	72	.529	15.5
Philadelphia	69	85	.448	28
Cincinnati	67	87	.435	30
Pittsburgh	63	91	.409	34
New York	61	93	.396	36

AMERICAN LEAGUE

	W	L	Pct.	GB
Boston	104	50	.675	—
Detroit	92	62	.597	12
New York	87	67	.565	17
Washington	76	78	.494	28
Chicago	74	80	.481	30
Cleveland	68	86	.442	36
St. Louis	66	88	.429	38
Philadelphia	49	105	.318	55

AWARDS

NL MVP: Stan Musial, STL
AL MVP: Ted Williams, BOS

ALL-STAR GAME

Fenway Park, Boston
July 9: AL 12, NL 0

POSTSEASON

WORLD SERIES
St. Louis Cardinals 4, Boston Red Sox 3
Oct. 6: Boston 3, ST. LOUIS 2
Oct. 7: ST. LOUIS 3, Boston 0
Oct. 9: BOSTON 4, St. Louis 0
Oct. 10: St. Louis 12, BOSTON 3
Oct. 11: BOSTON 6, St. Louis 3
Oct. 13: ST. LOUIS 4, Boston 1
Oct. 15: ST. LOUIS 4, Boston 3

Home team in CAPS

> "Most ballgames are lost, not won."
> — Casey Stengel

NATIONAL LEAGUE LEADERS

Home Runs
Kiner-Pit	23
Mize-NY	22
Slaughter-StL	18
Ennis-Phi	17

Runs Batted In
Slaughter-StL	130
Walker-Bro	116
Musial-StL	103
Kurowski-StL	89
Kiner-Pit	81

Batting Average
Musial-StL	.365
Hopp-Bos	.333
Walker-Bro	.319
Ennis-Phi	.313
Holmes-Bos	.310

On Base Percentage
Stanky-Bro	.436
Musial-StL	.434
Cavarretta-Chi	.401
Herman-Bro-Bos	.395
Walker-Bro	.391

Slugging Average
Musial-StL	.587
Ennis-Phi	.485
Slaughter-StL	.465
Kurowski-StL	.462
Walker-Bro	.448

Stolen Bases
Reiser-Bro	34
Haas-Cin	22
Hopp-Bos	21
Adams-Cin	16
Walker-Bro	14

Wins
Pollet-StL	21
Sain-Bos	20
Higbe-Bro	17
Dickson-StL	15
Brecheen-StL	15

Innings Pitched
Pollet-StL	266.0
Koslo-NY	265.1
Sain-Bos	265.0
Brecheen-StL	231.1
Schmitz-Chi	224.1

Saves
Raffensberger-Phi	6
Pollet-StL	5
Karl-Phi	5
Herring-Bro	5
Casey-Bro	5

Strikeouts
Schmitz-Chi	135
Higbe-Bro	134
Sain-Bos	129
Koslo-NY	121
Brecheen-StL	117

Earned Run Average
Pollet-StL	2.10
Sain-Bos	2.21
Beggs-Cin	2.32
Blackwell-Cin	2.45
Brecheen-StL	2.49

Complete Games
Sain-Bos	24
Pollet-StL	22
Koslo-NY	17
Ostermueller-Pit	16
Cooper-Bos	15

AMERICAN LEAGUE LEADERS

Home Runs
Greenberg-Det	44
Williams-Bos	38
Keller-NY	30
Seerey-Cle	26
DiMaggio-NY	25

Runs Batted In
Greenberg-Det	127
Williams-Bos	123
York-Bos	119
Doerr-Bos	116
Keller-NY	101

Batting Average
Vernon-Was	.353
Williams-Bos	.342
Pesky-Bos	.335
Kell-Phi-Det	.322
DiMaggio-Bos	.316

On Base Percentage
Williams-Bos	.497
Keller-NY	.405
Vernon-Was	.403
Pesky-Bos	.401
DiMaggio-Bos	.393

Slugging Average
Williams-Bos	.667
Greenberg-Det	.604
Keller-NY	.533
DiMaggio-NY	.511
Edwards-Cle	.509

Stolen Bases
Case-Cle	28
Stirnweiss-NY	18
Lake-Det	15

Wins
Newhouser-Det	26
Feller-Cle	26
Ferriss-Bos	25
Hughson-Bos	20
Chandler-NY	20

Innings Pitched
Feller-Cle	371.1
Newhouser-Det	292.2
Hughson-Bos	278.0
Trout-Det	276.1
Ferriss-Bos	274.0

Saves
Klinger-Bos	9
Caldwell-Chi	8
Murphy-NY	7
Ferrick-Cle-StL	6

Strikeouts
Feller-Cle	348
Newhouser-Det	275
Hughson-Bos	172
Trucks-Det	161
Trout-Det	151

Earned Run Average
Newhouser-Det	1.94
Chandler-NY	2.10
Feller-Cle	2.18
Bevens-NY	2.23
Flores-Phi	2.32

Complete Games
Feller-Cle	36
Newhouser-Det	29
Ferriss-Bos	26
Trout-Det	23
Hughson-Bos	21

THE YEAR IN BASEBALL

February 11: John Paciorek is born; he made debut as 18-year-old with Astros by reaching base in all five at-bats, scoring four runs and driving in five—and never played in big leagues again.

March 15: Bobby Bonds is born; he was the most frequent member of the "30-30" club (homers and steals) and came within one homer of going "40-40," a mark first reached by Oakland's Jose Canseco in 1988.

February 19: Giants outfielder Danny Gardella becomes the first major leaguer to announce he is jumping to the "outlaw" Mexican League.

April 14: Manager Mel Ott of the Giants hits his 511th, and final, home run.

April 18: Jackie Robinson debuts at second base for the Montreal Royals, hitting a home run and three singles.

April 18: Jim "Catfish" Hunter is born; he won 20 or more games in five straight years, taking Cy Young honors in 1974.

May 20: Claude Passeau of the Chicago Cubs makes his first error since September 21, 1941, ending his record streak for pitchers at 273 consecutive errorless chances.

May 28: In the first night game at Yankee Stadium, Washington beats New York 2-1.

June 22: Bill Veeck heads a syndicate that purchases the Cleveland Indians.

July 14: Player-manager Lou Boudreau sets a major league record by swatting five extra-base hits (four doubles and a home run). On the same day, the famous "Boudreau shift" is implemented to try to shut down Ted Williams.

July 22: Major league clubs are given the right to negotiate television rights to their ball games.

July 27: Rudy York hits two grand slams.

August 8: The Dreyfuss family, owners of the Pittsburgh Pirates since 1900, sell the club to a group that includes singer Bing Crosby for $2.5 million.

September 25: Bill Veeck, owner of Cleveland, offers free admission to a game with Chisox, and 12,800 show up to see Chicago win, 4-1.

October 3: The St. Louis Cardinals beat Brooklyn 8-4 at Ebbets Field to win an NL playoff two games to none.

October 15: In one of the most memorable World Series finishes ever, Enos Slaughter races home with the winning run from first base on a double by Harry Walker in the eighth inning of Game 7.

October 19: Allie Reynolds is traded to NY by Cleveland for Joe Gordon and Eddie Bockman. As an Indian, his won-lost record was 51-47; as a Yank, it was 131-60.

1947

Color barrier falls as Robinson debuts for Rickey's Dodgers

Between dramatic preseason developments and an especially vivid World Series, the regular 1947 season approached the humdrum. Brooklyn alone supplied endless headlines before Opening Day with the arrival of Jackie Robinson as the first black major leaguer since the 1880s, the endless sniping between Dodger general manager Branch Rickey and Yankees owner Larry MacPhail, and the year-long suspension of manager Leo Durocher for what Commissioner Happy Chandler termed "an accumulation of unpleasant incidents." Cleveland also riveted attention, especially for owner Bill Veeck's frantic attempts to appease fans after trying to trade off grandstand favorite Lou Boudreau and for the signing of Larry Doby as the AL's first African-American player.

Robinson wasted little time impressing Dodgers fans by taking Rookie-of-the-Year honors and animating Brooklyn's pennant win over St. Louis with his .297 mark and league-leading 29 steals. His

Jackie Robinson
The talented second baseman played through a season of endless taunts and occasional death threats as he won rookie-of-the-year honors and established himself as a Dodger mainstay and a national icon.

debut came on April 15, playing first base in front of 26,623 fans at Ebbets Field. Before the season was out, he faced a revolt by some teammates (quickly quashed by Rickey), vicious taunts from opponents, a threatened player strike in St. Louis and death threats in Cincinnati. He played through them all and became a sparkplug of the great Dodger teams of the '50s.

The Dodgers main mound presence was Ralph Branca with 21 wins. The Giants were the power story, establishing a new team record with their 221 home runs; first baseman Johnny Mize tied Pittsburgh's Ralph Kiner for tops in the department (51). Mize also led in RBIs (138). Other honors went to Harry Walker for the hitting title (.363) despite being traded by the Cardinals to the Phillies during the season, Boston's Warren Spahn for his 2.33 ERA, and Cincinnati's Ewell Blackwell for his 22 victories. Blackwell also came within two outs of emulating Johnny Vander Meer's 1938 feat of back-to-back no-hitters, and against the same teams (Boston and Brooklyn).

The Yankees made short work of the AL pennant race in spite of another Triple Crown for Boston's Ted Williams (.343-32-114) and season-long tensions in the clubhouse that came close to open revolt against owner MacPhail. Among other things, MacPhail was

given to fining players for negligible offenses and flying them around the league in an old C-54 transport that had several near-accidents. The club's 12-game bulge over the Tigers was achieved without a 20-game winner, without anybody driving in 100 runs, and with Joe DiMaggio's 20 homers the individual high. On the other hand, Joe Page hastened the approach of the full-time closer when he saved 17 games as well as winning 14. Only Cleveland's Bob Feller won 20 during the season, and Chicago's Joe Haynes led in ERA at 2.42.

Most World Series anthology films borrow heavily from 1947. In Game 3, New York's Yogi Berra hit the first pinch-homer in postseason history. In Game 4, Bill Bevens of the Yankees brought a no-hitter into the ninth inning, walked two batters, and then, with two out, surrendered a game-winning two-run double to pinch-hitter Cookie Lavagetto. In Game 6, Brooklyn left fielder Al Gionfriddo preserved a victory by snaring a blast off the bat of DiMaggio that is generally regarded as one of the top three World Series catches of all time. The Yankees came back in the final game to take the championship behind a fourth relief appearance by Page. Neither Bevens, Lavagetto, nor Gionfriddo ever played in the majors again after the Series.

1947 SEASON HIGHLIGHTS

NATIONAL LEAGUE

	W	L	Pct.	GB
Brooklyn	94	60	.610	—
St. Louis	89	65	.578	5
Boston	86	68	.558	8
New York	81	73	.526	13
Cincinnati	73	81	.474	21
Chicago	69	85	.448	25
Pittsburgh	62	92	.403	32
Philadelphia	62	92	.403	32

AMERICAN LEAGUE

	W	L	Pct.	GB
New York	97	57	.630	—
Detroit	85	69	.552	12
Boston	83	71	.539	14
Cleveland	80	74	.519	17
Philadelphia	78	76	.506	19
Chicago	70	84	.455	27
Washington	64	90	.416	33
St. Louis	59	95	.383	38

AWARDS
NL MVP: Bob Elliott, BOS
AL MVP: Joe DiMaggio, NY
NL Rookie: Jackie Robinson, BRO

ALL-STAR GAME
Wrigley Field, Chicago
July 8: AL 2, NL 1

POSTSEASON
WORLD SERIES
New York Yankees 4, Brooklyn Dodgers 3
Sep. 30: NEW YORK 5, Brooklyn 3
Oct. 1: NEW YORK 10, Brooklyn 3
Oct. 2: BROOKLYN 9, New York 8
Oct. 3: BROOKLYN 3, New York 2
Oct. 4: New York 2, BROOKLYN 1
Oct. 5: Brooklyn 8, NEW YORK 6
Oct. 6: NEW YORK 5, Brooklyn 2

Home team in CAPS

> "Jackie Robinson was the greatest competitor I ever saw. He didn't win. He triumphed."
>
> — Ralph Branca

NATIONAL LEAGUE LEADERS

Home Runs
Mize-NY	51
Kiner-Pit	51
Marshall-NY	36
W.Cooper-NY	35
Thomson-NY	29

Runs Batted In
Mize-NY	138
Kiner-Pit	127
W.Cooper-NY	122
B.Elliott-Bos	113
Marshall-NY	107

Batting Average
Walker-StL-Phi	.363
B.Elliott-Bos	.317
Galan-Cin	.314
Cavarretta-Chi	.314
Kiner-Pit	.313

On Base Percentage
Galan-Cin	.449
Walker-StL-Phi	.436
Kurowski-StL	.420
Kiner-Pit	.417
Walker-Bro	.415

Slugging Average
Kiner-Pit	.639
Mize-NY	.614
W.Cooper-NY	.586
Kurowski-StL	.544
Marshall-NY	.528

Stolen Bases
Robinson-Bro	29
Reiser-Bro	14
Walker-StL-Phi	13
Hopp-Bos	13
Torgeson-Bos	11

Wins
Blackwell-Cin	22
Spahn-Bos	21
Sain-Bos	21
Jansen-NY	21
Branca-Bro	21

Innings Pitched
Spahn-Bos	289.2
Branca-Bro	280.0
Blackwell-Cin	273.0
Sain-Bos	266.0
Jansen-NY	248.0

Saves
Casey-Bro	18
Trinkle-NY	10
Gumbert-Cin	10
Behrman-Bro-Pt-Bro	8

Strikeouts
Blackwell-Cin	193
Branca-Bro	148
Sain-Bos	132
Spahn-Bos	123
Munger-StL	123

Earned Run Average
Spahn-Bos	2.33
Blackwell-Cin	2.47
Branca-Bro	2.67
Leonard-Phi	2.68
Brazle-StL	2.84

Complete Games
Blackwell-Cin	23
Spahn-Bos	22
Sain-Bos	22
Jansen-NY	20
Leonard-Phi	19

AMERICAN LEAGUE LEADERS

Home Runs
Williams-Bos	32
Gordon-Cle	29
Heath-StL	27
Cullenbine-Det	24
York-Bos-Chi	21

Runs Batted In
Williams-Bos	114
Henrich-NY	98
DiMaggio-NY	97
Jones-Chi-Bos	96

Batting Average
Williams-Bos	.343
McCosky-Phi	.328
Pesky-Bos	.324
Kell-Det	.320
Mitchell-Cle	.316

On Base Percentage
Williams-Bos	.499
Fain-Phi	.414
Cullenbine-Det	.401
McCosky-Phi	.395
McQuinn-NY	.395

Slugging Average
Williams-Bos	.634
DiMaggio-NY	.522
Gordon-Cle	.496
Henrich-NY	.485
Heath-StL	.485

Stolen Bases
Dillinger-StL	34
Philley-Chi	21
Vernon-Was	12
Pesky-Bos	12

Wins
Feller-Cle	20
Reynolds-NY	19
Marchildon-Phi	19
Hutchinson-Det	18
Dobson-Bos	18

Innings Pitched
Feller-Cle	299.0
Newhouser-Det	285.0
Marchildon-Phi	276.2
Masterson-Was	253.0
Lopat-Chi	252.2

Saves
Page-NY	17
Klieman-Cle	17
Christopher-Phi	12
Ferrick-Was	9

Strikeouts
Feller-Cle	196
Newhouser-Det	176
Masterson-Was	135
Reynolds-NY	129
Marchildon-Phi	128

Earned Run Average
Haynes-Chi	2.42
Feller-Cle	2.68
Fowler-Phi	2.81
Lopat-Chi	2.81
Newhouser-Det	2.87

Complete Games
Newhouser-Det	24
Wynn-Was	22
Lopat-Chi	22
Marchildon-Phi	21
Feller-Cle	20

THE YEAR IN BASEBALL

January 8: Hank Greenberg is sold by Tigers to Pittsburgh, where he hits 25 homers and tutors Ralph Kiner.

January 20: Famed Negro League star Josh Gibson dies of a brain tumor at age 35.

January 21: Carl Hubbell, Lefty Grove, Frank Frisch, and Mickey Cochrane are elected to the Hall of Fame.

April 9: Leo Durocher is suspended for the entire season by commissioner Happy Chandler for consorting with people of dubious reputation.

April 15: Jackie Robinson plays his first major league game, at first base, for the Dodgers. He goes 0-for-3 at bat, but scores the deciding run in a 5-3 victory over the Boston Braves at Brooklyn. He becomes the first African-American to appear in the majors since 1884.

April 27: Babe Ruth Day is held at Yankee Stadium.

June 22: Ewell Blackwell almost duplicates the Vander Meer double no-hit record by following his June 18 gem over Boston with 8-1/3 hitless innings against the Dodgers before the bubble bursts.

July 5: Larry Doby breaks the color barrier in the American League, pinch hitting for Cleveland Indians against White Sox, 1947.

July 30: Ewell Blackwell's winning streak of 16 games is ended by a 6-5, 10-inning loss to Cincinnati.

September 12: Ralph Kiner smacks two homers to conclude a four-game stretch in which he hit eight.

September 29: A record World Series crowd of 73,365 at Yankee Stadium sees New York win the opening game 5-3 against Brooklyn.

October 3: Cookie Lavagetto's pinch double with two out and two aboard in the ninth inning of a World Series game at Ebbets Field ruins Bill Bevens' no-hitter and beats Yanks, 3 to 2.

October 7: Yankee general manager Larry MacPhail resigns and his interest in the club is purchased for $2 million by Dan Topping and Del Webb.

November 27: Joe DiMaggio is elected MVP over triple-crown winner Williams, 202 votes to 201. One writer fails to give Williams even a 10th-place vote, worth two points.

December 29: George Blaeholder dies.

1948

Durocher bolts;
Indians take Series
for showboat Veeck

The year 1948 was as close as Boston ever got to hosting an all-local World Series. The surprise was the NL Braves, whose third-place finish the year before had been the highest for the team since 1916. As late as early September, the club still seemed ready to fall under the charging Cardinals, but then a doubleheader sweep of the Dodgers kept it in first for good. Although associated with the despairing cry of "(Warren) Spahn, (Johnny) Sain, and pray for rain" where its rotation was concerned, the pitching was a lot more Sain (league-leading 24 wins) than Spahn (only 15 wins and a high 3.71 ERA). Other keys were rookie shortstop Alvin Dark (.322) and third baseman Bob Elliott (100 RBIs).

Around the rest of the league, Pittsburgh's Ralph Kiner and New York's Johnny Mize tied for the home-run leadership (40) for the second straight year, St. Louis' Stan Musial had both the highest average (.376) and the most RBIs (131), and Harry Brecheen of the Cardinals yielded the fewest runs at 2.24.

The NL's biggest off-field story was the move across the East River by Dodger manager Leo Durocher to take over as the dugout boss for the Giants. The switch came following Durocher's return from his 1947 suspension and his insecurity over replacement Burt Shotton's having won the pennant in his absence. When the Giants asked the Dodgers for permission to contact Shotton for their opening, they were told to take Durocher instead.

In the AL, Cleveland owner Bill Veeck rarely allowed the pennant race to get in the way of his promotions. Even with his Indians locked in a struggle with the Red Sox and Yankees for first place in the closing hours of the campaign, he couldn't pass up Joe Earley Night—festooning the Average Fan with gifts both valuable and ludicrous. The combination of the contending team and the grandstand come-ons brought an unprecedented 2,620,627 through the gates of Municipal Stadium.

On the field, another Veeck move to bring in the outfield fences helped second baseman Joe Gordon and third baseman Ken Keltner top the 30-homer mark; along with playing manager Lou Boudreau, the infielders also drove in more than 100 runs apiece. The pitching story was 20-game winners Bob Lemon and Gene Bearden and Negro Leagues legend Satchel Paige (6-1, 2.48 ERA). When the season ended in a tie between Cleveland and Boston, Boudreau chose Bearden, who neither before nor after 1948 won more than eight games, to start the one-game playoff against the Red Sox; supported by Boudreau's own two homers, the southpaw clinched the pennant. Bearden's 2.43 was the best ERA in the circuit, Hal Newhouser's 21 for the Tigers the most victories. The familiar names of Ted Williams (.369) and Joe DiMaggio (39 homers and 155 RBIs) dominated the hitting categories.

Cleveland's World Series win over Boston in six games featured brilliant pitching on both sides. In the opening game, Sain outdueled Bob Feller 1-0, with the run scoring in the eighth inning after the umpire blew a call on a pickoff of Braves catcher Phil Masi. In the fourth game, Bearden fashioned a 2-0 shutout. In Game 5, Sain lost 2-1 to Steve Gromek. The Indians' victory came despite a .199 team batting average.

Satchel Paige
In the twilight of a brilliant career, the former Negro Leagues star was signed by the Indians in mid-season, and he posted a 6-1 record.

1948 SEASON HIGHLIGHTS

NATIONAL LEAGUE

	W	L	Pct.	GB
Boston	91	62	.595	—
St. Louis	85	69	.552	6.5
Brooklyn	84	70	.545	7.5
Pittsburgh	83	71	.539	8.5
New York	78	76	.506	13.5
Philadelphia	66	88	.429	25.5
Cincinnati	64	89	.418	27
Chicago	64	90	.416	27.5

AMERICAN LEAGUE

	W	L	Pct.	GB
Cleveland	97	58	.626	—
Boston	96	59	.619	1
New York	94	60	.610	2.5
Philadelphia	84	70	.545	12.5
Detroit	78	76	.506	18.5
St. Louis	59	94	.386	37
Washington	56	97	.366	40
Chicago	51	101	.336	44.5

AWARDS

NL MVP: Stan Musial, STL
AL MVP: Lou Boudreau, CLE
NL Rookie: Alvin Dark, BOS

ALL-STAR GAME

Sportsman's Park, St. Louis
July 13: AL 5, NL 2

POSTSEASON
WORLD SERIES
Cleveland Indians 4, Boston Braves 2
Oct. 6: BOSTON 1, Cleveland 0
Oct. 7: Cleveland 4, BOSTON 1
Oct. 8: CLEVELAND 2, Boston 0
Oct. 9: CLEVELAND 2, Boston 1
Oct. 10: Boston 11, CLEVELAND 5
Oct. 11: Cleveland 4, BOSTON 3

Home team in CAPS

"I've always felt a lot of pitching coaches made a living out of running pitchers so they wouldn't have to spend that same time teaching them how to pitch."

— Johnny Sain

NATIONAL LEAGUE LEADERS

Home Runs
Mize-NY	40
Kiner-Pit	40
Musial-StL	39
Sauer-Cin	35

Runs Batted In
Musial-StL	131
Mize-NY	125
Kiner-Pit	123
Gordon-NY	107
Pafko-Chi	101

Batting Average
Musial-StL	.376
Ashburn-Phi	.333
Holmes-Bos	.325
Dark-Bos	.322
Slaughter-StL	.321

On Base Percentage
Musial-StL	.450
B.Elliott-Bos	.423
Ashburn-Phi	.410
Slaughter-StL	.409
Mize-NY	.395

Slugging Average
Musial-StL	.702
Mize-NY	.564
Gordon-NY	.537
Kiner-Pit	.533
Ennis-Phi	.525

Stolen Bases
Ashburn-Phi	32
Reese-Bro	25
Rojek-Pit	24
Robinson-Bro	22
Torgeson-Bos	19

Wins
Sain-Bos	24
Brecheen-StL	20
Schmitz-Chi	18
Jansen-NY	18
VanderMeer-Cin	17

Innings Pitched
Sain-Bos	314.2
Jansen-NY	277.0
Spahn-Bos	257.0
Dickson-StL	252.1
Barney-Bro	246.2

Saves
Gumbert-Cin	17
Wilks-StL	13
Higbe-Pit	10
Trinkle-NY	7
Behrman-Bro	7

Strikeouts
Brecheen-StL	149
Barney-Bro	138
Sain-Bos	137
Jansen-NY	126
Branca-Bro	122

Earned Run Average
Brecheen-StL	2.24
Leonard-Phi	2.51
Sain-Bos	2.60
Roe-Bro	2.63
Schmitz-Chi	2.64

Complete Games
Sain-Bos	28
Brecheen-StL	21
Schmitz-Chi	18
Spahn-Bos	16
Leonard-Phi	16

AMERICAN LEAGUE LEADERS

Home Runs
DiMaggio-NY	39
Gordon-Cle	32
Keltner-Cle	31
Stephens-Bos	29
Doerr-Bos	27

Runs Batted In
DiMaggio-NY	155
Stephens-Bos	137
Williams-Bos	127
Gordon-Cle	124
Majeski-Phi	120

Batting Average
Williams-Bos	.369
Boudreau-Cle	.355
Mitchell-Cle	.336
Zarilla-StL	.329
McCosky-Phi	.326

On Base Percentage
Williams-Bos	.497
Boudreau-Cle	.453
Appling-Chi	.423
Goodman-Bos	.414
Fain-Phi	.412

Slugging Average
Williams-Bos	.615
DiMaggio-NY	.598
Henrich-NY	.554
Boudreau-Cle	.534
Keltner-Cle	.522

Stolen Bases
Dillinger-StL	28
Coan-Was	23
Vernon-Was	15
Mitchell-Cle	13

Wins
Newhouser-Det	21
Lemon-Cle	20
Bearden-Cle	20
Raschi-NY	19
Feller-Cle	19

Innings Pitched
Lemon-Cle	293.2
Feller-Cle	280.1
Newhouser-Det	272.1
Dobson-Bos	245.1
Reynolds-NY	236.1

Saves
Christopher-Cle	17
Page-NY	16
Houtteman-Det	10
Ferrick-Was	10
Judson-Chi	8

Strikeouts
Feller-Cle	164
Lemon-Cle	147
Newhouser-Det	143
Brissie-Phi	127
Raschi-NY	124

Earned Run Average
Bearden-Cle	2.43
Scarborough-Was	2.82
Lemon-Cle	2.82
Newhouser-Det	3.01
Parnell-Bos	3.14

Complete Games
Lemon-Cle	20
Newhouser-Det	19
Raschi-NY	18
Feller-Cle	18

THE YEAR IN BASEBALL

May 20: In a 13-4 Cleveland win, the Indians tie an AL record by collecting 18 bases on balls.

May 27: Recently retired slugger Hank Greenberg buys an interest in the Indians, becoming the team's second largest stockholder.

June 13: The Yankees retire Babe Ruth's No. 3 in a ceremony that marks Ruth's final appearance at Yankee Stadium.

June 20: Cleveland draws a major league record 82,781 for a doubleheader.

July 7: The Indians sign former Negro League star Satchel Paige and, although the signing was ridiculed as a publicity stunt, Paige went 6-1.

July 16: Leo Durocher obtains his release from Brooklyn and promptly signs to manage the cross-town New York Giants, replacing Mel Ott.

August 3: Satchel Paige of the Indians makes first major league start.

August 13: A crowd of 51,013 flocks to Comiskey Park to see Satchel Paige and the Indians defeat Chicago 5-0.

August 16: Babe Ruth dies of cancer at age of 53.

August 17: Tom Henrich ties an AL record with his fourth grand-slam home run of the season.

September 22: Stan Musial has his fifth five-hit game of the season, tying Ty Cobb's record.

October 4: Cleveland shortstop, manager, and MVP Lou Boudreau goes 4 for 4 off Red Sox pitching as the Indians win the AL's first one-game playoff for a pennant.

October 10: A World Series record crowd of 86,228 in Cleveland sees the Braves beat the Indians 11-5.

November 30: Former pitching great Rube Foster organized the Negro National League, and on this date 28 years later it disbands.

1949

Stengel's Yankees limp to pennant then upset Dodgers

Both the Yankees and Dodgers reached the World Series by the barest of margins for their third postseason meeting of the decade. With the arrival of Casey Stengel at the helm of New York and the slotting of Duke Snider into center field at Ebbets Field, the two clubs also filled out the casts for most of baseball's prominent dramatics in the fifties. In Boston, the whites-only policy of the Red Sox front office found Willie Mays as lacking during a tryout as it had found Jackie Robinson a few years earlier.

The team that Stengel took over was beset by so many injuries that only shortstop Phil Rizzuto had 500 at bats, seven different players manned first base, and catcher Yogi Berra's 91 RBIs were the club high. Through deft platooning and a 21-win season from Vic Raschi, however, the Yankees arrived at the next to last day of the season only a game behind Boston. They overcame a 4-0 deficit to win the Saturday game, then on Sunday rode into the World Series on the strength of rookie second baseman Jerry Coleman's bases-loaded double, prevailing 5-3.

The Red Sox once again had to settle for the prizes handed out to Ted Williams, who was denied his third Triple Crown by an infinitesimal margin. The slugger topped the AL in homers with 43, tied teammate Vern Stephens with 159 RBIs, but lost the batting crown to Detroit's George Kell by the difference of .342911 to .342756. Mel Parnell of the Red Sox had the most victories with 25, Mike Garcia of the Indians the lowest ERA at 2.36.

Robinson's MVP year for the Dodgers was the difference in the NL race. In the first full season of what would become known as the Boys of Summer team, the second baseman led the league with his .342 mark and 37 steals, while scoring 122 runs and knocking in 124. The club also got 100-plus RBIs from first baseman Gil Hodges and right fielder Carl Furillo. Rookie Don Newcombe paced the pitchers with 17 victories.

Around the rest of the league, the loudest bat belonged to Pittsburgh's Ralph Kiner, who had the most homers (54) and RBIs (127). Warren Spahn of the Braves (21) and Howie Pollet of the Cardinals (20) were the only 20-game winners. New York's Dave Koslo had the lowest ERA (2.50). Tragedy was narrowly avoided in June when, in circumstances much like that involving Cubs shortstop Billy Jurges some years earlier, Phillies first baseman Eddie Waitkus was shot in a Chicago hotel room by a woman with a fixation on him. Waitkus eventually recovered to resume his career.

New York's World Series win in five games over Brooklyn wasn't

Ralph Kiner
Pittsburgh's slugger won seven consecutive NL home-run titles, including 1949 when he set career highs with 54 home runs and 127 RBIs.

quite as one-sided as it appeared. The first game was decided by the count of 1-0 when Tommy Henrich homered off Newcombe to lead off the ninth inning. Dodger southpaw Preacher Roe returned the compliment the next day with his own 1-0 win. The third game went to the ninth inning tied 1-1 before the Yankees scored three times and the Dodgers twice. In the fourth game, New York sprinted out to a 6-0 lead, but then Brooklyn came back for a four-run sixth inning before submitting to reliever Allie Reynolds. None of the pitchers did the batters favors. Berra went 1-for-16, Joe DiMaggio 2-for-18, Robinson 3-for-16, and Snider 3-for-21.

1949 SEASON HIGHLIGHTS

NATIONAL LEAGUE

	W	L	Pct.	GB
Brooklyn	97	57	.630	—
St. Louis	96	58	.623	1
Philadelphia	81	73	.526	16
Boston	75	79	.487	22
New York	73	81	.474	24
Pittsburgh	71	83	.461	26
Cincinnati	62	92	.403	35
Chicago	61	93	.396	36

AMERICAN LEAGUE

	W	L	Pct.	GB
New York	97	57	.630	—
Boston	96	58	.623	1
Cleveland	89	65	.578	8
Detroit	87	67	.565	10
Philadelphia	81	73	.526	16
Chicago	63	91	.409	34
St. Louis	53	101	.344	44
Washington	50	104	.325	47

AWARDS

NL MVP: Jackie Robinson, BRO
AL MVP: Ted Williams, BOS
NL Rookie: Don Newcombe, BRO
AL Rookie: Roy Sievers, STL

ALL-STAR GAME

Ebbets Field, Brooklyn
July 12: AL 11, NL 7

POSTSEASON
WORLD SERIES
New York Yankees 4, Brooklyn Dodgers 1
Oct. 5: NEW YORK 1, Brooklyn 0
Oct. 6: Brooklyn 1, NEW YORK 0
Oct. 7: New York 4, BROOKLYN 3
Oct. 8: New York 6, BROOKLYN 4
Oct. 9: New York 10, BROOKLYN 6

Home team in CAPS

> "If you don't win, you're going to be fired. If you do win, you've only put off the day you're going to be fired."
> — Leo Durocher

NATIONAL LEAGUE LEADERS

Home Runs
Kiner-Pit	54
Musial-StL	36
Sauer-Cin-Chi	31
Thomson-NY	27
Gordon-NY	26

Runs Batted In
Kiner-Pit	127
Robinson-Bro	124
Musial-StL	123
Hodges-Bro	115
Ennis-Phi	110

Batting Average
Robinson-Bro	.342
Musial-StL	.338
Slaughter-StL	.336
Furillo-Bro	.322
Kiner-Pit	.310

On Base Percentage
Musial-StL	.438
Robinson-Bro	.432
Kiner-Pit	.432
Slaughter-StL	.418
Stanky-Bos	.417

Slugging Average
Kiner-Pit	.658
Musial-StL	.624
Robinson-Bro	.528
Ennis-Phi	.525
Thomson-NY	.518

Stolen Bases
Robinson-Bro	37
Reese-Bro	26
Four tied	12

Wins
Spahn-Bos	21
Pollet-StL	20
Raffensberger-Cin	18

Innings Pitched
Spahn-Bos	302.1
Raffensberger-Cin	284.0
Jansen-NY	259.2
Heintzelman-Phi	250.0
Newcombe-Bro	244.1

Saves
Wilks-StL	9
Potter-Bos	7
Konstanty-Phi	7
Staley-StL	6
Palica-Bro	6

Strikeouts
Spahn-Bos	151
Newcombe-Bro	149
Jansen-NY	113
Roe-Bro	109
Branca-Bro	109

Earned Run Average
Koslo-NY	2.50
Staley-StL	2.73
Pollet-StL	2.77
Roe-Bro	2.79
Heintzelman-Phi	3.02

Complete Games
Spahn-Bos	25
Raffensberger-Cin	20
Newcombe-Bro	19
Pollet-StL	17
Jansen-NY	17

AMERICAN LEAGUE LEADERS

Home Runs
Williams-Bos	43
Stephens-Bos	39
Four tied	24

Runs Batted In
Williams-Bos	159
Stephens-Bos	159
Wertz-Det	133
Doerr-Bos	109
Chapman-Phi	108

Batting Average
Kell-Det	.343
Williams-Bos	.343
Dillinger-StL	.324
Mitchell-Cle	.317
Doerr-Bos	.309

On Base Percentage
Williams-Bos	.490
Appling-Chi	.439
Joost-Phi	.429
Kell-Det	.424
Michaels-Chi	.417

Slugging Average
Williams-Bos	.650
Stephens-Bos	.539
Henrich-NY	.526
Doerr-Bos	.497
Sievers-StL	.471

Stolen Bases
Dillinger-StL	20
Rizzuto-NY	18
Valo-Phi	14
Philley-Chi	13

Wins
Parnell-Bos	25
Kinder-Bos	23
Lemon-Cle	22
Raschi-NY	21
Kellner-Phi	20

Innings Pitched
Parnell-Bos	295.1
Newhouser-Det	292.0
Lemon-Cle	279.2
Trucks-Det	275.0
Raschi-NY	274.2

Saves
Page-NY	27
Benton-Cle	10
Ferrick-StL	6
Paige-Cle	5

Strikeouts
Trucks-Det	153
Newhouser-Det	144
Lemon-Cle	138
Kinder-Bos	138
Byrne-NY	129

Earned Run Average
Garcia-Cle	2.36
Parnell-Bos	2.77
Trucks-Det	2.81
Hutchinson-Det	2.96
Lemon-Cle	2.99

Complete Games
Parnell-Bos	27
Newhouser-Det	22
Lemon-Cle	22
Raschi-NY	21

THE YEAR IN BASEBALL

February 7: Joe DiMaggio, the Yankees star center fielder, signs a $100,000 contract, first in baseball.

April 19: The Yankees unveil a granite monument to Babe Ruth, along with plaques for Lou Gehrig and Miller Huggins, beyond center field in Yankee Stadium.

April 28: A New York fan charges Leo Durocher with assault, leading to Durocher being suspended.

June 15: Eddie Waitkus of the Phillies is shot by 19-year-old Ruth Steinhagen in a Chicago hotel, but recovers to play the next season.

July 18: Jackie Robinson testifies in front of the House of Un-American Activities committee, and later that day scores twice, once on a steal of home, in a 3-0 win.

August 21: For the first time in seven years, a game is forfeited after a barrage of bottles is hurled from the Philadelphia stands to protest a decision by umpire George Barr.

August 6: Luke Appling appears as a shortstop in his 2,154th game to break Rabbit Maranville's major league record.

September 15: Pirates pitcher Ernie Bonham dies following an appendectomy and stomach surgery.

September 30: Ralph Kiner hits his 54th home run and 16th in September in a 3-2 Pirates win over Cincinnati.

October 2: The Browns use a different pitcher in each of nine innings against White Sox.

October 29: The White Sox acquire young Nellie Fox from the Athletics for catcher Joe Tipton in what may be their best trade ever.

November 21: Bill Veeck sells the Indians for $2.2 million and the new owners install Hank Greenberg as general manager.

December 12: By a 7-1 vote, the AL rejects a proposal to bring back the legal spitball.

1950

Philly Whiz Kids end 35-year drought but fall to Yankees

October delivered what Philadelphia had been awaiting for a long time: the first pennant win by the Phillies since 1915 and the retirement of Connie Mack as the manager of the Athletics after 50 years. Among those who didn't get what they expected were Joe DiMaggio and Ted Williams. For DiMaggio, it was season-long troubles with manager Casey Stengel, who appeared to go out of his way to embarrass his biggest star, especially by moving him to first base. (The switch lasted a single game.) For Williams, it was a broken elbow in the All-Star game that sidelined him for the second half of the season.

Although the final NL standings separated the Phillies from the Dodgers by two games, it was more like two feet. In the ninth inning on the final day of the season, with Philadelphia holding a one-game lead, Brooklyn's Duke Snider singled in what appeared to be a tie-breaking run that would necessitate a playoff the following day. But center fielder Richie Ashburn threw out Cal Abrams at the plate, starter Robin Roberts recovered to get the next two batters, and Dick Sisler walloped a three-run homer in the 10th to give a young Phillies team, remembered today as the "Whiz Kids" their first pennant since 1915.

The main cogs in the triumph were Roberts with 20 wins, reliever Jim Konstanty with 16 wins and 22 saves in 74 tireless appearances (to earn the NL MVP award), and outfielder Del Ennis with 31 homers and an NL-best 126 RBIs. Pittsburgh's Ralph Kiner won his fifth straight homer title (47), St. Louis' Stan Musial won his fourth batting crown (.346), Warren Spahn of the Braves had the most wins with 21, and Jim Hearn divided his league-leading 2.49 ERA between the Cardinals and Giants.

For all his jerking around by Stengel, DiMaggio was able to put together his last big year for the Yankees (.301-32-122) in leading the club to the pennant. Catcher Yogi Berra had an even better season at .322-28-124, while handling a staff anchored by Vic Raschi (21 wins) and Ed Lopat (18). Although Williams was out of the picture in Boston after the All-Star game, the club remained in contention until the bitter end because of some ferocious hitting from Vern Stephens and Walt Dropo (co-RBI leaders at 144), Bobby Doerr (120 RBIs), and Billy Goodman, the only utility player in the 20th century to win a batting title (.354). Cleveland's Al Rosen had the most homers with 37, Cleveland's Bob Lemon the most wins with 23, and Early Wynn of the Indians the lowest ERA at 3.20.

During the season, the Browns became so disconcerted by the

George Kell
After winning his only batting championship in 1949, the Tigers third baseman followed up in 1950 by batting .340 and leading the AL with 218 hits and 56 doubles.

regular battering of their pitching that they hired a hypnotist to inspire self-confidence. The hypnotist, one David F. Tracy, sat around for two games, watched St. Louis lose by the scores of 20-4 and 29-4, and remembered nothing more about the Browns.

The biggest drama in the World Series came in Game 1 when the Phillies, hampered by injuries and the weariness of ace Roberts, were forced to start reliever Konstanty against Raschi. In his first start in four years, the right-hander lost 1-0. When Allie Reynolds came back the next day to defeat ace Roberts, 2-1, there was little to stop New York from a four-game sweep.

1950 SEASON HIGHLIGHTS

NATIONAL LEAGUE

	W	L	Pct.	GB
Philadelphia	91	63	.591	—
Brooklyn	89	65	.578	2
New York	86	68	.558	5
Boston	83	71	.539	8
St. Louis	78	75	.510	12.5
Cincinnati	66	87	.431	24.5
Chicago	64	89	.418	26.5
Pittsburgh	57	96	.373	33.5

AMERICAN LEAGUE

	W	L	Pct.	GB
New York	98	56	.636	—
Detroit	95	59	.617	3
Boston	94	60	.610	4
Cleveland	92	62	.597	6
Washington	67	87	.435	31
Chicago	60	94	.390	38
St. Louis	58	96	.377	40
Philadelphia	52	102	.338	46

AWARDS

NL MVP: Jim Konstanty, PHI
AL MVP: Phil Rizzuto, NY
NL Rookie: Sam Jethroe, BOS
AL Rookie: Walt Dropo, BOS

ALL-STAR GAME

Comiskey Park, Chicago
July 11: NL 4, AL 3

POSTSEASON
WORLD SERIES
New York Yankees 4, Philadelphia Phillies 0
Oct. 4: New York 1, PHILADELPHIA 0
Oct. 5: New York 2, PHILADELPHIA 1
Oct. 6: NEW YORK 3, Philadelphia 2
Oct. 7: NEW YORK 5, Philadelphia 2

Home team in CAPS

"The greatest thrill in the world is to end the game with a home run and watch everybody walk off the field while you're running the bases on air."

— Al Rosen

NATIONAL LEAGUE LEADERS

Home Runs
Kiner-Pit	47
Pafko-Chi	36
Sauer-Chi	32
Hodges-Bro	32

Runs Batted In
Ennis-Phi	126
Kiner-Pit	118
Hodges-Bro	113
Kluszewski-Cin	111
Musial-StL	109

Batting Average
Musial-StL	.346
Robinson-Bro	.328
Snider-Bro	.321
Ennis-Phi	.311
Kluszewski-Cin	.307

On Base Percentage
Stanky-NY	.460
Musial-StL	.437
Robinson-Bro	.423
Glaviano-StL	.421
Torgeson-Bos	.412

Slugging Average
Musial-StL	.596
Pafko-Chi	.591
Kiner-Pit	.590
Gordon-Bos	.557
Snider-Bro	.553

Stolen Bases
Jethroe-Bos	35
Reese-Bro	17
Snider-Bro	16
Torgeson-Bos	15
Ashburn-Phi	14

Wins
Spahn-Bos	21
Sain-Bos	20
Roberts-Phi	20

Innings Pitched
Bickford-Bos	311.2
Roberts-Phi	304.1
Spahn-Bos	293.0
Sain-Bos	278.1
Jansen-NY	275.0

Saves
Konstanty-Phi	22
Werle-Pit	8
Hogue-Bos	7
Branca-Bro	7

Strikeouts
Spahn-Bos	191
Blackwell-Cin	188
Jansen-NY	161
Simmons-Phi	146
Roberts-Phi	146

Earned Run Average
Maglie-NY	2.71
Blackwell-Cin	2.97
Jansen-NY	3.01
Roberts-Phi	3.02
Lanier-StL	3.13

Complete Games
Bickford-Bos	27
Spahn-Bos	25
Sain-Bos	25
Roberts-Phi	21
Jansen-NY	21

AMERICAN LEAGUE LEADERS

Home Runs
Rosen-Cle	37
Dropo-Bos	34
DiMaggio-NY	32
Stephens-Bos	30
Zernial-Chi	29

Runs Batted In
Stephens-Bos	144
Dropo-Bos	144
Berra-NY	124
Wertz-Det	123
DiMaggio-NY	122

Batting Average
Goodman-Bos	.354
Kell-Det	.340
DiMaggio-Bos	.328
Doby-Cle	.326
Zarilla-Bos	.325

On Base Percentage
Doby-Cle	.442
Yost-Was	.440
Pesky-Bos	.437
Fain-Phi	.430
Goodman-Bos	.427

Slugging Average
DiMaggio-NY	.585
Dropo-Bos	.583
Evers-Det	.551
Doby-Cle	.545
Rosen-Cle	.543

Stolen Bases
DiMaggio-Bos	15
Valo-Phi	12
Rizzuto-NY	12
Coan-Was	10
Lipon-Det	9

Wins
B.Lemon-Cle	23
Raschi-NY	21
Houtteman-Det	19

Innings Pitched
B.Lemon-Cle	288.0
Houtteman-Det	274.2
Garver-StL	260.0
Raschi-NY	256.2
Parnell-Bos	249.0

Saves
Harris-Was	15
Page-NY	13
Ferrick-StL-NY	11
Kinder-Bos	9
Brissie-Phi	8

Strikeouts
B.Lemon-Cle	170
Reynolds-NY	160
Raschi-NY	155
Wynn-Cle	143
Feller-Cle	119

Earned Run Average
Wynn-Cle	3.20
Garver-StL	3.39
Feller-Cle	3.43
Lopat-NY	3.47
Houtteman-Det	3.54

Complete Games
B.Lemon-Cle	22
Garver-StL	22
Parnell-Bos	21
Houtteman-Det	21

THE YEAR IN BASEBALL

January 26: Sluggers Jimmie Foxx (534 homers) and Mel Ott (511) are named to the Hall of Fame.

February 7: Ted Williams becomes the highest paid player in history at $125,000.

February 11: KiKi Cuyler dies; his bases-loaded double in the eighth inning of Game 7 won the 1925 World Series.

March 7: J.R. Richard is born; the 6-foot-8 pitcher had been amassing Hall of Fame calibre stats when he suffered a stroke during the 1980 season.

May 3: Baffled by a new rule, Vic Raschi of the Yanks commits a record four balks in one game, two less than the league record at that time for a full season.

June 8: At Fenway Park, the Red Sox slaughter the Browns 29-4. Bobby Doerr has three homers, Ted Williams and Walt Dropo two each, and Al Zarilla has four doubles.

July 4: Braves slugger Sid Gordon hits his fourth grand slam of the season to tie the major league record.

July 11: Ted Williams fractures his left elbow after smashing into the outfield wall while making a leaping catch at the All Star Game.

August 11: Hitting just .279 and mired in a 4-for-38 slump, Joe DiMaggio is benched for the first time in his career.

August 16: Playing at the Polo Grounds, Henry Thompson of the Giants hits two inside-the-park home runs, becoming the first player to do so since 1939.

August 19: Gillette pays $800,000 for TV rights to the World Series, while radio rights sell for $175,000.

August 31: Gil Hodges of the Dodgers hits four homers and a single and bats in nine runs in a 19-3 rout of the Braves at Brooklyn.

September 26: Phils reliever Jim Konstanty sets a major league record by making his 71st relief appearance of the season.

October 1: Dick Sisler's 10th-inning home run clinches the pennant for the Philadelphia Whiz Kids, the Phillies' first pennant in 35 years.

October 3: Phils lefty Curt Simmons is ruled ineligible for the World Series despite being on furlough from the army.

October 18: Connie Mack retires after 50 years as Philadelphia A's manager.

November 4: Grover Cleveland Alexander dies.

November 6: When Branch Rickey's contract as Dodger president is not renewed, he sells his 25 percent interest in the club for a reported $1.05 million and then becomes executive vice president of the Pirates.

December 11: By a 9-7 vote, owners decide the contract of commissioner Happy Chandler will not be renewed.

1951

Thomson big homer heard around world, and in Brooklyn, too

The scene for the most dramatic home run in baseball history was prepared by the Dodgers with a tear from the gate that brought them to a 13-1/2-game lead over the Giants by August 11. But then, following the callup of outfielder Willie Mays from the minors and some shuffling of defensive positions by manager Leo Durocher, the Giants mounted one of the sport's most startling comebacks. Without a great catch and extra-inning home run from Brooklyn's Jackie Robinson on the last day of the season against the Phillies, New York would have won the pennant in regulation time; instead, the two teams met in an improbable best-of-three playoff.

For the second time in five years, the Dodgers went down in an opening playoff contest, but then came back to paste New York, 10-0, behind Clem Labine. The do-or-die third game remained 1-1 until the eighth, when Brooklyn scored three times. But in the bottom of the ninth, against a quickly tiring Don Newcombe, the Giants put together two singles and a double to make it 4-2, runners on second and third with one out. Ralph Branca came out of the bullpen for Brooklyn, Bobby Thomson took a called strike, and then the third baseman launched the three-run homer that made for the Miracle at Coogan's Bluff. It was the second straight year Brooklyn had lost the flag on a home run on the final day of the season.

The key RBI bat in the Giants lineup belonged to Monte Irvin, who drove across a league-leading 121. Sal Maglie and Larry Jansen, who shared the third-game mound prior to the Thomson homer, also shared the most wins title (23). For the sixth consecutive year, the home-run honors went to Pittsburgh's Ralph Kiner with his 42, while Stan Musial of the Cardinals captured his fifth batting crown (.355). Boston's Chet Nichols registered the lowest ERA (2.88).

Compared to the NL, the AL race stopped few hearts, though it wasn't until September 17, when a suicide squeeze by Phil Rizzuto against the Indians put them in first place, that the Yankees took out the lease on their third straight pennant. The New York star was catcher Yogi Berra, not only for his 27 homers and .294 average, but for his handling of the team's Big Three—Ed Lopat (21), Vic Raschi (21), and Allie Reynolds (17). Berra was also behind the plate for the no-hitters thrown during the year by Reynolds against New York's chief rivals, Cleveland and then Boston. Others having big years were Cleveland's Bob Feller (22 wins), Philadelphia's Ferris Fain (.344), Gus Zernial in homers

Bobby Thomson
The third baseman became part of baseball lore with a bottom-of-the-ninth-inning home run that gave his New York Giants a 5-4 win over Brooklyn and a spot in the World Series.

(33) and RBIs (129) while moving between the White Sox and Athletics, and Saul Rogovin for an AL-best 2.78 ERA while shuttling between the Tigers and White Sox.

The Giants still had enough adrenalin going to win two of the first three World Series games, but then the Yankees battered both Maglie and Jansen during three straight wins. Lopat was the hill star with two complete-game victories. The Series marked the end of the career of Joe DiMaggio, who bowed out at 6-for-23, one home run and five RBIs. He was joined in the outfield during the Series by his successor Mickey Mantle.

1951 SEASON HIGHLIGHTS

NATIONAL LEAGUE

	W	L	Pct.	GB
New York	98	59	.624	—
Brooklyn	97	60	.618	1
St. Louis	81	73	.526	15.5
Boston	76	78	.494	20.5
Philadelphia	73	81	.474	23.5
Cincinnati	68	86	.442	28.5
Pittsburgh	64	90	.416	32.5
Chicago	62	92	.403	34.5

AMERICAN LEAGUE

	W	L	Pct.	GB
New York	98	56	.636	—
Cleveland	93	61	.604	5
Boston	87	67	.565	11
Chicago	81	73	.526	17
Detroit	73	81	.474	25
Philadelphia	70	84	.455	28
Washington	62	92	.403	36
St. Louis	52	102	.338	46

AWARDS

NL MVP: Roy Campanella, BRO
AL MVP: Yogi Berra, NY
NL Rookie: Willie Mays, NY
AL Rookie: Gil McDougald, NY

ALL-STAR GAME

Briggs Stadium, Detroit
July 10: NL 8, AL 3

POSTSEASON
WORLD SERIES
New York Yankees 4, New York Giants 2
Oct. 4: Giants 5, YANKEES 1
Oct. 5: YANKEES 3, Giants 1
Oct. 6: GIANTS 6, Yankees 2
Oct. 8: Yankees 6, GIANTS 2
Oct. 9: Yankees 13, GIANTS 1
Oct. 10: YANKEES 4, Giants 3

Home team in CAPS

> "I throw the ball right down the middle. The high-ball hitters swing over it and the low-ball hitters swing under it."
>
> — Saul Rogovin

NATIONAL LEAGUE LEADERS

Home Runs
Kiner-Pit	42
Hodges-Bro	40
Campanella-Bro	33
Thomson-NY	32
Musial-StL	32

Runs Batted In
Irvin-NY	121
Kiner-Pit	109
Gordon-Bos	109
Musial-StL	108
Campanella-Bro	108

Batting Average
Musial-StL	.355
Ashburn-Phi	.344
Robinson-Bro	.338
Campanella-Bro	.325
Irvin-NY	.312

On Base Percentage
Kiner-Pit	.452
Musial-StL	.449
Robinson-Bro	.429
Irvin-NY	.415
Stanky-NY	.401

Slugging Average
Kiner-Pit	.627
Musial-StL	.614
Campanella-Bro	.590
Thomson-NY	.562
Hodges-Bro	.527

Stolen Bases
Jethroe-Bos	35
Ashburn-Phi	29
Robinson-Bro	25
Torgeson-Bos	20
Reese-Bro	20

Wins
Maglie-NY	23
Jansen-NY	23
Spahn-Bos	22
Roe-Bro	22
Roberts-Phi	21

Innings Pitched
Roberts-Phi	315.0
Spahn-Bos	310.2
Maglie-NY	298.0
Dickson-Pit	288.2
Jansen-NY	278.2

Saves
Wilks-StL-Pit	13
Smith-Cin	11
Konstanty-Phi	9
Brazle-StL	7

Strikeouts
Spahn-Bos	164
Newcombe-Bro	164
Maglie-NY	146
Jansen-NY	145
Rush-Chi	129

Earned Run Average
Nichols-Bos	2.88
Maglie-NY	2.93
Spahn-Bos	2.98
Roberts-Phi	3.03
Jansen-NY	3.04

Complete Games
Spahn-Bos	26
Roberts-Phi	22
Maglie-NY	22
Roe-Bro	19
Dickson-Pit	19

AMERICAN LEAGUE LEADERS

Home Runs
Zernial-Chi-Phi	33
Williams-Bos	30
Robinson-Chi	29

Runs Batted In
Zernial-Chi-Phi	129
Williams-Bos	126
Robinson-Chi	117
Easter-Cle	103
Rosen-Cle	102

Batting Average
Fain-Phi	.344
Minoso-Cle-Chi	.326
Kell-Det	.319
Williams-Bos	.318
Fox-Chi	.313

On Base Percentage
Williams-Bos	.464
Fain-Phi	.451
Doby-Cle	.428
Yost-Was	.423
Minoso-Cle-Chi	.422

Slugging Average
Williams-Bos	.556
Doby-Cle	.512
Zernial-Chi-Phi	.511
Wertz-Det	.511
Minoso-Cle-Chi	.500

Stolen Bases
Minoso-Cle-Chi	31
Busby-Chi	26
Rizzuto-NY	18

Wins
Feller-Cle	22
Raschi-NY	21
Lopat-NY	21

Innings Pitched
Wynn-Cle	274.1
Lemon-Cle	263.1
Raschi-NY	258.1
Garcia-Cle	254.0
Feller-Cle	249.2

Saves
Kinder-Bos	14
Scheib-Phi	10
Brissie-Phi-Cle	9
Reynolds-NY	7
Garcia-Cle	6

Strikeouts
Raschi-NY	164
Wynn-Cle	133
Lemon-Cle	132
Gray-Det	131
McDermott-Bos	127

Earned Run Average
Rogovin-Det-Chi	2.78
Lopat-NY	2.91
Wynn-Cle	3.02
Pierce-Chi	3.03
Reynolds-NY	3.05

Complete Games
Garver-StL	24
Wynn-Cle	21
Lopat-NY	20
Pierce-Chi	18

THE YEAR IN BASEBALL

January 29: Baseball signs a six-year, $6 million All Star Game pact for TV-radio rights.

February 9: The St. Louis Browns sign pitcher Satchel Paige, 45, who hadn't played in the majors since 1949.

April 5: Rennie Stennett born; in a nine-inning game on September 16, 1975, he got seven hits in seven trips to the plate.

April 18: Mickey Mantle makes his major league debut, going 1-for-4.

May 25: Willie Mays, hitting .477 when called up from the minors, goes 0-for-5 in his major league debut with the Giants.

July 1: Bob Feller pitches the third no-hitter of his career to tie the major league record held by Cy Young and Larry Corcoran.

July 9: Harry Heilmann dies.

July 12: Allie Reynolds, the Super Chief of the Bronx Bombers, no-hits Cleveland, 1-0, the first of two such classics he will throw this year.

August 19: Eddie Gaedel, 43-inch midget, draws a walk as pinch hitter for Browns.

September 14: In his first big league game, Bob Nieman of the Browns homers in his first two at-bats.

September 20: The owners elect NL president Ford Frick as baseball's third commissioner at a salary of $65,000.

September 30: Jackie Robinson hits a home run in the 14th inning to give the Dodgers a 9-8 win over the Phils and a tie in the National League race with the Giants.

October 3: Bobby Thomson's dramatic homer off Ralph Branca in the ninth with two aboard gives Giants 5-4 victory over Dodgers in the third and final playoff game for pennant.

November 1: Catcher Roy Campanella of Brooklyn is voted the NL's MVP for the first of what will prove to be three times.

November 8: Yankee catcher Yogi Berra wins the first of his three MVP Awards.

1952

Army comes calling; Berra leads Yankees as Braves exit Boston

For the 50th and last time, the same 16 teams took the field Opening Day. Many also took it without key players because of the military draft.

In the NL, the Giants appeared indifferent to a severe ankle injury suffered by their RBI leader Monte Irvin in spring training, winning 16 of their first 18 games. But then the Army came calling for center fielder Willie Mays, and pitchers Sal Maglie and Larry Jansen took to the bench with bad backs, allowing the Dodgers to slip into first. Despite the loss of his own ace Don Newcombe to the military, Brooklyn manager Charlie Dressen tested the baseball gods (and ignored his club's fortunes in 1950 and 1951) when he shrugged off a midseason New York charge with the proclamation that "the Jints is dead." In fact, they were, and mainly because Dressen had found a replacement for Newcombe in Joe Black, a right-hander who notched 15 wins in 54 relief appearances and two starts. The biggest Dodger bat belonged to first baseman Gil Hodges, with 32 homers and 102 RBIs. Around the rest of the league, Ralph Kiner of the Pirates won his seventh straight home run title, tying with Hank Sauer of the Cubs at 37. Sauer also had the most RBIs (121). Stan Musial won his sixth batting title (.336), Robin Roberts of the Phillies had the most wins (28), and Giants fireman Hoyt Wilhelm posted the lowest ERA (2.43).

Cleveland boasted one of the AL's most formidable pitching rotations in decades, but still couldn't cope with New York manager Casey Stengel's ability to mix and match. Stengel's most reliable asset was Allie Reynolds, who completed 24 of his 29 starts, won 20, and led the league with his 2.06 ERA. Although no Yankee broke 100 RBIs, catcher Yogi Berra drove in 98 with 30 homers and Mickey Mantle put his imprint on center field by batting .311 and driving home 87. Cleveland was left with individual achievements—23 wins from Early Wynn, 22 from Bob Lemon and Mike Garcia, Larry Doby's unmatched 32 homers, and Al Rosen's league-best 105 RBIs. Much of the difference between the teams could be traced to Bob Feller's decline to nine wins. The other league honors went to Ferris Fain (second straight batting crown, at .327) and Bobby Shantz (24 victories) of the Athletics.

Home runs and brilliant outfield defense were the motifs of the seven-game World Series struggle won by the Yankees. With New York batting .216 and Brooklyn .215, the homers decided almost every game, with New York's Johnny Mize collecting three and Brooklyn's Duke Snider four. The most dramatic contest was

Bob Lemon
The Indians ace won 20 or more games seven times in 13 seasons, including 1952 when he won 22 and posted career highs with 28 complete games and 309 innings pitched.

Game 5, when Carl Erskine hung tough after surrendering five runs and, with the help of spectacular catches from Snider, Carl Furillo and Andy Pafko, completed an 11-inning victory. Reynolds and Vic Raschi won two each for New York. Brooklyn's biggest disappointment was Hodges, hitless in a record 21 at bats.

On September 21, the Dodgers also played (and won) the final game at Braves Field. Boston's move to Milwaukee for the 1953 season was the first franchise transfer since Baltimore's switch to New York in 1903. It would be far from the last one in the decade.

1952 SEASON HIGHLIGHTS

NATIONAL LEAGUE

	W	L	Pct.	GB
Brooklyn	96	57	.627	—
New York	92	62	.597	4.5
St. Louis	88	66	.571	8.5
Philadelphia	87	67	.565	9.5
Chicago	77	77	.500	19.5
Cincinnati	69	85	.448	27.5
Boston	64	89	.418	32
Pittsburgh	42	112	.273	54.5

AMERICAN LEAGUE

	W	L	Pct.	GB
New York	95	59	.617	—
Cleveland	93	61	.604	2
Chicago	81	73	.526	14
Philadelphia	79	75	.513	16
Washington	78	76	.506	17
Boston	76	78	.494	19
St. Louis	64	90	.416	31
Detroit	50	104	.325	45

AWARDS

NL MVP: Hank Sauer, CHI
AL MVP: Bobby Shantz, PHI
NL Rookie: Joe Black, BRO
AL Rookie: Harry Byrd, PHI

ALL-STAR GAME

Shibe Park, Philadelphia
July 8: NL 3, AL 2

POSTSEASON
WORLD SERIES
New York Yankees 4, Brooklyn Dodgers 3
Oct. 1: BROOKLYN 4, New York 2
Oct. 2: New York 7, BROOKLYN 1
Oct. 3: Brooklyn 5, NEW YORK 3
Oct. 4: NEW YORK 2, Brooklyn 0
Oct. 5: Brooklyn 6, NEW YORK 5
Oct. 6: New York 3, BROOKLYN 2
Oct. 7: New York 4, BROOKLYN 2

Home team in CAPS

"All pitchers are liars and crybabies."

— Yogi Berra

NATIONAL LEAGUE LEADERS

Home Runs		Runs Batted In		Batting Average	
Sauer-Chi	37	Sauer-Chi	121	Musial-StL	.336
Kiner-Pit	37	Thomson-NY	108	Kluszewski-Cin	.320
Hodges-Bro	32	Ennis-Phi	107	Robinson-Bro	.308
Mathews-Bos	25	Hodges-Bro	102	Snider-Bro	.303
Gordon-Bos	25	Slaughter-StL	101	Schoendienst-StL	.303

On Base Percentage		Slugging Average		Stolen Bases	
Robinson-Bro	.440	Musial-StL	.538	Reese-Bro	30
Musial-StL	.432	Sauer-Chi	.531	Jethroe-Bos	28
Hemus-StL	.392	Kluszewski-Cin	.509	Robinson-Bro	24
Hodges-Bro	.386	Kiner-Pit	.500	Ashburn-Phi	16
Slaughter-StL	.386	Hodges-Bro	.500		

Wins		Innings Pitched		Saves	
Roberts-Phi	28	Roberts-Phi	330.0	Brazle-StL	16
Maglie-NY	18	Spahn-Bos	290.0	Black-Bro	15
Staley-StL	17	Dickson-Pit	277.2	Wilhelm-NY	11
Rush-Chi	17	Rush-Chi	250.1	Leonard-Chi	11
Raffensberger-Cin	17	Raffensberger-Cin	247.0		

Strikeouts		Earned Run Average		Complete Games	
Spahn-Bos	183	Wilhelm-NY	2.43	Roberts-Phi	30
Rush-Chi	157	Hacker-Chi	2.58	Dickson-Pit	21
Roberts-Phi	148	Roberts-Phi	2.59	Spahn-Bos	19
Mizell-StL	146	Loes-Bro	2.69	Raffensberger-Cin	18
Simmons-Phi	141	Rush-Chi	2.70	Rush-Chi	17

AMERICAN LEAGUE LEADERS

Home Runs		Runs Batted In		Batting Average	
Doby-Cle	32	Rosen-Cle	105	Fain-Phi	.327
Easter-Cle	31	Robinson-Chi	104	Mitchell-Cle	.323
Berra-NY	30	Doby-Cle	104	Mantle-NY	.311
Dropo-Bos-Det	29	Zernial-Phi	100	Kell-Det-Bos	.311
Zernial-Phi	29	Berra-NY	98	Goodman-Bos	.306

On Base Percentage		Slugging Average		Stolen Bases	
Fain-Phi	.438	Doby-Cle	.541	Minoso-Chi	22
Valo-Phi	.432	Mantle-NY	.530	Rivera-StL-Chi	21
Mantle-NY	.394	Rosen-Cle	.524	Jensen-NY-Was	18
Joost-Phi	.388	Easter-Cle	.513	Rizzuto-NY	17
Rosen-Cle	.387	Wertz-Det-StL	.506	Throneberry-Bos	16

Wins		Innings Pitched		Saves	
Shantz-Phi	24	Lemon-Cle	309.2	Dorish-Chi	11
Wynn-Cle	23	Garcia-Cle	292.1	Paige-StL	10
Lemon-Cle	22	Wynn-Cle	285.2	Sain-NY	7
Garcia-Cle	22	Shantz-Phi	279.2		
Reynolds-NY	20	Pierce-Chi	255.1		

Strikeouts		Earned Run Average		Complete Games	
Reynolds-NY	160	Reynolds-NY	2.06	Lemon-Cle	28
Wynn-Cle	153	Garcia-Cle	2.37	Shantz-Phi	27
Shantz-Phi	152	Shantz-Phi	2.48	Reynolds-NY	24
Pierce-Chi	144	Lemon-Cle	2.50	Wynn-Cle	19
Garcia-Cle	143	Dobson-Chi	2.51	Garcia-Cle	19

THE YEAR IN BASEBALL

February 16: After 55 years as a player and coach, Honus Wagner, 77, retires.

April 23: Hoyt Wilhelm of the Giants wins his first major league game, and in the process hits a home run in his first at bat, followed by a triple. Although he pitched in 1,069 games after this day, he never hit another homer or triple.

April 30: In his last at-bat before heading off to Korea as a Marine fighter pilot, Ted Williams hits a game-winning, two-run home run.

May 15: Having pitched four no-hitters in the minors, Virgil Trucks of the Tigers hurls his first in the majors (against the Senators) and adds another before the season is out (August 25 against Yankees).

May 21: Nineteen successive Dodger batters reach base in the first inning against Cincinnati.

May 28: Willie Mays enters the army, and the Giants lose eight of their next 10 games.

June 14: Warren Spahn ties the NL record with 18 strikeouts in a 3-1, 15-inning loss to the Cubs.

July 30: Commissioner Ford Frick implements a rule to prevent interleague trades unless the player first clears waivers in his own league. He also bans trades after July 31.

August 25: Virgil Trucks of the Detroit Tigers gets credit for his second no-hitter of the season after a ball hit by Phil Rizzuto is initially ruled an error by Johnny Pesky, changed to a hit and then changed back to an error.

September 15: The Braves play their last game in Boston before moving to Milwaukee.

1953

Snider, Campanella each top 40 homers, but Yanks win again

The Braves moved not only from Boston to Milwaukee, but from the nether regions of the NL to second place. Although finishing well behind the Dodgers, the team drew a league-record 1,826,397 through the gates of County Stadium and animated other parks with large parties of traveling boosters.

With ace Don Newcombe still in the Army, the Dodgers concentrated on pulverizing the league offensively. Duke Snider and Roy Campanella became the league's first teammates to top 40 homers; the same pair plus Gil Hodges batted in over 100; Carl Furillo won the hitting title (.344); and five lineup regulars topped .300. Carl Erskine took over Newcombe's top spot in the rotation, winning 20. Milwaukee's ascent as Brooklyn's chief rival did little to dampen the routine furies between the Dodgers and Giants. On September 6, Furillo responded to an afternoon of beanballs and taunting by charging the New York dugout in search of manager Leo Durocher and broke his hand during a scuffle with several Giants. His compensation was being able to sit on his .344 average while Red Schoendienst and Stan Musial of the Cardinals sought vainly to overtake him.

Eddie Mathews of the Braves finally broke Ralph Kiner's grip on the home run title by belting 47, but had help from Pirates general manager Branch Rickey, who traded the Pittsburgh slugger to the Cubs during the season. Campanella's 142 RBIs were the most in the NL, as were the 23 wins by Warren Spahn of the Braves and Robin Roberts of the Phillies. Spahn also registered the lowest ERA (2.10).

In the AL, the Yankees won an unprecedented fifth straight pennant, and without much trouble following an 18-game winning streak in May. Catcher Yogi Berra produced the biggest offensive numbers for the fourth straight year (.296-27-108), but Mickey Mantle made the single biggest impression with a mammoth April home run off Chuck Stobbs in Washington. The blast, estimated as having traveled more than 500 feet by a Yankees publicist, popularized the use of tape measures for calculating home runs. Washington's Mickey Vernon won the batting title (.337) thanks in part to Senators baserunners who got themselves thrown out deliberately during the final game so the first baseman wouldn't have to make another plate appearance. The antics helped prevent Cleveland's Al Rosen (.336-43-145) from winning a Triple Crown. Bob Porterfield of the Senators racked up the most wins (22), Ed Lopat of the Yankees the lowest ERA (2.42).

Mantle and second baseman Billy Martin drove in 15 runs between them in New York's six-game World Series triumph over Brooklyn. The infielder's single (his 12th hit of the postseason) in the ninth inning of Game 6 erased a dramatic game-tying homer from Furillo in the top of the frame and made it five world titles in five tries for Stengel.

On September 27, the Browns played their final game, prior to a franchise shift to Baltimore for the 1954 season. Appropriately enough, the tattered franchise ran out of new balls during the game and was reduced to using a gash-dented batting practice ball. Also appropriately, St. Louis lost the contest to the White Sox, its 100th defeat of the year.

Roy Campanella
The standout Dodger catcher had a career year in 1953, swatting 41 home runs, batting .312 and leading the NL with 142 RBIs.

1953 SEASON HIGHLIGHTS

NATIONAL LEAGUE

	W	L	Pct.	GB
Brooklyn	105	49	.682	—
Milwaukee	92	62	.597	13
St. Louis	83	71	.539	22
Philadelphia	83	71	.539	22
New York	70	84	.455	35
Cincinnati	68	86	.442	37
Chicago	65	89	.422	40
Pittsburgh	50	104	.325	55

AMERICAN LEAGUE

	W	L	Pct.	GB
New York	99	52	.656	—
Cleveland	92	62	.597	8.5
Chicago	89	65	.578	11.5
Boston	84	69	.549	16
Washington	76	76	.500	23.5
Detroit	60	94	.390	40.5
Philadelphia	59	95	.383	41.5
St. Louis	54	100	.351	46.5

AWARDS

NL MVP: Roy Campanella, BRO
AL MVP: Al Rosen, CLE
NL Rookie: Jim Gilliam, BRO
AL Rookie: Harvey Kuenn, DET

ALL-STAR GAME
Crosley Field, Cincinnati
July 14: NL 5, AL 1

POSTSEASON
WORLD SERIES
New York Yankees 4, Brooklyn Dodgers 2
Sept. 30: NEW YORK 9, Brooklyn 5
Oct. 1: NEW YORK 4, Brooklyn 2
Oct. 2: BROOKLYN 3, New York 2
Oct. 3: BROOKLYN 7, New York 3
Oct. 4: New York 11, BROOKLYN 7
Oct. 5: NEW YORK 4, Brooklyn 3

Home team in CAPS

"Carrots might be good for my eyes, but they won't straighten out the curveball."

— Carl Furillo

NATIONAL LEAGUE LEADERS

Home Runs
Mathews-Mil	47
Snider-Bro	42
Campanella-Bro	41
Kluszewski-Cin	40
Kiner-Pit-Chi	35

Runs Batted In
Campanella-Bro	142
Mathews-Mil	135
Snider-Bro	126
Ennis-Phi	125
Hodges-Bro	122

Batting Average
Furillo-Bro	.344
Schoendienst-StL	.342
Musial-StL	.337
Snider-Bro	.336
Mueller-NY	.333

On Base Percentage
Musial-StL	.437
Robinson-Bro	.425
Snider-Bro	.419
Irvin-NY	.406
Mathews-Mil	.406

Slugging Average
Snider-Bro	.627
Mathews-Mil	.627
Campanella-Bro	.611
Musial-StL	.609
Furillo-Bro	.580

Stolen Bases
Bruton-Mil	26
Reese-Bro	22
Gilliam-Bro	21
Robinson-Bro	17
Snider-Bro	16

Wins
Spahn-Mil	23
Roberts-Phi	23
Haddix-StL	20
Erskine-Bro	20
Staley-StL	18

Innings Pitched
Roberts-Phi	346.2
Spahn-Mil	265.2
Haddix-StL	253.0
Erskine-Bro	246.2
Simmons-Phi	238.0

Saves
Brazle-StL	18
Wilhelm-NY	15
Hughes-Bro	9
Leonard-Chi	8
Burdette-Mil	8

Strikeouts
Roberts-Phi	198
Erskine-Bro	187
Mizell-StL	173
Haddix-StL	163
Spahn-Mil	148

Earned Run Average
Spahn-Mil	2.10
Roberts-Phi	2.75
Haddix-StL	3.06
Antonelli-Mil	3.18
Simmons-Phi	3.21

Complete Games
Roberts-Phi	33
Spahn-Mil	24
Simmons-Phi	19
Haddix-StL	19
Erskine-Bro	16

AMERICAN LEAGUE LEADERS

Home Runs
Rosen-Cle	43
Zernial-Phi	42
Doby-Cle	29
Berra-NY	27
Boone-Cle-Det	26

Runs Batted In
Rosen-Cle	145
Vernon-Was	115
Boone-Cle-Det	114
Zernial-Phi	108
Berra-NY	108

Batting Average
Vernon-Was	.337
Rosen-Cle	.336
Goodman-Bos	.313
Minoso-Chi	.313
Busby-Was	.312

On Base Percentage
Woodling-NY	.429
Rosen-Cle	.422
Minoso-Chi	.410
Fain-Chi	.405
Yost-Was	.403

Slugging Average
Rosen-Cle	.613
Zernial-Phi	.559
Berra-NY	.523
Boone-Cle-Det	.519
Vernon-Was	.518

Stolen Bases
Minoso-Chi	25
Rivera-Chi	22
Jensen-Was	18
Philley-Phi	13
Busby-Was	13

Wins
Porterfield-Was	22
Parnell-Bos	21
B.Lemon-Cle	21
Trucks-StL-Chi	20

Innings Pitched
B.Lemon-Cle	286.2
Garcia-Cle	271.2
Pierce-Chi	271.1
Trucks-StL-Chi	264.1
Porterfield-Was	255.0

Saves
Kinder-Bos	27
Dorish-Chi	18
Reynolds-NY	13
Paige-StL	11
Sain-NY	9

Strikeouts
Pierce-Chi	186
Trucks-StL-Chi	149
Wynn-Cle	138
Parnell-Bos	136
Garcia-Cle	134

Earned Run Average
Lopat-NY	2.42
Pierce-Chi	2.72
Trucks-StL-Chi	2.93
Sain-NY	3.00
Ford-NY	3.00

Complete Games
Porterfield-Was	24
B.Lemon-Cle	23
Garcia-Cle	21
Pierce-Chi	19
Trucks-StL-Chi	17

THE YEAR IN BASEBALL

February 19: Ted Williams safely crash lands his fighter jet while serving in Korea.

February 20: August A. Busch buys the Cardinals for $3.75 million and pledges to keep the team in St. Louis.

March 18: The Boston Braves move to Milwaukee, becoming the first franchise to move since 1903.

April 9: August A. Busch buys Sportsman's Park for $800,000.

April 13: For the first time in half a century, a new city is represented in the American and National Leagues. The Braves move from Boston to Milwaukee and open in Cincinnati where Max Surkont set down the Reds 2-0.

April 17: Mickey Mantle of the Yankees blasts the longest measured home run, clearing left-field wall in Washington for a flight of 565 feet.

April 29: Joe Adcock becomes the first player to homer into the center-field bleachers at the Polo Grounds, more than 475 feet away.

May 6: In his debut as a starting pitcher, Alva "Bobo" Holloman of the Browns pitches a no-hitter.

May 25: Ralph Kiner becomes the 12th player to hit 300 career home runs.

June 18: Red Sox rookie outfielder Gene Stephens becomes the first AL player to get three hits in the same inning.

August 6: Ted Williams returns to the Red Sox lineup after military service in Korea.

August 23: Phil Paine pitches in nine games in Japan while serving in the military, becoming the first ex-major leaguer to play in Japan.

September 6: Roy Campanella sets the major league, single season record for home runs by a catcher when he strokes No. 38 to pass Gabby Hartnett (1930).

October 29: The sale of the St. Louis AL franchise is completed, and the venerable Browns become the Baltimore Orioles.

November 24: Relative unknown Walter Alston signs a one-year contract to manage the Dodgers.

1954

Indians ride pitching to 111 wins but Mays steals the spotlight

The Indians finally got tired of playing runner-up and ended the Yankees streak of five consecutive pennants. To reach the postseason, however, they had to win a then-record 111 games, while New York won more (103) than during any of its five flag years.

Although outhit by the Yankees, Cleveland's staff ERA of 2.78 was the lowest in the AL since 1918. The chief contributors to the mark were righties Bob Lemon and Early Wynn, who each won a league-best 23; Mike Garcia, who paced the circuit with his 2.64 ERA (while winning another 19); and rookies Ray Narleski and Don Mossi, who came out of the bullpen for a combined 9 wins and 20 saves. The offense was concentrated around Al Rosen for his 102 RBIs and, especially, Bobby Avila for his .341 batting title and Larry Doby for the most homers (32) and RBIs (126).

In the NL, the return of Willie Mays from the Army and the acquisition of southpaw Johnny Antonelli from the Braves motored the Giants to a pennant. Mays put in his first serious bid as the best player of his era when he won the batting title (.345), clouted 33 doubles, 13 triples, and 41 homers, and drove in 110 runs. Antonelli's 21 wins and league-best 2.76 ERA anchored a staff heavily dependent on relievers Hoyt Wilhelm and Marv Grissom; between them, the knuckleballer Wilhelm and screwballer Grissom won 22 and saved 26. Brooklyn hopes of catching New York faded when catcher Roy Campanella broke his hand and Don Newcombe returned from the military much rustier than Mays, winning merely nine times. For the second year in a row, though, the Dodgers produced two 40-plus home run hitters—this time Duke Snider and Gil Hodges.

Next to Mays, the NL's loudest bat in 1954 belonged to Cincinnati's Ted Kluszewski, who led the way in both homers (49) and RBIs (141). Robin Roberts of the Phillies won 23—the third time in four years he registered the most victories. The trade that brought Antonelli to the Giants also had the unintended effect of hastening the arrival of another future Hall of Famer to the league. When the player obtained for the pitcher, 1951 playoff hero Bobby Thomson, broke his ankle in spring training, Milwaukee gave his outfield slot to Hank Aaron.

Against every expectation, the Giants swept the Indians in four games in the World Series. The highlight was The Catch in the first game—Mays' incredible over-the-shoulder grab of a Vic Wertz drive to the outer expanses of the Polo Grounds with two runners on for Cleveland. The grab, together with an equally improbable rocket throw back to the infield, aborted a big rally and set New York up for an extra-inning victory. In six at-bats, pinch-hitter and backup outfielder Dusty Rhodes had two singles, two homers, and seven RBIs.

On September 26, the Athletics defeated the Yankees in what turned out to be the final game played by the Philadelphia franchise in the AL; the following season, the A's called Kansas City home. A couple of months later, the Yankees were also involved in the biggest trade in major league history—a two-step, 18-player transaction that ultimately came down to New York acquiring right-handers Bob Turley and Don Larsen.

Willie Mays
Perhaps the greatest World Series catch ever, Mays corralled a Vic Wertz blast at the Polo Grounds in a Giants sweep of the Indians.

1954 SEASON HIGHLIGHTS

NATIONAL LEAGUE

	W	L	Pct.	GB
New York	97	57	.630	—
Brooklyn	92	62	.597	5
Milwaukee	89	65	.578	8
Philadelphia	75	79	.487	22
Cincinnati	74	80	.481	23
St. Louis	72	82	.468	25
Chicago	64	90	.416	33
Pittsburgh	53	101	.344	44

AMERICAN LEAGUE

	W	L	Pct.	GB
Cleveland	111	43	.721	—
New York	103	51	.669	8
Chicago	94	60	.610	17
Boston	69	85	.448	42
Detroit	68	86	.442	43
Washington	66	88	.429	45
Baltimore	54	100	.351	57
Philadelphia	51	103	.331	60

AWARDS

NL MVP: Willie Mays, NY
AL MVP: Yogi Berra, NY
NL Rookie: Wally Moon, STL
AL Rookie: Bob Grim, NY

ALL-STAR GAME
Municipal Stadium, Cleveland
July 13: AL 11, NL 9

POSTSEASON
WORLD SERIES
New York Giants 4, Cleveland Indians 0
Sep. 29: New York 5, Cleveland 2
Sep. 30: New York 3, Cleveland 1
Oct. 1: New York 6, Cleveland 4
Oct. 2: New York 7, Cleveland 4

Home team in CAPS

"I'm not sure I know what the hell charisma is, but I get the feeling it's Willie Mays."

— Ted Kluszewski

NATIONAL LEAGUE LEADERS

Home Runs
Kluszewski-Cin	49
Hodges-Bro	42
Sauer-Chi	41
Mays-NY	41

Runs Batted In
Kluszewski-Cin	141
Snider-Bro	130
Hodges-Bro	130
Musial-StL	126
Ennis-Phi	119

Batting Average
Mays-NY	.345
Mueller-NY	.342
Snider-Bro	.341
Musial-StL	.330
Kluszewski-Cin	.326

On Base Percentage
Ashburn-Phi	.442
Musial-StL	.433
Mathews-Mil	.428
Snider-Bro	.427
Mays-NY	.415

Slugging Average
Mays-NY	.667
Snider-Bro	.647
Kluszewski-Cin	.642
Musial-StL	.607
Mathews-Mil	.603

Stolen Bases
Bruton-Mil	34
Temple-Cin	21
Fondy-Chi	20
Moon-StL	18
Ashburn-Phi	11

Wins
Roberts-Phi	23
Spahn-Mil	21
Antonelli-NY	21
Haddix-StL	18
Erskine-Bro	18

Innings Pitched
Roberts-Phi	336.2
Spahn-Mil	283.1
Erskine-Bro	260.1
Haddix-StL	259.2
Antonelli-NY	258.2

Saves
Hughes-Bro	24
Smith-Cin	20
Grissom-NY	19
Jolly-Mil	10
Hetki-Pit	9

Strikeouts
Roberts-Phi	185
Haddix-StL	184
Erskine-Bro	166
Antonelli-NY	152
Spahn-Mil	136

Earned Run Average
Antonelli-NY	2.30
Burdette-Mil	2.76
Simmons-Phi	2.81
Gomez-NY	2.88
Conley-Mil	2.96

Complete Games
Roberts-Phi	29
Spahn-Mil	23
Simmons-Phi	21
Antonelli-NY	18

AMERICAN LEAGUE LEADERS

Home Runs
Doby-Cle	32
Williams-Bos	29
Mantle-NY	27
Jensen-Bos	25

Runs Batted In
Doby-Cle	126
Berra-NY	125
Jensen-Bos	117
Minoso-Chi	116

Batting Average
Williams-Bos	.345
Avila-Cle	.341
Minoso-Chi	.320
Noren-NY	.319
Fox-Chi	.319

On Base Percentage
Williams-Bos	.516
Minoso-Chi	.416
Rosen-Cle	.412
Mantle-NY	.411
Yost-Was	.406

Slugging Average
Williams-Bos	.635
Minoso-Chi	.535
Mantle-NY	.525
Rosen-Cle	.506
Vernon-Was	.492

Stolen Bases
Jensen-Bos	22
Rivera-Chi	18
Minoso-Chi	18
Jacobs-Phi	17
Busby-Was	17

Wins
Wynn-Cle	23
Lemon-Cle	23
Grim-NY	20
Trucks-Chi	19
Garcia-Cle	19

Innings Pitched
Wynn-Cle	270.2
Trucks-Chi	264.2
Garcia-Cle	258.2
Lemon-Cle	258.1
Gromek-Det	252.2

Saves
Sain-NY	22
Kinder-Bos	15
Narleski-Cle	13

Strikeouts
Turley-Bal	185
Wynn-Cle	155
Trucks-Chi	152
Pierce-Chi	148
Harshman-Chi	134

Earned Run Average
Garcia-Cle	2.64
Lemon-Cle	2.72
Wynn-Cle	2.73
Gromek-Det	2.74
Trucks-Chi	2.79

Complete Games
Porterfield-Was	21
Lemon-Cle	21
Wynn-Cle	20
Gromek-Det	17

THE YEAR IN BASEBALL

January 14: Joe DiMaggio and Marilyn Monroe get married.

January 30: Braves trade Johnny Antonelli, Don Liddle, Ebba St. Claire to NY for Bobby Thomson and Sam Calderone.

March 13: Bobby Thomson, newly acquired by the Braves, suffers a triple fracture of his right ankle against Yankees to open a spot in the lineup for Hank Aaron.

March 14: Aaron starts first exhibition game and gets three hits, including a homer, vs. Red Sox.

March 29: Phil Cavarretta becomes the first manager ever fired in spring training after he gives Cubs owner Phil Wrigely an honest assessment of the team's poor chances.

April 13: Returning to the Giants after two years in the army, Willie Mays hits a two-run homer that beats Brooklyn 4-3.

April 23: At Sportsman's Park, Hank Aaron hits the first home run of his career.

May 2: Stan Musial sets a major league mark with five homers in a doubleheader against the Giants (later tied by Nate Colbert).

July 28: Jim Bagby, Sr. dies; he won 31 games for the champion Indians of 1920

July 31: Joe Adcock of Milwaukee unloads on the Dodgers for a record 18 total bases—four homers and a two-bagger.

August 1: Joe Adcock's slugging rampage of the previous day is followed by his beaning by Clem Labine at Ebbets Field.

August 29: The Milwaukee Braves set an NL season attendance record of 1,841,666 on their way to a season total of 2,131,388.

September 10: Unable to handle Hoyt Wilhelm's knuckleball, catcher Ray Katt sets a major league record with four passed balls in one inning.

September 12: A record crowd of 86,587 jams Cleveland's Memorial Stadium to watch an Indians-Yankees doubleheader.

September 26: Karl Spooner hurls his second shutout in his second major league start, equaling the record of Al Spalding, John M. Ward, Jim Hughes, and Al Worthington.

September 29: In Game 1 of the World Series, Willie Mays makes one of the greatest catches in history as he tracks down a Vic Wertz line drive in deep center field.

October 28: Arnold Johnson buys a controlling interest in the Philadelphia Athletics from the Mack family for $3.5 million and moves the team to Kansas City.

November 27: Orioles and Yankees swap 18 players.

1955

The Boys of Summer pound out Series win over Berra's Yankees

After a decade-and-a-half of promising "Wait 'til Next Year," Dodger fans finally got the calendar they wanted, defeating the Yankees in the World Series. In getting there, Brooklyn streaked out of the gate with 10 straight wins and 22 victories in its first 24 games. In the AL, the New York path to the sixth postseason meeting with the Dodgers since 1941 was marked by the first black player (catcher Elston Howard) on the club roster and by immediate signs that the new Kansas City home of the Athletics was operating as a major league farm club for the Bronx.

Statistically, Brooklyn was led on the mound by Don Newcombe (20 wins) and Clem Labine (13 wins and 11 saves). But in midseason when the club hit its only big snag, it quickly recovered again thanks to rookies Roger Craig and Don Bessent, called up from the minors for a double-header they proceeded to sweep. The offense came from the bulwarks of the Boys of Summer—Duke Snider, Roy Campanella, Gil Hodges, and Carl Furillo all hitting at least 26 homers and all but Furillo driving home 100 runs. Snider's 136 RBIs paced the league. The club's September 8 clinching was the earliest in league history. Second-place Milwaukee's main consolation was the blossoming of Hank Aaron with his first 100-RBI season, while the Giants had to settle for Willie Mays' home run title (51). The other bests were Richie Ashburn of the Phillies for batting (.338), teammate Robin Roberts for victories (23), and Pittsburgh's Bob Friend for ERA (2.63).

In the AL, the Yankees again entrusted most of their offense to Yogi Berra (27 homers and 108 RBIs) and Mickey Mantle (a league-leading 37 homers). An almost totally reshaped rotation counted most heavily on Whitey Ford (18), Bob Turley (17), and comeback southpaw Tommy Byrne (16). Cleveland's ability to keep pace most of the year owed significantly to the emergence of Herb Score (16 wins and a league-tops 245 strikeouts) as a third arm to go with Bob Lemon and Early Wynn, but the fading of Mike Garcia and Bob Feller on the mound and just about everybody in the batter's box proved insurmountable. Ford, Lemon and Boston's Frank Sullivan had the most wins with 18, Chicago's Billy Pierce the best ERA at 1.97. At the age of 20, Detroit's Al Kaline became the game's youngest batting champion (.340), while Ray Boone of the Tigers and Jackie Jensen of the Red Sox tied at 116 RBIs.

The Yankees started off the World Series with two quick wins at Yankee Stadium. For the third game, Brooklyn manager Walter

Yogi Berra
The Yankees perennial all-star won his second consecutive MVP award after 27 home runs and 108 RBIs to lead New York to another World Series, won by Brooklyn.

Alstron went to southpaw Johnny Podres, whose season record had been an uninspiring 8-10. Not only did Podres pitch a complete-game victory, but Brooklyn won the next two, as well. After Ford evened the Series back in the Bronx, Podres took the hill in the showdown seventh game against Byrne. The title was ultimately decided by a Berra drive down the left-field line in the sixth inning with two runners on base; defensive replacement Sandy Amoros grabbed it while running full steam toward the stands, then started a relay back to the infield for a double play. Podres went on from there for another complete game, this one a 2-0 shutout.

1955 SEASON HIGHLIGHTS

NATIONAL LEAGUE

	W	L	Pct.	GB
Brooklyn	98	55	.641	—
Milwaukee	85	69	.552	13.5
New York	80	74	.519	18.5
Philadelphia	77	77	.500	21.5
Cincinnati	75	79	.487	23.5
Chicago	72	81	.471	26
St. Louis	68	86	.442	30.5
Pittsburgh	60	94	.390	38.5

AMERICAN LEAGUE

	W	L	Pct.	GB
New York	96	58	.623	—
Cleveland	93	61	.604	3
Chicago	91	63	.591	5
Boston	84	70	.545	12
Detroit	79	75	.513	17
Kansas City	63	91	.409	33
Baltimore	57	97	.370	39
Washington	53	101	.344	43

AWARDS

NL MVP: Roy Campanella, BRO
AL MVP: Yogi Berra, NY
NL Rookie: Bill Virdon, STL
AL Rookie: Herb Score, CLE

ALL-STAR GAME

County Stadium, Milwaukee
July 12: NL 6, AL 5

POSTSEASON
WORLD SERIES
Brooklyn Dodgers 4, New York Yankees 3
Sep. 28: New York 6, Brooklyn 5
Sep. 29: New York 4, Brooklyn 2
Sep. 30: Brooklyn 8, New York 3
Oct. 1: Brooklyn 8, New York 5
Oct. 2: Brooklyn 5, New York 3
Oct. 3: New York 5, Brooklyn 1
Oct. 4: Brooklyn 2, New York 0
MVP: Johnny Podres, Brooklyn

Home team in CAPS

> **"That's too bad. They're the only team I can beat."**
> — Dave Cole, after his trade to the Phillies in 1955

NATIONAL LEAGUE LEADERS

Home Runs
Mays-NY	51
Kluszewski-Cin	47
Banks-Chi	44
Snider-Bro	42
Mathews-Mil	41

Runs Batted In
Snider-Bro	136
Mays-NY	127
Ennis-Phi	120
Banks-Chi	117
Kluszewski-Cin	113

Batting Average
Ashburn-Phi	.338
Mays-NY	.319
Musial-StL	.319
Campanella-Bro	.318
Aaron-Mil	.314

On Base Percentage
Ashburn-Phi	.449
Snider-Bro	.421
Mathews-Mil	.417
Musial-StL	.411
Mays-NY	.404

Slugging Average
Mays-NY	.659
Snider-Bro	.628
Mathews-Mil	.601
Banks-Chi	.596
Kluszewski-Cin	.585

Stolen Bases
Bruton-Mil	25
Mays-NY	24
Boyer-StL	22
Temple-Cin	19
Gilliam-Bro	15

Wins
Roberts-Phi	23
Newcombe-Bro	20
Spahn-Mil	17
Nuxhall-Cin	17

Innings Pitched
Roberts-Phi	305.0
Nuxhall-Cin	257.0
Spahn-Mil	245.2
Jones-Chi	241.2
Antonelli-NY	235.1

Saves
Meyer-Phi	16
Roebuck-Bro	12
Labine-Bro	11
Freeman-Cin	11
Grissom-NY	8

Strikeouts
Jones-Chi	198
Roberts-Phi	160
Haddix-StL	150
Newcombe-Bro	143
Antonelli-NY	143

Earned Run Average
Friend-Pit	2.83
Newcombe-Bro	3.20
Buhl-Mil	3.21
Spahn-Mil	3.26
Roberts-Phi	3.28

Complete Games
Roberts-Phi	26
Newcombe-Bro	17
Spahn-Mil	16

AMERICAN LEAGUE LEADERS

Home Runs
Mantle-NY	37
Zernial-KC	30
Williams-Bos	28

Runs Batted In
Jensen-Bos	116
Boone-Det	116
Berra-NY	108
Sievers-Was	106
Kaline-Det	102

Batting Average
Kaline-Det	.340
Power-KC	.319
Kell-Chi	.312
Fox-Chi	.311
Kuenn-Det	.306

On Base Percentage
Mantle-NY	.433
Kaline-Det	.425
Smith-Cle	.411
Yost-Was	.410
Goodman-Bos	.397

Slugging Average
Mantle-NY	.611
Kaline-Det	.546
Doby-Cle	.505
Power-KC	.505
Sievers-Was	.489

Stolen Bases
Rivera-Chi	25
Minoso-Chi	19
Jensen-Bos	16
Busby-Was-Chi	12
Smith-Cle	11

Wins
F.Sullivan-Bos	18
Lemon-Cle	18
Ford-NY	18
Wynn-Cle	17
Turley-NY	17

Innings Pitched
F.Sullivan-Bos	260.0
Ford-NY	253.2
Turley-NY	246.2
Wilson-Bal	235.1
Lary-Det	235.0

Saves
Narleski-Cle	19
Kinder-Bos	18
Gorman-KC	18
Konstanty-NY	11
Morgan-NY	10

Strikeouts
Score-Cle	245
Turley-NY	210
Pierce-Chi	157
Ford-NY	137
Hoeft-Det	133

Earned Run Average
Pierce-Chi	1.97
Ford-NY	2.63
Wynn-Cle	2.82
Score-Cle	2.85
F.Sullivan-Bos	2.91

Complete Games
Ford-NY	18
Hoeft-Det	17
Five tied	16

THE YEAR IN BASEBALL

April 11: Chuck Tanner hits a homer on the first pitch he sees in the major leagues.

April 12: A crowd of 32,844 turns out to see the debut of the Kansas City A's.

May 12: Sam "Toothpick" Jones of the Cubs pitches a no-hit, no-run game. In the ninth against Pittsburgh, he walks the bases full and then fans the next three batters.

June 8: The Dodgers option Tommy Lasorda to Montreal to make room on the roster for Sandy Koufax.

June 24: Harmon Killebrew, 18, hits his first major league roundtripper off Billy Hoeft at Griffith Stadium.

July 19: Reliever Babe Birrer of Detroit pitches four innings and connects for two three-run homers.

August 15: A homer off Mel Wright in Sportsman's park gives pitcher Warren Spahn a home run in every National League stadium.

September 14: Herb Score of the Indians breaks Grover Cleveland Alexander's rookie record of 235 strikeouts. He finishes with 245.

September 19: Ernie Banks sets a major league record by hitting his fifth grand slam of the season.

September 20: Willie Mays becomes only the seventh player to record 50 home runs in a season.

September 25: Detroit's Al Kaline becomes the youngest batting champion in history, taking the AL crown at age 20.

October 4: The Brooklyn Dodgers win their first World Series with Johnny Podres blanking the Yankees 2-0 in the final game, aided by Sandy Amoros' great catch.

1956

Mantle outstanding and Larsen perfect as O'Malley bristles

The Dodgers and Braves were franchises going in opposite directions, but the former still had enough left to beat out the latter for the NL pennant. In the AL, Mickey Mantle put up the superstar numbers that had been predicted for him since his arrival in 1951.

Brooklyn played much of its season under the cloud of ultimatums from owner Walter O'Malley that he wanted out of Ebbets Field or else. To advance his cause for a new stadium, O'Malley transferred seven home games to Jersey City. On the field, the team wrestled all year with well-balanced Milwaukee and homer-happy Cincinnati. Despite tying the league record for team home runs (221), the Reds were on the sidelines as the Braves and Dodgers entered the final weekend with a single game between them. Then Brooklyn swept the Pirates and St. Louis took two of three from Milwaukee to keep the pennant in Ebbets Field. Don Newcombe blazed through the league with a 27-7 record, but a second Dodger pitcher, Sal Maglie, proved invaluable. Obtained from the Indians in late May, the one-time Dodger nemesis from the Giants won 13, including a no-hitter against the Phillies in the final week of the season. Duke Snider (an NL-tops 43 homers) was the only Dodger reaching 100 RBIs. Milwaukee stayed close on the strength of Hank Aaron's batting title (.328), 75 home runs between Eddie Mathews and Joe Adcock, 20 wins from Warren Spahn, and Lew Burdette's 2.70 ERA. In swatting their 221 homers, the Reds got at least 28 from five players. The RBI leader was Stan Musial of the Cardinals (109).

Mantle's Triple Crown performance (.353-52-130) steered New York past three 20-game winners on the Indians—Early Wynn, Herb Score and Bob Lemon. Catcher Yogi Berra chipped in with another big offensive year (30-105) while negotiating a staff that, after ace Whitey Ford (19 wins and an AL-best 2.47 ERA), was an ongoing experiment because of mediocre years from Bob Turley and Don Larsen. Ultimately, the salvation of the rotation were 22-year-old Johnny Kucks (22) and the previously untested Tom Sturdivant (16). Frank Lary of the Tigers had the league's most wins (21).

The seventh and last Brooklyn-Bronx World Series got off to an unusual start when the Dodgers won the first two games and the Yankees had to come back in the third and fourth contests. All that turned out to be a prelude to Game 5, when Larsen pitched the only no-hitter (and perfect game) in World Series history, defeating Maglie 2-0. The Dodgers came back in Game 6, when Jackie Robinson drove in the only run in the 10th inning to end a pitching duel between Turley and Clem Labine. But with the help of two home runs from Berra and a grand slam from Bill Skowron, Kucks ended matters the next day with a three-hit shutout.

Following the season, the Dodgers announced the trade of Robinson to the Giants for pitcher Dick Littlefield—a transaction voided when Robinson announced his retirement. For his part, however, O'Malley did not void his announced sale of Ebbets Field in stepping up pressures for a new stadium.

Don Larsen
Yogi Berra is the first to congratulate the Yankee pitcher after Larsen's perfect outing against Brooklyn in Game 5 of the World Series.

1956 SEASON HIGHLIGHTS

NATIONAL LEAGUE

	W	L	Pct.	GB
Brooklyn	93	61	.604	—
Milwaukee	92	62	.597	1
Cincinnati	91	63	.591	2
St. Louis	76	78	.494	17
Philadelphia	71	83	.461	22
New York	67	87	.435	26
Pittsburgh	66	88	.429	27
Chicago	60	94	.390	33

AMERICAN LEAGUE

	W	L	Pct.	GB
New York	97	57	.630	—
Cleveland	88	66	.571	9
Chicago	85	69	.552	12
Boston	84	70	.545	13
Detroit	82	72	.532	15
Baltimore	69	85	.448	28
Washington	59	95	.383	38
Kansas City	52	102	.338	45

AWARDS

NL MVP: Don Newcombe, BRO
AL MVP: Mickey Mantle, NY
Cy Young: Don Newcombe, BRO
NL Rookie: Frank Robinson, CIN
AL Rookie: Luis Aparicio, CHI

ALL-STAR GAME
Griffith Stadium, Washington
July 10: NL 7, AL 3

POSTSEASON
WORLD SERIES
New York Yankees 4, Brooklyn Dodgers 3
Oct. 3: Brooklyn 6, New York 3
Oct. 5: Brooklyn 13, New York 8
Oct. 6: New York 5, Brooklyn 3
Oct. 7: New York 6, Brooklyn 2
Oct. 8: New York 2, Brooklyn 0
Oct. 9: Brooklyn 1, New York 0
Oct. 10: New York 9, Brooklyn 0
MVP: Don Larsen, New York

Home team in CAPS

> "Guessing what the pitcher is going to throw is 80 percent of being a successful hitter. The other 20 percent is just execution."
>
> — Hank Aaron

NATIONAL LEAGUE LEADERS

Home Runs
Snider-Bro	43
Robinson-Cin	38
Adcock-Mil	38
Mathews-Mil	37

On Base Percentage
Snider-Bro	.402
Gilliam-Bro	.400
Musial-StL	.390
Moon-StL	.390
Jones-Phi	.387

Wins
Newcombe-Bro	27
Spahn-Mil	20
Antonelli-NY	20

Strikeouts
Jones-Chi	176
Haddix-StL-Phi	170
Friend-Pit	166
Roberts-Phi	157
Mizell-StL	153

Runs Batted In
Musial-StL	109
Adcock-Mil	103
Kluszewski-Cin	102
Snider-Bro	101
Boyer-StL	98

Slugging Average
Snider-Bro	.598
Adcock-Mil	.597
Aaron-Mil	.558
Robinson-Cin	.558
Mays-NY	.557

Innings Pitched
Friend-Pit	314.1
Roberts-Phi	297.1
Spahn-Mil	281.1
Newcombe-Bro	268.0
Kline-Pit	264.0

Earned Run Average
Burdette-Mil	2.70
Spahn-Mil	2.78
Antonelli-NY	2.86
Maglie-Bro	2.87
Newcombe-Bro	3.06

Batting Average
Aaron-Mil	.328
Virdon-StL-Pit	.319
Clemente-Pit	.311
Musial-StL	.310
Boyer-StL	.306

Stolen Bases
Mays-NY	40
Gilliam-Bro	21
White-NY	15
Temple-Cin	14
Reese-Bro	13

Saves
Labine-Bro	19
Freeman-Cin	18
Lown-Chi	13
Jackson-StL	9
Bessent-Bro	9

Complete Games
Roberts-Phi	22
Spahn-Mil	20
Friend-Pit	19
Newcombe-Bro	18
Burdette-Mil	16

AMERICAN LEAGUE LEADERS

Home Runs
Mantle-NY	52
Wertz-Cle	32
Berra-NY	30
Sievers-Was	29
Maxwell-Det	28

On Base Percentage
Williams-Bos	.479
Mantle-NY	.467
Nieman-Chi-Bal	.438
Minoso-Chi	.430
Maxwell-Det	.420

Wins
Lary-Det	21
Five tied	20

Strikeouts
Score-Cle	263
Pierce-Chi	192
Foytack-Det	184
Hoeft-Det	172
Lary-Det	165

Runs Batted In
Mantle-NY	130
Kaline-Det	128
Wertz-Cle	106
Simpson-KC	105
Berra-NY	105

Slugging Average
Mantle-NY	.705
Williams-Bos	.605
Maxwell-Det	.534
Berra-NY	.534
Kaline-Det	.530

Innings Pitched
Lary-Det	294.0
Wynn-Cle	277.2
Pierce-Chi	276.1
Foytack-Det	256.0
Lemon-Cle	255.1

Earned Run Average
Ford-NY	2.47
Score-Chi	2.53
Wynn-Cle	2.72
Lemon-Cle	3.03
Harshman-Chi	3.10

Batting Average
Mantle-NY	.353
Williams-Bos	.345
Kuenn-Det	.332
Maxwell-Det	.326
Nieman-Chi-Bal	.320

Stolen Bases
Aparicio-Chi	21
Rivera-Chi	20
Avila-Cle	17
Minoso-Chi	12

Saves
Zuverink-Bal	16
Mossi-Cle	11
Morgan-NY	11
Shantz-KC	9
Delock-Bos	9

Complete Games
Pierce-Chi	21
Lemon-Cle	21
Lary-Det	20

THE YEAR IN BASEBALL

February 8: Connie Mack, who was the A's field manager for 50 years, dies at age 93.

February 15: The Pirates and A's cancel an exhibition game in Birmingham, Ala. because of a local ordinance barring interracial competiton.

April 24: AL umpire Frank Umont is the first to wear glasses in a regular-season game.

May 18: Mickey Mantle homers from both sides of the plate for the third time in his career, breaking the mark held by Jim Russell.

May 28: Dale Long of the Pirates connects for his eighth home run in eight consecutive games, a record later tied by Don Mattingly.

July 6: Jim Busby hits second grand slam in two days; these are only two of his 13-year career.

July 6: Commissioner Ford Frick inaugurates the Cy Young Award to honor the outstanding pitcher each year as selected by the Baseball Writers Association of America.

August 7: The Boston Red Sox fine Ted Williams $5,000 for spitting at Boston fans, who had booed Williams after he misplayed a wind-blown fly ball by Mickey Mantle.

September 11: Frank Robinson ties the NL record for home runs by a rookie by swatting No. 38.

September 18: En route to a batting triple crown, Mickey Mantle hits his 50th home run of the season.

September 30: White Sox hurler Jim Derrington, 16 years, 10 months, becomes the youngest pitcher since 1900 to start a game, which he loses 7-6.

October 8: In what is still the only no-hitter in Series history, Don Larsen of the Yankees pitches a perfect game against Brooklyn.

November 14: Mickey Mantle is the unanimous MVP of the AL.

November 21: Brooklyn's Don Newcombe becomes first to win NL's MVP and Cy Young Award.

December 13: The Dodgers trade Jackie Robinson to the Giants for pitcher Dick Littlefield and $35,000, but Robinson retires.

1957

Aaron powers Braves in swan-song season for Dodgers, Giants

Ted Williams
At age 38 the Red Sox slugger flirted with .400 before winning his fifth AL batting crown with a .388 average, while hitting 38 home runs.

The Boys of Summer era ended in more ways than one. While the Braves took over the top rung from the Dodgers in on-field NL competition, Brooklyn owner Walter O'Malley completed arrangements for moving his club to Los Angeles for the 1958 season. Part of his preparations involved getting a commitment from the Giants (a condition imposed by the league for travel and scheduling reasons) that they would move at the same time to San Francisco.

Neither Brooklyn nor any other club posed much of a pennant challenge to Milwaukee. The Braves' drive was spearheaded by Hank Aaron (.322 with a league-best 44 homers and 132 RBIs) and Warren Spahn (most wins, 22). Equally important, the club was able to get key mideason reinforcements in second baseman Red Schoendienst (.310) from the Giants and outfielder Bob Hazle from the minors (.403 in 134 at bats). Stan Musial of the Cardinals won his seventh and last batting title (.351), Johnny Podres of the Dodgers registered the lowest ERA (2.66). The fourth-place Reds settled for being the most popular club. When Cincinnati fans stuffed All-Star ballot boxes to elect every home-team regular except first baseman George Crowe to the NL's starting lineup, league president Ford Frick stepped in to bench shortstop Roy McMillan and third baseman Don Hoak, as well. Frick used the ballot stuffing as an excuse to take All-Star voting away from fans for the next 12 years.

In the AL, the Yankees needed some weeks to overcome a fast start by the surprising White Sox, but thereafter had little trouble

winning their eighth flag in nine years. While the New York attack outside Mickey Mantle's 34 home runs registered few impressive numbers, manager Casey Stengel's adroit use of the bench and platoon players again proved decisive. Tom Sturdivant's 16 wins topped the staff. Cleveland, already on the decline because of the age of its veterans, suffered another blow in May, when its new ace Herb Score was struck in the eye by a line drive off the bat of New York's Gil McDougald; it was the beginning of the end for Score. The year's pitching honors went to Chicago's Billy Pierce and Detroit's Jim Bunning for their 20 wins and to New York's Bobby Shantz for his 2.45 ERA. At the age of 38, Ted Williams of the Red Sox won his fifth batting title (.388). Roy Sievers of the Senators had both the most homers (42) and most RBIs (114).

The seven-game World Series belonged to Lew Burdette, with the Braves right-hander throwing three complete-game victories, including two shutouts. Offensively, Aaron was the prominent story in a meager .209 team effort, clouting three homers and a triple among his 11 hits and driving in seven runs.

The end to NL ball in New York came on September 29, when the Giants were blown out by the Pirates at the Polo Grounds, 9-1, and the Dodgers bowed to the Phillies in Philadelphia, 2-1. Among those on hand for the last New York game was Jack Doyle, who had managed the club briefly in 1895. The defection of the Dodgers opened up decades of debate as to whether it was the chief agent of Brooklyn's ensuing social and economic problems.

1957 SEASON HIGHLIGHTS

NATIONAL LEAGUE

	W	L	Pct.	GB
Milwaukee	95	59	.617	—
St. Louis	87	67	.565	8
Brooklyn	84	70	.545	11
Cincinnati	80	74	.519	15
Philadelphia	77	77	.500	18
New York	69	85	.448	26
Pittsburgh	62	92	.403	33
Chicago	62	92	.403	33

AMERICAN LEAGUE

	W	L	Pct.	GB
New York	98	56	.636	—
Chicago	90	64	.584	8
Boston	82	72	.532	16
Detroit	78	76	.506	20
Baltimore	76	76	.500	21
Cleveland	76	77	.497	21.5
Kansas City	59	94	.386	38.5
Washington	55	99	.357	43

AWARDS

NL MVP: Hank Aaron, MIL
AL MVP: Mickey Mantle, NY
Cy Young: Warren Spahn, MIL
NL Rookie: Jack Sanford, PHI
AL Rookie: Tony Kubek, NY
GOLD GLOVES
ML: Bobby Shantz, P; Sherm Lollar, C; Gil Hodges, 1B; Nellie Fox, 2B; Frank Malzone, 3B; Roy McMillan, SS; Minnie Minoso, Al Kaline, Willie Mays, OF

ALL-STAR GAME
Sportsman's Park, St. Louis
July 9: AL 6, NL 5

POSTSEASON
WORLD SERIES
Milwaukee Braves 4, New York Yankees 3
Oct. 2: New York 3, Milwaukee 1
Oct. 3: Milwaukee 4, New York 2
Oct. 5: New York 12, Milwaukee 3
Oct. 6: Milwaukee 7, New York 5
Oct. 7: Milwaukee 1, New York 0
Oct. 9: New York 3, Milwaukee 2
Oct. 10: Milwaukee 5, New York 0
MVP: Lew Burdette, Milwaukee

Home team in CAPS

"If you don't catch the ball, you catch the bus."

— Rocky Bridges

NATIONAL LEAGUE LEADERS

Home Runs

Aaron-Mil	44
Banks-Chi	43
Snider-Bro	40
Mays-NY	35
Mathews-Mil	32

Runs Batted In

Aaron-Mil	132
Ennis-StL	105
Musial-StL	102
Banks-Chi	102
Hodges-Bro	98

Batting Average

Musial-StL	.351
Mays-NY	.333
Robinson-Cin	.322
Aaron-Mil	.322
Groat-Pit	.315

On Base Percentage

Musial-StL	.428
Mays-NY	.411
Bouchee-Phi	.396
Ashburn-Phi	.392
Temple-Cin	.391

Slugging Average

Mays-NY	.626
Musial-StL	.612
Aaron-Mil	.600
Snider-Bro	.587
Banks-Chi	.579

Stolen Bases

Mays-NY	38
Gilliam-Bro	26
Blasingame-StL	21
Temple-Cin	19
Fernandez-Phi	18

Wins

Spahn-Mil	21
Sanford-Phi	19
Buhl-Mil	18
Drysdale-Bro	17
Burdette-Mil	17

Innings Pitched

Friend-Pit	277.0
Spahn-Mil	271.0
Burdette-Mil	256.2
Lawrence-Cin	250.1
Roberts-Phi	249.2

Saves

Labine-Bro	17
Grissom-NY	14
Lown-Chi	12
Wilhelm-StL	11

Strikeouts

Sanford-Phi	188
Drott-Chi	170
Drabowsky-Chi	170
Jones-StL	154
Drysdale-Bro	148

Earned Run Average

Podres-Bro	2.66
Drysdale-Bro	2.69
Spahn-Mil	2.69
Buhl-Mil	2.74
Law-Pit	2.87

Complete Games

Spahn-Mil	18
Friend-Pit	17
Gomez-NY	16
Sanford-Phi	15

AMERICAN LEAGUE LEADERS

Home Runs

Sievers-Was	42
Williams-Bos	38
Mantle-NY	34
Wertz-Cle	28
Zernial-KC	27

Runs Batted In

Sievers-Was	114
Wertz-Cle	105
Minoso-Chi	103
Malzone-Bos	103
Jensen-Bos	103

Batting Average

Williams-Bos	.388
Mantle-NY	.365
Woodling-Cle	.321
Boyd-Bal	.318
Fox-Chi	.317

On Base Percentage

Williams-Bos	.528
Mantle-NY	.515
Minoso-Chi	.413
Woodling-Cle	.412
Fox-Chi	.404

Slugging Average

Williams-Bos	.731
Mantle-NY	.665
Sievers-Was	.579
Woodling-Cle	.521
Wertz-Cle	.485

Stolen Bases

Aparicio-Chi	28
Rivera-Chi	18
Minoso-Chi	18
Mantle-NY	16

Wins

Pierce-Chi	20
Bunning-Det	20
Sturdivant-NY	16
Donovan-Chi	16
Brewer-Bos	16

Innings Pitched

Bunning-Det	267.1
Wynn-Cle	263.0
Pierce-Chi	257.0
Johnson-Bal	242.0
F.Sullivan-Bos	240.2

Saves

Grim-NY	19
Narleski-Cle	16
Delock-Bos	11
Zuverink-Bal	9
Clevenger-Was	8

Strikeouts

Wynn-Cle	184
Bunning-Det	182
Johnson-Bal	177
Pierce-Chi	171
Turley-NY	152

Earned Run Average

Shantz-NY	2.45
Sturdivant-NY	2.54
Bunning-Det	2.69
Turley-NY	2.71
F.Sullivan-Bos	2.73

Complete Games

Pierce-Chi	16
Donovan-Chi	16
Brewer-Bos	15

THE YEAR IN BASEBALL

January 4: The Dodgers become the first major league team to own their own airplane when they purchase a 44-passenger, twin-engine plane for $750,000.

February 28: The U.S. Supreme Court decides 6-3 that baseball is the only professional sport exempt from antitrust laws.

May 7: Gil McDougald of the Yankees hits a line drive that hits Herb Score in the face, causing Score to leave the game on a stretcher with lacerations and a broken nose.

May 16: Celebrating Billy Martin's 29th birthday, several Yankees become embroiled in a brawl at Manhattan's Copacabana Club, leading to $5,500 in fines and the eventual trading of Martin to Kansas City.

May 28: The NL approves the transfer of the Dodgers and Giants to California, on condition they move at the same time.

June 12: Stan Musial sets an NL consecutive-game record by appearing in Game No. 823.

June 13: Ted Williams becomes the first AL player to hit three home runs in a game twice in the same season.

June 28: After Cincinnati fans stuff the ballot box to select eight Reds starters for the All Star Game, commissioner Ford Frick names Stan Musial, Willie Mays and Hank Aaron to replace Reds Gus Bell, George Crowe and Wally Post.

July 8: Commissioner Ford Frick is re-elected by the owners to a second seven-year term.

August 1: Gil Hodges sets an NL record by hitting his 13th career grand slam.

August 17: In the same at-bat by Richie Ashburn, spectator Alice Roth suffers a broken nose on a foul ball and is hit a second time while being loaded onto a stretcher.

September 3: Warren Spahn hurls his 41st career shutout, an NL record for left-handers.

September 22: Duke Snider hits his 40th home, the last ever at Ebbets Field, to tie Ralph Kiner's NL record of five-consecutive 40-homer seasons.

September 24: Ted Williams is retired by Hal Griggs, snapping a streak of 16 straight times on base, a record.

November 22: Mantle wins the AL MVP Award, 233 points to 232 by Williams, who hit .388 at age 39, the second time Williams lost MVP honors by one point.

1958

Dodgers toast of L.A., Mays forlorn in S.F. as Braves take pennant

The arrival of major league baseball in California didn't divert the Braves and Yankees from renewing their acquaintanceship in the postseason, but that was about all it didn't affect. With the bizarrely spacious Memorial Coliseum as its temporary home, Los Angeles shattered all NL attendance records, starting with an April 18 Opening Day crowd of 78,672. On the other hand, the Dodgers on the field showed little during their inaugural West Coast season but their age, dropping toward the bottom of the second division for the first time since World War II. Abetting the plunge was an off-season automobile accident that left star catcher Roy Campanella paralyzed for life. Another factor was the configuration of the home field—a 251-foot fence in left field, but a huge power alley in right that neutralized the offense of chief slugger Duke Snider. In San Francisco, Willie Mays discovered that his frequent laments about being forced to leave New York only encouraged Giants fans to embrace rookie Orlando Cepeda rather than him as their favorite son.

The Braves made relatively quick work of the pennant race, with only the surprising Pirates posing anything like a challenge. The Milwaukee effort was captained from the mound by Warren Spahn (a league-leading 22 wins) and Lew Burdette (20), while Hank Aaron and Eddie Mathews both topped the 30-homer mark. Pittsburgh, near the bottom of the league since the end of World War II, soared in the standings thanks largely to Bob Friend (tied with Spahn at 22 wins) on the mound and Frank Thomas (35 homers, 109 RBIs) at the plate. Aside from Thomas, the only NLer to reach 100 RBIs was Ernie Banks of Chicago, who led in both that department (129) and with his 47 homers. Richie Ashburn of the Phillies won the batting championship (.350), Stu Miller of the Giants had the lowest ERA (2.47).

In the AL, the Yankees won their fourth straight pennant behind four category leaders: Bob Turley for wins (21), Whitey Ford for ERA (2.01), fireballing Ryne Duren for saves (20), and Mickey Mantle for home runs (42). The other league leaders came from the Red Sox—Ted Williams with his sixth and last batting title (.328) and Jackie Jensen with the most RBIs (122). Suspicions about New York's control over Kansas City exploded in June when Cleveland sent star prospect Roger Maris to the Athletics in a five-player deal; under pressure from owners who predicted Maris would be quickly sent on to the Bronx, AL president Will Harridge warned the A's to keep the young slugger in a Kansas City uniform. They did what they were told—until after the 1959 season.

For one of the rare times in their history, the Yankees took the role of underdog in the World Series, and that was even before losing three of the first four games. But then Turley, who had been knocked out in the first inning of Game 2, ran up a shutout, two wins, and a save over the final three games for a comeback championship. New York's offensive star was out-fielder Hank Bauer, who had ten hits, four home runs, and eight runs batted in.

Ernie Banks
The popular Cubs shortstop led the NL with 47 home runs and 129 RBIs, as well as posting a league-best .614 slugging average.

1958 SEASON HIGHLIGHTS

NATIONAL LEAGUE

	W	L	Pct.	GB
Milwaukee	92	62	.597	—
Pittsburgh	84	70	.545	8
San Francisco	80	74	.519	12
Cincinnati	76	78	.494	16
St. Louis	72	82	.468	20
Chicago	72	82	.468	20
Los Angeles	71	83	.461	21
Philadelphia	69	85	.448	23

AMERICAN LEAGUE

	W	L	Pct.	GB
New York	92	62	.597	—
Chicago	82	72	.532	10
Boston	79	75	.513	13
Cleveland	77	76	.503	14.5
Detroit	77	77	.500	15
Baltimore	74	79	.484	17.5
Kansas City	73	81	.474	19
Washington	61	93	.396	31

AWARDS

NL MVP: Ernie Banks, CHI
AL MVP: Jackie Jensen, BOS
Cy Young: Bob Turley, NY
NL Rookie: Orlando Cepeda, SF
AL Rookie: Albie Pearson, WAS

GOLD GLOVES
NL: Harvey Haddix, P; Del Crandall, C; Gil Hodges, 1B; Bill Mazeroski, 2B; Ken Boyer, 3B; Roy McMillan, SS; Hank Aaron, Frank Robinson, Willie Mays, OF
AL: Bobby Shantz, P; Sherm Lollar, C; Vic Power, 1B; Frank Bolling, 2B; Frank Malzone, 3B; Luis Aparicio, SS; Norm Siebern, Al Kaline, Jim Piersall, OF

ALL-STAR GAME

Memorial Stadium, Baltimore
July 8: AL 4, NL 3

POSTSEASON
WORLD SERIES
New York Yankees 4, Milwaukee Braves 3

Oct. 1: Milwaukee 4, New York 3
Oct. 2: Milwaukee 13, New York 5
Oct. 4: New York 4, Milwaukee 0
Oct. 5: Milwaukee 3, New York 0
Oct. 6: New York 7, Milwaukee 0
Oct. 8: New York 4, Milwaukee 3
Oct. 9: New York 6, Milwaukee 2
MVP: Bob Turley, New York

Home team in CAPS

"The only way to prove that you're a good sport is to lose."

— Ernie Banks

NATIONAL LEAGUE LEADERS

Home Runs
Banks-Chi	47
Thomas-Pit	35
Robinson-Cin	31
Mathews-Mil	31
Aaron-Mil	30

Runs Batted In
Banks-Chi	129
Thomas-Pit	109
H.Anderson-Phi	97
Mays-SF	96
Cepeda-SF	96

Batting Average
Ashburn-Phi	.350
Mays-SF	.347
Musial-StL	.337
Aaron-Mil	.326
Skinner-Pit	.321

On Base Percentage
Ashburn-Phi	.441
Musial-StL	.426
Mays-SF	.423
Temple-Cin	.406
Skinner-Pit	.390

Slugging Average
Banks-Chi	.614
Mays-SF	.583
Aaron-Mil	.546
Thomas-Pit	.528
Musial-StL	.528

Stolen Bases
Mays-SF	31
Ashburn-Phi	30
T.Taylor-Chi	21
Blasingame-StL	20
Gilliam-LA	18

Wins
Spahn-Mil	22
Friend-Pit	22
Burdette-Mil	20
Roberts-Phi	17
Purkey-Cin	17

Innings Pitched
Spahn-Mil	290.0
Burdette-Mil	275.1
Friend-Pit	274.0
Roberts-Phi	269.2

Saves
Face-Pit	20
Labine-LA	14
Farrell-Phi	11

Strikeouts
Jones-StL	225
Spahn-Mil	150
Podres-LA	143
Antonelli-SF	143
Friend-Pit	135

Earned Run Average
Miller-SF	2.47
Jones-StL	2.88
Burdette-Mil	2.91
Spahn-Mil	3.07
Roberts-Phi	3.24

Complete Games
Spahn-Mil	23
Roberts-Phi	21
Burdette-Mil	19
Purkey-Cin	17
Friend-Pit	16

AMERICAN LEAGUE LEADERS

Home Runs
Mantle-NY	42
Colavito-Cle	41
Sievers-Was	39
Cerv-KC	38
Jensen-Bos	35

Runs Batted In
Jensen-Bos	122
Colavito-Cle	113
Sievers-Was	108
Cerv-KC	104
Mantle-NY	97

Batting Average
Williams-Bos	.328
Runnels-Bos	.322
Kuenn-Det	.319
Kaline-Det	.313
Power-KC-Cle	.312

On Base Percentage
Williams-Bos	.462
Mantle-NY	.445
Runnels-Bos	.418
Colavito-Cle	.407
Jensen-Bos	.398

Slugging Average
Colavito-Cle	.620
Cerv-KC	.592
Mantle-NY	.592
Williams-Bos	.584
Sievers-Was	.544

Stolen Bases
Aparicio-Chi	29
Rivera-Chi	21
Landis-Chi	19
Mantle-NY	18
Minoso-Cle	14

Wins
Turley-NY	21
Pierce-Chi	17
McLish-Cle	16
Lary-Det	16

Innings Pitched
Lary-Det	260.1
Ramos-Was	259.1
Donovan-Chi	248.0
Turley-NY	245.1
Pierce-Chi	245.0

Saves
Duren-NY	20
Hyde-Was	18
Kiely-Bos	12
Wall-Bos	10

Strikeouts
Wynn-Chi	179
Bunning-Det	177
Turley-NY	168
Harshman-Bal	161
Pascual-Was	146

Earned Run Average
Ford-NY	2.01
Pierce-Chi	2.68
Harshman-Bal	2.89
Lary-Det	2.90
O'Dell-Bal	2.97

Complete Games
Turley-NY	19
Pierce-Chi	19
Lary-Det	19
Harshman-Bal	17

THE YEAR IN BASEBALL

January 15: In a deal worth more than $1 million, the Yankees announce that they will televise 140 games in 1958.

January 29: Dodgers catcher Roy Campanella suffers a broken neck in an auto accident and is left permanently paralyzed below the waist.

January 30: Commissioner Ford Frick announces that players and coaches, not fans, will vote for the All Star teams.

February 6: Ted Williams becomes the highest paid player in baseball history when the Red Sox sign him for $135,000.

March 11: The league announces that, starting immediately, players will be required to wear batting helmets.

April 7: The Dodgers erect a 42-foot screen in left field to reduce home runs down the line, which measures just 250 feet.

April 15: Big league ball comes to California as the Giants defeat the Dodgers in their home opener at Seals Stadium in San Francisco.

April 18: Following a downtown parade in the morning, the Dodgers first game in Los Angeles draws a record crowd of 78,682 to the Coliseum.

May 13: Stan Musial becomes the eighth player in baseball history to collect 3,000 hits.

June 27: Billy Pierce of the White Sox retires 26 Washington batters in a row before pinch hitter Ed Fitzgerald doubles for the only hit. Pierce wins, 1-0.

August 14: Vic Power, Cleveland first baseman, steals home twice; he stole only one other base all year.

August 28: White Sox second baseman Nellie Fox sets a record for consecutive games without a strikeout (98).

September 13: Warren Spahn becomes the first lefty to win 20 or more games nine times.

September 20: Baltimore's Hoyt Wilhelm, still winless (0-6) as a starter after his relief career foundered, revives his fortunes by no-hitting New York.

1959

93,000 greet Campanella; Dodgers win playoff and top Sox in Series

The two California teams rebounded from their orientation problems to engage Milwaukee in a three-team NL pennant struggle down to the final days of the season. In the AL, Al Lopez, who as manager of the 1954 Indians had interrupted New York's five straight flags, stopped another Bronx skein at four from his role as the dugout boss of the White Sox.

With only eight games left on the NL schedule, the Giants held a two-game lead over Los Angeles and Milwaukee and were debating about whether or not to open still-unfinished Candlestick Park for the World Series. The question became moot when San Francisco blew seven of its remaining games, including three straight to the Dodgers. Los Angeles also had better luck in best-of-three playoffs than its Brooklyn forebears in 1946 and 1951: After finishing the season in a flat-footed tie with the Braves, the club parlayed some clutch hitting from its bench and an error by shortstop Felix Mantilla to finish off Milwaukee in two games. The key ingredients of the Los Angeles victory were 17 wins from Don Drysdale, comeback years from both Duke Snider and Gil Hodges, and, especially, veteran Wally Moon's ability to exploit the Coliseum's left-field screen with so-called "Moon Shots" in clutch situations. Milwaukee reached the playoffs thanks largely to its veterans—Hank Aaron who won the batting title (.355), Eddie Mathews who led in homers (46), their combined 85 homers and 237 RBIs, and the league-best 21 wins from both Warren Spahn and Lew Burdette. Sam Jones of the Giants not only tied Spahn and Burdette for victories, but also notched the lowest ERA (2.83). Ernie Banks of the Cubs drove in the most runs (143).

On May 7, an unprecedented 93,103 fans turned out at the Coliseum to pay tribute to paralyzed Brooklyn Dodger star Roy Campanella. On May 26, Harvey Haddix of the Pirates lost baseball's most magnificently pitched game when he hurled 12 perfect innings against the Braves, but was then victimized by an error, an intentional walk, and a Joe Adcock blast out of the park that was ruled a ground-rule double when Adcock passed Aaron on the basepaths.

Lopez's Go-Go Sox revolved around the ability of leadoff man Luis Aparicio to get on base and steal (he had 56 thefts), of second batter Nellie Fox (.306) to score him or at least move him to third for a fly ball, and of the league's best pitching staffs to hold a fragile lead. The rotation was anchored by Early Wynn's league-best 22 wins and Bob Shaw's 18; relievers Turk Lown and Gerry Staley combined for 127 appearances and 29 saves. The team's generally

Hank Aaron
Not only did Aaron bat .355 to win the NL batting title, he combined with Eddie Mathews for 85 home runs to lead Milwaukee into a playoff against Los Angeles.

anemic but opportunistic offense was dramatized on April 22, when Chicago scored 11 runs in one inning against Kansas City; the rally consisted of 10 walks, a hit batsman, three errors, and a lone single by Johnny Callison. The other league bests were Detroit's Harvey Kuenn (.353), Washington's Harmon Killebrew and Cleveland's Rocky Colavito (42 homers), Boston's Jackie Jensen (112 RBIs), and Baltimore's Hoyt Wilhelm (2.19 ERA).

The hero of the six-game World Series was Dodger reliever Larry Sherry, who won twice and racked up two saves in four appearances.

1959 SEASON HIGHLIGHTS

NATIONAL LEAGUE

	W	L	Pct.	GB
Los Angeles	88	68	.564	—
Milwaukee	86	70	.551	2
San Francisco	83	71	.539	4
Pittsburgh	78	76	.506	9
Cincinnati	74	80	.481	13
Chicago	74	80	.481	13
St. Louis	71	83	.461	16
Philadelphia	64	90	.416	23

AMERICAN LEAGUE

	W	L	Pct.	GB
Chicago	94	60	.610	—
Cleveland	89	65	.578	5
New York	79	75	.513	15
Detroit	76	78	.494	18
Boston	75	79	.487	19
Baltimore	74	80	.481	20
Kansas City	66	88	.429	28
Washington	63	91	.409	31

AWARDS
NL MVP: Ernie Banks, CHI
AL MVP: Nellie Fox, CHI
Cy Young: Early Wynn, CHI
NL Rookie: Willie McCovey, SF
AL Rookie: Bob Allison, WAS
GOLD GLOVES
NL: Harvey Haddix, P; Del Crandall, C; Gil Hodges, 1B; Charlie Neal, 2B; Ken Boyer, 3B; Roy McMillan, SS; Hank Aaron, Jackie Brandt, Willie Mays, OF
AL: Bobby Shantz, P; Sherm Lollar, C; Vic Power, 1B; Nellie Fox, 2B; Frank Malzone, 3B; Luis Aparicio, SS; Jackie Jensen, Al Kaline, Minnie Minoso, OF

ALL-STAR GAMES
Memorial Coliseum, Los Angeles
Aug. 3: AL 5, NL 3

Forbes Field, Pittsburgh
July 7: NL 5, AL 4

POSTSEASON
WORLD SERIES
Los Angeles Dodgers 4, Chicago White Sox 2
Oct. 1: Chicago 11, Los Angeles 0
Oct. 2: Los Angeles 4, Chicago 3
Oct. 4: Los Angeles 3, Chicago 1
Oct. 5: Los Angeles 5, Chicago 4
Oct. 6: Chicago 1, Los Angeles 0
Oct. 8: Los Angeles 9, Chicago 3
MVP: Larry Sherry, Los Angeles

Home team in CAPS

"I exploit the greed of all hitters."
— Lew Burdette

NATIONAL LEAGUE LEADERS

Home Runs
Mathews-Mil	46
Banks-Chi	45
Aaron-Mil	39
Robinson-Cin	36
Mays-SF	34

Runs Batted In
Banks-Chi	143
Robinson-Cin	125
Aaron-Mil	123
Bell-Cin	115
Mathews-Mil	114

Batting Average
Aaron-Mil	.355
Cunningham-StL	.345
Cepeda-SF	.317
Pinson-Cin	.316
Mays-SF	.313

On Base Percentage
Cunningham-StL	.456
Aaron-Mil	.406
Robinson-Cin	.397
Moon-LA	.396
Mathews-Mil	.391

Slugging Average
Aaron-Mil	.636
Banks-Chi	.596
Mathews-Mil	.593
Robinson-Cin	.583
Mays-SF	.583

Stolen Bases
Mays-SF	27
T.Taylor-Chi	23
Gilliam-LA	23
Cepeda-SF	23
Pinson-Cin	21

Wins
Spahn-Mil	21
S.Jones-SF	21
Burdette-Mil	21
Antonelli-SF	19

Innings Pitched
Spahn-Mil	292.0
Burdette-Mil	289.2
Antonelli-SF	282.0
S.Jones-SF	270.2
Drysdale-LA	270.2

Saves
McMahon-Mil	15
McDaniel-StL	15
Elston-Chi	13
Henry-Chi	12

Strikeouts
Drysdale-LA	242
S.Jones-SF	209
Koufax-LA	173
Antonelli-SF	165
McCormick-SF	151

Earned Run Average
S.Jones-SF	2.83
Miller-SF	2.84
Buhl-Mil	2.86
Spahn-Mil	2.96
Law-Pit	2.98

Complete Games
Spahn-Mil	21
Law-Pit	20
Burdette-Mil	20
Roberts-Phi	19

AMERICAN LEAGUE LEADERS

Home Runs
Killebrew-Was	42
Colavito-Cle	42
Lemon-Was	33
Maxwell-Det	31
Mantle-NY	31

Runs Batted In
Jensen-Bos	112
Colavito-Cle	111
Killebrew-Was	105
Lemon-Was	100
Maxwell-Det	95

Batting Average
Kuenn-Det	.353
Kaline-Det	.327
Runnels-Bos	.314
Fox-Chi	.306
Minoso-Cle	.302

On Base Percentage
Yost-Det	.437
Runnels-Bos	.415
Kaline-Det	.414
Woodling-Bal	.405
Kuenn-Det	.405

Slugging Average
Kaline-Det	.530
Killebrew-Was	.516
Mantle-NY	.514
Colavito-Cle	.512
Lemon-Was	.510

Stolen Bases
Aparicio-Chi	56
Mantle-NY	21
Landis-Chi	20
Jensen-Bos	20
Allison-Was	13

Wins
Wynn-Chi	22
McLish-Cle	19
Shaw-Chi	18

Innings Pitched
Wynn-Chi	255.2
Bunning-Det	249.2
Foytack-Det	240.1
Pascual-Was	238.2
McLish-Cle	235.1

Saves
Lown-Chi	15
Staley-Chi	14
Loes-Bal	14
Duren-NY	14
Fornieles-Bos	11

Strikeouts
Bunning-Det	201
Pascual-Was	185
Wynn-Chi	179
Score-Cle	147
Wilhelm-Bal	139

Earned Run Average
Wilhelm-Bal	2.19
Pascual-Was	2.64
Shaw-Chi	2.69
Ditmar-NY	2.90
Walker-Bal	2.92

Complete Games
Pascual-Was	17
Pappas-Bal	15
Mossi-Det	15
Wynn-Chi	14
Bunning-Det	14

THE YEAR IN BASEBALL

January 15: Joe Cronin is named AL president, the first player to reach such heights in the game's management.

January 22: Ken Williams dies; the St. Louis Browns' outfielder, who hit 39 homers in 1922, was one of only two men to snatch the home-run title from Babe Ruth in the period 1918-1931.

February 7: Nap Lajoie dies.

March 10: Bill Veeck buys control of the Chicago White Sox for $2.7 million.

May 1: Thirty-nine-year-old Early Wynn of the White Sox is the whole show against the Red Sox as he pitches a one-hitter, strikes out 14, and hit a double and home run in a 1-0 victory.

May 7: Roy Campanella Night at the Los Angeles Coliseum draws a record U.S. crowd of 93,103 to witness an exhibition game between the Dodgers and the Yankees.

May 26: Harvey Haddix of Pittsburgh pitches 12 perfect innings before losing to Milwaukee 1-0 in the 13th on an error, a sacrifice, and Joe Adcock's double.

June 2: Brooks Robinson hits into the first of his career record four triple plays.

June 10: Rocky Colavito of Cleveland hits four homers against the Baltimore Orioles.

July 30: Willie McCovey, just up from Phoenix, collects four hits in four trips in his debut with the San Francisco Giants. His hits included two triples in a 7-2 triumph over the Phillies, and they came off no patsy— future Hall of Famer Robin Roberts.

August 18: Branch Rickey resigns as chairman of the Pirates to become president of the proposed Continental League, which never plays a game.

November 4: Ernie Banks wins his second straight MVP Award; he led NL shortstops in fielding while poling out 45 homers and driving in 143 runs.

November 17: Willie McCovey of the Giants is named NL Rookie of the Year in a unanimous vote.

December 11: The Yanks acquire Roger Maris in a seven-player deal that also moves Don Larsen to Kansas City.

1960

Mantle, Maris united, Ted goes out in style as Maz blast ends Series

Racial integration finally reached baseball's Florida spring-training camps when the Cardinals demanded St. Petersburg put an end to separate housing for white and black players. The action followed protests by African-American first baseman Bill White over the exclusion of blacks from a public function attended by Cardinals and Yankees. Other kinds of protests were heard in Cleveland, where fan favorite Rocky Colavito had been traded to the Tigers during the offseason. Then there was the muttering from several AL team offices over Kansas City's predictable trade of rising slugger Roger Maris to the Yankees.

On the field, Maris wasted little time in showing what other teams had feared by belting 39 homers and driving in a league-leading 112 runs to complement Mickey Mantle's AL-best 40 homers. The power display by the two outfielders overcame a sluggish New York start that kept alive pennant hopes in Chicago and Baltimore until late summer. The Yankees ended the season by winning their last 15 games. Although Art Ditmar's 15 wins were the most on the staff, New York had the lowest team ERA. The single biggest winners were Chuck Estrada of the Orioles and Jim Perry of the Indians, with 18; Frank Baumann of the White Sox had the lowest ERA (2.67). Pete Runnels of Boston took the batting title (.320).

In the NL, the Pirates completed their two-year rise from the bottom by taking their first flag in 33 years. Pittsburgh's success owed much to manager Danny Murtaugh's ability to slide bench players into the lineup without slighting the egos of regulars. This paid off in a big way in September when batting titlist Dick Groat (.325) went down with a fractured wrist. His replacement, Dick Schofield, batted .403 down the stretch. The pitching was headed by Vern Law (20 wins), Bob Friend (18), and Roy Face (10 wins and 24 saves). Around the rest of the league, prominent production came from Ernie Banks of the Cubs (41 homers), Hank Aaron of the Braves (126 RBIs), Warren Spahn of the Braves and Ernie Broglio of the Cardinals (21 wins), and Mike McCormick of the Giants (2.70 ERA).

Bill Mazeroski
The second baseman became an instant hero when his Game 7, bottom-of-the-ninth home run gave the Pirates an unlikely World Series championship against the Yankees.

In their three wins over the first six games of the World Series, the Yankees outscored the Pirates, 38-3. But two wins by Law had gone a long way toward neutralizing that going into the showdown. The seesaw finale saw Pittsburgh take an early 4-0 lead, slip behind 5-4 in the middle innings, rally for five runs in the eighth inning with the big help of a three-run homer from backup catcher Hal Smith, then blow a 9-7 lead in the top of the ninth. Finally, Pirates second baseman Bill Mazeroski tagged New York's Ralph Terry for a homer leading off the bottom of the ninth. In their unlikely defeat, Bill Skowron and Bobby Richardson of the Yankees combined for 23 hits, Mantle and Richardson for 23 RBIs.

Immediately after the World Series, the Yankees fired Casey Stengel, who cracked he would "never again make the mistake of being 70." In Boston, Ted Williams also left the scene, homering in his final at bat. And in Washington, the Senators received permission to move to Minnesota as part of an expansion that brought another team to the District of Columbia and an AL entry into the Los Angeles market.

1960 SEASON HIGHLIGHTS

NATIONAL LEAGUE

	W	L	Pct.	GB
Pittsburgh	95	59	.617	—
Milwaukee	88	66	.571	7
St. Louis	86	68	.558	9
Los Angeles	82	72	.532	13
San Francisco	79	75	.513	16
Cincinnati	67	87	.435	28
Chicago	60	94	.390	35
Philadelphia	59	95	.383	36

AMERICAN LEAGUE

	W	L	Pct.	GB
New York	97	57	.630	—
Baltimore	89	65	.578	8
Chicago	87	67	.565	10
Cleveland	76	78	.494	21
Washington	73	81	.474	24
Detroit	71	83	.461	26
Boston	65	89	.422	32
Kansas City	58	96	.377	39

AWARDS

NL MVP: Dick Groat, PIT
AL MVP: Roger Maris, NY
Cy Young: Vern Law, PIT
NL Rookie: Frank Howard, LA
AL Rookie: Ron Hansen, BAL
GOLD GLOVES
NL: Harvey Haddix, P; Del Crandall, C; Bill White, 1B; Bill Mazeroski, 2B; Ken Boyer, 3B; Ernie Banks, SS; Hank Aaron, Wally Moon, Willie Mays, OF
AL: Bobby Shantz, P; Earl Battey, C; Vic Power, 1B; Nellie Fox, 2B; Brooks Robinson, 3B; Luis Aparicio, SS; Roger Maris, Jim Landis, Minnie Minoso, OF

ALL-STAR GAMES

Yankee Stadium, New York
July 13: NL 6, AL 0

Municipal Stadium, Kansas City
July 11: NL 5, AL 3

POSTSEASON
WORLD SERIES
Pittsburgh Pirates 4, New York Yankees 3
Oct. 5: Pittsburgh 6, New York 4
Oct. 6: New York 16, Pittsburgh 3
Oct. 8: New York 10, Pittsburgh 0
Oct. 9: Pittsburgh 3, New York 2
Oct. 10: Pittsburgh 5, New York 2
Oct. 12: New York 12, Pittsburgh 0
Oct. 13: Pittsburgh 10, New York 9
MVP: Bobby Richardson, New York

Home team in CAPS

> **"I wanted to be the greatest hitter who ever lived. A man has to have goals and that was mine, to have people say, 'There goes Ted Williams. The greatest hitter who ever lived.' "**
>
> — Ted Williams

NATIONAL LEAGUE LEADERS

Home Runs
Banks-Chi	41
Aaron-Mil	40
Mathews-Mil	39
Boyer-StL	32
Robinson-Cin	31

Runs Batted In
Aaron-Mil	126
Mathews-Mil	124
Banks-Chi	117
Mays-SF	103
Boyer-StL	97

Batting Average
Groat-Pit	.325
Larker-LA	.323
Mays-SF	.319
Clemente-Pit	.314
Boyer-StL	.304

On Base Percentage
Ashburn-Chi	.416
Robinson-Cin	.413
Mathews-Mil	.401
Moon-LA	.387
Mays-SF	.386

Slugging Average
Robinson-Cin	.595
Aaron-Mil	.566
Boyer-StL	.562
Mays-SF	.555
Banks-Chi	.554

Stolen Bases
Wills-LA	50
Pinson-Cin	32
T.Taylor-Chi-Phi	26
Mays-SF	25
Bruton-Mil	22

Wins
Spahn-Mil	21
Broglio-StL	21
Law-Pit	20
Burdette-Mil	19

Innings Pitched
Jackson-StL	282.0
Friend-Pit	275.2
Burdette-Mil	275.2
Law-Pit	271.2
Drysdale-LA	269.0

Saves
McDaniel-StL	26
Face-Pit	24
Henry-Cin	17
Brosnan-Cin	12

Strikeouts
Drysdale-LA	246
Koufax-LA	197
S.Jones-SF	190
Broglio-StL	188
Friend-Pit	183

Earned Run Average
McCormick-SF	2.70
Broglio-StL	2.74
Drysdale-LA	2.84
Williams-LA	3.00
Friend-Pit	3.00

Complete Games
Spahn-Mil	18
Law-Pit	18
Burdette-Mil	18
Hobbie-Chi	16
Friend-Pit	16

AMERICAN LEAGUE LEADERS

Home Runs
Mantle-NY	40
Maris-NY	39
Lemon-Was	38
Colavito-Det	35
Killebrew-Was	31

Runs Batted In
Maris-NY	112
Minoso-Chi	105
Wertz-Bos	103
Lemon-Was	100
Gentile-Bal	98

Batting Average
Runnels-Bos	.320
Smith-Chi	.315
Minoso-Chi	.311
Skowron-NY	.309
Kuenn-Cle	.308

On Base Percentage
Yost-Det	.416
Woodling-Bal	.403
Runnels-Bos	.403
Mantle-NY	.402
Sievers-Chi	.399

Slugging Average
Maris-NY	.581
Mantle-NY	.558
Killebrew-Was	.534
Sievers-Chi	.534
Skowron-NY	.528

Stolen Bases
Aparicio-Chi	51
Landis-Chi	23
Green-Was	21
Kaline-Det	19
Piersall-Cle	18

Wins
Perry-Cle	18
Estrada-Bal	18
B.Daley-KC	16

Innings Pitched
Lary-Det	274.1
Ramos-Was	274.0
Perry-Cle	261.1
Herbert-KC	252.2
Bunning-Det	252.0

Saves
Klippstein-Cle	14
Fornieles-Bos	14
Moore-Chi-Was	13
B.Shantz-NY	11

Strikeouts
Bunning-Det	201
Ramos-Was	160
Wynn-Chi	158
Lary-Det	149
Estrada-Bal	144

Earned Run Average
Baumann-Chi	2.67
Bunning-Det	2.79
Brown-Bal	3.06
Ditmar-NY	3.06
Ford-NY	3.08

Complete Games
Lary-Det	15
Ramos-Was	14
Herbert-KC	14
Wynn-Chi	13
B.Daley-KC	13

THE YEAR IN BASEBALL

January 24: Russ Ford dies.

January 29: At his own request, Stan Musial's pay is reduced from $100,000 to $80,000 based on his 1959 performance.

February 18: Walter O'Malley completes the purchase of the Chavez Ravine area in Los Angeles.

April 17: Eddie Mathews becomes the second youngest major leaguer to reach 300 home runs.

June 17: Ted Williams hits home run number 500.

July 19: Juan Marichal breaks in with the Giants by pitching a one-hit shutout, defeating Robin Roberts and the Phillies.

August 3: Detroit trades manager Jimmy Dykes to Cleveland for manager Joe Gordon.

September 2: Twenty years after homering off Thornton Lee, Ted Williams hits a home run off Lee's son, Don.

September 15: Willie Mays gets five hits and ties a modern-day record with three triples in one game.

September 16: Warren Spahn, 39, records his 11th 20-win season by no-hitting the Phillies.

September 26: In his final major league plate appearance, Ted Williams hits the 521st home run of his career. He is taken out of the game before the start of the ninth inning and, as he leaves the field to a thunderous standing ovation, refuses, as usual, to tip his cap

October 13: Bill Mazeroski opens the bottom of the ninth with a home run off Ralph Terry of the Yankees to give the Pirates a 10-9 victory and the championship.

October 17: At the Blackstone Hotel in Chicago, the NL awards franchises to New York and Houston for 1962.

October 26: The American League approves the transfer of the Senators to Minnesota and announces new franchises will be awarded to Washington and Los Angeles. This is the first expansion of the major leagues in this century.

November 9: Casey Stengel, fired as the Yankees' manager after his 10th pennant in 12 years, says, "I'll never make the mistake of being 70 years old again."

December 20: Charles Finley purchases 52 percent of the A's from the estate of Arnold Johnson.

December 20: Cubs owner P.K. Wrigley announces that Chicago will not hire a manager but will instead be run by a committee of coaches.

1961

Maris tops Ruth but haunted by asterisk and fan antipathy

The AL's expansion to 10 teams and a 162-game schedule gave those obsessed with accumulative statistics something new to brood about, and nobody brooded more than Commissioner Ford Frick. With New York outfielders Roger Maris and Mickey Mantle both taking aim at Babe Ruth's single-season home run mark of 60, Frick, a one-time ghostwriter for the Bambino, decreed that any 61st homer would be asterisked in the record book if not achieved within the old 154-game schedule. Among other things, this worked to guarantee relatively modest gates in September when the two sluggers drew closer to the Ruth standard.

The Maris-Mantle show was the centerpiece of a homer barrage against AL pitchers, with the Yankees trotting around the bases an unprecedented 240 times on their way to the pennant. Along the way, it became clear that grandstand sentiment tilted toward the homegrown Mantle, not the Kansas City-delivered Maris, for breaking the Ruth record. But as harassed as he was by fans and reporters, Maris maintained a lead over his teammate until a bad leg sidelined Mantle down the stretch. As it turned out, he reached only 59 homers within 154 games, not getting Number 60 until tagging Baltimore's Jack Fisher in Game 159 and reaching Boston's Tracy Stallard for his 61st in the 162nd contest. Only 23,154 were on hand at Yankee Stadium to see the last blow.

Mickey Mantle and Roger Maris
The Yankee sluggers took aim at Ruth's home run record, with Maris, right, emerging as an unpopular record breaker when he hit his 61st homer on the season's final day.

In addition to their firepower, the Yankees owed their flag to a combined 41-7 from Whitey Ford and Ralph Terry and to 15 wins and 29 saves from Luis Arroyo. Ford's 25 victories topped the league, as did the 2.40 ERA posted by Washington's Dick Donovan. Maris led the way with his 61 homers and 142 RBIs (one of these later disputed), while Detroit's Norm Cash won the batting championship (.361). Despite driving in 270 runs between them, Maris and Mantle were not the league's most productive tandem; that distinction went to Cash and Rocky Colavito, who plated 272 runs.

In the eight-team NL, the Reds overcame a 6-18 start to finish in the postseason for the first time in 21 years. Most of the heavy lifting came from left fielder Frank Robinson (.323-37-124) and right-hander Joey Jay (tied with Milwaukee's Warren Spahn for the most wins, 21). Cincinnati's major competition came from the Dodgers, where in his seventh big-league season southpaw Sandy Koufax finally broke through to win 18 and pace the league in strikeouts. The other category winners were San Francisco's Orlando Cepeda (46 homers and 142 RBIs) and Pittsburgh's Roberto Clemente (.351). In addition to tying Jay for victories, Spahn recorded the lowest ERA (3.02).

Even with Mantle mostly on the sidelines with a leg infection, the Yankees had little trouble putting the Reds away in a five-game World Series. Ford dominated on the mound, tossing a Game 1 two-hitter and throwing more blanks until an ankle injury forced his removal in Game 4; by then, he had passed Ruth's World Series record of 29-2/3 consecutive scoreless innings. Utility player Hector Lopez drove in seven runs in nine at bats.

1961 SEASON HIGHLIGHTS

NATIONAL LEAGUE

	W	L	Pct.	GB
Cincinnati	93	61	.604	—
Los Angeles	89	65	.578	4
San Francisco	85	69	.552	8
Milwaukee	83	71	.539	10
St. Louis	80	74	.519	13
Pittsburgh	75	79	.487	18
Chicago	64	90	.416	29
Philadelphia	47	107	.305	46

AMERICAN LEAGUE

	W	L	Pct.	GB
New York	109	53	.673	—
Detroit	101	61	.623	8
Baltimore	95	67	.586	14
Chicago	86	76	.531	23
Cleveland	78	83	.484	30.5
Boston	76	86	.469	33
Minnesota	70	90	.438	38
Los Angeles	70	91	.435	38.5
Washington	61	100	.379	47.5
Kansas City	61	100	.379	47.5

AWARDS

NL MVP: Frank Robinson, CIN
AL MVP: Roger Maris, NY
Cy Young: Whitey Ford, NY
NL Rookie: Billy Williams, CHI
AL Rookie: Don Schwall, BOS
GOLD GLOVES
NL: Bobby Shantz, P; Johnny Roseboro, C; Bill White, 1B; Bill Mazeroski, 2B; Ken Boyer, 3B; Maury Wills, SS; Roberto Clemente, Vada Pinson, Willie Mays, OF
AL: Frank Lary, P; Earl Battey, C; Vic Power, 1B; Bobby Richardson, 2B; Brooks Robinson, 3B; Luis Aparicio, SS; Jim Piersall, Jim Landis, Al Kaline, OF

ALL-STAR GAMES

Fenway Park, Boston
July 31: NL 1, AL 1

Candlestick Park, San Francisco
July 11: NL 5, AL 4

POSTSEASON
WORLD SERIES
New York Yankees 4, Cincinnati Reds 1
Oct. 4: New York 2, Cincinnati 0
Oct. 5: Cincinnati 6, New York 2
Oct. 7: New York 3, Cincinnati 2
Oct. 8: New York 7, Cincinnati 0
Oct. 9: New York 13, Cincinnati 5
MVP: Whitey Ford, New York

Home team in CAPS

"Now they talk on the radio about the records set by Ruth, and DiMaggio and Henry Aaron. But they rarely mention mine. Do you know what I have to show for the 61 home runs? Nothing."

— Roger Maris

NATIONAL LEAGUE LEADERS

Home Runs

Cepeda-SF	46
Mays-SF	40
Robinson-Cin	37
Stuart-Pit	35
Adcock-Mil	35

Runs Batted In

Cepeda-SF	142
Robinson-Cin	124
Mays-SF	123
Aaron-Mil	120
Stuart-Pit	117

Batting Average

Clemente-Pit	.351
Pinson-Cin	.343
Boyer-StL	.329
Moon-LA	.328
Aaron-Mil	.327

On Base Percentage

Moon-LA	.438
Robinson-Cin	.411
Mathews-Mil	.405
Boyer-StL	.400
Mays-SF	.395

Slugging Average

Robinson-Cin	.611
Cepeda-SF	.609
Aaron-Mil	.594
Mays-SF	.584
Stuart-Pit	.581

Stolen Bases

Wills-LA	35
Pinson-Cin	23
Robinson-Cin	22
Aaron-Mil	21
Mays-SF	18

Wins

Spahn-Mil	21
Jay-Cin	21
O'Toole-Cin	19

Innings Pitched

Burdette-Mil	272.1
Spahn-Mil	262.2
Cardwell-Chi	259.1
Koufax-LA	255.2
O'Toole-Cin	252.2

Saves

Miller-SF	17
Face-Pit	17
Henry-Cin	16
Brosnan-Cin	16
L.Sherry-LA	15

Strikeouts

Koufax-LA	269
Williams-LA	205
Drysdale-LA	182
O'Toole-Cin	178
Gibson-StL	166

Earned Run Average

Spahn-Mil	3.02
O'Toole-Cin	3.10
Simmons-StL	3.13
McCormick-SF	3.20
Gibson-StL	3.24

Complete Games

Spahn-Mil	21
Koufax-LA	15
Jay-Cin	14
Burdette-Mil	14

AMERICAN LEAGUE LEADERS

Home Runs

Maris-NY	61
Mantle-NY	54
Killebrew-Min	46
Gentile-Bal	46
Colavito-Det	45

Runs Batted In

Maris-NY	142
Gentile-Bal	141
Colavito-Det	140
Cash-Det	132
Mantle-NY	128

Batting Average

Cash-Det	.361
Kaline-Det	.324
Piersall-Cle	.322
Mantle-NY	.317
Gentile-Bal	.302

On Base Percentage

Cash-Det	.488
Mantle-NY	.452
Gentile-Bal	.428
Pearson-LA	.422
Killebrew-Min	.409

Slugging Average

Mantle-NY	.687
Cash-Det	.662
Gentile-Bal	.646
Maris-NY	.620
Killebrew-Min	.606

Stolen Bases

Aparicio-Chi	53
Howser-KC	37
Wood-Det	30
Hinton-Was	22
Bruton-Det	22

Wins

Ford-NY	25
Lary-Det	23
Barber-Bal	18
Bunning-Det	17
Terry-NY	16

Innings Pitched

Ford-NY	283.0
Lary-Det	275.1
Bunning-Det	268.0
Ramos-Min	264.1
Pascual-Min	252.1

Saves

Arroyo-NY	29
Wilhelm-Bal	18
Fornieles-Bos	15
Moore-Min	14
Fox-Det	12

Strikeouts

Pascual-Min	221
Ford-NY	209
Bunning-Det	194
Pizarro-Chi	188
McBride-LA	180

Earned Run Average

Donovan-Was	2.40
Stafford-NY	2.68
Mossi-Det	2.96
Pappas-Bal	3.04
Pizarro-Chi	3.05

Complete Games

Lary-Det	22
Pascual-Min	15
Barber-Bal	14

THE YEAR IN BASEBALL

January 29: Outfield greats and stolen-base kings Max Carey and Billy Hamilton are elected to the Hall of Fame. Between them they had 1,650 thefts, and in 1922 Carey stole 51 bases in 53 tries.

January 31: Houston voters approve a bond to finance a luxury domed stadium, paving the way for a NL franchise.

February 9: Willie Mays signs for $85,000, making him the highest paid player in the NL.

February 16: Dazzy Vance dies; he didn't notch his first big league victory until age 31, then won 197 and led the league in strikeouts seven straight seasons.

March 6: New York Metropolitan Baseball Club, Inc., receives certificate of membership in the NL.

March 14: George Weiss comes out of retirement to become president of the New York Mets.

April 28: Five days past his 40th birthday, Braves lefty Warren Spahn becomes the second oldest major leaguer (after Cy Young) to hurl a no-hitter.

April 30: Willie Mays wallops four home runs against the Braves in Milwaukee.

May 9: Jim Gentile of the Orioles hits consecutive grand slam homers in the first and second innings.

June 8: Eddie Mathews, Henry Aaron, Joe Adcock, and Frank Thomas of Milwaukee hit successive homers in the seventh inning against Cincinnati.

June 23: Stan Musial hits two home runs to pass Lou Gehrig on the all-time list for extra base hits.

July 17: Ty Cobb dies.

August 22: Roger Maris, en route to breaking Babe Ruth's home run record, becomes the first player to hit his 50th home run in August. He connected against the Angels, who beat the Yankees, 4-3.

September 22: Jim Gentile hits his fifth grand slam to tie the major league single-season record.

September 27: Sandy Koufax fans seven Phils to set an NL record of 269 strikeouts in a season.

October 1: Roger Maris sets a new season record for home runs when he hits his 61st off Tracy Stallard of the Red Sox to give the Yankees a 1-0 victory.

November 26: The Rules Committee votes 8-1 against legalizing the spitball.

1962

Wills eclipses Cobb amid Mets follies and Yankees triumph

The NL expanded into New York and Houston as an alternative to a war with a would-be third circuit, the Continental League. The creation of the Mets filled the East Coast void left by the departure of the Dodgers and Giants; it also filled the record books with folly when the squad of such graying veterans as Richie Ashburn, Gil Hodges and Frank Thomas lost 120 games, including streaks of 9 (to start the year), 11, 13, and 17. New York was officially eliminated from the pennant chase on August 7.

On the West Coast, one of the clubs that had abandoned New York broke other marks. In moving into Dodger Stadium, Los Angeles set an attendance record of 2,755,184. For his part, shortstop Maury Wills eclipsed a 47-year-old Ty Cobb standard by stealing 104 bases. But not even the thievery of Wills, a batting title (.346) and RBI crown (153) for Tommy Davis, a league-best 25 wins and 232 strikeouts from Don Drysdale, or a franchise-high 102 California wins managed to bring the Dodgers a pennant. The major reason was a hand circulatory problem that disabled ERA leader (2.54) Sandy Koufax as of mid-July. With Willie Mays blasting a league-best 49 homers and driving home 141 and Jack Sanford winning 24, San Francisco kept the pressure on to force a pennant playoff. Just as in 1951, the Giants won the first game, lost the second, and were only an inning away from going home for the winter when the Dodgers blew it. Instead of a Bobby Thomson home run, this time it was Los Angeles pitchers Ed Roebuck and Stan Williams walking and wild pitching the pennant runs around.

In the AL, the Yankees won yet another pennant, with most of the novelty coming from their closest runner-ups—the transferred Twins and expansion Angels. Mickey Mantle did the biggest hitting and Ralph Terry (a league-best 23 victories) the most consistent pitching. Minnesota stayed in the race on the strength of Harmon Killebrew's unmatched 48 homers and 126 RBIs, 20 wins from Camilo Pascual, and 18 from Jim Kaat. As much as the Angels surprised in the standings, they gained even more headlines from the *bon vivant* dalliances of rookie pitcher Bo Belinsky with Hollywood actresses. Belinsky, whose quick six wins included a no-hitter against Baltimore, ended up with merely 28 victories over eight years. The most impressively pitched game came in September from Washington's Tom Cheney, who struck out a never-equaled 21 batters in a 16-inning contest against the Orioles. Boston's Pete Runnels won his second batting title in three years (.326), and Detroit's Hank Aguirre was the hardest to score against (2.21 ERA).

Mickey Mantle
The great center fielder hit the 30-home-run plateau for the eighth straight season in leading the Yankees to the World Series, where they defeated the Giants in seven games.

The seven-game Giants-Yankees World Series was as tight as it could be. Over the first six games, the teams won alternately while enduring one five-day streak of idleness because of rain postponements and travel dates. In the third Sanford-Terry matchup of the Series, the New York right-hander took a 1-0 lead into the bottom of the ninth inning, then yielded a bunt single to Matty Alou and a double to Mays around two strikeouts. With the championship on the line, Willie McCovey ended matters by scorching a line drive to second baseman Bobby Richardson. New York's 20th championship would also be its last for 15 years.

1962 SEASON HIGHLIGHTS

NATIONAL LEAGUE

	W	L	Pct.	GB
San Francisco	103	62	.624	—
Los Angeles	102	63	.618	1
Cincinnati	98	64	.605	3.5
Pittsburgh	93	68	.578	8
Milwaukee	86	76	.531	15.5
St. Louis	84	78	.519	17.5
Philadelphia	81	80	.503	20
Houston	64	96	.400	36.5
Chicago	59	103	.364	42.5
New York	40	120	.250	60.5

AMERICAN LEAGUE

	W	L	Pct.	GB
New York	96	66	.593	—
Minnesota	91	71	.562	5
Los Angeles	86	76	.531	10
Detroit	85	76	.528	10.5
Chicago	85	77	.525	11
Cleveland	80	82	.494	16
Baltimore	77	85	.475	19
Boston	76	84	.475	19
Kansas City	72	90	.444	24
Washington	60	101	.373	35.5

AWARDS

NL MVP: Maury Wills, LA
AL MVP: Mickey Mantle, NY
Cy Young: Don Drysdale, LA
NL Rookie: Ken Hubbs, CHI
AL Rookie: Tom Tresh, NY
GOLD GLOVES
NL: Bobby Shantz, P; Del Crandall, C; Bill White, 1B; Ken Hubbs, 2B; Jim Davenport, 3B; Maury Wills, SS; Roberto Clemente, Bill Virdon, Willie Mays, OF
AL: Jim Kaat, P; Earl Battey, C; Vic Power, 1B; Bobby Richardson, 2B; Brooks Robinson, 3B; Luis Aparicio, SS; Mickey Mantle, Jim Landis, Al Kaline, OF

ALL-STAR GAMES

Wrigley Field, Chicago
July 30: AL 9, NL 4
MVP: Maury Wills, Los Angeles Dodgers

D.C. Stadium, Washington
July 10: NL 3, AL 1
MVP: Maury Wills, L.A. Dodgers and Leon Wagner, L.A. Angels

POSTSEASON
WORLD SERIES
New York Yankees 4, San Francisco Giants 3
Oct. 4: New York 6, San Francisco 2
Oct. 5: San Francisco 2, New York 0
Oct. 7: New York 3, San Francisco 2
Oct. 8: San Francisco 7, New York 3
Oct. 10: New York 5, San Francisco 3
Oct. 15: San Francisco 5, New York 2
Oct. 16: New York 1, San Francisco 0
MVP: Ralph Terry, New York

Home team in CAPS

"They've shown me ways to lose that I never knew existed."
— Casey Stengel, on the expansion Mets

NATIONAL LEAGUE LEADERS

Home Runs
Mays-SF 49
H.Aaron-Mil 45
Robinson-Cin 39
Banks-Chi 37
Cepeda-SF 35

Runs Batted In
T.Davis-LA 153
Mays-SF 141
Robinson-Cin 136
H.Aaron-Mil 128
Howard-LA 119

Batting Average
T.Davis-LA .346
Robinson-Cin .342
Musial-StL .330
White-StL .324
H.Aaron-Mil .323

On Base Percentage
Robinson-Cin .424
Musial-StL .420
Skinner-Pit .397
Altman-Chi .394
H.Aaron-Mil .393

Slugging Average
Robinson-Cin .624
H.Aaron-Mil .618
Mays-SF .615
Howard-LA .560
T.Davis-LA .535

Stolen Bases
Wills-LA 104
W.Davis-LA 32
Pinson-Cin 26
Javier-StL 26
Taylor-Phi 20

Wins
Drysdale-LA 25
Sanford-SF 24
Purkey-Cin 23
Jay-Cin 21

Innings Pitched
Drysdale-LA 314.1
Purkey-Cin 288.1
O'Dell-SF 280.2
Mahaffey-Phi 274.0
Jay-Cin 273.0

Saves
Face-Pit 28
Perranoski-LA 20
Miller-SF 19
McDaniel-StL 14

Strikeouts
Drysdale-LA 232
Koufax-LA 216
Gibson-StL 208
Farrell-Hou 203
O'Dell-SF 195

Earned Run Average
Koufax-LA 2.54
Shaw-Mil 2.80
Purkey-Cin 2.81
Drysdale-LA 2.83
Gibson-StL 2.85

Complete Games
Spahn-Mil 22
O'Dell-SF 20
Mahaffey-Phi 20
Drysdale-LA 19

AMERICAN LEAGUE LEADERS

Home Runs
Killebrew-Min 48
Cash-Det 39
Wagner-LA 37
Colavito-Det 37

Runs Batted In
Killebrew-Min 126
Siebern-KC 117
Colavito-Det 112
Robinson-Chi 109
Wagner-LA 107

Batting Average
Runnels-Bos .326
Mantle-NY .321
Robinson-Chi .312
Hinton-Was .310
Siebern-KC .308

On Base Percentage
Mantle-NY .488
Siebern-KC .416
Cunningham-Chi .415
Runnels-Bos .411
Robinson-Chi .387

Slugging Average
Mantle-NY .605
Killebrew-Min .545
Colavito-Det .514
Cash-Det .513
Allison-Min .511

Stolen Bases
Aparicio-Chi 31
Hinton-Was 28
Wood-Det 24
Charles-KC 20

Wins
Terry-NY 23
Pascual-Min 20
Herbert-Chi 20
Donovan-Cle 20
Bunning-Det 19

Innings Pitched
Terry-NY 298.2
Kaat-Min 269.0
Bunning-Det 258.0
Pascual-Min 257.2
Ford-NY 257.2

Saves
Radatz-Bos 24
Bridges-NY 18
Fox-Det 16
Wilhelm-Bal 15
Bell-Cle 12

Strikeouts
Pascual-Min 206
Bunning-Det 184
Terry-NY 176
Pizarro-Chi 173
Kaat-Min 173

Earned Run Average
Aguirre-Det 2.21
Roberts-Bal 2.78
Ford-NY 2.90
Chance-LA 2.96
Fisher-Chi 3.10

Complete Games
Pascual-Min 18
Kaat-Min 16
Donovan-Cle 16
Terry-NY 14

THE YEAR IN BASEBALL

April 11: The New York Mets play their first game and lose, 11-4, to the Cardinals at St. Louis.

April 13: The expansion Mets draw just 12,447 to their home debut, a 4-2 loss to Pittsburgh at the Polo Grounds.

April 30: Willie Mays becomes the ninth player in major league history to hit four home runs in a game.

April 24: Sandy Koufax ties the modern-day record with 18 strikeouts in nine innings against Chicago.

May 19: Stan Musial gets hit number 3,431 to break Honus Wagner's recognized NL record of 3,430 (subsequently revised to 3,415).

July 23: Jackie Robinson becomes the first African-American inducted into the Hall of Fame.

July 25: Stan Musial drives in two runs against the Dodgers to become the NL's all-time RBI leader at 1,862.

July 31: A recommendation for interleague play by commissioner Ford Frick is rejected by the owners.

September 5: Ken Hubbs of the Cubs sets major league records at second base for consecutive games without an error (78) and consecutive error-free chances (418).

September 12: Tom Cheney of the Senators sets a record by fanning 21 Orioles in a 16-inning game which he wins, 2-1.

September 18: Houston's Bob Aspromonte sets a NL record for third basemen with his 57th consecutive error-free game.

September 23: Maury Wills breaks Ty Cobb's record of 96 steals in a season, stealing two bases in a Dodger loss in St. Louis.

October 3: The Dodgers set a major league season attendance record of 2,755,184 by drawing a crowd of 45,693 on the final day.

November 20: Chisox release Early Wynn, who has 299 wins (he signs with Cleveland in June 1963 and wins one game).

November 21: Dick Stuart, who goes from Pittsburgh to Boston with Jack Lamabe, for Don Schwall and Jim Pagliaroni, hits 42 homers with 118 RBIs in first year in AL.

November 29: Owners and players agree to return to a single All-Star game in 1963, with 95 percent of proceeds earmarked for the players' pension fund.

1963

Koufax Triple Crown leads Dodger charge as Musial calls it quits

The circulation problems that had disabled Sandy Koufax in 1962 and cost the Dodgers a pennant were nowhere in evidence when the southpaw came back to win the pitching Triple Crown. None of his league-best 25 wins was more important than a mid-September blanking of the Cardinals after St. Louis had won 19 out of 20 and appeared on the verge of repeating the San Francisco comeback of the previous season. In the AL, the Yankees were able to plug in big efforts from catcher Elston Howard, first baseman Joe Pepitone, and right-hander Jim Bouton just when it appeared that injuries to Mickey Mantle and Roger Maris and the weight of years on Yogi Berra would doom the club to being an also-ran.

In asserting himself as the game's most dominant pitcher, Koufax tied San Francisco's Juan Marichal with his 25 victories, struck out 306, and posted an ERA of 1.88; one of the wins was the second of his four career no-hitters. His chief accomplices on the mound were Don Drysdale with 19 wins and Ron Perranoski with 16 wins and 21 saves. The pitching was needed because, with the exception of Tommy Davis' second straight batting title (.326), the Dodgers were no match offensively for St. Louis. Their biggest hit of the year was the only one picked up by rookie Dick Nen in eight at bats—a ninth-inning game-tying homer that helped put the Cardinals away the day after Koufax had shut them out.

The campaign's biggest sluggers were Willie McCovey of the Giants and Hank Aaron of the Braves with 44 homers; Aaron also drove in an NL-high 130 runs. On September 6, the Giants provided a footnote to the season by becoming the first club to have a trio of brothers—Felipe, Matty and Jesus Alou—play the outfield together.

Because of Mantle's fractured foot and Maris' bad back, the two New York outfielders played together only 30 times during the season. The slack was taken up by MVP Howard and Pepitone, who combined for 55 home runs. Bouton's 21 wins complemented a league-leading 25 racked up by Whitey Ford. The other honors were spread around the league—to Minnesota's Harmon Killebrew (45 homers), Boston's Dick Stuart (118 RBIs) and Carl Yastrzemski (.321), and Chicago's Gary Peters (2.33).

The Yankees-Dodgers World Series had little in common with the Bronx-Brooklyn duels on the East Coast. For one thing, it was a four-game sweep; for another, it wasn't New York doing the sweeping. The only familiar note was southpaw Johnny Podres taking the second game. Otherwise, it was Koufax pitching two complete-game wins, Drysdale outlasting Bouton 1-0, and the Yankees scoring only four runs and batting .171.

Following the season, St. Louis slugger Stan Musial announced his retirement, going off with some statistical oddities for his 17-year career. Among other things, the 3,630 hits that went into his lifetime .331 average were divided perfectly between those at home and those on the road. The lefty slugger also demonstrated his consistency by having batted at least .323 for every month of a baseball season.

Sandy Koufax
The southpaw led the NL in wins (25), ERA (1.88) and strikeouts (306) and added two complete-game World Series wins for the Dodgers.

1963 SEASON HIGHLIGHTS

NATIONAL LEAGUE

	W	L	Pct.	GB
Los Angeles	99	63	.611	—
St. Louis	93	69	.574	6
San Francisco	88	74	.543	11
Philadelphia	87	75	.537	12
Cincinnati	86	76	.531	13
Milwaukee	84	78	.519	15
Chicago	82	80	.506	17
Pittsburgh	74	88	.457	25
Houston	66	96	.407	33
New York	51	111	.315	48

AMERICAN LEAGUE

	W	L	Pct.	GB
New York	104	57	.646	—
Chicago	94	68	.580	10.5
Minnesota	91	70	.565	13
Baltimore	86	76	.531	18.5
Detroit	79	83	.488	25.5
Cleveland	79	83	.488	25.5
Boston	76	85	.472	28
Kansas City	73	89	.451	31.5
Los Angeles	70	91	.435	34
Washington	56	106	.346	48.5

AWARDS

NL MVP: Sandy Koufax, LA
AL MVP: Elston Howard, NY
Cy Young: Sandy Koufax, LA
NL Rookie: Pete Rose, CIN
AL Rookie: Gary Peters, CHI
GOLD GLOVES
NL: Bobby Shantz, P; Johnny Edwards, C; Bill White, 1B; Bill Mazeroski, 2B; Ken Boyer, 3B; Bobby Wine, SS; Roberto Clemente, Curt Flood, Willie Mays, OF
AL: Jim Kaat, P; Elston Howard, C; Vic Power, 1B; Bobby Richardson, 2B; Brooks Robinson, 3B; Zoilo Versalles, SS; Carl Yastrzemski, Jim Landis, Al Kaline, OF

ALL-STAR GAME

Municipal Stadium, Cleveland
July 9: NL 5, AL 3
MVP: Willie Mays, San Francisco

POSTSEASON

WORLD SERIES
Los Angeles Dodgers 4, New York Yankees 0
Oct. 2: Los Angeles 5, New York 2
Oct. 3: Los Angeles 4, New York 1
Oct. 5: Los Angeles 1, New York 0
Oct. 6: Los Angeles 2, New York 1
MVP: Sandy Koufax, Los Angeles

Home team in CAPS

> "I can see how he won 25 games. What I don't understand is how he lost five."
>
> — Yogi Berra after being swept by Sandy Koufax and the Dodgers in the 1963 World Series

NATIONAL LEAGUE LEADERS

Home Runs
McCovey-SF	44
H.Aaron-Mil	44
Mays-SF	38
Cepeda-SF	34
Howard-LA	28

Runs Batted In
H.Aaron-Mil	130
Boyer-StL	111
White-StL	109
Pinson-Cin	106
Mays-SF	103

Batting Average
T.Davis-LA	.326
Clemente-Pit	.320
Groat-StL	.319
H.Aaron-Mil	.319
Cepeda-SF	.316

On Base Percentage
Mathews-Mil	.400
H.Aaron-Mil	.394
Mays-SF	.384
Robinson-Cin	.381
Groat-StL	.380

Slugging Average
H.Aaron-Mil	.586
Mays-SF	.582
McCovey-SF	.566
Cepeda-SF	.563
Pinson-Cin	.514

Stolen Bases
Wills-LA	40
H.Aaron-Mil	31
Pinson-Cin	27
Robinson-Cin	26
W.Davis-LA	25

Wins
Marichal-SF	25
Koufax-LA	25
Spahn-Mil	23
Maloney-Cin	23
Ellsworth-Chi	22

Innings Pitched
Marichal-SF	321.1
Drysdale-LA	315.1
Koufax-LA	311.0
Ellsworth-Chi	290.2
Sanford-SF	284.1

Saves
McDaniel-Chi	22
Perranoski-LA	21
Face-Pit	16
Baldschun-Phi	16
Henry-Cin	14

Strikeouts
Koufax-LA	306
Maloney-Cin	265
Drysdale-LA	251
Marichal-SF	248
Gibson-StL	204

Earned Run Average
Koufax-LA	1.88
Ellsworth-Chi	2.11
Friend-Pit	2.34
Marichal-SF	2.41
Simmons-StL	2.48

Complete Games
Spahn-Mil	22
Koufax-LA	20
Ellsworth-Chi	19
Marichal-SF	18
Drysdale-LA	17

AMERICAN LEAGUE LEADERS

Home Runs
Killebrew-Min	45
Stuart-Bos	42
Allison-Min	35
Hall-Min	33
Howard-NY	28

Runs Batted In
Stuart-Bos	118
Kaline-Det	101
Killebrew-Min	96
Colavito-Det	91
Allison-Min	91

Batting Average
Yastrzemski-Bos	.321
Kaline-Det	.312
Rollins-Min	.307
Pearson-LA	.304
Ward-Chi	.295

On Base Percentage
Yastrzemski-Bos	.419
Pearson-LA	.403
Cash-Det	.388
Allison-Min	.381
Kaline-Det	.378

Slugging Average
Killebrew-Min	.555
Allison-Min	.533
Howard-NY	.528
Stuart-Bos	.521
Hall-Min	.521

Stolen Bases
Aparicio-Bal	40
Hinton-Was	25
Wood-Det	18
Snyder-Bal	18
Pearson-LA	17

Wins
Ford-NY	24
Pascual-Min	21
Bouton-NY	21
Monbouquette-Bos	20
Barber-Bal	20

Innings Pitched
Ford-NY	269.1
Terry-NY	268.0
Monbouquette-Bos	266.2
Barber-Bal	258.2
Roberts-Bal	251.1

Saves
S.Miller-Bal	27
Radatz-Bos	25
Wyatt-KC	21
Wilhelm-Chi	21
Dailey-Min	21

Strikeouts
Pascual-Min	202
Bunning-Det	196
Stigman-Min	193
Peters-Chi	189
Ford-NY	189

Earned Run Average
Peters-Chi	2.33
Pizarro-Chi	2.39
Pascual-Min	2.46
Bouton-NY	2.53
Downing-NY	2.56

Complete Games
Terry-NY	18
Pascual-Min	18
Stigman-Min	15
Herbert-Chi	14
Aguirre-Det	14

THE YEAR IN BASEBALL

January 26: The strike zone is expanded to its pre-1950 size, from the top of the shoulders to the bottom of the knees.

February 15: Bump Hadley dies.

February 28: Eppa Rixey dies; he pitched 21 years for poor clubs yet won 266 games.

March 10: Pete Rose, a non-roster player appearing in his first exhibition game, goes 2 for 2, both doubles.

April 1: Mets purchase outfielder Duke Snider from the Los Angeles Dodgers.

April 11: Warren Spahn's opening day 6-1 win is the 328th of his career, making him the winningest left-hander in major league history.

April 13: Pete Rose records his first major league hit, a triple off Pittsburgh's Bob Friend.

May 8: Stan Musial hits a home run against L.A. for his 1,357th extra-base hit, surpassing Babe Ruth's major league record.

July 13: Early Wynn, after struggling through six unsuccessful starts, attains his 300th and final win.

September 6: Baseball historian Lee Allen declares the Indians-Senators game is the 100,000th in major league history.

September 8: Warren Spahn wins his 20th game to tie Christy Mathewson's record of 13 20-win seasons.

September 15: The three Alou brothers—Felipe, Matty, and Jesus—play briefly in the Giant outfield at the same time in a regular game. This necessitated benching Willie Mays.

September 29: In what is both his debut and his finale, John Paciorek of Houston goes 3 for 3 with two walks, three RBIs, and four runs scored.

October 15: Sandy Koufax sets a World Series record with 15 strikeouts against the Yankees.

December 2: Oversized catcher's mitts are banned, effective in 1965.

1964

Boyer leads Cardinals as Yankees squabble and Phillies collapse

In one of the NL's most momentous collapses, Philadelphia stood at the top of the standings by 6-1/2 games with two weeks to go, then suddenly dropped ten in a row while the Reds reeled off nine consecutive wins, the Cardinals took eight in a row, and the Giants played at an .800 clip. The result was a final weekend in which every game had a domino effect on the rest of the schedule and in which the circuit's worst team—the Mets—ended up having a big say on who emerged with the flag.

The Phillies' breakdown was aided by manager Gene Mauch's almost exclusive (and panicky) reliance on Jim Bunning and Chris Short to start games down the stretch. The Reds were the sentimental favorite because of their fatally ailing manager Fred Hutchinson, but it was the Cardinals who were ultimately able to find all the right pieces at the right time. Two of the biggest pieces came from mid-season transactions—a June trade with the Cubs that netted outfielder Lou Brock (.348) and the August recall of reliever Barney Schultz (14 saves) from the minors. The additions of Brock and Schultz came amid executive-suite pressures to trade off veteran players for a rebuilding program and owner Gussie Busch's handshake deal with Leo Durocher to replace Johnny Keane as manager after the season. Those prospects were still alive on the final weekend, when the Mets stalled at 108 losses to defeat St. Louis aces Bob Gibson and Ray Sadecki. But then the Cardinals finally came back to win the season finale and the flag.

Aside from Brock, the Cardinals offense was largely MVP third baseman Ken Boyer (a league-best 119 RBIs) and first baseman Bill White (.303-21-102). Sadecki won 20, Gibson 19 and Curt Simmons 18. Bunning's 19 wins for the Phillies included the NL's first perfect game (against New York) since 1880. Willie Mays of the Giants had the most home runs (47), Roberto Clemente of the Pirates the highest average (.339), Larry Jackson of the Cubs the most wins (24), and Sandy Koufax of the Dodgers the lowest ERA (1.74).

Brooks Robinson
The Hall of Fame third baseman had a career year at the plate, leading the AL with 118 RBIs while batting .317 with 26 home runs.

The AL race was fought as much within the Yankees clubhouse as on the field. For a good part of the year, newly appointed manager Yogi Berra had problems asserting authority over a rambunctious crew used to him as an affable teammate. That ended in August when utility infielder Phil Linz was goaded into playing a harmonica on a team bus despite Berra's orders not to, the manager got in his face, and the club, in need of any inspiration at all, blew the incident up into the trigger for a 22-6 September and a fifth straight pennant. Individual league honors went to Harmon Killebrew (49 homers) and Tony Oliva (.323) of the Twins, Brooks Robinson of the Orioles (118 RBIs), Gary Peters of the White Sox (20 wins), and Dean Chance of the Angels (20 wins and a 1.65 ERA).

Despite big performances from Jim Bouton (two wins) and Bobby Richardson (13 hits), the Yankees went down in a seven-game World Series. Key St. Louis blows were a fourth-game grand slam from Boyer and a three-run homer in the 10th inning of the fifth game from Tim McCarver. The day after the Series, the Yankees fired Berra, replacing him with Keane, who felt unappreciated in St. Louis.

1964 SEASON HIGHLIGHTS

NATIONAL LEAGUE

	W	L	Pct.	GB
St. Louis	93	69	.574	—
Philadelphia	92	70	.568	1
Cincinnati	92	70	.568	1
San Francisco	90	72	.556	3
Milwaukee	88	74	.543	5
Pittsburgh	80	82	.494	13
Los Angeles	80	82	.494	13
Chicago	76	86	.469	17
Houston	66	96	.407	27
New York	53	109	.327	40

AMERICAN LEAGUE

	W	L	Pct.	GB
New York	99	63	.611	—
Chicago	98	64	.605	1
Baltimore	97	65	.599	2
Detroit	85	77	.525	14
Los Angeles	82	80	.506	17
Minnesota	79	83	.488	20
Cleveland	79	83	.488	20
Boston	72	90	.444	27
Washington	62	100	.383	37
Kansas City	57	105	.352	42

AWARDS

NL MVP: Ken Boyer, STL
AL MVP: Brooks Robinson, BAL
Cy Young: Dean Chance, LA
NL Rookie: Dick Allen, PHI
AL Rookie: Tony Oliva, MIN
GOLD GLOVES
NL: Bobby Shantz, P; Johnny Edwards, C; Bill White, 1B; Bill Mazeroski, 2B; Ron Santo, 3B; Ruben Amaro, SS; Roberto Clemente, Curt Flood, Willie Mays, OF
AL: Jim Kaat, P; Elston Howard, C; Vic Power, 1B; Bobby Richardson, 2B; Brooks Robinson, 3B; Luis Aparicio, SS; Vic Davalillo, Jim Landis, Al Kaline, OF

ALL-STAR GAME

Shea Stadium, New York
July 7: NL 7, AL 4
MVP: Johnny Callison, Philadelphia

POSTSEASON
WORLD SERIES
St. Louis Cardinals 4, New York Yankees 3
Oct. 7: ST. LOUIS 9, New York 5
Oct. 8: New York 8, ST. LOUIS 3
Oct. 10: NEW YORK 2, St. Louis 1
Oct. 11: St. Louis 4, NEW YORK 3
Oct. 12: St. Louis 5, NEW YORK 2
Oct. 14: New York 8, ST. LOUIS 3
Oct. 15: ST. LOUIS 7, New York 5
MVP: Bob Gibson, St. Louis

Home team in CAPS

> "I think I was the best baseball player I ever saw."
>
> — Willie Mays

NATIONAL LEAGUE LEADERS

Home Runs
Mays-SF	47
Williams-Chi	33
Hart-SF	31
Cepeda-SF	31
Callison-Phi	31

Runs Batted In
Boyer-StL	119
Santo-Chi	114
Mays-SF	111
Torre-Mil	109
Callison-Phi	104

Batting Average
Clemente-Pit	.339
Carty-Mil	.330
Aaron-Mil	.328
Torre-Mil	.321
Allen-Phi	.318

On Base Percentage
Santo-Chi	.401
Robinson-Cin	.399
Aaron-Mil	.394
Carty-Mil	.391
Clemente-Pit	.391

Slugging Average
Mays-SF	.607
Santo-Chi	.564
Allen-Phi	.557
Carty-Mil	.554
Robinson-Cin	.548

Stolen Bases
Wills-LA	53
Brock-Chi-StL	43
W.Davis-LA	42
Harper-Cin	24
Robinson-Cin	23

Wins
Jackson-Chi	24
Marichal-SF	21
Sadecki-StL	20

Innings Pitched
Drysdale-LA	321.1
Jackson-Chi	297.2
Gibson-StL	287.1
Bunning-Phi	284.1
Veale-Pit	279.2

Saves
Woodeshick-Hou	23
McBean-Pit	22
Baldschun-Phi	21
McDaniel-Chi	15

Strikeouts
Veale-Pit	250
Gibson-StL	245
Drysdale-LA	237
Koufax-LA	223
Bunning-Phi	219

Earned Run Average
Koufax-LA	1.74
Drysdale-LA	2.18
Short-Phi	2.20
Marichal-SF	2.48
Bunning-Phi	2.63

Complete Games
Marichal-SF	22
Drysdale-LA	21
Jackson-Chi	19
Gibson-StL	17
Ellsworth-Chi	16

AMERICAN LEAGUE LEADERS

Home Runs
Killebrew-Min	49
Powell-Bal	39
Mantle-NY	35
Colavito-KC	34
Stuart-Bos	33

Runs Batted In
B.Robinson-Bal	118
Stuart-Bos	114
Mantle-NY	111
Killebrew-Min	111
Colavito-KC	102

Batting Average
Oliva-Min	.323
B.Robinson-Bal	.317
Howard-NY	.313
Mantle-NY	.303
Robinson-Chi	.301

On Base Percentage
Mantle-NY	.426
Allison-Min	.406
Powell-Bal	.400
Robinson-Chi	.388
Kaline-Det	.385

Slugging Average
Powell-Bal	.606
Mantle-NY	.591
Oliva-Min	.557
Allison-Min	.553
Killebrew-Min	.548

Stolen Bases
Aparicio-Bal	57
Weis-Chi	22
Davalillo-Cle	21
Howser-Cle	20
Hinton-Was	17

Wins
Peters-Chi	20
Chance-LA	20
Wickersham-Det	19
Pizarro-Chi	19
Bunker-Bal	19

Innings Pitched
Chance-LA	278.1
Peters-Chi	273.2
Bouton-NY	271.1
Pascual-Min	267.1
Osteen-Was	257.0

Saves
Radatz-Bos	29
Wilhelm-Chi	27
Miller-Bal	23
Wyatt-KC	20
B.Lee-LA	19

Strikeouts
Downing-NY	217
Pascual-Min	213
Chance-LA	207
Peters-Chi	205
Lolich-Det	192

Earned Run Average
Chance-LA	1.65
Horlen-Chi	1.88
Ford-NY	2.13
Peters-Chi	2.50
Pizarro-Chi	2.56

Complete Games
Chance-LA	15
Pascual-Min	14
Pappas-Bal	13
Osteen-Was	13
Kaat-Min	13

THE YEAR IN BASEBALL

January 16: AL owners vote 9-1 against Charles Finley's proposal to move the A's to Louisville and order Finley to sign a lease in Kansas City or lose the franchise.

February 15: Cubs second baseman Ken Hubbs, 22, dies when his private plane crashed near Provo, Utah.

February 17: Luke Appling is elected to the Hall of Fame; "Old Aches and Pains" hit a homer in an Old Timers' Game at age 75.

February 27: Mickey Mantle signs his first $100,000 contract with the Yankees.

April 17: Pittsburgh's Willie Stargell hits the first home run at Shea Stadium.

April 24: Sandy Koufax strikes out 18 Chicago Cubs.

May 31: The Giants and Mets set a major league record by playing a game that lasts 7 hours, 22 minutes, won 8-6 by the Giants in 23 innings.

June 4: Sandy Koufax becomes just the fourth pitcher to hurl three no-hitters by blanking the Phillies 3-0.

June 21: Jim Bunning pitches a perfect game for the Phillies over the Mets.

August 5: Ford Frick tells the league presidents and club owners that he will not be seeking to stay on as commissioner at the end of his contract.

August 12: Mickey Mantle homers from each side of the plate in the same game for the 10th and final time, a major league record.

August 14: Bo Belinsky is suspended after attacking a sportswriter.

September 1: Southpaw relief pitcher Masanori Murakami becomes the first major league player from Japan.

September 26: The Braves and Phillies set a major league record by using 43 players in a nine-inning game.

October 17: After the Yankees lose the World Series, Yogi Berra is fired.

November 7: The NL gives the Braves permission to move to Atlanta for the 1966 season.

December 4: Baseball approves a free agent draft for players not included on any team's 40-man roster.

1965

Yanks, Cards plummet, Braves pack their bags; Koufax dominates

Baseball moved indoors to the Astrodome, William Eckert took over as commissioner, and the first amateur draft was held, but the most startling development for many was the plunge of the Yankees to their worst finish since 1925. In the NL, the world champion Cardinals went New York one worse by becoming the first 20th-century titlist to plummet all the way down to seventh place.

With New York out of the picture, Minnesota moved to the top of the AL, drawing only spasmodic challenges from Chicago and Baltimore. In a period of widened strike zones, the Twins batted only .254, the lowest in AL history for a team leading the league in that department. But they also had batting champion Tony Oliva (.321) and four players with more than 20 homers. With ace Camilo Pascual out for almost two months with a torn back muscle, Jim Grant led the staff (and the league) with 21 wins; Jim Kaat contributed another 18. Other honors around the AL went to Boston's 20-year-old Tony Conigliaro, the youngest player ever to lead in home runs with his 32; Rocky Colavito, who returned to Cleveland to drive in the most runs (108); and Sam McDowell of the Indians, who had the lowest ERA (2.18) and most strikeouts (325).

The NL season was played under the cloud of legal and public contentiousness in Milwaukee, where the Braves were forced to play a final lame-duck year after announcing plans to move to Atlanta. Disillusioned fans stayed away from County Stadium to the degree that a gate of 1,000 was not always assured. The club's final home game on September 22 drew 12,577—about the same number that had welcomed the first club's arrival at the Milwaukee train station in 1953.

The NL pennant race came down to the Dodgers and Giants again, and with some of the violence of their old East Coast rivalry. On August 22, San Francisco pitcher Juan Marichal decided Los Angeles catcher John Roseboro was returning the ball to pitcher Sandy Koufax by way of his ear, so he turned around and whacked the receiver with his bat. The attack and ensuing melee cost the Giants ace $1,750 and a nine-day suspension. The loss of at least two starts by the 22-game winner was recalled in the Bay Area when San Francisco finished two games behind the Dodgers. On the other hand, Koufax was all but unstoppable in a Triple Crown performance of 26 wins, 382 strikeouts, and a 2.04 ERA. In September, the left-hander threw in a perfect-game victory against the Cubs (and practically had to, since mound opponent Bob Hendley yielded only one hit). Also having big years were Willie Mays of the Giants (52 homers), Deron

Don Drysdale
The fiery right-hander combined with Sandy Koufax to give the Dodgers the best pitching tandem in baseball, winning a combined 49 games and the World Series.

Johnson of the Reds (130 RBIs) and Roberto Clemente of the Pirates (.329).

The Twins stunned World Series oddsmakers when they defeated 23-game winner Don Drysdale and Koufax in the first two games, but then Claude Osteen stopped the Dodger slide in Game 3. Before the seven games were over, Koufax came back to throw two shutouts to give Los Angeles the title.

Minnesota's aspirations to becoming the AL's new power in place of the Yankees effectively ended in December, when the Orioles obtained slugger Frank Robinson in a trade with the Reds.

1965 SEASON HIGHLIGHTS

NATIONAL LEAGUE

	W	L	Pct.	GB
Los Angeles	97	65	.599	—
San Francisco	95	67	.586	2
Pittsburgh	90	72	.556	7
Cincinnati	89	73	.549	8
Milwaukee	86	76	.531	11
Philadelphia	85	76	.528	11.5
St. Louis	80	81	.497	16.5
Chicago	72	90	.444	25
Houston	65	97	.401	32
New York	50	112	.309	47

AMERICAN LEAGUE

	W	L	Pct.	GB
Minnesota	102	60	.630	—
Chicago	95	67	.586	7
Baltimore	94	68	.580	8
Detroit	89	73	.549	13
Cleveland	87	75	.537	15
New York	77	85	.475	25
California	75	87	.463	27
Washington	70	92	.432	32
Boston	62	100	.383	40
Kansas City	59	103	.364	43

AWARDS

NL MVP: Willie Mays, SF
AL MVP: Zoilo Versalles, MIN
Cy Young: Sandy Koufax, LA
NL Rookie: Jim Lefebvre, LA
AL Rookie: Curt Blefary, BAL

GOLD GLOVES

NL: Bob Gibson, P; Joe Torre, C; Bill White, 1B; Bill Mazeroski, 2B; Ron Santo, 3B; Leo Cardenas, SS; Roberto Clemente, Curt Flood, Willie Mays, OF
AL: Jim Kaat, P; Bill Freehan, C; Joe Pepitone, 1B; Bobby Richardson, 2B; Brooks Robinson, 3B; Zoilo Versalles, SS; Carl Yastrzemski, Tom Tresh, Al Kaline, OF

ALL-STAR GAME

Metropolitan Stadium, Bloomington, Minnesota
July 13: NL 6, AL 5
MVP: Juan Marichal, San Francisco

POSTSEASON
WORLD SERIES
Los Angeles Dodgers 4, Minnesota Twins 3
Oct. 6: MINNESOTA 8, Los Angeles 2
Oct. 7: MINNESOTA 5, Los Angeles 1
Oct. 9: LOS ANGELES 4, Minnesota 0
Oct. 10: LOS ANGELES 7, Minnesota 2
Oct. 11: LOS ANGELES 7, Minnesota 0
Oct. 13: MINNESOTA 5, Los Angeles 1
Oct. 14: Los Angeles 2, MINNESOTA 0
MVP: Sandy Koufax, Los Angeles

Home team in CAPS

"In the end it all comes down to talent. You can talk all you want about intangibles, I just don't know what that means."

— Sandy Koufax

NATIONAL LEAGUE LEADERS

Home Runs
Mays-SF	52
McCovey-SF	39
Williams-Chi	34
Santo-Chi	33
Robinson-Cin	33

Runs Batted In
Johnson-Cin	130
Robinson-Cin	113
Mays-SF	112
Williams-Chi	108
Stargell-Pit	107

Batting Average
Clemente-Pit	.329
H.Aaron-Mil	.318
Mays-SF	.317
Williams-Chi	.315
Rose-Cin	.312

On Base Percentage
Mays-SF	.399
Robinson-Cin	.388
H.Aaron-Mil	.384
McCovey-SF	.383
Rose-Cin	.383

Slugging Average
Mays-SF	.645
H.Aaron-Mil	.560
Williams-Chi	.552
Robinson-Cin	.540
McCovey-SF	.539

Stolen Bases
Wills-LA	94
Brock-StL	63
Wynn-Hou	43
Harper-Cin	35
W.Davis-LA	25

Wins
Koufax-LA	26
Cloninger-Mil	24
Drysdale-LA	23
Marichal-SF	22
Ellis-Cin	22

Innings Pitched
Koufax-LA	335.2
Drysdale-LA	308.1
Gibson-StL	299.0
Short-Phi	297.1
Marichal-SF	295.1

Saves
Abernathy-Chi	31
McCool-Cin	21
Linzy-SF	21

Strikeouts
Koufax-LA	382
Veale-Pit	276
Gibson-StL	270
Bunning-Phi	268
Maloney-Cin	244

Earned Run Average
Koufax-LA	2.04
Marichal-SF	2.13
Law-Pit	2.15
Maloney-Cin	2.54
Bunning-Phi	2.60

Complete Games
Koufax-LA	27
Marichal-SF	24
Gibson-StL	20
Drysdale-LA	20
Cloninger-Mil	16

AMERICAN LEAGUE LEADERS

Home Runs
Conigliaro-Bos	32
Cash-Det	30
Horton-Det	29
Wagner-Cle	28

Runs Batted In
Colavito-Cle	108
Horton-Det	104
Oliva-Min	98
Mantilla-Bos	92
Whitfield-Cle	90

Batting Average
Oliva-Min	.321
Yastrzemski-Bos	.312
Davalillo-Cle	.301
Robinson-Bal	.297
Wagner-Cle	.294

On Base Percentage
Yastrzemski-Bos	.398
Colavito-Cle	.387
Oliva-Min	.384
Blefary-Bal	.382
Mantilla-Bos	.377

Slugging Average
Yastrzemski-Bos	.536
Conigliaro-Bos	.512
Cash-Det	.512
Wagner-Cle	.495
Oliva-Min	.491

Stolen Bases
Campaneris-KC	51
Cardenal-Cal	37
Versalles-Min	27
Davalillo-Cle	26
Aparicio-Bal	26

Wins
Grant-Min	21
Stottlemyre-NY	20
Kaat-Min	18
McDowell-Cle	17

Innings Pitched
Stottlemyre-NY	291.0
McDowell-Cle	273.0
Grant-Min	270.1
Kaat-Min	264.1
Newman-Cal	260.2

Saves
Kline-Was	29
S.Miller-Bal	24
Fisher-Chi	24
B.Lee-Cal	23
Radatz-Bos	22

Strikeouts
McDowell-Cle	325
Lolich-Det	226
McLain-Det	192
Siebert-Cle	191
Downing-NY	179

Earned Run Average
McDowell-Cle	2.18
Fisher-Chi	2.40
Siebert-Cle	2.43
Brunet-Cal	2.56
Richert-Was	2.60

Complete Games
Stottlemyre-NY	18
McDowell-Cle	14
Grant-Min	14
McLain-Det	13

THE YEAR IN BASEBALL

March 17: Jackie Robinson becomes the first African-American to work on a television broadcast when he is signed by ABC-TV.

April 9: The Houston Astrodome opens with an exhibition game between the Astros and Yankees.

May 16: Nineteen-year-old Jim Palmer wins his first major league game and hits his first homer as the Orioles beat the Yanks 7-5.

July 9: The Senators Frank Howard ties a major league record by striking out seven times in a doubleheader.

August 18: Henry Aaron of the Braves hits a Curt Simmons pitch on top of the pavilion roof at Sportsman's Park, St. Louis, for an apparent home run. However, umpire Chris Pelekoudas calls him out for being out of the batter's box when he connected.

August 19: Jim Maloney tosses his second no-hitter of the season, winning 1-0 over the Cubs, after fanning 12 and walking 10.

August 29: Willie Mays hits his 17th home run of August to set an NL record for homers in one month.

August 30: On the advice of his doctor, Casey Stengel, 75, steps down as manager of the Mets.

September 8: Bert Campaneris of the A's plays all 9 positions. Only Cesar Tovar of the Twins has matched this feat.

September 9: Sandy Koufax of the Dodgers pitches a perfect game against the Cubs, fanning 14 and winning 1-0. His opponent, Bob Hendley, allows the Dodgers only one hit, a double by Lou Johnson.

September 18: On Mickey Mantle Day at Yankee Stadium, 50,180 fans see Mantle play his 2,000th game.

September 25: Satchel Paige becomes at 59 the oldest to play in the majors vs. the Red Sox. He allows only one hit in his three innings of work.

October 25: Leo Durocher is named to manage the Cubs, ending Chicago's committee-of-coaches scheme.

November 10: Willie Mays of the Giants is named the NL's MVP.

November 17: Among 156 nominees, retired Air Force general William D. "Spike" Eckert is selected as the game's new commissioner, replacing Ford Frick.

November 23: The Mets acquire 44-year-old pitcher Warren Spahn from the Braves, for whom he had won 20 or more 13 times.

December 9: Beloved baseball executive and innovator Branch Rickey dies.

1966

Koufax's arm gives out, Robinson does it all as Orioles take Series

The Dodgers and Giants yet again battled down to the closing minutes of the NL campaign and could once again measure their final distance from one another by Sandy Koufax. But this time, Los Angeles also paid for the southpaw's stellar abilities—first before the season when he and moundmate Don Drysdale pulled a joint contract holdout, then after the year when over-reliance on the left-hander proved to have aggravated an arthritic elbow, forcing his premature retirement. In the AL, Frank Robinson, written off by Cincinnati as an "old 30" to justify trading him away, won the Triple Crown in leading the Orioles to the first of numerous postseason appointments extending over the next decade.

The Koufax-Drysdale holdout cost the pitchers significant spring-training time—a fact underlined by the Dodgers after the southpaw's retirement. But that didn't prevent Koufax from ringing up another Triple Crown of 27 wins, 317 strikeouts, and a 1.73 ERA. Nor did it prevent manager Walt Alston from using him on short rest down the stretch, particularly in view of Drysdale's poor 13-16 record. The other major ingredients in the Dodger pennant were reliever Phil Regan's 21 saves and "vulture" 14 wins, and the team's ability to manufacture just enough runs from an offense led by Jim Lefebvre's mere 74 RBIs. Hank Aaron warmed to his new setting in Atlanta by leading the league in homers (44) and RBIs (127), while Alou brothers Matty (.342) of the Pirates and Felipe (.327) of the Braves finished one-two in the batting race. The line of the year went to Leo Durocher, who took over the Cubs with the cocksure pronouncement that they weren't "an eighth-place club." They weren't; they finished tenth.

Robinson's Triple Crown (.316-49-122) highlighted an AL season in which the Orioles ran away with the pennant for the first few months and then, in the words of general manager Harry Dalton, "limped away with it." The team's main problem all year was a lack of healthy starters after Jim Palmer and Dave McNally. In addition to Frank Robinson, Brooks Robinson and Boog Powell also knocked in 100 runs. Runner-up Minnesota had the league's biggest winner in Jim Kaat (25) and another power season from Harmon Killebrew (39-110), but a crapshoot of a rotation and a spotty lineup otherwise. Chicago's Gary Peters won his second

Frank Robinson
In his first year in Baltimore, Robinson proved his Cincinnati critics wrong by winning a batting Triple Crown and leading the Orioles to a World Series championship.

ERA title (1.98).

The World Series turned out to be over in the third inning of the first game. After the two Robinsons homered off Drysdale in the first inning and the Dodgers had come back to trail 4-2 at the end of three, Los Angeles did not score another run in the four-game sweep. In the opener, reliever Moe Drabowsky struck out 11 in 6-2/3 innings. Palmer, Wally Bunker, and McNally, the only other pitchers used by Baltimore, then hurled shutouts. Koufax's last big-league appearance turned out to be a Game 2 debacle in which outfielder Willie Davis made three errors behind him in one inning.

The offseason was no smoother for the Dodgers. When shortstop Maury Wills flew back home during a team tour of Japan, claiming he needed to consult a doctor about his knee, an infuriated Walter O'Malley had him traded to the Pirates.

1966 SEASON HIGHLIGHTS

NATIONAL LEAGUE

	W	L	Pct.	GB
Los Angeles	95	67	.586	—
San Francisco	93	68	.578	1.5
Pittsburgh	92	70	.568	3
Philadelphia	87	75	.537	8
Atlanta	85	77	.525	10
St. Louis	83	79	.512	12
Cincinnati	76	84	.475	18
Houston	72	90	.444	23
New York	66	95	.410	28.5
Chicago	59	103	.364	36

AMERICAN LEAGUE

	W	L	Pct.	GB
Baltimore	97	63	.606	—
Minnesota	89	73	.549	9
Detroit	88	74	.543	10
Chicago	83	79	.512	15
Cleveland	81	81	.500	17
California	80	82	.494	18
Kansas City	74	86	.463	23
Washington	71	88	.447	25.5
Boston	72	90	.444	26
New York	70	89	.440	26.5

AWARDS

NL MVP: Roberto Clemente, PIT
AL MVP: Frank Robinson, BAL
Cy Young: Sandy Koufax, LA
NL Rookie: Tommy Helms, CIN
AL Rookie: Tommie Agee, CHI

GOLD GLOVES

NL: Bob Gibson, P; Johnny Roseboro, C; Bill White, 1B; Bill Mazeroski, 2B; Ron Santo, 3B; Gene Alley, SS; Roberto Clemente, Curt Flood, Willie Mays, OF

AL: Jim Kaat, P; Bill Freehan, C; Joe Pepitone, 1B; Bobby Knoop, 2B; Brooks Robinson, 3B; Luis Aparicio, SS; Tony Oliva, Tommie Agee, Al Kaline, OF

ALL-STAR GAME

Busch Memorial Stadium, St. Louis
July 12: NL 2, AL 1
MVP: Brooks Robinson, Baltimore

POSTSEASON

WORLD SERIES
Baltimore Orioles 4, Los Angeles Dodgers 0
Oct. 5: Baltimore 5, LOS ANGELES 2
Oct. 6: Baltimore 6, LOS ANGELES 0
Oct. 8: BALTIMORE 1, Los Angeles 0
Oct. 9: BALTIMORE 1, Los Angeles 0
MVP: Frank Robinson, Baltimore
Home team in CAPS

"Every time I look at my pocketbook, I see Jackie Robinson."

— Willie Mays

NATIONAL LEAGUE LEADERS

Home Runs		Runs Batted In		Batting Average	
Aaron-Atl	44	Aaron-Atl	127	Alou-Pit	.342
Allen-Phi	40	Clemente-Pit	119	Alou-Atl	.327
Mays-SF	37	Allen-Phi	110	Carty-Atl	.326
Torre-Atl	36	White-Phi	103	Allen-Phi	.317
McCovey-SF	36	Mays-SF	103	Clemente-Pit	.317

On Base Percentage		Slugging Average		Stolen Bases	
Santo-Chi	.417	Allen-Phi	.632	Brock-StL	74
Morgan-Hou	.412	McCovey-SF	.586	Jackson-Hou	49
Allen-Phi	.398	Stargell-Pit	.581	Wills-LA	38
Carty-Atl	.396	Torre-Atl	.560	Phillips-Phi-Chi	32
McCovey-SF	.394	Mays-SF	.556	Harper-Cin	29

Wins		Innings Pitched		Saves	
Koufax-LA	27	Koufax-LA	323.0	Regan-LA	21
Marichal-SF	25	Bunning-Phi	314.0	McCool-Cin	18
Perry-SF	21	Marichal-SF	307.1	Face-Pit	18
Gibson-StL	21	Gibson-StL	280.1	Raymond-Hou	16
Short-Phi	20	Drysdale-LA	273.2	Linzy-SF	16

Strikeouts		Earned Run Average		Complete Games	
Koufax-LA	317	Koufax-LA	1.73	Koufax-LA	27
Bunning-Phi	252	Cuellar-Hou	2.22	Marichal-SF	25
Veale-Pit	229	Marichal-SF	2.23	Gibson-StL	20
Gibson-StL	225	Bunning-Phi	2.41	Short-Phi	19
Marichal-SF	222	Gibson-StL	2.44	Bunning-Phi	16

AMERICAN LEAGUE LEADERS

Home Runs		Runs Batted In		Batting Average	
F.Robinson-Bal	49	F.Robinson-Bal	122	F.Robinson-Bal	.316
Killebrew-Min	39	Killebrew-Min	110	Oliva-Min	.307
Powell-Bal	34	Powell-Bal	109	Kaline-Det	.288
Cash-Det	32	B.Robinson-Bal	100	Powell-Bal	.287
Pepitone-NY	31	Horton-Det	100	Killebrew-Min	.281

On Base Percentage		Slugging Average		Stolen Bases	
F.Robinson-Bal	.415	F.Robinson-Bal	.637	Campaneris-KC	52
Kaline-Det	.396	Killebrew-Min	.538	Buford-Chi	51
Killebrew-Min	.393	Kaline-Det	.534	Agee-Chi	44
McAuliffe-Det	.375	Powell-Bal	.532	Aparicio-Bal	25
Powell-Bal	.374	McAuliffe-Det	.509	Cardenal-Cal	24

Wins		Innings Pitched		Saves	
Kaat-Min	25	Kaat-Min	304.2	Aker-KC	32
McLain-Det	20	McLain-Det	264.1	Kline-Was	23
Wilson-Bos-Det	18	Wilson-Bos-Det	264.0	Sherry-Det	20
Siebert-Cle	16	Chance-Cal	259.2	Fisher-Chi-Bal	19
Palmer-Bal	15	Bell-Cle	254.1	S.Miller-Bal	18

Strikeouts		Earned Run Average		Complete Games	
McDowell-Cle	225	Peters-Chi	1.98	Kaat-Min	19
Kaat-Min	205	Horlen-Chi	2.43	McLain-Det	14
Wilson-Bos-Det	200	Hargan-Cle	2.48	Wilson-Bos-Det	13
Richert-Was	195	Perry-Min	2.54	Bell-Cle	12
Bell-Cle	194	John-Chi	2.62		

THE YEAR IN BASEBALL

March 5: Marvin Miller is elected as president of the Major League Players Association.

March 8: Casey Stengel is elected to the Hall of Fame.

March 30: Sandy Koufax and Don Drysdale end a spring-training holdout, signing for $130,000 and $105,000 respectively.

April 3: The New York Mets give a reported signing bonus of $50,000 to University of Southern California pitcher Tom Seaver.

April 11: Emmett Ashford becomes the major leagues' first black umpire in a game witnessed by Vice President Hubert Humphrey.

April 12: The Braves play their first game in Atlanta in front of 50,761, losing 3-2 to Pittsburgh.

May 4: Willie Mays hits his 512th home run to break the NL record held by Mel Ott.

May 8: Orioles slugger Frank Robinson knocks the first ball ever hit completely out of Baltimore's Memorial Stadium, a shot measured at 451 feet.

May 12: The Cardinals open new Busch Stadium with a 12-inning, 4-3 win over the Braves.

July 3: Tony Cloninger of Atlanta hits two grand slams and a single, to drive in nine runs.

August 12: Art Shamsky of the Reds comes off the bench to pinch hit in the eighth and hits a home run. He stays in the game and connects again in the 10th and 11th innings, but Cincinnati still loses to Pittsburgh.

August 16: Willie Mays hits his 534th home run to tie Jimmie Foxx's record for righthanded batters.

September 17: Cleveland pitchers set an AL record by fanning 19 in the first nine innings of a 10-inning game in Detroit.

September 29: Sandy Koufax records 300 strikeouts to become the first pitcher in the 20th century with three 300 strikeout seasons.

October 6: Jim Palmer, 20, becomes the youngest pitcher to hurl a World Series shutout as the Orioles beat the Dodgers, 6-0. Sandy Koufax is the loser, and it marks his last appearance in a game.

November 18: Sandy Koufax announces his retirement due to an arthritic left elbow.

1967

Yaz wins Triple Crown but Bosox bats silenced by Gibson in Series

What the NL had done in 1964, the AL did in 1967—throwing a batch of teams into the final week with an equal chance of winning the flag. None of them was named New York or, more surprisingly in view of the 1966 World Series, Baltimore. Injuries to Frank Robinson, Jim Palmer, and just about any Orioles pitcher not named Tom Phoebus made Baltimore a spectator to a fight among Boston, Minnesota, Detroit, and Chicago.

With two exceptions, the Red Sox remained in the thick of things only because of manager Dick Williams' ability to thread journeymen and rookies into a cohesive unit. The exceptions were right-hander Jim Lonborg, whose 22 victories paced the league, and left fielder Carl Yastrzemski, whose 44 homers, 121 RBIs, and .326 average made him a worthy successor to Ted Williams by adding up to a Triple Crown. A prospective third star, 1965 home run king Tony Conigliaro, appeared on the way to another big power year when he was beaned by Jack Hamilton of the Angels in August; although he returned to action in 1969, Conigliaro never fully recovered his sight, developed other ailments, and was dead by 45. Minnesota's ace was slugger Harmon Killebrew (tied with Yastrzemski at 44 homers), Detroit's was right-hander Earl Wilson (tied with Lonborg at 22 wins), and Chicago's was ERA leader Joel Horlen (2.06).

By the final weekend, not even manager Eddie Stanky's season-long magic act could keep the .225-hitting White Sox in the race, but the Twins stood merely one game ahead of the Red Sox and Tigers. Then Boston, sealing its so-called "Impossible Dream," defeated Minnesota twice and the Angels dumped the Tigers in the final game to head off a playoff. That Detroit didn't have a better record was largely the result of a foot injury suffered by Denny McLain when the right-hander appeared on the verge of matching Wilson as a 20-game winner; a couple of years later, McLain's association with gamblers would raise questions about the seriousness of the injury. Not the least of Boston's satisfactions was that the franchise outdrew every other AL club for the first time in 52 years.

There was no such suspense in the NL, where the Cardinals shook off a broken leg suffered in June by ace Bob Gibson to roll over the Giants and other pretenders. St. Louis was led by first baseman Orlando Cepeda (.325 and a league-leading 111 RBIs) and Lou Brock (21 homers and 52 steals). The other league honors went to Hank Aaron of the Braves (39 homers), Roberto Clemente of the Pirates (.357), Mike McCormick of the Giants (22 wins), and Phil Niekro of the Braves (1.87 ERA).

Gibson and Lonborg were the story of the seven-game World Series. His broken leg a memory, Gibson won the opener, 2-1, then a Game 4 shutout; for Lonborg, it was a one-hit masterpiece in

Carl Yastrzemski
With 44 home runs, 121 RBIs and a .326 average, Yastrzemski won a batting Triple Crown and led Boston to the AL pennant.

Game 2 and a three-hitter in Game 5. In the finale, though, the Cardinals took advantage of Gibson's extra day of rest to back his third complete game with a pounding of Lonborg. Brock had 12 hits and Roger Maris' 7 RBIs for St. Louis.

After the season, owner Charles Finley was given permission to move his Athletics to Oakland. Lawsuit threats by Kansas City prompted the AL to promise a new team for the city within two years.

1967 SEASON HIGHLIGHTS

NATIONAL LEAGUE

	W	L	Pct.	GB
St. Louis	101	60	.627	—
San Francisco	91	71	.562	10.5
Chicago	87	74	.540	14
Cincinnati	87	75	.537	14.5
Philadelphia	82	80	.506	19.5
Pittsburgh	81	81	.500	20.5
Atlanta	77	85	.475	24.5
Los Angeles	73	89	.451	28.5
Houston	69	93	.426	32.5
New York	61	101	.377	40.5

AMERICAN LEAGUE

	W	L	Pct.	GB
Boston	92	70	.568	—
Minnesota	91	71	.562	1
Detroit	91	71	.562	1
Chicago	89	73	.549	3
California	84	77	.522	7.5
Washington	76	85	.472	15.5
Baltimore	76	85	.472	15.5
Cleveland	75	87	.463	17
New York	72	90	.444	20
Kansas City	62	99	.385	29.5

AWARDS

NL MVP: Orlando Cepeda, STL
AL MVP: Carl Yastrzemski, BOS
NL Cy Young: Mike McCormick, SF
AL Cy Young: Jim Lonborg, BOS
NL Rookie: Tom Seaver, NY
AL Rookie: Rod Carew, MIN
GOLD GLOVES
NL: Bob Gibson, P; Randy Hundley, C; Wes Parker, 1B; Bill Mazeroski, 2B; Ron Santo, 3B; Gene Alley, SS; Roberto Clemente, Curt Flood, Willie Mays, OF
AL: Jim Kaat, P; Bill Freehan, C; George Scott, 1B; Bobby Knoop, 2B; Brooks Robinson, 3B; Jim Fregosi, SS; Paul Blair, Carl Yastrzemski, Al Kaline, OF

ALL-STAR GAME

Anaheim Stadium, Anaheim, California
July 11: NL 2, AL 1
MVP: Tony Perez, Cincinnati

POSTSEASON
WORLD SERIES
St. Louis Cardinals 4, Boston Red Sox 3
Oct. 4: St. Louis 2, BOSTON 1
Oct. 5: BOSTON 5, St. Louis 0
Oct. 7: ST. LOUIS 5, Boston 2
Oct. 8: ST. LOUIS 6, Boston 0
Oct. 9: Boston 3, ST. LOUIS 1
Oct. 11: BOSTON 8, St. Louis 4
Oct. 12: St. Louis 7, BOSTON 2
MVP: Bob Gibson, St. Louis

Home team in CAPS

"A great catch is like watching girls go by. The last one you see is always the prettiest."

— Bob Gibson

NATIONAL LEAGUE LEADERS

Home Runs
Aaron-Atl	39
Wynn-Hou	37
Santo-Chi	31
McCovey-SF	31
Hart-SF	29

Runs Batted In
Cepeda-StL	111
Clemente-Pit	110
Aaron-Atl	109
Wynn-Hou	107
Perez-Cin	102

Batting Average
Clemente-Pit	.357
Gonzalez-Phi	.339
Alou-Pit	.338
Flood-StL	.335
Staub-Hou	.333

On Base Percentage
Allen-Phi	.404
Cepeda-StL	.403
Staub-Hou	.402
Clemente-Pit	.402
Santo-Chi	.401

Slugging Average
Aaron-Atl	.573
Allen-Phi	.566
Clemente-Pit	.554
McCovey-SF	.535
Cepeda-StL	.524

Stolen Bases
Brock-StL	52
Wills-Pit	29
Morgan-Hou	29
Pinson-Cin	26
Phillips-Chi	24

Wins
McCormick-SF	22
Jenkins-Chi	20
Osteen-LA	17
Bunning-Phi	17

Innings Pitched
Bunning-Phi	302.1
Perry-SF	293.0
Jenkins-Chi	289.1
Osteen-LA	288.1
Drysdale-LA	282.0

Saves
Abernathy-Cin	28
Linzy-SF	17
Face-Pit	17
Perranoski-LA	16
Hoerner-StL	15

Strikeouts
Bunning-Phi	253
Jenkins-Chi	236
Perry-SF	230
Nolan-Cin	206
Cuellar-Hou	203

Earned Run Average
Niekro-Atl	1.87
Bunning-Phi	2.29
Short-Phi	2.39
Nolan-Cin	2.58
Perry-SF	2.61

Complete Games
Jenkins-Chi	20
Seaver-NY	18
Perry-SF	18
Marichal-SF	18

AMERICAN LEAGUE LEADERS

Home Runs
Yastrzemski-Bos	44
Killebrew-Min	44
Howard-Was	36
F.Robinson-Bal	30

Runs Batted In
Yastrzemski-Bos	121
Killebrew-Min	113
F.Robinson-Bal	94
Howard-Was	89
Oliva-Min	83

Batting Average
Yastrzemski-Bos	.326
F.Robinson-Bal	.311
Kaline-Det	.308
Scott-Bos	.303
Blair-Bal	.293

On Base Percentage
Yastrzemski-Bos	.421
Kaline-Det	.415
Killebrew-Min	.413
F.Robinson-Bal	.408
Mantle-NY	.394

Slugging Average
Yastrzemski-Bos	.622
F.Robinson-Bal	.576
Killebrew-Min	.558
Kaline-Det	.541
Howard-Was	.511

Stolen Bases
Campaneris-KC	55
Buford-Chi	34
Agee-Chi	28
McCraw-Chi	24
Clarke-NY	21

Wins
Wilson-Det	22
Lonborg-Bos	22
Chance-Min	20
Horlen-Chi	19
McLain-Det	17

Innings Pitched
Chance-Min	283.2
Lonborg-Bos	273.1
Wilson-Det	264.0
Kaat-Min	263.1
Peters-Chi	260.0

Saves
Rojas-Cal	27
Wyatt-Bos	20
Locker-Chi	20
Womack-NY	18
Worthington-Min	16

Strikeouts
Lonborg-Bos	246
McDowell-Cle	236
Chance-Min	220
Tiant-Cle	219
Peters-Chi	215

Earned Run Average
Horlen-Chi	2.06
Peters-Chi	2.28
Siebert-Cle	2.38
John-Chi	2.47
Merritt-Min	2.53

Complete Games
Chance-Min	18
Lonborg-Bos	15
Hargan-Cle	15

THE YEAR IN BASEBALL

February 16: Red Ruffing is elected to the Hall of Fame.

May 6: Mickey Mantle hits the 500th home run of his career.

May 10: Hank Aaron hits the only inside-the-park home run of his career.

June 4: Curt Flood's record of 568 chances without an error ends when he drops a fly ball in a 4-1 Cardinals win over the Cubs.

July 12: Reds third baseman Tony Perez ends the longest All Star Game (15 innings, three hours, 41 minutes) with a home run off Catfish Hunter.

July 14: Eddie Mathews becomes the seventh member of baseball's 500 home run club.

July 25: Race riots in Detroit cause postponement of a Tigers-Orioles game.

August 6: Brooks Robinson hits into the fourth triple play of his career, setting a major league record.

August 18: Boston's Tony Conigliaro is beaned by the Angels' Jack Hamilton and is out of baseball until 1969.

October 11: Carl Yastrzemski, Reggie Smith and Rico Petrocelli set a World Series record with three consecutive home runs.

October 12: Lou Brock steals three bases in the Cardinals Game 7 victory to set a record of seven steals in the World Series.

November 27: Senators get Bill Denehy and $100,000 from Mets for manager Gil Hodges.

1968

McLain wins 31, but Lolich the hero as Tigers down Cards

The Yankees supplied all the evidence needed for the so-called Year of the Pitcher: as a team, they batted .214—and still finished four games over .500. With Denny McLain dominating in the AL and Bob Gibson in the NL, the widened strike zones introduced earlier in the decade exacted full vengeance for the offensive bloodbaths in both leagues around 1930. In April, the Mets and Astros played a six-hour, 24-inning game that Houston finally won, 1-0, on an error. In September, a San Francisco-St. Louis series featured back-to-back no-hitters from Gaylord Perry of the Giants and Ray Washburn of the Cardinals. Even the All-Star game was a 1-0 affair.

In becoming the first 30-game winner since Dizzy Dean in 1934, McLain spurred the Tigers into a rout of other AL clubs. The cherry on the cake was that the team also managed to sport three hitters (Willie Horton, Bill Freehan and Norm Cash) with at least 25 home runs. More typical of the season was that Detroit got along with a starting shortstop (Ray Oyler) batting a record-low .135 and a backup (Dick Tracewski) humming through at .156. Boston's Carl Yastrzemski saved the entire league from embarrassment by sneaking into the .300 circle (.301) to win the batting title, while teammate Ken Harrelson drove in the most runs (109) and Washington's Frank Howard poked the most long balls (44). Aside from McLain's 31 wins, the other big pitching star was Cleveland's Luis Tiant, who won 21 and surrendered a mere 1.60 runs every nine innings. None of the league's top five ERA pitchers yielded two runs.

But compared to Gibson, even the AL's stingiest came off as batting-practice pitchers. The St. Louis right-hander's invisible 1.12 ERA was the lowest since the use of the lively ball in 1920. It featured 13 shutouts, 22 wins and an NL-best 268 strikeouts. The Gibson effort was more than enough to lead the Cardinals to the pennant, but he still fell short of pitching's Triple Crown because of the 26 wins racked up by San Francisco's Juan Marichal. Willie McCovey of the Giants had the most home runs (36) and RBIs (105), while Pete Rose of the Reds won the batting crown (.335).

The anticipated World Series duel between McLain and Gibson was upstaged by Detroit southpaw Mickey Lolich. After Gibson threw a shutout in the opener, Lolich came back to even things in Game 2. Another Gibson complete-game victory in Game 4 put the Cardinals up 3-1, but Lolich came back again the next day to win. Finally, in Game 7, the two pitchers faced off, going six scoreless innings. But then the Tigers broke through for three runs in the seventh with what proved to be the margin for the world championship. The Detroit win was widely credited with cooling racial tensions in the city in the wake of the assassination of Martin Luther King.

During the 1968 season, the White Sox played nine home games in Milwaukee in a Walter O'Malley-like ploy to press demands for a new stadium in Chicago. But there were bigger moves than that on the horizon with the announcement that both leagues would add two clubs in 1969—Montreal and San Diego in the NL, Kansas City and Seattle in the AL.

Denny McLain
The Tigers ace would fall into disgrace for consorting with gamblers, but in 1968 he was baseball's first 30-game winner since 1934.

1968 SEASON HIGHLIGHTS

NATIONAL LEAGUE

	W	L	Pct.	GB
St. Louis	97	65	.599	—
San Francisco	88	74	.543	9
Chicago	84	78	.519	13
Cincinnati	83	79	.512	14
Atlanta	81	81	.500	16
Pittsburgh	80	82	.494	17
Philadelphia	76	86	.469	21
Los Angeles	76	86	.469	21
New York	73	89	.451	24
Houston	72	90	.444	25

AMERICAN LEAGUE

	W	L	Pct.	GB
Detroit	103	59	.636	—
Baltimore	91	71	.562	12
Cleveland	86	75	.534	16.5
Boston	86	76	.531	17
New York	83	79	.512	20
Oakland	82	80	.506	21
Minnesota	79	83	.488	24
California	67	95	.414	36
Chicago	67	95	.414	36
Washington	65	96	.404	37.5

AWARDS

NL MVP: Bob Gibson, STL
AL MVP: Denny McLain, DET
NL Cy Young: Bob Gibson, STL
AL Cy Young: Denny McLain, DET
NL Rookie: Johnny Bench, CIN
AL Rookie: Stan Bahnsen, NY

GOLD GLOVES

NL: Bob Gibson, P; Johnny Bench, C; Wes Parker, 1B; Glenn Beckert, 2B; Ron Santo, 3B; Dal Maxvill, SS; Roberto Clemente, Curt Flood, Willie Mays, OF
AL: Jim Kaat, P; Bill Freehan, C; George Scott, 1B; Bobby Knoop, 2B; Brooks Robinson, 3B; Luis Aparicio, SS; Mickey Stanley, Carl Yastrzemski, Reggie Smith, OF

ALL-STAR GAME

Astrodome, Houston
July 9: NL 1, AL 0
MVP: Willie Mays, San Francisco

POSTSEASON
WORLD SERIES
Detroit Tigers 4, St. Louis Cardinals 3
Oct. 2: ST. LOUIS 4, Detroit 0
Oct. 3: Detroit 8, ST. LOUIS 1
Oct. 5: St. Louis 7, DETROIT 3
Oct. 6: St. Louis 10, DETROIT 1
Oct. 7: DETROIT 5, St. Louis 3
Oct. 9: Detroit 13, ST. LOUIS 1
Oct. 10: Detroit 4, ST. LOUIS 1
MVP: Mickey Lolich, Detroit

Home team in CAPS

"Show me a guy who's afraid to look bad, and I'll show you a guy you can beat every time."

— Lou Brock

NATIONAL LEAGUE LEADERS

Home Runs
McCovey-SF	36
Allen-Phi	33
Banks-Chi	32
Williams-Chi	30
H.Aaron-Atl	29

Runs Batted In
McCovey-SF	105
Williams-Chi	98
Santo-Chi	98
Perez-Cin	92
Allen-Phi	90

Batting Average
Rose-Cin	.335
Alou-Pit	.332
Alou-Atl	.317
A.Johnson-Cin	.312
Flood-StL	.301

On Base Percentage
Rose-Cin	.394
McCovey-SF	.383
Wynn-Hou	.378
Mays-SF	.376
Staub-Hou	.376

Slugging Average
McCovey-SF	.545
Allen-Phi	.520
Williams-Chi	.500
H.Aaron-Atl	.498
Mays-SF	.488

Stolen Bases
Brock-StL	62
Wills-Pit	52
Davis-LA	36
H.Aaron-Atl	28
Jones-NY	23

Wins
Marichal-SF	26
Gibson-StL	22
Jenkins-Chi	20

Innings Pitched
Marichal-SF	326.0
Jenkins-Chi	308.0
Gibson-StL	304.2
Perry-SF	291.0
Seaver-NY	277.2

Saves
Regan-LA-Chi	25
Carroll-Atl-Cin	17
Hoerner-StL	17
Brewer-LA	14

Strikeouts
Gibson-StL	268
Jenkins-Chi	260
Singer-LA	227
Marichal-SF	218
Sadecki-SF	206

Earned Run Average
Gibson-StL	1.12
Bolin-SF	1.99
Veale-Pit	2.05
Koosman-NY	2.08
Blass-Pit	2.12

Complete Games
Marichal-SF	30
Gibson-StL	28
Jenkins-Chi	20
Perry-SF	19
Koosman-NY	17

AMERICAN LEAGUE LEADERS

Home Runs
F.Howard-Was	44
Horton-Det	36
Harrelson-Bos	35
Jackson-Oak	29

Runs Batted In
Harrelson-Bos	109
F.Howard-Was	106
Northrup-Det	90
Powell-Bal	85
Horton-Det	85

Batting Average
Yastrzemski-Bos	.301
Cater-Oak	.290
Oliva-Min	.289
Horton-Det	.285
Uhlaender-Min	.283

On Base Percentage
Yastrzemski-Bos	.429
F.Robinson-Bal	.391
Mantle-NY	.387
Monday-Oak	.373
Andrews-Bos	.369

Slugging Average
F.Howard-Was	.552
Horton-Det	.543
Harrelson-Bos	.518
Yastrzemski-Bos	.495
Oliva-Min	.477

Stolen Bases
Campaneris-Oak	62
Cardenal-Cle	40
Tovar-Min	35
Buford-Bal	27
Foy-Bos	26

Wins
McLain-Det	31
McNally-Bal	22
Tiant-Cle	21
Stottlemyre-NY	21
Hardin-Bal	18

Innings Pitched
McLain-Det	336.0
Chance-Min	292.0
Stottlemyre-NY	278.2
McNally-Bal	273.0
McDowell-Cle	269.0

Saves
Worthington-Min	18
Wood-Chi	16
Higgins-Was	13

Strikeouts
McDowell-Cle	283
McLain-Det	280
Tiant-Cle	264
Chance-Min	234
McNally-Bal	202

Earned Run Average
Tiant-Cle	1.60
McDowell-Cle	1.81
McNally-Bal	1.95
McLain-Det	1.96
John-Chi	1.98

Complete Games
McLain-Det	28
Tiant-Cle	19
Stottlemyre-NY	19
McNally-Bal	18
Hardin-Bal	16

THE YEAR IN BASEBALL

April 15: The Astros and Mets play 23-1/2 innings of scoreless ball before a bobble by Al Weis leads to a Houston run in the 24th frame.

May 8: Jim "Catfish" Hunter of Oakland pitches a perfect game against the Twins. There was not even a tough fielding play behind Hunter, who fanned 11. He also got three hits and four RBIs.

May 19: After hitting 10 home runs in six games, Frank Howard of the Senators is stopped by Detroit's Earl Wilson.

June 4: Don Drysdale of the Dodgers blanks the Pirates, 5-0, for his sixth straight shutout en route to a record 58 scoreless innings; twenty years later, his mark would be topped by Orel Hershiser.

June 29: Jim Northrup of Detroit hits a grand slam, his third in five days.

July 1: A first-inning wild pitch ends Bob Gibson's srtreak of 47-2/3 scoreless innings.

July 3: Luis Tiant registers 19 strikeouts in 10 innings to lead Cleveland to a 1-0 win over Minnesota.

July 14: Houston's Don Wilson fans 18 to tie the major league, nine inning record held by Bob Feller, and ties the major league record with eight consecutive strikeouts.

September 14: Denny McLain becomes baseball's first 30-game winner since Dizzy Dean in 1934.

September 18: After Gaylord Perry had pitched a no-hitter over the Cardinals the day before, Ray Washburn retaliates with a no-hitter over the Giants in the same San Francisco park.

September 19: With his 31st win in hand, Denny McLain admitted to feeding a belt-high fastball to Mickey Mantle, resulting in home run No. 535 to move Mantle to third on the all-time list.

October 2: Bob Gibson breaks Sandy Koufax's Series record by whiffing 17 Tigers while winning the first game.

November 5: Denny McLain takes MVP and Cy Young honors for his 31-6 record.

Chapter 18

Showman Bill Veeck and the Last Hurrah of the '48 Indians

Against a backdrop of Bill Veeck hullabaloo, a team of aging stars, journeymen and young players on the way up blended to treat their fans to an unforgettable season.

Bob Feller
Booed early in the season, Feller rebounded in the second half and finished with 19 wins as the Indians won the pennant in a playoff against Boston.

By Hal Lebovitz
SPORT Magazine, June 1965

On a chilly October 12, 1948, a crowd estimated at more than 300,000 lined Cleveland's main drag, Euclid Avenue, and cheered wildly as a caravan of convertibles went by. Inside the convertibles were the Cleveland Indians, world champions of baseball; they had just taken part in the wildest, wackiest, most dramatic—and melodramatic—season in the history of the American League and, possibly, in the history of all baseball.

This was a strange team, made up of a few stars, several young-sters, some old veterans and numerous castoffs. They had all blended together for one last hurrah, winning the pennant in an historic playoff game and then winning the World Series.

The following September, with proper funeral ceremony, coffin, hearse and all, the pennant was buried in the outfield at Cleveland's ballpark. This was a one-year team, and an unforgettable team.

Leading the cast of characters, literal characters, was the pro-ducer of this team of destiny: Bill Veeck, iconoclast. The picture of Veeck remains constant today: never a necktie, an open-necked sport shirt, sans overcoat, even in the coldest weather. Bill Veeck. Showboat, showman, carny man, con man, a man who admittedly will use chicanery and cajolery to reach his goal. A baseball man, who grew up as the son of a baseball man. And, above all, almost a genius.

Bill Veeck stormed into Cleveland in June, 1946. He bought an inept ballclub that received little acknowledgement from the fans and, suddenly, he had the fans acknowledging the club. He had them coming in crowds to see the Indians.

Almost every time they came, they saw different Indians. Veeck's gag line was: "We've got three teams—one here, one coming and one going." Finally, during the 1948 season, he had the team he wanted. It included:

LOU BOUDREAU: Became boy manager of the Indians in 1942 at age 24 ... a handsome former University of Illinois basketball star ... a brilliant shortstop, fine hitter and idol of every Cleveland fan ... even when the team floundered he could do no wrong in the fans' minds ... had weak ankles which required yards of tape before each game ... batted .355 and knocked in 106 runs to lead the team to the 1948 pennant and was voted the American League's Most Valuable Player almost unanimously.

JOE GORDON: The unofficial team captain ... obtained from the Yankees for Allie Reynolds prior to '47 season ... Loose, acrobatic second baseman ... generally easy-going disposition, but could rise in fury when riled ... once riled by a motorist, who cut in front of him, and punched the motorist ... obtained for immediate results, being near the end of his career ... responded in 1948 with 32 homers and 124 RBI, the best season of his life.

GENE BEARDEN: A throw-in in the Gordon deal ... Yanks gave Indians pick of several minor-league pitchers, and Casey Stengel, Veeck's friend, who was then managing Oakland, recommended 27-year-old knuckleballer Bearden ... Cleveland kept him in '48 only because there was a desperate need for a left-hander, any left-hander ... became a one-year phenom winning 20 and losing 7 ... lowest ERA, 2.34, in the league and was voted Rookie of the Year ... faded just as fast and the theory is that when Stengel took over the Yanks in '49 he advised his hitters to "lay off the knuckler," it being too low to be called a strike ... the information spread throughout the league and Bearden was finished ... happy-go-lucky and strikingly good-looking, he became the favorite of the bobby-soxers.

BOB FELLER: Came off Iowa farm in 1936 and became a strikeout pitcher supreme ... the best pitcher in all baseball most of his career and now a Hall of Famer ... was 20-11 in 1947 and was expected to be ace of the staff again in '48, but was not ... was 19-15 in '48.

BOB LEMON: Had kicked around with Indians as an infielder and outfielder ... finally was tried as a pitcher July 31, 1946, and had 4-5 season ... followed with 11-5 year and zoomed to 20-14 in 1948 ... great sense of humor ... always tugged at his cap before each pitch and once Joe McCarthy, Red Sox manager, falsely accused him of having "something" on the cap that helped him doctor the ball. Umpire made him change cap. Next day Lemon walked across diamond wearing Red Sox owner Tom Yawkey's fedora.

KEN KELTNER: Though only 31 in 1948, was near end of his career ... steady third baseman ... promised a $5,000 bonus by Veeck if he had good year in '47. Batted .257 and was surprised when Veeck called him into office and gave him the money. Many say bonus helped spur him to hit .297 in '48, with 31 homers and 119 RBI.

JIM HEGAN: Developed in Cleveland farm system ... picture-book catcher ... extremely popular with fans and pitchers ... Boudreau called pitching signals from shortstop early in '48, but when he discovered Bill Dickey of Yanks was intercepting them during a New York batting spree he returned the duty to Hegan ... proof of Hegan's success: eight Cleveland pitchers finished with ERAs under 3.00.

LARRY DOBY: Joined the Indians July 3, 1947 ... first Negro in American League ... had played second base for Newark Eagles in Negro League but was outfielder with Cleveland ... was 22 and highly sensitive ... subject to great pressure ... batted .156 first year and Indians planned to send him out for more seasoning, but had great spring in '48 and was kept as regular outfielder ... rose above the many obstacles to bat .301 with 14 homers, 66 RBI in '48.

STEVE GROMEK: Former infielder converted to pitcher ... excellent control ... Injured in 1947 and had 3-5 record ... was 9-3 in '48 ... enjoyed hiding reporters' typewriters, but stopped when one writer retaliated by hiding his baseball shoes.

DALE MITCHELL: As a rookie in '47, batted .316 ... batted .336 in '48 ... spray hitter ... fine speed ... left fielder ... hit safely in 21 straight games in '48.

EDDIE ROBINSON: First baseman with good power ... batted .254 in '48, his second year in majors.

THURMAN TUCKER: Obtained in trade with White Sox after '47 ... won center-field job, played there first 30 games, had finger broken by a pitch and sidelined full month ... started 53 games all season and team won 38 of these, a .719 average, nearly 100 points above season's average ... claim to fame: close resemblance to comic Joe E. Brown.

HAL PECK: Veeck's personal good-luck charm ... had played outfield for Veeck in Milwaukee and Bill asked for him to be included in deal with Yanks that brought Gordon to Cleveland ... shot off toes in hunting accident ... arm operation handicapped his throwing ... batted .286, coming through with key pinch hits.

HANK EDWARDS: Outfielder tabbed "hard luck Henry" because of repetition of injuries ... injured shoulder making fine, game-saving catch late in season and could not play in the World Series.

DON BLACK: Had played with Athletics, never reaching his potential because of a drinking problem ... Veeck promised to take him in '46 and give him a chance if he'd join Alcoholics Anonymous ... He joined and pitched no-hitter in '47 ... spot pitcher in '48 ... never pitched again.

JOHNNY BERARDINO: Now seen on TV as "Dr. Steve Hardy" in General Hospital ... Veeck gave St. Louis Browns $50,000 and a player for him to strengthen infield bench for '48 ... was a movie actor even then and one of Veeck's stunts was to have Johnny's face insured ... appeared in 66 games.

ALLIE CLARK: Wanting more power for the outfield, Veeck gave Yanks Red Embree, a good pitcher, for him ... an ironworker in off-season ... could squeeze a beer can flat with one hand ... played 81 games and batted .310.

WALT JUDNICH and BOB MUNCRIEF: Both obtained for '48 from the Browns for $25,000 and players ... Judnich was utility outfielder ... Muncrief was pitcher.

JOE TIPTON: Second-string catcher, behind Hegan, which was like being on vacation.

RUSS CHRISTOPHER: Had a heart condition and couldn't qualify for many jobs ... Veeck offered Athletics $25,000 for the tall, skinny, right-hander and Connie Mack didn't want to take the money because of Russ' poor health ... Russ desired to play, however, and insisted, "If I die, let me die pitching" ... Was used in relief, for an inning or a pitch at a time and became known as "one-

pitch Christopher" ... was under doctor's supervision all season ... Never pitched again and died in 1954.

BOB KENNEDY: Strong-armed outfielder obtained from the White Sox just before the '48 trade deadline ... was fiery leader.

SAM ZOLDAK: Left-handed pitcher obtained from Browns at trade deadline for $100,000 ... would sit in a clubhouse and say to teammates: "They paid $100,000 for me. How much are you worth?" ... used as starter and reliefer ... had 9-6 record.

SATCHEL PAIGE: Had barnstormed in Negro Leagues and elsewhere for years ... joined Cleveland July 9, 1948, started seven games, pitched two shutouts, helped in relief and finished 6-1, with a 2.47 ERA, second lowest in league.

Get any group of Clevelanders together, age 30 or over, mention 1948 and the above names tumble out as the memories come flooding back. Virtually every Clevelander of walking age saw at least one game at the ballpark that hectic, historic year. And some Clevelanders not yet able to walk saw games, too. Among Veeck's many gimmicks was a baby service at Municipal Stadium. Bring the baby, drop him off, then watch the game.

Game after game, fans jammed into the park to set attendance records. Incredibly the average crowd per home date was over 40,000. The final total—2,620,627—established an all-time high.

Cleveland lived and died with the team. A victory made it a cheery town. Gloom followed a loss. In offices and homes radio sets were tuned up to catch every pitch. On residential streets, the play-by-play blared from every window.

Ironically, before the season, the fans seemed ready to boycott the team. The anger began when the St. Louis Browns offered Veeck Vern Stephens, plus other players, for Boudreau. Veeck did not think Boudreau was an exceptional manager and he considered the deal. The story broke and the fans reacted with anger.

Veeck, extremely popular until then, suddenly was about to commit an unpardonable crime. One newspaper published a "Boudreau Ballot" and fans overwhelmingly voted for his retention.

Regardless, Bill was prepared to go through with the deal, firmly convinced it would strengthen the team. But the Browns withdrew the offer. Veeck then brilliantly turned the reversal to his advantage. He rushed back to Cleveland, hobbled from one street corner to another (one leg had been amputated the year before to prevent the spread of osteomyelitis caused by a war injury) to talk with the fans personally. "If you really want Lou, we'll keep him," was his theme.

Veeck became more popular than ever. He signed Boudreau to a two-year contract. Unknown to the fans, though, the fine print said that Lou could be demoted to player status only the second year if the team wasn't successful. Further, Veeck fired Boudreau's coaches and forced him to replace them with Bill McKechnie and Muddy Ruel, two wise and veteran baseball men.

Veeck soon discovered why the Browns had called off the deal. The Red Sox had made them a better offer. Boston got Stephens and pitcher Jack Kramer and became a top contender.

As the season opened the Indians didn't figure as contenders for the pennant. The most optimistic Cleveland writers picked them no higher than third. Gambling odds against Cleveland winning were a 20-1 shot. The Yanks and Red Sox were 5-6 and the Tigers 8-1.

A record opening day turnout of 73,163 saw Feller shut out the Browns on two hits. Lemon won the next one, beating the Tigers, 8-2, and Feller came back to beat them, 4-1. That was the beginning of six successive victories. The Indians then lost the next four. The hot team, one nobody had given a chance, was the Philadelphia Athletics.

Feller lost his effectiveness and someone—anyone—was needed. Boudreau gave Bearden his first start on May 8 and Gene responded with a three-hit, 8-1 victory over Washington.

Through the entire season it was a torrid four-team race. The A's refused to fall out until September when their veteran shortstop Eddie Joost was sidelined by injury. Feller's inconsistency until after the All-Star game kept the Indians from breaking far in front. They moved up and down until May 31 when they took over first place and stayed there until July 24. On that day they lost and fell to third, so tight was the race. They came back to hold the lead most of August, while Al Simmons, A's coach, was telling the world: "Don't worry about the Indians. They'll choke up. They always do."

From rival dugouts came the choke-up sign—forefinger and thumb to throat—and when on Labor Day the Indians fell 4-1/2 games out of first, people around the league were saying, "We told you so." Even the fickle fans in Cleveland agreed it was all over.

But the Indians kept trying. And everyone helped. Like groundskeeper Emil Bossard, who carefully custom built the diamond for every home game. Other teams did this, too, but Bossard was incomparable. The pick-and-shovel artist slanted the foul lines to favor the Indians. And because Keltner, Gordon and Boudreau were slow, Bossard made the infield soft and slow, giving them time to catch up to hard grounders.

The Indians put rookie pitcher Ernie Groth in the scoreboard. Armed with powerful binoculars, Groth picked off the catcher's signs, more than 500 feet away. Seated at the base of the scoreboard, wearing white trousers, was Marshall Bossard, Emil's son. Groth would tell him what the pitch would be and Bossard would signal the bench. For a fastball Bossard sat motionless. For a curve he crossed his legs. The Cleveland batters knew which pitches were coming.

There were many memorable moments through the season:

There was the day Boudreau had used up so many players in an effort to beat the White Sox he ran out of catchers and had to put himself behind the plate the final two innings.

There was the day Larry Doby camped under a fly, lost it in the sun and the ball hit him squarely on the top of his head, resulting in a loss to the A's. From then on, whenever the Indians visited Philadelphia, a loud-mouthed, imaginative A's fan sat behind the Tribe dugout wearing a steel helmet. Each time Doby came to the plate the fan would bang the helmet with a stick.

There was the day Doby hit a home run against the loud-speakers above the wall in deep center in Griffith Stadium, said at the time to be the hardest ball ever hit there. The ball bounced back into the playing field and Larry, not realizing it was an automatic homer, raced around the bases and slid into the plate.

There was the day Boudreau stole home on Red Sox catcher Matt Batts, who argued so violently with the umpire that he forgot Eddie Robinson was on first base. During the argument Robbie jogged to second, making Sox manager McCarthy so angry he came out of the dugout and kicked Batts squarely in the seat of the pants.

There was Bob Lemon's no-hitter, June 30, in Detroit. In the fourth inning George Kell hit a line drive down the left-field line

that was caught, miraculously, by Dale Mitchell. No one else came close to making a hit. Kell came up again with two outs in the ninth. Lemon's second pitch was so wide, Hegan merely waved at it. The catcher got a new ball from umpire Cal Hubbard and walked out to Bob.

"Lem was white as a sheet," Hegan recalled later. "I said, 'Let's get this guy out.' Lem didn't seem to hear me. I stood there until he finally muttered, 'Okay.' Kell hit the next pitch straight back to Bob. He ran three-fourths of the way to first before he threw the ball and it wasn't until the umpire motioned 'out' that he seemed to come out of shock."

There was the first crowd above 80,000—82,681 to be exact—that overflowed the Stadium to see a doubleheader against the A's. They saw the Indians win two, taking the second on a pinch-hit by Veeck's boy, Peck.

There was the doubleheader of August 8. Robinson hit three homers that day against the Yankees, but the fans walked out talking about a single. Boudreau had been badly injured a few days earlier and he was on the bench as the doubleheader began; only two points separated the Indians, A's and Yankees, the top three teams, and the Red Sox in fourth, 1-1/2 games out of first.

In the seventh inning of the first game, Cleveland trailed, 6-4. With the bases loaded and two out, Thurman Tucker came to bat. The Yanks brought in their ace reliever, Joe Page. Time was called. A pinch-hitter was coming in for Cleveland. Whom would Lou put in? He put himself in. He walked with a limp to the plate and singled to tie the score. The Indians won both games.

There was the night in Washington with the score tied 6-6 in the bottom of the tenth with one out; Ed Stewart of the Senators was on third base. Boudreau called time and sent Bob Kennedy in to play right field. The next hitter flied deep to right. Kennedy backed to the wall to get a running start, moved in toward the ball, caught it and rifled it home. Stewart was out at the plate and was so astonished by the throw he remained on the ground for a full minute after the inning was over. In the eleventh Kennedy singled home the winning run.

There was the afternoon Lemon pitched eight scoreless innings against the White Sox, then lost in the ninth, 3-2. A writer approached Lemon in the clubhouse afterward and asked, "What did you throw?" The usually pleasant pitcher replied in unprintable terms and the next day Boudreau called the reporters together.

"I don't want anything to happen to upset the team," Boudreau said. "I'd like to strike a bargain with you fellows. Would you agree not to come into the clubhouse after the games? I promise to meet you in my office, answer all questions and get any information you may want from the players."

In a rare pact the Cleveland writers, as eager for a pennant as Boudreau, agreed to cooperate.

There were Veeck's stunts: strolling bands, fireworks, orchids and nylons for the females. Something was going on at the Stadium every night and one rooter suggested facetiously in a letter: "Why not have a night for me, good old Joe Earley, just a fan?" Veeck proclaimed "Joe Earley Night," and gave old Joe a vanful of gifts, including assorted farm animals, from chickens to a swayback horse, plus numerous valuable household items. Not long afterward the customers held a night for Veeck, a unique honor for an owner.

There was the booing of Bob Feller. After the first few weeks of the season the great pitcher, once the favorite of the fans, couldn't win. Some fans began booing him. Publicly, Feller said nothing.

but at home his wife, Virginia, found him irritable and short with the children for the first time in his career. He confided to a writer: "Cleveland fans are bush. The whole team would rather play on the road."

The quote was published and attributed to an unnamed Cleveland player. Veeck quickly came to the defense of the fans, who were filling his park at record rates. Cheers soon drowned out the boos, but not for long. When Feller was named to the All-Star team (because of his reputation), Boudreau and Veeck met and decided Bob needed a rest. A vacation during the All-Star break, they decided, would revive him for the second half of the season. They called him in and asked him to withdraw from the All-Star Game. Bob reluctantly did.

Immediately editorials criticized him for this "shameful" act. Bob said it was his idea, refusing to reveal he was following orders from his superiors. Now he really heard boos, tormenting ones, the instant he showed his face in *any* park. But he remained silent. And the rest cure worked. The second half of the season he was again a great pitcher. The boos subsided.

There was the controversial signing of "ancient" Satchel Paige. Secretly, Veeck invited Paige to town, phoned Boudreau and said, "I've got a pitcher I want you to look over." Lou came down to the Stadium, blinked in disbelief when he saw Satch. "Leroy," as Veeck always called him, jogged a bit, said, "I'm ready." Lou caught him and batted against him. Remarkably, all but four of Paige's pitches were over the plate. "I'll take him," said Lou and Satch joined the club.

"This time Veeck has gone too far," people said. *The Sporting News* blistered Bill for signing the "old man" as, the papers said, a publicity stunt, pure and simple. Veeck remained silent.

In games, the tall, skinny right-hander would amble slowly to the mound. "Why hurry into trouble?" he would say. And, inevitably, he would easily handle the trouble.

Further, Paige was a great gate attraction. He drew a sell-out crowd when he pitched in Chicago. Detroit drew a standing-room-only crowd when it was erroneously announced he was scheduled to pitch. On August 20, his start against the last-place White Sox attracted 78,382 to Cleveland's ballpark, largest night crowd in the history of baseball. Satch pitched a 1-0 three-hitter, "for the folks."

Veeck added to the attraction by saying Paige "must be at least 50 or 60." Satch really was under 40 and offered to pay $500 to anyone who could prove he played ball before 1927. An enterprising fan went to Chattanooga to uncover a box score showing a "Satchell" had pitched in 1926.

"That's me," admitted Paige, "I must have slept out a year." Veeck was forced to pay off for his pitcher. Further evidence revealed Satch was 16 that year, making him 38 in 1948, but Veeck scoffed at it and said, "Even his mama doesn't know how old he is."

Satch, more inventive, added to the attraction, too. He told reporters he had a "be ball—because it be where I want it to be." Other pitches of his, he said, were "a whipsy-dipsy-do, a single curve, a double curve and a triple curve." Actually he had virtually no breaking pitch and was successful chiefly because of his amazing control. In warmups he would take the tobacco out of a cigarette butt, use the tiny paper for home plate, then throw strike after strike over it.

Satch helped keep the team loose. He called Feller "Bob Rapid" and Hegan "Big Catch." He said the Indians' goal was to play in the "World Serious."

Satch burped often, the result of a stomach condition he attrib-

uted to South American food. Once Hegan gave him the sign for a fastball. Satch leaned forward and stared at the signal. Then he stepped off the rubber. When he returned to position Hegan gave him the sign again. After another long look, Satch backed off once more. This time Hegan reluctantly gave the sign for a curve. Again Satch stared and stepped off.

Hegan went to the mound and said, "C'mon Satch. I've called everything you've got."

"I got gas, Big Catch," said Satch. He produced a giant belch. "Ah, I'm okay now." And he was.

Satch's pitching motions and mannerisms drove umpires and batters to distraction. He'd wiggle his fingers and occasionally he'd employ his delayed delivery, the "hesitation pitch." Often the umpires would call balks.

"They don't know the rules," Satch would say forgivingly.

But Boudreau didn't always see Satch as humorously as his teammates did. Satch had no conception of time, or space or place. He would report in the afternoon for a night game, and vice versa. Once he failed to show up at Yankee Stadium. Fortunately the game was called because of rain. "I knew it was gonna happen," explained Satch. Boudreau fined him $50.

He missed a train from New York to Boston and when the team arrived Satch was there waiting. "I took a bird," he said. Boudreau fined him again.

Finally, Lou handed him a schedule and said, "I'm going to ask you for this every day, Satch. If you're ever without it, it'll be an automatic $100 fine." But even Lou often had to walk away quickly so his smile wouldn't show. Satch was fun and games and simply too good a pitcher. Even *The Sporting News* eventually admitted its editorial comment might have been premature.

There was the day tragedy struck, September 13. Don Black was the Cleveland pitcher, and in the second inning he came to bat, swung, staggered, turned a small circle around umpire Bill Summers, muttered, "My God, Bill, what's happened?" and sagged to the ground, unconscious. The 31-year-old pitcher was rushed to Charity Hospital where examination revealed a hemorrhage on the brain. A blood vessel had snapped, causing blood to flood his skull.

Don hovered between life and death for weeks. He survived, but his days as an active athlete were over. Veeck announced a Don Black Night to be held on a date the Indians were scheduled to play a day game against the league-leading Red Sox. Veeck said he wanted the largest possible crowd to turn out for Black's benefit and he asked Joe Cronin, the Red Sox general manager, for permission to play the game at night. Cronin was in no position to refuse, although his manager Joe McCarthy fretted. "You watch, we'll have to face Feller under the lights," said McCarthy. "I'd much rather play him in the day-time."

Feller did pitch and, with 76,772 people looking on, he beat the Sox, 5-2, pulling the Indians into a first-place tie. The date was September 22 and the Indians, accused of choking up, had come back. Further, Veeck turned over the Indians' entire cut of the gate, $40,380, to the Black family. (Black died in 1959.)

There was the unprecedented playoff game. Shortly after the Don Black Night, the Indians, Red Sox and Yanks were tied for first, with just seven games to go. The Indians moved to two games in front with three remaining. It was cut to one, with two left. On the final Saturday, Cleveland beat the Tigers to clinch a tie and the Red Sox knocked off the Yankees. Cleveland was one game in front of Boston.

On Sunday, the last day of the season, Feller was named to pitch against the Tigers. A victory and the Indians were in.

Suddenly Veeck didn't trust himself. If the Cleveland game were called for any reason he would have the pennant, there being no provision for rescheduling at that time.

Veeck phoned Will Harridge, president of the American League. "Send somebody up here to take charge," he said. "I might be tempted to call the game if there's one cloud in the sky." Harridge sent Tommy Connolly, his umpire-in-chief.

Sunday turned out to be a beautiful day—in Boston, not Cleveland. Hal Newhouser of the Tigers beat Cleveland, 7-1. The Red Sox beat the Yankees, 10-5. A playoff game for the pennant would be played in Boston the following afternoon.

Boudreau called a squad meeting. "This is your game, men," he said. "I'd like to hear your suggestions about our pitcher for tomorrow."

Joe Gordon stood up. "Lou, you've taken us this far," said Gordon. "We're with you all the way. You name the pitcher."

Lemon had pitched Friday, Bearden Saturday and Feller had just finished working.

"It'll be Bearden," said Boudreau. "But don't tell anybody. Let's keep the Red Sox guessing."

On the overnight train ride to Boston, Keltner, taking a few extra beers to relax, had to be put to bed by his teammates. The unconcerned Bearden sat up late playing cards.

The next day Boston's Fenway Park was jammed. "Who's going to pitch for the Indians?" people asked. The Red Sox sent several spies into the Tribe clubhouse for clues. Lemon and Feller both had rubdowns. Only one day's rest behind him, Bearden nonchalantly sat on the dugout steps. Finally, shortly before game-time, Bearden began to warm up.

Meanwhile, the Sox starter proved a greater surprise. To this day manager McCarthy is being second guessed for his choice of Denny Galehouse. In truth, McCarthy had delegated his catcher Birdie Tebbetts to discover privately "who wants to pitch." Birdie found most of the regulars weren't about to volunteer.

Galehouse was eager to work. Several weeks earlier he had shut out the Indians in a lengthy relief victory. Galehouse's willingness, coupled with his earlier success, won him the nomination.

Amid thick tension, the Red Sox scored a run off Bearden in the first inning. Boudreau tied it up with a homer. After that Bearden settled down. In the fourth Boudreau singled, Gordon singled and Keltner hit a three-run homer. Boudreau hit a homer in the sixth and Cleveland won the pennant, 8-3.

That night a victory celebration was held in the Kenmore Hotel. The pressure finally was off, and the liquid flowed. Keltner reminded Tipton of a card debt he hadn't paid. Tipton's reply prompted Kenny to throw a punch. Tipton ducked and the punch hit Lemon.

But soon everybody became "the greatest guy in the world." An unforgettable scene was Zoldak, tears streaming down his face, bawling to Veeck: "Bill, I'm really not worth $100,000."

Boudreau called for a minute of silent prayer for Don Black, still on the critical list in Charity Hospital and reminded the players to report to Braves Field the next day for a workout prior to the World Series opener. They showed up, most of them in no condition to practice.

Cleveland won the World Series in six games. The only disappointment was Feller failing to realize his dream of a World Series

victory. He lost the opener, 1-0, because umpire Bill Stewart was unprepared for a pickoff play Feller and Boudreau had perfected. With Phil Masi on second, Boudreau rested his gloved hand on his left knee signaling the play was on. Feller, took his stretch, counted "one-thousand-one, one-thousand-two, one-thousand-three," wheeled and threw to second. Meanwhile, Lou, who had been counting, too, broke for the bag, caught the throw and tagged the surprised Masi sliding back. Stewart called him safe, a single scored him and the Braves took the opener.

In the fifth game Feller got his chance again, before 86,288 in Cleveland, but this time didn't have it, losing 11-5. The Indians won the series in Boston the next day. The pitching heroes of the World Series were Lemon (two victories), Bearden (one victory, a shutout, as a starter, and a great relief job) and Gromek (one victory). The hitting heroes were Doby (.318 and 11 total bases), Robinson (.300) and Boudreau (.273 and ten total bases). Kennedy

hit .500 as a pinch-hitter and Tucker hit .333 as a pinch-hitter.

The train ride home was wild. Veeck poured milk, water and champagne on everyone. Bottles of sparkling Burgundy were opened and aimed like guns. The entire dining car was a shambles and a worried conductor said, "You'll have to pay for this."

"Send the bill," replied traveling secretary Spud Goldstein. The bill came to $3,000.

When the players arrived at the Terminal they were greeted by a howling mob. Fortunately most of the players had topcoats to throw over their burgundy-stained clothes. Then the victory parade down Euclid Avenue began.

Said rookie Al Rosen: "There can't be another baseball city like this anywhere."

There wasn't. Not in 1948.

Chapter 19

The Summer of 1950: When Philadelphia Fell for the Whiz Kids

For years the Phillies were the sickliest team in the NL. And then in 1950 a group of youngsters seasoned beyond their years pestered their way to the pennant.

By Harry Paxton
SPORT Magazine, June 1964

Because Philadelphia is a tryout town on the theater circuit, its citizens have become accustomed to short runs. No matter how successful the play, Philadelphians know they'll have it to themselves for only a matter of days. They shouldn't have been surprised, then, when the most exciting National League baseball team the city ever had followed in that tradition. Like Shakespearean actors, the Phillies of 1950—the Whiz Kids—strutted and fretted their life upon the stage and then were seen no more.

No more, that is, until the evening of June 5, 1963. Like a belated curtain call, the players in that 1950 smash hit assembled in Connie Mack Stadium to take a nostalgic bow. They played an exhibition against the current Phillies and before the dewy eyes of 35,000 fans, the scrapbook came alive. Second-baseman Mike Goliat unconsciously grabbed a line drive high above his head. The Whiz Kids on the bench were hysterical with laughter. "That is exactly how it was in '50," said one.

Other things seemed to be the same, too. The fans were still in love with Robin Roberts. Catcher Andy Seminick homered into the upper deck. Russ (The Mad Monk) Meyer exploded and threw the resin bag in the air when manager Eddie Sawyer took him out. And in came Jim Konstanty, who relieved in almost half of the Phillies' 1950 games. This time, though, Jim was transported by a sign of the times—a helicopter. "If they had used a helicopter for Konstanty in 1950," said Seminick, "he would have run up one helluva gas bill."

Later, in the clubhouse, the reminiscing continued. "When people come to see me down in Apalachicola, Florida," Jimmy Bloodworth said to Dick Sisler, "I say, 'Welcome to the House that Sisler Built.' I took the $4,200 from the World Series and built it. Your homer, boy, bought every piece of lumber."

"Boy, I was nervous out there," first-baseman Eddie Waitkus said. "I hadn't touched a glove in eight years, and I was scared I'd disgrace myself."

"This team never disgraced itself," one-time coach Benny Bengough said to Waitkus. "I liked what (owner) Bob Carpenter said: 'They beat every team that was better than they were.' "

"All I remember," said Roberts, laughing, "was that every game seemed 2-1. Didn't we ever win one big?"

Seminick and Granny Hamner and a few others broke into barber-shop harmony on a hymn they had sung 13 years before. In another corner of the room, Sawyer walked by Meyer. "Hey, look at Skip," said Meyer. "He's going into the shower with his cigar lit again. How many managers have a waterproof cigar?"

Sawyer smiled wistfully. "Simmons pitches tomorrow," he said.

Robin Roberts
On the final day of the season, Roberts, 23, picked up his 20th win to bring Philadelphia just its second pennant since 1883.

This is how it had been.

If they didn't come to the majors directly from playpens (as some caustic wits insisted), they still weren't many years removed. Their hallmark was precociously skilled youth. Sportswriters borrowed the nickname "Whiz Kids" from a wartime teenage basket-

ball team at the University of Illinois. But that was one of the few things about them that wasn't original.

Cartoonist Willard Mullin symbolized them as brash little ragamuffins who went around showing up the big fellows. Sentimental favorites? The Whiz Kids couldn't miss, any more than David could against Goliath. Curt Simmons, 20. Richie Ashburn, 23. Robin Roberts, 23, Willie Jones, 24. Granny Hamner, 22. Del Ennis, 24. These were some of the names and ages of the regulars in the spring of 1950. Even the club owner was youthful—Bob Carpenter, 34.

Experts were aware that the Phils had the makings of a winner, but the consensus said: Give them a couple of years. The Whiz Kids either hadn't heard this or didn't believe it. They saw no reason why they couldn't win right now. They weren't overawed by the established stars and teams they faced. They assumed every time they took the field that they were going to wind up with more runs than the other club. Somehow, they very often did.

The fact that this was the Philadelphia Phillies gave a Cinderella tone to the whole affair. The Phils had been the epitome of baseball futility for as long as most fans could remember. Just as you could count on the Yankees to be in the pennant race in the American League, so you could rely on the Phillies to finish last or thereabouts in the National. From 1918 through 1948 they had escaped the second division only once—in 1932, when they placed fourth. Sixteen times they were last.

This was a major league franchise whose owners operated it like a minor-league one, spending little or nothing for players and selling off the best of what they had to wealthier clubs. The Phillies had losing teams. So they didn't draw many customers. So they peddled their occasional stars to balance the budget. So they kept on having losing teams. Finally, at the end of 1943, the Phils got an owner of great substance—Robert Ruliph Morgan Carpenter, a wealthy Du Pont official, who installed his sportsminded son Bob Jr., as president.

If people had been aware of Bob Jr.'s past history, they would have known that he relished the impossible. As a 16-year-old, Bob and his younger brother Bill, while on a hunting expedition in Alaska, went after a pretty big target. They took a small motorboat into a bay and began chasing a whale, shooting at it with small arms.

Still, no ownership ever began from farther out in left field. The club's "farm system" consisted of one lone working agreement, with Trenton in the Class B Interstate League. Carpenter recalls, "All we had to start out with were 25 second-division ballplayers and one minor-leaguer at Trenton, a fellow called Turkey Tyson."

This was almost no exaggeration, though the Phillies had acquired two players of lasting value in 1943: A 17-year-old high-school outfielder named Ennis and a minor-league catcher named Seminick.

Herb Pennock, who had been hired away from the Boston Red Sox as general manager, went on from there. Despite wartime transportation difficulties, his scouts began fanning out and looking for whatever talent the military hadn't already snatched away.

The payment of substantial bonuses to kids wasn't a widespread practice then, but the new Philadelphia organization seldom quibbled about the price when it came to landing a promising boy. In Virginia in 1944 the Phils paid $8,000 to shortstop Granny Hamner, 17, a quick-moving, quick-tempered bundle of nervous energy. In Nebraska in 1945 they gave a similar amount to blond speedboy Richie Ashburn, 18, who could have gotten more from the Yankees but correctly assumed that he'd advance faster with the Phils.

"He's another Ty Cobb without Cobb's meanness," a Philadelphia writer was to proclaim the first time he saw Richie in Florida.

It took $16,500 in 1946 to sign Willie (Puddinhead) Jones out of a Carolina semi-pro league at the age of 18. "A Pie Traynor with power," was the hopeful tag on the drawling, unhurried Jones.

Willie never seemed in a hurry, but he could fool you. During the period when the scouts were trailing him, one scout brought him to his hotel. The scout excused himself for a moment, went to his room and left Willie alone with the room clerk, a young lady named Carolyn Goodson. "Ah took one look at her," says Willie, "and Ah said, 'Ah'm gonna marry you!' She thought Ah was crazy. But four months later we were married."

While Willie and his bride were settling down together, the Phillies opened farms on which to rear their bonus babies. To Utica in the Class A Eastern League went Hamner, Ashburn and eventually Willie Jones. Also prepping for the majors at Utica was the manager, Eddie Sawyer, a well-educated, level-headed fellow who had never advanced beyond the minors as an outfielder because of injuries. Herb Pennock had handpicked him in 1944—when Sawyer was 33—as the Phils' pilot of the future.

By 1947 the baseball ivory market had become highly competitive again. The Phils did pick up a useful young pitcher named Bubba Church for $3,000, and they got infielder Mike Goliat for nothing—he simply showed up at their Class D farm in Vandergrift, Pennsylvania, and asked for a trial. But they had to go to $65,000 that spring for left-hander Curt Simmons of Egypt, Pennsylvania, who was sought by every club in the majors except one. With his high-kicking windup, his crackling fastball and his big-breaking curve, it was no wonder he attracted everyone's attention.

Late that summer the Phils got another pitching standout for $20,000—Robin Roberts, of Springfield, Illinois, and Michigan State. Roberts had less dazzling stuff than Simmons, but he was nearly three years older and more mature, with much sharper control.

Early in 1948 Pennock died suddenly of a stroke at 53. For the long-range future of the Phillies this was a disaster, but in the immediate future it made little difference. During his four-year stewardship all but one of the youngsters who were to contribute to the 1950 pennant drive were in the Phillie system.

The Whiz Kids weren't all kids, of course. There was a blending of older players at key spots. There was Eddie Waitkus, who had been acquired in 1948 deals with the Cubs, along with Russ Meyer and aging Bill Nicholson. There was Dick Sisler, picked up in a trade with the Cardinals. Most of all, there was Jim Konstanty, who was 31 when Eddie Sawyer spotted him at Toronto in 1948 after two other National League clubs had given up on him.

Konstanty had been mediocre as a starting pitcher, but as a relief man in Philadelphia he was sensational with his big windup and the deceptive palmball which he called his changeup.

The Phils had tied for last place in 1947, then advanced to sixth the following year. In 1949 they pulled into third place with a determined September drive. Such rapid progress by a youthful club should have impressed the oddsmakers, but it didn't. In the 1950 advance betting odds the Phillies ranked fourth at 8-to-1, behind the heavily favored Brooklyn Dodgers, St. Louis Cardinals and Boston Braves.

The Phils had a pleasant opening day, beating the Dodgers and Don Newcombe behind Robin Roberts, but lost five of the next six. Not until May 6, with an 11-7 victory in St. Louis, did they pull above .500 to stay. By the Fourth of July the Phils were in the middle of a four-team race (St. Louis, Philadelphia, Brooklyn and

Boston). By July 25 they were on top and starting to pull away.

They weren't doing it by overpowering the opposition, and this was part of their special appeal. In a great majority of their games they simply outlasted the other fellows. The Phils would finish fourth in the National League in runs scored, but they would allow the fewest runs in the majors. In 99 games the Phils would limit the enemy to four runs or less. On 76 occasions it would be three runs or less.

Their greatest strength, obviously, was pitching. Simmons, who had been too wild in previous years, suddenly developed big-league control. By July 27 he had won 14 games. He might have finished with 25 if he hadn't been called up for two weeks of National Guard duty at that stage. On September 13 he was recalled again by the Guard and missed the remainder of the season. Even so, his 1950 record was 17 and 8.

Robin Roberts, with better hitting and fielding support than he had ever had before, won 20 games for the first time. He kept pumping his live fastball into the strike zone, sometimes striking out batters, but more often making them pop up or hit in the dirt. And he was tireless—many days he was throwing harder in the ninth inning than in the first.

The biggest pitching surprise was Bob Miller, a 23-year-old sinkerball pitcher who had a nine-game winning streak and ended up at 11 and 6. Another unexpected lift during mid-season came from Bubba Church, 24, an eight-game winner. The only disappointments on the staff were non-Whiz Kids Russ Meyer, 26, and Ken Heintzelman, 35, and even they won big games down the stretch.

The most important member of the staff, though, was the man who never started a game until the World Series—Konstanty. Every winning pitcher except the strong-armed Roberts owed much of his success to Big Jim. Sawyer waved Konstanty in from the bullpen 74 times during the 154-game season—then the modern single-season record. Between July 19 and August 30 Jim appeared in 17 ballgames, worked 38 innings—and allowed only one run.

Sublimely confident that he had pitching down to an exact science—his supreme assurance sometimes irritated his teammates as well as his opponents—Konstanty was credited in 1950 with 16 wins and 24 saves. He won the Most Valuable Player award overwhelmingly, the first relief pitcher ever to win it.

As confident as Konstanty was of his ability, he wasn't above asking for advice and giving credit to the man who gave it. Strangely, the man Jim credited most in 1950 was not a Phillie, nor was he even in baseball. Konstanty's chief adviser was Andy Skinner, an undertaker from Worcester, New York. A close friend of Konstanty's, Skinner had caught the pitcher during the offseason and had learned the mechanics of each pitch. Then, in July, Konstanty felt his slider wasn't breaking right. Jim called Skinner down to Philadelphia, Skinner watched Jim throw and, Konstanty said, corrected him. Instead of the Phillies' pennant hopes being buried by an ineffective Konstanty, they had been revived—by an undertaker.

The Phillies also had a solid outfield. Del Ennis hit well and hard all season—a .311 average, 31 homers and a league-leading 126 RBI. Richie Ashburn slapped and hit-and-ran for a .303 average.

The biggest transformation—in both playing ability and attitude—was undergone by left fielder Dick Sisler. Finally overcoming the burden that had always faced him as the son of George Sisler, Dick hit .293. "And more importantly," said a club attache, "it's been wonderful to see Sisler's personality blossom out this year. He always was a nice guy, but he seemed to sort of hang back. Now that he's been having a good season, getting confidence in himself,

he's really bloomed. I think he's probably the best-liked fellow on the club."

In the infield Waitkus at first worked smoothly with a trio of Whiz Kids—Jones, Hamner and Goliat. All had superior years in the field, and all but Goliat (.234) hit for respectable averages. But Goliat did come through periodically with important hits. This was true of everybody in the lineup, including the balding Seminick (Grandpa Whiz), who batted .288. Behind the plate Seminick was no picture of grace, but he was a steady receiver.

Check through the rosters of championship teams and you'll almost always come up with the name of a "take-charge guy." Hamner played this role admirably for the Whiz Kids. Writer Frank O'Rourke described Hamner this way: "When he goes out there in that cocky walk, his chin out, arms swinging, you know what he's thinking—that Hamner can lick anybody and will prove it."

Granny always itched for the chance to prove it. When he was playing for Utica in the minors and the fans rode him for an error, he would challenge them to come down and fight. The Utica team frequently got in free-for-alls with Williamsport and Hamner always sought out the catcher, who was Williamsport's biggest man. Granny even went so far as to punch a captain in the Army. Supposedly, Hamner got away with it.

Sawyer learned quickly that when you have a battler like Hamner on your club, you utilize him, not repress him. Early in 1950 Hamner said to coach Benny Bengough, "Would you ask the Skipper if it would be all right for me to talk to the pitchers when they get in trouble?" Bengough relayed the request to Sawyer. "Tell him to go ahead," said the manager. "He does it anyway, doesn't he?"

Those were the principals. An appealing club? Yes. A colorful club? No. The only conspicuous personality on the squad was Russ Meyer, the terrible-tempered pitcher. He wasn't enough of a factor in 1950 to rate much attention, except from clubhouse custodian Unk Russell, whose head Meyer almost tore off with a flying hunk of soap.

To be sure, there was an occasional flare-up on the field—Jones vs. Connie Ryan of the Reds at one point, Seminick vs. Bill Rigney of the Giants at another. But by and large this was hardly a flamboyant crew.

A popular conception was that these were dedicated, clean-living young athletes who abstained from even the most minor vices. This was untrue of most of them as they grew older and more sophisticated, and it was an exaggeration even then. Nevertheless, the American Dairy Association would have been proud of these boys. It is said that the closest Ashburn ever came to blowing up was when his teammates once played a practical joke on him. "Who swiped my stinking milk?" yelled Richie.

Ennis wasn't as pink-cheeked as Ashburn, but he was of the same breed. During one road trip Del's stomach was acting up. It was suggested that his food might settle better if he took a glass of wine before dinner. "I can't stand the stuff," said Ennis. "I'd rather have stomach trouble."

The manager was even less hard-bitten than his ballplayers. Sawyer's only striking innovation was to establish a no-wives rule at training camp in 1950. Sawyer was affable with the press, but he just wouldn't dramatize himself. He gave stock answers to every question.

In good periods or bad, Sawyer was always unruffled, a quality that probably made him the ideal leader of this particular team. An intolerant manager could have undermined the confidence of the kids. Sawyer was patient and reassuring. He cracked down only if he thought a player wasn't trying his hardest. That seldom if ever hap-

pened in 1950, because this was a club headed toward the pennant.

Strangely, Sawyer's biggest task was to fend off over-confidence from the players and fans during the season's last month. On September 3 a mob of 30,000 cheered the team at the Philadelphia airport after it had won 11 of 14 on the road and opened a seven-game lead. "There are still 27 games left," Sawyer told the crowd. "We don't have this pennant won yet." He didn't know how right he was.

The next day the Giants shut them out twice, emphasizing the Phils' shortage of offensive power. The Whiz Kids had been winning games all year without many runs, but how long could it last?

The pattern carried over into a series with the second-place Dodgers. First they wasted a good pitching job by Bubba Church, 2-0. Then they wasted one by Curt Simmons, 3-2. And then they wasted one by Robin Roberts, again losing 3-2.

The Phillies' lead was down to four games and the seemingly pressure-proof old pros of the Dodgers began needling the Whiz Kids mercilessly. "The Whiz Kids are shaking," Jackie Robinson taunted. "They are contented and rich," said Branch Rickey.

Before the final game of the Dodger series Sawyer called a club-house meeting. He handed the ball to Meyer and said, "Rock 'em to sleep." If Meyer needed any further incentive, he got it when the Dodgers kept yelling "Choke-up" at him. The Mad Monk beat them, 4-3, to end the five-game losing streak.

Slowly and painfully, the Phillies' hitters started coming out of their slumps. On the day before Simmons was to return to active duty, Willie Jones decided there was only one way to break his own slump. "Ah tried different neckties, different shoe laces, and now Ah'm just gonna grab any bat I see to break this jinx," said Willie. The bat worked, and Willie hit a ninth-inning game-winning single.

The Phillies began playing like pennant-winners again and on September 16 they won a doubleheader against Cincinnati. The winning pitchers were Blix Donnelly and Heintzelman, both 35. "Some Whiz Kids!" said Blix. "They're taking us old men out of camphor to win." With 11 games left the Phillies had regained their seven-game lead and it appeared to be all over. But Sawyer was still saying that they didn't have the pennant won yet. And he was still so right. The Whiz Kids dropped two straight to the Dodgers, one out of three to the Braves, then four in a row to the Giants. They didn't choke up in the sense that they were kicking games away. But the earlier conviction that this was a team of destiny appeared to have evaporated. No longer did they come up with the big hits or the big plays in the clutch situations. Confided an insider: "They're all praying now that somebody else will get hot and win it for them."

Going into the final weekend the Phillies were only two games in front of the Dodgers with two games left—in Brooklyn. On Saturday, September 30, the Dodgers closed to within one game and a playoff with a 7-3 victory. Now the Phillies were being called the Fizz Kids.

For the finale on Sunday, October 1, a standing-room crowd of 35,073 packed Ebbets Field, with another 30,000 being turned away. Each club led with its top starter. Roberts vs. Newcombe. For Roberts it was the fourth start in nine days. He had won his 19th game on September 12 (Newcombe also had 19 wins), but had been unable to win since, although he had several near-misses.

In the first five innings Roberts limited the Dodgers to one hit—a fourth-inning double by Pee Wee Reese. The Phils got a man on first in every inning but the first, but the runners never advanced.

In the Philadelphia sixth, with two out and nobody on, Sisler bounced a hit between first and second. Ennis blooped a single to center. Jones drove another hit past second to give the Whiz Kids a 1-0 lead. It didn't last long. In the Dodger half Pee Wee Reese got his second hit, a bases-empty home run. It was a freak. The ball hit the screen in right field and instead of bouncing back into play, it got stuck on top of the scoreboard.

In the ninth inning the score was still 1-1. The Phils, who had collected eight hits off Newcombe, couldn't break the tie. It was the Dodgers' turn, and Roberts, who had a three-hitter up to then, quickly got in trouble.

Robin had issued his only base on balls to leadoff man Cal Abrams in the first. Now, leading off the ninth, Abrams worked Roberts for another base on balls. Reese followed with his third hit, a solid single to left that pushed Abrams to second. Then Duke Snider rifled another single to center.

Cal Abrams, racing around second, was waved home by third-base coach Milt Stock, who had little respect for the throwing arm of Richie Ashburn. But Richie came in fast to scoop up the ball and threw Abrams out at the plate by 15 feet.

That was the only break Roberts needed. After walking Jackie Robinson intentionally to load the bases, he got Carl Furillo on a pop foul and Gil Hodges on a fly to right.

In the Phillies' tenth Dick Sisler, who had already hit three singles, stepped up with two men on and one out and lofted the ball into the left-field seats for one of baseball's historic home runs. Now the score was 4-1, and it stayed that way. Back home at their radios thousands of Philadelphians went wild. The Whiz Kids had made it. This was only the second pennant for a club that had been operating in the National League since 1883—the other had come back in 1915.

After October 1 it was all anticlimactic. The Whiz Kids moved into the World Series against the heavily favored New York Yankees. Many people said the Kids wouldn't win a single game. Sure enough, they didn't. Their pitching and fielding held up—they limited the Yankees to 11 runs—but they could score only five themselves. The scores: 1-0, 2-1, 3-2, 5-2.

Nobody thought then that the Whiz Kids were a one-shot proposition. Maybe they'd been playing over their heads in 1950, but in the long run a youthful club like this was bound to get even better. Well, it didn't. Individually, a couple of Whiz Kids advanced to even bigger seasons—Roberts, Ashburn. But for men such as Del Ennis and Willie Jones, 1950 turned out to be the best year they would ever have.

Perhaps their September comedown in 1950 was a traumatic experience from which the Whiz Kids as a group never quite recovered. They sagged all the way to fifth place in 1951, playing less than .500 ball, and never finished higher than third thereafter. The Phillies' management kept handing out big bonuses to teenagers, the way Herb Pennock had done, but they didn't get the same results.

As the decade wore on the gang began breaking up. Some of the one-time Whiz Kids were traded away; others simply dropped from the majors or retired. The Phils settled into their old niche near the basement, where the Carpenter ownership had originally found them. Not until 1962, when they pulled above the .500 level after four straight cellar finishes, were there signs that the Phillies might have another hopeful crop of youngsters.

Not another crop of Whiz Kids, though. There'll never be another bunch quite like them. Their moment of glory was all too brief.

Duke Snider
Carl Furillo is the first to greet Snider (No. 4) upon his return to the dugout after hitting a three-run World Series homer.

Chapter 20

The '55 Dodgers: Delivering at Last on Years of Promise

For years the Dodgers refrain had been 'Wait till next year!' But that all changed with the team of '55 that dominated the NL and then downed the mighty Yankees.

By Frank Graham, Jr.
SPORT Magazine, June 1962

Approximately 2,000 screaming, starry-eyed Dodger fans, held in check by police lines, jammed the sidewalks in front of and across from Brooklyn's Hotel Bossert. Inside, this evening of October 4, 1955, the Dodgers were celebrating their first world championship. The crowd, which had started to gather in the late afternoon, roared with the arrival of each Brooklyn hero.

In the riotous hotel lounge where players, club officials, newspapermen and their families swarmed in an endless round of toasts and back-slapping, somebody pulled me aside and shouted into my ear:

"That crowd out on the street is yelling for Podres and Hodges. You work for the Dodgers. Why don't you give the fans a break and let them see a couple of the ballplayers?"

Good idea. I pulled Podres and Hodges from the center of a circle of admirers and asked them to come out and wave to the crowd. We pushed our way through a sort of advance guard that had managed to penetrate as far as the lobby, and moved out onto the steps. The two stars of the Dodgers' World Series victory waved to the fans. Hodges, called to by a little boy standing in front of the nearest police barricade, descended the steps to sign the boy's autograph album.

Then, before anybody realized what was happening, some 2,000 wildly excited fans pushed aside the restraining wall of cops, knocked over the barricades and came charging down on us. I pulled Podres back through the front door as the crowd stampeded past, but Gil and a couple of cops were well mauled before Hodges could fight his way, like a swimmer in heavy seas, through the surging, clutching mob into the safety of the lobby. As the police struggled to shepherd the fans back behind the barricades, a distraught sergeant glared at me through the front door and growled:

"Try that again, buddy, and I'll have you locked up."

This was the focal point of Brooklyn's hysteria, but it was only one of thousands of wild demonstrations which had begun as Pee Wee Reese scooped up Elston Howard's grounder and tossed to Hodges at first base to end the 1955 World Series. Frustration, building through years of failure, helped to detonate the explosion. But more, there was local pride in one of the most imposing teams in baseball history. Brooklyn dominated the National League that year as no other team has, before or since, then confirmed its greatness with an uphill victory over the mighty New York Yankees. Watching the strutting, childishly happy ballplayers at the Bossert that night, I found it hard to believe that this was the same group that had assembled, uncertain of themselves and their manager, only seven months before at spring training in Vero Beach, Florida.

The past always seemed to hang like a cloud over the Dodgers

("Wait till next year!" was simply a reflex statement) and the cloud never hung so threateningly as it did in the spring of 1955. The previous season had been a disaster. Walter Alston, hired by owner Walter O'Malley to bring the Dodgers a World Series victory, hadn't come close to piloting them as far as the Series; they ran a dreary second to Leo Durocher's Giants in the pennant race. One baseball writer called Alston "a cipher." The fans called him a lot worse.

The team itself no longer seemed to be a collection of superstars. Don Newcombe, the 6-foot-4, 225-pound pitcher who had won 17 games in 1949, 19 in '50 and 20 in '51, had returned to the Dodgers in 1954 after two years in the army and hadn't been able to get anybody out. Roy Campanella, the round, squeaky-voiced catcher whose hits from an unorthodox stance had twice made him the league's Most Valuable Player, had suffered a nerve injury in his hand that reduced him to uselessness. Swinging one-handed in 1954, Roy had batted .207. Jackie Robinson, whose speed and clutch hitting would eventually get him in the Hall of Fame, had bad legs. Pee Wee Reese, the team leader, was approaching 36. And nobody knew how young Johnny Podres would respond after having been operated on for appendicitis.

As spring training began, Alston had a full squad on hand with the exception of an unknown named Sandy Amoros. Amoros, a left fielder, was missing en route from his home in Cuba. But nobody was particularly upset. Sandy's chances of solving the Dodgers' left-field problem were so dim that Alston was thinking of shifting one of the veterans—Robinson, Hodges, Junior Gilliam—there from the infield. Finally Amoros arrived, three days late, to complete the squad.

"I got lost," Sandy blandly explained to vice-president Buzzie Bavasi.

"He must think I'm a damned fool," Bavasi said later. "He got off the boat in Miami and started to drive up here. How could he get lost? If he turned right he'd fall into the Atlantic Ocean and if he turned left he'd fall into the Everglades." Buzzie fined him $100.

Sandy smiled. Because his English wasn't very good, he thought Bavasi was *giving* him $100.

It was one of the few smiles of a grim spring. Those of us who were there will never forget Alston, sitting in the press lounge after a workout, trying to answer the writers' questions. Who would play first? It would be Hodges, the slugger who was known, too, as the finest fielding first baseman around, unless he played left field. Who would play second? It would be Gilliam, unless he was traded for another catcher or was shifted to left field, or it might be Don Zimmer unless Zimmer beat out Reese for shortstop, or it might be the highly rated rookie Charlie Neal if he could make the team. Who would play third? It might be Robinson if he weren't shifted to left field, or it might be tough Don Hoak, or it might be Reese

if somebody else played shortstop or it might be ...

Who would play left field? Could Newk regain his old form? Could Campy grip a bat well enough to hit? What about Podres' condition? How was Karl Spooner's sore arm?

"I don't know. I don't know." Alston repeated the phrase like a recording. He wasn't being evasive. At the time he *didn't* know, but he had made up his mind to find out. Only right fielder Carl Furillo, noted for his "rifle" arm and slashing line drives (he had led the National League in batting in 1953 with a .344 average) and center fielder Duke Snider, who had hit 42 home runs in '53 and 40 in '54, seemed secure at their positions.

Alston began a program of conditioning and experimenting that was designed to put a solid ball club on the field by the time the season opened. Meanwhile, it was to bring him as much abuse as any manager has ever been subjected to. As the Dodgers broke camp and moved north, Alston was still shifting his players around, trying to find out exactly what he had at his disposal. The writers, unable to tell their readers who would be playing for the Dodgers on opening day, grew restive. They began to say Alston was hesitant, unsure of himself and confused.

But it took Jackie Robinson to put the juggling into the headlines. "How can I get in condition to play ball if he won't let me in the lineup?" Jackie complained to the writers. Jackie's remarks were printed under "Robinson Blasts Alston" headlines, and the writers rushed to Alston.

"I know what Robinson can do," Alston said. "I'm trying to find out what Hoak can do."

Privately, Alston was furious. He wanted to know why Robinson hadn't come to him with his complaint before airing it in the press. The reports that the manager could be pushed around by his stars gained added credence.

"I can't talk to him man to man," Robinson told a friend. "I don't know why, but I just can't."

Taking their lead from Robinson, other players went to the writers with their complaints. Campanella was insulted because Alston had him batting eighth. Russ Meyer felt he wasn't getting enough pitching assignments. When the team got to Washington, Alston received further humiliation.

His predecessor as manager of the Dodgers, Charlie Dressen, had just taken over as manager of the Senators. The writers went to Dressen and asked, since Alston hadn't given them his opening-day lineup, would Charlie make out a Dodger lineup from his own knowledge of them? Sure, Dressen said. He told them how he would handle the Dodgers and it made a funny story. Alston didn't laugh.

Then the season opened and everything turned topsy-turvy. Alston, indefinite about his plans until then, had decided on the makeup of his team: Hodges, Gilliam, Reese and Robinson in the infield. Amoros, Snider and Furillo in the outfield, and Campy catching.

On April 13 the Dodgers opened the season at Ebbets Field and beat the Pirates, 6-1, before 6,999 fans. That day was to set a pattern for the rest of the season: the Dodgers, performing brilliantly in every department, outclassed their rivals and were watched by a disappointing number of Brooklyn fans.

One of the big doubts about Alston was answered in the next ten days. The Dodgers got off to the fastest start in National League history. Beautifully conditioned, they piled up a commanding lead before the rest of the league knew what had happened, and justified Alston's endless shuffling and tinkering during the exhibition tour. They won their first nine games to tie the league record, then broke the record on April 22 by slaughtering Robin Roberts and the Phillies, 14-4. Only 3,874 fans saw the game at Ebbets Field.

Nobody was more puzzled (or upset) by the absence of the fans than the players. While the Dodgers were slugging Roberts to the showers, O'Malley thought it would be a good idea to reward the few fans who had paid to see the team break the record. The fans were told over the PA system that an important announcement would be made after the game (the announcement said that souvenir ashtrays, commemorating the new record, would be sent to fans who turned in their rain checks). In the clubhouse after the game, the players were discussing the crowd and Snider said:

"When they said there'd be an important announcement after the game I thought they were going to announce that the franchise had been moved to Los Angeles."

But those prophetic words were swallowed up in the swirl of events. The next night 27,297 fans watched the Dodgers play the Giants and, despite another dashing performance by Robinson, the Dodgers' winning streak was broken. Somebody said they were frightened by all the people. But now the Dodgers were (temporarily, at least) snarling at somebody besides their manager. That night it was the umpires, as Alston and Zimmer were thrown out of the game. The next day it was the Giants' turn to absorb some beatings.

The fervor started, predictably, between Robinson and Sal Maglie. Maglie, not yet dreaming that he would become a Dodger within a year, was battling his mortal enemies. One of his pitches narrowly missed Robinson's head. On the next pitch Jackie bunted along the first-base line, trying to draw Maglie into a spot where he could be run down. Sal, however, let Whitey Lockman pick up the bunt. Whitey threw to Davey Williams, covering first, and Robinson went for the Giant uniform. He knocked Williams, still grimly clutching the ball, toward right field, and players from both teams flooded the field. Fists were brandished, hard words exchanged. Only quick work by the umpires prevented a riot.

The umpires had to go to work again in the fifth inning. Al Dark led off with a drive to right-center field that fell in for what normally would have been a double. But Dark kept right on running around second and headed for third. The throw beat him cleanly, but Dark crashed into Robinson, jarring the ball from Jackie's hand, and immediately the two players were on their feet and hurling curses at each other. Umpire Babe Pinelli got Dark out of there in a hurry, told Robinson not to make any trouble ("Who? Me?" Jackie asked, astonished) and a riot was again averted.

"I didn't see Williams covering first," Robinson said after the game.

"I thought it was an easy triple," Dark told other reporters at the same moment.

Everybody kept a straight face.

The second big doubt about Alston was cleared up on May 5. It was a quiet morning at Ebbets Field and the Dodger manager was pitching to some of the bench warmers as batting practice got under way. Then Joe Becker, the Dodgers' pitching coach, appeared on the field and beckoned to Alston.

"I told Newcombe you wanted him to pitch some batting practice today," Becker said, "but he says he doesn't want to. He only wants to pitch in games."

"Did you tell him that he's not going to start until we get to Chicago?"

"I told him," Becker said.

Alston went to the clubhouse and found the uniformed Newcombe sitting in front of his locker.

"I hear you don't want to pitch batting practice," Alston said.

"That's right," Newcombe said.

"Then take off that uniform and go home," Alston said. Then he turned to traveling secretary Lee Scott and said, "Tell Buzzie I want to talk to him right away."

Before Newcombe reached his home in New Jersey there was a telegram waiting for him from Buzzie Bavasi. Newcombe was suspended without pay until he complied with his manager's orders. The next day Newcombe was back on the scene, willing to pitch batting practice or do anything else that Alston asked. Alston emerged as the undisputed boss of the Dodgers.

This Dodger team thrived on trouble. Newcombe traveled with the team to Philadelphia, pitched brilliantly in relief and helped the Dodgers to their 22nd victory in 24 games. Three days later he pitched a one-hit shutout against the Cubs.

The pennant race had become a shambles. No longer unsure of himself or cramped by a weak bench, Alston managed with the flair of a Durocher or a Stengel. He inserted pinch-hitters and called on his bullpen with daring and skill; Newcombe, a terror on the mound now, also became a menacing pinch-hitter, while Clem Labine and Karl Spooner headed an effective staff of relievers. Campanella, long since promoted from eighth to the cleanup slot, once more joined Hodges, Snider and Furillo in walloping home runs. Robinson rose to the occasion in the big games, Reese was still the "Old Pro," and Gilliam and Amoros were the Dodgers' insurance that enemy pitchers would not find a breather in their lineup. On June 11, with the season one-third over, the Dodgers led the league by 10-1/2 games.

Reese's age, which had been a threat to the Dodgers' well-being in the spring, now became only an excuse for a party. July 22, his 36th birthday, was designated "Pee Wee Reese Day" at Ebbets Field and Brooklyn fans rose to the occasion. Over 30,000 jammed the ballpark to honor the Dodger captain. In the fifth inning all of the lights were turned out at Ebbets Field and the crowd, holding lighted matches aloft, sang "Happy Birthday to Pee Wee."

It was a welcome moment of pleasure in a period when matters had suddenly taken a turn for the worse. All of Brooklyn was talking about its heroes, but except for an occasional big event, it was watching them on television. Too often at Ebbets Field there were only islands of fans in an ocean of empty seats. Disturbed, O'Malley announced that the Dodgers would play seven home games (plus an exhibition) at Jersey City in 1956.

But this hop-and-skip that was to precede the big jump to Los Angeles was nearly overlooked at the time. The Dodgers had suddenly slumped. One of those incredible series of injuries that sometimes overtakes a healthy team had cropped up in Brooklyn. Robinson and Campanella were hobbled by knee injuries, Snider came down with a virus, Amoros hurt his back. Moving swiftly, Alston put Hoak at third, sent Gilliam to left field and Zimmer to second. The youngsters responded with outstanding performances.

More serious was the sudden decimation of their pitching staff. Alston arrived at the ballpark one day to find that five of his best pitchers—Erskine, Podres, Spooner, Billy Loes and Meyer—were hurt. It was July, and the Dodgers had a 13-game lead, but the spectre of 1951 still hung over them (then they had blown a 13-1/2-game lead in August).

Alston went to Bavasi with a plea for help. The Dodgers' farm system was equal to it. Roger Craig and Don Bessent arrived just in time for a doubleheader, each pitched and won, and another crisis had been passed.

In August, Robinson, who had played little since the All Star Game, returned to the lineup and for about a week put on one of the friskiest displays of his career—taking the extra base on hits, stealing bases, rattling enemy pitchers by dancing down off third. "My leg still bothers me," Jackie said to a friend, "but the club has been dead the last week or so, and I thought I could put a little life into it."

Mission accomplished, Jackie returned to the bench and concentrated on getting his leg in shape for the World Series. The pennant race itself was over. At Milwaukee on September 8 the Dodgers beat the Braves, 10-2, to clinch it. Then they went out and celebrated and made more news when Newcombe blew his stack: Snider had poured a can of beer into Newk's new Panama hat.

The Dodgers had reason to celebrate. They had clinched the pennant earlier than any other club in league history, and led at the time by 17 games (with Alston resting his regulars the lead dropped to 13-1/2 games at the end of the season).

There were heroes everywhere you looked. Campanella, the one-handed swinger of a year before, had come back to bat .318, hit 32 homers, drive in 107 runs and win his third Most Valuable Player Award. Snider, who led the majors in runs batted in with 136, clouted 42 homers and batted .309. Newcombe had come back to post the major leagues' best won-lost record, 20-5, batted .381 and hit seven home runs. Robinson and Reese were tremendous in the clutch. Labine, working in 60 games, was baseball's best relief pitcher. Furillo batted .314 (with 26 homers and 95 RBIs) and Hodges batted .290 (with 22 homers and 102 RBIs).

But other Dodger teams had won the pennant. The World Series had been a trap for all of them. When the Yankees clinched the American League pennant in an exciting finish, much of the earlier fan and press enthusiasm for the Dodgers began to fade. The Dodgers had already met the Yankees five times in the Series and each time had come out second best. Now the predictions of another disaster began to come in. It was all right when ex-Yankees like Joe DiMaggio and Tommy Henrich forecast a Yankee victory; it really hurt when ex-Dodger Billy Cox jumped on the Yankee bandwagon too.

"The Dodgers will choke up," Cox announced from his home in Pennsylvania. "I know. I was with them. They always choked up as soon as they heard they had to play the Yankees."

It was not really Billy's prediction that the Dodgers objected to. It was his use of the third person, rather than the first person, plural.

Brooklyn's worst fears seemed about to be realized when the Yankees bombed Newcombe in the Series opener at Yankee Stadium. Joe Collins hit two home runs and Newk's usual flawless control deserted him. He walked two Yankees at crucial moments, and both scored. Brooklyn's only bright spot was Robinson's daring steal of home in the eighth inning.

"It was a lousy play," grumbled the Yankees' tactician, Lawrence Peter Berra. "The Dodgers were two runs behind when he did it. That run didn't mean nuthin'."

If Yogi thought *that* would pass unnoticed, he didn't know Jackie Robinson. "Let Berra play his kind of game and I'll play mine," Jackie said. "They weren't looking for me to come in and I got a big jump on the pitcher. Any time they'll *give* me a run I'll take it."

But no matter how Robinson and the rest of the Dodgers huffed and puffed, they seemed to be getting nowhere. No left-handed pitcher had beaten them all season, but Whitey Ford had been the winning pitcher against them in the first game, and now lefty Tommy Byrne came back to throttle them in the second, 4-2. Loes pitched as badly for Brooklyn as Newcombe had the day before. As the two teams prepared for the third game at Ebbets Field the Dodgers' cause looked almost hopeless. No team had ever lost the first two games of a best-of-seven World Series and come back to win it.

Only Walter Alston seemed confident. "I feel as good as anybody can after losing two," he said.

The third game was the turning point. Alston decided to use young Johnny Podres in a park which was supposed to be fatal to left-handers. Podres, celebrating his 23rd birthday that afternoon, seemed to share his manager's confidence. Campanella, who had had no luck at all at the Stadium, hit a two-run homer in the first inning. The Yankees tied the score in the second on Mantle's homer and an error by Campy, but Jackie Robinson took over in the bottom of that inning.

With one out Jackie singled, and a moment later the bases were filled when Amoros was hit by a pitch and Podres beat out a bunt. Then Robbie went into his classic act. Moving up and down the third base line, feinting a dash toward home, pulling up suddenly, feinting again. Turley, obviously disturbed by the bravado, walked Gilliam on four pitches to force in Robinson. Another run came in before reliever Tom Morgan got the Dodgers out.

In the seventh Robinson (who had been playing well in the field too) humiliated the Yankees once more. He doubled to left, took a wide turn around second and feinted a dash to third. Elston Howard, who had retrieved the ball in the outfield, hesitated, then threw to second trying to nail Jackie before he could get back there. Instead Robinson wheeled and raced to third, sliding in under Billy Martin's high relay. A moment later Amoros dribbled a hit through the drawn-in infield and Brooklyn had another run. Podres, using his changeup beautifully, held on to win, 8-3.

Still, there was to be one more interlude of intra-team strife in Brooklyn. Zimmer, whose fine late-season play had earned him a job at second base in the Series (Gilliam moving to left field in place of Amoros), complained bitterly when Alston benched him again.

"I've earned my chance to play," Don told the writers. "The manager didn't even tell me I was out of there. I had to read it in the newspapers."

It was sweet music to those of us in the Brooklyn camp. A strife-torn Brooklyn team seemed to be a dangerous one.

Back on the field, the Dodgers were handling the Yankees as they had handled their National League opposition during the season. Labine's strong relief pitching and home runs by Campanella, Snider and Hodges gave the Dodgers a victory, 8-5, in the fourth game. Alston started rookie Craig in the fifth game and Roger, with the help of Labine's fourth relief job in five days and Snider's two homers, beat the Yankees, 5-3. As the two clubs went back to the Stadium, the Dodgers needed only one victory for their first world championship.

Brooklyn's anguished fans, fearful that their Dodgers would let the big one slip away once more, had to spend another day on the rack. Ford pitched a four-hitter, Spooner was clobbered for five runs in the first inning, and the Dodgers lost, 5-1. The Series was even.

Confident Podres was to pitch the final game. Zimmer was back at second for the Dodgers, Gilliam in left. Campy doubled off Byrne in the fourth inning and scored on Hodges' single. In the last of the fourth, Berra hit a looping fly ball into left-center. Gilliam yelled Snider off the ball, then stepped back and let it fall for a double. Podres, mixing his fastball with a curve and the change-up, got out of the inning.

Brooklyn scored its second run in the sixth on Hodges' sacrifice fly. It was then that Alston made the move that saved the game. He took out Zimmer for a pinch-hitter and sent Amoros to left and Gilliam back to second. In the bottom of that inning the Yankees got the first two men on base. Then Berra hit the ball that they still talk about in Brooklyn.

It was a high fly into the corner in left. Amoros, playing Yogi in left-center, had to run over 100 feet to catch up with it. Then, just before going into the railing, he stretched out his glove and caught the ball. Fending off the rail, he turned and fired to Reese, who in turn made a perfect throw to Hodges and doubled Gil McDougald off first.

The ninth inning was pure torture for Brooklyn fans. They groaned on each pitch as Podres fought to hold his 2-0 lead. He did. Bill Skowron grounded out, Bob Cerv flied out and Howard grounded out.

The Dodgers are gone from Brooklyn now. So are Ebbets Field and the Dodgers' old office building at 215 Montague Street. But the yell that went up when Hodges took Pee Wee's throw still seems to be around somewhere. It was a yell that had been held in for a long time, and there seemed to be a feeling in it that you'd better yell while you had the chance. Brooklyn's world champions had come along just in time.

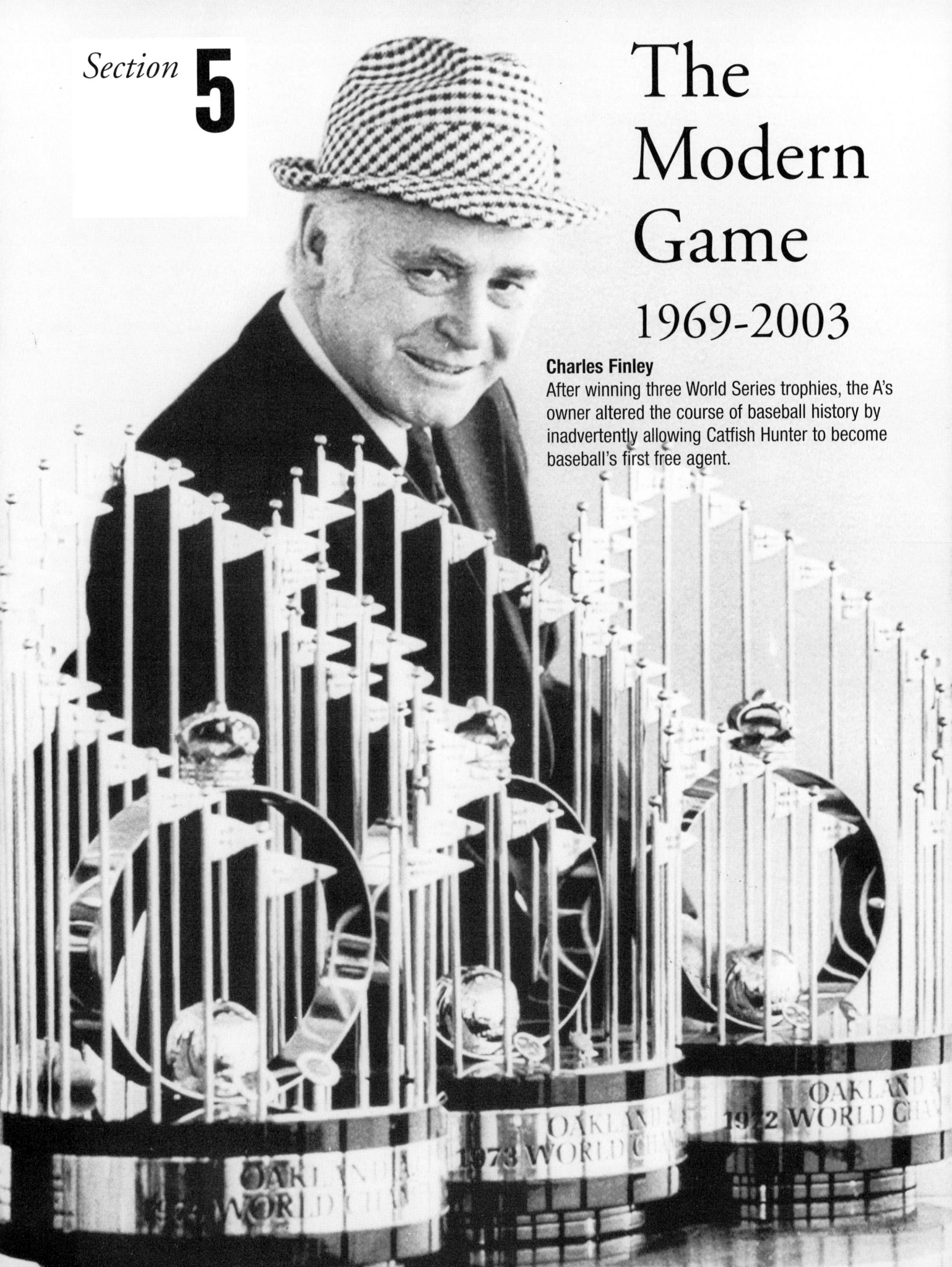

The Modern Game

1969-2003

Charles Finley
After winning three World Series trophies, the A's owner altered the course of baseball history by inadvertently allowing Catfish Hunter to become baseball's first free agent.

FAMOUS FIRSTS

1969: The first major league game outside the U.S. is played at Montreal's Jarry Park.

1972: The first major league player strike occurs and delays opening day by two weeks.

1973: The Yankees' Ron Blomberg becomes the major leagues' first designated hitter.

1973: Roberto Clemente becomes the first Hispanic player enshrined in the Hall of Fame.

1976: Andy Messersmith and Dave McNally become the first players to play out their options to become free agents.

1980: Nolan Ryan earns baseball's first $1 million annual salary (a four-year contract).

1982: Joel Youngblood becomes first major league player to get hits for two different teams (Mets and Expos) in two different cities (Chicago and Philadelphia) on the same day.

1989: Bill White becomes the first African-American league president (NL) and Ken Griffey, Sr. and Jr. become the first father-son duo to perform simultaneously.

1990: Kirby Puckett earns the first $3 million salary.

1997: The first regular-season interleague games are played.

Chapter 21

Freedom's Just Another Word …

Just as baseball seemed to be going the way of the dodo, with low scores and lousy teams in New York pushing other sports to the media forefront, the game was saved through innovation and inadvertent good fortune. Both leagues expanded to 12 teams in 1969. Amazingly, in this first year of divisional play, the New York Mets stormed from the cellar (actually, ninth place in 1968, their highest finish to that time) to win the World Series. Additionally, the game's officials intervened on behalf of the embattled hitters, reducing the strike zone, lowering the mound and even, in 1973, adding the designated hitter to the AL on a (hah!) experimental basis.

Thus restored to health, lumber characterized Earl Weaver's Baltimore Orioles (starring unrelated Robinsons Frank and Brooks, plus Boog Powell) and the Big Red Machine of Cincinnati (Pete Rose, Johnny Bench George Foster, Tony Perez). Along with the three-time world champion Oakland A's, these were the best teams of the 1970s and among the best ever. In 1975 the Reds narrowly defeated the Boston Red Sox in a fabulous World Series that featured a 12th-inning homer by Boston's Carlton Fisk that won Game 6 and captivated North America.

Before that momentous media event, baseball had been buoyed by Hank Aaron's pursuit of Babe Ruth's career home-run record, long thought unapproachable yet broken on April 8, 1974. Outstanding pitchers like Bob Gibson, Tom Seaver, Jim Palmer, and Steve Carlton continued to grab headlines throughout the decade, but the balance of the game had been restored.

Even the demise of the reserve clause, following challenges by Andy Messersmith and Dave McNally and formal burial by arbitrator Peter Seitz, turned out to be fortunate for baseball. Tilting the balance of power from the century-long dominance of owners to the 1870s dominance of players, free agency hurtled the game into a spending spree that saw the Yankees return to respectability, gave hope to bedraggled franchises with depleted farm system and—contrary to owner lamentations—created an unparalleled parity in the game.

Another league expansion took place in 1977 (this time AL-only, with the Toronto Blue Jays and the Seattle Mariners making for a 14-team circuit). But the big story in the American League in the late '70s took place in New York, with Catfish Hunter and Reggie Jackson leading the team on the field and George Steinbrenner and Billy Martin playing Punch and Judy off it; while George was hiring and firing Billy a preposterous five times, the Bronx Zoo filled the sports page with all the melodrama of a soap opera.

Fernandomania opened the 1980s and the exploits of Mike Schmidt, Rickey Henderson and Cal Ripken kept the fans fanatic. The strategic doctrine of the decade was Whiteyball, a speed-and-defense, Astroturf-oriented style pioneered by Cardinals manager Whitey Herzog. As Aaron had passed Ruth in 1974, Nolan Ryan blew past Walter Johnson's strikeout mark in 1983 while racking up, by career's end, an unprecedented seven no-hitters. But for better and worse, the decade truly belonged to Pete Rose, who in 1985 sur-

Catfish Hunter and Reggie Jackson
The pitcher and the slugger, who both left Oakland for Yankee riches, symbolize the change that arrived with the dawning of free agency.

passed Ty Cobb's all-time hit record and only four years later was banned from the game he loved for a range of improper associations. Rose did not confirm the loudly whispered accusation that he had bet on games while he managed the Reds until 15 years later.

Recurring labor strife and play stoppages had marred the game every few years ever since the 1970s, but 1994 provided something disastrously new: a player strike, precipitated by owner intransigence on the issue of a salary cap, that ended a glorious season on August 12. Incredibly, both sides dug in their heels and the play stoppage extended to a cancellation of the World Series and even a delayed start to the 1995 campaign. The game took years to recover both attendance and reputation and it may yet have some distance to travel to soften the hearts of its spurned fans.

The new century brought thrilling postseason play plus the amazing batting feats of Barry Bonds and Alex Rodriguez, and nasty rumors about steroid use by a range of big-name players.

1969

The Miracle Mets baseball's big story in a year of change

About the only thing that remained the same between 1968 and 1969 was the hitting of Willie McCovey and Pete Rose. The enlargement of both leagues to 12 teams added a postseason playoff tier. The firing of William Eckert brought a new commissioner in Bowie Kuhn. The suffocating tilt of the game toward pitching prompted moves to lower the mound and take other steps for aiding hitters. And the least likely team in the NL won its division, the pennant and, finally, the World Series.

The trigger behind the latest expansion was the panicky 1967 promise of AL president Joe Cronin that Kansas City would have a new franchise to replace the departed Athletics. The other new AL team, in Seattle, turned out to be a business fiasco, lasting only one year. The addition of Montreal in the NL brought the first big-league team based outside the United States, while San Diego created a regional rivalry with Los Angeles that would siphon off much of the heat of the Dodgers-Giants competitions.

In the NL West, the Braves surprised the favored Giants by rising from fifth to half a pennant on the backs of Hank Aaron (44 homers), new acquisition Orlando Cepeda (22-88) and Phil Niekro (23 wins). But the Surprise Braves were no match for the Miracle Mets. A year after finishing ninth, New York overcame a 9-1/2-game deficit to the Cubs as late as the second week of August, winning 38 of its last 49 games for a stunning turnaround. The main ingredients were a 25-win season from Tom Seaver, manager Gil Hodges' deft platooning of journeymen, and a defensive middle that kept the young pitching staff out of trouble. Juan Marichal of the Giants had the best ERA (2.10), while McCovey (45 homers and 126 RBIs) and Rose (.348) won their categories for the second year in a row.

In the AL division races, Baltimore took the East and Minnesota the West by big margins. The Orioles got 20 wins from Mike Cuellar and Dave McNally, the Twins from Jim Perry and Dave Boswell. Minnesota's Harmon Killebrew won MVP honors by setting the pace in homers (49) and RBIs (140), while Baltimore got 100-RBI seasons from Boog Powell and Frank Robinson. Rod Carew of the Twins won the batting title (.332), Denny McLain of the Tigers had the most wins (24), and Dick Bosman of the Senators proved the hardest to hit (2.19).

Both the Mets and Orioles swept their League Championship Series. New York overcame shaky pitching and three homers and seven RBIs by Aaron, mainly by batting .327 in the three games. In the AL, Baltimore needed to go to extra innings to win the first two games, then lathered the Twins, 11-2, in the finale.

Willie McCovey
For the second consecutive year the Giants slugger led the NL with 45 home runs and 126 RBIs, while also topping the league in slugging average and on-base percentage.

The favored Orioles were even more so after defeating Seaver in the World Series opener. But then New York came back for four straight wins made of many things. On the mound, Jerry Koosman won twice; at bat, Donn Clendenon provided three clutch homers and the light-hitting Al Weis three key RBIs; in the field, Tommie Agee made two spectacular catches in Game 3 and Ron Swoboda one in Game 4; on the basepaths, the Mets won a dubious interference call in Game 4 and a crucial hit-batsman call in Game 5. Baltimore's .146 average was the lowest ever by an AL team in the World Series.

1969 SEASON HIGHLIGHTS

NATIONAL LEAGUE

East	W	L	Pct.	GB
New York	100	62	.617	—
Chicago	92	70	.568	8
Pittsburgh	88	74	.543	12
St. Louis	87	75	.537	13
Philadelphia	63	99	.389	37
Montreal	52	110	.321	48

West	W	L	Pct.	GB
Atlanta	93	69	.574	—
San Francisco	90	72	.556	3
Cincinnati	89	73	.549	4
Los Angeles	85	77	.525	8
Houston	81	81	.500	12
San Diego	52	110	.321	41

AMERICAN LEAGUE

East	W	L	Pct.	GB
Baltimore	109	53	.673	—
Detroit	90	72	.556	19
Boston	87	75	.537	22
Washington	86	76	.531	23
New York	80	81	.497	28.5
Cleveland	62	99	.385	46.5

West	W	L	Pct.	GB
Minnesota	97	65	.599	—
Oakland	88	74	.543	9
California	71	91	.438	26
Kansas City	69	93	.426	28
Chicago	68	94	.420	29
Seattle	64	98	.395	33

AWARDS

NL MVP: Willie McCovey, SF
AL MVP: Harmon Killebrew, MIN
NL Cy Young: Tom Seaver, NY
AL Cy Young: Mike Cuellar, BAL; Denny McLain, DET
NL Rookie: Ted Sizemore, LA
AL Rookie: Lou Piniella, KC
GOLD GLOVES
NL: Bob Gibson, P; Johnny Bench, C; Wes Parker, 1B; Felix Millan, 2B; Clete Boyer, 3B; Don Kessinger, SS; Roberto Clemente, Curt Flood, Pete Rose, OF
AL: Jim Kaat, P; Bill Freehan, C; Joe Pepitone, 1B; Davey Johnson, 2B; Brooks Robinson, 3B; Mark Belanger, SS; Mickey Stanley, Carl Yastrzemski, Paul Blair, OF

ALL-STAR GAME
R.F.K. Memorial Stadium, Washington, D.C.
July 23: NL 9, AL 3
MVP: Willie McCovey, San Francisco

POSTSEASON
WORLD SERIES
New York Mets 4, Baltimore Orioles 1
Oct. 11: BALTIMORE 4, New York 1
Oct. 12: New York 2, BALTIMORE 1
Oct. 14: NEW YORK 5, Baltimore 0
Oct. 15: NEW YORK 2, Baltimore 1
Oct. 16: NEW YORK 5, Baltimore 3
MVP: Donn Clendenon, New York

NATIONAL LEAGUE
NLCS
New York Mets 3, Atlanta Braves 0
Oct. 4: New York 9, ATLANTA 5
Oct. 5: New York 11, ATLANTA 6
Oct. 6: NEW YORK 7, Atlanta 4

AMERICAN LEAGUE
ALCS
Baltimore Orioles 3, Minnesota Twins 0
Oct. 4: BALTIMORE 4, Minnesota 3
Oct. 5: BALTIMORE 1, Minnesota 0
Oct. 6: Baltimore 11, MINNESOTA 2

Home team in CAPS

> **"I didn't have evil intentions,
> but I guess I did have power."**
> — Harmon Killebrew

NATIONAL LEAGUE LEADERS

Home Runs	
McCovey-SF	45
H.Aaron-Atl	44
May-Cin	38
Perez-Cin	37
Wynn-Hou	33

Runs Batted In	
McCovey-SF	126
Santo-Chi	123
Perez-Cin	122
May-Cin	110
Banks-Chi	106

Batting Average	
Rose-Cin	.348
Clemente-Pit	.345
Jones-NY	.340
Alou-Pit	.331
McCovey-SF	.320

On Base Percentage	
McCovey-SF	.458
Wynn-Hou	.440
Rose-Cin	.432
Staub-Mon	.427
Jones-NY	.424

Slugging Average	
McCovey-SF	.656
H.Aaron-Atl	.607
Allen-Phi	.573
Stargell-Pit	.556
Clemente-Pit	.544

Stolen Bases	
Brock-StL	53
Morgan-Hou	49
Bonds-SF	45
Wills-Mon-LA	40
Tolan-Cin	26

Wins	
Seaver-NY	25
Niekro-Atl	23
Marichal-SF	21
Jenkins-Chi	21

Innings Pitched	
Perry-SF	325.1
Osteen-LA	321.0
Singer-LA	315.2
Gibson-StL	314.0
Jenkins-Chi	311.1

Saves	
Gladding-Hou	29
Upshaw-Atl	27
Granger-Cin	27
Brewer-LA	20
Regan-Chi	17

Strikeouts	
Jenkins-Chi	273
Gibson-StL	269
Singer-LA	247
Wilson-Hou	235
Perry-SF	233

Earned Run Average	
Marichal-SF	2.10
Carlton-StL	2.17
Gibson-StL	2.18
Seaver-NY	2.21
Koosman-NY	2.28

Complete Games	
Gibson-StL	28
Marichal-SF	27
Perry-SF	26
Jenkins-Chi	23
Niekro-Atl	21

AMERICAN LEAGUE LEADERS

Home Runs	
Killebrew-Min	49
Howard-Was	48
Jackson-Oak	47
Yastrzemski-Bos	40
Petrocelli-Bos	40

Runs Batted In	
Killebrew-Min	140
Powell-Bal	121
Jackson-Oak	118
Bando-Oak	113

Batting Average	
Carew-Min	.332
Smith-Bos	.309
Oliva-Min	.309
F.Robinson-Bal	.308
Powell-Bal	.304

On Base Percentage	
Killebrew-Min	.430
F.Robinson-Bal	.417
Jackson-Oak	.410
Petrocelli-Bos	.407
Howard-Was	.403

Slugging Average	
Jackson-Oak	.608
Petrocelli-Bos	.589
Killebrew-Min	.584
Howard-Was	.574
Powell-Bal	.559

Stolen Bases	
Harper-Sea	73
Campaneris-Oak	62
Tovar-Min	45
Kelly-KC	40
Foy-KC	37

Wins	
McLain-Det	24
Cuellar-Bal	23

Innings Pitched	
McLain-Det	325.0
Stottlemyre-NY	303.0
Cuellar-Bal	290.2
McDowell-Cle	285.0
Lolich-Det	280.2

Saves	
Perranoski-Min	31
K.Tatum-Cal	22
Lyle-Bos	17
Watt-Bal	16
Higgins-Was	16

Strikeouts	
McDowell-Cle	279
Lolich-Det	271
Messersmith-Cal	211
Boswell-Min	190

Earned Run Average	
Bosman-Was	2.19
Palmer-Bal	2.34
Cuellar-Bal	2.38
Messersmith-Cal	2.52
Peterson-NY	2.55

Complete Games	
Stottlemyre-NY	24
McLain-Det	23
McDowell-Cle	18
Cuellar-Bal	18
Peterson-NY	16

THE YEAR IN BASEBALL

January 24: Tom Zachary dies. He gave up Babe Ruth's 60th homer in 1927.

February 4: Bowie Kuhn is named baseball commissioner.

February 19: Doc White dies; the songwriting dentist was the left-handed ace of the "hitless wonder" White Sox.

February 21: Ted Williams is named manager of the Senators. In his debut year, they went from 31 games under .500 to 10 over.

March 1: Mickey Mantle announces his retirement; the three-time MVP hit 536 homers plus a record 18 in the World Series.

March 17: St. Louis Cardinals trade Orlando Cepeda to Atlanta for Joe Torre.

April 8: The Montreal Expos defeat the Mets, 10-9, in major league baseball's first international game.

April 11: Seattle Pilots play their first game, beating the White Sox, 7-0.

April 14: In the first major league game played outside the United States, the Montreal Expos defeat St. Louis, 8-7, at Jarry Park.

May 4: The Astros turn seven double plays against San Francisco.

June 14: Reggie Jackson of Oakland has his biggest batting day as he knocks in 10 runs with two homers, a double, and two singles against the Red Sox in Boston. Oakland won 21-7.

July 9: The Cubs' Jimmy Qualls singles off the Mets' Tom Seaver with one out in the ninth, breaking up a perfect game.

July 14: Joe Niekro of the Padres defeats Atlanta, 1-0; the losing pitcher is his brother Phil.

July 15: Rod Carew ties Pete Reiser's single-season record with his seventh steal of home.

September 12: Jerry Koosman and Don Cardwell of Mets each throw 1-0 shutouts over Pirates; each gets game-winning RBI.

September 15: Steve Carlton of the Cardinals fans 19 Mets but loses, 4-3, as Ron Swoboda drives in all four runs with two homers.

October 16: Behind Jerry Koosman and homers by Al Weis and Donn Clendenon, the Mets beat the Orioles to take the Series in five games.

October 29: Tom Seaver gets the first of three Cy Young Awards.

November 15: Billy Southworth dies.

1970

Flood, McLain, Bouton make off-field news in season of turmoil

There was more action off the field than on it in 1970. Cardinals outfielder Curt Flood sat out the season after refusing to accept a winter trade to the Phillies and filing suit against baseball's reserve clause. Although Flood himself would ultimately lose his case before the Supreme Court in 1972, his action proved to be the critical opening salvo for winning free agency for players. In February, Commissioner Bowie Kuhn announced the suspension of Tigers pitcher Denny McLain for association with bookmakers; before the year was out, the two-time Cy Young Award winner would also be idled for throwing ice water at reporters and for carrying a gun. Mere days before the start of the season, the AL authorized the transfer of the Seattle franchise to Milwaukee, leaving behind a cauldron of lawsuits that, as in the case of Kansas City in 1967, would eventually lead to the addition of a team for an abandoned community. The year also marked the publication of Jim Bouton's Ball Four and its embarrassing accounts of the game's racial policies and the endless chases of major league players after women.

On the field in the NL, the Reds and Pirates positioned themselves for the first of five League Championship Series encounters over the next 11 years. Cincinnati's first Big Red Machine team under Sparky Anderson was propelled by Johnny Bench's league-leading 45 homers and 148 RBIs, Tony Perez's 40 homers and 129 RBIs, 38 victories from Jim Merritt and Gary Nolan, and 35 saves from Wayne Granger. Pittsburgh's most potent bat belonged to Willie Stargell (31 homers), with only reliever Dave Giusti (nine wins and 26 saves) showing marked consistency from the mound. Rico Carty of the Braves won the batting title (.366), Tom Seaver of the Mets had the lowest ERA (2.82), and Gaylord Perry of the Giants and Bob Gibson of the Cardinals each posted 23 victories.

In the AL, the Orioles and Twins had little trouble repeating as division winners. Boog Powell wielded the most productive bat for Baltimore (35-114), while Mike Cuellar and Dave McNally each won 24 and Jim Palmer 20. For Minnesota, Harmon Killebrew and Tony Oliva drove in 220 runs between them and Jim Perry matched the 24 wins of Cuellar and McNally for the most in the circuit. The other category laurels went to Frank Howard of the Senators for his 44 homers and 126 RBIs, to Alex Johnson of the Angels for barely edging Carl Yastrzemski with his .329 average, and to Diego Segui of the Athletics for his 2.56 ERA.

As in 1969, both LCS matchups were three-game sweeps. Despite the hitting reputations of both teams, Cincinnati outscored Pittsburgh by the combined score of 9-3. Nobody pitched a complete game or drove in more than two runs on either club. In the AL, Baltimore battered Minnesota to a tune of .330, with Powell driving in six.

Baltimore's only problem in the World Series was Reds first baseman Lee May, whose seven hits were good for eight RBIs. Otherwise, the Orioles did everything better in their five-game victory, not least showcase the brilliant defense of third baseman Brooks Robinson. Robinson wasn't bad offensively, either, collecting nine hits and six runs batted in.

Johnny Bench
Cincinnati's all-star catcher fueled the Big Red Machine with an NL leading 45 home runs and 129 RBIs while helping the up-and-coming Reds to the pennant.

1970 SEASON HIGHLIGHTS

NATIONAL LEAGUE

East	W	L	Pct.	GB
Pittsburgh	89	73	.549	—
Chicago	84	78	.519	5
New York	83	79	.512	6
Atlanta	76	86	.469	13
Montreal	73	89	.451	16
Philadelphia	73	88	.453	15.5
West				
Cincinnati	102	60	.630	—
Los Angeles	87	74	.540	14.5
San Francisco	86	76	.531	16
Houston	79	83	.488	23
St. Louis	76	86	.469	26
San Diego	63	99	.389	39

AMERICAN LEAGUE

East	W	L	Pct.	GB
Baltimore	108	54	.667	—
New York	93	69	.574	15
Boston	87	75	.537	21
Detroit	79	83	.488	29
Cleveland	76	86	.469	32
Washington	70	92	.432	38
West				
Minnesota	98	64	.605	—
Oakland	89	73	.549	9
California	86	76	.531	12
Kansas City	65	97	.401	33
Milwaukee	65	97	.401	33
Chicago	56	106	.346	42

AWARDS
NL MVP: Johnny Bench, CIN
AL MVP: Boog Powell, BAL
NL Cy Young: Bob Gibson, STL
AL Cy Young: Jim Perry, MIN
NL Rookie: Carl Morton, MON
AL Rookie: Thurman Munson, NY
GOLD GLOVES
NL: Bob Gibson, P; Johnny Bench, C; Wes Parker, 1B; Tommy Helms, 2B; Doug Rader, 3B; Don Kessinger, SS; Roberto Clemente, Tommie Agee, Pete Rose, OF
AL: Jim Kaat, P; Ray Fosse, C; Jim Spencer, 1B; Davey Johnson, 2B; Brooks Robinson, 3B; Luis Aparicio, SS; Mickey Stanley, Ken Berry, Paul Blair, OF

ALL-STAR GAME
Riverfront Stadium, Cincinnati
July 14: NL 5, AL 4
MVP: Carl Yastrzemski, Boston
POSTSEASON
WORLD SERIES
Baltimore Orioles 4, Cincinnati Reds 1
Oct. 10: Baltimore 4, CINCINNATI 3
Oct. 11: Baltimore 6, CINCINNATI 5
Oct. 13: BALTIMORE 9, Cincinnati 3
Oct. 14: Cincinnati 6, BALTIMORE 5
Oct. 15: BALTIMORE 9, Cincinnati 3
MVP: Brooks Robinson, Baltimore

NATIONAL LEAGUE
NLCS
Cincinnati Reds 3, Pittsburgh Pirates 0
Oct. 3: Cincinnati 3, PITTSBURGH 0
Oct. 4: Cincinnati 3, PITTSBURGH 1
Oct. 5: CINCINNATI 3, Pittsburgh 2

AMERICAN LEAGUE
ALCS
Baltimore Orioles 3, Minnesota Twins 0
Oct. 3: Baltimore 10, MINNESOTA 6
Oct. 4: Baltimore 11, MINNESOTA 3
Oct. 5: BALTIMORE 6, Minnesota 1

Home team in CAPS

> "I don't want to embarrass any other catcher by comparing him with Johnny Bench."
> — Sparky Anderson

NATIONAL LEAGUE LEADERS

Home Runs		Runs Batted In		Batting Average	
Bench-Cin	45	Bench-Cin	148	Carty-Atl	.366
Williams-Chi	42	Williams-Chi	129	Torre-StL	.325
Perez-Cin	40	Perez-Cin	129	Sanguillen-Pit	.325
McCovey-SF	39	McCovey-SF	126	Williams-Chi	.322
		H.Aaron-Atl	118	Parker-LA	.319

On Base Percentage		Slugging Average		Stolen Bases	
Carty-Atl	.456	McCovey-SF	.612	Tolan-Cin	57
McCovey-SF	.446	Perez-Cin	.589	Brock-StL	51
Dietz-SF	.430	Bench-Cin	.587	Bonds-SF	48
Hickman-Chi	.421	Williams-Chi	.586	Morgan-Hou	42
Perez-Cin	.405	Carty-Atl	.584	Davis-LA	38

Wins		Innings Pitched		Saves	
Perry-SF	23	Perry-SF	328.2	Granger-Cin	35
Gibson-StL	23	Jenkins-Chi	313.0	Giusti-Pit	26
Jenkins-Chi	22	Gibson-StL	294.0	Brewer-LA	24
Merritt-Cin	20	Seaver-NY	290.2	Raymond-Mon	23
		Holtzman-Chi	287.2	Selma-Phi	22

Strikeouts		Earned Run Average		Complete Games	
Seaver-NY	283	Seaver-NY	2.82	Jenkins-Chi	24
Jenkins-Chi	274	Simpson-Cin	3.02	Perry-SF	23
Gibson-StL	274	Walker-Pit	3.04	Gibson-StL	23
Perry-SF	214	Gibson-StL	3.12	Seaver-NY	19
Holtzman-Chi	202	Koosman-NY	3.14	Dierker-Hou	17

AMERICAN LEAGUE LEADERS

Home Runs		Runs Batted In		Batting Average	
Howard-Was	44	Howard-Was	126	Johnson-Cal	.329
Killebrew-Min	41	T.Conigliaro-Bos	116	Yastrzemski-Bos	.329
Yastrzemski-Bos	40	Powell-Bal	114	Oliva-Min	.325
T.Conigliaro-Bos	36	Killebrew-Min	113	Aparicio-Chi	.313
Powell-Bal	35	Oliva-Min	107	F.Robinson-Bal	.306

On Base Percentage		Slugging Average		Stolen Bases	
Yastrzemski-Bos	.453	Yastrzemski-Bos	.592	Campaneris-Oak	42
Howard-Was	.420	Powell-Bal	.549	Harper-Mil	38
Powell-Bal	.417	Killebrew-Min	.546	Alomar-Cal	35
Killebrew-Min	.416	Howard-Was	.546	Kelly-KC	34
Buford-Bal	.409	Harper-Mil	.522	Otis-KC	33

Wins		Innings Pitched		Saves	
Perry-Min	24	Palmer-Bal	305.0	Perranoski-Min	34
McNally-Bal	24	McDowell-Cle	305.0	McDaniel-NY	29
Cuellar-Bal	24	Cuellar-Bal	297.2	Timmermann-Det	27
Wright-Cal	22	McNally-Bal	296.0	Knowles-Was	27
		Perry-Min	278.2	Grant-Oak	24

Strikeouts		Earned Run Average		Complete Games	
McDowell-Cle	304	Segui-Oak	2.56	Cuellar-Bal	21
Lolich-Det	230	Palmer-Bal	2.71	McDowell-Cle	19
Johnson-KC	206	Wright-Cal	2.83	Palmer-Bal	17
Palmer-Bal	199	Peterson-NY	2.90	McNally-Bal	16
Culp-Bos	197	McDowell-Cle	2.92	Culp-Bos	15

THE YEAR IN BASEBALL

January 16: Curt Flood, who refused to report to the Phillies after being traded by the Cardinals, files a civil lawsuit challenging baseball's reserve clause.

April 22: Tom Seaver of the Mets fans the last 10 Padres he faces for a 2-1 victory. He gave up only two hits while whiffing a total of 19 San Diego players.

May 10: Hoyt Wilhelm becomes the first pitcher to appear in 1,000 games.

May 12: Ernie Banks gets home run No. 500.

May 17: Hank Aaron becomes the ninth player to amass 3,000 hits.

May 30: All Star voting is returned to the fans as computerized punch-card ballots are distributed in ballparks and stores.

June 21: Detroit's Cesar Gutierrez goes 7 for 7 in a 12-inning game with Cleveland; the last to go 7-for-7 was Wilbert Robinson of the Baltimore Orioles in 1892.

June 26: Frank Robinson hits two grand slam homers for the Orioles as they clobber Washington 12-2.

July 14: Pete Rose ends one of baseball's most memorable All-Star games by crashing into catcher Ray Fosse to score the winning run.

July 18: Willie Mays joins Hank Aaron and eight others in the 3,000-hit club.

August 11: Jim Bunning becomes the first pitcher since Cy Young to win 100 games in each league.

August 12: Curt Flood loses his $4.1-million antitrust suit against baseball and the reserve clause is upheld.

September 2: Billy Williams of the Cubs plays his 1,117th consecutive game, a National League record.

October 3: Major League umpires return to work after a one-day walkout in quest of better pay.

1971

Rookie Blue takes Cy, Orioles staff all aces; Pirates win Series

The Dodgers and Giants staged another of their emotional pennant duels in 1971, but with a couple of changes in the script—it was San Francisco that blew the big lead, though it did manage to hold on to reach the postseason. In the AL, the Athletics of Charlie Finley put in their claim as a league power on the left arm of 22-year-old Vida Blue.

In the NL West, the Giants held an 8-1/2-game lead over the Dodgers in early September, then, hobbled by a knee injury to slugger Willie McCovey and the perceptible slowing of Willie Mays, saw Los Angeles charge to within a game. Only the hitting of Bobby Bonds (33 homers,102 RBIs) and the pitching of Juan Marichal and Gaylord Perry over the last two weeks staved off a lot of Bay Area baying. In the NL East, another big year from Willie Stargell (a league-leading 48 homers with 125 RBIs) helped the Pirates beat off an eleventh-hour rush from the Cardinals. The St. Louis attack was headed by Joe Torre, who won the batting title (.363) and drove in the most runs (137). Ferguson Jenkins of the Cubs registered the most wins (24), Tom Seaver of the Mets the lowest ERA (1.76).

In the AL West, Oakland all but coasted behind Blue's 24 wins and Catfish Hunter's 21. The left-handed Blue also posted a 1.82 ERA, good enough for both the MVP and Cy Young awards. Baltimore's third straight appearance in the postseason as the AL East representative owed to even more formidable pitching—the first staff since the 1920 White Sox to boast four 20-game winners (Dave McNally, Mike Cuellar, Pat Dobson, and Jim Palmer). But it was another hurler, Detroit's Mickey Lolich, who ended up with the most wins (25) and strikeouts (308). The hitting honors were spread around among Bill Melton of the White Sox (33 homers), Tony Oliva of the Twins (.337) and Minnesota teammate Harmon Killebrew, the only batter in the league to drive in 100 runs (119).

Vida Blue
The A's young left-hander had a dominant rookie season, winning 24 games and the Cy Young Award but pitching depth carried Baltimore to the World Series.

Baltimore kept up another habit by sweeping the ALCS for the third straight year, tagging Oakland pitchers for five runs in each game. In the NL, the Giants finally managed to send a playoff series beyond three games, but only for one day more. The highlight of the Pittsburgh victory was a Game 2 explosion by first baseman Bob Robertson, who had three home runs and a double to account for five runs.

The World Series showcased the offensive and defensive talents of Roberto Clemente and the pitching of Steve Blass. While the Pirates right fielder collected 12 hits, Blass threw two complete-game victories for the difference in the seven-game struggle.

No team made more news during the year than the Senators. First, owner Bob Short took on the Denny McLain problem by acquiring him from the Tigers in a disastrous trade; the seriously out-of-shape right-hander led the AL with his 22 losses. For more headlines, Short bought the rights to Curt Flood while the outfielder was awaiting a Supreme Court verdict on his challenge to the reserve clause; that lasted 35 at bats. Finally, Short ended the Washington run of his franchise altogether by winning permission to move it to Texas for the 1972 season.

1971 SEASON HIGHLIGHTS

NATIONAL LEAGUE

East	W	L	Pct.	GB
Pittsburgh	97	65	.599	—
San Francisco	90	72	.556	7
New York	83	79	.512	14
Chicago	83	79	.512	14
Montreal	71	90	.441	25.5
Philadelphia	67	95	.414	30
West				
St. Louis	90	72	.556	—
Los Angeles	89	73	.549	1
Atlanta	82	80	.506	8
Houston	79	83	.488	11
Cincinnati	79	83	.488	11
San Diego	61	100	.379	28.5

AMERICAN LEAGUE

East	W	L	Pct.	GB
Baltimore	101	57	.639	—
Detroit	91	71	.562	12
Boston	85	77	.525	18
New York	82	80	.506	21
Washington	63	96	.396	38.5
Cleveland	60	102	.370	43
West				
Oakland	101	60	.627	—
Kansas City	85	76	.528	16
Chicago	79	83	.488	22.5
California	76	86	.469	25.5
Minnesota	74	86	.463	26.5
Milwaukee	69	92	.429	32

AWARDS
NL MVP: Joe Torre, STL
AL MVP: Vida Blue, OAK
NL Cy Young: Fergie Jenkins, CHI
AL Cy Young: Vida Blue, OAK
NL Rookie: Earl Williams, ATL
AL Rookie: Chris Chambliss, CLE
GOLD GLOVES
NL: Bob Gibson, P; Johnny Bench, C; Wes Parker, 1B; Tommy Helms, 2B; Doug Rader, 3B; Bud Harrelson, SS; Roberto Clemente, Bobby Bonds, Willie Davis, OF
AL: Jim Kaat, P; Ray Fosse, C; George Scott, 1B; Davey Johnson, 2B; Brooks Robinson, 3B; Mark Belanger, SS; Carl Yastrzemski, Amos Otis, Paul Blair, OF

ALL-STAR GAME
Tiger Stadium, Detroit
July 13: AL 6, NL 4
MVP: Frank Robinson, Baltimore
POSTSEASON
WORLD SERIES
Pittsburgh Pirates 4, Baltimore Orioles 3
Oct. 9: BALTIMORE 5, Pittsburgh 3
Oct. 11: BALTIMORE 11, Pittsburgh 3
Oct. 12: PITTSBURGH 5, Baltimore 1
Oct. 13: PITTSBURGH 4, Baltimore 3
Oct. 14: PITTSBURGH 4, Baltimore 0
Oct. 16: BALTIMORE 3, Pittsburgh 2
Oct. 17: Pittsburgh 2, BALTIMORE 1
MVP: Roberto Clemente, Pittsburgh

NATIONAL LEAGUE
NLCS
Pittsburgh Pirates 3, San Francisco Giants 1
Oct. 2: SAN FRANCISCO 5, Pittsburgh 4
Oct. 3: Pittsburgh 9, SAN FRANCISCO 4
Oct. 5: PITTSBURGH 2, San Francisco 1
Oct. 6: PITTSBURGH 9, San Francisco 5

AMERICAN LEAGUE
ALCS
Baltimore Orioles 3, Oakland A's 0
Oct. 3: BALTIMORE 5, Oakland 3
Oct. 4: BALTIMORE 5, Oakland 1
Oct. 5: Baltimore 5, OAKLAND 3

"Bad baseball players make good managers."
— Earl Weaver

Home team in CAPS

NATIONAL LEAGUE LEADERS

Home Runs
Stargell-Pit 48
H.Aaron-Atl 47
May-Cin 39
Johnson-Phi 34

Runs Batted In
Torre-StL 137
Stargell-Pit 125
H.Aaron-Atl 118
Bonds-SF 102
Montanez-Phi 99

Batting Average
Torre-StL .363
Garr-Atl .343
Beckert-Chi .342
Clemente-Pit .341
H.Aaron-Atl .327

On Base Percentage
Mays-SF .429
Torre-StL .424
H.Aaron-Atl .414
Hunt-Mon .403
Stargell-Pit .401

Slugging Average
H.Aaron-Atl .669
Stargell-Pit .628
Torre-StL .555
May-Cin .532
Bonds-SF .512

Stolen Bases
Brock-StL 64
Morgan-Hou 40
Garr-Atl 30

Wins
Jenkins-Chi 24
Seaver-NY 20
Downing-LA 20
Carlton-StL 20
Ellis-Pit 19

Innings Pitched
Jenkins-Chi 325.0
Stoneman-Mon 294.2
Seaver-NY 286.1
Perry-SF 280.0
Marichal-SF 279.0

Saves
Giusti-Pit 30
Marshall-Mon 23
Brewer-LA 22
J.Johnson-SF 18
Upshaw-Atl 17

Strikeouts
Seaver-NY 289
Jenkins-Chi 263
Stoneman-Mon 251
Kirby-SD 231
Sutton-LA 194

Earned Run Average
Seaver-NY 1.76
Roberts-SD 2.10
Wilson-Hou 2.45
Forsch-Hou 2.53
Sutton-LA 2.54

Complete Games
Jenkins-Chi 30
Seaver-NY 21
Stoneman-Mon 20
Gibson-StL 20

AMERICAN LEAGUE LEADERS

Home Runs
Melton-Chi 33
Jackson-Oak 32
Cash-Det 32
Smith-Bos 30

Runs Batted In
Killebrew-Min 119
F.Robinson-Bal 99
Smith-Bos 96
Murcer-NY 94
Bando-Oak 94

Batting Average
Oliva-Min .337
Murcer-NY .331
Rettenmund-Bal .318
Tovar-Min .311
Carew-Min .307

On Base Percentage
Murcer-NY .429
Rettenmund-Bal .424
Kaline-Det .421
Buford-Bal .415
White-NY .399

Slugging Average
Oliva-Min .546
Murcer-NY .543
Cash-Det .531
F.Robinson-Bal .510
Jackson-Oak .508

Stolen Bases
Otis-KC 52
Patek-KC 49
Alomar-Cal 39
Campaneris-Oak 34

Wins
Lolich-Det 25
Blue-Oak 24
Wood-Chi 22
McNally-Bal 21
Hunter-Oak 21

Innings Pitched
Lolich-Det 376.0
Wood-Chi 334.0
Blue-Oak 312.0
Cuellar-Bal 292.1
Coleman-Det 286.0

Saves
Sanders-Mil 31
Abernathy-KC 23
Scherman-Det 20
Fingers-Oak 17
Burgmeier-KC 17

Strikeouts
Lolich-Det 308
Blue-Oak 301
Coleman-Det 236
Blyleven-Min 224
Wood-Chi 210

Earned Run Average
Blue-Oak 1.82
Wood-Chi 1.91
Palmer-Bal 2.68
Hedlund-KC 2.71
Blyleven-Min 2.81

Complete Games
Lolich-Det 29
Blue-Oak 24
Wood-Chi 22
Cuellar-Bal 21
Palmer-Bal 20

THE YEAR IN BASEBALL

January 11: Tigers pitcher John Hiller, 27, suffers a heart attack and sits out one season before making a remarkable comeback.
February 9: Satchel Paige becomes the first player to enter the Hall of Fame by virtue of his accomplishments in the Negro Baseball Leagues.
April 10: Veterans Stadium in Philadelphia opens.
April 27: Braves slugger Hank Aaron becomes the third player to hit 600 home runs.
May 29: Joe Morgan, Denis Menke, Cesar Geronimo, Jack Billingham, and Ed Armbrister come to the Reds from the Astros for Lee May, Tommy Helms, and Jimmy Stewart.
May 30: Willie Mays scores the 1,950th run of his career to break the NL record held by Stan Musial.
June 21: Ken Harrelson retires from baseball to become a pro golfer.
June 23: Rick Wise of the Phils hits a home run in the fourth consecutive game that he pitched in June.
June 27: Rick Wise of the Phils pitches a no-hitter against the Reds and hits two homers in 4-0 win.
August 10: Harmon Killebrew becomes the 10th player to hit 500 home runs.
September 26: Jim Palmer becomes the fourth member of the Orioles staff to win 20 games in 1971.
September 29: Ron Hunt sets a Major League record by being hit by a pitch 50 times in one season.
September 30: The Senators final game in Washington is forfeited with the Senators leading in the ninth inning when fans swarm the field.
November 29: Gaylord Perry and Frank Duffy are traded from San Francisco to Cleveland for Sam McDowell.

1972

Clemente dies in crash after A's upend Reds in strike-marred year

Cincinnati's Big Red Machine moved into high gear thanks to the off-season acquisition of second baseman Joe Morgan from Houston. The Giants ended more than two decades of ties with Willie Mays by sending him to the Mets in a midseason deal, but these were the least of off-the-field events. Most conspicuously, the Players Association struck spring-training camps to back up demands for a better pension plan; by the time a settlement was reached, 13 days and 86 games had been subtracted from the regular-season schedule. The campaign was also bracketed by the deaths of popular figures. In the spring, Mets manager Gil Hodges dropped dead of a heart attack on a golf course. On New Year's Eve at the end of the year, Pittsburgh star Roberto Clemente went down in a plane crash while on a mercy mission to earthquake victims in Nicaragua.

Morgan's contribution to Cincinnati's mauling of the NL West was to steal 58 bases and top the league in runs scored (122) while driving in 73 and batting .292. Johnny Bench paced the NL in both homers (40) and RBIs (125), while Clay Carroll made up for the club's circuit-low 25 complete games with 37 saves. In the NL East, Pittsburgh did some slapping around of its own behind such familiar figures as Willie Stargell (33-112) and Steve Blass (19 wins). Two of the biggest performers of the year were on abysmal teams. Not only did Steve Carlton's 27 victories account for 45 percent of Philadelphia's wins, but his 310 strikeouts and 1.97 ERA gave him a Triple Crown. In San Diego, Nate Colbert's 111 RBIs amounted to a record 23 percent of those knocked in by the Padres as a whole. Billy Williams of the Cubs won the batting title (.333).

The games lost during the spring strike came back to haunt the Red Sox when they lost the AL East to the Tigers by a mere half game. Detroit's most valuable player was 22-game-winner Mickey Lolich. Vida Blue's lengthy contract holdout cost Oakland any quick jump on the AL West, but the club prevailed anyway when Catfish Hunter and Ken Holtzman teamed up for 40 wins and Rollie Fingers anchored a solid bullpen with 21 saves and 11 victories. Minnesota's Rod Carew became the first AL batting champion (.318) not to hit a home run, Chicago's Dick Allen compiled the most homers (37) and RBIs (113), Chicago's Wilbur Wood and Cleveland's Gaylord Perry won 24, and Boston's Luis Tiant held hitters to a 1.91 ERA.

Both playoff series were tense five-game affairs. In the NL, Pittsburgh had Cincinnati on the ropes in the ninth inning of the clincher, but then Bench tied it with a homer and, a few batters later, Bob Moose wild-pitched home the pennant run. In the AL,

Roberto Clemente
The classy Pirates outfielder, the winner of four batting titles and 12 Gold Gloves, died in a December plane crash while on a mercy mission to Nicaragua earthquake victims.

only Oakland scored as many as five runs in any game, Blue Moon Odom won twice and Blue made up for a miserable year by coming out of the bullpen to shut out Detroit over the last four innings of the 2-1 finale.

Oakland overcame the absence of injured slugger Reggie Jackson to outlast Cincinnati in a seven-game World Series. Most of the slack was taken up by catcher Gene Tenace, who belted four homers and drove in nine runs. Hunter won twice and Fingers had a win and two saves. Only one of the seven games was decided by more than one run.

1972 SEASON HIGHLIGHTS

NATIONAL LEAGUE

	W	L	Pct.	GB
East				
Pittsburgh	96	59	.619	—
Chicago	85	70	.548	11
New York	83	73	.532	13.5
St. Louis	75	81	.481	21.5
Montreal	70	86	.449	26.5
Philadelphia	59	97	.378	37.5
West				
Cincinnati	95	59	.617	—
Los Angeles	85	70	.548	10.5
Houston	84	69	.549	10.5
Atlanta	70	84	.455	25
San Francisco	69	86	.445	26.5
San Diego	58	95	.379	36.5

AMERICAN LEAGUE

	W	L	Pct.	GB
East				
Detroit	86	70	.551	—
Boston	85	70	.548	0.5
Baltimore	80	74	.519	5
New York	79	76	.510	6.5
Cleveland	72	84	.462	14
Milwaukee	65	91	.417	21
West				
Oakland	93	62	.600	—
Chicago	87	67	.565	5.5
Minnesota	77	77	.500	15.5
Kansas City	76	78	.494	16.5
California	75	80	.484	18
Texas	54	100	.351	38.5

AWARDS

NL MVP: Johnny Bench, CIN
AL MVP: Dick Allen, CHI
NL Cy Young: Steve Carlton, PHI
AL Cy Young: Gaylord Perry, CLE
NL Rookie: Jon Matlack, NY
AL Rookie: Carlton Fisk, BOS
GOLD GLOVES
NL: Bob Gibson, P; Johnny Bench, C; Wes Parker, 1B; Felix Millan, 2B; Doug Rader, 3B; Larry Bowa, SS; Roberto Clemente, Cesar Cedeno, Willie Davis, OF
AL: Jim Kaat, P; Carlton Fisk, C; George Scott, 1B; Doug Griffin, 2B; Brooks Robinson, 3B; Ed Brinkman, SS; Ken Berry, Bobby Murcer, Paul Blair, OF

ALL-STAR GAME

Atlanta-Fulton County Stadium, Atlanta
July 25: NL 4, AL 3
MVP: Joe Morgan, Cincinnati

POSTSEASON
WORLD SERIES
Oakland Athletics 4, Cincinnati Reds 3
Oct. 14: Oakland 3, CINCINNATI 2
Oct. 15: Oakland 2, CINCINNATI 1
Oct. 18: Cincinnati 1, OAKLAND 0
Oct. 19: OAKLAND 3, Cincinnati 2
Oct. 20: Cincinnati 5, OAKLAND 4
Oct. 21: CINCINNATI 8, Oakland 1
MVP: Gene Tenace, Oakland

NATIONAL LEAGUE
NLCS
Cincinnati Reds 3, Pittsburgh Pirates 2
Oct. 7: PITTSBURGH 5, Cincinnati 1
Oct. 8: Cincinnati 5, PITTSBURGH 3
Oct. 9: Pittsburgh 3, CINCINNATI 2
Oct. 10: CINCINNATI 7, Pittsburgh 1
Oct. 11: CINCINNATI 4, Pittsburgh 3

AMERICAN LEAGUE
ALCS
Oakland A's 3, Detroit Tigers 2
Oct. 7: OAKLAND 3, Detroit 2
Oct. 8: OAKLAND 5, Detroit 0
Oct. 10: DETROIT 3, Oakland 0
Oct. 11: DETROIT 4, Oakland 3
Oct. 12: Oakland 2, DETROIT 1

> **"Why pitch nine innings when you can get just as famous pitching two?"**
> — Sparky Lyle, on relief pitching

Home team in CAPS

NATIONAL LEAGUE LEADERS

Home Runs		Runs Batted In		Batting Average	
Bench-Cin	40	Bench-Cin	125	Williams-Chi	.333
Colbert-SD	38	Williams-Chi	122	Garr-Atl	.325
Williams-Chi	37	Stargell-Pit	112	Baker-Atl	.321
Aaron-Atl	34	Colbert-SD	111	Cedeno-Hou	.320
Stargell-Pit	33	May-Hou	98	Watson-Hou	.312

On Base Percentage		Slugging Average		Stolen Bases	
Morgan-Cin	.419	Williams-Chi	.606	Brock-StL	63
Williams-Chi	.403	Stargell-Pit	.558	Morgan-Cin	58
Santo-Chi	.397	Bench-Cin	.541	Cedeno-Hou	55
Aaron-Atl	.391	Cedeno-Hou	.537	Bonds-SF	44
Wynn-Hou	.391	Aaron-Atl	.514	Tolan-Cin	42

Wins		Innings Pitched		Saves	
Carlton-Phi	27	Carlton-Phi	346.1	Carroll-Cin	37
Seaver-NY	21	Jenkins-Chi	289.1	McGraw-NY	27
Osteen-LA	20	Niekro-Atl	282.1	Giusti-Pit	22
Jenkins-Chi	20	Gibson-StL	278.0	Marshall-Mon	18
		Sutton-LA	272.2		

Strikeouts		Earned Run Average		Complete Games	
Carlton-Phi	310	Carlton-Phi	1.97	Carlton-Phi	30
Seaver-NY	249	Nolan-Cin	1.99	Jenkins-Chi	23
Gibson-StL	208	Sutton-LA	2.08	Gibson-StL	23
Sutton-LA	207	Matlack-NY	2.32	Wise-StL	20
Jenkins-Chi	184	Gibson-StL	2.46	Sutton-LA	18

AMERICAN LEAGUE LEADERS

Home Runs		Runs Batted In		Batting Average	
D.Allen-Chi	37	D.Allen-Chi	113	Carew-Min	.318
Murcer-NY	33	Mayberry-KC	100	Piniella-KC	.312
Killebrew-Min	26	Murcer-NY	96	D.Allen-Chi	.308
Epstein-Oak	26	Scott-Mil	88	May-Chi	.308
		Powell-Bal	81	Rudi-Oak	.305

On Base Percentage		Slugging Average		Stolen Bases	
D.Allen-Chi	.422	D.Allen-Chi	.603	Campaneris-Oak	52
May-Chi	.408	Fisk-Bos	.538	Nelson-Tex	51
Mayberry-KC	.396	Murcer-NY	.537	Patek-KC	33
White-NY	.385	Mayberry-KC	.507	Kelly-Chi	32
Scheinblum-KC	.385	Epstein-Oak	.490	Otis-KC	28

Wins		Innings Pitched		Saves	
Wood-Chi	24	Wood-Chi	376.2	Lyle-NY	35
Perry-Cle	24	Perry-Cle	342.2	Forster-Chi	29
Lolich-Det	22	Lolich-Det	327.1	Fingers-Oak	21
		Hunter-Oak	295.1	Granger-Min	19
		Blyleven-Min	287.1	Sanders-Mil	17

Strikeouts		Earned Run Average		Complete Games	
Ryan-Cal	329	Tiant-Bos	1.91	Perry-Cle	29
Lolich-Det	250	Perry-Cle	1.92	Lolich-Det	23
Perry-Cle	234	Hunter-Oak	2.04	Wood-Chi	20
Blyleven-Min	228	Palmer-Bal	2.07	Ryan-Cal	20
Coleman-Det	222	Nelson-KC	2.08	Palmer-Bal	18

THE YEAR IN BASEBALL

February 21: Tom Seaver becomes the highest paid pitcher in baseball history when he signs a $172,500-a-year contract with the Mets.

February 25: The Phillies obtain Steve Carlton from the Cardinals for Rick Wise; all Carlton does this year is win 27 games and the Cy Young Award.

February 28: Dizzy Trout dies.

March 11: Zack Wheat dies.

March 22: The Yankees obtain reliever Sparky Lyle from the Boston Red Sox for Danny Cater and Mario Guerrero.

April 1: The Seattle franchise transfers to Milwaukee.

April 13: First full major league player strike in history ends after 10 days.

August 1: Nate Colbert of San Diego drives in 13 runs in a doubleheader victory on five homers and two singles.

September 30: Roberto Clemente hits a double in the fourth inning against the Mets for his 3,000th hit in the majors. It proves to be his last hit as he would die in an airplane crash in December.

October 9: Oakland's Gene Tenace homers in his first two World Series at-bats.

November 28: Frank Robinson is traded from the Dodgers to the Angels, for whom he becomes that new phenomenon, the designated hitter.

December 31: Pittsburgh Pirate star Roberto Clemente is killed in the crash of a plane flying in relief supplies to Nicaraguan earthquake victims.

1973

Ryan breaks K record; Jackson, pitching power Oakland to title

Only an abstention by the Phillies prevented NL owners from joining those in the AL in adopting a designated hitter. One new owner who found the DH already in place was George Steinbrenner, who took over the Yankees in April with the pronouncement that he would "stick to building ships" for his Cleveland-based American Ship Building Company.

On the field, three of the four division races delivered familiar teams across the finish line first. In the AL West, Reggie Jackson's league-leading 32 homers and 117 RBIs along with 20-win seasons from Catfish Hunter, Ken Holtzman and Vida Blue overwhelmed opponents. In the AL East, Jim Palmer's 22 victories and AL-best 2.40 ERA kept Baltimore above a generally punchless division. For the second year in a row, Minnesota's Rod Carew won the batting title (.350) and Chicago's Wilbur Wood compiled the most wins (24). Nolan Ryan of the Angels satisfied himself with two no-hitters and a major league-record 383 strikeouts.

In the NL West, the equally predictable Reds rode an MVP season from batting champ Pete Rose (.338) and 100-RBI years from Johnny Bench and Tony Perez to a triumph over the Dodgers. But in the NL East, all six clubs spent the year worrying more about trying to reach .500 than indulging title dreams. Well into mid-September it was anybody's race, and even after superior Mets pitching had asserted itself, rainouts forced New York to go into the day after the scheduled end of the season before clinching matters. The Mets, the only division team to play better than .500, were driven by Tom Seaver (19 wins and a league-best 2.03 ERA), with the help of reliever Tug McGraw's 25 saves and the (originally sarcastic) slogan of "You gotta believe!" Willie Stargell of the Pirates had the most NL home runs (44) and RBIs (119), Ron Bryant of the Giants the most victories (24).

Clutch ALCS homers by Oakland's Bert Campaneris in Game 3 and by Baltimore's Andy Etchebarren and Bobby Grich in Game 4 set the stage for a second-straight pennant by the Athletics behind a Hunter shutout in the finale. In the NLCS, the heavily favored Reds could only get as far as Rose took them: with a murderous slide into Mets shortstop Bud Harrelson in Game 3 that precipitated field brawls and enough crowd disorders at Shea Stadium to threaten a forfeit win for Cincinnati; then with a 12th-inning home run in Game 4 that tied the teams at two wins apiece. But Seaver and McGraw had little trouble giving the Mets an unlikely pennant in the decisive fifth game.

Ailing Mets outfielder Rusty Staub looked to be the story of the

Willie Stargell
The veteran first baseman stepped up to fill the Pirates' leadership void caused by the death of Roberto Clemente by leading the NL with 44 home runs and 119 RBIs.

World Series against the even more heavily favored Athletics when he led both teams with 11 hits. But although out-pitched, out-hit, and out-scored, Oakland hung on for a second consecutive championship in seven games. Holtzman won twice and Rollie Fingers saved two games. Following Game 2, A's owner Charlie Finley tried to put second baseman Mike Andrews on the disabled list after his errors had helped the Mets win. Commissioner Bowie Kuhn stopped the move, but it prompted manager Dick Williams to announce he'd had enough of Finley and, win or lose, intended resigning after the Series. Williams did what he promised.

1973 SEASON HIGHLIGHTS

NATIONAL LEAGUE

	W	L	Pct.	GB
East				
Houston	82	80	.506	—
St. Louis	81	81	.500	1
Pittsburgh	80	82	.494	2
Montreal	79	83	.488	3
Chicago	77	84	.478	4.5
Philadelphia	71	91	.438	11
West				
Cincinnati	99	63	.611	—
Los Angeles	95	66	.590	3.5
San Francisco	88	74	.543	11
New York	82	79	.509	16.5
Atlanta	76	85	.472	22.5
San Diego	60	102	.370	39

AMERICAN LEAGUE

	W	L	Pct.	GB
East				
Baltimore	97	65	.599	—
Boston	89	73	.549	8
Detroit	85	77	.525	12
New York	80	82	.494	17
Milwaukee	74	88	.457	23
Cleveland	71	91	.438	26
West				
Oakland	94	68	.580	—
Kansas City	88	74	.543	6
Minnesota	81	81	.500	13
California	79	83	.488	15
Chicago	77	85	.475	17
Texas	57	105	.352	37

AWARDS

NL MVP: Pete Rose, CIN
AL MVP: Reggie Jackson, OAK
NL Cy Young: Tom Seaver, NY
AL Cy Young: Jim Palmer, BAL
NL Rookie: Gary Matthews, SF
AL Rookie: Al Bumbry, BAL

GOLD GLOVES
NL: Bob Gibson, P; Johnny Bench, C; Mike Jorgensen, 1B; Joe Morgan, 2B; Doug Rader, 3B; Roger Metzger, SS; Bobby Bonds, Cesar Cedeno, Willie Davis, OF
AL: Jim Kaat, P; Thurman Munson, C; George Scott, 1B; Bobby Grich, 2B; Brooks Robinson, 3B; Mark Belanger, SS; Amos Otis, Mickey Stanley, Paul Blair, OF

ALL-STAR GAME
Royals Stadium, Kansas City
July 24: NL 7, AL 1
MVP: Bobby Bonds, San Francisco

POSTSEASON
WORLD SERIES
Oakland Athletics 4, New York Mets 3
Oct. 13: OAKLAND 2, New York 1
Oct. 14: New York 10, OAKLAND 7
Oct. 16: Oakland 3, NEW YORK 2
Oct. 17: NEW YORK 6, Oakland 1
Oct. 18: NEW YORK 2, Oakland 0
Oct. 20: OAKLAND 3, New York 1
Oct. 21: OAKLAND 5, New York 2
MVP: Reggie Jackson, Oakland

NATIONAL LEAGUE
NLCS
New York Mets 3, Cincinnati Reds 2
Oct. 6: CINCINNATI 2, New York 1
Oct. 7: New York 5, CINCINNATI 0
Oct. 8: NEW YORK 9, Cincinnati 2
Oct. 9: Cincinnati 2, NEW YORK 1
Oct. 10: NEW YORK 7, Cincinnati 2

AMERICAN LEAGUE
ALCS
Oakland A's 3, Baltimore Orioles 2
Oct. 6: BALTIMORE 6, Oakland 0
Oct. 7: Oakland 6, BALTIMORE 3
Oct. 9: OAKLAND 2, Baltimore 1
Oct. 10: Baltimore 5, OAKLAND 4
Oct. 11: OAKLAND 3, Baltimore 0

"Blind people come to the park just to listen to him pitch."
— Reggie Jackson on Tom Seaver

Home team in CAPS

NATIONAL LEAGUE LEADERS

Home Runs
Stargell-Pit 44
Johnson-Atl 43
Evans-Atl 41
Aaron-Atl 40
Bonds-SF 39

Runs Batted In
Stargell-Pit 119
May-Hou 105
Evans-Atl 104
Bench-Cin 104
Singleton-Mon 103

Batting Average
Rose-Cin .338
Cedeno-Hou .320
Maddox-SF .319
Perez-Cin .314
Watson-Hou .312

On Base Percentage
Singleton-Mon .429
Fairly-Mon .422
Morgan-Cin .408
Evans-Atl .407
Watson-Hou .405

Slugging Average
Stargell-Pit .646
Evans-Atl .556
Johnson-Atl .546
Cedeno-Hou .537
Bonds-SF .530

Stolen Bases
Brock-StL 70
Morgan-Cin 67
Cedeno-Hou 56
Bonds-SF 43
Lopes-LA 36

Wins
Bryant-SF 24
Seaver-NY 19
Billingham-Cin 19
Sutton-LA 18
Gullett-Cin 18

Innings Pitched
Carlton-Phi 293.1
Billingham-Cin 293.1
Seaver-NY 290.0
Reuss-Hou 279.1
Jenkins-Chi 271.0

Saves
Marshall-Mon 31
McGraw-NY 25
Giusti-Pit 20
Brewer-LA 20

Strikeouts
Seaver-NY 251
Carlton-Phi 223
Matlack-NY 205
Sutton-LA 200

Earned Run Average
Seaver-NY 2.08
Sutton-LA 2.42
Twitchell-Phi 2.50
Marshall-Mon 2.66
Messersmith-LA 2.70

Complete Games
Seaver-NY 18
Carlton-Phi 18
Billingham-Cin 16

AMERICAN LEAGUE LEADERS

Home Runs
Jackson-Oak 32
Robinson-Cal 30
Burroughs-Tex 30
Bando-Oak 29

Runs Batted In
Jackson-Oak 117
Scott-Mil 107
Mayberry-KC 100
Bando-Oak 98
Robinson-Cal 97

Batting Average
Carew-Min .350
Scott-Mil .306
Davis-Bal .306
Murcer-NY .304
May-Mil .303

On Base Percentage
Mayberry-KC .420
Carew-Min .415
Yastrzemski-Bos .411
Tenace-Oak .391
Jackson-Oak .387

Slugging Average
Jackson-Oak .531
Bando-Oak .498
Robinson-Cal .489
Scott-Mil .488
Munson-NY .487

Stolen Bases
Harper-Bos 54
North-Oak 53
Nelson-Tex 43
Carew-Min 41
Patek-KC 36

Wins
Wood-Chi 24
Coleman-Det 23
Palmer-Bal 22

Innings Pitched
Wood-Chi 359.1
Perry-Cle 344.0
Ryan-Cal 326.0
Blyleven-Min 325.0
Singer-Cal 315.2

Saves
Hiller-Det 38
Lyle-NY 27
Fingers-Oak 22
Bird-KC 20
Acosta-Chi 18

Strikeouts
Ryan-Cal 383
Blyleven-Min 258
Singer-Cal 241
Perry-Cle 238
Lolich-Det 214

Earned Run Average
Palmer-Bal 2.40
Blyleven-Min 2.52
Lee-Bos 2.75
Ryan-Cal 2.87
Medich-NY 2.95

Complete Games
Perry-Cle 29
Ryan-Cal 26
Blyleven-Min 25
Tiant-Bos 23
Colborn-Mil 22

THE YEAR IN BASEBALL

February 25: A new three-year agreement is reached between the players and owners that provides a minimum salary of $15,000, salary arbitration and the "10-and-5" trade rule.

March 26: George Sisler dies.

April 6: Ron Blomberg of the Yankees becomes the first major league designated hitter.

July 21: Hank Aaron joins Babe Ruth as the only players to hit the 700 home-run plateau.

August 17: Willie Mays hits the 660th—and last—home run of his career.

August 29: Nolan Ryan of the Angels gives up one tainted hit in a 5-0 win over the Yankees. Two Angel infielders play Alphonse and Gaston with Thurman Munson's pop fly, and it drops between them.

September 27: Nolan Ryan fans 16, giving him 383 for the season, to pass Sandy Koufax's single-season strikeout record.

October 30: Tom Seaver wins his second Cy Young Award, becoming first non-20 game winner to take the honor.

November 13: Reggie Jackson of Oakland is voted MVP as he leads the AL in homers, RBIs, and slugging.

December 5: Montreal trades reliever Mike Marshall to the Dodgers—for whom he pitches in 106 games over two seasons and wins the Cy Young Award—for Willie Davis.

1974

Aaron belts No. 715 to break Ruth record as Brock swipes 118

Hank Aaron entered the season one short of Babe Ruth's career mark of 714 home runs, but not at all short on hate mail warning him not to break the "white man's record." For its part, the Braves ownership insisted the slugger sit out the first two games of the season in Cincinnati so the record quest could draw crowds to his home stadium. Commissioner Bowie Kuhn stepped in to order Aaron to appear in the Opening Day lineup against the Reds, and he promptly clouted No. 714 with the first swing of his bat. But Atlanta also got its piece of history when he waited until April 8, against Al Downing of the Dodgers at Fulton County Stadium, to collect No. 715.

In the pennant races, the Dodgers, anchored by reliever Mike Marshall's record 106 appearances (15 wins and 21 saves in a staggering 208 relief innings), slipped past Cincinnati to take the NL West. Also aiding the Los Angeles effort were a league-high 20 wins from Andy Messersmith and 19 from Don Sutton and 100-plus RBI seasons from Steve Garvey and Jim Wynn. In the NL East, Pittsburgh squeaked by St. Louis despite Lou Brock's record-shattering 118 steals. Messersmith's 20 victories were matched by Atlanta's Phil Niekro, while another Braves right-hander, Buzz Capra, posted the lowest ERA (2.28). Mike Schmidt of the Phillies had the most homers (36), Johnny Bench of the Reds the most RBIs (129), and Ralph Garr of the Braves the highest batting average (.353).

Baltimore and Oakland once again dominated the AL. In the East, the offensively anemic Orioles needed 15 one-run victories down the stretch to beat off the resurgent Yankees, who had shifted to Shea Stadium while Yankee Stadium was being overhauled. Mike Cuellar and Ross Grimsley contributed 40 wins between them for Baltimore. In the West, the Athletics had season-long clubhouse fights and animosities toward owner Charlie Finley to deal with, but they prevailed largely because of Catfish Hunter's AL-leading 25 wins and 2.49 ERA and another 36 victories from Ken Holtzman and Vida Blue. Ferguson Jenkins of Texas matched Hunter in the win column, with the other honors going to the Twins' Rod Carew (.364), the White Sox's Dick Allen (32 homers), and ther Rangers' Jeff Burroughs (118 RBIs). The Tigers' Al Kaline became the first ALer since Eddie Collins in 1925 to collect 3,000 hits.

In the NLCS, Sutton overpowered the Pirates, shutting them out in the opener and yielding only three hits over eight innings of the fourth-game pennant clincher. After a rude battering of Hunter in the opening game, the ALCS also showcased brilliant pitching, with the A's notching their third straight pennant behind shutouts by Holtzman and Blue and a fourth-game recovery by Hunter.

Oakland made it 3-for-3 in the World Series, though it wasn't

Hank Aaron
Despite all the hate mail he received as he neared Babe Ruth's all-time home-run record, Aaron was all smiles for the hometown Atlanta fans after No. 715.

as easy as the championship in five games might have appeared. Four of the contests were settled by the score of 3-2 and the team's .211 average provided minimal support for pitchers. A's hurlers were even called on for additional duties—Hunter to close the first game from the bullpen, Holtzman to spark a fourth-game win with a home run after two years of not swinging a bat. Concerning the continual tension with Finley, Reggie Jackson spoke for the team in saying it "took the fun out of winning."

1974 SEASON HIGHLIGHTS

NATIONAL LEAGUE

East	W	L	Pct.	GB
Atlanta	88	74	.543	—
St. Louis	86	75	.534	1.5
Philadelphia	80	82	.494	8
Montreal	79	82	.491	8.5
New York	71	91	.438	17
Chicago	66	96	.407	22

West	W	L	Pct.	GB
Los Angeles	102	60	.630	—
Cincinnati	98	64	.605	4
Pittsburgh	88	74	.543	14
Houston	81	81	.500	21
San Francisco	72	90	.444	30
San Diego	60	102	.370	42

AMERICAN LEAGUE

East	W	L	Pct.	GB
Baltimore	91	71	.562	—
New York	89	73	.549	2
Texas	84	76	.525	6
Kansas City	77	85	.475	14
Milwaukee	76	86	.469	15
Detroit	72	90	.444	19

West	W	L	Pct.	GB
Oakland	90	72	.556	—
Boston	84	78	.519	6
Minnesota	82	80	.506	8
Chicago	80	80	.500	9
Cleveland	77	85	.475	13
California	68	94	.420	22

AWARDS

NL MVP: Steve Garvey, LA
AL MVP: Jeff Burroughs, TEX
NL Cy Young: Mike Marshall, LA
AL Cy Young: Catfish Hunter, OAK
NL Rookie: Bake McBride, STL
AL Rookie: Mike Hargrove, TEX

GOLD GLOVES

NL: Andy Messersmith, P; Johnny Bench, C; Steve Garvey, 1B; Joe Morgan, 2B; Doug Rader, 3B; Dave Concepcion, SS; Bobby Bonds, Cesar Cedeno, Cesar Geronimo, OF

AL: Jim Kaat, P; Thurman Munson, C; George Scott, 1B; Bobby Grich, 2B; Brooks Robinson, 3B; Mark Belanger, SS; Amos Otis, Joe Rudi, Paul Blair, OF

ALL-STAR GAME

Three Rivers Stadium, Pittsburgh
July 23: NL 7, AL 2
MVP: Steve Garvey, Los Angeles

POSTSEASON
WORLD SERIES
Oakland Athletics 4, Los Angeles Dodgers 1
Oct. 12: Oakland 3, LA 2
Oct. 13: LA 3, Oakland 2
Oct. 15: OAKLAND 3, Los Angeles 2
Oct. 16: OAKLAND 5, Los Angeles 2
Oct. 17: OAKLAND 3, Los Angeles 2
MVP: Rollie Fingers, Oakland

NATIONAL LEAGUE
NLCS
Los Angeles Dodgers 3, Pittsburgh Pirates 1
Oct. 5: Los Angeles 3, PITTSBURGH 0
Oct. 6: Los Angeles 5, PITTSBURGH 2
Oct. 8: Pittsburgh 7, LOS ANGELES 0
Oct. 9: LOS ANGELES 12, Pittsburgh 1

AMERICAN LEAGUE
ALCS
Oakland A's 3, Baltimore Orioles 1
Oct. 5: Baltimore 6, OAKLAND 3
Oct. 6: OAKLAND 5, Baltimore 0
Oct. 8: Oakland 1, BALTIMORE 0
Oct. 9: Oakland 2, BALTIMORE 1

> **"The key to winning baseball games is pitching, fundamentals, and three-run homers."**
> — Earl Weaver

Home team in CAPS

NATIONAL LEAGUE LEADERS

Home Runs
Schmidt-Phi	36
Bench-Cin	33
Wynn-LA	32
Perez-Cin	28
Cedeno-Hou	26

Runs Batted In
Bench-Cin	129
Schmidt-Phi	116
Garvey-LA	111
Wynn-LA	108
Simmons-StL	103

Batting Average
Garr-Atl	.353
Oliver-Pit	.321
Gross-Hou	.314
Buckner-LA	.314
Madlock-Chi	.313

On Base Percentage
Morgan-Cin	.430
Stargell-Pit	.409
Bailey-Mon	.400
Schmidt-Phi	.398
Smith-StL	.394

Slugging Average
Schmidt-Phi	.546
Stargell-Pit	.537
Smith-StL	.528
Bench-Cin	.507
Garr-Atl	.503

Stolen Bases
Brock-StL	118
Lopes-LA	59
Morgan-Cin	58
Cedeno-Hou	57
Lintz-Mon	50

Wins
P.Niekro-Atl	20
Messersmith-LA	20
Sutton-LA	19
Billingham-Cin	19

Innings Pitched
P.Niekro-Atl	302.1
Messersmith-LA	292.1
Carlton-Phi	291.0
Lonborg-Phi	283.0
Sutton-LA	276.0

Saves
Marshall-LA	21
Moffitt-SF	15
Borbon-Cin	14
Giusti-Pit	12

Strikeouts
Carlton-Phi	240
Messersmith-LA	221
Seaver-NY	201
P.Niekro-Atl	195
Matlack-NY	195

Earned Run Average
Capra-Atl	2.28
P.Niekro-Atl	2.38
Matlack-NY	2.41
Marshall-LA	2.42
Messersmith-LA	2.59

Complete Games
P.Niekro-Atl	18
Carlton-Phi	17
Lonborg-Phi	16
Rooker-Pit	15

AMERICAN LEAGUE LEADERS

Home Runs
D.Allen-Chi	32
Jackson-Oak	29
Tenace-Oak	26
Darwin-Min	25
Burroughs-Tex	25

Runs Batted In
Burroughs-Tex	118
Bando-Oak	103
Rudi-Oak	99
K.Henderson-Chi	95
Darwin-Min	94

Batting Average
Carew-Min	.364
Orta-Chi	.316
McRae-KC	.310
Piniella-NY	.305
Maddox-NY	.303

On Base Percentage
Carew-Min	.435
Yastrzemski-Bos	.421
Burroughs-Tex	.405
Maddox-NY	.397
Jackson-Oak	.396

Slugging Average
D.Allen-Chi	.563
Jackson-Oak	.514
Burroughs-Tex	.504
Rudi-Oak	.484
Freehan-Det	.479

Stolen Bases
North-Oak	54
Carew-Min	38
Lowenstein-Cle	36
Campaneris-Oak	34
Patek-KC	33

Wins
Jenkins-Tex	25
Hunter-Oak	25

Innings Pitched
Ryan-Cal	332.2
Jenkins-Tex	328.1
G.Perry-Cle	322.1
Wood-Chi	320.1
Hunter-Oak	318.1

Saves
Forster-Chi	24
Murphy-Mil	20
Campbell-Min	19
Buskey-NY-Cle	18
Fingers-Oak	18

Strikeouts
Ryan-Cal	367
Blyleven-Min	249
Jenkins-Tex	225
G.Perry-Cle	216
Lolich-Det	202

Earned Run Average
Hunter-Oak	2.49
G.Perry-Cle	2.51
Hassler-Cal	2.61
Blyleven-Min	2.66
Fitzmorris-KC	2.79

Complete Games
Jenkins-Tex	29
G.Perry-Cle	28
Lolich-Det	27
Ryan-Cal	26
Tiant-Bos	25

THE YEAR IN BASEBALL

January 16: Whitey Ford and Mickey Mantle, teammates through the Yankees' glory years of the 1950s and 1960s, are elected to the Hall of Fame.

January 25: Ray Kroc, who made his millions from McDonald's, buys the Padres for $12 million.

April 3: The Dodgers receive 17-year-old Pedro Guerrero from Cleveland for pitcher Bruce Ellingsen.

April 4: In the earliest opening in major league history, the Cincinnati Reds defeat the Atlanta Braves 7-6 in 11 innings. In his first time at bat, Hank Aaron hits a three-run homer off Jack Billingham. It was his 714th, tying Babe Ruth's career record.

April 8: At Atlanta, Hank Aaron breaks Babe Ruth's career record by slugging his 715th home run, off southpaw Al Downing in the fourth inning.

July 3: Pitching in his major league record 13th consecutive game, Dodgers reliever Mike Marshall saves Tommy John's 4-1 win.

September 10: Lou Brock steals his 104th and 105th bases of the season to break Maury Wills' single-season record.

October 3: Frank Robinson is hired to manage the Cincinnati Reds for 1975, becoming the major leagues' first African-American manager.

November 2: Hank Aaron is traded to the Brewers for Dave May; in Japan, he defeats Sadaharu Oh in homer contest 10-9, at Korakuen Stadium in Tokyo.

December 31: The Yankees sign Catfish Hunter to a five-year, $3.75-million contract after he was declared a free agent as a result of a salary-payment dispute with Charles Finley of Oakland.

1975

Hunter joins Yankees, Robinson makes history; A's streak snapped

Some teams had money, others didn't; some had problems with minorities, others didn't. Because of Charlie Finley's breach of contract on an annuity payment, Oakland ace Catfish Hunter anticipated the free agency era by leaving the A's and signing a $3-million-multiyear contract with the Yankees. On the other side of the street from New York were the White Sox, who peddled catcher Ed Herrmann to the Bronx because they didn't have money to pay him, then dealt outfielder Buddy Bradford to the Cardinals to meet the payroll. Cleveland lowered another racial barrier by hiring Frank Robinson as the first black manager, but Milwaukee's Del Crandall was fired after season-long conflicts with Latin players.

The addition of rookie outfielders Fred Lynn and Jim Rice shoved Boston past Baltimore in the AL East. Lynn's .331-21-105 was good enough to net him both MVP and Rookie-of-the-Year nods, while Rice contributed a .309-22-102 performance. Oakland won its fifth straight division title within an air of expectancy that Hunter's departure would prompt Finley to sell out. The Athletics were spurred by Reggie Jackson's AL-best 36 homers, Vida Blue's 22 wins, and Rollie Fingers' 10 wins and 24 saves. Milwaukee's George Scott not only matched Jackson for home runs, but led the way with his 109 RBIs. Rod Carew of the Twins won his fourth consecutive batting crown and fifth overall (.359). Hunter started paying off for the Yankees right away by tying Baltimore's Jim Palmer for the most wins (23); Palmer also took the ERA title (2.09).

In the NL West, the Reds made up for 1974 by going 41-9 for one stretch before the All-Star game to sew up the title. The nimble double-play combination of Joe Morgan and Dave Concepcion also combined for 100 steals, Tony Perez and Johnny Bench topped 100 RBIs and Will McEnaney and Rawley Eastwick made for a lefty-righty bullpen tandem of 37 saves. In the East, the Pirates put off a challenge from the suddenly power-laden Phillies, in good part because of Dave Parker's .308-25-101 and Jerry Reuss' 18 wins. Philadelphia's drive was motored by home-run leader Mike Schmidt (38) and RBI king Greg Luzinski (120). Other bests went to Chicago's Bill Madlock (.354), New York's Tom Seaver (22 wins), and San Diego's Randy Jones (2.24). Houston's season was clouded by the January suicide of 30-year-old right-hander Don Wilson, who had won more than 100 games for the club.

The playoffs reverted to past sweeps with both the Red Sox and Reds securing pennants in three games. Luis Tiant set the tone in

Fred Lynn
After a 10-RBI game in Detroit, the Red Sox outfielder, on his way to being named the AL MVP and rookie of the year, accepts congratulations in the Tiger clubhouse.

the ALCS with a three-hitter in Game 1 while Boston beat up on Oakland lefty Ken Holtzman twice in four days. Cincinnati's romp over the Pirates featured a complete-game win from Don Gullett and a win and a save by Eastwick.

Tiant was a Red Sox hero in the World Series, as well, when he won twice and gutted through into the eighth of a third game. A second hero was Carlton Fisk, whose 12th-inning homer ended a classic Game 6. But the biggest heroes wore Cincinnati uniforms—Eastwick with two wins and a save and Morgan with a 10th-inning single that ended Game 3 and a ninth-inning safety in Game 7 that gave the Reds the championship.

1975 SEASON HIGHLIGHTS

NATIONAL LEAGUE

East	W	L	Pct.	GB
Pittsburgh	92	69	.571	—
Philadelphia	86	76	.531	6.5
New York	82	80	.506	10.5
St. Louis	82	80	.506	10.5
Montreal	75	87	.463	17.5
Chicago	75	87	.463	17.5

West	W	L	Pct.	GB
Cincinnati	108	54	.667	—
Los Angeles	88	74	.543	20
San Francisco	80	81	.497	27.5
San Diego	71	91	.438	37
Atlanta	67	94	.416	40.5
Houston	64	97	.398	43.5

AMERICAN LEAGUE

East	W	L	Pct.	GB
Boston	95	65	.594	—
Baltimore	90	69	.566	4.5
New York	83	77	.519	12
Texas	79	83	.488	17
Milwaukee	68	94	.420	28
Detroit	57	102	.358	37.5

West	W	L	Pct.	GB
Oakland	98	64	.605	—
Kansas City	91	71	.562	7
Cleveland	79	80	.497	17.5
Minnesota	76	83	.478	20.5
Chicago	75	86	.466	22.5
California	72	89	.447	25.5

AWARDS

NL MVP: Joe Morgan, CIN
AL MVP: Fred Lynn, BOS
NL Cy Young: Tom Seaver, NY
AL Cy Young: Jim Palmer, BAL
NL Rookie: John Montefusco, SF
AL Rookie: Fred Lynn, BOS
GOLD GLOVES
NL: Andy Messersmith, P; Johnny Bench, C; Steve Garvey, 1B; Joe Morgan, 2B; Ken Reitz, 3B; Dave Concepcion, SS; Garry Maddox, Cesar Cedeno, Cesar Geronimo, OF
AL: Jim Kaat, P; Thurman Munson, C; George Scott, 1B; Bobby Grich, 2B; Brooks Robinson, 3B; Mark Belanger, SS; Fred Lynn, Joe Rudi, Paul Blair, OF

ALL-STAR GAME

County Stadium, Milwaukee
July 15: NL 6, AL 3
MVPs: Bill Madlock, Chicago Cubs and Jon Matlack, N.Y. Mets

POSTSEASON
WORLD SERIES

Cincinnati Reds 4, Boston Red Sox 3
Oct. 11: BOSTON 6, Cincinnati 0
Oct. 12: Cincinnati 3, BOSTON 2
Oct. 14: CINCINNATI 6, Boston 5
Oct. 15: Boston 5, CINCINNATI 4
Oct. 16: CINCINNATI 6, Boston 2
Oct. 21: BOSTON 7, Cincinnati 6
Oct. 22: Cincinnati 4, BOSTON 3
MVP: Pete Rose, Cincinnati

NATIONAL LEAGUE
NLCS

Cincinnati Reds 3, Pittsburgh Pirates 0
Oct. 4: CINCINNATI 8, Pittsburgh 3
Oct. 5: CINCINNATI 6, Pittsburgh 1
Oct. 7: Cincinnati 5, PITTSBURGH 3

AMERICAN LEAGUE
ALCS

Boston Red Sox 3, Oakland A's 0
Oct. 4: BOSTON 7, Oakland 1
Oct. 5: BOSTON 6, Oakland 3
Oct. 7: Boston 5, OAKLAND 3

"Reggie (Jackson) is really a good guy. He'd give you the shirt off his back. Of course, he'd call a press conference to announce it."

—Catfish Hunter

Home team in CAPS

NATIONAL LEAGUE LEADERS

Home Runs
Schmidt-Phi	38
Kingman-NY	36
Luzinski-Phi	34
Bench-Cin	28

Runs Batted In
Luzinski-Phi	120
Bench-Cin	110
Perez-Cin	109
Staub-NY	105

Batting Average
Madlock-Chi	.354
Simmons-StL	.332
Sanguillen-Pit	.328
Morgan-Cin	.327
Watson-Hou	.324

On Base Percentage
Morgan-Cin	.471
Wynn-LA	.407
Rose-Cin	.407
Madlock-Chi	.406
Murcer-SF	.404

Slugging Average
Parker-Pit	.541
Luzinski-Phi	.540
Schmidt-Phi	.523
Bench-Cin	.519
Foster-Cin	.518

Stolen Bases
Lopes-LA	77
Morgan-Cin	67
Brock-StL	56
Cedeno-Hou	50
Cardenal-Chi	34

Wins
Seaver-NY	22
Jones-SD	20
Messersmith-LA	19
Hooton-Chi-LA	18
Reuss-Pit	18

Innings Pitched
Messersmith-LA	321.2
Jones-SD	285.0
Seaver-NY	280.1
Morton-Atl	277.2
Niekro-Atl	275.2

Saves
Hrabosky-StL	22
Eastwick-Cin	22
Giusti-Pit	17
McEnaney-Cin	15
Knowles-Chi	15

Strikeouts
Seaver-NY	243
Montefusco-SF	215
Messersmith-LA	213
Carlton-Phi	192
Richard-Hou	176

Earned Run Average
Jones-SD	2.24
Messersmith-LA	2.29
Seaver-NY	2.38
Reuss-Pit	2.54
Forsch-StL	2.86

Complete Games
Messersmith-LA	19
Jones-SD	18
Seaver-NY	15
Reuss-Pit	15

AMERICAN LEAGUE LEADERS

Home Runs
Scott-Mil	36
Jackson-Oak	36
Mayberry-KC	34
Bonds-NY	32

Runs Batted In
Scott-Mil	109
Mayberry-KC	106
Lynn-Bos	105
Jackson-Oak	104

Batting Average
Carew-Min	.359
Lynn-Bos	.331
Munson-NY	.318
Rice-Bos	.309
C.Washington-Oak	.308

On Base Percentage
Carew-Min	.428
Mayberry-KC	.419
Singleton-Bal	.418
Harrah-Tex	.406
Lynn-Bos	.405

Slugging Average
Lynn-Bos	.566
Mayberry-KC	.547
Powell-Cle	.524
Scott-Mil	.515
Bonds-NY	.512

Stolen Bases
Rivers-Cal	70
C.Washington-Oak	40
Otis-KC	39
Carew-Min	35
Remy-Cal	34

Wins
Palmer-Bal	23
Hunter-NY	23
Blue-Oak	22
Torrez-Bal	20
Kaat-Chi	20

Innings Pitched
Hunter-NY	328.0
Palmer-Bal	323.0
G.Perry-Cle-Tex	305.2
Kaat-Chi	303.2
Wood-Chi	291.1

Saves
Gossage-Chi	26
Fingers-Oak	24
Murphy-Mil	20
LaRoche-Cle	17
Drago-Bos	15

Strikeouts
Tanana-Cal	269
G.Perry-Cle-Tex	233
Blyleven-Min	233
Palmer-Bal	193
Blue-Oak	189

Earned Run Average
Palmer-Bal	2.09
Hunter-NY	2.58
Eckersley-Cle	2.60
Tanana-Cal	2.62
Figueroa-Cal	2.91

Complete Games
Hunter-NY	30
G.Perry-Cle-Tex	25
Palmer-Bal	25
Jenkins-Tex	22
Blyleven-Min	20

THE YEAR IN BASEBALL

March 13: Frank Robinson debuts as the majors' first black manager.

May 31: Spoiler Cesar Tovar registers the only hit off Catfish Hunter—the fifth time he has had his team's only hit in a game.

June 1: Nolan Ryan of the Angels pitches his fourth no-hitter, a 1-0 win over the Orioles. It was his 100th major league victory.

June 18: Red Sox rookie Fred Lynn drives in 10 runs against Detroit with three homers, a double, and a single; he won both Rookie of the Year and MVP awards.

July 21: Felix Millan of the Mets hits four singles, but each time is wiped out as Joe Torre grounds into a double play.

July 31: Max Flack dies.

August 9: Davey Lopes of the Dodgers steals his 32nd consecutive base without being caught in a win over the Mets to break Max Carey's 1922 record. Lopes tacked on six more steals before being nipped on August 24.

September 16: The Pirates annihilate the Cubs in Wrigley Field 22-0, in the most one-sided shutout since 1900. Rennie Stennett gets 7 hits in 7 at-bats.

October 21: The Reds use eight pitchers in the sixth game of the Series, but Carlton Fisk breaks up the thrilling contest with a homer in the 12th inning to give the Red Sox a 7-6 win.

October 22: Following a tense 12-inning loss in Boston the night before, the Reds get a ninth-inning single from Joe Morgan and win Game 7 and the World Series.

November 12: Tom Seaver wins his third Cy Young Award.

November 28: Steve Stone signs as free agent with Baltimore.

1976

Free agency arrives as Finley, Kuhn battle and Bench leads Reds

Owners resorted to a spring-training lockout after an arbitrator ruled during the winter that pitchers Andy Messersmith and Dave McNally were entitled to free agency and that the reserve clause had seen its day. Los Angeles owner Walter O'Malley's attempt to blacklist the hurlers was thwarted when Atlanta signed Messersmith and McNally retired. A subsequent agreement stipulated free-agency rights would kick in after six years of major league service.

In the AL East, the Yankees celebrated their return to their Bronx stadium by taking their first division title, behind MVP Thurman Munson (.302-17-105), home-run leader Graig Nettles (32), Ed Figueroa's 19 wins, and Sparky Lyle's 23 saves. New York's rotation would have been stronger if not for Commissioner Bowie Kuhn's veto of Oakland's proposed sale of Vida Blue to the Yankees. According to Kuhn, neither that deal nor the attempt by A's owner Charlie Finley to sell Joe Rudi and Rollie Fingers to Boston were in the "best interests of baseball." Finley's would-be fire sale of stars and his initial refusal to take them back after Kuhn's intervention provided just enough room for Kansas City to back into the AL West title.

The Royals also claimed the batting title for the year in George Brett (.333), but there was significant suspicion the honor should have gone to teammate Hal McRae. The difference was a misjudged fly ball by Minnesota outfielder Steve Brye in the ninth inning of the final game that was ruled an inside-the-park-home run for Brett. McRae accused Twins manager Gene Mauch of playing Brye out of position deliberately so a white man could win the batting crown. Lee May of the Orioles had the most RBIs (109), teammate Jim Palmer the most wins (22) and Mark Fidrych of the Tigers the lowest ERA (2.34). Fidrych, dubbed The Bird for a resemblance to a "Sesame Street" character, galvanized national attention for mound antics that included talking to the ball.

In the NL East, the Phillies knocked off the Pirates behind a circuit-best 38 homers from Mike Schmidt, Steve Carlton's 20 wins, and John Denny's 2.52 ERA. Joe Morgan (.320-27-111), George Foster (.306 with 29 homers and an NL-best 121 RBIs) and Rawley Eastwick (11 wins and 26 saves) helped Cincinnati coast in the NL West. Chicago's Bill Madlock won the hitting title (.339), San Diego's Randy Jones had the most wins (22).

The Reds had their problems with outfielder Jay Johnstone (7-for-9), but they handled the rest of the Phillies for a three-game NLCS sweep. The far more intense ALCS came down to a seesaw fifth game in which Brett clouted a tying three-run homer in the eighth inning, only to see New York first baseman Chris Chambliss

Big Bird and Mark Fidrych
The baseball world was captivated by Fidrych's colorful style and sparkling 2.34 ERA for the Detroit Tigers in the only complete season of his injury-shortened career.

lead off the ninth with his eleventh hit, second homer, and eighth RBI of the series.

The World Series was another Cincinnati blowout, with the Yankees going down in four straight. Led by Johnny Bench's eight hits and six RBIs, the Reds were so tidy about the rout that they sent only nine batters to the plate during the Series. New York's satisfaction came a few weeks later in the signing of Cincinnati ace Don Gullett as a free agent.

1976 SEASON HIGHLIGHTS

NATIONAL LEAGUE

	W	L	Pct.	GB
East				
Philadelphia	101	61	.623	—
Pittsburgh	92	70	.568	9
New York	86	76	.531	15
Chicago	75	87	.463	26
St. Louis	72	90	.444	29
Montreal	55	107	.340	46
West				
Cincinnati	102	60	.630	—
Los Angeles	92	70	.568	10
Houston	80	82	.494	22
San Francisco	74	88	.457	28
San Diego	73	89	.451	29
Atlanta	70	92	.432	32

AMERICAN LEAGUE

	W	L	Pct.	GB
East				
New York	97	62	.610	—
Baltimore	88	74	.543	10.5
Boston	83	79	.512	15.5
Cleveland	81	78	.509	16
Detroit	74	87	.460	24
Milwaukee	66	95	.410	32
West				
Kansas City	90	72	.556	—
Oakland	87	74	.540	2.5
Minnesota	85	77	.525	5
Texas	76	86	.469	14
California	76	86	.469	14
Chicago	64	97	.398	25.5

AWARDS

NL MVP: Joe Morgan, CIN
AL MVP: Thurman Munson, NY
NL Cy Young: Randy Jones, SD
AL Cy Young: Jim Palmer, BAL
NL Rookie: Butch Metzger, SD; Pat Zachry, CIN
AL Rookie: Mark Fidrych, DET
NL Relief Pitcher: Rawly Eastwick, CIN
AL Relief Pitcher: Bill Campbell, MIN
GOLD GLOVES
NL: Jim Kaat, P; Johnny Bench, C; Steve Garvey, 1B; Joe Morgan, 2B; Mike Schmidt, 3B; Dave Concepcion, SS; Garry Maddox, Cesar Cedeno, Cesar Geronimo, OF
AL: Jim Palmer, P; Jim Sundberg, C; George Scott, 1B; Bobby Grich, 2B; Aurelio Rodriguez, 3B; Mark Belanger, SS; Dwight Evans, Joe Rudi, Rick Manning, OF

ALL-STAR GAME
Veterans Stadium, Philadelphia
July 13: NL 7, AL 1
MVP: George Foster, Cincinnati
POSTSEASON
WORLD SERIES
Cincinnati Reds 4, New York Yankees 0
Oct. 16: CINCINNATI 5, New York 1
Oct. 17: CINCINNATI 4, New York 3
Oct. 19: Cincinnati 6, NEW YORK 2
Oct. 21: Cincinnati 7, NEW YORK 2
MVP: Johnny Bench, Cincinnati

NATIONAL LEAGUE
NLCS
Cincinnati Reds 3, Philadelphia Phillies 0
Oct. 9: Cincinnati 6, PHILADELPHIA 3
Oct. 10: Cincinnati 6, PHILADELPHIA 2
Oct. 12: CINCINNATI 7, Philadelphia 6

AMERICAN LEAGUE
ALCS
New York Yankees 3, Kansas City Royals 2
Oct. 9: New York 4, KANSAS CITY 1
Oct. 10: KANSAS CITY 7, New York 3
Oct. 12: NEW YORK 5, Kansas City 3
Oct. 13: Kansas City 7, NEW YORK 4
Oct. 14: NEW YORK 7, Kansas City 6

"When you're a winner you're always happy, but if you're happy as a loser you'll always be a loser."
—Mark Fidrych

Home team in CAPS

NATIONAL LEAGUE LEADERS

Home Runs

Schmidt-Phi	38
Kingman-NY	37
Monday-Chi	32
Foster-Cin	29
Morgan-Cin	27

Runs Batted In

Foster-Cin	121
Morgan-Cin	111
Schmidt-Phi	107
Watson-Hou	102
Luzinski-Phi	95

Batting Average

Madlock-Chi	.339
Griffey-Cin	.336
Maddox-Phi	.330
Rose-Cin	.323
Morgan-Cin	.320

On Base Percentage

Morgan-Cin	.453
Madlock-Chi	.415
Rose-Cin	.406
Griffey-Cin	.403
Cey-LA	.389

Slugging Average

Morgan-Cin	.576
Foster-Cin	.530
Schmidt-Phi	.524
Monday-Chi	.507
Kingman-NY	.506

Stolen Bases

Lopes-LA	63
Morgan-Cin	60
Taveras-Pit	58
Cedeno-Hou	58
Brock-StL	56

Wins

Jones-SD	22
Sutton-LA	21
Koosman-NY	21
Richard-Hou	20
Carlton-Phi	20

Innings Pitched

Jones-SD	315.1
Richard-Hou	291.0
Seaver-NY	271.0
Niekro-Atl	270.2
Sutton-LA	267.2

Saves

Eastwick-Cin	26
Lockwood-NY	19
Forsch-Hou	19
Hough-LA	18
Metzger-SD	16

Strikeouts

Seaver-NY	235
Richard-Hou	214
Koosman-NY	200
Carlton-Phi	195
Niekro-Atl	173

Earned Run Average

Denny-StL	2.52
Rau-LA	2.57
Seaver-NY	2.59
Koosman-NY	2.69
Zachry-Cin	2.74

Complete Games

Jones-SD	25
Koosman-NY	17
Matlack-NY	16
Sutton-LA	15
Richard-Hou	14

AMERICAN LEAGUE LEADERS

Home Runs

Nettles-NY	32
R.Jackson-Bal	27
Bando-Oak	27

Runs Batted In

L.May-Bal	109
Munson-NY	105
Yastrzemski-Bos	102

Batting Average

Brett-KC	.333
McRae-KC	.332
Carew-Min	.331
Bostock-Min	.323
LeFlore-Det	.316

On Base Percentage

McRae-KC	.412
Hargrove-Tex	.401
Carew-Min	.398
Staub-Det	.392
Carty-Cle	.384

Slugging Average

R.Jackson-Bal	.502
Rice-Bos	.482
Nettles-NY	.475
Lynn-Bos	.467
Carew-Min	.463

Stolen Bases

North-Oak	75
LeFlore-Det	58
Campaneris-Oak	54
Baylor-Oak	52
Patek-KC	51

Wins

Palmer-Bal	22
Tiant-Bos	21
Garland-Bal	20

Innings Pitched

Palmer-Bal	315.0
Hunter-NY	298.2
Blue-Oak	298.1
Blyleven-Min-Tex	297.2
Slaton-Mil	292.2

Saves

Lyle-NY	23
LaRoche-Cle	21
Fingers-Oak	20
Campbell-Min	20
Littell-KC	16

Strikeouts

Ryan-Cal	327
Tanana-Cal	261
Blyleven-Min-Tex	219
Eckersley-Cle	200
Hunter-NY	173

Earned Run Average

Fidrych-Det	2.34
Blue-Oak	2.35
Tanana-Cal	2.43
Torrez-Oak	2.50
Palmer-Bal	2.51

Complete Games

Fidrych-Det	24
Tanana-Cal	23
Palmer-Bal	23

THE YEAR IN BASEBALL

January 6: Ted Turner buys the Braves for $11 million.

March 11: Larry Gardner dies.

March 21: Toronto is granted AL franchise for 1977.

April 10: At Milwaukee, leading 9-6 in the bottom of ninth, Yankees' Sparky Lyle surrenders a grand slam to Don Money, but first-base ump James McKean called timeout before the pitch, and Brewers lose, 9-7.

April 15: Renovated Yankee Stadium is jammed with 52,613 fans for Opening Day ceremonies.

May 29: Joe Niekro hits the only home run of his career—off his brother Phil.

June 22: Pitcher Randy Jones ties Christy Mathewson's 63-year-old NL record by going 68 innings without allowing a base on balls.

July 20: Hank Aaron hits the 755th—and last—home run of his career.

September 12: Minnie Minoso becomes oldest player to get a hit in a regulation game. He is almost 54.

September 29: After 23 years and 2,040 victories, Walter Alston steps down as Dodgers' manager.

October 14: The Yankees win the pennant on Chris Chambliss' ninth-inning homer off Kansas City's Mark Littell in Game 5 of AL Playoffs.

November 4: The first free-agent draft is held, and Montreal selects Reggie Jackson with the first choice.

November 29: The Yankees sign free-agent outfielder Reggie Jackson for $3.5 million dollars.

1977

Seaver, Jackson move, Yankees' Mr. October a smash hit in Series

Turmoil characterized the first free-agent season, as much because of managers as free agents. The Yankees had a little of both in signing high-priced Reggie Jackson and then watching the slugger's ego scrape against that of fractious pilot Billy Martin all year. In Texas, infielder Lenny Randle sucker-punched dugout boss Frank Lucchesi, winning an immediate suspension and criminal charges. In Atlanta, it was owner Ted Turner trying to take over the team on the field; in Los Angeles, Walter Alston being squeezed out for Tom Lasorda after 23 one-year contracts. In New York, Joe Torre was given the reins of the Mets just in time to see the Midnight Massacre of the forced trade of ace Tom Seaver to the Reds after weeks of acrimony among the pitcher, the front office, and Daily News columnist Dick Young. Amidst all the commotion, the AL also fielded two new expansion teams, in Toronto and Seattle.

When he wasn't facing off against Martin, Jackson was hitting 32 homers and driving in 110 runs to team up with Graig Nettles (37-107) and Thurman Munson (18-100) for another AL East title-winning club. Boston stayed in the running because of four 100-RBI men in the lineup (including home-run king Jim Rice) and Bill Campbell, the very first re-entry draft free agent, who won 13 and saved 31. In the AL West, the Royals had an easier time behind the offense of Al Cowens (.312-23-112) and a rotation headed by 20-game-winner Dennis Leonard. Leonard tied Dave Goltz of Minnesota and Jim Palmer of Baltimore for most victories, while California's Frank Tanana recorded the lowest ERA (2.54). After flirting with .400 much of the season, Rod Carew of the Twins took hitting honors at .388; teammate Larry Hisle had the most RBIs (119).

In the NL West, Cincinnati's acquisition of Seaver came too late to surmount a lead built by the Dodgers in winning 17 of their first 20 games. The Los Angeles effort included 20 wins from Tommy John and 100-RBI years from Steve Garvey and Ron Cey. In the East, another Phillies title came with the help of Steve Carlton's league-leading 23 wins and power splurges by Greg Luzinski (39-130) and Mike Schmidt (38-101). The NL's most productive slugger was Cincinnati's George Foster, who hit 52 homers and drove in 149 runs. Two Pirates distinguished themselves: Dave Parker for batting (.338) and John Candelaria for ERA (2.34).

Kansas City manager Whitey Herzog didn't take another ALCS defeat from the Yankees gracefully. After once again losing the pennant in the ninth inning of the fifth game, Herzog blamed John Mayberry for the loss, suggesting the first baseman's 4-for-18 was due to drugs. The turning point to the NLCS came in Game 3 when, facing its second loss, Los Angeles rallied in the ninth inning

Reggie Jackson
With three homers in the final game of the World Series, including this blast off Dodger Elias Sosa, Jackson's first year as a Yankee ended as Mr. October.

on pinch hits from 38-year-old Vic Davalillo and 39-year-old Manny Mota. Dusty Baker drove in eight runs for the Dodger victory in four games.

The Yankees secured their first championship since 1962 when Jackson stepped forward as Mister October by belting three consecutive homers against the Dodgers in the concluding sixth game. The outfielder belted five round-trippers in all and finished with a .450 average and 8 RBIs. Mike Torrez won twice for New York.

1977 SEASON HIGHLIGHTS

NATIONAL LEAGUE

	W	L	Pct.	GB
East				
Philadelphia	101	61	.623	—
Pittsburgh	96	66	.593	5
St. Louis	83	79	.512	18
Houston	81	81	.500	20
Montreal	75	87	.463	26
New York	64	98	.395	37
West				
Los Angeles	98	64	.605	—
Cincinnati	88	74	.543	10
Chicago	81	81	.500	17
San Francisco	75	87	.463	23
San Diego	69	93	.426	29
Atlanta	61	101	.377	37

AMERICAN LEAGUE

	W	L	Pct.	GB
East				
New York	100	62	.617	—
Baltimore	97	64	.602	2.5
Boston	97	64	.602	2.5
California	74	88	.457	26
Cleveland	71	90	.441	28.5
Milwaukee	67	95	.414	33
Toronto	54	107	.335	45.5
West				
Kansas City	102	60	.630	—
Texas	94	68	.580	8
Chicago	90	72	.556	12
Minnesota	84	77	.522	17.5
Detroit	74	88	.457	28
Seattle	64	98	.395	38
Oakland	63	98	.391	38.5

AWARDS

NL MVP: George Foster, CIN
AL MVP: Rod Carew, MIN
NL Cy Young: Steve Carlton, PHI
AL Cy Young: Sparky Lyle, NY
NL Rookie: Andre Dawson, MON
AL Rookie: Eddie Murray, BAL
NL Relief Pitcher: Rollie Fingers, SD
AL Relief Pitcher: Bill Campbell, BOS
GOLD GLOVES
NL: Jim Kaat, P; Johnny Bench, C; Steve Garvey, 1B; Joe Morgan, 2B; Mike Schmidt, 3B; Dave Concepcion, SS; Garry Maddox, Dave Parker, Cesar Geronimo, OF
AL: Jim Palmer, P; Jim Sundberg, C; Jim Spencer, 1B; Frank White, 2B; Graig Nettles, 3B; Mark Belanger, SS; Al Cowens, Juan Beniquez, Carl Yastrzemski, OF

ALL-STAR GAME
Yankee Stadium, New York
July 19: NL 7, AL 5
MVP: Don Sutton, Los Angeles
POSTSEASON
WORLD SERIES
New York Yankees 4, Los Angeles Dodgers 2
Oct. 11: NEW YORK 4, Los Angeles 3
Oct. 12: Los Angeles 6, NEW YORK 1
Oct. 14: New York 5, LOS ANGELES 3
Oct. 15: New York 4, LOS ANGELES 2
Oct. 16: LOS ANGELES 10, New York 4
Oct. 18: NEW YORK 8, Los Angeles 4
MVP: Reggie Jackson, New York

NATIONAL LEAGUE
NLCS
Los Angeles Dodgers 3, Philadelphia Phillies 1
Oct. 4: Philadelphia 7, LOS ANGELES 5
Oct. 5: LOS ANGELES 7, Philadelphia 1
Oct. 7: Los Angeles 6, PHILADELPHIA 5
Oct. 8: Los Angeles 4, PHILADELPHIA 1
MVP: Dusty Baker, Los Angeles

AMERICAN LEAGUE
ALCS
New York Yankees 3, Kansas City Royals 2
Oct. 5: Kansas City 7, NEW YORK 2
Oct. 6: NEW YORK 6, Kansas City 2
Oct. 7: KANSAS CITY 6, New York 2
Oct. 8: New York 6, KANSAS CITY 4
Oct. 9: New York 5, KANSAS CITY 3

"You hit a four-ounce baseball with a 35-ounce bat and there's going to be some damage."
—George Foster

Home team in CAPS

NATIONAL LEAGUE LEADERS

Home Runs
Foster-Cin	52
Burroughs-Atl	41
Luzinski-Phi	39
Schmidt-Phi	38
Garvey-LA	33

Runs Batted In
Foster-Cin	149
Luzinski-Phi	130
Garvey-LA	115
Burroughs-Atl	114

Batting Average
Parker-Pit	.338
Templeton-StL	.322
Foster-Cin	.320
Griffey-Cin	.318
Simmons-StL	.318

On Base Percentage
Smith-LA	.432
Morgan-Cin	.420
Tenace-SD	.417
Simmons-StL	.410
Parker-Pit	.399

Slugging Average
Foster-Cin	.631
Luzinski-Phi	.594
Smith-LA	.576
Schmidt-Phi	.574
Bench-Cin	.540

Stolen Bases
Taveras-Pit	70
Cedeno-Hou	61
Richards-SD	56
Moreno-Pit	53
Morgan-Cin	49

Wins
Carlton-Phi	23
Seaver-NY-Cin	21

Innings Pitched
Niekro-Atl	330.1
Rogers-Mon	301.2
Carlton-Phi	283.0
Richard-Hou	267.0
Seaver-NY-Cin	261.1

Saves
Fingers-SD	35
Sutter-Chi	31
Gossage-Pit	26
Hough-LA	22

Strikeouts
Niekro-Atl	262
Richard-Hou	214
Rogers-Mon	206
Carlton-Phi	198
Seaver-NY-Cin	196

Earned Run Average
Candelaria-Pit	2.34
Seaver-NY-Cin	2.58
Hooton-LA	2.62
Carlton-Phi	2.64
John-LA	2.78

Complete Games
Niekro-Atl	20
Seaver-NY-Cin	19
Rogers-Mon	17
Carlton-Phi	17
Richard-Hou	13

AMERICAN LEAGUE LEADERS

Home Runs
Rice-Bos	39
Nettles-NY	37
Bonds-Cal	37
Scott-Bos	33
Jackson-NY	32

Runs Batted In
Hisle-Min	119
Bonds-Cal	115
Rice-Bos	114
Hobson-Bos	112
Cowens-KC	112

Batting Average
Carew-Min	.388
Bostock-Min	.336
Singleton-Bal	.328
Rivers-NY	.326
LeFlore-Det	.325

On Base Percentage
Carew-Min	.452
Singleton-Bal	.442
Hargrove-Tex	.424
Fisk-Bos	.408
Page-Oak	.407

Slugging Average
Rice-Bos	.593
Carew-Min	.570
Jackson-NY	.550
Hisle-Min	.533
Brett-KC	.532

Stolen Bases
Patek-KC	53
Page-Oak	42
Remy-Cal	41
Bonds-Cal	41
LeFlore-Det	39

Wins
Palmer-Bal	20
Leonard-KC	20
Goltz-Min	20
Ryan-Cal	19

Innings Pitched
Palmer-Bal	319.0
Goltz-Min	303.0
Ryan-Cal	299.0
Leonard-KC	292.2
Garland-Cle	282.2

Saves
Campbell-Bos	31
Lyle-NY	26
LaGrow-Chi	25
Kern-Cle	18
LaRoche-Cle-Cal	17

Strikeouts
Ryan-Cal	341
Leonard-KC	244
Tanana-Cal	205
Palmer-Bal	193
Eckersley-Cle	191

Earned Run Average
Tanana-Cal	2.54
Blyleven-Tex	2.72
Ryan-Cal	2.77
Guidry-NY	2.82
Palmer-Bal	2.91

Complete Games
Ryan-Cal	22
Palmer-Bal	22
Leonard-KC	21
Garland-Cle	21
Tanana-Cal	20

THE YEAR IN BASEBALL

January 2: Bowie Kuhn suspends Ted Turner for one year as a result of tampering charges related to the free-agency signing of Gary Matthews.

January 31: Joe Sewell is named to the Hall of Fame; the toughest strikeout in baseball history, he fanned only 114 times in a 14-year career.

March 21: Mark "The Bird" Fidrych, coming off a Rookie of the Year performance, hurts his left knee and never fully recovers.

March 28: The Rangers' Lenny Randle attacks 50-year-old manager Frank Lucchesi, breaking his cheekbone.

April 6: The Seattle Mariners lose 7-0 to the Angels in their franchise debut.

April 7: In the debut of the Toronto Blue Jays, Al Woods hits a pinch-hit home run in his first major league at-bat as Jays beat the White Sox 9-5.

July 11: Vida Blue starts for the NL to become the first pitcher to start for both leagues in the All Star Game.

August 29: Lou Brock records career steal No. 893 to break Ty Cobb's all-time stolen-base record.

September 3: Sadaharu Oh hits the 756th home run of his career to pass Hank Aaron as the all-time pro baseball home-run king.

September 9: Lou Whitaker and Alan Trammell make their debuts in the same game to begin 19 years together in Detroit.

October 18: Reggie Jackson hits three home runs on three pitches as the Yanks clinch the World Series with a Game 6 win over Los Angeles.

November 22: Goose Gossage leaves the Pirates as a free agent to sign a six-year contract for $2.75 million with the Yankees.

1978

Guidry rises above Bronx Zoo madness as Rose chases record

Bronx Zoo hysteria reached a new peak with Yankees slugger Reggie Jackson, manager Billy Martin, and owner George Steinbrenner going at one another while the Red Sox built up a 14-1/2 -game lead in the AL East by mid-July. When Martin was finally fired for Bob Lemon, the team began eating into the Boston lead, not least because of a dominating 25-3 (1.74) record compiled by southpaw Ron Guidry. In the NL, Pete Rose galvanized attention by going after Joe DiMaggio's 56-game hitting streak; he had to settle for recording his 3,000th hit and tying Willie Keeler's NL mark of 44 consecutive games with at least one safety. After three foiled attempts to sell Vida Blue for cash, Oakland's Charlie Finley completed the destruction of his franchise by dealing the ace southpaw to the Giants for the most players (seven) ever exchanged for one; San Francisco also threw in $300,000.

Under Lemon, the Yankees played at a 48-20 pace over the final two months, including a four-game September sweep at Fenway Park by the composite score of 42-9. But after blowing their lead and then some, the Red Sox did some rallying of their own with eight straight wins to force a division-title playoff. Leading 2-0 in the seventh inning, Boston's Mike Torrez gave up a three-run homer to New York shortstop Bucky Dent; after reliever Bob Stanley surrendered two more runs, the Yankees had half a pennant. In the AL West, Dennis Leonard and Paul Splittorff combined for 40 wins for Kansas City's third consecutive title. Rod Carew of the Twins won his seventh batting crown (.333) and Boston's Jim Rice topped the homer (46) and RBI (139) lists. Rice's 406 total bases were the most in baseball since Stan Musial in 1948 and the most in the AL since Joe DiMaggio in 1937.

Despite Rose's feats and season-long conflict in their clubhouse, the Dodgers took the NL West; Steve Garvey led the hitters with 113 RBIs, Burt Hooton the pitchers with 19 wins. In the East, the Phillies needed every one of Greg Luzinski's 35 homers and 101 RBIs to edge out Pittsburgh because of off years from other veterans. The league's hitting honors once again went to Dave Parker of the Pirates for average (.334) and to George Foster of the Reds for homers (40) and RBIs (120). Gaylord Perry of the Padres won 21, Craig Swan of the Mets had a 2.43 ERA, and J.R. Richard of the Astros became the first NL right-hander to strike out 300.

For the second year in a row, the Dodgers took the Phillies in a four-game NLCS, with Garvey hitting four homers and John spinning a Game 2 shutout. For the third straight season, it was the

Gaylord Perry
Ranked among baseball's finest spitballers, Perry won 21 games to lead the NL in the 17th season of a 22-year career that produced 314 wins and a place in Cooperstown.

Yankees over the Royals in the ALCS. The Royals were so ill-fated they even lost Game 3 despite three homers from George Brett.

The World Series faceoff between the Yankees and Dodgers ended as the one in 1977 had, with a New York championship in six games. Reggie Jackson was again center-stage and had two homers and eight RBIs, but it was his Game 4 baserunning, in throwing a hip at a potential double-play ball and not being called for interference, that turned both that contest and the entire Series. The usually light-hitting Dent and infield scrub Brian Doyle combined for 17 hits and 9 runs driven across.

1978 SEASON HIGHLIGHTS

NATIONAL LEAGUE

	W	L	Pct.	GB
East				
Philadelphia	90	72	.556	—
Pittsburgh	88	73	.547	1.5
Chicago	79	83	.488	11
Montreal	76	86	.469	14
St. Louis	69	93	.426	21
New York	66	96	.407	24
West				
Los Angeles	95	67	.586	—
Cincinnati	92	69	.571	2.5
San Francisco	89	73	.549	6
San Diego	84	78	.519	11
Houston	74	88	.457	21
Atlanta	69	93	.426	26

AMERICAN LEAGUE

	W	L	Pct.	GB
East				
New York	100	63	.613	—
Boston	99	64	.607	1
Milwaukee	93	69	.574	6.5
Baltimore	90	71	.559	9
Detroit	86	76	.531	13.5
Cleveland	69	90	.434	29
Toronto	59	102	.366	40
West				
Kansas City	92	70	.568	—
Texas	87	75	.537	5
California	87	75	.537	5
Minnesota	73	89	.451	19
Chicago	71	90	.441	20.5
Oakland	69	93	.426	23
Seattle	56	104	.350	35

AWARDS

NL MVP: Dave Parker, PIT
AL MVP: Jim Rice, BOS
NL Cy Young: Gaylord Perry, SD
AL Cy Young: Ron Guidry, NY
NL Rookie: Bob Horner, ATL
AL Rookie: Lou Whitaker, DET
NL Relief Pitcher: Rollie Fingers, SD
AL Relief Pitcher: Rich Gossage, NYY
GOLD GLOVES
NL: Phil Niekro, P; Bob Boone, C; Keith Hernandez, 1B; Davey Lopes, 2B; Mike Schmidt, 3B; Larry Bowa, SS; Garry Maddox, Dave Parker, Ellis Valentine, OF
AL: Jim Palmer, P; Jim Sundberg, C; Chris Chambliss, 1B; Frank White, 2B; Graig Nettles, 3B; Mark Belanger, SS; Fred Lynn, Dwight Evans, Rick Miller, OF

ALL-STAR GAME

San Diego Stadium
July 11: NL 7, AL 3
MVP: Steve Garvey, Los Angeles

POSTSEASON

WORLD SERIES
New York Yankees 4, Los Angeles Dodgers 2
Oct. 10: LOS ANGELES 11, New York 5
Oct. 11: LOS ANGELES 4, New York 3
Oct. 13: NEW YORK 5, Los Angeles 1
Oct. 14: NEW YORK 4, Los Angeles 3
Oct. 15: NEW YORK 12, Los Angeles 2
Oct. 17: New York 7, LOS ANGELES 2
MVP: Bucky Dent, New York

NATIONAL LEAGUE

NLCS
Los Angeles Dodgers 3, Philadelphia Phillies 1
Oct. 4: Los Angeles 9, PHILADELPHIA 5
Oct. 5: Los Angeles 4, PHILADELPHIA 0
Oct. 6: Philadelphia 9, LOS ANGELES 4
Oct. 7: LOS ANGELES 4, Philadelphia 3
MVP: Steve Garvey, Los Angeles

AMERICAN LEAGUE

ALCS
New York Yankees 3, Kansas City Royals 1
Oct. 3: New York 7, KANSAS CITY 1
Oct. 4: KANSAS CITY 10, New York 4
Oct. 6: NEW YORK 6, Kansas City 5
Oct. 7: NEW YORK 2, Kansas City 1

Home team in CAPS

> "(Thurman) Munson's not moody, he's just mean. When you're moody, you're nice sometimes."
> —Sparky Lyle

NATIONAL LEAGUE LEADERS

Home Runs		Runs Batted In		Batting Average	
Foster-Cin	40	Foster-Cin	120	Parker-Pit	.334
Luzinski-Phi	35	Parker-Pit	117	Garvey-LA	.316
Parker-Pit	30	Garvey-LA	113	Cruz-Hou	.315
Smith-LA	29	Luzinski-Phi	101	Madlock-SF	.309
		Clark-SF	98	Winfield-SD	.308

On Base Percentage		Slugging Average		Stolen Bases	
Burroughs-Atl	.436	Parker-Pit	.585	Moreno-Pit	71
Parker-Pit	.395	Smith-LA	.559	Taveras-Pit	46
Tenace-SD	.394	Foster-Cin	.546	Lopes-LA	45
Smith-LA	.392	Clark-SF	.537	DeJesus-Chi	41
Luzinski-Phi	.390	Burroughs-Atl	.529	Smith-SD	40

Wins		Innings Pitched		Saves	
Perry-SD	21	Niekro-Atl	334.1	Fingers-SD	37
Grimsley-Mon	20	Richard-Hou	275.1	Tekulve-Pit	31
Niekro-Atl	19	Grimsley-Mon	263.0	Bair-Cin	28
Hooton-LA	19	Perry-SD	260.2	Sutter-Chi	27
		Knepper-SF	260.0	Garber-Phi-Atl	25

Strikeouts		Earned Run Average		Complete Games	
Richard-Hou	303	Swan-NY	2.43	Niekro-Atl	22
Niekro-Atl	248	Rogers-Mon	2.47	Grimsley-Mon	19
Seaver-Cin	226	Vuckovich-StL	2.54	Richard-Hou	16
Blyleven-Pit	182	Knepper-SF	2.63	Knepper-SF	16
Montefusco-SF	177	Hooton-LA	2.71		

AMERICAN LEAGUE LEADERS

Home Runs		Runs Batted In		Batting Average	
Rice-Bos	46	Rice-Bos	139	Carew-Min	.333
Hisle-Mil	34	Staub-Det	121	Oliver-Tex	.324
Baylor-Cal	34	Hisle-Mil	115	Rice-Bos	.315
Thornton-Cle	33	Thornton-Cle	105	Piniella-NY	.314
Thomas-Mil	32			Oglivie-Mil	.303

On Base Percentage		Slugging Average		Stolen Bases	
Carew-Min	.415	Rice-Bos	.600	LeFlore-Det	68
Singleton-Bal	.410	Hisle-Mil	.533	Cruz-Sea	59
Hargrove-Tex	.391	DeCinces-Bal	.526	Wills-Tex	52
Otis-KC	.387	Otis-KC	.525	Dilone-Oak	50
Randolph-NY	.385	Thornton-Cle	.516	Wilson-KC	46

Wins		Innings Pitched		Saves	
Guidry-NY	25	Palmer-Bal	296.0	Gossage-NY	27
Caldwell-Mil	22	Leonard-KC	294.2	LaRoche-Cal	25
Palmer-Bal	21	Caldwell-Mil	293.1	Stanhouse-Bal	24
Leonard-KC	21	Flanagan-Bal	281.1	Marshall-Min	21
		Sorensen-Mil	280.2	Hrabosky-KC	20

Strikeouts		Earned Run Average		Complete Games	
Ryan-Cal	260	Guidry-NY	1.74	Caldwell-Mil	23
Guidry-NY	248	Matlack-Tex	2.27	Leonard-KC	20
Leonard-KC	183	Caldwell-Mil	2.36	Palmer-Bal	19
Flanagan-Bal	167	Palmer-Bal	2.46	Matlack-Tex	18
Eckersley-Bos	162	Goltz-Min	2.49		

THE YEAR IN BASEBALL

January 25: Gaylord Perry is traded from the Texas Rangers to San Diego for Dave Tomlin and $125,000; with the Padres he goes 21-6.

January 30: Bowie Kuhn voids a Vida Blue trade from Oakland to Cincinnati that involved a cash payment of $1.75 million.

April 23: Reds second baseman Joe Morgan commits an error to end a streak of 91 error-free games.

May 5: Pete Rose collects career hit No. 3,000.

June 16: Tom Seaver finaly hurls a no-hitter after several near misses in his splendid 12-year career.

June 17: Ron Guidry strikes out 18 batters in a four-hit, 4-0 shutout of the Angels to set an AL record for lefthanders.

June 30: Lary Doby becomes the second African-American manager in major league history when he is hired by the White Sox.

August 1: Pete Rose's hitting streak is halted at 44 games, tying Willie Keeler's NL mark.

September 14: Jim Bouton, 38, earns a 4-1 win for the Giants, his first win since 1970.

October 2: In a one-game season playoff, Bucky Dent of the Yankees hits a three-run homer in the seventh inning to help defeat the Red Sox 5-4 and give winning hurler Ron Guidry a remarkable 25-3 season.

October 25: Gaylord Perry becomes the first pitcher to win the Cy Young Award in both leagues.

November 7: After becoming the first AL player since Joe DiMaggio in 1937 to reach 400 total bases in a season, Jim Rice is named MVP.

1979

Pirates discover 'family,' as Rose, Carew traded, Munson killed in crash

New York hopes of a fourth straight AL East title sagged in April when closer Goose Gossage broke his finger in clubhouse jostling with teammate Cliff Johnson; then those hopes disappeared altogether in August when club captain Thurman Munson was killed flying his private plane. The hostilities between Minnesota owner Calvin Griffith and Rod Carew that forced the all-star infielder's trade to the Angels produced as many labored negotiating twists (including an intervention from the commissioner's office) as free-agent Pete Rose's public angling for a new team (ultimately the Phillies) generated variations on tackiness.

Carew's addition to the Angels lineup helped produce the expansion franchise's first division title. The team's three 100-plus RBI men included league leader Don Baylor (139). With the Yankees out of the picture, Baltimore surged to the top in the East, in good part because of Mike Flanagan's AL-best 23 wins, Ken Singleton's 35 homers and 111 RBIs, and manager Earl Weaver's ability to get super numbers out of an outfield platoon of John Lowenstein and Gary Roenicke (36 homers and 98 RBIs combined). The other circuit leaders were Boston's Fred Lynn (.333), Milwaukee's Gorman Thomas (45 homers), and New York's Ron Guidry (2.78 ERA). Mike Marshall, already in possession of the NL record for appearances in a year (106), added the AL mark by coming out of the bullpen 89 times and starting once for the Twins. In July, Bill Veeck's Disco Demolition Night in Chicago turned into riots, fires that all but ravaged Comiskey Park, and a forfeit loss for the home team. In September, Carl Yastrzemski of the Red Sox collected his 3,000th hit.

Despite a big year from Rose (.331 with 208 hits), Philadelphia finished well behind Pittsburgh in the NL East. While Dave Parker, Willie Stargell and Bill Madlock provided the offense, Kent Tekulve proved to be the big man on the mound for the Pirates, coming out of the bullpen for 10 wins and 31 saves in 94 appearances. In the West, Ray Knight's ability to hit .318 as Rose's replacement was the key to a surprise Cincinnati division win. Individually, Dave Kingman of the Cubs had the most homers (48), Dave Winfield of the Padres the most RBIs (118), Keith Hernandez of the Cardinals the highest average (.344), J.R. Richard of the Astros the lowest ERA (2.71), and the brothers Joe (Houston) and Phil (Atlanta) Niekro the most wins (21). Kingman's 48 homers were only one less than were hit by the entire Houston team.

The "We Are Family" Pirates swatted the Reds in three quick NLCS games, with Stargell homering twice and driving in six. In the ALCS, a 10th-inning pinch-homer by Lowenstein in Game 1 and a shutout by Scott McGregor in Game 4 were the bookends

Thurman Munson
While flying home on an off-day, Munson, a mainstay of the Yankee championship teams of 1977 and '78, died when his private plane crashed in Canton, Ohio.

for a Baltimore pennant.

Stargell and Tekulve starred in the sweaty seven-game World Series in which the Pirates rallied for the title after losing three of the first four games. The first baseman clouted three homers with seven RBIs, while the reliever picked up three saves in five appearances. Stargell was one of four Pirates to collect hits in double figures, the club as a whole slamming Baltimore pitching at a .323 clip.

After the season, Nolan Ryan became the first free agent to sign a million-dollar contract when he negotiated a four-year, $4.5 million deal with the Houston Astros.

1979 SEASON HIGHLIGHTS

NATIONAL LEAGUE

East	W	L	Pct.	GB
Pittsburgh	98	64	.605	—
Montreal	95	65	.594	2
St. Louis	86	76	.531	12
Philadelphia	84	78	.519	14
Chicago	80	82	.494	18
New York	63	99	.389	35

West	W	L	Pct.	GB
Cincinnati	90	71	.559	—
Houston	89	73	.549	1.5
Los Angeles	79	83	.488	11.5
San Francisco	71	91	.438	19.5
San Diego	68	93	.422	22
Atlanta	66	94	.413	23.5

AMERICAN LEAGUE

East	W	L	Pct.	GB
Baltimore	102	57	.642	—
Milwaukee	95	66	.590	8
Boston	91	69	.569	11.5
New York	89	71	.556	13.5
Kansas City	85	77	.525	18.5
Cleveland	81	80	.503	22
Toronto	53	109	.327	50.5

West	W	L	Pct.	GB
California	88	74	.543	—
Detroit	85	76	.528	2.5
Texas	83	79	.512	5
Minnesota	82	80	.506	6
Chicago	73	87	.456	14
Seattle	67	95	.414	21
Oakland	54	108	.333	34

AWARDS

NL MVP: Keith Hernandez, STL; Willie Stargell, PIT
AL MVP: Don Baylor, CAL
NL Cy Young: Bruce Sutter, CHI
AL Cy Young: Mike Flanagan, BAL
NL Rookie: Rick Sutcliffe, LA
AL Rookie: John Castino, MIN; Alfredo Griffin, TOR
NL Relief Pitcher: Bruce Sutter, CHI
AL Relief Pitcher: Jim Kern, TEX
GOLD GLOVES
NL: Phil Niekro, P; Bob Boone, C; Keith Hernandez, 1B; Manny Trillo, 2B; Mike Schmidt, 3B; Dave Concepcion, SS; Garry Maddox, Dave Parker, Dave Winfield, OF
AL: Jim Palmer, P; Jim Sundberg, C; Cecil Cooper, 1B; Frank White, 2B; Buddy Bell, 3B; Rick Burleson, SS; Fred Lynn, Dwight Evans, Sixto Lezcano, OF

ALL-STAR GAME
Kingdome, Seattle
July 17: NL 7, AL 6
MVP: Dave Parker, Pittsburgh
POSTSEASON
WORLD SERIES
Pittsburgh Pirates 4, Baltimore Orioles 3
Oct. 10: BALTIMORE 5, Pittsburgh 4
Oct. 11: Pittsburgh 3, BALTIMORE 2
Oct. 12: Baltimore 8, PITTSBURGH 4
Oct. 13: Baltimore 9, PITTSBURGH 6
Oct. 14: PITTSBURGH 7, Baltimore 1
Oct. 16: Pittsburgh 4, BALTIMORE 0
Oct. 17: Pittsburgh 4, BALTIMORE 1
MVP: Willie Stargell, Pittsburgh

NATIONAL LEAGUE
NLCS
Pittsburgh Pirates 3, Cincinnati Reds 0
Oct. 2: Pittsburgh 5, CINCINNATI 2
Oct. 3: Pittsburgh 3, CINCINNATI 2
Oct. 5: PITTSBURGH 7, Cincinnati 1
MVP: Willie Stargell, Pittsburgh

AMERICAN LEAGUE
ALCS
Baltimore Orioles 3, California Angels 1
Oct. 3: BALTIMORE 6, California 3
Oct. 4: BALTIMORE 9, California 8
Oct. 5: CALIFORNIA 4, Baltimore 3
Oct. 6: Baltimore 8, CALIFORNIA 0

> "It helps if the hitter thinks you're a little crazy."
>
> —Nolan Ryan

Home team in CAPS

NATIONAL LEAGUE LEADERS

Home Runs			Runs Batted In			Batting Average	
Kingman-Chi	48		Winfield-SD	118		Hernandez-StL	.344
Schmidt-Phi	45		Kingman-Chi	115		Rose-Phi	.331
Winfield-SD	34		Schmidt-Phi	114		Knight-Cin	.318
Horner-Atl	33		Garvey-LA	110		Garvey-LA	.315
Stargell-Pit	32		Hernandez-StL	105		Horner-Atl	.314

On Base Percentage			Slugging Average			Stolen Bases	
Hernandez-StL	.421		Kingman-Chi	.613		Moreno-Pit	77
Rose-Phi	.421		Schmidt-Phi	.564		North-SF	58
Tenace-SD	.407		Foster-Cin	.561		Taveras-Pit-NY	44
Mazzilli-NY	.397		Winfield-SD	.558		Lopes-LA	44
Winfield-SD	.396		Horner-Atl	.552		Scott-Mon	39

Wins			Innings Pitched			Saves	
Niekro-Atl	21		Niekro-Atl	342.0		Sutter-Chi	37
Niekro-Hou	21		Richard-Hou	292.1		Tekulve-Pit	31
Richard-Hou	18		Niekro-Hou	263.2		Garber-Atl	25
Reuschel-Chi	18		Jones-SD	263.0		Sambito-Hou	22
Carlton-Phi	18		Swan-NY	251.1		Lavelle-SF	20

Strikeouts			Earned Run Average			Complete Games	
Richard-Hou	313		Richard-Hou	2.71		Niekro-Atl	23
Carlton-Phi	213		Hume-Cin	2.76		Richard-Hou	19
Niekro-Atl	208		Schatzeder-Mon	2.83		Rogers-Mon	13
Blyleven-Pit	172		Hooton-LA	2.97		Carlton-Phi	13
McGlothen-Chi	147		Niekro-Hou	3.00		Hooton-LA	12

AMERICAN LEAGUE LEADERS

Home Runs			Runs Batted In			Batting Average	
Thomas-Mil	45		Baylor-Cal	139		Lynn-Bos	.333
Rice-Bos	39		Rice-Bos	130		Brett-KC	.329
Lynn-Bos	39		Thomas-Mil	123		Downing-Cal	.326
Baylor-Cal	36		Lynn-Bos	122		Rice-Bos	.325
Singleton-Bal	35		Porter-KC	112		Oliver-Tex	.323

On Base Percentage			Slugging Average			Stolen Bases	
Porter-KC	.429		Lynn-Bos	.637		Wilson-KC	83
Lynn-Bos	.426		Rice-Bos	.596		LeFlore-Det	78
Downing-Cal	.420		Lezcano-Mil	.573		Cruz-Sea	49
Lezcano-Mil	.420		Brett-KC	.563		Bumbry-Bal	37
Singleton-Bal	.409		Jackson-NY	.544		Wills-Tex	35

Wins			Innings Pitched			Saves	
Flanagan-Bal	23		D.Martinez-Bal	292.1		Marshall-Min	32
John-NY	21		John-NY	276.1		Kern-Tex	29
Koosman-Min	20		Flanagan-Bal	265.2		Stanhouse-Bal	21
Guidry-NY	18		Koosman-Min	263.2		Lopez-Det	21
			Jenkins-Tex	259.0		Monge-Cle	19

Strikeouts			Earned Run Average			Complete Games	
Ryan-Cal	223		Guidry-NY	2.78		D.Martinez-Bal	18
Guidry-NY	201		John-NY	2.96		Ryan-Cal	17
Flanagan-Bal	190		Eckersley-Bos	2.99		John-NY	17
Jenkins-Tex	164		Flanagan-Bal	3.08		Eckersley-Bos	17
Koosman-Min	157		Morris-Det	3.28			

THE YEAR IN BASEBALL

January 23: Willie Mays is elected to the Hall of Fame, receiving 409 of a possible 432 votes.

February 2: The Twins trade six-time batting champ Rod Carew to the Angels.

March 7: Semi-pro and sandlot umpires are used when major league umpires strike.

April 7: Ken Forsch of Houston pitches a no-hit, no-run game against Atlanta to duplicate the no-hitter hurled by his brother Bob of the Cardinals on April 16, 1978.

June 12: The Tigers fire manager Les Moss and hand the job to Sparky Anderson.

August 2: Yankee catcher Thurman Munson dies in the crash of a plane he was piloting at the Canton, Ohio, airport. He was 32.

September 23: St. Louis legend Lou Brock steals the 938th and final base of his career.

September 23: Pete Rose gets a single to give him 200 hits to break Ty Cobb's record of nine consecutive 200-hit seasons.

September 26: Atlanta's Phil Neikro notches his 20th win to match his brother, Joe, as they join Jim and Gaylord Perry as the second brother act to win 20 games in the same season.

October 23: Billy Martin fights a marshmallow salesman in a bar in Bloomington, Minnesota and is fired five days later.

November 19: Nolan Ryan is the first free agent to sign a million-dollar-a-year contract (Houston Astros).

1980

Brett flirts with .400, Phillies win Series after a 97-year wait

Ninety-seven years after entering the NL, the Phillies finally won a World Series. Eighteen years after entering the circuit, the Astros played a key supporting role in the most dramatic LCS held to date. Thirty-nine years after Ted Williams had done it, George Brett of the Royals made a serious bid to bat .400.

With veterans Mike Schmidt, Steve Carlton, Pete Rose, and Tug McGraw leading the way, Philadelphia held off the Expos on the final weekend of the season to take the NL East. To get that far, the Phillies had to overcome clubhouse simmerings fed by egos working in opposed directions; the turning point came in early September, when general manager Paul Owens lashed into the players for paying merely lip service to manager Dallas Green's We-Not-I preachings. Even then, it took an 11th-inning homer by Schmidt against Montreal on the next-to-last day to seal matters. The third baseman topped the NL in both home runs (48) and RBIs (121), while Carlton posted the most wins (24). In the NL West, the Astros were on the verge of joining the Hall of Blown Leads in going to Los Angeles with a three-game edge over the Dodgers on the final weekend and proceeding to lose three in a row. But then Joe Niekro came back for his 20th win in a division-title playoff. Bill Buckner of the Cubs won the batting title (.324), Don Sutton of the Dodgers had the lowest ERA (2.20).

Brett's quest for .400 was the focus of an AL West race that Kansas City won handily. The third baseman remained sharp at the plate despite knee and wrist injuries that sidelined him for 45 games; although he eventually had to settle for .390, his consolations were the batting crown, an MVP award, and the feat of being the first player in 30 years to have more RBIs (118) than games played (117). Other ingredients of the Royals triumph were 20 wins from Dennis Leonard and 33 saves and 12 wins from Dan Quisenberry. In the AL East, the Yankees parlayed big seasons from Reggie Jackson (.300-41-111), Tommy John (22 wins) and Goose Gossage (33 saves) into a title. Jackson's homers tied Milwaukee's Ben Oglivie for the most in the league; Cecil Cooper of the Brewers knocked in the most runs (122). Steve Stone of the Orioles had the most victories (25), Rudy May of the Yankees the lowest ERA (2.46).

Quisenberry (a win and a save) was better than Gossage (a blown save in the concluding third game) in the ALCS, so the Royals finally got past the Yankees for a pennant on their fourth try. But it was the NLCS that riveted attention, with four of the five games going into extra innings, Game 2 remaining scoreless until the 11th, only one home run hit in the entire series, an umpire

George Brett
The Royals third baseman took a run at the magical .400 batting mark before slipping back to .390 as Kansas City went to the World Series.

overruled on a triple-play call, Nolan Ryan blowing a 5-2 lead in the eighth inning of the finale, and bench players, pinch-hitters, and relievers proving decisive. The run that gave the Phillies the pennant was delivered on a 10th-inning double by Garry Maddox.

After picking up two saves against Houston in the NLCS, McGraw collected two more and a win in Philadelphia's six-game World Series victory over Kansas City. Carlton also won twice, amassing 17 strikeouts in 14 innings, while Schmidt and Bake McBride combined for 12 RBIs. Royals leadoff man Willie Wilson struck out a record 12 times.

1980 SEASON HIGHLIGHTS

NATIONAL LEAGUE

East	W	L	Pct.	GB
Philadelphia	91	71	.562	—
Montreal	90	72	.556	1
Pittsburgh	83	79	.512	8
St. Louis	74	88	.457	17
New York	67	95	.414	24
Chicago	64	98	.395	27

West	W	L	Pct.	GB
Houston	93	70	.571	—
Los Angeles	92	71	.564	1
Cincinnati	89	73	.549	3.5
Atlanta	81	80	.503	11
San Francisco	75	86	.466	17
San Diego	73	89	.451	19.5

AMERICAN LEAGUE

East	W	L	Pct.	GB
New York	103	59	.636	—
Baltimore	100	62	.617	3
Milwaukee	86	76	.531	17
Detroit	84	78	.519	19
Boston	83	77	.519	19
Cleveland	79	81	.494	23
Toronto	67	95	.414	36

West	W	L	Pct.	GB
Kansas City	97	65	.599	—
Oakland	83	79	.512	14
Minnesota	77	84	.478	19.5
Texas	76	85	.472	20.5
Chicago	70	90	.438	26
California	65	95	.406	31
Seattle	59	103	.364	38

AWARDS

NL MVP: Mike Schmidt, PHI
AL MVP: George Brett, KC
NL Cy Young: Steve Carlton, PHI
AL Cy Young: Steve Stone, BAL
NL Rookie: Steve Howe, LA
AL Rookie: Joe Charboneau, CLE
NL Relief Pitcher: Rollie Fingers, SD
AL Relief Pitcher: Dan Quisenberry, KC
GOLD GLOVES
NL: Phil Niekro, P; Gary Carter, C; Keith Hernandez, 1B; Doug Flynn, 2B; Mike Schmidt, 3B; Ozzie Smith, SS; Garry Maddox, Andre Dawson, Dave Winfield, OF
AL: Mike Norris, P; Jim Sundberg, C; Cecil Cooper, 1B; Frank White, 2B; Buddy Bell, 3B; Alan Trammell, SS; Fred Lynn, Willie Wilson, Dwayne Murphy, OF

ALL-STAR GAME

Dodger Stadium, Los Angeles
July 8: NL 4, AL 2
MVP: Ken Griffey Sr., Cincinnati

POSTSEASON
WORLD SERIES

Philadelphia Phillies 4, Kansas City Royals 2
Oct. 14: PHILADELPHIA 7, Kansas City 6
Oct. 15: PHILADELPHIA 6, Kansas City 4
Oct. 17: KANSAS CITY 4, Philadelphia 3
Oct. 18: KANSAS CITY 5, Philadelphia 3
Oct. 19: Philadelphia 4, KANSAS CITY 3
Oct. 21: PHILADELPHIA 4, Kansas City 1
MVP: Mike Schmidt, Philadelphia

NATIONAL LEAGUE
NLCS

Philadelphia Phillies 3, Houston Astros 2
Oct. 7: PHILADELPHIA 3, Houston 1
Oct. 8: Houston 7, PHILADELPHIA 4
Oct. 10: HOUSTON 1, Philadelphia 0
Oct. 11: Philadelphia 5, HOUSTON 3
Oct. 12: Philadelphia 8, HOUSTON 7
MVP: Manny Trillo, Philadelphia

Home team in CAPS

AMERICAN LEAGUE
ALCS

Kansas City Royals 3, New York Yankees 0
Oct. 8: KANSAS CITY 7, New York 2
Oct. 9: KANSAS CITY 3, New York 2
Oct. 10: Kansas City 4, NEW YORK 2
MVP: Frank White, Kansas City

> "If a tie is like kissing your sister, losing is like kissing your grandmother with her teeth out."
> —George Brett

NATIONAL LEAGUE LEADERS

Home Runs
Schmidt-Phi	48
Horner-Atl	35
Murphy-Atl	33
Carter-Mon	29
Baker-LA	29

Runs Batted In
Schmidt-Phi	121
Hendrick-StL	109
Garvey-LA	106
Carter-Mon	101
Hernandez-StL	99

Batting Average
Buckner-Chi	.324
Hernandez-StL	.321
Templeton-StL	.319
McBride-Phi	.309
Cedeno-Hou	.309

On Base Percentage
Hernandez-StL	.410
Cedeno-Hou	.390
Clark-SF	.390
Schmidt-Phi	.388
Driessen-Cin	.382

Slugging Average
Schmidt-Phi	.624
Clark-SF	.517
Murphy-Atl	.510
Simmons-StL	.505
Baker-LA	.503

Stolen Bases
LeFlore-Mon	97
Moreno-Pit	96
Collins-Cin	79
Scott-Mon	63
Richards-SD	61

Wins
Carlton-Phi	24
Niekro-Hou	20
Bibby-Pit	19
Reuss-LA	18
Ruthven-Phi	17

Innings Pitched
Carlton-Phi	304.0
Rogers-Mon	281.0
Niekro-Atl	275.0
Reuschel-Chi	257.0
Niekro-Hou	256.0

Saves
Sutter-Chi	28
Hume-Cin	25
Fingers-SD	23
Camp-Atl	22
Allen-NY	22

Strikeouts
Carlton-Phi	286
Ryan-Hou	200
Soto-Cin	182
Niekro-Atl	176
Blyleven-Pit	168

Earned Run Average
Sutton-LA	2.20
Carlton-Phi	2.34
Reuss-LA	2.51
Blue-SF	2.97
Rogers-Mon	2.98

Complete Games
Rogers-Mon	14
Carlton-Phi	13
Niekro-Atl	11
Niekro-Hou	11

AMERICAN LEAGUE LEADERS

Home Runs
Oglivie-Mil	41
Jackson-NY	41
Thomas-Mil	38
Armas-Oak	35
Murray-Bal	32

Runs Batted In
Cooper-Mil	122
Oglivie-Mil	118
G.Brett-KC	118
Oliver-Tex	117
Murray-Bal	116

Batting Average
G.Brett-KC	.390
Cooper-Mil	.352
Dilone-Cle	.341
Rivers-Tex	.333
Carew-Cal	.331

On Base Percentage
G.Brett-KC	.461
Randolph-NY	.429
Henderson-Oak	.422
Hargrove-Cle	.421
Thompson-Det-Cal	.402

Slugging Average
G.Brett-KC	.664
Jackson-NY	.597
Oglivie-Mil	.563
Cooper-Mil	.539
Yount-Mil	.519

Stolen Bases
Henderson-Oak	100
Wilson-KC	79
Dilone-Cle	61
Cruz-Sea	45
Bumbry-Bal	44

Wins
Stone-Bal	25
Norris-Oak	22
John-NY	22
McGregor-Bal	20
Leonard-KC	20

Innings Pitched
Langford-Oak	290.0
Norris-Oak	284.1
Gura-KC	283.1
Leonard-KC	280.1
John-NY	265.1

Saves
Quisenberry-KC	33
Gossage-NY	33
Farmer-Chi	30
Stoddard-Bal	26
Burgmeier-Bos	24

Strikeouts
Barker-Cle	187
Norris-Oak	180
Guidry-NY	166
Leonard-KC	155
Bannister-Sea	155

Earned Run Average
May-NY	2.46
Norris-Oak	2.53
Burns-Chi	2.84
Keough-Oak	2.92
Gura-KC	2.95

Complete Games
Langford-Oak	28
Norris-Oak	24
Keough-Oak	20
John-NY	16
Gura-KC	16

THE YEAR IN BASEBALL

February 15: Gaylord Perry is traded from the Padres to Texas with Tucker Ashford and Joe Carroll for Willie Montanez.

March 14: Chuck Klein is elected to the Hall of Fame; the slugging Phils' outfielder recorded 44 assists in 1930.

April 12: In the second inning of Milwaukee's 18-1 victory over the Red Sox, Cecil Cooper and Don Money each belt a grand-slam homer.

June 20: Freddie Patek, one of baseball's smallest players, hits three home runs and a double to lead California in a 20-2 trouncing of the Red Sox in Fenway Park.

July 30: Houston pitcher J.R. Richard's career ends after he suffers a stroke and undergoes life-saving surgery to remove a blood clot.

August 23: Charles Finley sells the A's for $12.7 million to the Haas family (of Levi jeans fame).

September 10: Montreal pitcher Bill Gullickson, 21, strikes out 18 to set a major league strikeout record for rookies.

October 10: With the Kansas City Royals down 2-1 in the seventh inning of the third AL championship playoff game, George Brett hits a three-run homer off relief ace Goose Gossage of the Yankees to give the Royals a 4-2 win and a three-game sweep of the Series.

November 16: George Brett of the Royals, coming off a .390 season, is named his league's MVP.

November 20: Mike Schmidt of the Phillies wins the first of his three MVP Awards.

December 15: Dave Winfield becomes the highest paid player in baseball by signing a 10-year, $15-million contract with the Yankees.

1981

Strike and split season create tainted champs, but Fernando shines

Heavy-handed attempts by the owners to win back compensation for what they had lost on free agency prompted a player strike on June 12. Before play resumed in August, 713 games had been burned. To deal with the depleted schedule, executives came up with a Rube Goldberg formula that split the season into first-half and second-half winners. What this meant in practice was that because they did not finish first in either half, the Reds (with baseball's best overall record), Cardinals, Orioles, Rangers, and White Sox did not qualify for the postseason while inferior clubs did. On the other hand, threats by fan groups to boycott games because of the strike came to little. The first Phillies home game after the walkout drew 60,561 to see Pete Rose pass Stan Musial for most hits by a NL player.

Cincinnati's exasperated effort in the NL West came up against the Dodgers in the first half and the Astros in the second. Los Angeles also had the player of the year in southpaw Fernando Valenzuela, who hurled five shutouts in his first seven games and eight overall on his way to rookie and Cy Young awards. Houston's chief cachet was Nolan Ryan, who turned in the best ERA at 1.69. In the NL East, the Phillies took the first half with the help of Mike Schmidt's league-best homers (31) and RBIs (91). To win the second half, the Expos got conspicuous production from Tim Raines (71 steals in 88 games), Andre Dawson (24 homers), and Steve Rogers (12 wins). Tom Seaver of the Reds had the most victories (14), Bill Madlock of the Pirates the highest average (.341).

Billy Martin's running game, epitomized by Rickey Henderson's 56 thefts, got the Athletics off to 18 wins in their first 20 games on their way to first-half eligibility in the AL West. The second half went to the Royals even though they finished three games under .500 overall. In the AL East, free agent Dave Winfield joined Reggie Jackson and Graig Nettles to power the Yankees for the first half, and the Brewers adopted a similar approach for the second half. Four pitchers won 14 games and four position players hit 22 homers to lead those categories. Carney Lansford of Boston won the batting crown (.336), Eddie Murray of Baltimore the RBI title (78). The official ERA leader was Steve McCatty of Oakland (2.33), but only because rules dictated the rounding off of the actually lower ERA of Sammy Stewart of the Orioles.

The Expos and Dodgers both won their division playoffs in five games, with Rogers (two wins) leading Montreal and Jerry Reuss (no earned runs in 18 innings) for L.A. But in the NLCS, Rogers surrendered a homer to Rick Monday in the ninth inning of Game 5 to give the Dodgers the pennant. In the AL, the A's ripped through the Royals in three straight with the help of a Mike Norris shutout, while the Yankees outlasted the Brewers in five thanks to two Dave Righetti wins and three Goose Gossage saves. New York then swept Oakland in the ALCS with the same formula plus nine RBIs from Nettles.

Dusty Baker and Pedro Guerrero drove in 13 runs between them to lead Los Angeles over New York in a six-game World Series. Yankees reliever George Frazier lost three of the games. Winfield's 1-for-22 drew sneers from George Steinbrenner that he had played like a "Mister May."

Fernando Valenzuela
The rookie left-hander had five shutouts in his first seven starts en route to winning Rookie of the Year and Cy Young honors.

1981 SEASON HIGHLIGHTS

NATIONAL LEAGUE

East	W	L	Pct.	GB
Montreal	60	48	.556	—
Philadelphia	59	48	.551	0.5
St. Louis	59	43	.578	-2
Pittsburgh	46	56	.451	11
New York	41	62	.398	16.5
Chicago	38	65	.369	19.5

West	W	L	Pct.	GB
Cincinnati	66	42	.611	—
Los Angeles	63	47	.573	4
Houston	61	49	.555	6
San Francisco	56	55	.505	11.5
Atlanta	50	56	.472	15
San Diego	41	69	.373	26

AMERICAN LEAGUE

East	W	L	Pct.	GB
Milwaukee	62	47	.569	—
Detroit	60	49	.550	2
New York	59	48	.551	2
Baltimore	59	46	.562	1
Boston	59	49	.546	2.5
Cleveland	52	51	.505	7
Toronto	37	69	.349	23.5

West	W	L	Pct.	GB
Oakland	64	45	.587	—
Texas	57	48	.543	5
Chicago	54	52	.509	8.5
California	51	59	.464	13.5
Kansas City	50	53	.485	11
Seattle	44	65	.404	20
Minnesota	41	68	.376	23

AWARDS

NL MVP: Mike Schmidt, PHI
AL MVP: Rollie Fingers, MIL
NL Cy Young: Fernando Valenzuela, LA
AL Cy Young: Rollie Fingers, MIL
NL Rookie: Fernando Valenzuela, LA
AL Rookie: Dave Righetti, NY
NL Relief Pitcher: Bruce Sutter, STL
AL Relief Pitcher: Rollie Fingers, MIL

GOLD GLOVES

NL: Steve Carlton, P; Gary Carter, C; Keith Hernandez, 1B; Manny Trillo, 2B; Mike Schmidt, 3B; Ozzie Smith, SS; Garry Maddox, Andre Dawson, Dusty Baker, OF

AL: Mike Norris, P; Jim Sundberg, C; Mike Squires, 1B; Frank White, 2B; Buddy Bell, 3B; Alan Trammell, SS; Dwight Evans, Rickey Henderson, Dwayne Murphy, OF

ALL-STAR GAME

Municipal Stadium, Cleveland
Aug. 9: NL 5, AL 4
MVP: Gary Carter, Montreal

POSTSEASON

WORLD SERIES

Los Angeles Dodgers 4, New York Yankees 2
Oct. 20: NEW YORK 5, Los Angeles 3
Oct. 21: NEW YORK 3, Los Angeles 0
Oct. 23: LOS ANGELES 5, New York 4
Oct. 24: LOS ANGELES 8, New York 7
Oct. 25: LOS ANGELES 2, New York 1
Oct. 28: Los Angeles 9, NEW YORK 2
MVPs: Ron Cey, Pedro Guerrero and Steve Yeager, Los Angeles

NATIONAL LEAGUE
NLCS

Los Angeles Dodgers 3, Montreal Expos 2
Oct. 13: LOS ANGELES 5, Montreal 1
Oct. 14: Montreal 3, LOS ANGELES 0
Oct. 16: MONTREAL 4, Los Angeles 1
Oct. 17: Los Angeles 7, MONTREAL 1
Oct. 19: Los Angeles 2, MONTREAL 1
MVP: Burt Hooton, Los Angeles

NL WEST, DIVISION PLAYOFF

Los Angeles Dodgers 3, Houston Astros 2
Oct. 6: HOUSTON 3, Los Angeles 1
Oct. 7: HOUSTON 1, Los Angeles 0
Oct. 9: LOS ANGELES 6, Houston 1
Oct. 10: LOS ANGELES 2, Houston 1
Oct. 11: LOS ANGELES 4, Houston 0

NL EAST, DIVISION PLAYOFF

Montreal Expos 3, Philadelphia Phillies 2
Oct. 7: MONTREAL 3, Philadelphia 1
Oct. 8: MONTREAL 3, Philadelphia 1
Oct. 9: PHILADELPHIA 6, Montreal 2
Oct. 10: PHILADELPHIA 6, Montreal 5
Oct. 11: Montreal 3, PHILADELPHIA 0

AMERICAN LEAGUE
ALCS

New York Yankees 3, Oakland A's 0
Oct. 13: NEW YORK 3, Oakland 1
Oct. 14: NEW YORK 13, Oakland 3
Oct. 15: New York 4, OAKLAND 0
MVP: Graig Nettles, New York

AL WEST, DIVISION PLAYOFF

Oakland Athletics 3, Kansas City Royals 0
Oct. 6: Oakland 4, KANSAS CITY 0
Oct. 7: Oakland 2, KANSAS CITY 1
Oct. 9: OAKLAND 4, Kansas City 1

AL EAST, DIVISION PLAYOFF

New York Yankees 3, Milwaukee Brewers 2
Oct. 7: New York 5, MILWAUKEE 3
Oct. 8: New York 3, MILWAUKEE 0
Oct. 9: Milwaukee 5, NEW YORK 3
Oct. 10: Milwaukee 2, NEW YORK 1
Oct. 11: NEW YORK 7, Milwaukee 3

Home team in CAPS

NATIONAL LEAGUE LEADERS

Home Runs
Schmidt-Phi	31
Dawson-Mon	24
Kingman-NY	22
Foster-Cin	22
Hendrick-StL	18

Runs Batted In
Schmidt-Phi	91
Foster-Cin	90
Buckner-Chi	75
Carter-Mon	68

Batting Average
Madlock-Pit	.341
Rose-Phi	.325
Baker-LA	.320
Schmidt-Phi	.316
Buckner-Chi	.311

On Base Percentage
Schmidt-Phi	.439
Madlock-Pit	.418
Hernandez-StL	.405
Matthews-Phi	.404
Raines-Mon	.394

Slugging Average
Schmidt-Phi	.644
Dawson-Mon	.553
Foster-Cin	.519
Madlock-Pit	.495
Hendrick-StL	.485

Stolen Bases
Raines-Mon	71
Moreno-Pit	39
Scott-Mon	30

Wins
Seaver-Cin	14
Valenzuela-LA	13
Carlton-Phi	13

Innings Pitched
Valenzuela-LA	192.1
Carlton-Phi	190.0
Soto-Cin	175.0
Seaver-Cin	166.1
Niekro-Hou	166.0

Saves
Sutter-StL	25
Minton-SF	21
Allen-NY	18
Camp-Atl	17

Strikeouts
Valenzuela-LA	180
Carlton-Phi	179
Soto-Cin	151
Ryan-Hou	140
Gullickson-Mon	115

Earned Run Average
Ryan-Hou	1.69
Knepper-Hou	2.18
Hooton-LA	2.28
Reuss-LA	2.30
Carlton-Phi	2.42

Complete Games
Valenzuela-LA	11
Soto-Cin	10
Carlton-Phi	10
Reuss-LA	8
Rogers-Mon	7

AMERICAN LEAGUE LEADERS

Home Runs
Murray-Bal	22
Grich-Cal	22
Evans-Bos	22
Armas-Oak	22

Runs Batted In
Murray-Bal	78
Armas-Oak	76
Oglivie-Mil	72
Evans-Bos	71
Winfield-NY	68

Batting Average
Lansford-Bos	.336
Paciorek-Sea	.326
Cooper-Mil	.320
Henderson-Oak	.319
Hargrove-Cle	.317

On Base Percentage
Hargrove-Cle	.432
Evans-Bos	.418
Henderson-Oak	.411
Kemp-Det	.393
Lansford-Bos	.391

Slugging Average
Grich-Cal	.543
Murray-Bal	.534
Evans-Bos	.522
Paciorek-Sea	.509
Cooper-Mil	.495

Stolen Bases
Henderson-Oak	56
Cruz-Sea	43
LeFlore-Chi	36
Wilson-KC	34
Dilone-Cle	29

Wins
Vuckovich-Mil	14
Morris-Det	14
McCatty-Oak	14
D.Martinez-Bal	14

Innings Pitched
Leonard-KC	201.2
Morris-Det	198.0
Langford-Oak	195.1
McCatty-Oak	185.2
Stieb-Tor	183.2

Saves
Fingers-Mil	28
Gossage-NY	20
Quisenberry-KC	18
Corbett-Min	17
Saucier-Det	13

Strikeouts
Barker-Cle	127
Burns-Chi	108
Leonard-KC	107
Blyleven-Cle	107
Guidry-NY	104

Earned Run Average
Righetti-NY	2.05
Stewart-Bal	2.32
McCatty-Oak	2.33
Lamp-Chi	2.41
John-NY	2.63

Complete Games
Langford-Oak	18
McCatty-Oak	16
Morris-Det	15
Norris-Oak	12
Gura-KC	12

THE YEAR IN BASEBALL

January 15: Johnny Mize is elected to the Hall of Fame.

April 9: Rookie Fernando Valenzuela shuts out the Astros on Opening Day; he went on to win the Rookie and Cy Young Awards.

April 19: The International League game between Rochester and Pawtucket which started at 8:00 the previous evening is suspended at 4:07 on Easter morning after 32 innings, with the score tied at 2-2. When the game was resumed on June 23, Pawtucket scored one run in the 33rd to win. It was easily the longest game in Organized Baseball history.

April 29: Steve Carlton gets strikeout number 3,000.

June 10: Pete Rose ties Stan Musial's NL record with his 3,630th hit.

September 26: Houston's Nolan Ryan pitches his fifth career no-hit, no-run game, a 5-0 victory over the Los Angeles Dodgers at the Astrodome.

October 21: The Cards get Willie McGee from the Yanks for Bob Sykes.

October 28: After losing the first two Series games to the Yankees, the Los Angeles Dodgers come back to sweep the final four for the Series.

December 10: St. Louis and San Diego trade shortstops, with Ozzie Smith going to the Cards and Garry Templeton to the Padres.

1982

Herzog's pinballers unable to keep up with Harvey's Wallbangers

None of the four division winners had been a preseason favorite, and they all waited until the final hours of the campaign to make the improbable into fact. Only the NL East Cardinals, in unveiling their artificial-turf, speed-and-defense game under manager Whitey Herzog, laid the foundations for more than a single year's success.

The St. Louis win owed a great deal to Herzog's trading acumen, and specifically to the acquisition of Ozzie Smith from San Diego, Lonnie Smith from Cleveland and Willie McGee from the Yankees. Their skill at pinball baseball, along with Bruce Sutter's 36 saves and George Hendrick's 104 RBIs, wore down the aging Phillies. In the NL West, the Braves won their first 13 games, but then did their best to squander a 10-game lead over the Dodgers at the end of July; at one point, they lost 19 of 21. With both Los Angeles and San Francisco a game behind on the final weekend, Atlanta finally backed into the postseason when the California clubs knocked each other off. Atlanta's main assets were Dale Murphy, whose 109 RBIs tied with Montreal's Al Oliver for the most in the NL; Phil Niekro, who went 17-4; and Gene Garber, who saved 30. Oliver also won the batting title (.331). Other bests were New York's Dave Kingman (37 homers), Philadelphia's Steve Carlton (23 wins), and Montreal's Steve Rogers (2.40 ERA).

Both the Brewers and Angels took their AL divisions by hitting the ball out of the park. In the East, the so-called Harvey's Wallbangers of manager Harvey Kuenn clouted 216 homers, including 39 from leader Gorman Thomas, 34 from Ben Oglivie, 32 from Cecil Cooper, and 29 from Robin Yount. All four hitters also drove in 100 runs, supporting 18 wins from Pete Vuckovich and 29 saves from Rollie Fingers. For all that, the club had to survive an eleventh-hour scare when the pursuing Orioles tied them on the next to last day of the season, necessitating two homers from Yount to win a showdown finale. In the West, the addition of free agent Reggie Jackson (tied with Thomas at 39 homers) made for six Angels lineup regulars with at least 19 homers. Although Oakland sank miserably in the division, outfielder Rickey Henderson obliterated the season-steal mark by swiping 130 bases. Others at the top were Hal McRae of Kansas City (133 RBIs), Willie Wilson of the Royals (.332), LaMarr Hoyt of Chicago (19 wins), and Rick Sutcliffe of the Indians (2.96 ERA).

With the help of rain washing out a 1-0 deficit to Niekro in the NLCS opener, the Cardinals swept the Braves in three. Bob Forsch pitched a three-hit shutout and McGee knocked in five. In the ALCS, the Brewers staked the Angels to two victories, then won

Rickey Henderson
One of the most dynamic baserunners and leadoff hitters in baseball history, Henderson shattered the major league record by stealing 130 bases.

three straight for the flag despite 10 RBIs from California designated hitter Don Baylor. Milwaukee's triumph was keyed by two saves from Pete Ladd, replacing the injured Fingers.

The World Series got off to an ideal start for the Brewers with a 10-0 rout that included a record five hits from Paul Molitor. But before the seven-game duel was over, St. Louis also enjoyed a romp (13-1) and got up off the floor to take the sixth and seventh games for the championship. Joaquin Andujar won twice, Sutter saved a pair, and Keith Hernandez drove in eight for the Cardinals. Molitor and Yount combined for 23 hits for the losers.

1982 SEASON HIGHLIGHTS

NATIONAL LEAGUE

	W	L	Pct.	GB
East				
St. Louis	92	70	.568	—
Philadelphia	89	73	.549	3
Montreal	86	76	.531	6
Pittsburgh	84	78	.519	8
Chicago	73	89	.451	19
New York	65	97	.401	27
West				
Atlanta	89	73	.549	—
Los Angeles	88	74	.543	1
San Francisco	87	75	.537	2
San Diego	81	81	.500	8
Houston	77	85	.475	12
Cincinnati	61	101	.377	28

AMERICAN LEAGUE

	W	L	Pct.	GB
East				
Milwaukee	95	67	.586	—
Baltimore	94	68	.580	1
Boston	89	73	.549	6
Detroit	83	79	.512	12
New York	79	83	.488	16
Cleveland	78	84	.481	17
Toronto	78	84	.481	17
West				
California	93	69	.574	—
Kansas City	90	72	.556	3
Chicago	87	75	.537	6
Seattle	76	86	.469	17
Oakland	68	94	.420	25
Texas	64	98	.395	29
Minnesota	60	102	.370	33

AWARDS

NL MVP: Dale Murphy, ATL
AL MVP: Robin Yount, MIL
NL Cy Young: Steve Carlton, PHI
AL Cy Young: Pete Vuckovich, MIL
NL Rookie: Steve Sax, LA
AL Rookie: Cal Ripken Jr., BAL
NL Relief Pitcher: Bruce Sutter, STL
AL Relief Pitcher: Dan Quisenberry, KC

GOLD GLOVES
NL: Phil Niekro, P; Gary Carter, C; Keith Hernandez, 1B; Manny Trillo, 2B; Mike Schmidt, 3B; Ozzie Smith, SS; Garry Maddox, Andre Dawson, Dale Murphy, OF
AL: Ron Guidry, P; Bob Boone, C; Eddie Murray, 1B; Frank White, 2B; Buddy Bell, 3B; Robin Yount, SS; Dwight Evans, Dave Winfield, Dwayne Murphy, OF

ALL-STAR GAME
Olympic Stadium, Montreal
July 13: NL 4, AL 1
MVP: Dave Concepcion, Cincinnati

POSTSEASON
WORLD SERIES
St. Louis Cardinals 4, Milwaukee Brewers 3
Oct. 12: Milwaukee 10, ST. LOUIS 0
Oct. 13: ST. LOUIS 5, Milwaukee 4
Oct. 15: St. Louis 6, MILWAUKEE 2
Oct. 16: MILWAUKEE 7, St. Louis 5
Oct. 17: MILWAUKEE 6, St. Louis 4
Oct. 19: ST. LOUIS 13, Milwaukee 1
Oct. 20: ST. LOUIS 6, Milwaukee 3
MVP: Darrell Porter, St. Louis

NATIONAL LEAGUE
NLCS
St. Louis Cardinals 3, Atlanta Braves 0
Oct. 7: ST. LOUIS 7, Atlanta 0
Oct. 9: ST. LOUIS 4, Atlanta 3
Oct. 10: St. Louis 6, ATLANTA 2
MVP: Darrell Porter, St. Louis

AMERICAN LEAGUE
ALCS
Milwaukee Brewers 3, California Angels 2
Oct. 5: CALIFORNIA 8, Milwaukee 3
Oct. 6: CALIFORNIA 4, Milwaukee 2
Oct. 8: MILWAUKEE 5, California 3
Oct. 9: MILWAUKEE 9, California 5
Oct. 10: MILWAUKEE 4, California 3
MVP: Fred Lynn, California

> **"Trying to hit Phil Niekro is like trying to eat Jell-O with chopsticks."**
> —Bobby Murcer

Home team in CAPS

NATIONAL LEAGUE LEADERS

Home Runs
Kingman-NY	37
Murphy-Atl	36
Schmidt-Phi	35
Horner-Atl	32
Guerrero-LA	32

Runs Batted In
Oliver-Mon	109
Murphy-Atl	109
Buckner-Chi	105
Hendrick-StL	104
Clark-SF	103

Batting Average
Oliver-Mon	.331
Madlock-Pit	.319
Durham-Chi	.312
L.Smith-StL	.307
Buckner-Chi	.306

On Base Percentage
Schmidt-Phi	.407
Hernandez-StL	.404
Morgan-SF	.402
Thompson-Pit	.397
Oliver-Mon	.394

Slugging Average
Schmidt-Phi	.547
Guerrero-LA	.536
Durham-Chi	.521
Oliver-Mon	.514
Thompson-Pit	.511

Stolen Bases
Raines-Mon	78
L.Smith-StL	68
Moreno-Pit	60
Wilson-NY	58
S.Sax-LA	49

Wins
Carlton-Phi	23
Valenzuela-LA	19
Rogers-Mon	19
Reuss-LA	18

Innings Pitched
Carlton-Phi	295.2
Valenzuela-LA	285.0
Rogers-Mon	277.0
Niekro-Hou	270.0
Andujar-StL	265.2

Saves
Sutter-StL	36
Minton-SF	30
Garber-Atl	30
Reardon-Mon	26
Tekulve-Pit	20

Strikeouts
Carlton-Phi	286
Soto-Cin	274
Ryan-Hou	245
Valenzuela-LA	199
Rogers-Mon	179

Earned Run Average
Rogers-Mon	2.40
Niekro-Hou	2.47
Andujar-StL	2.47
Soto-Cin	2.79
Valenzuela-LA	2.87

Complete Games
Carlton-Phi	19
Valenzuela-LA	18
Niekro-Hou	16
Rogers-Mon	14
Soto-Cin	13

AMERICAN LEAGUE LEADERS

Home Runs
Thomas-Mil	39
R.Jackson-Cal	39
Winfield-NY	37
Oglivie-Mil	34

Runs Batted In
McRae-KC	133
Cooper-Mil	121
Thornton-Cle	116
Yount-Mil	114
Thomas-Mil	112

Batting Average
Wilson-KC	.332
Yount-Mil	.331
Carew-Cal	.319
Murray-Bal	.316
Cooper-Mil	.313

On Base Percentage
Evans-Bos	.403
Harrah-Cle	.400
Henderson-Oak	.399
Carew-Cal	.399
Murray-Bal	.395

Slugging Average
Yount-Mil	.578
Winfield-NY	.560
Murray-Bal	.549
DeCinces-Cal	.548
McRae-KC	.542

Stolen Bases
Henderson-Oak	130
Garcia-Tor	54
J.Cruz-Sea	46
Molitor-Mil	41
Wilson-KC	37

Wins
Hoyt-Chi	19
Zahn-Cal	18
Vuckovich-Mil	18
Gura-KC	18

Innings Pitched
Stieb-Tor	288.1
Clancy-Tor	266.2
Morris-Det	266.1
Caldwell-Mil	258.0
D.Martinez-Bal	252.0

Saves
Quisenberry-KC	35
Gossage-NY	30
Fingers-Mil	29
Caudill-Sea	26
Davis-Min	22

Strikeouts
Bannister-Sea	209
Barker-Cle	187
Righetti-NY	163
Guidry-NY	162
Tudor-Bos	146

Earned Run Average
Sutcliffe-Cle	2.96
Stanley-Bos	3.10
Palmer-Bal	3.13
Petry-Det	3.22
Stieb-Tor	3.25

Complete Games
Stieb-Tor	19
Morris-Det	17
Langford-Oak	15
Hoyt-Chi	14

THE YEAR IN BASEBALL

April 1: Walt Terrell and Ron Darling are traded from Texas to the Mets for Lee Mazilli.

April 6: A blizzard in New York cancels Opening Day and the next three games.

May 6: Gaylord Perry gets win No. 300.

July 6: Indian Bob Johnson dies.

August 4: Outfielder Joel Youngblood knocks in the winning run in the New York Mets' 7-4 victory over the Cubs in Chicago. In the course of the day-game he is traded to the Montreal Expos, who are playing that night in Philadelphia. Youngblood catches a plane for Philly and appears in right field for the Expos in the fourth inning. He later contributes a single. He becomes the only person to play for two different teams in two different cities on the same day

August 23: With a reputation for doctoring the ball which dated back many years, 43-year-old Seattle pitcher Gaylord Perry is ejected in the seventh inning for throwing a spitball against the Red Sox.

August 27: Rickey Henderson not only breaks Lou Brock's season stolen base record of 118, but swipes three more bases in the A's 5-4 loss at Milwaukee. This gives Henderson 122 thefts in 127 games.

October 12: Paul Molitor of Milwaukee collects five hits, a Series record, in the 10-0 opener over the Cardinals in St. Louis. Mike Caldwell tosses the shutout for the Brewers.

December 16: The Mets reacquire Tom Seaver from the Reds for three players.

1983

Win Ugly Sox, pine tar, Phillie Wheeze Kids produce unsightly year

Whatever else the 1983 season had, it was distinctly short on grace. The fractured Red Sox ownership ran rival front offices, Cubs manager Lee Elia was fired after calling Wrigley Field fans "garbage," the White Sox were acclaimed for "winning ugly," and both the Orioles and Phillies won with aging teams operating on fumes. Then there was the noisiest incident of all at Yankee Stadium on July 24, when a George Brett home run was initially disallowed because he had used too much pine tar on his bat. When the Royals third baseman went berserk against umpires, AL president Lee MacPhail ruled against the arbiters to permit the home run, and the teams had to resume playing the game's final inning later in the season.

The Win Ugly White Sox stayed close to the rest of the AL West until August when they went on a 46-15 tear. Although their sobriquet was sometimes attributed to a hefty roster that seemed to have missed few meals, it actually took root in Texas manager Doug Rader's observation that "they win ugly—they get six hits, but they get six runs with them." LaMarr Hoyt anchored the staff with a league-leading 24 wins, with Rich Dotson winning another 22. Rookie Ron Kittle clouted 35 homers with 100 RBIs, while Greg Luzinski and Carlton Fisk teamed up for another 58 circuits. In the AL East, Eddie Murray and Cal Ripken, Jr. contributed 60 homers and 213 RBIs to a Baltimore title. Scott McGregor's 18 wins and rookie Mike Boddicker's 16 made up for a slew of injuries to the veteran staff. Boston had the big hitters on the year—Wade Boggs taking the batting crown (.361) and Jim Rice the home run (39) and RBI titles (126, shared with Milwaukee's Cecil Cooper). Rick Honeycutt of Texas earned ERA honors (2.42) despite being traded in midseason to the Dodgers.

With only outfielder Von Hayes still in his 20s and five key players 38 or older, Philadelphia picked up the monicker of Wheeze Kids as they struggled through the NL East and ongoing battles with management to win the division title. The effort, spearheaded by John Denny's league-best 19 wins and Mike Schmidt's unmatched 40 homers, couldn't save manager Pat Corrales, who was replaced by general manager Paul Owens in July even with the Phillies in first place. The Dodgers took the West, with Pedro Guerrero knocking in 103. Bill Madlock of the Pirates won his fourth batting crown (.323), Dale Murphy of the Braves drove in the most runs (121), and Atlee Hammaker of the Giants took the ERA honors (2.25).

The Phillies set the tone for the NLCS with a first-inning homer from Schmidt in the opening game, going on to defeat the

Mike Schmidt
The power-hitting third baseman led the NL in home runs eight times, including 1983 when he swatted 40 to lead the Phillies to the AL East title.

Dodgers in four. Steve Carlton won twice, and Gary Matthews drove in eight. Baltimore did a similar job on Chicago, holding the White Sox to three runs in four games. Boddicker pitched a Game 2 shutout, striking out 14.

Homers by Joe Morgan and Garry Maddox gave Philadelphia a Game 1 victory in the World Series, but that was it for the NLers. With neither team hitting much, Rick Dempsey's four doubles and a home run and two round-trippers from Murray drove four straight Baltimore wins. Within days, most of the Wheeze Kids were released, traded or simply not re-signed.

1983 SEASON HIGHLIGHTS

NATIONAL LEAGUE

East	W	L	Pct.	GB
Philadelphia	90	72	.556	—
Pittsburgh	84	78	.519	6
Montreal	82	80	.506	8
San Francisco	79	83	.488	11
Chicago	71	91	.438	19
New York	68	94	.420	22

West	W	L	Pct.	GB
Los Angeles	91	71	.562	—
Atlanta	88	74	.543	3
Houston	85	77	.525	6
San Diego	81	81	.500	10
St. Louis	79	83	.488	12
Cincinnati	74	88	.457	17

AMERICAN LEAGUE

East	W	L	Pct.	GB
Baltimore	98	64	.605	—
Detroit	92	70	.568	6
New York	91	71	.562	7
Toronto	89	73	.549	9
Milwaukee	87	75	.537	11
Boston	78	84	.481	20
Cleveland	70	92	.432	28

West	W	L	Pct.	GB
Chicago	99	63	.611	—
Kansas City	79	83	.488	20
Texas	77	85	.475	22
Oakland	74	88	.457	25
California	70	92	.432	29
Minnesota	70	92	.432	29
Seattle	60	102	.370	39

AWARDS

NL MVP: Dale Murphy, ATL
AL MVP: Cal Ripken Jr., BAL
NL Cy Young: John Denny, PHI
AL Cy Young: La Marr Hoyt, CHI
NL Rookie: Darryl Strawberry, NY
AL Rookie: Ron Kittle, CHI
NL Relief Pitcher: Al Holland, PHI
AL Relief Pitcher: Dan Quisenberry, KC
NL Manager: Tom Lasorda, LA
AL Manager: Tony LaRussa, CHI
GOLD GLOVES
NL: Phil Niekro, P; Tony Pena, C; Keith Hernandez, 1B; Ryne Sandberg, 2B; Mike Schmidt, 3B; Ozzie Smith, SS; Willie McGee, Andre Dawson, Dale Murphy, OF
AL: Ron Guidry, P; Lance Parrish, C; Eddie Murray, 1B; Lou Whitaker, 2B; Buddy Bell, 3B; Alan Trammell, SS; Dwight Evans, Dave Winfield, Dwayne Murphy, OF

ALL-STAR GAME

Comiskey Park, Chicago
July 6: AL 13, NL 3
MVP: Fred Lynn, California

POSTSEASON

WORLD SERIES
Baltimore Orioles 4, Philadelphia Phillies 1
Oct. 11: Philadelphia 2, BALTIMORE 1
Oct. 12: BALTIMORE 4, Philadelphia 1
Oct. 14: Baltimore 3, PHILADELPHIA 2
Oct. 15: Baltimore 5, PHILADELPHIA 4
Oct. 16: Baltimore 5, PHILADELPHIA 0
MVP: Rick Dempsey, Baltimore

NATIONAL LEAGUE

NLCS
Philadelphia Phillies 3, Los Angeles Dodgers 1
Oct. 4: Philadelphia 1, LOS ANGELES 0
Oct. 5: LOS ANGELES 4, Philadelphia 1
Oct. 7: PHILADELPHIA 7, Los Angeles 2
Oct. 8: PHILADELPHIA 7, Los Angeles 2
MVP: Gary Matthews, Philadelphia

Home team in CAPS

AMERICAN LEAGUE

ALCS
Baltimore Orioles 3, Chicago White Sox 1
Oct. 5: Chicago 2, BALTIMORE 1
Oct. 6: BALTIMORE 4, Chicago 0
Oct. 7: Baltimore 11, CHICAGO 1
Oct. 8: Baltimore 3, CHICAGO 0
MVP: Mike Boddicker, Baltimore

> "I've seen the future and it's much like the present, only longer."
>
> —Dan Quisenberry

NATIONAL LEAGUE LEADERS

Home Runs

Schmidt-Phi	40
Murphy-Atl	36
Guerrero-LA	32
Dawson-Mon	32
Evans-SF	30

Runs Batted In

Murphy-Atl	121
Dawson-Mon	113
Schmidt-Phi	109
Guerrero-LA	103
Kennedy-SD	98

Batting Average

Madlock-Pit	.323
L.Smith-StL	.321
Cruz-Hou	.318
Hendrick-StL	.318
Knight-Hou	.304

On Base Percentage

Schmidt-Phi	.402
Hernandez-StL-NY	.398
Murphy-Atl	.396
Raines-Mon	.395
Madlock-Pit	.389

Slugging Average

Murphy-Atl	.540
Dawson-Mon	.539
Guerrero-LA	.531
Schmidt-Phi	.524
Evans-SF	.516

Stolen Bases

Raines-Mon	90
Wiggins-SD	66
S.Sax-LA	56
Wilson-NY	54
L.Smith-StL	43

Wins

Denny-Phi	19
Soto-Cin	17
Rogers-Mon	17
Gullickson-Mon	17
Lea-Mon	16

Innings Pitched

Carlton-Phi	283.2
Soto-Cin	273.2
Rogers-Mon	273.0
Niekro-Hou	263.2
Valenzuela-LA	257.0

Saves

Smith-Chi	29
Holland-Phi	25
Minton-SF	22
Sutter-StL	21
Reardon-Mon	21

Strikeouts

Carlton-Phi	275
Soto-Cin	242
McWilliams-Pit	199
Valenzuela-LA	189
Ryan-Hou	183

Earned Run Average

Hammaker-SF	2.25
Denny-Phi	2.37
Welch-LA	2.65
Soto-Cin	2.70
Pena-LA	2.75

Complete Games

Soto-Cin	18
Rogers-Mon	13
Gullickson-Mon	10

AMERICAN LEAGUE LEADERS

Home Runs

Rice-Bos	39
Armas-Bos	36
Kittle-Chi	35
Murray-Bal	33

Runs Batted In

Rice-Bos	126
Cooper-Mil	126
Winfield-NY	116
Parrish-Det	114
Murray-Bal	111

Batting Average

Boggs-Bos	.361
Carew-Cal	.339
Whitaker-Det	.320
Trammell-Det	.319
Ripken-Bal	.318

On Base Percentage

Boggs-Bos	.449
Henderson-Oak	.415
Carew-Cal	.411
Murray-Bal	.398
Singleton-Bal	.395

Slugging Average

Brett-KC	.563
Rice-Bos	.550
Murray-Bal	.538
Fisk-Chi	.518
Ripken-Bal	.517

Stolen Bases

Henderson-Oak	108
R.Law-Chi	77
Wilson-KC	59
J.Cruz-Sea-Chi	57
Sample-Tex	44

Wins

Hoyt-Chi	24
Dotson-Chi	22
Guidry-NY	21
Morris-Det	20
Petry-Det	19

Innings Pitched

Morris-Det	293.2
Stieb-Tor	278.0
Petry-Det	266.1
Hoyt-Chi	260.2
McGregor-Bal	260.0

Saves

Quisenberry-KC	45
Stanley-Bos	33
Davis-Min	30
Caudill-Sea	26
Ladd-Mil	25

Strikeouts

Morris-Det	232
Bannister-Chi	193
Stieb-Tor	187
Righetti-NY	169
Sutcliffe-Cle	160

Earned Run Average

Honeycutt-Tex	2.42
Boddicker-Bal	2.77
Stieb-Tor	3.04
Hough-Tex	3.18
McGregor-Bal	3.18

Complete Games

Guidry-NY	21
Morris-Det	20
Stieb-Tor	14
Rawley-NY	13
McGregor-Bal	12

THE YEAR IN BASEBALL

March 3: Steve Carlton becomes the highest-paid player in baseball history when he signs a four-year, $4.15-million contract.

April 23: Milt Wilcox's perfect game at Chicago is ruined on a two-out ninth-inning single.

April 27: Nolan Ryan moves past Walter Johnson with strikeout No. 3,509 to become baseball's all-time leader.

May 20: Wildfire Schulte dies.

July 6: In the 50th anniversary All Star Game at Comiskey Park the AL routs the NL 13-3.

July 24: An apparent ninth-inning two-run homer by George Brett is disallowed because pine tar on his bat handle exceeds 17 inches, but the umpire's decision is overruled by AL president Lee MacPhail who orders the game resumed on August 18.

July 29: Steve Garvey's consecutive game steak of 1,207 is ended when he suffers a dislocated thumb.

August 24: Philadelphia first baseman Pete Rose's consecutive game streak ends at 745.

September 17: Johnny Bench night draws a record crowd of 53,790 in Cincinnati, and Bench responds with a two-run homer and a single.

October 10: The Detroit Tigers are purchased by Tom Monaghan, founder and president of Domino's Pizza.

November 15: After pleading guilty to attempting to purchase cocaine, Willie Wilson, Willie Aikens, Jerry Martin, and Vida Blue are sentenced to three months in prison.

December 8: Dr. Bobby Brown is elected president of the AL.

1984

Cubs blow Series shot as Sparky's Tigers lead from start to finish

There was more baseball than usual in Chicago. On the evening of May 8, the White Sox and Brewers undertook a 25-inning affair that lasted a record eight hours and six minutes before being settled the next day on a home run by Chicago's Harold Baines. On the other side of town, the Cubs turned an adroit June trade into their first postseason appearance since the 1945 World Series. On the other hand, they didn't have to protest a ruling that they would lose the NL's scheduled home-field advantage in the World Series because of Wrigley Field's lack of lights (and the need to appease NBC); they simply didn't get that far.

The deal that turned the Cubs around brought Rick Sutcliffe from the Indians in exchange for outfielders Joe Carter and Mel Hall; the right-hander went 16-1 to lead Chicago past the revived Mets for the NL East title. Other big contributors were MVP second baseman Ryne Sandberg (.314 with 84 RBIs) and Lee Smith (9 wins and 33 saves). In the West, the equally surprising Padres melded such homegrown talents as Tony Gwynn and Kevin McReynolds with veterans like Steve Garvey, Graig Nettles and Goose Gossage to run away from the division. Gwynn won the batting title (.351), while Philadelphia's Mike Schmidt and Atlanta's Dale Murphy had the most homers (36) and Schmidt tied with Montreal's Gary Carter in the RBI department (106). Joaquin Andujar of St. Louis recorded the most victories (20), Alejandro Pena of Los Angeles the lowest ERA (2.48). In April, Pete Rose of the Expos doubled off Philadelphia's Jerry Koosman to join Ty Cobb in the exclusive 4,000-hit club.

Sparky Anderson's Tigers made a joke of the AL East race, standing 35-5 by mid-May and becoming the first club since the 1927 Yankees to hold first place every day of the season. Although the Tigers led the league in most critical categories and Jack Morris and Dan Petry pitched in for 37 wins, the team MVP was reliever Willie Hernandez, who won 9 and saved 32 in 80 appearances. The Royals took a generally hapless West by being the only club to play better than .500. Like the Tigers, they could point to their closer, Dan Quisenberry with 6 wins and 44 saves, as their most indispensable man. Boston's Tony Armas posted the biggest slugging numbers (43 homers and 123 RBIs), New York's Don Mattingly the best average (.343), and Baltimore's Mike Boddicker the most victories (20) and best ERA (2.79).

The Cubs had three shots at winning their first pennant in 39 years, and blew them all. After winning the first two NLCS games,

Dwight Gooden
At age 19, Gooden arrived with a blazing fastball and devastating curve to set a rookie strikeout record (276) and become the youngest-ever All-Star Game participant.

they lost the third by not being able to hit San Diego's Ed Whitson, the fourth on a ninth-inning homer to Garvey, and the fifth on a combination of first baseman Leon Durham's error and comeback RBIs from Gwynn and Garvey. Garvey totaled eight RBIs on seven hits. In the ALCS, the Tigers blew away the Royals in three straight, holding Kansas City to a .170 average.

Detroit continued their dominance in the World Series, winning the championship in five games. The hitting stars were Kirk Gibson and Alan Trammell, who collected 15 hits and 13 RBIs between them. Morris won twice and Hernandez saved two.

1984 SEASON HIGHLIGHTS

NATIONAL LEAGUE

East	W	L	Pct.	GB
Chicago	96	65	.596	—
New York	90	72	.556	6.5
St. Louis	84	78	.519	12.5
Philadelphia	81	81	.500	15.5
Montreal	78	83	.484	18
Pittsburgh	75	87	.463	21.5
West				
San Diego	92	70	.568	—
Houston	80	82	.494	12
Atlanta	80	82	.494	12
Los Angeles	79	83	.488	13
Cincinnati	70	92	.432	22
San Francisco	66	96	.407	26

AMERICAN LEAGUE

East	W	L	Pct.	GB
Detroit	104	58	.642	—
Toronto	89	73	.549	15
New York	87	75	.537	17
Boston	86	76	.531	18
Baltimore	85	77	.525	19
Cleveland	75	87	.463	29
Milwaukee	67	94	.416	36.5
West				
Kansas City	84	78	.519	—
Minnesota	81	81	.500	3
California	81	81	.500	3
Oakland	77	85	.475	7
Chicago	74	88	.457	10
Seattle	74	88	.457	10
Texas	69	92	.429	14.5

AWARDS

NL MVP: Ryne Sandberg, CHI
AL MVP: Willie Hernandez, DET
NL Cy Young: Rick Sutcliffe, CHI
AL Cy Young: Willie Hernandez, DET
NL Rookie: Dwight Gooden, NY
AL Rookie: Alvin Davis, SEA
NL Relief Pitcher: Bruce Sutter, STL
AL Relief Pitcher: Dan Quisenberry, KC
NL Manager: Jim Frey, CHI
AL Manager: Sparky Anderson, DET

GOLD GLOVES

NL: Joaquin Andujar, P; Tony Pena, C; Keith Hernandez, 1B; Ryne Sandberg, 2B; Mike Schmidt, 3B; Ozzie Smith, SS; Bob Dernier, Andre Dawson, Dale Murphy, OF
AL: Ron Guidry, P; Lance Parrish, C; Eddie Murray, 1B; Lou Whitaker, 2B; Buddy Bell, 3B; Alan Trammell, SS; Dwight Evans, Dave Winfield, Dwayne Murphy, OF

ALL-STAR GAME

Candlestick Park, San Francisco
July 10: NL 3, AL 1
MVP: Gary Carter, Montreal

POSTSEASON

WORLD SERIES
Detroit Tigers 4, San Diego Padres 1
Oct. 9: Detroit 3, SAN DIEGO 2
Oct. 10: SAN DIEGO 5, Detroit 3
Oct. 12: DETROIT 5, San Diego 2
Oct. 13: DETROIT 4, San Diego 2
Oct. 14: DETROIT 8, San Diego 4
MVP: Alan Trammell, Detroit

NATIONAL LEAGUE

NLCS
San Diego Padres 3, Chicago Cubs 2
Oct. 2: CHICAGO 13, San Diego 0
Oct. 3: CHICAGO 4, San Diego 2
Oct. 4: SAN DIEGO 7, Chicago 1
Oct. 6: SAN DIEGO 7, Chicago 5
Oct. 7: SAN DIEGO 6, Chicago 3
MVP: Steve Garvey, San Diego

Home team in CAPS

AMERICAN LEAGUE

ALCS
Detroit Tigers 3, Kansas City Royals 0
Oct. 2: Detroit 6, KANSAS CITY 1
Oct. 3: Detroit 5, KANSAS CITY 3
Oct. 5: DETROIT 1, Kansas City 0
MVP: Kirk Gibson, Detroit

> **"There is one word in America that says it all, and that one word is 'You never know'."**
> —Joaquin Andujar

NATIONAL LEAGUE LEADERS

Home Runs
Schmidt-Phi	36
Murphy-Atl	36
Carter-Mon	27
Strawberry-NY	26
Cey-Chi	25

Runs Batted In
Schmidt-Phi	106
Carter-Mon	106
Murphy-Atl	100
Strawberry-NY	97
Cey-Chi	97

Batting Average
Gwynn-SD	.351
Lacy-Pit	.321
C.Davis-SF	.315
Sandberg-Chi	.314
Ray-Pit	.312

On Base Percentage
Matthews-Chi	.417
Hernandez-NY	.415
Gwynn-SD	.411
Raines-Mon	.395
Schmidt-Phi	.388

Slugging Average
Murphy-Atl	.547
Schmidt-Phi	.536
Sandberg-Chi	.520
C.Davis-SF	.507
Durham-Chi	.505

Stolen Bases
Raines-Mon	75
Samuel-Phi	72
Wiggins-SD	70
L.Smith-StL	50

Wins
Andujar-StL	20
Soto-Cin	18
Gooden-NY	17
Sutcliffe-Chi	16
Niekro-Hou	16

Innings Pitched
Andujar-StL	261.1
Valenzuela-LA	261.0
Niekro-Hou	248.1
Rhoden-Pit	238.1
Soto-Cin	237.1

Saves
Sutter-StL	45
Smith-Chi	33
Orosco-NY	31
Holland-Phi	29
Gossage-SD	25

Strikeouts
Gooden-NY	276
Valenzuela-LA	240
Ryan-Hou	197
Soto-Cin	185
Carlton-Phi	163

Earned Run Average
Pena-LA	2.48
Gooden-NY	2.60
Hershiser-LA	2.66
Rhoden-Pit	2.72
Candelaria-Pit	2.72

Complete Games
Soto-Cin	13
Valenzuela-LA	12
Andujar-StL	12
Knepper-Hou	11
Mahler-Atl	9

AMERICAN LEAGUE LEADERS

Home Runs
Armas-Bos	43
Kingman-Oak	35
Thornton-Cle	33
Parrish-Det	33
Murphy-Oak	33

Runs Batted In
Armas-Bos	123
Rice-Bos	122
Kingman-Oak	118
Davis-Sea	116

Batting Average
Mattingly-NY	.343
Winfield-NY	.340
Boggs-Bos	.325
Bell-Tex	.315
Trammell-Det	.314

On Base Percentage
Murray-Bal	.415
Boggs-Bos	.409
Henderson-Oak	.401
Winfield-NY	.397
Davis-Sea	.395

Slugging Average
Baines-Chi	.541
Mattingly-NY	.537
Evans-Bos	.532
Armas-Bos	.531
Hrbek-Min	.522

Stolen Bases
Henderson-Oak	66
Collins-Tor	60
Butler-Cle	52
Pettis-Cal	48
Wilson-KC	47

Wins
Boddicker-Bal	20
Morris-Det	19
Blyleven-Cle	19
Viola-Min	18
Petry-Det	18

Innings Pitched
Stieb-Tor	267.0
Hough-Tex	266.0
Alexander-Tor	261.2
Boddicker-Bal	261.1
Viola-Min	257.2

Saves
Quisenberry-KC	44
Caudill-Oak	36
Hernandez-Det	32
Righetti-NY	31
Davis-Min	29

Strikeouts
Langston-Sea	204
Stieb-Tor	198
Witt-Cal	196
Blyleven-Cle	170
Hough-Tex	164

Earned Run Average
Boddicker-Bal	2.79
Stieb-Tor	2.83
Blyleven-Cle	2.87
Niekro-NY	3.09
Zahn-Cal	3.12

Complete Games
Hough-Tex	17
Boddicker-Bal	16
Dotson-Chi	14
Blyleven-Cle	12
Beattie-Sea	12

THE YEAR IN BASEBALL

March 20: Stan Coveleski dies.

April 7: Jack Morris throws the first no-hitter by a Tiger in 26 years, winning 4-0 over Chicago.

April 13: Pete Rose gets hit No. 4,000—exactly 21 years after collecting his first hit.

May 9: The longest game in AL history ends in the 25th inning when Harold Baines homers to give Chicago a 7-6 win over Milwaukee.

May 11: Tigers run away to best start in major league history at 26-4.

June 24: Joe Morgan hits his 265th career home run to break Rogers Hornsby's record for second basemen.

June 27: Dwight Evans hits for the cycle.

July 10: Dwight Gooden, at 19 the youngest All-Star in history, combines with Fernando Valenzuela to fan six in a row to set an All-Star Game strikeout record.

August 16: Pete Rose is named player manager of the Reds after being traded by Philadelphia to Cincinnati.

September 12: Dwight Gooden fans 16 Phils in a 2-1 victory, equaling the number of Pirates fanned in his last outing—tying the record for strikeouts in consecutive starts.

September 17: Reggie Jackson, now with the California Angels, becomes the 13th player to hit 500 big league homers. His wallop against Kansas City's Bud Black came 17 years to the day after his first big league hit.

September 30: California's Mike Witt pitches a perfect game on the final day of the season, needing just 97 pitches to beat Texas, 1-0.

November 30: Ryne Sandberg becomes the first Cub since Ernie Banks in 1959 to win the NL MVP Award.

1985

Rose gets hit No. 4,192 as Carew, Seaver, Ryan also achieve milestones

In a year of hallmarks, the most significant came on September 11, when Reds playing manager Pete Rose surpassed Ty Cobb by singling off San Diego's Eric Show for his 4,192nd hit. The Rose safety was the centerpiece for such other lifetime achievements during the season as the 3,000th hit for Rod Carew, the 300th victories for Tom Seaver and Phil Niekro, and the 4,000th strikeout for Nolan Ryan. Less celebrated were a two-day players strike in August and a drug trial in September that named such stars as Keith Hernandez and Dave Parker as past users of cocaine.

In the NL West, Orel Hershiser's 19 wins and slugging from Pedro Guerrero (.320-33-87) and Mike Marshall (.293-28-95) led the Dodgers to a division title. In the East, the Cardinals and Mets went at each other all year before St. Louis finally emerged. The Cardinals running game featured an NL- record-shattering 110 steals by rookie Vince Coleman, 56 more and a batting championship from Willie McGee (.353), Tommy Herr's 110 RBIs on merely 8 home runs, and 21 wins apiece for John Tudor and Joaquin Andujar. New York's biggest response was in Dwight Gooden, who took the Triple Crown with 24 wins, a 1.53 ERA and 268 strikeouts. Dale Murphy of the Braves had the most homers (37), Parker of the Reds the most runs batted in (125).

In the AL East, expansion Toronto popped to the surface behind the lusty hitting of George Bell and Jesse Barfield and the pitching of Doyle Alexander and Dave Stieb (ERA leader, 2.48). With the Yankees breathing down their necks in mid-September, the Blue Jays lost the first game of a critical series in Yankee Stadium, but then won the next three to all but nail down the title. As late as September 30, the Royals trailed the Angels in the AL West, but then they beat California three-out-of-four for the difference. The Kansas City win was most prominently the work of George Brett (.335-30-112), Bret Saberhagen (20 wins) and Dan Quisenberry (37 saves). Boston's Wade Boggs won the Silver Bat (.368) and teammate Dwight Evans had the most homers (40), while New York's Don Mattingly led in RBIs (145) and his teammate Ron Guidry in wins (22).

With a format change to the best-of-seven, the Cardinals took the NLCS in six games when Los Angeles closer Tom Niedenfuer

Pete Rose
On his way to setting major league records for hits (4,256) and games played (3,562), Rose passed Ty Cobb as the all-time hits leader with hit No. 4,192.

served up crushing ninth-inning homers in Game 5 to Ozzie Smith and in Game 6 to Jack Clark. The switch-hitting Smith collected 10 hits in the series. In the ALCS, Toronto won three of the first four games, but then fell apart in the prolonged format as Brett led a charge back with the help of a Game 5 shutout by Royals southpaw Danny Jackson.

Kansas City spotted the Cardinals the same 3-1 lead in the World Series, and once again came back to triumph. Also again, Jackson fired a Game 5 beauty and Brett hammered opposing pitchers, but this time a critically bad umpiring call at first base in the ninth inning of the sixth game also helped to keep a Royals victory rally going. When the ALers bashed around aces Tudor and Andujar in the finale, the former smashed his hand through a window and the latter had to be removed from the field after seeking to start fights with both umpires and Royals.

1985 SEASON HIGHLIGHTS

NATIONAL LEAGUE

	W	L	Pct.	GB
East				
St. Louis	101	61	.623	—
New York	98	64	.605	3
Montreal	84	77	.522	16.5
Chicago	77	84	.478	23.5
Philadelphia	75	87	.463	26
Pittsburgh	57	104	.354	43.5
West				
Los Angeles	95	67	.586	—
Cincinnati	89	72	.553	5.5
San Diego	83	79	.512	12
Houston	83	79	.512	12
Atlanta	66	96	.407	29
San Francisco	62	100	.383	33

AMERICAN LEAGUE

	W	L	Pct.	GB
East				
Toronto	99	62	.615	—
New York	97	64	.602	2
Detroit	84	77	.522	15
Baltimore	83	78	.516	16
Boston	81	81	.500	18.5
Milwaukee	71	90	.441	28
Cleveland	60	102	.370	39.5
West				
Kansas City	91	71	.562	—
California	90	72	.556	1
Chicago	85	77	.525	6
Oakland	77	85	.475	14
Minnesota	77	85	.475	14
Seattle	74	88	.457	17
Texas	62	99	.385	28.5

AWARDS

NL MVP: Willie McGee, STL
AL MVP: Don Mattingly, NY
NL Cy Young: Dwight Gooden, NY
AL Cy Young: Bret Saberhagen, KC
NL Rookie: Vince Coleman, STL
AL Rookie: Ozzie Guillen, CHI
NL Relief Pitcher: Jeff Reardon, MON
AL Relief Pitcher: Dan Quisenberry, KC
NL Manager: Whitey Herzog, STL
AL Manager: Bobby Cox, TOR

GOLD GLOVES
NL: Rick Reuschel, P; Tony Pena, C; Keith Hernandez, 1B; Ryne Sandberg, 2B; Tim Wallach, 3B; Ozzie Smith, SS; Willie McGee, Andre Dawson, Dale Murphy, OF
AL: Ron Guidry, P; Lance Parrish, C; Don Mattingly, 1B; Lou Whitaker, 2B; George Brett, 3B; Alfredo Griffin, SS; Dwight Evans, Dave Winfield, Gary Pettis, Dwayne Murphy, OF

ALL-STAR GAME

H. Humphrey Metrodome, Minneapolis
July 16: NL 6, AL 1
MVP: Lamarr Hoyt, San Diego

POSTSEASON

WORLD SERIES
Kansas City Royals 4, St. Louis Cardinals 3
Oct. 19: St. Louis 3, KANSAS CITY 1
Oct. 20: St. Louis 4, KANSAS CITY 2
Oct. 22: Kansas City 6, ST. LOUIS 1
Oct. 23: ST. LOUIS 3, Kansas City 0
Oct. 24: Kansas City 6, ST. LOUIS 1
Oct. 26: KANSAS CITY 2, St. Louis 1
Oct. 27: KANSAS CITY 11, St. Louis 0
MVP: Bret Saberhagen, Kansas City

NATIONAL LEAGUE

NLCS
St. Louis Cardinals 4, Los Angeles Dodgers 2
Oct. 9: LOS ANGELES 4, St. Louis 1
Oct. 10: LOS ANGELES 8, St. Louis 2
Oct. 12: ST. LOUIS 4, Los Angeles 2
Oct. 13: ST. LOUIS 12, Los Angeles 2
Oct. 14: ST. LOUIS 3, Los Angeles 2
Oct. 16: St. Louis 7, LOS ANGELES 5
MVP: Ozzie Smith, St. Louis

Home team in CAPS

AMERICAN LEAGUE

ALCS
Kansas City Royals 4, Toronto Blue Jays 3
Oct. 8: TORONTO 6, Kansas City 1
Oct. 9: TORONTO 6, Kansas City 5
Oct. 11: KANSAS CITY 6, Toronto 5
Oct. 12: Toronto 3, KANSAS CITY 1
Oct. 13: KANSAS CITY 2, Toronto 0
Oct. 15: Kansas City 5, TORONTO 3
Oct. 16: Kansas City 6, TORONTO 22
MVP: George Brett, Kansas City

> **"I'd walk through hell in a gasoline suit to keep playing baseball."**
> —Pete Rose

NATIONAL LEAGUE LEADERS

Home Runs
Murphy-Atl	37
Parker-Cin	34
Schmidt-Phi	33
Guerrero-LA	33
Carter-NY	32

Runs Batted In
Parker-Cin	125
Murphy-Atl	111
Herr-StL	110
Moreland-Chi	106
Wilson-Phi	102

Batting Average
McGee-StL	.353
Guerrero-LA	.320
Raines-Mon	.320
Gwynn-SD	.317
Parker-Cin	.312

On Base Percentage
Guerrero-LA	.425
Scioscia-LA	.409
Raines-Mon	.407
Rose-Cin	.398
Clark-StL	.397

Slugging Average
Guerrero-LA	.577
Parker-Cin	.551
Murphy-Atl	.539
Schmidt-Phi	.532
Marshall-LA	.515

Stolen Bases
Coleman-StL	110
Raines-Mon	70
McGee-StL	56
Sandberg-Chi	54
Samuel-Phi	53

Wins
Gooden-NY	24
Tudor-StL	21
Andujar-StL	21
Browning-Cin	20
Hershiser-LA	19

Innings Pitched
Gooden-NY	276.2
Tudor-StL	275.0
Valenzuela-LA	272.1
Andujar-StL	269.2
Mahler-Atl	266.2

Saves
Reardon-Mon	41
Smith-Chi	33
Smith-Hou	27
Power-Cin	27
Gossage-SD	26

Strikeouts
Gooden-NY	268
Soto-Cin	214
Ryan-Hou	209
Valenzuela-LA	208
Fernandez-NY	180

Earned Run Average
Gooden-NY	1.53
Tudor-StL	1.93
Hershiser-LA	2.03
Reuschel-Pit	2.27
Welch-LA	2.31

Complete Games
Gooden-NY	16
Valenzuela-LA	14
Tudor-StL	14
Cox-StL	10
Andujar-StL	10

AMERICAN LEAGUE LEADERS

Home Runs
Evans-Det	40
Fisk-Chi	37
Balboni-KC	36
Mattingly-NY	35
G.Thomas-Sea	32

Runs Batted In
Mattingly-NY	145
Murray-Bal	124
Winfield-NY	114
Baines-Chi	113
Brett-KC	112

Batting Average
Boggs-Bos	.368
Brett-KC	.335
Mattingly-NY	.324
Henderson-NY	.314
Butler-Cle	.311

On Base Percentage
Boggs-Bos	.452
Brett-KC	.442
Harrah-Tex	.437
Henderson-NY	.422
Murray-Bal	.387

Slugging Average
Brett-KC	.585
Mattingly-NY	.567
Barfield-Tor	.536
Murray-Bal	.523
Evans-Det	.519

Stolen Bases
Henderson-NY	80
Pettis-Cal	56
Butler-Cle	47
Wilson-KC	43
Smith-KC	40

Wins
Guidry-NY	22
Saberhagen-KC	20
Viola-Min	18
Burns-Chi	18

Innings Pitched
Blyleven-Cle-Min	293.2
Boyd-Bos	272.1
Stieb-Tor	265.0
Alexander-Tor	260.2
Guidry-NY	259.0

Saves
Quisenberry-KC	37
James-Chi	32
Moore-Cal	31
Hernandez-Det	31

Strikeouts
Blyleven-Cle-Min	206
Bannister-Chi	198
Morris-Det	191
Hurst-Bos	189
Witt-Cal	180

Earned Run Average
Stieb-Tor	2.48
Leibrandt-KC	2.69
Saberhagen-KC	2.87
Key-Tor	3.00
Blyleven-Cle-Min	3.16

Complete Games
Blyleven-Cle-Min	24
Moore-Sea	14
Hough-Tex	14
Morris-Det	13
Boyd-Bos	13

THE YEAR IN BASEBALL

January 7: Lou Brock and Hoyt Wilhelm are elected to the Hall of Fame.

July 2: Joe Niekro wins his 200th career game to join Phil as the second brother tandem to reach 200 wins.

July 4: The Mets beat the Braves 16-3 in a game that endures two rain delays and six hours, 10 minutes of playing time.

August 20: Dwight Gooden passes the 200 strikeout mark to join Herb Score as the only pitchers this century to surpass 200 strikeouts in their first two seasons.

September 11: With a single off Eric Snow, Pete Rose passes Ty Cobb to become baseball's all-time hits leader at 4,192 before a crowd of 47,237 at Cincinnati's Riverfront Stadium.

October 6: Phil Niekro, 46, wins his 300th career game, 8-0 over Toronto, and becomes the oldest player to pitch a complete-game shutout.

October 27: The Yankees fire Billy Martin for an unprecedented fourth time and replace him with Lou Piniella.

November 15: Riggs Stephenson dies; for his 14-year career, he batted .336.

November 27: Vince Coleman, who stole 110 bases for the Cardinals, joins Frank Robinson, Orlando Cepada and Willie McCovey as the only unanimous winners of the league's Rookie of the Year Award.

1986

Buckner boots Series to make Amazin' Mets improbable champs

The Mets went into the season with bullseyes on their backs after manager Davey Johnson's vow not only to win, but to "dominate." By the end of the postseason, they had not only accomplished that, but had played the biggest role in the most thrilling fall in baseball history.

New York's 21-1/2-game lead over the Phillies in the NL East was such a team effort that Bob Ojeda's winning percentage of .783 (18-5) was the closest the club had to a league category leader. Nobody hit 30 homers, and only Gary Carter reached 100 RBIs. Of particular importance, though, were the 43 saves accumulated by Jesse Orosco and Roger McDowell. In the West, Mike Scott's Cy Young Award year (18 wins, an NL-best 2.22 ERA) and Glenn Davis' 31-101 drove the Astros to the title over injury-plagued rivals. The Expos' Tim Raines had the highest average (.334), the Phils' Mike Schmidt led the homer (37) and RBI (119) departments and the Dodgers' Fernando Valenzuela won the most (21).

Both the Red Sox and Angels built up big enough leads in their AL divisions to absorb September slumps. Boston's win was powered by Wade Boggs' batting crown (.357), 100-RBI seasons from Bill Buckner and Jim Rice, and designated hitter Don Baylor's 31 homers and 94 RBIs. On the mound, Roger Clemens secured MVP and Cy Young awards with his league-best 24 victories and 2.48 ERA. On the evening of April 18, the right-hander also struck out a record 20 Mariners. In the West, California kept surprising Texas at bay with a collection of aging veterans, 100 RBIs from Wally Joyner and 35 wins from Mike Witt and Kirk McCaskill. Jesse Barfield of the Blue Jays had the most homers (40), Joe Carter of the Indians the most RBIs (121).

In the ALCS, California took three of four games and held a 5-2 lead in the ninth of Game 5 when two-run homers from Baylor and Dave Henderson knotted things. After the Angels came back to retie the game, Henderson hit a decisive sacrifice fly in the 11th inning. Boston then pummeled Angels pitching in Games 6 and 7 for a comeback flag. Although one game shorter, the NLCS was even more dramatic. The first five games featured complete-game efforts from Scott for Houston's two wins, a come-from-behind ninth-inning homer from New York's Lenny Dykstra, and a 12-inning Mets win. With Scott looming again as the Game 7 starter, New York went into the final inning of the sixth game trailing 3-0, tied it, went ahead in the 14th, saw the Astros retie it,

Wade Boggs
The Red Sox third baseman won four consecutive batting titles in the 1980s, including 1986 when he batted .357 as Boston won the AL flag.

scored three in the 16th, and barely held on when Houston fell short by scoring only two in the bottom of the frame. Orosco accounted for three of the New York wins.

After five World Series games, the Red Sox held a 3-2 lead, then played the role of the Angels in encountering disaster. Up by a 5-3 score in the 10th inning of a tumultuous Game 6 and with the champagne on ice in their clubhouse, Red Sox relievers Calvin Schiraldi and Bob Stanley yielded two-out hits to Carter, Kevin Mitchell and Ray Knight, a game-tying wild pitch, and a Mookie Wilson bouncer that went through Buckner's legs for a stunning New York win. In Game 7, the Mets trailed 3-0 into the sixth inning before thrashing the Red Sox bullpen for an improbable victory and championship. Marty Barrett had thirteen hits for the losers, Carter nine RBIs and Orosco two saves for the winners.

1986 SEASON HIGHLIGHTS

NATIONAL LEAGUE

East	W	L	Pct.	GB
New York	108	54	.667	—
Cincinnati	86	76	.531	22
St. Louis	79	82	.491	28.5
Montreal	78	83	.484	29.5
Chicago	70	90	.438	37
Pittsburgh	64	98	.395	44

West	W	L	Pct.	GB
Houston	96	66	.593	—
Philadelphia	86	75	.534	9.5
San Francisco	83	79	.512	13
San Diego	74	88	.457	22
Los Angeles	73	89	.451	23
Atlanta	72	89	.447	23.5

AMERICAN LEAGUE

East	W	L	Pct.	GB
Boston	95	66	.590	—
New York	90	72	.556	5.5
Texas	87	75	.537	8.5
Toronto	86	76	.531	9.5
Cleveland	84	78	.519	11.5
Milwaukee	77	84	.478	18
Baltimore	73	89	.451	22.5

West	W	L	Pct.	GB
California	92	70	.568	—
Detroit	87	75	.537	5
Oakland	76	86	.469	16
Kansas City	76	86	.469	16
Chicago	72	90	.444	20
Minnesota	71	91	.438	21
Seattle	67	95	.414	25

AWARDS

NL MVP: Mike Schmidt, PHI
AL MVP: Roger Clemens, BOS
NL Cy Young: Mike Scott, HOU
AL Cy Young: Roger Clemens, BOS
NL Rookie: Todd Worrell, STL
AL Rookie: Jose Canseco, OAK
NL Relief Pitcher: Todd Worrell, STL
AL Relief Pitcher: Dave Righetti, NY
NL Manager: Hal Lanier, HOU
AL Manager: John McNamara, BOS

GOLD GLOVES

NL: Fernando Valenzuela, P; Jody Davis, C; Keith Hernandez, 1B; Ryne Sandberg, 2B; Mike Schmidt, 3B; Ozzie Smith, SS; Willie McGee, Tony Gwynn, Dale Murphy, OF

AL: Ron Guidry, P; Bob Boone, C; Don Mattingly, 1B; Frank White, 2B; Gary Gaetti, 3B; Tony Fernandez, SS; Kirby Puckett, Jesse Barfield, Gary Pettis, OF

ALL-STAR GAME

Astrodome, Houston
July 15: AL 3, NL 2
MVP: Roger Clemens, Boston

POSTSEASON

WORLD SERIES
New York Mets 4, Boston Red Sox 3
Oct. 18: Boston 1, NEW YORK 0
Oct. 19: Boston 9, NEW YORK 3
Oct. 21: New York 7, BOSTON 1
Oct. 22: NewYork 6, BOSTON 2
Oct. 23: BOSTON 4, New York 2
Oct. 25: NEW YORK 6, Boston 5
Oct. 27: NEW YORK 8, Boston 5
MVP: Ray Knight, New York

NATIONAL LEAGUE
NLCS
New York Mets 4, Houston Astros 2
Oct. 8: HOUSTON 1, New York 0
Oct. 9: New York 5, HOUSTON 1
Oct. 11: NEW YORK 6, Houston 5
Oct. 12: Houston 3, NEW YORK 1
Oct. 14: NEW YORK 2, Houston 1
Oct. 15: New York 7, HOUSTON 6
MVP: Mike Scott, Houston

Home team in CAPS

AMERICAN LEAGUE
ALCS
Boston Red Sox 4, California Angels 3
Oct. 7: California 8, BOSTON 1
Oct. 8: BOSTON 9, California 2
Oct. 10: CALIFORNIA 5, Boston 3
Oct. 11: CALIFORNIA 4, Boston 3
Oct. 12: Boston 7, CALIFORNIA 6
Oct. 14: BOSTON 10, California 4
Oct. 15: BOSTON 8, California 1
MVP: Marty Barrett, Boston

"You measure the value of a ballplayer by how many fannies he puts in the seats."
—George Steinbrenner

NATIONAL LEAGUE LEADERS

Home Runs
Schmidt-Phi	37
Parker-Cin	31
Davis-Hou	31
Murphy-Atl	29

Runs Batted In
Schmidt-Phi	119
Parker-Cin	116
Carter-NY	105
Davis-Hou	101
Hayes-Phi	98

Batting Average
Raines-Mon	.334
Sax-LA	.332
Gwynn-SD	.329
Bass-Hou	.311
Hernandez-NY	.310

On Base Percentage
Raines-Mon	.415
Hernandez-NY	.414
Schmidt-Phi	.395
Sax-LA	.391
Gwynn-SD	.382

Slugging Average
Schmidt-Phi	.547
Strawberry-NY	.507
McReynolds-SD	.504
Davis-Hou	.493
Bass-Hou	.486

Stolen Bases
Coleman-StL	107
Davis-Cin	80
Raines-Mon	70
Duncan-LA	48

Wins
Valenzuela-LA	21
Krukow-SF	20
Scott-Hou	18
Ojeda-NY	18

Innings Pitched
Scott-Hou	275.1
Valenzuela-LA	269.1
Knepper-Hou	258.0
Rhoden-Pit	253.2
Gooden-NY	250.0

Saves
Worrell-StL	36
Reardon-Mon	35
Smith-Hou	33
Smith-Chi	31

Strikeouts
Scott-Hou	306
Valenzuela-LA	242
Youmans-Mon	202
Gooden-NY	200
Fernandez-NY	200

Earned Run Average
Scott-Hou	2.22
Ojeda-NY	2.57
Darling-NY	2.81
Rhoden-Pit	2.84
Gooden-NY	2.84

Complete Games
Valenzuela-LA	20
Rhoden-Pit	12
Gooden-NY	12
Krukow-SF	10

AMERICAN LEAGUE LEADERS

Home Runs
Barfield-Tor	40
Kingman-Oak	35
Gaetti-Min	34
Deer-Mil	33
Canseco-Oak	33

Runs Batted In
Carter-Cle	121
Canseco-Oak	117
Mattingly-NY	113
Rice-Bos	110

Batting Average
Boggs-Bos	.357
Mattingly-NY	.352
Puckett-Min	.328
Tabler-Cle	.326
Rice-Bos	.324

On Base Percentage
Boggs-Bos	.455
P.Bradley-Sea	.406
Brett-KC	.404
Murray-Bal	.400
Mattingly-NY	.399

Slugging Average
Mattingly-NY	.573
Barfield-Tor	.559
Puckett-Min	.537
Bell-Tor	.532
Gaetti-Min	.518

Stolen Bases
Henderson-NY	87
Pettis-Cal	50
Cangelosi-Chi	50
Wilson-KC	34
Gibson-Det	34

Wins
Clemens-Bos	24
Morris-Det	21
Higuera-Mil	20
Witt-Cal	18
Rasmussen-NY	18

Innings Pitched
Blyleven-Min	271.2
Witt-Cal	269.0
Morris-Det	267.0
Moore-Sea	266.0
Clemens-Bos	254.0

Saves
Righetti-NY	46
Aase-Bal	34
Henke-Tor	27
Hernandez-Det	24
Moore-Cal	21

Strikeouts
Langston-Sea	245
Clemens-Bos	238
Morris-Det	223
Blyleven-Min	215
Witt-Cal	208

Earned Run Average
Clemens-Bos	2.48
Higuera-Mil	2.79
Witt-Cal	2.84
Hurst-Bos	2.99
D.Jackson-KC	3.20

Complete Games
Candiotti-Cle	17
Blyleven-Min	16
Morris-Det	15
Higuera-Mil	15
Witt-Cal	14

THE YEAR IN BASEBALL

March 27: Baseball's Rules Committee decides that the DH can, for the first time, be allowed in World Series games played in AL parks.

April 29: Roger Clemens, 23, sets a nine-inning major league record by striking out 20 Mariners in a 3-1 Red Sox win.

June 10: The NL announces that Yale University president A. Bartlett Giamatti will succeed Chub Feeney as president at the end of the year.

June 19: California's Don Sutton becomes the 19th pitcher to win 300 games.

June 21: Bo Jackson, the 1985 Heisman Trophy winner and first pick in the NFL draft, opts instead for baseball, signing with the Royals.

July 6: Atlanta slugger Bob Horner becomes the 11th player to hit four home runs in a game.

September 25: For the first time in major league history, a pennant is won by a no-hitter when Houston's Mike Scott no-hits the Giants.

October 15: The Mets defeat Houston in the NLCS, winning Game 6 by a score of 7-6 in 16 innings. In a game that lasted four hours, forty-two minutes, the Mets scored three in the ninth to tie the game at 3-3; and the Astros scored one in the 14th to stay alive at 4-4 and two in the bottom of the 16th to give the Mets a mighty scare.

October 25: Only one strike away from losing the World Series to the Boston Red Sox, the Mets stage a miraculous rally in the 10th inning of Game 6. Down 5-3 in the bottom of the tenth with two out, no one on, and two strikes on Gary Carter, the Mets go on to score the winning run on Bill Buckner's misplay of a Mookie Wilson grounder. New York will win Game 7 two days later.

1987

Mets ace enters rehab, Jays fold down stretch as Twins roar to top

Injuries, clutch home runs and midseason deals saw to it that none of the 1986 division winners repeated a year later. It was also a season of individual streaks and broken streaks: Paul Molitor hit in 39 straight for the Brewers, Don Mattingly homered in eight straight games for the Yankees and manager Cal Ripken, Sr. sat his son down in September after Cal, Jr. had played in 8,243 consecutive innings (904 games) for the Orioles.

In the NL East, New York ace Dwight Gooden's rehab for a cocaine problem, Bob Ojeda's slicing of a finger with garden shears and Roger McDowell's hernia ailment left first place open to the Cardinals for much of the year. The Mets still appeared on their way back until September 11, when St. Louis' Terry Pendleton hit a last-gasp three-run homer off McDowell in the ninth inning to revive the Cardinals. The St. Louis attack was led by Jack Clark and Willie McGee (both with 100 RBIs), Vince Coleman (109 steals) and Todd Worrell (33 saves). In the West, midseason deals for slugger Kevin Mitchell and pitchers Rick Reuschel and Dave Dravecky kept San Francisco above Cincinnati. Houston finished well behind despite Nolan Ryan's NL-leading 2.76 ERA (on a record of 8-16!). The Cubs produced both the top slugger in Andre Dawson (49 homers, 137 RBIs) and most successful pitcher in Rick Sutcliffe (18 wins), while Tony Gwynn of the Padres won the batting title (.370).

With a home record of 56-25, the Twins outpaced the Royals for the AL West title. Minnesota's offense produced three 30-homer hitters (Kent Hrbek, Gary Gaetti, Tom Brunansky) and a .332-28-99 year from Kirby Puckett, while trade acquisition Jeff Reardon settled the rotation with 31 saves. In the East, the Blue Jays appeared to have beaten off the Tigers by taking three of four from them with a week to go, but they then lost five a row. The sixth defeat came to Detroit on the last day of the campaign, when Frank Tanana bested Jimmy Key, 1-0. Detroit's comeback was oiled by late-season trades bringing in right-hander Doyle Alexander and four-time batting champ Bill Madlock. Toronto's consolations were Key's AL-best 2.76 and George Bell's

Tony Gwynn
A career .338 hitter, the San Diego outfielder won eight NL batting titles between 1984 and 1997, including 1987 when he batted .370 with 218 hits.

134 RBIs. Boston's Roger Clemens and Oakland's Dave Stewart won 20, Wade Boggs of the Red Sox won a fourth batting crown (.363), and Oakland's Mark McGwire poled the most homers (49).

In the NLCS, the Giants went up 3-2 after five, but then couldn't plate a single run over the final two games against Cardinals starters John Tudor and Danny Cox. St. Louis' winning effort came from so many directions that the series MVP trophy went to San Francisco's Jeffrey Leonard for his four homers and 10 hits. With howling Metrodome fans in the role of the 26th Player, the Twins finished off the Tigers in a five-game ALCS. Bert

Blyleven won twice and Brunansky drove in nine. Alexander was rattled for ten earned runs in nine innings.

The Twins played four World Series games in the Metrodome, so they became champions. Giving new meaning to home-field advantage, Minnesota outscored St. Louis 33-12 before their relentlessly roaring, hanky-waving fans. Puckett collected 10 hits, Hrbek and Dan Gladden hit grand slams, and Frank Viola won twice. After the Series, a St. Louis otolaryngolist claimed the Twins had not won fairly because Metrodome decibel levels had left the Cardinals disoriented.

1987 SEASON HIGHLIGHTS

NATIONAL LEAGUE

East	W	L	Pct.	GB
St. Louis	95	67	.586	—
New York	92	70	.568	3
Montreal	91	71	.562	4
Philadelphia	80	82	.494	15
Pittsburgh	80	82	.494	15
Houston	76	86	.469	19
West				
San Francisco	90	72	.556	—
Cincinnati	84	78	.519	6
Chicago	76	85	.472	13.5
Los Angeles	73	89	.451	17
Atlanta	69	92	.429	20.5
San Diego	65	97	.401	25

AMERICAN LEAGUE

East	W	L	Pct.	GB
Detroit	98	64	.605	—
Toronto	96	66	.593	2
Milwaukee	91	71	.562	7
New York	89	73	.549	9
Boston	78	84	.481	20
Baltimore	67	95	.414	31
Cleveland	61	101	.377	37
West				
Minnesota	85	77	.525	—
Kansas City	83	79	.512	2
Oakland	81	81	.500	4
Seattle	78	84	.481	7
Chicago	77	85	.475	8
Texas	75	87	.463	10
California	75	87	.463	10

AWARDS

NL MVP: Andre Dawson, CHI
AL MVP: George Bell, TOR
NL Cy Young: Steve Bedrosian, PHI
AL Cy Young: Roger Clemens, BOS
NL Rookie: Benito Santiago, SD
AL Rookie: Mark McGwire, OAK
NL Relief Pitcher: Steve Bedrosian, PHI
AL Relief Pitcher: Dave Righetti, NY
NL Manager: Buck Rodgers, MON
AL Manager: Sparky Anderson, DET
GOLD GLOVES
NL: Rick Reuschel, P; Mike LaValliere, C; Keith Hernandez, 1B; Ryne Sandberg, 2B; Terry Pendleton, 3B; Ozzie Smith, SS; Andre Dawson, Tony Gwynn, Eric Davis, OF
AL: Mark Langston, P; Bob Boone, C; Don Mattingly, 1B; Frank White, 2B; Gary Gaetti, 3B; Tony Fernandez, SS; Kirby Puckett, Jesse Barfield, Dave Winfield, OF

ALL-STAR GAME
Oakland-Alameda County Stadium, Oakland
July 14: NL 2, AL 0
MVP: Tim Raines, Montreal
POSTSEASON
WORLD SERIES
Minnesota Twins 4, St. Louis Cardinals 3
Oct. 17: MINNESOTA 10, St. Louis 1
Oct. 18: MINNESOTA 8, St. Louis 4
Oct. 20: ST. LOUIS 3, Minnesota 1
Oct. 21: ST. LOUIS 7, Minnesota 2
Oct. 22: ST. LOUIS 4, Minnesota 2
Oct. 24: MINNESOTA 11, St. Louis 5
Oct. 25: MINNESOTA 4, St. Louis 2
MVP: Frank Viola, Minnesota

NATIONAL LEAGUE
NLCS
St. Louis Cardinals 4, San Francisco Giants 3
Oct. 6: ST. LOUIS 5, San Francisco 3
Oct. 7: San Francisco 5, ST. LOUIS 0
Oct. 9: St. Louis 6, SAN FRANCISCO 5
Oct. 10: SAN FRANCISCO 4, St. Louis 2
Oct. 11: SAN FRANCISCO 6, St. Louis 3
Oct. 13: ST. LOUIS 1, San Francisco 0
Oct. 14: ST. LOUIS 6, San Francisco 0
MVP: Jeffrey Leonard, San Francisco

Home team in CAPS

AMERICAN LEAGUE
ALCS
Minnesota Twins 4, Detroit Tigers 1
Oct. 7: MINNESOTA 8, Detroit 5
Oct. 8: MINNESOTA 6, Detroit 3
Oct. 10: DETROIT 7, Minnesota 6
Oct. 11: Minnesota 5, DETROIT 3
Oct. 12: Minnesota 9, DETROIT 5
MVP: Gary Gaetti, Minnesota

"If it hadn't hit the scoreboard, it could have gone all the way around the world and hit me in the back of my head."
—Sandy Alomar Jr., on Mark McGwire home run

NATIONAL LEAGUE LEADERS

Home Runs			Runs Batted In			Batting Average	
Dawson-Chi	49		Dawson-Chi	137		Gwynn-SD	.370
Murphy-Atl	44		Wallach-Mon	123		Guerrero-LA	.338
Strawberry-NY	39		Schmidt-Phi	113		Raines-Mon	.330
Davis-Cin	37		Clark-StL	106		Kruk-SD	.313
Johnson-NY	36					James-Atl	.312

On Base Percentage			Slugging Average			Stolen Bases	
Clark-StL	.461		Clark-StL	.597		Coleman-StL	109
Gwynn-SD	.450		Davis-Cin	.593		Gwynn-SD	56
Raines-Mon	.431		Strawberry-NY	.583		Hatcher-Hou	53
Guerrero-LA	.421		Clark-SF	.580		Raines-Mon	50
Murphy-Atl	.420		Murphy-Atl	.580		Davis-Cin	50

Wins			Innings Pitched			Saves	
Sutcliffe-Chi	18		Hershiser-LA	264.2		Bedrosian-Phi	40
Rawley-Phi	17		Welch-LA	251.2		Smith-Chi	36
Scott-Hou	16		Valenzuela-LA	251.0		Worrell-StL	33
Hershiser-LA	16		Scott-Hou	247.2		Franco-Cin	32
			Z.Smith-Atl	242.0		McDowell-NY	25

Strikeouts			Earned Run Average			Complete Games	
Ryan-Hou	270		Ryan-Hou	2.76		Reuschel-Pit-SF	12
Scott-Hou	233		Dunne-Pit	3.03		Valenzuela-LA	12
Welch-LA	196		Hershiser-LA	3.06		Hershiser-LA	10
Valenzuela-LA	190		Reuschel-Pit-SF	3.09		Z.Smith-Atl	9
Hershiser-LA	190		Gooden-NY	3.21		Scott-Hou	8

AMERICAN LEAGUE LEADERS

Home Runs			Runs Batted In			Batting Average	
McGwire-Oak	49		Bell-Tor	134		Boggs-Bos	.363
Bell-Tor	47		Evans-Bos	123		Molitor-Mil	.353
			McGwire-Oak	118		Trammell-Det	.343
			Joyner-Cal	117		Puckett-Min	.332
			Mattingly-NY	115		Mattingly-NY	.327

On Base Percentage			Slugging Average			Stolen Bases	
Boggs-Bos	.467		McGwire-Oak	.618		Reynolds-Sea	60
Molitor-Mil	.438		Bell-Tor	.605		Wilson-KC	59
Evans-Bos	.422		Boggs-Bos	.588		Redus-Chi	52
Randolph-NY	.415		Evans-Bos	.569		Molitor-Mil	45
Trammell-Det	.406		Molitor-Mil	.566		Henderson-NY	41

Wins			Innings Pitched			Saves	
Stewart-Oak	20		Hough-Tex	285.1		Henke-Tor	34
Clemens-Bos	20		Clemens-Bos	281.2		Righetti-NY	31
Langston-Sea	19		Langston-Sea	272.0		Reardon-Min	31
			Blyleven-Min	267.0		Plesac-Mil	23
			Morris-Det	266.0		Buice-Cal	17

Strikeouts			Earned Run Average			Complete Games	
Langston-Sea	262		Key-Tor	2.76		Clemens-Bos	18
Clemens-Bos	256		Viola-Min	2.90		Saberhagen-KC	15
Higuera-Mil	240		Clemens-Bos	2.97		Hurst-Bos	15
Hough-Tex	223		Saberhagen-KC	3.36		Langston-Sea	14
Morris-Det	208		Morris-Det	3.38		Higuera-Mil	14

THE YEAR IN BASEBALL

April 8: The Dodgers fire vice president Al Campanis for racially insensitive comments he made on ABC TV.

June 22: Tom Seaver abandons a comeback attempt with the Mets and retires with a career record of 311-205.

July 14: The rookie of the year award is renamed in honor of Jackie Robinson.

July 18: Don Mattingly hits a home run in his eighth consecutive game to tie the major league record set by Dale Long in 1956.

August 10: Phillies pitcher Kevin Gross joins Joe Niekro as the second player suspended for 10 games in 1987 for scuffing the baseball.

August 26: Paul Molitor goes 0-for-4 to end a 39-game hitting streak, the longest in the AL since Joe DiMaggio's 56-game streak in 1941.

September 14: The Blue Jays hit a major league record 10 home runs in an 18-3 rout of the Orioles.

September 21: Darryl Strawberry joins Howard Johnson as the only teammates to achieve 30 home runs and 30 stolen bases in the same season.

September 29: Don Mattingly breaks a major league record with his sixth grand slam of the season.

October 17: A World Series game is played indoors for the first time (at the Metrodome in Minneapolis).

November 18: Cubs outfielder Andre Dawson becomes the first player from a last-place club since Ernie Banks to win an MVP award.

1988

Night ball for Wrigley, Canseco has 40-40 year; Gibson is homer hero

If 1987 had accented individual player streaks, 1988 highlighted team skeins. Atlanta started the season by losing its first 10 games, but Baltimore more than doubled that with a record 21 defeats from the starting gate. When Joe Morgan took over the Red Sox in midseason, they won their first 12 games, feeding into a run of 24 straight victories at Fenway Park. Wrigley Field's 74-year streak of day baseball only also ended when lights were installed for an August 8 game against the Phillies (rain forced the first Cubs home night game to be played the next day against the Mets).

In the AL East, the switch to Morgan from John McNamara helped propel Boston through a tight division race. The victory was keyed by Wade Boggs' batting title (.366), 100-RBI seasons from Dwight Evans and Mike Greenwell, and 18 wins from Bruce Hurst and Roger Clemens. Oakland had a much easier time of it in the West, largely thanks to Jose Canseco's 40-40 year, Dave Stewart's 21 wins and Dennis Eckersley's 45 saves. Aside from his 40 steals, Canseco's 42 homers and 124 RBIs led the AL. The pitching honors went to Minnesota, to Frank Viola's 24 wins and Alan Anderson's 2.45 ERA.

In the NL East, the Mets got off to a fast start, then coasted the rest of the way on their pitching. David Cone emerged as the rotation strong man with a 20-3 mark, Dwight Gooden and Ron Darling contributed another 35 wins, and Randy Myers and Roger McDowell saved 42. Darryl Strawberry posed the biggest offensive threat with his 39 homers (NL-best) and 101 RBIs. Driven by free-agent acquisition Kirk Gibson and right-hander Orel Hershiser, the Dodgers took the West. Hershiser, whose 23 wins tied Cincinnati's Danny Jackson for the most, threw a record 59 straight scoreless innings over the final four weeks of the season. Other NL leaders were San Francisco's Will Clark (109 RBIs), San Diego's Tony Gwynn (.313) and St. Louis' Joe Magrane

Kirk Gibson
Hobbled by injury, Gibson came off the bench to hit a bottom-of-the-ninth home run for L.A. that ranks among the most dramatic homers in World Series history.

(2.18). The year's rowdiest scene took place at Riverfront Stadium when a protracted argument between Pete Rose and umpire Dave Pallone provoked a near-riot, prompting a one-month suspension of the manager and the censuring of Cincinnati broadcasters Joe Nuxhall and Marty Brennaman for ridiculing the arbiter as "incompetent" and a "scab."

The NLCS was heavy on late-game comebacks, with New York winning the first and third games with rallies on their final turn at-bat and Los Angeles returning the favor in Game 4 with a two-out, game-tying homer by Mike Scioscia in the ninth and a winning cir-

cuit by Gibson in the 12th. Hershiser pitched a seventh-game shutout for the Los Angeles pennant. There was little suspense in the ALCS, where Oakland parlayed three Canseco homers and four Eckersley saves into a sweep of Boston.

The most dramatic moment of the World Series came in the bottom of the ninth inning of Game 1, when a hobbled Gibson came off the bench to pinch-hit a homer off Eckersley for a Dodger victory. From that point on, it was mainly Hershiser, with two complete-game victories, and the veteran Mickey Hatcher, with two homers and five key RBIs.

1988 SEASON HIGHLIGHTS

NATIONAL LEAGUE

	W	L	Pct.	GB
East				
New York	100	60	.625	—
Pittsburgh	85	75	.531	15
Montreal	81	81	.500	20
Chicago	77	85	.475	24
St. Louis	76	86	.469	25
Philadelphia	65	96	.404	35.5
West				
Los Angeles	94	67	.584	—
Cincinnati	87	74	.540	7
San Diego	83	78	.516	11
San Francisco	83	79	.512	11.5
Houston	82	80	.506	12.5
Atlanta	54	106	.338	39.5

AMERICAN LEAGUE

	W	L	Pct.	GB
East				
Boston	89	73	.549	—
Detroit	88	74	.543	1
Toronto	87	75	.537	2
Milwaukee	87	75	.537	2
New York	85	76	.528	3.5
Cleveland	78	84	.481	11
Baltimore	54	107	.335	34.5
West				
Oakland	104	58	.642	—
Minnesota	91	71	.562	13
Kansas City	84	77	.522	19.5
California	75	87	.463	29
Chicago	71	90	.441	32.5
Texas	70	91	.435	33.5
Seattle	68	93	.422	35.5

AWARDS

NL MVP: Kirk Gibson, LA
AL MVP: Jose Canseco, OAK
NL Cy Young: Orel Hershiser, LA
AL Cy Young: Frank Viola, MIN
NL Rookie: Chris Sabo, CIN
AL Rookie: Walt Weiss, OAK
NL Relief Pitcher: John Franco, CIN
AL Relief Pitcher: Dennis Eckersley, OAK
NL Manager: Tom Lasorda, LA
AL Manager: Tony LaRussa, OAK
GOLD GLOVES
NL: Orel Hershiser, P; Benito Santiago, C; Keith Hernandez, 1B; Ryne Sandberg, 2B; Tim Wallach, 3B; Ozzie Smith, SS; Andre Dawson, Andy Van Slyke, Eric Davis, OF
AL: Mark Langston, P; Bob Boone, C; Don Mattingly, 1B; Harold Reynolds, 2B; Gary Gaetti, 3B; Tony Fernandez, SS; Kirby Puckett, Devon White, Gary Pettis, OF

ALL-STAR GAME
Riverfront Stadium, Cincinnati
July 12: AL 2, NL 1
MVP: Terry Steinbach, Oakland

POSTSEASON
WORLD SERIES
Los Angeles Dodgers 4, Oakland Athletics 1
Oct. 15: LOS ANGELES 5, Oakland 4
Oct. 16: LOS ANGELES 6, Oakland 0
Oct. 18: OAKLAND 2, Los Angeles 1
Oct. 19: Los Angeles 4, OAKLAND 3
Oct. 20: Los Angeles 5, OAKLAND 2
MVP: Orel Hershiser, Los Angeles

NATIONAL LEAGUE
NLCS
Los Angeles Dodgers 4, New York Mets 3
Oct. 4: New York 3, LOS ANGELES 2
Oct. 5: LOS ANGELES 6, New York 3
Oct. 8: NEW YORK 8, Los Angeles 4
Oct. 9: Los Angeles 5, NEW YORK 4
Oct. 10: Los Angeles 7, NEW YORK 4
Oct. 11: New York 5, LOS ANGELES 1
Oct. 12: LOS ANGELES 6, New York 0
MVP: Orel Hershiser, Los Angeles

Home team in CAPS

AMERICAN LEAGUE
ALCS
Oakland Athletics 4, Boston Red Sox 0
Oct. 5: Oakland 2, BOSTON 1
Oct. 6: Oakland 4, BOSTON 3
Oct. 8: OAKLAND 10, Boston 6
Oct. 9: OAKLAND 4, Boston 1
MVP: Dennis Eckersley, Oakland

NATIONAL LEAGUE LEADERS

Home Runs
Strawberry-NY	39
Davis-Hou	30
Galarraga-Mon	29
Clark-SF	29
McReynolds-NY	27

Runs Batted In
Clark-SF	109
Strawberry-NY	101
VanSlyke-Pit	100
Bonilla-Pit	100

Batting Average
Gwynn-SD	.313
Palmeiro-Chi	.307
Dawson-Chi	.303
Galarraga-Mon	.302
Perry-Atl	.300

On Base Percentage
Daniels-Cin	.400
Butler-SF	.395
Clark-SF	.392
Gibson-LA	.381
Gwynn-SD	.374

Slugging Average
Strawberry-NY	.545
Galarraga-Mon	.540
Clark-SF	.508
VanSlyke-Pit	.506
Dawson-Chi	.504

Stolen Bases
Coleman-StL	81
Young-Hou	65
Smith-StL	57
Sabo-Cin	46
Nixon-Mon	46

Wins
Jackson-Cin	23
Hershiser-LA	23
Cone-NY	20
Reuschel-SF	19

Innings Pitched
Hershiser-LA	267.0
Jackson-Cin	260.2
Browning-Cin	250.2
Mahler-Atl	249.0
Maddux-Chi	249.0

Saves
Franco-Cin	39
Gott-Pit	34
Worrell-StL	32
Davis-SD	28
Bedrosian-Phi	28

Strikeouts
Ryan-Hou	228
Cone-NY	213
DeLeon-StL	208
Scott-Hou	190
Fernandez-NY	189

Earned Run Average
Magrane-StL	2.18
Cone-NY	2.22
Hershiser-LA	2.26
Tudor-StL-LA	2.32
Rijo-Cin	2.39

Complete Games
Jackson-Cin	15
Hershiser-LA	15
Show-SD	13
Sutcliffe-Chi	12
Gooden-NY	10

AMERICAN LEAGUE LEADERS

Home Runs
Canseco-Oak	42
McGriff-Tor	34
McGwire-Oak	32
Murray-Bal	28
Gaetti-Min	28

Runs Batted In
Canseco-Oak	124
Puckett-Min	121
Greenwell-Bos	119
Evans-Bos	111
Winfield-NY	107

Batting Average
Boggs-Bos	.366
Puckett-Min	.356
Greenwell-Bos	.325
Winfield-NY	.322
Molitor-Mil	.312

On Base Percentage
Boggs-Bos	.480
Greenwell-Bos	.420
Davis-Sea	.416
Winfield-NY	.398
Henderson-NY	.397

Slugging Average
Canseco-Oak	.569
McGriff-Tor	.552
Gaetti-Min	.551
Puckett-Min	.545
Greenwell-Bos	.531

Stolen Bases
Henderson-NY	93
Pettis-Det	44
Molitor-Mil	41
Canseco-Oak	40

Wins
Viola-Min	24
Stewart-Oak	21
Gubicza-KC	20

Innings Pitched
Stewart-Oak	275.2
Gubicza-KC	269.2
Clemens-Bos	264.0
Langston-Sea	261.1
Saberhagen-KC	260.2

Saves
Eckersley-Oak	45
Reardon-Min	42
Jones-Cle	37
Thigpen-Chi	34
Plesac-Mil	30

Strikeouts
Clemens-Bos	291
Langston-Sea	235
Viola-Min	193
Stewart-Oak	192
Higuera-Mil	192

Earned Run Average
Anderson-Min	2.45
Higuera-Mil	2.45
Viola-Min	2.64
Gubicza-KC	2.70
Clemens-Bos	2.93

Complete Games
Stewart-Oak	14
Clemens-Bos	14
Witt-Tex	13
Witt-Cal	12
Swindell-Cle	12

THE YEAR IN BASEBALL

February 23: The city of Chicago grants the Cubs permission to install lights and play up to 18 night games per year.

April 28: The Orioles set an AL record with their 21st straight loss.

May 14: Cardinals' infielder Jose Oquendo becomes the first non-pitcher in 20 years to get a major league decision, a loss, in a 16-inning game against the Braves.

June 25: Cal Ripken plays in his 1,000th consecutive game.

June 30: Alarmed by threats by the White Sox to move to Florida, Illinois lawmakers grant state subsidies for a new stadium to replace venerable Comiskey Park.

August 9: The Cubs and Mets play the first official night game at Wrigley Field

September 8: Bart Giamatti is unanimously elected as baseball's seventh commissioner to succeed Peter Ueberroth in 1989.

September 16: Tom Browning of the Reds becomes the 14th pitcher to throw a perfect game, defeating L.A. at Cincinnati, 1-0.

September 23: Jose Canseco steals two bases to become the first player to have 40 steals and 40 home runs in a season.

September 29: Orel Hershiser of the Dodgers throws 10 shutout innings against the Padres before departing the tie game, thus running his streak of scoreless frames to 59 and surpassing by one the record set in 1968 by Don Drysdale.

September 30: For the second consecutive time, Dave Stieb of Toronto is only one strike away from a no-hitter, then allows a dink hit and settles for a one-hitter.

October 15: in Game 1 of the World Series, pinch-hitter Kirk Gibson hits a two-out homer in the bottom of the ninth to give the Dodgers a 5-4 win.

1989

After Rose gets life ban, bad heart kills Giamatti; earthquake rocks Series

A season of shocks began in the spring when new commissioner A. Bartlett Giamatti revealed he was looking into charges that Reds manager Pete Rose had been systematically violating the game's statutes against gambling. Over the next few months, the sides swapped charges (and court briefs) until, in August, Rose agreed to accept a lifetime suspension without explicit admission of baseball bets. When the chain-smoking Giamatti died a week later of a heart attack, his successor and keeper of the flame Fay Vincent did little to discourage insinuations the commissioner had been left exhausted by the Rose investigation.

The surprise team was the NL East Cubs, who filled the vacuum left by a Mets squad riven by age, injuries and clubhouse rifts centered around Darryl Strawberry and rookie Gregg Jefferies. The Chicago push was led by Greg Maddux (19 wins), Mitch Williams (36 saves) and Ryne Sandberg (30 homers). In the West, the Giants benefited from big offensive seasons from home run (47) and RBI (125) leader Kevin Mitchell and Will Clark (.333-23-111) to edge a Padres club driven by Tony Gwynn's fourth batting crown (.336) and Mark Davis' 44 saves. Scott Garrelts of the Giants registered the lowest ERA (2.28), Mike Scott of the Astros the most wins (20). The underside of the San Francisco victory was an excruciating scene on August 15, when left-hander Dave Dravecky, making a comeback from cancer, cracked his structurally weakened arm bone to resounding effect around Olympic Stadium while delivering a pitch. The arm was later amputated.

In the AL East, the Blue Jays celebrated the opening of SkyDome and a baseball season attendance record of 3,375,573 by overtaking the revived Orioles down the stretch. Toronto's big bats were home run leader Fred McGriff (36) and George Bell (104 RBIs); Dave Stieb's 17 wins included three one-hitters. In the West, Oakland stayed with the pack while Jose Canseco recovered from a broken wrist, then pulled away over the final weeks. Dave Stewart won 21, Dennis Eckersley saved 33, and Mark McGwire slugged 33 homers. Ruben Sierra of the Rangers had the most RBIs (119), Kirby Puckett of the Twins the highest average (.339) and Bret Saberhagen of the Royals the most wins (23) and best ERA (2.16).

The NCLS turned into a duel between first basemen, with Clark of the Giants going 13-for-20 with 8 RBIs and Mark Grace

Dennis Eckersley
Ranked among the top relief pitchers of all time, Eckersley saved 33 games for a powerful A's team that went on to sweep San Francisco in the World Series.

of the Cubs going 11-for-17 with 8 RBIs. Beyond Grace, though, Chicago proved punchless against the San Francisco bullpen, especially Steve Bedrosian (three saves), losing in five games. Oakland needed the same amount of time to defeat Toronto, with Stewart winning twice, Eckersley adding three saves, and Rickey Henderson doing just about everything (6-for-15 with seven walks, two homers, five RBIs, and eight steals).

The Athletics were even more dominant in their World Series sweep over the Giants, but few remembered it because of a devastating earthquake that struck the Bay Area prior to Game 3. Sixty-seven people were killed by the tremors, and the Series was allowed to continue ten days later only after San Francisco and Oakland residents made clear they would welcome the games. Stewart and Mike Moore split the four victories.

1989 SEASON HIGHLIGHTS

NATIONAL LEAGUE

East

	W	L	Pct.	GB
Chicago	93	69	.574	—
New York	87	75	.537	6
Houston	86	76	.531	7
Montreal	81	81	.500	12
Pittsburgh	74	88	.457	19
Philadelphia	67	95	.414	26

West

	W	L	Pct.	GB
San Francisco	92	70	.568	—
San Diego	89	73	.549	3
St. Louis	86	76	.531	6
Los Angeles	77	83	.481	14
Cincinnati	75	87	.463	17
Atlanta	63	97	.394	28

AMERICAN LEAGUE

East

	W	L	Pct.	GB
Toronto	89	73	.549	—
Baltimore	87	75	.537	2
Texas	83	79	.512	6
Milwaukee	81	81	.500	8
New York	74	87	.460	14.5
Cleveland	73	89	.451	16
Detroit	59	103	.364	30

West

	W	L	Pct.	GB
Oakland	99	63	.611	—
Kansas City	92	70	.568	7
California	91	71	.562	8
Boston	83	79	.512	16
Minnesota	80	82	.494	19
Seattle	73	89	.451	26
Chicago	69	92	.429	29.5

AWARDS

NL MVP: Kevin Mitchell, SF
AL MVP: Robin Yount, MIL
NL Cy Young: Mark Davis, SD
AL Cy Young: Bret Saberhagen, KC
NL Rookie: Jerome Walton, CHI
AL Rookie: Gregg Olson, BAL
NL Relief Pitcher: Mark Davis, SD
AL Relief Pitcher: Jeff Russell, TEX
NL Manager: Don Zimmer, CHI
AL Manager: Frank Robinson, BAL

GOLD GLOVES
NL: Ron Darling, P; Benito Santiago, C; Andres Galarraga, 1B; Ryne Sandberg, 2B; Terry Pendleton, 3B; Ozzie Smith, SS; Tony Gwynn, Andy Van Slyke, Eric Davis, OF
AL: Bret Saberhagen, P; Bob Boone, C; Don Mattingly, 1B; Harold Reynolds, 2B; Gary Gaetti, 3B; Tony Fernandez, SS; Kirby Puckett, Devon White, Gary Pettis, OF

ALL-STAR GAME
Anaheim Stadium, Anaheim
July 11: AL 5, NL 3
MVP: Bo Jackson, Kansas City

POSTSEASON
WORLD SERIES
Oakland Athletics 4, San Francisco Giants 0
Oct. 14: OAKLAND 5, San Francisco 0
Oct. 15: OAKLAND 5, San Francisco 1
Oct. 27: Oakland 13, SAN FRANCISCO 7
Oct. 28: Oakland 9, SAN FRANCISCO 6
MVP: Dave Stewart, Oakland

NLCS
San Francisco Giants 4, Chicago Cubs 1
Oct. 4: San Francisco 11, CHICAGO 3
Oct. 5: CHICAGO 9, San Francisco 5
Oct. 7: SAN FRANCISCO 5, Chicago 4
Oct. 8: SAN FRANCISCO 6, Chicago 4
Oct. 9: SAN FRANCISCO 3, Chicago 2
MVP: Will Clark, San Francisco

AMERICAN LEAGUE
ALCS
Oakland Athletics 4, Toronto Blue Jays 1
Oct. 3: OAKLAND 7, Toronto 3
Oct. 4: OAKLAND 6, Toronto 3
Oct. 6: TORONTO 7, Oakland 3
Oct. 7: Oakland 6, TORONTO 5
Oct. 8: Oakland 4, TORONTO 3
MVP: Rickey Henderson, Oakland

Home team in CAPS

NATIONAL LEAGUE LEADERS

Home Runs		Runs Batted In		Batting Average	
Mitchell-SF	47	Mitchell-SF	125	Gwynn-SD	.336
Johnson-NY	36	Guerrero-StL	117	Clark-SF	.333
Davis-Hou	34	Clark-SF	111	L.Smith-Atl	.315
Davis-Cin	34	Johnson-NY	101	Grace-Chi	.314
Sandberg-Chi	30	Davis-Cin	101	Guerrero-StL	.311

On Base Percentage		Slugging Average		Stolen Bases	
L.Smith-Atl	.420	Mitchell-SF	.635	Coleman-StL	65
J.Clark-SD	.413	Johnson-NY	.559	Samuel-Phi-NY	42
Clark-SF	.412	Clark-SF	.546	R.Alomar-SD	42
Grace-Chi	.407	Davis-Cin	.541	Raines-Mon	41
Guerrero-StL	.398	L.Smith-Atl	.533	Johnson-NY	41

Wins		Innings Pitched		Saves	
Scott-Hou	20	Hershiser-LA	256.2	Davis-SD	44
Maddux-Chi	19	Browning-Cin	249.2	Williams-Chi	36
Magrane-StL	18	Hurst-SD	244.2	Franco-Cin	32
Bielecki-Chi	18	DeLeon-StL	244.2	Howell-LA	28
Reuschel-SF	17	Drabek-Pit	244.1	Burke-Mon	28

Strikeouts		Earned Run Average		Complete Games	
DeLeon-StL	201	Garrelts-SF	2.28	Hurst-SD	10
Belcher-LA	200	Hershiser-LA	2.31	Belcher-LA	10
Fernandez-NY	198	Langston-Mon	2.39	Scott-Hou	9
Cone-NY	190	Whitson-SD	2.66	Magrane-StL	9
Hurst-SD	179	Hurst-SD	2.69	Browning-Cin	9

AMERICAN LEAGUE LEADERS

Home Runs		Runs Batted In		Batting Average	
McGriff-Tor	36	Sierra-Tex	119	Puckett-Min	.339
Carter-Cle	35	Mattingly-NY	113	Lansford-Oak	.336
McGwire-Oak	33	Esasky-Bos	108	Boggs-Bos	.330
Jackson-KC	32	Jackson-KC	105	Yount-Mil	.318
Esasky-Bos	30	Carter-Cle	105	Franco-Tex	.316

On Base Percentage		Slugging Average		Stolen Bases	
Boggs-Bos	.434	Sierra-Tex	.543	R.Henderson-NY-Oak	77
Davis-Sea	.428	McGriff-Tor	.525	Espy-Tex	45
R.Henderson-NY-Oak	.413	Yount-Mil	.511	White-Cal	44
McGriff-Tor	.402	Esasky-Bos	.500	Sax-NY	43
Evans-Bos	.402	Davis-Sea	.496	Pettis-Det	43

Wins		Innings Pitched		Saves	
Saberhagen-KC	23	Saberhagen-KC	262.1	Russell-Tex	38
Stewart-Oak	21	Stewart-Oak	257.2	Thigpen-Chi	34
Moore-Oak	19	Gubicza-KC	255.0	Schooler-Sea	33
Davis-Oak	19	Clemens-Bos	253.1	Plesac-Mil	33
Ballard-Bal	18	Milacki-Bal	243.0	Eckersley-Oak	33

Strikeouts		Earned Run Average		Complete Games	
Ryan-Tex	301	Saberhagen-KC	2.16	Saberhagen-KC	12
Clemens-Bos	230	Finley-Cal	2.57	Morris-Det	10
Saberhagen-KC	193	Moore-Oak	2.61	Finley-Cal	9
Gubicza-KC	173	Blyleven-Cal	2.73		
Bosio-Mil	173	McCaskill-Cal	2.93		

THE YEAR IN BASEBALL

January 9: Johnny Bench and Carl Yastrzemski are elected to Hall of Fame.

February 2: Bill White, six-time All-Star and longtime Yankee broadcaster, is elected National League President.

April 3: The major league debut of Seattle's Ken Griffey, Jr. gives baseball its first father-son duo active simultaneously.

April 19: 329-game winner Steve Carlton announces his retirement.

May 29: Philadelphia's Mike Schmidt retires from baseball with 548 career home runs.

June 4: The Dodgers-Astros 22-inning, 7 hour and 14 minute marathon is the longest night game in major league history. Astros won 5-4.

July 28: St. Louis outfielder Vince Coleman's major league record of 50 straight stolen bases is ended by Montreal catcher Nelson Santovenia.

August 22: The Rangers' Nolan Ryan fans Rickey Henderson for his 5,000th career strikeout.

September 1: Commissioner Bart Giamatti dies of a heart attack while vacationing on Martha's Vineyard, Massachusetts. Francis T. "Fay" Vincent succeeds him 12 days later.

September 25: With a 4-for-5 day, Boston's Wade Boggs becomes the only player ever to record four consecutive 200-hit, 100-walk seasons. He also extends his modern major league record with his seventh straight 200-hit season.

October 9: With a game winning two-run single in the bottom of the 8th, Will Clark propels the Giants to their first NL pennant since 1962. Clark, the LCS Most Valuable Player, sets a record by hitting .650 (13-20).

October 17: At 5:04 PM Pacific time, just prior to the start of World Series Game 3 between the Athletics and the Giants, a deadly earthquake measuring 7.1 on the Richter scale strikes the Bay Area. The Series does not resume until October 27th. Oakland sweeps.

December 25: Billy Martin dies in an accident in Johnson City, N.Y.

1990

Jail sentence for Rose, exile for Steinbrenner as players face lockout

Pete Rose was hustled into jail for tax evasion, George Steinbrenner went into exile for paying a gambler to find grounds for getting him out of his contract with outfielder Dave Winfield and owners resorted to a spring-training lockout to force their terms on a new agreement with the Players Association. Rose was out after five months, Steinbrenner back after less than three years, and the players on the field again on their own terms in 32 days. No-no was also the main theme between the lines, with seven no-hitters (including Nolan Ryan's sixth) recorded in both leagues.

In the NL West, Cincinnati almost managed the impossible feat of leading the division for all but one day and not getting to the playoffs. But though they cringed before a late September rush by the Dodgers, the Reds held on thanks to their Nasty Boys bullpen of Randy Myers (31 saves), Rob Dibble (8 wins and 11 saves) and Norm Charlton (12 wins). In the East, Pittsburgh's Killer Bees dumped the favored Mets, mainly because of Barry Bonds (.301-33-114, plus 52 steals), Bobby Bonilla (32-120) and Doug Drabek (an NL-tops 22 wins). Other category leaders were Chicago's Ryne Sandberg (40 homers), San Francisco's Matt Williams (122 RBIs) and Houston's Danny Darwin (2.21). Willie McGee won the batting title (.335) despite being traded from the Cardinals to the Athletics in late August.

As in 1987, the Blue Jays gave away a title in the last week of the season, this time to Boston. The Red Sox had themselves blown a 6-1/2-game lead in early September, but clambered back to the top rung when Toronto lost six of its last eight. Roger Clemens won 21 and topped the AL with his 1.93 ERA for an otherwise unspectacular Boston club. In the West, Oakland produced a glut of superstar numbers: Jose Canseco and Mark McGwire combining for 76 homers and 209 RBIs; Rickey Henderson batting .325 and stealing 65 bases; Bob Welch winning a league-best 27; Dave Stewart winning 20 for the fourth straight year; and Dennis Eckersley saving 48. Chicago had kept relatively close much of the year thanks to Bobby Thigpen's record 57 saves. Detroit's Cecil Fielder had the most homers (51) and RBIs (132), Kansas City's George Brett the best average (.329).

With Myers saving three and the Nasty Boys prominent in every game, the Reds took the NLCS from the Pirates in six. The turning point was a Game 3 victory powered by home runs from Billy Hatcher and Mariano Duncan. In the ALCS, the Athletics embarrassed the Red Sox in four straight, holding them to one run in each game and so frustrating Clemens he was thrown out of the finale in the second inning after baiting the home-plate umpire. Stewart won twice and Eckersley saved two.

Ken Griffey, Jr.
Ken Griffey, Jr. made headlines when he teamed with his father, Ken Griffey, Sr., to become the first father-son combination to play together in the majors.

To the amazement of oddsmakers, however, it was Oakland that was swept in the World Series. The batting stars were Hatcher, who went 9-for-12 with six runs scored, and Chris Sabo, who went 9-for-16 with a couple of homers. Jose Rijo won twice. But it wasn't total joy for Cincinnati: In Game 4, star outfielder Eric Davis, already nursing shoulder and knee injuries, lacerated his kidney diving for a double and had to be taken to an Oakland hospital. It emerged later that Reds owner Marge Schott refused to fly him back to Ohio because he had missed the team flight.

1990 SEASON HIGHLIGHTS

NATIONAL LEAGUE

East	W	L	Pct.	GB
Pittsburgh	95	67	.586	—
New York	91	71	.562	4
San Francisco	85	77	.525	10
Philadelphia	77	85	.475	18
Chicago	77	85	.475	18
St. Louis	70	92	.432	25
West				
Cincinnati	91	71	.562	—
Los Angeles	86	76	.531	5
Montreal	85	77	.525	6
San Diego	75	87	.463	16
Houston	75	87	.463	16
Atlanta	65	97	.401	26

AMERICAN LEAGUE

East	W	L	Pct.	GB
Boston	88	74	.543	—
Toronto	86	76	.531	2
Detroit	79	83	.488	9
Seattle	77	85	.475	11
Baltimore	76	85	.472	11.5
Minnesota	74	88	.457	14
New York	67	95	.414	21
West				
Oakland	103	59	.636	—
Chicago	94	68	.580	9
Texas	83	79	.512	20
California	80	82	.494	23
Cleveland	77	85	.475	26
Kansas City	75	86	.466	27.5
Milwaukee	74	88	.457	29

AWARDS

NL MVP: Barry Bonds, PIT
AL MVP: Rickey Henderson, OAK
NL Cy Young: Doug Drabek, PIT
AL Cy Young: Bob Welch, OAK
NL Rookie: David Justice, ATL
AL Rookie: Sandy Alomar Jr., CLE
NL Relief Pitcher: John Franco, NY
AL Relief Pitcher: Bobby Thigpen, CHI
NL Manager: Jim Leyland, PIT
AL Manager: Jeff Torborg, CHI
GOLD GLOVES
NL: Greg Maddux, P; Benito Santiago, C; Andres Galarraga, 1B; Ryne Sandberg, 2B; Tim Wallach, 3B; Ozzie Smith, SS; Tony Gwynn, Andy Van Slyke, Barry Bonds, OF
AL: Mike Boddicker, P; Sandy Alomar Jr, C; Mark McGwire, 1B; Harold Reynolds, 2B; Kelly Gruber, 3B; Ozzie Guillen, SS; Ellis Burks, Ken Griffey Jr, Gary Pettis, OF

ALL-STAR GAME
Wrigley Field, Chicago
July 10: AL 2, NL 0
MVP: Julio Franco, Texas

POSTSEASON
WORLD SERIES
Cincinnati Reds 4, Oakland Athletics 0
Oct. 16: CINCINNATI 7, Oakland 0
Oct. 17: CINCINNATI 5, Oakland 4
Oct. 19: Cincinnati 5, OAKLAND 3
Oct. 20: Cincinnati 2, OAKLAND 1
MVP: Jose Rijo, Cincinnati

NATIONAL LEAGUE
NLCS
Cincinnati Reds 4, Pittsburgh Pirates 2
Oct. 4: Pittsburgh 4, CINCINNATI 3
Oct. 5: CINCINNATI 2, Pittsburgh 1
Oct. 8: Cincinnati 6, PITTSBURGH 3
Oct. 9: Cincinnati 5, PITTSBURGH 3
Oct. 10: PITTSBURGH 3, Cincinnati 2
Oct. 12: CINCINNATI 2, Pittsburgh 1
MVP: Rob Dibble and Randy Myers, Cincinnati

AMERICAN LEAGUE
ALCS
Oakland Athletics 4, Boston Red Sox 0
Oct. 6: Oakland 9, BOSTON 1
Oct. 7: Oakland 4, BOSTON 1
Oct. 9: OAKLAND 4, Boston 1
Oct. 10: OAKLAND 3, Boston 1
MVP: Dave Stewart, Oakland

Home team in CAPS

NATIONAL LEAGUE LEADERS

Home Runs
Sandberg-Chi	40
Strawberry-NY	37
Mitchell-SF	35
Williams-SF	33
Bonds-Pit	33

Runs Batted In
Williams-SF	122
Bonilla-Pit	120
Carter-SD	115
Bonds-Pit	114
Strawberry-NY	108

Batting Average
McGee-StL	.335
Murray-LA	.330
Magadan-NY	.328
Dykstra-Phi	.325
Dawson-Chi	.310

On Base Percentage
Magadan-NY	.425
Dykstra-Phi	.420
Murray-LA	.417
Bonds-Pit	.410
Butler-SF	.401

Slugging Average
Bonds-Pit	.565
Sandberg-Chi	.559
Mitchell-SF	.544
Gant-Atl	.539
Justice-Atl	.535

Stolen Bases
Coleman-StL	77
Yelding-Hou	64
Bonds-Pit	52
Butler-SF	51
Nixon-Mon	50

Wins
Drabek-Pit	22
Viola-NY	20
Martinez-LA	20
Gooden-NY	19

Innings Pitched
Viola-NY	249.2
Maddux-Chi	237.0
Martinez-LA	234.1
Gooden-NY	232.2

Saves
Franco-NY	33
Myers-Cin	31
L.Smith-StL	27
Smith-Hou	23
Lefferts-SD	23

Strikeouts
Cone-NY	233
Martinez-LA	223
Gooden-NY	223
Viola-NY	182
Fernandez-NY	181

Earned Run Average
Darwin-Hou	2.21
Smith-Mon-Pit	2.55
Whitson-SD	2.60
Viola-NY	2.67
Rijo-Cin	2.70

Complete Games
Martinez-LA	12
Hurst-SD	9
Drabek-Pit	9
Maddux-Chi	8

AMERICAN LEAGUE LEADERS

Home Runs
Fielder-Det	51
McGwire-Oak	39
J.Canseco-Oak	37
McGriff-Tor	35
Gruber-Tor	31

Runs Batted In
Fielder-Det	132
Gruber-Tor	118
McGwire-Oak	108
J.Canseco-Oak	101
Sierra-Tex	96

Batting Average
Brett-KC	.329
R.Henderson-Oak	.325
Palmeiro-Tex	.319
Trammell-Det	.304
Boggs-Bos	.302

On Base Percentage
R.Henderson-Oak	.441
McGriff-Tor	.403
E.Martinez-Sea	.399
Davis-Sea	.393
Brett-KC	.392

Slugging Average
Fielder-Det	.592
R.Henderson-Oak	.577
J.Canseco-Oak	.543
McGriff-Tor	.530
Brett-KC	.515

Stolen Bases
R.Henderson-Oak	65
Sax-NY	43
Kelly-NY	42
Cole-Cle	40
Pettis-Tex	38

Wins
Welch-Oak	27
Stewart-Oak	22
Clemens-Bos	21

Innings Pitched
Stewart-Oak	267.0
Morris-Det	249.2
Welch-Oak	238.0
Hanson-Sea	236.0
Finley-Cal	236.0

Saves
Thigpen-Chi	57
Eckersley-Oak	48
Jones-Cle	43
Olson-Bal	37
Righetti-NY	36

Strikeouts
Ryan-Tex	232
Witt-Tex	221
Hanson-Sea	211
Clemens-Bos	209
Langston-Cal	195

Earned Run Average
Clemens-Bos	1.93
Finley-Cal	2.40
Stewart-Oak	2.56
Appier-KC	2.76
Stieb-Tor	2.93

Complete Games
Stewart-Oak	11
Morris-Det	11

THE YEAR IN BASEBALL

January 9: Joe Morgan and Jim Palmer are elected to Hall of Fame.

February 15: Spring training camps fail to open due to the lack of a Basic Agreement between the owners and the Players Association. The opening of the season is delayed one week by the 32-day lockout.

February 24: Former Boston outfielder Tony Conigliaro, the youngest player to reach career 100 home runs and who was tragically beaned in 1967, dies of pneumonia and kidney failure at the age of 45.

April 9: Delino Deshields of Montreal with four hits ties the National League record for most hits in a major league debut.

May 18: In a 7-0 loss to the Astros, Chicago's Ryne Sandberg commits an error to end his major league record streak of errorless games at 123 and chances at 584.

May 29: In a 2-1 loss to Toronto, Oakland's Rickey Henderson passes Ty Cobb to becomes the AL's all-time stolen base leader with 893.

June 11: Texas' Nolan Ryan throws his sixth career no-hitter in a 5-0 victory over Oakland. He would win his 300th game on July 31.

June 12: Baltimore's Cal Ripken, Jr. plays in his 1,308th consecutive game to move past Everett Scott into second place on the all-time list.

July 1: Yankee Andy Hawkins becomes only the second pitcher to lose a complete game in which he allowed no hits (4-0 vs. the White Sox).

July 17: Minnesota accomplishes a major league first as they pull off two 5-4-3 triple plays in a 1-0 loss to Boston.

July 28: Cal Ripken's fifth-inning error in the first game of a doubleheader ends his record 95 straight errorless games.

August 17: Chicago White Sox's Carlton Fisk belts his 328th home run to surpass Johnny Bench's record for home runs by a catcher.

August 31: Seattle's Ken Griffey, Jr. and his father become the first father-son combo to play as teammates in a 5-2 victory over Kansas City.

September 3: In preserving a 4-2 win over Kansas City, White Sox reliever Bobby Thigpen breaks Dave Righetti's record with his 47th save.

1991

Rickey passes Brock, Braves lay foundation as Puckett leads Twins

The most successful management tandem for any team sport in the country came together when Bobby Cox dropped his second job as Atlanta general manager to concentrate on the dugout and was replaced in the front office by John Schuerholz. The pair proceeded to guide the Braves to a division title every completed season through 2003. In the AL, the Twins matched the Braves by going from last to first, but went them one better by adding a world championship to their comeback.

Atlanta's season-long duel with Los Angeles turned on which team had the fewer injuries, and the Braves, despite also losing leadoff man Otis Nixon to a failed drug test, prevailed. The key man on the field was third baseman Terry Pendleton, whose batting title (.319) was just one of the leadership elements that earned him an MVP trophy. Tom Glavine won a league-best 20, Steve Avery 18, and John Smoltz went 11-2 over the second half of the year. In the East, Pittsburgh's lethal combination of Barry Bonds and Bobby Bonilla combined for 216 RBIs and John Smiley equaled Glavine with 20 victories for an easy distancing of second-place St. Louis. Howard Johnson of the Mets led in both homers (38) and RBIs (117), with Montreal's Dennis Martinez yielding only 2.39 runs per nine innings.

Minnesota's climb back to the top in the AL West came in a division in which every team played at least .500. It was due to a league-high .280 batting average and significant mound work from Scott Erickson (20 wins), free agent pickup Jack Morris (18), and reliever Rick Aguilera (42 saves). In the East, the Blue Jays solved years of clubhouse troubles with a series of good-riddance trades that simultaneously brought in Roberto Alomar (.295 with 53 steals), Joe Carter (33-108), and Devon White (40 doubles, 10 triples) for a title. Detroit's Cecil Fielder and Oakland's Jose Canseco tied at 44 homers, Fielder had the most RBIs (133) and Julio Franco of the Rangers the highest average (.341). Detroit's Bill Gullickson matched Erickson's 20 wins, while Boston's Roger Clemens posted the lowest ERA (2.62). Oakland's Rickey Henderson stole his 939th base to break Lou Brock's career mark and Nolan Ryan of Texas hurled his seventh no-hitter.

The Braves victory in the seven-game NLCS featured four shutouts, including three 1-0 games. Avery teamed with closer Alejandro Pena in two of the blankings; Smoltz picked up the other two wins. Pittsburgh's Jay Bell collected 12 hits, but he also struck out 10 times and batted in only one run. In the ALCS, the Twins scraped through to two wins in the first three games, then battered Toronto pitching in the final two. Morris won twice, Aguilera

Nolan Ryan
Still going strong at age 44, the incomparable righthander had 203 strikeouts, passing 5,500 for his career, and pitched the seventh no-hitter of his career.

saved three, and Kirby Puckett drove in six.

The same trio figured prominently in a breathless seven-game World Series. But as in 1987, another conspicuous factor was the Metrodome, where incessantly shrieking fans punctuated with exclamation marks four Twins home victories. The finale, a scoreless matchup for nine innings between Morris and Smoltz, was one of the postseason's greatest games, ending on a 10th-inning single by pinch-hitter Gene Larkin off the Atlanta bullpen. Morris won twice, Aguilera had two saves and Puckett dominated the sixth game with a great catch and an 11th-inning homer.

1991 SEASON HIGHLIGHTS

NATIONAL LEAGUE

East	W	L	Pct.	GB
Pittsburgh	98	64	.605	—
St. Louis	84	78	.519	14
Philadelphia	78	84	.481	20
Chicago	77	83	.481	20
New York	77	84	.478	20.5
Montreal	71	90	.441	26.5

West	W	L	Pct.	GB
Atlanta	94	68	.580	—
Los Angeles	93	69	.574	1
San Diego	84	78	.519	10
San Francisco	75	87	.463	19
Cincinnati	74	88	.457	20
Houston	65	97	.401	29

AMERICAN LEAGUE

East	W	L	Pct.	GB
Toronto	91	71	.562	—
Boston	84	78	.519	7
Detroit	84	78	.519	7
Seattle	83	79	.512	8
New York	71	91	.438	20
Baltimore	67	95	.414	24
Cleveland	57	105	.352	34

West	W	L	Pct.	GB
Minnesota	95	67	.586	—
Chicago	87	75	.537	8
Texas	85	77	.525	10
Oakland	84	78	.519	11
Milwaukee	83	79	.512	12
Kansas City	82	80	.506	13
California	81	81	.500	14

AWARDS

NL MVP: Terry Pendleton, ATL
AL MVP: Cal Ripken Jr., BAL
NL Cy Young: Tom Glavine, ATL
AL Cy Young: Roger Clemens, BOS
NL Rookie: Jeff Bagwell, HOU
AL Rookie: Chuck Knoblauch, MIN
NL Relief Pitcher: Lee Smith, STL
AL Relief Pitcher: Bryan Harvey, CAL
NL Manager: Bobby Cox, ATL
AL Manager: Tom Kelly, MIN
GOLD GLOVES
NL: Greg Maddux, P; Tom Pagnozzi, C; Will Clark, 1B; Ryne Sandberg, 2B; Matt Williams, 3B; Ozzie Smith, SS; Tony Gwynn, Andy Van Slyke, Barry Bonds, OF
AL: Mark Langston, P; Tony Pena, C; Don Mattingly, 1B; Roberto Alomar, 2B; Robin Ventura, 3B; Cal Ripken Jr., SS; Kirby Puckett, Ken Griffey Jr., Devon White, OF

ALL-STAR GAME
SkyDome, Toronto
July 9: AL 4, NL 2
MVP: Cal Ripken Jr., Baltimore
POSTSEASON
WORLD SERIES
Minnesota Twins 4, Atlanta Braves 3
Oct. 19: MINNESOTA 5, Atlanta 2
Oct. 20: MINNESOTA 3, Atlanta 2
Oct. 22: ATLANTA 5, Minnesota 4
Oct. 23: ATLANTA 3, Minnesota 2
Oct. 24: ATLANTA 14, Minnesota 5
Oct. 26: MINNESOTA 4, Atlanta 3
Oct. 27: MINNESOTA 1, Atlanta 0
MVP: Jack Morris, Minnesota

NATIONAL LEAGUE
NLCS
Atlanta Braves 4, Pittsburgh Pirates 3
Oct. 9: PITTSBURGH 5, Atlanta 1
Oct. 10: Atlanta 1, PITTSBURGH 0
Oct. 12: ATLANTA 10, Pittsburgh 3
Oct. 13: Pittsburgh 3, ATLANTA 2
Oct. 14: Pittsburgh 1, ATLANTA 0
Oct. 16: Atlanta 1, PITTSBURGH 0
Oct. 17: Atlanta 4, PITTSBURGH 0
MVP: Steve Avery, Atlanta

AMERICAN LEAGUE
ALCS
Minnesota Twins 4, Toronto Blue Jays 1
Oct. 8: MINNESOTA 5, Toronto 4
Oct. 9: Toronto 5, MINNESOTA 2
Oct. 11: Minnesota 3, TORONTO 2
Oct. 12: Minnesota 9, TORONTO 3
Oct. 13: Minnesota 6, TORONTO 5
MVP: Kirby Puckett, Minnesota

Home team in CAPS

NATIONAL LEAGUE LEADERS

Home Runs			Runs Batted In			Batting Average	
Johnson-NY	38		Johnson-NY	117		Pendleton-Atl	.319
Williams-SF	34		Clark-SF	116		Morris-Cin	.318
Gant-Atl	32		Bonds-Pit	116		Gwynn-SD	.317
McGriff-SD	31		McGriff-SD	106		McGee-SF	.312
Dawson-Chi	31		Gant-Atl	105		Jose-StL	.305

On Base Percentage		Slugging Average			Stolen Bases	
Bonds-Pit	.419	Clark-SF	.536		Grissom-Mon	76
Butler-LA	.402	Johnson-NY	.535		Nixon-Atl	72
McGriff-SD	.400	Pendleton-Atl	.517		DeShields-Mon	56
Bonilla-Pit	.398	Bonds-Pit	.514		Lankford-StL	44
Bagwell-Hou	.391	Larkin-Cin	.506		Bonds-Pit	43

Wins		Innings Pitched			Saves	
Smiley-Pit	20	Maddux-Chi	263.0		L.Smith-StL	47
Glavine-Atl	20	Glavine-Atl	246.2		Dibble-Cin	31
Avery-Atl	18	Morgan-LA	236.1		Williams-Phi	30
Martinez-LA	17	Drabek-Pit	234.2		Franco-NY	30
		Cone-NY	232.2		Righetti-SF	24

Strikeouts		Earned Run Average			Complete Games	
Cone-NY	241	D.Martinez-Mon	2.39		D.Martinez-Mon	9
Maddux-Chi	198	Rijo-Cin	2.51		Glavine-Atl	9
Glavine-Atl	192	Glavine-Atl	2.55		Mulholland-Phi	8
Rijo-Cin	172	Belcher-LA	2.62		Maddux-Chi	7
Harnisch-Hou	172	Harnisch-Hou	2.70			

AMERICAN LEAGUE LEADERS

Home Runs			Runs Batted In			Batting Average	
Fielder-Det	44		Fielder-Det	133		Franco-Tex	.341
Canseco-Oak	44		Canseco-Oak	122		Boggs-Bos	.332
C.Ripken-Bal	34		Sierra-Tex	116		Randolph-Mil	.327
Carter-Tor	33		C.Ripken-Bal	114		K.Griffey-Sea	.327
Thomas-Chi	32		Thomas-Chi	109		Molitor-Mil	.325

On Base Percentage		Slugging Average			Stolen Bases	
Thomas-Chi	.454	Tartabull-KC	.593		R.Henderson-Oak	58
Randolph-Mil	.427	C.Ripken-Bal	.566		Alomar-Tor	53
Boggs-Bos	.425	Canseco-Oak	.556		Raines-Chi	51
Franco-Tex	.409	Thomas-Chi	.553		Polonia-Cal	48
E.Martinez-Sea	.407	Palmeiro-Tex	.532		Cuyler-Det	41

Wins		Innings Pitched			Saves	
Gullickson-Det	20	Clemens-Bos	271.1		Harvey-Cal	46
Erickson-Min	20	McDowell-Chi	253.2		Eckersley-Oak	43
Langston-Cal	19	Morris-Min	246.2		Aguilera-Min	42
		Langston-Cal	246.1		Reardon-Bos	40
		Tapani-Min	244.0		Montgomery-KC	33

Strikeouts		Earned Run Average			Complete Games	
Clemens-Bos	241	Clemens-Bos	2.62		McDowell-Chi	15
Johnson-Sea	228	Candiotti-Cle-Tor	2.65		Clemens-Bos	13
Ryan-Tex	203	Wegman-Mil	2.84		Navarro-Mil	10
McDowell-Chi	191	J.Abbott-Cal	2.89		Morris-Min	10
Langston-Cal	183	Ryan-Tex	2.91		Terrell-Det	8

THE YEAR IN BASEBALL

January 8: Ferguson Jenkins, Rod Carew, and Gaylord Perry are elected to the Hall of Fame.

April 18: On Opening Day at New Comiskey, a sell-out crowd of 42,191 watches the Tigers crush the White Sox 16-0.

May 1: Texas' Nolan Ryan pitches his seventh no-hitter in a 3-0 win over Toronto. Oakland's Rickey Henderson steals his 939th base to surpass Lou Brock as baseball's stolen-base king.

May 4: Cleveland's Chris James drives in 9 runs in 20-6 win over A's.

May 15: In the company of President Bush, Queen Elizabeth II attends her first major league baseball game, in Baltimore.

June 16: In a 7-6 loss to Expos, Atlanta's Otis Nixon steals six bases to tie the major league record.

July 9: In the American League's 4-2 victory, Tony LaRussa becomes the first manager to win three consecutive All-Star games. The A's Dennis Eckersley becomes first reliever to save three consecutive All-Star games.

July 28: Dennis Martinez of Montreal pitches the 13th perfect game in history in a 2-0 win over the Dodgers.

September 29: With a victory over the White Sox, Minnesota becomes the first AL team to go from last to first in one year.

October 6: New York Mets pitcher David Cone fans 19 Phillies to tie Steve Carlton's National League record for strikeouts in a game.

October 22: Gene Larkin's 10th-inning sacrifice fly gives Minnesota the World Championship, and ends the only scoreless extra-inning Game 7 in Series history. The Twins become the first team to go from last to World Champions in one year.

1992

In topsy-turvy season, World Series title goes to Canada's Jays

Several teams would have gladly eliminated 1992 from their histories. The Angels barely averted tragedy when a team bus plunged off a turnpike, injuring 11 and laying up manager Buck Rodgers for three months. The Mets attracted lurid spring training headlines that three players had raped a woman and that a fourth had exposed himself in public. The Yankees wrangled with Commissioner Fay Vincent over pitcher Steve Howe's relapse into drugs. Cincinnati manager Lou Piniella got into a videotaped punch-up with reliever Rob Dibble. The Astros had to stay on the road throughout August because the Astrodome had been rented out for the Republican convention. The Red Sox dropped to last place for the first time since 1932, the Dodgers for the first time since 1905.

The Braves and Pirates had little trouble repeating in the NL. Atlanta's effort was driven by Terry Pendleton's 105 RBIs, Tom Glavine's 20 wins, and John Smoltz's 15 victories and league-leading 215 strikeouts. In the East, Barry Bonds' .311-34-103 proved doubly valuable for Pittsburgh following the free-agent defection of Bobby Bonilla to the Mets. Knuckleballer Tim Wakefield rescued the pitching by going 8-1 after a late-season recall from the minors. Chicago's Greg Maddux equalled Glavine's NL-high 20 wins, while Billy Swift of the Giants had the lowest ERA (2.08). Fred McGriff of the Padres had the most homers (35), teammate Gary Sheffield the best average (.330) and Darren Daulton of the Phillies the most RBIs (109).

The Orioles had cause for celebration with the opening of Camden Yards, but they still finished well behind the Blue Jays. The big bat for Toronto was Joe Carter (34-119), the mound stopper Jack Morris, who tied Kevin Brown of the Rangers for an AL-best 21 wins. In the West, Oakland manager Tony La Russa's adroit use of an eight-man relief corps bridged the gap between a shaky rotation and a brilliant Dennis Eckersley (51 saves, 1.91) for an unexpected division win. Mark McGwire's 42 homers and 104 RBIs paced an offense shaken by an August swap of slugger Jose Canseco to Texas for Ruben Sierra. The league's biggest bats were Juan Gonzales of Texas (43 homers), Seattle's Edgar Martinez (.343), and Detroit's Cecil Fielder, who tied Babe Ruth's record for setting the pace in RBIs (124) three straight years. Boston's Roger Clemens led in ERA (2.41). Seattle's Bret Boone became the first third-generation major leaguer.

The Braves tantalized the Pirates down to the final out of the seventh game of the NLCS, then sent up pinch-hitter Francisco Cabrera to single in the tying and winning runs for a second-

Greg Maddux
In his final season in Chicago, Maddux tied future Atlanta teammate Tom Glavine with 20 wins to earn the first of four consecutive Cy Young Awards.

straight pennant. The blow off Stan Belinda came after Pittsburgh had apparently come back from a 3-games-to-2 deficit to take the flag. Led by Roberto Alomar's 11 hits, Juan Guzman's two wins and Tom Henke's three saves, Toronto disposed of Oakland in six games in the ALCS.

Catcher Pat Borders grabbed the limelight with nine hits, but Dave Winfield put the finishing touches on a six-game Blue Jays World Series triumph when he doubled in two runs in the 11th inning of the finale. Jimmy Key and setup man Duane Ward split the four wins over the Braves.

1992 SEASON HIGHLIGHTS

NATIONAL LEAGUE

East	W	L	Pct.	GB
Pittsburgh	96	66	.593	—
Montreal	87	75	.537	9
St. Louis	83	79	.512	13
Chicago	78	84	.481	18
New York	72	90	.444	24
Philadelphia	70	92	.432	26
West				
Atlanta	98	64	.605	—
Cincinnati	90	72	.556	8
San Diego	82	80	.506	16
Houston	81	81	.500	17
San Francisco	72	90	.444	26
Los Angeles	63	99	.389	35

AMERICAN LEAGUE

East	W	L	Pct.	GB
Toronto	96	66	.593	—
Milwaukee	92	70	.568	4
Baltimore	89	73	.549	7
New York	76	86	.469	20
Cleveland	76	86	.469	20
Detroit	75	87	.463	21
Boston	73	89	.451	23
West				
Oakland	96	66	.593	—
Minnesota	90	72	.556	6
Chicago	86	76	.531	10
Texas	77	85	.475	19
California	72	90	.444	24
Kansas City	72	90	.444	24
Seattle	64	98	.395	32

AWARDS

NL MVP: Barry Bonds, PIT
AL MVP: Dennis Eckersley, OAK
NL Cy Young: Greg Maddux, CHI
AL Cy Young: Dennis Eckersley, OAK
NL Rookie: Eric Karros, LA
AL Rookie: Pat Listach, MIL
NL Relief Pitcher: Lee Smith, STL
AL Relief Pitcher: Dennis Eckersley, OAK
NL Manager: Jim Leyland, PIT
AL Manager: Tony LaRussa, OAK
GOLD GLOVES
NL: Greg Maddux, P; Tom Pagnozzi, C; Mark Grace, 1B; Jose Lind, 2B; Terry Pendleton, 3B; Ozzie Smith, SS; Larry Walker, Andy Van Slyke, Barry Bonds, OF
AL: Mark Langston, P; Ivan Rodriguez, C; Don Mattingly, 1B; Roberto Alomar, 2B; Robin Ventura, 3B; Cal Ripken Jr., SS; Kirby Puckett, Ken Griffey Jr., Devon White, OF

ALL-STAR GAME

Jack Murphy Stadium, San Diego
July 14: AL 13, NL 6
MVP: Ken Griffey Jr., Seattle

POSTSEASON
WORLD SERIES
Toronto Blue Jays 4, Atlanta Braves 2
Oct. 17: ATLANTA 3, Toronto 1
Oct. 18: Toronto 5, ATLANTA 4
Oct. 20: TORONTO 3, Atlanta 2
Oct. 21: TORONTO 2, Atlanta 1
Oct. 22: Atlanta 7, TORONTO 2
Oct. 24: ATLANTA 4, Atlanta 3
MVP: Pat Borders, Toronto

NATIONAL LEAGUE
NLCS
Atlanta Braves 4, Pittsburgh Pirates 3
Oct. 6: ATLANTA 5, Pittsburgh 1
Oct. 7: ATLANTA 13, Pittsburgh 5
Oct. 9: PITTSBURGH 3, Atlanta 2
Oct. 10: Atlanta 6, PITTSBURGH 4
Oct. 11: PITTSBURGH 7, Atlanta 1
Oct. 13: Pittsburgh 13, ATLANTA 4
Oct. 14: ATLANTA 3, Pittsburgh 2
MVP: John Smoltz, Atlanta

AMERICAN LEAGUE
ALCS
Toronto Blue Jays 4, Oakland Athletics 2
Oct. 7: Oakland 4, TORONTO 3
Oct. 8: TORONTO 3, Oakland 1
Oct. 10: Toronto 7, OAKLAND 5
Oct. 11: Toronto 7, OAKLAND 6
Oct. 12: OAKLAND 6, Toronto 2
Oct. 14: TORONTO 9, Oakland 2
MVP: Roberto Alomar, Toronto

Home team in CAPS

NATIONAL LEAGUE LEADERS

Home Runs
McGriff-SD	35
Bonds-Pit	34
Sheffield-SD	33
Hollins-Phi	27
Daulton-Phi	27

Runs Batted In
Daulton-Phi	109
Pendleton-Atl	105
McGriff-SD	104
Bonds-Pit	103
Sheffield-SD	100

Batting Average
Sheffield-SD	.330
VanSlyke-Pit	.324
Kruk-Phi	.323
Roberts-Cin	.323
Gwynn-SD	.317

On Base Percentage
Bonds-Pit	.461
Kruk-Phi	.428
Butler-LA	.413
McGriff-SD	.396
Roberts-Cin	.396

Slugging Average
Bonds-Pit	.624
Sheffield-SD	.580
McGriff-SD	.556
Daulton-Phi	.524
Sandberg-Chi	.510

Stolen Bases
Grissom-Mon	78
DeShields-Mon	46
Roberts-Cin	44
Finley-Hou	44
O.Smith-StL	43

Wins
Maddux-Chi	20
Glavine-Atl	20

Innings Pitched
Maddux-Chi	268.0
Drabek-Pit	256.2
Smoltz-Atl	246.2
Morgan-Chi	240.0
Avery-Atl	233.2

Saves
L.Smith-StL	43
Myers-SD	38
Wetteland-Mon	37
D.Jones-Hou	36
M.Williams-Phi	29

Strikeouts
Smoltz-Atl	215
Cone-NY	214
Maddux-Chi	199
Fernandez-NY	193
Drabek-Pit	177

Earned Run Average
Swift-SF	2.08
Tewksbury-StL	2.16
Maddux-Chi	2.18
Schilling-Phi	2.35
Martinez-Mon	2.47

Complete Games
Mulholland-Phi	12
Schilling-Phi	10
Drabek-Pit	10
Smoltz-Atl	9
Maddux-Chi	9

AMERICAN LEAGUE LEADERS

Home Runs
Gonzalez-Tex	43
McGwire-Oak	42
Fielder-Det	35
Carter-Tor	34
Belle-Cle	34

Runs Batted In
Fielder-Det	124
Carter-Tor	119
Thomas-Chi	115
Belle-Cle	112
Bell-Chi	112

Batting Average
E.Martinez-Sea	.343
Puckett-Min	.329
Thomas-Chi	.323
Molitor-Mil	.320
Mack-Min	.315

On Base Percentage
Thomas-Chi	.446
Tartabull-NY	.410
E.Martinez-Sea	.408
Alomar-Tor	.406
Molitor-Mil	.396

Slugging Average
McGwire-Oak	.585
E.Martinez-Sea	.544
Thomas-Chi	.536
Griffey-Sea	.535
Gonzalez-Tex	.529

Stolen Bases
Lofton-Cle	66
Listach-Mil	54
Anderson-Bal	53
Polonia-Cal	51
Alomar-Tor	49

Wins
Morris-Tor	21
Brown-Tex	21
McDowell-Chi	20
Mussina-Bal	18
Clemens-Bos	18

Innings Pitched
Brown-Tex	265.2
Wegman-Mil	261.2
McDowell-Chi	260.2
Nagy-Cle	252.0
Perez-NY	247.2

Saves
Eckersley-Oak	51
Aguilera-Min	41
Montgomery-KC	39
Olson-Bal	36
Henke-Tor	34

Strikeouts
Johnson-Sea	241
Perez-NY	218
Clemens-Bos	208
Guzman-Tex	179
McDowell-Chi	178

Earned Run Average
Clemens-Bos	2.41
Appier-KC	2.46
Mussina-Bal	2.54
Guzman-Tor	2.64
Abbott-Cal	2.77

Complete Games
McDowell-Chi	13
Clemens-Bos	11
Brown-Tex	11
Perez-NY	10
Nagy-Cle	10

THE YEAR IN BASEBALL

January 7: Tom Seaver and Rollie Fingers are elected to the Hall of Fame. Seaver, named on 98.8% of ballots, breaks Ty Cobb's record of 98.2%.

April 6: Baltimore Orioles win the opening game at their new Camden Yards ballpark, 2-0 over the Indians.

August 18: Bret Boone's major league debut with the Mariners gives baseball its first three generational family of major leaguers.

August 23: With a 3-1 win over the Phillies, the Astros conclude a 28-day, 26-game road trip, caused by the Republican National Convention at the Astrodome. The trip, which spanned 9,186 miles and eight cities, saw Houston finish with a respectable 12-14 record.

August 28: Milwaukee collects an American League record 31 hits in a 22-2 rout of the Blue Jays.

September 3: Major League owners announce their request for Commissioner Fay Vincent's immediate resignation. He resigns on September 7, and Bud Selig, owner of the Brewers, is appointed Chairman of Major League Baseball's Executive Committee.

September 9: In a 5-4 loss to the Indians, Milwaukee's Robin Yount becomes the 17th player to attain 3,000 hits.

September 23: Against the Pirates, Phillies second baseman Mickey Morandini turns only the ninth unassisted triple play, and the first in the National League since May 30, 1927.

September 30: George Brett of the Royals becomes the 18th player to get 3,000 hits. After receiving congratulations, Brett is picked off first base.

October 22: Longtime Brooklyn Dodger and New York Yankee announcer Red Barber dies at the age of 84.

December 8: San Francisco signs free agent Barry Bonds.

1993

Carter dings Wild Thing with walk-off homer as Jays repeat in Series

The NL sought to create more fans with the expansion additions of Colorado and Florida, but otherwise did its best to alienate them. Reds owner Marge Schott's ongoing racial slurs and discriminatory hiring practices brought only a slap-on-the-wrist fine and suspension. The Padres landed in court when two fans accused the franchise of deceptive advertising in luring season ticket-holders with star players already slated to be traded away. The Mets had to release Vince Coleman after the outfielder threw a firecracker that injured a two-year-old girl. In the AL, a tragic spring training boating accident killed Cleveland pitchers Steve Olin and Tim Crews and seriously injured southpaw Bobby Ojeda.

The addition of Cy Young Award winner Greg Maddux and (in midseason) slugger Fred McGriff was supposed to have assured the Braves of a third straight NL West title, but the Giants kept them struggling to the final day, thanks mainly to free-agent acquisition Barry Bonds' NL-leading 46 homers and 123 RBIs. The difference turned out to be Giants rookie Salomon Torres, who lost the only four games dropped by his club over the last 18. Atlanta's big stick was David Justice, with 40 homers and 120 RBIs. Maddux not only won 20, but topped the league with his 2.36 ERA; the victories left him two behind Tom Glavine and San Francisco's John Burkett. In the East, the Phillies won 28 of their first 40 and were never seriously challenged. Their offensive spark was leadoff man Len Dykstra, whose 143 runs were the most scored in the league in 60 years. The erratic Wild Thing, Mitch Williams, saved 43. Another closer, Chicago's Randy Myers, saved 53, associating him with 65 percent of his club's wins. Colorado's Andres Galarraga captured the batting title (.370).

In the AL West, the Athletics were the first team to tumble from first to sole possession of the basement since their 1915 Philadelphia forbears, helping to clear the path for the White Sox. Chicago's win was largely the work of Frank Thomas (.317-41-128) and pitchers Jack McDowell (a league-high 22 wins) and Alex Fernandez (18). The hitting-happy Blue Jays made it three in a row in the East, with John Olerud (.363), Paul Molitor (.332) and Roberto Alomar (.326) finishing one-two-three in the batting race. Pat Hentgen won 19 and Duane Ward saved 45 for Toronto. Other league leaders were Juan Gonzalez of the Rangers (46 homers), Albert Belle of the Indians (129 RBIs) and Kevin Appier of the Royals (2.56 ERA).

The Phillies stunned the Braves in the NLCS by winning three in a row after losing two of the first three. The Wild Thing cemented his reputation nationally with hairbreadth escapes that still added up to two wins and two saves for a mere 51/3 innings of

Joe Carter
By hitting a walk-off, three-run homer in the bottom of the ninth inning to end the season, Carter secured a place in World Series lore.

pitching. Toronto stayed true to form by hitting .302 in its six-game ALCS triumph over Chicago. Juan Guzman and Dave Stewart each won twice, with Ward collecting two saves.

A slugfest of a six-game World Series featured 24 hits between Molitor and Yount, 4 homers and 8 RBIs by slap-hitter Dykstra, and an improbable Game 4 of 29 runs and 32 hits. Most of all, it featured Joe Carter's come-from-behind three-run homer in the bottom of the ninth of the finale off Williams for a Toronto championship. Ward was one of the few relatively unscathed pitchers, winning one and saving two.

1993 SEASON HIGHLIGHTS

NATIONAL LEAGUE

East	W	L	Pct.	GB
Philadelphia	97	65	.599	—
Montreal	94	68	.580	3
St. Louis	87	75	.537	10
Chicago	84	78	.519	13
Pittsburgh	75	87	.463	22
Florida	64	98	.395	33
New York	59	103	.364	38

West	W	L	Pct.	GB
Atlanta	104	58	.642	—
San Francisco	103	59	.636	1
Houston	85	77	.525	19
Los Angeles	81	81	.500	23
Cincinnati	73	89	.451	31
Colorado	67	95	.414	37
San Diego	61	101	.377	43

AMERICAN LEAGUE

East	W	L	Pct.	GB
Toronto	95	67	.586	—
New York	88	74	.543	7
Baltimore	85	77	.525	10
Detroit	85	77	.525	10
Boston	80	82	.494	15
Cleveland	76	86	.469	19
Milwaukee	69	93	.426	26

West	W	L	Pct.	GB
Chicago	94	68	.580	—
Texas	86	76	.531	8
Kansas City	84	78	.519	10
Seattle	82	80	.506	12
Minnesota	71	91	.438	23
California	71	91	.438	23
Oakland	68	94	.420	26

AWARDS

NL MVP: Barry Bonds, SF
AL MVP: Frank Thomas, CHI
NL Cy Young: Greg Maddux, ATL
AL Cy Young: Jack McDowell, CHI
NL Rookie: Mike Piazza, LA
AL Rookie: Tim Salmon, CAL
NL Relief Pitcher: Randy Myers, CHI
AL Relief Pitcher: Jeff Montgomery, KC
NL Manager: Dusty Baker, SF
AL Manager: Gene Lamont, CHI

GOLD GLOVES

NL: Greg Maddux, P; Kirt Manwaring, C; Mark Grace, 1B; Robby Thompson, 2B; Matt Williams, 3B; Jay Bell, SS; Larry Walker, Marquis Grissom, Barry Bonds, OF
AL: Mark Langston, P; Ivan Rodriguez, C; Don Mattingly, 1B; Roberto Alomar, 2B; Robin Ventura, 3B; Omar Vizquel, SS; Kenny Lofton, Ken Griffey Jr., Devon White, OF

ALL-STAR GAME

Oriole Park at Camden Yards, Baltimore
July 13: AL 9, NL 3
MVP: Kirby Puckett, Minnesota

POSTSEASON

WORLD SERIES

Toronto Blue Jays 4, Philadelphia Phillies 2
Oct. 16: TORONTO 8, Philadelphia 5
Oct. 17: Philadelphia 6, TORONTO 4
Oct. 19: Toronto 10, PHILADELPHIA 3
Oct. 20: Toronto 15, PHILADELPHIA 14
Oct. 21: PHILADELPHIA 2, Toronto 0
Oct. 23: TORONTO 8, Philadelphia 6
MVP: Paul Molitor, Toronto

NATIONAL LEAGUE
NLCS

Philadelphia Phillies 4, Atlanta Braves 2
Oct. 6: PHILADELPHIA 4, Atlanta 3
Oct. 7: Atlanta 14, PHILADELPHIA 3
Oct. 9: ATLANTA 9, Philadelphia 4
Oct. 10: Philadelphia 2, ATLANTA 1
Oct. 11: Philadelphia 4, ATLANTA 3
Oct. 13: PHILADELPHIA 6, Atlanta 3
MVP: Curt Schilling, Philadelphia

AMERICAN LEAGUE
ALCS

Toronto Blue Jays 4, Chicago White Sox 2
Oct. 5: Toronto 7, CHICAGO 3
Oct. 6: Toronto 3, CHICAGO 1
Oct. 8: Chicago 6, TORONTO 1
Oct. 9: Chicago 7, TORONTO 4
Oct. 10: TORONTO 5, Chicago 3
Oct. 12: Toronto 6, CHICAGO 3
MVP: Dave Stewart, Toronto

Home team in CAPS

NATIONAL LEAGUE LEADERS

Home Runs
Bonds-SF	46
Justice-Atl	40
Williams-SF	38
McGriff-SD-Atl	37
Gant-Atl	36

Runs Batted In
Bonds-SF	123
Justice-Atl	120
Gant-Atl	117
Piazza-LA	112
Williams-SF	110

Batting Average
Galarraga-Col	.370
Gwynn-SD	.358
Jefferies-StL	.342
Bonds-SF	.336
Grace-Chi	.325

On Base Percentage
Bonds-SF	.463
Kruk-Phi	.433
Dykstra-Phi	.423
Merced-Pit	.415
Jefferies-StL	.411

Slugging Average
Bonds-SF	.677
Galarraga-Col	.602
Williams-SF	.561
Piazza-LA	.561
McGriff-SD-Atl	.549

Stolen Bases
Carr-Fla	58
Grissom-Mon	53
Nixon-Atl	47
Lewis-SF	46
Jefferies-StL	46

Wins
Glavine-Atl	22
Burkett-SF	22
Swift-SF	21
Maddux-Atl	20

Innings Pitched
Maddux-Atl	267.0
Rijo-Cin	257.1
Smoltz-Atl	243.2
Glavine-Atl	239.1
Drabek-Hou	237.2

Saves
Myers-Chi	53
Beck-SF	48
Harvey-Fla	45

Strikeouts
Rijo-Cin	227
Smoltz-Atl	208
Maddux-Atl	197
Schilling-Phi	186
Harnisch-Hou	185

Earned Run Average
Maddux-Atl	2.36
Rijo-Cin	2.48
Portugal-Hou	2.77
Swift-SF	2.82
Avery-Atl	2.94

Complete Games
Maddux-Atl	8
Five tied	7

AMERICAN LEAGUE LEADERS

Home Runs
Gonzalez-Tex	46
Griffey-Sea	45
Thomas-Chi	41
Belle-Cle	38
Palmeiro-Tex	37

Runs Batted In
Belle-Cle	129
Thomas-Chi	128
Carter-Tor	121
Gonzalez-Tex	118
Fielder-Det	117

Batting Average
Olerud-Tor	.363
Molitor-Tor	.332
Alomar-Tor	.326
Lofton-Cle	.325
Baerga-Cle	.321

On Base Percentage
Olerud-Tor	.478
Phillips-Det	.446
Henderson-Oak-Tor	.435
Thomas-Chi	.434
Hoiles-Bal	.419

Slugging Average
Gonzalez-Tex	.632
Griffey-Sea	.617
Thomas-Chi	.607
Olerud-Tor	.599
Hoiles-Bal	.585

Stolen Bases
Lofton-Cle	70
Polonia-Cal	55
Alomar-Tor	55
Henderson-Oak-Tor	53
Curtis-Cal	48

Wins
McDowell-Chi	22
Johnson-Sea	19
Hentgen-Tor	19

Innings Pitched
Eldred-Mil	258.0
McDowell-Chi	256.2
Langston-Cal	256.1
Johnson-Sea	255.1
Cone-KC	254.0

Saves
D.Ward-Tor	45
Montgomery-KC	45
Henke-Tex	40
Hernandez-Chi	38
Eckersley-Oak	36

Strikeouts
Johnson-Sea	308
Langston-Cal	196
Guzman-Tor	194
Cone-KC	191
Finley-Cal	187

Earned Run Average
Appier-KC	2.56
Alvarez-Chi	2.95
Key-NY	3.00
Fernandez-Chi	3.13
Viola-Bos	3.14

Complete Games
Finley-Cal	13
Brown-Tex	12
McDowell-Chi	10
Johnson-Sea	10
Eldred-Mil	8

THE YEAR IN BASEBALL

January 5: Reggie Jackson is elected to the Hall of Fame.

March 22: Cleveland pitchers Steve Olin and Tim Crews are killed in a boating accident in Florida. Pitcher Bob Ojeda is injured but survived.

April 4: Pitcher Graeme Lloyd and Dave Nilsson of the Brewers become the first all-Australian battery in major league history.

April 5: In their first game, the Florida Marlins defeat the Dodgers 6-3.

April 9: After two road losses, the expansion Colorado Rockies, before a major league Opening Day and NL regular-season record crowd of 80,227, defeat the Expos for their first win.

April 13: The Cardinals' Lee Smith passes Jeff Reardon to become baseball's all-time save leader with 358.

June 22: White Sox catcher Carlton Fisk catches his 2,226th game to eclipse Bob Boone's major league record for games caught.

June 26: Hall of Fame catcher and three-time NL MVP Roy Campanella of the Dodgers dies of a heart attack at age 71.

July 2: Hall of Fame pitcher and 1962 Cy Young Award winner Don Drysdale dies of a heart attack at age 56.

July 28: The Mets' Anthony Young beats the Marlins 5-4 to end his record 27-game losing streak. His last win was on April 19, 1992.

September 4: The Yankees' Jim Abbott, born without a right hand, pitches a no-hitter in a 4-0 victory over Cleveland.

September 9: By a margin of 27-1, major league owners vote to realign each league into a three-division format and add a third round of playoffs beginning in 1994.

September 16: Minnesota's Dave Winfield becomes the 19th player to attain 3,000 career hits.

September 22: Texas' Nolan Ryan makes his 773rd and final career start, but fails to retire a batter. He walks four and allows two hits.

1994

Baseball's darkest hour: World Series cancelled due to players' strike

An August 12 players strike eclipsed the commotion around the creation of central divisions in both leagues for justifying an extra layer of (televised) postseason playoffs. The walkout was an inevitable response to ownership intentions of holding out for a salary cap and the rescinding of arbitration rights in a new Basic Agreement. When the impasse continued into September, postseason play was called off altogether for the first time since John McGraw had refused to play Boston in a 1904 World Series.

In the NL East, the curtailed season thwarted a drive by the Expos to end Atlanta's dominance. Under manager Felipe Alou, Montreal had compiled the best record in either league (.649) behind the hitting of his son Moises (.339) and Larry Walker (.322) and the pitching of Ken Hill (an NL-high 16 wins) and John Wetteland (25 saves). In the NL Central, Hal Morris' .335 and Kevin Mitchell's 30 homers had kept the Reds a whisper above the Astros, powered by RBI leader Jeff Bagwell (116). Mike Piazza (.319-24-92) had the big bat in the Dodgers' lead over the Giants in the West. Tony Gwynn's .394 for San Diego represented the highest average since Ted Williams had topped .400 in 1941, while Matt Williams clocked a league-leading 43 homers for the Giants. Atlanta's Greg Maddux not only matched Hill's 16 wins, but his 1.56 ERA was an unprecedented two-and-a-half runs less than the league as a whole.

If the abbreviated season prompted what-ifs where Gwynn's chances of hitting .400 were concerned, others thought it went on too long. Dwight Gooden's failure of a drug test ended his once-brilliant career with the Mets. Cubs outfielder Tuffy Rhodes tagged Gooden for three home runs on Opening Day, but Chicago lost that game and its next 11 at Wrigley Field, contributing to a decision by all-star second baseman Ryne Sandberg to retire in June. San Francisco center fielder Darren Lewis made the first error of his career after an astonishing 392 games.

The AL equivalent of Montreal was New York, which had a 6 1/2-game over Baltimore when play was stopped. The most productive Yankees were batting champion Paul O'Neill (.359), Wade Boggs (.342) and wins leader Jimmy Key (17). In the Central, Cleveland served notice it was finally awakening from a 50-year sleep in conjunction with its move into Jacobs Field. Although the team finished a game behind the White Sox, few would have bet on those final standings in a full season. Despite being suspended a week for using a corked bat, Indians slugger

Ozzie Smith
The Cardinals balletic shortstop, who holds the NL record with 13 gold gloves in a sparkling 19-year career, led the NL in fielding average for the eighth time.

Albert Belle still had 36 homers and 101 RBIs. Only three years after all its teams had played at least .500, the AL West couldn't come up with a club any better than 10 games below the break-even point. The best of the bad was Texas, with Jose Canseco clouting 31 homers and Kenny Rogers becoming the first AL southpaw to pitch a perfect game (against the Angels). Other league leaders were Ken Griffey of Seattle (40 homers), Kirby Puckett of Minnesota (112 RBIs), and Steve Ontiveros of Oakland (2.65 ERA). The league's biggest hullabaloo centered around Chicago's signing of basketball wizard Michael Jordan to play in its minor-league system. He quit the following year after the promotion had exhausted its usefulness.

1994 SEASON HIGHLIGHTS

NATIONAL LEAGUE

East	W	L	Pct.	GB
Montreal	74	40	.649	—
Atlanta	68	46	.596	6
San Francisco	55	60	.478	19.5
Philadelphia	54	61	.470	20.5
Florida	51	64	.443	23.5
Central				
Houston	66	49	.574	—
Cincinnati	66	48	.579	-0.5
Pittsburgh	53	61	.465	12.5
St. Louis	53	61	.465	12.5
Chicago	49	64	.434	16
West				
Los Angeles	58	56	.509	—
New York	55	58	.487	2.5
Colorado	53	64	.453	6.5
San Diego	47	70	.402	12.5

AMERICAN LEAGUE

East	W	L	Pct.	GB
New York	70	43	.619	—
Baltimore	63	49	.563	6.5
Toronto	55	60	.478	16
Boston	54	61	.470	17
Minnesota	53	60	.469	17
Central				
Chicago	67	46	.593	—
Cleveland	66	47	.584	1
Kansas City	64	51	.557	4
Milwaukee	53	62	.461	15
Detroit	53	62	.461	15
West				
Texas	52	62	.456	—
Oakland	51	63	.447	1
Seattle	49	63	.438	2
California	47	68	.409	5.5

AWARDS

NL MVP: Jeff Bagwell, HOU
AL MVP: Frank Thomas, CHI
NL Cy Young: Greg Maddux, ATL
AL Cy Young: David Cone, KC
NL Rookie: Raul Mondesi, LA
AL Rookie: Bob Hamelin, KC
NL Relief Pitcher: Rod Beck, SF
AL Relief Pitcher: Lee Smith, BAL
NL Manager: Felipe Alou, MON
AL Manager: Buck Showalter, NY

GOLD GLOVES
NL: Greg Maddux, P; Tom Pagnozzi, C; Jeff Bagwell, 1B; Craig Biggio, 2B; Matt Williams, 3B; Barry Larkin, SS; Darren Lewis, Marquis Grissom, Barry Bonds, OF
AL: Mark Langston, P; Ivan Rodriguez, C; Don Mattingly, 1B; Roberto Alomar, 2B; Wade Boggs, 3B; Omar Vizquel, SS; Kenny Lofton, Ken Griffey Jr., Devon White, OF

ALL-STAR GAME
Three Rivers Stadium, Pittsburgh
July 12: NL 8, AL 7
MVP: Fred McGriff, Atlanta

POSTSEASON
Cancelled by strike

"The way baseball players think about it is guys before us have sacrificed things to enable us to have a healthy game. We're a strong union because we're all on the same page. We need to keep it that way."

— Matt Williams

"I don't know if we gained very much. I don't know if the owners gained very much. I think that should be an example. I don't think a strike fixed anything."

— Tony Gwynn

NATIONAL LEAGUE LEADERS

Home Runs
Williams-SF	43
Bagwell-Hou	39
Bonds-SF	37
McGriff-Atl	34
Galarraga-Col	31

Runs Batted In
Bagwell-Hou	116
Williams-SF	96
Bichette-Col	95
McGriff-Atl	94
Piazza-LA	92

Batting Average
Gwynn-SD	.394
Bagwell-Hou	.367
Kingery-Col	.349
Alou-Mon	.339
Morris-Cin	.335

On Base Percentage
Gwynn-SD	.454
Bagwell-Hou	.451
Mitchell-Cin	.429
Justice-Atl	.427
Bonds-SF	.426

Slugging Average
Thomas-Chi	.729
Belle-Cle	.714
Griffey-Sea	.674
O'Neill-NY	.603
Hamelin-KC	.599

Stolen Bases
Biggio-Hou	39
Sanders-Atl-Cin	38
Grissom-Mon	36
Carr-Fla	32
Lewis-SF	30

Wins
Hill-Mon	16
Maddux-Atl	16
Jackson-Phi	14
Saberhagen-NY	14
Glavine-Atl	13

Innings Pitched
Maddux-Atl	202.0
Jackson-Phi	179.1
Saberhagen-NY	177.1
Benes-SD	172.1
Rijo-Cin	172.1

Saves
Franco-NY	30
Beck-SF	28
Jones-Phi	27
Wetteland-Mon	25

Strikeouts
Benes-SD	189
Rijo-Cin	171
Maddux-Atl	156
Saberhagen-NY	143
Martinez-Mon	142

Earned Run Average
Maddux-Atl	1.56
Saberhagen-NY	2.74
Drabek-Hou	2.84
Fassero-Mon	2.99
Reynolds-Hou	3.05

Complete Games
Maddux-Atl	10
Drabek-Hou	6
Candiotti-LA	5

AMERICAN LEAGUE LEADERS

Home Runs
Griffey Jr.-Sea	40
Thomas-Chi	38
Belle-Cle	36
Canseco-Tex	31
Fielder-Det	28

Runs Batted In
Puckett-Min	112
Carter-Tor	103
Belle-Cle	101
Thomas-Chi	101
Franco-Chi	98

Batting Average
O'Neill-NY	.359
Belle-Cle	.357
Thomas-Chi	.353
Lofton-Cle	.349
Boggs-NY	.342

On Base Percentage
Thomas-Chi	.487
O'Neill-NY	.461
Belle-Cle	.438
Boggs-NY	.433
Clark-Tex	.431

Slugging Average
Thomas-Chi	.729
Belle-Cle	.714
Griffey Jr.-Sea	.674
O'Neill-NY	.603
Hamelin-KC	.599

Stolen Bases
Lofton-Cle	60
Coleman-KC	50
Nixon-Bos	42
Knoblauch-Min	35
Anderson-Bal	31

Wins
Key-NY	17
Cone-KC	16
Mussina-Bal	16
McDonald-Bal	14

Innings Pitched
Finley-Cal	183.1
McDowell-Chi	181.0
Eldred-Mil	179.0
Martinez-Cle	176.2
Mussina-Bal	176.1

Saves
Smith-Bal	33
Montgomery-KC	27
Aguilera-Min	23
Eckersley-Oak	19
Ayala-Sea	18

Strikeouts
Johnson-Sea	204
Clemens-Bos	168
Finley-Cal	148
Hentgen-Tor	147
Appier-KC	145

Earned Run Average
Ontiveros-Oak	2.65
Clemens-Bos	2.85
Cone-KC	2.94
Mussina-Bal	3.06
Johnson-Sea	3.19

Complete Games
Johnson-Sea	9
Finley-Cal	7
Martinez-Cle	7

THE YEAR IN BASEBALL

April 8: Braves left-hander Kent Mercker no-hits the Dodgers, 6-0, in his first career complete game.

April 8: Chan Ho Park of the Dodgers becomes the first Korean-born player to appear in a major league game.

April 9: Basketball legend Michael Jordan makes his professional baseball debut with an 0-for-3 day for Birmingham.

April 21: Indians first baseman Eddie Murray hits home runs from both sides of the plate in a game for the 11th time in his career to break Mickey Mantle's record.

April 30: Blue Jays outfielder Joe Carter finishes April with 31 RBIs to set a record for the month, while Colorado's Andres Galarraga sets the NL mark with 30.

June 13: Ryne Sandberg of the Cubs, considered by many as one of the best second baseman in NL history, abruptly announces his retirement.

June 22: Mets reliever John Franco earns his 253rd career save to break Dave Righetti's record for most saves by a left-hander.

June 22: Seattle's Ken Griffey, Jr. breaks Babe Ruth's record for most home runs hit by the end of June when he connects for his 31st in a 12-3 win over the Angels.

July 9: Red Sox shortstop John Valentin records an unassisted triple play.

July 14: Cardinals shortstop Ozzie Smith breaks Luis Aparicio's record for assists by a shortstop with his 8,017th in an 8-1 loss to Colorado.

July 28: Kenny Rogers of the Rangers throws the 14th perfect game in major league history—and the first by a left-hander in AL history.

August 1: Orioles shortshop Cal Ripken, Jr. plays in his 2,000th consecutive game.

August 5: Fred McGriff becomes the seventh player to hit 30 or more home runs for seven consecutive seasons.

August 12: Major league players go on strike, the eighth work stoppage since 1972.

September 14: Major League Baseball cancels the World Series. It makes the first season without a World Series in 90 years.

1995

Ripken passes Gehrig, Nomo a hit in L.A. as Braves finally win

The 234-day players strike was settled in April with the owners getting nothing but court rulings that they had illegally sought to eliminate free agency and salary arbitration. Spring-training plans to field scab clubs came up against existing Ontario laws preventing Toronto from going along and quickly passed legislation in Maryland enforcing Baltimore's opposition to the tactic. The so-called "replacement players" nevertheless persisted as a problem in clubhouses for union members and in the media where they were usually presented as "little guys" trying to make a living. The little guys on the field were the wild-card clubs added to the three division winners to make for a three-tiered postseason.

Atlanta had little trouble qualifying from the NL East, with Greg Maddux again pacing the league in both wins (19) and ERA (1.63). The big story in the Central Division was MVP Barry Larkin, whose .319 and 51 stolen bases ignited Cincinnati's win. The West went to the Dodgers, where Mike Piazza and Eric Karros combined for 58 homers and Japan's Hideo Nomo became as much of a cultural sensation as Fernando Valenzuela in 1981. The Dodgers squeaked in ahead of the Rockies, who themselves had to win the last day of the season to avoid a playoff against Houston for the wild-card slot. The Colorado attack wasn't subtle: four players (Dante Bichette, Larry Walker, Andres Galarraga, Vinny Castilla) who topped 30 homers. Bichette, who also batted .340, led the NL in both homers (40) and RBIs (128). San Diego's Tony Gwynn took his sixth Silver Bat (.368).

Cal Ripken, Jr.
The Orioles shortstop was honored with a 22-minute ovation in Baltimore when he broke Lou Gehrig's record by appearing in his 2,131st consecutive game.

In the AL Central, Cleveland charred records by clinching on its 123rd game and finishing 30 ahead of Kansas City. Albert Belle topped the league with his 50 homers and 126 RBIs. In the East, Boston nosed out the Yankees while fitting uniforms for 50 different players during the year. Mo Vaughn put up MVP numbers with his .300, 39 homers and (tying Belle) 126 RBIs. In the West, the Angels staged one of the great collapses, squandering a 13-game August lead over the Mariners, finally losing to Seattle's Randy Johnson in a special showdown playoff game. Johnson had the AL's lowest ERA (2.48), teammate Edgar Martinez its highest batting mark (.356) and Baltimore's Mike Mussina the most wins (19). On September 6, Baltimore's Cal Ripken, Jr. broke Lou Gehrig's record of playing in 2,130 consecutive games.

Colorado's distinction as the expansion club to reach the postseason the quickest lasted four games. In the best-of-five Division Series, the Braves slammed Rockies pitching at a .331 clip, including 11 hits from Marquis Grissom. The Reds made even shorter work of the Dodgers, outscoring them 22-7 in a sweep. The Indians were equally brisk with Boston in one AL division set, leaving the Yankees and Mariners to provide most of the thrills in the new playoff tier. After losing the first two in New York, Seattle returned home to run the table, with Edgar Martinez's two-out, two-run double in the ninth inning of the finale deciding matters.

The NLCS was all Atlanta, with Cincinnati and its .209 average going down four straight. Orel Hershiser starred for Cleveland in the ALCS, winning twice and striking out 15 in 14 innings. Kenny Lofton had eleven hits and five steals for the Indians victory in six over the Mariners.

The Braves were also up to the task in the World Series, with Tom Glavine's 1-0 win in Game 6 the ribbon on the box. The lefty won twice, while Grissom continued his big postseason with nine more hits.

1995 SEASON HIGHLIGHTS

NATIONAL LEAGUE

East	W	L	Pct.	GB
Atlanta	90	54	.625	—
New York	69	75	.479	21
Philadelphia	69	75	.479	21
Florida	67	76	.469	22.5
Montreal	66	78	.458	24
Central				
Cincinnati	85	59	.590	—
Houston	76	68	.528	9
Chicago	73	71	.507	12
St. Louis	62	81	.434	22.5
Pittsburgh	58	86	.403	27
West				
Los Angeles	78	66	.542	—
Colorado	77	67	.535	1
San Diego	70	74	.486	8
San Francisco	67	77	.465	11

AMERICAN LEAGUE

East	W	L	Pct.	GB
Boston	86	58	.597	—
Seattle	79	66	.545	7.5
Baltimore	71	73	.493	15
Detroit	60	84	.417	26
Toronto	56	88	.389	30
Central				
Cleveland	100	44	.694	—
Kansas City	70	74	.486	30
Chicago	68	76	.472	32
Milwaukee	65	79	.451	35
Minnesota	56	88	.389	44
West				
New York	79	65	.549	—
California	78	67	.538	1.5
Texas	74	70	.514	5
Oakland	67	77	.465	12

AWARDS

NL MVP: Barry Larkin, CIN
AL MVP: Mo Vaughn, BOS
NL Cy Young: Greg Maddux, ATL
AL Cy Young: Randy Johnson, SEA
NL Rookie: Hideo Nomo, LA
AL Rookie: Marty Cordova, MIN
NL Relief Pitcher: Tom Henke, STL
AL Relief Pitcher: Jose Mesa, CLE
NL Manager: Don Baylor, COL
AL Manager: Lou Piniella, SEA
GOLD GLOVES
NL: Greg Maddux, P; Charles Johnson, C; Mark Grace, 1B; Craig Biggio, 2B; Ken Caminiti, 3B; Barry Larkin, SS; Raul Mondesi, Marquis Grissom, Steve Finley, OF
AL: Mark Langston, P; Ivan Rodriguez, C; J.T. Snow, 1B; Roberto Alomar, 2B; Wade Boggs, 3B; Omar Vizquel, SS; Kenny Lofton, Ken Griffey Jr., Devon White, OF

ALL-STAR GAME
The Ballpark at Arlington, Texas
July 11: NL 3, AL 2
MVP: Jeff Conine, Florida
POSTSEASON
WORLD SERIES
Atlanta Braves 4, Cleveland Indians 2
Oct. 21: Atlanta 3, Cleveland 2
Oct. 22: Atlanta 4, Cleveland 3
Oct. 24: CLEVELAND 7, Atlanta 6
Oct. 25: Atlanta 5, CLEVELAND 2
Oct. 26: CLEVELAND 5, Atlanta 4
Oct. 27: ATLANTA 1, Cleveland 0
MVP: Tom Glavine, Atlanta
NATIONAL LEAGUE
NLCS
Atlanta Braves 4, Cincinnati Reds 0
Oct. 10: Atlanta 2, CINCINNATI 1
Oct. 11: Atlanta 6, CINCINNATI 2

Oct. 13: ATLANTA 5, Cincinnati 2
Oct. 14: ATLANTA 6, Cincinnati 0
MVP: Mike Devereaux, Atlanta
NLDS
Cincinnati Reds 3, Los Angeles Dodgers 0
Oct. 3: Cincinnati 7, LOS ANGELES 2
Oct. 4: Cincinnati 5, LOS ANGELES 4
Oct. 6: CINCINNATI 10, Los Angeles 1
Atlanta Braves 3, Colorado Rockies 1
Oct. 3: Atlanta 5, COLORADO 4
Oct. 4: Atlanta 7, COLORADO 4
Oct. 6: Colorado 7, ATLANTA 5
Oct. 1: ATLANTA 10, Colorado 4
AMERICAN LEAGUE
ALCS
Cleveland Indians 4, Seattle Mariners 2
Oct. 10: SEATTLE 3, Cleveland 2
Oct. 11: Cleveland 5, SEATTLE 2
Oct. 13: Seattle 5, CLEVELAND 2

Oct. 14: CLEVELAND 7, Seattle 0
Oct. 15: CLEVELAND 3, Seattle 2
Oct. 17: Cleveland 4, SEATTLE 0
MVP: Orel Hershiser, Cleveland
ALDS
Seattle Mariners 3, New York Yankees 2
Oct. 3: NEW YORK 9, Seattle 6
Oct. 4: NEW YORK 7, Seattle 5
Oct. 6: SEATTLE 7, New York 4
Oct. 7: SEATTLE 11, New York 8
Oct. 8: SEATTLE 6, New York 5
Cleveland Indians 3, Boston Red Sox 0
Oct. 3: CLEVELAND 5, Boston 4
Oct. 4: CLEVELAND 4, Boston 0
Oct. 6: Cleveland 8, BOSTON 2

Home team in CAPS

NATIONAL LEAGUE LEADERS

Home Runs
Bichette-Col	40
Sosa-Chi	36
Walker-Col	36
Bonds-SF	33

Runs Batted In
Bichette-Col	128
Sosa-Chi	119
Galarraga-Col	106
Conine-Fla	105
Karros-LA	105

Batting Average
Gwynn-SD	.368
Piazza-LA	.346
Bichette-Col	.340
Bell-Hou	.334
Grace-Chi	.326

On Base Percentage
Bonds-SF	.431
Biggio-Hou	.406
Magadan-Hou	.428
Gwynn-SD	.404
Weiss-Col	.403

Slugging Average
Bichette-Col	.620
Walker-Col	.607
Piazza-LA	.606
R.Sanders-Cin	.579
Bonds-SF	.577

Stolen Bases
Veras-Fla	56
Larkin-Cin	51
DeShields-LA	39
Finley-SD	36
Sanders-Cin	36

Wins
Maddux-Atl	19
Schourek-Cin	18
Martinez-LA	17
Glavine-Atl	16

Innings Pitched
Maddux-Atl	209.2
Neagle-Pit	209.2
Martinez-LA	206.1
Hamilton-SD	204.1
Navarro-Chi	200.1

Saves
Myers-Chi	38
Henke-StL	36
Beck-SF	33
Slocumb-Phi	32
Worrell-LA	32

Strikeouts
Galarraga-Col	146
Sosa-Chi	134
Sanders-Cin	122
Karros-LA	115
Brogna-NY	111

Earned Run Average
Maddux-Atl	1.63
Nomo-LA	2.54
Ashby-SD	2.94
Valdes-LA	3.05
Glavine-Atl	3.08

Complete Games
Maddux-Atl	10
Leiter-SF	7
Valdes-LA	6
Neagle-Pit	5

AMERICAN LEAGUE LEADERS

Home Runs
Belle-Cle	50
Buhner-Sea	40
Thomas-Chi	40

Runs Batted In
Belle-Cle	126
Vaughn-Bos	126
Buhner-Sea	121
Martinez-Sea	113

Batting Average
Martinez-Sea	.356
Knoblauch-Min	.333
Salmon-Cal	.330
Boggs-NY	.324
Murray-Cle	.323

On Base Percentage
Martinez-Sea	.479
Thomas-Chi	.454
Thome-Cle	.438
Salmon-Cal	.429
Davis-Cal	.429

Slugging Average
Belle-Cle	.690
E.Martinez-Sea	.628
F.Thomas-Chi	.606
Salmon-Cal	.494
Palmeiro-Bal	.583

Stolen Bases
Lofton-Cle	54
Goodwin-KC	50
Nixon-Tex	50
Knoblauch-Min	46
Coleman-KC-Sea	42

Wins
Mussina-Bal	19
Cone-Tor-NY	18
Johnson-Sea	18
Rogers-Tex	17

Innings Pitched
Cone-Tor-NY	229.1
Mussina-Bal	221.2
McDowell-NY	217.2
Johnson-Sea	214.1
Gubicza-KC	213.1

Saves
Mesa-Cle	46
Smith-Cal	37
Aguilera-Min-Bos	32
Hernandez-Chi	32

Strikeouts
Johnson-Sea	294
Stottlemyre-Oak	205
Finley-Cal	195
Cone-Tor-NY	191
Appier-KC	185

Earned Run Average
Johnson-Sea	2.48
Wakefield-Bos	2.95
Martinez-Cle	3.08
Mussina-Bal	3.29
Rogers-Tex	3.38

Complete Games
McDowell-NY	8
Erickson-Min-Bal	7
Mussina-Bal	7

THE YEAR IN BASEBALL

March 31: The longest strike in sports history ends by order of a U.S. District court judge who forbids owners from implementing new financial working conditions.

May 3: When David Bell makes his debut at third base for the Indians he makes the Bells—with his father Buddy and his grandfather Gus—the second three-generation family in history (the Boones are the other).

May 28: The White Sox and Tigers combine for a major league record 12 home runs at Tiger Stadium in a 14-12 Chicago win.

September 6: Cal Ripken, Jr. breaks Lou Gehrig's record for consecutive games played before a home-town crowd at Camden Yards and receives an ovation that lasts for more than 22 minutes.

September 8: Cleveland ends a 41-year postseason drought by clinching the AL Central with a 3-2 win over the Orioles.

September 19: Andres Galarraga homers to makes the Rockies the second team to have four players hit 30 or more homers in a season.

September 30: Indians outfielder Albert Belle hits his 50th home run to become the first player ever to have 50 home runs and 50 doubles in the same season.

1996

Clemens strikes out 20, Yankees back on top in tough year for umps

It wasn't a good year to be an umpire. On Opening Day in Cincinnati, the very overweight John McSherry dropped dead of a heart attack, prompting belated moves for the better conditioning of arbiters. In September, Baltimore's Roberto Alomar spat in the face of John Hirschbeck during an argument, setting off (unsatisfied) demands he be disciplined severely and (brief) threats of an umpire walkout during the postseason.

In the NL East, Atlanta rolled to its customary division title with star turns from John Smoltz (a league-high 24 wins) and Ryan Klesko (34 homers). St. Louis took the Central largely thanks to Andy Benes (18 wins), Dennis Eckersley (30 saves), and Brian Jordan (.310 with 104 RBIs). San Diego had the two best hitters in the league outside Colorado in MVP Ken Caminiti (.326-40-130) and batting titlist Tony Gwynn (.353), helping it to the title in the West. The Padres clinched by sweeping their final series against the Dodgers, who ended up as the wild card anyway. A highlight of the Los Angeles season was a Hideo Nomo no-hitter in the improbable setting of Colorado. Andres Galarraga of the Rockies collected the most homers (47) and RBIs (150). In August, the Padres and Mets played the first regular-season games in Mexico, in Monterrey.

In the AL, Joe Torre debuted as Yankees manager with an East title built on 100-RBI seasons from Tino Martinez and Bernie Williams, Andy Pettitte's circuit-tops 21 wins and a brilliant bullpen tandem of setup man Mariano Rivera and closer John Wetteland (43 saves). The Indians trashed the Central, with Albert Belle leading the league with his 148 RBIs. Texas got big numbers in the West from Juan Gonzalez (.310-47-144) and Dean Palmer (38-107) to hold off a late surge by the Mariners. Seattle's Alex Rodriguez won the batting crown (.358), Oakland's Mark McGwire the homer category (52) and Toronto's Juan Guzman the ERA laurels (2.93). In September, Boston's Roger Clemens matched his ten-year-old mark of 20 strikeouts in a game, this time against the Tigers.

Both the Braves and Cardinals swept their division series. Atlanta's Mark Wohlers saved all three games against the Dodgers, with neither team batting .200. Gary Gaetti's three-run homer in the first inning of the opener (his only hit in the series) sent St. Louis off to its rout of San Diego; Eckersley saved all the wins. In the AL, Williams and Derek Jeter collected 14 hits between them in a four-game victory over the Rangers. Baltimore also closed out the Indians in four, the clincher coming on a 12th-inning home run from the incessantly booed Alomar.

In the NLCS, the Braves dropped three of the first four games, then came back to throttle the Cardinals by a margin of 32-1 over the last three. Javier Lopez and the usually light-hitting Mark Lemke teamed up for 25 hits and 11 RBIs, Smoltz won twice and Wohlers saved two more. In the ALCS, a controversial call on a first-game homer by Jeter gave the Yankees the break they needed

Alex Rodriguez
In his first full season as a starter, Rodriguez batted .358 (with 36 home runs) to become the first shortstop since 1944 to lead the AL in batting.

for an eventual five-game triumph over the Orioles. Jeter had 10 hits, Williams and Cecil Fielder 14 RBIs between them.

The World Series began with New York surrendering two homers in the opener to Atlanta rookie Andruw Jones and being blanked in Game 2 by Greg Maddux and Wohlers, but then the Yankees came back for four straight. The turning point was a Game 4 eighth-inning homer by Jim Leyritz against Wohlers that wiped out what had once been a 6-0 Braves lead. Wetteland saved all four victories.

1996 SEASON HIGHLIGHTS

NATIONAL LEAGUE

East

	W	L	Pct.	GB
Atlanta	96	66	.593	—
Montreal	88	74	.543	8
Florida	80	82	.494	16
New York	71	91	.438	25
Philadelphia	67	95	.414	29

Central

	W	L	Pct.	GB
St. Louis	88	74	.543	—
Houston	82	80	.506	6
Cincinnati	81	81	.500	7
Chicago	76	86	.469	12
Pittsburgh	73	89	.451	15

West

	W	L	Pct.	GB
San Diego	91	71	.562	—
Los Angeles	90	72	.556	1
Colorado	83	79	.512	8
San Francisco	68	94	.420	23

AMERICAN LEAGUE

East

	W	L	Pct.	GB
New York	92	70	.568	—
Baltimore	88	74	.543	4
Chicago	85	77	.525	7
Toronto	74	88	.457	18
Detroit	53	109	.327	39

Central

	W	L	Pct.	GB
Cleveland	99	62	.615	—
Seattle	85	76	.528	14
Milwaukee	80	82	.494	19.5
Minnesota	78	84	.481	21.5
Kansas City	75	86	.466	24

West

	W	L	Pct.	GB
Texas	90	72	.556	—
Boston	85	77	.525	5
Oakland	78	84	.481	12
California	70	91	.435	19.5

AWARDS

NL MVP: Ken Caminiti, SD
AL MVP: Juan Gonzalez, TEX
NL Cy Young: John Smoltz, ATL
AL Cy Young: Pat Hentgen, TOR
NL Rookie: Todd Hollandsworth, LA
AL Rookie: Derek Jeter, NY
NL Relief Pitcher: Jeff Brantley, CIN
AL Relief Pitcher: John Wetteland, NY
NL Manager: Bruce Bochy, SD
AL Manager: Johnny Oates, TEX; Joe Torre, NY
GOLD GLOVES
NL: Greg Maddux, P; Charles Johnson, C; Mark Grace, 1B; Craig Biggio, 2B; Ken Caminiti, 3B; Barry Larkin, SS; Barry Bonds, Marquis Grissom, Steve Finley, OF
AL: Mike Mussina, P; Ivan Rodriguez, C; J.T. Snow, 1B; Roberto Alomar, 2B; Robin Ventura, 3B; Omar Vizquel, SS; Kenny Lofton, Ken Griffey Jr., Jay Buhner, OF

ALL-STAR GAME
Veterans Stadium, Philadelphia
July 9: NL 6, AL 0
MVP: Mike Piazza, Los Angeles

POSTSEASON
WORLD SERIES
New York Yankees 4, Atlanta Braves 2
Oct. 20: Atlanta 12, NEW YORK 1
Oct. 21: Atlanta 4, NEW YORK 0
Oct. 22: New York 5, ATLANTA 2
Oct. 23: New York 8, ATLANTA 6
Oct. 24: New York 1, ATLANTA 0
Oct. 26: NEW YORK 3, Atlanta 2
MVP: John Wetteland, New York

NATIONAL LEAGUE
NLCS
Atlanta Braves 4, St. Louis Cardinals 3
Oct. 9: ATLANTA 4, St. Louis 2
Oct. 10: St. Louis 8, ATLANTA 3
Oct. 12: ST. LOUIS 3, Atlanta 2
Oct. 13: ST. LOUIS 4, Atlanta 3
Oct. 14: Atlanta 14, ST. LOUIS 0
Oct. 16: ATLANTA 3, St. Louis 1
Oct. 17: ATLANTA 15, St. Louis 0
MVP: Javy Lopez, Atlanta

NLDS
St. Louis Cardinals 3, San Diego Padres 0
Oct. 1: ST. LOUIS 3, San Diego 1
Oct. 3: ST. LOUIS 5, San Diego 4
Oct. 5: St. Louis 7, SAN DIEGO 5
Atlanta Braves 3, Los Angeles Dodgers 0
Oct. 2: Atlanta 2, LOS ANGELES 1
Oct. 3: Atlanta 3, LOS ANGELES 2
Oct. 5: ATLANTA 5, Los Angeles 2

AMERICAN LEAGUE
ALCS
New York Yankees 4, Baltimore Orioles 1
Oct. 9: NEW YORK 5, Baltimore 4
Oct. 10: Baltimore 5, NEW YORK 3
Oct. 11: New York 5, BALTIMORE 2
Oct. 12: New York 8, BALTIMORE 4
Oct. 13: New York 6, BALTIMORE 4
MVP: Bernie Williams, New York

ALDS
Baltimore Orioles 3, Cleveland Indians 1
Oct. 1: BALTIMORE 10, Cleveland 4
Oct. 2: BALTIMORE 7, Cleveland 4
Oct. 4: CLEVELAND 9, Baltimore 4
Oct. 5: Baltimore 4, CLEVELAND 3
New York Yankees 3, Texas Rangers 1
Oct. 1: Texas 6, NEW YORK 2
Oct. 2: NEW YORK 5, Texas 4
Oct. 4: New York 3, TEXAS 2
Oct. 5: New York 6, TEXAS 4

Home team in CAPS

NATIONAL LEAGUE LEADERS

Home Runs

Galarraga-Col	47
Bonds-SF	42
Sheffield-Fla	42
Hundley-NY	41

Runs Batted In

Galarraga-Col	150
Bichette-Col	141
Caminiti-SD	130
Bonds-SF	129
Burks-Col	128

Batting Average

Gwynn-SD	.353
Burks-Col	.344
Piazza-LA	.336
Johnson-NY	.333
Grace-Chi	.331

On Base Percentage

Sheffield-Fla	.465
Bonds-SF	.461
Bagwell-Hou	.451
Piazza-LA	.422
Henderson-SD	.410

Slugging Average

Burks-Col	.639
Galarraga-Col	.624
Finley-SD	.621
Castilla-Col	.615
Caminiti-SD	.601

Stolen Bases

Young-Col	53
Johnson-NY	50
DeShields-LA	48
Bonds-SF	40
Martin-Pit	38

Wins

Smoltz-Atl	24
Benes-StL	18
Brown-Fla	17
Ritz-Col	17

Innings Pitched

Smoltz-Atl	253.2
Maddux-Atl	245.0
Reynolds-Hou	239.0
Navarro-Chi	236.2
Glavine-Atl	235.1

Saves

Brantley-Cin	44
Worrell-LA	44
Hoffman-SD	42
Wohlers-Atl	39
Rojas-Mon	36

Strikeouts

Smoltz-Atl	276
Nomo-LA	234
Fassero-Mon	222
Martinez-Mon	222
Kile-Hou	219

Earned Run Average

Brown-Fla	1.89
Maddux-Atl	2.72
Leiter-Fla	2.93
Smoltz-Atl	2.94
Glavine-Atl	2.98

Complete Games

Schilling-Phi	8
Smoltz-Atl	6

AMERICAN LEAGUE LEADERS

Home Runs

McGwire-Oak	52
Anderson-Bal	50
Griffey Jr.-Sea	49
Belle-Cle	48
Gonzalez-Tex	47

Runs Batted In

Belle-Cle	148
Gonzalez-Tex	144
Vaughn-Bos	143
Palmeiro-Bal	142
Griffey Jr.-Sea	140

Batting Average

Rodriguez-Sea	.358
Thomas-Chi	.349
Molitor-Min	.341
Knoblauch-Min	.341
Greer-Tex	.332

On Base Percentage

McGwire-Oak	.467
Martinez-Sea	.464
Thomas-Chi	.459
Thome-Cle	.450
Knoblauch-Min	.448

Slugging Average

McGwire-Oak	.730
Gonzalez-Tex	.643
Anderson-Bal	.637
Rodriguez-Sea	.631
Griffey-Sea	.628

Stolen Bases

Lofton-Cle	75
Goodwin-KC	66
Nixon-Tor	54
Knoblauch-Min	45
Vizquel-Cle	35

Wins

Pettitte-NY	21
Hentgen-Tor	20
Mussina-Bal	19
Nagy-Cle	17

Innings Pitched

Hentgen-Tor	265.2
Fernandez-Chi	258.0
Hill-Tex	250.2
Mussina-Bal	243.1
Clemens-Bos	242.2

Saves

Wetteland-NY	43
Mesa-Cle	39
Hernandez-Chi	38
Percival-Cal	36
Fetters-Mil	32

Strikeouts

Clemens-Bos	257
Finley-Cal	215
Appier-KC	207
Mussina-Bal	204
Fernandez-Chi	200

Earned Run Average

Guzman-Tor	2.93
Hentgen-Tor	3.22
Nagy-Cle	3.41
Fernandez-Chi	3.45
Appier-KC	3.62

Complete Games

Hentgen-Tor	10
Hill-Tex	7
Pavlik-Tex	7

THE YEAR IN BASEBALL

March 31: Opening Day is in March for the first time.

April 27: Barry Bonds joins his father Bobby, godfather Willie Mays, and Andre Dawson as the only players with 300 homers and 300 steals.

July 12: Kirby Puckett retires due to a damaged retina.

July 29: Tom Lasorda calls it quits after 20 seasons as Dodger manager following a heart attack and an angioplasty in June.

August 16: The Padres and Mets play the first regular-season major league game ever played in Mexico.

September 6: Eddie Murray hits home run No. 500 to join Hank Aaron and Willie Mays as the only players with 500 home runs and 3,000 hits.

September 16: Paul Molitor of the Twins becomes the 21st player to reach 3,000 hits—and the first to reach the milestone with a triple.

September 18: Roger Clemens ties his own major league record with 20 strikeouts against the Tigers.

September 27: Baltimore's Roberto Alomar spits at home-plate umpire John Hirschbeck during an argument and is suspended five games.

October 9: The Yankees win the ALCS opener when a 12-year-old fan sticks his glove out and turns a fly ball into a home run to tie the game.

1997

Interleague games get mixed reviews as Marlins surprise

Interleague play brought box-office novelty, the 50th anniversary of Jackie Robinson's debut more rhetoric than opportunity for minorities in front offices, and a blockbuster trade genuine benefits for both teams.

Atlanta's path to the NL East title was marked by Denny Neagle's league-leading 20 wins, Greg Maddux's 19-4 mastery and Chipper Jones' 111 RBIs. Houston took the Central with Craig Biggio scoring the most runs in the league in 65 years (146), Jeff Bagwell knocking in 135, and Darryl Kile winning 19. A preseason deal sending slugger Matt Williams to the Indians paid off for the Giants in a West title when acquisition Jeff Kent broke out with a 29-121 effort, complementing Barry Bonds' 40-101 and 19 wins from Shawn Estes. Florida earned the wild card slot with one of the strongest rotations in the league and an offense led by Moises Alou's 115 RBIs. San Diego's Tony Gwynn won his eighth batting crown (.372), Colorado's Larry Walker the homer title (49), teammate Andres Galarraga the RBI primacy (140), and Montreal's Pedro Martinez the ERA low (1.90).

In the AL, Seattle claimed the two most electrifying players in the league when Randy Johnson and Ken Griffey, Jr. led the team to a title in the West. The lefty's 20 wins included two 19-strikeout games, while the outfielder had the most homers (56) and RBIs (147). Cleveland took another crown in the Central with power and timely defeatism from rival Chicago. The power came from ex-Giant Williams (32-105), Jim Thome (40-102) and David Justice (33-101); the defeatism from White Sox owner Jerry Reinsdorf, who scythed his pitching staff in a July trade when the club was only a few games behind the Indians. In the East, the Orioles stayed first all year with the aid of Rafael Palmeiro's 38-110 and Randy Myers' 45 saves. Tino Martinez's 44-141 helped boost the Yankees to the wild card. Frank Thomas of the White Sox won the batting title (.347), and free agent Roger Clemens settled into a new home in Toronto with a Cy Young Award-winning Triple Crown (21-2.05-292).

Both NL division playoffs were sweeps. The Marlins won their first two games with ninth-inning walk-off hits, then Devon White's grand slam finished off the Giants in Game 3. Atlanta pitching overwhelmed Houston, limiting top-of-the-order hitters Biggio, Derek Bell and Bagwell to two singles in 37 at bats while getting complete efforts from Maddux and John Smoltz. In the AL, the Yankees won two of the first three, but Sandy Alomar's game-tying homer off Mariano Rivera in Game 4 turned the tide for the Indians in a comeback victory. Baltimore beat Johnson twice and got two wins from Mike Mussina to put away Seattle in four.

The Marlins continued their unlikely march in the NLCS by taking the Braves in six. With the help of plate umpire Eric Gregg's vast strike zone, Livan Hernandez struck out 16 in 10 2/3 innings

Roger Clemens
Amid whispers he was washed up, Clemens bolted from Boston to Toronto and won a pitching Triple Crown and his first of two consecutive Cy Young Awards.

on his way to two wins and Kevin Brown won the other two, compensating for Florida's .199 batting average. The key to Cleveland's six-game win over the Orioles was two extra-inning victories—the first on a missed bunt that Baltimore catcher Lenny Webster mistakenly thought was a foul ball, the second on an 11th-inning homer by Tony Fernandez.

Florida's dream season climaxed when Edgar Renteria singled home an 11th-inning run in the seventh game of the World Series against Cleveland. Once again, Hernandez starred with two wins, with Alou providing three homers and nine runs batted in.

1997 SEASON HIGHLIGHTS

NATIONAL LEAGUE

East	W	L	Pct.	GB
Atlanta	101	61	.623	—
Florida	92	70	.568	9
New York	88	74	.543	13
Montreal	78	84	.481	23
Philadelphia	68	94	.420	33

Central	W	L	Pct.	GB
Houston	84	78	.519	—
Pittsburgh	79	83	.488	5
Cincinnati	76	86	.469	8
St. Louis	73	89	.451	11
Chicago	68	94	.420	16

West	W	L	Pct.	GB
San Francisco	90	72	.556	—
Los Angeles	88	74	.543	2
Colorado	83	79	.512	7
San Diego	76	86	.469	14

AMERICAN LEAGUE

East	W	L	Pct.	GB
Baltimore	98	64	.605	—
New York	96	66	.593	2
Detroit	79	83	.488	19
Boston	78	84	.481	20
Toronto	76	86	.469	22

Central	W	L	Pct.	GB
Cleveland	86	75	.534	—
Chicago	80	81	.497	6
Milwaukee	78	83	.484	8
Minnesota	68	94	.420	18.5
Kansas City	67	94	.416	19

West	W	L	Pct.	GB
Seattle	90	72	.556	—
Anaheim	84	78	.519	6
Texas	77	85	.475	13
Oakland	65	97	.401	25

AWARDS

NL MVP: Larry Walker, COL
AL MVP: Ken Griffey, Jr., SEA
NL Cy Young: Pedro Martinez, MON
AL Cy Young: Roger Clemens, TOR
NL Rookie: Scott Rolen, PHI
AL Rookie: Nomar Garciaparra, BOS
NL Relief Pitcher: Jeff Shaw, CIN
AL Relief Pitcher: Randy Myers, BAL
NL Manager: Dusty Baker, SF
AL Manager: Davey Johnson, BAL
GOLD GLOVES
NL: Greg Maddux, P; Charles Johnson, C; J.T. Snow, 1B; Craig Biggio, 2B; Ken Caminiti, 3B; Rey Ordonez, SS; Barry Bonds, Larry Walker, Raul Mondesi, OF
AL: Mike Mussina, P; Ivan Rodriguez, C; Rafael Palmeiro, 1B; Chuck Knoblauch, 2B; Matt Williams, 3B; Omar Vizquel, SS; Bernie Williams, Ken Griffey Jr., Jim Edmonds, OF

ALL-STAR GAME
Jacobs Field, Cleveland
July 8: AL 3, NL 1
MVP: Sandy Alomar Jr., Cleveland

POSTSEASON
WORLD SERIES
Florida Marlins 4, Cleveland Indians 3
Oct. 18: FLORIDA 7, Cleveland 4
Oct. 19: Cleveland 6, FLORIDA 1
Oct. 21: Florida 14, CLEVELAND 11
Oct. 22: CLEVELAND 10, Florida 3
Oct. 23: Florida 8, CLEVELAND 7
Oct. 25: Cleveland 4, FLORIDA 1
Oct. 26: FLORIDA 3, Cleveland 2
MVP: Livan Hernandez, Florida

NATIONAL LEAGUE
NLCS
Florida Marlins 4, Atlanta Braves 2
Oct. 7: Florida 5, ATLANTA 3

Oct. 8: ATLANTA 7, Florida 1
Oct. 10: FLORIDA 5, Atlanta 2
Oct. 11: Atlanta 4, FLORIDA 0
Oct. 12: FLORIDA 2, Atlanta 1
Oct. 14: Florida 7, ATLANTA 4
MVP: Livan Hernandez, Florida

NLDS
Atlanta Braves 3, Houston Astros 0
Sept. 30: ATLANTA 2, Houston 1
Oct. 1: ATLANTA 13, Houston 3
Oct. 3: Atlanta 4, HOUSTON 1

Florida Marlins 3, San Francisco Giants 0
Sept. 30: FLORIDA 2, San Francisco 1
Oct. 1: FLORIDA 7, San Francisco 6
Oct. 3: Florida 6, SAN FRANCISCO 2

AMERICAN LEAGUE
ALCS
Cleveland Indians 4, Baltimore Orioles 2
Oct. 8: BALTIMORE 3, Cleveland 0

Oct. 9: Cleveland 5, BALTIMORE 4
Oct. 11: CLEVELAND 2, Baltimore 1
Oct. 12: CLEVELAND 8, Baltimore 7
Oct. 13: Baltimore 4, CLEVELAND 2
Oct. 15: Cleveland 1, BALTIMORE 0
MVP: Marquis Grissom, Cleveland

ALDS
Baltimore Orioles 3, Seattle Mariners 1
Oct. 1: Baltimore 9, SEATTLE 3
Oct. 2: Baltimore 9, SEATTLE 3
Oct. 4: Seattle 4, BALTIMORE 2
Oct. 5: BALTIMORE 3, Seattle 1

Cleveland Indians 3, New York Yankees 2
Sept. 30: NEW YORK 8, Cleveland 6
Oct. 2: Cleveland 7, NEW YORK 5
Oct. 4: New York 6, CLEVELAND 1
Oct. 5: CLEVELAND 3, New York 2
Oct. 6: CLEVELAND 4, New York 3

Home team in CAPS

NATIONAL LEAGUE LEADERS

Home Runs
Walker-Col	49
Bagwell-Hou	43
Galarraga-Col	41

Runs Batted In
Galarraga-Col	140
Bagwell-Hou	135
Walker-Col	130
Piazza-LA	124
Kent-SF	121

Batting Average
Gwynn-SD	.372
Walker-Col	.366
Piazza-LA	.362
Lofton-Atl	.333
Joyner-SD	.327

On Base Percentage
Walker-Col	.452
Bonds-SF	.446
Piazza-LA	.431
Bagwell-Hou	.425
Sheffield-Fla	.424

Slugging Average
Walker-Col	.720
Piazza-LA	.638
Bagwell-Hou	.592
Galarraga-Col	.585
Lankford-StL	.585

Stolen Bases
Womack-Pit	60
Sanders-Cin	56
DeShields-StL	55
Biggio-Hou	47
Young-COL-LA	45

Wins
Neagle-Atl	20
Estes-SF	19
Kile-Hou	19
Maddux-Atl	19

Innings Pitched
Smoltz-Atl	256.0
Kile-Hou	255.2
Schilling-Phi	254.1
Martinez-Mon	241.1
Glavine-Atl	240.0

Saves
Shaw-Cin	42
Beck-SF	37
Hoffman-SD	37
Eckersley-StL	36
Franco-NY	36

Strikeouts
Sosa-Chi	174
Gant-StL	162
Rodriguez-Mon	149
Galarraga-Col	141
Rolen-Phi	138

Earned Run Average
Martinez-Mon	1.90
Maddux-Atl	2.20
Kile-Hou	2.57
Valdes-LA	2.65
Brown-Fla	2.69

Complete Games
Martinez-Mon	13
Perez-Mon	8
Hampton-Hou	7
Schilling-Phi	7
Smoltz-Atl	7

AMERICAN LEAGUE LEADERS

Home Runs
Griffey Jr.-Sea	56
Martinez-NY	44
Gonzalez-Tex	42
Buhner-Sea	40
Thome-Cle	40

Runs Batted In
Griffey Jr.-Sea	147
Martinez-NY	141
Gonzalez-Tex	131
Salmon-Ana	129
Thomas-Chi	125

Batting Average
Thomas-Chi	.347
Martinez-Sea	.330
Justice-Cle	.329
Williams-NY	.328
Ramirez-Cle	.328

On Base Percentage
Thomas-Chi	.456
Martinez-Sea	.456
Thome-Cle	.423
Vaughn-Bos	.420
Justice-Cle	.418

Slugging Average
Griffey-Sea	.646
F.Thomas-Chi	.611
Justice-Cle	.596
Gonzalez-Tex	.589
Thome-Cle	.579

Stolen Bases
Hunter-Det	74
Knoblauch-Min	62
Goodwin-KC-Tex	50
Nixon-Tor	47
Vizquel-Cle	43

Wins
Clemens-Tor	21
Johnson-Sea	20
Radke-Min	20
Pettitte-NY	18
Moyer-Sea	17

Innings Pitched
Clemens-Tor	264.0
Hentgen-Tor	264.0
Pettitte-NY	240.1
Radke-Min	239.2
Appier-KC	235.2

Saves
Myers-Bal	45
Rivera-NY	43
Jones-Mil	36
Jones-Det	31
Wetteland-Tex	31

Strikeouts
Clemens-Tor	292
Johnson-Sea	291
Cone-NY	222
Mussina-Bal	218
Appier-KC	196

Earned Run Average
Clemens-Tor	2.05
Johnson-Sea	2.28
Cone-NY	2.82
Pettitte-NY	2.88
Thompson-Det	3.02

Complete Games
Clemens-Tor	9
Hentgen-Tor	9
Johnson-Sea	5
Tewksbury-Min	5
Wells-NY	5

THE YEAR IN BASEBALL

April 15: On the 50th anniversary of Jackie Robinson breaking the color barrier, Robinson's No. 42 is retired in perpetuity for every team.

June 12: The first interleague game in the regular season is played in Texas, where the Giants beat the Rangers, 4-3.

July 31: The A's send Mark McGwire to St. Louis.

August 8: Seattle's Randy Johnson strikes out 19 White Sox batters in a 5-0 win to become the first pitcher to strike out 19 batters twice in one year.

September 16: Philadelphia's Curt Schilling becomes the 13th pitcher to strike out 300 batters in a season, fanning nine in a 3-2 win over the Mets.

September 28: Mark McGwire hits his 58th home run to tie Jimmie Foxx and Hank Greenberg for the most by a right-handed hitter.

October 14: Kevin Brown retires Chipper Jones with two runners on to make the Marlins the first expansion team to advance to the World Series after just five seasons.

November 1: Roger Clemens becomes the first AL pitcher to win the Cy Young Award four times.

November 12: Ken Griffey, Jr. becomes the ninth unanimous pick for AL MVP.

1998

Marlins hold fire sale as McGwire and Sosa chase home-run record

Yet another expansion moved Tampa Bay into the AL, Arizona into the NL, and Milwaukee from the former into the latter. Other preseason activity centered on Florida's fire sale of its world champions behind claims it had lost money in 1997. The campaign itself was consumed by the frantically publicized duel between St. Louis' Mark McGwire and Chicago's Sammy Sosa for eclipsing Roger Maris' 61-homer mark.

The Braves ran away from the Mets in the NL East, mainly because of Tom Glavine (a league-best 20 wins), Greg Maddux (a league-low 2.22 with 18 wins), and Andres Galarraga (44-121). Moises Alou, one of the bargains from the Marlins, energized the Astros to a Central title with his .312-33-124; at the trading deadline, Houston also picked up Randy Johnson, who proceeded to win 10 of his 11 decisions. Sosa's NL-tops 158 RBIs pushed the Cubs into the wild card, but only after a showdown playoff game with the Giants. Kevin Tapani anchored Chicago with 19 wins, and rookie Kerry Wood fanned 20 Astros in a May contest to tie the Roger Clemens record. On September 8, McGwire overtook Maris, then continued on to 70 homers (Sosa wound up with 66). San Diego took the West with Kevin Brown winning 18, Trevor Hoffman saving 53 and Greg Vaughn going 50-119. Colorado's Larry Walker won the hitting title (.363).

New York's franchise-record 114 wins made a joke of the AL East race. Bernie Williams won the batting crown (.339), Tino Martinez and Paul O'Neill drove in 100 and David Cone tied Toronto's Clemens and Rick Helling of Texas for the most wins (20). Boston took the wild card with Mo Vaughn and Nomar Garciaparra combining for 75 homers and Pedro Martinez winning 19. The Indians went wire-to-wire in the Central with Manny Ramirez driving in 145. Juan Gonzalez (.318-45-157) was the bellwether of the Texas win in the West, with Aaron Sele backing up Helling's 20 victories with 19 of his own. Seattle's Ken Griffey, Jr. topped the power departments again with 56 homers and 146 RBIs, and Toronto's Clemens took another Triple Crown (20-2.65-271). On September 20, Cal Ripken, Jr. volunteered to end his consecutive game streak at 2,632.

The Braves disposed of the Cubs in three straight NL division games, with a third-game grand slam by Eddie Perez clinching matters. Brown outdueled Johnson, 2-1, in the Padres-Astros opener, then pitched strongly again in Game 3, racking up 21 strikeouts altogether in San Diego's victory in four. Jim Leyritz collected three

Mark McGwire
In a celebrated year-long race, McGwire outslugged Sammy Sosa to break Roger Maris' single-season record of 61 home runs as he finished the year with 70.

homers and five RBIs in ten at bats for San Diego. In the AL, the Yankees held the Rangers to a single run in their sweep, with Mariano Rivera saving two. Cleveland lost the opener, but won the next three over Boston. Vaughn and Garciaparra clouted five homers and drove in 18 for the losers, but the Red Sox got only one RBI from anybody else. Mike Jackson saved all three wins for the Indians.

In the NLCS, San Diego won the first three, staggered for two games, then claimed the pennant on Sterling Hitchcock's second victory. In the ALCS, Jim Thome hit four homers and drove in eight for Cleveland, but Omar Vizquel's error in the sixth game opened the door to a three-run inning that gave New York the pennant in six.

A seventh-inning grand slam by Tino Martinez in the opening game put the Yankees on track for a sweep of the Padres in the World Series. Rivera saved three and Scott Brosius drove in six.

1998 SEASON HIGHLIGHTS

NATIONAL LEAGUE

	W	L	Pct.	GB
East				
Atlanta	106	56	.654	—
New York	88	74	.543	18
Philadelphia	75	87	.463	31
Arizona	65	97	.401	41
Florida	54	108	.333	52
Central				
Houston	102	60	.630	—
Chicago	90	73	.552	12.5
St. Louis	83	79	.512	19
Cincinnati	77	85	.475	25
Milwaukee	74	88	.457	28
Pittsburgh	69	93	.426	33
West				
San Diego	98	64	.605	—
San Francisco	89	74	.546	9.5
Los Angeles	83	79	.512	15
Colorado	77	85	.475	21
Montreal	65	97	.401	33

AMERICAN LEAGUE

	W	L	Pct.	GB
East				
New York	114	48	.704	—
Boston	92	70	.568	22
Toronto	88	74	.543	26
Baltimore	79	83	.488	35
Tampa Bay	63	99	.389	51
Central				
Cleveland	89	73	.549	—
Chicago	80	82	.494	9
Kansas City	72	89	.447	16.5
Minnesota	70	92	.432	19
Detroit	65	97	.401	24
West				
Texas	88	74	.543	—
Anaheim	85	77	.525	3
Seattle	76	85	.472	11.5
Oakland	74	88	.457	14

AWARDS

NL MVP: Sammy Sosa, CHI
AL MVP: Juan Gonzalez, TEX
NL Cy Young: Tom Glavine, ATL
AL Cy Young: Roger Clemens, TOR
NL Rookie: Kerry Wood, CHI
AL Rookie: Ben Grieve, OAK
NL Relief Pitcher: Trevor Hoffman, SD
AL Relief Pitcher: Tom Gordon, BOS
NL Manager: Larry Dierker, HOU
AL Manager: Joe Torre, NY
GOLD GLOVES
NL: Greg Maddux, P; Charles Johnson, C; J.T. Snow, 1B; Bret Boone, 2B; Scott Rolen, 3B; Rey Ordonez, SS; Barry Bonds, Larry Walker, Andruw Jones, OF
AL: Mike Mussina, P; Ivan Rodriguez, C; Rafael Palmeiro, 1B; Roberto Alomar, 2B; Robin Ventura, 3B; Omar Vizquel, SS; Bernie Williams, Ken Griffey Jr., Jim Edmonds, OF

ALL-STAR GAME
Coors Field, Denver
July 7: AL 13, NL 8
MVP: Roberto Alomar, Baltimore

POSTSEASON
WORLD SERIES
New York Yankees 4, San Diego Padres 0
Oct. 17: New York 9, San Diego 6
Oct. 18: New York 9, San Diego 3
Oct. 20: New York 5, San Diego 4
Oct. 21: New York 3, San Diego 0
MVP: Scott Brosius, New York
NATIONAL LEAGUE
NLCS
San Diego Padres 4, Atlanta Braves 2
Oct. 7: San Diego 3, ATLANTA 2
Oct. 8: San Diego 3, ATLANTA 0
Oct. 10: SAN DIEGO 4, Atlanta 1

Oct. 11: Atlanta 8, SAN DIEGO 3
Oct. 12: Atlanta 7, SAN DIEGO 6
Oct. 14: San Diego 5, ATLANTA 0
MVP: Sterling Hitchcock, San Diego
NLDS
Atlanta Braves 3, Chicago Cubs 0
Sept. 30: ATLANTA 7, Chicago 1
Oct. 1: ATLANTA 2, Chicago 1
Oct. 3: Atlanta 6, CHICAGO 2
San Diego Padres 3, Houston Astros 1
Sept. 29: San Diego 2, HOUSTON 1
Oct. 1: HOUSTON 5, San Diego 4
Oct. 3: SAN DIEGO 2, Houston 1
Oct. 4: SAN DIEGO 6, Houston 1
AMERICAN LEAGUE
ALCS
New York Yankees 4, Cleveland Indians 2
Oct. 6: NEW YORK 7, Cleveland 2

Oct. 7: Cleveland 4, NEW YORK 1
Oct. 9: CLEVELAND 6, New York 1
Oct. 10: New York 4, CLEVELAND 0
Oct. 11: New York 5, CLEVELAND 3
Oct. 13: NEW YORK 9, Cleveland 5
MVP: David Wells, New York
ALDS
New York Yankees 3, Texas Rangers 0
Sept. 29: NEW YORK 2, Texas 0
Sept. 30: NEW YORK 3, Texas 1
Oct. 2: New York 4, TEXAS 0
Cleveland Indians 3, Boston Red Sox 1
Sept. 29: Boston 11, CLEVELAND 3
Sept. 30: CLEVELAND 9, Boston 5
Oct. 2: Cleveland 4, BOSTON 3
Oct. 3: Cleveland 2, BOSTON 1

Home team in CAPS

NATIONAL LEAGUE LEADERS

Home Runs
McGwire-StL	70
Sosa-Chi	66
Vaughn-SD	50
Castilla-Col	46
Galarraga-Atl	44

On Base Percentage
McGwire-StL	.473
Olerud-NY	.452
Walker-Col	.446
Bonds-SF	.442
Sheffield-Fla-LA	.435

Wins
Glavine-Atl	20
Tapani-Chi	19
Reynolds-Hou	19
Maddux-Atl	18
Brown-SD	18

Strikeouts
Schilling-Phi	300
Brown-SD	257
Wood-Chi	233
Reynolds-Hou	209
Maddux-Atl	204

Runs Batted In
Sosa-Chi	158
McGwire-StL	147
Castilla-Col	144
Kent-SF	128
Burnitz-Mil	125

Slugging Average
McGwire-StL	.752
Sosa-Chi	.647
Walker-Col	.630
Bonds-SF	.609
Vaughn-SD	.597

Innings Pitched
Schilling-Phi	268.2
Brown-SD	257.0
Maddux-Atl	251.0
C.Perez-Mon-LA	241.0
Hernandez-Fla	234.1

Earned Run Average
Maddux-Atl	2.22
Brown-SD	2.38
Leiter-NY	2.47
Glavine-Atl	2.47
Daal-Ari	2.88

Batting Average
Walker-Col	.363
Olerud-NY	.354
Bichette-Col	.331
Piazza-LA-Fla-NY	.328
Kendall-Pit	.327

Stolen Bases
Womack-Pit	58
Biggio-Hou	50
Young-LA	42
Renteria-Fla	41
Bonds-SF	28

Saves
Hoffman-SD	53
Beck-Chi	51
Shaw-Cin-LA	48
Nen-SF	40
J.Franco-NY	38

Complete Games
Schilling-Phi	15
Maddux-Atl	9
Hernandez-Fla	9
C.Perez-Mon-LA	7
Brown-SD	7

AMERICAN LEAGUE LEADERS

Home Runs
Griffey Jr.-Sea	56
Belle-Chi	49
Canseco-Tor	46
Gonzalez-Tex	45
Ramirez-Cle	45

On Base Percentage
Martinez-Sea	.429
Williams-NY	.422
Thome-Cle	.413
Salmon-Ana	.410
Offerman-KC	.403

Wins
Clemens-Tor	20
Cone-NY	20
Helling-Tex	20
Martinez-Bos	19
Sele-Tex	19

Strikeouts
Clemens-Tor	271
Martinez-Bos	251
Johnson-Sea	213
Finley-Ana	212
Cone-NY	209

Runs Batted In
Gonzalez-Tex	157
Belle-Chi	152
Griffey Jr.-Sea	146
Ramirez-Cle	145
Rodriguez-Sea	124

Slugging Average
Belle-Chi	.655
Gonzalez-Tex	.630
Griffey-Sea	.611
M.Ramirez-Cle	.599
Delgado-Tor	.592

Innings Pitched
Erickson-Bal	251.1
Rogers-Oak	238.2
Clemens-Tor	234.2
Moyer-Sea	234.1
Belcher-KC	234.0

Earned Run Average
Clemens-Tor	2.65
Martinez-Bos	2.89
Rogers-Oak	3.17
Finley-Ana	3.39
Wells-NY	3.49

Batting Average
Williams-NY	.339
Vaughn-Bos	.337
Belle-Chi	.328
Davis-Bal	.327
Jeter-NY	.324

Stolen Bases
Henderson-Oak	66
Lofton-Cle	54
Stewart-Tor	51
Rodriguez-Sea	46
Offerman-KC	45

Saves
Gordon-Bos	46
Percival-Ana	42
Wetteland-Tex	42
Jackson-Cle	40
Aguilera-Min	38

Complete Games
Erickson-Bal	11
Wells-NY	8
Fassero-Sea	7
Rogers-Oak	7

THE YEAR IN BASEBALL

April 7: National League baseball returns to Milwaukee after an absence of 32 years as the Brewers switch leagues.

May 6: Kerry Wood sets an NL mark and ties the major league record with 20 strikeouts in a 2-0 win over the Astros.

May 17: David Wells pitches the 15th perfect game in modern history.

July 8: Bud Selig is unanimously elected the ninth commissioner.

August 23: Barry Bonds becomes the first player in major league history to hit at least 400 home runs and steal 400 bases.

September 8: Mark McGwire passes Roger Maris to become the single-season home run king with his 61st homer, a 341-foot drive off Cubs pitcher Steve Trachsel.

September 20: Cal Ripken's string of consecutive games ends at 2,632 when the Orioles third baseman asks to be taken out of the lineup before the final Orioles home game of the season.

September 27: Mark McGwire caps an amazing summer with two home runs in the final game to give him 70 for the year.

November 16: Roger Clemens wins his second consecutive AL Cy Young Award to become the first five-time winner.

1999

Martinez is dominant but Yankees repeat in World Series

Pedro Martinez chose a striking year to display his dominance, displacing Roger Clemens as an AL Triple Crown winner while the circuit's biggest hitters enjoyed garish seasons. In addition to going 23-4 with 313 strikeouts, the Boston right-hander's 2.07 ERA was almost a run-and-a-half better than runner-up David Cone and his strikeout-to-walk ratio was 8.5-1.

But even Martinez's superiority and Nomar Garciaparra's batting title (.357) could earn the Red Sox only a wild-card spot against another Yankees AL East win. New York's offensive onslaught was led by Derek Jeter (.349-24-102 with 219 hits); Paul O'Neill, Tino Martinez and Bernie Williams also drove in 100. Mariano Rivera saved 45. Manny Ramirez batted in the most runs (165) since Jimmie Foxx in 1938 and Roberto Alomar did everything (.323-24-120 with 37 steals and 138 runs scored) to motor Cleveland's rout in the Central. In the West, Ivan Rodriguez threw out 54 percent of would-be basestealers, then hit .332 with 35 homers and 113 RBIs with a bat in his hand to spark Texas; the catcher had plenty of help from Rafael Palmeiro (.324-47-148) and Juan Gonzalez (.326-39-128). Seattle's Ken Griffey won his third-straight home-run crown (48).

In the NL Central, Mark McGwire followed up his 70-homer outburst by pacing the league in both round-trippers (65) and RBIs (147), but once again St. Louis sat out the postseason. Houston's Central title was largely the work of Mike Hampton's league-best 22 wins, 21 more from Jose Lima and Billy Wagner's development as a closer (39 saves with an opposition batting average of .135). Arizona won the West with a record-breaking 35-game turnaround from the previous year. Randy Johnson struck out 364 and registered the league's lowest ERA (2.48); Matt Williams led the Diamondbacks offense at 35-142, with Jay Bell and Luis Gonzalez also driving home 100. Chipper Jones' 45 homers and Greg Maddux's 19 wins spurred Atlanta's NL East win. The Mets took the wild card by defeating the Reds in a winner-take-all playoff game. Colorado's Larry Walker hit .379 for his second batting title in a row.

For the second-straight year in the AL division series, the Yankees humiliated Texas by yielding a single run in a three-game sweep. Williams drove in six and Rivera saved two. Pedro Martinez contributed more heroics against Cleveland by throwing six no-hit relief innings in the fifth-game clincher. John Valentin drove in twelve runs and Troy O'Leary walloped two homers good for seven runs in the finale. In the NL, Atlanta took Houston in four, with Brian Jordan driving in seven. New York did the same to Arizona,

Pedro Martinez
A Cy Young winner in both leagues, Martinez earned a Triple Crown with 23 wins, 313 strikeouts and a 2.17 ERA as Boston took a wild-card playoff spot.

the clincher coming on a 10th-inning walkoff homer in the fourth game by backup catcher Todd Pratt.

Martinez could pitch only once in the ALCS, so the Red Sox won only once. Seven hits from Jeter and two more Rivera saves closed out Boston in five games. In the NLCS, the Braves took the Mets three in a row, but then New York pulled out a comeback win, setting the stage for two barn-burners. In Game 5, the teams paraded 15 pitchers to the mound before the Mets' Robin Ventura cleared the wall in the 12th inning with the bases loaded (the grand slam was ruled a single after he passed Pratt on the bases). In Game 6, Kenny Rogers walked home Atlanta's pennant run in the 11th inning after the clubs had marched 14 pitchers to the hill.

Clearly exhausted by the Mets series, the Braves went down four in a row to the Yankees in the World Series. Rivera had another two saves.

1999 SEASON HIGHLIGHTS

NATIONAL LEAGUE

East	W	L	Pct.	GB
Atlanta	103	59	.636	—
Houston	97	65	.599	6
Philadelphia	77	85	.475	26
Montreal	68	94	.420	35
Florida	64	98	.395	39
Central				
New York	97	66	.595	—
Cincinnati	96	67	.589	1
Pittsburgh	78	83	.484	18
St. Louis	75	86	.466	21
San Diego	74	88	.457	22.5
Chicago	67	95	.414	29.5
West				
Arizona	100	62	.617	—
San Francisco	86	76	.531	14
Los Angeles	77	85	.475	23
Milwaukee	74	87	.460	25.5
Colorado	72	90	.444	28

AMERICAN LEAGUE

East	W	L	Pct.	GB
New York	98	64	.605	—
Boston	94	68	.580	4
Toronto	84	78	.519	14
Baltimore	78	84	.481	20
Detroit	69	92	.429	28.5
Central				
Cleveland	97	65	.599	—
Chicago	75	86	.466	21.5
Tampa Bay	69	93	.426	28
Kansas City	64	97	.398	32.5
Minnesota	63	97	.394	33
West				
Texas	95	67	.586	—
Oakland	87	75	.537	8
Seattle	79	83	.488	16
Anaheim	70	92	.432	25

AWARDS

NL MVP: Chipper Jones, ATL
AL MVP: Ivan Rodriguez, TEX
NL Cy Young: Randy Johnson, ARI
AL Cy Young: Pedro Martinez, BOS
NL Rookie: Scott Williamson, CIN
AL Rookie: Carlos Beltran, KC
NL Relief Pitcher: Billy Wagner, HOU
AL Relief Pitcher: Mariano Rivera, NY
NL Manager: Jack McKeon, CIN
AL Manager: Jimy Williams, BOS
GOLD GLOVES
NL: Greg Maddux, P; Mike Lieberthal, C; J.T. Snow, 1B; Pokey Reese, 2B; Robin Ventura, 3B; Rey Ordonez, SS; Steve Finley, Larry Walker, Andruw Jones, OF
AL: Mike Mussina, P; Ivan Rodriguez, C; Rafael Palmeiro, 1B; Roberto Alomar, 2B; Scott Brosius, 3B; Omar Vizquel, SS; Bernie Williams, Ken Griffey Jr., Shawn Green, OF

ALL-STAR GAME
Fenway Park, Boston
July 13: AL 4, NL 1
MVP: Pedro Martinez, Boston

POSTSEASON
WORLD SERIES
New York Yankees 4, Atlanta Braves 0
Oct. 23: New York 4, Atlanta 1
Oct. 24: New York 7, Atlanta 2
Oct. 26: New York 6, Atlanta 5
Oct. 27: New York 4, Atlanta 1
MVP: Mariano Rivera, New York

NATIONAL LEAGUE
NLCS
Atlanta Braves 4, New York Mets 2
Oct. 12: ATLANTA 4, New York 2
Oct. 13: ATLANTA 4, New York 3
Oct. 15: Atlanta 1, NEW YORK 0
Oct. 16: NEW YORK 3, Atlanta 2

Oct. 17: NEW YORK 4, Atlanta 3
Oct. 19: ATLANTA 10, New York 9
MVP: Eddie Perez, Atlanta
NLDS
New York Mets 3, Arizona Diamondbacks 1
Oct. 5: New York 8, ARIZONA 4
Oct. 6: ARIZONA 7, New York 1
Oct. 8: NEW YORK 9, Arizona 2
Oct. 9: NEW YORK 4, Arizona 3
Atlanta Braves 3, Houston Astros 1
Oct. 5: Houston 6, ATLANTA 1
Oct. 6: ATLANTA 5, Houston 1
Oct. 8: Atlanta 5, HOUSTON 3
Oct. 9: Atlanta 7, HOUSTON 5
AMERICAN LEAGUE
ALCS
New York Yankees 4, Boston Red Sox 1
Oct. 13: NEW YORK 4, Boston 3
Oct. 14: NEW YORK 3, Boston 2

Oct. 16: BOSTON 13, New York 1
Oct. 17: New York 9, BOSTON 2
Oct. 18: New York 6, BOSTON 1
MVP: Orlando Hernandez, New York
ALDS
Boston Red Sox 3, Cleveland Indians 2
Oct. 6: CLEVELAND 3, Boston 2
Oct. 7: CLEVELAND 11, Boston 1
Oct. 9: BOSTON 9, Cleveland 3
Oct. 10: BOSTON 23, Cleveland 7
Oct. 11: Boston 12, CLEVELAND 8
New York Yankees 3, Texas Rangers 0
Oct. 5: NEW YORK 8, Texas 0
Oct. 7: NEW YORK 3, Texas 1
Oct. 9: New York 3, TEXAS 0

Home team in CAPS

NATIONAL LEAGUE LEADERS

Home Runs
McGwire-StL	65
Sosa-Chi	63
Jones-Atl	45
Vaughn-Cin	45

Runs Batted In
McGwire-StL	147
Williams-Ari	142
Sosa-Chi	141
Bichette-Col	133
Guerrero-Mon	131

Batting Average
Walker-Col	.379
Gonzalez-Ari	.336
Abreu-Phi	.335
Casey-Cin	.332
Cirillo-Mil	.326

On Base Percentage
Walker-Col	.458
Bagwell-Hou	.454
Abreu-Phi	.446
Jones-Atl	.441
Olerud-NY	.427

Slugging Average
Walker-Col	.710
McGwire-StL	.697
Sosa-Chi	.635
C.Jones-Atl	.633
Giles-Pit	.614

Stolen Bases
Womack-Ari	72
Cedeno-NY	66
Young-LA	51
Castillo-Fla	50

Wins
Hampton-Hou	22
Lima-Hou	21
Maddux-Atl	19

Innings Pitched
Johnson-Ari	271.2
Brown-LA	252.1
Lima-Hou	246.1
Hampton-Hou	239.0
Glavine-Atl	234.0

Saves
Urbina-Mon	41
Hoffman-SD	40
Wagner-Hou	39
Rocker-Atl	38

Strikeouts
Johnson-Ari	364
Brown-LA	221
Astacio-Col	210
Millwood-Atl	205
Reynolds-Hou	197

Earned Run Average
Johnson-Ari	2.48
Millwood-Atl	2.68
Hampton-Hou	2.90
Brown-LA	3.00
Smoltz-Atl	3.19

Complete Games
Johnson-Ari	12
Schilling-Phi	8
Astacio-Col	7
Brown-LA	5

AMERICAN LEAGUE LEADERS

Home Runs
Griffey Jr.-Sea	48
Palmeiro-Tex	47
Delgado-Tor	44
Ramirez-Cle	44

Runs Batted In
Ramirez-Cle	165
Palmeiro-Tex	148
Delgado-Tor	134
Griffey Jr.-Sea	134
Gonzalez-Tex	128

Batting Average
Garciaparra-Bos	.357
Jeter-NY	.349
Williams-NY	.342
Martinez-Sea	.337
Ramirez-Cle	.333

On Base Percentage
Martinez-Sea	.447
Ramirez-Cle	.442
Jeter-NY	.438
Williams-NY	.435
Fernandez-Tor	.427

Slugging Average
M.Ramirez-Cle	.663
Palmeiro-Text	.630
Garciaparra-Bos	.603
Gonzalez-Tex	.601
Green-Tor	.588

Stolen Bases
Hunter-Det-Sea	44
Vizquel-Cle	42
Goodwin-Tex	39
Alomar-Cle	37
Stewart-Tor	37

Wins
Martinez-Bos	23
Colon-Cle	18
Mussina-Bal	18
Sele-Tex	18

Innings Pitched
Wells-Tor	231.2
Erickson-Bal	230.1
Moyer-Sea	228.0
Burba-Cle	220.0
Helling-Tex	219.1

Saves
Rivera-NY	45
Hernandez-TB	43
Wetteland-Tex	43
Jackson-Cle	39
Mesa-Sea	33

Strikeouts
Martinez-Bos	313
Finley-Ana	200
Sele-Tex	186
Cone-NY	177
Burba-Cle	174

Earned Run Average
Martinez-Bos	2.07
Cone-NY	3.44
Mussina-Bal	3.50
Radke-Min	3.75
Rosado-KC	3.85

Complete Games
Wells-Tor	7
Erickson-Bal	6
Ponson-Bal	6
Martinez-Bos	5
Rosado-KC	5

THE YEAR IN BASEBALL

February 18: Roger Clemens, a five-time Cy Young Award winner, is traded from Toronto to the New York Yankees.

March 8: Former Yankee great Joe DiMaggio, 84, dies in Florida.

March 28: Baltimore becomes the first major league team in 40 years to play in Cuba, defeating the Cuban national team 3-2.

April 4: For the first time in history, the season opens outside of the U.S., with Colorado defeating San Diego 8-2 in Monterey, Mexico.

April 20: The Cincinnati Reds are sold for $67 million.

July 18: Yankees pitcher David Cone tosses a perfect game.

September 27: In the final game at Tiger Stadium, which opened in 1912, Detroit defeats Kansas City 8-2.

November 4: The Cleveland Indians are sold for $320 million to Larry Dolan.

November 11: Wade Boggs retires after an 18-year career.

November 30: Jeffrey Loria buys the Montreal Expos.

November 30: Major league umpires vote to dissolve their union.

2000

Bad blood in NY as Yankees down Mets in Subway Series

The Mets and Cubs opened the season with two games in Tokyo. The gesture toward internationalizing the game coincided with centralizing Commissioner Bud Selig's power by disbanding the separate National and American league offices.

The Mets didn't return from Japan with any better idea about how to beat the Braves in the NL East, but they gained the wild-card slot. Mike Piazza (.324-38-113) was the main relief for a turgid offense that went through 18 outfielders in search of another bat during the year. Atlanta's usual spot at the top of the East was underwritten by Tom Glavine (an NL-best 21 wins), Andruw Jones (.303-36-103), and Andres Galarraga (.302-28-100) making a striking recovery from lymphatic cancer. St. Louis took the Central after trades for Darryl Kile (20 wins) and Jim Edmonds (42-108). The Giants celebrated their move into Pac Bell Park by running away from the rest of the West. Barry Bonds delivered 49 homers and Jeff Kent earned the MVP nod for his .334-33-125. Other bests were Chicago's Sammy Sosa for 50 homers, Colorado's Todd Helton for both his .372 average and 147 RBIs and the Dodgers' Kevin Brown for his 2.58 ERA.

In the AL, the Yankees took the East, with Bernie Williams (.307-30-121) the biggest bat and Andy Pettitte winning 19. Chicago surprised Cleveland in the Central behind a comeback from Frank Thomas (.328-43-143) and the full flowering of Magglio Ordonez (.315-32-126). In the West, Tim Hudson won his league-best 20th game on the final day of the season to give Oakland the title and leave defeated Seattle with the wild card. The Athletics offense came primarily from Jason Giambi (.333-43-137) and Miguel Tejada (30-115), that of the Mariners from Edgar Martinez (.324 and 37 with an AL-high 145 RBIs). Toronto's David Wells tied Hudson for most wins, Boston's Pedro Martinez fashioned a 1.74 ERA, Anaheim's Troy Glaus had the most homers (47), and Nomar Garciaparra of the Red Sox won his second-straight batting championship (.372).

In the NL division series, the Cardinals belted Greg Maddux for six runs in the first inning of the opener on their way to a sweep of the Braves. Edmonds whacked two homers and drove in seven. The Mets went a fourth game with the Giants before they too advanced; in Game 4, New York's Bobby Jones threw a one-hit shutout. In the AL, Seattle held the White Sox to a .185 average in a sweep. The Yankees ended the drama quickly in the fifth game of their tied series against Oakland by scoring six in the first inning. Mariano Rivera saved all three New York wins.

In the NLCS, the Mets got to the St. Louis starter in the first inning of each game and claimed the pennant in five. Mike Hampton's second win was a three-hit shutout for the clincher. In the AL, the Yankees didn't score until the eighth inning of the second game, then exploded for seven and kept it up most of the rest of the way for a win in six. Orlando Hernandez won twice and David Justice drove in eight.

New York's first Subway Series since 1956 had its most furious moment in the first inning of Game 2, when Roger Clemens shat-

Derek Jeter
In the World Series, Jeter cemented his reputation as a clutch player by batting .409 with two homers and scoring six of the Yankees runs.

tered Piazza's bat and then threw its remains in his direction, prompting both benches to empty and the NLers to nurse a grudge for two years. Otherwise, the Yankees dominated for their late-inning hitting, especially a 12th-inning single from Jose Vizcaino in Game 1 and a two-run single from Luis Sojo in the ninth inning of the concluding Game 5.

2000 SEASON HIGHLIGHTS

NATIONAL LEAGUE

East	W	L	Pct.	GB
Atlanta	95	67	.586	—
New York	94	68	.580	1
Florida	79	82	.491	15.5
Montreal	67	95	.414	28
Chicago	65	97	.401	30

Central	W	L	Pct.	GB
St. Louis	95	67	.586	—
Cincinnati	85	77	.525	10
Milwaukee	73	89	.451	22
Houston	72	90	.444	23
Pittsburgh	69	93	.426	26
Philadelphia	65	97	.401	30

West	W	L	Pct.	GB
San Francisco	97	65	.599	—
Los Angeles	86	76	.531	11
Arizona	85	77	.525	12
Colorado	82	80	.506	15
San Diego	76	86	.469	21

AMERICAN LEAGUE

East	W	L	Pct.	GB
New York	87	74	.540	—
Boston	85	77	.525	2.5
Toronto	83	79	.512	4.5
Baltimore	74	88	.457	13.5
Minnesota	69	93	.426	18.5

Central	W	L	Pct.	GB
Chicago	95	67	.586	—
Cleveland	90	72	.556	5
Detroit	79	83	.488	16
Kansas City	77	85	.475	18
Tampa Bay	69	92	.429	25.5

West	W	L	Pct.	GB
Oakland	91	70	.565	—
Seattle	91	71	.562	0.5
Anaheim	82	80	.506	9.5
Texas	71	91	.438	20.5

AWARDS

NL MVP: Jeff Kent, SF
AL MVP: Jason Giambi, OAK
NL Cy Young: Randy Johnson, ARI
AL Cy Young: Pedro Martinez, BOS
NL Rookie: Rafael Furcal, ATL
AL Rookie: Kazuhiro Sasaki, SEA
NL Relief Pitcher: Antonio Alfonseca, FLA
AL Relief Pitcher: Todd Jones, DET
NL Manager: Dusty Baker, SF
AL Manager: Jerry Manuel, CHI

GOLD GLOVES
NL: Greg Maddux, P; Mike Matheny, C; J.T. Snow, 1B; Pokey Reese, 2B; Scott Rolen, 3B; Neifi Perez, SS; Steve Finley, Jim Edmonds, Andruw Jones, OF
AL: Kenny Rogers, P; Ivan Rodriguez, C; John Olerud, 1B; Roberto Alomar, 2B; Travis Fryman, 3B; Omar Vizquel, SS; Bernie Williams, Jermaine Dye, Darin Erstad, OF

ALL-STAR GAME
Turner Field, Atlanta
July 11: AL 6, NL 3
MVP: Derek Jeter, New York Yankees

POSTSEASON
WORLD SERIES
New York Yankees 4, New York Mets 1
Oct. 21: Yankees 4, Mets 3
Oct. 22: Yankees 6, Mets 5
Oct. 24: Mets 4, Yankees 2
Oct. 25: Yankees 3, Mets 2
Oct. 26: Yankees 4, Mets 2
MVP: Derek Jeter, New York

NATIONAL LEAGUE
NLCS
New York Mets 4, St. Louis Cardinals 1
Oct. 11: New York 6, ST. LOUIS 2
Oct. 12: New York 6, ST. LOUIS 5

Oct. 14: St. Louis 8, NEW YORK 2
Oct. 15: NEW YORK 10, St. Louis 6
Oct. 16: NEW YORK 7, St. Louis 0
MVP: Mike Hampton, New York
NLDS
New York Mets 3, San Francisco Giants 1
Oct. 4: SAN FRANCISCO 5, New York 1
Oct. 5: New York 5, SAN FRANCISCO 4
Oct. 7: NEW YORK 1, San Francisco 0
Oct. 8: NEW YORK 4, San Francisco 0
St. Louis Cardinals 3, Atlanta Braves 0
Oct. 3: ST. LOUIS 7, Atlanta 5
Oct. 5: ST. LOUIS 10, Atlanta 4
Oct. 7: St. Louis 7, ATLANTA 1
AMERICAN LEAGUE
ALCS
New York Yankees 4, Seattle Mariners 2
Oct. 10: Seattle 2, NEW YORK 0

Oct. 11: NEW YORK 7, Seattle 1
Oct. 13: New York 8, SEATTLE 2
Oct. 14: New York 5, SEATTLE 0
Oct. 15: SEATTLE 6, New York 2
Oct. 17: NEW YORK 9, Seattle 7
MVP: David Justice, New York
ALDS
New York Yankees 3, Oakland Athletics 2
Oct. 3: OAKLAND 5, New York 3
Oct. 4: New York 4, OAKLAND 0
Oct. 6: NEW YORK 4, Oakland 2
Oct. 7: Oakland 11, NEW YORK 1
Oct. 8: New York 7, OAKLAND 5
Seattle Mariners 3, Chicago White Sox 0
Oct. 3: Seattle 7, CHICAGO 4
Oct. 4: Seattle 5, CHICAGO 2
Oct. 6: SEATTLE 2, Chicago 1

Home team in CAPS

NATIONAL LEAGUE LEADERS

Home Runs
Sosa-CHC	50
Bonds-SFG	49
Bagwell-HOU	47
Guerrero-MON	44
Hidalgo-HOU	44

On Base Percentage
Helton-COL	.463
Bonds-SFG	.440
Sheffield-LAD	.438
Giles-PIT	.432
Alfonzo-NYM	.425

Wins
Glavine-ATL	21
Kile-STL	20
Johnson-ARI	19
Maddux-ATL	19
Park-LAD	18

Strikeouts
Johnson-ARI	347
Park-LAD	217
Brown-LAD	216
Dempster-FLA	209
Leiter-NYM	200

Runs Batted In
Helton-COL	147
Sosa-CHC	138
Bagwell-HOU	132
Kent-SFG	125

Slugging Average
Helton-COL	.698
Bonds-SF	.688
V.Guerrero-MON	.664
Sheffield-LA	.643
Hidalgo-HOU	.636

Innings Pitched
Lieber-CHC	251.0
Maddux-ATL	249.3
Johnson-ARI	248.7
Glavine-ATL	241.0
Hernandez-SFG	240.0

Earned Run Average
Brown-LAD	2.58
Johnson-ARI	2.64
D'Amico-MIL	2.66
Maddux-ATL	3.00
Hampton-NYM	3.14

Batting Average
Helton-COL	.372
Alou-HOU	.355
Guerrero-MON	.345
Hammonds-COL	.335
Castillo-FLA	.334

Stolen Bases
Castillo-FLA	62
Goodwin-TOT	55
Young-CHC	54
Womack-ARI	45
Furcal-ATL	40

Saves
Alfonseca-FLA	45
Hoffman-SDP	43
Benitez-NYM	41
Nen-SFG	41
Graves-CIN	30

Complete Games
Johnson-ARI	8
Schilling-TOT	8
Lieber-CHC	6
Maddux-ATL	6

AMERICAN LEAGUE LEADERS

Home Runs
Glaus-ANA	47
Giambi-OAK	43
Thomas-CHW	43
Four tied	41

On Base Percentage
Giambi-OAK	.476
Delgado-TOR	.470
Ramirez-CLE	.457
Thomas-CHW	.436
Garciaparra-BOS	.434

Wins
Hudson-OAK	20
Wells-TOR	20
Pettitte-NYY	19
Martinez-BOS	18
Sele-SEA	17

Strikeouts
Martinez-BOS	284
Colon-CLE	212
Mussina-BAL	210
Finley-CLE	189
Clemens-NYY	188

Runs Batted In
Martinez-SEA	145
Sweeney-KCR	144
Thomas-CHW	143
Delgado-TOR	137
Giambi-OAK	137

Slugging Average
M.Ramirez-CLE	.697
Delgado-TOR	.664
J.Giambi-OAK	.647
Thomas-CHI	.625
A.Rodriguez-SEA	.606

Innings Pitched
Mussina-BAL	237.7
Wells-TOR	229.7
Rogers-TEX	227.3
Radke-MIN	226.7
Ponson-BAL	222.0

Earned Run Average
Martinez-BOS	1.74
Clemens-NYY	3.70
Mussina-BAL	3.79
Sirotka-CHW	3.79
Colon-CLE	3.88

Batting Average
Garciaparra-BOS	.372
Erstad-ANA	.355
Ramirez-CLE	.351
Delgado-TOR	.344
Jeter-NYY	.339

Stolen Bases
Damon-KCR	46
Alomar-CLE	39
DeShields-BAL	37
Henderson-SEA	31

Saves
Jones-DET	42
Lowe-BOS	42
Sasaki-SEA	37
Rivera-NYY	36

Complete Games
Wells-TOR	9
Martinez-BOS	7
Mussina-BAL	6
Ponson-BAL	6

THE YEAR IN BASEBALL

January 19: The owners vote to expand the power of the commissioner's office, giving Bud Selig increased authority.

January 31: Atlanta pitcher John Rocker is suspended until May 1 and fined $20,000 for remarks attributed to him in a *Sports Illustrated* article. The suspension is later reduced by an arbitrator to two weeks.

February 10: Seattle slugger Ken Griffey, Jr. is traded to Cincinnati for four players.

March 29: In the earliest opening day in major league history, the season begins in Tokyo, with the Cubs defeating the Mets 5-3.

April 10: Ken Griffey, Jr., 30, becomes the youngest player to reach 400 home runs

May 24: 16 Dodger players and three coaches are suspended following an altercation with fans at Wrigley Field

May 29: The 11th unassisted triple play in regular season history is recorded by Oakland second baseman Randy Velarde.

September 4: A five-year labor agreement is reached between Major League Baseball and its umpires.

2001

Bonds shatters records, Suzuki gathers awards but A-Rod hits jackpot

Barry Bonds had the greatest offensive year in history: 73 home runs, a slugging percentage of .863, 107 extra-base hits, a .515 on-base average, and 177 walks to go with his .328 hitting and 137 RBIs. What the Giants outfielder didn't have was the most money, which was the $252 million for 10 years given to Alex Rodriguez by the Rangers, or the sympathetic buzz generated by Seattle's Ichiro Suzuki, the first Japanese position player in the U.S. and immediately the winner of the AL batting title.

Bonds or not, Arizona took the NL West, thanks to starters Curt Schilling (22 wins) and Randy Johnson (21 wins, a league-low 2.49 ERA, and 372 strikeouts) and slugger Luis Gonzalez (.325-57-142). Houston won the Central by adding Lance Berkman (.331-34-126) to runs-happy Enron Field, while St. Louis earned the wild card with Albert Pujols putting up rookie-of-the-year numbers (.329-37-130) and Matt Morris matching Schilling for victories. In the East, Atlanta became the first team to reach the postseason with a losing home record (40-41); Greg Maddux won 17. Colorado's Larry Walker took the batting crown (.350); Chicago's Sammy Sosa drove in the most runs (160). The season's most emotional moment on the field came on a game-turning Mike Piazza homer for the Mets in New York's first home contest after the September 11 terrorist attacks.

Ichiro's .350, Bret Boone's league-high 141 RBIs, Jamie Moyer's 20 wins, and Freddy Garcia's 3.05 ERA led the Mariners to the West division title with an AL-record 116 wins. Oakland settled for the wild card behind Mark Mulder's league-best 21 wins and Jason Giambi's .342-38-120. Cleveland got 84 homers and 264 RBIs from Jim Thome and Juan Gonzalez in taking the Central. Tino Martinez (34-113), Roger Clemens (20-3) and Mariano Rivera (50 saves) helped engineer New York's title in the East. Texas didn't go anywhere, but Rodriguez led the league with his 52 homers.

The Braves again swept the Astros in the Division series by limiting Houston's top hitters to a .196 mark. Schilling won twice in Arizona's five-game conquest of St. Louis. In the AL, Moyer's two wins were the difference in Seattle's triumph in five over Cleveland. The Yankees became the first postseason team to lose an opening pair at home, then go on to victory. The key was a Game 3 relay flip by Derek Jeter that prevented Oakland from tying the contest and continuing a rally.

In the NLCS, Johnson broke a string of seven consecutive post-season losses to lead Arizona twice over defensively shoddy Atlanta in a five-game series. The Yankees also needed only five to put away the Mariners in the ALCS; Andy Pettitte won twice and Rivera racked up a win and two saves.

Schilling and Johnson were to the fore again in the World Series when they quickly put the Yankees down 0-2. But then Arizona closer Byung Hyun Kim surrendered last-gasp tying ninth-inning homers on back-to-back nights to Martinez and Scott Brosius,

Barry Bonds
All smiles after setting major league records with 73 home runs and an .863 slugging percentage, Bonds easily won his fourth NL MVP Award.

helping New York to a 3-2 edge. After a sixth-game Diamondbacks thumping, the Series came down to the ninth inning of the finale, when Rivera made a crucial error on a sacrifice and Gonzalez ended up blooping a single for a comeback championship victory. Johnson won three of Arizona's games, the last one in relief.

After the season, Commissioner Bud Selig presided over ownership musical chairs with Montreal's Jeffrey Loria moving to Florida, Marlins owner John Henry joining a group to buy the Red Sox, and all 29 other teams taking over the Expos. Selig denied any conflict-of-interest problems.

2001 SEASON HIGHLIGHTS

NATIONAL LEAGUE

East	W	L	Pct.	GB
Chicago	88	74	.543	—
Los Angeles	86	76	.531	2
New York	82	80	.506	6
Florida	76	86	.469	12
Montreal	68	94	.420	20
Central				
St. Louis	93	69	.574	—
Houston	93	69	.574	—
Atlanta	88	74	.543	5
Milwaukee	68	94	.420	25
Cincinnati	66	96	.407	27
Pittsburgh	62	100	.383	31
West				
Arizona	92	70	.568	—
San Francisco	90	72	.556	2
Philadelphia	86	76	.531	6
San Diego	79	83	.488	13
Colorado	73	89	.451	19

AMERICAN LEAGUE

East	W	L	Pct.	GB
New York	95	65	.594	—
Boston	82	79	.509	13.5
Toronto	80	82	.494	16
Baltimore	63	98	.391	32.5
Tampa Bay	62	100	.383	34
Central				
Cleveland	91	71	.562	—
Minnesota	85	77	.525	6
Chicago	83	79	.512	8
Detroit	66	96	.407	25
Kansas City	65	97	.401	26
West				
Seattle	116	46	.716	—
Oakland	102	60	.630	14
Anaheim	75	87	.463	41
Texas	73	89	.451	43

AWARDS

NL MVP: Barry Bonds, SF
AL MVP: Ichiro Suzuki, SEA
NL Cy Young: Randy Johnson, ARI
AL Cy Young: Roger Clemens, NY
NL Rookie: Albert Pujols, STL
AL Rookie: Ichiro Suzuki, SEA
NL Relief Pitcher: Armando Benitez, NY
AL Relief Pitcher: Mariano Rivera, NY
NL Manager: Larry Bowa, PHI
AL Manager: Lou Piniella, SEA
GOLD GLOVES
NL: Greg Maddux, P; Brad Ausmus, C; Todd Helton, 1B; Fernando Vina, 2B; Scott Rolen, 3B; Orlando Cabrera, SS; Larry Walker, Jim Edmonds, Andruw Jones, OF
AL: Mike Mussina, P; Ivan Rodriguez, C; Doug Mientkiewicz, 1B; Roberto Alomar, 2B; Eric Chavez, 3B; Omar Vizquel, SS; Ichiro Suzuki, Torii Hunter, Mike Cameron, OF

ALL-STAR GAME
SAFECO Field, Seattle
July 10: AL 4, NL 1
MVP: Cal Ripken Jr., Baltimore

POSTSEASON
WORLD SERIES
Arizona Diamondbacks 4, New York Yankees 3
Oct. 27: ARIZONA 9, New York 1
Oct. 28: ARIZONA 4, New York 0
Oct. 30: NEW YORK 2, Arizona 1
Oct. 31: NEW YORK 4, Arizona 3
Nov. 1: NEW YORK 3, Arizona 2
Nov. 3: ARIZONA 15, New York 2
Nov. 4: ARIZONA 3, New York 2
MVP: Randy Johnson and Curt Schilling, Arizona

NATIONAL LEAGUE
NLCS
Arizona Diamondbacks 4, Atlanta Braves 1
Oct. 16: ARIZONA 2, Atlanta 0
Oct. 17: Atlanta 8, ARIZONA 1

Oct. 19: Arizona 5, ATLANTA 1
Oct. 20: Arizona 11, ATLANTA 4
Oct. 21: Arizona 3, ATLANTA 2
MVP: Craig Counsell, Arizona
NLDS
Arizona Diamondbacks 3, St. Louis Cardinals 2
Oct. 9: ARIZONA 1, St. Louis 0
Oct. 10: St. Louis 4, ARIZONA 1
Oct. 12: Arizona 5, ST. LOUIS 3
Oct. 13: ST. LOUIS 4, Arizona 1
Oct. 14: ARIZONA 2, St. Louis 1
Atlanta Braves 3, Houston Astros 0
Oct. 9: Atlanta 7, HOUSTON 4
Oct. 10: Atlanta 1, HOUSTON 0
Oct. 12: ATLANTA 6, Houston 2

AMERICAN LEAGUE
ALCS
New York Yankees 4, Seattle Mariners 1
Oct. 17: New York 4, SEATTLE 2
Oct. 18: New York 3, SEATTLE 2

Oct. 20: Seattle 14, NEW YORK 3
Oct. 21: NEW YORK 3, Seattle 1
Oct. 22: NEW YORK 12, Seattle 3
MVP: Andy Pettitte, New York
ALDS
New York Yankees 3, Oakland Athletics 2
Oct. 10: Oakland 5, NEW YORK 3
Oct. 11: Oakland 2, NEW YORK 0
Oct. 13: New York 1, OAKLAND 0
Oct. 14: New York 9, OAKLAND 2
Oct. 15: NEW YORK 5, Oakland 3
Seattle Mariners 3, Cleveland Indians 2
Oct. 9: Cleveland 5, SEATTLE 0
Oct. 11: SEATTLE 5, Cleveland 1
Oct. 13: CLEVELAND 17, Seattle 2
Oct. 14: Seattle 6, CLEVELAND 2
Oct. 15: SEATTLE 3, Cleveland 1

Home team in CAPS

NATIONAL LEAGUE LEADERS

Home Runs
Bonds-SF	73
Sosa-Chi	64
Gonzalez-Ari	57
Green-LA	49
Helton-Col	49

Runs Batted In
Sosa-Chi	160
Helton-Col	146
Gonzalez-Ari	142
Bonds-SF	137

Batting Average
Walker-Col	.350
Helton-Col	.336
Alou-Hou	.331
Berkman-Hou	.331
Jones-Atl	.330

On Base Percentage
Bonds-SF	.515
Walker-Col	.449
Sosa-Chi	.437
Helton-Col	.432
Berkman-Hou	.430

Slugging Average
Bonds-SF	.863
Sosa-Chi	.737
Gonzalez-Ari	.688
Helton-Col	.685
Walker-Col	.662

Stolen Bases
Pierre-Col	46
Rollins-Phi	46
Guerrero-Mon	37
Abreu-Phi	36
Castillo-Fla	33

Wins
Morris-StL	22
Schilling-Ari	22
Johnson-Ari	21
Lieber-Chi	20

Innings Pitched
Schilling-Ari	256.2
Johnson-Ari	249.2
Park-LA	234.0
Maddux-Atl	233.0
Lieber-Chi	232.1

Saves
Nen-SF	45
Benitez-NY	43
Hoffman-SD	43
Shaw-LA	43
Mesa-Phi	42

Strikeouts
Johnson-Ari	372
Schilling-Ari	293
Park-LA	218
Wood-Chi	217
Vazquez-Mon	208

Earned Run Average
Johnson-Ari	2.49
Schilling-Ari	2.98
Burkett-Atl	3.04
Maddux-Atl	3.05
Kile-StL	3.09

Complete Games
Schilling-Ari	6
Lieber-Chi	5
Vazquez-Mon	5

AMERICAN LEAGUE LEADERS

Home Runs
Rodriguez-Tex	52
Thome-Cle	49
Palmeiro-Tex	47
Glaus-Ana	41
Ramirez-Bos	41

Runs Batted In
Boone-Sea	141
Gonzalez-Cle	140
Rodriguez-Tex	135
Ramirez-Bos	125
Thome-Cle	124

Batting Average
Suzuki-Sea	.350
Giambi-Oak	.342
Alomar-Cle	.336
Boone-Sea	.331
Catalanotto-Tex	.330

On Base Percentage
Giambi-Oak	.477
Martinez-Sea	.423
Thome-Cle	.416
Alomar-Cle	.415
Delgado-Tor	.408

Slugging Average
Giambi-Oak	.660
Thome-Cle	.624
Rodriguez-Tex	.622
Ramirez-Bos	.609
Gonzalez-Cle	.590

Stolen Bases
Suzuki-Sea	56
Cedeno-Det	55
Soriano-NY	43
McLemore-Sea	39
Knoblauch-NY	38

Wins
Mulder-Oak	21
Clemens-NY	20
Moyer-Sea	20
Garcia-Sea	18
Hudson-Oak	18

Innings Pitched
Garcia-Sea	238.2
Hudson-Oak	235.0
Mays-Min	233.2
Sparks-Det	232.0

Saves
Rivera-NY	50
Sasaki-Sea	45
Foulke-Chi	42
Percival-Ana	39
Koch-Tor	36

Strikeouts
Nomo-Bos	220
Mussina-NY	214
Clemens-NY	213
Zito-Oak	205
Colon-Cle	201

Earned Run Average
Garcia-Sea	3.05
Mussina-NY	3.15
Mays-Min	3.16
Buehrle-Chi	3.29
Hudson-Oak	3.37

Complete Games
Sparks-Det	8
Mulder-Oak	6
Radke-Min	6
Weaver-Det	5

THE YEAR IN BASEBALL

April 1: In the season opener, Toronto defeats Texas, 8-1, in the first major league game played in Puerto Rico.

April 2: Yankee veteran Roger Clemens passes Walter Johnson with strikeout No. 3,509 to become the all-time AL career strikeout leader.

April 9: Willie Stargell, 61, dies from kidney failure.

April 25: Rickey Henderson earns his 2,063rd walk to break Babe Ruth's record; On October 4, he scores his 2,246th run to pass Ty Cobb and become the leading run-scorer.

September 11: All games are cancelled following terrorist attacks on New York and Washington.

September 29: Seattle's Ichiro Suzuki breaks Shoeless Joe Jackson's 1911 record of 234 hits in one season by a rookie.

October 5: Barry Bonds hits two home runs, Nos. 71 and 72, to break Mark McGwire's record for home runs in a season.

2002

Tragedy hits Cards as Selig criticized and Randy is dandy

From individual performances to winning streaks to division wins, the season was writ large. In the case of the Cardinals, it was tragically so with the mid-season death of pitching ace Darryl Kile from a coronary attack. In the case of Commissioner Bud Selig, it was embarrassingly so—first in his legally blocked and widely ridiculed attempts to contract Minnesota and Montreal out of existence, then in his decision to declare the All-Star game a tie after both sides had run out of players.

In the NL West, Barry Bonds became the oldest player (38) to win his first batting crown (.370), leading the Giants to a wild card. Arizona took the West behind a Triple Crown performance from Randy Johnson (24-2.32-334); together, the southpaw and Curt Schilling posted a 47-12 record with 650 strikeouts. Albert Pujols had another big year (.314-34-127) in helping St. Louis leave Houston 13 behind in the Central. The Braves were even more dominant in the East, outpacing the Expos by 19 games; the Atlanta bullpen received 55 saves from John Smoltz and an ERA of 0.95 from Chris Hammond. Chicago's Sammy Sosa had the most homers (49), Houston's Lance Berkman the most RBIs (128). Sean Green of Los Angeles had baseball's biggest offensive day when he hit four homers, a double, and a single, good for an all-time-high 19 total bases, against the Brewers in May.

In the AL Central, Selig's contraction-candidate Twins ran away from Chicago as of the second pitch of the season; when Jacque Jones hit it for a homer, Minnesota was on the way to staying in first place all year. Eddie Guardado saved 45. In the East, the Yankees had another laugher with Jason Giambi and Alfonso Soriano teaming up for 80 home runs and 224 RBIs. Oakland put a stranglehold on the West with an AL-record 20 straight victories between August 13 and September 4. Barry Zito won a league-high 23 games and Miguel Tejada earned the MVP for his .308-34-131. The wild-card Angels were steered by Garret Anderson's 123 RBIs, Jarrod Washburn's 18 wins and Troy Percival's 40 saves. Alex Rodriguez of the Rangers topped the home run (57) and RBI (142) columns, Boston's Manny Ramirez won the batting crown (.349), and nobody bettered Red Sox teammate Pedro Martinez's 2.26 ERA.

Bonds hit three homers and Russ Ortiz won twice in San Francisco's Division Series victory in five over Atlanta. Middle reliever Jeff Fassero won twice in St. Louis's sweep of Arizona. In the AL, Brad Radke outpitched Oakland twice in a Minnesota triumph adorned by BUD LITE signs all over the Metrodome. The Yankees and Angels exchanged home-run barrages in their first two of five games, then Anaheim did most of the hitting by itself. Tim Salmon drove in seven for the victors.

In the NLCS, the Cardinals tried to neutralize Bonds by

Randy Johnson
After capturing a Triple Crown with 24 wins, 334 strikeouts and a 2.34 ERA, Johnson was an overwhelming choice for his fifth Cy Young award.

walking him ten times, but that still gave him an opening for six RBIs and next batter Benito Santiago a chance for six more. San Francisco's win in five was capped by three Robb Nen saves. In the ALCS, the Twins took the opener, but then went down four straight to the Angels. Adam Kennedy's three homers in Game 5 were three more than Minnesota hit the entire series.

The World Series also revolved around Bonds, with the slugger reaching base 21 of 30 times and blasting 4 homers. But because that included 13 walks and Anaheim could tattoo Giants pitching at a .310 rate, the ALers emerged with the championship in seven. For the first time in a seven-game set, neither team had a pitcher complete seven innings.

2002 SEASON HIGHLIGHTS

NATIONAL LEAGUE

	W	L	Pct.	GB
East				
Atlanta	101	59	.631	—
Montreal	83	79	.512	19
Philadelphia	80	81	.497	21.5
Florida	79	83	.488	23
New York	75	86	.466	26.5
Central				
St. Louis	97	65	.599	—
Houston	84	78	.519	13
Cincinnati	78	84	.481	19
Pittsburgh	72	89	.447	24.5
Chicago	67	95	.414	30
Milwaukee	56	106	.346	41
West				
Arizona	98	64	.605	—
San Francisco	95	66	.590	2.5
Los Angeles	92	70	.568	6
Colorado	73	89	.451	25
San Diego	66	96	.407	32

AMERICAN LEAGUE

	W	L	Pct.	GB
East				
New York	103	58	.640	—
Boston	93	69	.574	10.5
Toronto	78	84	.481	25.5
Baltimore	67	95	.414	36.5
Tampa Bay	55	106	.342	48
Central				
Minnesota	94	67	.584	—
Chicago	81	81	.500	13.5
Cleveland	74	88	.457	20.5
Kansas City	62	100	.383	32.5
Detroit	55	106	.342	39
West				
Oakland	103	59	.636	—
Anaheim	99	63	.611	4
Seattle	93	69	.574	10
Texas	72	90	.444	31

AWARDS

NL MVP: Barry Bonds, SF
AL MVP: Miguel Tejada, OAK
NL Cy Young: Randy Johnson, ARI
AL Cy Young: Barry Zito, OAK
NL Rookie: Jason Jennings, COL
AL Rookie: Eric Hinske, TOR
NL Relief Pitcher: John Smoltz, ATL
AL Relief Pitcher: Billy Koch, OAK
NL Manager: Tony LaRussa, STL
AL Manager: Mike Scioscia, ANA
GOLD GLOVES
NL: Greg Maddux, P; Brad Ausmus, C; Todd Helton, 1B; Fernando Vina, 2B; Scott Rolen, 3B; Edgar Renteria, SS; Larry Walker, Jim Edmonds, Andruw Jones, OF
AL: Kenny Rogers, P; Ben Molina, C; John Olerud, 1B; Bret Boone, 2B; Eric Chavez, 3B; Alex Rodriguez, SS; Ichiro Suzuki, Torii Hunter, Darin Erstad, OF

ALL-STAR GAME
Miller Park, Milwaukee
July 9: NL 7, AL 7
MVP: None selected

POSTSEASON
WORLD SERIES
Anaheim Angels 4, San Francisco Giants 3
Oct. 19: San Francisco 4, ANAHEIM 3
Oct. 20: ANAHEIM 11, San Francisco 10
Oct. 22: Anaheim 10, SAN FRANCISCO 4
Oct. 23: SAN FRANCISCO 4, Anaheim 3
Oct. 24: SAN FRANCISCO 16, Anaheim 4
Oct. 26: ANAHEIM 6, San Francisco 5
Oct. 27: ANAHEIM 4, San Francisco 1
MVP: Troy Glaus, Anaheim

NATIONAL LEAGUE
NLCS
San Francisco Giants 4, St. Louis Cardinals 1
Oct. 9: San Francisco 9, ST. LOUIS 6
Oct. 10: San Francisco 4, ST. LOUIS 1

Oct. 12: St. Louis 5, SAN FRANCISCO 4
Oct. 13: SAN FRANCISCO 4, St. Louis 3
Oct. 14: SAN FRANCISCO 2, St. Louis 1
MVP: Benito Santiago, San Francisco
NLDS
St. Louis Cardinals 3, Arizona Diamondbacks 0
Oct. 1: St. Louis 12, ARIZONA 2
Oct. 3: St. Louis 2, ARIZONA 1
Oct. 5: ST. LOUIS 6, Arizona 3
San Francisco Giants 3, Atlanta Braves 2
Oct. 2: San Francisco 8, ATLANTA 5
Oct. 3: ATLANTA 7, San Francisco 3
Oct. 5: Atlanta 10, SAN FRANCISCO 2
Oct. 6: SAN FRANCISCO 8, Atlanta 3
Oct. 7: San Francisco 3, ATLANTA 1

AMERICAN LEAGUE
ALCS
Anaheim Angels 4, Minnesota Twins 1
Oct. 8: MINNESOTA 2, Anaheim 1
Oct. 9: Anaheim 6, MINNESOTA 3

Oct. 11: ANAHEIM 2, Minnesota 1
Oct. 12: ANAHEIM 7, Minnesota 1
Oct. 13: ANAHEIM 13, Minnesota 5
MVP: Adam Kennedy, Anaheim
ALDS
Minnesota Twins 3, Oakland Athletics 2
Oct. 1: Minnesota 7, OAKLAND 5
Oct. 2: OAKLAND 9, Minnesota 1
Oct. 4: Oakland 6, MINNESOTA 3
Oct. 5: MINNESOTA 11, Oakland 2
Oct. 6: Minnesota 5, OAKLAND 4
Anaheim Angels 3, New York Yankees 1
Oct. 1: NEW YORK 8, Anaheim 5
Oct. 2: Anaheim 8, NEW YORK 6
Oct. 4: ANAHEIM 9, New York 6
Oct. 5: ANAHEIM 9, New York 5

Home team in CAPS

NATIONAL LEAGUE LEADERS

Home Runs
Sosa-Chi	49
Bonds-SF	46
Berkman-Hou	42
Green-LA	42
Guerrero-Mon	39

Runs Batted In
Berkman-Hou	128
Pujols-StL	127
Burrell-Phi	116
Green-LA	114
Guerrero-Mon	111

Batting Average
Bonds-SF	.370
Walker-Col	.338
Guerrero-Mon	.336
Helton-Col	.329
Jones-Atl	.327

On Base Percentage
Bonds-SF	.582
Giles-Pit	.450
Jones-ATL	.435
Helton-Col	.429
Walker-Col	.421

Slugging Average
Bonds-SF	.799
Giles-Pit	.622
Walker-Col	.602
Sosa-Chi	.594
Guerrero-Mon	.593

Stolen Bases
Castillo-Fla	48
Pierre-Col	47
Roberts-LA	45
Guerrero-Mon	40
Sanchez-Mil	37

Wins
Johnson-Ari	24
Schilling-Ari	23
Oswalt-Hou	19
Glavine-Atl	18
Millwood-Atl	18

Innings Pitched
Johnson-Ari	260.0
Schilling-Ari	259.3
Oswalt-Hou	233.0
Vazquez-Mon	230.3
Glavine-Atl	224.7

Saves
Smoltz-Atl	55
Gagne-LA	52
Williams-Pit	46
Mesa-Phi	45
Nen-SF	43

Strikeouts
Johnson-Ari	334
Schilling-Ari	316
Wood-Chi	217
Clement-Chi	215
Oswalt-Hou	208

Earned Run Average
Johnson-Ari	2.32
Maddux-Atl	2.62
Glavine-Atl	2.96
Perez-LA	3.00
Oswalt-Hou	3.01

Complete Games
Johnson-Ari	8
Burnett-Fla	7
Hernandez-SF	5
Schilling-Ari	5

AMERICAN LEAGUE LEADERS

Home Runs
Rodriguez-Tex	57
Thome-Cle	52
Palmeiro-Tex	43
Giambi-NY	41
Soriano-NY	39

Runs Batted In
Rodriguez-Tex	142
Ordonez-Chi	135
Tejada-Oak	131
Anderson-Ana	123
Giambi-NY	122

Batting Average
Ramirez-Bos	.349
Sweeney-KC	.340
Williams-NY	.333
Suzuki-Sea	.321
Ordonez-Chi	.320

On Base Percentage
Ramirez-Bos	.450
Thome-Cle	.445
Giambi-NY	.435
Sweeney-KC	.417
Williams-NY	.415

Slugging Average
Thome-Cle	.677
Ramirez-Bos	.647
Rodriguez-Tex	.623
Giambi-NY	.598
Ordonez-Chi	.597

Stolen Bases
Soriano-NY	41
Beltran-KC	35
Jeter-NY	32

Wins
Zito-Oak	23
Lowe-Bos	21
Martinez-Bos	20

Innings Pitched
Halladay-Tor	239.3
Buehrle-Chi	239.0
Hudson-Oak	238.3
Moyer-Sea	230.7
Zito-Oak	229.3

Saves
Guardado-Min	45
Koch-Oak	44
Percival-Ana	40
Urbina-Bos	40
Escobar-Tor	38

Strikeouts
Martinez-Bos	239
Clemens-NY	192
Mussina-NY	182
Zito-Oak	182
Garcia-Sea	181

Earned Run Average
Martinez-Bos	2.26
Lowe-Bos	2.58
Zito-Oak	2.75
Wakefield-Bos	2.81
Halladay-Tor	2.93

Complete Games
Byrd-KC	7
Buehrle-Chi	5
Kennedy-TB	5

THE YEAR IN BASEBALL

April 30: New York Mets pitcher Al Leiter defeats Arizona 10-1 to become the first pitcher to record a victory against all 30 teams.

May 2: Seattle center fielder Mike Cameron becomes the first player in nine years to hit four home runs in a game. Three weeks later, Los Angeles right fielder Shawn Green hits four for the Dodgers.

June 18: Longtime Cardinals announcer Jack Buck, 77, dies.

June 21: Luis Castillo of the Marlins hits safely in this 35th straight game to break Rogers Hornsby's 80-year-old record for second basemen.

June 22: St. Louis pitcher Darryl Kile, 33, dies suddenly in his sleep in a Chicago hotel from heart disease.

July 2: A record 62 home runs are hit in the majors on a single day.

July 5: Hall of Fame slugger Ted Williams dies at his home in Florida.

August 9: Barry Bonds joins Hank Aaron, Babe Ruth and Willie Mays as players to hit 600 home runs.

2003

Sosa becomes uncorked in another cursed year for Cubs, Red Sox

Embarrassment surfaced on four fronts. The steroid-related death of Baltimore prospect Steve Bechler in spring training prompted tests that revealed much wider use of supplement drugs than anyone in baseball had wanted to admit. The 2002 All-Star game farce produced the idea that the winning league should have home-field advantage in the World Series. The dubious common ownership of the Expos and failure to sell the franchise inspired the notion of 22 "home" games for the team in Puerto Rico. Cubs slugger Sammy Sosa was discovered using a corked bat in a game.

For the sixth straight year, the AL East teams finished in the exact same order. The latest New York title featured 100-RBI seasons from Hideki Matsui, Jason Giambi, and Jorge Posada, and 21 wins from Andy Pettitte. Boston took the wild card with an offensive powerhouse that established a new team slugging record (.491). Bill Mueller won the batting title (.326) and Pedro Martinez took another ERA crown (2.22). In the Central, the midseason acquisition of Shannon Stewart woke up the Twins for a title. Oakland closer Keith Foulke (9 wins, 43 saves) picked up enough of the slack for an injured rotation to tow the A's into the playoffs. Alex Rodriguez of the Rangers won another homer crown (47), Toronto's Carlos Delgado drove in the most runs (145) and fellow Blue Jay Roy Halliday had the most wins (22). The Tigers set the AL record for losses (119).

Atlanta won the NL East with Javier Lopez and Gary Sheffield combining for 82 homers and 241 RBIs; Lopez's 43 blasts set a season mark for catchers. Russ Ortiz had the most wins in the league (21) and Greg Maddux became the only pitcher to win at least 15 games 16 times in a row. The Marlins turned around their season in June when they brought in 72-year-old Jack McKeon as manager and called up flamboyant rookie Dontrelle Willis (14 wins), going on to earn the wild card. Chicago captured the Central thanks to its young pitchers, especially Mark Prior (18-2.43-245) and Kerry Wood (14-3.20-266). Jason Schmidt's NL-best 2.34 ERA anchored San Francisco's staff in winning the West. St. Louis's Albert Pujols had the highest average (.359), Philadelphia's Jim Thome the most homers (47), and Colorado's Preston Wilson the most RBIs (141). Los Angeles reliever Eric Gagne saved 55 games in 55 tries.

The punchless Twins went down in four to the Yankees in the Division series; leadoff man Stewart was on base eight times but never scored. Manny Ramirez's homer in Game 5 completed Boston's 0-2 comeback against the Athletics; the Oakland loss made it nine times in a row the club was unable to close out a post-season series. On the other hand, the Cubs won their first post-

Eric Gagne
The Canadian-born reliever won the Cy Young after saving 55 games in 55 attempts and extending his overall major league record to 63-for-63 dating back to 2002.

season series since 1908 in eliminating the Braves in five. Ivan Rodriguez's offensive and defensive roughhouse around home plate led the Marlins over the Giants in four.

A fiercely fought ALCS centered around a Game 3 brawl between Boston's Martinez and New York coach Don Zimmer, Red Sox manager Grady Little's refusal to pull Martinez in Game 7, and an 11th-inning home run by Aaron Boone that gave the Yankees the pennant. A Cubs fan's reach for a foul ball in Game 6, Josh Beckett's starting and relief work and Rodriguez's 10 RBIs were the keynotes of a Florida comeback in a seven-game NLCS.

Beckett also starred in Florida's six-game World Series win over the Yankees, sealing matters with a shutout.

2003 SEASON HIGHLIGHTS

NATIONAL LEAGUE

	W	L	Pct.	GB
East				
Atlanta	101	61	.623	—
Florida	91	71	.562	10
Philadelphia	86	76	.531	15
Montreal	83	79	.512	18
New York	66	95	.410	34.5
Central				
Chicago	88	74	.543	—
Houston	87	75	.537	1
St. Louis	85	77	.525	3
Pittsburgh	75	87	.463	13
Cincinnati	69	93	.426	19
Milwaukee	68	94	.420	20
West				
San Francisco	100	61	.621	—
Los Angeles	85	77	.525	15.5
Arizona	84	78	.519	16.5
Colorado	74	88	.457	26.5
San Diego	64	98	.395	36.5

AMERICAN LEAGUE

	W	L	Pct.	GB
East				
New York	101	61	.623	—
Boston	95	67	.586	6
Toronto	86	76	.531	15
Baltimore	71	91	.438	30
Tampa Bay	63	99	.389	38
Central				
Minnesota	90	72	.556	—
Chicago	86	76	.531	4
Kansas City	83	79	.512	7
Cleveland	68	94	.420	22
Detroit	43	119	.265	47
West				
Oakland	96	66	.593	—
Seattle	93	69	.574	3
Anaheim	77	85	.475	19
Texas	71	91	.438	25

AWARDS

NL MVP: Barry Bonds, SF
AL MVP: Alex Rodriguez, TEX
NL Cy Young: Eric Gagne, LA
AL Cy Young: Roy Halladay, TOR
NL Rookie: Dontrelle Willis, FLA
AL Rookie: Angel Berroa, KC
NL Relief Pitcher: Eric Gagne, LA
AL Relief Pitcher: Keith Foulke, OAK
NL Manager: Jack McKeon, FLA
AL Manager: Tony Peña, KC
GOLD GLOVES
NL: Mike Hampton, P; Mike Matheny, C; Derrek Lee, 1B; Luis Castillo, 2B; Scott Rolen, 3B; Edgar Renteria, SS; Andruw Jones, Jose Cruz Jr., Jim Edmonds, OF
AL: Mike Mussina, P; Bengie Molina, C; John Olerud, 1B; Bret Boone, 2B; Eric Chavez, 3B; Alex Rodriguez, SS; Ichiro Suzuki, Mike Cameron, Torii Hunter, OF

ALL-STAR GAME
U.S. Cellular Field, Chicago
July 15: AL 7, NL 6
MVP: Garret Anderson, Anaheim

POSTSEASON
WORLD SERIES
Florida Marlins 4, New York Yankees 2
Oct. 18: Florida 3, NEW YORK 2
Oct. 19: NEW YORK 6, Florida 1
Oct. 21: New York 6, FLORIDA 1
Oct. 22: FLORIDA 4, New York 3
Oct. 23: FLORIDA 6, New York 4
Oct. 25: Florida 2, NEW YORK 0
MVP: Josh Beckett, Florida

NATIONAL LEAGUE
NLCS
Florida Marlins 4, Chicago Cubs 3
Oct. 7: Florida 9, CHICAGO 8
Oct. 8: CHICAGO 12, Florida 3
Oct. 10: Chicago 5, FLORIDA 4
Oct. 11: Chicago 8, FLORIDA 3
Oct. 12: FLORIDA 4, Chicago 0
Oct. 14: Florida 8, CHICAGO 3
Oct. 15: Florida 9, CHICAGO 6
MVP: Ivan Rodriguez, Florida

NLDS
Chicago Cubs 3, Atlanta Braves 2
Sept. 30: Chicago 4, ATLANTA 2
Oct. 1: ATLANTA 5, Chicago 3
Oct. 3: CHICAGO 3, Atlanta 1
Oct. 4: Atlanta 6, CHICAGO 4
Oct. 5: Chicago 5, ATLANTA 1

Florida Marlins 3, San Francisco Giants 1
Sept. 30: SAN FRANCISCO 2, Florida 0
Oct. 1: Florida 9, SAN FRANCISCO 5
Oct. 3: FLORIDA 4, San Francisco 3
Oct. 4: FLORIDA 7, San Francisco 6

AMERICAN LEAGUE
ALCS
New York Yankees 4, Boston Red Sox 3
Oct. 8: Boston 5, NEW YORK 2
Oct. 9: NEW YORK 6, Boston 2
Oct. 11: New York 4, BOSTON 3
Oct. 13: BOSTON 3, New York 2
Oct. 14: New York 4, BOSTON 2
Oct. 15: Boston 9, NEW YORK 6
Oct. 16: NEW YORK 6, Boston 5
MVP: Mariano Rivera, New York

ALDS
Boston Red Sox 3, Oakland Athletics 2
Oct. 1: OAKLAND 5, Boston 4
Oct. 2: OAKLAND 5, Boston 1
Oct. 4: BOSTON 3, Oakland 1
Oct. 5: BOSTON 5, Oakland 4
Oct. 6: Boston 4, OAKLAND 3

New York Yankees 3, Minnesota Twins 1
Sept. 30: Minnesota 3, NEW YORK 1
Oct. 2: NEW YORK 4, Minnesota 1
Oct. 4: New York 3, MINNESOTA 1
Oct. 5: New York 8, MINNESOTA 1

Home team in CAPS

NATIONAL LEAGUE LEADERS

Home Runs
Thome-Phi	47
Bonds-SF	45
Sexson-Mil	45
Lopez-Atl	43
Pujols-StL	43

Runs Batted In
Wilson-Col	141
Sheffield-Atl	132
Thome-Phi	131
Pujols-StL	124
Sexson-Mil	124

Batting Average
Pujols-StL	.359
Helton-Col	.358
Bonds-SF	.341
Renteria-StL	.330
Sheffield-Atl	.330

On Base Percentage
Bonds-SF	.529
Helton-Col	.458
Pujols-StL	.439
Giles-Pit-SD	.427
Walker-Col	.422

Slugging Average
Bonds-SF	.749
Lopez-Atl	.687
Pujols-StL	.667
Helton-Col	.629
Edmonds-StL	.617

Stolen Bases
Pierre-Fla	65
Podsednik-Mil	43
Roberts-LA	40
Renteria-StL	34
Lofton-Pit-Chi	30

Wins
Ortiz-Atl	21
Prior-Chi	18
Williams-StL	18
Schmidt-SF	17

Innings Pitched
Hernandez-Mon	233.1
Vazquez-Mon	230.2
Millwood-Phi	222.0
Sheets-Mil	220.2
Williams-StL	220.2

Saves
Gagne-LA	55
Smoltz-Atl	45
Wagner-Hou	44
Worrell-SF	38
Biddle-Mon	34

Strikeouts
Wood-Chi	266
Prior-Chi	245
Vazquez-Mon	241
Schmidt-SF	208
Schilling-Ari	194

Earned Run Average
Schmidt-SF	2.34
Brown-LA	2.39
Prior-Chi	2.43
Webb-Ari	2.84
Schilling-Ari	2.95

Complete Games
Hernandez-Mon	8
Millwood-Phi	5
Morris-StL	5
Schmidt-SF	5

AMERICAN LEAGUE LEADERS

Home Runs
Rodriguez-Tex	47
Delgado-Tor	42
Thomas-Chi	42
Giambi-NY	41

Runs Batted In
Delgado-Tor	145
Rodriguez-Tex	118
Boone-Sea	117
Wells-Tor	117
Anderson-Ana	116

Batting Average
Mueller-Bos	.326
Ramirez-Bos	.325
Jeter-NY	.324
Wells-Tor	.317
Ordonez-Chi	.317

On Base Percentage
Ramirez-Bos	.427
Delgado-Tor	.426
Giambi-NY	.412
Martinez-Sea	.406
Posada-NY	.405

Slugging Average
Rodriguez-Tex	.600
Delgado-Tor	.593
Ortiz-Bos	.592
Ramirez-Bos	.587
Nixon-Bos	.578

Stolen Bases
Crawford-TB	55
Sanchez-Det	44
Beltran-KC	41
Soriano-NY	35
Suzuki-Sea	34

Wins
Halladay-Tor	22
Loaiza-Chi	21
Moyer-Sea	21
Pettitte-NY	21

Innings Pitched
Halladay-Tor	266.0
Colon-Chi	242.0
Hudson-Oak	240.0
Zito-Oak	231.2
Buehrle-Chi	230.1

Saves
Foulke-Oak	43
Guardado-Min	41
Rivera-NY	40
Julio-Bal	36
Percival-Ana	33

Strikeouts
Loaiza-Chi	207
Martinez-Bos	206
Halladay-Tor	204
Mussina-NY	195
Clemens-NY	190

Earned Run Average
Martinez-Bos	2.22
Hudson-Oak	2.70
Loaiza-Chi	2.90
Mulder-Oak	3.13
Halladay-Tor	3.25

Complete Games
Colon-Chi	9
Halladay-Tor	9
Mulder-Oak	9

THE YEAR IN BASEBALL

June 6: Cubs slugger Sammy Sosa is suspended for eight games (later reduced to seven) after being caught on June 3 using a corked bat.

June 11: After Houston starter Roy Oswalt is injured, five relievers combine to preserve a no-hitter in an 8-0 win against the Yankees.

June 13: Yankees pitcher Roger Clemens becomes the 21st pitcher in history to win 300 games and the fourth to record 4,000 strikeouts.

June 18: Larry Doby, the AL's first African-American player, dies at 79.

June 27: Boston sets a record by scoring 10 runs before making an out in a 14-run first inning against Florida.

September 2: Dodgers reliever Eric Gagne sets a record by saving his 55th consecutive game in a 4-1 win over Montreal.

September 21: Greg Maddux beats Florida 8-0 to become the first major league pitcher to win at least 15 games for 16 conecutive seasons.

November 24: Hall of Fame pitcher Warren Spahn dies at 82.

Chapter 22

Curt Flood's Legacy: One Man's Struggle to Become Free

The former St. Louis Cardinals' star tells how his challenge of baseball authority changed his life—and, ultimately, the course of the game.

By Curt Flood with Stu Black
SPORT Magazine, November 1977

*I*t is an important moment in the 1977 preseason, the first meeting between the coach and his baseball team. In a soft voice, but firmly, quite firmly, he begins talking about what he expects of his players. They face him in a row along the third-base line, silent, attentive. Clearly, he has not only their command, but also their respect. They know that he was one of the most accomplished players of his time.

His time was the late '50s and the '60s. He batted .293 in a 15-year major league career and appeared on the cover of Sports Illustrated *in 1968 under the heading,* "Baseball's Best Center Fielder." He was known, too, for his intelligence and broad interests. He earned money by hitting baseballs, but also by taking photographs and painting portraits. He brought mental agility as well as physical skills to sport, overall perspective as well as concentration on his craft. It is no surprise, thus, to see him now, at 39, teaching, coaching.

Except. Except these are not professional ballplayers, but sandlotters, American Legion players. Their coach, Curt Flood, cannot get a job in "organized baseball." He has tried, but he has the reputation, after all, as "the man who started it all," the man whose 1969 lawsuit paved the way for the freedom and large salaries major league baseball players have today.

To validate his case, Curt Flood had to stay out of baseball a full season, sacrificing a salary of more than $100,000. And when he lost in the courts and tried to come back as a player, he was physically spent and emotionally beleaguered. Very quickly, he left baseball permanently and for seven years sought a new life in places like Denmark, mainland Spain, and the island of Majorca. Now he is back in the States, in Oakland, standing out here with his American Legion team, dedicated, happy to be involved again with his game.

Partly because of what he did in 1969, ballplayers today are making those millions. Curt Flood did not get a cent. The noted sports attorney, Bob Woolf, wrote in a recent book that "the legacy of Curt Flood will live on. The years ahead may prove that Flood left a greater imprint on sports than any Hall of Famer." Here, Flood tells the story behind that legacy. At a time when it has become reflex to criticize athletes in their fight for higher and higher pay, it is instructive to examine, through Flood's story, some of the very valid roots of those fights. His is the story of a battle for rights,

Curt Flood
Shown here with Marvin Miller of the Players' Association, Flood's failed lawsuit against Major League Baseball in 1970 later paved the way for free agency.

and its aftermath, the story of what can happen to someone who dares challenge wealth, authority and tradition.

I guess the thing I like most about major league baseball today is that finally, we, the athletes, are getting what we deserve. For 100 years the Buschs, the Ewing Kauffmans, the O'Malleys and the

George Steinbrenners have been making all the money. I don't mean petty cash either. Millions. Babe Ruth made $80,000. Willie Mays made $100,000. They were two of the greatest athletes of all time, but the only reason their salaries stood out was because everyone else's was so low. Today, a guy like Chris Speier is able to swing a deal for $2 million. What the hell is wrong with that? The athlete is the show so why shouldn't he make a compensatory wage? I hear people today saying that these kids today are all spoiled silly. I tell these people to sit down and shut up. You know what Johnny Carson makes a night? *Eighteen thousand dollars a night* to sit and interview people. Nobody complains about that. But they complained when I played and made $90,000 for six months.

Understand, money wasn't the reason I sued baseball. I sued because I'm a person, not a chattel and not owned by anyone. I sued for my freedom. How'd you like to think of yourself as owned? How'd you like to be controlled by a "reserve clause," to have no choice at all for the rest of your life in where you can work within your profession. For the rest of your life. Literally. That's the way it was. In an attempt to work out some settlement before I brought my case to court, the major league player representatives and I met with a number of owners and their aides. After a lot of haggling, one of the player reps, Jim Bouton of the New York Yankees, laughed and said, "Okay, we can resolve this thing right now. Let's make a man free agent when he's 65." All of us on our side of the table laughed. The owners didn't laugh. In fact, they said no. We couldn't believe it. So Bouton asked them why not. And John Gaherin, their chief negotiator, said, "Because you'll get your foot in the door, then you'll want to be free agents at 55." He was serious.

I was 17 when I signed my first baseball contract and 14 years later I was still bound by terms in it. So I fought back. And I'm still paying a price for that fight. Several months ago I wrote a letter, asking for a job in baseball. My sister sent a copy of that letter and a copy of my resume to every major league club, and I still haven't received even *one* reply. A reporter from CBS recently asked me if I thought I was being blackballed. Well, with the credentials I have, I certainly should have been offered some job in baseball, someplace, a job coaching in some capacity. I'd rather not travel continuously again, but I think I know enough about hitting and fielding where I could really help someone during spring training; let me stay on a kid's butt for six weeks and I'll either make a great fielder out of him or he'll end up hating my guts. Then the rest of the year I could scout the Oakland area, where I live.

But that's nothing more than a dream, I guess. And I've certainly learned, during my battle and its aftermath, about hard reality.

It was October, 1969, when Jim Toomey of the St. Louis Cardinals' front office called to tell me I'd been traded to the Phillies. I couldn't believe it. Twelve years with the team and I'd just been told I was fired. Really, being traded and being fired are synonymous. "We no longer want you" is what they're saying. Ego trip, right? I thought I was the greatest center fielder who ever lived and they didn't want me.

I sat down and thought about it for a while. I was supposed to forget 12 years of my life and just move to Philadelphia. Difficult to do. The next day I received an index card in the mail. On it was my name, "Flood, Curtis," then my contract number, then the words, "You have been," followed by a list of possible means of dispensation—"waived, sold, released, traded." Next to each was a square, to be checked off where appropriate. On my card the square next to "traded" had been checked. They had sent me a form. Twelve years was worth more than a form.

I started to think, "What the hell am I, a used car?" In the next couple of days I talked to a friend of mine, Allan Zerman, an attorney. Allan said I had three options: Either retire, go to Philadelphia or challenge the right of one man to own another. He said the reserve clause was illegal, but that I'd probably lose a court fight anyway, that baseball was too powerful to be damaged by someone like me. I guess I realized that, but I didn't care.

Now, when I decided to fight, a few people in the media, like Howard Cosell, gave me a fair hearing. Most, however, were like Bob Burnes, a St. Louis newspaper columnist, who wrote that here's Flood making all this money and bellyaching, a little spoiled brat; without baseball, Flood would be mopping floors someplace; what the hell does Flood want? What Flood wanted was not to be owned, not to be a slave. I said something like, "Being owned by a baseball team is like being a slave 100 years ago. No matter how much money you make, they just trade you from one plantation to another, depending on how they want the cotton chopped." The word "slave" really brought on ridicule. My adversaries thought it was hilariously funny. They never seemed to understand the philosophical point I was trying to make.

People always ask me if I have a history of being a rebel. The answer is no. I can't think of a time before the reserve-clause fight when I stood up against authority. And I wasn't moved by any psychological resentments toward the game, either. I've always loved baseball. I started playing when I was eight or nine, in Oakland. It was a mixed community, about 50-50 black and white, a working-class neighborhood. There was a park right across from my house and I played baseball there all the time. Frank Robinson and Vada Pinson played there, too. And Tommy Harper, although he was a little younger than us. And Bill Russell, the great basketball player. We had good times.

I still love the game of baseball. I have nothing but fond memories of the guys I played with. So many of them were wonderful companions and unique men. A few of them were geniuses and expressed themselves in that wacky way geniuses often do. Bob Gibson, who was my roommate for ten years, had his own view of pitching. "I pitch like I make love," he used to say. "I go for as long as I can as hard as I can and I don't want any relief." And I once asked Stan Musial his thoughts on hitting. I figured that was like hearing the Ten Commandments from Moses. Stan said, "Hitting is easy. When you get a ball in the strike zone, hit the shit out of it."

We not only had a great time together on the Cardinals, we were a helluva great team. We won pennants in 1964, 1967 and 1968, and two World Series. We were 25 high-strung athletes who would stay on each other. At that time Steve Carlton was with us and back then he had no idea what a great pitcher he was. We would tell him to go out there and just throw strikes, that they couldn't hit him, but he couldn't believe he was that good. One night, I think it was in Los Angeles, he pitched a fabulous game, but was beaten in the ninth when someone hit a ball out. He'd pitched such a great game that the radio guy had him on the post-game show anyway. The first question Steve got asked was, "What kind of pitch did the guy hit," and Steve, still in that pitcher's intensity fog, said, "It was a fastball about cock high." I could imagine those cats in the control room turning knobs and

shouting, *"Cut that off."* We were listening to it in the clubhouse and couldn't believe what we heard. We laughed like crazy and when Steve got back, we demanded an instant replay of the question, and especially the answer. For the next two weeks, we always picked Steve as our "star of the game" and wanted him on the post-game show. Whether he pitched or not.

Because of my love for the guys, and the great relationships I had with them, I was disappointed, I guess, that not one ballplayer came to court when my reserve-clause case went to trial. But I understood the reason. It was the same reason that made athletes accept the status quo for so long. Management could do anything it wanted to you.

Look, I was afraid to challenge management for years, too. From 1956 until 1958, when I was sent to the Cardinals, I was in the Cincinnati organization. My first year in Organized Ball I played in High Point, N.C., and led the league in batting with a .340 average, hit 29 homers, knocked in 128 runs, scored 133. Since I'd earned peanuts, I thought I'd surely get a raise. Wrong. I met with Gabe Paul, the Cincinnati general manager, and he said that while they'd like to give me more money, he couldn't. What you really ought to do, he advised, is go to Savannah, Georgia, have a good year, come back next year, and we'll talk about giving you more money. Right then, under any kind of logical circumstances, you would just say, "I'm going to work for someone else. Someone who will pay me some money now that I've proved some worth." But the reserve clause said I couldn't do that.

I was 19 years old when Gabe Paul told me to come back next year, a kid up against a man whose whole life had been sitting behind a desk and dealing with ballplayers. But in 1969, when the Cardinals traded me to the Phillies, I was 31, a man with numerous business ventures in St. Louis, who had a sense not only of his own individuality, but his worth. I called Marvin Miller, the executive director of the Major League Players Association, and told him I wasn't reporting to Philadelphia. I said I had discussed this at length with my attorney and had decided to sue in order to test the legality of the reserve clause. I said I wanted and needed the help of the association. Miller asked if I were sure I wanted to do this. He said it could end my career and bring me permanent enemies. I told him I didn't care, I knew what I wanted to do.

My attorney friend, Al Zerman, and I went to New York and met with Miller and Richard Moss, the Players Association's chief counsel. After we had talked long and hard, Miller said, "Go home and think about it some more. When you have, if you still want to sue, we'll talk about it again."

So I did that. I went back to St. Louis, thought about it, and decided it had to be done. Some guy making $10,000 a year wasn't going to do it. So two weeks later I went back to New York, alone, and convinced Miller that this was what I really wanted to do. When Miller was finally sure that I was sure, he invited me to the player representatives' meeting in Puerto Rico.

At the meeting, I answered questions from the player reps. They weren't sure what I really wanted. Hell, I was making $90,000 and they thought I might be trying to raise it to $125,000.

They questioned me for about an hour. Giants catcher Tom Haller asked if my suit was tied to black militancy. I told him it was related to the Constitution of this country. When the guys were convinced that I was sincere, they unanimously voted to support me and agreed to pay all the costs of a trial.

When I got back home I heard from John Quinn, the Phillies' general manager. He wanted to meet with me. I knew no amount of money could get me to play, but decided he deserved the courtesy of a meeting. And when we got together, it was a funny feeling. It was the first time I'd been with a baseball executive and felt I had options.

I started by telling Quinn that I had decided to go to litigation, but he still thought he could talk me out of it by offering a contract for over $100,000 a year. Every time I said, "No, money is not what I'm after," he would raise his offer. Then he began offering me automobiles. In his frame of reference ballplayers were only interested in shiny cars, cocktail bars and movie stars. I met with him several more times, out of respect for him, but we were talking different things. The only offer I could have possibly accepted would have been a contract without a reserve clause.

I made a number of attempts to reach an accord with baseball before a trial. In a civil series of telegrams and letters to Bowie Kuhn I said I was a human being and a free agent, not a piece of property. Kuhn, in a nice, friendly letter, agreed I was a human being and not a piece of property, but said I was owned by the Philadelphia team.

Soon after that exchange, the player representatives and I met with the owners to see if a court case could be avoided. For the first two hours, management people talked only about how long a player's sideburns should be. The argument grew hot and heavy over whether the hair should be allowed to come below the earlobe or whether it should remain above it. Someone actually pulled out *a ruler.* After the decision was put off, to be resolved in the future by a committee, we finally got to talk about the reserve clause. That's when Bouton laughingly suggested they let us become free agents at 65, and they let us know that they weren't backing off, that a trial was inevitable.

The trial was a blur. But some of the things that happened at it will always stay with me. I guess memory number one is that of Jackie Robinson coming to testify for me. Jackie wasn't just anybody. He had freed another group of slaves 80 years after Lincoln. He had taken an enormous amount of garbage for every black athlete who followed him. And there he was talking about me, saying, "It takes a great amount of courage for any individual—and that's why I admire Mr. Flood so much for what he's doing—to stand up against something that is appalling to him." That was worth everything to me.

I have other strong memories. Hank Greenberg testified on my behalf. And Bill Veeck. Their support, and Robinson's, was very important to me because you always wonder if you've done the right thing. They were saying I had. Miller said that, too, and so did Moss, and our chief attorney, Arthur Goldberg, the former justice of the Supreme Court. Goldberg and Miller had been colleagues at the Steelworkers union and because of their association and his personal interest in the case, Goldberg took on my case for no fee, only an agreement that expenses and his associates' time—which came to $200,000—would be paid.

I kept thinking, "Isn't this something, a former Supreme Court justice representing me." Because he was running for governor of New York, Goldberg could not spend as much time on the case as he would have liked, but he was around often enough to make an impression on me. I remember one tactic of his as particularly brilliant. He would hold a blank piece of paper in his hand while cross-examining a witness. He would say to the witness, "Didn't you say," then pause, refer to the paper and continue the alleged quote. The witness, who never knew the page was empty, would invariably be

disoriented.

I remember another of our attorneys, Jay Topkis, confronting Joe Cronin, then the president of the American League. Cronin had testified strongly in favor of the reserve clause, insisting it preserved the sanctity of the game. He said he had learned this from his uncle-in-law, Clark Griffith, an old-time player who later owned the Washington Senators. When Topkis opened his cross-examination, he asked if Cronin knew that Griffith had jumped his own reserve clause in 1901 and had become the center of a furor back then. Cronin's answer was a barely audible no.

With the exception of those who were now in management, only one ballplayer or former ballplayer testified against me. Joe Garagiola. First he told the judge, "I wish you were on a bubble-gum card." Then he said that baseball, just the way it was, had the best system anyone could devise.

More than the specifics of the trial, I remember the pressure. Insane. For months I'd been in a pressure cooker. I was constantly being badgered for interviews. I had no time for myself. I was so preoccupied I couldn't keep a close watch on the photography business I owned in St. Louis and while the trial was going on, the business went under. Talk about irony. Here I was in New York City, involved in the biggest court case in sports history, being defended by a former associate justice of the U.S. Supreme Court. and at the same time I'm being sued in some small claims court in St. Louis because my photography business went bust. I'm hearing major legal brains talking strategy during the day and talking to people back in St. Louis at night about paying the light-bulb bill. I felt warped. I had to get away. When the trial ended, I was told it could take months before a decision was handed down, before I'd know if I won. I needed to escape. I left the country.

I went to Denmark, a place I'd visited before. I knew no one cared about baseball there, that I would be left alone and could do absolutely nothing if I wished. When I got there I checked into a Copenhagen hotel and discovered that the Rolling Stones were staying there, too. By watching what was happening to them, I got a view of my own life. People beating on their door and calling them on the phone constantly. It was nuts.

Copenhagen was too hectic for me. I needed more quiet and privacy. I moved to a beautiful little town, Vaethbeck, 15 miles north of Copenhagen. I painted a little. I chased girls. I tried to sort out my thoughts.

About six months after I arrived in Denmark, I read in the international *Herald Tribune* that a decision had been reached in my case. I'd lost. I wasn't surprised. Not really. I'd thought all along—and I've never said this to anyone before, not even privately—that there was no way a black man was going to win that suit. Listen, it eventually took two white guys—Andy Messersmith and Dave McNally—to destroy the reserve clause. Their battles were appreciably the same as mine. I know that a main reason I lost was because I was too far ahead of my time, that before you change a tradition, you need a groundbreaker, need to make people think about the situation, understand it. Okay, I was the groundbreaker. But I don't think I'm being paranoid in also feeling that my color hurt me. You don't think they were going to allow a little black kid to walk away with $2 million, do you? That was the amount I'd sued for.

We appealed the decision and soon after that I got a call from Robert Short, the owner of the Washington Senators, who had bought the rights to talk to me about playing ball. Short said he wanted to talk about a contract. I told him no, the case was still in litigation, that we had an appeal going and I couldn't do anything until I consulted my lawyer. Short said he'd like to come up and see me. I thought, "Sonofabitch, he's in the lobby, he's downstairs." I said, "Come on up." He said no, he's still in Washington, but why don't we meet in New York? I felt tingly all over. I really wanted to play baseball again. It was December, 1970, and I hadn't played baseball in a year and a half.

I phoned Marvin Miller and told him about Short's call. Miller said that he had been the one who suggested that Short make the call. Miller had discussed the situation with Goldberg and they'd decided that because I had missed the 1970 season I had suffered enough damage to make my case viable whether I played the next year or not. Both Miller and Goldberg suggested I come to New York to meet with Short.

Short offered me a contract for well over $100,000. I accepted, but wanted an understanding: If I felt I couldn't make it, I could quit and go back to Denmark. He said, "Okay, that's a deal," and shook my hand.

Short is a first-class person. He assigned a man to spend a month with me in Florida before spring training. The guy's only duties were to help me get ready. He ran with me, pitched to me, hit fly balls to me, gave me as much work as I could handle in a month. Then, when the team came in, Ted Williams, the manager, wanted me to take over and act as sort of team captain, a link between him and the kids on the squad. It was difficult to do because I was in awe of Ted Williams, too; he was such a perfectionist, worked so hard.

Except for Short, no one in baseball—not umpires, players, managers, general managers or owners—ever brought up the lawsuit to me. It was as if 1,000 people had sworn an oath of silence on the subject. But while I heard nothing from the people in my business, I heard plenty from the fans. They really got on me, saying I was greedy. But what the fan doesn't understand is all the athlete wants is a fair share of the tremendous amounts of money people make off sports. When I sued baseball, I sued for modifications in the structure, so that the owner could still make a fair profit without owning a man's body. That's all I ever wanted.

I lasted eight weeks in the spring of '71. That's all. I saw that I couldn't keep up with the kids. I just didn't have the ability to play anymore. I was drained. I wasn't going to take money under those circumstances, so the day I reached my decision, I sent Short a telegram from the Washington airport, telling him I was leaving. Then I flew to New York to connect with a flight to Denmark. To show you how fast Short moves, he had two people waiting for me at the New York airport. They tried to talk me out of getting on the plane to Denmark. But I was gone.

I stayed in Vaethbeck for six months, then moved to Spain, where it was warmer. There I met a woman named Ann and we soon opened a bar in Majorca. We called it "The Rustic Inn" and catered to U.S. sailors from the Sixth Fleet. We did a fantastic business for a number of years. It was an American oasis, an American sports hangout. We had a videotape player in the bar and we showed major league baseball games, Muhammad Ali fights and other sports events. Howard Cosell would send me the tapes.

The Spanish police never understood what was happening. No one had ever heard of baseball in Spain, except the kids off the Sixth Fleet. When the Majorcan cops saw all those black people coming into my bar, they assumed I had to be doing something wrong. Selling dope or something. So they were on us from the

time we opened until we closed. They would search the place like you wouldn't believe. I got sick and tired of being rousted three nights a week. And after a few years I left Spain.

I went to Andorra, but only for a little while. I realized I was bloody homesick. I had long ago lost my case and the appeal, and—remember—I hadn't left the United States because I didn't think it was a great country. I had left because I needed peace of mind and couldn't get the privacy I needed here. But that was long ago. My roots are here. My parents are here. My children are here. People understand what you're saying here. I speak Spanish, but I'm never sure people really get the point of what I'm saying. I knew that for sure when I said to some girl, "Would you like to go to bed with me?" and she said, "I'm really not sleepy."

So I'm back. I've been back since early 1976. Back in Oakland, where I grew up. My mother is still living in the house I bought for her 15 years ago. And Sam Bercovich, whom I consider the world's finest human being, is still sponsoring an American Legion baseball team—the same team that Frank Robinson, Vada Pinson and I played on 25 years ago. Now I'm coaching that team and also coaching a Connie Mack League team that Sam sponsors. I'm working for Sam, too, doing public relations work and commercial lettering for his furniture store. And I'm also making money painting portraits for people.

I love coaching kids, working with them on mechanical skills and teaching them mental agility, teaching them, for example, to always think two plays ahead. I especially make them concentrate on their attitude about winning. All my life people have been telling me it's not whether you win or lose. Well, shoot, if you teach a kid how to lose, he'll be a loser for the rest of his life. You have to have an attitude about losing. You have to know where you made your mistakes, correct them, then kick yourself in the butt and try again.

I'm nearly 40 years old now, and I'd like to try again—in baseball. I hope they'll give me the chance. I did something I thought was right, but that's over now. I know that my action helped get money and freedom for ballplayers of these and future times, and that makes me feel good. But at the same time, over the past seven years I've not made that much money. I've been stripped of my security. You always have a little selfish thing in the back of your mind which asks, "Did I give up too much to do this?" I'll never know.

Curt Flood is sitting in the home he owns in Oakland, sipping beer and answering questions. Near him, tacked on a wall of the living room, is the 1968 Sports Illustrated *cover billing him as "Baseball's Best Center Fielder." It is a large living room and a pleasant house. He lives here alone, next door to his mother. His five children live in Los Angeles with his former wife and occasionally come up for visits.*

"Have you ever been given any award or any kind of recognition for what you did?" Flood is asked. "By, say, the Players Association?"

"No."

"No one has ever acknowledged that you did something?"

"Only my closest friends."

"When you go to major league games, do the players recognize you?"

"It's not like that. These kids don't have the slightest idea who I am."

"Doesn't anyone come up to you, acknowledge you at the games?"

"Fans, yeah. But the players ... " Curt Flood pauses. "The players couldn't care less who I am."

Epilogue

The year after this article appeared, Curt Flood was hired by the Oakland A's as part of their broadcast team. He spent one year with the A's and then set up a foundation for inner-city kids. He was diagnosed with throat cancer in 1996 and died on January 20, 1997 in Los Angeles. Dozens of former ballplayers attended his funeral, and many were dismayed that there was virtually no representation from the current generation of multi-millionaire players who owed so much to Flood.

<table>
<tr><td>*Chapter 23*</td><td># Henry Aaron's Pursuit of an Immortal and His Magic Number</td></tr>
</table>

The baseball world was in a tizzy in April 1974 as Hank Aaron moved to within a single swing of Babe Ruth's all-time home run record.

By Pat Conroy
SPORT Magazine, May 1974

So eager were they to find their own special approach to the Henry Aaron story a reporter and a photographer from *The Atlanta Journal* stationed themselves outside a men's room at Atlanta Stadium throughout the Braves' final game of the 1973 season. If some poor man's body had betrayed him, if he had been forced by nature to abandon his stadium seat at the very moment Aaron delivered his historic 714th home run, the reporter and photographer were going to have that exceedingly personal tragedy as their exclusive story.

The vigil was wasted. The Aaron story, with all its excesses and frequent absurdity, was pushed back till this season. Reporters, stone-eyed and babbling from writing about Henry's quick wrists, his consistency, his concentration and his quiet manner, had a chance to sit back and catch their breath before Aaron would finally depose Babe Ruth as the leading home-run hitter of all time.

The Braves' front office prepared for the inevitable event as though a virgin birth were scheduled at home plate. In an exhaustively detailed media guide, you could learn everything about Hank Aaron. You could learn that through 1973 Hank had hit 128 first-inning home runs, one 14th-inning home run, that Don Drysdale had served the most gopher balls to Hank (17), and that Hank had hit more home runs (36) on the third and 21st than any other days of the month, and the fewest (13) on the sixth day of the month. If this did not satisfy your need to know, you could find "Notable Quotes By Hank Aaron," "Notable Quotes About Hank Aaron," and "Fun With Hank Aaron." Under the magnifying glass of total coverage, Aaron could not pick his nose without it becoming a minor statistic, a footnote in the morning news.

There is something natural about all this. Baseball fans love numbers. They like to swirl them around their mouths like Bordeaux wine. Most statistics are modest, unassuming and without presumption. Other statistics have more body, and by their richness and bite, provide a substantial addition to the satisfaction and mystery surrounding the game. But of all the tonnage of statistics gathered and disseminated about baseball, one number has long stood out, a corona of achievement by which the sport defined and measured itself. The number 714 glowed in the consciousness of American sport like a pale ring around a planet. It was one of the inviolable, unreachable records, woven into the poetry and mythology of baseball, largely because the jockstrap hanging from this totem belonged to George Herman Ruth.

It is not that Hank Aaron is hitting 715 home runs that is news; the news is that Hank is toppling the colossus, surpassing that

Hank Aaron
With this swing on April 8, 1974, Hank Aaron hit career homer No. 715 to pass Babe Ruth and become baseball's all-time home-run leader.

strangely built and powerful man who extended the limits of this game to its furthest frontiers, the man who gave baseball its largest definitions and stretched its mythic dimensions. Hank is usurping the kingdom of the home run from the man who invented the home run. There is something about the home run that belongs uniquely to Babe Ruth and always will. If a man in 1913 could hit

12 home runs and be tagged with the sobriquet "Home Run" Baker, what do you call the man who in 1920 hit 54 home runs? You call him one of the greatest sports nicknames ever conjured up in a press box. You call him the "Sultan of Swat."

The stunning fact about Aaron's assault on The Babe was that he came on so suddenly. For years, Willie Mays was the leading pretender to the throne. Willie made a hard run for it until time sent its battalions up against his flesh. Those of us who loved Willie watched our hero backed against the outfield wall by the caprices of old age, by that semi-death of extraordinary athletes who dance too long, then stumble home in a last graceless waltz that is the cruelest, most public humiliation of sport. Years ago, the world knew that The Babe was safe from Willie. But in 1971, a 37-year-old man hit 47 home runs and the chase was on again. The next year Aaron hit 34. Last year he hit 40 and at the end of the season was staring eyeball-to-eyeball with Babe Ruth.

Aaron is 40 now. A 40-year-old man, in baseball time, should be caring for his sores and drooling in his spikes. But time has treated Aaron like a handmaiden. He, in turn, has taken very good care of his body. His career has been an extended lesson plan in the long-range benefits of consistency. He has always hit well, fielded well and run well. Never has he been flashy or electric. He has retained an animal's sense of pace. Hunters tell us that a pack of wolves can run down an elk, not because of greater speed, but because of a powerful endurance. For years, Aaron was the invisible man of the National League. He played the game extraordinarily well, but nobody seemed to care that much. But now, because of the number 714, and because of the oft-invoked ghost of Babe Ruth, Henry Louis Aaron is one of the most visible athletes in the world today. Even *Pravda* has taken note.

The breaking of the record is pure show business, an event orchestrated by Jaycees, PR men, writers, photographers, agents, owners and men who think they know instinctively that it is good for the grand old game. In the middle of February, the Atlanta front office announced that Aaron would not start in the opener at Cincinnati. "We owe the fans of Atlanta the opportunity to see Hank break Ruth's home run record," they announced. What they were really saying was, "We are going to make a hell of a lot of money during the 11-game home stand of the Braves." If Hank failed to break the record in those first 11 games, the Braves would conceivably pull in 500,000 fans. Furthermore, the event had profitable historical significance: Wherever Aaron's 715th home run landed, that stadium would gain an indelible position in the history of baseball. The exact spot the ball hit was assured of a bronze plaque. If it hit a seat in the left-field bleachers, then that seat would become a number on a tour guide. The pitcher who gave up that most famous of pitches would be a name prized for centuries by trivia aficionados and would probably even be good for a shaving cream commercial or two ("I got creamed"). An Atlanta bank paid 700 silver dollars to the boy who returned the baseball bruised by Hank's 700th home run. The ball that broke Ruth's record would be a far larger piece of history, and a considerably more valuable piece. In the mind of every fan sitting in the left-field stands would be the thought that maybe, just maybe, he would walk away from the park with the most famous baseball ever hit. It would ignite the fiercest scramble in bleacher history. For that ball could be a down payment on a condominium at Costa del Sol. It could send a kid to Harvard. The name of the man or woman who retrieved that ball would be a household word for a day or two. There was that much frenzy approaching the event.

It was also in many ways, one of the most boring sports stories of the century. Every sportswriter in the country searched the rills and slopes of his brain hoping to find the different angle, the fresh approach or a new way of looking at Hank's assault on Babe Ruth's record. They asked Hank every conceivable question. They interviewed every person who had known Hank in the past 40 years, from Vic Raschi, who surrendered Hank's first home run, to Aaron's daughter, sons, sisters, brothers, mother, father, managers, coaches, players, and friends. There was something about the obscenely crowded press conferences with Hank that made a reporter feel like a participant at an orgy. After each game last season, the flock gathered to ask Hank the same watered-down questions and Hank, salivating on cue, would render the same colorless, good-natured answers he had delivered the day before and the day before that. The chase ate up a lot of good words, and left a lot of semi-burned-out reporters staring into the outfield lights.

Last summer the hate mail made a good story. When the epistolary Klansmen took up their pens armed with malevolent rhetoric about a black man surpassing Babe Ruth, it was a grand focus that brought a cataract of mail from well-wishers rooting for Hank and the American way. It is hard to dislike Hank Aaron. Even Richard Nixon said on film that Aaron is what this country's all about. One thing sportswriters agreed upon was that what this country was not about was calling Hank a nigger.

Then the hate mail ended, stopped completely, and there was nothing much to write about anymore. You can describe a home run in just so many ways. And Hank is not the kind of athlete that generates stories by the nature of his personality. He does not get naked and dance on tables. He does not say things that provoke controversy or stimulate fever in the national press. It has become almost a game among sportswriters to farm the dry plains of Hank's personality for a memorable quote, a pungent one-liner or the quiet stinger that would flavor a news release or support a feature.

But Aaron is composed. As he talks to the press, his quotes are redolent with bland, undetectable smells; no condiments or sauces add dash to his spoken prose. He speaks carefully, modulating each word, a soft American voice coming out of the greatest smile in sports. It is a voice that would serve well at SALT talks, behind conference tables, in confessionals or at funerals. It is a voice that has peddled Brut, praised Life Buoy and savored Oh Henry candy bars. It is a voice that has joked with Flip Wilson, sung with Dinah Shore and philosophized with Mike Douglas. It is a voice without blood pressure, reduced and filtered to a cool drone, a voice acutely aware that each time it speaks, 100 typewriters hammer into action and invisible words hum through unseen wires and through the airspace of the world. Hank has a quiet elegance rare in the kingdom of the jock. He has prepared long and hard for his entrance into the limelight and the selling of Hank Aaron.

His chase of Babe Ruth's ghost is going to make him a remarkably wealthy man. In a year's time, he has become a conglomerate. The newly formed Menke-Riback Financial Corporation in Atlanta advises him on land purchases, cattle, office parks, and other tax shelters. After last season, Hank informed a press conference that the William Morris Agency would be handling everything else; they would have prime responsibility for turning Aaron into a national resource. They promised that in the next two years Hank would make more money than in his 20 previous years of baseball. They can afford to talk in such grandiose terms. Hank is the third major athlete William Morris has deigned to touch, following the luminous trails of Mark Spitz and Secretariat. The trinity will make a lot

of money, but you have to wonder at what price. Thus far William Morris has taken man and beast and turned them into straw. Despite what you see in commercials, you hold fast to the theorem that Mark is a more interesting, complex guy than he seems selling Schick razors, that he does, indeed, have a brain larger than a wood tick. You suspect that the William Morris people search for small pieces of personality in their clients and like, bone fragments, have them surgically stripped away. You can only cling to the hope that after Hank has been packaged, programmed, ticketed, and punched, a little of Mobile, Alabama, will linger along with a lot of the quiet, decent man who played this game so patiently and so well for so long. But even if Hank does undergo a William Morris lobotomy, the agency does a splendid job of making their clients very unlike you and me. At a winter press conference, Hank announced that he had sold himself lock, stock and jockstrap to Magnavox Corporation for one million dollars. Magnavox, in turn was humbly grateful to have purchased Hank to peddle their TV sets and record players. In the publicity release trumpeting their deal with Aaron, Magnavox said, "Perhaps most importantly, Henry Aaron is the type of person with whom Magnavox would be proud to associate in its business activities had he never hit a home run." Sure, Magnavox. After the consummation of that deal, no one except William Morris and perhaps Menke-Riback knows how much Hank Aaron is actually worth, but rumor has it that he has entered secret negotiations to buy England.

During the celebrated long winter, Hank was in the news every couple of weeks. Jimmy Carter, the governor of Georgia, made Hank an official Admiral in Georgia's unofficial Navy. Sammy Davis Jr. brought Hank to Hollywood to talk about a movie based on Aaron's life. Mobile, Alabama, the city that spawned Hank, embraced him in a joyous Henry Aaron Day which seemed both ironic and hopeful a decade after Selma. Somehow, all these stories, no matter how yeastless, helped us pass those months when Hank was not in uniform, when the quick wrists were not swinging a bat and when those dark eyes were not glowering at a pitcher 60 feet away. It is not in print but in the batters' box that Henry Aaron is finally interesting and devastatingly articulate. It is on the field that he lends his quiet fury to this often bloodless sport. The memory of the final Braves game of last season is one that goes a long way in explaining what the furor is all about.

On the last day of the 1973 season, 40,000 men, women and children came to Atlanta Stadium to cheer for Hank Aaron, to watch his last attempt to overtake Babe Ruth before the winter gap. The atmosphere hummed with excitement and each person in the ballpark caught the invisible vibrations that trembled through the crowd as though each fan were a tuning fork, sensitive to what only could be felt and not seen. In the press box, 200 reporters, infected by the audible enthusiasm of the crowd, hunched over typewriters. It was an overcast day, but everything in Atlanta seemed clear and bright as though the William Morris Agency represented the entire city and Mark Spitz was smiling just before sliding the whole city into a Schick injector razor.

At times, rare times, a crowd can sing with one voice, cry for the same thing, chant in the same tongue and hunger for the same moment. That is how it was on this day, when the crowd of 40,000 came to honor Hank Aaron. When he came to bat in the first inning, they rose to greet him in a delirious chorus. The city gleamed. The sportswriters tensed. He hit a slow roller between third and short that took a high, corpulent bounce. Aaron looked toward third and raced to beat it out on swift 39-year-old legs. He

beat it out and the crowd sang a hymn of joy.

The crowd relaxed after Aaron had hit. It became a party where people talked to each other. They barely watched the game. In the press box, the reporters fiddled with long columns of numbers like accountants.

Aaron singled twice more that day. Then in the eighth inning, he walked to bat for the last time in 1973. This was the moment of denouement when he would have his last chance before he turned 40 to tie Babe Ruth. The crowd tensed as one. The press box was a place of concentration and silence. Some people in the crowd could not bear to look, but looked anyway. Some screamed just to relieve the pressure. When Hank swung, the whole crowd and every reporter knew that the season had ended. That the chase of the Babe would have to wait until April of 1974. It was a lifeless, wooded pop-up that any of three fielders could have caught. But no one cared who caught it. Every eye on the stadium was fixed on Hank Aaron. Hank slowed up at first base, went past the bag, then ran toward the dugout. It was the final out of the inning. A teammate threw him his glove just as he passed the coach's box on the first-base line. Then Hank turned toward left field and jogged slowly toward his position with extraordinary dignity and grace.

It began in left field. The entire left-field bleachers leapt to their feet in a deafening ovation for this man who had just popped up. Aaron looked up appreciatively and smiled his magnificent smile. It was a moment when men realize why sport is such a powerful metaphor. Then the third-base side of the field was on its feet screaming out their appreciation. Then the upper mezzanines rose until in a matter of seconds 40,000 people had risen to honor this grand statesman of the game. There was an unimpeachable beauty, an untarnished moment when the game stopped and applause thundered in counterpointing waves around the stadium. Hank took off his cap and waved it first at left field, then spinning in a slow, unchoreographed circle he acknowledged the homage of the fans that had come to see only him. It was a translucent moment when a crowd decided to make love to an athlete and the athlete had the superb style to respond in kind. Without question, a man has never received so much applause for a pop-up in the history of baseball.

So the world looks and writes about Henry Aaron and Babe Ruth and this much is certain: A man's life is measured in many ways and all men come to demarcations, those profoundly meaningful points of reference between birth and death which provide memory a place to go back to. Some men remember where they were when they heard the news of Pearl Harbor or when they saw their first convertible. This generation will remember a window on the Texas School Depository and the triumph of the first men on the moon. But the people in the stands the day Henry Louis Aaron hit his 715th home run will bear witness to that moment for the rest of their lives. The memory will sustain and enrich them until that day when some unknown, perhaps even unborn, man who, because of his quick, powerful gifts, begins a long, tortuous chase of what will then be called the ghost of Henry Aaron.

Epilogue

Thirty years later, Aaron still holds baseball's most venerable record. He also holds on to some of the hate mail received during his pursuit of Ruth. After retiring he was hired as a Braves vice-president—where he still works—and became a frequent critic of baseball's poor record in hiring African-Americans to managing and executive jobs. In 1982 he fell nine votes shy of being the first unanimous selection to the Baseball Hall of Fame.

<table>
<tr><td>

Chapter 24

</td><td>

The Day the Yankees Sent a Kluttz Fishing to Bring in a Catfish

</td></tr>
</table>

In this excerpt from Now Pitching for the Yankees, *a former Yankees employee recounts the historic free-agent signing of Catfish Hunter on New Year's Eve, 1974.*

Jim (Catfish) Hunter
When A's owner Charles Finley was late to pay, the pitcher was declared a free agent and was signed by the Yankees to baseball's richest contract.

By Marty Appel

One of the great things about working for the Yankees was meeting people from all over, like Ron Guidry of Louisiana or James Augustus Hunter, the peanut farmer from Hertford, North Carolina. It was like having a free subscription to *National Geographic*.

Hunter was the youngest of nine children, and I give his parents a tremendous amount of credit for raising their youngest to emerge with such self-confidence, self-assurance and decency. No doubt his older siblings helped, and it was of interest to me that Nolan Ryan, a Hall of Fame contemporary with equal dignity, was the youngest of six. Tom Seaver was the youngest of four, Kirby Puckett the youngest of six.

Jimmy was raised to farm, and he hunted and fished, and his career almost ended before it started. His brother Pete accidentally misfired a shotgun while hunting and loaded his right foot with buckshot.

"You shot my damned foot off!" Jimmy yelled. They got him to a hospital, where he lost his small right toe and the use of the adjoining ones. Many thought his hopes for playing pro ball were dashed. (It was very much like Joe DiMaggio, a hot prospect in San Francisco 40 years earlier, badly injuring his knee. Everyone lost interest in him except the Yankees.)

But the Kansas City Athletics gave Jimmy a contract, and their owner, Charles O. Finley, gave him a nickname. Having signed a

Blue Moon Odom, a Jumbo Jim Nash and a Mudcat Grant, he was now bent on having a team with colorful nicknames. He told Jimmy, "You're now 'Catfish' Hunter. You got the name when you ran away from home and came back with catfish for dinner."

The scout who signed Hunter for the A's was another southern gentleman, with the unlikely name of Clyde Kluttz. Clyde had been an average ballplayer, a catcher, but, like Hunter, he was a man of his word, an honorable presence in baseball, and, in his long scouting and player-development career, everyone respected him.

We had the good fortune to have Clyde in our employ at the time. Lee MacPhail had brought him to the organization in 1971 to run our scouting operation. Aside from his unusual name (and he signed a center fielder named Mickey Klutts for us while he was there), he was a delightful man with a terrific wife named Wayne. Clyde and Wayne Kluttz. At work, Clyde shared an office with our farm-system administrator—a former Dodger catcher and Branch Rickey disciple named George Pfister. So it was Pfister and Kluttz. Great baseball names.

Details, details, details. Finley did not like to be bothered by them, but, as an insurance man, he should have been used to them. The whole insurance world was based on details. Actuarial tables, premium schedules, assigned-risk auto policies.

So it was odd that ol' Charlie simply "forgot" to make the final payment on Catfish's 1974 contract in time. And when Cat got himself an agent, Jerry Kapstein, to announce that he was considering himself a free agent because of the delay, Finley was sure he would set things right by just making the payment. It would be late, but it would be paid.

Charlie, for all of his rascally behavior, would lend players money, give them nice bonuses, and treat them to big parties at his ranch. But he could also cheap out on World Series rings, hotel selection, and so forth. You never knew which Charlie you were getting.

It was during the World Series of '74 that Kapstein was telling everyone that Hunter's contract had been voided. It wasn't really a distraction, because the A's themselves were controversial, and something was always going on with them. The '73 Series had been an embarrassment, and here they were, back for more. The Kapstein–Hunter story was just another sidebar.

But things had been going on in the labor movement since Curt Flood had challenged the reserve clause and gone all the way to the Supreme Court with it. Marvin Miller had coaxed the players into a more cohesive union, making them realize that there were more than pensions to be negotiated. The players had come to trust Miller, to appreciate the uncondescending style with which he addressed them, and the depth of his sincerity. Owners would call him an old-fashioned and dangerous zealot, but the players were uniting behind him because he shot straight from the hip and, with just the right touch, connected with them over their common enemy—baseball's reserve clause and those who administered it.

Now Hunter was saying he was free. What might this mean?

In 1967 Ken "Hawk" Harrelson had been released in midseason by Finley over a disciplinary dispute. Finley just cut him loose in the middle of the year. He was hitting .305, and, in an era of pitching dominance, he was one of the league's better hitters and more colorful characters.

Suddenly on the open market, he was able to turn himself into a $100,000 player, as the Red Sox picked him up and made him part of their "Impossible Dream" stretch run. The following year,

the "Year of the Pitcher," he led the league with 109 RBIs while belting 35 homers with his $100,000 contract. That was what free agency was worth then for an everyday position player.

What would it mean now?

It didn't seem to matter; most people thought that there was no way Finley would really lose the guy over just a late payment. But Miller had managed to negotiate a system of arbitration when a grievance was filed, and, as a result, this would not be a case of the commissioner fining Finley and sending Hunter back home. This time, the arbitrator, Peter Seitz, ruled that Hunter and Kapstein were correct—he was a free agent.

Chaos!

Commission Bowie Kuhn quickly instituted a cooling-down period of a few days to let teams decide what to do, but early indications were that the Harrelson days were long gone. We were about to be talking much bigger bucks here.

People looked at the Yankees and wondered whether the now-suspended George Steinbrenner could authorize Gabe Paul to bid for Hunter. (Steinbrenner had been suspended for two years by Kuhn after the Yankee owner pleaded guilty to five felony counts of violating campaign-contribution laws.)

Kuhn later said he had no doubt that Steinbrenner would be involved, and it was foolish to prohibit him from decision making after he'd spent $10 million (with his partners) on the whole franchise. So long as he wasn't publicly seen doing the negotiating, Kuhn let it be.

I was sitting with Gabe Paul and talking about our plans.

"Do you think," I asked, "that this could go over a million dollars?"

"Hell, yes!" he roared, "This is war! It's going to be a lot more than a million dollars!"

Good ol' Gabe. He was playing with someone else's money, and he was loving it.

One by one, teams flew to Ahoskie, North Carolina, to visit with Catfish's law firm, and the wizened old J. Carlton Cherry, Sr. Almost every team made an appearance—sometimes an owner, sometimes a pitching coach (San Diego's Bill Posedel, Hunter's old Oakland pitching coach), sometimes a player (Cleveland sent fellow Carolinian Gaylord Perry), and once even Finley went himself, not too embarrassed to try and re-sign his ace. For the Yankees, it was all in the hands of our director of player procurement and scouting, Clyde Kluttz.

This qualified as player procurement. And boy, did we have the right man on the case.

By today's standards, the numbers are small, but, in the context of 1974, this was an unqualified extravaganza. Baseball had barely made its way to the $200,000 annual salary at this point, with Hank Aaron achieving it. Six-digit territory was still reserved for the elite. Many young players were earning in the $25,000 to $40,000 range. Murcer had been our only $100,000 player since Mickey Mantle. Signing bonuses? Forget it. Multi-year contracts? We knew of one—Earl Wilson with Boston, through his agent, Bob Woolf.

Now the talk was millions.

The bidding war dominated the sports news for weeks. Hunter would take a break from farming or fishing to wander down to Ahoskie to greet visitors at his attorney's office. The media was, miserably, camped out at whatever cheap lodging they could get in Ahoskie, no hotspot for Marriotts, Sheratons or Hiltons.

I am positive that at no time did Catfish close the door to his

house, look at his wife, Helen, jump up and down, and yell, "We're gonna be rich! We're gonna be rich!" Jimmy Hunter took life as it came. Excitement for him might be a pennant, but that was the competitive juices flowing—the real rush of a great athlete.

He was a big kid, picked off the peanut farm, having some fun, playing some ball. If he'd been assigned to grounds crew duty, he'd have loved it—working the soil, having a beer with the guys after work. He could have dragged that infield and pumped his million-dollar arm to "YMCA" with the best of them.

One of my favorite Catfish stories involved him and a team-mate, Nelson Mathews, traveling with the Kansas City Athletics when they were just breaking in. The team found themselves killing time in the railroad depot in Cleveland. Wearing raincoats over their sport jackets, Mathews and Hunter fished out some quarters and had their pictures taken in one of those "four pictures for a quarter" booths. They turned up their collars and posed face-forward and in profile, trying to look as sinister as they could.

When they got their strips of pictures, they headed back into the big waiting room and came upon a little old lady, minding her own business. With Mathews looking to the side and standing a few feet away, Hunter went to the woman and, rapidly popping open his wallet, said, "Excuse me, ma'am, Cleveland Police, under-cover division. Can you tell me if you've seen this man?"

He flashed the strip of Mathews' photos. The woman studied them and then looked up to see Mathews standing a few feet behind Hunter, glancing nervously around the station.

The woman nearly fainted as she silently pointed over Hunter's shoulder, her eyes bulging. Cat turned around, recognized the sus-pect, and began chasing him all around the station as the woman yelled. It was one of the greatest moments in killing-time-in-a-rail-road-station history.

Now this big kid turned Cy Young winner was gonna be rich.

Showing absolutely no restraint, as though giving no thought to the consequences, the owners practically trampled each other with wheelbarrows full of money. What they were doing was not only making Catfish Hunter rich but sending a very clear message to Marvin Miller and the Players' Association: "Hey, this is what you guys are really worth without the reserve clause. This is what you could get on the open market if you were free agents."

The owners still blame the players today, or the arbitrator, but it was their own actions that got the ball rolling. Whatever had happened in baseball between Finley firing Hawk Harrelson in '67 and Finley breaching Catfish Hunter's contract seven years later, it was obvious that it was a call to arms for Miller. And his musket was ready.

I was going to be at a New Year's Eve party in New Jersey with Ron and Mara Blomberg, a date, and Ron's lawyer and his wife. But the plans began to unravel when my phone rang in Riverdale at 10 A.M.

"Better get in here," said Gabe. "We may be signing Hunter today."

I headed for our offices on the final day of 1974 and realized when I arrived that the trip might be for nothing. Clyde Kluttz had persuaded Hunter to fly to New York to meet with Gabe. They boarded George Steinbrenner's private jet and headed for LaGuardia. In the plane was Ed Greenwald, one of Steinbrenner's partners, and it was Greenwald who was writing out the details of an elaborate contract for Hunter and Paul to negotiate. Hunter's

three lawyers were aboard as well.

The Padres, Expos and Angels all offered more money to Catfish, but it was his trust in Clyde Kluttz, almost a father figure to him, that was winning the day for the Yankees.

In Gabe's office, our little elite team of commandos had gath-ered. Tal Smith, Elliot Wahle (the bright young minor-league administrator), and Mickey Morabito, my unofficial assistant without business cards, were present for history. Dave Weidler was there—someone had to be able to cut a check.

"We'll meet with him right here, and if he signs, we'll announce it immediately," Gabe told me. "No delay. As soon as he signs, I'll call you, and you call the press. You might as well start preparing a release, just in case."

We had entered the era of photocopying machines, so that in most places of business you would prepare the release and then run off however many you needed. Indeed, when I traveled with the Yankees, even to cheap Oakland, I would show up with my press notes on letterhead, and they would "Xerox" a hundred or so for me. It was standard procedure now, except at the Yankees.

Gabe had decided that the cost of photocopying was too high.

"Call A.B. Dick," he told me, "and tell them you're with the Yankees and you want their finest mimeograph machine. With a supply of stencils."

This had happened a few weeks before, and the machine had been delivered this very week. If Catfish wasn't jumping up and down when he was ruled a free agent, I am sure that the people at A.B. Dick were dancing when I called. It had to be their first sale in a year, and maybe their last ever.

So, on top of all the responsibility of assembling the sports world's biggest news conference on New Year's Eve, as snow was falling over New York, there I was, reading the instruction manual for the new mimeograph machine, and trying my best to type a stencil without making a mistake so that we might look "first class." All while we were about to pour millions onto Hunter.

The Hunter party arrived around two. Catfish was wearing a pullover shirt and carrying a cup to spit his tobacco juice into. He said "hi" to me, knowing me through our mutual buddy Jimmy Bank. I smiled back and gave him the thumbs-up, as in, "Make it happen, Catfish."

At four, Gabe called me and said, "Start calling the press."

"We have a deal?" I asked.

"No, but if we don't, we'll give them a statement anyway."

So I began calling the press. By this time, at least, we had moved on to touchtone telephones, and I didn't have to deal with the rotary dial any longer. And Mickey helped with the calls, as well as with the mimeographing.

No one was happy to receive my call. Everyone had New Year's Eve plans, and this was right smack in the middle of preparation. I heard groans and sighs and the voices of irate wives in the back-ground. In addition, the snow was falling harder and travel was dif-ficult. If we didn't have a signing to announce, this was going to be very embarrassing, and we were really going to piss people off.

The press began arriving around six. Still no signing. They knew that Hunter was down the hall in Gabe's corner office. We only had coffee to offer them.

My phone rang. It was Gabe. "Come on down," he said.

I went in, and there was Catfish, wearing a Yankee cap. There were about nine of us in the room, and Gabe had popped open some New Year's Eve champagne (cheap, but first class). The deal was done, and the Yankees were making baseball history, as this

great franchise had once been accustomed to doing.

The nine of us walked down the hall to the group-ticket-sales office, the biggest room we had, the one in which Steinbrenner had addressed the entire staff, the one in which we had introduced Tal Smith and then Bill Virdon to the press.

I spoke first.

"Gentlemen, I give you Gabe Paul for a very special announcement, on a very special New Year's Eve for the New York Yankees."

Gabe took center stage and proceeded to say that Catfish had signed literally 15 minutes before. He could think of no other transaction that had been announced so quickly. But this story could hardly keep, and, for tax reasons, they wanted the contract and some of the payments made in calendar year 1974.

The deal was said to be between $2.8 million and $3.5 million. It was still an age when such things were kept quiet. It was revealed years later that the package was actually worth $2,931,000, and that because part of it was deferred and part of it was insurance annuities for his two children, as well as college scholarships; it cost the Yankees only $1,762,836. The actual salary was, surprisingly, only $100,000 a year, plus a $50,000 annual signing bonus for five years, deferred. For all the talk of millions, Catfish was not about to move to a bigger house or buy everyone a new car. (He did get a new Buick for himself for each of the five years as part of the deal.)

Catfish was calm and poised throughout the press conference. He continued to spit tobacco juice into his cup. Neil Walsh, director of special events for New York City, presented him with a fishing pole on behalf of the City. Aside from the Yankee cap, it was the only prop we had for still photographers.

The six New York television stations each got its filmed interview, the written press got what they needed, and, by eight, everyone was departing. Catfish? He was getting right back on the plane for Hertford. He was going hunting in the morning; had to be up early.

I found myself alone with Gabe in his office, the last two left. I said, "This was a proud day for us. This is where the Yankees should be. This can be a real turnaround day for this team."

"Which pen did he use to sign the contract?" I asked.

"Well, this one right here," said Gabe.

It was a 19-cent Bic pen.

"Mind if I take it?" I asked. "I think I might like to give it to Cooperstown."

"No, be my guest," he said.

A few weeks later, at a winter sports banquet in Oneonta, I presented the pen to Kenny Smith, the old New York newspaperman who was now the public relations director at the Hall of Fame. And that little pen that started it all is still on display there.

* * *

The presence of Catfish Hunter on our roster overwhelmed the sports news as 1975 began. He was, for weeks, a household name, the biggest story in America. We decided to bring him back to New York early in January to do a round of media, making up for the haste with which we had hauled out a press conference on New Year's Eve.

Cat would have rather been hunting, but he was accommodating, and, in a way, I think he was enjoying it despite himself.

We booked him on *Good Morning America,* and, when we arrived, we found the Reverend Jesse Jackson in the green room, waiting his turn.

"You related to Reggie Jackson?" said Hunter. "You guys look alike."

I cringed.

Jesse just laughed and said something about wishing he could play ball like Reggie. And then he got Hunter's autograph. It was going to be a good day.

At midday we retreated to the Americana Hotel on Seventh Avenue for a rest and then an informal press luncheon over pastrami sandwiches from the Stage Deli. The New York beat writers who hadn't celebrated with us on New Year's Eve sat around on sofas and chairs and pummeled Catfish with good-natured questions. He took a few pops at Finley but mostly thanked him for the screwup that had allowed him to be a free agent. And he remembered to thank him for past favors, for indeed, cheap as he was, Finley was not beyond reaching into his pocket to help a player in need.

Someone asked him about his salary. In those days, salaries were still pretty personal and not automatically reported through the Players' Association so that everyone knew what everyone made. Hunter surprised everyone in the room by saying, "Well, it will come out eventually; it's $150,000 a year."

After all the talk of millions, that was a surprise.

* * *

You would have expected Catfish Hunter to be our Opening Day pitcher, but we opened in Cleveland, so Hunter was held back for our home opener. This was just as well, because that particular Opening Day in Cleveland was historic and would have far overshadowed anything we were doing.

It was the debut of Frank Robinson, the new player-manager of the Indians and, at long last, the first black manager in the major leagues.

Frank had been the logical candidate for this honor for some years. He had done all you had to do, even as a player, such as managing winter ball in Puerto Rico. He was testy, not the easiest guy to get along with, but he was a smart baseball man and, of course, a great player. Respect did not automatically come with that—a number of his players never accepted him—but the time for a black manager was long overdue, and, to the credit of Cleveland owner Ted Bonda, the time had finally come.

Bowie Kuhn played a big role in finally bringing this about. Jackie Robinson had pushed Kuhn hard on the issue. Jackie had sat with Kuhn in Cincinnati at the 1972 World Series, nearly blind, agreeing to participate in a 25th anniversary salute to his breaking the color line, as long as Kuhn pledged to lobby hard for blacks in management. And true to his word, Kuhn did just that.

Bonda was finally the guy who made it happen. Kuhn was present, along with Rachel Robinson, Jackie's beautiful and gracious widow, lending her blessing and, in a way, Jackie's. Jackie had died of diabetes just days after the '72 Series.

There was a press conference before the game, with Frank, Rachel, Kuhn, and Bonda all present, and one writer asked Bonda if Kuhn had played any role in bringing this about. If so, this would be one of the finest hours of the Kuhn administration.

"No, not at all," said Bonda.

Kuhn went to him later and said, "Frankly, Ted, I was a little surprised by your answer, after all the conversations we have had."

"Oh, commissioner," he replied, "I just didn't want to embarrass you."

The rain was falling hard on this day in miserable Municipal

Stadium, but 56,715 fans were on hand for history. I was really glad that the Yankees were—by the luck of the draw—the opposing team, so that I could witness it.

Cleveland was the last ballpark in which photographers were allowed on the field while the game was going on, and, when Robinson came to bat in the first inning, the scene was utter madness. There were 20 photographers hovering within 20 feet of the batter's box, like a scene from some old Babe Ruth newsreel. In most parks, this practice had ended with the advent of long camera lenses, "Big Berthas," some 25 years back!

Robinson was the designated hitter that afternoon, because he was one of the last playing managers baseball would see (Joe Torre with the '77 Mets and Pete Rose with the Reds in '85, until his banishment, were the last).

Robinson was batting against our Doc Medich, and, on a 2-2 pitch, damned if he didn't line a home run to left that absolutely turned the place into bedlam. Of all of the emotional events I have witnessed in person, this had to rank among the greatest. It was absolutely perfect that he would do that at that moment, and, a year later, when Cleveland fans joined others around the country in selecting the "greatest moment in team history," Robinson's home run was the winner.

We lost the game 5-3, and it seemed only right and proper for it to end that way.

We had only 26,000 on hand for our Catfish opener at Shea Stadium (Yankee Stadium was undergoing renovation), and a huge press corps turned out to see him lose 5-3 to Mickey Lolich. He then lost his next two starts, and suddenly he was 0-3 and everyone was wondering if we had made the blunder of the century, pouring millions into a has-been.

And in truth, because pitchers are human, and humans are fallible, it was certainly possible that he was not going to have a season like the one he had had in Oakland when he won the Cy Young Award in '74. (The Yankees would relive this anxiety with Roger Clemens in 1999.)

But Catfish was never worried, not for a second. He knew that losses were part of baseball, and they didn't bother him a bit. He was famous for being a home-run pitcher, and he had a way of admiring them and then moving on to the next batter.

Catfish didn't win his first game until April 27, when he beat the Brewers 10-1 before 42,000 at Shea. Johnny Carson had already started telling Hunter jokes at 0-3, but this win not only ended that, it set him up for a remarkable season in which he went 23-14 (23-11 after the bad start), hurling 328 innings and 30 complete games in 39 starts. By today's standards, these read like stats from the turn of the century. Some thought the Yankees were trying too hard to get their money's worth in the first year of his five-year deal. But Hunter knew his arm better than anyone, and people trusted his ability to say "enough" if he had to leave a game.

(Reprinted with permission, Sport Media Enterprises, Inc., 2004)

The Postseason

Johnny Bench, Will McEnaney, Pete Rose
After getting the final out for the Cincinnati Reds in the 1975 World Series, McEnaney is embraced by Bench with Rose looking on.

FAMOUS FIRSTS

1884: Providence of the National League is declared "Champions of the World" after defeating the New York Metropolitans of the American Association in three straight games in baseball's first world series.

1903: In the first World Series of the new century, Boston defeats Pittsburgh, five games to three.

1919: The first known World Series fix occurs when members of the Chicago White Sox conspire with gamblers.

1947: The first Little League World Series is played.

1951: Gil McDougald becomes the first rookie to hit a grand slam in the World Series.

1956: Don Larsen of the Yankees throws the first World Series no-hitter and perfect game.

1970: The first strike by major league umpires occurs during the playoffs.

1971: Baltimore plays in Pittsburgh in the first night World Series game.

1992: The Toronto Blue Jays become the first non-U.S. World Series champions.

1995: The wild cards are introduced for the first time in postseason play.

1997: The Florida Marlins become the first wild card team to win the World Series.

Chapter 25

Postseason Play

By Frederick Ivor-Campbell and David Pietrusza

When Major League Baseball and the striking players were unable to work out a settlement of their dispute in 1994, they interrupted a tradition of major league postseason play that traced back to 1871, the first year there was a professional league. National Association teams in the 1870s typically followed the conclusion of their championship (regularly scheduled) season with exhibition games against amateur clubs. In the 1880s nearly every major league club played a couple of weeks of postseason games, generally against major and minor league teams they hadn't faced during the regular season. In the 20th century there had been a World Series every year for 90 years, prefaced since 1969 by League Championship Series to determine the American and National League pennant winners.

Before there was a World Series there were city and regional series. In 1882 Cleveland defeated Cincinnati for the championship of Ohio, and the next year teams in Philadelphia and New York played for the championships of those cities. These were informal series, arranged by the clubs themselves without official league sanction, and varied in the number of games scheduled according to the desires of the clubs involved.

The same held true for the early World Series, which had their beginnings in 1884. Two years earlier, the champions of the National League and the brand-new American Association played a pair of postseason contests (in which each team recorded a shutout against the other). Some would like to call these games the first World Series, but no one in 1882 saw them as more than exhibition games. In fact, because the NL didn't yet recognize the legitimacy of the AA and forbade its clubs to play those of the new league, the NL champion Chicago White Stockings had to release their players from their season con-

Mickey Lolich
In leading Detroit past St. Louis in the 1968 World Series, Lolich was 3-0 with a 1.67 ERA, and also swatted the first home run of his career.

tracts so they could face AA champion Cincinnati as technically independent players.

That winter the two major leagues made their peace, and although a proposed series between the 1883 NL and AA titlists was called off, the 1884 champion Providence Grays (NL) and the Metropolitan Club of New York (AA) played three games "for the championship of the United States." The winning Grays were acclaimed in the press as "champions of the world," and the World Series was born.

The brief 1884 Series set the stage for more elaborate World Series to follow. From 1885 through 1890 the NL and AA pennant-winners met in Series that ranged in length from six games to fifteen.

The demise of the AA after the 1891 season caused a one-year gap in postseason championship play. When the National League expanded from eight clubs to 12 the next year (by absorbing four teams from the defunct AA), it divided the regular season into two halves, with the first-half winner playing the winner of the second half for the title. Boston defeated Cleveland in the postseason championship series, but the unpopular divided season was not repeated (that is, until the strike year of 1981).

Two years later a new postseason scheme was devised when one William C. Temple offered a prize cup to the winner of a post-season series between the first- and second-place finishers in the NL. For four years these best-of-seven Temple Cup games served as the officially recognized world championship. But by the end of four lopsided Series (only one of which was won by the pennant-winning club), fan interest—never robust—had declined so much that the trophy was returned to its donor and the series abandoned.

In 1900, partisans of second-place Pittsburgh felt that their Pirates were the equal of pennant-winning Brooklyn, and a Pittsburgh newspaper, the *Chronicle-Telegraph*, offered a silver trophy cup to the winner of a best-of-five series between the clubs, to be played entirely in Pittsburgh. Described in the press as the "world's championship series," the games confirmed the superiority of Brooklyn's Superbas, who needed only four games to subdue the hometown Pirates.

The upgrading of the American League from minor to major league status in 1901 made a return to inter-league World Series play theoretically possible, but it was not until after the NL and AL had made peace in 1903 that the first modern Series was contested. The owners of NL champion Pittsburgh and AL champion Boston arranged a best-of-nine postseason Series in 1903, which proved both popular and financially successful—a firm foundation for future Series. When the NL pennant-winning Giants refused to meet repeating AL titlist Boston in 1904, press and fan disappointment led baseball's National Commission to establish the World Series officially in 1905.

The end of the 1903 season saw not only the first modern World Series, but also a revival of city and regional series (which had lapsed when the AA folded) in Chicago, Philadelphia, St. Louis, and Ohio. In 1905 the National Commission offered to oversee these series, too, and give them the stability of official sanction. Until the manpower needs of the World War halted the 1918 season a month early (discouraging postseason play apart from the World Series), most of the city and regional series— and occasional series between other clubs, like Cleveland and Pittsburgh, and the Boston Red Sox and New York Giants—were played under National Commission auspices.

After the war's end, only Chicago's Cubs and White Sox resumed a city series; they played 16 series between 1921 and 1942, when World War II intervened. For 26 years thereafter the World Series alone remained of the once multifaceted major league postseason—until the AL and NL split into two divisions each in 1969 and ushered in a new layer of playoffs: the League Championship Series. (In 1981, to recoup some of the money and fan interest lost during a midseason players' strike that split the season in half, a one-time third layer of postseason playoffs was added, pitting the first-half and second-half winners in each division against each other for the division titles—an aberration that made the divisional races even more surreal than the strike itself had done.) From 1969 through 1984 the LCS were played as best-of-five series, but in 1985 they were expanded to match the best-of-seven World Series.

In 1993, the club owners voted to realign each league into three divisions—East, Central, and West—and to install a preliminary layer of playoffs for each league. The three divisional champions and the second-place team with the best record would determine, through a pair of best-of-five Division Series, which two teams would compete for the pennant in the League Championship Series. The first Division Series games were held in 1995.

Key to the Statistics

The statistics in this section of *Total Baseball* are standard—there is little point in applying newer analytical measures to performances that run to seven games or fewer. We do offer, however, stats that were not standard at the time, such as earned run averages for years before 1912 and runs batted in before 1920 (which were determined from box scores and play-by-plays) and saves before 1969. Beyond our powers of reconstruction were the following: runs batted in, stolen bases, and batter strikeouts for the World Series of 1885.

The length of the World Series varied from three games in 1884 all the way up to 15 in 1887 and 10 the following year. The best-of-seven format came in with the Temple Cup Series of 1894 and has been the norm for World Series ever since (excepting 1900, 1903, and 1919–1921). In recent years this format has become the norm for League Championship Series as well. The rules of the day are used for scoring methods, so walks are counted as hits in the 1887 World Series.

If a player appeared at more than one position during the Series, the number of games he played at each is noted (for example, a man who divided seven games at shortstop and third base would carry the notation *ss-4, 3b-3*).

Other abbreviations are as follows:

POS	Position	SB	Stolen Bases
AVG	Batting Average	W	Wins
G	Games	L	Losses
AB	At Bats	ERA	Earned Run Average
R	Runs	GS	Games Started
H	Hits	CG	Complete Games
2B	Doubles	SHO	Shutouts
3B	Triples	SV	Saves
HR	Home Runs	IP	Innings Pitched
RB	Runs Batted In	ER	Earned Runs
BB	Bases on Balls	SO	Strikeouts

PROVIDENCE GRAYS (NL) 3, NEW YORK METS (AA) 0

After a flurry of boasts and challenges, Mets manager Jim Mutrie and the Grays' Frank Bancroft arranged a three-game series in New York to determine which team was the nation's best. These were not the first games between NL and AA pennant winners. In 1882, the AA's first season, champion Cincinnati met NL titlist Chicago twice as part of its postseason schedule, in games viewed simply as exhibition contests. (Each team won one). The next year a postseason series was proposed between champions Boston (NL) and the Athletics of Philadelphia (AA), but the Athletics fared so poorly in exhibitions against lesser NL teams that they refused to face Boston.

The 1884 Series was touted as "for the championship of the United States," but the influential weekly *Sporting Life* established precedent for future Series hype by naming victorious Providence "Champions of the World." The weather turned cold and windy as the opening Series game got under way. A hardy crowd of 2,500 saw the Grays' great Charlie "Old Hoss" Radbourn blank the Mets on two singles. Mets pitcher Tim Keefe, wild at the start, paved the way for two first-inning Providence runs by hitting the first two men to face him and assisted them around the bases with a pair of wild pitches. Paul Hines singled in the third for the Grays' first hit and scored as a passed ball and two more wild pitches brought him home. Keefe yielded only four other hits, but they came back to back in the seventh to produce the Grays' final three runs.

The 1,000 spectators at Game 2 witnessed the Series' closest contest. Keefe and Radbourn overwhelmed their opposition for four innings, but in the top of the fifth the Grays bunched three of their five hits for three two-out runs as Jerry Denny homered over the center field fence. The Mets responded with a run in the last of the fifth, but scored no more before darkness ended the game after seven innings.

The Grays had clinched the championship with their second win, and when they saw only a few hundred diehards in the stands for Game 3, they wanted to go home. The Mets must have regretted their

insistence on playing the game. Although darkness halted it after only six innings, rookie New York pitcher Buck Becannon (replacing Keefe, who umpired) and awful Mets fielding gave Providence 11 or 12 runs (scorers disagreed), while Radbourn held the New Yorkers to a pair of unearned tallies.

PRO (N)

PLAYER/POS	AVG	G	AB	R	H	2B	3B	HR	RB	BB	SO	SB
Cliff Carroll, of	.100	3	10	2	1	0	0	0	1	0	1	0
Jerry Denny, 3b	.444	3	9	3	4	0	1	1	2	0	3	0
Jack Farrell, 2b	.444	3	9	3	4	2	0	0	0	0	0	1
Barney Gilligan, c	.444	3	9	3	4	2	0	0	2	0	1	0
Paul Hines, of	.375	3	8	5	3	0	0	0	1	1	0	2
Arthur Irwin, ss	.333	3	9	3	3	0	1	0	2	0	2	0
Charlie Radbourn, p	.100	3	10	1	1	0	0	0	2	1	3	0
Paul Radford, of	.000	3	7	1	0	0	0	0	0	1	1	0
Joe Start, 1b	.100	3	10	0	1	0	0	0	0	1	2	0
TOTAL	.259		81	21	21	4	2	1	12	3	13	3

PITCHER	W	L	ERA	G	GS	CG	SV	SHO	IP	H	ER	BB	SO
Charlie Radbourn	3	0	0.00	3	3	3	0	1	22.0	11	0	0	16
TOTAL	3	0	0.00	3	3	3	0	1	22.0	11	0	0	16

NY (A)

PLAYER/POS	AVG	G	AB	R	H	2B	3B	HR	RB	BB	SO	SB
Buck Becannon, p	.500	1	2	0	1	0	0	0	0	0	0	0
Steve Brady, of	.000	3	10	1	0	0	0	0	0	0	1	0
Dude Esterbrook, 3b	.300	3	10	0	3	1	0	0	0	0	3	1
Tom Forster, 2b	.000	1	3	0	0	0	0	0	0	0	1	0
Bill Holbert, c	.000	1	2	0	0	0	0	0	0	0	1	0
Tim Keefe, p	.200	2	5	0	1	0	0	0	0	0	4	0
Ed Kennedy, of	.000	3	7	0	0	0	0	0	0	0	2	0
Candy Nelson, ss	.100	3	10	0	1	0	0	0	0	0	1	0
Dave Orr, 1b	.111	3	9	0	1	0	0	0	0	0	0	0
Charlie Reipschlager, c	.000	2	5	1	0	0	0	0	0	0	1	0
Chief Roseman, of	.333	3	9	1	3	0	0	0	1	0	1	0
Dasher Troy, 2b	.200	2	5	0	1	0	0	0	1	0	1	0
TOTAL	.143		77	3	11	1	0	0	2	0	16	1

PITCHER	W	L	ERA	G	GS	CG	SV	SHO	IP	H	ER	BB	SO
Buck Becannon	0	1	10.50	1	1	1	0	0	6.0	9	7	2	1
Tim Keefe	0	2	3.60	2	2	2	0	0	15.0	10	6	3	12
TOTAL	0	3	5.57	3	3	3	0	0	21.0	19	13	5	13

GAME 1 AT NY OCT 23

```
NY   000 000 000    0  2  1
PRO  201 000 30X    6  5  3
```
Pitchers: KEEFE vs RADBOURN
Attendance: 2,500

GAME 2 AT NY OCT 24

```
PRO  000 030 0    3  5  3
NY   000 010 0    1  3  0
```
Pitchers: RADBOURN vs KEEFE
Home Runs: Denny-PRO
Attendance: 1,000
(Game called at end of seventh, darkness)

GAME 3 AT NY OCT 25

```
PRO  120 144    12  11  4
NY   000 011     2   5  9
```
Pitchers: RADBOURN vs BECANNON
Attendance: 300
(Game called at end of sixth, darkness)

CHICAGO WHITE STOCKINGS (NL) 3, ST. LOUIS BROWNS (AA) 3; TIE, 1

Before the start of the final game, the two clubs agreed to throw out Game 2, which had been forfeited to Chicago, leaving the Series tied at two wins apiece, plus the one tie. But after the Browns won the seventh game for their third victory, Chicago manager Cap Anson decided his club should retain its forfeit win after all, and a select committee agreed, leaving the Series in a tie instead of a White Stockings defeat.

Game 1, in Chicago, was called for darkness after eight innings, with the score tied 5–5. The Browns scored first with a run in the second and added four more in the top of the fourth. But Chicago came back with a run in the last of the fourth, and in the bottom of the eighth scored four more on a walk, two singles, and Fred Pfeffer's game-tying three-run homer.

The Series moved to St. Louis for the next three games. Chicago was leading 5–4 in the sixth inning of Game 2 when Browns manager Charlie Comiskey pulled his team off the field, objecting to the umpiring of David Sullivan. Umpire Sullivan later forfeited the game to the White Stockings; he worked no more in the Series. The Browns won Game 3, scoring five unearned runs with two out in the top of the first, and holding on for a 7–4 win. Chicago lost again the next day in a much closer game. The Browns scored first with a run in the third inning, but Abner Dalrymple's two-run homer in the fifth gave the White Stockings a 2–1 lead. In the bottom of the eighth, however, St. Louis scored twice and held on for the 3–2 win.

The Series took to the road for its final three games. In Pittsburgh for Game 5, Chicago overwhelmed the Browns 9–2, scoring four runs in the first inning, and their final three just before darkness ended the game after seven innings.

Game 6 and 7 were played in Cincinnati. The White Stockings won the sixth game by the same 9–2 score as Game 5. The Browns' two runs were unearned, as Chicago's Jim McCormick stopped St. Louis on just two singles. The Browns' victory in the finale was a runaway 13–4, called for darkness. St. Louis' six-run fourth inning typified the game's sloppy play, the runs scoring on five hits, four errors, and two passed balls.

CHI (N)

PLAYER/POS	AVG	G	AB	R	H	2B	3B	HR	RB	BB	SO	SB
Cap Anson, 1b	.423	7	26	8	11	1	1	0	7	2		
Tom Burns, ss-4,3b-3	.080	7	25	3	2	0	1	0	0	0		
John Clarkson, p-3, of-2	.125	5	16	1	2	1	0	0	1	0		
Abner Dalrymple, of	.269	7	26	4	7	2	0	1	3	2		
Silver Flint, c	.143	4	14	0	2	0	0	0	0	0		
George Gore, of	.000	1	3	1	0	0	0	0	0	1		
Bug Holliday, of	.000	1	4	0	0	0	0	0	0	0		
King Kelly, c-4, of-3	.346	7	26	9	9	3	1	0	4	2		
Jim McCormick, p	.214	4	14	1	3	0	0	0	2	0		
Fred Pfeffer, 2b	.407	7	27	5	11	2	0	1	7	0		
Billy Sunday, of	.273	6	22	5	6	2	0	0	1	2		
N. Williamson, 3b-4, ss-3	.087	7	23	1	2	0	0	0	3	4		
TOTAL	.243		226	38	55	11	3	2	28	13		

PITCHER	W	L	ERA	G	GS	CG	SV	SHO	IP	H	ER	BB	SO
John Clarkson	1	1	0.78	3	3	3	0	0	23.0	19	2	3	19
Jim McCormick	2	2	2.48	4	4	4	0	0	29.0	23	8	4	15
TOTAL	3	3	1.73	7	7	7	0	0	52.0	42	10	7	34

STL (A)

PLAYER/POS	AVG	G	AB	R	H	2B	3B	HR	RB	BB	SO	SB
Sam Barkley, 2b	.087	7	23	3	2	0	0	0	1	2		
Doc Bushong, c	.154	4	13	1	2	0	0	0	2	0		
Bob Caruthers, p-3, of-2	.200	5	15	1	3	0	1	0	6	1		
Charlie Comiskey, 1b	.292	7	24	6	7	0	0	0	1	0		
Dave Foutz, p	.167	4	12	1	2	0	0	0	0	0		
Bill Gleason, ss	.231	7	26	5	6	2	0	0	1	1		
Arlie Latham, 3b	.318	7	22	5	7	3	0	0	5	2		
Hugh Nicol, of	.000	1	2	0	0	0	0	0	0	0		
Tip O'Neill, of	.208	7	24	4	5	0	0	0	3	0		
Yank Robinson, of-4, c-3	.174	7	23	5	4	0	1	0	0	1		
Curt Welch, of	.148	7	27	5	4	1	1	0	2	0		
TOTAL	.199		211	36	42	6	3	0	21	7		

PITCHER	W	L	ERA	G	GS	CG	SV	SHO	IP	H	ER	BB	SO
Bob Caruthers	1	1	2.42	3	3	3	0	0	26.0	25	7	4	16
Dave Foutz	2	2	0.61	4	4	4	0	0	29.1	30	2	9	14
TOTAL	3	3	1.46	7	7	7	0	0	55.1	55	9	13	30

GAME 1 AT CHI OCT 14

```
STL  010 400 00    5 7 2
CHI  000 100 04    5 5 10
```
Pitchers: Caruthers vs Clarkson
Home Runs: Pfeffer-CHI
Attendance: 2,000
(Game called at end of eighth, darkness)

GAME 2 AT STL OCT 15

```
CHI  110 003       5 6 5
STL  300 10X       4 2 4
```
Pitchers: McCORMICK vs FOUTZ
Attendance: 2,000
(Game forfeited to Chicago in bottom of sixth)

GAME 3 AT STL OCT 16

```
CHI  111 000 001   4 8 7
STL  500 002 00X   7 8 4
```
Pitchers: CLARKSON vs CARUTHERS
Attendance: 3,000

GAME 4 AT STL OCT 17

```
CHI  000 020 000   2 8 3
STL  001 000 02X   3 6 7
```
Pitchers: McCORMICK vs FOUTZ
Home Runs: Dalrymple-CHI
Attendance: 3,000

GAME 5 AT PIT A OCT 22

```
CHI  400 110 3     9 7 1
STL  010 000 1     2 4 7
```
Pitchers: CLARKSON vs FOUTZ
Attendance: 500
(Game called at end of seventh, darkness)

GAME 6 AT CIN A OCT 23

```
CHI  200 111 040   9 11 7
STL  002 000 000   2 2 7
```
Pitchers: McCORMICK vs CARUTHERS
Attendance: 1,500

GAME 7 AT CIN A OCT 24

```
CHI  200 020 00    4 9 9
STL  004 621 0X   13 13 5
```
Pitchers: McCORMICK vs FOUTZ
Attendance: 1,200 (Game called in eighth, darkness)

ST. LOUIS BROWNS (AA) 4, CHICAGO WHITE STOCKINGS (NL) 2

It was a winner-take-all Series, with the club that won four games pocketing the entire proceeds. Attendance, very good for those days, averaged over 7,000 per game and brought the victorious Browns about $14,000.

The first three games were played in Chicago. The White Stockings won the opener on a sparkling five-hit shutout by their ace John Clarkson. But St. Louis's Bob Caruthers improved on Clarkson's performance the next day, blanking Chicago on just two singles as his Browns turned 13 hits and 13 Chicago errors into 12 runs (in a game shortened by darkness to eight innings). The White Stockings improved their fielding in the next game (which was also called after eight innings), and this time their bats came alive. With 11 hits (including home runs by Mike "King" Kelly and George Gore) combining with seven St. Louis errors, they regained the Series advantage with an easy 11–4 win.

When the venue shifted to St. Louis, though, the Browns battled back. In a back-and-forth battle in Game 4, Chicago tied the game at 5–5 with a pair of runs in the sixth, but St. Louis scored three final runs a half inning later, winning when darkness ended play in the middle of the seventh.

Game 5 repeated an innovation from the second game: two umpires (instead of the usual one), plus a "referee" who stood between the pitcher and second base. The umpiring satisfied everyone, but Chicago, handicapped by their scheduled pitcher's sore arm, lost when they sent shortstop Ned Williamson and right fielder Jimmy Ryan into the box. St. Louis got to Williamson and Ryan for 11 hits and 10 runs as their Nat Hudson held Chicago batters to three hits and three runs.

The finale proved to be the Series' best-played and closest game. Chicago's Clarkson shut out the Browns through seven innings as his mates built a three-run lead— one of them scored on Fred's Pfeffer's homer in the fourth. Rain (and a rowdy crowd which poured onto the field) halted play for a while in the fifth. But the game resumed and the rain subsided. In the last of the eighth, Charlie Comiskey scored the Browns' first run on a single, errant

throw and run-scoring fly out, and Arlie Latham tripled home two more runners later in the inning to tie the game. The score remained 3–3 into the last of the tenth, when the Browns' Curt Welch singled (for only the fourth St. Louis hit), went to second on an infield hit and took third on a sacrifice. Welch then attempted to steal home but catcher Kelly had smelled out the play and called for a pitchout. Clarkson's delivery was poor and bobbled by Kelly, allowing Welch to steal home with a "$15,000 slide" for the Browns' triumph.

STL (A)

PLAYER/POS	AVG	G	AB	R	H	2B	3B	HR	RB	BB	SO	SB
Doc Bushong, c	.188	6	16	4	3	1	0	0	2	4	5	0
Bob Caruthers, p-3, of-3	.250	6	24	6	6	1	2	0	5	1	4	1
Charlie Comiskey, 1b	.292	6	24	2	7	1	0	0	2	0	4	0
Dave Foutz, p-2, of-2	.200	4	15	2	3	1	1	0	3	0	3	0
Bill Gleason, ss	.208	6	24	3	5	0	0	0	5	1	3	0
Nat Hudson, p-1, of-1	.167	2	6	1	1	0	1	0	0	1	3	0
Arlie Latham, 3b-6, c-1	.174	6	23	4	4	0	1	0	3	3	4	2
Tip O'Neill, of	.400	6	20	4	8	0	2	2	5	4	5	2
Yank Robinson, 2b	.316	6	19	5	6	1	1	0	3	2	3	2
Curt Welch, of	.350	6	20	7	7	2	0	0	1	3	4	2
TOTAL	.262		191	38	50	7	8	2	29	19	38	9

PITCHER	W	L	ERA	G	GS	CG	SV	SHO	IP	H	ER	BB	SO
Bob Caruthers	2	1	2.42	3	3	3	0	1	26.0	18	7	6	12
Dave Foutz	1	1	3.60	2	2	2	0	0	15.0	16	6	6	7
Nat Hudson	1	0	2.57	1	1	1	0	0	7.0	3	2	3	3
TOTAL	4	2	2.81	6	6	6	0	1	48.0	37	15	15	22

CHI (N)

PLAYER/POS	AVG	G	AB	R	H	2B	3B	HR	RB	BB	SO	SB
Cap Anson, 1b-6, c-2	.238	6	21	3	5	1	0	0	1	4	0	1
Tom Burns, 3b-6, of-1	.286	6	21	2	6	2	1	0	1	0	2	0
John Clarkson, p-4, of-1	.067	4	15	0	1	0	0	0	1	0	2	1
Abner Dalrymple, of	.190	6	21	2	4	1	1	0	2	0	5	1
Silver Flint, c	.000	1	3	0	0	0	0	0	0	1	0	0
George Gore, of	.174	6	23	4	4	0	0	1	2	3	3	0
King Kelly, c-5, ss-1,3b-1	.208	6	24	4	5	0	0	1	1	2	2	1
Jim McCormick, p	.000	1	3	0	0	0	0	0	0	0	0	0
Fred Pfeffer, 2b	.286	6	21	7	6	0	0	1	4	2	1	2
Jimmy Ryan, of-6, p-1, ss-1	.250	6	20	4	5	1	0	0	2	0	1	1
Ned Williamson, ss-6, p-2, c-1, of-1	.056	6	18	2	1	0	1	0	3	4	5	1
TOTAL	.195		190	28	37	5	3	3	18	15	22	8

PITCHER	W	L	ERA	G	GS	CG	SV	SHO	IP	H	ER	BB	SO
John Clarkson	2	2	2.01	4	4	3	0	1	31.1	25	7	12	28
Jim McCormick	0	1	6.75	1	1	1	0	0	8.0	13	6	2	4
Jimmy Ryan	0	0	9.00	1	0	0	0	0	5.0	8	5	4	4
Ned Williamson	0	1	4.50	2	1	0	0	0	2.0	4	1	1	2
TOTAL	2	4	3.69	8	6	4	0	1	46.1	50	19	19	38

GAME 1 AT CHI OCT 18
```
STL  000 000 000   0  5 3
CHI  200 001 03X   6 10 4
```
Pitchers: FOUTZ vs CLARKSON
Attendance: 6,000

GAME 2 AT CHI OCT 19
```
STL  200 230 50   12 13 2
CHI  000 000 00    0  2 10
```
Pitchers: CARUTHERS vs McCORMICK
Home Runs: O'Neill-STL (2)
Attendance: 8,000
(Game called at end of eighth, darkness)

GAME 3 AT CHI OCT 20
```
CHI  200 112 32   11 11 2
STL  010 002 01    4  9 7
```
Pitchers: CLARKSON, Williamson (8) vs CARUTHERS
Home Runs: Kelly-CHI, Gore-CHI
Attendance: 6,000 (Game called at end of eighth, darkness)

GAME 4 AT STL OCT 21
```
CHI  300 002 0    5 6 4
STL  011 033 X    8 7 4
```
Pitchers: CLARKSON vs FOUTZ
Attendance: 8,000
(Game called in seventh, darkness)

GAME 5 AT STL OCT 22
```
CHI  011 100 00    3  3 3
STL  214 003 0X   10 11 3
```
Pitchers: WILLIAMSON, Ryan (2) vs HUDSON
Attendance: 10,000
(Game called in eighth, darkness)

GAME 6 AT STL OCT 23
```
CHI  010 101 0000   3 6 2
STL  000 000 3001   4 5 3
```
Pitchers: CLARKSON vs CARUTHERS
Home Runs: Pfeffer-CHI
Attendance: 8,000

DETROIT WOLVERINES (NL) 10, ST. LOUIS BROWNS (AA) 5

Even though their star slugger Dan Brouthers was sidelined for all but one game by a sprained ankle, the Wolverines—in baseball's longest World Series, played in 10 different cities—followed up their only pennant with an easy triumph over repeating AA champion St. Louis. The Browns won the opener at home, though, 6–1. They played errorless ball (rare in that era) as pitcher Bob Caruthers held Detroit scoreless until the ninth inning, and drove in the Browns' second run himself with a first-inning single.

The Wolverines came back to win the next three games. They took an early lead in Game 2 and held on for a 5–3 win in St. Louis to even the Series. Then, in the Series' tightest game (played in Detroit) the Wolverines defeated Caruthers 2–1 in the last of the 13th when their pitcher Charlie Getzien led off with a single, advanced to second and third on ground outs, and scored on an infield error. In Game 4 (in Pittsburgh) Detroit's Charles "Lady" Baldwin stopped the Browns on two hits.

Caruthers hurled a seven-hitter in Brooklyn for St. Louis' second win, but Detroit took the next four. Getzien contributed a two-hit shutout in New York, and Baldwin overcame Caruthers 3–1 in Philadelphia the next day. Getzien yielded eight hits the day after that in Boston, but Caruthers gave up thirteen, including two home runs to Sam Thompson, and Detroit took the game 9–2. Back in Philadelphia for Game 9, St. Louis broke a 1–1 tie with a run in the top of the sixth. But the Wolverines scored two in the seventh and a final run in the eighth. The win gave Detroit a 7–2 Series advantage.

Game 10, scheduled for the next day in Washington, was postponed because of rain until the following morning. Detroit's Hardy Richardson opened the game with a home run, but the Wolverines lost an opportunity to clinch the Series as the Browns overwhelmed Getzien with 16 hits for an 11–4 victory featuring a triple play. But that afternoon, in Baltimore, Detroit took the deciding game as decisively as they had lost in the morning, knocking the Browns' Dave Foutz for 14 hits (including four by Richardson and three—including a home run—by Larry Twitchell) as Baldwin held St.

Louis to two hits in a 13–3 win.

The Browns and Wolverines split the final four meaningless games, played in Brooklyn, Detroit, Chicago, and St. Louis.

DET (N)

PLAYER/POS	AVG	G	AB	R	H	2B	3B	HR	RB	BB	SO	SB
Lady Baldwin, p	.316	5	19	1	6	1	0	0	2	2	2	1
Charlie Bennett, c-10,1b-3	.311	11	45	6	14	2	1	0	9	3	5	5
Dan Brouthers, 1b	.667	1	3	0	2	0	0	0	0	0	0	0
Pete Conway, p	.000	4	12	0	0	0	0	0	0	0	2	0
Fred Dunlap, 2b	.150	11	40	5	6	0	1	0	1	0	4	4
Charlie Ganzel, 1b-10, c-7	.237	14	59	5	14	1	0	0	3	1	2	3
Charlie Getzien, p	.391	6	23	5	9	2	0	0	2	3	6	1
Ned Hanlon, of	.291	15	55	5	16	1	1	0	4	5	1	7
Hardy Richardson, of-10,2b-5,3b-1	.209	15	67	12	14	5	2	1	4	1	9	7
Jack Rowe, ss	.354	15	65	12	23	1	1	0	7	2	1	5
Cy Sutcliffe, 1b-3, c-1	.167	4	12	1	2	0	0	0	1	1	1	1
Sam Thompson, of	.393	15	61	8	24	2	0	2	8	3	3	5
Larry Twitchell, of	.250	6	20	5	5	1	0	1	3	0	1	1
Deacon White, 3b-14,1b-1	.233	15	60	8	14	1	1	0	5	2	0	2
TOTAL	.275		541	73	149	17	7	4	49	23	37	42

PITCHER	W	L	ERA	G	GS	CG	SV	SHO	IP	H	ER	BB	SO
Lady Baldwin	4	1	1.50	5	5	5	0	1	42.0	38	7	10	4
Pete Conway	2	2	3.00	4	4	4	0	0	33.0	37	11	6	10
Charlie Getzien	4	2	2.53	6	6	6	0	1	57.0	76	16	15	17
TOTAL	10	5	2.32	15	15	15	0	2	132.0	151	34	31	31

STL (A)

PLAYER/POS	AVG	G	AB	R	H	2B	3B	HR	RB	BB	SO	SB
Jack Boyle, c	.208	6	24	1	5	0	0	0	2	0	4	0
Doc Bushong, c	.333	9	33	3	11	0	0	0	1	4	1	0
Bob Caruthers, p-8, of-3	.255	10	47	2	12	0	0	0	3	1	1	3
Charlie Comiskey, 1b-14, of-1	.317	15	63	8	20	2	0	0	5	1	1	4
Dave Foutz, of-11, p-3,1b-1	.197	15	61	4	12	2	1	0	3	2	3	0
Bill Gleason, ss	.212	13	52	3	11	0	0	0	1	3	2	1
Silver King, p	.071	4	14	0	1	0	0	0	1	0	3	0
Arlie Latham, 3b	.388	15	67	12	26	1	0	1	2	9	2	15
Harry Lyons, ss	.375	2	8	3	3	0	0	0	2	1	0	0
Tip O'Neill, of	.200	15	65	7	13	2	1	1	9	0	2	0
Yank Robinson, 2b	.446	15	56	5	25	5	1	0	4	10	6	4
Curt Welch, of	.207	15	58	6	12	3	1	1	8	0	2	1
TOTAL	.276		548	54	151	15	4	3	41	31	27	28

PITCHER	W	L	ERA	G	GS	CG	SV	SHO	IP	H	ER	BB	SO
Bob Caruthers	4	4	2.13	8	8	8	0	0	71.2	76	17	12	19
Dave Foutz	0	3	3.46	3	3	3	0	0	26.0	45	10	9	6
Silver King	1	3	2.03	4	4	4	0	0	31.0	28	7	2	21
TOTAL	5	10	2.38	15	15	15	0	0	128.2	149	34	23	46

GAME 1 AT STL OCT 10
STL 200 040 000 6 16 0
DET 000 000 001 1 5 5
Pitchers: CARUTHERS vs GETZIEN
Attendance: 4,208

GAME 2 AT STL OCT 11
DET 022 000 100 5 12 2
STL 000 000 120 3 10 7
Pitchers: CONWAY vs FOUTZ
Attendance: 6,408

GAME 3 AT DET OCT 12
STL 010 000 000 000 0 1 16 7
DET 000 000 010 000 1 2 7 1
Pitchers: CARUTHERS vs GETZIEN
Attendance: 4,509

GAME 4 AT PIT OCT 13
DET 410 012 000 8 12 1
STL 000 000 000 0 5 6
Pitchers: BALDWIN vs KING
Attendance: 2,447

GAME 5 AT BRO OCT 14
STL 200 002 100 5 7 4
DET 000 020 000 2 8 5
Pitchers: CARUTHERS vs CONWAY
Attendance: 6,796

GAME 6 AT NY OCT 15
DET 330 000 003 9 15 1
STL 000 000 000 0 5 8
Pitchers: GETZIEN vs FOUTZ
Attendance: 5,797

GAME 7 AT PHI OCT 17
STL 000 000 001 1 10 1
DET 030 000 00X 3 7 1
Pitchers: CARUTHERS vs BALDWIN
Home Runs: O'Neill-STL
Attendance: 6,478

GAME 8 AT BOS OCT 18
DET 031 003 200 9 17 2
STL 100 001 000 2 10 5
Pitchers: GETZIEN vs CARUTHERS
Home Runs: Thompson-DET (2)
Attendance: 2,891

GAME 9 AT PHI OCT 19
STL 000 101 000 2 9 2
DET 000 100 21X 4 6 3
Pitchers: KING vs CONWAY
Attendance: 2,389

GAME 10 AT WAS OCT 21 (AM)
DET 200 010 001 4 9 3
STL 200 031 41X 11 19 5
Pitchers: GETZIEN vs CARUTHERS
Home Runs: Latham-STL, Welch-STL, Richardson-DET
Attendance: 1,261

GAME 11 AT BAL OCT 21 (PM)
STL 110 010 000 3 4 7
DET 100 344 10X 13 18 7
Pitchers: FOUTZ vs BALDWIN
Home Runs: Twitchell-DET
Attendance: 2,707
(Detroit wins best of 15 series 8 to 3)

GAME 12 AT BRO OCT 22
DET 000 100 0   1 6 3
STL 410 000 X   5 12 2
Pitchers: CONWAY vs KING
Attendance: 1,138
(Game called in seventh, darkness)

GAME 13 AT DET OCT 24
DET 020 100 120 6 14 3
STL 100 010 001 3 5 5
Pitchers: BALDWIN vs CARUTHERS
Attendance: 3,389

GAME 14 AT CHI OCT 25
STL 000 002 100 3 10 5
DET 300 100 00X 4 4 4
Pitchers: KING vs GETZIEN
Attendance: 378

GAME 15 AT STL OCT 26
STL 340 110   9 13 5
DET 011 000   2 9 7
Pitchers: CARUTHERS vs BALDWIN
Attendance: 659
(Game called after sixth, cold)

NEW YORK GIANTS (NL) 6, ST. LOUIS BROWNS (AA) 4

St. Louis, AA champions for the fourth straight year, battled the Giants closely through several games, but blowout losses in Games 6 and 8 undid them. The first three games were played in New York. In a splendidly pitched opener, Browns ace Charles "Silver" King held New York to two hits and a walk while Giants ace Tim Keefe limited the Browns to three hits and a walk, striking out nine on his way to a narrow 2–1 win. St. Louis evened the Series in Game 2 behind the shutout pitching of Elton "Icebox" Chamberlain. Tommy McCarthy scored the Browns' first run in the second inning when, after singling, he moved around to third on two passed balls by Giants catcher Buck Ewing and came home on Ewing's failed attempt to throw out a runner stealing second. Two more runs in the ninth gave St. Louis more than enough insurance for the win.

The Giants scored twice in the first inning of Game 3, and increased their lead to 4–0 before allowing St. Louis a pair of harmless runs in the final innings. They also scored first and led all the way in Game 4 (played in Brooklyn). The Browns took a 4–1 lead into the bottom of the eighth in Game 5 (in New York), but a five-run Giants rally reversed the lead—and the outcome—as the game was called for darkness with St. Louis at bat in the ninth.

Mickey Welch hurled a three-hitter (in Philadelphia) two days later, but St. Louis, capitalizing on walks and a questionable "safe" call at home, carried a 4–1 lead into the sixth inning. New York exploded in the late innings for 11 runs.

The final four games were played in St. Louis. The Browns spoiled New York's hope of quick victory in Game 7, coming from behind to tie the score with three runs in the fourth, and—after New York had scored twice in the sixth—recovering again with a four-run eighth for a 7–5 lead before darkness again halted play after eight innings. But the Browns' win only delayed the inevitable. The Giants hammered Icebox Chamberlain for 12 hits in Game 8 (including home runs by Buck Ewing and Mike Tiernan) to clinch their first world championship with an 11–3 win.

NY (N)

PLAYER/POS	AVG	G	AB	R	H	2B	3B	HR	RB	BB	SO	SB
Willard Brown, c	.375	2	8	1	3	1	0	0	0	0	0	0
Roger Connor, 1b	.304	7	23	7	7	1	2	0	3	4	0	4
Ed Crane, p	.143	2	7	1	1	0	0	0	2	0	1	0
Buck Ewing, c-6,1b-1	.346	7	26	9	9	0	2	1	6	1	3	5
Bill George, p-1,1b-1	.333	2	9	2	3	1	0	1	4	0	2	0
George Gore, of-2,3b-1	.455	3	11	5	5	1	0	0	0	2	2	2
Gil Hatfield, p-1,2b-1, ss-1	.250	2	8	2	2	0	0	0	1	1	2	1
Tim Keefe, p	.091	4	11	2	1	0	0	0	0	2	2	1
Pat Murphy, c	.100	3	10	1	1	0	0	0	1	0	0	0
Jim O'Rourke, of-7,1b-2, ss-1	.222	1	36	4	8	0	0	1	4	2	3
Danny Richardson, 2b	.167	9	36	6	6	2	0	0	6	3	5	3
Mike Slattery, of-10,2b-1	.205	10	39	6	8	2	0	0	5	0	5	6
Mike Tiernan, of	.342	1	38	8	13	0	0	1	6	8	2	5
Cannonball Titcomb, p-1, of-1	.500	1	4	1	2	1	0	0	1	0	0	0
John Ward, ss	.379	8	29	4	11	1	0	0	6	1	0	6
Mickey Welch, p	.286	2	7	2	2	0	0	0	1	0	0	0
Art Whitney, 3b-9, of-1	.324	1	37	7	12	0	1	0	12	1	4	2
TOTAL	.277		339	64	94	10	5	3	55	27	30	38

PITCHER	W	L	ERA	G	GS	CG	SV	SHO	IP	H	ER	BB	SO
Ed Crane	1	1	2.12	2	2	2	0	0	17.0	15	4	6	12
Bill George	0	1	7.20	1	1	1	0	0	10.0	15	8	3	4
Gil Hatfield	0	0	12.60	1	0	0	0	0	5.0	12	7	3	2
Tim Keefe	4	0	0.51	4	4	4	0	0	35.0	18	2	9	30
Cannonball Titcomb	0	1	6.75	1	1	0	0	0	4.0	5	3	2	2
Mickey Welch	1	1	2.65	2	2	2	0	0	17.0	10	5	9	2
TOTAL	6	4	2.97	11	10	9	0	0	88.0	75	29	32	52

STL (A)

PLAYER/POS	AVG	G	AB	R	H	2B	3B	HR	RB	BB	SO	SB
Jack Boyle, c-4, of-1	.438	4	16	4	7	0	1	0	4	2	2	3
Icebox Chamberlain, p	.000	5	13	3	0	0	0	0	0	4	3	1
Charlie Comiskey, 1b-10, of-1	.268	10	41	6	11	1	1	0	3	1	1	4
Jim Devlin, p	.000	1	3	0	0	0	0	0	0	0	0	0
Ed Herr, of	.091	3	11	2	1	0	0	0	0	0	5	1
Silver King, p	.067	5	15	1	1	0	0	0	0	1	6	0
Arlie Latham, 3b	.250	1	40	10	10	0	0	0	3	5	6	11
Harry Lyons, of	.118	5	17	0	2	0	0	0	1	1	5	0
Tommy McCarthy, of	.244	1	41	10	10	1	0	1	9	0	0	6
Jocko Milligan, c-8,1b-1	.400	8	25	5	10	2	1	0	4	3	3	0
Tip O'Neill, of	.243	10	37	8	9	1	0	2	11	6	3	0
Yank Robinson, 2b	.250	1	36	7	9	2	1	0	7	6	12	2
Bill White, ss	.143	10	35	4	5	1	0	0	4	3	6	1
TOTAL	.227		330	60	75	8	4	3	46	32	52	29

PITCHER	W	L	ERA	G	GS	CG	SV	SHO	IP	H	ER	BB	SO
Icebox Chamberlain	2	3	5.32	5	5	5	0	1	44.0	52	26	16	13
Jim Devlin	1	0	2.57	1	0	0	0	0	7.0	5	2	2	5
Silver King	1	3	2.31	5	5	4	0	0	35.0	37	9	9	12
TOTAL	4	6	3.87	11	10	9	0	1	86.0	94	37	27	30

The final two games meant nothing to the outcome, and both clubs used reserve pitchers in Game 9.

GAME 1 AT NY OCT 16
STL 001 000 000   1 3 5
NY 011 000 00X   2 2 4
Pitchers: KING vs KEEFE
Attendance: 4,876

GAME 2 AT NY OCT 17
STL 010 000 002   3 7 4
NY 000 000 001   1 6 1
Pitchers: CHAMBERLAIN vs WELCH
Attendance: 5,575

GAME 3 AT NY OCT 18
STL 000 000 011   2 5 5
NY 200 100 10X   4 5 2
Pitchers: KING vs KEEFE
Attendance: 5,780

GAME 4 AT BRO OCT 19
NY 104 010 000   6 8 2
STL 001 000 020   3 7 4
Pitchers: CRANE vs CHAMBERLAIN
Attendance: 3,062

GAME 5 AT NY OCT 20
STL 003 001 00   4 5 5
NY 100 000 05   6 9 2
Pitchers: KING vs KEEFE
Attendance: 9,124
(Game called at end of eighth, darkness)

GAME 6 AT PHI OCT 22
NY 000 103 35   12 13 5
STL 301 000 01   5 3 7
Pitchers: WELCH vs CHAMBERLAIN
Attendance: 3,281
(Game called at end of eighth, darkness)

GAME 7 AT STL OCT 24
NY 030 002 00   5 11 3
STL 000 300 04   7 8 3
Pitchers: CRANE vs KING
Attendance: 4,624
(Game called at end of eighth, darkness)

GAME 8 AT STL OCT 25
NY 103 100 006   11 12 2
STL 000 100 110   3 5 6
Pitchers: KEEFE vs CHAMBERLAIN
Home Runs: Ewing-NY, Tiernan-NY

GAME 9 AT STL OCT 26
STL 140 020 2023   14 15 4
NY 035 000 1200   11 14 5
Pitchers: King, DEVLIN (4) vs GEORGE
Home Runs: O'Neill-STL
Attendance: 711

GAME 10 AT STL OCT 27
STL 010 505 421   18 17 3
NY 310 000 021   7 13 8
Pitchers: CHAMBERLAIN vs TITCOMB, Hatfield (5)
Home Runs: George-NY, O'Neill-STL, McCarthy-STL
Attendance: 412

NEW YORK GIANTS (NL) 6, BROOKLYN BRIDEGROOMS (AA) 3

Six wins was the magic number this year, and it was agreed that—unlike most previous Series—play would not continue beyond the deciding game. The Giants wanted the opening game called for darkness after the seventh inning, when they led, 10–8. But the umpires held off until Brooklyn, in the deepening gloom, had scored four runs in the last of the eighth to go ahead, 12–10.

The next day, in Brooklyn before more than 16,000 spectators (by far the largest World Series crowd to that time), Ed "Cannonball" Crane held the Grooms to four hits as New York evened the Series. But Brooklyn won the next two for a 3–1 Series advantage. In Game 3, ahead 8–7 in the sixth inning, the Grooms began stalling, waiting for darkness to fall. The score was still 8–7 when the game was finally halted in the top of the ninth with one out and three Giants on base.

Darkness for a third time gave Brooklyn the victory in Game 4. New York overcame a 7–2 Bridegroom lead to tie the score with five runs in the top of the sixth, but in the bottom of the inning Brooklyn's Tom "Oyster" Burns homered in the dark for three runs. The umpires then halted the game.

The five remaining contests went the distance, and the Giants won them all. Crane in Game 5 gave up eight hits, but homered in his own behalf, driving in two runs in his Giants' 11–3 rout. In Game 6 the Grooms scored a run in the second inning, but New York tied the game with two outs in the last of the ninth (when John Ward singled, stole second and third, and scored on Roger Connor's single), and won it with two away in the 11th as Ward drove in Mike Slattery from second with an infield hit.

Back-to-back homers by Giants Dan Richardson and Jim O'Rourke highlighted an eight-run second inning in Game 7. The Giants' eventual 11–7 win gave them their first Series advantage. In Game 8 the Giants outscored the Grooms 12–2 over the first four innings and beat them, 16–7.

With their backs to the wall, the Bridegrooms scored first in Game 9 and held a 2–1 lead after five innings. But New York tied the score in the sixth and went ahead 3–2 on a passed ball in the seventh.

Meanwhile pitcher Hank O'Day blanked the Grooms on just two hits after the first inning to bring New York its second straight world championship.

NY (N)

PLAYER/POS	AVG	G	AB	R	H	2B	3B	HR	RB	BB	SO	SB
Willard Brown, c	.600	1	5	3	3	0	0	1	2	0	0	0
Roger Connor, 1b	.343	9	35	9	12	2	2	0	12	3	2	8
Ed Crane, p	.278	5	18	3	5	1	1	1	5	1	2	0
Buck Ewing, c	.250	8	36	5	9	4	0	0	7	2	5	1
George Gore, of	.333	5	21	5	7	1	1	0	1	3	0	2
Tim Keefe, p	.500	2	4	1	2	1	0	0	0	1	1	0
Hank O'Day, p	.167	3	6	0	1	0	0	0	0	2	2	0
Jim O'Rourke, of	.389	9	36	7	14	2	2	2	7	2	2	3
Danny Richardson, 2b	.314	9	35	8	11	1	1	3	8	3	5	3
Mike Slattery, of	.188	4	16	6	3	0	0	0	1	3	1	1
Mike Tiernan, of	.289	9	38	12	11	1	1	1	5	5	3	3
John Ward, ss	.417	9	36	10	15	0	1	0	7	5	2	10
Mickey Welch, p	.333	1	3	0	1	0	0	0	0	0	1	0
Art Whitney, 3b	.229	9	35	4	8	2	1	0	3	1	0	0
TOTAL	.315		324	73	102	16	10	8	58	31	26	31

PITCHER	W	L	ERA	G	GS	CG	SV	SHO	IP	H	ER	BB	SO
Ed Crane	4	1	3.72	5	5	4	0	0	38.2	29	16	32	19
Tim Keefe	0	1	8.18	2	1	1	1	0	11.0	17	10	2	4
Hank O'Day	2	0	1.17	3	2	2	0	0	23.0	10	3	14	12
Mickey Welch	0	1	9.00	1	1	0	0	0	5.0	11	5	3	1
TOTAL	6	3	3.94	11	9	7	1	0	77.2	67	34	51	36

BRO (A)

PLAYER/POS	AVG	G	AB	R	H	2B	3B	HR	RB	BB	SO	SB
Oyster Burns, of	.229	9	35	8	8	3	0	2	11	5	6	0
Doc Bushong, c	.000	3	8	0	0	0	0	0	0	1	0	0
Bob Caruthers, p	.250	4	8	1	2	0	0	0	1	3	3	0
Bob Clark, c	.417	4	12	3	5	2	0	0	3	2	2	0
Hub Collins, 2b	.371	9	35	13	13	3	0	1	2	7	5	6
Pop Corkhill, of	.208	9	24	4	5	1	0	1	5	6	2	1
Jumbo Davis, ss	.000	1	4	0	0	0	0	0	0	0	0	0
Dave Foutz, 1b-9, p-1	.286	9	35	7	10	2	0	1	9	4	2	3
Mickey Hughes, p	.333	1	3	1	1	1	0	0	0	1	2	0
Tom Lovett, p	.000	1	1	0	0	0	0	0	0	0	0	0
Darby O'Brien, of	.161	9	31	8	5	0	1	0	4	12	6	6
George Pinckney, 3b	.258	9	31	2	8	2	0	0	3	4	2	2
Germany Smith, ss	.172	8	29	2	5	2	1	0	2	3	2	2
Adonis Terry, p-5, 1b-1	.167	5	18	1	3	0	0	0	1	1	1	1
Joe Visner, c-3, of-2	.125	5	16	2	2	1	0	0	0	2	3	0
TOTAL	.231		290	52	67	17	2	5	41	51	36	21

PITCHER	W	L	ERA	G	GS	CG	SV	SHO	IP	H	ER	BB	SO
Bob Caruthers	0	2	3.75	4	2	2	1	0	24.0	28	10	6	6
Dave Foutz	0	0	7.20	1	0	0	0	0	5.0	5	4	2	2
Mickey Hughes	1	0	7.71	1	1	0	0	0	7.0	14	6	3	3
Tom Lovett	0	1	24.00	1	1	0	0	0	3.0	8	8	2	1
Adonis Terry	2	3	5.97	5	5	4	0	0	37.2	47	25	18	14
TOTAL	3	6	6.22	12	9	6	1	0	76.2	102	53	31	26

GAME 1 AT NY OCT 18

```
NY   020 210 50    10 12 2
BRO  510 000 24    12 16 3
```
Pitchers: KEEFE vs TERRY
Home Runs: Collins-BRO, Richardson-NY
Attendance: 8,848
(Game called at end of eighth, darkness)

GAME 2 AT BRO OCT 19

```
NY   111 120 000    6 10 4
BRO  110 000 000    2  4 8
```
Pitchers: CRANE vs CARUTHERS
Attendance: 16,172

GAME 3 AT NY OCT 22

```
NY   200 032 00    7 15 2
BRO  023 120 00    8 12 3
```
Pitchers: WELCH, O'Day (6) vs HUGHES, Caruthers (8)
Home Runs: Corkhill-BRO, O'Rourke-NY
Attendance: 5,181
(Game called at end of eighth, darkness)

GAME 4 AT BRO OCT 23

```
NY   001 105      7 9 8
BRO  202 033     10 7 1
```
Pitchers: CRANE vs TERRY
Home Runs: Burns-BRO
Attendance: 3,045
(Game called at end of sixth, darkness)

GAME 5 AT BRO OCT 24

```
NY   004 040 021   11 12 2
BRO  000 111 000    3  8 2
```
Pitchers: CRANE vs CARUTHERS
Home Runs: Brown-NY, Richardson-NY, Crane-NY
Attendance: 2,901

GAME 6 AT NY OCT 25

```
BRO 010 00 000 00    1 6 4
NY  000 00 000 01    2 7 1
```
Pitchers: TERRY vs O'DAY
Attendance: 2,556

GAME 7 AT NY OCT 26

```
BRO 004 030 000    7  5 3
NY  180 001 10X   11 14 4
```
Pitchers: LOVETT, Caruthers (4) vs CRANE, Keefe (5)
Home Runs: Richardson-NY, O'Rourke-NY
Attendance: 3,312

GAME 8 AT BRO OCT 28

```
NY  541 203 001   16 15 4
BRO 200 000 023    7  5 4
```
Pitchers: CRANE vs TERRY, Foutz (5)
Home Runs: Foutz-BRO, Tiernan-NY, Burns-BRO
Attendance: 2,584

GAME 9 AT NY OCT 29

```
BRO 200 000 000    2 4 2
NY  100 001 10X    3 8 5
```
Pitchers: TERRY vs O'DAY
Attendance: 3,067

BROOKLYN BRIDEGROOMS (NL) 3, LOUISVILLE CYCLONES (AA) 3; TIE, 1

The Bridegrooms, AA pennant winners in 1889, switched to the NL and returned to World Series play as champions of their new league. Louisville, meanwhile, rose from a last-place finish in 1889 to replace Brooklyn at the top of the AA. The Series, though, seemed meaningless to many who believed that pennant-winning Boston of the outlaw Players League (which had drawn off many of the best NL and AA players) could beat both Louisville and Brooklyn if given the opportunity.

The first four games of the Series were played in Louisville before an ever decreasing number of spectators. The largest crowd—5,600—saw the Cyclones humiliated in the opener 9–0 as Brooklyn's Adonis Terry stopped them on two singles. The Grooms won the second game, too, breaking a 2–2 tie with a pair of runs in the fourth and holding on for a 5–3 win.

Louisville played catch-up throughout Game 3 and entered the last of the eighth still behind 7–4. But a walk, three hits, a sacrifice fly, and a passed ball tied the score before darkness ended the game. Only 1,050 spectators attended the final contest in Louisville, but they saw the first Louisville win. The Cyclones scored three runs in the first inning, but Brooklyn countered with three an inning later, and both teams scored single runs in the third. Louisville's Red Ehret blanked the Grooms the rest of the way, but Brooklyn's Tom Lovett yielded the Cyclones a winning run in the seventh when Tim Shinnick tripled and was sacrificed home.

Rain postponed the first game in Brooklyn for two days, but when it was played—on a cold, muddy day before a small crowd of 1,000—the Grooms took the lead on Oyster Burns's two-run homer in the first inning and held it all the way for their third win. As the weather grew colder, the crowds declined for the final two games. Louisville captured its second win by a 9–8 margin when a three-run Brooklyn rally in the eighth inning of Game 6 stalled one run short of a tie. Only abut 300 diehards saw the Cyclones even the Series in the finale, 6–2 behind Red Ehret's four-hitter. A tie-breaking eighth game seemed called for, but there

was not enough interest in playing any further in the bitter cold.

BRO (N)

PLAYER/POS	AVG	G	AB	R	H	2B	3B	HR	RB	BB	SO	SB
Oyster Burns, of-4,3b-3	.222	7	27	6	6	2	0	1	5	3	4	0
Doc Bushong, c	.000	2	6	0	0	0	0	0	0	0	1	0
Bob Caruthers, of	.000	2	6	0	0	0	0	0	0	2	0	0
Bob Clark, c	.667	1	3	2	2	0	1	0	1	0	0	0
Hub Collins, 2b	.310	7	29	7	9	0	1	0	1	3	0	2
Tom Daly, c-6,1b-1	.182	6	22	1	4	2	0	0	3	0	4	2
Patsy Donovan, of	.471	5	17	5	8	1	0	0	3	2	1	3
Dave Foutz, 1b-7, of-1	.300	7	30	6	9	2	1	0	4	0	1	1
Tom Lovett, p-4, of-1	.067	5	15	0	1	0	0	0	0	0	4	0
Darby O'Brien, of	.125	6	24	3	3	0	1	0	3	1	5	3
George Pinkney, 3b	.357	4	14	4	5	0	2	0	3	2	1	1
Germany Smith, ss	.276	7	29	3	8	0	2	0	7	0	3	1
Adonis Terry, p-3, of-3	.050	6	20	5	1	1	0	0	0	6	3	1
TOTAL	.231		242	42	56	8	8	1	30	19	27	14

PITCHER	W	L	ERA	G	GS	CG	SV	SHO	IP	H	ER	BB	SO
Tom Lovett	2	2	2.83	4	4	4	0	0	35.0	29	11	6	14
Adonis Terry	1	1	3.60	3	3	3	0	1	25.0	25	10	10	8
TOTAL	3	3	3.15	7	7	7	0	1	60.0	54	21	16	22

LOU (A)

PLAYER/POS	AVG	G	AB	R	H	2B	3B	HR	RB	BB	SO	SB
Ned Bligh, c	.000	2	3	0	0	0	0	0	0	0	1	0
Ed Daily, of-4, p-2	.136	6	22	1	3	1	1	0	3	1	2	2
Red Ehret, p	.429	3	7	1	3	0	1	0	0	0	0	0
Charlie Hamburg, of	.269	7	26	3	7	1	0	0	2	0	3	0
George Meakim, p	.500	1	2	0	1	0	0	0	0	0	0	0
Harry Raymond, ss-5, ss-3	.148	7	27	5	4	1	1	0	1	2	5	1
John Ryan, c	.053	6	19	0	1	0	0	0	2	0	1	1
Tim Shinnick, 2b	.292	7	24	3	7	1	1	0	3	2	2	2
Scott Stratton, p-3, of-1	.222	4	9	4	2	1	0	0	0	2	1	3
Harry Taylor, 1b	.300	7	30	6	9	1	0	0	2	2	3	3
Phil Tomney, ss	.200	3	5	1	1	0	0	0	0	3	1	0
Farmer Weaver, of	.259	7	27	4	7	1	0	0	4	1	2	5
Pete Weckbecker, c	.000	1	4	0	0	0	0	0	0	0	1	0
Jimmy 'Chicken' Wolf, 3b-5, of-3	.360	7	25	4	9	3	1	0	8	3	0	2
TOTAL	.235		230	32	54	10	5	0	25	16	22	19

PITCHER	W	L	ERA	G	GS	CG	SV	SHO	IP	H	ER	BB	SO
Ed Daily	0	2	2.65	2	2	2	0	0	17.0	12	5	8	5
Red Ehret	2	0	1.35	3	2	2	1	0	20.0	12	3	6	13
George Meakim	0	0	0.00	1	0	0	0	0	4.0	6	0	1	1
Scott Stratton	1	1	2.37	3	3	1	0	0	19.0	26	5	4	8
TOTAL	3	3	1.95	9	7	5	1	0	60.0	56	13	19	27

GAME 1 AT LOU OCT 17
BRO 300 030 30   9 11 1
LOU 000 000 00   0 2 6
Pitchers: TERRY vs STRATTON
Attendance: 5,600

GAME 2 AT LOU OCT 18
BRO 020 201 000 5 5 3
LOU 101 000 001 3 6 5
Pitchers: LOVETT vs DAILY
Attendance: 2,860

GAME 3 AT LOU OCT 20
BRO 020 130 10 7 10 2
LOU 001 012 03 7 11 3
Pitchers: Terry vs Stratton, Meakim (4)
Attendance: 2,500
(Game called at end of eighth, darkness)

GAME 4 AT LOU OCT 21
BRO 031 000 000 4 7 2
LOU 301 000 10X 5 9 2
Pitchers: LOVETT vs EHRET
Attendance: 1,050

GAME 5 AT BRO OCT 25
LOU 010 010 000 2 5 6
BRO 210 000 20X 7 7 0
Pitchers: DAILY vs LOVETT
Home Runs: Burns-BRO
Attendance: 1,000

GAME 6 AT BRO OCT 27
LOU 012 101 220 9 13 3
BRO 100 004 030 8 12 3
Pitchers: STRATTON, Ehret (7) vs TERRY
Attendance: 600

GAME 7 AT BRO OCT 28
LOU 103 000 020 6 8 3
BRO 200 000 000 2 4 1
Pitchers: EHRET vs LOVETT
Attendance: 300

BOSTON BEANEATERS 5, CLEVELAND SPIDERS 0; TIE, 1

Interleague squabbling prevented a World Series in 1891, and the AA folded before the next season. Four AA clubs were taken into the NL, expanding the NL to 12 teams. To create a postseason championship series, the regular season was divided in half, with first-half winner Boston meeting second-half victor Cleveland for both the league and world titles.

The first game, in Cleveland, was a pitching and fielding classic. Boston's Jack Stivetts and Cleveland's Cy Young blanked the opposition for 11 innings before darkness halted the game. Young yielded just six hits and Stivetts four—all singles. Just as remarkable in an era when errors were commonplace, Cleveland committed only one and Boston none; several outstanding plays were made in the field.

Boston center fielder Hugh Duffy was the offensive and defensive star of Game 2. He drove in three of the Beaneaters' four runs (with a fly out, a triple, and a double), and scored the fourth himself after tripling a second time. And in the bottom of the ninth he snared a leadoff liner with a great running catch. As it was, Cleveland scored once in the inning to pull within a run of a tie; Duffy's catch prevented a certain tie and a possible Cleveland win. Game 3 was just as close. Pitchers Stivetts and Young each gave up two early runs, but then blanked their foes until the seventh inning, when Boston's Tommy McCarthy singled in Stivetts (who had doubled) with what proved the winning run.

The Series moved to Boston for the next three games. In Game 4, Boston ace Kid Nichols shut out the Spiders, scattering seven hits and fanning eight. Cleveland's Nig Cuppy yielded only six hits, but one was a home run ball to Hugh Duffy for two runs in the third inning, and another was a two-run single to Joe Quinn in the sixth. Cleveland pitcher John Clarkson helped his own cause the next day with a three-run homer in a six-run second inning. But Boston pitcher Jack Stivetts—with the score now 7–5 Cleveland in the sixth—tripled in a run and scored the tying run. In the seventh, Stivetts scored Boston's twelfth (and final) run after singling, while holding

Cleveland scoreless through the final four innings.

Two days later the Beaneaters brought the Series to an end with their fifth straight win. The Spiders scored first, with a three-run third, but pitcher Kid Nichols held them scoreless after that and singled home Boston's tying and go-ahead runs himself as the Beaneaters tagged Cy Young for eight runs over the final six innings.

BOS (N)

PLAYER/POS	AVG	G	AB	R	H	2B	3B	HR	RB	BB	SO	SB
Charlie Bennett, c	.286	2	7	2	2	0	0	1	1	0	2	1
Hugh Duffy, of	.462	6	26	3	12	3	2	1	9	1	0	3
Charlie Ganzel, c	.500	2	8	1	4	0	0	0	2	1	0	0
King Kelly, c	.000	2	8	0	0	0	0	0	0	0	2	1
Herman Long, ss	.222	6	27	4	6	0	0	0	1	0	0	2
Bobby Lowe, of	.130	6	23	8	3	0	0	0	0	1	2	1
Tommy McCarthy, of	.381	6	21	2	8	2	0	0	2	6	1	3
Billy Nash, 3b	.167	6	24	3	4	0	0	0	4	2	3	2
Kid Nichols, p	.286	6	7	1	2	0	0	0	2	0	1	1
Joe Quinn, 2b	.286	6	21	2	6	1	1	0	4	1	2	0
Harry Staley, p	.000	1	4	0	0	0	0	0	0	0	3	0
Jack Stivetts, p	.250	3	12	3	3	1	1	0	1	0	2	0
Tommy Tucker, 1b	.261	6	23	2	6	0	0	1	2	0	1	0
TOTAL	.265		211	31	56	7	4	3	28	12	19	14

PITCHER	W	L	ERA	G	GS	CG	SV	SHO	IP	H	ER	BB	SO
Kid Nichols	2	0	1.00	2	2	2	0	1	18.0	17	2	4	13
Harry Staley	1	0	3.00	1	1	1	0	0	9.0	10	3	1	0
Jack Stivetts	2	0	0.93	3	3	3	0	1	29.0	21	3	7	17
TOTAL	5	0	1.29	6	6	6	0	2	56.0	48	8	12	30

CLE (N)

PLAYER/POS	AVG	G	AB	R	H	2B	3B	HR	RB	BB	SO	SB
Jesse Burkett, of	.320	6	25	3	8	1	0	0	1	0	2	4
Cupid Childs, 2b	.409	6	22	3	9	0	2	0	0	5	1	0
John Clarkson, p	.250	2	8	1	2	0	0	1	3	0	1	0
Nig Cuppy, p	.000	1	3	0	0	0	0	0	0	0	2	0
George Davis, 3b-2	.167	3	6	0	1	0	0	0	0	0	1	0
Jimmy McAleer, of	.182	6	22	0	4	0	0	0	1	2	2	1
Ed McKean, ss	.440	6	25	2	11	0	0	0	6	1	3	0
Jack O'Connor, of	.136	6	22	1	3	0	0	0	0	2	3	0
Patsy Tebeau, 3b	.000	5	18	1	0	0	0	0	0	0	2	1
Jake Virtue, 1b	.125	6	24	1	3	0	0	0	0	0	5	1
Cy Young, p	.091	3	11	1	1	0	0	0	0	0	5	0
Chief Zimmer, c	.261	6	23	2	6	1	1	0	2	0	3	0
TOTAL	.230		209	15	48	2	3	1	13	12	30	7

PITCHER	W	L	ERA	G	GS	CG	SV	SHO	IP	H	ER	BB	SO
John Clarkson	0	2	5.29	2	2	2	0	0	17.0	24	10	5	9
Nig Cuppy	0	1	1.13	1	1	1	0	0	8.0	6	1	4	1
Cy Young	0	2	3.00	3	3	3	0	1	27.0	26	9	3	9
TOTAL	0	5	3.46	6	6	6	0	1	52.0	56	20	12	19

GAME 1 AT CLE OCT 17
CLE 00000000000　0 4 1
BOS 00000000000　0 6 0
Pitchers: Young vs Stivetts
Attendance: 6,000
(Game called at end of eleventh, darkness)

GAME 2 AT CLE OCT 18
BOS 1 0 1 0 1 0　0 1 0　4 10 2
CLE 0 0 1 1 0 0　0 0 1　3 10 2
Pitchers: STALEY vs CLARKSON
Attendance: 6,700

GAME 3 AT CLE OCT 19
CLE 2 0 0 0 0 0　0 0 0　2 8 0
BOS 1 1 0 0 0 0　1 0 X　3 9 2
Pitchers: YOUNG vs STIVETTS
Attendance: 5,000

GAME 4 AT BOS OCT 21
CLE 0 0 0 0 0 0　0 0 0　0 7 3
BOS 0 0 2 0 0 2　0 0 X　4 6 0
Pitchers: CUPPY vs NICHOLS
Home Runs: Duffy-BOS
Attendance: 6,547

GAME 5 AT BOS OCT 22
CLE 0 6 0 0 1 0　0 0 0　7 9 4
BOS 0 0 0 3 2 4　3 0 X　12 14 3
Pitchers: CLARKSON vs STIVETTS
Home Runs: Clarkson-CLE, Tucker-BOS
Attendance: 3,466

GAME 6 AT BOS OCT 24
CLE 0 0 3 0 0 0　0 0 0　3 10 5
BOS 0 0 2 2 1 1　1 X　8 11 5
Pitchers: YOUNG vs NICHOLS
Home Runs: Bennett-BOS
Attendance: 2,300

NEW YORK GIANTS 4, BALTIMORE ORIOLES 0

As the divided season of 1892 was not repeated, no postseason championship games were held in 1893. But in 1894 Pittsburgh sportsman William C. Temple offered an elegant trophy to the winner of a series between the NL's first- and second-place finishers. For four years the Temple Cup games determined the world championship. In this first matchup, second-place New York swept the feisty pennant-winning Orioles.

Game 1, in Baltimore, was a shutout through four innings as New York's Amos Rusie and Baltimore's Duke Esper held their opponents at bay. But New York's George Van Haltren tripled in the fifth inning and scored the game's first run on a fly to left. The Giants also scored single runs in the sixth, seventh, and eighth innings, while Rusie continued his shutout pitching through the eighth. In the ninth John McGraw singled, and he came around on a sacrifice, stolen base, and single to spoil the shutout. But the effort was too little to deprive Rusie of his win.

Some 200 policemen patrolled the second game the next day to protect the umpires and New York's players and fans from the abusive Orioles and the crowd. Baltimore scored first with two runs in the second and, after losing and regaining the lead, completed the eighth inning tied 5–5. But in the top of the ninth, the Giants put together their second four-run inning of the game. Once again the Orioles came up with a run in the last of the ninth, but once again came up short.

More than 22,000 spectators showed up for Game 3 as the Series shifted to New York—a huge crowd for that era, even for a Saturday. As in the first game, the Giants' Amos Rusie hurled a 4–1 victory. New York broke a 1–1 tie with a run in the fifth on a throwing error and a ground out, and scored the game's final runs an inning later. Threatening weather held down attendance at Game 4 to about 12,000. Baltimore jumped to a quick lead with two runs in the top of the first, but New York pitcher Jouett Meekin held the Orioles to just one run after that as the Giants piled up runs for a 16–3 advantage by the time darkness forced an end to play after eight innings. Meekin, in

winning his second game of the Series, con-nected for three hits himself—half as many as he permitted the whole Baltimore team.

NY (N)

PLAYER/POS	AVG	G	AB	R	H	2B	3B	HR	RB	BB	SO	SB
Eddie Burke, of	.389	4	18	3	7	1	0	0	2	1	0	1
George Davis, 3b	.313	4	16	5	5	2	2	0	5	2	0	2
Jack Doyle, 1b	.588	4	17	4	10	1	1	0	6	1	1	6
Duke Farrell, c	.400	4	15	5	6	0	0	0	2	1	1	1
Shorty Fuller, ss	.286	4	14	4	4	0	0	0	2	2	0	1
Jouett Meekin, p	.556	2	9	2	5	0	0	0	3	0	1	0
Yale Murphy, of	.000	1	1	0	0	0	0	0	0	0	0	0
Amos Rusie, p	.429	2	7	1	3	1	0	0	1	0	1	0
Mike Tiernan, of	.294	4	17	5	5	0	1	0	3	2	2	0
George Van Haltren, of	.500	4	14	3	7	1	1	0	0	2	2	2
John Ward, 2b	.294	4	17	1	5	0	0	0	6	0	0	0
TOTAL	.393		145	33	57	6	5	0	30	11	8	13

PITCHER	W	L	ERA	G	GS	CG	SV	SHO	IP	H	ER	BB	SO
Jouett Meekin	2	0	1.59	2	2	2	0	0	17.0	13	3	8	6
Amos Rusie	2	0	0.50	2	2	2	0	0	18.0	14	1	3	9
TOTAL	4	0	1.03	4	4	4	0	0	35.0	27	4	11	15

BAL (N)

PLAYER/POS	AVG	G	AB	R	H	2B	3B	HR	RB	BB	SO	SB
Frank Bonner, ss-1, of-1	.000	2	5	0	0	0	0	0	0	0	2	0
Steve Brodie, of	.000	4	15	2	0	0	0	0	0	2	1	1
Dan Brouthers, 1b	.188	4	16	2	3	0	0	0	0	1	0	3
Duke Esper, p	.000	1	2	0	0	0	0	0	0	1	0	0
Kid Gleason, p	.200	2	5	0	1	0	1	0	1	0	1	0
Bill Hawke, p	.000	1	2	0	0	0	0	0	0	0	1	0
George Hemming, p	.000	1	3	0	0	0	0	0	0	1	1	0
Hughie Jennings, ss	.143	4	14	0	2	0	0	0	1	0	2	0
Willie Keeler, of	.250	3	12	1	3	0	0	0	1	1	0	1
Joe Kelley, of	.333	4	15	2	5	1	1	0	0	3	2	1
John McGraw, 3b	.250	4	16	2	4	0	0	0	2	0	0	1
Heinie Reitz, 2b	.333	4	15	1	5	0	0	0	4	1	3	1
Wilbert Robinson, c	.267	4	15	1	4	0	0	0	1	1	1	1
TOTAL	.200		135	11	27	1	2	0	10	11	15	8

PITCHER	W	L	ERA	G	GS	CG	SV	SHO	IP	H	ER	BB	SO
Duke Esper	0	1	4.00	1	1	1	0	0	9.0	13	4	1	3
Kid Gleason	0	1	9.69	2	1	1	0	0	13.0	25	14	6	3
Bill Hawke	0	1	9.00	1	1	0	0	0	4.0	9	4	1	0
George Hemming	0	1	1.13	1	1	1	0	0	8.0	10	1	3	2
TOTAL	0	4	6.09	5	4	3	0	0	34.0	57	23	11	8

GAME 1 AT BAL OCT 4

NY   000 011 110   4 13 2
BAL   000 000 001   1 7 1
Pitchers: RUSIE vs ESPER
Attendance: 9,000

GAME 2 AT BAL OCT 5

NY   004 000 014   9 14 3
BAL   022 000 101   6 7 2
Pitchers: MEEKIN vs GLEASON
Attendance: 11,000

GAME 3 AT NY OCT 6

BAL   000 100 000   1 7 4
NY   100 012 00X   4 10 4
Pitchers: HEMMING vs RUSIE
Attendance: 22,000

GAME 4 AT NY OCT 8

BAL   201 000 00   3 6 3
NY   101 351 50   16 20 4
Pitchers: HAWKE, Gleason (5) vs MEEKIN
Attendance: 12,000
(Game called at end of eighth, darkness)

CLEVELAND SPIDERS 4, BALTIMORE ORIOLES 1

Baltimore, repeating as NL pennant winner, returned to Temple Cup play against new runner-up Cleveland. The first half of the opener—played in Cleveland—featured a scoreless duel between Baltimore veteran John "Sadie" McMahon and the Spiders' great Cy Young. After Cleveland scored the game's first run in the last of the fifth, the teams traded runs and the lead, completing the eighth inning tied 3–3. In the top of the ninth, doubles by Wilbert Robinson and John McGraw restored the edge to Baltimore. But in the bottom of the inning, four straight Cleveland hits pushed across the tying run and filled the bases. One runner was forced at home for the first out, but a grounder that just missed being a double-play ball drove in the winning Cleveland run.

The next three games were not so closely contested. A large and enthusiastic Cleveland crowd watched its Spiders jump on Baltimore for three runs in the bottom of the first inning of Game 2 and coast to a 7–2 win behind the strong pitching of Nig Cuppy, who held the Orioles to five singles. Cleveland repeated itself in Game 3, again exploding for three runs in the bottom of the first on the way to a seven-run total. Cy Young was just as effective in the box as Cuppy had been, scattering four hits over seven shutout innings be-fore Baltimore put together three singles in the eighth for their only run.

When the teams shifted to Baltimore for Game 4, the Orioles came to life. While their pitcher Duke Esper strangled the Spiders on just five singles—only two Cleveland runners advanced as far as second base—Baltimore batters tagged Nig Cuppy for five runs and their first Temple Cup win in two years of trying.

It proved to be their only win of the Series. The next day, in the first close struggle since the opener, Cy Young and Baltimore's rookie ace Bill Hoffer dueled scorelessly through six innings. But in the top of the seventh, Young doubled to start what became a three-run rally, and an inning later the Spiders scored twice more. Baltimore scored a single run in the last of the seventh, and, with two out in the ninth, loaded the bases on two walks and a hit batsman. A Cleve-

land error brought in the Orioles' second run as the bases remained full for Steve Brodie. But despite the pleas of Baltimore partisans to hit a homer or triple, Brodie didn't deliver and Cleveland copped the cup.

CLE (N)

PLAYER/POS	AVG	G	AB	R	H	2B	3B	HR	RB	BB	SO	SB
Harry Blake, of	.250	5	20	1	5	3	0	0	2	0	2	0
Jesse Burkett, of	.450	5	20	3	9	2	0	0	2	0	0	1
Cupid Childs, 2b	.190	5	21	4	4	1	0	0	2	1	0	1
Nig Cuppy, p	.167	2	6	1	1	1	0	0	1	0	0	0
Jimmy McAleer, of	.286	5	21	2	6	0	0	0	2	0	0	1
Chippy McGarr, 3b	.368	5	19	3	7	2	0	0	1	1	1	2
Ed McKean, ss	.300	5	20	2	6	1	1	0	4	3	0	1
Patsy Tebeau, 1b	.286	5	21	3	6	1	0	0	3	1	0	0
Cy Young, p	.250	3	12	3	3	1	0	0	1	0	1	0
Chief Zimmer, c	.333	4	18	2	6	2	0	0	3	3	5	0
TOTAL	.298		178	24	53	14	1	0	21	9	9*	6

PITCHER	W	L	ERA	G	GS	CG	SV	SHO	IP	H	ER	BB	SO
Nig Cuppy	1	1	3.18	2	2	2	0	0	17.0	14	6	4	6
Cy Young	3	0	2.33	3	3	3	0	0	27.0	28	7	4	2
TOTAL	4	1	2.66	5	5	5	0	0	44.0	42	13	8	8

BAL (N)

PLAYER/POS	AVG	G	AB	R	H	2B	3B	HR	RB	BB	SO	SB
Steve Brodie, of	.200	5	20	1	4	0	0	0	2	0	0	0
Scoops Carey, 1b	.263	5	19	0	5	1	0	0	1	0	0	0
Boileryard Clarke, c	.286	2	7	1	2	0	0	0	0	0	0	2
Duke Esper, p	.000	1	3	0	0	0	0	0	0	1	2	0
Kid Gleason, 2b	.105	5	19	0	2	0	0	0	0	0	1	0
Bill Hoffer, p	.000	2	7	0	0	0	0	0	0	0	2	0
Hughie Jennings, ss	.368	5	19	3	7	2	0	0	2	1	0	1
Willie Keeler, of	.235	5	17	3	4	0	0	0	1	3	1	0
Joe Kelley, of	.368	5	19	1	7	0	0	0	5	1	1	1
John McGraw, 3b	.400	5	20	4	8	2	0	0	1	2	0	2
Sadie McMahon, p	.000	2	7	0	0	0	0	0	0	0	0	0
Wilbert Robinson, c	.250	3	12	1	3	1	0	0	0	0	1	0
TOTAL	.249		169	14	42	6	0	0	12	8	8	6

PITCHER	W	L	ERA	G	GS	CG	SV	SHO	IP	H	ER	BB	SO
Duke Esper	1	0	0.00	1	1	1	0	1	9.0	5	0	0	3
Bill Hoffer	0	2	4.24	2	2	2	0	0	17.0	21	8	6	4
Sadie McMahon	0	2	5.94	2	2	2	0	0	16.2	27	11	3	2
TOTAL	1	4	4.01	5	5	5	0	1	42.2	53	19	9	9

GAME 1 AT CLE OCT 2

BAL   000 001 021   4 12 0
CLE   000 011 012   5 14 3
Pitchers: McMAHON vs YOUNG
Attendance: 8,000

GAME 2 AT CLE OCT 3

BAL   010 001 000   2 5 4
CLE   300 012 10X   7 10 5
Pitchers: HOFFER vs CUPPY
Attendance: 10,000

GAME 3 AT CLE OCT 5

BAL   000 000 010   1 7 1
CLE   300 000 31X   7 13 1
Pitchers: McMAHON vs YOUNG
Attendance: 12,000

GAME 4 AT BAL OCT 7

CLE   000 000 000   0 5 1
BAL   012 000 20X   5 9 1
Pitchers: CUPPY vs ESPER
Attendance: 9,100

GAME 5 AT BAL OCT 8

CLE   000 000 320   5 11 3
BAL   000 000 101   2 9 5
Pitchers: YOUNG vs HOFFER

BALTIMORE ORIOLES 4, CLEVELAND SPIDERS 0

Baltimore captured its third consecutive pennant and for the second year in a row faced runner-up Cleveland in the Temple Cup games. But this time the Orioles emerged triumphant—with a sweep in which their margin of victory was never less than four runs.

Aces Bill Hoffer of Baltimore and the Spiders' Cy Young faced each other in the opener, in Baltimore. Hoffer walked four men, but gave up only five hits while the Orioles bombarded Young for 13. When the game ended, Hoffer and Baltimore had a 7–1 win.

Bobby Wallace (who had not yet discovered his role at shortstop that would propel him into the Hall of Fame) pitched for Cleveland in Game 2. He lost the game in the first inning when two Spider errors, a hit batsman, three hits, and a steal of home put four Baltimore runs on the board. The Orioles added two runs in the third and another in the fifth, while their promising 20-year-old pitcher Joe Corbett held the Spiders to two runs on seven hits.

The Orioles' Hoffer gave up 10 hits to Cleveland in Game 3—two more than the Birds made off Nig Cuppy. But all the hits off Hoffer were singles, and he walked only one. Half of Cleveland's hits went toward producing just two runs. Their second run tied the score in the fifth inning, but in the sixth Baltimore regained the lead as John McGraw singled, stole second, took third on an error, and came home on an outfield fly. In the eighth the Orioles bunched four of their eight hits for three insurance runs.

The Series moved to Cleveland for the fourth game. Young Joe Corbett was again sent into the box for Baltimore, this time to face Nig Cuppy. For six innings the game was a scoreless duel. Baltimore hit safely in every inning but the second, but failed to score until the seventh, when Joe Kelley's double and Jack Doyle's single scored the only run they would need. But the Orioles added a second run in that inning and three more in the eighth. Two of the four Cleveland hits against Corbett put men on base in the eighth inning, and Corbett walked two in the ninth to raise Cleveland's hopes. But no Spider scored, and with the 5–0

win the Orioles were world champions at last.

BAL (N)

PLAYER/POS	AVG	G	AB	R	H	2B	3B	HR	RB	BB	SO	SB
Steve Brodie, of	.067	4	15	1	1	0	0	0	3	0	0	1
Joe Corbett, p	.500	2	6	1	3	1	0	0	0	1	1	0
Jack Doyle, 1b	.294	4	17	3	5	1	0	0	4	0	0	2
Bill Hoffer, p	.286	2	7	1	2	0	2	0	0	0	1	0
Hughie Jennings, ss	.333	4	15	5	5	2	0	0	3	1	2	1
Willie Keeler, of	.471	4	17	4	8	1	2	0	4	0	0	1
Joe Kelley, of	.471	4	17	3	8	1	0	0	4	0	1	2
John McGraw, 3b	.267	4	15	4	4	0	0	0	1	0	0	4
Joe Quinn, 3b	.000	1	3	0	0	0	0	0	0	0	0	0
Heinie Reitz, 2b	.133	4	15	1	2	0	0	0	2	1	0	0
Wilbert Robinson, c	.267	4	15	1	4	1	0	0	2	0	3	0
TOTAL	.296		142	25	42	7	4	0	23	3	8	11

PITCHER	W	L	ERA	G	GS	CG	SV	SHO	IP	H	ER	BB	SO
Joe Corbett	2	0	0.50	2	2	2	0	1	18.0	11	1	7	10
Bill Hoffer	2	0	1.50	2	2	2	0	0	18.0	15	3	5	10
TOTAL	4	0	1.00	4	4	4	0	1	36.0	26	4	12	20

CLE (N)

PLAYER/POS	AVG	G	AB	R	H	2B	3B	HR	RB	BB	SO	SB
Harry Blake, of	.071	4	14	1	1	0	0	0	0	1	1	1
Jesse Burkett, of	.333	4	15	1	5	0	0	0	0	2	3	0
Cupid Childs, 2b	.231	4	13	2	3	0	0	0	0	4	0	1
Nig Cuppy, p	.143	2	7	0	1	0	0	0	0	0	1	0
Jimmy McAleer, of	.133	4	15	0	2	0	0	0	1	1	2	1
Chippy McGarr, 3b	.063	4	16	0	1	0	0	0	0	0	3	2
Ed McKean, ss	.313	4	16	0	5	1	1	0	1	1	2	1
Jack O'Connor, 1b	.286	4	14	1	4	0	0	0	1	1	2	0
Patsy Tebeau, 1b	.000	1	1	0	0	0	0	0	0	0	0	0
Bobby Wallace, p-1	.200	3	5	0	1	0	0	0	0	0	0	0
Cy Young, p	.000	1	3	0	0	0	0	0	0	0	0	0
Chief Zimmer, c	.214	4	14	0	3	1	0	0	1	2	6	0
TOTAL	.195		133	5	26	2	1	0	4	12	20	6

PITCHER	W	L	ERA	G	GS	CG	SV	SHO	IP	H	ER	BB	SO
Nig Cuppy	0	2	4.76	2	2	2	0	0	17.0	19	9	0	4
Bobby Wallace	0	1	4.50	1	1	1	0	0	8.0	10	4	2	4
Cy Young	0	1	6.00	1	1	1	0	0	9.0	13	6	1	0
TOTAL	0	4	5.03	4	4	4	0	0	34.0	42	19	3	8

GAME 1 AT BAL OCT 2

BAL 0 0 2   0 0 1   3 1 0   7 13 1
CLE 0 0 0   0 0 1   0 0 0   1 5 4
Pitchers: HOFFER vs YOUNG
Attendance: 4,000

GAME 2 AT BAL OCT 3

BAL 4 0 2   0 1 0   0 0   7 10 3
CLE 0 0 1   0 0 1   0 0   2 7 3
Pitchers: CORBETT vs WALLACE
Attendance: 3,100
(Game called at end of eighth, darkness)

GAME 3 AT BAL OCT 5

BAL 0 1 1   0 0 1   0 3 0   6 8 2
CLE 0 0 1   0 1 0   0 0 0   2 7 3
Pitchers: HOFFER vs CUPPY
Attendance: 2,000

GAME 4 AT CLE OCT 8

CLE 0 0 0   0 0 0   0 0 0   0 4 2
BAL 0 0 0   0 0 0   2 3 X   5 11 1
Pitchers: CUPPY vs CORBETT
Attendance: 1,500

BALTIMORE ORIOLES 4, BOSTON BEANEATERS 1

Boston had edged Baltimore in a close race for the NL pennant, but the Orioles turned the tables on the Beaneaters in Temple Cup play. The Series was a high-scoring affair with an average score of 11-8 for each game.

The opener, in Boston, set the tone for the games. Baltimore sent four runners across the plate in the top of the first inning, and Boston followed in its half with three. The Beaneaters recorded only 12 hits in the game to the Orioles' 20, but they also received seven walks from Baltimore hurler Jerry Nops, and five of those runners scored. The lead switched back and forth in the middle innings, but Boston scored two final runs in the eighth and hung on for a 13–12 win.

Baltimore's Joe Corbett gave up 16 hits (one a home run) and four walks in Game 2 as Boston scored 11 times. But Boston's two pitchers, Fred Klobedanz and Jack Stivetts, were even more generous, handing out 17 hits (including three homers—one of them to opposing pitcher Corbett, who also hit a double and two singles) and five walks as the Orioles evened the Series with their thirteen-run attack.

Game 3 was the Series' lowest in run production, with Baltimore scoring four in the second inning and another four in the third for an 8–3 win. But rain ended the game before Boston could complete its time at bat in the last of the eighth, which erased from the record four more Orioles runs scored earlier in the inning. Rather than waste the two free days before the Series resumed in Baltimore, the two clubs stayed in Massachusetts and played a pair of exhibition games in Worcester and Springfield. Baltimore won them both, 11–10, and 8–6.

The Orioles continued their roll in Series Game 4, with another close but high-scoring victory, 12–11. It looked at first like a blowout as Baltimore scored six runs in the first inning and five more in the second. But Ted Lewis relieved Boston starter Jack Stivetts and held Baltimore to just one further run as the Beaneaters fought back to within one run of a tie before faltering in the ninth.

Boston batters hit Bill Hoffer safely 15 times in Game 5, but only three Beaneaters scored. Baltimore,

with two fewer hits, garnered six more runs than Boston and, with their fourth win, the right to hold the cup for another year. But attendance at the final game was so small the embarrassed Baltimore management refused to release the figures, and the league gave the cup back to Mr. Temple rather than sponsor another unprofitable Series. There was no postseason championship contest in 1898 or 1899.

BAL (N)

PLAYER/POS	AVG	G	AB	R	H	2B	3B	HR	RB	BB	SO	SB
Frank Bowerman, 1,1b-1	.500	2	8	2	4	0	1	0	4	0	0	0
Boileryard Clarke, c	.563	4	16	5	9	1	1	1	4	1	0	0
Joe Corbett, p	.667	2	6	2	4	1	0	1	2	0	1	0
Jack Doyle, 1b	.526	5	19	7	10	2	0	0	9	0	1	2
Bill Hoffer, p	.250	2	8	2	2	1	0	0	0	0	0	0
Hughie Jennings, ss	.318	5	22	5	7	2	0	0	3	4	0	0
Willie Keeler, of	.391	5	23	5	9	2	0	0	2	4	0	0
Joe Kelley, of	.313	4	16	7	5	3	0	0	5	5	0	0
John McGraw, 3b	.300	5	20	6	6	1	1	0	6	7	0	0
Jerry Nops, p	.286	2	7	0	2	0	0	0	1	1	5	0
Tom O'Brien, of	.400	1	5	2	2	1	0	0	0	0	0	0
Heinie Reitz, 2b	.250	5	20	4	5	1	0	1	4	2	0	0
Jake Stenzel, of	.381	5	21	7	8	1	1	0	3	2	0	2
TOTAL	.382		191	54	73	16	4	3	43	26	7	4

PITCHER	W	L	ERA	G	GS	CG	SV	SHO	IP	H	ER	BB	SO
Joe Corbett	1	0	9.00	2	1	1	0	0	12.0	21	12	8	5
Bill Hoffer	2	0	3.38	2	2	2	0	0	16.0	25	6	4	2
Jerry Nops	1	1	12.86	2	2	1	0	0	14.0	23	20	9	3
TOTAL	4	1	8.14	6	5	4	0	0	42.0	69	38	21	10

BOS (N)

PLAYER/POS	AVG	G	AB	R	H	2B	3B	HR	RB	BB	SO	SB
Marty Bergen, c	.500	1	4	0	2	0	0	0	1	0	1	1
Jimmy Collins, 3b	.182	5	22	2	4	0	0	0	4	1	0	0
Hugh Duffy, of	.524	5	21	6	11	2	0	0	7	1	0	0
Billy Hamilton, of	.500	4	16	6	8	1	0	0	2	5	3	2
Charlie Hickman, p-1, of-1	.250	1	4	0	1	1	0	0	1	0	0	0
Fred Klobedanz, p	1.000	2	5	3	5	0	0	0	0	0	0	0
Fred Lake, c	.000	1	3	0	0	0	0	0	0	0	1	0
Ted Lewis, p	.500	3	6	1	3	1	0	0	1	1	0	0
Herman Long, ss	.286	5	21	4	6	1	1	1	5	2	2	1
Bobby Lowe, 2b	.391	5	23	6	9	2	0	0	6	1	0	1
Kid Nichols, p	.000	1	3	0	0	0	0	0	1	0	0	0
Chick Stahl, of	.381	5	21	6	8	1	0	0	6	3	2	2
Jack Stivetts, p-2, of-1	.000	3	7	1	0	0	0	0	0	1	0	1
Jim Sullivan, p	.000	1	1	0	0	0	0	0	0	0	0	0
Fred Tenney, 1b	.286	5	21	4	6	0	0	0	2	4	1	2
George Yeager, c	.500	3	12	2	6	1	1	0	2	2	0	0
TOTAL	.365		189	41	69	10	2	1	38	21	10	10

PITCHER	W	L	ERA	G	GS	CG	SV	SHO	IP	H	ER	BB	SO
Charlie Hickman	0	1	3.60	1	1	0	0	0	5.0	7	2	2	0
Fred Klobedanz	0	1	9.35	2	1	0	0	0	8.2	12	9	8	0
Ted Lewis	1	1	6.00	3	1	0	0	0	12.0	18	8	9	4
Kid Nichols	0	0	12.00	1	1	0	0	0	6.0	14	8	0	3
Jack Stivetts	0	1	18.47	2	1	0	0	0	6.1	16	13	7	0
Jim Sullivan	0	0	3.00	1	0	0	0	0	3.0	6	1	0	0
TOTAL	1	4	9.00	10	5	0	0	0	41.0	73	41	26	7

GAME 1 AT BOS OCT 4

BAL 4 0 1 0 2 3 2 0 0   12 20 4
BOS 3 0 0 1 2 5 0 2 X   13 12 4
Pitchers: NOPS vs Nichols, LEWIS (7)
Attendance: 9,600

GAME 2 AT BOS OCT 5

BAL 1 3 0 1 6 0 1 1 0   13 17 2
BOS 0 0 2 6 2 0 1 0 0   11 16 3
Pitchers: CORBETT vs KLOBEDANZ, Stivetts (5)
Home Runs: Reitz-BAL, Clarke-BAL, Corbett-BAL, Long-BOS
Attendance: 6,500

GAME 3 AT BOS OCT 6

BAL 0 4 4 0 0 0 0   8 9 2
BOS 0 0 3 0 0 0 0   3 10 2
Pitchers: HOFFER vs LEWIS, Klobedanz (3)
Attendance: 5,000
(Game called in eighth, rain)

GAME 4 AT BAL OCT 9

BOS 0 0 0 0 2 4 3 2 0   11 16 3
BAL 6 5 0 0 0 1 0 0 X   12 14 3
Pitchers: STIVETTS, Lewis (2) vs NOPS, Corbett (7)
Attendance: 2,500

GAME 5 AT BAL OCT 11

BOS 0 2 0 0 0 0 0 0 1   3 15 3
BAL 0 2 3 0 0 0 2 2 X   9 13 2
Pitchers: HICKMAN, Sullivan (7) vs HOFFER
Attendance: 700

BROOKLYN SUPERBAS 3, PITTSBURGH PIRATES 1

Pennant-winning Brooklyn led the NL in hitting, but runner-up Pittsburgh claimed the best pitching. Honus Wagner was the only Pittsburgh regular to hit over .300, but he enjoyed what turned out to be his finest season offensively, leading the league with a .381 batting average. Pittsburghers believed their club superior to Brooklyn and a best-of-five "world championship" series was arranged, with all the games to be played in Pittsburgh for a silver cup donated by the Pittsburgh *Chronicle-Telegraph*. Brooklyn, however, proved that its pennant was no fluke.

Two of the game's best pitchers faced off in the opener: Pittsburgh's Rube Waddell, who had led the league in ERA, and Joe "Iron Man" McGinnity, whose 28 regular-season more than those wins of totaled the league's eight runners-up. McGinnity prevailed, shutting out the Pirates until two unearned runs came across in the top of the ninth. Pirates errors also gave Brooklyn a pair of unearned runs, hits—13 but in Waddell all, including lost the six game in the on Superbas' three-run third inning.

In Game 2, Brooklyn's Frank Kitson held Pittsburgh to four hits, and although his Superbas scored only one earned run, six Pirate errors gave them their second win, 4–2. The Pirates staved off a Series sweep with sharp pitching and heavy hitting in Game 3. Deacon Phillippe shut out Brooklyn on six hits as the Pirates jumped on Harry Howell for 13. All Pittsburgh's hits were singles, but combined with Brooklyn errors they were good for ten runs, seven of them unearned.

Three Brooklyn singles and a fumble by Pirates pitcher Sam Leever in the fourth inning of Game 4 gave the Superbas three runs and a 4–0 lead the Pirates could not overcome. Brooklyn hurler McGinnity scattered nine hits and, supported by flawless fielding, held Pittsburgh to a single run to bring Brooklyn its first World Series triumph in three tries—and its last until 1955. The Brooklyn players voted to award their trophy to McGinnity for his fine pitching. The cup may be seen today—along with the Temple Cup and the current World Series trophy—at the Baseball Hall of Fame in Cooperstown.

BRO (N)

PLAYER/POS	AVG	G	AB	R	H	2B	3B	HR	RB	BB	SO	SB
Lave Cross, 3b	.278	4	18	2	5	0	1	0	1	0	0	1
Bill Dahlen, ss	.176	4	17	3	3	0	1	0	2	0	3	1
Tom Daly, 2b	.154	4	13	2	2	1	0	0	1	3	1	0
Duke Farrell, c	.375	2	8	0	3	0	0	0	1	0	0	1
Harry Howell, p	.000	1	3	0	0	0	0	0	0	0	2	0
Hughie Jennings, 1b	.167	4	18	1	3	1	0	0	2	1	1	0
Fielder Jones, of	.278	4	18	3	5	0	0	0	4	1	1	1
Willie Keeler, of	.353	4	17	0	6	0	0	0	0	1	0	0
Joe Kelley, of	.176	4	17	2	3	0	0	0	1	2	3	0
Frank Kitson, p	.000	1	3	0	0	0	0	0	0	1	2	0
Joe McGinnity, p	.143	2	7	1	1	0	0	0	1	0	2	0
Deacon McGuire, c	.375	2	8	1	3	1	0	0	0	0	1	0
TOTAL	.231		147	15	34	3	2	0	13	9	16	4

PITCHER	W	L	ERA	G	GS	CG	SV	SHO	IP	H	ER	BB	SO
Harry Howell	0	1	3.38	1	1	1	0	0	8.0	13	3	2	3
Frank Kitson	1	0	1.00	1	1	1	0	0	9.0	4	1	1	2
Joe McGinnity	2	0	0.00	2	2	2	0	0	18.0	14	0	3	5
TOTAL	3	1	1.03	4	4	4	0	0	35.0	31	4	6	10

PIT (N)

PLAYER/POS	AVG	G	AB	R	H	2B	3B	HR	RB	BB	SO	SB
Ginger Beaumont, of	.267	4	15	2	4	0	0	0	1	1	0	1
Fred Ely, ss	.286	4	14	1	4	1	0	0	0	1	1	2
Tommy Leach, of	.176	4	17	4	3	0	0	0	1	1	2	0
Sam Leever, p	.250	2	4	0	1	0	0	0	0	0	1	1
Tom O'Brien, 1b	.125	4	16	1	2	1	0	0	2	0	1	0
Jack O'Connor, c	.250	2	4	0	1	0	0	0	1	1	0	0
Deacon Phillippe, p	.000	1	4	1	0	0	0	0	0	0	1	0
Claude Ritchey, 2b	.333	4	15	3	5	1	0	0	1	1	0	0
Pop Schriver, ph	.000	1	1	0	0	0	0	0	0	0	0	0
Rube Waddell, p	.200	2	5	0	1	0	0	0	0	0	1	0
Honus Wagner, of	.400	4	15	2	6	1	0	0	3	0	1	2
Jimmy Williams, 3b	.214	4	14	0	3	0	0	0	0	1	0	0
Chief Zimmer, c	.111	3	9	1	1	0	0	0	1	0	2	1
TOTAL	.233		133	15	31	4	0	0	10	6	10	7

PITCHER	W	L	ERA	G	GS	CG	SV	SHO	IP	H	ER	BB	SO
Sam Leever	0	2	1.38	2	2	1	0	0	13.0	13	2	4	4
Deacon Phillippe	1	0	0.00	1	1	1	0	1	9.0	6	0	2	5
Rube Waddell	0	1	1.93	2	1	1	0	0	14.0	15	3	3	7
TOTAL	1	3	1.25	5	4	3	0	1	36.0	34	5	9	16

GAME 1 AT PIT OCT 15

```
BRO  003 101 000   5 13 1
PIT  000 000 002   2  5 4
```
Pitchers: McGINNITY vs WADDELL
Attendance: 4,000

GAME 2 AT PIT OCT 16

```
BRO  010 003 000   4 7 0
PIT  000 100 100   2 4 6
```
Pitchers: KITSON vs LEEVER
Attendance: 1,800

GAME 3 AT PIT OCT 17

```
BRO  000 000 000   0  6 3
PIT  310 020 13X  10 13 1
```
Pitchers: HOWELL vs PHILLIPPE
Attendance: 2,500

GAME 4 AT PIT OCT 18

```
BRO  100 311 000   6 8 0
PIT  000 001 000   1 9 3
```
Pitchers: McGINNITY vs LEEVER, Waddell (5)
Attendance: 2,335

BOSTON PILGRIMS (AL) 5, PITTSBURGH PIRATES (NL) 3

When the Boston Pilgrims of the young American League accepted a challenge from owner Barney Dreyfuss of the National League Pirates, the modern World Series was born. (In 1901 and 1902, the National and American Leagues were warring, and did not stage a postseason series.) Pittsburgh was favored to win but entered the Series weakened by injuries to pitching ace Sam Leever and shortstop Honus Wagner, and by the loss of pitcher Ed Doheny to mental illness.

Deacon Phillippe, the Pirates' one healthy starter, faced Cy Young in the opener, winning handily as the Pirates, with two out in the top of the first, jumped on Young (and a porous defense) for four runs. Right fielder Jimmy Sebring starred offensively for the Pirates, with four RBIs and the Series' first home run. Boston came back in Game 2 as Bill Dinneen shut out the Pirates on three hits. His teammates scored three runs off the sore-armed Leever and reliever Bucky Veil, two coming on homers by Patsy Dougherty. (They were the last World Series home runs for five years.)

Phillippe, with only a day's rest, started Game 3 and again pitched Pittsburgh into the Series lead, holding Boston to four hits. After a Sunday travel day to Pittsburgh and a day of rain, Phillippe defeated Boston a third time, though he yielded three ninth-inning runs before emerging with a 5–4 win.

The tide began to turn against the Pirates the next day, as Boston knocked five ground-rule triples into the overflow crowd, scoring 10 runs in the sixth and seventh innings to give Young an 11–2 victory. Dinneen bested Leever for a second time in Game 6, holding the Pirates scoreless in eight of their nine innings for a 6–3 win. And in Game 7, Phillippe finally lost and Young won.

After another travel Sunday and another rainout, Phillippe faced the Pilgrims for the fifth time. He pitched well, giving up three runs (only two of them earned). But Bill Dinneen pitched better, holding the Pirates to four hits as he shut them out for the second time to give Boston the Series.

BOS (A)

PLAYER/POS	AVG	G	AB	R	H	2B	3B	HR	RB	BB	SO	SB
Jimmy Collins, 3b	.250	8	36	5	9	1	2	0	1	1	1	3
Lou Criger, c	.231	8	26	1	6	0	0	0	4	2	3	0
Bill Dinneen, p	.250	4	12	1	3	0	0	0	0	2	2	0
Patsy Dougherty, of	.235	8	34	3	8	0	2	2	5	2	6	0
Duke Farrell, ph	.000	2	2	0	0	0	0	0	1	0	0	0
Hobe Ferris, 2b	.290	8	31	3	9	0	1	0	5	0	6	0
Buck Freeman, of	.281	8	32	6	9	0	3	0	4	2	2	0
Tom Hughes, p	.000	1	0	0	0	0	0	0	0	0	0	0
Candy La Chance, 1b	.222	8	27	5	6	2	1	0	4	3	2	0
Jack O'Ben, ph	.000	2	2	0	0	0	0	0	0	0	1	0
Freddy Parent, ss	.281	8	32	8	9	0	3	0	4	1	1	0
Chick Stahl, of	.303	8	33	6	10	1	3	0	3	1	2	2
Cy Young, p	.133	4	15	1	2	0	1	0	3	0	3	0
TOTAL	.252		282	39	71	4	16	2	34	14	29	5

PITCHER	W	L	ERA	G	GS	CG	SV	SHO	IP	H	ER	BB	SO
Bill Dinneen	3	1	2.06	4	4	4	0	2	35.0	29	8	8	28
Tom Hughes	0	1	9.00	1	1	0	0	0	2.0	4	2	2	0
Cy Young	2	1	1.85	4	3	3	0	0	34.0	31	7	4	17
TOTAL	5	3	2.15	9	8	7	0	2	71.0	64	17	14	45

PIT (N)

PLAYER/POS	AVG	G	AB	R	H	2B	3B	HR	RB	BB	SO	SB
Ginger Beaumont, of	.265	8	34	6	9	0	1	0	1	2	4	2
Kitty Bransfield, 1b	.207	8	29	3	6	0	2	0	1	1	6	1
Fred Clarke, of	.265	8	34	3	9	2	1	0	2	1	5	1
Brickyard Kennedy, p	.500	1	2	0	1	1	0	0	0	0	0	0
Tommy Leach, 3b	.273	8	33	3	9	0	4	0	7	1	4	1
Sam Leever, p	.000	2	4	0	0	0	0	0	0	0	0	0
Ed Phelps, c-7	.231	8	26	1	6	2	0	0	1	1	6	0
Deacon Phillippe, p	.222	5	18	1	4	0	0	0	1	0	3	0
Claude Ritchey, 2b	.111	8	27	2	3	1	0	0	2	4	7	1
Jimmy Sebring, of	.367	8	30	3	11	0	1	1	3	1	4	0
Harry Smith, c	.000	1	3	0	0	0	0	0	0	0	0	0
Gus Thompson, p	.000	1	1	0	0	0	0	0	0	0	2	0
Bucky Veil, p	.000	1	2	0	0	0	0	0	0	0	2	0
Honus Wagner, ss	.222	8	27	2	6	1	0	0	3	3	4	3
TOTAL	.237		270	24	64	7	9	1	21	14	45	9

PITCHER	W	L	ERA	G	GS	CG	SV	SHO	IP	H	ER	BB	SO
Brickyard Kennedy	0	1	5.14	1	1	0	0	0	7.0	11	4	3	3
Sam Leever	0	2	5.40	2	2	1	0	0	10.0	13	6	3	2
Deacon Phillippe	3	2	2.86	5	5	5	0	0	44.0	38	14	3	22
Gus Thompson	0	0	4.50	1	0	0	0	0	2.0	3	1	0	1
Bucky Veil	0	0	1.29	1	0	0	0	0	7.0	6	1	5	1
TOTAL	3	5	3.34	10	8	6	0		0.0	71	26	14	29

GAME 1 AT BOS OCT 1

PIT 4 0 1 1 0 0 1 0 0   7 12 2
BOS 0 0 0 0 0 0 2 0 1   3 6 4
Pitchers: PHILLIPPE vs YOUNG
Home Runs: Sebring-PIT
Attendance: 16,242

GAME 2 AT BOS OCT 2

PIT 0 0 0 0 0 0 0 0 0   0 3 2
BOS 2 0 0 0 0 1 0 0 X   3 9 0
Pitchers: LEEVER, Veil (2) vs DINNEEN
Home Runs: Dougherty-BOS (2)
Attendance: 9,415

GAME 3 AT BOS OCT 3

PIT 0 1 2 0 0 0 0 1 0   4 7 0
BOS 0 0 0 1 0 0 0 1 0   2 4 2
Pitchers: PHILLIPPE vs HUGHES, Young (3)
Attendance: 18,801

GAME 4 AT PIT OCT 6

BOS 0 0 0 0 1 0 0 0 3   4 9 1
PIT 1 0 0 0 1 0 3 0 X   5 12 1
Pitchers: DINNEEN vs PHILLIPPE
Attendance: 7,600

GAME 5 AT PIT OCT 7

BOS 0 0 0 0 0 6 4 1 0   11 14 2
PIT 0 0 0 0 0 0 2 0 0   2 6 4
Pitchers: YOUNG vs KENNEDY, Thompson (8)
Attendance: 12,322

GAME 6 AT PIT OCT 8

BOS 0 0 3 0 2 0 1 0 0   6 10 1
PIT 0 0 0 0 0 0 3 0 0   3 10 3
Pitchers: DINNEEN vs LEEVER
Attendance: 11,556

GAME 7 AT PIT OCT 10

BOS 2 0 0 2 0 2 0 1 0   7 11 4
PIT 0 0 0 1 0 1 0 0 1   3 10 3
Pitchers: YOUNG vs PHILLIPPE
Attendance: 17,038

GAME 8 AT BOS OCT 13

PIT 0 0 0 0 0 0 0 0 0   0 4 3
BOS 0 0 0 2 0 1 0 0 X   3 8 0
Pitchers: PHILLIPPE vs DINNEEN
Attendance: 7,455

NEW YORK GIANTS (NL) 4, PHILADELPHIA ATHLETICS (AL) 1

After a year's gap caused by the Giants' refusal to play the American League champion Boston Pilgrims, the World Series—now established on an official and permanent basis (and reduced to a best-of-seven format)—resumed with a pitching classic. Even though ERA league leader Rube Waddell had ostensibly injured his shoulder and could not pitch in the Series for the A's—rumor had it that gamblers had reached him—the Philadelphia staff recorded a Series ERA of only 1.47. But the Giants' staff—led by Christy Mathewson's three shutouts—registered a matchless ERA of 0.00, permitting only three unearned runs to score in their only Series loss. Every victory in the Series was a shutout.

Mathewson, a 31-game winner in the regular season, continued his winning ways in the Series opener. Though three of the four hits he yielded were doubles, he permitted no more than one hit in any inning, and stopped the only scoring threat, fielding a squeeze bunt to throw out the runner at the plate in the sixth inning.

The A's came back to tie the Series the next day. This time it was Chief Bender's turn to hurl a four-hit shutout. Joe McGinnity also pitched well for the Giants, but New York errors in the third and eighth innings let in three unearned runs—the only runs, as it turned out, to be scored against the Giants in the Series.

Mathewson, pitching with only two days' rest in Game 3, once again permitted only four hits (all singles this time), and Philadelphia's flawed fielding let in seven unearned runs to help give Matty an easy 9–0 win. In Game 4, McGinnity, the hard-luck loser of Game 2, tried again. This time the Giants supported him almost flawlessly, while he gave up only five singles on his way to victory in the Series' tightest game. An A's error led to a single Giants run, and a loss for Eddie Plank, who had pitched even better than McGinnity, giving up only four hits while fanning six.

Chief Bender, the A's winner in Game 2, pitched a five-hitter in Game 6, but he also yielded three walks, all of which contributed to the two New York runs. Mathewson, though he gave up six

hits, walked none, retiring the final ten batters to conclude his record third shutout—and the Series.

NY (N)

PLAYER/POS	AVG	G	AB	R	H	2B	3B	HR	RB	BB	SO	SB
Red Ames, p	.000	1	0	0	0	0	0	0	0	0	0	0
Roger Bresnahan, c	.313	5	16	3	5	2	0	0	1	4	0	1
George Browne, of	.182	5	22	2	4	0	0	0	1	0	2	2
Bill Dahlen, ss	.000	5	15	1	0	0	0	0	1	3	2	3
Art Devlin, 3b	.250	5	16	0	4	1	0	0	1	1	3	3
Mike Donlin, of	.263	5	19	4	5	1	0	0	1	2	1	2
Billy Gilbert, 2b	.235	5	17	1	4	0	0	0	2	0	2	1
Christy Mathewson, p	.250	3	8	1	2	0	0	0	0	1	1	0
Dan McGann, 1b	.235	5	17	1	4	2	0	0	4	2	7	0
Joe McGinnity, p	.000	2	5	0	0	0	0	0	0	0	2	0
Sam Mertes, of	.176	5	17	2	3	1	0	0	2	2	5	0
Sammy Strang, ph	.000	1	1	0	0	0	0	0	0	0	1	0
TOTAL	.203		153	15	31	7	0	0	13	15	26	12

PITCHER	W	L	ERA	G	GS	CG	SV	SHO	IP	H	ER	BB	SO
Red Ames	0	0	0.00	1	0	0	0	0	1.0	1	0	1	1
Christy Mathewson	3	0	0.00	3	3	3	0	3	27.0	14	0	1	18
Joe McGinnity	1	1	0.00	2	2	1	0	1	17.0	10	0	3	6
TOTAL	4	1	0.00	6	5	4	0	4	45.0	25	0	5	25

PHI (A)

PLAYER/POS	AVG	G	AB	R	H	2B	3B	HR	RB	BB	SO	SB
Chief Bender, p	.000	2	5	0	0	0	0	0	0	0	1	0
Andy Coakley, p	.000	1	2	0	0	0	0	0	0	0	1	0
Lave Cross, 3b	.105	5	19	0	2	0	0	0	0	1	1	0
Monte Cross, ss	.176	5	17	0	3	0	0	0	0	0	7	0
Harry Davis, 1b	.200	5	20	0	4	1	0	0	0	0	1	0
Topsy Hartsel, of	.294	5	17	1	5	1	0	0	0	2	1	2
Danny Hoffman, ph	.000	1	1	0	0	0	0	0	0	0	1	0
Bris Lord, of	.100	5	20	0	2	0	0	0	2	0	5	0
Danny Murphy, 2b	.188	5	16	0	3	1	0	0	0	0	2	0
Eddie Plank, p	.167	2	6	0	1	0	0	0	0	0	2	0
Mike Powers, c	.143	3	7	0	1	1	0	0	0	0	0	0
Ossee Schreckengost, c	.222	3	9	2	2	1	0	0	0	0	0	0
Socks Seybold, of	.125	5	16	0	2	0	0	0	0	2	3	0
TOTAL	.161		155	3	25	5	0	0	2	5	25	2

PITCHER	W	L	ERA	G	GS	CG	SV	SHO	IP	H	ER	BB	SO
Chief Bender	1	1	1.06	2	2	2	0	1	17.0	9	2	6	13
Andy Coakley	0	1	2.00	1	1	1	0	0	9.0	8	2	5	2
Eddie Plank	0	2	1.59	2	2	2	0	0	17.0	14	3	4	11
TOTAL	1	4	1.47	5	5	5	0	1	43.0	31	7	15	26

GAME 1 AT PHI OCT 9
NY   000 020 001   3 10 1
PHI 000 000 000   0 4 0
Pitchers: MATHEWSON vs PLANK
Attendance: 17,955

GAME 2 AT NY OCT 10
PHI 001 000 020   3 6 2
NY   000 000 000   0 4 2
Pitchers: BENDER vs McGINNITY, Ames (9)
Attendance: 24,992

GAME 3 AT PHI OCT 12
NY   200 050 002   9 9 1
PHI 000 000 000   0 4 5
Pitchers: MATHEWSON vs COAKLEY
Attendance: 10,991

GAME 4 AT NY OCT 13
PHI 000 000 000   0 5 2
NY   000 100 00X   1 4 1
Pitchers: PLANK vs McGINNITY
Attendance: 13,598

GAME 5 AT NY OCT 14
PHI 000 000 000   0 6 0
NY   000 010 01X   2 5 1
Pitchers: BENDER vs MATHEWSON
Attendance: 24,187

CHICAGO WHITE SOX (AL) 4, CHICAGO CUBS (NL) 2

The Cubs and White Sox have played more postseason City Series than any other clubs, but this was their only all-Chicago World Series. The Cubs were the clear favorites: league leaders in batting, fielding, and pitching (with a team ERA of only 1.76). They were one of baseball's greatest teams ever, with a still-record 116 wins, finishing 20 games ahead of the second-place Giants. The White Sox, by contrast, although their pitching and fielding were good enough to rank second in the American League, were the junior circuit's weakest hitters, batting as a team only .230, 32 points below the Cubs. But in the Series the "hitless wonders" prevailed. Though they hit only .198 and yielded eight unearned runs, the Sox bunched their hits for 20 earned runs—double the Cubs' total. Meanwhile, Sox pitchers held the Cubs to a .196 BA, and produced a team ERA less than half that of Cub pitchers.

Game 1 was a pitcher's duel as the Cubs' Mordecai "Three Finger" Brown and Nick Altrock traded four-hitters and one earned run apiece. But Brown lost the game when his error in the seventh led to the second run for the Sox. The Cubs snapped back to take Game 2 on Ed Reulbach's one-hit 7–1 win. Although Reulbach issued six walks, he didn't really need the five unearned runs handed his club by Sox errors.

In Game 3 the Sox regained the Series lead as Ed Walsh two-hit the Cubs, fanning 12 for the Series' first shutout. The Cubs' Jack Pfiester also pitched shutout ball in eight of his nine innings, but George Rohe's bases-loaded triple in the sixth gave the Sox more than enough to defeat him. Brown brought the Cubs back the next day, evening the Series with a two-hit shutout of his own, winning when Altrock yielded his only run on pairs of singles and sacrifice bunts in the seventh.

The rest of the Series belonged to the hitless wonders, who rocked three Cub pitchers for 12 hits and eight runs to take Game 5, and buried Brown and Orval Overall under 14 hits and another eight runs in Game 6 to capture their first world championship

CHI (A)

PLAYER/POS	AVG	G	AB	R	H	2B	3B	HR	RB	BB	SO	SB
Nick Altrock, p	.250	2	4	0	1	0	0	0	0	1	1	0
George Davis, ss	.308	3	13	4	4	3	0	0	6	0	1	1
Jiggs Donahue, 1b	.333	6	18	0	6	2	1	0	4	3	3	0
Patsy Dougherty, of	.100	6	20	1	2	0	0	0	1	3	4	2
Eddie Hahn, of	.273	6	22	4	6	0	0	0	0	1	1	0
Frank Isbell, 2b	.308	6	26	4	8	4	0	0	4	0	6	1
Fielder Jones, of	.095	6	21	4	2	0	0	0	0	3	3	0
Ed McFarland, ph	.000	1	1	0	0	0	0	0	0	0	0	0
Bill O'Neill, of	.000	1	1	1	0	0	0	0	0	0	0	0
Frank Owen, p	.000	1	2	0	0	0	0	0	0	0	1	0
George Rohe, 3b	.333	6	21	2	7	1	2	0	4	3	1	2
Billy Sullivan, c	.000	6	21	0	0	0	0	0	0	0	9	0
Lee Tannehill, ss	.111	3	9	1	1	0	0	0	0	0	2	0
Babe Towne, ph	.000	1	1	0	0	0	0	0	0	0	0	0
Ed Walsh, p	.000	2	4	1	0	0	0	0	0	0	3	0
Doc White, p	.000	3	3	0	0	0	0	0	0	0	1	0
TOTAL	.198		187	22	37	10	3	0	19	18	35	6

PITCHER	W	L	ERA	G	GS	CG	SV	SHO	IP	H	ER	BB	SO
Nick Altrock	1	1	1.00	2	2	2	0	0	18.0	11	2	2	5
Frank Owen	0	0	3.00	1	0	0	0	0	6.0	6	2	3	2
Ed Walsh	2	0	1.20	2	2	1	0	1	15.0	7	2	6	17
Doc White	1	1	1.80	3	2	1	1	0	15.0	12	3	7	4
TOTAL	4	2	1.50	8	6	4	1	1	54.0	36	9	18	28

CHI (N)

PLAYER/POS	AVG	G	AB	R	H	2B	3B	HR	RB	BB	SO	SB
Mordecai Brown, p	.333	3	6	0	2	0	0	0	0	0	4	0
Frank Chance, 1b	.238	6	21	3	5	1	0	0	0	2	1	2
Johnny Evers, 2b	.150	6	20	2	3	1	0	0	1	1	3	2
Doc Gessler, ph	.000	2	1	0	0	0	0	0	0	1	0	0
Solly Hofman, of	.304	6	23	3	7	1	0	0	2	3	5	1
Johnny Kling, c	.176	6	17	2	3	1	0	0	0	4	3	0
Pat Moran, ph	.000	2	2	0	0	0	0	0	0	0	0	0
Orval Overall, p	.250	2	4	1	1	1	0	0	0	1	1	0
Jack Pfiester, p	.000	2	2	0	0	0	0	0	0	0	1	0
Ed Reulbach, p	.000	2	3	0	0	0	0	0	0	1	0	0
Frank Schulte, of	.269	6	26	1	7	3	0	0	3	1	3	0
Jimmy Sheckard, of	.000	6	21	0	0	0	0	0	0	1	2	4	1
Harry Steinfeldt, 3b	.250	6	20	2	5	1	0	0	2	1	0	0
Joe Tinker, ss	.167	6	18	4	3	0	0	0	1	2	2	3
TOTAL	.196		184	18	36	9	0	0	11	18	28	9

PITCHER	W	L	ERA	G	GS	CG	SV	SHO	IP	H	ER	BB	SO
Mordecai Brown	1	2	3.20	3	3	2	0	1	19.2	14	7	4	12
Orval Overall	0	0	2.25	2	0	0	0	0	12.0	10	3	3	8
Jack Pfiester	0	2	6.10	2	1	1	0	0	10.1	7	7	3	11
Ed Reulbach	1	0	2.45	2	2	1	0	0	11.0	6	3	8	4
TOTAL	2	4	3.40	9	6	4	0	1	53.0	37	20	18	35

GAME 1 AT CHI-N OCT 9

CHI-A 000 011 000　2 4 1
CHI-N 000 001 000　1 4 2
Pitchers: ALTROCK vs BROWN
Attendance: 12,693

GAME 2 AT CHI-A OCT 10

CHI-N 031 001 020　7 10 2
CHI-A 000 010 000　1 1 2
Pitchers: REULBACH vs WHITE, Owen (4)
Attendance: 12,595

GAME 3 AT CHI-N OCT 11

CHI-A 000 003 000　3 4 1
CHI-N 000 000 000　0 2 2
Pitchers: WALSH vs PFIESTER
Attendance: 13,667

GAME 4 AT CHI-A OCT 12

CHI-N 000 000 100　1 7 1
CHI-A 000 000 000　0 2 1
Pitchers: BROWN vs ALTROCK
Attendance: 18,385

GAME 5 AT CHI-N OCT 13

CHI-A 102 401 000　8 12 6
CHI-N 300 102 000　6 6 0
Pitchers: WALSH, White (7) vs Reulbach, PFIESTER (3), Overall (4)
Attendance: 23,257

GAME 6 AT CHI-A OCT 14

CHI-N 100 010 001　3 7 0
CHI-A 340 000 01X　8 14 3
Pitchers: BROWN, Overall (2) vs WHITE
Attendance: 19,249

CHICAGO CUBS (NL) 4, DETROIT TIGERS (AL) 0; TIE, 1

The two-run lead that Detroit took into the bottom of the ninth inning of Game 1 proved to be its biggest of the Series. And it was shortlived, as Chicago—after Frank Chance's leadoff single—took advantage of a hit batsman, a fumble at third base, and a dropped third strike to even the score. Three scoreless extra innings later, darkness ended the game in a 3–3 tie.

The Tigers pitched well enough in the Series. Wild Bill Donovan and George Mullin, who provided more than 80 percent of Detroit's pitching, allowed only four earned runs each for a combined 1.89 ERA. But Cubs pitchers gave up only four earned runs as a team, suffocating the Tigers with a team ERA of 0.75. And while Tiger fielders made one less error than the Cubs, their misplays proved more costly, permitting eight unearned runs to the Cubs' two.

Detroit's three-run eighth in the opener provided half of their Series scoring. Nine Detroit hits in Game 2 produced only one run, while the Cubs bunched six of their nine hits into two innings for three runs and the Series' first win. In Games 3 and 4, while the Tigers were twice again limited to a single run, the Cubs increased their run production to five and six, clustering 40 percent of their hits into two three-run innings, "Three one Finger" in each Brown game.

Mordecai wrapped up the Series for Chicago with a shutout, as his Cubs blended a hit in each of the first two innings with three stolen bases and a Detroit error for the game's only two runs.

Detroit's 20-year-old Ty Cobb, the American League batting, RBI, and stolen base leader in his first full big league season, hit an anemic .200 in the World Series, stealing no bases and driving in no runs. If there was an offensive hero, it was Cubs centerfielder Jimmy Slagle. At age 34, nearing the end of a 10-year major league career, he led both clubs with four RBIs (nearly quadruple his season's per-game output) and six stolen bases.

CHI (N)

PLAYER/POS	AVG	G	AB	R	H	2B	3B	HR	RB	BB	SO	SB
Mordecai Brown, p	.000	1	3	0	0	0	0	0	0	1	0	0
Frank Chance, 1b	.214	4	14	3	3	1	0	0	0	3	2	3
Johnny Evers, 2b-5, ss-1	.350	5	20	2	7	2	0	0	1	0	1	3
Del Howard, 1b-1	.200	2	5	0	1	0	0	0	0	0	2	1
Johnny Kling, c	.211	5	19	2	4	0	0	0	1	1	4	0
Pat Moran, ph	.000	1	0	0	0	0	0	0	0	0	0	0
Orval Overall, p	.200	2	5	0	1	0	0	0	2	0	1	0
Jack Pfiester, p	.000	1	2	0	0	0	0	0	0	0	1	0
Ed Reulbach, p	.200	2	5	0	1	0	0	0	1	0	0	0
Frank Schulte, of	.250	5	20	3	5	0	0	0	2	1	2	0
Jimmy Sheckard, of	.238	5	21	0	5	2	0	0	2	0	4	1
Jimmy Slagle, of	.273	5	22	3	6	0	0	0	4	2	3	6
Harry Steinfeldt, 3b	.471	5	17	2	8	1	1	0	2	1	2	1
Joe Tinker, ss	.154	5	13	4	2	0	0	0	1	3	3	1
Heinie Zimmerman, 2b	.000	1	1	0	0	0	0	0	0	0	1	0
TOTAL	.257		167	19	43	6	1	0	16	12	26	16

PITCHER	W	L	ERA	G	GS	CG	SV	SHO	IP	H	ER	BB	SO
Mordecai Brown	1	0	0.00	1	1	1	0	1	9.0	7	0	1	4
Orval Overall	1	0	1.00	2	2	1	0	0	18.0	14	2	4	11
Jack Pfiester	1	0	1.00	1	1	1	0	0	9.0	9	1	1	3
Ed Reulbach	1	0	0.75	2	1	1	0	0	12.0	6	1	3	4
TOTAL	4	0	0.75	6	5	4	0	1	48.0	36	4	9	22

DET (A)

PLAYER/POS	AVG	G	AB	R	H	2B	3B	HR	RB	BB	SO	SB
Jimmy Archer, c	.000	1	3	0	0	0	0	0	0	0	1	0
Ty Cobb, of	.200	5	20	1	4	0	1	0	0	0	3	0
Bill Coughlin, 3b	.250	5	20	0	5	0	0	0	0	1	4	1
Sam Crawford, of	.238	5	21	1	5	1	0	0	3	0	3	0
Bill Donovan, p	.000	2	8	0	0	0	0	0	0	0	3	0
Davy Jones, of	.353	5	17	1	6	0	0	0	0	4	0	3
Ed Killian, p	.500	1	2	1	1	0	0	0	0	0	0	0
George Mullin, p	.000	2	6	0	0	0	0	0	0	0	1	0
Charley O'Leary, ss	.059	5	17	0	1	0	0	0	0	1	3	0
Fred Payne, c-1	.250	2	4	0	1	0	0	0	1	0	0	1
Claude Rossman, 1b	.400	5	20	1	8	0	1	0	2	1	0	1
Germany Schaefer, 2b	.143	5	21	1	3	0	0	0	0	0	3	0
Boss Schmidt, c-3	.167	4	12	0	2	0	0	0	0	2	1	0
Ed Siever, p	.000	1	1	0	0	0	0	0	0	0	0	0
TOTAL	.209		172	6	36	1	2	0	6	9	22	6

PITCHER	W	L	ERA	G	GS	CG	SV	SHO	IP	H	ER	BB	SO
Bill Donovan	0	1	1.71	2	2	2	0	0	21.0	17	4	5	16
Ed Killian	0	0	2.25	1	0	0	0	0	4.0	3	1	1	1
George Mullin	0	2	2.12	2	2	2	0	0	17.0	16	4	6	8
Ed Siever	0	1	4.50	1	1	0	0	0	4.0	7	2	0	1
TOTAL	0	4	2.15	6	5	4	0	0	46.0	43	11	12	26

GAME 1 AT CHI OCT 8

```
DET  000 000 030 0003  9 3
CHI  000 100 002 0003 10 5
```
Pitchers: Donovan vs Overall, Reulbach (10)
Attendance: 24,377
(Game called at end of twelfth, darkness)

GAME 2 AT CHI OCT 9

```
DET  010 000 000  1 9 1
CHI  010 200 00X  3 9 1
```
Pitchers: MULLIN vs PFIESTER
Attendance: 21,901

GAME 3 AT CHI OCT 10

```
DET  000 001 000  1 6 1
CHI  010 310 00X  5 10 1
```
Pitchers: SIEVER, Killian (5) vs REULBACH
Attendance: 13,114

GAME 4 AT DET OCT 11

```
CHI  000 020 301  6 7 2
DET  000 100 000  1 5 2
```
Pitchers: OVERALL vs DONOVAN
Attendance: 11,306

GAME 5 AT DET OCT 12

```
CHI  110 000 000  2 7 1
DET  000 000 000  0 7 2
```
Pitchers: Brown vs Mullin
Attendace: 7,370

CHICAGO CUBS (NL) 4, DETROIT TIGERS (AL) 1

The Tigers won their final game of the season to take their second straight pennant, and the Cubs won their third pennant in a row by defeating the Giants in a replay of an earlier tie. Ty Cobb and Detroit improved on their 1907 Series performance, as Cobb led his club in batting, hits, and RBIs, and the Tigers won a game. But the Cubs as a team hit 90 percentage points higher than Detroit, and outscored them 24–15, to take the Series with relative ease.

In Game 1, the Tigers took advantage of the Cubs' ragged fielding to score two runs in the eighth for a 6–5 lead. But in the top of the ninth the Cubs erupted for five runs on six consecutive singles and a double steal to win the game. The next day Chicago's Orval Overall held Detroit to four hits and one ninth-inning run. The Tigers' Wild Bill Donovan pitched even better for seven innings, holding Chicago to a single in the sixth. But in the eighth, Joe Tinker's two-run homer—the first in a World Series since 1903—began an assault that ended only after six Cubs had crossed the plate.

Detroit finally manufactured a Series win, pummeling Jack Pfiester in Game 3 for 10 hits (six of them in the sixth inning) and an 8–3 victory. But that was their last burst. As the Series moved to Detroit for Games 4 and 5, the Tiger offense collapsed. Three Finger Brown, the winner as a reliever in Game 1, won Game 4 as a starter, shutting out the Tigers on four hits. The Cubs needed only three of their 10 hits, combining them with a couple of walks and stolen bases, and a muffed fly ball, to score twice in the third inning and once in the ninth.

Only 6,210 spectators—the smallest World Series crowd of the century—saw Overall strike out four Tigers in the first inning of Game 5 (one reached first on a wild pitch) in what became a three-hit shutout. Meanwhile, his Cubs unloaded for 10 hits, defeating Donovan a second time, scoring runs in the first and fifth innings. Overall—after yielding a leadoff walk to Cobb in the fifth—retired Cobb on a force play and set down the final 11 men to face him.

CHI (N)

PLAYER/POS	AVG	G	AB	R	H	2B	3B	HR	RB	BB	SO	SB
Mordecai Brown, p	.000	2	4	0	0	0	0	0	0	0	2	0
Frank Chance, 1b	.421	5	19	4	8	0	0	0	2	3	1	5
Johnny Evers, 2b	.350	5	20	5	7	1	0	0	2	1	2	2
Solly Hofman, of	.316	5	19	2	6	0	1	0	4	1	4	2
Del Howard, ph	.000	1	1	0	0	0	0	0	0	0	0	0
Johnny Kling, c	.250	5	16	2	4	1	0	0	2	2	2	0
Orval Overall, p	.333	3	6	0	2	0	0	0	0	0	1	0
Jack Pfiester, p	.000	1	2	0	0	0	0	0	0	0	2	0
Ed Reulbach, p	.000	2	3	0	0	0	0	0	0	0	1	0
Frank Schulte, of	.389	5	18	4	7	0	1	0	2	2	1	2
Jimmy Sheckard, of	.238	5	21	2	5	2	0	0	1	2	3	1
Harry Steinfeldt, 3b	.250	5	16	3	4	0	0	0	3	2	5	1
Joe Tinker, ss	.263	5	19	2	5	0	0	1	4	0	2	2
TOTAL	.293		164	24	48	4	2	1	20	13	26	15

PITCHER	W	L	ERA	G	GS	CG	SV	SHO	IP	H	ER	BB	SO
Mordecai Brown	2	0	0.00	2	1	1	0	1	11.0	6	0	1	5
Orval Overall	2	0	0.98	3	2	2	0	1	18.1	7	2	7	15
Jack Pfiester	0	1	7.87	1	1	0	0	0	8.0	10	7	3	1
Ed Reulbach	0	0	4.70	2	1	0	0	0	7.2	9	4	1	5
TOTAL	4	1	2.60	8	5	3	0	2	45.0	32	13	12	26

DET (A)

PLAYER/POS	AVG	G	AB	R	H	2B	3B	HR	RB	BB	SO	SB
Ty Cobb, of	.368	5	19	3	7	1	0	0	4	1	2	2
Bill Coughlin, 3b	.125	3	8	0	1	0	0	0	1	0	1	0
Sam Crawford, of	.238	5	21	2	5	1	0	0	1	1	2	0
Bill Donovan, p	.000	2	4	0	0	0	0	0	0	1	1	1
Red Downs, 2b	.167	2	6	1	1	1	0	0	1	1	2	0
Davy Jones, ph	.000	3	2	1	0	0	0	0	0	1	1	0
Ed Killian, p	.000	1	0	0	0	0	0	0	0	0	0	0
Matty McIntyre, of	.222	5	18	2	4	1	0	0	0	3	2	1
George Mullin, p	.333	1	3	1	1	0	0	0	1	1	0	0
Charley O'Leary, ss	.158	5	19	2	3	0	0	0	0	0	3	0
Claude Rossman, 1b	.211	5	19	3	4	0	0	0	3	1	4	1
Germany Schaefer, 2b-3,3b-2	.125	5	16	0	2	0	0	0	0	1	4	1
Boss Schmidt, c	.071	4	14	0	1	0	0	0	1	0	2	0
Ed Summers, p	.200	2	5	0	1	0	0	0	1	0	2	0
Ira Thomas, c-1	.500	2	4	0	2	1	0	0	1	1	0	0
George Winter, p-1	.000	2	0	0	0	0	0	0	0	0	0	0
TOTAL	.203		158	15	32	5	0	0	14	12	26	6

PITCHER	W	L	ERA	G	GS	CG	SV	SHO	IP	H	ER	BB	SO
Bill Donovan	0	2	4.24	2	2	2	0	0	17.0	17	8	4	10
Ed Killian	0	0	11.57	1	1	0	0	0	2.1	5.0	3	3	1
George Mullin	1	0	0.00	1	1	1	0	0	9.0	7	0	1	8
Ed Summers	0	2	4.30	2	1	0	0	0	14.2	18	7	4	7
George Winter	0	0	0.00	1	0	0	0	0	1.0	1	0	1	0
TOTAL	1	4	3.68	7	5	3	0	0	44.0	48	18	13	26

GAME 1 AT DET OCT 10

```
CHI  0 0 4  0 0 0  1 0 5   10 14 2
DET  1 0 0  0 0 0  3 2 0    6 10 4
```
Pitchers: Reulbach, Overall (7), BROWN (8) vs Killian, SUMMERS (3)
Attendance: 10,812

GAME 2 AT CHI OCT 11

```
DET  0 0 0  0 0 0  0 0 1    1 4 1
CHI  0 0 0  0 0 0  0 6 X    6 7 1
```
Pitchers: DONOVAN vs OVERALL
Home Runs: Tinker-CHI Attendance: 17,760

GAME 3 AT CHI OCT 12

```
DET  1 0 0  0 0 5  0 2 0    8 11 4
CHI  0 0 0  3 0 0  0 0 0    3 7 2
```
Pitchers: MULLIN vs PFIESTER, Reulbach (9)
Attendance: 14,543

GAME 4 AT DET OCT 13

```
CHI  0 0 2  0 0 0  0 0 1    3 10 0
DET  0 0 0  0 0 0  0 0 0    0 4 1
```
Pitchers: BROWN vs SUMMERS, Winter (9)
Attendance: 12,907

GAME 5 AT DET OCT 14

```
CHI  1 0 0  0 1 0  0 0 0    2 10 0
DET  0 0 0  0 0 0  0 0 0    0 3 0
```
Pitchers: OVERALL vs DONOVAN
Attendance: 6,210

PITTSBURGH PIRATES (NL) 4, DETROIT TIGERS (AL) 3

Babe Adams, a 27-year-old rookie pitcher, was only the fifth biggest winner on the Pittsburgh staff. But his fine 12–3 record was supported by a team-best 1.11 ERA, and manager Fred Clarke started him in the Series opener against Detroit's ace George Mullin (who had led the American League with a career-high 29 wins). Mullin pitched well, giving up only one earned run—manager/outfielder Clarke's homer in the fourth inning. But four Tiger errors led to three Pittsburgh runs in the fifth and sixth. Meanwhile, Adams, after yielding a run in the first, pitched shutout ball the rest of the way for the win.

Detroit came back in Game 2 with seven runs (including Ty Cobb's theft of home) as Wild Bill Donovan held the Pirates to two runs on five hits. In Game 3 the Pirates took an early lead, which Detroit, despite rallies in the seventh and ninth innings, was unable to overcome. Errors determined most of the scoring, as only one of Detroit's six runs and two of Pittsburgh's eight were earned.

Mullin shut out the Pirates on five hits in Game 4, striking out 10 men as Detroit scored five runs (all earned, despite Pittsburgh's six errors) to drive out starter Lefty Leifield after four innings. The seesaw Series continued in Game 5, with Babe Adams winning his second game behind his Pirates' 10-hit, eight-run attack. Adams gave up leadoff homers to Davy Jones in the first and Sam Crawford in the eighth. But Pittsburgh's Clarke more than countered these with his three-run shot in the seventh. (All three homers were hit into temporary seats in center field.)

Back in Detroit for Game 6, the Tigers evened the Series for the third time, Mullin winning his second game in a close contest that saw Pittsburgh pull within a run of tying the game in the ninth before a runner thrown out at home and a game-ending double play cut their rally dead.

In the finale it was Babe Adams once again, scattering six hits for an easy 8–0 win, his third of the Series. Detroit had done better than ever, but still lost their third World Series in three consecutive attempts. A quarter century would pass before they would have a chance to try again.

PIT (N)

PLAYER/POS	AVG	G	AB	R	H	2B	3B	HR	RB	BB	SO	SB
Ed Abbaticchio, ph	.000	1	1	0	0	0	0	0	0	0	0	0
Bill Abstein, 1b	.231	7	26	3	6	2	0	0	2	3	10	1
Babe Adams, p	.000	3	9	0	0	0	0	0	0	1	1	0
Bobby Byrne, 3b	.250	7	24	5	6	1	0	0	0	1	4	1
Howie Camnitz, p	.000	2	1	0	0	0	0	0	0	0	0	0
Fred Clarke, of	.211	7	19	7	4	0	0	2	7	5	3	3
George Gibson, c	.240	7	25	2	6	2	0	0	2	1	1	2
Ham Hyatt, of-1	.000	2	4	1	0	0	0	0	1	1	0	0
Tommy Leach, of-7,3b-1	.360	7	25	8	9	4	0	0	2	2	1	1
Lefty Leifield, p	.000	1	1	0	0	0	0	0	0	0	1	0
Nick Maddox, p	.000	1	4	0	0	0	0	0	0	0	1	0
Dots Miller, 2b	.250	7	28	2	7	1	0	0	4	2	5	3
Paddy O'Connor, ph	.000	1	1	0	0	0	0	0	0	0	1	0
Deacon Phillippe, p	.000	2	1	0	0	0	0	0	0	0	1	0
Honus Wagner, ss	.333	7	24	4	8	2	1	0	6	4	2	6
Vic Willis, p	.000	2	4	0	0	0	0	0	0	0	1	0
Chief Wilson, of	.154	7	26	2	4	1	0	0	1	0	2	1
TOTAL	.224		223	34	50	13	1	2	25	20	34	18

PITCHER	W	L	ERA	G	GS	CG	SV	SHO	IP	H	ER	BB	SO
Babe Adams	3	0	1.33	3	3	3	0	1	27.0	18	4	6	11
Howie Camnitz	0	1	9.82	2	1	0	0	0	3.2	8	4	2	2
Lefty Leifield	0	1	11.25	1	1	0	0	0	4.0	7	5	1	0
Nick Maddox	1	0	1.00	1	1	1	0	0	9.0	10	1	2	4
Deacon Phillippe	0	0	0.00	2	0	0	0	0	6.0	2	0	1	2
Vic Willis	0	1	3.97	2	1	0	0	0	11.1	10	5	8	3
TOTAL	4	3	2.80	11	7	4	0	1	61.0	55	19	20	22

DET (A)

PLAYER/POS	AVG	G	AB	R	H	2B	3B	HR	RB	BB	SO	SB
Donie Bush, ss	.261	7	23	5	6	1	0	0	3	5	3	1
Ty Cobb, of	.231	7	26	3	6	3	0	0	5	2	2	2
Sam Crawford, of-7,1b-1	.250	7	28	4	7	3	0	1	4	1	1	1
Jim Delahanty, 2b	.346	7	26	2	9	4	0	0	4	2	5	0
Bill Donovan, p	.000	2	4	0	0	0	0	0	0	0	1	0
Davy Jones, of	.233	7	30	6	7	0	0	1	1	2	1	1
Tom Jones, 1b	.250	7	24	3	6	1	0	0	2	2	0	1
Matty McIntyre, of-1	.000	4	3	0	0	0	0	0	0	0	1	0
George Moriarty, 3b	.273	7	22	4	6	1	0	0	1	3	1	0
George Mullin, p-4	.188	6	16	1	3	1	0	0	0	1	3	0
Charley O'Leary, 3b	.000	1	3	0	0	0	0	0	0	0	0	0
Boss Schmidt, c	.222	6	18	0	4	2	0	0	4	2	0	0
Oscar Stanage, c	.200	2	5	0	1	0	0	0	0	2	0	0
Ed Summers, p	.000	2	3	0	0	0	0	0	0	0	0	0
Ed Willett, p	.000	2	2	0	0	0	0	0	0	0	0	0
Ralph Works, p	.000	1	0	0	0	0	0	0	0	0	0	0
TOTAL	.236		233	28	55	16	0	2	26	20	22	6

PITCHER	W	L	ERA	G	GS	CG	SV	SHO	IP	H	ER	BB	SO
Bill Donovan	1	1	3.00	2	2	1	0	0	12.0	7	4	8	7
George Mullin	2	1	2.25	4	3	3	0	1	32.0	23	8	8	20
Ed Summers	0	2	8.59	2	2	0	0	0	7.1	13	7	4	4
Ed Willett	0	0	0.00	2	0	0	0	0	7.2	3	0	0	1
Ralph Works	0	0	9.00	1	0	0	0	0	2.0	4	2	0	2
TOTAL	3	4	3.10	11	7	4	0	1	61.0	50	21	20	34

GAME 1 AT PIT OCT 8

```
DET  1 0 0  0 0 0  0 0 0    1  6  4
PIT  0 0 0  1 2 1  0 0 X    4  5  0
```
Pitchers: MULLIN vs ADAMS
Home Runs: Clarke-PIT
Attendance: 29,264

GAME 2 AT PIT OCT 9

```
DET  0 2 3  0 2 0  0 0 0    7  9  3
PIT  2 0 0  0 0 0  0 0 0    2  5  1
```
Pitchers: DONOVAN vs CAMNITZ, Willis (3)
Attendance: 30,915

GAME 3 AT DET OCT 11

```
PIT  5 1 0  0 0 0  0 0 2    8 10  3
DET  0 0 0  0 0 0  4 0 2    6 10  5
```
Pitchers: MADDOX vs SUMMERS, Willett (1), Works (8)
Attendance: 18,277

GAME 4 AT DET OCT 12

```
PIT  0 0 0  0 0 0  0 0 0    0  5  6
DET  0 2 0  3 0 0  0 0 X    5  8  0
```
Pitchers: LEIFIELD, Phillippe (5) vs MULLIN
Attendance: 17,036

GAME 5 AT PIT OCT 13

```
DET  1 0 0  0 0 2  0 1 0    4  6  1
PIT  1 1 1  0 0 0  4 1 X    8 10  2
```
Pitchers: SUMMERS, Willett (8) vs ADAMS
Home Runs: D.Jones-DET, Crawford-DET, Clarke-PIT
Attendance: 21,706

GAME 6 AT DET OCT 14

```
PIT  3 0 0  0 0 0  0 0 1    4  7  3
DET  1 0 0  2 1 1  0 0 X    5 10  3
```
Pitchers: WILLIS, Camnitz (6), Phillippe (7) vs MULLIN
Attendance: 10,535

GAME 7 AT DET OCT 16

```
PIT  0 2 0  2 0 3  0 1 0    8  7  0
DET  0 0 0  0 0 0  0 0 0    0  6  3
```
Pitchers: ADAMS vs DONOVAN, Mullin (4)
Attendance: 17,562

PHILADELPHIA ATHLETICS (AL) 4, CHICAGO CUBS (NL) 1

Pitcher Jack Coombs burst into stardom in 1910, emerging as the ace of a Philadelphia pitching staff which dominated the American League with an ERA of only 1.79. Coombs himself led league pitchers with 31 wins and 13 shutouts, and finished second to Chicago's Ed Walsh with an ERA of 1.30—all career bests. He continued his domination into the World Series, pitching three complete-game victories in the Athletics' surprisingly easy triumph over the Cubs.

The Series' finest pitching performance, though, was turned in by the A's Chief Bender in the opener. Only two batters reached base over the first eight innings—on a single and walk—and both of them were cut down trying to steal second. In the ninth, two Cubs singles and two A's errors produced an unearned run, but as the A's had scored four runs (Bender himself providing the margin of victory with the game's second RBI in the second inning), the Cubs' run did no damage.

Coombs started Game 2 and gave up a run in the top of the first inning. But Philadelphia bats were hot in the Series (their team .316 batting average stood as a Series record for 50 years), and their 14 hits in this game (including four doubles and six runs in the seventh) sank Three Finger Brown and gave Coombs an easy win. Connie Mack also started Coombs in Game 3, two days later, and again the result was a lopsided win. Coombs himself drove in three of his team's 12 runs, and right fielder Danny Murphy added three more with the Series' only home run.

Bender pitched Game 4 and suffered the A's only loss, as the Cubs tied the game at 3–3 with a run in the bottom of the ninth, and won it for reliever Three Finger Brown with a two-out RBI single an inning later.

Coombs faced Brown a second time in Game 5. Both clubs made nine hits, but the A's put four of them together with a walk, a wild pitch, and two stolen bases for five runs in the eighth to sink Brown as they had in Game 2, breaking a tight game wide open for Coombs' third win and the Athletics' first world championship

PHI (A)

PLAYER/POS	AVG	G	AB	R	H	2B	3B	HR	RB	BB	SO	SB
Frank Baker, 3b	.409	5	22	6	9	3	0	0	4	2	1	0
Jack Barry, ss	.235	5	17	3	4	2	0	0	3	1	3	0
Chief Bender, p	.333	2	6	1	2	0	0	0	1	1	1	0
Eddie Collins, 2b	.429	5	21	5	9	4	0	0	3	2	0	4
Jack Coombs, p	.385	3	13	0	5	1	0	0	3	0	3	0
Harry Davis, 1b	.353	5	17	5	6	3	0	0	2	3	4	0
Topsy Hartsel, of	.200	1	5	2	1	0	0	0	0	0	1	2
Jack Lapp, c	.250	1	4	0	1	0	0	0	1	0	2	0
Bris Lord, of	.182	5	22	3	4	2	0	0	1	1	3	0
Danny Murphy, of	.350	5	20	6	7	3	0	1	9	1	0	1
Amos Strunk, of	.278	4	18	2	5	1	1	0	2	2	5	0
Ira Thomas, c	.250	4	12	2	3	0	0	0	1	4	1	0
TOTAL	.316		177	35	56	19	1	1	30	17	24	7

PITCHER	W	L	ERA	G	GS	CG	SV	SHO	IP	H	ER	BB	SO
Chief Bender	1	1	1.93	2	2	2	0	0	18.2	12	4	4	14
Jack Coombs	3	0	3.33	3	3	3	0	0	27.0	23	10	14	17
TOTAL	4	1	2.76	5	5	5	0	0	45.2	35	14	18	31

CHI (N)

PLAYER/POS	AVG	G	AB	R	H	2B	3B	HR	RB	BB	SO	SB
Jimmy Archer, c-2,1b-1	.182	3	11	1	2	1	0	0	0	0	3	0
Ginger Beaumont, ph	.000	3	2	1	0	0	0	0	0	1	1	0
Mordecai Brown, p	.000	3	7	0	0	0	0	0	0	0	1	0
Frank Chance, 1b	.353	5	17	1	6	1	1	0	4	0	3	0
King Cole, p	.000	1	2	0	0	0	0	0	0	0	2	0
Solly Hofman, of	.267	5	15	2	4	0	0	0	2	4	3	0
Johnny Kane, pr	.000	1	0	0	0	0	0	0	0	0	0	0
Johnny Kling, c-3	.077	5	13	0	1	0	0	0	1	1	2	0
Harry McIntire, p	.000	2	1	0	0	0	0	0	0	0	1	0
Tom Needham, ph	.000	1	1	0	0	0	0	0	0	0	0	0
Orval Ovall, p	.000	1	1	0	0	0	0	0	0	0	0	0
Jack Pfiester, p	.000	2	0	0	0	0	0	0	0	0	1	0
Ed Reulbach, p	.000	1	0	0	0	0	0	0	0	0	0	0
Lew Richie, p	.000	1	0	0	0	0	0	0	0	0	0	0
Frank Schulte, of	.353	5	17	3	6	3	0	0	2	2	3	0
Jimmy Sheckard, of	.286	5	14	5	4	2	0	0	1	7	2	1
Harry Steinfeldt, 3b	.100	5	20	2	2	1	0	0	1	0	4	0
Joe Tinker, ss	.333	5	18	2	6	2	0	0	0	2	2	1
Heinie Zimmerman, 2b	.235	5	17	0	4	1	0	0	2	1	3	1
TOTAL	.222		158	15	35	11	1	0	13	18	31	3

PITCHER	W	L	ERA	G	GS	CG	SV	SHO	IP	H	ER	BB	SO
Mordecai Brown	1	2	5.50	3	2	1	0	0	18.0	23	11	7	14
King Cole	0	0	3.38	1	1	0	0	0	8.0	10	3	3	5
Harry McIntire	0	1	6.75	2	0	0	0	0	5.1	4	4	3	3
Orval Overall	0	1	9.00	1	1	0	0	0	3.0	6	3	1	1
Jack Pfiester	0	0	0.00	1	0	0	0	0	6.2	9	0	1	1
Ed Reulbach	0	0	9.00	1	1	0	0	0	2.0	3	2	2	0
Lew Richie	0	0	0.00	1	0	0	0	0	1.0	1	0	0	0
TOTAL	1	4	4.70	10	5	1	0	0	44.0	56	23	17	24

GAME 1 AT PHI OCT 17

```
CHI  000 000 001   1 3 1
PHI  021 000 01X   4 7 2
```
Pitchers: OVERALL, McIntire (4) vs BENDER
Attendance: 26,891

GAME 2 AT PHI OCT 18

```
CHI  100 000 101   3 8 3
PHI  002 010 60X   4 7 2
```
Pitchers: BROWN, Richie (8) vs COOMBS
Attendance: 24,597

GAME 3 AT CHI OCT 20

```
PHI  125 000 400  12 15 1
CHI  120 000 020   5  6 5
```
Pitchers: COOMBS vs Reulbach, McINTIRE (3), Pfiester (3)
Home Runs: Murphy-PHI
Attendance: 26,210

GAME 4 AT CHI OCT 22

```
PHI  001 200 000 0  3 11 3
CHI  100 100 001 1  4  9 1
```
Pitchers: BENDER vs Cole, BROWN (9)
Attendance: 19,150

GAME 5 AT CHI OCT 23

```
PHI  100 010 050   7 9 1
CHI  010 000 010   2 9 2
```
Pitchers: COOMBS vs BROWN
Attendance: 27,374

PHILADELPHIA ATHLETICS (AL) 4, NEW YORK GIANTS (NL) 2

Connie Mack's pitching aces outdueled Christy Mathewson, and Frank Baker hit two crucial home runs to become "Home Run" Baker forever more, as the A's avenged their 1905 Series loss to the Giants. Game 1, though, belonged to Matty and New York. Philadelphia scored first, but the Giants tied the game with an unearned run in the fourth inning, and won it with two doubles in the seventh, setting at naught Chief Bender's otherwise splendid 11-strikeout performance.

The A's came back to take three in a row. In Game 2 Eddie Plank held the Giants to one run and Baker hit the first of his homers, breaking a tie in the sixth with a two-run blast off Rube Marquard. The next day, the A's and Jack Coombs handed Mathewson his first World Series loss. Both pitchers went the distance in an 11-inning duel that saw Matty hold the A's scoreless through eight, only to give up a game-tying home run to Baker in the ninth, and two unearned runs in the 11th. Coombs, meanwhile, pitched two-hit, one-run ball through 10 innings. In the last of the 11th, a third Giants hit and an A's error let in a second run, but the rally died when Beals Becker was cut down for the final out trying to steal second.

After a week of rain, Mathewson and Bender squared off in Game 4. The Giants jumped on Bender for two runs in the first, and held the lead until the fourth. But in the last of the fourth, three successive A's doubles and a run-scoring fly put the A's in front to stay as Bender held New York scoreless over the final eight innings.

In Game 5, a three-run homer by the A's Rube Oldring off Rube Marquard in the third provided the only scoring through 6-1/2 innings. But the Giants crept back with one run in the seventh, and two more in the last of the ninth tied the score. Plank replaced Coombs for the A's in the 10th and took the loss as Larry Doyle led off with a double, took third on a missed force play, and scored on Fred Merkle's fly to deep right.

After five closely contested games, Game 6 was a laugher. It, too, was close at first—tied 1-1 after 3-1/2 innings. But the A's

scored four runs in the fourth on singles and errors, once in the sixth, and seven times in the seventh on a barrage of hits, an error, and a two-run wild pitch. Chief Bender, who gave up only four hits and two unearned runs, was the beneficiary of this largesse, taking his second win of the Series and giving the A's their second consecutive world title.

PHI (A)

PLAYER/POS	AVG	G	AB	R	H	2B	3B	HR	RB	BB	SO	SB
Frank Baker, 3b	.375	6	24	7	9	2	0	2	5	1	5	0
Jack Barry, ss	.368	6	19	2	7	4	0	0	2	0	2	2
Chief Bender, p	.091	3	11	0	1	0	0	0	0	0	1	0
Eddie Collins, 2b	.286	6	21	4	6	1	0	0	1	2	2	2
Jack Coombs, p	.250	2	8	1	2	0	0	0	0	0	0	0
Harry Davis, 1b	.208	6	24	3	5	1	0	0	5	0	3	0
Jack Lapp, c	.250	2	8	1	2	0	0	0	0	0	1	0
Bris Lord, of	.185	6	27	2	5	2	0	0	1	0	5	0
Stuffy McInnis, 1b	.000	1	0	0	0	0	0	0	0	0	0	0
Danny Murphy, of	.304	6	23	4	7	3	0	0	3	0	3	0
Rube Oldring, of	.200	6	25	2	5	2	0	1	3	0	5	0
Eddie Plank, p	.000	2	3	0	0	0	0	0	0	0	2	0
Amos Strunk, pr	.000	1	0	0	0	0	0	0	0	0	0	0
Ira Thomas, c	.083	4	12	1	1	0	0	0	0	1	1	2	0
TOTAL	.244		205	27	50	15	0	3	21	4	31	4

PITCHER	W	L	ERA	G	GS	CG	SV	SHO	IP	H	ER	BB	SO
Chief Bender	2	1	1.04	3	3	3	0	0	26.0	16	3	8	20
Jack Coombs	1	0	1.35	2	2	1	0	0	20.0	11	3	6	16
Eddie Plank	1	1	1.86	2	1	1	0	0	9.2	6	2	0	8
TOTAL	4	2	1.29	7	6	5	0	0	55.2	33	8	14	44

NY (N)

PLAYER/POS	AVG	G	AB	R	H	2B	3B	HR	RB	BB	SO	SB
Red Ames, p	.500	2	2	0	1	0	0	0	0	0	1	0
Beals Becker, ph	.000	3	3	0	0	0	0	0	0	0	0	0
Doc Crandall, p-2	.500	3	2	1	1	1	0	0	1	2	0	0
Josh Devore, of	.167	6	24	1	4	1	0	0	3	1	8	0
Larry Doyle, 2b	.304	6	23	3	7	3	1	0	1	2	1	2
Art Fletcher, ss	.130	6	23	1	3	1	0	0	1	0	4	0
Buck Herzog, 3b	.190	6	21	3	4	2	0	0	0	2	3	2
Rube Marquard, p	.000	3	2	0	0	0	0	0	0	0	2	0
Christy Mathewson, p	.286	3	7	0	2	0	0	0	0	1	3	0
Fred Merkle, 1b	.150	6	20	1	3	1	0	0	1	2	6	0
Chief Meyers, c	.300	6	20	2	6	2	0	0	2	0	3	0
Red Murray, of	.000	6	21	0	0	0	0	0	0	2	5	0
Fred Snodgrass, of	.105	6	19	1	2	0	0	0	1	2	7	0
Art Wilson, c	.000	1	1	0	0	0	0	0	0	0	0	0
Hooks Wiltse, p	.000	2	1	0	0	0	0	0	0	0	1	0
TOTAL	.175		189	13	33	11	1	0	10	14	44	4

PITCHER	W	L	ERA	G	GS	CG	SV	SHO	IP	H	ER	BB	SO
Red Ames	0	1	2.25	2	1	0	0	0	8.0	6	2	1	6
Doc Crandall	1	0	0.00	2	0	0	0	0	4.0	2	0	0	2
Rube Marquard	0	1	1.54	3	2	0	0	0	11.2	9	2	1	8
Christy Mathewson	1	2	2.00	3	3	2	0	0	27.0	25	6	2	13
Hooks Wiltse	0	0	18.90	2	0	0	0	0	3.1	8	7	0	2
TOTAL	2	4	2.83	12	6	2	0	0	54.0	50	17	4	31

GAME 1 AT NY OCT 14

```
PHI  010 000 000   1 6 2
NY   000 100 10X   2 5 0
```
Pitchers: BENDER vs MATHEWSON
Attendance: 38,281

GAME 2 AT PHI OCT 16

```
NY   010 000 000   1 5 3
PHI  100 002 00X   3 4 0
```
Pitchers: MARQUARD, Crandall (8) vs PLANK
Home Runs: Baker-PHI
Attendance: 26,286

GAME 3 AT NY OCT 17

```
PHI  000 000 010 2   3 9 2
NY   001 000 000 1   2 3 5
```
Pitchers: COOMBS vs MATHEWSON
Home Runs: Baker-PHI
Attendance: 37,216

GAME 4 AT PHI OCT 24

```
NY   200 000 000   2 7 3
PHI  000 310 00X   4 11 1
```
Pitchers: MATHEWSON, Wiltse (8) vs BENDER
Attendance: 24,355

GAME 5 AT NY OCT 25

```
PHI  003 000 000 0   3 7 1
NY   000 000 102 1   4 9 2
```
Pitchers: Coombs, PLANK (10) vs Marquard, Ames (4), CRANDALL (8)
Home Runs: Oldring-PHI
Attendance: 33,228

GAME 6 AT PHI OCT 26

```
NY   100 000 001   2 4 3
PHI  001 401 70X  13 13 5
```
Pitchers: AMES, Wiltse (5), Marquard (7) vs BENDER
Attendance: 20,485

BOSTON RED SOX (AL) 4, NEW YORK GIANTS (NL) 3; TIE, 1

The Giants outhit the Red Sox by 50 percentage points, and their pitchers let in one less earned run per game. But this was the Series in which Fred Snodgrass' famous muff of a routine fly to center in the 10th inning of the final game helped turn a slim Giants lead into a Red Sox world championship. In all fairness, it must be admitted that Snodgrass followed his muff with a brilliant catch off the next batter, and indecision by the catcher and first baseman permitted a pop foul to drop, keeping the Sox alive to score the tying and winning runs. For that matter, this final game might not have been needed at all if Snodgrass and Beals Becker hadn't both been cut down trying to steal second in the 11th inning of Game 2, which ended in a tie because of darkness. If either had gone on to score, the Giants would have won the Series in seven games.

Boston's Smokey Joe Wood followed up his spectacular 34–5 regular season with Series wins in Games 1 and 4, before being rocked for six runs in the first inning of Game 7 for a loss. Relieving in the eighth inning of the finale, he stopped the Giants for two innings, but gave up what would have been the losing run in the 10th had not the Giants' fielding in the last of the inning turned the game around, giving Wood the win and the Sox the Series.

Although Wood won three games, the best pitching of the Series was turned in by the Giants' Rube Marquard and Boston's Hugh Bedient. Marquard (who in the regular season had tied a major league record with 19 consecutive wins) won two of his club's three victories (Games 3 and 6), allowing three runs—only one of them earned. Bedient, in two starts and two relief appearances, matched Marquard's 0.50 earned run average, winning a duel with Christy Mathewson in Game 5, and hurling seven effective innings against Matty in the finale.

Mathewson was the Series' hard-luck pitcher: his one tie and two losses were all decided by unearned runs.

BOS (A)

PLAYER/POS	AVG	G	AB	R	H	2B	3B	HR	RB	BB	SO	SB
Neal Ball, ph	.000	1	1	0	0	0	0	0	0	0	1	0
Hugh Bedient, p	.000	4	6	0	0	0	0	0	0	0	0	0
Hick Cady, c	.136	7	22	1	3	0	0	0	1	0	3	0
Bill Carrigan, c	.000	2	7	0	0	0	0	0	0	0	0	0
Ray Collins, p	.000	2	5	0	0	0	0	0	0	0	2	0
Clyde Engle, ph	.333	3	3	1	1	1	0	0	2	0	0	0
Larry Gardner, 3b	.179	8	28	4	5	2	1	1	5	2	5	0
Charley Hall, p	.750	2	4	0	3	1	0	0	0	1	0	0
Olaf Henriksen, ph	1.000	2	1	0	1	1	0	0	1	0	0	0
Harry Hooper, of	.290	8	31	3	9	2	1	0	1	4	4	2
Duffy Lewis, of	.156	8	32	4	5	3	0	0	2	2	2	0
Buck O'Brien, p	.000	2	2	0	0	0	0	0	0	0	2	0
Tris Speaker, of	.300	8	30	4	9	1	2	0	2	4	2	1
Jake Stahl, 1b	.281	8	32	3	9	2	0	0	2	0	6	2
Heinie Wagner, ss	.167	8	30	1	5	1	0	0	0	3	6	1
Joe Wood, p	.286	4	7	1	2	0	0	0	1	1	0	0
Steve Yerkes, 2b	.250	8	32	3	8	0	2	0	4	2	3	0
TOTAL	.220		273	25	60	14	6	1	21	19	36	6

PITCHER	W	L	ERA	G	GS	CG	SV	SHO	IP	H	ER	BB	SO
Hugh Bedient	1	0	0.50	4	2	1	0	0	18.0	10	1	7	7
Ray Collins	0	0	1.26	2	1	0	0	0	14.1	14	2	0	6
Charley Hall	0	0	3.38	2	1	0	0	0	10.2	11	4	9	1
Buck O'Brien	0	2	5.00	2	2	0	0	0	9.0	12	5	3	4
Joe Wood	3	1	3.68	4	3	2	0	0	22.0	27	9	3	21
TOTAL	4	3	2.55	14	8	3	0	0	74.0	74	21	22	39

NY (N)

PLAYER/POS	AVG	G	AB	R	H	2B	3B	HR	RB	BB	SO	SB
Red Ames, p	.000	1	0	0	0	0	0	0	0	0	0	0
Beals Becker, of-1	.000	2	4	1	0	0	0	0	0	2	0	0
Doc Crandall, p	.000	1	1	0	0	0	0	0	0	0	1	0
Josh Devore, of	.250	7	24	4	6	0	0	0	0	7	5	4
Larry Doyle, 2b	.242	8	33	5	8	1	0	1	2	3	2	2
Art Fletcher, ss	.179	8	28	1	5	1	0	0	3	1	4	1
Buck Herzog, 3b	.400	8	30	6	12	4	1	0	5	1	3	2
Rube Marquard, p	.000	2	4	0	0	0	0	0	0	1	0	0
Christy Mathewson, p	.167	3	12	0	2	0	0	0	0	0	4	0
Moose McCormick, ph	.250	5	4	0	1	0	0	0	1	0	0	0
Fred Merkle, 1b	.273	8	33	5	9	2	1	0	3	0	7	1
Chief Meyers, c	.357	8	28	2	10	0	1	0	3	2	3	1
Red Murray, of	.323	8	31	5	10	4	1	0	4	2	2	0
Tillie Shafer, ss	.000	3	0	0	0	0	0	0	0	0	0	0
Fred Snodgrass, of	.212	8	33	2	7	2	0	0	2	2	5	1
Jeff Tesreau, p	.375	3	8	0	3	0	0	0	0	2	1	0
Art Wilson, c	1.000	2	1	0	1	0	0	0	0	0	0	0
TOTAL	.270		274	31	74	14	4	1	25	22	39	12

PITCHER	W	L	ERA	G	GS	CG	SV	SHO	IP	H	ER	BB	SO
Red Ames	0	0	4.50	1	0	0	0	0	2.0	3	1	1	0
Doc Crandall	0	0	0.00	1	0	0	0	0	2.0	1	0	0	2
Rube Marquard	2	0	0.50	2	2	2	0	0	18.0	14	1	2	9
Christy Mathewson	0	2	1.26	3	3	3	0	0	28.2	23	4	5	10
Jeff Tesreau	1	2	3.13	3	3	1	0	0	23.0	19	8	11	15
TOTAL	3	4	1.71	10	8	6	0	0	73.2	60	14	19	36

GAME 1 AT NY OCT 8

```
BOS   000 001 300    4 6 1
NY    002 000 001    3 8 1
```
Pitchers: WOOD vs TESREAU, Crandall (8)
Attendance: 35,730

GAME 2 AT BOS OCT 9

```
NY    010 100 030 10   6 11 5
BOS   300 010 001 0    6 10 1
```
Pitchers: Mathewson vs Collins, Hall (8), Bedient (11)
Attendance: 30,148
(Game called at end of eleventh, darkness)

GAME 3 AT BOS OCT 10

```
NY    010 010 000    2 7 1
BOS   000 000 001    1 7 0
```
Pitchers: MARQUARD vs O'BRIEN, Bedient (9)
Attendance: 34,624

GAME 4 AT NY OCT 11

```
BOS   010 100 001    3 8 1
NY    000 000 100    1 9 1
```
Pitchers: WOOD vs TESREAU, Ames (8)
Attendance: 36,502

GAME 5 AT BOS OCT 12

```
NY    000 000 100    1 3 1
BOS   002 000 00X    2 5 1
```
Pitchers: MATHEWSON vs BEDIENT
Attendance: 34,683

GAME 6 AT NY OCT 14

```
BOS   020 000 000    2 7 2
NY    500 000 00X    5 11 2
```
Pitchers: O'BRIEN, Collins (2) vs MARQUARD
Attendance: 30,622

GAME 7 AT BOS OCT 15

```
NY    610 002 101   11 16 4
BOS   010 000 210    4 9 3
```
Pitchers: TESREAU vs WOOD, Hall (2)
Home Runs: Doyle-NY, Gardner-BOS
Attendance: 32,694

GAME 8 AT BOS OCT 16

```
NY    001 0000 01    2 9 2
BOS   000 000 100 2  3 8 5
```
Pitchers: MATHEWSON vs Bedient, WOOD (8)
Attendance: 17,034

PHILADELPHIA ATHLETICS (AL) 4, NEW YORK GIANTS (NL) 1

Third baseman Frank Baker and catcher Wally Schang drove in more than 60 percent of the Athletics' runs, as Philadelphia dispatched the Giants in five games. Chief Bender led A's pitchers with two wins, and rookie Bullet Joe Bush hurled a nifty five-hitter in Game 3, but the Series highlights were two duels between the A's Eddie Plank and Christy Mathewson of the Giants. The A's heavy hitting made Bender's wins possible and Bush's win easy, but pitching dominated the Plank-Matty games.

Bender yielded 11 hits in the opener, as did the Giants' pitchers. But five of the game's six extrabase hits belonged to the A's—including Baker's two-run homer and triples by Schang and Eddie Collins—and Bender emerged victorious. In Game 2, Plank and Mathewson pitched shutout ball through nine innings, but in the top of the 10th Matty himself singled in the game's first run and scored the second. Taking a 3–0 lead into the bottom of the inning, he set the A's down in order for New York's only Series win.

In Game 3, Schang's solo homer and Collins' three hits (including his second Series triple) and three RBIs led a 12-hit A's attack which, with Bush's fine pitching, put Philadelphia back into the Series lead. Bender won again in Game 4, shutting out the Giants through six innings as his A's scored six runs. But in the seventh, New York's Fred Merkle homered for three runs, and a single, double, and triple in the eighth brought in two more runs. With his lead cut to a single run, Bender bore down in the ninth and retired the side in order.

Plank avenged his earlier loss with a brilliant two-hitter in Game 5, facing the minimum three batters in eight of the nine innings. (His own error in the fifth—a dropped pop-up—led to the Giants' only run.) Mathewson pitched well, too, yielding only six singles. But four of them came in the first and third innings, combining with two sacrifice flies and an error for three runs. Only one Philadelphia batter reached base in the final six innings, but with Plank pitching as he was, the game and the title were in Philadelphia's pocket.

PHI (A)

PLAYER/POS	AVG	G	AB	R	H	2B	3B	HR	RB	BB	SO	SB
Frank Baker, 3b	.450	5	20	2	9	0	0	1	7	0	2	1
Jack Barry, ss	.300	5	20	3	6	3	0	0	1	0	0	0
Chief Bender, p	.000	2	8	0	0	0	0	0	1	0	1	0
Joe Bush, p	.250	1	4	0	1	0	0	0	0	0	1	0
Eddie Collins, 2b	.421	5	19	5	8	0	2	0	3	1	2	3
Jack Lapp, c	.250	1	4	0	1	0	0	0	0	0	1	0
Stuffy McInnis, 1b	.118	5	17	1	2	1	0	0	2	0	2	0
Eddie Murphy, of	.227	5	22	2	5	0	0	0	0	2	0	0
Rube Oldring, of	.273	5	22	5	6	0	1	0	0	0	1	1
Eddie Plank, p	.143	2	7	0	1	0	0	0	0	0	0	0
Wally Schang, c	.357	4	14	2	5	0	1	1	7	2	4	0
Amos Strunk, of	.118	5	17	3	2	0	0	0	0	2	2	0
TOTAL	.264		174	23	46	4	4	2	21	7	16	5

PITCHER	W	L	ERA	G	GS	CG	SV	SHO	IP	H	ER	BB	SO
Chief Bender	2	0	4.00	2	2	2	0	0	18.0	19	8	1	9
Joe Bush	1	0	1.00	1	1	1	0	0	9.0	5	1	4	3
Eddie Plank	1	1	0.95	2	2	2	0	0	19.0	9	2	3	7
TOTAL	4	1	2.15	5	5	5	0	0	46.0	33	11	8	19

NY (N)

PLAYER/POS	AVG	G	AB	R	H	2B	3B	HR	RB	BB	SO	SB
George Burns, of	.158	5	19	2	3	2	0	0	2	1	5	1
Claude Cooper, pr	.000	2	0	0	0	0	0	0	0	0	0	1
Doc Crandall, p-2	.000	4	4	0	0	0	0	0	0	0	0	0
Al Demaree, p	.000	1	1	0	0	0	0	0	0	0	0	0
Larry Doyle, 2b	.150	5	20	1	3	0	0	0	2	0	1	0
Art Fletcher, ss	.278	5	18	1	5	0	0	0	3	1	1	1
Eddie Grant, ph	.000	2	1	0	0	0	0	0	0	0	0	0
Buck Herzog, 3b	.053	5	19	1	1	0	0	0	0	0	1	0
Rube Marquard, p	.000	2	1	0	0	0	0	0	0	0	0	0
Christy Mathewson, p	.600	2	5	1	3	0	0	0	1	1	0	0
Moose McCormick, ph	.500	2	2	1	1	0	0	0	0	0	0	0
Larry McLean, c-4	.500	5	12	0	6	0	0	0	2	0	0	0
Fred Merkle, 1b	.231	4	13	3	3	0	0	1	3	1	2	0
Chief Meyers, c	.000	1	4	0	0	0	0	0	0	0	0	0
Red Murray, of	.250	5	16	2	4	0	0	0	1	2	2	2
Tillie Shafer, of-5,3b-1	.158	5	19	2	3	1	1	0	1	2	3	0
Fred Snodgrass, 1b-1, of-1	.333	2	3	0	1	0	0	0	0	0	0	0
Jeff Tesreau, p	.000	2	2	0	0	0	0	0	0	0	1	0
Art Wilson, c	.000	3	3	0	0	0	0	0	0	0	2	0
Hooks Wiltse, 1b	.000	2	2	0	0	0	0	0	0	0	1	0
TOTAL	.201		164	15	33	3	1	1	15	8	19	5

PITCHER	W	L	ERA	G	GS	CG	SV	SHO	IP	H	ER	BB	SO
Doc Crandall	0	0	3.86	2	0	0	0	0	4.2	4	2	0	2
Al Demaree	0	1	4.50	1	1	0	0	0	4.0	7	2	1	0
Rube Marquard	0	1	7.00	2	1	0	0	0	9.0	10	7	3	3
Christy Mathewson	1	1	0.95	2	2	2	0	1	19.0	14	2	2	7
Jeff Tesreau	0	1	6.48	2	1	0	0	0	8.1	11	6	1	4
TOTAL	1	4	3.80	9	5	2	0	1	45.0	46	19	7	16

GAME 1 AT NY OCT 7

PHI 000 320 010   6 11 1
NY   001 030 000   4 11 0
Pitchers: BENDER vs MARQUARD, Crandall (6), Tesreau (8)
Home Runs: Baker-PHI
Attendance: 36,291

GAME 2 AT PHI OCT 8

NY   000 000 000 3   3 7 2
PHI 000 000 000 0   0 8 2
Pitchers: MATHEWSON vs PLANK
Attendance: 20,563

GAME 3 AT NY OCT 9

PHI 320 000 210   8 12 1
NY   000 010 100   2 5 1
Pitchers: BUSH vs TESREAU, Crandall (7)
Home Runs: Schang-PHI
Attendance: 36,896

GAME 4 AT PHI OCT 10

NY   000 000 320   5 8 2
PHI 010 320 00X   6 9 0
Pitchers: DEMAREE, Marquard (5) vs BENDER
Home Runs: Merkle-NY
Attendance: 20,568

GAME 5 AT NY OCT 11

PHI 102 000 000   3 6 1
NY   000 010 000   1 2 2
Pitchers: PLANK vs MATHEWSON
Attendance: 36,682

BOSTON BRAVES (NL) 4, PHILADELPHIA ATHLETICS (AL) 0

The Athletics, easy winners of their fourth pennant in five years, were clear favorites over Boston. But the "Miracle Braves"—who moved from last place to first between July 18 and Aug. 25 and kept going to take the pennant by 10-1/2 games—had the momentum and swept the Series.

Boston pitcher Dick Rudolph (who won 27 games during the season) limited the A's to five hits and an unearned run, to take the opener behind the Braves' heavy hitting, 7–1. But the rest of the games were not won so easily. Philadelphia's Eddie Plank held the Braves scoreless through eight innings of Game 2, and gave up only one run in the ninth. But the Braves' Bill James (26–7 during the season) allowed only two hits and no runs at all.

Game 3 was a seesaw affair not settled until the 12th inning. Through 10 innings, starters Lefty Tyler of Boston and Joe Bush of the A's traded runs. Philadelphia scored one in the top of the first, but Braves' catcher Hank Gowdy doubled in the tying run in the second. The teams traded runs again in the fourth, but no one else crossed the plate until the 10th, when Frank Baker's bases-loaded single drove in two. For the third time, the Braves came back to tie it up. Gowdy opened the last of the 10th with the Series' only home run, and after a walk and single, a sacrifice fly knotted the score. Bill James came on to pitch no-hit ball through the 11th and 12th. Bush remained in for the A's, retiring the side in the 11th. But an inning later Gowdy opened with his third crucial hit of the game, a double. Les Mann replaced him as runner, and after a walk, bunt, and wild throw to third, Mann scampered home with the winning run.

Two of Connie Mack's most promising young pitchers, Bob Shawkey and Herb Pennock (who would later find stardom as New York Yankees), shared the A's pitching in Game 4, and gave up only six hits between them. But a walk and an error led to a Boston run in the fourth, and although Shawkey himself doubled in the tying run a half inning later, two more Braves scored in the last of the fifth on Johnny Evers' single. Pennock came on to pitch three innings of shutout relief, but

Rudolph held the A's hitless over the final four innings to preserve his second win and the Braves' crown.

GAME 1 AT PHI OCT 9
BOS 020 013 010 7 11 2
PHI 010 000 000 1 5 0
Pitchers: RUDOLPH vs BENDER, Wyckoff (6)
Attendance: 20,562

GAME 2 AT PHI OCT 10
BOS 000 000 001 1 7 1
PHI 000 000 000 0 2 1
Pitchers: JAMES vs PLANK
Attendance: 20,562

GAME 3 AT BOS OCT 12
PHI 100 100 000 200 4 8 2
BOS 010 100 000 201 5 9 1
Pitchers: BUSH vs Tyler, JAMES (11)
Home Runs: Gowdy-BOS
Attendance: 35,520

GAME 4 AT BOS OCT 13
PHI 000 010 000 1 7 0
BOS 000 120 00X 3 6 0
Pitchers: SHAWKEY, Pennock (6) vs RUDOLPH
Attendance: 34,365

BOS (N)

PLAYER/POS	AVG	G	AB	R	H	2B	3B	HR	RB	BB	SO	SB
Ted Cather, of	.000	1	5	0	0	0	0	0	0	0	1	0
Joe Connolly, of	.111	3	9	1	1	0	0	0	1	1	1	0
Charlie Deal, 3b	.125	4	16	1	2	2	0	0	0	0	0	2
Josh Devore, ph	.000	1	1	0	0	0	0	0	0	0	1	0
Johnny Evers, 2b	.438	4	16	2	7	0	0	0	2	2	2	1
Larry Gilbert, ph	.000	1	0	0	0	0	0	0	0	1	0	0
Hank Gowdy, c	.545	4	11	3	6	3	1	1	3	5	1	1
Bill James, p	.000	2	4	0	0	0	0	0	0	0	4	0
Les Mann, of-2	.286	3	7	1	2	0	0	0	1	0	1	0
Rabbit Maranville, ss	.308	4	13	1	4	0	0	0	3	1	1	2
Herbie Moran, of	.077	3	13	2	1	1	0	0	0	1	1	1
Dick Rudolph, p	.333	2	6	1	2	0	0	0	0	1	1	0
Butch Schmidt, 1b	.294	4	17	2	5	0	0	0	2	0	2	1
Lefty Tyler, p	.000	1	3	0	0	0	0	0	0	0	1	0
Possum Whitted, of	.214	4	14	2	3	0	1	0	2	3	1	1
TOTAL	.244		135	16	33	6	2	1	14	15	18	9

PITCHER	W	L	ERA	G	GS	CG	SV	SHO	IP	H	ER	BB	SO
Bill James	2	0	0.00	2	1	1	0	1	11.0	2	0	6	9
Dick Rudolph	2	0	0.50	2	2	2	0	0	18.0	12	1	4	15
Lefty Tyler	0	0	3.60	1	1	0	0	0	10.0	8	4	3	4
TOTAL	4	0	1.15	5	4	3	0	1	39.0	22	5	13	28

PHI (A)

PLAYER/POS	AVG	G	AB	R	H	2B	3B	HR	RB	BB	SO	SB
Frank Baker, 3b	.250	4	16	0	4	2	0	0	2	1	3	0
Jack Barry, ss	.071	4	14	1	1	0	0	0	0	1	3	1
Chief Bender, p	.000	1	2	0	0	0	0	0	0	0	0	0
Joe Bush, p	.000	1	5	0	0	0	0	0	0	0	2	0
Eddie Collins, 2b	.214	4	14	0	3	0	0	0	1	2	1	1
Jack Lapp, c	.000	1	1	0	0	0	0	0	0	0	0	0
Stuffy McInnis, 1b	.143	4	14	2	2	1	0	0	0	3	3	0
Eddie Murphy, of	.188	4	16	2	3	2	0	0	0	2	2	0
Rube Oldring, of	.067	4	15	0	1	0	0	0	0	0	5	0
Herb Pennock, p	.000	1	1	0	0	0	0	0	0	0	0	0
Eddie Plank, p	.000	1	2	0	0	0	0	0	0	0	1	0
Wally Schang, c	.167	4	12	1	2	1	0	0	0	1	4	0
Bob Shawkey, p	.500	1	2	0	1	1	0	0	1	0	1	0
Amos Strunk, of	.286	2	7	0	2	0	0	0	0	0	2	0
Jimmy Walsh, of-2	.333	3	6	0	2	1	0	0	1	3	1	0
Weldon Wyckoff, p	1.000	1	1	0	1	1	0	0	0	0	0	0
TOTAL	.172		128	6	22	9	0	0	5	13	28	2

PITCHER	W	L	ERA	G	GS	CG	SV	SHO	IP	H	ER	BB	SO
Chief Bender	0	1	10.13	1	1	0	0	0	5.1	8	6	2	3
Joe Bush	0	1	3.27	1	1	1	0	0	11.0	9	4	4	4
Herb Pennock	0	0	0.00	1	0	0	0	0	3.0	2	0	2	3
Eddie Plank	0	1	1.00	1	1	1	0	0	9.0	7	1	4	6
Bob Shawkey	0	1	3.60	1	1	0	0	0	5.0	4	2	2	0
Weldon Wyckoff	0	0	2.45	1	0	0	0	0	3.2	3	1	1	2
TOTAL	0	4	3.41	6	4	2	0	0	37.0	33	14	15	18

BOSTON RED SOX (AL) 4, PHILADELPHIA PHILLIES (NL) 1

In a Series characterized by outstanding pitching, Boston's five runs in Game 5 were the most scored by either team. It was also one of the most closely contested Series: the deciding run was not scored until the ninth inning in three of the games, and only in Game 1 was the margin of victory as much as two runs.

Grover Cleveland Alexander pitched the opener for the Phillies, and while the Red Sox tagged him for eight hits, they were all singles, and not until the eighth inning did one manage to drive a runner home. Boston's Ernie Shore pitched just as well, giving up only five singles and four walks. But two Philadelphia hits produced a run in the fourth, and an alternating pair of walks and infield hits in the eighth broke the tie with two runs for the Phillies' only win.

The next three games were 2–1 Boston victories. Rube Foster held the Phillies to three hits in Game 2, and led his team at the bat, going 3-for-4, including a double in the fifth. But it was his single in the ninth with a man on second that produced what proved to be the winning run as he retired the side in the bottom of the ninth to preserve his win. Dutch Leonard duplicated Foster's three-hit pitching two days later as the Series moved to Boston's spacious new Braves Field for Game 3. Before a new Series record crowd of 42,300, Leonard defeated the great Alexander, as Boston's Duffy Lewis—with his third hit of the game—singled over second base to score Harry Hooper from third with two out in the bottom of the ninth.

Ernie Shore returned to the mound for Boston in Game 4, and although he gave up more hits (seven) than he had in Game 1, his Sox had scored their two runs before the Phillies put across their one in the eighth.

Rube Foster was not as effective in Game 5 as he had been in Game 2, twice giving the Phillies a tworun lead as Phillie first baseman Fred Luderus drove in three runs with a double and a home run. But from the fifth inning on, Foster held Philadelphia scoreless on two hits, while Duffy Lewis evened the score with a two-run homer in the eighth, and Harry Hooper (who had tied the score earlier with a

home run in the third) won the game and the Series with a second homer in the top of the ninth

BOS (A)

PLAYER/POS	AVG	G	AB	R	H	2B	3B	HR	RB	BB	SO	SB
Jack Barry, 2b	.176	5	17	1	3	0	0	0	1	1	2	0
Hick Cady, c	.333	4	6	0	2	0	0	0	0	1	2	0
Bill Carrigan, c	.000	1	2	0	0	0	0	0	0	1	1	0
Rube Foster, p	.500	2	8	0	4	1	0	0	1	0	2	0
Del Gainer, 1b	.333	1	3	1	1	0	0	0	0	0	0	0
Larry Gardner, 3b	.235	5	17	2	4	1	0	1	0	0	1	0
Olaf Henriksen, ph	.000	2	2	0	0	0	0	0	0	0	0	0
Dick Hoblitzel, 1b	.313	5	16	1	5	0	0	0	1	0	1	1
Harry Hooper, of	.350	5	20	4	7	0	0	2	3	2	4	0
Hal Janvrin, ss	.000	1	1	0	0	0	0	0	0	0	0	0
Dutch Leonard, p	.000	1	3	0	0	0	0	0	0	0	2	0
Duffy Lewis, of	.444	5	18	1	8	1	0	1	5	1	4	0
Babe Ruth, ph	.000	1	1	0	0	0	0	0	0	0	0	0
Everett Scott, ss	.056	5	18	0	1	0	0	0	0	0	3	0
Ernie Shore, p	.200	2	5	0	1	0	0	0	0	0	3	0
Tris Speaker, of	.294	5	17	2	5	0	1	0	0	4	1	0
Pinch Thomas, c	.200	2	5	0	1	0	0	0	0	0	0	0
TOTAL	.264		159	12	42	2	2	3	11	11	25	1

PITCHER	W	L	ERA	G	GS	CG	SV	SHO	IP	H	ER	BB	SO
Rube Foster	2	0	2.00	2	2	2	0	0	18.0	12	4	2	13
Dutch Leonard	1	0	1.00	1	1	1	0	0	9.0	3	1	0	6
Ernie Shore	1	1	2.12	2	2	2	0	0	17.0	12	4	8	6
TOTAL	4	1	1.84	5	5	5	0	0	44.0	27	9	10	25

PHI (N)

PLAYER/POS	AVG	G	AB	R	H	2B	3B	HR	RB	BB	SO	SB
G.C. Alexander, p	.200	2	5	0	1	0	0	0	0	0	1	0
Dave Bancroft, ss	.294	5	17	2	5	0	0	0	1	2	2	0
Beals Becker, of	.000	2	0	0	0	0	0	0	0	0	0	0
Ed Burns, c	.188	5	16	1	3	0	0	0	0	1	2	0
Bobby Byrne, ph	.000	1	1	0	0	0	0	0	0	0	0	0
George Chalmers, p	.333	2	3	0	1	0	0	0	0	0	1	0
Gavvy Cravath, of	.125	5	16	2	2	1	1	0	1	2	6	0
Oscar Dugey, pr	.000	2	0	0	0	0	0	0	0	0	0	1
Bill Killefer, ph	.000	1	1	0	0	0	0	0	0	0	0	0
Fred Luderus, 1b	.438	5	16	1	7	2	0	1	6	1	4	0
Erskine Mayer, p	.000	2	4	0	0	0	0	0	0	0	2	0
Bert Niehoff, 2b	.063	5	16	1	1	0	0	0	0	1	5	0
Dode Paskert, of	.158	5	19	2	3	0	0	0	0	1	2	0
Eppa Rixey, p	.500	1	2	0	1	0	0	0	0	0	0	0
Milt Stock, 3b	.118	5	17	1	2	1	0	0	0	1	0	0
Possum Whitted, of-5,1b-1	.067	5	15	0	1	0	0	0	1	1	0	1
TOTAL	.182		148	10	27	4	1	1	9	10	25	2

PITCHER	W	L	ERA	G	GS	CG	SV	SHO	IP	H	ER	BB	SO
G.C. Alexander	1	1	1.53	2	2	2	0	0	17.2	14	3	4	10
George Chalmers	0	1	2.25	1	1	1	0	0	8.0	8	2	3	6
Erskine Mayer	0	1	2.38	2	2	1	0	0	11.1	16	3	2	7
Eppa Rixey	0	1	4.05	1	0	0	0	0	6.2	4	3	2	2
TOTAL	1	4	2.27	6	5	4	0	0	43.2	42	11	11	25

GAME 1 AT PHI OCT 8

```
BOS 000 000 010   1 8 1
PHI 000 100 02X   3 5 1
```
Pitchers: SHORE vs ALEXANDER
Attendance: 19,343

GAME 2 AT PHI OCT 9

```
BOS 100 000 001   2 10 0
PHI 000 010 000   1 3 1
```
Pitchers: FOSTER vs MAYER
Attendance: 20,306

GAME 3 AT BOS OCT 11

```
PHI 001 000 000   1 3 0
BOS 000 100 001   2 6 1
```
Pitchers: ALEXANDER vs LEONARD
Attendance: 42,300

GAME 4 AT BOS OCT 12

```
PHI 000 000 010   1 7 0
BOS 001 001 00X   2 8 1
```
Pitchers: CHALMERS vs SHORE
Attendance: 41,096

GAME 5 AT PHI OCT 13

```
BOS 011 000 021   5 10 1
PHI 200 200 000   4 9 1
```
Pitchers: FOSTER vs Mayer, RIXEY (3)
Home Runs: Hooper-BOS (2),
 Lewis-BOS, Luderus-PHI
Attendance: 20,306

BOSTON RED SOX (AL) 4, BROOKLYN ROBINS (NL) 1

In close pennant races, the Red Sox repeated as league champions and Brooklyn won its first pennant since 1900. The first three games of the Series were tightly contested, and the outcomes were determined by only one run apiece. For 6-1/2 innings in the opener, Brooklyn's Rube Marquard dueled Boston's Ernie Shore about equally. But in the last of the seventh the Sox capitalized on a double, some sloppy Brooklyn fielding, and a couple of sacrifice hits for three runs, adding another off reliever Jeff Pfeffer in the eighth for a 6–1 lead. The Robins fought back in the ninth, driving out Shore and drawing within one run of a tie before reliever Carl Mays retired the final man with the bases loaded.

Game 2 was even tighter. Boston starter Babe Ruth gave up a first-inning inside-the-park homer to Hy Myers, but in the third he drove in Everett Scott (who had tripled) to tie the game at 1–1. Then for the next 10 innings he and Robins pitcher Sherry Smith shut off all scoring. Ruth continued to blank Brooklyn in the 14th, and in the last of the inning a walk, sacrifice, and single over the head of the third baseman gave Boston and Ruth the victory.

Brooklyn veteran Jack Coombs took a 4–0 lead into the sixth inning of Game 3 before weakening. But after giving up a third Boston run on Larry Gardner's one-out homer in the seventh, he was relieved by Jeff Pfeffer, who set the Sox down in order the rest of the way. In saving what proved to be Coombs' last World Series appearance (as well as the Robins' only Series win), Pfeffer preserved Coombs' perfect Series won-lost record at 5–0.

Games 4 and 5 proved anticlimactic. In Game 4, Gardner's second homer of the Series—inside-the-park for three runs in the second inning—overcame the Robins' two runs in the first. The Sox added a run here and there to increase their lead, while Sox starter Dutch Leonard shut Brooklyn out through the final eight innings for a comfortable 6–2 win. And in what became the Series finale, Ernie Shore held the Robins to three singles and one unearned run as his Sox took advantage of a bad-hop triple in the second and two third-inning errors by Robin short-stop Ivy Olson to take the lead—and their fourth world championship.

BOS (A)

PLAYER/POS	AVG	G	AB	R	H	2B	3B	HR	RB	BB	SO	SB
Hick Cady, c	.250	2	4	1	1	0	0	0	0	3	0	0
Bill Carrigan, c	.667	1	3	0	2	0	0	0	1	0	1	0
Rube Foster, p	.000	1	1	0	0	0	0	0	0	0	1	0
Del Gainer, ph	1.000	1	1	0	1	0	0	0	1	0	0	0
Larry Gardner, 3b	.176	5	17	2	3	0	0	2	6	0	2	0
Olaf Henriksen, ph	.000	1	0	1	0	0	0	0	0	1	0	0
Dick Hoblitzel, 1b	.235	5	17	3	4	1	0	0	2	6	0	0
Harry Hooper, of	.333	5	21	6	7	1	1	0	1	3	1	1
Hal Janvrin, 2b	.217	5	23	2	5	3	0	0	1	0	6	0
Dutch Leonard, p	.000	1	3	0	0	0	0	0	0	1	3	0
Duffy Lewis, of	.353	5	17	3	6	2	1	0	1	2	1	0
Carl Mays, p	.000	2	1	0	0	0	0	0	0	0	1	0
Mike McNally, pr	.000	1	0	1	0	0	0	0	0	0	0	0
Babe Ruth, p	.000	1	5	0	0	0	0	0	1	0	2	0
Everett Scott, ss	.125	5	16	1	2	0	1	0	1	1	1	0
Ernie Shore, p	.000	2	7	0	0	0	0	0	0	0	2	0
Chick Shorten, of	.571	2	7	0	4	0	0	0	2	0	1	0
Pinch Thomas, c	.143	3	7	0	1	0	1	0	0	0	1	0
Tilly Walker, of	.273	3	11	1	3	0	1	0	1	1	2	0
Jimmy Walsh, of	.000	1	3	0	0	0	0	0	0	0	0	0
TOTAL	.238		164	21	39	7	6	2	18	18	25	1

PITCHER	W	L	ERA	G	GS	CG	SV	SHO	IP	H	ER	BB	SO
Rube Foster	0	0	0.00	1	0	0	0	0	3.0	3	0	0	1
Dutch Leonard	1	0	1.00	1	1	1	0	0	9.0	5	1	4	3
Carl Mays	0	1	5.06	2	1	0	1	0	5.1	8	3	3	2
Babe Ruth	1	0	0.64	1	1	1	0	0	14.0	6	1	3	4
Ernie Shore	2	0	1.53	2	2	1	0	0	17.2	12	3	4	9
TOTAL	4	1	1.47	7	5	3	1	0	49.0	34	8	14	19

BRO (N)

PLAYER/POS	AVG	G	AB	R	H	2B	3B	HR	RB	BB	SO	SB
Larry Cheney, p	.000	1	0	0	0	0	0	0	0	0	0	0
Jack Coombs, p	.333	1	3	0	1	0	0	0	1	0	0	0
George Cutshaw, 2b	.105	5	19	2	2	1	0	0	2	1	1	0
Jake Daubert, 1b	.176	4	17	1	3	0	1	0	0	2	3	0
Wheezer Dell, p	.000	1	0	0	0	0	0	0	0	0	0	0
Gus Getz, ph	.000	1	1	0	0	0	0	0	0	0	0	0
Jimmy Johnston, of-2	.300	3	10	1	3	0	1	0	0	1	0	0
Rube Marquard, p	.000	2	3	0	0	0	0	0	0	0	1	0
Fred Merkle, 1b-1	.250	3	4	0	1	0	0	0	1	2	0	0
Chief Meyers, c	.200	3	10	0	2	0	1	0	0	1	0	0
Otto Miller, c	.125	2	8	0	1	0	0	0	0	0	1	0
Mike Mowrey, 3b	.176	5	17	2	3	0	0	0	1	3	2	0
Hy Myers, of	.182	5	22	2	4	0	0	1	3	0	3	0
Ivy Olson, ss	.250	5	16	1	4	0	1	0	2	2	2	0
Ollie O'Mara, ph	.000	1	1	0	0	0	0	0	0	0	0	0
Jeff Pfeffer, p-3	.250	4	4	0	1	0	0	0	0	0	2	0
Nap Rucker, p	.000	1	0	0	0	0	0	0	0	0	0	0
Sherry Smith, p	.200	1	5	0	1	1	0	0	0	0	0	0
Casey Stengel, of-3	.364	4	11	2	4	0	0	0	0	0	1	0
Zack Wheat, of	.211	5	19	2	4	0	1	0	1	2	2	1
TOTAL	.200		170	13	34	2	5	1	11	14	19	1

PITCHER	W	L	ERA	G	GS	CG	SV	SHO	IP	H	ER	BB	SO
Larry Cheney	0	0	3.00	1	0	0	0	0	3.0	4	1	1	5
Jack Coombs	1	0	4.26	1	1	0	0	0	6.1	7	3	1	1
Wheezer Dell	0	0	0.00	1	0	0	0	0	1.0	1	0	0	0
Rube Marquard	0	2	5.73	2	2	0	0	0	11.0	12	7	6	9
Jeff Pfeffer	0	1	1.69	3	1	0	1	0	10.2	7	2	4	5
Nap Rucker	0	0	0.00	1	0	0	0	0	2.0	1	0	0	3
Sherry Smith	0	1	1.35	1	1	1	0	0	13.1	7	2	6	2
TOTAL	1	4	2.85	10	5	1	1	0	47.1	39	15	18	25

GAME 1 AT BOS OCT 7
BRO 000 100 004   5 10 4
BOS 001 010 31X   6 8 1
Pitchers: MARQUARD, Pfeffer (8) vs SHORE, Mays (9)
Attendance: 36,117

GAME 2 AT BOS OCT 9
BRO 100 000 000 000 00   1 6 2
BOS 001 000 000 000 01   2 7 1
Pitchers: SMITH vs RUTH
Home Runs: H.Myers-BRO
Attendance: 41,373

GAME 3 AT BRO OCT 10
BOS 000 002 100   3 7 1
BRO 001 120 00X   4 10 0
Pitchers: MAYS, Foster (6) vs COOMBS, Pfeffer (7)
Home Runs: Gardner-BOS
Attendance: 21,087

GAME 4 AT BRO OCT 11
BOS 030 110 100   6 10 1
BRO 200 000 000   2 5 4
Pitchers: LEONARD vs MARQUARD, Cheney (5), Rucker (8)
Home Runs: Gardner-BOS
Attendance: 21,662

GAME 5 AT BOS OCT 12
BRO 010 000 000   1 3 3
BOS 012 010 00X   4 7 2
Pitchers: PFEFFER, Dell (8) vs SHORE
Attendance: 42,620

CHICAGO WHITE SOX (AL) 4, NEW YORK GIANTS (NL) 2

Easy winners in their pennant races, the White Sox and Giants traded pairs of victories in the Series before the Sox came up with a second pair to take the title in six games. In the opener, Happy Felsch's solo homer in the fourth inning gave Sox starter Eddie Cicotte the margin he needed to defeat Slim Sallee, 2–1, and in Game 2 Red Faber went all the way, as his Sox broke a 2–2 tie in the fourth inning with five runs on six singles for Chicago's second win.

The clubs traveled to New York for Games 3 and 4, and Giants pitchers rewarded their fans with a pair of shutouts to even the Series. In Game 3, a triple, double, and single against the Sox' Cicotte in the fourth inning produced the only scoring, as Giant Rube Benton blanked the Sox on five hits, walking none. Giant ace Ferdie Schupp (a 21-game winner during the season) did the honors in Game 4, scattering seven hits, as teammate Benny Kauff, with his first Series hit in the fourth inning, homered inside the park to deep center against Red Faber for the deciding run. Two later runs against Faber and two more in the eighth (on Kauff's second homer) against reliever Dave Danforth made Schupp's win easy.

But Faber, the loser in Game 4, came in to pitch two innings of perfect relief two days later in Chicago for his second win, as the Sox rebounded from a 5–2 deficit with three runs in the bottom of the seventh to tie the game and three more an inning later to win it.

After a day of rest and a return to New York, Faber was given his third start. He pitched well enough, but his third win and the Series clincher was really the gift of some infamous Giants fielding. In the fourth inning, the first two Sox batters—Eddie Collins and Joe Jackson—reached on a high throw to first and a dropped fly. Happy Felsch, the third man up, reached on a fielder's choice as Giants third baseman Heinie Zimmerman chased Collins across the plate in a botched rundown. Jackson and Felsch scored the second and third unearned runs as Chick Gandil singled off the hapless Rube Benton. The Giants recovered to score two runs an inning later, but Faber shut them out the rest of the way to give his Sox the Series.

CHI (A)

PLAYER/POS	AVG	G	AB	R	H	2B	3B	HR	RB	BB	SO	SB
Eddie Cicotte, p	.143	3	7	0	1	0	0	0	0	1	2	0
Eddie Collins, 2b	.409	6	22	4	9	1	0	0	2	2	3	3
Shano Collins, of	.286	6	21	2	6	1	0	0	0	0	2	0
Dave Danforth, p	.000	1	0	0	0	0	0	0	0	0	0	0
Red Faber, p	.143	4	7	0	1	0	0	0	0	0	3	0
Happy Felsch, of	.273	6	22	4	6	1	0	1	3	1	5	0
Chick Gandil, 1b	.261	6	23	1	6	1	0	0	5	0	2	1
Joe Jackson, of	.304	6	23	4	7	0	0	0	2	1	0	1
Nemo Leibold, of	.400	2	5	1	2	0	0	0	1	1	1	0
Byrd Lynn, ph	.000	1	1	0	0	0	0	0	0	0	1	0
Fred McMullin, 3b	.125	6	24	1	3	1	0	0	2	1	6	0
Swede Risberg, ph	.500	2	2	0	1	0	0	0	1	0	0	0
Reb Russell, p	.000	1	0	0	0	0	0	0	0	0	0	0
Ray Schalk, c	.263	6	19	1	5	0	0	0	2	1	1	1
Buck Weaver, ss	.333	6	21	3	7	1	0	0	1	0	2	0
Lefty Williams, p	.000	1	0	0	0	0	0	0	0	0	0	0
TOTAL	.274		197	21	54	6	0	1	17	11	28	6

PITCHER	W	L	ERA	G	GS	CG	SV	SHO	IP	H	ER	BB	SO
Eddie Cicotte	1	1	1.96	3	2	2	0	0	23.0	23	5	2	13
Dave Danforth	0	0	18.00	1	0	0	0	0	1.0	3.0	2	0	2
Red Faber	3	1	2.33	4	3	2	0	0	27.0	21	7	3	9
Reb Russell	0	0	∞	1	1	0	0	0	0.0	2	1	1	0
Lefty Williams	0	0	9.00	1	0	0	0	0	1.0	2	1	0	3
TOTAL	4	2	2.77	10	6	4	0	0	52.0	51	16	6	27

NY (N)

PLAYER/POS	AVG	G	AB	R	H	2B	3B	HR	RB	BB	SO	SB
Fred Anderson, p	.000	1	0	0	0	0	0	0	0	0	0	0
Rube Benton, p	.000	2	4	0	0	0	0	0	0	0	3	0
George Burns, of	.227	6	22	3	5	0	0	0	2	3	6	1
Art Fletcher, ss	.200	6	25	2	5	1	0	0	0	0	2	0
Buck Herzog, 2b	.250	6	24	1	6	0	1	0	2	0	4	0
Walter Holke, 1b	.286	6	21	2	6	2	0	0	1	0	6	0
Benny Kauff, of	.160	6	25	2	4	1	0	2	5	0	2	1
Lew McCarty, c-2	.400	3	5	1	2	0	1	0	1	0	0	0
Pol Perritt, p	1.000	3	2	0	2	0	0	0	0	0	0	0
Bill Rariden, c	.385	5	13	2	5	0	0	0	2	2	1	0
Dave Robertson, of	.500	6	22	3	11	1	1	0	1	0	0	2
Slim Sallee, p	.167	2	6	0	1	0	0	0	0	1	2	0
Ferdie Schupp, p	.250	2	4	0	1	0	0	0	0	1	0	1
Jeff Tesreau, p	.000	1	0	0	0	0	0	0	0	0	0	0
Jim Thorpe, of	.000	1	0	0	0	0	0	0	0	0	0	0
Joe Wilhoit, ph	.000	2	1	0	0	0	0	0	0	1	0	0
Heinie Zimmerman, 3b	.120	6	25	1	3	0	1	0	0	0	0	0
TOTAL	.256		199	17	51	5	4	2	16	6	27	4

PITCHER	W	L	ERA	G	GS	CG	SV	SHO	IP	H	ER	BB	SO
Fred Anderson	0	1	18.00	1	0	0	0	0	2 5.0	4	0	3	
Rube Benton	1	1	0.00	2	2	1	0	1	14.0	9	0	1	8
Pol Perritt	0	0	1.08	3	0	0	0	0	8.1	9	1	3	3
Slim Sallee	0	2	5.28	2	2	1	0	0	15.1	20	9	4	4
Ferdie Schupp	1	0	1.74	2	2	1	0	1	10.1	11	2	2	9
Jeff Tesreau	0	0	0.00	1	0	0	0	0	1.0	0	0	1	1
TOTAL	2	4	2.82	11	6	3	0	2	51.0	54	16	11	28

GAME 1 AT CHI OCT 6

NY   000 010 000   1 7 1
CHI 001 100 00X   2 7 1
Pitchers: SALLEE vs CICOTTE
Home Runs: Felsch-CHI
Attendance: 32,000

GAME 2 AT CHI OCT 7

NY   020 000 000   2 8 1
CHI 020 500 00X   7 14 1
Pitchers: Schupp, ANDERSON (2), Perritt (4), Tesreau (8) vs FABER
Attendance: 32,000

GAME 3 AT NY OCT 10

CHI 000 000 000   0 5 3
NY   000 200 00X   2 8 2
Pitchers: CICOTTE vs BENTON
Attendance: 33,616

GAME 4 AT NY OCT 11

CHI 000 000 000   0 7 0
NY   000 110 12X   5 10 1
Pitchers: FABER, Danforth (8) vs SCHUPP
Home Runs: Kauff-NY (2)
Attendance: 27,746

GAME 5 AT CHI OCT 13

NY   200 200 100   5 12 3
CHI 001 001 33X   8 14 6
Pitchers: SALLEE, Perritt (8) vs Russell, Cicotte (1), Williams (7), FABER (8)
Attendance: 27,323

GAME 6 AT NY OCT 15

CHI 000 300 001   4 7 1
NY   000 020 000   2 6 3
Pitchers: FABER vs BENTON, Perritt (6)
Attendance: 33,969

BOSTON RED SOX (AL) 4, CHICAGO CUBS (NL) 2

Although both clubs had lost key players to military service, so had other major league teams, and after a season shortened by a month because of the war, the Red Sox and Cubs found themselves opponents in an early-September World Series.

In the opener, Babe Ruth pushed his string of consecutive scoreless World Series innings to 22, holding the Cubs to six singles as he went the distance. The Cubs' Hippo Vaughn pitched just as well, but two of the five singles he yielded followed a leadoff walk in the fourth and produced the game's only run. Chicago evened the Series in Game 2, bunching four of their seven hits after a walk in the second inning to take a 3–0 lead. Successive triples in Boston's ninth spoiled Lefty Tyler's shutout but not his victory.

Hippo Vaughn lost another close one in Game 3 when he gave up two runs in the fourth inning on a hit batsman and a succession of singles. The Cubs got him one run back in the fifth, but Boston's Carl Mays held Chicago to that one run as he hurled Boston back into the Series lead. Ruth pushed the Sox farther ahead in another squeaker in Game 4. As he continued his mastery over Cubs hitters, he drove Boston into the lead with a two-run triple in the fourth inning (his only Series hit). But in the eighth a runscoring ground out ended his record setting string of scoreless innings at 29-2/3, and a single drove in another run to tie the game. The Sox, though, scored a third run on a Chicago error in the last of the eighth, and reliever Bullet Joe Bush shut down a threat in the ninth to save Ruth's win.

Vaughn, in his third start, finally found what was needed for victory—a shutout, on five hits, as the Cubs added hits to walks from Boston's Sad Sam Jones in the third and eighth to push across their three runs. But in Game 6 the Sox scored two unearned runs on a dropped line drive to right in the third inning. It was their only scoring off Lefty Tyler, but Boston's Carl Mays was on his way to a one-run three-hitter that brought the Red Sox their fifth world championship in five tries. To date, although they have tried four more times, they have not won a sixth.

BOS (A)

PLAYER/POS	AVG	G	AB	R	H	2B	3B	HR	RB	BB	SO	SB
Sam Agnew, c	.000	4	9	0	0	0	0	0	0	0	0	0
Joe Bush, p	.000	2	2	0	0	0	0	0	0	1	0	0
Jean Dubuc, ph	.000	1	1	0	0	0	0	0	0	0	1	0
Harry Hooper, of	.200	6	20	0	4	0	0	0	0	2	2	0
Sam Jones, p	.000	1	1	0	0	0	0	0	0	1	0	0
Carl Mays, p	.200	2	5	1	1	0	0	0	0	0	1	0
Stuffy McInnis, 1b	.250	6	20	2	5	0	0	0	1	1	1	0
Hack Miller, ph	.000	1	1	0	0	0	0	0	0	0	0	0
Babe Ruth, p-2, of-2	.200	3	5	0	1	0	1	0	2	0	2	0
Wally Schang, c	.444	5	9	1	4	0	0	0	1	2	3	1
Everett Scott, ss	.100	6	20	0	2	0	0	0	1	1	1	0
Dave Shean, 2b	.211	6	19	2	4	1	0	0	0	4	3	1
Amos Strunk, of	.174	6	23	1	4	1	1	0	0	0	5	0
Fred Thomas, 3b	.118	6	17	0	2	0	0	0	0	1	2	0
George Whiteman, of	.250	6	20	2	5	0	1	0	1	2	1	1
TOTAL	.186		172	9	32	2	3	0	6	16	21	3

PITCHER	W	L	ERA	G	GS	CG	SV	SHO	IP	H	ER	BB	SO
Joe Bush	0	1	3.00	2	1	1	1	0	9.0	7	3	3	0
Sam Jones	0	1	3.00	1	1	1	0	0	9.0	7	3	5	5
Carl Mays	2	0	1.00	2	2	2	0	0	18.0	10	2	3	5
Babe Ruth	2	0	1.06	2	2	1	0	1	17.0	13	2	7	4
TOTAL	4	2	1.70	7	6	5	1	1	53.0	37	10	18	14

CHI (N)

PLAYER/POS	AVG	G	AB	R	H	2B	3B	HR	RB	BB	SO	SB
Turner Barber, ph	.000	3	2	0	0	0	0	0	0	0	0	0
Charlie Deal, 3b	.176	6	17	0	3	0	0	0	0	0	1	0
Phil Douglas, p	.000	1	0	0	0	0	0	0	0	0	0	0
Max Flack, of	.263	6	19	2	5	0	0	0	0	4	1	1
Claude Hendrix, p-1	1.000	2	1	0	1	0	0	0	0	0	0	0
Charlie Hollocher, ss	.190	6	21	2	4	0	1	0	1	1	1	1
Bill Killefer, c	.118	6	17	2	2	1	0	0	2	2	0	0
Les Mann, of	.227	6	22	0	5	2	0	0	2	0	0	0
Bill McCabe, ph	.000	3	1	1	0	0	0	0	0	0	0	0
Fred Merkle, 1b	.278	6	18	1	5	0	0	0	1	4	3	0
Bob O'Farrell, c-1	.000	3	3	0	0	0	0	0	0	0	0	0
Dode Paskert, of	.190	6	21	0	4	1	0	0	2	2	2	0
Charlie Pick, 2b	.389	6	18	2	7	1	0	0	0	1	1	1
Lefty Tyler, p	.200	3	5	0	1	0	0	0	2	2	0	0
Hippo Vaughn, p	.000	3	10	0	0	0	0	0	0	0	5	0
Chuck Wortman, 2b	.000	1	1	0	0	0	0	0	0	0	0	0
Rollie Zeider, 3b	.000	2	0	0	0	0	0	0	0	2	0	0
TOTAL	.210		176	10	37	5	1	0	10	18	14	3

PITCHER	W	L	ERA	G	GS	CG	SV	SHO	IP	H	ER	BB	SO
Phil Douglas	0	1	0.00	1	0	0	0	0	1.0	1	0	0	0
Claude Hendrix	0	0	0.00	1	0	0	0	0	1.0	0	0	0	0
Lefty Tyler	1	1	1.17	3	3	1	0	0	23.0	14	3	11	4
Hippo Vaughn	1	2	1.00	3	3	3	0	1	27.0	17	3	5	17
TOTAL	2	4	1.04	8	6	4	0	1	52.0	32	6	16	21

GAME 1 AT CHI SEPT 5
```
BOS  000 100 000   1 5 0
CHI  000 000 000   0 6 0
```
Pitchers: RUTH vs VAUGHN
Attendance: 19,274

GAME 2 AT CHI SEPT 6
```
BOS  000 000 001   1 6 1
CHI  030 000 00X   3 7 1
```
Pitchers: BUSH vs TYLER
Attendance: 20,040

GAME 3 AT CHI SEPT 7
```
BOS  000 200 000   2 7 0
CHI  000 010 000   1 7 1
```
Pitchers: MAYS vs VAUGHN
Attendance: 27,054

GAME 4 AT BOS SEPT 9
```
CHI  000 000 020   2 7 1
BOS  000 200 01X   3 4 0
```
Pitchers: Tyler, DOUGLAS (8) vs RUTH, Bush (9)
Attendance: 22,183

GAME 5 AT BOS SEPT 10
```
CHI  001 000 002   3 7 0
BOS  000 000 000   0 5 0
```
Pitchers: VAUGHN vs JONES
Attendance: 24,694

GAME 6 AT BOS SEPT 11
```
CHI  000 100 000   1 3 2
BOS  002 000 00X   2 5 0
```
Pitchers: TYLER, Hendrix (8) vs MAYS
Attendance: 15,238

CINCINNATI REDS (NL) 5, CHICAGO WHITE SOX (AL) 3

In the bottom of the first inning of Game 1, White Sox pitcher Eddie Cicotte hit the first batter to face him, a prearranged signal to gamblers that "the fix was on"—that the Sox would throw the Series. The eight Chicago conspirators—pitching aces Cicotte and Lefty Williams, outfielders Joe Jackson and Happy Felsch, and infielders Chick Gandil, Buck Weaver, Fred McMullin and Swede Risberg—received no more than a fraction of the $100,000 promised them but "honored" their end of the deal. Cicotte (winner of 29 regular-season games, with a 1.82 ERA) gave up seven hits and six runs in the opening innings of Game 1 en route to a 9–1 loss. Williams, though he held the Reds to four hits in Game 2, uncharacteristically walked six and fanned only one, a performance bad enough for a 4–2 loss.

Dickie Kerr, Chicago's third-best pitcher and not in on the fix, won Game 3 with a three-hit shutout. But although Cicotte pitched well in Game 4, Chicago lost a third time as the Reds' Jimmy Ring hurled a three-hit shutout of his own (all three hits coming, ironically, off the bats of conspirators Jackson, Felsch, and Gandil).

Cincinnati's Hod Eller beat Chicago in Game 5 with the Series' third successive three-hit shutout. Loser Lefty Williams once again yielded only four hits, but three came in a four-run sixth inning which also saw a walk and a throwing error by Felsch. (The win, the Reds' fourth, did not decide the Series, which had been expanded to the best five of nine in the exuberance which followed the end of the Great War.)

Chicago exerted itself to win the next two games. In Game 6, Kerr's second win depended on crucial hits by Jackson and Gandil in the tenth inning; and in Game 7 Cicotte held the Reds to one run as Jackson and Felsch drove in all of Chicago's four runs.

But in Game 8, Williams gave up two singles and two doubles before being pulled with only one away in the first. Jackson homered in the third. And he doubled and Gandil tripled to drive in three Chicago runs in the eighth. But by then the Reds had scored 10 runs on their way to an easy win and their tainted world title.

CIN (N)

PLAYER/POS	AVG	G	AB	R	H	2B	3B	HR	RB	BB	SO	SB
Jake Daubert, 1b	.241	8	29	4	7	0	1	0	1	1	2	1
Pat Duncan, of	.269	8	26	3	7	2	0	0	8	2	2	0
Hod Eller, p	.286	2	7	2	2	1	0	0	0	0	2	0
Ray Fisher, p	.500	2	2	0	1	0	0	0	0	0	0	0
Heinie Groh, 3b	.172	8	29	6	5	2	0	0	2	6	4	0
Larry Kopf, ss	.222	8	27	3	6	0	2	0	2	3	2	0
Dolf Luque, p	.000	2	1	0	0	0	0	0	0	0	1	0
Sherry Magee, ph	.500	2	2	0	1	0	0	0	0	0	0	0
Greasy Neale, of	.357	8	28	3	10	1	1	0	4	2	5	1
Bill Rariden, c	.211	5	19	0	4	0	0	0	2	0	0	1
Morrie Rath, 2b	.226	8	31	5	7	1	0	0	2	4	1	2
Jimmy Ring, p	.000	2	5	0	0	0	0	0	0	0	2	0
Edd Roush, of	.214	8	28	6	6	2	1	0	7	3	0	2
Dutch Ruether, p-2	.667	3	6	2	4	1	2	0	4	1	0	0
Slim Sallee, p	.000	2	4	0	0	0	0	0	0	0	0	0
Jimmy Smith, pr	.000	1	0	0	0	0	0	0	0	0	0	0
Ivey Wingo, c	.571	3	7	1	4	0	0	0	1	3	1	0
TOTAL	.255		251	35	64	10	7	0	33	25	22	7

PITCHER	W	L	ERA	G	GS	CG	SV	SHO	IP	H	ER	BB	SO
Hod Eller	2	0	2.00	2	2	2	0	1	18.0	13	4	2	15
Ray Fisher	0	1	2.35	2	1	0	0	0	7.2	7	2	2	2
Dolf Luque	0	0	0.00	2	0	0	0	0	5.0	1	0	0	6
Jimmy Ring	1	1	0.64	2	1	1	0	1	14.0	7	1	6	4
Dutch Ruether	1	0	2.57	2	2	1	0	0	14.0	12	4	4	1
Slim Sallee	1	1	1.35	2	2	1	0	0	13.1	19	2	1	2
TOTAL	5	3	1.63	12	8	5	0	2	72.0	59	13	15	30

CHI (A)

PLAYER/POS	AVG	G	AB	R	H	2B	3B	HR	RB	BB	SO	SB
Eddie Cicotte, p	.000	3	8	0	0	0	0	0	0	0	3	0
Eddie Collins, 2b	.226	8	31	2	7	1	0	0	1	1	2	1
Shano Collins, of	.250	4	16	2	4	1	0	0	0	0	0	0
Happy Felsch, of	.192	8	26	2	5	1	0	0	3	1	4	0
Chick Gandil, 1b	.233	8	30	1	7	0	1	0	5	1	3	1
Joe Jackson, of	.375	8	32	5	12	3	0	1	6	1	2	0
Bill James, p	.000	1	2	0	0	0	0	0	0	0	1	0
Dickie Kerr, p	.167	2	6	0	1	0	0	0	0	0	0	0
Nemo Leibold, of	.056	5	18	0	1	0	0	0	0	2	3	1
Grover Lowdermilk, p	.000	1	0	0	0	0	0	0	0	0	0	0
Byrd Lynn, c	.000	1	1	0	0	0	0	0	0	0	0	0
Erskine Mayer, p	.000	1	0	0	0	0	0	0	0	0	0	0
Fred McMullin, ph	.500	2	2	0	1	0	0	0	0	0	0	0
Eddie Murphy, ph	.000	3	2	0	0	0	0	0	0	0	1	0
Swede Risberg, ss	.080	8	25	3	2	1	0	1	0	5	3	1
Ray Schalk, c	.304	8	23	1	7	0	0	0	2	4	2	1
Buck Weaver, 3b	.324	8	34	4	11	4	1	0	0	0	2	0
Roy Wilkinson, p	.000	2	2	0	0	0	0	0	0	0	1	0
Lefty Williams, p	.200	3	5	0	1	0	0	0	0	0	3	0
TOTAL	.224		263	20	59	10	3	1	17	15	30	5

PITCHER	W	L	ERA	G	GS	CG	SV	SHO	IP	H	ER	BB	SO
Eddie Cicotte	1	2	2.91	3	3	2	0	0	21.2	19	7	5	7
Bill James	0	0	5.79	1	0	0	0	0	4.2	8	3	3	2
Dickie Kerr	2	0	1.42	2	2	2	0	1	19.0	14	3	3	6
Grover Lowdermilk	0	0	9.00	1	0	0	0	0	1.0	2	1	1	0
Erskine Mayer	0	0	0.00	1	0	0	0	0	1.0	0	0	1	0
Roy Wilkinson	0	0	1.23	2	0	0	0	0	7.1	9	1	4	3
Lefty Williams	0	3	6.61	3	3	1	0	0	16.1	12	12	8	4
TOTAL	3	5	3.42	13	8	5	0	1	71.0	64	27	25	22

GAME 1 AT CIN OCT 1
```
CHI  010 000 000    1  6  1
CIN  100 500 21X    9 14  1
```
Pitchers: CICOTTE, Wilkinson (4), Lowdermilk (8) vs RUETHER
Attendance: 30,511

GAME 2 AT CIN OCT 2
```
CHI  000 000 200    2 10  1
CIN  000 301 00X    4  4  2
```
Pitchers: WILLIAMS vs SALLEE
Attendance: 29,690

GAME 3 AT CHI OCT 3
```
CIN  000 000 000    0  3  1
CHI  020 100 00X    3  7  0
```
Pitchers: FISHER, Luque (8) vs KERR
Attendance: 29,126

GAME 4 AT CHI OCT 4
```
CIN  000 020 000    2  5  2
CHI  000 000 000    0  3  2
```
Pitchers: RING vs CICOTTE
Attendance: 34,363

GAME 5 AT CHI OCT 6
```
CIN  000 004 001    5  4  0
CHI  000 000 000    0  3  3
```
Pitchers: ELLER vs WILLIAMS, Mayer (9)
Attendance: 34,379

GAME 6 AT CIN OCT 7
```
CHI  000 013 000 1  5 10  3
CIN  002 200 000 0  4 11  0
```
Pitchers: KERR vs Ruether, RING (6)
Attendance: 32,006

GAME 7 AT CIN OCT 8
```
CHI  101 020 000    4 10  1
CIN  000 001 000    1  7  4
```
Pitchers: CICOTTE vs SALLEE, Fisher (5), Luque (6)
Attendance: 13,923

GAME 8 AT CHI OCT 9
```
CIN  410 013 010   10 16  2
CHI  001 000 040    5 10  1
```
Pitchers: ELLER vs WILLIAMS, James (1), Wilkinson (6)
Home Runs: Jackson-CHI
Attendance: 32,930

CLEVELAND INDIANS (AL) 5, BROOKLYN ROBINS (NL) 2

The Indians outscored the Robins in the Series, 21-8. Yet after losing the opener in Brooklyn, the Robins fought back to take the next two, and held the Series lead as the teams traveled to Cleveland for the next four games.

Both clubs garnered five hits in Game 1, but an error, walk, single, and double gave the Indians two runs in the second and a lead they never yielded, as Stan Coveleski outlasted Rube Marquard for the win. In Game 2, both clubs increased their hit totals to seven, but the Robins bunched six of theirs into three innings for three runs, while Burleigh Grimes, only once yielding two hits in an inning, shut the Indians out. The two runs Brooklyn scored in the first inning of Game 3 were all Sherry Smith needed to give the Robins their second win behind his three-hit pitching. But Brooklyn scored only twice more in the Series as the Indians swept to the championship with four wins in Cleveland.

With the Indians scoring four runs in Game 4 before Brooklyn put its one run on the board, Coveleski breezed to his second five-hit Series run. Jim Bagby had it even easier the next day. The Robins tagged him for 13 hits, but not until the ninth inning were they able to put them together for a run. Meanwhile Bagby and his teammates were registering a couple of Series firsts as they moved to an eight-run lead. Right fielder Elmer Smith opened the scoring in the first inning with the first World Series grand slam, and Bagby himself homered for three more in the fourth—the first pitcher to hit a Series home run.

But the 1920 Series is best remembered for second baseman Bill Wambsganss' unassisted triple play in the fifth inning. With runners on first and second going on pitcher Clarence Mitchell's liner, Wambsganss snared the ball for the first out, stepped on second to force one runner, and tagged the runner coming in from first to retire the side.

In Game 6 Duster Mails, a late-season addition to the team, shut out Brooklyn on three hits in a 1–0 squeaker over Sherry Smith. Coveleski won the clincher the next day, also via the shutout, with his third five-hitter of the Series and his third Series win.

CLE (A)

PLAYER/POS	AVG	G	AB	R	H	2B	3B	HR	RB	BB	SO	SB
Jim Bagby, p	.333	2	6	1	2	0	0	1	3	0	0	0
George Burns, 1b-4	.300	5	10	1	3	1	0	0	3	3	3	0
Ray Caldwell, p	.000	1	0	0	0	0	0	0	0	0	0	0
Stan Coveleski, p	.100	3	10	2	1	0	0	0	0	0	4	0
Joe Evans, of	.308	4	13	0	4	0	0	0	0	1	0	0
Larry Gardner, 3b	.208	7	24	1	5	1	0	0	2	1	1	0
Jack Graney, of-2	.000	3	3	0	0	0	0	0	0	0	2	0
Charlie Jamieson, of-5	.333	6	15	2	5	1	0	0	1	1	0	1
Doc Johnston, 1b	.273	5	11	1	3	0	0	0	0	2	1	1
Harry Lunte, 2b	.000	1	0	0	0	0	0	0	0	0	0	0
Duster Mails, p	.000	2	5	0	0	0	0	0	0	0	1	0
Les Nunamaker, c-1	.500	2	2	0	1	0	0	0	0	0	0	0
Steve O'Neill, c	.333	7	21	1	7	3	0	0	2	4	3	0
Joe Sewell, ss	.174	7	23	0	4	0	0	0	0	2	1	0
Elmer Smith, of	.308	5	13	1	4	0	1	1	5	1	1	0
Tris Speaker, of	.320	7	25	6	8	2	1	0	1	3	1	0
Pinch Thomas, c	.000	1	0	0	0	0	0	0	0	0	0	0
George Uhle, p	.000	2	0	0	0	0	0	0	0	0	0	0
Bill Wambsganss, 2b	.154	7	26	3	4	0	0	0	1	2	1	0
Joe Wood, of	.200	4	10	2	2	1	0	0	0	1	2	0
TOTAL	.244		217	21	53	9	2	2	18	21	21	2

PITCHER	W	L	ERA	G	GS	CG	SV	SHO	IP	H	ER	BB	SO
Jim Bagby	1	1	1.80	2	2	1	0	0	15.0	20	3	1	3
Ray Caldwell	0	1	27.00	1	1	0	0	0	0.1	2	1	1	0
Stan Coveleski	3	0	0.67	3	3	3	0	1	27.0	15	2	2	8
Duster Mails	1	0	0.00	2	1	1	0	1	15.2	6	0	6	6
George Uhle	0	0	0.00	2	0	0	0	0	3.0	1	0	0	3
TOTAL	5	2	0.89	10	7	5	0	2	61.0	44	6	10	20

BRO (N)

PLAYER/POS	AVG	G	AB	R	H	2B	3B	HR	RB	BB	SO	SB
Leon Cadore, p	.000	2	0	0	0	0	0	0	0	0	0	0
Tommy Griffith, of	.190	7	21	1	4	2	0	0	3	0	2	0
Burleigh Grimes, p	.333	3	6	1	2	0	0	0	0	0	0	0
Jimmy Johnston, 3b	.214	4	14	2	3	0	0	0	0	0	2	1
Pete Kilduff, 2b	.095	7	21	0	2	0	0	0	1	1	4	0
Ed Konetchy, 1b	.174	7	23	0	4	0	1	0	2	3	2	0
Ernie Krueger, c-3	.167	4	6	0	1	0	0	0	0	0	0	0
Bill Lamar, ph	.000	3	3	0	0	0	0	0	0	0	0	0
Al Mamaux, p	.000	3	1	0	0	0	0	0	0	0	1	0
Rube Marquard, p	.000	2	1	0	0	0	0	0	0	0	0	0
Bill McCabe, pr	.000	1	0	0	0	0	0	0	0	0	0	0
Otto Miller, c	.143	6	14	0	2	0	0	0	0	1	2	0
Clarence Mitchell, p-1	.333	2	3	0	1	0	0	0	0	0	0	0
Hy Myers, of	.231	7	26	0	6	0	0	0	1	0	1	0
Bernie Neis, of-2	.000	4	5	0	0	0	0	0	0	1	0	0
Ivy Olson, ss	.320	7	25	2	8	1	0	0	0	3	1	0
Jeff Pfeffer, p	.000	1	1	0	0	0	0	0	0	0	0	0
Ray Schmandt, ph	.000	1	1	0	0	0	0	0	0	0	1	0
Jack Sheehan, 3b	.182	3	11	0	2	0	0	0	0	0	1	0
Sherry Smith, p	.000	2	6	0	0	0	0	0	0	0	2	0
Zack Wheat, of	.333	7	27	2	9	2	0	0	2	1	2	0
TOTAL	.205		215	8	44	5	1	0	8	10	20	1

PITCHER	W	L	ERA	G	GS	CG	SV	SHO	IP	H	ER	BB	SO
Leon Cadore	0	1	9.00	2	1	0	0	0	2.0	4	2	1	1
Burleigh Grimes	1	2	4.19	3	3	1	0	1	19.1	23	9	9	4
Al Mamaux	0	0	4.50	3	0	0	0	0	4.0	2	2	0	5
Rube Marquard	0	1	3.00	2	1	0	0	0	9.0	7	3	3	6
Clarence Mitchell	0	0	0.00	1	0	0	0	0	4.2	3	0	3	1
Jeff Pfeffer	0	0	3.00	1	0	0	0	0	3.0	4	1	2	1
Sherry Smith	1	1	0.53	2	2	2	0	0	17.0	10	1	3	3
TOTAL	2	5	2.75	14	7	3	0	1	59.0	53	18	21	21

GAME 1 AT BRO OCT 5

CLE 0 2 0 1 0 0 0 0 0   3 5 0
BRO 0 0 0 0 0 0 1 0 0   1 5 1
Pitchers: COVELESKI vs MARQUARD, Mamaux (7), Cadore (9)
Attendance: 23,753

GAME 2 AT BRO OCT 6

CLE 0 0 0 0 0 0 0 0 0   0 7 1
BRO 1 0 1 0 1 0 0 0 X   3 7 0
Pitchers: BAGBY, Uhle (7) vs GRIMES
Attendance: 22,559

GAME 3 AT BRO OCT 7

CLE 0 0 0 1 0 0 0 0 0   1 3 1
BRO 2 0 0 0 0 0 0 0 X   2 6 1
Pitchers: CALDWELL, Mails (1), Uhle (8) vs SMITH
Attendance: 25,088

GAME 4 AT CLE OCT 9

BRO 0 0 0 1 0 0 0 0 0   1 5 1
CLE 2 0 2 0 0 1 0 0 X   5 12 2
Pitchers: CADORE, Mamaux (2), Marquard (3), Pfeffer (6) vs COVELESKI
Attendance: 25,734

GAME 5 AT CLE OCT 10

BRO 0 0 0 0 0 0 0 0 1   1 13 1
CLE 4 0 0 3 1 0 0 0 X   8 12 2
Pitchers: GRIMES, Mitchell (4) vs BAGBY
Home Runs: E.Smith-CLE, Bagby-CLE
Attendance: 26,884

GAME 6 AT CLE OCT 11

BRO 0 0 0 0 0 0 0 0 0   0 3 0
CLE 0 0 0 0 0 1 0 0 X   1 7 3
Pitchers: SMITH vs MAILS
Attendance: 27,194

GAME 7 AT CLE OCT 12

BRO 0 0 0 0 0 0 0 0 0   0 5 2
CLE 0 0 0 1 1 0 1 0 X   3 7 3
Pitchers: GRIMES, Mamaux (8) vs COVELESKI
Attendance: 27,525

NEW YORK GIANTS (NL) 5, NEW YORK YANKEES (AL) 3

Since both the Giants and Yankees called the Polo Grounds home, all eight games were played there, with the two clubs alternating from game to game as the home team. Pitching dominated the first two games—especially Yankees pitching. In Game 1, Giant third baseman Frank Frisch went 4-for-4 against Carl Mays. But Mays gave up only one other hit and walked no one, to fashion a shutout. The next day Art Nehf of the Giants allowed the Yankees only three singles. But the Yankees capitalized on two of them, together with one of Nehf's seven walks, a couple of Giants errors, and Bob Meusel's steal of home to score three times, as pitcher Waite Hoyt shut out the Giants on two singles to put the Yanks two up in the Series.

In Game 3 the hitters finally came alive. With the score tied 4–4 in the last of the seventh, the Giants unloaded for eight hits which, with two walks and a sacrifice fly, produced eight runs and the first Giants win. They evened the Series the next day, scoring three runs in the eighth to take a 3–1 lead, adding another in the ninth. Babe Ruth's first World Series home run, a solo shot in the bottom of the ninth, thrilled the fans but had no effect on the game's outcome.

The Yankees regained the Series lead in Game 5. Waite Hoyt was not as sharp as he had been in the opener, yielding ten hits. But the only run scored against him came as the result of a first-inning error, a deficit his Yankees teammates overcame for a 3–1 win. In Game 6 the Yankees took a quick 3–0 lead in the first. The Giants tied it in the top of the second on home runs by Irish Meusel and Frank Snyder, but Chick Fewster hit a two-run shot a half inning later to restore the Yankees lead. In the fourth inning, though, the Giants parlayed four singles and an error into four runs and a lead that held up for a Series-tying win.

The Yankees scored only one run the rest of the way as the Giants took the final two games on unearned runs. In Game 7, Mays and the Giants' Phil Douglas dueled into the seventh tied 1–1. But in the last of the seventh, Frank Snyder's double drove in Johnny Rawlings, who had reached on an

error, for the game's deciding run. In Game 8, Hoyt held the Giants to six hits and completed his third game without giving up an earned run. But a Giants runner had scored in the first inning when a grounder shot through the legs of shortstop Roger Peckinpaugh. It turned out to be the game's only run, as Art Nehf and his Giants' flawless fielding blanked the Yankees to give manager John McGraw his first world championship since 1905.

NY (N)

PLAYER/POS	AVG	G	AB	R	H	2B	3B	HR	RB	BB	SO	SB
Dave Bancroft, ss	.152	8	33	3	5	1	0	0	3	1	5	0
Jesse Barnes, p	.444	3	9	3	4	0	0	0	0	0	0	0
George Burns, of	.333	8	33	2	11	4	1	0	2	3	5	1
Phil Douglas, p	.000	3	7	0	0	0	0	0	0	0	2	0
Frankie Frisch, 3b	.300	8	30	5	9	0	1	0	1	4	3	3
George Kelly, 1b	.233	8	30	3	7	1	0	0	4	3	10	0
Irish Meusel, of	.345	8	29	4	10	2	1	1	7	2	3	1
Art Nehf, p	.000	3	9	0	0	0	0	0	0	1	3	0
Johnny Rawlings, 2b	.333	8	30	2	10	3	0	0	4	0	3	0
Earl Smith, c-2	.000	3	7	0	0	0	0	0	0	0	1	0
Frank Snyder, c-6	.364	7	22	4	8	1	0	1	3	0	2	0
Fred Toney, p	.000	2	0	0	0	0	0	0	0	0	0	0
Ross Youngs, of	.280	8	25	3	7	1	1	0	4	7	2	2
TOTAL	.269		264	29	71	13	4	2	28	22	38	7

PITCHER	W	L	ERA	G	GS	CG	SV	SHO	IP	H	ER	BB	SO
Jesse Barnes	2	0	1.65	3	0	0	0	0	16.1	10	3	6	18
Phil Douglas	2	1	2.08	3	3	2	0	0	26.0	20	6	5	17
Art Nehf	1	2	1.38	3	3	3	0	1	26.0	13	4	13	8
Fred Toney	0	0	23.63	2	2	0	0	0	2.2	7	7	3	1
TOTAL	5	3	2.54	11	8	5	0	1	71.0	50	20	27	44

NY (A)

PLAYER/POS	AVG	G	AB	R	H	2B	3B	HR	RB	BB	SO	SB
Frank Baker, 3b-2	.250	4	8	0	2	0	0	0	0	1	0	0
Rip Collins, p	.000	1	0	0	0	0	0	0	0	0	0	0
Al DeVormer, c-1	.000	2	1	0	0	0	0	0	0	0	0	0
Chick Fewster, of	.200	4	10	3	2	0	0	1	2	3	3	0
Harry Harper, p	.000	1	0	0	0	0	0	0	0	0	0	0
Waite Hoyt, p	.222	3	9	0	2	0	0	0	1	0	1	0
Carl Mays, p	.111	3	9	0	1	0	0	0	0	0	1	0
Mike McNally, 3b	.200	7	20	3	4	1	0	0	1	1	3	2
Bob Meusel, of	.200	8	30	3	6	2	0	0	3	2	5	1
Elmer Miller, of	.161	8	31	3	5	1	0	0	2	2	5	0
Roger Peckinpaugh, ss	.179	8	28	2	5	1	0	0	0	4	3	0
Bill Piercy, p	.000	1	0	0	0	0	0	0	0	0	0	0
Wally Pipp, 1b	.154	8	26	1	4	1	0	0	2	2	3	1
Jack Quinn, p	.000	1	2	0	0	0	0	0	0	0	1	0
Tom Rogers, p	.000	1	0	0	0	0	0	0	0	0	0	0
Babe Ruth, of	.313	6	16	3	5	0	0	1	4	5	8	2
Wally Schang, c	.286	8	21	1	6	1	1	0	1	5	4	0
Bob Shawkey, p	.500	2	4	2	2	0	0	0	0	0	1	0
Aaron Ward, 2b	.231	8	26	1	6	0	0	0	4	2	6	0
TOTAL	.207		24	122	50	7	1	2	20	27	44	6

PITCHER	W	L	ERA	G	GS	CG	SV	SHO	IP	H	ER	BB	SO
Rip Collins	0	0	54.00	1	0	0	0	0	0.2	4	4	1	0
Harry Harper	0	0	20.25	1	1	0	0	0	1.1	3	3	2	1
Waite Hoyt	2	1	0.00	3	3	3	0	1	27.0	18	0	11	18
Carl Mays	1	2	1.73	3	3	3	0	1	26.0	20	5	0	9
Bill Piercy	0	0	0.00	1	0	0	0	0	1.0	2	0	0	2
Jack Quinn	0	1	9.82	1	0	0	0	0	3.2	8	4	2	2
Tom Rogers	0	0	6.75	1	0	0	0	0	1.1	3	1	0	1
Bob Shawkey	0	1	7.00	2	1	0	0	0	9.0	13	7	6	5
TOTAL	3	5	3.09	13	8	6	0	2	70.0	71	24	22	38

GAME 1 AT NY-N OCT 5
NY-A 1 0 0 0 1 1 0 0 0   3 7 0
NY-N 0 0 0 0 0 0 0 0 0   0 5 0
Pitchers: MAYS vs DOUGLAS,
Barnes (9)
Attendance: 30,202

GAME 2 AT NY-A OCT 6
NY-N 0 0 0 0 0 0 0 0 0   0 2 3
NY-A 0 0 0 1 0 0 0 2X   3 3 0
Pitchers: NEHF vs HOYT
Attendance: 34,939

GAME 3 AT NY-N OCT 7
NY-A 0 0 4 0 0 0 0 1 0   5 8 0
NY-N 0 0 4 0 0 0 8 1X 13 20 0
Pitchers: Shawkey, QUINN (3),
Collins (7), Rogers (8) vs Toney,
BARNES (3)
Attendance: 36,509

GAME 4 AT NY-A OCT 9
NY-N 0 0 0 0 0 0 0 3 1   4 9 1
NY-A 0 0 0 0 1 0 0 0 1   2 7 1
Pitchers: DOUGLAS vs MAYS
Home Runs: Ruth-NY(A)
Attendance: 36,372

GAME 5 AT NY-N OCT 10
NY-A 0 0 1 2 0 0 0 0 0   3 6 1
NY-N 0 0 0 0 0 0 1 1 0   1 10 1
Pitchers: HOYT vs NEHF
Attendance: 35,758

GAME 6 AT NY-A OCT 11
NY-N 0 3 0 4 0 1 0 0 0   8 13 0
NY-A 3 2 0 0 0 0 0 0 2   5 7 2
Pitchers: Toney, BARNES (1) vs Harper,
SHAWKEY (2), Piercy (9)
Home Runs: E.Meusel-NY(N),
Snyder-NY(N), Fewster-NY(A)
Attendance: 34,283

GAME 7 AT NY-N OCT 12
NY-A 0 1 0 0 0 0 0 0 0   1 8 1
NY-N 0 0 0 1 0 0 1 0X   2 6 0
Pitchers: MAYS vs DOUGLAS
Attendance: 36,503

GAME 8 AT NY-A OCT 13
NY-N 1 0 0 0 0 0 0 0 0   1 6 0
NY-A 0 0 0 0 0 0 0 0 0   0 4 1
Pitchers: NEHF vs HOYT
Attendance: 25,410

NEW YORK GIANTS (NL) 4, NEW YORK YANKEES (AL) 0; TIE, 1

The Giants didn't quite sweep the Series—a tie in Game 2 interrupted their string of victories—but they shut down the Yankees offense, holding Yankees to three runs or less per game, and Babe Ruth to two hits and a .118 batting average. This Series restored the best-of-seven-games format after three years of best-of-nine.

The Giants had to come from behind to take Game 1. Bullet Joe Bush and Art Nehf hurled shutout ball through five innings before the Yankees scored single runs in the sixth and seventh innings (Ruth driving in the Series' first run for the second year in a row with his single in the sixth). But in the eighth, Bush gave up four straight singles and two runs before Waite Hoyt relieved him with the score tied and men on first and third. Hoyt set down all three men he faced, but the first out—Ross Youngs' fly to center—drove in what proved to be the Giants' winning run.

The Giants led off Game 2 with three first-inning runs on Irish Meusel's home run, but scored no more as Bob Shawkey stopped them for nine innings while his Yankees picked up runs in the first, fourth (on Aaron Ward's homer), and eighth to tie it all up. At the end of the 10th, with 45 minutes left before sundown, the umpires called the game for darkness and provoked a storm of seat cushions and bottles from the stands.

The Giants resumed their winning ways in Game 3 behind Jack Scott's shutout. Scott—picked up by the Giants in midseason—gave up only four hits, walking one, in the Series' top pitching performance. In Game 4 the Yankees scored twice in the first inning, but in the fifth the Giants pounced on Carl Mays for four hits and two runs before the first out was recorded. Before the inning ended, a ground out and another hit had brought two more Giants across the plate, enough to survive Aaron Ward's second Series home run for a 4–3 win.

Game 5, the clincher, showed Nehf the winner by two runs at game's end, but the game went back and forth before the outcome was decided. Nehf gave up only five hits—all singles—but all of them contributed toward scoring Yankees runs in the first, fifth, and

seventh innings. The Giants took the lead in the second with a pair of runs, but again fell behind until four hits and a walk in the eighth undid pitcher Joe Bush's fine effort, giving the Giants three additional runs and John McGraw his third world title.

NY (N)

PLAYER/POS	AVG	G	AB	R	H	2B	3B	HR	RB	BB	SO	SB
Dave Bancroft, ss	.211	5	19	4	4	0	0	0	2	2	1	0
Jesse Barnes, p	.000	1	4	0	0	0	0	0	0	0	1	0
Bill Cunningham, of	.200	4	10	0	2	0	0	0	2	2	1	0
Frankie Frisch, 2b	.471	5	17	3	8	1	0	0	2	1	0	1
Heinie Groh, 3b	.474	5	19	4	9	0	1	0	0	2	1	0
George Kelly, 1b	.278	5	18	0	5	0	0	0	2	0	3	0
Lee King, of	1.000	2	1	0	1	0	0	0	1	0	0	0
Hugh McQuillan, p	.250	1	4	1	1	1	0	0	0	0	1	0
Irish Meusel, of	.250	5	20	3	5	0	0	1	7	0	1	0
Art Nehf, p	.000	2	3	0	0	0	0	0	0	2	0	0
Rosy Ryan, p	.000	1	0	0	0	0	0	0	0	0	0	0
Jack Scott, p	.250	1	4	0	1	0	0	0	0	0	1	0
Earl Smith, c-1	.143	4	7	0	1	0	0	0	0	0	2	0
Frank Snyder, c	.333	4	15	1	5	0	0	0	0	0	1	0
Casey Stengel, of	.400	2	5	0	2	0	0	0	0	0	0	0
Ross Youngs, of	.375	5	16	2	6	0	0	0	2	3	1	0
TOTAL	.309		162	18	50	2	1	1	18	12	15	1

PITCHER	W	L	ERA	G	GS	CG	SV	SHO	IP	H	ER	BB	SO
Jesse Barnes	0	0	1.80	1	1	1	0	0	10.0	8	2	2	6
Hugh McQuillan	1	0	3.00	1	1	1	0	0	9.0	8	3	2	4
Art Nehf	1	0	2.25	2	2	1	0	0	16.0	11	4	3	6
Rosy Ryan	1	0	0.00	1	0	0	0	0	2.0	1	0	0	2
Jack Scott	1	0	0.00	1	1	1	0	1	9.0	4	0	1	2
TOTAL	4	0	1.76	6	5	4	0	1	46.0	32	9	8	20

NY (A)

PLAYER/POS	AVG	G	AB	R	H	2B	3B	HR	RB	BB	SO	SB
Frank Baker, ph	.000	1	1	0	0	0	0	0	0	0	0	0
Joe Bush, p	.167	2	6	0	1	0	0	0	1	0	0	0
Joe Dugan, 3b	.250	5	20	4	5	1	0	0	0	0	1	0
Waite Hoyt, p	.500	2	2	0	1	0	0	0	0	0	0	0
Sam Jones, p	.000	2	0	0	0	0	0	0	0	0	0	0
Carl Mays, p	.000	1	2	0	0	0	0	0	0	0	0	0
Norm McMillan, of	.000	1	2	0	0	0	0	0	0	0	0	0
Mike McNally, 2b	.000	1	0	0	0	0	0	0	0	0	0	0
Bob Meusel, of	.300	5	20	2	6	1	0	0	2	1	3	1
Wally Pipp, 1b	.286	5	21	0	6	1	0	0	3	0	2	1
Babe Ruth, of	.118	5	17	1	2	1	0	0	1	2	3	0
Wally Schang, c	.188	5	16	0	3	1	0	0	0	0	3	0
Everett Scott, ss	.143	5	14	0	2	0	0	0	1	1	0	0
Bob Shawkey, p	.000	1	4	0	0	0	0	0	0	0	1	0
Elmer Smith, ph	.000	2	2	0	0	0	0	0	0	0	2	0
Aaron Ward, 2b	.154	5	13	3	2	0	0	2	3	3	3	0
Whitey Witt, of	.222	5	18	1	4	1	1	0	0	1	2	0
TOTAL	.203		158	11	32	6	1	2	11	8	20	2

PITCHER	W	L	ERA	G	GS	CG	SV	SHO	IP	H	ER	BB	SO
Joe Bush	0	2	4.80	2	2	1	0	0	15.0	21	8	5	6
Waite Hoyt	0	1	1.13	2	1	0	0	0	8.0	11	1	2	4
Sam Jones	0	0	0.00	2	0	0	0	0	2.0	1	0	1	0
Carl Mays	0	1	4.50	1	1	0	0	0	8.0	9	4	2	1
Bob Shawkey	0	0	2.70	1	1	1	0	0	10.0	8	3	2	4
TOTAL	0	4	3.35	8	5	2	0	0	43.0	50	16	12	15

GAME 1 AT NY-N OCT 4
NY-A 000 001 100 2 7 0
NY-N 000 000 03X 3 11 3
Pitchers: BUSH, Hoyt (8) vs Nehf, RYAN (8)
Attendance: 36,514

GAME 2 AT NY-A OCT 5
NY-N 300 000 000 0 3 8 1
NY-A 100 100 100 0 3 8 0
Pitchers: Barnes vs Shawkey
Home Runs: E.Meusel-NY (N), Ward-NY (A)
Attendance: 37,020

GAME 3 AT NY-N OCT 6
NY-A 000 000 000 0 4 1
NY-N 002 000 10X 3 12 1
Pitchers: HOYT, Jones (8) vs J.SCOTT
Attendance: 37,620

GAME 4 AT NY-A OCT 7
NY-N 000 040 000 4 9 1
NY-A 200 000 100 3 8 0
Pitchers: McQUILLAN vs MAYS, Jones (9)
Home Runs: Ward-NY(A)
Attendance: 36,242

GAME 5 AT NY-N OCT 8
NY-A 100 010 100 3 5 0
NY-N 020 000 03X 5 10 0
Pitchers: BUSH vs NEHF
Attendance: 38,551

NEW YORK YANKEES (AL) 4, NEW YORK GIANTS (NL) 2

After two Series played entirely in the Polo Grounds, the Giants and Yankees in 1923 had Yankee Stadium across the river to play alternate games in. Celebrating the opener in the new "house that Ruth built," the Yankees took an early three-run lead. In the third inning, though, the Giants drove out starter Waite Hoyt, emerging with four runs. Reliever Joe Bush prevented further scoring for several innings as the Yankees picked up a tying run in the seventh. But with the game still knotted in the top of the ninth, Casey Stengel legged out an inside-the-park homer to win it for the Giants.

Babe Ruth gave Herb Pennock his first World Series win with a pair of homers in Game 2. The first, a solo blast over the roof in right, broke a 1–1 tie in the fourth, and the second, an inning later, concluded the Yankees scoring in their 4–2 win that evened the Series. Stengel sent the Giants ahead in the seventh inning of Game 3, lifting a home run over the fence for the game's only score. The run gave Art Nehf the win in his duel with Sad Sam Jones, and again gave the Giants the Series lead.

Ross Youngs' fourth hit of Game 4, an inside-the-park homer into the Polo Grounds' deep outfield, gave the Giants a fourth run to lead off the bottom of the ninth, but as a rally it fell short; the Yankees, took the game to even the Series. In Game 5 Joe Bush gave up only three Giant hits—a single, double, and triple to Irish Meusel. Irish scored the only Giant run, but his Yankee brother Bob drove in three runs with his three hits—sharing RBI honors with Joe Dugan, whose four hits included the Series' third inside-the-park home run, a three-run shot in the second inning. Final score: 8–1.

In Game 6 Yankees starter Herb Pennock yielded four runs in his seven innings on the mound and seemed on the edge of defeat. But in the top of the eighth, Art Nehf (who had pitched one-hit ball since Ruth homered in the first) lost his stuff. With one out, two singles followed by two walks (on eight pitches) forced in a run. Rosy Ryan replaced Nehf and walked in another run. Ruth struck out, but Bob Meusel's single and a wild throw from center cleared the bases

to put the Yankees ahead 6–4, where they remained to game's end for their first world championship.

NY (A)

PLAYER/POS	AVG	G	AB	R	H	2B	3B	HR	RB	BB	SO	SB
Joe Bush, p-3	.429	4	7	2	3	1	0	0	1	1	1	0
Joe Dugan, 3b	.280	6	25	5	7	2	1	1	5	3	0	0
Hinky Haines, of	.000	2	1	1	0	0	0	0	0	0	0	0
Harvey Hendrick, ph	.000	1	1	0	0	0	0	0	0	0	0	0
Fred Hofmann, ph	.000	2	1	0	0	0	0	0	0	1	0	0
Waite Hoyt, p	.000	1	1	0	0	0	0	0	0	0	1	0
Ernie Johnson, ss-1	.000	2	0	1	0	0	0	0	0	0	0	0
Sam Jones, p	.000	2	2	0	0	0	0	0	0	0	1	0
Bob Meusel, of	.269	6	26	1	7	1	2	0	8	0	3	0
Herb Pennock, p	.000	3	6	0	0	0	0	0	0	0	2	0
Wally Pipp, 1b	.250	6	20	2	5	0	0	0	2	4	1	0
Babe Ruth, of-6,1b-1	.368	6	19	8	7	1	1	3	3	8	6	0
Wally Schang, c	.318	6	22	3	7	0	0	0	0	1	2	0
Everett Scott, ss	.318	6	22	2	7	0	0	0	3	0	1	0
Bob Shawkey, p	.333	1	3	0	1	0	0	0	1	0	0	0
Aaron Ward, 2b	.417	6	24	4	10	0	0	1	2	1	3	1
Whitey Witt, of	.240	6	25	1	6	2	0	0	4	1	1	0
TOTAL	.293		205	30	60	8	4	5	29	20	22	1

PITCHER	W	L	ERA	G	GS	CG	SV	SHO	IP	H	ER	BB	SO
Joe Bush	1	1	1.08	3	1	1	0	0	16.2	7	2	4	5
Waite Hoyt	0	0	15.43	1	1	0	0	0	2.1	4	4	1	0
Sam Jones	0	1	0.90	2	1	0	0	0	10.0	5	1	2	3
Herb Pennock	2	0	3.63	3	2	1	1	0	17.1	19	7	1	8
Bob Shawkey	1	0	3.52	1	1	0	0	0	7.2	12	3	4	2
TOTAL	4	2	2.83	10	6	2	2	0	54.0	47	17	12	18

NY (N)

PLAYER/POS	AVG	G	AB	R	H	2B	3B	HR	RB	BB	SO	SB
Dave Bancroft, ss	.083	6	24	1	2	0	0	0	1	1	2	1
Virgil Barnes, p	.000	2	1	0	0	0	0	0	0	0	1	0
Jack Bentley, p-2	.600	5	5	0	3	1	0	0	0	0	0	0
Bill Cunningham, of-3	.143	4	7	0	1	0	0	0	1	0	1	0
Frankie Frisch, 2b	.400	6	25	2	10	0	1	0	1	0	0	0
Dinty Gearin, pr	.000	1	0	0	0	0	0	0	0	0	0	0
Hank Gowdy, c-2	.000	3	4	0	0	0	0	0	0	1	0	0
Heinie Groh, 3b	.182	6	22	3	4	0	1	0	2	3	1	0
Travis Jackson, ph	.000	1	1	0	0	0	0	0	0	0	0	0
Claude Jonnard, p	.000	2	0	0	0	0	0	0	0	0	0	0
George Kelly, 1b	.182	6	22	1	4	0	0	0	1	1	2	0
Freddie Maguire, pr	.000	2	0	1	0	0	0	0	0	0	0	0
Hugh McQuillan, p	.000	2	3	0	0	0	0	0	0	0	1	0
Irish Meusel, of	.280	6	25	3	7	1	1	1	2	0	2	0
Art Nehf, p	.167	2	6	0	1	0	0	0	0	0	4	0
Jimmy O'Connell, ph	.000	2	1	0	0	0	0	0	0	0	1	0
Rosy Ryan, p	.000	3	2	0	0	0	0	0	0	0	1	0
Jack Scott, p	.000	2	1	0	0	0	0	0	0	0	0	0
Frank Snyder, c	.118	5	17	1	2	0	0	1	2	0	2	0
Casey Stengel, of	.417	6	12	3	5	0	0	2	4	4	0	0
Mule Watson, p	.000	1	0	0	0	0	0	0	0	0	0	0
Ross Youngs, of	.348	6	23	2	8	0	0	1	3	2	0	1
TOTAL	.234		201	17	47	2	3	5	17	12	18	1

PITCHER	W	L	ERA	G	GS	CG	SV	SHO	IP	H	ER	BB	SO
Virgil Barnes	0	0	0.00	2	0	0	0	0	4.2	4	0	0	4
Jack Bentley	0	1	9.45	2	1	0	0	0	6.2	10	7	4	1
Claude Jonnard	0	0	0.00	2	0	0	0	0	2.0	1	0	1	1
Hugh McQuillan	0	1	5.00	2	1	0	0	0	9.0	11	5	4	3
Art Nehf	1	1	2.76	2	2	1	0	1	16.1	10	5	6	7
Rosy Ryan	1	0	0.96	3	0	0	0	0	9.1	11	1	3	3
Jack Scott	0	1	12.00	2	1	0	0	0	3.0	9	4	1	2
Mule Watson	0	0	13.50	1	1	0	0	0	2.0	4	3	1	1
TOTAL	2	4	4.25	16	6	1	0	1	53.0	60	25	20	22

GAME 1 AT NY-A OCT 10

NY-N 004 000 001 5 8 0
NY-A 120 000 100 4 12 1
Pitchers: Watson, RYAN (3) vs Hoyt, BUSH (3)
Home Runs: Stengel-NY(N)
Attendance: 55,307

GAME 2 AT NY-N OCT 11

NY-A 010 210 000 4 10 0
NY-N 010 001 000 2 9 2
Pitchers: PENNOCK vs McQUILLAN, Bentley (4)
Home Runs: Ward-NY (A), E.Meusel-NY (N), Ruth-NY (A) (2)
Attendance: 40,402

GAME 3 AT NY-A OCT 12

NY-N 000 000 100 1 4 0
NY-A 000 000 000 0 6 1
Pitchers: NEHF vs JONES, Bush (9)
Home Runs: Stengel-NY (N)
Attendance: 62,430

GAME 4 AT NY-N OCT 13

NY-A 061 100 000 8 13 1
NY-N 000 000 031 4 13 1
Pitchers: SHAWKEY, Pennock (8) vs J.SCOTT, Ryan (2), McQuillan (2), Jonnard (8), Barnes (9)
Home Runs: Youngs-NY (N)
Attendance: 46,302

GAME 5 AT NY-A OCT 14

NY-N 010 000 000 1 3 2
NY-A 340 100 00X 8 14 0
Pitchers: BENTLEY, J.Scott (2), Barnes (4), Jones (8) vs BUSH
Home Runs: Dugan-NY(A)
Attendance: 62,817

GAME 6 AT NY-N OCT 15

NY-A 100 000 050 6 5 0
NY-N 100 111 000 4 10 1
Pitchers: PENNOCK, Jones (8) vs NEHF, Ryan (8)
Home Runs: Ruth-NY(A), Snyder-NY(N)
Attendance: 34,172

WASHINGTON SENATORS (AL) 4, NEW YORK GIANTS (NL) 3

Four of the seven games in this exciting Series were decided by one run—two of them after 12 innings. Pitcher Walter Johnson, in his first World Series after 18 big-league seasons and 376 victories, opened for Washington against the Giants' Art Nehf. Although 14 Giants reached base on hits or walks in the first nine innings, only two scored—George Kelly and Bill Terry, both of whom homered. In the bottom of the ninth, the Senators scored their second run to send the game into extra innings. Johnson shut out the Giants for two more frames, but in the top of the 12th, two walks and three singles put New York ahead by two. Washington came back with a run and had a man on third. But Kelly, making his only appearance at second, stopped Goose Goslin's grounder with his bare hand, and Nehf had the Giants' first win.

Goslin and manager/second baseman Bucky Harris homered in Game 2 to give the Senators a 3–0 lead through six innings. The Giants scored once in the seventh and drove out starter Tom Zachary with two more in the ninth to tie the game, but in the last of the ninth Roger Peckinpaugh doubled in the tie breaker to even the Series.

The Giants took an early lead in Game 3 and held it to retake the Series lead, but Washington (led by Goslin's three-run homer in the third) unleashed a 13-hit, seven-run attack the next day to even the Series once more. In Game 5, though, New York pulled ahead again, defeating Johnson a second time as winning pitcher Jack Bentley put the Giants into the lead for good with a two-run homer in the fifth. In Game 6, Washington's two runs in the fifth inning overcame a first-inning Giant run and gave Tom Zachary all he needed for the Senators' third win, which set the stage for one of the most memorable games in Series history.

Washington scored first in Game 7 on manager Harris' homer in the fourth inning, but the Giants scored three runs in the sixth (two of them on Senator errors) to go ahead, 3–1. In the last of the eighth, though, Harris' grounder to third bounced over the head of rookie Freddie Lindstrom for two more runs and a 3–3 tie. Walter Johnson came in to face the Giants in the ninth, and shut them out through

the 12th, fanning five. Then in the bottom of the 12th, with one out, Muddy Ruel (given a second chance after Giants catcher Hank Gowdy caught his foot in his mask and missed Ruel's pop foul) doubled to left. Pitcher Johnson then reached first when shortstop Travis Jackson bobbled what should have been a third-out grounder. With men on second and first, Earl McNeely bounced to Lindstrom at third. But again the ball bounced over Lindstrom's head, and Ruel raced home with Johnson's first Series win and Washington's only world championship.

WAS (A)

PLAYER/POS	AVG	G	AB	R	H	2B	3B	HR	RB	BB	SO	SB
Ossie Bluege, ss-5,3b-4	.192	7	26	2	5	0	0	0	3	3	4	1
Goose Goslin, of	.344	7	32	4	11	1	0	3	7	0	7	0
Bucky Harris, 2b	.333	7	33	5	11	0	0	2	7	1	4	0
Walter Johnson, p	.111	3	9	0	1	0	0	0	0	0	0	0
Joe Judge, 1b	.385	7	26	4	10	1	0	0	0	5	2	0
Nemo Leibold, of-1	.167	3	6	1	1	1	0	0	0	1	0	0
Firpo Marberry, p	.000	4	2	0	0	0	0	0	0	0	0	0
Joe Martina, p	.000	1	0	0	0	0	0	0	0	0	0	0
Earl McNeely, of	.222	7	27	4	6	3	0	0	1	4	4	1
Ralph Miller, 3b	.182	4	11	0	2	0	0	0	2	1	0	0
George Mogridge, p	.000	2	5	0	0	0	0	0	0	0	5	0
Curly Ogden, p	.000	1	0	0	0	0	0	0	0	0	0	0
Roger Peckinpaugh, ss	.417	4	12	1	5	2	0	0	2	1	0	1
Sam Rice, of	.207	7	29	2	6	0	0	0	1	3	2	2
Muddy Ruel, c	.095	7	21	2	2	1	0	0	0	6	1	0
Allan Russell, p	.000	1	0	0	0	0	0	0	0	0	0	0
Mule Shirley, ph	.500	3	2	1	1	0	0	0	0	1	0	0
By Speece, p	.000	1	0	0	0	0	0	0	0	0	0	0
Bennie Tate, ph	.000	3	0	0	0	0	0	0	0	1	3	0
Tommy Taylor, 3b	.000	3	2	0	0	0	0	0	0	0	2	0
Tom Zachary, p	.000	2	5	0	0	0	0	0	0	1	3	0
TOTAL	.246		248	26	61	9	0	5	25	29	34	5

PITCHER	W	L	ERA	G	GS	CG	SV	SHO	IP	H	ER	BB	SO
Walter Johnson	1	2	2.25	3	2	2	0	0	24.0	30	6	11	20
Firpo Marberry	0	1	1.13	4	1	0	2	0	8.0	9	1	4	10
Joe Martina	0	0	0.00	1	0	0	0	0	1.0	0	0	0	1
George Mogridge	1	0	2.25	2	1	0	0	0	12.0	7	3	6	5
Curly Ogden	0	0	0.00	1	1	0	0	0	0.1	0	0	1	1
Allan Russell	0	0	3.00	1	0	0	0	0	3.0	4	1	0	0
By Speece	0	0	9.00	1	0	0	0	0	1.0	3	1	0	0
Tom Zachary	2	0	2.04	2	2	1	0	0	17.2	13	4	3	3
TOTAL	4	3	2.15	15	7	3	2	0	67.0	66	16	25	40

NY (N)

PLAYER/POS	AVG	G	AB	R	H	2B	3B	HR	RB	BB	SO	SB
Harry Baldwin, p	.000	1	0	0	0	0	0	0	0	0	0	0
Virgil Barnes, p	.000	2	4	0	0	0	0	0	0	1	2	0
Jack Bentley, p-3	.286	5	7	1	2	0	0	1	2	1	1	0
Wayland Dean, p	.000	1	0	0	0	0	0	0	0	0	0	0
Frankie Frisch, 2b-7,3b-1	.333	7	30	1	10	4	1	0	4	1	1	1
Hank Gowdy, c	.259	7	27	4	7	0	0	0	1	2	2	0
Heinie Groh, ph	1.000	1	1	0	1	0	0	0	0	0	0	0
Travis Jackson, ss	.074	7	27	3	2	0	0	0	1	1	4	1
Claude Jonnard, p	.000	1	0	0	0	0	0	0	0	0	0	0
George Kelly, 1b-4, of-4,2b-1	.290	7	31	7	9	1	0	1	4	1	8	0
Fred Lindstrom, 3b	.333	7	30	1	10	2	0	0	4	3	6	0
Hugh McQuillan, p	1.000	3	1	0	1	0	0	0	1	1	0	0
Irish Meusel, of	.154	4	13	0	2	1	0	0	1	2	0	0
Art Nehf, p	.429	3	7	1	3	0	0	0	0	0	0	0
Rosy Ryan, p	.500	2	2	1	1	0	0	1	2	0	0	0
Frank Snyder, ph	.000	1	1	0	0	0	0	0	0	0	0	0
Billy Southworth, of-2	.000	5	1	1	0	0	0	0	0	0	0	0
Bill Terry, 1b-4	.429	5	14	3	6	0	1	1	1	3	1	0
Mule Watson, p	.000	1	0	0	0	0	0	0	0	0	0	0
Hack Wilson, of	.233	7	30	1	7	1	0	0	3	1	9	0
Ross Youngs, of	.185	7	27	3	5	1	0	0	1	5	6	1
TOTAL	.261		253	27	66	9	2	4	21	25	40	3

PITCHER	W	L	ERA	G	GS	CG	SV	SHO	IP	H	ER	BB	SO
Harry Baldwin	0	0	0.00	1	0	0	0	0	2.0	1	0	0	1
Virgil Barnes	0	1	5.68	2	2	0	0	0	12.2	15	8	1	9
Jack Bentley	1	2	3.18	3	2	1	0	0	17.0	18	6	8	10
Wayland Dean	0	0	4.50	1	0	0	0	0	2.0	3	1	0	2
Claude Jonnard	0	0	—	1	0	0	0	0	0.0	0	0	1	0
Hugh McQuillan	0	1	2.57	3	1	0	1	0	7.0	2	2	6	2
Art Nehf	1	1	1.83	3	2	1	0	0	19.2	15	4	9	7
Rosy Ryan	0	0	3.18	2	0	0	0	0	5.2	7	2	4	3
Mule Watson	0	0	0.00	1	0	0	1	0	0.2	0	0	0	0
TOTAL	3	4	3.10	17	7	2	2	0	66.2	61	23	29	34

GAME 1 AT WAS OCT 4

NY 010 100 000 002 4 14 1
WAS 000 001 001 001 3 10 1
Pitchers: NEHF vs JOHNSON
Home Runs: Kelly-NY, Terry-NY
Attendance: 35,760

GAME 2 AT WAS OCT 5

NY 000 000 102 3 6 0
WAS 200 010 001 4 6 1
Pitchers: BENTLEY vs ZACHARY, Marberry (9)
Home Runs: Goslin-WAS, Harris-WAS
Attendance: 35,922

GAME 3 AT NY OCT 6

WAS 000 200 011 4 9 2
NY 021 101 01X 6 12 0
Pitchers: MARBERRY, Russell (4), Martina (7), Speece (8) vs McQUILLAN, Ryan (4), Jonnard (9), Watson (9)
Home Runs: Ryan-NY
Attendance: 47,608

GAME 4 AT NY OCT 7

WAS 003 020 020 7 13 3
NY 100 001 011 4 6 1
Pitchers: MOGRIDGE, Marberry (8) vs BARNES, Baldwin (6), Dean (8)
Home Runs: Goslin-WAS
Attendance: 49,243

GAME 5 AT NY OCT 8

WAS 000 100 010 2 9 1
NY 001 020 03X 6 13 0
Pitchers: JOHNSON vs BENTLEY, McQuillan (8)
Home Runs: Bentley-NY, Goslin-WAS
Attendance: 49,211

GAME 6 AT WAS OCT 9

NY 100 000 000 1 7 1
WAS 000 020 00X 2 4 0
Pitchers: NEHF, Ryan (8) vs ZACHARY
Attendance: 34,254

GAME 7 AT WAS OCT 10

NY 000 003 000 000 3 8 3
WAS 000 100 020 001 4 10 4
Pitchers: Barnes, McQuillan (8), Nehf (10), BENTLEY (11) vs Ogden, Mogridge (1), Marberry (6), JOHNSON (9)
Home Runs: Harris-WAS
Attendance: 31,667

PITTSBURGH PIRATES (NL) 4, WASHINGTON SENATORS (AL) 3

Repeating as pennant winners, the Senators found themselves again locked in a tight Series, this time with the Pirates, who hadn't won a pennant since 1909. Again Walter Johnson pitched the Series opener, winning this time with a strong five-hit, 10-strikeout performance, giving up only one run on Pie Traynor's homer in the fifth. Home runs by Pirates Kiki Cuyler and Glenn Wright and Senator Joe Judge accounted for four of the five runs scored in Game 2, in which Vic Aldridge dueled Stan Coveleski to a narrow 3–2 Pittsburgh win, evening the Series.

Washington took Games 3 and 4, though, for a 3–1 Series advantage, Goose Goslin's solo homer in the sixth inning providing the margin of victory in Game 3, and homers by Goslin (for three runs) and Joe Harris the next day providing all the scoring as Johnson shut the Pirates out.

Harris hit his third Series homer in Game 5, but Pittsburgh overwhelmed Coveleski as he lost to Aldridge for a second time. And although Goslin's third homer gave the Senators an early lead in Game 6, Pittsburgh's Ray Kremer shut Washington out from the third inning on as his teammates pulled even with two runs in the bottom of the third, and Eddie Moore's homer in the fifth gave him the run he needed for a win that sent the Series into a seventh game.

Both clubs went with their best in the finale as Johnson, winner of Games 1 and 4, faced Aldridge, victor in Games 2 and 5. But Aldridge was wild, issuing three walks and two wild pitches in addition to two hits before being yanked with only one out in the top of the first. Johnson was hardly more effective: although he lasted the whole game, he gave up 15 hits and five earned runs. But if there was a Series goat, it would have to be Washington shortstop Roger Peckinpaugh, the American League MVP. Though he drove in a run in the first and homered for another in the eighth, his dropped pop fly in the seventh and wild throw in the eighth (his seventh and eighth errors of the Series) opened the way to four unearned runs and Pittsburgh's 9–7 triumph.

PIT (N)

PLAYER/POS	AVG	G	AB	R	H	2B	3B	HR	RB	BB	SO	SB
Babe Adams, p	.000	1	0	0	0	0	0	0	0	0	0	0
Vic Aldridge, p	.000	3	7	0	0	0	0	0	0	0	0	0
Clyde Barnhart, of	.250	7	28	1	7	1	0	0	5	3	5	1
Carson Bigbee, of-1	.333	4	3	1	1	1	0	0	1	0	0	1
Max Carey, of	.458	7	24	6	11	4	0	0	2	2	3	3
Kiki Cuyler, of	.269	7	26	3	7	3	0	1	6	1	4	0
Johnny Gooch, c	.000	3	3	0	0	0	0	0	0	0	0	0
George Grantham, 1b-4	.133	5	15	0	2	0	0	0	0	0	3	1
Ray Kremer, p	.143	3	7	0	1	0	0	0	0	1	5	0
Stuffy McInnis, 1b-3	.286	4	14	0	4	0	0	0	0	1	0	2
Lee Meadows, p	.000	1	1	0	0	0	0	0	0	1	1	0
Eddie Moore, 2b	.231	7	26	7	6	1	0	1	2	5	2	0
Johnny Morrison, p	.500	3	2	1	1	0	0	0	0	0	0	0
Red Oldham, p	.000	1	0	0	0	0	0	0	0	0	0	0
Earl Smith, c	.350	6	20	0	7	1	0	0	0	1	2	0
Pie Traynor, 3b	.346	7	26	2	9	0	2	1	4	3	1	1
Glenn Wright, ss	.185	7	27	3	5	1	0	1	3	1	4	0
Emil Yde, p-1	.000	2	1	1	0	0	0	0	0	0	0	0
TOTAL	.265		230	25	61	12	2	4	25	17	32	7

PITCHER	W	L	ERA	G	GS	CG	SV	SHO	IP	H	ER	BB	SO
Babe Adams	0	0	0.00	1	0	0	0	0	1.0	2	0	0	0
Vic Aldridge	2	0	4.42	3	3	2	0	0	18.1	18	9	9	9
Ray Kremer	2	1	3.00	3	2	2	0	0	21.0	17	7	4	9
Lee Meadows	0	1	3.38	1	1	0	0	0	8.0	6	3	0	4
Johnny Morrison	0	0	2.89	3	0	0	0	0	9.1	11	3	1	7
Red Oldham	0	0	0.00	1	0	0	1	0	1.0	0	0	0	2
Emil Yde	0	1	11.57	1	1	0	0	0	2.1	5	3	3	1
TOTAL	4	1	3.69	13	7	4	1	0	61.0	59	25	17	32

WAS (A)

PLAYER/POS	AVG	G	AB	R	H	2B	3B	HR	RB	BB	SO	SB
Spencer Adams, 2b-1	.000	2	1	0	0	0	0	0	0	0	0	0
Win Ballou, p	.000	2	0	0	0	0	0	0	0	0	0	0
Ossie Bluege, 3b	.278	5	18	2	5	1	0	0	2	0	4	0
Stan Coveleski, p	.000	2	3	0	0	0	0	0	0	1	2	0
Alex Ferguson, p	.000	2	4	0	0	0	0	0	0	0	3	0
Goose Goslin, of	.308	7	26	6	8	1	0	3	6	3	3	0
Joe Harris, of	.440	7	25	5	11	2	0	3	6	3	4	0
Bucky Harris, 2b	.087	7	23	2	2	0	0	0	0	1	3	0
Walter Johnson, p	.091	3	11	0	1	0	0	0	0	0	3	0
Joe Judge, 1b	.174	7	23	2	4	1	0	1	4	3	2	0
Nemo Leibold, ph	.500	3	2	1	1	1	0	0	0	1	0	0
Firpo Marberry, p	.000	4	0	0	0	0	0	0	0	0	0	0
Earl McNeely, of-2	.000	4	2	0	0	0	0	0	0	0	0	1
Buddy Myer, 3b	.250	3	8	0	2	0	0	0	0	1	2	0
Roger Peckinpaugh, ss	.250	7	24	1	6	1	0	1	3	1	2	1
Sam Rice, of	.364	7	33	5	12	0	0	0	3	0	1	0
Muddy Ruel, c	.316	7	19	0	6	1	0	0	1	3	2	0
Dutch Ruether, ph	.000	1	1	0	0	0	0	0	0	0	1	0
Hank Severeid, c	.333	1	3	0	1	0	0	0	0	0	0	0
Bobby Veach, ph	.000	2	1	0	0	0	0	0	0	1	0	0
Tom Zachary, p	.000	1	0	0	0	0	0	0	0	0	0	0
TOTAL	.262		225	26	59	8	0	8	26	17	32	2

PITCHER	W	L	ERA	G	GS	CG	SV	SHO	IP	H	ER	BB	SO
Win Ballou	0	0	0.00	2	0	0	0	0	1.2	0	0	1	1
Stan Coveleski	0	2	3.77	2	2	1	0	0	14.1	16	6	5	3
Alex Ferguson	1	1	3.21	2	2	0	0	0	14.0	13	5	6	11
Walter Johnson	2	1	2.08	3	3	3	0	1	26.0	26	6	4	15
Firpo Marberry	0	0	0.00	4	0	0	1	0	2.1	3	0	0	2
Tom Zachary	0	0	10.80	1	0	0	0	0	1.2	3	2	1	0
TOTAL	3	4	2.85	12	7	4	1	1	60.0	61	19	17	32

GAME 1 AT PIT OCT 7

WAS 010 020 001   4 8 1
PIT 000 010 000   1 5 0
Pitchers: JOHNSON vs MEADOWS, Morrison (9)
Home Runs: J.Harris-WAS, Traynor-PIT
Attendance: 41,723

GAME 2 AT PIT OCT 8

WAS 010 000 001   2 8 2
PIT 000 100 02X   3 7 0
Pitchers: COVELESKI vs ALDRIDGE
Home Runs: Judge-WAS, Wright-PIT, Cuyler-PIT
Attendance: 43,364

GAME 3 AT WAS OCT 10

PIT 010 101 000   3 8 3
WAS 001 001 20X   4 10 1
Pitchers: KREMER vs FERGUSON, Marberry (8)
Home Runs: Goslin-WAS
Attendance: 36,495

GAME 4 AT WAS OCT 11

PIT 000 000 000   0 6 1
WAS 004 000 00X   4 12 0
Pitchers: YDE, Morrison (3), Adams (8) vs JOHNSON
Home Runs: Goslin-WAS, J.Harris-WAS
Attendance: 38,701

GAME 5 AT WAS OCT 12

PIT 002 000 211   6 13 0
WAS 100 100 100   3 8 1
Pitchers: ALDRIDGE vs COVELESKI, Ballou (7), Zachary (8), Marberry (9)
Home Runs: J.Harris-WAS
Attendance: 35,899

GAME 6 AT PIT OCT 13

WAS 110 000 000   2 6 2
PIT 002 010 00X   3 7 1
Pitchers: FERGUSON, Ballou (8) vs KREMER
Home Runs: Goslin-WAS, Moore-PIT
Attendance: 43,810

GAME 7 AT PIT OCT 15

WAS 400 200 010   7 7 2
PIT 003 010 23X   9 15 2
Pitchers: JOHNSON vs Aldridge, Morrison (1), KREMER (5), Oldham (9)
Home Runs: Peckinpaugh-WAS
Attendance: 42,856

ST. LOUIS CARDINALS (NL) 4, NEW YORK YANKEES (AL) 3

The Yankees, returning to the World Series after a two-year absence, faced the Cardinals, who had won their first pennant since joining the National League in 1892. Both clubs led their league in slugging and runs scored; this power erupted occasionally in the Series, but over all, pitching dominated as each staff bettered its regular-season earned run average by nearly a run per game.

Herb Pennock of the Yankees pitched a splendid three-hitter in the opener. After yielding two hits and a run in the first inning, he shut out the Cards the rest of the way, holding them hitless until the ninth. St. Louis starter Bill Sherdel also pitched effectively, but three walks in the first and a hit-sacrifice-hit sandwich in the sixth brought in enough runs to beat him.

In Game 2, the veteran Grover Cleveland Alexander evened the Series, striking out 10 and holding the Yankees to four singles (three of them in the two-run second) as Billy Southworth and Tommy Thevenow homered for four of St. Louis' six runs. Two days later Jesse Haines put the Cards into the lead, winning the game both ways with a five-hit shutout and a two-run homer.

New York's big bats finally awoke in Game 4. Five Yankees doubled, and Babe Ruth hit three home runs (a World Series record) in a 14-hit, 10-run assault. Yankees pitcher Waite Hoyt also gave up 14 hits, but 12 were singles and only five runs scored. In contrast, Game 5 was a pitchers' duel. Pennock and Sherdel again faced each other and held the opposition to two runs apiece through nine innings. But in the 10th, rookie Tony Lazzeri's sacrifice fly gave New York a 3–2 lead, which Pennock held in the last of the 10th for his second win.

With St. Louis down three games to two, the Series moved to hostile New York for the final games. This didn't seem to trouble the Cardinals, who erupted in Game 6 for their own 10-run game, four of them driven in by Les Bell's first-inning single and seventh-inning home run. Alexander pitched a complete game for his second Series win, and came back the next day to relieve Haines in the seventh with a 3–2 lead and the bases full. He struck out Lazzeri

to end the inning and kept the Yankees off the bases until he issued Babe Ruth his 11th Series walk with two away in the ninth. But Ruth, trying to steal second, was caught, and the Cards were world champions.

STL (N)

PLAYER/POS	AVG	G	AB	R	H	2B	3B	HR	RB	BB	SO	SB
G.C. Alexander, p	.000	3	7	1	0	0	0	0	0	0	2	0
Hi Bell, p	.000	1	0	0	0	0	0	0	0	0	0	0
Les Bell, 3b	.259	7	27	4	7	1	0	1	6	2	5	0
Jim Bottomley, 1b	.345	7	29	4	10	3	0	0	5	1	2	0
Taylor Douthit, of	.267	4	15	3	4	2	0	0	1	3	2	0
Jake Flowers, ph	.000	3	3	0	0	0	0	0	0	0	1	0
Chick Hafey, of	.185	7	27	2	5	2	0	0	0	0	7	0
Jesse Haines, p	.600	3	5	1	3	0	0	1	2	0	1	0
Bill Hallahan, p	.000	1	0	0	0	0	0	0	0	0	0	0
Wattie Holm, of-4	.125	5	16	1	2	0	0	0	1	1	2	0
Rogers Hornsby, 2b	.250	7	28	2	7	1	0	0	4	2	2	1
Vic Keen, p	.000	1	0	0	0	0	0	0	0	0	0	0
Bob O'Farrell, c	.304	7	23	2	7	1	0	0	2	2	2	0
Art Reinhart, p	.000	1	0	0	0	0	0	0	0	0	0	0
Flint Rhem, p	.000	1	1	0	0	0	0	0	0	0	1	0
Bill Sherdel, p	.000	2	5	0	0	0	0	0	0	0	2	0
Billy Southworth, of	.345	7	29	6	10	1	1	1	4	0	0	1
Tommy Thevenow, ss	.417	7	24	5	10	1	0	1	4	0	1	0
Specs Toporcer, ph	.000	1	0	0	0	0	0	0	0	1	0	0
TOTAL	.272		239	31	65	12	1	4	30	11	30	2

PITCHER	W	L	ERA	G	GS	CG	SV	SHO	IP	H	ER	BB	SO
G.C. Alexander	2	0	1.33	3	2	2	1	0	20.1	12	3	4	17
Hi Bell	0	0	9.00	1	0	0	0	0	2.0	4	2	1	1
Jesse Haines	2	0	1.08	3	2	1	0	1	16.2	13	2	9	5
Bill Hallahan	0	0	4.50	1	0	0	0	0	2.0	2	1	3	1
Vic Keen	0	0	0.00	1	0	0	0	0	1.0	0	0	0	0
Art Reinhart	0	1	∞	1	0	0	0	0	0.0	1	4	4	0
Flint Rhem	0	0	6.75	1	1	0	0	0	4.0	7	3	2	4
Bill Sherdel	0	2	2.12	2	2	1	0	0	17.0	15	4	8	3
TOTAL	4	3	2.71	13	7	4	1	1	63.0	54	19	31	31

NY (A)

PLAYER/POS	AVG	G	AB	R	H	2B	3B	HR	RB	BB	SO	SB
Spencer Adams, ph	.000	2	0	0	0	0	0	0	0	0	0	0
Pat Collins, c	.000	3	2	0	0	0	0	0	0	0	1	0
Earle Combs, of	.357	7	28	3	10	2	0	0	2	5	2	0
Joe Dugan, 3b	.333	7	24	2	8	1	0	0	2	1	1	0
Mike Gazella, 3b	.000	1	0	0	0	0	0	0	0	0	0	0
Lou Gehrig, 1b	.348	7	23	1	8	2	0	0	4	5	4	0
Waite Hoyt, p	.000	2	6	0	0	0	0	0	0	0	1	0
Sam Jones, p	.000	1	0	0	0	0	0	0	0	0	0	0
Mark Koenig, ss	.125	7	32	2	4	1	0	0	2	0	6	0
Tony Lazzeri, 2b	.192	7	26	2	5	1	0	0	3	1	6	0
Bob Meusel, of	.238	7	21	3	5	1	1	0	0	6	1	0
Ben Paschal, ph	.250	5	4	0	1	0	0	0	0	1	2	0
Herb Pennock, p	.143	3	7	1	1	1	0	0	0	0	0	0
Dutch Ruether, p-1	.000	3	4	0	0	0	0	0	0	0	0	0
Babe Ruth, of	.300	7	20	6	6	0	0	4	5	11	2	1
Hank Severeid, c	.273	7	22	1	6	1	0	0	1	1	2	0
Bob Shawkey, p	.000	3	2	0	0	0	0	0	0	0	1	0
Urban Shocker, p	.000	2	2	0	0	0	0	0	0	0	2	0
Myles Thomas, p	.000	2	0	0	0	0	0	0	0	0	0	0
TOTAL	.242		223	21	54	10	1	4	20	31	31	1

PITCHER	W	L	ERA	G	GS	CG	SV	SHO	IP	H	ER	BB	SO
Waite Hoyt	1	1	1.20	2	2	1	0	0	15.0	19	2	1	10
Sam Jones	0	0	9.00	1	0	0	0	0	1.0	2	1	2	1
Herb Pennock	2	0	1.23	3	2	2	0	0	22.0	13	3	4	8
Dutch Ruether	0	1	8.31	1	1	0	0	0	4.1	7	4	2	1
Bob Shawkey	0	1	5.40	3	1	0	0	0	10.0	8	6	2	7
Urban Shocker	0	1	5.87	2	1	0	0	0	7.2	13	5	0	3
Myles Thomas	0	0	3.00	2	0	0	0	0	3.0	3	1	0	0
TOTAL	3	4	3.14	14	7	3	0	0	63.0	65	22	11	30

GAME 1 AT NY OCT 2

STL 100 000 000   1 3 1
NY 100 001 00X   2 6 0
Pitchers: SHERDEL, Haines (8) vs PENNOCK
Attendance: 61,658

GAME 2 AT NY OCT 3

STL 002 000 301   6 12 1
NY 020 000 000   2 4 0
Pitchers: ALEXANDER vs SHOCKER, Shawkey (8), Jones (9)
Home Runs: Southworth-STL, Thevenow-STL
Attendance: 63,600

GAME 3 AT STL OCT 5

NY 000 000 000   0 5 1
STL 000 310 00X   4 8 0
Pitchers: RUETHER, Shawkey (5), Thomas (8) vs HAINES
Home Runs: Haines-STL
Attendance: 37,708

GAME 4 AT STL OCT 6

NY 101 142 100   10 14 1
STL 100 300 001   5 14 0
Pitchers: HOYT vs Rhem, REINHART (5), H.Bell (5), Hallahan (7), Keen (9)
Home Runs: Ruth-NY (3)
Attendance: 38,825

GAME 5 AT STL OCT 7

NY 000 001 001 1   3 9 1
STL 000 100 001 0   2 7 1
Pitchers: PENNOCK vs SHERDEL
Attendance: 39,552

GAME 6 AT NY OCT 9

STL 300 010 501   10 13 2
NY 000 100 100   2 8 1
Pitchers: ALEXANDER vs SHAWKEY, Shocker (7), Thomas (8)
Home Runs: L.Bell-STL
Attendance: 48,615

GAME 7 AT NY OCT 10

STL 000 300 000   3 8 0
NY 001 001 000   2 8 3
Pitchers: HAINES, Alexander (7) vs HOYT, Pennock (7)
Home Runs: Ruth-NY
Attendance: 38,093

NEW YORK YANKEES (AL) 4, PITTSBURGH PIRATES (NL) 0

The Pirates, who struggled to a narrow pennant win in a four-team race, were no slouches at the bat. Their team batting average of .305 led the National League, and in the Waner brothers—Paul and Lloyd—and Pie Traynor they had three of the league's five top hitters. But in the World Series they came up against a Yankees team that is still widely regarded as the game's greatest ever. With 110 season victories and a 19-game margin over second-place Philadelphia, the Yankees led the American League in nearly every offensive category. Three Yankees—Earle Combs, Lou Gehrig, and Babe Ruth—hit over .350, and divided among them league crowns in runs, hits, doubles, triples, home runs (Ruth's 60), RBIs, and slugging average. The Yankees not only hit, but their pitching staff boasted the league's lowest earned run average.

In the Series, though, it was Pittsburgh's erratic play that brought about the first American League sweep. The Pirates scored four times off Waite Hoyt in Game 1, and might have won the game. But Paul Waner misplayed a Gehrig fly for a run-scoring triple in the first, and in the third, two Pirates errors led to three more runs. A final run in the fifth was all New York needed to win, 5–4.

The Yankees won the next two games more convincingly, with strong pitching and timely hitting. George Pipgras held Pittsburgh to two runs in Game 2 as his Yankees bunched seven of their 11 hits into the third and eighth innings (also taking advantage of two walks and a hit batsman in the eighth) for their six runs. And in Game 3—as Herb Pennock pitched perfectly into the eighth inning before yielding two hits and a run—the Yankees again bunched most of their hits into two innings, scoring two runs on Gehrig's first-inning triple and six more in the seventh, climaxed by Ruth's three-run homer.

Pittsburgh took advantage of two Yankees errors in the seventh inning of Game 4 to score two runs and tie the game at three-all. But in the last of the ninth, after the Pirates' Johnny Miljus had struck out Gehrig and Bob Meusel with the bases loaded, his second wild pitch of the inning undid him— Combs scored from third with the Series' winning run.

NY (A)

PLAYER/POS	AVG	G	AB	R	H	2B	3B	HR	RB	BB	SO	SB
Benny Bengough, c	.000	2	4	1	0	0	0	0	0	1	0	0
Pat Collins, c	.600	2	5	0	3	1	0	0	0	3	0	0
Earle Combs, of	.313	4	16	6	5	0	0	0	2	1	2	0
Joe Dugan, 3b	.200	4	15	2	3	0	0	0	0	0	0	0
Cedric Durst, ph	.000	1	1	0	0	0	0	0	0	0	0	0
Lou Gehrig, 1b	.308	4	13	2	4	2	2	0	4	3	3	0
Johnny Grabowski, c	.000	1	2	0	0	0	0	0	0	0	0	0
Waite Hoyt, p	.000	1	3	0	0	0	0	0	0	0	0	0
Mark Koenig, ss	.500	4	18	5	9	2	0	0	2	0	2	0
Tony Lazzeri, 2b	.267	4	15	1	4	1	0	0	2	1	4	0
Bob Meusel, of	.118	4	17	1	2	0	0	0	1	1	7	1
Wilcy Moore, p	.200	2	5	0	1	0	0	0	0	0	3	0
Herb Pennock, p	.000	1	4	1	0	0	0	0	0	1	0	0
George Pipgras, p	.333	1	3	0	1	0	0	0	0	0	1	0
Babe Ruth, of	.400	4	15	4	6	0	0	2	7	2	2	1
TOTAL	.279		136	23	38	6	2	2	19	13	25	2

PITCHER	W	L	ERA	G	GS	CG	SV	SHO	IP	H	ER	BB	SO
Waite Hoyt	1	0	4.91	1	1	0	0	0	7.1	8	4	1	2
Wilcy Moore	1	0	0.84	2	1	1	1	0	10.2	11	1	2	2
Herb Pennock	1	0	1.00	1	1	1	0	0	9.0	3	1	0	1
George Pipgras	1	0	2.00	1	1	1	0	0	9.0	7	2	1	2
TOTAL	4	0	2.00	5	4	3	1	0	36.0	29	8	4	7

PIT (N)

PLAYER/POS	AVG	G	AB	R	H	2B	3B	HR	RB	BB	SO	SB
Vic Aldridge, p	.000	1	2	0	0	0	0	0	0	0	0	0
Clyde Barnhart, of	.313	4	16	0	5	1	0	0	4	0	0	0
Fred Brickell, ph	.000	2	2	1	0	0	0	0	0	0	0	0
Mike Cvengros, p	.000	2	0	0	0	0	0	0	0	0	0	0
Joe Dawson, p	.000	1	0	0	0	0	0	0	0	0	0	0
Johnny Gooch, c	.000	3	5	0	0	0	0	0	0	1	1	0
George Grantham, 2b	.364	3	11	0	4	1	0	0	0	1	1	0
Heinie Groh, ph	.000	1	1	0	0	0	0	0	0	0	0	0
Joe Harris, 1b	.200	4	15	0	3	0	0	0	1	0	0	0
Carmen Hill, p	.000	1	1	0	0	0	0	0	0	1	0	0
Ray Kremer, p	.500	1	2	1	1	1	0	0	0	0	1	0
Lee Meadows, p	.000	1	2	0	0	0	0	0	0	0	0	0
Johnny Miljus, p	.000	2	2	0	0	0	0	0	0	0	2	0
Hal Rhyne, 2b	.000	1	4	0	0	0	0	0	0	0	0	0
Earl Smith, c-2	.000	3	8	0	0	0	0	0	0	0	0	0
Roy Spencer, c	.000	1	1	0	0	0	0	0	0	0	0	0
Pie Traynor, 3b	.200	4	15	1	3	1	0	0	0	0	1	0
Lloyd Waner, of	.400	4	15	5	6	1	1	0	0	1	0	0
Paul Waner, of	.333	4	15	0	5	1	0	0	3	0	1	0
Glenn Wright, ss	.154	4	13	1	2	0	0	0	2	0	0	0
Emil Yde, pr	.000	1	0	1	0	0	0	0	0	0	0	0
TOTAL	.223		130	10	29	6	1	0	10	4	7	0

PITCHER	W	L	ERA	G	GS	CG	SV	SHO	IP	H	ER	BB	SO
Vic Aldridge	0	1	7.36	1	1	0	0	0	7.1	10	6	4	4
Mike Cvengros	0	0	3.86	2	0	0	0	0	2.1	3	1	0	2
Joe Dawson	0	0	0.00	1	0	0	0	0	1.0	0	0	0	0
Carmen Hill	0	0	4.50	1	1	0	0	0	6.0	9	3	1	6
Ray Kremer	0	1	3.60	1	1	0	0	0	5.0	5	2	3	1
Lee Meadows	0	1	9.95	1	1	0	0	0	6.1	7	7	1	6
Johnny Miljus	0	1	1.35	2	0	0	0	0	6.2	4	1	4	6
TOTAL	0	4	5.19	9	4	0	0	0	34.2	38	20	13	25

GAME 1 AT PIT OCT 5

```
NY   103 010 000   5 6 1
PIT  101 010 010   4 9 2
```
Pitchers: HOYT, Moore (8) vs KREMER, Miljus (6)
Attendance: 41,467

GAME 2 AT PIT OCT 6

```
NY   003 000 030   6 11 0
PIT  100 000 010   2 7 2
```
Pitchers: PIPGRAS vs ALDRIDGE, Cvengros (8), Dawson (9)
Attendance: 41,634

GAME 3 AT NY OCT 7

```
PIT  000 000 010   1 3 1
NY   200 000 60X   8 9 0
```
Pitchers: MEADOWS, Cvengros (7) vs PENNOCK
Home Runs: Ruth-NY
Attendance: 60,695

GAME 4 AT NY OCT 8

```
PIT  100 000 200   3 10 1
NY   100 020 001   4 12 2
```
Pitchers: Hill, MILJUS (7) vs MOORE
Home Runs: Ruth-NY
Attendance: 57,909

NEW YORK YANKEES (AL) 4, ST. LOUIS CARDINALS (NL) 0

After squandering a 13-1/2-game lead and falling briefly behind the Athletics in early September, the Yankees recovered to meet the Cardinals—winners of another tight National League race—in the Series. With Herb Pennock lost to arm trouble, the Yankees made do with just three pitchers in extending their Series win streak to eight games.

The four games offered little suspense, but for Yankees fans there were thrills aplenty. The Bronx Bombers' nine home runs (including four by Lou Gehrig and three by Babe Ruth) nearly equalled St. Louis' total scoring (10 runs), and Gehrig himself drove in as many runs (nine) as the entire Cardinals offense. Ruth and Gehrig started things off with successive doubles and a run in the first inning of the opener, and when Bob Meusel followed Ruth's second double with a home run in the fourth, the Yanks had more than they would need to support Waite Hoyt's three-hitter. The Cardinals' Jim Bottomley homered off Hoyt in the seventh, but successive singles by Mark Koenig, Ruth, and Gehrig produced a fourth Yankee run and concluded the scoring.

Gehrig homered in the first inning of Game 2 to get New York off to a 3–0 lead against 41-year-old Grover Cleveland Alexander. The Cards snapped back to tie the game, but the Yankees retook the lead with a run in the last of the second and put together four hits, two walks, and a hit batsman for four more in the third. A final Yankees run in the seventh capped a 9–3 four-hit win for pitcher George Pipgras.

Jim Bottomley gave St. Louis its first lead of the Series with a two-run triple in the first inning of Game 3. But Tom Zachary gave up only one more run, taking the third Yankees win as Gehrig drove in three runs with homers in the second and fourth, and his teammates scored three more in the sixth (thanks in large part to two Cardinals errors and Meusel's steal of home) and a final (unearned) run an inning later.

New York completed its second straight Series sweep with another 7–3 win two days later. Waite Hoyt gained his second victory, mostly on the strength of five solo Yankees

homers, including three by Babe Ruth.

NY (A)

PLAYER/POS	AVG	G	AB	R	H	2B	3B	HR	RB	BB	SO	SB
Benny Bengough, c	.231	4	13	1	3	0	0	0	1	1	1	0
Pat Collins, c	1.000	1	1	0	1	1	0	0	0	0	0	0
Earle Combs, ph	.000	1	0	0	0	0	0	0	1	0	0	0
Joe Dugan, 3b	.167	3	6	0	1	0	0	0	0	0	0	0
Leo Durocher, 2b	.000	4	2	0	0	0	0	0	0	0	1	0
Cedric Durst, of	.375	4	8	3	3	0	0	1	2	0	1	0
Lou Gehrig, 1b	.545	4	11	5	6	1	0	4	9	6	0	0
Waite Hoyt, p	.143	2	7	0	1	0	0	0	0	0	0	0
Mark Koenig, ss	.158	4	19	1	3	0	0	0	0	0	1	0
Tony Lazzeri, 2b	.250	4	12	2	3	1	0	0	0	1	0	2
Bob Meusel, of	.200	4	15	5	3	1	0	1	3	2	5	2
Ben Paschal, of	.200	3	10	0	2	0	0	0	0	1	1	0
George Pipgras, p	.000	1	2	0	0	0	0	0	0	1	0	1
Gene Robertson, 3b	.125	3	8	1	1	0	0	0	0	2	1	0
Babe Ruth, of	.625	4	16	9	10	3	0	3	4	1	2	0
Tom Zachary, p	.000	1	4	0	0	0	0	0	0	0	1	0
TOTAL	.276		134	27	37	7	0	9	25	13	13	4

PITCHER	W	L	ERA	G	GS	CG	SV	SHO	IP	H	ER	BB	SO
Waite Hoyt	2	0	1.50	2	2	2	0	0	18.0	14	3	6	14
George Pipgras	1	0	2.00	1	1	1	0	0	9.0	4	2	4	8
Tom Zachary	1	0	3.00	1	1	1	0	0	9.0	9	3	1	7
TOTAL	4	0	2.00	4	4	4	0	0	36.0	27	8	11	29

STL (N)

PLAYER/POS	AVG	G	AB	R	H	2B	3B	HR	RB	BB	SO	SB
G.C. Alexander, p	.000	2	1	0	0	0	0	0	0	1	0	0
Ray Blades, ph	.000	1	1	0	0	0	0	0	0	0	1	0
Jim Bottomley, 1b	.214	4	14	1	3	0	1	1	3	2	6	0
Taylor Douthit, of	.091	3	11	1	1	0	0	0	1	1	1	0
Frankie Frisch, 2b	.231	4	13	1	3	0	0	0	1	2	2	2
Chick Hafey, of	.200	4	15	0	3	0	0	0	0	1	4	0
Jesse Haines, p	.000	1	2	0	0	0	0	0	0	0	0	0
George Harper, of	.111	3	9	1	1	0	0	0	0	2	2	0
Andy High, 3b	.294	4	17	1	5	2	0	0	1	1	3	0
Wattie Holm, of-1	.167	3	6	0	1	0	0	0	1	0	1	0
Syl Johnson, p	.000	2	0	0	0	0	0	0	0	0	0	0
Rabbit Maranville, ss	.308	4	13	2	4	1	0	0	0	1	1	1
Pepper Martin, pr	.000	1	0	1	0	0	0	0	0	0	0	0
Clarence Mitchell, p	.000	1	2	0	0	0	0	0	0	0	0	0
Ernie Orsatti, of-1	.286	4	7	1	2	1	0	0	0	1	3	0
Flint Rhem, p	.000	1	0	0	0	0	0	0	0	0	0	0
Bill Sherdel, p	.000	2	5	0	0	0	0	0	0	0	2	0
Earl Smith, c	.750	1	4	0	3	0	0	0	0	0	0	0
Tommy Thevenow, ss	.000	1	0	0	0	0	0	0	0	0	0	0
Jimmie Wilson, c	.091	3	11	1	1	1	0	0	1	0	3	0
TOTAL	.206		131	10	27	5	1	1	9	11	29	3

PITCHER	W	L	ERA	G	GS	CG	SV	SHO	IP	H	ER	BB	SO
G.C. Alexander	0	1	19.80	2	1	0	0	0	5.0	10	11	4	2
Jesse Haines	0	1	4.50	1	1	0	0	0	6.0	6	3	3	3
Syl Johnson	0	0	4.50	2	0	0	0	0	2.0	4	1	1	1
Clarence Mitchell	0	0	1.59	1	0	0	0	0	5.2	2	1	2	3
Flint Rhem	0	0	0.00	1	0	0	0	0	2.0	0	0	0	1
Bill Sherdel	0	2	4.72	2	2	0	0	0	13.1	15	7	3	3
TOTAL	0	4	6.09	9	4	0	0	0	34.0	37	23	13	13

GAME 1 AT NY OCT 4

```
STL  000 000 100    1  3  1
NY   100 200 01X    4  7  0
```
Pitchers: SHERDEL, Johnson (8) vs HOYT
Home Runs: Meusel-NY, Bottomley-STL
Attendance: 61,425

GAME 2 AT NY OCT 5

```
STL  030 000 000    3  4  1
NY   314 000 10X    9  8  2
```
Pitchers: ALEXANDER, Mitchell (3) vs PIPGRAS
Home Runs: Gehrig-NY
Attendance: 60,714

GAME 3 AT STL OCT 7

```
NY   010 203 100    7  7  2
STL  200 010 000    3  9  3
```
Pitchers: ZACHARY vs HAINES, Johnson (7), Rhem (8)
Home Runs: Gehrig-NY (2)
Attendance: 39,602

GAME 4 AT STL OCT 9

```
NY   000 100 420    7 15  2
STL  001 100 001    3 11  0
```
Pitchers: HOYT vs SHERDEL, Alexander (7)
Home Runs: Ruth-NY (3), Durst-NY, Gehrig-NY
Attendance: 37,331

PHILADELPHIA ATHLETICS (AL) 4, CHICAGO CUBS (NL) 1

The surprising success of a surprise starter and the ultimate in big innings highlighted the return of the Athletics to World Series play after a gap of 15 years. In the opener, A's manager Connie Mack passed over the aces of his pitching staff in favor of Howard Ehmke, an aging journeyman who that season had started only eight times and pitched under 55 innings. But Ehmke, who (per Mack's instructions) had studied the Cubs' hitters in a series of late-season games, held the Cubs scoreless through the first eight innings of Game 1 (yielding an unearned run in the last of the ninth) while fanning 13 batters for a new Series record. Chicago's Charlie Root also pitched effectively until Jimmie Foxx's solo homer in the seventh gave the A's the game's first score. A pair of errors by Cubs shortstop Woody English in the ninth set up two unearned runs against reliever Guy Bush and gave Ehmke and the A's all the lead they needed.

Home runs by Foxx and Al Simmons drove in five of the A's nine runs in Game 2 as Philadelphia took a 2–0 Series lead. But Guy Bush held Mack's sluggers to nine singles and one run in Game 3 as his Cubs scored three runs in the sixth to take their first win.

The Cubs seemed well on their way to tying the Series in Game 4 as they entered the last of the seventh with an 8–0 lead. But Simmons led off with a homer to erase Charlie Root's shutout, and five of the next six batters singled. Art Nehf relieved Root, but the first batter to face him—Mule Haas—lofted a fly to center which Hack Wilson lost in the sun for a three-run inside-the-park homer, and the score was 8–7. After walking Mickey Cochrane, Nehf was replaced by Sheriff Blake, who gave up two singles and saw the tying run come home before Pat Malone took the mound with two men still on base and only one away. Malone struck out two in a row to end the inning—but not until he first hit a batter and gave up a double by Jimmy Dykes for the two runs that gave the A's a 10–8 win and a 3–1 Series advantage.

Game 5, although inevitably anticlimactic, was not decided until the final at bat. Chicago scored twice off Ehmke in the fourth as Malone shut out the A's with only two hits through eight. But in the last of the ninth a single and Haas' home run tied the score, and—with two men out—Simmons doubled, Foxx was walked intentionally, Bing Miller doubled, and the Series was history.

GAME 1 AT CHI OCT 8

PHI	0 0 0	0 0 0	1 0 2	3	6	1
CHI	0 0 0	0 0 0	0 0 1	1	8	2

Pitchers: EHMKE vs ROOT, Bush (8)
Home Runs: Foxx-PHI
Attendance: 50,740

GAME 2 AT CHI OCT 9

PHI	0 0 3	3 0 0	1 2 0	9	12	0
CHI	0 0 0	0 3 0	0 0 0	3	11	1

Pitchers: EARNSHAW, Grove (5) vs MALONE, Blake (4), Carlson (6), Nehf (9)
Home Runs: Simmons-PHI, Foxx-PHI
Attendance: 49,987

GAME 3 AT PHI OCT 11

CHI	0 0 0	0 0 3	0 0 0	3	6	1
PHI	0 0 0	0 1 0	0 0 0	1	9	1

Pitchers: BUSH vs EARNSHAW
Attendance: 29,921

GAME 4 AT PHI OCT 12

CHI	0 0 0	2 0 5	1 0 0	8	10	2
PHI	0 0 0	0 0 0	1 0 0 x	10	15	2

Pitchers: Root, Nehf (7), BLAKE (7), Malone (7), Carlson (8) vs Quinn, Walberg (6), ROMMEL (7), Grove (8)
Home Runs: Grimm-CHI, Haas-PHI, Simmons-PHI
Attendance: 29,921

GAME 5 AT PHI OCT 14

CHI	0 0 2	0 0 0	0 0 0	2	8	1
PHI	0 0 0	0 0 0	0 0 3	3	6	0

Pitchers: MALONE vs Ehmke, WALBERG (4)
Home Runs: Haas-PHI
Attendance: 29,921

PHI (A)

PLAYER/POS	AVG	G	AB	R	H	2B	3B	HR	RB	BB	SO	SB
Max Bishop, 2b	.190	5	21	2	4	0	0	0	1	2	3	0
Joe Boley, ss	.235	5	17	1	4	0	0	0	1	0	3	0
George Burns, ph	.000	1	2	0	0	0	0	0	0	0	1	0
Mickey Cochrane, c	.400	5	15	5	6	1	0	0	0	7	0	0
Jimmy Dykes, 3b	.421	5	19	2	8	1	0	0	4	1	1	0
George Earnshaw, p	.000	2	5	1	0	0	0	0	0	0	4	0
Howard Ehmke, p	.200	2	5	0	1	0	0	0	0	0	0	0
Jimmie Foxx, 1b	.350	5	20	5	7	1	0	2	5	1	1	0
Walter French, ph	.000	1	1	0	0	0	0	0	0	0	1	0
Lefty Grove, p	.000	2	0	0	0	0	0	0	0	0	0	0
Mule Haas, of	.238	5	21	3	5	0	0	2	6	1	3	0
Bing Miller, of	.368	5	19	1	7	1	0	0	4	0	2	0
Jack Quinn, p	.000	1	2	0	0	0	0	0	0	0	2	0
Eddie Rommel, p	.000	1	0	0	0	0	0	0	0	0	0	0
Al Simmons, of	.300	5	20	6	6	1	0	2	5	1	4	0
Homer Summa, ph	.000	1	1	0	0	0	0	0	0	0	1	0
Rube Walberg, p	.000	2	1	0	0	0	0	0	0	0	0	0
TOTAL	.281		171	26	48	5	0	6	26	13	27	0

PITCHER	W	L	ERA	G	GS	CG	SV	SHO	IP	H	ER	BB	SO
George Earnshaw	1	1	2.63	2	2	1	0	0	13.2	14	4	6	17
Howard Ehmke	1	0	1.42	2	2	1	0	0	12.2	14	2	3	13
Lefty Grove	0	0	0.00	2	0	0	2	0	6.1	3	0	1	10
Jack Quinn	0	0	9.00	1	1	0	0	0	5.0	7	5	2	2
Eddie Rommel	1	0	9.00	1	0	0	0	0	1.0	2	1	1	0
Rube Walberg	1	0	0.00	2	0	0	0	0	6.1	3	0	0	8
TOTAL	4	1	2.40	10	5	2	2	0	45.0	43	12	13	50

CHI (N)

PLAYER/POS	AVG	G	AB	R	H	2B	3B	HR	RB	BB	SO	SB
Footsie Blair, ph	.000	1	1	0	0	0	0	0	0	0	0	0
Sheriff Blake, p	1.000	2	1	0	1	0	0	0	0	0	0	0
Guy Bush, p	.000	2	3	1	0	0	0	0	0	1	3	0
Hal Carlson, p	.000	2	0	0	0	0	0	0	0	0	0	0
Kiki Cuyler, of	.300	5	20	4	6	1	0	0	4	1	7	0
Woody English, ss	.190	5	21	1	4	2	0	0	0	1	6	0
Mike Gonzalez, c-1	.000	2	1	0	0	0	0	0	0	0	1	0
Charlie Grimm, 1b	.389	5	18	2	7	0	0	1	4	1	2	0
Gabby Hartnett, ph	.000	3	3	0	0	0	0	0	0	0	3	0
Cliff Heathcote, ph	.000	2	1	0	0	0	0	0	0	0	0	0
Rogers Hornsby, 2b	.238	5	21	4	5	1	1	0	1	1	8	0
Pat Malone, p	.250	3	4	0	1	1	0	0	0	0	2	0
Norm McMillan, 3b	.100	5	20	0	2	0	0	0	0	2	6	1
Art Nehf, p	.000	2	0	0	0	0	0	0	0	0	0	0
Charlie Root, p	.000	2	5	0	0	0	0	0	0	0	3	0
Riggs Stephenson, of	.316	5	19	3	6	1	0	0	3	2	2	0
Zack Taylor, c	.176	5	17	0	3	0	0	0	3	0	3	0
Chick Tolson, ph	.000	1	1	0	0	0	0	0	0	0	1	0
Hack Wilson, of	.471	5	17	2	8	0	1	0	0	4	3	0
TOTAL	.249		173	17	43	6	2	1	15	13	50	1

PITCHER	W	L	ERA	G	GS	CG	SV	SHO	IP	H	ER	BB	SO
Sheriff Blake	0	1	13.50	2	0	0	0	0	1.1	4	2	0	1
Guy Bush	1	0	0.82	2	1	1	0	0	11.0	12	1	2	4
Hal Carlson	0	0	6.75	2	0	0	0	0	4.0	7	3	1	3
Pat Malone	0	2	4.15	3	2	1	0	0	13.0	12	6	7	11
Art Nehf	0	0	18.00	2	0	0	0	0	1.0	1	2	1	0
Charlie Root	0	1	4.72	2	2	0	0	0	13.1	12	7	2	8
TOTAL	1	4	4.33	13	5	2	0	0	43.2	48	21	13	27

PHILADELPHIA ATHLETICS (AL) 4, ST. LOUIS CARDINALS (NL) 2

Pitching 85 percent of the Series with a combined ERA of 1.02, Philadelphia aces George Earnshaw and Lefty Grove chilled the hot Cardinals, who had hit .314 and averaged more than six runs per game during the season. The A's hit only .197 themselves in the Series, but more than half their hits went for extra bases as they out-scored St. Louis 21–12 and took their second consecutive world championship in six games.

Grove faced Cardinals spitballer Burleigh Grimes in the opener, giving up nine hits, including four singles in the Cards' two-run third. The Athletics, for their part, touched Grimes for only five hits, all in separate innings. But every hit—a double, two triples, and home runs by Al Simmons and Mike Cochrane—resulted in a run, and Grove and the A's emerged 5–2 victors. In the first inning of Game 2, Cochrane again homered, sending Earnshaw on his way to Philadelphia's second win, 6–1.

When the Series moved to St. Louis, though, the Cards came alive. Wild Bill Hallahan (their leading winner during the season, with 15) spaced seven hits for a shutout. Taylor Douthit's fourth inning home run off Rube Walberg was the first St. Louis hit, but the Cards knocked out nine more for four more runs before they were finished. A pair of unearned runs evened the Series the next day when A's third baseman Jimmy Dykes' wild throw to first in the fourth inning let in a tie-breaking run and led to a third against the ultimate loser Lefty Grove. Meanwhile, Cardinals veteran Jesse Haines, after yielding three Philadelphia hits and a run in the first inning, shut out the A's on one hit the rest of the way.

Earnshaw and Grove combined to restore the Series lead to the Athletics in Game 5 with a three-hit shutout. Grove, who took over when Earnshaw left for a pinch hitter in the eighth, garnered his second Series win as Jimmie Foxx homered off Grimes in the top of the ninth for the game's only runs. After a travel day to Philadelphia, Earnshaw pitched again for the A's in Game 6, and pushed the Cardinals' scoreless streak to 21 innings before allowing them a token run in the ninth. But by then seven A's had crossed the plate and the Series was theirs.

PHI (A)

PLAYER/POS	AVG	G	AB	R	H	2B	3B	HR	RB	BB	SO	SB
Max Bishop, 2b	.222	6	18	5	4	0	0	0	0	7	3	0
Joe Boley, ss	.095	6	21	1	2	0	0	0	1	0	1	0
Mickey Cochrane, c	.222	6	18	5	4	1	0	2	4	5	2	0
Jimmy Dykes, 3b	.222	6	18	2	4	3	0	1	5	5	3	0
George Earnshaw, p	.000	3	9	0	0	0	0	0	0	0	5	0
Jimmie Foxx, 1b	.333	6	21	3	7	2	1	1	3	2	4	0
Lefty Grove, p	.000	3	6	0	0	0	0	0	0	0	3	0
Mule Haas, of	.111	6	18	1	2	0	1	0	1	1	3	0
Eric McNair, ph	.000	1	1	0	0	0	0	0	0	0	0	0
Bing Miller, of	.143	6	21	0	3	2	0	0	3	0	4	0
Jim Moore, of-1	.333	3	3	0	1	0	0	0	0	1	1	0
Jack Quinn, p	.000	1	0	0	0	0	0	0	0	0	0	0
Bill Shores, p	.000	1	0	0	0	0	0	0	0	0	1	0
Al Simmons, of	.364	6	22	4	8	2	0	2	4	2	2	0
Rube Walberg, p	.000	1	2	0	0	0	0	0	0	0	0	0
TOTAL	.197		178	21	35	10	2	6	21	24	32	0

PITCHER	W	L	ERA	G	GS	CG	SV	SHO	IP	H	ER	BB	SO
George Earnshaw	2	0	0.72	3	3	2	0	0	25.0	13	2	7	19
Lefty Grove	2	1	1.42	3	2	2	0	0	19.0	15	3	3	10
Jack Quinn	0	0	4.50	1	0	0	0	0	2.0	3	1	0	1
Bill Shores	0	0	13.50	1	0	0	0	0	1.1	3	2	0	0
Rube Walberg	0	1	3.86	1	1	0	0	0	4.2	4	2	1	3
TOTAL	4	2	1.73	9	6	4	0	0	52.0	38	10	11	33

STL (N)

PLAYER/POS	AVG	G	AB	R	H	2B	3B	HR	RB	BB	SO	SB
Sparky Adams, 3b	.143	6	21	0	3	0	0	0	1	0	4	0
Hi Bell, p	.000	1	0	0	0	0	0	0	0	0	0	0
Ray Blades, of-3	.111	5	9	2	1	0	0	0	0	2	2	0
Jim Bottomley, 1b	.045	6	22	1	1	1	0	0	0	2	9	0
Taylor Douthit, of	.083	6	24	1	2	0	0	1	2	0	2	0
George Fisher, ph	.500	2	2	0	1	1	0	0	0	0	1	0
Frankie Frisch, 2b	.208	6	24	0	5	2	0	0	0	0	1	1
Charlie Gelbert, ss	.353	6	17	2	6	0	1	0	2	3	3	0
Burleigh Grimes, p	.400	2	5	0	2	0	0	0	0	0	1	0
Chick Hafey, of	.273	6	22	2	6	5	0	0	2	1	3	0
Jesse Haines, p	.500	1	2	0	1	0	0	0	0	1	0	0
Bill Hallahan, p	.000	2	2	0	0	0	0	0	0	1	1	0
Andy High, 3b	.500	1	2	1	1	0	0	0	0	0	0	0
Syl Johnson, p	.000	2	0	0	0	0	0	0	0	0	0	0
Jim Lindsey, p	1.000	2	1	0	1	0	0	0	0	0	0	0
Gus Mancuso, c	.286	2	7	1	2	0	0	0	0	1	2	0
Ernie Orsatti, ph	.000	1	1	0	0	0	0	0	0	0	0	0
George Puccinelli, ph	.000	1	1	0	0	0	0	0	0	0	0	0
Flint Rhem, p	.000	1	1	0	0	0	0	0	0	0	1	0
George Watkins, of	.167	4	12	2	2	2	0	1	1	1	3	0
Jimmie Wilson, c	.267	4	15	0	4	1	0	0	2	0	1	0
TOTAL	.200		190	12	38	10	1	2	11	11	33	1

PITCHER	W	L	ERA	G	GS	CG	SV	SHO	IP	H	ER	BB	SO
Hi Bell	0	0	0.00	1	0	0	0	0	1.0	0	0	0	0
Burleigh Grimes	0	2	3.71	2	2	2	0	0	17.0	10	7	6	13
Jesse Haines	1	0	1.00	1	1	1	0	0	9.0	4	1	4	2
Bill Hallahan	1	1	1.64	2	2	1	0	1	11.0	9	2	8	8
Syl Johnson	0	0	7.20	2	0	0	0	0	5.0	4	4	3	4
Jim Lindsey	0	0	1.93	2	0	0	0	0	4.2	1	1	1	2
Flint Rhem	0	1	10.80	1	1	0	0	0	3.1	7	4	2	3
TOTAL	2	4	3.35	11	6	4	0	1	51.0	35	19	24	32

GAME 1 AT PHI OCT 1

```
STL  0 0 2 0 0 0 0 0 0    2  9  0
PHI  0 1 0 1 0 1 1 1 X    5  5  0
```
Pitchers: GRIMES vs GROVE
Home Runs: Cochrane-PHI, Simmons-PHI
Attendance: 32,295

GAME 2 AT PHI OCT 2

```
STL  0 1 0 0 0 0 0 0 0    1  6  2
PHI  2 0 2 2 0 0 0 0 X    6  7  2
```
Pitchers: RHEM, Lindsey (4), Johnson (7) vs EARNSHAW
Home Runs: Cochrane-PHI, Watkins-STL
Attendance: 32,295

GAME 3 AT STL OCT 4

```
PHI  0 0 0 0 0 0 0 0 0    0  7  0
STL  0 0 0 1 1 0 2 1 X    5 10  0
```
Pitchers: WALBERG, Shores (5), Quinn (7) vs HALLAHAN
Home Runs: Douthit-STL
Attendance: 36,944

GAME 4 AT STL OCT 5

```
PHI  1 0 0 0 0 0 0 0 0    1  4  1
STL  0 0 1 2 0 0 0 0 X    3  5  1
```
Pitchers: GROVE vs HAINES
Attendance: 39,946

GAME 5 AT STL OCT 6

```
PHI  0 0 0 0 0 0 0 0 2    2  5  0
STL  0 0 0 0 0 0 0 0 0    0  3  1
```
Pitchers: Earnshaw, GROVE (8) vs GRIMES
Home Runs: Foxx-PHI
Attendance: 38,844

GAME 6 AT PHI OCT 8

```
STL  0 0 0 0 0 0 0 0 1    1  5  1
PHI  2 0 1 2 1 1 0 0 X    7  7  0
```
Pitchers: HALLAHAN, Johnson (3), Lindsey (6), Bell (8) vs EARNSHAW
Home Runs: Dykes-PHI, Simmons-PHI
Attendance: 32,295

ST. LOUIS CARDINALS (NL) 4, PHILADELPHIA ATHLETICS (AL) 3

For the second year in a row, the A's met the Cardinals in the Series, and once again pitchers Lefty Grove and George Earnshaw provided more than 80 percent of the Athletics' pitching, performing splendidly and winning three games between them. But this time Cardinals pitchers Wild Bill Hallahan and Burleigh Grimes outshone them, winning two games apiece to bring St. Louis the world championship.

Grove gave up four hits and two runs in the first inning of the opener, but shut out the Cards the rest of the way as the A's scored six off Paul Derringer to take the Series lead. Earnshaw also held St. Louis to two runs the next day—both manufactured by Pepper Martin's daring baserunning. But they were more than enough for Hallahan, who shut out the A's on three singles.

The Cardinals took their first Series lead in Game 3, scoring five times off Grove and reliever Roy Mahaffey while Grimes held the A's hitless through seven innings and scoreless through eight before giving up a harmless two-run homer to Al Simmons in the bottom of the ninth. But the A's came back to even the Series the next day on Earnshaw's two-hit shutout.

Pepper Martin, hero of Game 2, homered for two runs in Game 5, and drove in two more of St. Louis' five runs with a sacrifice fly and a single. Meanwhile pitcher Hallahan held Philadelphia to a lone run, returning the Series lead to the Cardinals with his second win.

Game 6 pitted Grove and Derringer against each other again as in the opener, and again Grove emerged the victor, holding the Cardinals to one run and five hits. The Athletics scored four unearned runs in the fifth off the unfortunate Derringer. After an error put a runner on base to open the inning, he allowed two singles and walked four, including two with the bases full, before leaving the game. Four more Philadelphia runs in the seventh (two of them scoring on a dropped fly ball) gave the A's the Series' only lopsided win.

In the finale, Grimes once again held the A's scoreless through eight before giving up two runs in the ninth. And once again the runs

proved harmless against an early Cardinals lead, as Hallahan came on to retire Max Bishop for the final out.

GAME 1 AT STL OCT 1

PHI 004 000 200 6 11 0
STL 200 000 000 2 12 0
Pitchers: GROVE vs DERRINGER, Johnson (8)
Home Runs: Simmons-PHI
Attendance: 38,529

GAME 2 AT STL OCT 2

PHI 000 000 000 0 3 0
STL 010 000 10X 2 6 1
Pitchers: EARNSHAW vs HALLAHAN
Attendance: 35,947

GAME 3 AT PHI OCT 5

STL 020 200 001 5 12 0
PHI 000 000 002 2 2 0
Pitchers: GRIMES vs GROVE, Mahaffey (9)
Home Runs: Simmons-PHI
Attendance: 32,295

GAME 4 AT PHI OCT 6

STL 000 000 000 0 2 1
PHI 100 002 00X 3 10 0
Pitchers: JOHNSON, Lindsey (6), Derringer (8) vs EARNSHAW
Home Runs: Foxx-PHI
Attendance: 32,295

GAME 5 AT PHI OCT 7

STL 100 002 011 5 12 0
PHI 000 000 100 1 9 0
Pitchers: HALLAHAN vs HOYT, Walberg (7), Rommel (9)
Home Runs: Martin-STL, Watkins-STL
Attendance: 32,295

GAME 6 AT STL OCT 9

PHI 000 040 400 8 8 1
STL 000 001 000 1 5 2
Pitchers: GROVE vs DERRINGER, Johnson (5), Lindsey (7), Rhem (9)
Attendance: 39,401

GAME 7 AT STL OCT 10

PHI 000 000 002 2 7 1
STL 202 000 00X 4 5 0
Pitchers: EARNSHAW, Walberg (8) vs GRIMES, Hallahan (9)
Attendance: 20,805

STL (N)

PLAYER/POS	AVG	G	AB	R	H	2B	3B	HR	RB	BB	SO	SB
Sparky Adams, 3b	.250	2	4	0	1	0	0	0	0	0	1	0
Ray Blades, ph	.000	2	2	0	0	0	0	0	0	0	2	0
Jim Bottomley, 1b	.160	7	25	2	4	1	0	0	2	2	5	0
Ripper Collins, ph	.000	2	2	0	0	0	0	0	0	0	1	0
Paul Derringer, p	.000	3	2	0	0	0	0	0	0	0	1	0
Jake Flowers, 3b-4	.091	5	11	1	1	1	0	0	0	1	0	0
Frankie Frisch, 2b	.259	7	27	2	7	2	0	0	1	1	2	1
Charlie Gelbert, ss	.261	7	23	0	6	1	0	0	3	0	4	0
Burleigh Grimes, p	.286	2	7	0	2	0	0	0	2	0	2	0
Chick Hafey, of	.167	6	24	1	4	0	0	0	0	0	5	1
Bill Hallahan, p	.000	3	6	0	0	0	0	0	0	0	3	0
Andy High, 3b	.267	4	15	3	4	0	0	0	0	0	2	0
Syl Johnson, p	.000	3	2	0	0	0	0	0	0	0	2	0
Jim Lindsey, p	.000	2	0	0	0	0	0	0	0	0	0	0
Gus Mancuso, c-1	.000	2	1	0	0	0	0	0	0	0	0	0
Pepper Martin, of	.500	7	24	5	12	4	0	1	5	2	3	5
Ernie Orsatti, of	.000	1	3	0	0	0	0	0	0	0	3	0
Flint Rhem, p	.000	1	0	0	0	0	0	0	0	0	0	0
Wally Roettger, of	.286	3	14	1	4	1	0	0	0	0	3	0
George Watkins, of	.286	5	14	4	4	1	0	1	2	2	1	1
Jimmie Wilson, c	.217	7	23	0	5	0	0	0	2	1	1	0
TOTAL	.236		229	19	54	11	0	2	17	9	41	8

PITCHER	W	L	ERA	G	GS	CG	SV	SHO	IP	H	ER	BB	SO
Paul Derringer	0	2	4.26	3	2	0	0	0	12.2	14	6	7	14
Burleigh Grimes	2	0	2.04	2	2	1	0	0	17.2	9	4	9	11
Bill Hallahan	2	0	0.49	3	2	2	1	1	18.1	12	1	8	12
Syl Johnson	0	1	3.00	3	1	0	0	0	9.0	10	3	1	6
Jim Lindsey	0	0	5.40	2	0	0	0	0	3.1	4	2	3	2
Flint Rhem	0	0	0.00	1	0	0	0	0	1.0	1	0	0	1
TOTAL	4	3	2.32	14	7	3	1	1	62.0	50	16	28	46

PHI (A)

PLAYER/POS	AVG	G	AB	R	H	2B	3B	HR	RB	BB	SO	SB
Max Bishop, 2b	.148	7	27	4	4	0	0	0	0	3	5	0
Joe Boley, ph	.000	1	1	0	0	0	0	0	0	0	1	0
Mickey Cochrane, c	.160	7	25	2	4	0	0	0	1	5	2	0
Doc Cramer, ph	.500	2	2	0	1	0	0	0	2	0	0	0
Jimmy Dykes, 3b	.227	7	22	2	5	0	0	0	2	5	1	0
George Earnshaw, p	.000	3	8	0	0	0	0	0	0	0	2	0
Jimmie Foxx, 1b	.348	7	23	3	8	0	0	1	3	6	5	0
Lefty Grove, p	.000	3	10	0	0	0	0	0	0	0	7	0
Mule Haas, of	.130	7	23	1	3	1	0	0	2	3	5	0
Johnnie Heving, ph	.000	1	1	0	0	0	0	0	0	0	0	0
Waite Hoyt, p	.000	1	2	0	0	0	0	0	0	0	0	0
Roy Mahaffey, p	.000	1	0	0	0	0	0	0	0	0	0	0
Eric McNair, 2b-1	.000	2	2	1	0	0	0	0	0	0	1	0
Bing Miller, of	.269	7	26	3	7	1	0	0	1	0	4	0
Jim Moore, of-1	.333	2	3	0	1	0	0	0	0	0	1	0
Eddie Rommel, p	.000	1	0	0	0	0	0	0	0	0	0	0
Al Simmons, of	.333	7	27	4	9	2	0	2	8	3	3	0
Phil Todt, ph	.000	1	0	0	0	0	0	0	0	1	0	0
Rube Walberg, p	.000	2	0	0	0	0	0	0	0	0	0	0
Dib Williams, ss	.320	7	25	2	8	1	0	1	2	1	9	0
TOTAL	.220		227	22	50	6	0	3	20	28	46	0

PITCHER	W	L	ERA	G	GS	CG	SV	SHO	IP	H	ER	BB	SO
George Earnshaw	1	2	1.88	3	3	2	0	1	24.0	12	5	4	20
Lefty Grove	2	1	2.42	3	3	2	0	0	26.0	28	7	2	16
Waite Hoyt	0	1	4.50	1	1	0	0	0	6.0	7	3	0	1
Roy Mahaffey	0	0	9.00	1	0	0	0	0	1.0	1	1	1	0
Eddie Rommel	0	0	9.00	1	0	0	0	0	1.0	3	1	0	0
Rube Walberg	0	0	3.00	2	0	0	0	0	3.0	3	1	2	4
TOTAL	3	4	2.66	11	7	4	0	1	61.0	54	18	9	41

NEW YORK YANKEES (AL) 4, CHICAGO CUBS (NL) 0

Lou Gehrig, who hit .529 and scored nearly a quarter of New York's runs, led both clubs in batting, slugging, hits, runs, and RBIs as the Yankees crushed the Cubs in four games. But the Series is best remembered for Babe Ruth's "called" shot in Game 3, when he pointed his bat at pitcher Charlie Root in the fifth inning and broke the game's 4–4 tie a moment later with a massive home run into the center field bleachers. Debate has raged ever since about whether Ruth intended his gesture as a home run prediction. Whether intended or not, it erased from public memory Gehrig's home run that followed Ruth's (and the homers both men had hit earlier in the game), and made memorable an otherwise undistinguished Series.

Chicago scored in the first inning of each game, taking early leads in three of the four, but held no lead beyond the sixth inning. In the opener the Cubs connected for ten hits to the Yankees' eight, but managed to score only half as many runs as the New Yorkers, who put what had been a close game out of reach with five runs in the sixth (on four walks, two singles, and a ground out) and three more in the seventh (a walk, two singles, a hit batsman, a sacrifice fly, and a wild pitch).

Chicago's Lon Warneke walked four batters in Game 2, and three of them went on to score as the Yankees countered single Chicago runs in the first and third with pairs of their own on two walks and two singles in each frame. (A fifth Yankees run—on two singles without bases on balls—concluded the scoring for the game.)

Game 3 featured not only the two homers each by Ruth and Gehrig, but home runs by the Cubs' Kiki Cuyler and Gabby Hartnett. Hartnett's solo shot in the last of the ninth brought Chicago to within two runs of New York for the Series' closest finish.

Four first-inning singles, Frank Demaree's three-run homer, and a Yankees error gave the Cubs a 4–1 advantage early in Game 4—their biggest lead of the Series—but by game's end, 19 Yankees hits (including two home runs by Tony Lazzeri and one by Earle Combs) had created 13 runs, and the world title belonged to the Yankees.

NY (A)

PLAYER/POS	AVG	G	AB	R	H	2B	3B	HR	RB	BB	SO	SB
Johnny Allen, p	.000	1	0	0	0	0	0	0	0	0	0	0
Sammy Byrd, of	.000	1	0	0	0	0	0	0	0	0	0	0
Ben Chapman, of	.294	4	17	1	5	2	0	0	6	2	4	0
Earle Combs, of	.375	4	16	8	6	1	0	1	4	4	3	0
Frankie Crosetti, ss	.133	4	15	2	2	1	0	0	0	2	3	0
Bill Dickey, c	.438	4	16	2	7	0	0	0	4	2	1	0
Lou Gehrig, 1b	.529	4	17	9	9	1	0	3	8	2	1	0
Lefty Gomez, p	.000	1	3	0	0	0	0	0	0	0	2	0
Myril Hoag, pr	.000	1	0	1	0	0	0	0	0	0	0	0
Tony Lazzeri, 2b	.294	4	17	4	5	0	0	2	5	2	1	0
Wilcy Moore, p	.333	1	3	0	1	0	0	0	0	0	2	0
Herb Pennock, p	.000	2	1	0	0	0	0	0	0	0	0	0
George Pipgras, p	.000	1	5	0	0	0	0	0	0	0	5	0
Red Ruffing, p-1	.000	2	4	0	0	0	0	0	0	1	1	0
Babe Ruth, of	.333	4	15	6	5	0	0	2	6	4	3	0
Joe Sewell, 3b	.333	4	15	4	5	1	0	0	3	4	0	0
TOTAL	.313		144	37	45	6	0	8	36	23	26	0

PITCHER	W	L	ERA	G	GS	CG	SV	SHO	IP	H	ER	BB	SO
Johnny Allen	0	0	40.50	1	1	0	0	0	0.2	5	3	0	0
Lefty Gomez	1	0	1.00	1	1	1	0	0	9.0	9	1	1	8
Wilcy Moore	1	0	0.00	1	0	0	0	0	5.1	2	0	0	1
Herb Pennock	0	0	2.25	2	0	0	2	0	4.0	2	1	1	4
George Pipgras	1	0	4.50	1	1	0	0	0	8.0	9	4	3	1
Red Ruffing	1	0	3.00	1	1	1	0	0	9.0	10	3	6	10
TOTAL	4	0	3.00	7	4	2	2	0	36.0	37	12	11	24

CHI (N)

PLAYER/POS	AVG	G	AB	R	H	2B	3B	HR	RB	BB	SO	SB
Guy Bush, p	.000	2	1	0	0	0	0	0	0	1	0	0
Kiki Cuyler, of	.278	4	18	2	5	1	1	1	2	0	3	1
Frank Demaree, of	.286	2	7	1	2	0	0	1	4	1	0	0
Woody English, 3b	.176	4	17	2	3	0	0	0	1	2	2	0
Burleigh Grimes, p	.000	2	1	0	0	0	0	0	0	0	1	0
Charlie Grimm, 1b	.333	4	15	2	5	2	0	0	1	2	2	0
Marv Gudat, ph	.000	2	2	0	0	0	0	0	0	0	1	0
Stan Hack, ph	.000	1	0	0	0	0	0	0	0	0	0	0
Gabby Hartnett, c	.313	4	16	2	5	2	0	1	1	1	3	0
Rollie Hemsley, c-1	.000	3	3	0	0	0	0	0	0	0	3	0
Billy Herman, 2b	.222	4	18	5	4	1	0	0	1	1	3	0
Billy Jurges, ss	.364	3	11	1	4	1	0	0	1	0	1	2
Mark Koenig, ss-1	.250	2	4	1	1	0	1	0	1	1	0	0
Pat Malone, p	.000	1	0	0	0	0	0	0	0	0	0	0
Jakie May, p	.000	2	2	0	0	0	0	0	0	0	0	0
Johnny Moore, of	.000	2	7	1	0	0	0	0	0	2	1	0
Charlie Root, p	.000	1	2	0	0	0	0	0	0	0	1	0
Bob Smith, p	.000	1	0	0	0	0	0	0	0	0	0	0
Riggs Stephenson, of	.444	4	18	2	8	1	0	0	4	0	0	0
Bud Tinning, p	.000	2	0	0	0	0	0	0	0	0	0	0
Lon Warneke, p	.000	2	4	0	0	0	0	0	0	0	3	0
TOTAL	.253		14 619	37	8	2	3		16	11	24	3

PITCHER	W	L	ERA	G	GS	CG	SV	SHO	IP	H	ER	BB	SO
Guy Bush	0	1	14.29	2	2	0	0	0	5.2	5	9	6	2
Burleigh Grimes	0	0	23.63	2	0	0	0	0	2.2	7	7	2	0
Pat Malone	0	0	0.00	1	0	0	0	0	2.2	1	0	4	4
Jakie May	0	1	11.57	2	0	0	0	0	4.2	9	6	3	4
Charlie Root	0	1	10.38	1	1	0	0	0	4.1	6	5	3	4
Bob Smith	0	0	9.00	1	0	0	0	0	1.0	2	1	0	1
Bud Tinning	0	0	0.00	2	0	0	0	0	2.1	0	0	0	3
Lon Warneke	0	1	5.91	2	1	1	0	0	10.2	15	7	5	8
TOTAL	0	4	9.26	13	4	1	0	0	34.0	45	35	23	26

GAME 1 AT NY SEPT 28
CHI 200 000 220   6 10 1
NY   000 305 31X 12 8 2
Pitchers: BUSH, Grimes (6), Smith (8) vs RUFFING
Home Runs: Gehrig-NY
Attendance: 41,459

GAME 2 AT NY SEPT 29
CHI 101 000 000   2 9 0
NY   202 010 00X   5 10 1
Pitchers: WARNEKE vs GOMEZ
Attendance: 50,709

GAME 3 AT CHI OCT 1
NY   301 020 001   7 8 1
CHI 102 100 001   5 9 4
Pitchers: PIPGRAS, Pennock (9) vs ROOT, Malone (5), May (7), Tinning (9)
Home Runs: Ruth-NY (2), Gehrig-NY (2), Cuyler-CHI, Hartnett-CHI
Attendance: 49,986

GAME 4 AT CHI OCT 2
NY   102 002 404 13 19 4
CHI 400 001 001   6 9 1
Pitchers: Allen, MOORE (1), Pennock (7) vs Bush, Warneke (1), MAY (4), Tinning (7), Grimes (9)
Home Runs: Demaree-CHI, Lazzeri-NY (2), Combs-NY
Attendance: 49,844

NEW YORK GIANTS (NL) 4, WASHINGTON SENATORS (AL) 1

Although John McGraw had retired from managing the Giants in 1932, he continued to regard them as "his" team. Led now by first baseman Bill Terry, the Giants faced a club also led by an active player, shortstop Joe Cronin in his rookie managerial season.

Giants ace Carl Hubbell dominated the first game, striking out 10 while limiting the Senators to five singles and a pair of unearned runs. Mel Ott set the tone for New York with a two-out two-run homer in the first inning, and singled home a third run in the third to build a lead Washington would not overcome. The next day the Senators scored first, on Goose Goslin's solo homer in the third. But that was the only run scored off Hal Schumacher, and when the Giants drove out Senators starter Alvin Crowder with six runs in the sixth they had their second win well in hand.

The Senators revived when the Series moved to Washington for Game 3. Each of second baseman Buddy Myer's three hits scored or drove in a run, providing a growing cushion for pitcher Earl Whitehill, who recorded the Series' only shutout.

Games 4 and 5 went to New York, but not without a struggle. In the fourth game, manager Terry's home run broke the ice in the fourth inning, but Hubbell muffed a bunt in the seventh which led to the tying run. Hubbell and Senators starter Monty Weaver dueled without further scoring until shortstop Blondy Ryan's single in the top of the 11th put New York up by one. Hubbell let men reach second and third with one out in the last of the 11th, but an intentional walk set up the hoped-for double play to end the game.

New York had built a three-run lead in Game 5 when Fred Schulte evened the score in the last of the sixth with a three-run homer. Relievers Jack Russell and Dolf Luque then dueled scorelessly into the 10th, when Mel Ott (whose homer had begun the Series' scoring in the first inning of Game One) homered once again for what proved the Series' final run. Luque shut down the Senators in their half of the 10th, and "McGraw's Giants" were for the fourth time the world's finest. But before the advent of another spring, McGraw was dead.

NY (N)

PLAYER/POS	AVG	G	AB	R	H	2B	3B	HR	RBI	BB	SO	SB
Hi Bell, p	.000	1	0	0	0	0	0	0	0	0	0	0
Hughie Critz, 2b	.136	5	22	2	3	0	0	0	0	1	0	0
Kiddo Davis, of	.368	5	19	1	7	1	0	0	0	0	3	0
Freddie Fitzsimmons, p	.500	1	2	0	1	0	0	0	0	0	0	0
Carl Hubbell, p	.286	2	7	0	2	0	0	0	0	0	0	0
Travis Jackson, 3b	.222	5	18	3	4	1	0	0	2	1	3	0
Dolf Luque, p	1.000	1	1	0	1	0	0	0	0	0	0	0
Gus Mancuso, c	.118	5	17	2	2	1	0	0	2	3	0	0
Jo-Jo Moore, of	.227	5	22	1	5	1	0	0	1	1	3	0
Lefty O'Doul, ph	1.000	1	1	0	1	0	0	0	2	0	0	0
Mel Ott, of	.389	5	18	3	7	0	0	2	4	4	4	0
Homer Peel, of-1	.500	2	2	0	1	0	0	0	0	0	0	0
Blondy Ryan, ss	.278	5	18	0	5	0	0	0	1	1	5	0
Hal Schumacher, p	.286	2	7	0	2	0	0	0	0	3	3	0
Bill Terry, 1b	.273	5	22	3	6	1	0	1	1	1	0	0
TOTAL	.267		176	16	47	5	0	3	16	11	21	0

PITCHER	W	L	ERA	G	GS	CG	SV	SHO	IP	H	ER	BB	SO
Hi Bell	0	0	0.00	1	0	0	0	0	1.0	0	0	0	0
Freddie Fitzsimmons	0	1	5.14	1	1	0	0	0	7.0	9	4	0	2
Carl Hubbell	2	0	0.00	2	2	2	0	0	20.0	13	0	6	15
Dolf Luque	1	0	0.00	1	0	0	0	0	4.1	2	0	2	5
Hal Schumacher	1	0	2.45	2	2	1	0	0	14.2	13	4	5	3
TOTAL	4	1	1.53	7	5	3	0	0	47.0	37	8	13	25

WAS (A)

PLAYER/POS	AVG	G	AB	R	H	2B	3B	HR	RBI	BB	SO	SB
Ossie Bluege, 3b	.125	5	16	1	2	1	0	0	0	1	6	0
Cliff Bolton, ph	.000	2	2	0	0	0	0	0	0	0	0	0
Joe Cronin, ss	.318	5	22	1	7	0	0	0	2	0	2	0
General Crowder, p	.250	2	4	0	1	0	0	0	0	0	0	0
Goose Goslin, of	.250	5	20	2	5	1	0	1	1	1	3	0
Dave Harris, of-1	.000	3	2	0	0	0	0	0	0	2	0	0
John Kerr, pr	.000	1	0	0	0	0	0	0	0	0	0	0
Joe Kuhel, 1b	.150	5	20	1	3	0	0	0	1	1	4	0
Heinie Manush, of	.111	5	18	2	2	0	0	0	0	2	1	0
Alex McColl, p	.000	1	0	0	0	0	0	0	0	0	0	0
Buddy Myer, 2b	.300	5	20	2	6	1	0	0	2	2	3	0
Sam Rice, ph	1.000	1	1	0	1	0	0	0	0	0	0	0
Jack Russell, p	.000	3	2	0	0	0	0	0	0	1	2	0
Fred Schulte, of	.333	5	21	0	7	1	0	1	4	1	1	0
Luke Sewell, c	.176	5	17	1	3	0	0	0	1	2	0	1
Lefty Stewart, p	.000	1	1	0	0	0	0	0	0	0	1	0
Tommy Thomas, p	.000	2	0	0	0	0	0	0	0	0	0	0
Monte Weaver, p	.000	1	4	0	0	0	0	0	0	0	2	0
Earl Whitehill, p	.000	1	3	0	0	0	0	0	0	0	0	0
TOTAL	.214		173	11	37	4	0	2	11	13	25	1

PITCHER	W	L	ERA	G	GS	CG	SV	SHO	IP	H	ER	BB	SO
General Crowder	0	1	7.36	2	2	0	0	0	11.0	16	9	5	7
Alex McColl	0	0	0.00	1	0	0	0	0	2.0	0	0	0	0
Jack Russell	0	1	0.87	3	0	0	0	0	10.1	8	1	0	7
Lefty Stewart	0	1	9.00	1	1	0	0	0	2.0	6	2	0	0
Tommy Thomas	0	0	0.00	2	0	0	0	0	1.1	1	0	0	2
Monte Weaver	0	1	1.74	1	1	0	0	0	10.1	11	2	4	3
Earl Whitehill	1	0	0.00	1	1	1	0	1	9.0	5	0	2	2
TOTAL	1	4	2.74	11	5	1	0	1	46.0	47	14	11	21

GAME 1 AT NY OCT 3

WAS 000 100 001   2 5 3
NY 202 000 00X   4 10 2
Pitchers: STEWART, Russell (3), Thomas (8) vs HUBBELL
Home Runs: Ott-NY
Attendance: 46,672

GAME 2 AT NY OCT 4

WAS 001 000 000   1 5 0
NY 000 006 00X   6 10 0
Pitchers: CROWDER, Thomas (6), McColl (7) vs SCHUMACHER
Home Runs: Goslin-WAS
Attendance: 35,461

GAME 3 AT WAS OCT 5

NY 000 000 000   0 5 0
WAS 210 000 10X   4 9 1
Pitchers: FITZSIMMONS, Bell (8) vs WHITEHILL
Attendance: 25,727

GAME 4 AT WAS OCT 6

NY 000 100 000 01 2 11 1
WAS 000 000 100 00 1 8 0
Pitchers: HUBBELL vs WEAVER, Russell (11)
Home Runs: Terry-NY
Attendance: 26,762

GAME 5 AT WAS OCT 7

NY 020 001 000 1   4 11 1
WAS 000 003 000 0   3 10 0
Pitchers: Schumacher, LUQUE (6) vs Crowder, RUSSELL (6)
Home Runs: Schulte-WAS, Ott-NY
Attendance: 28,454

ST. LOUIS CARDINALS (NL) 4, DETROIT TIGERS (AL) 3

Pitching brothers Dizzy and Paul Dean won seven games in 10 days to give the Cardinals the pennant on the final day of the season. In the Series they continued their winning ways, chalking up all four Cardinals victories. Dizzy pitched the opener in Detroit. Given a 3–0 lead, thanks to five Detroit errors in the first three innings, he breezed to an 8–3 win.

Detroit's Schoolboy Rowe brought the Tigers back with a pitching masterpiece in Game 2. After giving up single runs in the second and third innings, he allowed only one runner to reach base over the next nine as his Tigers tied the score in the ninth, and won it on two walks and a single in the 12th.

Paul Dean nearly pitched a shutout in Game 3, yielding a harmless run with two out in the ninth after the Cards had built him a 4–0 lead. Brother Diz figured in a curious and painful play in Game 4. Pinch-running in the fourth inning, he was beaned by a would-be double-play throw as he ran to second. The tying run scored from third on the play, but Detroit's pitcher Elden Auker shut out the Cards through the final five innings, and his teammates scored six more runs to bury St. Louis 10–4, evening the Series at two apiece. Diz was rushed to the hospital, but as no damage was found he started Game 5 the next day. He pitched well enough, but Detroit's Tommy Bridges pitched better, giving the Cardinals only one run to the Tigers' three.

Paul Dean evened the Series again with a win against Rowe in a closely contested sixth game. A grounder through Dean's legs allowed the Tigers to tie the game in the sixth inning, but Paul redeemed his error in the seventh when he singled in the tie-breaking run. Dizzy came back after only a day's rest to hurl a six-hit shutout in the finale. He also scored the game's first run and drove in the sixth with a double and single in his team's seven-run third. Three innings later, frustrated Tigers fans, angered by Joe Medwick's rough slide into their third baseman, pelted Medwick with food and bottles, halting the game for 20 minutes until Commissioner Landis ordered St. Louis from the game. The delay only forestalled Detroit's

STL (N)

PLAYER/POS	AVG	G	AB	R	H	2B	3B	HR	RB	BB	SO	SB
Tex Carleton, p	.000	2	1	0	0	0	0	0	0	0	0	0
Ripper Collins, 1b	.367	7	30	4	11	1	0	0	3	1	2	0
Pat Crawford, ph	.000	2	2	0	0	0	0	0	0	0	0	0
Spud Davis, ph	1.000	2	2	0	2	0	0	0	1	0	0	0
Dizzy Dean, p-3	.250	4	12	3	3	2	0	0	1	0	3	0
Paul Dean, p	.167	2	6	0	1	0	0	0	2	0	1	0
Bill DeLancey, c	.172	7	29	3	5	3	0	1	4	2	8	0
Leo Durocher, ss	.259	7	27	4	7	1	1	0	0	0	0	0
Frankie Frisch, 2b	.194	7	31	2	6	1	0	0	4	0	1	0
Chick Fullis, of	.400	3	5	0	2	0	0	0	0	0	0	0
Jesse Haines, p	.000	1	0	0	0	0	0	0	0	0	0	0
Bill Hallahan, p	.000	1	3	0	0	0	0	0	0	0	1	0
Pepper Martin, 3b	.355	7	31	8	11	3	1	0	4	3	3	2
Joe Medwick, of	.379	7	29	4	11	0	1	1	5	1	7	0
Jim Mooney, p	.000	1	0	0	0	0	0	0	0	0	1	0
Ernie Orsatti, of	.318	7	22	3	7	0	1	0	2	3	1	0
Jack Rothrock, of	.233	7	30	3	7	3	1	0	6	1	2	0
Dazzy Vance, p	.000	1	0	0	0	0	0	0	0	0	0	0
Bill Walker, p	.000	2	2	0	0	0	0	0	0	0	2	0
Burgess Whitehead, ss	.000	1	0	0	0	0	0	0	0	0	0	0
TOTAL	.279		262	34	73	14	5	2	32	11	31	2

PITCHER	W	L	ERA	G	GS	CG	SV	SHO	IP	H	ER	BB	SO
Tex Carleton	0	0	7.36	2	1	0	0	0	3.2	5	3	2	2
Dizzy Dean	2	1	1.73	3	3	2	0	1	26.0	20	5	5	17
Paul Dean	2	0	1.00	2	2	2	0	0	18.0	15	2	7	11
Jesse Haines	0	0	0.00	1	0	0	0	0	0.2	1	0	0	2
Bill Hallahan	0	0	2.16	1	1	0	0	0	8.1	6	2	4	6
Jim Mooney	0	0	0.00	1	0	0	0	0	1.0	1	0	0	0
Dazzy Vance	0	0	0.00	1	0	0	0	0	1.1	2	0	1	3
Bill Walker	0	2	7.11	2	0	0	0	0	6.1	6	5	6	2
TOTAL	4	3	2.34	13	7	4	0	1	65.1	56	17	25	43

DET (A)

PLAYER/POS	AVG	G	AB	R	H	2B	3B	HR	RB	BB	SO	SB
Elden Auker, p	.000	2	4	0	0	0	0	0	0	0	2	0
Tommy Bridges, p	.143	3	7	0	1	0	0	0	0	1	4	0
Mickey Cochrane, c	.214	7	28	2	6	1	0	0	1	4	3	0
General Crowder, p	.000	2	1	0	0	0	0	0	0	0	0	0
Frank Doljack, of-1	.000	2	2	0	0	0	0	0	0	0	0	0
Pete Fox, of	.286	7	28	1	8	6	0	0	2	1	4	0
Charlie Gehringer, 2b	.379	7	29	5	11	1	0	1	2	3	0	1
Goose Goslin, of	.241	7	29	2	7	1	0	0	2	3	1	0
Hank Greenberg, 1b	.321	7	28	4	9	2	1	1	7	4	9	1
Ray Hayworth, c	.000	1	0	0	0	0	0	0	0	0	0	0
Chief Hogsett, p	.000	3	3	0	0	0	0	0	0	0	1	0
Firpo Marberry, p	.000	2	0	0	0	0	0	0	0	0	0	0
Marv Owen, 3b	.069	7	29	0	2	0	0	0	1	0	5	1
Billy Rogell, ss	.276	7	29	3	8	1	0	0	4	1	4	1
Schoolboy Rowe, p	.000	3	7	0	0	0	0	0	0	0	5	0
Gee Walker, ph	.333	3	3	0	1	0	0	0	1	0	1	0
Jo-Jo White, of	.130	7	23	6	3	0	0	0	0	8	4	1
TOTAL	.224		250	23	56	12	1	2	20	25	43	5

PITCHER	W	L	ERA	G	GS	CG	SV	SHO	IP	H	ER	BB	SO
Elden Auker	1	1	5.56	2	2	1	0	0	11.1	16	7	5	2
Tommy Bridges	1	1	3.63	3	2	1	0	0	17.1	21	7	1	12
General Crowder	0	1	1.50	2	1	0	0	0	6.0	6	1	1	2
Chief Hogsett	0	0	1.23	3	0	0	0	0	7.1	6	1	3	3
Firpo Marberry	0	0	21.60	2	0	0	0	0	1.2	5	4	1	0
Schoolboy Rowe	1	1	2.95	3	2	2	0	0	21.1	19	7	0	12
TOTAL	3	4	3.74	15	7	4	0	0	65.0	73	27	11	31

defeat, as the Cards took the title game, 11–0.

GAME 1 AT DET OCT 3
STL 021 014 000   8 13 2
DET 001 001 010   3 8 5
Pitchers: J.DEAN vs CROWDER, Marberry (6), Hogsett (6)
Home Runs: Medwick-STL, Greenberg-DET
Attendance: 42,505

GAME 2 AT DET OCT 4
STL 011 000 000 000   2 7 3
DET 000 100 001 001   3 7 0
Pitchers: Hallahan, W.WALKER (9) vs ROWE
Attendance: 43,451

GAME 3 AT STL OCT 5
DET 000 000 001   1 8 2
STL 110 020 00X   4 9 1
Pitchers: BRIDGES, Hogsett (5) vs P.DEAN
Attendance: 34,073

GAME 4 AT STL OCT 6
DET 003 100 150   10 13 1
STL 011 200 000   4 10 5
Pitchers: AUKER vs Carleton, Vance (3), W.WALKER (5), Haines (8), Mooney (9)
Attendance: 37,492

GAME 5 AT STL OCT 7
DET 010 002 000   3 7 0
STL 000 000 100   1 7 1
Pitchers: BRIDGES vs J.DEAN, Carleton (9)
Home Runs: Gehringer-DET, DeLancey-STL
Attendance: 38,536

GAME 6 AT DET OCT 8
STL 100 020 100   4 10 2
DET 001 002 000   3 7 1
Pitchers: P.DEAN vs ROWE
Attendance: 44,551

GAME 7 AT DET OCT 9
STL 007 002 200   11 17 1
DET 000 000 000   0 6 3
Pitchers: J.DEAN vs AUKER, Rowe (3), Hogsett (3), Bridges (4), Marberry (8), Crowder (9)
Attendance: 40,902

DETROIT TIGERS (AL) 4, CHICAGO CUBS (NL) 2

With a 21-game September winning streak, the Cubs vaulted over the Giants and Cardinals to face Detroit in the Series, and for a moment it seemed as if their momentum might carry them past the Tigers as well. Chicago scored two runs off Schoolboy Rowe in the top of the first in the opener, and right fielder Frank Demaree homered to open the ninth as Lon Warneke blanked the Tigers on four hits. But Detroit retaliated quickly in Game 2, driving out starter Charlie Root in the first inning with four runs (including Hank Greenberg's two-run homer) before Root had had a chance to record even one out. Tigers pitcher Rocky Bridges gained an easy 8–3 win, but Greenberg broke a wrist and was finished for the Series.

In Game 3 the Cubs scored three times before Detroit countered with their first run in the sixth. But a walk and four Tiger hits in the eighth put the Bengals ahead, 4–3. Billy Rogell turned a foiled steal into a rundown to allow a fifth Tiger to cross the plate. Two Cubs runs in the last of the ninth tied the score, but Detroit pulled out the victory in the 11th as a pair of singles sandwiched Fred Lindstrom's error at third to give them an unearned run.

Detroit's Alvin "General" Crowder followed up the Tigers' advantage the next day with a neat five-hit 2–1 win. Once again the Cubs bobbled away the game, this time with two sixth-inning errors that enabled Detroit to score the winning run without a hit. Chuck Klein's two-run homer saved Chicago from elimination in Game Five as Lon Warneke and Bill Lee shut out the Tigers through eight before letting in a harmless run in the ninth.

Chicago's Larry French and Tiger Rocky Bridges yielded 12 hits apiece in Game 6. Cubs second baseman Billy Herman singled in a run in the third to tie the score, and homered for two more runs in the fifth to put the Cubs ahead. But the Tigers tied it up an inning later, and took their first world title ever when Goose Goslin singled in Mickey Cochrane with two out in the bottom of the ninth.

DET (A)

PLAYER/POS	AVG	G	AB	R	H	2B	3B	HR	RB	BB	SO	SB
Elden Auker, p	.000	1	2	0	0	0	0	0	0	0	1	0
Tommy Bridges, p	.125	2	8	1	1	0	0	0	1	0	3	0
Flea Clifton, 3b	.000	4	16	1	0	0	0	0	0	2	4	0
Mickey Cochrane, c	.292	6	24	3	7	1	0	0	1	4	1	0
General Crowder, p	.333	1	3	1	1	0	0	0	0	1	0	0
Pete Fox, of	.385	6	26	1	10	3	1	0	4	0	1	0
Charlie Gehringer, 2b	.375	6	24	4	9	3	0	0	4	2	1	1
Goose Goslin, of	.273	6	22	2	6	1	0	0	3	5	0	0
Hank Greenberg, 1b	.167	2	6	1	1	0	0	1	2	1	0	0
Chief Hogsett, p	.000	1	0	0	0	0	0	0	0	0	0	0
Marv Owen, 1b-4,3b-2	.050	6	20	2	1	0	0	0	1	2	3	0
Billy Rogell, ss	.292	6	24	1	7	2	0	0	1	2	5	0
Schoolboy Rowe, p	.250	3	8	0	2	1	0	0	0	0	1	0
Gee Walker, of-1	.250	3	4	1	1	0	0	0	0	1	0	0
Jo-Jo White, of	.263	5	19	3	5	0	0	0	1	5	7	0
TOTAL	.248		206	21	51	11	1	1	18	25	27	1

PITCHER	W	L	ERA	G	GS	CG	SV	SHO	IP	H	ER	BB	SO
Elden Auker	0	0	3.00	1	1	0	0	0	6.0	6	2	2	1
Tommy Bridges	2	0	2.50	2	2	2	0	0	18.0	18	5	4	9
General Crowder	1	0	1.00	1	1	1	0	0	9.0	5	1	3	5
Chief Hogsett	0	0	0.00	1	0	0	0	0	1.0	0	0	1	0
Schoolboy Rowe	1	2	2.57	3	2	2	0	0	21.0	19	6	1	14
TOTAL	4	2	2.29	8	6	5	0	0	55.0	48	14	11	29

CHI (N)

PLAYER/POS	AVG	G	AB	R	H	2B	3B	HR	RB	BB	SO	SB
Tex Carleton, p	.000	1	1	0	0	0	0	0	0	1	1	0
Phil Cavarretta, 1b	.125	6	24	3	3	0	0	0	0	0	5	0
Frank Demaree, of	.250	6	24	2	6	1	0	2	2	1	4	0
Larry French, p	.250	2	4	1	1	0	0	0	0	0	2	0
Augie Galan, of	.160	6	25	2	4	1	0	0	2	2	2	0
Stan Hack, 3b-6, ss-1	.227	6	22	2	5	1	1	0	0	2	2	1
Gabby Hartnett, c	.292	6	24	1	7	0	0	1	2	0	3	0
Roy Henshaw, p	.000	1	1	0	0	0	0	0	0	0	0	0
Billy Herman, 2b	.333	6	24	3	8	2	1	1	6	0	2	0
Billy Jurges, ss	.250	6	16	3	4	0	0	0	1	4	4	0
Chuck Klein, of-3	.333	5	12	2	4	0	0	1	2	0	0	0
Fabian Kowalik, p	.500	1	2	1	1	0	0	0	0	0	0	0
Bill Lee, p	.000	2	1	0	0	0	0	0	1	0	0	0
Fred Lindstrom, of-4,3b-1	.200	4	15	0	3	1	0	0	0	1	1	0
Ken O'Dea, ph	1.000	1	1	0	1	0	0	0	1	0	0	0
Charlie Root, p	.000	2	0	0	0	0	0	0	0	0	0	0
Walter Stephenson, ph	.000	1	1	0	0	0	0	0	0	0	1	0
Lon Warneke, p	.200	3	5	0	1	0	0	0	0	0	0	0
TOTAL	.238		202	18	48	6	2	5	17	11	29	1

PITCHER	W	L	ERA	G	GS	CG	SV	SHO	IP	H	ER	BB	SO
Tex Carleton	0	1	1.29	1	1	0	0	0	7.0	6	1	7	4
Larry French	0	2	3.38	2	1	1	0	0	10.2	15	4	2	8
Roy Henshaw	0	0	7.36	1	0	0	0	0	3.2	2	3	5	2
Fabian Kowalik	0	0	2.08	1	0	0	0	0	4.1	3	1	1	1
Bill Lee	0	0	4.35	2	1	0	1	0	10.1	11	5	5	5
Charlie Root	0	1	18.00	2	1	0	0	0	2.0	5	4	1	2
Lon Warneke	2	0	0.54	3	2	1	0	1	16.2	9	1	4	5
TOTAL	2	4	3.13	12	6	2	1	1	54.2	51	19	25	27

GAME 1 AT DET OCT 2

CHI	2 0 0	0 0 0	0 0 1		3	7	0
DET	0 0 0	0 0 0	0 0 0		0	4	3

Pitchers: WARNEKE vs ROWE
Home Runs: Demaree-CHI
Attendance: 47,391

GAME 2 AT DET OCT 3

CHI	0 0 0	0 1 0	2 0 0		3	6	1
DET	4 0 0	3 0 0	1 0 X		8	9	2

Pitchers: ROOT, Henshaw (1), Kowalik (4) vs BRIDGES
Home Runs: Greenberg-DET
Attendance: 46,742

GAME 3 AT CHI OCT 4

DET	0 0 0	0 0 1	0 4 0 0 1		6	12	2
CHI	0 2 0	0 1 0	0 0 2 0 0		5	10	3

Pitchers: Auker, Hogsett (7), ROWE (8) vs Lee, FRENCH (10)
Home Runs: Demaree-CHI
Attendance: 45,532

GAME 4 AT CHI OCT 5

DET	0 0 1	0 0 1	0 0 0		2	7	0
CHI	0 0 0	0 0 0	0 0 0		1	5	2

Pitchers: CROWDER vs CARLETON, Root (8)
Home Runs: Hartnett-CHI
Attendance: 49,350

GAME 5 AT CHI OCT 6

DET	0 0 0	0 0 0	0 0 1		1	7	1
CHI	0 0 2	0 0 0	1 0 X		3	8	0

Pitchers: ROWE vs WARNEKE, Lee (7)
Home Runs: Klein-CHI
Attendance: 49,237

GAME 6 AT DET OCT 7

CHI	0 0 1	0 2 0	0 0 0		3	12	0
DET	1 0 0	1 0 1	0 0 1		4	12	1

Pitchers: FRENCH vs BRIDGES
Home Runs: Herman-CHI
Attendance: 48,420

NEW YORK YANKEES (AL) 4, NEW YORK GIANTS (NL) 2

The Giants managed to win two games, but this first Series between the cross-river rivals in 13 years was really no contest. Babe Ruth was gone, but Lou Gehrig was still there, and Joe DiMaggio had arrived. The Yankees outhit the Giants by 56 percentage points and outscored them by 20 runs.

Giants ace Carl Hubbell, who had won his final 16 decisions of the regular season, continued his streak in the Series opener. The Yankees scored first on George Selkirk's third-inning homer, but Giants shortstop Dick Bartell homered to even things in the fifth. Hubbell held the Yankees to that one run, but the Giants roughed up Red Ruffing for five more runs, to give the Polo Grounders a brief Series advantage.

Game 2 was a blowout, as the Yankees hammered five Giants pitchers for 18 runs—four of them on Tony Lazzeri's grand slam in the third—to give Lefty Gomez an easy win. By contrast, Game 3 was a pitchers' duel. Although the Giants touched Bump Hadley and Pat Malone for 11 hits, only Jimmy Ripple's fifth-inning homer produced a run. Freddie Fitzsimmons was much more stingy with hits, yielding only four. But one was Gehrig's home run in the second inning, and another was Frank Crosetti's game-winning RBI single in the eighth.

Gehrig homered again in the third inning of Game 4 to give the Yankees an insurmountable lead—and Hubbell his first loss in months. Down three games to one, the Giants struggled back in Game 5. They took a first-inning 3–0 lead, but the Yankees clawed their way back, and by the end of six the score was 4–4. There it stayed until the 10th, when a double, sacrifice, and fly to center put the Giants ahead by a run. Hal Schumacher, who had pitched the whole game, held the Yankees scoreless one more time for the win.

Fitzsimmons, who had pitched so well in his third-game loss, didn't last four innings in Game 6. Though the Giants scored first, Jake Powell (who led all Series hitters at .455) tied the game with a two-run homer in the top of the second for the Yankees. Two more runs in the fourth drove out Fitzsimmons, but the game stayed close until the top of the ninth,

NY (A)

PLAYER/POS	AVG	G	AB	R	H	2B	3B	HR	RB	BB	SO	SB
Frankie Crosetti, ss	.269	6	26	5	7	2	0	0	3	3	5	0
Bill Dickey, c	.120	6	25	5	3	0	0	1	5	3	4	0
Joe DiMaggio, of	.346	6	26	3	9	3	0	0	3	1	3	0
Lou Gehrig, 1b	.292	6	24	5	7	1	0	2	7	3	2	0
Lefty Gomez, p	.250	2	8	1	2	0	0	0	3	0	3	0
Bump Hadley, p	.000	1	2	0	0	0	0	0	0	0	1	0
Roy Johnson, ph	.000	2	1	0	0	0	0	0	0	0	1	0
Tony Lazzeri, 2b	.250	6	20	4	5	0	0	1	7	4	4	0
Pat Malone, p	1.000	2	1	0	1	0	0	0	0	0	0	0
Johnny Murphy, p	.500	1	2	1	1	0	0	0	1	0	1	0
Monte Pearson, p	.500	1	4	0	2	1	0	0	0	0	0	0
Jake Powell, of	.455	6	22	8	10	1	0	1	5	4	4	1
Red Rolfe, 3b	.400	6	25	5	10	0	0	0	4	3	1	0
Red Ruffing, p-2	.000	3	5	0	0	0	0	0	0	1	2	0
Bob Seeds, pr	.000	1	0	0	0	0	0	0	0	0	0	0
George Selkirk, of	.333	6	24	6	8	0	1	2	3	4	4	0
TOTAL	.302		215	43	65	8	1	7	41	26	35	1

PITCHER	W	L	ERA	G	GS	CG	SV	SHO	IP	H	ER	BB	SO
Lefty Gomez	2	0	4.70	2	2	1	0	0	15.1	14	8	11	9
Bump Hadley	1	0	1.13	1	1	0	0	0	8.0	10	1	1	2
Pat Malone	0	1	1.80	2	0	0	1	0	5.0	2	1	1	2
Johnny Murphy	0	0	3.38	1	0	0	1	0	2.2	1	1	1	1
Monte Pearson	1	0	2.00	1	1	1	0	0	9.0	7	2	2	7
Red Ruffing	0	1	5.14	2	2	1	0	0	14.0	16	8	5	12
TOTAL	4	2	3.50	9	6	3	2	0	54.0	50	21	21	33

NY (N)

PLAYER/POS	AVG	G	AB	R	H	2B	3B	HR	RB	BB	SO	SB
Dick Bartell, ss	.381	6	21	5	8	3	0	1	3	4	4	0
Slick Castleman, p	.500	1	2	0	1	0	0	0	0	0	0	0
Dick Coffman, p	.000	2	0	0	0	0	0	0	0	0	0	0
Harry Danning, c-1	.000	2	2	0	0	0	0	0	0	0	1	0
Kiddo Davis, ph	.500	4	2	2	1	0	0	0	0	0	0	0
Freddie Fitzsimmons, p	.500	2	4	0	2	0	0	0	0	0	1	0
Frank Gabler, p	.000	2	0	0	0	0	0	0	0	1	0	0
Harry Gumbert, p	.000	2	0	0	0	0	0	0	0	0	0	0
Carl Hubbell, p	.333	2	6	0	2	0	0	0	1	0	0	0
Travis Jackson, 3b	.190	6	21	1	4	0	0	0	1	1	3	0
Mark Koenig, 2b-1	.333	3	3	0	1	0	0	0	0	0	1	0
Hank Leiber, of	.000	2	6	0	0	0	0	0	0	2	2	0
Sam Leslie, ph	.667	4	3	0	2	0	0	0	0	0	0	0
Gus Mancuso, c	.263	6	19	3	5	2	0	0	1	3	3	0
Eddie Mayo, 3b	.000	1	1	0	0	0	0	0	0	0	0	0
Jo-Jo Moore, of	.214	6	28	4	6	2	0	1	1	1	4	0
Mel Ott, of	.304	6	23	4	7	2	0	1	3	3	1	0
Jimmy Ripple, of	.333	5	12	2	4	0	0	1	3	3	3	0
Hal Schumacher, p	.000	2	4	0	0	0	0	0	0	1	3	0
Al Smith, p	.000	1	0	0	0	0	0	0	0	0	0	0
Bill Terry, 1b	.240	6	25	1	6	0	0	0	5	1	4	0
Burgess Whitehead, 2b	.048	6	21	1	1	0	0	0	0	2	1	0
TOTAL	.246		20 323	50	9	0	4	20	21	33	0

PITCHER	W	L	ERA	G	GS	CG	SV	SHO	IP	H	ER	BB	SO
Slick Castleman	0	0	2.08	1	0	0	0	0	4.1	3	1	2	5
Dick Coffman	0	0	32.40	2	0	0	0	0	1.2	5	6	1	1
Freddie Fitzsimmons	0	2	5.40	2	2	1	0	0	11.2	13	7	2	6
Frank Gabler	0	0	7.20	2	0	0	0	0	5.0	7	4	4	0
Harry Gumbert	0	0	36.00	2	0	0	0	0	2.0	7	8	4	2
Carl Hubbell	1	1	2.25	2	2	1	0	0	16.0	15	4	2	10
Hal Schumacher	1	1	5.25	2	2	1	0	0	12.0	13	7	10	11
Al Smith	0	0	81.00	1	0	0	0	0	0.1	2	3	1	0
TOTAL	2	4	6.79	14	6	3	0	0	53.0	65	40	26	35

when five Yankees singles and three walks produced seven runs and a Series-ending 13–5 rout.

GAME 1 AT NY-N SEPT 30
NY-A   0 0 1   0 0 0   0 0 0   1 7 2
NY-N   0 0 0   0 1 1   0 4 X   6 9 1
Pitchers: RUFFING vs HUBBELL
Home Runs: Bartell-NY(N), Selkirk-NY(A)
Attendance: 39,419

GAME 2 AT NY-N OCT 2
NY-A   2 0 7   0 0 1   2 0 6   18 17 0
NY-N   0 1 0   3 0 0   0 0 0   4 6 1
Pitchers: GOMEZ vs SCHUMACHER, Smith (3), Coffman (3), Gabler (5), Gumbert (9)
Home Runs: Dickey-NY (A), Lazzeri-NY (A)
Attendance: 43,543

GAME 3 AT NY-A OCT 3
NY-N   0 0 0   0 1 0   0 0 0   1 11 0
NY-A   0 1 0   0 0 0   0 1 X   2 4 0
Pitchers: FITZSIMMONS vs HADLEY, Malone (9)
Home Runs: Gehrig-NY (A), Ripple-NY (N)
Attendance: 64,842

GAME 4 AT NY-A OCT 4
NY-N   0 0 0   1 0 0   0 1 0   2 7 1
NY-A   0 1 3   0 0 0   0 1 X   5 10 1
Pitchers: HUBBELL, Gabler (8) vs PEARSON
Home Runs: Gehrig-NY (A)
Attendance: 66,669

GAME 5 AT NY-A OCT 5
NY-N   3 0 0   0 0 1 0 0 0 1   5 8 3
NY-A   0 1 1   0 0 2 0 0 0 0   4 10 1
Pitchers: SCHUMACHER vs Ruffing, MALONE (7)
Home Runs: Selkirk-NY (A)
Attendance: 50,024

GAME 6 AT NY-N OCT 6
NY-A   0 2 1   2 0 0   0 1 7   13 17 2
NY-N   2 0 0   0 1 0   1 1 0   5 9 1
Pitchers: GOMEZ, Murphy (7) vs FITZSIMMONS, Castleman (4), Coffman (9), Gumbert (9)
Home Runs: Moore-NY(N), Ott-NY(N), Powell-NY(A)
Attendance: 38,427

NEW YORK YANKEES (AL) 4, NEW YORK GIANTS (NL) 1

For the second year in a row, the Yankees overwhelmed the Giants, this time in just five games. Giants ace Carl Hubbell, who took the opener in 1936, was unable to repeat this time. For five innings he held the Yankees to one hit. But in the sixth everything fell apart. Before Hubbell was taken out, two walks, five singles, and an error had led in five runs. And the two runners Hubbell left on base scored later on a second Giants error and two walks by reliever Dick Coffman. The Yankees' Lefty Gomez also yielded six hits, but wider spacing and better field support held the Giants to one run in the fifth. Tony Lazzeri's homer in the eighth made the final score 8–1.

The Yankees spread their runs a bit more evenly in Game 2. For the second time the Giants gained a 1–0 lead. Rookie phenom Cliff Melton held the Yankees scoreless through four, but four straight hits for two runs at the start of the fifth drove him out. Reliever Ad Gumbert stopped the Yankees in the rest of the inning but gave up four more hits—and four more runs—in the sixth before Coffman stepped in to stop the assault. But Coffman gave up two final Yankees runs in the seventh, to complete a second straight 8–1 win, as Red Ruffing held the Giants scoreless through the final eight innings.

The Yankees had scored five times off Hal Schumacher in Game 3 before the Giants got their one run in the seventh. But Yankees starter Monte Pearson made the game tighter as he yielded a single and two walks to load the bases in the ninth before Johnny Murphy came on to record the final out.

The Giants' bats finally came alive in the second inning of Game 4. Seven singles, plus a walk and a missed play at the plate gave the club a 6–1 lead, which starter Hubbell protected for the only Giants win of the Series.

Solo homers by Myril Hoag in the second and Joe DiMaggio in the third gave the Yankees a 2–0 lead early in Game 5, but Giants slugger Mel Ott tied it up with a two-run shot off Lefty Gomez in the last of the third. But Gomez shut the Giants down the rest of the way, and singled in Lazzeri in the fifth with what proved the

game winner (scoring himself on Lou Gehrig's double for the final run of the Series).

NY (A)

PLAYER/POS	AVG	G	AB	R	H	2B	3B	HR	RB	BB	SO	SB
Ivy Andrews, p	.000	1	2	0	0	0	0	0	0	0	1	0
Frankie Crosetti, ss	.048	5	21	2	1	0	0	0	0	3	2	0
Bill Dickey, c	.211	5	19	3	4	0	1	0	3	2	2	0
Joe DiMaggio, of	.273	5	22	2	6	0	0	1	4	0	3	0
Lou Gehrig, 1b	.294	5	17	4	5	1	1	1	3	5	4	0
Lefty Gomez, p	.167	2	6	2	1	0	0	0	1	2	1	0
Bump Hadley, p	.000	1	0	0	0	0	0	0	0	0	0	0
Myril Hoag, of	.300	5	20	4	6	1	0	1	2	0	1	0
Tony Lazzeri, 2b	.400	5	15	3	6	0	1	1	2	3	3	0
Johnny Murphy, p	.000	1	0	0	0	0	0	0	0	0	0	0
Monte Pearson, p	.000	1	3	0	0	0	0	0	0	1	1	0
Jake Powell, ph	.000	1	1	0	0	0	0	0	0	0	1	0
Red Rolfe, 3b	.300	5	20	3	6	2	1	0	1	3	2	0
Red Ruffing, p	.500	1	4	0	2	1	0	0	3	0	0	0
George Selkirk, of	.263	5	19	5	5	1	0	0	6	2	0	0
Kemp Wicker, p	.000	1	0	0	0	0	0	0	0	0	0	0
TOTAL	.249		169	28	42	6	4	4	25	21	21	0

PITCHER	W	L	ERA	G	GS	CG	SV	SHO	IP	H	ER	BB	SO
Ivy Andrews	0	0	3.18	1	0	0	0	0	5.2	6	2	4	1
Lefty Gomez	2	0	1.50	2	2	2	0	0	18.0	16	3	2	8
Bump Hadley	0	1	33.75	1	1	0	0	0	1.1	6	5	0	0
Johnny Murphy	0	0	0.00	1	0	0	1	0	0.1	0	0	0	0
Monte Pearson	1	0	1.04	1	1	0	0	0	8.2	5	1	2	4
Red Ruffing	1	0	1.00	1	1	1	0	0	9.0	7	1	3	8
Kemp Wicker	0	0	0.00	1	0	0	0	0	1.0	0	0	0	0
TOTAL	4	1	2.45	8	5	3	1	0	44.0	40	12	11	21

NY (N)

PLAYER/POS	AVG	G	AB	R	H	2B	3B	HR	RB	BB	SO	SB
Dick Bartell, ss	.238	5	21	3	5	1	0	0	1	0	3	0
Wally Berger, ph	.000	3	3	0	0	0	0	0	0	0	1	0
Don Brennan, p	.000	2	0	0	0	0	0	0	0	0	0	0
Lou Chiozza, of	.286	2	7	0	2	0	0	0	0	1	1	0
Dick Coffman, p	.000	2	1	0	0	0	0	0	0	0	1	0
Harry Danning, c	.250	3	12	0	3	1	0	0	2	0	2	0
Harry Gumbert, p	.000	2	0	0	0	0	0	0	0	0	0	0
Carl Hubbell, p	.000	2	6	1	0	0	0	0	1	0	0	0
Hank Leiber, of	.364	3	11	2	4	0	0	0	2	1	1	0
Sam Leslie, ph	.000	2	1	0	0	0	0	0	0	1	0	0
Gus Mancuso, c-2	.000	3	8	0	0	0	0	0	1	0	1	0
Johnny McCarthy, 1b	.211	5	19	1	4	1	0	0	1	1	2	0
Cliff Melton, p	.000	3	2	0	0	0	0	0	0	1	1	0
Jo-Jo Moore, of	.391	5	23	1	9	1	0	0	1	0	1	0
Mel Ott, 3b	.200	5	20	1	4	0	0	1	3	1	4	0
Jimmy Ripple, of	.294	5	17	2	5	0	0	0	3	3	1	0
Blondy Ryan, ph	.000	1	1	0	0	0	0	0	0	0	1	0
Hal Schumacher, p	.000	1	1	0	0	0	0	0	0	0	1	0
Al Smith, p	.000	2	0	0	0	0	0	0	0	0	0	0
Burgess Whitehead, 2b	.250	5	16	1	4	2	0	0	0	2	0	1
TOTAL	.237		169	12	40	6	0	1	12	11	21	1

PITCHER	W	L	ERA	G	GS	CG	SV	SHO	IP	H	ER	BB	SO
Don Brennan	0	0	0.00	2	0	0	0	0	3.0	1	0	1	1
Dick Coffman	0	0	4.15	2	0	0	0	0	4.1	2	2	5	1
Harry Gumbert	0	0	27.00	2	0	0	0	0	1.1	4	4	1	1
Carl Hubbell	1	1	3.77	2	2	1	0	0	14.1	12	6	4	7
Cliff Melton	0	2	4.91	3	2	0	0	0	11.0	12	6	6	7
Hal Schumacher	0	1	6.00	1	1	0	0	0	6.0	9	4	4	3
Al Smith	0	0	3.00	2	0	0	0	0	3.0	2	1	0	1
TOTAL	1	4	4.81	14	5	1	0	0	43.0	42	23	21	21

GAME 1 AT NY-A OCT 6

```
NY-N  000 010 000  1 6 2
NY-A  000 007 01X  8 7 0
```
Pitchers: HUBBELL, Gumbert (6), Coffman (6), Smith (8) vs GOMEZ
Home Runs: Lazzeri-NY (A)
Attendance: 60,573

GAME 2 AT NY-A OCT 7

```
NY-N  100 000 000  1 7 0
NY-A  000 024 20X  8 12 0
```
Pitchers: MELTON, Gumbert (5), Coffman (6) vs RUFFING
Attendance: 57,675

GAME 3 AT NY-N OCT 8

```
NY-A  012 110 000  5 9 0
NY-N  000 000 100  1 5 4
```
Pitchers: PEARSON, Murphy (9) vs SCHUMACHER, Melton (7), Brennan (9)
Attendance: 37,385

GAME 4 AT NY-N OCT 9

```
NY-A  101 000 001  3 6 0
NY-N  060 000 10X  7 12 3
```
Pitchers: HADLEY, Andrews (2), Wicker (8) vs HUBBELL
Home Runs: Gehrig-NY (A)
Attendance: 44,293

GAME 5 AT NY-N OCT 10

```
NY-A  011 020 000  4 8 0
NY-N  002 000 000  2 10 0
```
Pitchers: GOMEZ vs MELTON, Smith (6), Brennan (8)
Home Runs: DiMaggio-NY (A), Hoag-NY(A), Ott-NY(N)
Attendance: 38,216

NEW YORK YANKEES (AL) 4, CHICAGO CUBS (NL) 0

As they had six years earlier, the Cubs faced the Yankees in the World Series, and as they had six years earlier, New York swept the Series in four games. Although Cubs batters made nearly as many hits as the Yankees, they did much less damage, driving in 13 fewer runs. In Game 1, Yankees ace Red Ruffing scattered nine hits, holding Chicago to a single run. The Cubs' Bill Lee was nearly as effective in scattering hits, but a base on balls in the second (the game's only walk) followed by a pair of singles sandwiched around an error accounted for two runs—all the Yankees would need for the win (though they scored once more in the sixth).

In Game 2 the Cubs outhit the Yankees 11 to 7, but scored only half as many runs as the New Yorkers. Chicago's Dizzy Dean, pitching on craft and guile with his fastball gone, managed to keep the game close until the final innings. With a 3–2 lead going into the eighth, though, he gave up a two-run homer to Frank Crosetti, and the same to Joe DiMaggio in the ninth before being relieved. Yankees fireman Johnny Murphy, meanwhile, held Chicago scoreless over the final two innings to preserve Lefty Gomez's win.

Utility outfielder Joe Marty drove in both Chicago runs in Game 3 with a grounder to third in the fifth and a homer in the eighth. (His .500 batting average was tops for both teams, and he drove in five of the Cubs' nine Series runs.) But again the Cubs fell short, as rookie second baseman Joe Gordon homered to tie the score in the bottom of the fifth with the first of what would be five Yankees runs by the time Bill Dickey's homer in the eighth ended the scoring for the day.

Cubs second baseman Billy Herman's wild throw with two out in the second inning of Game 4 led to three unearned runs, and a lead the Yankees would not relinquish. Though their lead was cut to one run (4–3) when Chicago scored twice in the top of the eighth, the Yankees took advantage of two wild pitches and two walks to turn their four hits into four runs that crushed Chicago hopes and gave the New Yorkers a record third consecutive world championship.

NY (A)

PLAYER/POS	AVG	G	AB	R	H	2B	3B	HR	RB	BB	SO	SB
Frankie Crosetti, ss	.250	4	16	1	4	2	1	1	6	2	4	0
Bill Dickey, c	.400	4	15	2	6	0	0	1	2	1	0	1
Joe DiMaggio, of	.267	4	15	4	4	0	0	1	2	1	1	0
Lou Gehrig, 1b	.286	4	14	4	4	0	0	0	0	2	3	0
Lefty Gomez, p	.000	1	2	0	0	0	0	0	0	0	0	0
Joe Gordon, 2b	.400	4	15	3	6	2	0	1	6	1	3	0
Tommy Henrich, of	.250	4	16	3	4	1	0	1	1	0	1	0
Myril Hoag, of-1	.400	2	5	3	2	1	0	0	1	0	0	0
Johnny Murphy, p	.000	1	0	0	0	0	0	0	0	0	0	0
Monte Pearson, p	.333	1	3	1	1	0	0	0	0	0	1	0
Jake Powell, of	.000	1	0	0	0	0	0	0	0	0	0	0
Red Rolfe, 3b	.167	4	18	0	3	0	0	0	1	0	3	1
Red Ruffing, p	.167	2	6	1	1	0	0	0	1	1	0	0
George Selkirk, of	.200	3	10	0	2	0	0	0	1	2	1	0
TOTAL	.274		135	22	37	6	1	5	21	11	16	3

PITCHER	W	L	ERA	G	GS	CG	SV	SHO	IP	H	ER	BB	SO
Lefty Gomez	1	0	3.86	1	1	0	0	0	7.0	9	3	1	5
Johnny Murphy	0	0	0.00	1	0	0	1	0	2.0	2	0	1	1
Monte Pearson	1	0	1.00	1	1	1	0	0	9.0	5	1	2	9
Red Ruffing	2	0	1.50	2	2	2	0	0	18.0	17	3	2	11
TOTAL	4	0	1.75	5	4	3	1	0	36.0	33	7	6	26

CHI (N)

PLAYER/POS	AVG	G	AB	R	H	2B	3B	HR	RB	BB	SO	SB
Clay Bryant, p	.000	1	2	0	0	0	0	0	0	0	1	0
Tex Carleton, p	.000	1	0	0	0	0	0	0	0	0	0	0
Phil Cavarretta, of-3	.462	4	13	1	6	1	0	0	0	0	1	0
Ripper Collins, 1b	.133	4	15	1	2	0	0	0	0	0	3	0
Dizzy Dean, p	.667	2	3	0	2	0	0	0	0	0	0	0
Frank Demaree, of	.100	3	10	1	1	0	0	0	0	1	2	0
Larry French, p	.000	3	0	0	0	0	0	0	0	0	0	0
Augie Galan, ph	.000	2	2	0	0	0	0	0	0	0	1	0
Stan Hack, 3b	.471	4	17	3	8	1	0	0	1	1	2	0
Gabby Hartnett, c	.091	3	11	0	1	0	1	0	0	0	2	0
Billy Herman, 2b	.188	4	16	1	3	0	0	0	0	1	4	0
Billy Jurges, ss	.231	4	13	0	3	1	0	0	0	1	3	0
Tony Lazzeri, ph	.000	2	2	0	0	0	0	0	0	0	1	0
Bill Lee, p	.000	2	3	0	0	0	0	0	0	0	1	0
Joe Marty, of	.500	3	12	1	6	1	0	1	5	0	2	0
Ken O'Dea, c-1	.200	3	5	1	1	0	0	1	2	1	0	0
Vance Page, p	.000	1	0	0	0	0	0	0	0	0	0	0
Carl Reynolds, of-3	.000	4	12	0	0	0	0	0	0	1	3	0
Charlie Root, p	.000	1	0	0	0	0	0	0	0	0	0	0
Jack Russell, p	.000	2	0	0	0	0	0	0	0	0	0	0
TOTAL	.243		136	9	33	4	1	2	8	6	26	0

PITCHER	W	L	ERA	G	GS	CG	SV	SHO	IP	H	ER	BB	SO
Clay Bryant	0	1	6.75	1	1	0	0	0	5.1	6	4	5	3
Tex Carleton	0	0	∞	1	0	0	0	0	0.0	1	2	2	0
Dizzy Dean	0	1	6.48	2	1	0	0	0	8.1	8	6	1	2
Larry French	0	0	2.70	3	0	0	0	0	3.1	1	1	1	2
Bill Lee	0	2	2.45	2	2	0	0	0	11.0	15	3	1	8
Vance Page	0	0	13.50	1	0	0	0	0	1.1	2	2	0	0
Charlie Root	0	0	3.00	1	0	0	0	0	3.0	3	1	0	1
Jack Russell	0	0	0.00	2	0	0	0	0	1.2	1	0	1	0
TOTAL	0	4	5.03	13	4	0	0	0	34.0	37	19	11	16

GAME 1 AT CHI OCT 5

NY   020 000 100   3 12 1
CHI 001 000 000   1 9 1
Pitchers: RUFFING vs LEE, Russell (9)
Attendance: 43,642

GAME 2 AT CHI OCT 6

NY   020 000 022   6 7 2
CHI 102 000 000   3 11 0
Pitchers: GOMEZ, Murphy (8) vs
J.DEAN, French (9)
Home Runs: Crosetti-NY,
DiMaggio-NY
Attendance: 42,108

GAME 3 AT NY OCT 8

CHI 000 010 010   2 5 1
NY   000 022 01X   5 7 2
Pitchers: BRYANT, Russell (6),
French (7) vs PEARSON
Home Runs: Dickey-NY, Gordon-NY,
Marty-CHI
Attendance: 55,236

GAME 4 AT NY OCT 9

CHI 000 100 020   3 8 1
NY   030 001 04X   8 11 1
Pitchers: LEE, Root (4), Page (7),
French (8), Carleton (8), J.Dean (8) vs
RUFFING
Home Runs: Henrich-NY, O'Dea-CHI
Attendance: 59,847

NEW YORK YANKEES (AL) 4, CINCINNATI REDS (NL) 0

The Yankees won their fourth consecutive World Series with their second sweep in a row. This time the victim was Cincinnati, in the Series for the first time since their tainted triumph over the Black Sox two decades earlier. New York had lost the power of Lou Gehrig (whose illness forced his retirement early in the season), but in the Series rookie outfielder Charlie Keller took up the slack. He led both clubs in batting, slugging, home runs, RBIs, hits, and runs, and hit one of the Series' two triples. His eight runs scored equal-led those of the whole Cincinnati team.

The Yankees' Red Ruffing and Cincinnati's Paul Derringer hurled matching four-hitters through eight innings of Game 1. With the score tied 1–1, Ruffing set the Reds down in order in the ninth. But in the bottom of the ninth Keller tripled off Derringer with one away, and scored the deciding run on catcher Bill Dickey's single.

Babe Dahlgren, Gehrig's replacement at first base, doubled in the third and later scored the Yankees' first run in Game 2, and homered in the next inning for New York's fourth and final run of the game. Reds starter Bucky Walters stopped the Yankees after that, but they had more than enough runs for the win, as Monte Pearson held the Reds hitless through seven and wound up with a two-hit shutout.

Keller provided the margin of victory with a pair of two-run homers in the first and fifth innings of Game 3. Joe DiMaggio's two-run homer in the third and Bill Dickey's solo shot that followed Keller's homer in the fifth accounted for the rest of New York's runs in their 7–3 win.

No one scored through six innings of Game 4. Keller and Dickey then homered in the top of the seventh, but Red Rolfe's error at third in the last of the inning opened the way for the Reds to go ahead with three unearned runs. They earned a fourth run an inning later, but the Yankees tied it up with two in the ninth (one unearned) and took the lead in the 10th with three more runs (two unearned) on a walk, a single, and three more Reds errors. Reliever Johnny Murphy held off a Cincinnati threat in the last of the 10th and the Series was over.

NY (A)

PLAYER/POS	AVG	G	AB	R	H	2B	3B	HR	RB	BB	SO	SB
Frankie Crosetti, ss	.063	4	16	2	1	0	0	0	1	2	2	0
Babe Dahlgren, 1b	.214	4	14	2	3	2	0	1	2	0	4	0
Bill Dickey, c	.267	4	15	2	4	0	0	2	5	1	2	0
Joe DiMaggio, of	.313	4	16	3	5	0	0	1	3	1	1	0
Lefty Gomez, p	.000	1	1	0	0	0	0	0	0	0	1	0
Joe Gordon, 2b	.143	4	14	1	2	0	0	0	1	0	2	0
Bump Hadley, p	.000	1	3	0	0	0	0	0	0	0	0	0
Oral Hildebrand, p	.000	1	1	0	0	0	0	0	0	0	1	0
Charlie Keller, of	.438	4	16	8	7	1	1	3	6	1	2	0
Johnny Murphy, p	.000	1	2	0	0	0	0	0	0	0	1	0
Monte Pearson, p	.000	1	2	0	0	0	0	0	0	0	1	0
Red Rolfe, 3b	.125	4	16	2	2	0	0	0	0	0	0	0
Red Ruffing, p	.333	1	3	0	1	0	0	0	0	0	1	0
George Selkirk, of	.167	4	12	0	2	1	0	0	0	3	2	0
Steve Sundra, p	.000	1	0	0	0	0	0	0	0	1	0	0
TOTAL	.206		13	120	27	4	1	7	18	9	20	0

PITCHER	W	L	ERA	G	GS	CG	SV	SHO	IP	H	ER	BB	SO
Lefty Gomez	0	0	9.00	1	1	0	0	0	1.0	3	1	0	1
Bump Hadley	1	0	2.25	1	0	0	0	0	8.0	7	2	3	2
Oral Hildebrand	0	0	0.00	1	1	0	0	0	4.0	2	0	0	3
Johnny Murphy	1	0	2.70	1	0	0	0	0	3.1	5	1	0	2
Monte Pearson	1	0	0.00	1	1	1	0	1	9.0	2	0	1	8
Red Ruffing	1	0	1.00	1	1	1	0	0	9.0	4	1	1	4
Steve Sundra	0	0	0.00	1	0	0	0	0	2.2	4	0	1	2
TOTAL	4	0	1.22	7	4	2	0	1	37.0	27	5	6	22

CIN (N)

PLAYER/POS	AVG	G	AB	R	H	2B	3B	HR	RB	BB	SO	SB
Wally Berger, of	.000	4	15	0	0	0	0	0	0	1	0	4	0
Nino Bongiovanni, ph	.000	1	1	0	0	0	0	0	0	0	0	0
Frenchy Bordagaray, pr	.000	2	0	0	0	0	0	0	0	0	0	0
Harry Craft, of	.091	4	11	0	1	0	0	0	0	0	6	0
Paul Derringer, p	.200	2	5	0	1	0	0	0	0	0	0	0
Lonny Frey, 2b	.000	4	17	0	0	0	0	0	0	0	1	4	0
Lee Gamble, ph	.000	1	1	0	0	0	0	0	0	0	1	0
Ival Goodman, of	.333	4	15	3	5	1	0	0	1	1	2	1
Lee Grissom, p	.000	1	0	0	0	0	0	0	0	0	0	0
Willard Hershberger, c-2	.500	3	2	0	1	0	0	0	1	0	0	0
Ernie Lombardi, c	.214	4	14	0	3	0	0	0	2	0	1	0
Frank McCormick, 1b	.400	4	15	1	6	1	0	0	1	0	1	0
Whitey Moore, p	.000	1	1	0	0	0	0	0	0	0	0	0
Billy Myers, ss	.333	4	12	2	4	0	1	0	0	2	3	0
Al Simmons, of	.250	1	4	1	1	1	0	0	0	0	0	0
Junior Thompson, p	1.000	1	1	0	1	0	0	0	0	0	0	0
Bucky Walters, p	.000	2	3	0	0	0	0	0	0	0	0	0
Billy Werber, 3b	.250	4	16	1	4	0	0	0	2	2	0	0
TOTAL	.203		133	8	27	3	1	0	8	6	22	1

PITCHER	W	L	ERA	G	GS	CG	SV	SHO	IP	H	ER	BB	SO
Paul Derringer	0	1	2.35	2	2	1	0	0	15.1	9	4	3	9
Lee Grissom	0	0	0.00	1	0	0	0	0	1.1	0	0	1	0
Whitey Moore	0	0	0.00	1	0	0	0	0	3.0	0	0	0	2
Junior Thompson	0	1	13.50	1	1	0	0	0	4.2	5	7	4	3
Bucky Walters	0	2	4.91	2	1	1	0	0	11.0	13	6	1	6
TOTAL	0	4	4.33	7	4	2	0	0	35.1	27	17	9	20

GAME 1 AT NY OCT 4

```
CIN  000 100 000   1 4 0
NY   000 010 001   2 6 0
```
Pitchers: DERRINGER vs RUFFING
Attendance: 58,541

GAME 2 AT NY OCT 5

```
CIN  000 000 000   0 2 0
NY   003 100 00X   4 9 0
```
Pitchers: WALTERS vs PEARSON
Home Runs: Dahlgren-NY
Attendance: 59,791

GAME 3 AT CIN OCT 7

```
NY   202 030 000   7 5 1
CIN  120 000 000   3 10 0
```
Pitchers: Gomez, HADLEY (2) vs THOMPSON, Grissom (5), Moore (7)
Home Runs: Keller-NY (2), DiMaggio-NY, Dickey-NY
Attendance: 32,723

GAME 4 AT CIN OCT 8

```
NY   000 000 202 3   7 7 1
CIN  000 000 310 0   4 11 4
```
Pitchers: Hildebrand, Sundra (5), MURPHY (7) vs Derringer, WALTERS (8)
Home Runs: Keller-NY, Dickey-NY
Attendance: 32,794

CINCINNATI REDS (NL) 4, DETROIT TIGERS (AL) 3

The Tigers outpitched and outslugged the Reds, and scored six more runs than the Reds did. What they failed to do was win the Series.

Tigers ace Bobo Newsom, who had enjoyed what would be his finest season in a long career, carried his mastery into the Series opener. Detroit gave him an early lead, driving out Reds starter Paul Derringer with five runs in the second inning, and added a pair of runs in the fifth on Bruce Campbell's home run. Newsom, meanwhile, held the Reds to single runs in the fourth and eighth.

Cincinnati's Bucky Walters walked the first two Tigers he faced in Game 2, and both scored. But two Reds runs in the second tied the game, Jimmy Ripple's two-run homer an inning later gave them the lead, and pitcher Walters scored an insurance run in the fourth after doubling. Another Tigers walk in the sixth led to their third run, but Walters retired the remaining Tigers in order.

Detroit's Rocky Bridges yielded 10 hits and four runs in Game 3, but his teammates responded with 13 hits and seven runs, including a pair of two-run homers by Rudy York and Pinky Higgins in the seventh. Cincinnati again evened the Series the next day, though, with five runs to support Derringer's five-hit, two-run pitching. Although Newsom's father had suffered a fatal heart attack the day after seeing his son win the opener, the son pitched Game 5, and improved on his previous performance with a three-hit shutout. Hank Greenberg's homer in the third inning accounted for the first three of the Tigers' eight runs in their lopsided win.

The Reds returned home needing to win the final two games. Like Newsom, Bucky Walters bettered his earlier win with a shutout in Game 6, and drove in two of the Reds' four runs, one with a solo homer in the eighth. In the Series finale, Newsom and Derringer found themselves evenly matched. The Tigers scored a run in the third, while Newsom held Cincinnati scoreless through six. But in the seventh, leadoff doubles by Frank McCormick and Jimmy Ripple, plus a successful bunt and a fly to deep center, gave the Reds two runs—all they needed as Derringer stopped the Tigers

CIN (N)

PLAYER/POS	AVG	G	AB	R	H	2B	3B	HR	RB	BB	SO	SB
Morrie Arnovich, of	.000	1	1	0	0	0	0	0	0	0	0	0
Bill Baker, c	.250	3	4	1	1	0	0	0	0	0	1	0
Joe Beggs, p	.000	1	0	0	0	0	0	0	0	0	0	0
Harry Craft, ph	.000	1	1	0	0	0	0	0	0	0	0	0
Paul Derringer, p	.000	3	7	0	0	0	0	0	0	0	1	0
Lonny Frey, ph	.000	3	2	0	0	0	0	0	0	0	0	0
Ival Goodman, of	.276	7	29	5	8	2	0	0	5	0	3	0
Johnny Hutchings, p	.000	1	0	0	0	0	0	0	0	0	0	0
Eddie Joost, 2b	.200	7	25	0	5	0	0	0	2	1	2	0
Ernie Lombardi, c-1	.333	2	3	0	1	1	0	0	0	1	0	0
Frank McCormick, 1b	.214	7	28	2	6	1	0	0	0	1	1	0
Mike McCormick, of	.310	7	29	1	9	3	0	0	2	1	6	0
Whitey Moore, p	.000	3	2	0	0	0	0	0	0	0	1	0
Billy Myers, ss	.130	7	23	0	3	0	0	0	2	2	5	0
Elmer Riddle, p	.000	1	0	0	0	0	0	0	0	0	0	0
Lew Riggs, ph	.000	3	3	1	0	0	0	0	0	0	2	0
Jimmy Ripple, of	.333	7	21	3	7	2	0	1	6	4	2	0
Junior Thompson, p	.000	1	1	0	0	0	0	0	0	0	1	0
Jim Turner, p	.000	1	2	0	0	0	0	0	0	0	0	0
Johnny Vander Meer, p	.000	1	0	0	0	0	0	0	0	0	0	0
Bucky Walters, p	.286	2	7	2	2	1	0	1	2	0	1	0
Billy Werber, 3b	.370	7	27	5	10	4	0	0	2	4	2	0
Jimmie Wilson, c	.353	6	17	2	6	0	0	0	0	1	2	1
TOTAL	.250		232	22	58	14	0	2	21	15	30	

PITCHER	W	L	ERA	G	GS	CG	SV	SHO	IP	H	ER	BB	SO
Joe Beggs	0	0	9.00	1	0	0	0	0	1.0	3	1	0	1
Paul Derringer	2	1	2.79	3	3	2	0	0	19.1	17	6	10	6
Johnny Hutchings	0	0	9.00	1	0	0	0	0	1.0	2	1	1	0
Whitey Moore	0	0	3.24	3	0	0	0	0	8.1	8	3	6	7
Elmer Riddle	0	0	0.00	1	0	0	0	0	1.0	0	0	0	2
Junior Thompson	0	1	16.20	1	1	0	0	0	3.1	8	6	4	2
Jim Turner	0	1	7.50	1	1	0	0	0	6.0	8	5	0	4
J. Vander Meer	0	0	0.00	1	0	0	0	0	3.0	2	0	3	2
Bucky Walters	2	0	1.50	2	2	2	0	1	18.0	8	3	6	6
TOTAL	4	3	3.69	14	7	4	0	1	61.0	56	25	30	30

DET (A)

PLAYER/POS	AVG	G	AB	R	H	2B	3B	HR	RB	BB	SO	SB
Earl Averill, ph	.000	3	3	0	0	0	0	0	0	0	0	0
Dick Bartell, ss	.269	7	26	2	7	2	0	0	3	3	3	0
Tommy Bridges, p	.000	1	3	0	0	0	0	0	0	0	1	0
Bruce Campbell, of	.360	7	25	4	9	1	0	1	5	4	4	0
Frank Croucher, ss	.000	1	0	0	0	0	0	0	0	0	0	0
Pete Fox, ph	.000	1	1	0	0	0	0	0	0	0	0	0
Charlie Gehringer, 2b	.214	7	28	3	6	0	0	0	1	2	0	0
Johnny Gorsica, p	.000	2	4	0	0	0	0	0	0	0	2	0
Hank Greenberg, of	.357	7	28	5	10	2	1	1	6	2	5	0
Pinky Higgins, 3b	.333	7	24	2	8	3	1	1	6	3	3	0
Fred Hutchinson, p	.000	1	0	0	0	0	0	0	0	0	0	0
Barney McCosky, of	.304	7	23	5	7	1	0	0	1	7	0	0
Archie McKain, p	.000	1	0	0	0	0	0	0	0	0	0	0
Bobo Newsom, p	.100	3	10	1	1	0	0	0	0	0	1	0
Schoolboy Rowe, p	.000	2	1	0	0	0	0	0	0	0	1	0
Clay Smith, p	.000	1	1	0	0	0	0	0	0	0	1	0
Billy Sullivan, c-4	.154	5	13	3	2	0	0	0	0	5	2	0
Birdie Tebbetts, c-3	.000	4	11	0	0	0	0	0	0	0	0	0
Dizzy Trout, p	.000	1	1	0	0	0	0	0	0	0	0	0
Rudy York, 1b	.231	7	26	3	6	0	1	1	2	4	7	0
TOTAL	.246		228	28	56	9	3	4	24	30	30	0

PITCHER	W	L	ERA	G	GS	CG	SV	SHO	IP	H	ER	BB	SO
Tommy Bridges	1	0	3.00	1	1	1	0	0	9.0	10	3	1	5
Johnny Gorsica	0	0	0.79	2	0	0	0	0	11.1	6	1	4	4
Fred Hutchinson	0	0	9.00	1	0	0	0	0	1.0	1	1	1	1
Archie McKain	0	0	3.00	1	0	0	0	0	3.0	4	1	0	0
Bobo Newsom	2	1	1.38	3	3	3	0	1	26.0	18	4	4	17
Schoolboy Rowe	0	2	17.18	2	2	0	0	0	3.2	12	7	1	1
Clay Smith	0	0	2.25	1	0	0	0	0	4.0	1	1	3	1
Dizzy Trout	0	1	9.00	1	1	0	0	0	2.0	6	2	1	1
TOTAL	3	4	3.00	12	7	4	0	1	60.0	58	20	15	30

through the final six innings for the victory.

GAME 1 AT CIN OCT 2
DET 050 020 000   7 10 1
CIN 000 100 010   2 8 3
Pitchers: NEWSOM vs DERRINGER, Moore (2), Riddle (9)
Home Runs: Campbell-DET
Attendance: 31,793

GAME 2 AT CIN OCT 3
DET 200 001 000   3 3 1
CIN 022 100 00X   5 9 0
Pitchers: ROWE, Gorsica (4) vs WALTERS
Home Runs: Ripple-CIN
Attendance: 30,640

GAME 3 AT DET OCT 4
CIN 100 000 012   4 10 1
DET 000 100 42X   7 13 1
Pitchers: TURNER, Moore (7), Beggs (8) vs BRIDGES
Home Runs: York-DET, Higgins-DET
Attendance: 52,877

GAME 4 AT DET OCT 5
CIN 201 100 010   5 11 1
DET 001 001 000   2 5 1
Pitchers: DERRINGER vs TROUT, Smith (3), McKain (7)
Attendance: 54,093

GAME 5 AT DET OCT 6
CIN 000 000 000   0 3 0
DET 003 400 01X   8 13 0
Pitchers: THOMPSON, Moore (4), Vander Meer (5), Hutchings (8) vs NEWSOM
Home Runs: Greenberg-DET
Attendance: 55,189

GAME 6 AT CIN OCT 7
DET 000 000 000   0 5 0
CIN 200 001 01X   4 10 2
Pitchers: ROWE, Gorsica (1), Hutchinson (8) vs WALTERS
Home Runs: Walters-CIN
Attendance: 30,481

GAME 7 AT CIN OCT 8
DET 001 000 000   1 7 0
CIN 000 000 20X   2 7 1
Pitchers: NEWSOM vs DERRINGER
Attendance: 26,854

NEW YORK YANKEES (AL) 4, BROOKLYN DODGERS (NL) 1

Dodgers catcher Mickey Owen's dropped third strike in Game 4 was the Series' memorable boner, but it was not the chief cause of Brooklyn's downfall. Yankees pitching was. Three Yankees hurled complete-game wins, with each giving the Dodgers only one earned run. And relief ace Johnny Murphy hurled two-hit shutout ball in six innings over two games, winning one.

Joe Gordon opened the Series scoring with a solo homer in the second inning for the Yankees in Game 1, and the Yankees added runs in the fourth and sixth. Owen tripled in the Dodgers' first run in the fifth, and pinch hitter Lew Riggs singled in an unearned run in the seventh. But Yankees starter Red Ruffing held on to his slim lead through the final two innings for the win.

Dodgers ace Whitlow Wyatt gave the Yankees single runs in the second and third innings of Game 2, but held them scoreless the rest of the way. Meanwhile, the Dodgers tied the game in the fifth, and scored an unearned run in the sixth to finish the scoring and give Brooklyn its only win of the Series.

Freddie Fitzsimmons, with the Dodgers' best pitching of the Series, dueled Marius Russo through seven scoreless innings in Game 3. But Fitzsimmons' final out of the seventh—a line drive by Russo that bounced off Fitzsimmons' leg into the glove of shortstop Pee Wee Reese—broke his kneecap. Hugh Casey, who replaced Fitzsimmons in the eighth, retired the first batter, but then gave up four straight singles for two runs before being removed. The Yankees scored no more, and Brooklyn came up with a run in the last of the eighth. But Russo stopped the Dodgers in order in the ninth to preserve his lead for the Yankees' second win.

In Game 4, for the first time in the Series, the margin of victory was more than one run, thanks to catcher Owen's famous boner. Brooklyn held the lead 4–3 with two out in the top of the ninth. Dodgers reliever Casey, who had shut out the Yankees since coming on in the fifth inning, then struck out Tommy Henrich for what should have been the game-ending out. But Owen let the ball get by him, and before the third out was

recorded Casey had given up a single, two doubles, and two walks—and four runs, for Brooklyn's third loss.

The Yankees scored twice off Wyatt in the second inning of Game 5, and once more in the fifth (on Henrich's home run), as Tiny Bonham held Brooklyn to four hits and a single run to clinch the ninth Yankees world title.

NY (A)

PLAYER/POS	AVG	G	AB	R	H	2B	3B	HR	RB	BB	SO	SB
Tiny Bonham, p	.000	1	4	0	0	0	0	0	0	0	4	0
Frenchy Bordagaray, pr	.000	1	0	0	0	0	0	0	0	0	0	0
Marv Breuer, p	.000	1	1	0	0	0	0	0	0	0	0	0
Spud Chandler, p	.500	1	2	0	1	0	0	0	1	0	0	0
Bill Dickey, c	.167	5	18	3	3	1	0	0	1	3	1	0
Joe DiMaggio, of	.263	5	19	1	5	0	0	0	1	2	2	0
Atley Donald, p	.000	1	2	0	0	0	0	0	0	0	1	0
Joe Gordon, 2b	.500	5	14	2	7	1	1	1	5	7	0	0
Tommy Henrich, of	.167	5	18	4	3	1	0	1	1	3	3	0
Charlie Keller, of	.389	5	18	5	7	2	0	0	5	3	1	0
Johnny Murphy, p	.000	2	2	0	0	0	0	0	0	0	1	0
Phil Rizzuto, ss	.111	5	18	0	2	0	0	0	0	3	1	1
Red Rolfe, 3b	.300	5	20	2	6	0	0	0	0	2	1	0
Buddy Rosar, c	.000	1	0	0	0	0	0	0	0	0	0	0
Red Ruffing, p	.000	1	3	0	0	0	0	0	0	0	0	0
Marius Russo, p	.000	1	4	0	0	0	0	0	0	0	1	0
George Selkirk, ph	.500	2	2	0	1	0	0	0	0	0	0	0
Johnny Sturm, 1b	.286	5	21	0	6	0	0	0	2	0	2	1
TOTAL	.247		166	17	41	5	1	2	16	23	18	2

PITCHER	W	L	ERA	G	GS	CG	SV	SHO	IP	H	ER	BB	SO
Tiny Bonham	1	0	1.00	1	1	1	0	0	9.0	4	1	2	2
Marv Breuer	0	0	0.00	1	0	0	0	0	3.0	3	0	1	2
Spud Chandler	0	1	3.60	1	1	0	0	0	5.0	4	2	2	2
Atley Donald	0	0	9.00	1	1	0	0	0	4.0	6	4	3	2
Johnny Murphy	1	0	0.00	2	0	0	0	0	6.0	2	0	1	3
Red Ruffing	1	0	1.00	1	1	1	0	0	9.0	6	1	3	5
Marius Russo	1	0	1.00	1	1	1	0	0	9.0	4	1	2	5
TOTAL	4	1	1.80	8	5	3	0	0	45.0	29	9	14	21

BRO (N)

PLAYER/POS	AVG	G	AB	R	H	2B	3B	HR	RB	BB	SO	SB
Johnny Allen, p	.000	3	0	0	0	0	0	0	0	0	0	0
Dolph Camilli, 1b	.167	5	18	1	3	1	0	0	1	1	6	0
Hugh Casey, p	.500	3	2	0	1	0	0	0	0	0	1	0
Pete Coscarart, 2b	.000	3	7	1	0	0	0	0	0	1	2	0
Curt Davis, p	.000	1	2	0	0	0	0	0	0	0	0	0
Freddie Fitzsimmons, p	.000	1	2	0	0	0	0	0	0	0	0	0
Herman Franks, c	.000	1	1	0	0	0	0	0	0	0	0	0
Larry French, p	.000	2	0	0	0	0	0	0	0	0	0	0
Augie Galan, ph	.000	2	2	0	0	0	0	0	0	0	1	0
Billy Herman, 2b	.125	4	8	0	1	0	0	0	0	2	0	0
Kirby Higbe, p	1.000	1	1	0	1	0	0	0	0	0	0	0
Cookie Lavagetto, 3b	.100	3	10	1	1	0	0	0	0	2	0	0
Joe Medwick, of	.235	5	17	1	4	1	0	0	0	1	2	0
Mickey Owen, c	.167	5	12	1	2	0	1	0	2	3	0	0
Pee Wee Reese, ss	.200	5	20	1	4	0	0	0	2	0	0	0
Pete Reiser, of	.200	5	20	1	4	1	1	1	3	1	6	0
Lew Riggs, 3b-2	.250	3	8	0	2	0	0	0	1	1	1	0
Dixie Walker, of	.222	5	18	3	4	2	0	0	0	2	1	0
Jimmy Wasdell, of-1	.200	3	5	0	1	1	0	0	2	0	0	0
Whit Wyatt, p	.167	2	6	1	1	1	0	0	0	0	1	0
TOTAL	.182		159	11	29	7	2	1	11	14	21	0

PITCHER	W	L	ERA	G	GS	CG	SV	SHO	IP	H	ER	BB	SO
Johnny Allen	0	0	0.00	3	0	0	0	0	3.2	1	0	3	0
Hugh Casey	0	2	3.38	3	0	0	0	0	5.1	9	2	2	1
Curt Davis	0	1	5.06	1	1	0	0	0	5.1	6	3	3	1
Freddie Fitzsimmons	0	0	0.00	1	1	0	0	0	7.0	4	0	3	1
Larry French	0	0	0.00	2	0	0	0	0	1.0	0	0	0	0
Kirby Higbe	0	0	7.36	1	1	0	0	0	3.2	6	3	2	1
Whit Wyatt	1	1	2.50	2	2	2	0	0	18.0	15	5	10	14
TOTAL	1	4	2.66	13	5	2	0	0	44.0	41	13	23	18

GAME 1 AT NY OCT 1
BRO 000 010 100   2 6 0
NY 010 101 00X   3 6 1
Pitchers: DAVIS, Casey (6), Allen (7) vs RUFFING
Home Runs: Gordon-NY
Attendance: 68,540

GAME 2 AT NY OCT 2
BRO 000 021 000   3 6 2
NY 011 000 000   2 9 1
Pitchers: WYATT vs CHANDLER, Murphy (6)
Attendance: 66,248

GAME 3 AT BRO OCT 4
NY 000 000 020   2 8 0
BRO 000 000 010   1 4 0
Pitchers: RUSSO vs Fitzsimmons, CASEY (8), French (8), Allen (9)
Attendance: 33,100

GAME 4 AT BRO OCT 5
NY 100 200 004   7 12 0
BRO 000 220 000   4 9 1
Pitchers: Donald, Breuer (5), MURPHY (8) vs Higbe, French (4), Allen (5), CASEY (5)
Home Runs: Reiser-BRO
Attendance: 33,813

GAME 5 AT BRO OCT 6
NY 020 010 000   3 6 0
BRO 001 000 000   1 4 1
Pitchers: BONHAM vs WYATT
Home Runs: Henrich-NY
Attendance: 34,072

ST. LOUIS CARDINALS (NL) 4, NEW YORK YANKEES (AL) 1

Rookies Stan Musial and Whitey Kurowski drove in game-winning runs for rookie-pitcher Johnny Beazley in Games 2 and 5 as the major leagues' youngest team upset the Yankees. New York won only the opener, building a seven-run lead for starter Red Ruffing, who shut out St. Louis on one hit through 8-1/3 innings before giving up four hits and four harmless runs in the last of the ninth.

The Cardinals scored first in Game 2 on catcher Walker Cooper's two-run double in the first inning. Kurowski tripled in a third run in the seventh, but pitcher Beazley, after holding the Yankees scoreless through seven innings, gave up three runs in the eighth on two singles and Charlie Keller's two-run homer. St. Louis regained the lead a half inning later when Musial singled home Enos Slaughter (who had doubled), and stifled a threat in the ninth as Slaughter's great throw from right field nailed a runner at third.

Second-year Cardinals pitcher Ernie White turned in the Series' top mound performance with a six-single, no-walk shutout in Game 3 (aided by outfielders Musial and Slaughter, who hauled in a pair of potential home run blasts in the seventh inning). The Cards managed only five singles themselves, but they combined one with a walk, sacrifice, and ground out for a run in the third, and sandwiched a Yankees error with two hits in the ninth for an unearned insurance run.

Game 4 saw the Series' heaviest hitting. New York scored once in the first, but the Cards exploded in the fourth for six runs on six hits and two walks. The Yankees tied it up two innings later, with Keller's three-run homer the feature of the five-run inning. St. Louis took the lead for good with two runs in the seventh, and added a ninth run in the ninth.

Beazley and Ruffing tangled in Game 5. Phil Rizzuto's solo homer put New York ahead in the first inning. Slaughter's fourth-inning home run tied the score, but the Yankees regained the lead with a run later in the inning. The Cards tied the game again in the sixth, and took the final lead when Kurowski homered for two runs in the top of the ninth. The Yankees

threatened in the last of the ninth, putting their first two men on with a single and error. But catcher Cooper picked a runner off second, second baseman Jimmy Brown redeemed his earlier error with a sparkling catch, then fielded a routine grounder for the final out.

STL (N)

PLAYER/POS	AVG	G	AB	R	H	2B	3B	HR	RB	BB	SO	SB
Johnny Beazley, p	.143	2	7	0	1	0	0	0	0	0	5	0
Jimmy Brown, 2b	.300	5	20	2	6	0	0	0	1	3	0	0
Mort Cooper, p	.200	2	5	1	1	0	0	0	2	0	1	0
Walker Cooper, c	.286	5	21	3	6	1	0	0	4	0	1	0
Creepy Crespi, pr	.000	1	0	1	0	0	0	0	0	0	0	0
Harry Gumbert, p	.000	2	0	0	0	0	0	0	0	0	0	0
Johnny Hopp, 1b	.176	5	17	3	3	0	0	0	0	1	1	0
Whitey Kurowski, 3b	.267	5	15	3	4	0	1	1	5	2	3	0
Max Lanier, p	1.000	2	1	0	1	0	0	0	1	0	0	0
Marty Marion, ss	.111	5	18	2	2	0	1	0	3	1	2	0
Terry Moore, of	.294	5	17	2	5	1	0	0	2	2	3	0
Stan Musial, of	.222	5	18	2	4	1	0	0	2	4	0	0
Ken O'Dea, ph	1.000	1	1	0	1	0	0	0	1	0	0	0
Howie Pollet, p	.000	1	0	0	0	0	0	0	0	0	0	0
Ray Sanders, ph	.000	2	1	1	0	0	0	0	0	1	0	0
Enos Slaughter, of	.263	5	19	3	5	1	0	1	2	3	2	0
Harry Walker, ph	.000	1	1	0	0	0	0	0	0	0	1	0
Ernie White, p	.000	1	2	0	0	0	0	0	0	0	0	0
TOTAL	.239		163	23	39	4	2	2	23	17	19	0

PITCHER	W	L	ERA	G	GS	CG	SV	SHO	IP	H	ER	BB	SO
Johnny Beazley	2	0	2.50	2	2	2	0	0	18.0	17	5	3	6
Mort Cooper	0	1	5.54	2	2	0	0	0	13.0	17	8	4	9
Harry Gumbert	0	0	0.00	2	0	0	0	0	0.2	1	0	0	0
Max Lanier	1	0	0.00	2	0	0	0	0	4.0	3	0	1	1
Howie Pollet	0	0	0.00	1	0	0	0	0	0.1	0	0	0	0
Ernie White	1	0	0.00	1	1	1	0	1	9.0	6	0	0	6
TOTAL	4	1	2.60	10	5	3	0	1	45.0	44	13	8	22

NY (A)

PLAYER/POS	AVG	G	AB	R	H	2B	3B	HR	RB	BB	SO	SB
Tiny Bonham, p	.000	2	2	0	0	0	0	0	0	1	0	0
Hank Borowy, p	.000	1	1	0	0	0	0	0	0	0	1	0
Marv Breuer, p	.000	1	0	0	0	0	0	0	0	0	0	0
Spud Chandler, p	.000	2	2	0	0	0	0	0	0	0	1	0
Frankie Crosetti, 3b	.000	1	3	0	0	0	0	0	0	0	1	0
Roy Cullenbine, of	.263	5	19	3	5	1	0	0	2	1	2	1
Bill Dickey, c	.263	5	19	1	5	0	0	0	0	1	0	0
Joe DiMaggio, of	.333	5	21	3	7	0	0	0	3	0	1	0
Atley Donald, p	.000	1	2	0	0	0	0	0	0	0	0	0
Joe Gordon, 2b	.095	5	21	1	2	1	0	0	0	0	7	0
Buddy Hassett, 1b	.333	3	9	1	3	1	0	0	2	0	1	0
Charlie Keller, of	.200	5	20	2	4	0	0	2	5	1	3	0
Jerry Priddy, 1b-3,3b-1	.100	3	10	0	1	1	0	0	1	1	0	0
Phil Rizzuto, ss	.381	5	21	2	8	0	0	1	1	2	1	2
Red Rolfe, 3b	.353	4	17	5	6	2	0	0	0	1	2	0
Buddy Rosar, ph	1.000	1	1	0	1	0	0	0	0	0	0	0
Red Ruffing, p-2	.222	4	9	0	2	0	0	0	0	0	2	0
George Selkirk, ph	.000	1	1	0	0	0	0	0	0	0	0	0
Tuck Stainback, pr	.000	2	0	0	0	0	0	0	0	0	0	0
Jim Turner, p	.000	1	0	0	0	0	0	0	0	0	0	0
TOTAL	.247		178	18	44	6	0	3	14	8	22	3

PITCHER	W	L	ERA	G	GS	CG	SV	SHO	IP	H	ER	BB	SO
Tiny Bonham	0	1	4.09	2	1	1	0	0	11.0	9	5	3	3
Hank Borowy	0	0	18.00	1	1	0	0	0	3.0	6	6	3	1
Marv Breuer	0	0	—	1	0	0	0	0	0.0	2	0	0	0
Spud Chandler	0	1	1.08	2	1	0	1	0	8.1	5	1	1	3
Atley Donald	0	1	6.00	1	0	0	0	0	3.0	3	2	2	1
Red Ruffing	1	1	4.08	2	2	1	0	0	17.2	14	8	7	11
Jim Turner	0	0	0.00	1	0	0	0	0	1.0	0	0	1	0
TOTAL	1	4	4.50	10	5	2	1	0	44.0	39	22	17	19

GAME 1 AT STL SEPT 30
NY 000 110 032   7 11 0
STL 000 000 004   4 7 4
Pitchers: RUFFING, Chandler (9) vs M.COOPER, Gumbert (8), Lanier (9)
Attendance: 34,769

GAME 2 AT STL OCT 1
NY 000 000 030   3 10 2
STL 200 000 11X   4 6 0
Pitchers: BONHAM vs BEAZLEY
Home Runs: Keller-NY
Attendance: 34,255

GAME 3 AT NY OCT 2
STL 001 000 001   2 5 1
NY 000 000 000   0 6 1
Pitchers: WHITE vs CHANDLER, Breuer (9), Turner (9)
Attendance: 69,123

GAME 4 AT NY OCT 4
STL 000 600 201   9 12 1
NY 100 005 000   6 10 1
Pitchers: M.Cooper, Gumbert (6), Pollet (6), LANIER (7) vs Borowy, DONALD (4), Bonham (7)
Home Runs: Keller-NY
Attendance: 69,902

GAME 5 AT NY OCT 5
STL 000 101 002   4 9 4
NY 100 100 000   2 7 1
Pitchers: BEAZLEY vs RUFFING
Home Runs: Rizzuto-NY, Slaughter-STL, Kurowski-STL
Attendance: 69,052

NEW YORK YANKEES (AL) 4, ST. LOUIS CARDINALS (NL) 1

Although both clubs had lost players to military service since the previous World Series, history seemed to be repeating itself. The Cardinals lost to the Yankees in the opener and won the second game, as they had the previous year. But this year it was the Yankees who took the next three games and the Series, as fine Cardinal pitching gave way to even finer mound work by New York.

Yankees pitcher Spurgeon (Spud) Chandler, coming off his finest season (20–4, 1.64 ERA), continued to overwhelm the opposition in the Series. He held the Cards to two runs (only one earned) in Game 1, and the Yankees took advantage of a wild pitch to score two runs of their own in the sixth inning, breaking a 2–2 tie for a 4–2 win. Cardinals short-stop Marty Marion homered in the third inning for the first run the next day, and first baseman Ray Sanders homered for two more runs in a three-run fourth. Cardinals ace Mort Cooper held New York to one run on four hits through eight innings, but he weakened in the last of the ninth, giving up a double and triple to the first two batters. But only two runs scored as he retired the next three men for St. Louis' only victory.

The Cardinals carried a 2–1 lead into the last of the eighth inning of Game 3, when a pair of errors, two walks, and five hits (including Billy Johnson's three-run triple) undid them. Yankees fireman Johnny Murphy retired the Cards in order in the ninth to save Hank Borowy's win. Max Lanier and Harry Brecheen held New York to just two runs (and six hits) in Game 4, but Yankees pitcher Marius Russo gave up only one run—and that was scored only because of two Yankees errors in the seventh inning.

In the fifth and (as it turned out) final game, St. Louis couldn't score, although they knocked Spud Chandler for 10 hits. But they were all singles and were spaced harmlessly over eight of the nine innings. Three St. Louis pitchers held the Yankees to just seven hits, six of them singles. But in the sixth inning Bill Dickey followed one of the singles with the game's only extra-base hit—a home run—to produce the game's only scoring, and bring the Yankees yet another world championship, their 10th.

NY (A)

PLAYER/POS	AVG	G	AB	R	H	2B	3B	HR	RB	BB	SO	SB
Tiny Bonham, p	.000	1	2	0	0	0	0	0	0	0	1	0
Hank Borowy, p	.500	1	2	1	1	1	0	0	0	0	1	0
Spud Chandler, p	.167	2	6	0	1	0	0	0	0	0	2	0
Frankie Crosetti, ss	.278	5	18	4	5	0	0	0	1	2	3	1
Bill Dickey, c	.278	5	18	1	5	0	0	1	4	2	2	0
Nick Etten, 1b	.105	5	19	0	2	0	0	0	2	1	2	0
Joe Gordon, 2b	.235	5	17	2	4	1	0	1	2	3	3	0
Billy Johnson, 3b	.300	5	20	3	6	1	1	0	3	0	3	0
Charlie Keller, of	.222	5	18	3	4	0	1	0	2	2	5	1
Johnny Lindell, of	.111	4	9	1	1	0	0	0	0	1	4	0
Bud Metheny, of	.125	2	8	0	1	0	0	0	0	0	2	0
Johnny Murphy, p	.000	2	0	0	0	0	0	0	0	0	0	0
Marius Russo, p	.667	1	3	1	2	2	0	0	0	1	1	0
Tuck Stainback, of	.176	5	17	0	3	0	0	0	0	0	2	0
Snuffy Stirnweiss, ph	.000	1	1	1	0	0	0	0	0	0	0	0
Roy Weatherly, ph	.000	1	1	0	0	0	0	0	0	0	0	0
TOTAL	.220		159	17	35	5	2	2	14	12	30	2

PITCHER	W	L	ERA	G	GS	CG	SV	SHO	IP	H	ER	BB	SO
Tiny Bonham	0	1	4.50	1	1	0	0	0	8.0	6	4	3	9
Hank Borowy	1	0	2.25	1	1	0	0	0	8.0	6	2	3	4
Spud Chandler	2	0	0.50	2	2	2	0	1	18.0	17	1	3	10
Johnny Murphy	0	0	0.00	2	0	0	1	0	2.0	1	0	1	1
Marius Russo	1	0	0.00	1	1	1	0	0	9.0	7	0	1	2
TOTAL	4	1	1.40	7	5	3	1	1	45.0	37	7	11	26

STL (N)

PLAYER/POS	AVG	G	AB	R	H	2B	3B	HR	RB	BB	SO	SB
Al Brazle, p	.000	1	3	0	0	0	0	0	0	0	1	0
Harry Brecheen, p	.000	3	2	0	0	0	0	0	0	0	0	0
Mort Cooper, p	.000	2	5	0	0	0	0	0	0	0	3	0
Walker Cooper, c	.294	5	17	1	5	0	0	0	0	0	1	0
Frank Demaree, ph	.000	1	1	0	0	0	0	0	0	0	0	0
Murry Dickson, p	.000	1	0	0	0	0	0	0	0	0	0	0
Debs Garms, of-1	.000	2	5	0	0	0	0	0	0	0	2	0
Johnny Hopp, of	.000	1	4	0	0	0	0	0	0	0	1	0
Lou Klein, 2b	.136	5	22	0	3	0	0	0	0	1	2	0
Howie Krist, p	.000	1	0	0	0	0	0	0	0	0	0	0
Whitey Kurowski, 3b	.222	5	18	2	4	1	0	0	1	0	3	0
Max Lanier, p	.250	3	4	0	1	0	0	0	1	0	0	0
Danny Litwhiler, of-4	.267	5	15	0	4	1	0	0	2	2	4	0
Marty Marion, ss	.357	5	14	1	5	2	0	1	2	3	1	1
Stan Musial, of	.278	5	18	2	5	0	0	0	0	2	2	0
Sam Narron, ph	.000	1	1	0	0	0	0	0	0	0	0	0
Ken O'Dea, c-1	.667	2	3	0	2	0	0	0	0	0	0	0
Ray Sanders, 1b	.294	5	17	3	5	0	0	1	2	3	4	0
Harry Walker, of	.167	5	18	0	3	1	0	0	0	0	2	0
Ernie White, pr	.000	1	0	0	0	0	0	0	0	0	0	0
TOTAL	.224		165	9	37	5	0	2	8	11	26	1

PITCHER	W	L	ERA	G	GS	CG	SV	SHO	IP	H	ER	BB	SO
Al Brazle	0	1	3.68	1	1	0	0	0	7.1	5	3	2	4
Harry Brecheen	0	1	2.45	3	0	0	0	0	3.2	5	1	3	3
Mort Cooper	1	1	2.81	2	2	1	0	0	16.0	11	5	3	10
Murry Dickson	0	0	0.00	1	0	0	0	0	0.2	0	0	1	0
Howie Krist	0	0	–	1	0	0	0	0	0.0	1	0	0	0
Max Lanier	0	1	1.76	3	2	0	0	0	15.1	13	3	3	13
TOTAL	1	4	2.51	11	5	1	0	0	43.0	35	12	12	30

GAME 1 AT NY OCT 5
```
STL  010 010 000   2 7 2
NY   000 202 00X   4 8 2
```
Pitchers: LANIER, Brecheen (8) vs CHANDLER
Home Runs: Gordon-NY
Attendance: 68,676

GAME 2 AT NY OCT 6
```
STL  001 300 000   4 7 2
NY   000 100 002   3 6 0
```
Pitchers: M.COOPER vs BONHAM, Murphy (9)
Home Runs: Marion-STL, Sanders-STL
Attendance: 68,578

GAME 3 AT NY OCT 7
```
STL  000 200 000   2 6 4
NY             6   6 8 0
```
Pitchers: BRAZLE, Krist (8), Brecheen (8) vs BOROWY, Murphy (9)
Attendance: 69,990

GAME 4 AT STL OCT 10
```
NY   000 100 010   2 6 2
STL  000 000 100   1 7 1
```
Pitchers: RUSSO vs Lanier, BRECHEEN (8)
Attendance: 36,196

GAME 5 AT STL OCT 11
```
NY   000 002 000   2 7 1
STL  000 000 000   0 10 1
```
Pitchers: CHANDLER vs M.COOPER, Lanier (8), Dickson (9)
Home Runs: Dickey-NY
Attendance: 33,872

ST. LOUIS CARDINALS (NL) 4, ST. LOUIS BROWNS (AL) 2

The Cardinals entered the World Series as clear favorites against their landlord Browns (who owned Sportsman's Park, where both teams played). They won the Series in six games, but if the Browns' fielding had been as good as their pitching the outcome might have been different.

The Browns won the opener on Denny Galehouse's strong pitching. Galehouse gave up seven hits and four walks, but held the Cards scoreless before yielding a run in the ninth. Cardinals ace Mort Cooper also pitched well in six of his seven innings. He allowed the Browns only two hits, but they came back to back in the fourth inning—a single followed by George McQuinn's home run—to give the Browns all the scoring they needed.

Browns pitcher Nelson Potter's two errors (a fumble and a wild throw) on a bunt in the third inning of Game 2 led to an unearned run, and third baseman Mark Christman's bobble an inning later set up a second unearned run. The Browns tied the score with a pair of runs on three two-out hits in the seventh—enough to have won an error-free game—but lost when the Cardinals singled a run across in the last of the eleventh.

Two errors by the Browns led to a pair of unearned runs in Game 3, but Jack Kramer held the Cards scoreless apart from that, striking out 10. Meanwhile, the Browns tied together five singles with two out in the third inning for three runs, adding a fourth run on a wild pitch before the inning ended. In the seventh the Browns tacked on two more runs for a comfortable win and a 2–1 Series advantage.

The Cardinals came back to earn victory in Games 4 and 5, knocking three Browns pitchers for 12 hits in Game 4 (including Stan Musial's two-run homer in the first) and a 5–1 win for pitcher Harry Brecheen, then rapping Denny Galehouse for two solo homers in Game 5 (by Danny Litwhiler and Ray Sanders) for the game's only scoring as Mort Cooper fanned 12 Browns while shutting them out.

Two of the Cardinals' three runs in the fourth inning of Game 6 were made possible by Browns shortstop Vern Stephens' throwing error. They provided the margin of victory, as Cardinals pitchers Max Lanier and Ted Wilks held the Browns to three hits and a single run, and brought the Cards their second world title in three years.

STL (N)

PLAYER/POS	AVG	G	AB	R	H	2B	3B	HR	RB	BB	SO	SB
Augie Bergamo, of-2	.000	3	6	0	0	0	0	0	0	1	2	3	0
Harry Brecheen, p	.000	1	4	0	0	0	0	0	0	0	1	0
Bud Byerly, p	.000	1	0	0	0	0	0	0	0	0	0	0
Mort Cooper, p	.000	2	4	0	0	0	0	0	0	0	2	0
Walker Cooper, c	.318	6	22	1	7	2	1	0	2	3	2	0
Blix Donnelly, p	.000	2	1	0	0	0	0	0	0	0	1	0
George Fallon, 2b	.000	2	2	0	0	0	0	0	0	0	1	0
Debs Garms, ph	.000	2	2	0	0	0	0	0	0	0	0	0
Johnny Hopp, of	.185	6	27	2	5	0	0	0	0	0	8	0
Al Jurisich, p	.000	1	0	0	0	0	0	0	0	0	0	0
Whitey Kurowski, 3b	.217	6	23	2	5	1	0	0	1	1	4	0
Max Lanier, p	.500	2	4	0	2	0	0	0	1	0	0	0
Danny Litwhiler, of	.200	5	20	2	4	1	0	1	1	2	7	0
Marty Marion, ss	.227	6	22	1	5	3	0	0	2	2	3	0
Stan Musial, of	.304	6	23	2	7	2	0	1	2	2	0	0
Ken O'Dea, ph	.333	3	3	0	1	0	0	0	2	0	0	0
Ray Sanders, 1b	.286	6	21	5	6	0	0	1	1	5	8	0
Freddy Schmidt, p	.000	1	0	0	0	0	0	0	0	0	1	0
Emil Verban, 2b	.412	6	17	1	7	0	0	0	2	2	0	0
Ted Wilks, p	.000	2	2	0	0	0	0	0	0	0	2	0
TOTAL	.240		204	16	49	9	1	3	15	19	43	0

PITCHER	W	L	ERA	G	GS	CG	SV	SHO	IP	H	ER	BB	SO
Harry Brecheen	1	0	1.00	1	1	1	0	0	9.0	9	1	4	4
Bud Byerly	0	0	0.00	1	0	0	0	0	1.1	0	0	0	1
Mort Cooper	1	1	1.13	2	2	1	0	1	16.0	9	2	5	16
Blix Donnelly	1	0	0.00	2	0	0	0	0	6.0	2	0	1	9
Al Jurisich	0	0	27.00	1	0	0	0	0	0.2	2	2	1	0
Max Lanier	1	0	2.19	2	2	0	0	0	12.1	8	3	8	11
Freddy Schmidt	0	0	0.00	1	0	0	0	0	3.1	1	0	1	1
Ted Wilks	0	1	5.68	2	1	0	1	0	6.1	5	4	3	7
TOTAL	4	2	1.96	12	6	2	1	1	55.0	36	12	23	49

STL (A)

PLAYER/POS	AVG	G	AB	R	H	2B	3B	HR	RB	BB	SO	SB
Floyd Baker, 2b	.000	2	2	0	0	0	0	0	0	0	2	0
Milt Byrnes, ph	.000	3	2	0	0	0	0	0	0	1	2	0
Mike Chartak, ph	.000	2	2	0	0	0	0	0	0	0	2	0
Mark Christman, 3b	.091	6	22	0	2	0	0	0	1	0	6	0
Ellis Clary, ph	.000	1	1	0	0	0	0	0	0	0	0	0
Denny Galehouse, p	.200	2	5	0	1	0	0	0	0	1	1	0
Don Gutteridge, 2b	.143	6	21	1	3	1	0	0	0	3	5	0
Red Hayworth, c	.118	6	17	1	2	1	0	0	1	3	1	0
Al Hollingsworth, p	.000	1	1	0	0	0	0	0	0	0	0	0
Sig Jakucki, p	.000	1	0	0	0	0	0	0	0	0	0	0
Jack Kramer, p	.000	2	4	0	0	0	0	0	0	0	2	0
Mike Kreevich, of	.231	6	26	0	6	3	0	0	0	0	5	0
Chet Laabs, of-4	.200	5	15	1	3	1	1	0	0	2	6	0
Frank Mancuso, c-1	.667	2	3	0	2	0	0	0	1	0	0	0
George McQuinn, 1b	.438	6	16	2	7	2	0	1	5	7	2	0
Gene Moore, of	.182	6	22	4	4	0	0	0	0	3	6	0
Bob Muncrief, p	.000	2	1	0	0	0	0	0	0	0	1	0
Nelson Potter, p	.000	2	4	0	0	0	0	0	0	0	1	0
Tex Shirley, p-1	.000	2	0	0	0	0	0	0	0	0	0	0
Vern Stephens, ss	.227	6	22	2	5	1	0	0	0	3	3	0
Tom Turner, ph	.000	1	1	0	0	0	0	0	0	0	0	0
Al Zarilla, of-3	.100	4	10	1	1	0	0	0	1	0	4	0
TOTAL	.183		197	12	36	9	1	1	9	23	49	0

PITCHER	W	L	ERA	G	GS	CG	SV	SHO	IP	H	ER	BB	SO
Denny Galehouse	1	1	1.50	2	2	2	0	0	18.0	13	3	5	15
Al Hollingsworth	0	0	2.25	1	0	0	0	0	4.0	5	1	2	1
Sig Jakucki	0	1	9.00	1	1	0	0	0	3.0	5	3	0	4
Jack Kramer	1	0	0.00	2	1	1	0	0	11.0	9	0	4	12
Bob Muncrief	0	1	1.35	2	0	0	0	0	6.2	5	1	4	4
Nelson Potter	0	1	0.93	2	2	0	0	0	9.2	10	1	3	6
Tex Shirley	0	0	0.00	1	0	0	0	0	2.0	2	0	1	1
TOTAL	2	4	1.49	11	6	3	0	0	54.1	49	9	19	43

GAME 1 AT STL-N OCT 4

STL-A 000 200 000 2 2 0
STL-N 000 000 001 1 7 0
Pitchers: GALEHOUSE vs M.COOPER, Donnelly (8)
Home Runs: McQuinn-STL (A)
Attendance: 33,242

GAME 2 AT STL-N OCT 5

STL-A 000000 20000 2 7 4
STL-N 001100 00001 3 7 0
Pitchers: Potter, MUNCRIEF (7) vs Lanier, DONNELLY (8)
Attendance: 35,076

GAME 3 AT STL-A OCT 6

STL-N 100 000 100 2 7 0
STL-A 004 000 20X 6 8 2
Pitchers: WILKS, Schmidt (3), Jurisich (7), Byerly (7) vs KRAMER
Attendance: 34,737

GAME 4 AT STL-A OCT 7

STL-N 202 001 000 5 12 0
STL-A 000 000 010 1 9 1
Pitchers: BRECHEEN vs JAKUCKI, Hollingsworth (4), Shirley (8)
Home Runs: Musial-STL (N)
Attendance: 35,455

GAME 5 AT STL-A OCT 8

STL-N 000 001 010 2 6 1
STL-A 000 000 000 0 7 1
Pitchers: M.COOPER vs GALEHOUSE
Home Runs: Sanders-STL (N), Litwhiler-STL (N)
Attendance: 36,568

GAME 6 AT STL-N OCT 9

STL-A 010 000 000 1 3 2
STL-N 000 300 00X 3 10 0
Pitchers: POTTER, Muncrief (4), Kramer (7) vs LANIER, Wilks (6)
Attendance: 31,630

DETROIT TIGERS (AL) 4, CHICAGO CUBS (NL) 3

As World War II ended during the summer, military major leaguers began returning to their clubs. Hank Greenberg's return in July provided the spark needed for Detroit's narrow pennant victory, and his three-run homer in Game 2 of the World Series proved to be the decisive blow in the Tigers' successful struggle for the world title.

Chicago started strong as Cubs ace Hank Borowy shut out the Tigers on six singles while his teammates drove out Hal Newhouser with seven runs in the first three innings and won. Chicago continued its assault the next day with a run in the top of the fourth, but in the fifth inning Doc Cramer—with two out and two on—singled in the tying run, and Greenberg followed with his tiebreaking homer for three additional runs. Detroit pitcher Virgil Trucks (who had returned from the Navy in time to pitch in the regular-season finale) held the Cubs scoreless after the fourth inning for the win.

Chicago's Claude Passeau moved the Cubs back into the Series lead with a one-hit shutout in Game 3, but Dizzy Trout's five-hitter in Game 4 again evened the Series. The Tigers bunched four of their seven hits in the fourth inning for all four of their runs.

Detroit took the Series lead for the first time with an 8–4 win in Game 5. Borowy and Newhouser faced each other as they had in the opener, but this time Borowy was hit hard. Driven out when four Tigers opened the sixth inning with safe hits, he took the loss as Newhouser went the distance for the win.

In Game 6, Chicago concluded the seventh inning of a heavy-hitting game with a 7–3 lead. Detroit tied the score with four runs in the top of the eighth (capped by Greenberg's home run), but in the last of the 12th the Cubs' Stan Hack doubled home the winning run to keep Chicago's hopes alive.

Two days later in the finale, Cubs manager Charlie Grimm started Borowy, who had relieved for four shutout innings to win Game 6. But this third appearance in four days proved too much. Removed after the first three batters to face him singled, he took the loss, as the Tigers went on to score nine runs to win the World Series for the second time

DET (A)

PLAYER/POS	AVG	G	AB	R	H	2B	3B	HR	RB	BB	SO	SB
Al Benton, p	.000	3	0	0	0	0	0	0	0	0	0	0
Red Borom, ph	.000	2	1	0	0	0	0	0	0	0	0	0
Tommy Bridges, p	.000	1	0	0	0	0	0	0	0	0	0	0
George Caster, p	.000	1	0	0	0	0	0	0	0	0	0	0
Doc Cramer, of	.379	7	29	7	11	0	0	0	4	1	0	1
Roy Cullenbine, of	.227	7	22	5	5	2	0	0	4	8	2	1
Zeb Eaton, ph	.000	1	1	0	0	0	0	0	0	0	1	0
Hank Greenberg, of	.304	7	23	7	7	3	0	2	7	6	5	0
Joe Hoover, ss	.333	1	3	1	1	0	0	0	1	0	0	0
Chuck Hostetler, ph	.000	3	3	0	0	0	0	0	0	0	0	0
Bob Maier, ph	1.000	1	1	0	1	0	0	0	0	0	0	0
Eddie Mayo, 2b	.250	7	28	4	7	1	0	0	2	3	2	0
John McHale, ph	.000	3	1	0	0	0	0	0	0	0	1	0
Ed Mierkowicz, of	.000	1	0	0	0	0	0	0	0	0	0	0
Les Mueller, p	.000	1	0	0	0	0	0	0	0	0	0	0
Hal Newhouser, p	.000	3	8	0	0	0	0	0	0	1	1	0
Jimmy Outlaw, 3b	.179	7	28	1	5	0	0	0	3	2	1	0
Stubby Overmire, p	.000	1	1	0	0	0	0	0	0	0	0	0
Paul Richards, c	.211	7	19	0	4	2	0	0	6	4	3	0
Bob Swift, c	.250	3	4	1	1	0	0	0	0	2	0	0
Jim Tobin, p	.000	1	1	0	0	0	0	0	0	0	0	0
Dizzy Trout, p	.167	2	6	0	1	0	0	0	0	0	0	0
Virgil Trucks, p	.000	2	4	0	0	0	0	0	0	0	1	0
Hub Walker, ph	.500	2	2	1	1	1	0	0	0	0	0	0
Skeeter Webb, ss	.185	7	27	4	5	0	0	0	1	2	1	0
Rudy York, 1b	.179	7	28	1	5	1	0	0	3	3	4	0
TOTAL	.223		242	32	54	10	0	2	32	33	22	3

PITCHER	W	L	ERA	G	GS	CG	SV	SHO	IP	H	ER	BB	SO
Al Benton	0	0	1.93	3	0	0	0	0	4.2	6	1	0	5
Tommy Bridges	0	0	16.20	1	0	0	0	0	1.2	3	3	3	1
George Caster	0	0	0.00	1	0	0	0	0	0.2	0	0	0	1
Les Mueller	0	0	0.00	1	0	0	0	0	2.0	0	0	1	1
Hal Newhouser	2	1	6.10	3	3	2	0	0	20.2	25	14	4	22
Stubby Overmire	0	1	3.00	1	1	0	0	0	6.0	4	2	2	2
Jim Tobin	0	0	6.00	1	0	0	0	0	3.0	4	2	1	0
Dizzy Trout	1	1	0.66	2	1	1	0	0	13.2	9	1	3	9
Virgil Trucks	1	0	3.38	2	2	1	0	0	13.1	14	5	5	7
TOTAL	4	3	3.84	15	7	4	0	0	65.2	65	28	19	48

CHI (N)

PLAYER/POS	AVG	G	AB	R	H	2B	3B	HR	RB	BB	SO	SB
Heinz Becker, ph	.500	3	2	0	1	0	0	0	0	1	1	0
Cy Block, pr	.000	1	0	0	0	0	0	0	0	0	0	0
Hank Borowy, p	.167	4	6	1	1	1	0	0	0	0	3	0
Phil Cavarretta, 1b	.423	7	26	7	11	2	0	1	5	4	3	0
Bob Chipman, p	.000	1	0	0	0	0	0	0	0	0	0	0
Paul Derringer, p	.000	3	0	0	0	0	0	0	0	0	0	0
Paul Erickson, p	.000	4	0	0	0	0	0	0	0	0	0	0
Paul Gillespie, c-1	.000	3	6	0	0	0	0	0	0	0	0	0
Stan Hack, 3b	.367	7	30	1	11	3	0	0	4	4	2	0
Roy Hughes, ss	.294	6	17	1	5	1	0	0	3	4	5	0
Don Johnson, 2b	.172	7	29	4	5	2	1	0	0	0	8	1
Mickey Livingston, c	.364	6	22	3	8	3	0	0	4	1	1	0
Peanuts Lowrey, of	.310	7	29	4	9	1	0	0	0	1	2	0
Clyde McCullough, ph	.000	1	1	0	0	0	0	0	0	0	1	0
Lennie Merullo, ss	.000	3	2	0	0	0	0	0	0	0	1	0
Bill Nicholson, of	.214	7	28	1	6	1	1	0	8	2	5	0
Andy Pafko, of	.214	7	28	5	6	2	1	0	2	2	5	1
Claude Passeau, p	.000	3	7	1	0	0	0	0	1	0	4	0
Ray Prim, p	.000	2	0	0	0	0	0	0	0	0	0	0
Ed Sauer, ph	.000	2	2	0	0	0	0	0	0	0	2	0
Bill Schuster, ss-1	.000	2	1	1	0	0	0	0	0	0	0	0
Frank Secory, ph	.400	5	5	0	2	0	0	0	0	0	2	0
Hy Vandenberg, p	.000	3	1	0	0	0	0	0	0	0	0	0
Dewey Williams, c-1	.000	2	2	0	0	0	0	0	0	0	2	0
Hank Wyse, p	.000	3	3	0	0	0	0	0	0	0	1	0
TOTAL	.263		247	29	65	16	3	1	27	19	48	2

PITCHER	W	L	ERA	G	GS	CG	SV	SHO	IP	H	ER	BB	SO
Hank Borowy	2	2	4.00	4	3	1	0	1	18.0	21	8	6	8
Bob Chipman	0	0	0.00	1	0	0	0	0	0.1	0	0	1	0
Paul Derringer	0	0	6.75	3	0	0	0	0	5.1	5	4	7	1
Paul Erickson	0	0	3.86	4	0	0	0	0	7.0	8	3	3	5
Claude Passeau	1	0	2.70	3	2	1	0	1	16.2	7	5	8	3
Ray Prim	0	1	9.00	2	1	0	0	0	4.0	4	4	1	1
Hy Vandenberg	0	0	0.00	3	0	0	0	0	6.0	1	0	3	3
Hank Wyse	0	1	7.04	3	1	0	0	0	7.2	8	6	4	1
TOTAL	3	4	4.15	23	7	2	0	2	65.0	54	30	33	22

GAME 1 AT DET OCT 3
CHI 4 0 3 0 0 0 2 0 0   9 13 0
DET 0 0 0 0 0 0 0 0 0   0 6 0
Pitchers: BOROWY vs NEWHOUSER, Benton (3), Tobin (5), Mueller (8)
Home Runs: Cavarretta-CHI
Attendance: 54,637

GAME 2 AT DET OCT 4
CHI 0 0 0 1 0 0 0 0 0   1 7 0
DET 0 0 0 0 4 0 0 0 X   4 7 0
Pitchers: WYSE, Erickson (7) vs TRUCKS
Home Runs: Greenberg-DET
Attendance: 53,636

GAME 3 AT DET OCT 5
CHI 0 0 0 2 0 0 1 0 0   3 8 0
DET 0 0 0 0 0 0 0 0 0   0 1 2
Pitchers: PASSEAU vs OVERMIRE, Benton (7)
Attendance: 55,500

GAME 4 AT CHI OCT 6
DET 0 0 0 4 0 0 0 0 0   4 7 1
CHI 0 0 0 0 0 1 0 0 0   1 5 1
Pitchers: TROUT vs PRIM, Derringer (4), Vandenberg (6), Erickson (8)
Attendance: 42,923

GAME 5 AT CHI OCT 7
DET 0 0 1 0 0 4 1 0 2   8 11 0
CHI 0 0 1 0 0 0 2 0 1   4 7 2
Pitchers: NEWHOUSER vs BOROWY, Vandenberg (6), Chipman (6), Derringer (7), Erickson (9)
Attendance: 43,463

GAME 6 AT CHI OCT 8
DET 0 1 0 0 0 0 2 4 0 0 0 0   7 13 1
CHI 0 0 0 0 4 1 2 0 0 0 0 1   8 15 3
Pitchers: Trucks, Caster (5), Bridges (6), Benton (7), TROUT (8) vs Passeau, Wyse (7), Prim (8), BOROWY (9)
Home Runs: Greenberg-DET
Attendance: 41,708

GAME 7 AT CHI OCT 10
DET 5 1 0 0 0 0 1 2 0   9 9 1
CHI 1 0 0 1 0 0 0 1 0   3 10 0
Pitchers: NEWHOUSER vs BOROWY, Derringer (1), Vandenberg (2), Erickson (6), Passeau (8), Wyse (9)
Attendance: 41,590

ST. LOUIS CARDINALS (NL) 4, BOSTON RED SOX (AL) 3

With World War II over, the majors were at full strength for the first time in five years. Boston's big bats were back, and the Sox ran away with the American League pennant. St. Louis had Stan Musial back, but they struggled to their pennant, finishing the regular schedule tied with Brooklyn, and defeating them in the first major league tie-breaker playoff, two games to none.

Favored Boston edged St. Louis in the opener, but it took a home run by Rudy York in the top of the 10th to spoil Howie Pollet's strong showing. Harry Brecheen brought the Cards back the next day with the first of his three Series wins—a four-hit shutout.

Boston regained the lead in Game 3. Sox ace Dave Ferriss spaced six hits and a walk, one per inning, in shutting out the Cardinals, and Rudy York hit his second game-winning homer, this time a three-run shot in the first inning. The next day, though, St. Louis exploded for a record-tying 20 hits—four apiece by Enos Slaughter, Joe Garagiola, and Whitey Kurowski—to give pitcher George Munger (who had completed only two of his seven regular-season starts) an easy complete-game 12–3 victory.

For the third time the Red Sox took the Series lead, winning Game 5 behind Joe Dobson's four-hit pitching (the Cards' three runs in the 6–3 loss were unearned), but St. Louis tied the Series for the third time with a win in Game 6. Brecheen, in his second start, again pitched splendidly, holding Boston to a single run in the seventh inning, long after the Cards had driven out Sox starter Mickey Harris with three runs in the third.

The final game, like the Series itself, was a seesaw battle. Boston scored the first run in the top of the first, but St. Louis tied the score an inning later. The Cards took a two-run lead on three hits in the fifth, but the Sox came back in the eighth to tie it up as Dom DiMaggio doubled off reliever Brecheen to drive in a pair of pinch hitters who had singled and doubled off starter Murry Dickson. The Series' final run came a half inning later. Slaughter opened with a single, but moved no farther as the next two batters were retired. Then Harry Walker hit a liner over

short. Slaughter, off with the crack of the bat, never paused and beat the relay to the plate with what proved the winning run, as Brecheen held the Sox in the ninth for his third win of the Series to give the Cardinals their third world title in five seasons.

STL (N)

PLAYER/POS	AVG	G	AB	R	H	2B	3B	HR	RB	BB	SO	SB
Johnny Beazley, p	.000	1	0	0	0	0	0	0	0	0	0	0
Al Brazle, p	.000	1	2	0	0	0	0	0	0	0	0	0
Harry Brecheen, p	.125	3	8	2	1	0	0	0	1	0	1	0
Murry Dickson, p	.400	2	5	1	2	2	0	0	1	0	1	0
Erv Dusak, p	.250	4	4	0	1	1	0	0	0	2	2	0
Joe Garagiola, c	.316	5	19	2	6	2	0	0	4	0	3	0
Nippy Jones, ph	.000	1	1	0	0	0	0	0	0	0	1	0
Whitey Kurowski, 3b	.296	7	27	5	8	3	0	0	2	0	3	0
Marty Marion, ss	.250	7	24	1	6	2	0	0	4	1	1	0
Terry Moore, of	.148	7	27	1	4	0	0	0	2	2	6	0
Red Munger, p	.250	1	4	0	1	0	0	0	0	0	2	0
Stan Musial, 1b	.222	7	27	3	6	4	1	0	4	4	2	1
Howie Pollet, p	.000	2	4	0	0	0	0	0	0	0	1	0
Del Rice, c	.500	3	6	2	3	1	0	0	0	2	0	0
Red Schoendienst, 2b	.233	7	30	3	7	1	0	0	1	0	2	1
Dick Sisler, ph	.000	2	2	0	0	0	0	0	0	0	0	0
Enos Slaughter, of	.320	7	25	5	8	1	1	1	2	4	3	0
Harry Walker, of	.412	7	17	3	7	2	0	0	6	4	2	0
Ted Wilks, p	.000	1	0	0	0	0	0	0	0	0	0	0
TOTAL	.259		232	28	60	19	2	1	27	19	30	3

PITCHER	W	L	ERA	G	GS	CG	SV	SHO	IP	H	ER	BB	SO
Johnny Beazley	0	0	0.00	1	0	0	0	0	1.0	1	0	0	1
Al Brazle	0	1	5.40	1	0	0	0	0	6.2	7	4	6	4
Harry Brecheen	3	0	0.45	3	2	2	0	1	20.0	14	1	5	11
Murry Dickson	0	1	3.86	2	2	0	0	0	14.0	11	6	4	7
Red Munger	1	0	1.00	1	1	1	0	0	9.0	9	1	3	2
Howie Pollet	0	1	3.48	2	2	1	0	0	10.1	12	4	4	3
Ted Wilks	0	0	0.00	1	0	0	0	0	1.0	2	0	0	0
TOTAL	4	3	2.32	11	7	4	0	1	62.0	56	16	22	28

BOS (A)

PLAYER/POS	AVG	G	AB	R	H	2B	3B	HR	RB	BB	SO	SB
Jim Bagby, p	.000	1	1	0	0	0	0	0	0	0	0	0
Mace Brown, p	.000	1	0	0	0	0	0	0	0	0	0	0
Paul Campbell, pr	.000	1	0	0	0	0	0	0	0	0	0	0
Leon Culberson, of-3	.222	5	9	1	2	0	0	1	1	1	2	1
Dom DiMaggio, of	.259	7	27	2	7	3	0	0	3	2	2	0
Joe Dobson, p	.000	3	3	0	0	0	0	0	0	0	2	0
Bobby Doerr, 2b	.409	6	22	1	9	1	0	1	3	2	2	0
Clem Dreisewerd, p	.000	1	0	0	0	0	0	0	0	0	0	0
Dave Ferriss, p	.000	2	6	0	0	0	0	0	0	0	1	0
Don Gutteridge, 2b-2	.400	3	5	1	2	0	0	0	0	1	0	0
Mickey Harris, p	.333	2	3	0	1	0	0	0	0	0	1	0
Pinky Higgins, 3b	.208	7	24	1	5	1	0	0	2	2	0	0
Tex Hughson, p	.333	3	3	0	1	0	0	0	0	1	0	0
Earl Johnson, p	.000	3	1	0	0	0	0	0	0	0	0	0
Bob Klinger, p	.000	1	0	0	0	0	0	0	0	0	0	0
Tom McBride, of-2	.167	5	12	0	2	0	0	0	1	0	1	0
Catfish Metkovich, ph	.500	2	2	1	1	1	0	0	0	0	0	0
Wally Moses, of	.417	4	12	1	5	0	0	0	0	1	2	0
Roy Partee, c	.100	5	10	1	1	0	0	0	1	1	2	0
Johnny Pesky, ss	.233	7	30	2	7	0	0	0	0	1	3	1
Rip Russell, 3b-1	1.000	2	2	1	2	0	0	0	0	0	0	0
Mike Ryba, p	.000	1	0	0	0	0	0	0	0	0	0	0
Hal Wagner, c	.000	5	13	0	0	0	0	0	0	0	1	0
Ted Williams, of	.200	7	25	2	5	0	0	0	1	5	5	0
Rudy York, 1b	.261	7	23	6	6	1	1	2	5	6	4	0
Bill Zuber, p	.000	1	0	0	0	0	0	0	0	0	0	0
TOTAL	.240		233	20	56	7	1	4	18	22	28	2

PITCHER	W	L	ERA	G	GS	CG	SV	SHO	IP	H	ER	BB	SO
Jim Bagby	0	0	3.00	1	0	0	0	0	3.0	6	1	1	1
Mace Brown	0	0	27.00	1	0	0	0	0	1.0	4	3	1	0
Joe Dobson	1	0	0.00	3	1	1	0	0	12.2	4	0	3	10
Clem Dreisewerd	0	0	0.00	1	0	0	0	0	0.1	0	0	0	0
Dave Ferriss	1	0	2.03	2	2	1	0	1	13.1	13	3	2	4
Mickey Harris	0	2	3.72	2	2	0	0	0	9.2	11	4	4	5
Tex Hughson	0	1	3.14	3	2	0	0	0	14.1	14	5	3	8
Earl Johnson	1	0	2.70	3	0	0	0	0	3.1	1	1	2	1
Bob Klinger	0	1	13.50	1	0	0	0	0	0.2	2	1	1	0
Mike Ryba	0	0	13.50	1	0	0	0	0	0.2	2	1	1	0
Bill Zuber	0	0	4.50	1	0	0	0	0	2.0	3	1	1	1
TOTAL	3	4	2.95	19	7	2	0	1	61.0	60	20	19	30

GAME 1 AT STL OCT 6

```
BOS  010 000 001 1   3 9 2
STL  000 001 0100     2 7 0
```
Pitchers: Hughson, JOHNSON (9) vs POLLET
Home Runs: York-BOS
Attendance: 36,218

GAME 2 AT STL OCT 7

```
BOS  000 000 000   0 4 1
STL  001 020 00X   3 6 0
```
Pitchers: HARRIS, Dobson (8) vs BRECHEEN
Attendance: 35,815

GAME 3 AT BOS OCT 9

```
STL  000 000 000   0 6 1
BOS  300 000 01X   4 8 0
```
Pitchers: DICKSON, Wilks (8) vs FERRISS
Home Runs: York-BOS
Attendance: 34,500

GAME 4 AT BOS OCT 10

```
STL  033 010 104   12 20 1
BOS  000 100 020    3  9 4
```
Pitchers: MUNGER vs HUGHSON, Bagby (3), Zuber (6), Brown (8), Ryba (9), Dreiseward (9)
Home Runs: Slaughter-STL, Doerr-BOS
Attendance: 35,645

GAME 5 AT BOS OCT 11

```
STL  010 000 002   3 4 1
BOS  110 001 30X   6 11 3
```
Pitchers: Pollet, BRAZLE (1), Beazley (8) vs DOBSON
Home Runs: Culberson-BOS
Attendance: 35,982

GAME 6 AT STL OCT 13

```
BOS  000 000 100   1 7 0
STL  003 000 01X   4 8 0
```
Pitchers: HARRIS, Hughson (3), Johnson (8) vs BRECHEEN
Attendance: 35,768

GAME 7 AT STL OCT 15

```
BOS  100 000 020   3 8 0
STL  010 020 01X   4 9 1
```
Pitchers: Ferriss, Dobson (5), KLINGER (8), Johnson (8) vs Dickson, BRECHEEN (8)
Attendance: 36,143

NEW YORK YANKEES (AL) 4, BROOKLYN DODGERS (NL) 3

Two of the most memorable plays in World Series history brought Brooklyn victory in Games 4 and 6, but when the Series had ended the Yankees were world champions for the 11th time. Dodgers ace Ralph Branca set New York down in order through the first four innings of Game 1, but the first five batters to face him in the fifth inning reached base. Branca was lifted, but before the inning was over five Yankees had crossed the plate—more than enough for their first win.

The Yankees won again the next day, rocking four Brooklyn pitchers for 15 hits and an easy 10–3 win. Brooklyn finally made its presence felt in Game 3, another heavy-hitting affair, scoring six times in the second inning to establish a lead the Yankees could not overcome. Both teams recorded 13 hits, but Dodgers fireman Hugh Casey extinguished the last flame in the seventh inning, and preserved a narrow 9–8 Brooklyn lead the rest of the way.

Shortstop Pee Wee Reese's error and a bases-loaded walk gave the Yankees an unearned run in the first inning of Game 4, and they earned a second run in the fourth. Meanwhile, Yankees pitcher Bill Bevens, although he averaged a walk an inning, had allowed no hits and only one run as the game entered the last of the ninth. Bevens retired two in the ninth, but walked his ninth and 10th batters (one intentionally), then lost both his no-hitter and the game as Dodgers pinch hitter Cookie Lavagetto doubled home the two baserunners to even the Series.

Spec Shea (the winning pitcher in Game 1) held Brooklyn to four hits and one run in Game 5. Joe DiMaggio homered in the fifth inning for New York's second run, enough to put the Yankees back in the Series lead. The Dodgers rebounded in Game 6 to build an early 4–0 lead, but the Yankees tied the score in the last of the third and took a lead in the fourth. Brooklyn regained the lead in the sixth with four runs, but when DiMaggio hit a long fly to left with two on in the bottom half of the inning, it looked as if the score would be tied. But substitute left fielder Al Gionfriddo (in what turned out to be his last big league game) raced to the bullpen fence 415 feet out to rob

DiMag of the home run. New York scored a run in the ninth, but thanks to Gionfriddo's catch it was not enough.

Brooklyn scored first in the finale with a pair of second-inning runs, but relievers Bill Bevens and Joe Page shut them out through the final seven innings as their teammates gradually built a Series-clinching 5–2 victory.

NY (A)

PLAYER/POS	AVG	G	AB	R	H	2B	3B	HR	RB	BB	SO	SB
Yogi Berra, c-4, of-2	.158	6	19	2	3	0	0	1	2	1	2	0
Bill Bevens, p	.000	2	4	0	0	0	0	0	0	0	2	0
Bobby Brown, ph	1.000	4	3	2	3	2	0	0	3	1	0	0
Spud Chandler, p	.000	1	0	0	0	0	0	0	0	0	0	0
Allie Clark, of-1	.500	3	2	1	1	0	0	0	1	1	0	0
Joe DiMaggio, of	.231	7	26	4	6	0	0	2	5	6	2	0
Karl Drews, p	.000	2	2	0	0	0	0	0	0	0	2	0
Lonny Frey, ph	.000	1	1	0	0	0	0	0	0	1	0	0
Tommy Henrich, of	.323	7	31	2	10	2	0	1	5	2	3	0
Ralph Houk, ph	1.000	1	1	0	1	0	0	0	0	0	0	0
Billy Johnson, 3b	.269	7	26	8	7	0	3	0	2	3	4	0
Johnny Lindell, of	.500	6	18	3	9	3	1	0	7	5	2	0
Sherm Lollar, c	.750	2	4	3	3	2	0	0	1	0	0	0
George McQuinn, 1b	.130	7	23	3	3	0	0	0	1	5	8	0
Bobo Newsom, p	.000	2	0	0	0	0	0	0	0	0	0	0
Joe Page, p	.000	4	4	0	0	0	0	0	0	0	1	0
Jack Phillips, 1b-1	.000	2	2	0	0	0	0	0	0	0	0	0
Vic Raschi, p	.000	2	0	0	0	0	0	0	0	0	0	0
Allie Reynolds, p	.500	2	4	2	2	0	0	0	1	0	0	0
Phil Rizzuto, ss	.308	7	26	3	8	1	0	0	2	4	0	2
Aaron Robinson, c	.200	3	10	2	2	0	0	0	1	2	1	0
Spec Shea, p	.400	3	5	0	2	1	0	0	1	0	2	0
Snuffy Stirnweiss, 2b	.259	7	27	3	7	0	1	0	3	8	8	0
Butch Wensloff, p	.000	1	0	0	0	0	0	0	0	0	0	0
TOTAL	.282		238	38	67	11	5	4	36	38	37	2

PITCHER	W	L	ERA	G	GS	CG	SV	SHO	IP	H	ER	BB	SO
Bill Bevens	0	1	2.38	2	1	1	0	0	11.1	3	3	11	7
Spud Chandler	0	0	9.00	1	0	0	0	0	2.0	2	2	3	1
Karl Drews	0	0	3.00	2	0	0	0	0	3.0	2	1	1	0
Bobo Newsom	0	1	19.29	2	1	0	0	0	2.1	6	5	2	0
Joe Page	1	1	4.15	4	0	0	1	0	13.0	12	6	2	7
Vic Raschi	0	0	6.75	2	0	0	0	0	1.1	2	1	0	1
Allie Reynolds	1	0	4.76	2	2	1	0	0	11.1	15	6	3	6
Spec Shea	2	0	2.35	3	3	1	0	0	15.1	10	4	8	10
Butch Wensloff	0	0	0.00	1	0	0	0	0	2.0	0	0	0	0
TOTAL	4	3	4.09	19	7	3	1	0	61.2	52	28	30	32

BRO (N)

PLAYER/POS	AVG	G	AB	R	H	2B	3B	HR	RB	BB	SO	SB
Dan Bankhead, pr	.000	1	0	1	0	0	0	0	0	0	0	0
Rex Barney, p	.000	3	1	0	0	0	0	0	0	0	0	0
Hank Behrman, p	.000	5	0	0	0	0	0	0	0	0	0	0
Bobby Bragan, ph	1.000	1	1	0	1	1	0	0	1	0	0	0
Ralph Branca, p	.000	3	4	0	0	0	0	0	0	0	1	0
Hugh Casey, p	.000	6	1	0	0	0	0	0	0	0	1	0
Bruce Edwards, c	.222	7	27	3	6	1	0	0	2	2	7	0
Carl Furillo, of	.353	6	17	2	6	0	0	0	3	3	0	0
Al Gionfriddo, of-1	.000	4	3	2	0	0	0	0	0	1	0	1
Hal Gregg, p	.000	3	3	0	0	0	0	0	0	1	1	0
Joe Hatten, p	.333	4	3	1	1	0	0	0	0	0	0	0
Gene Hermanski, of	.158	7	19	4	3	0	1	0	1	3	3	0
Gil Hodges, ph	.000	1	1	0	0	0	0	0	0	0	1	0
Spider Jorgensen, 3b	.200	7	20	1	4	3	0	0	3	2	4	0
Cookie Lavagetto, 3b-3	.143	5	7	0	1	1	0	0	3	0	2	0
Vic Lombardi, p-2	.000	3	3	0	0	0	0	0	0	0	1	0
Eddie Miksis, 2b-1, of-1	.250	5	4	1	1	0	0	0	0	0	1	0
Pee Wee Reese, ss	.304	7	23	5	7	1	0	0	4	6	3	3
Pete Reiser, of-3	.250	5	8	1	2	0	0	0	0	3	1	0
Jackie Robinson, 1b	.259	7	27	3	7	2	0	0	3	2	4	2
Eddie Stanky, 2b	.240	7	25	4	6	1	0	0	2	3	2	0
Harry Taylor, p	.000	1	0	0	0	0	0	0	0	0	0	0
Arky Vaughan, ph	.500	3	2	0	1	0	0	0	0	1	0	0
Dixie Walker, of	.222	7	27	1	6	1	0	1	4	3	1	1
TOTAL	.230		226	29	52	13	1	1	26	30	32	7

PITCHER	W	L	ERA	G	GS	CG	SV	SHO	IP	H	ER	BB	SO
Rex Barney	0	1	2.70	3	1	0	0	0	6.2	4	2	10	3
Hank Behrman	0	0	7.11	5	0	0	0	0	6.1	9	5	3	3
Ralph Branca	1	1	8.64	3	1	0	0	0	8.1	12	8	5	8
Hugh Casey	2	0	0.87	6	0	0	1	0	10.1	5	1	1	3
Hal Gregg	0	1	3.55	3	1	0	0	0	12.2	9	5	8	10
Joe Hatten	0	0	7.00	4	1	0	0	0	9.0	12	7	7	5
Vic Lombardi	0	1	12.15	2	2	0	0	0	6.2	14	9	1	5
Harry Taylor	0	0	–	1	1	0	0	0	0.0	2	0	1	0
TOTAL	3	4	5.55	27	7	0	1	0	60.0	67	37	38	37

GAME 1 AT NY SEPT 30

```
BRO 1 0 0 0 0 1   1 0 0    3 6 0
NY  0 0 0 0 5 0   0 0 X    5 4 0
```
Pitchers: BRANCA, Behrman (5), Casey (7) vs SHEA, Page (6)
Attendance: 73,365

GAME 2 AT NY OCT 1

```
BRO 0 0 1 1 0 0   0 0 1    3 9 2
NY  1 0 1 1 2 1   4 0 X   10 15 1
```
Pitchers: LOMBARDI, Gregg (5), Behrman (7), Barney (7) vs REYNOLDS
Home Runs: Walker-BRO, Henrich-NY
Attendance: 69,865

GAME 3 AT BRO OCT 2

```
NY  0 0 2 2 2 1   1 0 0    8 13 0
BRO 0 6 1 2 0 0   0 0 X    9 13 1
```
Pitchers: NEWSOM, Raschi (2), Drews (3), Chandler (4), Page (6) vs Hatten, Branca (5), CASEY (7)
Home Runs: DiMaggio-NY, Berra-NY
Attendance: 33,098

GAME 4 AT BRO OCT 3

```
NY  1 0 0 1 0 0   0 0 0    2 8 1
BRO 0 0 0 0 0 0   0 0 2    1 3 3
```
Pitchers: BEVENS vs Taylor, Gregg (1), Behrman (8), CASEY (9)
Attendance: 33,443

GAME 5 AT BRO OCT 4

```
NY  0 0 0 1 1 0   0 0 0    2 5 0
BRO 0 0 0 0 0 1   0 0 0    1 4 1
```
Pitchers: SHEA vs BARNEY, Hatten (5), Behrman (7), Casey (8)
Home Runs: DiMaggio-NY
Attendance: 34,379

GAME 6 AT NY OCT 5

```
BRO 2 0 2 0 0 4   0 0 0    8 12 1
NY  0 0 4 1 0 0   0 0 1    6 15 2
```
Pitchers: Lombardi, BRANCA (3), Hatten (6), Drews (3), PAGE (5) vs Newsom (6), Raschi (7), Wensloff (8)
Attendance: 74,065

GAME 7 AT NY OCT 6

```
BRO 0 2 0 0 0 0   0 0 0    2 7 0
NY  0 1 0 2 0 1   1 0 X    5 7 0
```
Pitchers: GREGG, Behrman (4), Hatten (6), Barney (6), Casey (7) vs Shea, Bevens (2), PAGE (5)
Attendance: 71,548

CLEVELAND INDIANS (AL) 4, BOSTON BRAVES (NL) 2

Boston outpitched and outhit Cleveland, and the clubs tied in runs scored. But the Braves scored most of their runs in one game, and the Indians, spreading theirs more evenly, took the Series. Boston ace Johnny Sain dueled Bob Feller in the opener. Feller gave up only two singles, but one of them followed a walk and a sacrifice (and a controversial pickoff play at second, in which the Boston runner was ruled safe although photos later showed him clearly out). Both teams registered eight hits in Game 2, but Cleveland's led to four runs, while Indians hurler Bob Lemon held Boston to just one—and that was unearned.

Cleveland's rookie sensation Gene Bearden shut out the Braves on five hits in Game 3 as the Series moved to Cleveland's huge Municipal Stadium. Bearden himself, after doubling in the third, scored on a Boston error what proved to be the winning run. A record 81,897 fans saw Sain face Steve Gromek in Game 4. Only five Indians hit Sain safely, but a first-inning single and double put Cleveland on the board, and Larry Doby's home run two innings later made the score 2–0. Boston's Marv Rickert homered in the seventh to narrow Cleveland's lead, but that ended the scoring.

Another attendance record was set at Game 5 as 86,288 fans gathered to watch Bob Feller sew up the title for Cleveland. They went home disappointed. In a game that featured five of the Series' eight home runs, Boston jumped ahead on Bob Elliott's three-run blast in the first. Dale Mitchell opened Cleveland's half of the inning with a home run, but Elliott neutralized it in the third with his second homer. The Indians drove out Boston starter Nelson Potter with four runs in the fourth inning (three coming on Jim Hegan's homer). But Warren Spahn (who had lost Game 2) hurled one-hit shutout relief over the final five frames as his Braves tied the game on Bill Salkeld's homer in the sixth, and blew out Feller and two relievers with six runs in the seventh. The fourth Indians pitcher, Satchel Paige (in his only World Series appearance), retired two batters to end the inning, but the damage had been done.

A day later though, back in Boston, Cleveland edged the Braves 4–3 for the title. Gene Bearden's relief pitching allowed two inherited baserunners to score in the eighth, but halted Boston's rally one run short of a tie.

CLE (A)

PLAYER/POS	AVG	G	AB	R	H	2B	3B	HR	RB	BB	SO	SB
Gene Bearden, p	.500	2	4	1	2	1	0	0	0	0	1	0
Ray Boone, ph	.000	1	1	0	0	0	0	0	0	0	0	0
Lou Boudreau, ss	.273	6	22	1	6	4	0	0	3	1	1	0
Russ Christopher, p	.000	1	0	0	0	0	0	0	0	0	0	0
Allie Clark, of	.000	1	3	0	0	0	0	0	0	0	1	0
Larry Doby, of	.318	6	22	1	7	1	0	1	2	2	4	0
Bob Feller, p	.000	2	4	0	0	0	0	0	0	0	2	0
Joe Gordon, 2b	.182	6	22	3	4	0	0	1	2	1	2	1
Steve Gromek, p	.000	1	3	0	0	0	0	0	0	0	1	0
Jim Hegan, c	.211	6	19	2	4	0	0	1	5	1	4	1
Wally Judnich, of	.077	4	13	1	1	0	0	0	1	1	4	0
Ken Keltner, 3b	.095	6	21	3	2	0	0	0	0	2	3	0
Bob Kennedy, of	.500	3	2	0	1	0	0	0	1	0	1	0
Ed Klieman, p	.000	1	0	0	0	0	0	0	0	0	0	0
Bob Lemon, p	.000	2	7	0	0	0	0	0	0	0	0	0
Dale Mitchell, of	.174	6	23	4	4	1	0	1	1	2	0	0
Bob Muncrief, p	.000	1	0	0	0	0	0	0	0	0	0	0
Satchel Paige, p	.000	1	0	0	0	0	0	0	0	0	0	0
Hal Peck, of	.000	1	0	0	0	0	0	0	0	0	0	0
Eddie Robinson, 1b	.300	6	20	0	6	0	0	0	0	1	1	0
Al Rosen, ph	.000	1	1	0	0	0	0	0	0	0	0	0
Joe Tipton, ph	.000	1	1	0	0	0	0	0	0	0	1	0
Thurman Tucker, of	.333	1	3	1	1	0	0	0	0	0	1	0
TOTAL	.199		191	17	38	7	0	4	16	12	26	2

PITCHER	W	L	ERA	G	GS	CG	SV	SHO	IP	H	ER	BB	SO
Gene Bearden	1	0	0.00	2	1	1	1	1	10.2	6	0	1	4
Russ Christopher	0	0	∞	1	0	0	0	0	0.0	2	1	0	0
Bob Feller	0	2	5.02	2	2	1	0	0	14.1	10	8	5	7
Steve Gromek	1	0	1.00	1	1	1	0	0	9.0	7	1	1	2
Ed Klieman	0	0	∞	1	0	0	0	0	0.0	1	3	2	0
Bob Lemon	2	0	1.65	2	2	1	0	0	16.1	16	3	7	6
Bob Muncrief	0	0	0.00	1	0	0	0	0	2.0	1	0	0	0
Satchel Paige	0	0	0.00	1	0	0	0	0	0.2	0	0	0	0
TOTAL	4	2	2.72	11	6	4	1	1	53.0	43	16	16	19

BOS (N)

PLAYER/POS	AVG	G	AB	R	H	2B	3B	HR	RB	BB	SO	SB
Red Barrett, p	.000	2	0	0	0	0	0	0	0	0	0	0
Vern Bickford, p	.000	1	0	0	0	0	0	0	0	0	0	0
Clint Conatser, of	.000	2	4	0	0	0	0	0	1	0	0	0
Alvin Dark, ss	.167	6	24	2	4	1	0	0	0	0	2	0
Bob Elliott, 3b	.333	6	21	4	7	0	0	2	5	2	2	0
Tommy Holmes, of	.192	6	26	3	5	0	0	0	1	0	0	0
Phil Masi, c	.125	5	8	1	1	1	0	0	1	0	0	0
Frank McCormick, 1b-1	.200	3	5	0	1	0	0	0	0	0	2	0
Mike McCormick, of	.261	6	23	1	6	0	0	0	2	0	4	0
Nelson Potter, p	.500	2	2	0	1	0	0	0	0	0	1	0
Marv Rickert, of	.211	5	19	2	4	0	0	1	2	0	4	0
Connie Ryan, ph	.000	2	1	0	0	0	0	0	0	0	1	0
Johnny Sain, p	.200	2	5	0	1	0	0	0	0	0	0	0
Bill Salkeld, c	.222	5	9	2	2	0	0	1	1	5	1	0
Ray Sanders, ph	.000	1	1	0	0	0	0	0	0	0	0	0
Sibby Sisti, 2b	.000	2	1	0	0	0	0	0	0	0	0	0
Warren Spahn, p	.000	3	4	0	0	0	0	0	1	0	1	0
Eddie Stanky, 2b	.286	6	14	0	4	1	0	0	1	7	0	0
Earl Torgeson, 1b	.389	5	18	2	7	3	0	0	1	2	1	1
Bill Voiselle, p	.000	2	2	0	0	0	0	0	0	0	0	0
TOTAL	.230		187	17	43	6	0	4	16	16	19	1

PITCHER	W	L	ERA	G	GS	CG	SV	SHO	IP	H	ER	BB	SO
Red Barrett	0	0	0.00	2	0	0	0	0	3.2	1	0	0	1
Vern Bickford	0	1	2.70	1	1	0	0	0	3.1	4	1	5	1
Nelson Potter	0	0	8.44	2	1	0	0	0	5.1	6	5	2	1
Johnny Sain	1	1	1.06	2	2	2	0	1	17.0	9	2	0	9
Warren Spahn	1	1	3.00	3	1	0	0	0	12.0	10	4	3	12
Bill Voiselle	0	1	2.53	2	1	0	0	0	10.2	8	3	2	2
TOTAL	2	4	2.60	12	6	2	0	1	52.0	38	15	12	26

GAME 1 AT BOS OCT 6

```
CLE 000 000 000   0 4 0
BOS 000 000 01X   1 2 2
```
Pitchers: FELLER vs SAIN
Attendance: 40,135

GAME 2 AT BOS OCT 7

```
CLE 000 210 001   4 8 1
BOS 100 000 000   1 8 3
```
Pitchers: LEMON vs SPAHN, Barrett (5), Potter (8)
Attendance: 39,633

GAME 3 AT CLE OCT 8

```
BOS 000 000 000   0 5 1
CLE 001 100 00X   2 5 0
```
Pitchers: BICKFORD, Voiselle (4), Barrett (8) vs BEARDEN
Attendance: 70,306

GAME 4 AT CLE OCT 9

```
BOS 000 000 100   1 7 0
CLE 101 000 00X   2 5 0
```
Pitchers: SAIN vs GROMEK
Home Runs: Doby-CLE, Rickert-BOS
Attendance: 81,897

GAME 5 AT CLE OCT 10

```
BOS 301 001 600   11 12 0
CLE 100 400 000    5 6 2
```
Pitchers: Potter, SPAHN (4) vs FELLER, Klieman (7), Christopher (7), Paige (7), Muncrief (8)
Home Runs: Elliott-BOS (2), Mitchell-CLE, Hegan-CLE, Salkeld-BOS
Attendance: 86,288

GAME 6 AT BOS OCT 11

```
CLE 001 002 010   4 10 0
BOS 000 100 020   3 9 0
```
Pitchers: LEMON, Bearden (8) vs VOISELLE, Spahn (8)
Home Runs: Gordon-CLE
Attendance: 40,103

NEW YORK YANKEES (AL) 4, BROOKLYN DODGERS (NL) 1

Casey Stengel, in the first of his 12 years as Yankees manager, edged his team past the Boston Red Sox for his first of 10 American League pennants, then past the Dodgers for his first of seven world championships. New York and Brooklyn traded 1–0 wins to begin the Series. In Game 1 Allie Reynolds dueled rookie Don Newcombe scorelessly through 8-1/2 innings—until Tommy Henrich led off the last of the ninth with a home run to win the game for the Yankees. Jackie Robinson scored after doubling off Vic Raschi in the second inning of Game 2 for that game's only score, while Dodgers ace Preacher Roe permitted just six scattered hits—never more than one per inning.

The teams entered the ninth inning of Game 3 tied 1–1. But in the top of the ninth, Dodgers starter Ralph Branca, after loading the bases on two walks and a single, gave up another single to pinch hitter Johnny Mize for two runs. Jerry Coleman's single off reliever Jack Banta drove in another run before the third out was made. In the last of the ninth, Yankees fireman Joe Page (who had held Brooklyn scoreless since coming on with the bases loaded in the fourth) finally weakened. But after yielding solo homers to Luis Olmo and Roy Campanella, he struck out pinch hitter Bruce Edwards for New York's second win.

The Yankees' victory in Game 4 came a little easier. They scored first, driving out starter Don Newcombe with three runs in the fourth, and rapping reliever Joe Hatten for three more runs an inning later. Brooklyn retaliated in the sixth, sending Yankees starter Ed Lopat to the showers with seven singles for four runs. But Allie Reynolds came on for 3-1/3 innings of no-hit relief to preserve the Yankees lead—and his Series 0.00 earned run average.

After four closely contested games, the Yankees erupted in Game 5 for 10 runs in the first six innings as Brooklyn was held to just two. In the last of the seventh, the Dodgers came back, driving out starter Vic Raschi with a four-run rally, capped by Gil Hodges' three-run homer. But Joe Page came on to get the final out of the seventh, and held the Dodgers

scoreless over the final two innings to bring the Yankees' world titles to an even dozen.

NY (A)

PLAYER/POS	AVG	G	AB	R	H	2B	3B	HR	RB	BB	SO	SB
Hank Bauer, of	.167	3	6	0	1	0	0	0	0	0	0	0
Yogi Berra, c	.063	4	16	2	1	0	0	0	1	1	3	0
Bobby Brown, 3b-3	.500	4	12	4	6	1	2	0	5	2	2	0
Tommy Byrne, p	1.000	1	1	0	1	0	0	0	0	0	0	0
Gerry Coleman, 2b	.250	5	20	0	5	3	0	0	4	0	4	0
Joe DiMaggio, of	.111	5	18	2	2	0	0	1	2	3	5	0
Tommy Henrich, 1b	.263	5	19	4	5	0	0	1	1	3	0	0
Billy Johnson, 3b	.143	2	7	0	1	0	0	0	0	0	2	1
Johnny Lindell, of	.143	2	7	0	1	0	0	0	0	0	2	0
Ed Lopat, p	.333	1	3	0	1	1	0	0	1	0	0	0
Cliff Mapes, of	.100	4	10	3	1	1	0	0	2	2	4	0
Johnny Mize, ph	1.000	2	2	0	2	0	0	0	2	0	0	0
Gus Niarhos, c	.000	1	0	0	0	0	0	0	0	0	0	0
Joe Page, p	.000	3	4	0	0	0	0	0	0	0	2	0
Vic Raschi, p	.200	2	5	0	1	0	0	0	1	1	1	0
Allie Reynolds, p	.500	2	4	0	2	1	0	0	0	0	1	0
Phil Rizzuto, ss	.167	5	18	2	3	0	0	0	1	3	1	1
Charlie Silvera, c	.000	1	2	0	0	0	0	0	0	0	0	0
Snuffy Stirnweiss, ph	.000	1	0	0	0	0	0	0	0	0	0	0
Gene Woodling, of	.400	3	10	4	4	3	0	0	0	3	0	0
TOTAL	.226		164	21	37	10	2	2	20	18	27	2

PITCHER	W	L	ERA	G	GS	CG	SV	SHO	IP	H	ER	BB	SO
Tommy Byrne	0	0	2.70	1	1	0	0	0	3.1	2	1	2	1
Ed Lopat	1	0	6.35	1	1	0	0	0	5.2	9	4	1	4
Joe Page	1	0	2.00	3	0	0	1	0	9.0	6	2	3	8
Vic Raschi	1	1	4.30	2	2	0	0	0	14.2	15	7	5	11
Allie Reynolds	1	0	0.00	2	1	1	1	1	12.1	2	0	4	14
TOTAL	4	1	2.80	9	5	1	2	1	45.0	34	14	15	38

BRO (N)

PLAYER/POS	AVG	G	AB	R	H	2B	3B	HR	RB	BB	SO	SB
Jack Banta, p	.000	3	1	0	0	0	0	0	0	0	0	0
Rex Barney, p	.000	1	0	0	0	0	0	0	0	0	0	0
Ralph Branca, p	.000	1	3	0	0	0	0	0	0	0	3	0
Tommy Brown, ph	.000	2	2	0	0	0	0	0	0	0	1	0
Roy Campanella, c	.267	5	15	2	4	1	0	1	2	3	1	0
Billy Cox, 3b-1	.333	2	3	0	1	0	0	0	0	0	1	0
Bruce Edwards, ph	.500	2	2	0	1	0	0	0	0	1	0	0
Carl Erskine, p	.000	2	0	0	0	0	0	0	0	0	0	0
Carl Furillo, of-2	.125	3	8	0	1	0	0	0	1	0	0	0
Joe Hatten, p	.000	2	0	0	0	0	0	0	0	0	0	0
Gene Hermanski, of	.308	4	13	1	4	0	1	0	2	3	3	0
Gil Hodges, 1b	.235	5	17	2	4	0	0	1	4	1	4	0
Spider Jorgensen, 3b-3	.182	4	11	1	2	2	0	0	0	2	2	0
Mike McCormick, of	.000	1	0	0	0	0	0	0	0	0	0	0
Eddie Miksis, 3b-2	.286	3	7	0	2	1	0	0	0	0	1	0
Paul Minner, p	.000	1	0	0	0	0	0	0	0	0	0	0
Don Newcombe, p	.000	2	4	0	0	0	0	0	0	0	3	0
Luis Olmo, of	.273	4	11	2	3	0	0	1	2	0	2	0
Erv Palica, p	.000	1	0	0	0	0	0	0	0	0	0	0
Marv Rackley, of	.000	2	5	0	0	0	0	0	0	0	2	0
Pee Wee Reese, ss	.316	5	19	2	6	1	0	1	2	1	0	1
Jackie Robinson, 2b	.188	5	16	2	3	1	0	0	2	4	2	0
Preacher Roe, p	.000	1	3	0	0	0	0	0	0	0	3	0
Duke Snider, of	.143	5	21	2	3	1	0	0	0	0	8	0
Dick Whitman, ph	.000	1	1	0	0	0	0	0	0	0	1	0
TOTAL	.210		162	14	34	7	1	4	14	15	38	1

PITCHER	W	L	ERA	G	GS	CG	SV	SHO	IP	H	ER	BB	SO
Jack Banta	0	0	3.18	3	0	0	0	0	5.2	5	2	1	4
Rex Barney	0	1	16.88	1	1	0	0	0	2.2	3	5	6	2
Ralph Branca	0	1	4.15	1	1	0	0	0	8.2	4	4	4	6
Carl Erskine	0	0	16.20	2	0	0	0	0	1.2	3	3	1	0
Joe Hatten	0	0	16.20	2	0	0	0	0	1.2	4	3	2	0
Paul Minner	0	0	0.00	1	0	0	0	0	1.0	1	0	0	0
Don Newcombe	0	2	3.09	2	2	1	0	0	11.2	10	4	3	11
Erv Palica	0	0	0.00	1	0	0	0	0	2.0	1	0	1	1
Preacher Roe	1	0	0.00	1	1	1	0	1	9.0	6	0	0	3
TOTAL	1	4	4.30	14	5	2	0	1	44.0	37	21	18	27

GAME 1 AT NY OCT 5

```
BRO 000 000 000   0 2 0
NY  000 000 001   1 5 1
```
Pitchers: NEWCOMBE vs REYNOLDS
Home Runs: Henrich-NY
Attendance: 66,224

GAME 2 AT NY OCT 6

```
BRO 010 000 000   1 7 2
NY  000 000 000   0 6 1
```
Pitchers: ROE vs RASCHI, Page (9)
Attendance: 70,053

GAME 3 AT BRO OCT 7

```
NY  001 000 003   4 5 0
BRO 000 100 002   3 5 0
```
Pitchers: Byrne, PAGE (4) vs BRANCA, Banta (9)
Home Runs: Reese-BRO, Olmo-BRO, Campanella-BRO
Attendance: 32,788

GAME 4 AT BRO OCT 8

```
NY  000 330 000   6 10 0
BRO 000 004 000   4 9 1
```
Pitchers: LOPAT, Reynolds (6) vs NEWCOMBE, Hatten (4), Erskine (6), Banta (7)
Attendance: 33,934

GAME 5 AT BRO OCT 9

```
NY  203 113 000   10 11 1
BRO 001 001 400    6 11 2
```
Pitchers: RASCHI, Page (7) vs BARNEY, Banta (3), Erskine (6), Hatten (6), Palica (7), Minner (9)
Home Runs: DiMaggio-NY, Hodges-BRO
Attendance: 33,711

NEW YORK YANKEES (AL) 4, PHILADELPHIA PHILLIES (NL) 0

Philadelphia's Whiz Kids, who had capped an exciting pennant race with the Phillies' first flag in 35 years, carried the excitement into the World Series but couldn't quite catch up with the Yankees. New York scored only one run in the opener; Philadelphia didn't score any. The Phillies did score a run in the second game, but the Yankees scored two. In Game 3 the Phillies scored two runs, the Yankees three.

Jim Konstanty, the National League's ace reliever (and MVP), started his first major league game in four years to lead off the Series, and held the Yankees to just four hits in eight innings of work. But Bobby Brown's double in the fourth was followed by two long flies which moved Brown around to the plate—all the scoring New York needed as Vic Raschi held the Phillies to two singles and a walk.

Robin Roberts and Allie Reynolds dueled in Game 2. New York scored first with a run on a walk and two singles in the second inning, but two Philadelphia singles and a fly to left tied the game in the last of the fifth. There matters stood until the top of the tenth, when Joe DiMaggio led off with a home run to the upper deck in left. Reynolds held the Phillies in the bottom of the tenth for the second Yankees win.

The Phillies took a lead for the only time in the Series when they broke a 1–1 tie with a run in the seventh inning of Game 3. But New York scored on a Phillies error to tie the game again in the eighth, and in the last of the ninth—with two outs—Yankees Gene Woodling, Phil Rizzuto, and Jerry Coleman singled to produce the winning run.

Rookie sensation Whitey Ford started Game 4 and held Philadelphia scoreless into the ninth inning as his Yankees scored twice in the first and three more times in the sixth. He was taken out with two away in the ninth after two singles, a hit batsman, and a Yankee error had permitted two Phillies to score. But reliever Allie Reynolds struck out the final batter to secure a Series sweep for the Yankees.

NY (A)

PLAYER/POS	AVG	G	AB	R	H	2B	3B	HR	RB	BB	SO	SB
Hank Bauer, of	.133	4	15	0	2	0	0	0	1	0	0	0
Yogi Berra, c	.200	4	15	2	3	0	0	1	2	2	1	0
Bobby Brown, 3b	.333	4	12	2	4	1	1	0	1	0	0	0
Gerry Coleman, 2b	.286	4	14	2	4	1	0	0	3	2	0	0
Joe Collins, 1b	.000	1	0	0	0	0	0	0	0	0	0	0
Joe DiMaggio, of	.308	4	13	2	4	1	0	1	2	3	1	0
Tom Ferrick, p	.000	1	0	0	0	0	0	0	0	0	0	0
Whitey Ford, p	.000	1	3	0	0	0	0	0	0	0	2	0
Johnny Hopp, 1b	.000	3	2	0	0	0	0	0	0	0	0	0
Jackie Jensen, pr	.000	1	0	0	0	0	0	0	0	0	0	0
Billy Johnson, 3b	.000	4	6	0	0	0	0	0	0	0	3	0
Ed Lopat, p	.500	1	2	0	1	0	0	0	0	0	1	0
Cliff Mapes, of	.000	1	4	0	0	0	0	0	0	0	1	0
Johnny Mize, 1b	.133	4	15	0	2	0	0	0	0	0	0	0
Vic Raschi, p	.333	1	3	0	1	0	0	0	0	0	0	0
Allie Reynolds, p	.333	2	3	0	1	0	0	0	0	1	2	0
Phil Rizzuto, ss	.143	4	14	1	2	0	0	0	0	3	0	1
Gene Woodling, of	.429	4	14	2	6	0	0	0	1	2	0	0
TOTAL	.222		135	11	30	3	1	2	10	13	12	1

PITCHER	W	L	ERA	G	GS	CG	SV	SHO	IP	H	ER	BB	SO
Tom Ferrick	1	0	0.00	1	0	0	0	0	1.0	1	0	1	0
Whitey Ford	1	0	0.00	1	1	0	0	0	8.2	7	0	1	7
Ed Lopat	0	0	2.25	1	1	0	0	0	8.0	9	2	0	5
Vic Raschi	1	0	0.00	1	1	1	0	1	9.0	2	0	1	5
Allie Reynolds	1	0	0.87	2	1	1	1	0	10.1	7	1	4	7
TOTAL	4	0	0.73	6	4	2	1	1	37.0	26	3	7	24

PHI (N)

PLAYER/POS	AVG	G	AB	R	H	2B	3B	HR	RB	BB	SO	SB
Richie Ashburn, of	.176	4	17	0	3	1	0	0	1	0	4	0
Jimmy Bloodworth, 2b	.000	1	0	0	0	0	0	0	0	0	0	0
Putsy Caballero, ph	.000	3	1	0	0	0	0	0	0	0	1	0
Del Ennis, of	.143	4	14	1	2	1	0	0	0	0	0	0
Mike Goliat, 2b	.214	4	14	1	3	0	0	0	1	1	2	0
Granny Hamner, ss	.429	4	14	1	6	2	1	0	0	1	2	1
Ken Heintzelman, p	.000	1	2	0	0	0	0	0	0	0	0	0
Ken Johnson, pr	.000	1	0	1	0	0	0	0	0	0	0	0
Willie Jones, 3b	.286	4	14	1	4	1	0	0	0	0	3	0
Jim Konstanty, p	.250	3	4	0	1	0	0	0	0	0	1	0
Stan Lopata, c-1	.000	2	1	0	0	0	0	0	0	0	1	0
Jackie Mayo, of-1	.000	3	0	0	0	0	0	0	0	1	0	0
Russ Meyer, p	.000	2	0	0	0	0	0	0	0	0	0	0
Bob Miller, p	.000	1	0	0	0	0	0	0	0	0	0	0
Robin Roberts, p	.000	2	2	0	0	0	0	0	0	0	1	0
Andy Seminick, c	.182	4	11	0	2	0	0	0	0	1	3	0
Ken Silvestri, c	.000	1	0	0	0	0	0	0	0	0	0	0
Dick Sisler, of	.059	4	17	0	1	0	0	0	1	0	5	0
Eddie Waitkus, 1b	.267	4	15	0	4	1	0	0	0	2	0	0
Dick Whitman, ph	.000	3	2	0	0	0	0	0	0	0	1	0
TOTAL	.203		128	5	26	6	1	0	3	7	24	1

PITCHER	W	L	ERA	G	GS	CG	SV	SHO	IP	H	ER	BB	SO
Ken Heintzelman	0	0	1.17	1	1	0	0	0	7.2	4	1	6	3
Jim Konstanty	0	1	2.40	3	1	0	0	0	15.0	9	4	4	3
Russ Meyer	0	1	5.40	2	0	0	0	0	1.2	4	1	0	1
Bob Miller	0	1	27.00	1	1	0	0	0	0.1	2	1	0	0
Robin Roberts	0	1	1.64	2	1	1	0	0	11.0	11	2	3	5
TOTAL	0	4	2.27	9	4	1	0	0	35.2	30	9	13	12

GAME 1 AT PHI OCT 4

NY	000 100 000	1	5 0
PHI	000 000 000	0	2 1

Pitchers: RASCHI vs KONSTANTY, Meyer (9)
Attendance: 30,746

GAME 2 AT PHI OCT 5

NY	010 000 0001	2	10 0
PHI	000 010 0000	1	7 0

Pitchers: REYNOLDS vs ROBERTS
Home Runs: DiMaggio-NY
Attendance: 32,660

GAME 3 AT NY OCT 6

PHI	000 001 100	2	10 2
NY	001 000 011	3	7 0

Pitchers: Heintzelman, Konstanty (8), MEYER (9) vs Lopat, FERRICK (9)
Attendance: 64,505

GAME 4 AT NY OCT 7

PHI	000 000 002	2	7 1
NY	200 003 00X	5	8 2

Pitchers: MILLER, Konstanty (1), Roberts (8) vs FORD, Reynolds (9)
Attendance: 68,098

NEW YORK YANKEES (AL) 4, NEW YORK GIANTS (NL) 2

The Giants—who caught Brooklyn with a tremendous late-season drive, then defeated them for the pennant on Bobby Thomson's ninth-inning home run in Game 3 of the tie-breaker playoff series—carried their momentum through Game 3 of the World Series before bowing to the Yankees. Dave Koslo (the only Giants starter not to see action in the playoff) pitched the Series opener and held the Yankees to one run. Monte Irvin's steal of home for the Giants' second run in the top of the first was enough for the win, but Alvin Dark made Koslo's lead more secure with a three-run homer in the sixth.

The Yankees evened the Series in Game 2, scoring two early runs (one of them Joe Collins' home run) off Larry Jansen, and holding on for the win behind Ed Lopat's five-hit pitching. But the Giants regained the lead in Game 3 with five unearned runs (three of them on Whitey Lockman's homer) in a fifth inning prolonged by two Yankees errors, as pitchers Jim Hearn and Sheldon Jones combined to hold the Bronx Bombers to five hits and a pair of runs (though Hearn issued eight walks).

But that was the end of the Giants' drive. Although they scored first in both Games 4 and 5 with first-inning runs, they couldn't hold the lead either time. In Game 4 Allie Reynolds held the Giants to two runs as his Yankees scored six—including a two-run homer by Joe DiMaggio in the fifth inning that proved to be the last home run of his career. DiMag drove in three more runs in Game 5, as did Phil Rizzuto, and rookie infielder Gil McDougald contributed a grand slam as the Bombers earned their nickname in obliterating Giants pitching with 13 runs. Ed Lopat, meanwhile, hurled his second five-hitter in four days to give the Yanks the Series lead.

Hank Bauer tripled with the bases full in the sixth inning of Game 6 to break a tie and give the Yankees a 4–1 lead. The Giants loaded the bases with three straight singles to open the top of the ninth, and scored two runners on successive flies to left, to come within one run of a tie. But pinch hitter Sal Yvars (in his only Series at bat) lined out to right and the Yankees had their 14th world title.

NY (A)

PLAYER/POS	AVG	G	AB	R	H	2B	3B	HR	RB	BB	SO	SB
Hank Bauer, of	.167	6	18	0	3	0	1	0	3	1	1	0
Yogi Berra, c	.261	6	23	4	6	1	0	0	0	2	1	0
Bobby Brown, 3b-4	.357	5	14	1	5	1	0	0	0	2	1	0
Gerry Coleman, 2b	.250	5	8	2	2	0	0	0	0	1	2	0
Joe Collins, 1b-6, of-1	.222	6	18	2	4	0	0	1	3	2	1	0
Joe DiMaggio, of	.261	6	23	3	6	2	0	1	5	2	4	0
Bobby Hogue, p	.000	2	0	0	0	0	0	0	0	0	0	0
Johnny Hopp, ph	.000	1	0	0	0	0	0	0	0	1	0	0
Bob Kuzava, p	.000	1	0	0	0	0	0	0	0	0	0	0
Ed Lopat, p	.125	2	8	0	1	0	0	0	1	0	2	0
Mickey Mantle, of	.200	2	5	1	1	0	0	0	0	2	1	0
Billy Martin, pr	.000	1	0	1	0	0	0	0	0	0	0	0
Gil McDougald, 3b-5,2b-4	.261	6	23	2	6	1	0	1	7	2	2	0
Johnny Mize, 1b-2	.286	4	7	2	2	1	0	0	1	2	0	0
Tom Morgan, p	.000	1	0	0	0	0	0	0	0	0	0	0
Joe Ostrowski, p	.000	1	0	0	0	0	0	0	0	0	0	0
Vic Raschi, p	.000	2	2	0	0	0	0	0	0	0	2	0
Allie Reynolds, p	.333	2	6	0	2	0	0	0	1	0	1	0
Phil Rizzuto, ss	.320	6	25	5	8	0	0	1	3	2	3	0
Johnny Sain, p	.000	1	1	0	0	0	0	0	0	0	0	0
Gene Woodling, of-5	.167	6	18	6	3	1	1	1	1	5	3	0
TOTAL	.246		199	29	49	7	2	5	25	26	23	0

PITCHER	W	L	ERA	G	GS	CG	SV	SHO	IP	H	ER	BB	SO
Bobby Hogue	0	0	0.00	2	0	0	0	0	2.2	1	0	0	0
Bob Kuzava	0	0	0.00	1	0	0	1	0	1.0	0	0	0	0
Ed Lopat	2	0	0.50	2	2	2	0	0	18.0	10	1	3	4
Tom Morgan	0	0	0.00	1	0	0	0	0	2.0	2	0	1	3
Joe Ostrowski	0	0	0.00	1	0	0	0	0	2.0	1	0	0	1
Vic Raschi	1	1	0.87	2	2	0	0	0	10.1	12	1	8	4
Allie Reynolds	1	1	4.20	2	2	1	0	0	15.0	16	7	11	8
Johnny Sain	0	0	9.00	1	0	0	0	0	2.0	4	2	2	2
TOTAL	4	2	1.87	12	6	3	1	0	53.0	46	11	25	22

NY (N)

PLAYER/POS	AVG	G	AB	R	H	2B	3B	HR	RB	BB	SO	SB
Al Corwin, p	.000	1	0	0	0	0	0	0	0	0	0	0
Alvin Dark, ss	.417	6	24	5	10	3	0	1	4	2	3	0
Clint Hartung, of	.000	2	4	0	0	0	0	0	0	0	0	0
Jim Hearn, p	.000	2	3	0	0	0	0	0	0	0	1	0
Monte Irvin, of	.458	6	24	3	11	0	1	0	2	2	1	2
Larry Jansen, p	.000	3	2	0	0	0	0	0	0	0	0	0
Sheldon Jones, p	.000	2	0	0	0	0	0	0	0	0	0	0
Monte Kennedy, p	.000	2	0	0	0	0	0	0	0	0	0	0
Alex Konikowski, p	.000	1	0	0	0	0	0	0	0	0	0	0
Dave Koslo, p	.000	2	5	0	0	0	0	0	0	0	2	0
Whitey Lockman, 1b	.240	6	25	1	6	2	0	1	4	1	2	0
Jack Lohrke, ph	.000	2	2	0	0	0	0	0	0	0	1	0
Sal Maglie, p	.000	1	1	0	0	0	0	0	0	0	1	0
Willie Mays, of	.182	6	22	1	4	0	0	0	1	2	2	0
Ray Noble, c	.000	2	2	0	0	0	0	0	0	0	1	0
Bill Rigney, ph	.250	4	4	0	1	0	0	0	1	0	1	0
Hank Schenz, pr	.000	1	0	0	0	0	0	0	0	0	0	0
George Spencer, p	.000	2	0	0	0	0	0	0	0	0	0	0
Eddie Stanky, 2b	.136	6	22	3	3	0	0	0	1	3	2	0
Hank Thompson, of	.143	5	14	3	2	0	0	0	0	5	2	0
Bobby Thomson, 3b	.238	6	21	1	5	1	0	0	2	5	0	0
Wes Westrum, c	.235	6	17	1	4	1	0	0	0	5	3	0
Davey Williams, ph	.000	2	1	0	0	0	0	0	0	0	0	0
Sal Yvars, ph	.000	1	1	0	0	0	0	0	0	0	0	0
TOTAL	.237		194	18	46	7	1	2	15	25	22	2

PITCHER	W	L	ERA	G	GS	CG	SV	SHO	IP	H	ER	BB	SO
Al Corwin	0	0	0.00	1	0	0	0	0	1.2	1	0	0	1
Jim Hearn	1	0	1.04	2	1	0	0	0	8.2	5	1	8	1
Larry Jansen	0	2	6.30	3	2	0	0	0	10.0	8	7	4	6
Sheldon Jones	0	0	2.08	2	0	0	1	0	4.1	5	1	1	2
Monte Kennedy	0	0	6.00	2	0	0	0	0	3.0	3	2	1	4
Alex Konikowski	0	0	0.00	1	0	0	0	0	1.0	1	0	0	0
Dave Koslo	1	1	3.00	2	2	1	0	0	15.0	12	5	7	6
Sal Maglie	0	1	7.20	1	1	0	0	0	5.0	8	4	2	3
George Spencer	0	0	18.90	2	0	0	0	0	3.1	6	7	3	0
TOTAL	2	4	4.67	16	6	1	1	0	52.0	49	27	26	23

GAME 1 AT NY-A OCT 4

NY-N 2 0 0   0 0 3   0 0 0   5 10 1
NY-A 0 0 0   0 0 0   0 0 1   1 7 1
Pitchers: KOSLO vs REYNOLDS, Hogue (7), Morgan (8)
Home Runs: Dark-NY(N)
Attendance: 65,673

GAME 2 AT NY-A OCT 5

NY-N 0 0 0   0 0 0   1 0 0   1 5 1
NY-A 1 1 0   0 0 0   0 1 X   3 6 0
Pitchers: JANSEN, Spencer (7) vs LOPAT
Home Runs: Collins-NY(A)
Attendance: 66,018

GAME 3 AT NY-N OCT 6

NY-A 0 0 0   0 0 0   0 1 1   2 5 2
NY-N 0 1 0   0 5 0   0 0 X   6 7 2
Pitchers: RASCHI, Ostrowski (7) vs HEARN, Jones (8)
Home Runs: Lockman-NY(N), Woodling-NY(A)
Attendance: 52,035

GAME 4 AT NY-N OCT 8

NY-A 0 1 0   1 2 0   2 0 0   6 12 0
NY-N 1 0 0   0 0 0   0 0 1   2 8 2
Pitchers: REYNOLDS vs MAGLIE, Jones (6), Kennedy (9)
Home Runs: DiMaggio-NY(A)
Attendance: 49,010

GAME 5 AT NY-N OCT 9

NY-A 0 0 5   2 0 2   4 0 0   13 12 1
NY-N 1 0 0   0 0 0   0 0 0   1 5 3
Pitchers: LOPAT vs JANSEN, Kennedy (4), Spencer (6), Corwin (7), Konikowski (9)
Home Runs: McDougald-NY(A), Rizzuto-NY(A)
Attendance: 47,530

GAME 6 AT NY-A OCT 10

NY-N 0 0 0   0 1 0   0 0 2   3 11 1
NY-A 1 0 0   0 0 3   0 0 X   4 7 0
Pitchers: KOSLO, Hearn (7), Jansen (8) vs RASCHI, Sain (7), Kuzava (9)
Attendance: 61,711

NEW YORK YANKEES (AL) 4, BROOKLYN DODGERS (NL) 3

In four of the seven games, home runs provided the margin of victory. Homers accounted for five of the six runs scored in the opener, with Duke Snider's two-run blast in the sixth putting Brooklyn ahead to stay. Star Dodgers reliever Joe Black, in only his third start of the year, held New York to six hits and two runs in defeating Yankees ace Allie Reynolds.

In Game 2 Billy Martin's three-run shot was the centerpiece. Vic Raschi tossed a three-hitter. Brooklyn needed no homers to regain the Series advantage in Game 3. In the top of the ninth, with the Dodgers leading by a run, Pee Wee Reese and Jackie Robinson singled (driving out starter Ed Lopat) and pulled a double steal. Both then scored on a passed ball. Yankees pinch hitter Johnny Mize homered in the last of the ninth, but Preacher Roe escaped without further scoring for a complete-game 5–3 win.

Black opposed Reynolds again in Game 4 and bettered his earlier performance, holding New York to three hits and one run (a Mize homer) in seven innings. But Reynolds improved even more, fanning 10 as he shut the Dodgers out.

Snider hit his second homer of the Series and Mize his third in the fifth inning of Game 5. Mize's shot put New York ahead, but Brooklyn tied the game in the seventh and took a 6–5 lead when Snider doubled home a run in the 11th. Right fielder Carl Furillo's leaping catch in the last of the 11th robbed Mize of another home run, and starter Carl Erskine held on for the win, giving Brooklyn a 3–2 Series lead.

Snider's home run in the last of the sixth ended Vic Raschi's shutout in Game 6, but Yogi Berra, the first Yankee up in the seventh, tied the game and spoiled Billy Loes' shutout with his home run, and pitcher Raschi singled home the go-ahead run two outs later. Mickey Mantle's blast in the eighth (the first of his record 18 World Series home runs) made the score 3–1. Snider's fourth homer of the Series gave the Dodgers a second run in the eighth, but Allie Reynolds relieved Raschi and prevented further scoring, sending the Series to a seventh game.

Joe Black traded three shutout innings with Ed Lopat in the finale

before both clubs scored single runs in the fourth and fifth innings. Mantle homered off Black in the sixth for a third run that proved the Series winner, as three Yankees relievers held Brooklyn scoreless through the final four frames.

NY (A)

PLAYER/POS	AVG	G	AB	R	H	2B	3B	HR	RB	BB	SO	SB
Hank Bauer, of	.056	7	18	2	1	0	0	0	1	4	3	0
Yogi Berra, c	.214	7	28	2	6	1	0	2	3	2	4	0
Ewell Blackwell, p	.000	1	1	0	0	0	0	0	0	0	0	0
Joe Collins, 1b	.000	6	12	1	0	0	0	0	0	1	3	0
Tom Gorman, p	.000	1	0	0	0	0	0	0	0	0	0	0
Ralph Houk, ph	.000	1	1	0	0	0	0	0	0	0	0	0
Bob Kuzava, p	.000	1	1	0	0	0	0	0	0	0	0	0
Ed Lopat, p	.333	2	3	0	1	0	0	0	1	1	1	0
Mickey Mantle, of	.345	7	29	5	10	1	1	2	3	3	4	0
Billy Martin, 2b	.217	7	23	2	5	0	0	1	4	2	2	0
Gil McDougald, 3b	.200	7	25	5	5	0	0	1	3	5	2	1
Johnny Mize, 1b-4	.400	5	15	3	6	1	0	3	6	3	1	0
Irv Noren, of-3	.300	4	10	0	3	0	0	0	1	1	3	0
Vic Raschi, p	.167	3	6	0	1	0	0	0	1	1	2	0
Allie Reynolds, p	.000	4	7	0	0	0	0	0	0	0	2	0
Phil Rizzuto, ss	.148	7	27	2	4	1	0	0	0	0	5	0
Johnny Sain, p-1	.000	2	3	0	0	0	0	0	0	0	0	0
Ray Scarborough, p	.000	1	0	0	0	0	0	0	0	0	0	0
Gene Woodling, of-6	.348	7	23	4	8	1	1	1	1	3	3	0
TOTAL	.216		232	26	50	5	2	10	24	31	32	1

PITCHER	W	L	ERA	G	GS	CG	SV	SHO	IP	H	ER	BB	SO
Ewell Blackwell	0	0	7.20	1	1	0	0	0	5.0	4	4	3	4
Tom Gorman	0	0	0.00	1	0	0	0	0	0.2	1	0	0	0
Bob Kuzava	0	0	0.00	1	0	0	1	0	2.2	0	0	0	2
Ed Lopat	0	1	4.76	2	2	0	0	0	11.1	14	6	4	3
Vic Raschi	2	0	1.59	3	2	1	0	0	17.0	12	3	8	18
Allie Reynolds	2	1	1.77	4	2	1	1	1	20.1	12	4	6	18
Johnny Sain	0	1	3.00	1	1	0	0	0	6.0	6	2	3	3
Ray Scarborough	0	0	9.00	1	0	0	0	0	1.0	1	1	0	1
TOTAL	4	3	2.81	14	7	2	2	1	64.0	50	20	24	49

BRO (N)

PLAYER/POS	AVG	G	AB	R	H	2B	3B	HR	RB	BB	SO	SB
Sandy Amoros, ph	.000	1	0	0	0	0	0	0	0	0	0	0
Joe Black, p	.000	3	6	0	0	0	0	0	0	1	6	0
Roy Campanella, c	.214	7	28	0	6	0	0	0	1	1	6	0
Billy Cox, 3b	.296	7	27	4	8	2	0	0	3	3	4	0
Carl Erskine, p	.000	3	6	1	0	0	0	0	0	0	1	0
Carl Furillo, of	.174	7	23	1	4	2	0	0	0	3	3	0
Gil Hodges, 1b	.000	7	21	1	0	0	0	0	1	5	6	0
Tommy Holmes, of	.000	3	1	0	0	0	0	0	0	0	0	0
Ken Lehman, p	.000	1	0	0	0	0	0	0	0	0	0	0
Billy Loes, p	.333	2	3	0	1	0	0	0	0	0	1	1
Bobby Morgan, 3b	.000	2	1	0	0	0	0	0	0	0	0	0
Rocky Nelson, ph	.000	4	3	0	0	0	0	0	0	1	2	0
Andy Pafko, of-5	.190	7	21	0	4	0	0	0	2	0	4	0
Pee Wee Reese, ss	.345	7	29	4	10	1	0	0	1	4	2	1
Jackie Robinson, 2b	.174	7	23	4	4	0	0	1	2	7	5	2
Preacher Roe, p	.000	3	2	0	0	0	0	0	0	0	0	0
Johnny Rutherford, p	.000	1	0	0	0	0	0	0	0	0	0	0
George Shuba, of-3	.300	4	10	0	3	1	0	0	0	0	4	0
Duke Snider, of	.345	7	29	5	10	2	0	4	8	1	5	1
TOTAL	.215		233	20	50	7	0	6	18	24	49	5

PITCHER	W	L	ERA	G	GS	CG	SV	SHO	IP	H	ER	BB	SO
Joe Black	1	2	2.53	3	3	1	0	0	21.1	15	6	8	9
Carl Erskine	1	1	4.50	3	2	1	0	0	18.0	12	9	10	10
Ken Lehman	0	0	0.00	1	0	0	0	0	2.0	2	0	1	0
Billy Loes	0	1	4.35	2	1	0	0	0	10.1	11	5	5	5
Preacher Roe	1	0	3.18	3	1	1	0	0	11.1	9	4	6	7
Johnny Rutherford	0	0	9.00	1	1	0	0	0	1.0	1	1	1	1
TOTAL	3	4	3.52	13	7	3	0	0	64.0	50	25	31	32

GAME 1 AT BRO OCT 1

NY 010 000 010   2 6 2
BRO 010 002 01X   4 6 0
Pitchers: REYNOLDS, Scarborough (8) vs BLACK
Home Runs: Robinson-BRO, Snider-BRO, Reese-BRO, McDougald-NY
Attendance: 34,861

GAME 2 AT BRO OCT 2

NY 000 115 000   7 10 0
BRO 001 000 000   1 3 1
Pitchers: RASCHI vs ERSKINE, Loes (6), Lehman (8)
Home Runs: Martin-NY
Attendance: 33,792

GAME 3 AT NY OCT 3

BRO 001 010 012   5 11 0
NY 010 000 011   3 6 2
Pitchers: ROE vs LOPAT, Gorman (9)
Home Runs: Berra-NY, Mize-NY
Attendance: 66,698

GAME 4 AT NY OCT 4

BRO 000 000 000   0 4 1
NY 000 100 01X   2 4 1
Pitchers: BLACK, Rutherford (8) vs REYNOLDS
Home Runs: Mize-NY
Attendance: 71,787

GAME 5 AT NY OCT 5

BRO 010 030 100 01   6 10 0
NY 000 050 000 00   5 5 1
Pitchers: ERSKINE vs Blackwell, SAIN (6)
Home Runs: Snider-BRO, Mize-NY
Attendance: 70,536

GAME 6 AT BRO OCT 6

NY 000 000 210   3 9 0
BRO 000 001 010   2 8 1
Pitchers: RASCHI, Reynolds (8) vs LOES, Roe (9)
Home Runs: Snider-BRO (2), Berra-NY, Mantle-NY
Attendance: 30,037

GAME 7 AT BRO OCT 7

NY 000 111 100   4 10 4
BRO 000 110 000   2 8 1
Pitchers: Lopat, REYNOLDS (4), Raschi (7), Kuzava (7) vs BLACK, Roe (6), Erskine (8)
Home Runs: Woodling-NY, Mantle-NY
Attendance: 33,195

NEW YORK YANKEES (AL) 4, BROOKLYN DODGERS (NL) 2

Although the Yankees easily won the American League pennant, the Dodgers seemed even more overwhelming, with a team batting average of .285 and a club-record 105 wins. But when the Series was over, the Yankees had added a record fifth straight world championship to their record fifth straight pennant.

Dodgers ace Carl Erskine lasted only one inning of the Series opener, giving up three walks and two triples for four runs. By the middle of the seventh inning, the Dodgers had tied the score at 5–5. But Joe Collins homered for the Yanks to break the tie in the last of the seventh, and reliever Johnny Sain ensured his own win with a two-run double an inning later. The Dodgers outhit New York in Game 2, and held a 2–1 lead entering the bottom of the seventh. Billy Martin (who hit .500 and slugged .958 in the Series) tied the game with a leadoff homer in the seventh, and Mickey Mantle won it with a two-run blast in the eighth.

Brooklyn evened the Series at home with victories in Games 3 and 4. Erskine redeemed his poor start in Game 1 with a record-setting 14-strikeout performance in Game 3. But it was a narrow win, settled only when Roy Campanella homered in the last of the eighth to break a 2–2 tie. In Game 4, Duke Snider made Billy Loes' three-run pitching a winning performance, driving in four of the Dodgers' seven runs with two doubles and a homer.

But Brooklyn never held the lead in the final two games. Four home runs (including a Mantle grand slam) rocked Dodgers pitching in Game 5 as the Bombers built a lead which Dodger home runs in the eighth and ninth were unable to overcome. In Game 6 the Yankees built a 3–0 lead over Erskine in the first two innings. Brooklyn fought back with a run in the sixth, and tied the game on Carl Furillo's two-run homer in the top of the ninth. But with men on first and second in the last of the ninth, Billy Martin singled in the game-ending, Series-winning run. It was Martin's 12th hit, a new record for a six-game Series.

NY (A)

PLAYER/POS	AVG	G	AB	R	H	2B	3B	HR	RB	BB	SO	SB
Hank Bauer, of	.261	6	23	6	6	0	1	0	1	2	4	0
Yogi Berra, c	.429	6	21	3	9	1	0	1	4	3	3	0
Don Bollweg, 1b-1	.000	3	2	0	0	0	0	0	0	0	2	0
Joe Collins, 1b	.167	6	24	4	4	1	0	1	2	3	8	0
Whitey Ford, p	.333	2	3	0	1	0	0	0	0	0	0	0
Tom Gorman, p	.000	1	1	0	0	0	0	0	0	0	1	0
Bob Kuzava, p	.000	1	1	0	0	0	0	0	0	0	1	0
Ed Lopat, p	.000	1	3	0	0	0	0	0	0	0	2	0
Mickey Mantle, of	.208	6	24	3	5	0	0	2	7	3	8	0
Billy Martin, 2b	.500	6	24	5	12	1	2	2	8	1	2	1
Jim McDonald, p	.500	1	2	0	1	1	0	0	1	1	1	0
Gil McDougald, 3b	.167	6	24	2	4	0	1	2	4	1	3	0
Johnny Mize, ph	.000	3	3	0	0	0	0	0	0	0	1	0
Irv Noren, ph	.000	2	1	0	0	0	0	0	0	1	0	0
Vic Raschi, p	.000	1	2	0	0	0	0	0	0	0	1	0
Allie Reynolds, p	.500	3	2	0	1	0	0	0	0	0	1	0
Phil Rizzuto, ss	.316	6	19	4	6	1	0	0	0	3	2	1
Johnny Sain, p	.500	2	2	1	1	0	0	0	2	0	1	0
Art Schallock, p	.000	1	0	0	0	0	0	0	0	0	0	0
Gene Woodling, of	.300	6	20	5	6	0	0	1	3	6	2	0
TOTAL	.279		201	33	56	6	4	9	32	25	43	2

PITCHER	W	L	ERA	G	GS	CG	SV	SHO	IP	H	ER	BB	SO
Whitey Ford	0	1	4.50	2	2	0	0	0	8.0	9	4	2	7
Tom Gorman	0	0	3.00	1	0	0	0	0	3.0	4	1	0	1
Bob Kuzava	0	0	13.50	1	0	0	0	0	0.2	2	1	0	1
Ed Lopat	1	0	2.00	1	1	1	0	0	9.0	9	2	4	3
Jim McDonald	1	0	5.87	1	1	0	0	0	7.2	12	5	0	3
Vic Raschi	0	1	3.38	1	1	1	0	0	8.0	9	3	3	4
Allie Reynolds	1	0	6.75	3	1	0	1	·0	8.0	9	6	4	9
Johnny Sain	1	0	4.76	2	0	0	0	0	5.2	8	3	1	1
Art Schallock	0	0	4.50	1	0	0	0	0	2.0	2	1	1	1
TOTAL	4	2	4.50	13	6	2	1	0	52.0	64	26	15	30

BRO (N)

PLAYER/POS	AVG	G	AB	R	H	2B	3B	HR	RB	BB	SO	SB
Wayne Belardi, ph	.000	2	2	0	0	0	0	0	0	0	1	0
Joe Black, p	.000	1	0	0	0	0	0	0	0	0	0	0
Roy Campanella, c	.273	6	22	6	6	0	0	1	2	2	3	0
Billy Cox, 3b	.304	6	23	3	7	3	0	1	6	1	4	0
Carl Erskine, p	.250	3	4	0	1	0	0	0	0	0	1	0
Carl Furillo, of	.333	6	24	4	8	2	0	1	4	1	3	0
Jim Gilliam, 2b	.296	6	27	4	8	3	0	2	4	2	2	0
Gil Hodges, 1b	.364	6	22	3	8	0	0	1	1	3	3	1
Jim Hughes, p	.000	1	1	0	0	0	0	0	0	0	1	0
Clem Labine, p	.000	3	2	0	0	0	0	0	0	0	1	0
Billy Loes, p	.667	1	3	0	2	0	0	0	0	0	0	0
Russ Meyer, p	.000	1	1	0	0	0	0	0	0	0	1	0
Bob Milliken, p	.000	1	0	0	0	0	0	0	0	0	0	0
Bobby Morgan, ph	.000	1	1	0	0	0	0	0	0	0	0	0
Johnny Podres, p	1.000	1	1	0	1	0	0	0	0	0	0	0
Pee Wee Reese, ss	.208	6	24	0	5	0	1	0	0	4	1	0
Jackie Robinson, of	.320	6	25	3	8	2	0	0	2	1	0	1
Preacher Roe, p	.000	1	3	0	0	0	0	0	0	0	2	0
George Shuba, ph	1.000	2	1	1	1	0	0	1	2	0	0	0
Duke Snider, of	.320	6	25	3	8	3	0	1	5	2	6	0
Don Thompson, of	.000	2	0	0	0	0	0	0	0	0	0	0
Ben Wade, p	.000	2	0	0	0	0	0	0	0	0	0	0
Dick Williams, ph	.500	3	2	0	1	0	0	0	0	0	1	0
TOTAL	.300		213	27	64	13	1	8	26	15	30	2

PITCHER	W	L	ERA	G	GS	CG	SV	SHO	IP	H	ER	BB	SO
Joe Black	0	0	9.00	1	0	0	0	0	1.0	1	1	0	2
Carl Erskine	1	0	5.79	3	3	1	0	0	14.0	14	9	9	16
Jim Hughes	0	0	2.25	1	0	0	0	0	4.0	3	1	1	3
Clem Labine	0	2	3.60	3	0	0	1	0	5.0	10	2	1	3
Billy Loes	1	0	3.38	1	1	0	0	0	8.0	8	3	2	8
Russ Meyer	0	0	6.23	1	0	0	0	0	4.1	8	3	4	5
Bob Milliken	0	0	0.00	1	0	0	0	0	2.0	2	0	1	0
Johnny Podres	0	1	3.38	1	1	0	0	0	2.2	1	1	2	0
Preacher Roe	0	1	4.50	1	1	1	0	0	8.0	5	4	4	4
Ben Wade	0	0	15.43	2	0	0	0	0	2.1	4	4	1	2
TOTAL	2	4	4.91	15	6	2	1	0	51.1	56	28	25	43

GAME 1 AT NY SEPT 30

BRO 000 013 100   5 12 2
NY 400 010 13X   9 12 0
Pitchers: Erskine, Hughes (2), LABINE (6), Wade (8) vs Reynolds, SAIN (6)
Home Runs: Gilliam-BRO, Hodges-BRO, Shuba-BRO, Berra-NY, Collins-NY
Attendance: 69,374

GAME 2 AT NY OCT 1

BRO 000 200 000   2 9 1
NY 100 000 12X   4 5 0
Pitchers: ROE vs LOPAT
Home Runs: Martin-NY, Mantle-NY
Attendance: 66,786

GAME 3 AT BRO OCT 2

NY 000 010 010   2 6 0
BRO 000 011 01X   3 9 0
Pitchers: RASCHI vs ERSKINE
Home Runs: Campanella-BRO
Attendance: 35,270

GAME 4 AT BRO OCT 3

NY 000 020 001   3 9 0
BRO 300 102 10X   7 12 0
Pitchers: FORD, Gorman (2), Sain (5), Schallock (7) vs LOES, Labine (9)
Home Runs: McDougald-NY Snider-BRO
Attendance: 36,775

GAME 5 AT BRO OCT 4

NY 105 000 311   11 11 1
BRO 010 000 041   7 14 1
Pitchers: McDONALD, Kuzava (8), Reynolds (9) vs PODRES, Meyer (3), Wade (8), Black (9)
Home Runs: Woodling-NY, Mantle-NY, Martin-NY, McDougald-NY, Cox-BRO, Gilliam-BRO
Attendance: 36,775

GAME 6 AT NY OCT 5

BRO 000 001 002   3 8 3
NY 210 000 001   4 13 0
Pitchers: Erskine, Milliken (5), LABINE (7) vs Ford, REYNOLDS (8)
Home Runs: Furillo-BRO
Attendance: 62,370

NEW YORK GIANTS (NL) 4, CLEVELAND INDIANS (AL) 0

The Indians, who had won a league-record 111 games to break the American League domination of the New York Yankees, entered the World Series as strong favorites to humble the Giants. It was not to be.

Cleveland would have won the opener had it not been played in New York's Polo Grounds, with their short foul lines and deep center field. Most of the game was a pitchers' duel. Vic Wertz (the only Indian to hit safely in all four games) tripled off Sal Maglie to give Cleveland a two-run lead in the top of the first, but three singles and a walk in the third off Bob Lemon tied the score. Lemon then settled down to hold New York scoreless through the ninth. Cleveland threatened in the eighth when the first two batters reached base, bringing Wertz to the plate. As Wertz had already hit Maglie safely three times, Don Liddle was brought in to pitch to him. Wertz responded with a fly to deep center that would have been a home run in Cleveland, but in New York turned into the most famous catch in World Series history as Willie Mays raced out and tracked down the ball about 425 feet from the plate. Marv Grissom replaced Liddle on the mound and issued a walk to load the bases, but he retired the next two batters and (despite Wertz's double in the top of the 10th) held Cleveland scoreless the rest of the way. In the last of the 10th, Lemon retired the first batter, but Mays walked and stole second, and Hank Thompson was walked intentionally to set up the double play. Pinch hitter Dusty Rhodes then entered the hall of heroes with a short fly to right that—though it would have been an out in Cleveland—fell into the Polo Grounds stands for three runs and a Giants victory.

The rest of the Series was anticlimax. In the second game Rhodes, with half the Giants' four hits, drove in two runs on a single and another homer, providing the margin of victory for ace Johnny Antonelli, who allowed only one of Cleveland's 14 baserunners to score. Game 3 was no contest. New York had scored all six of its runs before the Indians managed to come up with single runs in both the seventh and eighth. Pinch hitter Hank Majeski's three-run

homer put Cleveland on the board in the fifth inning of Game 4. But as New York had already scored seven times, even a fourth Cleveland run in the seventh proved too little to prevent a shocking sweep by the Giants.

GAME 1 AT NY SEPT 29

CLE   2 0 0   0 0 0   0 0 0   2   8   0
NY   0 0 2   0 0 0   0 0 3   5   9   3
Pitchers: LEMON vs Maglie, Liddle (8), GRISSOM (8)
Home Runs: Rhodes-NY
Attendance: 52,751

GAME 2 AT NY SEPT 30

CLE   1 0 0   0 0 0   0 0 0   1   8   0
NY   0 0 0   0 2 0   1 0 X   3   4   0
Pitchers: WYNN, Mossi (8) vs ANTONELLI
Home Runs: Smith-CLE, Rhodes-NY
Attendance: 49,099

GAME 3 AT CLE OCT 1

NY   1 0 3   0 1 1   0 0 0   6   10   1
CLE   0 0 0   0 0 0   1 1 0   2   4   2
Pitchers: GOMEZ, Wilhelm (7) vs GARCIA, Houtteman (4), Narleski (6), Mossi (9)
Home Runs: Wertz-CLE
Attendance: 71,555

GAME 4 AT CLE OCT 2

NY   0 2 1   0 4 0   0 0 0   7   10   3
CLE   0 0 0   0 3 0   1 0 0   4   6   2
Pitchers: LIDDLE, Wilhelm (7), Antonelli (8) vs LEMON, Newhouser (5), Narleski (5), Mossi (6), Garcia (8)
Home Runs: Majeski-CLE
Attendance: 78,102

NY (N)

PLAYER/POS	AVG	G	AB	R	H	2B	3B	HR	RBI	BB	SO	SB
Johnny Antonelli, p	.000	2	3	0	0	0	0	0	0	1	0	0
Alvin Dark, ss	.412	4	17	2	7	0	0	0	0	1	1	0
Ruben Gomez, p	.000	1	4	0	0	0	0	0	0	0	2	0
Marv Grissom, p	.000	1	1	0	0	0	0	0	0	0	1	0
Monte Irvin, of	.222	4	9	1	2	1	0	0	2	0	3	0
Don Liddle, p	.000	2	3	0	0	0	0	0	0	0	2	0
Whitey Lockman, 1b	.111	4	18	2	2	0	0	0	0	1	2	0
Sal Maglie, p	.000	1	3	0	0	0	0	0	0	0	2	0
Willie Mays, of	.286	4	14	4	4	1	0	0	3	4	1	1
Don Mueller, of	.389	4	18	4	7	0	0	0	1	0	1	0
Dusty Rhodes, of-2	.667	3	6	2	4	0	0	2	7	1	2	0
Hank Thompson, 3b	.364	4	11	6	4	1	0	0	2	7	1	0
Wes Westrum, c	.273	4	11	0	3	0	0	0	3	1	3	0
Hoyt Wilhelm, p	.000	2	1	0	0	0	0	0	0	0	1	0
Davey Williams, 2b	.000	4	11	0	0	0	0	0	1	2	2	0
TOTAL	.254		130	21	33	3	0	2	20	17	24	1

PITCHER	W	L	ERA	G	GS	CG	SV	SHO	IP	H	ER	BB	SO
Johnny Antonelli	1	0	0.84	2	1	1	1	0	10.2	8	1	7	12
Ruben Gomez	1	0	2.45	1	1	0	0	0	7.1	4	2	3	2
Marv Grissom	1	0	0.00	1	0	0	0	0	2.2	1	0	3	2
Don Liddle	1	0	1.29	2	1	0	0	0	7.0	5	1	1	2
Sal Maglie	0	0	2.57	1	1	0	0	0	7.0	7	2	2	2
Hoyt Wilhelm	0	0	0.00	2	0	0	1	0	2.1	1	0	0	3
TOTAL	4	0	1.46	9	4	1	2	0	37.0	26	6	16	23

CLE (A)

PLAYER/POS	AVG	G	AB	R	H	2B	3B	HR	RBI	BB	SO	SB
Bobby Avila, 2b	.133	4	15	1	2	0	0	0	0	2	1	0
Sam Dente, ss	.000	3	3	1	0	0	0	0	0	1	0	0
Larry Doby, of	.125	4	16	0	2	0	0	0	0	2	4	0
Mike Garcia, p	.000	2	0	0	0	0	0	0	0	0	0	0
Bill Glynn, 1b-1	.500	2	2	1	1	1	0	0	0	0	1	0
Mickey Grasso, c	.000	1	0	0	0	0	0	0	0	0	0	0
Jim Hegan, c	.154	4	13	1	2	1	0	0	0	1	1	0
Art Houtteman, p	.000	1	0	0	0	0	0	0	0	0	0	0
Bob Lemon, p-2	.000	3	6	0	0	0	0	0	0	1	1	0
Hank Majeski, 3b-1	.167	4	6	1	1	0	0	1	3	0	1	0
Dale Mitchell, ph	.000	3	2	0	0	0	0	0	0	1	0	0
Don Mossi, p	.000	3	0	0	0	0	0	0	0	0	0	0
Hal Naragon, c	.000	1	0	0	0	0	0	0	0	0	0	0
Ray Narleski, p	.000	2	0	0	0	0	0	0	0	0	0	0
Hal Newhouser, p	.000	1	0	0	0	0	0	0	0	0	0	0
Dave Philley, of-2	.125	4	8	0	1	0	0	0	0	1	3	0
Dave Pope, of-2	.000	3	3	0	0	0	0	0	0	1	1	0
Rudy Regalado, 3b-1	.333	4	3	0	1	0	0	0	1	0	0	0
Al Rosen, 3b	.250	3	12	0	3	0	0	0	0	1	0	0
Al Smith, of	.214	4	14	2	3	0	0	1	2	2	2	0
George Strickland, ss	.000	3	9	0	0	0	0	0	0	0	2	0
Vic Wertz, 1b	.500	4	16	2	8	2	1	1	3	2	2	0
Wally Westlake, of	.143	2	7	0	1	0	0	0	0	0	3	0
Early Wynn, p	.500	1	2	0	1	1	0	0	0	0	1	0
TOTAL	.190		137	9	26	5	1	3	9	16	23	0

PITCHER	W	L	ERA	G	GS	CG	SV	SHO	IP	H	ER	BB	SO
Mike Garcia	0	1	5.40	2	1	0	0	0	5.0	6	3	4	4
Art Houtteman	0	0	4.50	1	0	0	0	0	2.0	2	1	1	1
Bob Lemon	0	2	6.75	2	2	1	0	0	13.1	16	10	8	11
Don Mossi	0	0	0.00	3	0	0	0	0	4.0	3	0	0	1
Ray Narleski	0	0	2.25	2	0	0	0	0	4.0	1	1	1	2
Hal Newhouser	0	0	∞	1	0	0	0	0	0.0	1	1	1	0
Early Wynn	0	1	3.86	1	1	0	0	0	7.0	4	3	2	5
TOTAL	0	4	4.84	12	4	1	0	0	35.1	33	19	17	24

BROOKLYN DODGERS (NL) 4, NEW YORK YANKEES (AL) 3

The Dodgers and Yankees, after a year's absence, faced each other again in the World Series—their sixth Series confrontation in 15 years. And after Brooklyn had lost the first two games it began to look as though 1955 might also mark the Yankees' sixth Series triumph over the Dodgers. But this was Brooklyn's year.

The opener was a hitters' game, but closely contested. Both teams scored twice in the second inning and once in the third, but first baseman Joe Collins' leadoff homer in the last of the fourth gave New York its first lead of the game, and his two-run blast in the sixth made the score 6–3. Brooklyn clawed back in the eighth for two runs—including Jackie Robinson's steal of home—to pull within one run of a tie, but they came no closer. In Game 2, Tommy Byrne held the Dodgers to five hits and two runs, and won his own game at the bat with a two-run single that capped the Yankees' four-run fourth.

The Series turned around as the Dodgers captured the next three games in Brooklyn. Roy Campanella's two-run homer in the first inning of Game 3 gave Brooklyn a quick lead. New York tied the game with a pair of runs in the second (one of them a homer by Mickey Mantle, who appeared in only three Series games because of a leg injury). But two more runs in the last of the second drove out New York starter Bob Turley and put them ahead to stay as Dodgers hurler Johnny Podres held the Yankees to three runs. Home runs by Campanella, Gil Hodges, and Duke Snider accounted for six of Brooklyn's eight runs in Game 4 as the Dodgers evened the Series. Sandy Amoros' second-inning homer initiated the scoring in Game 5, and Snider's blasts in the third and fifth (which made him the first player to hit four home runs in two different Series) gave Brooklyn a 4–1 lead, which even late-inning Yankees homers by Bob Cerv and Yogi Berra could not overcome.

New York bounced back in Game 6, scoring all five of their runs in the first inning (including three on Bill Skowron's homer) to give Whitey Ford a comfortable lead, which he held with a one-run four-hitter. But in the finale, Gil Hodges drove in both Brooklyn

BRO (N)

PLAYER/POS	AVG	G	AB	R	H	2B	3B	HR	RB	BB	SO	SB
Sandy Amoros, of	.333	5	12	3	4	0	0	1	3	4	4	0
Don Bessent, p	.000	3	1	0	0	0	0	0	0	0	1	0
Roy Campanella, c	.259	7	27	4	7	3	0	2	4	3	3	0
Roger Craig, p	.000	1	0	0	0	0	0	0	0	1	0	0
Carl Erskine, p	.000	1	1	0	0	0	0	0	0	0	0	0
Carl Furillo, of	.296	7	27	4	8	1	0	1	3	3	5	0
Jim Gilliam, 2b-5, of-4	.292	7	24	2	7	1	0	0	3	8	1	1
Don Hoak, 3b-1	.333	3	3	0	1	0	0	0	0	2	0	0
Gil Hodges, 1b	.292	7	24	2	7	0	0	1	5	3	2	0
Frank Kellert, ph	.333	3	3	0	1	0	0	0	0	1	0	0
Clem Labine, p	.000	4	4	0	0	0	0	0	0	0	3	0
Billy Loes, p	.000	1	1	0	0	0	0	0	0	0	0	0
Russ Meyer, p	.000	1	2	0	0	0	0	0	0	0	1	0
Don Newcombe, p	.000	1	3	0	0	0	0	0	0	0	0	0
Johnny Podres, p	.143	2	7	1	1	0	0	0	0	0	1	0
Pee Wee Reese, ss	.296	7	27	5	8	1	0	0	2	3	5	0
Jackie Robinson, 3b	.182	6	22	5	4	1	1	0	1	2	1	1
Ed Roebuck, p	.000	1	0	0	0	0	0	0	0	0	0	0
George Shuba, ph	.000	1	1	0	0	0	0	0	0	0	0	0
Duke Snider, of	.320	7	25	5	8	1	0	4	7	2	6	0
Karl Spooner, p	.000	2	0	0	0	0	0	0	0	0	0	0
Don Zimmer, 2b	.222	4	9	0	2	0	0	0	2	2	5	0
TOTAL	.260		223	31	58	8	1	9	30	33	38	2

PITCHER	W	L	ERA	G	GS	CG	SV	SHO	IP	H	ER	BB	SO
Don Bessent	0	0	0.00	3	0	0	0	0	3.1	3	0	1	1
Roger Craig	1	0	3.00	1	1	0	0	0	6.0	4	2	5	4
Carl Erskine	0	0	9.00	1	1	0	0	0	3.0	3	3	2	3
Clem Labine	1	0	2.89	4	0	0	1	0	9.1	6	3	2	2
Billy Loes	0	1	9.82	1	1	0	0	0	3.2	7	4	1	5
Russ Meyer	0	0	0.00	1	0	0	0	0	5.2	4	0	2	4
Don Newcombe	0	1	9.53	1	1	0	0	0	5.2	8	6	2	4
Johnny Podres	2	0	1.00	2	2	2	0	1	18.0	15	2	4	10
Ed Roebuck	0	0	0.00	1	0	0	0	0	2.0	1	0	0	0
Karl Spooner	0	1	13.50	2	1	0	0	0	3.1	4	5	3	6
TOTAL	3	3	3.75	17	7	2	1	1	60.0	55	25	22	39

NY (A)

PLAYER/POS	AVG	G	AB	R	H	2B	3B	HR	RB	BB	SO	SB
Hank Bauer, of-5	.429	6	14	1	6	0	0	0	1	0	1	0
Yogi Berra, c	.417	7	24	5	10	1	0	1	2	3	1	0
Tommy Byrne, p-2	.167	3	6	0	1	0	0	0	2	0	2	0
Andy Carey, ph	.500	2	2	0	1	0	1	0	1	0	0	0
Tom Carroll, pr	.000	2	0	0	0	0	0	0	0	0	0	0
Bob Cerv, of-4	.125	5	16	1	2	0	0	1	1	0	4	0
Gerry Coleman, ss	.000	3	3	0	0	0	0	0	0	0	1	0
Rip Coleman, p	.000	1	0	0	0	0	0	0	0	0	0	0
Joe Collins, 1b-5, of-1	.167	5	12	6	2	0	0	2	3	6	4	1
Whitey Ford, p	.000	2	6	1	0	0	0	0	0	1	1	0
Bob Grim, p	.000	3	2	0	0	0	0	0	0	0	0	0
Elston Howard, of	.192	7	26	3	5	0	0	1	3	1	8	0
Johnny Kucks, p	.000	2	0	0	0	0	0	0	0	0	0	0
Don Larsen, p	.000	1	2	0	0	0	0	0	0	0	0	0
Mickey Mantle, of-2	.200	3	10	1	2	0	0	1	1	0	2	0
Billy Martin, 2b	.320	7	25	2	8	1	1	0	4	1	5	0
Gil McDougald, 3b	.259	7	27	2	7	0	0	1	1	2	6	0
Tom Morgan, p	.000	2	0	0	0	0	0	0	0	0	0	0
Irv Noren, of	.063	5	16	0	1	0	0	0	1	1	1	0
Phil Rizzuto, ss	.267	7	15	2	4	0	0	0	1	5	1	2
Eddie Robinson, 1b-1	.667	4	3	0	2	0	0	0	1	2	1	0
Bill Skowron, 1b-3	.333	5	12	2	4	2	0	1	3	0	1	0
Tom Sturdivant, p	.000	2	0	0	0	0	0	0	0	0	0	0
Bob Turley, p	.000	3	1	0	0	0	0	0	0	0	0	0
TOTAL	.248		222	26	55	4	2	8	25	22	39	3

PITCHER	W	L	ERA	G	GS	CG	SV	SHO	IP	H	ER	BB	SO
Tommy Byrne	1	1	1.88	2	2	1	0	0	14.1	8	3	8	8
Rip Coleman	0	0	9.00	1	0	0	0	0	1.0	5	1	0	1
Whitey Ford	2	0	2.12	2	2	1	0	0	17.0	13	4	8	10
Bob Grim	0	1	4.15	3	1	0	1	0	8.2	8	4	5	8
Johnny Kucks	0	0	6.00	2	0	0	0	0	3.0	4	2	1	1
Don Larsen	0	1	11.25	1	1	0	0	0	4.0	5	5	2	2
Tom Morgan	0	0	4.91	2	0	0	0	0	3.2	3	2	3	1
Tom Sturdivant	0	0	6.00	2	0	0	0	0	3.0	5	2	2	0
Bob Turley	0	1	8.44	3	1	0	0	0	5.1	7	5	4	7
TOTAL	3	4	4.20	18	7	2	1	0	60.0	58	28	33	38

runs with a single in the fourth and a sacrifice fly in the sixth. They were all Brooklyn got, but they proved more than enough to carry the Dodgers to their first world title in 55 years, as left fielder Sandy Amoros stifled New York's only real scoring threat with a spectacular running catch in the sixth that started a double play and preserved Johnny Podres' second Series win.

GAME 1 AT NY SEPT 28
```
BRO  021 000 020   5 10 0
NY   021 102 00X   6  9 1
```
Pitchers: NEWCOMBE, Bessent (6), Labine (8) vs FORD, Grim (9)
Home Runs: Furillo-BRO, Snider-BRO, Howard-NY, Collins-NY (2)
Attendance: 63,869

GAME 2 AT NY SEPT 29
```
BRO  000 110 000   2 5 2
NY   000 400 00X   4 8 0
```
Pitchers: LOES, Bessent (4), Spooner (5), Labine (8) vs BYRNE
Attendance: 64,707

GAME 3 AT BRO SEPT 30
```
NY   020 000 100   3  7 0
BRO  220 200 20X   8 11 1
```
Pitchers: TURLEY, Morgan (2), Kucks (5), Sturdivant (7) vs PODRES
Home Runs: Campanella-BRO, Mantle-NY
Attendance: 34,209

GAME 4 AT BRO OCT 1
```
NY   110 102 000   5  9 0
BRO  001 330 10X   8 14 0
```
Pitchers: LARSEN, Kucks (5), R.Coleman (6), Morgan (7), Sturdivant (8) vs Erskine, Bessent (4), LABINE (5)
Home Runs: McDougald-NY, Campanella-BRO, Hodges-BRO, Snider-BRO
Attendance: 36,242

GAME 5 AT BRO OCT 2
```
NY   000 100 110   3 6 0
BRO  021 010 01X   5 9 2
```
Pitchers: GRIM, Turley (7) vs CRAIG, Labine (7)
Home Runs: Cerv-NY, Berra-NY, Amoros-BRO, Snider-BRO (2)
Attendance: 36,796

GAME 6 AT NY OCT 3
```
BRO  000 100 000   1 4 1
NY   500 000 00X   5 8 0
```
Pitchers: SPOONER, Meyer (1), Roebuck (7) vs FORD
Home Runs: Skowron-NY
Attendance: 64,022

GAME 7 AT NY OCT 4
```
BRO  000 101 000   2 5 0
NY   000 000 000   0 8 1
```
Pitchers: PODRES vs BYRNE, Grim (6), Turley (8)
Attendance: 62,465

NEW YORK YANKEES (AL) 4, BROOKLYN DODGERS (NL) 3

With both teams repeaters as league champions, the Yankees followed Brooklyn's winning pattern of the previous Series: losing the first two games, winning the next three, then splitting the final pair.

Sal Maglie outlasted Yankees ace Whitey Ford in the opener. Maglie gave up nine hits and three runs (on homers by Mickey Mantle and Billy Martin), but struck out 10 and took the win as Jackie Robinson and Gil Hodges contrib-uted homers for four of Brooklyn's six runs. Dodgers ace Don Newcombe was blown out by six Yankees runs (capped by Yogi Berra's grand slam) in the first two innings of Game 2. But Brooklyn came back with six unearned runs in their half of the second (three of them on Duke Snider's homer) and proceeded to run through seven Yankees pitchers for a 13–8 win and a two-game Series edge.

Whitey Ford tried again in Game 3, and this time held on for a complete-game 5–3 win, supported by Billy Martin's game-tying solo homer in the second and 40-yearold Enos Slaughter's go-ahead three-run shot in the sixth. Tom Sturdivant duplicated Ford's effec-tiveness and success the next day with a six-hit 6–2 win to even the Series.

Sal Maglie pitched Game 5 for Brooklyn and improved on his winning performance of Game 1, yielding only two runs and holding New York hitless until Mantle's two-out homer in the fourth inning. But no one was a match for Yankees pitcher Don Larsen that day. There was a close out on a deflected Dodger liner in the second inning, and center fielder Mantle made a fine running catch to prevent a hit in the fifth. But Larsen retired the rest routinely, and when Dale Mitchell fanned in the ninth Larsen had his perfect game—a feat still unique in World Series history.

Brooklyn reliever Clem Labine started in Game 6 against Bob Turley. No runner scored for either side until the last of the 10th inning when, with two out, Jackie Robinson lined a Turley pitch over the head of the left fielder, scoring Jim Gilliam from second and forcing New York into a seventh game.

The finale proved an anticli-mactic disaster for Brooklyn. Once

again Newcombe was driven out— this time by Yogi Berra's two two-run homers and Elston Howard's solo shot. By the time it was over, Bill Skowron had increased the Yankee run total to nine with a grand slam, and Johnny Kucks had shut Brooklyn out on three singles. For New York it was world title number 17.

NY (A)

PLAYER/POS	AVG	G	AB	R	H	2B	3B	HR	RB	BB	SO	SB
Hank Bauer, of	.281	7	32	3	9	0	0	1	3	0	5	1
Yogi Berra, c	.360	7	25	5	9	2	0	3	10	4	1	0
Tommy Byrne, p-1	.000	2	1	0	0	0	0	0	0	0	0	0
Andy Carey, 3b	.158	7	19	2	3	0	0	0	0	1	6	0
Bob Cerv, ph	1.000	1	1	0	1	0	0	0	0	0	0	0
Gerry Coleman, 2b	.000	2	2	0	0	0	0	0	0	0	0	0
Joe Collins, 1b-5	.238	6	21	2	5	2	0	0	2	2	3	0
Whitey Ford, p	.000	2	4	0	0	0	0	0	0	0	3	0
Elston Howard, of	.400	1	5	1	2	1	0	1	1	0	0	0
Johnny Kucks, p	.000	3	3	0	0	0	0	0	0	0	1	0
Don Larsen, p	.333	2	3	1	1	0	0	0	1	0	1	0
Mickey Mantle, of	.250	7	24	6	6	1	0	3	4	6	5	1
Billy Martin, 2b-7,3b-1	.296	7	27	5	8	0	0	2	3	1	6	0
Maury McDermott, p	1.000	1	1	0	1	0	0	0	0	0	0	0
Gil McDougald, ss	.143	7	21	0	3	0	0	0	1	3	6	0
Tom Morgan, p	1.000	2	1	1	1	0	0	0	0	0	0	0
Norm Siebern, ph	.000	1	1	0	0	0	0	0	0	0	0	0
Bill Skowron, 1b-2	.100	3	10	1	1	0	0	1	4	0	3	0
Enos Slaughter, of	.350	6	20	6	7	0	0	1	4	4	0	0
Tom Sturdivant, p	.333	2	3	0	1	0	0	0	0	0	1	0
Bob Turley, p	.000	3	4	0	0	0	0	0	0	0	1	0
George Wilson, ph	.000	1	1	0	0	0	0	0	0	0	1	0
TOTAL	.253		229	33	58	6	0	12	33	21	43	2

PITCHER	W	L	ERA	G	GS	CG	SV	SHO	IP	H	ER	BB	SO
Tommy Byrne	0	0	0.00	1	0	0	0	0	0.1	1	0	0	1
Whitey Ford	1	1	5.25	2	2	1	0	0	12.0	14	7	2	8
Johnny Kucks	1	0	0.82	3	1	1	0	1	11.0	6	1	3	2
Don Larsen	1	0	0.00	2	2	1	0	1	10.2	1	0	4	7
Maury McDermott	0	0	3.00	1	0	0	0	0	3.0	2	1	3	3
Tom Morgan	0	1	9.00	2	0	0	0	0	4.0	6	4	4	3
Tom Sturdivant	1	0	2.79	2	1	1	0	0	9.2	8	3	8	9
Bob Turley	0	1	0.82	3	1	1	0	0	11.0	4	1	8	14
TOTAL	4	3	2.48	16	7	5	0	2	61.2	42	17	32	47

BRO (N)

PLAYER/POS	AVG	G	AB	R	H	2B	3B	HR	RB	BB	SO	SB
Sandy Amoros, of	.053	6	19	1	1	0	0	0	1	2	4	0
Don Bessent, p	.500	2	2	0	1	0	0	0	0	1	1	0
Roy Campanella, c	.182	7	22	2	4	1	0	0	3	3	7	0
Gino Cimoli, of	.000	1	0	0	0	0	0	0	0	0	0	0
Roger Craig, p	.500	2	2	0	1	0	0	0	0	0	0	0
Don Drysdale, p	.000	1	0	0	0	0	0	0	0	0	0	0
Carl Erskine, p	.000	2	1	0	0	0	0	0	0	0	1	0
Carl Furillo, of	.240	7	25	2	6	2	0	0	1	2	3	0
Jim Gilliam, 2b-6, of-1	.083	7	24	2	2	0	0	0	2	7	3	1
Gil Hodges, 1b	.304	7	23	5	7	2	0	1	8	4	4	0
Ransom Jackson, ph	.000	3	3	0	0	0	0	0	0	0	2	0
Clem Labine, p	.250	2	4	0	1	1	0	0	0	0	2	0
Sal Maglie, p	.000	2	5	0	0	0	0	0	0	0	2	0
Dale Mitchell, ph	.000	4	4	0	0	0	0	0	0	0	1	0
Charlie Neal, 2b	.000	1	4	0	0	0	0	0	0	0	1	0
Don Newcombe, p	.000	2	1	0	0	0	0	0	0	0	0	0
Pee Wee Reese, ss	.222	7	27	3	6	0	1	0	2	2	6	0
Jackie Robinson, 3b	.250	7	24	5	6	1	0	1	2	5	2	0
Ed Roebuck, p	.000	3	0	0	0	0	0	0	0	0	0	0
Duke Snider, of	.304	7	23	5	7	1	0	1	4	6	8	0
Rube Walker, ph	.000	2	2	0	0	0	0	0	0	0	0	0
TOTAL	.195		215	25	42	8	1	3	24	32	47	1

PITCHER	W	L	ERA	G	GS	CG	SV	SHO	IP	H	ER	BB	SO
Don Bessent	1	0	1.80	2	0	0	0	0	10.0	8	2	3	5
Roger Craig	0	1	12.00	2	1	0	0	0	6.0	10	8	3	4
Don Drysdale	0	0	9.00	1	0	0	0	0	2.0	2	2	1	1
Carl Erskine	0	1	5.40	2	1	0	0	0	5.0	4	3	2	2
Clem Labine	1	0	0.00	2	1	1	0	1	12.0	8	0	3	7
Sal Maglie	1	1	2.65	2	2	2	0	0	17.0	14	5	6	15
Don Newcombe	0	1	21.21	2	2	0	0	0	4.2	11	11	3	4
Ed Roebuck	0	0	2.08	3	0	0	0	0	4.1	1	1	0	5
TOTAL	3	4	4.72	16	7	3	0	1	61.0	58	32	21	43

GAME 1 AT BRO OCT 3

```
NY   200 100 000   3 9 1
BRO  023 100 00X   6 9 0
```
Pitchers: FORD, Kucks (4), Morgan (6), Turley (8) vs MAGLIE
Home Runs: Mantle-NY, Robinson-BRO, Hodges-BRO, Martin-NY
Attendance: 34,479

GAME 2 AT BRO OCT 5

```
NY   150 100 001   8 12 2
BRO  061 220 02X  13 12 0
```
Pitchers: Larsen, Kucks (2), Byrne (2), Sturdivant (3), MORGAN (3), Turley (5), McDermott (6) vs Newcombe, Roebuck (2), BESSENT (3)
Home Runs: Berra-NY, Snider-BRO
Attendance: 36,217

GAME 3 AT NY OCT 6

```
BRO  010 001 100   3 8 1
NY   010 003 01X   5 8 1
```
Pitchers: CRAIG, Labine (7) vs FORD
Home Runs: Martin-NY, Slaughter-NY
Attendance: 73,977

GAME 4 AT NY OCT 7

```
BRO  000 100 001   2 6 0
NY   100 201 02X   6 7 2
```
Pitchers: ERSKINE, Roebuck (5), Drysdale (7) vs STURDIVANT
Home Runs: Mantle-NY, Bauer-NY
Attendance: 69,705

GAME 5 AT NY OCT 8

```
BRO  000 000 000   0 0 0
NY   000 101 00X   2 5 0
```
Pitchers: MAGLIE vs LARSEN
Home Runs: Mantle-NY
Attendance: 64,519

GAME 6 AT BRO OCT 9

```
NY   000 000 0000 0  0 7 0
BRO  000 000 0001 1  1 4 0
```
Pitchers: TURLEY vs LABINE
Attendance: 33,224

GAME 7 AT BRO OCT 10

```
NY   202 100 400   9 10 0
BRO  000 000 000   0 3 1
```
Pitchers: KUCKS vs NEWCOMBE, Bessent (4), Craig (7), Roebuck (7), Erskine (9)
Home Runs: Berra-NY (2), Howard-NY, Skowron-NY
Attendance: 33,782

MILWAUKEE BRAVES (NL) 4, NEW YORK YANKEES (AL) 3

Overall, the Yankees played better than the Braves, but the Braves had Lew Burdette, who was better than anybody in the Series.

The opener pitted the Braves' established great Warren Spahn against New York's Whitey Ford. Ford prevailed, with a five-hit 3–1 win as Spahn was chased in the sixth. Burdette, winner of 17 regular-season games, started Game 2 against veteran Bobby Shantz, the American League ERA leader. After a scoreless first inning, both pitchers gave up a run in the second and another in the third. Two goahead runs in the top of the fourth ended the Braves' scoring, but they were enough, as Burdette blanked New York through the final six innings to even the Series. Before he was finished, Burdette would stretch his consecutive scoreless innings streak to 24.

The Yankees exploded in Game 3, in Milwaukee, running through six Braves pitchers in a 12–3 rout. Braves fans even ended up cheering Yankees rookie Tony Kubek—a Milwaukee native—who opened the scoring with a solo homer in the first, scored again after singling in the fourth (on Mickey Mantle's home run), and concluded the Yankee scoring in the seventh with his second homer, with two aboard.

Warren Spahn carried a 4–1 Braves lead into the ninth inning of Game 4, but after retiring the first two batters in the ninth, he gave up singles to Yogi Berra and Gil McDougald, and a game-tying home run to Elston Howard. In the top of the 10th, Hank Bauer tripled in a go-ahead run, but Milwaukee's Johnny Logan doubled to tie it up in the last of the 10th, and Eddie Mathews homered to give Spahn a shaky victory.

Burdette faced Ford in Game 5. In the sixth inning the Braves put half their hits—three singles—back to back for a run. It was all they needed as Burdette spaced seven singles for the shutout. Back in New York two days later, all the scoring came on home runs. Each club hit a pair, but Berra's in the third was the only one with a man aboard. Braves blasts in the fifth (Frank Torre) and seventh (Hank Aaron) tied the score, but Bauer answered Aaron's homer in the last of the seventh with what proved the winning shot. Bob Turley, who yielded just four hits while fanning

eight (the Series high) claimed the victory.

In the finale, Burdette, with only two days' rest, scattered four hits over the first eight innings as the Braves gave him a 5–0 lead. In the bottom of the ninth, though, three Yankees singles loaded the bases with two out. But third baseman Eddie Mathews snared Bill Skowron's sharp grounder and stepped on the bag for a force out that preserved Burdette's second shutout and gave Milwaukee its first world championship.

MIL (N)

PLAYER/POS	AVG	G	AB	R	H	2B	3B	HR	RB	BB	SO	SB
Hank Aaron, of	.393	7	28	5	11	0	1	3	7	1	6	0
Joe Adcock, 1b	.200	5	15	1	3	0	0	0	2	0	2	0
Bob Buhl, p	.000	2	1	0	0	0	0	0	0	0	1	0
Lew Burdette, p	.000	3	8	0	0	0	0	0	0	1	2	0
Gene Conley, p	.000	1	0	0	0	0	0	0	0	0	0	0
Wes Covington, of	.208	7	24	1	5	1	0	0	1	2	6	1
Del Crandall, c	.211	6	19	1	4	0	0	1	1	1	1	0
John DeMerit, pr	.000	1	0	0	0	0	0	0	0	0	0	0
Bob Hazle, of	.154	4	13	2	2	0	0	0	0	1	2	0
Ernie Johnson, p	.000	3	1	0	0	0	0	0	0	0	1	0
Nippy Jones, ph	.000	3	2	0	0	0	0	0	0	0	0	0
Johnny Logan, ss	.185	7	27	5	5	1	0	1	2	3	6	0
Felix Mantilla, 2b-3	.000	4	10	1	0	0	0	0	0	1	0	0
Eddie Mathews, 3b	.227	7	22	4	5	3	0	1	4	8	5	0
Don McMahon, p	.000	3	0	0	0	0	0	0	0	0	0	0
Andy Pafko, of-5	.214	6	14	1	3	0	0	0	0	0	1	0
Juan Pizarro, p	.000	1	1	0	0	0	0	0	0	0	0	0
Del Rice, c	.167	2	6	0	1	0	0	0	0	1	2	0
Carl Sawatski, ph	.000	2	2	0	0	0	0	0	0	0	2	0
Red Schoendienst, 2b	.278	5	18	0	5	1	0	0	2	0	1	0
Warren Spahn, p	.000	2	4	0	0	0	0	0	0	0	1	0
Frank Torre, 1b	.300	7	10	2	3	0	0	2	3	2	0	0
Bob Trowbridge, p	.000	1	0	0	0	0	0	0	0	0	0	0
TOTAL	.209		225	23	47	6	1	8	22	22	40	1

PITCHER	W	L	ERA	G	GS	CG	SV	SHO	IP	H	ER	BB	SO
Bob Buhl	0	1	10.80	2	2	0	0	0	3.1	6	4	6	4
Lew Burdette	3	0	0.67	3	3	3	0	2	27.0	21	2	4	13
Gene Conley	0	0	10.80	1	0	0	0	0	1.2	2	2	1	0
Ernie Johnson	0	1	1.29	3	0	0	0	0	7.0	2	1	1	8
Don McMahon	0	0	0.00	3	0	0	0	0	5.0	3	0	3	5
Juan Pizarro	0	0	10.80	1	0	0	0	0	1.2	3	2	2	1
Warren Spahn	1	1	4.70	2	2	1	0	0	15.1	18	8	2	2
Bob Trowbridge	0	0	45.00	1	0	0	0	0	1.0	2	5	3	1
TOTAL	4	3	3.48	16	7	4	0	2	62.0	57	24	22	34

NY (A)

PLAYER/POS	AVG	G	AB	R	H	2B	3B	HR	RB	BB	SO	SB
Hank Bauer, of	.258	7	31	3	8	2	1	2	6	1	6	0
Yogi Berra, c	.320	7	25	5	8	1	0	1	2	4	0	0
Tommy Byrne, p	.500	2	2	0	1	0	0	0	0	0	1	0
Andy Carey, 3b	.286	2	7	0	2	1	0	0	0	1	1	0
Gerry Coleman, 2b	.364	7	22	2	8	2	0	0	2	3	1	0
Joe Collins, 1b-5	.000	6	5	0	0	0	0	0	0	0	3	0
Art Ditmar, p	.000	2	1	0	0	0	0	0	0	0	0	0
Whitey Ford, p	.000	2	5	0	0	0	0	0	0	0	1	0
Bob Grim, p	.000	2	0	0	0	0	0	0	0	0	0	0
Elston Howard, 1b-3	.273	6	11	2	3	0	0	1	3	1	3	0
Tony Kubek, of-5,3b-2	.286	7	28	4	8	0	0	2	4	0	4	0
Johnny Kucks, p	.000	1	0	0	0	0	0	0	0	0	0	0
Don Larsen, p	.000	2	2	1	0	0	0	0	0	0	2	0
Jerry Lumpe, 3b-3	.286	6	14	0	4	0	0	0	2	1	1	0
Mickey Mantle, of-5	.263	6	19	3	5	0	0	1	2	3	1	0
Gil McDougald, ss	.250	7	24	3	6	0	0	0	2	3	3	1
Bobby Richardson, 2b-1	.000	2	0	0	0	0	0	0	0	0	0	0
Bobby Shantz, p	.000	3	1	0	0	0	0	0	0	0	0	0
Harry Simpson, 1b-4	.083	5	12	0	1	0	0	0	1	0	4	0
Bill Skowron, 1b	.000	2	4	0	0	0	0	0	0	0	0	0
Enos Slaughter, of	.250	5	12	2	3	1	0	0	0	3	2	0
Tom Sturdivant, p	.000	2	1	0	0	0	0	0	0	0	0	0
Bob Turley, p	.000	3	4	0	0	0	0	0	0	0	2	0
TOTAL	.248		230	25	57	7	1	7	25	22	34	1

PITCHER	W	L	ERA	G	GS	CG	SV	SHO	IP	H	ER	BB	SO
Tommy Byrne	0	0	5.40	2	0	0	0	0	3.1	1	2	2	1
Art Ditmar	0	0	0.00	2	0	0	0	0	6.0	2	0	0	2
Whitey Ford	1	1	1.13	2	2	1	0	0	16.0	11	2	5	7
Bob Grim	0	1	7.71	2	0	0	0	0	2.1	3	2	0	2
Johnny Kucks	0	0	0.00	1	0	0	0	0	0.2	1	0	1	1
Don Larsen	1	1	3.72	2	1	0	0	0	9.2	8	4	5	6
Bobby Shantz	0	1	4.05	3	1	0	0	0	6.2	8	3	2	7
Tom Sturdivant	0	0	6.00	2	1	0	0	0	6.0	6	4	1	2
Bob Turley	1	0	2.31	3	2	1	0	0	11.2	7	3	6	12
TOTAL	3	4	2.89	19	7	2	0	0	62.1	47	20	22	40

GAME 1 AT NY OCT 2

MIL	000 000 100	1	5	0
NY	000 012 00X	3	9	1

Pitchers: SPAHN, Johnson (6), McMahon (7) vs FORD
Attendance: 69,476

GAME 2 AT NY OCT 3

MIL	011 200 000	4	8	0
NY	011 000 000	2	7	2

Pitchers: BURDETTE vs SHANTZ, Ditmar (4), Grim (8)
Home Runs: Logan-MIL, Bauer-NY
Attendance: 65,202

GAME 3 AT MIL OCT 5

NY	302 200 500	12	9	0
MIL	010 020 000	3	8	1

Pitchers: Turley, LARSEN (2) vs BUHL, Pizarro (1), Conley (3), Johnson (5), Trowbridge (7), McMahon (8)
Home Runs: Kubek-NY (2), Mantle-NY, Aaron-MIL
Attendance: 45,804

GAME 4 AT MIL OCT 6

NY	100 000 003 1	5	11	0
MIL	000 400 000 3	7	7	0

Pitchers: Sturdivant, Shantz (5), Kucks (8), Byrne (8), GRIM (10) vs SPAHN
Home Runs: Aaron-MIL, Torre-MIL, Howard-NY, Mathews-MIL
Attendance: 45,804

GAME 5 AT MIL OCT 7

NY	000 000 000	0	7	0
MIL	000 001 00X	1	6	1

Pitchers: FORD, Turley (8) vs BURDETTE
Attendance: 45,811

GAME 6 AT NY OCT 9

MIL	000 010 100	2	4	0
NY	002 000 10X	3	7	0

Pitchers: Buhl, JOHNSON (3), McMahon (8) vs TURLEY
Home Runs: Berra-NY, Torre-MIL, Aaron-MIL, Bauer-NY
Attendance: 61,408

GAME 7 AT NY OCT 10

MIL	004 000 010	5	9	1
NY	000 000 000	0	7	3

Pitchers: BURDETTE vs LARSEN, Shantz (3), Ditmar (4), Sturdivant (6), Byrne (8)
Home Runs: Crandall-MIL
Attendance: 61,207

NEW YORK YANKEES (AL) 4, MILWAUKEE BRAVES (NL) 3

After four games, Milwaukee held a 3–1 Series advantage, but New York rebounded to take the final three games and avenge their loss to the Braves the year before. As in the previous series, Warren Spahn faced Whitey Ford in the opener. The durable Spahn emerged the victor when Bill Bruton singled home the Braves' winning run off reliever Ryne Duren in the last of the 10th. In Game 2, home runs by Bruton and pitcher Lew Burdette (for three runs) helped the Braves take a 7–1 lead in the first inning. Milwaukee scored off five Yankees hurlers in their eventual 13–5 win.

Don Larsen and Ryne Duren combined for a shutout in Game 3 to give New York its first victory. Hank Bauer drove in all four runs with a two-run single in the fifth and his third home run in three games in the seventh. Warren Spahn held Bauer hitless in Game 4, blanking New York on two hits to defeat Whitey Ford and bring Milwaukee within a win of the championship.

Bob Turley came up with a shutout of his own the next day, though, fanning 10 men along the way. Gil McDougald's solo homer in the third inning was all the offense Turley needed, but as insurance the Yankees bunched six of their 10 hits into the sixth inning for six more runs.

Spahn and Ford, with only two days' rest, confronted each other a third time in Game 6. Ford lasted less than two innings, but Spahn (despite Hank Bauer's fourth Series home run in the first inning) endured into extra innings, when McDougald put New York ahead with a leadoff homer in the 10th. Two outs and two hits later, Spahn was removed, and Bill Skowron's single off reliever Don McMahon drove home another Yankees run. Milwaukee scored once in the last of the 10th and threatened further damage with men on first and third. But Bob Turley came on to retire the final batter and send the Series to a seventh game.

In the sixth inning of the finale, the Braves' Del Crandall homered against Turley (who had relieved Don Larsen in the third) to tie the game 2–2. But four runs off starter Lew Burdette in the top of the eighth (including Skowron's three-run homer) made the score 6–2,

where it remained, as Turley held on to bring Casey Stengel his seventh (and last) Series triumph—and the Yankees their 18th world title.

NY (A)

PLAYER/POS	AVG	G	AB	R	H	2B	3B	HR	RB	BB	SO	SB
Hank Bauer, of	.323	7	31	6	10	0	0	4	8	0	5	0
Yogi Berra, c	.222	7	27	3	6	3	0	0	2	1	0	0
Andy Carey, 3b	.083	5	12	1	1	0	0	0	0	0	3	0
Murry Dickson, p	.000	2	0	0	0	0	0	0	0	0	0	0
Art Ditmar, p	.000	1	1	0	0	0	0	0	0	0	0	0
Ryne Duren, p	.000	3	3	0	0	0	0	0	0	0	2	0
Whitey Ford, p	.000	3	4	1	0	0	0	0	0	2	2	0
Elston Howard, c	.222	6	18	4	4	0	0	0	2	1	4	1
Tony Kubek, ss	.048	7	21	0	1	0	0	0	1	1	7	0
Johnny Kucks, p	1.000	2	1	0	1	0	0	0	0	0	0	0
Don Larsen, p	.000	2	2	0	0	0	0	0	0	1	0	0
Jerry Lumpe, 3b-3, ss-2	.167	6	12	0	2	0	0	0	0	1	2	0
Duke Maas, p	.000	1	0	0	0	0	0	0	0	0	0	0
Mickey Mantle, of	.250	7	24	4	6	0	1	2	3	7	4	0
Gil McDougald, 2b	.321	7	28	5	9	2	0	2	4	2	4	0
Zach Monroe, p	.000	1	0	0	0	0	0	0	0	0	0	0
Bobby Richardson, 3b	.000	4	5	0	0	0	0	0	0	0	0	0
Norm Siebern, of	.125	3	8	1	1	0	0	0	0	3	2	0
Bill Skowron, 1b	.259	7	27	3	7	0	0	2	7	1	4	0
Enos Slaughter, ph	.000	4	3	1	0	0	0	0	0	1	1	0
Marv Throneberry, ph	.000	1	1	0	0	0	0	0	0	0	1	0
Bob Turley, p	.200	4	5	0	1	0	0	0	0	2	0	0
TOTAL	.210		233	29	49	5	1	10	29	21	42	1

PITCHER	W	L	ERA	G	GS	CG	SV	SHO	IP	H	ER	BB	SO
Murry Dickson	0	0	4.50	2	0	0	0	0	4.0	4	2	0	1
Art Ditmar	0	0	0.00	1	0	0	0	0	3.2	2	0	0	2
Ryne Duren	1	1	1.93	3	0	0	1	0	9.1	7	2	6	14
Whitey Ford	0	1	4.11	3	3	0	0	0	15.1	19	7	5	16
Johnny Kucks	0	0	2.08	2	0	0	0	0	4.1	4	1	1	0
Don Larsen	1	0	0.96	2	2	0	0	0	9.1	9	1	6	9
Duke Maas	0	0	81.00	1	0	0	0	0	0.1	2	3	1	0
Zach Monroe	0	0	27.00	1	0	0	0	0	1.0	3	3	1	1
Bob Turley	2	1	2.76	4	2	1	1	1	16.1	10	5	7	13
TOTAL	4	3	3.39	19	7	1	2	1	63.2	60	24	27	56

MIL (N)

PLAYER/POS	AVG	G	AB	R	H	2B	3B	HR	RB	BB	SO	SB
Hank Aaron, of	.333	7	27	3	9	2	0	0	2	4	6	0
Joe Adcock, 1b	.308	4	13	1	4	0	0	0	0	1	3	0
Billy Bruton, of	.412	7	17	2	7	0	0	1	2	5	5	0
Lew Burdette, p	.111	3	9	1	1	0	0	1	3	0	3	0
Wes Covington, of	.269	7	26	2	7	0	0	0	4	2	4	0
Del Crandall, c	.240	7	25	4	6	0	0	1	3	3	10	0
Harry Hanebrink, ph	.000	2	2	0	0	0	0	0	0	0	0	0
Johnny Logan, ss	.120	7	25	3	3	2	0	0	2	2	4	0
Felix Mantilla, ss-1	.000	4	0	1	0	0	0	0	0	0	0	0
Eddie Mathews, 3b	.160	7	25	3	4	2	0	0	3	6	11	1
Don McMahon, p	.000	3	0	0	0	0	0	0	0	0	0	0
Andy Pafko, of	.333	4	9	0	3	1	0	0	0	1	0	0
Juan Pizarro, p	.000	1	0	0	0	0	0	0	0	0	0	0
Bob Rush, p	.000	1	2	0	0	0	0	0	0	0	2	0
Red Schoendienst, 2b	.300	7	30	5	9	3	1	0	0	2	1	0
Warren Spahn, p	.333	3	12	0	4	0	0	0	3	0	6	0
Frank Torre, 1b	.176	7	17	0	3	0	0	0	1	2	0	0
Carl Willey, p	.000	1	0	0	0	0	0	0	0	0	0	0
Casey Wise, ph	.000	2	1	0	0	0	0	0	0	0	1	0
TOTAL	.250		240	25	60	10	1	3	24	27	56	1

PITCHER	W	L	ERA	G	GS	CG	SV	SHO	IP	H	ER	BB	SO
Lew Burdette	1	2	5.64	3	3	1	0	0	22.1	22	14	4	12
Don McMahon	0	0	5.40	3	0	0	0	0	3.1	3	2	3	5
Juan Pizarro	0	0	5.40	1	0	0	0	0	1.2	2	1	1	3
Bob Rush	0	1	3.00	1	1	0	0	0	6.0	3	2	5	2
Warren Spahn	2	1	2.20	3	3	2	0	1	28.2	19	7	8	18
Carl Willey	0	0	0.00	1	0	0	0	0	1.0	0	0	0	2
TOTAL	3	4	3.71	12	7	3	0	1	63.0	49	26	21	42

GAME 1 AT MIL OCT 1

```
NY  000 120 000 0   3 8 1
MIL 000 200 010 1   4 10 0
```
Pitchers: Ford, DUREN (8) vs SPAHN
Home Runs: Skowron-NY, Bauer-NY
Attendance: 46,367

GAME 2 AT MIL OCT 2

```
NY  100 100 003   5 7 0
MIL 710 023X      13 15 1
```
Pitchers: TURLEY, Maas (1), Kucks (1), Dickson (5), Monroe (8) vs BURDETTE
Home Runs: Bruton-MIL, Burdette-MIL, Mantle-NY (2), Bauer-NY
Attendance: 46,367

GAME 3 AT NY OCT 4

```
MIL 000 000 000   0 6 0
NY  000 020 20X   4 4 0
```
Pitchers: RUSH, McMahon (7) vs LARSEN, Duren (8)
Home Runs: Bauer-NY
Attendance: 71,599

GAME 4 AT NY OCT 5

```
MIL 000 001 110   3 9 0
NY  000 000 000   0 2 1
```
Pitchers: SPAHN vs FORD, Kucks (8), Dickson (9)
Attendance: 71,563

GAME 5 AT NY OCT 6

```
MIL 000 000 000   0 5 0
NY  001 006 00X   7 10 0
```
Pitchers: BURDETTE, Pizarro (6), Willey (8) vs TURLEY
Home Runs: McDougald-NY
Attendance: 65,279

GAME 6 AT MIL OCT 8

```
NY  100 001 000 2   4 10 1
MIL 110 000 000 1   3 10 4
```
Pitchers: Ford, Ditmar (2), DUREN (6), Turley (10) vs SPAHN, McMahon (10)
Home Runs: Bauer-NY, McDougald-NY
Attendance: 46,367

GAME 7 AT MIL OCT 9

```
NY  020 000 040   6 8 0
MIL 100 100 000   2 5 2
```
Pitchers: Larsen, TURLEY (3) vs BURDETTE, McMahon (8)
Home Runs: Crandall-MIL, Skowron-NY
Attendance: 46,367

LOS ANGELES DODGERS (NL) 4, CHICAGO WHITE SOX (AL) 2

It took a nosedive from first to third by San Francisco and a Dodgers playoff victory over Milwaukee (who had finished the season tied with the Dodgers), to bring Los Angeles the city's first major league pennant. But once they had made it to the Series, the Dodgers dispatched the White Sox in six games.

The opener, though, belonged to Chicago. In their first World Series in 40 years, the White Sox overwhelmed Los Angeles with 11 runs in the first four innings as pitchers Early Wynn and Gerry Staley combined to blank the Dodgers. Chicago's big gun was veteran slugger Ted Kluszewski (acquired from Pittsburgh in late August), whose single and two homers drove in five runs. Chicago scored twice in the first inning the next day, but Dodgers starter Johnny Podres settled down to blank the Sox over the next five innings as home runs by Charlie Neal in the fifth and pinch hitter Chuck Essegian and Neal (again) in the seventh put the Dodgers ahead by two. Rookie reliever Larry Sherry gave up a third Chicago run in the eighth on Al Smith's double, but a second runner was nailed at the plate, and Sherry set down the side in the ninth to save Podres' win.

When the Series moved to Los Angeles' cavernous Coliseum for the West Coast's first World Series games ever, fans turned out in record numbers, setting a new Series mark in each of the next three games. Dodgers starter Don Drysdale yielded 11 hits and four walks in Game 3, but the only run scored against him came on a double play after Larry Sherry had relieved him with two men on in the eighth. As Los Angeles had already scored twice, and added a third run in their half of the eighth, Drysdale emerged with the win and Sherry with his second save. In Game 4, the Sox's Sherm Lollar's three-run homer had tied the score by the time Sherry relieved Dodgers starter Roger Craig in the eighth, so Gil Hodges' solo homer in the last of the eighth gave Sherry the win this time—and Los Angeles a 3–1 Series advantage.

Chicago's Bob Shaw dueled Dodger Sandy Koufax through seven innings of Game 5 before 92,706 spectators (still a Series high). The Sox scored only once off Koufax, but one run was enough for their second win as a pair of Sox relievers continued Shaw's shutout through the final two innings.

Back in Chicago for Game 6, the Dodgers unloaded on Early Wynn and Dick Donovan for eight runs in the third and fourth innings. Ted Kluszewski's three-run homer in the last of the fourth led to Larry Sherry's fourth relief appearance—and his second Series win, as he held the Sox scoreless the rest of the game to bring the world championship to the West Coast for the first time.

LA (N)

PLAYER/POS	AVG	G	AB	R	H	2B	3B	HR	RB	BB	SO	SB
Chuck Churn, p	.000	1	0	0	0	0	0	0	0	0	0	0
Roger Craig, p	.000	2	3	0	0	0	0	0	0	0	2	0
Don Demeter, of	.250	6	12	2	3	0	0	0	0	1	3	0
Don Drysdale, p	.000	1	2	0	0	0	0	0	0	0	0	0
Chuck Essegian, ph	.667	4	3	2	2	0	0	2	2	1	1	0
Ron Fairly, of-4	.000	6	3	0	0	0	0	0	0	0	1	0
Carl Furillo, of-1	.250	4	4	0	1	0	0	0	2	0	1	0
Jim Gilliam, 3b	.240	6	25	2	6	0	0	0	0	2	2	2
Gil Hodges, 1b	.391	6	23	2	9	0	1	1	2	1	2	0
Johnny Klippstein, p	.000	1	0	0	0	0	0	0	0	0	0	0
Sandy Koufax, p	.000	2	2	0	0	0	0	0	0	0	1	0
Clem Labine, p	.000	1	0	0	0	0	0	0	0	0	0	0
Norm Larker, of	.188	6	16	2	3	0	0	0	0	0	3	0
Wally Moon, of	.261	6	23	3	6	0	0	1	2	2	2	1
Charlie Neal, 2b	.370	6	27	4	10	2	0	2	6	0	1	1
Joe Pignatano, c	.000	1	0	0	0	0	0	0	0	0	0	0
Johnny Podres, p-2	.500	3	4	1	2	1	0	0	1	0	0	0
Rip Repulski, ph	.000	1	0	0	0	0	0	0	0	1	0	0
Johnny Roseboro, c	.095	6	21	0	2	0	0	0	1	0	2	0
Larry Sherry, p-4	.500	5	4	0	2	0	0	0	0	0	1	0
Duke Snider, of-3	.200	4	10	1	2	0	0	1	2	2	0	0
Stan Williams, p	.000	1	0	0	0	0	0	0	0	0	0	0
Maury Wills, ss	.250	6	20	2	5	0	0	0	1	0	3	1
Don Zimmer, ss	.000	1	1	0	0	0	0	0	0	0	0	0
TOTAL	.261		203	21	53	3	1	7	19	12	27	5

PITCHER	W	L	ERA	G	GS	CG	SV	SHO	IP	H	ER	BB	SO
Chuck Churn	0	0	27.00	1	0	0	0	0	0.2	5	2	0	0
Roger Craig	0	1	8.68	2	2	0	0	0	9.1	15	9	5	8
Don Drysdale	1	0	1.29	1	1	0	0	0	7.0	11	1	4	5
Johnny Klippstein	0	0	0.00	1	0	0	0	0	2.0	1	0	0	2
Sandy Koufax	0	1	1.00	2	1	0	0	0	9.0	5	1	1	7
Clem Labine	0	0	0.00	1	0	0	0	0	1.0	0	0	0	1
Johnny Podres	1	0	4.82	2	2	0	0	0	9.1	7	5	6	4
Larry Sherry	2	0	0.71	4	0	0	2	0	12.2	8	1	2	5
Stan Williams	0	0	0.00	1	0	0	0	0	2.0	0	0	2	1
TOTAL	4	2	3.23	15	6	0	2	0	53.0	52	19	20	33

CHI (A)

PLAYER/POS	AVG	G	AB	R	H	2B	3B	HR	RB	BB	SO	SB
Luis Aparicio, ss	.308	6	26	1	8	1	0	0	2	2	3	1
Norm Cash, ph	.000	4	4	0	0	0	0	0	0	0	2	0
Dick Donovan, p	.333	3	3	0	1	0	0	0	0	0	1	0
Sammy Esposito, 3b	.000	2	2	0	0	0	0	0	0	0	1	0
Nellie Fox, 2b	.375	6	24	4	9	3	0	0	0	4	1	0
Billy Goodman, 3b	.231	5	13	1	3	0	0	0	1	0	5	0
Ted Kluszewski, 1b	.391	6	23	5	9	1	0	3	10	2	0	0
Jim Landis, of	.292	6	24	6	7	0	0	0	1	1	7	1
Sherm Lollar, c	.227	6	22	3	5	0	0	1	5	1	3	0
Turk Lown, p	.000	3	0	0	0	0	0	0	0	0	0	0
Jim McAnany, of	.000	3	5	0	0	0	0	0	0	1	0	0
Ray Moore, p	.000	1	0	0	0	0	0	0	0	0	0	0
Bubba Phillips, 3b-3, of-1	.300	3	10	0	3	1	0	0	0	0	0	0
Billy Pierce, p	.000	3	0	0	0	0	0	0	0	0	0	0
Jim Rivera, of	.000	5	11	1	0	0	0	0	0	3	1	0
Johnny Romano, ph	.000	1	1	0	0	0	0	0	0	0	0	0
Bob Shaw, p	.250	2	4	0	1	0	0	0	0	0	2	0
Al Smith, of	.250	6	20	1	5	3	0	0	1	4	4	0
Gerry Staley, p	.000	4	1	0	0	0	0	0	0	1	1	0
Earl Torgeson, 1b-1	.000	3	1	1	0	0	0	0	0	1	0	0
Early Wynn, p	.200	3	5	0	1	1	0	0	0	0	2	0
TOTAL	.261		199	23	52	10	0	4	19	20	33	2

PITCHER	W	L	ERA	G	GS	CG	SV	SHO	IP	H	ER	BB	SO
Dick Donovan	0	1	5.40	3	1	0	1	0	8.1	4	5	3	5
Turk Lown	0	0	0.00	3	0	0	0	0	3.1	2	0	1	3
Ray Moore	0	0	9.00	1	0	0	0	0	1.0	1	1	0	1
Billy Pierce	0	0	0.00	3	0	0	0	0	4.0	2	0	2	3
Bob Shaw	1	1	2.57	2	2	0	0	0	14.0	17	4	2	2
Gerry Staley	0	1	2.16	4	0	0	1	0	8.1	8	2	0	3
Early Wynn	1	1	5.54	3	3	0	0	0	13.0	19	8	4	10
TOTAL	2	4	3.46	19	6	0	2	0	52.0	53	20	12	27

GAME 1 AT CHI OCT 1

```
LA   000 000 000    0  8  3
CHI  207 200 00X   11 11  0
```
Pitchers: CRAIG, Churn (3), Labine (4), Koufax (5), Klippstein (7) vs WYNN, Staley (8)
Home Runs: Kluszewski-CHI (2)
Attendance: 48,013

GAME 2 AT CHI OCT 2

```
LA   000 010 300    4  9  1
CHI  200 000 010    3  8  0
```
Pitchers: PODRES, Sherry (7) vs SHAW, Lown (7)
Home Runs: Neal-LA (2), Essegian-LA
Attendance: 47,368

GAME 3 AT LA OCT 4

```
CHI  000 000 010    1 12  0
LA   000 000 21X    3  5  0
```
Pitchers: DONOVAN, Staley (7) vs DRYSDALE, Sherry (8)
Attendance: 92,394

GAME 4 AT LA OCT 5

```
CHI  000 000 400    4 10  3
LA   004 000 01X    5  9  0
```
Pitchers: Wynn, Lown (3), Pierce (4), STALEY (7) vs Craig, SHERRY (8)
Home Runs: Lollar-CHI, Hodges-LA
Attendance: 92,650

GAME 5 AT LA OCT 6

```
CHI  000 100 000    1  5  0
LA   000 000 000    0  9  0
```
Pitchers: SHAW, Pierce (7), Donovan (8) vs KOUFAX, Williams (8)
Attendance: 92,706

GAME 6 AT CHI OCT 8

```
LA   002 600 001    9 13  0
CHI  000 300 000    3  6  1
```
Pitchers: Podres, SHERRY (4) vs WYNN, Donovan (4), Lown (4), Staley (5), Pierce (8), Moore (9)
Home Runs: Snider-LA, Moon-LA, Kluszewski-CHI, Essegian-LA
Attendance: 47,653

PITTSBURGH PIRATES (NL) 4, NEW YORK YANKEES (AL) 3

Through six games and 8-1/2 innings of the seventh, the Yankees had outscored the Pirates by 29 runs. But as Pirates second baseman Bill Mazeroski stepped to the plate to open the last of the ninth, the Series was even at three games apiece, and Game 7 was tied 9–9. The stage was set for Mazeroski to fulfill that ultimate baseball fantasy, and he did, on pitcher Ralph Terry's second pitch.

Roger Maris opened the Series with a solo homer in the first inning of Game 1, and Elston Howard added two more runs with a homer in the ninth for the Yankees. But between the home runs New York scored only one run to the Pirates' six (including a two-run homer by Mazeroski in the fourth).

The Yankees avenged their firstgame loss with a blowout in Game 2. Pittsburgh hit safely 13 times, but scored only three runs. New York, though, turned 19 hits (and a Pirates error) into 16 runs— five of them driven in by Mickey Mantle's two home runs. Continuing their assault in New York the next day, the Bronx Bombers scored six runs in the first inning and four in the fourth as Whitey Ford blanked the Pirates on four hits. Mantle homered again, and second baseman Bobby Richardson drove in a Series single-game record six runs with a grand slam and a single.

Pirates ace Vernon Law—the winner of Game 1—started Game 4 and, with relief help once again from Roy Face, held the Yankees to two runs to even the Series. Law's bat proved crucial, too, as he doubled in Pittsburgh's first run and scored the third in a three-run fifth that provided all the Pirate scoring. In Game 5, the Pirates' Mazeroski doubled in what proved the two decisive runs in a three-run second as Harvey Haddix and Roy Face (who recorded his third save of the Series) duplicated the previous day's achievement of limiting New York to two runs.

But once again the Yankees came back. Bobby Richardson drove in three of New York's 12 runs with two triples to establish a new Series record of 12 RBIs as the Yankees, behind Whitey Ford's second shutout, sent the Series into a seventh game.

Home runs dominated the finale. Rocky Nelson's two-run shot

PIT (N)

PLAYER/POS	AVG	G	AB	R	H	2B	3B	HR	RB	BB	SO	SB
Gene Baker, ph	.000	3	3	0	0	0	0	0	0	0	1	0
Smoky Burgess, c	.333	5	18	2	6	1	0	0	0	2	1	0
Tom Cheney, p	.000	3	0	0	0	0	0	0	0	0	0	0
Joe Christopher, ph	.000	3	0	2	0	0	0	0	0	0	0	0
Gino Cimoli, of-6	.250	7	20	4	5	0	0	0	1	2	4	0
Roberto Clemente, of	.310	7	29	1	9	0	0	0	3	0	4	0
Roy Face, p	.000	4	3	0	0	0	0	0	0	0	2	0
Bob Friend, p	.000	3	1	0	0	0	0	0	0	0	0	0
Joe Gibbon, p	.000	2	0	0	0	0	0	0	0	0	0	0
Fred Green, p	.000	3	1	0	0	0	0	0	0	0	0	0
Dick Groat, ss	.214	7	28	3	6	2	0	0	2	0	1	0
Harvey Haddix, p	.333	2	3	0	1	0	0	0	0	0	1	0
Don Hoak, 3b	.217	7	23	3	5	2	0	0	3	4	1	0
Clem Labine, p	.000	3	0	0	0	0	0	0	0	0	0	0
Vern Law, p	.333	3	6	1	2	1	0	0	1	0	1	0
Bill Mazeroski, 2b	.320	7	25	4	8	2	0	2	5	0	3	0
Vinegar Bend Mizell, p	.000	2	0	0	0	0	0	0	0	0	0	0
Rocky Nelson, 1b-3	.333	4	9	2	3	0	0	1	2	1	1	0
Bob Oldis, c	.000	2	0	0	0	0	0	0	0	0	0	0
Dick Schofield, ss-2	.333	3	3	0	1	0	0	0	0	1	0	0
Bob Skinner, of	.200	2	5	2	1	0	0	0	1	1	0	1
Hal Smith, c	.375	3	8	1	3	0	0	1	3	0	0	0
Dick Stuart, 1b	.150	5	20	0	3	0	0	0	0	0	3	0
Bill Virdon, of	.241	7	29	2	7	3	0	0	5	1	3	1
George Witt, p	.000	3	0	0	0	0	0	0	0	0	0	0
TOTAL	.256		234	27	60	11	0	4	26	12	26	2

PITCHER	W	L	ERA	G	GS	CG	SV	SHO	IP	H	ER	BB	SO
Tom Cheney	0	0	4.50	3	0	0	0	0	4.0	4	2	1	6
Roy Face	0	0	5.23	4	0	0	3	0	10.1	9	6	2	4
Bob Friend	0	2	13.50	3	2	0	0	0	6.0	13	9	3	7
Joe Gibbon	0	0	9.00	2	0	0	0	0	3.0	4	3	1	2
Fred Green	0	0	22.50	3	0	0	0	0	4.0	11	10	1	3
Harvey Haddix	2	0	2.45	2	1	0	0	0	7.1	6	2	2	6
Clem Labine	0	0	13.50	3	0	0	0	0	4.0	13	6	1	2
Vern Law	2	0	3.44	3	3	0	0	0	18.1	22	7	3	8
Vinegar Bend Mizell	0	1	15.43	2	1	0	0	0	2.1	4	4	2	1
George Witt	0	0	0.00	3	0	0	0	0	2.2	5	0	2	1
TOTAL	4	3	7.11	28	7	0	3	0	62.0	91	49	18	40

NY (A)

PLAYER/POS	AVG	G	AB	R	H	2B	3B	HR	RB	BB	SO	SB
Luis Arroyo, p	.000	1	1	0	0	0	0	0	0	0	0	0
Yogi Berra, of-4, c-3	.318	7	22	6	7	0	0	1	8	2	0	0
Johnny Blanchard, c-2	.455	5	11	2	5	2	0	0	2	0	0	0
Clete Boyer, 3b-4, ss-1	.250	4	12	1	3	2	1	0	1	0	1	0
Bob Cerv, of-3	.357	4	14	1	5	0	0	0	0	0	3	0
Jim Coates, p	.000	3	1	0	0	0	0	0	0	0	1	0
Joe De Maestri, ss-3	.500	4	2	1	1	0	0	0	0	0	1	0
Art Ditmar, p	.000	2	0	0	0	0	0	0	0	0	0	0
Ryne Duren, p	.000	2	0	0	0	0	0	0	0	0	0	0
Whitey Ford, p	.250	2	8	1	2	0	0	0	0	2	2	0
Eli Grba, pr	.000	1	0	0	0	0	0	0	0	0	0	0
Elston Howard, c-4	.462	5	13	4	6	1	1	1	4	1	4	0
Tony Kubek, ss-7, of-2	.333	7	30	6	10	1	0	0	3	3	2	0
Dale Long, ph	.333	3	3	0	1	0	0	0	0	0	0	0
Hector Lopez, of-1	.429	3	7	0	3	0	0	0	0	0	0	0
Duke Maas, p	.000	1	0	0	0	0	0	0	0	0	0	0
Mickey Mantle, of	.400	7	25	8	10	1	0	3	11	8	9	0
Roger Maris, of	.267	7	30	6	8	1	0	2	2	2	4	0
Gil McDougald, 3b	.278	6	18	4	5	1	0	0	2	3	0	0
Bobby Richardson, 2b	.367	7	30	8	11	2	2	1	12	1	1	0
Bobby Shantz, p	.333	3	3	0	1	0	0	0	0	0	0	0
Bill Skowron, 1b	.375	7	32	7	12	2	0	2	6	0	6	0
Bill Stafford, p	.000	2	1	0	0	0	0	0	0	0	1	0
Ralph Terry, p	.000	2	2	0	0	0	0	0	0	0	1	0
Bob Turley, p	.250	2	4	0	1	0	0	0	0	1	1	0
TOTAL	.338		269	55	91	13	4	10	54	18	40	0

PITCHER	W	L	ERA	G	GS	CG	SV	SHO	IP	H	ER	BB	SO
Luis Arroyo	0	0	13.50	1	0	0	0	0	0.2	2	1	0	1
Jim Coates	0	0	5.68	3	0	0	0	0	6.1	6	4	1	3
Art Ditmar	0	2	21.60	2	2	0	0	0	1.2	6	4	1	0
Ryne Duren	0	0	2.25	2	0	0	0	0	4.0	2	1	1	5
Whitey Ford	2	0	0.00	2	2	2	0	2	18.0	11	0	2	8
Duke Maas	0	0	4.50	1	0	0	0	0	2.0	2	1	0	1
Bobby Shantz	0	0	4.26	3	0	0	0	0	6.1	4	3	1	1
Bill Stafford	0	0	1.50	2	0	0	0	0	6.0	5	1	1	2
Ralph Terry	0	2	5.40	2	1	0	0	0	6.2	7	4	1	5
Bob Turley	1	0	4.82	2	2	0	0	0	9.1	15	5	4	0
TOTAL	3	4	3.54	20	7	2	1	2	61.0	60	24	12	26

in the first opened the scoring, and homers by Bill Skowron in the fifth and Yogi Berra in the sixth contributed four of the five runs that put New York ahead 5–4. Hal Smith's three-run homer in the bottom of the eighth restored the lead to Pittsburgh, 9–7, and after the Yankees had tied the game in the top of the ninth (on three singles and a ground out), Mazeroski's immortal shot over the wall in left gave Pittsburgh its first world championship in 35 years.

GAME 1 AT PIT OCT 5

NY 100 100 002   4 13 2
PIT 300 201 00X   6 8 0
Pitchers: DITMAR, Coates (1), Maas (5), Duren (7) vs LAW, Face (8)
Home Runs: Maris-NY, Mazeroski-PIT, Howard-NY
Attendance: 36,676

GAME 2 AT PIT OCT 6

NY 002 127 301   16 19 1
PIT 000 100 002   3 13 1
Pitchers: TURLEY, Shantz (9) vs FRIEND, Green (5), Labine (6), Witt (6), Gibbon (7), Cheney (9)
Home Runs: Mantle-NY (2)
Attendance: 37,308

GAME 3 AT NY OCT 8

PIT 000 000 000   0 4 0
NY 600 400 00X   10 16 1
Pitchers: MIZELL, Labine (1), Green (1), Witt (4), Cheney (6), Gibbon (8) vs FORD
Home Runs: Richardson-NY, Mantle-NY
Attendance: 70,001

GAME 4 AT NY OCT 9

PIT 000 030 000   3 7 0
NY 000 100 100   2 8 0
Pitchers: LAW, Face (7) vs TERRY, Shantz (7), Coates (8)
Home Runs: Skowron-NY
Attendance: 67,812

GAME 5 AT NY OCT 10

PIT 031 000 001   5 10 2
NY 011 000 000   2 5 2
Pitchers: HADDIX, Face (7) vs DITMAR, Arroyo (2), Stafford (3), Duren (8)
Home Runs: Maris-NY
Attendance: 62,753

GAME 6 AT PIT OCT 12

NY 015 002 220   12 17 1
PIT 000 000 000   0 7 1
Pitchers: FORD vs FRIEND, Cheney (3), Mizell (4), Green (6), Labine (6), Witt (9)
Attendance: 38,580

GAME 7 AT PIT OCT 13

NY 000 014 022   9 13 1
PIT 220 000 051   10 11 0
Pitchers: Turley, Stafford (2), Shantz (3), Coates (8), TERRY (8) vs Law, Face (6), Friend (9), HADDIX (9)
Home Runs: Nelson-PIT, Skowron-NY, Berra-NY, Smith-PIT, Mazeroski-PIT
Attendance: 36,683

NEW YORK YANKEES (AL) 4, CINCINNATI REDS (NL) 1

Slugger Mickey Mantle sat out most of the Series with a thigh infection, but rookie manager Ralph Houk enjoyed an otherwise splendid finish to a splendid season as his Yankees mauled the Reds, 27 runs to 13. Yankees ace Whitey Ford, coming off one of his finest seasons (25–4), carried his mound mastery into the Series opener, holding Cincinnati to two singles and a walk as he hurled his third straight World Series shutout. New York recorded only six hits, but two of them were home runs by Elston Howard and Bill Skowron.

Gordy Coleman's two-run homer the next day in the top of the fourth inning broke Cincinnati's scoring drought and gave the Reds a 2–0 lead. Yogi Berra tied the score half an inning later with a two-run blast for New York, but that was all they would get. Reds starter Joey Jay blanked the Yankees the rest of the way as his teammates put across four more runs to even the Series. Bob Purkey pitched for the Reds in Game 3 and blanked New York on one hit through the first six innings, taking a 1–0 lead into the top of the seventh. A pair of singles sandwiched around a passed ball evened the score, but the Reds regained the lead with a run in the last of the seventh. But pinch hitter Johnny Blanchard homered to retie the game in the eighth and—while Yankees relief ace Luis Arroyo stopped the Reds through the final two innings—Roger Maris, who set the major league record with 61 home runs during the season, added another to win the game and regain the Series lead for New York.

Cincinnati never again threatened. In Game 4, Whitey Ford held the Reds to four harmless singles until he was removed in the sixth because of an ankle injury. (In the third inning he passed Babe Ruth's World Series record of 29-2/3 consecutive scoreless innings.) Reliever Jim Coates continued Ford's shutout as the Yankees scored seven runs for the decisive win. The fifth and final game also was no contest. Cincinnati did score five runs—three on Frank Robinson's third-inning home run and two on Wally Post's shot in the fifth. But the Yankees ran through eight Cincinnati pitchers, scoring 13 times. Seven of their 15 hits went for extra bases, including Johnny Blanchard's second home run of the Series, and a triple and homer by utility outfielder Hector Lopez.

NY (A)

PLAYER/POS	AVG	G	AB	R	H	2B	3B	HR	RB	BB	SO	SB
Luis Arroyo, p	.000	2	0	0	0	0	0	0	0	0	0	0
Yogi Berra, of	.273	4	11	2	3	0	0	1	3	5	1	0
Johnny Blanchard, of-2	.400	4	10	4	4	1	0	2	3	2	0	0
Clete Boyer, 3b	.267	5	15	0	4	2	0	0	3	4	0	0
Jim Coates, p	.000	1	1	0	0	0	0	0	0	0	1	0
Buddy Daley, p	.000	2	1	0	0	0	0	0	1	0	0	0
Whitey Ford, p	.000	2	5	1	0	0	0	0	0	0	1	0
Billy Gardner, ph	.000	1	1	0	0	0	0	0	0	0	0	0
Elston Howard, c	.250	5	20	5	5	3	0	1	1	2	3	0
Tony Kubek, ss	.227	5	22	3	5	0	0	0	1	1	4	0
Hector Lopez, of-3	.333	4	9	3	3	0	1	1	7	2	3	0
Mickey Mantle, of	.167	2	6	0	1	0	0	0	0	0	2	0
Roger Maris, of	.105	5	19	4	2	1	0	1	2	4	6	0
Jack Reed, of	.000	3	0	0	0	0	0	0	0	0	0	0
Bobby Richardson, 2b	.391	5	23	2	9	1	0	0	0	0	0	1
Bill Skowron, 1b	.353	5	17	3	6	0	0	1	5	3	4	0
Bill Stafford, p	.000	1	2	0	0	0	0	0	0	0	0	0
Ralph Terry, p	.000	2	3	0	0	0	0	0	0	0	1	0
TOTAL	.255		165	27	42	8	1	7	26	24	25	1

PITCHER	W	L	ERA	G	GS	CG	SV	SHO	IP	H	ER	BB	SO
Luis Arroyo	1	0	2.25	2	0	0	0	0	4.0	4	1	2	3
Jim Coates	0	0	0.00	1	0	0	1	0	4.0	1	0	1	2
Buddy Daley	1	0	0.00	2	0	0	0	0	7.0	5	0	0	3
Whitey Ford	2	0	0.00	2	2	1	0	1	14.0	6	0	1	7
Bill Stafford	0	0	2.70	1	1	0	0	0	6.2	7	2	2	5
Ralph Terry	0	1	4.82	2	2	0	0	0	9.1	12	5	2	7
TOTAL	4	1	1.60	10	5	1	1	1	45.0	35	8	8	27

NY (A)

PLAYER/POS	AVG	G	AB	R	H	2B	3B	HR	RB	BB	SO	SB
Gus Bell, ph	.000	3	3	0	0	0	0	0	0	0	0	0
Don Blasingame, 2b	.143	3	7	1	1	0	0	0	0	0	3	0
Jim Brosnan, p	.000	3	0	0	0	0	0	0	0	0	0	0
Leo Cardenas, ph	.333	3	3	0	1	1	0	0	0	0	1	0
Elio Chacon, 2b-3	.250	4	12	2	3	0	0	0	0	1	2	0
Gordie Coleman, 1b	.250	5	20	2	5	0	0	1	2	0	1	0
Johnny Edwards, c	.364	3	11	1	4	2	0	0	2	0	0	0
Gene Freese, 3b	.063	5	16	0	1	1	0	0	0	3	4	0
Dick Gernert, ph	.000	4	4	0	0	0	0	0	0	0	1	0
Bill Henry, p	.000	2	0	0	0	0	0	0	0	0	0	0
Ken Hunt, p	.000	1	0	0	0	0	0	0	0	0	0	0
Joey Jay, p	.000	2	4	0	0	0	0	0	0	0	2	0
Darrell Johnson, c	.500	2	4	0	2	0	0	0	0	0	0	0
Ken Johnson, p	.000	1	0	0	0	0	0	0	0	0	0	0
Sherman Jones, p	.000	1	0	0	0	0	0	0	0	0	0	0
Eddie Kasko, ss	.318	5	22	1	7	0	0	0	1	0	2	0
Jerry Lynch, ph	.000	4	3	0	0	0	0	0	0	1	1	0
Jim Maloney, p	.000	1	0	0	0	0	0	0	0	0	0	0
Jim O'Toole, p	.000	2	3	0	0	0	0	0	0	0	1	0
Vada Pinson, of	.091	5	22	0	2	1	0	0	0	0	1	0
Wally Post, of	.333	5	18	3	6	1	0	1	2	0	1	0
Bob Purkey, p	.000	2	3	0	0	0	0	0	0	0	3	0
Frank Robinson, of	.200	5	15	3	3	2	0	1	4	3	4	0
Jerry Zimmerman, c	.000	2	0	0	0	0	0	0	0	0	0	0
TOTAL	.206		170	13	35	8	0	3	11	8	27	0

PITCHER	W	L	ERA	G	GS	CG	SV	SHO	IP	H	ER	BB	SO
Jim Brosnan	0	0	7.50	3	0	0	0	0	6.0	9	5	4	5
Bill Henry	0	0	19.29	2	0	0	0	0	2.1	4	5	2	3
Ken Hunt	0	0	0.00	1	0	0	0	0	1.0	0	0	1	1
Joey Jay	1	1	5.59	2	2	1	0	0	9.2	8	6	6	6
Ken Johnson	0	0	0.00	1	0	0	0	0	0.2	0	0	0	0
Sherman Jones	0	0	0.00	1	0	0	0	0	0.2	0	0	0	0
Jim Maloney	0	0	27.00	1	0	0	0	0	0.2	4	2	1	1
Jim O'Toole	0	2	3.00	2	2	0	0	0	12.0	11	4	7	4
Bob Purkey	0	1	1.64	2	1	1	0	0	11.0	6	2	3	5
TOTAL	1	4	4.91	15	5	2	0	0	44.0	42	24	24	25

GAME 1 AT NY OCT 4

CIN 000 000 000   0 2 0
NY 000 101 00X   2 6 0
Pitchers: O'TOOLE, Brosnan (8) vs FORD
Home Runs: Howard-NY, Skowron-NY
Attendance: 62,397

GAME 2 AT NY OCT 5

CIN 000 211 020   6 9 0
NY 000 200 000   2 4 3
Pitchers: JAY vs TERRY, Arroyo (8)
Home Runs: Coleman-CIN, Berra-NY
Attendance: 63,083

GAME 3 AT CIN OCT 7

NY 000 000 111   3 6 1
CIN 001 000 100   2 8 0
Pitchers: Stafford, Daley (7), ARROYO (8) vs PURKEY
Home Runs: Blanchard-NY, Maris-NY
Attendance: 32,589

GAME 4 AT CIN OCT 8

NY 000 112 300   7 11 0
CIN 000 000 000   0 5 1
Pitchers: FORD, Coates (6) vs O'TOOLE, Brosnan (6), Henry (9)
Attendance: 32,589

GAME 5 AT CIN OCT 9

NY 510 502 000   13 15 1
CIN 003 020 000   5 11 3
Pitchers: Terry, DALEY (3) vs JAY, Maloney (1), K.Johnson (2), Henry (3), Jones (4), Purkey (5), Brosnan (7), Hunt (9)
Home Runs: Blanchard-NY, Robinson-CIN, Lopez-NY, Post-CIN
Attendance: 32,589

NEW YORK YANKEES (AL) 4, SAN FRANCISCO GIANTS (NL) 3

After edging Los Angeles for the pennant in a three-game playoff to break a regular-season tie, San Francisco battled to the final out of Game 7 before falling to New York in the World Series. The teams alternated wins throughout the Series. In the opener Roger Maris doubled two runs home for a quick lead. Whitey Ford gave up a run in the second (ending his record streak for consecutive scoreless World Series innings pitched at 33-2/3) and a tying run an inning later. But he blanked the Giants after that, and won the game on Clete Boyer's homer in the seventh.

Jack Sanford blanked the Yankees on three hits in Game 2, but in Game 3 Bill Stafford restored the Series edge to New York with a four-hit 3–2 win (a shutout until Ed Bailey's ninth-inning home run). Both clubs hit safely nine times in Game 4. But one of the Giants' hits was Chuck Hiller's tie-breaking grand slam in the seventh—more than enough for a Giants win and another Series tie. In Game 5 Sanford brought a three-hit 2–2 tie into the last of the eighth. But after he had notched his 10th strikeout, two singles and Tom Tresh's home run drove him out and gave Ralph Terry all the margin he needed to avenge his second-game loss to Sanford, and put the Yankees ahead in the Series for the third time.

When play resumed in San Francisco after several days of rain, Billy Pierce held New York to just three hits. One was Roger Maris' solo homer in the fifth, but Pierce's Giants unloaded on Whitey Ford for five runs, driving Ford out and keeping Giant hopes alive.

The finale pitted Terry against Sanford for the third time. Both pitched effectively, but Terry carried a 1–0 lead into the last of the ninth. Pinch hitter Matty Alou led off with a bunt single, but Terry fanned the next two batters. Then Willie Mays doubled to right, but Maris' slick fielding stopped Alou at third. As Terry faced Willie McCovey (who had homered off him in Game 2), he pondered the home run he had given up to Bill Mazeroski two years earlier to lose the 1960 World Series to Pittsburgh. McCovey lined Terry's third pitch toward right—but right at second baseman Bobby

Richardson, who grabbed it for the Yankees' 20th world title. It would be 15 years before they saw another.

NY (A)

PLAYER/POS	AVG	G	AB	R	H	2B	3B	HR	RB	BB	SO	SB
Yogi Berra, c-1	.000	2	2	0	0	0	0	0	0	2	0	0
Johnny Blanchard, ph	.000	1	1	0	0	0	0	0	0	0	1	0
Clete Boyer, 3b	.318	7	22	2	7	1	0	1	4	1	3	0
Marshall Bridges, p	.000	2	0	0	0	0	0	0	0	0	0	0
Jim Coates, p	.000	2	0	0	0	0	0	0	0	0	0	0
Buddy Daley, p	.000	1	0	0	0	0	0	0	0	0	0	0
Whitey Ford, p	.000	3	7	0	0	0	0	0	0	1	3	0
Elston Howard, c	.143	6	21	1	3	1	0	0	1	1	4	0
Tony Kubek, ss	.276	7	29	2	8	1	0	0	1	1	3	0
Dale Long, 1b	.200	2	5	0	1	0	0	0	1	0	1	0
Hector Lopez, ph	.000	2	2	0	0	0	0	0	0	0	0	0
Mickey Mantle, of	.120	7	25	2	3	1	0	0	0	4	5	2
Roger Maris, of	.174	7	23	4	4	1	0	1	5	5	2	0
Bobby Richardson, 2b	.148	7	27	3	4	0	0	0	0	3	1	0
Bill Skowron, 1b	.222	6	18	1	4	0	1	0	1	1	5	0
Bill Stafford, p	.000	1	3	0	0	0	0	0	0	0	1	0
Ralph Terry, p	.125	3	8	0	1	0	0	0	0	0	6	0
Tom Tresh, of	.321	7	28	5	9	1	0	1	4	1	4	2
TOTAL	.199		221	20	44	6	1	3	17	21	39	4

PITCHER	W	L	ERA	G	GS	CG	SV	SHO	IP	H	ER	BB	SO
Marshall Bridges	0	0	4.91	2	0	0	0	0	3.2	4	2	2	3
Jim Coates	0	1	6.75	2	0	0	0	0	2.2	1	2	1	3
Buddy Daley	0	0	0.00	1	0	0	0	0	1.0	1	0	1	0
Whitey Ford	1	1	4.12	3	3	1	0	0	19.2	24	9	4	12
Bill Stafford	1	0	2.00	1	1	1	0	0	9.0	4	2	2	5
Ralph Terry	2	1	1.80	3	3	2	0	1	25.0	17	5	2	16
TOTAL	4	3	2.95	12	7	4	0	1	61.0	51	20	12	39

SF (N)

PLAYER/POS	AVG	G	AB	R	H	2B	3B	HR	RB	BB	SO	SB
Felipe Alou, of	.269	7	26	2	7	1	1	0	1	1	4	0
Matty Alou, of-4	.333	6	12	2	4	1	0	0	1	0	1	0
Ed Bailey, c-3	.071	6	14	1	1	0	0	1	2	0	3	0
Bobby Bolin, p	.000	2	0	0	0	0	0	0	0	0	0	0
Ernie Bowman, ss-1	.000	2	1	1	0	0	0	0	0	0	0	0
Orlando Cepeda, 1b	.158	5	19	1	3	1	0	0	2	0	4	0
Jim Davenport, 3b	.136	7	22	1	3	1	0	0	1	4	7	0
Tom Haller, c	.286	4	14	1	4	1	0	1	3	0	2	0
Chuck Hiller, 2b	.269	7	26	4	7	3	0	1	5	3	4	0
Harvey Kuenn, of	.083	3	12	1	1	0	0	0	0	1	1	0
Don Larsen, p	.000	3	0	0	0	0	0	0	0	0	0	0
Juan Marichal, p	.000	1	2	0	0	0	0	0	0	0	1	0
Willie Mays, of	.250	7	28	3	7	2	0	0	1	1	5	1
Willie McCovey, 1b-2, of-2	.200	4	15	2	3	0	1	1	1	1	3	0
Stu Miller, p	.000	2	0	0	0	0	0	0	0	0	0	0
Bob Nieman, ph	.000	1	0	0	0	0	0	0	0	1	0	0
Billy O'Dell, p	.333	3	3	0	1	0	0	0	0	0	1	0
John Orsino, c	.000	1	1	0	0	0	0	0	0	0	0	0
Jose Pagan, ss	.368	7	19	2	7	0	0	1	2	0	1	0
Billy Pierce, p	.000	2	5	0	0	0	0	0	0	0	1	0
Jack Sanford, p	.429	3	7	0	3	0	0	0	0	0	2	0
TOTAL	.226		226	21	51	10	2	5	19	12	39	1

PITCHER	W	L	ERA	G	GS	CG	SV	SHO	IP	H	ER	BB	SO
Bobby Bolin	0	0	6.75	2	0	0	0	0	2.2	4	2	2	2
Don Larsen	1	0	3.86	3	0	0	0	0	2.1	1	1	2	0
Juan Marichal	0	0	0.00	1	1	0	0	0	4.0	2	0	2	4
Stu Miller	0	0	0.00	2	0	0	0	0	1.1	1	0	2	0
Billy O'Dell	0	1	4.38	3	1	0	1	0	12.1	12	6	3	9
Billy Pierce	1	1	2.40	2	2	1	0	0	15.0	8	4	2	5
Jack Sanford	1	2	1.93	3	3	1	0	1	23.1	16	5	8	19
TOTAL	3	4	2.66	16	7	2	1	1	61.0	44	18	21	39

GAME 1 AT SF OCT 4

NY	200 000 121	6 11 0
SF	011 000 000	2 10 0

Pitchers: FORD vs O'DELL, Larsen (7), Miller (9)
Home Runs: Boyer-NY
Attendance: 43,852

GAME 2 AT SF OCT 5

NY	000 000 000	0 3 1
SF	100 000 10X	2 6 0

Pitchers: TERRY, Daley (8) vs SANFORD
Home Runs: McCovey-SF
Attendance: 43,910

GAME 3 AT NY OCT 7

SF	000 000 002	2 4 3
NY	000 000 30X	3 5 1

Pitchers: PIERCE, Larsen (7), Bolin (8) vs STAFFORD
Home Runs: Bailey-SF
Attendance: 71,434

GAME 4 AT NY OCT 8

SF	020 000 401	7 9 1
NY	000 002 001	3 9 1

Pitchers: Marichal, Bolin (5), LARSEN (6), O'Dell (7) vs Ford, COATES (7), Bridges (7)
Home Runs: Haller-SF, Hiller-SF
Attendance: 66,607

GAME 5 AT NY OCT 10

SF	001 010 001	3 8 2
NY	000 101 03X	5 6 0

Pitchers: SANFORD, Miller (8) vs TERRY
Home Runs: Pagan-SF, Tresh-NY
Attendance: 63,165

GAME 6 AT SF OCT 15

NY	000 010 010	2 3 2
SF	000 320 00X	5 10 1

Pitchers: FORD, Coates (5), Bridges (8) vs PIERCE
Home Runs: Maris-NY
Attendance: 43,948

GAME 7 AT SF OCT 16

NY	000 100 000	1 7 0
SF	000 000 000	0 4 1

Pitchers: TERRY vs SANFORD, O'Dell (8)
Attendance: 43,948

LOS ANGELES DODGERS (NL) 4, NEW YORK YANKEES (AL) 0

The Yankees won the American League pennant by 10-1/2 games, but in the Series they were overwhelmed by Dodgers pitching. The opener pitted two all-time greats against each other: Whitey Ford (24–7 that season) and Sandy Koufax (25–5). For an inning it was close. Ford fanned two of the first three batters to face him, and Koufax struck out the side. But in the top of the second the Dodgers' Frank Howard doubled with one out, and before Ford could record the second out, two singles and John Roseboro's home run had put four Dodgers across home plate. Koufax ran his consecutive Ks to five and had tied the Series single-game record of 14 by the time Tom Tresh tagged him for a two-run homer in the eighth. That was New York's only scoring, and Koufax ended the game with a new-record 15th strikeout an inning later.

Veteran Johnny Podres pitched shutout ball through 8-1/3 innings of Game 2 as his Dodgers built him a four-run lead (one of the runs a homer by ex-Yankee Bill Skowron). New York scored a run in the last of the ninth, but it was not enough to keep the Dodgers from returning to Los Angeles with a 2–0 Series advantage.

A first-inning walk, a wild pitch, and a single moved Dodger Jim Gilliam around the bases for the only scoring in Game 3 as Jim Bouton hooked up in a duel with Don Drysdale. Bouton left after seven innings for Yankees relief ace Hal Reniff, who held Los Angeles hitless through the final frames. When Drysdale completed his shutout, only three singles had been hit against him, and he had struck out nine.

Ford and Koufax tangled again in the fourth game. Ford pitched much more impressively than he had in the opener, walking just one and yielding only two hits in seven innings. One of the hits was Frank Howard's solo homer in the fifth inning, but Mickey Mantle evened the score with a home run off Koufax in the seventh. In the last of the seventh, Yankee first baseman Joe Pepitone lost sight of a throw from the third baseman for an error that sent batter Jim Gilliam all the way to third, and Willie Davis followed with a fly to center that scored Gilliam with the go-ahead run. No one else scored against

Ford (or Reniff, who relieved him in the eighth), but no other Yankee scored against Koufax either, and the Dodgers, with just two hits, captured the game and the Series.

GAME 1 AT NY OCT 2

LA 041 000 000   5 9 0
NY 000 000 020   2 6 0
Pitchers: KOUFAX vs FORD, Williams (6), Hamilton (9)
Home Runs: Roseboro-LA, Tresh-NY
Attendance: 69,000

GAME 2 AT NY OCT 3

LA 200 100 010   4 10 1
NY 000 000 001   1 7 0
Pitchers: PODRES, Perranoski (9) vs DOWNING, Terry (6), Reniff (9)
Home Runs: Skowron-LA
Attendance: 66,455

GAME 3 AT LA OCT 5

NY 000 000 000   0 3 0
LA 100 000 00X   1 4 1
Pitchers: BOUTON, Reniff (8) vs DRYSDALE
Attendance: 55,912

GAME 4 AT LA OCT 6

NY 000 000 100   1 6 1
LA 000 010 10X   2 2 1
Pitchers: FORD, Reniff (8) vs KOUFAX
Home Runs: F.Howard-LA, Mantle-NY
Attendance: 55,912

LA (N)

PLAYER/POS	AVG	G	AB	R	H	2B	3B	HR	RB	BB	SO	SB
Tommy Davis, of	.400	4	15	0	6	0	2	0	2	0	2	1
Willie Davis, of	.167	4	12	2	2	2	0	0	3	0	6	0
Don Drysdale, p	.000	1	1	0	0	0	0	0	0	0	2	0
Ron Fairly, of	.000	4	1	0	0	0	0	0	0	0	3	0
Jim Gilliam, 3b	.154	4	13	3	2	0	0	0	0	0	3	1
Frank Howard, of	.300	3	10	2	3	1	0	1	1	0	2	0
Sandy Koufax, p	.000	2	6	0	0	0	0	0	0	0	2	0
Ron Perranoski, p	.000	1	0	0	0	0	0	0	0	0	0	0
Johnny Podres, p	.250	1	4	0	1	0	0	0	0	0	0	0
Johnny Roseboro, c	.143	4	14	1	2	0	0	1	3	0	4	0
Bill Skowron, 1b	.385	4	13	2	5	0	0	1	3	1	3	0
Dick Tracewski, 2b	.154	4	13	1	2	0	0	0	0	1	2	0
Maury Wills, ss	.133	4	15	1	2	0	0	0	0	1	3	1
TOTAL	.214		117	12	25	3	2	3	12	11	25	2

PITCHER	W	L	ERA	G	GS	CG	SV	SHO	IP	H	ER	BB	SO
Don Drysdale	1	0	0.00	1	1	1	0	1	9.0	3	0	1	9
Sandy Koufax	2	0	1.50	2	2	2	0	0	18.0	12	3	3	23
Ron Perranoski	0	0	0.00	1	0	0	1	0	0.2	1	0	0	1
Johnny Podres	1	0	1.08	1	1	0	0	0	8.1	6	1	1	4
TOTAL	4	0	1.00	5	4	3	1	1	36.0	22	4	5	37

NY (A)

PLAYER/POS	AVG	G	AB	R	H	2B	3B	HR	RB	BB	SO	SB
Yogi Berra, ph	.000	1	1	0	0	0	0	0	0	0	0	0
Johnny Blanchard, of-1	.000	1	3	0	0	0	0	0	0	0	0	0
Jim Bouton, p	.000	1	2	0	0	0	0	0	0	0	2	0
Clete Boyer, 3b	.077	4	13	0	1	0	0	0	0	1	6	0
Harry Bright, ph	.000	2	2	0	0	0	0	0	0	0	2	0
Al Downing, p	.000	1	1	0	0	0	0	0	0	0	1	0
Whitey Ford, p	.000	2	3	0	0	0	0	0	0	0	0	0
Steve Hamilton, p	.000	1	0	0	0	0	0	0	0	0	0	0
Elston Howard, c	.333	4	15	0	5	0	0	0	1	0	3	0
Tony Kubek, ss	.188	4	16	1	3	0	0	0	0	0	3	0
Phil Linz, ph	.333	3	3	0	1	0	0	0	0	0	1	0
Hector Lopez, of-2	.250	3	8	1	2	2	0	0	0	1	1	0
Mickey Mantle, of	.133	4	15	1	2	0	0	1	1	1	5	0
Roger Maris, of	.000	2	5	0	0	0	0	0	0	0	1	0
Joe Pepitone, 1b	.154	4	13	0	2	0	0	0	0	1	3	0
Hal Reniff, p	.000	3	0	0	0	0	0	0	0	0	0	0
Bobby Richardson, 2b	.214	4	14	0	3	1	0	0	0	1	3	0
Ralph Terry, p	.000	1	0	0	0	0	0	0	0	0	0	0
Tom Tresh, of	.200	4	15	1	3	0	0	1	2	1	6	0
Stan Williams, p	.000	1	0	0	0	0	0	0	0	0	0	0
TOTAL	.171		129	4	22	3	0	2	4	5	37	0

PITCHER	W	L	ERA	G	GS	CG	SV	SHO	IP	H	ER	BB	SO
Jim Bouton	0	1	1.29	1	1	0	0	0	7.0	4	1	5	4
Al Downing	0	1	5.40	1	1	0	0	0	5.0	7	3	1	6
Whitey Ford	0	2	4.50	2	2	0	0	0	12.0	10	6	3	8
Steve Hamilton	0	0	0.00	1	0	0	0	0	1.0	0	0	0	1
Hal Reniff	0	0	0.00	3	0	0	0	0	3.0	0	0	1	1
Ralph Terry	0	0	3.00	1	0	0	0	0	3.0	3	1	1	0
Stan Williams	0	0	0.00	1	0	0	0	0	3.0	1	0	0	5
TOTAL	0	4	2.91	10	4	0	0	0	34.0	25	11	11	25

ST. LOUIS CARDINALS (NL) 4, NEW YORK YANKEES (AL) 3

With late-season spurts the Cardinals edged the Reds and Phillies for their first pennant in 18 years and the Yankees overtook the White Sox and Orioles for their 15th in 18 years and their 29th over all. But when the Series was over, the long era of Yankee dominance had come to an end.

St. Louis won the opener, a 24-hit slugfest in which Curt Flood's RBI triple in the sixth proved the decisive blow. But New York came back to take the next two games. Rookie Mel Stottlemyre won Game 2, holding the Cards to three runs as his Yankees scored eight. (Loser Bob Gibson struck out nine, though, on his way to a new Series record of 31.) Game 3, by contrast, featured a pitchers' duel between Jim Bouton and veteran Curt Simmons. Cards reliever Barney Schultz, who replaced Simmons for the last of the ninth with the score 1–1, lost the game on his first pitch when Mickey Mantle homered to deep right (his 16th World Series home run, which moved him ahead of Babe Ruth into the all-time lead).

Ray Sadecki (the winner in Game 1) left with one out in the first inning of Game 4 after four Yankees hit safely, but relievers Roger Craig and Ron Taylor stopped New York on just two singles the rest of the way. The Cards were also held to six hits, but one was Ken Boyer's grand slam in the sixth, which erased a 3–0 Yankees lead and gave St. Louis enough runs to even the Series.

Gibson and Stottlemyre faced off a second time in Game 5. Gibson carried a 2–0 lead into the last of the ninth, when with two out Tom Tresh tagged him for a game-tying home run. In the top of the 10th, though, the Cards regained the lead on Tim McCarver's three-run homer and held on for the win as Gibson notched his 13th K of the game.

Bouton and Simmons tangled again in Game 6. Another 1–1 duel was shattered, this time in the top of the sixth when Roger Maris and Mantle tagged Simmons for back-to-back home runs. New York put the game away in the eighth with five runs off Cards relievers—four of them on Joe Pepitone's grand slam.

With the series tied 3–3, Gibson and Stottlemyre were called upon to settle the title. Gibson pitched the whole game, striking

out nine. Mantle touched him for a three-run homer in the sixth inning, and Clete Boyer and Phil Linz hit solo shots in the ninth. But as St. Louis had scored six times off Stottlemyre and his replacement Al Downing before the Yankees scored their first runs, the game ended with the Cards victors and world champions. Yogi Berra, New York's rookie manager, was fired the next day. The following season the Yankees finished sixth under Johnny Keane, who left St. Louis to manage New York.

STL (N)

PLAYER/POS	AVG	G	AB	R	H	2B	3B	HR	RBI	BB	SO	SB
Ken Boyer, 3b	.222	7	27	5	6	1	0	2	6	1	5	0
Lou Brock, of	.300	7	30	2	9	2	0	1	5	0	3	0
Gerry Buchek, 2b	1.000	4	1	1	1	0	0	0	0	0	0	0
Roger Craig, p	.000	2	1	0	0	0	0	0	0	0	0	0
Curt Flood, of	.200	7	30	5	6	0	1	0	3	3	1	0
Bob Gibson, p	.222	3	9	1	2	0	0	0	0	0	3	0
Dick Groat, ss	.192	7	26	3	5	1	1	0	1	4	3	0
Bob Humphreys, p	.000	1	0	0	0	0	0	0	0	0	0	0
Charlie James, ph	.000	3	3	0	0	0	0	0	0	0	1	0
Julian Javier, 2b	.000	1	0	1	0	0	0	0	0	0	0	0
Dal Maxvill, 2b	.200	7	20	0	4	1	0	0	1	1	4	0
Tim McCarver, c	.478	7	23	4	11	1	1	1	5	5	1	1
Gordie Richardson, p	.000	2	0	0	0	0	0	0	0	0	0	0
Ray Sadecki, p	.500	2	2	0	1	0	0	0	1	0	1	0
Barney Schultz, p	.000	4	1	0	0	0	0	0	0	0	0	0
Mike Shannon, of	.214	7	28	6	6	0	0	1	2	0	9	1
Curt Simmons, p	.500	2	4	0	2	0	0	0	1	0	1	0
Bob Skinner, ph	.667	4	3	0	2	1	0	0	1	1	0	0
Ron Taylor, p	.000	2	1	0	0	0	0	0	0	0	1	0
Carl Warwick, ph	.750	5	4	2	3	0	0	0	1	1	0	0
Bill White, 1b	.111	7	27	3	3	1	0	0	2	2	6	1
TOTAL	.254		240	32	61	8	3	5	29	18	39	3

PITCHER	W	L	ERA	G	GS	CG	SV	SHO	IP	H	ER	BB	SO
Roger Craig	1	0	0.00	2	0	0	0	0	5.0	2	0	3	9
Bob Gibson	2	1	3.00	3	3	2	0	0	27.0	23	9	8	31
Bob Humphreys	0	0	0.00	1	0	0	0	0	1.0	0	0	0	1
Gordie Richardson	0	0	40.50	2	0	0	0	0	0.2	3	3	2	0
Ray Sadecki	1	0	8.53	2	2	0	0	0	6.1	12	6	5	2
Barney Schultz	0	1	18.00	4	0	0	1	0	4.0	9	8	3	1
Curt Simmons	0	1	2.51	2	2	0	0	0	14.1	11	4	3	8
Ron Taylor	0	0	0.00	2	0	0	1	0	4.2	0	0	1	2
TOTAL	4	3	4.29	18	7	2	2	0	63.0	60	30	25	54

NY (A)

PLAYER/POS	AVG	G	AB	R	H	2B	3B	HR	RBI	BB	SO	SB
Johnny Blanchard, ph	.250	4	4	0	1	0	0	0	0	0	1	0
Jim Bouton, p	.143	2	7	0	1	0	0	0	1	0	2	0
Clete Boyer, 3b	.208	7	24	2	5	1	0	1	3	1	5	1
Al Downing, p	.000	3	2	0	0	0	0	0	0	0	2	0
Whitey Ford, p	1.000	1	1	0	1	0	0	0	1	2	0	0
Pedro Gonzalez, 3b	.000	1	1	0	0	0	0	0	0	0	0	0
Steve Hamilton, p	.000	2	0	0	0	0	0	0	0	0	0	0
Mike Hegan, ph	.000	3	1	1	0	0	0	0	0	1	1	0
Elston Howard, c	.292	7	24	5	7	1	0	0	2	4	6	0
Phil Linz, ss	.226	7	31	5	7	1	0	2	2	2	5	0
Hector Lopez, of-1	.000	3	2	0	0	0	0	0	0	0	2	0
Mickey Mantle, of	.333	7	24	8	8	2	0	3	8	6	8	0
Roger Maris, of	.200	7	30	4	6	0	0	1	1	1	4	0
Pete Mikkelsen, p	.000	4	0	0	0	0	0	0	0	0	0	0
Joe Pepitone, 1b	.154	7	26	1	4	1	0	1	5	2	3	0
Hal Reniff, p	.000	1	0	0	0	0	0	0	0	0	0	0
Bobby Richardson, 2b	.406	7	32	3	13	2	0	0	3	0	2	1
Rollie Sheldon, p	.000	2	0	0	0	0	0	0	0	0	0	0
Mel Stottlemyre, p	.125	3	8	0	1	0	0	0	0	0	6	0
Ralph Terry, p	.000	1	0	0	0	0	0	0	0	0	0	0
Tom Tresh, of	.273	7	22	4	6	2	0	2	7	6	7	0
TOTAL	.251		239	33	60	11	0	10	33	25	54	2

PITCHER	W	L	ERA	G	GS	CG	SV	SHO	IP	H	ER	BB	SO
Jim Bouton	2	0	1.56	2	2	1	0	0	17.1	15	3	5	7
Al Downing	0	1	8.22	3	1	0	0	0	7.2	9	7	2	5
Whitey Ford	0	1	8.44	1	1	0	0	0	5.1	8	5	1	4
Steve Hamilton	0	0	4.50	2	0	0	1	0	2.0	3	1	0	2
Pete Mikkelsen	0	1	5.79	4	0	0	0	0	4.2	4	3	2	4
Hal Reniff	0	0	0.00	1	0	0	0	0	0.1	2	0	0	0
Rollie Sheldon	0	0	0.00	2	0	0	0	0	2.2	0	0	2	2
Mel Stottlemyre	1	1	3.15	3	3	1	0	0	20.0	18	7	6	12
Ralph Terry	0	0	0.00	1	0	0	0	0	2.0	2	0	0	3
TOTAL	3	4	3.77	19	7	2	1	0	62.0	61	26	18	39

GAME 1 AT STL OCT 7
```
NY  030 010 010   5 12 2
STL 110 004 03X   9 12 0
```
Pitchers: FORD, Downing (6), Sheldon (8), Mikkelsen (9) vs SADECKI, Schultz (7)
Home Runs: Tresh-NY, Shannon-STL
Attendance: 30,805

GAME 2 AT STL OCT 8
```
NY  000 101 204   8 12 0
STL 001 000 011   3  7 0
```
Pitchers: STOTTLEMYRE vs GIBSON, Schultz (9), Craig (9), Richardson (9)
Home Runs: Linz-NY
Attendance: 30,805

GAME 3 AT NY OCT 10
```
STL 000 010 000   1 6 0
NY  010 000 001   2 5 2
```
Pitchers: Simmons, SCHULTZ (9) vs BOUTON
Home Runs: Mantle-NY
Attendance: 67,101

GAME 4 AT NY OCT 11
```
STL 000 004 000   4 6 1
NY  300 000 000   3 6 1
```
Pitchers: Sadecki, CRAIG (1), Taylor (6) vs DOWNING, Mikkelsen (7), Terry (8)
Home Runs: K.Boyer-STL
Attendance: 66,312

GAME 5 AT NY OCT 12
```
STL 000 020 000 3   5 10 1
NY  000 000 020 2   2  6 2
```
Pitchers: GIBSON vs Stottlemyre, Reniff (8), MIKKELSEN (8)
Home Runs: Tresh-NY, McCarver-STL
Attendance: 65,633

GAME 6 AT STL OCT 14
```
NY  000 012 050   8 10 0
STL 100 000 011   3 10 1
```
Pitchers: BOUTON, Hamilton (9) vs SIMMONS, Taylor (7), Schultz (8), Richardson (8), Humphreys (9)
Home Runs: Maris-NY, Mantle-NY, Pepitone-NY
Attendance: 30,805

GAME 7 AT STL OCT 15
```
NY  000 003 002   5 9 2
STL 000 330 10X   7 10 1
```
Pitchers: STOTTLEMYRE, Downing (5), Sheldon (5), Hamilton (7), Mikkelsen (8) vs GIBSON
Home Runs: Brock-STL, Mantle-NY, K.Boyer-STL, C.Boyer-NY, Linz-NY
Attendance: 30,346

LOS ANGELES DODGERS (NL) 4, MINNESOTA TWINS (AL) 3

The Twins (bringing the World Series to Minnesota for the first time ever) featured heavy hitting, while Dodgers hopes rested on great pitching and speed on the bases. For a while it looked as if power would triumph as the Twins took the first two games at home. They drove out starter Don Drysdale with seven runs in the first three innings of the opener—including home runs by Don Mincher and Zoilo Versalles—on the way to a convincing 8–2 win, and followed up with a 5–1 triumph the next day over Dodgers ace Sandy Koufax (who had declined to pitch Game 1 on Yom Kippur, the holiest day of the Jewish year) and star reliever Ron Perranoski, who was tagged for three of the Twins' runs.

But when the Series moved to Los Angeles, Dodgers pitching began to assert itself. Claude Osteen held Minnesota to five hits and no runs, while Los Angeles bunched seven of their 10 hits in the middle three innings for four runs. Drysdale evened the Series in Game 4, avenging his first-game pounding with a five-hitter. Twins Harmon Killebrew and Tony Oliva tagged him for a pair of solo homers, but that was Minnesota's only scoring—more than balanced by seven Dodgers runs, including homers by Wes Parker and Lou Johnson. In Game 5 the next day, Koufax avenged his earlier loss, carrying Los Angeles to its first Series lead with a shutout in which he allowed only four singles and a walk, while fanning 10 Twins. Speedster Willie Davis stole three bases and Maury Wills stole another as the Dodgers parlayed 14 hits into a 7–0 victory.

Back in Minnesota for Game 6, the Twins rallied, using the long ball to even the Series again with a 5–1 win. Bob Allison opened the scoring with a two-run shot off Claude Osteen in the fourth, and Minnesota pitcher Mudcat Grant insured his own win with a three-run blast two innings later.

In the finale, though, the visiting team won for the only time in the Series. Koufax again struck out 10, stopping the Twins on three hits for his second shutout. Lou Johnson's second Series homer (a fourth-inning solo shot to left off Twins starter Jim Kaat that was barely fair) was all the Dodgers

needed for their fifth world championship, but Ron Fairly followed Johnson with a double and Wes Parker singled home an insurance run that drove Kaat from the game and concluded the Series scoring.

LA (N)

PLAYER/POS	AVG	G	AB	R	H	2B	3B	HR	RB	BB	SO	SB
Jim Brewer, p	.000	1	0	0	0	0	0	0	0	0	0	0
Willie Crawford, ph	.500	2	2	0	1	0	0	0	0	0	1	0
Willie Davis, of	.231	7	26	3	6	0	0	0	0	0	2	3
Don Drysdale, p-2	.000	3	5	0	0	0	0	0	0	0	4	0
Ron Fairly, of	.379	7	29	7	11	3	0	2	6	0	1	0
Jim Gilliam, 3b	.214	7	28	2	6	1	0	0	2	1	0	0
Lou Johnson, of	.296	7	27	3	8	2	0	2	4	1	3	0
John Kennedy, 3b	.000	4	1	0	0	0	0	0	0	0	0	0
Sandy Koufax, p	.111	3	9	0	1	0	0	0	0	1	5	0
Jim Lefebvre, 2b	.400	3	10	2	4	0	0	0	0	0	0	0
Don LeJohn, ph	.000	1	1	0	0	0	0	0	0	0	1	0
Bob Miller, p	.000	2	0	0	0	0	0	0	0	0	0	0
Wally Moon, ph	.000	2	2	0	0	0	0	0	0	0	0	0
Claude Osteen, p	.333	2	3	0	1	0	0	0	0	0	0	0
Wes Parker, 1b	.304	7	23	3	7	0	1	1	2	3	3	2
Ron Perranoski, p	.000	2	0	0	0	0	0	0	0	0	0	0
Howie Reed, p	.000	2	0	0	0	0	0	0	0	0	0	0
Johnny Roseboro, c	.286	7	21	1	6	1	0	0	3	5	3	1
Dick Tracewski, 2b	.118	6	17	0	2	0	0	0	0	1	5	0
Maury Wills, ss	.367	7	30	3	11	3	0	0	3	1	3	3
TOTAL	.274		234	24	64	10	1	5	21	13	31	9

PITCHER	W	L	ERA	G	GS	CG	SV	SHO	IP	H	ER	BB	SO
Jim Brewer	0	0	4.50	1	0	0	0	0	2.0	3	1	0	1
Don Drysdale	1	1	3.86	2	2	1	0	0	11.2	12	5	3	15
Sandy Koufax	2	1	0.38	3	3	2	0	2	24.0	13	1	5	29
Bob Miller	0	0	0.00	2	0	0	0	0	1.1	0	0	0	0
Claude Osteen	1	1	0.64	2	2	1	0	1	14.0	9	1	5	4
Ron Perranoski	0	0	7.36	2	0	0	0	0	3.2	3	3	4	1
Howie Reed	0	0	8.10	2	0	0	0	0	3.1	2	3	2	4
TOTAL	4	3	2.10	14	7	4	0	3	60.0	42	14	19	54

MIN (A)

PLAYER/POS	AVG	G	AB	R	H	2B	3B	HR	RB	BB	SO	SB
Bob Allison, of	.125	5	16	3	2	1	0	1	2	2	9	1
Earl Battey, c	.120	7	25	1	3	0	1	0	2	0	5	0
Dave Boswell, p	.000	1	0	0	0	0	0	0	0	0	0	0
Mudcat Grant, p	.250	3	8	3	2	1	0	1	3	0	1	0
Jimmie Hall, of	.143	2	7	0	1	0	0	0	0	1	5	0
Jim Kaat, p	.167	3	6	0	1	0	0	0	2	0	5	0
Harmon Killebrew, 3b	.286	7	21	2	6	0	0	1	2	6	4	0
Johnny Klippstein, p	.000	2	0	0	0	0	0	0	0	0	0	0
Jim Merritt, p	.000	2	0	0	0	0	0	0	0	0	0	0
Don Mincher, 1b	.130	7	23	3	3	0	0	1	1	2	7	0
Joe Nossek, of-5	.200	6	20	0	4	0	0	0	0	0	1	0
Tony Oliva, of	.192	7	26	2	5	1	0	1	2	1	6	0
Camilo Pascual, p	.000	1	1	0	0	0	0	0	0	0	0	0
Jim Perry, p	.000	2	0	0	0	0	0	0	0	0	0	0
Bill Pleis, p	.000	1	0	0	0	0	0	0	0	0	0	0
Frank Quilici, 2b	.200	7	20	2	4	2	0	0	1	4	3	0
Rich Rollins, ph	.000	3	2	0	0	0	0	0	0	1	0	0
Sandy Valdespino, of-2	.273	5	11	1	3	1	0	0	0	0	1	0
Zoilo Versalles, ss	.286	7	28	3	8	1	1	1	4	2	7	1
Al Worthington, p	.000	2	0	0	0	0	0	0	0	0	0	0
Jerry Zimmerman, c	.000	2	1	0	0	0	0	0	0	0	0	0
TOTAL	.195		215	20	42	7	2	6	19	19	54	2

PITCHER	W	L	ERA	G	GS	CG	SV	SHO	IP	H	ER	BB	SO
Dave Boswell	0	0	3.38	1	0	0	0	0	2.2	3	1	2	3
Mudcat Grant	2	1	2.74	3	3	2	0	0	23.0	22	7	2	12
Jim Kaat	1	2	3.77	3	3	1	0	0	14.1	18	6	2	6
Johnny Klippstein	0	0	0.00	2	0	0	0	0	2.2	2	0	2	3
Jim Merritt	0	0	2.70	2	0	0	0	0	3.1	2	1	0	1
Camilo Pascual	0	1	5.40	1	1	0	0	0	5.0	8	3	1	0
Jim Perry	0	0	4.50	2	0	0	0	0	4.0	5	2	2	4
Bill Pleis	0	0	9.00	1	0	0	0	0	1.0	2	1	0	0
Al Worthington	0	0	0.00	2	0	0	0	0	4.0	2	0	2	2
TOTAL	3	4	3.15	17	7	3	0	0	60.0	64	21	13	31

GAME 1 AT MIN OCT 6
LA 010 000 001 2 10 1
MIN 016 001 00X 8 10 0
Pitchers: DRYSDALE, Reed (3),
  Brewer (5), Perranoski (7) vs GRANT
Home Runs: Fairly-LA, Mincher-MIN,
  Versalles-MIN
Attendance: 47,797

GAME 2 AT MIN OCT 7
LA 000 000 100 1 7 3
MIN 000 002 12X 5 9 0
Pitchers: KOUFAX, Perranoski (7),
  Miller (8) vs KAAT
Attendance: 48,700

GAME 3 AT LA OCT 9
MIN 000 000 000 0 5 0
LA 000 211 00X 4 10 1
Pitchers: PASCUAL, Merritt (6),
  Klippstein (8) vs OSTEEN
Attendance: 55,934

GAME 4 AT LA OCT 10
MIN 000 101 000 2 5 2
LA 110 103 01X 7 10 0
Pitchers: GRANT, Worthington (6),
  Pleis (8) vs DRYSDALE
Home Runs: Killebrew-MIN, Parker-LA,
  Oliva-MIN, Johnson-LA
Attendance: 55,920

GAME 5 AT LA OCT 11
MIN 000 000 000 0 4 1
LA 202 100 20X 7 14 0
Pitchers: KAAT, Boswell (3), Perry (6)
  vs KOUFAX
Attendance: 55,801

GAME 6 AT MIN OCT 13
LA 000 000 100 1 6 1
MIN 000 203 00X 5 6 1
Pitchers: OSTEEN, Reed (6), Miller (8)
  vs GRANT
Home Runs: Allison-MIN, Grant-MIN,
  Fairly-LA
Attendance: 49,578

GAME 7 AT MIN OCT 14
LA 000 200 000 2 7 0
MIN 000 000 000 0 3 1
Pitchers: KOUFAX vs KAAT
  Worthington (4), Klippstein (6),
  Merritt (7), Perry (9)
Home Runs: Johnson-LA
Attendance: 50,596

BALTIMORE ORIOLES (AL) 4, LOS ANGELES DODGERS (NL) 0

The Orioles, with their first pennant since moving from St. Louis in 1954, won the franchise's first World Series ever, crushing NL repeater Los Angeles in four games. Back-to-back home runs by Frank and Brooks Robinson in the top of the first inning of the opener gave Baltimore a quick three-run lead, and the O's added a fourth run an inning later before the Dodgers attempted to come back with single runs in the second and third innings. But by then Orioles reliever Moe Drabowsky had come on to pitch, and he stopped the Dodgers on one hit the rest of the way, striking out 11 (including six in a row in the fourth and fifth innings). The Dodgers would not score again in the Series.

Sophomore Jim Palmer (a week shy of his 21st birthday) hurled a four-hit shutout at Los Angeles in Game 2, defeating the great— but critically sore-armed—Sandy Koufax, who, though only 30 years old, was pitching the final game of his career. Three errors by center fielder Willie Davis in the fifth (including a pair of flies lost in the sun) led to three unearned runs— the first scoring against Koufax. Frank Robinson's leadoff triple in the sixth and Boog Powell's single gave the Orioles an earned run before a double play ended the inning. Koufax was replaced after the inning by a succession of Dodgers relievers as Baltimore went on to win, 6–0.

Wally Bunker did the honors for the Orioles in Game 3, emerging the victor of a pitching duel with Claude Osteen on the strength of a fifth-inning home run by Paul Blair, a tremendous 430-foot shot to left. Osteen yielded only two other Orioles hits—both singles—in his seven innings, and Dodger reliever Phil Regan retired the side in the eighth. But one run was all Bunker needed for his shutout win.

Dave McNally, who had given up the Dodgers' only Series runs in Game 1, mended his ways with a four-hit shutout in Game 4. He needed the shutout for the sweep, for Don Drysdale was also in top form. Drysdale, too, gave up only four hits. But one of them was Frank Robinson's second home run of the Series, a fourth-inning solo shot to left for the game's only scoring.

BAL (A)

PLAYER/POS	AVG	G	AB	R	H	2B	3B	HR	RB	BB	SO	SB
Luis Aparicio, ss	.250	4	16	0	4	1	0	0	2	0	0	0
Paul Blair, of	.167	4	6	2	1	0	0	1	1	1	0	0
Curt Blefary, of	.077	4	13	0	1	0	0	0	0	0	2	3	0
Wally Bunker, p	.000	1	2	0	0	0	0	0	0	0	1	0
Moe Drabowsky, p	.000	1	2	0	0	0	0	0	0	0	1	0
Andy Etchebarren, c	.083	4	12	2	1	0	0	0	0	2	4	0
Davey Johnson, 2b	.286	4	14	1	4	1	0	0	1	0	1	0
Dave McNally, p	.000	2	3	0	0	0	0	0	0	0	1	0
Jim Palmer, p	.000	1	4	0	0	0	0	0	0	0	2	0
Boog Powell, 1b	.357	4	14	1	5	1	0	0	1	0	1	0
Brooks Robinson, 3b	.214	4	14	2	3	0	0	1	1	1	0	0
Frank Robinson, of	.286	4	14	4	4	0	1	2	3	2	3	0
Russ Snyder, of	.167	3	6	1	1	0	0	0	1	2	0	0
TOTAL	.200		120	13	24	3	1	4	10	11	17	0

PITCHER	W	L	ERA	G	GS	CG	SV	SHO	IP	H	ER	BB	SO
Wally Bunker	1	0	0.00	1	1	1	0	1	9.0	6	0	1	6
Moe Drabowsky	1	0	0.00	1	0	0	0	0	6.2	1	0	2	11
Dave McNally	1	0	1.59	2	2	1	0	1	11.1	6	2	7	5
Jim Palmer	1	0	0.00	1	1	1	0	1	9.0	4	0	3	6
TOTAL	4	0	0.50	5	4	3	0	3	36.0	17	2	13	28

LA (N)

PLAYER/POS	AVG	G	AB	R	H	2B	3B	HR	RB	BB	SO	SB
Jim Barbieri, ph	.000	1	1	0	0	0	0	0	0	0	1	0
Jim Brewer, p	.000	1	0	0	0	0	0	0	0	0	0	0
Wes Covington, ph	.000	1	1	0	0	0	0	0	0	0	1	0
Tommy Davis, of-3	.250	4	8	0	2	0	0	0	0	1	1	0
Willie Davis, of	.063	4	16	0	1	0	0	0	0	0	4	0
Don Drysdale, p	.000	2	2	0	0	0	0	0	0	0	1	0
Ron Fairly, of-2,1b-1	.143	3	7	0	1	0	0	0	0	2	4	0
Al Ferrara, ph	1.000	1	1	0	1	0	0	0	0	0	0	0
Jim Gilliam, 3b	.000	2	6	0	0	0	0	0	1	2	0	0
Lou Johnson, of	.267	4	15	1	4	1	0	0	0	1	1	0
John Kennedy, 3b	.200	2	5	0	1	0	0	0	0	0	0	0
Sandy Koufax, p	.000	1	2	0	0	0	0	0	0	0	0	0
Jim Lefebvre, 2b	.167	4	12	1	2	0	0	1	1	3	4	0
Bob Miller, p	.000	1	0	0	0	0	0	0	0	0	0	0
Joe Moeller, p	.000	1	0	0	0	0	0	0	0	0	0	0
Nate Oliver, pr	.000	1	0	0	0	0	0	0	0	0	0	0
Claude Osteen, p	.000	1	2	0	0	0	0	0	0	0	1	0
Wes Parker, 1b	.231	4	13	0	3	2	0	0	0	1	3	0
Ron Perranoski, p	.000	2	0	0	0	0	0	0	0	0	0	0
Phil Regan, p	.000	2	0	0	0	0	0	0	0	0	0	0
Johnny Roseboro, c	.071	4	14	0	1	0	0	0	0	0	3	0
Dick Stuart, ph	.000	2	2	0	0	0	0	0	0	0	1	0
Maury Wills, ss	.077	4	13	0	1	0	0	0	0	3	3	1
TOTAL	.142		120	2	17	3	0	1	2	13	28	1

PITCHER	W	L	ERA	G	GS	CG	SV	SHO	IP	H	ER	BB	SO
Jim Brewer	0	0	0.00	1	0	0	0	0	1.0	0	0	0	1
Don Drysdale	0	2	4.50	2	2	1	0	0	10.0	8	5	3	6
Sandy Koufax	0	1	1.50	1	1	0	0	0	6.0	6	1	2	2
Bob Miller	0	0	0.00	1	0	0	0	0	3.0	2	0	2	1
Joe Moeller	0	0	4.50	1	0	0	0	0	2.0	1	1	1	0
Claude Osteen	0	1	1.29	1	1	0	0	0	7.0	3	1	1	3
Ron Perranoski	0	0	5.40	2	0	0	0	0	3.1	4	2	1	2
Phil Regan	0	0	0.00	2	0	0	0	0	1.2	0	0	1	2
TOTAL	0	4	2.65	11	4	1	0	0	34.0	24	10	11	17

GAME 1 AT LA OCT 5

BAL 310 100 000   5 9 0
LA 011 000 000   2 3 0
Pitchers: McNally, DRABOWSKY (3) vs DRYSDALE, Moeller (3), Miller (5), Perranoski (8)
Home Runs: F.Robinson-BAL, B.Robinson-BAL, Lefebvre-LA
Attendance: 55,941

GAME 2 AT LA OCT 6

BAL 000 031 020   6 8 0
LA 000 000 000   0 4 6
Pitchers: PALMER vs KOUFAX, Perranoski (7), Regan (8), Brewer (9)
Attendance: 55,947

GAME 3 AT BAL OCT 8

LA 000 000 000   0 6 0
BAL 000 010 00X   1 3 0
Pitchers: OSTEEN, Regan (8) vs BUNKER
Home Runs: Blair-BAL
Attendance: 54,445

GAME 4 AT BAL OCT 9

LA 000 000 000   0 4 0
BAL 000 100 00X   1 4 0
Pitchers: DRYSDALE vs McNALLY
Home Runs: F.Robinson-BAL
Attendance: 54,458

ST. LOUIS CARDINALS (NL) 4, BOSTON RED SOX (AL) 3

The Cardinals cruised into the Series leading by 10-1/2 games, whereas the Red Sox eked out their pennant over Minnesota and Detroit only by a dramatic win at season's end. The Sox continued to claw their way through six games of the Series before finally falling to superior pitching and hitting in the seventh game. Cardinals hurler Bob Gibson (who had missed a third of the season with a broken leg) edged Boston in the opener 2–1 with a six-hitter that included 10 strikeouts. The only run against him came on a solo homer by opposing pitcher Jose Santiago in the third that tied the game. But Santi-ago was undone when Lou Brock singled off him to open the seventh, then stole second, and moved around to score on a pair of ground outs.

Boston ace Jim Lonborg evened the Series the next day with a brilliant one-hit shutout. Triple Crown winner Carl Yastrzemski accounted for four of Boston's five runs with homers in the fourth and seventh innings. Cardinal Nelson Briles outlasted a succession of Boston pitchers for a go-ahead 5–2 win in Game 3, and Gibson, with a five-hit shutout in Game 4, put St. Louis up three games to one.

But Boston's Lonborg kept Red Sox hopes alive with another pitching gem—a three-hitter in which the only extra-base hit was Roger Maris' harmless home run in the last of the ninth, after the Sox had already scored three runs (two of them unearned). Boston's bats came alive as the Series moved to Boston for Game 6, and the Sox evened the Series with an 8–4 win. The Cards used eight pitchers in a futile effort to hold off the Boston assault. Boston's score would have been greater had not all four Boston homers (including three in the fourth inning by Yastrzemski, Reggie Smith, and Rico Petrocelli—his second of the game) been solo shots.

With the Series tied, the Series' two-game winners, Gibson and Lonborg, faced off in Game 7. It turned out to be no contest. Lonborg gave up 10 hits and seven runs (including a homer by pitcher Gibson in the fifth and a three-run blast by Julian Javier an inning later) in six innings. Four Boston relievers held the Cards scoreless

the rest of the game, but it was too late. Gibson's three-hitter included 10 strikeouts and, as he had in 1964, Gibson walked off the mound a winner in the seventh game.

STL (N)

PLAYER/POS	AVG	G	AB	R	H	2B	3B	HR	RB	BB	SO	SB
Eddie Bressoud, ss	.000	2	0	0	0	0	0	0	0	0	0	0
Nelson Briles, p	.000	2	3	0	0	0	0	0	0	0	0	0
Lou Brock, of	.414	7	29	8	12	2	1	1	3	2	3	7
Steve Carlton, p	.000	1	1	0	0	0	0	0	0	0	0	0
Orlando Cepeda, 1b	.103	7	29	1	3	2	0	0	1	0	4	0
Curt Flood, of	.179	7	28	2	5	1	0	0	3	3	3	0
Phil Gagliano, ph	.000	1	1	0	0	0	0	0	0	0	0	0
Bob Gibson, p	.091	3	11	1	1	0	0	1	1	1	2	0
Joe Hoerner, p	.000	2	0	0	0	0	0	0	0	0	0	0
Dick Hughes, p	.000	2	3	0	0	0	0	0	0	0	3	0
Larry Jaster, p	.000	1	0	0	0	0	0	0	0	0	0	0
Julian Javier, 2b	.360	7	25	2	9	3	0	1	4	0	6	0
Jack Lamabe, p	.000	3	0	0	0	0	0	0	0	0	0	0
Roger Maris, of	.385	7	26	3	10	1	0	1	7	3	1	0
Dal Maxvill, ss	.158	7	19	1	3	0	1	0	1	4	1	0
Tim McCarver, c	.125	7	24	3	3	1	0	0	2	2	2	0
Dave Ricketts, c	.000	3	3	0	0	0	0	0	0	0	0	0
Mike Shannon, 3b	.208	7	24	3	5	1	0	1	2	1	4	0
Ed Spiezio, ph	.000	1	1	0	0	0	0	0	0	0	0	0
Bobby Tolan, ph	.000	3	2	1	0	0	0	0	0	1	1	0
Ray Washburn, p	.000	2	0	0	0	0	0	0	0	0	0	0
Ron Willis, p	.000	3	0	0	0	0	0	0	0	0	0	0
Hal Woodeshick, p	.000	1	0	0	0	0	0	0	0	0	0	0
TOTAL	.223		229	25	51	11	2	5	24	17	30	7

PITCHER	W	L	ERA	G	GS	CG	SV	SHO	IP	H	ER	BB	SO
Nelson Briles	1	0	1.64	2	1	1	0	0	11.0	7	2	1	4
Steve Carlton	0	1	0.00	1	1	0	0	0	6.0	3	0	2	5
Bob Gibson	3	0	1.00	3	3	3	0	1	27.0	14	3	5	26
Joe Hoerner	0	0	40.50	2	0	0	0	0	0.2	4	3	1	0
Dick Hughes	0	1	5.00	2	2	0	0	0	9.0	9	5	3	7
Larry Jaster	0	0	0.00	1	0	0	0	0	0.1	2	0	0	0
Jack Lamabe	0	1	6.75	3	0	0	0	0	2.2	5	2	0	4
Ray Washburn	0	0	0.00	2	0	0	0	0	2.1	1	0	1	2
Ron Willis	0	0	27.00	3	0	0	0	0	1.0	2	3	4	1
Hal Woodeshick	0	0	0.00	1	0	0	0	0	1.0	1	0	0	0
TOTAL	4	3	2.66	20	7	4	0	1	61.0	48	18	17	49

BOS (A)

PLAYER/POS	AVG	G	AB	R	H	2B	3B	HR	RB	BB	SO	SB
Jerry Adair, 2b-4	.125	5	16	0	2	0	0	0	1	0	3	1
Mike Andrews, 2b-3	.308	5	13	2	4	0	0	0	1	0	1	0
Gary Bell, p	.000	3	0	0	0	0	0	0	0	0	0	0
Ken Brett, p	.000	2	0	0	0	0	0	0	0	0	0	0
Joe Foy, 3b-3	.133	6	15	2	2	1	0	0	1	1	5	0
Russ Gibson, c	.000	2	2	0	0	0	0	0	0	0	2	0
Ken Harrelson, of	.077	4	13	0	1	0	0	0	1	1	3	0
Elston Howard, c	.111	7	18	0	2	0	0	0	1	1	2	0
Dalton Jones, 3b-4	.389	6	18	2	7	0	0	0	1	1	3	0
Jim Lonborg, p	.000	3	9	0	0	0	0	0	0	0	7	0
Dave Morehead, p	.000	2	0	0	0	0	0	0	0	0	0	0
Dan Osinski, p	.000	2	0	0	0	0	0	0	0	0	0	0
Rico Petrocelli, ss	.200	7	20	3	4	1	0	2	3	3	8	0
Mike Ryan, c	.000	1	2	0	0	0	0	0	0	0	1	0
Jose Santiago, p	.500	3	2	1	1	0	0	1	1	0	1	0
George Scott, 1b	.231	7	26	3	6	1	1	0	0	3	6	0
Norm Siebern, of-1	.333	3	3	0	1	0	0	0	0	0	0	0
Reggie Smith, of	.250	7	24	3	6	1	0	2	3	2	2	0
Lee Stange, p	.000	1	0	0	0	0	0	0	0	0	0	0
Jerry Stephenson, p	.000	1	0	0	0	0	0	0	0	0	0	0
Jose Tartabull, of-6	.154	7	13	1	2	0	0	0	0	1	2	0
George Thomas, of-1	.000	2	2	0	0	0	0	0	0	0	1	0
Gary Waslewski, p	.000	2	1	0	0	0	0	0	0	0	1	0
John Wyatt, p	.000	2	0	0	0	0	0	0	0	0	0	0
Carl Yastrzemski, of	.400	7	25	4	10	2	0	3	5	4	1	0
TOTAL	.216		222	21	48	6	1	8	19	17	49	1

PITCHER	W	L	ERA	G	GS	CG	SV	SHO	IP	H	ER	BB	SO
Gary Bell	0	1	5.06	3	1	0	1	0	5.1	8	3	1	1
Ken Brett	0	0	0.00	2	0	0	0	0	1.1	0	0	1	1
Jim Lonborg	2	1	2.63	3	3	2	0	1	24.0	14	7	2	11
Dave Morehead	0	0	0.00	2	0	0	0	0	3.1	0	0	4	3
Dan Osinski	0	0	6.75	2	0	0	0	0	1.1	2	1	0	0
Jose Santiago	0	2	5.59	3	2	0	0	0	9.2	16	6	3	6
Lee Stange	0	0	0.00	1	0	0	0	0	2.0	3	0	0	0
Jerry Stephenson	0	0	9.00	1	0	0	0	0	2.0	3	2	1	0
Gary Waslewski	0	0	2.16	2	1	0	0	0	8.1	4	2	2	7
John Wyatt	1	0	4.91	2	0	0	0	0	3.2	1	2	3	1
TOTAL	34	4	3.39	21	7	2	1	1	61.0	51	23	17	30

GAME 1 AT BOS OCT 4

STL 001 000 100   2 10 0
BOS 001 000 000   1 6 0
Pitchers: GIBSON vs SANTIAGO, Wyatt (8)
Home Runs: Santiago-BOS
Attendance: 34,796

GAME 2 AT BOS OCT 5

STL 000 000 000   0 1 1
BOS 000 101 30X   5 9 0
Pitchers: HUGHES, Willis (6), Hoerner (7), Lamabe (7) vs LONBORG
Home Runs: Yastrzemski-BOS (2)
Attendance: 35,188

GAME 3 AT STL OCT 7

BOS 000 001 100   2 7 1
STL 120 001 01X   5 10 0
Pitchers: BELL, Waslewski (3), Stange (6), Osinski (8) vs BRILES
Home Runs: Shannon-STL, Smith-BOS
Attendance: 54,575

GAME 4 AT STL OCT 8

BOS 000 000 000   0 5 0
STL 402 000 00X   6 9 0
Pitchers: SANTIAGO, Bell (1), Stephenson (3), Morehead (5), Brett (8) vs GIBSON
Attendance: 54,575

GAME 5 AT STL OCT 9

BOS 001 000 002   3 6 1
STL 000 000 001   1 3 2
Pitchers: LONBORG vs CARLTON, Washburn (7), Willis (9), Lamabe (9)
Home Runs: Maris-STL
Attendance: 54,575

GAME 6 AT BOS OCT 11

STL 002 000 200   4 8 0
BOS 010 300 40X   8 12 1
Pitchers: Hughes, Willis (4), Briles (5), LAMABE (7), Hoerner (7), Jaster (7), Washburn (7), Woodeshick (8) vs Waslewski, WYATT (6), Bell (8)
Home Runs: Petrocelli-BOS (2), Yastrzemski-BOS, Smith-BOS, Brock-STL
Attendance: 35,188

GAME 7 AT BOS OCT 12

STL 002 023 000   7 10 1
BOS 000 010 010   2 3 1
Pitchers: GIBSON vs LONBORG, Santiago (7), Morehead (9), Osinski (9), Brett (9)
Home Runs: Gibson-STL, Javier-STL
Attendance: 35,188

DETROIT TIGERS (AL) 4, ST. LOUIS CARDINALS (NL) 3

In this "year of the pitcher," Tiger Denny McLain's 31 wins were the most for a major leaguer in 37 years. Cardinal Bob Gibson's 1.12 ERA was the majors' best since Dutch Leonard's 1.01 in 1914, and his 13 season shutouts tied for third best all time. In the Series, though, Detroit's second-best pitcher, Mickey Lolich, was the hero.

McLain came off second-best against Gibson in the opener. He yielded only three hits in his five innings, but two singles in the fourth combined with a pair of walks and an error accounted for three runs. Gibson, meanwhile, was in the process of striking out a Series-record 17 batters on the way to a five-hit shutout. But Lolich brought Detroit back in Game 2. He struck out nine, and his third-inning home run (the only one of his major league career) provided all the scoring needed for a Detroit victory, although the Tigers kept putting runs across for an 8–1 win.

Home runs accounted for most of the scoring in Game 3. Veteran Al Kaline's two-run shot in the third opened the scoring, but Tim McCarver's three-run blast in the fifth put St. Louis ahead. Dick McAuliffe's solo shot later in the inning brought Detroit within one, but the Cards put the game away on Orlando Cepeda's three-run homer in the seventh.

McLain faced Gibson again in Game 4, and again came off second-best. Lou Brock led off the game with a home run, and before the end of the third inning McLain was gone. Gibson gave up a solo homer to Jim Northrup in the fourth, but that was the only run he allowed. Gibson homered and struck out 10 in a 10–1 win.

Down three games to one, the Tigers were saved from elimination by Lolich. Although three hits in the top of the first (including Cepeda's second homer of the Series) gave St. Louis a quick three runs, Lolich held the Cards scoreless the rest of the game as his Tigers fought back with two runs in the fourth and three more in the seventh. McLain finally came through in Game 6, evening the Series with an easy 13–1 victory, in which Northrup's grand slam provided the big blow of a 10-run third inning.

Lolich and Gibson—both 2–0 in the Series—faced off in the

finale. Gibson broke his own World Series strikeout record in the third inning (finishing with 8 for the game and 35 for the Series), and both pitchers hurled shutout ball through six innings. But four two-out Tigers hits in the top of the seventh—including a misplayed flyball in center field—put three runs on the board, and another run in the ninth made the score 4–0. In the last of the ninth, Mike Shannon's solo homer spoiled Lolich's shutout, but not his third Series win—or the Tigers' comeback world title.

DET (A)

PLAYER/POS	AVG	G	AB	R	H	2B	3B	HR	RB	BB	SO	SB
Gates Brown, ph	.000	1	1	0	0	0	0	0	0	0	0	0
Norm Cash, 1b	.385	7	26	5	10	0	0	1	5	3	5	0
Wayne Comer, ph	1.000	1	1	0	1	0	0	0	0	0	0	0
Pat Dobson, p	.000	3	0	0	0	0	0	0	0	0	0	0
Bill Freehan, c	.083	7	24	0	2	1	0	0	2	4	8	0
John Hiller, p	.000	2	0	0	0	0	0	0	0	0	0	0
Willie Horton, of	.304	7	23	6	7	1	1	1	3	5	6	0
Al Kaline, of	.379	7	29	6	11	2	0	2	8	0	7	0
Fred Lasher, p	.000	1	0	0	0	0	0	0	0	0	0	0
Mickey Lolich, p	.250	3	12	2	3	0	0	1	2	1	5	0
Tom Matchick, ph	.000	3	3	0	0	0	0	0	0	0	1	0
Eddie Mathews, 3b-1	.333	2	3	0	1	0	0	0	0	1	1	0
Dick McAuliffe, 2b	.222	7	27	5	6	0	0	1	3	4	6	0
Denny McLain, p	.000	3	6	0	0	0	0	0	0	0	4	0
Don McMahon, p	.000	2	0	0	0	0	0	0	0	0	0	0
Jim Northrup, of	.250	7	28	4	7	0	1	2	8	1	5	0
Ray Oyler, ss	.000	4	0	0	0	0	0	0	0	0	0	0
Daryl Patterson, p	.000	2	0	0	0	0	0	0	0	0	0	0
Jim Price, ph	.000	2	2	0	0	0	0	0	0	0	1	0
Joe Sparma, p	.000	1	0	0	0	0	0	0	0	0	0	0
Mickey Stanley, ss-7, of-4	.214	7	28	4	6	0	1	0	0	2	4	0
Dick Tracewski, 3b-1	.000	2	0	1	0	0	0	0	0	0	0	0
Don Wert, 3b	.118	6	17	1	2	0	0	0	2	6	5	0
Earl Wilson, p	.000	1	1	0	0	0	0	0	0	0	1	0
TOTAL	.242		231	34	56	4	3	8	33	27	59	0

PITCHER	W	L	ERA	G	GS	CG	SV	SHO	IP	H	ER	BB	SO
Pat Dobson	0	0	3.86	3	0	0	0	0	4.2	5	2	1	0
John Hiller	0	0	13.50	2	0	0	0	0	2.0	6	3	3	1
Fred Lasher	0	0	0.00	1	0	0	0	0	2.0	1	0	0	1
Mickey Lolich	3	0	1.67	3	3	3	0	0	27.0	20	5	6	21
Denny McLain	1	2	3.24	3	3	1	0	0	16.2	18	6	4	13
Don McMahon	0	0	13.50	2	0	0	0	0	2.0	4	3	0	1
Daryl Patterson	0	0	0.00	2	0	0	0	0	3.0	1	0	1	0
Joe Sparma	0	0	54.00	1	0	0	0	0	0.1	2	2	0	0
Earl Wilson	0	1	6.23	1	1	0	0	0	4.1	4	3	6	3
TOTAL	4	3	3.48	18	7	4	0	0	62.0	61	24	21	40

STL (N)

PLAYER/POS	AVG	G	AB	R	H	2B	3B	HR	RB	BB	SO	SB
Nelson Briles, p	.000	2	4	0	0	0	0	0	0	0	4	0
Lou Brock, of	.464	7	28	6	13	3	1	2	5	3	4	7
Steve Carlton, p	.000	2	0	0	0	0	0	0	0	0	0	0
Orlando Cepeda, 1b	.250	7	28	2	7	0	0	2	6	2	3	0
Ron Davis, of	.000	2	7	0	0	0	0	0	0	0	2	0
Johnny Edwards, ph	.000	1	1	0	0	0	0	0	0	0	1	0
Curt Flood, of	.286	7	28	4	8	1	0	0	2	2	3	3
Phil Gagliano, ph	.000	3	3	0	0	0	0	0	0	0	0	0
Bob Gibson, p	.125	3	8	2	1	0	0	1	2	1	2	0
Wayne Granger, p	.000	1	0	0	0	0	0	0	0	0	0	0
Joe Hoerner, p	.500	3	2	0	1	0	0	0	0	0	1	0
Dick Hughes, p	.000	1	0	0	0	0	0	0	0	0	0	0
Larry Jaster, p	.000	1	0	0	0	0	0	0	0	0	0	0
Julian Javier, 2b	.333	7	27	1	9	1	0	0	3	3	4	1
Roger Maris, of-5	.158	6	19	5	3	1	0	0	1	3	3	0
Dal Maxvill, ss	.000	7	22	1	0	0	0	0	0	3	5	0
Tim McCarver, c	.333	7	27	3	9	0	2	1	4	3	2	0
Mel Nelson, p	.000	1	0	0	0	0	0	0	0	0	0	0
Dave Ricketts, ph	1.000	1	1	0	1	0	0	0	0	0	0	0
Dick Schofield, ss-1	.000	2	0	0	0	0	0	0	0	0	0	0
Mike Shannon, 3b	.276	7	29	3	8	1	0	1	4	1	5	0
Ed Spiezio, ph	1.000	1	1	0	1	0	0	0	0	0	0	0
Bobby Tolan, ph	.000	1	1	0	0	0	0	0	0	0	1	0
Ray Washburn, p	.000	2	3	0	0	0	0	0	0	0	0	0
Ron Willis, p	.000	3	0	0	0	0	0	0	0	0	0	0
TOTAL	.255		239	27	61	7	3	7	27	21	40	11

PITCHER	W	L	ERA	G	GS	CG	SV	SHO	IP	H	ER	BB	SO
Nelson Briles	0	1	5.56	2	2	0	0	0	11.1	13	7	4	7
Steve Carlton	0	0	6.75	2	0	0	0	0	4.0	7	3	1	3
Bob Gibson	2	1	1.67	3	3	3	0	1	27.0	18	5	4	35
Wayne Granger	0	0	0.00	1	0	0	0	0	2.0	0	0	1	1
Joe Hoerner	0	1	3.86	3	0	0	1	0	4.2	5	2	5	3
Dick Hughes	0	0	0.00	1	0	0	0	0	0.1	2	0	0	0
Larry Jaster	0	0	∞	1	0	0	0	0	0.0	2	3	1	0
Mel Nelson	0	0	0.00	1	0	0	0	0	1.0	0	0	1	1
Ray Washburn	1	1	9.82	2	2	0	0	0	7.1	7	8	7	6
Ron Willis	0	0	8.31	3	0	0	0	0	4.1	2	4	4	3
TOTAL	3	4	4.65	19	7	3	1	1	62.0	56	32	27	59

GAME 1 AT STL OCT 2

DET 000 000 000 0 5 3
STL 000 300 10X 4 6 0
Pitchers: McLAIN, Dobson (6), McMahon (8) vs GIBSON
Home Runs: Brock-STL
Attendance: 54,692

GAME 2 AT STL OCT 3

DET 011 003 102 8 13 1
STL 000 001 000 1 6 1
Pitchers: LOLICH vs BRILES, Carlton (6), Willis (7), Hoerner (9)
Home Runs: Horton-DET, Lolich-DET, Cash-DET
Attendance: 54,692

GAME 3 AT DET OCT 5

STL 000 040 300 7 13 0
DET 002 010 000 3 4 0
Pitchers: WASHBURN, Hoerner (6) vs WILSON, Dobson (5), McMahon (6), Patterson (7), Hiller (8)
Home Runs: Kaline-DET, McCarver-STL, McAuliffe-DET, Cepeda-STL
Attendance: 53,634

GAME 4 AT DET OCT 6

STL 202 200 040 10 13 0
DET 000 100 000 1 5 4
Pitchers: GIBSON vs McLAIN, Sparma (3), Patterson (4), Lasher (6), Hiller (8), Dobson (9)
Home Runs: Brock-STL, Gibson-STL, Northrup-DET
Attendance: 53,634

GAME 5 AT DET OCT 7

STL 300 000 000 3 9 0
DET 000 200 30X 5 9 1
Pitchers: Briles, HOERNER (7), Willis (7) vs LOLICH
Home Runs: Cepeda-STL
Attendance: 53,634

GAME 6 AT STL OCT 9

DET 02 100 10 0 13 12 1
STL 000 000 001 1 9 1
Pitchers: McLAIN vs WASHBURN, Jaster (3), Willis (3), Hughes (3), Carlton (4), Granger (7), Nelson (9)
Home Runs: Northrup-DET, Kaline-DET
Attendance: 54,692

GAME 7 AT STL OCT 10

DET 000 000 301 4 8 1
STL 000 000 001 1 5 0
Pitchers: LOLICH vs GIBSON
Home Runs: Shannon-STL
Attendance: 54,692

NEW YORK METS (EAST) 3, ATLANTA BRAVES (WEST) 0

Atlanta's Hank Aaron homered in each game and drove in a series-high seven runs. But the "Miracle Mets" as a team outhomered the Braves six to five, outhit them by 72 percentage points, and scored nearly twice as many runs.

Twice in the first game the Braves came from behind to lead by a run, but in the top of the eighth, five New York hits and poor Atlanta fielding buried starter Phil Niekro under five runs. In Game 2, home runs by Tommie Agee and Ken Boswell helped New York take an early 8–0 lead that even Aaron's three-run homer in the fifth couldn't threaten.

In the third game the lead changed hands three times on home runs. Aaron began the barrage with a two-run shot in the first inning. Agee's homer in the third followed by Boswell's for two runs in the fourth put the Mets ahead—until Orlando Cepeda's two-run homer in the fifth gave Atlanta another lead. But in the bottom of the fifth, Mets rookie Wayne Garrett's two-run blast reversed the lead one last time and, after four final shutout innings by 22-year-old reliever Nolan Ryan, the Mets had swept to their first pennant.

NY (E)

PLAYER/POS	AVG	G	AB	R	H	2B	3B	HR	RB	BB	SO	SB
Tommie Agee, of	.357	3	14	4	5	1	0	2	4	2	5	2
Ken Boswell, 2b	.333	3	12	4	4	0	0	2	5	1	2	0
Wayne Garrett, 3b	.385	3	13	3	5	2	0	1	3	2	2	1
Rod Gaspar, of	.000	3	0	0	0	0	0	0	0	0	0	0
Gary Gentry, p	.000	1	0	0	0	0	0	0	0	0	0	0
Jerry Grote, c	.167	3	12	3	2	1	0	0	1	1	4	0
Bud Harrelson, ss	.182	3	11	2	2	1	1	0	3	1	2	0
Cleon Jones, of	.429	3	14	4	6	2	0	1	4	1	2	2
Jerry Koosman, p	.000	1	2	1	0	0	0	0	0	0	1	0
Ed Kranepool, 1b	.250	3	12	2	3	1	0	0	1	1	2	0
J. C. Martin, ph	.500	2	2	0	1	0	0	0	2	0	0	0
Tug McGraw, p	.000	1	0	0	0	0	0	0	0	0	0	0
Nolan Ryan, p	.500	1	4	1	2	0	0	0	0	0	1	0
Tom Seaver, p	.000	1	3	0	0	0	0	0	0	0	0	0
Art Shamsky, of	.538	3	13	3	7	0	0	0	1	0	3	0
Ron Taylor, p	.000	2	0	0	0	0	0	0	0	0	0	0
Al Weis, 2b	.000	3	1	0	0	0	0	0	0	0	0	0
TOTAL	.327		113	27	37	8	1	6	24	10	25	5

PITCHER	W	L	ERA	G	GS	CG	SV	SHO	IP	H	ER	BB	SO
Gary Gentry	0	0	9.00	1	1	0	0	0	2.0	5	2	1	1
Jerry Koosman	0	0	11.57	1	1	0	0	0	4.2	7	6	4	5
Tug McGraw	0	0	0.00	1	0	0	1	0	3.0	1	0	1	1
Nolan Ryan	1	0	2.57	1	0	0	0	0	7.0	3	2	2	7
Tom Seaver	1	0	6.43	1	1	0	0	0	7.0	8	5	3	2
Ron Taylor	1	0	0.00	2	0	0	1	0	3.1	3	0	0	4
TOTAL	3	0	5.00	7	3	0	2	0	27.0	27	15	11	20

ATL (W)

PLAYER/POS	AVG	G	AB	R	H	2B	3B	HR	RB	BB	SO	SB
Hank Aaron, of	.357	3	14	3	5	2	0	3	7	0	1	0
Tommie Aaron, ph	.000	1	1	0	0	0	0	0	0	0	0	0
Felipe Alou, ph	.000	1	1	0	0	0	0	0	0	0	0	0
Bob Aspromonte, ph	.000	3	3	0	0	0	0	0	0	0	0	0
Clete Boyer, 3b	.111	3	9	0	1	0	0	0	3	2	3	0
Jim Britton, p	.000	1	0	0	0	0	0	0	0	0	0	0
Rico Carty, of	.300	3	10	4	3	2	0	0	0	3	1	0
Orlando Cepeda, 1b	.455	3	11	2	5	2	0	1	3	1	2	1
Bob Didier, c	.000	3	11	0	0	0	0	0	0	0	2	0
Paul Doyle, p	.000	1	0	0	0	0	0	0	0	0	0	0
Gil Garrido, ss	.200	3	10	0	2	0	0	0	0	1	1	0
Tony Gonzalez, of	.357	3	14	4	5	1	0	1	2	1	4	0
Sonny Jackson, ss	.000	1	0	0	0	0	0	0	0	0	0	0
Pat Jarvis, p	.000	1	2	0	0	0	0	0	0	0	2	0
Mike Lum, of-1	1.000	2	2	0	2	1	0	0	0	0	0	0
Felix Millan, 2b	.333	3	12	2	4	1	0	0	0	3	0	0
Gary Neibauer, p	.000	1	0	0	0	0	0	0	0	0	0	0
Phil Niekro, p	.000	1	3	0	0	0	0	0	0	0	1	0
Milt Pappas, p	.000	1	1	0	0	0	0	0	0	0	1	0
Ron Reed, p	.000	1	0	0	0	0	0	0	0	0	0	0
George Stone, p	.000	1	1	0	0	0	0	0	0	0	1	0
Bob Tillman, c	.000	1	0	0	0	0	0	0	0	0	0	0
Cecil Upshaw, p	.000	3	1	0	0	0	0	0	0	0	0	0
TOTAL	.255		106	15	27	9	0	5	15	11	20	1

PITCHER	W	L	ERA	G	GS	CG	SV	SHO	IP	H	ER	BB	SO
Jim Britton	0	0	0.00	1	0	0	0	0	0.1	0	0	1	0
Paul Doyle	0	0	0.00	1	0	0	0	0	1.0	2	0	1	3
Pat Jarvis	0	1	12.46	1	1	0	0	0	4.1	10	6	0	6
Gary Neibauer	0	0	0.00	1	0	0	0	0	1.0	0	0	0	1
Phil Niekro	0	1	4.50	1	1	0	0	0	8.0	9	4	4	4
Milt Pappas	0	0	11.57	1	0	0	0	0	2.1	4	3	0	4
Ron Reed	0	1	21.60	1	1	0	0	0	1.2	5	4	3	3
George Stone	0	0	9.00	1	0	0	0	0	1.0	2	1	0	0
Cecil Upshaw	0	0	2.84	3	0	0	0	0	6.1	5	2	1	4
TOTAL	0	3	6.92	11	3	0	0	0	26.0	37	20	10	25

GAME 1 AT ATL OCT 4

```
NY   020 200 050   9 10 1
ATL  012 010 100   5 10 2
```
Pitchers: SEAVER, Taylor (8) vs NIEKRO, Upshaw (9)
Home Runs: Gonzalez-ATL, H.Aaron-ATL
Attendance: 50,122

GAME 2 AT ATL OCT 5

```
NY   132 210 200   11 13 1
ATL  000 150 000    6  9 3
```
Pitchers: Koosman, TAYLOR (5), McGraw (7) vs REED, Doyle (2), Pappas (3), Britton (6), Upshaw (6), Neibauer (9)
Home Runs: Agee-NY, Boswell-NY, H.Aaron-ATL, Jones-NY
Attendance: 50,270

GAME 3 AT NY OCT 6

```
ATL  200 020 000   4  8 1
NY   001 231 00X   7 14 0
```
Pitchers: JARVIS, Stone (5), Upshaw (6) vs Gentry, RYAN (3)
Home Runs: H.Aaron-ATL, Agee-NY, Boswell-NY, Cepeda-ATL, Garrett-NY
Attendance: 53,195

BALTIMORE ORIOLES (EAST) 3, MINNESOTA TWINS (WEST) 0

Minnesota led the league in batting, Baltimore in pitching. In the ALCS, pitching prevailed as the Twins were held to a series batting average 113 points below their season mark.

Still, Minnesota nearly won the first game with three runs on only four hits. But the Orioles tied the score on Boog Powell's homer in the bottom of the ninth and won the game three innings later on Paul Blair's suicide squeeze bunt with two away. In Game 2, Minnesota's Dave Boswell scattered seven Baltimore hits over 10-2/3 scoreless innings before giving way to Ron Perranoski in the 11th. But Orioles pitcher Dave McNally was more than a match for Boswell. He gave up only three hits—none in the final 7-2/3 innings of the 11 he pitched—and took the win when Baltimore pinch hitter Curt Motton lined a single off Perranoski to score Powell from second with the game's only run.

In the third game, the Twins fell apart as the Orioles battered seven Minnesota pitchers for 18 hits. Baltimore's Jim Palmer gave up more than a hit an inning himself, but coasted to the pennant 11–2.

BAL (E)

PLAYER/POS	AVG	G	AB	R	H	2B	3B	HR	RB	BB	SO	SB
Mark Belanger, ss	.267	3	15	4	4	0	1	1	1	0	0	0
Paul Blair, of	.400	3	15	1	6	2	0	1	6	2	2	0
Don Buford, of	.286	3	14	3	4	1	0	0	1	3	0	0
Mike Cuellar, p	.000	1	2	0	0	0	0	0	0	0	1	0
Andy Etchebarren, c	.000	2	4	0	0	0	0	0	0	0	0	0
Dick Hall, p	.000	1	0	0	0	0	0	0	0	0	0	0
Elrod Hendricks, c	.250	3	8	2	2	2	0	0	3	1	2	0
Davey Johnson, 2b	.231	3	13	2	3	0	0	0	0	2	1	0
Marcelino Lopez, p	.000	1	0	0	0	0	0	0	0	0	0	0
Dave May, ph	.000	1	1	0	0	0	0	0	0	0	0	0
Dave McNally, p	.000	1	4	0	0	0	0	0	0	0	2	0
Curt Motton, ph	.500	2	2	0	1	0	0	0	1	0	0	0
Jim Palmer, p	.000	1	5	0	0	0	0	0	0	0	3	0
Boog Powell, 1b	.385	3	13	2	5	0	0	1	1	2	0	0
Merv Rettenmund, ph	.000	1	0	0	0	0	0	0	0	0	0	0
Pete Richert, p	.000	1	0	0	0	0	0	0	0	0	0	0
Brooks Robinson, 3b	.500	3	14	1	7	1	0	0	0	0	0	0
Frank Robinson, of	.333	3	12	1	4	2	0	1	2	3	3	0
Chico Salmon, ph	.000	1	1	0	0	0	0	0	0	0	0	0
Eddie Watt, p	.000	1	0	0	0	0	0	0	0	0	0	0
TOTAL	.293		123	16	36	8	1	4	15	13	14	0

PITCHER	W	L	ERA	G	GS	CG	SV	SHO	IP	H	ER	BB	SO
Mike Cuellar	0	0	2.25	1	1	0	0	0	8.0	3	2	1	7
Dick Hall	1	0	0.00	1	0	0	0	0	0.2	0	0	0	1
Marcelino Lopez	0	0	0.00	1	0	0	0	0	0.1	1	0	2	0
Dave McNally	1	0	0.00	1	1	1	0	1	11.0	3	0	5	11
Jim Palmer	1	0	2.00	1	1	1	0	0	9.0	10	2	2	4
Pete Richert	0	0	0.00	1	0	0	0	0	1.0	0	0	2	2
Eddie Watt	0	0	0.00	1	0	0	0	0	2.0	0	0	0	2
TOTAL	3	0	1.13	7	3	2	0	1	32.0	17	4	12	27

MIN (W)

PLAYER/POS	AVG	G	AB	R	H	2B	3B	HR	RB	BB	SO	SB
Bob Allison, of	.000	2	8	0	0	0	0	0	0	1	0	0
Dave Boswell, p	.000	1	4	0	0	0	0	0	0	0	4	0
Leo Cardenas, ss	.154	3	13	0	2	0	1	0	0	0	7	0
Rod Carew, 2b	.071	3	14	0	1	0	0	0	0	1	4	0
Dean Chance, p	.000	1	0	0	0	0	0	0	0	0	0	0
Joe Grzenda, p	.000	1	0	0	0	0	0	0	0	0	0	0
Tom Hall, p	.000	1	0	0	0	0	0	0	0	0	0	0
Harmon Killebrew, 3b	.125	3	8	2	1	1	0	0	6	2	0
Chuck Manuel, ph	.000	1	0	0	0	0	0	0	0	1	0	0
Bob Miller, p	.000	1	0	0	0	0	0	0	0	0	0	0
George Mitterwald, c	.143	2	7	0	1	0	0	0	0	1	3	0
Graig Nettles, ph	1.000	1	1	0	1	0	0	0	0	0	0	0
Tony Oliva, of	.385	3	13	3	5	2	0	1	2	1	3	1
Ron Perranoski, p	.000	3	1	0	0	0	0	0	0	0	1	0
Jim Perry, p	.000	1	3	0	0	0	0	0	0	0	0	0
Rich Reese, 1b	.167	3	12	0	2	0	0	0	2	1	1	0
Rich Renick, ph	.000	1	1	0	0	0	0	0	0	0	0	0
John Roseboro, c	.200	2	5	0	1	0	0	0	0	0	0	0
Cesar Tovar, of	.077	3	13	0	1	0	0	0	0	1	2	1
Ted Uhlaender, of	.167	2	6	0	1	0	0	0	0	0	0	0
Dick Woodson, p	1.000	1	1	0	1	0	0	0	0	0	0	0
Al Worthington, p	.000	1	0	0	0	0	0	0	0	0	0	0
TOTAL	.155		110	5	17	3	1	1	5	12	27	2

PITCHER	W	L	ERA	G	GS	CG	SV	SHO	IP	H	ER	BB	SO
Dave Boswell	0	1	0.84	1	1	0	0	0	10.2	7	1	7	4
Dean Chance	0	0	13.50	1	0	0	0	0	2.0	4	3	0	2
Joe Grzenda	0	0	0.00	1	0	0	0	0	0.2	0	0	0	0
Tom Hall	0	0	0.00	1	0	0	0	0	0.2	0	0	0	0
Bob Miller	0	1	5.40	1	1	0	0	0	1.2	5	1	0	0
Ron Perranoski	0	1	5.79	3	0	0	0	0	4.2	8	3	0	2
Jim Perry	0	0	3.38	1	1	0	0	0	8.0	6	3	3	3
Dick Woodson	0	0	10.80	1	0	0	0	0	1.2	3	2	3	2
Al Worthington	0	0	6.75	1	0	0	0	0	1.1	3	1	0	1
TOTAL	0	3	4.02	11	3	0	0	0	31.1	36	14	13	14

GAME 1 AT BAL OCT 4

MIN 0 0 0 0 1 0 2 0 0   3 4 2
BAL 0 0 0 1 1 0 0 0 1 0 0 1   4 10 1
Pitchers: Perry, PERRANOSKI (9) vs Cuellar, Richert (9), Watt (10), Lopez (12), HALL (12)
Home Runs: F.Robinson-BAL, Belanger-BAL, Oliva-MIN, Powell-BAL
Attendance: 39,324

GAME 2 AT BAL OCT 5

MIN 0 0 0 0 0 0 0 0 0 0 0   0 3 1
BAL 0 0 0 0 0 0 0 0 0 1   1 8 0
Pitchers: BOSWELL, Perranoski (11) vs McNALLY
Attendance: 41,704

GAME 3 AT MIN OCT 6

BAL 0 3 0 2 0 1 0 2 3   11 18 0
MIN 1 0 0 0 1 0 0 0 0   2 10 2
Pitchers: PALMER vs MILLER, Woodson (2), Hall (4), Worthington (5), Grzenda (6), Chance (7), Perranoski (9)
Home Runs: Blair-BAL
Attendance: 32,735

NEW YORK METS (NL) 4, BALTIMORE ORIOLES (AL) 1

The heavy-hitting, slick-fielding Orioles, who also boasted the majors' top pitching staff, entered the Series clear favorites against the upstart Mets. But the "Miracle Mets," after losing the opener, polished off Baltimore with four straight wins.

Tom Seaver (25–7) and Mike Cuellar (23–11) faced each other in the opener. Baltimore's leadoff batter, Don Buford, greeted Seaver with a home run, and a three-run rally with two out in the fourth made the score 4–0 before the Mets scored their first Series run in the seventh. Cuellar held New York to that one run for the victory.

No one scored for three innings of Game 2 off Oriole Dave McNally or even hit Met Jerry Koosman safely. But Donn Clendenon led off the fourth with a home run for the Mets as Koosman continued to no-hit Baltimore for three more innings. In the seventh, though, Baltimore's Paul Blair spoiled Koosman's no-hitter with a leadoff single, and after stealing second, scored the tying run on Brooks Robinson's single. But those were the only hits the O's would get, and in the top of the ninth three successive two-out singles produced what proved to be the winning run.

Mets pitchers Gary Gentry and Nolan Ryan (with the assist of two spectacular catches by center fielder Tommie Agee that saved a total of five runs) combined for a shutout in Game 3. Agee's leadoff homer against Jim Palmer in the first was all the scoring the Mets would need, but they added four more runs before the game ended. Game 4 was the Series' tightest. Seaver went the distance for the win, holding a 1–0 lead until a sacrifice fly scored the tying Baltimore run in the top of the ninth (Ron Swoboda's diving catch kept it from being an extra base hit). In the bottom of the 10th, the Mets finally won it as a bunt thrown to first hit the runner and bounded away, allowing pinch runner Rod Gaspar to score all the way from second.

Dave McNally and Jerry Koosman tangled a second time in Game 5, and again Koosman and the Mets emerged victorious. McNally's two-run homer in the third gave him a lead which Frank Robinson expanded with a solo

shot. But in an eerie sixth inning reprise of Game 4 of the 1957 World Series featuring Nippy Jones, the Mets' Cleon Jones was struck by a pitch on the foot and awarded first base after inspection by the home plate umpire revealed tell-tale shoe polish on the ball. Similar to the episode of 12 years earlier, Cleon Jones scored a key run on Donn Clendenon's home run which followed immediately.

Al Weis homered in the seventh for a 3–3 tie. With McNally now gone, two doubles off Eddie Watt in the eighth brought in the go-ahead run, and a pair of errors let in a run for insurance. Koosman held Baltimore scoreless in the ninth and the Mets miracle was complete.

NY (N)

PLAYER/POS	AVG	G	AB	R	H	2B	3B	HR	RB	BB	SO	SB
Tommie Agee, of	.167	5	18	1	3	0	0	1	1	1	2	5	1
Ken Boswell, 2b	.333	1	3	1	1	0	0	0	0	0	0	0
Don Cardwell, p	.000	1	0	0	0	0	0	0	0	0	0	0
Ed Charles, 3b	.133	4	15	1	2	1	0	0	0	0	2	0
Donn Clendenon, 1b	.357	4	14	4	5	1	0	3	4	2	6	0
Duffy Dyer, ph	.000	1	1	0	0	0	0	0	0	0	0	0
Wayne Garrett, 3b	.000	2	1	0	0	0	0	0	0	2	1	0
Rod Gaspar, of-1	.000	3	2	1	0	0	0	0	0	0	0	0
Gary Gentry, p	.333	1	3	0	1	1	0	0	0	0	2	0
Jerry Grote, c	.211	5	19	1	4	2	0	0	1	1	3	0
Bud Harrelson, ss	.176	5	17	1	3	0	0	0	0	3	4	0
Cleon Jones, of	.158	5	19	2	3	1	0	0	0	0	1	0
Jerry Koosman, p	.143	2	7	0	1	1	0	0	0	0	4	0
Ed Kranepool, 1b	.250	1	4	1	1	0	0	1	1	0	0	0
J. C. Martin, ph	.000	1	0	0	0	0	0	0	0	0	0	0
Nolan Ryan, p	.000	1	0	0	0	0	0	0	0	0	0	0
Tom Seaver, p	.000	2	4	0	0	0	0	0	0	0	2	0
Art Shamsky, of-1	.000	3	6	0	0	0	0	0	0	0	0	0
Ron Swoboda, of	.400	4	15	1	6	1	0	0	1	1	3	0
Ron Taylor, p	.000	2	0	0	0	0	0	0	0	0	0	0
Al Weis, 2b	.455	5	11	1	5	0	0	1	3	4	2	0
TOTAL	.220		159	15	35	8	0	6	13	15	35	1

PITCHER	W	L	ERA	G	GS	CG	SV	SHO	IP	H	ER	BB	SO
Don Cardwell	0	0	0.00	1	0	0	0	0	1.0	0	0	0	0
Gary Gentry	1	0	0.00	1	1	0	0	0	6.2	3	0	5	4
Jerry Koosman	2	0	2.04	2	2	1	0	0	17.2	7	4	4	9
Nolan Ryan	0	0	0.00	1	0	0	1	0	2.1	1	0	2	3
Tom Seaver	1	1	3.00	2	2	1	0	0	15.0	12	5	3	9
Ron Taylor	0	0	0.00	2	0	0	1	0	2.1	0	0	1	3
TOTAL	4	1	1.80	9	5	2	2	0	45.0	23	9	15	28

BAL (A)

PLAYER/POS	AVG	G	AB	R	H	2B	3B	HR	RB	BB	SO	SB
Mark Belanger, ss	.200	5	15	2	3	0	0	0	1	2	1	0
Paul Blair, of	.100	5	20	1	2	0	0	0	0	2	5	1
Don Buford, of	.100	5	20	1	2	1	0	1	2	2	4	0
Mike Cuellar, p	.400	2	5	0	2	0	0	0	1	0	3	0
Clay Dalrymple, ph	1.000	2	2	0	2	0	0	0	0	0	0	0
Andy Etchebarren, c	.000	2	6	0	0	0	0	0	0	0	1	0
Dick Hall, p	.000	1	0	0	0	0	0	0	0	0	0	0
Elrod Hendricks, c	.100	3	10	1	1	0	0	0	0	1	0	0
Davey Johnson, 2b	.063	5	16	1	1	0	0	0	0	2	1	0
Dave Leonhard, p	.000	1	0	0	0	0	0	0	0	0	0	0
Dave May, ph	.000	2	1	0	0	0	0	0	0	1	1	0
Dave McNally, p	.200	2	5	1	1	0	0	1	2	0	2	0
Curt Motton, ph	.000	1	1	0	0	0	0	0	0	0	0	0
Jim Palmer, p	.000	1	2	0	0	0	0	0	0	0	0	0
Boog Powell, 1b	.263	5	19	0	5	0	0	0	0	1	4	0
Merv Rettenmund, pr	.000	1	0	0	0	0	0	0	0	0	0	0
Pete Richert, p	.000	1	0	0	0	0	0	0	0	0	0	0
Brooks Robinson, 3b	.053	5	19	0	1	0	0	0	2	0	3	0
Frank Robinson, of	.188	5	16	2	3	0	0	1	1	4	3	0
Chico Salmon, pr	.000	2	0	0	0	0	0	0	0	0	0	0
Eddie Watt, p	.000	2	0	0	0	0	0	0	0	0	0	0
TOTAL	.146		157	9	23	1	0	3	9	15	28	1

PITCHER	W	L	ERA	G	GS	CG	SV	SHO	IP	H	ER	BB	SO
Mike Cuellar	1	0	1.13	2	2	1	0	0	16.0	13	2	4	13
Dick Hall	0	1	–	1	0	0	0	0	0.0	1	0	1	0
Dave Leonhard	0	0	4.50	1	0	0	0	0	2.0	1	1	1	1
Dave McNally	0	1	2.81	2	2	1	0	0	16.0	11	5	5	13
Jim Palmer	0	1	6.00	1	1	0	0	0	6.0	5	4	4	5
Pete Richert	0	0	–	1	0	0	0	0	0.0	0	0	0	0
Eddie Watt	0	1	3.00	2	0	0	0	0	3.0	4	1	0	3
TOTAL	1	4	2.72	10	5	2	0	0	43.0	35	13	15	35

GAME 1 AT BAL OCT 11

```
NY   000 000 100   1 6 1
BAL  100 300 00X   4 6 0
```
Pitchers: SEAVER, Cardwell (6), Taylor (7) vs CUELLAR
Home Runs: Buford-BAL
Attendance: 50,429

GAME 2 AT BAL OCT 12

```
NY   000 100 001   2 6 0
BAL  000 000 100   1 2 0
```
Pitchers: KOOSMAN, Taylor (9) vs McNALLY
Home Runs: Clendenon-NY
Attendance: 50,850

GAME 3 AT NY OCT 14

```
BAL  000 000 000   0 4 1
NY   120 001 01X   5 6 0
```
Pitchers: PALMER, Leonhard (7) vs GENTRY, Ryan (7)
Home Runs: Agee-NY, Kranepool-NY
Attendance: 56,335

GAME 4 AT NY OCT 15

```
BAL  000 000 001 0   1 6 1
NY   010 000 000 1   2 10 1
```
Pitchers: Cuellar, Watt (8), HALL (10), Richert (10) vs SEAVER
Home Runs: Clendenon-NY
Attendance: 57,367

GAME 5 AT NY OCT 16

```
BAL  003 000 000   3 5 2
NY   000 002 12X   5 7 0
```
Pitchers: McNALLY, WATT (8) vs KOOSMAN
Home Runs: McNally-BAL, F.Robinson-BAL, Clendenon-NY, Weis-NY
Attendance: 57,397

CINCINNATI REDS (WEST) 3, PITTSBURGH PIRATES (EAST) 0

Pitching was the name of the game and three the magic number, as Cincinnati swept Pittsburgh, scoring three runs in each game while holding the Pirates to just three runs for the whole series.

Pirates pitcher Dock Ellis matched the Reds' Gary Nolan for nine scoreless innings in Game 1 before a pinch-hit triple, a single, and a double undid him for three runs in the top of the 10th. In Game 2 Pittsburgh scored its first series run, but center fielder Bobby Tolan scored three for the Reds—including a home run—to give Cincinnati its second win.

The Pirates took a lead for the only time in the series with a run in the top of the first inning of Game 3. But Tony Perez and Johnny Bench homered in the bottom of the inning to put the Reds up 2–1. The Pirates tied the score in the fifth, but three Cincinnati relievers combined to shut them out over the final four innings. Tolan sank the Pirates ship with his second game-winner in two days: a single in the eighth that drove in Cincinnati's third—and final— run.

CIN (W)

PLAYER/POS	AVG	G	AB	R	H	2B	3B	HR	RB	BB	SO	SB
Johnny Bench, c	.222	3	9	2	2	0	0	1	1	3	1	0
Angel Bravo, ph	.000	1	1	0	0	0	0	0	0	0	0	0
Bernie Carbo, of	.000	2	6	0	0	0	0	0	0	1	2	0
Clay Carroll, p	.000	2	0	0	0	0	0	0	0	0	0	0
Ty Cline, of-1	1.000	2	1	2	1	0	1	0	0	1	0	0
Tony Cloninger, p	.000	1	1	0	0	0	0	0	0	0	0	0
Dave Concepcion, ss	.000	3	0	0	0	0	0	0	0	0	0	0
Wayne Granger, p	.000	1	0	0	0	0	0	0	0	0	0	0
Don Gullett, p	.000	2	1	0	0	0	0	0	0	0	0	0
Tommy Helms, 2b	.273	3	11	0	3	0	0	0	0	0	1	0
Lee May, 1b	.167	3	12	0	2	1	0	0	2	0	2	0
Hal McRae, of-1	.000	2	4	0	0	0	0	0	0	0	2	0
Jim Merritt, p	.000	1	2	0	0	0	0	0	0	0	2	0
Gary Nolan, p	.333	1	3	0	1	0	0	0	0	0	0	0
Tony Perez, 3b-3,1b-1	.333	3	12	1	4	2	0	1	2	1	1	0
Pete Rose, of	.231	3	13	1	3	0	0	0	1	0	0	0
Jimmy Stewart, of	.000	1	2	0	0	0	0	0	0	0	0	0
Bobby Tolan, of	.417	3	12	3	5	0	0	1	2	1	1	1
Milt Wilcox, p	.000	1	0	0	0	0	0	0	0	0	0	0
Woody Woodward, ss-3,3b-3	.100	3	10	0	1	0	0	0	0	1	0	0
TOTAL	.220		100	9	22	3	1	3	8	8	12	1

PITCHER	W	L	ERA	G	GS	CG	SV	SHO	IP	H	ER	BB	SO
Clay Carroll	0	0	0.00	2	0	0	1	0	1.1	2	0	0	2
Tony Cloninger	0	0	3.60	1	1	0	0	0	5.0	7	2	4	1
Wayne Granger	0	0	0.00	1	0	0	0	0	0.2	1	0	0	0
Don Gullett	0	0	0.00	2	0	0	2	0	3.2	1	0	2	3
Jim Merritt	1	0	1.69	1	1	0	0	0	5.1	3	1	0	2
Gary Nolan	1	0	0.00	1	1	0	0	0	9.0	8	0	4	6
Milt Wilcox	1	0	0.00	1	0	0	0	0	3.0	1	0	2	5
TOTAL	3	0	0.96	9	3	0	3	0	28.0	23	3	12	19

PIT (E)

PLAYER/POS	AVG	G	AB	R	H	2B	3B	HR	RB	BB	SO	SB
Gene Alley, ss	.000	2	7	0	0	0	0	0	0	1	2	0
Matty Alou, of	.250	3	12	1	3	1	0	0	0	2	1	0
Dave Cash, 2b	.125	2	8	1	1	1	0	0	0	1	1	0
Roberto Clemente, of	.214	3	14	1	3	0	0	0	1	0	4	0
Dock Ellis, p	.000	1	2	0	0	0	0	0	0	0	1	0
Joe Gibbon, p	.000	2	0	0	0	0	0	0	0	0	0	0
Dave Giusti, p	.000	2	0	0	0	0	0	0	0	0	0	0
Richie Hebner, 3b	.667	2	6	0	4	2	0	0	0	2	1	0
Johnny Jeter, of-1	.000	3	2	0	0	0	0	0	0	0	2	0
Bill Mazeroski, 2b	.000	1	2	0	0	0	0	0	0	2	0	0
Bob Moose, p	.000	1	4	0	0	0	0	0	0	0	1	0
Al Oliver, 1b	.250	2	8	0	2	0	0	0	1	1	0	0
Jose Pagan, 3b	.333	1	3	0	1	0	0	0	0	1	1	0
Freddie Patek, ss	.000	1	3	0	0	0	0	0	0	1	2	0
Bob Robertson, 1b-1	.200	2	5	0	1	1	0	0	0	0	0	0
Manny Sanguillen, c	.167	3	12	0	2	0	0	0	0	0	1	0
Willie Stargell, of	.500	3	12	0	6	1	0	0	1	1	1	0
Luke Walker, p	.000	1	2	0	0	0	0	0	0	0	1	0
TOTAL	.225		102	3	23	6	0	0	3	12	19	0

PITCHER	W	L	ERA	G	GS	CG	SV	SHO	IP	H	ER	BB	SO
Dock Ellis	0	1	2.79	1	1	0	0	0	9.2	9	3	4	1
Joe Gibbon	0	0	0.00	2	0	0	0	0	0.1	1	0	0	1
Dave Giusti	0	0	3.86	2	0	0	0	0	2.1	3	1	1	1
Bob Moose	0	1	3.52	1	1	0	0	0	7.2	4	3	2	4
Luke Walker	0	1	1.29	1	1	0	0	0	7.0	5	1	1	5
TOTAL	0	3	2.67	7	3	0	0	0	27.0	22	8	8	12

GAME 1 AT PIT OCT 3

CIN 0 0 0 0 0 0 0 0 0 3   3 9 0
PIT 0 0 0 0 0 0 0 0 0 0   0 8 0
Pitchers: NOLAN, Carroll (10) vs ELLIS, Gibbon (10)
Attendance: 33,088

GAME 2 AT PIT OCT 4

CIN 0 0 1 0 1 0 0 1 0   3 8 1
PIT 0 0 0 0 0 1 0 0 0   1 5 2
Pitchers: MERRITT, Carroll (6), Gullett (6) vs WALKER, Giusti (8)
Home Runs: Tolan-CIN
Attendance: 39,317

GAME 3 AT CIN OCT 5

PIT 1 0 0 0 1 0 0 0 0   2 10 0
CIN 2 0 0 0 0 0 1 X   3 5 0
Pitchers: MOOSE, Giusti (8) vs Cloninger, WILCOX (6), Granger (9), Gullett (9)
Home Runs: Perez-CIN, Bench-CIN
Attendance: 40,538

BALTIMORE ORIOLES (EAST) 3, MINNESOTA TWINS (WEST) 0

For the second year in a row, Baltimore swept Minnesota in the ALCS. In the first two games the Orioles' attack featured the big inning. The score was tied 2–2 in the first game as the Orioles came to bat in the top of the fourth. But by the time the Twins came to bat in the inning, they were seven runs behind—thanks in part to a grand slam by Baltimore pitcher Mike Cuellar. Harmon Killebrew's tworun homer in the fifth helped bring the Twins within three, but they came no closer.

Except for home runs to Killebrew and Tony Oliva in the fourth inning, Orioles pitcher Dave McNally stopped the Twins in Game 2, and Baltimore held a close 4–3 lead after eight. If they had been playing at home, they wouldn't have needed to bat at all in the ninth. But they did come to bat in the top of the ninth, and they once again buried Minnesota under a seven-run inning.

In the third game, for the second year in a row, pitcher Jim Palmer breezed through the series clincher. Baltimore scored five runs for him in the first three innings, and another in the eighth—four more than he needed to carry his club to another pennant.

BAL (E)

PLAYER/POS	AVG	G	AB	R	H	2B	3B	HR	RB	BB	SO	SB
Mark Belanger, ss	.333	3	12	5	4	0	0	0	1	1	0	0
Paul Blair, of	.077	3	13	0	1	0	0	0	0	1	4	0
Don Buford, of	.429	2	7	2	3	1	0	1	3	2	0	0
Mike Cuellar, p	.500	1	2	1	1	0	0	1	4	0	1	0
Andy Etchebarren, c	.111	2	9	1	1	0	0	0	0	0	3	0
Dick Hall, p	.500	1	2	1	1	0	0	0	0	0	1	0
Elrod Hendricks, c	.400	1	5	2	2	0	0	0	0	0	1	0
Davey Johnson, 2b	.364	3	11	4	4	0	0	2	4	1	1	0
Dave McNally, p	.400	1	5	1	2	1	0	0	1	0	1	0
Jim Palmer, p	.250	1	4	1	1	1	0	0	1	0	0	0
Boog Powell, 1b	.429	3	14	2	6	2	0	1	6	0	3	0
Merv Rettenmund, of	.333	1	3	1	1	0	0	0	1	2	1	1
Brooks Robinson, 3b	.583	3	12	3	7	2	0	0	1	0	1	0
Frank Robinson, of	.200	3	10	3	2	0	0	1	2	5	2	0
TOTAL	.330		109	27	36	7	0	6	24	12	19	1

PITCHER	W	L	ERA	G	GS	CG	SV	SHO	IP	H	ER	BB	SO
Mike Cuellar	0	0	12.46	1	1	0	0	0	4.1	10	6	1	2
Dick Hall	1	0	0.00	1	0	0	0	0	4.2	1	0	0	3
Dave McNally	1	0	3.00	1	1	1	0	0	9.0	6	3	5	5
Jim Palmer	1	0	1.00	1	1	1	0	0	9.0	7	1	3	12
TOTAL	3	0	3.33	4	3	2	0	0	27.0	24	10	9	22

MIN (W)

PLAYER/POS	AVG	G	AB	R	H	2B	3B	HR	RB	BB	SO	SB
Bob Allison, ph	.000	3	2	0	0	0	0	0	0	0	1	0
Brant Alyea, of-2	.000	3	7	1	0	0	0	0	0	2	3	0
Bert Blyleven, p	.000	1	0	0	0	0	0	0	0	0	0	0
Leo Cardenas, ss	.182	3	11	1	2	0	0	0	1	1	1	0
Rod Carew, ph	.000	2	2	0	0	0	0	0	0	0	1	0
Tom Hall, p	.000	2	1	0	0	0	0	0	0	0	1	0
Jim Holt, of	.000	3	5	0	0	0	0	0	0	0	2	0
Jim Kaat, p	.000	1	1	0	0	0	0	0	0	0	1	0
Harmon Killebrew, 3b-2,1b-1	.273	3	11	2	3	0	0	2	4	2	4	0
Chuck Manuel, ph	.000	1	1	0	0	0	0	0	0	0	1	0
George Mitterwald, c	.500	2	8	2	4	1	0	0	2	0	2	0
Tony Oliva, of	.500	3	12	2	6	2	0	1	1	0	1	0
Ron Perranoski, p	.000	2	0	0	0	0	0	0	0	0	0	0
Jim Perry, p	.000	2	1	0	0	0	0	0	0	1	0	0
Frank Quilici, 2b-2	.000	3	2	0	0	0	0	0	0	0	1	0
Paul Ratliff, c	.250	1	4	0	1	0	0	0	0	0	1	0
Rich Reese, 1b	.143	2	7	0	1	0	0	0	0	1	1	0
Rich Renick, 3b-1	.200	2	5	0	1	0	0	0	0	0	1	0
Danny Thompson, 2b	.125	3	8	0	1	1	0	0	0	1	0	0
Luis Tiant, p-1, pr-1	.000	2	0	0	0	0	0	0	0	0	0	0
Cesar Tovar, of-3,2b-1	.385	3	13	2	5	0	1	0	1	0	0	0
Stan Williams, p	.000	2	0	0	0	0	0	0	0	1	0	0
Dick Woodson, p	.000	1	0	0	0	0	0	0	0	0	0	0
Bill Zepp, p	.000	2	0	0	0	0	0	0	0	0	0	0
TOTAL	.238		101	10	24	4	1	3	10	9	22	0

PITCHER	W	L	ERA	G	GS	CG	SV	SHO	IP	H	ER	BB	SO
Bert Blyleven	0	0	0.00	1	0	0	0	0	2.0	2	0	0	2
Tom Hall	0	1	6.75	2	1	0	0	0	5.1	6	4	4	6
Jim Kaat	0	1	9.00	1	1	0	0	0	2.0	6	2	2	1
Ron Perranoski	0	0	19.29	2	0	0	0	0	2.1	5	5	1	3
Jim Perry	0	1	13.50	2	1	0	0	0	5.1	10	8	1	3
Luis Tiant	0	0	13.50	1	0	0	0	0	0.2	1	1	0	0
Stan Williams	0	0	0.00	2	0	0	0	0	6.0	2	0	1	2
Dick Woodson	0	0	9.00	1	0	0	0	0	1.0	2	1	1	0
Bill Zepp	0	0	6.75	2	0	0	0	0	1.1	2	1	2	2
TOTAL	0	3	7.62	14	3	0	0	0	26.0	36	22	12	19

GAME 1 AT MIN OCT 3

```
BAL   020 701 000   10 13 0
MIN   110 130 000    6 11 2
```
Pitchers: Cuellar, HALL (5) vs PERRY, Zepp (4), Woodson (5), Williams (6), Perranoski (9)
Home Runs: Cuellar-BAL, Buford-BAL, Powell-BAL, Killebrew-MIN
Attendance: 26,847

GAME 2 AT MIN OCT 4

```
BAL   102 100 007   11 13 0
MIN   000 300 000    3  6 2
```
Pitchers: McNally vs HALL, Zepp (4), Williams (5), Perranoski (8), Tiant (9)
Home Runs: F.Robinson-BAL, Killebrew-MIN, Oliva-MIN, Johnson-BAL
Attendance: 27,490

GAME 3 AT BAL OCT 5

```
MIN   000 010 000   1 7 2
BAL   113 000 10X   6 10 0
```
Pitchers: KAAT, Blyleven (3), Hall (5), Perry (7) vs PALMER
Home Runs: Johnson-BAL
Attendance: 27,608

BALTIMORE ORIOLES (AL) 4, CINCINNATI REDS (NL) 1

With a near-sweep of the Reds, the Orioles helped Baltimore fans forget their 1969 Series humiliation by the New York Mets. Baltimore's first two wins, though, were closely contested. In the opener in Cincinnati (the first World Series game played on artificial grass), a run in the first inning and Lee May's third-inning two-run homer off Orioles starter Jim Palmer gave Cincinnati a 3–0 lead. But Orioles Boog Powell and Elrod Hendricks tagged Gary Nolan for home runs in the fourth and fifth that evened the score, and Brooks Robinson—whose other-worldly defense at third gave Reds righthanded hitters nightmares throughout the Series—homered in the seventh for a one-run Baltimore lead that held up as Palmer settled down to pitch one-hit ball from the fourth inning until he was relieved for the final out of the ninth.

Game 2 was just as close. The Reds scored four runs in the first three innings, but Baltimore came back with six in the fourth and fifth. Johnny Bench's leadoff homer in the last of the sixth brought the Reds within one, but that was the end of the scoring for either side. In Game 3 Dave McNally gave up nine hits and three runs. But he himself hit a grand slam in the sixth inning to cement what became a 9–3 Baltimore victory.

On the verge of a Series sweep, the Orioles scored three runs in the last of the third inning of Game 4 to take a 4–2 lead. But the Reds' Pete Rose homered in the fifth, and although Baltimore got the run back in the sixth, Lee May's three-run blast in the eighth overcame the Orioles lead and gave the Reds a narrow 6–5 win as Reds reliever Clay Carroll permitted only one Oriole to hit safely over the final 3-2/3 innings.

Mike Cuellar, driven out of Game 2 in the third inning, hurled the complete game for Baltimore in Game 5, even though Cincinnati hammered him for four hits (three of them doubles) and three runs in the top of the first inning. But as Orioles home runs by Frank Robinson and Merv Rettenmund highlighted a Baltimore onslaught that produced 15 hits and nine runs, Cuellar settled down, holding Cincinnati to a walk and a pair of harmless singles over the final eight

innings to bring Baltimore its second world title in five years.

BAL (A)

PLAYER/POS	AVG	G	AB	R	H	2B	3B	HR	RB	BB	SO	SB
Mark Belanger, ss	.200	5	15	2	3	0	0	0	1	2	1	0
Paul Blair, of	.100	5	20	1	2	0	0	0	0	2	5	1
Don Buford, of	.100	5	20	1	2	1	0	1	2	2	4	0
Mike Cuellar, p	.400	2	5	0	2	0	0	0	1	0	3	0
Clay Dalrymple, ph	1.000	2	2	0	2	0	0	0	0	0	0	0
Andy Etchebarren, c	.000	2	6	0	0	0	0	0	0	0	1	0
Dick Hall, p	.000	1	0	0	0	0	0	0	0	0	0	0
Elrod Hendricks, c	.100	3	10	1	1	0	0	0	0	0	1	0
Davey Johnson, 2b	.063	5	16	1	1	0	0	0	0	2	1	0
Dave Leonhard, p	.000	1	0	0	0	0	0	0	0	0	0	0
Dave May, ph	.000	2	1	0	0	0	0	0	0	1	1	0
Dave McNally, p	.200	2	5	1	1	0	0	1	2	0	0	0
Curt Motton, ph	.000	1	1	0	0	0	0	0	0	0	0	0
Jim Palmer, p	.000	1	2	0	0	0	0	0	0	0	0	0
Boog Powell, 1b	.263	5	19	0	5	0	0	0	0	1	4	0
Merv Rettenmund, pr	.000	1	0	0	0	0	0	0	0	0	0	0
Pete Richert, p	.000	1	0	0	0	0	0	0	0	0	0	0
Brooks Robinson, 3b	.053	5	19	0	1	0	0	0	2	0	3	0
Frank Robinson, of	.188	5	16	2	3	0	0	1	1	4	3	0
Chico Salmon, pr	.000	2	0	0	0	0	0	0	0	0	0	0
Eddie Watt, p	.000	2	0	0	0	0	0	0	0	0	0	0
TOTAL	.146		157	9	23	1	0	3	9	15	28	1

PITCHER	W	L	ERA	G	GS	CG	SV	SHO	IP	H	ER	BB	SO
Mike Cuellar	1	0	3.18	2	2	1	0	0	11.1	10	4	2	5
Moe Drabowsky	0	0	2.70	2	0	0	0	0	3.1	2	1	1	1
Dick Hall	0	0	0.00	1	0	0	1	0	2.1	0	0	0	0
Marcelino Lopez	0	0	0.00	1	0	0	0	0	0.1	0	0	0	0
Dave McNally	1	0	3.00	1	1	1	0	0	9.0	9	3	2	5
Jim Palmer	1	0	4.60	2	2	0	0	0	15.2	11	8	9	9
Tom Phoebus	1	0	0.00	1	0	0	0	0	1.2	1	0	0	0
Pete Richert	0	0	0.00	1	0	0	1	0	0.1	0	0	0	0
Eddie Watt	0	1	9.00	1	0	0	0	0	1.0	2	1	1	3
TOTAL	4	1	3.40	12	5	2	2	0	45.0	35	17	15	23

CIN (N)

PLAYER/POS	AVG	G	AB	R	H	2B	3B	HR	RB	BB	SO	SB
Johnny Bench, c	.211	5	19	3	4	0	0	1	3	1	2	0
Angel Bravo, ph	.000	4	2	0	0	0	0	0	0	1	1	0
Bernie Carbo, of-2	.000	4	8	0	0	0	0	0	0	2	3	0
Clay Carroll, p	.000	4	1	0	0	0	0	0	0	0	1	0
Darrel Chaney, ss	.000	3	1	0	0	0	0	0	0	0	1	0
Ty Cline, ph	.333	3	3	0	1	0	0	0	0	0	0	0
Tony Cloninger, p	.000	2	2	0	0	0	0	0	0	0	1	0
Dave Concepcion, ss	.333	3	9	0	3	0	1	0	3	0	0	0
Pat Corrales, ph	.000	1	1	0	0	0	0	0	0	0	0	0
Wayne Granger, p	.000	2	0	0	0	0	0	0	0	0	0	0
Don Gullett, p	.000	3	1	0	0	0	0	0	0	0	1	0
Tommy Helms, 2b	.222	5	18	1	4	0	0	0	0	0	1	0
Lee May, 1b	.389	5	18	6	7	2	0	2	8	2	2	0
Jim McGlothlin, p	.000	1	2	0	0	0	0	0	0	0	1	0
Hal McRae, of	.455	3	11	1	5	2	0	0	3	0	1	0
Jim Merritt, p	.000	1	1	0	0	0	0	0	0	0	1	0
Gary Nolan, p	.000	2	3	0	0	0	0	0	0	0	0	0
Tony Perez, 3b	.056	5	18	2	1	0	0	0	0	3	4	0
Pete Rose, of	.250	5	20	2	5	1	0	1	2	2	0	0
Jimmy Stewart, ph	.000	2	2	0	0	0	0	0	0	0	1	0
Bobby Tolan, of	.211	5	19	5	4	1	0	1	1	3	2	1
Ray Washburn, p	.000	1	0	0	0	0	0	0	0	0	0	0
Milt Wilcox, p	.000	2	0	0	0	0	0	0	0	0	0	0
Woody Woodward, ss-3	.200	4	5	0	1	0	0	0	0	0	0	0
TOTAL	.213		164	20	35	6	1	5	20	15	23	1

PITCHER	W	L	ERA	G	GS	CG	SV	SHO	IP	H	ER	BB	SO
Clay Carroll	1	0	0.00	4	0	0	0	0	9.0	5	0	2	11
Tony Cloninger	0	1	7.36	2	1	0	0	0	7.1	10	6	5	4
Wayne Granger	0	0	33.75	2	0	0	0	0	1.1	7	5	1	1
Don Gullett	0	0	1.35	3	0	0	0	0	6.2	5	1	4	4
Jim McGlothlin	0	0	8.31	1	1	0	0	0	4.1	6	4	2	2
Jim Merritt	0	1	21.60	1	1	0	0	0	1.2	3	4	1	0
Gary Nolan	0	1	7.71	2	2	0	0	0	9.1	9	8	3	9
Ray Washburn	0	0	13.50	1	0	0	0	0	1.1	2	2	2	0
Milt Wilcox	0	1	9.00	2	0	0	0	0	2.0	3	2	0	2
TOTAL	1	4	6.70	18	5	0	0	0	43.0	50	32	20	33

GAME 1 AT CIN OCT 10

BAL 0 0 0 2 1 0 1 0 0   4 7 2
CIN 1 0 2 0 0 0 0 0 0   3 5 0
Pitchers: PALMER, Richert (9) vs NOLAN, Carroll (7)
Home Runs: May-CIN, Powell-BAL, Hendricks-BAL, B.Robinson-BAL
Attendance: 51,531

GAME 2 AT CIN OCT 11

BAL 0 0 0 1 5 0 0 0 0   6 10 2
CIN 3 0 1 0 0 1 0 0 0   5 7 0
Pitchers: Cuellar, PHOEBUS (3), Drabowsky (5), Lopez (7), Hall (7) vs McGlothlin, WILCOX (5), Carroll (5), Gullett (8)
Home Runs: Tolan-CIN, Powell-BAL, Bench-CIN
Attendance: 51,531

GAME 3 AT BAL OCT 13

CIN 0 1 0 0 0 0 2 0 0   3 9 0
BAL 2 0 1 0 1 4 1 0 X   9 10 1
Pitchers: CLONINGER, Granger (6), Gullett (7) vs McNALLY
Home Runs: F.Robinson-BAL, Buford-BAL, McNally-BAL
Attendance: 51,773

GAME 4 AT BAL OCT 14

CIN 0 1 1 0 1 0 0 3 0   6 8 3
BAL 0 1 3 0 0 1 0 0 0   5 8 0
Pitchers: Nolan, Gullett (3), CARROLL (6) vs Palmer, WATT (8), Drabowsky (9)
Home Runs: B.Robinson-BAL, Rose-CIN, May-CIN
Attendance: 53,007

GAME 5 AT BAL OCT 15

CIN 3 0 0 0 0 0 0 0 0   3 6 0
BAL 2 2 2 0 1 0 0 2 X   9 15 0
Pitchers: MERRITT, Granger (2), Wilcox (3), Cloninger (5), Washburn (7), Carroll (8) vs CUELLAR
Home Runs: F.Robinson-BAL, Rettenmund-BAL
Attendance: 45,341

PITTSBURGH PIRATES (EAST) 3, SAN FRANCISCO GIANTS (WEST) 1

For the first time, an LCS went more than the minimum three games, as Pittsburgh rebounded from a loss in the opener to take the next three from San Francisco.

The Pirates scored first, with two runs in the third inning of Game 1, but the Giants came back with a run in the bottom of the inning and put the game away in the fifth as Tito Fuentes and Willie McCovey both hit two-out two-run homers. Pirates first baseman Bob Robertson avenged his club's opening-game defeat the next day, battering four of the Giants' six pitchers for three home runs and a double—and five RBIs—in the Pirates' 9–5 win. Robertson continued his assault in Game 3, homering off Juan Marichal in the second. The Giants came back with a run in the sixth, but third baseman Richie Hebner put the game away with a second Pirates home run off Marichal in the eighth.

Both clubs scored five times in the first two innings of Game 4. But Pirates relievers Bruce Kison and Dave Giusti then pinned the Giants down for the final seven innings, while Roberto Clemente and Al Oliver combined for four RBIs in the sixth to capture the flag.

PIT (E)

PLAYER/POS	AVG	G	AB	R	H	2B	3B	HR	RB	BB	SO	SB
Gene Alley, ss	.500	1	2	1	1	0	0	0	0	0	0	0
Steve Blass, p	.000	2	1	0	0	0	0	0	0	0	1	0
Dave Cash, 2b	.421	4	19	5	8	2	0	0	1	0	1	1
Roberto Clemente, of	.333	4	18	2	6	0	0	0	4	1	6	0
Gene Clines, of	.333	1	3	1	1	0	0	1	1	0	1	0
Vic Davalillo, ph	.000	2	2	0	0	0	0	0	0	0	1	0
Dock Ellis, p	.000	1	3	0	0	0	0	0	0	0	2	0
Dave Giusti, p	.000	4	1	0	0	0	0	0	0	0	0	0
Richie Hebner, 3b	.294	4	17	3	5	1	0	2	4	0	4	0
Jackie Hernandez, ss	.231	4	13	2	3	0	0	0	1	0	4	0
Bob Johnson, p	.000	1	2	0	0	0	0	0	0	0	1	0
Bruce Kison, p	.000	1	2	0	0	0	0	0	0	0	0	0
Milt May, ph	.000	1	1	0	0	0	0	0	0	0	0	0
Bill Mazeroski, ph	1.000	1	1	1	1	0	0	0	0	0	0	0
Bob Miller, p	.000	1	1	0	0	0	0	0	0	0	0	0
Bob Moose, p	.000	1	0	0	0	0	0	0	0	0	0	0
Al Oliver, of	.250	4	12	2	3	0	0	1	5	1	3	0
Jose Pagan, 3b	.000	1	0	1	0	0	0	0	0	0	0	0
Bob Robertson, 1b	.438	4	16	5	7	1	0	4	6	0	2	0
Manny Sanguillen, c	.267	4	15	1	4	0	0	0	1	1	1	1
Willie Stargell, of	.000	4	14	1	0	0	0	0	0	2	6	0
TOTAL	.271		144	24	39	4	0	8	23	5	33	2

PITCHER	W	L	ERA	G	GS	CG	SV	SHO	IP	H	ER	BB	SO
Steve Blass	0	1	11.57	2	2	0	0	0	7.0	14	9	2	11
Dock Ellis	1	0	3.60	1	1	0	0	0	5.0	6	2	4	1
Dave Giusti	0	0	0.00	4	0	0	3	0	5.1	1	0	2	3
Bob Johnson	1	0	0.00	1	1	0	0	0	8.0	5	0	3	7
Bruce Kison	1	0	0.00	1	0	0	0	0	4.2	2	0	2	3
Bob Miller	0	0	6.00	1	0	0	0	0	3.0	3	2	3	3
Bob Moose	0	0	0.00	1	0	0	0	0	2.0	0	0	0	0
TOTAL	3	1	3.34	11	4	0	3	0	35.0	31	13	16	28

SF (W)

PLAYER/POS	AVG	G	AB	R	H	2B	3B	HR	RB	BB	SO	SB
Jim Barr, p	.000	1	1	0	0	0	0	0	0	0	0	0
Bobby Bonds, of	.250	3	8	0	2	0	0	0	0	2	4	0
Ron Bryant, p	.000	1	0	0	0	0	0	0	0	0	0	0
Don Carrithers, p	.000	1	0	0	0	0	0	0	0	0	0	0
John Cumberland, p	.000	1	0	0	0	0	0	0	0	0	0	0
Dick Dietz, c	.067	4	15	0	1	0	0	0	0	2	5	0
Frank Duffy, ph	.000	1	1	0	0	0	0	0	0	0	1	0
Tito Fuentes, 2b	.313	4	16	4	5	1	0	1	2	1	3	0
Alan Gallagher, 3b	.100	4	10	0	1	0	0	0	0	0	2	0
Steve Hamilton, p	.000	1	0	0	0	0	0	0	0	0	0	0
Jim Ray Hart, 3b-1	.000	3	5	0	0	0	0	0	0	0	2	0
Ken Henderson, of	.313	4	16	3	5	1	0	0	2	2	1	1
Jerry Johnson, p	.000	1	0	0	0	0	0	0	0	0	0	0
Dave Kingman, of-2	.111	4	9	0	1	0	0	0	0	1	3	0
Hal Lanier, 3b	.000	1	1	0	0	0	0	0	0	0	0	0
Juan Marichal, p	.000	1	3	0	0	0	0	0	0	0	1	0
Willie Mays, of	.267	4	15	2	4	2	0	1	3	3	3	1
Willie McCovey, 1b	.429	4	14	2	6	0	0	2	6	4	2	0
Don McMahon, p	.000	2	0	0	0	0	0	0	0	0	0	0
Gaylord Perry, p	.250	2	4	0	1	0	0	0	0	0	0	0
Jimmy Rosario, pr	.000	1	0	0	0	0	0	0	0	0	0	0
Chris Speier, ss	.357	4	14	4	5	1	0	1	1	1	1	0
TOTAL	.235		132	15	31	5	0	5	14	16	28	2

PITCHER	W	L	ERA	G	GS	CG	SV	SHO	IP	H	ER	BB	SO
Jim Barr	0	0	9.00	1	0	0	0	0	1.0	3	1	0	2
Ron Bryant	0	0	4.50	1	0	0	0	0	2.0	1	1	1	2
Don Carrithers	0	0	∞	1	0	0	0	0	0.0	3	3	0	0
John Cumberland	0	1	9.00	1	1	0	0	0	3.0	7	3	0	4
Steve Hamilton	0	0	9.00	1	0	0	0	0	1.0	1	1	0	3
Jerry Johnson	0	0	13.50	1	0	0	0	0	1.1	1	2	1	2
Juan Marichal	0	1	2.25	1	1	1	0	0	8.0	4	2	0	6
Don McMahon	0	0	0.00	2	0	0	0	0	3.0	0	0	0	3
Gaylord Perry	1	1	6.14	2	2	1	0	0	14.2	19	10	3	11
TOTAL	1	3	6.09	11	4	2	0	0	34.0	39	23	5	33

GAME 1 AT SF OCT 2

```
PIT   002 000 200    4 9 0
SF    001 040 00X    5 7 2
```
Pitchers: BLASS, Moose (6), Giusti (8) vs PERRY
Home Runs: Fuentes-SF, McCovey-SF
Attendance: 40,977

GAME 2 AT SF OCT 3

```
PIT   010 210 401    9 15 0
SF    110 000 002    4 9 0
```
Pitchers: ELLIS, Miller (6), Giusti (9) vs CUMBERLAND, Barr (4), McMahon (5), Carrithers (7), Bryant (7), Hamilton (9)
Home Runs: Robertson-PIT (3), Clines-PIT, Mays-SF
Attendance: 42,562

GAME 3 AT PIT OCT 5

```
SF    000 001 000    1 5 2
PIT   010 000 01X    2 4 1
```
Pitchers: MARICHAL vs JOHNSON, Giusti (9)
Home Runs: Robertson-PIT, Hebner-PIT Attendance: 38,322

GAME 4 AT PIT OCT 6

```
SF    140 000 000    5 10 0
PIT   230 004 00X    9 11 2
```
Pitchers: PERRY, Johnson (6), McMahon (8) vs Blass, KISON (3), Giusti (7)
Home Runs: Speier-SF, McCovey-SF, Hebner-PIT, Oliver-PIT
Attendance: 35,487

BALTIMORE ORIOLES (EAST) 3, OAKLAND A'S (WEST) 0

Baltimore, dividing its 15 runs evenly among the three games, swept the ALCS for the third year in a row.

Oakland's Vida Blue took a 3–1 lead into the seventh inning of Game 1, but with two away and men on first and third, a single and two doubles pushed across four runs to beat him, 5–3. Orioles starter Dave McNally and reliever Eddie Watt held the A's scoreless from the fifth inning on. In the second game Oakland managed only one run off Mike Cuellar, while the Orioles hammered Catfish Hunter for five runs on four homers—two of them by Boog Powell, including one in the eighth with a man aboard.

Reggie Jackson retaliated for the A's in Game 3 with two home runs off Jim Palmer, and Sal Bando added a third. But Palmer permitted no other A's to score, and—supported by a Baltimore run in the first and two each in the fifth and seventh—preserved the lead throughout the game. For the third year in a row Palmer clinched the pennant for Baltimore with a complete-game victory.

BAL (E)

PLAYER/POS	AVG	G	AB	R	H	2B	3B	HR	RB	BB	SO	SB
Mark Belanger, ss	.250	3	8	1	2	0	0	0	1	3	2	0
Paul Blair, of	.333	3	9	1	3	1	0	0	2	0	3	0
Don Buford, of	.429	2	7	1	3	0	1	0	0	2	1	0
Mike Cuellar, p	.333	1	3	0	1	0	0	0	0	0	2	0
Andy Etchebarren, c	.000	2	5	0	0	0	0	0	0	0	0	0
Elrod Hendricks, c	.500	2	4	1	2	0	0	1	2	1	1	0
Davey Johnson, 2b	.300	3	10	2	3	2	0	0	0	3	1	0
Dave McNally, p	.000	1	2	0	0	0	0	0	0	0	0	0
Curt Motton, ph	1.000	1	1	0	1	0	0	0	1	0	0	0
Jim Palmer, p-1	.200	2	5	1	1	0	0	0	0	0	1	0
Boog Powell, 1b	.300	3	10	4	3	0	0	2	3	3	3	0
Merv Rettenmund, of	.250	3	8	0	2	1	0	0	1	0	3	0
Brooks Robinson, 3b	.364	3	11	2	4	1	0	1	3	0	1	0
Frank Robinson, of	.083	3	12	2	1	1	0	0	1	1	4	0
Eddie Watt, p	.000	1	0	0	0	0	0	0	0	0	0	0
TOTAL	.274		95	15	26	7	1	4	14	13	22	0

PITCHER	W	L	ERA	G	GS	CG	SV	SHO	IP	H	ER	BB	SO
Mike Cuellar	1	0	1.00	1	1	1	0	0	9.0	6	1	1	2
Dave McNally	1	0	3.86	1	1	0	0	0	7.0	7	3	1	5
Jim Palmer	1	0	3.00	1	1	1	0	0	9.0	7	3	3	8
Eddie Watt	0	0	0.00	1	0	0	1	0	2.0	2	0	0	1
TOTAL	3	0	2.33	4	3	2	1	0	27.0	22	7	5	16

OAK (W)

PLAYER/POS	AVG	G	AB	R	H	2B	3B	HR	RB	BB	SO	SB
Sal Bando, 3b	.364	3	11	3	4	2	0	1	1	1	0	0
Curt Blefary, ph	.000	1	1	0	0	0	0	0	0	0	1	0
Vida Blue, p	.000	1	3	0	0	0	0	0	0	0	3	0
Bert Campaneris, ss	.167	3	12	0	2	1	0	0	0	0	1	0
Tommy Davis, 1b-2	.375	3	8	1	3	1	0	0	0	0	0	0
Dave Duncan, c	.500	2	6	0	3	1	0	0	2	0	0	0
Mike Epstein, 1b-1	.200	2	5	0	1	0	0	0	0	0	3	0
Rollie Fingers, p	.000	2	0	0	0	0	0	0	0	0	0	0
Mudcat Grant, p	.000	1	0	0	0	0	0	0	0	0	0	0
Dick Green, 2b	.286	3	7	0	2	0	0	0	0	1	1	0
Mike Hegan, ph	.000	1	1	0	0	0	0	0	0	0	1	0
Catfish Hunter, p	.000	1	3	0	0	0	0	0	0	0	1	0
Reggie Jackson, of	.333	3	12	2	4	1	0	2	2	0	1	0
Darold Knowles, p	.000	1	0	0	0	0	0	0	0	0	0	0
Bob Locker, p	.000	1	0	0	0	0	0	0	0	0	0	0
Angel Mangual, of	.167	3	12	1	2	1	1	0	2	0	1	0
Rick Monday, of	.000	1	3	0	0	0	0	0	0	1	2	0
Joe Rudi, of	.143	2	7	0	1	1	0	0	0	1	0	0
Diego Segui, p	.000	1	2	0	0	0	0	0	0	0	0	0
Gene Tenace, c	.000	1	3	0	0	0	0	0	0	1	1	0
TOTAL	.229		96	7	22	8	1	3	7	5	16	0

PITCHER	W	L	ERA	G	GS	CG	SV	SHO	IP	H	ER	BB	SO
Vida Blue	0	1	6.43	1	1	0	0	0	7.0	7	5	2	8
Rollie Fingers	0	0	7.71	2	0	0	0	0	2.1	2	2	1	2
Mudcat Grant	0	0	0.00	1	0	0	0	0	2.0	3	0	0	2
Catfish Hunter	0	1	5.63	1	1	1	0	0	8.0	7	5	2	6
Darold Knowles	0	0	0.00	1	0	0	0	0	0.1	1	0	0	0
Bob Locker	0	0	0.00	1	0	0	0	0	0.2	0	0	2	0
Diego Segui	0	1	5.79	1	1	0	0	0	4.2	6	3	6	4
TOTAL	0	3	5.40	8	3	1	0	0	25.0	26	15	13	22

GAME 1 AT BAL OCT 3

OAK 0 2 0 1 0 0 0 0 0   3 9 0
BAL 0 0 0 1 0 0 4 0 X   5 7 1
Pitchers: BLUE, Fingers (8) vs McNALLY, Watt (8)
Attendance: 42,621

GAME 2 AT BAL OCT 4

OAK 0 0 0 1 0 0 0 0 0   1 6 0
BAL 0 1 1 0 0 0 1 2 X   5 7 0
Pitchers: HUNTER vs CUELLAR
Home Runs: B.Robinson-BAL, Powell-BAL (2), Hendricks-BAL
Attendance: 35,003

GAME 3 AT OAK OCT 5

BAL 1 0 0 0 2 0 2 0 0   5 12 0
OAK 0 0 1 0 0 1 0 1 0   3 7 0
Pitchers: PALMER vs SEGUI, Fingers (5), Knowles (7), Locker (7), Grant (8)
Home Runs: Jackson-OAK (2), Bando-OAK
Attendance: 33,176

PITTSBURGH PIRATES (NL) 4, BALTIMORE ORIOLES (AL) 3

In its third successive Series, Baltimore faced its third different opponent and beat the Pirates in the first two games. A walk, a wild pitch, two Baltimore errors, and a single in the second inning of the opener gave Pittsburgh an early 3–0 lead. But Dave McNally shut out the Pirates on two hits the rest of the game as Frank Robinson, Merv Rettenmund, and Don Buford homered to give Baltimore a 5–3 victory. Jim Palmer took the win in Game 2 as Baltimore hammered Pirates pitching for 14 hits and 11 runs before Palmer issued Richie Hebner a three-run homer, Pittsburgh's only scoring, in the eighth.

The Pirates overtook the Orioles when the Series moved to Pittsburgh. Steve Blass pitched a three-hitter in Game 3, and while Frank Robinson's solo homer in the seventh ended Blass' shutout, a three-run shot by Bob Robertson in the last of the inning cemented a 5–1 Pittsburgh win. The next evening (in the first World Series night game ever), Baltimore scored three times in the top of the first inning, but two Pirates runs later in the inning and another run in the third tied the game. It remained tied until Pirates pinch hitter Milt May singled home the game winner with two away in the seventh.

With the Series now even at two wins apiece, Pittsburgh's Nelson Briles stopped the Orioles in Game 5 on a pair of singles. Bob Robertson's leadoff homer in the second proved all the Pirates needed for the win, but Briles himself drove in an insurance run later in the inning and Pittsburgh went on to win, 4–0.

The Pirates tried to win it all in Game 6, scoring single runs against the O's Jim Palmer in the second inning and the third (Roberto Clemente's home run). But Pirates starter Bob Moose was replaced after giving up a solo homer to Don Buford in the sixth, and a tying Baltimore run came home an inning later. A ninth-inning pinch hitter for Palmer produced nothing, but Baltimore won in the last of the 10th, when Frank Robinson scored on Brooks Robinson's sacrifice fly to shallow center.

Steve Blass, who had defeated Mike Cuellar in Game 3, faced him again in the finale and again emerged the victor of a pitching duel. Clemente's two-out homer in the fourth inning provided the game's only run until the eighth, when both teams scored single runs. Blass retired Baltimore in order in the ninth and the Pirates were world champions.

PIT (N)

PLAYER/POS	AVG	G	AB	R	H	2B	3B	HR	RB	BB	SO	SB
Gene Alley, ss	.000	2	2	0	0	0	0	0	0	1	0	0
Steve Blass, p	.000	2	7	0	0	0	0	0	0	0	1	0
Nelson Briles, p	.500	1	2	0	1	0	0	0	1	0	1	0
Dave Cash, 2b	.133	7	30	2	4	1	0	0	1	3	1	1
Roberto Clemente, of	.414	7	29	3	12	2	1	2	4	2	2	0
Gene Clines, of	.091	3	11	2	1	0	1	0	0	1	1	1
Vic Davalillo, of-2	.333	3	3	1	1	0	0	0	0	0	0	0
Dock Ellis, p	.000	1	1	0	0	0	0	0	0	0	1	0
Dave Giusti, p	.000	3	0	0	0	0	0	0	0	0	0	0
Richie Hebner, 3b	.167	3	12	2	2	0	0	1	3	3	3	0
Jackie Hernandez, ss	.222	7	18	2	4	0	0	0	1	2	5	1
Bob Johnson, p	.000	2	3	0	0	0	0	0	0	0	2	0
Bruce Kison, p	.000	2	2	0	0	0	0	0	0	1	2	0
Milt May, ph	.500	2	2	0	1	0	0	0	1	0	0	0
Bill Mazeroski, ph	.000	1	1	0	0	0	0	0	0	0	0	0
Bob Miller, p	.000	3	0	0	0	0	0	0	0	0	0	0
Bob Moose, p	.000	3	2	0	0	0	0	0	0	0	1	0
Al Oliver, of-4	.211	5	19	1	4	2	0	0	2	2	5	0
Jose Pagan, 3b	.267	4	15	0	4	2	0	0	2	0	1	0
Bob Robertson, 1b	.240	7	25	4	6	0	0	2	5	4	8	0
Charlie Sands, ph	.000	1	1	0	0	0	0	0	0	0	1	0
Manny Sanguillen, c	.379	7	29	3	11	1	0	0	0	0	3	2
Willie Stargell, of	.208	7	24	3	5	1	0	0	1	7	9	0
Bob Veale, p	.000	1	0	0	0	0	0	0	0	0	0	0
Luke Walker, p	.000	1	0	0	0	0	0	0	0	0	0	0
TOTAL	.235		238	23	56	9	2	5	21	26	47	5

PITCHER	W	L	ERA	G	GS	CG	SV	SHO	IP	H	ER	BB	SO
Steve Blass	2	0	1.00	2	2	2	0	0	18.0	7	2	4	13
Nelson Briles	1	0	0.00	1	1	1	0	1	9.0	2	0	2	2
Dock Ellis	0	1	15.43	1	1	0	0	0	2.1	4	4	1	1
Dave Giusti	0	0	0.00	3	0	0	1	0	5.1	3	0	2	4
Bob Johnson	0	1	9.00	2	1	0	0	0	5.0	5	5	3	3
Bruce Kison	1	0	0.00	2	0	0	0	0	6.1	1	0	2	3
Bob Miller	0	1	3.86	3	0	0	0	0	4.2	7	2	1	2
Bob Moose	0	0	6.52	3	1	0	0	0	9.2	12	7	2	7
Bob Veale	0	0	13.50	1	0	0	0	0	0.2	1	1	2	0
Luke Walker	0	0	40.50	1	1	0	0	0	0.2	3	3	1	0
TOTAL	4	3	3.50	19	7	3	1	1	61.2	45	24	20	35

BAL (A)

PLAYER/POS	AVG	G	AB	R	H	2B	3B	HR	RB	BB	SO	SB
Mark Belanger, ss	.238	7	21	4	5	0	1	0	0	5	2	1
Paul Blair, of-3	.333	4	9	2	3	1	0	0	0	0	1	0
Don Buford, of	.261	6	23	3	6	1	0	2	4	3	3	0
Mike Cuellar, p	.000	2	3	0	0	0	0	0	0	0	1	0
Pat Dobson, p	.000	3	2	0	0	0	0	0	0	0	2	0
Tom Dukes, p	.000	2	0	0	0	0	0	0	0	0	0	0
Andy Etchebarren, c	.000	1	2	0	0	0	0	0	0	0	0	0
Dick Hall, p	.000	1	0	0	0	0	0	0	0	0	0	0
Elrod Hendricks, c	.263	6	19	3	5	1	0	0	1	3	3	0
Grant Jackson, p	.000	1	0	0	0	0	0	0	0	0	0	0
Davy Johnson, 2b	.148	7	27	1	4	0	0	0	3	0	1	0
Dave Leonhard, p	.000	1	0	0	0	0	0	0	0	0	0	0
Dave McNally, p	.000	4	4	0	0	0	0	0	0	0	3	0
Jim Palmer, p	.000	2	4	0	0	0	0	0	0	2	2	0
Boog Powell, 1b	.111	7	27	1	3	0	0	1	1	1	3	0
Merv Rettenmund, of-6	.185	7	27	3	5	0	0	1	4	0	4	0
Pete Richert, p	.000	1	0	0	0	0	0	0	0	0	0	0
Brooks Robinson, 3b	.318	7	22	2	7	0	0	0	5	3	1	0
Frank Robinson, of	.280	7	25	5	7	0	0	2	2	2	8	0
Tom Shopay, ph	.000	5	4	0	0	0	0	0	0	0	0	0
Eddie Watt, p	.000	2	0	0	0	0	0	0	0	0	0	0
TOTAL	.205		219	24	45	3	1	5	22	20	35	1

PITCHER	W	L	ERA	G	GS	CG	SV	SHO	IP	H	ER	BB	SO
Mike Cuellar	0	2	3.86	2	2	0	0	0	14.0	11	6	6	10
Pat Dobson	0	0	4.05	3	1	0	0	0	6.2	13	3	4	6
Tom Dukes	0	0	0.00	2	0	0	0	0	4.0	2	0	0	1
Dick Hall	0	0	0.00	1	0	0	1	0	1.0	1	0	0	0
Grant Jackson	0	0	0.00	1	0	0	0	0	0.2	0	0	1	0
Dave Leonhard	0	0	0.00	1	0	0	0	0	1.0	0	0	1	0
Dave McNally	2	1	1.98	4	2	1	0	0	13.2	10	3	5	12
Jim Palmer	1	0	2.65	2	2	0	0	0	17.0	15	5	9	15
Pete Richert	0	0	0.00	1	0	0	0	0	0.2	0	0	0	1
Eddie Watt	0	1	3.86	2	0	0	0	0	2.1	4	1	0	2
TOTAL	3	4	2.66	19	7	1	1	1	56.0	18	26	47	

GAME 1 AT BAL OCT 9

PIT 030 000 000   3 3 0
BAL 013 010 00X   5 10 3
Pitchers: ELLIS, Moose (3), Miller (7) vs McNALLY
Home Runs: F.Robinson-BAL, Rettenmund-BAL, Buford-BAL
Attendance: 53,229

GAME 2 AT BAL OCT 11

PIT 000 000 030   3 8 1
BAL 010 361 00X   11 14 1
Pitchers: R.JOHNSON, Kison (4), Moose (4), Veale (5), Miller (6), Giusti (8) vs PALMER, Hall (9)
Home Runs: Hebner-PIT
Attendance: 53,239

GAME 3 AT PIT OCT 12

BAL 000 000 100   1 3 3
PIT 100 001 30X   5 7 0
Pitchers: CUELLAR, Dukes (7), Watt (8) vs BLASS
Home Runs: F.Robinson-BAL, Robertson-PIT
Attendance: 50,403

GAME 4 AT PIT OCT 13

BAL 300 000 000   3 4 1
PIT 201 000 10X   4 14 0
Pitchers: Dobson, Jackson (6), WATT (7), Richert (8) vs Walker, KISON (1), Giusti (8)
Attendance: 51,378

GAME 5 AT PIT OCT 14

BAL 000 000 000   0 2 1
PIT 021 010 00X   4 9 0
Pitchers: McNALLY, Leonhard (5), Dukes (6) vs BRILES
Home Runs: Robertson-PIT
Attendance: 51,377

GAME 6 AT BAL OCT 16

PIT 011 000 000 0   2 9 1
BAL 000 001 100 1   3 8 0
Pitchers: Moose, R.Johnson (6), Giusti (7), MILLER (10) vs Palmer, Dobson (10), McNALLY (10)
Home Runs: Clemente-PIT, Buford-BAL
Attendance: 44,174

GAME 7 AT BAL OCT 17

PIT 000 100 010   2 6 1
BAL 000 000 010   1 4 0
Pitchers: BLASS vs CUELLAR, Dobson (9), McNally (9)
Home Runs: Clemente-PIT
Attendance: 47,291

CINCINNATI REDS (WEST) 3, PITTSBURGH PIRATES (EAST) 2

Pittsburgh traded wins with Cincinnati through the first four games—winning the first and third—and took a lead into the ninth inning of the fifth game before a home run and a wild pitch undid them.

Cincinnati got eight hits in each of the first two games. In the first game, though, only Joe Morgan's first-inning homer produced a run, and the Reds lost, 5–1. But the next day, five first-inning hits gave the Reds four runs and a lead the Pirates could not overcome.

Pirates catcher Manny Sanguillen brought Pittsburgh back in Game 3 with a home run in the fifth and the game-winning RBI in the eighth. But Reds pitcher Ross Grimsley evened the series for Cincinnati the next day with a two-hitter, in the series' only complete-game performance.

Game 5 was Pittsburgh's for 8-1/2 innings. The Pirates scored first, and held the lead into the bottom of the ninth. But Johnny Bench opened the Reds' half of the ninth with a game-tying home run, and Tony Perez and Denis Menke followed him with singles. Bob Moose came in and retired the next two men, though George Foster (running for Perez) took third on a fly to right. Moose then threw away the pennant with a run-scoring, series-ending wild pitch.

CIN (W)

PLAYER/POS	AVG	G	AB	R	H	2B	3B	HR	RB	BB	SO	SB
Johnny Bench, c	.333	5	18	3	6	1	1	1	2	1	3	2
Jack Billingham, p	.000	1	2	0	0	0	0	0	0	0	1	0
Pedro Borbon, p	.000	3	0	0	0	0	0	0	0	0	0	0
Clay Carroll, p	.000	2	0	0	0	0	0	0	0	0	0	0
Darrel Chaney, ss	.188	5	16	3	3	0	0	0	1	1	1	1
Dave Concepcion, ss-1	.000	3	2	0	0	0	0	0	0	0	0	0
George Foster, pr	.000	1	0	1	0	0	0	0	0	0	0	0
Cesar Geronimo, of	.100	5	20	2	2	0	0	1	1	1	2	0
Ross Grimsley, p	.500	1	4	0	2	1	0	0	1	0	1	0
Don Gullett, p	.500	2	2	0	1	0	0	0	0	0	0	0
Joe Hague, ph	.000	3	1	0	0	0	0	0	0	2	1	0
Tom Hall, p	.000	2	1	0	0	0	0	0	0	0	0	0
Jim McGlothlin, p	.000	1	0	0	0	0	0	0	0	0	0	0
Hal McRae, ph	.000	1	0	0	0	0	0	0	0	0	0	0
Denis Menke, 3b	.250	5	16	1	4	1	0	0	0	4	3	0
Joe Morgan, 2b	.263	5	19	5	5	0	0	2	3	1	2	1
Gary Nolan, p	.000	1	2	0	0	0	0	0	0	0	1	0
Tony Perez, 1b	.200	5	20	2	4	1	0	0	2	0	7	0
Pete Rose, of	.450	5	20	1	9	4	0	0	2	1	2	0
Bobby Tolan, of	.238	5	21	3	5	1	1	0	4	0	4	0
Ted Uhlaender, ph	.500	2	2	0	1	0	0	0	0	0	0	0
TOTAL	.253		166	19	42	9	2	4	16	10	28	4

PITCHER	W	L	ERA	G	GS	CG	SV	SHO	IP	H	ER	BB	SO
Jack Billingham	0	0	3.86	1	1	0	0	0	4.2	5	2	2	4
Pedro Borbon	0	0	2.08	3	0	0	0	0	4.1	2	1	0	1
Clay Carroll	1	1	3.38	2	0	0	0	0	2.2	2	1	3	0
Ross Grimsley	1	0	1.00	1	1	1	0	0	9.0	2	1	0	5
Don Gullett	0	1	8.00	2	2	0	0	0	9.0	12	8	0	5
Tom Hall	1	0	1.23	2	0	0	0	0	7.1	3	1	3	8
Jim McGlothlin	0	0	0.00	1	0	0	0	0	1.0	0	0	0	0
Gary Nolan	0	0	1.50	1	1	0	0	0	6.0	4	1	1	4
TOTAL	3	2	3.07	13	5	1	0	0	44.0	30	15	9	27

PIT (E)

PLAYER/POS	AVG	G	AB	R	H	2B	3B	HR	RB	BB	SO	SB
Gene Alley, ss	.000	5	16	1	0	0	0	0	0	0	3	0
Steve Blass, p	.000	2	6	0	0	0	0	0	0	0	3	0
Nelson Briles, p	.000	1	2	0	0	0	0	0	0	0	1	0
Dave Cash, 2b	.211	5	19	0	4	0	0	0	3	0	0	0
Roberto Clemente, of	.235	5	17	1	4	1	0	1	2	3	5	0
Gene Clines, ph	.000	3	2	1	0	0	0	0	0	0	1	0
Vic Davalillo, ph	.000	1	0	0	0	0	0	0	0	1	0	0
Dock Ellis, p-1	.000	2	0	0	0	0	0	0	0	0	0	0
Dave Giusti, p	.000	3	1	0	0	0	0	0	0	0	0	0
Richie Hebner, 3b	.188	5	16	2	3	1	0	0	1	1	3	0
Ramon Hernandez, p	.000	3	0	0	0	0	0	0	0	0	1	0
Bob Johnson, p	.000	2	1	0	0	0	0	0	0	0	1	0
Bruce Kison, p	.000	2	0	0	0	0	0	0	0	0	0	0
Milt May, c	.500	1	2	0	1	0	0	0	1	0	0	0
Bill Mazeroski, ph	.500	2	2	0	1	0	0	0	0	0	1	0
Bob Miller, p	.000	1	0	0	0	0	0	0	0	0	0	0
Bob Moose, p	.000	2	0	0	0	0	0	0	0	0	0	0
Al Oliver, of	.250	5	20	3	5	2	1	1	3	0	4	0
Bob Robertson, 1b	.000	4	0	0	0	0	0	0	0	1	0	0
Manny Sanguillen, c	.313	5	16	4	5	1	0	1	2	0	0	0
Willie Stargell, 1b-5, of-1	.063	5	16	1	1	1	0	0	0	2	5	0
Rennie Stennett, of-5,2b-1	.286	5	21	2	6	0	0	0	1	1	0	0
Luke Walker, p	.000	1	0	0	0	0	0	0	0	0	0	0
TOTAL	.190		158	15	30	6	1	3	14	9	27	0

PITCHER	W	L	ERA	G	GS	CG	SV	SHO	IP	H	ER	BB	SO
Steve Blass	1	0	1.72	2	2	0	0	0	15.2	12	3	6	5
Nelson Briles	0	0	3.00	1	1	0	0	0	6.0	6	2	1	3
Dock Ellis	0	1	0.00	1	1	0	0	0	5.0	5	0	1	3
Dave Giusti	0	1	6.75	3	0	0	1	0	2.2	5	2	0	3
Ramon Hernandez	0	0	2.70	3	0	0	1	0	3.1	1	1	0	3
Bob Johnson	0	0	3.00	2	0	0	0	0	6.0	4	2	2	7
Bruce Kison	1	0	0.00	2	0	0	0	0	2.1	1	0	0	3
Bob Miller	0	0	0.00	1	0	0	0	0	1.0	0	0	0	1
Bob Moose	0	1	54.00	2	1	0	0	0	0.2	5	4	0	0
Luke Walker	0	0	18.00	1	0	0	0	0	1.0	3	2	0	0
TOTAL	2	3	3.30	18	5	0	2	0	43.2	42	16	10	28

GAME 1 AT PIT OCT 7

CIN 1 0 0 0 0 0 0 0 0   1 8 0
PIT 3 0 0 0 2 0 0 0 X   5 6 0
Pitchers: GULLETT, Borbon (7) vs BLASS, R.Hernandez (9)
Home Runs: Morgan-CIN, Oliver-PIT
Attendance: 50,476

GAME 2 AT PIT OCT 8

CIN 4 0 0 0 0 0 0 1 0   5 8 1
PIT 0 0 0 1 1 1 0 0 0   3 7 1
Pitchers: Billingham, HALL (5) vs MOOSE, Kison (6), R.Hernandez (7), Giusti (9)
Home Runs: Morgan-CIN
Attendance: 50,584

GAME 3 AT CIN OCT 9

PIT 0 0 0 0 1 1 0   3 7 0
CIN 0 0 2 0 0 0 0 0 0   2 8 1
Pitchers: Briles, KISON (7), Giusti (8) vs Nolan, Borbon (7), CARROLL (7), McGlothlin (9)
Home Runs: Sanguillen-PIT
Attendance: 52,420

GAME 4 AT CIN OCT 10

PIT 0 0 0 0 0 0 1 0 0   1 2 3
CIN 1 0 0 2 0 2 2 0 X   7 11 1
Pitchers: ELLIS, Johnson (6), Walker (7), Miller (8) vs GRIMSLEY
Home Runs: Clemente-PIT
Attendance: 39,447

GAME 5 AT CIN OCT 11

PIT 0 2 0 1 0 0 0 0 0   3 8 0
CIN 0 0 1 0 1 0 0 0 2   4 7 1
Pitchers: Blass, R.Hernandez (8), GIUSTI (9), Moose (9) vs Gullett, Borbon (4), Hall (6), CARROLL (9)
Home Runs: Geronimo-CIN, Bench-CIN
Attendance: 41,887

OAKLAND A'S (WEST) 3, DETROIT TIGERS (EAST) 2

Oakland turned back the Tigers in the first two games, but Detroit evened the series before succumbing in the fifth game.

In Game 1 Al Kaline homered off Rollie Fingers in the 11th to give Detroit starter Mickey Lolich a 2–1 lead. But in the last of the inning, pinch hitter Gonzalo Marquez singled off Tigers reliever Chuck Seelbach with two on to drive in the tying run, and Gene Tenace scored to win it on the same play as right fielder Kaline threw the ball away. Blue Moon Odom increased the A's series lead with a three-hit shutout in Game 2, but Detroit's Joe Coleman retaliated with 14 strikeouts and a shutout of his own to save the Tigers from elimination in Game 3.

In Game 4 the A's pulled out of a 1–1 tie with two runs in the top of the 10th. But Detroit in its half of the inning went through three Oakland relievers for three runs and the win. In the finale, after Odom, the A's starter, had given Detroit a run and a brief lead in the first, he and Vida Blue divided eight shutout innings between them as the A's scored twice to capture their first pennant since Connie Mack won his last in Philadelphia 41 years earlier.

OAK (W)

PLAYER/POS	AVG	G	AB	R	H	2B	3B	HR	RB	BB	SO	SB
Matty Alou, of	.381	5	21	2	8	4	0	0	2	0	2	1
Sal Bando, 3b	.200	5	20	0	4	0	0	0	0	0	3	0
Vida Blue, p	.000	4	1	0	0	0	0	0	0	0	0	0
Bert Campaneris, ss	.429	2	7	3	3	0	0	0	0	1	0	2
Tim Cullen, ss	.000	2	1	0	0	0	0	0	0	0	0	0
Dave Duncan, c	.000	2	2	0	0	0	0	0	0	1	1	0
Mike Epstein, 1b	.188	5	16	1	3	0	0	1	1	4	5	1
Rollie Fingers, p	.000	3	1	0	0	0	0	0	0	0	0	0
Dick Green, 2b	.125	5	8	0	1	1	0	0	0	0	0	0
Dave Hamilton, p	.000	1	0	0	0	0	0	0	0	0	0	0
Mike Hegan, 1b-1	.000	3	1	1	0	0	0	0	0	0	0	0
George Hendrick, of-1	.143	5	7	2	1	0	0	0	0	0	1	0
Ken Holtzman, p	.000	1	1	0	0	0	0	0	0	0	1	0
Joe Horlen, p	.000	1	0	0	0	0	0	0	0	0	0	0
Catfish Hunter, p	.167	2	6	0	1	0	0	0	0	0	2	0
Reggie Jackson, of	.278	5	18	1	5	1	0	0	2	1	6	2
Ted Kubiak, 2b-3, ss-1	.500	4	4	0	2	0	0	0	1	0	0	0
Bob Locker, p	.000	2	0	0	0	0	0	0	0	0	0	0
Angel Mangual, ph	.000	3	3	0	0	0	0	0	0	0	1	0
Gonzalo Marquez, ph	.667	3	3	1	2	0	0	0	1	0	0	0
Dal Maxvill, ss-4,2b-1	.125	5	8	0	1	0	0	0	0	1	2	1
Don Mincher, ph	.000	1	1	0	0	0	0	0	0	0	1	0
Blue Moon Odom, p-2	.250	3	4	0	1	1	0	0	0	0	1	0
Joe Rudi, of	.250	5	20	1	5	1	0	0	2	1	4	0
Gene Tenace, c-5,2b-2	.059	5	17	1	1	0	0	0	1	3	5	0
TOTAL	.224		170	13	38	8	0	1	10	12	35	7

PITCHER	W	L	ERA	G	GS	CG	SV	SHO	IP	H	ER	BB	SO
Vida Blue	0	0	0.00	4	0	0	1	0	5.1	4	0	1	5
Rollie Fingers	1	0	1.69	3	0	0	0	0	5.1	4	1	1	3
Dave Hamilton	0	0	∞	1	0	0	0	0	0.0	1	0	1	0
Ken Holtzman	0	1	4.50	1	1	0	0	0	4.0	4	2	2	2
Joe Horlen	0	1	∞	1	0	0	0	0	0.0	1	1	0	0
Catfish Hunter	0	0	1.17	2	2	0	0	0	15.1	10	2	5	9
Bob Locker	0	0	13.50	2	0	0	0	0	2.0	4	3	0	1
Blue Moon Odom	2	0	0.00	2	2	1	0	1	14.0	5	0	2	5
TOTAL	3	2	1.76	16	5	1	1	1	46.0	32	9	13	25

DET (E)

PLAYER/POS	AVG	G	AB	R	H	2B	3B	HR	RB	BB	SO	SB
Ed Brinkman, ss	.250	1	4	0	1	1	0	0	0	0	0	0
Ike Brown, 1b	.500	1	2	0	1	0	0	0	2	0	1	0
Gates Brown, ph	.000	3	2	1	0	0	0	0	0	1	0	0
Norm Cash, 1b	.267	5	15	1	4	0	0	1	2	2	3	0
Joe Coleman, p	.500	1	2	0	1	0	0	0	0	0	1	0
Bill Freehan, c	.250	3	12	2	3	1	0	1	3	0	1	0
Woody Fryman, p	.000	2	3	0	0	0	0	0	0	0	0	0
Tom Haller, ph	.000	1	1	0	0	0	0	0	0	0	0	0
John Hiller, p	.000	3	0	0	0	0	0	0	0	0	0	0
Willie Horton, of-3	.100	5	10	0	1	0	0	0	0	1	3	0
Al Kaline, of	.263	5	19	3	5	0	0	1	1	2	2	0
John Knox, pr	.000	1	0	0	0	0	0	0	0	0	0	0
Lerrin LaGrow, p	.000	1	0	0	0	0	0	0	0	0	0	0
Mickey Lolich, p	.000	2	7	0	0	0	0	0	0	0	2	0
Dick McAuliffe, ss-4,2b-1	.200	5	20	3	4	0	0	1	1	1	4	0
Joe Niekro, pr	.000	1	0	0	0	0	0	0	0	0	0	0
Jim Northrup, of	.357	5	14	0	5	0	0	0	1	2	3	0
Aurelio Rodriguez, 3b	.000	5	16	0	0	0	0	0	0	2	2	0
Fred Scherman, p	.000	1	0	0	0	0	0	0	0	0	0	0
Chuck Seelbach, p	.000	2	0	0	0	0	0	0	0	0	0	0
Duke Sims, c-2, of-2	.214	4	14	0	3	2	1	0	0	1	2	0
Mickey Stanley, of-3	.333	4	6	0	2	0	0	0	0	0	0	0
Tony Taylor, 2b	.133	4	15	0	2	2	0	0	0	0	2	0
Chris Zachary, p	.000	1	0	0	0	0	0	0	0	0	0	0
TOTAL	.198		162	10	32	6	1	4	10	13	25	0

PITCHER	W	L	ERA	G	GS	CG	SV	SHO	IP	H	ER	BB	SO
Joe Coleman	1	0	0.00	1	1	1	0	1	9.0	7	0	3	14
Woody Fryman	0	2	3.65	2	2	0	0	0	12.1	11	5	2	8
John Hiller	1	0	0.00	3	0	0	0	0	3.1	1	0	1	1
Lerrin La Grow	0	0	0.00	1	0	0	0	0	1.0	0	0	0	1
Mickey Lolich	0	1	1.42	2	2	0	0	0	19.0	14	3	5	10
Fred Scherman	0	0	0.00	1	0	0	0	0	0.2	1	0	0	1
Chuck Seelbach	0	0	18.00	2	0	0	0	0	1.0	4	2	0	0
Chris Zachary	0	0	∞	1	0	0	0	0	0.0	0	1	1	0
TOTAL	2	3	2.14	13	5	1	0	1	46.1	38	11	12	35

GAME 1 AT OAK OCT 7

DET 0 1 0 0 0 0 0 0 0 1   2 6 2
OAK 0 0 1 0 0 0 0 0 2   3 10 1
Pitchers: LOLICH, Seelbach (11) vs Hunter, Blue (9), FINGERS (9)
Home Runs: Cash-DET, Kaline-DET
Attendance: 29,536

GAME 2 AT OAK OCT 8

DET 0 0 0 0 0 0 0 0 0   0 3 1
OAK 1 0 0 0 4 0 0 0 X   5 8 0
Pitchers: FRYMAN, Zachary (5), Scherman (5), LaGrow (6), Hiller (7) vs ODOM
Attendance: 31,088

GAME 3 AT DET OCT 10

OAK 0 0 0 0 0 0 0 0 0   0 7 0
DET 0 0 0 2 0 0 0 1 X   3 8 1
Pitchers: HOLTZMAN, Fingers (5), Blue (6), Locker (7) vs COLEMAN
Home Runs: Freehan-DET
Attendance: 41,156

GAME 4 AT DET OCT 11

OAK 0 0 0 0 0 0 1 0 0 2   3 9 2
DET 0 0 1 0 0 0 0 0 3   4 10 1
Pitchers: Hunter, Fingers (8), Blue (9), Locker (10), HORLEN (10), Hamilton (10) vs Lolich, Seelbach (10), HILLER (10)
Home Runs: McAuliffe-DET, Epstein-OAK
Attendance: 37,615

GAME 5 AT DET OCT 12

OAK 0 1 0 1 0 0 0 0 0   2 4 0
DET 1 0 0 0 0 0 0 0 0   1 5 2
Pitchers: ODOM, Blue (6) vs FRYMAN, Hiller (9)
Attendance: 50,276

OAKLAND A'S (AL) 4, CINCINNATI REDS (NL) 3

Oakland slugger Reggie Jackson missed the Series with a pulled hamstring, but Gene Tenace (the A's backup catcher during the season) took up the slack, hitting four of the club's five homers and driving in nine of their 16 runs.

Six of the seven games were decided by a single run. Oakland won the first two in Cincinnati, 3–2, and 2–1. Tenace made the difference in the opener, driving in all the A's runs with a two-run homer in the second inning and a solo shot in the fifth. In the second game, A's starting pitcher Catfish Hunter singled in a run in the second inning which proved the margin of his victory. His 8-2/3-inning performance was the longest mound outing in a Series which saw the two clubs together use nearly seven pitchers per game.

Cincinnati took the first game in Oakland, 1–0. Blue Moon Odom held the Reds to one hit through six innings before giving up the game's only run on two singles and a sacrifice in the seventh. Cincinnati's Jack Billingham, too, yielded only three hits in eight-plus innings before yielding to ace reliever Clay Carroll, who retired the side in the ninth.

Game 4 went to Oakland, 3–2. Tenace opened the scoring with a solo homer in the fifth. The Reds' Bobby Tolan doubled in a pair in the eighth to put Cincinnati ahead, but in the last of the ninth four successive A's singles scored two runs, with Tenace scoring the game winner on pinch hitter Angel Mangual's hit. Tenace homered again in Game 5 for three runs, but it wasn't enough as the Reds tied the score in the eighth and won on Pete Rose's RBI single in the ninth.

The Reds produced the Series' only blowout with five runs in the seventh inning of Game 6 to make the score, 8–1. The finale saw Tenace drive in a run in the top of the first for a narrow Oakland lead which held until the Reds tied the game in the fifth. In the sixth the A's scored twice—Tenace doubling in the go-ahead run. Cincinnati scored once more in the eighth as a runner inherited by A's reliever Rollie Fingers came home on a sacrifice fly. But Fingers permitted no other runs to score, and the A's took the crown with their fourth one-run victory.

OAK (A)

PLAYER/POS	AVG	G	AB	R	H	2B	3B	HR	RB	BB	SO	SB
Matty Alou, of	.042	7	24	0	1	0	0	0	0	0	3	1
Sal Bando, 3b	.269	7	26	2	7	1	0	0	1	2	5	0
Vida Blue, p	.000	4	1	0	0	0	0	0	0	0	2	1	0
Bert Campaneris, ss	.179	7	28	1	5	0	0	0	0	1	4	0
Dave Duncan, c-1	.200	3	5	0	1	0	0	0	0	1	3	0
Mike Epstein, 1b	.000	6	16	1	0	0	0	0	0	5	3	0
Rollie Fingers, p	.000	6	1	0	0	0	0	0	0	0	0	0
Dick Green, 2b	.333	7	18	0	6	2	0	0	1	0	4	0
Dave Hamilton, p	.000	2	0	0	0	0	0	0	0	0	0	0
Mike Hegan, 1b-5	.200	6	5	0	1	0	0	0	0	0	2	0
George Hendrick, of	.133	5	15	3	2	0	0	0	0	1	2	0
Ken Holtzman, p	.000	3	5	0	0	0	0	0	0	0	0	0
Joe Horlen, p	.000	1	0	0	0	0	0	0	0	0	0	0
Catfish Hunter, p	.200	3	5	0	1	0	0	0	1	2	1	0
Ted Kubiak, 2b	.333	4	3	0	1	0	0	0	0	0	0	0
Allan Lewis, pr	.000	6	0	2	0	0	0	0	0	0	0	0
Bob Locker, p	.000	1	0	0	0	0	0	0	0	0	0	0
Angel Mangual, of-2	.300	4	10	1	3	0	0	0	1	0	0	0
Gonzalo Marquez, ph	.600	5	5	0	3	0	0	0	1	0	0	0
Don Mincher, ph	1.000	3	1	0	1	0	0	0	1	0	0	0
Blue Moon Odom, p-2	.000	4	4	0	0	0	0	0	0	0	3	0
Joe Rudi, of	.240	7	25	1	6	0	0	1	1	2	5	0
Gene Tenace, c-6,1b-1	.348	7	23	5	8	1	0	4	9	2	4	0
TOTAL	.209		220	16	46	4	0	5	16	21	37	1

PITCHER	W	L	ERA	G	GS	CG	SV	SHO	IP	H	ER	BB	SO
Vida Blue	0	1	4.15	4	1	0	1	0	8.2	8	4	5	5
Rollie Fingers	1	1	1.74	6	0	0	2	0	10.1	4	2	4	11
Dave Hamilton	0	0	27.00	2	0	0	0	0	1.1	3	4	1	1
Ken Holtzman	1	0	2.13	3	2	0	0	0	12.2	11	3	3	4
Joe Horlen	0	0	6.75	1	0	0	0	0	1.1	2	1	2	1
Catfish Hunter	2	0	2.81	3	2	0	0	0	16.0	12	5	6	11
Bob Locker	0	0	0.00	1	0	0	0	0	0.1	1	0	0	0
Blue Moon Odom	0	1	1.59	2	2	0	0	0	11.1	5	2	6	13
TOTAL	4	3	3.05	22	7	0	3	0	62.0	46	21	27	46

CIN (N)

PLAYER/POS	AVG	G	AB	R	H	2B	3B	HR	RB	BB	SO	SB
Johnny Bench, c	.261	7	23	4	6	1	0	1	1	5	5	2
Jack Billingham, p	.000	3	5	0	0	0	0	0	0	0	4	0
Pedro Borbon, p	.000	6	0	0	0	0	0	0	0	0	0	0
Clay Carroll, p	.000	5	0	0	0	0	0	0	0	0	0	0
Darrel Chaney, ss-3	.000	4	7	0	0	0	0	0	0	2	2	0
Dave Concepcion, ss-5	.308	6	13	2	4	0	1	0	2	2	2	1
George Foster, of-1	.000	2	0	0	0	0	0	0	0	0	0	0
Cesar Geronimo, of	.158	7	19	1	3	0	0	0	3	1	4	1
Ross Grimsley, p	.000	4	2	0	0	0	0	0	0	0	2	0
Don Gullett, p	.000	1	2	0	0	0	0	0	0	0	0	0
Joe Hague, of-1	.000	3	3	0	0	0	0	0	0	4	0	0
Tom Hall, p	.000	4	2	0	0	0	0	0	0	0	1	0
Julian Javier, ph	.000	4	2	0	0	0	0	0	0	0	0	0
Jim McGlothlin, p	.000	1	1	0	0	0	0	0	0	0	0	0
Hal McRae, of-2	.444	5	9	1	4	1	0	0	2	0	1	0
Denis Menke, 3b	.083	7	24	1	2	0	0	1	2	2	6	0
Joe Morgan, 2b	.125	7	24	4	3	2	0	0	1	6	3	2
Gary Nolan, p	.000	2	3	0	0	0	0	0	0	0	3	0
Tony Perez, 1b	.435	7	23	3	10	2	0	0	2	4	4	0
Pete Rose, of	.214	7	28	3	6	0	0	1	2	4	4	1
Bobby Tolan, of	.269	7	26	2	7	1	0	0	6	1	4	5
Ted Uhlaender, ph	.250	4	4	0	1	1	0	0	0	0	1	0
TOTAL	.209		220	21	46	8	1	3	21	27	46	12

PITCHER	W	L	ERA	G	GS	CG	SV	SHO	IP	H	ER	BB	SO
Jack Billingham	1	0	0.00	3	2	0	1	0	13.2	6	0	4	11
Pedro Borbon	0	1	3.86	6	0	0	0	0	7.0	7	3	2	4
Clay Carroll	0	1	1.59	5	0	0	1	0	5.2	6	1	4	3
Ross Grimsley	2	1	2.57	4	1	0	0	0	7.0	7	2	3	2
Don Gullett	0	0	1.29	1	1	0	0	0	7.0	5	1	2	4
Tom Hall	0	0	0.00	4	0	0	1	0	8.1	6	0	2	7
Jim McGlothlin	0	0	12.00	1	1	0	0	0	3.0	2	4	2	3
Gary Nolan	0	1	3.38	2	2	0	0	0	10.2	7	4	2	3
TOTAL	3	4	2.17	26	7	0	3	0	62.1	46	15	21	37

GAME 1 AT CIN OCT 14

OAK	020 010 000	3	7	0
CIN	010 100 000	2	4	0

Pitchers: HOLTZMAN, Fingers (6), Blue (7) vs NOLAN, Borbon (7), Carroll (8)
Home Runs: Tenace-OAK (2)
Attendance: 52,918

GAME 2 AT CIN OCT 15

OAK	011 000 000	2	9	2
CIN	000 000 001	1	6	0

Pitchers: HUNTER, Fingers (9) vs GRIMSLEY, Borbon (6), Hall (8)
Home Runs: Rudi-OAK
Attendance: 53,224

GAME 3 AT OAK OCT 18

CIN	000 000 100	1	4	2
OAK	000 000 000	0	3	2

Pitchers: BILLINGHAM, Carroll (9) vs ODOM, Blue (8), Fingers (8)
Attendance: 49,410

GAME 4 AT OAK OCT 19

CIN	000 000 020	2	7	1
OAK	000 010 002	3	10	1

Pitchers: Gullett, Borbon (8), CARROLL (9) vs Holtzman, Blue (8), FINGERS (9)
Home Runs: Tenace-OAK
Attendance: 49,410

GAME 5 AT OAK OCT 20

CIN	100 110 011	5	8	0
OAK	030 100 000	4	7	2

Pitchers: McGlothlin, Borbon (4), Hall (5), Carroll (7), GRIMSLEY (8), Billingham (9) vs Hunter, FINGERS (5), Hamilton (9)
Home Runs: Rose-CIN, Tenace-OAK, Menke-CIN
Attendance: 49,410

GAME 6 AT CIN OCT 21

OAK	000 010 000	1	7	1
CIN	000 111 50X	8	10	0

Pitchers: BLUE, Locker (6), Hamilton (7), Horlen (7) vs Nolan, GRIMSLEY (5), Borbon (6), Hall (7)
Home Runs: Bench-CIN
Attendance: 52,737

GAME 7 AT CIN OCT 22

OAK	100 002 000	3	6	1
CIN	000 010 010	2	4	2

Pitchers: Odom, HUNTER (5), Holtzman (8), Fingers (8) vs Billingham, BORBON (6), Carroll (6), Grimsley (7), Hall (8)
Attendance: 56,040

NEW YORK METS (EAST) 3, CINCINNATI REDS (WEST) 2

The Mets received strong pitching throughout the series, and their offense came through just often enough to defeat Cincinnati in five games.

Though three Reds pitchers held New York to three hits in Game 1, the single Mets run in the second seemed for a time enough for a win. But Tom Seaver gave up a home run to Pete Rose in the eighth and lost the game in the ninth when Johnny Bench homered. Not wanting another last-inning loss in Game 2, the Mets unloaded for four runs in the top of the ninth to add to their one in the fourth. But this time one would have been enough as Jon Matlack blanked the Reds on two hits.

The Mets made it easy for Jerry Koosman in Game 3 in New York, scoring nine times in the first four innings. Things were more difficult for shortstop Bud Harrelson, who exchanged blows with Pete Rose following Rose's hard slide in the fifth inning. A bench-clearing melee ensued, and fans in the left field stands showered Rose with debris until a delegation of Tom Seaver, Willie Mays, and Rusty Staub visited the area to calm nerves and eliminate the threat of a forfeit. In Game 4, though, Mets bats were stifled once again as four Reds pitchers combined for a 12-inning three-hitter. The Reds won the game and tied the series on Rose's sweetly vengeful 12th-inning homer.

In the finale the Mets took a quick two-run lead. Cincinnati tied the game in the top of the fifth, but New York retaliated with four more in the bottom of the inning. Seaver—and Tug McGraw in the ninth—held the Reds scoreless the rest of the way.

NY (E)

PLAYER/POS	AVG	G	AB	R	H	2B	3B	HR	RB	BB	SO	SB
Ken Boswell, ph	.000	1	1	0	0	0	0	0	0	0	0	0
Wayne Garrett, 3b	.087	5	23	1	2	1	0	0	1	0	5	0
Jerry Grote, c	.211	5	19	2	4	0	0	0	2	1	3	0
Don Hahn, of	.235	5	17	2	4	0	0	0	1	2	4	0
Bud Harrelson, ss	.167	5	18	1	3	0	0	0	2	1	1	0
Cleon Jones, of	.300	5	20	3	6	2	0	0	3	2	4	0
Jerry Koosman, p	.500	1	4	1	2	0	0	0	1	0	0	0
Ed Kranepool, of	.500	1	2	0	1	0	0	0	0	2	0	0
Jon Matlack, p	.000	1	2	0	0	0	0	0	0	1	2	0
Willie Mays, of	.333	1	3	1	1	0	0	0	0	1	0	0
Tug McGraw, p	.000	2	1	0	0	0	0	0	0	0	1	0
Felix Millan, 2b	.316	5	19	5	6	0	0	0	2	2	1	0
John Milner, 1b	.176	5	17	2	3	0	0	0	1	5	3	0
Harry Parker, p	.000	1	0	0	0	0	0	0	0	0	0	0
Tom Seaver, p	.333	2	6	1	2	2	0	0	1	1	1	0
Rusty Staub, of	.200	4	15	4	3	0	0	3	5	3	2	0
George Stone, p	.000	1	1	0	0	0	0	0	0	1	1	0
TOTAL	.220		168	23	37	5	0	3	22	19	28	0

PITCHER	W	L	ERA	G	GS	CG	SV	SHO	IP	H	ER	BB	SO
Jerry Koosman	1	0	2.00	1	1	1	0	0	9.0	8	2	0	9
Jon Matlack	1	0	0.00	1	1	1	0	1	9.0	2	0	3	9
Tug McGraw	0	0	0.00	2	0	0	1	0	5.0	4	0	3	3
Harry Parker	0	1	9.00	1	0	0	0	0	1.0	1	1	0	0
Tom Seaver	1	1	1.62	2	2	1	0	0	16.2	13	3	5	17
George Stone	0	0	1.35	1	1	0	0	0	6.2	3	1	2	4
TOTAL	3	2	1.33	8	5	3	1	1	47.1	31	7	13	42

CIN (W)

PLAYER/POS	AVG	G	AB	R	H	2B	3B	HR	RB	BB	SO	SB
Ed Armbrister, of-1	.167	3	6	0	1	0	0	0	0	0	5	0
Johnny Bench, c	.263	5	19	1	5	2	0	1	1	2	3	0
Jack Billingham, p	.000	2	3	0	0	0	0	0	0	0	1	0
Pedro Borbon, p	.000	4	0	0	0	0	0	0	0	0	0	0
Clay Carroll, p	.000	3	0	0	0	0	0	0	0	0	0	0
Darrel Chaney, ph	.000	5	9	0	0	0	0	0	0	3	4	0
Ed Crosby, ss-2	.500	3	2	0	1	0	0	0	0	0	1	0
Dan Driessen, 3b	.167	4	12	0	2	1	0	0	1	0	2	0
Phil Gagliano, ph	.000	3	3	0	0	0	0	0	0	0	1	0
Cesar Geronimo, of	.067	4	15	0	1	0	0	0	0	0	7	0
Ken Griffey, of-2	.143	3	7	0	1	1	0	0	0	0	1	0
Ross Grimsley, p	.000	2	0	0	0	0	0	0	0	0	0	0
Don Gullett, p	.000	3	1	0	0	0	0	0	0	0	0	0
Tom Hall, p	.000	3	0	0	0	0	0	0	0	0	0	0
Hal King, ph	.500	3	2	0	1	0	0	0	0	1	1	0
Andy Kosco, of	.300	3	10	0	3	0	0	0	0	2	3	0
Denis Menke, ss-2,3b-2	.222	3	9	1	2	0	0	1	1	1	2	0
Joe Morgan, 2b	.100	5	20	1	2	1	0	0	1	2	2	0
Roger Nelson, p	.000	1	1	0	0	0	0	0	0	0	1	0
Fred Norman, p	.000	1	1	0	0	0	0	0	0	0	1	0
Tony Perez, 1b	.091	5	22	1	2	0	0	1	2	0	4	0
Pete Rose, of	.381	5	21	3	8	1	0	2	2	2	2	0
Larry Stahl, ph	.500	4	4	1	2	0	0	0	0	0	1	0
Dave Tomlin, p	.000	1	0	0	0	0	0	0	0	0	0	0
TOTAL	.186		167	8	31	6	0	5	8	13	42	0

PITCHER	W	L	ERA	G	GS	CG	SV	SHO	IP	H	ER	BB	SO
Jack Billingham	0	1	4.50	2	2	0	0	0	12.0	9	6	4	9
Pedro Borbon	1	0	0.00	4	0	0	1	0	4.2	3	0	0	3
Clay Carroll	1	0	1.29	3	0	0	0	0	7.0	5	1	1	2
Ross Grimsley	0	1	12.27	2	1	0	0	0	3.2	7	5	2	3
Don Gullett	0	1	2.00	3	1	0	0	0	9.0	4	2	3	6
Tom Hall	0	0	67.50	3	0	0	0	0	0.2	3	5	4	1
Roger Nelson	0	0	0.00	1	0	0	0	0	2.1	0	0	1	0
Fred Norman	0	0	1.80	1	1	0	0	0	5.0	1	1	3	3
Dave Tomlin	0	0	16.20	1	0	0	0	0	1.2	5	3	1	1
TOTAL	2	3	4.50	20	5	0	1	0	46.0	37	23	19	28

GAME 1 AT CIN OCT 6

```
NY   010 000 000   1 3 0
CIN  000 000 011   2 6 0
```
Pitchers: SEAVER vs Billingham, Hall (9), BORBON (9)
Home Runs: Rose-CIN, Bench-CIN
Attendance: 53,431

GAME 2 AT CIN OCT 7

```
NY   000 100 004   5 7 0
CIN  000 000 000   0 2 0
```
Pitchers: MATLACK vs GULLETT, Carroll (6), Hall (9), Borbon (9)
Home Runs: Staub-NY
Attendance: 54,041

GAME 3 AT NY OCT 8

```
CIN  002 000 000   2 8 1
NY   151 200 00X   9 11 1
```
Pitchers: GRIMSLEY, Hall (2), Tomlin (3), Nelson (4), Borbon (7) vs KOOSMAN
Home Runs: Staub-NY (2), Menke-CIN
Attendance: 53,967

GAME 4 AT NY OCT 9

```
CIN  000000 100 001 2  8 0
NY   001000 000 000 1  3 2
```
Pitchers: Norman, Gullett (6), CARROLL (10), Borbon (12) vs Stone, McGraw (7), PARKER (12)
Home Runs: Perez-CIN, Rose-CIN
Attendance: 50,786

GAME 5 AT NY OCT 10

```
CIN  001 010 000   2 7 1
NY   200 041 00X   7 13 1
```
Pitchers: BILLINGHAM, Gullett (5), Carroll (5), Grimsley (7) vs SEAVER, McGraw (9)
Attendance: 50,323

OAKLAND A'S (WEST) 3, BALTIMORE ORIOLES (EAST) 2

The Orioles finally met their match in an ALCS as Oakland took its second consecutive pennant. Baltimore started strong, chasing A's starter Vida Blue with four runs in the first inning as Jim Palmer—pitching the series opener for a change—blanked the A's on five hits. But Oakland snapped back in Game 2, with five of their six runs coming on homers by Sal Bando (two, for three runs), Joe Rudi, and Bert Campaneris.

Oriole Mike Cuellar and the A's Ken Holtzman cut down opposing batters for 10-1/2 innings in Game 3 before Oakland's Campaneris broke the 1–1 tie in the bottom of the 11th with a leadoff home run. The next day Palmer was driven out in the second inning by three Oakland runs, and the A's added to their lead with another run in the sixth. But Andy Etchebarren led a four-run Orioles comeback in the seventh with a three-run homer, and Bobby Grich's solo shot in the next inning gave the Orioles the margin they needed to win the game and tie the series.

The A's took it all in the finale, though, needing only one of their three runs as Catfish Hunter stopped Baltimore cold on five scattered hits.

OAK (W)

PLAYER/POS	AVG	G	AB	R	H	2B	3B	HR	RB	BB	SO	SB
Jesus Alou, dh-1	.333	4	6	0	2	0	0	0	1	0	1	0
Mike Andrews, 1b-1, dh-1	.000	2	1	0	0	0	0	0	0	0	0	0
Sal Bando, 3b	.167	5	18	2	3	0	0	2	3	3	6	0
Vida Blue, p	.000	2	0	0	0	0	0	0	0	0	0	0
Pat Bourque, dh	.000	2	1	0	0	0	0	0	0	2	1	0
Bert Campaneris, ss	.333	5	21	3	7	1	0	2	3	2	2	3
Billy Conigliaro, of	.000	1	4	0	0	0	0	0	0	0	2	0
Vic Davalillo, 1b-2, of-2	.625	4	8	2	5	1	1	0	1	1	0	0
Rollie Fingers, p	.000	3	0	0	0	0	0	0	0	0	0	0
Ray Fosse, c	.091	5	11	2	1	1	0	0	3	2	2	0
Dick Green, 2b	.077	5	13	0	1	1	0	0	1	0	4	0
Ken Holtzman, p	.000	1	0	0	0	0	0	0	0	0	0	0
Catfish Hunter, p	.000	2	0	0	0	0	0	0	0	0	0	0
Reggie Jackson, of	.143	5	21	0	3	0	0	0	0	0	6	0
Deron Johnson, dh	.100	4	10	0	1	0	0	0	0	2	6	0
Ted Kubiak, 2b	.000	3	2	0	0	0	0	0	0	0	1	0
Allan Lewis, pr	.000	2	0	1	0	0	0	0	0	0	0	0
Angel Mangual, of	.111	3	9	1	1	0	0	0	0	0	3	0
Blue Moon Odom, p	.000	1	0	0	0	0	0	0	0	0	0	0
Horacio Pina, p	.000	1	0	0	0	0	0	0	0	0	0	0
Joe Rudi, of	.222	5	18	1	4	0	0	1	3	3	1	0
Gene Tenace, 1b-5, c-3	.235	5	17	3	4	1	0	0	0	2	4	0
TOTAL	.200		160	15	32	5	1	5	15	17	39	3

PITCHER	W	L	ERA	G	GS	CG	SV	SHO	IP	H	ER	BB	SO
Vida Blue	0	1	10.29	2	2	0	0	0	7.0	8	8	5	3
Rollie Fingers	0	1	1.93	3	0	0	1	0	4.2	4	1	2	4
Ken Holtzman	1	0	0.82	1	1	1	0	0	11.0	3	1	1	7
Catfish Hunter	2	0	1.65	2	2	1	0	1	16.1	12	3	5	6
Blue Moon Odom	0	0	1.80	1	0	0	0	0	5.0	6	1	2	4
Horacio Pina	0	0	0.00	1	0	0	0	0	2.0	3	0	1	1
TOTAL	3	2	2.74	10	5	2	1	1	46.0	36	14	16	25

BAL (E)

PLAYER/POS	AVG	G	AB	R	H	2B	3B	HR	RB	BB	SO	SB
Doyle Alexander, p	.000	1	0	0	0	0	0	0	0	0	0	0
Frank Baker, ss	.000	2	0	0	0	0	0	0	0	0	0	0
Don Baylor, of-3	.273	4	11	3	3	0	0	0	1	3	5	0
Mark Belanger, ss	.125	5	16	0	2	0	0	0	1	1	1	0
Paul Blair, of	.167	5	18	2	3	0	0	0	0	1	5	0
Larry Brown, 3b	.000	1	0	0	0	0	0	0	0	0	0	0
Al Bumbry, of	.000	2	7	1	0	0	0	0	0	2	2	1
Rich Coggins, of	.444	2	9	1	4	1	0	0	0	0	0	0
Terry Crowley, of-1	.000	2	2	0	0	0	0	0	0	0	0	0
Mike Cuellar, p	.000	1	0	0	0	0	0	0	0	0	0	0
Tommy Davis, dh	.286	5	21	1	6	1	0	0	2	1	0	0
Andy Etchebarren, c	.357	4	14	1	5	1	0	1	4	0	1	0
Bobby Grich, 2b	.100	5	20	1	2	0	0	1	1	2	5	0
Don Hood, pr	.000	1	0	0	0	0	0	0	0	0	0	0
Grant Jackson, p	.000	2	0	0	0	0	0	0	0	0	0	0
Dave McNally, p	.000	1	0	0	0	0	0	0	0	0	0	0
Jim Palmer, p	.000	3	0	0	0	0	0	0	0	0	0	0
Boog Powell, 1b	.000	1	4	1	0	0	0	0	0	0	1	0
Merv Rettenmund, of	.091	3	11	1	1	0	0	0	0	3	2	0
Bob Reynolds, p	.000	2	0	0	0	0	0	0	0	0	0	0
Brooks Robinson, 3b	.250	5	20	1	5	2	0	0	2	1	1	0
Eddie Watt, p	.000	1	0	0	0	0	0	0	0	0	0	0
Earl Williams, 1b-4, c-1	.278	5	18	2	5	2	0	1	4	2	2	0
TOTAL	.211		171	15	36	7	0	3	15	16	25	1

PITCHER	W	L	ERA	G	GS	CG	SV	SHO	IP	H	ER	BB	SO
Doyle Alexander	0	1	4.91	1	1	0	0	0	3.2	5	2	0	1
Mike Cuellar	0	1	1.80	1	1	1	0	0	10.0	4	2	3	11
Grant Jackson	1	0	0.00	2	0	0	0	0	3.0	0	0	1	0
Dave McNally	0	1	5.87	1	1	0	0	0	7.2	7	5	2	7
Jim Palmer	1	0	1.84	3	2	1	0	1	14.2	11	3	8	15
Bob Reynolds	0	0	3.18	2	0	0	0	0	5.2	5	2	3	5
Eddie Watt	0	0	0.00	1	0	0	0	0	0.1	0	0	0	0
TOTAL	2	3	2.80	11	5	2	0	1	45.0	32	14	17	39

GAME 1 AT BAL OCT 6
OAK 000 000 000   0 5 1
BAL 400 000 11X   6 12 0
Pitchers: BLUE, Pina (1), Odom (3), Fingers (8) vs PALMER
Attendance: 41,279

GAME 2 AT BAL OCT 7
OAK 100 002 021   6 9 0
BAL 100 001 010   3 8 0
Pitchers: HUNTER, Fingers (8) vs McNALLY, Reynolds (8), G.Jackson (9)
Home Runs: Campaneris-OAK, Rudi-OAK, Bando-OAK (2)
Attendance: 48,425

GAME 3 AT OAK OCT 9
BAL 010 000 000 001   3 0
OAK 000 000 010 012   4 3
Pitchers: CUELLAR vs HOLTZMAN
Home Runs: Williams-BAL, Campaneris-OAK
Attendance: 34,367

GAME 4 AT OAK OCT 10
BAL 000 000 410   5 8 0
OAK 030 001 000   4 7 0
Pitchers: Palmer, Reynolds (2), Watt (7), G.JACKSON (7) vs Blue, FINGERS (7)
Home Runs: Etchebarren-BAL, Grich-BAL
Attendance: 27,497

GAME 5 AT OAK OCT 11
BAL 000 000 000   0 5 2
OAK 001 200 00X   3 7 0
Pitchers: ALEXANDER, Palmer (4) vs HUNTER
Attendance: 24,265

OAKLAND A'S (AL) 4, NEW YORK METS (NL) 3

For the second year in a row, the A's were outpitched and outscored by their Series opposition, and this time they were outhit as well. But again, when the dust of Game 7 had settled, they still wore the crown. A's starter Ken Holtzman, who because of the American League's new designated hitter rule had not batted all season, doubled for the A's first hit in the third inning of Game 1 and scored the first Oakland run on an error. The A's scored again in the inning, enough for the win as Holtzman and two relievers held New York to a single run.

The Mets evened things in a Game 2 that lasted a then-record 4 hours 13 minutes. New York scored four runs with two out in the top of the 12th inning for a lead the A's were not able to overcome. (Three of the runs scored on a pair of errors by second baseman Mike Andrews, prompting a flap that rocked the baseball world as A's owner Charlie Finley tried—unsuccessfully—to "fire" Andrews by declaring him injured.) Final score of the slugfest: 10–7.

In a somewhat more normal third game, the Mets grabbed an early lead on Wayne Garrett's lead-off homer in the bottom of the first and scored a second run on two singles and wild pitch for a 2–0 lead that held up until Oakland tied the game in the eighth. In the 11th, the A's Ted Kubiak worked his way around the bases on a walk, passed ball, and single for a lead that reliever Rollie Fingers held in the bottom of the inning.

New York evened the Series on Rusty Staub's three-run homer in the first inning of Game 4 (scoring three more times later for a 6–1 win). The Mets moved in front on a sparkling 2–0 three-hitter by Jerry Koosman and Tug McGraw in Game 5, but lost their edge as the Series returned to Oakland for Game 6, losing when Reggie Jackson's doubles in the first and third drove in two runs to give the A's a lead New York was unable to overtake.

Oakland made the finale look easy. Bert Campaneris and Jackson both hit two-run homers in the third inning, and Campaneris scored a fifth run two innings later before New York finally got on the board in the sixth. In the ninth inning the Mets scored a second

run with two outs, but reliever Darold Knowles came on for a record seventh pitching appearance and retired the final batter for his second Series save.

OAK (A)

PLAYER/POS	AVG	G	AB	R	H	2B	3B	HR	RBI	BB	SO	SB
Jesus Alou, of-6	.158	7	19	0	3	1	0	0	3	0	0	0
Mike Andrews, 2b-1	.000	2	3	0	0	0	0	0	0	1	1	0
Sal Bando, 3b	.231	7	26	5	6	1	1	0	1	4	7	0
Vida Blue, p	.000	2	4	0	0	0	0	0	0	0	4	0
Pat Bourque, 1b	.500	2	2	0	1	0	0	0	0	0	0	0
Bert Campaneris, ss	.290	7	31	6	9	0	1	1	3	1	7	3
Billy Conigliaro, ph	.000	3	3	0	0	0	0	0	0	0	1	0
Vic Davalillo, of-4,1b-1	.091	6	11	0	1	0	0	0	0	2	1	0
Rollie Fingers, p	.333	6	3	0	1	0	0	0	0	0	1	0
Ray Fosse, c	.158	7	19	0	3	1	0	0	0	1	4	0
Dick Green, 2b	.063	7	16	0	1	0	0	0	0	1	6	0
Ken Holtzman, p	.667	3	3	2	2	2	0	0	0	0	0	0
Catfish Hunter, p	.000	2	5	0	0	0	0	0	0	0	3	0
Reggie Jackson, of	.310	7	29	3	9	3	1	1	6	2	7	0
Deron Johnson, 1b-2	.300	6	10	0	3	1	0	0	0	1	4	0
Darold Knowles, p	.000	7	0	0	0	0	0	0	0	0	0	0
Ted Kubiak, 2b	.000	4	3	1	0	0	0	0	0	1	1	0
Allan Lewis, pr	.000	3	0	1	0	0	0	0	0	0	0	0
Paul Lindblad, p	.000	3	1	0	0	0	0	0	0	0	0	0
Angel Mangual, of-1	.000	5	6	0	0	0	0	0	0	0	3	0
Blue Moon Odom, p-2	.000	3	1	0	0	0	0	0	0	0	1	0
Horacio Pina, p	.000	2	0	0	0	0	0	0	0	0	0	0
Joe Rudi, of	.333	7	27	3	9	2	0	0	4	3	4	0
Gene Tenace, 1b-7, c-3	.158	7	19	0	3	1	0	0	3	11	7	0
TOTAL	.212		241	21	51	12	3	2	20	28	62	3

PITCHER	W	L	ERA	G	GS	CG	SV	SHO	IP	H	ER	BB	SO
Vida Blue	0	1	4.91	2	2	0	0	0	11.0	10	6	3	8
Rollie Fingers	0	1	0.66	6	0	0	2	0	13.2	13	1	4	8
Ken Holtzman	2	1	4.22	3	3	0	0	0	10.2	13	5	5	6
Catfish Hunter	1	0	2.03	2	2	0	0	0	13.1	11	3	4	6
Darold Knowles	0	0	0.00	7	0	0	2	0	6.1	4	0	5	5
Paul Lindblad	1	0	0.00	3	0	0	0	0	3.1	4	0	1	1
Blue Moon Odom	0	0	3.86	2	0	0	0	0	4.2	5	2	2	2
Horacio Pina	0	0	0.00	2	0	0	0	0	3.0	6	0	2	0
TOTAL	4	3	2.32	27	7	0	4	0	66.0	66	17	26	36

NY (N)

PLAYER/POS	AVG	G	AB	R	H	2B	3B	HR	RBI	BB	SO	SB
Jim Beauchamp, ph	.000	4	4	0	0	0	0	0	0	0	1	0
Ken Boswell, ph	1.000	3	3	1	3	0	0	0	0	0	0	0
Wayne Garrett, 3b	.167	7	30	4	5	0	0	2	2	5	11	0
Jerry Grote, c	.267	7	30	2	8	0	0	0	0	0	1	0
Don Hahn, of	.241	7	29	2	7	1	1	0	2	1	6	0
Bud Harrelson, ss	.250	7	24	2	6	1	0	0	1	5	3	0
Ron Hodges, ph	.000	1	0	0	0	0	0	0	0	1	0	0
Cleon Jones, of	.286	7	28	5	8	2	0	1	1	4	2	0
Jerry Koosman, p	.000	2	4	0	0	0	0	0	0	0	3	0
Ed Kranepool, ph	.000	4	3	0	0	0	0	0	0	0	0	0
Ted Martinez, pr	.000	2	0	0	0	0	0	0	0	0	0	0
Jon Matlack, p	.250	3	4	0	1	0	0	0	0	2	1	0
Willie Mays, of-2	.286	3	7	1	2	0	0	0	1	0	1	0
Tug McGraw, p	.333	5	3	1	1	0	0	0	0	0	1	0
Felix Millan, 2b	.188	7	32	3	6	1	1	0	1	1	1	0
John Milner, 1b	.296	7	27	2	8	0	0	0	2	5	1	0
Harry Parker, p	.000	3	0	0	0	0	0	0	0	0	0	0
Ray Sadecki, p	.000	4	0	0	0	0	0	0	0	0	0	0
Tom Seaver, p	.000	2	5	0	0	0	0	0	0	0	2	0
Rusty Staub, of	.423	7	26	1	11	2	0	1	6	2	2	0
George Stone, p	.000	2	0	0	0	0	0	0	0	0	0	0
George Theodore, of-1	.000	2	2	0	0	0	0	0	0	0	0	0
TOTAL	.253		261	24	66	7	2	4	16	26	36	0

PITCHER	W	L	ERA	G	GS	CG	SV	SHO	IP	H	ER	BB	SO
Jerry Koosman	1	0	3.12	2	2	0	0	0	8.2	9	3	7	8
Jon Matlack	1	2	2.16	3	3	0	0	0	16.2	10	4	5	11
Tug McGraw	1	0	2.63	5	0	0	1	0	13.2	8	4	9	14
Harry Parker	0	1	0.00	3	0	0	0	0	3.1	2	0	2	2
Ray Sadecki	0	0	1.93	4	0	0	1	0	4.2	5	1	1	6
Tom Seaver	0	1	2.40	2	2	0	0	0	15.0	13	4	3	18
George Stone	0	0	0.00	2	0	0	1	0	3.0	4	0	1	3
TOTAL	3	4	2.22	21	7	0	3	0	65.0	51	16	28	62

GAME 1 AT OAK OCT 13

```
NY    000 100 000   1 7 2
OAK   002 000 00X   2 4 0
```
Pitchers: MATLACK, McGraw (7) vs HOLTZMAN, Fingers (6), Knowles (9)
Attendance: 46,021

GAME 2 AT OAK OCT 14

```
NY    011 004 000 004  10 15 1
OAK   210 000 102 001   7 13 5
```
Pitchers: Koosman, Sadecki (3), Parker (5), McGRAW (6), Stone (12) vs Blue, Pina (6), Knowles (6), Odom (8), FINGERS (10), Lindblad (12)
Home Runs: Jones-NY, Garrett-NY
Attendance: 49,151

GAME 3 AT NY OCT 16

```
OAK   000 001 010 001   3 10 1
NY    200 000 000 00    2 10 2
```
Pitchers: Hunter, LINDBLAD (9), Fingers (11) vs Seaver, Sadecki (9), McGraw (9), PARKER (11)
Home Runs: Garrett-NY
Attendance: 54,817

GAME 4 AT NY OCT 17

```
OAK   000 100 000   1 5 1
NY    300 300 00X   6 13 1
```
Pitchers: HOLTZMAN, Odom (1), Knowles (4), Pina (5), Lindblad (8) vs MATLACK, Sadecki (9)
Home Runs: Staub-NY
Attendance: 54,817

GAME 5 AT NY OCT 18

```
OAK   000 000 000   0 3 1
NY    010 001 00X   2 7 1
```
Pitchers: BLUE, Knowles (6), Fingers (7) vs KOOSMAN, McGraw (7)
Attendance: 54,817

GAME 6 AT OAK OCT 20

```
NY    000 000 010   1 6 2
OAK   101 000 01X   3 7 0
```
Pitchers: SEAVER, McGraw (8) vs HUNTER, Knowles (8), Fingers (8)
Attendance: 49,333

GAME 7 AT OAK OCT 21

```
NY    000 001 001   2 8 1
OAK   004 010 00X   5 9 1
```
Pitchers: MATLACK, Parker (3), Sadecki (7), Stone (7) vs HOLTZMAN, Fingers (6), Knowles (9)
Home Runs: Campaneris-OAK, Jackson-OAK
Attendance: 49,333

LOS ANGELES DODGERS (WEST) 3, PITTSBURGH PIRATES (EAST) 1

Dodgers pitcher Don Sutton—who had brought his won-lost record from 10–9 to 19–9 with a nine-game winning streak in the regular season—continued his winning ways in the NLCS, surrendering only seven hits and one run in 17 innings and taking both the opener and clincher of the four-game series. Los Angeles' Andy Messersmith followed up Sutton's opening-game shutout with six shutout innings of his own in Game 2 before Pittsburgh scored its first two runs of the series in the seventh. They tied the score, but the Dodgers countered with three more in the top of the eighth to assure their second win.

The Pirates captured their only victory in Game 3, as Richie Hebner and Willie Stargell homered for five of the Bucs' seven runs, while Bruce Kison and Ramon Hernandez shut out the Dodgers on four hits.

Pittsburgh finally got to Sutton for a run when Stargell homered in the seventh inning of Game 4. But it was too little, and too late to stem a 12-run attack led by Steve Garvey's four hits (two of them home runs) and four RBIs for the Dodgers.

LA (W)

PLAYER/POS	AVG	G	AB	R	H	2B	3B	HR	RB	BB	SO	SB
Rick Auerbach, ph	1.000	1	1	0	1	1	0	0	0	0	0	0
Bill Buckner, of	.167	4	18	0	3	1	0	0	0	0	2	0
Ron Cey, 3b	.313	4	16	2	5	3	0	1	1	3	2	0
Willie Crawford, of	.250	2	4	1	1	0	0	0	1	1	1	0
Al Downing, p	.000	1	1	0	0	0	0	0	0	0	0	0
Joe Ferguson, of-3, c-2	.231	4	13	3	3	0	0	0	2	5	1	0
Steve Garvey, 1b	.389	4	18	4	7	1	0	2	5	1	1	0
Charlie Hough, p	.000	1	0	0	0	0	0	0	0	0	0	0
Von Joshua, ph	.000	1	0	0	0	0	0	0	0	1	0	0
Lee Lacy, pr	.000	1	0	0	0	0	0	0	0	0	0	0
Davey Lopes, 2b	.267	4	15	4	4	0	1	0	3	5	1	3
Mike Marshall, p	.000	2	0	0	0	0	0	0	0	0	0	0
Ken McMullen, ph	.000	1	1	0	0	0	0	0	0	0	1	0
Andy Messersmith, p	.000	1	3	0	0	0	0	0	0	0	1	0
Manny Mota, of-1	.333	3	3	0	1	0	0	0	1	0	0	0
Tom Paciorek, of	1.000	1	1	0	1	0	0	0	0	0	0	0
Doug Rau, p	.000	1	0	0	0	0	0	0	0	0	0	0
Bill Russell, ss	.389	4	18	1	7	0	0	0	3	1	0	0
Eddie Solomon, p	.000	1	0	0	0	0	0	0	0	0	0	0
Don Sutton, p	.286	2	7	0	2	0	0	0	1	1	2	0
Jimmy Wynn, of	.200	4	10	4	2	2	0	0	2	9	1	1
Steve Yeager, c	.000	3	9	1	0	0	0	0	0	3	3	1
TOTAL	.268		138	20	37	8	1	3	19	30	16	5

PITCHER	W	L	ERA	G	GS	CG	SV	SHO	IP	H	ER	BB	SO
Al Downing	0	0	0.00	1	0	0	0	0	4.0	1	0	1	0
Charlie Hough	0	0	7.71	1	0	0	0	0	2.1	4	2	0	2
Mike Marshall	0	0	0.00	2	0	0	0	0	3.0	3	0	0	1
Andy Messersmith	1	0	2.57	1	1	0	0	0	7.0	8	2	3	0
Doug Rau	0	1	40.50	1	1	0	0	0	0.2	3	3	1	0
Eddie Solomon	0	0	0.00	1	0	0	0	0	2.0	2	0	1	1
Don Sutton	2	0	0.53	2	2	1	0	1	17.0	7	1	2	13
TOTAL	3	1	2.00	9	4	1	0	1	36.0	25	8	8	17

PIT (E)

PLAYER/POS	AVG	G	AB	R	H	2B	3B	HR	RB	BB	SO	SB
Ken Brett, p	.000	1	1	0	0	0	0	0	0	0	1	0
Gene Clines, of	.000	2	1	1	0	0	0	0	0	0	0	0
Larry Demery, p	.000	2	0	0	0	0	0	0	0	0	0	0
Dave Giusti, p	.000	3	0	0	0	0	0	0	0	0	0	0
Richie Hebner, 3b	.231	4	13	1	3	0	0	1	4	1	4	0
Ramon Hernandez, p	.000	2	1	0	0	0	0	0	0	0	1	0
Art Howe, ph	.000	1	1	0	0	0	0	0	0	0	0	0
Ed Kirkpatrick, 1b	.000	3	9	0	0	0	0	0	0	2	0	0
Bruce Kison, p	.000	1	3	0	0	0	0	0	0	0	2	0
Mario Mendoza, ss	.200	3	5	0	1	0	0	0	1	1	0	0
Al Oliver, of	.143	4	14	1	2	0	0	0	1	2	2	0
Dave Parker, of-2	.125	3	8	0	1	0	0	0	0	0	1	0
Juan Pizarro, p	.000	1	0	0	0	0	0	0	0	0	0	0
Paul Popovich, ss	.600	3	5	1	3	0	0	0	0	0	0	0
Jerry Reuss, p	.000	2	2	0	0	0	0	0	0	0	0	0
Bob Robertson, 1b	.000	1	5	1	0	0	0	0	0	0	0	0
Jim Rooker, p	.500	1	2	0	1	0	0	0	0	0	0	0
Manny Sanguillen, c	.250	4	16	0	4	1	0	0	0	0	0	0
Willie Stargell, of	.400	4	15	3	6	0	0	2	4	1	2	0
Rennie Stennett, 2b	.063	4	16	1	1	0	0	0	0	1	1	0
Frank Taveras, ss	.000	2	2	0	0	0	0	0	0	0	0	1
Richie Zisk, of-2	.300	3	10	1	3	0	0	0	0	0	3	0
TOTAL	.194		129	10	25	1	0	3	10	8	17	1

PITCHER	W	L	ERA	G	GS	CG	SV	SHO	IP	H	ER	BB	SO
Ken Brett	0	0	7.71	1	0	0	0	0	2.1	3	2	2	1
Larry Demery	0	0	36.00	2	0	0	0	0	1.0	3	4	2	0
Dave Giusti	0	1	21.60	3	0	0	0	0	3.1	13	8	5	1
Ramon Hernandez	0	0	0.00	2	0	0	0	0	4.1	3	0	1	2
Bruce Kison	1	0	0.00	1	1	0	0	0	6.2	2	0	6	5
Juan Pizarro	0	0	0.00	1	0	0	0	0	0.2	0	0	1	0
Jerry Reuss	0	2	3.72	2	2	0	0	0	9.2	7	4	8	3
Jim Rooker	0	0	2.57	1	1	0	0	0	7.0	6	2	5	4
TOTAL	1	3	5.14	13	4	0	0	0	35.0	37	20	30	16

GAME 1 AT PIT OCT 5

LA   010 000 002   3 9 2
PIT   000 000 000   0 4 0
Pitchers: SUTTON vs REUSS, Giusti (8)
Attendance: 40,638

GAME 2 AT PIT OCT 6

LA   100 100 030   5 12 0
PIT   000 000 200   2 8 3
Pitchers: MESSERSMITH, Marshall (8) vs Rooker, GIUSTI (8), Demery (8), Hernandez (8)
Home Runs: Cey-LA
Attendance: 49,247

GAME 3 AT LA OCT 8

PIT   502 000 000   7 10 0
LA   000 000 000   0 4 5
Pitchers: KISON, Hernandez (7) vs RAU, Hough (1), Downing (4), Solomon (8)
Home Runs: Stargell-PIT, Hebner-PIT
Attendance: 55,953

GAME 4 AT LA OCT 9

PIT   000 000 100   1 3 1
LA   102 022 23X   12 12 0
Pitchers: REUSS, Brett (3), Demery (6), Giusti (7), Pizarro (8) vs SUTTON, Marshall (9)
Home Runs: Garvey-LA (2), Stargell-PIT
Attendance: 54,424

OAKLAND A'S (WEST) 3, BALTIMORE ORIOLES (EAST) 1

After spotting Baltimore a win in the opener, Oakland took the next three games and their third consecutive pennant. Although the A's got nine hits in Game 1—their series high—the Orioles hit harder, burying Oakland under home runs by Paul Blair, Brooks Robinson, and Bobby Grich. In Game 2, though, Ken Holtzman shut out Baltimore on five hits as Sal Bando and Ray Fosse homered. Bando homered again in the third game for the only Oakland run as Jim Palmer limited the A's to four hits. But one run was enough to defeat Baltimore, for Vida Blue shut them out on a masterful two-hitter.

Orioles starter Mike Cuellar walked nine men in 4-2/3 innings of Game 4, including four in the fifth to force in Oakland's first run. Two innings later Reggie Jackson's double (the only Oakland hit of the game) off reliever Ross Grimsley drove in Oakland's second run, while starter Catfish Hunter was blanking the O's through seven-plus innings. After failing to score for 30 consecutive innings, the Orioles got to reliever Rollie Fingers for a run with two out in the bottom of the ninth. But Fingers then struck out Don Baylor, and the A's had their pennant.

OAK (W)

PLAYER/POS	AVG	G	AB	R	H	2B	3B	HR	RB	BB	SO	SB
Jesus Alou, ph	1.000	1	1	0	1	0	0	0	0	0	0	0
Sal Bando, 3b	.231	4	13	4	3	0	0	2	2	4	0	0
Vida Blue, p	.000	1	0	0	0	0	0	0	0	0	0	0
Bert Campaneris, ss	.176	4	17	0	3	0	0	0	0	3	0	1
Rollie Fingers, p	.000	2	0	0	0	0	0	0	0	0	0	0
Ray Fosse, c	.333	4	12	1	4	1	0	1	3	1	2	0
Dick Green, 2b	.222	4	9	0	2	0	0	0	0	2	1	0
Jim Holt, 1b-1	.000	2	0	0	0	0	0	0	0	1	0	0
Ken Holtzman, p	.000	1	0	0	0	0	0	0	0	0	0	0
Catfish Hunter, p	.000	2	0	0	0	0	0	0	0	0	0	0
Reggie Jackson, dh-3, of-1	.167	4	12	0	2	1	0	0	1	5	2	0
Angel Mangual, dh	.250	1	4	0	1	0	0	0	0	0	0	0
Dal Maxvill, 2b	.000	1	1	0	0	0	0	0	0	0	1	0
Billy North, of	.063	4	16	3	1	1	0	0	0	2	1	1
Blue Moon Odom, p-1	.000	3	0	0	0	0	0	0	0	0	0	0
Joe Rudi, of	.154	4	13	0	2	0	1	0	1	3	2	0
Gene Tenace, 1b	.000	4	11	1	0	0	0	0	0	1	4	1
Manny Trillo, pr	.000	1	0	1	0	0	0	0	0	0	0	0
Claudell Washington, of-3	.273	4	11	1	3	1	0	0	0	0	0	0
Herb Washington, pr	.000	2	0	0	0	0	0	0	0	0	0	0
TOTAL	.183		120	11	22	4	1	3	11	22	16	3

PITCHER	W	L	ERA	G	GS	CG	SV	SHO	IP	H	ER	BB	SO
Vida Blue	1	0	0.00	1	1	1	0	1	9.0	2	0	0	7
Rollie Fingers	0	0	3.00	2	0	0	1	0	3.0	3	1	1	3
Ken Holtzman	1	0	0.00	1	1	1	0	1	9.0	5	0	2	3
Catfish Hunter	1	1	4.63	2	2	0	0	0	11.2	11	6	2	6
Blue Moon Odom	0	0	0.00	1	0	0	0	0	3.1	1	0	0	1
TOTAL	3	1	1.75	7	4	2	1	2	36.0	22	7	5	20

BAL (E)

PLAYER/POS	AVG	G	AB	R	H	2B	3B	HR	RB	BB	SO	SB
Frank Baker, ss	.000	2	0	0	0	0	0	0	0	0	0	0
Don Baylor, of	.267	4	15	0	4	0	0	0	0	0	2	0
Mark Belanger, ss	.000	4	9	0	0	0	0	0	0	1	3	0
Paul Blair, of	.286	4	14	3	4	0	0	1	2	2	2	0
Al Bumbry, ph	.000	2	1	0	0	0	0	0	0	0	1	0
Enos Cabell, of-1	.250	3	4	0	1	0	0	0	0	0	2	0
Rich Coggins, of	.000	3	11	0	0	0	0	0	0	0	3	0
Mike Cuellar, p	.000	2	0	0	0	0	0	0	0	0	0	0
Tommy Davis, dh	.267	4	15	0	4	0	0	0	1	0	1	0
Andy Etchebarren, c	.333	2	6	0	2	0	0	0	0	0	0	0
Wayne Garland, p	.000	1	0	0	0	0	0	0	0	0	0	0
Bobby Grich, 2b	.250	4	16	2	4	1	0	1	2	0	1	0
Ross Grimsley, p	.000	2	0	0	0	0	0	0	0	0	0	0
Elrod Hendricks, c	.167	3	6	1	1	0	0	0	0	1	3	0
Grant Jackson, p	.000	1	0	0	0	0	0	0	0	0	0	0
Dave McNally, p	.000	1	0	0	0	0	0	0	0	0	0	0
Curt Motton, ph	.000	1	1	0	0	0	0	0	0	0	0	0
Jim Palmer, p-1	.000	2	0	0	0	0	0	0	0	0	0	0
Boog Powell, 1b	.125	2	8	0	1	0	0	0	1	0	0	0
Bob Reynolds, p	.000	1	0	0	0	0	0	0	0	0	0	0
Brooks Robinson, 3b	.083	4	12	1	1	0	0	1	1	1	0	0
Earl Williams, 1b	.000	2	6	0	0	0	0	0	0	0	2	0
TOTAL	.177		124	7	22	1	0	3	7	5	20	0

PITCHER	W	L	ERA	G	GS	CG	SV	SHO	IP	H	ER	BB	SO
Mike Cuellar	1	1	2.84	2	2	0	0	0	12.2	9	4	13	6
Wayne Garland	0	0	0.00	1	0	0	0	0	0.2	1	0	1	0
Ross Grimsley	0	0	1.69	2	0	0	0	0	5.1	1	1	2	2
Grant Jackson	0	0	0.00	1	0	0	0	0	0.1	1	0	0	1
Dave McNally	0	1	1.59	1	1	0	0	0	5.2	6	1	2	2
Jim Palmer	0	1	1.00	1	1	1	0	0	9.0	4	1	1	4
Bob Reynolds	0	0	0.00	1	0	0	0	0	1.1	0	0	3	1
TOTAL	1	3	1.80	9	4	1	0	0	35.0	22	7	22	16

GAME 1 AT OAK OCT 5

```
BAL   1 0 0 1 4 0  0 0 0   6 10 0
OAK   0 0 1 0 1 0  0 0 1   3  9 0
```
Pitchers: CUELLAR, Grimsley (9) vs HUNTER, Odom (5), Fingers (9)
Home Runs: Blair-BAL, Robinson-BAL, Grich-BAL
Attendance: 41,609

GAME 2 AT OAK OCT 6

```
BAL   0 0 0 0 0 0  0 0 0   0 5 2
OAK   0 0 0 1 0 1  0 3 X   5 8 0
```
Pitchers: McNALLY, Garland (6), Reynolds (7), G.Jackson (8) vs HOLTZMAN
Home Runs: Bando-OAK, Fosse-OAK
Attendance: 42,810

GAME 3 AT BAL OCT 8

```
OAK   0 0 0 1 0 0  0 0 0   1 4 2
BAL   0 0 0 0 0 0  0 0 0   0 2 1
```
Pitchers: BLUE vs PALMER
Home Runs: Bando-OAK
Attendance: 32,060

GAME 4 AT BAL OCT 9

```
OAK   0 0 0 0 1 0  1 0 0   2 1 0
BAL   0 0 0 0 0 0  0 0 1   1 5 1
```
Pitchers: HUNTER, Fingers (8) vs CUELLAR, Grimsley (5)
Attendance: 28,136

OAKLAND A'S (AL) 4, LOS ANGELES DODGERS (NL) 1

Although the A's were in a turmoil of dislike for owner Charlie Finley—and for each other—they played well enough together to take their third consecutive world championship in just five games. Still, victory didn't come easily, as three of Oakland's wins came by identical 3–2 scores (as did the Dodgers' one victory), and their biggest winning margin was three runs in Game 4. It was the first World Series held entirely on the West Coast.

The A's and Dodgers split the first two games in Los Angeles. Oakland won the opener on the strength of Reggie Jackson's home run in the second inning, pitcher Ken Holtzman's double in the fifth (he moved around on a wild pitch and squeeze bunt), and a Dodgers throwing error in the eighth. The Dodgers evened the Series on Joe Ferguson's two-run homer in the sixth inning of the second game, which gave Los Angeles a 3–0 lead that an Oakland rally in the ninth failed to catch.

Los Angeles outhit Oakland in Game 3, but two of the A's runs were unearned, coming after Dodgers catcher Ferguson bobbled what should have been a third-out play in the third inning.

Pitcher Ken Holtzman, who had now gone two regular seasons without a time at bat, produced in Game 4 his second hit of the Series, this one a homer in the third inning for the game's first run. The Dodgers' Bill Russell tripled off him for two runs a half inning later, but in the last of the sixth inning Oakland regained the lead on three walks interspersed with a pair of singles and an RBI grounder to short. Four runs scored—more in this one inning than either team scored in any of the other four games.

Oakland took an early 2–0 lead in Game 5, with single runs in the first and second innings (the latter a Ray Fosse home run). The Dodgers put together a pinch-hit double, a walk, a pair of sacrifices (bunt and fly), and a single to tie the score in the sixth. But Joe Rudi hit the first pitch of Oakland's half of the seventh into the stands in left for the run that decided the game and the Series.

OAK (A)

PLAYER/POS	AVG	G	AB	R	H	2B	3B	HR	RB	BB	SO	SB
Jesus Alou, ph	.000	1	1	0	0	0	0	0	0	0	1	0
Sal Bando, 3b	.063	5	16	3	1	0	0	0	2	2	5	0
Vida Blue, p	.000	2	4	0	0	0	0	0	0	0	4	0
Bert Campaneris, ss	.353	5	17	1	6	2	0	0	2	0	2	1
Rollie Fingers, p	.000	4	2	0	0	0	0	0	0	0	1	0
Ray Fosse, c	.143	5	14	1	2	0	0	1	1	1	5	0
Dick Green, 2b	.000	5	13	1	0	0	0	0	1	1	4	0
Larry Haney, c	.000	2	0	0	0	0	0	0	0	0	0	0
Jim Holt, 1b-1	.667	4	3	0	2	0	0	0	2	0	0	0
Ken Holtzman, p	.500	2	4	2	2	1	0	1	1	1	1	0
Catfish Hunter, p	.000	2	2	0	0	0	0	0	0	0	2	0
Reggie Jackson, of	.286	5	14	3	4	1	0	1	1	5	3	1
Angel Mangual, ph	.000	1	1	0	0	0	0	0	0	0	1	0
Dal Maxvill, 2b	.000	2	0	0	0	0	0	0	0	0	0	0
Billy North, of	.059	5	17	3	1	0	0	0	0	2	5	1
Blue Moon Odom, p	.000	2	0	0	0	0	0	0	0	0	0	0
Joe Rudi, of-5,1b-2	.333	5	18	1	6	0	0	1	4	0	3	0
Gene Tenace, 1b	.222	5	9	0	2	0	0	0	0	3	4	0
Claudell Washington, of	.571	5	7	1	4	0	0	0	0	1	1	0
Herb Washington, pr	.000	3	0	0	0	0	0	0	0	0	0	0
TOTAL	.211		142	16	30	4	0	4	14	16	42	3

PITCHER	W	L	ERA	G	GS	CG	SV	SHO	IP	H	ER	BB	SO
Vida Blue	0	1	3.29	2	2	0	0	0	13.2	10	5	7	9
Rollie Fingers	1	0	1.93	4	0	0	2	0	9.1	8	2	2	6
Ken Holtzman	1	0	1.50	2	2	0	0	0	12.0	13	2	4	10
Catfish Hunter	1	0	1.17	2	1	0	1	0	7.2	5	1	2	5
Blue Moon Odom	1	0	0.00	2	0	0	0	0	1.1	0	0	1	2
TOTAL	4	1	2.05	12	5	0	3	0	44.0	36	10	16	32

LA (N)

PLAYER/POS	AVG	G	AB	R	H	2B	3B	HR	RB	BB	SO	SB
Rick Auerbach, pr	.000	1	0	0	0	0	0	0	0	0	0	0
Jim Brewer, p	.000	1	0	0	0	0	0	0	0	0	0	0
Bill Buckner, of	.250	5	20	1	5	1	0	1	1	1	1	0
Ron Cey, 3b	.176	5	17	1	3	0	0	0	0	3	3	0
Willie Crawford, of-2	.333	3	6	1	2	0	0	1	1	1	0	0
Al Downing, p	.000	1	1	0	0	0	0	0	0	0	0	0
Joe Ferguson, of-4, c-2	.125	5	16	2	2	0	0	1	2	4	6	1
Steve Garvey, 1b	.381	5	21	2	8	0	0	0	1	0	3	0
Charlie Hough, p	.000	1	0	0	0	0	0	0	0	0	0	0
Von Joshua, ph	.000	4	4	0	0	0	0	0	0	0	0	0
Lee Lacy, ph	.000	1	1	0	0	0	0	0	0	0	1	0
Davey Lopes, 2b	.111	5	18	2	2	0	0	0	0	3	4	2
Mike Marshall, p	.000	5	0	0	0	0	0	0	0	1	0	0
Andy Messersmith, p	.500	2	4	0	2	0	0	0	0	0	2	0
Tom Paciorek, ph	.500	3	2	1	1	1	0	0	0	0	0	0
Bill Russell, ss	.222	5	18	0	4	0	1	0	2	0	2	0
Don Sutton, p	.000	2	3	0	0	0	0	0	0	0	2	0
Jimmy Wynn, of	.188	5	16	1	3	1	0	1	2	4	4	0
Steve Yeager, c	.364	4	11	0	4	1	0	0	1	1	4	0
TOTAL	.228		158	11	36	4	1	4	10	16	32	3

PITCHER	W	L	ERA	G	GS	CG	SV	SHO	IP	H	ER	BB	SO
Jim Brewer	0	0	0.00	1	0	0	0	0	0.1	0	0	0	1
Al Downing	0	1	2.45	1	1	0	0	0	3.2	4	1	4	3
Charlie Hough	0	0	0.00	1	0	0	0	0	2.0	0	0	1	4
Mike Marshall	0	1	1.00	5	0	0	1	0	9.0	6	1	1	10
Andy Messersmith	0	2	4.50	2	2	0	0	0	14.0	11	7	7	12
Don Sutton	1	0	2.77	2	2	0	0	0	13.0	9	4	3	12
TOTAL	1	4	2.79	12	5	0	1	0	42.0	30	13	16	42

GAME 1 AT LA OCT 12

```
OAK  010 010 010    3 6 2
LA   000 010 001    2 11 1
```
Pitchers: Holtzman, FINGERS (5), Hunter (9) vs MESSERSMITH, Marshall (9)
Home Runs: Jackson-OAK, Wynn-LA
Attendance: 55,974

GAME 2 AT LA OCT 13

```
OAK  000 000 002    2 6 0
LA   010 002 00X    3 6 1
```
Pitchers: BLUE, Odom (8) vs SUTTON, Marshall (9)
Home Runs: Ferguson-LA
Attendance: 55,989

GAME 3 AT OAK OCT 15

```
LA   000 000 011    2 7 2
OAK  002 100 00X    3 5 2
```
Pitchers: DOWNING, Brewer (4), Hough (5), Marshall (7) vs HUNTER, Fingers (8)
Home Runs: Buckner-LA, Crawford-LA
Attendance: 49,347

GAME 4 AT OAK OCT 16

```
LA   000 200 000    2 7 1
OAK  001 004 00X    5 7 0
```
Pitchers: MESSERSMITH, Marshall (7) vs HOLTZMAN, Fingers (8)
Home Runs: Holtzman-OAK
Attendance: 49,347

GAME 5 AT OAK OCT 17

```
LA   000 002 000    2 5 1
OAK  110 010 10X    3 6 1
```
Pitchers: Sutton, MARSHALL (6) vs Blue, ODOM (7), Fingers (8)
Home Runs: Fosse-OAK, Rudi-OAK
Attendance: 49,347

CINCINNATI REDS (WEST) 3, PITTSBURGH PIRATES (EAST) 0

The Reds, who had steamrolled the National League during the season, continued their roll in the NLCS. Reds pitcher Don Gullett gave up three Pirate runs in the first game, but he drove in three himself with a home run and a single. Pitching the series' only complete game, he won easily behind his club's 12-hit, eight-run attack. The Reds won just as handily in Game 2, with Fred Norman and reliever Rawley Eastwick holding the Pirates to one run as Tony Perez drove in half the Reds' six runs—two of them with a first-inning homer.

In Game 3 the Pirates struggled gamely against elimination. Cincinnati scored first in the second, but in the sixth Al Oliver put Pittsburgh ahead with a two-run homer. In the eighth, though, Pete Rose restored the Reds' lead (and nullified rookie John Candelaria's 14-strikeout effort over 7-2/3 innings) with his two-run shot. The Pirates were granted a brief reprieve when Reds reliever Eastwick walked in the tying run in the bottom of the ninth. But in the 10th the Reds scored twice on three hits, and when Eastwick's replacement Pedro Borbon shut the Pirates down in the bottom of the tenth, Cincinnati had its series sweep.

CIN (W)

PLAYER/POS	AVG	G	AB	R	H	2B	3B	HR	RB	BB	SO	SB
Ed Armbrister, ph	.000	2	0	0	0	0	0	0	0	1	0	0
Johnny Bench, c	.077	3	13	1	1	0	0	0	0	1	6	1
Pedro Borbon, p	.000	1	0	0	0	0	0	0	0	0	0	0
Clay Carroll, p	.000	1	0	0	0	0	0	0	0	0	0	0
Dave Concepcion, ss	.455	3	11	2	5	0	0	1	1	1	2	2
Terry Crowley, ph	.000	1	0	0	0	0	0	0	0	0	0	0
Rawly Eastwick, p	.000	2	0	0	0	0	0	0	0	0	0	0
George Foster, of	.364	3	11	3	4	0	0	0	0	1	2	1
Cesar Geronimo, of	.000	3	10	0	0	0	0	0	0	1	1	7	0
Ken Griffey, of	.333	3	12	3	4	1	0	0	4	0	3	3
Don Gullett, p	.500	1	4	1	2	0	0	1	3	0	0
Will McEnaney, p	.000	1	0	0	0	0	0	0	0	0	0	0
Joe Morgan, 2b	.273	3	11	2	3	3	0	0	1	3	2	4
Gary Nolan, p	.000	1	2	0	0	0	0	0	0	0	2	0
Fred Norman, p	.000	1	1	0	0	0	0	0	0	1	0	0
Tony Perez, 1b	.417	3	12	3	5	0	0	1	4	1	2	0
Merv Rettenmund, ph	.000	2	1	1	0	0	0	0	0	1	0	0
Pete Rose, 3b	.357	3	14	3	5	0	0	1	2	0	2	0
TOTAL	.284		102	19	29	4	0	4	18	9	28	11

PITCHER	W	L	ERA	G	GS	CG	SV	SHO	IP	H	ER	BB	SO
Pedro Borbon	0	0	0.00	1	0	0	1	0	1.0	0	0	0	1
Clay Carroll	0	0	0.00	1	0	0	0	0	1.0	0	0	1	1
Rawly Eastwick	1	0	0.00	2	0	0	1	0	3.2	2	0	2	1
Don Gullett	1	0	3.00	1	1	1	0	0	9.0	8	3	2	5
Will McEnaney	0	0	6.75	1	0	0	0	0	1.1	1	1	0	1
Gary Nolan	0	0	3.00	1	1	0	0	0	6.0	5	2	0	5
Fred Norman	1	0	1.50	1	1	0	0	0	6.0	4	1	5	4
TOTAL	3	0	2.25	8	3	1	2	0	28.0	20	7	10	18

PIT (E)

PLAYER/POS	AVG	G	AB	R	H	2B	3B	HR	RB	BB	SO	SB
Ken Brett, p	.000	2	0	0	0	0	0	0	0	0	0	0
John Candelaria, p	.000	1	3	0	0	0	0	0	0	0	3	0
Larry Demery, p	.000	1	0	0	0	0	0	0	0	0	0	0
Duffy Dyer, ph	.000	1	0	0	0	0	0	0	0	1	1	0
Dock Ellis, p	.000	1	0	0	0	0	0	0	0	0	0	0
Dave Giusti, p	.000	1	0	0	0	0	0	0	0	0	0	0
Richie Hebner, 3b	.333	3	12	2	4	1	0	0	2	1	1	0
Ramon Hernandez, p	.000	1	0	0	0	0	0	0	0	0	0	0
Ed Kirkpatrick, ph	.000	2	2	0	0	0	0	0	0	0	0	0
Bruce Kison, p	.000	1	0	0	0	0	0	0	0	0	0	0
Al Oliver, of	.182	3	11	1	2	0	0	1	2	2	0	0
Dave Parker, of	.000	3	10	2	0	0	0	0	0	1	3	0
Willie Randolph, 2b-1	.000	2	2	1	0	0	0	0	0	0	1	0
Jerry Reuss, p	.000	1	1	0	0	0	0	0	0	0	0	0
Craig Reynolds, ss-1	.000	2	1	0	0	0	0	0	0	0	0	0
Bob Robertson, 1b-1	.500	3	2	0	1	0	0	0	1	1	0	0
Bill Robinson, ph	.000	2	2	0	0	0	0	0	0	0	1	0
Jim Rooker, p	.000	1	1	0	0	0	0	0	0	0	1	0
Manny Sanguillen, c	.167	3	12	0	2	0	0	0	0	0	0	0
Willie Stargell, 1b	.182	3	11	1	2	1	0	0	0	1	3	0
Rennie Stennett, 2b-3, ss-1	.214	3	14	0	3	0	0	0	0	0	1	0
Frank Taveras, ss	.143	3	7	0	1	0	0	0	1	1	2	0
Kent Tekulve, p	.000	2	0	0	0	0	0	0	0	0	0	0
Richie Zisk, of	.500	3	10	0	5	1	0	0	0	2	2	0
TOTAL	.198		101	7	20	3	0	1	7	10	18	0

PITCHER	W	L	ERA	G	GS	CG	SV	SHO	IP	H	ER	BB	SO
Ken Brett	0	0	0.00	2	0	0	0	0	2.1	1	0	0	1
John Candelaria	0	0	3.52	1	1	0	0	0	7.2	3	3	2	14
Larry Demery	0	0	18.00	1	0	0	0	0	2.0	4	4	1	1
Dock Ellis	0	0	0.00	1	0	0	0	0	2.0	2	0	0	2
Dave Giusti	0	0	0.00	1	0	0	0	0	1.1	0	0	0	1
Ramon Hernandez	0	1	27.00	1	0	0	0	0	0.2	3	2	0	0
Bruce Kison	0	0	4.50	1	0	0	0	0	2.0	2	1	1	1
Jerry Reuss	0	1	13.50	1	1	0	0	0	2.2	4	4	4	1
Jim Rooker	0	1	9.00	1	1	0	0	0	4.0	7	4	0	5
Kent Tekulve	0	0	6.75	2	0	0	0	0	1.1	3	1	1	2
TOTAL	0	3	6.58	12	3	0	0	0	26.0	29	19	9	28

GAME 1 AT CIN OCT 4

```
PIT  020 000 001   3  8 0
CIN  013 040 00X   8 11 0
```
Pitchers: REUSS, Brett (3), Demery (5), Ellis (7) vs GULLETT
Home Runs: Gullett-CIN
Attendance: 54,633

GAME 2 AT CIN OCT 5

```
PIT  000 100 000   1  5 0
CIN  200 201 10X   6 12 1
```
Pitchers: ROOKER, Tekulve (5), Brett (6), Kison (7) vs NORMAN, Eastwick (7)
Home Runs: Perez-CIN
Attendance: 54,752

GAME 3 AT PIT OCT 7

```
CIN  010 000 0202   5 6 0
PIT  000 002 0010   3 7 2
```
Pitchers: Nolan, C.Carroll (7), McEnaney (8), EASTWICK (9), Borbon (10) vs Candelaria, Giusti (8), HERNANDEZ (10), Tekulve (10)
Home Runs: Concepcion-CIN, Oliver-PIT, Rose-CIN
Attendance: 46,355

BOSTON RED SOX (EAST) 3, OAKLAND A'S (WEST) 0

The Oakland A's ran their domination of the American League West to five years, but an aroused Boston team stifled their try for a fourth straight pennant.

In the first game Luis Tiant held Oakland to three hits as his teammates—aided by four Oakland errors—scored seven times before giving the A's an unearned run in the eighth. Oakland scored first in Game 2 on Reggie Jackson's two-run homer in the first inning and added a run in the fourth. But Carl Yastrzemski's two-run shot in the last of the fourth, followed by a Carlton Fisk double and a Fred Lynn single, drove out A's starter Vida Blue, and the tying run scored on a double play. Single Boston runs in the sixth, seventh, and eighth put the game away.

The A's started Ken Holtzman for the second time in Game 3, after only two days of rest. He held the Sox scoreless for three innings, but was driven from the game in the fifth. Boston scored four times before Oakland put a run on the board, and retained the lead to the game's conclusion.

BOS (E)

PLAYER/POS	AVG	G	AB	R	H	2B	3B	HR	RB	BB	SO	SB
Juan Beniquez, dh	.250	3	12	2	3	0	0	0	1	0	1	2
Rick Burleson, ss	.444	3	9	2	4	2	0	0	1	1	0	0
Reggie Cleveland, p	.000	1	0	0	0	0	0	0	0	0	0	0
Cecil Cooper, 1b	.400	3	10	0	4	2	0	0	1	0	2	0
Denny Doyle, 2b	.273	3	11	3	3	0	0	0	1	0	1	0
Dick Drago, p	.000	2	0	0	0	0	0	0	0	0	0	0
Dwight Evans, of	.100	3	10	1	1	1	0	0	1	1	2	0
Carlton Fisk, c	.417	3	12	4	5	1	0	0	2	0	2	1
Fred Lynn, of	.364	3	11	1	4	1	0	0	3	0	0	0
Roger Moret, p	.000	1	0	0	0	0	0	0	0	0	0	0
Rico Petrocelli, 3b	.167	3	12	1	2	0	0	1	2	0	3	0
Luis Tiant, p	.000	1	0	0	0	0	0	0	0	0	0	0
Rick Wise, p	.000	1	0	0	0	0	0	0	0	0	0	0
Carl Yastrzemski, of	.455	3	11	4	5	1	0	1	2	1	1	0
TOTAL	.316		98	18	31	8	0	2	14	3	12	3

PITCHER	W	L	ERA	G	GS	CG	SV	SHO	IP	H	ER	BB	SO
Reggie Cleveland	0	0	5.40	1	1	0	0	0	5.0	7	3	1	2
Dick Drago	0	0	0.00	2	0	0	2	0	4.2	2	0	1	2
Roger Moret	1	0	0.00	1	0	0	0	0	1.0	1	0	1	0
Luis Tiant	1	0	0.00	1	1	1	0	0	9.0	3	0	3	8
Rick Wise	1	0	2.45	1	1	0	0	0	7.1	6	2	3	2
TOTAL	3	0	1.67	6	3	1	2	0	27.0	19	5	9	14

OAK (W)

PLAYER/POS	AVG	G	AB	R	H	2B	3B	HR	RB	BB	SO	SB
Glenn Abbott, p	.000	1	0	0	0	0	0	0	0	0	0	0
Sal Bando, 3b	.500	3	12	1	6	2	0	0	2	0	3	0
Vida Blue, p	.000	1	0	0	0	0	0	0	0	0	0	0
Dick Bosman, p	.000	1	0	0	0	0	0	0	0	0	0	0
Bert Campaneris, ss	.000	3	11	1	0	0	0	0	0	1	1	0
Rollie Fingers, p	.000	1	0	0	0	0	0	0	0	0	0	0
Ray Fosse, c	.000	1	2	0	0	0	0	0	0	0	1	0
Phil Garner, 2b	.000	3	5	0	0	0	0	0	0	0	1	0
Tommy Harper, ph	.000	1	0	0	0	0	0	0	0	1	0	0
Jim Holt, 1b-1	.333	3	3	0	1	1	0	0	0	0	0	0
Ken Holtzman, p	.000	2	0	0	0	0	0	0	0	0	0	0
Don Hopkins, dh	.000	1	0	0	0	0	0	0	0	0	0	0
Reggie Jackson, of	.417	3	12	1	5	0	0	1	3	0	2	0
Paul Lindblad, p	.000	2	0	0	0	0	0	0	0	0	0	0
Ted Martinez, 2b	.000	3	0	0	0	0	0	0	0	0	0	0
Billy North, of	.000	3	10	0	0	0	0	0	1	2	0	0
Joe Rudi, 1b-2, of-1	.250	3	12	1	3	2	0	0	0	0	1	0
Gene Tenace, c-3,1b-1	.000	3	9	0	0	0	0	0	0	3	2	0
Jim Todd, p	.000	3	0	0	0	0	0	0	0	0	0	0
Cesar Tovar, 2b-1	.500	2	2	2	1	0	0	0	0	1	0	0
Claudell Washington, of-2, dh-1	.250	3	12	1	3	1	0	0	1	0	2	0
Billy Williams, dh-2	.000	3	8	0	0	0	0	0	0	1	1	0
TOTAL	.194		98	7	19	6	0	1	7	9	14	0

PITCHER	W	L	ERA	G	GS	CG	SV	SHO	IP	H	ER	BB	SO
Glenn Abbott	0	0	0.00	1	0	0	0	0	1.0	0	0	0	0
Vida Blue	0	0	9.00	1	1	0	0	0	3.0	6	3	0	2
Dick Bosman	0	0	0.00	1	0	0	0	0	0.1	0	0	0	0
Rollie Fingers	0	1	6.75	1	0	0	0	0	4.0	5	3	1	3
Ken Holtzman	0	2	4.09	2	2	0	0	0	11.0	12	5	1	7
Paul Lindblad	0	0	0.00	2	0	0	0	0	4.2	5	0	1	0
Jim Todd	0	0	9.00	3	0	0	0	0	1.0	3	1	0	0
TOTAL	0	3	4.32	11	3	0	0	0	25.0	31	12	3	12

GAME 1 AT BOS OCT 4

OAK 000 000 010   1 3 4
BOS 200 000 50X   7 8 3
Pitchers: HOLTZMAN, Todd (7), Lindblad (7), Bosman (7), Abbott (8) vs TIANT
Attendance: 35,578

GAME 2 AT BOS OCT 5

OAK 200 100 000   3 10 0
BOS 000 301 11X   6 12 0
Pitchers: Blue, Todd (4), FINGERS (5) vs Cleveland, MORET (6), Drago (7)
Home Runs: Jackson-OAK, Yastrzemski-BOS, Petrocelli-BOS
Attendance: 35,578

GAME 3 AT OAK OCT 7

BOS 000 130 010   5 11 1
OAK 000 001 020   3 6 2
Pitchers: WISE, Drago (8) vs HOLTZMAN, Todd (5), Lindblad (5)
Attendance: 49,358

CINCINNATI REDS (NL) 4, BOSTON RED SOX (AL) 3

The Red Sox entered the Series as underdogs to the mighty Reds, who had won 108 regular-season games. In the opening game, though, the Reds were surprised by veteran Sox starter Luis Tiant, who shut them out on five hits with the Series' first complete game in four years.

Boston took a 2–1 lead into the ninth inning of Game 2 before Johnny Bench doubled to drive out starter Bill Lee, and Dave Concepcion and Ken Griffey drove in runs off reliever Dick Drago to turn the tide for Cincinnati. The Reds moved ahead in the Series with a 10-inning victory in Game 3, a slugfest in which each club hit three home runs and used five pitchers. Boston tied the score on Dwight Evans's two-run homer in the ninth, but in the last of the 10th, the Reds' Joe Morgan drove one over the center fielder's head with the bases full to end the game.

Tiant pitched Game 4 for Boston. Four of the nine hits against him went for extra bases, and each drove in a run. But the Sox bunched six of their 11 hits in the fourth inning for five runs—their only scoring, but enough for the win. The Reds moved nearer the title in Game 5, though, as Tony Perez homered twice for four runs in a 6–2 win for a 3–2 Series advantage.

A day of travel to Boston and three days of rain between Games 5 and 6 brought Tiant back to the mound for a third time. Rookie standout Fred Lynn gave Tiant a three-run lead with a first-inning homer, but Ken Griffey's triple and Johnny Bench's long single drove in the tying runs in the fifth. Two more runs in the seventh and Cesar Geronimo's leadoff homer in the eighth drove out Tiant, but Boston pinch hitter Bernie Carbo homered to center in the last of the eighth for three runs that tied the score again. After a trio of Boston relievers had held Cincinnati in check through the top of the 12th inning, the Sox leadoff hitter in the last of the 12th, Carlton Fisk, ended the game dramatically with a home run to left on the first pitch that came within inches of being foul.

After the pyrotechnics of Game 6 (ranked by some as the greatest World Series game ever), the seventh game, close as it was, came as an anticlimax. Boston scored three runs in the third, but the Reds began their comeback with Tony Perez's two-run homer in the sixth, tied the game an inning later, and took a 4–3 lead on Morgan's bloop RBI single in the ninth. Reliever Will McEnaney set the Sox down in order in the last of the ninth, and the Reds went home with their first title in 35 years.

CIN (N)

PLAYER/POS	AVG	G	AB	R	H	2B	3B	HR	RB	BB	SO	SB
Ed Armbrister, ph	.000	4	1	1	0	0	0	0	0	2	0	0
Johnny Bench, c	.207	7	29	5	6	2	0	1	4	2	4	0
Jack Billingham, p	.000	3	2	0	0	0	0	0	0	0	0	0
Pedro Borbon, p	.000	3	1	0	0	0	0	0	0	0	0	0
Clay Carroll, p	.000	5	0	0	0	0	0	0	0	0	0	0
Darrel Chaney, ph	.000	2	2	0	0	0	0	0	0	0	1	0
Dave Concepcion, ss	.179	7	28	3	5	1	0	1	4	0	1	3
Terry Crowley, ph	.500	2	2	0	1	0	0	0	0	0	1	0
Pat Darcy, p	.000	2	1	0	0	0	0	0	0	0	1	0
Dan Driessen, ph	.000	2	2	0	0	0	0	0	0	0	0	0
Rawly Eastwick, p	.000	5	1	0	0	0	0	0	0	0	0	0
George Foster, of	.276	7	29	1	8	1	0	0	2	1	1	0
Cesar Geronimo, of	.280	7	25	3	7	0	1	2	3	3	5	0
Ken Griffey, of	.269	7	26	4	7	3	1	0	4	4	2	0
Don Gullett, p	.286	3	7	1	2	0	0	0	0	0	2	0
Will McEnaney, p	1.000	5	1	0	1	0	0	0	0	0	0	0
Joe Morgan, 2b	.259	7	27	4	7	1	0	0	3	5	1	2
Gary Nolan, p	.000	2	1	0	0	0	0	0	0	0	0	0
Fred Norman, p	.000	2	1	0	0	0	0	0	0	0	0	0
Tony Perez, 1b	.179	7	28	4	5	0	0	3	7	3	9	1
Merv Rettenmund, ph	.000	3	3	0	0	0	0	0	0	0	1	0
Pete Rose, 3b	.370	7	27	3	10	1	1	0	2	5	1	0
TOTAL	.242		244	29	59	9	3	7	29	25	30	9

PITCHER	W	L	ERA	G	GS	CG	SV	SHO	IP	H	ER	BB	SO
Jack Billingham	0	0	1.00	3	1	0	0	0	9.0	8	1	5	7
Pedro Borbon	0	0	6.00	3	0	0	0	0	3.0	3	2	2	1
Clay Carroll	1	0	3.18	5	0	0	0	0	5.2	4	2	2	3
Pat Darcy	0	1	4.50	2	0	0	0	0	4.0	3	2	2	1
Rawly Eastwick	2	0	2.25	5	0	0	1	0	8.0	6	2	3	4
Don Gullett	1	1	4.34	3	3	0	0	0	18.2	19	9	10	15
Will McEnaney	0	0	2.70	5	0	0	1	0	6.2	3	2	2	5
Gary Nolan	0	0	6.00	2	2	0	0	0	6.0	6	4	1	2
Fred Norman	0	1	9.00	2	1	0	0	0	4.0	8	4	3	2
TOTAL	4	3	3.88	30	7	0	2	0	65.0	60	28	30	40

BOS (A)

PLAYER/POS	AVG	G	AB	R	H	2B	3B	HR	RB	BB	SO	SB
Juan Beniquez, of-2	.125	3	8	0	1	0	0	0	1	1	1	0
Rick Burleson, ss	.292	7	24	1	7	1	0	0	2	4	2	0
Jim Burton, p	.000	2	0	0	0	0	0	0	0	0	0	0
Bernie Carbo, of-2	.429	4	7	3	3	1	0	2	4	1	1	0
Reggie Cleveland, p	.000	3	2	0	0	0	0	0	0	0	0	0
Cecil Cooper, 1b	.053	5	19	0	1	1	0	0	1	0	3	0
Denny Doyle, 2b	.267	7	30	3	8	1	1	0	0	2	1	0
Dick Drago, p	.000	2	0	0	0	0	0	0	0	0	0	0
Dwight Evans, of	.292	7	24	3	7	1	1	1	5	3	4	0
Carlton Fisk, c	.240	7	25	5	6	0	0	2	4	7	7	0
Doug Griffin, ph	.000	1	1	0	0	0	0	0	0	0	0	0
Bill Lee, p	.167	2	6	0	1	0	0	0	0	0	3	0
Fred Lynn, of	.280	7	25	3	7	1	0	1	5	3	5	0
Rick Miller, of-2	.000	3	2	0	0	0	0	0	0	0	0	0
Bob Montgomery, ph	.000	1	1	0	0	0	0	0	0	0	0	0
Roger Moret, p	.000	3	0	0	0	0	0	0	0	0	0	0
Rico Petrocelli, 3b	.308	7	26	3	8	1	0	0	4	3	6	0
Dick Pole, p	.000	1	0	0	0	0	0	0	0	0	0	0
Diego Segui, p	.000	1	0	0	0	0	0	0	0	0	0	0
Luis Tiant, p	.250	3	8	2	2	0	0	0	0	2	4	0
Jim Willoughby, p	.000	3	0	0	0	0	0	0	0	0	0	0
Rick Wise, p	.000	2	2	0	0	0	0	0	0	0	0	0
Carl Yastrzemski, 1b-4, of-4	.310	7	29	7	9	0	0	0	4	4	1	0
TOTAL	.251		239	30	60	7	2	6	30	30	40	0

PITCHER	W	L	ERA	G	GS	CG	SV	SHO	IP	H	ER	BB	SO
Jim Burton	0	1	9.00	2	0	0	0	0	1.0	1	1	3	0
Reggie Cleveland	0	1	6.75	3	1	0	0	0	6.2	7	5	3	5
Dick Drago	0	1	2.25	2	0	0	0	0	4.0	3	1	1	1
Bill Lee	0	0	3.14	2	2	0	0	0	14.1	12	5	3	7
Roger Moret	0	0	0.00	3	0	0	0	0	1.2	2	0	3	1
Dick Pole	0	0	INF	1	0	0	0	0	0.0	0	1	2	0
Diego Segui	0	0	0.00	1	0	0	0	0	1.0	0	0	0	0
Luis Tiant	2	0	3.60	3	3	2	0	1	25.0	25	10	8	12
Jim Willoughby	0	1	0.00	3	0	0	0	0	6.1	3	0	0	2
Rick Wise	1	0	8.44	2	1	0	0	0	5.1	6	5	2	2
TOTAL	3	4	3.86	22	7	2	0	1	65.1	59	28	25	30

GAME 1 AT BOS OCT 11

CIN	000	000	000	0	5	0
BOS	000	000	60X	6	12	0

Pitchers: GULLETT, Carroll (7), McEnaney (7) vs TIANT
Attendance: 35,205

GAME 2 AT BOS OCT 12

CIN	000	100	002	3	7	1
BOS	100	001	000	2	7	0

Pitchers: Billingham, Borbon (6), McEnaney (7), EASTWICK (8) vs Lee, DRAGO (9)
Attendance: 35,205

GAME 3 AT CIN OCT 14

BOS	010	001	1020	5	10	2
CIN	000	230	0001	6	7	0

Pitchers: Wise, Burton (5), Cleveland (5), WILLOUGHBY (7), Moret (10) vs Nolan, Darcy (5), Carroll (7), McEnaney (7), EASTWICK (9)
Home Runs: Fisk-BOS, Bench-CIN, Concepcion-CIN, Geronimo-CIN, Carbo-BOS, Evans-BOS
Attendance: 55,392

GAME 4 AT CIN OCT 15

BOS	000	500	000	5	11	1
CIN	200	200	000	4	9	1

Pitchers: TIANT vs NORMAN, Borbon (4), Carroll (5), Eastwick (7)
Attendance: 55,667

GAME 5 AT CIN OCT 16

BOS	100	000	001	2	5	0
CIN	000	110	01X	6	8	0

Pitchers: CLEVELAND, Willoughby (6), Pole (8), Segui (8) vs GULLETT, Eastwick (9)
Home Runs: Perez-CIN (2)
Attendance: 56,393

GAME 6 AT BOS OCT 21

CIN	000	030	210 000	6	14	0
BOS	300	000	030 001	7	10	1

Pitchers: Nolan, Norman (3), Billingham (3), Carroll (5), Borbon (6), Eastwick (8), McEnaney (9), DARCY (10) vs Tiant, Moret (8), Drago (9), WISE (12)
Home Runs: Lynn-BOS, Geronimo-CIN, Carbo-BOS, Fisk-BOS
Attendance: 35,205

GAME 7 AT BOS OCT 22

CIN	000	002	101	4	9	0
BOS	003	000	000	3	5	2

Pitchers: Gullett, Billingham (5), CARROLL (7), McEnaney (9) vs Lee, Moret (7), Willoughby (7), BURTON (9), Cleveland (9)
Home Runs: Perez-CIN
Attendance: 35,205

CINCINNATI REDS (WEST) 3, PHILADELPHIA PHILLIES (EAST) 0

Philadelphia outhit Cincinnati in two of the three games, but couldn't turn enough hits into runs, as the Reds for the second year in a row swept the NLCS. The Phillies scored first in Game 1 with a run in the first inning. But pitcher Don Gullett held them scoreless for the next seven innings as his Reds caught up in the third, moved ahead in the sixth, and took a five-run lead into the last of the ninth. The Phillies scored twice in their half of the inning, but the rally fell short.

In the second game the Phillies outhit the Reds (10–6), scoring the game's first two runs while their starter Jim Lonborg threw a no-hitter for five innings. But in the sixth a walk and two singles drove Lonborg out and set the Reds off on a two-inning six-run spree for their second win.

Again in Game 3 the Phillies outhit the Reds, this time going into the last of the ninth ahead by two runs. But George Foster and Johnny Bench hit back-to-back homers off Ron Reed to tie the score, and two relievers (and a single and two walks) later, the Reds brought home another pennant as Ken Griffey's high-bouncing chop glanced off first baseman Bobby Tolan's outstretched glove.

CIN (W)

PLAYER/POS	AVG	G	AB	R	H	2B	3B	HR	RB	BB	SO	SB
Ed Armbrister, ph	.000	1	0	0	0	0	0	0	0	0	0	0
Johnny Bench, c	.333	3	12	3	4	1	0	1	1	1	2	1
Pedro Borbon, p	.000	2	2	1	0	0	0	0	0	0	2	0
Dave Concepcion, ss	.200	3	10	4	2	1	0	0	0	2	1	0
Dan Driessen, ph	.000	1	1	0	0	0	0	0	0	0	0	0
Rawly Eastwick, p	.000	2	0	0	0	0	0	0	0	0	0	0
Doug Flynn, 2b	.000	1	0	0	0	0	0	0	0	0	0	0
George Foster, of	.167	3	12	2	2	0	0	2	4	0	4	0
Cesar Geronimo, of	.182	3	11	0	2	0	1	0	2	1	3	0
Ken Griffey, of	.385	3	13	2	5	0	1	0	2	2	1	2
Don Gullett, p	.500	1	4	1	2	1	0	0	3	0	0	0
Mike Lum, ph	.000	1	1	0	0	0	0	0	0	0	0	0
Joe Morgan, 2b	.000	3	7	2	0	0	0	0	0	6	1	2
Gary Nolan, p	.000	1	0	0	0	0	0	0	0	1	0	0
Tony Perez, 1b	.200	3	10	1	2	0	0	0	3	1	2	0
Pete Rose, 3b	.429	3	14	3	6	2	1	0	2	1	0	0
Manny Sarmiento, p	.000	1	1	0	0	0	0	0	0	0	0	0
Pat Zachry, p	.000	1	1	0	0	0	0	0	0	0	0	0
TOTAL	.253		99	19	25	5	3	3	17	15	16	5

PITCHER	W	L	ERA	G	GS	CG	SV	SHO	IP	H	ER	BB	SO
Pedro Borbon	0	0	0.00	2	0	0	1	0	4.1	4	0	1	0
Rawly Eastwick	1	0	12.00	2	0	0	0	0	3.0	7	4	2	1
Don Gullett	1	0	1.13	1	1	0	0	0	8.0	2	1	3	4
Gary Nolan	0	0	1.59	1	1	0	0	0	5.2	6	1	2	1
Manny Sarmiento	0	0	18.00	1	0	0	0	0	1.0	2	2	1	0
Pat Zachry	1	0	3.60	1	1	0	0	0	5.0	6	2	3	3
TOTAL	3	0	3.33	8	3	0	1	0	27.0	27	10	12	9

PHI (E)

PLAYER/POS	AVG	G	AB	R	H	2B	3B	HR	RB	BB	SO	SB
Richie Allen, 1b	.222	3	9	1	2	0	0	0	0	3	2	0
Bob Boone, c	.286	3	7	0	2	0	0	0	1	1	0	0
Larry Bowa, ss	.125	3	8	1	1	1	0	0	1	3	0	0
Ollie Brown, of	.000	1	2	0	0	0	0	0	0	1	1	0
Steve Carlton, p	.000	1	2	0	0	0	0	0	0	0	0	0
Dave Cash, 2b	.308	3	13	1	4	1	0	0	1	0	0	0
Gene Garber, p	.000	2	0	0	0	0	0	0	0	0	0	0
Terry Harmon, pr	.000	1	0	1	0	0	0	0	0	0	0	0
Tom Hutton, ph	.000	1	1	0	0	0	0	0	0	0	0	0
Jay Johnstone, of-2	.778	3	9	1	7	1	1	0	2	1	0	0
Jim Kaat, p	.500	1	2	0	1	0	0	0	0	0	0	0
Jim Lonborg, p	.000	1	1	0	0	0	0	0	0	0	0	0
Greg Luzinski, of	.273	3	11	2	3	2	0	1	3	1	4	0
Garry Maddox, of	.231	3	13	2	3	1	0	0	1	1	0	0
Jerry Martin, of	.000	1	1	1	0	0	0	0	0	0	0	0
Tim McCarver, c-1	.000	2	4	0	0	0	0	0	0	0	1	0
Tug McGraw, p	.000	2	0	0	0	0	0	0	0	0	0	0
Johnny Oates, c	.000	1	1	0	0	0	0	0	0	0	0	0
Ron Reed, p	.000	2	1	0	0	0	0	0	0	0	0	0
Mike Schmidt, 3b	.308	3	13	1	4	2	0	0	2	0	1	0
Bobby Tolan, 1b-1, of-1	.000	3	2	0	0	0	0	0	0	1	0	0
Tom Underwood, p	.000	1	0	0	0	0	0	0	0	0	0	0
TOTAL	.270		100	11	27	8	1	1	11	12	9	0

PITCHER	W	L	ERA	G	GS	CG	SV	SHO	IP	H	ER	BB	SO
Steve Carlton	0	1	5.14	1	1	0	0	0	7.0	8	4	5	6
Gene Garber	0	1	13.50	2	0	0	0	0	0.2	2	1	1	0
Jim Kaat	0	0	3.00	1	1	0	0	0	6.0	2	2	2	1
Jim Lonborg	0	1	1.69	1	1	0	0	0	5.1	2	1	2	2
Tug McGraw	0	0	11.57	2	0	0	0	0	2.1	4	3	1	5
Ron Reed	0	0	7.71	2	0	0	0	0	4.2	6	4	2	2
Tom Underwood	0	0	0.00	1	0	0	0	0	0.1	1	0	2	0
TOTAL	0	3	5.13	10	3	0	0	0	26.1	25	15	15	16

GAME 1 AT PHI OCT 9

CIN 0 0 1 0 0 2 0 3 0   6 10 0
PHI 1 0 0 0 0 0 0 0 2   3 6 1
Pitchers: GULLETT, Eastwick (9) vs CARLTON, McGraw (8)
Home Runs: Foster-CIN
Attendance: 62,640

GAME 2 AT PHI OCT 10

CIN 0 0 0 0 0 4 2 0 0   6 6 0
PHI 0 1 0 0 1 0 0 0 0   2 10 1
Pitchers: ZACHRY, Borbon (6) vs LONBORG, Garber (6), McGraw (7), Reed (7)
Home Runs: Luzinski-PHI
Attendance: 62,651

GAME 3 AT CIN OCT 12

PHI 0 0 0 1 0 0 2 2 1   6 11 0
CIN 0 0 0 0 0 0 4 0 3   7 9 2
Pitchers: Kaat, Reed (7), GARBER (9), Underwood (9) vs Nolan, Sarmiento (6), Borbon (7), EASTWICK (8)
Home Runs: Foster-CIN, Bench-CIN
Attendance: 55,047

NEW YORK YANKEES (EAST) 3, KANSAS CITY ROYALS (WEST) 2

Returning to postseason play after a dozen years' absence, the Yankees found themselves evenly matched with the first-time-champion Royals. They didn't really need their two ninth-inning runs in the first game: the two they scored in the first inning proved cushion enough for Catfish Hunter's five-hitter. But Kansas City came back the next day, scoring first, losing the lead in the third, then regaining it for good in the sixth to gain a split in Kansas City.

The Royals again took a first-inning lead in Game 3, but this time the Yankees, once they went ahead in the sixth, didn't let go. Kansas City held on to its early lead in Game 4, building on it throughout the game for a second win, despite Graig Nettles' two home runs for New York.

But Game 5—like the series itself—was a seesaw affair. For the fourth time the Royals scored first, with a pair in the first on John Mayberry's home run. But the Yankees tied the game when they came to bat, and K.C. retook the lead in the second. New York went ahead again in the third and increased its lead to 6–3 in the sixth. But in the top of the eighth, George Brett's three-run homer tied the score once again, setting the stage for Chris Chambliss to win the 30th American League pennant for the Yankees with his first-pitch home run in the bottom of the ninth

NY (E)

PLAYER/POS	AVG	G	AB	R	H	2B	3B	HR	RB	BB	SO	SB
Sandy Alomar, dh-1	.000	2	1	0	0	0	0	0	0	0	0	0
Chris Chambliss, 1b	.524	5	21	5	11	1	1	2	8	0	1	2
Dock Ellis, p	.000	1	0	0	0	0	0	0	0	0	0	0
Ed Figueroa, p	.000	2	0	0	0	0	0	0	0	0	0	0
Oscar Gamble, of	.250	3	8	1	2	1	0	0	1	1	1	0
Ron Guidry, p	.000	1	0	0	0	0	0	0	0	0	0	0
Elrod Hendricks, ph	1.000	1	1	0	1	0	0	0	0	0	0	0
Catfish Hunter, p	.000	2	0	0	0	0	0	0	0	0	0	0
Grant Jackson, p	.000	2	0	0	0	0	0	0	0	0	0	0
Sparky Lyle, p	.000	1	0	0	0	0	0	0	0	0	0	0
Elliott Maddox, of	.222	3	9	0	2	1	0	0	1	0	1	0
Jim Mason, ss	.000	2	0	0	0	0	0	0	0	0	0	0
Carlos May, dh	.200	3	10	1	2	1	0	0	0	1	4	0
Thurman Munson, c	.435	5	23	3	10	2	0	0	3	0	1	0
Graig Nettles, 3b	.235	5	17	2	4	1	0	2	4	3	3	0
Lou Piniella, dh-3	.273	4	11	1	3	1	0	0	0	0	1	0
Willie Randolph, 2b	.118	5	17	0	2	0	0	0	1	3	1	1
Mickey Rivers, of	.348	5	23	5	8	0	1	0	0	1	1	0
Fred Stanley, ss	.333	5	15	1	5	2	0	0	0	2	0	0
Dick Tidrow, p	.000	3	0	0	0	0	0	0	0	0	0	0
Otto Velez, ph	.000	1	1	0	0	0	0	0	0	0	0	0
Roy White, of	.294	5	17	4	5	3	0	0	3	5	1	1
TOTAL	.316		174	23	55	13	2	4	21	16	15	4

PITCHER	W	L	ERA	G	GS	CG	SV	SHO	IP	H	ER	BB	SO
Dock Ellis	1	0	3.38	1	1	0	0	0	8.0	6	3	2	5
Ed Figueroa	0	1	5.84	2	2	0	0	0	12.1	14	8	2	5
Catfish Hunter	1	1	4.50	2	2	1	0	0	12.0	10	6	1	5
Grant Jackson	0	0	8.10	2	0	0	0	0	3.1	4	3	1	3
Sparky Lyle	0	0	0.00	1	0	0	1	0	1.0	0	0	1	0
Dick Tidrow	1	0	3.68	3	0	0	0	0	7.1	6	3	4	0
TOTAL	3	2	4.70	11	5	1	1	0	44.0	40	23	11	18

KC (W)

PLAYER/POS	AVG	G	AB	R	H	2B	3B	HR	RB	BB	SO	SB
Doug Bird, p	.000	1	0	0	0	0	0	0	0	0	0	0
George Brett, 3b	.444	5	18	4	8	1	1	1	5	2	1	0
Al Cowens, of	.190	5	21	3	4	0	1	0	0	1	1	2
Larry Gura, p	.000	2	0	0	0	0	0	0	0	0	0	0
Tom Hall, p	.000	1	0	0	0	0	0	0	0	0	0	0
Andy Hassler, p	.000	2	0	0	0	0	0	0	0	0	0	0
Dennis Leonard, p	.000	2	0	0	0	0	0	0	0	0	0	0
Mark Littell, p	.000	3	0	0	0	0	0	0	0	0	0	0
Buck Martinez, c	.333	5	15	0	5	0	0	0	4	1	3	0
John Mayberry, 1b	.222	5	18	4	4	0	0	1	3	1	0	0
Hal McRae, dh-3, of-2	.118	5	17	2	2	1	1	0	1	1	4	0
Steve Mingori, p	.000	3	0	0	0	0	0	0	0	0	0	0
Dave Nelson, dh-1	.000	2	2	0	0	0	0	0	0	0	1	0
Amos Otis, of	.000	1	1	0	0	0	0	0	0	0	0	0
Freddie Patek, ss	.389	5	18	2	7	2	0	0	4	0	1	0
Marty Pattin, p	.000	2	0	0	0	0	0	0	0	0	0	0
Tom Poquette, of	.188	5	16	1	3	2	0	0	4	2	3	0
Jamie Quirk, dh-2	.143	4	7	1	1	0	1	0	2	0	2	0
Cookie Rojas, 2b	.333	4	9	2	3	0	0	0	1	0	0	1
Paul Splittorff, p	.000	2	0	0	0	0	0	0	0	0	0	0
Bob Stinson, c-1	.000	2	1	0	0	0	0	0	0	0	0	0
John Wathan, c	.000	1	0	0	0	0	0	0	0	0	0	0
Frank White, 2b	.125	4	8	2	1	0	0	0	0	0	1	0
Jim Wohlford, of	.182	5	11	3	2	0	0	0	0	3	1	2
TOTAL	.247		162	24	40	6	4	2	24	11	18	5

PITCHER	W	L	ERA	G	GS	CG	SV	SHO	IP	H	ER	BB	SO
Doug Bird	1	0	1.93	1	0	0	0	0	4.2	4	1	0	1
Larry Gura	0	1	4.22	2	2	0	0	0	10.2	18	5	1	4
Tom Hall	0	0	0.00	1	0	0	0	0	0.1	1	0	0	0
Andy Hassler	0	1	6.14	2	1	0	0	0	7.1	8	5	6	4
Dennis Leonard	0	0	19.29	2	2	0	0	0	2.1	9	5	2	0
Mark Littell	0	1	1.93	3	0	0	0	0	4.2	4	1	1	3
Steve Mingori	0	0	2.70	3	0	0	1	0	3.1	4	1	0	1
Marty Pattin	0	0	27.00	2	0	0	0	0	0.1	0	1	1	0
Paul Splittorff	1	0	1.93	2	0	0	0	0	9.1	7	2	5	2
TOTAL	2	3	4.40	18	5	0	1	0	43.0	55	21	16	15

GAME 1 AT KC OCT 9

NY	200 000 002	4	12	0
KC	000 000 010	1	5	2

Pitchers: HUNTER vs GURA, Littell (9)
Attendance: 41,077

GAME 2 AT KC OCT 10

NY	012 000 000	3	12	5
KC	200 002 03X	7	9	0

Pitchers: FIGUEROA, Tidrow (6) vs Leonard, SPLITTORFF (3), Mingori (9)
Attendance: 41,091

GAME 3 AT NY OCT 12

KC	300 000 000	3	6	0
NY	000 204 00X	5	8	0

Pitchers: HASSLER, Pattin (6), Hall (6), Mingori (6), Littell (6) vs ELLIS, Lyle (9)
Home Runs: Chambliss-NY
Attendance: 56,808

GAME 4 AT NY OCT 13

KC	030 201 010	7	9	1
NY	020 000 101	4	11	0

Pitchers: Gura, BIRD (3), Mingori (7) vs HUNTER, Tidrow (4), Jackson (7)
Home Runs: Nettles-NY (2)
Attendance: 56,355

GAME 5 AT NY OCT 14

KC	210 000 030	6	11	1
NY	202 002 001	7	11	1

Pitchers: Leonard, Splittorff (1), Pattin (4), Hassler (5), LITTELL (7) vs Figueroa, Jackson (8), TIDROW (9)
Home Runs: Mayberry-KC, Brett-KC, Chambliss-NY
Attendance: 56,821

CINCINNATI REDS (NL) 4, NEW YORK YANKEES (AL) 0

The Reds led the National League in virtually every offensive category and in fielding as well. In the Series (which, incidentally, was the first to employ the designated hitter), the Big Red Machine continued its roll over the Yankees to become the first National League club in 54 years to repeat as world champions, as well as the first team to sweep both an LCS and World Series. Reds catcher Johnny Bench led the attack with eight hits, half of them for extra bases, for a batting average of .533 and a 1.133 average in slugging.

Joe Morgan's home run for Cincinnati in the first inning of Game 1 was the first hit of the Series, but New York pushed across a tying run half an inning later on a sacrifice fly. Pitchers Don Gullett and Pedro Borbon held the Yankees scoreless after that as the Reds regained the lead with a run in the third and extended it in the sixth and seventh for a 5–1 win.

Game 2 turned out to be the Reds' only narrow victory. They scored first, with three runs in the second inning. In the fourth the Yankees scored their first run, and they tied the score with two more runs in the seventh. But with two men out in the last of the ninth, a throwing error by Yankee shortstop Fred Stanley allowed Ken Griffey to reach second. Griffey then scored the winning run on Tony Perez's line single to left.

In Game 3, four hits and a pair of stolen bases put Cincinnati ahead 3–0 in the second inning, and Dan Driessen homered in the fourth to make it 4–0 before the Yankees scored their first run. Another quartet of hits in the eighth gave the Reds two more runs and a 6–2 win.

New York took the lead for the only time in the Series when Chris Chambliss doubled in Thurman Munson in the first inning of Game 4. (Munson had singled with the third of what became six straight hits.) But the Reds' George Foster drove in a tying run in the fourth, and Johnny Bench followed him with a two-run homer. New York scored again an inning later to come close, but Bench's second home run, a three-run blast in the ninth, put the game out of reach, and a pair of ground-rule doubles touched by New York fans put a lid on Cincinnati's sweep.

CIN (N)

PLAYER/POS	AVG	G	AB	R	H	2B	3B	HR	RB	BB	SO	SB
Johnny Bench, c	.533	4	15	4	8	1	1	2	6	0	1	0
Jack Billingham, p	.000	1	0	0	0	0	0	0	0	0	0	0
Pedro Borbon, p	.000	1	0	0	0	0	0	0	0	0	0	0
Dave Concepcion, ss	.357	4	14	1	5	1	1	0	3	1	3	1
Dan Driessen, dh	.357	4	14	4	5	2	0	1	1	2	0	1
George Foster, of	.429	4	14	3	6	1	0	0	4	2	3	0
Cesar Geronimo, of	.308	4	13	3	4	2	0	0	1	2	2	2
Ken Griffey, of	.059	4	17	2	1	0	0	0	1	0	1	1
Don Gullett, p	.000	1	0	0	0	0	0	0	0	0	0	0
Will McEnaney, p	.000	2	0	0	0	0	0	0	0	0	0	0
Joe Morgan, 2b	.333	4	15	3	5	1	1	1	2	2	2	2
Gary Nolan, p	.000	1	0	0	0	0	0	0	0	0	0	0
Fred Norman, p	.000	1	0	0	0	0	0	0	0	0	0	0
Tony Perez, 1b	.313	4	16	1	5	1	0	0	2	1	2	0
Pete Rose, 3b	.188	4	16	1	3	1	0	0	1	2	2	0
Pat Zachry, p	.000	1	0	0	0	0	0	0	0	0	0	0
TOTAL	.313		134	22	42	10	3	4	21	12	16	7

PITCHER	W	L	ERA	G	GS	CG	SV	SHO	IP	H	ER	BB	SO
Jack Billingham	1	0	0.00	1	0	0	0	0	2.2	0	0	0	1
Pedro Borbon	0	0	0.00	1	0	0	0	0	1.2	0	0	0	0
Don Gullett	1	0	1.23	1	1	0	0	0	7.1	5	1	3	4
Will McEnaney	0	0	0.00	2	0	0	2	0	4.2	2	0	1	2
Gary Nolan	1	0	2.70	1	1	0	0	0	6.2	8	2	1	1
Fred Norman	0	0	4.26	1	1	0	0	0	6.1	9	3	2	2
Pat Zachry	1	0	2.70	1	1	0	0	0	6.2	6	2	5	6
TOTAL	4	0	2.00	8	4	0	2	0	36.0	30	8	12	16

NY (A)

PLAYER/POS	AVG	G	AB	R	H	2B	3B	HR	RB	BB	SO	SB
Doyle Alexander, p	.000	1	0	0	0	0	0	0	0	0	0	0
Chris Chambliss, 1b	.313	4	16	1	5	1	0	0	1	0	2	0
Dock Ellis, p	.000	1	0	0	0	0	0	0	0	0	0	0
Ed Figueroa, p	.000	1	0	0	0	0	0	0	0	0	0	0
Oscar Gamble, of-2	.125	3	8	0	1	0	0	0	1	0	0	0
Elrod Hendricks, ph	.000	2	2	0	0	0	0	0	0	0	0	0
Catfish Hunter, p	.000	1	0	0	0	0	0	0	0	0	0	0
Grant Jackson, p	.000	1	0	0	0	0	0	0	0	0	0	0
Sparky Lyle, p	.000	2	0	0	0	0	0	0	0	0	0	0
Elliott Maddox, of-1, dh-1	.200	2	5	0	1	0	1	0	0	1	2	0
Jim Mason, ss	1.000	3	1	1	1	0	0	1	1	0	0	0
Carlos May, dh	.000	4	9	0	0	0	0	0	0	0	1	0
Thurman Munson, c	.529	4	17	2	9	0	0	0	2	0	1	0
Graig Nettles, 3b	.250	4	12	0	3	0	0	0	2	3	1	0
Lou Piniella, of-2, dh-2	.333	4	9	1	3	1	0	0	0	0	0	0
Willie Randolph, 2b	.071	4	14	1	1	0	0	0	0	1	3	0
Mickey Rivers, of	.167	4	18	1	3	0	0	0	0	1	2	1
Fred Stanley, ss	.167	4	6	1	1	1	0	0	1	3	1	0
Dick Tidrow, p	.000	2	0	0	0	0	0	0	0	0	0	0
Otto Velez, ph	.000	3	3	0	0	0	0	0	0	0	3	0
Roy White, of	.133	4	15	0	2	0	0	0	0	3	0	0
TOTAL	.222		135	8	30	3	1	1	8	12	16	1

PITCHER	W	L	ERA	G	GS	CG	SV	SHO	IP	H	ER	BB	SO
Doyle Alexander	0	1	7.50	1	1	0	0	0	6.0	9	5	2	1
Dock Ellis	0	1	10.80	1	1	0	0	0	3.1	7	4	0	1
Ed Figueroa	0	1	5.63	1	1	0	0	0	8.0	6	5	5	2
Catfish Hunter	0	1	3.12	1	1	1	0	0	8.2	10	3	4	5
Grant Jackson	0	0	4.91	1	0	0	0	0	3.2	4	2	0	3
Sparky Lyle	0	0	0.00	2	0	0	0	0	2.2	1	0	0	3
Dick Tidrow	0	0	7.71	2	0	0	0	0	2.1	5	2	1	1
TOTAL	0	4	5.45	9	4	1	0	0	34.2	42	21	12	16

GAME 1 AT CIN OCT 16

```
NY   0 1 0 0 0 0 0 0 0    1  5  1
CIN  1 0 1 0 0 1 2 0 X    5 10  1
```
Pitchers: ALEXANDER, Lyle (7) vs GULLETT, Borbon (8)
Home Runs: Morgan-CIN
Attendance: 54,826

GAME 2 AT CIN OCT 17

```
NY   0 0 0 1 0 0 2 0 0    3  9  1
CIN  0 3 0 0 0 0 0 0 1    4 10  0
```
Pitchers: HUNTER vs Norman, BILLINGHAM (7)
Attendance: 54,816

GAME 3 AT NY OCT 19

```
CIN  0 3 0 1 0 0 0 2 0    6 13  2
NY   0 0 0 1 0 0 1 0 0    2  8  0
```
Pitchers: ZACHRY, McEnaney (7) vs ELLIS, Jackson (4), Tidrow (8)
Home Runs: Driessen-CIN, Mason-NY
Attendance: 56,667

GAME 4 AT NY OCT 21

```
CIN  0 0 0 3 0 0 0 0 4    7  9  2
NY   1 0 0 0 1 0 0 0 0    2  8  0
```
Pitchers: NOLAN, McEnaney (7) vs FIGUEROA, Tidrow (9), Lyle (9)
Home Runs: Bench-CIN (2)
Attendance: 56,700

LOS ANGELES DODGERS (WEST) 3, PHILADELPHIA PHILLIES (EAST) 1

The Phillies took the first game, but the Dodgers proved better at turning hits into runs and swept the next three. Philadelphia jumped ahead in the first inning of Game 1, and had built a 5–1 lead by the seventh, when Ron Cey tied the score with a grand slam. But the Phillies came back with two runs on three singles in the top of the ninth and held on for the win. As in Game 1, both clubs again got nine hits apiece in Game 2, but this time Dodgers pitcher Don Sutton scattered the Phillies' hits for a single run over nine innings, while Phillies starter Jim Lonborg—in the four innings he pitched— yielded five runs, including a grand slam to Dusty Baker.

In Game 3 Los Angeles outhit the Phillies, but the Dodgers were nearly undone when starter Burt Hooton walked in three Philadelphia runs in the second inning. The Phillies took a two-run lead into the ninth, but after two men were out the Dodgers rebounded, thanks largely to a couple of old pros. Pinch hitter Vic Davalillo, age 38, beat out a drag bunt on a disputed call, and 39-year-old Manny Mota doubled to deep left. Two more singles scored three runs that proved enough for the win.

The Dodgers didn't even need all of their five hits to take the final game behind Tommy John's one-run seven-hitter, for one of those hits was another Dusty Baker home run with a man aboard

LA (W)

PLAYER/POS	AVG	G	AB	R	H	2B	3B	HR	RB	BB	SO	SB
Dusty Baker, of	.357	4	14	4	5	1	0	2	8	2	3	0
Glenn Burke, of	.000	4	7	0	0	0	0	0	0	0	3	0
Ron Cey, 3b	.308	4	13	4	4	1	0	1	4	2	4	1
Vic Davalillo, ph	1.000	1	1	1	1	0	0	0	0	0	0	0
Mike Garman, p	.000	2	0	0	0	0	0	0	0	0	0	0
Steve Garvey, 1b	.308	4	13	2	4	0	0	0	0	2	1	1
Ed Goodson, ph	.000	1	1	0	0	0	0	0	0	0	0	0
Jerry Grote, c-1	.000	2	0	0	0	0	0	0	0	1	0	0
Burt Hooton, p	1.000	1	1	0	1	1	0	0	0	0	0	0
Charlie Hough, p	.000	1	0	0	0	0	0	0	0	0	0	0
Tommy John, p	.200	2	5	0	1	0	0	0	0	0	2	0
Lee Lacy, ph	1.000	1	1	1	1	0	0	0	0	0	0	0
Davey Lopes, 2b	.235	4	17	2	4	0	0	0	3	2	0	0
Rick Monday, of	.286	3	7	1	2	1	0	0	0	2	1	0
Manny Mota, ph	1.000	1	1	1	1	1	0	0	0	0	0	0
Doug Rau, p	.000	1	0	0	0	0	0	0	0	0	0	0
Lance Rautzhan, p	.000	1	0	0	0	0	0	0	0	0	0	0
Rick Rhoden, p	.000	1	1	0	0	0	0	0	0	0	0	0
Bill Russell, ss	.278	4	18	3	5	1	0	0	2	0	0	0
Reggie Smith, of	.188	4	16	2	3	0	1	0	1	2	5	1
Elias Sosa, p	.000	2	1	0	0	0	0	0	0	0	0	0
Don Sutton, p	.000	1	3	0	0	0	0	0	0	0	0	0
Steve Yeager, c	.231	4	13	1	3	0	0	0	2	1	3	0
TOTAL	.263		133	22	35	6	1	3	20	14	22	3

PITCHER	W	L	ERA	G	GS	CG	SV	SHO	IP	H	ER	BB	SO
Mike Garman	0	0	0.00	2	0	0	1	0	1.1	0	0	0	1
Burt Hooton	0	0	16.20	1	1	0	0	0	1.2	2	3	4	1
Charlie Hough	0	0	4.50	1	0	0	0	0	2.0	2	1	0	3
Tommy John	1	0	0.66	2	2	1	0	0	13.2	11	1	5	11
Doug Rau	0	0	0.00	1	0	0	0	0	1.0	0	0	0	1
Lance Rautzhan	1	0	0.00	1	0	0	0	0	0.1	0	0	0	0
Rick Rhoden	0	0	0.00	1	0	0	0	0	4.1	2	0	2	0
Elias Sosa	0	1	10.13	2	0	0	0	0	2.2	5	3	0	0
Don Sutton	1	0	1.00	1	1	1	0	0	9.0	9	1	0	4
TOTAL	3	1	2.25	12	4	2	1	0	36.0	31	9	11	21

PHI (E)

PLAYER/POS	AVG	G	AB	R	H	2B	3B	HR	RB	BB	SO	SB
Bob Boone, c	.400	4	10	1	4	0	0	0	0	0	0	0
Larry Bowa, ss	.118	4	17	2	2	0	0	0	1	1	0	0
Ollie Brown, ph	.000	2	2	0	0	0	0	0	0	0	1	0
Warren Brusstar, p	.000	2	0	0	0	0	0	0	0	0	0	0
Steve Carlton, p	.500	2	4	0	2	0	0	0	1	0	2	0
Larry Christenson, p	.000	1	0	0	0	0	0	0	1	1	0	0
Gene Garber, p	.000	3	0	0	0	0	0	0	0	0	0	0
Richie Hebner, 1b-3	.357	4	14	2	5	2	0	0	0	0	1	0
Tom Hutton, 1b-1	.000	3	3	0	0	0	0	0	0	0	0	0
Davey Johnson, 1b	.250	1	4	0	1	0	0	0	2	0	1	0
Jay Johnstone, of	.200	2	5	0	1	0	0	0	0	0	1	0
Jim Lonborg, p	.000	1	1	0	0	0	0	0	0	0	0	0
Greg Luzinski, of	.286	4	14	2	4	1	0	1	2	3	3	1
Garry Maddox, of	.429	2	7	1	3	0	0	0	2	0	1	0
Jerry Martin, of-1	.000	3	4	0	0	0	0	0	0	0	2	0
Bake McBride, of	.222	4	18	2	4	0	0	1	2	1	2	0
Tim McCarver, c-2	.167	3	6	1	1	0	0	0	0	1	3	0
Tug McGraw, p	.000	2	0	0	0	0	0	0	0	0	0	0
Ron Reed, p	.000	3	0	0	0	0	0	0	0	0	0	0
Mike Schmidt, 3b	.063	4	16	2	1	0	0	0	1	2	3	0
Ted Sizemore, 2b	.231	4	13	1	3	0	0	0	0	2	0	0
TOTAL	.225		138	14	31	3	0	2	12	11	21	1

PITCHER	W	L	ERA	G	GS	CG	SV	SHO	IP	H	ER	BB	SO
Warren Brusstar	0	0	3.38	2	0	0	0	0	2.2	2	1	1	2
Steve Carlton	0	1	6.94	2	2	0	0	0	11.2	13	9	8	6
Larry Christenson	0	0	8.10	1	1	0	0	0	3.1	7	3	0	2
Gene Garber	1	1	3.38	3	0	0	0	0	5.1	4	2	0	3
Jim Lonborg	0	1	11.25	1	1	0	0	0	4.0	5	5	1	1
Tug McGraw	0	0	0.00	2	0	0	1	0	3.0	1	0	2	3
Ron Reed	0	0	1.80	3	0	0	0	0	5.0	3	1	2	5
TOTAL	1	3	5.40	14	4	0	1	0	35.0	35	21	14	22

GAME 1 AT LA OCT 4

```
PHI  200 021 002   7 9 0
LA   000 010 400   5 9 2
```
Pitchers: Carlton, GARBER (7), McGraw (9) vs John, Garman (5), Hough (6), SOSA (8)
Home Runs: Luzinski-PHI, Cey-LA
Attendance: 55,968

GAME 2 AT LA OCT 5

```
PHI  001 000 000   1 9 1
LA   001 401 10X   7 9 1
```
Pitchers: LONBORG, Reed (5), Brusstar (7) vs SUTTON
Home Runs: McBride-PHI, Baker-LA
Attendance: 55,973

GAME 3 AT PHI OCT 7

```
LA   020 100 003   6 12 2
PHI  030 000 020   5 6 2
```
Pitchers: Hooton, Rhoden (2), Rau (7), Sosa (8), RAUTZHAN (8), Garman (9) vs Christenson, Brusstar (4), Reed (5), GARBER (7)
Attendance: 63,719

GAME 4 AT PHI OCT 8

```
LA   020 020 000   4 5 0
PHI  000 100 000   1 7 0
```
Pitchers: JOHN vs CARLTON, Reed (6), McGraw (7), Garber (9)
Home Runs: Baker-LA
Attendance: 64,924

NEW YORK YANKEES (EAST) 3, KANSAS CITY ROYALS (WEST) 2

As in 1976 the Royals met the Yankees in the ALCS, and as in 1976 the series went five games, with the Royals outscoring New York by a single run. But this time Kansas City won the first game, and as the teams traded victories through the first four games and K.C. took a lead into the ninth inning of Game 5, it began to look as though this year the Royals might take the pennant.

Royals hitters began things with a bang, scoring six of their seven runs in Game 1 in the first three innings for an insurmountable lead. New York came back to take the second game 6–2 behind Ron Guidry's three-hitter, but the Royals reversed the score the next day as Dennis Leonard limited the Yankees to four hits. Yankees reliever Sparky Lyle shut K.C. down over the final five innings of Game 4 after the Royals had drawn within a run of New York in the fourth inning, and the series was tied.

In the finale, Kansas City drew first blood with two runs in the bottom of the first and led by one run after eight. But with the pennant in sight, the Royals gave up three runs in the top of the ninth, scoring nothing themselves as reliever Lyle held them off to give the Yankees their 31st flag.

NY (E)

PLAYER/POS	AVG	G	AB	R	H	2B	3B	HR	RB	BB	SO	SB
Paul Blair, of	.400	3	5	1	2	0	0	0	0	0	0	0
Chris Chambliss, 1b	.059	5	17	0	1	0	0	0	0	3	4	0
Bucky Dent, ss	.214	5	14	1	3	1	0	0	2	1	0	0
Ed Figueroa, p	.000	1	0	0	0	0	0	0	0	0	0	0
Ron Guidry, p	.000	2	0	0	0	0	0	0	0	0	0	0
Don Gullett, p	.000	1	0	0	0	0	0	0	0	0	0	0
Reggie Jackson, of-4, dh-1	.125	5	16	1	2	0	0	0	1	2	2	1
Cliff Johnson, dh-4	.400	5	15	2	6	2	0	1	2	1	2	0
Sparky Lyle, p	.000	4	0	0	0	0	0	0	0	0	0	0
Thurman Munson, c	.286	5	21	3	6	1	0	1	5	0	2	0
Graig Nettles, 3b	.150	5	20	1	3	0	0	0	1	0	3	0
Lou Piniella, of-4, dh-1	.333	5	21	1	7	3	0	0	2	0	1	0
Willie Randolph, 2b	.278	5	18	4	5	1	0	0	2	1	0	0
Mickey Rivers, of	.391	5	23	5	9	2	0	0	2	0	2	1
Fred Stanley, ss	.000	2	0	0	0	0	0	0	0	0	0	0
Dick Tidrow, p	.000	2	0	0	0	0	0	0	0	0	0	0
Mike Torrez, p	.000	2	0	0	0	0	0	0	0	0	0	0
Roy White, of-1, dh-1	.400	4	5	2	2	2	0	0	0	1	0	0
TOTAL	.263		175	21	46	12	0	2	17	9	16	2

PITCHER	W	L	ERA	G	GS	CG	SV	SHO	IP	H	ER	BB	SO
Ed Figueroa	0	0	10.80	1	1	0	0	0	3.1	5	4	2	3
Ron Guidry	1	0	3.97	2	2	1	0	0	11.1	9	5	3	8
Don Gullett	0	1	18.00	1	1	0	0	0	2.0	4	4	2	0
Sparky Lyle	2	0	0.96	4	0	0	0	0	9.1	7	1	0	3
Dick Tidrow	0	0	3.86	2	0	0	0	0	7.0	6	3	3	3
Mike Torrez	0	1	4.09	2	1	0	0	0	11.0	11	5	5	5
TOTAL	3	2	4.50	12	5	1	0	0	44.0	42	22	15	22

KC (W)

PLAYER/POS	AVG	G	AB	R	H	2B	3B	HR	RB	BB	SO	SB
Doug Bird, p	.000	3	0	0	0	0	0	0	0	0	0	0
George Brett, 3b	.300	5	20	2	6	0	2	0	2	1	0	0
Al Cowens, of	.263	5	19	2	5	0	0	1	5	1	3	0
Larry Gura, p	.000	2	0	0	0	0	0	0	0	0	0	0
Andy Hassler, p	.000	1	0	0	0	0	0	0	0	0	0	0
Pete LaCock, 1b	.000	1	0	0	0	0	0	0	0	1	1	0
Joe Lahoud, dh	.000	1	1	2	0	0	0	0	0	2	0	0
Dennis Leonard, p	.000	2	0	0	0	0	0	0	0	0	0	0
Mark Littell, p	.000	2	0	0	0	0	0	0	0	0	0	0
John Mayberry, 1b	.167	4	12	1	2	1	0	1	3	1	2	0
Hal McRae, dh-3, of-2	.444	5	18	6	8	3	0	1	2	3	1	0
Steve Mingori, p	.000	3	0	0	0	0	0	0	0	0	0	0
Amos Otis, of	.125	5	16	1	2	1	0	0	2	2	3	2
Freddie Patek, ss	.389	5	18	4	7	3	1	0	5	1	2	0
Marty Pattin, p	.000	1	0	0	0	0	0	0	0	0	0	0
Tom Poquette, of	.167	2	6	0	1	0	0	0	0	0	0	0
Darrell Porter, c	.333	5	15	3	5	0	0	0	0	3	0	0
Cookie Rojas, dh	.250	1	4	0	1	0	0	0	0	0	1	1
Paul Splittorff, p	.000	2	0	0	0	0	0	0	0	0	0	0
John Wathan, 1b-2, c-1, dh-1	.000	4	6	0	0	0	0	0	0	0	3	0
Frank White, 2b	.278	5	18	1	5	1	0	0	2	0	4	1
Joe Zdeb, of	.000	4	9	0	0	0	0	0	0	0	2	1
TOTAL	.258		163	22	42	9	3	3	21	15	22	5

PITCHER	W	L	ERA	G	GS	CG	SV	SHO	IP	H	ER	BB	SO
Doug Bird	0	0	0.00	3	0	0	0	0	2.0	4	0	0	1
Larry Gura	0	1	18.00	2	1	0	0	0	2.0	7	4	1	2
Andy Hassler	0	1	4.76	1	1	0	0	0	5.2	5	3	0	3
Dennis Leonard	1	1	3.00	2	1	1	0	0	9.0	5	3	2	4
Mark Littell	0	0	3.00	2	0	0	0	0	3.0	5	1	3	1
Steve Mingori	0	0	0.00	3	0	0	0	0	1.1	0	0	0	1
Marty Pattin	0	0	1.50	1	0	0	0	0	6.0	6	1	0	0
Paul Splittorff	1	0	2.40	2	2	0	0	0	15.0	14	4	3	4
TOTAL	2	3	3.27	16	5	1	0	0	44.0	46	16	9	16

GAME 1 AT NY OCT 5

```
KC   222 000 010   7 9 0
NY   002 000 000   2 9 0
```
Pitchers: SPLITTORFF, Bird (9) vs GULLETT. Tidrow (3), Lyle (9)
Home Runs: McRae-KC, Mayberry-KC, Munson-NY, Cowens-KC
Attendance: 54,930

GAME 2 AT NY OCT 6

```
KC   001 001 000   2 3 1
NY   000 023 01X   6 10 1
```
Pitchers: HASSLER, Littell (6), Mingori (8) vs GUIDRY
Home Runs: Johnson-NY
Attendance: 56,230

GAME 3 AT KC OCT 7

```
NY   000 010 001   2 4 1
KC   011 012 10X   6 12 1
```
Pitchers: TORREZ, Lyle (6) vs LEONARD
Attendance: 41,285

GAME 4 AT KC OCT 8

```
NY   121 100 001   6 13 0
KC   002 200 000   4 8 2
```
Pitchers: Figueroa, Tidrow (4), LYLE (4) vs GURA, Pattin (3), Mingori (9), Bird (9)
Attendance: 41,135

GAME 5 AT KC OCT 9

```
NY   001 000 013   5 10 0
KC   201 000 000   3 10 1
```
Pitchers: Guidry, Torrez (3), LYLE (8) vs Splittorff, Bird (8), Mingori (9), LEONARD (9), Gura (9), Littell (9)
Attendance: 41,133

NEW YORK YANKEES (AL) 4, LOS ANGELES DODGERS (NL) 2

This was the Series in which Reggie Jackson established his reputation as "Mr. October" with a record five home runs, including three in successive at bats in the final game, and the Yankees showed that after a decade or so of decline they were once again the world's best. Los Angeles scored first in the opening game with a pair of first-inning runs. But New York gained back half the ground in the bottom of the first and tied the game on Willie Randolph's leadoff homer in the sixth. The clubs traded runs in the eighth and ninth to take the game into extra innings. The impasse was not breached until the last of the 12th, when Randolph doubled and Paul Blair singled him home.

Game 2, by contrast, was a runaway Dodgers victory. Home runs in the first three innings by Ron Cey, Steve Yeager, and Reggie Smith made the score 5–0 before New York scored its lone run in the fourth. Burt Hooton got the win with a five-hitter, and for good measure, Steve Garvey homered in the ninth inning. The Yankees returned to form two days later in Los Angeles, though, scoring three runs in the top of the first on pairs of doubles and singles (and a Dodgers error). Dusty Baker's three-run homer tied the game in the third, but single runs in the next two innings provided Yankees pitcher Mike Torrez with runs enough for the win.

Two of the four hits yielded by emerging Yankees ace Ron Guidry in Game 4 were pitcher Rick Rhoden's double followed by Davey Lopes' home run in the third inning. But the Yankees had already scored three times in the second, and Reggie Jackson homered in the sixth as Guidry held Los Angeles scoreless after the third for a 4–2 win. New York's assault against pitcher Don Sutton in Game 5 included back-to-back home runs by Thurman Munson and Jackson in the eighth inning. But Los Angeles rocked Yankees pitching even harder, with homers by Steve Yeager and Reggie Smith producing five of the Dodgers' 10 runs as the club evaded elimination with its second win.

The Dodgers scored first in the sixth game when Steve Garvey's first-inning triple drove in two runners. Chris Chambliss matched

that an inning later for the Yankees with a two-run homer. Smith restored the lead to Los Angeles with a solo shot in the third inning, but Jackson put the Yankees back in front with the first of his three home runs, a two-run blast in the fourth. By the time he had homered again for two in the fifth and for the third time in the eighth, the Yankees' 21st world title was well in hand.

NY (A)

PLAYER/POS	AVG	G	AB	R	H	2B	3B	HR	RB	BB	SO	SB
Paul Blair, of-3	.250	4	4	0	1	0	0	0	1	0	0	0
Chris Chambliss, 1b	.292	6	24	4	7	2	0	1	4	0	2	0
Ken Clay, p	.000	2	0	0	0	0	0	0	0	0	0	0
Bucky Dent, ss	.263	6	19	0	5	0	0	0	2	2	1	0
Ron Guidry, p	.000	1	2	0	0	0	0	0	0	0	1	0
Don Gullett, p	.000	2	2	0	0	0	0	0	0	0	2	0
Catfish Hunter, p	.000	2	0	0	0	0	0	0	0	0	0	0
Reggie Jackson, of	.450	6	20	10	9	1	0	5	8	3	4	0
Cliff Johnson, c-1	.000	2	1	0	0	0	0	0	0	0	0	0
Sparky Lyle, p	.000	2	2	0	0	0	0	0	0	0	2	0
Thurman Munson, c	.320	6	25	4	8	2	0	1	3	2	8	0
Graig Nettles, 3b	.190	6	21	1	4	1	0	0	2	2	3	0
Lou Piniella, of	.273	6	22	1	6	0	0	0	3	0	3	0
Willie Randolph, 2b	.160	6	25	5	4	2	0	1	1	2	2	0
Mickey Rivers, of	.222	6	27	1	6	2	0	0	1	0	2	1
Fred Stanley, ss	.000	1	0	0	0	0	0	0	0	0	0	0
Dick Tidrow, p	.000	2	1	0	0	0	0	0	0	0	1	0
Mike Torrez, p	.000	2	6	0	0	0	0	0	0	0	4	0
Roy White, ph	.000	2	2	0	0	0	0	0	0	0	0	0
George Zeber, ph	.000	2	2	0	0	0	0	0	0	0	2	0
TOTAL	.244		205	26	50	10	0	8	25	11	37	1

PITCHER	W	L	ERA	G	GS	CG	SV	SHO	IP	H	ER	BB	SO
Ken Clay	0	0	2.45	2	0	0	0	0	3.2	2	1	1	0
Ron Guidry	1	0	2.00	1	1	1	0	0	9.0	4	2	3	7
Don Gullett	0	1	6.39	2	2	0	0	0	12.2	13	9	7	10
Catfish Hunter	0	1	10.38	2	1	0	0	0	4.1	6	5	0	1
Sparky Lyle	1	0	1.93	2	0	0	0	0	4.2	2	1	0	2
Dick Tidrow	0	0	4.91	2	0	0	0	0	3.2	5	2	0	1
Mike Torrez	2	0	2.50	2	2	2	0	0	18.0	16	5	5	15
TOTAL	4	2	4.02	13	6	3	0	0	56.0	48	25	16	36

LA (N)

PLAYER/POS	AVG	G	AB	R	H	2B	3B	HR	RB	BB	SO	SB
Dusty Baker, of	.292	6	24	4	7	0	0	1	5	0	2	0
Glenn Burke, of	.200	3	5	0	1	0	0	0	0	0	1	0
Ron Cey, 3b	.190	6	21	2	4	1	0	1	3	3	5	0
Vic Davalillo, ph	.333	3	3	0	1	0	0	0	1	0	0	0
Mike Garman, p	.000	2	0	0	0	0	0	0	0	0	0	0
Steve Garvey, 1b	.375	6	24	5	9	1	1	1	3	1	4	0
Ed Goodson, ph	.000	1	1	0	0	0	0	0	0	0	1	0
Jerry Grote, c	.000	1	1	0	0	0	0	0	0	0	0	0
Burt Hooton, p	.000	2	5	0	0	0	0	0	0	0	2	0
Charlie Hough, p	.000	2	0	0	0	0	0	0	0	0	0	0
Tommy John, p	.000	1	2	0	0	0	0	0	0	0	2	0
Lee Lacy, of-2	.429	4	7	1	3	0	0	0	0	2	1	0
Rafael Landestoy, pr	.000	1	0	0	0	0	0	0	0	0	0	0
Davey Lopes, 2b	.167	6	24	3	4	0	1	1	2	4	3	2
Rick Monday, of	.167	4	12	0	2	0	0	0	0	0	3	0
Manny Mota, ph	.000	3	3	0	0	0	0	0	0	0	1	0
Johnny Oates, c	.000	1	1	0	0	0	0	0	0	0	0	0
Doug Rau, p	.000	2	0	0	0	0	0	0	0	0	0	0
Lance Rautzhan, p	.000	1	0	0	0	0	0	0	0	0	0	0
Rick Rhoden, p	.500	2	2	1	1	1	0	0	0	0	0	0
Bill Russell, ss	.154	6	26	3	4	0	1	0	2	1	3	0
Reggie Smith, of	.273	6	22	7	6	1	0	3	5	4	3	0
Elias Sosa, p	.000	2	0	0	0	0	0	0	0	0	0	0
Don Sutton, p	.000	2	6	0	0	0	0	0	0	0	4	0
Steve Yeager, c	.316	6	19	2	6	1	0	2	5	1	1	0
TOTAL	.231		208	28	48	5	3	9	28	16	36	2

PITCHER	W	L	ERA	G	GS	CG	SV	SHO	IP	H	ER	BB	SO
Mike Garman	0	0	0.00	2	0	0	0	0	4.0	2	0	1	3
Burt Hooton	1	1	3.75	2	2	1	0	0	12.0	8	5	2	9
Charlie Hough	0	0	1.80	2	0	0	0	0	5.0	3	1	0	5
Tommy John	0	1	6.00	1	1	0	0	0	6.0	9	4	3	7
Doug Rau	0	1	11.57	2	1	0	0	0	2.1	4	3	0	1
Lance Rautzhan	0	0	0.00	1	0	0	0	0	0.1	0	0	2	0
Rick Rhoden	0	1	2.57	2	0	0	0	0	7.0	4	2	1	5
Elias Sosa	0	0	11.57	2	0	0	0	0	2.1	3	3	1	1
Don Sutton	1	0	3.94	2	2	1	0	0	16.0	17	7	1	6
TOTAL	2	4	4.09	16	6	2	0	0	55.0	50	25	11	37

GAME 1 AT NY OCT 11

LA 200 000 001 000 3 6 0
NY 100 001 010 001 4 11 0
Pitchers: Sutton, Rautzhan (8), Sosa (8), Garman (9), RHODEN (12) vs Gullett, LYLE (9)
Home Runs: Randolph-NY
Attendance: 56,668

GAME 2 AT NY OCT 12

LA 212 000 001 6 9 0
NY 000 100 000 1 5 0
Pitchers: HOOTON vs HUNTER, Tidrow (3), Clay (6), Lyle (9)
Home Runs: Cey-LA, Yeager-LA, Smith-LA, Garvey-LA
Attendance: 56,691

GAME 3 AT LA OCT 14

NY 300 110 000 5 10 0
LA 003 000 000 3 7 1
Pitchers: TORREZ vs JOHN, Hough (7)
Home Runs: Baker-LA
Attendance: 55,992

GAME 4 AT LA OCT 15

NY 030 001 000 4 7 0
LA 002 000 000 2 4 0
Pitchers: GUIDRY vs RAU, Rhoden (2), Garman (9)
Home Runs: Lopes-LA, Jackson-NY
Attendance: 55,995

GAME 5 AT LA OCT 16

NY 000 000 220 4 9 2
LA 100 432 00X 10 13 0
Pitchers: GULLETT, Clay (5), Tidrow (6), Hunter (7) vs SUTTON
Home Runs: Yeager-LA, Smith-LA, Munson-NY, Jackson-NY
Attendance: 55,955

GAME 6 AT NY OCT 18

LA 201 000 001 4 9 0
NY 020 320 01X 8 8 1
Pitchers: HOOTON, Sosa (4), Rau (5), Hough (7) vs TORREZ
Home Runs: Chambliss-NY, Smith-LA, Jackson-NY (3)
Attendance: 56,407

LOS ANGELES DODGERS (WEST) 3, PHILADELPHIA PHILLIES (EAST) 1

Steve Garvey hit half the Dodgers' eight home runs and Tommy John hurled the first LCS shutout in four years as Los Angeles, for the second year in a row, defeated the Phillies for the pennant in four games. Philadelphia's five runs in Game 1 would have been enough to win any of the other games, but not this one as the Dodgers out-homered the Phillies four to one (including two by Garvey) and scored nine times. Dodger Davey Lopes hit the game's only home run the next day (with a man aboard), but it was more than enough support for John's four-hit shutout.

The series' most decisive win went to the Phillies in Game 3. Steve Carlton allowed four runs to score, but he made up for it by driving four runs of his own on a homer and sacrifice fly. His teammates added five more, rendering futile Garvey's third series home run.

But Garvey's fourth homer, in Game 4, helped carry the Dodgers into the 10th inning, when Bill Russell—capitalizing on Gary Maddox's muff of Ron Cey's fly to center—singled home Cey with the Dodgers' unearned pennant winner.

LA (W)

PLAYER/POS	AVG	G	AB	R	H	2B	3B	HR	RB	BB	SO	SB
Dusty Baker, of	.467	4	15	1	7	2	0	0	1	3	0	0
Ron Cey, 3b	.313	4	16	4	5	1	0	1	3	2	4	0
Joe Ferguson, ph	.000	2	2	0	0	0	0	0	0	0	1	0
Terry Forster, p	.000	1	0	0	0	0	0	0	0	0	0	0
Steve Garvey, 1b	.389	4	18	6	7	1	1	4	7	0	1	0
Jerry Grote, c	.000	1	0	0	0	0	0	0	0	0	0	0
Burt Hooton, p	.000	1	2	0	0	0	0	0	0	0	1	0
Charlie Hough, p	.000	1	0	0	0	0	0	0	0	0	0	0
Tommy John, p	.000	1	3	0	0	0	0	0	0	0	0	0
Lee Lacy, ph	.000	2	2	0	0	0	0	0	0	0	0	0
Davey Lopes, 2b	.389	4	18	3	7	1	1	2	5	0	1	1
Rick Monday, of	.200	3	10	2	2	0	1	0	0	1	5	0
Manny Mota, ph	1.000	2	1	0	1	1	0	0	0	0	0	0
Billy North, of	.000	4	8	0	0	0	0	0	0	1	1	0
Doug Rau, p	.000	1	1	0	0	0	0	0	0	0	0	0
Lance Rautzhan, p	.000	1	0	0	0	0	0	0	0	0	0	0
Rick Rhoden, p	.000	1	1	0	0	0	0	0	0	0	0	0
Bill Russell, ss	.412	4	17	1	7	1	0	0	2	1	1	0
Reggie Smith, of	.188	4	16	2	3	1	0	0	1	0	2	0
Don Sutton, p	.000	1	2	0	0	0	0	0	0	0	2	0
Bob Welch, p	.000	1	2	0	0	0	0	0	0	0	1	0
Steve Yeager, c	.231	4	13	2	3	0	0	1	2	2	2	1
TOTAL	.286		147	21	42	8	3	8	21	9	22	2

PITCHER	W	L	ERA	G	GS	CG	SV	SHO	IP	H	ER	BB	SO
Terry Forster	1	0	0.00	1	0	0	0	0	1.0	1	0	0	2
Burt Hooton	0	0	7.71	1	1	0	0	0	4.2	10	4	0	5
Charlie Hough	0	0	4.50	1	0	0	0	0	2.0	1	1	0	1
Tommy John	1	0	0.00	1	1	1	0	1	9.0	4	0	2	4
Doug Rau	0	0	3.60	1	1	0	0	0	5.0	5	2	2	1
Lance Rautzhan	0	0	6.75	1	0	0	0	0	1.1	3	1	2	0
Rick Rhoden	0	0	2.25	1	0	0	0	0	4.0	2	1	1	3
Don Sutton	0	1	6.35	1	1	0	0	0	5.2	7	4	2	0
Bob Welch	1	0	2.08	1	0	0	0	0	4.1	2	1	0	5
TOTAL	3	1	3.41	9	4	1	0	1	37.0	35	14	9	21

PHI (E)

PLAYER/POS	AVG	G	AB	R	H	2B	3B	HR	RB	BB	SO	SB
Bob Boone, c	.182	3	11	0	2	0	0	0	0	0	1	0
Larry Bowa, ss	.333	4	18	2	6	0	0	0	0	1	2	0
Warren Brusstar, p	.000	3	0	0	0	0	0	0	0	0	0	0
Jose Cardenal, 1b	.167	2	6	0	1	0	0	0	0	1	1	0
Steve Carlton, p	.500	1	4	2	2	0	0	1	4	0	0	0
Larry Christenson, p	.000	1	1	0	0	0	0	0	0	0	1	0
Rawly Eastwick, p	.000	1	0	0	0	0	0	0	0	0	0	0
Barry Foote, ph	.000	1	1	0	0	0	0	0	0	0	0	0
Orlando Gonzalez, ph	.000	1	1	0	0	0	0	0	0	0	1	0
Richie Hebner, 1b-2	.111	3	9	0	1	0	0	0	1	0	0	0
Randy Lerch, p	.000	1	2	0	0	0	0	0	0	0	0	0
Greg Luzinski, of	.375	4	16	3	6	0	1	2	3	1	2	0
Garry Maddox, of	.263	4	19	1	5	0	0	0	2	0	3	0
Jerry Martin, of-3	.222	4	9	1	2	1	0	1	2	1	3	0
Bake McBride, of-2	.222	3	9	2	2	0	0	1	1	0	2	0
Tim McCarver, c-1	.000	2	4	2	0	0	0	0	1	2	0	0
Tug McGraw, p	.000	3	0	0	0	0	0	0	0	0	0	0
Jim Morrison, ph	.000	1	1	0	0	0	0	0	0	0	1	0
Ron Reed, p	.000	2	0	0	0	0	0	0	0	0	0	0
Dick Ruthven, p	.000	1	1	0	0	0	0	0	0	0	1	0
Mike Schmidt, 3b	.200	4	15	1	3	2	0	0	1	2	2	0
Ted Sizemore, 2b	.385	4	13	3	5	0	1	0	1	1	0	0
TOTAL	.250		140	17	35	3	2	5	16	9	21	0

PITCHER	W	L	ERA	G	GS	CG	SV	SHO	IP	H	ER	BB	SO
Warren Brusstar	0	0	0.00	3	0	0	0	0	2.2	2	0	1	0
Steve Carlton	1	0	4.00	1	1	1	0	0	9.0	8	4	2	8
Larry Christenson	0	1	12.46	1	1	0	0	0	4.1	7	6	1	3
Rawly Eastwick	0	0	9.00	1	0	0	0	0	1.0	3	1	0	1
Randy Lerch	0	0	5.06	1	1	0	0	0	5.1	7	3	0	0
Tug McGraw	0	1	1.59	3	0	0	0	0	5.2	3	1	5	5
Ron Reed	0	0	2.25	2	0	0	0	0	4.0	6	1	0	2
Dick Ruthven	0	1	5.79	1	1	0	0	0	4.2	6	3	0	3
TOTAL	1	3	4.66	13	4	1	0	0	36.2	42	19	9	22

GAME 1 AT PHI OCT 4

```
LA   004 211 001   9 13 1
PHI  010 030 001   5 12 1
```
Pitchers: Hooton, WELCH (5) vs CHRISTENSON, Brusstar (5), Eastwick (6), McGraw (7)
Home Runs: Garvey-LA (2), Lopes-LA, Yeager-LA, Martin-PHI
Attendance: 63,460

GAME 2 AT PHI OCT 5

```
LA   000 120 100   4 8 0
PHI  000 000 000   0 4 0
```
Pitchers: JOHN vs RUTHVEN, Brusstar (5), Reed (7), McGraw (9)
Home Runs: Lopes-LA
Attendance: 60,642

GAME 3 AT LA OCT 6

```
PHI  040 003 101   9 11 1
LA   012 000 010   4 8 2
```
Pitchers: CARLTON vs SUTTON, Rautzhan (6), Hough (8)
Home Runs: Carlton-PHI, Luzinski-PHI, Garvey-LA
Attendance: 55,043

GAME 4 AT LA OCT 7

```
PHI  002 000 1000   3 8 2
LA   010 101 0001   4 13 0
```
Pitchers: Lerch, Brusstar (6), Reed (7), McGRAW (9) vs Rau, Rhoden (6), FORSTER (10)
Home Runs: Luzinski-PHI, Cey-LA, Garvey-LA, McBride-PHI
Attendance: 55,124

NEW YORK YANKEES (EAST) 3, KANSAS CITY ROYALS (WEST) 1

It took Bucky Dent's pop-fly home run against Boston in an Eastern Division tiebreaker to carry the Yankees into the ALCS. But once there they took the pennant, downing the Royals for the third year in a row. Reggie Jackson's three-run homer in the eighth inning of Game 1 capped a 16-hit attack that scored seven runs as pitchers Jim Beattie and Ken Clay combined to limit Kansas City to two hits and a single run. The Royals, though, made it look just as easy the next day as their own 16 hits and ten runs evened the series.

Twice in Game 3 George Brett gave the Royals a lead with a home run, and he tied the game with a third homer in the fifth. But Jackson's two-run homer in the fourth brought the Yankees back, and Thurman Munson's two-run shot in the eighth gave New York a close win. Game 4 was just as close, but more of a pitcher's duel. Dennis Leonard, who went the distance, gave up only four hits, but two of them were home runs to Graig Nettles and Roy White. Yankees starter Ron Guidry allowed a run in the first, but shut out the Royals for the next seven innings. Goose Gossage preserved Guidry's good work—and the pennant—in the ninth.

NY (E)

PLAYER/POS	AVG	G	AB	R	H	2B	3B	HR	RB	BB	SO	SB
Jim Beattie, p	.000	1	0	0	0	0	0	0	0	0	0	0
Paul Blair, of-3,2b-1	.000	4	6	1	0	0	0	0	0	0	1	0
Chris Chambliss, 1b	.400	4	15	1	6	0	0	0	2	0	4	0
Ken Clay, p	.000	1	0	0	0	0	0	0	0	0	0	0
Bucky Dent, ss	.200	4	15	0	3	0	0	0	4	0	0	0
Brian Doyle, 2b	.286	3	7	0	2	0	0	0	1	1	1	0
Ed Figueroa, p	.000	1	0	0	0	0	0	0	0	0	0	0
Rich Gossage, p	.000	2	0	0	0	0	0	0	0	0	0	0
Ron Guidry, p	.000	1	0	0	0	0	0	0	0	0	0	0
Catfish Hunter, p	.000	1	0	0	0	0	0	0	0	0	0	0
Reggie Jackson, dh-3, of-1	.462	4	13	5	6	1	0	2	6	3	4	0
Cliff Johnson, ph	.000	1	1	0	0	0	0	0	0	0	0	0
Sparky Lyle, p	.000	1	0	0	0	0	0	0	0	0	0	0
Thurman Munson, c	.278	4	18	2	5	1	0	1	2	0	0	0
Graig Nettles, 3b	.333	4	15	3	5	0	1	1	2	0	1	0
Lou Piniella, of	.235	4	17	2	4	0	0	0	0	0	3	0
Mickey Rivers, of	.455	4	11	0	5	0	0	0	0	2	0	0
Fred Stanley, 2b	.200	2	5	0	1	0	0	0	0	0	2	0
Gary Thomasson, of	.000	3	1	0	0	0	0	0	0	0	0	0
Dick Tidrow, p	.000	1	0	0	0	0	0	0	0	0	0	0
Roy White, of-3, dh-1	.313	4	16	5	5	1	0	1	1	1	2	0
TOTAL	.300		140	19	42	3	1	5	18	7	18	0

PITCHER	W	L	ERA	G	GS	CG	SV	SHO	IP	H	ER	BB	SO
Jim Beattie	1	0	1.69	1	1	0	0	0	5.1	2	1	5	3
Ken Clay	0	0	0.00	1	0	0	1	0	3.2	0	0	3	2
Ed Figueroa	0	1	27.00	1	1	0	0	0	1.0	5	3	0	0
Rich Gossage	1	0	4.50	2	0	0	1	0	4.0	3	2	0	3
Ron Guidry	1	0	1.13	1	1	0	0	0	8.0	7	1	1	7
Catfish Hunter	0	0	4.50	1	1	0	0	0	6.0	7	3	3	5
Sparky Lyle	0	0	13.50	1	0	0	0	0	1.1	3	2	0	0
Dick Tidrow	0	0	4.76	1	0	0	0	0	5.2	8	3	2	1
TOTAL	3	1	3.86	9	4	0	2	0	35.0	35	15	14	21

KC (W)

PLAYER/POS	AVG	G	AB	R	H	2B	3B	HR	RB	BB	SO	SB
Doug Bird, p	.000	2	0	0	0	0	0	0	0	0	0	0
Steve Braun, of-1	.000	2	5	0	0	0	0	0	0	1	1	0
George Brett, 3b	.389	4	18	7	7	1	1	3	3	0	1	0
Al Cowens, of	.133	4	15	2	2	0	0	0	1	0	2	0
Larry Gura, p	.000	1	0	0	0	0	0	0	0	0	0	0
Al Hrabosky, p	.000	3	0	0	0	0	0	0	0	0	0	0
Clint Hurdle, of-2	.375	4	8	1	3	0	1	0	1	2	3	0
Pete LaCock, 1b-3	.364	4	11	1	4	2	1	0	1	3	1	1
Dennis Leonard, p	.000	2	0	0	0	0	0	0	0	0	0	0
Hal McRae, dh	.214	4	14	0	3	0	0	0	2	2	2	1
Steve Mingori, p	.000	1	0	0	0	0	0	0	0	0	0	0
Amos Otis, of	.429	4	14	2	6	2	0	0	1	3	5	4
Freddie Patek, ss	.077	4	13	2	1	0	0	1	2	1	4	0
Marty Pattin, p	.000	1	0	0	0	0	0	0	0	0	0	0
Tom Poquette, ph	.000	1	1	0	0	0	0	0	0	0	0	0
Darrell Porter, c	.357	4	14	1	5	1	0	0	3	2	0	0
Paul Splittorff, p	.000	1	0	0	0	0	0	0	0	0	0	0
John Wathan, 1b	.000	1	3	0	0	0	0	0	0	0	0	0
Frank White, 2b	.231	4	13	1	3	0	0	0	2	0	0	0
Willie Wilson, of	.250	3	4	0	1	0	0	0	0	0	2	0
TOTAL	.263		133	17	35	6	3	4	16	14	21	6

PITCHER	W	L	ERA	G	GS	CG	SV	SHO	IP	H	ER	BB	SO
Doug Bird	0	1	9.00	2	0	0	0	0	1.0	2	1	0	1
Larry Gura	1	0	2.84	1	1	0	0	0	6.1	8	2	2	2
Al Hrabosky	0	0	3.00	3	0	0	0	0	3.0	3	1	0	2
Dennis Leonard	0	2	3.75	2	2	1	0	0	12.0	13	5	2	11
Steve Mingori	0	0	7.36	1	0	0	0	0	3.2	5	3	3	0
Marty Pattin	0	0	27.00	1	0	0	0	0	0.2	2	2	0	0
Paul Splittorff	0	0	4.91	1	1	0	0	0	7.1	9	4	0	2
TOTAL	1	3	4.76	11	4	1	0	0	34.0	42	18	7	18

GAME 1 AT KC OCT 3

NY 011 020 030   7 16 0
KC 000 001 000   1 2 2
Pitchers: BEATTIE, Clay (6) vs LEONARD, Mingori (5), Hrabosky (8), Bird (9)
Home Runs: Jackson-NY
Attendance: 41,143

GAME 2 AT KC OCT 4

NY 000 000 220   4 12 1
KC 140 000 32X   10 16 1
Pitchers: FIGUEROA, Tidrow (2), Lyle (7) vs GURA, Pattin (7), Hrabosky (8)
Home Runs: Patek-KC
Attendance: 41,158

GAME 3 AT NY OCT 6

KC 101 010 020   5 10 1
NY 010 201 02X   6 10 0
Pitchers: Splittorff, BIRD (8), Hrabosky (8) vs Hunter, GOSSAGE (7)
Home Runs: Brett-KC (3), Jackson-NY, Munson-NY
Attendance: 55,535

GAME 4 AT NY OCT 7

KC 100 000 000   1 7 0
NY 010 001 00X   2 4 0
Pitchers: LEONARD vs GUIDRY, Gossage (9)
Home Runs: Nettles-NY, R.White-NY
Attendance: 56,356

NEW YORK YANKEES (AL) 4, LOS ANGELES DODGERS (NL) 2

The outcome was the same as in 1977: the Yankees over the Dodgers in six games. But this year New York overcame a two-game deficit by sweeping the next four, a feat never before achieved in a World Series.

Los Angeles overwhelmed New York in the opener. Home runs in the second and fourth innings by Dusty Baker and Davey Lopes (who had two homers and five RBIs) and another run in the fifth, gave the Dodgers a 7–0 lead before Reggie Jackson's leadoff homer in the seventh gave New York its first score. The Yankees scored four more times, but so did the Dodgers for an 11–5 win. Game 2 was closer. The Yankees scored first and held a lead through the top of the sixth, but Ron Cey's three-run homer in the bottom of the inning gave Los Angeles the runs they needed to win 4–3.

Ron Guidry, coming off a spectacular 25–3 regular season, gave up eight hits and issued seven walks. But only one baserunner scored, thanks in large part to several memorable stops and throws by third baseman Graig Nettles. Meanwhile, Roy White's home run in the first inning began the scoring in what would become a 5–1 Yankees' win.

It took 10 innings for New York to win Game 4. Starters Tommy John and Ed Figueroa hurled shutout ball until Reggie Smith tagged Figueroa for a three-run homer in the top of the fifth. The Yankees clawed back in the sixth. Reggie Jackson singled in one run, then—in a play that stirred great controversy (the Dodgers claimed intentionally) of a throw from second on an attempted double play, deflecting the ball to the outfield and permitting a second run to score. In the eighth, Thurman Munson doubled home the tying run, and in the last of the 10th Lou Piniella's two-out drive to center scored baserunner Roy White with the game winner.

Game 5 was a blowout. No one hit home runs, but the Yankees hit 16 singles (a Series record) and two doubles for 12 runs (five of them driven in by Munson's three hits) to give Jim Beattie (nine hits, two runs) an easy win. Back in Los Angeles for the sixth game, the Yankees won the crown on the hitting of two men at the bottom of

the batting order: Brian Doyle and Bucky Dent. With three hits each, they combined for five RBIs in the 7–2 win. For good measure, Reggie Jackson concluded the Series scoring with a mighty two-run homer in the seventh.

NY (A)

PLAYER/POS	AVG	G	AB	R	H	2B	3B	HR	RB	BB	SO	SB
Jim Beattie, p	.000	1	0	0	0	0	0	0	0	0	0	0
Paul Blair, of	.375	6	8	2	3	1	0	0	0	1	4	0
Chris Chambliss, 1b	.182	3	11	1	2	0	0	0	0	1	1	0
Ken Clay, p	.000	1	0	0	0	0	0	0	0	0	0	0
Bucky Dent, ss	.417	6	24	3	10	1	0	0	7	1	2	0
Brian Doyle, 2b	.438	6	16	4	7	1	0	0	2	0	0	0
Ed Figueroa, p	.000	2	0	0	0	0	0	0	0	0	0	0
Rich Gossage, p	.000	3	0	0	0	0	0	0	0	0	0	0
Ron Guidry, p	.000	1	0	0	0	0	0	0	0	0	0	0
Mike Heath, c	.000	1	0	0	0	0	0	0	0	0	0	0
Catfish Hunter, p	.000	2	0	0	0	0	0	0	0	0	0	0
Reggie Jackson, dh	.391	6	23	2	9	1	0	2	8	3	7	0
Cliff Johnson, ph	.000	2	2	0	0	0	0	0	0	0	1	0
Jay Johnstone, of	.000	2	0	0	0	0	0	0	0	0	0	0
Paul Lindblad, p	.000	1	0	0	0	0	0	0	0	0	0	0
Thurman Munson, c	.320	6	25	5	8	3	0	0	7	3	7	1
Graig Nettles, 3b	.160	6	25	2	4	0	0	0	1	0	6	0
Lou Piniella, of	.280	6	25	3	7	0	0	0	4	0	0	1
Mickey Rivers, of-4	.333	5	18	2	6	0	0	0	1	0	2	1
Jim Spencer, 1b-3	.167	4	12	3	2	0	0	0	0	2	4	0
Fred Stanley, 2b	.200	3	5	0	1	1	0	0	0	1	0	0
Gary Thomasson, of	.250	3	4	0	1	0	0	0	0	0	1	0
Dick Tidrow, p	.000	2	0	0	0	0	0	0	0	0	0	0
Roy White, of	.333	6	24	9	8	0	0	1	4	4	5	2
TOTAL	.306		222	36	68	8	0	3	34	16	40	5

PITCHER	W	L	ERA	G	GS	CG	SV	SHO	IP	H	ER	BB	SO
Jim Beattie	1	0	2.00	1	1	1	0	0	9.0	9	2	4	8
Ken Clay	0	0	11.57	1	0	0	0	0	2.1	4	3	2	2
Ed Figueroa	0	1	8.10	2	2	0	0	0	6.2	9	6	5	2
Rich Gossage	1	0	0.00	3	0	0	0	0	6.0	1	0	1	4
Ron Guidry	1	0	1.00	1	1	1	0	0	9.0	8	1	7	4
Catfish Hunter	1	1	4.15	2	2	0	0	0	13.0	13	6	1	5
Paul Lindblad	0	0	11.57	1	0	0	0	0	2.1	4	3	0	1
Dick Tidrow	0	0	1.93	2	0	0	0	0	4.2	4	1	0	5
TOTAL	4	2	3.74	13	6	2	0	0	53.0	52	22	20	31

LA (N)

PLAYER/POS	AVG	G	AB	R	H	2B	3B	HR	RB	BB	SO	SB
Dusty Baker, of	.238	6	21	2	5	0	0	1	1	1	3	0
Ron Cey, 3b	.286	6	21	2	6	0	0	1	4	3	3	0
Vic Davalillo, dh-1	.333	2	3	0	1	0	0	0	0	0	0	0
Joe Ferguson, c	.500	2	4	1	2	2	0	0	0	0	1	0
Terry Forster, p	.000	3	0	0	0	0	0	0	0	0	0	0
Steve Garvey, 1b	.208	6	24	1	5	1	0	0	0	1	7	1
Jerry Grote, c	.000	2	0	0	0	0	0	0	0	0	0	0
Burt Hooton, p	.000	2	0	0	0	0	0	0	0	0	0	0
Charlie Hough, p	.000	2	0	0	0	0	0	0	0	0	0	0
Tommy John, p	.000	2	0	0	0	0	0	0	0	0	0	0
Lee Lacy, dh	.143	4	14	0	2	0	0	0	1	1	3	0
Davey Lopes, 2b	.308	6	26	7	8	0	0	3	7	2	1	2
Rick Monday, of-4, dh-1	.154	5	13	2	2	1	0	0	0	4	3	0
Manny Mota, ph	.000	1	1	0	0	0	0	0	0	1	0	0
Billy North, of	.125	4	8	2	1	1	0	0	2	1	0	1
Johnny Oates, c	1.000	1	1	0	1	0	0	0	0	1	0	0
Doug Rau, p	.000	1	0	0	0	0	0	0	0	0	0	0
Lance Rautzhan, p	.000	2	0	0	0	0	0	0	0	0	0	0
Bill Russell, ss	.423	6	26	1	11	2	0	0	2	2	2	1
Reggie Smith, of	.200	6	25	3	5	0	0	1	5	2	6	0
Don Sutton, p	.000	2	0	0	0	0	0	0	0	0	0	0
Bob Welch, p	.000	3	0	0	0	0	0	0	0	0	0	0
Steve Yeager, c	.231	5	13	2	3	1	0	0	0	1	2	0
TOTAL	.261		199	23	52	8	0	6	22	20	31	5

PITCHER	W	L	ERA	G	GS	CG	SV	SHO	IP	H	ER	BB	SO
Terry Forster	0	0	0.00	3	0	0	0	0	4.0	5	0	1	6
Burt Hooton	1	1	6.48	2	2	0	0	0	8.1	13	6	3	6
Charlie Hough	0	0	8.44	2	0	0	0	0	5.1	10	5	2	5
Tommy John	1	0	3.07	2	2	0	0	0	14.2	14	5	4	6
Doug Rau	0	0	0.00	1	0	0	0	0	2.0	1	0	0	3
Lance Rautzhan	0	0	13.50	2	0	0	0	0	2.0	4	3	0	0
Don Sutton	0	2	7.50	2	2	0	0	0	12.0	17	10	4	8
Bob Welch	0	1	6.23	3	0	0	1	0	4.1	4	3	2	6
TOTAL	2	4	5.47	17	6	0	1	0	52.2	68	32	16	40

GAME 1 AT LA OCT 10

NY 000 000 320 5 9 1
LA 030 310 31X 11 15 2
Pitchers: FIGUEROA, Clay (2), Lindblad (5), Tidrow (7) vs JOHN, Forster (8)
Home Runs: Baker-LA, Lopes-LA (2), Jackson-NY
Attendance: 55,997

GAME 2 AT LA OCT 11

NY 002 000 100 3 11 0
LA 000 103 00X 4 7 0
Pitchers: HUNTER, Gossage (7) vs HOOTON, Forster (7), Welch (9)
Home Runs: Cey-LA
Attendance: 55,982

GAME 3 AT NY OCT 13

LA 001 000 000 1 8 0
NY 110 030 30X 5 10 1
Pitchers: SUTTON, Rautzhan (7), Hough (8) vs GUIDRY
Home Runs: White-NY
Attendance: 56,447

GAME 4 AT NY OCT 14

LA 000 030 0000 3 6 1
NY 000 002 0101 4 9 0
Pitchers: John, Forster (8), WELCH (8) vs Figueroa, Tidrow (6), GOSSAGE (9)
Home Runs: Smith-LA
Attendance: 56,445

GAME 5 AT NY OCT 15

LA 101 000 000 2 9 3
NY 004 300 41X 12 18 0
Pitchers: HOOTON, Rautzhan (3), Hough (4) vs BEATTIE
Attendance: 56,448

GAME 6 AT LA OCT 17

NY 030 002 200 7 11 0
LA 101 000 000 2 7 1
Pitchers: HUNTER, Gossage (8) vs SUTTON, Welch (7), Rau (8)
Home Runs: Lopes-LA, Jackson-NY
Attendance: 55,985

PITTSBURGH PIRATES (EAST) 3, CINCINNATI REDS (WEST) 0

The Pirates—with a better season's record than Cincinnati and stronger hitting and pitching—proved their superiority in the NLCS as well, dominating the statistics and sweeping the series. Yet the games were closer than the stats alone would suggest. Pittsburgh won the first game by three runs—but they didn't come until Willie Stargell's homer in the 11th inning broke a 2–2 tie.

In Game 2, Cincinnati scored first. The Pirates tied the game with a run in the fourth and took a narrow lead with another in the fifth. But the Reds came back on a game-tying pair of doubles in the ninth, and it wasn't until the 10th that Pittsburgh eked out its victory with a run on two singles and Don Robinson's shutout relief.

Only in the third game did the Pirates take a commanding lead, with six runs in the first four innings (two of them on home runs by Stargell and Bill Madlock). The Reds outhit Pittsburgh, but only Johnny Bench's homer brought them a run, as Bert Blyleven overcame them in the series' only complete-game pitching performance. The Pirates, who had lost to the Reds three times in the NLCS in the 1970s, ended the decade by overcoming Cincinnati for the pennant.

PIT (E)

PLAYER/POS	AVG	G	AB	R	H	2B	3B	HR	RB	BB	SO	SB
Matt Alexander, pr	.000	1	0	1	0	0	0	0	0	0	0	0
Jim Bibby, p	.000	1	0	0	0	0	0	0	0	1	0	0
Bert Blyleven, p	.333	1	3	1	1	0	0	0	0	0	1	0
John Candelaria, p	.000	1	3	0	0	0	0	0	0	0	2	0
Mike Easler, ph	.000	1	1	0	0	0	0	0	0	0	0	0
Tim Foli, ss	.333	3	12	1	4	1	0	0	3	0	0	0
Phil Garner, 2b-3, ss-1	.417	3	12	4	5	0	1	1	1	1	0	0
Grant Jackson, p	.000	2	1	0	0	0	0	0	0	0	0	0
Bill Madlock, 3b	.250	3	12	1	3	0	0	1	2	2	0	2
John Milner, of	.000	3	9	0	0	0	0	0	0	2	0	0
Omar Moreno, of	.250	3	12	3	3	0	1	0	0	2	1	0
Ed Ott, c	.231	3	13	0	3	0	0	0	0	0	2	0
Dave Parker, of	.333	3	12	2	4	0	0	0	2	2	3	0
Dave Roberts, p	.000	1	0	0	0	0	0	0	0	0	0	0
Don Robinson, p	.000	2	0	0	0	0	0	0	0	0	0	0
Bill Robinson, of	.000	3	3	0	0	0	0	0	0	0	0	0
Enrique Romo, p	.000	2	0	0	0	0	0	0	0	0	0	0
Willie Stargell, 1b	.455	3	11	2	5	2	0	2	6	3	2	0
Rennie Stennett, 2b	.000	1	0	0	0	0	0	0	0	0	0	0
Kent Tekulve, p	.000	2	1	0	0	0	0	0	0	0	1	0
TOTAL	.267		105	15	28	3	2	4	14	13	13	4

PITCHER	W	L	ERA	G	GS	CG	SV	SHO	IP	H	ER	BB	SO
Jim Bibby	0	0	1.29	1	1	0	0	0	7.0	4	1	4	5
Bert Blyleven	1	0	1.00	1	1	1	0	0	9.0	8	1	0	9
John Candelaria	0	0	2.57	1	1	0	0	0	7.0	5	2	1	4
Grant Jackson	1	0	0.00	2	0	0	0	0	2.0	1	0	1	2
Dave Roberts	0	0	∞	1	0	0	0	0	0.0	0	0	1	0
Don Robinson	1	0	0.00	2	0	0	1	0	2.0	0	0	1	3
Enrique Romo	0	0	0.00	2	0	0	0	0	0.1	3	0	1	1
Kent Tekulve	0	0	3.38	2	0	0	0	0	2.2	2	1	2	2
TOTAL	3	0	1.50	12	3	1	1	0	30.0	23	5	11	26

CIN (W)

PLAYER/POS	AVG	G	AB	R	H	2B	3B	HR	RB	BB	SO	SB
Rick Auerbach, ph	.000	2	2	0	0	0	0	0	0	0	1	0
Doug Bair, p	.000	1	0	0	0	0	0	0	0	0	0	0
Johnny Bench, c	.250	3	12	1	3	0	1	1	1	2	2	0
Dave Collins, of	.357	3	14	0	5	1	0	0	1	0	2	2
Dave Concepcion, ss	.429	3	14	1	6	1	0	0	0	0	3	0
Hector Cruz, of-1	.200	2	5	1	1	1	0	0	0	0	1	0
Dan Driessen, 1b	.083	3	12	1	1	0	0	0	0	1	3	0
George Foster, of	.200	3	10	1	2	0	0	1	2	4	3	0
Cesar Geronimo, of	.143	2	7	0	1	0	0	0	0	0	5	0
Tom Hume, p	.000	3	1	0	0	0	0	0	0	0	1	0
Ray Knight, 3b	.286	3	14	0	4	1	0	0	0	0	2	1
Mike LaCoss, p	.000	1	0	0	0	0	0	0	0	0	0	0
Charlie Leibrandt, p	.000	1	0	0	0	0	0	0	0	0	0	0
Joe Morgan, 2b	.000	3	11	0	0	0	0	0	0	3	1	1
Fred Norman, p	.000	1	1	0	0	0	0	0	0	0	1	0
Frank Pastore, p	.000	1	0	0	0	0	0	0	1	1	0	0
Tom Seaver, p	.000	1	2	0	0	0	0	0	0	0	1	0
Mario Soto, p	.000	1	0	0	0	0	0	0	0	0	0	0
Harry Spilman, ph	.000	2	2	0	0	0	0	0	0	0	0	0
Dave Tomlin, p	.000	3	0	0	0	0	0	0	0	0	0	0
TOTAL	.215		107	5	23	4	1	2	5	11	26	4

PITCHER	W	L	ERA	G	GS	CG	SV	SHO	IP	H	ER	BB	SO
Doug Bair	0	1	9.00	1	0	0	0	0	1.0	2	1	1	0
Tom Hume	0	1	6.75	3	0	0	0	0	4.0	6	3	0	2
Mike LaCoss	0	1	10.80	1	1	0	0	0	1.2	1	2	4	0
Charlie Leibrandt	0	0	0.00	1	0	0	0	0	0.1	0	0	0	0
Fred Norman	0	0	18.00	1	0	0	0	0	2.0	4	4	1	1
Frank Pastore	0	0	2.57	1	1	0	0	0	7.0	7	2	3	1
Tom Seaver	0	0	2.25	1	1	0	0	0	8.0	5	2	2	5
Mario Soto	0	0	0.00	1	0	0	0	0	2.0	0	0	1	1
Dave Tomlin	0	0	0.00	3	0	0	0	0	3.0	3	0	2	3
TOTAL	0	3	4.34	13	3	0	0	0	29.0	28	14	13	13

GAME 1 AT CIN OCT 2

```
PIT  0 0 2 0 0 0 0 0 0 3   5 10 0
CIN  0 0 0 2 0 0 0 0 0 0   2  7 0
```
Pitchers: Candelaria, Romo (8), Tekulve (8), JACKSON (10), D.Robinson (11) vs Seaver, HUME (9), Tomlin (11)
Home Runs: Garner-PIT, Foster-CIN, Stargell-PIT
Attendance: 55,006

GAME 2 AT CIN OCT 3

```
PIT  0 0 0 1 1 0 0 0 0 1   3 11 0
CIN  0 1 0 0 0 0 0 1 0 0   2  8 0
```
Pitchers: Bibby, Jackson (8), Romo (8), Tekulve (8), Roberts (9), D.ROBINSON (9) vs Pastore, Tomlin (8), Hume (8), BAIR (10)
Attendance: 55,000

GAME 3 AT PIT OCT 5

```
CIN  0 0 0 0 0 1 0 0 0   1  8 1
PIT  1 1 2 2 0 0 0 1 X   7  7 0
```
Pitchers: LaCOSS, Norman (2), Leibrandt (4), Soto (5), Tomlin (7), Hume (8) vs BLYLEVEN
Home Runs: Stargell-PIT, Madlock-PIT, Bench-CIN
Attendance: 42,240

BALTIMORE ORIOLES (EAST) 3, CALIFORNIA ANGELS (WEST) 1

Baltimore, returning to post-season play after a four-year absence, struggled with first-timer California through three games before blowing them away in the fourth. Game 1 went into the last of the 10th tied 3–3, when Oriole pinch hitter John Lowenstein, up with two men on, ended it with a two-out, two-strike shot that just cleared the left-field wall.

Game 2 looked like a blowout for Baltimore. Eddie Murray drove in four runs, and the rest of the team added five more to give the O's a 9–1 lead by the end of three. But California chipped away at the lead in the latter half of the game and drew within one in the ninth, before Brian Downing hit into a forceout with the bases full to end their scoring.

The Angels' late rally in Game 3 was more successful. Down by a run in the bottom of the ninth, they scored twice, on a walk, a dropped outfield fly, and Larry Harlow's game-winning double. The final game, though, was all Baltimore's, as Scott McGregor—pitching the series' only complete game—blanked the Angels on six hits. The Orioles scored two in the third and another in the fourth, before Pat Kelly put California pennant hopes out of reach with a three-run homer in the O's five-run seventh.

BAL (E)

PLAYER/POS	AVG	G	AB	R	H	2B	3B	HR	RB	BB	SO	SB
Mark Belanger, ss	.200	3	5	0	1	0	0	0	1	0	2	0
Al Bumbry, of	.250	4	16	5	4	0	1	0	0	4	3	2
Terry Crowley, ph	.500	2	2	0	1	0	0	0	1	0	0	0
Rich Dauer, 2b	.182	4	11	0	2	0	0	0	0	0	1	0
Doug DeCinces, 3b	.308	4	13	4	4	1	0	0	3	1	1	0
Rick Dempsey, c	.400	3	10	3	4	2	0	0	2	1	0	1
Mike Flanagan, p	.000	1	0	0	0	0	0	0	0	0	0	0
Kiko Garcia, ss	.273	3	11	1	3	0	0	0	2	2	4	0
Pat Kelly, dh-2, of-1	.364	3	11	3	4	0	0	1	4	1	3	2
John Lowenstein, of-3	.167	4	6	2	1	0	0	1	3	2	2	0
Dennis Martinez, p	.000	1	0	0	0	0	0	0	0	0	0	0
Lee May, dh	.143	2	7	0	1	0	0	0	1	1	3	0
Scott McGregor, p	.000	1	0	0	0	0	0	0	0	0	0	0
Eddie Murray, 1b	.417	4	12	3	5	0	0	1	5	5	2	0
Jim Palmer, p	.000	1	0	0	0	0	0	0	0	0	0	0
Gary Roenicke, of	.200	2	5	1	1	0	0	0	1	0	0	0
Ken Singleton, of	.375	4	16	4	6	2	0	0	2	1	2	0
Dave Skaggs, c	.000	1	4	0	0	0	0	0	0	0	0	0
Billy Smith, 2b	.000	1	4	0	0	0	0	0	0	0	1	0
Don Stanhouse, p	.000	3	0	0	0	0	0	0	0	0	0	0
TOTAL	.278		133	26	37	5	1	3	25	18	24	5

PITCHER	W	L	ERA	G	GS	CG	SV	SHO	IP	H	ER	BB	SO
Mike Flanagan	1	0	5.14	1	1	0	0	0	7.0	6	4	1	2
Dennis Martinez	0	0	3.24	1	0	0	0	0	8.1	8	3	0	4
Scott McGregor	1	0	0.00	1	1	1	0	1	9.0	6	0	1	4
Jim Palmer	0	0	3.00	1	1	0	0	0	9.0	7	3	2	3
Don Stanhouse	1	1	6.00	3	0	0	0	0	3.0	5	2	3	0
TOTAL	3	1	2.97	7	4	1	0	1	36.1	32	12	7	13

CAL (W)

PLAYER/POS	AVG	G	AB	R	H	2B	3B	HR	RB	BB	SO	SB
Don Aase, p	.000	2	0	0	0	0	0	0	0	0	0	0
Jim Anderson, ss	.091	4	11	0	1	0	0	0	0	0	1	0
Mike Barlow, p	.000	1	0	0	0	0	0	0	0	0	0	0
Don Baylor, dh-3, of-1	.188	4	16	2	3	0	0	1	2	1	2	0
Bert Campaneris, ss	.000	1	0	0	0	0	0	0	0	0	0	0
Rod Carew, 1b	.412	4	17	4	7	3	0	0	1	0	0	1
Bobby Clark, of	.000	1	3	0	0	0	0	0	0	0	2	0
Mark Clear, p	.000	1	0	0	0	0	0	0	0	0	0	0
Willie Davis, ph	.500	2	2	1	1	1	0	0	0	0	0	0
Brian Downing, c	.200	4	15	1	3	0	0	0	1	1	1	0
Dan Ford, of	.294	4	17	2	5	1	0	2	4	0	0	0
Dave Frost, p	.000	2	0	0	0	0	0	0	0	0	0	0
Bobby Grich, 2b	.154	4	13	0	2	1	0	0	2	1	1	0
Larry Harlow, of-2	.125	3	8	0	1	1	0	0	1	1	2	0
Chris Knapp, p	.000	1	0	0	0	0	0	0	0	0	0	0
Carney Lansford, 3b	.294	4	17	2	5	0	0	0	3	1	2	1
Dave LaRoche, p	.000	1	0	0	0	0	0	0	0	0	0	0
Rick Miller, of	.250	4	16	2	4	0	0	0	0	0	1	0
John Montague, p	.000	2	0	0	0	0	0	0	0	0	0	0
Merv Rettenmund, dh	.000	2	2	0	0	0	0	0	0	2	1	0
Nolan Ryan, p	.000	1	0	0	0	0	0	0	0	0	0	0
Frank Tanana, p	.000	1	0	0	0	0	0	0	0	0	0	0
Dickie Thon, ss	.000	1	0	1	0	0	0	0	0	0	0	0
TOTAL	.234		137	15	32	7	0	3	14	7	13	2

PITCHER	W	L	ERA	G	GS	CG	SV	SHO	IP	H	ER	BB	SO
Don Aase	1	0	1.80	2	0	0	0	0	5.0	4	1	2	6
Mike Barlow	0	0	0.00	1	0	0	0	0	1.0	0	0	0	0
Mark Clear	0	0	4.76	1	0	0	0	0	5.2	4	3	2	3
Dave Frost	0	1	18.69	2	1	0	0	0	4.1	8	9	5	1
Chris Knapp	0	1	7.71	1	1	0	0	0	2.1	5	2	1	0
Dave LaRoche	0	0	6.75	1	0	0	0	0	1.1	2	1	1	1
John Montague	0	1	9.00	2	0	0	0	0	4.0	4	4	2	2
Nolan Ryan	0	0	1.29	1	1	0	0	0	7.0	4	1	3	8
Frank Tanana	0	0	3.60	1	1	0	0	0	5.0	6	2	2	3
TOTAL	1	3	5.80	12	4	0	0	0	35.2	37	23	18	24

GAME 1 AT BAL OCT 3

```
CAL  101 001 0000   3  7 1
BAL  002 100 0003   6  6 0
```
Pitchers: Ryan, MONTAGUE (8) vs Palmer, STANHOUSE (10)
Home Runs: Ford-CAL, Lowenstein-BAL
Attendance: 52,787

GAME 2 AT BAL OCT 4

```
CAL  100 001 132   8 10 1
BAL  441 000 00X   9 11 1
```
Pitchers: FROST, Clear (2), Aase (8) vs FLANAGAN, Stanhouse (8)
Home Runs: Ford-CAL, Murray-BAL
Attendance: 52,108

GAME 3 AT CAL OCT 5

```
BAL  000 101 100   3  8 3
CAL  100 100 002   4  9 0
```
Pitchers: D.Martinez, STANHOUSE (9) vs Tanana, AASE (9)
Home Runs: Baylor-CAL
Attendance: 43,199

GAME 4 AT CAL OCT 6

```
BAL  002 100 500   8 12 1
CAL  000 000 000   0  6 0
```
Pitchers: McGREGOR vs KNAPP, LaRoche (3), Frost (4), Montague (7), Barlow (9)
Home Runs: Kelly-BAL
Attendance: 43,199

PITTSBURGH PIRATES (NL) 4, BALTIMORE ORIOLES (AL) 3

Veteran Willie Stargell was "Pops," and in the Series showed his Pirate "family" the way. Seven of his 12 hits went for extra bases, and he drove in a Series-high seven runs. What Stargell began, submarine reliever Kent Tekulve finished, appearing in five of the seven games and earning three saves.

Stargell drove in a pair of runs in the opener—one of them with an eighth-inning homer—but Pittsburgh's four runs fell short of the five Baltimore had scored in the first inning. The only extra-base hits in Game 2 came from the bat of Eddie Murray, who homered and doubled to drive in both Baltimore runs. But three singles and a sacrifice fly had already given Pittsburgh two runs in the second inning, and two more singles and a walk in the top of the ninth made the score 3–2. Tekulve came on in the last of the ninth to preserve the lead, fanning two as he retired the side in order.

Baltimore bounced back, though, to take the next two games in convincing fashion. The score favored the Orioles 8–4 when Tekulve came on to set the O's down in order over the final two innings. But Baltimore starter Scott McGregor had by then settled into his groove, retiring the final 11 Pirates with relative ease to preserve his lead and the win. It took four Orioles pitchers to hold the Pirates in Game 4. Stargell led the Bucs' 17-hit attack with a homer, double, and single, and the Pirates led 6–3 entering the eighth inning. But Baltimore loaded the bases in the top of the eighth, prompting Pirates manager Chuck Tanner to bring Tekulve in again. This one time the strategy failed, as Tekulve saw six runs score before he retired his first batter.

Down three games to one, the Pirates rebounded in Game 5, scoring seven times in the final three innings for a 7–1 victory. Baltimore starter Jim Palmer matched John Candelaria's shutout pitching through six innings of Game 6 before the Pirates tagged him for pairs of runs in the seventh and eighth. Tekulve, meanwhile, continued Candelaria's shutout through the final three innings, retiring the last seven men in order, four by strikeout. Baltimore scored first in the finale on Rich Dauer's leadoff home run in the third inning, but

Stargell put the Pirates ahead with a two-run homer in the sixth. Tekulve came in with two Orioles on base in the eighth to stifle the threat, and (after the Pirates had scored a pair of insurance runs in the top of the ninth) set Baltimore down in order to complete his team's comeback.

PIT (N)

PLAYER/POS	AVG	G	AB	R	H	2B	3B	HR	RB	BB	SO	SB
Matt Alexander, of	.000	1	0	0	0	0	0	0	0	0	0	0
Jim Bibby, p	.000	2	4	0	0	0	0	0	0	0	1	0
Bert Blyleven, p	.000	2	3	0	0	0	0	0	0	0	0	0
John Candelaria, p	.333	2	3	0	1	0	0	0	0	0	2	0
Mike Easler, ph	.000	2	1	0	0	0	0	0	0	1	0	0
Tim Foli, ss	.333	7	30	6	10	1	1	0	3	2	0	0
Phil Garner, 2b	.500	7	24	4	12	4	0	0	5	3	1	0
Grant Jackson, p	.000	4	1	0	0	0	0	0	0	0	0	0
Bruce Kison, p	.000	1	0	0	0	0	0	0	0	0	0	0
Lee Lacy, ph	.250	4	4	0	1	0	0	0	0	0	1	0
Bill Madlock, 3b	.375	7	24	2	9	1	0	0	3	5	1	0
John Milner, of	.333	3	9	2	3	1	0	0	1	2	0	0
Omar Moreno, of	.333	7	33	4	11	2	0	0	3	1	7	0
Steve Nicosia, c	.063	4	16	1	1	0	0	0	0	0	2	0
Ed Ott, c	.333	3	12	2	4	1	0	0	3	0	2	0
Dave Parker, of	.345	7	29	2	10	3	0	0	4	2	7	0
Don Robinson, p	.000	4	0	0	0	0	0	0	0	0	0	0
Bill Robinson, of-6	.263	7	19	2	5	1	0	0	2	0	4	0
Enrique Romo, p	.000	2	1	0	0	0	0	0	0	0	0	0
Jim Rooker, p	.000	2	2	0	0	0	0	0	0	0	1	0
Manny Sanguillen, ph	.333	3	3	0	1	0	0	0	0	1	0	0
Willie Stargell, 1b	.400	7	30	7	12	4	0	3	7	0	6	0
Rennie Stennett, ph	1.000	1	1	0	1	0	0	0	0	0	0	0
Kent Tekulve, p	.000	5	2	0	0	0	0	0	0	0	0	0
TOTAL	.323		251	32	81	18	1	3	32	16	35	0

PITCHER	W	L	ERA	G	GS	CG	SV	SHO	IP	H	ER	BB	SO
Jim Bibby	0	0	2.61	2	2	0	0	0	10.1	10	3	2	10
Bert Blyleven	1	0	1.80	2	1	0	0	0	10.0	8	2	3	4
John Candelaria	1	1	5.00	2	2	0	0	0	9.0	14	5	2	4
Grant Jackson	1	0	0.00	4	0	0	0	0	4.2	1	0	2	2
Bruce Kison	0	1	1108.00	1	1	0	0	0	0.1	3	4	2	0
Don Robinson	1	0	5.40	4	0	0	0	0	5.0	4	3	6	3
Enrique Romo	0	0	3.86	2	0	0	0	0	4.2	5	2	3	4
Jim Rooker	0	0	1.04	2	1	0	0	0	8.2	5	1	3	4
Kent Tekulve	0	1	2.89	5	0	0	3	0	9.1	4	3	3	10
TOTAL	4	3	3.34	24	7	0	3	0	62.0	54	23	26	41

BAL (A)

PLAYER/POS	AVG	G	AB	R	H	2B	3B	HR	RB	BB	SO	SB
Benny Ayala, of-3	.333	4	6	1	2	0	0	1	2	1	0	0
Mark Belanger, ss-4	.000	5	6	1	0	0	0	0	0	1	1	0
Al Bumbry, of	.143	7	21	3	3	0	0	0	1	2	1	0
Terry Crowley, ph	.250	5	4	0	1	1	0	0	2	1	0	0
Rich Dauer, 2b-5	.294	6	17	2	5	1	0	1	1	0	1	0
Doug DeCinces, 3b	.200	7	25	2	5	0	0	1	3	5	5	1
Rick Dempsey, c-6	.286	7	21	3	6	2	0	0	1	3	0	0
Mike Flanagan, p	.000	3	5	0	0	0	0	0	0	1	2	0
Kiko Garcia, ss	.400	6	20	4	8	2	1	0	6	1	3	0
Pat Kelly, ph	.250	5	4	0	1	0	0	0	0	1	1	0
John Lowenstein, of-3	.231	6	13	2	3	1	0	0	3	1	3	0
Tippy Martinez, p	.000	3	0	0	0	0	0	0	0	0	0	0
Dennis Martinez, p	.000	2	0	0	0	0	0	0	0	0	0	0
Lee May, ph	.000	2	1	0	0	0	0	0	0	1	1	0
Scott McGregor, p	.000	2	4	1	0	0	0	0	0	2	1	0
Eddie Murray, 1b	.154	7	26	3	4	1	0	1	2	4	4	1
Jim Palmer, p	.000	2	4	0	0	0	0	0	0	0	3	0
Gary Roenicke, of-5	.125	6	16	1	2	1	0	0	0	0	6	0
Ken Singleton, of	.357	7	28	3	10	1	0	0	2	2	5	0
Dave Skaggs, c	.333	1	3	1	1	0	0	0	0	0	0	0
Billy Smith, 2b-2	.286	4	7	1	2	0	0	0	0	2	0	0
Don Stanhouse, p	.000	3	0	0	0	0	0	0	0	0	0	0
Sammy Stewart, p	.000	1	1	0	0	0	0	0	0	0	0	0
Tim Stoddard, p	1.000	4	1	0	1	0	0	0	0	1	0	0
Steve Stone, p	.000	1	0	0	0	0	0	0	0	0	0	0
TOTAL	.232		233	26	54	10	1	4	23	26	41	2

PITCHER	W	L	ERA	G	GS	CG	SV	SHO	IP	H	ER	BB	SO
Mike Flanagan	1	1	3.00	3	2	1	0	0	15.0	18	5	2	13
Tippy Martinez	0	0	6.75	3	0	0	0	0	1.1	3	1	0	1
Dennis Martinez	0	0	18.00	2	1	0	0	0	2.0	6	4	0	0
Scott McGregor	1	1	3.18	2	2	1	0	0	17.0	16	6	2	8
Jim Palmer	0	1	3.60	2	2	0	0	0	15.0	18	6	5	8
Don Stanhouse	0	1	13.50	3	0	0	0	0	2.0	6	3	3	0
Sammy Stewart	0	0	0.00	1	0	0	0	0	2.2	4	0	1	0
Tim Stoddard	1	0	5.40	4	0	0	0	0	5.0	6	3	1	3
Steve Stone	0	0	9.00	1	0	0	0	0	2.0	4	2	2	2
TOTAL	3	4	4.35	21	7	2	0	0	62.0	81	30	16	35

GAME 1 AT BAL OCT 10

PIT 000 102 010 4 11 3
BAL 500 000 000 5 6 3
Pitchers: KISON, Rooker (1), Romo (5), D.Robinson (6), Jackson (8) vs FLANAGAN
Home Runs: Stargell-PIT, DeCinces-BAL
Attendance: 53,735

GAME 2 AT BAL OCT 11

PIT 020 000 001 3 11 2
BAL 010 001 000 2 6 1
Pitchers: Blyleven, D.ROBINSON (7), Tekulve (9) vs Palmer, T.Martinez (8), STANHOUSE (9)
Home Runs: Murray-BAL
Attendance: 53,739

GAME 3 AT PIT OCT 12

BAL 002 500 100 8 13 0
PIT 120 001 000 4 9 2
Pitchers: McGREGOR vs CANDELARIA, Romo (4), Jackson (7), Tekulve (8)
Home Runs: Ayala-BAL
Attendance: 50,848

GAME 4 AT PIT OCT 13

BAL 003 000 060 9 12 0
PIT 040 011 000 6 17 1
Pitchers: D.Martinez, Stewart (2), Stone (5), STODDARD (7) vs Bibby, Jackson (6), D.Robinson (8), TEKULVE (8)
Home Runs: Stargell-PIT
Attendance: 50,883

GAME 5 AT PIT OCT 14

BAL 000 010 000 1 6 2
PIT 000 002 23X 7 13 1
Pitchers: FLANAGAN, Stoddard (7), T.Martinez (7), Stanhouse (8) vs Rooker, BLYLEVEN (6)
Attendance: 50,920

GAME 6 AT BAL OCT 16

PIT 000 000 220 4 10 0
BAL 000 000 000 0 7 1
Pitchers: CANDELARIA, Tekulve (7) vs PALMER, Stoddard (9)
Attendance: 53,739

GAME 7 AT BAL OCT 17

PIT 000 002 002 4 10 0
BAL 001 000 000 1 4 2
Pitchers: Bibby, D.Robinson (5), JACKSON (5), Tekulve (8) vs McGREGOR, Stoddard (9), Flanagan (9), Stanhouse (9), T.Martinez (9), D.Martinez (9)
Home Runs: Stargell-PIT, Dauer-BAL
Attendance: 53,733

PHILADELPHIA PHILLIES (EAST) 3, HOUSTON ASTROS (WEST) 2

In the tightest LCS yet, the Phillies took the opener 3–1 on the series' only home run—Greg Luzinski's two-run blast in the sixth inning. It was the only game not to go into extra innings.

The Astros evened the series in Game 2—demolishing a 3–3 tie with four runs in the 10th—and took the series lead in a Game 3 pitchers' duel that saw Joe Niekro hurl ten scoreless innings for Houston. Reliever Dave Smith continued the shutout and took the win as Joe Morgan's triple and Denny Walling's sacrifice fly off Phillies reliever Tug McGraw scored the game's only run in the bottom of the 11th.

The Phillies rebounded, though, with their own set of extra-inning victories. In Game 4, a single and two doubles pushed across two goahead runs in the top of the tenth, and McGraw preserved the edge for his second series save. And in the finale—which saw the lead change hands three times—after Del Unser scored on Garry Maddox's 10th-inning double, Dick Ruthven held off Houston to bring the Phillies their first pennant in 30 years.

PHI (E)

PLAYER/POS	AVG	G	AB	R	H	2B	3B	HR	RB	BB	SO	SB
Ramon Aviles, pr	.000	1	0	1	0	0	0	0	0	0	0	0
Bob Boone, c	.222	5	18	1	4	0	0	0	2	1	2	0
Larry Bowa, ss	.316	5	19	2	6	0	0	0	0	3	3	1
Warren Brusstar, p	.000	2	1	0	0	0	0	0	0	0	1	0
Marty Bystrom, p	.000	1	2	0	0	0	0	0	0	0	1	0
Steve Carlton, p	.000	2	4	0	0	0	0	0	0	0	1	0
Larry Christenson, p	.000	1	2	0	0	0	0	0	0	0	1	0
Greg Gross, of-1	.750	4	4	2	3	0	0	0	1	0	0	0
Greg Luzinski, of	.294	5	17	3	5	2	0	1	4	0	6	0
Garry Maddox, of	.300	5	20	2	6	2	0	0	3	2	2	2
Bake McBride, of	.238	5	21	0	5	0	0	0	0	1	5	2
Tug McGraw, p	.000	5	1	0	0	0	0	0	0	0	0	0
Keith Moreland, c-1	.000	2	1	0	0	0	0	0	1	0	0	0
Dickie Noles, p	.000	2	0	0	0	0	0	0	0	0	0	0
Ron Reed, p	.000	3	0	0	0	0	0	0	0	0	0	0
Pete Rose, 1b	.400	5	20	3	8	0	0	0	2	5	3	0
Dick Ruthven, p	.000	2	2	0	0	0	0	0	0	0	2	0
Kevin Saucier, p	.000	2	0	0	0	0	0	0	0	0	0	0
Mike Schmidt, 3b	.208	5	24	1	5	1	0	0	1	1	6	1
Lonnie Smith, of-2	.600	3	5	2	3	0	0	0	0	0	0	1
Manny Trillo, 2b	.381	5	21	1	8	2	1	0	4	0	2	0
Del Unser, of-2	.400	5	5	2	2	1	0	0	1	0	2	0
George Vukovich, of-1	.000	4	3	0	0	0	0	0	0	0	0	0
TOTAL	.289		190	20	55	8	1	1	19	13	37	7

PITCHER	W	L	ERA	G	GS	CG	SV	SHO	IP	H	ER	BB	SO
Warren Brusstar	1	0	3.38	2	0	0	0	0	2.2	1	1	1	0
Marty Bystrom	0	0	1.69	1	1	0	0	0	5.1	7	1	2	1
Steve Carlton	1	0	2.19	2	2	0	0	0	12.1	11	3	8	6
Larry Christenson	0	0	4.05	1	1	0	0	0	6.2	5	3	5	2
Tug McGraw	0	1	4.50	5	0	0	2	0	8.0	8	4	4	5
Dickie Noles	0	0	0.00	2	0	0	0	0	2.2	1	0	3	0
Ron Reed	0	1	18.00	3	0	0	0	0	2.0	3	4	1	1
Dick Ruthven	1	0	2.00	2	1	0	0	0	9.0	3	2	5	4
Kevin Saucier	0	0	0.00	2	0	0	0	0	0.2	1	0	2	0
TOTAL	3	2	3.28	20	5	0	2	0	49.1	40	18	31	19

HOU (W)

PLAYER/POS	AVG	G	AB	R	H	2B	3B	HR	RB	BB	SO	SB
Joaquin Andujar, p	.000	1	0	0	0	0	0	0	0	0	0	0
Alan Ashby, c	.125	2	8	0	1	0	0	0	1	0	0	0
Dave Bergman, 1b	.333	4	3	0	1	0	1	0	2	0	0	0
Bruce Bochy, c	.000	1	1	0	0	0	0	0	0	0	0	0
Enos Cabell, 3b	.238	5	21	1	5	1	0	0	0	1	3	0
Cesar Cedeno, of	.182	3	11	1	2	0	0	0	1	1	0	0
Jose Cruz, of	.400	5	15	3	6	1	1	0	4	8	1	0
Ken Forsch, p	1.000	2	2	0	2	0	0	0	0	0	0	0
Danny Heep, ph	.000	1	1	0	0	0	0	0	0	0	0	0
Art Howe, 1b-4	.200	5	15	0	3	1	1	0	2	2	2	0
Frank LaCorte, p	.000	2	1	0	0	0	0	0	0	0	0	0
Rafael Landestoy, 2b-3, ss-1	.222	5	9	3	2	0	0	0	2	1	0	1
Jeffrey Leonard, of-1	.000	3	3	0	0	0	0	0	0	0	2	0
Joe Morgan, 2b	.154	4	13	2	2	1	1	0	0	6	1	0
Joe Niekro, p	.000	1	3	0	0	0	0	0	0	0	1	0
Terry Puhl, of-4	.526	5	19	4	10	2	0	0	3	3	2	2
Luis Pujols, c	.100	4	10	1	1	0	1	0	0	3	0	0
Craig Reynolds, ss	.154	4	13	2	2	1	0	0	0	3	1	0
Vern Ruhle, p	.000	1	3	0	0	0	0	0	0	0	1	0
Nolan Ryan, p	.000	2	4	1	0	0	0	0	0	1	2	0
Joe Sambito, p	.000	3	0	0	0	0	0	0	0	0	0	0
Dave Smith, p	.000	3	0	0	0	0	0	0	0	0	0	0
Denny Walling, of-2, 1b-1	.111	3	9	2	1	0	0	0	2	1	0	0
Gary Woods, of-3	.250	4	8	0	2	0	0	0	1	1	3	1
TOTAL	.233		172	19	40	7	5	0	18	31	19	4

PITCHER	W	L	ERA	G	GS	CG	SV	SHO	IP	H	ER	BB	SO
Joaquin Andujar	0	0	0.00	1	0	0	1	0	1.0	0	0	1	0
Ken Forsch	0	1	4.15	2	1	1	0	0	8.2	10	4	1	6
Frank LaCorte	1	1	3.00	2	0	0	0	0	3.0	7	1	2	2
Joe Niekro	0	0	0.00	1	1	0	0	0	10.0	6	0	1	2
Vern Ruhle	0	0	3.86	1	1	0	0	0	7.0	8	3	1	3
Nolan Ryan	0	0	5.40	2	2	0	0	0	13.1	16	8	3	14
Joe Sambito	0	1	4.91	3	0	0	0	0	3.2	4	2	2	6
Dave Smith	1	0	3.86	3	0	0	0	0	2.1	4	1	2	4
TOTAL	2	3	3.49	15	5	1	1	0	49.0	55	19	13	37

GAME 1 AT PHI OCT 7

```
HOU  0 0 1  0 0 0  0 0 0    1  7  0
PHI  0 0 0  0 0 2  1 0 X    3  8  1
```
Pitchers: FORSCH vs CARLTON, McGraw (8)
Home Runs: Luzinski-PHI
Attendance: 65,277

GAME 2 AT PHI OCT 8

```
HOU  0 0 1  0 0 0  1 1 0 4    7  8  1
PHI  0 0 0  2 0 0  0 1 0 1    4 14  2
```
Pitchers: Ryan, Sambito (7), D.Smith (7), LaCORTE (9), Andujar (10) vs Ruthven, McGraw (8), REED (9), Saucier (10)
Attendance: 65,476

GAME 3 AT HOU OCT 10

```
PHI  0 0 0 0 0  0 0 0 0 0 0    0  7  1
HOU  0 0 0 0 0  0 0 0 0 0 1    1  6  1
```
Pitchers: Christenson, Noles (7), McGRAW (8) vs Niekro, D.SMITH (11)
Attendance: 44,443

GAME 4 AT HOU OCT 11

```
PHI  000  000  030  2    5 13  0
HOU  000  110  001  0    3  5  1
```
Pitchers: Carlton, Noles (6), Saucier (7), Reed (7), BRUSSTAR (8), McGraw (10) vs Ruhle, D.Smith (8), SAMBITO (8)
Attendance: 44,952

GAME 5 AT HOU OCT 12

```
PHI  0 2 0  0 0 0  5 0 1    8 13  2
HOU  1 0 0  0 1 3  2 0 0    7 14  0
```
Pitchers: Bystrom, Brusstar (6), Christenson (7), Reed (7), McGraw (8), RUTHVEN (9) vs Ryan, Sambito (8), Forsch (8), LaCORTE (9)
Attendance: 44,802

KANSAS CITY ROYALS (WEST) 3, NEW YORK YANKEES (EAST) 0

Kansas City and New York met for the fourth time in the ALCS, and this time the Royals swept to their first pennant. In the first game the Yankees scored first, with second-inning home runs by Rick Cerone and Lou Piniella, but the Royals' Frank White doubled in a pair later in the inning to tie it, and Willie Aikens' hit in the third gave K.C. the lead. They held it to the end as Larry Gura shut out New York the rest of the way.

The Royals scored three runs in the third inning of Game 2, on Willie Wilson's two-run triple and an RBI double by U. L. Washington. Yankees starter Rudy May stopped K.C. after that, but the Royals already had enough for the win as Dennis Leonard held New York to two runs in eight innings. Dan Quisenberry kept the lid on in the ninth for the save.

Game 3 was decided by home runs. White scored first for the Royals with a solo shot in the fifth. New York took the lead briefly with a two-run sixth, but lost it—and the pennant—in the top of the seventh when Goose Gossage, relieving starter Tommy John with two outs and a man on, gave up an infield single to Washington and a home run to George Brett.

KC (W)

PLAYER/POS	AVG	G	AB	R	H	2B	3B	HR	RB	BB	SO	SB
Willie Aikens, 1b	.364	3	11	0	4	0	0	0	2	0	1	0
George Brett, 3b	.273	3	11	3	3	1	0	2	4	1	0	0
Larry Gura, p	.000	1	0	0	0	0	0	0	0	0	0	0
Clint Hurdle, of	.000	3	2	0	0	0	0	0	0	0	1	0
Pete LaCock, 1b	.000	1	0	0	0	0	0	0	0	0	0	0
Dennis Leonard, p	.000	1	0	0	0	0	0	0	0	0	0	0
Hal McRae, dh	.200	3	10	0	2	0	0	0	0	1	3	0
Amos Otis, of	.333	3	12	2	4	1	0	0	0	0	3	2
Darrell Porter, c	.100	3	10	2	1	0	0	0	0	1	0	0
Dan Quisenberry, p	.000	2	0	0	0	0	0	0	0	0	0	0
Paul Splittorff, p	.000	1	0	0	0	0	0	0	0	0	0	0
U. L. Washington, ss	.364	3	11	1	4	1	0	0	1	2	3	0
John Wathan, of	.000	3	6	1	0	0	0	0	0	3	1	0
Frank White, 2b	.545	3	11	3	6	1	0	1	3	0	1	1
Willie Wilson, of	.308	3	13	2	4	2	1	0	4	1	2	0
TOTAL	.289		97	14	28	6	1	3	14	9	15	3

PITCHER	W	L	ERA	G	GS	CG	SV	SHO	IP	H	ER	BB	SO
Larry Gura	1	0	2.00	1	1	1	0	0	9.0	10	2	1	4
Dennis Leonard	1	0	2.25	1	1	0	0	0	8.0	7	2	1	8
Dan Quisenberry	1	0	0.00	2	0	0	1	0	4.2	4	0	2	1
Paul Splittorff	0	0	1.69	1	1	0	0	0	5.1	5	1	2	3
TOTAL	3	0	1.67	5	3	1	1	0	27.0	26	5	6	16

NY (E)

PLAYER/POS	AVG	G	AB	R	H	2B	3B	HR	RB	BB	SO	SB
Bobby Brown, of	.000	3	10	1	0	0	0	0	0	0	2	0
Rick Cerone, c	.333	3	12	1	4	0	0	1	2	0	1	0
Ron Davis, p	.000	1	0	0	0	0	0	0	0	0	0	0
Bucky Dent, ss	.182	3	11	0	2	0	0	0	0	0	1	0
Oscar Gamble, of-1, dh-1	.200	2	5	1	1	0	0	0	0	1	1	0
Rich Gossage, p	.000	1	0	0	0	0	0	0	0	0	0	0
Ron Guidry, p	.000	1	0	0	0	0	0	0	0	0	0	0
Reggie Jackson, of	.273	3	11	1	3	1	0	0	1	4	0	0
Tommy John, p	.000	1	0	0	0	0	0	0	0	0	0	0
Joe Lefebvre, of	.000	1	0	0	0	0	0	0	0	0	0	0
Rudy May, p	.000	1	0	0	0	0	0	0	0	0	0	0
Bobby Murcer, dh	.000	1	4	0	0	0	0	0	0	0	2	0
Graig Nettles, 3b	.167	2	6	1	1	0	0	1	1	0	1	0
Lou Piniella, of	.200	2	5	1	1	0	0	1	1	2	1	0
Willie Randolph, 2b	.385	3	13	0	5	2	0	0	1	1	3	0
Aurelio Rodriguez, 3b	.333	2	6	0	2	1	0	0	0	0	0	0
Eric Soderholm, dh	.167	2	6	0	1	0	0	0	0	0	0	0
Jim Spencer, ph	.000	1	1	0	0	0	0	0	0	0	0	0
Tom Underwood, p	.000	2	0	0	0	0	0	0	0	0	0	0
Bob Watson, 1b	.500	3	12	0	6	3	1	0	3	5	6	0
TOTAL	.255		102	6	26	7	1	3	5	6	16	0

PITCHER	W	L	ERA	G	GS	CG	SV	SHO	IP	H	ER	BB	SO
Ron Davis	0	0	2.25	1	0	0	0	0	4.0	3	1	1	3
Rich Gossage	0	1	54.00	1	0	0	0	0	0.1	3	2	0	0
Ron Guidry	0	1	12.00	1	1	0	0	0	3.0	5	4	4	2
Tommy John	0	0	2.70	1	1	0	0	0	6.2	8	2	1	3
Rudy May	0	1	3.38	1	1	1	0	0	8.0	6	3	3	4
Tom Underwood	0	0	0.00	2	0	0	0	0	3.0	3	0	0	3
TOTAL	0	3	4.32	7	3	1	0	0	25.0	28	12	9	15

GAME 1 AT KC OCT 8

```
NY   020 000 000    2 10 1
KC   022 000 12X    7 10 0
```
Pitchers: GUIDRY, Davis (4), Underwood (8) vs GURA
Home Runs: Cerone-NY, Piniella-NY, G.Brett-KC
Attendance: 42,598

GAME 2 AT KC OCT 9

```
NY   000 020 000    2 8 0
KC   003 000 00X    3 6 0
```
Pitchers: MAY vs LEONARD, Quisenberry (9)
Home Runs: Nettles-NY
Attendance: 42,633

GAME 3 AT NY OCT 10

```
KC   000 010 300    4 12 1
NY   000 002 000    2 8 0
```
Pitchers: Splittorff, QUISENBERRY (6) vs John, GOSSAGE (7), Underwood (8)
Home Runs: White-KC, G.Brett-KC
Attendance: 56,588

PHILADELPHIA PHILLIES (NL) 4, KANSAS CITY ROYALS (AL) 2

Both clubs had won divisional titles three years in a row—1976–1978—only to lose the League Championship Series. But both overcame the jinx in 1980 to face off in the World Series—the Phillies for the first time in 30 years, the Royals for the first time ever. Kansas City began with a rush in the opener, scoring two runs on Amos Otis' homer in the second inning and two more on Willie Aikens' blast an inning later. But the Phillies came back to take the lead in their half of the third with a five-run rally capped by Bake McBride's three-run homer. Single runs in each of the next two innings kept the Phillies out of reach of Aikens' second two-run shot in the eighth for a narrow 7–6 win. The Phillies extended their Series advantage with a 6–4 win in the second game, rebounding from a two-run deficit with four runs in the eighth inning.

The two clubs traded single runs throughout Game 3. George Brett's first-inning homer began the scoring. The Phillies got the run back in the second inning, the Royals took the lead back in the fourth, Mike Schmidt homered to tie it again in the fifth, Amos Otis countered with a homer in the seventh, and Pete Rose singled in another tying run for Philadelphia in the eighth. Phillies reliever Tug McGraw (who had a save in the opening game) came on to pitch the last of the 10th inning, but couldn't hold the tie, though two men were out before Aikens singled in the Royals' winning run. The Royals evened the Series with their second victory the next day, scoring four times in the first inning and once in the second (with Aikens for the second time in the Series hitting two home runs in a game), then holding on for a 5–3 win.

But the Phillies recovered to win the next two, and their first world crown. Mike Schmidt's fourth-inning two-run homer began the Phillies' scoring in Game 5. The Royals replied with one run in the fifth, and Amos Otis' home run an inning later tied the game. A second K.C. run in the inning put the Royals ahead until the top of the ninth, when pinch hitter Del Unser doubled home Schmidt to tie the game, and Manny Trillo drove home Unser with the go-ahead run. Tug McGraw, who had

held K.C. scoreless through two innings of relief, loaded the bases in the last of the ninth with three walks, but at last fanned Jose Cardenal for the final out. In Game 6, with the Phillies ahead 4–0 in the eighth inning, McGraw relieved starter Steve Carlton with two men on, and loaded the bases with a walk. One Royal scored on a sacrifice fly before McGraw got his third out. In the ninth, another McGraw walk and two singles again loaded the bases with only one away. Frank White popped up in foul territory, and the ball bounced off Bob Boone's catcher's mitt into Pete Rose's hand. Willie Wilson then struck out for the 12th time to end the Series and give the Phillies their first world championship.

PHI (N)

PLAYER/POS	AVG	G	AB	R	H	2B	3B	HR	RB	BB	SO	SB
Bob Boone, c	.412	6	17	3	7	2	0	0	4	4	0	0
Larry Bowa, ss	.375	6	24	3	9	1	0	0	2	0	0	3
Warren Brusstar, p	.000	1	0	0	0	0	0	0	0	0	0	0
Marty Bystrom, p	.000	1	0	0	0	0	0	0	0	0	0	0
Steve Carlton, p	.000	2	0	0	0	0	0	0	0	0	0	0
Larry Christenson, p	.000	1	0	0	0	0	0	0	0	0	0	0
Greg Gross, of-3	.000	4	2	0	0	0	0	0	0	0	0	0
Greg Luzinski, dh-2, of-1	1.000	3	9	0	0	0	0	0	0	1	5	0
Garry Maddox, of	.227	6	22	1	5	2	0	0	1	1	3	0
Bake McBride, of	.304	6	23	3	7	1	0	1	5	2	1	0
Tug McGraw, p	.000	4	0	0	0	0	0	0	0	0	0	0
Keith Moreland, dh	.333	3	12	1	4	0	0	0	1	0	1	0
Dickie Noles, p	.000	1	0	0	0	0	0	0	0	0	0	0
Ron Reed, p	.000	2	0	0	0	0	0	0	0	0	0	0
Pete Rose, 1b	.261	6	23	2	6	1	0	0	1	2	2	0
Dick Ruthven, p	.000	1	0	0	0	0	0	0	0	0	0	0
Kevin Saucier, p	.000	1	0	0	0	0	0	0	0	0	0	0
Mike Schmidt, 3b	.381	6	21	6	8	1	0	2	7	4	3	0
Lonnie Smith, of-5, dh-1	.263	6	19	2	5	1	0	0	1	1	1	0
Manny Trillo, 2b	.217	6	23	4	5	2	0	0	2	0	0	0
Del Unser, of	.500	3	6	2	3	2	0	0	2	0	1	0
Bob Walk, p	.000	1	0	0	0	0	0	0	0	0	0	0
TOTAL	.294		201	27	59	13	0	3	26	15	17	3

PITCHER	W	L	ERA	G	GS	CG	SV	SHO	IP	H	ER	BB	SO
Warren Brusstar	0	0	0.00	1	0	0	0	0	2.1	0	0	1	0
Marty Bystrom	0	0	5.40	1	1	0	0	0	5.0	10	3	1	4
Steve Carlton	2	0	2.40	2	2	0	0	0	15.0	14	4	9	17
Larry Christenson	0	0	1108.00	1	1	0	0	0	0.1	5	4	0	0
Tug McGraw	1	1	1.17	4	0	0	2	0	7.2	7	1	8	10
Dickie Noles	0	0	1.93	1	0	0	0	0	4.2	5	1	2	6
Ron Reed	0	0	0.00	2	0	0	1	0	2.0	2	0	0	2
Dick Ruthven	0	0	3.00	1	1	0	0	0	9.0	9	3	0	7
Kevin Saucier	0	0	0.00	1	0	0	0	0	0.2	0	0	2	0
Bob Walk	1	0	7.71	1	1	0	0	0	7.0	8	6	3	3
TOTAL	4	2	3.69	15	6	0	3	0	53.2	60	22	26	49

KC (A)

PLAYER/POS	AVG	G	AB	R	H	2B	3B	HR	RB	BB	SO	SB
Willie Aikens, 1b	.400	6	20	5	8	0	1	4	8	6	8	0
George Brett, 3b	.375	6	24	3	9	2	1	1	3	2	4	1
Jose Cardenal, of	.200	4	10	0	2	0	0	0	0	0	3	0
Dave Chalk, 3b	.000	1	0	1	0	0	0	0	0	1	0	1
Onix Concepcion, pr	.000	3	0	0	0	0	0	0	0	0	0	0
Rich Gale, p	.000	2	0	0	0	0	0	0	0	0	0	0
Larry Gura, p	.000	2	0	0	0	0	0	0	0	0	0	0
Clint Hurdle, of	.417	4	12	1	5	1	0	0	0	2	1	1
Pete LaCock, 1b	.000	1	0	0	0	0	0	0	0	0	0	0
Dennis Leonard, p	.000	2	0	0	0	0	0	0	0	0	0	0
Renie Martin, p	.000	3	0	0	0	0	0	0	0	0	0	0
Hal McRae, dh	.375	6	24	3	9	3	0	0	1	2	2	0
Amos Otis, of	.478	6	23	4	11	2	0	3	7	3	3	0
Marty Pattin, p	.000	1	0	0	0	0	0	0	0	0	0	0
Darrell Porter, c-4	.143	5	14	1	2	0	0	0	0	3	4	0
Dan Quisenberry, p	.000	6	0	0	0	0	0	0	0	0	0	0
Paul Splittorff, p	.000	1	0	0	0	0	0	0	0	0	0	0
U L Washington, ss	.273	6	22	1	6	0	0	0	2	0	6	0
John Wathan, c-2, of-1	.286	3	7	1	2	0	0	0	1	2	1	0
Frank White, 2b	.080	6	25	1	2	0	0	0	0	1	5	1
Willie Wilson, of	.154	6	26	3	4	1	0	0	0	4	12	2
TOTAL	.290		207	23	60	9	2	8	22	26	49	6

PITCHER	W	L	ERA	G	GS	CG	SV	SHO	IP	H	ER	BB	SO
Rich Gale	0	1	4.26	2	2	0	0	0	6.1	11	3	4	4
Larry Gura	0	0	2.19	2	2	0	0	0	12.1	8	3	3	4
Dennis Leonard	1	1	6.75	2	2	0	0	0	10.2	15	8	2	5
Renie Martin	0	0	2.79	3	0	0	0	0	9.2	11	3	3	2
Marty Pattin	0	0	0.00	1	0	0	0	0	1.0	0	0	0	2
Dan Quisenberry	1	2	5.23	6	0	0	1	0	10.1	10	6	3	0
Paul Splittorff	0	0	5.40	1	0	0	0	0	1.2	4	1	0	0
TOTAL	2	4	4.15	17	6	0	1	0	52.0	59	24	15	17

GAME 1 AT PHI OCT 14

KC 0 2 2 0 0 0 0 2 0   6 9 1
PHI 0 0 5 1 1 0 0 0 X   7 11 0
Pitchers: LEONARD, Martin (4), Quisenberry (8) vs WALK, McGraw (8)
Home Runs: Otis-KC, Aikens-KC (2), McBride-PHI
Attendance: 65,791

GAME 2 AT PHI OCT 15

KC 0 0 0 0 0 1 3 0 0   4 11 0
PHI 0 0 0 0 2 0 0 4 X   6 8 1
Pitchers: Gura, QUISENBERRY (7) vs CARLTON, Reed (9)
Attendance: 65,775

GAME 3 AT KC OCT 17

PHI 0 1 0 0 1 0 0 1 0 0   3 14 0
KC 1 0 0 1 0 0 1 0 0 1   4 11 0
Pitchers: Ruthven, McGRAW (10) vs Gale, Martin (5), QUISENBERRY (8)
Home Runs: Schmidt-PHI, G.Brett-KC, Otis-KC
Attendance: 42,380

GAME 4 AT KC OCT 18

PHI 0 1 0 0 0 0 1 1 0   3 10 1
KC 4 1 0 0 0 0 0 0 X   5 10 2
Pitchers: CHRISTENSON, Noles (1), Saucier (6), Brusstar (6) vs LEONARD, Quisenberry (8)
Home Runs: Aikens-KC (2)
Attendance: 42,363

GAME 5 AT KC OCT 19

PHI 0 0 0 2 0 0 0 0 2   4 7 0
KC 0 0 0 0 1 2 0 0 0   3 12 2
Pitchers: Bystrom, Reed (6), McGRAW (7) vs Gura, QUISENBERRY (7)
Home Runs: Schmidt-PHI, Otis-KC
Attendance: 42,369

GAME 6 AT PHI OCT 21

KC 0 0 0 0 0 0 0 1 0   1 7 2
PHI 0 0 2 0 1 1 0 0 X   4 9 0
Pitchers: GALE, Martin (3), Splittorff (5), Pattin (7), Quisenberry (8) vs CARLTON, McGraw (8)
Attendance: 65,838

MONTREAL EXPOS 3, PHILADELPHIA PHILLIES 2

The Expos, who triumphed over the NL East in the second half of the season, won the first two play-off games at home by identical 3–1 scores over the first-half champion Phillies. In the first postseason game played in Canada the Phillies rapped Expos ace Steve Rogers for 10 hits in Game 1, but Keith Moreland's solo home run in the second was the only hit to produce a run. The homer tied the score briefly, but the Expos regained the lead in the last of the second inning on Chris Speier's double and increased it to 3–1 two innings later. The Expos scored their three runs early in Game 2 on Speier's second-inning single and Gary Carter's two-run homer an inning later. Expos starter Bill Gullickson blanked the Phillies on three hits through 7-2/3 innings, but three two-out hits in the eighth scored a run and brought on reliever Jeff Reardon, who ended the threat for his second save in as many days.

When the Series moved to Philadelphia, the Phillies recovered to even things with a pair of wins. After an easy 13-hit 6–2 victory in Game 3, they took a 4–0 lead into the fourth inning of Game 4. Montreal fought back to tie the game, fell behind again, then re-tied the score at 5–5 in the top of the seventh. The final innings featured a duel between relievers Tug McGraw and Jeff Reardon. McGraw stopped the Expos on one hit through three innings, and took the win when Reardon, after retiring eight Phillies in a row, gave up a leadoff homer to pinch hitter George Vukovich in the bottom of the 10th.

Steve Rogers won the division title for Montreal in the finale, hurling a six-hit shutout against the Phillies and driving in the first two of Montreal's three runs with a bases-loaded single through the box in the fifth inning.

MON (E)

PLAYER/POS	AVG	G	AB	R	H	2B	3B	HR	RB	BB	SO	SB
Stan Bahnsen, p	.000	1	0	0	0	0	0	0	0	0	0	0
Ray Burris, p	.000	1	2	0	0	0	0	0	0	0	2	0
Gary Carter, c	.421	5	19	3	8	3	0	2	6	1	1	0
Warren Cromartie, 1b	.227	5	22	1	5	2	0	0	1	0	9	0
Andre Dawson, of	.300	5	20	1	6	0	1	0	0	1	6	2
Terry Francona, of	.333	5	12	0	4	0	0	0	0	2	2	2
Woody Fryman, p	.000	1	0	0	0	0	0	0	0	0	0	0
Bill Gullickson, p	.000	1	3	0	0	0	0	0	0	0	1	0
Wallace Johnson, ph	.500	2	2	0	1	0	0	0	0	1	0	0
Bill Lee, p	.000	1	0	0	0	0	0	0	0	0	0	0
Jerry Manuel, 2b	.071	5	14	0	1	0	0	0	0	0	2	5
Brad Mills, ph	.000	1	0	0	0	0	0	0	0	0	1	0
John Milner, ph	.500	2	2	0	1	0	0	0	0	1	0	0
Larry Parrish, 3b	.150	5	20	3	3	1	0	0	1	1	3	0
Mike Phillips, 2b	.000	1	1	0	0	0	0	0	0	0	0	0
Jeff Reardon, p	.000	3	1	0	0	0	0	0	0	0	1	0
Steve Rogers, p	.400	2	5	0	2	0	0	0	2	0	1	0
Scott Sanderson, p	.000	1	1	0	0	0	0	0	0	0	1	0
Elias Sosa, p	.000	2	0	0	0	0	0	0	0	0	0	0
Chris Speier, ss	.400	5	15	4	6	2	0	0	3	4	2	0
Tim Wallach, of-3	.250	4	4	1	1	1	0	0	0	0	4	0
Jerry White, of	.167	5	18	3	3	1	0	0	1	2	2	3
TOTAL	.255		161	16	41	10	1	2	16	18	36	7

PITCHER	W	L	ERA	G	GS	CG	SV	SHO	IP	H	ER	BB	SO
Stan Bahnsen	0	0	0.00	1	0	0	0	0	1.1	1	0	1	1
Ray Burris	0	1	5.06	1	1	0	0	0	5.1	7	3	4	4
Woody Fryman	0	0	6.75	1	0	0	0	0	1.1	3	1	1	0
Bill Gullickson	1	0	1.17	1	1	0	0	0	7.2	6	1	1	3
Bill Lee	0	0	0.00	1	0	0	0	0	0.2	0	0	0	1
Jeff Reardon	0	1	2.08	3	0	0	2	0	4.1	1	1	1	2
Steve Rogers	2	0	0.51	2	2	1	0	1	17.2	16	1	3	5
Scott Sanderson	0	0	6.75	1	1	0	0	0	2.2	4	2	2	2
Elias Sosa	0	0	3.00	2	0	0	0	0	3.0	4	1	0	1
TOTAL	3	2	2.05	13	5	1	2	1	44.0	44	10	13	19

PHI (E)

PLAYER/POS	AVG	G	AB	R	H	2B	3B	HR	RB	BB	SO	SB
Luis Aguayo, pr	.000	2	0	1	0	0	0	0	0	0	0	0
Ramon Aviles, ph	.000	1	0	0	0	0	0	0	0	1	0	0
Bob Boone, c	.000	3	5	0	0	0	0	0	0	0	0	0
Larry Bowa, ss	.176	5	17	0	3	1	0	0	1	0	0	0
Warren Brusstar, p	.000	2	0	0	0	0	0	0	0	0	0	0
Steve Carlton, p	.250	2	4	0	1	0	0	0	0	0	0	0
Larry Christenson, p	.000	1	2	0	0	0	0	0	0	0	1	0
Dick Davis, of	.000	1	2	0	0	0	0	0	0	0	1	0
Greg Gross, of-2	.000	4	4	0	0	0	0	0	0	0	0	0
Sparky Lyle, p	.000	3	0	0	0	0	0	0	0	0	0	0
Garry Maddox, of	.333	2	3	0	1	1	0	0	0	0	0	0
Gary Matthews, of	.400	5	20	3	8	0	1	1	1	0	2	0
Bake McBride, of	.200	4	15	1	3	1	0	0	0	0	5	0
Tug McGraw, p	.000	2	0	0	0	0	0	0	0	0	0	0
Keith Moreland, c	.462	4	13	2	6	0	0	1	3	1	1	0
Dickie Noles, p	.000	1	0	0	0	0	0	0	0	1	0	0
Ron Reed, p	.000	4	0	0	0	0	0	0	0	0	0	0
Pete Rose, 1b	.300	5	20	1	6	1	0	0	2	2	0	0
Dick Ruthven, p	.000	1	1	0	0	0	0	0	0	0	0	0
Mike Schmidt, 3b	.250	5	16	3	4	1	0	1	2	4	2	0
Lonnie Smith, of	.263	5	19	1	5	1	0	0	0	0	4	0
Manny Trillo, 2b	.188	5	16	1	3	0	0	0	1	4	0	0
George Vukovich, of-3	.444	5	9	1	4	0	0	1	2	0	3	0
TOTAL	.265		166	14	44	6	1	4	12	13	19	0

PITCHER	W	L	ERA	G	GS	CG	SV	SHO	IP	H	ER	BB	SO
Warren Brusstar	0	0	4.91	2	0	0	0	0	3.2	5	2	1	3
Steve Carlton	0	2	3.86	2	2	0	0	0	14.0	14	6	8	13
Larry Christenson	1	0	1.50	1	1	0	0	0	6.0	4	1	1	8
Sparky Lyle	0	0	0.00	3	0	0	0	0	2.1	4	0	2	1
Tug McGraw	1	0	0.00	2	0	0	0	0	4.0	2	0	0	2
Dickie Noles	0	0	4.50	1	1	0	0	0	4.0	4	2	2	5
Ron Reed	0	0	3.00	4	0	0	0	0	6.0	5	2	3	4
Dick Ruthven	0	1	4.50	1	1	0	0	0	4.0	3	2	1	0
TOTAL	2	3	3.07	16	5	0	0	0	44.0	41	15	18	36

GAME 1 AT MON OCT 7

```
PHI  010 000 000   1 10 1
MON  110 100 00X   3  3 10 0
```
Pitchers: CARLTON, R.Reed (7) vs ROGERS, Reardon (9)
Home Runs: Moreland-PHI
Attendance: 34,327

GAME 2 AT MON OCT 8

```
PHI  000 000 010   1 6 2
MON  012 000 00X   3 7 0
```
Pitchers: RUTHVEN, Brusstar (5), Lyle (7), McGraw (8) vs GULLICKSON, Reardon (8)
Home Runs: Carter-MON
Attendance: 45,896

GAME 3 AT PHI OCT 9

```
MON  010 000 010   2  8 4
PHI  020 002 20X   6 13 0
```
Pitchers: BURRIS, Lee (6), Sosa (7) vs CHRISTENSON, Lyle (7), R.Reed (8)
Attendance: 36,835

GAME 4 AT PHI OCT 10

```
MON  000 112 1000   5 10 1
PHI  202 001 0001   6  9 0
```
Pitchers: Sanderson, Bahnsen (3), Sosa (5), Fryman (6), REARDON (7) vs Noles, Brusstar (5), Lyle (6), R.Reed (7), McGRAW (8)
Home Runs: Carter-MON, Schmidt-PHI, Matthews-PHI, G.Vukovich-PHI
Attendance: 38,818

GAME 5 AT PHI OCT 11

```
MON  000 021 000   3 8 1
PHI  000 000 000   0 6 0
```
Pitchers: ROGERS vs CARLTON, R.Reed (9)
Attendance: 47,384

LOS ANGELES DODGERS 3, HOUSTON ASTROS 2

Cincinnati, with the league's best overall season record, failed to win either half season in the NL West, and watched from the sidelines as first-half winner Los Angeles, down two games to none, recovered to win the final three games—and the division title—from second-half victor Houston. In the opener, Alan Ashby's two-run homer in the last of the ninth broke a 1–1 tie and gave Nolan Ryan a two-hit victory. The next day, Denny Walling's two-out bases-loaded single in the last of the 11th scored Phil Garner with the game's only run.

When the clubs shifted to Los Angeles for the remainder of the series, the Dodgers came alive. In Game 3, a first-inning double by Dusty Baker and home run by Steve Garvey drove in three runs. Pitcher Burt Hooton and two relievers held Houston to three hits in what became a 6–1 Dodgers victory. The next day, Fernando Valenzuela and Vern Ruhle hurled matching four-hitters. But Pedro Guerrero's home run in the fifth inning and a pair of singles sandwiched around a sacrifice and intentional walk in the seventh gave Los Angeles two runs, while Valenzuela held Houston to a single run in the ninth. In the finale, Jerry Reuss blanked the Astros on five hits while his Dodgers blended three of their seven hits with a walk and an Astros error for three runs in the sixth. Two more hits produced a final run an inning later.

LA (W)

PLAYER/POS	AVG	G	AB	R	H	2B	3B	HR	RB	BB	SO	SB
Dusty Baker, of	.167	5	18	2	3	1	0	0	1	2	0	0
Terry Forster, p	.000	1	0	0	0	0	0	0	0	0	0	0
Steve Garvey, 1b	.368	5	19	4	7	0	1	2	4	0	2	0
Pedro Guerrero, 3b	.176	5	17	1	3	1	0	1	1	2	4	1
Burt Hooton, p	.000	1	3	0	0	0	0	0	0	0	0	0
Steve Howe, p	.000	2	0	0	0	0	0	0	0	0	0	0
Jay Johnstone, ph	.000	1	1	0	0	0	0	0	0	0	0	0
Ken Landreaux, of	.200	5	20	1	4	1	0	0	1	0	1	0
Davey Lopes, 2b	.200	5	20	1	4	1	0	0	3	7	1	4
Mike Marshall, ph	.000	1	1	0	0	0	0	0	0	0	1	0
Rick Monday, of	.214	5	14	1	3	0	0	0	1	2	4	0
Tom Niedenfuer, p	.000	1	0	0	0	0	0	0	0	0	0	0
Jerry Reuss, p	.000	2	8	0	0	0	0	0	0	0	8	0
Bill Russell, ss	.250	5	16	1	4	1	0	0	2	3	1	0
Steve Sax, 2b	.000	1	0	0	0	0	0	0	0	0	0	0
Mike Scioscia, c	.154	4	13	0	2	0	0	0	1	1	2	0
Reggie Smith, ph	.000	2	1	0	0	0	0	0	0	1	0	0
Dave Stewart, p	.000	2	0	0	0	0	0	0	0	0	0	0
Derrel Thomas, of	.000	4	2	1	0	0	0	0	0	0	1	0
Fernando Valenzuela, p	.000	2	4	0	0	0	0	0	0	0	1	0
Bob Welch, p	.000	2	0	0	0	0	0	0	0	0	0	0
Steve Yeager, c	.400	2	5	1	2	1	0	0	0	0	1	0
TOTAL	.198		162	13	32	6	1	3	12	13	34	2

PITCHER	W	L	ERA	G	GS	CG	SV	SHO	IP	H	ER	BB	SO
Terry Forster	0	0	0.00	1	0	0	0	0	0.1	0	0	0	0
Burt Hooton	1	0	1.29	1	1	0	0	0	7.0	3	1	3	2
Steve Howe	0	0	0.00	2	0	0	0	0	2.0	1	0	0	2
Tom Niedenfuer	0	0	0.00	1	0	0	0	0	0.1	1	0	1	1
Jerry Reuss	1	0	0.00	2	2	1	0	1	18.0	10	0	5	7
Dave Stewart	0	2	40.50	2	0	0	0	0	0.2	4	3	0	1
Fernando Valenzuela	1	0	1.06	2	2	1	0	0	17.0	10	2	3	10
Bob Welch	0	0	0.00	1	0	0	0	0	1.0	0	0	1	1
TOTAL	3	2	1.17	12	5	2	0	1	46.1	29	6	13	24

HOU (W)

PLAYER/POS	AVG	G	AB	R	H	2B	3B	HR	RB	BB	SO	SB
Alan Ashby, c	.111	3	9	1	1	0	0	1	2	2	0	0
Cesar Cedeno, 1b	.231	4	13	0	3	1	0	0	0	2	2	2
Jose Cruz, of	.300	5	20	0	6	1	0	0	0	1	3	1
Kiko Garcia, ss-1	.000	2	4	0	0	0	0	0	0	0	1	0
Phil Garner, 2b	.111	5	18	1	2	0	0	0	0	3	3	0
Art Howe, 3b	.235	5	17	1	4	0	0	1	1	2	1	0
Bob Knepper, p	.000	1	1	0	0	0	0	0	0	0	0	0
Frank LaCorte, p	.000	2	0	0	0	0	0	0	0	0	0	0
Joe Niekro, p	.000	1	2	0	0	0	0	0	0	0	0	0
Joe Pittman, ph	.000	2	2	0	0	0	0	0	0	0	0	0
Terry Puhl, of	.190	5	21	2	4	1	0	0	0	0	1	1
Luis Pujols, c	.000	2	6	0	0	0	0	0	0	0	1	0
Craig Reynolds, ss-1	.333	2	3	1	1	0	0	0	0	0	0	0
Dave Roberts, ph	.000	1	1	0	0	0	0	0	0	0	1	0
Vern Ruhle, p	.000	1	1	0	0	0	0	0	0	0	1	0
Nolan Ryan, p	.250	2	4	0	1	0	0	0	0	1	1	0
Joe Sambito, p	.000	2	0	0	0	0	0	0	0	0	0	0
Tony Scott, of	.150	5	20	0	3	0	0	0	2	1	6	0
Billy Smith, p	.000	1	0	0	0	0	0	0	0	0	0	0
Dave Smith, p	.000	2	0	0	0	0	0	0	0	0	0	0
Harry Spilman, ph	.000	1	1	0	0	0	0	0	0	0	0	0
Dickie Thon, ss	.182	4	11	0	2	0	0	0	0	1	0	0
Denny Walling, 1b-2	.333	3	6	0	2	0	0	0	1	0	1	0
Gary Woods, ph	.000	2	2	0	0	0	0	0	0	0	1	0
TOTAL	.179		162	6	29	3	0	2	6	13	24	4

PITCHER	W	L	ERA	G	GS	CG	SV	SHO	IP	H	ER	BB	SO
Bob Knepper	0	1	5.40	1	1	0	0	0	5.0	6	3	2	4
Frank LaCorte	0	0	0.00	2	0	0	0	0	3.2	2	0	1	5
Joe Niekro	0	0	0.00	1	1	0	0	0	8.0	7	0	3	4
Vern Ruhle	0	1	2.25	1	1	1	0	0	8.0	4	2	2	1
Nolan Ryan	1	1	1.80	2	2	1	0	0	15.0	6	3	3	14
Joe Sambito	1	0	16.20	2	0	0	0	0	1.2	5	3	2	2
Billy Smith	0	0	0.00	1	0	0	0	0	0.1	0	0	0	0
Dave Smith	0	0	3.86	2	0	0	0	0	2.1	2	1	0	4
TOTAL	2	3	2.45	12	5	2	0	0	44.0	32	12	13	34

GAME 1 AT HOU OCT 6

```
LA   000 000 100   1 2 0
HOU  000 001 002   3 8 0
```
Pitchers: Valenzuela, STEWART (9) vs RYAN
Home Runs: Garvey-LA, Ashby-HOU
Attendance: 44,836

GAME 2 AT HOU OCT 7

```
LA   000 000 00000  0 9 1
HOU  000 000 00001  1 9 0
```
Pitchers: Reuss, S.Howe (10), STEWART (11), Forster (11), Niedenfuer (11) vs Niekro, D.Smith (9), SAMBITO (11)
Attendance: 42,398

GAME 3 AT LA OCT 9

```
HOU  001 000 000   1 3 2
LA   300 000 03X    6 10 0
```
Pitchers: KNEPPER, LaCorte (6), Sambito (8), B.Smith (8) vs HOOTON, S.Howe (8), Welch (9)
Home Runs: Garvey-LA, A.Howe-HOU
Attendance: 46,820

GAME 4 AT LA OCT 10

```
HOU  000 000 001   1 4 0
LA   000 010 10X    2 4 0
```
Pitchers: RUHLE vs VALENZUELA
Home Runs: Guerrero-LA
Attendance: 55,983

GAME 5 AT LA OCT 11

```
HOU  000 000 000    0 5 3
LA   000 003 10X    4 7 2
```
Pitchers: RYAN, D.Smith (7), LaCorte (7) vs REUSS
Attendance: 55,979

NEW YORK YANKEES 3, MILWAUKEE BREWERS 2

The home field didn't seem to offer any advantage in this series. First-half winner New York captured both games played in Milwaukee, but when the Series moved to Yankee Stadium for the final three games, the second-half champion Brewers evened the series.

Milwaukee took a 2–0 lead early in the opener, but New York erupted for four runs in the fourth on Oscar Gamble's two-run homer and Rick Cerone's double, and held on to win, 5–3. In Game 2 rookie starter Dave Righetti fanned 10 Brewers in his six innings and Goose Gossage's brilliant relief earned him his second save in two days as the Yankees took a 3–0 win on homers by Lou Piniella and Reggie Jackson.

Milwaukee, struggling against elimination, took the lead in the seventh inning of Game 3 on Ted Simmons' two-run homer. New York tied the score at 3–3 in their half of the inning, but Paul Molitor broke the tie in the eighth with a solo homer. Simmons doubled home an insurance run later in the inning for a 5–3 Brewers win. The Brewers managed only four hits in Game 4, but three of them came in the fourth inning and combined with a sacrifice fly to produce the Brewers' two runs. New York scored once in the sixth, but baserunning errors an inning later ended their only other scoring threat.

In the finale Milwaukee scored two early runs, but the Yankees (as they had done in the opener) took the lead with a four-run fourth— this time on home runs by Reggie Jackson and Oscar Gamble, and Rick Cerone's single. Cerone later hit an insurance homer, as the home team finally won a game— and captured the series.

NY (E)

PLAYER/POS	AVG	G	AB	R	H	2B	3B	HR	RB	BB	SO	SB
Bobby Brown, pr	.000	1	0	0	0	0	0	0	0	0	0	0
Rick Cerone, c	.333	5	18	1	6	2	0	1	5	0	2	0
Ron Davis, p	.000	3	0	0	0	0	0	0	0	0	0	0
Barry Foote, ph	.000	1	0	0	0	0	0	0	0	0	0	0
Oscar Gamble, dh	.556	4	9	2	5	1	0	2	3	1	2	0
Rich Gossage, p	.000	3	0	0	0	0	0	0	0	0	0	0
Ron Guidry, p	.000	2	0	0	0	0	0	0	0	0	0	0
Reggie Jackson, of	.300	5	20	4	6	0	0	2	4	1	5	0
Tommy John, p	.000	1	0	0	0	0	0	0	0	0	0	0
Rudy May, p	.000	1	0	0	0	0	0	0	0	0	0	0
Larry Milbourne, ss	.316	5	19	4	6	1	0	0	0	0	1	0
Jerry Mumphrey, of	.095	5	21	2	2	0	0	0	0	0	1	1
Bobby Murcer, ph	.000	2	1	0	0	0	0	0	0	1	0	0
Graig Nettles, 3b	.059	5	17	1	1	0	0	0	1	3	1	0
Lou Piniella, dh	.200	4	10	1	2	1	0	1	3	0	0	0
Willie Randolph, 2b	.200	5	20	0	4	0	0	0	1	4	0	0
Rick Reuschel, p	.000	1	0	0	0	0	0	0	0	0	0	0
Dave Revering, 1b	.000	2	0	0	0	0	0	0	0	0	0	0
Dave Righetti, p	.000	2	0	0	0	0	0	0	0	0	0	0
Bob Watson, 1b	.438	5	16	2	7	0	0	0	1	1	1	0
Dave Winfield, of	.350	5	20	2	7	3	0	0	0	1	5	0
TOTAL	.269		171	19	46	8	0	6	18	9	22	1

PITCHER	W	L	ERA	G	GS	CG	SV	SHO	IP	H	ER	BB	SO
Ron Davis	1	0	0.00	3	0	0	0	0	6.0	1	0	2	6
Rich Gossage	0	0	0.00	3	0	0	3	0	6.2	3	0	2	8
Ron Guidry	0	0	5.40	2	2	0	0	0	8.1	11	5	3	8
Tommy John	0	1	6.43	1	1	0	0	0	7.0	8	5	2	0
Rudy May	0	0	0.00	1	0	0	0	0	2.0	1	0	0	1
Rick Reuschel	0	1	3.00	1	1	0	0	0	6.0	4	2	1	3
Dave Righetti	2	0	1.00	2	1	0	0	0	9.0	8	1	3	13
TOTAL	3	2	2.60	13	5	0	3	0	45.0	36	13	13	39

MIL (E)

PLAYER/POS	AVG	G	AB	R	H	2B	3B	HR	RB	BB	SO	SB
Sal Bando, 3b	.294	5	17	1	5	3	0	0	1	2	3	0
Dwight Bernard, p	.000	2	0	0	0	0	0	0	0	0	0	0
Thad Bosley, dh	.000	1	0	0	0	0	0	0	0	0	0	0
Mike Caldwell, p	.000	2	0	0	0	0	0	0	0	0	0	0
Cecil Cooper, 1b	.222	5	18	1	4	0	0	0	3	1	3	0
Jamie Easterly, p	.000	2	0	0	0	0	0	0	0	0	0	0
Marshall Edwards, of	.000	2	1	0	0	0	0	0	0	0	1	0
Rollie Fingers, p	.000	3	0	0	0	0	0	0	0	0	0	0
Jim Gantner, 2b	.143	4	14	1	2	1	0	0	0	0	2	0
Moose Haas, p	.000	2	0	0	0	0	0	0	0	0	0	0
Roy Howell, dh-3	.400	4	5	0	2	0	0	0	0	2	2	0
Randy Lerch, p	.000	1	0	0	0	0	0	0	0	0	0	0
Bob McClure, p	.000	3	0	0	0	0	0	0	0	0	0	0
Paul Molitor, of	.250	5	20	2	5	0	0	1	1	2	5	0
Don Money, 2b-1, dh-1	.000	2	3	0	0	0	0	0	0	0	0	0
Charlie Moore, of-2, dh-2	.222	4	9	0	2	0	0	0	1	1	2	0
Ben Oglivie, of	.167	5	18	0	3	1	0	0	1	0	7	0
Ed Romero, 2b	.500	1	2	1	1	0	0	0	0	0	1	0
Ted Simmons, c	.222	5	18	1	4	1	0	1	4	2	2	0
Jim Slaton, p	.000	4	0	0	0	0	0	0	0	0	0	0
Gorman Thomas, of-3, dh-2	.111	5	18	2	2	0	0	1	1	1	9	0
Pete Vuckovich, p	.000	2	0	0	0	0	0	0	0	0	0	0
Robin Yount, ss	.316	5	19	4	6	0	1	0	1	2	2	1
TOTAL	.222		162	13	36	6	1	3	13	13	39	1

PITCHER	W	L	ERA	G	GS	CG	SV	SHO	IP	H	ER	BB	SO
Dwight Bernard	0	0	0.00	2	0	0	0	0	2.1	0	0	0	0
Mike Caldwell	0	1	4.32	2	1	0	0	0	8.1	9	4	0	4
Jamie Easterly	0	0	6.75	2	0	0	0	0	1.1	2	1	0	1
Rollie Fingers	1	0	3.86	3	0	0	1	0	4.2	7	2	1	5
Moose Haas	0	2	9.45	2	2	0	0	0	6.2	13	7	1	1
Randy Lerch	0	0	1.50	1	1	0	0	0	6.0	3	1	4	3
Bob McClure	0	0	0.00	3	0	0	0	0	3.1	4	0	0	2
Jim Slaton	0	0	3.00	4	0	0	0	0	6.0	6	2	0	2
Pete Vuckovich	1	0	0.00	2	1	0	0	0	5.1	2	0	3	4
TOTAL	2	3	3.48	21	5	0	1	0	44.0	46	17	9	22

GAME 1 AT MIL OCT 7

NY 000 400 001 5 13 1
MIL 011 010 000 3 8 3
Pitchers: Guidry, DAVIS (5), Gossage (8) vs HAAS, Bernard (4), McClure (5), Slaton (6), Fingers (8)
Home Runs: Gamble-NY
Attendance: 35,064

GAME 2 AT MIL OCT 8

NY 000 100 002 3 7 0
MIL 000 000 000 0 7 0
Pitchers: RIGHETTI, Davis (7), Gossage (7) vs CALDWELL, Slaton (9)
Home Runs: Piniella-NY, Jackson-NY
Attendance: 26,395

GAME 3 AT NY OCT 9

MIL 000 000 320 5 9 0
NY 000 100 200 3 8 2
Pitchers: Lerch, FINGERS (7) vs JOHN, May (8)
Home Runs: Simmons-MIL, Molitor-MIL
Attendance: 56,411

GAME 4 AT NY OCT 10

MIL 000 200 000 2 4 2
NY 000 001 000 1 5 0
Pitchers: VUCKOVICH, Easterly (6), Slaton (7), McClure (8), Fingers (9) vs REUSCHEL, Davis (7)
Attendance: 52,077

GAME 5 AT NY OCT 11

MIL 011 000 100 3 8 0
NY 000 400 12X 7 13 0
Pitchers: HAAS, Caldwell (4), Bernard (4), McClure (6), Slaton (7), Easterly (8), Vuckovich (8) vs Guidry, RIGHETTI (5), Gossage (8)
Home Runs: Thomas-MIL, Jackson-NY, Gamble-NY, Cerone-NY
Attendance: 47,505

OAKLAND A'S 3, KANSAS CITY ROYALS 0

First-half winner Oakland, with the league's best win-loss record over the full season, swept the division title from second-half champ Kansas City (who, with a full-season record of 50–53, had become the only club in major-league history to qualify for post-season play with a losing record). Twice in the opener the Royals loaded the bases against Mike Norris with fewer than two outs, but both times failed to score. Meanwhile, after a Royals error had prolonged the A's fourth inning, Wayne Gross homered for three unearned Oakland runs. Dwayne Murphy's eighth-inning solo shot gave the A's a fourth run. The game ended with Norris possessor of a four-hit shutout.

Game 2 was closer. Oakland's Tony Armas doubled in a run in the top of the first, and doubled home another in the eighth (his fourth hit of the game) to break a 1–1 tie and provide the margin needed for pitcher Steve McCatty's six-hit win. Oakland's Rick Langford yielded 10 hits in Game 3 (including Kansas City's only extra-base hit of the series, a double), but only one Royal scored. The A's, meanwhile, were sending four runs across the plate—three of them by Rickey Henderson, who reached base four times on pairs of hits and walks.

OAK (W)

PLAYER/POS	AVG	G	AB	R	H	2B	3B	HR	RB	BB	SO	SB
Tony Armas, of	.545	3	11	1	6	2	0	0	3	1	1	0
Dave Beard, p	.000	1	0	0	0	0	0	0	0	0	0	0
Rick Bosetti, of	.000	1	0	0	0	0	0	0	0	0	0	0
Keith Drumright, dh	.250	1	4	0	1	0	0	0	0	0	0	0
Wayne Gross, 3b-1	.400	2	5	1	2	0	0	1	3	0	0	0
Mike Heath, c	.000	2	8	0	0	0	0	0	0	0	1	0
Rickey Henderson, of	.182	3	11	3	2	0	0	0	0	2	0	2
Cliff Johnson, dh	.286	2	7	0	2	1	0	0	0	0	1	0
Mickey Klutts, 3b	.143	2	7	0	1	0	0	0	0	0	1	0
Rick Langford, p	.000	1	0	0	0	0	0	0	0	0	0	0
Steve McCatty, p	.000	1	0	0	0	0	0	0	0	0	0	0
Dave McKay, 2b	.273	3	11	1	3	0	0	1	1	1	1	0
Kelvin Moore, 1b	.000	2	8	0	0	0	0	0	0	0	2	0
Dwayne Murphy, of	.545	3	11	4	6	1	0	1	2	1	1	0
Jeff Newman, c	.000	1	3	0	0	0	0	0	0	0	1	0
Mike Norris, p	.000	1	0	0	0	0	0	0	0	0	0	0
Rob Picciolo, ss	.333	1	3	0	1	0	0	0	0	0	0	0
Jim Spencer, 1b	.250	1	4	0	1	1	0	0	0	0	0	0
Fred Stanley, ss	.000	3	6	0	0	0	0	0	0	1	1	0
Tom Underwood, p	.000	1	0	0	0	0	0	0	0	0	0	0
TOTAL	.253		99	10	25	5	0	3	9	6	10	2

PITCHER	W	L	ERA	G	GS	CG	SV	SHO	IP	H	ER	BB	SO
Dave Beard	0	0	0.00	1	0	0	1	0	1.1	0	0	0	2
Rick Langford	1	0	1.23	1	1	0	0	0	7.1	10	1	0	3
Steve McCatty	1	0	1.00	1	1	1	0	0	9.0	6	1	4	3
Mike Norris	1	0	0.00	1	1	1	0	1	9.0	4	0	3	2
Tom Underwood	0	0	0.00	1	0	0	0	0	0.1	0	0	0	1
TOTAL	3	0	0.67	5	3	2	1	1	27.0	20	2	7	11

KC (W)

PLAYER/POS	AVG	G	AB	R	H	2B	3B	HR	RB	BB	SO	SB
Willie Aikens, 1b	.333	3	9	0	3	0	0	0	0	3	2	0
George Brett, 3b	.167	3	12	0	2	0	0	0	0	0	0	0
Cesar Geronimo, pr	.000	1	0	0	0	0	0	0	0	0	0	0
Larry Gura, p	.000	1	0	0	0	0	0	0	0	0	0	0
Clint Hurdle, of	.273	3	11	0	3	0	0	0	0	1	1	0
Mike Jones, p	.000	1	0	0	0	0	0	0	0	0	0	0
Dennis Leonard, p	.000	1	0	0	0	0	0	0	0	0	0	0
Renie Martin, p	.000	2	0	0	0	0	0	0	0	0	0	0
Lee May, 1b	.000	1	0	0	0	0	0	0	0	0	0	0
Hal McRae, dh	.091	3	11	0	1	1	0	0	0	1	1	0
Amos Otis, of	.000	3	12	0	0	0	0	0	1	0	4	0
Dan Quisenberry, p	.000	1	0	0	0	0	0	0	0	0	0	0
U. L. Washington, ss	.222	3	9	0	2	0	0	0	0	0	1	0
John Wathan, c	.300	3	10	1	3	0	0	0	0	1	1	0
Frank White, 2b	.182	3	11	1	2	0	0	0	0	1	1	0
Willie Wilson, of	.308	3	13	0	4	0	0	0	1	0	0	0
TOTAL	.204		98	2	20	1	0	0	2	7	11	0

PITCHER	W	L	ERA	G	GS	CG	SV	SHO	IP	H	ER	BB	SO
Larry Gura	0	1	7.36	1	1	0	0	0	3.2	7	3	3	3
Mike Jones	0	1	2.25	1	1	0	0	0	8.0	9	2	0	2
Dennis Leonard	0	1	1.13	1	1	0	0	0	8.0	7	1	1	3
Renie Martin	0	0	0.00	2	0	0	0	0	5.1	1	0	2	2
Dan Quisenberry	0	0	0.00	1	0	0	0	0	1.0	1	0	0	0
TOTAL	0	3	2.08	6	3	0	0	0	26.0	25	6	6	10

GAME 1 AT KC OCT 6

```
OAK  000 300 010   4 8 2
KC   000 000 000   0 4 1
```
Pitchers: NORRIS vs LEONARD, Martin (9)
Home Runs: Gross-OAK, Murphy-OAK
Attendance: 40,592

GAME 2 AT KC OCT 7

```
OAK  100 000 010   2 10 1
KC   000 010 000   1 6 0
```
Pitchers: McCATTY vs JONES, Quisenberry (9)
Attendance: 40,274 10 1

GAME 3 AT OAK OCT 9

```
KC   000 100 000   1 10 3
OAK  101 200 00X   4 7 0
```
Pitchers: GURA, Martin (4) vs LANGFORD, Underwood (8), Beard (8)
Home Runs: McKay-OAK
Attendance: 40,002

LOS ANGELES DODGERS (WEST) 3, MONTREAL EXPOS (EAST) 2

Fine pitching characterized the series, with the losing team held to one run in four of the five games. In the exception Ray Burris hurled a shutout for the Expos.

Montreal put men on base in each inning of the opener. But the pitching of Burt Hooton and Bob Welch—plus some fine Dodgers fielding—kept the Expos from scoring until the ninth, when their one run was too little to overcome the Dodger's four-run cushion. Burris' shutout evened the series in Game 2 as the Expos scored three times against rookie sensation Fernando Valenzuela. The Expos took the series lead in Game 3, overcoming a 1–0 deficit with a two-out four-run burst in the sixth (capped by Jerry White's three-run homer).

In the end, though, the Dodgers prevailed. Through seven innings of Game 4, Hooton and the Expos' Bill Gullickson dueled at 1–1. But in the top of the eighth, Steve Garvey homered with a man aboard, and four more Dodger runs in the ninth put the game away. The finale—Burris vs. Valenzuela again—featured another 1–1 duel, this one reaching into the top of the ninth when, with two out, Rick Monday homered off Steve Rogers, who came on in relief of Burris. In the bottom of the ninth, Valenzuela walked two batters after retiring two, but Welch came on to save the game and the pennant.

LA (W)

PLAYER/POS	AVG	G	AB	R	H	2B	3B	HR	RB	BB	SO	SB
Dusty Baker, of	.316	5	19	3	6	1	0	0	3	1	0	0
Bobby Castillo, p	.000	1	0	0	0	0	0	0	0	0	0	0
Ron Cey, 3b	.278	5	18	1	5	1	0	0	3	3	2	0
Terry Forster, p	.000	1	0	0	0	0	0	0	0	0	0	0
Steve Garvey, 1b	.286	5	21	2	6	0	0	1	2	0	4	0
Pedro Guerrero, of	.105	5	19	1	2	0	0	1	2	1	4	0
Burt Hooton, p	.000	2	5	0	0	0	0	0	0	0	2	0
Steve Howe, p	.000	2	0	0	0	0	0	0	0	0	0	0
Jay Johnstone, ph	.000	2	2	0	0	0	0	0	0	0	0	0
Ken Landreaux, of-3	.100	5	10	0	1	1	0	0	0	3	2	0
Davey Lopes, 2b	.278	5	18	0	5	0	0	0	0	1	3	5
Rick Monday, of-2	.333	3	9	2	3	0	0	1	1	0	4	0
Tom Niedenfuer, p	.000	1	0	0	0	0	0	0	0	0	0	0
Alejandro Pena, p	.000	2	0	0	0	0	0	0	0	0	0	0
Jerry Reuss, p	.000	1	2	0	0	0	0	0	0	0	0	0
Bill Russell, ss	.313	5	16	2	5	0	1	0	1	1	1	0
Steve Sax, 2b	.000	1	0	0	0	0	0	0	0	0	0	0
Mike Scioscia, c	.133	5	15	1	2	0	0	1	1	2	1	0
Reggie Smith, ph	1.000	1	1	0	1	0	0	0	1	0	0	0
Derrel Thomas, 3b-1, of-1	1.000	2	1	2	1	0	0	0	0	1	0	0
Fernando Valenzuela, p	.000	2	5	0	0	0	0	0	1	0	0	0
Bob Welch, p	.000	3	0	0	0	0	0	0	0	0	0	0
Steve Yeager, c	.500	1	2	1	1	0	0	0	0	0	0	0
TOTAL	.233		163	15	38	3	1	4	15	12	23	5

PITCHER	W	L	ERA	G	GS	CG	SV	SHO	IP	H	ER	BB	SO
Bobby Castillo	0	0	0.00	1	0	0	0	0	1.0	0	0	0	1
Terry Forster	0	0	0.00	1	0	0	0	0	0.1	0	0	0	1
Burt Hooton	2	0	0.00	2	2	0	0	0	14.2	11	0	6	7
Steve Howe	0	0	0.00	2	0	0	0	0	2.0	1	0	0	2
Tom Niedenfuer	0	0	0.00	1	0	0	0	0	0.1	2	0	0	0
Alejandro Pena	0	0	0.00	2	0	0	0	0	2.1	1	0	0	0
Jerry Reuss	0	1	5.14	1	1	0	0	0	7.0	7	4	1	2
Fernando Valenzuela	1	1	2.45	2	2	0	0	0	14.2	10	4	5	10
Bob Welch	0	0	5.40	3	0	0	1	0	1.2	2	1	0	2
TOTAL	3	2	1.84	15	5	0	1	0	44.0	34	9	12	25

MON (E)

PLAYER/POS	AVG	G	AB	R	H	2B	3B	HR	RB	BB	SO	SB
Ray Burris, p	.000	2	6	0	0	0	0	0	0	0	4	0
Gary Carter, c	.438	5	16	3	7	1	0	0	0	0	2	0
Warren Cromartie, 1b	.167	5	18	0	3	1	0	0	2	0	2	0
Andre Dawson, of	.150	5	20	2	3	0	0	0	0	0	4	0
Terry Francona, of-1	.000	2	1	0	0	0	0	0	0	0	1	0
Woody Fryman, p	.000	1	0	0	0	0	0	0	0	0	0	0
Bill Gullickson, p	.000	2	3	0	0	0	0	0	0	1	2	0
Bill Lee, p	.000	1	0	0	0	0	0	0	0	0	0	0
Jerry Manuel, pr	.000	1	0	0	0	0	0	0	0	0	0	0
John Milner, ph	.000	1	1	0	0	0	0	0	0	0	1	0
Larry Parrish, 3b	.263	5	19	2	5	2	0	0	2	1	1	0
Tim Raines, of	.238	5	21	1	5	2	0	0	1	0	3	0
Jeff Reardon, p	.000	1	0	0	0	0	0	0	0	0	0	0
Steve Rogers, p	.000	2	2	0	0	0	0	0	0	0	1	0
Rodney Scott, 2b	.167	5	18	0	3	0	0	0	0	1	3	1
Elias Sosa, p	.000	1	0	0	0	0	0	0	0	0	0	0
Chris Speier, ss	.188	5	16	0	3	0	0	0	0	2	0	0
Tim Wallach, ph	.000	1	1	0	0	0	0	0	0	0	0	0
Jerry White, of	.313	5	16	2	5	1	0	1	3	3	1	1
TOTAL	.215		158	10	34	7	0	1	8	12	25	2

PITCHER	W	L	ERA	G	GS	CG	SV	SHO	IP	H	ER	BB	SO
Ray Burris	1	0	0.53	2	2	1	0	1	17.0	10	1	3	4
Woody Fryman	0	0	36.00	1	0	0	0	0	1.0	3	4	1	1
Bill Gullickson	0	2	2.51	2	2	0	0	0	14.1	12	4	6	12
Bill Lee	0	0	0.00	1	0	0	0	0	0.1	1	0	0	0
Jeff Reardon	0	0	27.00	1	0	0	0	0	1.0	3	3	0	0
Steve Rogers	1	1	1.80	2	1	1	0	0	10.0	8	2	1	6
Elias Sosa	0	0	0.00	1	0	0	0	0	0.1	1	0	1	0
TOTAL	2	3	2.86	10	5	2	0	1	44.0	38	14	12	23

GAME 1 AT LA OCT 13

```
MON 000 000 001   1  9 0
LA  020 000 03X   5  8 0
```
Pitchers: GULLICKSON, Reardon (8) vs HOOTON, Welch (8), Howe (9)
Home Runs: Guerrero-LA, Scioscia-LA
Attendance: 51,273

GAME 2 AT LA OCT 14

```
MON 020 001 000   3 10 1
LA  000 000 000   0  5 1
```
Pitchers: BURRIS vs VALENZUELA, Niedenfuer (7), Forster (7), Pena (7), Castillo (9)
Attendance: 53,463

GAME 3 AT MON OCT 16

```
LA  000 100 000   1  7 0
MON 000 004 00X   4  7 1
```
Pitchers: REUSS, Pena (8) vs ROGERS
Home Runs: White-MON
Attendance: 54,372

GAME 4 AT MON OCT 17

```
LA  001 000 024   7 12 1
MON 000 100 000   1  5 1
```
Pitchers: HOOTON, Welch (8), Howe (9) vs GULLICKSON, Fryman (8), Sosa (9), Lee (9)
Home Runs: Garvey-LA
Attendance: 54,499

GAME 5 AT MON OCT 19

```
LA  000 010 001   2  6 0
MON 100 000 000   1  3 1
```
Pitchers: VALENZUELA, Welch (9) vs Burris, ROGERS (9)
Home Runs: Monday-LA
Attendance: 36,491

NEW YORK YANKEES (EAST) 3, OAKLAND A'S (WEST) 0

The A's scored only four runs to their opponents' 20 as the Yankees swept the series. And only two of New York's six pitchers permitted an Oakland runner to score, while not one of Oakland's eight pitchers held New York scoreless. Even so, two of the three games were closely contested.

Oakland's Mike Norris gave up a bases-loaded double to Graig Nettles in the first inning of Game 1 before settling down to pitch shutout ball. But the three runs Nettles drove in were more than enough, as Tommy John and two relievers held the A's to a single run.

Game 2 was the series' only blowout, and even it remained close for three innings. But, led by a pair of three-run homers from Nettles and Lou Piniella, the Yankees parlayed 19 hits into 13 runs as Yankee reliever George Frazier held the A's scoreless over the final five frames.

Game 3 remained tight until the ninth. Through eight innings the only run came on Willie Randolph's homer off Oakland starter Matt Keough. But in the top of the ninth, Graig Nettles tagged reliever Tom Underwood for his second bases-clearing double of the series. The three runs weren't really needed, as Dave Righetti, Ron Davis, and Goose Gossage combined to shut out the A's for the full nine.

NY (E)

PLAYER/POS	AVG	G	AB	R	H	2B	3B	HR	RB	BB	SO	SB
Bobby Brown, of-2	1.000	3	1	2	1	0	0	0	0	0	0	0
Rick Cerone, c	.100	3	10	1	1	0	0	0	0	0	0	0
Ron Davis, p	.000	2	0	0	0	0	0	0	0	0	0	0
Barry Foote, c-1	1.000	2	1	0	1	0	0	0	0	0	0	0
George Frazier, p	.000	1	0	0	0	0	0	0	0	0	0	0
Oscar Gamble, dh-2, of-1	.167	3	6	2	1	0	0	0	0	1	5	3	0
Rich Gossage, p	.000	2	0	0	0	0	0	0	0	0	0	0
Reggie Jackson, of	.000	2	4	1	0	0	0	0	0	1	1	0	1
Tommy John, p	.000	1	0	0	0	0	0	0	0	0	0	0
Rudy May, p	.000	1	0	0	0	0	0	0	0	0	0	0
Larry Milbourne, ss	.462	3	13	4	6	0	0	0	1	0	0	0
Jerry Mumphrey, of	.500	3	12	2	6	1	0	0	0	3	2	0
Bobby Murcer, dh	.333	1	3	0	1	0	0	0	0	0	1	1	0
Graig Nettles, 3b	.500	3	12	2	6	2	0	1	9	1	0	0
Lou Piniella, dh-2, of-1	.600	3	5	2	3	0	0	1	3	0	0	0
Willie Randolph, 2b	.333	3	12	2	4	0	0	1	2	0	1	0
Dave Revering, 1b	.500	2	2	0	1	0	0	0	0	0	0	0
Dave Righetti, p	.000	1	0	0	0	0	0	0	0	0	0	0
Andre Robertson, ss	.000	1	1	0	0	0	0	0	0	0	0	0
Aurelio Rodriguez, 3b	.000	1	0	0	0	0	0	0	0	0	0	0
Bob Watson, 1b	.250	3	12	0	3	0	0	0	0	1	0	1	0
Dave Winfield, of	.154	3	13	2	2	1	0	0	2	2	2	1
TOTAL	.336		107	20	36	4	0	3	20	13	10	2

PITCHER	W	L	ERA	G	GS	CG	SV	SHO	IP	H	ER	BB	SO
Ron Davis	0	0	0.00	2	0	0	0	0	3.1	0	0	2	4
George Frazier	1	0	0.00	1	0	0	0	0	5.2	5	0	1	5
Rich Gossage	0	0	0.00	2	0	0	1	0	2.2	1	0	0	2
Tommy John	1	0	1.50	1	1	0	0	0	6.0	6	1	1	3
Rudy May	0	0	8.10	1	0	0	0	0	3.1	6	3	0	5
Dave Righetti	1	0	0.00	1	1	0	0	0	6.0	4	0	2	4
TOTAL	3	0	1.33	8	2	0	1	0	27.0	22	4	6	23

OAK (W)

PLAYER/POS	AVG	G	AB	R	H	2B	3B	HR	RB	BB	SO	SB
Tony Armas, of	.167	3	12	0	2	0	0	0	0	0	5	0
Dave Beard, p	.000	1	0	0	0	0	0	0	0	0	0	0
Rick Bosetti, of-1, dh-1	.250	2	4	1	1	1	0	0	0	0	1	0
Mike Davis, ph	1.000	1	1	0	1	0	0	0	0	0	0	0
Keith Drumright, dh-1	.000	3	4	0	0	0	0	0	0	1	0	0
Wayne Gross, 3b	.000	3	5	0	0	0	0	0	0	0	0	0
Mike Heath, c-2, of-1	.333	3	6	1	2	0	0	0	0	0	1	0
Rickey Henderson, of	.364	3	11	0	4	2	1	0	1	1	2	2
Cliff Johnson, dh	.000	2	6	0	0	0	0	0	0	2	2	0
Jeff Jones, p	.000	1	0	0	0	0	0	0	0	0	0	0
Matt Keough, p	.000	1	0	0	0	0	0	0	0	0	0	0
Brian Kingman, p	.000	1	0	0	0	0	0	0	0	0	0	0
Mickey Klutts, 3b	.429	3	7	1	3	0	0	0	0	0	1	0
Steve McCatty, p	.000	1	0	0	0	0	0	0	0	0	0	0
Dave McKay, 2b	.273	3	11	0	3	0	0	0	1	0	2	0
Kelvin Moore, 1b	.250	3	8	0	2	0	0	0	0	0	1	0
Dwayne Murphy, of	.250	3	8	0	2	1	0	0	1	2	3	0
Jeff Newman, c	.000	2	5	0	0	0	0	0	0	0	2	0
Mike Norris, p	.000	1	0	0	0	0	0	0	0	0	0	0
Bob Owchinko, p	.000	1	0	0	0	0	0	0	0	0	0	0
Rob Picciolo, ss	.200	2	5	1	1	0	0	0	0	0	2	0
Jim Spencer, 1b	.000	2	3	0	0	0	0	0	0	0	0	0
Fred Stanley, ss	.333	2	3	0	1	0	0	0	0	1	0	1
Tom Underwood, p	.000	2	0	0	0	0	0	0	0	0	0	0
TOTAL	.222		99	4	22	4	1	0	4	6	23	2

PITCHER	W	L	ERA	G	GS	CG	SV	SHO	IP	H	ER	BB	SO
Dave Beard	0	0	40.50	1	0	0	0	0	0.2	5	3	0	0
Jeff Jones	0	0	4.50	1	0	0	0	0	2.0	2	1	1	0
Matt Keough	0	1	1.08	1	1	0	0	0	8.1	7	1	6	4
Brian Kingman	0	0	81.00	1	0	0	0	0	0.1	3	3	0	0
Steve McCatty	0	1	13.50	1	1	0	0	0	3.1	6	5	2	2
Mike Norris	0	1	3.68	1	1	0	0	0	7.1	6	3	2	4
Bob Owchinko	0	0	5.40	1	0	0	0	0	1.2	3	1	0	0
Tom Underwood	0	0	13.50	2	0	0	0	0	1.1	4	2	2	0
TOTAL	0	3	6.84	9	3	0	0	0	25.0	36	19	13	10

GAME 1 AT NY OCT 13

```
OAK  000 010 000   1  6  1
NY   300 000 00X   3  7  1
```
Pitchers: NORRIS, Underwood (8) vs JOHN, Davis (7), Gossage (8)
Attendance: 55,740

GAME 2 AT NY OCT 14

```
OAK  001 200 000   3 11  1
NY   100 701 40X  13 19  0
```
Pitchers: McCATTY, Beard (4), Jones (5), Kingman (7), Owchinko (7) vs May, FRAZIER (4)
Home Runs: Piniella-NY, Nettles-NY
Attendance: 48,497

GAME 3 AT OAK OCT 15

```
NY   000 001 003   4 10  0
OAK  000 000 000   0  5  2
```
Pitchers: RIGHETTI, Davis (7), Gossage (9) vs KEOUGH, Underwood (9)
Home Runs: Randolph-NY
Attendance: 47,302

LOS ANGELES DODGERS (NL) 4, NEW YORK YANKEES (AL) 2

What the Yankees had done to the Dodgers three years earlier, the Dodgers now did to the Yankees in this, their 11th meeting in the Series: they took the crown with four straight wins after losing the first two games. In the opener Bob Watson's first-inning three-run homer gave New York an insurmountable lead. Yankees starter Ron Guidry pitched seven strong innings, yielding just one run on a Steve Yeager homer, but two eighth-inning Dodgers runs charged to reliever Ron Davis made things exciting until Yankees third baseman Graig Nettles dampened the rally with a splendid diving catch of Steve Garvey's line drive. In Game 2, Tommy John (now a Yankee) shut out his old teammates on three hits for seven innings. Reliever Goose Gossage completed the shutout, earning his second save in two days in the 3–0 Yankees victory.

But as the Series moved to Los Angeles, the Dodgers took the upper hand. Rookie ace Fernando Valenzuela experienced rocky going in the early innings of Game 3, yielding six hits (including home runs to Bob Watson and Rick Cerone) and four runs in the second and third innings. But Ron Cey's first-inning home run had given Los Angeles three early runs, and the Dodgers added two more in the fifth as Valenzuela settled down to blank New York on three hits over the final six innings. The next day the Dodgers evened the Series with another close win. New York scored four times before the Dodgers got their first runs, but L.A. tied the game at 6–6 in the sixth and took an 8–6 lead an inning later. Reggie Jackson homered in the eighth to bring New York within one run of a tie, but they came no closer.

In Game 5, for the third day in a row, the Dodgers overcame a Yankees lead to claim a one-run victory. Jerry Reuss gave the Yankees a run on two hits in the second inning, but shut them out on just three additional hits the rest of the way. Yankees starter Ron Guidry, meanwhile, stopped the Dodgers on two hits through the first six innings, but then gave up back-to-back homers to Pedro Guerrero and Steve Yeager in the seventh—runs enough for a 2–1 Dodgers win. The final game was

close for four innings, but in the fifth and sixth the Dodgers broke it open with seven runs and coasted in on Steve Howe's 3-2/3 innings of shutout relief to a 9–2 win and, including 1900, their sixth world championship.

LA (N)

PLAYER/POS	AVG	G	AB	R	H	2B	3B	HR	RB	BB	SO	SB
Dusty Baker, of	.167	6	24	3	4	0	0	0	1	1	6	0
Bobby Castillo, p	.000	1	0	0	0	0	0	0	0	0	0	0
Ron Cey, 3b	.350	6	20	3	7	0	0	1	6	3	3	0
Terry Forster, p	.000	2	0	0	0	0	0	0	0	0	0	0
Steve Garvey, 1b	.417	6	24	3	10	1	0	0	0	2	5	0
Dave Goltz, p	.000	2	0	0	0	0	0	0	0	0	0	0
Pedro Guerrero, of	.333	6	21	2	7	1	1	2	7	2	6	0
Burt Hooton, p	.000	2	4	1	0	0	0	0	0	1	3	0
Steve Howe, p	.000	3	2	0	0	0	0	0	0	0	2	0
Jay Johnstone, ph	.667	3	3	1	2	0	0	1	3	0	0	0
Ken Landreaux, of-3	.167	5	6	1	1	1	0	0	0	0	2	1
Davey Lopes, 2b	.227	6	22	6	5	1	0	0	2	4	3	4
Rick Monday, of-4	.231	5	13	1	3	1	0	0	0	3	6	0
Tom Niedenfuer, p	.000	2	0	0	0	0	0	0	0	0	0	0
Jerry Reuss, p	.000	2	3	0	0	0	0	0	0	0	1	0
Bill Russell, ss	.240	6	25	1	6	0	0	0	2	0	1	1
Steve Sax, 2b-1	.000	2	1	0	0	0	0	0	0	0	0	0
Mike Scioscia, c	.250	3	4	1	1	0	0	0	0	0	1	0
Reggie Smith, ph	.500	2	2	0	1	0	0	0	0	0	1	0
Dave Stewart, p	.000	2	0	0	0	0	0	0	0	0	0	0
Derrel Thomas, of-3, 3b-2, ss-1	.000	5	7	2	0	0	0	0	1	1	2	0
Fernando Valenzuela, p	.000	1	3	0	0	0	0	0	0	0	1	0
Bob Welch, p	.000	1	0	0	0	0	0	0	0	0	0	0
Steve Yeager, c	.286	6	14	2	4	1	0	2	4	0	2	0
TOTAL	.258		198	27	51	6	1	6	26	20	44	6

PITCHER	W	L	ERA	G	GS	CG	SV	SHO	IP	H	ER	BB	SO
Bobby Castillo	0	0	9.00	1	0	0	0	0	1.0	0	1	5	0
Terry Forster	0	0	0.00	2	0	0	0	0	2.0	1	0	3	0
Dave Goltz	0	0	5.40	2	0	0	0	0	3.1	4	2	1	2
Burt Hooton	1	1	1.59	2	2	0	0	0	11.1	8	2	9	3
Steve Howe	0	0	3.86	3	0	0	1	0	7.0	7	3	1	4
Tom Niedenfuer	0	0	0.00	2	0	0	0	0	5.0	3	0	1	0
Jerry Reuss	1	1	3.86	2	2	1	0	0	11.2	10	5	3	8
Dave Stewart	0	0	0.00	2	0	0	0	0	1.2	1	0	2	1
F. Valenzuela	1	0	4.00	1	1	1	0	0	9.0	9	4	7	6
Bob Welch	0	0	∞	1	1	0	0	0	0.0	3	2	1	0
TOTAL	4	2	3.29	18	6	2	1	0	52.0	46	19	33	24

NY (A)

PLAYER/POS	AVG	G	AB	R	H	2B	3B	HR	RB	BB	SO	SB
Bobby Brown, of-2	.000	4	1	1	0	0	0	0	0	0	1	0
Rick Cerone, c	.190	6	21	2	4	1	0	1	3	4	2	0
Ron Davis, p	.000	4	0	0	0	0	0	0	0	0	0	0
Barry Foote, ph	.000	1	1	0	0	0	0	0	0	0	1	0
George Frazier, p	.000	3	2	0	0	0	0	0	0	0	1	0
Oscar Gamble, of-2	.333	3	6	1	2	0	0	0	1	1	0	0
Rich Gossage, p	.000	3	1	0	0	0	0	0	0	1	1	0
Ron Guidry, p	.000	2	5	0	0	0	0	0	0	0	3	0
Reggie Jackson, of	.333	3	12	3	4	1	0	1	1	2	3	0
Tommy John, p	.000	3	2	0	0	0	0	0	0	0	0	0
Dave LaRoche, p	.000	1	0	0	0	0	0	0	0	0	0	0
Rudy May, p	.000	3	1	0	0	0	0	0	0	0	0	0
Larry Milbourne, ss	.250	6	20	2	5	2	0	0	3	4	0	0
Jerry Mumphrey, of	.200	5	15	2	3	0	0	0	0	3	2	1
Bobby Murcer, ph	.000	4	3	0	0	0	0	0	0	0	0	0
Graig Nettles, 3b	.400	3	10	1	4	1	0	0	1	1	0	0
Lou Piniella, of-3	.438	6	16	2	7	1	0	0	3	0	1	0
Willie Randolph, 2b	.222	6	18	5	4	1	1	2	3	9	0	1
Rick Reuschel, p	.000	2	2	0	0	0	0	0	0	0	1	0
Dave Righetti, p	.000	1	1	0	0	0	0	0	0	0	0	0
Andre Robertson, pr	.000	1	0	0	0	0	0	0	0	0	0	0
Aurelio Rodriguez, 3b-3	.417	4	12	1	5	0	0	0	0	1	2	0
Bob Watson, 1b	.318	6	22	2	7	1	0	2	7	3	0	0
Dave Winfield, of	.045	6	22	1	1	0	0	0	1	5	4	1
TOTAL	.238		193	22	46	8	1	6	22	33	24	4

PITCHER	W	L	ERA	G	GS	CG	SV	SHO	IP	H	ER	BB	SO
Ron Davis	0	0	23.14	4	0	0	0	0	2.1	4	6	5	4
George Frazier	0	3	17.18	3	0	0	0	0	3.2	9	7	3	2
Rich Gossage	0	0	0.00	3	0	0	2	0	5.0	2	0	2	5
Ron Guidry	1	1	1.93	2	2	0	0	0	14.0	8	3	4	15
Tommy John	1	0	0.69	3	2	0	0	0	13.0	11	1	0	8
Dave LaRoche	0	0	0.00	1	0	0	0	0	1.0	0	0	0	2
Rudy May	0	0	2.84	3	0	0	0	0	6.1	5	2	1	5
Rick Reuschel	0	0	4.91	2	0	0	0	0	3.2	7	2	3	2
Dave Righetti	0	0	13.50	1	1	0	0	0	2.0	5	3	2	1
TOTAL	2	4	4.24	22	6	0	2	0	51.0	51	24	20	44

GAME 1 AT NY OCT 20

```
LA  000 010 020   3 5 0
NY  301 100 00X   5 6 0
```
Pitchers: REUSS, Castillo (3), Goltz (4), Niedenfuer (5), Stewart (8) vs GUIDRY, Davis (8), Gossage (8)
Home Runs: Watson-NY, Yeager-LA
Attendance: 56,470

GAME 2 AT NY OCT 21

```
LA  000 000 000   0 4 2
NY  000 010 02X   3 6 1
```
Pitchers: HOOTON, Forster (7), Howe (8), Stewart (8) vs JOHN, Gossage (8)
Attendance: 56,505

GAME 3 AT LA OCT 23

```
NY  022 000 000   4 9 0
LA  300 020 00X   5 11 1
```
Pitchers: Righetti, FRAZIER (3), May (5), Davis (8) vs VALENZUELA
Home Runs: Cey-LA, Watson-NY Cerone-NY
Attendance: 56,236

GAME 4 AT LA OCT 24

```
NY  211 002 010   7 13 1
LA  002 013 20X   8 14 2
```
Pitchers: Reuschel, May (4), Davis (5), FRAZIER (5), John (7) vs Welch, Goltz (1), Forster (4), Niedenfuer (5), HOWE (7)
Home Runs: Johnstone-LA, Randolph-NY, Jackson-NY
Attendance: 56,242

GAME 5 AT LA OCT 25

```
NY  010 000 000   1 5 0
LA  000 000 20X   2 4 3
```
Pitchers: GUIDRY, Gossage (8) vs REUSS
Home Runs: Guerrero-LA, Yeager-LA
Attendance: 56,115

GAME 6 AT NY OCT 28

```
LA  000 134 010   9 13 1
NY  001 001 000   2 7 2
```
Pitchers: HOOTON, Howe (6) vs John, FRAZIER (5), Davis (6), Reuschel (6), May (7), LaRoche (9)
Home Runs: Guerrero-LA, Randolph-NY
Attendance: 56,513

ST. LOUIS CARDINALS (EAST) 3, ATLANTA BRAVES (WEST) 0

The official records show Atlanta ahead only once in a three-game series swept by the Cardinals. But in the original Game 1, Phil Niekro held a slim 1–0 Atlanta lead in the fifth inning when rain wiped out the game just before it could become official.

In the first official game, the Braves scored nothing at all as Bob Forsch held them to three hits. Atlanta's Pascual Perez gave up only one run through the first five innings, but the Cardinals exploded for five runs in the sixth to put the game away. Following another rainout, Niekro tried again in Game 2. He gave up a run in the first, but Atlanta came back with three before he yielded a second run in the sixth. Gene Garber, who relieved Niekro, gave up the tying run in the eighth and lost the game in the bottom of the ninth on Ken Oberkfell's RBI liner over the center fielder's head.

Joaquin Andujar shut out the Braves through six innings of Game 3 before giving up two runs in the seventh. But by then St. Louis had scored five times. Bruce Sutter retired the last seven Braves in relief of Andujar, and the Cardinals had their pennant

STL (E)

PLAYER/POS	AVG	G	AB	R	H	2B	3B	HR	RB	BB	SO	SB
Joaquin Andujar, p	.000	1	1	0	0	0	0	0	0	0	1	0
Doug Bair, p	.000	1	0	0	0	0	0	0	0	0	0	0
Steve Braun, ph	.000	1	1	0	0	0	0	0	0	0	0	0
Bob Forsch, p	.667	1	3	1	2	0	0	0	1	0	0	0
David Green, of	1.000	2	1	1	1	0	0	0	0	0	0	0
George Hendrick, of	.308	3	13	2	4	0	0	0	2	1	2	0
Keith Hernandez, 1b	.333	3	12	3	4	0	0	0	1	2	3	0
Tommy Herr, 2b	.231	3	13	1	3	1	0	0	0	1	2	0
Willie McGee, of	.308	3	13	4	4	0	2	1	5	0	5	0
Ken Oberkfell, 3b	.200	3	15	1	3	0	0	0	2	0	0	0
Darrell Porter, c	.556	3	9	3	5	3	0	0	1	5	2	0
Lonnie Smith, of	.273	3	11	1	3	0	0	0	1	0	1	0
Ozzie Smith, ss	.556	3	9	0	5	0	0	0	3	3	0	1
John Stuper, p	.000	1	1	0	0	0	0	0	0	0	0	0
Bruce Sutter, p	.000	2	1	0	0	0	0	0	0	0	0	0
TOTAL	.330		103	17	34	4	2	1	16	12	16	1

PITCHER	W	L	ERA	G	GS	CG	SV	SHO	IP	H	ER	BB	SO
Joaquin Andujar	1	0	2.70	1	1	0	0	0	6.2	6	2	2	4
Doug Bair	0	0	0.00	1	0	0	0	0	1.0	2	0	3	0
Bob Forsch	1	0	0.00	1	1	1	0	1	9.0	3	0	0	6
John Stuper	0	0	3.00	1	1	0	0	0	6.0	4	2	1	4
Bruce Sutter	1	0	0.00	2	0	0	1	0	4.1	0	0	0	1
TOTAL	3	0	1.33	6	3	1	1	1	27.0	15	4	6	15

ATL (W)

PLAYER/POS	AVG	G	AB	R	H	2B	3B	HR	RB	BB	SO	SB
Steve Bedrosian, p	.000	2	0	0	0	0	0	0	0	0	0	0
Bruce Benedict, c	.250	3	8	1	2	1	0	0	0	2	1	0
Brett Butler, of-1	.000	2	1	0	0	0	0	0	0	0	0	0
Rick Camp, p	.000	1	0	0	0	0	0	0	0	0	0	0
Chris Chambliss, 1b	.000	3	10	0	0	0	0	0	0	1	0	0
Gene Garber, p	.000	2	1	0	0	0	0	0	0	0	0	0
Terry Harper, of	.000	1	1	1	0	0	0	0	0	0	0	0
Bob Horner, 3b	.091	3	11	0	1	0	0	0	0	0	2	0
Glenn Hubbard, 2b	.222	3	9	1	2	0	0	0	1	0	3	0
Rick Mahler, p	.000	1	0	0	0	0	0	0	0	0	0	0
Donnie Moore, p	.000	2	0	0	0	0	0	0	0	0	0	0
Dale Murphy, of	.273	3	11	1	3	0	0	0	0	0	2	1
Phil Niekro, p	.000	1	0	0	0	0	0	0	1	0	0	0
Pascual Perez, p	.000	2	3	0	0	0	0	0	0	0	1	0
Biff Pocoroba, ph	.000	1	1	0	0	0	0	0	0	0	0	0
Rafael Ramirez, ss	.182	3	11	1	2	0	0	0	1	1	1	0
Jerry Royster, of-3,3b-1	.182	3	11	0	2	0	0	0	0	0	2	0
Bob Walk, p	.000	1	0	0	0	0	0	0	0	0	0	0
Claudell Washington, of	.333	3	9	0	3	0	0	0	0	2	2	0
Larry Whisenton, ph	.000	2	2	0	0	0	0	0	0	0	1	0
TOTAL	.169		89	5	15	1	0	0	3	6	15	1

PITCHER	W	L	ERA	G	GS	CG	SV	SHO	IP	H	ER	BB	SO
Steve Bedrosian	0	0	18.00	2	0	0	0	0	1.0	3	2	1	2
Rick Camp	0	1	36.00	1	1	0	0	0	1.0	4	4	1	0
Gene Garber	0	1	8.10	2	0	0	0	0	3.1	4	3	1	3
Rick Mahler	0	0	0.00	1	0	0	0	0	1.2	3	0	2	0
Donnie Moore	0	0	0.00	2	0	0	0	0	2.2	2	0	0	1
Phil Niekro	0	0	3.00	1	1	0	0	0	6.0	6	2	4	5
Pascual Perez	0	1	5.19	2	1	0	0	0	8.2	10	5	2	4
Bob Walk	0	0	9.00	1	0	0	0	0	1.0	2	1	1	1
TOTAL	0	3	6.04	12	3	0	0	0	25.1	34	17	12	16

GAME 1 AT STL OCT 7
ATL 0 0 0 0 0 0 0 0 0　　0 3 0
STL 0 0 1 0 0 5 0 1 X　　7 13 1
Pitchers: PEREZ, Bedrosian (6), Moore (6), Walk (8) vs FORSCH
Attendance: 53,008

GAME 2 AT STL OCT 9
ATL 0 0 2 0 1 0 0 0 0　　3 6 0
STL 1 0 0 0 0 1 0 1 1　　4 9 1
Pitchers: Niekro, GARBER (7) vs Stuper, Bair (7), SUTTER (8)
Attendance: 53,408

GAME 3 AT ATL OCT 10
STL 0 4 0 0 1 0 0 0 1　　6 12 0
ATL 0 0 0 0 0 0 2 0 0　　2 6 1
Pitchers: ANDUJAR, Sutter (7) vs CAMP, Perez (2), Moore (5), Mahler (7), Bedrosian (8), Garber (9)
Home Runs: McGee-STL
Attendance: 52,173

MILWAUKEE BREWERS (EAST) 3, CALIFORNIA ANGELS (WEST) 2

For the first time in LCS play, a club won the first two games but lost the series. The Angels overcame a 3–1 deficit to take Game 1, with four runs in the third and three more later, while starter Tommy John settled down to stop the Brewers through the final six innings. In Game 2 Bruce Kison prevailed, as the Angels built a 4–0 lead over Milwaukee and Pete Vuckovich before Kison gave up what proved to be a harmless two-run homer to Paul Molitor in the fifth.

With three chances to clinch the pennant, California three times fell short. In the third game, their three eighth-inning runs couldn't catch the Brewers, who already had five. In Game 4, Don Baylor's eighth-inning grand slam completed California scoring at five runs, but Milwaukee had already scored seven, and they added two more. In the finale, Kison held a 3–2 lead when he was relieved after five innings. But Cecil Cooper singled off Luis Sanchez in the seventh (with two out and the bases loaded) for two runs and a Brewers lead. Bob McClure and Pete Ladd held off the Angels through the final two innings, and the Brewers were on their way to their first World Series.

MIL (E)

PLAYER/POS	AVG	G	AB	R	H	2B	3B	HR	RB	BB	SO	SB
Dwight Bernard, p	.000	1	0	0	0	0	0	0	0	0	0	0
Mark Brouhard, of	.750	1	4	4	3	1	0	1	3	0	0	0
Mike Caldwell, p	.000	1	0	0	0	0	0	0	0	0	0	0
Cecil Cooper, 1b	.150	5	20	1	3	2	0	0	4	0	6	0
Marshall Edwards, dh-2, of-1	.000	3	1	2	0	0	0	0	0	0	0	1
Jim Gantner, 2b	.188	5	16	1	3	0	0	0	2	1	1	0
Moose Haas, p	.000	1	0	0	0	0	0	0	0	0	0	0
Roy Howell, dh	.000	1	3	0	0	0	0	0	0	0	1	0
Pete Ladd, p	.000	3	0	0	0	0	0	0	0	0	0	0
Bob McClure, p	.000	1	0	0	0	0	0	0	0	0	0	0
Paul Molitor, 3b	.316	5	19	4	6	1	0	2	5	2	3	1
Don Money, dh	.182	4	11	2	2	0	0	0	1	3	1	0
Charlie Moore, of	.462	5	13	3	6	0	0	0	1	2	0	0
Ben Oglivie, of	.133	4	15	1	2	0	0	1	1	0	3	0
Ted Simmons, c	.167	5	18	3	3	0	0	0	1	1	4	0
Jim Slaton, p	.000	2	0	0	0	0	0	0	0	0	0	0
Don Sutton, p	.000	1	0	0	0	0	0	0	0	0	0	0
Gorman Thomas, of	.067	5	15	1	1	0	0	1	3	2	7	0
Pete Vuckovich, p	.000	2	0	0	0	0	0	0	0	0	5	0
Robin Yount, ss	.250	5	16	1	4	0	0	0	0	0	5	0
TOTAL	.219		151	23	33	4	0	5	20	15	28	2

PITCHER	W	L	ERA	G	GS	CG	SV	SHO	IP	H	ER	BB	SO
Dwight Bernard	0	0	0.00	1	0	0	0	0	1.0	0	0	0	0
Mike Caldwell	0	1	15.00	1	1	0	0	0	3.0	7	5	1	2
Moose Haas	1	0	4.91	1	1	0	0	0	7.1	5	4	5	7
Pete Ladd	0	0	0.00	3	0	0	2	0	3.1	0	0	0	5
Bob McClure	1	0	0.00	1	0	0	0	0	1.2	2	0	0	0
Jim Slaton	0	0	1.93	2	0	0	1	0	4.2	3	1	1	3
Don Sutton	1	0	3.52	1	1	0	0	0	7.2	8	3	2	9
Pete Vuckovich	0	1	4.40	2	2	1	0	0	14.1	15	7	7	8
TOTAL	3	2	4.19	12	5	1	3	0	43.0	40	20	16	34

CAL (W)

PLAYER/POS	AVG	G	AB	R	H	2B	3B	HR	RB	BB	SO	SB
Don Baylor, dh	.294	5	17	2	5	1	1	1	10	2	0	0
Juan Beniquez, of	.000	2	0	0	0	0	0	0	0	0	0	0
Bob Boone, c	.250	5	16	3	4	0	0	1	4	0	2	0
Rod Carew, 1b	.176	5	17	2	3	1	0	0	0	4	4	1
Bobby Clark, of	.000	2	0	0	0	0	0	0	0	0	0	0
Doug De Cinces, 3b	.316	5	19	5	6	2	0	0	0	1	5	0
Brian Downing, of	.158	5	19	4	3	1	0	0	0	3	2	0
Tim Foli, ss	.125	5	16	0	2	0	0	0	1	0	3	0
Dave Goltz, p	.000	1	0	0	0	0	0	0	0	0	0	0
Bobby Grich, 2b	.200	5	15	1	3	1	0	0	1	2	7	0
Andy Hassler, p	.000	2	0	0	0	0	0	0	0	0	0	0
Reggie Jackson, of	.111	5	18	2	2	0	0	1	2	2	7	0
Ron Jackson, ph	1.000	1	1	0	1	0	0	0	0	0	0	0
Tommy John, p	.000	2	0	0	0	0	0	0	0	0	0	0
Bruce Kison, p	.000	2	0	0	0	0	0	0	0	0	0	0
Fred Lynn, of	.611	5	18	4	11	2	0	1	5	2	3	0
Luis Sanchez, p	.000	2	0	0	0	0	0	0	0	0	0	0
Rob Wilfong, ph	.000	2	1	0	0	0	0	0	0	0	1	0
Mike Witt, p	.000	1	0	0	0	0	0	0	0	0	0	0
Geoff Zahn, p	.000	1	0	0	0	0	0	0	0	0	0	0
TOTAL	.255		157	23	40	8	1	4	23	16	34	1

PITCHER	W	L	ERA	G	GS	CG	SV	SHO	IP	H	ER	BB	SO
Dave Goltz	0	0	7.36	1	0	0	0	0	3.2	4	3	2	2
Andy Hassler	0	0	0.00	2	0	0	0	0	2.2	0	0	0	2
Tommy John	1	1	5.11	2	2	1	0	0	12.1	11	7	6	6
Bruce Kison	1	0	1.93	2	2	1	0	0	14.0	8	3	3	12
Luis Sanchez	0	1	6.75	2	0	0	0	0	2.2	4	2	1	1
Mike Witt	0	0	6.00	1	0	0	0	0	3.0	2	2	2	3
Geoff Zahn	0	1	7.36	1	1	0	0	0	3.2	4	3	1	2
TOTAL	2	3	4.29	11	5	2	0	0	42.0	33	20	15	28

GAME 1 AT CAL OCT 5

MIL 021 000 000   3 7 2
CAL 104 210 00X   8 10 0
Pitchers: CALDWELL, Slaton (4), Ladd (7), Bernard (8) vs JOHN
Home Runs: Thomas-MIL, Lynn-CAL
Attendance: 64,406

GAME 2 AT CAL OCT 6

MIL 000 020 000   2 5 0
CAL 021 100 00X   4 6 0
Pitchers: VUCKOVICH vs KISON
Home Runs: Re.Jackson-CAL, Molitor-MIL
Attendance: 64,179

GAME 3 AT MIL OCT 8

CAL 000 000 030   3 8 0
MIL 000 300 20X   5 6 0
Pitchers: ZAHN, Witt (4), Hassler (7) vs SUTTON, Ladd (8)
Home Runs: Molitor-MIL, Boone-CAL
Attendance: 50,135

GAME 4 AT MIL OCT 9

CAL 000 001 040   5 5 3
MIL 030 301 02X   9 9 2
Pitchers: JOHN, Goltz (4), Sanchez (8) vs HAAS, Slaton (8)
Home Runs: Baylor-CAL, Brouhard-MIL
Attendance: 51,003

GAME 5 AT MIL OCT 10

CAL 101 100 000   3 11 1
MIL 100 100 20X   4 6 4
Pitchers: Kison, SANCHEZ (6), Hassler (7) vs Vuckovich, McCLURE (7), Ladd (9)
Home Runs: Oglivie-MIL
Attendance: 54,968

ST. LOUIS CARDINALS (NL) 4, MILWAUKEE BREWERS (NL) 3

The Series was anticipated as a matchup of Cardinals speed and Brewers power. In the event, though, St. Louis outslugged the Brewers and wound up as world champions.

The Brewers, in their first World Series, looked unstoppable in the opening game. Hammering four Cardinals pitchers for 17 hits (including a record five for Paul Molitor), they scored 10 runs while pitcher Mike Caldwell was shutting out the Cards on three hits. In the second game Milwaukee continued the onslaught, building an early 3–0 lead. But St. Louis finally got on the scoreboard with two runs in the last of the third, and tied the game at 4–4 in the sixth on Darrell Porter's two-run double. And the Cards won the game on a bases-loaded walk in the eighth as relievers Doug Bair and Bruce Sutter held the Brewers scoreless over the final four innings.

St. Louis pushed into the Series lead in Game 3, thanks mostly to the 6-1/3 shutout innings of starter Joaquin Andujar and the fielding and batting of center fielder Willie McGee. McGee drove in four of the six Cardinal runs with a pair of homers and prevented an extrabase hit and a two-run Brewers homer with leaping catches in the first and final innings. The Cards pressed their advantage in Game 4 with four early runs. But in the last of the seventh (with the score now 5–1), an error by Cardinals pitcher Dave LaPoint opened the way for Milwaukee to win the game with six two-out runs on a barrage of hits (and the added assistance of a pair of walks and a wild pitch).

Mike Caldwell wasn't as effective in Game 5 as he had been in the opener, yielding 14 hits and four runs in 8-1/3 innings of work. But he was never behind in the game as his teammates, with 11 hits of their own (four of them by Robin Yount, including a home run) and several fielding gems put Milwaukee ahead again in the Series with a 6–4 win.

The Cards had their backs to the wall as the Series moved to St. Louis for the final games. But in Game 6 the Cards responded to their opening-game humiliation with a laugher of their own, 13–1, on John Stuper's four-hitter. And in the finale they rocked Brewers ace Pete Vuckovich and three relievers

for 15 hits and a 6–3 victory that gave starter Joaquin Andujar his second Series win and reliever Bruce Sutter his second save.

STL (N)

PLAYER/POS	AVG	G	AB	R	H	2B	3B	HR	RB	BB	SO	SB
Joaquin Andujar, p	.000	2	0	0	0	0	0	0	0	0	0	0
Doug Bair, p	.000	3	0	0	0	0	0	0	0	0	0	0
Steve Braun, dh	.500	2	2	0	1	0	0	0	2	1	0	0
Glenn Brummer, c	.000	1	0	0	0	0	0	0	0	0	0	0
Bob Forsch, p	.000	2	0	0	0	0	0	0	0	0	0	0
David Green, of-4, dh-3	.200	7	10	3	2	1	1	0	0	1	3	0
George Hendrick, of	.321	7	28	5	9	0	0	0	5	2	2	0
Keith Hernandez, 1b	.259	7	27	4	7	2	0	1	8	4	2	0
Tommy Herr, 2b	.160	7	25	2	4	2	0	0	5	3	3	0
Dane Iorg, dh	.529	5	17	4	9	4	1	0	1	0	0	0
Jim Kaat, p	.000	4	0	0	0	0	0	0	0	0	0	0
Jeff Lahti, p	.000	2	0	0	0	0	0	0	0	0	0	0
Dave LaPoint, p	.000	2	0	0	0	0	0	0	0	0	0	0
Willie McGee, of	.240	6	25	6	6	0	0	2	5	1	3	2
Ken Oberkfell, 3b	.292	7	24	4	7	1	0	0	1	2	1	0
Darrell Porter, c	.286	7	28	1	8	2	0	1	5	1	4	0
Mike Ramsey, 3b-2	.000	3	1	1	0	0	0	0	0	0	1	0
Lonnie Smith, of-6, dh-1	.321	7	28	6	9	4	1	0	1	1	5	2
Ozzie Smith, ss	.208	7	24	3	5	0	0	0	1	3	0	1
John Stuper, p	.000	2	0	0	0	0	0	0	0	0	0	0
Bruce Sutter, p	.000	4	0	0	0	0	0	0	0	0	0	0
Gene Tenace, dh-1	.000	5	6	0	0	0	0	0	0	1	2	0
TOTAL	.273		245	39	67	16	3	4	34	20	26	7

PITCHER	W	L	ERA	G	GS	CG	SV	SHO	IP	H	ER	BB	SO
Joaquin Andujar	2	0	1.35	2	2	0	0	0	13.1	10	2	1	4
Doug Bair	0	1	9.00	3	0	0	0	0	2.0	2	2	2	3
Bob Forsch	0	2	4.97	2	2	0	0	0	12.2	18	7	3	4
Jim Kaat	0	0	3.86	4	0	0	0	0	2.1	4	1	2	2
Jeff Lahti	0	0	10.80	2	0	0	0	0	1.2	4	2	1	1
Dave LaPoint	0	0	3.24	2	1	0	0	0	8.1	10	3	2	3
John Stuper	1	0	3.46	2	2	1	0	0	13.0	10	5	5	5
Bruce Sutter	1	0	4.70	4	0	0	2	0	7.2	6	4	3	6
TOTAL	4	3	3.84	21	7	1	2	0	61.0	64	26	19	28

MIL (A)

PLAYER/POS	AVG	G	AB	R	H	2B	3B	HR	RB	BB	SO	SB
Dwight Bernard, p	.000	1	0	0	0	0	0	0	0	0	0	0
Mike Caldwell, p	.000	3	0	0	0	0	0	0	0	0	0	0
Cecil Cooper, 1b	.286	7	28	3	8	1	0	1	6	1	1	0
Marshall Edwards, of	.000	1	0	0	0	0	0	0	0	0	0	0
Jim Gantner, 2b	.333	7	24	5	8	4	1	0	4	1	1	0
Moose Haas, p	.000	2	0	0	0	0	0	0	0	0	0	0
Roy Howell, dh	.000	4	11	1	0	0	0	0	0	0	3	0
Pete Ladd, p	.000	1	0	0	0	0	0	0	0	0	0	0
Bob McClure, p	.000	5	0	0	0	0	0	0	0	0	0	0
Doc Medich, p	.000	1	0	0	0	0	0	0	0	0	0	0
Paul Molitor, 3b	.355	7	31	5	11	0	0	0	3	2	4	1
Don Money, dh-4	.231	5	13	4	3	1	0	0	1	2	3	0
Charlie Moore, of	.346	7	26	3	9	3	0	0	2	1	0	0
Ben Oglivie, of	.222	7	27	4	6	0	1	1	1	2	4	0
Ted Simmons, c	.174	7	23	2	4	0	0	2	3	5	3	0
Jim Slaton, p	.000	2	0	0	0	0	0	0	0	0	0	0
Don Sutton, p	.000	2	0	0	0	0	0	0	0	0	0	0
Gorman Thomas, of	.115	7	26	0	3	0	0	0	0	3	2	7
Pete Vuckovich, p	.000	2	0	0	0	0	0	0	0	0	0	0
Ned Yost, c	.000	1	0	0	0	0	0	0	0	1	0	0
Robin Yount, ss	.414	7	29	6	12	3	0	1	6	2	2	0
TOTAL	.269		238	33	64	12	2	5	29	19	28	1

PITCHER	W	L	ERA	G	GS	CG	SV	SHO	IP	H	ER	BB	SO
Dwight Bernard	0	0	0.00	1	0	0	0	0	1.0	0	0	0	1
Mike Caldwell	2	0	2.04	3	2	1	0	1	17.2	19	4	3	6
Moose Haas	0	0	7.36	2	1	0	0	0	7.1	8	6	3	4
Pete Ladd	0	0	0.00	1	0	0	0	0	0.2	1	0	2	0
Bob McClure	0	2	4.15	5	0	0	2	0	4.1	5	2	3	5
Doc Medich	0	0	18.00	1	0	0	0	0	2.0	5	4	1	0
Jim Slaton	1	0	0.00	2	0	0	0	0	2.2	1	0	2	1
Don Sutton	0	1	7.84	2	2	0	0	0	10.1	12	9	1	5
Pete Vuckovich	0	1	4.50	2	2	0	0	0	14.0	16	7	5	4
TOTAL	3	4	4.80	19	7	1	2	1	60.0	67	32	20	26

GAME 1 AT STL OCT 12

```
MIL  200 112 004   10 17 0
STL  000 000 000    0  3 1
```
Pitchers: CALDWELL vs FORSCH, Kaat (6), LaPoint (8), Lahti (9)
Home Runs: Simmons-MIL
Attendance: 53,723

GAME 2 AT STL OCT 13

```
MIL  012 010 000   4 10 1
STL  002 002 01X   5  8 0
```
Pitchers: Sutton, McCLURE (7), Ladd (8) vs Stuper, Kaat (5), Bair (5), SUTTER (7)
Home Runs: Simmons-MIL
Attendance: 53,723

GAME 3 AT MIL OCT 15

```
STL  000 030 201   6 6 1
MIL  000 000 020   2 5 3
```
Pitchers: ANDUJAR, Kaat (7), Bair (7), Sutter (7) vs VUCKOVICH, McClure (9)
Home Runs: McGee-STL (2), Cooper-MIL
Attendance: 56,556

GAME 4 AT MIL OCT 16

```
STL  130 001 000   5 8 1
MIL  000 010 60X   7 10 2
```
Pitchers: LaPoint, BAIR (7), Kaat (7), Lahti (7) vs Haas, SLATON (6), McClure (8)
Attendance: 56,560

GAME 5 AT MIL OCT 17

```
STL  001 000 102   4 15 2
MIL  101 010 12X   6 11 1
```
Pitchers: FORSCH, Sutter (8) vs CALDWELL, McClure (9)
Home Runs: Yount-MIL
Attendance: 56,562

GAME 6 AT STL OCT 19

```
MIL  000 000 001    1  4 4
STL  020 326 00X   13 12 1
```
Pitchers: SUTTON, Slaton (5), Medich (6), Bernard (8) vs STUPER
Home Runs: Porter-STL, Hernandez-STL
Attendance: 53,723

GAME 7 AT STL OCT 20

```
MIL  000 012 000   3 7 0
STL  000 103 02X   6 15 1
```
Pitchers: Vuckovich, McCLURE (6), Haas (6), Caldwell (8) vs ANDUJAR, Sutter (8)
Home Runs: Oglivie-MIL
Attendance: 53,723

PHILADELPHIA PHILLIES (EAST) 3, LOS ANGELES DODGERS (WEST) 1

The Dodgers earned only four runs off Philadelphia pitching, and even though they doubled their run total to eight on unearned runs, the Phillies scored twice that number to take the pennant in four games.

Mike Schmidt homered off Jerry Reuss in the first inning of the opener for the game's only run. Phillies starter Steve Carlton loaded the bases in the eighth, but Al Holland came on to get the third out and preserve the shutout. The Phillies also scored only one run in the second game, on Gary Matthews' homer off Fernando Valenzuela in the second. But this time the run only tied the score, and in the fifth Pedro Guerrero trip-led in two unearned runs to give Valenzuela the Dodgers' only win.

The Phillies' Charlie Hudson hurled the series' only complete game, a four-hitter, to win Game 3. Gary Matthews' four hits in Game 3 and 4 included his second and third series homers, and drove in half the Phillies' 14 runs as they took the two games by identical 7–2 scores.

PHI (E)

PLAYER/POS	AVG	G	AB	R	H	2B	3B	HR	RB	BB	SO	SB
Steve Carlton, p	.200	2	5	0	1	0	0	0	0	0	3	0
Ivan DeJesus, ss	.250	4	12	0	3	0	0	0	1	3	3	0
John Denny, p	.000	1	1	0	0	0	0	0	0	0	0	0
Bob Dernier, of	.000	1	0	0	0	0	0	0	0	0	0	0
Bo Diaz, c	.154	4	13	0	2	1	0	0	0	2	1	0
Greg Gross, of-3	.000	4	5	1	0	0	0	0	0	2	2	0
Von Hayes, of-1	.000	2	2	0	0	0	0	0	0	0	0	0
Al Holland, p	.000	2	0	0	0	0	0	0	0	0	0	0
Charles Hudson, p	.000	1	4	0	0	0	0	0	0	0	3	0
Joe Lefebvre, of-1	.000	2	2	0	0	0	0	0	0	1	0	0
Sixto Lezcano, of	.308	4	13	2	4	0	0	1	2	1	1	0
Garry Maddox, of	.273	3	11	0	3	1	0	0	1	0	1	0
Gary Matthews, of	.429	4	14	4	6	0	0	3	8	2	1	1
Joe Morgan, 2b	.067	4	15	1	1	0	0	0	0	2	1	0
Tony Perez, ph	1.000	1	1	0	1	0	0	0	0	0	0	0
Ron Reed, p	.000	2	0	0	0	0	0	0	0	0	0	0
Pete Rose, 1b	.375	4	16	3	6	0	0	0	0	1	1	1
Juan Samuel, pr	.000	1	0	0	0	0	0	0	0	0	0	0
Mike Schmidt, 3b	.467	4	15	5	7	2	0	1	2	2	3	0
Ossie Virgil, ph	.000	1	1	0	0	0	0	0	0	0	1	0
TOTAL	.262		130	16	34	4	0	5	15	15	22	2

PITCHER	W	L	ERA	G	GS	CG	SV	SHO	IP	H	ER	BB	SO
Steve Carlton	2	0	0.66	2	2	0	0	0	13.2	13	1	5	13
John Denny	0	1	0.00	1	1	0	0	0	6.0	5	0	3	3
Al Holland	0	0	0.00	2	0	0	1	0	3.0	1	0	0	3
Charles Hudson	1	0	2.00	1	1	1	0	0	9.0	4	2	2	9
Ron Reed	0	0	2.70	2	0	0	0	0	3.1	4	1	1	3
TOTAL	3	1	1.03	8	4	1	1	0	35.0	27	4	11	31

LA (W)

PLAYER/POS	AVG	G	AB	R	H	2B	3B	HR	RB	BB	SO	SB
Dusty Baker, of	.357	4	14	4	5	1	0	1	1	2	0	0
Joe Beckwith, p	.000	2	0	0	0	0	0	0	0	0	0	0
Greg Brock, 1b	.000	3	9	1	0	0	0	0	0	0	3	0
Jack Fimple, c	.143	3	7	0	1	0	0	0	0	1	3	0
Pedro Guerrero, 3b	.250	4	12	1	3	1	1	0	2	3	3	0
Rick Honeycutt, p	.000	2	0	0	0	0	0	0	0	0	0	0
Rafael Landestoy, ph	.000	2	2	0	0	0	0	0	0	0	1	0
Ken Landreaux, of	.143	4	14	0	2	0	0	0	1	1	3	0
Candy Maldonado, ph	.000	2	2	0	0	0	0	0	0	0	1	0
Mike Marshall, 1b-3, of-2	.133	4	15	1	2	1	0	1	2	1	6	0
Rick Monday, ph	.000	1	0	0	0	0	0	0	0	0	0	0
Jose Morales, ph	.000	2	2	0	0	0	0	0	0	0	1	0
Tom Niedenfuer, p	.000	2	0	0	0	0	0	0	0	0	0	0
Alejandro Pena, p	1.000	1	1	0	1	0	0	0	0	0	0	0
Jerry Reuss, p	.000	2	3	0	0	0	0	0	0	0	3	0
Bill Russell, ss	.286	4	14	1	4	0	0	0	0	2	4	1
Steve Sax, 2b	.250	4	16	0	4	0	0	0	0	1	0	1
Derrel Thomas, of	.444	4	9	0	4	1	0	0	0	0	3	1
Fernando Valenzuela, p	.000	1	3	0	0	0	0	0	0	1	0	0
Bob Welch, p	.000	1	0	0	0	0	0	0	0	0	0	0
Steve Yeager, c	.167	2	6	0	1	1	0	0	0	0	0	0
Pat Zachry, p	.000	2	0	0	0	0	0	0	0	0	0	0
TOTAL	.209		129	8	27	5	1	2	7	11	31	3

PITCHER	W	L	ERA	G	GS	CG	SV	SHO	IP	H	ER	BB	SO
Joe Beckwith	0	0	0.00	2	0	0	0	0	2.1	1	0	2	3
Rick Honeycutt	0	0	21.60	2	0	0	0	0	1.2	4	4	0	2
Tom Niedenfuer	0	0	0.00	2	0	0	1	0	2.0	0	0	1	3
Alejandro Pena	0	0	6.75	1	0	0	0	0	2.2	4	2	1	3
Jerry Reuss	0	2	4.50	2	2	0	0	0	12.0	14	6	3	4
F. Valenzuela	1	0	1.13	1	1	0	0	0	8.0	7	1	4	5
Bob Welch	0	1	6.75	1	1	0	0	0	1.1	0	1	2	0
Pat Zachry	0	0	2.25	2	0	0	0	0	4.0	4	1	2	2
TOTAL	1	3	3.97	13	4	0	1	0	34.0	34	15	15	22

GAME 1 AT LA OCT 4

```
PHI  100 000 000   1 5 1
LA   000 000 000   0 7 0
```
Pitchers: CARLTON, Holland (8) vs REUSS, Niedenfuer (9)
Home Runs: Schmidt-PHI
Attendance: 49,963

GAME 2 AT LA OCT 5

```
PHI  010 000 000   1 7 2
LA   100 020 00X   4 6 1
```
Pitchers: DENNY, Reed (7) vs VALENZUELA, Niedenfuer (9)
Home Runs: Matthews-PHI
Attendance: 55,967

GAME 3 AT PHI OCT 7

```
LA   000 200 000   2 4 0
PHI  021 120 01X   7 9 1
```
Pitchers: WELCH, Pena (2), Honeycutt (5), Beckwith (5), Zachry (7) vs HUDSON
Home Runs: Marshall-LA, Matthews-PHI
Attendance: 53,490

GAME 4 AT PHI OCT 8

```
LA   000 100 010   2 10 0
PHI  300 022 00X   7 13 1
```
Pitchers: REUSS, Beckwith (5), Honeycutt (5), Zachry (7) vs CARLTON, Reed (7), Holland (8)
Home Runs: Matthews-PHI, Baker-LA, Lezcano-PHI
Attendance: 64,494

BALTIMORE ORIOLES (EAST) 3, CHICAGO WHITE SOX (WEST) 1

The White Sox and Orioles entered the ALCS evenly matched, with similar season's records and stats. But Baltimore all but shut down Chicago's run production in this quick four-game meeting. Both teams had 28 hits, but the Sox, held to four for extra bases, found themselves outslugged by 116 percentage points and outscored by 16 runs.

Chicago won the first game, scoring two of their three series runs as LaMarr Hoyt shut out Baltimore for eight innings before letting in a run in the ninth. But the White Sox had concluded their effective scoring. In Game 2, Orioles rookie Mike Boddicker shut them out on five hits, striking out 14. In Game 3 the Sox scored their final run. The Orioles got only two more hits than Chicago but blended them with nine walks, a hit batsman, and a Sox error to score 11 runs.

In the fourth game, Orioles pitchers Storm Davis and Tippy Martinez saw to it that ten Chicago hits scored no runs. Britt Burns held Baltimore scoreless, too, through nine innings. But Tito Landrum's solo homer in the top of the 10th drove Burns out, and two more Orioles runs provided more than enough scoring to win Baltimore the flag.

BAL (E)

PLAYER/POS	AVG	G	AB	R	H	2B	3B	HR	RB	BB	SO	SB
Benny Ayala, dh	.000	1	0	0	0	0	0	0	0	1	0	0
Mike Boddicker, p	.000	1	0	0	0	0	0	0	0	0	0	0
Al Bumbry, of	.125	3	8	0	1	1	0	0	1	0	2	0
Todd Cruz, 3b	.133	4	15	0	2	0	0	0	1	0	5	0
Rich Dauer, 2b	.000	4	14	0	0	0	0	0	0	1	0	0
Storm Davis, p	.000	1	0	0	0	0	0	0	0	0	0	0
Rick Dempsey, c	.167	4	12	1	2	0	0	0	0	1	1	0
Jim Dwyer, of-1	.250	2	4	1	1	1	0	0	0	1	0	0
Mike Flanagan, p	.000	1	0	0	0	0	0	0	0	0	0	0
Dan Ford, of-1	.200	2	5	0	1	1	0	0	0	0	1	0
Tito Landrum, of-3	.200	4	10	2	2	0	0	1	1	0	2	0
John Lowenstein, of-2	.167	3	6	0	1	1	0	0	2	1	2	0
Tippy Martinez, p	.000	2	0	0	0	0	0	0	0	0	0	0
Scott McGregor, p	.000	1	0	0	0	0	0	0	0	0	0	0
Eddie Murray, 1b	.267	4	15	5	4	0	0	1	3	3	3	1
Joe Nolan, ph	.000	1	0	0	0	0	0	0	1	0	0	0
Jim Palmer, pr	.000	1	0	0	0	0	0	0	0	0	0	0
Cal Ripken, ss	.400	4	15	5	6	2	0	0	1	2	3	0
Gary Roenicke, of	.750	3	4	4	3	1	0	1	4	5	0	0
John Shelby, of-2	.222	3	9	1	2	0	0	0	0	1	3	1
Ken Singleton, dh	.250	4	12	0	3	2	0	0	1	2	2	0
Sammy Stewart, p	.000	2	0	0	0	0	0	0	0	0	0	0
TOTAL	.217		129	19	28	9	0	3	17	16	24	2

PITCHER	W	L	ERA	G	GS	CG	SV	SHO	IP	H	ER	BB	SO
Mike Boddicker	1	0	0.00	1	1	1	0	1	9.0	5	0	3	14
Storm Davis	0	0	0.00	1	1	0	0	0	6.0	5	0	2	2
Mike Flanagan	1	0	1.80	1	1	0	0	0	5.0	5	1	0	1
Tippy Martinez	1	0	0.00	2	0	0	0	0	6.0	5	0	3	5
Scott McGregor	0	1	1.35	1	1	0	0	0	6.2	6	1	3	2
Sammy Stewart	0	0	0.00	2	0	0	1	0	4.1	2	0	1	2
TOTAL	3	1	0.49	8	4	1	1	1	37.0	28	2	12	26

CHI (W)

PLAYER/POS	AVG	G	AB	R	H	2B	3B	HR	RB	BB	SO	SB
Juan Agosto, p	.000	1	0	0	0	0	0	0	0	0	0	0
Harold Baines, of	.125	4	16	0	2	0	0	0	0	1	3	0
Floyd Bannister, p	.000	1	0	0	0	0	0	0	0	0	0	0
Salome Barojas, p	.000	2	0	0	0	0	0	0	0	0	0	0
Britt Burns, p	.000	1	0	0	0	0	0	0	0	0	0	0
Julio Cruz, 2b	.333	4	12	0	4	0	0	0	0	3	4	2
Richard Dotson, p	.000	1	0	0	0	0	0	0	0	0	0	0
Jerry Dybzinski, ss	.250	2	4	0	1	0	0	0	0	0	0	0
Carlton Fisk, c	.176	4	17	0	3	1	0	0	0	1	3	0
Scott Fletcher, ss	.000	3	7	0	0	0	0	0	0	1	0	0
Jerry Hairston, of	.000	2	3	0	0	0	0	0	0	1	1	0
LaMarr Hoyt, p	.000	1	0	0	0	0	0	0	0	0	0	0
Ron Kittle, of	.286	3	7	1	2	1	0	0	0	1	2	0
Jerry Koosman, p	.000	1	0	0	0	0	0	0	0	0	0	0
Dennis Lamp, p	.000	3	0	0	0	0	0	0	0	0	0	0
Rudy Law, of	.389	4	18	1	7	1	0	0	0	0	1	2
Vance Law, 3b	.182	4	11	0	2	0	0	0	1	1	3	0
Greg Luzinski, dh	.133	4	15	0	2	1	0	0	0	1	5	0
Tom Paciorek, 1b-3, of-2	.250	4	16	1	4	0	0	0	1	1	2	0
Aurelio Rodriguez, 3b	.000	2	0	0	0	0	0	0	0	0	0	0
Mike Squires, 1b-3	.000	4	4	0	0	0	0	0	0	0	0	0
Dick Tidrow, p	.000	1	0	0	0	0	0	0	0	0	0	0
Greg Walker, 1b-1	.333	2	3	0	1	0	0	0	0	1	2	0
TOTAL	.211		133	3	28	4	0	0	2	12	26	4

PITCHER	W	L	ERA	G	GS	CG	SV	SHO	IP	H	ER	BB	SO
Juan Agosto	0	0	0.00	1	0	0	0	0	0.1	0	0	0	0
Floyd Bannister	0	1	4.50	1	1	0	0	0	6.0	5	3	1	5
Salome Barojas	0	0	18.00	2	0	0	0	0	1.0	4	2	0	0
Britt Burns	0	1	0.96	1	1	0	0	0	9.1	6	1	5	8
Richard Dotson	0	1	10.80	1	1	0	0	0	5.0	6	6	3	3
LaMarr Hoyt	1	0	1.00	1	1	1	0	0	9.0	5	1	0	4
Jerry Koosman	0	0	54.00	1	0	0	0	0	0.1	1	2	2	0
Dennis Lamp	0	0	0.00	3	0	0	0	0	2.0	0	0	2	1
Dick Tidrow	0	0	3.00	1	0	0	0	0	3.0	1	1	3	3
TOTAL	1	3	4.00	12	4	1	0	0	36.0	28	16	16	24

GAME 1 AT BAL OCT 5

CHI 001 001 000   2 7 0
BAL 000 000 001   1 5 1
Pitchers: HOYT vs McGREGOR, Stewart (7), T.Martinez (8)
Attendance: 51,289

GAME 2 AT BAL OCT 6

CHI 000 000 000   0 5 2
BAL 010 102 00X   4 6 0
Pitchers: BANNISTER, Barojas (7), Lamp (8) vs BODDICKER
Home Runs: Roenicke-BAL
Attendance: 52,347

GAME 3 AT CHI OCT 7

BAL 310 020 014   11 8 1
CHI 010 000 000   1 6 1
Pitchers: FLANAGAN, Stewart (6) vs DOTSON, Tidrow (6), Koosman (9), Lamp (9)
Home Runs: Murray-BAL
Attendance: 46,635

GAME 4 AT CHI OCT 8

BAL 000 000 0003   3 9 0
CHI 000 000 0000   0 10 0
Pitchers: Davis, T.MARTINEZ (7) vs BURNS, Barojas (10), Agosto (10), Lamp (10)
Home Runs: Landrum-BAL
Attendance: 45,477

BALTIMORE ORIOLES (AL) 4, PHILADELPHIA PHILLIES (NL) 1

Near neighbors Baltimore and Philadelphia met in a World Series for the first time. Both clubs were led by new managers: Baltimore by Joe Altobelli, who inherited a team built under longtime Orioles manager Earl Weaver, and the Phillies by general manager Paul Owens, who replaced Pat Corrales with himself in midseason.

Both started their top winners in the opener, and the result was a pitchers' duel, with all three runs scored on solo homers. John Denny gave up the first to Jim Dwyer in the first inning, but after that (with late-inning help from Al Holland) he blanked the Orioles, while Baltimore's Scott McGregor, after five and two thirds scoreless innings gave up home runs to Joe Morgan and (the deciding blast two innings later) to Garry Maddox.

The Orioles swept the next four games. In Game 2, Mike Boddicker yielded just three singles (and no walks) to Philadelphia. Though one of the singles led to a run in the fourth inning, giving the Phillies a 1–0 lead, John Lowenstein tied the score with a home run in the fifth. Three more hits in the inning and a sacrifice fly gave the Orioles the lead, 3–1, and three two-out singles in the seventh inning brought in a fourth Baltimore run.

Philadelphia again scored first in Game 3, on leadoff home runs in the second and third innings by Gary Matthews and Joe Morgan. But the Orioles finally got to veteran starter Steve Carlton in the sixth for one run and drove him out after a second run scored an inning later. Carlton suffered the loss when the baserunner he left scored the tie-breaking run from second on an error by shortstop Ivan DeJesus.

The Phillies also lost Game 4 by a single run. Baltimore scored first with two runs in the top of the fourth, but Philadelphia recovered with one run in the fourth and two an inning later. They would not lead again in the Series. Baltimore scored twice in the sixth to go ahead again, and once more in the seventh. The Phillies scored once more with two down in the last of the ninth to draw within one run of a tie, but Joe Morgan lined out to second to end the game.

Home runs by Rick Dempsey and Eddie Murray (who hit two)

accounted for four of Baltimore's five runs in the final game—more than enough to support Scott McGregor's five-hit shutout pitching.

BAL (A)

PLAYER/POS	AVG	G	AB	R	H	2B	3B	HR	RB	BB	SO	SB
Benny Ayala, ph	1.000	1	1	1	1	0	0	0	1	0	0	0
Mike Boddicker, p	.000	1	3	0	0	0	0	0	0	1	0	1	0
Al Bumbry, of	.091	4	11	0	1	1	0	0	1	0	1	0
Todd Cruz, 3b	.125	5	16	1	2	0	0	0	0	1	3	0
Rich Dauer, 2b	.211	5	19	2	4	1	0	0	3	0	3	0
Storm Davis, p	.000	1	2	0	0	0	0	0	0	0	2	0
Rick Dempsey, c	.385	5	13	3	5	4	0	1	2	2	2	0
Jim Dwyer, of	.375	2	8	3	3	1	0	1	1	0	0	0
Mike Flanagan, p	.000	1	1	0	0	0	0	0	0	0	1	0
Dan Ford, of-4	.167	5	12	1	2	0	0	1	1	1	5	0
Tito Landrum, of	.000	3	0	0	0	0	0	0	0	0	0	1
John Lowenstein, of	.385	4	13	2	5	1	0	1	1	0	3	0
Tippy Martinez, p	.000	3	0	0	0	0	0	0	0	0	0	0
Scott McGregor, p	.000	2	5	0	0	0	0	0	0	0	0	0
Eddie Murray, 1b	.250	5	20	2	5	0	0	2	3	1	4	0
Joe Nolan, c	.000	2	2	0	0	0	0	0	0	1	0	0
Jim Palmer, p	.000	1	0	0	0	0	0	0	0	0	0	0
Cal Ripken, ss	.167	5	18	2	3	0	0	0	1	3	4	0
Gary Roenicke, of-2	.000	3	7	0	0	0	0	0	0	0	2	0
Len Sakata, 2b	.000	1	1	0	0	0	0	0	0	0	0	0
John Shelby, of	.444	5	9	1	4	0	0	0	1	0	4	0
Ken Singleton, ph	.000	2	1	0	0	0	0	0	0	1	1	0
Sammy Stewart, p	.000	3	2	0	0	0	0	0	0	0	1	0
TOTAL	.213		164	18	35	8	0	6	17	10	37	1

PITCHER	W	L	ERA	G	GS	CG	SV	SHO	IP	H	ER	BB	SO
Mike Boddicker	1	0	0.00	1	1	1	0	0	9.0	3	0	0	6
Storm Davis	1	0	5.40	1	1	0	0	0	5.0	6	3	1	3
Mike Flanagan	0	0	4.50	1	1	0	0	0	4.0	6	2	1	1
Tippy Martinez	0	0	3.00	3	0	0	2	0	3.0	3	1	0	0
Scott McGregor	1	1	1.06	2	2	1	0	1	17.0	9	2	2	12
Jim Palmer	1	0	0.00	1	0	0	0	0	2.0	2	0	1	1
Sammy Stewart	0	0	0.00	3	0	0	0	0	5.0	2	0	2	6
TOTAL	4	1	1.60	12	5	2	2	1	45.0	31	8	7	29

PHI (N)

PLAYER/POS	AVG	G	AB	R	H	2B	3B	HR	RB	BB	SO	SB
Larry Andersen, p	.000	2	0	0	0	0	0	0	0	0	0	0
Marty Bystrom, p	.000	1	0	0	0	0	0	0	0	0	0	0
Steve Carlton, p	.000	1	3	0	0	0	0	0	0	0	1	0
Ivan DeJesus, ss	.125	5	16	0	2	0	0	0	0	1	2	0
John Denny, p	.200	2	5	1	1	0	0	0	1	0	1	0
Bob Dernier, pr	.000	1	0	1	0	0	0	0	0	0	0	0
Bo Diaz, c	.333	5	15	1	5	1	0	0	0	1	2	0
Greg Gross, of	.000	2	6	0	0	0	0	0	0	0	0	0
Von Hayes, of-1	.000	4	3	0	0	0	0	0	0	0	1	0
Willie Hernandez, p	.000	3	0	0	0	0	0	0	0	0	0	0
Al Holland, p	.000	2	0	0	0	0	0	0	0	0	0	0
Charles Hudson, p	.000	2	2	0	0	0	0	0	0	0	1	0
Joe Lefebvre, of-2	.200	3	5	0	1	1	0	0	2	0	1	0
Sixto Lezcano, of-3	.125	4	8	0	1	0	0	0	0	0	2	0
Garry Maddox, of-3	.250	4	12	1	3	1	0	1	1	0	2	0
Gary Matthews, of	.250	5	16	1	4	0	0	1	1	1	2	0
Joe Morgan, 2b	.263	5	19	3	5	0	1	2	2	2	3	1
Tony Perez, 1b-2	.200	4	10	0	2	0	0	0	0	0	2	0
Ron Reed, p	.000	3	0	0	0	0	0	0	0	0	0	0
Pete Rose, 1b-3, of-1	.313	5	16	1	5	1	0	0	1	1	3	0
Juan Samuel, ph	.000	3	1	0	0	0	0	0	0	0	0	0
Mike Schmidt, 3b	.050	5	20	0	1	0	0	0	0	0	6	0
Ossie Virgil, c-1	.500	3	2	0	1	0	0	0	1	0	0	0
TOTAL	.195		159	9	31	4	1	4	9	7	29	1

PITCHER	W	L	ERA	G	GS	CG	SV	SHO	IP	H	ER	BB	SO
Larry Andersen	0	0	2.25	2	0	0	0	0	4.0	4	1	0	1
Marty Bystrom	0	0	0.00	1	0	0	0	0	1.0	0	0	0	1
Steve Carlton	0	1	2.70	1	1	0	0	0	6.2	5	2	3	7
John Denny	1	1	3.46	2	2	0	0	0	13.0	12	5	3	9
Willie Hernandez	0	0	0.00	3	0	0	0	0	4.0	0	0	1	4
Al Holland	0	0	0.00	2	0	0	1	0	3.2	1	0	0	5
Charles Hudson	0	2	8.64	2	2	0	0	0	8.1	9	8	1	6
Ron Reed	0	0	2.70	3	0	0	0	0	3.1	4	1	2	4
TOTAL	1	4	3.48	16	5	0	1	0	44.0	35	17	10	37

GAME 1 AT BAL OCT 11

PHI 000 001 010   2 5 0
BAL 100 000 000   1 5 1
Pitchers: DENNY, Holland (8) vs McGREGOR, Stewart (9), T.Martinez (9)
Home Runs: Morgan-PHI, Maddox-PHI, Dwyer-BAL
Attendance: 52,204

GAME 2 AT BAL OCT 12

PHI 000 100 000   1 3 0
BAL 000 030 10X   4 9 1
Pitchers: HUDSON, Hernandez (5), Andersen (6), Reed (8) vs BODDICKER
Home Runs: Lowenstein-BAL
Attendance: 52,132

GAME 3 AT PHI OCT 14

BAL 000 001 200   3 6 1
PHI 011 000 000   2 8 2
Pitchers: Flanagan, PALMER (5), Stewart (7), T.Martinez (9) vs CARLTON, Holland (7)
Home Runs: Matthews-PHI, Morgan-PHI, Ford-BAL
Attendance: 65,792

GAME 4 AT PHI OCT 15

BAL 000 202 100   5 10 1
PHI 000 120 001   4 10 0
Pitchers: DAVIS, Stewart (6), T.Martinez (8) vs DENNY, Hernandez (6), Reed (6), Andersen (8)
Attendance: 66,947

GAME 5 AT PHI OCT 16

BAL 011 210 000   5 5 0
PHI 000 000 000   0 5 1
Pitchers: McGREGOR vs HUDSON, Bystrom (5), Hernandez (6), Reed (9)
Home Runs: Murray-BAL (2), Dempsey-BAL
Attendance: 67,064

SAN DIEGO PADRES (WEST) 3, CHICAGO CUBS (EAST) 2

After two games in Chicago, the Cubs appeared headed for their first pennant in 39 years. Rick Sutcliffe and Warren Brusstar shut out the Padres, 13–0, in an opener enlivened by five Cubs home runs, including two homers by Gary Matthews and one by Sutcliffe. In a quieter second game, the Cubs built a 4–1 lead over the first four innings and held on for the win.

When the series moved to San Diego, though, the Padres came to life. In the fifth and sixth innings of Game 3, they obliterated a 1–0 Cubs lead with seven runs, as Ed Whitson and Goose Gossage held the Cubs scoreless after the second inning for what turned into an easy Padres win.

Game 4 was not so easy. San Diego scored first in the third inning, lost their lead in the fourth, tied it in the fifth, went ahead in the seventh, and fell back into a 5–5 tie in the eighth. But in the bottom of the ninth, Steve Garvey's two-run homer sent the series into a fifth game.

Leon Durham put the Cubs ahead with a two-run homer in the first inning of the finale, and Jody Davis added to the lead with a solo shot in the second. Rick Sutcliffe, meanwhile, was setting down Padres as he added five shutout innings to his seven from Game 1. But he gave up two runs in the sixth, and after first baseman Durham allowed a grounder go through his legs to let in the tying run in the seventh, the Cubs watched the pennant slip away as Tony Gwynn's double and Garvey's single drove in the game's final three runs.

SD (W)

PLAYER/POS	AVG	G	AB	R	H	2B	3B	HR	RB	BB	SO	SB
Kurt Bevacqua, ph	.000	2	2	0	0	0	0	0	0	0	0	0
Greg Booker, p	.000	1	0	0	0	0	0	0	0	0	0	0
Bobby Brown, of	.000	3	4	1	0	0	0	0	0	1	2	1
Dave Dravecky, p	.000	3	0	0	0	0	0	0	0	0	0	0
Tim Flannery, ph	.500	3	2	2	1	0	0	0	0	0	0	0
Steve Garvey, 1b	.400	5	20	1	8	1	0	1	7	1	2	0
Rich Gossage, p	.000	3	0	0	0	0	0	0	0	0	0	0
Tony Gwynn, of	.368	5	19	6	7	3	0	0	3	1	2	0
Greg Harris, p	.000	1	0	0	0	0	0	0	0	0	0	0
Andy Hawkins, p	.000	3	0	0	0	0	0	0	0	0	0	0
Terry Kennedy, c	.222	5	18	2	4	0	0	0	1	1	3	0
Craig Lefferts, p	.000	3	0	0	0	0	0	0	0	0	0	0
Tim Lollar, p	.000	1	1	0	0	0	0	0	0	0	1	0
Carmelo Martinez, of	.176	5	17	1	3	0	0	0	0	2	4	0
Kevin McReynolds, of	.300	4	10	2	3	0	0	1	4	3	1	0
Graig Nettles, 3b	.143	4	14	1	2	0	0	0	2	1	1	0
Mario Ramirez, ph	.000	2	2	0	0	0	0	0	0	0	0	0
Luis Salazar, of-2,3b-1	.200	3	5	0	1	0	1	0	0	0	1	0
Eric Show, p	.000	2	1	0	0	0	0	0	0	0	0	0
Champ Summers, ph	.000	2	2	0	0	0	0	0	0	0	1	0
Garry Templeton, ss	.333	5	15	2	5	1	0	0	2	2	0	1
Mark Thurmond, p	1.000	1	1	0	1	0	0	0	0	0	0	0
Ed Whitson, p	.000	1	3	0	0	0	0	0	0	0	1	0
Alan Wiggins, 2b	.316	5	19	4	6	0	0	0	1	2	2	0
TOTAL	.265		155	22	41	5	1	2	20	14	22	2

PITCHER	W	L	ERA	G	GS	CG	SV	SHO	IP	H	ER	BB	SO
Greg Booker	0	0	0.00	1	0	0	0	0	2.0	2	0	1	2
Dave Dravecky	0	0	0.00	3	0	0	0	0	6.0	2	0	0	5
Rich Gossage	0	0	4.50	3	0	0	1	0	4.0	5	2	1	5
Greg Harris	0	0	31.50	1	0	0	0	0	2.0	9	7	3	2
Andy Hawkins	0	0	0.00	3	0	0	0	0	3.2	0	0	2	1
Craig Lefferts	2	0	0.00	3	0	0	0	0	4.0	1	0	1	1
Tim Lollar	0	0	6.23	1	1	0	0	0	4.1	3	3	4	3
Eric Show	0	1	13.50	2	2	0	0	0	5.1	8	8	4	2
Mark Thurmond	0	1	9.82	1	1	0	0	0	3.2	7	4	2	1
Ed Whitson	1	0	1.13	1	1	0	0	0	8.0	5	1	2	6
TOTAL	3	2	5.23	19	5	0	1	0	43.0	42	25	20	28

CHI (E)

PLAYER/POS	AVG	G	AB	R	H	2B	3B	HR	RB	BB	SO	SB
Thad Bosley, ph	.000	2	2	0	0	0	0	0	0	0	2	0
Larry Bowa, ss	.200	5	15	1	3	1	0	0	1	1	0	0
Warren Brusstar, p	.000	3	1	0	0	0	0	0	0	0	0	0
Ron Cey, 3b	.158	5	19	3	3	1	0	1	3	3	3	0
Henry Cotto, of	1.000	3	1	1	1	0	0	0	0	0	0	0
Jody Davis, c	.389	5	18	3	7	2	0	2	6	0	3	0
Bob Dernier, of	.235	5	17	5	4	2	0	1	1	5	4	2
Leon Durham, 1b	.150	5	20	3	3	0	0	2	4	1	4	0
Dennis Eckersley, p	.000	1	2	0	0	0	0	0	0	0	1	0
George Frazier, p	.000	1	0	0	0	0	0	0	0	0	0	0
Richie Hebner, ph	.000	2	1	0	0	0	0	0	0	0	0	0
Steve Lake, c	1.000	1	1	0	1	1	0	0	0	0	0	0
Davey Lopes, of-1	.000	2	1	0	0	0	0	0	0	0	0	0
Gary Matthews, of	.200	5	15	4	3	0	0	2	5	6	4	1
Keith Moreland, of	.333	5	18	3	6	2	0	0	2	1	1	0
Ryne Sandberg, 2b	.368	5	19	3	7	2	0	0	2	3	2	3
Scott Sanderson, p	.000	1	2	0	0	0	0	0	0	0	1	0
Lee Smith, p	.000	2	0	0	0	0	0	0	0	0	0	0
Tim Stoddard, p	.000	2	0	0	0	0	0	0	0	0	0	0
Rick Sutcliffe, p	.500	2	6	1	3	0	0	1	1	0	2	0
Steve Trout, p	.500	2	2	0	1	0	0	0	0	0	0	0
Tom Veryzer, ss-2,3b-1	.000	3	1	0	0	0	0	0	0	0	0	0
Gary Woods, of	.000	1	1	0	0	0	0	0	0	0	1	0
TOTAL	.259		162	26	42	11	0	9	25	20	28	6

PITCHER	W	L	ERA	G	GS	CG	SV	SHO	IP	H	ER	BB	SO
Warren Brusstar	0	0	0.00	3	0	0	0	0	4.1	6	0	0	1
Dennis Eckersley	0	1	8.44	1	1	0	0	0	5.1	9	5	0	0
George Frazier	0	0	10.80	1	0	0	0	0	1.2	2	2	0	1
Scott Sanderson	0	0	5.79	1	1	0	0	0	4.2	6	3	1	2
Lee Smith	0	1	9.00	2	0	0	1	0	2.0	3	2	0	3
Tim Stoddard	0	0	4.50	2	0	0	0	0	2.0	1	1	2	2
Rick Sutcliffe	1	1	3.38	2	2	0	0	0	13.1	9	5	8	10
Steve Trout	1	0	2.00	2	1	0	0	0	9.0	5	2	3	3
TOTAL	2	3	4.25	14	5	0	1	0	42.1	41	20	14	22

GAME 1 AT CHI OCT 2

```
SD   000 000 000    0  6  1
CHI  203 062 00X   13 16  0
```
Pitchers: SHOW, Harris (5), Booker (7) vs SUTCLIFFE, Brusstar (8)
Home Runs: Dernier-CHI, Matthews-CHI (2), Sutcliffe-CHI, Cey-CHI
Attendance: 36,282

GAME 2 AT CHI OCT 3

```
SD   000 101 000    2  5  0
CHI  102 100 00X    4  8  1
```
Pitchers: THURMOND, Hawkins (4), Dravecky (6), Lefferts (8) vs TROUT, Smith (9)
Attendance: 36,282

GAME 3 AT SD OCT 4

```
CHI  010 000 000    1  5  0
SD   000 034 00X    7 11  0
```
Pitchers: ECKERSLEY, Frazier (6), Stoddard (8) vs WHITSON, Gossage (9)
Home Runs: McReynolds-SD
Attendance: 58,346

GAME 4 AT SD OCT 6

```
CHI  000 300 020    5  8  1
SD   002 010 202    7 11  0
```
Pitchers: Sanderson, Brusstar (5), Stoddard (7), SMITH (8) vs Lollar, Hawkins (5), Dravecky (6), Gossage (8), LEFFERTS (9)
Home Runs: Davis-CHI, Durham-CHI, Garvey-SD
Attendance: 58,354

GAME 5 AT SD OCT 7

```
CHI  210 000 000    3  5  1
SD   000 002 40X    6  8  0
```
Pitchers: SUTCLIFFE, Trout (7), Brusstar (8) vs Show, Hawkins (2), Dravecky (4), LEFFERTS (6), Gossage (8)
Home Runs: Durham-CHI, Davis-CHI
Attendance: 58,359

DETROIT TIGERS (EAST) 3, KANSAS CITY ROYALS (WEST) 0

The heavily favored Tigers swept the series, but not without difficulty, despite a 14-hit, three-homer, 8–1 romp in the opener.

Games 2 and 3 were much tighter. In the second game, after Detroit had built a 3–0 lead over the first three innings, rookie starter Bret Saberhagen settled down and blanked the Tigers for the next five innings as K.C. inched its way to a tie with runs in the fourth, seventh, and eighth. Through the ninth and 10th innings, Tigers reliever Aurelio Lopez and Dan Quisenberry of the Royals dueled scorelessly, but in the top of the 11th Johnny Grubb doubled home two Tigers runs. Lopez struggled but held the Royals scoreless in the last of the 11th for the win.

In Game 3 the Royals' Charlie Leibrandt and Tigers' Milt Wilcox and Willie Hernandez hurled matching three-hitters. But the Tigers secured the game—and the pennant—when Chet Lemon scored on a broken double play in the second inning for the game's only run.

DET (E)

PLAYER/POS	AVG	G	AB	R	H	2B	3B	HR	RB	BB	SO	SB
Doug Baker, ss	.000	1	0	0	0	0	0	0	0	0	0	0
Dave Bergman, 1b-1	1.000	2	1	1	1	0	0	0	0	0	0	1
Tom Brookens, 2b-1,3b-1	.000	2	2	0	0	0	0	0	0	0	1	0
Marty Castillo, 3b	.250	3	8	0	2	0	0	0	2	0	3	1
Darrell Evans, 1b-3,3b-1	.300	3	10	1	3	1	0	0	1	1	0	1
Barbaro Garbey, dh-2	.333	3	9	1	3	0	0	0	0	0	1	0
Kirk Gibson, of	.417	3	12	2	5	1	0	1	2	2	1	1
Johnny Grubb, dh	.250	1	4	0	1	1	0	0	2	0	0	0
Willie Hernandez, p	.000	3	0	0	0	0	0	0	0	0	0	0
Larry Herndon, of	.200	2	5	1	1	0	0	1	1	1	2	0
Ruppert Jones, of	.000	2	5	1	0	0	0	0	0	1	1	0
Rusty Kuntz, of	.000	1	1	0	0	0	0	0	0	0	0	0
Chet Lemon, of	.000	3	13	1	0	0	0	0	0	0	1	0
Aurelio Lopez, p	.000	1	0	0	0	0	0	0	0	0	0	0
Jack Morris, p	.000	1	0	0	0	0	0	0	0	0	0	0
Lance Parrish, c	.250	3	12	1	3	1	0	1	3	0	3	0
Dan Petry, p	.000	1	0	0	0	0	0	0	0	0	0	0
Alan Trammell, ss	.364	3	11	2	4	0	1	1	3	3	1	0
Lou Whitaker, 2b	.143	3	14	3	2	0	0	0	0	0	3	0
Milt Wilcox, p	.000	1	0	0	0	0	0	0	0	0	0	0
TOTAL	.234		107	14	25	4	1	4	14	8	17	4

PITCHER	W	L	ERA	G	GS	CG	SV	SHO	IP	H	ER	BB	SO
Willie Hernandez	0	0	2.25	3	0	0	1	0	4.0	3	1	1	3
Aurelio Lopez	1	0	0.00	1	0	0	0	0	3.0	4	0	1	2
Jack Morris	1	0	1.29	1	1	0	0	0	7.0	5	1	1	4
Dan Petry	0	0	2.57	1	1	0	0	0	7.0	4	2	1	4
Milt Wilcox	1	0	0.00	1	1	0	0	0	8.0	2	0	2	8
TOTAL	3	0	1.24	7	3	0	1	0	29.0	18	4	6	21

KC (W)

PLAYER/POS	AVG	G	AB	R	H	2B	3B	HR	RB	BB	SO	SB
Steve Balboni, 1b	.091	3	11	0	1	0	0	0	0	1	*4	0
Buddy Biancalana, ss	.000	2	1	0	0	0	0	0	0	0	1	0
Bud Black, p	.000	1	0	0	0	0	0	0	0	0	0	0
George Brett, 3b	.231	3	13	0	3	0	0	0	0	0	2	0
Onix Concepcion, ss	.000	3	7	0	0	0	0	0	0	0	0	0
Mark Huismann, p	.000	1	0	0	0	0	0	0	0	0	0	0
Dane Iorg, ph	.500	2	2	0	1	0	0	0	1	0	0	0
Lynn Jones, of-2	.200	3	5	1	1	0	0	0	0	0	0	0
Mike Jones, p	.000	1	0	0	0	0	0	0	0	0	0	0
Charlie Leibrandt, p	.000	1	0	0	0	0	0	0	0	0	0	0
Hal McRae, ph	1.000	2	2	0	2	1	0	0	1	0	0	0
Darryl Motley, of	.167	3	12	0	2	0	0	0	0	1	1	0
Jorge Orta, dh	.100	3	10	1	1	0	1	0	1	0	2	0
Greg Pryor, 3b	.000	1	0	0	0	0	0	0	0	0	0	0
Dan Quisenberry, p	.000	1	0	0	0	0	0	0	0	0	0	0
Bret Saberhagen, p	.000	1	0	0	0	0	0	0	0	0	0	0
Pat Sheridan, of	.000	3	6	1	0	0	0	0	0	3	3	0
Don Slaught, c	.364	3	11	0	4	0	0	0	0	0	0	0
U. L. Washington, ph	.000	2	1	0	0	0	0	0	0	0	1	0
John Wathan, dh	.000	1	1	0	0	0	0	0	0	0	0	0
Frank White, 2b	.091	3	11	1	1	0	0	0	0	0	3	0
Willie Wilson, of	.154	3	13	0	2	0	0	0	0	1	2	0
TOTAL	.170		106	4	18	1	1	0	4	6	21	0

PITCHER	W	L	ERA	G	GS	CG	SV	SHO	IP	H	ER	BB	SO
Bud Black	0	1	7.20	1	1	0	0	0	5.0	7	4	1	3
Mark Huismann	0	0	6.75	1	0	0	0	0	2.2	6	2	1	2
Mike Jones	0	0	6.75	1	0	0	0	0	1.1	1	1	0	0
Charlie Leibrandt	0	1	1.13	1	1	1	0	0	8.0	3	1	4	6
Dan Quisenberry	0	1	3.00	1	0	0	0	0	3.0	2	1	1	1
Bret Saberhagen	0	0	2.25	1	1	0	0	0	8.0	6	2	1	5
TOTAL	0	3	3.54	6	3	1	0	0	28.0	25	11	8	17

GAME 1 AT KC OCT 2

DET 200 110 121   8 14 0
KC   000 000 100   1 5 1
Pitchers: MORRIS, Hernandez (8) vs
  BLACK, Huismann (6), M.Jones (8)
Home Runs: Herndon-DET,
  Trammell-DET, Parrish-DET
Attendance: 41,973

GAME 2 AT KC OCT 3

DET 201 000 000 2   5 8 1
KC   000 100 110 0   3 10 3
Pitchers: Petry, Hernandez (8),
  LOPEZ (9) vs Saberhagen,
  QUISENBERRY (9)
Home Runs: Gibson-DET
Attendance: 42,019

GAME 3 AT DET OCT 5

KC   000 000 000   0 3 3
DET 010 000 00X   1 3 0
Pitchers: LEIBRANDT vs WILCOX,
  Hernandez (9)
Attendance: 52,168

DETROIT TIGERS (AL) 4, SAN DIEGO PADRES (NL) 1

Few objective observers expected the Padres (playing in their first World Series) to best the mighty Tigers—and they didn't. Detroit's first two batters in Game 1 hit safely to produce the Series' first scoring before an out had been recorded. San Diego countered with three two-out hits in their half of the first to go ahead, 2–1. But Detroit starter Jack Morris settled down to shut out the Padres over the final eight innings, and his Tigers scored the tying and winning runs in the fifth on Larry Herndon's two-run homer.

The Tigers scored again in Game 2 before the first out was recorded and drove out Ed Whitson with three first-inning runs on five singles. But this time Detroit was shut out (by relievers Andy Hawkins and Craig Lefferts) over the final eight, while San Diego scored single runs in the first and fourth and the winning runs in the fifth on a three-run homer by the normally light-hitting Kurt Bevacqua.

The Tigers won Game 3 on walks—a Series-record 11—as the Series moved to Detroit. After scoring their first two runs in the second on a single and Marty Castillo's home run, they put across two more in the inning on a pair of hits alternated with three walks (the last with the bases full). Three more walks an inning later, followed by a hit batsman, gave Detroit its final run in what became a 5–2 win.

Alan Trammell's two-run homer in the first inning of Game 4 put the Tigers ahead to stay. Jack Morris gave up a solo home run to Terry Kennedy in the second, but Trammell swatted a second two-run shot an inning later for a 4–1 lead. Morris let a second run score on a wild pitch in the ninth, but then retired Kennedy for the third out and his second Series win.

Kirk Gibson's two home runs framed Detroit's scoring in the final game. His two-run shot in the first inning opened the game's scoring. San Diego tied it up with runs in the third and fourth, but Detroit took a 5–3 lead with runs in the fifth and seventh (the latter on Lance Parrish's homer). The unlikely Kurt Bevacqua brought the Padres within a run of tying the game with his second Series homer in the eighth (doubling his regular-season total), but Gibson ended the scoring—and Padres hopes—with a three-run blast half an inning later.

DET (A)

PLAYER/POS	AVG	G	AB	R	H	2B	3B	HR	RB	BB	SO	SB
Doug Bair, p	.000	1	0	0	0	0	0	0	0	0	0	0
Dave Bergman, 1b	.000	5	5	0	0	0	0	0	0	0	1	0
Tom Brookens, 3b	.000	3	3	0	0	0	0	0	0	0	1	0
Marty Castillo, 3b	.333	3	9	2	3	0	0	1	2	2	1	0
Darrell Evans, 1b-4,3b-2	.067	5	15	1	1	0	0	0	1	4	4	0
Barbaro Garbey, dh-3	.000	4	12	0	0	0	0	0	0	0	2	0
Kirk Gibson, of	.333	5	18	4	6	0	0	2	7	4	4	3
Johnny Grubb, dh-2	.333	4	3	0	1	0	0	0	0	0	0	0
Willie Hernandez, p	.000	3	0	0	0	0	0	0	0	0	0	0
Larry Herndon, of	.333	5	15	1	5	0	0	1	3	3	2	0
Howard Johnson, ph	.000	1	1	0	0	0	0	0	0	0	0	0
Ruppert Jones, of	.000	2	3	0	0	0	0	0	0	0	1	0
Rusty Kuntz, ph	.000	2	1	0	0	0	0	0	0	1	1	0
Chet Lemon, of	.294	5	17	1	5	0	0	0	1	2	2	2
Aurelio Lopez, p	.000	2	0	0	0	0	0	0	0	0	0	0
Jack Morris, p	.000	2	0	0	0	0	0	0	0	0	0	0
Lance Parrish, c	.278	5	18	3	5	1	0	2	3	2	1	1
Dan Petry, p	.000	2	0	0	0	0	0	0	0	0	0	0
Bill Scherrer, p	.000	3	0	0	0	0	0	0	0	0	0	0
Alan Trammell, ss	.450	5	20	5	9	1	0	2	6	2	2	1
Lou Whitaker, 2b	.278	5	18	6	5	2	0	0	4	4	0	0
Milt Wilcox, p	.000	1	0	0	0	0	0	0	0	0	0	0
TOTAL	.253		158	23	40	4	0	7	23	24	27	7

PITCHER	W	L	ERA	G	GS	CG	SV	SHO	IP	H	ER	BB	SO
Doug Bair	0	0	0.00	1	0	0	0	0	0.2	0	0	0	1
Willie Hernandez	0	0	1.69	3	0	0	2	0	5.1	4	1	0	1
Aurelio Lopez	1	0	0.00	2	0	0	0	0	3.0	1	0	1	4
Jack Morris	2	0	2.00	2	2	2	0	0	18.0	13	4	3	13
Dan Petry	0	1	9.00	2	2	0	0	0	8.0	14	8	5	4
Bill Scherrer	0	0	3.00	3	0	0	0	0	3.0	5	1	0	0
Milt Wilcox	1	0	1.50	1	1	0	0	0	6.0	7	1	2	4
TOTAL	4	1	3.07	14	5	2	2	0	44.0	44	15	11	26

SD (N)

PLAYER/POS	AVG	G	AB	R	H	2B	3B	HR	RB	BB	SO	SB
Kurt Bevacqua, dh	.412	5	17	4	7	2	0	2	4	1	2	0
Bruce Bochy, ph	1.000	1	1	0	1	0	0	0	0	0	0	0
Greg Booker, p	.000	1	0	0	0	0	0	0	0	0	0	0
Bobby Brown, of	.067	5	15	1	1	0	0	0	2	0	4	0
Dave Dravecky, p	.000	2	0	0	0	0	0	0	0	0	0	0
Tim Flannery, 2b	1.000	1	1	0	1	0	0	0	0	0	0	0
Steve Garvey, 1b	.200	5	20	2	4	2	0	0	2	0	2	0
Rich Gossage, p	.000	2	0	0	0	0	0	0	0	0	0	0
Tony Gwynn, of	.263	5	19	1	5	0	0	0	0	3	2	1
Greg Harris, p	.000	1	0	0	0	0	0	0	0	0	0	0
Andy Hawkins, p	.000	3	0	0	0	0	0	0	0	0	0	0
Terry Kennedy, c	.211	5	19	2	4	1	0	1	3	1	1	0
Craig Lefferts, p	.000	3	0	0	0	0	0	0	0	0	0	0
Tim Lollar, p	.000	1	0	0	0	0	0	0	0	0	0	0
Carmelo Martinez, of	.176	5	17	0	3	0	0	0	0	1	9	0
Graig Nettles, 3b	.250	5	12	2	3	0	0	0	2	5	0	0
Ron Roenicke, of-1	.000	2	0	0	0	0	0	0	0	0	0	0
Luis Salazar, of-2,3b-1	.333	4	3	0	1	0	0	0	0	0	0	0
Eric Show, p	.000	1	0	0	0	0	0	0	0	0	0	0
Champ Summers, ph	.000	1	1	0	0	0	0	0	0	0	1	0
Garry Templeton, ss	.316	5	19	1	6	1	0	0	0	0	3	0
Mark Thurmond, p	.000	2	0	0	0	0	0	0	0	0	0	0
Ed Whitson, p	.000	1	0	0	0	0	0	0	0	0	0	0
Alan Wiggins, 2b	.364	5	22	2	8	1	0	0	1	0	2	1
TOTAL	.265		166	15	44	7	0	3	14	11	26	2

PITCHER	W	L	ERA	G	GS	CG	SV	SHO	IP	H	ER	BB	SO
Greg Booker	0	0	9.00	1	0	0	0	0	1.0	0	1	4	0
Dave Dravecky	0	0	0.00	2	0	0	0	0	4.2	3	0	1	5
Rich Gossage	0	0	13.50	2	0	0	0	0	2.2	3	4	1	2
Greg Harris	0	0	0.00	1	0	0	0	0	5.1	3	0	3	5
Andy Hawkins	1	1	0.75	3	0	0	0	0	12.0	4	1	6	4
Craig Lefferts	0	0	0.00	3	0	0	1	0	6.0	2	0	1	7
Tim Lollar	0	1	21.60	1	1	0	0	0	1.2	4	4	4	0
Eric Show	0	0	10.13	1	1	0	0	0	2.2	4	3	1	2
Mark Thurmond	0	1	10.13	2	2	0	0	0	5.1	12	6	3	2
Ed Whitson	0	0	40.50	1	1	0	0	0	0.2	5	3	0	0
TOTAL	1	4	4.71	17	5	0	1	0	42.0	40	22	24	27

GAME 1 AT SD OCT 9

```
DET  100 020 000    3 8 0
SD   200 000 000    2 8 1
```
Pitchers: MORRIS vs THURMOND, Hawkins (6), Dravecky (8)
Home Runs: Herndon-DET
Attendance: 57,908

GAME 2 AT SD OCT 10

```
DET  300 000 000    3 7 3
SD   100 130 00X    5 11 0
```
Pitchers: PETRY, Lopez (5), Scherrer (6), Bair (7), Hernandez (8) vs Whitson, HAWKINS (1), Lefferts (7)
Home Runs: Bevacqua-SD
Attendance: 57,911

GAME 3 AT DET OCT 12

```
SD   001 000 100    2 5 0
DET  041 000 00X    5 7 0
```
Pitchers: LOLLAR, Booker (2), Harris (3) vs WILCOX, Scherrer (7), Hernandez (7)
Home Runs: Castillo-DET
Attendance: 51,970

GAME 4 AT DET OCT 13

```
SD   010 000 001    2 10 2
DET  202 000 00X    4 7 0
```
Pitchers: SHOW, Dravecky (3), Lefferts (7), Gossage (8) vs MORRIS
Home Runs: Trammell-DET (2), Kennedy-SD
Attendance: 52,130

GAME 5 AT DET OCT 14

```
SD   001 200 010    4 10 1
DET  300 010 13X    8 11 1
```
Pitchers: Thurmond, HAWKINS (1), Lefferts (5), Gossage (7) vs Petry, Scherrer (4), LOPEZ (5), Hernandez (8)
Home Runs: Gibson-DET (2), Parrish-DET, Bevacqua-SD
Attendance: 51,901

ST. LOUIS CARDINALS (EAST) 4, LOS ANGELES DODGERS (WEST) 2

The Dodgers' league-leading pitchers held St. Louis to three runs over the first two games, even though the Cardinals recorded eight hits per game. But the Cards' league-leading hitters put their blows to better advantage in the next four games of the expanded NLCS, scoring 26 times for four wins and the pennant.

Fernando Valenzuela captured Game 1 for the Dodgers, thanks in part to some ragged fielding by the usually sharp Cardinals infield. And as Orel Hershiser was holding St. Louis to two runs in Game 2, an errant Cardinals pickoff throw and heavy Dodgers hitting gave him an increasingly comfortable lead.

When the series shifted to St. Louis for Game 3, the Cardinals revived, scoring twice in each of the first two innings for a quick lead, which they held for their first win. In Game 4 they unloaded for nine runs in the second inning, and in Game 5—with the game and series tied in the bottom of the ninth—Ozzie Smith hit his first left-handed home run ever to give St. Louis the series lead.

Back in Los Angeles, the Dodgers scored first in Game 6, and held a 4–1 lead after six innings. But three Cardinals scored on four hits in the seventh, and though Mike Marshall's eighth-inning home run restored the lead to Los Angeles, Jack Clark settled things for St. Louis with a three-run homer in the ninth.

STL (E)

PLAYER/POS	AVG	G	AB	R	H	2B	3B	HR	RB	BB	SO	SB
Joaquin Andujar, p	.250	2	4	1	1	1	0	0	0	0	1	0
Steve Braun, ph	.000	2	2	0	0	0	0	0	0	0	0	0
Bill Campbell, p	.000	3	0	0	0	0	0	0	0	0	0	0
Cesar Cedeno, of-4	.167	5	12	2	2	1	0	0	2	2	3	0
Jack Clark, 1b	.381	6	21	4	8	0	0	1	4	5	5	0
Vince Coleman, of	.286	3	14	2	4	0	0	0	1	0	2	1
Danny Cox, p	.000	1	2	0	0	0	0	0	0	1	1	0
Ken Dayley, p	.500	5	2	0	1	0	0	0	0	0	0	0
Bob Forsch, p	.000	1	0	0	0	0	0	0	0	0	0	0
Brian Harper, ph	.000	1	1	0	0	0	0	0	0	0	0	0
Tommy Herr, 2b	.333	6	21	2	7	4	0	1	6	5	2	1
Rick Horton, p	.000	3	0	0	0	0	0	0	0	0	0	0
Mike Jorgensen, ph	.000	2	2	0	0	0	0	0	0	0	1	0
Jeff Lahti, p	.000	2	0	0	0	0	0	0	0	0	0	0
Tito Landrum, of-4	.429	5	14	2	6	0	0	0	4	1	1	0
Willie McGee, of	.269	6	26	6	7	1	0	0	3	3	6	2
Tom Nieto, c	.000	1	3	0	0	0	0	0	0	1	2	0
Terry Pendleton, 3b	.208	6	24	2	5	1	0	0	4	1	3	0
Darrell Porter, c	.267	5	15	1	4	1	0	0	0	5	4	0
Ozzie Smith, ss	.435	6	23	4	10	1	1	1	3	3	1	0
John Tudor, p	.000	2	4	1	0	0	0	0	0	1	1	0
Andy Van Slyke, of	.091	5	11	1	1	0	0	0	1	2	1	0
Todd Worrell, p	.000	4	0	0	0	0	0	0	0	0	0	0
TOTAL	.279		201	29	56	10	1	3	26	30	34	6

PITCHER	W	L	ERA	G	GS	CG	SV	SHO	IP	H	ER	BB	SO
Joaquin Andujar	0	1	6.97	2	2	0	0	0	10.1	14	8	4	9
Bill Campbell	0	0	0.00	3	0	0	0	0	2.1	3	0	0	2
Danny Cox	1	0	3.00	1	1	0	0	0	6.0	4	2	5	4
Ken Dayley	0	0	0.00	5	0	0	2	0	6.0	2	0	1	3
Bob Forsch	0	0	5.40	1	1	0	0	0	3.1	3	2	2	0
Rick Horton	0	0	9.00	3	0	0	0	0	3.0	4	3	2	1
Jeff Lahti	1	0	0.00	2	0	0	0	0	2.0	2	0	0	1
John Tudor	1	1	2.84	2	2	0	0	0	12.2	10	4	3	8
Todd Worrell	1	0	1.42	4	0	0	0	0	6.1	4	1	2	3
TOTAL	4	2	3.46	23	6	0	2	0	52.0	46	20	19	31

LA (W)

PLAYER/POS	AVG	G	AB	R	H	2B	3B	HR	RB	BB	SO	SB
Dave Anderson, ss-3,3b-1	.000	4	5	1	0	0	0	0	0	3	1	0
Bob Bailor, 3b	.000	2	1	0	0	0	0	0	0	0	0	0
Greg Brock, 1b-4	.083	5	12	2	1	0	0	1	2	2	2	0
Enos Cabell, 1b-3	.077	5	13	1	1	0	0	0	0	0	3	0
Bobby Castillo, p	.000	1	2	0	0	0	0	0	0	0	1	0
Carlos Diaz, p	.000	2	0	0	0	0	0	0	0	0	0	0
Mariano Duncan, ss	.222	5	18	2	4	2	1	0	1	1	3	1
Pedro Guerrero, of	.250	6	20	2	5	1	0	0	4	5	2	0
Orel Hershiser, p	.286	2	7	1	2	0	0	0	1	0	2	0
Rick Honeycutt, p	.000	2	0	0	0	0	0	0	0	0	0	0
Ken Howell, p	.000	1	0	0	0	0	0	0	0	0	0	0
Jay Johnstone, ph	.000	1	1	0	0	0	0	0	0	0	0	0
Ken Landreaux, of	.389	5	18	4	7	3	0	0	2	1	1	0
Bill Madlock, 3b	.333	6	24	5	8	1	0	3	7	0	2	1
Candy Maldonado, of-3	.143	4	7	0	1	0	0	0	1	0	3	0
Mike Marshall, of	.217	6	23	1	5	2	0	1	3	1	3	0
Len Matuszek, 1b-1, of-1	1.000	3	1	1	1	0	0	0	0	0	0	0
Tom Niedenfuer, p	.000	3	1	0	0	0	0	0	0	0	1	0
Jerry Reuss, p	.000	1	0	0	0	0	0	0	0	0	0	0
Steve Sax, 2b	.300	6	20	1	6	3	0	0	1	1	5	0
Mike Scioscia, c	.250	6	16	2	4	0	0	0	1	4	0	0
Fernando Valenzuela, p	.200	2	5	0	1	0	0	0	0	0	1	0
Bob Welch, p	.000	1	1	0	0	0	0	0	0	0	1	0
Terry Whitfield, ph	.000	1	0	0	0	0	0	0	0	0	0	0
Steve Yeager, c	.000	1	2	0	0	0	0	0	0	0	1	0
TOTAL	.234		197	23	46	12	1	5	23	19	31	4

PITCHER	W	L	ERA	G	GS	CG	SV	SHO	IP	H	ER	BB	SO
Bobby Castillo	0	0	3.38	1	0	0	0	0	5.1	4	2	2	4
Carlos Diaz	0	0	3.00	2	0	0	0	0	3.0	5	1	1	2
Orel Hershiser	1	0	3.52	2	2	1	0	0	15.1	17	6	6	5
Rick Honeycutt	0	0	13.50	2	0	0	0	0	1.1	4	2	2	1
Ken Howell	0	0	0.00	1	0	0	0	0	2.0	0	0	0	2
Tom Niedenfuer	0	2	6.35	3	0	0	1	0	5.2	5	4	2	5
Jerry Reuss	0	1	10.80	1	1	0	0	0	1.2	5	2	1	0
F. Valenzuela	1	0	1.88	2	2	0	0	0	14.1	11	3	10	13
Bob Welch	0	1	6.75	1	1	0	0	0	2.2	5	2	6	2
TOTAL	2	4	3.86	15	6	1	1	0	51.1	56	22	30	34

GAME 1 AT LA OCT 9

```
STL  000 000 100   1 8 1
LA   000 103 00X   4 4 0
```
Pitchers: TUDOR, Dayley (6), Campbell (7), Worrell (8) vs VALENZUELA, Niedenfuer (7)
Attendance: 55,270

GAME 2 AT LA OCT 10

```
STL  001 000 001   2 8 1
LA   003 212 00X   8 13 1
```
Pitchers: ANDUJAR, Horton (5), Campbell (6), Dayley (7), Lahti (8) vs HERSHISER
Home Runs: Brock-LA
Attendance: 55,222

GAME 3 AT STL OCT 12

```
LA   000 100 100   2 7 2
STL  220 000 00X   4 8 0
```
Pitchers: WELCH, Honeycutt (3), Diaz (5), Howell (7) vs COX, Horton (7), Worrell (7), Dayley (9)
Home Runs: Herr-STL
Attendance: 53,708

GAME 4 AT STL OCT 13

```
LA   000 000 110   2 5 2
STL  090 110 01X   12 15 0
```
Pitchers: REUSS, Honeycutt (2), Castillo (2), Diaz (8) vs TUDOR, Horton (8), Campbell (9)
Home Runs: Madlock-LA
Attendance: 53,708

GAME 5 AT STL OCT 14

```
LA   000 200 000   2 5 1
STL  200 000 001   3 5 1
```
Pitchers: Valenzuela, NIEDENFUER (9) vs Forsch, Dayley (4), Worrell (7), LAHTI (9)
Home Runs: Madlock-LA, Smith-STL
Attendance: 53,708

GAME 6 AT LA OCT 16

```
STL  001 000 303   7 12 1
LA   110 020 010   5 8 0
```
Pitchers: Andujar, WORRELL (7), Dayley (9) vs Hershiser, NIEDENFUER (7)
Home Runs: Madlock-LA, Marshall-LA, Clark-STL
Attendance: 55,208

KANSAS CITY ROYALS (WEST) 4, TORONTO BLUE JAYS (EAST) 3

Were it not for the expansion of the ALCS to a best-of-seven series, the Blue Jays would have won the pennant. But after winning three of the first four games, the Jays lost their steam, and K.C. swept to their second pennant.

The pitching of Toronto ace Dave Stieb proved a key to the club's fortunes. Three times he started for the Jays. In the opener he threw eight shutout innings as the Jays won easily. In Game 4 he continued to dominate batters, though three walks in the sixth helped the Royals score a go-ahead run before Toronto pulled it out (for reliever Tom Henke) with a three-run ninth.

Had the series ended there, Stieb would have been a hero. But it didn't, and he was called upon again for Game 7—perhaps with inadequate rest. This time he faltered. After giving up single runs in the second and fourth innings, he loaded the bases in the sixth with two walks and a hit bats-man. Jim Sundberg unloaded them with a wind-blown triple, later scoring himself, and the Royals were on the road to victory.

George Brett keyed Kansas City's triumph. His four hits in Game 3 (including two home runs) gave the club its first victory, and his RBI ground out in Game 5 and go-ahead homer in Game 6 proved game-winners in contests the Royals had to win.

KC (W)

PLAYER/POS	AVG	G	AB	R	H	2B	3B	HR	RBI	BB	SO	SB
Steve Balboni, 1b	.120	7	25	1	3	0	0	0	1	2	8	0
Buddy Biancalana, ss	.222	7	18	2	4	1	0	0	1	1	6	0
Bud Black, p	.000	3	0	0	0	0	0	0	0	0	0	0
George Brett, 3b	.348	7	23	6	8	2	0	3	5	7	5	0
Onix Concepcion, ss	.000	4	1	0	0	0	0	0	0	0	0	0
Steve Farr, p	.000	2	0	0	0	0	0	0	0	0	0	0
Mark Gubicza, p	.000	2	0	0	0	0	0	0	0	0	0	0
Dane Iorg, ph	.500	4	2	0	1	1	0	0	0	2	0	0
Danny Jackson, p	.000	2	0	0	0	0	0	0	0	0	0	0
Lynn Jones, of	.000	5	0	0	0	0	0	0	0	0	0	0
Charlie Leibrandt, p	.000	3	0	0	0	0	0	0	0	0	0	0
Hal McRae, dh	.261	6	23	1	6	2	0	0	3	1	6	0
Darryl Motley, of	.333	2	3	1	1	0	0	0	1	1	2	0
Jorge Orta, dh-1	.000	2	5	0	0	0	0	0	0	0	1	0
Jamie Quirk, ph	.000	1	1	0	0	0	0	0	0	0	0	0
Dan Quisenberry, p	.000	4	0	0	0	0	0	0	0	0	0	0
Bret Saberhagen, p	.000	2	0	0	0	0	0	0	0	0	0	0
Pat Sheridan, of	.150	7	20	4	3	0	0	2	3	2	3	0
Lonnie Smith, of	.250	7	28	2	7	2	0	0	1	3	6	1
Jim Sundberg, c	.167	7	24	3	4	1	1	1	6	1	7	0
Frank White, 2b	.200	7	25	1	5	0	0	0	3	1	2	0
Willie Wilson, of	.310	7	29	5	9	0	0	1	2	1	5	1
TOTAL	.225		227	26	51	9	1	7	26	22	51	2

PITCHER	W	L	ERA	G	GS	CG	SV	SHO	IP	H	ER	BB	SO
Bud Black	0	0	1.69	3	1	0	0	0	10.2	11	2	4	8
Steve Farr	1	0	1.42	2	0	0	0	0	6.1	4	1	1	3
Mark Gubicza	1	0	3.24	2	1	0	0	0	8.1	4	3	4	4
Danny Jackson	1	0	0.00	2	1	1	0	1	10.0	10	0	1	7
Charlie Leibrandt	1	2	5.28	3	2	0	0	0	15.1	17	9	4	6
Dan Quisenberry	0	1	3.86	4	0	0	1	0	4.2	7	2	0	3
Bret Saberhagen	0	0	6.14	2	2	0	0	0	7.1	12	5	2	6
TOTAL	4	3	3.16	18	7	1	1	1	62.2	65	22	16	37

TOR (E)

PLAYER/POS	AVG	G	AB	R	H	2B	3B	HR	RBI	BB	SO	SB
Jim Acker, p	.000	2	0	0	0	0	0	0	0	0	0	0
Doyle Alexander, p	.000	2	0	0	0	0	0	0	0	0	0	0
Jesse Barfield, of	.280	7	25	3	7	1	0	1	4	3	7	1
George Bell, of	.321	7	28	4	9	3	0	0	1	0	4	0
Jeff Burroughs, ph	.000	1	1	0	0	0	0	0	0	0	0	0
Jim Clancy, p	.000	1	0	0	0	0	0	0	0	0	0	0
Tony Fernandez, ss	.333	7	24	2	8	2	0	0	2	1	2	0
Cecil Fielder, ph	.333	3	3	0	1	1	0	0	0	0	1	0
Damaso Garcia, 2b	.233	7	30	4	7	4	0	0	1	3	3	0
Jeff Hearron, c	.000	2	0	0	0	0	0	0	0	0	0	0
Tom Henke, p	.000	3	0	0	0	0	0	0	0	0	0	0
Garth Iorg, 3b	.133	6	15	1	2	0	0	0	0	1	3	0
Cliff Johnson, dh	.368	7	19	1	7	2	0	0	2	1	4	0
Jimmy Key, p	.000	2	0	0	0	0	0	0	0	0	0	0
Dennis Lamp, p	.000	3	0	0	0	0	0	0	0	0	0	0
Gary Lavelle, p	.000	1	0	0	0	0	0	0	0	0	0	0
Manny Lee, 2b	.000	5	0	0	0	0	0	0	0	0	0	0
Lloyd Moseby, of	.226	7	31	5	7	1	0	0	4	2	3	1
Rance Mulliniks, 3b	.364	5	11	1	4	1	0	1	3	2	2	0
Al Oliver, dh	.375	5	8	0	3	1	0	0	3	0	0	0
Dave Stieb, p	.000	3	0	0	0	0	0	0	0	0	0	0
Lou Thornton, pr	.000	2	0	1	0	0	0	0	0	0	0	0
Willie Upshaw, 1b	.231	7	26	2	6	2	0	0	1	1	4	0
Ernie Whitt, c	.190	7	21	1	4	1	0	0	2	2	4	0
TOTAL	.269		242	25	65	19	0	2	23	16	37	2

PITCHER	W	L	ERA	G	GS	CG	SV	SHO	IP	H	ER	BB	SO
Jim Acker	0	0	0.00	2	0	0	0	0	6.0	2	0	0	5
Doyle Alexander	0	1	8.71	2	2	0	0	0	10.1	14	10	3	9
Jim Clancy	0	1	9.00	1	0	0	0	0	1.0	2	1	1	0
Tom Henke	2	0	4.26	3	0	0	0	0	6.1	5	3	4	4
Jimmy Key	0	1	5.19	2	2	0	0	0	8.2	15	5	2	5
Dennis Lamp	0	0	0.00	3	0	0	0	0	9.1	2	0	1	10
Gary Lavelle	0	0	–	1	0	0	0	0	0.0	0	0	1	0
Dave Stieb	1	1	3.10	3	3	0	0	0	20.1	11	7	10	18
TOTAL	3	4	3.77	17	7	0	0	0	62.0	51	26	22	51

GAME 1 AT TOR OCT 8

```
KC    000 000 001    1  5  1
TOR   023 100 00X    6 11  0
```
Pitchers: LEIBRANDT, Farr (3), Gubicza (5), Jackson (8) vs STIEB, Henke (9)
Attendance: 39,115

GAME 2 AT TOR OCT 9

```
KC    002 100 0011   5 10  3
TOR   000 102 0102   6 10  0
```
Pitchers: Black, QUISENBERRY (8) vs Key, Lamp (4), Lavelle (8), HENKE (8)
Home Runs: Wilson-KC, Sheridan-KC
Attendance: 34,029

GAME 3 AT KC OCT 11

```
TOR   000 050 000    5 13  1
KC    100 112 01X    6 10  1
```
Pitchers: Alexander, Lamp (6), CLANCY (8) vs Saberhagen, Black (5), FARR (5)
Home Runs: Brett-KC (2), Barfield-TOR, Mulliniks-TOR, Sundberg-KC
Attendance: 40,224

GAME 4 AT KC OCT 12

```
TOR   000 000 003    3  7  0
KC    000 001 000    1  2  0
```
Pitchers: Stieb, HENKE (7) vs LEIBRANDT, Quisenberry (9)
Attendance: 41,112

GAME 5 AT KC OCT 13

```
TOR   000 000 000    0  8  0
KC    110 000 00X    2  8  0
```
Pitchers: KEY, Acker (6) vs JACKSON
Attendance: 40,046

GAME 6 AT TOR OCT 15

```
KC    101 012 000    5  8  1
TOR   101 001 000    3  8  2
```
Pitchers: GUBICZA, Black (6), Quisenberry (9) vs ALEXANDER, Lamp (6)
Home Runs: Brett-KC
Attendance: 37,557

GAME 7 AT TOR OCT 16

```
KC    010 104 000    6  8  0
TOR   000 010 001    2  8  1
```
Pitchers: Saberhagen, LEIBRANDT (4), Quisenberry (9) vs STIEB, Acker (6)
Home Runs: Sheridan-KC
Attendance: 32,084

KANSAS CITY ROYALS (AL) 4, ST. LOUIS CARDINALS (NL) 3

The underdog Royals surprised St. Louis with superior hitting and pitching and even outstole the speedy Cards, six bases to two. Still, had an umpire not muffed a call at first base in Game 6, St. Louis might have emerged from the game wearing the world crown.

The Cardinals broke a 1–1 tie in the fourth inning of the opener with back-to-back doubles off Danny Jackson and held on behind the strong pitching of John Tudor and reliever Todd Worrell for a 3–1 win. In Game 2, except for the fourth inning, when he yielded a single and two doubles (for two runs) before retiring his first batter, Cardinals starter Danny Cox held the Royals in check. Royals starter Charlie Leibrandt hurled even more effectively, holding St. Louis to two hits—until the ninth inning, when four hits (three of them doubles) produced four runs and a second Card victory.

Kansas City finally demonstrated its punch in Game 3. Frank White hit a two-run homer in the fifth, and the Royals scored four more times to win behind the six-hit hurling of sophomore sensation Bret Saberhagen. The next day, though, Royals bats died again against John Tudor, who shut them out on five hits. Three Royals pitchers yielded only six hits, but two were home runs to Tito Landrum and Willie McGee, and one was a triple to Terry Pendleton, who scored on a squeeze play.

Down three games to one, the Royals hammered 11 hits in Game 5 for six runs to win behind Danny Jackson's five-hitter. Seven hits in the first eight innings of Game 6, though, scored no runs against Cardinals starter Danny Cox and reliever Ken Dayley. But in the last of the ninth, with the Cards ahead, 1–0, and Todd Worrell now pitching, Royals pinch hitter Jorge Orta was ruled safe at first on what the cameras showed clearly as an out. This miscall, followed by a pop foul that first baseman Jack Clark should have caught but didn't, opened the door to disintegration by St. Louis. A single and passed ball put Royals at second and third, and, after an intentional walk to set up the double play, pinch hitter Dane Iorg singled home the tying and winning runs for the Royals.

The Cardinals threw seven pitchers at Kansas City in the finale in a vain attempt to halt the Royals' 14-hit, 11-run attack, while Bret Saberhagen stopped the Cards cold on five hits to bring the Royals their first world title.

KC (A)

PLAYER/POS	AVG	G	AB	R	H	2B	3B	HR	RB	BB	SO	SB
Steve Balboni, 1b	.320	7	25	2	8	0	0	0	3	5	4	0
Joe Beckwith, p	.000	1	0	0	0	0	0	0	0	0	0	0
Buddy Biancalana, ss	.278	7	18	2	5	0	0	0	2	5	4	0
Bud Black, p	.000	2	1	0	0	0	0	0	0	0	1	0
George Brett, 3b	.370	7	27	5	10	1	0	0	1	4	7	1
Onix Concepcion, ss-2	.000	3	0	1	0	0	0	0	0	0	0	0
Dane Iorg, ph	.500	2	2	0	1	0	0	0	2	0	0	0
Danny Jackson, p	.000	2	6	0	0	0	0	0	0	0	5	0
Lynn Jones, of-4	.667	6	3	0	2	1	1	0	0	0	0	0
Charlie Leibrandt, p	.000	2	4	0	0	0	0	0	0	0	2	0
Hal McRae, ph	.000	3	1	0	0	0	0	0	0	1	0	0
Darryl Motley, of-4	.364	5	11	1	4	0	0	1	3	0	1	0
Jorge Orta, of	.333	3	3	0	1	0	0	0	0	0	0	0
Greg Pryor, 3b	.000	1	0	0	0	0	0	0	0	0	0	0
Dan Quisenberry, p	.000	4	0	0	0	0	0	0	0	0	0	0
Bret Saberhagen, p	.000	2	7	1	0	0	0	0	0	0	4	0
Pat Sheridan, of-4	.222	5	18	0	4	2	0	0	1	0	7	0
Lonnie Smith, of	.333	7	27	4	9	3	0	0	4	3	8	2
Jim Sundberg, c	.250	7	24	6	6	2	0	0	1	6	4	0
John Wathan, ph	.000	2	1	0	0	0	0	0	0	0	1	0
Frank White, 2b	.250	7	28	4	7	3	0	1	6	3	4	1
Willie Wilson, of	.367	7	30	2	11	0	1	0	3	1	4	3
TOTAL	.288		236	28	68	12	2	2	26	28	56	7

PITCHER	W	L	ERA	G	GS	CG	SV	SHO	IP	H	ER	BB	SO
Joe Beckwith	0	0	0.00	1	0	0	0	0	2.0	1	0	0	3
Bud Black	0	1	5.06	2	1	0	0	0	5.1	4	3	5	4
Danny Jackson	1	1	1.69	2	2	1	0	0	16.0	9	3	5	12
Charlie Leibrandt	0	1	2.76	2	2	0	0	0	16.1	10	5	4	10
Dan Quisenberry	1	0	2.08	4	0	0	0	0	4.1	5	1	3	3
Bret Saberhagen	2	0	0.50	2	2	2	0	1	18.0	11	1	1	10
TOTAL	4	3	1.89	13	7	3	0	1	62.0	40	13	18	42

STL (N)

PLAYER/POS	AVG	G	AB	R	H	2B	3B	HR	RB	BB	SO	SB
Joaquin Andujar, p	.000	2	1	0	0	0	0	0	0	0	1	0
Steve Braun, ph	.000	1	1	0	0	0	0	0	0	0	0	0
Bill Campbell, p	.000	3	0	0	0	0	0	0	0	0	0	0
Cesar Cedeno, of	.133	5	15	1	2	1	0	0	1	2	2	0
Jack Clark, 1b	.240	7	25	1	6	2	0	0	4	3	9	0
Danny Cox, p	.000	2	4	0	0	0	0	0	0	0	2	0
Ken Dayley, p	.000	4	0	0	0	0	0	0	0	0	0	0
Ivan DeJesus, ph	.000	1	1	0	0	0	0	0	0	0	0	0
Bob Forsch, p	.000	2	0	0	0	0	0	0	0	0	0	0
Brian Harper, ph	.250	4	4	0	1	0	0	0	1	0	1	0
Tommy Herr, 2b	.154	7	26	2	4	2	0	0	0	2	2	0
Rick Horton, p	.000	3	1	0	0	0	0	0	0	0	1	0
Mike Jorgensen, of-1	.000	2	3	0	0	0	0	0	0	0	0	0
Jeff Lahti, p	.000	3	0	0	0	0	0	0	0	0	0	0
Tito Landrum, of	.360	7	25	3	9	2	0	1	1	0	2	0
Tom Lawless, pr	.000	1	0	0	0	0	0	0	0	0	0	0
Willie McGee, of	.259	7	27	2	7	2	0	1	2	1	3	1
Tom Nieto, c	.000	2	5	0	0	0	0	0	0	1	2	0
Terry Pendleton, 3b	.261	7	23	3	6	1	1	0	3	3	2	0
Darrell Porter, c	.133	5	15	0	2	0	0	0	0	2	5	0
Ozzie Smith, ss	.087	7	23	1	2	0	0	0	0	4	0	1
John Tudor, p	.000	3	5	0	0	0	0	0	0	0	4	0
Andy Van Slyke, of	.091	6	11	0	1	0	0	0	0	0	5	0
Todd Worrell, p	.000	3	1	0	0	0	0	0	0	0	1	0
TOTAL	.185		216	13	40	10	1	2	13	18	42	2

PITCHER	W	L	ERA	G	GS	CG	SV	SHO	IP	H	ER	BB	SO
Joaquin Andujar	0	1	9.00	2	1	0	0	0	4.0	10	4	4	3
Bill Campbell	0	0	2.25	3	0	0	0	0	4.0	4	1	2	5
Danny Cox	0	0	1.29	2	2	0	0	0	14.0	14	2	4	13
Ken Dayley	1	0	0.00	4	0	0	0	0	6.0	1	0	3	5
Bob Forsch	0	1	12.00	2	1	0	0	0	3.0	6	4	1	3
Rick Horton	0	0	6.75	3	0	0	0	0	4.0	4	3	5	5
Jeff Lahti	0	0	12.27	3	0	0	1	0	3.2	10	5	0	2
John Tudor	2	1	3.00	3	3	1	0	1	18.0	15	6	7	14
Todd Worrell	0	1	3.86	3	0	0	1	0	4.2	4	2	2	6
TOTAL	3	4	3.96	25	7	1	2	1	61.1	68	27	28	56

GAME 1 AT KC OCT 19

STL 001 100 001   3 7 1
KC   010 010 000   1 8 0
Pitchers: TUDOR, Worrell (7) vs JACKSON, Quisenberry (8), Black (9)
Attendance: 41,650

GAME 2 AT KC OCT 20

STL 000 000 004   4 6 0
KC   000 200 000   2 9 0
Pitchers: Cox, DAYLEY (8), Lahti (9) vs LEIBRANDT, Quisenberry (9)
Attendance: 41,656

GAME 3 AT STL OCT 22

KC   000 220 200   6 11 0
STL 000 001 000   1 6 0
Pitchers: SABERHAGEN vs ANDUJAR, Campbell (5), Horton (6), Dayley (8)
Home Runs: White-KC
Attendance: 53,634

GAME 4 AT STL OCT 23

KC   000 000 000   0 5 1
STL 011 010 00X   3 6 0
Pitchers: BLACK, Beckwith (6) Quisenberry (8) vs TUDOR
Home Runs: Landrum-STL, McGee-STL
Attendance: 53,634

GAME 5 AT STL OCT 24

KC   130 000 011   6 11 2
STL 100 000 000   1 5 1
Pitchers: JACKSON vs FORSCH, Horton (2), Campbell (4), Worrell (6), Lahti (8)
Attendance: 53,634

GAME 6 AT KC OCT 26

STL 000 000 010   1 5 0
KC   000 000 002   2 10 0
Pitchers: Cox, Dayley (8), WORRELL (9) vs Leibrandt, QUISENBERRY (8)
Attendance: 41,628

GAME 7 AT KC OCT 27

STL 000 000 000   0 5 0
KC   023 060 00X   11 14 0
Pitchers: TUDOR, Campbell (3), Lahti (5), Horton (5), Andujar (5), Forsch (5), Dayley (7) vs SABERHAGEN
Home Runs: Motley-KC
Attendance: 41,658

NEW YORK METS (EAST) 4, HOUSTON ASTROS (WEST) 2

Houston pitcher Mike Scott overwhelmed the Mets in Games 1 and 4, and would have faced them a third time in Game 7 if the Astros had won Game 6. They tried, scoring three runs in the first as Bob Knepper shut out the Mets on two hits through eight innings of the sixth game. But in the top of the ninth New York tied the game and held on into extra innings. No one scored again until the Mets put a run across in the 14th. Billy Hatcher tied it up again later in the 14th with a home run just inside the left-field foul pole. Two innings later the Mets (aided by a pair of wild pitches) scored three runs. Again the Astros came back, scoring twice, but fell just short as Jesse Orosco struck out Kevin Bass with two men on base to win his third game of the series and give New York the pennant.

In the series opener Houston scored just one run off Dwight Gooden, but it was enough, as Mike Scott, fanning 14, shut out the Mets on five hits. New York came back with five runs in Game 2 to win behind Bob Ojeda, who gave up 10 hits but only one run. In Game 3 the Astros held the lead into the last of the sixth, when New York tied the score with four runs. Houston retook the lead in the seventh with a run, but Len Dykstra won it for New York with a two-run homer in the bottom of the ninth.

The Astros' win in Game 4 evened the series. Houston had scored three runs by the time Scott (on his way to a three-hitter) gave the Mets their only run in the eighth. Houston's Nolan Ryan gave up only two hits in the first nine innings of Game 5 (one of them Darryl Strawberry's game-tying solo homer in the fifth), striking out 12. But New York's Gooden also yielded only one run in 10 innings of work. Charlie Kerfeld shut out the Mets in the 10th and 11th, and the Mets' Orosco stopped Houston in the 11th and 12th. But in the last of the 12th, Gary Carter singled home a run off Kerfeld to end the game (and his series-long batting slump)—setting the stage for the 16-inning marathon the next day.

NY (E)

PLAYER/POS	AVG	G	AB	R	H	2B	3B	HR	RB	BB	SO	SB
Rick Aguilera, p	.000	2	0	0	0	0	0	0	0	0	0	0
Wally Backman, 2b	.238	6	21	5	5	0	0	0	2	2	4	1
Gary Carter, c	.148	6	27	1	4	1	0	0	2	2	5	0
Ron Darling, p	.000	1	1	0	0	0	0	0	0	0	0	0
Lenny Dykstra, of	.304	6	23	3	7	1	1	1	3	2	4	1
Kevin Elster, ss	.000	4	3	0	0	0	0	0	0	0	1	0
Sid Fernandez, p	.000	1	1	0	0	0	0	0	0	0	0	0
Dwight Gooden, p	.000	2	5	0	0	0	0	0	0	0	2	0
Danny Heep, of-1	.250	5	4	0	1	0	0	0	1	0	2	0
Keith Hernandez, 1b	.269	6	26	3	7	1	1	0	3	3	6	0
Howard Johnson, ph	.000	2	2	0	0	0	0	0	0	0	0	0
Ray Knight, 3b	.167	6	24	1	4	0	0	0	2	1	5	0
Lee Mazzilli, ph	.200	5	5	0	1	0	0	0	0	0	3	0
Roger McDowell, p	.000	2	1	0	0	0	0	0	0	0	0	0
Kevin Mitchell, of	.250	2	8	1	2	0	0	0	0	0	1	0
Bob Ojeda, p	.000	2	5	1	0	0	0	0	0	0	2	0
Jesse Orosco, p	.000	4	0	0	0	0	0	0	0	0	0	0
Rafael Santana, ss	.176	6	17	0	3	0	0	0	0	0	3	0
Doug Sisk, p	.000	1	0	0	0	0	0	0	0	0	0	0
Darryl Strawberry, of	.227	6	22	4	5	1	0	2	5	3	12	1
Tim Teufel, 2b	.167	2	6	0	1	0	0	0	0	0	0	0
Mookie Wilson, of	.115	6	26	2	3	0	0	0	1	1	7	1
TOTAL	.189		227	21	43	4	2	3	19	14	57	4

PITCHER	W	L	ERA	G	GS	CG	SV	SHO	IP	H	ER	BB	SO
Rick Aguilera	0	0	0.00	2	0	0	0	0	5.0	2	0	2	2
Ron Darling	0	0	7.20	1	1	0	0	0	5.0	6	4	2	5
Sid Fernandez	0	1	4.50	1	1	0	0	0	6.0	3	3	1	5
Dwight Gooden	0	1	1.06	2	2	0	0	0	17.0	16	2	5	9
Roger McDowell	0	0	0.00	2	0	0	0	0	7.0	1	0	0	3
Bob Ojeda	1	0	2.57	2	2	1	0	0	14.0	15	4	4	6
Jesse Orosco	3	0	3.38	4	0	0	0	0	8.0	5	3	2	10
Doug Sisk	0	0	0.00	1	0	0	0	0	1.0	1	0	1	0
TOTAL	4	2	2.29	15	6	1	0	0	63.0	49	16	17	40

HOU (W)

PLAYER/POS	AVG	G	AB	R	H	2B	3B	HR	RB	BB	SO	SB
Larry Andersen, p	.000	2	0	0	0	0	0	0	0	0	0	0
Alan Ashby, c	.130	6	23	2	3	1	0	1	2	2	1	0
Kevin Bass, of	.292	6	24	0	7	2	0	0	0	4	4	2
Jeff Calhoun, p	.000	1	0	0	0	0	0	0	0	0	0	0
Jose Cruz, of	.192	6	26	0	5	0	0	0	2	1	8	0
Glenn Davis, 1b	.269	6	26	3	7	1	0	1	3	1	3	0
Bill Doran, 2b	.222	6	27	3	6	0	0	1	3	2	2	2
Phil Garner, 3b	.222	3	9	1	2	1	0	0	2	1	2	0
Billy Hatcher, of	.280	6	25	4	7	0	0	1	2	3	2	3
Charlie Kerfeld, p	.000	3	0	0	0	0	0	0	0	0	0	0
Bob Knepper, p	.000	2	5	0	0	0	0	0	0	1	2	0
Davey Lopes, ph	.000	3	2	1	0	0	0	0	0	1	0	0
Aurelio Lopez, p	.000	2	0	0	0	0	0	0	0	0	0	0
Jim Pankovits, ph	.000	2	2	0	0	0	0	0	0	0	1	0
Terry Puhl, ph	.667	3	3	0	2	0	0	0	0	0	0	1
Craig Reynolds, ss	.333	4	12	1	4	0	0	0	1	1	3	0
Nolan Ryan, p	.000	2	4	0	0	0	0	0	0	0	2	0
Mike Scott, p	.000	2	6	0	0	0	0	0	0	0	5	0
Dave Smith, p	.000	2	0	0	0	0	0	0	0	0	0	0
Dickie Thon, ss	.250	6	12	1	3	0	0	0	1	1	0	0
Denny Walling, 3b	.158	5	19	1	3	1	0	0	2	0	4	0
TOTAL	.218		225	17	49	6	0	5	17	17	40	8

PITCHER	W	L	ERA	G	GS	CG	SV	SHO	IP	H	ER	BB	SO
Larry Andersen	0	0	0.00	2	0	0	0	0	5.0	1	0	2	3
Jeff Calhoun	0	0	9.00	1	0	0	0	0	1.0	1	1	1	0
Charlie Kerfeld	0	1	2.25	3	0	0	0	0	4.0	2	1	1	4
Bob Knepper	0	0	3.52	2	2	0	0	0	15.1	13	6	1	9
Aurelio Lopez	0	1	8.10	2	0	0	0	0	3.1	7	3	4	3
Nolan Ryan	0	1	3.86	2	2	0	0	0	14.0	9	6	1	17
Mike Scott	2	0	0.50	2	2	2	0	1	18.0	8	1	1	19
Dave Smith	0	1	9.00	2	0	0	0	0	2.0	2	2	3	2
TOTAL	2	4	2.87	16	6	2	0	1	62.2	43	20	14	57

GAME 1 AT HOU OCT 8

```
NY  000 000 000   0 5 0
HOU 010 000 00X   1 7 1
```
Pitchers: GOODEN, Orosco (8) vs SCOTT
Home Runs: Davis-HOU
Attendance: 44,131

GAME 2 AT HOU OCT 9

```
NY  000 230 000   5 10 0
HOU 000 000 100   1 10 2
```
Pitchers: OJEDA vs RYAN, Andersen (6), Lopez (8), Kerfeld (9)
Attendance: 44,391

GAME 3 AT NY OCT 11

```
HOU 220 000 100   5 8 1
NY  000 004 002   6 10 1
```
Pitchers: Knepper, Kerfeld (8), SMITH (9) vs Darling, Aguilera (6), OROSCO (9)
Home Runs: Doran-HOU, Strawberry-NY, Dykstra-NY
Attendance: 55,052

GAME 4 AT NY OCT 12

```
HOU 020 010 000   3 4 1
NY  000 000 010   1 3 0
```
Pitchers: SCOTT vs FERNANDEZ, McDowell (7), Sisk (9)
Home Runs: Ashby-HOU, Thon-HOU
Attendance: 55,038

GAME 5 AT NY OCT 14

```
HOU 000 010 000 000 0   1 9 1
NY  000 010 000 000 1   2 4 0
```
Pitchers: Ryan, KERFELD (10) vs Gooden, OROSCO (11)
Home Runs: Strawberry-NY
Attendance: 54,986

GAME 6 AT HOU OCT 15

```
NY  000 000 003 000 0103   7 11 0
HOU 300 000 000 000 0102   6 11 1
```
Pitchers: Ojeda, Aguilera (6), McDowell (9), OROSCO (14) vs Knepper, Smith (9), Andersen (11), LOPEZ (14), Calhoun (16)
Home Runs: Hatcher-HOU
Attendance: 45,718

BOSTON RED SOX (EAST) 4, CALIFORNIA ANGELS (WEST) 3

For the second time in the two years of the expanded ALCS, a club that would have been eliminated in a five-game series came back to take the pennant in seven games. The first two games were one-sided. California scored five early runs off Roger Clemens and breezed to an easy 8–1 win in the opener. Boston retaliated in Game 2 with nine runs, breaking the game open with six unanswered runs in the seventh and eighth innings.

Game 3 was close until the Angels homered twice for three runs with two out in the seventh to break a 1–1 tie. In Game 4, the Angels were handed a tie in the last of the ninth when Boston reliever Calvin Schiraldi hit a batter with the bases loaded and won in the 11th on Bobby Grich's RBI single.

The Red Sox, down three games to one, were on the brink of elimination in Game Five, with two outs in the ninth, when Dave Henderson, after fouling off one third-strike pitch, hit the next for a two-run homer that gave Boston a one-run lead. The Angels tied the game in the last of the ninth, but Henderson's sacrifice fly in the 11th put the Sox ahead for good.

Boston needed two more wins and got them with surprising ease, 10–4 and 8–1, as Oil Can Boyd and Clemens redeemed their earlier losses.

BOS (E)

PLAYER/POS	AVG	G	AB	R	H	2B	3B	HR	RB	BB	SO	SB
Tony Armas, of	.125	5	16	1	2	1	0	0	0	0	2	0
Marty Barrett, 2b	.367	7	30	4	11	2	0	0	5	2	2	0
Don Baylor, dh	.346	7	26	6	9	3	0	1	2	4	5	0
Wade Boggs, 3b	.233	7	30	3	7	1	1	0	2	4	1	0
Oil Can Boyd, p	.000	2	0	0	0	0	0	0	0	0	0	0
Bill Buckner, 1b	.214	7	28	3	6	1	0	0	3	0	2	0
Roger Clemens, p	.000	3	0	0	0	0	0	0	0	0	0	0
Steve Crawford, p	.000	1	0	0	0	0	0	0	0	0	0	0
Dwight Evans, of	.214	7	28	2	6	1	0	1	4	3	3	0
Rich Gedman, c	.357	7	28	4	10	1	0	1	6	0	4	0
Mike Greenwell, ph	.500	2	2	0	1	0	0	0	0	0	0	0
Dave Henderson, of	.111	5	9	3	1	0	0	1	4	2	2	0
Bruce Hurst, p	.000	2	0	0	0	0	0	0	0	0	0	0
Spike Owen, ss	.429	7	21	5	9	0	1	0	3	2	2	1
Jim Rice, of	.161	7	31	8	5	1	0	2	6	1	8	0
Ed Romero, ss	.000	1	2	0	0	0	0	0	0	0	0	0
Joe Sambito, p	.000	3	0	0	0	0	0	0	0	0	0	0
Calvin Schiraldi, p	.000	4	0	0	0	0	0	0	0	0	0	0
Bob Stanley, p	.000	3	0	0	0	0	0	0	0	0	0	0
Dave Stapleton, 1b	.667	4	3	2	2	0	0	0	0	0	1	0
TOTAL	.272		254	41	69	11	2	6	35	19	31	1

PITCHER	W	L	ERA	G	GS	CG	SV	SHO	IP	H	ER	BB	SO
Oil Can Boyd	1	1	4.61	2	2	0	0	0	13.2	17	7	3	8
Roger Clemens	1	1	4.37	3	3	0	0	0	22.2	22	11	7	17
Steve Crawford	1	0	0.00	1	0	0	0	0	1.2	1	0	2	1
Bruce Hurst	1	0	2.40	2	2	1	0	0	15.0	18	4	1	8
Joe Sambito	0	0	0.00	3	0	0	0	0	0.2	1	0	0	0
Calvin Schiraldi	0	1	1.50	4	0	0	1	0	6.0	5	1	3	9
Bob Stanley	0	0	4.76	3	0	0	0	0	5.2	7	3	3	1
TOTAL	4	3	3.58	18	7	1	1	0	65.1	71	26	20	44

CAL (W)

PLAYER/POS	AVG	G	AB	R	H	2B	3B	HR	RB	BB	SO	SB
Bob Boone, c	.455	7	22	4	10	0	0	1	2	1	3	0
Rick Burleson, 2b-2, dh-1	.273	4	11	0	3	0	0	0	0	0	0	0
John Candelaria, p	.000	2	0	0	0	0	0	0	0	0	0	0
Doug Corbett, p	.000	3	0	0	0	0	0	0	0	0	0	0
Doug DeCinces, 3b	.281	7	32	2	9	3	0	1	3	0	2	0
Brian Downing, of	.222	7	27	2	6	0	0	1	7	4	5	0
Chuck Finley, p	.000	3	0	0	0	0	0	0	0	0	0	0
Bobby Grich, 2b-3,1b-3	.208	6	24	1	5	0	0	1	3	0	8	0
George Hendrick, of-2,1b-1	.083	3	12	0	1	0	0	0	0	0	2	0
Jack Howell, ph	.000	2	1	0	0	0	0	0	0	1	1	0
Reggie Jackson, dh	.192	6	26	2	5	2	0	0	2	2	7	0
Ruppert Jones, of-5	.176	6	17	4	3	1	0	0	2	5	2	0
Wally Joyner, 1b	.455	3	11	3	5	2	0	1	2	2	0	0
Gary Lucas, p	.000	4	0	0	0	0	0	0	0	0	0	0
Kirk McCaskill, p	.000	2	0	0	0	0	0	0	0	0	0	0
Donnie Moore, p	.000	3	0	0	0	0	0	0	0	0	0	0
Jerry Narron, c-3	.500	4	2	1	1	0	0	0	0	1	1	0
Gary Pettis, of	.346	7	26	4	9	1	0	1	4	3	5	0
Vern Ruhle, p	.000	1	0	0	0	0	0	0	0	0	0	0
Dick Schofield, ss	.300	7	30	4	9	1	0	1	2	1	5	1
Don Sutton, p	.000	2	0	0	0	0	0	0	0	0	1	0
Devon White, of-3	.500	4	2	2	1	0	0	0	0	0	1	0
Rob Wilfong, 2b	.308	4	13	1	4	1	0	0	2	0	2	0
Mike Witt, p	.000	2	0	0	0	0	0	0	0	0	0	0
TOTAL	.277		256	30	71	11	0	7	29	20	44	1

PITCHER	W	L	ERA	G	GS	CG	SV	SHO	IP	H	ER	BB	SO
John Candelaria	1	1	0.84	2	2	0	0	0	10.2	11	1	6	7
Doug Corbett	1	0	5.40	3	0	0	0	0	6.2	9	4	2	2
Chuck Finley	0	0	0.00	3	0	0	0	0	2.0	1	0	0	1
Gary Lucas	0	0	11.57	4	0	0	0	0	2.1	3	3	1	2
Kirk McCaskill	0	2	7.71	2	2	0	0	0	9.1	16	8	5	7
Donnie Moore	0	1	7.20	3	0	0	1	0	5.0	8	4	2	0
Vern Ruhle	0	0	13.50	1	0	0	0	0	0.2	2	1	0	0
Don Sutton	0	0	1.86	2	2	1	0	0	9.2	6	2	1	4
Mike Witt	1	0	2.55	2	2	1	0	0	17.2	13	5	2	8
TOTAL	3	4	3.94	22	7	1	1	0	64.0	69	28	19	31

GAME 1 AT BOS OCT 7

```
CAL  0 4 1  0 0 0  0 3 0    8 11 0
BOS  0 0 0  0 0 1  0 0 0    1  5 1
```
Pitchers: WITT vs CLEMENS, Sambito (8), Stanley (8)
Attendance: 32,993

GAME 2 AT BOS OCT 8

```
CAL  0 0 0  1 1 0  0 0 0    2 11 3
BOS  1 1 0  0 1 0  3 3 X    9 13 2
```
Pitchers: McCASKILL, Lucas (8), Corbett (8) vs HURST
Home Runs: Joyner-CAL, Rice-BOS
Attendance: 32,786

GAME 3 AT CAL OCT 10

```
BOS  0 1 0  0 0 0  0 2 0    3 9 1
CAL  0 0 0  0 0 1  3 1 X    5 8 0
```
Pitchers: BOYD, Sambito (7), Schiraldi (8) vs CANDELARIA, Moore (8)
Home Runs: Schofield-CAL, Pettis-CAL
Attendance: 64,206

GAME 4 AT CAL OCT 11

```
BOS  0 0 0  0 0 1  0 2 0 0 0    3  6 1
CAL  0 0 0  0 0 0  0 0 3 0 1    4 11 2
```
Pitchers: Clemens, SCHIRALDI (9) vs Sutton, Lucas (7), Ruhle (7), Finley (8), CORBETT (8)
Home Runs: DeCinces-CAL
Attendance: 64,223

GAME 5 AT CAL OCT 12

```
BOS  0 2 0  0 0 0  0 0 4 0 1    7 12 0
CAL  0 0 1  0 2 2  0 0 1 0 0    6 13 0
```
Pitchers: Hurst, Stanley (7), Sambito (9), CRAWFORD (9), Schiraldi (11) vs Witt, Lucas (9), MOORE (9), Finley (11)
Home Runs: Gedman-BOS, Boone-CAL, Grich-CAL, Baylor-BOS, Henderson-BOS
Attendance: 64,223

GAME 6 AT BOS OCT 14

```
CAL  2 0 0  0 0 0  1 1 0     4 11 1
BOS  2 0 5  0 1 0  2 0 X    10 16 1
```
Pitchers: McCASKILL, Lucas (3), Corbett (4), Finley (7) vs BOYD, Stanley (8)
Home Runs: Downing-CAL
Attendance: 32,998

GAME 7 AT BOS OCT 15

```
CAL  0 0 0  0 0 0  0 1 0    1 6 2
BOS  0 3 0  4 0 0  1 0 X    8 8 1
```
Pitchers: CANDELARIA, Sutton (4), Moore (8) vs CLEMENS, Schiraldi (8)
Home Runs: Rice-BOS, Evans-BOS
Attendance: 33,001

NEW YORK METS (NL) 4, BOSTON RED SOX (AL) 3

In their three most recent Series appearances—1946, 1967, and 1975—the Red Sox had battled to a seventh game, only to lose. This time they came within one strike of winning the crown in the sixth game—and lost again in Game 7.

Boston surprised the favored Mets by taking the first two games in New York. Bruce Hurst (with relief from Calvin Schiraldi in the ninth) pitched a four-hitter. New York's Ron Darling hurled just as well but lost when a seventh-inning walk, a wild pitch, and an error by second baseman Tim Teufel moved Jim Rice around the bases with the game's only run. Game 2, close for three innings, turned into a 9–3 Boston blowout as the Sox racked New York pitching for 18 hits, including home runs by Dave Henderson and Dwight Evans.

When the Series moved to Boston, though, the Mets revived to rap Sox starter Oil Can Boyd and two relievers for 13 hits and seven runs (starting with Len Dykstra's leadoff home run in the first inning) as former Sox pitcher Bob Ojeda subdued his old teammates, giving up just one run on five hits in his seven innings of work. The next day Ron Darling redeemed his first-game loss with seven shutout innings as his teammates built him a 6–0 lead (five of the runs scoring on homers by Dykstra and a pair by Gary Carter). The game ended at 6–2, with the Series even at two wins apiece.

Boston recovered in its final home appearance, taking a 4–0 lead and holding it until Teufel spoiled Bruce Hurst's try for a second shutout by homering in the eighth inning. Hurst yielded a second run with two outs in the ninth, but struck out Len Dykstra on three pitches to seal his second win.

The ninth inning of Game 6 ended with the score tied, 3–3. Boston's Dave Henderson led off the 10th with a home run and two more Sox hits made the score, 5–3. Boston reliever Calvin Schiraldi retired the first two Mets in the last of the 10th on long flies, but then three Mets singled, driving in one run and driving out Schiraldi. Bob Stanley, his replacement, had two strikes on Mookie Wilson when a wild pitch let in the tying run, and then Wilson's grounder went through first baseman Bill Buckner's legs as the winning run bounded

across the plate for the Mets.

The Red Sox nearly recovered in Game 7. Second-inning home runs by Dwight Evans and Rich Gedman, a walk, sacrifice, and single gave Boston a 3–0 lead which they held into the sixth inning. But then starter Bruce Hurst lost his touch: four hits and a walk later the score was tied. A succession of five Sox relievers tried to hold the line, but the Mets scored five runs to Boston's two in the final innings for an 8–5 triumph.

NY (N)

PLAYER/POS	AVG	G	AB	R	H	2B	3B	HR	RB	BB	SO	SB
Rick Aguilera, p	.000	2	0	0	0	0	0	0	0	0	0	0
Wally Backman, 2b	.333	6	18	4	6	0	0	0	1	3	2	1
Gary Carter, c	.276	7	29	4	8	2	0	2	9	0	4	0
Ron Darling, p	.000	3	3	0	0	0	0	0	0	0	1	0
Lenny Dykstra, of	.296	7	27	4	8	0	0	2	3	2	7	0
Kevin Elster, ss	.000	1	1	0	0	0	0	0	0	0	0	0
Sid Fernandez, p	.000	3	0	0	0	0	0	0	0	0	0	0
Dwight Gooden, p	.500	2	2	1	1	0	0	0	0	0	0	0
Danny Heep, dh-2, of-1	.091	5	11	0	1	0	0	0	2	1	1	0
Keith Hernandez, 1b	.231	7	26	1	6	0	0	0	4	5	1	0
Howard Johnson, 3b-1, ss-1	.000	2	5	0	0	0	0	0	0	0	2	0
Ray Knight, 3b	.391	6	23	4	9	1	0	1	5	2	2	0
Lee Mazzilli, of-1	.400	4	5	2	2	0	0	0	0	0	0	0
Roger McDowell, p	.000	5	0	0	0	0	0	0	0	0	0	0
Kevin Mitchell, of-2, dh-1	.250	5	8	1	2	0	0	0	0	0	3	0
Bob Ojeda, p	.000	2	2	0	0	0	0	0	0	0	1	0
Jesse Orosco, p	1.000	4	1	0	1	0	0	0	1	0	0	0
Rafael Santana, ss	.250	7	20	3	5	0	0	0	2	2	5	0
Doug Sisk, p	.000	1	0	0	0	0	0	0	0	0	0	0
Darryl Strawberry, of	.208	7	24	4	5	1	0	1	1	4	6	3
Tim Teufel, 2b	.444	3	9	1	4	1	0	1	1	1	2	0
Mookie Wilson, of	.269	7	26	3	7	1	0	0	1	1	6	3
TOTAL	.271		240	32	65	6	0	7	29	21	43	7

PITCHER	W	L	ERA	G	GS	CG	SV	SHO	IP	H	ER	BB	SO
Rick Aguilera	1	0	12.00	2	0	0	0	0	3.0	8	4	1	4
Ron Darling	1	1	1.53	3	3	0	0	0	17.2	13	3	10	12
Sid Fernandez	0	0	1.35	3	0	0	0	0	6.2	6	1	1	10
Dwight Gooden	0	2	8.00	2	2	0	0	0	9.0	17	8	4	9
Roger McDowell	1	0	4.91	5	0	0	0	0	7.1	10	4	6	2
Bob Ojeda	1	0	2.08	2	2	0	0	0	13.0	13	3	5	9
Jesse Orosco	0	0	0.00	4	0	0	2	0	5.2	2	0	0	6
Doug Sisk	0	0	0.00	1	0	0	0	0	0.2	0	0	1	1
TOTAL	4	3	3.29	22	7	0	2	0	63.0	69	23	28	53

BOS (A)

PLAYER/POS	AVG	G	AB	R	H	2B	3B	HR	RB	BB	SO	SB
Tony Armas, ph	.000	1	1	0	0	0	0	0	0	0	1	0
Marty Barrett, 2b	.433	7	30	1	13	2	0	0	4	5	2	0
Don Baylor, dh-3	.182	4	11	1	2	1	0	0	1	1	3	0
Wade Boggs, 3b	.290	7	31	3	9	3	0	0	3	4	2	0
Oil Can Boyd, p	.000	1	0	0	0	0	0	0	0	0	0	0
Bill Buckner, 1b	.188	7	32	2	6	0	0	0	1	0	3	0
Roger Clemens, p	.000	2	4	1	0	0	0	0	0	0	1	0
Steve Crawford, p	.000	3	0	0	0	0	0	0	0	0	0	0
Dwight Evans, of	.308	7	26	4	8	2	0	2	9	4	3	0
Rich Gedman, c	.200	7	30	1	6	1	0	1	1	0	10	0
Mike Greenwell, ph	.000	4	3	0	0	0	0	0	0	1	2	0
Dave Henderson, of	.400	7	25	6	10	1	1	2	5	2	6	0
Bruce Hurst, p	.000	3	3	0	0	0	0	0	0	0	3	0
Al Nipper, p	.000	2	0	0	0	0	0	0	0	0	0	0
Spike Owen, ss	.300	7	20	2	6	0	0	0	2	5	6	0
Jim Rice, of	.333	7	27	6	9	1	1	0	6	9	0	0
Ed Romero, ss	.000	3	1	0	0	0	0	0	0	0	0	0
Joe Sambito, p	.000	2	0	0	0	0	0	0	0	0	0	0
Calvin Schiraldi, p	.000	3	1	0	0	0	0	0	0	0	1	0
Bob Stanley, p	.000	5	1	0	0	0	0	0	0	0	1	0
Dave Stapleton, 1b	.000	3	1	0	0	0	0	0	0	0	0	0
TOTAL	.278		248	27	69	11	2	5	26	28	53	0

PITCHER	W	L	ERA	G	GS	CG	SV	SHO	IP	H	ER	BB	SO
Oil Can Boyd	0	1	7.71	1	1	0	0	0	7.0	9	6	1	3
Roger Clemens	0	0	3.18	2	2	0	0	0	11.1	9	4	6	11
Steve Crawford	1	0	6.23	3	0	0	0	0	4.1	5	3	0	4
Bruce Hurst	2	0	1.96	3	3	1	0	0	23.0	18	5	6	17
Al Nipper	0	1	7.11	2	1	0	0	0	6.1	10	5	2	2
Joe Sambito	0	0	27.00	2	0	0	0	0	0.1	2	1	2	0
Calvin Schiraldi	0	2	13.50	3	0	0	1	0	4.0	7	6	3	2
Bob Stanley	0	0	0.00	5	0	0	1	0	6.1	5	0	1	4
TOTAL	3	4	4.31	21	7	1	2	0	62.2	65	30	21	43

GAME 1 AT NY OCT 18

BOS 000 000 100   1 5 0
NY 000 000 000   0 4 1
Pitchers: HURST, Schiraldi (9) vs DARLING, McDowell (8)
Attendance: 55,076

GAME 2 AT NY OCT 19

BOS 003 120 201   9 18 0
NY 002 010 000   3 8 1
Pitchers: Clemens, CRAWFORD (5), Stanley (7) vs GOODEN, Aguilera (6), Orosco (7), Fernandez (9), Sisk (9)
Home Runs: Henderson-BOS, Evans-BOS
Attendance: 55,063

GAME 3 AT BOS OCT 21

NY 400 000 210   7 13 0
BOS 001 000 000   1 5 0
Pitchers: OJEDA, McDowell (8) vs BOYD, Sambito (8), Stanley (8)
Home Runs: Dykstra-NY
Attendance: 33,595

GAME 4 AT BOS OCT 22

NY 000 300 210   6 12 0
BOS 000 000 020   2 7 1
Pitchers: DARLING, McDowell (7), Orosco (7) vs NIPPER, Crawford (7), Stanley (9)
Home Runs: Dykstra-NY, Carter-NY (2)
Attendance: 33,920

GAME 5 AT BOS OCT 23

NY 000 000 011   2 10 1
BOS 011 020 00X   4 12 0
Pitchers: GOODEN, Fernandez (5) vs HURST
Home Runs: Teufel-NY
Attendance: 34,010

GAME 6 AT NY OCT 25

BOS 110 000 100 2   5 13 3
NY 000 020 010 3   6 8 2
Pitchers: Clemens, SCHIRALDI (8), Stanley (10) vs Ojeda, McDowell (7), Orosco (8), AGUILERA (9)
Home Runs: Henderson-BOS
Attendance: 55,078

GAME 7 AT NY OCT 27

BOS 030 000 020   5 9 0
NY 000 003 32X   8 10 0
Pitchers: Hurst, SCHIRALDI (7), Sambito (7), Stanley (7), Nipper (8), Crawford (8) vs Darling, Fernandez (4), McDOWELL (8), Orosco (9)
Home Runs: Evans-BOS, Gedman-BOS, Knight-NY, Strawberry-NY
Attendance: 55,032

ST. LOUIS CARDINALS (EAST) 4, SAN FRANCISCO GIANTS (WEST) 3

The Giants scored four times in the fourth inning of Game 5, winning the game and taking a 3–2 series advantage. But Cardinals pitchers shut them out the rest of the series (an NLCS record 22 innings) to capture the flag.

St. Louis won the opener, 5–3, with pitcher Greg Mathews' two-run single in the sixth providing his margin of victory. The Giants came back in Game 2, supporting Dave Dravecky's two-hit shutout with home runs by Will Clark and Jeffrey Leonard. But the Cards retook the series lead in Game 3, overcoming a 4–0 deficit with two runs on Jim Lindeman's homer in the sixth and four more in the seventh (capped by Lindeman's sacrifice fly) for an eventual 6–5 win.

The Giants snapped back with a pair of wins, scoring four runs on three homers in Game 4 (including Leonard's fourth in successive games—an LCS record), and six runs in Game 5. But Dravecky and the Giants lost a heartbreaker in Game 6 when right fielder Candy Maldonado lost Tony Pena's fly in the lights for a triple. Pena scored on a sacrifice fly for the game's only run, as John Tudor and two late-inning relievers blanked the Giants. Danny Cox pitched an easier shutout in the finale as his Cardinals hammered seven San Francisco pitchers for 12 hits and six runs.

STL (E)

PLAYER/POS	AVG	G	AB	R	H	2B	3B	HR	RB	BB	SO	SB
Jack Clark, ph	.000	1	1	0	0	0	0	0	0	0	1	0
Vince Coleman, of	.269	7	26	3	7	1	0	0	4	4	6	1
Danny Cox, p	.333	2	6	0	2	0	0	0	1	0	2	0
Ken Dayley, p	.000	3	0	0	0	0	0	0	0	0	0	0
Dan Driessen, 1b-4	.250	5	12	1	3	2	0	0	1	1	1	0
Curt Ford, of	.333	4	9	2	3	0	0	0	0	1	1	0
Bob Forsch, p	.000	3	0	0	0	0	0	0	0	0	0	0
Tommy Herr, 2b	.222	7	27	0	6	0	0	0	3	0	1	1
Rick Horton, p	.000	1	0	0	0	0	0	0	0	0	0	0
Lance Johnson, pr	.000	1	0	1	0	0	0	0	0	0	0	1
Tom Lawless, 3b-2, of-1	.333	3	6	0	2	0	0	0	0	1	1	0
Jim Lindeman, 1b	.308	5	13	1	4	0	0	1	3	0	3	0
Joe Magrane, p	.000	1	1	0	0	0	0	0	0	0	0	0
Greg Mathews, p	1.000	2	2	0	2	0	0	0	2	0	0	0
Willie McGee, of	.308	7	26	2	8	1	1	0	2	0	5	0
John Morris, of	.000	2	3	0	0	0	0	0	0	0	0	0
Jose Oquendo, of-5,3b-1	.167	5	12	3	2	0	0	1	4	3	2	0
Tom Pagnozzi, ph	.000	1	1	0	0	0	0	0	0	0	0	0
Tony Pena, c	.381	7	21	5	8	0	1	0	3	4	1	0
Terry Pendleton, 3b	.211	6	19	3	4	0	1	0	1	0	6	0
Ozzie Smith, ss	.200	7	25	2	5	0	1	0	1	3	4	0
John Tudor, p	.000	2	4	0	0	0	0	0	0	0	4	0
Todd Worrell, p-3, of-1	.000	3	1	0	0	0	0	0	0	0	1	0
TOTAL	.260		215	23	56	4	4	2	22	16	42	4

PITCHER	W	L	ERA	G	GS	CG	SV	SHO	IP	H	ER	BB	SO
Danny Cox	1	1	2.12	2	2	2	0	1	17.0	17	4	3	11
Ken Dayley	0	0	0.00	3	0	0	2	0	4.0	1	0	2	4
Bob Forsch	1	1	12.00	3	0	0	0	0	3.0	4	4	1	3
Rick Horton	0	0	0.00	1	0	0	0	0	3.0	2	0	0	2
Joe Magrane	0	0	9.00	1	1	0	0	0	4.0	4	4	2	3
Greg Mathews	1	0	3.48	2	2	0	0	0	10.1	6	4	3	10
John Tudor	1	1	1.76	2	2	0	0	0	15.1	16	3	5	12
Todd Worrell	0	0	2.08	3	0	0	1	0	4.1	4	1	1	6
TOTAL	4	3	2.95	17	7	2	3	1	61.0	54	20	17	51

SF (W)

PLAYER/POS	AVG	G	AB	R	H	2B	3B	HR	RB	BB	SO	SB
Mike Aldrete, of-3	.100	5	10	0	1	0	0	0	1	0	2	0
Bob Brenly, c	.235	6	17	3	4	1	0	1	2	3	7	0
Will Clark, 1b	.360	7	25	3	9	2	0	1	3	3	6	1
Chili Davis, of	.150	6	20	2	3	1	0	0	0	1	4	0
Kelly Downs, p	.000	1	0	0	0	0	0	0	0	0	0	0
Dave Dravecky, p	.167	2	6	0	1	0	0	0	0	0	1	0
Scott Garrelts, p	.000	2	0	0	0	0	0	0	0	0	0	0
Atlee Hammaker, p	.000	2	3	0	0	0	0	0	0	0	0	0
Mike Krukow, p	.000	1	2	0	0	0	0	0	0	1	0	0
Mike LaCoss, p	.000	2	0	0	0	0	0	0	0	0	0	0
Craig Lefferts, p	.000	3	0	0	0	0	0	0	0	0	0	0
Jeffrey Leonard, of	.417	7	24	5	10	0	0	4	5	3	4	0
Candy Maldonado, of	.211	5	19	2	4	1	0	0	2	0	3	0
Bob Melvin, c-2	.429	3	7	0	3	0	0	0	0	1	1	0
Eddie Milner, of-4	.143	6	7	0	1	0	0	0	0	0	3	0
Kevin Mitchell, 3b	.267	7	30	2	8	1	0	1	2	0	3	1
Joe Price, p	.000	2	1	0	0	0	0	0	0	0	1	0
Rick Reuschel, p	.000	2	2	0	0	0	0	0	0	0	1	0
Don Robinson, p	.000	3	0	0	0	0	0	0	0	0	0	0
Chris Speier, 2b-1	.000	3	5	0	0	0	0	0	0	0	2	0
Harry Spilman, ph	.500	3	2	1	1	0	0	1	1	0	0	0
Rob Thompson, 2b-6	.100	7	20	4	2	0	1	0	1	2	5	2
Jose Uribe, ss	.269	7	26	1	7	1	0	0	0	2	4	1
TOTAL	.239		226	23	54	7	1	9	20	17	51	5

PITCHER	W	L	ERA	G	GS	CG	SV	SHO	IP	H	ER	BB	SO
Kelly Downs	0	0	0.00	1	0	0	0	0	1.1	1	0	0	0
Dave Dravecky	1	1	0.60	2	2	1	0	1	15.0	7	1	4	14
Scott Garrelts	0	0	6.75	2	0	0	0	0	2.2	2	2	4	4
Atlee Hammaker	0	1	7.87	2	2	0	0	0	8.0	12	7	0	7
Mike Krukow	1	0	2.00	1	1	1	0	0	9.0	9	2	1	3
Mike LaCoss	0	0	0.00	2	0	0	0	0	3.1	1	0	3	2
Craig Lefferts	0	0	0.00	3	0	0	0	0	2.0	3	0	1	0
Joe Price	1	0	0.00	2	0	0	0	0	5.2	3	0	1	7
Rick Reuschel	0	1	6.30	2	2	0	0	0	10.0	15	7	2	2
Don Robinson	0	1	9.00	3	0	0	0	0	3.0	3	3	0	3
TOTAL	3	4	3.30	20	7	2	0	1	60.0	56	22	16	42

GAME 1 AT STL OCT 6

```
SF   100 100 010   3 7 1
STL  001 103 00X   5 10 1
```
Pitchers: REUSCHEL, Lefferts (7), Garrelts (8) vs MATHEWS, Worrell (8), Dayley (8)
Home Runs: Leonard-SF
Attendance: 55,331

GAME 2 AT STL OCT 7

```
SF   020 100 020   5 10 0
STL  000 000 000   0 2 1
```
Pitchers: DRAVECKY vs TUDOR, Forsch (9)
Home Runs: Clark-SF, Leonard-SF
Attendance: 55,331

GAME 3 AT SF OCT 9

```
STL  000 002 400   6 11 1
SF   031 000 001   5 7 1
```
Pitchers: Magrane, FORSCH (5), Worrell (7) vs Hammaker, D.ROBINSON (7), Lefferts (7), LaCoss (8)
Home Runs: Lindeman-STL, Leonard-SF, Spilman-SF
Attendance: 57,913

GAME 4 AT SF OCT 10

```
STL  020 000 000   2 9 0
SF   000 120 01X   4 9 2
```
Pitchers: COX vs KRUKOW
Home Runs: Thompson-SF, Leonard-SF, Brenly-SF
Attendance: 57,997

GAME 5 AT SF OCT 11

```
STL  101 100 000   3 7 0
SF   101 400 00X   6 7 1
```
Pitchers: Mathews, FORSCH (4), Horton (4), Dayley (7) vs Reuschel, PRICE (5)
Home Runs: Mitchell-SF
Attendance: 59,363

GAME 6 AT STL OCT 13

```
SF   000 000 000   0 6 0
STL  010 000 00X   1 5 0
```
Pitchers: DRAVECKY, D.Robinson (7) vs TUDOR, Worrell (8), Dayley (9)
Attendance: 55,331

GAME 7 AT STL OCT 14

```
SF   000 000 000   0 8 1
STL  040 002 00X   6 12 0
```
Pitchers: HAMMAKER, Price (3), Downs (3), Garrelts (5), Lefferts (6), LaCoss (6), D.Robinson (8) vs COX
Home Runs: Oquendo-STL
Attendance: 55,331

MINNESOTA TWINS (WEST) 4, DETROIT TIGERS (EAST) 1

The Tigers, with the best overall won-lost record in the majors, were favored to defeat the Twins, whose record was the ninth best in baseball. Minnesota, however, held the home field advantage and the major leagues' best record at home. Tigers pitcher Doyle Alexander—he had been 9–0 since joining Detroit in mid-August—took a 5–4 lead into the last of the eighth in Game 1. But a single and double drove him out, and before the inning was over three more Twins had scored to sew up their first win. Detroit scored twice in the second inning the next day, but the Twins responded later in the inning with three runs, two on Tim Laudner's double off Tigers ace Jack Morris, and increased their lead in the fourth and fifth to seal Morris' first loss in Minnesota after 11 wins.

The Tigers won a game after the series moved to Detroit, when Pat Sheridan's two-run homer in the eighth inning of Game 3 restored a lead they had squandered in the middle innings. But that was it for Detroit, as the Twins surprised everyone by subduing the Tigers in their den. In Game 4 they took the lead for good on Greg Gagne's fourth-inning home run. And in Game 5, after initiating the scoring with four runs in the second, Minnesota pushed on to a 9–5 win and their first pennant in 22 years.

MIN (W)

PLAYER/POS	AVG	G	AB	R	H	2B	3B	HR	RB	BB	SO	SB
Keith Atherton, p	.000	1	0	0	0	0	0	0	0	0	0	0
Don Baylor, dh	.400	2	5	0	2	0	0	0	1	0	0	0
Juan Berenguer, p	.000	4	0	0	0	0	0	0	0	0	0	0
Bert Blyleven, p	.000	2	0	0	0	0	0	0	0	0	0	0
Tom Brunansky, of	.412	5	17	5	7	4	0	2	9	4	3	0
Randy Bush, dh	.250	4	12	4	3	0	1	0	2	3	2	3
Sal Butera, c	.667	1	3	0	2	0	0	0	0	0	0	0
Mark Davidson, pr	.000	1	0	0	0	0	0	0	0	0	0	0
Gary Gaetti, 3b	.300	5	20	5	6	1	0	2	5	1	3	0
Greg Gagne, ss	.278	5	18	5	5	3	0	2	3	3	4	0
Dan Gladden, of	.350	5	20	5	7	2	0	0	5	2	1	0
Kent Hrbek, 1b	.150	5	20	4	3	0	0	1	1	3	0	0
Gene Larkin, ph	1.000	1	1	0	1	1	0	0	1	0	0	0
Tim Laudner, c	.071	5	14	1	1	1	0	0	2	2	5	0
Steve Lombardozzi, 2b	.267	5	15	2	4	0	0	0	1	2	2	0
Al Newman, 2b	.000	1	2	0	0	0	0	0	0	0	0	0
Kirby Puckett, of	.208	5	24	3	5	1	0	1	3	0	5	1
Jeff Reardon, p	.000	4	0	0	0	0	0	0	0	0	0	0
Dan Schatzeder, p	.000	2	0	0	0	0	0	0	0	0	0	0
Les Straker, p	.000	1	0	0	0	0	0	0	0	0	0	0
Frank Viola, p	.000	2	0	0	0	0	0	0	0	0	0	0
TOTAL	.269		171	34	46	13	1	8	33	20	25	4

PITCHER	W	L	ERA	G	GS	CG	SV	SHO	IP	H	ER	BB	SO
Keith Atherton	0	0	0.00	1	0	0	0	0	0.1	1	0	0	0
Juan Berenguer	0	0	1.50	4	0	0	1	0	6.0	1	1	3	6
Bert Blyleven	2	0	4.05	2	2	0	0	0	13.1	12	6	3	9
Jeff Reardon	1	1	5.06	4	0	0	2	0	5.1	7	3	3	5
Dan Schatzeder	0	0	0.00	2	0	0	0	0	4.1	2	0	0	5
Les Straker	0	0	16.88	1	1	0	0	0	2.2	3	5	4	1
Frank Viola	1	0	5.25	2	2	0	0	0	12.0	14	7	5	9
TOTAL	4	1	4.50	16	5	0	3	0	44.0	40	22	18	35

DET (E)

PLAYER/POS	AVG	G	AB	R	H	2B	3B	HR	RB	BB	SO	SB
Doyle Alexander, p	.000	2	0	0	0	0	0	0	0	0	0	0
Dave Bergman, 1b-1, dh-1	.250	4	4	0	1	0	0	0	0	2	1	0
Tom Brookens, 3b	.000	5	13	0	0	0	0	0	0	0	3	0
Darrell Evans, 1b-5,3b-1	.294	5	17	0	5	0	0	0	0	4	2	0
Kirk Gibson, of	.286	5	21	4	6	1	0	1	4	3	8	3
Johnny Grubb, dh-1	.571	4	7	0	4	0	0	0	0	0	1	0
Mike Heath, c	.286	3	7	1	2	0	0	1	2	0	0	0
Mike Henneman, p	.000	3	0	0	0	0	0	0	0	0	0	0
Willie Hernandez, p	.000	1	0	0	0	0	0	0	0	0	0	0
Larry Herndon, of-2, dh-1	.333	3	9	1	3	1	0	0	2	1	1	0
Eric King, p	.000	2	0	0	0	0	0	0	0	0	0	0
Chet Lemon, of	.278	5	18	4	5	0	0	2	4	1	4	0
Bill Madlock, dh	.000	1	5	0	0	0	0	0	0	0	3	0
Jack Morris, p-1, dh-1	.000	2	0	1	0	0	0	0	0	0	0	0
Jim Morrison, 3b-1, dh-1	.400	2	5	1	2	0	0	0	0	0	1	0
Matt Nokes, c-3, dh-2	.143	5	14	2	2	0	0	1	2	1	4	0
Dan Petry, p	.000	1	0	0	0	0	0	0	0	0	0	0
Jeff Robinson, p	.000	1	0	0	0	0	0	0	0	0	0	0
Pat Sheridan, of-4	.300	5	10	2	3	1	0	1	2	0	2	1
Frank Tanana, p	.000	1	0	0	0	0	0	0	0	0	0	0
Walt Terrell, p	.000	1	0	0	0	0	0	0	0	0	0	0
Mark Thurmond, p	.000	1	0	0	0	0	0	0	0	0	0	0
Alan Trammell, ss	.200	5	20	3	4	1	0	0	2	1	2	0
Lou Whitaker, 2b	.176	5	17	4	3	0	0	1	1	1	7	1
TOTAL	.240		167	23	40	4	0	7	21	18	35	5

PITCHER	W	L	ERA	G	GS	CG	SV	SHO	IP	H	ER	BB	SO
Doyle Alexander	0	2	10.00	2	2	0	0	0	9.0	14	10	1	5
Mike Henneman	1	0	10.80	3	0	0	0	0	5.0	6	6	6	3
Willie Hernandez	0	0	0.00	1	0	0	0	0	0.1	2	0	0	0
Eric King	0	0	1.69	2	0	0	0	0	5.1	3	1	2	4
Jack Morris	0	1	6.75	1	1	1	0	0	8.0	6	6	3	7
Dan Petry	0	0	0.00	1	0	0	0	0	3.1	1	0	0	1
Jeff Robinson	0	0	0.00	1	0	0	0	0	0.1	1	0	0	0
Frank Tanana	0	1	5.06	1	1	0	0	0	5.1	6	3	4	1
Walt Terrell	0	0	9.00	1	1	0	0	0	6.0	7	6	4	4
Mark Thurmond	0	0	0.00	1	0	0	0	0	0.1	0	0	0	0
TOTAL	1	4	6.70	14	5	1	0	0	43.0	46	32	20	25

GAME 1 AT MIN OCT 7

DET 0 0 1 0 0 1 1 2 0   5 10 0
MIN 0 1 0 0 3 0 0 4 X   8 10 0
Pitchers: ALEXANDER, Henneman (8), Hernandez (8), King (8) vs Viola, REARDON (8)
Home Runs: Heath-DET, Gibson-DET, Gaetti-MIN (2)
Attendance: 53,269

GAME 2 AT MIN OCT 8

DET 0 2 0 0 0 0 0 1 0   3 7 1
MIN 0 3 0 2 1 0 0 0 X   6 6 0
Pitchers: MORRIS vs BLYLEVEN, Berenguer (8)
Home Runs: Lemon-DET, Whitaker-DET, Hrbek-MIN
Attendance: 55,245

GAME 3 AT DET OCT 10

MIN 0 0 0 2 0 2 2 0 0   6 8 1
DET 0 0 5 0 0 0 0 2 X   7 7 0
Pitchers: Straker, Schatzeder (3), Berenguer (7), REARDON (8) vs Terrell, HENNEMAN (7)
Home Runs: Gagne-MIN, Brunansky-MIN, Sheridan-DET
Attendance: 49,730

GAME 4 AT DET OCT 11

MIN 0 0 1 1 1 1 0 1 0   5 7 1
DET 1 0 0 0 1 1 0 0 0   3 7 3
Pitchers: VIOLA, Atherton (6), Berenguer (6), Reardon (9) vs TANANA, Petry (6), Thurmond (9)
Home Runs: Puckett-MIN, Gagne-MIN
Attendance: 51,939

GAME 5 AT DET OCT 12

MIN 0 4 0 0 0 0 1 1 3   9 15 1
DET 0 0 0 3 0 0 1 0 0   5 9 1
Pitchers: BLYLEVEN, Schatzeder (7), Berenguer (8), Reardon (8) vs ALEXANDER, King (2), Henneman (7), Robinson (9)
Home Runs: Brunansky-MIN, Nokes-DET, Lemon-DET
Attendance: 47,448

MINNESOTA TWINS (AL) 4, ST. LOUIS CARDINALS (NL) 3

Although the Twins compiled a dismal record on the road during the season (29–52), their play at home (56–25) topped the majors. In postseason play they won all six games played in their Metrodome, including the four that won them the world championship. They overwhelmed St. Louis in the Series opener, the first World Series game ever played indoors. The Cardinals scored first, in the second inning, but Twins ace Frank Viola (with relief from Keith Atherton in the ninth) stopped them after that as his teammates unloaded for seven runs in the fourth inning (capped by Dan Gladden's grand slam) on their way to a 10–1 win. The Cardinals scored four runs in Game 2, but again the Twins enjoyed a big fourth inning—bunching six of their 10 hits together for six runs—and scored two other runs on homers by Gary Gaetti and Tim Laudner.

When the Series moved to St. Louis, the Cardinals grabbed the home advantage to post their three wins. In Game 3, Cardinal pitchers John Tudor and Todd Worrell combined for a five-hitter as the Cards came from behind with a three-run seventh to win, 3–1. The next day St. Louis broke a 1–1 tie with their own fourth-inning explosion, for six runs. The big blow was a three-run homer by utility infielder Tom Lawless—only the second home run of his big league career—as the Cards won, 7–2. After five scoreless innings in Game 5, St. Louis moved out to a 4–0 lead in the sixth and seventh innings. Gaetti's eighth-inning triple put two Minnesota runs across, but the Cards held on for a 4–2 win.

Back in Minneapolis, St. Louis built up a 5–2 lead in Game 6 before the Twins retaliated with four runs in the fifth inning (with Don Baylor's three-run homer providing the tying runs) and four more an inning later on Kent Hrbek's grand slam. A final Twins run in the eighth ended the scoring at 11–5.

The Cardinals scored first in Game 7, with a pair of runs in the second inning, but the Twins edged their way to a tie with single runs in the second and fifth, and an inning later took the lead on three walks and an infield single. As Twins starter Frank Viola held St. Louis scoreless on two hits after the

second inning, Minnesota made the score 4–2 with a final run in the eighth, and ace reliever Jeff Reardon retired the Cards in order in the ninth to bring Minnesota its first world championship.

GAME 1 AT MIN OCT 17

```
STL 010 000 000    1 5 1
MIN 000 720 10X   10 11 0
```
Pitchers: MAGRANE, Forsch (4), Horton (7) vs VIOLA, Atherton (9)
Home Runs: Gladden-MIN, Lombardozzi-MIN
Attendance: 55,171

GAME 2 AT MIN OCT 18

```
STL 000 010 120    4 9 0
MIN 010 601 00X    8 10 0
```
Pitchers: COX, Tunnell (4), Dayley (7), Worrell (8) vs BLYLEVEN, Berenguer (8), Reardon (9)
Home Runs: Gaetti-MIN, Laudner-MIN
Attendance: 55,257

GAME 3 AT STL OCT 20

```
MIN 000 001 000    1 5 1
STL 000 000 30X    3 9 1
```
Pitchers: Straker, BERENGUER (7), Schatzeder (7) vs TUDOR, Worrell (8)
Attendance: 55,347

GAME 4 AT STL OCT 21

```
MIN 001 010 000    2 7 1
STL 001 600 00X    7 10 1
```
Pitchers: VIOLA, Schatzeder (4), Niekro (5), Frazier (7) vs Mathews, FORSCH (4), Dayley (7)
Home Runs: Gagne-MIN, Lawless-STL
Attendance: 55,347

GAME 5 AT STL OCT 22

```
MIN 000 000 020    2 6 1
STL 000 003 10X    4 10 0
```
Pitchers: BLYLEVEN, Atherton (7), Reardon (7) vs COX, Dayley (8), Worrell (8)
Attendance: 55,347

GAME 6 AT MIN OCT 24

```
STL 110 210 000    5 11 2
MIN 200 044 01X   11 15 0
```
Pitchers: TUDOR, Horton (5), Forsch (6), Dayley (6), Tunnell (7) vs Straker, SCHATZEDER (4), Berenguer (6), Reardon (9)
Home Runs: Herr-STL, Baylor-MIN, Hrbek-MIN
Attendance: 55,293

GAME 7 AT MIN OCT 25

```
STL 020 000 000    2 6 1
MIN 010 011 01X    4 10 0
```
Pitchers: Magrane, COX (5), Worrell (6) vs VIOLA, Reardon (9)
Attendance: 55,376

MIN (A)

PLAYER/POS	AVG	G	AB	R	H	2B	3B	HR	RB	BB	SO	SB
Keith Atherton, p	.000	2	0	0	0	0	0	0	0	0	0	0
Don Baylor, dh-3	.385	5	13	3	5	0	0	1	3	1	1	0
Juan Berenguer, p	.000	3	0	0	0	0	0	0	0	0	0	0
Bert Blyleven, p	.000	2	1	0	0	0	0	0	0	0	1	0
Tom Brunansky, of	.200	7	25	5	5	0	0	0	2	4	4	1
Randy Bush, dh-2	.167	4	6	1	1	1	0	0	2	0	1	0
Sal Butera, c	.000	1	0	0	0	0	0	0	0	0	0	0
Mark Davidson, of-1	.000	2	1	0	0	0	0	0	0	0	0	0
George Frazier, p	.000	1	0	0	0	0	0	0	0	0	0	0
Gary Gaetti, 3b	.259	7	27	4	7	2	1	1	4	2	5	2
Greg Gagne, ss	.200	7	30	5	6	1	0	1	3	1	6	0
Dan Gladden, of	.290	7	31	3	9	2	1	1	7	3	4	2
Kent Hrbek, 1b	.208	7	24	4	5	0	0	1	6	5	3	0
Gene Larkin, 1b-1, dh-1	.000	5	3	1	0	0	0	0	0	1	0	0
Tim Laudner, c	.318	7	22	4	7	1	0	1	4	5	4	0
Steve Lombardozzi, 2b	.412	6	17	3	7	1	0	1	4	2	2	0
Al Newman, 2b-3	.200	4	5	0	1	0	0	0	0	1	1	0
Joe Niekro, p	.000	1	0	0	0	0	0	0	0	0	0	0
Kirby Puckett, of	.357	7	28	5	10	1	1	0	3	2	1	0
Jeff Reardon, p	.000	4	0	0	0	0	0	0	0	0	0	0
Dan Schatzeder, p	.000	3	0	0	0	0	0	0	0	0	0	0
Roy Smalley, ph	.500	4	2	0	1	1	0	0	0	0	2	0
Les Straker, p	.000	2	2	0	0	0	0	0	0	0	2	0
Frank Viola, p	.000	3	1	0	0	0	0	0	0	0	1	0
TOTAL	.269		238	38	64	10	3	7	38	29	36	6

PITCHER	W	L	ERA	G	GS	CG	SV	SHO	IP	H	ER	BB	SO
Keith Atherton	0	0	6.75	2	0	0	0	0	1.1	0	1	1	0
Juan Berenguer	0	1	10.38	3	0	0	0	0	4.1	10	5	0	1
Bert Blyleven	1	1	2.77	2	2	0	0	0	13.0	13	4	2	12
George Frazier	0	0	0.00	1	0	0	0	0	2.0	1	0	0	2
Joe Niekro	0	0	0.00	1	0	0	0	0	2.0	1	0	1	1
Jeff Reardon	0	0	0.00	4	0	0	1	0	4.2	5	0	0	3
Dan Schatzeder	1	0	6.23	3	0	0	0	0	4.1	4	3	3	3
Les Straker	0	0	4.00	2	2	0	0	0	9.0	9	4	3	6
Frank Viola	2	1	3.72	3	3	0	0	0	19.1	17	8	3	16
TOTAL	4	3	3.75	21	7	0	1	0	60.0	60	25	13	44

STL (N)

PLAYER/POS	AVG	G	AB	R	H	2B	3B	HR	RB	BB	SO	SB
Vince Coleman, of	.143	7	28	5	4	2	0	0	2	2	10	6
Danny Cox, p	.000	3	2	0	0	0	0	0	0	0	1	0
Ken Dayley, p	.000	4	1	0	0	0	0	0	0	0	1	0
Dan Driessen, 1b	.231	4	13	3	3	2	0	0	1	1	0	0
Curt Ford, of-4	.308	5	13	1	4	0	0	0	2	1	1	0
Bob Forsch, p	.000	3	2	0	0	0	0	0	0	0	0	0
Tommy Herr, 2b	.250	7	28	2	7	0	0	1	1	2	2	0
Rick Horton, p	.000	2	0	0	0	0	0	0	0	0	0	0
Lance Johnson, pr	.000	1	0	0	0	0	0	0	0	0	0	1
Steve Lake, c	.333	3	3	0	1	0	0	0	1	0	0	0
Tom Lawless, 3b	.100	3	10	1	1	0	0	1	3	0	4	0
Jim Lindeman, 1b-6, of-1	.333	6	15	3	5	1	0	0	2	0	3	0
Joe Magrane, p	.000	2	0	0	0	0	0	0	0	0	0	0
Greg Mathews, p	.000	1	1	0	0	0	0	0	0	0	0	0
Willie McGee, of	.370	7	27	2	10	2	0	0	4	0	9	0
John Morris, of	.000	1	2	0	0	0	0	0	0	0	0	0
Jose Oquendo, 3b-4, of-3	.250	7	24	2	6	0	0	0	2	1	4	0
Tom Pagnozzi, dh-1	.250	2	4	0	1	0	0	0	0	0	0	0
Tony Pena, c-6, dh-1	.409	7	22	2	9	1	0	0	4	3	2	1
Terry Pendleton, dh-2	.429	3	7	2	3	0	0	0	1	1	1	2
Ozzie Smith, ss	.214	7	28	3	6	0	0	0	2	2	3	2
John Tudor, p	.000	2	2	0	0	0	0	0	0	0	2	0
Lee Tunnell, p	.000	2	0	0	0	0	0	0	0	0	0	0
Todd Worrell, p	.000	4	0	0	0	0	0	0	0	0	0	0
TOTAL	.259		232	26	60	8	0	2	25	13	44	12

PITCHER	W	L	ERA	G	GS	CG	SV	SHO	IP	H	ER	BB	SO
Danny Cox	1	2	7.71	3	2	0	0	0	11.2	13	10	8	9
Ken Dayley	0	0	1.93	4	0	0	1	0	4.2	2	1	0	3
Bob Forsch	1	0	9.95	3	0	0	0	0	6.1	8	7	5	3
Rick Horton	0	0	6.00	2	0	0	0	0	3.0	3	2	0	1
Joe Magrane	0	1	8.59	2	2	0	0	0	7.1	9	7	5	5
Greg Mathews	0	0	2.45	1	1	0	0	0	3.2	2	1	2	3
John Tudor	1	1	5.73	2	2	0	0	0	11.0	15	7	3	8
Lee Tunnell	0	0	2.08	2	0	0	0	0	4.1	4	1	2	1
Todd Worrell	0	0	1.29	4	0	0	2	0	7.0	6	1	4	3
TOTAL	3	4	5.64	23	7	0	3	0	59.0	64	37	29	36

LOS ANGELES DODGERS (WEST) 4, NEW YORK METS (EAST) 3

The Mets had defeated the Dodgers in 10 of 11 regular season games, but in the NLCS the pitching of Dodger ace Orel Hershiser and rookie Tim Belcher, and the timely hitting of Mike Scioscia and Kirk Gibson, propelled L.A. to the pennant. The Dodgers scored a first-inning run in the opener and carried a 2–0 lead into the ninth. But three Mets runs in the top of the ninth (the final two scoring with two outs on a fly to short center that bounced off the glove of a diving John Shelby) gave New York the victory.

Dodgers pitcher Tim Belcher singled with two away in the second inning of Game 2 to start a four-run rally—the margin of victory in Belcher's 6–3 win. In Game 3 (played in a steady downpour after a rainout the night before), the Mets overcame a 4–3 deficit, rapping four Dodgers pitchers for five runs in the last of the eighth to take the series lead.

Kirk Gibson's 12th-inning solo homer the next night put the Dodgers ahead, 5–4, after Mike Scioscia's ninth-inning home run had pulled them into a tie. In the last of the 12th, Orel Hershiser (who had pitched seven innings to no decision in the previous game) took the mound with two outs and the bases full, and saved the game as center fielder Shelby, on the run, snared Kevin McReynolds' looping fly.

Gibson homered again in Game 5—for three runs that provided the winning margin in a 7–4 Dodgers victory. One game from the pennant, as the series moved back to Los Angeles, the Dodgers for the first time failed to score first and saw the series evened a third time as David Cone held them to five hits and one run while the Mets scored five. But in the finale, the Dodgers unloaded on Ron Darling for six runs in the first two innings and Hershiser blanked the Mets on five hits

LA (W)

PLAYER/POS	AVG	G	AB	R	H	2B	3B	HR	RB	BB	SO	SB
Tim Belcher, p	.125	2	8	1	1	0	0	0	0	0	3	0
Mike Davis, ph	.000	4	2	0	0	0	0	0	0	1	0	0
Rick Dempsey, c-3	.400	4	5	1	2	2	0	0	2	1	0	0
Kirk Gibson, of	.154	7	26	2	4	0	0	2	6	3	6	2
Jose Gonzalez, of-4	.000	5	0	2	0	0	0	0	0	0	0	0
Alfredo Griffin, ss	.160	7	25	1	4	1	0	0	3	0	5	0
Jeff Hamilton, 3b	.217	7	23	2	5	0	0	0	1	3	4	0
Mickey Hatcher, 1b-6, of-1	.238	6	21	4	5	2	0	0	3	3	0	0
Danny Heep, ph	.000	3	1	0	0	0	0	0	0	1	1	0
Orel Hershiser, p	.000	4	9	1	0	0	0	0	0	1	2	0
Brian Holton, p	1.000	3	1	1	1	0	0	0	1	1	0	0
Rick Horton, p	.000	4	0	0	0	0	0	0	0	0	0	0
Jay Howell, p	.000	2	0	0	0	0	0	0	0	0	0	0
Tim Leary, p	.000	2	1	0	0	0	0	0	0	0	0	0
Mike Marshall, of	.233	7	30	3	7	1	1	0	5	2	9	0
Jesse Orosco, p	.000	4	0	0	0	0	0	0	0	0	0	0
Alejandro Pena, p	.000	3	0	0	0	0	0	0	0	0	0	0
Steve Sax, 2b	.267	7	30	7	8	0	0	0	3	3	3	5
Mike Scioscia, c	.364	7	22	3	8	1	0	1	2	1	2	0
Mike Sharperson, ss-1,3b-1	.000	2	1	0	0	0	0	0	0	1	1	0
John Shelby, of	.167	7	24	3	4	0	0	0	3	5	12	2
Franklin Stubbs, 1b-3	.250	4	8	0	2	0	0	0	0	0	4	0
John Tudor, p	.000	1	2	0	0	0	0	0	0	0	2	0
Tracy Woodson, 1b	.250	3	4	0	1	0	0	0	0	0	1	0
TOTAL	.214		243	31	52	7	1	3	30	25	54	9

PITCHER	W	L	ERA	G	GS	CG	SV	SHO	IP	H	ER	BB	SO
Tim Belcher	2	0	4.11	2	2	0	0	0	15.1	12	7	4	16
Orel Hershiser	1	0	1.09	4	3	1	1	1	24.2	18	3	7	15
Brian Holton	0	0	2.25	3	0	0	1	0	4.0	2	1	1	2
Rick Horton	0	0	0.00	4	0	0	0	0	4.1	4	0	2	3
Jay Howell	0	1	27.00	2	0	0	0	0	0.2	1	2	2	1
Tim Leary	0	1	6.23	2	1	0	0	0	4.1	8	3	3	3
Jesse Orosco	0	0	7.71	4	0	0	0	0	2.1	4	2	3	0
Alejandro Pena	1	1	4.15	3	0	0	1	0	4.1	1	2	5	1
John Tudor	0	0	7.20	1	1	0	0	0	5.0	8	4	1	1
TOTAL	4	3	3.32	25	7	1	3	1	65.0	58	24	28	42

NY (E)

PLAYER/POS	AVG	G	AB	R	H	2B	3B	HR	RB	BB	SO	SB
Rick Aguilera, p	.000	3	1	0	0	0	0	0	0	0	1	0
Wally Backman, 2b	.273	7	22	2	6	1	0	0	2	2	5	1
Gary Carter, c	.222	7	27	0	6	1	1	0	4	1	3	0
David Cone, p	.000	3	4	0	0	0	0	0	0	0	0	0
Ron Darling, p-2	.000	2	3	0	0	0	0	0	0	0	2	0
Lennie Dykstra, of	.429	7	14	6	6	3	0	1	3	4	0	0
Kevin Elster, ss	.250	5	8	1	2	1	0	0	1	3	0	0
Sid Fernandez, p	.000	1	1	0	0	0	0	0	0	0	0	0
Dwight Gooden, p	.200	3	5	0	1	0	0	0	0	0	2	0
Keith Hernandez, 1b	.269	7	26	2	7	0	0	1	5	6	7	1
Gregg Jefferies, 3b	.333	7	27	2	9	2	0	0	1	4	0	0
Howard Johnson, ss-5,3b-1	.056	6	18	3	1	0	0	0	0	1	6	1
Terry Leach, p	.000	3	0	0	0	0	0	0	0	0	0	0
Dave Magadan, ph	.000	3	3	0	0	0	0	0	0	0	2	0
Lee Mazzilli, ph	.500	3	2	0	1	0	0	0	0	0	0	1
Roger McDowell, p	.000	4	0	0	0	0	0	0	0	0	0	0
Kevin McReynolds, of	.250	7	28	4	7	2	0	2	4	3	5	2
Randy Myers, p	.000	3	0	0	0	0	0	0	0	0	0	0
Mackey Sasser, c-1	.200	4	5	0	1	0	0	0	0	0	1	0
Darryl Strawberry, of	.300	7	30	5	9	2	0	1	6	2	5	0
Tim Teufel, 2b	.000	1	3	0	0	0	0	0	0	0	1	0
Mookie Wilson, of-3	.154	4	13	2	2	0	0	0	0	1	2	0
TOTAL	.242		240	27	58	12	1	5	27	28	42	6

PITCHER	W	L	ERA	G	GS	CG	SV	SHO	IP	H	ER	BB	SO
Rick Aguilera	0	0	1.29	3	0	0	0	0	7.0	3	1	2	4
David Cone	1	1	4.50	3	2	1	0	0	12.0	10	6	5	9
Ron Darling	0	1	7.71	2	2	0	0	0	7.0	11	6	4	7
Sid Fernandez	0	1	13.50	1	1	0	0	0	4.0	7	6	1	5
Dwight Gooden	0	0	2.95	3	2	0	0	0	18.1	10	6	8	20
Terry Leach	0	0	0.00	3	0	0	0	0	5.0	4	0	1	4
Roger McDowell	0	1	4.50	4	0	0	0	0	6.0	6	3	2	5
Randy Myers	2	0	0.00	3	0	0	0	0	4.2	1	0	2	0
TOTAL	3	4	3.94	22	7	1	0	0	64.0	52	28	25	54

GAME 1 AT LA OCT 4

```
NY   000 000 003   3 8 1
LA   100 000 100   2 4 0
```
Pitchers: Gooden, MYERS (8) vs Hershiser, HOWELL (9)
Attendance: 55,582

GAME 2 AT LA OCT 5

```
NY   000 200 001   3 6 0
LA   140 010 00X   6 7 0
```
Pitchers: Cone, Myers (3), Leach (6), McDowell (8) vs BELCHER, Orosco (9), Pena (9)
Home Runs: Hernandez-NY
Attendance: 55,780

GAME 3 AT NY OCT 8

```
LA   021 000 010   4 7 2
NY   001 002 05X   8 9 2
```
Pitchers: Hershiser, Howell (8), PENA (8), Orosco (8), Horton (8) vs Darling, McDowell (7), MYERS (8), Cone (9)
Attendance: 44,672

GAME 4 AT NY OCT 9

```
LA   2 0 0 0 0 0 0 0 2 0 0 1 5 7 1
NY   0 0 0 3 0 1 0 0 0 0 0 0 4 10 2
```
Pitchers: Tudor, Holton (6), Horton (7), PENA (9), Leary (12), Orosco (12), Hershiser (12) vs Gooden, Myers (9), McDOWELL (11)
Home Runs: Strawberry-NY, McReynolds-NY, Scioscia-LA, Gibson-LA
Attendance: 54,014

GAME 5 AT NY OCT 10

```
LA   000 330 001   7 12 0
NY   000 030 010   4 9 1
```
Pitchers: BELCHER, Horton (8), Holton (8) vs FERNANDEZ, Leach (5), Aguilera (6), McDowell (8)
Home Runs: Gibson-LA, Dykstra-NY
Attendance: 52,069

GAME 6 AT LA OCT 11

```
NY   101 021 000   5 11 0
LA   000 000 000   1 5 2
```
Pitchers: CONE vs LEARY, Holton (5), Horton (6), Orosco (8)
Home Runs: McReynolds-NY
Attendance: 55,885

GAME 7 AT LA OCT 12

```
NY   000 000 000   0 5 2
LA   150 000 00X   6 10 0
```
Pitchers: DARLING, Gooden (2), Leach (5), Aguilera (7) vs HERSHISER
Attendance: 55,693

OAKLAND A'S (WEST) 4, BOSTON RED SOX (EAST) 0

Jose Canseco's three home runs and Dennis Eckersley's sparkling relief pitching highlighted Oakland's sweep to the pennant. In his six shutout innings, Eckersley gave up just one hit and a pair of walks while fanning five, to record an ALCS record four saves.

Canseco's fourth-inning solo shot off Bruce Hurst put the A's out in front in Game 1. Boston tied it up in the seventh, but two former Boston players—Carney Lansford, who doubled, and Dave Henderson, who singled him home—put Oakland back in front in the eighth, and Eckersley (also an ex-Bostonian) held the Sox through the final two innings.

Oakland's Storm Davis and Boston's Roger Clemens dueled scorelessly through five innings of Game 2. The Sox took advantage of an Oakland error to score twice in the sixth, but four Oakland hits in the seventh (including a two-run homer by Canseco), a balk, and a wild pitch put the A's up, 3–2. Rich Gedman's home run for Boston in the last of the seventh tied the score, but in the ninth Oakland's rookie shortstop Walt Weiss singled home what proved the game winner off Sox ace reliever Lee Smith.

Boston unloaded for five runs in the first two innings of Game 3. But Weiss' double and home runs by Mark McGwire and Carney Lansford in the last of the second brought the A's within one run of a tie, and Ron Hassey's two-run homer an inning later gave the A's a lead that they held to the end. Dave Henderson's two-run blast in the eighth capped Oakland's 10–6 victory.

Canseco's first-inning homer in Game 4 put the A's ahead to stay, as starter Dave Stewart and relievers Rick Honeycutt and Eckersley combined for a four-hit, 4–1 pennant clincher.

OAK (W)

PLAYER/POS	AVG	G	AB	R	H	2B	3B	HR	RB	BB	SO	SB
Don Baylor, dh	.000	2	6	0	0	0	0	0	0	1	2	0
Greg Cadaret, p	.000	1	0	0	0	0	0	0	0	0	0	0
Jose Canseco, of	.313	4	16	4	5	1	0	3	4	1	2	1
Storm Davis, p	.000	1	0	0	0	0	0	0	0	0	0	0
Dennis Eckersley, p	.000	4	0	0	0	0	0	0	0	0	0	0
Mike Gallego, 2b	.083	4	12	1	1	0	0	0	0	0	3	0
Ron Hassey, c	.500	4	8	2	4	1	0	1	3	1	1	0
Dave Henderson, of	.375	4	16	2	6	1	0	1	4	1	7	0
Rick Honeycutt, p	.000	3	0	0	0	0	0	0	0	0	0	0
Stan Javier, of	.500	2	4	0	2	0	0	0	1	1	0	0
Carney Lansford, 3b	.294	4	17	4	5	1	0	1	2	0	2	0
Mark McGwire, 1b	.333	4	15	4	5	0	0	1	3	1	5	0
Gene Nelson, p	.000	2	0	0	0	0	0	0	0	0	0	0
Dave Parker, dh-2, of-1	.250	3	12	1	3	1	0	0	0	0	4	0
Tony Phillips, of-2,2b-1	.286	2	7	0	2	1	0	0	0	0	1	3	0
Eric Plunk, p	.000	1	0	0	0	0	0	0	0	0	0	0
Luis Polonia, of-1	.400	3	5	0	2	0	0	0	0	1	2	0
Terry Steinbach, c	.250	2	4	0	1	0	0	0	0	0	2	0
Dave Stewart, p	.000	2	0	0	0	0	0	0	0	0	0	0
Walt Weiss, ss	.333	4	15	2	5	2	0	0	2	0	4	0
Bob Welch, p	.000	1	0	0	0	0	0	0	0	0	0	0
Curt Young, p	.000	1	0	0	0	0	0	0	0	0	0	0
TOTAL	.299		137	20	41	8	0	7	20	10	35	1

PITCHER	W	L	ERA	G	GS	CG	SV	SHO	IP	H	ER	BB	SO
Greg Cadaret	0	0	27.00	1	0	0	0	0	0.1	1	1	0	0
Storm Davis	0	0	0.00	1	1	0	0	0	6.1	2	0	5	4
Dennis Eckersley	0	0	0.00	4	0	0	4	0	6.0	1	0	2	5
Rick Honeycutt	1	0	0.00	3	0	0	0	0	2.0	0	0	2	0
Gene Nelson	2	0	0.00	2	0	0	0	0	4.2	5	0	1	0
Eric Plunk	0	0	0.00	1	0	0	0	0	0.1	1	0	0	1
Dave Stewart	1	0	1.35	2	2	0	0	0	13.1	9	2	6	11
Bob Welch	0	0	27.00	1	1	0	0	0	1.2	6	5	2	0
Curt Young	0	0	0.00	1	0	0	0	0	1.1	1	0	0	2
TOTAL	4	0	2.00	16	4	0	4	0	36.0	26	8	18	23

BOS (E)

PLAYER/POS	AVG	G	AB	R	H	2B	3B	HR	RB	BB	SO	SB
Marty Barrett, 2b	.067	4	15	2	1	0	0	0	0	1	0	0
Todd Benzinger, 1b-3	.091	4	11	0	1	0	0	0	0	1	3	0
Mike Boddicker, p	.000	1	0	0	0	0	0	0	0	0	0	0
Wade Boggs, 3b	.385	4	13	2	5	0	0	0	3	3	4	0
Ellis Burks, of	.235	4	17	2	4	1	0	0	1	0	3	0
Roger Clemens, p	.000	1	0	0	0	0	0	0	0	0	0	0
Dwight Evans, of	.167	4	12	1	2	1	0	0	1	3	5	0
Wes Gardner, p	.000	1	0	0	0	0	0	0	0	0	0	0
Rich Gedman, c	.357	4	14	1	5	0	0	1	1	2	1	0
Mike Greenwell, of	.214	4	14	2	3	1	0	1	3	3	0	0
Bruce Hurst, p	.000	2	0	0	0	0	0	0	0	0	0	0
Spike Owen, dh	.000	1	0	0	0	0	0	0	0	1	0	0
Larry Parrish, 1b-2	.000	4	6	0	0	0	0	0	0	0	2	0
Jody Reed, ss	.273	4	11	0	3	1	0	0	0	2	1	0
Jim Rice, dh	.154	4	13	0	2	0	0	0	1	2	4	0
Ed Romero, pr	.000	1	0	0	0	0	0	0	0	0	0	0
Kevin Romine, pr	.000	2	0	1	0	0	0	0	0	0	0	0
Lee Smith, p	.000	2	0	0	0	0	0	0	0	0	0	0
Mike Smithson, p	.000	1	0	0	0	0	0	0	0	0	0	0
Bob Stanley, p	.000	2	0	0	0	0	0	0	0	0	0	0
TOTAL	.206		126	11	26	4	0	2	10	18	23	0

PITCHER	W	L	ERA	G	GS	CG	SV	SHO	IP	H	ER	BB	SO
Mike Boddicker	0	1	20.25	1	1	0	0	0	2.2	8	6	1	2
Roger Clemens	0	0	3.86	1	1	0	0	0	7.0	6	3	0	8
Wes Gardner	0	0	5.79	1	0	0	0	0	4.2	6	3	2	8
Bruce Hurst	0	2	2.77	2	2	1	0	0	13.0	10	4	5	12
Lee Smith	0	1	8.10	2	0	0	0	0	3.1	6	3	1	4
Mike Smithson	0	0	0.00	1	0	0	0	0	2.1	3	0	0	1
Bob Stanley	0	0	9.00	2	0	0	0	0	1.0	2	1	1	0
TOTAL	0	4	5.29	10	4	1	0	0	34.0	41	20	10	35

GAME 1 AT BOS OCT 5

OAK 000 100 010 — 2 6 0
BOS 000 000 100 — 1 6 0
Pitchers: Stewart, HONEYCUTT (7), Eckersley (8) vs HURST
Home Runs: Canseco-OAK
Attendance: 34,104

GAME 2 AT BOS OCT 6

OAK 000 000 301 — 4 10 1
BOS 000 002 100 — 3 4 1
Pitchers: Davis, Cadaret (7), NELSON (7), Eckersley (9) vs Clemens, Stanley (8), SMITH (8)
Home Runs: Canseco-OAK, Gedman-BOS
Attendance: 34,605

GAME 3 AT OAK OCT 8

BOS 320 000 100 — 6 12 0
OAK 042 010 12X — 10 15 1
Pitchers: BODDICKER, Gardner (3), Stanley (8) vs Welch, NELSON (2), Young (6), Plunk (7), Honeycutt (7), Eckersley (8)
Home Runs: Greenwell-BOS, McGwire-OAK, Lansford-OAK, Hassey-OAK, Henderson-OAK
Attendance: 49,261

GAME 4 AT OAK OCT 9

BOS 000 001 000 — 1 4 0
OAK 101 000 02X — 4 10 1
Pitchers: HURST, Smithson (5), Smith (7) vs STEWART, Honeycutt (8), Eckersley (9)
Home Runs: Canseco-OAK
Attendance: 49,406

LOS ANGELES DODGERS (NL) 4, OAKLAND A'S (AL) 1

Mickey Hatcher's home run in the first inning of Game 1 set the tone for the Dodgers' surprising triumph over Oakland's mighty A's. Hatcher, who homered only once during the season, initiated the Series scoring with a two-run blast to left center. Half an inning later the A's Jose Canseco—baseball's leading slugger, with 42 homers—erased the Dodger lead with his first career grand slam. But while Hatcher went on to hit safely six more times in the Series—including another home run—Canseco's first hit was also his last, as he went 0-for-19 the rest of the way. The Dodgers scored once in the sixth inning to draw within one run of a tie, but remained behind until the last of the ninth when, with two outs and one on, Kirk Gibson pinch hit for pitcher Alejandro Pena. Gibson, the Dodgers' top source of power during the season, was so hobbled by leg injuries that he had, till that moment, sat out the game in the training room. But with two strikes on him he belted a home run off baseball's premier reliever, Dennis Eckersley, to win the game. It was Gibson's only Series appearance.

Dodgers ace Orel Hershiser blanked the A's on three hits in Game 2 and led the offense with three hits of his own. His single in the third inning began a five-run rally (capped by Mike Marshall's three-run homer), and his fourth-inning double drove in the Dodgers' sixth and final run.

When the Series moved to Oakland, the A's recovered for a dramatic win in Game 3, as Mark McGwire (who had homered 32 times during the season) broke a 1–1 tie with his only Series hit, a solo homer in the last of the ninth. In Game 4, Dodgers reliever Jay Howell, who had yielded the losing home run the day before, got McGwire to pop up with the bases full to end the seventh inning, and blanked the A's the rest of the way to preserve a narrow 4–3 victory.

Hershiser returned to pitch Game 5. He allowed two runs in his four-hitter, but Mickey Hatcher had given the Dodgers the lead with a two-run homer in the first inning, and Mike Davis (who had homered just twice during the season) drove a 3–0 pitch into the stands for two more runs in the fourth. Veteran catcher Rick

Dempsey (substituting for injured first-stringer Mike Scioscia) doubled home a fifth Los Angeles run in the sixth, and the Dodgers were on their way to a seventh world title.

GAME 1 AT LA OCT 15
```
OAK 040 000 000    4 7 0
LA  200 001 002    5 7 0
```
Pitchers: Stewart, ECKERSLEY (9) vs Belcher, Leary (3), Holton (6), PENA (8)
Home Runs: Hatcher-LA, Canseco-OAK, Gibson-LA
Attendance: 55,983

GAME 2 AT LA OCT 16
```
OAK 000 000 000    0 3 0
LA  005 100 00X    6 10 1
```
Pitchers: DAVIS, Nelson (4), Young (6), Plunk (7), Honeycutt (8) vs HERSHISER
Home Runs: Marshall-LA
Attendance: 56,051

GAME 3 AT OAK OCT 18
```
LA  000 010 000    1 8 1
OAK 001 000 001    2 5 0
```
Pitchers: Tudor, Leary (2), Pena (6), J.HOWELL (9) vs Welch, Cadaret (6), Nelson (6), HONEYCUTT (8)
Home Runs: McGwire-OAK
Attendance: 49,316

GAME 4 AT OAK OCT 19
```
LA  201 000 100    4 8 1
OAK 100 001 100    3 9 2
```
Pitchers: BELCHER, J.Howell (7) vs STEWART, Cadaret (7), Eckersley (9)
Attendance: 49,317

GAME 5 AT OAK OCT 20
```
LA  200 201 000    5 8 0
OAK 001 000 010    2 4 0
```
Pitchers: HERSHISER vs DAVIS, Cadaret (5), Nelson (5), Honeycutt (8), Plunk (9), Burns (9)
Home Runs: Hatcher-LA, Davis-LA
Attendance: 49,317

LA (N)

PLAYER/POS	AVG	G	AB	R	H	2B	3B	HR	RB	BB	SO	SB
Dave Anderson, dh	.000	1	1	0	0	0	0	0	0	0	1	0
Tim Belcher, p	.000	2	0	0	0	0	0	0	0	0	0	0
Mike Davis, dh-2, of-1	.143	4	7	3	1	0	0	1	2	4	0	2
Rick Dempsey, c	.200	2	5	0	1	1	0	0	1	1	2	0
Kirk Gibson, ph	1.000	1	1	1	1	0	0	1	2	0	0	0
Jose Gonzalez, of-3	.000	4	2	0	0	0	0	0	0	0	2	0
Alfredo Griffin, ss	.188	5	16	2	3	0	0	0	0	2	4	0
Jeff Hamilton, 3b	.105	5	19	1	2	0	0	0	0	1	4	0
Mickey Hatcher, of	.368	5	19	5	7	1	0	2	5	1	3	0
Danny Heep, of-1, dh-1	.250	3	8	0	2	1	0	0	0	0	2	0
Orel Hershiser, p	1.000	2	3	1	3	2	0	0	1	0	0	0
Brian Holton, p	.000	1	0	0	0	0	0	0	0	0	0	0
Jay Howell, p	.000	2	0	0	0	0	0	0	0	0	0	0
Tim Leary, p	.000	2	0	0	0	0	0	0	0	0	0	0
Mike Marshall, of	.231	5	13	2	3	0	0	1	3	0	5	0
Alejandro Pena, p	.000	2	0	0	0	0	0	0	0	0	0	0
Steve Sax, 2b	.300	5	20	3	6	0	0	0	0	1	1	0
Mike Scioscia, c	.214	4	14	0	3	0	0	0	1	0	2	0
John Shelby, of	.222	5	18	0	4	1	0	0	1	2	7	1
Franklin Stubbs, 1b	.294	5	17	3	5	2	0	0	2	1	3	0
John Tudor, p	.000	1	0	0	0	0	0	0	0	0	0	0
Tracy Woodson, 1b-3	.000	4	4	0	0	0	0	0	0	1	0	0
TOTAL	.246		167	21	41	8	1	5	19	13	36	4

PITCHER	W	L	ERA	G	GS	CG	SV	SHO	IP	H	ER	BB	SO
Tim Belcher	1	0	6.23	2	2	0	0	0	8.2	10	6	6	10
Orel Hershiser	2	0	1.00	2	2	2	0	1	18.0	7	2	6	17
Brian Holton	0	0	0.00	1	0	0	0	0	2.0	0	0	1	0
Jay Howell	0	1	3.38	2	0	0	1	0	2.2	3	1	1	2
Tim Leary	0	0	1.35	2	0	0	0	0	6.2	6	1	2	4
Alejandro Pena	1	0	0.00	2	0	0	0	0	5.0	2	0	1	7
John Tudor	0	0	0.00	1	1	0	0	0	1.1	0	0	0	1
TOTAL	4	1	2.03	12	5	2	1	1	44.1	28	10	17	41

OAK (A)

PLAYER/POS	AVG	G	AB	R	H	2B	3B	HR	RB	BB	SO	SB
Don Baylor, ph	.000	1	1	0	0	0	0	0	0	0	1	0
Todd Burns, p	.000	1	0	0	0	0	0	0	0	0	0	0
Greg Cadaret, p	.000	3	0	0	0	0	0	0	0	0	0	0
Jose Canseco, of	.053	5	19	1	1	0	0	1	5	2	5	1
Storm Davis, p	.000	2	1	0	0	0	0	0	0	0	1	0
Dennis Eckersley, p	.000	2	0	0	0	0	0	0	0	0	0	0
Mike Gallego, 2b	.000	1	0	0	0	0	0	0	0	0	0	0
Ron Hassey, c-4	.250	5	8	0	2	0	0	0	1	3	3	0
Dave Henderson, of	.300	5	20	1	6	2	0	0	1	2	7	0
Rick Honeycutt, p	.000	3	0	0	0	0	0	0	0	0	0	0
Glenn Hubbard, 2b	.250	4	12	2	3	0	0	0	0	1	2	1
Stan Javier, of-2	.500	3	4	0	2	0	0	0	0	2	1	0
Carney Lansford, 3b	.167	5	18	2	3	0	0	0	1	2	2	0
Mark McGwire, 1b	.059	5	17	1	1	0	0	1	1	3	4	0
Gene Nelson, p	.000	3	0	0	0	0	0	0	0	0	0	0
Dave Parker, of-2, dh-2	.200	4	15	0	3	0	0	0	0	2	4	0
Tony Phillips, 2b-1, of-1	.250	2	4	1	1	0	0	0	0	1	2	0
Eric Plunk, p	.000	2	0	0	0	0	0	0	0	0	0	0
Luis Polonia, of-2	.111	3	9	1	1	0	0	0	0	0	2	0
Terry Steinbach, c-2, dh-1	.364	3	11	0	4	1	0	0	0	0	2	0
Dave Stewart, p	.000	2	3	1	0	0	0	0	0	0	1	0
Walt Weiss, ss	.063	5	16	1	1	0	0	0	0	0	2	1
Bob Welch, p	.000	1	0	0	0	0	0	0	0	0	0	0
Curt Young, p	.000	1	0	0	0	0	0	0	0	0	0	0
TOTAL	.177		158	11	28	3	0	2	11	17	41	3

PITCHER	W	L	ERA	G	GS	CG	SV	SHO	IP	H	ER	BB	SO
Todd Burns	0	0	0.00	1	0	0	0	0	0.1	0	0	0	0
Greg Cadaret	0	0	0.00	3	0	0	0	0	2.0	2	0	0	3
Storm Davis	0	2	11.25	2	2	0	0	0	8.0	14	10	1	7
Dennis Eckersley	0	1	10.80	2	0	0	0	0	1.2	2	2	1	2
Rick Honeycutt	1	0	0.00	3	0	0	0	0	3.1	2	0	0	5
Gene Nelson	0	0	1.42	3	0	0	0	0	6.1	4	1	3	3
Eric Plunk	0	0	0.00	2	0	0	0	0	1.2	0	0	0	3
Dave Stewart	0	1	3.14	2	2	0	0	0	14.1	12	5	5	5
Bob Welch	0	0	1.80	1	1	0	0	0	5.0	6	1	3	8
Curt Young	0	0	0.00	1	0	0	0	0	1.0	1	0	0	0
TOTAL	1	4	3.92	20	5	0	0	0	43.2	41	19	13	36

SAN FRANCISCO GIANTS (WEST) 4, CHICAGO CUBS (EAST) 1

From the first inning of Game 1 when they drove in their teams' first runs, first basemen Will Clark of the Giants and Mark Grace of the Cubs dominated the offense, finishing with eight RBIs apiece and NLCS record-shattering batting average of .650 and .647, respectively. Although Grace homered for two Chicago runs in the opener, the game belonged to Clark, whose four hits—two of them home runs, one a grand slam—drove in six of the 11 San Francisco runs.

Grace led the Cubs' retaliation the next day with his second three-hit game, driving in four of Chicago's nine runs with doubles in the first and sixth innings. Kevin Mitchell, Matt Williams, and Robby Thompson—runners-up to Clark for Giants offensive honors in the series—all homered in the losing cause.

Chicago scored first in the next three games but lost them all narrowly. Thompson's two-run homer in the last of the seventh put the Giants ahead for good in Game 3. The next day, Williams's two-run single in the third inning overcame Chicago's lead, and his two-run homer in the fifth broke a 4–4 tie to conclude the scoring.

Cubs starter Mike Bielecki stopped San Francisco on a pair of singles through six innings of Game 5; he carried a 1–0 lead into the seventh, when Clark's triple and Mitchell's sacrifice fly tied the score. An inning later, after Bielecki loaded the bases with three two-out walks, relief ace Mitch Williams was called on to face Clark and got two strikes on him. But after fouling off a slider and fastball, Clark lined a single up the middle for two go-ahead runs. San Francisco closer Steve Bedrosian yielded Chicago a second run in the ninth on a trio of two-out singles, but Ryne Sandberg (until then batting .421 in the series) grounded out, and the Giants owned their first pennant in 27 years.

SF (W)

PLAYER/POS	AVG	G	AB	R	H	2B	3B	HR	RB	BB	SO	SB
Bill Bathe, ph	.000	2	1	0	0	0	0	0	0	0	1	0
Steve Bedrosian, p	.000	4	0	0	0	0	0	0	0	0	0	0
Jeff Brantley, p	.000	3	0	0	0	0	0	0	0	1	0	0
Brett Butler, of	.211	5	19	6	4	0	0	0	0	3	3	0
Will Clark, 1b	.650	5	20	8	13	3	1	2	8	2	2	0
Kelly Downs, p	.000	2	3	0	0	0	0	0	0	0	1	0
Scott Garrelts, p	.000	2	4	0	0	0	0	0	0	0	1	0
Atlee Hammaker, p	.000	1	0	0	0	0	0	0	0	0	0	0
Terry Kennedy, c	.188	5	16	0	3	1	0	0	0	1	4	0
Mike LaCoss, p	.000	1	1	0	0	0	0	0	0	0	0	0
Craig Lefferts, p	.000	2	0	0	0	0	0	0	0	0	0	0
Greg Litton, 3b	1.000	1	1	0	1	0	0	0	0	0	0	0
Candy Maldonado, of	.000	3	3	1	0	0	0	0	1	2	0	0
Kirt Manwaring, c	.000	3	2	0	0	0	0	0	0	0	0	0
Kevin Mitchell, of	.353	5	17	5	6	0	0	2	7	3	3	0
Donell Nixon, of-2	.000	3	3	0	0	0	0	0	0	0	1	1
Ken Oberkfell, 3b-1	.000	3	4	0	0	0	0	0	0	0	0	0
Rick Reuschel, p	.000	2	2	0	0	0	0	0	0	0	0	0
Ernest Riles, ph	.000	1	1	0	0	0	0	0	0	0	0	0
Don Robinson, p	.000	1	0	0	0	0	0	0	0	0	0	0
Pat Sheridan, of	.154	5	13	1	2	0	1	0	0	0	4	0
Robby Thompson, 2b	.278	5	18	5	5	0	0	2	3	3	2	0
Jose Uribe, ss	.235	5	17	2	4	1	0	0	1	1	5	1
Matt Williams, 3b-5, ss-1	.300	5	20	2	6	1	0	2	9	0	2	0
TOTAL	.267		165	30	44	6	2	8	29	17	29	2

PITCHER	W	L	ERA	G	GS	CG	SV	SHO	IP	H	ER	BB	SO
Steve Bedrosian	0	0	2.70	4	0	0	3	0	3.1	4	1	2	2
Jeff Brantley	0	0	0.00	3	0	0	0	0	5.0	1	0	2	3
Kelly Downs	1	0	3.12	2	0	0	0	0	8.2	8	3	6	6
Scott Garrelts	1	0	5.40	2	2	0	0	0	11.2	16	7	2	8
Atlee Hammaker	0	0	0.00	1	0	0	0	0	1.0	1	0	0	0
Mike LaCoss	0	0	9.00	1	1	0	0	0	3.0	7	3	0	2
Craig Lefferts	0	0	9.00	2	0	0	0	0	1.0	1	1	2	1
Rick Reuschel	1	1	5.19	2	2	0	0	0	8.2	12	5	2	5
Don Robinson	1	0	0.00	1	0	0	0	0	1.2	3	0	0	0
TOTAL	4	1	4.09	18	5	0	3	0	44.0	53	20	16	27

CHI (E)

PLAYER/POS	AVG	G	AB	R	H	2B	3B	HR	RB	BB	SO	SB
Paul Assenmacher, p	.000	2	0	0	0	0	0	0	0	0	0	0
Mike Bielecki, p	.200	2	5	0	1	0	0	0	2	0	2	0
Andre Dawson, of	.105	5	19	0	2	1	0	0	3	2	6	0
Shawon Dunston, ss	.316	5	19	2	6	0	0	0	0	1	1	1
Joe Girardi, c	.100	4	10	1	1	0	0	0	0	1	2	0
Mark Grace, 1b	.647	5	17	3	11	3	1	1	8	4	1	1
Paul Kilgus, p	.000	1	0	0	0	0	0	0	0	0	0	0
Lester Lancaster, p	.000	3	1	0	0	0	0	0	0	0	1	0
Vance Law, 3b-1	.000	2	3	0	0	0	0	0	0	0	3	0
Greg Maddux, p-2	.000	3	3	1	0	0	0	0	0	0	0	0
Lloyd McClendon, c-2, of-1	.667	3	3	0	2	0	0	0	0	1	0	0
Domingo Ramos, ph	.000	1	1	0	0	0	0	0	0	0	0	0
Luis Salazar, 3b	.368	5	19	2	7	0	1	1	2	0	0	0
Ryne Sandberg, 2b	.400	5	20	6	8	3	1	1	4	3	4	0
Scott Sanderson, p	.000	1	0	0	0	0	0	0	0	0	0	0
Dwight Smith, of	.200	4	15	2	3	1	0	0	0	2	2	1
Rick Sutcliffe, p	.500	1	2	0	1	1	0	0	0	0	1	0
Jerome Walton, of	.364	5	22	4	8	0	0	0	2	2	2	0
Mitch Webster, of-2	.333	3	3	0	1	0	0	0	0	0	0	0
Curtis Wilkerson, 3b-1	.500	3	2	1	1	0	0	0	0	0	0	0
Mitch Williams, p	.000	2	0	0	0	0	0	0	0	0	0	0
Steve Wilson, p	.000	2	0	0	0	0	0	0	0	0	0	0
Rick Wrona, c	.000	2	5	0	0	0	0	0	0	0	3	0
Marvell Wynne, of-2	.167	4	6	0	1	0	0	0	0	0	0	0
TOTAL	.303		175	22	53	9	3	3	21	16	27	3

PITCHER	W	L	ERA	G	GS	CG	SV	SHO	IP	H	ER	BB	SO
P. Assenmacher	0	0	13.50	2	0	0	0	0	0.2	3	1	0	0
Mike Bielecki	0	1	3.65	2	2	0	0	0	12.1	7	5	6	11
Paul Kilgus	0	0	0.00	1	0	0	0	0	3.0	4	0	1	1
Lester Lancaster	1	1	6.00	3	0	0	0	0	6.0	6	4	1	3
Greg Maddux	0	1	13.50	2	2	0	0	0	7.1	13	11	4	5
Scott Sanderson	0	0	0.00	1	0	0	0	0	2.0	2	0	0	1
Rick Sutcliffe	0	0	4.50	1	1	0	0	0	6.0	5	3	4	2
Mitch Williams	0	0	0.00	2	0	0	0	0	1.0	1	0	0	2
Steve Wilson	0	1	4.91	2	0	0	0	0	3.2	3	2	1	4
TOTAL	1	4	5.57	16	5	0	0	0	42.0	44	26	17	29

GAME 1 AT CHI OCT 4

SF 301 400 030 11 13 0
CHI 201 000 000 3 10 1
Pitchers: GARRELTS, Brantley (8), Hammaker (9) vs MADDUX, Kilgus (5), Wilson (8)
Home Runs: Grace-CHI, Clark-SF (2), Sandberg-CHI, Mitchell-SF
Attendance: 39,195

GAME 2 AT CHI OCT 5

SF 000 200 021 5 10 0
CHI 600 003 00X 9 11 0
Pitchers: REUSCHEL, Downs (1), Lefferts (6), Brantley (7), Bedrosian (8) vs Bielecki, Assenmacher (5), LANCASTER (6)
Home Runs: Mitchell-SF, Williams-SF, Thompson-SF
Attendance: 39,195

GAME 3 AT SF OCT 7

CHI 200 100 100 4 10 0
SF 300 000 20X 5 8 3
Pitchers: Sutcliffe, Assenmacher (7), LANCASTER (7) vs LaCoss, Brantley (4), ROBINSON (7), Lefferts (8), Bedrosian (9)
Home Runs: Thompson-SF
Attendance: 62,065

GAME 4 AT SF OCT 8

CHI 110 020 000 4 12 1
SF 102 120 00X 6 9 1
Pitchers: Maddux, WILSON (4), Sanderson (6), Williams (8) vs Garrelts, DOWNS (5), Bedrosian (9)
Home Runs: Salazar-CHI, Williams-SF
Attendance: 62,078

GAME 5 AT SF OCT 9

CHI 001 000 001 2 10 1
SF 000 000 12X 3 4 1
Pitchers: BIELECKI, Williams (8), Lancaster (8) vs REUSCHEL, Bedrosian (9)
Attendance: 62,084

OAKLAND A'S (WEST) 4, TORONTO BLUE JAYS (EAST) 1

The awesome A's produced their share of heroes. Jose Canseco powered a truly heroic home run into the top deck of Toronto's SkyDome in Game 4; Dave Parker, in his seventh postseason series, at last hit his first postseason homer (and later his second); closer Dennis Eckersley added three saves to his four from 1988 to establish a new LCS record; and Carney Lansford was batting .455, with four RBIs, when a hamstring pull in Game 3 ended his series play. But the hero of heroes was leadoff batter Rickey Henderson.

Oakland might have won the opener without Henderson, even though his hard slide into second in the sixth inning broke up a double play and forced a wide throw that gave the A's two runs and their first lead of the game. And the A's might also have won the next day even if Henderson had not rattled Toronto with four stolen bases. The A's suffered their loss in Game 3 despite an early 2–0 lead with Henderson scoring both runs—the first after walking, the second after a double and stolen base.

But in the final two games, Rickey Henderson's contribution made the difference between defeat and victory. A pair of two-run Henderson homers (together with Canseco's memorable blast and later RBI single) gave the A's their 6–5 win in Game 4. And in the first inning of Game 5, Henderson, after walking, stole his eighth base—a postseason series record—before Canseco singled him home with the A's first run. Two innings later Henderson tripled home the second Oakland run. The A's scored twice more in the seventh, but Toronto had narrowed Oakland's lead to one run when Eckersley fanned a final Blue Jay to secure the second straight Oakland pennant. Rickey Henderson was the unanimous choice for series MVP.

OAK (W)

PLAYER/POS	AVG	G	AB	R	H	2B	3B	HR	RB	BB	SO	SB
Lance Blankenship, 2b	.000	1	0	0	0	0	0	0	0	0	0	0
Jose Canseco, of	.294	5	17	1	5	0	0	1	3	3	7	0
Storm Davis, p	.000	1	0	0	0	0	0	0	0	0	0	0
Dennis Eckersley, p	.000	4	0	0	0	0	0	0	0	0	0	0
Mike Gallego, 2b-2, ss-2	.273	4	11	3	3	1	0	0	1	0	2	0
Ron Hassey, c	.167	2	6	0	1	0	0	0	0	1	1	2
Dave Henderson, of	.263	5	19	4	5	3	0	1	1	2	5	0
Rickey Henderson, of	.400	5	15	8	6	1	1	2	5	7	0	8
Rick Honeycutt, p	.000	3	0	0	0	0	0	0	0	0	0	0
Stan Javier, of	.000	1	2	0	0	0	0	0	0	0	1	0
Carney Lansford, 3b	.455	3	11	2	5	0	0	0	4	2	1	2
Mark McGwire, 1b	.389	5	18	3	7	1	0	1	3	1	4	0
Mike Moore, p	.000	1	0	0	0	0	0	0	0	0	0	0
Gene Nelson, p	.000	1	0	0	0	0	0	0	0	0	0	0
Dave Parker, dh	.188	4	16	2	3	0	0	2	3	0	0	0
Ken Phelps, ph	1.000	1	1	0	1	1	0	0	0	0	0	0
Tony Phillips, 2b-3,3b-3	.167	5	18	1	3	1	0	0	1	2	4	2
Terry Steinbach, c-3, dh-1	.200	4	15	0	3	0	0	0	1	1	5	0
Dave Stewart, p	.000	2	0	0	0	0	0	0	0	0	0	0
Walt Weiss, ss	.111	4	9	2	1	1	0	0	0	1	1	1
Bob Welch, p	.000	1	0	0	0	0	0	0	0	0	0	0
Matt Young, p	.000	1	0	0	0	0	0	0	0	0	2	0
TOTAL	.272		158	26	43	9	1	7	23	20	32	13

PITCHER	W	L	ERA	G	GS	CG	SV	SHO	IP	H	ER	BB	SO
Storm Davis	0	1	7.11	1	1	0	0	0	6.1	5	5	2	3
Dennis Eckersley	0	0	1.59	4	0	0	3	0	5.2	4	1	0	2
Rick Honeycutt	0	0	32.40	3	0	0	0	0	1.2	6	6	5	1
Mike Moore	1	0	0.00	1	1	0	0	0	7.0	3	0	2	3
Gene Nelson	0	0	0.00	1	0	0	0	0	1.1	1	0	0	2
Dave Stewart	2	0	2.81	2	2	0	0	0	16.0	13	5	3	9
Bob Welch	1	0	3.18	1	1	0	0	0	5.2	8	2	1	4
Matt Young	0	0	0.00	1	0	0	0	0	0.1	0	0	2	0
TOTAL	4	1	3.89	14	5	0	3	0	44.0	40	19	15	24

TOR (E)

PLAYER/POS	AVG	G	AB	R	H	2B	3B	HR	RB	BB	SO	SB
Jim Acker, p	.000	5	0	0	0	0	0	0	0	0	0	0
George Bell, dh-3, of-2	.200	5	20	2	4	0	0	1	2	0	3	0
Pat Borders, c	1.000	1	1	0	1	0	0	0	1	0	0	0
John Cerutti, p	.000	2	0	0	0	0	0	0	0	0	0	0
Junior Felix, of	.273	3	11	0	3	1	0	0	3	0	2	0
Tony Fernandez, ss	.350	5	20	6	7	3	0	0	1	1	2	5
Mike Flanagan, p	.000	1	0	0	0	0	0	0	0	0	0	0
Kelly Gruber, 3b	.294	5	17	2	5	1	0	0	1	3	2	1
Tom Henke, p	.000	3	0	0	0	0	0	0	0	0	0	0
Jimmy Key, p	.000	1	0	0	0	0	0	0	0	0	0	0
Manny Lee, 2b	.250	2	8	2	2	0	0	0	0	0	1	0
Nelson Liriano, 2b	.429	3	7	1	3	0	0	0	1	2	0	3
Lee Mazzilli, dh-2	.000	3	8	0	0	0	0	0	0	0	2	0
Fred McGriff, 1b	.143	5	21	1	3	0	0	0	3	0	4	0
Lloyd Moseby, of	.313	5	16	4	5	0	0	1	2	5	2	1
Rance Mulliniks, ph	.000	1	1	0	0	0	0	0	0	0	1	0
Dave Stieb, p	.000	2	0	0	0	0	0	0	0	0	0	0
Todd Stottlemyre, p	.000	1	0	0	0	0	0	0	0	0	0	0
Duane Ward, p	.000	2	0	0	0	0	0	0	0	0	0	0
David Wells, p	.000	1	0	0	0	0	0	0	0	0	0	0
Ernie Whitt, c	.125	5	16	1	2	0	0	1	3	2	3	0
Mookie Wilson, of	.263	5	19	2	5	0	0	0	2	2	2	1
TOTAL	.242		165	21	40	5	0	3	19	15	24	11

PITCHER	W	L	ERA	G	GS	CG	SV	SHO	IP	H	ER	BB	SO
Jim Acker	0	0	1.42	5	0	0	0	0	6.1	4	1	1	4
John Cerutti	0	0	0.00	2	0	0	0	0	2.2	0	0	3	1
Mike Flanagan	0	1	10.38	1	1	0	0	0	4.1	7	5	1	3
Tom Henke	0	0	0.00	3	0	0	0	0	2.2	0	0	0	3
Jimmy Key	1	0	4.50	1	1	0	0	0	6.0	7	3	2	2
Dave Stieb	0	2	6.35	2	2	0	0	0	11.1	12	8	6	10
Todd Stottlemyre	0	1	7.20	1	1	0	0	0	5.0	7	4	2	3
Duane Ward	0	0	7.36	2	0	0	0	0	3.2	6	3	3	5
David Wells	0	0	0.00	1	0	0	0	0	1.0	0	0	2	1
TOTAL	1	4	5.02	18	5	0	0	0	43.0	43	24	20	32

GAME 1 AT OAK OCT 3

```
TOR  020 100 000   3 5 1
OAK  010 013 02X   7 11 0
```
Pitchers: STIEB, Acker (6), Ward (8) vs STEWART, Eckersley (9)
Home Runs: D.Henderson-OAK, Whitt-TOR, McGwire-OAK
Attendance: 49,435

GAME 2 AT OAK OCT 4

```
TOR  001 000 020   3 5 1
OAK  000 203 10X   6 9 1
```
Pitchers: STOTTLEMYRE, Acker (6), Wells (6), Henke (7), Cerutti (8) vs MOORE, Honeycutt (8), Eckersley (8)
Home Runs: Parker-OAK
Attendance: 49,444

GAME 3 AT TOR OCT 6

```
OAK  101 100 000   3 8 1
TOR  000 400 30X   7 8 0
```
Pitchers: DAVIS, Honeycutt (7), Nelson (7), M.Young (8) vs KEY, Acker (7), Henke (9)
Home Runs: Parker-OAK
Attendance: 50,268

GAME 4 AT TOR OCT 7

```
OAK  003 020 100   6 11 1
TOR  000 101 120   5 13 0
```
Pitchers: WELCH, Honeycutt (7), Eckersley (8) vs FLANAGAN, Ward (5), Cerutti (8), Acker (9)
Home Runs: R.Henderson-OAK (2), Canseco-OAK
Attendance: 50,076

GAME 5 AT TOR OCT 8

```
OAK  101 000 200   4 4 0
TOR  000 000 012   3 9 0
```
Pitchers: STEWART, Eckersley (9) vs STIEB, Acker (7), Henke (9)
Home Runs: Moseby-TOR, Bell-TOR
Attendance: 50,024

OAKLAND A'S (AL) 4, SAN FRANCISCO GIANTS (NL) 0

Not even the devastating earthquake that blindsided baseball's first San Francisco Bay World Series could halt the Oakland juggernaut. The A's scored first in every game and, except for an inning and a half of Game 2 in which the score stood at 1–1, held their lead to the finish.

A's ace Dave Stewart shut out the Giants on five hits in the opener. Three second-inning Oakland runs initiated the Series scoring, and Dave Parker and Walt Weiss expanded Stewart's margin of comfort with solo homers in the third and fourth. In Game 2, doubles by Carney Lansford in the first inning and Parker in the fourth drove home the two runs the A's would need for victory; Terry Steinbach's three-run blast later in the fourth added frosting to Oakland's cake. A's starter Mike Moore yielded a pair of singles and the first San Francisco run of the Series in the third inning but held the Giants to just two more singles in his seven-plus innings of work. Relievers Rick Honeycutt and Dennis Eckersley hurled perfect ball in the eighth and ninth.

After a day off, the Series shifted 11 miles across the Bay to San Francisco for Game 3. But just as fans were settling into their seats, the earthquake struck, knocking out power to Candlestick Park and (as gradually became known) killing 67 people in scattered pockets of destruction throughout the Bay Area. The fans were sent home, but despite the pleas of a few Eastern reporters that the rest of the Series be cancelled, the overwhelming desire of Bay Area residents prevailed, and Game 3 came off at last, 10 days late. Starter Dave Stewart gave up three runs in seven innings, but by the time he was relieved, his A's had sent nine men across the plate. Four more runs in the eighth completed the Oakland scoring. The Giants put together their first big inning of the Series, scoring four runs in the last of the ninth. Although the Giants' effort fell far short of what was needed, pinch hitter Bill Bathe's home run—the game's seventh, including five by the A's—set a new World Series record.

Oakland's Rickey Henderson led off Game 4 with a home run, and by the time Kevin Mitchell homered in San Francisco's first

pair of runs in the sixth inning, the A's had scored eight times. The Giants struggled back, though, scoring four times in the seventh on a walk and a cycle of hits—home run, triple, double, and single—to draw within two runs of a tie. But they came no closer. Todd Burns and Eckersley hurled the Series to its conclusion.

OAK (A)

PLAYER/POS	AVG	G	AB	R	H	2B	3B	HR	RB	BB	SO	SB
Lance Blankenship, 2b	.500	1	2	1	1	0	0	0	0	0	0	0
Todd Burns, p	.000	2	0	0	0	0	0	0	0	0	0	0
Jose Canseco, of	.357	4	14	5	5	0	0	1	3	4	3	1
Dennis Eckersley, p	.000	2	0	0	0	0	0	0	0	0	0	0
Mike Gallego, 2b-1,3b-1	.000	2	1	0	0	0	0	0	0	0	0	0
Dave Henderson, of	.308	4	13	6	4	2	0	2	4	4	3	0
Rickey Henderson, of	.474	4	19	4	9	1	2	1	3	2	2	3
Rick Honeycutt, p	.000	3	0	0	0	0	0	0	0	0	0	0
Stan Javier, of	.000	1	0	0	0	0	0	0	0	0	0	0
Carney Lansford, 3b	.438	4	16	5	7	1	0	1	4	3	1	0
Mark McGwire, 1b	.294	4	17	0	5	1	0	0	1	1	3	0
Mike Moore, p	.333	2	3	1	1	1	0	0	2	0	1	0
Gene Nelson, p	.000	2	0	0	0	0	0	0	0	0	0	0
Dave Parker, dh-2	.222	3	9	2	2	1	0	1	2	0	2	0
Ken Phelps, ph	.000	1	1	0	0	0	0	0	0	0	0	0
Tony Phillips, 2b-3,3b-2, of-1	.235	4	17	2	4	1	0	1	3	0	3	0
Terry Steinbach, c	.250	4	16	3	4	0	1	1	7	2	1	0
Dave Stewart, p	.000	2	3	0	0	0	0	0	0	0	1	0
Walt Weiss, ss	.133	4	15	3	2	0	0	1	1	2	2	0
TOTAL	.301		146	32	44	8	3	9	30	18	22	4

PITCHER	W	L	ERA	G	GS	CG	SV	SHO	IP	H	ER	BB	SO
Todd Burns	0	0	0.00	2	0	0	0	0	1.2	1	0	1	0
Dennis Eckersley	0	0	0.00	2	0	0	1	0	1.2	0	0	0	0
Rick Honeycutt	0	0	6.75	3	0	0	0	0	2.2	4	2	0	2
Mike Moore	2	0	2.08	2	2	0	0	0	13.0	9	3	3	10
Gene Nelson	0	0	54.00	2	0	0	0	0	1.0	4	6	2	1
Dave Stewart	2	0	1.69	2	2	1	0	1	16.0	10	3	2	14
TOTAL	4	0	3.50	13	4	1	1	1	36.0	28	14	8	27

SF (N)

PLAYER/POS	AVG	G	AB	R	H	2B	3B	HR	RB	BB	SO	SB
Bill Bathe, ph	.500	2	2	1	1	0	0	1	3	0	0	0
Steve Bedrosian, p	.000	2	0	0	0	0	0	0	0	0	0	0
Jeff Brantley, p	.000	3	0	0	0	0	0	0	0	0	0	0
Brett Butler, of	.286	4	14	1	4	1	0	0	1	2	1	2
Will Clark, 1b	.250	4	16	2	4	1	0	0	0	1	3	0
Kelly Downs, p	.000	3	0	0	0	0	0	0	0	0	0	0
Scott Garrelts, p	.000	2	1	0	0	0	0	0	0	0	1	0
Atlee Hammaker, p	.000	2	0	0	0	0	0	0	0	0	0	0
Terry Kennedy, c	.167	4	12	1	2	0	0	0	2	1	3	0
Mike LaCoss, p	.000	2	1	0	0	0	0	0	0	0	0	0
Craig Lefferts, p	.000	3	0	0	0	0	0	0	0	0	0	0
Greg Litton, 2b-2,3b-1	.500	2	6	1	3	1	0	1	3	0	0	0
Candy Maldonado, of-3	.091	4	11	1	1	0	1	0	0	0	4	0
Kirt Manwaring, c	1.000	1	1	1	1	1	0	0	0	0	0	0
Kevin Mitchell, of	.294	4	17	2	5	0	0	1	2	0	3	0
Donell Nixon, of	.200	2	5	1	1	0	0	0	0	1	1	0
Ken Oberkfell, 3b	.333	4	6	1	2	0	0	0	0	3	0	0
Rick Reuschel, p	.000	1	0	0	0	0	0	0	0	0	0	0
Ernie Riles, dh-2	.000	4	8	0	0	0	0	0	0	0	1	0
Don Robinson, p	.000	1	0	0	0	0	0	0	0	0	0	0
Pat Sheridan, of	.000	1	2	0	0	0	0	0	0	0	0	0
Robby Thompson, 2b	.091	4	11	0	1	0	0	0	0	2	4	0
Jose Uribe, ss	.200	3	5	1	1	0	0	0	0	0	0	0
Matt Williams, ss-4,3b-3	.125	4	16	1	2	0	0	1	1	0	6	0
TOTAL	.209		134	14	28	4	1	4	14	8	27	2

PITCHER	W	L	ERA	G	GS	CG	SV	SHO	IP	H	ER	BB	SO
Steve Bedrosian	0	0	0.00	2	0	0	0	0	2.2	0	0	2	2
Jeff Brantley	0	0	4.15	3	0	0	0	0	4.1	5	2	3	1
Kelly Downs	0	0	7.71	3	0	0	0	0	4.2	3	4	2	4
Scott Garrelts	0	2	9.82	2	2	0	0	0	7.1	13	8	1	8
Atlee Hammaker	0	0	15.43	2	0	0	0	0	2.1	8	4	0	2
Mike LaCoss	0	0	6.23	2	0	0	0	0	4.1	4	3	3	2
Craig Lefferts	0	0	3.38	3	0	0	0	0	2.2	2	1	2	1
Rick Reuschel	0	1	11.25	1	1	0	0	0	4.0	5	5	4	2
Don Robinson	0	1	21.60	1	1	0	0	0	1.2	4	4	1	0
TOTAL	0	4	8.21	19	4	0	0	0	34.0	44	31	18	22

GAME 1 AT OAK OCT 14

```
SF   000 000 000   0  5  1
OAK  031 100 00X   5 11  1
```
Pitchers: GARRELTS, Hammaker (5), Brantley (6), LaCoss (8) vs STEWART
Home Runs: Parker-OAK, Weiss-OAK
Attendance: 49,385

GAME 2 AT OAK OCT 15

```
SF   001 000 000   1  4  0
OAK  100 400 00X   5  7  0
```
Pitchers: REUSCHEL, Downs (5), Lefferts (7), Bedrosian (8) vs MOORE, Honeycutt (8), Eckersley (9)
Home Runs: Steinbach-OAK
Attendance: 49,388

GAME 3 AT SF OCT 27

```
OAK  200 241 040   13 14  0
SF   010 200 004    7 10  3
```
Pitchers: STEWART, Honeycutt (8), Nelson (9), Burns (9) vs GARRELTS, Downs (4), Brantley (5), Hammaker (8), Lefferts (9)
Home Runs: Williams-SF, D.Henderson-OAK (2), Phillips-OAK, Canseco-OAK, Lansford-OAK, Bathe-SF
Attendance: 62,038

GAME 4 AT SF OCT 28

```
OAK  130 031 010   9 12  0
SF   000 002 400   6  9  0
```
Pitchers: MOORE, Nelson (7), Honeycutt (7), Burns (7), Eckersley (9) vs ROBINSON, LaCoss (2), Brantley (6), Downs (6), Lefferts (8), Bedrosian (8)
Home Runs: R.Henderson-OAK, Mitchell-SF, Litton-SF
Attendance: 62,032

CINCINNATI REDS (WEST) 4, PITTSBURGH PIRATES (EAST) 2

Fielding plays and misplays provided some of the most crucial moments of the series. After the Pirates had overcome a three-run deficit to tie the score in Game 1, they won the game when Eric Davis misplayed Andy Van Slyke's fly to left field for a run-scoring double. Cincinnati right fielder Paul O'Neill evened the series in Game 2 by singling home the game's first run in the first inning, then (with the game tied 1–1 in the fifth) doubling in the go-ahead—and final—run on a fly Pirates left fielder Barry Bonds lost in the late afternoon sun. Finally, O'Neill gunned down Pittsburgh's potential tying run at third base when Van Slyke attempted to move up after Bonds' fly-out to right.

Two- and three-run homers by Reds Billy Hatcher and Mariano Duncan gave Cincinnati the series advantage in Game 3, and Chris Sabo's sacrifice fly and two-run blast proved the decisive blows a day later as the Reds pushed their series lead to 3–1. In that game left fielder Eric Davis, backing up Bobby Bonilla's double off the center field wall, prevented what would have become a game-tying run when, with a perfect throw to third, he nailed Bonilla trying for a triple.

The Pirates staved off elimination with a narrow 3–2 win in Game 5, a win preserved by a spectacular bases-loaded game-ending double play. But in Game 6, Pittsburgh's uncertain fielding in the first inning gave the Reds their first and, as it turned out, decisive run. In the ninth inning, with the Reds ahead 2–1, Reds right fielder Glen Braggs snared a deep fly with a leaping catch that prevented at least one, and perhaps two, Pirates runs from scoring. One strikeout later the Reds had snared the National League pennant.

CIN (W)

PLAYER/POS	AVG	G	AB	R	H	2B	3B	HR	RB	BB	SO	SB
Billy Bates, pr	.000	2	0	1	0	0	0	0	0	0	0	0
Todd Benzinger, 1b-2	.333	5	9	0	3	0	0	0	0	2	0	0
Glenn Braggs, of	.200	2	5	0	1	0	0	0	0	0	1	0
Tom Browning, p	.000	2	3	0	0	0	0	0	0	0	1	0
Norm Charlton, p	.000	4	0	0	0	0	0	0	0	0	0	0
Eric Davis, of	.174	6	23	2	4	1	0	0	2	1	9	0
Rob Dibble, p	.000	4	2	0	0	0	0	0	0	0	1	0
Mariano Duncan, 2b	.300	6	20	1	6	0	0	1	4	0	8	0
Billy Hatcher, of	.333	4	15	2	5	1	0	1	2	0	2	0
Danny Jackson, p	.000	2	3	0	0	0	0	0	0	0	2	0
Barry Larkin, ss	.261	6	23	5	6	2	0	0	1	3	1	3
Rick Mahler, p	.000	1	0	0	0	0	0	0	0	0	0	0
Hal Morris, 1b-4	.417	5	12	3	5	1	0	0	1	1	0	0
Randy Myers, p	.000	4	0	0	0	0	0	0	0	0	0	0
Ron Oester, 2b-2	.333	4	3	1	1	0	0	0	0	0	1	0
Joe Oliver, c	.143	5	14	1	2	0	0	0	0	0	2	0
Paul O'Neill, of	.471	5	17	1	8	3	0	1	4	1	1	1
Luis Quinones, ph	.500	3	2	1	1	0	0	0	0	2	0	1
Jeff Reed, c	.000	4	7	0	0	0	0	0	0	0	2	0
Jose Rijo, p	.000	2	5	0	0	0	0	0	0	0	1	0
Chris Sabo, 3b	.227	6	22	1	5	0	0	1	3	1	4	0
Scott Scudder, p	.000	1	0	0	0	0	0	0	0	0	0	0
Herm Winningham, of-2	.286	3	7	1	2	1	0	0	1	1	1	1
TOTAL	.255		192	20	49	9	0	4	20	10	37	6

PITCHER	W	L	ERA	G	GS	CG	SV	SHO	IP	H	ER	BB	SO
Tom Browning	1	1	3.27	2	2	0	0	0	11.0	9	4	6	5
Norm Charlton	1	1	1.80	4	0	0	0	0	5.0	4	1	3	3
Rob Dibble	0	0	0.00	4	0	0	1	0	5.0	0	0	1	10
Danny Jackson	1	0	2.38	2	2	0	0	0	11.1	8	3	7	8
Rick Mahler	0	0	0.00	1	0	0	0	0	1.2	2	0	0	0
Randy Myers	0	0	0.00	4	0	0	3	0	5.2	2	0	3	7
Jose Rijo	1	0	4.38	2	2	0	0	0	12.1	10	6	7	15
Scott Scudder	0	0	0.00	1	0	0	0	0	1.0	1	0	0	1
TOTAL	4	2	2.38	20	6	0	4	0	53.0	36	14	27	49

PIT (E)

PLAYER/POS	AVG	G	AB	R	H	2B	3B	HR	RB	BB	SO	SB
Wally Backman, 3b-2	.143	3	7	1	1	1	0	0	0	1	3	1
Stan Belinda, p	.000	3	0	0	0	0	0	0	0	0	0	0
Jay Bell, ss	.250	6	20	3	5	1	0	1	1	4	3	0
Barry Bonds, of	.167	6	18	4	3	0	0	0	1	6	5	2
Bobby Bonilla, of-5,3b-3	.190	6	21	0	4	1	0	0	1	3	1	0
Sid Bream, 1b	.500	4	8	1	4	1	0	1	3	2	3	0
Doug Drabek, p	.167	2	6	0	1	0	0	0	0	0	2	0
Jeff King, 3b-4	.100	5	10	0	1	0	0	0	0	1	5	0
Bill Landrum, p	.000	2	0	0	0	0	0	0	0	0	0	0
Mike LaValliere, c	.000	3	6	1	0	0	0	0	0	3	1	0
Jose Lind, 2b	.238	6	21	1	5	1	1	1	2	1	4	0
Carmelo Martinez, 1b	.250	2	8	0	2	2	0	0	2	0	1	0
Bob Patterson, p	.000	2	0	0	0	0	0	0	0	0	0	0
Ted Power, p	.000	3	1	0	0	0	0	0	0	0	1	0
Gary Redus, 1b-2	.250	5	8	1	2	0	0	0	0	1	3	1
R. J. Reynolds, of-3	.200	6	10	0	2	0	0	0	0	2	2	1
Don Slaught, c	.091	4	11	0	1	1	0	0	1	2	3	0
John Smiley, p	.000	1	0	0	0	0	0	0	0	0	0	0
Zane Smith, p	.000	2	3	0	0	0	0	0	0	0	1	0
Andy Van Slyke, of	.208	6	24	3	5	1	1	0	3	1	7	1
Bob Walk, p	.000	2	4	0	0	0	0	0	0	0	4	0
TOTAL	.194		186	15	36	9	2	3	14	27	49	6

PITCHER	W	L	ERA	G	GS	CG	SV	SHO	IP	H	ER	BB	SO
Stan Belinda	0	0	2.45	3	0	0	0	0	3.2	3	1	0	4
Doug Drabek	1	1	1.65	2	2	1	0	0	16.1	12	3	3	13
Bill Landrum	0	0	0.00	2	0	0	0	0	2.0	0	0	0	1
Bob Patterson	0	0	0.00	2	0	0	1	0	1.0	1	0	2	0
Ted Power	0	0	3.60	3	1	0	1	0	5.0	6	2	2	3
John Smiley	0	0	0.00	1	0	0	0	0	2.0	2	0	0	0
Zane Smith	0	2	6.00	2	1	0	0	0	9.0	14	6	1	8
Bob Walk	1	1	4.85	2	2	0	0	0	13.0	11	7	2	8
TOTAL	2	4	3.29	17	6	1	2	0	52.0	49	19	10	37

GAME 1 AT CIN OCT 4

```
PIT  001 200 100   4 7 1
CIN  300 000 000   3 5 0
```
Pitchers: WALK, Belinda (7), Patterson (9), Power (9) vs Rijo, CHARLTON (6), Dibble (9)
Home Runs: Bream-PIT
Attendance: 55,700

GAME 2 AT CIN OCT 5

```
PIT  000 010 000   1 6 0
CIN  100 010 00X'  2 5 0
```
Pitchers: DRABEK vs BROWNING, Dibble (7), Myers (8)
Home Runs: Lind-PIT
Attendance: 54,456

GAME 3 AT PIT OCT 8

```
CIN  020 030 001   6 13 1
PIT  000 200 010   3 8 0
```
Pitchers: JACKSON, Dibble (8), Charlton (8), Myers (9) vs SMITH, Landrum (6), Smiley (7), Belinda (9)
Home Runs: Duncan-CIN, Hatcher-CIN
Attendance: 45,611

GAME 4 AT PIT OCT 9

```
CIN  000 200 201   5 10 1
PIT  100 100 010   3 8 0
```
Pitchers: RIJO, Myers (8), Dibble (9) vs WALK, Power (8)
Home Runs: O'Neill-CIN, Sabo-CIN, Bell-PIT
Attendance: 50,461

GAME 5 AT PIT OCT 10

```
CIN  100 000 010   2 7 0
PIT  200 100 00X   3 6 1
```
Pitchers: BROWNING, Mahler (6), Charlton (7), Scudder (8) vs DRABEK, Patterson (9)
Attendance: 48,221

GAME 6 AT CIN OCT 12

```
PIT  000 010 000   1 1 3
CIN  100 000 10X   2 9 0
```
Pitchers: Power, SMITH (3), Belinda (7), Landrum (8) vs Jackson, CHARLTON (7), Myers (8)
Attendance: 56,079

OAKLAND A'S (WEST) 4, BOSTON RED SOX (EAST) 0

The ejection of Boston ace Roger Clemens from Game 4 for mouthing off to an umpire provided a moment of raucous counterpoint to the surgical precision with which Oakland dismembered the Red Sox. While the A's pitchers anesthetized Boston's hitters, parceling out just one run per game, their batters sliced up the Sox with singles, steals, and sacrifices.

In the fourth inning of Game 1, Boston's Wade Boggs interrupted a pitchers' duel between Clemens and Oakland's Dave Stewart with the series' only home run. But in the top of the seventh—after a tiring Clemens had been relieved—the A's evened the score with a walk, single, and sacrifice fly, took the lead an inning later with a pair of singles sandwiched around a bunt and stolen base, then buried the Sox with seven runs in the ninth. DH Harold Baines provided Oakland's most productive offense in the second game, singling home the tying run in the fourth inning, driving in the tiebreaker with a groundout in the seventh, and doubling home a third run in the ninth. In Game 3, a double steal by Baines and Jose Canseco set up the A's tying and tiebreaking runs, which scored on a sacrifice fly and a single.

The A's scored first for the only time in the series in Game 4, on a pair of singles and a grounder to short in the second inning. Following the shouting match between the Sox and umpires that erupted when pitcher Clemens was thrown out for disputing a walk, Mike Gallego doubled home two more Oakland runs. A trio of Boston relievers stopped the A's the rest of the way, and a pair of Red Sox hits in the ninth ended Dave Stewart's shutout bid. But Rick Honeycutt came on to preserve Stewart's second win of the series and sew up Oakland's third successive American League championship.

OAK (W)

PLAYER/POS	AVG	G	AB	R	H	2B	3B	HR	RB	BB	SO	SB
Harold Baines, dh	.357	4	14	2	5	1	0	0	3	2	1	1
Lance Blankenship, dh	.000	3	0	1	0	0	0	0	0	0	0	1
Jose Canseco, of	.182	4	11	3	2	0	0	0	1	5	5	2
Dennis Eckersley, p	.000	3	0	0	0	0	0	0	0	0	0	0
Mike Gallego, ss-3,2b-2	.400	4	10	1	4	1	0	0	2	1	1	0
Ron Hassey, c-1, dh-1	.333	2	3	0	1	0	0	0	0	2	0	0
Dave Henderson, of	.167	2	6	0	1	0	0	0	1	0	2	1
Rickey Henderson, of	.294	4	17	1	5	0	0	0	3	1	2	2
Rick Honeycutt, p	.000	3	0	0	0	0	0	0	0	0	0	0
Doug Jennings, of	.000	1	1	0	0	0	0	0	0	0	0	0
Carney Lansford, 3b	.438	4	16	2	7	1	0	0	2	0	1	0
Willie McGee, of-2, dh-1	.222	3	9	3	2	1	0	0	0	1	2	2
Mark McGwire, 1b	.154	4	13	2	2	0	0	0	2	3	3	0
Mike Moore, p	.000	1	0	0	0	0	0	0	0	0	0	0
Gene Nelson, p	.000	1	0	0	0	0	0	0	0	0	0	0
Jamie Quirk, p	1.000	1	1	0	1	0	0	0	0	0	0	0
Willie Randolph, 2b	.375	4	8	1	3	0	0	0	3	1	0	0
Terry Steinbach, c	.455	3	11	2	5	0	0	0	1	1	2	0
Dave Stewart, p	.000	2	0	0	0	0	0	0	0	0	0	0
Walt Weiss, ss	.000	2	7	2	0	0	0	0	0	2	2	0
Bob Welch, p	.000	1	0	0	0	0	0	0	0	0	0	0
TOTAL	.299		127	20	38	4	0	0	18	19	21	9

PITCHER	W	L	ERA	G	GS	CG	SV	SHO	IP	H	ER	BB	SO
Dennis Eckersley	0	0	0.00	3	0	0	2	0	3.1	2	0	0	3
Rick Honeycutt	0	0	0.00	3	0	0	1	0	1.2	0	0	0	0
Mike Moore	1	0	1.50	1	1	0	0	0	6.0	4	1	1	5
Gene Nelson	0	0	0.00	1	0	0	0	0	1.2	3	0	0	0
Dave Stewart	2	0	1.13	2	2	0	0	0	16.0	8	2	2	4
Bob Welch	1	0	1.23	1	1	0	0	0	7.1	6	1	3	4
TOTAL	4	0	1.00	11	4	0	3	0	36.0	23	4	6	16

BOS (E)

PLAYER/POS	AVG	G	AB	R	H	2B	3B	HR	RB	BB	SO	SB
Larry Andersen, p	.000	3	0	0	0	0	0	0	0	0	0	0
Marty Barrett, 2b	.000	3	0	0	0	0	0	0	0	0	0	0
Mike Boddicker, p	.000	1	0	0	0	0	0	0	0	0	0	0
Wade Boggs, 3b	.438	4	16	1	7	1	0	1	1	0	3	0
Tom Bolton, p	.000	2	0	0	0	0	0	0	0	0	0	0
Tom Brunansky, of	.083	4	12	0	1	0	0	0	1	1	3	0
Ellis Burks, of	.267	4	15	1	4	2	0	0	0	1	1	1
Roger Clemens, p	.000	2	0	0	0	0	0	0	0	0	0	0
Dwight Evans, dh	.231	4	13	0	3	1	0	0	0	1	3	0
Jeff Gray, p	.000	2	0	0	0	0	0	0	0	0	0	0
Mike Greenwell, of	.000	4	14	1	0	0	0	0	0	2	2	0
Greg Harris, p	.000	1	0	0	0	0	0	0	0	0	0	0
Danny Heep, ph	.000	2	2	0	0	0	0	0	0	0	0	0
Dana Kiecker, p	.000	1	0	0	0	0	0	0	0	0	0	0
Randy Kutcher, pr	.000	2	0	0	0	0	0	0	0	0	0	0
Dennis Lamp, p	.000	1	0	0	0	0	0	0	0	0	0	0
Mike Marshall, ph	.333	3	3	0	1	0	0	0	0	0	0	0
Rob Murphy, p	.000	1	0	0	0	0	0	0	0	0	0	0
Tony Pena, c	.214	4	14	0	3	0	0	0	0	0	0	0
Carlos Quintana, 1b	.000	4	13	0	0	0	0	0	1	1	0	0
Jeff Reardon, p	.000	1	0	0	0	0	0	0	0	0	0	0
Jody Reed, 2b-4, ss-3	.133	4	15	0	2	0	0	0	1	0	2	0
Luis Rivera, ss	.222	4	9	1	2	1	0	0	0	0	2	0
TOTAL	.183		126	4	23	5	0	1	4	6	16	1

PITCHER	W	L	ERA	G	GS	CG	SV	SHO	IP	H	ER	BB	SO
Larry Andersen	0	1	6.00	3	0	0	0	0	3.0	3	2	3	3
Mike Boddicker	0	1	2.25	1	1	1	0	0	8.0	6	2	3	7
Tom Bolton	0	0	0.00	2	0	0	0	0	3.0	2	0	2	3
Roger Clemens	0	1	3.52	2	2	0	0	0	7.2	7	3	5	4
Jeff Gray	0	0	2.70	2	0	0	0	0	3.1	4	1	1	2
Greg Harris	0	1	27.00	1	0	0	0	0	0.1	3	1	0	0
Dana Kiecker	0	0	1.59	1	1	0	0	0	5.2	6	1	1	2
Dennis Lamp	0	0	108.00	1	0	0	0	0	0.1	2	4	2	0
Rob Murphy	0	0	13.50	1	0	0	0	0	0.2	2	1	1	0
Jeff Reardon	0	0	9.00	1	0	0	0	0	2.0	3	2	1	0
TOTAL	0	4	4.50	15	4	1	0	0	34.0	38	17	19	21

GAME 1 AT BOS OCT 6

```
OAK 000 000 117    9 13 0
BOS 000 100 000    1  5 1
```
Pitchers: STEWART, Eckersley (9) vs Clemens, ANDERSEN (7), Bolton (8), Gray (8), Lamp (9), Murphy (9)
Home Runs: Boggs-BOS
Attendance: 35,192

GAME 2 AT BOS OCT 7

```
OAK 000 100 102    4 13 1
BOS 001 000 000    1  6 0
```
Pitchers: WELCH, Honeycutt (8), Eckersley (8) vs Kiecker, HARRIS (6), Andersen (7), Reardon (8)
Attendance: 35,070

GAME 3 AT OAK OCT 9

```
BOS 010 000 000    1  8 3
OAK 000 202 00X    4  6 0
```
Pitchers: BODDICKER vs MOORE, Nelson (7), Honeycutt (8), Eckersley (9)
Attendance: 49,026

GAME 4 AT OAK OCT 10

```
BOS 000 000 001    1  4 1
OAK 030 000 00X    3  6 0
```
Pitchers: CLEMENS, Bolton (2), Gray (5), Andersen (8) vs STEWART, Honeycutt (9)
Attendance: 49,052

CINCINNATI REDS (NL) 4, OAKLAND A'S (WEST) 0

In the most stunning World Series sweep since 1954, Cincinnati's fired-up Reds roasted the team many were proclaiming baseball's newest dynasty. Reds left fielder Eric Davis, playing despite shoulder and knee injuries, provided the A's their first hint of what was to come when—on the first pitch thrown to him in the first inning—he homered over the center field wall for two runs. Billy Hatcher, on base with a walk, scored ahead of Davis, the first of his Series-high six runs. Hatcher would not be retired at the plate until Game 3. For Oakland starter Dave Stewart, the 7-0 loss in Game 1 ended a personal postseason six-game win streak. For the club, the loss ended a streak of 10 postseason wins in a row.

The A's put up their best fight of the Series in Game 2, scoring first, then overcoming a 2–1 deficit in the third inning with three more runs for a 4–2 lead. Cincinnati narrowed the gap with a run in the fourth and tied the score in the eighth when Hatcher tripled—setting a World Series record with his seventh straight hit—and came home on a grounder to short. The A's held on until the 10th inning, when ace reliever Dennis Eckersley gave up three straight hits to lose the game.

Game 3 was another Cincinnati blowout, an 8–3 contest in which all 11 runs were scored in the second and third innings. Chris Sabo led the Reds assault with two home runs, and handled a Series-record 10 chances at third base.

For seven innings of Game 4 the tide of battle seemed to be turning in Oakland's favor. Billy Hatcher —who was batting .750— left the game after a pitch hit his hand in the first inning. Later in the inning Eric Davis tore a kidney diving for a Willie McGee shot that went for a double. McGee went on to score, and Davis departed for the hospital. A renewed Dave Stewart, supported by sharp fielding, seemed capable of sustaining his 1–0 lead to the finish. But in the eighth the Reds, with just one solid hit, eked out the two runs they would need for victory. After loading the bases with a leadoff single, a third-strike bunt that went for a hit, and a sacrifice bunt that Stewart misplayed for an error, the

Reds drove home the tying run with a grounder to short and took the lead on a sacrifice fly. Meanwhile Reds starter Jose Rijo held the A's hitless after the first inning, leveling 20 men in order from the second into the ninth, when ace closer Randy Myers relieved him for the final two outs of the sweep.

CIN (N)

PLAYER/POS	AVG	G	AB	R	H	2B	3B	HR	RB	BB	SO	SB
Jack Armstrong, p	.000	1	0	0	0	0	0	0	0	0	0	0
Billy Bates, ph	1.000	1	1	1	1	0	0	0	0	0	0	0
Todd Benzinger, 1b-3	.182	4	11	1	2	0	0	0	0	0	0	0
Glenn Braggs, of-1	.000	2	4	0	0	0	0	0	2	1	0	0
Tom Browning, p	.000	1	0	0	0	0	0	0	0	0	0	0
Norm Charlton, p	.000	1	0	0	0	0	0	0	0	0	0	0
Eric Davis, of	.286	4	14	3	4	0	0	1	5	0	0	0
Rob Dibble, p	.000	3	0	0	0	0	0	0	0	0	0	0
Mariano Duncan, 2b	.143	4	14	1	2	0	0	0	1	2	2	1
Billy Hatcher, of	.750	4	12	6	9	4	1	0	2	2	0	0
Danny Jackson, p	.000	1	1	0	0	0	0	0	0	0	1	0
Barry Larkin, ss	.353	4	17	3	6	1	1	0	1	2	0	0
Hal Morris, 1b-2, dh-2	.071	4	14	0	1	0	0	0	2	1	1	0
Randy Myers, p	.000	3	0	0	0	0	0	0	0	0	0	0
Ron Oester, ph	1.000	1	1	0	1	0	0	0	0	1	0	0
Joe Oliver, c	.333	4	18	2	6	3	0	0	2	0	1	0
Paul O'Neill, of	.083	4	12	2	1	0	0	0	1	5	2	1
Jose Rijo, p	.333	2	3	0	1	0	0	0	0	0	0	0
Chris Sabo, 3b	.563	4	16	2	9	1	0	2	5	2	2	0
Scott Scudder, p	.000	1	0	0	0	0	0	0	0	0	0	0
Herm Winningham, of-1	.500	2	4	1	2	0	0	0	0	0	0	0
TOTAL	.317		142	22	45	9	2	3	22	15	9	2

PITCHER	W	L	ERA	G	GS	CG	SV	SHO	IP	H	ER	BB	SO
Jack Armstrong	0	0	0.00	1	0	0	0	0	3.0	1	0	0	3
Tom Browning	1	0	4.50	1	1	0	0	0	6.0	6	3	2	2
Norm Charlton	0	0	0.00	1	0	0	0	0	1.0	1	0	0	0
Rob Dibble	1	0	0.00	3	0	0	0	0	4.2	3	0	1	4
Danny Jackson	0	0	10.13	1	1	0	0	0	2.2	6	3	2	0
Randy Myers	0	0	0.00	3	0	0	1	0	3.0	2	0	0	3
Jose Rijo	2	0	0.59	2	2	0	0	0	15.1	9	1	5	14
Scott Scudder	0	0	0.00	1	0	0	0	0	1.1	0	0	2	2
TOTAL	4	0	1.70	13	4	0	1	0	37.0	28	7	12	28

OAK (A)

PLAYER/POS	AVG	G	AB	R	H	2B	3B	HR	RB	BB	SO	SB
Harold Baines, dh-2	.143	3	7	1	1	0	0	1	2	1	2	0
Lance Blankenship, ph	.000	1	1	0	0	0	0	0	0	0	1	0
Mike Bordick, ss	.000	3	0	0	0	0	0	0	0	0	0	0
Todd Burns, p	.000	2	0	0	0	0	0	0	0	0	0	0
Jose Canseco, of-3, dh-1	.083	4	12	1	1	0	0	1	2	2	3	0
Dennis Eckersley, p	.000	2	0	0	0	0	0	0	0	0	0	0
Mike Gallego, ss	.091	4	11	0	1	0	0	0	1	1	3	1
Ron Hassey, c-1	.333	3	6	0	2	0	0	0	1	0	0	0
Dave Henderson, of-3	.231	4	13	2	3	1	0	0	0	1	3	0
Rickey Henderson, of	.333	4	15	2	5	2	0	1	1	3	4	3
Rick Honeycutt, p	.000	1	0	0	0	0	0	0	0	0	0	0
Doug Jennings, ph	1.000	1	1	0	1	0	0	0	0	0	0	0
Joe Klink, p	.000	1	0	0	0	0	0	0	0	0	0	0
Carney Lansford, 3b	.267	4	15	0	4	0	0	0	1	1	0	0
Willie McGee, of-3	.200	4	10	1	2	1	0	0	0	0	2	1
Mark McGwire, 1b	.214	4	14	1	3	0	0	0	0	2	4	0
Mike Moore, p	.000	1	0	0	0	0	0	0	0	0	0	0
Gene Nelson, p	.000	2	0	0	0	0	0	0	0	0	0	0
Jamie Quirk, c	.000	1	3	0	0	0	0	0	0	0	2	0
Willie Randolph, 2b	.267	4	15	0	4	0	0	0	0	1	0	1
Scott Sanderson, p	.000	2	0	0	0	0	0	0	0	0	0	0
Terry Steinbach, c	.125	3	8	0	1	0	0	0	0	0	1	0
Dave Stewart, p	.000	2	1	0	0	0	0	0	0	0	1	0
Bob Welch, p	.000	1	3	0	0	0	0	0	0	0	2	0
Curt Young, p	.000	1	0	0	0	0	0	0	0	0	0	0
TOTAL	.207		135	8	28	4	0	3	8	12	28	7

PITCHER	W	L	ERA	G	GS	CG	SV	SHO	IP	H	ER	BB	SO
Todd Burns	0	0	16.20	2	0	0	0	0	1.2	5	3	2	0
Dennis Eckersley	0	1	6.75	2	0	0	0	0	1.1	3	1	0	1
Rick Honeycutt	0	0	0.00	1	0	0	0	0	1.2	2	0	1	0
Joe Klink	0	0	—	1	0	0	0	0	0.0	0	0	1	0
Mike Moore	0	1	6.75	1	1	0	0	0	2.2	8	2	0	1
Gene Nelson	0	0	0.00	2	0	0	0	0	5.0	3	0	2	0
Scott Sanderson	0	0	10.80	2	0	0	0	0	1.2	4	2	1	0
Dave Stewart	0	2	3.46	2	2	1	0	0	13.0	10	5	6	5
Bob Welch	0	0	4.91	1	1	0	0	0	7.1	9	4	2	2
Curt Young	0	0	0.00	1	0	0	0	0	1.0	1	0	0	0
TOTAL	0	4	4.33	15	4	1	0	0	35.1	45	17	15	9

GAME 1 AT CIN OCT 16
```
OAK 000 000 000   0  9 1
CIN 202 030 00X   7 10 0
```
Pitchers: STEWART, Burns (5), Nelson (5), Sanderson (7), Eckersley (8) vs RIJO, Dibble (8), Myers (9)
Home Runs: Davis-CIN
Attendance: 55,830

GAME 2 AT CIN OCT 17
```
OAK 103 000 000 0   4 10 2
CIN 200 100 010 1   5 14 2
```
Pitchers: Welch, Honeycutt (8), ECKERSLEY (10) vs Jackson, Scudder (3), Armstrong (5), Charlton (8), DIBBLE (9)
Home Runs: Canseco-OAK
Attendance: 55,832

GAME 3 AT OAK OCT 19
```
CIN 017 000 000   8 14 1
OAK 021 000 000   3  7 1
```
Pitchers: BROWNING, Dibble (7), Myers (8) vs MOORE, Sanderson (3), Klink (4), Nelson (4), Burns (8), Young (9)
Home Runs: Sabo-CIN (2), Baines-OAK, R.Henderson-OAK
Attendance: 48,269

GAME 4 AT OAK OCT 20
```
CIN 000 000 020   2  7 1
OAK 100 000 000   1  2 1
```
Pitchers: RIJO, Myers (9) vs STEWART
Attendance: 48,613

ATLANTA BRAVES (WEST) 4, PITTSBURGH PIRATES (EAST) 3

Pitching dominated this back-and-forth series which featured four shutouts, including three 1–0 games. Three times Atlanta hurlers blanked Pittsburgh on the Pirates' home grounds. Andy Van Slyke opened the series scoring with a first-inning home run. Pirates starter Doug Drabek held the Braves scoreless through six innings of the opener, before injuring himself on the basepaths. By the time David Justice homered in the ninth for Atlanta's only score, the Pirates had the game well in hand.

Atlanta evened the series in Game 2 behind the pitching of Steve Avery and Alejandro Pena, and the bat and glove of Mark Lemke. The Braves' second baseman doubled home that game's only run in the sixth inning and prevented a Pittsburgh run from scoring in the eighth with a diving stop of a grounder up the middle. In Atlanta for Game 3, the Braves took the series lead with a 10–3 rout that featured home runs by Ron Gant, Greg Olson, and Sid Bream. (Orlando Merced and Jay Bell homered for Pittsburgh.)

Game 4 was much closer. The Braves took a quick lead with two first-inning runs, but Pittsburgh scored once in the second and tied the game in the fifth on a throwing error. In the top of the 10th, Andy Van Slyke led off with a walk. With two away he stole second, and then scored what proved the winning run on Don Slaught's double. With the series even again, Atlanta lost a run in Game 5 when David Justice was ruled out for missing third base as he dashed home from second. An inning later the Pirates parlayed a walk and a pair of singles into the only run they would need to carry the series advantage back to Pittsburgh.

In Game 6, though, the Braves returned the favor, tying the series once more with a gem of their own. Avery and Pena combined for their second 1–0 victory, while Drabek held the Braves scoreless into the ninth, when Olson doubled home the game's only run.

In the finale, John Smoltz enjoyed a three-run lead when he took the mound in the bottom of the first inning. Rookie first baseman Brian Hunter (who had homered for two of the first-inning runs) doubled in an additional Atlanta run in the fifth. Meanwhile

Smoltz stopped the Pirates on six hits to bring the Braves their first pennant since their move to Atlanta in 1966.

ATL (W)

PLAYER/POS	AVG	G	AB	R	H	2B	3B	HR	RB	BB	SO	SB
Steve Avery, p	.143	2	7	0	1	0	0	0	0	0	4	0
Rafael Belliard, ss	.211	7	19	0	4	0	0	0	1	3	3	0
Jeff Blauser, ss	.000	2	2	0	0	0	0	0	0	0	0	0
Sid Bream, 1b	.300	4	10	1	3	0	0	1	3	0	1	0
Jim Clancy, p	.000	1	0	0	0	0	0	0	0	0	0	0
Ron Gant, of	.259	7	27	4	7	1	0	1	3	2	4	7
Tom Glavine, p	.250	2	4	0	1	0	0	0	0	0	2	0
Tommy Gregg, ph	.250	4	4	0	1	0	0	0	0	0	2	0
Brian Hunter, 1b	.333	5	18	2	6	2	0	1	4	0	2	0
David Justice, of	.200	7	25	4	5	1	0	1	2	3	7	0
Charlie Leibrandt, p	.000	1	1	0	0	0	0	0	0	0	0	0
Mark Lemke, 2b	.200	7	20	1	4	1	0	0	1	4	0	0
Kent Mercker, p	.000	1	0	0	0	0	0	0	0	0	0	0
Keith Mitchell, of	.000	5	4	0	0	0	0	0	0	0	1	0
Greg Olson, c	.333	7	24	3	8	1	0	1	4	4	3	1
Alejandro Pena, p	.000	4	0	0	0	0	0	0	0	0	0	0
Terry Pendleton, 3b	.167	7	30	1	5	1	1	0	1	1	3	0
Lonnie Smith, of	.250	7	24	3	6	3	0	0	4	5	1	4
John Smoltz, p	.200	2	5	0	1	0	0	0	1	4	1	0
Mike Stanton, p	.000	3	0	0	0	0	0	0	0	0	0	0
Jeff Treadway, 2b	.333	1	3	0	1	0	0	0	0	0	0	0
Jerry Willard, ph	.000	2	2	0	0	0	0	0	0	0	1	0
Mark Wohlers, p	.000	3	0	0	0	0	0	0	0	0	0	0
TOTAL	.231		229	19	53	10	1	5	19	22	42	10

PITCHER	W	L	ERA	G	GS	CG	SV	SHO	IP	H	ER	BB	SO
Steve Avery	2	0	0.00	2	2	0	0	0	16.1	9	0	4	17
Jim Clancy	0	0	0.00	1	0	0	0	0	0.1	0	0	0	0
Tom Glavine	0	2	3.21	2	2	0	0	0	14.0	12	5	6	11
Charlie Leibrandt	0	0	1.35	1	1	0	0	0	6.2	8	1	3	6
Kent Mercker	0	1	13.50	1	0	0	0	0	0.2	0	1	2	0
Alejandro Pena	0	0	0.00	4	0	0	3	0	4.1	1	0	0	4
John Smoltz	2	0	1.76	2	2	1	0	1	15.1	14	3	3	15
Mike Stanton	0	0	2.45	3	0	0	0	0	3.2	4	1	3	3
Mark Wohlers	0	0	0.00	3	0	0	0	0	1.2	3	0	1	1
TOTAL	4	3	1.57	19	7	1	3	1	63.0	51	11	22	57

PIT (E)

PLAYER/POS	AVG	G	AB	R	H	2B	3B	HR	RB	BB	SO	SB
Stan Belinda, p	.000	3	0	0	0	0	0	0	0	0	0	0
Jay Bell, ss	.414	7	29	2	12	2	0	1	1	0	10	0
Barry Bonds, of	.148	7	27	1	4	1	0	0	0	2	4	3
Bobby Bonilla, of	.304	7	23	2	7	2	0	0	1	6	2	0
Steve Buechele, 3b	.304	7	23	2	7	2	0	0	0	4	6	0
Doug Drabek, p	.200	2	5	0	1	1	0	0	1	0	2	0
Cecil Espy, of	.000	2	2	0	0	0	0	0	0	0	2	0
Bob Kipper, p	.000	1	0	0	0	0	0	0	0	0	0	0
Bill Landrum, p	.000	1	0	0	0	0	0	0	0	0	0	0
Mike LaValliere, c	.333	3	6	0	2	0	0	0	1	2	0	0
Jose Lind, 2b	.160	7	25	0	4	0	0	0	3	0	6	0
Roger Mason, p	.000	3	1	0	0	0	0	0	0	0	1	0
Lloyd McClendon, 1b-1	.000	3	2	0	0	0	0	0	0	1	0	0
Orlando Merced, 1b-2	.222	3	9	1	2	0	0	1	1	0	1	0
Bob Patterson, p	.000	1	0	0	0	0	0	0	0	0	0	0
Gary Redus, 1b	.158	5	19	1	3	0	0	0	0	1	4	2
Rosario Rodriguez, p	.000	1	0	0	0	0	0	0	0	0	0	0
Don Slaught, c	.235	6	17	0	4	1	0	0	1	1	4	0
John Smiley, p	.000	2	0	0	0	0	0	0	0	0	0	0
Zane Smith, p	.000	2	5	0	0	0	0	0	0	0	4	0
Randy Tomlin, p	.000	1	2	0	0	0	0	0	0	0	0	0
Andy Van Slyke, of	.160	7	25	3	4	2	0	1	2	5	5	1
Gary Varsho, ph	.500	2	2	0	1	0	0	0	0	0	1	0
Bob Walk, p	.000	3	2	0	0	0	0	0	0	0	2	0
Curtis Wilkerson, ph	.000	4	4	0	0	0	0	0	0	0	3	0
TOTAL	.224		228	12	51	10	0	3	11	22	57	6

PITCHER	W	L	ERA	G	GS	CG	SV	SHO	IP	H	ER	BB	SO
Stan Belinda	1	0	0.00	3	0	0	0	0	5.0	0	0	3	4
Doug Drabek	1	1	0.60	2	2	1	0	0	15.0	10	1	5	10
Bob Kipper	0	0	4.50	1	0	0	0	0	2.0	2	1	0	1
Bill Landrum	0	0	9.00	1	0	0	0	0	1.0	2	1	2	2
Roger Mason	0	0	0.00	3	0	0	1	0	4.1	3	0	1	2
Bob Patterson	0	0	0.00	1	0	0	0	0	2.0	1	0	0	3
Rosario Rodriguez	0	0	27.00	1	0	0	0	0	1.0	1	3	2	1
John Smiley	0	2	23.63	2	2	0	0	0	2.2	8	7	1	3
Zane Smith	1	1	0.61	2	2	0	0	0	14.2	15	1	3	10
Randy Tomlin	0	0	3.00	1	1	0	0	0	6.0	6	2	2	1
Bob Walk	0	0	1.93	3	0	0	1	0	9.1	5	2	3	5
TOTAL	3	4	2.57	20	7	1	2	0	63.0	53	18	22	42

GAME 1 AT PIT OCT 9

```
ATL  000 000 001   1 5 1
PIT  102 001 01X   5 8 1
```
Pitchers: GLAVINE, Wohlers (7), Stanton (8) vs DRABEK, Walk (7)
Home Runs: Van Slyke-PIT, Justice-ATL
Attendance: 57,347

GAME 2 AT PIT OCT 10

```
ATL  000 001 000   1 8 0
PIT  000 000 000   0 6 0
```
Pitchers: AVERY, Pena (9) vs SMITH, Mason (8), Belinda (9)
Attendance: 57,533

GAME 3 AT ATL OCT 12

```
PIT  100 100 100   3 10 2
ATL  411 000 13X  10 11 0
```
Pitchers: SMILEY, Landrum (3), Patterson (4, Kipper (6), Rodriguez (8) vs SMOLTZ, Stanton (7), Wohlers (8), Pena (8)
Home Runs: Merced-PIT, Bell-PIT, Gant-ATL, Olson-ATL, Bream-ATL
Attendance: 50,905

GAME 4 AT ATL OCT 13

```
PIT  010 010 000 1   3 11 1
ATL  200 000 000 0   2 7 1
```
Pitchers: Tomlin, Walk (7), BELINDA (9) vs Leibrandt, Clancy (7), Stanton (8), MERCKER (10), Wohlers (10)
Attendance: 51,109

GAME 5 AT ATL OCT 14

```
PIT  000 010 000   1 6 2
ATL  000 000 000   0 9 1
```
Pitchers: SMITH, Mason (8) vs GLAVINE, Pena (9)
Attendance: 51,109

GAME 6 AT PIT OCT 16

```
ATL  000 000 001   1 7 0
PIT  000 000 000   0 4 0
```
Pitchers: AVERY, Pena (9) vs DRABEK
Attendance: 54,508

GAME 7 AT PIT OCT 17

```
ATL  300 010 000   4 6 1
PIT  000 000 000   0 6 0
```
Pitchers: SMOLTZ vs SMILEY, Walk (1), Mason (6), Belinda (8)
Home Runs: Hunter-ATL
Attendance: 46,932

MINNESOTA TWINS (WEST) 4, TORONTO BLUE JAYS (EAST) 1

Minnesota struggled to achieve a 2–1 advantage in the first three games, then blew the Jays out of the SkyDome in the next two. Game 1 looked as though it would be an easy win for the Twins, who drove out starter Tom Candiotti with five runs on eight hits in the first two and two thirds innings. But Toronto scored once in the fourth and chased Twins starter Jack Morris in the sixth with five straight singles and three more runs. Relievers Carl Willis and Rick Aguilera, though, held Toronto to just one more single to preserve the victory for Minnesota.

The Jays scored three times in Game 2 before Minnesota put its first run across in the last of the third, and scored twice more in the seventh, taking their first—and, as it turned out, only—win behind the strong pitching of rookie Juan Guzman and relievers Tom Henke and Duane Ward. Toronto again scored early in Game 3, with a pair of two-out runs (one of them Joe Carter's homer) in the first inning. Jays starter Jimmy Key held the Twins scoreless until they got to him for a run in the fifth, and another in the sixth which evened the score. Meanwhile a string of Minnesota pitchers stifled the Blue Jays from the second inning on. In the 10th, pinch hitter Mike Pagliarulo won it for the Twins with a home run to right.

For the third game in a row, Toronto scored first, with a run in the second inning of Game 4. But Minnesota's Kirby Puckett homered in the fourth to tie the score, and by the time Toronto scored again two innings later, the Twins had upped its run total to six. Puckett's home run in the first inning of Game 5 gave the Twins the first of two early runs, but the Jays came back with three runs in the third and two more in the fourth to drive out starter Kevin Tapani. They scored no more, however, as three Twins relievers held them to one single in the final five frames. In the sixth inning, Minnesota reawakened to tie the game with a trio of runs, and salted it—and the pennant—away in the eighth: with two out, Puckett doubled home the go-ahead run, and Kent Hrbek singled in two more for insurance.

MIN (W)

PLAYER/POS	AVG	G	AB	R	H	2B	3B	HR	RB	BB	SO	SB
Rick Aguilera, p	.000	3	0	0	0	0	0	0	0	0	0	0
Steve Bedrosian, p	.000	2	0	0	0	0	0	0	0	0	0	0
Jarvis Brown, dh	.000	1	0	1	0	0	0	0	0	0	0	0
Chili Davis, dh	.294	5	17	3	5	2	0	0	2	5	8	1
Scott Erickson, p	.000	1	0	0	0	0	0	0	0	0	0	0
Greg Gagne, ss	.235	5	17	1	4	0	0	0	1	1	5	0
Dan Gladden, of	.261	5	23	4	6	0	0	0	3	1	3	3
Mark Guthrie, p	.000	2	0	0	0	0	0	0	0	0	0	0
Brian Harper, c	.278	5	18	1	5	2	0	0	1	0	2	0
Kent Hrbek, 1b	.143	5	21	0	3	0	0	0	3	1	3	0
Chuck Knoblauch, 2b	.350	5	20	5	7	2	0	0	3	3	3	2
Gene Larkin, ph	.000	3	3	0	0	0	0	0	0	0	1	0
Scott Leius, 3b	.000	3	4	0	0	0	0	0	0	1	1	0
Shane Mack, of	.333	5	18	4	6	1	1	0	3	2	4	2
Jack Morris, p	.000	2	0	0	0	0	0	0	0	0	0	0
Al Newman, 2b-1,3b-1	.000	2	0	0	0	0	0	0	0	0	0	0
Junior Ortiz, c	.000	3	3	0	0	0	0	0	0	0	0	0
Mike Pagliarulo, 3b	.333	5	15	4	5	1	0	1	3	0	2	0
Kirby Puckett, of	.429	5	21	4	9	1	0	2	6	1	4	0
Paul Sorrento, ph	.000	1	1	0	0	0	0	0	0	0	1	0
Kevin Tapani, p	.000	2	0	0	0	0	0	0	0	0	0	0
David West, p	.000	2	0	0	0	0	0	0	0	0	0	0
Carl Willis, p	.000	3	0	0	0	0	0	0	0	0	0	0
TOTAL	.276		181	27	50	9	1	3	25	15	37	8

PITCHER	W	L	ERA	G	GS	CG	SV	SHO	IP	H	ER	BB	SO
Rick Aguilera	0	0	0.00	3	0	0	3	0	3.1	1	0	0	3
Steve Bedrosian	0	0	0.00	2	0	0	0	0	1.1	3	0	2	2
Scott Erickson	0	0	4.50	1	1	0	0	0	4.0	3	2	5	2
Mark Guthrie	1	0	0.00	2	0	0	0	0	2.2	0	0	0	0
Jack Morris	2	0	4.05	2	2	0	0	0	13.1	17	6	1	7
Kevin Tapani	0	1	7.84	2	2	0	0	0	10.1	16	9	3	9
David West	1	0	0.00	2	0	0	0	0	5.2	1	0	4	4
Carl Willis	0	0	0.00	3	0	0	0	0	5.1	2	0	0	3
TOTAL	4	1	3.33	17	5	0	3	0	46.0	43	17	15	30

TOR (E)

PLAYER/POS	AVG	G	AB	R	H	2B	3B	HR	RB	BB	SO	SB
Jim Acker, p	.000	1	0	0	0	0	0	0	0	0	0	0
Roberto Alomar, 2b	.474	5	19	3	9	0	0	0	4	2	3	2
Pat Borders, c	.263	5	19	0	5	1	0	0	2	0	0	0
Tom Candiotti, p	.000	2	0	0	0	0	0	0	0	0	0	0
Joe Carter, of-3, dh-2	.263	5	19	3	5	2	0	1	4	1	5	0
Rob Ducey, of	.000	1	1	0	0	0	0	0	0	0	0	0
Rene Gonzales, 1b-1, ss-1	.000	2	0	0	0	0	0	0	0	0	0	0
Kelly Gruber, 3b	.286	5	21	1	6	1	0	0	4	0	4	1
Juan Guzman, p	.000	1	0	0	0	0	0	0	0	0	0	0
Tom Henke, p	.000	2	0	0	0	0	0	0	0	0	0	0
Jimmy Key, p	.000	1	0	0	0	0	0	0	0	0	0	0
Manuel Lee, ss	.125	5	16	3	2	0	0	0	0	1	5	0
Rob MacDonald, p	.000	1	0	0	0	0	0	0	0	0	0	0
Candy Maldonado, of	.100	5	20	1	2	1	0	0	1	1	6	0
Rance Mulliniks, dh-3	.125	5	8	1	1	0	0	0	0	3	0	0
John Olerud, 1b	.158	5	19	1	3	0	0	0	3	3	1	0
Todd Stottlemyre, p	.000	1	0	0	0	0	0	0	0	0	0	0
Pat Tabler, dh	.000	2	1	0	0	0	0	0	0	1	0	0
Mike Timlin, p	.000	4	0	0	0	0	0	0	0	0	0	0
Duane Ward, p	.000	2	0	0	0	0	0	0	0	0	0	0
David Wells, p	.000	4	0	0	0	0	0	0	0	0	0	0
Devon White, of	.364	5	22	5	8	1	0	0	0	2	3	3
Mookie Wilson, of-2	.250	3	8	1	2	0	0	0	0	1	3	1
TOTAL	.249		173	19	43	6	0	1	18	15	30	7

PITCHER	W	L	ERA	G	GS	CG	SV	SHO	IP	H	ER	BB	SO
Jim Acker	0	0	0.00	1	0	0	0	0	0.2	1	0	0	1
Tom Candiotti	0	1	8.22	2	2	0	0	0	7.2	17	7	2	5
Juan Guzman	1	0	3.18	1	1	0	0	0	5.2	4	2	4	2
Tom Henke	0	0	0.00	2	0	0	0	0	2.2	0	0	1	5
Jimmy Key	0	0	3.00	1	1	0	0	0	6.0	5	2	1	1
Rob MacDonald	0	0	9.00	1	0	0	0	0	1.0	1	1	1	0
Todd Stottlemyre	0	1	9.82	1	1	0	0	0	3.2	7	4	1	3
Mike Timlin	0	1	3.18	4	0	0	0	0	5.2	5	2	2	5
Duane Ward	0	1	6.23	2	0	0	1	0	4.1	4	3	1	6
David Wells	0	0	2.35	4	0	0	0	0	7.2	6	2	2	9
TOTAL	1	4	4.60	19	5	0	1	0	45.0	50	23	15	37

GAME 1 AT MIN OCT 8

TOR 000 103 000   4 9 3
MIN 221 000 00X   5 11 0
Pitchers: CANDIOTTI, Wells (3), Timlin (6) vs MORRIS, Willis (6), Aguilera (8)
Attendance: 54,766

GAME 2 AT MIN OCT 9

TOR 102 000 200   5 9 0
MIN 001 001 000   2 5 1
Pitchers: GUZMAN, Henke (6), Ward (8) vs TAPANI, Bedrosian (7), Guthrie (7)
Attendance: 54,816

GAME 3 AT TOR OCT 13

MIN 000 011 0001   3 7 0
TOR 200 000 0000   2 5 1
Pitchers: Erickson, West (5), Willis (7), GUTHRIE (9), Aguilera (10) vs Key, Wells (7), Henke (8), TIMLIN (10)
Home Runs: Carter-TOR, Pagliarulo-MIN
Attendance: 51,454

GAME 4 AT TOR OCT 12

MIN 000 402 111   9 13 1
TOR 010 001 001   3 11 2
Pitchers: MORRIS, Bedrosian (9) vs STOTTLEMYRE, Wells (4), Acker (6), Timlin (7), MacDonald (9)
Home Runs: Puckett-MIN
Attendance: 51,526

GAME 5 AT TOR OCT 13

MIN 110 003 030   8 14 2
TOR 003 200 000   5 9 1
Pitchers: Tapani, WEST (5), Willis (8), Aguilera (9) vs Candiotti, Timlin (6), WARD (6), Wells (8)
Home Runs: Puckett-MIN
Attendance: 51,425

MINNESOTA TWINS (AL) 4, ATLANTA BRAVES (NL) 3

By any measure, this World Series was one of the great ones. Five of the seven games were decided by a single run, three of them—including Games 6 and 7—in extra innings. The opener in Minnesota gave no indication of the suspense to come, as the Twins opened up a 4–0 lead in the fifth inning en route to a 5–2 win. Game 2 proved more difficult. Chili Davis put the Twins in front with a two-run homer in the first inning, but in the fifth Atlanta tied the score. Braves hurler Tom Glavine lost the game when the Twins' Scott Leius lofted a homer to lead off the eighth.

Minnesota took a quick lead in Game 3, but Atlanta tied the game an inning later, and went ahead on solo homers by David Justice in the fourth inning and Lonnie Smith in the fifth. Home runs by Kirby Puckett and Chili Davis in the fifth and sixth re-tied the score, which remained at 4–4 into the last of the 11th inning, when Justice scored from second on Mark Lemke's two-out single. Lemke's heroics also made the difference in Game 4. Mike Pagliarulo drove in a pair of runs for Minnesota with a single in the second and a home run in the seventh, but Braves Terry Pendleton and Lonnie Smith neutralized the runs with solo homers in the third and seventh. Lemke came to bat in the bottom of the ninth with one out and the score still 2–2. He tripled, and scored in a tight play to even the Series.

In Game 5 the Braves assaulted five Minnesota pitchers for 14 runs and the Series lead, but when play returned to Minnesota for Game 6 the Twins revived with two first inning runs. In the third inning Puckett prevented two Atlanta runs with a leaping catch above the wall, but in the fifth, Atlanta's Terry Pendleton evened the score with a two-run homer. Later in the inning the Twins regained the lead on Puckett's sacrifice fly. Atlanta knotted the score again in the seventh. In the last of the 11th, Puckett lined the ball over the wall.

No one scored through 9-1/2 innings of Game 7 as Minnesota's Jack Morris dueled John Smoltz, Mike Stanton, and Alejandro Pena. Thus the game was still scoreless in the last of the 10th when Dan Gladden hustled his way into a broken-bat double and moved to

third on Chuck Knoblauch's sacrifice bunt. Then, after the bases were loaded intentionally, pinch hitter Gene Larkin lobbed a hit over the head of the drawn-in left fielder. Gladden came home with the title for Minnesota.

MIN (A)

PLAYER/POS	AVG	G	AB	R	H	2B	3B	HR	RB	BB	SO	SB
Rick Aguilera, p	.000	4	1	0	0	0	0	0	0	0	0	0
Steve Bedrosian, p	.000	3	0	0	0	0	0	0	0	0	0	0
Jarvis Brown, of-2, dh-1	.000	3	2	0	0	0	0	0	0	0	0	0
Randy Bush, of-2	.250	3	4	0	1	0	0	0	0	0	1	0
Chili Davis, dh-4, of-1	.222	6	18	4	4	0	0	2	4	2	3	0
Scott Erickson, p	.000	2	1	0	0	0	0	0	0	0	1	0
Greg Gagne, ss	.167	7	24	1	4	1	0	1	3	0	7	0
Dan Gladden, of	.233	7	30	5	7	2	2	0	0	3	4	2
Mark Guthrie, p	.000	4	0	0	0	0	0	0	0	0	0	0
Brian Harper, c	.381	7	21	2	8	2	0	0	1	2	2	0
Kent Hrbek, 1b	.115	7	26	2	3	1	0	1	2	2	6	0
Chuck Knoblauch, 2b	.308	7	26	3	8	1	0	0	2	4	2	4
Gene Larkin, dh-1	.500	4	4	0	2	0	0	0	1	0	0	0
Terry Leach, p	.000	2	0	0	0	0	0	0	0	0	0	0
Scott Leius, 3b	.357	7	14	2	5	0	0	1	2	1	2	0
Shane Mack, of	.130	6	23	0	3	1	0	0	1	0	7	0
Jack Morris, p	.000	3	2	0	0	0	0	0	0	0	1	0
Al Newman, 3b-2,2b-1, ss-1	.500	4	2	0	1	0	1	0	1	0	0	0
Junior Ortiz, c	.200	3	5	0	1	0	0	0	1	0	1	0
Mike Pagliarulo, 3b	.273	6	11	1	3	0	0	1	2	1	2	0
Kirby Puckett, of	.250	7	24	4	6	0	1	2	4	5	7	1
Paul Sorrento, 1b-1	.000	3	2	0	0	0	0	0	0	1	2	0
Kevin Tapani, p	.000	2	1	0	0	0	0	0	0	0	0	0
David West, p	.000	2	0	0	0	0	0	0	0	0	0	0
Carl Willis, p	.000	4	0	0	0	0	0	0	0	0	0	0
TOTAL	.232		241	24	56	8	4	8	24	21	48	7

PITCHER	W	L	ERA	G	GS	CG	SV	SHO	IP	H	ER	BB	SO
Rick Aguilera	1	1	1.80	4	0	0	2	0	5.0	6	1	1	3
Steve Bedrosian	0	0	5.40	3	0	0	0	0	3.1	3	2	0	2
Scott Erickson	0	0	5.06	2	2	0	0	0	10.2	10	6	4	5
Mark Guthrie	0	1	2.25	4	0	0	0	0	4.0	3	1	4	3
Terry Leach	0	0	3.86	2	0	0	0	0	2.1	2	1	0	2
Jack Morris	2	0	1.17	3	3	1	0	1	23.0	18	3	9	15
Kevin Tapani	1	1	4.50	2	2	0	0	0	12.0	13	6	2	7
David West	0	0	∞	2	0	0	0	0	0.0	2	4	4	0
Carl Willis	0	0	5.14	4	0	0	0	0	7.0	6	4	2	2
TOTAL	4	3	3.74	26	7	1	2	1	67.1	63	28	26	39

ATL (N)

PLAYER/POS	AVG	G	AB	R	H	2B	3B	HR	RB	BB	SO	SB
Steve Avery, p	.000	2	3	0	0	0	0	0	0	0	2	0
Rafael Belliard, ss	.375	7	16	0	6	1	0	0	4	1	2	0
Jeff Blauser, ss	.167	5	6	0	1	0	0	0	0	1	1	0
Sid Bream, 1b	.125	7	24	0	3	2	0	0	0	3	4	0
Francisco Cabrera, c-1	.000	3	1	0	0	0	0	0	0	0	0	0
Jim Clancy, p	.000	3	1	0	0	0	0	0	0	0	1	0
Ron Gant, of	.267	7	30	3	8	0	1	0	4	2	3	1
Tom Glavine, p	.000	2	2	0	0	0	0	0	0	0	2	0
Tommy Gregg, ph	.000	4	3	0	0	0	0	0	0	0	2	0
Brian Hunter, 1b-4, of-4	.190	7	21	2	4	1	0	1	3	0	2	0
David Justice, of	.259	7	27	5	7	0	0	2	6	5	5	2
Charlie Leibrandt, p	.000	2	0	0	0	0	0	0	0	0	0	0
Mark Lemke, 2b	.417	6	24	4	10	1	3	0	4	2	4	0
Kent Mercker, p	.000	5	0	0	0	0	0	0	0	0	0	0
Keith Mitchell, of	.000	3	2	0	0	0	0	0	0	0	1	0
Greg Olson, c	.222	7	27	3	6	2	0	0	1	5	4	1
Alejandro Pena, p	.000	3	0	0	0	0	0	0	0	0	0	0
Terry Pendleton, 3b	.367	7	30	6	11	3	0	2	3	3	1	0
Randy St. Claire, p	.000	1	0	0	0	0	0	0	0	0	0	0
Lonnie Smith, dh-4, of-3	.231	7	26	5	6	0	0	3	3	3	4	1
John Smoltz, p	.000	2	2	0	0	0	0	0	0	0	1	0
Mike Stanton, p	.000	5	0	0	0	0	0	0	0	0	0	0
Jeff Treadway, 2b-1	.250	3	4	1	1	0	0	0	0	1	2	0
Jerry Willard, ph	.000	1	0	0	0	0	0	0	1	0	0	0
Mark Wohlers, p	.000	3	0	0	0	0	0	0	0	0	0	0
TOTAL	.253		249	29	63	10	4	8	29	26	39	5

PITCHER	W	L	ERA	G	GS	CG	SV	SHO	IP	H	ER	BB	SO
Steve Avery	0	0	3.46	2	2	0	0	0	13.0	10	5	1	8
Jim Clancy	1	0	4.15	3	0	0	0	0	4.1	3	2	4	2
Tom Glavine	1	1	2.70	2	2	1	0	0	13.1	8	4	7	8
Charlie Leibrandt	0	2	11.25	2	1	0	0	0	4.0	8	5	1	3
Kent Mercker	0	0	0.00	5	0	0	0	0	1.0	0	0	0	1
Alejandro Pena	0	1	3.38	3	0	0	0	0	5.1	6	2	3	7
Randy St. Claire	0	0	9.00	1	0	0	0	0	1.0	1	1	0	0
John Smoltz	0	0	1.26	2	2	0	0	0	14.1	13	2	1	11
Mike Stanton	0	0	0.00	5	0	0	0	0	7.1	5	0	2	4
Mark Wohlers	0	0	0.00	3	0	0	0	0	1.2	2	0	2	1
TOTAL	3	4	2.89	25	7	1	0	0	65.1	56	21	21	48

GAME 1 AT MIN OCT 19

ATL 000 001 010   2 6 1
MIN 001 031 00X   5 9 1
Pitchers: LEIBRANDT, Clancy (5), Wohlers (7), Stanton (8) vs MORRIS, Guthrie (8), Aguilera (8)
Home Runs: Gagne-MIN, Hrbek-MIN
Attendance: 55,108

GAME 2 AT MIN OCT 20

ATL 010 010 000   2 8 1
MIN 200 000 01X   3 4 1
Pitchers: GLAVINE vs TAPANI, Aguilera (9)
Home Runs: Davis-MIN, Leius-MIN
Attendance: 55,145

GAME 3 AT ATL OCT 22

MIN 1 0000 01 2 0000 4 10 1
ATL 0 1010 20 0001 5 8 2
Pitchers: Erickson, West (5), Leach (5), Bedrosian (6), Willis (8), Guthrie (10), AGUILERA (12) vs Avery, Pena (8), Stanton (10), Wohlers (12), Mercker (12), CLANCY (12)
Home Runs: Justice-ATL, Smith-ATL, Puckett-MIN, Davis-ATL
Attendance: 50,878

GAME 4 AT ATL OCT 23

MIN 010 000 100   2 7 0
ATL 001 000 101   3 8 0
Pitchers: Morris, Willis (7), GUTHRIE (8), Bedrosian (9) vs Smoltz, Wohlers (8), STANTON (9)
Home Runs: Pendleton-ATL, Pagliarulo-MIN, Smith-ATL
Attendance: 50,878

GAME 5 AT ATL OCT 24

MIN 000 003 011   5 7 1
ATL 000 410 63X   14 17 1
Pitchers: TAPANI, Leach (5), West (7), Bedrosian (7), Willis (8) vs GLAVINE, Mercker (6), Clancy (7), St. Claire (9)
Home Runs: Justice-ATL, Smith-ATL, Hunter-ATL
Attendance: 50,878

GAME 6 AT MIN OCT 26

ATL 000 020 100 003 9 1
MIN 200 001 000 014 9 0
Pitchers: Avery, Stanton (7), Pena (9), LEIBRANDT (11) vs Erickson, Guthrie (7), Willis (7), AGUILERA (10)
Home Runs: Pendleton-ATL, Puckett-MIN
Attendance: 55,155

GAME 7 AT MIN OCT 27

ATL 000 000 0000 0 7 0
MIN 000 000 0001 1 10 0
Pitchers: Smoltz, Stanton (8), PENA (9) vs MORRIS
Attendance: 55,118

ATLANTA BRAVES (WEST) 4, PITTSBURGH PIRATES (EAST) 3

Atlanta opened the series with a pair of one-sided wins but Pittsburgh pulled out a close victory in Game 3. After a third loss, the Pirates pummelled the Braves for two wins even more lopsided than their losses in the first two games. With the series now even, the stage was set for what turned out to be one of the most dramatic finishes in postseason history.

Jose Lind spoiled John Smoltz's Game 1 shutout with his first home run of the season in the eighth inning. But by then the Braves had scored five times and held victory firmly in hand. Game 2 was even easier. By the time the Pirates came up with four runs in the sev-enth inning (ending Steve Avery's LCS-record streak of scoreless innings at 22-1/3), Atlanta had already compiled two four-run innings of their own (one of them on Ron Gant's grand slam). The Braves added five more runs in the last of the seventh to put the game out of reach.

At home for Game 3, the Pirates pulled themselves together behind the five-hit pitching of rookie knuckleballer Tim Wakefield. Sid Bream's solo homer in the fourth inning gave Atlanta a 1–0 lead, but Don Slaught homered to even the score an inning later and a pair of sixth-inning doubles put the Pirates ahead. Ron Gant's homer for Atlanta in the top of the seventh tied the score again, but a single, double, and sacrifice fly in the bottom of the inning put Pittsburgh on top to stay.

A 6–4 loss in Game 4 brought the Pirates to the brink of elimination, but in Game 5 they counter-attacked, driving out Atlanta starter Steve Avery in the first inning with five hits (four of them doubles) and four runs, on their way to a 7–1 victory. The Pirates unloaded on Atlanta's Tom Glavine for eight runs in the second inning of Game 6 before the first out was recorded, and pushed the assault to a 13–4 conclusion and a tied series.

While the Pirates scored single runs in the first and sixth innings of the final game, Pirates starter Doug Drabek (who had taken losses in Games 1 and 4) held Atlanta scoreless through eight innings. Then, in the last of the ninth, leadoff Brave Terry Pendleton doubled. He moved to third as David Justice reached on a grounder bobbled by the usually sure-handed second baseman Jose

Lind. A walk to Sid Bream filled the bases. Stan Belinda replaced Drabek on the mound and retired Ron Gant on a fly to left, but Pendleton scored Atlanta's first run after the catch. Damon Berryhill walked to reload the bases, and pinch hitter Brian Hunter popped out. Had there been no error, the game would have been over, with the Pirates waving the pennant. Instead, little-used pinch hitter Francisco Cabrera lined the ball safely to left, scoring Justice and Bream for a repeat pennant.

GAME 1 AT ATL OCT 6

```
PIT  000 000 010   1 5 1
ATL  010 210 10X   5 8 0
```
Pitchers: DRABEK, Patterson (5), Neagle (7), Cox (8) vs SMOLTZ, Stanton (9)
Home Runs: Lind-PIT, Blauser-ATL
Attendance: 51,971

GAME 2 AT ATL OCT 7

```
PIT  000 040 410   5 7 0
ATL  040 040 50X  13 14 0
```
Pitchers: JACKSON, Mason (2), Walk (3), Tomlin (5), Neagle (7), Patterson (7), Belinda (8) vs AVERY, Freeman (7), Stanton (7), Wohlers (8), Reardon (9)
Home Runs: Gant-ATL
Attendance: 51,975

GAME 3 AT PIT OCT 9

```
ATL  000 100 100   2 5 0
PIT  000 011 10X   3 8 1
```
Pitchers: GLAVINE, Stanton (7), Wohlers (8) vs WAKEFIELD
Home Runs: Bream-ATL, Gant-ATL, Slaught-PIT
Attendance: 56,610

GAME 4 AT PIT OCT 10

```
ATL  020 022 000   6 11 1
PIT  021 000 100   4 6 1
```
Pitchers: SMOLTZ, Stanton (7), Reardon (9) vs DRABEK, Tomlin (5), Cox (6), Mason (7)
Attendance: 57,164

GAME 5 AT PIT OCT 11

```
ATL  000 000 010   1 3 0
PIT  401 001 10X   7 13 0
```
Pitchers: AVERY, Smith (1), Leibrandt (5), Freeman (6), Mercker (8) vs WALK
Attendance: 52,929

GAME 6 AT ATL OCT 13

```
PIT  080 041 000  13 13 1
ATL  000 100 102   4 9 1
```
Pitchers: WAKEFIELD vs GLAVINE, Leibrandt (2), Freeman (5), Mercker (7), Wohlers (9)
Home Runs: Bell-PIT, Bonds-PIT, McClendon-PIT, Justice-ATL (2)
Attendance: 51,975

GAME 7 AT ATL OCT 14

```
PIT  100 001 000   2 7 1
ATL  000 000 003   3 7 0
```
Pitchers: DRABEK, Belinda (9) vs Smoltz, Stanton (7), Smith (7), Avery (7), REARDON (9)
Attendance: 51,975

ATL (W)

PLAYER/POS	AVG	G	AB	R	H	2B	3B	HR	RB	BB	SO	SB
Steve Avery, p	.000	3	2	0	0	0	0	0	0	1	0	0
R. Belliard, ss-3,2b-1	.000	4	2	1	0	0	0	0	0	0	1	0
Damon Berryhill, c	.167	7	24	1	4	1	0	0	1	3	2	0
Jeff Blauser, ss	.208	7	24	3	5	0	1	1	4	3	2	0
Sid Bream, 1b	.273	7	22	5	6	3	0	1	2	3	0	0
Francisco Cabrera, ph	.500	2	2	0	1	0	0	0	2	0	0	0
Marvin Freeman, p	.000	3	0	0	0	0	0	0	0	0	0	0
Ron Gant, of	.182	7	22	5	4	0	0	2	6	4	4	1
Tom Glavine, p	.000	2	2	0	0	0	0	0	0	0	0	0
Brian Hunter, 1b-2	.200	3	5	1	1	0	0	0	0	0	1	0
David Justice, of	.280	7	25	5	7	1	0	2	6	6	2	0
Charlie Leibrandt, p	.000	2	1	0	0	0	0	0	0	0	1	0
Mark Lemke, 2b-7,3b-1	.333	7	21	2	7	1	0	0	2	5	3	0
Javier Lopez, c	.000	1	1	0	0	0	0	0	0	0	0	0
Kent Mercker, p	.000	2	0	0	0	0	0	0	0	0	0	0
Otis Nixon, of	.286	7	28	5	8	2	0	0	2	4	4	3
Terry Pendleton, 3b	.233	7	30	2	7	2	0	0	3	0	2	0
Jeff Reardon, p	.000	3	0	0	0	0	0	0	0	0	0	0
Deion Sanders, of-3	.000	4	5	0	0	0	0	0	0	0	3	0
Lonnie Smith, ph	.333	6	6	1	2	0	1	0	1	0	0	0
Pete Smith, p	.000	2	1	0	0	0	0	0	0	0	0	0
John Smoltz, p	.286	3	7	1	2	0	0	0	0	1	0	2	1
Mike Stanton, p	1.000	5	1	1	1	1	0	0	1	0	0	0
Jeff Treadway, 2b-1	.667	3	3	1	2	0	0	0	0	0	1	0
Mark Wohlers, p	.000	3	0	0	0	0	0	0	0	0	0	0
TOTAL	.244		234	34	57	11	2	6	32	29	28	5

PITCHER	W	L	ERA	G	GS	CG	SV	SHO	IP	H	ER	BB	SO
Steve Avery	1	1	9.00	3	2	0	0	0	8.0	13	8	2	3
Marvin Freeman	0	0	14.73	3	0	0	0	0	3.2	8	6	2	1
Tom Glavine	0	2	12.27	2	2	0	0	0	7.1	13	10	3	2
Charlie Leibrandt	0	0	1.93	2	0	0	0	0	4.2	4	1	3	3
Kent Mercker	0	0	0.00	2	0	0	0	0	3.0	1	0	1	1
Jeff Reardon	1	0	0.00	3	0	0	1	0	3.0	0	0	2	3
Pete Smith	0	0	2.45	2	0	0	0	0	3.2	2	1	3	3
John Smoltz	2	0	2.66	3	3	0	0	0	20.1	14	6	10	19
Mike Stanton	0	0	0.00	5	0	0	0	0	4.1	2	0	2	5
Mark Wohlers	0	0	0.00	3	0	0	0	0	3.0	2	0	1	2
TOTAL	4	3	4.72	28	7	0	1	0	61.0	59	32	29	42

PIT (E)

PLAYER/POS	AVG	G	AB	R	H	2B	3B	HR	RB	BB	SO	SB
Stan Belinda, p	.000	2	0	0	0	0	0	0	0	0	0	0
Jay Bell, ss	.172	7	29	3	5	2	0	1	4	3	4	0
Barry Bonds, of	.261	7	23	5	6	1	0	1	2	6	4	1
Alex Cole, of	.200	4	10	2	2	0	0	0	1	3	2	0
Danny Cox, p	.000	2	0	0	0	0	0	0	0	0	0	0
Doug Drabek, p	.000	3	6	0	0	0	0	0	0	1	4	0
Cecil Espy, of-2	.667	4	3	0	2	0	0	0	0	0	1	0
Carlos Garcia, 2b	.000	1	1	0	0	0	0	0	0	0	0	0
Danny Jackson, p	.000	1	0	0	0	0	0	0	0	0	0	0
Jeff King, 3b	.241	7	29	4	7	4	0	0	2	0	1	0
Mike LaValliere, c	.200	3	10	1	2	0	0	0	0	0	3	0
Jose Lind, 2b	.222	7	27	5	6	2	1	1	5	1	4	0
Roger Mason, p	.000	2	0	0	0	0	0	0	0	0	0	0
Lloyd McClendon, of	.727	5	11	4	8	2	0	1	4	4	1	0
Orlando Merced, 1b	.100	4	10	0	1	1	0	0	2	2	4	0
Denny Neagle, p	.000	2	0	0	0	0	0	0	0	0	0	0
Bob Patterson, p	.000	2	0	0	0	0	0	0	0	0	0	0
Gary Redus, 1b	.438	5	16	4	7	4	1	0	3	2	3	0
Don Slaught, c	.333	5	12	5	4	1	0	1	5	6	3	0
Randy Tomlin, p	.000	2	0	0	0	0	0	0	0	0	0	0
Andy Van Slyke, of	.276	7	29	1	8	3	1	0	4	1	5	0
Gary Varsho, of-1	.500	3	2	0	1	0	0	0	0	0	0	0
Tim Wakefield, p	.000	2	6	1	0	0	0	0	0	0	0	0
Bob Walk, p	.000	2	5	0	0	0	0	0	0	0	1	0
John Wehner, ph	.000	2	2	0	0	0	0	0	0	0	2	0
TOTAL	.255		231	35	59	20	3	5	32	29	42	1

PITCHER	W	L	ERA	G	GS	CG	SV	SHO	IP	H	ER	BB	SO
Stan Belinda	0	0	0.00	2	0	0	0	0	1.2	2	0	1	2
Danny Cox	0	0	0.00	2	0	0	0	0	1.1	1	0	1	1
Doug Drabek	0	3	3.71	3	3	0	0	0	17.0	18	7	6	10
Danny Jackson	0	1	21.60	1	1	0	0	0	1.2	4	4	2	0
Roger Mason	0	0	0.00	2	0	0	0	0	3.1	0	0	2	1
Denny Neagle	0	0	27.00	2	0	0	0	0	1.2	4	5	3	0
Bob Patterson	0	0	5.40	2	0	0	0	0	1.2	3	1	1	1
Randy Tomlin	0	0	6.75	2	0	0	0	0	2.2	5	2	1	0
Tim Wakefield	2	0	3.00	2	2	2	0	0	18.0	14	6	5	7
Bob Walk	1	0	3.86	2	1	1	0	0	11.2	6	5	7	6
TOTAL	3	4	4.45	20	7	3	0	0	60.2	57	30	29	28

TORONTO BLUE JAYS (EAST) 4, OAKLAND A'S (WEST) 2

Oakland had competed in three ALCS in the previous four years and won them all. Toronto in its first 15 seasons of existence had competed three times in the ALCS and never won. In the first game of the 1992 matchup, the Athletics scored first on Mark McGwire's two-run homer and the next batter, Terry Steinbach, pushed the score to 3–0 with another home run. Toronto's Pat Borders and Dave Winfield retaliated with solo homers in the fifth and sixth innings to narrow the gap, and the Blue Jays tied the score in the eighth when Winfield, who had doubled with two outs, came home on John Olerud's single. But in the top of the ninth, Harold Baines led off with the game's fifth home run to put Oakland back into the lead, and A's reliever Dennis Eckersley preserved it for his 10th ALCS save.

After this encouraging beginning, though, the A's went into a three-game decline. In Game 2, fireballer David Cone held Oakland scoreless through eight innings while the Jays built a 3–0 lead on Kelly Gruber's two-run homer in the fifth inning and a third score two innings later. Oakland finally touched Cone for a run in the ninth, but reliever Tom Henke smothered the threat. The A's recovered from an early deficit in Game 3 to tie the score in the fourth inning, but fell behind on Candy Maldonado's leadoff homer in the sixth and never regained the lead. In Game 4 the A's rocked Toronto starter Jack Morris for five runs in the fifth, and added another in the sixth to take a 6–1 lead. But in the eighth, reliever Eckersley, who came on with one run in and two on, yielded singles on his first two pitches to let in two more runs, and in the ninth gave up a leadoff single and a game-tying home run to Roberto Alomar. Toronto finally took the lead in the eleventh as Derek Bell fouled off several pitches before drawing a walk, took third on Maldonado's single, and scored on Pat Borders' fly to left. Reliever Tom Henke held the lead.

Down three games to one, Oakland came out slugging in Game 5. Ruben Sierra homered for a pair of runs in the first inning and the A's added a third run two innings later. Dave Winfield

homered in the Toronto fourth, but the A's took advantage of two Toronto errors to score three more runs an inning later. But they couldn't sustain their comeback. Joe Carter's two-run homer in the first inning of Game 6, and Candy Maldonado's three-run blast two innings later, highlighted a 9–2 Toronto romp that ended the team's string of failed opportunities and carried the American League pennant to Canada for the first time.

TOR (E)

PLAYER/POS	AVG	G	AB	R	H	2B	3B	HR	RB	BB	SO	SB
Roberto Alomar, 2b	.423	6	26	4	11	1	0	2	4	2	1	5
Derek Bell, of	.000	2	0	1	0	0	0	0	0	1	0	0
Pat Borders, c	.318	6	22	3	7	0	0	1	3	1	1	0
Joe Carter, of-6,1b-2	.192	6	26	2	5	0	0	1	3	2	4	2
David Cone, p	.000	2	0	0	0	0	0	0	0	0	0	0
Mark Eichhorn, p	.000	1	0	0	0	0	0	0	0	0	0	0
Alfredo Griffin, ss-1	.000	2	2	0	0	0	0	0	0	0	0	0
Kelly Gruber, 3b	.091	6	22	3	2	1	0	1	2	2	3	0
Juan Guzman, p	.000	2	0	0	0	0	0	0	0	0	0	0
Tom Henke, p	.000	4	0	0	0	0	0	0	0	0	0	0
Jimmy Key, p	.000	1	0	0	0	0	0	0	0	0	0	0
Manuel Lee, ss	.278	6	18	2	5	1	1	0	3	1	2	0
Candy Maldonado, of	.273	6	22	3	6	0	0	2	6	2	4	0
Jack Morris, p	.000	2	0	0	0	0	0	0	0	0	0	0
John Olerud, 1b	.348	6	23	4	8	2	0	1	4	2	5	0
Ed Sprague, ph	.500	2	2	0	1	0	0	0	0	0	1	0
Todd Stottlemyre, p	.000	1	0	0	0	0	0	0	0	0	0	0
Mike Timlin, p	.000	2	0	0	0	0	0	0	0	0	0	0
Duane Ward, p	.000	3	0	0	0	0	0	0	0	0	0	0
Devon White, of	.348	6	23	2	8	2	0	0	2	5	6	0
Dave Winfield, dh	.250	6	24	7	6	1	0	2	3	5	2	0
TOTAL	.281		210	31	59	8	1	10	30	23	29	7

PITCHER	W	L	ERA	G	GS	CG	SV	SHO	IP	H	ER	BB	SO
David Cone	1	1	3.00	2	2	0	0	0	12.0	11	4	5	9
Mark Eichhorn	0	0	0.00	1	0	0	0	0	1.0	0	0	0	0
Juan Guzman	2	0	2.08	2	2	0	0	0	13.0	12	3	5	11
Tom Henke	0	0	0.00	4	0	0	3	0	4.2	3	0	2	2
Jimmy Key	0	0	0.00	1	0	0	0	0	3.0	2	0	2	1
Jack Morris	0	1	6.57	2	2	1	0	0	12.1	11	9	9	6
Todd Stottlemyre	0	0	2.45	1	0	0	0	0	3.2	3	1	0	1
Mike Timlin	0	0	6.75	2	0	0	0	0	1.1	4	1	0	1
Duane Ward	1	0	6.75	3	0	0	0	0	4.0	6	3	1	2
TOTAL	4	2	3.44	18	6	1	3	0	55.0	52	21	24	33

OAK (W)

PLAYER/POS	AVG	G	AB	R	H	2B	3B	HR	RB	BB	SO	SB
Harold Baines, dh	.440	6	25	6	11	2	0	1	4	0	3	0
Lance Blankenship, 2b	.231	5	13	2	3	0	0	0	0	3	4	1
Mike Bordick, ss-4,2b-2	.053	6	19	1	1	0	0	0	0	1	2	1
Jerry Browne, 3b-2, of-1	.400	4	10	3	4	0	0	0	2	2	0	0
Jim Corsi, p	.000	3	0	0	0	0	0	0	0	0	0	0
Ron Darling, p	.000	1	0	0	0	0	0	0	0	0	0	0
Kelly Downs, p	.000	2	0	0	0	0	0	0	0	0	0	0
Dennis Eckersley, p	.000	3	0	0	0	0	0	0	0	0	0	0
Eric Fox, of-1, dh-1	.000	4	1	0	0	0	0	0	0	1	0	2
Rickey Henderson, of	.261	6	23	5	6	0	0	0	1	4	4	2
Rick Honeycutt, p	.000	2	0	0	0	0	0	0	0	0	0	0
Carney Lansford, 3b	.167	5	18	0	3	0	0	0	1	1	1	0
Mark McGwire, 1b	.150	6	20	1	3	0	0	1	3	5	4	0
Mike Moore, p	.000	2	0	0	0	0	0	0	0	0	0	0
Jeff Parrett, p	.000	3	0	0	0	0	0	0	0	0	0	0
Jamie Quirk, ph	.000	1	1	0	0	0	0	0	0	0	0	0
Randy Ready, ph	.000	1	1	0	0	0	0	0	0	0	1	0
Jeff Russell, p	.000	3	0	0	0	0	0	0	0	0	0	0
Ruben Sierra, of	.333	6	24	4	8	2	1	1	7	2	1	1
Terry Steinbach, c	.292	6	24	1	7	0	0	1	5	2	7	0
Dave Stewart, p	.000	2	0	0	0	0	0	0	0	0	0	0
Walt Weiss, ss	.167	3	6	1	1	0	0	0	0	2	1	2
Bob Welch, p	.000	1	0	0	0	0	0	0	0	0	0	0
Willie Wilson, of	.227	6	22	0	5	1	0	0	0	1	5	7
Bobby Witt, p	.000	1	0	0	0	0	0	0	0	0	0	0
TOTAL	.251		207	24	52	5	1	4	23	24	33	16

PITCHER	W	L	ERA	G	GS	CG	SV	SHO	IP	H	ER	BB	SO
Jim Corsi	0	0	0.00	3	0	0	0	0	2.0	2	0	3	0
Ron Darling	0	1	3.00	1	1	0	0	0	6.0	4	2	2	3
Kelly Downs	0	1	3.86	2	0	0	0	0	2.1	3	1	1	0
Dennis Eckersley	0	0	6.00	3	0	0	1	0	3.0	8	2	0	2
Rick Honeycutt	0	0	0.00	2	0	0	0	0	2.0	0	0	1	0
Mike Moore	0	2	7.45	2	2	0	0	0	9.2	11	8	5	7
Jeff Parrett	0	0	11.57	3	0	0	0	0	2.1	6	3	0	1
Jeff Russell	1	0	9.00	3	0	0	0	0	2.0	2	2	4	0
Dave Stewart	1	0	2.70	2	2	1	0	0	16.2	14	5	6	7
Bob Welch	0	0	2.57	1	1	0	0	0	7.0	7	2	1	7
Bobby Witt	0	0	18.00	1	0	0	0	0	1.0	2	2	1	1
TOTAL	2	4	4.50	23	6	1	1	0	54.0	59	27	23	29

GAME 1 AT TOR OCT 7

OAK 030 000 001   4 6 1
TOR 000 011 010   3 9 0
Pitchers: Stewart, RUSSELL (8), Eckersley (9) vs MORRIS
Home Runs: Baines-OAK, McGwire-OAK, Steinbach-OAK, Winfield-TOR, Borders-TOR
Attendance: 51,039

GAME 2 AT TOR OCT 8

OAK 000 000 001   1 6 0
TOR 000 020 10X   3 4 0
Pitchers: MOORE, Corsi (8), Parrett (8) vs CONE, Henke (9)
Home Runs: Gruber-TOR
Attendance: 51,114

GAME 3 AT OAK OCT 10

TOR 010 110 211   7 9 1
OAK 000 200 210   5 13 3
Pitchers: GUZMAN, Ward (7), Timlin (8), Henke (8) vs DARLING, Downs (7), Corsi (8), Russell (8), Honeycutt (9), Eckersley (9)
Home Runs: Alomar-TOR, Maldonado-TOR
Attendance: 46,911

GAME 4 AT OAK OCT 11

TOR 010 000 032 01 7 17 4
OAK 005 001 000 00 6 12 2
Pitchers: Morris, Stottlemyre (8), Timlin (8), WARD (9), Henke (11) vs Welch, Parrett (8), Eckersley (8), Corsi (9), DOWNS (10)
Home Runs: Alomar-TOR, Olerud-TOR
Attendance: 47,732

GAME 5 AT OAK OCT 12

TOR 000 100 100   2 7 3
OAK 201 030 00X   6 8 0
Pitchers: CONE, Key (5), Eichhorn (8) vs STEWART
Home Runs: Winfield-TOR, Sierra-OAK
Attendance: 44,955

GAME 6 AT TOR OCT 14

OAK 000 001 010   2 7 1
TOR 204 010 02X   9 13 0
Pitchers: MOORE, Parrett (3), Honeycutt (5), Russell (7), Witt (8) vs GUZMAN, Ward (8), Henke (9)
Home Runs: Carter-TOR, Maldonado-TOR
Attendance: 51,335

TORONTO BLUE JAYS (AL) 4, ATLANTA BRAVES (NL) 2

Atlanta outscored Toronto in the Series, 20 runs to 16, but the Blue Jays eked out four one-run victories to bring Canada its first baseball world championship.

In the fourth inning of Game 1, Atlanta's Tom Glavine gave up a leadoff homer to Joe Carter for the game's first run, but held the Jays to just one single the rest of the way. Meanwhile, Toronto starter Jack Morris shut out the Braves for five innings. But in the top of the sixth he gave up a deciding three-run homer to catcher Damon Berryhill. The next night, though, down 4–5 in the ninth inning, Toronto pinch hitter Derek Bell drew a walk from Braves closer Jeff Reardon, and pinch hitter Ed Sprague lined Reardon's first pitch over the left field wall.

Toronto moved ahead with another close victory in Game 3, the first World Series game ever played outside the United States. Atlanta threatened in the fourth inning when, with two on and none out, David Justice flied deep to center Devon White leaped high to snare it. Baserunner Terry Pendleton was ruled out for passing Deion Sanders on the basepath, and third baseman Kelly Gruber tagged Sanders, who was diving back into second base, to complete what seemed to be a triple play. The umpire didn't see the tag, how-ever, and called Sanders safe. Still, no Braves scored, and Joe Carter homered for the game's first run in the last of the fourth. Atlanta tied the game in the sixth and took the lead in the top of the eighth. Gruber homered to re-tie it in the bottom of the inning, and after the Jays had filled the bases in the last of the ninth, Candy Maldonado tagged Reardon for a hit over the drawn-in outfield to bring home the winning run.

The Jays pushed their Series advantage to 3–1 in Game 4. Catcher Pat Borders opened the Toronto third with a home run, and Gruber scored from second on Devon White's seventh-inning single. The Braves got to Toronto starter Jimmy Key for a run in the eighth, but relievers Duane Ward and Tom Henke shut them down.

In the fifth game the Blue Jays twice came from one run down to even the score. But in the fifth inning, after the Braves had once again built a one-run lead, Lonnie

Smith extended it with a grand slam that sent the Series back to Atlanta.

Toronto scored a run in the first inning of Game 6. Atlanta tied the game in the third, but Candy Maldonado's leadoff homer in the fourth restored the Jays' advantage. In the bottom of the ninth, the Braves scrabbled back to tie it up again. The score was 2–2 until the top of the 11th, when Toronto's Dave Winfield delivered two run-ners with a two-out double into the left-field corner. As it turned out, the Jays needed both runs, for Atlanta scored in the bottom of the 11th. But with two out and the potential tying run on third, Otis Nixon, was out at first attempting a bunt, and the Series was over.

TOR (A)

PLAYER/POS	AVG	G	AB	R	H	2B	3B	HR	RB	BB	SO	SB
Roberto Alomar, 2b	.208	6	24	3	5	1	0	0	0	3	3	3
Derek Bell, ph	.000	2	1	1	0	0	0	0	0	1	0	0
Pat Borders, c	.450	6	20	2	9	3	0	1	3	2	1	0
Joe Carter, of-4	.273	6	22	2	6	2	0	2	3	3	2	1
David Cone, p	.500	2	4	0	2	0	0	0	1	1	0	0
Mark Eichhorn, p	.000	1	0	0	0	0	0	0	0	0	0	0
Alfredo Griffin, ss	.000	2	0	0	0	0	0	0	0	0	0	0
Kelly Gruber, 3b	.105	6	19	2	2	0	0	1	1	2	5	1
Juan Guzman, p	.000	1	0	0	0	0	0	0	0	0	0	0
Tom Henke, p	.000	3	0	0	0	0	0	0	0	0	0	0
Jimmy Key, p	.000	2	1	0	0	0	0	0	0	0	0	0
Manuel Lee, ss	.105	6	19	1	2	0	0	0	0	1	2	0
Candy Maldonado, of-5	.158	6	19	1	3	0	0	1	2	2	5	0
Jack Morris, p	.000	2	2	0	0	0	0	0	0	0	0	0
John Olerud, 1b	.308	4	13	2	4	0	0	0	0	0	4	0
Ed Sprague, 1b-1	.500	3	2	1	1	0	0	1	2	1	0	0
Todd Stottlemyre, p	.000	4	0	0	0	0	0	0	0	0	0	0
Pat Tabler, ph	.000	2	2	0	0	0	0	0	0	0	0	0
Mike Timlin, p	.000	2	0	0	0	0	0	0	0	0	0	0
Duane Ward, p	.000	4	0	0	0	0	0	0	0	0	0	0
David Wells, p	.000	4	0	0	0	0	0	0	0	0	0	0
Devon White, of	.231	6	26	2	6	1	0	0	2	0	6	1
Dave Winfield, of-3, dh-3	.227	6	22	0	5	1	0	0	3	2	3	0
TOTAL	.230		196	17	45	8	0	6	17	18	33	6

PITCHER	W	L	ERA	G	GS	CG	SV	SHO	IP	H	ER	BB	SO
David Cone	0	0	3.48	2	2	0	0	0	10.1	9	4	8	8
Mark Eichhorn	0	0	0.00	1	0	0	0	0	1.0	0	0	0	1
Juan Guzman	0	0	1.13	1	1	0	0	0	8.0	8	1	1	7
Tom Henke	0	0	2.70	3	0	0	2	0	3.1	2	1	2	1
Jimmy Key	2	0	1.00	2	1	0	0	0	9.0	6	1	0	6
Jack Morris	0	2	8.44	2	2	0	0	0	10.2	13	10	6	12
Todd Stottlemyre	0	0	0.00	4	0	0	0	0	3.2	4	0	0	4
Mike Timlin	0	0	0.00	2	0	0	1	0	1.1	0	0	0	0
Duane Ward	2	0	0.00	4	0	0	0	0	3.1	1	0	1	6
David Wells	0	0	0.00	4	0	0	0	0	4.1	1	0	2	3
TOTAL	4	2	2.78	25	6	0	3	0	55.0	44	17	20	48

ATL (N)

PLAYER/POS	AVG	G	AB	R	H	2B	3B	HR	RB	BB	SO	SB
Steve Avery, p	.000	2	1	0	0	0	0	0	0	0	1	0
Rafael Belliard, ss-3, 2b-1	.000	4	0	0	0	0	0	0	0	0	0	0
Damon Berryhill, c	.091	6	22	1	2	0	0	1	3	1	11	0
Jeff Blauser, ss	.250	6	24	2	6	0	0	0	0	1	9	2
Sid Bream, 1b	.200	5	15	1	3	0	0	0	0	4	0	0
Francisco Cabrera, ph	.000	1	1	0	0	0	0	0	0	0	0	0
Ron Gant, of-3	.125	4	8	2	1	1	0	0	0	1	2	2
Tom Glavine, p	.000	2	2	0	0	0	0	0	0	1	0	0
Brian Hunter, 1b-3	.200	4	5	0	1	0	0	0	2	0	1	0
David Justice, of	.158	6	19	4	3	0	0	1	3	6	5	1
Charlie Leibrandt, p	.000	1	0	0	0	0	0	0	0	0	0	0
Mark Lemke, 2b	.211	6	19	0	4	0	0	0	2	1	3	0
Otis Nixon, of	.296	6	27	3	8	1	0	0	1	1	3	5
Terry Pendleton, 3b	.240	6	25	2	6	2	0	0	2	1	5	0
Jeff Reardon, p	.000	2	0	0	0	0	0	0	0	0	0	0
Deion Sanders, of	.533	4	15	4	8	2	0	0	1	2	1	5
Lonnie Smith, dh-3	.167	5	12	1	2	0	0	1	5	1	4	0
Pete Smith, p	.000	1	1	0	0	0	0	0	0	0	1	0
John Smoltz, p-2	.000	3	3	0	0	0	0	0	0	0	2	0
Mike Stanton, p	.000	4	0	0	0	0	0	0	0	0	0	0
Jeff Treadway, ph	.000	1	1	0	0	0	0	0	0	0	0	0
Mark Wohlers, p	.000	2	0	0	0	0	0	0	0	0	0	0
TOTAL	.220		200	20	44	6	0	3	19	20	48	15

PITCHER	W	L	ERA	G	GS	CG	SV	SHO	IP	H	ER	BB	SO
Steve Avery	0	1	3.75	2	2	0	0	0	12.0	11	5	3	11
Tom Glavine	1	1	1.59	2	2	2	0	0	17.0	10	3	4	8
Charlie Leibrandt	0	1	9.00	1	0	0	0	0	2.0	3	2	0	0
Jeff Reardon	0	1	13.50	2	0	0	0	0	1.1	2	2	1	1
Pete Smith	0	0	0.00	1	0	0	0	0	3.0	3	0	0	0
John Smoltz	1	0	2.70	2	2	0	0	0	13.1	13	4	7	12
Mike Stanton	0	0	0.00	4	0	0	1	0	5.0	3	0	2	1
Mark Wohlers	0	0	0.00	2	0	0	0	0	0.2	0	0	1	0
TOTAL	2	4	2.65	16	6	2	1	0	54.1	45	16	18	33

GAME 1 AT ATL OCT 17

TOR 000 100 000   1 4 0
ATL 000 003 00X   3 4 0
Pitchers: MORRIS, Stottlemyre (7), Wells (8) vs GLAVINE
Home Runs: Carter-TOR, Berryhill-ATL
Attendance: 51,763

GAME 2 AT ATL OCT 18

TOR 000 020 012   5 9 2
ATL 010 120 000   4 5 1
Pitchers: Cone, Wells (5), Stottlemyre (7), WARD (8), Henke (9) vs Smoltz, Stanton (8), REARDON (8)
Home Runs: Sprague-TOR
Attendance: 51,763

GAME 3 AT TOR OCT 20

ATL 000 001 010   2 9 0
TOR 000 100 011   3 6 1
Pitchers: AVERY, Wohlers (9), Stanton (9), Reardon (9) vs Guzman, WARD (9)
Home Runs: Carter-TOR, Gruber-TOR
Attendance: 51,813

GAME 4 AT TOR OCT 21

ATL 000 000 010   1 5 0
TOR 001 000 10X   2 6 0
Pitchers: GLAVINE vs KEY, Ward (8), Stanton (9), Reardon (9) vs Guzman, WARD (9)
Home Runs: Carter-TOR, Gruber-TOR
Attendance: 51,813

GAME 5 AT TOR OCT 22

ATL 100 150 000   7 13 0
TOR 010 100 000   2 6 0
Pitchers: SMOLTZ, Stanton (7) vs MORRIS, Wells (5), Timlin (7), Eichhorn (8), Stottlemyre (9)
Home Runs: Justice-ATL, L.Smith-ATL
Attendance: 52,268

GAME 6 AT ATL OCT 24

TOR 1 0 0 1 0 0 0 0 0 2 4 14 1
ATL 0 0 1 0 0 0 0 0 0 1 0 1 3 8 1
Pitchers: Cone, Stottlemyre (7), Wells (7), Ward (8), Henke (9), Timlin (11) vs Avery, P.Smith (5), Stanton (9), Wohlers (9), LEIBRANDT (10)
Home Runs: Maldonado-TOR
Attendance: 51,763

PHILADELPHIA PHILLIES (EAST) 4, ATLANTA BRAVES (WEST) 2

Atlanta outhit the Phillies by 47 percentage points, outscored them by 10 runs, and yielded 1.6 fewer earned runs per game. But the Phillies won the pennant. In the opener, Philadelphia starter Curt Schilling fanned 10 batters—including the first five he faced—and left the game after eight innings with a 3–2 lead. An errant throw by Phillies third baseman Kim Batiste (who had just entered the game to strengthen the defense) set up an unearned tying run in the ninth inning. But in the last of the 10th, after John Kruk had doubled, Batiste redeemed himself with a game-winning hit down the left field line.

While the Philadelphia offense remained steady over the next two games, the Braves erupted for 23 runs. By the time Philadelphia scored its first runs in the fourth inning of Game 2, Atlanta had already sent eight men across the plate. In Game 3 the Phillies scored first, and held a 2–0 lead before the Braves destroyed them with five runs in the sixth inning and four more in the seventh.

Game 4 featured only four fewer hits than Game 3, but 10 fewer runs, as Philadelphia evened the series with its second close win. Phillies starter Danny Jackson yielded nine hits and a pair of walks, but only one second-inning run. In the top of the fourth, Darren Daulton, who had reached on an infield error, took third on Milt Thompson's double and scored on Kevin Stocker's two-out single. Pitcher Jackson then singled home Thompson with what proved the winning run.

In the fifth game, Curt Schilling held Atlanta to four hits through eight innings, and carried a 3–0 lead into the bottom of the ninth. But when a walk and infield error put the first two men on, Mitch Williams relieved Schilling and gave up a trio of singles which tied the game. In the top of the 10th inning, though, Lenny Dykstra's solo homer restored the Phillies' lead, and veteran reliever Larry Andersen blanked the Braves in the bottom of the 10th—striking out the final two batters—to preserve the win.

After their two narrow wins on the road, the Phillies clinched the pennant with relative ease when the series returned to Philadelphia

for Game 6. Darren Daulton's two-out double in the third inning put the Phillies up 2–0. Atlanta scored once in the fifth, but Dave Hollins' two-run homer in the last of the fifth increased Philadelphia's lead to three runs, and Mickey Morandini's two-out, two-run triple an inning later pushed the score to 6–1. Atlanta's Jeff Blauser brought the score to 6–3 with a home run in the seventh inning, but Phillies relievers David West and Mitch Williams set the Braves down in order in the final two innings.

PHI (E)

PLAYER/POS	AVG	G	AB	R	H	2B	3B	HR	RB	BB	SO	SB
Larry Andersen, p	.000	3	0	0	0	0	0	0	0	0	0	0
Kim Batiste, 3b	1.000	4	1	0	1	0	0	0	0	1	0	0
Wes Chamberlain, of-2	.364	4	11	1	4	3	0	0	1	1	3	0
Darren Daulton, c	.263	6	19	2	5	1	0	1	3	6	3	0
Mariano Duncan, 2b	.267	3	15	3	4	0	2	0	0	0	5	0
Lenny Dykstra, of	.280	6	25	5	7	1	0	2	2	5	8	0
Jim Eisenreich, of-5	.133	6	15	0	2	1	0	0	1	0	2	0
Tommy Greene, p	.000	2	0	1	0	0	0	0	0	1	0	0
Dave Hollins, 3b	.200	6	20	2	4	1	0	2	4	5	4	1
Pete Incaviglia, of	.167	3	12	2	2	0	0	1	1	0	3	0
Danny Jackson, p	.250	1	4	0	1	0	0	0	1	0	3	0
Ricky Jordan, ph	.000	2	1	0	0	0	0	0	0	1	0	0
John Kruk, 1b	.250	6	24	4	6	2	1	1	5	4	5	0
Tony Longmire, ph	.000	1	1	0	0	0	0	0	0	0	1	0
Roger Mason, p	.000	2	0	0	0	0	0	0	0	0	0	0
Mickey Morandini, 2b	.250	4	16	1	4	0	1	0	2	0	3	1
Terry Mulholland, p	.000	1	2	0	0	0	0	0	0	0	1	0
Todd Pratt, c	.000	1	1	0	0	0	0	0	0	0	1	0
Ben Rivera, p	.000	1	0	0	0	0	0	0	0	0	0	0
Curt Schilling, p	.000	2	5	0	0	0	0	0	0	0	2	0
Kevin Stocker, ss	.182	6	22	0	4	1	0	0	1	2	5	0
Bobby Thigpen, p	.000	2	0	0	0	0	0	0	0	0	0	0
Milt Thompson, of-5	.231	6	13	2	3	1	0	0	1	0	2	0
David West, p	.000	3	0	0	0	0	0	0	0	0	0	0
Mitch Williams, p	.000	4	0	0	0	0	0	0	0	0	0	0
TOTAL	.227		207	23	47	11	4	7	22	26	51	2

PITCHER	W	L	ERA	G	GS	CG	SV	SHO	IP	H	ER	BB	SO
Larry Andersen	0	0	15.43	3	0	0	1	0	2.1	4	4	1	3
Tommy Greene	1	1	9.64	2	2	0	0	0	9.1	12	10	7	7
Danny Jackson	1	0	1.17	1	1	0	0	0	7.2	9	1	2	6
Roger Mason	0	0	0.00	2	0	0	0	0	3.0	1	0	0	2
Terry Mulholland	0	1	7.20	1	1	0	0	0	5.0	9	4	1	2
Ben Rivera	0	0	4.50	1	0	0	0	0	2.0	1	1	1	2
Curt Schilling	0	0	1.69	2	2	0	0	0	16.0	11	3	5	19
Bobby Thigpen	0	0	5.40	2	0	0	0	0	1.2	1	1	1	3
David West	0	0	13.50	3	0	0	0	0	2.2	5	4	2	5
Mitch Williams	2	0	1.69	4	0	0	2	0	5.1	6	1	2	5
TOTAL	4	2	4.75	21	6	0	3	0	55.0	59	29	22	54

ATL (W)

PLAYER/POS	AVG	G	AB	R	H	2B	3B	HR	RB	BB	SO	SB
Steve Avery, p	.500	2	4	1	2	1	0	0	0	0	1	0
Rafael Belliard, 2b-1, ss-1	.000	2	1	1	0	0	0	0	0	0	1	0
Damon Berryhill, c	.211	6	19	2	4	0	0	1	3	1	5	0
Jeff Blauser, ss	.280	6	25	5	7	1	0	2	4	4	7	0
Sid Bream, 1b	1.000	1	1	1	1	0	0	0	0	0	0	0
Francisco Cabrera, c-1	.667	3	3	0	2	0	0	0	1	0	1	0
Ron Gant, of	.185	6	27	4	5	3	0	0	3	2	9	0
Tom Glavine, p	.000	1	3	0	0	0	0	0	0	0	1	0
David Justice, of	.143	6	21	2	3	1	0	0	4	3	3	0
Mark Lemke, 2b	.208	6	24	2	5	2	0	0	4	1	6	0
Greg Maddux, p	.250	2	4	1	1	0	0	0	0	0	1	0
Fred McGriff, 1b	.435	6	23	6	10	2	0	1	4	4	7	0
Greg McMichael, p	.000	4	0	0	0	0	0	0	0	0	0	0
Kent Mercer, p	.000	5	0	0	0	0	0	0	0	0	0	0
Otis Nixon, of	.348	6	23	3	8	2	0	0	4	5	6	0
Greg Olson, c	.333	2	3	0	1	1	0	0	0	0	1	0
Bill Pecota, ph	.333	4	3	1	1	0	0	0	0	1	1	0
Terry Pendleton, 3b	.346	6	26	4	9	1	0	1	5	0	2	0
Deion Sanders, of-1	.000	5	3	0	0	0	0	0	0	0	1	0
John Smoltz, p	.000	1	1	0	0	0	0	0	0	0	1	0
Mike Stanton, p	.000	1	0	0	0	0	0	0	0	0	0	0
Tony Tarasco, of	.000	2	1	0	0	0	0	0	0	0	1	0
Mark Wohlers, p	.000	4	0	0	0	0	0	0	0	0	0	0
TOTAL	.274		215	33	59	14	0	5	32	22	54	0

PITCHER	W	L	ERA	G	GS	CG	SV	SHO	IP	H	ER	BB	SO
Steve Avery	0	0	2.77	2	2	0	0	0	13.0	9	4	6	10
Tom Glavine	1	0	2.57	1	1	0	0	0	7.0	6	2	0	5
Greg Maddux	1	0	4.97	2	2	0	0	0	12.2	11	7	7	11
Greg McMichael	0	1	6.75	4	0	0	0	0	4.0	7	3	2	1
Kent Mercer	0	0	1.80	5	0	0	0	0	5.0	3	1	2	4
John Smoltz	0	1	0.00	1	1	0	0	0	6.1	8	0	5	10
Mike Stanton	0	0	0.00	1	0	0	0	0	1.0	1	0	1	0
Mark Wohlers	0	1	3.38	4	0	0	0	0	5.1	2	2	3	10
TOTAL	2	4	3.15	20	6	0	0	0	54.1	47	19	26	51

GAME 1 AT PHI OCT 6
ATL 001 1000 010   3 9 0
PHI 100 101 000 1   4 9 1
Pitchers: Avery, Mercker (7), McMICHAEL (9) vs Schilling, WILLIAMS (9)
Home Runs: Incaviglia-PHI
Attendance: 62,012

GAME 2 AT PHI OCT 7
ATL 206 010 041   14 16 0
PHI 000 200 001   3 7 2
Pitchers: MADDUX, Stanton (8), Wohlers (9) vs GREENE, Thigpen (3), Rivera (4), Mason (6), West (8), Andersen
Home Runs: Blauser-ATL, McGriff-ATL, Pendleton-ATL, Berryhill-ATL, Dykstra-PHI, Hollins-PHI
Attendance: 62,436

GAME 3 AT ATL OCT 9
PHI 000 101 011   4 10 1
ATL 000 005 40X   9 12 0
Pitchers: MULHOLLAND, Mason (6), Andersen (7), West (7), Thigpen (8) vs GLAVINE, Mercker (8), McMichael (9)
Home Runs: Kruk-PHI
Attendance: 52,032

GAME 4 AT ATL OCT 10
PHI 000 200 000   2 8 1
ATL 010 000 000   1 10 1
Pitchers: JACKSON, Williams (8) vs SMOLTZ, Mercker (7), Wohlers (8)
Attendance: 52,032

GAME 5 AT ATL OCT 11
PHI 100 100 001 1   4 6 1
ATL 000 000 030   3 7 1
Pitchers: Schilling, WILLIAMS (9), Andersen (10) vs Avery, Mercker (8), McMichael (9), WOHLERS (9)
Home Runs: Dykstra-PHI, Daulton-PHI
Attendance: 52,032

GAME 6 AT PHI OCT 13
ATL 000 010 200   3 5 3
PHI 002 022 00X   6 7 1
Pitchers: MADDUX, Mercker (6), McMichael (7), Wohlers (7) vs GREENE, West (8), Williams (9)
Home Runs: Blauser-ATL, Hollins-PHI
Attendance: 62,502

TORONTO BLUE JAYS (EAST) 4, CHICAGO WHITE SOX (WEST) 2

The visiting team won the first four games of the series, but in Game 5, home team Toronto held off a ninth-inning White Sox rally to take a 3–2 series lead. Then, in Chicago two days later, the Jays put the Sox away.

In Chicago for the series opener, Toronto scored first when Ed Sprague tripled home a pair of runs in the fourth inning. The White Sox bounced ahead with three runs in the last of the fourth, but the Blue Jays regained the lead a half inning later on John Olerud's two-run double, then pulled away to a 17-hit, 7–3 win. Toronto also scored first in Game 2, with an unearned run in the first inning. But in the last of the inning, Dave Stewart walked the bases full, then handed Chicago the tying run with a wild pitch. With two out in the fourth inning, though, back-to-back doubles by Paul Molitor and Tony Fernandez restored the lead to Toronto, and a walk, an infield hit and an error increased the Jays' lead to 3–1. This ended the scoring, although the White Sox loaded the bases in the sixth before Stewart retired the next three batters.

The White Sox leaped to life when the series moved to Toronto for Game 3. After the first two men had been retired in the third inning, Sox batters combined five singles with a pair of walks for a 5–0 lead, which Chicago starter Wilson Alvarez held for a 6–1 complete game victory. Lance Johnson's two-run homer in the second inning of Game 4 put Chicago ahead. The Jays overtook them with three runs an inning later, but in the sixth inning Frank Thomas homered to even the score at 3–3, and after two batters walked, Johnson's two-out triple put the Sox ahead to stay.

The Blue Jays finally broke the visiting team's lock on victory, scoring single runs in each of the first four innings, and another in the seventh, while starter Juan Guzman held Chicago to three hits and a single run in his seven innings. Robin Ventura's two-run homer off Jays' reliever Duane Ward in the Chicago ninth narrowed Toronto's lead to 5–3, but Ward then retired Bo Jackson with his third strikeout.

Errors ended the White Sox season in Game 6. With the score tied 2–2 in the fourth inning, a

bobble by Chicago third baseman Robin Ventura put Paul Molitor on base. Molitor subsequently scored the go-ahead run when second base-man Joey Cora threw a ball into the dugout. Devon White homered in the ninth inning to stretch Toronto's lead to 4–2, and an error by Sox reliever Scott Radinsky on what should have been the third out set the stage for Molitor to triple home a pair of baserunners. Warren Newson's leadoff homer against Toronto reliever Duane Ward in the bottom of the ninth narrowed the score to 6–3, but the White Sox came no closer. The win, starter Dave Stewart's second of the series, was his eighth triumph without a loss in LCS play.

TOR (E)

PLAYER/POS	AVG	G	AB	R	H	2B	3B	HR	RB	BB	SO	SB
Roberto Alomar, 2b	.292	6	24	3	7	1	0	0	4	4	3	4
Pat Borders, c	.250	6	24	1	6	1	0	0	3	0	6	1
Joe Carter, of	.259	6	27	2	7	0	0	0	2	1	5	0
Tony Castillo, p	.000	2	0	0	0	0	0	0	0	0	0	0
Danny Cox, p	.000	2	0	0	0	0	0	0	0	0	0	0
Mark Eichhorn, p	.000	1	0	0	0	0	0	0	0	0	0	0
Tony Fernandez, ss	.318	6	22	1	7	0	0	0	1	2	4	0
Juan Guzman, p	.000	2	0	0	0	0	0	0	0	0	0	0
Rickey Henderson, of	.120	6	25	4	3	2	0	0	0	4	5	2
Pat Hentgen, p	.000	1	0	0	0	0	0	0	0	0	0	0
Al Leiter, p	.000	2	0	0	0	0	0	0	0	0	0	0
Paul Molitor, dh	.391	6	23	7	9	2	1	1	5	3	3	0
John Olerud, 1b	.348	6	23	5	8	1	0	0	3	4	1	0
Ed Sprague, 3b	.286	6	21	0	6	0	1	0	4	2	4	0
Dave Stewart, p	.000	2	0	0	0	0	0	0	0	0	0	0
Todd Stottlemyre, p	.000	1	0	0	0	0	0	0	0	0	0	0
Mike Timlin, p	.000	1	0	0	0	0	0	0	0	0	0	0
Duane Ward, p	.000	4	0	0	0	0	0	0	0	0	0	0
Devon White, of	.444	6	27	3	12	1	1	1	2	1	5	0
TOTAL	.301		216	26	65	8	3	2	24	21	36	7

PITCHER	W	L	ERA	G	GS	CG	SV	SHO	IP	H	ER	BB	SO
Tony Castillo	0	0	0.00	2	0	0	0	0	2.0	0	0	1	1
Danny Cox	0	0	0.00	2	0	0	0	0	5.0	3	0	2	5
Mark Eichhorn	0	0	0.00	1	0	0	0	0	2.0	1	0	1	1
Juan Guzman	2	0	2.08	2	2	0	0	0	13.0	8	3	9	9
Pat Hentgen	0	1	18.00	1	1	0	0	0	3.0	9	6	2	3
Al Leiter	0	0	3.38	2	0	0	0	0	2.2	4	1	2	2
Dave Stewart	2	0	2.03	2	2	0	0	0	13.1	8	3	8	8
Todd Stottlemyre	0	1	7.50	1	1	0	0	0	6.0	6	5	4	4
Mike Timlin	0	0	3.86	1	0	0	0	0	2.1	3	1	0	2
Duane Ward	0	0	5.79	4	0	0	2	0	4.2	4	3	3	8
TOTAL	4	2	3.67	18	6	0	2	0	54.0	46	22	32	43

CHI (W)

PLAYER/POS	AVG	G	AB	R	H	2B	3B	HR	RB	BB	SO	SB
Wilson Alvarez, p	.000	1	0	0	0	0	0	0	0	0	0	0
Tim Belcher, p	.000	1	0	0	0	0	0	0	0	0	0	0
Jason Bere, p	.000	1	0	0	0	0	0	0	0	0	0	0
Ellis Burks, of	.304	6	23	4	7	1	0	1	3	3	5	0
Joey Cora, 2b	.136	6	22	1	3	0	0	0	1	3	6	0
Jose DeLeon, p	.000	2	0	0	0	0	0	0	0	0	0	0
Alex Fernandez, p	.000	2	0	0	0	0	0	0	0	0	0	0
Craig Grebeck, 3b	1.000	1	1	0	1	0	0	0	0	0	0	0
Ozzie Guillen, ss	.273	6	22	4	6	1	0	0	2	0	2	1
Roberto Hernandez, p	.000	4	0	0	0	0	0	0	0	0	0	0
Bo Jackson, dh	.000	3	10	1	0	0	0	0	0	3	6	0
Lance Johnson, of	.217	6	23	2	5	1	1	1	6	2	1	0
Ron Karkovice, c	.000	6	15	0	0	0	0	0	0	1	7	0
Mike LaValliere, c	.333	2	3	0	1	0	0	0	0	1	0	0
Kirk McCaskill, p	.000	3	0	0	0	0	0	0	0	0	0	0
Jack McDowell, p	.000	2	0	0	0	0	0	0	0	0	0	0
Warren Newson, dh-1	.200	2	5	1	1	0	0	1	1	0	1	0
Dan Pasqua, dh	.000	2	6	1	0	0	0	0	0	1	2	0
Scott Radinsky, p	.000	4	0	0	0	0	0	0	0	0	0	0
Tim Raines, of	.444	6	27	5	12	3	0	0	1	2	2	1
Frank Thomas, 1b-4, dh-2	.353	6	17	2	6	0	0	1	3	10	5	0
Robin Ventura, 3b-6,1b-1	.200	6	20	2	4	0	0	1	5	6	6	0
TOTAL	.237		194	23	46	6	1	5	22	32	43	3

PITCHER	W	L	ERA	G	GS	CG	SV	SHO	IP	H	ER	BB	SO
Wilson Alvarez	1	0	1.00	1	1	1	0	0	9.0	7	1	2	6
Tim Belcher	1	0	2.45	1	0	0	0	0	3.2	3	1	3	1
Jason Bere	0	0	11.57	1	1	0	0	0	2.1	5	3	2	3
Jose DeLeon	0	0	1.93	2	0	0	0	0	4.2	7	1	1	6
Alex Fernandez	0	2	1.80	2	2	0	0	0	15.0	15	3	6	10
R. Hernandez	0	0	0.00	4	0	0	1	0	4.0	4	0	0	1
Kirk McCaskill	0	0	0.00	3	0	0	0	0	3.2	3	0	1	3
Jack McDowell	0	2	10.00	2	2	0	0	0	9.0	18	10	5	5
Scott Radinsky	0	0	10.80	4	0	0	0	0	1.2	3	2	1	1
TOTAL	1	4	3.57	20	6	1	1	0	53.0	65	21	21	36

GAME 1 AT CHI OCT 5
TOR 000 230 200   7 17 1
CHI 000 300 000   3 6 1
Pitchers: GUZMAN, Cox (7), Ward (9) vs McDOWELL, DeLeon (7), Radinsky (8), McCaskill (9)
Home Runs: Molitor-TOR
Attendance: 46,246

GAME 2 AT CHI OCT 6
TOR 100 200 000   3 8 0
CHI 100 000 000   1 7 2
Pitchers: STEWART, Leiter (7), Ward (9) vs FERNANDEZ, Hernandez (9)
Attendance: 46,101

GAME 3 AT TOR OCT 8
CHI 005 100 000   6 12 0
TOR 001 000 000   1 7 1
Pitchers: ALVAREZ vs HENTGEN, Cox (4), Eichhorn (7), Castillo (9)
Attendance: 51,783

GAME 4 AT TOR OCT 9
CHI 020 003 101   7 11 0
TOR 003 001 000   4 9 0
Pitchers: Bere, BELCHER (3), McCaskill (7), Radinsky (8), Hernandez (9) vs STOTTLEMYRE, Leiter (7), Timlin (7)
Home Runs: Thomas-CHI, Johnson-CHI
Attendance: 51,889

GAME 5 AT TOR OCT 10
CHI 000 010 002   3 5 1
TOR 111 100 10X   5 14 0
Pitchers: McDOWELL, DeLeon (3), Radinsky (7), Hernandez (7) vs GUZMAN, Castillo (8), Ward (9)
Home Runs: Ventura-CHI, Burks-CHI
Attendance: 51,375

GAME 6 AT CHI OCT 12
TOR 020 100 003   6 10 0
CHI 002 000 001   3 5 3
Pitchers: STEWART, Ward (8) vs FERNANDEZ, McCaskill (8), Radinsky (9), Hernandez (9)
Home Runs: White-TOR, Newson-CHI
Attendance: 45,527

TORONTO BLUE JAYS (AL) 4, PHILADELPHIA PHILLIES (NL) 2

The Phillies and Blue Jays split the first two games, played in Toronto. But the defending champs captured the lead when play moved to Philadelphia. In a contest delayed more than an hour by rain, Paul Molitor tripled home two Blue Jay runs before the first out had been recorded, and the Jays cruised to an easy 10–3 win.

By just about any measure except pitching effectiveness, Game 4—played in a steady drizzle that for a time increased to a downpour—was one of the great ones. At 4 hours 14 minutes, it was the longest in World Series history, and its 29 total runs scored set a record for major league postseason championship play, as did Philadelphia's 14 runs for a losing team. Toronto scored three times after two men had been retired in the top of the first inning, but Philadelphia retaliated immediately with four two-out runs in the bottom of the inning. Lenny Dykstra's two-run homer an inning later pushed the Phillies' lead to 6–3, but Toronto scrambled back to regain a 7–6 advantage in the third inning. Philadelphia scored a tying run in the fourth inning, then scored five times an inning later with a barrage of hits highlighted by Darren Daulton's two-run homer and Dykstra's second two-run blast of the game. Toronto scored twice in the sixth inning, but single runs in the sixth and seventh restored Philadelphia's five-run lead. Then, in the top of the eighth, the Blue Jays parlayed two walks, two singles and a two-base error (later changed by the official scorer to a double) into a pair of runs and a diamond full of baserunners. Rickey Henderson lined a two-run single to center to bring the Jays within one run of a tie, and Devon White looped a triple to right center for the tying and go-ahead runs. Relievers Mike Timlin and Duane Ward retired the final seven Phillies on five strikeouts and a pair of pop flies.

The Phillies salvaged their final home game, scoring single runs in the first two innings as Curt Schilling shut out the Blue Jays and forced the Series back to Toronto for a sixth game. Paul Molitor's RBI triple gave the Jays a first-inning lead, and his solo homer in the fifth stretched it to 5–1. Lenny Dykstra's three-run shot in the seventh (his fourth home run of the Series) brought Philadelphia to within a run of Toronto and Mariano Duncan scored the tying run on Dave Hollins' single. Pinch hitter Pete Incaviglia's sacrifice fly gave the Phillies their first lead of the game, 6–5. In the bottom of the ninth, Mitch Williams walked Rickey Henderson and, with one away, gave up a single to Molitor (which raised his Series batting average to .500). Molitor scored the Series-winning run when Joe Carter, the next man up, lined Williams' would-be third strike over the left-field fence for an 8–6 victory and Toronto's second straight world championship.

TOR (A)

PLAYER/POS	AVG	G	AB	R	H	2B	3B	HR	RB	BB	SO	SB
Roberto Alomar, 2b	.480	6	25	5	12	2	1	0	6	2	3	4
Pat Borders, c	.304	6	23	2	7	0	0	0	0	1	2	0
Rob Butler, ph	.500	2	2	1	1	0	0	0	0	0	0	0
Willie Canate, pr	.000	1	0	0	0	0	0	0	0	0	0	0
Joe Carter, of	.280	6	25	6	7	1	0	2	8	0	4	0
Tony Castillo, p	.000	2	1	0	0	0	0	0	0	0	1	0
Danny Cox, p	.000	3	1	0	0	0	0	0	0	0	0	0
Mark Eichhorn, p	.000	1	0	0	0	0	0	0	0	0	0	0
Tony Fernandez, ss	.333	6	21	2	7	1	0	0	9	3	3	0
Alfredo Griffin, 3b-2	.000	3	0	0	0	0	0	0	0	0	0	0
Juan Guzman, p	.000	2	2	0	0	0	0	0	0	0	1	0
Rickey Henderson, of	.227	6	22	6	5	2	0	0	2	5	2	1
Pat Hentgen, p	.000	1	3	0	0	0	0	0	0	0	1	0
Randy Knorr, c	.000	1	0	0	0	0	0	0	0	0	0	0
Al Leiter, p	1.000	3	1	0	1	1	0	0	0	0	0	0
Paul Molitor, dh-3	.500	6	24	10	12	2	2	2	8	3	0	1
John Olerud, 1b	.235	5	17	5	4	1	0	1	2	4	1	0
Ed Sprague, 3b-4,1b-1	.067	5	15	0	1	0	0	0	2	1	6	0
Dave Stewart, p	.000	2	0	0	0	0	0	0	0	0	0	0
Todd Stottlemyre, p	.000	1	0	0	0	0	0	0	0	0	1	0
Mike Timlin, p	.000	2	0	0	0	0	0	0	0	0	0	0
Duane Ward, p	.000	4	0	0	0	0	0	0	0	0	0	0
Devon White, of	.292	6	24	8	7	3	2	1	7	4	7	1
TOTAL	.311		206	45	64	13	5	6	45	25	30	7

PITCHER	W	L	ERA	G	GS	CG	SV	SHO	IP	H	ER	BB	SO
Tony Castillo	1	0	8.10	2	0	0	0	0	3.1	6	3	3	1
Danny Cox	0	0	8.10	3	0	0	0	0	3.1	6	3	5	6
Mark Eichhorn	0	0	0.00	1	0	0	0	0	0.1	1	0	1	0
Juan Guzman	0	1	3.75	2	2	0	0	0	12.0	10	5	8	12
Pat Hentgen	1	0	1.50	1	1	0	0	0	6.0	5	1	3	6
Al Leiter	1	0	7.71	3	0	0	0	0	7.0	12	6	2	5
Dave Stewart	0	1	6.75	2	2	0	0	0	12.0	10	9	8	8
Todd Stottlemyre	0	0	27.00	1	1	0	0	0	2.0	3	6	4	1
Mike Timlin	0	0	0.00	2	0	0	0	0	2.1	2	0	0	4
Duane Ward	1	0	1.93	4	0	0	2	0	4.2	3	1	0	7
TOTAL	4	2	5.77	21	6	0	2	0	53.0	58	34	34	50

PHI (N)

PLAYER/POS	AVG	G	AB	R	H	2B	3B	HR	RB	BB	SO	SB
Larry Andersen, p	.000	4	0	0	0	0	0	0	0	0	0	0
Kim Batiste,	.000	3	0	0	0	0	0	0	0	0	0	0
Wes Chamberlain, ph	.000	2	2	0	0	0	0	0	0	0	1	0
Darren Daulton, c	.217	6	23	4	5	2	0	1	4	4	5	0
Mariano Duncan, 2b-5, dh-1	.345	6	29	5	10	0	1	0	2	1	7	3
Lenny Dykstra, of	.348	6	23	9	8	1	0	4	8	7	4	4
Jim Eisenreich, of	.231	6	26	3	6	0	0	1	7	2	4	0
Tommy Greene, p	1.000	1	1	1	1	0	0	0	0	0	0	0
Dave Hollins, 3b	.261	6	23	5	6	1	0	0	2	6	5	0
Pete Incaviglia, of	.125	4	8	0	1	0	0	0	1	0	4	0
Danny Jackson, p	.000	1	1	0	0	0	0	0	0	0	1	0
Ricky Jordan, dh-2	.200	3	10	0	2	0	0	0	0	0	2	0
John Kruk, 1b	.348	6	23	4	8	1	0	0	4	7	7	0
Roger Mason, p	.000	4	1	0	0	0	0	0	0	0	2	0
Mickey Morandini, 2b-1	.200	3	5	1	1	0	0	0	0	1	2	0
Terry Mulholland, p	.000	2	0	0	0	0	0	0	0	0	0	0
Ben Rivera, p	.000	1	0	0	0	0	0	0	0	0	0	0
Curt Schilling, p	.500	2	2	0	1	0	0	0	0	0	1	0
Kevin Stocker, ss	.211	6	19	1	4	1	0	0	1	5	5	0
Bobby Thigpen, p	.000	2	0	0	0	0	0	0	0	0	0	0
Milt Thompson, of	.313	6	16	3	5	1	1	1	6	1	2	0
David West, p	.000	3	0	0	0	0	0	0	0	0	0	0
Mitch Williams, p	.000	3	0	0	0	0	0	0	0	0	0	0
TOTAL	.274		212	36	58	7	2	7	35	34	50	7

PITCHER	W	L	ERA	G	GS	CG	SV	SHO	IP	H	ER	BB	SO
Larry Andersen	0	0	12.27	4	0	0	0	0	3.2	5	5	3	3
Tommy Greene	0	0	27.00	1	1	0	0	0	2.1	7	7	4	1
Danny Jackson	0	1	7.20	1	1	0	0	0	5.0	6	4	1	1
Roger Mason	0	0	1.17	4	0	0	0	0	7.2	4	1	1	7
Terry Mulholland	1	0	6.75	2	2	0	0	0	10.2	14	8	3	5
Ben Rivera	0	0	27.00	1	0	0	0	0	1.1	4	4	2	3
Curt Schilling	1	1	3.52	2	2	1	0	1	15.1	13	6	5	9
Bobby Thigpen	0	0	0.00	2	0	0	0	0	2.2	1	0	1	0
David West	0	0	27.00	3	0	0	0	0	1.0	5	3	1	0
Mitch Williams	0	2	20.25	3	0	0	0	1	2.2	5	6	4	1
TOTAL	2	4	7.57	23	6	0	0	1	52.1	64	44	25	30

GAME 1 AT TOR OCT 16

```
PHI   2 0 1 0 1 0 0 0 1    5 11 1
TOR   0 2 1 0 1 1 3 0 X    8 10 3
```
Pitchers: SCHILLING, West (7), Andersen (7), Mason (8) vs Guzman, LEITER (6), Ward (8)
Home Runs: White-TOR, Olerud-TOR
Attendance: 52,011

GAME 2 AT TOR OCT 17

```
PHI   0 0 5 0 0 0 1 0 0    6 12 0
TOR   0 0 0 2 0 1 0 1 0    4  8 0
```
Pitchers: MULHOLLAND, Mason (6), Williams (7) vs STEWART, Castillo (7), Eichhorn (8), Timlin (8)
Home Runs: Dykstra-PHI, Eisenreich-PHI, Carter-TOR
Attendance: 52,062

GAME 3 AT PHI OCT 19

```
TOR   3 0 1 0 0 1 3 0 2   10 13 1
PHI   0 0 0 0 1 0 1 0 1    3  9 0
```
Pitchers: HENTGEN, Cox (7), Ward (9) vs JACKSON, Rivera (6), Thigpen (7), Andersen (9)
Home Runs: Molitor-TOR, Thompson-PHI
Attendance: 62,689

GAME 4 AT PHI OCT 20

```
TOR   3 0 4 0 0 2 0 6 0   15 18 0
PHI   4 2 0 1 5 1 1 0 0   14 14 0
```
Pitchers: Stottlemyre, Leiter (3), CASTILLO (5), Timlin (8), Ward (8) vs Greene, Mason (3), West (6), Andersen (7), WILLIAMS (8), Thigpen (9)
Home Runs: Dykstra-PHI (2), Daulton-PHI
Attendance: 62,731

GAME 5 AT PHI OCT 21

```
TOR   0 0 0 0 0 0 0 0 0    0 5 1
PHI   1 1 0 0 0 0 0 0 X    2 5 1
```
Pitchers: GUZMAN, Cox (8) vs SCHILLING
Attendance: 62,706

GAME 6 AT TOR OCT 23

```
PHI   0 0 0 1 0 0 5 0 0    6  7 0
TOR   3 0 0 1 1 0 0 0 3    8 10 2
```
Pitchers: Mulholland, Mason (6), West (8), Andersen (8), WILLIAMS (9) vs Stewart, Cox (7), Leiter (7), WARD (9)
Home Runs: Molitor-TOR, Dykstra-PHI, Carter-TOR
Attendance: 52,195

ATLANTA BRAVES (EAST) 3, COLORADO ROCKIES (WILD CARD) 1

Pitching-rich Atlanta's appearance in the division playoffs surprised few, but the hard-hitting expansion Rockies made history by reaching the postseason in just their third year of existence.

Two individuals shared the spotlight in Game 1: Braves rookie third baseman Chipper Jones and Rockies manager Don Baylor, but for wildly different reasons. Jones collected two homers and made a spectacular stop to rob Andres Galarraga of a double. Baylor was less fortunate. He ran out of hitters in the bottom of the ninth—having to use pitcher Lance Painter as his last batter—after Jones homered with two outs in the top of the inning. Atlanta won, 5–4.

Atlanta trailed, 4–3, going into the top of the ninth in Game 2, but they came thundering back with four runs as Mike Mordecai pinch homered, and Rockies second baseman Eric Young botched a routine ground ball. The Braves triumphed, 7–4, taking a 2–0 lead in the series.

In Game 3 Atlanta came through in the ninth once more on pinchhitter Luis Polonia's two-strike run-scoring single, and the game went into extra innings. But Colorado bounced back to score twice in the 10th on Dante Bichette's double down the left field line and run-scoring singles by Andres Galarraga and Vinny Castilla (who had homered in the sixth).

Cy Young Award winners battled in Game 4 as Greg Maddux and Bret Saberhagen started, but Saberhagen was ineffective and Atlanta eliminated the Rockies with a 10–4 win. Maddux struck out seven and walked none before leaving for a pinch hitter in the seventh inning. Not helping Saberhagen was a controversial "safe" call on a play in which he attempted to cover first. Fred McGriff followed with the first of his two homers in the contest.

ATL (E)

PLAYER/POS	AVG	G	AB	R	H	2B	3B	HR	RB	BB	SO	SB
Steve Avery, p	.000	1	0	0	0	0	0	0	0	0	0	0
Rafael Belliard, ss	.000	4	5	1	0	0	0	0	0	0	1	0
Jeff Blauser, ss	.000	3	6	0	0	0	0	0	0	1	3	0
Pedro Borbon, p	.000	1	0	0	0	0	0	0	0	0	0	0
Brad Clontz, p	.000	1	0	0	0	0	0	0	0	0	0	0
Mike Devereaux, of-3	.200	4	5	1	1	0	0	0	0	0	0	0
Tom Glavine, p	.333	1	3	0	1	0	0	0	0	0	1	0
Marquis Grissom, of	.524	4	21	5	11	2	0	3	4	0	3	2
Chipper Jones, 3b	.389	4	18	4	7	2	0	2	4	2	2	0
David Justice, of	.231	4	13	2	3	0	0	0	0	5	2	0
Ryan Klesko, of	.467	4	15	5	7	1	0	0	1	0	3	0
Mark Lemke, 2b	.211	4	19	3	4	1	0	0	1	1	3	0
Javy Lopez, c	.444	3	9	0	4	0	0	0	3	0	3	0
Greg Maddux, p	.167	2	6	1	1	0	0	0	0	0	1	0
Fred McGriff, 1b	.333	4	18	4	6	0	0	2	6	2	3	0
Greg McMichael, p	.000	2	0	0	0	0	0	0	0	0	0	0
Kent Mercker, p	.000	1	0	0	0	0	0	0	0	0	0	0
Mike Mordecai, ss-1	.667	2	3	1	2	1	0	1	2	0	0	0
Charlie O'Brien, c	.200	2	5	0	1	0	0	0	0	1	1	0
Alejandro Pena, p	.000	3	0	0	0	0	0	0	0	0	0	0
Luis Polonia, ph	.333	3	3	0	1	0	0	0	0	2	0	1
Dwight Smith, ph	.667	4	3	0	2	1	0	0	1	0	0	0
John Smoltz, p	.000	1	2	0	0	0	0	0	0	0	0	0
Mark Wohlers, p	.000	3	0	0	0	0	0	0	0	0	0	0
TOTAL	.331		154	27	51	8	0	7	24	12	27	3

PITCHER	W	L	ERA	G	GS	CG	SV	SHO	IP	H	ER	BB	SO
Steve Avery	0	0	13.50	1	0	0	0	0	0.2	1	1	0	1
Pedro Borbon	0	0	0.00	1	0	0	0	0	1.0	1	0	0	3
Brad Clontz	0	0	0.00	1	0	0	0	0	1.1	0	0	0	2
Tom Glavine	0	0	2.57	1	1	0	0	0	7.0	5	2	1	3
Greg Maddux	1	0	4.50	2	2	0	0	0	14.0	19	7	2	7
Greg McMichael	0	0	6.75	2	0	0	0	0	1.1	1	1	2	1
Kent Mercker	0	0	0.00	1	0	0	0	0	0.1	0	0	0	0
Alejandro Pena	2	0	0.00	3	0	0	0	0	3.0	3	0	1	2
John Smoltz	0	0	7.94	1	1	0	0	0	5.2	5	5	1	6
Mark Wohlers	0	1	6.75	3	0	0	2	0	2.2	6	2	2	4
TOTAL	3	1	4.38	16	4	0	2	0	37.0	41	18	9	29

COL (WC)

PLAYER/POS	AVG	G	AB	R	H	2B	3B	HR	RB	BB	SO	SB
Jason Bates, 2b-1,3b-1	.250	4	4	0	1	0	0	0	0	0	0	0
Dante Bichette, of	.588	4	17	6	10	3	0	1	3	1	3	0
Ellis Burks, of	.333	2	6	1	2	1	0	0	2	0	1	0
Vinny Castilla, 3b	.467	4	15	3	7	1	0	3	6	0	1	0
Andres Galarraga, 1b	.278	4	18	5	5	1	0	0	2	0	6	0
Joe Girardi, c	.125	4	16	0	2	0	0	0	0	0	2	0
Darren Holmes, p	.000	3	0	0	0	0	0	0	0	0	0	0
Trenidad Hubbard, ph	.000	3	2	0	0	0	0	0	0	0	0	0
Mike Kingery, of	.200	4	10	1	2	0	0	0	0	0	1	0
Curt Leskanic, p	.000	3	0	0	0	0	0	0	0	0	0	0
Mike Munoz, p	.000	4	0	0	0	0	0	0	0	0	0	0
J Owens, c	.000	1	1	0	0	0	0	0	0	0	1	0
Lance Painter, p-1	.000	2	2	0	0	0	0	0	0	0	1	0
Steve Reed, p	.000	3	0	0	0	0	0	0	0	0	0	0
Armando Reynoso, p	.000	1	0	0	0	0	0	0	0	0	0	0
Kevin Ritz, p	.000	2	2	0	0	0	0	0	0	0	1	0
Bruce Ruffin, p	.000	4	0	0	0	0	0	0	0	0	0	0
Bret Saberhagen, p	.000	1	1	0	0	0	0	0	0	0	0	0
Bill Swift, p	.000	1	3	0	0	0	0	0	0	0	2	0
Mark Thompson, p	.000	1	0	0	0	0	0	0	0	0	0	0
John Vander Wal, ph	.000	4	4	0	0	0	0	0	0	0	2	0
Larry Walker, of	.214	4	14	3	3	0	0	1	3	3	4	1
Walt Weiss, ss	.167	4	12	1	2	0	0	0	0	3	3	1
Eric Young, 2b	.438	4	16	3	7	1	0	1	2	2	2	1
TOTAL	.287		143	19	41	7	0	6	18	9	29	3

PITCHER	W	L	ERA	G	GS	CG	SV	SHO	IP	H	ER	BB	SO
Darren Holmes	1	0	0.00	3	0	0	0	0	1.2	6	0	0	2
Curt Leskanic	0	1	6.00	3	0	0	0	0	3.0	3	2	0	4
Mike Munoz	0	1	13.50	4	0	0	0	0	1.1	4	2	1	0
Lance Painter	0	0	5.40	1	1	0	0	0	5.0	5	3	2	4
Steve Reed	0	0	0.00	3	0	0	0	0	2.2	2	0	1	3
Armando Reynoso	0	0	0.00	1	0	0	0	0	1.0	2	0	0	0
Kevin Ritz	0	0	7.71	2	1	0	0	0	7.0	12	6	3	5
Bruce Ruffin	0	0	2.70	4	0	0	0	0	3.1	3	1	2	2
Bret Saberhagen	0	1	11.25	1	1	0	0	0	4.0	7	5	1	3
Bill Swift	0	0	6.00	1	1	0	0	0	6.0	7	4	2	3
Mark Thompson	0	0	0.00	1	0	0	0	1	1.0	0	0	0	0
TOTAL	1	3	5.75	24	4	0	1	0	36.0	51	23	12	27

GAME 1 AT COL OCT 3

ATL 001 002 011 5 12 1
COL 000 300 010 4 13 4
Pitchers: Maddux, McMichael (8), PENA (8), Wohlers (9) vs Ritz, Reed (6), Ruffin (7), Munoz (8), Holmes (8), LESKANIC (9)
Home Runs: Grissom-ATL, Jones-ATL (2), Castilla-COL
Attendance: 50,040

GAME 2 AT COL OCT 4

ATL 101 100 004 7 13 1
COL 000 003 010 4 8 2
Pitchers: Glavine, Avery (8), PENA (8), Wohlers (9) vs Painter, Reed (6), Ruffin (7), Leskanic (8), MUNOZ (9), Holmes (9)
Home Runs: Grissom-ATL (2), Walker-COL
Attendance: 50,040

GAME 3 AT ATL OCT 6

COL 102 002 000 2 7 9 0
ATL 000 300 101 0 5 11 0
Pitchers: Swift, Reed] (7), Munoz (7), Leskanic (7), Ruffin (8), HOLMES (9), Thompson (10) vs Smoltz, Clontz (6), Borbon (8), McMichael (9), WOHLERS (10), Mercker (10)
Home Runs: Young-COL, Castilla-COL
Attendance: 51,300

GAME 4 AT ATL OCT 7

COL 003 001 000 4 11 1
ATL 004 213 00X 10 15 0
Pitchers: SABERHAGEN, Ritz (5), Munoz (6), Reynoso (7), Ruffin (8) vs MADDUX, Pena (8)
Home Runs: Bichette-COL, Castilla-COL, McGriff-ATL (2)
Attendance: 50,027

CINCINNATI REDS (CENTRAL) 3, LOS ANGELES DODGERS (WEST) 0

Davey Johnson's Cincinnati Reds made short work of Tommy Lasorda's Los Angeles Dodgers in the 1995 NL division series, sweeping them, 3–0, and outscoring them, 22–7.

Game 1 saw the Reds score four times in the first inning as they walloped the Dodgers, 7–2. Los Angeles starter Ramon Martinez was ineffective, being cuffed for 10 hits and two walks in just four and a third innings.

Game 2 was a more even affair until the Los Angeles bullpen went to work. Barry Larkin's eighth-inning single to right broke open a 2–2 tie, and in the top of the ninth the Reds added two insurance runs.

The Reds wrapped up the series by humiliating the Dodgers 10–1 in Game 3. The Dodgers had their chances in the contest, but squandered their opportunities, leaving 11 runners on base. The Reds broke the game open in the sixth as pinch hitter Mark Lewis delivered a grand slam to left-center off Mark Guthrie.

CIN (C)

PLAYER/POS	AVG	G	AB	R	H	2B	3B	HR	RB	BB	SO	SB
Bret Boone, 2b	.300	3	10	4	3	1	0	1	1	1	3	1
Jeff Branson, 3b	.286	3	7	0	2	1	0	0	2	2	0	0
Jeff Brantley, p	.000	3	0	0	0	0	0	0	0	0	0	0
Dave Burba, p	.000	1	0	0	0	0	0	0	0	0	0	0
Mariano Duncan, 2b-1	.667	2	3	1	2	0	0	0	1	0	0	0
Ron Gant, of	.231	3	13	3	3	0	0	1	2	0	3	0
Thomas Howard, of	.100	3	10	0	1	1	0	0	0	0	2	0
Mike Jackson, p	1.000	3	1	0	1	1	0	0	3	0	0	0
Barry Larkin, ss	.385	3	13	2	5	0	0	0	1	1	2	4
Darren Lewis, of	.000	3	3	0	0	0	0	0	0	0	1	0
Mark Lewis, 3b	.500	2	2	2	1	0	0	1	5	1	0	0
Hal Morris, 1b	.500	3	10	5	5	1	0	0	2	3	1	1
Reggie Sanders, of	.154	3	13	3	2	1	0	1	2	1	9	2
Benito Santiago, c	.333	3	9	2	3	0	0	1	3	3	3	0
Pete Schourek, p	.000	1	2	0	0	0	0	0	0	0	1	0
John Smiley, p	.000	1	2	0	0	0	0	0	0	0	1	0
Jerome Walton, of	.000	3	3	0	0	0	0	0	0	1	1	0
David Wells, p	.333	1	3	0	1	0	0	0	0	0	1	0
TOTAL	.279		104	22	29	6	0	5	22	13	28	9

PITCHER	W	L	ERA	G	GS	CG	SV	SHO	IP	H	ER	BB	SO
Jeff Brantley	0	0	6.00	3	0	0	1	0	3.0	5	2	0	2
Dave Burba	1	0	0.00	1	0	0	0	0	1.0	2	0	1	0
Mike Jackson	0	0	0.00	3	0	0	0	0	3.2	4	0	0	1
Pete Schourek	1	0	2.57	1	1	0	0	0	7.0	5	2	3	5
John Smiley	0	0	3.00	1	1	0	0	0	6.0	9	2	0	1
David Wells	1	0	0.00	1	1	0	0	0	6.1	6	0	1	8
TOTAL	3	0	2.00	10	3	0	1	0	27.0	31	6	5	17

LA (W)

PLAYER/POS	AVG	G	AB	R	H	2B	3B	HR	RB	BB	SO	SB
Billy Ashley, ph	.000	1	0	0	0	0	0	0	0	1	0	0
Pedro Astacio, p	.000	3	0	0	0	0	0	0	0	0	0	0
Brett Butler, of	.267	3	15	1	4	0	0	0	1	0	3	0
John Cummings, p	.000	2	0	0	0	0	0	0	0	0	0	0
Delino DeShields, 2b	.250	3	12	1	3	0	0	0	0	1	3	0
Chad Fonville, ss	.500	3	12	1	6	0	0	0	0	0	1	0
Mark Guthrie, p	.000	3	0	0	0	0	0	0	0	0	0	0
Chris Gwynn, ph	.000	1	1	0	0	0	0	0	0	0	1	0
Dave Hansen, ph	.667	3	3	0	2	0	0	0	0	0	0	0
Todd Hollandsworth, of	.000	2	2	0	0	0	0	0	0	0	0	0
Eric Karros, 1b	.500	3	12	3	6	1	0	2	4	1	0	0
Roberto Kelly, of	.364	3	11	0	4	0	0	0	1	1	0	0
Ramon Martinez, p	.000	1	1	0	0	0	0	0	0	0	0	0
Raul Mondesi, of	.222	3	9	0	2	0	0	0	1	0	2	0
Hideo Nomo, p	.000	1	2	0	0	0	0	0	0	0	2	0
Jose Offerman, pr	.000	1	0	0	0	0	0	0	0	0	0	0
Antonio Osuna, p	.000	3	0	0	0	0	0	0	0	0	0	0
Mike Piazza, c	.214	3	14	1	3	1	0	1	1	0	2	0
Kevin Tapani, p	.000	2	0	0	0	0	0	0	0	0	0	0
Ismael Valdes, p	.000	1	3	0	0	0	0	0	0	0	0	0
Tim Wallach, 3b	.083	3	12	0	1	0	0	0	0	1	3	0
Mitch Webster, ph	.000	2	2	0	0	0	0	0	0	0	0	0
TOTAL	.279		111	7	31	2	0	3	7	5	17	0

PITCHER	W	L	ERA	G	GS	CG	SV	SHO	IP	H	ER	BB	SO
Pedro Astacio	0	0	0.00	3	0	0	0	0	3.1	1	0	0	5
John Cummings	0	0	20.25	2	0	0	0	0	1.1	3	3	2	3
Mark Guthrie	0	0	6.75	3	0	0	0	0	1.1	2	1	1	1
Ramon Martinez	0	1	14.54	1	1	0	0	0	4.1	10	7	2	3
Hideo Nomo	0	1	9.00	1	1	0	0	0	5.0	7	5	2	6
Antonio Osuna	0	1	2.70	3	0	0	0	0	3.1	3	1	1	3
Kevin Tapani	0	0	81.00	2	0	0	0	0	0.1	0	3	4	1
Ismael Valdes	0	0	0.00	1	1	0	0	0	7.0	3	0	1	6
TOTAL	0	3	6.92	16	3	0	0	0	26.0	29	20	13	28

GAME 1 AT LA OCT 3

CIN 4 0 0 0 3 0 0 0 0   7 12 0
LA   0 0 0 0 1 1 0 0 0   2 8 0
Pitchers: SCHOUREK, Jackson (8), Brantley (9) vs MARTINEZ, Cummings (5), Astacio (6), Guthrie (8), Osuna (9)
Home Runs: Santiago-CIN, Piazza-LA
Attendance: 44,199

GAME 2 AT LA OCT 4

CIN 0 0 0 2 0 0 0 1 2   5 6 0
LA   1 0 0 1 0 0 0 0 2   4 14 2
Pitchers: Smiley, BURBA (7), Jackson (8), Brantley (9) vs Valdes, OSUNA (8), Tapani (9), Guthrie (9), Astacio (9)
Home Runs: Sanders-CIN, Karros-LA (2)
Attendance: 46,051

GAME 3 AT CIN OCT 6

LA   0 0 0 1 0 0 0 0 0   1 9 1
CIN 0 0 2 1 0 4 3 0 X   10 11 2
Pitchers: NOMO, Tapani (6), Guthrie (6), Astacio (6), Cummings (7), Osuna (7) vs WELLS, Jackson (7), Brantley (9)
Home Runs: Gant-CIN, Boone-CIN, M.Lewis-CIN
Attendance: 53,276

CLEVELAND INDIANS (CENTRAL) 3, BOSTON RED SOX (EAST) 0

The Cleveland Indians had enjoyed a 100–44 record in the strike-shortened 1995 season and captured the AL's new Central Division by a record 30 games. Not surprisingly, they were heavily favored against the AL East champion Red Sox. And not surprisingly, the Curse of Rocky Colavito fell in three straight to the Curse of the Bambino—in other words, the Tribe won.

Yet there were moments of high drama in the series. Game 1 was a titanic struggle that had nearly everything: two rain delays (39 minutes at the start and 23 minutes in the eighth), three extra inning homers, and a controversial piece of lumber. The five-hour and one-minute game ended at 2:08 a.m. the next day. But no one in Cleveland was complaining.

Boston jumped off to a 2–0 lead on John Valentin's two-run homer, but Red Sox starter Roger Clemens surrendered three runs in the sixth. Boston's Luis Alicea evened the score up with a leadoff homer in the eighth. In the top of the 11th, Tim Naehring homered to give the Sox the lead, but Albert Belle retaliated in the bottom of the frame with a homer of his own. The next move was Boston's, which contended Belle's bat was corked. AL authorities confiscated it and sawed it in half but found no cork. In the 12th the Indians loaded the bases with one out but did not score. In the 13th former Red Sox catcher Tony Pena ended it all with an improbable homer off a 3–0 pitch from Zane Smith.

Game 2 was a much easier win as veteran Orel Hershiser faced Boston's Erik Hanson. Omar Vizquel doubled in two runs in the fifth. Eddie Murray added a two-run homer off Hanson in the eighth. That was more than Hershiser needed as he struck out seven in seven and a third innings while walking just two and allowing three hits.

Game 3 moved from Jacobs Field to Fenway Park, but the home field proved to be no advantage. Red Sox knuckleballer Tim Wakefield surrendered seven runs in five and a third innings as the Indians, behind Charles Nagy, eliminated Boston with an 8–2 win. Mo Vaughn and Jose Canseco went hitless, running their record to 0-for-27, with nine strikeouts in

the series. But Boston's defeat was not the duo's fault entirely. Overall, Sox batters were 2-for-28 with runners in scoring position.

GAME 1 AT CLE OCT 3

BOS 002 000 010 010 0   4 11 2
CLE 000 003 000 010 1   5 10 2
Pitchers: Clemens, Cormier (8), Belinda (8), Stanton (8), Aguilera (11), Maddux (11), SMITH (12) vs Martinez, Tavarez (7), Assenmacher (8), Plunk (8), Mesa (10), Poole (11), HILL (12)
Home Runs: Valentin-BOS, Alicea-BOS, Naehring-BOS, Belle-CLE, Pena-CLE
Attendance: 44,218

GAME 2 AT CLE OCT 4

BOS 000 000 000   0 3 1
CLE 000 02 0002X   4 4 2
Pitchers: HANSON vs HERSHISER, Tavarez (8), Assenmacher (8), Mesa (9)
Home Runs: Murray-CLE
Attendance: 44,264

GAME 3 AT BOS OCT 6

BOS 000 100 010   2 7 1
CLE 021 005 000   8 11 2
Pitchers: NAGY, Tavarez (8), Assenmacher (9) vs WAKEFIELD, Cormier (6), Maddux (6), Hudson (9)
Home Runs: Thome-CLE
Attendance: 34,211

CLE (C)

PLAYER/POS	AVG	G	AB	R	H	2B	3B	HR	RB	BB	SO	SB
Sandy Alomar, c	.182	3	11	1	2	1	0	0	1	0	1	0
Paul Assenmacher, p	.000	3	0	0	0	0	0	0	0	0	0	0
Carlos Baerga, 2b	.286	3	14	2	4	1	0	0	1	0	1	0
Albert Belle, of	.273	3	11	3	3	1	0	1	3	4	3	0
Alvaro Espinoza, 3b	.000	1	1	0	0	0	0	0	0	0	0	0
Orel Hershiser, p	.000	1	0	0	0	0	0	0	0	0	0	0
Ken Hill, p	.000	1	0	0	0	0	0	0	0	0	0	0
Wayne Kirby, of-2	1.000	3	1	0	1	0	0	0	0	0	0	0
Kenny Lofton, of	.154	3	13	1	2	0	0	0	0	1	3	0
Dennis Martinez, p	.000	1	0	0	0	0	0	0	0	0	0	0
Jose Mesa, p	.000	2	0	0	0	0	0	0	0	0	0	0
Eddie Murray, dh	.385	3	13	3	5	0	1	1	3	2	1	0
Charles Nagy, p	.000	1	0	0	0	0	0	0	0	0	0	0
Tony Pena, c	.500	2	2	1	1	0	0	1	1	0	0	0
Herb Perry, ph	.000	1	1	0	0	0	0	0	0	0	0	0
Eric Plunk, p	.000	1	0	0	0	0	0	0	0	0	0	0
Jim Poole, p	.000	1	0	0	0	0	0	0	0	0	0	0
Manny Ramirez, of	.000	3	12	1	0	0	0	0	0	1	2	0
Paul Sorrento, 1b	.300	3	10	2	3	0	0	0	1	2	3	0
Julian Tavarez, p	.000	3	0	0	0	0	0	0	0	0	0	0
Jim Thome, 3b	.154	3	13	1	2	0	0	1	3	1	6	0
Omar Vizquel, ss	.167	3	12	2	2	1	0	0	4	2	2	1
TOTAL	.219		114	17	25	4	1	4	17	13	22	1

PITCHER	W	L	ERA	G	GS	CG	SV	SHO	IP	H	ER	BB	SO
Paul Assenmacher	0	0	0.00	3	0	0	0	0	1.2	0	0	0	3
Orel Hershiser	1	0	0.00	1	1	0	0	0	7.1	3	0	2	7
Ken Hill	1	0	0.00	1	0	0	0	0	1.1	1	0	0	2
Dennis Martinez	0	0	3.00	1	1	0	0	0	6.0	5	2	0	2
Jose Mesa	0	0	0.00	2	0	0	0	0	2.0	0	0	2	0
Charles Nagy	1	0	1.29	1	1	0	0	0	7.0	4	1	5	6
Eric Plunk	0	0	0.00	1	0	0	0	0	1.1	1	0	1	1
Jim Poole	0	0	5.40	1	0	0	0	0	1.2	2	1	1	2
Julian Tavarez	0	0	6.75	3	0	0	0	0	2.2	5	2	0	3
TOTAL	3	0	1.74	14	3	0	0	0	31.0	21	6	11	26

BOS (E)

PLAYER/POS	AVG	G	AB	R	H	2B	3B	HR	RB	BB	SO	SB
Rick Aguilera, p	.000	1	0	0	0	0	0	0	0	0	0	0
Luis Alicea, 2b	.600	3	10	1	6	1	0	1	1	2	2	1
Stan Belinda, p	.000	1	0	0	0	0	0	0	0	0	0	0
Jose Canseco, dh-2, of-1	.000	3	13	0	0	0	0	0	0	2	2	0
Roger Clemens, p	.000	1	0	0	0	0	0	0	0	0	0	0
Rheal Cormier, p	.000	2	0	0	0	0	0	0	0	0	0	0
Mike Greenwell, of	.200	3	15	0	3	0	0	0	0	0	1	0
Erik Hanson, p	.000	1	0	0	0	0	0	0	0	0	0	0
Bill Haselman, c	.000	1	2	0	0	0	0	0	0	0	0	0
Dwayne Hosey, of	.000	3	12	1	0	0	0	0	0	2	3	1
Joe Hudson, p	.000	1	0	0	0	0	0	0	0	0	0	0
Reggie Jefferson, dh	.250	1	4	1	1	0	0	0	0	0	1	0
Mike Macfarlane, c	.333	3	9	0	3	0	0	0	1	0	3	0
Mike Maddux, p	.000	2	0	0	0	0	0	0	0	0	0	0
Willie McGee, of	.250	2	4	0	1	0	0	0	1	0	2	0
Tim Naehring, 3b	.308	3	13	2	4	0	0	1	1	0	1	0
Zane Smith, p	.000	1	0	0	0	0	0	0	0	0	0	0
Matt Stairs, ph	.000	1	1	0	0	0	0	0	0	0	1	0
Mike Stanton, p	.000	1	0	0	0	0	0	0	0	0	0	0
Lee Tinsley, of	.000	1	5	0	0	0	0	0	0	1	2	0
John Valentin, ss	.250	3	12	1	3	1	0	1	2	3	1	0
Mo Vaughn, 1b	.000	3	14	0	0	0	0	0	0	1	7	0
Tim Wakefield, p	.000	1	0	0	0	0	0	0	0	0	0	0
TOTAL	.184		114	6	21	2	0	3	6	11	26	2

PITCHER	W	L	ERA	G	GS	CG	SV	SHO	IP	H	ER	BB	SO
Rick Aguilera	0	0	13.50	1	0	0	0	0	0.2	3	1	0	1
Stan Belinda	0	0	0.00	1	0	0	0	0	0.1	0	0	0	0
Roger Clemens	0	0	3.86	1	1	0	0	0	7.0	5	3	1	5
Rheal Cormier	0	0	13.50	2	0	0	0	0	0.2	2	1	1	2
Erik Hanson	0	1	4.50	1	1	1	0	0	8.0	4	4	4	5
Joe Hudson	0	0	0.00	1	0	0	0	0	1.0	2	0	1	0
Mike Maddux	0	0	0.00	2	0	0	0	0	3.0	2	0	1	1
Zane Smith	0	1	6.75	1	0	0	0	0	1.1	1	1	0	0
Mike Stanton	0	0	0.00	1	0	0	0	0	2.1	1	0	0	4
Tim Wakefield	0	1	11.81	1	1	0	0	0	5.1	5	7	5	4
TOTAL	0	3	5.16	12	3	1	0	0	29.2	25	17	13	22

SEATTLE MARINERS (WEST) 3, NEW YORK YANKEES (WILD CARD) 2

The hitherto laughable Seattle Mariners shocked the New York Yankees in a gritty, exciting fivegame division series that could only be likened to two prize fighters standing toe-to-toe and slugging it out.

Seattle found its rotation askew after being forced into a one-game playoff against California to determine the AL West championship. In Game 1 the Yankees' David Cone started against Seattle's Chris Bosio and triumphed 9–6 despite Ken Griffey, Jr.'s two homers. Ultimately, Griffey would hit five in the series.

The Yankees won Game 2 by breaking up a 5–5 marathon on a two-run Jim Leyritz homer in the bottom of the 15th. In the 12th Griffey had homered to right-center on a 3–1 pitch to give Seattle the lead, but New York evened it in the bottom of the inning on Ruben Sierra's run-scoring double to left.

Seattle's ace, Cy Young Award winner Randy Johnson, finally appeared in Game 3, striking out 10 as Seattle won, 7–6, before a delirious Kingdome crowd. New York jumped off to a 5–0 lead in Game 4, but Seattle battled back to even the series at 2–2. The big blow was Edgar Martinez's grand-slam to center in the Mariners' five-run eighth inning. The game went down to the last out as New York left runners on second and third in the ninth.

After Seattle scored twice in the eighth to deadlock deciding Game 5 at 4–4, Mariners manager Lou Piniella brought in Randy Johnson (who had pitched seven innings just two days before) to shut the door on New York. Not to be outdone, Yankees manager Buck Showalter countered with starter Jack McDowell. Once again, Edgar Martinez (series average of .571) came through in the clutch, hitting a two-run double down the left field line to end the game—and the series.

SEA (W)

PLAYER/POS	AVG	G	AB	R	H	2B	3B	HR	RB	BB	SO	SB
Bobby Ayala, p	.000	2	0	0	0	0	0	0	0	0	0	0
Tim Belcher, p	.000	2	0	0	0	0	0	0	0	0	0	0
Andy Benes, p	.000	2	0	0	0	0	0	0	0	0	0	0
Mike Blowers, 3b-5,1b-1	.167	5	18	0	3	0	0	0	1	3	7	0
Chris Bosio, p	.000	2	0	0	0	0	0	0	0	0	0	0
Jay Buhner, of	.458	5	24	2	11	1	0	1	3	2	4	0
Norm Charlton, p	.000	4	0	0	0	0	0	0	0	0	0	0
Vince Coleman, of	.217	5	23	6	5	0	1	1	1	2	4	1
Joey Cora, 2b	.316	5	19	7	6	1	0	1	1	3	0	1
Alex Diaz, of-1	.333	2	3	0	1	0	0	0	0	1	1	0
Felix Fermin, ss-2,2b-1	.000	3	1	0	0	0	0	0	0	0	1	0
Ken Griffey, of	.391	5	23	9	9	0	0	5	7	2	4	1
Randy Johnson, p	.000	2	0	0	0	0	0	0	0	0	0	0
Tino Martinez, 1b	.409	5	22	4	9	1	0	1	5	3	4	0
Edgar Martinez, dh	.571	5	21	6	12	3	0	2	10	6	2	0
Jeff Nelson, p	.000	3	0	0	0	0	0	0	0	0	0	0
Warren Newson, ph	.000	1	1	0	0	0	0	0	0	0	1	0
Bill Risley, p	.000	4	0	0	0	0	0	0	0	0	0	0
Alex Rodriguez, ss	.000	1	1	1	0	0	0	0	0	0	0	0
Luis Sojo, ss	.250	5	20	0	5	0	0	0	3	0	3	0
Doug Strange, 3b	.000	2	4	0	0	0	0	0	0	1	1	0
Bob Wells, p	.000	1	0	0	0	0	0	0	0	0	0	0
Chris Widger, c	.000	2	3	0	0	0	0	0	0	0	3	0
Dan Wilson, c	.118	5	17	0	2	0	0	0	1	2	6	0
TOTAL	.315		200	35	63	6	1	11	33	25	41	3

PITCHER	W	L	ERA	G	GS	CG	SV	SHO	IP	H	ER	BB	SO
Bobby Ayala	0		54.00	2	0	0	0	0	0.2	6	4	1	0
Tim Belcher	0	1	6.23	2	0	0	0	0	4.1	4	3	5	0
Andy Benes	0	0	5.40	2	2	0	0	0	11.2	10	7	9	8
Chris Bosio	0	0	10.57	2	2	0	0	0	7.2	10	9	4	2
Norm Charlton	1	0	2.45	4	0	0	1	0	7.1	4	2	3	9
Randy Johnson	2	0	2.70	2	1	0	0	0	10.0	5	3	6	16
Jeff Nelson	0	1	3.18	3	0	0	0	0	5.2	7	2	3	7
Bill Risley	0	0	6.00	4	0	0	1	0	3.0	2	2	0	1
Bob Wells	0	0	9.00	1	0	0	0	0	1.0	2	1	1	0
TOTAL	3	2	5.79	22	5	0	2	0	51.1	50	33	32	43

NY (WC)

PLAYER/POS	AVG	G	AB	R	H	2B	3B	HR	RB	BB	SO	SB
Wade Boggs, 3b	.263	4	19	4	5	2	0	1	3	3	5	0
David Cone, p	.000	2	0	0	0	0	0	0	0	0	0	0
Russ Davis, 3b	.200	2	5	0	1	0	0	0	0	0	2	0
Tony Fernandez, ss	.238	5	21	0	5	2	0	0	0	2	2	0
Sterling Hitchcock, p	.000	2	0	0	0	0	0	0	0	0	0	0
Steve Howe, p	.000	2	0	0	0	0	0	0	0	0	0	0
Dion James, of	.083	4	12	0	1	0	0	0	0	1	1	0
Scott Kamieniecki, p	.000	1	0	0	0	0	0	0	0	0	0	0
Pat Kelly, 2b-4	.000	5	3	3	0	0	0	0	0	1	1	3	0
Jim Leyritz, c	.143	2	7	1	1	0	0	1	2	0	1	0
Don Mattingly, 1b	.417	5	24	3	10	4	0	1	6	1	5	0
Jack McDowell, p	.000	2	0	0	0	0	0	0	0	0	0	0
Paul O'Neill, of	.333	5	18	5	6	0	0	3	6	5	5	0
Andy Pettitte, p	.000	1	0	0	0	0	0	0	0	0	0	0
Jorge Posada, pr	.000	1	0	1	0	0	0	0	0	0	0	0
Mariano Rivera, p	.000	3	0	0	0	0	0	0	0	0	0	0
Ruben Sierra, dh	.174	5	23	2	4	2	0	2	5	2	7	0
Mike Stanley, c	.313	5	16	2	5	0	0	1	3	2	1	0
Darryl Strawberry, ph	.000	2	2	0	0	0	0	0	0	0	1	0
Randy Velarde, 2b-4, 3b-2, of-2	.176	5	17	3	3	0	0	0	1	6	4	0
John Wetteland, p	.000	3	0	0	0	0	0	0	0	0	0	0
Bob Wickman, p	.000	3	0	0	0	0	0	0	0	0	0	0
Bernie Williams, of	.429	5	21	8	9	2	0	2	5	7	3	1
Gerald Williams, of	.000	5	5	1	0	0	0	0	0	2	3	0
TOTAL	.259		193	33	50	12	0	11	32	32	43	1

PITCHER	W	L	ERA	G	GS	CG	SV	SHO	IP	H	ER	BB	SO
David Cone	1	0	4.60	2	2	0	0	0	15.2	15	8	9	14
Sterling Hitchcock	0	0	5.40	2	0	0	0	0	1.2	2	1	2	1
Steve Howe	0	0	18.00	2	0	0	0	0	1.0	4	2	0	0
Scott Kamieniecki	0	0	7.20	1	1	0	0	0	5.0	9	4	4	4
Jack McDowell	0	2	9.00	2	1	0	0	0	7.0	8	7	4	6
Andy Pettitte	0	0	5.14	1	1	0	0	0	7.0	9	4	3	0
Mariano Rivera	1	0	0.00	3	0	0	0	0	5.1	3	0	1	8
John Wetteland	0	1	14.54	3	0	0	0	0	4.1	8	7	2	5
Bob Wickman	0	0	0.00	3	0	0	0	0	3.0	5	0	0	3
TOTAL	2	3	5.94	19	5	0	0	0	50.0	63	33	25	41

GAME 1 AT NY OCT 3

```
SEA  000 101 202   6  9  0
NY   002 002 41X   9 13  0
```
Pitchers: Bosio, NELSON (6), Ayala (7), Risley (7), Wells (8) vs CONE, Wetteland (9)
Home Runs: Griffey-SEA (2), Boggs-NY, Sierra-NY
Attendance: 57,178

GAME 2 AT NY OCT 4

```
SEA  001 001 200 001 000   5 16  2
NY   000 012 100 001 002   7 11  0
```
Pitchers: Benes, Risley (6), Charlton (7), Nelson (11), BELCHER (12) vs Pettitte, Wickman (8), Wetteland (9), RIVERA (12)
Home Runs: Coleman-SEA, Griffey-SEA, Sierra-NY, Mattingly-NY, O'Neill-NY, Leyritz-NY
Attendance: 57,126

GAME 3 AT SEA OCT 6

```
NY   000 100 120   4  6  2
SEA  000 024 10X   7  7  0
```
Pitchers: McDOWELL, Howe (6), Wickman (6), Hitchcock (7), Rivera (7) vs JOHNSON, Risley (8), Charlton (8)
Home Runs: B.Williams-NY (2), Stanley-NY, T.Martinez-SEA
Attendance: 57,944

GAME 4 AT SEA OCT 7

```
NY   302 000 012   8 14  1
SEA  004 011 05X  11 16  0
```
Pitchers: Kamieniecki, Hitchcock (6), Wickman (7), WETTELAND (7), Howe (8) vs Bosio, Nelson (3), Belcher (7), CHARLTON (8), Ayala (9), Risley (9)
Home Runs: O'Neill-NY, E.Martinez-SEA (2), Griffey-SEA, Buhner-SEA
Attendance: 57,180

GAME 5 AT SEA OCT 8

```
NY   000 202 000 01   5  6  0
SEA  001 100 002 002   6 15  0
```
Pitchers: Cone, Rivera (8), McDOWELL (9) vs Benes, Charlton (7), JOHNSON (9)
Home Runs: O'Neill-NY, Cora-SEA, Griffey-SEA
Attendance: 57,411

ATLANTA BRAVES (EAST) 4, CINCINNATI REDS (CENTRAL) 0

Both the Braves and the Reds had moved through the National League's first-ever division series with ease, with Atlanta knocking off Colorado, 3–1, and Cincinnati sweeping the Dodgers in three games as the Reds made their first postseason appearance since 1990. The Braves, meanwhile, became the first team to play in the NLCS four straight times.

In Game 1 of the NLCS, a scant crowd of only 40,382 Riverfront Stadium patrons saw the Braves edge the Reds, 2–1. Atlanta prevailed despite failing to move a runner past second until the ninth inning, as the Reds' Pete Schourek held the Braves to four singles through eight. Atlanta broke through in the 11th on Mike Devereaux's pinch-hit single, a feat which helped earn him NLCS MVP honors.

Game 2 was another extra inning affair as Atlanta cracked the game open with four in the 10th to triumph, 6–2. In that inning the Braves loaded the bases, scoring their first run on Mark Portugal's wild pitch. Javier Lopez followed with a three-run homer off the left-field foul screen. Game 3 remained scoreless until the sixth, when catcher Charlie O'Brien homered to left off David Wells, scoring Fred McGriff and Mike Devereaux. Chipper Jones followed with a two-run homer to complete the Braves' scoring.

Game 4 saw a 6–0 Atlanta win, completing the first sweep since 1982. Steve Avery allowed just three singles, two of which failed to make it out of the infield. Mike Devereaux delivered the key blow, a three-run homer to left in the seventh. Atlanta, seeking its first Series win since 1957, would now face Cleveland, making its first Fall Classic appearance since 1954.

ATL (E)

PLAYER/POS	AVG	G	AB	R	H	2B	3B	HR	RB	BB	SO	SB
Steve Avery, p	.500	2	2	0	1	0	0	0	0	0	0	0
Rafael Belliard, ss	.273	4	11	1	3	0	0	0	0	0	3	0
Jeff Blauser, ss	.000	1	4	0	0	0	0	0	0	1	2	0
Brad Clontz, p	.000	1	0	0	0	0	0	0	0	0	0	0
Mike Devereaux, of	.308	4	13	2	4	1	0	1	5	1	2	0
Tom Glavine, p	.000	1	1	0	0	0	0	0	0	0	0	0
Marquis Grissom, of	.263	4	19	2	5	0	1	0	0	1	4	0
Chipper Jones, 3b	.438	4	16	3	7	0	0	1	3	3	1	1
David Justice, of	.273	3	11	1	3	0	0	0	1	2	1	0
Ryan Klesko, of-3	.000	4	7	0	0	0	0	0	0	3	4	0
Mark Lemke, 2b	.167	4	18	2	3	0	0	0	1	1	0	0
Javy Lopez, c	.357	3	14	2	5	1	0	1	3	0	1	0
Greg Maddux, p	.000	1	3	0	0	0	0	0	0	0	1	0
Fred McGriff, 1b	.438	4	16	5	7	4	0	0	3	3	0	0
Greg McMichael, p	.000	3	0	0	0	0	0	0	0	0	0	0
Mike Mordecai, ss-1	.000	2	2	0	0	0	0	0	0	0	1	0
Charlie O'Brien, c-1	.400	2	5	1	2	0	0	1	3	0	1	0
Alejandro Pena, p	.000	3	0	0	0	0	0	0	0	0	0	0
Luis Polonia, of-1	.500	3	2	0	1	0	0	0	1	0	0	0
Dwight Smith, ph	.000	2	2	0	0	0	0	0	0	0	0	0
John Smoltz, p	.333	1	3	0	1	0	0	0	0	0	1	0
Mark Wohlers, p	.000	4	0	0	0	0	0	0	0	0	0	0
TOTAL	.282		149	19	42	6	1	4	17	16	22	2

PITCHER	W	L	ERA	G	GS	CG	SV	SHO	IP	H	ER	BB	SO
Steve Avery	1	0	0.00	2	1	0	0	0	6.0	2	0	4	6
Brad Clontz	0	0	0.00	1	0	0	0	0	0.1	1	0	0	0
Tom Glavine	0	0	1.29	1	1	0	0	0	7.0	7	1	2	5
Greg Maddux	1	0	1.13	1	1	0	0	0	8.0	7	1	2	4
Greg McMichael	1	0	0.00	3	0	0	0	1	2.2	0	0	1	2
Alejandro Pena	0	0	0.00	3	0	0	0	0	3.0	2	0	1	4
John Smoltz	0	0	2.57	1	1	0	0	0	7.0	7	2	2	2
Mark Wohlers	1	0	1.80	4	0	0	0	0	5.0	2	1	0	8
TOTAL	4	0	1.15	16	4	0	1	0	39.0	28	5	12	31

CIN (C)

PLAYER/POS	AVG	G	AB	R	H	2B	3B	HR	RB	BB	SO	SB
Eric Anthony, ph	.000	2	1	0	0	0	0	0	0	1	1	0
Bret Boone, 2b	.214	4	14	1	3	0	0	0	0	1	2	0
Jeff Branson, 3b	.111	4	9	2	1	1	0	0	0	0	2	1
Jeff Brantley, p	.000	2	0	0	0	0	0	0	0	0	0	0
Dave Burba, p	.000	2	0	0	0	0	0	0	0	0	0	0
Hector Carrasco, p	.000	1	0	0	0	0	0	0	0	0	0	0
Mariano Duncan, 1b-1	.000	3	3	0	0	0	0	0	0	1	1	0
Ron Gant, of	.188	4	16	1	3	0	0	0	1	0	3	0
Lenny Harris, ph	1.000	3	2	0	2	0	0	0	1	0	0	1
Xavier Hernandez, p	.000	1	0	0	0	0	0	0	0	0	0	0
Thomas Howard, of-3	.250	4	8	0	2	1	0	0	1	2	0	0
Mike Jackson, p	.000	3	0	0	0	0	0	0	0	0	0	0
Barry Larkin, ss	.389	4	18	1	7	2	1	0	0	1	1	1
Darren Lewis, of	.000	2	1	0	0	0	0	0	0	0	0	0
Mark Lewis, 3b	.250	2	4	0	1	0	0	0	0	1	1	0
Hal Morris, 1b	.167	4	12	0	2	1	0	0	1	1	1	1
Mark Portugal, p	.000	1	0	0	0	0	0	0	0	0	0	0
Reggie Sanders, of	.125	4	16	0	2	0	0	0	0	2	10	0
Benito Santiago, c	.231	4	13	0	3	0	0	0	0	2	3	0
Pete Schourek, p	.000	2	5	0	0	0	0	0	0	0	4	0
John Smiley, p	.000	1	1	0	0	0	0	0	0	0	0	0
Eddie Taubensee, c-1	.500	2	2	0	1	0	0	0	0	0	0	0
Jerome Walton, of	.000	2	7	0	0	0	0	0	0	0	2	0
David Wells, p	.500	1	2	0	1	0	0	0	0	0	0	0
TOTAL	.209		134	5	28	5	1	0	4	12	31	4

PITCHER	W	L	ERA	G	GS	CG	SV	SHO	IP	H	ER	BB	SO
Jeff Brantley	0	0	0.00	2	0	0	0	0	2.2	0	0	2	1
Dave Burba	0	0	0.00	2	0	0	0	0	3.2	3	0	4	0
Hector Carrasco	0	0	0.00	1	0	0	0	0	1.1	1	0	0	3
Xavier Hernandez	0	0	27.00	1	0	0	0	0	0.2	3	2	0	0
Mike Jackson	0	1	23.14	3	0	0	0	0	2.1	5	6	4	1
Mark Portugal	0	1	36.00	1	0	0	0	0	1.0	3	4	1	0
Pete Schourek	0	1	1.26	2	2	0	0	0	14.1	14	2	3	13
John Smiley	0	0	3.60	1	1	0	0	0	5.0	5	2	0	1
David Wells	0	1	4.50	1	1	0	0	0	6.0	8	3	2	3
TOTAL	0	4	4.62	14	4	0	0	0	37.0	42	19	16	22

GAME 1 AT CIN OCT 10

```
ATL  0 0 0 0 0 0 0 0 1 0 1   2 7 0
CIN  0 0 0 1 0 0 0 0 0 0 0   1 8 0
```
Pitchers: Glavine, Pena (8), WOHLERS (9), Clontz (11), Avery (11), McMichael (11) vs Schourek, Brantley (9), JACKSON (11)
Attendance: 40,382

GAME 2 AT CIN OCT 11

```
ATL  1 0 0 1 0 0 0 0 4   6 11 1
CIN  0 0 0 0 2 0 0 0 0   2 9 1
```
Pitchers: Smoltz, Pena (8), McMICHAEL (9), Wohlers (10) vs Smiley, Burba (6), Jackson (8), Brantley (9), PORTUGAL (10)
Home Runs: Lopez-ATL
Attendance: 44,624

GAME 3 AT ATL OCT 13

```
CIN  0 0 0 0 0 0 0 1 1   2 8 0
ATL  0 0 0 0 0 3 2 0 X   5 12 1
```
Pitchers: WELLS, Hernandez (7), Carrasco (7) vs MADDUX, Wohlers (9)
Home Runs: O'Brien-ATL, Jones-ATL
Attendance: 51,424

GAME 4 AT ATL OCT 14

```
CIN  0 0 0 0 0 0 0 0 0   0 3 1
ATL  0 0 1 0 0 0 5 0 X   6 12 1
```
Pitchers: SCHOUREK, Jackson (7), Burba (7) vs AVERY, McMichael (7), Pena (8), Wohlers (9)
Home Runs: Devereaux-ATL
Attendance: 52,067

CLEVELAND INDIANS (CENTRAL) 4, SEATTLE MARINERS (WEST) 2

Cleveland had romped in a threegame sweep of Boston. Seattle had engaged in a thrilling, exhausting five-game series against New York, fraying their pitching—and probably their nerves—in the process.

Most observers expected the Tribe to take Game 1. Seattle's rotation had been decimated in defeating the Yankees, and Mariners manager Lou Piniella had to start rookie Bob Wolcott rather than ace Randy Johnson. Wolcott gave up a game-tying seventh inning homer to Albert Belle, but otherwise Piniella had nothing to complain about. Seattle answered in the bottom of that frame and made the run hold up.

Cleveland stranded 10 runners in Game 2 (making a total of 22 left on in the first two contests) but still triumphed, 5–2. Manny Ramirez came into the game mired in a 1-for-16 postseason slump but went 4-for-4 with solo homers in the sixth and eighth innings.

Randy Johnson finally appeared in the series in Game 3 but wasn't around for a decision. The Mariners jumped off to a 2–0 lead thanks to two Cleveland errors, but at the end of eight the score was tied. In the top of the 11th an intentional walk to Tino Martinez backfired as Jay Buhner followed with a threerun homer.

In Game 4 Cleveland evened the series with a 7–0 triumph against an ineffective Andy Benes, aided by Eddie Murray's two-run first inning homer, Jim Thome's two-run third inning homer, and Omar Vizquel's run-scoring sixth inning double.

In Game 5 Orel Hershiser ran his career postseason record to 7–0 as he struck out eight and walked only two. He needed help, however, leaving the game with a 3–2 lead that Paul Assenmacher and Jose Mesa protected skillfully.

In the final game, the Indians' Dennis Martinez defeated Randy Johnson, 4–0. Through eight innings only one run had scored (an unearned one by Cleveland), but in that inning Mariners hopes unraveled. Johnson surrendered a leadoff double to Tony Pena, then an infield single to Kenny Lofton, who stole second. Next came a wild pitch. Ruben Amaro (running for Pena) scored, but so did Lofton, motoring all the way from second,

embarrassing Mariners catcher Dan Wilson. That play sealed the Mariners' doom. Carlos Baerga then homered, and, two innings later, the Indians had their first AL pennant in 41 years.

GAME 1 AT SEA OCT 10
CLE 001 000 100 2 10 1
SEA 020 010 10X 3 7 0
Pitchers: MARTINEZ, Tavarez (7), Assenmacher (8), Plunk (8) vs WOLCOTT, Nelson (8), Charlton (8)
Home Runs: Belle-CLE, Blowers-SEA
Attendance: 57,065

GAME 2 AT SEA OCT 11
CLE 000 022 010 5 12 0
SEA 000 001 001 2 6 1
Pitchers: HERSHISER, Mesa (9) vs BELCHER, Ayala (9), Risley (9)
Home Runs: Ramirez-CLE (2), Griffey-SEA, Buhner-SEA
Attendance: 58,144

GAME 3 AT CLE OCT 13
SEA 011 000 000 03 5 9 1
CLE 000 100 001 000 2 4 2
Pitchers: Johnson, CHARLTON (9) vs Nagy, Mesa (9), TAVAREZ (10), Assenmacher (11), Plunk (11)
Home Runs: Buhner-SEA (2)
Attendance: 43,643

GAME 4 AT CLE OCT 14
SEA 000 000 000 0 6 1
CLE 312 001 00X 7 9 0
Pitchers: BENES, Wells (3), Ayala (6), Nelson (7), Risley (8) vs HILL, Poole (8), Ogea (9), Embree (9)
Home Runs: Murray-CLE, Thome-CLE
Attendance: 43,686

GAME 5 AT CLE OCT 15
SEA 001 010 000 2 5 2
CLE 100 002 00X 3 10 4
Pitchers: BOSIO, Nelson (6), Risley (7) vs HERSHISER, Tavarez (7), Assenmacher (7), Plunk (8), Mesa (9)
Home Runs: Thome-CLE
Attendance: 43,607

GAME 6 AT SEA OCT 17
CLE 000 010 030 4 8 0
SEA 000 000 000 0 4 1
Pitchers: MARTINEZ, Tavarez (8), Mesa (9) vs JOHNSON, Charlton (8)
Home Runs: Baerga-CLE
Attendance: 58,489

CLE (C)

PLAYER/POS	AVG	G	AB	R	H	2B	3B	HR	RB	BB	SO	SB
Sandy Alomar, c	.267	5	15	0	4	1	1	0	1	1	1	0
Ruben Amaro, dh-1	.000	3	1	1	0	0	0	0	0	0	0	0
Paul Assenmacher, p	.000	3	0	0	0	0	0	0	0	0	0	0
Carlos Baerga, 2b	.400	6	25	3	10	0	0	1	4	2	3	0
Albert Belle	.222	5	18	1	4	1	0	1	1	3	5	0
Alan Embree, p	.000	1	0	0	0	0	0	0	0	0	0	0
Alvaro Espinoza, 3b	.125	4	8	1	1	0	0	0	0	0	3	0
Orel Hershiser, p	.000	2	0	0	0	0	0	0	0	0	0	0
Ken Hill, p	.000	1	0	0	0	0	0	0	0	0	0	0
Wayne Kirby, of	.200	5	5	2	1	0	0	0	0	0	0	1
Kenny Lofton, of	.458	6	24	4	11	0	2	0	3	4	6	5
Dennis Martinez, p	.000	2	0	0	0	0	0	0	0	0	0	0
Jose Mesa, p	.000	4	0	0	0	0	0	0	0	0	0	0
Eddie Murray, dh	.250	6	24	2	6	1	0	1	3	2	3	0
Charles Nagy, p	.000	1	0	0	0	0	0	0	0	0	0	0
Chad Ogea, p	.000	1	0	0	0	0	0	0	0	0	0	0
Tony Pena, c	.333	4	6	1	2	1	0	0	0	0	1	0
Herb Perry, 1b	.000	3	8	0	0	0	0	0	0	1	3	0
Eric Plunk, p	.000	3	0	0	0	0	0	0	0	0	0	0
Jim Poole, p	.000	1	0	0	0	0	0	0	0	0	0	0
Manny Ramirez, of	.286	6	21	2	6	0	0	2	2	2	5	0
Paul Sorrento, 1b	.154	4	13	2	2	1	0	0	0	2	3	0
Julian Tavarez, p	.000	4	0	0	0	0	0	0	0	0	0	0
Jim Thome, 3b	.267	5	15	2	4	0	0	2	5	2	3	0
Omar Vizquel, ss	.087	6	23	2	2	1	0	0	2	5	2	3
TOTAL	.257		206	23	53	6	3	7	21	25	37	9

PITCHER	W	L	ERA	G	GS	CG	SV	SHO	IP	H	ER	BB	SO
Paul Assenmacher	0	0	0.00	3	0	0	0	0	1.1	0	0	1	2
Alan Embree	0	0	0.00	1	0	0	0	0	0.1	0	0	0	1
Orel Hershiser	2	0	1.29	2	2	0	0	0	14.0	9	2	3	15
Ken Hill	1	0	0.00	1	1	0	0	0	7.0	5	0	3	6
Dennis Martinez	1	1	2.03	2	2	0	0	0	13.1	10	3	3	7
Jose Mesa	0	0	2.25	4	0	0	1	0	4.0	3	1	1	1
Charles Nagy	0	0	1.13	1	1	0	0	0	8.0	5	1	0	6
Chad Ogea	0	0	0.00	1	0	0	0	0	0.2	1	0	0	2
Eric Plunk	0	0	9.00	3	0	0	0	0	2.0	1	2	3	2
Jim Poole	0	0	0.00	1	0	0	0	0	1.0	0	0	0	2
Julian Tavarez	0	1	2.70	4	0	0	0	0	3.1	3	1	1	2
TOTAL	4	2	1.64	23	6	0	1	0	55.0	37	10	15	46

SEA (W)

PLAYER/POS	AVG	G	AB	R	H	2B	3B	HR	RB	BB	SO	SB
Rich Amaral, ph	.000	2	2	0	0	0	0	0	0	0	1	0
Bobby Ayala, p	.000	2	0	0	0	0	0	0	0	0	0	0
Tim Belcher, p	.000	1	0	0	0	0	0	0	0	0	0	0
Andy Benes, p	.000	1	0	0	0	0	0	0	0	0	0	0
Mike Blowers, 3b	.222	6	18	1	4	0	0	1	2	0	4	0
Chris Bosio, p	.000	1	0	0	0	0	0	0	0	0	0	0
Jay Buhner, of	.304	6	23	5	7	2	0	3	5	2	8	0
Norm Charlton, p	.000	3	0	0	0	0	0	0	0	0	0	0
Vince Coleman, of-5	.100	6	20	0	2	0	0	0	0	2	6	4
Joey Cora, 2b	.174	6	23	3	4	1	0	0	0	1	0	2
Alex Diaz, of-3	.429	4	7	0	3	1	0	0	1	1	1	0
Felix Fermin, 2b-1, ss-1	.000	2	0	0	0	0	0	0	0	0	0	0
Ken Griffey, of	.333	6	21	2	7	2	0	1	2	4	4	2
Randy Johnson, p	.000	2	0	0	0	0	0	0	0	0	0	0
Tino Martinez, 1b	.136	6	22	1	3	0	0	0	0	3	7	0
Edgar Martinez, dh	.087	6	23	0	2	0	0	0	0	2	5	1
Jeff Nelson, p	.000	3	0	0	0	0	0	0	0	0	0	0
Bill Risley, p	.000	3	0	0	0	0	0	0	0	0	0	0
Alex Rodriguez, ph	.000	1	1	0	0	0	0	0	0	0	1	0
Luis Sojo, ss	.250	6	20	0	5	2	0	0	1	0	2	0
Doug Strange, 3b-2	.000	4	4	0	0	0	0	0	0	0	2	0
Bob Wells, p	.000	1	0	0	0	0	0	0	0	0	0	0
Chris Widger, c	.000	3	1	0	0	0	0	0	0	0	1	0
Dan Wilson, c	.000	6	16	0	0	0	0	0	0	0	4	0
Bob Wolcott, p	.000	1	0	0	0	0	0	0	0	0	0	0
TOTAL	.184		201	12	37	8	0	5	10	15	46	9

PITCHER	W	L	ERA	G	GS	CG	SV	SHO	IP	H	ER	BB	SO
Bobby Ayala	0	0	2.45	2	0	0	0	0	3.2	3	1	3	3
Tim Belcher	0	1	6.35	1	1	0	0	0	5.2	9	4	2	1
Andy Benes	0	1	23.14	1	1	0	0	0	2.1	6	6	2	3
Chris Bosio	0	1	3.38	1	1	0	0	0	5.1	7	2	2	3
Norm Charlton	1	0	0.00	3	0	0	1	0	6.0	1	0	1	5
Randy Johnson	0	1	2.35	2	2	0	0	0	15.1	12	4	2	13
Jeff Nelson	0	0	0.00	3	0	0	0	0	3.0	3	0	5	3
Bill Risley	0	0	0.00	3	0	0	0	0	2.2	2	0	1	2
Bob Wells	0	0	3.00	1	0	0	0	0	3.0	2	1	2	2
Bob Wolcott	1	0	2.57	1	1	0	0	0	7.0	8	2	5	2
TOTAL	2	4	3.33	18	6	0	1	0	54.0	53	20	25	37

ATLANTA BRAVES (NL) 4, CLEVELAND INDIANS (AL) 2

The Indians and Braves met for a rematch of their tussle in the 1948 World Series, but this time the transplanted Braves went home with the honors. Game 1 quickly established that Atlanta's vaunted pitching staff was no myth. Perennial Cy Young Award winner Greg Maddux used just 95 pitches in shutting down the hard-hitting Indians. Only three runners reached against him, on opposite field singles by Kenny Lofton and Jim Thome, and on an error by Rafael Belliard. Cleveland starter Orel Hershiser tired in the seventh and walked two, leading to the second and third Atlanta runs and his first loss after seven straight postseason victories.

In Game 2 Atlanta took a 2–0 Series lead as catcher Javier Lopez anticipated a Dennis Martinez fastball on the outside part of the plate. He hammered it to straightaway center field for a two-run homer, shattering a 2–2 tie and providing the Braves with all the margin they would need for a 4–3 win.

The Indians bats finally came alive in Game 3. It looked like the Tribe would be facing a 3–0 deficit, as they trailed 6–5 in the bottom of the eighth. But in that inning Kenny Lofton (who reached base six times in the contest) scored the tying run on Sandy Alomar's first hit of the series. In the 11th Murray singled off Alejandro Pena's first pitch to score pinch-runner Alvaro Espinoza with the winning run.

Atlanta's Ryan Klesko and Cleveland's Albert Belle traded solo sixth-inning homers in Game 4 to set up a 1–1 tie going into the top of the seventh. Atlanta then scored three runs on Luis Polonia's run-scoring double and David Justice's two-out, two-run single to center to break the contest open and ultimately give Atlanta a 5–2 win.

The Tribe stayed alive in Game 5 as Jim Thome singled in the go-ahead run in the sixth and provided a crucial insurance run with an eighth inning homer. Ryan Klesko nicked Jose Mesa for a two-run homer in the ninth—the third straight game in which he'd homered—but it wasn't enough.

The keys to Game 6 were two players with something to prove: Tom Glavine, who had survived Atlanta's horrible days in the late 1980s, and David Justice, who was

taking heat for comments he had made about Atlanta fans' lack of spirit. Glavine allowed only a sixth inning single to Tony Pena, walked three and struck out eight. Justice brought home the game's only run with a sixth inning homer off reliever Jim Poole. The Braves now had their first world championship since 1957 and had become the first franchise to win the crown in three different cities—Boston, Milwaukee, and Atlanta.

ATL (N)

PLAYER/POS	AVG	G	AB	R	H	2B	3B	HR	RB	BB	SO	SB
Steve Avery, pn	.000	1	0	0	0	0	0	0	0	0	0	0
Rafael Belliard, ss	.000	6	16	0	0	0	0	0	0	1	4	0
Pedro Borbon, p	.000	1	0	0	0	0	0	0	0	0	0	0
Brad Clontz, p	.000	2	0	0	0	0	0	0	0	0	0	0
Mike Devereaux, of-4, dh-1	.250	5	4	0	1	0	0	0	1	2	1	0
Tom Glavine, p	.000	2	4	0	0	0	0	0	0	1	2	0
Marquis Grissom, of	.360	6	25	3	9	1	0	0	1	1	3	3
Chipper Jones, 3b	.286	6	21	3	6	3	0	0	4	4	3	0
David Justice, of	.250	6	20	3	5	1	0	1	5	5	5	0
Ryan Klesko, of-3, dh-3	.313	6	16	4	5	0	0	3	4	3	4	0
Mark Lemke, 2b	.273	6	22	1	6	0	0	0	0	3	2	0
Javy Lopez, c	.176	6	17	1	3	2	0	1	3	1	1	0
Greg Maddux, p	.000	2	3	0	0	0	0	0	0	0	1	0
Fred McGriff, 1b	.261	6	23	5	6	2	0	2	3	3	7	1
Greg McMichael, p	.000	3	0	0	0	0	0	0	0	0	0	0
Kent Mercker, p	.000	1	0	0	0	0	0	0	0	0	0	0
Mike Mordecai, ss-2, dh-1	.333	3	3	0	1	0	0	0	0	0	1	0
Charlie O'Brien, c	.000	2	3	0	0	0	0	0	0	0	1	0
Alejandro Pena, p	.000	2	0	0	0	0	0	0	0	0	0	0
Luis Polonia, of-4	.286	6	14	3	4	1	0	1	4	1	3	1
Dwight Smith, ph	.500	3	2	0	1	0	0	0	0	1	0	0
John Smoltz, p	.000	1	0	0	0	0	0	0	0	0	0	0
Mark Wohlers, p	.000	4	0	0	0	0	0	0	0	0	0	0
TOTAL	.244		193	23	47	10	0	8	23	25	34	5

PITCHER	W	L	ERA	G	GS	CG	SV	SHO	IP	H	ER	BB	SO
Steve Avery	1	0	1.50	1	1	0	0	0	6.0	3	1	5	3
Pedro Borbon	0	0	0.00	1	0	0	1	0	1.0	0	0	0	2
Brad Clontz	0	0	2.70	2	0	0	0	0	3.1	2	1	0	2
Tom Glavine	2	0	1.29	2	2	0	0	0	14.0	4	2	6	11
Greg Maddux	1	1	2.25	2	2	1	0	0	16.0	9	4	3	8
Greg McMichael	0	0	2.70	3	0	0	0	0	3.1	3	1	2	2
Kent Mercker	0	0	4.50	1	0	0	0	0	2.0	1	1	2	2
Alejandro Pena	0	1	9.00	2	0	0	0	0	1.0	3	1	2	0
John Smoltz	0	0	15.43	1	1	0	0	0	2.1	6	4	2	4
Mark Wohlers	0	0	1.80	4	0	0	2	0	5.0	4	1	3	3
TOTAL	4	2	2.67	19	6	1	3	0	54.0	35	16	25	37

CLE (A)

PLAYER/POS	AVG	G	AB	R	H	2B	3B	HR	RB	BB	SO	SB
Sandy Alomar, c	.200	5	15	0	3	2	0	0	1	0	2	0
Ruben Amaro, of-1	.000	2	2	0	0	0	0	0	0	0	1	0
Paul Assenmacher, p	.000	4	0	0	0	0	0	0	0	0	0	0
Carlos Baerga, 2b	.192	6	26	1	5	2	0	0	4	1	1	0
Albert Belle, of	.235	6	17	4	4	0	0	2	4	7	5	0
Alan Embree, p	.000	4	0	0	0	0	0	0	0	0	0	0
Alvaro Espinoza, 3b-1	.500	2	2	1	1	0	0	0	0	0	0	0
Orel Hershiser, p	.000	2	2	0	0	0	0	0	0	0	0	0
Ken Hill, p	.000	2	0	0	0	0	0	0	0	0	0	0
Wayne Kirby, of-2	.000	3	1	0	0	0	0	0	0	0	1	0
Kenny Lofton, of	.200	6	25	6	5	1	0	0	0	3	1	6
Dennis Martinez, p	.000	2	3	0	0	0	0	0	0	0	1	0
Jose Mesa, p	.000	3	0	0	0	0	0	0	0	0	0	0
Eddie Murray, 1b-3, dh-3	.105	6	19	1	2	0	0	1	3	5	4	0
Charles Nagy, p	.000	1	0	0	0	0	0	0	0	0	0	0
Tony Pena, c	.167	2	6	0	1	0	0	0	0	0	0	0
Herb Perry, 1b	.000	3	5	0	0	0	0	0	0	0	2	0
Jim Poole, p	.000	2	1	0	0	0	0	0	0	0	0	0
Manny Ramirez, of	.222	6	18	2	4	0	0	1	2	4	5	1
Paul Sorrento, 1b-3	.182	6	11	0	2	1	0	0	0	0	4	0
Julian Tavarez, p	.000	5	0	0	0	0	0	0	0	0	0	0
Jim Thome, 3b	.211	6	19	1	4	1	0	1	2	5	5	0
Omar Vizquel, ss	.174	6	23	3	4	0	1	0	1	3	5	1
TOTAL	.179		195	19	35	7	1	5	17	25	37	8

PITCHER	W	L	ERA	G	GS	CG	SV	SHO	IP	H	ER	BB	SO
Paul Assenmacher	0	0	6.75	4	0	0	0	0	1.1	1	1	3	3
Alan Embree	0	0	2.70	4	0	0	0	0	3.1	2	1	2	2
Orel Hershiser	1	1	2.57	2	2	0	0	0	14.0	8	4	4	13
Ken Hill	0	1	4.26	2	1	0	0	0	6.1	7	3	4	1
Dennis Martinez	0	1	3.48	2	2	0	0	0	10.1	12	4	8	5
Jose Mesa	1	0	4.50	2	0	0	1	0	4.0	5	2	1	4
Charles Nagy	0	0	6.43	1	1	0	0	0	7.0	8	5	1	4
Jim Poole	0	1	3.86	2	0	0	0	0	2.1	1	1	0	1
Julian Tavarez	0	0	0.00	5	0	0	0	0	4.1	3	0	2	1
TOTAL	2	4	3.57	24	6	0	1	0	53.0	47	21	25	34

GAME 1 AT ATL OCT 21
CLE 1 0 0 0 0 0 0 0 1   2 2 0
ATL 0 1 0 0 0 0 2 0 X   3 3 2
Pitchers: HERSHISER, Assenmacher (7), Tavarez (7), Embree (8) vs MADDUX
Home Runs: McGriff-ATL
Attendance: 51,876

GAME 2 AT ATL OCT 22
CLE 0 2 0 0 0 0 1 0 0   3 6 2
ATL 0 0 2 0 0 2 0 0 X   4 8 2
Pitchers: MARTINEZ, Poole (7), Tavarez (8) vs GLAVINE, McMichael (7), Pena (7), Wohlers (8)
Home Runs: Murray-CLE, Lopez-ATL
Attendance: 51,877

GAME 3 AT CLE OCT 24
ATL 1 0 0 0 0 1 1 3 0 0 0   6 12 1
CLE 2 0 2 0 0 0 1 1 0 0 1   7 12 2
Pitchers: Smoltz, Clontz (3), Mercker (5), McMichael (7), Wohlers (8), PENA (11) vs Nagy, Assenmacher (8), Tavarez (8), MESA (9)
Home Runs: McGriff-ATL, Klesko-ATL
Attendance: 43,584

GAME 4 AT CLE OCT 25
ATL 0 0 0 0 0 1 3 0 1   5 11 1
CLE 0 0 0 0 0 1 0 0 1   2 6 0
Pitchers: AVERY, McMichael (7), Wohlers (9), Borbon (9) vs HILL, Assenmacher (7), Tavarez (8), Embree (8)
Home Runs: Belle-CLE, Ramirez-CLE, Klesko-ATL
Attendance: 43,578

GAME 5 AT CLE OCT 26
ATL 0 0 0 1 1 0 0 0 2   4 7 0
CLE 2 0 0 0 0 2 0 1 X   5 8 1
Pitchers: MADDUX, Clontz (8) vs HERSHISER, Mesa (9)
Home Runs: Belle-CLE, Thome-CLE, Polonia-ATL, Klesko-ATL
Attendance: 43,595

GAME 6 AT ATL OCT 28
CLE 0 0 0 0 0 0 0 0 0   0 1 1
ATL 0 0 0 0 0 1 0 0 X   1 6 0
Pitchers: Martinez, POOLE (5), Hill (7), Embree (7), Tavarez (8), Assenmacher (8) vs GLAVINE, Wohlers (9)
Home Runs: Justice-ATL
Attendance: 51,875

ATLANTA BRAVES (EAST) 3, LOS ANGELES DODGERS (WILD CARD) 0

The Braves became the first National League team to make five consecutive postseason appearances. The Braves struggled in mid-September, but their opponents in the Division Series, the Dodgers, had really stumbled into the post-season. Los Angeles lost its last four regular-season games, but still captured the wild card. Dodger Stadium was abuzz when the Division Series began and the two starting pitchers, LA's Ramon Martinez and Atlanta's John Smoltz, were equal to the task. Martinez allowed just one run and three hits through eight innings while Smoltz pitched nine innings with only one run and four hits against him. Smoltz and the Braves caught the break they needed in the 10th when Javier Lopez homered to right-center for a 2–1 lead. Reliever Mark Wohlers made it hold up with two strikeouts in the tenthth inning.

Pitching was the name of the game again the next night. While Greg Maddux's four-year streak of Cy Young Awards would end in 1996, he reminded the country that his trophy collection was well-deserved. Maddux, however, was touched for unearned runs in the first and fourth innings as the Dodgers took a 2–1 lead into the seventh inning despite just three hits. Dodgers starter Ismael Valdes limited the Braves to three hits as well through six innings, including a home run by Ryan Klesko, but that changed in a span of seven pitches in the seventh inning. Fred McGriff hit a line-drive home run to center field to tie the score. After Valdes recorded his fifth strikeout, Jermaine Dye hit the first pitch he saw over the left field wall for a 3–2 lead. Greg McMichael and Mark Wohlers each had a scoreless inning to close out the win.

A club-record crowd greeted the Braves at Fulton County Stadium for Game 3, but the fans fidgeted in their seats when Hideo Nomo struck out the first two Braves he faced. They were soon on their feet, however, when Chipper Jones singled and McGriff doubled him home. Nomo retired the first two batters he faced in the fourth inning, but he was on his way to the showers by the time the third out was recorded. Pitcher Tom Glavine started the rally with a double and Marquis Grissom

walked before Mark Lemke doubled home both runners. Chipper Jones followed with a two-run home run to give Atlanta a 5–0 lead. To their credit, the Dodgers nicked Glavine for a run in the seventh inning and McMichael for another in the eighth, but Mike Bielecki and Mark Wohlers allowed nothing more and the Braves had another opportunity to celebrate.

ATL (E)

PLAYER/POS	AVG	G	AB	R	H	2B	3B	HR	RB	BB	SO	SB
Rafael Belliard, ss	.000	3	0	0	0	0	0	0	0	0	0	0
Mike Bielecki, p	.000	1	0	0	0	0	0	0	0	0	0	0
Jeff Blauser, ss	.111	3	9	0	1	0	0	0	0	1	3	0
Jermaine Dye, of	.182	3	11	1	2	0	0	1	1	0	6	1
Tom Glavine, p	.500	1	2	1	1	1	0	0	0	0	0	0
Marquis Grissom, of	.083	3	12	2	1	0	0	0	0	1	2	1
Andruw Jones, of	.000	3	0	0	0	0	0	0	0	1	0	0
Chipper Jones, 3b	.222	3	9	2	2	0	0	1	2	3	4	1
Ryan Klesko, of	.125	3	8	1	1	0	0	1	1	3	4	1
Mark Lemke, 2b	.167	3	12	1	2	1	0	0	2	0	1	0
Javy Lopez, c	.286	2	7	1	2	0	0	1	1	1	0	1
Greg Maddux, p	.000	1	2	0	0	0	0	0	0	0	1	0
Fred McGriff, 1b	.333	3	9	1	3	1	0	1	3	2	1	0
Greg McMichael, p	.000	2	0	0	0	0	0	0	0	0	0	0
Terry Pendleton, ph	.000	1	1	0	0	0	0	0	0	0	1	0
Eddie Perez, c	.333	1	3	0	1	0	0	0	0	0	0	0
Luis Polonia, ph	.000	2	2	0	0	0	0	0	0	0	1	0
John Smoltz, p	.000	1	2	0	0	0	0	0	0	0	1	0
Mark Wohlers, p	.000	3	0	0	0	0	0	0	0	0	0	0
TOTAL	.180		89	10	16	3	0	5	10	12	24	5

PITCHER	W	L	ERA	G	GS	CG	SV	SHO	IP	H	ER	BB	SO
Mike Bielecki	0	0	0.00	1	0	0	0	0	0.2	0	0	1	1
Tom Glavine	1	0	1.35	1	1	0	0	0	6.2	5	1	3	7
Greg Maddux	1	0	0.00	1	1	0	0	0	7.0	3	0	0	7
Greg McMichael	0	0	6.75	2	0	0	0	0	1.1	1	1	1	3
John Smoltz	1	0	1.00	1	1	0	0	0	9.0	4	1	2	7
Mark Wohlers	0	0	0.00	3	0	0	3	0	3.1	1	0	0	4
TOTAL	3	0	0.96	9	3	0	3	0	28.0	14	3	7	29

LA (WC)

PLAYER/POS	AVG	G	AB	R	H	2B	3B	HR	RB	BB	SO	SB
Billy Ashley, ph	.000	2	2	0	0	0	0	0	0	0	2	0
Pedro Astacio, p	.000	1	0	0	0	0	0	0	0	0	0	0
Tom Candiotti, p	.000	1	0	0	0	0	0	0	0	0	0	0
Juan Castro, 2b	.200	2	5	0	1	1	0	0	1	1	1	0
Dave Clark, ph	.000	2	2	0	0	0	0	0	0	0	2	0
Chad Curtis, of	.000	1	2	0	0	0	0	0	0	1	1	0
Delino DeShields, 2b	.000	2	4	0	0	0	0	0	0	0	1	0
Darren Dreifort, p	.000	1	0	0	0	0	0	0	0	0	0	0
Greg Gagne, ss	.273	3	11	2	3	1	0	0	0	0	5	0
Mark Guthrie, p	.000	1	0	0	0	0	0	0	0	0	0	0
Dave Hansen, ph	.000	2	2	0	0	0	0	0	0	0	0	0
Todd Hollandsworth, of	.333	3	12	1	4	3	0	0	1	0	3	0
Eric Karros, 1b	.000	3	9	0	0	0	0	0	0	2	3	0
Wayne Kirby, of	.125	3	8	1	1	0	0	0	0	2	1	0
Ramon Martinez, p	.000	1	3	0	0	0	0	0	0	0	2	0
Raul Mondesi, of	.182	3	11	0	2	2	0	0	1	0	4	0
Hideo Nomo, p	.000	1	1	0	0	0	0	0	0	0	1	0
Antonio Osuna, p	.000	2	0	0	0	0	0	0	0	0	0	0
Mike Piazza, c	.300	3	10	1	3	0	0	0	2	1	2	0
Scott Radinsky, p	.000	2	0	0	0	0	0	0	0	0	0	0
Ismael Valdes, p	.000	1	2	0	0	0	0	0	0	0	0	0
Tim Wallach, 3b	.000	3	11	0	0	0	0	0	0	0	1	0
Todd Worrell, p	.000	1	0	0	0	0	0	0	0	0	0	0
TOTAL	.147		95	5	14	7	0	0	5	7	29	0

PITCHER	W	L	ERA	G	GS	CG	SV	SHO	IP	H	ER	BB	SO
Pedro Astacio	0	0	0.00	1	0	0	0	0	1.2	0	0	0	1
Tom Candiotti	0	0	0.00	1	0	0	0	0	2.0	0	0	0	1
Darren Dreifort	0	0	0.00	1	0	0	0	0	0.2	0	0	0	0
Mark Guthrie	0	0	0.00	1	0	0	0	0	0.1	0	0	1	1
Ramon Martinez	0	0	1.13	1	1	0	0	0	8.0	3	1	3	6
Hideo Nomo	0	1	12.27	1	1	0	0	0	3.2	5	5	5	3
Antonio Osuna	0	1	4.50	2	0	0	0	0	2.0	3	1	1	4
Scott Radinsky	0	0	0.00	2	0	0	0	0	1.1	0	0	1	2
Ismael Valdes	0	1	4.26	1	1	0	0	0	6.1	5	3	0	5
Todd Worrell	0	0	0.00	1	0	0	0	0	1.0	0	0	1	1
TOTAL	0	3	3.33	12	3	0	0	0	27.0	16	10	12	24

GAME 1 AT LA OCT 2

ATL 000 100 000 1　2 4 1
LA　000 010 000 0　1 5 0
Pitchers: SMOLTZ, Wohlers (10) vs Martinez, Radinsky (9), OSUNA (9)
Home Runs: Lopez-ATL
Attendance: 47,428

GAME 2 AT LA OCT 3

ATL 010 000 200　3 5 2
LA　100 100 000　2 3 0
Pitchers: MADDUX, McMichael (8), Wohlers (9) vs VALDES, Astacio (7), Worrell (9)
Home Runs: Klesko-ATL, McGriff-ATL, Dye-ATL
Attendance: 51,916

GAME 3 AT ATL OCT 5

LA　000 000 110　2 6 1
ATL 100 400 00X　5 7 0
Pitchers: NOMO, Guthrie (4), Candiotti (5), Radinsky (7), Osuna (8), Dreifort (8) vs GLAVINE, McMichael (7), Bielecki (8), Wohlers (8)
Home Runs: C.Jones-ATL

ST. LOUIS CARDINALS (CENTRAL) 3, SAN DIEGO PADRES (WEST) 0

St. Louis finished 19 games under .500 in 1995, but with new manager Tony LaRussa and 14 new players, the Cards of 1996 won 88 games and captured the NL Central by six games. San Diego's storybook season ended with a three-game sweep over the Dodgers to claim the NL West title with a 91–71 mark. The Cardinals took control of the Division Series at Busch Stadium when Gary Gaetti hit a three-run home run, his only hit of the series, to give the Cards a first-inning lead against Joey Hamilton. St. Louis made it hold up. Todd Stottlemyre, who entered the game with a postseason ERA of 7.50, allowed only a Rickey Henderson home run in 6-2/3 innings. Then LaRussa's veteran bullpen of Rick Honeycutt and Dennis Eckersley, with 40 years of major league experience between them, kept the Padres at bay.

Game 2 was another well-played contest as the two teams matched each other run for run through the first seven and a half innings in front of a record crowd in St. Louis. Willie McGee singled in the first run of the game for the Cards in the third, but Ken Caminiti answered back with a home run to right field to tie the score at 1–1 in the top of the fifth. St. Louis rallied for three runs in the bottom of the frame when Ron Gant hit a bases-clearing double. The Padres scored twice in the sixth when Tony Gwynn singled in one run and a throwing error allowed another run to score. San Diego tied the game in the top of the eighth on a groundout by Steve Finley, but Tom Pagnozzi's line drive in the bottom of the inning ticked off the glove of reliever Trevor Hoffman and brought home the winning run. Eckersley retired the side in order in the ninth to make a winner of Honeycutt.

In San Diego's only other playoff appearance in 1984, the Padres dropped the first two games in Chicago and then won the last three at home for the pennant. The Padres were looking for that magic again as they took a 4–1 lead after four innings against Cardinals starter Donovan Osborne. The Cards rallied to tie matters in the sixth. St. Louis pushed across a run in the seventh after the Padres misplayed a bunt, but Caminiti hit his

second home run of the game—and third of the series—to tie the game in the eighth. San Diego had a chance to take the lead later in the inning, but right fielder Brian Jordan made a sensational diving catch to end the threat. With his shoulder still aching from the catch, Jordan crushed a home run to left off Hoffman for a 7–5 lead in the ninth. Eckersley made the sweep official by earning the save.

STL (C)

PLAYER/POS	AVG	G	AB	R	H	2B	3B	HR	RB	BB	SO	SB
Luis Alicea, 2b	.182	3	11	1	2	2	0	0	0	1	4	0
Andy Benes, p	.500	1	2	1	1	0	0	0	0	0	1	0
Royce Clayton, ss	.333	2	6	1	2	0	0	0	0	3	1	0
Dennis Eckersley, p	.000	3	0	0	0	0	0	0	0	0	0	0
Gary Gaetti, 3b	.091	3	11	1	1	0	0	1	3	0	3	0
Mike Gallego, 2b-1, 3b-1	.000	2	1	0	0	0	0	0	0	0	1	0
Ron Gant, of	.400	3	10	3	4	1	0	1	4	2	0	2
Rick Honeycutt, p	.000	3	1	0	0	0	0	0	0	0	1	0
Brian Jordan, of	.333	3	12	4	4	0	0	1	3	1	3	1
Ray Lankford, of	.500	1	2	1	1	0	0	0	0	1	0	0
John Mabry, 1b	.300	3	10	1	3	0	1	0	1	1	1	0
T. J. Mathews, p	.000	1	0	0	0	0	0	0	0	0	0	0
Willie McGee, of	.100	3	10	1	1	0	0	0	1	1	3	0
Miguel Mejia, pr	.000	1	0	0	0	0	0	0	0	0	0	0
Donovan Osborne, p	.000	1	1	0	0	0	0	0	0	0	0	0
Tom Pagnozzi, c	.273	3	11	0	3	0	0	0	2	1	3	0
Mark Petkovsek, p	.000	1	0	0	0	0	0	0	0	0	0	0
Ozzie Smith, ss-1	.333	2	3	1	1	0	0	0	0	2	0	0
Todd Stottlemyre, p	.000	1	2	0	0	0	0	0	0	0	2	0
Mark Sweeney, ph	1.000	1	1	0	1	0	0	0	0	0	0	0
TOTAL	.255		94	15	24	3	1	3	14	13	23	3

PITCHER	W	L	ERA	G	GS	CG	SV	SHO	IP	H	ER	BB	SO
Andy Benes	0	0	5.14	1	1	0	0	0	7.0	6	4	1	9
Dennis Eckersley	0	0	0.00	3	0	0	3	0	3.2	3	0	0	2
Rick Honeycutt	1	0	3.38	3	0	0	0	0	2.2	3	1	1	2
T. J. Mathews	1	0	0.00	1	0	0	0	0	1.0	1	0	0	2
Donovan Osborne	0	0	9.00	1	1	0	0	0	4.0	7	4	0	5
Mark Petkovsek	0	0	0.00	1	0	0	0	0	2.0	0	0	0	1
Todd Stottlemyre	1	0	1.35	1	1	0	0	0	6.2	5.0	1	2	7
TOTAL	3	0	3.33	11	3	0	3	0	27.0	25	10	4	28

SD (W)

PLAYER/POS	AVG	G	AB	R	H	2B	3B	HR	RB	BB	SO	SB
Andy Ashby, p	.000	1	1	0	0	0	0	0	0	0	1	0
Willie Blair, p.	.000	1	0	0	0	0	0	0	0	0	0	0
Doug Bochtler, p	.000	1	0	0	0	0	0	0	0	0	0	0
Ken Caminiti, 3b	.300	3	10	3	3	0	0	3	3	2	5	0
Archi Cianfrocco, 1b	.333	3	3	1	1	0	0	0	0	0	1	0
Steve Finley, of	.083	3	12	0	1	0	0	0	1	0	4	1
John Flaherty, c	.000	2	4	0	0	0	0	0	0	0	1	0
Chris Gomez, ss	.167	3	12	0	2	0	0	0	1	0	4	0
Tony Gwynn, of	.308	3	13	0	4	1	0	0	1	0	2	1
Chris Gwynn, ph	1.000	2	2	1	2	0	0	0	0	0	0	0
Joey Hamilton, p	.000	1	2	0	0	0	0	0	0	0	2	0
Rickey Henderson, of	.333	3	12	2	4	0	0	1	1	2	3	0
Trevor Hoffman, p	.000	2	0	0	0	0	0	0	0	0	0	0
Brian Johnson, c	.375	2	8	2	3	1	0	0	0	0	1	0
Wally Joyner, 1b	.111	3	9	0	1	0	0	0	0	0	2	0
Scott Livingstone, ph	.500	2	2	1	1	0	0	0	0	0	0	0
Luis Lopez, pr	.000	1	0	0	0	0	0	0	0	0	0	0
Jody Reed, 2b	.273	3	11	0	3	1	0	0	2	0	1	0
Scott Sanders, p	.000	1	1	0	0	0	0	0	0	0	0	0
Fernando Valenzuela, p	.000	1	0	0	0	0	0	0	0	0	0	0
Greg Vaughn, ph	.000	3	3	0	0	0	0	0	0	0	1	0
Dario Veras, p	.000	2	0	0	0	0	0	0	0	0	0	0
Tim Worrell, p	.000	2	0	0	0	0	0	0	0	0	0	0
TOTAL	.238		105	10	25	3	0	4	9	4	28	2

PITCHER	W	L	ERA	G	GS	CG	SV	SHO	IP	H	ER	BB	SO
Andy Ashby	0	0	6.75	1	1	0	0	0	5.1	7	4	1	5
Willie Blair	0	0	0.00	1	0	0	0	0	2.0	1	0	2	3
Doug Bochtler	0	1	27.00	1	0	0	0	0	1.0	1	2	0	2
Joey Hamilton	0	1	4.50	1	1	0	0	0	6.0	5	3	0	6
Trevor Hoffman	0	1	10.80	2	0	0	0	0	1.2	3	2	1	2
Scott Sanders	0	0	8.31	1	1	0	0	0	4.1	3	4	4	4
F. Valenzuela	0	0	0.00	1	0	0	0	0	0.2	0	0	2	0
Dario Veras	0	0	0.00	2	0	0	0	0	1.0	1	0	0	1
Tim Worrell	0	0	2.45	2	0	0	0	0	3.2	4	1	1	2
TOTAL	0	3	5.40	12	3	0	0	0	25.0	24	15	13	23

GAME 1 AT STL OCT 1

SD 000 001 000   1 8 1
STL 300 000 00X   3 6 0
Pitchers: HAMILTON, Blair (7) vs STOTTLEMYRE, Honeycutt (7), Eckersley (8)
Home Runs: Henderson-SD, Gaetti-STL
Attendance: 54,193

GAME 2 AT STL OCT 3

SD 000 012 010   4 6 0
STL 001 030 01X   5 5 1
Pitchers: Sanders, Veras (5), Worrell (6), BOCHTLER (8), Hoffman (8) vs An.Benes, HONEYCUTT (8), Eckersley (9)
Home Runs: Caminiti-SD
Attendance: 56,752

GAME 3 AT SD OCT 5

STL 100 003 102   7 13 1
SD 021 100 010   5 11 2
Pitchers: Osborne, Petkovsek (5), Honeycutt (7), MATHEWS (8), Eckersley (9) vs Ashby, Worrell (6), Valenzuela (8), Veras (8), HOFFMAN (9)
Home Runs: Gant-STL, Jordan-STL, Caminiti-SD (2)
Attendance: 53,899

NEW YORK YANKEES (EAST) 3, TEXAS RANGERS (WEST) 1

The Rangers jumped out to a lead in all four games of the Division Series, but the difference was Yankees relief pitching—and Bernie Williams. The New York bullpen allowed just one earned run in 19-2/3 innings of relief while Texas relievers failed to hold the lead in all three losses. Williams hit three home runs in the series, including two in decisive Game 4. Juan Gonzalez hit five home runs and drove in nine runs for the Rangers, but the Yankees won by corralling the rest of the Texas bats in the series.

John Burkett, a late-season acquisition, quieted the boisterous Yankee Stadium crowd with a complete-game effort in Game 1. Gonzalez and Dean Palmer both homered off David Cone in the fifth inning for a 6–2 Ranger win. Texas jumped out to a 4–1 lead in Game 2 against Andy Pettitte, courtesy of a pair of Gonzalez home runs, but the Rangers' failure to convert two tailor-made double-play grounders in the fourth inning gave the Yankees a key run. The Yankees tied it against the Texas bullpen and the Rangers defense gave New York the game when Palmer threw away Charlie Hayes' bunt in the 12th inning to score Derek Jeter with the winner.

In Game 3 Williams homered to the opposite field in the top of the first inning and then reached over the fence to rob Rusty Greer of a home run in the bottom of the inning. In the first home postseason game in the history of the franchise, Darren Oliver gave the crowd plenty to cheer about as he held the Yankees to four hits through eight innings. Texas scored two runs off Jimmy Key as Gonzalez provided the expected power with a fourth-inning home run and the other run was set up when no one covered second base on a steal. Rangers manager Johnny Oates knew the shaky state of his bullpen, so he let Oliver start the ninth and yanked him only after the first two runners reached base. Mike Henneman allowed a game-tying sacrifice fly and surrendered a single by Mariano Duncan for a 3–2 Yankees lead. John Wetteland retired the side in the ninth to give New York a two games to one lead.

The Rangers jumped out to a 4–0 lead the next afternoon in Game 4. Gonzalez, as usual, added

a home run, but timely hits by Mickey Tettleton, Ivan Rodriguez, and Mark McLemore scored three more runs and ended the Yankees' streak of bullpen dominance. New York simply started a new streak. David Weathers pitched three scoreless innings of relief and wound up with the win when Mariano Rivera and Wetteland also pitched scoreless baseball. The Rangers, meanwhile, tried eight pitchers and still couldn't stop the Yankees. Cecil Fielder, Duncan, and Jeter each drove in runs in the fourth to cut the lead to 4–3. Switch-hitting Williams led off the fifth with a home run from the left side to tie the game and—after Fielder had given the Yankees the lead in the seventh—Williams clinched it with a homer from the right side in the ninth inning.

NY (E)

PLAYER/POS	AVG	G	AB	R	H	2B	3B	HR	RB	BB	SO	SB
Brian Boehringer, p	.000	2	0	0	0	0	0	0	0	0	0	0
Wade Boggs, 3b	.083	3	12	0	1	1	0	0	0	0	2	0
David Cone, p	.000	1	0	0	0	0	0	0	0	0	0	0
Mariano Duncan, 2b	.313	4	16	0	5	0	0	0	3	0	4	0
Cecil Fielder, dh	.364	3	11	2	4	0	0	1	4	1	2	0
Andy Fox, dh-1	.000	2	0	0	0	0	0	0	0	0	0	0
Joe Girardi, c	.222	4	9	1	2	0	0	0	0	4	1	0
Charlie Hayes, 3b-2	.200	3	5	0	1	0	0	0	1	0	0	0
Derek Jeter, ss	.412	4	17	2	7	1	0	0	1	0	2	0
Jimmy Key, p	.000	1	0	0	0	0	0	0	0	0	0	0
Jim Leyritz, c-1	.000	2	3	0	0	0	0	0	0	1	1	0
Graeme Lloyd, p	.000	2	0	0	0	0	0	0	0	0	0	0
Tino Martinez, 1b	.267	4	15	3	4	2	0	0	0	3	1	0
Jeff Nelson, p	.000	2	0	0	0	0	0	0	0	0	0	0
Paul O'Neill, of	.133	4	15	0	2	0	0	0	0	0	2	0
Andy Pettitte, p	.000	1	0	0	0	0	0	0	0	0	0	0
Tim Raines, of	.250	4	16	3	4	0	0	0	0	3	1	0
Mariano Rivera, p	.000	2	0	0	0	0	0	0	0	0	0	0
Ruben Rivera, of	.000	2	1	0	0	0	0	0	0	0	1	0
Kenny Rogers, p	.000	2	0	0	0	0	0	0	0	0	0	0
Luis Sojo, 2b	.000	2	0	0	0	0	0	0	0	0	0	0
Darryl Strawberry, dh	.000	2	5	0	0	0	0	0	0	0	2	0
Dave Weathers, p	.000	2	0	0	0	0	0	0	0	0	0	0
John Wetteland, p	.000	3	0	0	0	0	0	0	0	0	0	0
Bernie Williams, of	.467	4	15	5	7	0	0	3	5	2	1	1
TOTAL	.264		140	16	37	4	0	4	15	13	20	1

PITCHER	W	L	ERA	G	GS	CG	SV	SHO	IP	H	ER	BB	SO
Brian Boehringer	1	0	6.75	2	0	0	0	0	1.1	3	1	2	0
David Cone	0	1	9.00	1	1	0	0	0	6.0	8	6	2	8
Jimmy Key	0	0	3.60	1	1	0	0	0	5.0	5	2	1	3
Graeme Lloyd	0	0	0.00	2	0	0	0	0	1.0	1	0	0	0
Jeff Nelson	1	0	0.00	2	0	0	0	0	3.2	2	0	2	5
Andy Pettitte	0	0	5.68	1	1	0	0	0	6.1	4	4	6	3
Mariano Rivera	0	0	0.00	2	0	0	0	0	4.2	0	0	1	1
Kenny Rogers	0	0	9.00	2	1	0	0	0	2.0	5	2	2	1
Dave Weathers	1	0	0.00	2	0	0	0	0	5.0	1	0	0	5
John Wetteland	0	0	0.00	3	0	0	2	0	4.0	2	0	4	4
TOTAL	3	1	3.46	18	4	0	2	0	39.0	31	15	20	30

TEX (W)

PLAYER/POS	AVG	G	AB	R	H	2B	3B	HR	RB	BB	SO	SB
Damon Buford, pr	.000	2	0	0	0	0	0	0	0	0	0	0
John Burkett, p	.000	1	0	0	0	0	0	0	0	0	0	0
Will Clark, 1b	.125	4	16	1	2	0	0	0	0	3	2	0
Dennis Cook, p	.000	2	0	0	0	0	0	0	0	0	0	0
Kevin Elster, ss	.333	4	12	2	4	2	0	0	0	3	2	1
Rene Gonzales, ss	.000	1	0	0	0	0	0	0	0	0	0	0
Juan Gonzalez, of	.438	4	16	5	7	0	0	5	9	3	2	0
Rusty Greer, of	.125	4	16	2	2	0	0	0	0	3	3	0
Darryl Hamilton, of	.158	4	19	0	3	0	0	0	0	0	2	0
Mike Henneman, p	.000	3	0	0	0	0	0	0	0	0	0	0
Ken Hill, p	.000	1	0	0	0	0	0	0	0	0	0	0
Mark McLemore, 2b	.133	4	15	1	2	0	0	0	2	0	4	0
Warren Newson, ph	.000	2	1	0	0	0	0	0	0	1	0	0
Darren Oliver, p	.000	1	0	0	0	0	0	0	0	0	0	0
Dean Palmer, 3b	.211	4	19	3	4	1	0	1	2	0	5	0
Danny Patterson, p	.000	1	0	0	0	0	0	0	0	0	0	0
Roger Pavlik, p	.000	1	0	0	0	0	0	0	0	0	0	0
Ivan Rodriguez, c	.375	4	16	1	6	1	0	0	2	2	3	0
Jeff Russell, p	.000	2	0	0	0	0	0	0	0	0	0	0
Mike Stanton, p	.000	3	0	0	0	0	0	0	0	0	0	0
Mickey Tettleton, dh	.083	4	12	1	1	0	0	0	1	5	7	0
Ed Vosberg, p	.000	1	0	0	0	0	0	0	0	0	0	0
Bobby Witt, p	.000	1	0	0	0	0	0	0	0	0	0	0
TOTAL	.218		142	16	31	4	0	6	16	20	30	1

PITCHER	W	L	ERA	G	GS	CG	SV	SHO	IP	H	ER	BB	SO
John Burkett	1	0	2.00	1	1	1	0	0	9.0	10	2	1	7
Dennis Cook	0	0	0.00	2	0	0	0	0	1.1	0	0	1	0
Mike Henneman	0	0	0.00	3	0	0	0	0	1.0	1	0	1	1
Ken Hill	0	0	4.50	1	1	0	0	0	6.0	5	3	3	1
Darren Oliver	0	1	3.38	1	1	0	0	0	8.0	6	3	2	3
Danny Patterson	0	0	0.00	1	0	0	0	0	0.1	1	0	0	0
Roger Pavlik	0	1	6.75	1	0	0	0	0	2.2	4	2	0	1
Jeff Russell	0	0	3.00	2	0	0	0	0	3.0	3	1	0	1
Mike Stanton	0	1	2.70	3	0	0	0	0	3.1	2	1	3	3
Ed Vosberg	0	0	∞	1	0	0	0	0	0.0	1	0	0	0
Bobby Witt	0	0	8.10	1	1	0	0	0	3.1	4	3	2	3
TOTAL	1	3	3.55	17	4	1	0	0	38.0	37	15	13	20

GAME 1 AT NY OCT 1

TEX 000 501 000   6 8 0
NY 100 100 000   2 19 0
Pitchers: BURKETT vs CONE, Lloyd (7), Weathers (8)
Home Runs: Gonzalez-TEX, Palmer-TEX
Attendance: 57,205

GAME 2 AT NY OCT 2

TEX 013 000 000 000   4 8 1
NY 010 100 110 001   5 8 0
Pitchers: Hill, Cook (7), Russell (8), STANTON (10), Henneman (12) vs Pettitte, Rivera (7), Wetteland (10), Lloyd (12), Nelson (12), Rogers (12), BOEHRINGER (12)
Home Runs: Gonzalez-TEX (2), Fielder-NY
Attendance: 57,156

GAME 3 AT TEX OCT 4

NY 100 000 002   3 7 1
TEX 000 110 000   2 6 1
Pitchers: Key, NELSON (6), Wetteland (9) vs OLIVER, Henneman (9), Stanton (9)
Home Runs: Williams-NY, Gonzalez-TEX
Attendance: 50,860

GAME 4 AT TEX OCT 5

NY 000 310 101   6 12 1
TEX 022 000 000   4 9 0
Pitchers: Rogers, Boehringer (3), WEATHERS (4), Rivera (7), Wetteland (9) vs Witt, Patterson (4), Cook (4), PAVLIK (5), Vosberg (7), Russell (7), Stanton (8), Henneman (9)
Home Runs: Williams-NY (2), Gonzalez-TEX
Attendance: 50,066

BALTIMORE ORIOLES (WILD CARD) 3, CLEVELAND INDIANS (CENTRAL) 1

An ugly spitting incident by Roberto Alomar overshadowed Baltimore's first trip to the postseason since 1983. Alomar spit at umpire John Hirschbeck during the last series of the regular season and that led the umpires to threaten to strike the postseason if Alomar was not suspended immediately. He was not suspended, the umpires (thanks to a court order) did not strike, and the fans both cheered Alomar (in Baltimore) and booed him (in Cleveland). But in the end, Alomar was the hero in the Orioles' unlikely win over the team with the best record in baseball.

Roberto Alomar was not the only player to come through with a big home run. Brady Anderson, the poster boy for "Year of the Home Run" with 50 regular-season clouts, started the series with a home run to lead off Game 1. The Orioles followed suit three more times, including a grand slam by Bobby Bonilla and two home runs by B.J. Surhoff, as the Orioles cruised to a 10–4 win. The Indians battled back from a 4–0 deficit to tie Game 2, but the difference was the way relief pitchers handled bases loaded situations in the eighth inning. In the top of the inning, the Indians had the bases loaded with no one out and the five-six-seven batters due up. Julio Franco hit a long sacrifice fly to tie the game, but reliever Armando Benitez came back to strike out Manny Ramirez and Sandy Alomar Jr. to end the threat. In the bottom of the eighth, the Orioles loaded the bases with none out and Indians reliever Paul Assenmacher got Surhoff to ground back to the mound. Assenmacher got the force out at home, but catcher Sandy Alomar's return throw to first bounced and could not be handled by Jeff Kent as Cal Ripken crossed the plate. The Indians argued that Surhoff ran on the inside route to the base and should have been ruled out automatically. This time, the umpires were on Baltimore's side and the O's went on to win, 7–4, to take a two games to none lead.

Relief pitching was again the difference in Game 3, but it was the Indians, not the Orioles who got the better of it at Jacobs Field. Jesse Orosco walked the bases loaded in the seventh inning and Benitez entered a 4–4 game with the chance to douse another Tribe

rally. Albert Belle's grand slam broke the tie and shattered Baltimore's bid for a sweep. Game 4 was an uncharacteristic pitcher's duel. Charles Nagy, who had been hit hard by the O's in the opener, fanned 12 batters in six innings and four relievers held Baltimore to two runs through eight innings.

Cleveland closer Jose Mesa had a 3–2 lead and a chance to force Game 5, but Roberto Alomar came through with a single to tie the game in the ninth. Mesa faced Alomar again in the 12th and he responded with a 402-foot home run to center for a 4–3 lead. Third baseman Todd Zeile, a converted catcher and a late-season pickup, made a great play on a bunt by Jose Vizcaino to get the first out in the bottom of the 12th and reliever Randy Myers did the rest. The Orioles, who struck out a postseason-record 23 times in the game, still found a way to get the bat on the ball when it counted.

BAL (WC)

PLAYER/POS	AVG	G	AB	R	H	2B	3B	HR	RB	BB	SO	SB
Manny Alexander, dh-1	.000	3	0	2	0	0	0	0	0	0	0	0
Roberto Alomar, 2b	.294	4	17	2	5	0	0	1	4	2	3	0
Brady Anderson, of	.294	4	17	3	5	0	0	2	4	2	3	0
Armando Benitez, p	.000	3	0	0	0	0	0	0	0	0	0	0
Bobby Bonilla, of	.200	4	15	4	3	0	0	2	5	4	6	0
Mike Devereaux, of-3	.000	4	1	0	0	0	0	0	0	0	0	0
Scott Erickson, p	.000	1	0	0	0	0	0	0	0	0	0	0
Chris Hoiles, c	.143	4	7	1	1	0	0	0	0	3	3	0
Pete Incaviglia, of	.200	2	5	1	1	0	0	0	0	0	4	0
Terry Mathews, p	.000	3	0	0	0	0	0	0	0	0	0	0
Eddie Murray, dh	.400	4	15	1	6	1	0	0	1	3	4	1
Mike Mussina, p	.000	1	0	0	0	0	0	0	0	0	0	0
Randy Myers, p	.000	3	0	0	0	0	0	0	0	0	0	0
Jesse Orosco, p	.000	4	0	0	0	0	0	0	0	0	0	0
Rafael Palmeiro, 1b	.176	4	17	4	3	1	0	1	2	1	6	0
Mark Parent, c	.200	4	5	0	1	0	0	0	0	0	2	0
Arthur Lee Rhodes, p	.000	2	0	0	0	0	0	0	0	0	0	0
Cal Ripken, ss	.444	4	18	2	8	3	0	0	2	0	3	0
B. J. Surhoff, of-3	.385	4	13	3	5	0	0	3	5	0	1	0
David Wells, p	.000	2	0	0	0	0	0	0	0	0	0	0
Todd Zeile, 3b	.263	4	19	2	5	1	0	0	0	2	5	0
TOTAL	.289		149	25	43	6	0	9	23	17	40	1

PITCHER	W	L	ERA	G	GS	CG	SV	SHO	IP	H	ER	BB	SO
Armando Benitez	2	0	2.25	3	0	0	0	0	4.0	1	1	2	6
Scott Erickson	0	0	4.05	1	1	0	0	0	6.2	6	3	2	6
Terry Mathews	0	0	0.00	3	0	0	0	0	2.2	3	0	1	2
Mike Mussina	0	0	4.50	1	1	0	0	0	6.0	7	3	2	6
Randy Myers	0	0	0.00	3	0	0	2	0	3.0	0	0	0	3
Jesse Orosco	0	1	36.00	4	0	0	0	0	1.0	2	4	3	2
Arthur Lee Rhodes	0	0	9.00	2	0	0	0	0	1.0	1	1	1	1
David Wells	1	0	4.61	2	2	0	0	0	13.2	15	7	4	6
TOTAL	3	1	4.50	19	4	0	2	0	38.0	35	19	15	32

CLE (C)

PLAYER/POS	AVG	G	AB	R	H	2B	3B	HR	RB	BB	SO	SB
Sandy Alomar, c	.125	4	16	0	2	0	0	0	3	0	2	0
Paul Assenmacher, p	.000	3	0	0	0	0	0	0	0	0	0	0
Albert Belle, of	.200	4	15	2	3	0	0	2	6	3	2	1
Casey Candaele, dh-1	.000	2	0	1	0	0	0	0	0	1	0	0
Alan Embree, p	.000	3	0	0	0	0	0	0	0	0	0	0
Julio Franco, 1b-3, dh-1	.133	4	15	1	2	0	0	0	1	1	6	0
Brian Giles, ph	.000	1	1	0	0	0	0	0	0	0	1	0
Orel Hershiser, p	.000	1	0	0	0	0	0	0	0	0	0	0
Jeff Kent, 3b-2,1b-1, 2b-1	.125	4	8	2	1	1	0	0	0	0	0	0
Kenny Lofton, of	.167	4	18	3	3	0	0	0	1	2	3	5
Jack McDowell, p	.000	1	0	0	0	0	0	0	0	0	0	0
Jose Mesa, p	.000	2	0	0	0	0	0	0	0	0	0	0
Charles Nagy, p	.000	2	0	0	0	0	0	0	0	0	0	0
Chad Ogea, p	.000	1	0	0	0	0	0	0	0	0	0	0
Tony Pena, c	.000	1	0	0	0	0	0	0	0	0	0	0
Eric Plunk, p	.000	3	0	0	0	0	0	0	0	0	0	0
Manny Ramirez, of	.375	4	16	4	6	2	0	2	2	1	4	0
Kevin Seitzer, dh-3,1b-1	.294	4	17	1	5	1	0	0	4	2	4	1
Paul Shuey, p	.000	3	0	0	0	0	0	0	0	0	0	0
Julian Tavarez, p	.000	2	0	0	0	0	0	0	0	0	0	0
Jim Thome, 3b	.300	4	10	1	3	0	0	0	1	5	0	0
Jose Vizcaino, 2b	.333	3	12	1	4	2	0	0	1	1	1	0
Omar Vizquel, ss	.429	4	14	4	6	1	0	0	2	3	4	4
Nigel Wilson, ph	.000	1	1	0	0	0	0	0	0	0	0	0
TOTAL	.245		143	20	35	7	0	4	20	15	32	11

PITCHER	W	L	ERA	G	GS	CG	SV	SHO	IP	H	ER	BB	SO
Paul Assenmacher	1	0	0.00	3	0	0	0	0	1.2	0	0	1	2
Alan Embree	0	0	9.00	3	0	0	0	0	1.0	0	1	0	1
Orel Hershiser	0	0	5.40	1	1	0	0	0	5.0	7	3	3	3
Jack McDowell	0	0	6.35	1	1	0	0	0	5.2	6	4	1	5
Jose Mesa	0	1	3.86	2	0	0	0	0	4.2	8	2	0	7
Charles Nagy	0	1	7.15	2	2	0	0	0	11.1	15	9	5	13
Chad Ogea	0	0	0.00	1	0	0	0	0	1.0	0	0	1	0
Eric Plunk	0	1	6.75	3	0	0	0	0	4.0	1	3	2	6
Paul Shuey	0	0	9.00	3	0	0	0	0	2.0	5	2	2	2
Julian Tavarez	0	0	0.00	2	0	0	0	0	1.1	1	0	2	1
TOTAL	1	3	5.84	21	4	0	0	0	37.0	43	24	17	40

GAME 1 AT BAL OCT 1

CLE 010 200 100   4 10 0
BAL 112 005 10X   10 10 1
Pitchers: NAGY, Embree (6), Shuey (6), Tavarez (8) vs WELLS, Orosco (7), Mathews (7), Rhodes (8), Myers (9)
Home Runs: Ramirez-CLE, Anderson-BAL, Surhoff-BAL (2), Bonilla-BAL
Attendance: 47,644

GAME 2 AT BAL OCT 2

CLE 000 003 010   4 8 2
BAL 100 030 00X   7 9 0
Pitchers: Hershiser, PLUNK (6), Assenmacher (8), Tavarez (8) vs Erickson, Orosco (7), BENITEZ (8), Myers (9)
Home Runs: Belle-CLE, Anderson-BAL
Attendance: 48,970

GAME 3 AT CLE OCT 4

BAL 010 300 000   4 8 2
CLE 120 100 41X   9 10 0
Pitchers: Mussina, OROSCO (7), Benitez (7), Rhodes (8), Mathews (8) vs McDowell, Embree (6), Shuey (7), ASSENMACHER (7), Plunk (8), Mesa (9)
Home Runs: Surhoff-BAL, Ramirez-CLE, Belle-CLE
Attendance: 44,250

GAME 4 AT CLE OCT 5

BAL 020 000 001 001   4 14 1
CLE 000 210 000 000   3 7 1
Pitchers: Wells, Mathews (8), Orosco (9), BENITEZ (10), Myers (12) vs Nagy, Embree (7), Shuey (7), Assenmacher (7), Plunk (8), MESA (9), Ogea (12)
Home Runs: Palmeiro-BAL, Bonilla-BAL, R.Alomar-BAL
Attendance: 44,280

ATLANTA BRAVES (EAST) 4, ST. LOUIS CARDINALS (CENTRAL) 3

The Cards and Braves last met in the NLCS in 1982—a 3–0 Cardinals sweep. Fourteen years later, the Cardinals were just as tough, but John Smoltz beat the Cards in the opener in Atlanta, 4–2. In Game 2, St. Louis turned the tables. Four-time Cy Young winner Greg Maddux was touched for three runs in the first three innings, but the Braves rallied to tie the game on a two-run home run by Marquis Grissom and a single by Ryan Klesko. After the Cards took a 4–3 lead in the seventh on a Ray Lankford sacrifice fly, Maddux fanned Ron Gant and intentionally walked Brian Jordan to pitch to Gary Gaetti. Gaetti hit the first pitch for a grand slam and finished the scoring at 8–3.

The Cards kept the pressure on St. Louis. Gant hit a pair of home runs off Tom Glavine and Cardinals starter Donovan Osborne pitched seven strong innings in Game 3. Dennis Eckersley came on in the ninth to earn his fourth save of the postseason in the 3–2 Cards win. The Braves handed Denny Neagle a 3–0 lead in Game 4 on home runs by Klesko and Mark Lemke plus an RBI single by Jermaine Dye. But the Cards came back. Neagle got the first two outs in the seventh, but John Mabry singled and Tom Pagnozzi walked. Dmitri Young greeted reliever Greg McMichael with triple that plated two runs. Luis Alicea, followed with a walk and the Cards evened the score on an infield hit by Royce Clayton. In the eighth, Jordan lined a 2–1 pitch over the wall for a 4–3 lead.

The series' second part commenced in Game 5—and it was all Atlanta. The Braves had a 5–0 lead after half an inning and that was more than enough for John Smoltz. But they kept on hitting, collecting 22 hits and sending Stottlemyre to the showers in the second. McGriff and Javier Lopez added home runs in the 14–0 rout to send the series back to Atlanta. In Game 6 the only run the Cards got came on a wild pitch by Mark Wohlers in relief of Greg Maddux.

The Cards never even had a chance to do any damage against Glavine in Game 7. Osborne allowed three runs on RBIs by McGriff, Dye, and Andruw Jones, but the crushing blow came off the bat of Glavine. His line drive to left went for a three-run triple and a 6–0

lead. Atlanta added nine more runs, including home runs by MVP Lopez and Andruw Jones, who, at 19, became the youngest player to hit a postseason round-tripper. The Braves also became the first team to come back from a 3–1 deficit to win the NLCS. From Game 5 on, the Braves outscored the Cards, 32–1.

ATL (E)

PLAYER/POS	AVG	G	AB	R	H	2B	3B	HR	RB	BB	SO	SB
Steve Avery, p	.000	2	0	0	0	0	0	0	0	0	0	0
Rafael Belliard, ss	.667	4	6	0	4	0	0	0	2	0	0	0
Mike Bielecki, p	.000	3	0	0	0	0	0	0	0	0	0	0
Jeff Blauser, ss	.176	7	17	5	3	0	1	0	2	4	6	0
Brad Clontz, p	.000	1	0	0	0	0	0	0	0	0	0	0
Jermaine Dye, of	.214	7	28	2	6	1	0	0	4	1	7	0
Tom Glavine, p	.167	2	6	0	1	0	1	0	3	0	3	0
Marquis Grissom, of	.286	7	35	6	10	1	0	1	3	0	8	2
Andruw Jones, of	.222	5	9	3	2	0	0	1	3	3	2	0
Chipper Jones, 3b	.440	7	25	6	11	2	0	0	4	3	1	1
Ryan Klesko, of	.250	6	16	1	4	0	0	1	3	2	6	0
Mark Lemke, 2b	.444	7	27	4	12	2	0	1	5	4	2	0
Javy Lopez, c	.542	7	24	8	13	5	0	2	6	3	1	1
Greg Maddux, p	.000	2	4	0	0	0	0	0	0	0	2	0
Fred McGriff, 1b	.250	7	28	6	7	0	1	2	7	3	5	0
Greg McMichael, p	.000	3	0	0	0	0	0	0	0	0	0	0
Mike Mordecai, 2b-2, 3b-1	.250	4	4	1	1	0	0	0	0	0	1	0
Denny Neagle, p	.500	2	2	0	1	0	0	0	0	0	0	0
Terry Pendleton, 3b-2	.000	6	6	0	0	0	0	0	0	1	3	0
Eddie Perez, c	.000	4	1	0	0	0	0	0	0	0	0	0
Luis Polonia, ph	.000	3	3	0	0	0	0	0	0	0	0	0
John Smoltz, p	.286	2	7	1	2	0	0	0	1	0	3	0
Terrell Wade, p	.000	1	0	0	0	0	0	0	0	0	0	0
Mark Wohlers, p	.000	3	1	0	0	0	0	0	0	0	1	0
TOTAL	.309		249	44	77	11	3	8	43	25	51	4

PITCHER	W	L	ERA	G	GS	CG	SV	SHO	IP	H	ER	BB	SO
Steve Avery	0	0	0.00	2	0	0	0	0	2.0	2	0	1	1
Mike Bielecki	0	0	0.00	3	0	0	0	0	3.0	0	0	1	3
Brad Clontz	0	0	0.00	1	0	0	0	0	0.2	0	0	0	0
Tom Glavine	1	1	2.08	2	2	0	0	0	13.0	10	3	0	9
Greg Maddux	1	1	2.51	2	2	0	0	0	14.1	15	4	2	10
Greg McMichael	0	1	9.00	3	0	0	0	0	2.0	4	2	1	2
Denny Neagle	0	0	2.35	2	1	0	0	0	7.2	2	2	3	8
John Smoltz	2	0	1.20	2	2	0	0	0	15.0	12	2	3	12
Terrell Wade	0	0	0.00	1	0	0	0	0	0.1	0	0	0	1
Mark Wohlers	0	0	0.00	3	0	0	0	2	3.0	0	0	0	4
TOTAL	4	3	1.92	21	7	0	0	2	61.0	45	13	11	53

STL (C)

PLAYER/POS	AVG	G	AB	R	H	2B	3B	HR	RB	BB	SO	SB
Luis Alicea, 2b	.000	5	8	0	0	0	0	0	0	2	1	0
Alan Benes, p	.000	2	1	0	0	0	0	0	0	0	1	0
Andy Benes, p	.250	3	4	0	1	1	0	0	0	1	2	0
Royce Clayton, ss	.350	5	20	4	7	0	0	0	1	1	4	0
Dennis Eckersley, p	.000	3	0	0	0	0	0	0	0	0	0	0
Tony Fossas, p	.000	5	0	0	0	0	0	0	0	0	0	0
Gary Gaetti, 3b	.292	7	24	1	7	0	0	1	4	1	5	0
Mike Gallego, 2b-5, 3b-2	.143	7	14	1	2	0	0	0	0	1	3	0
Ron Gant, of	.240	7	25	3	6	1	0	2	4	2	6	0
Rick Honeycutt, p	.000	5	0	0	0	0	0	0	0	0	0	0
Danny Jackson, p	.000	1	1	0	0	0	0	0	0	0	0	0
Brian Jordan, of	.240	7	25	3	6	1	1	1	2	1	3	0
Ray Lankford, of-3	.000	5	13	1	0	0	0	0	1	1	4	0
John Mabry, 1b-6, of-2	.261	7	23	1	6	0	0	0	0	0	6	0
T. J. Mathews, p	.000	2	0	0	0	0	0	0	0	0	0	0
Willie McGee, of-5	.333	6	15	0	5	0	0	0	0	0	3	0
Miguel Mejia, of-2	.000	3	1	1	0	0	0	0	0	0	1	0
Donovan Osborne, p	.000	2	3	0	0	0	0	0	0	0	3	0
Tom Pagnozzi, c	.158	7	19	1	3	1	0	0	1	1	4	0
Mark Petkovsek, p	.000	6	0	0	0	0	0	0	0	0	0	0
Danny Sheaffer, c	.000	2	3	0	0	0	0	0	0	0	1	0
Ozzie Smith, ss-2	.000	3	9	0	0	0	0	0	0	0	1	0
Todd Stottlemyre, p	.000	3	2	0	0	0	0	0	0	0	0	0
Mark Sweeney, of-2	.000	5	4	1	0	0	0	0	0	0	2	0
Dmitri Young, 1b-2	.286	4	7	1	2	0	1	0	2	0	2	0
TOTAL	.204		221	18	45	4	2	4	15	11	53	1

PITCHER	W	L	ERA	G	GS	CG	SV	SHO	IP	H	ER	BB	SO
Alan Benes	0	1	2.84	2	1	0	0	0	6.1	3	2	2	5
Andy Benes	0	0	5.28	3	2	0	0	0	15.1	19	9	3	9
Dennis Eckersley	1	0	0.00	3	0	0	1	0	3.1	2	0	0	4
Tony Fossas	0	0	2.08	5	0	0	0	0	4.1	1	1	3	1
Rick Honeycutt	0	0	9.00	5	0	0	0	0	4.0	5	4	3	3
Danny Jackson	0	0	9.00	1	0	0	0	0	3.0	7	3	3	3
T. J. Mathews	0	0	0.00	2	0	0	0	0	0.2	2	0	1	2
Donovan Osborne	1	1	9.39	2	2	0	0	0	7.2	12	8	4	6
Mark Petkovsek	0	1	7.36	6	0	0	0	0	7.1	11	6	3	7
Todd Stottlemyre	1	1	12.38	3	2	0	0	0	8.0	15	11	3	11
TOTAL	3	4	6.60	32	7	0	0	0	60.0	77	44	25	51

GAME 1 AT ATL OCT 9

```
STL 010 000 100    2 5 1
ATL 000 020 02X    4 9 0
```
Pitchers: An.Benes, PETKOVSEK (7), Fossas (8), Mathews (8) vs SMOLTZ, Wohlers (9)
Attendance: 48,686

GAME 2 AT ATL OCT 10

```
STL 102 000 500    8 11 2
ATL 002 001 000    3 5 2
```
Pitchers: STOTTLEMYRE, Petkovsek (7), Honeycutt (8), Eckersley (8) vs MADDUX, McMichael (7), Neagle (8), Avery (9)
Home Runs: Gaetti-STL, Grissom-ATL
Attendance: 52,067

GAME 3 AT STL OCT 12

```
ATL 100 000 010    2 8 1
STL 200 001 00X    3 7 0
```
Pitchers: GLAVINE, Bielecki (7), McMichael (8) vs OSBORNE, Petkovsek (7), Honeycutt (9), Eckersley (9)
Home Runs: Gant-STL (2)
Attendance: 56,769

GAME 4 AT STL OCT 13

```
ATL 010 002 000    3 9 1
STL 000 000 31X    4 5 0
```
Pitchers: Neagle, McMICHAEL (7), Wohlers (8) vs An.Benes, Fossas (6), Mathews (6), Al.Benes (6), Honeycutt (8), ECKERSLEY (9)
Home Runs: Klesko-ATL, Lemke-ATL, Jordan-STL
Attendance: 56,764

GAME 5 AT STL OCT 14

```
ATL 520 310 012   14 22 0
STL 000 000 000    0 7 0
```
Pitchers: SMOLTZ, Bielecki (8), Wade (9), Clontz (9) vs STOTTLEMYRE, Jackson (2), Fossas (5), Petkovsek (7), Honeycutt (9)
Home Runs: Lopez-ATL, McGriff-ATL
Attendance: 56,782

GAME 6 AT ATL OCT 16

```
STL 000 000 010    1 6 1
ATL 010 010 01X    3 7 0
```
Pitchers: Al.BENES, Fossas (6), Petkovsek (6), Stottlemyre (9) vs MADDUX, Wohlers (8)
Attendance: 52,067

GAME 7 AT ATL OCT 17

```
STL 000 000 000    0 4 2
ATL 600 403 20X   15 17 0
```
Pitchers: OSBORNE, An.Benes (1), Petkovsek (6), Honeycutt (6), Fossas (8) vs GLAVINE, Bielecki (8), Avery (9)
Home Runs: Lopez-ATL, A.Jones-ATL, McGriff-ATL
Attendance: 52,067

NEW YORK YANKEES (EAST) 4, BALTIMORE ORIOLES (WILD CARD) 1

The Yankees and the Orioles had gone a combined 28 years without a pennant, but that was going to change in 1996—for one team at least. The Orioles had the early advantage in Game 1 on home runs from Brady Anderson and Rafael Palmeiro, but the Yankees cut the lead to 4–3 after seven. Derek Jeter led off the eighth with a long fly to right that Tony Tarasco seemed to have lined up at the wall, but fate—in the form of a 12-year-old boy—intervened. Yankees fan Jeff Maier reached over the fence and knocked the ball into the stands. Right-field umpire Rich Garcia ruled it a home run despite protests from several Orioles, including manager Davey Johnson, who was ejected. (Upon seeing a replay, Garcia admitted he made the wrong call, but AL president Gene Budig denied Baltimore's protest.) The Orioles got out of further trouble in the eighth, but Game 1 was tied at 4–4. With Randy Myers pitching in the bottom of the 11th, Bernie Williams hit a 1–1 pitch deep to left to give the Yanks the win.

Baltimore bounced back in Game 2. Orioles southpaw David Wells spotted the Yanks a pair of first inning runs, but Wells improved to 10–1 at Yankee Stadium. Todd Zeile's two-run home run off David Cone tied the game in the third and Palmeiro's two-run shot off reliever Jeff Nelson gave Baltimore the lead in the seventh. The Orioles added a run in the eighth to go up 5–3, but Benitez retired Cecil Fielder and Tino Martinez with two on in the ninth to even the series at one game apiece.

The teams traveled to Camden Yards for the next three games. Zeile's two-run home run in the first looked like it might stand up as Mike Mussina was masterful through seven and two thirds innings. He never got that last out, though. The Yanks rallied to tie in the eighth then Martinez doubled to left field and Williams dashed home with the go-ahead run.

Darryl Strawberry took Game 4 of the ALCS into his own hands. His solo home run in the second gave the Yanks a 3–1 lead and his two-run blast in the eighth capped off New York's 8–4 victory.

Jim Leyritz started the decisive third-inning rally in Game 5 with a

NY (E)

PLAYER/POS	AVG	G	AB	R	H	2B	3B	HR	RB	BB	SO	SB
Mike Aldrete, ph	.000	1	0	0	0	0	0	0	0	0	0	0
Wade Boggs, 3b	.133	3	15	1	2	0	0	0	0	1	3	0
David Cone, p	.000	1	0	0	0	0	0	0	0	0	0	0
Mariano Duncan, 2b	.200	4	15	0	3	2	0	0	0	0	3	0
Cecil Fielder, dh	.167	5	18	3	3	0	0	2	8	4	5	0
Andy Fox, dh	.000	2	0	0	0	0	0	0	0	0	0	0
Joe Girardi, c	.250	4	12	1	3	0	1	0	0	1	3	0
Charlie Hayes, 3b-2, dh-1	.143	4	7	0	1	0	0	0	0	2	2	0
Derek Jeter, ss	.417	5	24	5	10	2	0	1	1	0	5	2
Jimmy Key, p	.000	1	0	0	0	0	0	0	0	0	0	0
Jim Leyritz, c-2, of-1	.250	3	8	1	2	0	0	1	2	1	4	0
Graeme Lloyd, p	.000	2	0	0	0	0	0	0	0	0	0	0
Tino Martinez, 1b	.182	5	22	3	4	1	0	0	0	0	2	0
Jeff Nelson, p	.000	2	0	0	0	0	0	0	0	0	0	0
Paul O'Neill, of	.273	4	11	1	3	0	0	1	2	3	2	0
Andy Pettitte, p	.000	2	0	0	0	0	0	0	0	0	0	0
Tim Raines, of	.267	5	15	2	4	1	0	0	0	1	1	0
Mariano Rivera, p	.000	2	0	0	0	0	0	0	0	0	0	0
Kenny Rogers, p	.000	1	0	0	0	0	0	0	0	0	0	0
Luis Sojo, 2b	.200	3	5	0	1	0	0	0	0	0	1	0
Darryl Strawberry, of	.417	4	12	4	5	0	0	3	5	2	2	0
Dave Weathers, p	.000	2	0	0	0	0	0	0	0	0	0	0
John Wetteland, p	.000	4	0	0	0	0	0	0	0	0	0	0
Bernie Williams, of	.474	5	19	6	9	3	0	2	6	5	4	1
TOTAL	.273		183	27	50	9	1	10	24	20	37	3

PITCHER	W	L	ERA	G	GS	CG	SV	SHO	IP	H	ER	BB	SO
David Cone	0	0	3.00	1	1	0	0	0	6.0	5	2	5	5
Jimmy Key	1	0	2.25	1	1	0	0	0	8.0	3	2	1	5
Graeme Lloyd	0	0	0.00	2	0	0	0	0	1.2	0	0	0	1
Jeff Nelson	0	1	11.57	2	0	0	0	0	2.1	5	3	0	2
Andy Pettitte	1	0	3.60	2	2	0	0	0	15.0	10	6	5	7
Mariano Rivera	1	0	0.00	2	0	0	0	0	4.0	6	0	1	5
Kenny Rogers	0	0	12.00	1	1	0	0	0	3.0	5	4	2	3
Dave Weathers	1	0	0.00	2	0	0	0	0	3.0	3	0	4	0
John Wetteland	0	0	4.50	4	0	0	1	0	4.0	2	2	1	5
TOTAL	4	1	3.64	17	5	0	1	0	47.0	39	19	15	33

BAL (WC)

PLAYER/POS	AVG	G	AB	R	H	2B	3B	HR	RB	BB	SO	SB
Roberto Alomar, 2b	.217	5	23	2	5	2	0	0	1	0	4	0
Brady Anderson, of	.190	5	21	5	4	1	0	1	1	3	5	0
Armando Benitez, p	.000	3	0	0	0	0	0	0	0	0	0	0
Bobby Bonilla, of	.050	5	20	1	1	0	0	1	2	1	4	0
Rocky Coppinger, p	.000	1	0	0	0	0	0	0	0	0	0	0
Mike Devereaux, of	.000	3	2	0	0	0	0	0	0	0	1	0
Scott Erickson, p	.000	2	0	0	0	0	0	0	0	0	0	0
Chris Hoiles, c	.167	4	12	1	2	0	0	1	2	1	3	0
Pete Incaviglia, dh	.500	1	2	1	1	0	0	0	0	0	0	0
Terry Mathews, p	.000	3	0	0	0	0	0	0	0	0	0	0
Alan Mills, p	.000	3	0	0	0	0	0	0	0	0	0	0
Eddie Murray, dh	.267	5	15	1	4	0	0	1	2	2	2	0
Mike Mussina, p	.000	1	0	0	0	0	0	0	0	0	0	0
Randy Myers, p	.000	3	0	0	0	0	0	0	0	0	0	0
Jesse Orosco, p	.000	4	0	0	0	0	0	0	0	0	0	0
Rafael Palmeiro, 1b	.235	5	17	4	4	0	0	2	4	4	4	0
Mark Parent, c	.167	2	6	0	1	0	0	0	0	0	2	0
Arthur Lee Rhodes, p	.000	3	0	0	0	0	0	0	0	0	0	0
Cal Ripken, ss	.250	5	20	1	5	1	0	0	0	1	4	0
B. J. Surhoff, of	.267	5	15	0	4	0	0	0	2	1	2	0
Tony Tarasco, of	.000	2	1	0	0	0	0	0	0	0	1	0
David Wells, p	.000	1	0	0	0	0	0	0	0	0	1	0
Todd Zeile, 3b	.364	5	22	3	8	0	0	3	5	2	1	0
TOTAL	.222		176	19	39	4	0	9	19	15	33	0

PITCHER	W	L	ERA	G	GS	CG	SV	SHO	IP	H	ER	BB	SO
Armando Benitez	0	0	7.71	3	0	0	1	0	2.1	3	2	3	2
Rocky Coppinger	0	1	8.44	1	1	0	0	0	5.1	6	5	1	3
Scott Erickson	0	1	2.38	2	2	0	0	0	11.1	14	3	4	8
Terry Mathews	0	0	0.00	3	0	0	0	0	2.1	0	0	2	3
Alan Mills	0	0	3.86	3	0	0	0	0	2.1	3	1	1	3
Mike Mussina	0	1	5.87	1	1	0	0	0	7.2	8	5	2	6
Randy Myers	0	1	2.25	3	0	0	0	0	4.0	4	1	3	2
Jesse Orosco	0	0	4.50	4	0	0	0	0	2.0	2	1	1	2
Arthur Lee Rhodes	0	0	0.00	3	0	0	0	0	2.0	2	0	0	2
David Wells	1	0	4.05	1	1	0	0	0	6.2	8	3	3	6
TOTAL	1	4	4.11	24	5	0	1	0	46.0	50	21	20	37

home run off Scott Erickson. Jeter singled and Wade Boggs ended an 0-for-23 playoff skid with an infield hit to set the stage for the rally that put the Birds away for good. Series MVP Bernie Williams then sent a tailor-made double-play grounder to Roberto Alomar, but the second baseman let it go through his legs. One out later, Fielder cleared the basepaths with a three-run home run for a 5–0 lead. Strawberry followed with a 446-foot drive to tie the 1993 Blue Jays for the most home runs (10) in an LCS. Andy Pettitte and John Wetteland held off Baltimore to bring the World Series back to Yankee Stadium for the first time since 1981 and send manager Joe Torre to the Fall Classic for the first time after a record 4,272 games as a player and manager.

GAME 1 AT NY OCT 9

BAL	0 1 1 1 0 1 0 0 0 0 0	4	11 1
NY	1 1 0 0 0 0 1 1 0 0 1	5	11 0

Pitchers: Erickson, Orosco (7), Benitez (7), Rhodes (8), Mathews (9), MYERS (9) vs Pettitte, Nelson (8), Wetteland (9), RIVERA (10)
Home Runs: Anderson-BAL, Palmeiro-BAL, Jeter-NY, Williams-NY
Attendance: 56,495

GAME 2 AT NY OCT 10

BAL	0 0 2 0 0 0 2 1 0	5	10 0
NY	2 0 0 0 0 0 1 0 0	3	11 1

Pitchers: WELLS, Mills (7), Orosco (7), Myers (9), Benitez (9) vs Cone, NELSON (7), Lloyd (8), Weathers (9)
Home Runs: Zeile-BAL, Palmeiro-BAL
Attendance: 56,432

GAME 3 AT BAL OCT 11

NY	0 0 0 1 0 0 0 4 0	5	8 0
BAL	2 0 0 0 0 0 0 0 0	2	3 2

Pitchers: KEY, Wetteland (9) vs MUSSINA, Orosco (8), Mathews (9)
Home Runs: Fielder-NY, Zeile-BAL
Attendance: 48,635

GAME 4 AT BAL OCT 12

NY	2 1 0 2 0 0 0 3 0	8	9 0
BAL	1 0 1 2 0 0 0 0 0	4	11 0

Pitchers: Rogers, WEATHERS (4), Lloyd (6), Rivera (7), Wetteland (9) vs COPPINGER, Rhodes (6), Mills (7), Orosco (8), Benitez (8), Mathews (9)
Home Runs: Williams-NY, Strawberry-NY (2), O'Neill-NY, Hoiles-BAL
Attendance: 48,974

GAME 5 AT BAL OCT 13

NY	0 0 6 0 0 0 0 0 0	6	11 0
BAL	0 0 0 0 0 1 0 1 2	4	4 1

Pitchers: PETTITTE, Wetteland (9) vs ERICKSON, Rhodes (6), Mills (7), Myers (8)
Home Runs: Leyritz-NY, Fielder-NY, Strawberry-NY, Zeile-BAL, Murray-BAL, Bonilla-BAL
Attendance: 48,718

NEW YORK YANKEES (AL) 4, ATLANTA BRAVES (NL) 2

New York looked disoriented in the opener, squandering opportunities early against John Smoltz, but it wasn't long before the Braves took advantage of Andy Pettitte. Andruw Jones, 19, became the youngest player in Series history to hit a homer in the second, and, an inning later, joined Gene Tenace as the second player to homer his first two times up in the Series. It was 9–0 before Wade Boggs broke up the no-hit bid by Smoltz in the fifth. Things didn't get much better for the Yanks the next night. Greg Maddux handcuffed New York on six hits in eight innings as Fred McGriff drove in three runs. The Braves steamrolled New York 16–1 in the first two games.

Things changed in Atlanta. David Cone allowed just four hits through six, and RBI singles by Bernie Williams and Darryl Strawberry gave the Yankees a 2–1 lead against Tom Glavine. The Yankees got insurance in the form of a two-run home run by Williams and an RBI single by Luis Sojo in the eighth. The Braves battered Kenny Rogers for five runs in two-plus innings in Game 4 and Andruw Jones doubled off David Weathers for a 6–0 lead in the fifth. Right field umpire Tim Welke got in the way of Jermaine Dye and kept Derek Jeter's foul fly from being caught. Then Jeter singled; two hits, a walk and an error followed to cut Atlanta's lead in half. Closer Mark Wohlers came in to start the eighth and promptly gave up two hits. It looked like the Braves might escape when Mariano Duncan hit a double-play grounder to Rafael Belliard, but the shortstop botched it and only one out was recorded. Jim Leyritz then homered to tie the game. With runners on first and second in the 10th, Braves manager Bobby Cox opted to walk Williams to load the bases for Boggs. Steve Avery walked Boggs, to bring in the go-ahead run. The Yankees scored again and held on for the biggest comeback in the team's World Series history.

Things continued to go New York's way in Game 5. Pettitte won the last game ever played at Fulton County Stadium because one of the game's best outfielders, Marquis Grissom, dropped a ball, and two gimpy outfielders, Strawberry and Paul O'Neill, made great catches to preserve the 1–0 win.

The Yankees got good news on the only off-day of the Series. Manager Joe Torre's brother Frank, who won a World Series ring with the 1957 Braves, received a heart transplant after months of waiting for a donor. The good luck continued for Game 6. O'Neill doubled to start the third and Joe Girardi tripled him home; Jeter and Williams followed with RBI singles against Maddux. The Braves got a run when Dye walked with the bases loaded in the fourth, but Terry Pendleton grounded into a double play to end the threat. Key pitched into the sixth and Weathers, Lloyd, and Rivera got the Yanks to the ninth. Series MVP John Wetteland allowed a run but gained his fourth save of the Series when Mark Lemke popped up to Hayes in foul ground.

NY (A)

PLAYER/POS	AVG	G	AB	R	H	2B	3B	HR	RB	BB	SO	SB
Mike Aldrete, of-1	.000	2	1	0	0	0	0	0	0	0	0	0
Brian Boehringer, p	.000	2	0	0	0	0	0	0	0	0	0	0
Wade Boggs, 3b	.273	4	11	0	3	1	0	0	2	1	0	0
David Cone, p	.000	1	2	0	0	0	0	0	0	0	1	0
Mariano Duncan, 2b	.053	6	19	1	1	0	0	0	0	0	4	1
Cecil Fielder, 1b-3, dh-3	.391	6	23	1	9	2	0	0	2	2	2	0
Andy Fox, 2b-1,3b-1	.000	4	0	1	0	0	0	0	0	0	0	0
Joe Girardi, c	.200	4	10	1	2	0	1	0	1	1	2	0
Charlie Hayes, 3b-4, 1b-1	.188	5	16	2	3	0	0	0	1	1	5	0
Derek Jeter, ss	.250	6	20	5	5	0	0	0	1	4	6	1
Jimmy Key, p	.000	2	0	0	0	0	0	0	0	0	0	0
Jim Leyritz, c-3	.375	4	8	1	3	0	0	1	3	3	2	1
Graeme Lloyd, p	.000	4	1	0	0	0	0	0	0	0	0	0
Tino Martinez, 1b-5	.091	6	11	0	1	0	0	0	0	2	5	0
Jeff Nelson, p	.000	3	0	0	0	0	0	0	0	0	0	0
Paul O'Neill, of-4	.167	5	12	1	2	2	0	0	0	3	2	0
Andy Pettitte, p	.000	2	4	0	0	0	0	0	0	0	1	0
Tim Raines, of	.214	4	14	2	3	0	0	0	0	2	1	0
Mariano Rivera, p	.000	4	1	0	0	0	0	0	0	0	0	0
Kenny Rogers, p	1.000	1	1	0	1	0	0	0	0	0	0	0
Luis Sojo, 2b-3	.600	5	5	0	3	1	0	0	1	0	0	0
Darryl Strawberry, of	.188	5	16	0	3	0	0	1	1	4	6	0
Dave Weathers, p	.000	3	0	0	0	0	0	0	0	0	0	0
John Wetteland, p	.000	5	0	0	0	0	0	0	0	0	0	0
Bernie Williams, of	.167	6	24	3	4	0	0	1	4	3	6	0
TOTAL	.216		199	18	43	6	1	2	16	26	43	4

PITCHER	W	L	ERA	G	GS	CG	SV	SHO	IP	H	ER	BB	SO
Brian Boehringer	0	0	5.40	2	0	0	0	0	5.0	5	3	0	5
David Cone	1	0	1.50	1	1	0	0	0	6.0	4	1	4	3
Jimmy Key	1	1	3.97	2	2	0	0	0	11.1	15	5	5	1
Graeme Lloyd	1	0	0.00	4	0	0	0	0	2.2	0	0	0	4
Jeff Nelson	0	0	0.00	3	0	0	0	0	4.1	1	0	1	5
Andy Pettitte	1	1	5.91	2	2	0	0	0	10.2	11	7	4	5
Mariano Rivera	0	0	1.59	4	0	0	0	0	5.2	4	1	3	4
Kenny Rogers	0	0	22.50	1	1	0	0	0	2.0	5	5	2	0
Dave Weathers	0	0	3.00	3	0	0	0	0	3.0	2	1	3	3
John Wetteland	0	0	2.08	5	0	0	4	0	4.1	4	1	1	6
TOTAL	4	2	3.93	27	6	0	4	0	55.0	51	24	23	36

ATL (N)

PLAYER/POS	AVG	G	AB	R	H	2B	3B	HR	RB	BB	SO	SB
Steve Avery, p	.000	1	0	0	0	0	0	0	0	0	0	0
Rafael Belliard, ss-3	.000	4	0	0	0	0	0	0	0	0	0	0
Mike Bielecki, p	.000	2	1	0	0	0	0	0	0	0	1	0
Jeff Blauser, ss	.167	6	18	2	3	1	0	0	1	1	4	0
Brad Clontz, p	.000	3	0	0	0	0	0	0	0	0	0	0
Jermaine Dye, of	.118	5	17	0	2	0	0	0	1	1	1	0
Tom Glavine, p	.000	1	1	1	0	0	0	0	0	1	1	0
Marquis Grissom, of	.444	6	27	4	12	2	1	0	5	1	2	1
Andruw Jones, of	.400	6	20	4	8	1	0	2	6	3	6	1
Chipper Jones, 3b-6, ss-1	.286	6	21	3	6	3	0	0	3	4	2	1
Ryan Klesko, of-2, 1b-1, dh-1	.100	5	10	2	1	0	0	0	1	2	4	0
Mark Lemke, 2b	.231	6	26	2	6	1	0	0	2	0	3	0
Javy Lopez, c	.190	6	21	3	4	0	0	0	1	3	4	0
Greg Maddux, p	.000	2	0	0	0	0	0	0	0	0	0	0
Fred McGriff, 1b	.300	6	20	4	6	0	0	2	6	5	4	0
Greg McMichael, p	.000	2	0	0	0	0	0	0	0	0	0	0
Mike Mordecai, ph	.000	1	1	0	0	0	0	0	0	0	1	0
Denny Neagle, p	.000	2	1	0	0	0	0	0	0	0	1	0
Terry Pendleton, dh-2,3b-1	.222	4	9	1	2	1	0	0	0	1	1	0
Eddie Perez, c	.000	2	1	0	0	0	0	0	0	0	0	0
Luis Polonia, ph	.000	6	5	0	0	0	0	0	0	1	2	0
John Smoltz, p	.500	2	2	0	1	0	0	0	0	0	0	0
Terrell Wade, p	.000	2	0	0	0	0	0	0	0	0	0	0
Mark Wohlers, p	.000	4	0	0	0	0	0	0	0	0	0	0
TOTAL	.254		201	26	51	9	1	4	26	23	36	3

PITCHER	W	L	ERA	G	GS	CG	SV	SHO	IP	H	ER	BB	SO
Steve Avery	0	1	13.50	1	0	0	0	0	0.2	1	1	3	0
Mike Bielecki	0	0	0.00	2	0	0	0	0	3.0	0	0	3	6
Brad Clontz	0	0	0.00	3	0	0	0	0	1.2	1	0	1	2
Tom Glavine	0	1	1.29	1	1	0	0	0	7.0	4	1	3	8
Greg Maddux	1	1	1.72	2	2	0	0	0	15.2	14	3	1	8
Greg McMichael	0	0	27.00	2	0	0	0	0	1.0	5	3	0	1
Denny Neagle	0	0	3.00	2	1	0	0	0	6.0	5	2	4	3
John Smoltz	1	1	0.64	2	2	0	0	0	14.0	6	1	8	14
Terrell Wade	0	0	0.00	2	0	0	0	0	0.2	0	0	1	0
Mark Wohlers	0	0	6.23	4	0	0	0	0	4.1	7	3	2	4
TOTAL	2	4	2.33	21	6	0	0	0	54.0	43	14	26	43

GAME 1 AT NY OCT 20

ATL 026 013 000 — 12 13 0
NY 000 010 000 — 1 4 1
Pitchers: SMOLTZ, McMichael (7), Neagle (8), Wade (9), Clontz (9) vs PETTITTE, Boehringer (3), Weathers (6), Nelson (8), Wetteland (9)
Home Runs: A.Jones-ATL (2), McGriff-ATL
Attendance: 56,365

GAME 2 AT NY OCT 21

ATL 101 011 000 — 4 10 0
NY 000 000 000 — 0 7 1
Pitchers: MADDUX, Wohlers (9) vs KEY, Lloyd (7), Nelson (7), Rivera (9)
Attendance: 56,340

GAME 3 AT ATL OCT 22

NY 100 100 030 — 5 8 1
ATL 000 001 010 — 2 6 1
Pitchers: CONE, Rivera (7), Lloyd (8), Wetteland (9) vs GLAVINE, McMichael (8), Clontz (8), Bielecki (9)
Home Runs: Williams-NY
Attendance: 51,843

GAME 4 AT ATL OCT 23

NY 000 003 0302 — 8 12 0
ATL 041 010 0000 — 6 9 2
Pitchers: Rogers, Boehringer (3), Weathers (6), Nelson (6), Rivera (8), LLOYD (9), Wetteland (10) vs Neagle, Wade (6), Bielecki (6), Wohlers (8), AVERY (10), Clontz (10)
Home Runs: Leyritz-NY, McGriff-ATL
Attendance: 51,881

GAME 5 AT ATL OCT 24

NY 000 100 000 — 1 4 1
ATL 000 000 000 — 0 5 1
Pitchers: PETTITTE, Wetteland (9) vs SMOLTZ, Wohlers (9)
Attendance: 51,881

GAME 6 AT NY OCT 26

ATL 000 100 001 — 2 8 0
NY 003 000 00X — 3 8 1
Pitchers: MADDUX, Wohlers (8) vs KEY, Weathers (6), Lloyd (6), Rivera (7), Wetteland (9)
Attendance: 56,375

FLORIDA MARLINS (WILD CARD) 3, SAN FRANCISCO GIANTS (WEST) 0

The Giants went from last place in 1996 to first place in 1997, but Florida got the key hits late in each game to key a sweep of the division series. The Marlins became the first expansion team to win a postseason series, in their fifth year of existence. Kirk Reuter and Kevin Brown each threw seven innings of four-hit ball and each pitcher was nicked for a run in their last inning in Game 1. Bill Mueller homered for the Giants leading off the top of the seventh, and Charles Johnson answered with a home run in the bottom of the inning. In the last of the ninth, the Marlins loaded the bases with one out, but Devon White grounded into a force play at the plate. Reliever Roberto Hernandez fell behind Edgar Renteria and the Marlins shortstop grounded a single to right to win the game.

Game 2 was a battle of the bullpens; starters Shawn Estes and Al Leiter were both out of the game by the fifth inning. Stan Javier had four hits, and Barry Bonds, who had three RBIs in 21 career postseason games, drove home two runs. Bobby Bonilla's three RBIs and Gary Sheffield's home run gave the Marlins a 6–5 lead entering the ninth, but two errors and a broken bat hit against Robb Nen tied the game. In the bottom of the ninth, Moises Alou singled with two runners on against Hernandez, and center fielder Dante Powell's strong throw hit the pitcher's mound and bounced straight up in the air, allowing Sheffield to score the winning run.

Wilson Alvarez, who came with Hernandez in a late season blockbuster deal with the White Sox, sailed through the first five and two thirds innings of Game 3, but then he filled the bases. Devon White, batting eighth, just missed getting hit by a pitch, then launched a grand slam to left field. Jeff Kent homered twice, the second coming just after Mueller was thrown out trying to steal, but Alex Fernandez, Dennis Cook, and Nen limited San Francisco to just five more hits.

FL (WC)

PLAYER/POS	AVG	G	AB	R	H	2B	3B	HR	RB	BB	SO	SB
Kurt Abbott, 2b-2	.250	3	8	0	2	0	0	0	0	0	0	0
Moises Alou, of	.214	3	14	1	3	1	0	0	1	0	3	0
Alex Arias, ph	1.000	1	1	1	1	0	0	0	1	0	0	0
Bobby Bonilla, 3b	.333	3	12	1	4	0	0	1	3	2	1	0
Kevin Brown, p	.000	1	2	0	0	0	0	0	0	0	2	0
John Cangelosi, ph	.000	1	1	0	0	0	0	0	0	0	0	0
Jeff Conine, 1b	.364	3	11	3	4	1	0	0	0	1	0	0
Dennis Cook, p	.000	2	0	0	0	0	0	0	0	0	0	0
Craig Counsell, 2b	.400	3	5	0	2	1	0	0	1	1	0	0
Jim Eisenreich, ph	.000	2	0	0	0	0	0	0	0	0	2	0
Alex Fernandez, p	.000	1	2	0	0	0	0	0	0	0	1	1
Livan Hernandez, p	.000	1	1	0	0	0	0	0	0	0	0	0
Charles Johnson, c	.250	3	8	5	2	1	0	1	2	3	2	0
Al Leiter, p	.000	1	1	0	0	0	0	0	0	0	0	0
Robb Nen, p	.000	2	0	0	0	0	0	0	0	0	0	0
Edgar Renteria, ss	.154	3	13	1	2	0	0	0	1	2	4	0
Gary Sheffield, of	.556	3	9	2	5	1	0	1	1	5	0	0
John Wehner, of	.000	1	0	0	0	0	0	0	0	0	0	0
Devon White, of	.182	3	11	1	2	0	0	1	4	2	3	0
TOTAL	.273		99	15	27	5	0	4	14	19	16	1

PITCHER	W	L	ERA	G	GS	CG	SV	SHO	IP	H	ER	BB	SO
Kevin Brown	0	0	1.29	1	1	0	0	0	7.0	4	1	0	5
Dennis Cook	1	0	0.00	2	0	0	0	0	3.0	0	0	1	3
Alex Fernandez	1	0	2.57	1	1	0	0	0	7.0	7	2	0	5
Livan Hernandez	0	0	2.25	1	0	0	0	0	4.0	3	1	0	3
Al Leiter	0	0	9.00	1	1	0	0	0	4.0	7	4	3	3
Robb Nen	1	0	0.00	2	0	0	0	0	2.0	1	0	2	2
TOTAL	3	0	2.67	8	3	0	0	0	27.0	22	8	6	21

SF (W)

PLAYER/POS	AVG	G	AB	R	H	2B	3B	HR	RB	BB	SO	SB
Wilson Alvarez, p	.000	1	2	0	0	0	0	0	0	0	0	0
Rod Beck, p	.000	1	0	0	0	0	0	0	0	0	0	0
Marvin Benard, ph	.000	2	2	0	0	0	0	0	0	0	1	0
Damon Berryhill, ph	.000	1	1	0	0	0	0	0	0	0	0	0
Barry Bonds, of	.250	3	12	0	3	2	0	0	2	0	3	1
Shawn Estes, p	.000	1	1	0	0	0	0	0	0	0	1	0
Darryl Hamilton, of	.000	2	5	1	0	0	0	0	0	0	1	0
Doug Henry, p	.000	1	0	0	0	0	0	0	0	0	0	0
Roberto Hernandez, p	.000	3	0	0	0	0	0	0	0	0	0	0
Glenallen Hill, of-2	.000	3	7	0	0	0	0	0	0	2	2	0
Stan Javier, of	.417	3	12	2	5	1	0	0	1	0	2	1
Brian Johnson, c	.100	3	10	2	1	0	0	1	1	1	4	0
Jeff Kent, 2b-3,1b-1	.300	3	10	2	3	0	0	2	2	2	1	0
Mark Lewis, 2b	.600	1	5	0	3	0	0	0	1	0	0	0
Bill Mueller, 3b	.250	3	12	1	3	0	0	1	1	0	0	0
Dante Powell, of	.000	1	0	0	0	0	0	0	0	0	0	0
Rich Rodriguez, p	.000	2	0	0	0	0	0	0	0	0	0	0
Kirk Rueter, p	.500	1	2	1	1	0	0	0	0	0	0	0
J. T. Snow, 1b	.167	3	6	0	1	0	0	0	0	1	1	0
Julian Tavarez, p	.000	3	0	0	0	0	0	0	0	0	0	0
Jose Vizcaino, ss	.182	3	11	1	2	1	0	0	0	0	5	0
TOTAL	.224		98	9	22	4	0	4	8	6	21	2

PITCHER	W	L	ERA	G	GS	CG	SV	SHO	IP	H	ER	BB	SO
Wilson Alvarez	0	1	6.00	1	1	0	0	0	6.0	6	4	4	4
Rod Beck	0	0	0.00	1	0	0	0	0	1.1	1	0	0	1
Shawn Estes	0	0	15.00	1	1	0	0	0	3.0	5	5	4	3
Doug Henry	0	0	0.00	1	0	0	0	0	2.0	1	0	3	2
R. Hernandez	0	1	20.25	3	0	0	0	0	1.1	5	3	3	1
Rich Rodriguez	0	0	0.00	2	0	0	0	0	1.0	1	0	0	0
Kirk Rueter	0	0	1.29	1	1	0	0	0	7.0	4	1	3	5
Julian Tavarez	0	1	4.50	3	0	0	0	0	4.0	4	2	2	0
TOTAL	0	3	5.26	13	3	0	0	0	25.2	27	15	19	16

GAME 1 AT FLA SEPT 30

```
SF   000 000 100   1  4 0
FLA  000 000 101   2  7 0
```
Pitchers: Rueter, TAVAREZ (8), Hernandez (9) vs Brown, COOK (8)
Home Runs: Mueller-SF, Johnson-FLA
Attendance: 42,167

GAME 2 AT FLA OCT 1

```
SF   111 100 101   6 11 0
FLA  201 201 001   7 10 2
```
Pitchers: Estes, Henry (4), Tavarez (6), Rodriguez (8), HERNANDEZ (9) vs Leiter, Hernandez (5), NEN (9)
Home Runs: Bonilla-FLA, Johnson-SF, Sheffield-FLA
Attendance: 41,283

GAME 3 AT SF OCT 3

```
FLA  000 004 020   6 10 2
SF   000 101 000   2  7 0
```
Pitchers: FERNANDEZ, Cook (8), Nen (8) vs ALVAREZ, Tavarez (7), Hernandez (8), Rodriguez (8), Beck (8)
Home Runs: Kent-SF (2), White-FLA
Attendance: 57,188

ATLANTA BRAVES (EAST) 3, HOUSTON ASTROS (CENTRAL) 0

The Astros had the worst record of any team to reach the 1997 postseason while the Braves had the best record in baseball. It was a mismatch on paper, and it played out that way on the field, too. The Braves outscored the Astros, 19–5, and their pitching proved to be so dominant that 20-game winner Denny Neagle didn't even get a start in the series for Atlanta.

The handwriting was on the wall in Game 1 when Darryl Kile pitched a two-hitter and still lost, 2–1. Kile was also Houston's only hitter in the clutch, driving in the team's run. Kenny Lofton doubled to start the game and two fly outs brought him home. Ryan Klesko homered to lead off the second and that was it for the scoring and the hitting for the Braves, but Greg Maddux scattered seven hits for the complete-game victory.

Even in a 13–3 second game, the pitchers again had a lot to say about the outcome—although much of it was with their bats. Tom Glavine's single in the bottom of the third sparked a three-run Braves rally and Mike Hampton's single in the top of the fourth drove in the tying run. In the fifth inning Hampton got the first two outs, but then walked four straight batters. His replacement, Mike Magnante, allowed a two-run single to pinch hitter Greg Colrunn that gave the Braves a 6–3 lead. Glavine's single started a five-run rally in the sixth inning.

Game 3 belonged to John Smoltz, who pitched a three-hitter for his 10th career postseason victory. Shane Reynolds, starting the first postseason game in the Astrodome since 1986, had early chances to pitch out of trouble. He picked off Kenny Lofton in the first inning, then allowed a home run to Chipper Jones. In the second, he had a base open with Smoltz on deck, but he pitched instead to Jeff Blauser, who singled in the second run. Smoltz, meanwhile, struck out 11 Astros and silenced "The Killer B's." For the series, the top of the Astros order—Craig Biggio, Derek Bell, and Jeff Bagwell—batted a combined .054 (2-for-37).

ATL (E)

PLAYER/POS	AVG	G	AB	R	H	2B	3B	HR	RB	BB	SO	SB
Danny Bautista, of	.333	3	3	0	1	0	0	0	0	2	0	1
Jeff Blauser, ss	.300	3	10	2	3	0	0	1	4	2	2	0
Mike Cather, p	.000	1	1	0	0	0	0	0	0	0	1	0
Greg Colbrunn, ph	1.000	1	1	0	1	0	0	0	2	0	0	0
Tom Glavine, p	.667	1	3	2	2	0	0	0	0	0	0	0
Tony Graffanino, 2b	.000	3	3	0	0	0	0	0	0	0	2	1
Andruw Jones, of	.000	3	5	1	0	0	0	0	0	1	1	0
Chipper Jones, 3b	.500	3	8	3	4	0	0	1	2	3	2	1
Ryan Klesko, of	.250	3	8	2	2	1	0	1	1	0	2	0
Keith Lockhart, 2b	.000	2	6	0	0	0	0	0	0	0	1	0
Kenny Lofton, of	.154	3	13	2	2	1	0	0	0	1	2	0
Javy Lopez, c	.286	2	7	3	2	2	0	0	1	2	1	0
Greg Maddux, p	.000	1	2	0	0	0	0	0	0	0	1	0
Fred McGriff, 1b	.222	3	9	4	2	0	0	0	1	3	2	0
Eddie Perez, c	.000	1	3	0	0	0	0	0	0	0	1	0
John Smoltz, p	.000	1	4	0	0	0	0	0	0	0	1	0
Michael Tucker, of	.167	2	6	1	1	0	0	0	0	1	1	0
Mark Wohlers, p	.000	1	0	0	0	0	0	0	0	0	0	0
TOTAL	.217		92	19	20	4	0	3	15	15	20	1

PITCHER	W	L	ERA	G	GS	CG	SV	SHO	IP	H	ER	BB	SO
Mike Cather	0	0	0.00	1	0	0	0	0	2.0	0	0	1	2
Tom Glavine	1	0	4.50	1	1	0	0	0	6.0	5	3	5	4
Greg Maddux	1	0	1.00	1	1	1	0	0	9.0	7	1	1	6
John Smoltz	1	0	1.00	1	1	1	0	0	9.0	3	1	1	11
Mark Wohlers	0	0	0.00	1	0	0	0	0	1.0	1	0	0	1
TOTAL	3	0	1.67	5	3	2	0	0	27.0	16	5	8	24

HOU (C)

PLAYER/POS	AVG	G	AB	R	H	2B	3B	HR	RB	BB	SO	SB
Bob Abreu, ph	.333	3	3	0	1	0	0	0	0	0	2	1
Brad Ausmus, c	.400	2	5	1	2	1	0	0	2	0	1	0
Jeff Bagwell, 1b	.083	3	12	0	1	0	0	0	0	1	5	0
Derek Bell, of	.000	3	13	0	0	0	0	0	0	0	3	0
Sean Berry, ph	.000	1	1	0	0	0	0	0	0	0	0	0
Craig Biggio, 2b	.083	3	12	0	1	0	0	0	0	1	0	0
Chuck Carr, of	.250	2	4	1	1	0	0	1	1	1	3	0
Raul Eusebio, c	.667	1	3	1	2	0	0	0	0	0	1	1
Ramon Garcia, p	.000	2	0	0	0	0	0	0	0	0	0	0
Luis Gonzalez, of	.333	3	12	0	4	0	0	0	0	0	1	0
Ricky Gutierrez, ss	.125	3	8	0	1	0	0	0	0	2	1	0
Mike Hampton, p	.500	1	2	0	1	0	0	0	1	0	0	0
Richard Hidalgo, of	.000	2	5	1	0	0	0	0	0	1	2	0
Thomas Howard, ph	.000	2	1	0	0	0	0	0	0	1	1	0
Russ Johnson, ph	.000	1	1	0	0	0	0	0	0	0	1	0
Darryl Kile, p	1.000	1	2	0	2	0	0	0	1	0	0	0
Jose Lima, p	.000	1	0	0	0	0	0	0	0	0	0	0
Mike Magnante, p	.000	2	0	0	0	0	0	0	0	0	0	0
Tom Martin, p	.000	2	0	0	0	0	0	0	0	0	0	0
Tony Pena, c	.000	2	0	0	0	0	0	0	0	0	0	0
Shane Reynolds, p	.000	1	1	0	0	0	0	0	0	0	1	0
Bill Spiers, 3b	.000	3	11	1	0	0	0	0	0	1	2	0
Russ Springer, p	.000	2	0	0	0	0	0	0	0	0	0	0
Billy Wagner, p	.000	1	0	0	0	0	0	0	0	0	0	0
TOTAL	.167		96	5	16	1	0	1	5	8	24	2

PITCHER	W	L	ERA	G	GS	CG	SV	SHO	IP	H	ER	BB	SO
Ramon Garcia	0	0	0.00	2	0	0	0	0	1.0	1	0	1	1
Mike Hampton	0	1	11.57	1	1	0	0	0	4.2	2	6	8	2
Darryl Kile	0	1	2.57	1	1	0	0	0	7.0	2	2	2	4
Jose Lima	0	0	0.00	1	0	0	0	0	1.0	0	0	1	1
Mike Magnante	0	0	4.50	2	0	0	0	0	2.0	4	1	0	2
Tom Martin	0	0	0.00	2	0	0	0	0	0.2	1	0	1	0
Shane Reynolds	0	1	3.00	1	1	0	0	0	6.0	5	2	1	5
Russ Springer	0	0	5.40	2	0	0	0	0	1.2	2	1	1	3
Billy Wagner	0	0	18.00	1	0	0	0	0	1.0	3	2	0	2
TOTAL	0	3	5.04	13	3	0	0	0	25.0	20	14	15	20

GAME 1 AT ATL SEPT 30

```
HOU  000 010 000   1 7 1
ATL  110 000 00X   2 2 0
```
Pitchers: KILE, Springer (8), Martin (8) vs MADDUX
Home Runs: Klesko-ATL
Attendance: 46,467

GAME 2 AT ATL OCT 1

```
HOU  000 300 000    3 6 2
ATL  003 035 02X   13 10 1
```
Pitchers: HAMPTON, Magnante (5), Garcia (6), Lima (7), Wagner (8) vs GLAVINE, Cather (7), Wohlers (9)
Home Runs: Blauser-ATL
Attendance: 49,200

GAME 3 AT HOU OCT 3

```
ATL  110 000 110   4 8 2
HOU  000 000 100   1 3 1
```
Pitchers: SMOLTZ vs REYNOLDS, Springer (7), Martin (8), Garcia (8), Magnante (9)
Home Runs: C.Jones-ATL, Carr-HOU
Attendance: 53,688

CLEVELAND INDIANS (CENTRAL) 3, NEW YORK YANKEES (WILD CARD) 2

The predetermined postseason matchup seemed to favor the wild card Yankees, who drew the Indians in the Division Series while the AL East champion Orioles got the power-packed Mariners. The Indians had the worst record of any American League postseason club, but Cleveland got off to a 5–0 lead in the first inning of Game 1. Cleveland held a 6–1 lead by the time David Cone was chased from the mound, and Cone's injured shoulder made it his only appearance of the series. But Orel Hershiser, who came into the series with an 8–1 record with a 1.83 ERA in the postseason, didn't last through the fifth inning. In the sixth inning, Tim Raines, Derek Jeter, and Paul O'Neill hit successive home runs—a first in postseason history—to give the Yankees an 8–6 victory.

In Game 2 the Yankees couldn't hold the lead. New York reached 21-year-old rookie Jaret Wright for three runs in the first inning, but a two-out rally off Andy Pettitte in the fourth inning gave the Indians a 5–3 lead. Matt Williams homered in the fifth inning, and a trio of relievers held off a late Yankees comeback. David Wells pitched a five-hitter in Game 3 to win a Division Series game for the third straight year for his third different team. New York chased Cleveland starter Charles Nagy in the fourth inning, and Paul O'Neill greeted Chad Ogea with a grand slam. It was the last run the Indians bullpen would allow.

In Game 4 Orel Hershiser and Dwight Gooden looked a lot like they did when they faced each other in the 1988 playoffs. Hershiser was good for seven innings, but Gooden left with a 2–1 lead in the sixth. The Yankees were four outs from winning the series with their closer Mariano Rivera on the mound when Sandy Alomar hit an opposite-field home run to tie the game. In the ninth inning Omar Vizquel's hard grounder up the middle glanced off reliever Ramiro Mendoza and rolled into left field, allowing Marquis Grissom to score from second with the winning run.

Manny Ramirez stepped to the plate in the third inning of Game 5 batting .111 for the series, but he hit a ground-rule double on a twostrike pitch from Pettitte to

score Grissom and Vizquel. The Indians took a 4–0 lead, but the Yankees made it a one-run game in the sixth inning against Wright. Jose Mesa snuffed a Yankees rally in the eighth, and, after a two-out double by O'Neill in the ninth, he retired Bernie Williams on a flyball to left to end the series.

CLE (C)

PLAYER/POS	AVG	G	AB	R	H	2B	3B	HR	RB	BB	SO	SB
Sandy Alomar, c	.316	5	19	4	6	1	0	2	5	0	2	0
Paul Assenmacher, p	.000	4	0	0	0	0	0	0	0	0	0	0
Tony Fernandez, 2b	.182	4	11	0	2	1	0	0	4	0	0	0
Brian Giles, of	.143	3	7	0	1	0	0	0	0	0	1	0
Marquis Grissom, of	.235	5	17	3	4	0	1	0	0	1	2	0
Orel Hershiser, p	.000	2	0	0	0	0	0	0	0	0	0	0
Mike Jackson, p	.000	4	0	0	0	0	0	0	0	0	0	0
David Justice, dh	.263	5	19	3	5	2	0	1	2	2	3	0
Jose Mesa, p	.000	2	0	0	0	0	0	0	0	0	0	0
Alvin Morman, p	.000	1	0	0	0	0	0	0	0	0	0	0
Charles Nagy, p	.000	1	0	0	0	0	0	0	0	0	0	0
Chad Ogea, p	.000	1	0	0	0	0	0	0	0	0	0	0
Eric Plunk, p	.000	1	0	0	0	0	0	0	0	0	0	0
Manny Ramirez, of	.143	5	21	2	3	1	0	0	3	0	3	0
Bip Roberts, of-4,2b-2	.316	5	19	1	6	0	0	0	1	2	2	2
Kevin Seitzer, 1b	.000	1	4	0	0	0	0	0	0	0	0	0
Jim Thome, 1b	.200	5	15	1	3	0	0	0	1	0	5	0
Omar Vizquel, ss	.500	5	18	3	9	0	0	0	1	2	1	4
Matt Williams, 3b	.235	5	17	4	4	1	0	1	3	3	3	0
Jaret Wright, p	.000	2	0	0	0	0	0	0	0	0	0	0
TOTAL	.257		167	21	43	6	1	4	20	10	22	6

PITCHER	W	L	ERA	G	GS	CG	SV	SHO	IP	H	ER	BB	SO
Paul Assenmacher	0	0	5.40	4	0	0	0	0	3.1	2	2	2	2
Orel Hershiser	0	0	3.97	2	2	0	0	0	11.1	14	5	2	4
Mike Jackson	1	0	0.00	4	0	0	0	0	4.1	3	0	1	5
Jose Mesa	0	0	2.70	2	0	0	1	0	3.1	5	1	1	2
Alvin Morman	0	0	∞	1	0	0	0	0	0.0	0	0	1	0
Charles Nagy	0	1	9.82	1	1	0	0	0	3.2	2	4	6	1
Chad Ogea	0	0	1.69	1	0	0	0	0	5.1	2	1	0	1
Eric Plunk	0	1	27.00	1	0	0	0	0	0.1	4	4	0	1
Jaret Wright	2	0	3.97	2	2	0	0	0	11.1	11	5	7	10
TOTAL	3	2	4.50	18	5	0	1	0	44.0	43	22	20	26

NY (WC)

PLAYER/POS	AVG	G	AB	R	H	2B	3B	HR	RB	BB	SO	SB
Brian Boehringer, p	.000	1	0	0	0	0	0	0	0	0	0	0
Wade Boggs, 3b-2	.429	3	7	1	3	0	0	0	0	2	0	0
David Cone, p	.000	1	0	0	0	0	0	0	0	0	0	0
Chad Curtis, of	.167	4	6	0	1	0	0	0	0	3	1	0
Cecil Fielder, dh	.125	2	8	0	1	0	0	0	1	0	3	0
Andy Fox, 2b	.000	2	0	0	0	0	0	0	0	0	0	0
Joe Girardi, c	.133	5	15	2	2	0	0	0	0	1	3	0
Dwight Gooden, p	.000	1	0	0	0	0	0	0	0	0	0	0
Charlie Hayes, 3b-5, 2b-1	.333	5	15	0	5	0	0	0	1	0	2	0
Derek Jeter, ss	.333	5	21	6	7	1	0	2	2	3	5	1
Graeme Lloyd, p	.000	2	0	0	0	0	0	0	0	0	0	0
Tino Martinez, 1b	.222	5	18	1	4	1	0	1	4	2	4	0
Ramiro Mendoza, p	.000	2	0	0	0	0	0	0	0	0	0	0
Jeff Nelson, p	.000	4	0	0	0	0	0	0	0	0	0	0
Paul O'Neill, of	.421	5	19	5	8	5	0	2	7	3	0	0
Andy Pettitte, p	.000	2	0	0	0	0	0	0	0	0	0	0
Jorge Posada, c	.000	2	2	0	0	0	0	0	0	0	1	0
Scott Pose, pr	.000	1	0	0	0	0	0	0	0	0	0	0
Tim Raines, of-3, dh-2	.211	5	19	4	4	0	0	1	3	3	1	2
Mariano Rivera, p	.000	2	0	0	0	0	0	0	0	0	0	0
Rey Sanchez, 2b	.200	5	15	1	3	1	0	0	1	1	2	0
Mike Stanley, dh-1	.750	2	4	1	3	1	0	0	1	0	1	0
Mike Stanton, p	.000	3	0	0	0	0	0	0	0	0	0	0
David Wells, p	.000	1	0	0	0	0	0	0	0	0	0	0
Bernie Williams, of	.118	5	17	3	2	1	0	1	1	4	3	0
TOTAL	.259		166	24	43	7	0	6	23	20	26	3

PITCHER	W	L	ERA	G	GS	CG	SV	SHO	IP	H	ER	BB	SO
Brian Boehringer	0	0	0.00	1	0	0	0	0	1.2	1	0	1	2
David Cone	0	0	16.20	1	1	0	0	0	3.1	7	6	2	2
Dwight Gooden	0	0	1.59	1	1	0	0	0	5.2	5	1	3	5
Graeme Lloyd	0	0	0.00	2	0	0	0	0	1.1	0	0	0	1
Ramiro Mendoza	1	1	2.45	2	0	0	0	0	3.2	3	1	0	2
Jeff Nelson	0	0	0.00	4	0	0	0	0	4.0	4	0	2	0
Andy Pettitte	0	2	8.49	2	2	0	0	0	11.2	15	11	1	5
Mariano Rivera	0	0	4.50	2	0	0	1	0	2.0	2	1	0	1
Mike Stanton	0	0	0.00	3	0	0	0	0	1.0	1	0	1	3
David Wells	1	0	1.00	1	1	1	0	0	9.0	5	1	0	1
TOTAL	2	3	4.36	19	5	1	1	0	43.1	43	21	10	22

GAME 1 AT NY SEPT 30

```
CLE 500 100 000   6 11 0
NY  010 115 00X   8 11 0
```
Pitchers: Hershiser, Morman (5), PLUNK (5), Assenmacher (7), Jackson (7) vs Cone, MENDOZA (4), Nelson (7), Rivera (8)
Home Runs: Alomar-BAL, Martinez-NY, Raines-NY, Jeter-NY, O'Neill-NY
Attendance: 57,398

GAME 2 AT NY OCT 2

```
CLE 000 520 000   7 11 1
NY  300 000 011   5  7 2
```
Pitchers: WRIGHT, Jackson (7), Assenmacher (7), Mesa (8) vs PETTITTE, Boehringer (6), Lloyd (7), Nelson (9)
Home Runs: Williams-CLE, Jeter-NY
Attendance: 57,360

GAME 3 AT CLE OCT 4

```
NY  101 400 000   6 4 1
CLE 010 000 000   1 5 1
```
Pitchers: WELLS vs NAGY, Ogea (4)
Home Runs: O'Neill-NY
Attendance: 45,274

GAME 4 AT CLE OCT 5

```
NY  200 000 000   2 9 1
CLE 010 000 011   3 9 0
```
Pitchers: Gooden, Lloyd (6), Nelson (6), Stanton (7), Rivera (8), MENDOZA (9) vs Hershiser, Assenmacher (8), JACKSON (8)
Home Runs: Justice-CLE, Alomar-CLE
Attendance: 45,231

GAME 5 AT CLE OCT 6

```
NY  000 021 000   3 12 0
CLE 003 100 00X   4  7 2
```
Pitchers: PETTITTE, Nelson (7), Stanton (8) vs WRIGHT, Jackson (6), Assenmacher (7), Mesa (8)
Attendance: 45,203

BALTIMORE ORIOLES (EAST) 3, SEATTLE MARINERS (WEST) 1

The Orioles found an antidote to Randy Johnson, and they used it twice to beat the Mariners. Meanwhile, Mike Mussina found a way to silence Seattle's powerful lineup twice and that was the difference. Orioles manager Davey Johnson raised eyebrows when he rested Roberto Alomar, Rafael Palmeiro, and B.J. Surhoff against southpaw Randy Johnson, but their replacements and the rest of the Baltimore lineup had little trouble in Game 1. Johnson left in the fifth inning trailing 5–1, and the much-maligned Mariners bullpen lived up to its reputation as the Orioles coasted behind Mussina. Jamie Moyer had a 2–1 lead when he was forced to leave Game 2 with an injured left elbow in the fifth inning. Paul Spoljaric relieved and the next batter, Roberto Alomar, doubled off Ken Griffey's glove in center field to give the Orioles a 3–2 lead. Brady Anderson homered and doubled against two more Mariners relievers, and the Orioles left Seattle with their second straight 9–3 laugher.

Roberto Kelly doubled in a run in the first inning, and Griffey singled in a run in the fifth to stake Jeff Fassero to a 2–0 lead in Game 3. Fassero pitched a brilliant threehitter for eight innings, but manager Lou Piniella brought in Heathcliff Slocumb to close the game when the Mariners took a 4–0 lead into the bottom of the ninth. Jeffrey Hammonds doubled home two runs, but Harold Baines popped out to end the game.

Mussina, who pitched a five-hitter for seven innings in the series opener, allowed just two hits in seven innings in Game 4. The Orioles helped him out by scoring twice in the first inning on a home run by Jeff Reboulet (Alomar's replacement in Davey Johnson's lineup against Randy Johnson) and a run-scoring single by Cal Ripken. Edgar Martinez led off the second inning with a home run, and Seattle followed that with a walk and a single. Mussina did not allow another hit and fanned seven.

BAL (E)

PLAYER/POS	AVG	G	AB	R	H	2B	3B	HR	RB	BB	SO	SB
Roberto Alomar, 2b	.300	4	10	1	3	2	0	0	2	1	1	0
Brady Anderson, of	.353	4	17	3	6	1	0	1	4	1	4	1
Harold Baines, dh-1	.400	2	5	2	2	0	0	1	1	1	0	0
Armando Benitez, p	.000	3	0	0	0	0	0	0	0	0	0	0
Geronimo Berroa, dh-3, of-1	.385	4	13	4	5	1	0	2	2	2	2	0
Mike Bordick, ss	.400	4	10	4	4	1	0	0	4	4	2	0
Eric Davis, of	.222	3	9	0	2	0	0	0	2	0	5	0
Scott Erickson, p	.000	1	0	0	0	0	0	0	0	0	0	0
Jeffrey Hammonds, of	.100	4	10	3	1	1	0	0	2	2	2	1
Chris Hoiles, c	.143	3	7	1	1	0	0	1	1	2	1	0
Jimmy Key, p	.000	1	0	0	0	0	0	0	0	0	0	0
Terry Mathews, p	.000	1	0	0	0	0	0	0	0	0	0	0
Alan Mills, p	.000	1	0	0	0	0	0	0	0	0	0	0
Mike Mussina, p	.000	2	0	0	0	0	0	0	0	0	0	0
Randy Myers, p	.000	2	0	0	0	0	0	0	0	0	0	0
Jesse Orosco, p	.000	2	0	0	0	0	0	0	0	0	0	0
Rafael Palmeiro, 1b	.250	4	12	2	3	2	0	0	0	0	2	0
Jeff Reboulet, 2b	.200	2	5	1	1	0	0	1	1	0	2	0
Arthur Lee Rhodes, p	.000	1	0	0	0	0	0	0	0	0	0	0
Cal Ripken, 3b	.438	4	16	1	7	2	0	0	1	2	2	0
B. J. Surhoff, of	.273	3	11	0	3	1	0	0	2	0	2	0
Jerome Walton, 1b	.000	2	4	0	0	0	0	0	0	0	2	0
Lenny Webster, c	.167	3	6	1	1	0	0	0	1	1	0	0
TOTAL	.289		135	23	39	11	0	6	23	16	27	2

PITCHER	W	L	ERA	G	GS	CG	SV	SHO	IP	H	ER	BB	SO
Armando Benitez	0	0	3.00	3	0	0	0	0	3.0	3	1	2	4
Scott Erickson	1	0	4.05	1	1	0	0	0	6.2	7	3	2	6
Jimmy Key	0	1	3.86	1	1	0	0	0	4.2	8	2	0	4
Terry Mathews	0	0	18.00	1	0	0	0	0	1.0	2	2	0	1
Alan Mills	0	0	0.00	1	0	0	0	0	1.0	1	0	0	1
Mike Mussina	2	0	1.93	2	2	0	0	0	14.0	7	3	3	16
Randy Myers	0	0	0.00	2	0	0	1	0	2.0	0	0	0	5
Jesse Orosco	0	0	0.00	2	0	0	0	0	1.1	1	0	0	1
Arthur Lee Rhodes	0	0	0.00	1	0	0	0	0	2.1	0	0	0	4
TOTAL	3	1	2.75	14	4	0	1	0	36.0	29	11	7	42

SEA (W)

PLAYER/POS	AVG	G	AB	R	H	2B	3B	HR	RB	BB	SO	SB
Rich Amaral, 1b	.500	2	4	2	2	0	0	0	0	0	1	0
Bobby Ayala, p	.000	1	0	0	0	0	0	0	0	0	0	0
Mike Blowers, 3b	.200	3	5	0	1	0	0	0	0	0	3	0
Jay Buhner, of	.231	4	13	2	3	0	0	2	2	3	6	0
Norm Charlton, p	.000	2	0	0	0	0	0	0	0	0	0	0
Joey Cora, 2b	.176	4	17	1	3	0	0	0	0	0	4	0
Rob Ducey, of-1	.500	2	4	0	2	0	0	0	1	0	0	0
Jeff Fassero, p	.000	1	0	0	0	0	0	0	0	0	0	0
Brent Gates, 3b	.000	2	4	0	0	0	0	0	0	0	0	0
Ken Griffey, of	.133	4	15	0	2	0	0	0	2	1	3	2
Randy Johnson, p	.000	2	0	0	0	0	0	0	0	0	0	0
Roberto Kelly, of-3	.308	4	13	1	4	3	0	0	1	0	0	0
Edgar Martinez, dh	.188	4	16	2	3	0	0	2	3	0	3	0
Jamie Moyer, p	.000	1	0	0	0	0	0	0	0	0	0	0
Alex Rodriguez, ss	.313	4	16	1	5	1	0	1	1	0	5	0
Andy Sheets, 3b	.333	2	3	0	1	0	0	0	0	0	2	0
Heathcliff Slocumb, p	.000	2	0	0	0	0	0	0	0	0	0	0
Paul Sorrento, 1b	.300	4	10	2	3	1	0	1	1	2	3	0
Paul Spoljaric, p	.000	2	0	0	0	0	0	0	0	0	0	0
Mike Timlin, p	.000	1	0	0	0	0	0	0	0	0	0	0
Bob Wells, p	.000	1	0	0	0	0	0	0	0	0	0	0
Rick Wilkins, c	.000	1	0	0	0	0	0	0	0	1	0	0
Dan Wilson, c	.000	4	13	0	0	0	0	0	0	0	9	0
TOTAL	.218		133	11	29	5	0	6	11	7	42	2

PITCHER	W	L	ERA	G	GS	CG	SV	SHO	IP	H	ER	BB	SO
Bobby Ayala	0	0	40.50	1	0	0	0	0	1.1	4	6	1	3
Norm Charlton	0	0	0.00	2	0	0	0	0	2.1	2	0	0	1
Jeff Fassero	1	0	1.13	1	1	0	0	0	8.0	3	1	4	3
Randy Johnson	0	2	5.54	2	2	1	0	0	13.0	14	8	6	16
Jamie Moyer	0	1	5.79	1	1	0	0	0	4.2	5	3	1	2
Heathcliff Slocumb	0	0	4.50	2	0	0	0	0	2.0	3	1	1	0
Paul Spoljaric	0	0	0.00	2	0	0	0	0	1.2	4	0	0	1
Mike Timlin	0	0	54.00	1	0	0	0	0	0.2	3	4	1	1
Bob Wells	0	0	0.00	1	0	0	0	0	1.1	1	0	0	1
TOTAL	1	3	5.91	13	4	1	0	0	35.0	39	23	14	28

GAME 1 AT SEA OCT 1

BAL 001 044 000   9 13 0
SEA 000 100 101   3 7 1
Pitchers: MUSSINA, Orosco (8), Benitez (9) vs JOHNSON, Timlin (6), Spoljaric (6), Wells (7), Charlton (8)
Home Runs: Martinez-SEA, Berroa-BAL, Hoiles-BAL, Buhner-SEA, Rodriguez-SEA
Attendance: 59,579

GAME 2 AT SEA OCT 2

BAL 010 020 240   9 14 0
SEA 200 000 100   3 9 0
Pitchers: ERICKSON, Benitez (7), Orosco (8), Myers (9) vs MOYER, Spoljaric (5), Ayala (7), Charlton (8), Slocumb (9)
Home Runs: Baines-BAL, Anderson-BAL
Attendance: 59,309

GAME 3 AT BAL OCT 4

SEA 001 010 002   4 11 0
BAL 000 000 002   2 5 0
Pitchers: FASSERO, Slocumb (9) vs KEY, Mills (5), Rhodes (6), Mathews (9)
Home Runs: Buhner-SEA, Sorrento-SEA
Attendance: 49,137

GAME 4 AT BAL OCT 5

SEA 010 000 000   1 2 0
BAL 200 010 00X   3 7 0
Pitchers: JOHNSON vs MUSSINA, Benitez (8), Myers (9)
Home Runs: Reboulet-BAL, Martinez-SEA, Berroa-BAL
Attendance: 48,766

FLORIDA MARLINS (WILD CARD) 4, ATLANTA BRAVES (EAST) 2

The Marlins didn't even exist the last time Jim Leyland led a team to the NLCS against the Braves; since then Atlanta had become the first team in history to win six straight division titles (minus the 1994 strike season). Leyland watched as his Pirates lost to the Braves in the bottom of the ninth in Game 7 of the 1992 NLCS in Fulton County Stadium, but now he was with a different team; the Braves had a different stadium (Turner Field), and the results were different, too.

The fifth-year Marlins struck for five unearned runs off Greg Maddux in the opener, and Kevin Brown and three relievers made it hold up. Charles Johnson, who was the first catcher in major league history to go through an entire season without an error, threw a ball into center field on a stolen base attempt by Kenny Lofton in the first inning of Game 2. Keith Lockhart tripled Lofton home and Ryan Klesko hit his second home run in as many nights. Lockhart singled in the third inning and Chipper Jones followed with his second home run in two games. Alex Fernandez left after two and two thirds innings; it was later revealed that he had a torn rotator cuff and would not pitch for a year.

Fernandez's replacement, Livan Hernandez, made his first appearance of the series in relief in Game 3 in Florida and picked up the win. This time poor defense and bad baserunning cost Atlanta. After Chipper Jones got caught in a rundown at second base with the bases loaded in the top of the sixth inning, Andruw Jones misplayed a flyball in right to tie the game. Johnson, who was hitless in 10 career at bats against John Smoltz, doubled in three runs and chased him from the game. Denny Neagle was masterful for the Braves in Game 4, pitching the first complete game in the NLCS since 1992. Series MVP Hernandez followed with an even more remarkable performance with 15 strikeouts, tying an LCS record set the day before by Baltimore's Mike Mussina in Cleveland. Maddux again pitched in bad luck. He allowed just four hits, but Jeff Conine's single in the seventh drove in Bobby Bonilla with the deciding run.

The Braves, who complained

about umpire Eric Gregg's liberal strike zone in Game 5, could only complain about their inability to get timely hits in Game 6. The Marlins batted around and scored four runs in the first inning off Tom Glavine, but the Braves cut the lead to 4–3 by the second inning. Brown, whose start was pushed back three days because of a stomach virus, talked Leyland out of removing him after the sixth inning. He remained in the contest despite a two-out Braves rally in the ninth inning that brought the tying run to the plate. Chipper Jones grounded a ball up the middle but Craig Counsell went behind second base and flipped to Edgar Renteria for the force play to give the Marlins the pennant exactly five years after the Braves had rallied in the ninth to take the flag away from Leyland's Pirates.

FL (WC)

PLAYER/POS	AVG	G	AB	R	H	2B	3B	HR	RB	BB	SO	SB
Kurt Abbott, 2b	.375	2	8	0	3	1	0	0	0	0	2	0
Moises Alou, of-4	.067	5	15	0	1	1	0	0	5	1	3	0
Alex Arias, 3b-2	1.000	3	1	0	1	0	0	0	0	0	0	0
Bobby Bonilla, 3b	.261	6	23	3	6	1	0	0	4	1	6	0
Kevin Brown, p	.000	2	6	0	0	0	0	0	0	0	3	0
John Cangelosi, of-1	.200	3	5	0	1	0	0	0	0	1	0	0
Jeff Conine, 1b	.111	6	18	1	2	0	0	0	1	1	4	0
Dennis Cook, p	.000	2	0	0	0	0	0	0	0	0	0	0
Craig Counsell, 2b-4	.429	5	14	0	6	0	0	0	2	3	3	0
Darren Daulton, 1b-2	.250	3	4	1	1	1	0	0	1	1	2	0
Jim Eisenreich, of	.000	1	3	0	0	0	0	0	0	0	0	0
Alex Fernandez, p	.000	1	1	0	0	0	0	0	0	0	1	0
Felix Heredia, p	.000	2	0	0	0	0	0	0	0	0	0	0
Livan Hernandez, p	.000	2	3	0	0	0	0	0	0	0	1	0
Charles Johnson, c	.118	6	17	1	2	2	0	0	5	3	8	0
Al Leiter, p	.000	2	1	0	0	0	0	0	0	0	0	0
Robb Nen, p	.000	2	0	0	0	0	0	0	0	0	0	0
Jay Powell, p	.000	1	0	0	0	0	0	0	0	0	0	0
Edgar Renteria, ss	.227	6	22	4	5	1	0	0	0	3	6	1
Tony Saunders, p	.000	1	2	0	0	0	0	0	0	0	2	0
Gary Sheffield, of	.235	6	17	6	4	0	0	1	1	7	3	0
Ed Vosberg, p	.000	2	0	0	0	0	0	0	0	0	0	0
Devon White, of	.190	6	21	4	4	1	0	0	1	2	7	1
Greg Zaun, c	.000	1	0	0	0	0	0	0	0	0	0	0
TOTAL	.199		181	20	36	8	0	1	20	23	52	2

PITCHER	W	L	ERA	G	GS	CG	SV	SHO	IP	H	ER	BB	SO
Kevin Brown	2	0	4.20	2	2	1	0	0	15.0	16	7	5	11
Dennis Cook	0	0	0.00	2	0	0	0	0	2.1	0	0	0	2
Alex Fernandez	0	1	16.88	1	1	0	0	0	2.2	6	5	1	3
Felix Heredia	0	0	5.40	2	0	0	0	0	3.1	3	2	2	4
Livan Hernandez	2	0	0.84	2	1	1	0	0	10.2	5	1	2	16
Al Leiter	0	1	4.32	2	1	0	0	0	8.1	13	4	2	6
Robb Nen	0	0	0.00	2	0	0	2	0	2.0	0	0	0	1
Jay Powell	0	0	0.00	1	0	0	0	0	0.2	0	0	0	0
Tony Saunders	0	0	3.38	1	1	0	0	0	5.1	4	2	3	3
Ed Vosberg	0	0	0.00	2	0	0	0	0	2.2	2	0	1	3
TOTAL	4	2	3.57	17	6	2	2	0	53.0	49	21	16	49

ATL (E)

PLAYER/POS	AVG	G	AB	R	H	2B	3B	HR	RB	BB	SO	SB
Danny Bautista, of	.250	2	4	0	1	0	0	0	0	0	0	0
Jeff Blauser, ss	.300	6	20	5	6	0	0	1	1	3	6	0
Mike Cather, p	.000	4	0	0	0	0	0	0	0	0	0	0
Greg Colbrunn, ph	.667	3	3	0	2	0	0	0	0	0	0	0
Alan Embree, p	.000	1	0	0	0	0	0	0	0	0	0	0
Tom Glavine, p	.333	2	3	0	1	0	0	0	0	0	2	0
Tony Graffanino, 2b	.250	3	8	1	2	1	0	0	0	0	3	0
Tommy Gregg, ph	.000	4	4	0	0	0	0	0	0	0	1	0
Andruw Jones, of	.444	5	9	0	4	0	0	0	1	1	1	0
Chipper Jones, 3b	.292	6	24	5	7	1	0	2	4	2	3	0
Ryan Klesko, of	.235	5	17	2	4	0	0	2	4	2	3	0
Kerry Ligtenberg, p	.000	2	0	0	0	0	0	0	0	0	0	0
Keith Lockhart, 2b	.500	5	16	4	8	1	1	0	3	1	1	0
Kenny Lofton, of	.185	6	27	3	5	0	1	0	1	1	7	1
Javy Lopez, c	.059	5	17	0	1	1	0	0	2	1	7	0
Greg Maddux, p	.000	2	3	0	0	0	0	0	0	0	2	0
Fred McGriff, 1b	.333	6	21	0	7	1	0	0	4	2	7	0
Denny Neagle, p	.000	2	3	0	0	0	0	0	0	0	1	0
Eddie Perez, c	.000	2	2	0	0	0	0	0	0	0	0	0
John Smoltz, p	.000	1	2	0	0	0	0	0	0	0	1	0
Michael Tucker, of-4	.100	5	10	1	1	0	0	1	1	3	4	0
Mark Wohlers, p	.000	1	0	0	0	0	0	0	0	0	0	0
TOTAL	.253		194	21	49	5	2	6	21	16	49	1

PITCHER	W	L	ERA	G	GS	CG	SV	SHO	IP	H	ER	BB	SO
Mike Cather	0	0	0.00	4	0	0	0	0	2.2	3	0	0	3
Alan Embree	0	0	0.00	1	0	0	0	0	1.0	0	0	1	1
Tom Glavine	1	1	5.40	2	2	0	0	0	13.1	13	8	11	9
Kerry Ligtenberg	0	0	0.00	2	0	0	0	0	3.0	1	0	0	4
Greg Maddux	0	2	1.38	2	2	0	0	0	13.0	9	2	4	16
Denny Neagle	1	0	0.00	2	1	1	0	0	12.0	5	0	1	9
John Smoltz	0	1	7.50	1	1	0	0	0	6.0	5	5	5	9
Mark Wohlers	0	0	0.00	1	0	0	0	0	1.0	0	0	1	1
TOTAL	2	4	2.60	15	6	1	0	0	52.0	36	15	23	52

GAME 1 AT ATL OCT 7

FLA 302 000 000 5 6 0
ATL 101 001 000 3 5 2
Pitchers: BROWN, Cook (7), Powell (8), Nen (9) vs MADDUX, Neagle (7)
Home Runs: C.Jones-ATL, Klesko-ATL
Attendance: 49,244

GAME 2 AT ATL OCT 8

FLA 000 000 010 1 3 1
ATL 302 000 20X 7 13 0
Pitchers: FERNANDEZ, Leiter (3), Heredia (6), Vosberg (8) vs GLAVINE, Cather (8), Wohlers (9)
Home Runs: Klesko-ATL, C.Jones-ATL
Attendance: 48,933

GAME 3 AT FLA OCT 10

ATL 000 101 000 2 6 1
FLA 000 104 00X 5 8 1
Pitchers: SMOLTZ, Cather (7), Ligtenberg (8) vs Saunders, HERNANDEZ (6), Cook (8), Nen (9)
Home Runs: Sheffield-FLA
Attendance: 53,857

GAME 4 AT FLA OCT 11

ATL 101 020 000 4 11 0
FLA 000 000 000 0 4 0
Pitchers: NEAGLE vs LEITER, Heredia (7), Vosberg (9)
Home Runs: Blauser-ATL
Attendance: 54,890

GAME 5 AT FLA OCT 12

ATL 010 000 000 1 3 0
FLA 100 000 10X 2 5 0
Pitchers: MADDUX, Cather (8) vs HERNANDEZ
Home Runs: Tucker-ATL
Attendance: 51,982

GAME 6 AT ATL OCT 14

FLA 400 003 000 7 10 1
ATL 120 000 001 4 11 1
Pitchers: BROWN vs GLAVINE, Cather (6), Ligtenberg (7), Embree (9)
Attendance: 50,446

CLEVELAND INDIANS (CENTRAL) 4, BALTIMORE ORIOLES (EAST) 2

In a series dominated by pitching, Baltimore's starters were brilliant, but it was Cleveland's relief corps that won the day. Brady Anderson, who made a leaping catch at the wall to end the top of the first inning of Game 1, hit Chad Ogea's first pitch for a home run to lead off the bottom of the inning. Scott Erickson tossed a four-hitter for eight innings, and Randy Myers earned the save. The Indians got off to a solid start in Game 2 with a two-run home run by Manny Ramirez, but Cal Ripken matched it with a two-run homer in the second inning. Mike Bordick broke the tie with a two-run single in the sixth inning. Armando Benitez surrendered a three-run home run to ninth-place hitter Marquis Grissom in the eighth inning to even the series.

Game 3 was a bizarre contest played in the twilight of Jacobs Field that haunted batters and fielders alike. Baltimore's Mike Mussina struck out an LCS-record 15 batters, but a run-scoring single by Matt Williams gave Cleveland a 1–0 lead heading into the ninth. With a runner on second and one out, Grissom misplayed a fly ball to allow the tying run to score. The oddest play of the day was the one that finally ended the game in the 12th inning. On a suicide squeeze, Omar Vizquel missed the bunt attempt and catcher Lenny Webster missed the ball. Webster, thinking it was a foul ball, walked after it and ALCS MVP Grissom slid across the plate with the winning run.

A wild pitch resulted in two runs on one play in Game 4, one on a wild pitch by Arthur Rhodes and the second on Webster's throwing error. Rafael Palmiero's single in the top of the ninth tied the game, but Sandy Alomar singled home Ramirez with the winning run in the bottom of the inning. The Orioles kept the series alive with a 4–2 win in Game 5, but the Indians had the tying runs on base left to end the game.

Mussina's performance in Game 6 was actually better than his Game 3 gem, but again the Orioles could not score for him. Charles Nagy was not as sharp for Cleveland, but 14 Baltimore baserunners were stranded. The play of the game was a perfectly executed rotation play on Roberto

Alomar's bunt in the seventh inning with Williams throwing to Vizquel for the out at third. Tony Fernandez, who got the start at second base because his batting practice line drive damaged the thumb of teammate Bip Roberts, homered to right field in the top of the 11th inning. The Indians bullpen earned all four wins in the series.

CLE (C)

PLAYER/POS	AVG	G	AB	R	H	2B	3B	HR	RB	BB	SO	SB
Sandy Alomar, c	.125	6	24	3	3	0	0	1	4	1	3	0
Brian Anderson, p	.000	3	0	0	0	0	0	0	0	0	0	0
Paul Assenmacher, p	.000	5	0	0	0	0	0	0	0	0	0	0
Jeff Branson, dh	.000	1	2	0	0	0	0	0	0	0	2	0
Tony Fernandez, 2b	.357	5	14	1	5	1	0	1	2	1	2	0
Brian Giles, of	.188	6	16	1	3	3	0	0	0	2	6	0
Marquis Grissom, of	.261	6	23	2	6	0	0	1	4	1	9	3
Orel Hershiser, p	.000	1	0	0	0	0	0	0	0	0	0	0
Mike Jackson, p	.000	5	0	0	0	0	0	0	0	0	0	0
Jeff Juden, p	.000	3	0	0	0	0	0	0	0	0	0	0
David Justice, dh	.333	6	21	3	7	1	0	0	0	2	4	0
Jose Mesa, p	.000	4	0	0	0	0	0	0	0	0	0	0
Alvin Morman, p	.000	2	0	0	0	0	0	0	0	0	0	0
Charles Nagy, p	.000	2	0	0	0	0	0	0	0	0	0	0
Chad Ogea, p	.000	2	0	0	0	0	0	0	0	0	0	0
Eric Plunk, p	.000	1	0	0	0	0	0	0	0	0	0	0
Manny Ramirez, of	.286	6	21	3	6	1	0	2	3	5	5	0
Bip Roberts, 2b-4, of-2	.150	5	20	0	3	1	0	0	0	0	8	1
Kevin Seitzer, 1b-3	.000	4	4	0	0	0	0	0	0	1	2	0
Jim Thome, 1b	.071	6	14	3	1	0	0	0	0	5	4	0
Omar Vizquel, ss	.040	6	25	1	1	0	0	0	0	2	10	0
Matt Williams, 3b	.217	6	23	1	5	1	0	0	2	3	7	1
Jaret Wright, p	.000	1	0	0	0	0	0	0	0	0	0	0
TOTAL	.193		207	18	40	8	0	5	15	23	62	5

PITCHER	W	L	ERA	G	GS	CG	SV	SHO	IP	H	ER	BB	SO
Brian Anderson	1	0	1.42	3	0	0	0	0	6.1	1	1	3	7
Paul Assenmacher	1	0	9.00	5	0	0	0	0	2.0	5	2	1	3
Orel Hershiser	0	0	0.00	1	1	0	0	0	7.0	4	0	1	7
Mike Jackson	0	0	0.00	5	0	0	0	0	4.1	1	0	1	7
Jeff Juden	0	0	0.00	3	0	0	0	0	1.0	2	0	2	2
Jose Mesa	1	0	3.38	4	0	0	2	0	5.1	5	2	3	5
Alvin Morman	0	0	0.00	2	0	0	0	0	1.1	0	0	0	1
Charles Nagy	0	0	2.77	2	2	0	0	0	13.0	17	4	5	5
Chad Ogea	0	2	3.21	2	2	0	0	0	14.0	12	5	5	7
Eric Plunk	1	0	0.00	1	0	0	0	0	0.2	1	0	0	0
Jaret Wright	0	0	15.00	1	1	0	0	0	3.0	6	5	2	3
TOTAL	4	2	2.95	29	6	0	2	0	58.0	54	19	23	47

BAL (E)

PLAYER/POS	AVG	G	AB	R	H	2B	3B	HR	RB	BB	SO	SB
Roberto Alomar, 2b	.182	6	22	2	4	0	0	1	2	7	3	0
Brady Anderson, of	.360	6	25	5	9	2	0	2	3	4	4	2
Harold Baines, dh	.353	6	17	1	6	0	0	1	2	2	1	0
Armando Benitez, p	.000	4	0	0	0	0	0	0	0	0	0	0
Geronimo Berroa, of-4, dh-2	.286	6	21	1	6	2	0	0	3	0	3	0
Mike Bordick, ss	.158	6	19	0	3	1	0	0	2	0	6	0
Eric Davis, of-3, dh-3	.154	6	13	1	2	0	0	1	1	1	3	0
Scott Erickson, p	.000	2	0	0	0	0	0	0	0	0	0	0
Jeffrey Hammonds, of-4	.000	5	3	0	0	0	0	0	0	1	2	1
Chris Hoiles, c	.143	4	14	1	2	0	0	0	0	2	5	0
Scott Kamieniecki, p	.000	2	0	0	0	0	0	0	0	0	0	0
Jimmy Key, p	.000	2	0	0	0	0	0	0	0	0	0	0
Alan Mills, p	.000	3	0	0	0	0	0	0	0	0	0	0
Mike Mussina, p	.000	2	0	0	0	0	0	0	0	0	0	0
Randy Myers, p	.000	4	0	0	0	0	0	0	0	0	0	0
Jesse Orosco, p	.000	2	0	0	0	0	0	0	0	0	0	0
Rafael Palmeiro, 1b	.280	6	25	3	7	2	0	1	2	0	10	0
Jeff Reboulet, ss	.000	1	2	1	0	0	0	0	0	0	0	0
Arthur Lee Rhodes, p	.000	2	0	0	0	0	0	0	0	0	0	0
Cal Ripken, 3b	.348	6	23	3	8	2	0	1	3	4	6	0
B.J. Surhoff, of-6,1b-1	.200	6	25	1	5	2	0	0	1	2	2	0
Jerome Walton, of	.000	1	0	0	0	0	0	0	0	0	0	0
Lenny Webster, c-3	.222	4	9	0	2	0	0	0	0	0	1	0
TOTAL	.248		218	19	54	11	0	7	19	23	47	3

PITCHER	W	L	ERA	G	GS	CG	SV	SHO	IP	H	ER	BB	SO
Armando Benitez	0	2	12.00	4	0	0	0	0	3.0	3	4	4	6
Scott Erickson	1	0	4.26	2	2	0	0	0	12.2	15	6	1	6
Scott Kamieniecki	1	0	0.00	2	1	0	0	0	8.0	4	0	2	5
Jimmy Key	0	0	2.57	2	1	0	0	0	7.0	5	2	3	7
Alan Mills	0	1	2.70	3	0	0	0	0	3.1	1	1	2	3
Mike Mussina	0	0	0.60	2	2	0	0	0	15.0	4	1	4	25
Randy Myers	0	1	5.06	4	0	0	1	0	5.1	6	3	3	7
Jesse Orosco	0	0	0.00	2	0	0	0	0	1.1	0	0	1	1
Arthur Lee Rhodes	0	0	0.00	2	0	0	0	0	2.1	2	0	3	2
TOTAL	2	4	2.64	23	6	0	1	0	58.0	40	17	23	62

GAME 1 AT BAL OCT 8

CLE 000 000 000   0 4 1
BAL 102 000 00X   3 6 1
Pitchers: OGEA, Anderson (7) vs ERICKSON, Myers (9)
Home Runs: Anderson-BAL, Alomar-BAL
Attendance: 49,029

GAME 2 AT BAL OCT 9

CLE 200 000 030   5 6 3
BAL 020 002 000   4 8 1
Pitchers: Nagy, Morman (6), Juden (6), ASSENMACHER (6), Jackson (8), Mesa (9) vs Key, Kamienecki (5), BENITEZ (9)
Home Runs: Ramirez-CLE, Ripken-BAL, Grissom-CLE
Attendance: 49,131

GAME 3 AT CLE OCT 11

BAL 000 000 001 000   1 8 1
CLE 000 000 100 001   2 6 0
Pitchers: Mussina, Benitez (8), Orosco (9), Mills (9), Rhodes (10), MYERS (11) vs Hershiser, Assenmacher (8), Jackson (8), Mesa (9), Juden (11), Morman (11), PLUNK (12)
Attendance: 45,047

GAME 4 AT CLE OCT 12

BAL 014 000 101   7 12 2
CLE 020 140 001   8 13 0
Pitchers: Erickson, Rhodes (5), MILLS (7), Orosco (9), Benitez (9) vs Wright, Anderson (4), Juden (7), Assenmacher (7), Jackson (7), MESA (8)
Home Runs: Alomar-CLE, Anderson-BAL, Baines-BAL, Palmiero-BAL, Ramirez-CLE
Attendance: 45,081

GAME 5 AT CLE OCT 13

BAL 002 000 002   4 10 0
CLE 000 000 002   2 8 1
Pitchers: KAMIENIECKI, Key (6), Myers (9) vs OGEA, Assenmacher (9), Jackson (9)
Home Runs: Davis-BAL
Attendance: 45,068

GAME 6 AT BAL OCT 15

CLE 000 000 000 01   1 3 0
BAL 000 000 000 00   0 10 0
Pitchers: Nagy, Assenmacher (8), Jackson (8), ANDERSON (10), Mesa (11) vs Mussina, Myers (9), BENITEZ (11)
Home Runs: Fernandez-CLE
Attendance: 49,075

FLORIDA MARLINS (NL) 4, CLEVELAND INDIANS (AL) 3

Back-to-back home runs by Moises Alou and Charles Johnson in the fifth inning off Orel Hershiser helped the Marlins to a 7–4 win in Game 1 of the World Series. Florida starter Livan Hernandez didn't make it out of the sixth, but a trio of Marlins relievers finished off the Tribe before the first of four crowds of 67,000-plus in Miami. The home crowd didn't have much to cheer about in Game 2 as Bip Roberts and Sandy Alomar each drove in two runs and Chad Ogea pitched the Indians to a 6–1 win.

The temperature in Cleveland for Game 3 was 30 degrees lower and the wind blew almost 20 miles per hour harder than in Miami. The biggest change, though, was on the scorebook. The 25 combined runs and 17 walks were just shy of setting World Series marks, but a defensive play by the not-so-slick-fielding Gary Sheffield was as crucial as any hit. The Marlins right fielder, who had five RBIs in the game, leaped to grab Jim Thome's seventh-inning drive at the wall to keep the score tied at 7–7. Cleveland's bullpen and defense collapsed in the ninth, resulting in seven runs. Marlins closer Rob Nen surrendered four runs in the bottom of the ninth, but Florida hung on for the ugly 14–11 win.

The 15-degree wind chill for Game 4 made it the coldest World Series in history, and home runs by Manny Ramirez and Matt Williams made it a long night for the Marlins. Jaret Wright outdistanced Tony Saunders amid snow flurries as the Indians evened the World Series with a 10–3 win. In Game 5 Alou hit his second three-run home run off Orel Hershiser, his third homer of the Series. Hernandez, who would be named Series MVP, pitched into the ninth inning of Florida's 8–7 win. In Game 6 Ogea had two hits, two RBIs, scored a run, and also earned the 4–1 win for the Indians to set the stage for a seventh game.

Starters Al Leiter and Jaret Wright both pitched well, but Game 7 came down to the bullpen. The Indians were within two outs of their first world championship since 1948 when Craig Counsell's sacrifice fly drove in the tying run in the ninth inning off Jose Mesa. Edgar Renteria ended the second-longest seventh game in World Series history with a bases-loaded

single over the glove of Indians pitcher Charles Nagy with two outs in the 11th inning. Counsell crossed home plate with the deciding run in Florida's 3–2 win to make the Marlins the first wild card team to win the World Series. Tony Fernandez drove in both Cleveland runs, but his crucial error prolonged the deciding rally.

FLA (N)

PLAYER/POS	AVG	G	AB	R	H	2B	3B	HR	RB	BB	SO	SB
Kurt Abbott, dh-1	.000	3	3	0	0	0	0	0	0	0	1	0
Antonio Alfonseca, p	.000	3	0	0	0	0	0	0	0	0	0	0
Moises Alou, of	.321	7	28	6	9	2	0	3	9	3	6	1
Alex Arias, 3b-1, dh-1	.000	2	1	1	0	0	0	0	0	0	0	0
Bobby Bonilla, 3b	.207	7	29	5	6	1	0	1	3	3	5	0
Kevin Brown, p	.000	2	3	0	0	0	0	0	0	0	1	0
John Cangelosi, ph	.333	3	3	0	1	0	0	0	0	0	2	0
Jeff Conine, 1b	.231	6	13	1	3	0	0	0	2	0	0	0
Dennis Cook, p	.000	3	0	0	0	0	0	0	0	0	0	0
Craig Counsell, 2b	.182	7	22	4	4	1	0	0	2	6	5	1
Darren Daulton, 1b-5, dh-1	.389	7	18	7	7	2	0	1	2	3	0	1
Jim Eisenreich, 1b-2, dh-2	.500	5	8	1	4	0	0	1	3	3	1	0
Cliff Floyd, dh-1	.000	4	2	1	0	0	0	0	0	1	1	0
Felix Heredia, p	.000	4	0	0	0	0	0	0	0	0	0	0
Livan Hernandez, p	.000	2	2	0	0	0	0	0	0	0	0	0
Charles Johnson, c	.357	7	28	4	10	0	0	1	3	1	6	0
Al Leiter, p	.000	2	0	0	0	0	0	0	0	2	0	0
Robb Nen, p	.000	4	0	0	0	0	0	0	0	0	0	0
Jay Powell, p	.000	4	0	0	0	0	0	0	0	0	0	0
Edgar Renteria, ss	.290	7	31	3	9	2	0	0	3	3	5	0
Tony Saunders, p	.000	1	0	0	0	0	0	0	0	0	0	0
Gary Sheffield, of	.292	7	24	4	7	1	0	1	5	8	5	0
Ed Vosberg, p	.000	2	0	0	0	0	0	0	0	0	0	0
Devon White, of	.242	7	33	0	8	3	1	0	2	3	10	1
Greg Zaun, c-1	.000	2	2	0	0	0	0	0	0	0	0	0
TOTAL	.272		250	37	68	12	1	8	34	36	48	4

PITCHER	W	L	ERA	G	GS	CG	SV	SHO	IP	H	ER	BB	SO
Antonio Alfonseca	0	0	0.00	3	0	0	0	0	6.1	6	0	1	5
Kevin Brown	0	2	8.18	2	2	0	0	0	11.0	15	10	5	6
Dennis Cook	1	0	0.00	3	0	0	0	0	3.2	1	0	1	5
Felix Heredia	0	0	0.00	4	0	0	0	0	5.1	2	0	1	5
Livan Hernandez	2	0	5.27	2	2	0	0	0	13.2	15	8	10	7
Al Leiter	0	0	5.06	2	2	0	0	0	10.2	10	6	10	10
Robb Nen	0	0	7.71	4	0	0	2	0	4.2	8	4	2	7
Jay Powell	1	0	7.36	4	0	0	0	0	3.2	5	3	4	2
Tony Saunders	0	1	27.00	1	1	0	0	0	2.0	7	6	3	2
Ed Vosberg	0	0	6.00	2	0	0	0	0	3.0	3	2	3	2
TOTAL	4	3	5.40	827	7	0	2	0	64.0	72	39	40	51

CLE (A)

PLAYER/POS	AVG	G	AB	R	H	2B	3B	HR	RB	BB	SO	SB
Sandy Alomar, c	.367	7	30	5	11	1	0	2	10	2	3	0
Brian Anderson, p	.000	3	0	0	0	0	0	0	0	0	0	0
Paul Assenmacher, p	.000	5	0	0	0	0	0	0	0	0	0	0
Jeff Branson, ph	.000	1	1	0	0	0	0	0	0	0	1	0
Tony Fernandez, 2b	.471	5	17	1	8	1	0	0	4	0	1	0
Brian Giles, of-2	.500	5	4	1	2	1	0	0	2	4	1	0
Marquis Grissom, of	.360	7	25	5	9	1	0	0	2	4	4	0
Orel Hershiser, p	.000	2	2	0	0	0	0	0	0	0	1	0
Mike Jackson, p	.000	4	2	0	0	0	0	0	0	0	1	0
Jeff Juden, p	.000	2	0	0	0	0	0	0	0	0	0	0
David Justice, of-4, dh-3	.185	7	27	4	5	0	0	0	4	6	8	0
Jose Mesa, p	.000	5	0	0	0	0	0	0	0	0	0	0
Alvin Morman, p	.000	2	0	0	0	0	0	0	0	0	0	0
Charles Nagy, p	.000	2	0	0	0	0	0	0	0	0	0	0
Chad Ogea, p	.500	2	4	1	2	1	0	0	2	0	1	0
Eric Plunk, p	.000	3	0	0	0	0	0	0	0	0	0	0
Manny Ramirez, of	.154	7	26	3	4	0	0	2	6	6	5	0
Bip Roberts, 2b-4, of-2	.273	6	22	3	6	4	0	0	4	3	5	0
Kevin Seitzer, ph	.000	1	1	0	0	0	0	0	0	0	0	0
Jim Thome, 1b	.286	7	28	8	8	0	0	1	2	4	5	0
Omar Vizquel, ss	.233	7	30	5	7	2	0	0	1	3	5	5
Matt Williams, 3b	.385	7	26	8	10	1	0	1	3	7	6	0
Jaret Wright, p	.000	2	2	0	0	0	0	0	0	0	2	0
TOTAL	.291		247	44	72	12	1	7	42	40	51	5

PITCHER	W	L	ERA	G	GS	CG	SV	SHO	IP	H	ER	BB	SO
Brian Anderson	0	0	2.45	3	0	0	1	0	3.2	2	1	0	2
Paul Assenmacher	0	0	0.00	5	0	0	0	0	4.0	5	0	0	6
Orel Hershiser	0	2	11.70	2	2	0	0	0	10.0	15	13	6	5
Mike Jackson	0	0	1.93	4	0	0	0	0	4.2	5	1	3	4
Jeff Juden	0	0	4.50	2	0	0	0	0	2.0	2	1	2	0
Jose Mesa	0	0	5.40	5	0	0	0	0	5.0	10	3	1	5
Alvin Morman	0	0	0.00	2	0	0	0	0	0.1	0	0	2	1
Charles Nagy	0	1	6.43	2	1	0	0	0	7.0	8	5	5	5
Chad Ogea	2	0	1.54	2	2	0	0	0	11.2	11	2	3	5
Eric Plunk	0	1	9.00	3	0	0	0	0	3.0	3	3	4	3
Jaret Wright	1	0	2.92	2	2	0	0	0	12.1	7	4	10	12
TOTAL	3	4	4.66	32	7	0	2	0	63.2	68	33	36	48

GAME 1 AT FLA OCT 18

CLE 1 0 0 0 1 1 0 1 0   4 11 0
FLA 0 0 1 4 2 0   0 0 X   7 7 1
Pitchers: HERSHISER, Juden (5), Plunk (6), Assenmacher (8) vs HERNANDEZ, Cook (6), Powell (8), Nen (9)
Home Runs: Alou-FLA, Johnson-FLA, Ramirez-CLE, Thome-CLE
Attendance: 67,245

GAME 2 AT FLA OCT 19

CLE 1 0 0 0 3 2 0 0 0   6 14 0
FLA 1 0 0 0 0 0 0 0 0   1 8 0
Pitchers: OGEA, Jackson (7), Mesa (9) vs BROWN, Heredia (7), Alfonseca (8)
Home Runs: Alomar-CLE
Attendance: 67,025

GAME 3 AT CLE OCT 21

FLA 1 0 1 1 0 2 2 0 7   14 16 3
CLE 2 0 0 3 2 0 0 0 4   11 10 3
Pitchers: Leiter, Heredia (5), COOK (8), Nen (9) vs Nagy, Anderson (7), Jackson (7), Assenmacher (8), PLUNK (8), Morman (9), Mesa (9)
Home Runs: Sheffield-FLA, Daulton-FLA, Thome-CLE, Eisenreich-FLA
Attendance: 44,880

GAME 4 AT CLE OCT 22

FLA 0 0 0 1 0 2 0 0 0   3 6 2
CLE 3 0 3 0 0 1 1 2 X   10 15 0
Pitchers: SAUNDERS, Alfonseca (3), Vosberg (6), Powell (8) vs WRIGHT, Anderson (7)
Home Runs: Ramirez-CLE, Alou-FLA, Williams-CLE
Attendance: 44,877

GAME 5 AT CLE OCT 23

FLA 0 2 0 0 0 4 0 1 1   8 15 2
CLE 0 1 3 0 0 0 0 0 3   7 9 0
Pitchers: HERNANDEZ, Nen (9) vs HERSHISER, Morman (6), Plunk (7), Juden (7), Assenmacher (8), Mesa (9)
Home Runs: Alomar-CLE, Alou-FLA
Attendance: 44,888

GAME 6 AT FLA OCT 25

CLE 0 2 0 1 0 1 0 0 0   4 7 0
FLA 0 0 0 0 1 0 0 0 0   1 8 0
Pitchers: OGEA, Jackson (6), Assenmacher (8), Mesa (9) vs BROWN, Heredia (6), Powell (8), Vosberg (9)
Attendance: 67,498

GAME 7 AT FLA OCT 26

CLE 0 0 2 0 0 0 0 0 0 0 0   2 6 2
FLA 0 0 0 0 0 0 1 0 1 0 1   3 8 0
Pitchers: Wright, Assenmacher (7), Jackson (8), Anderson (8), Mesa (9), NAGY (10) vs Leiter, Cook (7), Alfonseca (8), Heredia (9), Nen (9), POWELL (11)
Home Runs: Bonilla-FLA
Attendance: 67,204

SAN DIEGO PADRES (WEST) 3, HOUSTON ASTROS (CENTRAL) 1

The Astros and Padres had both won division titles by comfortable margins, but Houston was given the pre-series edge because they had won more games and held advantages in many offensive and defensive categories. Plus, the Astros had Randy Johnson, the 6-foot-10 left-hander obtained from Seattle who went 10–1 with a 1.28 ERA down the stretch. The Astros also had home-field advantage in the Division Series. Yet none of that prepared the Astros for Kevin Brown or Jim Leyritz. Brown struck out 16 and limited Houston to just two hits in eight innings in Game 1; Leyritz, who drove in at least one run in each game of the series, brought in the first run with a sacrifice fly in the sixth inning. Greg Vaughn added a home run off Johnson in the eighth and the Padres held on for the 2–1 win.

The Astros led Game 2 from the first inning as Jeff Bagwell drove in three runs and Derek Bell added a home run to take a 4–2 lead into the top of the ninth. Leyritz, who hit dramatic post-season home runs for the Yankees in 1995 and '96, lofted an opposite-field, two-run home run just inside the right-field foul pole to tie the game. Houston's Ricky Gutierrez stole third base in the bottom of the ninth and then scored when Bill Spiers singled to end the game and tie the series.

With an extra off day on the schedule, Padres manager Bruce Bochy moved Brown up in the rotation to pitch Game 3. Brown lowered his ERA for the series to 0.61 and reliever Dan Miceli came in with the bases loaded in the top of the seventh to strike out Spiers and keep the game tied at 1–1. Leyritz homered off Scott Elarton in the bottom of the seventh as the Padres took a 2–1 lead in the game and the series. The second consecutive crowd of more than 64,000 in San Diego watched Leyritz hit his third home run of the series in Game 4. Padres left-hander Sterling Hitchcock struck out 11 of the 21 batters he faced and earned the win when Sean Berry threw away Ken Caminiti's grounder to bring in the go-ahead run in the sixth. The Padres tacked on four insurance runs in the eighth on a two-run triple by John Vander Wal and a two-run homer by Wally

Joyner. Trevor Hoffman, who pitched in all four games, set down the Astros in the ninth inning.

GAME 1 AT HOU SEPT 29

SD 000 001 010 2 9 1
HOU 000 000 001 1 4 0
Pitchers: BROWN, Hoffman (9) vs JOHNSON, Powell (9), Henry (9)
Home Runs: Vaughn-SD
Attendance: 50,080

GAME 2 AT HOU OCT 1

SD 000 002 002 4 8 1
HOU 102 000 011 5 11 1
Pitchers: Ashby, Hamilton (5), Wall (8), MICELI (9), Hoffman (9) vs Reynolds, Powell (8), WAGNER (9)
Home Runs: Leyritz-SD, Bell-HOU
Attendance: 45,550

GAME 3 AT SD OCT 3

HOU 000 000 100 1 4 0
SD 000 001 10X 2 3 0
Pitchers: Hampton, ELARTON (7) vs Brown, MICELI (7), Hoffman (9)
Home Runs: Leyritz-SD
Attendance: 65,235

GAME 4 AT SD OCT 4

HOU 000 100 000 1 3 1
SD 010 001 04X 6 7 1
Pitchers: JOHNSON, Miller (7), Henry (7), Powell (8) vs HITCHCOCK, Hamilton (7), Miceli (7), Hoffman (9)
Home Runs: Leyritz-SD, Joyner-SD
Attendance: 64,898

SD (W)

PLAYER/POS	AVG	G	AB	R	H	2B	3B	HR	RB	BB	SO	SB
George Arias, ph	.000	1	1	0	0	0	0	0	0	0	1	0
Andy Ashby, p	.000	1	1	0	0	0	0	0	0	0	0	0
Kevin Brown, p	.000	2	3	0	0	0	0	0	0	0	2	0
Ken Caminiti, 3b	.143	4	14	2	2	0	0	0	0	1	3	0
Steve Finley, of	.100	4	10	2	1	1	0	0	1	1	4	0
Chris Gomez, ss	.273	4	11	1	3	0	0	0	0	4	1	0
Tony Gwynn, of	.200	4	15	1	3	2	0	0	2	0	2	0
Joey Hamilton, p	.000	2	0	0	0	0	0	0	0	0	0	0
Carlos Hernandez, c	.417	4	12	0	5	0	0	0	0	0	0	0
Sterling Hitchcock, p	.000	1	2	0	0	0	0	0	0	0	1	0
Trevor Hoffman, p	.000	4	0	0	0	0	0	0	0	0	0	0
Wally Joyner, 1b	.167	4	6	1	1	0	0	1	2	1	2	0
Jim Leyritz, 1b-3, c-1	.400	4	10	3	4	0	0	3	5	0	2	0
Dan Miceli, p	.000	3	0	0	0	0	0	0	0	0	0	0
Greg Myers, c	.000	1	0	0	0	0	0	0	0	0	0	0
Ruben Rivera, of	.000	3	6	0	0	0	0	0	0	0	3	0
Andy Sheets, 2b-1	.000	2	0	0	0	0	0	0	0	0	0	0
Mark Sweeney, ph	.000	2	1	0	0	0	0	0	0	1	0	0
John Vander Wal, ph	.333	3	3	1	1	0	1	0	2	0	1	0
Greg Vaughn, of	.333	4	15	2	5	1	0	1	1	0	4	0
Quilvio Veras, 2b	.133	4	15	1	2	0	0	0	0	1	6	0
Donne Wall, p	.000	1	0	0	0	0	0	0	0	0	0	0
TOTAL	.216		125	14	27	4	1	5	13	9	32	0

PITCHER	W	L	ERA	G	GS	CG	SV	SHO	IP	H	ER	BB	SO
Andy Ashby	0	0	6.75	1	1	0	0	0	4.0	6	3	1	4
Kevin Brown	1	0	0.61	2	2	0	0	0	14.2	5	1	7	21
Joey Hamilton	0	0	0.00	2	0	0	0	0	3.1	1	0	2	3
Sterling Hitchcock	1	0	1.50	1	1	0	0	0	6.0	3	1	0	11
Trevor Hoffman	0	0	0.00	4	0	0	2	0	3.0	3	0	1	4
Dan Miceli	1	1	2.70	3	0	0	0	0	3.1	2	1	0	4
Donne Wall	0	0	9.00	1	0	0	0	0	1.0	2	1	0	2
TOTAL	3	1	1.78	14	4	0	2	0	35.1	22	7	11	49

HOU (C)

PLAYER/POS	AVG	G	AB	R	H	2B	3B	HR	RB	BB	SO	SB
Moises Alou, of	.188	4	16	0	3	0	0	0	0	0	2	0
Brad Ausmus, c	.222	4	9	0	2	0	0	0	0	0	4	0
Jeff Bagwell, 1b	.143	4	14	0	2	0	0	0	4	1	6	0
Derek Bell, of	.125	4	16	1	2	0	0	1	1	0	7	0
Sean Berry, 3b	.000	1	2	0	0	0	0	0	0	0	1	0
Craig Biggio, 2b	.182	4	11	3	2	1	0	0	1	4	4	0
Dave Clark, ph	.000	2	0	0	0	0	0	0	0	2	0	0
Scott Elarton, p	.000	1	0	0	0	0	0	0	0	0	0	0
Raul Eusebio, c	.333	1	3	0	1	1	0	0	0	0	2	0
Carl Everett, of-3	.154	4	13	1	2	0	0	0	0	0	4	0
Ricky Gutierrez, ss	.300	4	10	1	3	0	0	0	0	3	7	1
Mike Hampton, p	.000	1	2	0	0	0	0	0	0	0	2	0
Doug Henry, p	.000	2	0	0	0	0	0	0	0	0	0	0
Richard Hidalgo, of	.250	1	4	0	1	0	0	0	0	0	1	0
Pete Incaviglia, ph	.000	1	1	0	0	0	0	0	0	0	1	0
Randy Johnson, p	.000	2	4	0	0	0	0	0	0	0	4	0
Trever Miller, p	.000	1	0	0	0	0	0	0	0	0	0	0
Jay Powell, p	.000	3	0	0	0	0	0	0	0	0	0	0
Shane Reynolds, p	.000	1	2	0	0	0	0	0	0	0	1	0
Bill Spiers, 3b	.286	4	14	2	4	3	0	0	1	1	3	0
Billy Wagner, p	.000	1	0	0	0	0	0	0	0	0	0	0
TOTAL	.182		121	82	2	5	0	1	7	11	49	1

PITCHER	W	L	ERA	G	GS	CG	SV	SHO	IP	H	ER	BB	SO
Scott Elarton	0	1	4.50	1	0	0	0	0	2.0	1	1	1	3
Mike Hampton	0	0	1.50	1	1	0	0	0	6.0	2	1	1	2
Doug Henry	0	0	5.40	2	0	0	0	0	1.2	2	1	0	1
Randy Johnson	0	2	1.93	2	2	0	0	0	14.0	12	3	2	17
Trever Miller	0	0	∞	1	0	0	0	0	0.0	0	0	1	0
Jay Powell	0	0	11.57	3	0	0	0	0	2.1	2	3	3	3
Shane Reynolds	0	0	2.57	1	1	0	0	0	7.0	4	2	1	5
Billy Wagner	1	0	18.00	1	0	0	0	0	1.0	4	2	0	1
TOTAL	1	3	3.44	12	4	0	0	0	34.0	27	13	9	32

ATLANTA BRAVES (EAST) 3, CHICAGO CUBS (WILD CARD) 0

The Cubs had just completed a remarkable season that included Sammy Sosa's home run chase with Mark McGwire and a three-way wild card race, while the Braves were just getting ready for business as usual in October. Atlanta, making its seventh consecutive trip to the postseason, was coming off a regular season that included a franchise-best 106 wins. By contrast, the Cubs had won 90 games, and they needed a one-game playoff victory over the Giants to secure a postseason berth for the first time in nine years.

The teams started even in Game 1, but the Braves still had great pitching. John Smoltz, who went 17–3 during the season, handcuffed the Cubs on five hits. Atlanta took the lead on Michael Tucker's home run in the second inning following a two-out error. A grand slam by Ryan Klesko in the seventh put the game out of reach.

Chicago's Kevin Tapani, a 19-game winner, outpitched 20-game winner Tom Glavine in Game 2. Tapani had a four-hit shutout through eight innings, and manager Jim Riggleman, hoping to save an exhausted bullpen, let the right-hander pitch the ninth inning with a 1–0 lead. Javier Lopez homered to left with one out to tie the game. Terry Mulholland relieved in the 10th, but he missed the first base bag on a bunt play to put runners on first and second for Chipper Jones. Jones hit a line drive that landed just inside the left field line to bring in the winning run.

Atlanta's Greg Maddux, who won the first of his four Cy Young Awards as a Cub in 1992, had the task of quieting the raucous crowd at Wrigley Field in Game 3. Maddux outdid Cubs phenom Kerry Wood on the mound and on the basepaths. A superb slide enabled Maddux to stretch a double in the third inning, and, after he crossed to third on a groundout, he scored on a passed ball. In the top of the eighth, Gerald Williams singled in Atlanta's second run, and Eddie Perez lifted a grand slam to left off Rod Beck. Maddux was charged with two runs in the eighth, but Kerry Ligtenberg relieved and finished off the Cubs. Atlanta pitching held Chicago to just three extra-base hits and four runs in the series, while Sosa, who clubbed 66

home runs during the season, was one of six Cubs regulars to bat under .200 in Atlanta's sweep.

ATL (E)

PLAYER/POS	AVG	G	AB	R	H	2B	3B	HR	RB	BB	SO	SB
Danny Bautista, of	.500	2	2	0	1	1	0	0	0	0	0	0
Greg Colbrunn, ph	.000	2	2	0	0	0	0	0	0	0	0	0
Andres Galarraga, 1b	.250	3	12	1	3	0	0	0	0	1	3	0
Tom Glavine, p	.000	1	1	0	0	0	0	0	0	0	0	0
Tony Graffanino, ph	.000	1	0	0	0	0	0	0	0	0	0	0
Ozzie Guillen, ph	.000	1	1	0	0	0	0	0	0	0	0	0
Andruw Jones, of	.000	3	9	2	0	0	0	0	1	3	2	2
Chipper Jones, 3b	.200	2	10	2	2	0	0	0	1	4	3	0
Ryan Klesko, of	.273	3	11	1	3	0	0	1	4	0	3	0
Kerry Ligtenberg, p	.000	3	0	0	0	0	0	0	0	0	0	0
Keith Lockhart, 2b	.333	3	12	2	4	0	0	0	0	1	0	0
Javy Lopez, c	.286	2	7	1	2	0	0	1	1	1	1	0
Greg Maddux, p	.250	1	4	1	1	1	0	0	0	0	1	0
Eddie Perez, c	.200	1	5	1	1	0	0	1	4	0	2	0
Odaliz Perez, p	.000	1	0	0	0	0	0	0	0	0	0	0
John Rocker, p	.000	2	0	0	0	0	0	0	0	0	0	0
Rudy Seanez, p	.000	1	0	0	0	0	0	0	0	0	0	0
John Smoltz, p	.500	1	2	0	1	0	0	0	0	0	1	0
Michael Tucker, of	.250	3	8	1	2	0	0	1	2	2	0	1
Walt Weiss, ss	.154	3	13	2	2	0	0	0	0	1	3	0
Gerald Williams, of	.500	2	2	1	1	0	0	0	1	0	1	0
TOTAL	.228		101	15	23	2	0	4	14	14	20	3

PITCHER	W	L	ERA	G	GS	CG	SV	SHO	IP	H	ER	BB	SO
Tom Glavine	0	0	1.29	1	1	0	0	0	7.0	3	1	1	8
Kerry Ligtenberg	0	0	0.00	3	0	0	0	0	3.1	1	0	4	3
Greg Maddux	1	0	2.57	1	1	0	0	0	7.0	7	2	0	4
Odaliz Perez	1	0	0.00	1	0	0	0	0	0.2	0	0	0	1
John Rocker	0	0	0.00	2	0	0	0	0	1.1	1	0	0	2
Rudy Seanez	0	0	0.00	1	0	0	0	0	1.0	0	0	0	0
John Smoltz	1	0	1.17	1	1	0	0	0	7.2	5	1	0	6
TOTAL	3	0	1.29	10	3	0	0	0	28.0	17	4	5	24

CHI (WC)

PLAYER/POS	AVG	G	AB	R	H	2B	3B	HR	RB	BB	SO	SB
Manny Alexander, ss-1	.000	2	5	0	0	0	0	0	0	0	1	0
Rod Beck, p	.000	1	0	0	0	0	0	0	0	0	0	0
Jeff Blauser, ph	.000	2	2	0	0	0	0	0	0	0	1	0
Brant Brown, ph	.000	1	1	0	0	0	0	0	0	0	0	0
Mark Clark, p	.500	1	2	0	1	0	0	0	0	0	0	0
Gary Gaetti, 3b	.091	3	11	0	1	0	0	0	0	0	4	0
Mark Grace, 1b	.083	3	12	0	1	0	0	0	1	0	2	0
Felix Heredia, p	.000	1	0	0	0	0	0	0	0	0	0	0
Jose Hernandez, ss	.286	2	7	1	2	0	0	0	0	0	2	0
Glenallen Hill, of	.333	1	3	0	1	0	0	0	0	1	2	1
Tyler Houston, c	.167	3	6	1	1	0	0	1	1	0	3	0
Lance Johnson, of	.167	3	12	0	2	0	0	0	1	0	1	0
Matt Karchner, p	.000	1	0	0	0	0	0	0	0	0	0	0
Angel Martinez, c	1.000	1	1	1	1	0	0	0	0	0	0	0
Mickey Morandini, 2b	.222	3	9	1	2	0	0	0	1	2	2	0
Mike Morgan, p	.000	2	0	0	0	0	0	0	0	0	0	0
Terry Mulholland, p	.000	2	0	0	0	0	0	0	0	0	0	0
Henry Rodriguez, of-2	.143	3	7	0	1	1	0	0	0	1	2	0
Scott Servais, c	.667	1	3	0	2	0	0	0	0	0	0	0
Sammy Sosa, of	.182	3	11	0	2	1	0	0	0	1	4	0
Kevin Tapani, p	.000	1	1	0	0	0	0	0	0	0	0	0
Kerry Wood, p	.000	1	1	0	0	0	0	0	0	0	0	0
TOTAL	.181		94	4	17	2	0	1	4	5	24	1

PITCHER	W	L	ERA	G	GS	CG	SV	SHO	IP	H	ER	BB	SO
Rod Beck	0	0	16.20	1	0	0	0	0	1.2	5	3	2	1
Mark Clark	0	1	3.00	1	1	0	0	0	6.0	7	2	1	4
Felix Heredia	0	0	54.00	1	0	0	0	0	0.1	0	2	2	0
Matt Karchner	0	0	13.50	1	0	0	0	0	0.2	1	1	0	1
Mike Morgan	0	0	0.00	2	0	0	0	0	1.1	0	0	0	1
Terry Mulholland	0	1	11.57	2	0	0	0	0	2.1	2	3	2	2
Kevin Tapani	0	0	1.00	1	1	0	0	0	9.0	5	1	3	6
Kerry Wood	0	1	1.80	1	1	0	0	0	5.0	3	1	4	5
TOTAL	0	3	4.44	10	3	0	0	0	26.1	23	13	14	20

GAME 1 AT ATL SEPT 30

CHI 000 000 010   1 5 1
ATL 020 001 40X   7 8 0
Pitchers: CLARK, Heredia (7), Karchner (7), Morgan (8) vs SMOLTZ, Rocker (8), Ligtenberg (9)
Home Runs: Tucker-ATL, Klesko-ATL, Houston-CHI
Attendance: 45,598

GAME 2 AT ATL OCT 1

CHI 000 001 0000   1 4 1
ATL 000 000 001 1   2 6 0
Pitchers: Tapani, MULHOLLAND (10) vs Glavine, Rocker (8), Seanez (9), Ligtenberg (10), O.Perez (10)
Home Runs: Lopez-ATL
Attendance: 51,713

GAME 3 AT CHI OCT 3

ATL 001 000 050   6 9 0
CHI 000 000 020   2 8 2
Pitchers: MADDUX, Ligtenberg (8) vs WOOD, Mulholland (6), Beck (8), Morgan (9)
Home Runs: E.Perez-ATL
Attendance: 39,597

CLEVELAND INDIANS (CENTRAL) 3, BOSTON RED SOX (WILD CARD) 1

The Boston Red Sox had to go back to Game 5 of the 1986 World Series for the team's last postseason win, but they broke out of their postseason slump in a big way. Their string of 13 straight postseason losses (two World Series games, eight Championship Series games, and three Division Series games) ended quickly against the Indians in the opening game of the 1998 Division Series. Mo Vaughn launched a home run to left field with two men on in the first inning, then homered again with a runner on in the sixth, before he capped the day with a two-run double in the eighth. Nomar Garciaparra added a home run and a sacrifice fly as the two Boston sluggers drove in each run of their team's 11–3 win. For the series, the pair combined for 19 runs batted in, while the rest of the team drove in just one run.

The Red Sox jumped out to a quick 2–0 lead in the first inning of Game 2 as both Cleveland manager Mike Hargrove and starting pitcher Dwight Gooden were ejected after separate arguments with umpire Joe Brinkman. The Indians were a new team after that. They chased Boston starter Tim Wakefield in a five-run second inning, Dave Burba pitched five and a third innings of relief for the win, and Mike Jackson tossed the final two innings to even the series. In the third game the Indians managed just five hits, but four of those were solo home runs as Cleveland held on for a 4–3 win in Boston. The home run that wound up being the most important was Manny Ramirez's second of the game in the top of the ninth. Garciaparra's two-run home run in the bottom of the ninth cut the lead to 4–3, but two groundouts ended the game.

Both the fans and the press alike were critical of Boston manager Jimy Williams for not starting his ace, Pedro Martinez, on three day's rest in Game 4. Martinez, who won Game 1, watched as Pete Schourek pitched five and a third strong innings and left with a 1–0 lead supplied by Garciaparra's third home run of the series. Boston closer Tom Gordon had not blown a save since April 14, but he surrendered the lead in the eighth inning on a two-run double by left fielder David Justice, who had also thrown out John Valentin at the

plate in the sixth inning. Jackson earned his third save in as many games as the Indians defeated the Red Sox in the postseason for the second time in three years.

GAME 1 AT CLE SEPT 29

```
BOS  300 032 030  11 12 0
CLE  000 002 100   3  7 0
```
Pitchers: MARTINEZ, Corsi (8) vs WRIGHT, Jones (5), Reed (8), Assenmacher (8), Poole (8), Shuey (8), Assenmacher (9)
Home Runs: Vaughn-BOS (2), Garciaparra-BOS, Lofton-CLE, Thome-CLE
Attendance: 45,185

GAME 2 AT CLE SEPT 30

```
BOS  201 002 000   5 10 0
CLE  151 001 01X   9  9 1
```
Pitchers: WAKEFIELD, Wasdin (2), Lowe (4), Swindell (6), Gordon (8) vs Gooden, BURBA (1), Shuey (6), Assenmacher (8), Jackson (8)
Home Runs: Justice-CLE
Attendance: 45,229

GAME 3 AT BOS OCT 2

```
CLE  000 011 101   4  5 0
BOS  000 100 002   3  6 0
```
Pitchers: NAGY, Jackson (9) vs SABERHAGEN, Corsi (8), Eckersley (9)
Home Runs: Thome-CLE, Lofton-CLE, Ramirez-CLE (2), Garciaparra-BOS
Attendance: 33,114

GAME 4 AT BOS OCT 3

```
CLE  000 000 020   2  5 0
BOS  000 100 000   1  6 0
```
Pitchers: Colon, Poole (6), REED (7), Shuey (8), Jackson (9) vs Schourek, Lowe (6), GORDON (8)
Home Runs: Garciaparra-BOS
Attendance: 33,537

CLE (C)

PLAYER/POS	AVG	G	AB	R	H	2B	3B	HR	RB	BB	SO	SB
Sandy Alomar, c	.231	4	13	2	3	3	0	0	2	1	4	0
Paul Assenmacher, p	.000	3	0	0	0	0	0	0	0	0	0	0
Dave Burba, p	.000	1	0	0	0	0	0	0	0	0	0	0
Bartolo Colon, p	.000	1	0	0	0	0	0	0	0	0	0	0
Joey Cora, 2b	.000	4	10	2	0	0	0	0	0	3	2	0
Travis Fryman, 3b	.154	4	13	1	2	1	0	0	0	3	4	1
Brian Giles, of-2, dh-1	.200	3	10	1	2	1	0	0	0	1	4	0
Dwight Gooden, p	.000	1	0	0	0	0	0	0	0	0	0	0
Mike Jackson, p	.000	3	0	0	0	0	0	0	0	0	0	0
Doug Jones, p	.000	1	0	0	0	0	0	0	0	0	0	0
David Justice, of-2, dh-2	.313	4	16	2	5	4	0	1	6	0	1	0
Kenny Lofton, of	.375	4	16	5	6	1	0	2	4	1	1	2
Charles Nagy, p	.000	1	0	0	0	0	0	0	0	0	0	0
Jim Poole, p	.000	2	0	0	0	0	0	0	0	0	0	0
Manny Ramirez, of	.357	4	14	2	5	2	0	2	3	1	4	0
Steve Reed, p	.000	2	0	0	0	0	0	0	0	0	0	0
Richie Sexson, 1b	.000	3	2	0	0	0	0	0	0	2	1	0
Paul Shuey, p	.000	3	0	0	0	0	0	0	0	0	0	0
Jim Thome, 1b-3, dh-1	.133	4	15	2	2	0	0	2	2	2	5	0
Omar Vizquel, ss	.067	4	15	1	1	0	0	0	0	1	0	0
Enrique Wilson, 2b	.000	1	2	0	0	0	0	0	0	0	0	0
Jaret Wright, p	.000	1	0	0	0	0	0	0	0	0	0	0
TOTAL	.206		126	18	26	12	0	7	17	15	26	3

PITCHER	W	L	ERA	G	GS	CG	SV	SHO	IP	H	ER	BB	SO
Paul Assenmacher	0	0	0.00	3	0	0	0	0	1.0	2	0	0	2
Dave Burba	1	0	5.06	1	0	0	0	0	5.1	4	3	2	4
Bartolo Colon	0	0	1.59	1	1	0	0	0	5.2	5	1	3	3
Dwight Gooden	0	0	54.00	1	1	0	0	0	0.1	1	2	2	1
Mike Jackson	0	0	4.50	3	0	0	3	0	4.0	3	2	1	1
Doug Jones	0	0	6.75	1	0	0	0	0	2.2	3	2	1	1
Charles Nagy	1	0	1.13	1	1	0	0	0	8.0	4	1	0	3
Jim Poole	0	0	0.00	2	0	0	0	0	1.0	1	0	1	2
Steve Reed	1	0	40.50	2	0	0	0	0	0.2	1	3	1	1
Paul Shuey	0	0	0.00	3	0	0	0	0	3.0	3	0	1	4
Jaret Wright	0	1	12.46	1	1	0	0	0	4.1	7	6	2	6
TOTAL	3	1	5.00	19	4	0	3	0	36.0	34	20	14	28

BOS (WC)

PLAYER/POS	AVG	G	AB	R	H	2B	3B	HR	RB	BB	SO	SB
M. Benjamin, 2b-4, 1b-1	.091	4	11	1	1	0	0	0	0	1	3	0
Darren Bragg, of	.083	3	12	0	1	0	0	0	0	0	5	0
D. Buford, of-1, dh-1	.000	3	1	2	0	0	0	0	0	0	0	0
Jim Corsi, p	.000	2	0	0	0	0	0	0	0	0	0	0
Midre Cummings, ph	.000	3	3	0	0	0	0	0	0	0	0	0
Dennis Eckersley, p	.000	1	0	0	0	0	0	0	0	0	0	0
Nomar Garciaparra, ss	.333	4	15	4	5	1	0	3	11	1	0	0
Tom Gordon, p	.000	2	0	0	0	0	0	0	0	0	0	0
Scott Hatteberg, c	.111	3	9	0	1	0	0	0	0	3	1	0
Darren Lewis, of	.357	4	14	4	5	2	0	0	1	1	3	1
Derek Lowe, p	.000	2	0	0	0	0	0	0	0	0	0	0
Pedro Martinez, p	.000	1	0	0	0	0	0	0	0	0	0	0
Trot Nixon, of	.333	2	3	0	1	0	0	0	0	1	0	0
Troy O'Leary, of	.063	4	16	0	1	0	0	0	0	1	4	0
Bret Saberhagen, p	.000	1	0	0	0	0	0	0	0	0	0	0
Donnie Sadler, 2b	.000	3	0	0	0	0	0	0	0	0	0	0
Pete Schourek, p	.000	1	0	0	0	0	0	0	0	0	0	0
Mike Stanley, dh	.267	4	15	1	4	0	0	0	0	2	5	0
Greg Swindell, p	.000	1	0	0	0	0	0	0	0	0	0	0
John Valentin, 3b	.467	4	15	5	7	1	0	0	3	1	0	0
Jason Varitek, c	.250	1	4	0	1	0	0	0	1	0	1	0
Mo Vaughn, 1b	.412	4	17	3	7	2	0	2	7	1	5	0
Tim Wakefield, p	.000	1	0	0	0	0	0	0	0	0	0	0
John Wasdin, p	.000	1	0	0	0	0	0	0	0	0	0	0
TOTAL	.252		135	20	34	6	0	5	19	14	28	1

PITCHER	W	L	ERA	G	GS	CG	SV	SHO	IP	H	ER	BB	SO
Jim Corsi	0	0	0.00	2	0	0	0	0	3.0	1	0	1	2
Dennis Eckersley	0	0	9.00	1	0	0	0	0	1.0	1	1	0	1
Tom Gordon	0	1	9.00	2	0	0	0	0	3.0	4	3	4	1
Derek Lowe	0	0	2.08	2	0	0	0	0	4.1	3	1	1	2
Pedro Martinez	1	0	3.86	1	1	0	0	0	7.0	6	3	0	8
Bret Saberhagen	0	1	3.86	1	1	0	0	0	7.0	4	3	1	7
Pete Schourek	0	0	0.00	1	1	0	0	0	5.1	2	0	4	1
Greg Swindell	0	0	0.00	1	0	0	0	0	1.1	0	0	1	1
Tim Wakefield	0	1	33.75	1	1	0	0	0	1.1	3	5	2	1
John Wasdin	0	0	10.80	1	0	0	0	0	1.2	2	2	1	2
TOTAL	1	3	4.63	13	4	0	0	0	35.0	26	18	15	26

NEW YORK YANKEES (EAST) 3, TEXAS RANGERS (WEST) 0

Despite an AL-record 114 wins by the Yankees, the Rangers actually batted higher than New York during the regular season (.289 to .288). They were second in the league to New York in runs (965 to 940), but pitching stole the show in the Division Series. The Rangers received three good performances from their starters, but Texas scored just one run in three games and batted a meager .141. David Wells set the tone in Game 1 with a five-hitter through eight innings. Texas starter Todd Stottlemyre, son of Yankees pitching coach Mel Stottlemyre, nearly matched Wells with six hits in eight innings, but the two runs the Yankees scratched out in the second inning proved to be his downfall. With one out in the second, Jorge Posada walked and Chad Curtis doubled him to third. Scott Brosius singled in one run and then got in a rundown on an attempted steal of second while Curtis crossed the plate.

Shane Spencer, who hit 10 home runs in just 67 at bats in August and September for the Yankees, homered in the second inning off Rick Helling in Game 2. Spencer singled to start the fourth inning and Brosius followed with a home run. Andy Pettitte rose to the occasion—although he allowed the Rangers' lone run of the series—as he permitted just three hits in seven innings.

Not even a violent lightning storm and torrential rain could save the Rangers in Game 3. The Yankees scored four times in the sixth inning on homers by Paul O'Neill and Spencer before the weather forced a 3-hour, 16-minute delay in Texas. The Yankees, already drained from the news that teammate Darryl Strawberry had been diagnosed with colon cancer, showed no signs of fatigue when Game 3 finally resumed. The Rangers managed just three hits off four New York pitchers as the Yankees beat Texas in the Division Series for the second time in three years.

NY (E)

PLAYER/POS	AVG	G	AB	R	H	2B	3B	HR	RB	BB	SO	SB
Scott Brosius, 3b	.400	3	10	1	4	0	0	1	3	0	3	0
Homer Bush, dh	.000	1	0	0	0	0	0	0	0	0	0	1
David Cone, p	.000	1	0	0	0	0	0	0	0	0	0	0
Chad Curtis, of	.667	3	3	1	2	1	0	0	1	1	1	1
Chili Davis, dh	.167	2	6	0	1	0	0	0	0	0	2	0
Joe Girardi, c	.429	2	7	0	3	0	0	0	0	0	1	0
Derek Jeter, ss	.111	3	9	0	1	0	0	0	0	2	2	0
Chuck Knoblauch, 2b	.091	3	11	0	1	0	0	0	0	0	4	0
Graeme Lloyd, p	.000	1	0	0	0	0	0	0	0	0	0	0
Tino Martinez, 1b	.273	3	11	1	3	2	0	0	0	0	2	0
Jeff Nelson, p	.000	2	0	0	0	0	0	0	0	0	0	0
Paul O'Neill, of	.364	3	11	1	4	2	0	1	1	1	1	0
Andy Pettitte, p	.000	1	0	0	0	0	0	0	0	0	0	0
Jorge Posada, c	.000	1	2	1	0	0	0	0	0	1	2	0
Tim Raines, dh-1	.250	2	4	1	1	1	0	0	0	1	1	0
Mariano Rivera, p	.000	3	0	0	0	0	0	0	0	0	0	0
Shane Spencer, of	.500	2	6	3	3	0	0	2	4	0	1	0
David Wells, p	.000	1	0	0	0	0	0	0	0	0	0	0
Bernie Williams, of	.000	3	11	0	0	0	0	0	0	1	4	0
TOTAL	.253		91	9	23	6	0	4	8	7	24	2

PITCHER	W	L	ERA	G	GS	CG	SV	SHO	IP	H	ER	BB	SO
David Cone	1	0	0.00	1	1	0	0	0	5.2	2	0	1	6
Graeme Lloyd	0	0	0.00	1	0	0	0	0	0.1	0	0	0	0
Jeff Nelson	0	0	0.00	2	0	0	0	0	2.2	2	0	1	2
Andy Pettitte	1	0	1.29	1	1	0	0	0	7.0	3	1	0	8
Mariano Rivera	0	0	0.00	3	0	0	2	0	3.1	1	0	1	2
David Wells	1	0	0.00	1	1	0	0	0	8.0	5	0	1	9
TOTAL	3	0	0.33	9	3	0	2	0	27.0	13	1	4	27

TEX (W)

PLAYER/POS	AVG	G	AB	R	H	2B	3B	HR	RB	BB	SO	SB
Luis Alicea, ph	.000	1	1	0	0	0	0	0	0	0	0	0
Will Clark, 1b	.091	3	11	0	1	0	0	0	0	1	2	0
Royce Clayton, ss	.222	3	9	0	2	0	0	0	0	0	4	0
Tim Crabtree, p	.000	2	0	0	0	0	0	0	0	0	0	0
Juan Gonzalez, of	.083	3	12	1	1	1	0	0	0	0	3	0
Tom Goodwin, of	.250	2	4	0	1	0	0	0	0	0	1	0
Rusty Greer, of	.091	3	11	0	1	0	0	0	0	1	2	0
Rick Helling, p	.000	1	0	0	0	0	0	0	0	0	0	0
Roberto Kelly, of	.143	1	7	0	1	1	0	0	0	0	2	0
Mark McLemore, 2b	.100	3	10	0	1	1	0	0	0	2	3	0
Ivan Rodriguez, c	.100	3	10	0	1	0	0	0	1	0	5	0
Aaron Sele, p	.000	1	0	0	0	0	0	0	0	0	0	0
Mike Simms, dh	.200	2	5	0	1	0	0	0	0	0	2	0
Lee Stevens, dh	.000	1	3	0	0	0	0	0	0	0	1	0
Todd Stottlemyre, p	.000	1	0	0	0	0	0	0	0	0	0	0
John Wetteland, p	.000	1	0	0	0	0	0	0	0	0	0	0
Todd Zeile, 3b	.333	3	9	0	3	0	0	0	0	0	2	0
TOTAL	.141		92	1	13	3	0	0	1	4	27	0

PITCHER	W	L	ERA	G	GS	CG	SV	SHO	IP	H	ER	BB	SO
Tim Crabtree	0	0	0.00	2	0	0	0	0	4.0	1	0	0	2
Rick Helling	0	1	4.50	1	1	0	0	0	6.0	8	3	1	9
Aaron Sele	0	1	6.00	1	1	0	0	0	6.0	8	4	1	4
Todd Stottlemyre	0	1	2.25	1	1	1	0	0	8.0	6	2	4	8
John Wetteland	0	0	0.00	1	0	0	0	0	1.0	0	0	1	1
TOTAL	0	3	3.24	6	3	1	0	0	25.0	23	9	7	24

GAME 1 AT NY SEPT 29

```
TEX  000 000 000   0 5 0
NY   020 000 00X   2 6 0
```
Pitchers: STOTTLEMYRE vs WELLS, Rivera (9)
Attendance: 57,362

GAME 2 AT NY SEPT 30

```
TEX  000 010 000   1 5 0
NY   010 200 00X   3 8 0
```
Pitchers: HELLING, Crabtree (7) vs PETTITTE, Nelson (8), Rivera (8)
Home Runs: Spencer-NY, Brosius-NY
Attendance: 57,360

GAME 3 AT TEX OCT 2

```
NY   000 004 000   4 9 1
TEX  000 000 000   0 3 1
```
Pitchers: CONE, Lloyd (6), Nelson (7), Rivera (9) vs SELE, Crabtree (7), Wetteland (9)
Home Runs: O'Neill-NY, Spencer-NY
Attendance: 49,450

SAN DIEGO PADRES (WEST) 4, ATLANTA BRAVES (EAST) 2

Good pitching and timely hitting sent the Padres to their first World Series in 14 years. The Braves, who were appearing in their seventh consecutive NLCS, missed the World Series after winning 100 games for the third time in five seasons. The first of four errors in the NLCS by first baseman Andres Galarraga gave the Padres a 2–1 lead against John Smoltz in the seventh inning of Game 1. But Trevor Hoffman, who had 53 saves during the season, could not hold the lead as Andruw Jones drove in the tying run in the ninth. Ken Caminiti homered in the 10th, and the Padres held on for the 3–2 win. Game 2 was all Kevin Brown. Not only did he pitch a three-hit shutout, he also had two hits and in the ninth scored an important insurance run.

The series shifted to the West Coast and the momentum stayed with the Padres. While Sterling Hitchcock labored through five innings, he trailed only 1–0 thanks to John Vander Wal, who threw out Walt Weiss at the plate to end the third inning. Hitchcock singled to open the bottom of the fifth and he came around to score on Steve Finley's double. Finley then scored on a single by Tony Gwynn. The Braves threatened in the top of the sixth, but Donne Wall came out of the bullpen and struck out pinch-hitters Ryan Klesko and Michael Tucker with three men on—one of three innings in which Atlanta left the bases loaded. The Braves were down, 3–2, in the seventh inning of Game 4 and were looking at the wrong end of a sweep when they finally exploded. Javier Lopez homered off a tiring Joey Hamilton to tie the game, and Galarraga capped the six-run seventh with a grand slam.

The Padres had a 4–2 lead in Game 5 when manager Bruce Bochy brought in his scheduled Game 6 starter, Kevin Brown, to pitch out of a jam in the seventh inning. He retired all three batters, but, in the eighth he surrendered a three-run home run to Michael Tucker, who drove in five runs. Atlanta added two more runs in the inning, which became crucial when Jim Leyritz hit a two-run homer off Kerry Ligtenberg in the ninth to make it 7–6. Greg Maddux, with four Cy Young Awards but no saves in his 12-year career, got the last

three outs. The Braves became the first team in postseason history to force a sixth game after trailing three games to none.

Tom Glavine and Hitchcock were locked in a scoreless pitcher's duel when the Padres bunched six hits for five runs in the sixth inning. The decisive play, however, occurred when left fielder Danny Bautista dropped Hitchcock's sinking line drive allowing two runs to score. Hitchcock, who combined with four relievers for a two-hitter, earned series MVP.

SD (W)

PLAYER/POS	AVG	G	AB	R	H	2B	3B	HR	RB	BB	SO	SB
Andy Ashby, p	.000	2	4	0	0	0	0	0	0	0	4	0
Brian Boehringer, p	.000	3	0	0	0	0	0	0	0	0	0	0
Kevin Brown, p	.500	2	4	1	2	0	0	0	0	0	1	0
Ken Caminiti, 3b	.273	6	22	3	6	0	0	2	4	5	4	0
Steve Finley, of	.333	6	21	3	7	1	0	0	2	6	2	1
Chris Gomez, ss	.150	6	20	2	3	0	0	0	0	2	5	0
Tony Gwynn, of	.231	6	26	1	6	1	0	0	2	1	2	0
Joey Hamilton, p	.000	2	2	0	0	0	0	0	0	0	1	0
Carlos Hernandez, c	.333	6	18	2	6	2	0	0	0	1	5	0
Sterling Hitchcock, p	.200	2	5	1	1	0	0	0	0	0	0	0
Trevor Hoffman, p	.000	3	0	0	0	0	0	0	0	0	0	0
Wally Joyner, 1b	.313	6	16	3	5	0	0	0	2	4	3	0
Mark Langston, p	.000	3	0	0	0	0	0	0	0	0	0	0
Jim Leyritz, 1b-3, c-2	.167	5	12	1	2	0	0	1	4	0	2	0
Dan Miceli, p	.000	3	0	0	0	0	0	0	0	0	0	0
Greg Myers, ph	1.000	2	1	1	1	0	0	1	2	1	0	0
Randy Myers, p	.000	4	0	0	0	0	0	0	0	0	0	0
Ruben Rivera, of	.231	6	13	1	3	2	0	0	0	0	7	1
Andy Sheets, ss-2	.000	3	3	0	0	0	0	0	0	0	1	0
Mark Sweeney, ph	.000	3	2	1	0	0	0	0	0	1	1	0
John Vander Wal, of-2	.429	3	7	1	3	0	0	1	2	0	2	0
Greg Vaughn, of-2	.250	3	8	1	2	0	0	0	0	1	1	0
Quilvio Veras, 2b	.250	6	24	2	6	1	0	0	0	5	7	0
Donne Wall, p	.000	3	0	0	0	0	0	0	0	0	0	0
TOTAL	.255		208	24	53	7	0	5	20	27	48	2

PITCHER	W	L	ERA	G	GS	CG	SV	SHO	IP	H	ER	BB	SO
Andy Ashby	0	0	2.08	2	2	0	0	0	13.0	14	3	2	5
Brian Boehringer	0	0	0.00	3	0	0	0	0	3.0	3	0	1	1
Kevin Brown	1	1	2.61	2	1	1	0	0	10.1	5	3	4	12
Joey Hamilton	0	1	4.91	2	1	0	0	0	7.1	7	4	3	6
Sterling Hitchcock	2	0	0.90	2	2	0	0	0	10.0	5	1	8	14
Trevor Hoffman	1	0	2.08	3	0	0	0	1	4.1	2	1	2	7
Mark Langston	0	0	0.00	3	0	0	0	0	1.1	1	0	0	1
Dan Miceli	0	0	13.50	3	0	0	0	0	0.2	4	1	0	1
Randy Myers	0	0	13.50	4	0	0	0	0	2.0	3	3	2	3
Donne Wall	0	0	3.00	3	0	0	0	1	3.0	3	1	4	4
TOTAL	4	2	2.78	27	6	1	2	0	55.0	47	17	26	54

ATL (E)

PLAYER/POS	AVG	G	AB	R	H	2B	3B	HR	RB	BB	SO	SB
Danny Bautista, of-4	.000	5	5	0	0	0	0	0	0	0	1	0
Greg Colbrunn, ph	.333	6	6	0	2	0	0	0	0	0	2	0
Andres Galarraga, 1b	.095	6	21	1	2	0	0	1	4	6	6	0
Tom Glavine, p-2	.250	3	4	0	1	0	0	0	0	1	2	0
Tony Graffanino, 2b-3	.333	4	3	2	1	1	0	0	1	2	1	0
Ozzie Guillen, ss-3	.417	4	12	1	5	0	0	0	1	0	1	0
Andruw Jones, of	.273	6	22	3	6	0	0	1	2	1	4	1
Chipper Jones, 3b	.208	6	24	2	5	1	0	0	1	4	5	0
Ryan Klesko, of	.083	5	12	2	1	0	0	0	1	6	3	0
Kerry Ligtenberg, p	.000	4	0	0	0	0	0	0	0	0	0	0
Keith Lockhart, 2b	.235	6	17	2	4	1	1	0	0	0	4	0
Javy Lopez, c	.300	6	20	2	6	0	0	1	1	0	7	0
Greg Maddux, p	.000	2	1	0	0	0	0	0	0	0	0	0
Marty Malloy, 2b-1	.000	4	1	1	0	0	0	0	0	0	0	0
Dennis Martinez, p	.000	4	0	0	0	0	0	0	0	0	0	0
Denny Neagle, p	.000	2	2	0	0	0	0	0	0	0	0	0
Eddie Perez, c	.750	3	4	0	3	0	0	0	0	0	0	0
Odaliz Perez, p	.000	2	0	0	0	0	0	0	0	0	0	0
John Rocker, p	.000	6	0	1	0	0	0	0	0	1	0	0
Rudy Seanez, p	.000	4	0	0	0	0	0	0	0	0	0	0
John Smoltz, p	.200	2	5	0	1	0	0	0	0	0	1	0
Michael Tucker, of-5	.385	6	13	1	5	1	0	1	5	2	5	0
Walt Weiss, ss	.200	4	15	0	3	0	0	0	1	2	5	1
Gerald Williams, of	.154	5	13	0	2	0	0	0	0	1	6	1
TOTAL	.235		200	18	47	4	1	4	17	26	54	3

PITCHER	W	L	ERA	G	GS	CG	SV	SHO	IP	H	ER	BB	SO
Tom Glavine	0	2	2.31	2	2	0	0	0	11.2	13	3	9	8
Kerry Ligtenberg	0	1	7.36	4	0	0	0	0	3.2	3	3	2	5
Greg Maddux	0	1	3.00	2	1	0	0	0	6.0	5	2	3	4
Dennis Martinez	1	0	0.00	4	0	0	0	0	3.1	1	0	1	0
Denny Neagle	0	0	3.52	2	1	0	0	0	7.2	8	3	2	9
Odaliz Perez	0	0	54.00	2	0	0	0	0	0.1	5	2	2	0
John Rocker	1	0	0.00	6	0	0	0	0	4.2	3	0	1	5
Rudy Seanez	0	0	6.00	4	0	0	0	0	3.0	2	2	1	4
John Smoltz	0	0	3.95	2	2	0	0	0	13.2	13	6	6	13
TOTAL	2	4	3.50	28	6	0	0	0	54.0	53	21	27	48

GAME 1 AT ATL OCT 7

SD 0 0 0 0 1 0 0 1 0 1   3 7 0
ATL 0 0 1 0 0 0 0 0 1 0   2 8 3
Pitchers: Ashby, R.Myers (8), Miceli (8), HOFFMAN (8), Wall (10) vs Smoltz, Rocker (8), Martinez (8), LIGTENBERG (9)
Home Runs: A.Jones-ATL, Caminiti-SD
Attendance: 42,117

GAME 2 AT ATL OCT 8

SD 0 0 0 0 0 1 0 0 2   3 11 0
ATL 0 0 0 0 0 0 0 0 0   0 3 1
Pitchers: BROWN vs GLAVINE, Rocker (7), Seanez (8), O.Perez (9), Ligtenberg (9)
Attendance: 43,083

GAME 3 AT SD OCT 10

ATL 0 0 1 0 0 0 0 0 0   1 8 2
SD 0 0 0 0 2 0 0 2 X   4 7 0
Pitchers: MADDUX, Martinez (6), Rocker (7), Seanez (8) vs HITCHCOCK, Wall (6), Miceli (8), R.Myers (8), Hoffman (8)
Attendance: 62,799

GAME 4 AT SD OCT 11

ATL 0 0 0 1 0 1 6 0 0   8 12 0
SD 0 0 2 0 0 1 0 0 0   3 8 0
Pitchers: Neagle, MARTINEZ (6), Rocker (7), O.Perez (8), Seanez (8), Ligtenberg (9) vs HAMILTON, Myers (7), Miceli (7), Boehringer (8), Langston (9)
Home Runs: Leyritz-SD, Lopez-ATL, Galarraga-ATL
Attendance: 65,042

GAME 5 AT SD OCT 12

ATL 0 0 0 1 0 1 0 5 0   7 14 1
SD 2 0 0 0 0 2 0 0 2   6 10 1
Pitchers: Smoltz, ROCKER (7), Seanez (8), Ligtenberg (9), Maddux (9) vs Ashby, Langston (7), BROWN (7), Wall (8), Boehringer (9), R.Myers (9)
Home Runs: Caminiti-SD, Vander Wal-SD, Tucker-ATL, G.Myers-SD
Attendance: 58,988

GAME 6 AT ATL OCT 14

SD 0 0 0 5 0 0 0 0 0   5 10 0
ATL 0 0 0 0 0 0 0 0 0   0 2 1
Pitchers: HITCHCOCK, Boehringer (6), Langston (7), Hamilton (7), Hoffman (9) vs GLAVINE, Rocker (6), Martinez (6), Neagle (8)
Attendance: 50,988

NEW YORK YANKEES (EAST) 4, CLEVELAND INDIANS (CENTRAL) 2

The Yankees, coming off a three-game sweep of Texas in the Division Series, handled the Indians easily to start the ALCS. New York scored five times in the first inning of Game 1 of the ALCS to knock out Indians starter Jaret Wright, who had been 2–0 against the Yankees in the 1997 Division Series. That was more than enough for David Wells, who pitched into the ninth inning of the 7–2 victory. Pitching and defense kept the Yankees and Indians tied at 1–1 through 11 innings the next afternoon, but it all fell apart for the Yankees in the top of the 12th. After a leadoff single by Jim Thome, Enrique Wilson came in to pinch run. Travis Fryman laid down a bunt that Tino Martinez errantly fired into Fryman's back. Chuck Knoblauch argued that Fryman had been out of the baseline and should be called out, but the Yankees second baseman made his protest while the play was still going on. By the time Knoblauch picked up the ball and threw home, Wilson had scored. The Indians won the argument and the game.

Bartolo Colon allowed just four hits in Game 3 to record the Tribe's first complete postseason game since the opening game of the 1954 World Series. Three home runs in the fifth inning (by Manny Ramirez, Jim Thome, and Mark Whiten) provided the power to give Cleveland a 2–1 series lead. The Yankees came back with a pitching gem of their own in Game 4 as rookie Orlando Hernandez teamed with two relievers to blank the Indians to even the ALCS. David Wells didn't have his best stuff and he wasn't in a good mood, but he still got the big outs when he needed to in Game 5. Angered by comments made by Cleveland fans as he warmed up, Wells shook off a rocky first inning to give the Yankees the lead in the series with a 5–3 win. Chili Davis drove in three runs in support of ALCS MVP Wells.

David Cone and Charles Nagy had both pitched splendidly in Game 2, but the hitters took charge in their rematch in Game 6. The Yankees grabbed a 6–0 lead after three innings as Cleveland played poor defense, and the Yankees took advantage of the wet grass to advance extra bases. The Indians nearly caught up with one

NY (E)

PLAYER/POS	AVG	G	AB	R	H	2B	3B	HR	RB	BB	SO	SB
Scott Brosius, 3b	.300	6	20	2	6	1	0	1	6	2	4	0
Homer Bush, dh-1	.000	2	0	1	0	0	0	0	0	0	0	1
David Cone, p	.000	2	0	0	0	0	0	0	0	0	0	0
Chad Curtis, of	.000	2	4	0	0	0	0	0	0	1	2	0
Chili Davis, dh	.286	5	14	2	4	1	0	1	5	2	3	0
Joe Girardi, c	.250	3	8	2	2	0	0	0	0	1	0	0
Orlando Hernandez, p	.000	1	0	0	0	0	0	0	0	0	0	0
Derek Jeter, ss	.200	6	25	3	5	1	1	0	2	2	5	3
Chuck Knoblauch, 2b	.200	6	25	4	5	1	0	0	0	4	2	0
Ricky Ledee, dh-1	.000	3	5	0	0	0	0	0	0	0	0	0
Graeme Lloyd, p	.000	1	0	0	0	0	0	0	0	0	0	0
Tino Martinez, 1b	.105	6	19	1	2	1	0	0	1	6	8	2
Ramiro Mendoza, p	.000	2	0	0	0	0	0	0	0	0	0	0
Jeff Nelson, p	.000	3	0	0	0	0	0	0	0	0	0	0
Paul O'Neill, of	.280	6	25	6	7	2	0	1	3	3	4	2
Andy Pettitte, p	.000	1	0	0	0	0	0	0	0	0	0	0
Jorge Posada, c	.182	5	11	1	2	0	0	1	2	4	2	0
Tim Raines, dh-2, of-1	.100	3	10	0	1	0	0	0	1	2	5	0
Mariano Rivera, p	.000	4	0	0	0	0	0	0	0	0	0	0
Luis Sojo, 1b	.000	1	0	0	0	0	0	0	0	0	0	0
Shane Spencer, of	.100	3	10	1	1	0	0	0	0	1	3	0
Mike Stanton, p	.000	3	0	0	0	0	0	0	0	0	0	0
David Wells, p	.000	2	0	0	0	0	0	0	0	0	0	0
Bernie Williams, of	.381	6	21	4	8	1	0	0	5	7	4	1
TOTAL	.218		197	27	43	8	1	4	25	35	42	9

PITCHER	W	L	ERA	G	GS	CG	SV	SHO	IP	H	ER	BB	SO
David Cone	1	0	4.15	2	2	0	0	0	13.0	12	6	6	13
O. Hernandez	1	0	0.00	1	1	0	0	0	7.0	3	0	2	6
Graeme Lloyd	0	0	0.00	1	0	0	0	0	0.2	1	0	0	0
Ramiro Mendoza	0	0	0.00	2	0	0	0	0	4.1	4	0	0	1
Jeff Nelson	0	1	20.25	3	0	0	0	0	1.1	3	3	1	3
Andy Pettitte	0	1	11.57	1	1	0	0	0	4.2	8	6	3	1
Mariano Rivera	0	0	0.00	4	0	0	1	0	5.2	0	0	1	5
Mike Stanton	0	0	0.00	3	0	0	0	0	3.2	2	0	1	4
David Wells	2	0	2.87	2	2	0	0	0	15.2	12	5	2	18
TOTAL	4	2	3.21	19	6	0	1	0	56.0	45	20	16	51

CLE (C)

PLAYER/POS	AVG	G	AB	R	H	2B	3B	HR	RB	BB	SO	SB
Sandy Alomar, c	.063	5	16	1	1	0	0	0	0	0	2	0
Paul Assenmacher, p	.000	3	0	0	0	0	0	0	0	0	0	0
Jeff Branson, ph	.000	1	1	0	0	0	0	0	0	0	0	0
Dave Burba, p	.000	3	0	0	0	0	0	0	0	0	0	0
Bartolo Colon, p	.000	1	0	0	0	0	0	0	0	0	0	0
Joey Cora, 2b	.143	2	7	1	1	0	0	0	0	2	1	0
Einar Diaz, c	.000	5	4	0	0	0	0	0	0	0	1	0
Travis Fryman, 3b	.174	6	23	2	4	0	0	0	0	1	5	1
Brian Giles, of	.083	4	12	0	1	0	0	0	0	1	3	0
Dwight Gooden, p	.000	1	0	0	0	0	0	0	0	0	0	0
Mike Jackson, p	.000	1	0	0	0	0	0	0	0	0	0	0
David Justice, dh-4, of-1	.158	6	19	2	3	0	0	1	2	3	3	0
Kenny Lofton, of	.185	6	27	2	5	1	0	1	3	1	7	1
Charles Nagy, p	.000	2	0	0	0	0	0	0	0	0	0	0
Chad Ogea, p	.000	2	0	0	0	0	0	0	0	0	0	0
Jim Poole, p	.000	4	0	0	0	0	0	0	0	0	0	0
Manny Ramirez, of	.333	6	21	2	7	1	0	2	4	4	9	0
Steve Reed, p	.000	5	0	0	0	0	0	0	0	0	0	0
Richie Sexson, 1b	.000	3	6	0	0	0	0	0	0	0	3	0
Paul Shuey, p	.000	5	0	0	0	0	0	0	0	0	0	0
Jim Thome, 1b-4, dh-2	.304	6	23	4	7	0	0	4	8	1	8	0
Omar Vizquel, ss	.440	6	25	2	11	0	1	0	0	1	3	4
Mark Whiten, of	.286	2	7	2	2	1	0	1	1	1	3	0
Enrique Wilson, 2b	.214	5	14	2	3	0	0	0	1	1	3	0
Jaret Wright, p	.000	2	0	0	0	0	0	0	0	0	0	0
TOTAL	.220		205	20	45	3	1	9	19	16	51	6

PITCHER	W	L	ERA	G	GS	CG	SV	SHO	IP	H	ER	BB	SO
Paul Assenmacher	0	0	0.00	3	0	0	0	0	2.0	0	0	0	3
Dave Burba	1	0	3.00	3	0	0	0	0	6.0	3	2	5	8
Bartolo Colon	1	0	1.00	1	1	1	0	0	9.0	4	1	4	3
Dwight Gooden	0	1	5.79	1	1	0	0	0	4.2	3	3	3	3
Mike Jackson	0	0	0.00	1	0	0	1	0	1.0	0	0	0	2
Charles Nagy	0	1	3.72	2	2	0	0	0	9.2	13	4	1	6
Chad Ogea	0	1	8.10	2	1	0	0	0	6.2	9	6	5	4
Jim Poole	0	0	0.00	4	0	0	0	0	1.1	0	0	1	2
Steve Reed	0	0	0.00	5	0	0	0	0	1.2	0	0	1	0
Paul Shuey	0	0	0.00	5	0	0	0	0	6.1	4	0	7	7
Jaret Wright	0	1	8.10	2	1	0	0	0	6.2	7	6	8	4
TOTAL	2	4	3.60	27	6	1	1	0	55.0	43	22	35	42

swing on a grand slam by Thome, his fourth homer of the series, to make it 6–5 in the fifth inning. Omar Vizquel's wild throw after a record-tying 74 postseason games without an error set up a three-run sixth inning that put the game, and the Yankees' 35th AL pennant, on ice.

GAME 1 AT NY OCT 6

```
CLE 000 000 002    2 5 0
NY  500 001 10X    7 11 0
```
Pitchers: WRIGHT, Ogea (1), Poole (7), Reed (7), Shuey (8) vs WELLS, Nelson (9)
Home Runs: Posada-NY, Ramirez-CLE
Attendance: 57,138

GAME 2 AT NY OCT 7

```
CLE 000 100 000003 4 8 1
NY  000 000 100000 1 7 1
```
Pitchers: Nagy, Reed (7), Poole (8), Shuey (8), Assenmacher (10), BURBA (11), Jackson (12) vs Cone, Rivera (9), Stanton (11), NELSON (11), Lloyd (12)
Home Runs: Justice-CLE
Attendance: 57,128

GAME 3 AT CLE OCT 9

```
NY  100 000 000    1 4 0
CLE 020 040 00X    6 12 0
```
Pitchers: PETTITTE, Mendoza (5), Stanton (7) vs COLON
Home Runs: Thome-CLE (2), Ramirez-CLE, Whiten-CLE
Attendance: 44,904

GAME 4 AT CLE OCT 10

```
NY  100 200 001    4 4 0
CLE 000 000 000    0 4 3
```
Pitchers: HERNANDEZ, Stanton (8), Rivera (9) vs GOODEN, Poole (5), Burba (6), Shuey (9)
Home Runs: O'Neill-NY
Attendance: 44,981

GAME 5 AT CLE OCT 11

```
NY  310 100 000    5 6 0
CLE 200 001 000    3 8 0
```
Pitchers: WELLS, Nelson (8), Rivera (8) vs OGEA, Wright (2), Reed (8), Assenmacher (8), Shuey (9)
Home Runs: Lofton-CLE, Davis-NY, Thome-CLE
Attendance: 44,966

GAME 6 AT NY OCT 13

```
CLE 000 050 000    5 8 3
NY  213 003 00X    9 11 1
```
Pitchers: NAGY, Burba (4), Poole (6), Shuey (6), Assenmacher (8) vs CONE, Mendoza (6), Rivera (9)
Home Runs: Brosius-NY, Thome-CLE
Attendance: 57,142

NEW YORK YANKEES (AL) 4, SAN DIEGO PADRES (NL) 0

The World Series opened with the two hottest pitchers of the postseason facing each other, but neither New York's David Wells nor San Diego's Kevin Brown had their best stuff. The Yankees struck for two runs off Brown in the second inning, but three home runs—two by Greg Vaughn and one by Tony Gwynn—staked the Padres to a 5–2 lead. In the seventh Donne Wall relieved Brown with two runners on and Chuck Knoblauch promptly tied the game with a home run. A few batters later Tino Martinez launched a grand slam off Mark Langston to cap New York's seven-run seventh.

The Yankees jumped on the Padres for seven runs in the first three innings of Game 2. Paul O'Neill made a running catch to rob Wally Joyner of a hit with two runners on base in the top of the first, and a walk and a throwing error by San Diego set up New York for three runs in the bottom of the inning. Bernie Williams capped off a three-run second with a home run and Jorge Posada added a two-run shot of his own three innings later.

The Padres returned home and put the first three runs of the game across the plate in the sixth inning against David Cone. Padres pitcher Sterling Hitchcock started the rally with a single, and a throwing error by O'Neill kept it going. Scott Brosius led off the seventh with a home run, and a passed ball and an error made it a 3–2 game. With closer Trevor Hoffman pitching in the eighth with two runners aboard, Brosius hit his second homer in as many innings and the Yankees held on for a 5–4 win.

Andy Pettitte, pitching for the first time in 10 days, combined with Jeff Nelson and Mariano Rivera to blank the Padres on seven hits in Game 4. The Yankees, showing that they could win in a variety of ways, scored once on a groundout in the sixth and added two insurance runs off Brown on Brosius' sixth RBI in four games plus a sacrifice fly by Ricky Ledee. Mark Sweeney ended the game, fittingly, with a grounder to MVP Brosius, and the Yankees had their 24th world championship.

NY (A)

PLAYER/POS	AVG	G	AB	R	H	2B	3B	HR	RB	BB	SO	SB
Scott Brosius, 3b	.471	4	17	3	8	0	0	2	6	0	4	0
Homer Bush, dh-1	.000	2	0	0	0	0	0	0	0	0	0	0
David Cone, p	.500	1	2	0	1	0	0	0	0	0	0	0
Chili Davis, dh-2	.286	3	7	3	2	0	0	0	2	3	2	0
Joe Girardi, c	.000	2	6	0	0	0	0	0	0	0	2	0
Orlando Hernandez, p	.000	1	0	0	0	0	0	0	0	0	0	0
Derek Jeter, ss	.353	4	17	4	6	0	0	0	1	3	3	0
Chuck Knoblauch, 2b	.375	4	16	3	6	0	0	1	3	3	2	1
Ricky Ledee, of	.600	4	10	1	6	3	0	0	4	2	1	0
Graeme Lloyd, p	.000	1	0	0	0	0	0	0	0	0	0	0
Tino Martinez, 1b	.385	4	13	4	5	0	0	1	4	4	2	0
Ramiro Mendoza, p	.000	1	1	0	0	0	0	0	0	0	0	0
Jeff Nelson, p	.000	3	0	0	0	0	0	0	0	0	0	0
Paul O'Neill, of	.211	4	19	3	4	1	0	0	0	1	2	0
Andy Pettitte, p	.000	1	2	0	0	0	0	0	0	0	2	0
Jorge Posada, c	.333	3	9	2	3	0	0	1	2	2	2	0
Mariano Rivera, p	.000	3	1	0	0	0	0	0	0	0	0	0
Shane Spencer, of	.333	1	3	1	1	1	0	0	0	0	2	0
Mike Stanton, p	.000	1	0	0	0	0	0	0	0	0	0	0
David Wells, p	.000	1	0	0	0	0	0	0	0	0	0	0
Bernie Williams, of	.063	4	16	2	1	0	0	1	3	2	5	0
TOTAL	.309		139	26	43	5	0	6	25	20	29	1

PITCHER	W	L	ERA	G	GS	CG	SV	SHO	IP	H	ER	BB	SO
David Cone	0	0	3.00	1	1	0	0	0	6.0	2	2	3	4
O. Hernandez	1	0	1.29	1	1	0	0	0	7.0	6	1	3	7
Graeme Lloyd	0	0	0.00	1	0	0	0	0	0.1	0	0	0	0
Ramiro Mendoza	1	0	9.00	1	0	0	0	0	1.0	2	1	0	1
Jeff Nelson	0	0	0.00	3	0	0	0	0	2.1	2	0	1	4
Andy Pettitte	1	0	0.00	1	1	0	0	0	7.1	5	0	3	4
Mariano Rivera	0	0	0.00	3	0	0	3	0	4.1	5	0	0	4
Mike Stanton	0	0	27.00	1	0	0	0	0	0.2	3	2	0	1
David Wells	1	0	6.43	1	1	0	0	0	7.0	7	5	2	4
TOTAL	4	0	2.75	13	4	0	3	0	36.0	32	11	12	29

SD (N)

PLAYER/POS	AVG	G	AB	R	H	2B	3B	HR	RB	BB	SO	SB
Andy Ashby, p	.000	1	0	0	0	0	0	0	0	0	0	0
Brian Boehringer, p	.000	2	0	0	0	0	0	0	0	0	0	0
Kevin Brown, p	.500	2	2	0	1	0	0	0	0	0	0	0
Ken Caminiti, 3b	.143	4	14	1	2	1	0	0	1	2	7	0
Steve Finley, of	.083	3	12	0	1	1	0	0	0	0	2	1
Chris Gomez, ss	.364	4	11	2	4	0	0	1	0	1	1	0
Tony Gwynn, of	.500	4	16	2	8	0	0	1	3	1	0	0
Joey Hamilton, p	.000	1	0	0	0	0	0	0	0	0	0	0
Carlos Hernandez, c	.200	4	10	0	2	0	0	0	0	0	3	0
Sterling Hitchcock, p	.500	1	2	1	1	0	0	0	0	0	0	0
Trevor Hoffman, p	.000	1	0	0	0	0	0	0	0	0	0	0
Wally Joyner, 1b	.000	3	8	0	0	0	0	0	0	3	1	0
Mark Langston, p	.000	1	0	0	0	0	0	0	0	0	0	0
Jim Leyritz, 1b-2, c-1, dh-1	.000	4	10	0	0	0	0	0	0	1	4	0
Dan Miceli, p	.000	2	0	0	0	0	0	0	0	0	0	0
Greg Myers, c-1	.000	2	4	0	0	0	0	0	0	0	2	0
Randy Myers, p	.000	3	0	0	0	0	0	0	0	0	0	0
Ruben Rivera, of	.800	3	5	1	4	2	0	0	1	0	0	0
Andy Sheets, ss	.000	2	2	0	0	0	0	0	0	0	1	0
Mark Sweeney, ph	.667	3	3	0	2	0	0	0	1	0	0	0
John Vander Wal, of-1	.400	4	5	0	2	1	0	0	0	0	0	0
Greg Vaughn, of-3, dh-1	.133	4	15	3	2	0	0	2	4	1	2	0
Quilvio Veras, 2b	.200	4	15	3	3	2	0	0	1	3	4	0
Donne Wall, p	.000	2	0	0	0	0	0	0	0	0	0	0
TOTAL	.239		134	13	32	7	1	3	11	12	29	1

PITCHER	W	L	ERA	G	GS	CG	SV	SHO	IP	H	ER	BB	SO
Andy Ashby	0	1	13.50	1	1	0	0	0	2.2	10	4	1	1
Brian Boehringer	0	0	9.00	2	0	0	0	0	2.0	4	2	2	3
Kevin Brown	0	1	4.40	2	2	0	0	0	14.1	14	7	6	13
Joey Hamilton	0	0	0.00	1	0	0	0	0	1.0	0	0	1	1
Sterling Hitchcock	0	0	1.50	1	1	0	0	0	6.0	7	1	1	7
Trevor Hoffman	1	9	1.00	0	0	0	0	0	2.0	2	2	1	0
Mark Langston	0	4	0.50	1	0	0	0	0	0.2	1	3	2	0
Dan Miceli	0	0	0.00	2	0	0	0	0	1.2	2	0	2	1
Randy Myers	0	0	9.00	3	0	0	0	0	1.0	0	1	1	2
Donne Wall	0	1	6.75	2	0	0	0	0	2.2	3	2	3	1
TOTAL	0	4	5.82	16	4	0	0	0	34.0	43	22	20	29

GAME 1 AT NY OCT 17

```
SD  002 030 010  6 8 1
NY  020 000 70X  9 9 1
```
Pitchers: Brown, WALL (7), Langston (7), Boehringer (8), R.Myers (8) vs WELLS, Nelson (8), Rivera (8)
Home Runs: Vaughn-SD (2), Gwynn-SD, Knoblauch-NY, Martinez-NY
Attendance: 56,712

GAME 2 AT NY OCT 18

```
SD  000 010 020  3 10 1
NY  331 020 00X  9 16 0
```
Pitchers: ASHBY, Boehringer (3), Wall (5), Miceli (8) vs HERNANDEZ, Stanton (8), Nelson (8)
Home Runs: Williams-NY, Posada-NY
Attendance: 56,692

GAME 3 AT SD OCT 20

```
NY  000 000 230  5 9 1
SD  000 003 010  4 7 1
```
Pitchers: Cone, Lloyd (7), MENDOZA (7), Rivera (9) vs Hitchcock, Hamilton (7), R. Myers (8), HOFFMAN (8)
Home Runs: Brosius-NY (2)
Attendance: 64,667

GAME 4 AT SD OCT 21

```
NY  000 001 020  3 9 0
SD  000 000 000  0 7 0
```
Pitchers: PETTITTE, Nelson (8), Rivera (8) vs BROWN, Miceli (9), R. Myers (9)
Attendance: 65,427

ATLANTA BRAVES (EAST) 3, HOUSTON ASTROS (CENTRAL) 1

The Atlanta Braves, with eight consecutive division titles to their credit, had won 10 consecutive Division Series games heading into Game 1 at Turner Field. Houston's Daryle Ward broke a 1–1 tie in the sixth inning with a home run off Greg Maddux, and Ken Caminiti's three-run homer in the ninth wrapped up the scoring. Shane Reynolds pitched out of several jams to earn the win for the Astros.

Caminiti homered in the second inning of Game 2; Kevin Millwood allowed nothing else. He struck out eight and walked none in his first postseason appearance. In contrast to Houston's one hit, the Braves had 11 hits, including three by Ryan Klesko.

In Game 3 the Braves wriggled out of trouble in inning after inning at the Astrodome. Starter Tom Glavine allowed an RBI-single to Caminiti and walked a run in the first, but a line drive out ended the inning. The Astros tied it in the seventh on a single by Bill Spiers, but Mike Remlinger struck out Caminiti and Matt Mieske flied out to end the threat. The Astros loaded the bases on two hits and a walk with none out in the 10th. Reliever John Rocker induced Carl Everett to ground into a force play at home for the first out. With the infield in, Tony Eusebio hit a bullet up the middle that knocked Walt Weiss' glove off, but the shortstop grabbed the ball and threw home for a force play. Rocker fanned Ricky Gutierrez to end the inning. Brian Jordan doubled home two runs in the top of the 12th for a 5–3 lead. Millwood, like Maddux earlier in the game, made a rare bullpen appearance. He retired the side in order for the save.

The Braves scored five times on seven singles in the sixth inning in Game 5. Houston crawled back in the game on Eusebio's solo homer in the seventh and Caminiti's three-run shot in the eighth. Rocker came on to strike out Craig Biggio with a runner on third to end the threat. The Braves held on for the 7–5 win to take the series in the final game played at the Astrodome.

ATL (E)

PLAYER/POS	AVG	G	AB	R	H	2B	3B	HR	RB	BB	SO	SB
Howard Battle, ph	.000	1	1	0	0	0	0	0	0	0	0	0
Bret Boone, 2b	.474	4	19	3	9	1	0	0	1	0	4	1
Tom Glavine, p	.000	1	2	0	0	0	0	0	0	0	1	0
Ozzie Guillen, ph	.000	1	1	0	0	0	0	0	0	0	0	0
Jose Hernandez, ss	.091	4	11	1	1	0	0	0	0	1	3	1
Brian Hunter, 1b	.000	3	4	0	0	0	0	0	0	1	3	0
Andruw Jones, of	.222	4	18	1	4	1	0	0	2	1	3	0
Chipper Jones, 3b	.231	4	13	2	3	0	0	0	1	5	2	0
Brian Jordan, of	.471	4	17	2	8	1	0	1	7	1	2	0
Ryan Klesko, 1b	.333	4	12	3	4	0	0	0	1	1	4	0
Keith Lockhart, 2b-1	.000	3	1	0	0	0	0	0	0	0	1	0
Greg Maddux, p	.000	2	1	0	0	0	0	0	0	0	0	0
Kevin McGlinchy, p	.000	1	0	0	0	0	0	0	0	0	0	0
Kevin Millwood, p	.250	2	4	0	1	0	0	0	0	0	3	0
Terry Mulholland, p	.000	2	0	0	0	0	0	0	0	0	0	0
Otis Nixon, of	1.000	1	1	1	1	0	0	0	0	0	0	1
Eddie Perez, c	.250	0	16	1	4	0	0	0	3	0	3	0
Mike Remlinger, p	.000	2	0	0	0	0	0	0	0	0	0	0
John Rocker, p	.000	2	0	0	0	0	0	0	0	0	1	0
John Smoltz, p	.667	1	3	1	2	1	0	0	0	0	1	0
Russ Springer, p	.000	1	0	0	0	0	0	0	0	0	0	0
Walt Weiss, ss	.167	3	6	1	1	0	0	0	0	0	2	0
Gerald Williams, of	.389	4	18	2	7	1	0	0	3	0	3	1
TOTAL	.304		148	18	45	5	0	1	18	11	35	4

PITCHER	W	L	ERA	G	GS	CG	SV	SHO	IP	H	ER	BB	SO
Tom Glavine	0	0	3.00	1	1	0	0	0	6.0	5	2	3	6
Greg Maddux	0	1	2.57	2	1	0	0	0	7.0	10	2	5	5
Kevin McGlinchy	0	0	0.00	1	0	0	0	0	0.1	0	0	0	0
Kevin Millwood	1	0	0.90	2	1	1	1	0	10.0	1	1	0	9
Terry Mulholland	0	0	27.00	2	0	0	0	0	0.2	3	2	0	0
Mike Remlinger	0	0	9.82	2	0	0	0	0	3.2	4	4	3	4
John Rocker	1	0	0.00	2	0	0	1	0	3.1	0	0	2	5
John Smoltz	1	0	5.14	1	1	0	0	0	7.0	6	4	3	3
Russ Springer	0	0	0.00	1	0	0	0	0	1.0	2	0	1	1
TOTAL	3	1	3.46	14	4	1	2	0	39.0	31	15	17	33

HOU (C)

PLAYER/POS	AVG	G	AB	R	H	2B	3B	HR	RB	BB	SO	SB
Jeff Bagwell, 1b	.154	4	13	3	2	0	0	0	0	5	4	0
Glen Barker, of	.000	2	3	1	0	0	0	0	0	0	2	1
Derek Bell, of-1	.333	2	3	0	1	0	0	0	0	0	0	0
Craig Biggio, 2b	.105	4	19	1	2	0	0	0	0	1	5	0
Tim Bogar, ss-1	.750	2	4	0	3	1	0	0	1	1	0	0
Jose Cabrera, p	.000	1	0	0	0	0	0	0	0	0	0	0
Ken Caminiti, 3b	.471	4	17	3	8	0	0	3	8	2	1	0
Scott Elarton, p	.000	2	0	0	0	0	0	0	0	0	0	0
Tony Eusebio, c	.267	4	15	2	4	0	0	1	3	1	2	0
Carl Everett, of	.133	4	15	2	2	0	0	0	1	2	8	0
Ricky Gutierrez, ss	.000	3	10	0	0	0	0	0	0	2	5	0
Mike Hampton, p	.000	1	2	0	0	0	0	0	0	0	1	0
Doug Henry, p	.000	2	0	0	0	0	0	0	0	0	0	0
Chris Holt, p	.000	1	0	0	0	0	0	0	0	0	0	0
Stan Javier, of	.273	4	11	1	3	0	0	0	0	1	1	0
Russ Johnson, ph	1.000	2	1	0	1	1	0	0	0	1	0	0
Jose Lima, p	.000	1	2	0	0	0	0	0	0	0	1	0
Matt Mieske, of-1	.000	2	4	1	0	0	0	0	0	1	0	0
Trever Miller, p	.000	2	0	0	0	0	0	0	0	0	0	0
Jay Powell, p	.000	3	0	0	0	0	0	0	0	0	0	0
Shane Reynolds, p	.250	2	4	0	1	0	0	0	0	0	1	0
Bill Spiers, of-3	.273	4	11	0	3	0	0	0	1	0	1	1
Billy Wagner, p	.000	1	0	0	0	0	0	0	0	0	0	0
Daryle Ward, of-2	.143	3	7	1	1	0	0	1	1	0	2	0
TOTAL	.220		141	15	31	2	0	5	15	17	33	2

PITCHER	W	L	ERA	G	GS	CG	SV	SHO	IP	H	ER	BB	SO
Jose Cabrera	0	0	0.00	1	0	0	0	0	2.0	2	0	0	6
Scott Elarton	0	0	3.86	2	0	0	0	0	2.1	4	1	1	3
Mike Hampton	0	0	3.86	1	1	0	0	0	7.0	6	3	1	9
Doug Henry	0	0	0.00	2	0	0	0	0	3.2	1	0	3	2
Chris Holt	0	0	∞	1	0	0	0	0	0.0	3	3	0	0
Jose Lima	0	1	5.40	1	1	0	0	0	6.2	9	4	2	4
Trever Miller	0	0	0.00	2	0	0	0	0	1.1	1	0	0	2
Jay Powell	0	1	6.00	3	0	0	0	0	3.0	3	2	1	3
Shane Reynolds	1	1	4.09	2	2	0	0	0	11.0	16	5	3	5
Billy Wagner	0	0	0.00	1	0	0	0	0	1.0	0	0	0	1
TOTAL	1	3	4.26	16	4	0	0	0	38.0	45	18	11	35

GAME 1 AT ATL OCT 5

```
HOU 010 001 004    6 13 0
ATL 000 010 000    1  7 0
```
Pitchers: REYNOLDS, Miller (7), Henry (7), Wagner (9) vs MADDUX, Remlinger (8)
Home Runs: Ward-HOU, Caminiti-HOU
Attendance: 39,119

GAME 2 AT ATL OCT 6

```
HOU 010 000 000    1  1 1
ATL 100 001 30X    5 11 1
```
Pitchers: LIMA, Elarton (7), Powell (8) vs MILLWOOD
Home Runs: Caminiti-HOU
Attendance: 41,913

GAME 3 AT HOU OCT 8

```
ATL 000000 000 002 5 12 0
HOU 200000 100 000 3  9 2
```
Pitchers: Glavine, Mulholland (7), Maddux (8), Remlinger (7), Springer (9), ROCKER (10), Millwood (12) vs Hampton, Cabrera (8), Henry (10), POWELL (12)
Home Runs: Jordan-ATL
Attendance: 48,625

GAME 4 AT HOU OCT 9

```
ATL 101 005 000    7 15 1
HOU 000 000 140    5  8 1
```
Pitchers: SMOLTZ, Mulholland (8), McGlinchy (8), Rocker (8) vs REYNOLDS, Holt (6), Elarton (6), Miller (8), Powell (9)
Home Runs: Eusebio-HOU, Caminiti-HOU
Attendance: 48,553

NEW YORK METS (WILD CARD) 3, ARIZONA DIAMONDBACKS (WEST) 1

The New York Mets had to win their last four games, including a one-game playoff in Cincinnati, to earn their first postseason berth since 1988. The Arizona Diamondbacks, only in their second year of existence, won 100 games and cruised to the National League West title.

Randy Johnson had early problems against the Mets in Game 1 of the Division Series, yet the Diamondbacks rallied to tie the score against Masato Yoshii. Johnson filled the bases in the ninth and left in favor of rookie Bobby Chouinard. Matt Williams made a diving stop and threw home for the force play for the second out, but Edgardo Alfonzo followed with his second home run of the game. Johnson suffered his sixth consecutive postseason loss.

Todd Stottlemyre, pitching with a 70 percent tear of his rotator cuff, allowed just four hits in 6-2/3 innings to win Game 2. Steve Finley drove in five runs and Matt Williams had three hits in Arizona's first postseason victory. Mike Piazza was on the bench in Game 3 because of a bad reaction to a cortisone shot to his left hand. The Mets made up for his absence with 11 hits and eight walks in a 9–2 victory. Rickey Henderson added his sixth stolen base in three games to set a Division Series record.

Al Leiter nursed a 2–1 lead into the eighth inning of Game 4. He left after Tony Womack's infield hit, and Jay Bell followed with a two-run double off Armando Benitez. The inning ended when defensive replacement Melvin Mora threw out Bell trying to score on a single. In the bottom of the inning, Womack, who had just moved from shortstop to right field, dropped a flyball. The Mets tied the game on Roger Cedeno's sacrifice fly. Piazza's replacement Todd Pratt homered off Matt Mantei in the bottom of the 10th inning to set off a raucous celebration at Shea Stadium.

NY (WC)

PLAYER/POS	AVG	G	AB	R	H	2B	3B	HR	RBI	BB	SO	SB
Benny Agbayani, of	.300	4	10	1	3	1	0	0	1	0	3	0
Edgardo Alfonzo, 2b	.250	4	16	6	4	1	0	3	6	3	2	0
Armando Benitez, p	.000	2	0	0	0	0	0	0	0	0	0	0
Bobby Bonilla, ph	.000	2	1	1	0	0	0	0	0	1	0	0
Roger Cedeno, of	.286	4	7	1	2	0	0	0	2	1	1	1
Dennis Cook, p	.000	1	0	0	0	0	0	0	0	0	0	0
Octavio Dotel, p	.000	1	0	0	0	0	0	0	0	0	0	0
Shawon Dunston, of-2	.167	4	6	0	1	0	0	0	0	0	1	0
John Franco, p	.000	3	0	0	0	0	0	0	0	0	0	0
Matt Franco, ph	.000	1	0	0	0	0	0	0	0	1	0	0
Darryl Hamilton, of	.125	4	8	0	1	0	0	0	2	2	0	0
Rickey Henderson, of	.400	4	15	5	6	0	0	0	1	3	1	6
Orel Hershiser, p	.000	1	0	0	0	0	0	0	0	0	0	0
Al Leiter, p	.000	1	3	0	0	0	0	0	0	0	2	0
Pat Mahomes, p	.000	1	0	0	0	0	0	0	0	0	0	0
Melvin Mora, of	.000	3	1	1	0	0	0	0	0	1	0	0
John Olerud, 1b	.438	4	16	3	7	0	0	1	6	3	2	0
Rey Ordonez, ss	.286	4	14	1	4	1	0	0	2	0	5	1
Mike Piazza, c	.222	2	9	0	2	0	0	0	0	0	4	0
Todd Pratt, c-2	.125	3	8	2	1	0	0	1	1	2	1	0
Rick Reed, p	.000	1	1	0	0	0	0	0	0	0	1	0
Kenny Rogers, p	.000	1	2	0	0	0	0	0	0	0	1	0
Robin Ventura, 3b	.214	4	14	1	3	2	0	0	1	4	2	0
Turk Wendell, p	.000	2	1	0	0	0	0	0	0	0	1	0
Masato Yoshii, p	.000	2	2	0	0	0	0	0	0	0	1	0
TOTAL	.254		134	22	34	5	0	5	22	21	28	8

PITCHER	W	L	ERA	G	GS	CG	SV	SHO	IP	H	ER	BB	SO
Armando Benitez	0	0	0.00	2	0	0	0	0	2.1	2	0	1	2
Dennis Cook	0	0	0.00	1	0	0	0	0	1.2	1	0	1	1
Octavio Dotel	0	0	54.00	1	0	0	0	0	0.1	1	2	2	0
John Franco	1	0	0.00	3	0	0	0	0	3.2	1	0	0	2
Orel Hershiser	0	0	0.00	1	0	0	0	0	1.0	0	0	0	1
Al Leiter	0	0	3.52	1	1	0	0	0	7.2	3	3	3	4
Pat Mahomes	0	0	5.40	1	0	0	0	0	1.2	3	1	0	1
Rick Reed	1	0	3.00	1	1	0	0	0	6.0	4	2	3	2
Kenny Rogers	0	1	8.31	1	1	0	0	0	4.1	5	4	2	6
Turk Wendell	1	0	0.00	2	0	0	0	0	2.0	0	0	2	0
Masato Yoshii	0	0	6.75	1	1	0	0	0	5.1	6	4	0	3
TOTAL	3	1	4.00	15	4	0	0	0	36.0	26	16	14	22

ARI (W)

PLAYER/POS	AVG	G	AB	R	H	2B	3B	HR	RBI	BB	SO	SB
Brian Anderson, p	.000	1	2	0	0	0	0	0	0	0	0	0
Jay Bell, 2b	.286	4	14	3	4	1	0	0	3	1	0	0
Bobby Chouinard, p	.000	2	0	0	0	0	0	0	0	0	0	0
Greg Colbrunn, 1b	.400	2	5	1	2	1	0	1	2	2	2	0
Omar Daal, p	.000	1	1	0	0	0	0	0	0	0	1	0
Erubiel Durazo, 1b	.143	2	7	1	1	0	0	1	1	1	1	0
Steve Finley, of	.385	4	13	0	5	1	0	0	5	3	1	0
Andy Fox, ss	.000	1	3	0	0	0	0	0	0	0	1	0
Hanley Frias, ss	.000	4	7	0	0	0	0	0	0	0	3	0
Bernard Gilkey, of	.000	2	6	0	0	0	0	0	0	0	0	0
Luis Gonzalez, of	.200	4	10	3	2	1	0	1	2	5	1	0
Lenny Harris, 3b-1	.000	2	2	0	0	0	0	0	0	0	0	0
Darren Holmes, p	.000	1	0	0	0	0	0	0	0	0	0	0
Randy Johnson, p	.333	1	3	0	1	1	0	0	0	0	1	0
Matt Mantei, p	.000	1	0	0	0	0	0	0	0	0	0	0
Gregg Olson, p	.000	2	0	0	0	0	0	0	0	0	0	0
Dan Plesac, p	.000	1	0	0	0	0	0	0	0	0	0	0
Kelly Stinnett, c	.143	4	14	1	2	1	0	0	0	1	4	0
Todd Stottlemyre, p	.000	1	3	0	0	0	0	0	0	0	1	0
Greg Swindell, p	.000	3	0	0	0	0	0	0	0	0	0	0
Turner Ward, ph	.500	3	2	2	1	0	0	1	3	1	0	0
Matt Williams, 3b	.375	4	16	3	6	1	0	0	0	0	1	0
Tony Womack, of-4, ss-2	.111	4	18	2	2	0	1	0	0	0	6	0
TOTAL	.206		126	16	26	7	1	4	16	14	22	0

PITCHER	W	L	ERA	G	GS	CG	SV	SHO	IP	H	ER	BB	SO
Brian Anderson	0	0	2.57	1	1	0	0	0	7.0	7	2	0	4
Bobby Chouinard	0	0	4.50	2	0	0	0	0	2.0	3	1	0	1
Omar Daal	0	1	6.75	1	1	0	0	0	4.0	6	3	3	4
Darren Holmes	0	0	27.00	1	0	0	0	0	1.1	1	4	3	0
Randy Johnson	0	1	7.56	1	1	0	0	0	8.1	8	7	3	11
Matt Mantei	0	1	4.50	1	0	0	0	0	2.0	1	1	3	1
Gregg Olson	0	0	0.00	2	0	0	0	0	0.1	0	0	1	0
Dan Plesac	0	0	54.00	1	0	0	0	0	0.1	3	2	0	0
Todd Stottlemyre	1	0	1.35	1	1	0	0	0	6.2	4	1	5	6
Greg Swindell	0	0	0.00	3	0	0	0	0	3.1	1	0	3	1
TOTAL	1	3	5.35	15	4	0	0	0	35.1	34	21	21	28

GAME 1 AT ARI OCT 5

```
NY   102 100 004   8 10 0
ARI  001 102 000   4  7 0
```
Pitchers: Yoshii, Cook (6), WENDELL (8), Benitez (9) vs JOHNSON, Chouinard (9)
Home Runs: Alfonzo-NY (2), Olerud-NY, Durazo-ARI, Gonzalez-ARI
Attendance: 49,584

GAME 2 AT ARI OCT 6

```
NY   001 000 000   1 5 0
ARI  003 020 20X   7 9 1
```
Pitchers: ROGERS, Mahomes (5), Dotel (7), J.Franco (7) vs STOTTLEMYRE, Olson (7), Swindell (8)
Attendance: 49,328

GAME 3 AT NY OCT 8

```
ARI  000 020 000   2  5 3
NY   012 006 00X   9 11 0
```
Pitchers: DAAL, Holmes (5), Plesac (6), Chouinard (6), Swindell (8) vs REED, Wendell (7), J.Franco (8), Hershiser (9)
Home Runs: Ward-ARI
Attendance: 56,180

GAME 4 AT NY OCT 9

```
ARI  000 010 0200    3 5 1
NY   000 101 0101    4 8 0
```
Pitchers: Anderson, Olson (8), Swindell (8), MANTEI (8) vs Leiter, Benitez (8), J.FRANCO (10)
Home Runs: Alfonzo-NY, Colbrunn-ARI, Pratt-NY
Attendance: 56,177

NEW YORK YANKEES (EAST) 3, TEXAS RANGERS (WEST) 0

The New York Yankees limited the Texas Rangers to one run in three games for the second straight year. After losing their first Division Series game to Texas in 1996, the Yankees won nine consecutive postseason games against the Rangers. Orlando Hernandez made easy work of Texas in Game 1. He and two relievers combined on a two-hit shutout. Bernie Williams drove in six runs with three hits and added a sliding catch to stymie the Rangers.

Texas scored its lone run of the series in fourth inning of Game 2 on a home run by Juan Gonzalez. Scott Brosius tied the game with a double in the sixth, Ricky Ledee gave New York the lead with a seventh-inning double, and a bases-loaded walk added a third run in the eighth. Andy Pettitte survived seven hits to gain the victory.

Roger Clemens clinched the series for the Yankees in his native Texas. He allowed only three hits in seven innings, and Mariano Rivera pitched two scoreless innings for his second save of the series. Darryl Strawberry provided all the offensive support with a two-out, three-run home run in the first inning against Esteban Loaiza.

NY (E)

PLAYER/POS	AVG	G	AB	R	H	2B	3B	HR	RB	BB	SO	SB
Clay Bellinger, dh	.000	1	0	0	0	0	0	0	0	0	0	0
Scott Brosius, 3b	.100	3	10	0	1	1	0	0	1	0	0	0
Roger Clemens, p	.000	1	0	0	0	0	0	0	0	0	0	0
Chad Curtis, of	.000	3	3	1	0	0	0	0	0	0	0	0
Chili Davis, dh	.333	1	3	0	1	0	0	0	0	0	2	0
Joe Girardi, c	.000	2	6	0	0	0	0	0	0	0	1	0
Orlando Hernandez, p	.000	1	0	0	0	0	0	0	0	0	0	0
Derek Jeter, ss	.455	3	11	3	5	1	1	0	0	2	3	0
Chuck Knoblauch, 2b	.167	3	12	1	2	0	0	0	0	1	3	0
Ricky Ledee, of	.273	3	11	1	3	2	0	0	2	1	5	0
Jim Leyritz, dh	.000	2	2	0	0	0	0	0	0	1	1	0
Tino Martinez, 1b	.182	3	11	2	2	0	0	0	0	2	2	0
Jeff Nelson, p	.000	3	0	0	0	0	0	0	0	0	0	0
Paul O'Neill, of	.250	3	8	2	2	0	0	0	0	0	1	0
Andy Pettitte, p	.000	1	0	0	0	0	0	0	0	0	0	0
Jorge Posada, c	.250	1	4	0	1	1	0	0	0	0	0	0
Mariano Rivera, p	.000	2	0	0	0	0	0	0	0	0	0	0
Darryl Strawberry, dh	.333	2	6	2	2	0	0	1	3	1	0	0
Bernie Williams, of	.364	3	11	2	4	1	0	1	6	1	2	0
TOTAL	.235		98	14	23	6	1	2	13	10	19	0

PITCHER	W	L	ERA	G	GS	CG	SV	SHO	IP	H	ER	BB	SO
Roger Clemens	1	0	0.00	1	1	0	0	0	7.0	3	0	2	2
O. Hernandez	1	0	0.00	1	1	0	0	0	8.0	2	0	6	4
Jeff Nelson	0	0	0.00	3	0	0	0	0	1.2	1	0	1	3
Andy Pettitte	1	0	1.23	1	1	0	0	0	7.1	7	1	0	5
Mariano Rivera	0	0	0.00	2	0	0	2	0	3.0	1	0	0	3
TOTAL	3	0	0.33	8	3	0	2	0	27.0	14	1	9	17

TEX (W)

PLAYER/POS	AVG	G	AB	R	H	2B	3B	HR	RB	BB	SO	SB
Royce Clayton, ss	.000	3	10	0	0	0	0	0	0	0	1	0
Tim Crabtree, p	.000	2	0	0	0	0	0	0	0	0	0	0
Jeff Fassero, p	.000	1	0	0	0	0	0	0	0	0	0	0
Juan Gonzalez, of	.182	3	11	1	2	0	0	1	1	1	3	0
Tom Goodwin, of	.143	3	7	0	1	0	0	0	0	0	1	0
Rusty Greer, of	.111	3	9	0	1	0	0	0	0	3	1	0
Rick Helling, p	.000	1	0	0	0	0	0	0	0	0	0	0
Roberto Kelly, of	.333	1	3	0	1	0	0	0	0	0	2	0
Esteban Loaiza, p	.000	1	0	0	0	0	0	0	0	0	0	0
Mark McLemore, 2b	.100	3	10	0	1	0	0	0	0	1	3	0
Rafael Palmeiro, dh	.273	3	11	0	3	0	0	0	0	1	1	0
Danny Patterson, p	.000	1	0	0	0	0	0	0	0	0	0	0
Ivan Rodriguez, c	.250	3	12	0	3	1	0	0	0	0	2	1
Aaron Sele, p	.000	1	0	0	0	0	0	0	0	0	0	0
Lee Stevens, 1b	.111	3	9	0	1	1	0	0	0	1	2	0
Mike Venafro, p	.000	2	0	0	0	0	0	0	0	0	0	0
John Wetteland, p	.000	1	0	0	0	0	0	0	0	0	0	0
Todd Zeile, 3b	.100	3	10	0	1	0	0	0	0	2	1	0
Jeff Zimmerman, p	.000	1	0	0	0	0	0	0	0	0	0	0
TOTAL	.152		92	1	14	2	0	1	1	9	17	1

PITCHER	W	L	ERA	G	GS	CG	SV	SHO	IP	H	ER	BB	SO
Tim Crabtree	0	0	5.40	2	0	0	0	0	1.2	1	1	1	1
Jeff Fassero	0	0	9.00	1	0	0	0	0	1.0	2	1	1	1
Rick Helling	0	1	2.84	1	1	0	0	0	6.1	5	2	1	8
Esteban Loaiza	0	1	3.86	1	1	0	0	0	7.0	5	3	1	4
Danny Patterson	0	0	0.00	1	0	0	0	0	1.0	1	0	0	0
Aaron Sele	0	1	5.40	1	1	0	0	0	5.0	6	3	5	3
Mike Venafro	0	0	0.00	2	0	0	0	0	1.0	2	0	1	0
John Wetteland	0	0	0.00	1	0	0	0	0	1.0	0	0	0	1
Jeff Zimmerman	0	0	0.00	1	0	0	0	0	1.0	1	0	0	1
TOTAL	0	3	3.60	11	3	0	0	0	25.0	23	10	10	19

GAME 1 AT NY OCT 5

```
TEX  000 000 000   0  2 1
NY   010 024 01X   8 10 0
```
Pitchers: SELE, Crabtree (6), Venafro (6), Patterson (7), Fassero (8) vs HERNANDEZ, Nelson (9)
Home Runs: Williams-NY
Attendance: 57,099

GAME 2 AT NY OCT 7

```
TEX  000 100 000   1  7 0
NY   000 010 11X   3  7 2
```
Pitchers: HELLING, Crabtree (7), Venafro (8) vs PETTITTE, Nelson (8), Rivera (9)
Home Runs: Gonzalez-TEX
Attendance: 57,485

GAME 3 AT TEX OCT 9

```
NY   300 000 000   3  6 0
TEX  000 000 000   0  5 1
```
Pitchers: CLEMENS, Nelson (8), Rivera (8) vs LOAIZA, Zimmerman (8), Wetteland (9)
Home Runs: Strawberry-NY
Attendance: 50,269

BOSTON RED SOX (WILD CARD) 3, CLEVELAND INDIANS (CENTRAL) 2

The Boston Red Sox had lost 18 of their last 19 postseason games and were one game away from elimination when the club rallied to win the Division Series. From the seventh inning of Game 3 to the end of the series, Boston outscored the Cleveland Indians, 41–15.

Things looked bad for Boston after Pedro Martinez left Game 1 with a strained back muscle. Cleveland trailed 2–0, but John Valentin's throwing error kept the sixth inning alive and Jim Thome followed with a home run. Travis Fryman singled in the bottom of the ninth to win the game. The next afternoon the Indians scored six runs in the third inning and five runs in the fourth to walk away with an 11–1 win and two games to none lead.

The Red Sox led 3–2 after six innings in Game 3, but the Indians tied it in the seventh on Valentin's second throwing error of the series. After reliever Ricardo Rincon got two outs in the seventh inning, Valentin doubled to drive in two runs. Brian Daubach followed with a home run.

The fourth game of the series was the greatest scoring display in postseason history. Bartolo Colon, pitching on three days' rest, did not make it out of the second inning. The Red Sox scored multiple runs in seven of eight innings. Valentine homered twice and drove in seven runs, Mike Stanley had five hits, and Jason Varitek scored five times in the 23–7 shellacking.

The Indians and Red Sox traded longballs for the first three innings of Game 5 in Cleveland. Thome hit two mammoth home runs and Fryman added another, but the game took a decided turn after Boston forged an 8-all tie in the top of the fourth inning. Pedro Martinez came out of the bullpen and pitched six innings of no-hit relief. Sean DePaula, who pitched three innings of hitless relief for Cleveland, was removed in favor of Paul Shuey to start the seventh. Troy O'Leary, who had hit a grand slam earlier following an intentional walk to Nomar Garciaparra, ripped a three-run shot after another intentional pass to Garciaparra.

BOS (WC)

PLAYER/POS	AVG	G	AB	R	H	2B	3B	HR	RB	BB	SO	SB
Rod Beck, p	.000	2	0	0	0	0	0	0	0	0	0	0
Damon Buford, of	.000	1	3	0	0	0	0	0	0	0	1	0
Rheal Cormier, p	.000	2	0	0	0	0	0	0	0	0	0	0
Brian Daubach,dh-4,1b-1	.250	4	16	3	4	2	0	1	3	0	7	0
Rich Garces, p	.000	2	0	0	0	0	0	0	0	0	0	0
Nomar Garciaparra, ss	.417	5	12	6	5	2	0	2	4	3	3	0
Tom Gordon, p	.000	2	0	0	0	0	0	0	0	0	0	0
Scott Hatteberg, c	1.000	1	1	1	1	0	0	0	1	0	0	0
Butch Huskey, dh	.200	2	5	0	1	0	0	0	0	0	1	0
Darren Lewis, of	.375	4	16	5	6	1	0	0	2	0	2	1
Derek Lowe, p	.000	3	0	0	0	0	0	0	0	0	0	0
Pedro Martinez, p	.000	2	0	0	0	0	0	0	0	0	0	0
Ramon Martinez, p	.000	1	0	0	0	0	0	0	0	0	0	0
Kent Mercker, p	.000	1	0	0	0	0	0	0	0	0	0	0
Lou Merloni, ss	.333	3	6	1	2	0	0	0	1	1	1	0
Trot Nixon, of	.214	5	14	5	3	3	0	0	6	4	5	0
Jose Offerman, 2b	.389	5	18	4	7	1	0	1	6	7	0	0
Troy O'Leary, of	.200	5	20	4	4	0	0	2	7	2	3	0
Bret Saberhagen, p	.000	2	0	0	0	0	0	0	0	0	0	0
Donnie Sadler, 3b-1, dh-1	.500	2	2	1	1	0	0	0	0	0	1	0
Mike Stanley, 1b	.500	5	20	4	10	2	1	0	2	2	3	0
John Valentin, 3b	.318	5	22	6	7	2	0	3	12	0	4	0
Jason Varitek, c	.238	5	21	7	5	3	0	1	3	0	4	0
Tim Wakefield, p	.000	2	0	0	0	0	0	0	0	0	0	0
John Wasdin, p	.000	2	0	0	0	0	0	0	0	0	0	0
TOTAL	.318		176	47	56	17	1	10	47	19	35	1

PITCHER	W	L	ERA	G	GS	CG	SV	SHO	IP	H	ER	BB	SO
Rod Beck	0	0	0.00	2	0	0	0	0	2.0	2	0	0	2
Rheal Cormier	0	0	0.00	2	0	0	0	0	4.0	2	0	1	4
Rich Garces	1	0	3.86	2	0	0	0	0	2.1	2	1	3	2
Tom Gordon	0	0	4.50	2	0	0	0	0	2.0	1	1	1	3
Derek Lowe	1	1	4.32	3	0	0	0	0	8.1	6	4	1	7
Pedro Martinez	1	0	0.00	2	1	0	0	0	10.0	3	0	4	11
Ramon Martinez	0	0	3.18	1	1	0	0	0	5.2	5	2	3	6
Kent Mercker	0	0	10.80	1	1	0	0	0	1.2	3	2	1	1
Bret Saberhagen	0	1	27.00	2	2	0	0	0	3.2	9	11	4	2
Tim Wakefield	0	0	13.50	2	0	0	0	0	2.0	3	3	4	4
John Wasdin	0	0	27.00	2	0	0	0	0	1.2	5	4	1	1
TOTAL	3	2	6.02	21	5	0	0	0	43.1	38	29	28	43

CLE (C)

PLAYER/POS	AVG	G	AB	R	H	2B	3B	HR	RB	BB	SO	SB
Roberto Alomar, 2b	.368	5	19	4	7	4	0	0	3	2	3	2
Sandy Alomar, c	.143	5	14	1	2	0	0	0	1	2	6	0
Paul Assenmacher, p	.000	1	0	0	0	0	0	0	0	0	0	0
Harold Baines, dh	.357	4	14	1	5	0	0	1	4	2	1	0
Dave Burba, p	.000	1	0	0	0	0	0	0	0	0	0	0
Bartolo Colon, p	.000	2	0	0	0	0	0	0	0	0	0	0
Wil Cordero, dh-2, of-1	.556	3	9	3	5	0	0	1	2	1	2	0
Sean DePaula, p	.000	3	0	0	0	0	0	0	0	0	0	0
Einar Diaz, c	.000	2	1	0	0	0	0	0	0	0	0	0
Travis Fryman, 3b	.267	5	15	2	4	0	0	1	4	3	2	1
Mike Jackson, p	.000	2	0	0	0	0	0	0	0	0	0	0
David Justice, of	.000	3	8	0	0	0	0	0	1	2	2	0
Steve Karsay, p	.000	2	0	0	0	0	0	0	0	0	0	0
Kenny Lofton, of	.125	5	16	5	2	1	0	0	1	5	6	2
Charles Nagy, p	.000	2	0	0	0	0	0	0	0	0	0	0
Manny Ramirez, of	.056	5	18	5	1	1	0	0	1	4	8	0
Steve Reed, p	.000	2	0	0	0	0	0	0	0	0	0	0
Ricardo Rincon, p	.000	1	0	0	0	0	0	0	0	0	0	0
Dave Roberts, of	.000	2	3	0	0	0	0	0	0	0	2	0
Richie Sexson, 1b-1, of-1	.167	3	6	1	1	0	0	0	1	1	3	0
Paul Shuey, p	.000	3	0	0	0	0	0	0	0	0	0	0
Jim Thome, 1b	.353	5	17	7	6	0	0	4	10	4	5	0
Omar Vizquel, ss	.238	5	21	3	5	1	1	0	3	2	3	0
Enrique Wilson, 2b-2	.000	3	2	0	0	0	0	0	0	1	0	0
Jaret Wright, p	.000	1	0	0	0	0	0	0	0	0	0	0
TOTAL	.233		163	32	38	7	1	7	31	28	43	5

PITCHER	W	L	ERA	G	GS	CG	SV	SHO	IP	H	ER	BB	SO
Paul Assenmacher	0	0	27.00	1	0	0	0	0	1.0	5	3	0	0
Dave Burba	0	0	0.00	1	1	0	0	0	4.0	1	0	1	0
Bartolo Colon	0	1	9.00	2	2	0	0	0	9.0	11	9	4	12
Sean DePaula	0	0	1.80	3	0	0	0	0	5.0	2	1	3	5
Mike Jackson	0	0	4.50	2	0	0	0	0	2.0	2	1	1	1
Steve Karsay	0	0	9.00	2	0	0	0	0	3.0	5	3	1	3
Charles Nagy	1	0	7.20	2	2	0	0	0	10.0	11	8	2	6
Steve Reed	0	0	30.86	2	0	0	0	0	2.1	9	8	1	1
Ricardo Rincon	0	0	40.50	1	0	0	0	0	0.2	2	3	1	1
Paul Shuey	1	1	11.25	3	0	0	0	0	4.0	5	4	5	4
Jaret Wright	0	1	22.50	1	0	0	0	0	2.0	4	5	1	1
TOTAL	2	3	9.63	20	5	0	0	0	43.0	56	46	19	35

GAME 1 AT CLE OCT 6

```
BOS  010 100 000   2 5 1
CLE  000 002 001   3 6 1
```
Pitchers: P.Martinez, LOWE (5), Cormier (9), Garces (9) vs Colon, SHUEY (9)
Home Runs: Garciaparra-BOS, Thome-CLE
Attendance: 45,182

GAME 2 AT CLE OCT 7

```
BOS  001 000 000   1 6 0
CLE  006 500 00X  11 8 0
```
Pitchers: SABERHAGEN, Wasdin (3), Wakefield (5), Gordon (7), Beck (8) vs NAGY, Karsay (8), Jackson (9)
Home Runs: Baines-CLE, Thome-CLE
Attendance: 45,184

GAME 3 AT BOS OCT 9

```
CLE  000 101 100   3 9 1
BOS  000 021 60X   9 11 2
```
Pitchers: Burba, WRIGHT (5), Rincon (7), DePaula (7), Reed (8) vs R.Martinez, LOWE (6), Beck (9)
Home Runs: Valentin-BOS, Daubach-BOS
Attendance: 33,539

GAME 4 AT BOS OCT 10

```
CLE  110 040 001   7 8 0
BOS  253 530 32X  23 24 0
```
Pitchers: COLON, Karsay (2), Reed (4), DePaula (5), Assenmacher (7), Shuey (8) vs Mercker, GARCES (2), Wakefield (5), Wasdin (5), Cormier (5), Gordon (9)
Home Runs: Valentin-BOS (2), Offerman-BOS, Varitek-BOS, Cordero-CLE
Attendance: 33,898

GAME 5 AT CLE OCT 11

```
BOS  205 100 301  12 10 0
CLE  323 000 000   8 7 1
```
Pitchers: Saberhagen, Lowe (2), P.MARTINEZ (4) vs Nagy, DePaula (4), SHUEY (7), Jackson (9)
Home Runs: Garciaparra-BOS, Thome-CLE (2), Fryman-CLE, O'Leary-BOS (2)
Attendance: 45,114

ATLANTA BRAVES (EAST) 4, NEW YORK METS (WILD CARD) 2

Atlanta, playing in its eighth consecutive NLCS, rolled past the Mets in the opener as Greg Maddux outpitched Masato Yoshii. The next afternoon Kenny Rogers took a 2–0 lead into the bottom of the sixth, but two-run homers by Brian Jordan and Eddie Perez put the Braves in front. After closer John Rocker squashed a Mets rally in the eighth, John Smoltz, making his first major league relief appearance, earned the save. First-inning throwing errors by the Mets battery of Al Leiter and Mike Piazza allowed Atlanta to push across a first-inning run in Game 3. Tom Glavine and two relievers made it stand up in a 1–0 win at Shea.

The Mets grabbed a 1–0 lead in Game 4 on John Olerud's home run, but back-to-back homers by Jordan and Ryan Klesko in the eighth inning spoiled a brilliant outing by New York starter Rick Reed. In the bottom of the eighth, however, Olerud's grounder up the middle drove in the tying and go-ahead runs.

Olerud homered in the first inning of Game 5. The Braves tied it with consecutive hits by Jordan and Chipper Jones to chase Yoshii in the fourth. Orel Hershiser came on in relief and started a string of 10 straight scoreless innings by the Mets bullpen. Not to be outdone, the Braves blanked the Mets for 13 consecutive innings. The Braves finally broke through in the 15th inning on a run-scoring triple by Keith Lockhart. Shawon Dunston led off the bottom of the inning with a single. Rookie Kevin McGlinchy walked three of the next four batters, including Todd Pratt to tie the game. Robin Ventura, in a 1-for-18 slump, cleared the fence in right for an apparent game-ending grand slam, but he was mobbed by teammates before he reached second base. There was confusion over what the final score should be; after several minutes a 4–3 verdict was posted, and Ventura was credited with a game-winning single.

Leiter did not retire a batter in Game 6. The Braves took a 5–0 lead, highlighted by a two-run single by series Most Valuable Player Eddie Perez. Although Darryl Hamilton's two-run single in the sixth pulled the Mets within two runs, a pinch-hit single by Jose Hernandez upped Atlanta's lead to 7–3. Mike Piazza, who later left the

game because of a slight concussion, slammed a home run in the seventh off Smoltz to tie the game. Melvin Mora singled in a run in the eighth to give the Mets the lead, but Brian Hunter's single in the bottom of the inning tied the game. After New York took another lead in the 10th, Guillen's single again knotted the score. When Jordan reached third with one out in the 11th, Kenny Rogers walked the next two batters intentionally. He then walked Andruw Jones to bring in the series-ending run.

ATL (E)

PLAYER/POS	AVG	G	AB	R	H	2B	3B	HR	RB	BB	SO	SB
Howard Battle, 1b-1	.000	3	2	0	0	0	0	0	0	0	2	1
Bret Boone, 2b	.182	6	22	2	4	1	0	0	1	1	7	2
Jorge Fabregas, ph	.000	2	2	0	0	0	0	0	0	0	1	0
Tom Glavine, p	.000	1	2	0	0	0	0	0	0	0	1	0
Ozzie Guillen, ss-2	.333	3	3	0	1	0	0	0	1	0	0	0
Jose Hernandez, ph	.500	2	2	0	1	0	0	0	2	0	1	0
Brian Hunter, 1b	.100	6	10	1	1	0	0	0	2	5	2	1
Andruw Jones, of	.217	6	23	5	5	0	0	0	1	4	3	0
Chipper Jones, 3b	.263	6	19	3	5	2	0	0	1	9	7	1
Brian Jordan, of	.200	6	25	3	5	0	0	2	5	3	5	0
Ryan Klesko, 1b	.125	4	8	1	1	0	0	1	1	2	1	0
Keith Lockhart, 2b-1	.400	3	5	0	2	0	1	0	1	0	2	0
Greg Maddux, p	.000	2	5	0	0	0	0	0	0	0	4	0
Kevin McGlinchy, p	.000	1	1	0	0	0	0	0	0	0	1	0
Kevin Millwood, p	.000	2	4	0	0	0	0	0	0	1	0	0
Terry Mulholland, p	.000	2	0	0	0	0	0	0	0	0	0	0
Greg Myers, c	.000	2	2	0	0	0	0	0	0	1	1	0
Otis Nixon, pr	.000	2	0	1	0	0	0	0	0	0	0	2
Eddie Perez, c	.500	6	20	2	10	2	0	2	5	1	3	0
Mike Remlinger, p	.000	5	0	0	0	0	0	0	0	0	0	0
John Rocker, p	.000	6	0	0	0	0	0	0	0	0	0	0
John Smoltz, p	.000	3	2	0	0	0	0	0	0	0	0	0
Russ Springer, p	.000	2	0	0	0	0	0	0	0	0	0	0
Walt Weiss, ss	.286	6	21	2	6	2	0	0	1	2	4	2
Gerald Williams, of	.179	6	28	4	5	2	0	0	1	2	2	3
TOTAL	.223		206	24	46	9	1	5	22	31	47	14

PITCHER	W	L	ERA	G	GS	CG	SV	SHO	IP	H	ER	BB	SO
Tom Glavine	1	0	0.00	1	1	0	0	0	7.0	7	0	1	8
Greg Maddux	1	0	1.93	2	2	0	0	0	14.0	12	3	1	7
Kevin McGlinchy	0	1	18.00	1	0	0	0	0	1.0	2	2	4	1
Kevin Millwood	1	0	3.55	2	2	0	0	0	12.2	13	5	1	9
Terry Mulholland	0	0	0.00	2	0	0	0	0	2.2	1	0	1	2
Mike Remlinger	0	1	3.18	5	0	0	0	0	5.2	3	2	3	4
John Rocker	0	0	0.00	6	0	0	1	0	6.2	3	0	2	9
John Smoltz	0	0	6.23	3	1	0	1	0	8.2	8	6	0	8
Russ Springer	1	0	0.00	2	0	0	0	0	2.0	0	0	1	1
TOTAL	4	2	2.69	24	6	0	2	0	60.1	49	18	14	49

NY (WC)

PLAYER/POS	AVG	G	AB	R	H	2B	3B	HR	RB	BB	SO	SB
Benny Agbayani, of-3	.143	4	7	2	1	0	0	0	0	4	2	1
Edgardo Alfonzo, 2b	.222	6	27	2	6	4	0	0	1	1	9	0
Armando Benitez, p	.000	5	0	0	0	0	0	0	0	0	0	0
Bobby Bonilla, ph	.333	3	3	0	1	0	0	0	0	0	2	0
Roger Cedeno, of-4	.500	5	12	2	6	1	0	0	1	0	1	2
Dennis Cook, p	.000	3	0	0	0	0	0	0	0	0	0	0
Octavio Dotel, p	.000	1	0	0	0	0	0	0	0	0	0	0
Shawon Dunston, of-1	.143	5	7	2	1	0	0	0	0	0	2	1
John Franco, p	.000	3	0	0	0	0	0	0	0	0	0	0
Matt Franco, ph	.500	5	2	1	1	0	0	0	0	1	0	0
Darryl Hamilton, of	.353	5	17	0	6	1	0	0	2	0	4	0
Rickey Henderson, of	.174	6	23	2	4	1	0	0	1	0	5	1
Orel Hershiser, p	.000	2	1	0	0	0	0	0	0	0	0	0
Al Leiter, p	.000	2	2	0	0	0	0	0	0	0	1	0
Pat Mahomes, p	.000	3	2	0	0	0	0	0	0	0	0	0
Melvin Mora, of-5	.429	6	14	3	6	0	0	1	2	2	2	2
John Olerud, 1b	.296	6	27	4	8	0	0	2	6	2	3	0
Rey Ordonez, ss	.042	6	24	0	1	0	0	0	0	2	0	0
Mike Piazza, c	.167	6	24	1	4	0	0	1	4	1	6	0
Todd Pratt, c-2	.500	4	2	0	1	0	0	0	3	1	1	0
Rick Reed, p	.000	1	2	0	0	0	0	0	0	0	0	0
Kenny Rogers, p	.000	3	1	0	0	0	0	0	0	0	1	0
Robin Ventura, 3b	.120	6	25	2	3	1	0	1	5	2	5	0
Turk Wendell, p	.000	5	0	0	0	0	0	0	0	0	0	0
Masato Yoshii, p	.000	2	3	0	0	0	0	0	0	0	1	0
TOTAL	.218		225	21	49	9	0	4	21	14	49	7

PITCHER	W	L	ERA	G	GS	CG	SV	SHO	IP	H	ER	BB	SO
Armando Benitez	0	0	1.35	5	0	0	1	0	6.2	3	1	2	9
Dennis Cook	0	0	0.00	3	0	0	0	0	1.1	1	0	2	1
Octavio Dotel	1	0	3.00	1	0	0	0	0	3.0	4	1	2	5
John Franco	0	0	3.38	3	0	0	0	0	2.2	3	1	1	3
Orel Hershiser	0	0	0.00	2	0	0	0	0	4.1	1	0	3	5
Al Leiter	0	1	6.43	2	2	0	0	0	7.0	5	5	4	5
Pat Mahomes	0	0	1.42	3	0	0	0	0	6.1	4	1	3	3
Rick Reed	0	0	2.57	1	1	0	0	0	7.0	3	2	0	5
Kenny Rogers	0	2	5.87	3	1	0	0	0	7.2	11	5	7	2
Turk Wendell	1	0	4.76	5	0	0	0	0	5.2	2	3	4	5
Masato Yoshii	0	1	4.70	2	2	0	0	0	7.2	9	4	3	4
TOTAL	2	4	3.49	30	6	0	1	0	59.1	46	23	31	47

GAME 1 AT ATL OCT 12

NY 000 100 001 2 6 2
ATL 100 011 01X 4 8 2
Pitchers: YOSHII, Mahomes (5), Cook (7), Wendell (8) vs MADDUX, Remlinger (8), Rocker (8)
Home Runs: Perez-ATL
Attendance: 44,172

GAME 2 AT ATL OCT 13

NY 010 010 010 3 5 1
ATL 000 004 00X 4 9 1
Pitchers: ROGERS, Wendell (6), Benitez (8) vs MILLWOOD, Rocker (8), Smoltz (9)
Home Runs: Mora-NY, Jordan-ATL, Perez-ATL
Attendance: 44,624

GAME 3 AT NY OCT 15

ATL 100 000 000 1 3 1
NY 000 000 000 0 7 2
Pitchers: GLAVINE, Remlinger (8), Rocker (9) vs LEITER, J.Franco (8), Benitez (8)
Attendance: 55,911

GAME 4 AT NY OCT 16

ATL 000 000 020 2 3 0
NY 000 001 02X 3 5 0
Pitchers: Smoltz, REMLINGER (8), Rocker (8) vs Reed, WENDELL (8), Benitez (9)
Home Runs: Olerud-NY, Jordan-ATL, Klesko-ATL
Attendance: 55,872

GAME 5 AT NY OCT 17

ATL 000 200 000 000 001 3 13 2
NY 200 000 000 000 002 4 11 1
Pitchers: Maddux, Mulholland (8), Remlinger (10), Springer (12), Rocker (13), McGLINCHY (14) vs Yoshii, Hershiser (4), Wendell (7), Cook (7), Mahomes (7), J.Franco (8), Benitez (10), Rogers (11), DOTEL (13)
Home Runs: Olerud-NY
Attendance: 55,723

GAME 6 AT ATL OCT 19

NY 000 003 410 10 9 15 2
ATL 500 002 010 11 10 10 1
Pitchers: Leiter, Mahomes (1), Wendell (5), Cook (6), Hershiser (7), J.Franco (8), Benitez (8), ROGERS (11) vs Millwood, Mulholland (6), Smoltz (7), Remlinger (7), Rocker (9), SPRINGER (10)
Home Runs: Piazza-NY
Attendance: 52,335

NEW YORK YANKEES (EAST) 4, BOSTON RED SOX (WILD CARD) 1

The only thing missing in the nearly century-long rivalry between the New York Yankees and Boston Red Sox was a postseason chapter. The addition of the wild card enabled the pair to meet in the 1999 Championship Series.

The Red Sox arrived in New York fresh off a dramatic win over the Cleveland Indians in the Division Series. Boston got off to a solid start in the ALCS by taking an early 3–0 lead over New York in Game 1. Scott Brosius homered off Kent Merker to cut the lead to 3–2, and New York tied the game on Derek Jeter's RBI-single in the seventh inning as Brosius jarred the ball from the grasp of catcher Jason Varitek. Bernie Williams homered off Rod Beck in the 10th to give the Yankees the win. Boston took an early lead again in Game 2, but the Yankees rallied in the seventh on two-out hits by Chuck Knoblauch and Paul O'Neill for the win. It was the Yanks' 12th consecutive postseason win, tying a their own record set between 1927 and 1932.

Fenway Park was not kind to the Yanks, or former favorite son Roger Clemens, in Game 3. The Sox rocked Clemens for five runs in two innings and he left to the hoots of the raucous Fenway crowd. Boston ace Pedro Martinez allowed just two hits in seven innings. John Valentin knocked in five runs and Nomar Garciaparra drove in three runs in a 13–1 rout. The Red Sox took an early lead for the fourth straight game the following night, but mistakes and blown chances cost Boston a chance to even the series. Two errors in the fourth inning allowed the Yanks to gain the lead. A Boston rally was snuffed in the eighth inning when umpire Tim Tschida called Jose Offerman out as part of a double play, even though Offerman was never tagged. Although Ricky Ledee's pinch-hit grand slam in the ninth inning put the game away, Fenway fans littered the field with debris and halted play following the ejection of manager Jimy Williams.

Jeter homered in the first inning of Game 5 to send the Yankees on their way to the pennant. Boston committed its LCS record 10th error and left 11 runners on bases against series Most Valuable Player Orlando Hernandez and four relievers.

NY (E)

PLAYER/POS	AVG	G	AB	R	H	2B	3B	HR	RB	BB	SO	SB
Clay Bellinger, dh-2, ss-1	.000	3	1	0	0	0	0	0	0	0	1	0
Scott Brosius, 3b	.222	5	18	3	4	0	1	2	3	1	4	0
Roger Clemens, p	.000	1	0	0	0	0	0	0	0	0	0	0
David Cone, p	.000	1	0	0	0	0	0	0	0	0	0	0
Chad Curtis, of-2, dh-1	.000	3	6	1	0	0	0	0	0	0	2	1
Chili Davis, dh	.091	5	11	0	1	0	0	0	1	3	4	0
Joe Girardi, c	.250	3	8	0	2	0	0	0	0	0	2	0
Orlando Hernandez, p	.000	2	0	0	0	0	0	0	0	0	0	0
Hideki Irabu, p	.000	1	0	0	0	0	0	0	0	0	0	0
Derek Jeter, ss	.350	5	20	3	7	1	0	1	3	2	3	0
Chuck Knoblauch, 2b	.333	5	18	3	6	1	0	0	1	3	0	1
Ricky Ledee, of-2	.250	3	8	2	2	0	0	1	4	1	4	0
Tino Martinez, 1b	.263	5	19	3	5	1	0	1	3	2	4	0
Ramiro Mendoza, p	.000	2	0	0	0	0	0	0	0	0	0	0
Jeff Nelson, p	.000	2	0	0	0	0	0	0	0	0	0	0
Paul O'Neill, of	.286	5	21	2	6	0	0	0	1	1	5	0
Andy Pettitte, p	.000	1	0	0	0	0	0	0	0	0	0	0
Jorge Posada, c	.100	3	10	1	1	0	0	1	2	1	2	0
Mariano Rivera, p	.000	3	0	0	0	0	0	0	0	0	0	0
Luis Sojo, 2b	.000	2	1	0	0	0	0	0	0	0	0	0
Shane Spencer, of	.111	3	9	1	1	0	0	0	0	1	6	0
Mike Stanton, p	.000	3	0	0	0	0	0	0	0	0	0	0
Darryl Strawberry, dh	.333	3	6	1	2	0	0	1	1	1	2	0
Allen Watson, p	.000	3	0	0	0	0	0	0	0	0	0	0
Bernie Williams, of	.250	5	20	3	5	1	0	1	2	2	5	1
TOTAL	.239		176	23	42	4	1	8	21	18	44	3

PITCHER	W	L	ERA	G	GS	CG	SV	SHO	IP	H	ER	BB	SO
Roger Clemens	0	1	22.50	1	1	0	0	0	2.0	6	5	2	2
David Cone	1	0	2.57	1	1	0	0	0	7.0	7	2	3	9
O. Hernandez	1	0	1.80	2	2	0	0	0	15.0	12	3	6	13
Hideki Irabu	0	0	13.50	1	0	0	0	0	4.2	13	7	0	3
Ramiro Mendoza	0	0	0.00	2	0	0	1	0	2.1	0	0	0	2
Jeff Nelson	0	0	0.00	2	0	0	0	0	0.2	0	0	0	0
Andy Pettitte	1	0	2.45	1	1	0	0	0	7.1	8	2	1	5
Mariano Rivera	1	0	0.00	3	0	0	2	0	4.2	5	0	0	3
Mike Stanton	0	0	0.00	3	0	0	0	0	0.1	1	0	1	0
Allen Watson	0	0	0.00	3	0	0	0	0	1.0	2	0	2	1
TOTAL	4	1	3.80	19	5	0	3	0	45.0	54	19	15	38

BOS (WC)

PLAYER/POS	AVG	G	AB	R	H	2B	3B	HR	RB	BB	SO	SB
Rod Beck, p	.000	2	0	0	0	0	0	0	0	0	0	0
Damon Buford, of	.400	4	5	1	2	0	0	0	0	0	2	1
Rheal Cormier, p	.000	4	0	0	0	0	0	0	0	0	0	0
Brian Daubach, dh-5, 1b-1	.176	5	17	2	3	1	0	1	3	1	4	0
Rich Garces, p	.000	2	0	0	0	0	0	0	0	0	0	0
Nomar Garciaparra, ss	.400	5	20	2	8	2	0	2	5	2	2	1
Tom Gordon, p	.000	3	0	0	0	0	0	0	0	0	0	0
Scott Hatteberg, c-1	.000	3	1	0	0	0	0	0	0	0	1	0
Butch Huskey, dh-3	.200	4	5	1	1	1	0	0	0	1	1	0
Darren Lewis, of	.118	5	17	2	2	1	0	0	1	1	3	1
Derek Lowe, p	.000	3	0	0	0	0	0	0	0	0	0	0
Pedro Martinez, p	.000	1	0	0	0	0	0	0	0	0	0	0
Ramon Martinez, p	.000	1	0	0	0	0	0	0	0	0	0	0
Kent Mercker, p	.000	2	0	0	0	0	0	0	0	0	0	0
Lou Merloni, ph	.000	1	0	0	0	0	0	0	0	1	0	0
Trot Nixon, of	.286	5	14	2	4	2	0	0	0	1	5	0
Jose Offerman, 2b	.458	5	24	4	11	0	1	0	2	1	3	1
Troy O'Leary, of	.350	5	20	2	7	3	0	0	1	2	5	0
Pat Rapp, p	.000	1	0	0	0	0	0	0	0	0	0	0
Bret Saberhagen, p	.000	1	0	0	0	0	0	0	0	0	0	0
Donnie Sadler, of-1, dh-1	.000	2	0	0	0	0	0	0	0	0	0	0
Mike Stanley, 1b	.222	5	18	1	4	0	0	0	1	2	4	0
John Valentin, 3b	.348	5	23	3	8	2	0	1	5	2	4	0
Jason Varitek, c	.200	5	20	1	4	1	1	1	1	1	4	0
TOTAL	.293		184	21	54	13	2	5	19	15	38	4

PITCHER	W	L	ERA	G	GS	CG	SV	SHO	IP	H	ER	BB	SO
Rod Beck	0	1	27.00	2	0	0	0	0	0.2	2	2	0	1
Rheal Cormier	0	0	0.00	4	0	0	0	0	3.2	3	0	3	4
Rich Garces	0	0	12.00	2	0	0	0	0	3.0	3	4	1	2
Tom Gordon	0	0	13.50	3	0	0	0	0	2.0	3	3	1	3
Derek Lowe	0	0	1.42	3	0	0	0	0	6.1	6	1	2	7
Pedro Martinez	1	0	0.00	1	1	0	0	0	7.0	2	0	2	12
Ramon Martinez	0	0	4.05	1	1	0	0	0	6.2	6	3	3	5
Kent Mercker	0	1	4.70	2	2	0	0	0	7.2	12	4	4	5
Pat Rapp	0	0	0.00	1	0	0	0	0	1.0	0	0	1	0
Bret Saberhagen	0	1	1.50	1	1	0	0	0	6.0	5	1	1	5
TOTAL	1	4	3.68	20	5	0	0	0	44.0	42	18	18	44

GAME 1 AT NY OCT 13

```
BOS  210 000 0000  3 8 2
NY   020 000 1001  4 10 1
```
Pitchers: Mercker, Garces (5), Lowe (7), Cormier (9), BECK (10) vs Hernandez, RIVERA (9)
Home Runs: Brosius-NY, Williams-NY
Attendance: 57,181

GAME 2 AT NY OCT 14

```
BOS  000 020 000  2 10 0
NY   000 100 20X  3 7 0
```
Pitchers: R.MARTINEZ, Gordon (7), Cormier (7) vs CONE, Stanton (8), Nelson (8), Watson (8), Mendoza (8), Rivera (9)
Home Runs: Martinez-NY, Garciaparra-BOS
Attendance: 57,180

GAME 3 AT BOS OCT 16

```
NY   000 000 010  1 3 3
BOS  222 021 40X  13 21 1
```
Pitchers: CLEMENS, Irabu (3), Stanton (7), Watson (8) vs P.MARTINEZ, Gordon (8), Rapp (9)
Home Runs: Valentin-BOS, Daubach-BOS, Garciaparra-BOS, Brosius-NY
Attendance: 33,190

GAME 4 AT BOS OCT 17

```
NY   010 200 006  9 11 0
BOS  011 000 103  2 10 3
```
Pitchers: PETTITTE, Rivera (8) vs SABERHAGEN, Lowe (7), Cormier (8), Garces (8), Beck (9)
Home Runs: Strawberry-NY, Ledee-NY
Attendance: 33,586

GAME 5 AT BOS OCT 18

```
NY   200 000 202  6 11 1
BOS  000 000 010  1 5 2
```
Pitchers: HERNANDEZ, Stanton (8), Nelson (8), Watson (8), Mendoza (8) vs MERCKER, Lowe (4), Cormier (7), Gordon (9)
Home Runs: Jeter-NY, Varitek-BOS, Posada-NY
Attendance: 33,589

NEW YORK YANKEES (AL) 4, ATLANTA BRAVES (NL) 0

The Yankees steamrolled the Braves for their 25th world championship and second consecutive World Series sweep. Atlanta's only hit against Orlando Hernandez in Game 1 was a fourth-inning home run by Chipper Jones. Greg Maddux made that run stand up until a single, a walk, and an error loaded the bases with none out in the eighth inning. Derek Jeter singled to tie the game and force Maddux to the bench. Atlanta southpaw John Rocker came in to face Paul O'Neill, but the lefthanded-hitting outfielder grounded a single to bring in two runs. Yanks closer Mariano Rivera made the lead stand up. Atlanta got just one hit against New York's Game 2 starter, David Cone, and the Yanks knocked Braves starter Kevin Milwood from the game in the third inning at Turner Field.

The Braves jumped out to a 5–1 lead in Game 3 as Bret Boone had three doubles off starter Andy Pettitte. The Braves had 10 hits in less than four innings against Pettitte, and had several other chances to score throughout the game, but never got the hit that blew the game open. New York's bullpen blanked Atlanta for the final 6-1/3 innings. Meanwhile, solo home runs by Chad Curtis and Tino Martinez brought the Yankees within 5–3. With starter Tom Glavine still pitching in the bottom of the eighth inning, Chuck Knoblauch launched a flyball to right that tipped off right fielder Brian Jordan's glove for a game-tying two-run home run. Curtis, who hit just five home runs all season, led off the 10th inning with his second home run of the game to give the Yankees the victory.

Roger Clemens, who had struggled for much of the season, outdueled John Smoltz in Game 4. A single by Jeter followed an infield hit by Knoblauch in the decisive third inning. After Jeter stole second, Bernie Williams was intentionally walked, to set up a force with Tino Martinez at the plate. Smoltz induced a hard-hit grounder, but it caromed off first baseman Ryan Klesko into right field for a two-run single. With the Yanks leading 3–1 in the eighth inning, Jim Leyritz homered to left. Rivera, with two saves and a win in the sweep, retired the side in the ninth to earn Most Valuable Player honors.

NY (A)

PLAYER/POS	AVG	G	AB	R	H	2B	3B	HR	RB	BB	SO	SB
Scott Brosius, 3b	.375	4	16	2	6	1	0	0	1	0	5	0
Roger Clemens, p	.000	1	0	0	0	0	0	0	0	0	0	0
David Cone, p	.000	1	4	0	0	0	0	0	0	0	0	0
Chad Curtis, of	.333	3	6	3	2	0	0	2	2	0	0	0
Chili Davis, dh	.000	1	4	0	0	0	0	0	0	0	2	0
Joe Girardi, c	.286	2	7	1	2	0	0	0	0	0	1	0
Jason Grimsley, p	.000	1	0	0	0	0	0	0	0	0	0	0
Orlando Hernandez, p	.000	1	1	0	0	0	0	0	0	0	0	0
Derek Jeter, ss	.353	4	17	4	6	1	0	0	1	1	3	3
Chuck Knoblauch, 2b	.313	4	16	5	5	1	0	1	3	1	3	1
Ricky Ledee, of	.200	3	10	0	2	1	0	0	1	1	4	0
Jim Leyritz, dh-1	1.000	2	1	1	1	0	0	1	2	1	0	0
Tino Martinez, 1b	.267	4	15	3	4	0	0	1	5	2	4	0
Ramiro Mendoza, p	.000	1	1	0	0	0	0	0	0	0	0	0
Jeff Nelson, p	.000	4	0	0	0	0	0	0	0	0	0	0
Paul O'Neill, of	.200	4	15	0	3	0	0	0	4	2	2	0
Andy Pettitte, p	.000	1	0	0	0	0	0	0	0	0	0	0
Jorge Posada, c	.250	2	8	0	2	1	0	0	1	0	3	0
Mariano Rivera, p	.000	3	0	0	0	0	0	0	0	0	0	0
Luis Sojo, 2b	.000	1	0	0	0	0	0	0	0	0	0	0
Mike Stanton, p	.000	1	0	0	0	0	0	0	0	0	0	0
Darryl Strawberry, dh-1	.333	2	3	0	1	0	0	0	0	0	1	0
Bernie Williams, of	.231	4	13	2	3	0	0	0	0	4	2	1
TOTAL	.270		137	21	37	5	0	5	20	13	31	5

PITCHER	W	L	ERA	G	GS	CG	SV	SHO	IP	H	ER	BB	SO
Roger Clemens	1	0	1.17	1	1	0	0	0	7.2	4	1	2	4
David Cone	1	0	0.00	1	1	0	0	0	7.0	1	0	5	4
Jason Grimsley	0	0	0.00	1	0	0	0	0	2.1	2	0	2	0
O. Hernandez	1	0	1.29	1	1	0	0	0	7.0	1	1	2	10
Ramiro Mendoza	0	0	10.80	1	0	0	0	0	1.2	3	2	1	0
Jeff Nelson	0	0	0.00	4	0	0	0	0	2.2	2	0	1	3
Andy Pettitte	0	0	12.27	1	1	0	0	0	3.2	10	5	1	1
Mariano Rivera	1	0	0.00	3	0	0	2	0	4.2	3	0	1	3
Mike Stanton	0	0	0.00	1	0	0	0	0	0.1	0	0	0	1
TOTAL	4	0	2.19	14	4	0	2	0	37.0	26	9	15	26

ATL (N)

PLAYER/POS	AVG	G	AB	R	H	2B	3B	HR	RB	BB	SO	SB
Howard Battle, ph	.000	1	0	0	0	0	0	0	0	0	0	0
Bret Boone, 2b-3	.538	4	13	1	7	4	0	0	3	1	3	0
Jorge Fabregas, ph	.000	1	1	0	0	0	0	0	0	0	1	0
Tom Glavine, p	.000	1	0	0	0	0	0	0	0	0	0	0
Ozzie Guillen, ss-1, dh-1	.000	3	5	0	0	0	0	0	0	0	1	0
Jose Hernandez, ss-1, dh-1	.200	2	5	0	1	1	0	0	2	0	2	1
Brian Hunter, 1b	.250	2	4	0	1	0	0	0	0	0	1	0
Andruw Jones, of	.077	4	13	1	1	0	0	0	0	1	3	0
Chipper Jones, 3b	.231	4	13	2	3	0	0	1	2	4	2	0
Brian Jordan, of	.077	4	13	1	1	0	0	0	1	4	2	0
Ryan Klesko, 1b	.167	4	12	0	2	0	0	0	0	0	1	0
Keith Lockhart, 2b-2, dh-1	.143	4	7	1	1	0	0	0	0	2	0	0
Greg Maddux, p	.000	1	2	0	0	0	0	0	0	0	2	0
Kevin McGlinchy, p	.000	1	0	0	0	0	0	0	0	0	0	0
Kevin Millwood, p	.000	1	0	0	0	0	0	0	0	0	0	0
Terry Mulholland, p	.000	2	0	0	0	0	0	0	0	1	0	0
Greg Myers, c-3	.333	4	6	0	2	0	0	0	1	1	0	0
Otis Nixon, of-1	.500	2	2	0	1	0	0	0	0	0	0	0
Eddie Perez, c	.125	3	8	0	1	0	0	0	0	1	3	0
Mike Remlinger, p	.000	2	0	0	0	0	0	0	0	0	0	0
John Rocker, p	.000	2	0	0	0	0	0	0	0	0	0	0
John Smoltz, p	.000	1	0	0	0	0	0	0	0	0	0	0
Russ Springer, p	.000	2	0	0	0	0	0	0	0	0	0	0
Walt Weiss, ss	.222	3	9	1	2	0	0	0	0	0	1	0
Gerald Williams, of	.176	4	17	2	3	0	1	0	0	0	4	0
TOTAL	.200		130	9	26	5	1	1	9	15	26	1

PITCHER	W	L	ERA	G	GS	CG	SV	SHO	IP	H	ER	BB	SO
Tom Glavine	0	0	5.14	1	1	0	0	0	7.0	7	4	0	3
Greg Maddux	0	1	2.57	1	1	0	0	0	7.0	5	2	3	5
Kevin McGlinchy	0	0	0.00	1	0	0	0	0	2.0	2	0	1	2
Kevin Millwood	0	1	18.00	1	1	0	0	0	2.0	8	4	2	2
Terry Mulholland	0	0	7.36	2	0	0	0	0	3.2	5	3	1	3
Mike Remlinger	0	1	9.00	2	0	0	0	0	1.0	1	1	1	0
John Rocker	0	0	0.00	2	0	0	0	0	3.0	2	0	2	4
John Smoltz	0	1	3.86	1	1	0	0	0	7.0	6	3	3	11
Russ Springer	0	0	0.00	2	0	0	0	0	2.1	1	0	0	1
TOTAL	0	4	4.37	13	4	0	0	0	35.0	37	17	13	31

GAME 1 AT ATL OCT 23

NY	0 0 0 0 0 0 0 4 0	4 6 0
ATL	0 0 0 1 0 0 0 0 0	1 2 2

Pitchers: HERNANDEZ, Nelson (8), Stanton (8), Rivera (8) vs MADDUX, Rocker (8), Remlinger (9)
Home Runs: C.Jones-ATL
Attendance: 51,342

GAME 2 AT ATL OCT 24

NY	3 0 2 1 1 0 0 0 0	7 14 1
ATL	0 0 0 0 0 0 0 0 2	2 5 1

Pitchers: CONE, Mendoza (8), Nelson (9) vs MILLWOOD, Mulholland (3), Springer (6), McGlinchy (8)
Attendance: 51,226

GAME 3 AT NY OCT 26

ATL	1 0 3 1 0 0 0 0 0	5 14 1
NY	1 0 0 0 1 0 1 2 0 1	6 9 0

Pitchers: Glavine, Rocker (8), REMLINGER (10) vs Pettitte, Grimsley (4), Nelson (7), RIVERA (9)
Home Runs: Curtis-NY (2), Martinez-NY, Knoblauch-NY
Attendance: 56,794

GAME 4 AT NY OCT 27

ATL	0 0 0 0 0 0 0 1 0	1 5 0
NY	0 0 3 0 0 0 0 1 X	4 8 0

Pitchers: SMOLTZ, Mulholland (8), Springer (8) vs CLEMENS, Nelson (8), Rivera (8)
Home Runs: Leyritz-NY
Attendance: 56,752

ST. LOUIS CARDINALS (CENTRAL) 3, ATLANTA BRAVES (EAST) 0

The Braves had lost just two Division Series games over the previous five seasons, including three sweeps, but this time it was Atlanta that was swept. The Cardinals, who had secured home-field advantage for the series on the last day of the season, made the most of it by scoring six times in the bottom of the first inning of the opener against Greg Maddux. Staked to a 6–0 lead, hard-throwing rookie Rick Ankiel suddenly—and disturbingly—fell apart. He issued a post-season-record five wild pitches in the third inning before being relieved. Mike James helped protect the 6–4 lead and earned the victory.

Atlanta scored twice in the top of the first inning in Game 2, but it was wiped out by a three-run home run by Will Clark. Ray Lankford's two-run double capped another outburst and forced Tom Glavine from the game. The 10–4 win marked the most runs scored in a postseason game against Atlanta since 1992.

Although the Braves managed to get out the first inning of Game 3 with a 1–1 tie, the Cards took the lead on a home run by Jim Edmonds in the third. When St. Louis starter Garrett Stephenson was forced to leave the game with elbow tendonitis, Britt Reames came out of the bullpen and combined with three relievers to keep Atlanta hitless for the rest of the game.

STL (C)

PLAYER/POS	AVG	G	AB	R	H	2B	3B	HR	RB	BB	SO	SB
Rick Ankiel, p	.000	1	1	0	0	0	0	0	0	0	0	0
Jason Christiansen, p	.000	1	0	0	0	0	0	0	0	0	0	0
Will Clark, 1b	.250	3	12	3	3	0	0	1	4	1	3	0
Eric Davis, of-1	.000	2	4	0	0	0	0	0	0	0	2	0
J. D. Drew, of	.167	2	6	1	1	0	0	0	0	2	1	2
Shawon Dunston, ph	1.000	1	1	0	1	0	0	0	0	0	0	0
Jim Edmonds, of	.571	3	14	5	8	4	0	2	7	1	2	1
Carlos Hernandez, c	.273	3	11	3	3	0	0	1	1	1	2	0
Mike James, p	.000	2	1	0	0	0	0	0	0	0	1	0
Darryl Kile, p-1	.000	2	3	0	0	0	0	0	0	0	1	0
Ray Lankford, of	.200	3	10	2	2	1	0	0	3	2	5	0
Mark McGwire, ph	.500	3	2	1	1	0	0	1	1	1	0	0
Matt Morris, p	.000	2	0	0	0	0	0	0	0	0	0	0
Craig Paquette, 3b-1, of-1	.000	2	2	0	0	0	0	0	0	0	0	0
Placido Polanco, 3b	.300	3	10	1	3	0	0	0	3	1	0	1
Britt Reames, p	.000	2	0	0	0	0	0	0	0	0	0	0
Edgar Renteria, ss	.200	3	10	5	2	0	0	0	0	4	1	2
Garrett Stephenson, p	.000	1	1	0	0	0	0	0	0	0	0	0
Mike Timlin, p	.000	2	0	0	0	0	0	0	0	0	0	0
Dave Veres, p	.000	2	0	0	0	0	0	0	0	0	0	0
Fernando Vina, 2b	.308	3	13	3	4	0	0	1	3	1	1	0
TOTAL	.277		101	24	28	5	0	6	22	14	19	6

PITCHER	W	L	ERA	G	GS	CG	SV	SHO	IP	H	ER	BB	SO
Rick Ankiel	0	0	13.50	1	1	0	0	0	2.2	4	4	6	3
Jason Christiansen	0	0	0.00	1	0	0	0	0	0.1	0	0	0	0
Mike James	1	0	0.00	2	0	0	0	0	4.1	1	0	1	1
Darryl Kile	1	0	2.57	1	1	0	0	0	7.0	4	2	2	6
Matt Morris	0	0	0.00	2	0	0	0	0	2.0	0	0	1	0
Britt Reames	1	0	0.00	2	0	0	0	0	3.1	0	0	3	2
G. Stephenson	0	0	2.45	1	1	0	0	0	3.2	3	1	2	2
Mike Timlin	0	0	10.80	2	0	0	0	0	1.2	5	2	1	2
Dave Veres	0	0	0.00	2	0	0	0	0	2.0	1	0	0	4
TOTAL	3	0	3.00	14	3	0	0	0	27.0	18	9	16	20

ATL (E)

PLAYER/POS	AVG	G	AB	R	H	2B	3B	HR	RB	BB	SO	SB
Andy Ashby, p	.000	2	0	0	0	0	0	0	0	0	0	0
Paul Bako, c	.000	2	1	0	0	0	0	0	0	0	1	0
Bobby Bonilla, of-1	.000	3	2	0	0	0	0	0	0	2	0	0
John Burkett, p	.000	1	0	0	0	0	0	0	0	0	0	0
Rafael Furcal, ss-3	.091	3	11	2	1	0	0	0	0	3	0	1
Andres Galarraga, 1b	.200	3	10	1	2	1	0	0	1	2	4	0
Tom Glavine, p	.000	1	1	0	0	0	0	0	0	0	1	0
Andruw Jones, of	.111	3	9	3	1	0	0	1	1	4	1	0
Chipper Jones, 3b	.333	3	12	2	4	1	0	0	1	1	4	0
Brian Jordan, of	.364	3	11	1	4	1	0	0	4	1	1	0
Wally Joyner, ph	.333	3	3	0	1	1	0	0	0	0	0	0
Kerry Ligtenberg, p	.000	3	0	0	0	0	0	0	0	0	0	0
Keith Lockhart, 2b	.125	3	8	0	1	0	0	0	0	0	1	0
Javy Lopez, c	.091	3	11	0	1	0	0	0	0	0	1	0
Greg Maddux, p-1	.000	2	1	1	0	0	0	0	0	1	0	0
Kevin Millwood, p	.000	1	1	0	0	0	0	0	0	1	0	0
Terry Mulholland, p	.000	3	0	0	0	0	0	0	0	0	0	0
Mike Remlinger, p	.000	3	0	0	0	0	0	0	0	0	0	0
John Rocker, p	.000	1	0	0	0	0	0	0	0	0	0	0
Reggie Sanders, of	.000	3	9	0	0	0	0	0	0	2	5	0
B. J. Surhoff, ph	.500	2	2	0	1	0	0	0	0	0	0	0
Walt Weiss, ss	.667	1	3	0	2	1	0	0	2	0	0	0
TOTAL	.189		95	10	18	5	0	1	9	16	20	1

PITCHER	W	L	ERA	G	GS	CG	SV	SHO	IP	H	ER	BB	SO
Andy Ashby	0	0	2.45	2	0	0	0	0	3.2	1	1	3	5
John Burkett	0	0	6.75	1	0	0	0	0	1.1	1	1	0	0
Tom Glavine	0	1	27.00	1	1	0	0	0	2.1	6	7	1	2
Kerry Ligtenberg	0	0	5.40	3	0	0	0	0	1.2	0	1	1	3
Greg Maddux	0	1	11.25	1	1	0	0	0	4.0	9	5	3	2
Kevin Millwood	0	1	7.71	1	1	0	0	0	4.2	4	4	3	3
Terry Mulholland	0	0	5.40	3	0	0	0	0	3.1	1.0	2	2	1
Mike Remlinger	0	0	2.70	3	0	0	0	0	3.1	6	1	0	3
John Rocker	0	0	0.00	1	0	0	0	0	0.2	0	0	1	0
TOTAL	0	3	7.92	16	3	0	0	0	25.0	28	22	14	19

GAME 1 AT STL OCT 3

											R	H	E
ATL	0	0	4	0	0	0	0	0	1		5	8	3
STL	6	0	0	1	0	0	0	0	X		7	11	1

Pitchers: MADDUX, Remlinger (5), Mulholland (6), Rocker (8), Ligtenberg (8) vs Ankiel, JAMES (3), Timlin (6), Reames (7), Veres (9)
Home Runs: Edmonds-STL
Attendance: 52,378

GAME 2 AT STL OCT 5

											R	H	E
ATL	2	0	0	0	0	0	0	2	0		4	7	1
STL	1	0	9	0	0	0	0	0	X		10	9	0

Pitchers: GLAVINE, Ashby (3), Burkett (5), Mulholland (6), Ligtenberg (7), Remlinger (8) vs KILE, Christiansen (8), Timlin (8), Morris (9)
Home Runs: Clark-STL, Hernandez-STL, A.Jones-ATL, McGwire-STL
Attendance: 52,389

GAME 3 AT ATL OCT 7

											R	H	E
STL	1	0	2	0	1	3	0	0	0		7	8	0
ATL	1	0	0	0	0	0	0	0	0		1	3	1

Pitchers: Stephenson, REAMES (4), James (6), Morris (8), Veres (9) vs MILLWOOD, Mulholland (5), Ligtenberg (6), Remlinger (6), Ashby (8)
Home Runs: Vina-STL, Edmonds-STL
Attendance: 49,898

NEW YORK METS (WILD CARD) 3, SAN FRANCISCO GIANTS (WEST) 1

The Giants, who had swept New York in a four-game series at Pac Bell Park in May, continued their dominance of the Mets in their new stadium in Game 1. A two-out triple by Barry Bonds in the fourth inning gave the Giants a 2–1 lead—and resulted in a season-ending injury to right fielder Derek Bell. Ellis Burks launched a three-run home run to cap the inning and the scoring.

Al Leiter allowed just one run and five hits in eight innings in Game 2, but he watched from the dugout as J.T. Snow's pinch-hit three-run homer off Armando Benitez tied the game in the ninth inning. In the top of the 10th, however, Felix Rodriguez surrendered a two-out single by Jay Payton to score Darryl Hamilton with the go ahead run. The game ended when Bonds was caught looking at a 3–2 changeup from John Franco.

Russ Ortiz kept the Mets hitless until the sixth inning of Game 3, but right fielder Timo Perez followed Hamilton's single with a run-scoring hit to make the score 2–1. Edgardo Alfonzo doubled home the tying run against closer Robb Nen in the eighth inning. Five innings later Benny Agbayani homered to left to win the game. The next day Robin Ventura smacked a two-run home run in the first inning and Bobby Jones had the Giants completely under control, except for one inning. Jeff Kent led off the fifth with a double for San Francisco's only hit of the day. Two outs and two walks followed but manager Dusty Baker sent pitcher Mark Gardner to bat. He popped up and Jones did not allow another baserunner.

NY (WC)

PLAYER/POS	AVG	G	AB	R	H	2B	3B	HR	RB	BB	SO	SB
Kurt Abbott, ss	.000	1	2	0	0	0	0	0	0	0	1	0
Benny Agbayani, of	.333	4	15	1	5	1	0	1	1	3	3	0
Edgardo Alfonzo, 2b	.278	4	18	1	5	2	0	1	5	1	2	0
Derek Bell, of	.000	1	1	0	0	0	0	0	0	0	0	0
Armando Benitez, p	.000	2	0	0	0	0	0	0	0	0	0	0
Mike Bordick, ss	.167	4	12	3	2	0	0	0	0	3	4	0
Dennis Cook, p	.000	2	0	0	0	0	0	0	0	0	0	0
John Franco, p	.000	2	0	0	0	0	0	0	0	0	0	0
Darryl Hamilton, of-2	.500	3	4	1	2	1	0	0	0	1	1	0
Mike Hampton, p	.500	1	2	0	1	0	0	0	0	0	1	0
Lenny Harris, ph	.000	2	2	1	0	0	0	0	0	0	0	1
Bobby J. Jones, p	.000	1	4	1	0	0	0	0	0	0	3	0
Al Leiter, p	.000	1	4	0	0	0	0	0	0	0	2	0
Joe McEwing,of-3,3b-1	1.000	4	1	0	1	0	0	0	0	0	0	0
Jay Payton, of	.176	4	17	1	3	0	0	0	2	0	4	1
Timo Perez, of	.294	4	17	2	5	1	0	0	3	0	2	1
Mike Piazza, c	.214	4	14	1	3	1	0	0	0	4	3	0
Todd Pratt, c	.000	1	1	0	0	0	0	0	0	0	0	0
Rick Reed, p	.000	1	1	0	0	0	0	0	0	0	0	0
Glendon Rusch, p	.000	1	0	0	0	0	0	0	0	0	0	0
Robin Ventura, 3b	.143	4	14	1	2	0	0	1	2	4	1	0
Turk Wendell, p	.000	2	0	0	0	0	0	0	0	0	0	0
Rick White, p	.000	2	0	0	0	0	0	0	0	0	0	0
Todd Zeile, 1b	.071	4	14	0	1	1	0	0	0	4	3	0
TOTAL	.210		143	13	30	7	0	3	13	20	30	3

PITCHER	W	L	ERA	G	GS	CG	SV	SHO	IP	H	ER	BB	SO
Armando Benitez	1	0	6.00	2	0	0	0	0	3.0	4	2	1	3
Dennis Cook	0	0	0.00	2	0	0	0	0	1.1	0	0	2	1
John Franco	0	0	0.00	2	0	0	1	0	2.0	1	0	0	2
Mike Hampton	0	1	8.44	1	1	0	0	0	5.1	6	5	3	2
Bobby J. Jones	1	0	0.00	1	1	1	0	1	9.0	1	0	2	5
Al Leiter	0	0	2.25	1	1	0	0	0	8.0	5	2	3	6
Rick Reed	0	0	3.00	1	1	0	0	0	6.0	7	2	2	6
Glendon Rusch	0	0	0.00	1	0	0	0	0	0.2	0	0	0	2
Turk Wendell	0	0	0.00	2	0	0	0	0	2.0	0	0	1	5
Rick White	1	0	0.00	2	0	0	0	0	2.2	6	0	2	4
TOTAL	3	1	2.48	15	4	1	1	1	40.0	30	11	16	36

SF (W)

PLAYER/POS	AVG	G	AB	R	H	2B	3B	HR	RB	BB	SO	SB
Rich Aurilia, ss	.133	4	15	0	2	1	0	0	0	0	3	0
Marvin Benard, of-3	.071	4	14	0	1	0	0	0	1	1	7	0
Barry Bonds, of	.176	4	17	2	3	1	1	0	1	3	4	1
Ellis Burks, of	.231	4	13	2	3	1	0	1	4	4	2	0
Felipe Crespo, ph	.250	4	4	0	1	0	0	0	0	0	0	0
Russ Davis, ph	.000	2	2	0	0	0	0	0	0	0	1	0
Miguel Del Toro, p	.000	1	0	0	0	0	0	0	0	0	0	0
Alan Embree, p	.000	2	0	0	0	0	0	0	0	0	0	0
Bobby Estalella, c	.083	4	12	1	1	0	0	0	1	0	2	0
Shawn Estes, p	.000	1	0	0	0	0	0	0	0	1	0	0
Aaron Fultz, p	.000	1	0	0	0	0	0	0	0	0	0	0
Mark Gardner, p	.000	1	2	0	0	0	0	0	0	0	1	0
Doug Henry, p	.000	3	0	0	0	0	0	0	0	0	0	0
Livan Hernandez, p	.000	1	3	0	0	0	0	0	0	0	1	0
Jeff Kent, 2b-4,1b-1	.375	4	16	3	6	1	0	0	1	1	3	1
Ramon Martinez,2b-1,ss-1	.333	2	6	0	2	0	0	0	0	0	2	0
Doug Mirabelli, c	.000	1	2	0	0	0	0	0	0	1	1	0
Bill Mueller, 3b	.250	4	20	2	5	2	0	0	0	0	3	0
Calvin Murray, of	.200	3	5	0	1	0	0	0	0	0	4	0
Robb Nen, p	.000	2	0	0	0	0	0	0	0	0	0	0
Russ Ortiz, p	.000	1	3	0	0	0	0	0	0	0	1	0
Armando Rios, ph	.500	2	2	0	1	0	0	0	0	0	0	0
Felix Rodriguez, p	.000	3	0	0	0	0	0	0	0	0	0	0
Kirk Rueter, p	.000	1	0	0	0	0	0	0	0	1	0	0
J. T. Snow, 1b	.400	4	10	1	4	0	0	1	3	4	1	0
TOTAL	.205		146	11	30	6	1	2	11	16	36	2

PITCHER	W	L	ERA	G	GS	CG	SV	SHO	IP	H	ER	BB	SO
Miguel Del Toro	0	0	0.00	1	0	0	0	0	1.0	1	0	0	2
Alan Embree	0	0	0.00	2	0	0	0	0	1.2	0	0	0	0
Shawn Estes	0	0	6.00	1	1	0	0	0	3.0	3	2	3	3
Aaron Fultz	0	1	6.75	1	0	0	0	0	1.1	3	1	0	0
Mark Gardner	0	1	8.31	1	1	0	0	0	4.1	4	4	2	5
Doug Henry	0	0	2.25	3	0	0	0	0	4.0	1	1	3	1
Livan Hernandez	1	0	1.17	1	1	0	0	0	7.2	5	1	5	5
Robb Nen	0	0	0.00	2	0	0	0	0	2.1	2	0	1	3
Russ Ortiz	0	0	1.69	1	1	0	0	0	5.1	2	1	4	4
Felix Rodriguez	0	1	6.23	3	0	0	0	0	4.1	6	3	1	6
Kirk Rueter	0	0	0.00	1	1	0	0	0	4.1	3	0	1	1
TOTAL	1	3	2.97	17	4	0	0	0	39.1	30	13	20	30

GAME 1 AT SF OCT 4

NY	001 000 000	1 5 0
SF	104 000 00X	5 10 0

Pitchers: HAMPTON, Wendell (6), Cook (7), White (7), Rusch (8) vs HERNANDEZ, Rodriguez (8), Nen (9)
Home Runs: Burks-SF
Attendance: 40,430

GAME 2 AT SF OCT 5

NY	020 000 002 1	5 10 0
SF	010 000 030 0	4 8 0

Pitchers: Leiter, BENITEZ (9), J.Franco (10) vs Estes, Rueter (4), Henry (8), RODRIGUEZ (9)
Home Runs: Alfonzo-NY, Snow-SF
Attendance: 40,430

GAME 3 AT NY OCT 7

SF	000 200 000 000 0	2 11 0
NY	000 001 010 000 1	3 9 0

Pitchers: Ortiz, Embree (6), Henry (7), Nen (8), Rodriguez (10), FULTZ (12) vs Reed, Cook (7), Wendell (7), J.Franco (9), Benitez (10), WHITE (12)
Home Runs: Agbayani-NY
Attendance: 56,270

GAME 4 AT NY OCT 8

SF	000 000 000	0 1 1
NY	200 020 00X	4 6 0

Pitchers: GARDNER, Henry (5), Embree (7), Del Toro (8) vs B.J.JONES
Home Runs: Ventura-NY
Attendance: 52,888

SEATTLE MARINERS (WILD CARD) 3, CHICAGO WHITE SOX (CENTRAL) 0

Seattle clinched the wild card on the final day of the season, while the White Sox had wrapped up the American League Central Division several weeks earlier. The Mariners, however, twice received game-winning hits in their final at bat to gain the sweep.

Seattle took a 3–0 lead in the opener, but Chicago, keyed by RBI-triples in the second and third innings, forged a 4–3 lead. Mike Cameron tied the game in the seventh with a single against Chad Bradford. After Seattle squelched a Chicago rally in the bottom of the ninth, Edgar Martinez and John Olerud hit back-to-back home runs in the 10th inning. The Mariners won the next day behind Paul Abbott and three relievers to take a two-game advantage.

James Baldwin, pitching with a slight rotator cuff tear, held Seattle to one run in six innings in Game 3; Aaron Sele held Chicago to one run in 7-1/3 innings. Olerud led off the bottom of the ninth with a line drive that struck reliever Kelly Wunsch, whose wild throw allowed Olerud to reach second base. Stan Javier bunted pinch runner Rickey Henderson to third, and with the infield in, pinch hitter Carlos Guillen bunted past first baseman Frank Thomas to win the game and the series.

SEA (WC)

PLAYER/POS	AVG	G	AB	R	H	2B	3B	HR	RB	BB	SO	SB
Paul Abbott, p	.000	1	0	0	0	0	0	0	0	0	0	0
David Bell, 3b	.364	3	11	0	4	1	0	0	1	2	2	0
Jay Buhner, of	.200	2	5	1	1	0	0	1	1	2	0	0
Mike Cameron, of	.250	3	12	2	3	0	0	0	2	0	0	1
Freddy Garcia, p	.000	1	0	0	0	0	0	0	0	0	0	0
Carlos Guillen, ph	1.000	1	1	0	1	0	0	0	1	0	0	0
Rickey Henderson, of-2	.400	3	5	3	2	0	0	0	0	1	0	1
Raul Ibanez, of	.375	3	8	2	3	0	0	0	0	0	0	0
Stan Javier, of	.167	3	6	0	1	0	0	0	1	0	3	0
Al Martin, ph	.000	1	1	0	0	0	0	0	0	0	0	0
Edgar Martinez, dh	.364	3	11	2	4	1	0	1	2	2	1	0
Mark McLemore, 2b	.111	3	9	1	1	0	0	0	0	2	1	0
Jose Mesa, p	.000	2	0	0	0	0	0	0	0	0	0	0
John Olerud, 1b	.300	3	10	2	3	0	0	1	2	2	1	0
Joe Oliver, c	.250	3	4	1	1	0	0	1	1	0	1	0
Jose Paniagua, p	.000	2	0	0	0	0	0	0	0	0	0	0
Arthur Lee Rhodes, p	.000	3	0	0	0	0	0	0	0	0	0	0
Alex Rodriguez, ss	.308	3	13	0	4	0	0	0	2	0	2	0
Kazuhiro Sasaki, p	.000	2	0	0	0	0	0	0	0	0	0	0
Aaron Sele, p	.000	1	0	0	0	0	0	0	0	0	0	0
Brett Tomko, p	.000	1	0	0	0	0	0	0	0	0	0	0
Dan Wilson, c	.000	2	3	0	0	0	0	0	1	1 .	2	0
TOTAL	.283		99	14	28	2	0	4	14	12	13	2

PITCHER	W	L	ERA	G	GS	CG	SV	SHO	IP	H	ER	BB	SO
Paul Abbott	1	0	1.59	1	1	0	0	0	5.2	5	1	3	1
Freddy Garcia	0	0	10.80	1	1	0	0	0	3.1	6	4	3	2
Jose Mesa	1	0	0.00	2	0	0	0	0	2.0	0	0	1	2
Jose Paniagua	1	0	0.00	2	0	0	0	0	2.1	1	0	2	3
Arthur Lee Rhodes	0	0	0.00	3	0	0	0	0	2.2	0	0	2	2
Kazuhiro Sasaki	0	0	0.00	2	0	0	2	0	2.0	1	0	0	5
Aaron Sele	0	0	1.23	1	1	0	0	0	7.1	3	1	3	1
Brett Tomko	0	0	0.00	1	0	0	0	0	2.2	1	0	1	0
TOTAL	3	0	1.93	13	3	0	2	0	28.0	17	6	15	16

CHI (C)

PLAYER/POS	AVG	G	AB	R	H	2B	3B	HR	RB	BB	SO	SB
Jeff Abbott, of	.000	1	1	0	0	0	0	0	0	0	0	0
Harold Baines, dh-1	.250	2	4	1	1	1	0	0	0	0	1	0
James Baldwin, p	.000	1	0	0	0	0	0	0	0	0	0	0
Lorenzo Barcelo, p	.000	1	0	0	0	0	0	0	0	0	0	0
Chad Bradford, p	.000	1	0	0	0	0	0	0	0	0	0	0
Mark Buehrle, p	.000	1	0	0	0	0	0	0	0	0	0	0
McKay Christensen, of	.000	1	0	0	0	0	0	0	0	0	0	0
Ray Durham, 2b	.200	3	10	2	2	1	0	1	1	3	3	0
Keith Foulke, p	.000	1	0	0	0	0	0	0	0	0	0	0
Tony Graffanino, 3b	.000	1	0	0	0	0	0	0	0	0	0	0
Bobby Howry, p	.000	1	0	0	0	0	0	0	0	0	0	0
Charles Johnson, c	.333	3	9	0	3	0	0	0	0	1	1	0
Paul Konerko, 1b-2	.000	3	9	1	0	0	0	0	0	1	1	0
Carlos Lee, of	.091	3	11	0	1	1	0	0	1	0	2	0
Magglio Ordonez, of	.182	3	11	0	2	0	1	0	1	2	2	1
Jim Parque, p	.000	1	0	0	0	0	0	0	0	0	0	0
Josh Paul, c	.000	1	0	0	0	0	0	0	0	0	0	0
Herb Perry, 3b	.444	3	9	0	4	1	0	0	1	2	2	0
Bill Simas, p	.000	2	0	0	0	0	0	0	0	0	0	0
Chris Singleton, of	.111	3	9	1	1	0	1	0	1	0	2	0
Mike Sirotka, p	.000	1	0	0	0	0	0	0	0	0	0	0
Frank Thomas, dh-2,1b-1	.000	3	9	0	0	0	0	0	0	4	0	0
Jose Valentin, ss	.300	3	10	2	3	2	0	0	1	2	2	3
Kelly Wunsch, p	.000	3	0	0	0	0	0	0	0	0	0	0
TOTAL	.185		92	71	7	6	2	1	6	15	16	4

PITCHER	W	L	ERA	G	GS	CG	SV	SHO	IP	H	ER	BB	SO
James Baldwin	0	0	1.50	1	1	0	0	0	6.0	3	1	3	2
Lorenzo Barcelo	0	0	0.00	1	0	0	0	0	1.2	0	0	1	0
Chad Bradford	0	0	0.00	1	0	0	0	0	0.2	2	0	0	0
Mark Buehrle	0	0	0.00	1	0	0	0	0	0.1	2	0	0	1
Keith Foulke	0	1	11.57	2	0	0	0	0	2.1	4	3	2	2
Bobby Howry	0	0	3.38	2	0	0	0	0	2.2	1	2	4	4
Jim Parque	0	0	4.50	1	0	0	0	0	6.0	6	3	1	2
Bill Simas	0	0	6.75	2	0	0	0	0	1.1	0	1	1	2
Mike Sirotka	0	1	4.76	1	0	0	0	0	5.2	7	3	2	0
Kelly Wunsch	0	1	0.00	3	0	0	0	0	0.2	2	0	0	0
TOTAL	0	3	3.95	15	1	0	0	0	27.1	28	12	12	13

GAME 1 AT CHI OCT 3

SEA	2	1	0	0	0	0	1	0	0	3	7	13	0
CHI	0	2	2	0	0	0	0	0	0	4	9	0	

Pitchers: Garcia, Tomko (4), Paniagua (7), Rhodes (9), MESA (9), Sasaki (10) vs Parque (7), Bradford (7), Wunsch (8), Simas (8), FOULKE (9)
Home Runs: Oliver-SEA, Durham-CHI, Martinez-SEA, Olerud-SEA
Attendance: 45,290

GAME 2 AT CHI OCT 4

SEA	0	2	0	1	1	0	0	0	1	5	9	1
CHI	1	0	1	0	0	0	0	0	0	2	5	1

Pitchers: ABBOTT, Mesa (7), Sasaki (9) vs SIROTKA, Barcelo (6), Wunsch (8), Simas (8), Buehrle (9)
Home Runs: Buhner-SEA
Attendance: 45,383

GAME 3 AT SEA OCT 6

CHI	0	1	0	0	0	0	0	0	0	1	3	1
SEA	0	0	0	1	0	0	0	0	1	2	6	2

Pitchers: Baldwin, Howry (7), WUNSCH (9), Foulke (9) vs Sele, Rhodes (8), PANIAGUA (9)
Attendance: 48,010

NEW YORK YANKEES (EAST) 3, OAKLAND A'S (WEST) 2

Oakland, playing its first post-season game since 1992, strung together three runs in the fifth inning of the opener to take a 3–2 lead against the two-time defending world champions. After New York tied the game in the top of the sixth, Ramon Hernandez doubled in his second run of the game to give Oakland back the lead. Jeff Tam, Jim Mecir, and Jason Isringhausen held the Yankees hitless over the last three innings in relief of Gil Heredia.

In Game 2 Glenallen Hill broke a scoreless tie with a single in the sixth inning. Paul O'Neill, who had been intentionally walked, scored along with Hill when Luis Sojo doubled. Andy Pettitte and Mariano Rivera combined on the shutout to even the series. The A's nicked Orlando Hernandez for a run in the second inning of Game 3, but the Yankees scored twice in the bottom of the inning on a fielder's choice and an infield single off Tim Hudson. Sojo, whose diving stop resulted in a key double play in the seventh inning, drove in an insurance run in the eighth.

Olmeda Saenz launched a threerun home run in the first inning of Game 4, and Oakland rolled to an 11–1 win. The second loss by Roger Clemens in four days resulted in an all-night flight back to Oakland for Game 5 the next afternoon. Leadoff hitter Chuck Knoblauch collected two hits in the first inning as New York exploded for six runs against Heredia. Pettitte could not make it out of the fourth inning, but four relievers—including Orlando Hernandez—held the A's scoreless the rest of the way.

NY (E)

PLAYER/POS	AVG	G	AB	R	H	2B	3B	HR	RB	BB	SO	SB
Clay Bellinger, of	1.000	2	1	0	1	1	0	0	1	0	0	0
Scott Brosius, 3b	.176	5	17	0	3	1	0	0	1	1	4	0
Randy Choate, p	.000	1	0	0	0	0	0	0	0	0	0	0
Roger Clemens, p	.000	2	0	0	0	0	0	0	0	0	0	0
Dwight Gooden, p	.000	1	0	0	0	0	0	0	0	0	0	0
Orlando Hernandez, p	.000	2	0	0	0	0	0	0	0	0	0	0
Glenallen Hill, dh-3	.083	4	12	1	1	0	0	0	2	1	5	0
Derek Jeter, ss	.211	5	19	1	4	0	0	0	2	2	3	0
David Justice, of	.222	5	18	2	4	0	0	1	1	3	4	0
Chuck Knoblauch, dh-2	.333	3	9	1	3	0	0	0	1	0	2	1
Tino Martinez, 1b	.421	5	19	2	8	2	0	0	4	1	3	0
Jeff Nelson, p	.000	2	0	0	0	0	0	0	0	0	0	0
Paul O'Neill, of	.211	5	19	4	4	1	0	0	0	2	4	0
Andy Pettitte, p	.000	2	0	0	0	0	0	0	0	0	0	0
Luis Polonia, ph	1.000	1	1	0	1	0	0	0	0	0	0	0
Jorge Posada, c	.235	5	17	2	4	2	0	0	1	3	5	0
Mariano Rivera, p	.000	3	0	0	0	0	0	0	0	0	0	0
Luis Sojo, 2b	.188	5	16	2	3	2	0	0	5	2	1	0
Mike Stanton, p	.000	3	0	0	0	0	0	0	0	0	0	0
Jose Vizcaino, 2b	.000	1	0	1	0	0	0	0	0	0	0	0
Bernie Williams, of	.250	5	20	3	5	3	0	0	1	1	4	0
TOTAL	.244		168	19	41	12	0	1	19	16	35	1

PITCHER	W	L	ERA	G	GS	CG	SV	SHO	IP	H	ER	BB	SO
Randy Choate	0	0	6.75	1	0	0	0	0	1.1	0	1	1	1
Roger Clemens	0	2	8.18	2	2	0	0	0	11.0	13	10	8	10
Dwight Gooden	0	0	21.60	1	0	0	0	0	1.2	4	4	1	1
O. Hernandez	1	0	2.45	2	1	0	0	0	7.1	5	2	5	5
Jeff Nelson	0	0	0.00	2	0	0	0	0	2.0	0	0	0	2
Andy Pettitte	1	0	3.97	2	2	0	0	0	11.1	15	5	3	7
Mariano Rivera	0	0	0.00	3	0	0	3	0	5.0	2	0	0	2
Mike Stanton	1	0	2.08	3	0	0	0	0	4.1	5	1	1	3
TOTAL	3	2	4.70	16	5	0	3	0	44.0	44	23	19	31

OAK (W)

PLAYER/POS	AVG	G	AB	R	H	2B	3B	HR	RB	BB	SO	SB
Kevin Appier, p	.000	2	0	0	0	0	0	0	0	0	0	0
Eric Chavez, 3b	.333	5	21	4	7	3	0	0	4	0	5	0
Ryan Christenson, of	.500	2	2	0	1	0	0	0	1	0	1	0
Sal Fasano, c	.000	1	0	0	0	0	0	0	0	0	0	0
Jason Giambi, 1b	.286	5	14	2	4	0	0	0	1	7	2	1
Jeremy Giambi, of-2, 2	.333	4	9	1	3	0	0	0	1	2	2	0
Ben Grieve, of	.118	5	17	1	2	0	0	0	2	3	7	0
Gil Heredia, p	.000	2	0	0	0	0	0	0	0	0	0	0
Ramon Hernandez, c	.375	5	16	3	6	2	0	0	3	0	3	0
Tim Hudson, p	.000	1	0	0	0	0	0	0	0	0	0	0
Jason Isringhausen, p	.000	1	0	0	0	0	0	0	0	0	0	0
Doug Jones, p	.000	2	0	0	0	0	0	0	0	0	0	0
Terrence Long, of	.158	5	19	2	3	0	0	1	1	3	2	0
Mike Magnante, p	.000	2	0	0	0	0	0	0	0	0	0	0
Jim Mecir, p	.000	3	0	0	0	0	0	0	0	0	0	0
Frank Menechino, 2b	.000	1	0	0	0	0	0	0	0	0	0	0
Adam Piatt, of-2	.167	3	6	2	1	0	0	0	0	0	1	0
Bo Porter, of	1.000	2	1	0	1	0	0	0	1	0	0	0
Olmedo Saenz, dh-3	.231	4	13	1	3	0	0	1	4	0	2	0
Matt Stairs, of-2	.111	3	9	0	1	1	0	0	0	0	1	0
Jeff Tam, p	.000	3	0	0	0	0	0	0	0	0	0	0
Miguel Tejada, ss	.350	5	20	5	7	2	0	0	1	2	2	1
Randy Velarde, 2b	.250	5	20	2	5	1	0	0	3	2	3	1
Barry Zito, p	.000	1	0	0	0	0	0	0	0	0	0	0
TOTAL	.263		167	23	44	9	0	2	22	19	31	3

PITCHER	W	L	ERA	G	GS	CG	SV	SHO	IP	H	ER	BB	SO
Kevin Appier	0	1	3.48	2	1	0	0	0	10.1	10	4	6	13
Gil Heredia	1	1	12.79	2	2	0	0	0	6.1	11	9	3	3
Tim Hudson	0	1	3.38	1	1	1	0	0	8.0	6	3	4	5
J. Isringhausen	0	0	0.00	2	0	0	1	0	2.0	1	0	0	3
Doug Jones	0	0	0.00	2	0	0	0	0	1.1	1	0	0	1
Mike Magnante	0	0	0.00	2	0	0	0	0	3.0	1	0	0	2
Jim Mecir	0	0	0.00	3	0	0	0	0	5.1	1	0	0	2
Jeff Tam	0	0	0.00	3	0	0	0	0	2.0	3	0	1	1
Barry Zito	1	0	1.59	1	1	0	0	0	5.2	7	1	2	5
TOTAL	2	3	3.48	18	5	1	1	0	44.0	41	17	16	35

GAME 1 AT OAK OCT 3

NY   0 2 0 0 0 1   0 0 0   3 7 0
OAK 0 0 0 0 3 1   0 1 X   5 10 2
Pitchers: CLEMENS, Stanton (7), Nelson (8) vs HEREDIA, Tam (7), Mecir (7), Isringhausen (9)
Attendance: 47,360

GAME 2 AT OAK OCT 4

NY   0 0 0 0 0 3   0 0 1   4 8 1
OAK 0 0 0 0 0 0   0 0 0   0 6 1
Pitchers: PETTITTE, Rivera (8) vs APPIER, Magnante (7), Tam (9), Jones (9)
Attendance: 47,860

GAME 3 AT NY OCT 6

OAK 0 1 0 0 1 0   0 0 0   2 4 2
NY   0 2 0 0 0 0   0 0 1   4 6 1
Pitchers: HUDSON vs HERNANDEZ, Rivera (8)
Home Runs: Long-OAK
Attendance: 56,606

GAME 4 AT NY OCT 7

OAK 3 0 0 0 0 3   0 1 4   11 11 0
NY   0 0 0 0 0 1   0 0 0   1 8 0
Pitchers: ZITO, Mecir (6), Magnante (7), Jones (9) vs CLEMENS, Stanton (6), Choate (7), Gooden (8)
Home Runs: Saenz-OAK
Attendance: 56,915

GAME 5 AT OAK OCT 8

NY   6 0 0 1 0 0   0 0 0   7 12 0
OAK 0 2 1 2 0 0   0 0 0   5 13 0
Pitchers: Pettitte, STANTON (4), Nelson (6), Hernandez (8), Rivera (8) vs HEREDIA, Tam (1), Appier (2), Mecir (6), Isringhausen (9)
Home Runs: Justice-NY
Attendance: 41,170

NEW YORK METS (WILD CARD) 4, ST. LOUIS CARDINALS (CENTRAL) 1

Some critics claimed the Cardinals did the Mets a favor by knocking the arch-rival Braves out of the postseason; New York returned the favor by defeating St. Louis in five games. The Mets scored in the first inning of each game and their pitching staff made the leads hold up.

Timo Perez, who had made his major league debut against the Cardinals just six weeks earlier, doubled to start the series and scored the first of his League Championship Series record-tying eight runs. Mike Hampton allowed just six hits in seven innings for the win. Rick Ankiel, who had been bafflingly wild in the Division Series, could not find the plate in Game 2. He walked three, threw two wild pitches, and was replaced by Britt Reames following a run-scoring double by Benny Agbayani in the first inning. The Cardinals rallied to tie the game in the fifth and again in the eighth, but Jay Payton singled in the go-ahead run in the ninth.

Jim Edmonds doubled in two runs in the first inning of Game 3, and Edgar Renteria scored twice and drove in two runs in an 8–2 win. Andy Benes allowed only six hits in eight innings, with both runs against him scoring on double plays. Darryl Kile, pitching on three days' rest, was drilled for seven runs in three innings in Game 4. The Cardinals pulled to within 10–6 and had two runners on base in the eighth, but manager Tony La Russa selected Craig Paquette to bat instead of All-Star Mark McGwire, who was relegated to pinch hitter because of knee tendonitis. Paquette grounded out to end the inning.

Pat Hentgen, who had not pitched in more than two weeks, surrendered three runs on four hits (plus two errors) in the first inning of Game 5. Todd Zeile drove Hentgen from the game with a three-run double in the fourth. Ankiel made another wobbly performance, issuing two walks and two wild pitches in two-thirds of an inning. A pitch from Dave Veres glanced off Payton's head in the eighth and caused both benches to empty, but order was restored quickly. NLCS Most Valuable Player Hampton retired the side in the ninth for the Mets' first National League pennant in 14 years.

NY (WC)

PLAYER/POS	AVG	G	AB	R	H	2B	3B	HR	RB	BB	SO	SB
Kurt Abbott, ss	.000	2	3	0	0	0	0	0	0	0	2	0
Benny Agbayani, of	.353	5	17	0	6	2	0	0	3	4	0	0
Edgardo Alfonzo, 2b	.444	5	18	5	8	1	1	0	4	4	1	0
Armando Benitez, p	.000	3	0	0	0	0	0	0	0	0	0	0
Mike Bordick, ss	.077	5	13	2	1	0	0	0	0	3	1	0
Dennis Cook, p	.000	1	0	0	0	0	0	0	0	0	0	0
John Franco, p	.000	3	0	0	0	0	0	0	0	0	0	0
Matt Franco, 1b-1	.000	2	3	0	0	0	0	0	0	0	1	0
Darryl Hamilton, ph	.000	3	2	0	0	0	0	0	0	0	0	0
Mike Hampton, p	.167	2	6	1	1	0	0	0	0	0	1	0
Lenny Harris, ph	.000	2	1	0	0	0	0	0	0	0	1	0
Bobby J. Jones, p	.000	1	2	0	0	0	0	0	0	0	1	0
Al Leiter, p	.000	1	3	0	0	0	0	0	0	0	2	0
Joe McEwing, of-3,3b-1	.000	4	0	2	0	0	0	0	0	0	0	0
Jay Payton, of	.158	5	19	1	3	0	0	1	3	2	5	0
Timo Perez, of	.304	5	23	8	7	2	0	0	0	1	3	2
Mike Piazza, c	.412	5	17	7	7	3	0	2	4	5	0	0
Rick Reed, p	.000	1	1	0	0	0	0	0	0	0	0	0
Glendon Rusch, p	.000	2	0	0	0	0	0	0	0	0	0	0
Bubba Trammell, ph	.000	3	3	0	0	0	0	0	0	0	2	0
Robin Ventura, 3b	.214	5	14	4	3	1	0	0	5	6	0	0
Turk Wendell, p	.000	2	0	0	0	0	0	0	0	0	0	0
Rick White, p	.000	1	0	0	0	0	0	0	0	0	0	0
Todd Zeile, 1b	.368	5	19	1	7	3	0	1	8	2	4	0
TOTAL	.262		164	31	43	12	1	4	27	27	24	2

PITCHER	W	L	ERA	G	GS	CG	SV	SHO	IP	H	ER	BB	SO
Armando Benitez	0	0	0.00	3	0	0	1	0	3.0	3	0	2	2
Dennis Cook	0	0	0.00	1	0	0	0	0	1.0	1	0	0	2
John Franco	0	0	6.75	3	0	0	0	0	2.2	3	2	2	2
Mike Hampton	2	0	0.00	2	2	1	0	1	16.0	9	0	4	12
Bobby J. Jones	0	0	13.50	1	1	0	0	0	4.0	6	6	0	2
Al Leiter	0	0	3.86	1	1	0	0	0	7.0	8	3	0	9
Rick Reed	0	1	10.80	1	1	0	0	0	3.1	8	4	1	4
Glendon Rusch	1	0	0.00	2	0	0	0	0	3.2	3	0	0	3
Turk Wendell	1	0	0.00	2	0	0	0	0	1.1	1	0	1	2
Rick White	0	0	9.00	1	0	0	0	0	3.0	5	3	1	1
TOTAL	4	1	3.60	17	5	1	1	1	45.0	47	18	11	39

STL (C)

PLAYER/POS	AVG	G	AB	R	H	2B	3B	HR	RB	BB	SO	SB
Rick Ankiel, p	.000	2	0	0	0	0	0	0	0	0	0	0
Alan Benes, p	.333	1	3	1	1	0	0	0	0	0	2	0
Jason Christiansen, p	.000	2	0	0	0	0	0	0	0	0	0	0
Will Clark, 1b	.412	5	17	3	7	2	0	1	1	2	1	0
Eric Davis, of-3	.200	4	10	1	2	1	0	0	1	0	2	0
J. D. Drew, of	.333	5	12	2	4	1	0	0	1	0	3	0
Shawon Dunston, of-2	.333	4	6	1	2	1	0	0	0	0	0	0
Jim Edmonds, of	.227	5	22	1	5	1	0	1	5	1	9	0
Pat Hentgen, p	1.000	1	1	0	1	0	0	0	0	0	0	0
Carlos Hernandez, c	.250	5	16	3	4	0	0	0	1	1	1	0
Mike James, p	.000	4	0	0	0	0	0	0	0	0	0	0
Darryl Kile, p-2	.000	3	2	0	0	0	0	0	0	1	0	0
Ray Lankford, of-4	.333	5	12	1	4	1	0	0	1	1	5	0
Eli Marrero, c-3	.000	4	4	0	0	0	0	0	0	1	0	0
Mark McGwire, ph	.000	3	2	0	0	0	0	0	0	1	0	0
Matt Morris, p	.000	2	0	0	0	0	0	0	0	0	0	0
Craig Paquette, of-2,3b-1	.167	4	6	0	1	0	0	0	0	0	2	0
Placido Polanco, 3b-2	.200	4	5	0	1	0	0	0	0	2	1	0
Britt Reames, p	.000	2	1	0	0	0	0	0	0	0	1	0
Edgar Renteria, ss	.300	5	20	4	6	1	0	0	4	0	2	3
Fernando Tatis, 3b-4	.231	5	13	1	3	2	0	0	2	1	5	0
Mike Timlin, p	.000	3	0	0	0	0	0	0	0	0	0	0
Dave Veres, p	.000	3	0	0	0	0	0	0	0	0	0	0
Fernando Vina, 2b	.261	5	23	3	6	1	0	0	1	1	4	0
Rick Wilkins, ph	.000	2	2	0	0	0	0	0	0	0	0	0
TOTAL	.266		177	21	47	11	0	2	18	11	39	3

PITCHER	W	L	ERA	G	GS	CG	SV	SHO	IP	H	ER	BB	SO
Rick Ankiel	0	0	20.25	2	1	0	0	0	1.1	1	3	5	2
Alan Benes	1	0	2.25	1	1	0	0	0	8.0	6	2	3	5
J. Christiansen	0	0	0.00	2	0	0	0	0	2.0	0	0	0	1
Pat Hentgen	0	1	14.73	1	1	0	0	0	3.2	7	6	5	2
Mike James	0	0	15.43	4	0	0	0	0	2.1	5	4	1	0
Darryl Kile	0	2	9.00	2	2	0	0	0	10.0	13	10	5	3
Matt Morris	0	0	4.91	2	0	0	0	0	3.2	3	2	2	2
Britt Reames	0	0	1.42	2	0	0	0	0	6.1	5	1	4	6
Mike Timlin	0	1	0.00	3	0	0	0	0	3.1	1	0	0	0
Dave Veres	0	0	0.00	3	0	0	0	0	2.1	2	0	0	3
TOTAL	1	4	5.86	22	5	0	0	0	43.0	43	28	27	24

GAME 1 AT STL OCT 11

NY	200 010 003	6	8	3
STL	000 000 002	2	9	0

Pitchers: HAMPTON, J.Franco (8), Benitez (9) vs KILE, James (8), Christiansen (9)
Home Runs: Zeile-NY, Payton-NY
Attendance: 52,255

GAME 2 AT STL OCT 12

NY	201 000 021	6	9	0
STL	010 020 020	5	10	3

Pitchers: Leiter, J.Franco (8), WENDELL (8), Benitez (9) vs Ankiel, Reames (1), Morris (6), Veres (8), TIMLIN (9)
Home Runs: Piazza-NY
Attendance: 52,250

GAME 3 AT NY OCT 14

STL	202 130 000	8	14	0
NY	100 100 000	2	7	1

Pitchers: AN.BENES, James (9), Veres (9) vs REED, Rusch (5), White (5), Cook (8), Wendell (9)
Attendance: 55,693

GAME 4 AT NY OCT 15

STL	200 130 000	6	11	2
NY	430 102 00X	10	9	0

Pitchers: KILE, James (4), Timlin (5), Morris (7), Christiansen (8) vs B.J.Jones, RUSCH (5), J.Franco (8), Benitez (9)
Home Runs: Edmonds-STL, Clark-STL, Piazza-NY
Attendance: 55,665

GAME 5 AT NY OCT 16

STL	000 000 000	0	3	2
NY	300 300 10X	7	10	0

Pitchers: HENTGEN, Timlin (4), Reames (5), Ankiel (7), James (7), Veres (8) vs HAMPTON
Attendance: 55,695

ALCS 2000

NEW YORK YANKEES (EAST) 4, SEATTLE MARINERS (WILD CARD) 2

The Yankees entered the American League Championship Series in a batting slump, and Seattle's Freddy Garcia did not help matters with 6-2/3 shutout innings in Game 1. Denny Neagle, who had not pitched in the Division Series, allowed only an RBI-single by Rickey Henderson and a home run by Alex Rodriguez. Three relievers helped keep the Yanks off the scoreboard. New York did not score for the first seven innings of Game 2, but Bernie Williams plated the club's first run of the series with a game-tying single in the eighth. Six more hits followed, capped by Derek Jeter's home run.

The Yankees continued hitting when the series shifted to Seattle. Back-to-back home runs by Williams and Tino Martinez erased a 1–0 Mariners lead. Andy Pettitte allowed nine hits, but he got outs at key moments and helped New York nurse a 4–2 lead into the seventh. The Yankees assured victory with four runs in the ninth inning, led by a two-run double by David Justice.

New York needed little offense in Game 4, but Derek Jeter and Justice accounted for five runs with home runs in support of Roger Clemens. Clemens allowed only Al Martin's seventh-inning double, which glanced off Tino Martinez's glove, and two walks. His masterful 15-strikeout performance was the first complete-game shutout in the ALCS in 15 years. Neagle had a 2–1 lead when he was relieved with two runners on in the fifth inning of Game 5. Jeff Nelson surrendered a two-run single, followed by consecutive home runs by Edgar Martinez and John Olerud. Garcia beat the Yankees for the second time, again with shutout relief from Jose Paniagua, Arthur Rhodes, and Kazuhiro Sasaki.

Seattle's bullpen was its undoing in Game 6. The Mariners took a 4–0 lead on a pair of doubles in the first inning and a two-run home run by Carlos Guillen, but starter John Halama could not get out of the fourth inning. After Brett Tomko's 2-1/3 shutout innings in relief, the Yankees put together another big rally. Rhodes surrendered a three-run homer to Justice, the ALCS Most Valuable Player. Orlando Hernandez, who had benefited from a late rally in Game 2, earned the win again.

Although Mariano Rivera's string of 34 consecutive scoreless post-season innings ended, he preserved the victory and assured New York of its first Subway Series since 1956.

NY (E)

PLAYER/POS	AVG	G	AB	R	H	2B	3B	HR	RB	BB	SO	SB
Clay Bellinger, of	.000	5	0	0	0	0	0	0	0	0	0	0
Scott Brosius, 3b	.222	6	18	2	4	0	0	0	0	0	2	3	0
Randy Choate, p	.000	1	0	0	0	0	0	0	0	0	0	0
Roger Clemens, p	.000	1	0	0	0	0	0	0	0	0	0	0
David Cone, p	.000	1	0	0	0	0	0	0	0	0	0	0
Dwight Gooden, p	.000	1	0	0	0	0	0	0	0	0	0	0
Jason Grimsley, p	.000	2	0	0	0	0	0	0	0	0	0	0
Orlando Hernandez, p	.000	2	0	0	0	0	0	0	0	0	0	0
Glenallen Hill, ph	.000	2	2	0	0	0	0	0	0	0	2	0
Derek Jeter, ss	.318	6	22	6	7	0	0	2	5	6	7	1
David Justice, of	.231	6	26	4	6	2	0	2	8	2	7	0
Chuck Knoblauch, dh	.261	6	23	3	6	2	0	0	2	3	4	0
Tino Martinez, 1b	.320	6	25	5	8	2	0	1	1	2	4	0
Denny Neagle, p	.000	2	0	0	0	0	0	0	0	0	0	0
Jeff Nelson, p	.000	3	0	0	0	0	0	0	0	0	0	0
Paul O'Neill, of	.250	6	20	0	5	0	0	0	0	5	1	2	0
Andy Pettitte, p	.000	1	0	0	0	0	0	0	0	0	0	0
Luis Polonia, ph	.000	2	2	0	0	0	0	0	0	0	1	0
Jorge Posada, c	.158	6	19	2	3	1	0	0	3	5	5	0
Mariano Rivera, p	.000	3	0	0	0	0	0	0	0	0	0	0
Luis Sojo, 2b-6,3b-2	.261	6	23	1	6	1	0	0	2	2	3	0
Jose Vizcaino, 2b-3	1.000	4	2	3	2	1	0	0	2	0	0	2
Bernie Williams, of	.435	6	23	5	10	1	0	1	3	2	3	1
TOTAL	.279		204	31	57	10	0	6	31	25	41	4

PITCHER	W	L	ERA	G	GS	CG	SV	SHO	IP	H	ER	BB	SO
Randy Choate	0	0	0.00	1	0	0	0	0	0.1	0	0	0	1
Roger Clemens	1	0	0.00	1	1	1	0	0	9.0	1	0	2	15
David Cone	0	0	0.00	1	0	0	0	0	1.0	0	0	0	0
Dwight Gooden	0	0	0.00	1	0	0	0	0	2.1	1	0	0	1
Jason Grimsley	0	0	0.00	2	0	0	0	0	1.0	2	0	3	1
O. Hernandez	2	0	4.20	2	2	0	0	0	15.0	13	7	8	14
Denny Neagle	0	2	4.50	2	2	0	0	0	10.0	6	5	7	7
Jeff Nelson	0	0	9.00	3	0	0	0	0	3.0	5	3	0	6
Andy Pettitte	1	0	2.70	1	1	0	0	0	6.2	9	2	1	2
Mariano Rivera	0	0	1.93	3	0	0	1	0	4.2	4	1	0	1
TOTAL	4	2	3.06	17	6	1	1	0	53.0	41	18	21	48

SEA (WC)

PLAYER/POS	AVG	G	AB	R	H	2B	3B	HR	RB	BB	SO	SB
Paul Abbott, p	.000	1	0	0	0	0	0	0	0	0	0	0
David Bell, 3b-4,2b-1	.222	5	18	0	4	0	0	0	0	0	0	0
Jay Buhner, of-3	.182	4	11	0	2	0	0	0	0	1	6	0
Mike Cameron, of	.111	6	18	3	2	0	0	0	1	2	7	1
Freddy Garcia, p	.000	2	0	0	0	0	0	0	0	0	0	0
Charles Gipson, of	.000	2	0	0	0	0	0	0	0	0	0	0
Carlos Guillen, 3b	.200	2	5	1	1	0	0	1	2	2	2	0
John Halama, p	.000	2	0	0	0	0	0	0	0	0	0	0
Rickey Henderson, of	.222	3	9	2	2	1	0	0	1	2	2	0
Raul Ibanez, of-3	.000	6	9	0	0	0	0	0	0	0	2	0
Stan Javier, of	.071	4	14	0	1	0	0	0	0	1	4	0
Al Martin, of-3	.182	4	11	2	2	2	0	0	0	2	3	0
Edgar Martinez, dh	.238	6	21	2	5	1	0	1	4	3	5	0
Mark McLemore, 2b	.250	5	16	2	4	3	0	0	2	2	1	0
Jose Mesa, p	.000	3	0	0	0	0	0	0	0	0	0	0
John Olerud, 1b	.350	6	20	2	7	3	0	1	2	2	2	1
Joe Oliver, c	.167	4	6	0	1	0	0	0	0	1	1	0
Jose Paniagua, p	.000	5	0	0	0	0	0	0	0	0	0	0
Robert Ramsay, p	.000	2	0	0	0	0	0	0	0	0	0	0
Arthur Lee Rhodes, p	.000	4	0	0	0	0	0	0	0	0	0	0
Alex Rodriguez, ss	.409	6	22	4	9	0	0	2	5	3	8	1
Kazuhiro Sasaki, p	.000	2	0	0	0	0	0	0	0	0	0	0
Aaron Sele, p	.000	1	0	0	0	0	0	0	0	0	0	0
Brett Tomko, p	.000	2	0	0	0	0	0	0	0	0	0	0
Dan Wilson, c	.091	4	11	0	1	0	0	0	0	1	5	0
TOTAL	.215		191	18	41	12	0	5	18	21	48	3

PITCHER	W	L	ERA	G	GS	CG	SV	SHO	IP	H	ER	BB	SO
Paul Abbott	0	1	5.40	1	1	0	0	0	5.0	3	3	3	3
Freddy Garcia	2	0	1.54	2	2	0	0	0	11.2	10	2	4	11
John Halama	0	0	2.89	2	2	0	0	0	9.1	10	3	5	3
Jose Mesa	0	0	12.46	3	0	0	0	0	4.1	5	6	3	3
Jose Paniagua	0	1	4.15	5	0	0	0	0	4.1	4	2	1	4
Robert Ramsay	0	0	0.00	2	0	0	0	0	1.2	2	0	0	1
Arthur Lee Rhodes	0	1	31.50	4	0	0	0	0	2.0	8	7	4	5
Kazuhiro Sasaki	0	0	0.00	2	0	0	1	0	2.2	3	0	1	3
Aaron Sele	0	1	6.00	1	1	0	0	0	6.0	9	4	0	4
Brett Tomko	0	0	7.20	2	0	0	0	0	5.0	3	4	4	4
TOTAL	2	4	5.37	24	6	0	1	0	52.0	57	31	25	41

GAME 1 AT NY OCT 10

```
SEA  000 011 000   2 5 0
NY   000 000 000   0 6 1
```
Pitchers: GARCIA, Paniagua (7), Rhodes (8), Sasaki (9) vs NEAGLE, Nelson (6), Choate (9), Grimsley (9)
Home Runs: Rodriguez-SEA
Attendance: 54,481

GAME 2 AT NY OCT 11

```
SEA  001 000 000   1 7 2
NY   000 000 07X   7 14 0
```
Pitchers: Halama, Paniagua (7), RHODES (8), Mesa (8) vs HERNANDEZ, Rivera (9)
Home Runs: Jeter-NY
Attendance: 55,317

GAME 3 AT SEA OCT 13

```
NY   021 001 004   8 13 0
SEA  100 010 000   2 10 1
```
Pitchers: PETTITTE, Nelson (7), Rivera (8) vs SELE, Tomko (7), Ramsay (9)
Home Runs: Williams-NY, Martinez-NY
Attendance: 47,827

GAME 4 AT SEA OCT 14

```
NY   000 030 020   5 5 0
SEA  000 000 000   0 1 0
```
Pitchers: CLEMENS vs ABBOTT, Ramsay (6), Mesa (7), Paniagua (9)
Home Runs: Jeter-NY, Justice-NY
Attendance: 47,803

GAME 5 AT SEA OCT 15

```
NY   000 200 000   2 8 0
SEA  100 050 00X   6 8 0
```
Pitchers: NEAGLE, Nelson (5), Grimsley (5), Gooden (5), Cone (8) vs GARCIA, Paniagua (6), Rhodes (7), Sasaki (8)
Home Runs: Martinez-SEA, Olerud-SEA
Attendance: 47,802

GAME 6 AT NY OCT 17

```
SEA  200 200 030   7 10 0
NY   000 300 60X   9 11 0
```
Pitchers: Halama, Tomko (4), PANIAGUA (7), Rhodes (7), Mesa (7) vs HERNANDEZ, Rivera (8)
Home Runs: Guillen-SEA, Justice-NY, Rodriguez-SEA
Attendance: 56,598

NEW YORK YANKEES (AL) 4, NEW YORK METS (NL) 1

Gripped by its first Subway Series in 44 years, New York was split in its favoritism for its two teams. The Mets made two key baserunning mistakes in the opener in the Bronx, but they still held a 3–2 lead heading into the bottom of the ninth inning thanks to a two-run pinch-hit single by Bubba Trammel and an infield hit by Edgardo Alfonzo. Paul O'Neill fouled off four two-strike offerings before walking against Armando Benitez with one out in the ninth. Two successive singles and Chuck Knoblauch's sacrifice fly tied the game. The Mets wriggled out of jams the next two innings, but Jose Vizcaino's fourth hit of the game plated the winning run for the Yanks in the 12th.

In the first inning of Game 2 Mike Piazza's bat shattered, hurling the sheared barrel at the feet of Roger Clemens. The pitcher threw the bat, nearly hitting Piazza and causing both benches to empty. When play resumed, Piazza grounded out and Clemens allowed just two hits over eight innings. By the time Piazza and Jay Payton homered in the ninth inning, the Yankees had built a large enough lead to hold on for the 6–5 win.

Game 3 was the highlight of the Series for Queens. In the bottom of the eighth inning of a tie game, Benny Agbayani doubled to score Todd Zeile. In the process the Mets handed Orlando Hernandez his first postseason loss after nine decisions, and John Franco earned his first World Series win after 17 major league seasons. The next night Series Most Valuable Player Derek Jeter homered on the first pitch of the game. Triples in the second and third innings provided two more runs. With two outs in the fifth and no one on, Yankees manager Joe Torre replaced Denny Neagle with David Cone. Piazza, who had homered in his last at bat, popped up. Jeff Nelson, Mike Stanton, and Mariano Rivera retired the Mets on two hits the rest of the way.

Al Leiter pitched brilliantly in Game 5, and his two-out bunt spurred his team's only rally. Home runs by Bernie Williams and Jeter kept the game even until two outs in the ninth when the Mets southpaw tired. Luis Sojo, whose grounder had plated the go-ahead run in Game 4, singled in Jorge Posada in the ninth inning. Another run scored when the throw was deflected out of play. After Piazza flied out to deep center field, the Yankees had become the first team since 1972–74 Oakland A's to win three straight world championships.

GAME 1 AT NY-A OCT 21

NY-N 000 000 300 000 3 10 0
NY-A 000 002 001 001 4 12 0
Pitchers: Leiter, J.Franco (8), Benitez (9), Cook (10), Rusch (10), WENDELL (11) vs Pettitte, Nelson (7), Rivera (9), STANTON (11)
Attendance: 55,913

GAME 2 AT NY-A OCT 22

NY-N 000 000 005 5 7 3
NY-A 210 010 11X 6 12 1
Pitchers: HAMPTON, Rusch (7), White (7), Cook (8) vs CLEMENS, Nelson (9), Rivera (9)
Home Runs: Brosius-NY-A, Piazza-NY-N, Payton-NY-N
Attendance: 56,059

GAME 3 AT NY-N OCT 24

NY-A 001 100 000 2 8 0
NY-N 010 001 02X 4 9 0
Pitchers: HERNANDEZ, Stanton (8) vs Reed, Wendell (7), Cook (7), J.FRANCO (8), Benitez (9)
Home Runs: Ventura-NY-N
Attendance: 55,299

GAME 4 AT NY-N OCT 25

NY-A 111 000 000 3 8 0
NY-N 002 000 000 2 6 1
Pitchers: Neagle, Cone (5), NELSON (6), Stanton (7), Rivera (8) vs B.J.JONES, Rusch (6), J.Franco (9), Benitez (9)
Home Runs: Jeter-NY-A, Piazza-NY-N
Attendance: 55,290

GAME 5 AT NY-N OCT 26

NY-A 010 001 002 4 7 1
NY-N 020 000 000 2 8 1
Pitchers: Pettitte, STANTON (8), Rivera (9) vs LEITER, J.Franco (9)
Home Runs: Williams-NY-A, Jeter-NY-A
Attendance: 55,292

NY (A)

PLAYER/POS	AVG	G	AB	R	H	2B	3B	HR	RB	BB	SO	SB
Clay Bellinger, of	.000	4	0	0	0	0	0	0	0	0	0	0
Scott Brosius, 3b	.308	5	13	2	4	0	0	1	3	2	2	0
Jose Canseco, ph	.000	1	1	0	0	0	0	0	0	0	1	0
Roger Clemens, p	.000	1	0	0	0	0	0	0	0	0	0	0
David Cone, p	.000	1	0	0	0	0	0	0	0	0	0	0
Orlando Hernandez, p	.000	1	2	0	0	0	0	0	0	0	2	0
Glenallen Hill, dh-of	.000	3	3	0	0	0	0	0	0	0	0	0
Derek Jeter, ss	.409	5	22	6	9	2	1	2	2	3	8	0
David Justice, of	.158	5	19	1	3	2	0	0	3	3	2	0
Chuck Knoblauch, dh-2	.100	4	10	1	1	0	0	0	1	1	2	1
Tino Martinez, 1b	.364	5	22	3	8	1	0	0	2	1	4	0
Denny Neagle, p	.000	1	2	0	0	0	0	0	0	0	1	0
Jeff Nelson, p	.000	3	0	0	0	0	0	0	0	0	0	0
Paul O'Neill, of	.474	5	19	2	9	2	2	0	2	3	4	0
Andy Pettitte, p	.000	2	3	0	0	0	0	0	0	0	1	0
Luis Polonia, ph	.500	2	2	0	1	0	0	0	0	0	0	0
Jorge Posada, c	.222	5	18	2	4	1	0	0	1	5	4	0
Mariano Rivera, p	.000	4	1	0	0	0	0	0	0	0	0	0
Luis Sojo, 2b-2,3b-2	.286	4	7	0	2	0	0	0	2	1	0	1
Mike Stanton, p	.000	4	0	0	0	0	0	0	0	0	0	0
Jose Vizcaino, 2b	.235	4	17	0	4	0	0	0	1	0	5	0
Bernie Williams, of	.111	5	18	2	2	0	0	1	1	5	5	0
TOTAL	.263		179	19	47	8	3	4	18	25	40	1

PITCHER	W	L	ERA	G	GS	CG	SV	SHO	IP	H	ER	BB	SO
Roger Clemens	1	0	0.00	1	1	0	0	0	8.0	2	0	0	9
David Cone	0	0	0.00	1	0	0	0	0	0.1	0	0	0	0
O. Hernandez	0	1	4.91	1	1	0	0	0	7.1	9	4	3	12
Denny Neagle	0	0	3.86	1	1	0	0	0	4.2	4	2	2	3
Jeff Nelson	1	0	10.13	3	0	0	0	0	2.2	5	3	1	1
Andy Pettitte	0	0	1.98	2	2	0	0	0	13.2	16	3	4	9
Mariano Rivera	0	0	3.00	4	0	0	2	0	6.0	4	2	1	7
Mike Stanton	2	0	0.00	4	0	0	0	0	4.1	0	0	0	7
TOTAL	4	1	2.68	17	5	0	2	0	47.0	40	14	11	48

NY (N)

PLAYER/POS	AVG	G	AB	R	H	2B	3B	HR	RB	BB	SO	SB
Kurt Abbott, ss	.250	5	8	0	2	1	0	0	0	1	3	0
Benny Agbayani, of	.278	5	18	2	5	2	0	0	2	3	6	0
Edgardo Alfonzo, 2b	.143	5	21	1	3	0	0	0	1	1	5	0
Armando Benitez, p	.000	3	0	0	0	0	0	0	0	0	0	0
Mike Bordick, ss	.125	4	8	0	1	0	0	0	0	0	3	0
Dennis Cook, p	.000	3	0	0	0	0	0	0	0	0	0	0
John Franco, p	.000	4	0	0	0	0	0	0	0	0	0	0
Matt Franco, 1b	.000	1	1	0	0	0	0	0	0	0	1	0
Darryl Hamilton, ph	.000	4	3	0	0	0	0	0	0	2	0	0
Mike Hampton, p	.000	1	0	0	0	0	0	0	0	0	0	0
Lenny Harris, dh-1	.000	3	4	1	0	0	0	0	0	1	1	0
Bobby Jones, p	.000	1	2	0	0	0	0	0	0	0	1	0
Al Leiter, p	.000	2	2	0	0	0	0	0	0	0	0	0
Joe McEwing, of-2	.000	3	1	1	0	0	0	0	0	0	0	0
Jay Payton, of	.333	5	21	3	7	0	0	1	3	0	5	0
Timo Perez, of	.125	5	16	1	2	0	0	0	0	1	4	0
Mike Piazza, c-4, dh	.273	5	22	3	6	2	0	2	4	4	4	0
Todd Pratt, c	.000	1	2	1	0	0	0	0	0	1	2	0
Rick Reed, p	1.000	1	1	0	1	0	0	0	0	0	0	0
Glendon Rusch, p	.000	3	0	0	0	0	0	0	0	0	0	0
Bubba Trammell, of-2	.400	4	5	1	2	0	0	0	3	1	1	0
Robin Ventura, 3b	.150	5	20	1	3	1	0	1	1	1	5	0
Turk Wendell, p	.000	2	0	0	0	0	0	0	0	0	0	0
Rick White, p	.000	1	0	0	0	0	0	0	0	0	0	0
Todd Zeile, 1b	.400	5	20	1	8	2	0	0	1	1	5	0
TOTAL	.229		175	16	40	8	0	4	15	11	48	0

PITCHER	W	L	ERA	G	GS	CG	SV	SHO	IP	H	ER	BB	SO
Armando Benitez	0	0	3.00	3	0	0	1	0	3.0	3	1	2	2
Dennis Cook	0	0	0.00	3	0	0	0	0	0.2	1	0	3	1
John Franco	1	0	0.00	4	0	0	0	0	3.1	3	0	0	1
Mike Hampton	0	1	6.00	1	1	0	0	0	6.0	8	4	5	4
Bobby Jones	0	1	5.40	1	1	0	0	0	5.0	4	3	3	3
Al Leiter	0	1	2.87	2	2	0	0	0	15.2	12	5	6	16
Rick Reed	0	0	3.00	1	1	0	0	0	6.0	6	2	1	8
Glendon Rusch	0	0	2.25	3	0	0	0	0	4.0	6	1	2	2
Turk Wendell	0	1	5.40	2	0	0	0	0	1.2	3	1	2	2
Rick White	0	0	6.75	1	0	0	0	0	1.1	1	1	1	1
TOTAL	1	4	3.47	21	5	0	1	0	46.2	47	18	25	40

ARIZONA DIAMONDBACKS (WEST) 3, ST. LOUIS CARDINALS (WILD CARD) 2

Arizona, led by twin towers Randy Johnson (21–6) and Curt Schilling (22–6), edged the Giants by two games to win the NL West. The Cardinals tied the Astros for the best record in the league, but Houston was awarded the NL Central title based on a 9–7 head-to-head record, leaving St. Louis the wild-card spot.

Schilling pitched a three-hit shutout, striking out nine, to out-duel the Cards' Matt Morris, 1–0, in Game 1. The only run scored in the fifth on a hit batsman, a sacrifice, and a basehit by Steve Finley.

The Cardinals came back to beat Johnson and the D'backs, 4–1, the next day. Woody Williams pitched seven strong innings, surrendering just four hits, and rookie Albert Pujols hit a two-run homer in the first inning to give him all the runs he would need. It was Johnson's seventh straight post-season loss—but it would be his last one this year.

Craig Counsell—who had hit only four home runs, none off a southpaw, all season—belted a three-run blast in the seventh to break a 2–2 tie, as Arizona took Game 3 by a score of 5–3. Continuing the pattern, the Cardinals won the next game, 4–1. Fernando Vina went 3-for-3, including a homer, helping rookie Bud Smith to victory. Dustin Hermanson retired all nine batters he faced in relief of Smith.

The deciding game was a Schilling-Morris rematch, and the results were much the same: Schilling gave up just one run in nine innings, Morris one in eight. But after Morris was forced out of the game by a blister, the Diamondbacks tallied the winning run with two out in the bottom of the ninth. Tony Womack's single scored pinch-runner Danny Bautista from second base, sending the Diamondbacks to a 2–1 victory and their first Championship Series.

Lost in the shuffle, Mark McGwire had gone 0-for-3 in his last major-league game. The Cardinals' slugger, who had been benched in Games 2 and 3, faxed his retirement notice to the baseball world shortly after the Series.

ARI (W)

PLAYER/POS	AVG	G	AB	R	H	2B	3B	HR	RB	BB	SO	SB
Brian Anderson, p	.000	2	0	0	0	0	0	0	0	0	0	0
Rod Barajas, c	.000	1	0	0	0	0	0	0	0	0	0	0
Miguel Batista, p	.000	2	1	0	0	0	0	0	0	0	0	0
Danny Bautista, of-2	.000	3	6	1	0	0	0	0	1	0	1	0
Jay Bell, 2b-1	.250	2	4	0	1	0	0	0	0	0	1	0
Greg Colbrunn, 1b-1	.333	4	6	0	2	0	0	0	1	1	0	0
Craig Counsell, 2b	.187	5	16	2	3	0	0	1	3	2	2	0
Midre Cummings, pr	.000	2	0	1	0	0	0	0	0	0	0	0
David Dellucci, ph	.000	2	0	0	0	0	0	0	0	0	0	0
Erubiel Durazo, ph	.000	1	1	0	0	0	0	0	0	0	0	0
Steve Finley, of	.421	5	19	1	8	1	0	0	2	0	2	0
Luis Gonzalez, of	.263	5	19	1	5	0	0	1	1	2	4	0
Mark Grace, 1b	.214	4	14	0	3	1	0	0	0	2	3	0
Randy Johnson, p	.000	1	2	0	0	0	0	0	0	0	2	0
Byung-Hyun Kim, p	.000	1	0	0	0	0	0	0	0	0	0	0
Albie Lopez, p	.000	1	1	0	0	0	0	0	0	0	0	0
Damian Miller, c	.267	5	15	1	4	0	0	0	0	1	3	0
Mike Morgan, p	.000	3	0	0	0	0	0	0	0	0	0	0
Reggie Sanders, of	.357	5	14	2	5	1	0	1	1	3	3	1
Curt Schilling, p	.000	2	5	0	0	0	0	0	0	0	2	0
Greg Swindell, p	.000	2	0	0	0	0	0	0	0	0	0	0
Matt Williams, 3b	.062	5	16	0	1	1	0	0	0	4	4	0
Tony Womack, ss	.294	5	17	1	5	1	0	0	1	3	2	0
TOTAL	.237		156	10	37	5	0	3	10	18	29	1

PITCHER	W	L	ERA	G	GS	CG	SV	SHO	IP	H	ER	BB	SO
Brian Anderson	0	0	2.25	2	0	0	0	0	4.0	3	1	0	3
Miguel Batista	1	0	2.70	2	1	0	0	0	6.7	3	2	1	4
Randy Johnson	0	1	3.38	1	1	0	0	0	8.0	6	3	2	9
Byung-Hyun Kim	0	0	0.00	1	0	0	1	0	1.3	1	0	2	1
Albie Lopez	0	1	12.00	1	1	0	0	0	3.0	4	4	3	0
Mike Morgan	0	0	4.50	3	0	0	0	0	2.0	2	1	2	1
Curt Schilling	2	0	0.50	2	2	2	0	1	18.0	9	1	2	18
Greg Swindell	0	0	0.00	2	0	0	0	0	1.7	1	0	0	2
TOTAL	3	2	2.42	14	5	2	1	1	44.7	29	12	12	38

STL (WC)

PLAYER/POS	AVG	G	AB	R	H	2B	3B	HR	RB	BB	SO	SB
Miguel Cairo, of-2	.200	3	5	0	1	0	0	0	0	0	1	1
J.D. Drew, of	.154	5	13	1	2	0	0	1	2	3	1	0
Jim Edmonds, of	.235	5	17	3	4	1	0	2	3	6	0	0
Dustin Hermanson, p	.000	1	1	0	0	0	0	0	0	0	1	0
Darryl Kile, p	.000	1	2	0	0	0	0	0	0	0	2	0
Steve Kline, p	.000	4	0	0	0	0	0	0	0	0	0	0
Eli Marrero, c	.000	3	7	0	0	0	0	0	0	0	0	0
Mike Matheny, c	.200	4	10	0	2	0	0	0	0	0	3	0
Mike Matthews, p	.000	1	0	0	0	0	0	0	0	0	0	0
Mark McGwire, 1b-3	.091	4	11	0	1	0	0	0	0	0	6	0
Matt Morris, p	.000	2	4	0	0	0	0	0	0	0	3	0
Craig Paquette, of-2, 3b-1	.143	2	7	0	1	0	0	0	0	0	5	0
Placido Polanco, 3b	.267	5	15	1	4	0	0	0	1	1	1	1
Albert Pujols, of-3, 1b-4	.111	5	18	1	2	0	0	1	2	2	2	0
Edgar Renteria, ss	.235	5	17	2	4	1	0	1	1	2	4	0
Kerry Robinson, of-3	.500	4	2	0	1	0	0	0	0	1	0	0
Bud Smith, p	.000	1	1	1	0	0	0	0	0	1	1	0
Gene Stechschulte, p	.000	2	0	0	0	0	0	0	0	0	0	0
Mike Timlin, p	.000	1	0	0	0	0	0	0	0	0	0	0
Dave Veres, p	.000	2	0	0	0	0	0	0	0	0	0	0
Fernando Vina, 2b	.316	5	19	2	6	0	0	1	2	0	1	1
Woody Williams, p	.333	1	3	1	1	1	0	0	0	0	1	0
TOTAL	.191		152	12	29	3	0	6	12	12	38	3

PITCHER	W	L	ERA	G	GS	CG	SV	SHO	IP	H	ER	BB	SO
Dustin Hermanson	0	0	0.00	1	0	0	0	0	3.0	0	0	0	0
Darryl Kile	0	0	3.00	1	1	0	0	0	6.0	3	2	5	5
Steve Kline	0	1	2.08	4	0	0	2	0	4.3	4	1	2	0
Mike Matthews	0	1	40.50	1	0	0	0	0	0.7	4	3	0	0
Matt Morris	0	1	1.20	2	2	0	0	0	15.0	13	2	5	12
Bud Smith	1	0	1.80	1	1	0	0	0	5.0	4	1	4	2
G. Stechschulte	0	0	0.00	2	0	0	0	0	0.3	3	0	0	0
Mike Timlin	0	0	0.00	1	0	0	0	0	1.3	1	0	0	0
Dave Veres	0	0	0.00	2	0	0	0	0	1.0	1	0	1	1
Woody Williams	1	0	1.29	1	1	0	0	0	7.0	4	1	1	9
TOTAL	2	3	2.06	16	5	0	2	0	43.7	37	10	18	29

GAME 1 AT ARI OCT 9

```
STL  000 000 000   0 3 1
ARI  000 010 00X   1 8 1
```
Pitchers: MORRIS, Stechschulte (8), Veres (8) vs SCHILLING
Attendance: 42,251

GAME 2 AT ARI OCT 10

```
STL  201 000 001   4 7 0
ARI  000 000 010   1 5 2
```
Pitchers: W WILLIAMS, Kline (8) vs JOHNSON, Morgan (9), Swindell (9), Batista (9)
Home Runs: Pujols-STL
Attendance: 41,793

GAME 3 AT STL OCT 12

```
ARI  000 001 400   5 9 0
STL  000 200 100   3 6 0
```
Pitchers: BATISTA, Anderson (7), Morgan (8), Kim (8) vs Kile, MATTHEWS (7), Timlin (7), Stechschulte (9), Kline (9)
Home Runs: Gonzalez-ARI, Counsell-ARI, Edmonds-STL, Renteria-STL
Attendance: 52,273

GAME 4 AT STL OCT 13

```
ARI  100 000 000   1 6 0
STL  112 000 00X   4 7 1
```
Pitchers: LOPEZ, Anderson (4), Swindell (7), Morgan (8) vs SMITH, Hermanson (6), Kline (9)
Home Runs: Edmonds-STL, Vina-STL
Attendance: 52,194

GAME 5 AT ARI OCT 14

```
STL  000 000 010   1 6 1
ARI  000 100 001   2 9 1
```
Pitchers: Morris, Veres (9), KLINE (9) vs SCHILLING
Home Runs: Drew-STL, Sanders-ARI
Attendance: 42,810

ATLANTA BRAVES (EAST) 3, HOUSTON ASTROS (CENTRAL) 0

The Astros won the National League Central Division on a technicality, tying the Cardinals for the NL's best record, but beating them 9-of-16 head-to-head; since both teams qualified for postseason, no playoff was needed. The Braves, meanwhile, finally had to battle for the NL East title, winning a modest 88 games to edge the Phillies by two.

Atlanta didn't have to battle as much in the NLDS, though. They outscored Houston, 14-6, in sweeping the series in three straight. Atlanta out-hit their opponents, .303 to .200, and out-pitched them, 1.67 to 4.15, not allowing a single hit with runners in scoring position.

It started with a 7-4 win in Game 1. Chipper Jones' three-run homer off Billy Wagner's first pitch in the eighth was the death-blow. Jones had been hitless in eight previous at bats against Wagner, with six strikeouts. Brian Jordan and Andruw Jones also homered for Atlanta, while Vinny Castilla and Brad Ausmus connected for Houston.

Tom Glavine and John Smoltz combined to shut out the Astros, 1-0 in Game 2. The game's only run was unearned, scoring on a second-inning double play following an error. Atlanta's Andruw Jones hit safely his first three times up in this game, giving him five straight hits en route to a .500 Series average.

Reserve catcher Paul Bako was the hero of Game 3. Bako drove in three runs—one on his first homer since June 1, another on a double, and the third on a squeeze bunt—to pace the Braves' 6-2 victory. Julio Franco and Chipper Jones also homered for Atlanta, and John Burkett went 6-1/3 innings for the win. For the fourth time in five years, the Astros had won their division, only to get flattened in the Divisional Series, by an aggregate count of twelve games to two.

ATL (E)

PLAYER/POS	AVG	G	AB	R	H	2B	3B	HR	RB	BB	SO	SB
Paul Bako, c	.286	3	7	1	2	1	0	1	3	1	0	0
John Burkett, p	.000	1	2	0	0	0	0	0	0	0	1	0
Ken Caminiti, ph	.000	2	2	0	0	0	0	0	0	0	1	0
Mark DeRosa, ss	1.000	1	1	0	1	0	0	0	0	0	0	0
Julio Franco, 1b	.308	3	13	3	4	0	0	1	1	0	1	0
Marcus Giles, 2b	.250	3	12	2	3	1	0	0	1	0	3	0
Tom Glavine, p	.333	1	3	0	1	0	0	0	0	0	0	0
Andruw Jones, of	.500	3	12	2	6	0	0	1	1	0	3	0
Chipper Jones, 3b	.444	3	9	2	4	0	0	2	5	3	1	0
Brian Jordan, of	.182	3	11	1	2	0	0	1	2	0	5	0
Steve Karsay, p	.000	1	0	0	0	0	0	0	0	0	0	0
Keith Lockhart, 2b	.500	1	2	1	1	1	0	0	0	0	0	0
Greg Maddux, p	.000	1	2	0	0	0	0	0	0	0	1	0
Dave Martinez, ph	.000	1	1	0	0	0	0	0	0	0	0	0
Steve Reed, p	.000	1	0	0	0	0	0	0	0	0	0	0
Mike Remlinger, p	.000	1	0	0	0	0	0	0	0	0	0	0
Rey Sanchez, ss	.222	3	9	1	2	1	0	0	0	0	2	0
Rudy Seanez, p	.000	1	0	0	0	0	0	0	0	0	0	0
John Smoltz, p	.000	3	1	0	0	0	0	0	0	0	0	0
B.J. Surhoff, of	.273	3	11	1	3	1	0	0	0	0	0	1
Steve Torrealba, c	1.000	1	1	0	1	1	0	0	0	0	0	0
TOTAL	.303		99	14	30	6	0	6	13	4	18	1

PITCHER	W	L	ERA	G	GS	CG	SV	SHO	IP	H	ER	BB	SO
John Burkett	1	0	2.84	1	1	0	0	0	6.3	6	2	2	4
Tom Glavine	1	0	0.00	1	1	0	0	0	8.0	6	0	2	3
Steve Karsay	0	0	0.00	1	0	0	0	0	1.0	0	0	0	1
Greg Maddux	0	0	3.00	1	1	0	0	0	6.0	4	2	3	5
Steve Reed	0	0	0.00	1	0	0	0	0	0.3	0	0	0	0
Mike Remlinger	0	0	0.00	1	0	0	0	0	0.3	0	0	0	0
Rudy Seanez	1	0	0.00	1	0	0	0	0	1.0	0	0	1	0
John Smoltz	0	0	2.25	3	0	0	2	0	4.0	3	1	0	3
TOTAL	3	0	1.67	10	3	0	2	0	27.0	19	5	8	16

HOU (C)

PLAYER/POS	AVG	G	AB	R	H	2B	3B	HR	RB	BB	SO	SB
Moises Alou, of	.167	3	12	0	2	1	0	0	1	0	1	0
Brad Ausmus, c-2	.250	3	8	1	2	0	0	1	2	0	0	0
Jeff Bagwell, 1b	.429	3	7	0	3	0	0	0	0	5	1	0
Lance Berkman, of	.167	3	12	0	2	0	0	0	0	0	4	0
Craig Biggio, 2b	.167	3	12	0	2	0	0	0	0	0	1	0
Vinny Castilla, 3b	.273	3	11	1	3	0	0	1	1	0	3	0
Nelson Cruz, p	.000	2	0	0	0	0	0	0	0	0	0	0
Octavio Dotel, p	.000	2	0	0	0	0	0	0	0	0	0	0
Tony Eusebio, c	.667	1	3	1	2	1	0	0	0	0	0	0
Richard Hidalgo, of	.125	3	8	1	1	0	0	0	0	3	2	0
Mike Jackson, p	.000	2	0	0	0	0	0	0	0	0	0	0
Julio Lugo, ss-2	.000	3	8	1	0	0	0	0	0	0	2	0
Orlando Merced, ph	.000	1	1	0	0	0	0	0	0	0	0	0
Wade Miller, p	.000	1	2	0	0	0	0	0	0	0	0	0
Dave Mlicki, p	.000	1	1	0	0	0	0	0	0	0	0	0
Shane Reynolds, p	.000	1	1	0	0	0	0	0	0	0	0	0
Chris Truby, ph	.000	1	1	0	0	0	0	0	0	0	1	0
Ron Villone, p	.000	1	0	0	0	0	0	0	0	0	0	0
Jose Vizcaino, ss-2	.167	3	6	0	1	0	0	0	0	0	1	0
Billy Wagner, p	.000	2	0	0	0	0	0	0	0	0	0	0
Daryle Ward, ph	.500	2	2	1	1	0	0	1	2	0	0	0
Mike Williams, p	.000	1	0	0	0	0	0	0	0	0	0	0
TOTAL	.200		95	6	19	2	0	3	6	8	16	0

PITCHER	W	L	ERA	G	GS	CG	SV	SHO	IP	H	ER	BB	SO
Nelson Cruz	0	0	0.00	2	0	0	0	0	2.7	1	0	1	1
Octavio Dotel	0	0	5.40	2	0	0	0	0	3.3	5	2	0	5
Mike Jackson	0	1	27.00	2	0	0	0	0	0.7	3	2	0	1
Wade Miller	0	0	2.57	1	1	0	0	0	7.0	7	2	0	6
Dave Mlicki	0	1	0.00	1	1	0	0	0	5.0	4	0	2	0
Shane Reynolds	0	1	9.00	1	1	0	0	0	4.0	6	4	1	1
Ron Villone	0	0	0.00	1	0	0	0	0	0.7	0	0	0	0
Billy Wagner	0	0	5.40	2	0	0	0	0	1.7	1	1	0	3
Mike Williams	0	0	9.00	1	0	0	0	0	1.0	3	1	0	1
TOTAL	0	3	4.15	13	3	0	0	0	26.0	30	12	4	18

GAME 1 AT HOU

```
ATL  1 0 0  1 0 0  0 4 1   7 13 1
HOU  0 0 0  0 2 1  0 0 1   4  6 1
```
Pitchers: Maddux, SEANEZ (7), Smoltz (9) vs Miller, M JACKSON (8), B Wagner (8), Mi Williams (9)
Home Runs: Jordan-ATL, C Jones-ATL, A Jones-ATL, Ausmus-HOU, Castilla-HOU
Attendance: 35,553

GAME 2 AT HOU OCT 10

```
ATL  0 1 0  0 0 0  0 0 0   1 7 0
HOU  0 0 0  0 0 0  0 0 0   0 7 2
```
Pitchers: GLAVINE, Smoltz (9) vs MLICKI, Dotel (6), Jackson (8), Cruz (8), Wagner (9)
Attendance: 35,704

GAME 3 AT ATL OCT 12

```
HOU  0 0 0  0 0 0  2 0 0   2  6 0
ATL  0 2 1  1 0 0  0 2 X   6 10 0
```
Pitchers: REYNOLDS, Cruz (5), Dotel (7), Villone (8) vs BURKETT, Reed (7), Remlinger (7), Karsay (8), Smoltz (9)
Home Runs: Ward-HOU, Bako-ATL, Franco-ATL, C Jones-ATL
Attendance: 39,923

SEATTLE MARINERS (WEST) 3, CLEVELAND INDIANS (CENTRAL) 2

Seattle had run up an amazing 116–46 record, setting an American League record—and tying the major-league mark—for wins in a season. Cleveland had totaled a modest 91 victories in taking the mediocre Central Division. Nonetheless, the two teams would go down to the wire in the ALDS.

Cleveland opened things with a 5–0 win in Game 1. The Indians' Bartolo Colon fanned ten and scattered six hits in eight innings, while his team supported him with a well-balanced attack, including a home run by Ellis Burks. Seattle came back with a 5–1 victory in Game 2. Mike Cameron and Edgar Martinez clubbed two-run homers within the first fourteen pitches of the game, and Jamie Moyer and three relievers stymied the Cleveland offense.

There was nothing wrong with the Cleveland offense in Game 3. Happy to be in their home park, the Indians erupted for a 17–2 massacre. Omar Vizquel led the attack with two singles, a double, a triple, and six RBI, and Juan Gonzalez also had four hits, including two doubles and a homer. It made for an easy night for 21-year-old rookie pitcher C. C. Sabathia. "This is probably the worst game we've played all year," said Seattle manager Lou Piniella. "If we're good enough, we'll win tomorrow. If we're not, we'll congratulate Cleveland and go home."

Cleveland took a 1–0 lead into the seventh inning of Game 4, but Seattle staved off elimination with six runs in the last three frames for a 6–2 win. The Mariners finished the job at Seattle the next day, as Moyer earned his second victory, 3–1. Rookie Ichiro Suzuki had three hits, making him 12-for-20 for the five-game series. Despite being outscored in the Series, 26–16, out-hit (.260 to .247), out-pitched (3.35 to 4.70), and out-fielded (.984 to .972), the M's were on their way to the American League Championship Series.

SEA (W)

PLAYER/POS	AVG	G	AB	R	H	2B	3B	HR	RB	BB	SO	SB
Paul Abbott, p	.000	0	0	0	0	0	0	0	0	0	0	0
David Bell, 3b	.312	5	16	2	5	1	0	1	2	1	6	0
Bret Boone, 2b	.095	5	21	1	2	0	0	0	0	1	11	1
Jay Buhner, of	.000	2	3	0	0	0	0	0	0	2	1	0
Mike Cameron, of	.222	5	18	2	4	3	0	1	3	2	7	0
Norm Charlton, p	.000	0	0	0	0	0	0	0	0	0	0	0
Freddy Garcia, p	.000	0	0	0	0	0	0	0	0	0	0	0
Charles Gipson, ph	.000	1	1	0	0	0	0	0	0	0	0	0
John Halama, p	.000	0	0	0	0	0	0	0	0	0	0	0
Stan Javier, of	.250	4	8	2	2	1	0	0	0	2	1	0
Tom Lampkin, c	.000	2	2	0	0	0	0	0	0	0	2	0
Al Martin, ph	.000	3	2	1	0	0	0	0	0	0	0	0
Edgar Martinez, dh	.312	5	16	3	5	1	0	2	5	5	2	1
Mark McLemore, ss-4, of-1	.167	5	18	0	3	0	0	0	3	1	8	0
Jamie Moyer, p	.000	0	0	0	0	0	0	0	0	0	0	0
Jeff Nelson, p	.000	0	0	0	0	0	0	0	0	0	0	0
John Olerud, 1b	.176	5	17	1	3	0	0	0	1	3	5	0
Jose Paniagua, p	.000	0	0	0	0	0	0	0	0	0	0	0
Arthur Rhodes, p	.000	0	0	0	0	0	0	0	0	0	0	0
Kazuhiro Sasaki, p	.000	0	0	0	0	0	0	0	0	0	0	0
Aaron Sele, p	.000	0	0	0	0	0	0	0	0	0	0	0
Ed Sprague, ph	.000	1	1	0	0	0	0	0	0	0	0	0
Ichiro Suzuki, of	.600	5	20	4	12	1	0	0	2	1	0	1
Ramon Vazquez, ss	.000	1	0	0	0	0	0	0	0	0	0	0
Dan Wilson, c	.200	5	15	0	3	1	0	0	0	0	5	0
TOTAL	.247		158	16	39	8	0	4	16	18	48	3

PITCHER	W	L	ERA	G	GS	CG	SV	SHO	IP	H	ER	BB	SO
Paul Abbott	0	0	24.00	1	0	0	0	0	3.0	9	8	5	3
Norm Charlton	0	0	0.00	1	0	0	0	0	1.7	0	0	0	2
Freddy Garcia	1	1	3.86	2	2	0	0	0	11.7	13	5	3	13
John Halama	0	0	0.00	2	0	0	0	0	3.0	3	0	0	3
Jamie Moyer	2	0	1.50	2	2	0	0	0	12.0	8	2	2	10
Jeff Nelson	0	0	0.00	3	0	0	0	0	3.0	1	0	1	5
Jose Paniagua	0	0	27.00	1	0	0	0	0	2.0	4	6	2	1
Arthur Rhodes	0	0	0.00	3	0	0	0	0	2.7	1	0	0	1
Kazuhiro Sasaki	0	0	0.00	3	0	0	1	0	3.0	1	0	0	5
Aaron Sele	0	1	9.00	1	1	0	0	0	2.0	5	2	0	0
TOTAL	3	2	4.70	20	5	0	1	0	44.0	45	23	13	43

CLE (C)

PLAYER/POS	AVG	G	AB	R	H	2B	3B	HR	RB	BB	SO	SB
Roberto Alomar, 2b	.190	5	21	3	4	3	0	0	3	2	5	0
Danys Baez, p	.000	0	0	0	0	0	0	0	0	0	0	0
Russ Branyan, of-1	.333	2	3	1	1	0	0	0	0	0	1	0
Dave Burba, p	.000	0	0	0	0	0	0	0	0	0	0	0
Ellis Burks, dh	.316	5	19	4	6	1	0	1	1	1	3	0
Jolbert Cabrera, of	1.000	2	1	1	1	0	0	0	1	0	0	0
Bartolo Colon, p	.000	0	0	0	0	0	0	0	0	0	0	0
Wil Cordero, of	.000	1	1	0	0	0	0	0	0	0	0	0
Marty Cordova, of	.250	4	12	0	3	0	0	0	1	0	5	0
Einar Diaz, c	.312	5	16	3	5	0	0	0	2	2	1	0
Chuck Finley, p	.000	0	0	0	0	0	0	0	0	0	0	0
Travis Fryman, 3b	.176	5	17	4	3	1	0	0	2	2	7	0
Juan Gonzalez, of	.348	5	23	4	8	3	0	2	5	0	7	0
Kenny Lofton, of	.105	5	19	2	2	0	0	1	3	3	5	0
Ricardo Rincon, p	.000	0	0	0	0	0	0	0	0	0	0	0
David Riske, p	.000	0	0	0	0	0	0	0	0	0	0	0
John Rocker, p	.000	0	0	0	0	0	0	0	0	0	0	0
C.C. Sabathia, p	.000	0	0	0	0	0	0	0	0	0	0	0
Paul Shuey, p	.000	0	0	0	0	0	0	0	0	0	0	0
Jim Thome, 1b	.158	5	19	2	3	0	0	1	1	2	8	0
Omar Vizquel, ss	.409	5	22	2	9	1	1	0	6	1	1	1
Bob Wickman, p	.000	0	0	0	0	0	0	0	0	0	0	0
TOTAL	.260		173	26	45	9	1	5	25	13	43	1

PITCHER	W	L	ERA	G	GS	CG	SV	SHO	IP	H	ER	BB	SO
Danys Baez	0	0	2.45	3	0	0	0	0	3.7	4	1	0	6
Dave Burba	0	0	0.00	1	0	0	0	0	1.0	0	0	0	1
Bartolo Colon	1	1	1.84	2	2	0	0	0	14.7	12	3	6	13
Chuck Finley	0	2	7.27	2	2	0	0	0	8.7	9	7	6	10
Ricardo Rincon	0	0	9.00	3	0	0	0	0	2.0	2	2	0	3
David Riske	0	0	0.00	3	0	0	0	0	3.7	2	0	1	5
John Rocker	0	0	0.00	1	0	0	0	0	1.0	1	0	0	1
C.C. Sabathia	1	0	3.00	1	1	0	0	0	6.0	6	2	5	5
Paul Shuey	0	0	6.75	2	0	0	0	0	1.3	3	1	0	2
Bob Wickman	0	0	0.00	1	0	0	0	0	1.0	0	0	0	2
TOTAL	2	3	3.35	19	5	0	0	0	43.0	39	16	18	48

GAME 1 AT SEA OCT 9

CLE 000 301 010   5 11 1
SEA 000 000 000   0 6 1
Pitchers: COLON, Wickman (9) vs F. GARCIA, Charlton (6), Paniagua (8), Halama (9)
Home Runs: E Burks-CLE
Attendance: 48,033

GAME 2 AT SEA OCT 11

CLE 000 000 100   1 6 0
SEA 400 010 00X   5 6 0
Pitchers: FINLEY, Riske (5), Shuey (7), Baez (8) vs MOYER, Nelson (7), Rhodes (8), Sasaki (9)
Home Runs: Cameron-SEA, E. Martinez-SEA, Bell-SEA
Attendance: 48,052

GAME 3 AT CLE OCT 13

SEA 100 000 100   2 7 3
CLE 224 013 05X   17 19 0
Pitchers: SELE, Abbott (3), Halama (6), Paniagua (8) vs SABATHIA, Riske (7), Rincon (7), Burba (8), Rocker (9)
Home Runs: Gonzalez-CLE, Lofton-CLE, Thome-CLE
Attendance: 45,069

GAME 4 AT CLE OCT 14

SEA 000 000 312   6 11 0
CLE 010 000 100   2 5 2
Pitchers: GARCIA, Nelson (7), Rhodes (7), Sasaki (9) vs COLON, Baez (7), Rincon (8), Shuey (9)
Home Runs: E Martinez-SEA, Gonzalez-CLE
Attendance: 45,025

GAME 5 AT SEA OCT 15

CLE 001 000 000   1 4 0
SEA 020 000 10X   3 9 1
Pitchers: FINLEY, Riske (5), Rincon (6), Baez (7) vs MOYER, Nelson (7), Rhodes (8), Sasaki (9)
Attendance: 47,867

NEW YORK YANKEES (EAST) 3, OAKLAND A'S (WILD CARD) 2

Besides their postseason-experience advantage, the Yankees were emotional favorites this year, due to New York's human tragedies in the 9/11 attacks of the previous month. The Yanks had won the AL East by a whopping 13-1/2 games, while the A's finished 14 games behind the Mariners in the AL West, getting to the postseason only via the wild card. Nevertheless, Oakland won seven more games than New York, and had the second-best record in the major leagues, so this was anyone's series.

The A's put the Yankees deep in the hole by winning the first two games in New York. Oakland was never behind in either contest, winning 5–3 and 2–0 behind Mark Mulder and Tim Hudson.

Looking to complete the sweep, Oakland's Barry Zito pitched a masterpiece in Game 3, allowing just two hits in eight innings. But one of them was a fifth-inning home run by Jorge Posada, and it turned out to be the only run of the game. Mike Mussina tossed seven innings of four-hit ball for the victory. A remarkable play came in the seventh, when Oakland's Jeremy Giambi was thrown out at home plate by shortstop Derek Jeter, who had come from nowhere to intercept a throw by right fielder Shane Spencer between first base and home plate. Though Jeter was deified for his heads-up play and Giambi was skewered for coming in standing up, in truth the baserunner probably would have been out even if Jeter had let the ball go through and Giambi had slid.

The Yankees got an easy 9–2 win in Game 4. Bernie Williams knocked in five runs with two doubles and a single, and Orlando Hernandez and two relievers stranded eleven Oakland baserunners. To add injury to insult, Oakland lost the services of outfielder Jermaine Dye, who suffered a broken leg on his own foul tip.

The Yankees came from behind to win the clincher at home, 5–3. The go-ahead run scored after Williams struck out for what appeared to be the end of a 1-2-3 third inning, but reached on backup catcher Greg Myers' error. A hit batsman, walk, and a second error followed, and another unearned run in the fourth sealed Oakland's fate.

NY (E)

PLAYER/POS	AVG	G	AB	R	H	2B	3B	HR	RB	BB	SO	SB
Clay Bellinger, pr	.000	1	0	0	0	0	0	0	0	0	0	0
Scott Brosius, 3b	.059	5	17	0	1	0	0	0	1	0	3	0
Roger Clemens, p	.000	0	0	0	0	0	0	0	0	0	0	0
Orlando Hernandez, p	.000	0	0	0	0	0	0	0	0	0	0	0
Sterling Hitchcock, p	.000	0	0	0	0	0	0	0	0	0	0	0
Derek Jeter, ss	.444	5	18	2	8	1	0	0	1	1	0	0
David Justice, of-2, dh-2	.231	4	13	3	3	0	1	1	1	2	5	0
Chuck Knoblauch, of	.273	5	22	1	6	1	0	0	1	0	0	1
Tino Martinez, 1b	.111	5	18	1	2	0	0	1	2	1	6	0
Ramiro Mendoza, p	.000	0	0	0	0	0	0	0	0	0	0	0
Mike Mussina, p	.000	0	0	0	0	0	0	0	0	0	0	0
Paul O'Neill, of-1, dh-2	.091	3	11	1	1	1	0	0	0	0	0	0
Jorge Posada, c	.444	5	18	3	8	1	0	1	2	2	2	1
Andy Pettitte, p	.000	0	0	0	0	0	0	0	0	0	0	0
Mariano Rivera, p	.000	0	0	0	0	0	0	0	0	0	0	0
Alfonso Soriano, 2b	.222	5	18	2	4	0	0	0	3	1	5	2
Shane Spencer, of	.250	3	8	1	2	1	0	0	0	1	4	0
Mike Stanton, p	.000	0	0	0	0	0	0	0	0	0	0	0
Randy Velarde, dh	.200	2	5	0	1	0	0	0	0	0	1	0
Bernie Williams, of	.222	5	18	4	4	3	0	0	5	3	3	0
Jay Witasick, p	.000	0	0	0	0	0	0	0	0	0	0	0
TOTAL	.241		166	18	40	8	1	3	16	11	29	4

PITCHER	W	L	ERA	G	GS	CG	SV	SHO	IP	H	ER	BB	SO
Roger Clemens	0	1	5.40	2	2	0	0	0	8.3	9	5	4	6
O. Hernandez	1	0	3.18	1	1	0	0	0	5.7	8	2	2	5
Sterling Hitchcock	0	0	6.00	1	0	0	0	0	3.0	5	2	0	2
Ramiro Mendoza	0	0	0.00	3	0	0	0	0	4.3	2	0	1	5
Mike Mussina	1	0	0.00	1	1	0	0	0	7.0	4	0	1	4
Andy Pettitte	0	1	1.42	1	1	0	0	0	6.3	7	1	2	4
Mariano Rivera	0	0	0.00	3	0	0	2	0	5.0	4	0	0	4
Mike Stanton	1	0	0.00	3	0	0	0	0	4.7	3	0	0	1
Jay Witasick	0	0	13.50	1	0	0	0	0	0.7	1	1	1	0
TOTAL	3	2	2.20	16	5	0	2	0	45.0	43	11	11	31

OAK (WC)

PLAYER/POS	AVG	G	AB	R	H	2B	3B	HR	RB	BB	SO	SB
Chad Bradford, p	.000	0	0	0	0	0	0	0	0	0	0	0
Eric Byrnes, ph	.000	2	2	0	0	0	0	0	0	0	1	0
Eric Chavez, 3b	.143	5	21	0	3	1	0	0	0	0	5	0
Johnny Damon, of	.409	5	22	3	9	2	1	0	0	1	1	2
Jermaine Dye, of	.231	4	13	0	3	2	0	0	0	2	2	0
Ron Gant, of-1, dh-2	.182	4	11	1	2	0	0	1	1	0	3	0
Jason Giambi, 1b	.353	5	17	2	6	0	0	1	4	4	2	0
Jeremy Giambi, dh	.308	5	13	0	4	1	0	0	2	1	0	1
Mark Guthrie, p	.000	0	0	0	0	0	0	0	0	0	0	0
Ramon Hernandez, c	.000	5	10	0	0	0	0	0	0	1	4	0
Erik Hiljus, p	.000	0	0	0	0	0	0	0	0	0	0	0
Tim Hudson, p	.000	0	0	0	0	0	0	0	0	0	0	0
Jason Isringhausen, p	.000	0	0	0	0	0	0	0	0	0	0	0
Cory Lidle, p	.000	0	0	0	0	0	0	0	0	0	0	0
Terrence Long, of	.389	5	18	3	7	3	0	2	3	1	2	0
Mike Magnante, p	.000	0	0	0	0	0	0	0	0	0	0	0
Jim Mecir, p	.000	0	0	0	0	0	0	0	0	0	0	0
Frank Menechino, 2b	.083	4	12	2	1	0	0	0	0	1	4	0
Mark Mulder, p	.000	0	0	0	0	0	0	0	0	0	0	0
Greg Myers, c	.143	3	7	0	1	0	0	0	0	0	3	0
Olmedo Saenz, dh-1	.000	3	4	0	0	0	0	0	0	0	1	0
F.P. Santangelo, 2b	.333	2	3	0	1	1	0	0	0	0	0	0
Jeff Tam, p	.000	0	0	0	0	0	0	0	0	0	0	0
Miguel Tejada, ss	.286	5	21	1	6	3	0	0	1	0	3	0
Barry Zito, p	.000	0	0	0	0	0	0	0	0	0	0	0
TOTAL	.247		174	12	43	13	1	4	11	11	31	3

PITCHER	W	L	ERA	G	GS	CG	SV	SHO	IP	H	ER	BB	SO
Chad Bradford	0	0	0.00	1	0	0	0	0	1.0	0	0	0	1
Mark Guthrie	0	0	0.00	2	0	0	0	0	3.0	0	0	0	2
Erik Hiljus	0	0	27.00	1	0	0	0	0	0.3	0	1	2	0
Tim Hudson	1	0	0.93	2	1	0	0	0	9.7	8	1	1	5
Jason Isringhausen	0	0	0.00	2	0	0	2	0	2.0	1	0	1	3
Cory Lidle	0	1	10.80	1	1	0	0	0	3.3	5	4	3	0
Mike Magnante	0	0	0.00	1	0	0	0	0	1.3	3	0	1	1
Jim Mecir	0	0	5.40	2	0	0	0	0	3.3	4	2	0	4
Mark Mulder	1	1	2.45	2	2	0	0	0	11.0	14	3	2	7
Jeff Tam	0	0	18.00	1	0	0	0	0	1.0	3	2	0	0
Barry Zito	0	1	1.12	1	1	0	0	0	8.0	2	1	1	6
TOTAL	2	3	2.86	16	5	0	2	0	44.0	40	14	11	29

GAME 1 AT NY OCT 10
OAK 1 0 0 1 0 0 1 2 0   5 10 1
NY 0 0 0 0 1 0 0 2 0   3 10 1
Pitchers: MULDER, Mecir (7), Isringhausen (9) vs CLEMENS, Hitchcock(5), Witasick (8), Stanton (8)
Home Runs: Long-OAK (2), Ja. Giambi-OAK, T Martinez-NY
Attendance: 56,697

GAME 2 AT NY OCT 11
OAK 0 0 0 1 0 0 0 0 1   2 9 1
NY 0 0 0 0 0 0 0 0 0   0 7 0
Pitchers: HUDSON, Isringhausen (9) vs PETTITTE, Mendoza (7), Rivera (9)
Home Runs: Gant-OAK
Attendance: 56,684

GAME 3 AT OAK OCT 13
NY 0 0 0 0 1 0 0 0 0   1 2 0
OAK 0 0 0 0 0 0 0 0 0   0 6 1
Pitchers: MUSSINA, Rivera (8) vs ZITO, Guthrie (9)
Home Runs: Posada-NY
Attendance: 55,861

GAME 4 AT OAK OCT 14
NY 0 2 2 3 0 0 0 0 2   9 11 1
OAK 0 0 2 0 0 0 0 0 0   2 11 1
Pitchers: O. HERNANDEZ, Stanton (6), Mendoza (8) vs LIDLE, Hiljus (4), Magnante (4), Guthrie (6), Bradford (8), Tam (9)
Attendance: 43,681

GAME 5 AT NY OCT 15
OAK 1 1 0 0 1 0 0 0 0   3 7 3
NY 0 2 1 1 0 1 0 0 X   5 10 1
Pitchers: MULDER, Hudson (5), Mecir (7) vs Clemens, STANTON (5), Mendoza (7), Rivera (8)
Home Runs: Justice-NY
Attendance: 56,642

ARIZONA DIAMONDBACKS (WEST) 4, ATLANTA BRAVES (EAST) 1

The Diamondbacks, looking for their first pennant ever, showed little respect to the Braves, in the postseason for the tenth straight time. Randy Johnson set the tone in Game 1 with a three-hit shutout, striking out 11 and retiring 20 straight at one point, as Arizona won, 2–0. For Johnson in post-season play, the win broke a seven-game losing skid. Anticipating he would be asked if it were a monkey off his back, Johnson said "This is more like a gorilla: King Kong." Little did anyone know Johnson had just started a five-game post-season winning streak.

Atlanta came back with an 8–1 victory in Game 2, as Tom Glavine pitched seven strong innings and Marcus Giles, Javy Lopez and B. J. Surhoff homered. Giles' dinger was on the game's first pitch, Lopez's two-run shot in the seventh gave the Braves a 3–1 lead, and Surhoff's homer was part of a five-run eighth.

But Game 3 went to the Diamondbacks, as Curt Schilling tossed his third complete-game victory of the postseason, permitting just four hits and fanning twelve to win, 5–1. Schilling also figured in a key offensive moment, scoring on a fifth-inning infield grounder and knocking catcher Lopez out of commission, allowing Tony Womack to score as well.

Arizona drove Greg Maddux out of the box and took advantage of shoddy Atlanta defense to win Game 4, 11–4. Craig Counsell led the attack with three hits and four RBI. The D'backs then took the clincher, 3–2, behind Johnson's second win of the Series, Byung-Hyun Kim's second save and Erubiel Durazo's two-run homer. For Durazo, batting for the injured Mark Grace, it was his only hit of the Series.

In just their fourth season of existence, Arizona would be playing in the World Series. Counsell, who batted .381 with three doubles and five runs, was named NLCS MVP.

ARI (W)

PLAYER/POS	AVG	G	AB	R	H	2B	3B	HR	RB	BB	SO	SB
Brian Anderson, p	.000	1	1	0	0	0	0	0	0	0	1	0
Miguel Batista, p	.000	2	2	0	0	0	0	0	0	0	1	0
Danny Bautista, of	.250	2	4	1	1	0	0	0	1	1	1	0
Jay Bell, 2b	.000	1	4	0	0	0	0	0	0	0	0	0
Greg Colbrunn, ph	.000	1	1	0	0	0	0	0	0	0	0	0
Craig Counsell, 2b-4, ss-1	.381	5	21	5	8	3	0	0	4	0	3	1
Midre Cummings, ph	.000	1	1	0	0	0	0	0	0	0	0	0
David Dellucci, ph	.500	2	2	1	1	0	0	0	0	0	0	0
Erubiel Durazo, 1b-1	.333	2	3	1	1	0	0	1	2	0	1	0
Steve Finley, of	.286	5	14	1	4	1	0	0	5	3	1	1
Luis Gonzalez, of	.211	5	19	4	4	0	0	1	4	3	3	0
Mark Grace, 1b	.375	5	16	1	6	0	0	0	1	2	1	0
Randy Johnson, p	.000	2	6	0	0	0	0	0	0	0	2	0
Byung-Hyun Kim, p	.000	3	1	0	0	0	0	0	0	0	0	0
Albie Lopez, p	.000	1	1	0	0	0	0	0	0	0	1	0
Damian Miller, c	.176	5	17	0	3	0	0	0	0	2	5	0
Mike Morgan, p	.000	2	0	0	0	0	0	0	0	0	0	0
Reggie Sanders, of	.118	5	17	2	2	0	0	0	1	5	5	1
Curt Schilling, p	.250	1	4	1	1	0	0	0	0	0	2	0
Greg Swindell, p	.000	2	0	0	0	0	0	0	0	0	0	0
Matt Williams, 3b	.278	5	18	1	5	1	0	0	3	2	3	0
Bobby Witt, p	.000	1	0	0	0	0	0	0	0	0	0	0
Tony Womack, ss	.200	4	20	4	4	1	0	0	0	0	2	0
TOTAL	.233		172	22	40	6	0	2	21	18	32	3

PITCHER	W	L	ERA	G	GS	CG	SV	SHO	IP	H	ER	BB	SO
Brian Anderson	1	0	2.70	1	0	0	0	0	3.3	4	1	1	0
Miguel Batista	0	1	5.14	2	1	0	0	0	7.0	5	4	2	3
Randy Johnson	2	0	1.12	2	2	1	0	1	16.0	10	2	3	19
Byung-Hyun Kim	0	0	0.00	3	0	0	2	0	5.0	0	0	1	3
Albie Lopez	0	0	6.00	1	1	0	0	0	3.0	5	2	1	1
Mike Morgan	0	0	27.00	2	0	0	0	0	1.0	3	3	1	1
Curt Schilling	1	0	1.00	1	1	1	0	0	9.0	4	1	2	12
Greg Swindell	0	0	27.00	2	0	0	0	0	0.3	1	1	0	0
Bobby Witt	0	0	27.00	1	0	0	0	0	0.3	3	1	0	0
TOTAL	4	1	3.00	15	5	2	2	1	45.0	35	15	11	39

ATL (E)

PLAYER/POS	AVG	G	AB	R	H	2B	3B	HR	RB	BB	SO	SB
Paul Bako, c	.000	3	3	0	0	0	0	0	0	0	0	0
John Burkett, p	.000	1	1	0	0	0	0	0	0	0	1	0
Mark DeRosa, ss-1	.000	4	4	0	0	0	0	0	0	0	1	0
Julio Franco, 1b	.261	5	23	2	6	0	0	1	2	0	2	0
Marcus Giles, 2b	.200	5	20	4	4	1	0	1	1	3	4	0
Bernard Gilkey, of-2	.200	3	5	0	1	0	0	0	0	2	1	0
Tom Glavine, p	.000	2	3	0	0	0	0	0	0	0	2	0
Andruw Jones, of	.176	5	17	4	3	0	0	1	1	1	5	0
Chipper Jones, 3b	.263	5	19	1	5	1	0	0	2	3	6	0
Brian Jordan, of	.190	5	21	1	4	2	0	0	3	0	6	0
Steve Karsay, p	.000	4	0	0	0	0	0	0	0	0	0	0
Kerry Ligtenberg, p	.000	2	0	0	0	0	0	0	0	0	0	0
Keith Lockhart, ph	.000	2	1	0	0	0	0	0	0	1	0	0
Javy Lopez, c	.143	5	14	1	2	0	0	1	2	1	4	0
Greg Maddux, p	.333	2	3	0	1	0	0	0	0	0	2	0
Jason Marquis, p	.000	4	0	0	0	0	0	0	0	0	0	0
Dave Martinez, of-1	.200	4	5	0	1	0	0	0	0	0	1	0
Kevin Millwood, p	.000	1	0	0	0	0	0	0	0	0	0	0
Steve Reed, p	.000	1	0	0	0	0	0	0	0	0	0	0
Mike Remlinger, p	.000	3	0	0	0	0	0	0	0	0	0	0
Rey Sanchez, ss	.294	5	17	1	5	1	0	0	1	0	4	0
Rudy Seanez, p	.000	2	0	0	0	0	0	0	0	0	0	0
John Smoltz, p	.000	2	0	0	0	0	0	0	0	0	0	0
B.J. Surhoff, of-3	.231	4	13	1	3	0	0	1	2	0	1	0
TOTAL	.207		169	15	35	6	0	5	14	11	39	0

PITCHER	W	L	ERA	G	GS	CG	SV	SHO	IP	H	ER	BB	SO
John Burkett	0	1	8.31	1	1	0	0	0	4.3	7	4	2	2
Tom Glavine	1	1	1.50	2	2	0	0	0	12.0	10	2	5	5
Steve Karsay	0	0	2.08	4	0	0	0	0	4.3	3	1	1	6
Kerry Ligtenberg	0	0	0.00	2	0	0	0	0	3.0	0	0	1	2
Greg Maddux	0	2	5.40	2	2	0	0	0	10.0	14	6	2	7
Jason Marquis	0	0	0.00	2	0	0	0	0	2.0	2	0	2	3
Kevin Millwood	0	0	0.00	1	0	0	0	0	1.0	0	0	0	1
Steve Reed	0	0	∞	1	0	0	0	0	0.0	0	0	0	0
Mike Remlinger	0	0	0.00	3	0	0	0	0	2.3	3	0	2	2
Rudy Seanez	0	0	0.00	2	0	0	0	0	2.0	1	0	3	3
John Smoltz	0	0	0.00	2	0	0	0	0	3.0	0	0	0	1
TOTAL	1	4	2.66	22	5	0	0	0	44.0	40	13	18	32

GAME 1 AT ARI OCT 16

```
ATL  000 000 000    0 6 1
ARI  100 010 00X    2 8 0
```
Pitchers: MADDUX, Remlinger (8), Karsay (8) vs R. JOHNSON
Attendance: 37,729

GAME 2 AT ARI OCT 17

```
ATL  100 000 250    8 8 0
ARI  000 001 000    1 5 1
```
Pitchers: GLAVINE, Karsay (8), Smoltz (9) vs BATISTA, Morgan (8), Swindell (8), Witt (8), Kim (9)
Home Runs: Giles-ATL, Lopez-ATL, Surhoff-ATL
Attendance: 49,334

GAME 3 AT ATL OCT 19

```
ARI  002 030 000    5 9 1
ATL  000 100 000    1 4 1
```
Pitchers: SCHILLING vs BURKETT, Reed (5), Remlinger (5), Ligtenberg (8), Seanez (7), Millwood (8), Marquis (9)
Attendance: 41,624

GAME 4 AT ATL

```
ARI  004 200 014   11 12 0
ATL  110 000 110    4 13 4
```
Pitchers: Lopez, ANDERSON (4), Morgan (7), Swindell (7), Batista (8), Kim (8) vs MADDUX, Remlinger (4), Ligtenberg (5), Seanez (7), Karsay (8), Marquis (9)
Home Runs: Gonzalez-ARI, A. Jones-ATL
Attendance: 42,291

GAME 5 AT ATL OCT 21

```
ARI  000 120 000    3 6 1
ATL  000 100 100    2 7 1
```
Pitchers: R. JOHNSON, Kim (8) vs GLAVINE, Karsay (6), Smoltz (8)
Home Runs: Durazo-ARI, Franco-ATL
Attendance: 35,652

NEW YORK YANKEES (EAST) 4, SEATTLE MARINERS (WEST) 1

It was a match-up between the Yankees, who had set the American League record with 114 wins just three years ago, and the Mariners, who had broken it with 116 this year. But, while New York had put an exclamation point on their season with an 11–2 record in the playoffs, the Mariners would limp home having gone just 4–6 after their amazing regular season.

The Yankees never trailed in winning the first two games at Seattle. In Game 1, Andy Pettitte gave up just three hits and one run in eight innings, and Paul O'Neill homered, as New York prevailed, 4–2. In Game 2, the Yanks scored three runs in the second inning and Mike Mussina, Ramiro Mendoza and Mariano Rivera made them stand up for a 3–2 victory.

Down 2–0 after four innings of Game 3, Seattle erupted for 14 runs the rest of the game to roll to a 14–3 triumph. Jamie Moyer pitched seven strong innings for the win, and John Olerud, Bret Boone (five RBI) and Jay Buhner homered.

Game 4 started as a sloppy pitchers' duel, with Seattle's Paul Abbott tossing five hitless innings but walking eight, while Roger Clemens allowed just one hit in the same span but walked four and threw a wild pitch. Both were lifted after five, but the game remained scoreless until the eighth, when homers by Seattle's Boone and New York's Bernie Williams made it 1–1. Finally, Alfonso Soriano hit a two-run shot—only the sixth hit of the game by both teams combined—in the bottom of the ninth to give the Yanks a 3–1 win.

Game 5 was all New York. Williams, O'Neill and Tino Martinez homered, and Series MVP Pettitte notched his second win as the Yankees cruised, 12–3. The 2001 Mariners might have won two more games than the 1998 Yankees, but when the '01 versions of both teams met for the league pennant, it was New York that won three more games than their foes.

NY (E)

PLAYER/POS	AVG	G	AB	R	H	2B	3B	HR	RB	BB	SO	SB
Clay Bellinger, of	.000	1	1	0	0	0	0	0	0	0	0	0
Scott Brosius, 3b	.187	5	16	3	3	2	0	0	2	0	6	0
Roger Clemens, p	.000	0	0	0	0	0	0	0	0	0	0	0
Todd Greene, c	.000	1	1	0	0	0	0	0	0	0	0	0
Orlando Hernandez, p	.000	0	0	0	0	0	0	0	0	0	0	0
Derek Jeter, ss	.118	5	17	0	2	0	0	0	2	2	2	0
David Justice, dh	.278	5	18	3	5	1	0	0	4	3	1	0
Chuck Knoblauch, of	.333	5	18	0	6	1	0	0	3	2	3	0
Tino Martinez, 1b	.250	5	20	3	5	1	0	1	3	0	4	0
Ramiro Mendoza, p	.000	0	0	0	0	0	0	0	0	0	0	0
Mike Mussina, p	.000	0	0	0	0	0	0	0	0	0	0	0
Paul O'Neill, of	.417	5	12	2	5	0	0	2	3	1	0	0
Andy Pettitte, p	.000	0	0	0	0	0	0	0	0	0	0	0
Jorge Posada, c	.214	5	14	4	3	1	0	0	0	6	7	0
Mariano Rivera, p	.000	0	0	0	0	0	0	0	0	0	0	0
Luis Sojo, 1b	.000	1	1	0	0	0	0	0	0	0	0	0
Alfonso Soriano, 2b	.400	5	15	5	6	0	0	1	2	3	3	2
Shane Spencer, of	.286	5	7	1	2	1	0	0	1	1	1	1
Mike Stanton, p	.000	0	0	0	0	0	0	0	0	0	0	0
Randy Velarde, 3b	.000	1	1	0	0	0	0	0	0	0	0	0
Bernie Williams, of	.235	5	17	4	4	0	0	3	5	5	4	0
Enrique Wilson, ss	1.000	1	1	0	1	0	0	0	0	0	0	0
Jay Witasick, p	.000	0	0	0	0	0	0	0	0	0	0	0
Mark Wohlers, p	.000	0	0	0	0	0	0	0	0	0	0	0
TOTAL	.264	159	25	42	7	0	7	24	23	31	3	

PITCHER	W	L	ERA	G	GS	CG	SV	SHO	IP	H	ER	BB	SO
Roger Clemens	0	0	0.00	1	1	0	0	0	5.0	1	0	4	7
O. Hernandez	0	1	7.20	1	1	0	0	0	5.0	4	5	7	7
Ramiro Mendoza	0	0	1.69	3	0	0	0	0	5.3	3	1	2	4
Mike Mussina	1	0	3.00	1	1	0	0	0	6.0	4	2	1	3
Andy Pettitte	2	0	2.51	2	2	0	0	0	14.3	11	4	2	8
Mariano Rivera	1	0	1.93	4	0	0	2	0	4.7	2	1	1	3
Mike Stanton	0	0	27.00	2	0	0	0	0	1.0	1	3	2	0
Jay Witasick	0	0	9.00	1	0	0	0	0	3.0	6	3	0	2
Mark Wohlers	0	0	13.50	1	0	0	0	0	0.7	3	1	1	1
TOTAL	4	1	3.80	16	5	0	2	0	45.0	36	19	18	35

SEA (W)

PLAYER/POS	AVG	G	AB	R	H	2B	3B	HR	RB	BB	SO	SB
Paul Abbott, p	.000	0	0	0	0	0	0	0	0	0	0	0
David Bell, 3b	.187	5	16	1	3	0	0	0	4	0	3	0
Bret Boone, 2b	.316	5	19	2	6	0	0	2	6	2	2	0
Jay Buhner, of	.333	3	6	2	2	0	0	1	1	1	3	0
Mike Cameron, of	.176	5	17	3	3	2	0	0	0	4	4	0
Norm Charlton, p	.000	0	0	0	0	0	0	0	0	0	0	0
Freddy Garcia, p	.000	0	0	0	0	0	0	0	0	0	0	0
Charles Gipson, dh-1, of-1	.000	2	1	1	0	0	0	0	0	0	0	0
Carlos Guillen, ss	.250	3	8	1	2	0	0	0	0	0	1	0
John Halama, p	.000	0	0	0	0	0	0	0	0	0	0	0
Stan Javier, of-4	.214	5	14	2	3	0	0	1	2	1	3	1
Tom Lampkin, c	.250	2	4	0	1	0	0	0	0	1	2	0
Al Martin, dh-1	.500	2	2	1	1	0	1	0	0	0	0	0
Edgar Martinez, dh	.150	5	20	1	3	1	0	0	0	1	6	0
Mark McLemore, ss-3, of-1, 2b-1	.143	5	14	1	2	0	1	0	3	2	2	0
Jamie Moyer, p	.000	0	0	0	0	0	0	0	0	0	0	0
Jeff Nelson, p	.000	0	0	0	0	0	0	0	0	0	0	0
John Olerud, 1b	.211	5	19	2	4	0	0	1	3	2	4	0
Jose Paniagua, p	.000	0	0	0	0	0	0	0	0	0	0	0
Joel Pineiro, p	.000	0	0	0	0	0	0	0	0	0	0	0
Arthur Rhodes, p	.000	0	0	0	0	0	0	0	0	0	0	0
Kazuhiro Sasaki, p	.000	0	0	0	0	0	0	0	0	0	0	0
Aaron Sele, p	.000	0	0	0	0	0	0	0	0	0	0	0
Ichiro Suzuki, of	.222	5	18	3	4	1	0	0	1	4	4	2
Dan Wilson, c	.154	4	13	2	2	0	0	0	1	0	1	0
TOTAL	.211	171	22	36	4	2	5	20	18	35	3	

PITCHER	W	L	ERA	G	GS	CG	SV	SHO	IP	H	ER	BB	SO
Paul Abbott	0	0	0.00	1	1	0	0	0	5.0	0	0	8	2
Norm Charlton	0	0	0.00	2	0	0	0	0	1.7	1	0	2	2
Freddy Garcia	0	1	3.68	1	1	0	0	0	7.3	7	3	4	6
John Halama	0	0	13.50	2	0	0	0	0	2.0	3	3	0	0
Jamie Moyer	1	0	2.57	1	1	0	0	0	7.0	4	2	1	5
Jeff Nelson	0	0	0.00	2	0	0	0	0	2.3	1	0	1	3
Jose Paniagua	0	0	12.27	3	0	0	0	0	3.7	7	5	1	1
Joel Pineiro	0	0	4.50	1	0	0	0	0	2.0	4	1	2	5
Arthur Rhodes	0	0	4.50	2	0	0	0	0	2.0	2	1	0	2
Kazuhiro Sasaki	0	1	54.00	1	0	0	0	0	0.3	2	2	0	0
Aaron Sele	0	2	3.60	2	2	0	0	0	10.0	11	4	4	5
TOTAL	1	4	4.36	18	5	0	0	0	43.3	42	21	23	31

GAME 1 AT SEA OCT 17

NY	0 1 0 2 0 0 0 0 1	4 9 0
SEA	0 0 0 0 1 0 0 0 1	2 4 0

Pitchers: PETTITTE, Rivera (9) vs SELE, Charlton (7), Paniagua (8)
Home Runs: O'Neill-NY
Attendance: 47,644

GAME 2 AT SEA OCT 18

NY	0 3 0 0 0 0 0 0 0	3 9 1
SEA	0 0 0 2 0 0 0 0 0	2 6 0

Pitchers: MUSSINA, Mendoza (7), Rivera (8) vs GARCIA, Rhodes (8), Nelson (9)
Home Runs: Javier-SEA
Attendance: 47,791

GAME 3 AT NY OCT 20

SEA	0 0 0 0 2 7 2 1 2	14 15 0
NY	2 0 0 0 0 0 0 1 0	3 7 2

Pitchers: MOYER, Paniagua (8), Halama (9) vs HERNANDEZ, Stanton (6), Wohlers (6), Witasick (7)
Home Runs: Olerud-SEA, Boone-SEA, Buhner-SEA, B. Williams-NY
Attendance: 56,517

GAME 4 AT NY OCT 21

SEA	0 0 0 0 0 0 0 1 0	1 2 0
NY	0 0 0 0 0 0 0 1 2	3 4 0

Pitchers: ABBOTT, Charlton (6), Nelson (6), Rhodes (8), SASAKI (9) vs Clemens, Mendoza (6), RIVERA (9)
Home Runs: Boone-SEA, B. Williams-NY, Soriano-NY
Attendance: 56,375

GAME 5 AT NY OCT 22

SEA	0 0 0 0 0 0 3 0 0	3 9 1
NY	0 0 4 1 0 4 0 3 X	12 13 1

Pitchers: SELE, Halama (5), Pineiro (6), Paniagua (8) vs PETTITTE, Mendoza (7), Stanton (8), Rivera (9)
Home Runs: B. Williams-NY, O'Neill-NY, T. Martinez-NY
Attendance: 56,370

ARIZONA DIAMONDBACKS (NL) 4, NEW YORK YANKEES (AL) 3

The Yankees were looking for their fourth straight world championship and 27th of their storied history. The Diamondbacks had never even been in a World Series. Nevertheless, the D'backs—with fearsome pitchers Randy Johnson and Curt Schilling anchoring their rotation—were not to be underestimated.

Schilling made that clear in Game 1, pitching seven innings of three-hit ball as Arizona rolled, 9–1. And Johnson made it even clearer in Game 2, hurling a three-hit shutout and whiffing 11 to beat the Yanks, 4–0. Matt Williams' three-run homer in the seventh iced it.

As the Series moved to New York, President George W. Bush threw out the first ball, and Roger Clemens took it from there as the Yankees eked out a 2–1 victory. Clemens and Mariano Rivera combined on a three-hitter with 13 strikeouts.

Schilling had another brilliant outing in Game 4, allowing three hits in seven innings, while striking out nine. Diamondbacks' closer Byung-Hyun Kim took over, and brought the Diamondbacks within one out of winning, 3–1, and taking a commanding 3–1 advantage in the Series. Instead, Tino Martinez belted a two-run homer in the ninth, Derek Jeter slugged a solo shot in the tenth, and the Series was tied. Both blasts came off Kim, and the second came just after midnight—making this the first World Series to extend into November.

Game 5 was more of the same. Again, Arizona took a two-run lead into the bottom of the ninth, and again Kim surrendered a two-out, two-run homer, this time to Scott Brosius. The Yankees won, 3–2, on a single by Alfonso Soriano in the 12th.

Back in Arizona, the Diamondbacks stopped the Yankees' momentum. They scored 15 runs in the first four innings, collected a World Series record 22 hits, and allowed Johnson to coast to a 15–2 victory. Although Arizona had outscored New York, 34–12, the Series was tied, and it all came down to Game 7: Schilling against his mentor, Clemens. Both pitched well, but Soriano's eighth-inning homer gave New York the lead, 2–1. In came Rivera—who had converted 23-straight postseason save opportunities—to nail it down. He struck out three in the eighth.

Then, the unthinkable happened in the ninth. Two hits, a throwing error by Rivera, and a hit batsman left the score tied with the bases loaded and only one out. With the infield in, Luis Gonzalez blooped a ball just over shortstop Jeter's head, plating the winning run. Johnson, who had retired all four batters he faced on zero days' rest, got his third win, and he and Schilling were named co-MVPs of the Series.

ARI (N)

PLAYER/POS	AVG	G	AB	R	H	2B	3B	HR	RB	BB	SO	SB
Rod Barajas, c	.400	2	5	1	2	0	0	1	1	0	0	0
Miguel Batista, p	.000	2	0	0	0	0	0	0	0	0	0	0
Danny Bautista, of-4, dh-1	.583	5	12	1	7	2	0	0	7	1	1	0
Jay Bell, 2b-1	.143	3	7	3	1	0	0	0	1	0	2	0
Troy Brohawn, p	.000	1	0	0	0	0	0	0	0	0	0	0
Greg Colbrunn, 1b	.400	1	5	2	2	0	0	0	1	1	1	0
Craig Counsell, 2b	.083	6	24	1	2	0	0	1	1	0	7	0
Midre Cummings, pr	.000	2	0	2	0	0	0	0	0	0	0	0
David Dellucci, of-1	.500	2	2	0	1	0	0	0	0	0	0	0
Erubiel Durazo, dh-3	.364	4	11	0	4	1	0	0	1	3	4	0
Steve Finley, of	.368	6	19	5	7	0	0	1	2	4	5	0
Luis Gonzalez, of	.259	7	27	4	7	2	0	1	5	1	11	0
Mark Grace, 1b	.263	6	19	1	5	1	0	1	3	4	1	0
Randy Johnson, p	.143	3	7	2	1	0	0	0	1	0	2	0
Damian Miller, c	.190	6	21	3	4	2	0	0	2	1	11	0
Mike Morgan, p	.000	3	0	0	0	0	0	0	0	0	0	0
Reggie Sanders, of	.304	6	23	6	7	1	0	0	1	1	7	1
Curt Schilling, p	.000	3	6	0	0	0	0	0	0	0	5	0
Greg Swindell, p	.000	3	0	0	0	0	0	0	0	0	0	0
Matt Williams, 3b	.269	7	26	3	7	2	0	1	7	0	6	0
Bobby Witt, p	.000	1	0	0	0	0	0	0	0	0	0	0
Tony Womack, ss	.250	7	32	3	8	3	0	0	3	1	7	1
TOTAL	.264		246	37	65	14	0	6	36	17	70	2

PITCHER	W	L	ERA	G	GS	CG	SV	SHO	IP	H	ER	BB	SO
Brian Anderson	0	1	3.38	1	1	0	0	0	5.3	5	2	3	1
Miguel Batista	0	0	0.00	2	1	0	0	0	8.0	5	0	5	6
Troy Brohawn	0	0	0.00	1	0	0	0	0	1.0	1	0	0	1
Randy Johnson	3	0	1.04	3	2	1	0	1	17.3	9	2	3	19
Byung-Hyun Kim	0	1	13.50	2	0	0	0	0	3.3	6	5	1	6
Albie Lopez	0	0	27.00	1	0	0	0	0	0.3	2	1	0	0
Mike Morgan	0	0	0.00	3	0	0	0	0	4.7	1	0	0	1
Curt Schilling	1	0	1.69	3	3	0	0	0	21.3	12	4	2	26
Greg Swindell	0	0	0.00	3	0	0	0	0	2.7	1	0	1	2
Bobby Witt	0	0	0.00	1	0	0	0	0	1.0	0	0	1	1
TOTAL	4	3	1.94	20	7	1	0	1	65.0	42	14	16	63

NY (A)

PLAYER/POS	AVG	G	AB	R	H	2B	3B	HR	RB	BB	SO	SB
Clay Bellinger, of	.000	2	2	0	0	0	0	0	0	0	2	0
Scott Brosius, 3b	.167	7	24	1	4	2	0	1	3	0	8	0
Randy Choate, p	.000	2	1	0	0	0	0	0	0	0	1	0
Roger Clemens, p	.000	2	2	0	0	0	0	0	0	0	1	0
Todd Greene, c	.500	1	2	1	1	1	0	0	0	0	0	0
Sterling Hitchcock, p	.000	2	0	0	0	0	0	0	0	0	0	0
Derek Jeter, ss	.148	7	27	3	4	0	0	1	1	0	6	0
David Justice, of-2, dh-2	.167	5	12	0	2	0	0	0	0	1	9	0
Chuck Knoblauch, of-3, dh-2	.056	6	18	1	1	0	0	0	0	0	2	0
Tino Martinez, 1b	.190	6	21	1	4	0	0	1	3	2	2	0
Mike Mussina, p	.000	2	1	0	0	0	0	0	0	0	1	0
Paul O'Neill, of-4	.333	5	15	1	5	1	0	0	0	2	2	1
Andy Pettitte, p	.333	2	3	0	1	0	0	0	0	0	1	0
Jorge Posada, c	.174	7	23	2	4	1	0	1	1	3	8	0
Mariano Rivera, p	.000	4	0	0	0	0	0	0	0	0	0	0
Luis Sojo, 1b-1	.333	2	3	0	1	0	0	0	0	1	0	0
Alfonso Soriano, 2b	.240	7	25	1	6	0	0	1	2	0	7	0
Shane Spencer, of-5	.200	7	20	1	4	0	0	1	2	2	6	0
Mike Stanton, p	.000	5	0	0	0	0	0	0	0	0	0	0
Randy Velarde, 1b	.000	1	3	0	0	0	0	0	0	1	1	0
Bernie Williams, of	.208	7	24	2	5	1	0	0	2	4	6	0
Enrique Wilson, ss-1	.000	2	3	0	0	0	0	0	0	0	0	0
Jay Witasick, p	.000	1	0	0	0	0	0	0	0	0	0	0
TOTAL	.183		229	14	42	6	0	6	14	16	63	1

PITCHER	W	L	ERA	G	GS	CG	SV	SHO	IP	H	ER	BB	SO
Randy Choate	0	0	2.45	2	0	0	0	0	3.7	7	1	1	2
Roger Clemens	1	0	1.35	2	2	0	0	0	13.3	10	2	4	19
O. Hernandez	0	0	1.42	1	1	0	0	0	6.3	4	1	4	5
Sterling Hitchcock	1	0	0.00	2	0	0	0	0	4.0	1	0	0	6
Ramiro Mendoza	0	0	0.00	2	0	0	0	0	2.7	1	0	0	1
Mike Mussina	0	1	4.09	2	2	0	0	0	11.0	11	5	4	14
Andy Pettitte	0	2	10.00	2	2	0	0	0	9.0	12	10	2	9
Mariano Rivera	1	1	1.42	4	0	0	0	0	6.3	6	1	1	7
Mike Stanton	0	0	3.18	5	0	0	0	0	5.7	5	2	1	3
Jay Witasick	0	0	54.00	1	0	0	0	0	1.3	10	8	0	4
TOTAL	3	4	4.26	23	7	0	0	1	63.3	65	30	17	70

GAME 1 AT NY OCT 27

```
NY   100 000 000    1  3  2
ARI  104 400 00X    9 10  0
```
Pitchers: MUSSINA, Choate (4), Hitchcock (5), Stanton (8) vs SCHILLING, Morgan (8), Swindell (9)
Home Runs: Counsell-ARI, Gonzalez-ARI
Attendance: 49,646

GAME 2 AT ARI OCT 28

```
NY   000 000 000    0  3  0
ARI  010 000 30X    4  5  0
```
Pitchers: PETTITTE, Stanton (8) vs JOHNSON
Home Runs: M. Williams-ARI
Attendance: 49,646

GAME 3 AT NY OCT 30

```
ARI  000 100 000    1  3  3
NY   010 001 00X    2  7  1
```
Pitchers: ANDERSON, Morgan (6), Swindell (7) vs CLEMENS, Rivera (8)
Home Runs: Posada-NY
Attendance: 55,820

GAME 4 AT NY OCT 31

```
ARI  000 100 0200    3  6  0
NY   001 000 021     4  7  0
```
Pitchers: Schilling, KIM (8) vs Hernandez, Stanton (7), Mendoza (8), RIVERA (10)
Home Runs: Grace-ARI, Spencer-NY, T. Martinez-NY, Jeter-NY
Attendance: 55,863

GAME 5 AT NY NOV 1

```
ARI  000 020 000 000    2  8  0
NY   000 000 002 001    3  9  1
```
Pitchers: Batista, Swindell (8), Kim (9), Morgan (9), LOPEZ (12) vs Mussina, Mendoza (9), Rivera (10), HITCHCOCK (12)
Home Runs: Finley-ARI, Barajas-ARI, Brosius-NY
Attendance: 56,018

GAME 6 AT ARI NOV 3

```
NY   000 002 000     2  7  1
ARI  138 300 00X    15 22  0
```
Pitchers: PETTITTE, Witasick (3), Choate (4), Stanton (7) vs JOHNSON, Witt (8), Brohawn (9)
Attendance: 49,707

GAME 7 AT ARI NOV 4

```
NY   000 000 110    2  6  3
ARI  000 001 002    3 11  0
```
Pitchers: Clemens, Stanton (7), RIVERA (8) vs Schilling, Batista (8), JOHNSON (8)
Home Runs: Soriano-NY
Attendance: 49,589

SAN FRANCISCO GIANTS (WILD CARD) 3, ATLANTA BRAVES (EAST) 2

The perennial powerhouse Braves won the NL East for the eighth straight season, this time by 19 games over Montreal. Atlanta's first-round opponents, the Giants, took the National League's wild-card spot behind Barry Bonds' second straight MVP season. But Bonds entered the fray with a reputation as an autumn choker, with a .196 lifetime postseason batting average and just one homer in 97 at bats.

The Giants drew first blood, torching Tom Glavine for an 8–2 lead by the sixth inning of Game 1, and holding on for an 8–5 win. Bonds was a quiet 1-for-4, but Russ Ortiz pitched seven strong innings for the victory. The Braves answered with a 7–3 triumph, as Kevin Millwood allowed just three hits and no walks in six innings, Javy Lopez and Vinny Castilla homered and Mark DeRosa cracked a double and triple. Bonds—after going hitless in his first three at bats—sent a message with a solo home run in the ninth inning.

The Braves won Game 3, 10–2, despite another home run by Bonds. Greg Maddux got the win, backed by Keith Lockhart's three-run shot. But the Giants KO'd Glavine again the next day, evening the series, 8–3. Rich Aurilia knocked in four runs with two singles and a homer, giving him seven RBIs for the series. It all came down to Game 5, back in Atlanta.

Bonds started the scoring in the second inning, singling, advancing to second on a ground-out, and tallying on Reggie Sanders' single. Two innings later, Bonds drilled his third homer of the series, driving in what proved to be the winning run. Five Giants hurlers held the Braves to one run, and the Giants completed the upset, 3–1. Ortiz earned his second victory, and Bonds was quieting his critics day by day.

SF (WC)

PLAYER/POS	AVG	G	AB	R	H	2B	3B	HR	RB	BB	SO	SB
Rich Aurilia, ss	.238	5	21	4	5	1	0	2	7	1	5	0
Manuel Aybar, p	.000	2	0	0	0	0	0	0	0	0	0	0
David Bell, 3b	.187	5	16	3	3	0	0	0	1	3	4	0
Barry Bonds, of	.294	5	17	5	5	0	0	3	4	4	1	0
Shawon Dunston, ph	.000	2	1	0	0	0	0	0	0	0	1	0
Scott Eyre, p	.000	3	0	0	0	0	0	0	0	0	0	0
Pedro Feliz, ph	.000	1	1	0	0	0	0	0	0	0	1	0
Aaron Fultz, ph	.000	2	0	0	0	0	0	0	0	0	0	0
Tom Goodwin, ph	.000	2	2	0	0	0	0	0	0	0	2	0
Livan Hernandez, p	.000	1	2	0	0	0	0	0	0	0	0	0
Jeff Kent, 2b	.263	5	19	1	5	2	0	0	1	2	7	0
Kenny Lofton, of	.350	5	20	5	7	1	0	0	2	2	3	1
Ramon Martinez, ph	.000	1	0	0	0	0	0	0	0	1	0	0
Robb Nen, p	.000	4	0	0	0	0	0	0	0	0	0	0
Russ Ortiz, p	.167	2	6	1	1	0	0	0	0	0	4	0
Felix Rodriguez, p	.000	3	0	0	0	0	0	0	0	0	0	0
Kirk Rueter, p	.000	1	1	0	0	0	0	0	0	0	1	0
Reggie Sanders, of	.222	5	18	1	4	1	0	0	1	3	5	0
Benito Santiago, c	.238	5	21	1	5	2	0	0	5	1	5	0
Jason Schmidt, p	.000	1	2	0	0	0	0	0	0	0	1	0
J.T. Snow, 1b	.316	5	19	3	6	2	0	1	3	1	5	0
Jay Witasick, p	.000	2	0	0	0	0	0	0	0	0	0	0
Tim Worrell, p	.000	3	0	0	0	0	0	0	0	0	0	0
TOTAL	.247		166	24	41	9	0	6	24	18	45	1

PITCHER	W	L	ERA	G	GS	CG	SV	SHO	IP	H	ER	BB	SO
Manuel Aybar	0	0	6.75	2	0	0	0	0	2.7	2	2	1	3
Scott Eyre	0	0	0.00	3	0	0	0	0	1.3	1	0	0	0
Aaron Fultz	0	0	∞	2	0	0	0	0	0.0	2	1	0	0
Livan Hernandez	1	0	3.24	1	1	0	0	0	8.3	8	3	2	6
Robb Nen	0	0	0.00	4	0	0	2	0	2.7	4	0	1	1
Russ Ortiz	2	0	2.19	2	2	0	0	0	12.3	9	3	8	8
Felix Rodriguez	0	0	0.00	3	0	0	0	0	3.0	1	0	2	2
Kirk Rueter	0	1	18.00	1	1	0	0	0	3.0	7	6	2	1
Jason Schmidt	0	1	6.75	1	1	0	0	0	5.3	3	4	4	5
Jay Witasick	0	0	0.00	2	0	0	0	0	2.3	0	0	0	1
Tim Worrell	0	0	12.00	3	0	0	0	0	3.0	7	4	2	3
TOTAL	3	2	4.70	24	5	0	2	0	44.0	44	23	22	30

ATL (E)

PLAYER/POS	AVG	G	AB	R	H	2B	3B	HR	RB	BB	SO	SB
Henry Blanco, c	.167	2	6	0	1	0	0	0	0	0	2	0
Darren Bragg, of-1	.000	4	3	0	0	0	0	0	0	0	0	0
Vinny Castilla, 3b	.389	5	18	5	7	0	0	1	4	2	2	0
Mark DeRosa, 2b-3	.429	4	7	2	3	1	1	0	3	1	1	0
Julio Franco, 1b	.182	5	22	2	4	0	0	0	1	2	3	1
Matt Franco, ph	.000	4	2	0	0	0	0	0	0	0	0	0
Rafael Furcal, ss	.250	5	24	2	6	1	1	0	2	0	5	1
Marcus Giles, ph	.500	3	2	0	1	0	0	0	0	0	0	0
Tom Glavine, p	.500	2	2	0	1	0	0	0	0	2	0	0
Kevin Gryboski, p	.000	3	0	0	0	0	0	0	0	0	0	0
Chris Hammond, p	.000	3	0	0	0	0	0	0	0	0	0	0
Wes Helms, 1b	.000	1	0	0	0	0	0	0	0	0	0	0
Darren Holmes, p	.000	3	0	0	0	0	0	0	0	0	0	0
Andruw Jones, of	.316	5	19	4	6	1	0	0	2	2	3	0
Chipper Jones, of	.294	5	17	3	5	0	0	0	2	5	2	0
Kerry Ligtenberg, p	.000	1	0	0	0	0	0	0	0	0	0	0
Keith Lockhart, 2b	.333	5	12	1	4	0	0	1	4	2	4	0
Javy Lopez, c	.333	4	15	4	5	1	0	2	4	1	3	0
Greg Maddux, p	.000	1	3	0	0	0	0	0	0	0	1	0
Kevin Millwood, p	.000	2	2	0	0	0	0	0	0	0	0	0
Damian Moss, p	.000	2	0	0	0	0	0	0	0	0	0	0
Mike Remlinger, p	.000	3	0	0	0	0	0	0	0	0	0	0
Gary Sheffield, of	.062	5	16	3	1	0	0	1	1	7	3	0
John Smoltz, p	.000	2	0	0	0	0	0	0	0	0	0	0
TOTAL	.259		170	26	44	4	2	5	25	22	30	2

PITCHER	W	L	ERA	G	GS	CG	SV	SHO	IP	H	ER	BB	SO
Tom Glavine	0	2	15.26	2	2	0	0	0	7.7	17	13	7	4
Kevin Gryboski	0	0	0.00	3	0	0	0	0	3.7	2	0	2	3
Chris Hammond	0	0	6.75	3	0	0	0	0	2.7	2	2	3	2
Darren Holmes	0	0	0.00	3	0	0	0	0	2.7	1	0	0	5
Kerry Ligtenberg	0	0	0.00	1	0	0	0	0	2.0	0	0	0	1
Greg Maddux	1	0	3.00	1	1	0	0	0	6.0	5	2	1	3
Kevin Millwood	1	1	3.27	2	2	0	0	0	11.0	7	4	0	14
Damian Moss	0	0	3.00	2	0	0	0	0	3.0	2	1	1	3
Mike Remlinger	0	0	4.50	3	0	0	0	0	2.0	3	1	2	3
John Smoltz	0	0	2.70	2	0	0	0	0	3.3	2	1	2	7
TOTAL	2	3	4.91	22	5	0	0	0	44.0	41	24	18	45

GAME 1 AT ATL OCT 2

SF 030 302 000 8 12 2
ATL 020 000 030 5 10 0
Pitchers: ORTIZ, Worrell (8), Eyre (8), Nen (9) vs GLAVINE, Hammond (6), Gryboski (6), Moss (8), Holmes (9)
Home Runs: Sheffield-ATL, Lopez-ATL
Attendance: 41,903

GAME 2 AT ATL OCT 3

SF 010 001 001 3 7 0
ATL 130 300 00X 7 8 0
Pitchers: RUETER, Aybar (4), Witasick (6), Rodriguez (8) vs MILLWOOD, Remlinger (7), Holmes (8), Smoltz (8)
Home Runs: Snow-SF, Aurilia-SF, Bonds-SF, Lopez-ATL, Castilla-ATL
Attendance: 47,167

GAME 3 AT SF OCT 5

ATL 001 005 004 10 10 0
SF 100 001 000 2 5 0
Pitchers: MADDUX, Hammond (7), Remlinger (8), Gryboski (9) vs SCHMIDT, Aybar (6), Rodriguez (7), Eyre (8), Worrell (9), Fultz (9), Nen (9), Witasick (9)
Home Runs: Lockhart-ATL, Bonds-SF
Attendance: 43,043

GAME 4 AT SF OCT 6

ATL 000 012 000 3 9 0
SF 223 010 00X 8 11 0
Pitchers: GLAVINE, Gryboski (3), Moss (5), Ligtenberg (7) vs HERNANDEZ, Eyre (9), Nen (9)
Home Runs: Aurilia-SF
Attendance: 43,070

GAME 5 AT ATL OCT 7

SF 010 100 100 3 6 2
ATL 000 001 000 1 7 0
Pitchers: ORTIZ, Fultz (6), Rodriguez (6), Worrell (7), Nen (9) vs MILLWOOD, Hammond (6), Remlinger (7), Holmes (7), Smoltz (8)
Home Runs: Bonds-SF
Attendance: 45,203

ST. LOUIS CARDINALS (CENTRAL) 3, ARIZONA DIAMONDBACKS (WEST) 0

The Cardinals won the NL Central Division handily, with a 13-game cushion over the Astros, though it was a difficult year for them, due particularly to the sudden death of their 33-year-old pitcher, Darryl Kile, on June 22 (his five-year-old son, Kannon, was a visible presence throughout the Cards' autumn run). The defending world champion Diamondbacks had to work a little harder to return to the postseason, but 98 wins—including 47 by their pair of aces, Randy Johnson and Curt Schilling—got it done. The dynamic duo had been unstoppable in last year's postseason, going 9–1 with 103 strikeouts, just 14 walks, and a 1.30 ERA. But this year they would have to take a backseat to another team's pitching.

In Game 1 at Arizona, the Cards showed Johnson no respect, pounding him for ten hits and six runs in six innings, and cruising to a 12–2 victory. Jim Edmonds started things with a two-run homer in the first inning, Scott Rolen added another in the fourth, and three other Cardinals drove in two runs apiece. Winner Matt Morris allowed just one earned run in seven innings.

St. Louis got another pitching gem in Game 2, permitting Arizona only six hits and one unearned run. Chuck Finley worked 6-1/3 scoreless innings, and he had to, as Schilling allowed only one run—a J.D. Drew homer—in seven innings of work. The D'backs tied the score in the eighth on an error and a two-out double by Quinton McCracken, but the Cards tallied the winner in the ninth on a single by Edgar Renteria, a sacrifice, and a basehit by Miguel Cairo, who batted 1.000 (4-for-4) in the series. Fernando Vina had four hits for the winners, en route to a .600 series average.

The Cardinals completed the sweep in St. Louis with a 6–3 win in Game 3. St. Louis pitchers held Arizona to four hits, and Jeff Fassero picked up his second victory in relief. Overall, the Cards' pitching corps held Arizona to a .184 batting average, posting a 1.33 ERA in the series.

STL (C)

PLAYER/POS	AVG	G	AB	R	H	2B	3B	HR	RB	BB	SO	SB
Andy Benes, p	.000	1	1	0	0	0	0	0	0	1	0	0
Miguel Cairo, 3b	1.000	2	4	2	4	1	0	0	3	0	0	0
Mike Crudale, p	.000	1	0	0	0	0	0	0	0	0	0	0
J.D. Drew, of	.222	2	9	1	2	0	0	1	1	1	2	0
Jim Edmonds, of	.273	3	11	1	3	0	0	1	2	2	4	0
Jeff Fassero, p	.000	3	0	0	0	0	0	0	0	0	0	0
Chuck Finley, p	.000	1	3	0	0	0	0	0	0	0	2	0
Jason Isringhausen, p	.000	2	0	0	0	0	0	0	0	0	0	0
Steve Kline, p	.000	2	0	0	0	0	0	0	0	0	0	0
Eli Marrero, of	.000	2	6	0	0	0	0	0	1	0	1	0
Tino Martinez, 1b	.000	3	11	2	0	0	0	0	0	2	1	0
Mike Matheny, c	.444	3	9	3	4	1	0	0	2	2	1	0
Matt Morris, p	.250	1	4	1	1	0	0	0	2	0	2	0
Eduardo Perez, ph	.000	1	1	0	0	0	0	0	0	0	0	0
Albert Pujols,												
1b-1, 3b-1, of-3	.300	3	10	3	3	0	1	0	3	3	1	0
Edgar Renteria, ss	.250	3	12	3	3	0	0	0	0	1	1	2
Kerry Robinson, ph	.500	2	2	0	1	0	0	0	1	0	0	0
Scott Rolen, 3b	.429	2	7	1	3	0	0	1	2	0	2	0
Fernando Vina, 2b	.600	3	15	3	9	0	0	0	1	1	0	0
Rick White, p	.000	2	0	0	0	0	0	0	0	0	0	0
TOTAL	.314		105	20	33	2	1	3	19	12	17	2

PITCHER	W	L	ERA	G	GS	CG	SV	SHO	IP	H	ER	BB	SO
Andy Benes	0	0	5.79	1	1	0	0	0	4.7	2	3	4	5
Mike Crudale	0	0	0.00	1	0	0	0	0	1.0	0	0	1	2
Jeff Fassero	2	0	0.00	3	0	0	0	0	2.7	3	0	0	2
Chuck Finley	0	0	0.00	1	1	0	0	0	6.3	4	0	2	7
J. Isringhausen	0	0	0.00	2	0	0	2	0	2.0	0	0	0	1
Steve Kline	0	0	0.00	2	0	0	0	0	1.3	1	0	1	0
Matt Morris	1	0	1.29	1	1	0	0	0	7.0	7	1	2	3
Rick White	0	0	0.00	2	0	0	0	0	2.0	1	0	1	1
TOTAL	3	0	1.33	13	3	0	2	0	27.0	18	4	11	21

ARI (W)

PLAYER/POS	AVG	G	AB	R	H	2B	3B	HR	RB	BB	SO	SB
Rod Barajas, c	.250	2	4	1	1	0	0	1	1	0	1	0
Miguel Batista, p	.000	1	1	0	0	0	0	0	0	0	1	0
Alex Cintron, 3b-1	.000	2	0	0	0	0	0	0	0	0	0	0
Greg Colbrunn, 1b	.000	1	3	1	0	0	0	0	0	1	1	0
David Dellucci, of	.286	3	7	1	2	0	0	1	2	0	1	0
Chris Donnels, ph	.000	3	2	0	0	0	0	0	0	1	0	0
Erubiel Durazo, 1b-1	.000	2	4	0	0	0	0	0	0	1	1	0
Mike Fetters, p	.000	1	0	0	0	0	0	0	0	0	0	0
Steve Finley, of	.222	3	9	1	2	0	0	0	1	2	2	1
Mark Grace, 1b	.250	2	4	0	1	0	0	0	0	1	0	0
Rick Helling, p	.000	2	0	0	0	0	0	0	0	0	0	0
Randy Johnson, p	.000	1	2	0	0	0	0	0	0	0	2	0
Byung-Hyun Kim, p	.000	1	0	0	0	0	0	0	0	0	0	0
Mike Koplove, p	.000	1	0	0	0	0	0	0	0	0	0	0
Mark Little, of	.000	2	4	0	0	0	0	0	0	0	2	0
Matt Mantei, p	.000	1	0	0	0	0	0	0	0	0	0	0
Quinton McCracken, of	.364	3	11	1	4	1	0	0	2	1	2	0
Damian Miller, c	.500	1	2	0	1	1	0	0	0	2	0	0
Chad Moeller, c-1	.400	3	5	0	2	0	0	0	0	0	1	0
Mike Myers, p	.000	2	0	0	0	0	0	0	0	0	0	0
Curt Schilling, p	.000	1	2	0	0	0	0	0	0	0	0	0
Junior Spivey, 2b	.154	3	13	0	2	0	0	0	0	1	3	0
Greg Swindell, p	.000	2	0	0	0	0	0	0	0	0	0	0
Matt Williams, 3b	.083	3	12	0	1	0	0	0	0	0	3	0
Tony Womack, ss	.154	3	13	1	2	0	0	0	0	1	1	0
TOTAL	.184		98	6	18	2	0	2	6	11	21	1

PITCHER	W	L	ERA	G	GS	CG	SV	SHO	IP	H	ER	BB	SO
Miguel Batista	0	1	9.82	1	1	0	0	0	3.7	5	4	3	1
Mike Fetters	0	0	0.00	1	0	0	0	0	0.7	1	0	1	1
Rick Helling	0	0	0.00	2	0	0	0	0	4.0	1	0	0	2
Randy Johnson	0	1	7.50	1	1	0	0	0	6.0	10	5	2	4
Byung-Hyun Kim	0	0	18.00	1	0	0	0	0	1.0	2	2	3	0
Mike Koplove	0	1	6.75	1	0	0	0	0	1.3	2	1	0	1
Matt Mantei	0	0	54.00	1	0	0	0	0	0.3	1	2	1	0
Mike Myers	0	0	0.00	2	0	0	0	0	1.7	2	0	0	1
Curt Schilling	0	0	1.29	1	1	0	0	0	7.0	7	1	1	7
Greg Swindell	0	0	27.00	2	0	0	0	0	0.3	2	1	0	0
TOTAL	0	3	5.54	13	3	0	0	0	26.0	33	16	12	17

GAME 1 AT ARI OCT 1

STL   200 301 600   12 14 1
ARI   101 000 000   2 8 2
Pitchers: MORRIS, Fassero (8), Crudale (9) vs JOHNSON, Mantei (7), Swindell (7), Fetters (7), Helling (8)
Home Runs: Edmonds-STL, Rolen-STL
Attendance: 49,154

GAME 2 AT ARI OCT 3

STL   001 000 001   2 10 1
ARI   000 000 010   1 6 0
Pitchers: Finley, Kline (7), White (7), FASSERO (8), Isringhausen (9) vs Schilling, KOPLOVE (8), Myers (9)
Home Runs: Drew-STL
Attendance: 48,856

GAME 3 AT STL OCT 5

ARI   020 010 000   3 4 0
STL   011 200 02X   6 9 0
Pitchers: BATISTA, Swindell (4), Helling (5), Myers (7), Kim (8) vs Benes, FASSERO (7), White (7), Kline (8), Isringhausen (9)
Home Runs: Dellucci-ARI, Barajas-ARI
Attendance: 52,189

ANAHEIM ANGELS (WILD CARD) 3, NEW YORK YANKEES (EAST) 1

The Yankees easily won their fifth-straight eastern division crown, and were looking ahead to their fifth-straight World Series appearance, once they phoned in their Divisional and Championship Series wins. The never-say-die Angels, who won the 2002 AL wild card after having finished 41 games out of first place in 2001, had other ideas.

Game 1 was a see-saw battle. Derek Jeter homered for the Yankees in the first inning, but the Angels manufactured a run in the third on two singles, a stolen base and an error. Jason Giambi's two-run homer in the fourth gave the Yanks the lead again; however, the Angels answered with Garret Anderson's two-run double in the fifth. Rondell White homered for New York in the bottom of that frame, but the Angels tied it again on a sixth-inning dinger by Troy Glaus. Glaus homered again two innings later to give Anaheim its first lead, but Bernie Williams' three-run blast capped off a four-run eighth as the Yankees pulled out an 8–5 win. It was to be their last one of the year.

Anaheim built up a 4–0 advantage in Game 2, but by the sixth the Yankees had taken the lead, 5–4. Back-to-back jacks by Anderson and Glaus put the Angels back on top, and they held on to win, 8–6, as the Yankees left the tying runs on base.

The series moved to California, but the results were the same, as Game 3 was another back-and-forth slugfest. The Yankees jumped to a 6–1 lead in the third, but the Angels pecked away until it was tied after seven. In the eighth, doubles by Adam Kennedy and Darin Erstad and a homer by Tim Salmon gave Anaheim three runs and the game, 9–6.

The Yanks led Game 4, 2–1, until the bottom of the fifth, when the floodgates opened. Anaheim scored eight runs on ten hits, and coasted in to win the game, 9–5, and the series.

Anaheim's offensive statistics in the series were staggering. The club batted .376 with a .624 slugging percentage, and Salmon's .263 BA was the lowest on the entire team!

ANA (WC)

PLAYER/POS	AVG	G	AB	R	H	2B	3B	HR	RB	BB	SO	SB
Garret Anderson, of	.389	4	18	5	7	2	0	1	4	1	3	0
Kevin Appier, p	.000	1	0	0	0	0	0	0	0	0	0	0
Brendan Donnelly, p	.000	3	0	0	0	0	0	0	0	0	0	0
David Eckstein, ss	.278	4	18	2	5	0	0	0	1	0	0	1
Darin Erstad, of	.421	4	19	4	8	2	0	0	2	0	1	1
Chone Figgins, dh	.000	1	0	1	0	0	0	0	0	0	0	1
Brad Fullmer, dh	.286	3	7	1	2	1	0	0	1	1	1	0
Benji Gil, 2b	.800	2	5	1	4	0	0	0	1	0	0	0
Troy Glaus, 3b	.312	4	16	4	5	0	0	3	3	3	1	3	0
Adam Kennedy, 2b	.500	4	8	4	4	1	0	1	3	1	2	1
John Lackey, p	.000	1	0	0	0	0	0	0	0	0	0	0
Ben Molina, c	.267	4	15	0	4	2	0	0	2	0	1	0
Alex Ochoa, of	.000	3	0	0	0	0	0	0	0	0	0	0
Ramon Ortiz, p	.000	1	0	0	0	0	0	0	0	0	0	0
Troy Percival, p	.000	3	0	0	0	0	0	0	0	0	0	0
Francisco Rodriguez, p	.000	3	0	0	0	0	0	0	0	0	0	0
Tim Salmon, of	.263	4	19	3	5	1	0	2	7	1	5	0
Scott Schoeneweis, p	.000	3	0	0	0	0	0	0	0	0	0	0
Scott Spiezio, 1b	.400	4	15	2	6	1	0	1	6	2	1	0
Jarrod Washburn, p	.000	2	0	0	0	0	0	0	0	0	0	0
Ben Weber, p	.000	2	0	0	0	0	0	0	0	0	0	0
Shawn Wooten, dh	.667	3	9	4	6	0	0	1	2	0	1	0
TOTAL	.376		149	31	56	10	0	9	31	7	18	4

PITCHER	W	L	ERA	G	GS	CG	SV	SHO	IP	H	ER	BB	SO
Kevin Appier	0	0	5.40	1	1	0	0	0	5.0	5	3	3	3
Brendan Donnelly	0	0	13.50	3	0	0	0	0	2.0	3	3	1	2
John Lackey	0	0	0.00	1	0	0	0	0	3.0	3	0	1	3
Ramon Ortiz	0	0	20.25	1	1	0	0	0	2.7	3	6	4	1
Troy Percival	0	0	5.40	3	0	0	2	0	3.3	6	2	0	4
F. Rodriguez	2	0	3.18	3	0	0	0	0	5.7	2	2	2	8
S. Schoeneweis	0	0	27.00	3	0	0	0	0	0.3	2	1	0	0
Jarrod Washburn	1	0	3.75	2	2	0	0	0	12.0	12	5	3	4
Ben Weber	0	1	18.00	2	0	0	0	0	1.0	2	2	2	0
TOTAL	3	1	6.17	19	4	0	2	0	35.0	38	24	16	25

NY (E)

PLAYER/POS	AVG	G	AB	R	H	2B	3B	HR	RB	BB	SO	SB
Roger Clemens, p	.000	1	0	0	0	0	0	0	0	0	0	0
Ron Coomer, dh	.500	1	2	0	1	0	0	0	0	0	0	0
Jason Giambi, 1b-3, dh-1	.357	4	14	5	5	0	0	1	3	4	1	0
Orlando Hernandez, p	.000	2	0	0	0	0	0	0	0	0	0	0
Derek Jeter, ss	.500	4	16	6	8	0	0	2	3	2	3	0
Nick Johnson, 1b-1, dh-2	.182	3	11	1	2	0	0	0	1	1	5	0
Steve Karsay, p	.000	4	0	0	0	0	0	0	0	0	0	0
Ramiro Mendoza, p	.000	2	0	0	0	0	0	0	0	0	0	0
Raul Mondesi, of	.250	4	12	1	3	0	0	0	1	3	1	0
Mike Mussina, p	.000	1	0	0	0	0	0	0	0	0	0	0
Andy Pettitte, p	.000	1	0	0	0	0	0	0	0	0	0	0
Jorge Posada, c	.235	4	17	2	4	0	0	1	3	0	3	0
Juan Rivera, of	.250	4	12	2	3	0	0	0	3	1	3	0
Mariano Rivera, p	.000	1	0	0	0	0	0	0	0	0	0	0
Alfonso Soriano, 2b	.118	4	17	2	2	1	0	1	2	1	4	1
Shane Spencer, of	.000	1	0	0	0	0	0	0	0	0	0	0
Mike Stanton, p	.000	3	0	0	0	0	0	0	0	0	0	0
John Vander Wal, of-1	.000	2	2	0	0	0	0	0	0	0	1	0
Robin Ventura, 3b	.286	4	14	1	4	2	0	0	4	1	2	0
Jeff Weaver, p	.000	2	0	0	0	0	0	0	0	0	0	0
David Wells, p	.000	1	0	0	0	0	0	0	0	0	0	0
Rondell White, dh	.333	1	3	1	1	0	0	1	1	0	0	0
Bernie Williams, of	.333	4	15	4	5	1	0	1	3	3	2	0
Enrique Wilson, pr	.000	1	0	0	0	0	0	0	0	0	0	0
TOTAL	.281		135	25	38	4	0	7	24	16	25	1

PITCHER	W	L	ERA	G	GS	CG	SV	SHO	IP	H	ER	BB	SO
Roger Clemens	0	0	6.35	1	1	0	0	0	5.7	8	4	3	5
O. Hernandez	0	1	2.84	2	0	0	0	0	6.3	5	2	0	7
Steve Karsay	1	0	6.75	4	0	0	0	0	2.7	3	2	0	1
Ramiro Mendoza	0	0	13.50	2	0	0	0	0	1.3	5	2	0	0
Mike Mussina	0	0	9.00	1	1	0	0	0	4.0	6	4	0	2
Andy Pettitte	0	0	12.00	1	1	0	0	0	3.0	8	4	0	1
Mariano Rivera	0	0	0.00	1	0	0	1	0	1.0	1	0	0	0
Mike Stanton	0	1	10.12	3	0	0	0	0	2.7	6	3	1	1
Jeff Weaver	0	0	6.75	2	0	0	0	0	2.7	4	2	3	1
David Wells	0	1	15.43	1	1	0	0	0	4.7	10	8	0	0
TOTAL	1	3	8.21	18	4	0	1	0	34.0	56	31	7	18

GAME 1 AT NY OCT 1

```
ANA  0 0 1  0 2 1  0 1 0    5 12 0
NY   1 0 0  2 1 0  0 4 X    8  8 1
```
Pitchers: Washburn, WEBER (8), Schoeneweis (8), Donnelly (8) vs Clemens, Mendoza (6), KARSAY (8), Rivera (9)
Home Runs: Glaus-ANA (2), Jeter-NY, Giambi-NY, White-NY, Williams-NY
Attendance: 56,710

GAME 2 AT NY OCT 2

```
ANA  1 2 1  0 0 0  0 3 1    8 17 1
NY   0 0 1  2 0 2  0 0 1    6 12 1
```
Pitchers: Appier, RODRIGUEZ (6), Weber (8), Donnelly (8), Percival (8) vs Pettitte, HERNANDEZ (4), Karsay (8), Stanton (8), Weaver (9)
Home Runs: Salmon-ANA, Spiezio-ANA, Anderson-ANA, Glaus-ANA, Jeter-NY, Soriano-NY
Attendance: 56,695

GAME 3 AT ANA OCT 4

```
NY   3 0 3  0 0 0  0 0 0    6  6 0
ANA  0 1 2  1 0 1  1 3 X    9 12 0
```
Pitchers: Mussina, STANTON (6), Karsay (8) vs Ortiz, Lackey (3), Schoeneweis (6), RODRIGUEZ (7), Percival (9)
Home Runs: Kennedy-ANA, Salmon-ANA
Attendance: 45,072

GAME 4 AT ANA OCT 5

```
NY   0 1 0  0 1 1  1 0 1    5 12 2
ANA  0 0 1  0 8 0  0 0 X    9 15 1
```
Pitchers: WELLS, Mendoza (5), Hernandez (5), Karsay (8), Stanton (8) vs WASHBURN, Donnelly (6), Schoeneweis (7), Rodriguez (7), Percival (9)
Home Runs: Posada-NY, Wooten-ANA
Attendance: 45,067

MINNESOTA TWINS (CENTRAL) 3, OAKLAND A'S (WEST) 2

Oakland, led by an outstanding pitching staff, won 103 games to prevail in the tough AL West. Meanwhile, the low-budget Twins won their first division title in 11 years, and should have been just happy to be in the playoffs. But just as in the other three Division Series this year, things didn't go according to script.

Thanks to three crucial errors, Oakland jumped to a 5–1 lead behind ace Tim Hudson in Game 1. But Twins' pitchers held them scoreless the rest of the way and scratched and clawed until they had come away with a 7–5 victory.

The A's answered with two straight big wins. In Game 2 they gave Mark Mulder nine runs, three on a homer by Eric Chavez and three more on a triple by David Justice, and coasted to a 9–1 triumph. In Game 3, four Oakland home runs gave Barry Zito all the runs he needed for a 6–3 victory.

Doug Mientkiewicz led the Game 4 assault as the Twins knotted the series with an 11–2 win. Mientkiewicz drove in three runs with three hits, including his second homer of the series. Eric Milton was the easy winner.

The deciding game was a nail-biter. Minnesota scored single runs in the second and third, and Oakland got one back on a Ray Durham homer in the third. There the score stood until the ninth inning, when the Twins seemingly put the game away against ace reliever Billy Koch. A.J. Pierzynski cranked a two-run homer, and David Ortiz added an RBI double to make it 5–1.

Chavez started Oakland's last gasp with an infield hit, and one out later Justice doubled. Mark Ellis then homered to right to close the gap to 5–4. With two out, Randy Velarde singled, bringing up Durham—who had five extra-base hits in the series—as the potential winning run. But Durham fouled out, sending the Twins to the ALCS.

MIN (C)

PLAYER/POS	AVG	G	AB	R	H	2B	3B	HR	RB	BB	SO	SB
Mike Cuddyer, of	.385	5	13	1	5	1	0	0	1	3	3	0
Tony Fiore, p	.000	1	0	0	0	0	0	0	0	0	0	0
Eddie Guardado, p	.000	2	0	0	0	0	0	0	0	0	0	0
Cristian Guzman, ss	.286	5	21	5	6	2	0	1	2	2	4	2
La Troy Hawkins, p	.000	3	0	0	0	0	0	0	0	0	0	0
Dennis Hocking, 2b-1,of-1	.500	3	6	0	3	1	0	0	1	0	1	0
Torii Hunter, of	.300	5	20	4	6	4	0	0	2	1	4	0
Mike Jackson, p	.000	1	0	0	0	0	0	0	0	0	0	0
Jacque Jones, of	.250	5	20	3	5	3	0	0	1	1	8	0
Bobby Kielty, of-2, dh-1	.000	3	4	0	0	0	0	0	0	0	1	0
Corey Koskie, 3b	.143	5	21	3	3	0	1	1	5	2	6	0
Matt LeCroy, dh	.444	3	9	1	4	0	0	0	1	0	3	0
Kyle Lohse, p	.000	2	0	0	0	0	0	0	0	0	0	0
Joe Mays, p	.000	1	0	0	0	0	0	0	0	0	0	0
Doug Mientkiewicz, 1b	.250	5	20	3	5	0	0	2	4	1	1	0
Eric Milton, p	.000	1	0	0	0	0	0	0	0	0	0	0
Dustan Mohr, of	1.000	4	2	1	2	1	0	0	0	1	0	0
David Ortiz, dh	.231	4	13	0	3	2	0	0	2	0	5	0
A.J. Pierzynski, c	.437	5	16	4	7	0	1	1	4	2	2	0
Tom Prince, c	.000	1	2	0	0	0	0	0	0	0	2	0
Brad Radke, p	.000	2	0	0	0	0	0	0	0	0	0	0
Rick Reed, p	.000	1	0	0	0	0	0	0	0	0	0	0
Luis Rivas, 2b	.250	4	12	2	3	1	0	0	0	1	2	0
J.C. Romero, p	.000	3	0	0	0	0	0	0	0	0	0	0
Johan Santana, p	.000	2	0	0	0	0	0	0	0	0	0	0
Total	.291		179	27	52	15	2	5	23	14	42	2

PITCHER	W	L	ERA	G	GS	CG	SV	SHO	IP	H	ER	BB	SO
Tony Fiore	0	0	20.25	1	0	0	0	0	1.3	4	3	2	0
Eddie Guardado	0	0	13.50	2	0	0	1	0	2.0	5	3	1	1
La Troy Hawkins	0	0	0.00	3	0	0	0	0	2.3	0	0	0	5
Mike Jackson	0	0	0.00	1	0	0	0	0	0.7	1	0	0	0
Kyle Lohse	0	0	0.00	2	0	0	0	0	4.0	2	0	0	5
Joe Mays	0	1	14.73	1	1	0	0	0	3.7	9	6	2	1
Eric Milton	1	0	2.57	1	1	0	0	0	7.0	6	2	1	3
Brad Radke	2	0	1.54	2	2	0	0	0	11.7	14	2	1	7
Rick Reed	0	1	7.20	1	1	0	0	0	5.0	6	4	2	8
J.C. Romero	0	0	0.00	3	0	0	0	0	3.3	3	0	1	2
Johan Santana	0	0	6.00	2	0	0	0	0	3.0	3	2	2	2
TOTAL	3	2	4.50	19	5	0	1	0	44.0	53	22	12	34

OAK (W)

PLAYER/POS	AVG	G	AB	R	H	2B	3B	HR	RB	BB	SO	SB
Micah Bowie, p	.000	1	0	0	0	0	0	0	0	0	0	0
Chad Bradford, p	.000	2	0	0	0	0	0	0	0	0	0	0
Eric Byrnes, of-1	.000	2	1	0	0	0	0	0	0	0	1	0
Eric Chavez, 3b	.381	5	21	3	8	0	0	1	5	2	1	0
Ray Durham, dh	.333	5	21	7	7	3	0	2	2	2	4	1
Jermaine Dye, of	.400	5	20	3	8	2	0	1	1	1	5	0
Mark Ellis, 2b	.368	5	19	1	7	2	0	1	4	1	2	0
Scott Hatteberg, 1b	.500	5	14	5	7	2	0	1	3	3	0	0
Ramon Hernandez, c	.059	5	17	0	1	0	0	0	0	0	4	0
Tim Hudson, p	.000	2	0	0	0	0	0	0	0	0	0	0
David Justice, of	.238	5	21	2	5	1	1	0	4	0	4	0
Billy Koch, p	.000	3	0	0	0	0	0	0	0	0	0	0
Cory Lidle, p	.000	1	0	0	0	0	0	0	0	0	0	0
Ted Lilly, p	.000	2	0	0	0	0	0	0	0	0	0	0
Terrence Long, of	.167	5	18	1	3	0	0	1	1	1	2	0
John Mabry, 1b-1, of-1	.000	2	2	0	0	0	0	0	0	0	1	0
Jim Mecir, p	.000	1	0	0	0	0	0	0	0	0	0	0
Mark Mulder, p	.000	2	0	0	0	0	0	0	0	0	0	0
Greg Myers, c	.000	2	1	0	0	0	0	0	0	0	0	0
Adam Piatt, of-1	.333	3	3	0	1	1	0	0	0	0	1	0
Ricardo Rincon, p	.000	2	0	0	0	0	0	0	0	0	0	0
Olmedo Saenz, 1b	.000	1	0	0	0	0	0	0	0	0	1	0
Miguel Tejada, ss	.143	5	21	3	3	1	0	1	4	1	7	0
Randy Velarde, 1b-3, 2b-1	.600	4	5	1	3	1	0	1	0	1	0	0
Barry Zito, p	.000	1	0	0	0	0	0	0	0	0	0	0
TOTAL	.288		184	26	53	13	1	8	25	12	34	1

PITCHER	W	L	ERA	G	GS	CG	SV	SHO	IP	H	ER	BB	SO
Micah Bowie	0	0	0.00	1	0	0	0	0	1.3	0	0	0	3
Chad Bradford	0	0	0.00	2	0	0	0	0	3.0	1	0	0	1
Tim Hudson	0	1	6.23	2	2	0	0	0	8.7	13	6	4	8
Billy Koch	0	0	9.00	3	0	0	1	0	3.0	5	3	2	3
Cory Lidle	0	0	9.00	1	0	0	0	0	1.0	2	1	0	0
Ted Lilly	0	1	13.50	2	0	0	0	0	4.0	10	6	1	3
Jim Mecir	0	0	0.00	1	0	0	0	0	1.0	0	0	0	2
Mark Mulder	1	1	2.08	2	2	0	0	0	13.0	14	3	3	12
Ricardo Rincon	0	0	0.00	2	0	0	0	0	3.0	2	0	0	2
Barry Zito	1	0	4.50	1	1	0	0	0	6.0	5	3	4	8
TOTAL	2	3	4.50	17	5	0	1	0	44.0	52	22	14	42

GAME 1 AT OAK OCT 1

```
MIN  0 1 2 0 0 3  1 0 0    7 13 3
OAK  3 2 0 0 0 0  0 0 0    5 12 0
```
Pitchers: RADKE, Romero (7), Guardado (9) vs Hudson, LILLY (6), Lidle (7), Rincon (8), Mecir (9)
Home Runs: Koskie-MIN, Mientkiewicz-MIN
Attendance: 34,853

GAME 2 AT OAK OCT 2

```
MIN  0 0 0 0 0 1  0 0 0    1 7 1
OAK  3 0 0 5 1 0  0 X      9 14 0
```
Pitchers: MAYS, Fiore (4), Lohse (6), Hawkins (8) vs MULDER, Bradford (7), Koch (9)
Home Runs: Guzman-MIN, Chavez-OAK
Attendance: 31,953

GAME 3 AT MIN OCT 4

```
OAK  2 0 0 1 0 1  2 0 0    6 9 1
MIN  0 0 0 1 2 0  0 0 0    3 8 0
```
Pitchers: ZITO, Rincon (7), Koch (9) vs REED, Santana (6), Jackson (7), Romero (8), Hawkins (9)
Home Runs: Durham-OAK, Hatteberg-OAK, Long-OAK, Dye-OAK
Attendance: 55,932

GAME 4 AT MIN OCT 5

```
OAK  0 0 2 0 0 0  0 0 0    2 7 2
MIN  0 0 2 7 0 0  2 0 X   11 12 0
```
Pitchers: HUDSON, Lilly (4), Bowie (7) vs MILTON, Lohse (8)
Home Runs: Tejada-OAK, Mientkiewicz-MIN
Attendance: 55,960

GAME 5 AT OAK OCT 6

```
MIN  0 1 1 0 0 0  0 0 3    5 12 0
OAK  0 0 1 0 0 0  0 0 3    4 11 0
```
Pitchers: RADKE, Romero (7), Hawkins (8), Guardado (9) vs MULDER, Bradford (8), Koch (9)
Home Runs: Pierzynski-MIN, Durham-OAK, Ellis-OAK
Attendance: 32,146

SAN FRANCISCO GIANTS (WILD CARD) 4, ST. LOUIS CARDINALS (CENTRAL) 1

Cardinals' pitching, which carried them through the Divisional Series, betrayed them in Game 1 of the LCS. Their strategy of pitching around Barry Bonds backfired, as Benito Santiago knocked in four runs, three of them following walks to Bonds. Pitching to Bonds proved no smarter, as he drilled a two-run triple in the second inning. When the dust settled, the Giants had scored a 9–6 victory, with Santiago, David Bell and Kenny Lofton contributing homers.

There was less offense in Game 2, but the outcome was the same: a Giants' victory. San Francisco got just seven hits, but two were home runs by Rich Aurilia. Jason Schmidt, meanwhile, gave up just four hits and one run in seven-plus innings for a 4–1 win.

The Series moved to San Francisco, where the Cardinals finally got a "W." Home runs by Mike Matheny, Jim Edmonds and Eli Marrero offset Bonds' prodigious three-run bomb into McCovey Cove, and St. Louis won, 5–4.

The Cards took a 2–0 lead in the first inning of Game 4, then squandered several opportunities to extend it. The Giants tied it on J.T. Snow's two-run double in the sixth, then took the lead on Santiago's two-run homer in the eighth. Both blows came after walks to Bonds, the second one intentional. Although the Cardinals out-hit them 12–4, the Giants won 4–3.

Game 5 was a pitching duel between the Cardinals' Matt Morris and the Giants' Kirk Rueter. The two matched goose-eggs until the seventh, when the Cards scored. But the Giants tied it on Bonds' sacrifice fly in the eighth and won it on Lofton's third hit of the game with two out in the ninth. The final was 2–1, with Tim Worrell picking up his second win in relief. Although Bonds finished the NLCS with a .591 on-base percentage, a .727 slugging percentage, and six RBIs, Santiago was named Series MVP.

SF (WC)

PLAYER/POS	AVG	G	AB	R	H	2B	3B	HR	RB	BB	SO	SB
Rich Aurilia, ss	.333	5	15	4	5	1	0	2	5	2	2	0
David Bell, 3b	.412	5	17	4	7	1	0	1	1	2	3	0
Barry Bonds, of	.273	5	11	5	3	0	1	1	6	10	2	0
Shawon Dunston, of-1	.500	2	2	0	1	0	0	0	0	0	1	0
Scott Eyre, p	.000	4	0	0	0	0	0	0	0	0	0	0
Pedro Feliz, ph	.000	1	1	0	0	0	0	0	0	0	0	0
Aaron Fultz, p	.000	1	0	0	0	0	0	0	0	0	0	0
Tom Goodwin, of	.000	2	3	0	0	0	0	0	0	0	2	0
Livan Hernandez, p	.000	1	1	0	0	0	0	0	0	0	1	0
Jeff Kent, 2b	.263	5	19	3	5	0	0	0	0	2	4	0
Kenny Lofton, of	.238	5	21	4	5	0	0	1	2	2	4	1
Ramon Martinez, ss-1	.000	2	1	0	0	0	0	0	1	0	0	0
Robb Nen, p	.000	3	1	0	0	0	0	0	0	0	1	0
Russ Ortiz, p	1.000	1	1	0	1	0	0	0	0	0	0	0
Felix Rodriguez, p	.000	4	1	0	0	0	0	0	0	0	1	0
Kirk Rueter, p	.000	2	5	0	0	0	0	0	0	0	1	0
Reggie Sanders, of	.062	4	16	0	1	0	0	0	0	0	4	0
Benito Santiago, c	.300	5	20	2	6	0	0	2	6	2	4	0
Jason Schmidt, p	.000	1	2	0	0	0	0	0	0	0	2	0
Tsuyoshi Shinjo, of	.000	1	1	0	0	0	0	0	0	0	0	0
J.T. Snow, 1b	.250	5	20	1	5	1	1	0	2	1	4	0
Jay Witasick, p	.000	1	0	0	0	0	0	0	0	0	0	0
Tim Worrell, p	.000	4	0	0	0	0	0	0	0	0	0	0
TOTAL	.247		158	23	39	3	2	7	23	21	36	1

PITCHER	W	L	ERA	G	GS	CG	SV	SHO	IP	H	ER	BB	SO
Scott Eyre	0	0	0.00	4	0	0	0	0	1.7	2	0	0	0
Aaron Fultz	0	0	0.00	1	0	0	0	0	0.3	0	0	0	0
Livan Hernandez	0	0	2.84	1	1	0	0	0	6.3	9	2	1	0
Robb Nen	0	0	2.70	3	0	0	3	0	3.3	3	1	1	4
Russ Ortiz	0	0	7.71	1	1	0	0	0	4.7	5	4	3	3
Felix Rodriguez	0	0	1.93	4	0	0	0	0	4.7	3	1	2	2
Kirk Rueter	1	0	4.09	2	2	0	0	0	11.0	15	5	2	3
Jason Schmidt	1	0	1.17	1	1	0	0	0	7.7	4	1	1	8
Jay Witasick	0	1	9.00	1	0	0	0	0	1.0	1	1	0	0
Tim Worrell	2	0	2.08	4	0	0	0	0	4.3	2	1	0	3
TOTAL	4	1	3.20	22	5	0	3	0	45.0	44	16	10	23

STL (C)

PLAYER/POS	AVG	G	AB	R	H	2B	3B	HR	RB	BB	SO	SB
Andy Benes, p	.000	1	2	0	0	0	0	0	0	0	0	0
Miguel Cairo, 3b	.385	3	13	2	5	0	0	1	2	0	2	0
Mike Crudale, p	.000	1	0	0	0	0	0	0	0	0	0	0
Mike Difelice, ph	.000	1	1	0	0	0	0	0	0	0	0	0
J.D. Drew, of-4	.385	5	13	1	5	0	0	1	1	1	2	0
Jim Edmonds, of	.400	5	20	2	8	2	0	1	4	2	5	0
Jeff Fassero, p	.000	1	0	0	0	0	0	0	0	0	0	0
Chuck Finley, p	.000	1	2	1	0	0	0	0	0	0	1	0
Jason Isringhausen, p	.000	2	0	0	0	0	0	0	0	0	0	0
Steve Kline, p	.000	4	0	0	0	0	0	0	0	0	0	0
Eli Marrero, of	.187	4	16	1	3	1	0	1	1	1	1	0
Tino Martinez, 1b	.143	4	14	1	2	0	0	0	1	2	1	1
Mike Matheny, c	.316	5	19	2	6	2	0	1	1	0	2	0
Matt Morris, p	.000	2	4	0	0	0	0	0	0	0	1	0
Eduardo Perez, of-1	.250	3	4	1	1	0	0	1	1	1	0	0
Albert Pujols, of-2,3b-2,1b-1	.263	5	19	2	5	1	0	1	2	2	5	0
Edgar Renteria, ss	.158	5	19	0	3	0	0	0	1	0	2	0
Kerry Robinson, of-1	.000	3	2	1	0	0	0	0	0	1	1	0
Dave Veres, p	.000	2	0	0	0	0	0	0	0	0	0	0
Fernando Vina, 2b	.261	5	23	2	6	2	0	0	2	0	0	0
Rick White, p	.000	3	0	0	0	0	0	0	0	0	0	0
Woody Williams, p	.000	1	0	0	0	0	0	0	0	0	0	0
TOTAL	.257		171	16	44	8	0	7	16	10	23	1

PITCHER	W	L	ERA	G	GS	CG	SV	SHO	IP	H	ER	BB	SO
Andy Benes	0	0	3.38	1	1	0	0	0	5.3	2	2	4	5
Mike Crudale	0	0	10.80	1	0	0	0	0	1.7	1	2	1	2
Jeff Fassero	0	0	0.00	1	0	0	0	0	0.7	0	0	2	1
Chuck Finley	1	0	7.20	1	1	0	0	0	5.0	7	4	3	1
J. Isringhausen	0	0	4.50	2	0	0	1	0	2.0	1	1	3	3
Steve Kline	0	0	0.00	4	0	0	0	0	2.3	2	0	0	1
Matt Morris	0	2	6.23	2	2	0	0	0	13.0	16	9	6	6
Dave Veres	0	0	0.00	2	0	0	0	0	3.7	2	0	1	5
Rick White	0	1	4.50	3	0	0	0	0	4.0	2	2	2	5
Woody Williams	0	1	4.50	1	1	0	0	0	6.0	6	3	1	7
TOTAL	1	4	4.74	18	5	0	1	0	43.7	39	23	21	36

GAME 1 AT STL OCT 9

```
SF   141 012 000   9 11 0
STL  010 022 010   6 11 0
```
Pitchers: RUETER, Rodriguez (6), Worrell (8), Nen (9) vs MORRIS, Crudale (5), Veres (7), Kline (9)
Home Runs: Lofton-SF, Bell-SF, Santiago-SF, Pujols-STL, Cairo-STL, Drew-STL
Attendance: 52,175

GAME 2 AT STL OCT 10

```
SF   100 020 001   4 7 0
STL  000 000 010   1 6 0
```
Pitchers: SCHMIDT, Eyre (8), Nen (8) vs WILLIAMS, White (7), Fassero (8), Isringhausen (9)
Home Runs: Aurilia (2)-SF, Perez-STL
Attendance: 52,195

GAME 3 AT SF OCT 12

```
STL  002 111 000   5 6 1
SF   010 030 000   4 10 0
```
Pitchers: FINLEY, Veres (6), Kline (7), White (8), Isringhausen (9) vs Ortiz, Fultz (5), WITASICK (6), Rodriguez (7), Eyre (8), Worrell (9)
Home Runs: Matheny-STL, Edmonds-STL, Marrero-STL, Bonds-SF
Attendance: 42,177

GAME 4 AT SF OCT 13

```
STL  200 000 001   3 12 0
SF   000 002 02X   4 4 1
```
Pitchers: Benes, WHITE (6), Kline (8) vs Hernandez, Rodriguez (7), Eyre (8), WORRELL (8), Nen (9)
Home Runs: Santiago-SF
Attendance: 42,676

GAME 5 AT SF OCT 14

```
STL  000 001 000   1 9 0
SF   000 000 011   2 7 0
```
Pitchers: MORRIS, Kline (9) vs Reuter, Rodriguez (7), Eyre (8), WORRELL (8)
Attendance: 42,673

ANAHEIM ANGELS (WILD CARD) 4, MINNESOTA TWINS (CENTRAL) 1

With a 4–8 record in the regular season, Joe Mays didn't fit the profile of a Game 1 starter. But after holding the Angels to just four hits, no walks and one unearned run in eight innings, he had written his own profile. The Twins got just five hits themselves, but key doubles by Torii Hunter and Corey Koskie gave Mays all the support he needed for a 2–1 victory.

The Angels evened the Series with a 6–3 win in Game 2. Darin Erstad's first-inning homer opened the scoring, and Brad Fullmer's two-run shot in the sixth made it 6–0, before Ramon Ortiz weakened. Three Anaheim relievers shut down the Twins the rest of the way.

With their "rally monkeys" in full swing, the Angels then took the lead with a 2–1 triumph in Anaheim. Garret Anderson's second-inning home run started the scoring, and Troy Glaus' eighth-inning blast ended it. Jarrod Washburn pitched seven strong innings, Francisco Rodriguez picked up the win with a scoreless eighth, and Troy Percival recorded the save, thanks to a diving catch by Alex Ochoa.

Game 4 was shaping up as a pitchers' duel between the Twins' Brad Radke and the Angels' John Lackey, matching zeroes for six innings. But the rally monkeys struck again, as the Haloes erupted for two runs in the seventh and five in the eighth to secure a 7–1 win.

Trying to stay alive, Minnesota took a 5–3 lead into the bottom of the seventh of Game 5. But ninth-place hitter Adam Kennedy—who had hit just seven home runs all season—connected for his third of the game, a three-run shot. That opened the floodgates, as the Angels added another seven runs before the inning was over to put it away, 13–5. Kennedy, who was named Series MVP, finished the day 4-for-4 with five RBI, and Scott Spiezio added two singles and a homer. The Angels were on their way to their first World Series.

ANA (WC)

PLAYER/POS	AVG	G	AB	R	H	2B	3B	HR	RB	BB	SO	SB
Garret Anderson, of	.250	5	20	3	5	1	0	1	3	1	0	0
Kevin Appier, p	.000	2	0	0	0	0	0	0	0	0	0	0
Brendan Donnelly, p	.000	3	0	0	0	0	0	0	0	0	0	0
David Eckstein, ss	.286	5	21	1	6	0	0	0	2	0	2	0
Darin Erstad, of	.364	5	22	4	8	0	0	1	2	0	3	1
Chone Figgins, pr	1.000	3	1	2	1	0	0	0	0	0	0	0
Brad Fullmer, dh	.333	4	12	2	4	2	0	1	4	0	2	0
Benji Gil, 2b	.000	1	2	0	0	0	0	0	0	0	1	0
Troy Glaus, 3b	.316	5	19	4	6	0	1	1	2	2	5	0
Adam Kennedy, 2b	.357	4	14	5	5	0	0	3	5	0	2	1
John Lackey, p	.000	1	0	0	0	0	0	0	0	0	0	0
Ben Molina, c	.214	5	14	0	3	0	1	0	2	1	2	0
Jose Molina, c	.000	3	1	0	0	0	0	0	0	0	0	0
Alex Ochoa, of	.000	4	4	2	0	0	0	0	0	0	3	0
Ramon Ortiz, p	.000	1	0	0	0	0	0	0	0	0	0	0
Orlando Palmeiro, of-1	.000	2	2	0	0	0	0	0	0	0	1	0
Troy Percival, p	.000	3	0	0	0	0	0	0	0	0	0	0
Francisco Rodriguez, p	.000	4	0	0	0	0	0	0	0	0	0	0
Tim Salmon, of	.214	5	14	0	3	0	0	0	0	3	1	0
Scott Schoeneweis, p	.000	1	0	0	0	0	0	0	0	0	0	0
Scott Spiezio, 1b	.353	5	17	5	6	2	0	1	5	2	1	1
Jarrod Washburn, p	.000	1	0	0	0	0	0	0	0	0	0	0
Ben Weber, p	.000	3	0	0	0	0	0	0	0	0	0	0
Shawn Wooten, dh	.250	3	8	1	2	0	0	0	1	0	3	0
TOTAL	.287		171	29	49	5	2	8	26	9	26	3

PITCHER	W	L	ERA	G	GS	CG	SV	SHO	IP	H	ER	BB	SO
Kevin Appier	0	1	3.48	2	2	0	0	0	10.3	10	4	4	3
Brendan Donnelly	0	0	8.10	3	0	0	0	0	3.3	3	3	0	5
John Lackey	1	0	0.00	1	1	0	0	0	7.0	3	0	0	7
Ramon Ortiz	1	0	5.06	1	1	0	0	0	5.3	10	3	1	3
Troy Percival	0	0	0.00	3	0	0	2	0	3.3	0	0	0	3
F. Rodriguez	2	0	0.00	4	0	0	0	0	4.3	2	0	2	7
S. Schoeneweis	0	0	0.00	1	0	0	0	0	0.7	0	0	0	0
Jarrod Washburn	0	0	1.29	1	1	0	0	0	7.0	6	1	0	7
Ben Weber	0	0	3.38	3	0	0	0	0	2.7	3	1	0	3
TOTAL	4	1	2.45	19	5	0	2	0	44.0	37	12	7	38

MIN (C)

PLAYER/POS	AVG	G	AB	R	H	2B	3B	HR	RB	BB	SO	SB
Mike Cuddyer, of	.200	3	5	0	1	0	0	0	0	1	1	0
Eddie Guardado, p	.000	1	0	0	0	0	0	0	0	0	0	0
Cristian Guzman, ss	.167	5	18	1	3	1	0	0	0	0	3	0
La Troy Hawkins, p	.000	4	0	0	0	0	0	0	0	0	0	0
Torii Hunter, cf	.167	5	18	2	3	2	0	0	0	1	3	0
Mike Jackson, p	.000	3	0	0	0	0	0	0	0	0	0	0
Jacque Jones, of	.100	5	20	0	2	1	0	0	2	0	4	0
Bobby Kielty, dh-2, of-1	.000	4	3	0	0	0	0	0	1	1	2	0
Corey Koskie, 3b	.278	5	18	3	5	2	0	0	2	2	8	0
David Lamb, 2b	.000	2	0	0	0	0	0	0	0	0	0	0
Matt LeCroy, dh	.333	1	3	0	1	0	0	0	0	0	1	0
Kyle Lohse, p	.000	1	0	0	0	0	0	0	0	0	0	0
Joe Mays, p	.000	2	0	0	0	0	0	0	0	0	0	0
Doug Mientkiewicz, 1b	.278	5	18	1	5	1	0	0	2	1	2	0
Eric Milton, p	.000	1	0	0	0	0	0	0	0	0	0	0
Dustan Mohr, ph	.417	5	12	3	5	1	0	0	0	0	4	1
David Ortiz, dh	.312	5	16	0	5	1	0	0	2	5	0	0
A.J. Pierzynski, c	.250	5	16	1	4	0	0	0	2	0	2	0
Tom Prince, c	.000	1	1	0	0	0	0	0	0	0	0	0
Brad Radke, p	.000	1	0	0	0	0	0	0	0	0	0	0
Rick Reed, p	.000	1	0	0	0	0	0	0	0	0	0	0
Luis Rivas, 2b	.250	5	12	1	3	0	0	0	0	1	3	0
J.C. Romero, p	.000	4	0	0	0	0	0	0	0	0	0	0
Johan Santana, p	.000	4	0	0	0	0	0	0	0	0	0	0
Bob Wells, p	.000	2	0	0	0	0	0	0	0	0	0	0
TOTAL	.231		160	12	37	9	0	0	11	7	38	1

PITCHER	W	L	ERA	G	GS	CG	SV	SHO	IP	H	ER	BB	SO
Eddie Guardado	0	0	0.00	1	0	0	1	0	1.0	0	0	1	2
La Troy Hawkins	0	0	20.25	4	0	0	0	0	1.3	4	3	1	1
Mike Jackson	0	0	27.00	3	0	0	0	0	1.0	5	3	2	2
Kyle Lohse	0	0	0.00	1	0	0	0	0	1.0	0	0	0	1
Joe Mays	1	0	2.03	2	2	0	0	0	13.3	12	3	0	3
Eric Milton	0	0	1.50	1	1	0	0	0	6.0	5	1	2	4
Brad Radke	0	1	2.70	1	1	0	0	0	6.7	5	2	1	4
Rick Reed	0	1	10.12	1	1	0	0	0	5.3	8	6	0	0
J.C. Romero	0	1	22.50	4	0	0	0	0	2.0	4	5	2	3
Johan Santana	0	1	10.80	4	0	0	0	0	3.3	4	4	0	4
Bob Wells	0	0	9.00	2	0	0	0	0	1.0	2	1	0	2
TOTAL	1	4	6.00	24	5	0	1	0	42.0	49	28	9	26

GAME 1 AT MIN OCT 8

ANA 001 000 000   1 4 0
MIN 010 010 00X   2 5 1
Pitchers: APPIER, Donnelly (6), Schoeneweis (7), Weber (8) vs MAYS, Guardado (9)
Attendance: 55,562

GAME 2 AT MIN OCT 9

ANA 130 002 000   6 10 0
MIN 000 003 000   3 11 1
Pitchers: ORTIZ, Donnelly (6), Rodriguez (7), Percival (8) vs REED, Santana (6), Romero (8), Hawkins (8), Jackson (9)
Home Runs: Erstad-ANA, Fullmer-ANA
Attendance: 55,990

GAME 3 AT ANA OCT 11

MIN 000 000 100   1 6 0
ANA 010 000 01X   2 7 2
Pitchers: Milton, Hawkins (7), Santana (7), Jackson (7), ROMERO (7) vs WASHBURN, RODRIGUEZ (8), Percival (9)
Home Runs: Anderson-ANA, Glaus-ANA
Attendance: 44,234

GAME 4 AT ANA OCT 12

MIN 000 000 001   1 6 2
ANA 000 000 25X   7 10 0
Pitchers: RADKE, Santana (7), Hawkins (8), Romero (8), Jackson (8), Wells (8) vs LACKEY, Rodriguez (8), Weber (9)
Attendance: 44,830

GAME 5 AT ANA OCT 13

MIN 110 000 300   5 9 0
ANA 001 020 10X   13 18 0
Pitchers: Mays, SANTANA (7), Hawkins (7), Romero (7), Wells (7), Lohse (8) vs Appier, Donnelly (6), RODRIGUEZ (7), Weber (8), Percival (9)
Home Runs: Kennedy (3)-ANA, Spiezio-ANA
Attendance: 44,835

ANAHEIM ANGELS (AL) 4, SAN FRANCISCO GIANTS (NL) 3

The Angels finally made it to the World Series, in their 42nd year of existence. The Giants, making it an all-California Series, hadn't had much more success during that period, not appearing in the Fall Classic since 1989, nor winning a Series game since 1962.

Barry Bonds homered in his first career World Series at bat to start the Giants to a 4–3 win. Troy Glaus, en route to the Series MVP Award, hit two homers in a losing cause. Game 2 was a slugfest from the get-go. Anaheim scored five in the first inning, but San Francisco took a 9–7 lead with four runs in the fifth. The Angels retook the lead on Tim Salmon's fourth hit—and second two-run homer—in the eighth. Bonds hit a long homer in the ninth but it was not enough, as the Angels held on, 11–10.

The Haloes continued their heavy hitting at San Francisco in Game 3. Though they hit no homers, they amassed 16 hits of other varieties for a 10–4 victory. Lost in the shuffle was another Bonds bomb. San Francisco then evened things with a 4–3 win. Bonds was intentionally walked his first three times up as the Angels sought to protect an early 3–0 lead, built with the help of Glaus' two-run homer. However, one of the walks set up the tying run in the fifth, and David Bell drove in the game-winner in the eighth. The Giants took no prisoners in a 16–4 win the next day. Jeff Kent bashed two homers and a double, and Bonds also had three hits.

Back in Anaheim, with Bonds hitting yet another homer, San Francisco opened up a 5–0 lead by the seventh. Russ Ortiz was cruising along, and the Giants were eight outs away from the world championship. But Scott Spiezio hit a three-run homer, and the Angels added three more in the eighth—two on Glaus' double—to escape with a stunning 6–5 victory.

Garret Anderson's bases-clearing double in the third inning of Game 7 broke a 1–1 tie and scored the final runs of the 2002 season. Four Angels' pitchers shut down the Giants the rest of the way, and the Angels were world champs. Bonds finished the postseason with 8 homers in just 45 at bats, 27 walks in 17 games, a .581 on-base percentage, and a .978 slugging percentage.

ANA (A)

PLAYER/POS	AVG	G	AB	R	H	2B	3B	HR	RB	BB	SO	SB
Garret Anderson, of	.281	7	32	3	9	1	0	0	6	0	3	0
Brendan Donnelly, p	.000	5	0	0	0	0	0	0	0	0	0	0
David Eckstein, ss	.310	7	29	6	9	0	0	0	3	3	2	1
Darin Erstad, of	.300	7	30	6	9	3	0	1	3	1	4	1
Chone Figgins, pr	.000	2	0	1	0	0	0	0	0	0	0	0
Brad Fullmer, dh-4	.267	5	15	3	4	0	0	0	1	2	2	0
Benji Gil, 2b-1	.800	3	5	1	4	1	0	0	0	0	1	0
Troy Glaus, 3b	.385	7	26	7	10	3	0	3	8	4	6	0
Adam Kennedy, 2b-6	.280	7	25	1	7	2	0	2	0	0	7	0
John Lackey, p	.500	3	2	0	1	0	0	0	0	0	0	0
Ben Molina, c	.286	7	21	2	6	2	0	0	2	3	1	0
Jose Molina, c	.000	3	0	0	0	0	0	0	0	0	0	0
Alex Ochoa, of	.000	5	1	0	0	0	0	0	0	0	0	0
Ramon Ortiz, p	.000	1	3	0	0	0	0	0	0	0	2	0
Orlando Palmeiro, ph	.250	4	4	1	1	1	0	0	0	0	2	0
Francisco Rodriguez, p	.000	4	0	0	0	0	0	0	0	0	0	0
Tim Salmon, of	.346	7	26	7	9	1	0	2	5	4	7	1
Scott Schoeneweis, p	.000	2	0	0	0	0	0	0	0	0	0	0
Scot Shields, p	.000	1	0	0	0	0	0	0	0	0	0	0
Scott Spiezio, 1b	.261	7	23	3	6	1	1	1	8	6	1	1
Jarrod Washburn, p	.000	2	1	0	0	0	0	0	0	0	0	0
Ben Weber, p	.000	4	0	0	0	0	0	0	0	0	0	0
Shawn Wooten, 1b-2	.500	3	2	0	1	0	0	0	0	0	0	0
TOTAL	.310		245	41	76	15	1	7	38	23	38	6

PITCHER	W	L	ERA	G	GS	CG	SV	SHO	IP	H	ER	BB	SO
Kevin Appier	0	0	11.37	2	2	0	0	0	6.3	9	8	5	4
Brendan Donnelly	1	0	0.00	5	0	0	0	0	7.7	1	0	4	6
John Lackey	1	0	4.38	3	2	0	0	0	12.3	15	6	5	7
Ramon Ortiz	0	1	7.20	1	1	0	0	0	5.0	5	4	4	3
Troy Percival	0	0	3.00	3	0	0	3	0	3.0	2	1	1	3
F. Rodriguez	1	1	2.08	4	0	0	0	0	8.7	6	2	1	13
S. Schoeneweis	0	0	0.00	2	0	0	0	0	2.0	1	0	1	2
Scot Shields	0	0	5.40	1	0	0	0	0	1.7	5	1	0	1
Jarrod Washburn	0	2	9.31	2	2	0	0	0	9.7	12	10	7	6
Ben Weber	0	0	13.50	4	0	0	0	0	4.7	10	7	2	5
TOTAL	4	3	5.75	27	7	0	3	0	61.0	66	39	30	50

SF (N)

PLAYER/POS	AVG	G	AB	R	H	2B	3B	HR	RB	BB	SO	SB
Rich Aurilia, ss	.250	7	32	5	8	2	0	2	5	1	9	0
David Bell, 3b	.304	7	23	4	7	0	0	1	4	5	4	0
Barry Bonds, of	.471	7	17	8	8	2	0	4	6	13	3	0
Shawon Dunston, dh-2	.222	4	9	1	2	0	0	1	3	0	1	0
Scott Eyre, p	.000	3	0	0	0	0	0	0	0	0	0	0
Pedro Feliz, dh-1	.000	3	5	0	0	0	0	0	0	0	0	0
Aaron Fultz, p	.000	2	0	0	0	0	0	0	0	0	0	0
Tom Goodwin, dh-1, of-2	.000	5	4	0	0	0	0	0	0	1	2	1
Livan Hernandez, p	.000	2	0	0	0	0	0	0	0	0	0	0
Jeff Kent, 2b	.276	7	29	6	8	1	0	3	7	1	7	0
Kenny Lofton, of	.290	7	31	9	9	1	1	0	2	2	2	3
Ramon Martinez, ph	.000	2	2	0	0	0	0	0	0	0	2	0
Robb Nen, p	.000	3	0	0	0	0	0	0	0	0	0	0
Felix Rodriguez, p	.000	6	0	0	0	0	0	0	0	0	0	0
Kirk Rueter, p	.500	2	2	1	1	0	0	0	0	0	0	0
Reggie Sanders, of	.238	7	21	3	5	0	0	2	6	2	9	0
Benito Santiago, c	.231	7	26	2	6	0	0	0	5	3	4	0
Jason Schmidt, p	.000	2	1	0	0	0	0	0	0	0	1	0
Tsuyoshi Shinjo, dh-1, of-1	.167	3	6	1	1	0	0	0	0	0	3	0
J.T. Snow, 1b	.407	7	27	6	11	1	0	1	4	2	1	0
Jay Witasick, p	.000	2	0	0	0	0	0	0	0	0	0	0
Tim Worrell, p	.000	6	0	0	0	0	0	0	0	0	0	0
Chad Zerbe, p	.000	3	0	0	0	0	0	0	0	0	0	0
TOTAL	.281		235	44	66	7	1	14	42	30	50	5

PITCHER	W	L	ERA	G	GS	CG	SV	SHO	IP	H	ER	BB	SO
Scott Eyre	0	0	0.00	3	0	0	0	0	3.0	5	0	1	2
Aaron Fultz	0	0	3.86	2	0	0	0	0	2.3	4	1	1	0
Livan Hernandez	0	2	14.29	2	2	0	0	0	5.7	9	9	9	4
Robb Nen	0	0	0.00	3	0	0	2	0	3.0	2	0	1	3
Russ Ortiz	0	0	10.12	2	2	0	0	0	8.0	13	9	2	2
Felix Rodriguez	0	1	4.76	6	0	0	0	0	5.7	4	3	1	3
Kirk Rueter	0	0	2.70	2	1	0	0	0	10.0	10	3	1	5
Jason Schmidt	1	0	5.23	2	2	0	0	0	10.3	16	6	4	14
Jay Witasick	0	0	54.00	2	0	0	0	0	0.3	3	2	1	1
Tim Worrell	1	1	3.18	6	0	0	0	0	5.7	4	2	1	4
Chad Zerbe	1	0	3.00	3	0	0	0	0	6.0	6	2	0	0
TOTAL	3	4	5.55	33	7	0	2	0	60.0	76	37	23	38

GAME 1 AT ANA OCT 19

SF 020 002 000   4 6 0
ANA 010 002 000   3 9 0
Pitchers: SCHMIDT, Fe. Rodriguez (6), Worrell (8), Nen (9) vs WASHBURN, Donnelly (6), Schoeneweis (8), Weber (8)
Home Runs: Bonds-SF, Sanders-SF, Snow-SF, Glaus-ANA (2)
Attendance: 44,603

GAME 2 AT ANA OCT 20

SF 041 040 001   10 12 1
ANA 520 011 02X   11 16 1
Pitchers: Ru. Ortiz, Zerbe (2), Witasick (6), Fultz (6), FE. RODRIGUEZ (7), Worrell (8) vs Appier, Lackey (3), Weber (5), FR. RODRIGUEZ (6), Percival (9)
Home Runs: Sanders-SF, Bell-SF, Kent-SF, Bonds-SF, Salmon-ANA (2)
Attendance: 44,584

GAME 3 AT SF OCT 22

ANA 004 401 010   10 16 0
SF 100 030 000   4 6 2
Pitchers: RA. ORTIZ, Donnelly (6), Schoeneweis (8) vs HERNANDEZ, Witasick (4), Fultz (5), Fe. Rodriguez (7), Eyre (8)
Home Runs: Bonds-SF
Attendance: 42,707

GAME 4 AT SF OCT 23

ANA 012 000 000   3 10 1
SF 000 030 01X   4 12 1
Pitchers: Lackey, Weber (6), FR. RODRIGUEZ (7) vs Reuter, Fe. Rodriguez (7), WORRELL (8), Nen (9)
Home Runs: Glaus-ANA
Attendance: 42,703

GAME 5 AT SF OCT 24

ANA 000 031 000   4 10 2
SF 330 002 44X   16 16 0
Pitchers: WASHBURN, Donnelly (5), Weber (6), Shields (7) vs Schmidt, ZERBE (5), Fe. Rodriguez (6), Worrell (7), Eyre (9)
Home Runs: Kent-SF (2), Aurilia-SF
Attendance: 42,713

GAME 6 AT ANA OCT 26

SF 000 031 100   5 8 1
ANA 000 000 33X   6 10 1
Pitchers: Ru. Ortiz, Fe. Rodriguez (7), Eyre (7), WORRELL (7), Nen (8) vs Appier, Rodriguez (5), DONNELLY (8), Percival (9)
Home Runs: Dunston-SF, Bonds-SF, Spiezio-ANA, Erstad-ANA
Attendance: 44,506

GAME 7 AT ANA OCT 27

SF 010 000 000   1 6 0
ANA 013 000 00X   4 5 0
Pitchers: HERNANDEZ, Zerbe (3), Rueter (4), Worrell (8) vs LACKEY, Donnelly (6), Fr. Rodriguez (8), Percival (9)
Attendance: 44,598

FLORIDA MARLINS (WILD CARD) 3, SAN FRANCISCO GIANTS (WEST) 1

With the incomparable Barry Bonds winning his third straight MVP Award, the Giants had notched 100 victories, winning the West by a whopping 15-1/2 games. Meanwhile, the upstart Marlins— still having never won a division title—had snuck into the postseason via the wild-card route. But everyone starts the postseason with a 0-0 record.

Game 1 was a true pitchers' duel, as each team managed only three hits. Marlins' youngster Josh Beckett hurled seven innings of two-hit ball, but the Giants' Jason Schmidt was even better, going the distance for a 2-0 shutout.

Game 2 was a different story. The Giants took a 4-1 lead into the fifth inning, but the Marlins ravaged seven pitchers for eight runs from that point on, winning 9-5. Juan Pierre was the offensive star with four hits, including a double, scoring three runs and driving in three others.

The two teams battled 11 innings in Game 3. Florida's Ivan Rodriguez started the scoring with a two-run homer in the first inning, and ended it with a two-run single in the 11th. He accounted for all of Florida's runs as they scored a 4-3 victory and took a 2-1 lead in the Series. Edgardo Alfonzo had four hits for the losers, en route to a .529 Series average.

The Marlins finished things off with a 7-6 triumph in Game 4, and Rodriguez was again the central figure. He put Florida ahead with an RBI double in the third, and scored the tie-breaking run in the eighth, knocking the ball out of the mitt of Giants' catcher Yorvit Torrealba. Then, in the ninth, J.T. Snow came homeward with the Giants' potential tying run, barreling over Rodriguez. But I-Rod held the ball, ending the game and Series in spectacular fashion.

FLA (WC)

PLAYER/POS	AVG	G	AB	R	H	2B	3B	HR	RB	BB	SO	SB
Brian Banks, ph	.000	2	2	0	0	0	0	0	0	0	0	0
Josh Beckett, p	.000	1	1	0	0	0	0	0	0	0	1	0
Miguel Cabrera, 3b	.286	4	14	1	4	2	0	0	3	1	6	0
Luis Castillo, 2b	.294	4	17	2	5	3	0	0	1	3	3	0
Jeff Conine, of	.267	4	15	2	4	0	0	0	2	2	1	0
Juan Encarnacion, of	.133	4	15	1	2	0	0	1	1	2	3	0
Chad Fox, p	.000	3	0	0	0	0	0	0	0	0	0	0
Alex Gonzalez, ss	.062	4	16	2	1	0	0	0	0	1	3	0
Lenny Harris, ph	.500	2	2	0	1	0	0	0	0	0	0	0
Rick Helling, p	.000	1	0	0	0	0	0	0	0	0	0	0
Todd Hollandsworth, ph	.333	3	3	1	1	0	0	0	0	0	2	0
Derrek Lee, 1b	.250	4	16	2	4	1	0	0	2	1	2	1
Braden Looper, p	.000	2	0	0	0	0	0	0	0	0	0	0
Mike Lowell, 3b	.000	2	3	0	0	0	0	0	0	0	1	0
Carl Pavano, p	.000	3	0	0	0	0	0	0	0	0	0	0
Brad Penny, p	1.000	2	1	0	1	0	0	0	0	0	0	0
Juan Pierre, of	.263	4	19	5	5	1	0	0	3	1	1	1
Mark Redman, p	.000	1	2	0	0	0	0	0	0	0	0	0
Ivan Rodriguez, c	.353	4	17	3	6	1	0	1	6	3	1	0
Ugueth Urbina, p	.000	3	0	0	0	0	0	0	0	0	0	0
Dontrelle Willis, p	1.000	2	3	1	3	0	1	0	1	0	0	0
TOTAL	.253		146	20	37	8	1	2	18	14	25	2

PITCHER	W	L	ERA	G	GS	CG	SV	SHO	IP	H	ER	BB	SO
Josh Beckett	0	1	1.29	1	1	0	0	0	7.0	2	1	5	9
Chad Fox	0	0	1.80	3	0	0	0	0	5.0	3	1	3	3
Rick Helling	0	0	27.00	1	0	0	0	0	0.3	2	1	2	0
Braden Looper	1	0	0.00	2	0	0	0	0	1.7	1	0	2	0
Carl Pavano	2	0	0.00	3	0	0	0	0	2.7	1	0	1	1
Brad Penny	0	0	6.35	2	1	0	0	0	5.7	5	4	1	6
Mark Redman	0	0	3.00	1	1	0	0	0	6.0	7	2	3	4
Ugueth Urbina	0	0	3.00	3	0	0	1	0	3.0	4	1	1	2
Dontrelle Willis	0	0	7.94	2	1	0	0	0	5.7	7	5	2	3
TOTAL	3	1	3.65	18	4	0	1	0	37.0	32	15	20	28

SF (W)

PLAYER/POS	AVG	G	AB	R	H	2B	3B	HR	RB	BB	SO	SB
Edgardo Alfonzo, 3b	.529	4	17	3	9	4	0	0	5	1	1	0
Rich Aurilia, ss	.133	4	15	4	2	1	0	0	1	3	3	0
Barry Bonds, of	.222	4	9	3	2	1	0	0	2	8	0	1
Jim Brower, p	.000	2	0	0	0	0	0	0	0	0	0	0
Jason Christiansen, p	.000	1	0	0	0	0	0	0	0	0	0	0
Jose Cruz Jr., of	.000	4	11	0	0	0	0	0	1	2	4	0
Ray Durham, 2b	.235	4	17	2	4	0	0	0	0	1	5	0
Scott Eyre, p	.000	1	0	0	0	0	0	0	0	0	0	0
Pedro Feliz, ph	.667	3	3	1	2	0	1	0	1	0	1	0
Andres Galarraga, 1b-1	.000	2	5	0	0	0	0	0	0	0	1	0
Marquis Grissom, of	.143	4	14	1	2	0	0	0	1	2	5	0
Jeffrey Hammonds, of-1	.400	3	5	1	2	0	0	0	0	1	0	0
Matt Herges, p	.000	3	0	0	0	0	0	0	0	0	0	0
Dustin Hermanson, p	.000	1	0	0	0	0	0	0	0	0	0	0
Joe Nathan, p	.000	2	0	0	0	0	0	0	0	0	0	0
Neifi Perez, 2b-1	.333	3	3	1	1	1	0	0	0	1	0	0
Sidney Ponson, p	.000	1	1	0	0	0	0	0	0	0	0	0
Felix Rodriguez, p	.000	3	0	0	0	0	0	0	0	0	0	0
Kirk Rueter, p	.500	1	2	0	1	0	0	0	0	0	0	0
Benito Santiago, c-3	.182	4	11	0	2	0	0	0	0	0	2	0
Jason Schmidt, p	.000	1	3	0	0	0	0	0	0	0	2	0
J.T. Snow, 1b	.312	4	16	0	5	0	0	0	3	0	3	0
Yorvit Torrealba, c	.000	2	3	0	0	0	0	0	1	0	0	0
Jerome Williams, p	.000	1	1	0	0	0	0	0	0	0	1	0
Tim Worrell, p	.000	2	0	0	0	0	0	0	0	0	0	0
TOTAL	.235		136	16	32	7	1	0	15	20	28	1

PITCHER	W	L	ERA	G	GS	CG	SV	SHO	IP	H	ER	BB	SO
Jim Brower	0	0	6.00	2	0	0	0	0	3.0	5	2	3	3
J. Christiansen	0	0	∞	1	0	0	0	0	0.0	1	0	0	0
Scott Eyre	0	0	0.00	1	0	0	0	0	0.3	0	0	0	0
Matt Herges	0	0	0.00	3	0	0	0	0	4.3	1	0	2	5
D. Hermanson	0	0	0.00	1	0	0	0	0	1.0	1	0	1	0
Joe Nathan	0	1	81.00	2	0	0	0	0	0.3	4	3	1	1
Sidney Ponson	0	0	7.20	1	1	0	0	0	5.0	7	4	0	3
Felix Rodriguez	0	1	2.25	3	0	0	0	0	4.0	4	1	1	5
Kirk Rueter	0	0	3.60	1	1	0	0	0	5.0	3	2	2	2
Jason Schmidt	1	0	0.00	1	1	1	0	1	9.0	3	0	0	5
Jerome Williams	0	0	13.50	1	1	0	0	0	2.0	5	3	1	1
Tim Worrell	0	1	0.00	2	0	0	0	0	2.7	3	0	3	0
TOTAL	1	3	3.68	19	4	1	0	1	36.7	37	15	14	25

GAME 1 at SF SEP 30

```
FLA  000 000 000    0  3  1
SF   000 100 01X    2  3  2
```
Pitchers: BECKETT, Fox (8) vs SCHMIDT
Attendance: 43,704

GAME 2 at SF OCT 1

```
FLA  100 033 110    9 14  0
SF   100 310 000    5  8  2
```
Pitchers: Penny, Helling (5), PAVANO (5), Fox (6), Willis (8), Looper (8), Urbina (9) vs Ponson, NATHAN (6), Christiansen (6), Herges (6), Rodriguez (7), Brower (8), Worrell (9)
Home Runs: Encarnacion-FLA
Attendance: 43,766

GAME 3 at FLA OCT 3

```
SF   00000 200001    3 12  1
FLA  20000 000002    4  8  1
```
Pitchers: Rueter, Herges (6), Eyre (7), Nathan (8), Rodriguez (8), WORRELL (10) vs Redman, Fox (7), Urbina (9), Pavano (10), LOOPER (11)
Home Runs: Rodriguez-FLA
Attendance: 61,488

GAME 4 at FLA OCT 4

```
SF   010 004 001    6  9  2
FLA  012 200 02X    7 12  0
```
Pitchers: Williams, Brower (3), Hermanson (5), Herges (6), RODRIGUEZ (8) vs Willis, Penny (6), PAVANO (8), Urbina (9)
Attendance: 65,464

CHICAGO CUBS (CENTRAL) 3, ATLANTA BRAVES (EAST) 2

The Braves had won yet another NL East title with 101 victories, 10 more than their nearest rival; the Cubs had taken their first divisional title since 1989, winning a three-team dogfight with just 88 wins.

Game 1 was all Kerry Wood. The Cubs' pitcher collected as many hits (two) as he gave up, while striking out 11 batters in 7-1/3 innings. Wood's two-run double in the sixth broke a 1–1 tie, and the Cubs held on to win, 4–2.

The Cubs threatened to break Game 2 open early. Five batters into the game, they had the bases loaded, no outs, and two runs in. But Braves' pitcher Mike Hampton settled down, and Chicago didn't score again until the eighth. Atlanta tallied two in the bottom of that frame, evening the Series with a 5–3 win.

Game 3 featured Cubs' youthful ace Mark Prior against four-time Cy Young Award-winner Greg Maddux, who had been the Cubs' ace the last time they reached the postseason. The young gun came out on top this time, as Prior fired a two-hitter to win, 3–1.

The see-saw battle continued in Game 4. Chipper Jones hit a pair of two-run homers for Atlanta, but the outcome was in doubt until the final pitch. It was Braves' relief ace John Smoltz against Cubs' super-slugger Sammy Sosa, representing the tying run with two out and a 3–2 count in the ninth. Sosa launched a long fly ball, but not long enough, and the Braves had evened the Series, 6–4.

Game 5 was Wood against Hampton. Wood went eight innings, allowing only one run, and homers by Alex Gonzalez and Aramis Ramirez gave him all the support he needed. The Cubs won, 5–1, to complete the upset.

CHI (C)

PLAYER/POS	AVG	G	AB	R	H	2B	3B	HR	RB	BB	SO	SB
Antonio Alfonseca, p	.000	1	0	0	0	0	0	0	0	0	0	0
Moises Alou, of	.500	5	20	3	10	1	0	0	3	1	4	1
Paul Bako, c	.000	3	4	0	0	0	0	0	1	2	2	0
Joe Borowski, p	.000	2	0	0	0	0	0	0	0	0	0	0
Matt Clement, p	.000	1	2	0	0	0	0	0	0	0	1	0
Juan Cruz, p	.000	1	0	0	0	0	0	0	0	0	0	0
Kyle Farnsworth, p	.000	3	0	0	0	0	0	0	0	0	0	0
Doug Glanville, ph	.000	2	1	1	0	0	0	0	0	0	0	0
Alex Gonzalez, ss	.250	5	12	1	3	0	0	1	1	2	3	0
Tom Goodwin, ph	1.000	2	1	0	1	1	0	0	2	0	0	0
Mark Grudzielanek, 2b	.150	5	20	2	3	0	0	0	0	3	4	0
Mark Guthrie, p	.000	1	0	0	0	0	0	0	0	0	0	0
Eric Karros, 1b	.375	4	16	4	6	0	0	2	2	0	3	0
Kenny Lofton, of	.286	5	21	3	6	1	0	0	1	2	2	3
Ramon Martinez, ss	.000	2	4	0	0	0	0	0	0	0	2	0
Damian Miller, c-4, ph-1	.091	4	11	0	1	1	0	0	1	2	5	0
Troy O'Leary, ph	.000	1	1	0	0	0	0	0	0	0	0	0
Mark Prior, p	.000	1	3	0	0	0	0	0	0	0	2	0
Aramis Ramirez, 3b	.278	5	18	2	5	1	0	1	3	2	2	0
Mike Remlinger, p	.000	2	0	0	0	0	0	0	0	0	0	0
Randall Simon, 1b-3	.429	4	7	1	3	1	0	0	2	0	2	0
Sammy Sosa, of	.187	5	16	1	3	1	0	0	1	6	4	1
Dave Veres, p	.000	2	0	0	0	0	0	0	0	0	0	0
Kerry Wood, p	.286	2	7	1	2	1	0	0	2	0	2	0
Carlos Zambrano, p	.000	1	3	0	0	0	0	0	0	0	2	0
TOTAL	.257		167	19	43	8	0	4	19	20	38	5

PITCHER	W	L	ERA	G	GS	CG	SV	SHO	IP	H	ER	BB	SO
Antonio Alfonseca	0	0	0.00	1	0	0	0	0	1.0	1	0	0	0
Joe Borowski	0	0	0.00	2	0	0	1	0	2.0	1	0	0	5
Matt Clement	0	1	7.71	1	1	0	0	0	4.7	8	4	4	3
Juan Cruz	0	0	0.00	1	0	0	0	0	1.0	0	0	1	2
Kyle Farnsworth	0	0	0.00	3	0	0	0	0	2.7	1	0	1	2
Mark Guthrie	0	0	27.00	1	0	0	0	0	0.7	2	2	1	0
Mark Prior	1	0	1.00	1	1	1	0	0	9.0	2	1	4	7
Mike Remlinger	0	0	0.00	2	0	0	0	0	0.7	0	0	1	1
Dave Veres	0	1	13.50	2	0	0	0	0	1.3	2	2	2	0
Kerry Wood	2	0	1.76	2	2	0	0	0	15.3	7	3	7	18
Carlos Zambrano	0	0	4.76	1	1	0	0	0	5.7	11	3	0	4
TOTAL	3	2	3.07	17	5	1	1	0	44.0	35	15	21	42

ATL (E)

PLAYER/POS	AVG	G	AB	R	H	2B	3B	HR	RB	BB	SO	SB
Darren Bragg, of-1	.000	2	5	0	0	0	0	0	0	1	0	1
Vinny Castilla, 3b	.250	5	16	0	4	0	0	0	1	3	6	0
Will Cunnane, p	.000	2	0	0	0	0	0	0	0	0	0	0
Mark DeRosa, 2b-2, 3b-1	.429	4	7	1	3	2	0	0	2	1	2	0
Robert Fick, 1b-3	.000	4	11	0	0	0	0	0	0	1	2	0
Julio Franco, 1b-3	.500	4	8	1	4	1	0	0	0	2	2	0
Matt Franco, ph	.000	2	2	1	0	0	0	0	0	0	1	0
Rafael Furcal, ss	.211	5	19	3	4	0	0	0	0	3	5	1
Jesse Garcia, 2b-2	.000	2	0	1	0	0	0	0	0	0	0	0
Marcus Giles, 2b-4	.357	5	14	3	5	0	0	1	3	2	2	0
Kevin Gryboski, p	.000	5	0	0	0	0	0	0	0	0	0	0
Mike Hampton, p	.250	2	4	0	1	0	0	0	0	0	2	0
Roberto Hernandez, p	.000	1	0	0	0	0	0	0	0	0	0	0
Andruw Jones, of	.059	5	17	1	1	0	0	0	0	1	4	0
Chipper Jones, of	.167	5	18	3	3	0	0	2	6	3	4	0
Ray King, p	.000	4	0	0	0	0	0	0	0	0	0	0
Javy Lopez, c	.333	5	21	1	7	2	0	0	0	0	6	0
Greg Maddux, p	.000	1	2	0	0	0	0	0	0	0	0	0
Kent Mercker, p	.000	1	0	0	0	0	0	0	0	0	0	0
Russ Ortiz, p	.200	2	5	0	1	0	0	0	0	0	2	0
Gary Sheffield, of	.143	4	14	0	2	0	0	0	1	2	0	0
John Smoltz, p	.000	2	0	0	0	0	0	0	0	0	0	0
Jaret Wright, p	.000	4	0	0	0	0	0	0	0	0	0	0
TOTAL	.215		163	15	35	5	0	3	15	21	42	1

PITCHER	W	L	ERA	G	GS	CG	SV	SHO	IP	H	ER	BB	SO
Will Cunnane	0	0	5.40	2	0	0	0	0	1.7	3	1	0	2
Kevin Gryboski	0	0	3.00	5	0	0	0	0	3.0	2	1	2	4
Mike Hampton	0	0	4.26	2	2	0	0	0	12.7	11	6	6	16
R. Hernandez	0	0	0.00	1	0	0	0	0	1.0	1	0	0	0
Ray King	0	0	0.00	4	0	0	0	0	1.0	1	0	1	0
Greg Maddux	0	0	3.00	1	1	0	0	0	6.0	6	2	1	1
Kent Mercker	0	0	0.00	1	0	0	0	0	1.0	0	0	1	1
Russ Ortiz	0	0	5.06	2	2	0	0	0	10.7	15	6	7	9
John Smoltz	0	0	6.00	2	0	0	1	0	3.0	4	2	0	1
Jaret Wright	0	0	0.00	4	0	0	0	0	4.0	0	0	2	4
TOTAL	0	0	3.68	24	5	0	1	0	44.0	43	18	20	38

GAME 1 at ATL SEP 30

```
CHI  000 004 000    4 10 0
ATL  001 000 010    2  3 1
```
Pitchers: WOOD, Remlinger (8), Farnsworth (8), Borowski (9) vs ORTIZ, King (6), Gryboski (6), Wright (7), Mercker (8), Hernandez (9)
Home Runs: Giles-ATL
Attendance: 52,043

GAME 2 at ATL OCT 1

```
CHI  200 000 010    3  6 0
ATL  100 101 02X    5 13 0
```
Pitchers: Zambrano, Farnsworth (6), VERES (6) vs Hampton, King (7), Gryboski (7), SMOLTZ (8)
Attendance: 52,743

GAME 3 at CHI OCT 3

```
ATL  000 000 010    1  2 4
CHI  200 000 01X    3  8 0
```
Pitchers: MADDUX, Wright (7), Gryboski (8) vs PRIOR
Attendance: 39,982

GAME 4 at CHI OCT 4

```
ATL  000 130 020    6 12 0
CHI  001 001 011    4 10 0
```
Pitchers: ORTIZ, King (6), Gryboski (6), Wright (7), Cunnane (8), Smoltz (9) vs CLEMENT, Alfonseca (5), Remlinger (6), Veres (7), Farnsworth (7), Guthrie (8), Cruz (9)
Home Runs: C. Jones-ATL (2), Karros-CHI (2)
Attendance: 39,983

GAME 5 at CHI OCT 5

```
CHI  110 002 001    5  9 0
ATL  000 001 000    1  5 1
```
Pitchers: WOOD, Borowski (9) vs HAMPTON, Gryboski (7), Wright (8), Cunnane (9), King (9)
Home Runs: Gonzalez-CHI, Ramirez-CHI
Attendance: 54,357

NEW YORK YANKEES (EAST) 3, MINNESOTA TWINS (CENTRAL) 1

The Yankees returned to the postseason on the strength of 101 victories, most in the American League; the Twins were back, too, but it took only 90 wins to win the weak AL Central.

When the Twins surprised their hosts with a 3–1 win in Game 1, the New York media went into a frenzy, predicting whose heads would be rolling after the dust settled. After all, the Yanks had lost the World Series in 2001 and the American League Divisional Series in 2002; owner George Steinbrenner wasn't going to sit idly by while they bowed to another inferior team.

He didn't have to, at least not in this Series. After team captain Derek Jeter subtly guaranteed a Yanks' comeback (saying that Andy Pettitte's Game 2 start wouldn't be his last of the year), New York's pitchers quieted the media and the Twins' bats, holding them to just three runs in the last 30 innings of the ALDS.

Pettitte did his part to make Jeter's prediction come true, pitching seven strong innings, allowing just four hits and one run, while striking out ten. Jason Giambi's two-run single in the seventh was the big hit for the Yankees, who evened the Series with a 4–1 triumph.

The teams shuttled to Minnesota for Game 3, with Roger Clemens duplicating Pettitte's effort: one run allowed in seven innings. Hideki Matsui's two-run homer in the third gave him all the support he needed, and Mariano Rivera retired all six batters he faced for the second game in a row. New York won, 3–1.

David Wells gave the Yanks yet another strong pitching performance, going 7-2/3 innings in an 8–1 victory. New York hung up a "6" on the scoreboard in the fourth—as many runs in one inning as Minnesota scored in the entire Series—to put it away. Jeter homered and finished as the team's top hitter at .429.

NY (E)

PLAYER/POS	AVG	G	AB	R	H	2B	3B	HR	RB	BB	SO	SB
Aaron Boone, 3b	.200	4	15	1	3	1	0	0	0	0	3	1
Roger Clemens, p	.000	1	0	0	0	0	0	0	0	0	0	0
David Dellucci, dh	.000	1	0	0	0	0	0	0	0	0	0	0
Jason Giambi, dh	.250	4	16	1	4	2	0	0	2	2	5	0
Felix Heredia, p	.000	1	0	0	0	0	0	0	0	0	0	0
Derek Jeter, ss	.429	4	14	2	6	0	0	1	1	4	2	1
Nick Johnson, 1b	.077	4	13	2	1	1	0	0	2	3	2	0
Hideki Matsui, of	.267	4	15	2	4	1	0	1	3	2	3	0
Mike Mussina, p	.000	1	0	0	0	0	0	0	0	0	0	0
Jeff Nelson, p	.000	1	0	0	0	0	0	0	0	0	0	0
Andy Pettitte, p	.000	1	0	0	0	0	0	0	0	0	0	0
Jorge Posada, c	.176	4	17	1	3	1	0	0	0	0	6	0
Juan Rivera, of	.333	4	12	2	4	0	0	0	0	1	0	0
Mariano Rivera, p	.000	2	0	0	0	0	0	0	0	0	0	0
Ruben Sierra, of	.000	1	2	0	0	0	0	0	0	0	0	0
Alfonso Soriano, 2b	.368	4	19	2	7	1	0	0	4	0	6	2
David Wells, p	.000	1	0	0	0	0	0	0	0	0	0	0
Gabe White, p	.000	1	0	0	0	0	0	0	0	0	0	0
Bernie Williams, of	.400	4	15	3	6	2	0	0	3	2	2	0
TOTAL	.275		138	16	38	9	0	2	15	14	29	4

PITCHER	W	L	ERA	G	GS	CG	SV	SHO	IP	H	ER	BB	SO
Roger Clemens	1	0	1.29	1	1	0	0	0	7.0	5	1	1	6
Felix Heredia	0	0	0.00	1	0	0	0	0	2.0	1	0	1	1
Mike Mussina	0	1	3.86	1	1	0	0	0	7.0	7	3	3	6
Jeff Nelson	0	0	∞	1	0	0	0	0	0.0	0	0	1	0
Andy Pettitte	1	0	1.29	1	1	0	0	0	7.0	4	1	3	10
Mariano Rivera	0	0	0.00	2	0	0	2	0	4.0	0	0	0	4
David Wells	1	0	1.17	1	1	0	0	0	7.7	8	1	0	5
Gabe White	0	0	0.00	1	0	0	0	0	1.3	1	0	0	1
TOTAL	3	1	1.50	9	4	0	2	0	36.0	26	6	9	33

MIN (C)

PLAYER/POS	AVG	G	AB	R	H	2B	3B	HR	RB	BB	SO	SB
Mike Cuddyer, dh	.250	1	4	0	1	0	0	0	0	1	3	0
Lew Ford, ph	.000	1	1	0	0	0	0	0	0	0	1	0
Chris Gomez, 2b	.000	1	0	0	0	0	0	0	0	0	0	0
Eddie Guardado, p	.000	2	0	0	0	0	0	0	0	0	0	0
Cristian Guzman, ss	.154	4	13	1	2	0	0	0	0	1	2	0
La Troy Hawkins, p	.000	3	0	0	0	0	0	0	0	0	0	0
Dennis Hocking, 2b	.000	1	0	0	0	0	0	0	0	0	0	0
Torii Hunter, of	.429	4	14	3	6	0	1	1	2	2	2	0
Jacque Jones, of	.125	4	16	0	2	0	0	0	0	0	5	0
Corey Koskie, 3b	.200	4	15	0	3	1	0	0	0	0	5	0
Matt LeCroy, dh	.091	3	11	1	1	0	0	0	0	1	4	0
Kyle Lohse, p	.000	1	0	0	0	0	0	0	0	0	0	0
Doug Mientkiewicz, 1b	.133	4	15	0	2	0	0	0	0	1	2	0
Brad Radke, p	.000	1	0	0	0	0	0	0	0	0	0	0
A.J. Pierzynski, c	.231	4	13	1	3	0	0	1	1	2	0	0
Rick Reed, p	.000	1	0	0	0	0	0	0	0	0	0	0
Juan Rincon, p	.000	3	0	0	0	0	0	0	0	0	0	0
Luis Rivas, 2b	.000	4	13	0	0	0	0	0	1	0	4	0
Kenny Rogers, p	.000	1	0	0	0	0	0	0	0	0	0	0
J.C. Romero, p	.000	3	0	0	0	0	0	0	0	0	0	0
Michael Ryan, ph	.000	1	1	0	0	0	0	0	0	0	1	0
Johan Santana, p	.000	2	0	0	0	0	0	0	0	0	0	0
Shannon Stewart, of	.400	4	15	0	6	2	0	0	0	2	4	1
TOTAL	.198		131	6	26	3	1	2	5	9	33	1

PITCHER	W	L	ERA	G	GS	CG	SV	SHO	IP	H	ER	BB	SO
Eddie Guardado	0	0	9.00	2	0	0	1	0	2.0	5	2	0	2
La Troy Hawkins	1	0	6.00	3	0	0	0	0	3.0	5	2	0	5
Kyle Lohse	0	1	5.40	1	1	0	0	0	5.0	6	3	2	5
Eric Milton	0	0	0.00	1	0	0	0	0	3.3	2	0	0	2
Brad Radke	0	1	2.84	1	1	0	0	0	6.3	5	2	2	4
Rick Reed	0	0	0.00	1	0	0	0	0	0.7	1	0	0	0
Juan Rincon	0	0	0.00	3	0	0	0	0	2.3	1	0	4	1
Kenny Rogers	0	0	0.00	1	0	0	0	0	1.3	1	0	1	3
J.C. Romero	0	0	0.00	3	0	0	0	0	3.3	3	0	2	1
Johan Santana	0	1	7.04	2	2	0	0	0	7.7	9	6	3	6
TOTAL	1	3	3.86	18	4	0	1	0	35.0	38	15	14	29

GAME 1 at NY SEP 30

MIN 001 002 000   3 8 0
NY   000 000 001   1 9 1
Pitchers: Santana, Reed (5), Romero (5), HAWKINS (7), Guardado (9) vs MUSSINA, Nelson (8), Heredia (8)
Attendance: 56,292

GAME 2 at NY OCT 2

MIN 000 010 000   1 4 1
NY   100 000 30X   4 8 1
Pitchers: RADKE, Hawkins (7), Romero (7), Rincon (8) vs PETTITTE, Rivera (8)
Home Runs: Hunter-MIN
Attendance: 56,479

GAME 3 at MIN OCT 4

NY   021 000 000   3 8 1
MIN 001 000 000   1 5 0
Pitchers: CLEMENS, Rivera (8) vs LOHSE, Rogers (6), Romero (7), Rincon (8)
Home Runs: Matsui-NY, Pierzynski-MIN
Attendance: 55,915

GAME 4 at MIN OCT 5

NY   000 600 011   8 13 0
MIN 000 100 000   1 9 1
Pitchers: WELLS, White (8) vs SANTANA, Rincon (4), Milton (4), Hawkins (8), Guardado (9)
Home Runs: Jeter-NY
Attendance: 55,875

BOSTON RED SOX (WILD CARD) 3, OAKLAND A'S (WEST) 2

Both the Red Sox and A's had to beat out the Mariners to make the American League Divisional Series. The M's won 93 games; Oakland won 96 to claim the AL West title, while Boston—perennial second-place finishers behind the Yankees—won 95 to grab the wild card.

Game 1 went back and forth. Boston scored first, but Oakland went on top with three runs off ace Pedro Martinez in the third. The Red Sox retook the lead, 4–3 in the seventh, but the A's tied it in the ninth as Byung-Hyun Kim blew the save. Oakland finally won it in the 12th, 5–4.

The Athletics ripped Tim Wakefield for five runs in the second inning of Game 2, and Barry Zito cruised to a 5–1 victory. For the fourth straight year, Oakland was one win away from the American League Championship Series, this time with three chances to get it.

At Fenway Park, Boston's Derek Lowe and Oakland's Ted Lilly engaged in a pitchers' duel. The game went into extra innings tied at one, but Trot Nixon's pinch-hit, two-run homer off Rich Harden won it for Boston in the 11th.

The A's were four outs away from winning the Series in Game 4, with a one-run lead and the American League's top closer, Keith Foulke, on the mound. But David Ortiz came through with a two-run double to keep the Sox alive with a 5–4 win.

Back on the west coast, the deciding game was Martinez vs. Zito. Oakland started things with a run in the fourth, but sixth-inning homers by Boston's Jason Varitek and Manny Ramirez—the latter with two on base—gave the Sox a 4–1 lead. The A's wouldn't quit, tallying in the sixth and eighth to creep within one, and loading the bases with two out in the bottom of the ninth. But when Lowe struck out Terrence Long, the A's had lost Game 5 of the ALDS for the fourth year in a row.

BOS (WC)

PLAYER/POS	AVG	G	AB	R	H	2B	3B	HR	RB	BB	SO	SB
Adrian Brown, of-1, dh-1	.000	4	2	0	0	0	0	0	0	0	1	0
John Burkett, p	.000	1	0	0	0	0	0	0	0	0	0	0
Johnny Damon, of	.316	5	19	2	6	2	0	1	3	2	1	2
Alan Embree, p	.000	3	0	0	0	0	0	0	0	0	0	0
Nomar Garciaparra, ss	.300	5	20	2	6	1	0	0	0	3	2	1
Damian Jackson, 2b	.000	4	5	0	0	0	0	0	0	0	2	0
Gabe Kapler, of-3, dh-1	.000	4	9	0	0	0	0	0	0	0	3	0
Byung-Hyun Kim, p	.000	1	0	0	0	0	0	0	0	0	0	0
Derek Lowe, p	.000	3	0	0	0	0	0	0	0	0	0	0
Pedro Martinez, p	.000	2	0	0	0	0	0	0	0	0	0	0
David McCarty, ph	.000	1	0	0	0	0	0	0	0	0	0	0
Kevin Millar, 1b	.238	5	21	0	5	0	0	0	0	2	4	0
Doug Mirabelli, c	.500	2	4	2	2	1	0	0	0	0	0	0
Bill Mueller, 3b	.105	5	19	0	2	1	0	0	0	3	4	0
Trot Nixon, of-3	.200	4	10	1	2	0	0	1	2	1	3	0
David Ortiz, dh	.095	5	21	0	2	1	0	0	2	2	7	0
Manny Ramirez, of	.200	5	20	2	4	0	0	1	3	3	7	0
Mike Timlin, p	.000	3	0	0	0	0	0	0	0	0	0	0
Jason Varitek, c-4	.286	5	14	4	4	0	0	2	2	2	2	0
Tim Wakefield, p	.000	2	0	0	0	0	0	0	0	0	0	0
Todd Walker, 2b	.312	5	16	4	5	0	0	3	4	0	1	0
Scott Williamson, p	.000	5	0	0	0	0	0	0	0	0	0	0
TOTAL	.211		180	17	38	6	0	8	16	18	39	3

PITCHER	W	L	ERA	G	GS	CG	SV	SHO	IP	H	ER	BB	SO
John Burkett	0	0	6.75	1	1	0	0	0	5.3	9	4	2	1
Alan Embree	0	0	0.00	3	0	0	0	0	2.0	1	0	0	0
Byung-Hyun Kim	0	0	13.50	1	0	0	0	0	0.7	0	1	1	1
Derek Lowe	0	1	0.93	3	1	0	0	1	9.7	7	1	7	6
Pedro Martinez	1	0	3.86	2	2	0	0	0	14.0	13	6	5	9
Mike Timlin	0	0	0.00	3	0	0	0	0	4.3	0	0	0	5
Tim Wakefield	0	1	3.52	2	1	0	0	0	7.7	6	3	3	7
Scott Williamson	2	0	0.00	5	0	0	0	0	5.0	2	0	3	8
TOTAL	0	0	2.77	20	5	0	1	0	48.7	38	15	21	37

OAK (W)

PLAYER/POS	AVG	G	AB	R	H	2B	3B	HR	RB	BB	SO	SB
Chad Bradford, p	.000	4	0	0	0	0	0	0	0	0	0	0
Eric Byrnes, of-4	.462	5	13	2	6	1	0	0	2	0	5	1
Eric Chavez, 3b	.045	5	22	1	1	1	0	0	0	3	1	1
Erubiel Durazo, dh	.238	5	21	3	5	2	0	0	3	3	4	0
Jermaine Dye, of	.231	4	13	2	3	0	0	1	3	0	2	0
Mark Ellis, 2b	.118	5	17	2	2	0	0	0	0	4	7	0
Keith Foulke, p	.000	3	0	0	0	0	0	0	0	0	0	0
Jose Guillen, of	.455	4	11	1	5	1	0	0	1	3	2	0
Rich Harden, p	.000	2	0	0	0	0	0	0	0	0	0	0
Scott Hatteberg, 1b	.176	5	17	3	3	0	0	0	0	5	5	0
Ramon Hernandez, c	.200	4	15	1	3	0	0	0	2	2	1	0
Tim Hudson, p	.000	2	0	0	0	0	0	0	0	0	0	0
Ted Lilly, p	.000	2	0	0	0	0	0	0	0	0	0	0
Terrence Long, of-3	.250	4	8	0	2	0	0	0	0	1	3	0
Billy McMillon, of-1	.167	3	6	0	1	0	0	0	0	1	1	0
Jim Mecir, p	.000	1	0	0	0	0	0	0	0	0	0	0
Adam Melhuse, c-1	.600	2	5	1	3	0	0	1	1	0	1	0
Frank Menechino, 2b	.000	1	0	0	0	0	0	0	0	0	0	0
Ricardo Rincon, p	.000	4	0	0	0	0	0	0	0	0	0	0
Chris Singleton, of	.286	2	7	2	2	2	0	0	1	1	1	1
Steve Sparks, p	.000	1	0	0	0	0	0	0	0	0	0	0
Miguel Tejada, ss	.087	5	23	0	2	1	0	0	2	0	4	0
Barry Zito, p	.000	2	0	0	0	0	0	0	0	0	0	0
TOTAL	.213		178	18	38	8	1	1	15	21	37	3

PITCHER	W	L	ERA	G	GS	CG	SV	SHO	IP	H	ER	BB	SO
Chad Bradford	0	0	0.00	4	0	0	0	0	3.7	4	0	2	5
Keith Foulke	0	1	3.60	3	0	0	0	0	5.0	4	2	2	3
Rich Harden	1	1	13.50	2	0	0	0	0	1.3	2	2	2	1
Tim Hudson	0	0	3.52	2	2	0	0	0	7.7	10	3	1	6
Ted Lilly	0	0	0.00	2	1	0	0	0	9.0	2	0	2	7
Jim Mecir	0	0	0.00	1	0	0	0	0	0.7	1	0	1	0
Ricardo Rincon	0	0	4.50	4	0	0	0	0	4.0	4	2	1	3
Steve Sparks	0	0	4.50	1	0	0	0	0	4.0	2	2	3	1
Barry Zito	1	1	3.46	2	2	0	0	0	13.0	9	5	4	13
TOTAL	2	3	2.98	21	5	0	0	0	48.3	38	16	18	39

GAME 1 at OAK OCT 1

BOS 100 010 200 000 4 12 2
OAK 003 000 001 001 5 8 0
Pitchers: Martinez, Timlin (8), Kim (9), Embree (9), Williamson (10), LOWE (11) vs Hudson, Rincon (7), Bradford (8), Foulke (9), HARDEN (12)
Home Runs: Walker-BOS (2), Varitek-BOS
Attendance: 50,606

GAME 2 at OAK OCT 2

BOS 001000 000 1 6 1
OAK 050000 00X 5 6 0
Pitchers: WAKEFIELD, Embree (7), Williamson (8) vs ZITO, Bradford (8), Foulke (9)
Attendance: 36,305

GAME 3 at BOS OCT 4

OAK 000 001 000 00 1 6 4
BOS 010 000 000 02 3 7 2
Pitchers: Lilly, Bradford (8), Rincon (9), Mecir (10), HARDEN (11) vs Lowe, Timlin (8), WILLIAMSON (11)
Attendance: 35,460

GAME 4 at BOS OCT 5

OAK 010 003 000 4 11 1
BOS 002 001 02X 5 7 0
Pitchers: Hudson, Sparks (2), Rincon (6), FOULKE (8), Burkett, Wakefield (6), WILLIAMSON (8)
Home Runs: Dye-OAK, Damon-BOS, Walker-BOS
Attendance: 35,048

GAME 5 at OAK OCT 6

BOS 000 004 000 4 6 0
OAK 000 101 010 3 7 0
Pitchers: MARTINEZ, Embree (8), Timlin (8), Williamson (9), Lowe (9) vs ZITO, Lilly (7), Bradford (9), Rincon (9)
Home Runs: Varitek-BOS, Ramirez-BOS
Attendance: 49,397

FLORIDA MARLINS (WILD CARD) 4, CHICAGO CUBS (CENTRAL) 3

The Cubs were striving to overcome the legendary "Billy Goat Curse" and advance to their first World Series since 1945. They started auspiciously, hammering Josh Beckett for four runs in the first inning of Game 1, but the Marlins answered with five in the third. Chicago tied it in the sixth, and the teams scored two apiece in the ninth to send it into extra innings. Finally, Mike Lowell's pinch-homer in the 11th won it for Florida, 9–8. Ivan Rodriguez, on his way to the Series MVP Award, knocked in five runs.

Behind two homers by Alex Gonzalez (not to be confused with the Florida shortstop of the same name), Chicago built up an 11–0 lead in Game 2, giving ace Mark Prior an easy 12–3 victory. The Cubs had to work harder for a Game 3 win in Florida, but got it when pinch hitter Doug Glanville ripped an RBI triple in the 11th inning, making the final 5–4, Cubs.

The fourth game was much like the second: Chicago built up a big lead (7–0) early, and a strong-armed pitcher (Matt Clement) cruised to victory. Aramis Ramirez (2 HR, 6 RBIs) was the hitting star as the Cubs won their third straight, 8–3.

Beckett kept the Marlins alive with a brilliant two-hit shutout—the first complete game of his pro career. He struck out 11 in the 4–0 victory. Prior was working on a shutout of his own in Game 6. The Cubs led, 3–0 in the eighth inning and were four outs away from the World Series. Then came one of those moments that baseball lore is made of.

Luis Castillo lifted a foul toward the left-field stands. Moises Alou appeared poised to make the catch, but Chicago fan Steven Bartman reached out and deflected the ball. No interference was called and, given new life, Castillo walked. Prior and the Cubs then proceeded into meltdown. By the time the inning ended, the Marlins had scored eight runs for a Series-tying 8–3 victory.

The Cubs built Kerry Wood a 5–3 lead in the finale, but he let it slip away in the fifth. In came Beckett, on just two days' rest. He gave the Fish four more strong innings to carry them to a 9–6 triumph. The Marlins were on to their second World Series, and the Cubs were still cursed.

FLA (WC)

PLAYER/POS	AVG	G	AB	R	H	2B	3B	HR	RB	BB	SO	SB
Brian Banks, ph	.000	2	1	1	0	0	0	0	0	1	0	0
Josh Beckett, p	.250	3	8	0	2	0	0	0	0	0	1	3	0
Nate Bump, p	.000	2	0	0	0	0	0	0	0	0	0	0
Miguel Cabrera, 3b-3, ss-1, of-5	.333	7	30	9	10	0	0	3	6	2	6	0
Luis Castillo, 2b	.214	7	28	3	6	1	0	0	2	5	2	2
Jeff Conine, of	.458	7	24	4	11	1	1	1	3	4	2	0
Juan Encarnacion, of	.250	5	12	1	3	1	0	1	1	0	4	0
Chad Fox, p	.000	3	0	0	0	0	0	0	0	0	0	0
Alex Gonzalez, ss	.125	7	24	1	3	2	0	0	4	0	6	0
Lenny Harris, p	.000	3	2	0	0	0	0	0	0	1	0	0
Rick Helling, p	.000	2	1	0	0	0	0	0	0	0	0	0
Todd Hollandsworth, ph	1.000	4	3	2	3	1	0	0	2	1	0	0
Derrek Lee, 1b	.187	7	32	2	6	2	0	1	4	1	8	1
Braden Looper, p	.000	2	0	0	0	0	0	0	0	0	0	0
Mike Lowell, 3b	.200	7	20	5	4	0	0	2	3	3	4	0
Mike Mordecai, 2b-1, ss-1	.200	3	5	1	1	0	0	0	3	0	0	0
Carl Pavano, p	.000	3	2	0	0	0	0	0	0	0	1	0
Brad Penny, p	.000	3	1	0	0	0	0	0	0	0	1	0
Juan Pierre, of	.303	7	33	5	10	1	2	0	1	2	1	1
Mark Redman, p	.000	2	2	0	0	0	0	0	0	0	1	0
Mike Redmond, p	.000	1	0	1	0	0	0	0	0	0	1	0
Ivan Rodriguez, c	.321	7	28	5	9	2	0	2	10	5	7	0
Michael Tejera, p	.000	2	0	0	0	0	0	0	0	0	0	0
Ugueth Urbina, p	.000	4	0	0	0	0	0	0	0	0	0	0
Dontrelle Willis, p	.000	2	0	0	0	0	0	0	0	0	0	0
TOTAL	.266		256	40	68	12	3	10	39	28	45	4

PITCHER	W	L	ERA	G	GS	CG	SV	SHO	IP	H	ER	BB	SO
Josh Beckett	1	0	3.26	3	2	1	0	1	19.3	11	7	2	19
Nate Bump	0	0	6.00	2	0	0	0	0	3.0	3	2	0	3
Chad Fox	1	0	5.40	3	0	0	0	0	3.3	5	2	2	2
Rick Helling	0	0	6.35	2	0	0	0	0	5.7	7	4	4	5
Braden Looper	0	0	0.00	2	0	0	1	0	1.7	1	0	1	1
Carl Pavano	0	0	2.35	3	1	0	0	0	7.7	8	2	1	8
Brad Penny	1	1	15.75	3	1	0	0	0	4.0	9	7	3	0
Mark Redman	0	0	6.52	2	2	0	0	0	9.7	13	7	4	4
Michael Tejera	0	1	6.75	2	0	0	0	0	1.3	2	1	0	1
Ugueth Urbina	1	0	2.57	4	0	0	1	0	7.0	2	2	0	10
Dontrelle Willis	0	1	18.90	2	1	0	0	0	3.3	4	7	6	4
TOTAL	4	3	5.59	28	7	1	2	1	66.0	65	41	23	57

CHI (C)

PLAYER/POS	AVG	G	AB	R	H	2B	3B	HR	RB	BB	SO	SB
Antonio Alfonseca, p	.000	3	0	0	0	0	0	0	0	0	0	0
Moises Alou, of	.310	7	29	4	9	1	0	2	5	2	1	0
Paul Bako, c	.250	6	16	4	4	1	0	0	1	1	7	0
Joe Borowski, p	.000	3	0	0	0	0	0	0	0	0	0	0
Matt Clement, p	.000	1	4	0	0	0	0	0	0	1	0	0
Kyle Farnsworth, p	.000	5	0	0	0	0	0	0	0	0	0	0
Doug Glanville	1.000	1	1	0	1	0	1	0	1	0	0	0
Alex Gonzalez, ss	.286	7	28	5	8	2	0	3	7	2	7	0
Tom Goodwin, of-1	.250	5	4	1	1	0	1	0	0	0	3	0
Mark Grudzielanek, 2b	.200	7	30	2	6	1	1	0	3	0	5	0
Mark Guthrie, p	.000	2	0	0	0	0	0	0	0	0	0	0
Eric Karros, 1b	.231	5	13	2	3	0	0	0	0	2	3	0
Kenny Lofton, of	.323	7	31	8	10	1	0	0	2	3	4	1
Ramon Martinez, ss-3, 2b-1	.000	4	4	0	0	0	0	0	0	0	1	0
Damian Miller, c	.200	4	10	0	2	1	0	0	1	2	2	0
Troy O'Leary, of-1	.333	3	3	1	1	0	0	1	1	0	0	0
Mark Prior, p	.000	2	4	0	0	0	0	0	0	0	2	0
Aramis Ramirez, 3b	.231	7	26	4	6	0	1	3	7	5	6	0
Mike Remlinger, p	.000	5	0	0	0	0	0	0	0	0	0	0
Randall Simon, 1b-5	.294	6	17	3	5	2	0	1	4	0	3	0
Sammy Sosa, of	.308	7	26	7	8	1	0	2	6	6	9	0
Dave Veres, p	.000	3	0	0	0	0	0	0	0	0	0	0
Kerry Wood, p	.333	2	3	1	1	0	0	1	3	0	0	0
Carlos Zambrano, p	.000	2	3	0	0	0	0	0	0	0	3	0
TOTAL	.258		252	42	65	10	4	13	41	23	57	1

PITCHER	W	L	ERA	G	GS	CG	SV	SHO	IP	H	ER	BB	SO
Antonio Alfonseca	0	0	0.00	3	0	0	0	0	2.3	2	0	2	0
Joe Borowski	1	0	1.59	3	0	0	0	0	5.7	5	1	3	1
Matt Clement	1	0	3.52	1	1	0	0	0	7.7	5	3	2	3
Kyle Farnsworth	0	0	10.12	5	0	0	0	0	5.3	6	6	2	7
Mark Guthrie	0	1	9.00	2	0	0	0	0	1.0	1	1	0	0
Mark Prior	1	1	3.14	2	2	0	0	0	14.3	14	5	5	11
Mike Remlinger	0	0	2.70	5	0	0	1	0	3.3	3	1	1	2
Dave Veres	0	0	3.00	3	0	0	0	0	3.0	4	1	1	0
Kerry Wood	0	1	7.30	2	2	0	0	0	12.3	14	10	7	13
Carlos Zambrano	0	1	5.73	2	2	0	0	0	11.0	14	7	5	8
TOTAL	3	4	4.77	28	7	0	1	0	66.0	68	35	28	45

GAME 1 at CHI OCT 7
FLA 0 0 5 0 0 1 0 0 2 0 1   9 14 1
CHI 4 0 0 0 0 2 0 0 2 0 0   8 11 1
Pitchers: Beckett, Fox (7), URBINA (9), Looper (11) vs Zambrano, Remlinger (7), Farnsworth (7), Borowski (9), GUTHRIE (11), Alfonseca (11)
Home Runs: Rodriguez-FLA, Cabrera-FLA, Encarnacion-FLA, Lowell-FLA, Alou-CHI, Gonzalez-CHI, Sosa-CHI
Attendance: 39,567

GAME 2 at CHI OCT 8
FLA 0 0 0 0 0 2 0 1 0   3 9 1
CHI 2 3 3 0 3 1 0 0 X   12 16 1
Pitchers: PENNY, Bump (3), Helling (4), Pavano (7), Tejera (8) vs PRIOR, Veres (8), Guthrie (9)
Home Runs: Lee-FLA, Cabrera-FLA, Sosa-CHI, Ramirez-CHI, Gonzalez-CHI (2)
Attendance: 39,562

GAME 3 at FLA OCT 7
CHI 1 1 0 0 0 0 0 2 0 0 1   5 12 0
FLA 0 1 0 0 0 0 2 1 0 0 0   4 10 0
Pitchers: Wood, Farnsworth (7), BOROWSKI (8), Remlinger (11) vs Redman, Fox (7), Urbina (9), TEJERA (11), Looper (11)
Home Runs: Simon-CHI
Attendance: 65,115

GAME 4 at FLA OCT 11
CHI 4 0 2 1 0 0 1 0 0   8 8 0
FLA 0 0 0 0 2 0 0 1 0   3 6 1
Pitchers: CLEMENT, Farnsworth (8) vs WILLIS, Helling (3), Bump (6), Penny (8), Pavano (9)
Home Runs: Ramirez-CHI (2)
Attendance: 65,829

GAME 5 at FLA OCT 12
CHI 0 0 0 0 0 0 0 0 0   0 2 0
FLA 0 0 0 0 2 0 1 1 X   4 8 0
Pitchers: ZAMBRANO, Veres (6), Alfonseca (7), Remlinger (8) vs BECKETT
Home Runs: Lowell-FLA, Rodriguez-FLA, Conine-FLA
Attendance: 65,279

GAME 6 at CHI OCT 14
FLA 0 0 0 0 0 0 0 8 0   8 9 0
CHI 1 0 0 0 0 1 1 0 0   3 10 2
Pitchers: Pavano, Willis (6), FOX (7), Urbina (8) vs PRIOR, Farnsworth (8), Remlinger (8), Alfonseca (9)
Attendance: 39,577

GAME 7 at CHI OCT 15
FLA 3 0 0 0 3 1 2 0 0   9 12 0
CHI 0 3 2 0 0 0 1 0 0   6 6 0
Pitchers: Redman, PENNY (4), Beckett (5), Urbina (9) vs WOOD, Farnsworth (6), Veres (7), Remlinger (8), Borowski (8)
Home Runs: Cabrera-FLA, Wood-CHI, Alou-CHI, O'Leary-CHI
Attendance: 39,574

NEW YORK YANKEES (EAST) 4, BOSTON RED SOX (WILD CARD) 3

Baseball's fiercest rivalry was showcased, as the mighty Yankees hosted the Red Sox. Like the Cubs, the Sox suffered from a media-concocted "curse," dating back to their 1920 sale of Babe Ruth to the Yanks. Boston came out on top in the first game, however, as Tim Wakefield shut out the Yanks until the seventh and, backed by three homers, earned a 5–2 win.

Andy Pettitte continued his Game 2 mastery, evening the ALCS with a 6–2 victory. Then, as the Series moved to Boston, came the showdown: Boston's Pedro Martinez against New York's Roger Clemens. The two notorious brushback artists had nine Cy Young Awards between them. To add to the drama, it figured to be the final career appearance for Clemens in Boston, where he had spent his first 13 seasons.

Predictably, there was a bench-clearing melee, punctuated by the bizarre spectacle of Martinez decking Yankees' beloved 72-year-old coach Don Zimmer. But Clemens kept his head, holding the lead until he left in the seventh inning to a mixed ovation. The Yankees won, 4–3.

Wakefield evened the Series with his second victory, 3–2. The knuckleballer gave up just one run in seven frames, and Trot Nixon's fifth-inning homer gave the Sox the lead for good. David Wells put New York back on top with seven strong innings in Game 5, a 4–2 Yankees win. Back in New York, the Yanks built a 6–4 lead, but the Red Sox overcame it for a 9–6 triumph. It all came down to Game 7, again Martinez against Clemens.

This time, Martinez took control as Boston staked him to a 4–0 lead. Pedro gave up two homers to Jason Giambi, but still led, 5–2 in the eighth. Boston was five outs away from the Fall Classic. Though Martinez was still throwing in the mid-90s, the Yankees started chipping away at him. The media wanted manager Grady Little to replace Martinez (2.22 ERA for the season) with Alan Embree (4.25), but the skipper—in a decision reminiscent of Johnny Keane's in the 1964 World Series—stuck with his ace. It would cost Little his job; the Yanks tied the score in the eighth, and Aaron Boone's 11th-inning homer off Wakefield won it for

New York, 6–5. Mariano Rivera, who pitched three scoreless innings for the win, was named Series MVP.

NY (E)

PLAYER/POS	AVG	G	AB	R	H	2B	3B	HR	RB	BB	SO	SB
Aaron Boone, 3b	.176	7	17	2	3	0	0	1	2	1	6	1
Roger Clemens, p	.000	2	0	0	0	0	0	0	0	0	0	0
Jose Contreras, p	.000	4	0	0	0	0	0	0	0	0	0	0
David Dellucci, dh-2,of-1	.333	3	3	2	1	0	0	0	0	0	1	1
Karim Garcia, of	.250	5	16	1	4	0	0	0	3	2	4	0
Jason Giambi, dh	.231	7	26	4	6	0	0	3	3	4	7	0
Felix Heredia, p	.000	5	0	0	0	0	0	0	0	0	0	0
Derek Jeter, ss	.233	7	30	3	7	2	0	1	2	2	4	1
Nick Johnson, 1b	.231	7	26	4	6	1	0	1	3	2	4	0
Hideki Matsui, of	.308	7	26	3	8	3	0	0	4	1	3	0
Mike Mussina, p	.000	3	0	0	0	0	0	0	0	0	0	0
Jeff Nelson, p	.000	4	0	0	0	0	0	0	0	0	0	0
Andy Pettitte, p	.000	2	0	0	0	0	0	0	0	0	0	0
Jorge Posada, c	.296	7	27	5	8	4	0	1	6	3	4	0
Juan Rivera, of	.000	2	2	0	0	0	0	0	0	0	1	0
Mariano Rivera, p	.000	4	0	0	0	0	0	0	0	0	0	0
Ruben Sierra, of-1	.500	3	2	1	1	0	0	1	1	1	0	0
Alfonso Soriano, 2b	.133	7	30	0	4	1	0	0	3	1	11	2
David Wells, p	.000	2	0	0	0	0	0	0	0	0	0	0
Gabe White, p	.000	2	0	0	0	0	0	0	0	0	0	0
Bernie Williams, of	.192	7	26	5	5	1	0	0	2	4	3	0
Enrique Wilson, 3b	.143	2	7	0	1	0	0	0	0	0	1	0
TOTAL	.227		238	30	54	12	0	8	29	21	49	5

PITCHER	W	L	ERA	G	GS	CG	SV	SHO	IP	H	ER	BB	SO
Roger Clemens	1	0	5.00	2	2	0	0	0	9.0	11	5	2	8
Jose Contreras	0	1	5.79	4	0	0	0	0	4.7	6	3	2	7
Felix Heredia	0	0	3.38	5	0	0	0	0	2.7	0	1	3	3
Mike Mussina	0	2	4.11	3	2	0	0	0	15.3	16	7	4	17
Jeff Nelson	0	0	6.00	4	0	0	0	0	3.0	4	2	0	3
Andy Pettitte	1	0	4.63	2	2	0	0	0	11.7	17	6	4	10
Mariano Rivera	1	0	1.12	4	0	0	2	0	8.0	5	1	0	6
David Wells	1	0	2.35	2	1	0	0	0	7.7	5	2	2	5
Gabe White	0	0	4.50	2	0	0	0	0	2.0	4	1	0	1
TOTAL	4	3	3.94	28	7	0	2	0	64.0	68	28	17	60

BOS (WC)

PLAYER/POS	AVG	G	AB	R	H	2B	3B	HR	RB	BB	SO	SB
Bronson Arroyo, p	.000	3	0	0	0	0	0	0	0	0	0	0
John Burkett, p	.000	1	0	0	0	0	0	0	0	0	0	0
Johnny Damon, of	.200	5	20	1	4	1	0	0	1	3	3	1
Alan Embree, p	.000	5	0	0	0	0	0	0	0	0	0	0
Nomar Garciaparra, ss	.241	7	29	2	7	0	1	0	1	2	8	0
Damian Jackson, 2b-4	.333	5	3	0	1	0	0	0	1	0	1	0
Todd Jones, p	.000	1	0	0	0	0	0	0	0	0	1	0
Gabe Kapler, of-2, dh-1	.125	3	8	0	1	0	0	0	0	0	3	0
Derek Lowe, p	.000	2	0	0	0	0	0	0	0	0	0	0
Pedro Martinez, p	.000	2	0	0	0	0	0	0	0	0	0	0
David McCarty, ph	.000	1	1	0	0	0	0	0	0	0	1	0
Kevin Millar, 1b	.241	7	29	3	7	0	0	1	3	1	9	0
Doug Mirabelli, c	.286	3	7	0	2	0	0	0	0	0	2	0
Bill Mueller, 3b	.222	7	27	1	6	2	0	0	0	2	7	0
Trot Nixon, of	.333	7	24	8	8	1	0	3	5	5	7	1
David Ortiz, dh	.269	7	26	4	7	1	0	2	6	3	8	0
Manny Ramirez, of	.310	7	29	6	9	1	0	2	4	1	4	0
Mike Timlin, p	.000	5	0	0	0	0	0	0	0	0	0	0
Jason Varitek, c	.300	6	20	4	6	2	0	2	3	1	5	0
Tim Wakefield, p	.000	3	0	0	0	0	0	0	0	0	0	0
Scott Williamson, p	.000	3	0	0	0	0	0	0	0	0	0	0
Todd Walker, 2b	.370	7	27	5	10	1	1	2	2	1	2	0
TOTAL	.272		250	29	68	9	2	12	26	17	60	2

PITCHER	W	L	ERA	G	GS	CG	SV	SHO	IP	H	ER	BB	SO
Bronson Arroyo	0	0	2.70	3	0	0	0	0	3.3	2	1	2	5
John Burkett	0	0	7.36	1	1	0	0	0	3.7	7	3	0	1
Alan Embree	1	0	0.00	5	0	0	0	0	4.7	3	0	0	1
Todd Jones	0	0	0.00	1	0	0	0	0	0.3	1	0	1	1
Derek Lowe	0	2	6.43	2	2	0	0	0	14.0	14	10	7	5
Pedro Martinez	0	1	5.65	2	2	0	0	0	14.3	16	9	2	14
Scott Sauerbeck	0	0	0.00	1	0	0	0	0	0.3	1	0	1	0
Mike Timlin	0	0	0.00	5	0	0	0	0	5.3	1	0	2	6
Tim Wakefield	2	1	2.57	3	2	0	0	0	14.0	8	4	6	10
Scott Williamson	0	0	3.00	3	0	0	3	0	3.0	1	1	0	6
TOTAL	3	4	4.00	26	7	0	3	0	63.0	54	28	21	49

GAME 1 at NY OCT 8

BOS 000 220 100   5 13 0
NY   000 000 200   2 3 0
Pitchers: WAKEFIELD, Embree (7), Timlin (8), Williamson (9) vs MUSSINA, Heredia (6), Nelson (7), White (7), Contreras (9)
Home Runs: Ortiz-BOS, Walker-BOS, Ramirez-BOS
Attendance: 56,281

GAME 2 at NY OCT 9

BOS 010 001 000   2 10 1
NY   021 010 20X   6 8 0
Pitchers: LOWE, Sauerbeck (7), Arroyo (8) vs PETTITTE, Contreras (7), Rivera (9)
Home Runs: Varitek-BOS, Johnson-NY
Attendance: 56,295

GAME 3 at BOS OCT 11

NY   011 200 000   4 7 0
BOS 200 000 100   3 6 0
Pitchers: CLEMENS, Heredia (7), Contreras (7), Rivera (8) vs MARTINEZ, Timlin (8), Embree (9)
Home Runs: Jeter-NY
Attendance: 34,209

GAME 4 at BOS OCT 13

NY   000 010 001   2 6 1
BOS 000 110 10X   3 6 0
Pitchers: MUSSINA, Heredia (7), Nelson (8) vs WAKEFIELD, Timlin (8), Williamson (9)
Home Runs: Sierra-NY, Walker-BOS, Nixon-BOS
Attendance: 34,599

GAME 5 at BOS OCT 14

NY   030 000 010   4 7 1
BOS 000 100 010   2 6 1
Pitchers: WELLS, Rivera (8) vs LOWE, Embree (8), Arroyo (9)
Home Runs: Ramirez-BOS
Attendance: 34,619

GAME 6 at NY OCT 15

BOS 004 000 302   9 16 1
NY   100 410 000   6 12 2
Pitchers: Burkett, Arroyo (4), Jones (6), EMBREE (6), Timlin (8), Williamson vs Pettitte, CONTRERAS (6), Heredia (7), Nelson (8), White (9)
Home Runs: Varitek-BOS, Nixon-BOS, Giambi-NY, Posada-NY
Attendance: 56,277

GAME 7 at NY OCT 16

BOS 030 100 010 00   5 11 0
NY   000 010 130 01   6 11 1
Pitchers: Martinez, Embree (8), Timlin (8), WAKEFIELD (10) vs Clemens, Mussina (4), Heredia (7), Nelson (7), Wells (8), RIVERA (9)
Home Runs: Nixon-BOS, Millar-BOS, Ortiz-BOS, Giambi-NY (2), Boone-NY
Attendance: 56,279

FLORIDA MARLINS (NL) 4, NEW YORK YANKEES (AL) 2

The 2003 Marlins were trying to become just the second wild-card team ever to win it all. The first? The 1997 Marlins, the only other Florida team to finish above .500 since the team's inception. The Yankees, meanwhile, were back in the World Series for the sixth time in eight years, looking for their 27th world championship.

The Series opened in New York, thanks to the AL's victory in the All-Star Game. With Brad Penny outdueling David Wells, the Marlins pulled out a 3–2 victory. Yanks' third baseman Aaron Boone, the hero of the final ALCS game, got the goat-horns in this one. He went 0-for-4 and inexplicably cut off a throw that seemed destined to prevent Florida's third run from scoring.

The Yankees roared back with two straight 6–1 victories. Behind Hideki Matsui's three-run homer, Andy Pettitte again followed a Game 1 Yankees' loss with a Game 2 win. Mike Mussina was the victor in Game 3, though he had to sweat it out. He and Florida's Josh Beckett—an NLCS hero—locked into a 1–1 duel until the eighth inning, when Beckett was lifted. New York then stomped on the Florida bullpen to put the game away. The Yankees were halfway home, and there looked to be no stopping them.

Game 4 figured to be Roger Clemens' farewell, as the all-time great had announced his impending retirement. When Clemens was lifted after seven innings, trailing 3–1, even the Marlins' players respectfully stood and applauded. They stopped cheering when New York tied it up in the ninth, but Alex Gonzalez's 12th-inning homer gave Florida an emotional 4–3 win.

After a perfect first inning in which he threw just eight pitches, big-game pitcher Wells was forced to leave Game 5 due to back spasms. The Yanks had to rush in rookie spot-starter Jose Contreras, and Florida pounced on him for three quick runs, never falling behind and going on to a 6–4 win.

Game 6 was all Josh Beckett. The cocky 22-year-old shut down New York on just five hits to win, 2–0. It was only his second career complete game in the pros, following his NLCS shutout of the Cubs 13 days earlier. Beckett was named Series MVP, and the Marlins were world champions for the second time—even though they had yet to win a divisional title.

FLA (N)

PLAYER/POS	AVG	G	AB	R	H	2B	3B	HR	RB	BB	SO	SB
Josh Beckett, p	.000	1	2	0	0	0	0	0	0	0	2	0
Miguel Cabrera, of	.167	6	24	1	4	0	0	1	3	1	7	0
Luis Castillo, 2b	.154	6	26	1	4	0	0	0	1	0	7	1
Jeff Conine, dh-3, of-3	.333	6	21	4	7	1	0	0	0	3	2	0
Juan Encarnacion, of-5	.182	6	11	1	2	0	0	0	1	1	5	0
Chad Fox, p	.000	2	0	0	0	0	0	0	0	0	0	0
Alex Gonzalez, ss	.273	6	22	3	6	2	0	1	2	0	7	0
Todd Hollandsworth, ph	.000	2	2	0	0	0	0	0	0	0	1	0
Derrek Lee, 1b	.208	6	24	2	5	0	0	0	2	1	7	0
Braden Looper, p	.000	3	0	0	0	0	0	0	0	0	0	0
Mike Lowell, 3b	.217	6	23	1	5	1	0	0	2	2	3	0
Carl Pavano, p	.000	2	2	0	0	0	0	0	0	0	1	0
Brad Penny, p	.500	1	2	0	1	0	0	0	2	0	0	0
Juan Pierre, of	.333	6	21	2	7	2	0	0	3	5	2	1
Mike Redmond, p	.000	1	1	0	0	0	0	0	0	0	0	0
Ivan Rodriguez, c	.273	6	22	2	6	2	0	0	1	1	4	0
Ugueth Urbina, p	.000	2	0	0	0	0	0	0	0	0	0	0
Dontrelle Willis, p	.000	2	0	0	0	0	0	0	0	0	0	0
TOTAL	.232		203	17	47	8	0	2	17	14	48	2

PITCHER	W	L	ERA	G	GS	CG	SV	SHO	IP	H	ER	BB	SO
Josh Beckett	1	1	1.10	2	2	1	0	1	16.3	8	2	5	19
Chad Fox	0	0	6.00	3	0	0	0	0	3.0	4	2	4	4
Rick Helling	0	0	6.75	1	0	0	0	0	2.7	2	2	0	2
Braden Looper	1	0	9.82	4	0	0	0	0	3.7	6	4	0	4
Carl Pavano	0	0	1.00	2	1	0	0	0	9.0	8	1	1	6
Brad Penny	2	0	2.19	2	2	0	0	0	12.3	15	3	5	7
Mark Redman	0	1	15.43	1	1	0	0	0	2.3	5	4	2	2
Ugueth Urbina	0	0	6.00	3	0	0	2	0	3.0	2	2	3	2
Dontrelle Willis	0	0	0.00	3	0	0	0	0	3.7	4	0	2	3
TOTAL	4	2	3.21	21	6	1	2	1	56.0	54	20	22	49

NY (A)

PLAYER/POS	AVG	G	AB	R	H	2B	3B	HR	RB	BB	SO	SB
Aaron Boone, 3b	.143	6	21	1	3	0	0	1	2	0	6	0
Roger Clemens, p	.500	1	2	0	1	0	0	0	0	0	0	0
David Dellucci, of-2	.000	4	2	1	0	0	0	0	0	0	0	0
John Flaherty, c	.000	1	2	0	0	0	0	0	0	0	0	0
Karim Garcia, of	.286	5	14	1	4	0	0	0	0	0	3	0
Jason Giambi, 1b-1, dh-3	.235	6	17	2	4	1	0	1	1	4	3	0
Derek Jeter, ss	.346	6	26	5	9	3	0	0	2	1	7	0
Nick Johnson, 1b-5	.294	6	17	3	5	1	0	0	0	2	3	0
Hideki Matsui, of	.261	6	23	1	6	0	0	1	4	3	2	0
Mike Mussina, p	.000	1	3	0	0	0	0	0	0	0	3	0
Jorge Posada, c	.158	6	19	0	3	1	0	0	1	5	7	1
Juan Rivera, p	.167	4	6	0	1	1	0	0	1	1	1	0
Ruben Sierra, of-1	.250	5	4	0	1	0	1	0	2	1	3	0
Alfonso Soriano, 2b-5, of-1	.227	6	22	2	5	0	0	1	2	2	9	1
Bernie Williams, of	.400	6	25	5	10	2	0	2	5	2	2	0
Enrique Wilson, 2b-1, 3b-1	.500	2	4	0	2	1	0	0	1	1	0	0
TOTAL	.261		207	21	54	10	1	6	21	22	49	2

PITCHER	W	L	ERA	G	GS	CG	SV	SHO	IP	H	ER	BB	SO
Roger Clemens	0	0	3.86	1	1	0	0	0	7.0	8	3	0	5
Jose Contreras	0	1	5.68	4	0	0	0	0	6.3	5	4	5	10
Chris Hammond	0	0	0.00	2	0	0	0	0	2.0	2	0	0	0
Mike Mussina	1	0	1.29	1	1	0	0	0	7.0	7	1	1	9
Jeff Nelson	0	0	0.00	3	0	0	0	0	4.0	4	0	2	5
Andy Pettitte	1	1	0.57	2	2	0	0	0	15.7	12	1	4	14
Mariano Rivera	0	0	0.00	4	0	0	1	0	4.0	2	0	0	4
Jeff Weaver	0	1	9.00	1	0	0	0	0	1.0	1	1	0	0
David Wells	0	1	3.38	2	2	0	0	0	8.0	6	3	2	1
TOTAL	2	4	2.13	17	6	0	1	0	55.0	47	13	14	48

namned Series MVP, and the Marlins were world champions for the second time—even though they had yet to win a divisional title.

GAME 1 at NY OCT 18

FLA 100 020 000   3 7 1
NY 001 001 000   2 9 0
Pitchers: PENNY, Willis (6), Urbina (8) vs WELLS, Nelson (8), Contreras (9)
Home Runs: Williams-NY
Attendance: 55,769

GAME 2 at NY OCT 19

FLA 000 000 001   1 6 0
NY 310 200 00X   6 10 2
Pitchers: REDMAN, Helling (3), Fox (6), Pavano (7), Looper (8) vs PETTITTE, Contreras (9)
Home Runs: Matsui-NY, Soriano-NY
Attendance: 55,750

GAME 3 at FLA OCT 21

NY   000 100 014   6 6 1
FLA 100 000 000   1 8 0
Pitchers: MUSSINA, Rivera (8) vs BECKETT, Willis (8), Fox (8), Looper (9)
Home Runs: Boone-NY, Williams-NY
Attendance: 65,731

GAME 4 at FLA OCT 22

NY   010 000 002 000 3 12 0
FLA 300 000 000 001 4 10 0
Pitchers: Clemens, Nelson (8), Contreras (9), WEAVER (11) vs Pavano, Urbina (9), Fox (10), LOOPER (11)
Home Runs: Cabrera-FLA, Gonzalez-FLA
Attendance: 65,934

GAME 5 at FLA OCT 23

NY   100 000 102   4 12 1
FLA 030 120 00X   6 9 1
Pitchers: Wells, CONTRERAS (2), Hammond (5), Nelson (7) vs PENNY, Willias (8), Looper (9), Urbina (9)
Home Runs: Giambi-NY
Attendance: 65,975

GAME 6 at NY OCT 25

FLA 000 011 000   2 7 0
NY   000 000 000   0 5 1
Pitchers: BECKETT vs PETTITTE
Attendance: 55,773

Chapter 26

The Tiebreakers: One and Three Game Playoffs

By Bruce Markusen

Sometimes a 162-game schedule—or in the case of days gone by, a 154-game docket—is simply not enough to determine the best team in the league, the division, or even among the wild card contenders. Sometimes an extra game (or two, or even three) is needed to determine who should go to the postseason—and who should go home for a long winter of contemplation and regret. In those instances, the ultimate tiebreaking mechanism is required. For that, baseball calls upon a playoff.

Tiebreaker playoff games should not be confused with the term playoffs, which has long been used as an alternate name for the League Championship Series—and later the Division Series. League Championship Series have taken place since 1969, when both the American and National Leagues split into two divisions. In 1994 Major League Baseball initiated three divisions, a wild card qualifying team, and the corresponding Division Series, effectively creating another round of playoffs. These series, however, are on Major League Baseball's annual calendar; no one knows if a playoff will be required to break a tie until the last week—and usually the last day—of the regular season. Just in case, MLB always keeps the Monday after the season ends available for a playoff.

On 10 different occasions, extra games have been needed to break ties between teams that finished the regular season with identical records. Until the divisional format began, these playoffs were needed to determine the league champion. Since then the one-game format has been needed to decide divisional championships and wild card berths. While the games have the distinct feel of the postseason, these tiebreakers are considered regular-season games. All records accrued on these fateful days count toward the players' regular-season totals. Occasionally it has resulted in a home run crown (Eddie Mathews in 1959) or a 20th win (Joe Niekro in 1980), but winning is all that really matters when extra games are put on the schedule.

Sometimes the identity of playoff games can become confusing. For example, some might think that the season-ending 1908 game between the Chicago Cubs and New York Giants was a playoff game, but it was actually a *replaying* of an earlier game that had been suspended and declared a tie because of Fred Merkle's failure to touch second base on an apparent game-winning hit. The first tiebreaking playoff did not take place until 38 years later, when 154 games proved insufficient in determining superiority in the National League. That tie, between the St. Louis Cardinals and Brooklyn Dodgers, resulted in the first best-of-three playoff for the NL pennant. When the American League season ended in a tie between the Boston Red Sox and Cleveland Indians two years later, a one-game playoff was used to settle the score. The NL continued to use three-game playoffs to determine ties until the start of divisional play in 1969. In 1980 the first one-game playoff took place in the National League. That game, however, had one thing in

Gil Hodges
In 1959 the Dodgers first baseman scored the winning run in the 12th inning of Game 2 as Los Angeles swept Milwaukee in a playoff.

common with the first four NL tiebreakers: It involved the Dodgers. And for the fourth time, the Dodgers lost.

Although there were no ties that needed to be broken during the 19th century or for most of the first half of the 20th century, 10 tiebreakers have been required to break deadlocks between pennant-contending teams: seven in the National League and three in the American League. What follows is a recap of those games, as well as the down-to-the-wire events that led to these unscheduled and unforgettable climaxes to the season.

1946: St. Louis vs. Brooklyn

Tiebreaking playoffs were unheard of for the first several decades of the game's history. That unusual trend did not end until 1946, when the Brooklyn Dodgers and St. Louis Cardinals staged one of most memorable races in National League history.

On August 21 the Cardinals tied the Dodgers in the standings, thanks to a doubleheader sweep of the Philadelphia Phillies coupled with Brooklyn's loss to the Cincinnati Reds. The two teams remained deadlocked for four days, until the Redbirds jumped ahead. The Cardinals fell back into a tie the following day, but regained the lead on August 28.

The Cardinals remained in first place until a mid-September series with the Dodgers. After a split of the first two games of the series, Brooklyn manager Leo Durocher surprisingly called upon rookie right-hander Ralph Branca to pitch the rubber match. Under Durocher's original plan, Branca would pitch to only one batter before giving way to a left-hander, thus giving the Dodgers the platoon advantage.

Durocher altered his master plan after watching Branca pitch impressively to his first batter. "The Lip" allowed his rookie pitcher to remain in the game for another batter, and then another inning, and eventually the rest of the game. Branca finished with a three-hit shutout. His unexpected fortune brought the Dodgers within a half-game of the Cardinals.

On Friday, September 27, the Dodgers made up the half-game difference and moved into a first-place tie. Brooklyn won again on Saturday, as did St. Louis. With the pennant now resting on the final day of the regular season, both the Dodgers and the Cardinals lost, prompting the first tiebreaking playoff in major league history.

According to the National League's constitution at the time, the two teams would not be permitted to play a single game, but would have to play a series of games to determine the league's champion. Under the best two-out-of-three format, the Cardinals would host the first game at Sportsman's Park, followed by two games (if necessary) at Ebbets Field in Brooklyn.

Lefthander Howie Pollet pitched Game 1 for St. Louis despite a torn muscle in his throwing shoulder. Working in and out of trouble, he scattered eight hits and held the Dodgers to two runs. Pollet received ample offensive support from 20-year-old catcher Joe Garagiola, who had three hits and two RBIs. Veteran outfielder Terry Moore added three hits, as the Cardinals knocked Branca from the game in the third inning. Buoyed by Moore, Garagiola, and Pollet, the Cardinals claimed the first game of the playoff, 4–2.

In Game 2 the Cardinals erased an early 1–0 deficit by scoring a pair of runs in the top of the second. The Redbirds built up a 5–1 lead with a three-run rally in the fifth, then added three more runs in the seventh and eighth. With an 8–1 advantage and Murry Dickson efficiently striking down the Brooklyn offense, a sweep of the series seemed inevitable.

Then, in the bottom of the ninth, the Dodgers counterpunched. A three-run rally knocked Dickson from the game. With the bases loaded and only one out, the Dodgers brought the tying run to the plate. Relief pitcher Harry "The Cat" Brecheen fanned leadoff hitter Eddie Stanky and pinch hitter Howie Schultz to end the game. The 8–4 win gave the Cardinals a two-game sweep, launching them into the World Series. Furthermore, the tiebreaking playoff turned out to be a harbinger of good things to come, as the Cardinals defeated the Boston Red Sox on Slaughter's memorable "Mad Dash" in Game 7 of the World Series.

GAME 1 AT SPORTSMAN'S PARK, ST. LOUIS, OCTOBER 1, 1946

BROOKLYN	AB	R	H	2B	3B	HR	RBI
Stanky, 2B	3	0	1	0	0	0	0
Lavagetto, 3b	3	0	0	0	0	0	0
Medwick, lf	4	0	1	0	0	0	0
Tepsic, pr	0	0	0	0	0	0	0
Whitman, lf	0	0	0	0	0	0	0
F. Walker, rf	4	0	0	0	0	0	0
Furillo, cf	4	0	0	0	0	0	0
Reese, ss	4	1	2	0	0	0	0
Edwards, c	4	0	2	0	0	0	0
Schultz, 1b	3	1	2	0	0	1	2
Branca, p	1	0	0	0	0	0	0
Higbe, p	0	0	0	0	0	0	0
Rojek, ph	0	0	0	0	0	0	0
Gregg, p	0	0	0	0	0	0	0
Ramazzotti, ph	1	0	0	0	0	0	0
Lombardi, p	0	0	0	0	0	0	0
Melton, p	0	0	0	0	0	0	0

ST. LOUIS	AB	R	H	2B	3B	HR	RBI
Schoendienst, 2b	5	0	2	0	0	0	0
Moore, cf	5	1	3	0	0	0	0
Musial, 1b	4	2	1	0	1	0	0
Slaughter, rf	4	0	2	0	0	0	0
Kurowski, 3b	2	1	0	0	0	0	1
Garagiola, c	4	0	3	0	0	0	2
H. Walker, lf	3	0	1	0	0	0	1
Walker, ss	4	0	0	0	0	0	0
Pollet, p	4	0	0	0	0	0	0

BRO	0 0 1	0 0 0	1 0 0	2	8	0
STL	1 0 2	0 0 0	1 0 x	4	12	1

Bases on balls—Kurowski 2, Musial, Rojek, Lavagetto, Stanky. Sacrifice hit—Schultz. Left on base—Brooklyn 6, St. Louis 11. Error—Pollet. Wild pitch—Melton. Umpires—Reardon, Pinelli, Goetz, Boggess. Time of game—2:48. Attendance—26,012.

PITCHING BROOKLYN	IP	H	R	ER	BB	SO
Branca (L, 3–1)	2.2	6	3	3	2	3
Higbe	1.1	1	0	0	0	0
Gregg	2	1	0	0	1	1
Lombardi	.1	1	1	1	0	0
Melton	1.2	3	0	0	1	0
ST. LOUIS						
Pollet (W, 21–10)	9	8	2	2	3	2

GAME 2 AT EBBETS FIELD, BROOKLYN, OCTOBER 3, 1946

ST. LOUIS	AB	R	H	2B	3B	HR	RBI
Schoendienst, 2b	5	1	1	0	0	0	0
Moore, cf	5	1	2	1	0	0	0
Musial, 1b	4	1	1	1	0	0	0
Kurowski, 3b	2	2	1	0	0	0	2
Slaughter, rf	3	1	1	0	1	0	2
Dusak, lf	3	1	2	0	1	0	1
H. Walker, ph-lf	1	0	0	0	0	0	0
Marion, ss	3	0	1	0	0	0	2
Dickson, p	5	0	2	0	1	0	0
Brecheen, p	0	0	0	0	0	0	0

BROOKLYN	AB	R	H	2B	3B	HR	RBI
Stanky, 2b	5	0	0	0	0	0	0
Whitman, lf	4	0	0	0	0	0	0
Schultz, ph	1	0	0	0	0	0	0
Galan, 3b	4	2	2	1	0	0	0
F. Walker, rf	3	0	0	0	0	0	0
Stevens, 1b	4	1	2	0	1	0	2
Furillo, cf	4	1	1	0	0	0	1
Reese, ss	2	0	0	0	0	0	0
Edwards, c	2	0	1	0	0	0	1
Hatten, p	1	0	0	0	0	0	0
Behrman, p	0	0	0	0	0	0	0
Hermanski, ph	1	0	0	0	0	0	0
Lombardi, p	0	0	0	0	0	0	0
Higbe, p	0	0	0	0	0	0	0
Melton, p	0	0	0	0	0	0	0
Medwick, ph	1	0	0	0	0	0	0
Taylor, p	0	0	0	0	0	0	0
Lavagetto, ph	1	0	0	0	0	0	0

STL	0 2 0	0 3 0	1 2 0	8	13	0
BRO	1 0 0	0 0 0	0 0 3	4	6	0

Bases on balls—F. Walker, Edwards 2, Reese 2, Kurowski 3, Marion, Musial, Slaughter, Lavagetto. Sacrifice hits—Schoendienst, Dusak, Marion. Left on base—St. Louis 11, Brooklyn 7. Wild pitch—Dickson. Umpires—Pinelli, Goetz, Boggess, Reardon. Time of game—2:44. Attendance—31,437.

PITCHING	IP	H	R	ER	BB	SO
ST. LOUIS						
Dickson (W, 15–6)	8.1	5	4	4	5	3
Brecheen	.2	1	0	0	1	2
BROOKLYN						
Hatten (L, 14–11)	4.2	7	5	5	3	0
Behrman	.1	1	0	0	0	0
Lombardi	1.1	1	1	1	2	0
Higbe	1	3	2	2	2	1
Melton	.2	0	0	0	0	0
Taylor	1	1	0	0	0	1

1948: Cleveland vs. Boston

With the Boston Red Sox, Cleveland Indians, and New York Yankees fighting for first place in the American League, a three-way tie at season's end was a distinct possibility. As the season moved into its second-to-last day, the Indians found themselves in first place, with the Red Sox and Yankees each a single game behind.

The Yankees were scheduled to continue a season-ending series against the Red Sox on Saturday, October 2. When the Red Sox defeated the Yankees to push them two games out, they officially eliminated New York from contention. Meanwhile, the Indians won their game against the Tigers to maintain a one-game lead. With Sunday the last day remaining on the regular-season schedule, the Indians needed only to win their final game to clinch the pennant.

That win did not figure to come easily, not with future Hall of Famer Hal Newhouser on the mound for the Tigers. Newhouser allowed only five hits and defeated another future Hall of Famer—Bob Feller—in a 7–1 Detroit win. Coupled with Boston's 10–5 pounding of the Yankees, the loss dropped the Indians into a first-place tie, each team sporting a record of 96–58.

In contrast to the National League's constitution, the American League's rules called for a one-game playoff to break any ties between teams at season's end. Since the Red Sox had won a coin flip conducted by American League president Will Harridge on September 24, Fenway Park would be the site of the AL's first playoff.

Both managers made surprising pitching choices. Indians player-manager Lou Boudreau tabbed rookie Gene Bearden, despite the fact that he had started only two days earlier and would be pitching on one day's rest. Red Sox skipper Joe McCarthy made an even more stunning choice: journeyman Denny Galehouse, a 36-year-old right-hander who had posted a mediocre record of 8–7. Critics wondered why "Marse Joe" hadn't selected left-hander Mel Parnell, whose credentials seemed stronger than those of Galehouse.

Pitching in front of a capacity crowd of 33,957, Galehouse ran into immediate first-inning trouble. After retiring the first two batters, Galehouse surrendered a home run to Boudreau, who reached the screen atop Fenway's Green Monster in left field. The Red Sox countered quickly against Bearden. With one out in the bottom of the first, Johnny Pesky doubled to right-center field and came home on Vern Stephens' single to left. With the game tied in the top of the fourth, Boudreau singled, then moved up to second on Joe Gordon's hit. Ken Keltner followed with a three-run homer to knock Galehouse from the game. Veteran Ellis Kinder promptly allowed a double to Larry Doby, who eventually came around to score on Jim Hegan's infield grounder. The Indians now led by four runs.

The Indians scored another run in the fifth on Boudreau's second home run, but the Red Sox showed signs of life in the bottom of the sixth. After Joe Gordon mishandled a popup by Ted

Williams, Bobby Doerr launched a two-out, two-run homer.

The Sox remained within striking distance until the eighth, when Larry Doby doubled against Kinder and scored on an error by Williams, who failed to handle a long fly ball by Bearden. The Indians added another run in the top of the ninth and Bearden finished off the Red Sox for Cleveland's first pennant since 1920. It also set the stage for a championship performance in the World Series, something the Indians would not duplicate for the next half-century and beyond.

AT FENWAY PARK, BOSTON, OCTOBER 4, 1948

CLEVELAND	AB	R	H	2B	3B	HR	RBI
Mitchell, lf	5	0	1	0	0	0	0
Clark, 1b	2	0	0	0	0	0	0
Robinson, 1b	2	1	1	0	0	0	0
Boudreau, ss	4	3	4	0	0	2	2
Gordon, 2b	4	1	1	0	0	0	0
Keltner, 3b	5	1	3	1	0	1	3
Doby, cf	5	1	2	2	0	0	0
Kennedy, rf	2	0	0	0	0	0	1
Hegan, c	3	1	0	0	0	0	1
Bearden, p	3	0	1	0	0	0	0

BOSTON	AB	R	H	2B	3B	HR	RBI
DiMaggio, cf	4	0	0	0	0	0	0
Pesky, 3b	4	1	1	1	0	0	0
Williams, lf	4	1	1	0	0	0	0
Stephens, ss	4	0	1	0	0	1	2
Doerr, 2b	4	1	1	0	0	1	2
Spence, rf	1	0	0	0	0	0	0
Hitchcock, ph	0	0	0	0	0	0	0
Wright, pr	0	0	0	0	0	0	0
Goodman, 1b	3	0	0	0	0	0	0
Tebbetts, c	4	0	1	0	0	0	0
Galehouse, p	0	0	0	0	0	0	0
Kinder, p	2	0	0	0	0	0	0

CLE	1 0 0	4 1 0	0 1 1	8	13	1
BOS	1 0 0	0 0 2	0 0 0	3	5	1

Bases on balls—Spence 2, Galehouse, Goodman, Hitchcock, Bearden, Boudreau, Hegan, Gordon. Sacrifice hits—Kennedy 2, Robinson. Left on base—Cleveland 7, Boston 5. Errors—Gordon, Williams. Wild pitch—Kinder. Umpires—McGowan, Summers, Rommel, Berry. Time of game—2:24. Attendance—33,957.

PITCHING	IP	H	R	ER	BB	SO
CLEVELAND						
Bearden (W, 20–7)	9	5	3	2	5	6
BOSTON						
Galehouse (L, 8–8)	3	5	4	4	1	1
Kinder	6	8	4	3	3	2

1951: Brooklyn vs. New York

By mid-August, the National League pennant race seemed like a foregone conclusion. With a 13-1/2-game lead over the rival New York Giants, the Brooklyn Dodgers only needed to play a fair brand of ball over the season's final weeks to insure the National League pennant. Or so it seemed.

By September 20 the Giants had managed to cut the lead to a more manageable 4-1/2 games. Still, New York trailed the Dodgers by six full games in the loss column. With only seven games remaining on the schedule, the prospect of catching the Dodgers could be classified as a pipe dream.

The Giants swept a three-game series with the Boston Braves while the Dodgers lost two of three to the Phillies. The sudden developments narrowed the margin to only 2-1/2 games. On September 25 the Dodgers showed more signs of slippage by dropping a doubleheader to the Braves. In the meantime, the Giants took advantage of Brooklyn's woes by winning in Philadelphia. The lead, incredibly, was now down to a single game.

As the Giants took the next two days off, they gleefully watched the Dodgers stumble against Boston and then Philadelphia. Two more Brooklyn losses had left the Dodgers in a flat-footed tie with

the Giants for first place in the National League. Both teams sported identical records of 94–58.

The next day—the final Saturday of the regular season—both the Giants and the Dodgers won, courtesy of shutouts by Sal Maglie and Don Newcombe, respectively. Although the Dodgers had managed to break their losing streak, they remained tied with the Giants—with their regular-season finales scheduled for the next day.

On Sunday, September 30, the Giants posted a 3–2 victory over the Braves behind a five-hitter by Larry Jansen. The Dodgers, needing to win their game against the Phillies to force a tiebreaking playoff series, were in trouble early. Preacher Roe was out of the game and Philadelphia had a 6–1 lead after three innings. The Dodgers fought back over the next two innings, but still trailed, 8–5, as the game moved to the eighth inning.

Knowing that the Giants were on the verge of victory, the Dodgers promptly rallied to score three runs in the eighth to tie, eventually forcing extra innings. In the bottom of the 14th, an injured Jackie Robinson (who had hurt his elbow making a diving catch just two innings earlier) belted a solo home run against Robin Roberts. The blast gave the Dodgers a 9–8 win, preserving a share of first place with the Giants and setting up a best-of-three playoff.

The Dodgers took a 1–0 lead in Game 1 on Andy Pafko's home run in the second inning at Ebbets Field. The Giants retaliated in the fourth, as Bobby Thomson clubbed a two-run homer against Ralph Branca. Monte Irvin added a solo blast of his own in the eighth inning, increasing the advantage to 3–1. Jim Hearn pitched a complete-game five-hitter.

The second game, staged on an overcast day at the Polo Grounds, took on a more offensive-minded tone. The Dodgers reached Sam Jones for two runs on Jackie Robinson's first-inning home run. The Giants responded by putting early-game pressure on Clem Labine, picking up five hits in the first four innings. Labine worked his way out of several jams, stranding eight runners along the way.

The score remained 2–0 until the top of the fifth, when the Dodgers added another run. They scored three more in the sixth, highlighted by a Gil Hodges home run. Unfazed by a 41-minute rain delay in the sixth, Labine returned to the mound with a 6–0 lead in tow and continued to shut down the Giants' attack.

The Dodgers piled on additional runs in the seventh and ninth—spearheaded by Andy Pafko's second home run of the series. Rube Walker, filling in for an injured Roy Campanella behind the plate, added a homer in Brooklyn's 10–0 win.

Still, the Giants had the advantage of playing the final game at the Polo Grounds, giving them the tangible benefit of having the last at bat and the intangible help of a supportive crowd. Brooklyn struck first, however. Giants starter Sal Maglie walked two Dodgers and surrendered a single to Jackie Robinson to produce the first run of the day.

Twenty-game winner Don Newcombe shut out the Giants over the first six innings, but then had to face the middle of New York's order in the seventh. Monte Irvin pounded out a double and moved up to third on a sacrifice bunt by Whitey Lockman. With one out, Bobby Thomson lifted a sacrifice fly to score Irvin with the tying run. Maglie retired leadoff man Carl Furillo for the first out in the eighth, but then yielded singles to Pee Wee Reese and Duke Snider. With runners on first and third, an erratic Maglie uncorked a wild pitch, allowing Reese to score the go-ahead run. Maglie's wayward pitching continued when he walked Jackie

Robinson, once again putting runners on first and third. Pafko and Billy Cox followed with singles, adding two more runs to Brooklyn's total and raising the Dodgers' lead to three runs.

Newcombe, who retired the Giants without incident in the eighth, still looked strong. He entered the ninth with a four-hitter and needed just three outs to put the Dodgers' late-season stumble behind them. The fateful inning began with an infield hit by Alvin Dark. Newk then surrendered a single to Don Mueller, putting runners on first and third while bringing the tying run to the plate in Monte Irvin. Irvin swung underneath a Newcombe delivery, popping it up on the infield for one out. Whitey Lockman followed with a double, bringing home one run and putting the potential tying runs in scoring position.

The game paused for several moments, as an injured Mueller left the game, the result of breaking his ankle during his run to third base. Leo Durocher inserted Clint Hartung as the pinch runner for Mueller. Brooklyn skipper Charlie Dressen also made a change, removing Newcombe. After calling down to the bullpen and conferring with coach Clyde Sukeforth, Dressen called on Ralph Branca, the starter in Game 1.

Branca jumped ahead in the count with a first-pitch strike to Bobby Thomson, who had been a part-time player earlier in the season before Durocher decided to convert him to third base. Since the move from the outfield to the infield, Thomson had batted a scalding .357; Thomson had also homered against Branca in the first game of the playoff series.

As Rookie of the Year Willie Mays waited his turn in the on-deck circle, Branca delivered his second pitch to the plate. Thomson swung and swung hard, prompting a breathless description from longtime Giants broadcaster Russ Hodges:

> There's a long drive! It's going to be, I believe. . . ! The Giants win the pennant! The Giants win the pennant! The Giants win the pennant! The Giants win the pennant! The Giants win the pennant! Bobby Thomson hits into the lower deck of the left-field stands! The Giants win the pennant! And they're going crazy! They're going crazy! Oh-ho! . . . I don't believe it! I don't believe it! I do not believe it! Bobby Thomson . . . hit a line drive into the lower deck of the left-field stands. And this whole place is going crazy!

This frenetic description conveyed, at least in part, the shocking drama of arguably the most famous home run in the history of the game. With one swing, Thomson had enabled the Giants to move on to the World Series, while crushing the hopes of the Dodgers. Unlike the other two playoffs that had occurred over the past five years, the 1951 tiebreaker produced one of the game's truly indelible moments. A half-century later it was still considered by some to be the greatest moment in New York sports history, even though both the Dodgers and Giants moved to California after the 1957 season.

GAME 1 AT EBBETS FIELD, BROOKLYN, OCTOBER 1, 1951

NEW YORK	AB	R	H	2B	3B	HR	RBI
Stanky, 3b	5	0	2	0	0	0	0
Dark, ss	4	0	1	1	0	0	0
Mueller, rf	5	0	0	0	0	0	0
Irvin, lf	4	2	1	0	0	1	1
Lockman, 1b	4	0	1	0	0	0	0
Thomson, 3b	2	1	1	0	0	1	2
Mays, cf	3	0	0	0	0	0	0
Westrum, c	2	0	0	0	0	0	0
Hearn, p	3	0	0	0	0	0	0

BROOKLYN	AB	R	H	2B	3B	HR	RBI
Furillo, rf	4	0	0	0	0	0	0
Reese, ss	3	0	1	0	0	0	0
Snider, cf	4	0	1	0	0	0	0
Robinson, 2b	3	0	1	0	0	0	0
Campanella, c	3	0	0	0	0	0	0
Pafko, lf	3	1	1	0	0	1	1
Hodges, 1b	2	0	0	0	0	0	0
Cox, 3b	3	0	1	0	0	0	0
Branca, p	2	0	0	0	0	0	0
Russell, ph	1	0	0	0	0	0	0
Podbielan, p	0	0	0	0	0	0	0

NY	000	200	010	3	6	1
BRO	010	000	000	1	5	1

Bases on balls—Mays, Thomson, Westrum 2, Dark, Hodges, Reese. Sacrifice hits—Hearn, Thomson. Left on base—New York 10, Brooklyn 2. Errors—Dark, Snider. Hit by pitcher—Branca (Irvin). Umpires—Stewart, Goetz, Jorda, Conlan. Time of game—2:39. Attendance—30,707.

PITCHING NEW YORK	IP	H	R	ER	BB	SO
Hearn (W, 17–9)	9	5	1	1	2	5
BROOKLYN						
Branca (L, 13–11)	8	5	3	3	5	5
Podbielan	1	1	0	0	0	0

GAME 2 AT POLO GROUNDS, NEW YORK, OCTOBER 2, 1951

BROOKLYN	AB	R	H	2B	3B	HR	RBI
Furillo, rf	5	0	0	0	0	0	0
Reese, ss	5	1	2	0	0	0	0
Snider, cf	4	1	2	1	0	0	1
Robinson, 2b	5	1	3	0	0	1	3
Pafko, lf	5	1	1	0	0	1	1
Hodges, 1b	4	2	2	0	0	1	1
Cox, 3b	3	2	0	0	0	0	0
Walker, c	5	1	3	0	0	1	2
Labine, p	4	1	0	0	0	0	0

NEW YORK	AB	R	H	2B	3B	HR	RBI
Stanky, 2b	5	0	1	0	0	0	0
Dark, ss	5	0	0	0	0	0	0
Mueller, rf	4	0	1	0	0	0	0
Irvin, lf	4	0	1	0	0	0	0
Lockman, 1b	3	0	1	0	0	0	0
Thomson, 3b	4	0	1	1	0	0	0
Mays, cf	4	0	1	0	0	0	0
Westrum, c	3	0	0	0	0	0	0
Williams, pr	0	0	0	0	0	0	0
Jones, p	1	0	0	0	0	0	0
Spencer, p	1	0	1	0	0	0	0
Rigney, ph	0	0	0	0	0	0	0
Corwin, p	0	0	0	0	0	0	0
Thompson, ph	1	0	0	0	0	0	0

BRO	200	013	202	10	13	2
NY	000	000	000	0	6	5

Bases on balls—Snider, Labine, Hodges, Cox, Lockman, Rigney, Westrum. Sacrifice hit—Cox. Left on base—New York 11, Brooklyn 8. Errors—Reese, Hodges, Thomson, Mays, Jones, Spencer 2. Umpires—Goetz, Jorda, Conlan, Stewart. Time of game—3:25. Attendance—38,609.

PITCHING BROOKLYN	IP	H	R	ER	BB	SO
Labine (W, 5–1)	9	6	0	0	3	3
NEW YORK						
Jones (L, 6–11)	2.1	4	2	2	1	2
Spencer	3.2	6	4	2	1	0
Corwin	3	3	4	3	2	2

GAME 3 AT POLO GROUNDS, NEW YORK, OCTOBER 3, 1951

BROOKLYN	AB	R	H	2B	3B	HR	RBI
Furillo, rf	5	0	0	0	0	0	0
Reese, ss	4	2	1	0	0	0	0
Snider, cf	3	1	2	0	0	0	0
Robinson, 2b	2	1	1	0	0	0	1
Pafko, lf	4	0	1	0	0	0	1
Hodges, 1b	4	0	0	0	0	0	0
Cox, 3b	4	0	2	0	0	0	1
Walker, c	4	0	1	0	0	0	0
Newcombe, p	4	0	0	0	0	0	0
Branca, p	0	0	0	0	0	0	0

NEW YORK	AB	R	H	2B	3B	HR	RBI
Stanky, 2b	4	0	0	0	0	0	0
Dark, ss	4	1	1	0	0	0	0
Mueller, rf	4	0	1	0	0	0	0
Hartung, pr	0	1	0	0	0	0	0

Irvin, lf	4	1	1	1	0	0	0
Lockman, 1b	3	1	2	1	0	0	1
*Thomson, 3b	4	1	3	1	0	1	4
Mays, cf	3	0	0	0	0	0	0
Westrum, c	0	0	0	0	0	0	0
Rigney, ph	1	0	0	0	0	0	0
Noble, c	0	0	0	0	0	0	0
Maglie, p	2	0	0	0	0	0	0
Thompson, ph	1	0	0	0	0	0	0
Jansen, p	0	0	0	0	0	0	0

BRO	100	000	030	4	8	0
NY	000	000	104	5	8	0

*One out when winning run scored on Thomson's home run. Bases on balls—Reese, Snider, Robinson 2, Westrum 2. Left on base—Brooklyn 7, New York 3. Wild pitch—Maglie. Umpires—Jorda, Conlan, Stewart, Goetz. Time of game—2:28. Attendance—34,320.

PITCHING BROOKLYN	IP	H	R	ER	BB	SO
Newcombe	8.1	7	4	4	2	2
Branca (L, 13–12)	0	1	1	1	0	0
NEW YORK						
Maglie	8	8	4	4	4	6
Jansen (W, 23–11)	1	0	0	0	0	0

1959: Los Angeles vs. Milwaukee

It was only fitting that the 1959 National League pennant race required a tiebreaking playoff game to decide its champion. After all, NL fans had enjoyed one of the most compelling races in the game's history that fall, with the league's lead changing hands seven times in the final nine days of the regular season. Three teams—the Los Angeles Dodgers, Milwaukee Braves, and San Francisco Giants—found themselves in a bizarre tangle over the final week and a half of the season and only narrowly avoided an unprecedented three-way tie at the top of the standings.

Heading into the final day of the regular season, the Braves and Dodgers stood tied for first place, with the Giants a game and a half back but still hopeful because of the potential of sweeping a doubleheader against the Cardinals. The Dodgers soon crushed San Francisco's pennant hopes by clubbing the Chicago Cubs, 7–1, behind the pitching of Roger Craig. That victory rendered the Giants' twinbill meaningless, but only tightened the pressure on the Braves, who were scheduled to host the Philadelphia Phillies. Bob Buhl—a 14-game winner—pitched Milwaukee to a 5–2 win, deadlocking the pennant race after 154 games.

The best-of-three-game playoff opened in Milwaukee the next day, but early-afternoon rain showers caused a 47-minute delay before the start of the game. The rain also damaged the Braves' home-field advantage by limiting the crowd to just over 18,000 at 50,000-seat County Stadium.

Both teams had used their best starting pitchers in the final days of the regular season, forcing managers Walter Alston and Fred Haney to rely on unappealing options in the opener. Alston tabbed left-hander Danny McDevitt, a 10-game winner for Los Angeles but a far less intimidating hurler than either Don Drysdale or Sandy Koufax, and less experienced than Roger Craig. Haney countered with an even more shadowy choice in Carlton Willey, who had won only five of 13 decisions and had not started a game since August 3.

The Dodgers touched Willey early, as Charlie Neal led off with a single, moved up to second on a infield grounder, and came home to score on Norm Larker's hit. After producing a scoreless bottom of the first, the Braves rallied for two runs in the second. McDevitt allowed a walk and two consecutive singles, which tied the game, and then missed badly with his first two pitches to Willey. The sudden ineffectiveness against the bottom of the Braves' order convinced Alston to make a change. He lifted Willey and replaced him with rookie reliever Larry Sherry. He induced a groundball, but

shortstop Maury Wills bobbled it and all runners were safe. Bobby Avila plated the Braves' second run with an infield grounder. Sherry escaped further trouble, but the Braves now led, 2–1.

Willey immediately surrendered singles to Neal, Larker and Gil Hodges in the top of the third to tie the game. Catcher John Roseboro, best known for his defense, hit his 10th home run of the year in the sixth inning to give the Dodgers a 3–2 lead. Sherry made the run stand up as he pitched scoreless ball from the third through the ninth inning.

While the first game had spotlighted the bottom end of each team's starting rotation, Game 2 at the Dodgers' new home at Los Angeles Memorial Coliseum offered a matchup of established aces: Lew Burdette for the Braves and Don Drysdale for the Dodgers. Now on the verge of elimination, the Braves handled Drysdale early, scoring two runs in the first inning. A walk, a double by Hank Aaron, and a single by Frank Torre accounted for the Braves' early rally.

The Dodgers cut the lead in half in the bottom of the first, but the Braves applied more pressure to Drysdale in the second. Johnny Logan singled and moved into scoring position on a base hit by Burdette. Duke Snider's errant throw from center field allowed Logan to score Milwaukee's third run.

Charlie Neal's solo home run in the fourth inning made it a one-run game, but Eddie Mathews countered with his 46th homer. His blast gave him the National League home-run crown, breaking a tie with Chicago's Ernie Banks; more important, his homer boosted Milwaukee's advantage back to two runs. The Braves added another run in the top of the eighth. Given the pitching of Burdette, who had not permitted a Dodger past first base since Neal's fourth-inning blast, a 5–2 lead seemed nearly insurmountable.

Wally Moon opened the bottom of the ninth with a single, followed by a hit by Snider. Hodges then walked to load the bases and push a suddenly vulnerable Burdette from the game. With no one out, Haney called on veteran right-hander Don McMahon.

Norm Larker, one of the heroes in Game 1, dented Milwaukee's lead with a two-run single to draw L.A. within one run and push the tying run to third base. McMahon then gave way to Warren Spahn, who surrendered a sacrifice fly to Carl Furillo that tied the game.

Alston turned the ball over to Stan Williams in the 10th. The hard-throwing right-hander kept the Braves off the board for three innings. In the 12th, Bob Rush, Milwaukee's fifth pitcher of the day, retired the first two Dodgers. He then walked Hodges and allowed a single to Joe Pignatano. Furillo followed by hitting a high bouncer up the middle. Felix Mantilla, who had moved from second base to shortstop following a seventh-inning injury to Johnny Logan, fielded the ball behind the second-base bag. Mantilla's off-balance throw short-hopped Frank Torre at first base. The ball took an unexpected hop to Torre's right and bounced past the first baseman, allowing Hodges to score the winning run.

GAME 1 AT COUNTY STADIUM, MILWAUKEE, SEPTEMBER 28, 1959

LOS ANGELES	AB	R	H	2B	3B	HR	RBI
Gilliam, 3b	4	0	0	0	0	0	0
Neal, 2b	5	1	3	0	0	0	0
Moon, lf	4	1	1	0	0	0	0
Larker, rf	4	0	3	0	0	0	1
Lillis, pr	0	0	0	0	0	0	0
Fairly, rf	0	0	0	0	0	0	0
Hodges, 1b	3	0	1	0	0	0	1
Demeter, cf	4	0	1	0	0	0	0
Roseboro, c	4	1	1	0	0	1	1
Wills, ss	4	0	0	0	0	0	0
McDevitt, p	1	0	0	0	0	0	0
L. Sherry, p	2	0	0	0	0	0	0

MILWAUKEE	AB	R	H	2B	3B	HR	RBI
Avila, 2b	5	0	0	0	0	0	1
Mathews, 3b	4	0	0	0	0	0	0
Aaron, rf	2	0	0	0	0	0	0
Adcock, 1b	3	0	0	0	0	0	0
Pafko, lf	2	0	0	0	0	0	0
Maye, ph-lf	2	0	1	0	0	0	0
Logan, ss	3	1	1	0	0	0	0
Crandall, c	4	1	2	0	0	0	0
Bruton, cf	4	0	1	0	0	0	1
Willey, p	2	0	1	0	0	0	0
Slaughter, ph	1	0	0	0	0	0	0
McMahon, p	0	0	0	0	0	0	0
Torre, ph	1	0	0	0	0	0	0

				R	H	E
LA	1 0 1	0 0 1	0 0 0	3	10	1
MIL	0 2 0	0 0 0	0 0 0	2	6	0

Bases on balls—Aaron 2, Logan, Adcock, Hodges, L. Sherry, Gilliam. Left on base—Los Angeles 8, Milwaukee 8. Errors—Wills. Umpires—Conlan, Barlick, Boggess, Donatelli, Gorman, Jackowski. Time of game—2:40. Attendance—18,297.

PITCHING LOS ANGELES	IP	H	R	ER	BB
McDevitt	1.1	2	2	2	2
L.Sherry (W, 7-2)	7.2	4	0	0	2
MILWAUKEE					
Willey (L, 5–9)	6	8	3	3	2
McMahon	3	2	0	0	1

GAME 2 AT MEMORIAL COLISEUM, LOS ANGELES, SEPTEMBER 29, 1959

MILWAUKEE	AB	R	H	2B	3B	HR	RBI
Bruton, cf	6	0	0	0	0	0	0
Mathews, 3b	4	2	2	0	0	1	1
Aaron, rf	4	1	2	1	0	0	0
Torre, 1b	3	0	1	0	0	0	2
Maye, lf	2	0	0	0	0	0	0
Pafko, ph-lf	1	0	0	0	0	0	0
Slaughter, ph	1	0	0	0	0	0	0
DeMerit, lf	0	0	0	0	0	0	0
Spangler, ph-lf	0	0	0	0	0	0	0
Logan, ss	3	1	2	0	0	0	0
Schoendienst, 2b	1	0	0	0	0	0	0
Vernon, ph	1	0	0	0	0	0	0
Cottier, 2b	0	0	0	0	0	0	0
Adcock, ph	1	0	0	0	0	0	0
Avila, 2b	0	0	0	0	0	0	0
Crandall, c	6	1	1	0	1	0	0
Mantilla, 2b-ss	5	0	1	0	0	0	1
Burdette, p	4	0	1	0	0	0	0
McMahon, p	0	0	0	0	0	0	0
Spahn, p	0	0	0	0	0	0	0
Jay, p	1	0	0	0	0	0	0
Rush, p	1	0	0	0	0	0	0

LOS ANGELES	AB	R	H	2B	3B	HR	RBI
Gilliam, 3b	5	0	1	0	0	0	0
Neal, 2b	6	2	2	0	1	1	1
Moon, rf-lf	6	1	3	0	0	0	1
Snider, cf	4	0	1	0	0	0	0
Lillis, pr	0	1	0	0	0	0	0
Williams, p	2	0	0	0	0	0	0
Hodges, 1b	5	2	2	0	0	0	0
Larker, lf	4	0	2	0	0	0	2
Pignatano, pr-c	1	0	1	0	0	0	0
Roseboro, c	3	0	0	0	0	0	0
*Furillo, ph-rf	2	0	2	0	0	0	1
Wills, ss	5	0	1	0	0	0	0
Drysdale, p	1	0	0	0	0	0	0
Podres, p	1	0	0	0	0	0	0
Churn, p	0	0	0	0	0	0	0
Demeter, ph	1	0	0	0	0	0	0
Koufax, p	0	0	0	0	0	0	0
Labine, p	0	0	0	0	0	0	0
Essegian, ph	0	0	0	0	0	0	0
Fairly, ph	2	0	0	0	0	0	0

					R	H	E
MIL	2 1 0	0 1 0	0 1 0	0 0 0	5	10	0
LA	1 0 0	1 0 0	0 0 3	0 0 1	6	15	0

*Two out when winning run scored on Furillo's ground ball in the bottom of the 12th. Bases on balls—Mathews 2, Aaron 2, Torre 3, DeMerit, Spangler, Gilliam, Hodges. Hit by pitcher—By Jay (Pignatano). Wild pitch—Podres. Passed ball—Pignatano. Umpires—Barlick, Boggess, Donatelli, Conlan, Jackowski, Gorman. Time of game—4:06. Attendance—36,853.

PITCHING	IP	H	R	ER	BB	SO
MILWAUKEE						
Burdette	8	10	5	5	0	4
McMahon	0	1	0	0	0	0
Spahn	.1	1	0	0	0	0
Jay	2.1	1	0	0	1	1
Rush (L, 5–6)	1	2	1	0	1	0
LOS ANGELES						
Drysdale	4.1	6	4	3	2	3
Podres	2.1	3	0	0	1	1
Churn	1.1	1	1	1	0	0
Koufax	.2	0	0	0	3	1
Labine	.1	0	0	0	0	1
Williams (W, 5–5)	3	0	0	0	3	3

1962: San Francisco vs. Los Angeles

After playing outstanding baseball all summer, the Los Angeles Dodgers and San Francisco Giants both stumbled to the finish line. With only two weeks to go in the 1962 season, San Francisco won only six of their next 12 games, but received a major break when the rival Dodgers ran into a slump. Los Angeles went just 3–9 during the same stretch. As a result, the Dodgers held a mere one-game lead over the Giants going into the final day of the season.

With the National League pennant on the line, San Francisco manager Alvin Dark decided that star first baseman Orlando Cepeda didn't give the Giants their best chance of winning the last game. Dark felt Cepeda was exhausted from having played so many games during the regular season after another year of winter ball. As a result Dark benched Cepeda, the same player who had batted over .300 and belted 35 home runs for him during the season. Orlando cried in reaction to the news that he would not start. "That was the worst day of my life," he told Stan Isaacs of *Newsday*.

It wouldn't be a very good day for teammate Felipe Alou, either. San Francisco's starting right fielder also sat out the game—the result of another controversial decision by Dark. Yet the absence of both Cepeda and Alou did not stop the Giants from winning the game. Willie Mays hit a dramatic home run in the bottom of the eighth inning to give the Giants a 2–1 victory over the expansion Houston Colt .45s. With the Dodgers losing their game to the St. Louis Cardinals, the Giants tied Los Angeles atop the National League with a mark of 101–61. Eleven years earlier the same two teams had been forced to play a heart-stopping three-game playoff, but that was when the two clubs were based in New York; now the California clubs would battle it out again—and the series would again be decided by a ninth-inning rally.

Courtesy of a coin flip conducted by National League president Warren Giles, the series opened at San Francisco's Candlestick Park. The Dodgers actually won the flip, but opted to play the second and third games at home, rather than open the series with a single home game at Dodger Stadium. The Giants opened up an early 3–0 lead against a fatigued Sandy Koufax, who allowed a double to Felipe Alou and home runs to Mays and Jim Davenport before departing with no one out in the second.

In the bottom of the sixth inning, Mays and Cepeda hit back-to-back home runs against reliever Larry Sherry to put the game away. San Francisco southpaw Billy Pierce, meanwhile, continued his mastery by the Bay. Pierce's 8–0 complete game was his 12th consecutive win at Candlestick. For the Dodgers, it was their fifth consecutive loss—and their third straight shutout defeat.

Los Angeles hoped that the backdrop of Dodger Stadium would help the team in Game 2, but a disappointing crowd of only 25,321 and a heavy layer of smog hanging over the stadium greeted the club. The Giants scored four runs against Don Drysdale in the sixth to open up a five-run lead. San Francisco starter Jack Sanford blanked the Dodgers for the first five innings, extending the team's scoreless streak to 35 innings.

Without warning, the Dodgers awakened. Jim "Junior" Gilliam reached Sanford for a leadoff walk in the sixth, prompting Alvin Dark to remove his starter. Duke Snider rapped a double against Stu Miller, pushing Gilliam to third and marking the beginning of a hit parade that included three consecutive pinch hits—by Doug Camilli, Andy Carey and Lee Walls. By the time the Giants employed their third reliever of the inning, the Dodgers had managed to score seven times to take a two-run lead.

The Giants rallied to tie the game with a pair of runs in the eighth, but Los Angeles reliever Stan Williams stopped that rally short. The game remained deadlocked until the bottom of the ninth, when Maury Wills and Gilliam both drew walks. With backup outfielder Daryl Spencer scheduled to bat in a clear-cut bunting situation, Dark summoned Gaylord Perry from the bullpen.

Spencer bunted the ball right to Perry, as Jose Pagan raced to cover third base from his regular position at shortstop. Perry appeared to have time to throw to Pagan and eliminate the lead runner, but opted to throw to first instead. With the game-winning run now standing on third, Dark replaced Perry with left-hander Mike McCormick.

McCormick intentionally walked Tommy Davis, loading the bases and bringing lefty Ron Fairly to the plate. A few moments later, Fairly lofted a fly ball to short center field. Although the ball was not hit deep, the fleet Wills was able to score to give the Dodgers a thrilling 8–7 victory.

A much larger crowd of 45,693 fans showed up to watch the visiting Giants open up a 2–0 lead in Game 3. The Giants capitalized on shoddy fielding, which included three errors in the third inning behind starter Johnny Podres. As they had done in the second game, the Dodgers staged a comeback.

Los Angeles scored a run in the fourth and two more in the sixth on a home run by Tommy Davis, with Duke Snider picking up hits in the midst of each rally. The Dodgers added to the lead in the seventh, when Wills collected his fourth straight hit, stole second and third, and came home on Ed Bailey's wild throw down the left-field line. The Dodgers took their 4–2 lead into the ninth inning, but pitching—the club's strength throughout the year—cost them the pennant.

Facing reliever Ed Roebuck, the slap-hitting Matty Alou led off the ninth with a pinch-hit single. With one out, Willie McCovey and Felipe Alou—Matty's brother—each drew walks, loading the bases. Willie Mays followed by hitting a ferocious line drive up the middle, off the hand of Roebuck. The infield hit brought home a run and knocked Roebuck from the game.

Los Angeles manager Walter Alston called on Stan Williams, his intimidating right-hander who liked to throw inside pitches. Most scouts considered Williams one of the toughest pitchers—and perhaps the meanest—in the major leagues.

With the bases still loaded, Orlando Cepeda swung and missed at a rising fastball. Cepeda drove the next pitch deep toward right field. Frank Howard, the Dodgers' 6-foot-9 giant in the outfield, made a reaching stab of the drive, but it was far enough to score pinch runner Ernie Bowman from third base to tie the game.

The Giants then took the lead, scoring a run on a pair of walks (an intentional pass to Ed Bailey and an unintentional one to Jim Davenport). Jose Pagan followed by hitting a groundball that second baseman Larry Burright bobbled, allowing an insurance run to score.

Billy Pierce came on to retire the Dodgers in order in the bottom of the ninth, sealing an incredible 6–4 win—and the first pennant for Horace Stoneham's Giants since 1954. With a dramatic comeback victory in their possession, the Giants were also headed to the World Series for the first time since moving to San Francisco.

GAME 1 AT CANDLESTICK PARK, SAN FRANCISCO, OCTOBER 1, 1962

LOS ANGELES	AB	R	H	2B	3B	HR	RBI
Wills, ss	4	0	0	0	0	0	0
Gilliam, 2b	3	0	0	0	0	0	0
T. Davis, lf	4	0	0	0	0	0	0
Howard, rf	4	0	0	0	0	0	0
Walls, 1b	3	0	0	0	0	0	0
Carey, 3b	3	0	1	0	0	0	0
W. Davis, cf	3	0	0	0	0	0	0
Koufax, p	0	0	0	0	0	0	0
Roebuck, p	1	0	0	0	0	0	0
McMullen, ph	1	0	1	0	0	0	0
Tracewski, pr	0	0	0	0	0	0	0
L. Sherry, p	0	0	0	0	0	0	0
Smith, p	0	0	0	0	0	0	0
Camilli, ph	1	0	1	1	0	0	0
Ortega, p	0	0	0	0	0	0	0
Perranoski, p	0	0	0	0	0	0	0

SAN FRANCISCO	AB	R	H	2B	3B	HR	RBI
Kuenn, lf	5	0	0	0	0	0	0
Hiller, 2b	4	0	1	0	0	0	0
F. Alou, rf	4	1	1	1	0	0	0
Mays, cf	3	3	3	0	0	2	3
Cepeda, 1b	4	1	1	0	0	1	1
Davenport, 3b	3	2	2	0	0	1	1
Bailey, c	2	1	1	0	0	0	0
Pagan, ss	3	0	1	1	0	0	2
Pierce, p	4	0	0	0	0	0	0

```
LA  000  000  000   0  3  1
SF  210  002  03x   8 10  0
```
Bases on balls—Bailey 2, Mays, Davenport, Gilliam. Stolen base—Mays. Sacrifice hit—Pagan. Error—Howard. Umpires—Conlan, Boggess, Donatelli, Landes. Time of game—2:39. Attendance—32,652.

PITCHING LOS ANGELES	IP	H	R	ER	BB	SO
Koufax (L, 14–7)	1	4	3	3	0	0
Roebuck	4	1	0	0	0	2
L.Sherry	.1	3	2	2	1	0
Smith	1.2	1	0	0	0	2
Ortega	.1	0	2	2	2	0
Perranoski	.2	1	1	0	1	0
SAN FRANCISCO						
Pierce (W, 16–6)	9	3	0	0	1	6

GAME 2 AT DODGER STADIUM, LOS ANGELES, OCTOBER 2, 1962

SAN FRANCISCO	AB	R	H	2B	3B	HR	RBI
Hiller, 2b	3	1	1	0	0	0	1
Nieman, ph	1	0	0	0	0	0	0
Bowman, 2b	1	0	0	0	0	0	0
Davenport, 3b	6	1	2	0	0	0	1
Mays, cf	5	0	1	0	0	0	0
McCovey, lf	2	0	1	0	0	0	1
Miller, p	0	0	0	0	0	0	0
O'Dell, p	0	0	0	0	0	0	0
Larsen, p	0	0	0	0	0	0	0
Bailey, ph	1	0	1	0	0	0	1
Boles, pr	0	1	0	0	0	0	0
Bolin, p	0	0	0	0	0	0	0
LeMay, p	0	0	0	0	0	0	0
Perry, p	0	0	0	0	0	0	0
McCormick, p	0	0	0	0	0	0	0
Cepeda, 1b	5	1	1	0	0	0	0
F. Alou, rf	4	0	2	1	0	0	1
Haller, c	1	1	0	0	0	0	0
Orsino, c	1	0	1	0	0	0	1
Pagan, ss	5	1	3	1	0	0	0
Sanford, p	3	1	0	0	0	0	0
M. Alou, lf	0	0	0	0	0	0	0
Kuenn, ph-lf	2	0	0	0	0	0	0

LOS ANGELES	AB	R	H	2B	3B	HR	RBI
Wills, ss	4	1	0	0	0	0	0
Gilliam, 2b-3b	3	1	0	0	0	0	0
Snider, lf	3	1	1	1	0	0	0
Spencer, ph	0	0	0	0	0	0	0
T. Davis, 3b-cf	3	0	1	0	0	0	1
Moon, 1b	2	1	1	0	0	0	0
Fairly, 1b	1	0	1	0	0	0	1
Howard, rf	3	1	1	0	0	0	1
Roseboro, c	2	0	0	0	0	0	0
Camilli, ph-c	2	1	1	0	0	0	0
W. Davis, cf	2	0	0	0	0	0	0
Carey, ph	0	0	0	0	0	0	1
Burright, pr-2b	0	1	0	0	0	0	0
Drysdale, p	2	0	0	0	0	0	0
Roebuck, p	0	0	0	0	0	0	0
Walls, ph	1	1	1	1	0	0	3
Perranoski, p	0	0	0	0	0	0	0
Smith, p	0	0	0	0	0	0	0
Williams, p	1	0	0	0	0	0	0

```
SF  010  004  020   7 13  1
LA  000  007  001   8  7  2
```
Bases on balls—Snider, Howard, Gilliam 2, Moon, Burright, Wills, T. Davis, Haller 2, McCovey 2, F. Alou. Stolen base—Wills. Sacrifice hit—Spencer. Sacrifice flies—T. Davis, Orsino, Fairly. Left on base—San Francisco 13, Los Angeles 7. Errors—Haller, Howard, Drysdale.
Hit by pitcher—By Drysdale (Hiller), by O'Dell (Carey). Umpires—Barlick, Boggess, Donatelli, Conlan. Time of game—4:18. Attendance—25,321.

PITCHING SAN FRANCISCO	IP	H	R	ER	BB	SO
Sanford	5	2	1	1	3	4
Miller	.1	2	3	3	1	0
O'Dell	0	2	3	2	0	0
Larsen	1.2	1	0	0	0	1
Bolin (L, 7–3)	1	0	1	1	2	2
LeMay	0	0	0	0	1	0
Perry	.1	0	0	0	0	0
McCormick	.1	0	0	0	1	0
LOS ANGELES						
Drysdale	5.1	7	5	3	4	4
Roebuck	.2	1	0	0	0	0
Perranoski	1	4	1	1	0	0
Smith	.1	1	1	0	0	0
Williams (W, 14–12)	1.2	0	0	0	1	2

GAME 3 AT DODGER STADIUM, LOS ANGELES, OCTOBER 3, 1962

SAN FRANCISCO	AB	R	H	2B	3B	HR	RBI
Kuenn, lf	5	1	2	0	0	0	1
Hiller, 2b	3	0	1	1	0	0	0
McCovey, ph	0	0	0	0	0	0	0
Bowman, pr-2b	0	1	0	0	0	0	0
F. Alou, rf	4	1	1	0	0	0	0
Mays, cf	3	1	1	0	0	0	1
Cepeda, 1b	4	0	1	0	0	0	1
Bailey, c	4	0	2	0	0	0	0
Davenport, 3b	4	0	1	0	0	0	1
Pagan, ss	5	1	2	0	0	0	0
Marichal, p	2	1	1	0	0	0	0
Larsen, p	0	0	0	0	0	0	0
M. Alou, ph	1	0	1	0	0	0	0
Nieman, ph	1	0	0	0	0	0	0
Pierce, p	0	0	0	0	0	0	0

LOS ANGELES	AB	R	H	2B	3B	HR	RBI
Wills, ss	5	1	4	0	0	0	0
Gilliam, 2b-3b	5	0	0	0	0	0	0
Snider, lf	3	2	2	1	0	0	0
Burright, 2b	1	0	0	0	0	0	0
Walls, ph	1	0	0	0	0	0	0
T. Davis, 3b-lf	3	1	2	0	0	1	2
Moon, 1b	3	0	0	0	0	0	0
Fairly, 1b-rf	0	0	0	0	0	0	0
Howard, rf	4	0	0	0	0	0	1
Harkness, 1b	0	0	0	0	0	0	0
Roseboro, c	3	0	0	0	0	0	0
W. Davis, cf	3	0	0	0	0	0	0
Podres, p	2	0	0	0	0	0	0
Roebuck, p	2	0	0	0	0	0	0
Williams, p	0	0	0	0	0	0	0
Perranoski, p	0	0	0	0	0	0	0

```
SF  002  000  004   6 13  3
LA  000  102  100   4  8  4
```
Bases on balls—T. Davis, Roseboro, W. Davis, Mays 2, McCovey, F. Alou, Bailey, Davenport. Stolen bases—Wills 3, T. Davis. Sacrifice hits—Hiller, Marichal, Fairly. Sacrifice fly—Cepeda. Left on base—San Francisco 12, Los Angeles 8.

Errors—Bailey, Pagan, Marichal, Gilliam, Burright, Roseboro, Podres.
Wild pitch—Williams. Umpires—Boggess, Donatelli, Conlan, Barlick.
Time of game—3:00. Attendance—45,693.

PITCHING	IP	H	R	ER	BB	SO
SAN FRANCISCO						
Marichal	7	8	4	3	1	2
Larsen (W, 5–4)	1	0	0	0	2	1
Pierce	1	0	0	0	0	0
LOS ANGELES						
Podres	5	9	2	1	1	0
Roebuck (L, 10–2)	3.1	4	4	3	3	0
Williams	.1	0	0	0	2	0
Perranoski	.1	0	0	0	0	1

1978: New York vs. Boston

Perhaps the most memorable one-game playoff took place in 1978, when the Boston Red Sox and New York Yankees met in Fenway Park's October twilight to decide the championship of the American League East. It was the culmination of one of baseball's greatest divisional races.

Riddled with injuries to key players like Rich Gossage, and laden with controversies involving the triumvirate of Reggie Jackson, Billy Martin and George Steinbrenner, the Yankees had endured a miserable first half of the 1978 season. On July 19 the Yankees reached a low-water mark when they fell 14 games behind Boston. Martin's decision to resign four days later paved the way for the hiring of Bob Lemon, who had recently been fired by the White Sox. Lemon, a Hall of Fame pitcher during his playing days, quickly restored order by ignoring a tantrum thrown by Jackson and fining Mickey Rivers and Roy White for breaking team rules. Under Lemon's calming leadership, and aided by the continuing domination of ace left-hander Ron Guidry, the Yankees regrouped and slowly climbed back into contention in the East. (A New York City newspaper strike didn't hurt, either; beat writers were no longer around to fan the flames of controversy that had marked the first half of the season.)

By early September the Yankees moved within four games of the Red Sox, just in time for the start of a quartet of head-to-head games. Four days and one famed "Boston Massacre" later, there was a tie for first place in the AL East.

The Yankees eventually moved past the Red Sox, but Boston reeled off seven straight wins to close within one game of first place heading into the final day of the season. When Cleveland's Rick Waits blanked the Yankees in the Sunday finale, Boston found the door to the pennant ajar. The Red Sox shut out the Toronto Blue Jays, forcing a one-game playoff.

Having won a coin toss in September, the Red Sox enjoyed the advantage of hosting the matchup with the Yankees at Fenway Park. Red Sox manager Don Zimmer selected right-hander Mike Torrez, who had won the final game of the previous season's World Series for the Yankees before departing as a free agent. Guidry, who had won 24 of 27 decisions, took the mound for New York.

Carl Yastrzemski started the scoring by driving one of Guidry's pitches inside the right-field foul pole. In the sixth inning the Red Sox added to the lead. Leadoff batter Rick Burleson pounded a double and moved up to third on Jerry Remy's sacrifice bunt. Jim Rice, who would win the American League's Most Valuable Player Award over Guidry, followed with a single to center field. Rice's 139th RBI of the season gave the Sox a seemingly safe 2–0 lead.

Torrez still looked strong as he retired Graig Nettles to start the seventh inning, but Chris Chambliss and Roy White followed with back-to-back singles. Bob Lemon then sent veteran Jim Spencer to the plate as a pinch hitter for Brian Doyle, a light-hitting second baseman. Spencer failed to deliver, managing only a harmless fly

ball. With two on and two out, ninth-place hitter Bucky Dent stepped to the plate.

Second-guessers were already wondering why Lemon wasn't lifting Dent for a pinch hitter. The Yankees could have called on any one of three formidable veterans in the pinch: Jay Johnstone, Gary Thomasson, or Cliff Johnson. Since Lemon had already pinch hit for Doyle, and with Fred Stanley scheduled to come into the game to take his place at second base, Lemon had no other middle infielders at his disposal. The situation seemed to favor the Red Sox.

When Torrez delivered his second pitch, Dent fouled it directly off his left foot. Dent hobbled back to the dugout, changed his bat, and returned to the plate. On the next pitch he lifted a fly ball toward left field. If Dent had hit a ball of such moderate depth at Yankee Stadium, it would have been caught well in front of the warning track. But at Fenway Park the ball had plenty of depth to reach the park's famed left-field fence. But did it have enough height to clear the wall and land in the netting above the Green Monster?

Fans watching the game on television back in New York struggled to see the ball against the October background of late afternoon sun and shadows. "Deep to left," cried Bill White, announcing the game on WPIX-TV in New York. "That ball is . . . gone! Home run!" It was just Dent's fifth home run of the year and the defining moment in his career—as well as Torrez's.

There were several critical moments still to come. Later that same inning, Thurman Munson provided an insurance run with an RBI double. In the top of the eighth, Jackson gave the Yankees a three-run lead with a monster home run to center field. The Red Sox rallied for two runs in the bottom of the eighth against Gossage and continued to apply pressure in the ninth. With Burleson on first, Jerry Remy lined a ball solidly toward right field. Draped and blinded by the Fenway sun, Lou Piniella had no idea of the ball's location. He didn't see the ball until it landed on the outfield grass, and then stabbed at it with his glove. Somehow Piniella fielded the ball cleanly, holding Burleson at second base. Instead of having the tying run on third with only one out, the Red Sox still needed to advance their lead runner two more bases to even the game.

Jim Rice followed with a fly ball to right field, which would have scored Burleson easily had he already been on third base. As it was, Burleson had to settle for advancing from second to third. With two outs, Yastrzemski came to the plate. Gossage tried to throw his best pitch—a rising fastball—past the slowed swing of the aging Yaz. Down to his final strike, Yastrzemski swung late and lofted a popup down the third base line. Straddling the foul line, Graig Nettles cradled the ball with two hands, ending one of baseball's most classic pressure-filled games as well as one of its most thrilling races.

AT FENWAY PARK, BOSTON, OCTOBER 2, 1978

NEW YORK	AB	R	H	2B	3B	HR	RBI
Rivers, cf	2	1	1	1	0	0	0
Blair, ph-cf	1	0	1	0	0	0	0
Munson, c	5	0	1	1	0	0	1
Piniella, rf	4	0	1	0	0	0	0
Jackson, dh	4	1	1	0	0	1	1
Nettles, 3b	4	0	0	0	0	0	0
Chambliss, 1b	4	1	1	0	0	0	0
White, lf	3	1	1	0	0	0	0
Thomasson, lf	0	0	0	0	0	0	0
Doyle, 2b	2	0	0	0	0	0	0
Spencer, ph	1	0	0	0	0	0	0
F. Stanley, 2b	1	0	0	0	0	0	0
Dent, ss	4	1	1	0	0	1	3
Guidry, p	0	0	0	0	0	0	0
Gossage, p	0	0	0	0	0	0	0
BOSTON	**AB**	**R**	**H**	**2B**	**3B**	**HR**	**RBI**
Burleson, ss	4	1	1	1	0	0	0
Remy, 2b	4	1	2	1	0	0	0

Rice, rf	5	0	1	0	0	0	1
Yastrzemski, lf	5	2	2	0	0	1	2
Fisk, c	3	0	1	0	0	0	0
Lynn, cf	4	0	1	0	0	0	1
Hobson, dh	4	0	1	0	0	0	0
Scott, 1b	4	0	2	1	0	0	0
Brohamer, 3b	1	0	0	0	0	0	0
Bailey, ph	1	0	0	0	0	0	0
Duffy, 3b	0	0	0	0	0	0	0
Evans, ph	1	0	0	0	0	0	0
Torrez, p	0	0	0	0	0	0	0
B. Stanley, p	0	0	0	0	0	0	0
Hassler, p	0	0	0	0	0	0	0
Drago, p	0	0	0	0	0	0	0

NY	000	000	410	5	8	0
BOS	010	001	020	4	11	0

Bases on balls—Rivers 2, White, Burleson, Fisk. Stolen bases—Rivers 2. Sacrifice hits—Brohamer, Remy. Left on base—New York 6, Boston 9. Passed ball—Munson. Umpires—Denkinger, Evans, Clark, Palermo. Time of game—2:52. Attendance—32,925.

PITCHING NEW YORK	IP	H	R	ER	BB	SO
Guidry (W, 25–3)	6.1	6	2	2	1	5
Gossage (Save 27)	2.2	5	2	2	1	2
BOSTON						
Torrez (L, 16–13)	6.2	5	4	4	3	4
Stanley	.1	2	1	1	0	0
Hassler	1.2	1	0	0	0	2
Drago	.1	0	0	0	0	0

1980: Houston vs. Los Angeles

The identity of the first-place finisher in the National League West seemed like a foregone conclusion. The Houston Astros held a three-game lead over the second-place Los Angeles Dodgers with only three games to play in the regular season. Of course, it helped the Dodgers that they were scheduled to play those three games against the Astros. Additionally, Los Angeles would have the comfort of playing at Dodger Stadium. Still, the Dodgers faced a daunting task; they would have to sweep the Astros in the weekend three-game set just to force a tiebreaking game on Monday afternoon.

The Dodgers won Friday's game in extra innings, thanks to a masterful pitching relief effort by recently recalled left-hander Fernando Valenzuela. Los Angeles also won Saturday's game, 2–1, as veteran southpaw Jerry Reuss outdueled Nolan Ryan. And then on Sunday, rookie Steve Howe notched a victory in relief as the Dodgers again scraped by the Astros, 4–3. Somehow, the Dodgers had won all three games—all by one-run margins. A one-game playoff would now be needed to determine the winner of the National League's crown—and an earlier coin flip had determined the game would be played in Los Angeles. Unlike the first four National League tiebreakers played before the start of divisional play in 1969, this would be the first one-game playoff—the others had all been best-of-three-game series. It would, however, be the same in one respect: For the fifth time it would involve the Dodgers.

In spite of having momentum and home-field advantage in their favor, the Dodgers experienced moments of uncertainty early in the tiebreaking game. Second baseman Davey Lopes bobbled Terry Puhl's leadoff grounder for an error. Later in the inning, catcher Joe Ferguson dropped a throw at the plate, enabling Puhl to score the first run of the game. Cesar Cedeno followed with another run-scoring ground ball, giving the Astros a 2–0 jump.

Having capitalized on the Dodgers' unsettled defense, Astros hitters took on a more threatening pose in the third. Enos Cabell singled against starter Dave Goltz and then came home to score on an unlikely home run by Art Howe, Houston's singles-hitting first baseman. Houston continued to expand its lead in the fourth, knocking a wobbling Goltz from the game. Puhl led off with a single and then stole both second and third base. After walks to

Cabell and Joe Morgan, Jose Cruz lofted a sacrifice fly to score Puhl. Two batters later, Howe added to his clutch-hitting resume by depositing a single into center field, increasing Houston's advantage to seven runs.

In the bottom of the fourth, veteran knuckleballer Joe Niekro showed small signs of cracking by allowing the Dodgers to score their first run of the afternoon on a single by Rick Monday. Niekro tossed scoreless ball over the final five innings. His complete-game six-hitter gave him his second consecutive 20-win season—and clinched the first division title in the history of the Houston franchise. The victory also set the stage for one of the league's most dramatic Championship Series: a taut five-game struggle between Houston and Philadelphia.

HOUSTON	AB	R	H	2B	3B	HR	RBI
Puhl, rf	5	2	1	0	0	0	0
Cabell, 3b	4	2	2	0	0	0	0
Bergman, 1b	0	0	0	0	0	0	0
Morgan, 2b	2	1	0	0	0	0	0
Landestoy, 2b	2	0	0	0	0	0	0
Cruz, lf	4	0	1	0	0	0	1
Cedeno, cf	4	1	1	0	0	0	1
A.Howe, 1b-3b	5	1	3	0	0	1	4
Ashby, c	4	0	1	0	0	0	0
Reynolds, ss	4	0	3	1	0	0	0
Niekro, p	2	0	0	0	0	0	0

LOS ANGELES	AB	R	H	2B	3B	HR	RBI
Lopes, 2b	4	0	0	0	0	0	0
S.Howe, p	0	0	0	0	0	0	0
Johnstone, rf	4	0	0	0	0	0	0
Baker, lf	4	1	1	0	0	0	0
Garvey, 1b	4	0	0	0	0	0	0
Monday, cf	3	0	1	0	0	0	1
Ferguson, c	4	0	1	0	0	0	0
Hatcher, 3b	3	0	1	0	0	0	0
Thomasson, ph	1	0	0	0	0	0	0
Thomas, ss	3	0	2	0	0	0	0
Goltz, p	0	0	0	0	0	0	0
Law, ph	1	0	0	0	0	0	0
Sutcliffe, p	0	0	0	0	0	0	0
Beckwith, p	0	0	0	0	0	0	0
Castillo, p	0	0	0	0	0	0	0
Davalillo, ph	1	0	0	0	0	0	0
Valenzuela, p	0	0	0	0	0	0	0
Perconte, ph-2b	2	0	0	0	0	0	0

HOU	202	300	000	7	12	1
LA	000	100	000	1	6	2

Bases on balls—Cabell, Morgan, Cedeno, Ashby, Monday, Thomas. Stolen bases—Cabell, Cedeno, Puhl 2. Sacrifice hits—Niekro 2. Sacrifice flies—Cruz. Passed ball—Ashby. Umpires—Harvey, Colosi, Runge, Dale. Time of game—3:10. Attendance—51,127.

PITCHING HOUSTON	IP	H	R	ER	BB	SO
Niekro (W, 20–12)	9	6	1	0	2	6
LOS ANGELES						
Goltz (L, 7–11)	3	8	4	2	0	2
Sutcliffe	.1	1	3	3	2	0
Beckwith	.1	1	0	0	1	0
Castillo	1.1	1	0	0	1	2
Valenzuela	2	1	0	0	0	1
S.Howe	2	0	0	0	0	0

1995: Seattle vs. California

After tiebreaking playoff games had occurred twice in a three-year span, there were none for a decade and a half. And for most of the strike-shortened 1995 season, the possibility of a tiebreaking game seemed remote, at best, in the American League West. By August 9 the California Angels led the second-place Seattle Mariners by 11 games. By August 20 they had stretched their cushion to 12-1/2 games—the largest lead in the team's checkered history.

Unfortunately for the Angels, the final two months of the regular season would reflect the futility of a franchise that had repeatedly failed in its quest to make beloved owner Gene Autry a World

Series participant. From August 25 to September 26 the Angels won a grand total of six games. A pair of nine-game losing streaks contributed to California's collapse, which saw the Angels' lead completely disintegrate into a three-game deficit.

The Angels rallied to win their final five games, allowing them to draw into a deadlock with the Mariners at the end of the regular-season schedule. The Angels, however, faced two imposing obstacles in trying to win a tiebreaking playoff game. First, the club would have to play the elimination game at the Kingdome, where the Mariners had developed a powerful home-field advantage thanks to their suddenly clamorous fans and an ear-numbing sound system. More important, the Angels would have to overcome the extraordinary pitching of Cy Young Award favorite Randy Johnson, winner of 17 of 19 decisions.

Ironically, the Angels countered with veteran left-hander Mark Langston, who had been the Mariners' ace during the late 1980s. From 1984 to mid-1989, Langston had won 79 games as one of the Mariners' few bright spots. Then came a trade to the pennant-contending Montreal Expos, whose return package featured three players, including a wild and uncertain prospect named Randy Johnson.

Over the first four innings, Langston matched Johnson in a scoreless duel. Seattle's offense finally broke through in the fifth, pushing across a single run against a stingy Langston. Given Johnson's domination during the regular season, a 1–0 lead seemed monumental. Still, the Angels had managed to keep the game close, giving their dangerous lineup (one of only two AL teams during the shortened 1995 season to score more than 800 runs) a reasonable chance to draw even.

The Angels needed only one swing of the bat to tie the game, but California could not even reach base against an impervious Johnson. The 6-foot-10 southpaw retired the first 17 batters he faced until California's ninth-place hitter, the pesky Rex Hudler, finally managed a two-out single. Hudler was left stranded when Johnson retired leadoff man Tony Phillips.

With their 1–0 lead still intact, Mike Blowers led off the bottom of the seventh with a single. Seattle manager Lou Piniella asked Tino Martinez to lay down a sacrifice bunt, but second baseman Hudler made a last-minute break in covering first, forcing a late throw by Langston. Dan Wilson followed with another sacrifice bunt, moving both runners up. After Langston hit Joey Cora with a pitch, Vince Coleman laced a line drive to right field, where Tim Salmon made the catch. To the surprise of some Mariners (especially an irate Coleman), Blowers did not tag. The bases remained loaded as the slap-hitting Luis Sojo waddled to the plate.

Just one out away from escaping what had seemed like a hopeless jam, Langston made a good pitch to Sojo, breaking his bat. Sojo fought off the pitch with his typical opposite-field swing, resulting in a line drive down the right-field line. As the ball skirted into the bullpen, both Blowers and Martinez scored. Cora also rounded third and decided to challenge the arm of Langston, who had fielded the relay from Tim Salmon in right. Langston, a seven-time Gold Glove winner, double-pumped and then made a poor throw past catcher Andy Allanson. By the time Allanson had retrieved the ball and thrown to Langston at the plate, not only had Cora scored, but Sojo had raced home as well.

The Mariners added four more runs in the eighth, expanding their lead to 9–0. Johnson allowed a home run to Phillips in the ninth, but it mattered little, other than denying Johnson a shutout. The 9–1 victory put the Mariners in the postseason for the first

time in the franchise's 19-year history and set the stage for a stunning five-game Division Series conquest of the New York Yankees.

As for the fallen Angels, they could not even console themselves with the newly created avenue to the postseason: the wild card. California's 76–67 record left the team 1-1/2 games behind the Yankees. Gene Autry never saw his Angels reach the World Series; the club was sold the following year and the Hollywood legend died in 1998.

AT THE KINGDOME, SEATTLE, OCTOBER 2, 1995

CALIFORNIA	AB	R	H	2B	3B	HR	RBI
Phillips, 3b	4	1	1	0	0	1	1
DiSarcina, ss	3	0	0	0	0	0	0
Owen, ph	1	0	0	0	0	0	0
Edmonds, cf	3	0	0	0	0	0	0
Perez, ph	1	0	0	0	0	0	0
Salmon, rf	4	0	0	0	0	0	0
Davis, dh	2	0	0	0	0	0	0
Snow, 1b	3	0	0	0	0	0	0
Anderson, lf	2	0	0	0	0	0	0
Gallagher, ph-lf	1	0	0	0	0	0	0
Allanson, c	2	0	0	0	0	0	0
Gonzales, ph	1	0	1	1	0	0	0
Fabregas, c	0	0	0	0	0	0	0
Hudler, 2b	3	0	1	0	0	0	0
Langston, p	0	0	0	0	0	0	0
Patterson, p	0	0	0	0	0	0	0
James, p	0	0	0	0	0	0	0
Holzemer, p	0	0	0	0	0	0	0
Habyan, p	0	0	0	0	0	0	0

SEATTLE	AB	R	H	2B	3B	HR	RBI
Coleman, lf	5	0	2	0	0	0	1
Sojo, ss	3	1	2	1	0	0	3
Griffey, cf	3	0	0	0	0	0	0
E. Martinez, dh	3	1	2	0	0	0	0
Buhner, rf	4	1	1	0	0	0	0
Blowers, 3b	3	2	2	0	0	0	1
T. Martinez, 1b	2	2	1	0	0	0	0
Wilson, c	3	1	1	1	0	0	2
Cora, 2b	2	1	1	0	0	0	1
Johnson, p	0	0	0	0	0	0	0

CAL	000	000	001	1	3	1	
SEA	000	010	44x	9	12	0	

Bases on balls—Davis, Griffey, E. Martinez, Blowers, T. Martinez. Sacrifice hits—Sojo, T. Martinez, Wilson. Sacrifice fly—Cora. Left on base—California 3, Seattle 4. Error—Langston. Hit by pitch—By Langston (Cora). Umpires—Shulock, Evans, Young, Kosc, Johnson, Kaiser. Time of game—2:50. Attendance—52,356.

PITCHING	IP	H	R	ER	BB	SO
CALIFORNIA						
Langston (L, 15–7)	6.2	8	5	4	3	2
Patterson	.1	0	0	0	0	1
James	0	2	3	3	1	0
Holzemer	0	1	1	1	0	0
Habyan	1	1	0	0	0	1
SEATTLE						
Johnson (W, 18–2)	9	3	1	1	1	12

1998: Chicago vs. San Francisco

While tiebreaking playoff games had been needed to determine the winners of pennant races and divisional races, the 1998 season created the necessity for a different kind of tiebreaker: one that would determine the wild card, which had been introduced only three years earlier. Two surprising second-place teams, the Chicago Cubs from the Central Division and the San Francisco Giants from the Western Division, finished the regular season with identical records. The two teams arrived at that record in vastly different ways, as the Cubs dropped five of their last seven games, while the Giants won six of their last seven. Yet the Giants easily could have won the wild card without a tiebreaker, if only they had been able to maintain a 7–0 lead over Colorado in their 162nd game of the season. Instead, the Giants blew the lead and lost an 8–7 heartbreaker on a home run by Neifi Perez, mandating a one-game playoff against the Cubs. It could have been weirder—if the New

York Mets had beaten the Atlanta Braves on the final day of the season, it would have created the first playoff involving three teams.

In addition to making history as the first wild-card tiebreaker, the one-game matchup between the Cubs and Giants represented the first time that a tiebreaker would be played at night. Ironically, the backdrop would be provided by the historic presence of Wrigley Field, the last existing ballpark to install lights. Chicago's Steve Trachsel opposed San Francisco's Mark Gardner in a matchup of veteran right-handers.

During the regular season, Trachsel had gained unwanted notoriety by allowing Mark McGwire's record-breaking 62nd home run. Now, less than a month later, Trachsel was taking a no-hitter into the seventh inning. With one out in the top of the seventh, Giants catcher Brent Mayne broke through with a single, but was left stranded when Matt Karchner picked up the third out in relief of Trachsel.

By the time Trachsel's no-hit bid came to an end, the Cubs had built up a 4–0 lead. The ageless Gary Gaetti—who had been signed in midseason after being released by the Cardinals—had kick-started Chicago's offense with a two-run homer in the bottom of the fifth. The Cubs added to their advantage in the bottom of the sixth, when they loaded the bases and set the stage for a two-run single by pinch hitter Matt Mieske.

The offensive fireworks of supporting cast members like Mieske and Gaetti overshadowed the performance of Sammy Sosa, whose season-long pursuit with McGwire of the 37-year-old home run record of Roger Maris had helped rejuvenate the sport. Sosa did not homer in the tiebreaker against the Giants, leaving him with 66 home runs, four shy of McGwire's total but still the second-highest total ever. Sosa nonetheless had two hits in four at bats against San Francisco pitching.

With a 4–0 lead in tow, Cubs manager Jim Riggleman turned to his bullpen, but not his regular relievers. Lacking confidence in his usual corps of middle men, Riggleman called on a pair of starting pitchers—Kevin Tapani and Terry Mulholland—to pitch the seventh and eighth. The decision to use Mulholland was surprising, given that the veteran wild card had thrown 121 pitches in an eight-inning stint the previous day.

Neither Tapani nor Mulholland pitched well, prompting Riggleman to call on another overworked pitcher, closer Rod Beck. With one out in the ninth inning and the Giants in the midst of a three-run rally, Beck retired the dangerous Jeff Kent. Beck would now have to face veteran slugger Joe Carter, who was hitless in three official at bats. Ironically, the 1993 World Series hero had started his career at Wrigley Field with the Cubs, only to be traded to the Indians as part of the famed 1984 deal that brought Rick Sutcliffe and his division-winning pitching to the Windy City. Now on the verge of retirement, Carter hoped he had enough bat speed left to hit a two-run homer, which would tie the game. Carter swung hard at a Beck delivery but popped the ball up meekly on the infield. Chicago's 5–3 victory earned the franchise its first trip to the postseason since 1989.

AT WRIGLEY FIELD, CHICAGO, SEPTEMBER 28, 1998

SAN FRANCISCO	AB	R	H	2B	3B	HR	RBI
Javier, cf	3	1	1	1	0	0	0
Aurilia, ss	3	0	0	0	0	0	0
Dunston, ph-ss	1	0	1	0	0	0	0
Burks, ph	0	0	0	0	0	0	0
Sanchez, pr	0	0	0	0	0	0	0
Bonds, lf	4	0	0	0	0	0	1
Kent, 2b	4	0	0	0	0	0	1
Carter, rf	4	0	0	0	0	0	0

	AB	R	H	2B	3B	HR	RBI
Snow, 1b	3	0	1	0	1	0	0
Hayes, 3b	3	0	0	0	0	0	0
Mesa, p	0	0	0	0	0	0	0
B. Johnson, c	2	0	0	0	0	0	0
Mayne, ph-c	2	1	2	0	0	0	0
Gardner, p	2	0	0	0	0	0	0
Rodriguez, p	0	0	0	0	0	0	0
Johnstone, p	0	0	0	0	0	0	0
Rios, ph	0	0	0	0	0	0	0
Ortiz, p	0	0	0	0	0	0	0
Morman, p	0	0	0	0	0	0	0
Mueller, 3b	1	1	1	0	0	0	0

CHICAGO	AB	R	H	2B	3B	HR	RBI
L. Johnson, cf	4	1	1	0	0	0	0
Morandini, 2b	4	0	1	0	0	0	0
Sosa, rf	4	2	2	0	0	0	0
Grace, 1b	3	0	2	1	0	0	0
Rodriguez, lf	2	1	1	0	0	0	0
Mieske, ph-lf	1	0	1	0	0	0	2
Karchner, p	0	0	0	0	0	0	0
Heredia, p	0	0	0	0	0	0	0
Tapani, p	1	0	0	0	0	0	0
Mulholland, p	0	0	0	0	0	0	0
Beck, p	0	0	0	0	0	0	0
Gaetti, 3b	4	1	1	0	0	1	2
Houston, c	3	0	0	0	0	0	0
Hernandez, ss	2	0	1	0	0	0	0
Trachsel, p	1	0	0	0	0	0	0
Merced, lf	1	0	0	0	0	0	0

SF	000	000	003	3	6	0	
CHI	000	022	01X	5	10	0	

Bases on balls—Javier 2, Burks, Carter, Snow, Hayes, Rios, Grace, Hernandez. Sacrifice—Trachsel. Sacrifice fly—Bonds. Stolen base—Hernandez. Left on base—San Francisco 11, Chicago 4. Umpires—Froemming, Rippley, Darling, Winters, Poncino, Vanover. Time of game—3:41. Attendance—39,556.

PITCHING SAN FRANCISCO	IP	H	R	ER	BB	SO
Gardner (L, 13–6)	5.1	6	4	4	1	2
R. Rodriguez	0	1	0	0	1	0
Johnstone	.2	0	0	0	0	0
Ortiz	.2	1	0	0	0	0
Morman	.2	0	0	0	0	1
Mesa	.2	2	1	1	0	0
CHICAGO						
Trachsel (W, 15–8)	6.1	1	0	0	6	6
Karchner	.1	1	0	0	0	0
Heredia	.1	0	0	0	0	0
Tapani	1.0	3	2	2	0	0
Mulholland	.1	1	1	1	1	0
Beck (Save 51)	.2	0	0	0	0	0

1999: New York vs. Cincinnati

On September 19, 1999, the New York Mets opened up a four-game lead over the Cincinnati Reds for the wild-card berth in the National League playoff race. With only 10 days remaining in the regular season, the identity of the final playoff team in the NL seemed certain. Well, not quite so certain.

The Mets suddenly lost seven consecutive games, spurring rumors that embattled manager Bobby Valentine might be fired *before* the season came to an end. Just as the Mets reached the depths of depression, Valentine remained aboard and the team rebounded. After sweeping the final three regularly scheduled games against the Pittsburgh Pirates, the Mets insured themselves of at least a tie with the Cincinnati Reds.

In the meantime, the Reds experienced a rollercoaster conclusion to their season. They swept a four-game weekend series from the St. Louis Cardinals, but followed that up with a split of a two-game set with the Houston Astros. Cincinnati then lost the first two games of their final series to the lowly Milwaukee Brewers. On the final Sunday, the Reds had to wait out a 347-minute rain delay. By the time the rain had subsided and the game had been played to a 7–1 finish, an exhausted group of Reds prepared for a sudden-death winner-take-all match with the rejuvenated Mets.

As fortune would have it, the Mets could confidently hand the

ball to their left-handed ace, Al Leiter, who would pitch on his usual four days' rest. In contrast, the latest turn in Cincinnati's starting rotation fell upon journeyman Steve Parris. Although Parris had surprised observers by winning 11 of 14 decisions during the season, his pedigree lacked the impressiveness of Leiter, who had once started the seventh game of a World Series.

Playing in front of a capacity crowd of 54,621 at Cincinnati's Cinergy Field, the Mets took advantage of a shaky Parris from the opening pitch. After Rickey Henderson reached on a leadoff single, Edgardo Alfonzo clubbed the right-hander's sixth pitch of the night over the left-field wall. The two-run homer—Alfonzo's 27th of the season—placed immediate pressure on the Reds. The Mets added a single run in the third (knocking a wild Parris from the game in favor of Denny Neagle), then padded the lead further on Henderson's solo home run in the fifth. The Mets rounded out the scoring with a single run in the sixth.

Such ample run support proved more than enough for Leiter, who pitched his finest game of the season. Leiter allowed only two hits—a single to Jeffrey Hammonds and a double to Pokey Reese—in shutting down one of the National League's most prolific offensive lineups. When Dmitri Young hit Leiter's 133rd pitch right at Alfonzo, the left-hander's night—and Cincinnati's season—came to an official end.

The Mets poured onto the field to celebrate the 5–0 whitewash and the franchise's first trip to the postseason since 1988. No one had played as vital a role as Leiter, whose 13th win of the season seemed almost as momentous as his performance in Game 7 of the 1997 World Series.

AT CINERGY FIELD, CINCINNATI, OCTOBER 4, 1999

NEW YORK	AB	R	H	2B	3B	HR	RBI
Henderson, lf	5	2	2	0	0	1	1
Mora, lf	0	0	0	0	0	0	0
Alfonzo, 2b	4	2	2	1	0	1	3
Olerud, 1b	5	0	2	1	0	0	0
Piazza, c	2	0	0	0	0	0	0
Ventura, 3b	3	0	1	0	0	0	1
Hamilton, cf	4	0	1	0	0	0	0
Cedeno, rf	4	0	1	0	0	0	0
Ordonez, ss	3	1	0	0	0	0	0
Leiter, p	3	0	0	0	0	0	0

CINCINNATI	AB	R	H	2B	3B	HR	RBI
Reese, 2b	3	0	1	1	0	0	0
Larkin, ss	3	0	0	0	0	0	0
Casey, 1b	4	0	0	0	0	0	0
Vaughn, lf	3	0	0	0	0	0	0
Young, rf	4	0	0	0	0	0	0
Hammonds, cf	3	0	1	0	0	0	0
Taubensee, c	2	0	0	0	0	0	0
Boone, 3b	3	0	0	0	0	0	0
Parris, p	0	0	0	0	0	0	0
Neagle, p	1	0	0	0	0	0	0
Stynes, ph	1	0	0	0	0	0	0
Graves, p	0	0	0	0	0	0	0
Lewis, ph	1	0	0	0	0	0	0
Reyes, p	0	0	0	0	0	0	0

NY	201	011	000	5	9	0	
CIN	000	000	000	0	2	0	

Bases on balls—Alfonzo, Piazza 3, Ventura 2, Hamilton, Ordonez, Reese, Larkin, Vaughn, Taubensee. Sacrifice—Leiter. Left on base—New York 10, Cincinnati 5. Umpires—Froemming, G. Davis, M. Hirschbeck, Rapuano, Rieker, Nelson. Time of game—3:03. Attendance—54,621.

PITCHING	IP	H	R	ER	BB	SO
NEW YORK						
Leiter (W, 13–12)	9	2	0	0	4	7
CINCINNATI						
Parris (L, 11–4)	2.2	3	3	3	3	1
Neagle	2.1	2	1	1	3	2
Graves	3	2	1	1	2	2
Reyes	1	2	0	0	0	0

Features

Section **7**

Brooks Robinson
Orioles shortstop Mark Belanger looks on as Robinson demonstrates the defensive skill that made him one of baseball's top third basemen.

FAMOUS FIRSTS

1892: The National League allows Sunday baseball for the first time.

1921: Baseball hires Kenesaw Mountain Landis as its first commissioner.

1926: Amplifiers are used at the Polo Grounds for the first time in the majors.

1936: The Cincinnati Reds take a plane to St. Louis to become the first team to fly.

1941: The Los Angeles Dodgers become the first club to wear batting helmets.

1948: Satchel Paige records his first major league shutout in his first major league game.

1960: Player names are placed on the back of jerseys for the first time.

1963: The Alou brothers, Matty, Felipe and Jesus, appear in a major league outfield together for the first time.

Chapter 27

The Business of Baseball

By David Pietrusza and Rob Neyer

Baseball has been a business almost from its outset. When it was not a business, it was barely recognizable as baseball. And even before players received compensation and owners charged admissions, the games were played for money—in the form of widespread fan gambling.

While Harry Wright's 1869 Cincinnati Red Stockings were baseball's first *fully* professional team, players had been compensated both openly and covertly for at least ten years before that. In May 1862 William H. Cammeyer had charged admissions at his enclosed field, Brooklyn's Union Grounds, thus, as Michael Gershman pointed out in *Diamonds*, commencing "the true beginning of professional baseball as a spectator sport."

In 1870 the governing body of baseball, the National Association of Base Ball Players, heard a resolution ("that this Association regard the custom of hiring men to play the game of baseball as reprehensible and injurious to the best interests of the game") proposed by a Mr. Cantwell of Albany, New York, which would ban professionalism in the sport. It was the last gasp of the "gentleman's game." The resolution failed to pass; the old amateur association soon collapsed, and the National Association of *Professional* Base Ball Players, the first major league, formed for the following year.

This new National Association, a jerrybuilt league, collapsed in 1876 and was replaced by William Hulbert's more structured National League of Professional Base Ball Clubs. That circuit quickly moved to elevate baseball's organization as well as its tone. Gambling, Sunday ball and the sale of alcohol on the grounds were banned. The new league created territorial rights (i.e., geographic monopolies) and imposed minimum ticket prices of 50 cents. "A good game is worth 50 cts, a poor one is dear at 25," contended Harry Wright.

But soon the American Association, "The Beer and Whiskey League," challenged the National League, and, for competitive reasons, alcohol would again be sold at NL parks. Attendance increased as the range of concessions widened and moralistic restrictions eased (Sunday ball took hold in a few cities and by the turn of the century became the norm). At the Polo Grounds, around the turn of the century, English-born Harry Mosely

Bruce Sutter
After winning the 1979 Cy Young Award, the relief ace won a landmark $700,000 salary arbitration decision that one owner called "an atom bomb for our industry."

Stevens, the inventor of the scorecard, also gave the world the hot dog. Harry Payne Whitney once remarked that Stevens had "parlayed a bag of peanuts into millions." (The concessions business was so good for Stevens that, when the Polo Grounds burnt in 1911, owner John T. Brush turned to him for a loan to rebuild it.)

As money came in, it also flowed out. Players had to eat, and being the best in their profession, were not going to be satisfied with hot dogs. From the earliest days of the game, players sold—or, more precisely, rented—their services to the highest bidder. The

inflation of players' salaries as they moved from club to club ("revolving") helped collapse the National Association. The National League would not follow the same path. "It is ridiculous to pay ballplayers $2,000 a year," complained Hulbert in the 1870s, "when the $800 boys often do just as well."

The Reserve Clause

Before long the National League was "reserving" players' services. On September 29, 1879, it created a secret "reserve list" of five players per club with whom other teams would not "contract with, employ, engage or negotiate." At first players did not mind being reserved, for it signified their stature and guaranteed employment for the upcoming season.

Before long entire rosters were reserved, and the basis of major league labor relations was set for a century. Even in an age of few labor rights, management, however, knew the reserve clause stood on woefully weak legal ground. When players revolted in 1890 and formed their own Players National League, management went to court to compel their return. Their efforts failed. During the birth of the American League and, during the Federal League war of 1914 and 1915, similar judgments went against the reserve clause.

As the Federal League collapsed, however, the outlaw circuit's Baltimore Terrapins were unhappy with the terms of the settlement that terminated their league. In 1917 they sued in Federal Court, charging Organized Baseball with violation of the Clayton Antitrust Act. The United States Supreme Court, however, not only ruled against Baltimore, but surprisingly provided Organized Baseball with legal protection far beyond what it could have realistically hoped: antitrust exemption.

On May 22, 1922, speaking for the court's majority, Justice Oliver Wendell Holmes held that baseball was not interstate commerce. He further held that the reserve clause, "intended to protect the rights of clubs … to retain the services of sufficient players," was legal.

With the exception of gradually increasing revenues from radio, and then from television, baseball's business practices remained remarkably static for the next few decades. Not until after World War II was there a significant legal challenge to the reserve clause, and that was settled out of court. In the 1950s, however, the pace of change quickened. Franchise shifts moved teams into Milwaukee, Kansas City, Baltimore, Los Angeles and San Francisco. And New York City's abandonment of the National League led to the Continental League challenge and then to expansion.

A Peculiar Institution

Baseball, indeed any sports league, operates in a universe far different from that of normal commerce. On the one hand there is fierce competition—for fans, labor, advertising, etc. On the other hand there must be a balance between competing entities.

This is not the case with baseball, and never has been. The New York Yankees or Los Angeles Dodgers need competition. On the most basic level, both clubs require opponents in order to play games, and baseball needs healthy rivalries to attract crowds both at home and away. (Of the several reasons for the collapse of the old National Association, an important one was the overwhelming dominance of the Boston Red Stockings.)

On a deeper level, however, a national network of clubs is necessary to create a national base of fans as opposed to a local or regional one, as Hulbert recognized from the dawn of professional league play. Such a need for a national fan base now mandates expansion into areas of growing population, while striving to protect existing franchises in older cities.

This need to succeed at the cost of one's competitor without crushing him entirely forms some of the basis of the current "big market-small market" controversy. In fact, though, the paradox is decades old and produced such implausible results as the continued existence of chronically impoverished franchises like the St. Louis Browns. It also led to the imposition of the amateur-free-agent draft in the 1960s, which aimed at equalizing the talent pool as it first came into Organized Baseball (and also to stop the upward spiral of bonuses).

As television contracts, particularly cable contracts, grew larger, so did the disparity in club resources. Once free agency came upon the scene such disparity would help fuel bidding wars for talent not seen since Federal League days.

The MLBPA

In 1946 an abortive attempt at a players' union, the American Baseball Guild, failed. Nevertheless, the group did obtain a $5,000 minimum salary for ballplayers. In 1954 big league players, led by Allie Reynolds and Ralph Kiner, formed the Major League Baseball Players' Association (MLBPA). Although not originally a union in the true sense of the word, the MLBPA secured 60 percent of television revenues from both the World Series and the All-Star Game for player pensions. Not until 1966, when the MLBPA selected as its chief Marvin Miller—a veteran of the U.S. Department of Labor, the International Association of Machinists, the United Auto Workers, and the United Steelworkers of America—did baseball labor-management negotiations enter the modern era.

The following season ownership responded by creating the Player Relations Committee (PRC), consisting of both league presidents and three owners from each league. Named as the PRC's first head was John J. Gaherin, former president of the New York City Newspapers Association.

By February 1968 the MLBPA and the PRC had hammered out Major League Baseball's first Basic Agreement. It raised the minimum major league salary from $6,000 to $10,000 but, more significantly for the future, created a grievance procedure and promised a review of the reserve clause.

Events rapidly accelerated. In 1969 the MLBPA threatened to strike, but was dissuaded from that course of action when management conceded to Miller increases in the pension fund and in the minimum major league salary along with the right of players to employ agents. Key to reaching that settlement was the National League's attorney, Bowie Kuhn. Six months later management rewarded Kuhn for his efforts by tendering him an eight-year contract as Commissioner.

A new Basic Agreement was arrived at in 1970. It raised the minimum player salary from $10,000 to $15,000, restricted salary cuts to 20 percent, and—most importantly—set up a system of impartial arbitration.

Strike One

In 1972 the Players Association staged the first general work stoppage in baseball history, delaying the start of the season for 13 days and forcing the cancellation of 86 regular season games.

Prior to the 1972 season opening, players requested a 25 percent raise in pension benefits, but then reduced their demand to 17 percent. This lower amount created an $800,000 cost to ownership, but represented only the amount necessary to keep pace with

the cost of living since enactment of the last Basic Agreement in 1969. The Players Association also wanted $400,000 to cover increased medical and health-care benefits.

The owners agreed to pick up this latter cost, but later produced a lower bid of $250,000 from Blue Cross-Blue Shield. Miller charged that management had not bargained in "good faith" and had decreased the amount of money previously offered. This issue galvanized player support for a work stoppage, with the MLBPA voting 663-10 (with two abstentions) to authorize a strike. Finally the MLBPA's Executive Board authorized a strike by a vote of 47-0.

Major League Baseball (MLB) suffered its first general strike on April 1, 1972, five days before the start of the regular season. As the stoppage unfolded, Miller developed a compromise solution that eventually led to a return to work, although management's Player Relations Committee at first dismissed the idea as "imprudent."

At this point President Richard Nixon suggested that both parties be brought together by the Federal Mediation and Reconciliation Service.

Miller eventually won an increased management contribution of $490,000 to the players' benefit plan, plus a transfer of $400,000 in surplus pension funds to improve players' retirement benefits and maintain their health benefits. However, the players did lose 4.9 percent in their salaries for the season because of the strike. Management wanted lost games to be made up, but Miller rejected the idea unless that 4.9 percent salary loss was likewise recovered.

And so baseball's first player strike came to an end at 4:15 p.m. on April 13, with play to resume two days later. Players lost $600,000 in salaries. Owners lost an estimated $5.2 in revenue from the canceled games.

Lost amid the dollar figures in the newspaper stories was a very important concession granted labor—the right to arbitrate grievances. In just a few years that right would turn baseball on its head.

Curt Flood Tests the Waters

Coming hard on the heels of these events was the United States Supreme Court's June 19, 1972, ruling in the Curt Flood case. By a 5-3 majority the high court reluctantly reaffirmed both the game's antitrust exemption and the reserve clause. (See "Baseball and The Law" and "Curt Flood's Legacy" in this volume.)

A third Basic Agreement was negotiated following the 1972 season. The MLBPA accepted management's proposal that players with two years plus one day of major league service could have their salary disputes arbitrated. The MLBPA also gained the so-called five-and-ten-year rule. Any player with ten years of service in the major leagues and five years of service with his current club could veto a proposed trade. Had that rule been in effect in 1970 Curt Flood would not have sought recourse in the courts.

The Seitz Decisions

Since the signing of the Basic Agreement of 1972, players had had the right to arbitration of grievances before a three-person panel, consisting of labor, management and an impartial arbitrator. In practice, since the labor representative would always uphold the labor view, and management that of its side, the impartial arbitrator held immense power.

In 1974 Peter Seitz, a graduate of New York University and a man with decades of experience in the arbitration field but "only a passing interest in spectator sports," was named baseball's fourth arbitrator. He replaced Gabriel Alexander of Detroit.

Wrote Bowie Kuhn: "There were some misgivings on the PRC in selecting Seitz because he was thought to favor the labor side of issues. But he had served in the same role for the NBA with no disastrous results."

However, Marvin Miller had detected something else in Seitz's record. In one NBA opinion Seitz cited a 1969 California Court of Appeals ruling allowing San Francisco's Rick Barry to sign with an American Basketball Association team after finishing his NBA option year. MLB and NBA option clauses were identical. If a similar case were to come before Seitz would he rule in the same way?

On December 13, 1973, Seitz gave a hint of the changes he would unleash, when he found that A's owner Charles Finley had failed to comply with the terms of pitcher Catfish Hunter's 1973 contract. It was "pellucidly clear," Seitz stated, that under article 7A of the Standard Player Contract a player could terminate his contract—including the reserve clause—if management failed to live up to its terms. Seitz's decision set off an unprecedented bidding war by 15 clubs which resulted in Hunter's signing an estimated $3.75 million, five-year contract with the Yankees.

The following year the Expos' Dave McNally and the Dodgers' Andy Messersmith, dissatisfied with their contracts, refused to sign new ones. Their respective clubs exercised their rights to renew their agreements for an additional year without the player's signature. At season's end both pitchers claimed free agency.

On December 23, 1975, Seitz ruled for McNally and Messersmith, and the very basis of the reserve clause—to bind a player in perpetuity to a single club—was overturned. Organized Baseball reacted with anger. Seitz was immediately dismissed by the owners, as was their right, although it was the first time either management or labor had exercised that privilege.

The owners appealed Seitz's decision regarding McNally and Messersmith, but it was affirmed in Federal District Court on February 4, 1976, and on appeal one month later.

The Fourth Basic Agreement

By this time the Third Basic Agreement had expired. In the spring of 1976, it was ownership's turn to bring play to a halt, locking players out of the spring-training camps. After 24 days of the shutdown, Commissioner Bowie Kuhn ordered the camps reopened. Even though no Basic Agreement existed, the season began anyway. It was not until July that an agreement was reached. The Fourth Basic Agreement granted free agency to all players with six or more seasons of major league service. Under the Fourth Basic Agreement, the average player salary increased nearly threefold from 1976 ($51,501) to 1980 ($143,756).

Two factors fueled the increase: bidding wars for established stars and salary arbitration. The pivotal arbitration case involved Cubs relief ace Bruce Sutter. Following the 1979 season, Sutter (who then had only four years of major league service) went to arbitration. The Cubs offered him $350,000. Sutter wanted $700,000, then a staggering amount for a player with such relatively limited service. In February an arbitrator ruled in Sutter's favor. Previously, only longtime (and often somewhat past their prime) stars had reaped the really big salaries, but now the floodgates were opening.

Strike Two

The strike of 1972 was replayed with greater volume in 1981, when the Players Association staged baseball's first midseason work

stoppage. A strike had been narrowly averted in May 1980 but was not to be halted in 1981.

The Fourth Basic Agreement expired on December 31, 1979. Despite—or perhaps because of—numerous owners' measures to protect themselves from a work stoppage (including $50 million in Lloyds of London strike insurance, purchased at a cost of $2.2 million in premiums, and a $15 million strike fund), no strike occurred in 1980.

The issue now at stake was free-agent compensation. Miller staked out a position that he wanted to expand free agency, cutting its threshold from six years of service to four. Ownership (represented by PRC head Ray Grebey) pressed for increased compensation for clubs losing free agents. Management wanted clubs which had lost such players to receive major league players in return, instead of extra selections in the June amateur draft.

In February 1981 management invoked its right to implement this plan unilaterally. Less than a week later labor indicated a strike was possible if they did. In May 1981, Miller filed a brief with the National Labor Relations Board asking that club financial data be turned over to the union, to validate management's claim that free agency was causing financial havoc. His request was refused.

In June, ownership proposed a variant on the idea of free-agent compensation, but Miller again rejected it. On June 11, Miller removed himself from the bargaining process, and the next day the strike began. Unlike the clubs, the Players Association had no strike insurance. Miller himself forswore his estimated $160,000 salary during the work stoppage.

Miller personally returned to the bargaining table on July 1. The strike ended on July 31, and the settlement involved complex compensation formulas, an increase in the minimum major league salary to $40,000, and a myriad of provisions involving the strike-shortened season itself, including the use of a split-season format for 1981 and an extra round of postseason play.

The settlement's key provision provided for clubs to receive a player in compensation for better talent (so called "Class A" free agents) that was lost. Clubs could protect up to 24 players from being chosen as compensation. Clubs eligible for compensation need not select a player from the club that had signed their free agent, but clubs could exempt themselves from the risk of losing players in this fashion by voluntarily electing not to sign Class A free agents themselves for the term of this Basic Agreement.

Players ratified the settlement by a vote of 627 to 37; clubs approved it, 21-2, with St. Louis and Cincinnati casting negative votes and three franchises abstaining.

The strike cost players (now earning a minimum of $32,000 per season and an average of $193,000 annually) between $28 million and $34 million in lost salaries. Estimates for management losses ranged from a low of $1.6 million to a high of $7.6 million in revenues, although in many cases losses were offset by the aforementioned $50 million in strike insurance.

The Ueberroth Era

This new Basic Agreement was set to expire on December 31, 1984. As it did, major league finances strained to the breaking point.

Former Olympics organizer Peter V. Ueberroth replaced Bowie Kuhn as Commissioner in October 1984 and was soon faced with the crisis. At the Los Angeles Olympics Ueberroth had turned an impressive $215 million profit. MLB, on the other hand, seemed headed for bankruptcy. It turned to Ueberroth for salvation and to

lure him to the job significantly strengthened the Commissioner's powers.

In early 1985 MLB opened its books and revealed the full dimensions of the situation. Of the 26 clubs, 22 had lost money in 1984, totaling an aggregate deficit of $42 million. If the trend continued, MLB's accounting firm of Ernst & Whinney warned, the red ink would total $58 million in 1985, $94 million in 1986, $113 million in 1987 and $155 million in 1988. Management figures also contended that, as a whole, MLB had enjoyed a positive balance sheet just once in the previous nine seasons—in 1978, and that was only a mere $4,586.

The MLBPA disputed these figures, contending that MLB had actually turned a $9.3 million profit in 1984. Figures reported a full decade later by the Associated Press, however, largely reiterated Ernst & Whinney's claims.

Several other events of 1984 served to emphasize management's claim that the game was financially unsound. In June the Mariners' George Argyros, reportedly seeking bankruptcy protection, renegotiated his lease on the Kingdome. In September, the A's received similar concessions at the Oakland-Alameda County Coliseum and even obtained a $15 million loan from Coliseum authorities to deal with existing debt. Across the Bay, Bob Lurie's Giants faced defeat in efforts to secure a new ballpark and mulled playing at the Coliseum. That October the Galbreath family sold the Pittsburgh Pirates. They sought $35-$40 million for the club; they received just $22 million.

Greatly aggravating management's financial woes was the huge increase in player salaries following the institution of free agency and arbitration. In 1976 the average major league salary was $51,501. It jumped to $76,066 in 1977 and had grown to $371,571 by 1985.

Ueberroth swung into action and recreated his Olympic strategy of securing lucrative corporate sponsorships, such as designating IBM the official computer of Major League Baseball or Chevrolet the official car. Successful marketing and a terrific pennant race (15 clubs were still contenders on September 1) caused attendance to skyrocket in 1986. For the first time, every major league club exceeded the million mark in paid attendance. The result was the end of red ink. In 1986 MLB turned a net operating profit of $11.5 million. It was a modest profit, but it presaged far greater ones, peaking at a 1989 level of $214 million.

In the Ronald Reagan boom years, baseball also succeeded in negotiating a lucrative six-season (1984-89) television contract with NBC and ABC generating $1.125 billion in revenue for MLB. That translated into $8 million per year per club and tripled the revenue flow from the previous TV contract.

Aiding Ueberroth was a turnaround in baseball's popularity that had been building for some time. Starting back in 1968, the Harris poll had identified football as the nation's most popular spectator sport. In the late 1970s baseball began climbing back, overtaking the National Football League in the polls. Attendance steadily climbed and so did telecasting of individual team broadcasts. In 1982 the Los Angeles Dodgers had been the first club to attract 3 million fans. In 1987 they were joined by the Cards and Mets; in 1988 by the Twins (who had drawn just 469,000 paying customers in the strike-shortened 1981 season); and in 1989 by Toronto. In 1991, aided by SkyDome, the Blue Jays smashed through the 4-million-fan level. In 1993 the expansion Rockies pushed the attendance record even higher.

At work was the new technology of cable television. "Super-

stations" such as WTBS (Braves), WGN (Cubs), WPIX (Yankees), WOR (Mets), and WKTV (Rangers) brought baseball into millions of homes on a daily basis, strengthening fan loyalties. Although a positive development in making baseball more widely available, the superstations, which are based in major markets, increased the historical disparity between "have" and "have not" teams.

The Strikes of 1984-85

As Ueberroth took office, major league umpires threatened to strike during the 1984 postseason. Ueberroth stepped in, appointed himself sole mediator and avoided a work stoppage, but he faced a far more difficult challenge as baseball's Basic Agreement expired on December 31 of that year. Three issues dominated events: pension-plan contributions, free-agent compensation, and salary arbitration. As the agreement expired, players were receiving $15.5 million annually toward their pension plan. Donald Fehr wanted one-third of Ueberroth's new television contract, a sum equivalent to $62.5 million annually.

The MLBPA also desired elimination of the free-agent compensation plan adopted back in 1981, but counterbalancing that was management's agenda for curtailing salary arbitration. As negotiations continued in 1985, ownership proposed a freeze in both salaries and pension levels, as they opened their books to display red ink.

As negotiations progressed, the union set an August 6, 1985, strike deadline. Management countered with an increase in pension contributions to $25 million annually but tied its offer to stability in salary levels (i.e., pension contributions would rise to that level only if salaries increased by no more than $13 million). For example, if salaries rose by $14 million, only $24 million in pension contributions would result. Some projected that this method would produce an actual *reduction* in pension contributions.

On August 2, Ueberroth proposed a compromise settlement but players went out on strike as threatened. Despite tough talk from both sides, a settlement was reached just two days later. Only 25 games were lost, 14 in the American League, 11 in the National. All contests were eventually rescheduled.

On the larger issues, both sides received some satisfaction. Management obtained gains on the arbitration front. Instead of going to arbitration after two seasons, players would now wait three years before exercising that option. This provision would translate into major savings for management, most notably in the case of 1986 Cy Young Award winner Roger Clemens. Ownership also received concessions regarding arbitration mechanisms.

On the other hand, the MLBPA received what it wanted in regard to free agency. Limitations on the number of clubs eligible to negotiate with a free agent were now lifted. Compensation for signing a free agent was no longer to be in the form of major league players. Instead, teams signing free agents would now forfeit amateur draft picks.

On a more basic level, the major league minimum salary was raised from $40,000 to $60,000 with cost of living adjustments promised for 1987 and 1989. Players also gained in regard to pensions and World Series shares. Owners would retroactively contribute $25 million toward 1984 pension accounts, with payments rising to $39 million by 1989. In terms of what an average player would net from this settlement, a ten-year veteran could now collect $91,000 per year starting at age 62. The previous Basic Agreement called for such players to receive $57,000 at age 65.

A little-noted provision of the Sixth Basic Agreement provided for what proved to be an increasingly debated concept: revenue sharing. Of the ABC-NBC television contract money, $20 million dollars would be set aside for financially troubled franchises.

Collusion or Fiscal Restraint?

As the smoke cleared from the August 1985 strike, ownership looked for ways to control labor costs. In September 1984, Ueberroth had personally addressed ownership and urged fiscal restraint. Salaries had continued to escalate. The average major league salary rose from $329,408 in 1984 to $371,157 in 1985. Forty-three players now had million-dollar contracts, headed by Mike Schmidt at $2,130,000 and Gary Carter at $2,028,571. Ueberroth's message was simple: "It is not smart to sign long-term contracts."

That advice soon translated into a far more controversial outcome. As the 1985 season ended, 62 major league players (including Detroit's All-Star outfielder Kirk Gibson) filed for arbitration. Few of them received offers from new clubs. Gibson did not receive contract offers from any club other than Detroit. Hoping to receive an $8 million, five-year pact, he instead agreed to a three-year, $4-million contract. Only five players changed clubs, and all five had been virtually cut loose by their previous teams.

The MLBPA charged "collusion" and filed grievances against all 26 clubs, noting that the Basic Agreement included a clause stating that "Players shall not act in concert with other Players and Clubs shall not act in concert with the other Clubs" in regard to player signings. Oddly enough, that clause had been inserted at ownership's behest to prevent dual holdouts, such as the celebrated one staged by Don Drysdale and Sandy Koufax in 1966.

In the middle of the case, the PRC fired arbitrator Thomas Tuttle Roberts because of its displeasure over Roberts' decision voiding player drug testing. The dismissal was hardly unprecedented; the MLBPA had four times dismissed arbitrators and the PRC had exercised that option once previously. But no dismissal had ever occurred while a decision was ongoing. The union grieved once more, and Roberts was reinstated.

Before Roberts reached a decision, another crop of free agents emerged at the close of the 1986 season. Unlike the largely lackluster contingent of the previous season, this crop of 79 free agents included such stars as Jack Morris, Ron Guidry, Dale Murphy, Lance Parrish, Tim Raines, Bob Horner, and Andre Dawson. Again, only players unwanted by their original team received offers from competing clubs. Parrish, Horner and Ray Knight signed with new clubs; Dawson had to sign a blank contract to join the Cubs. Parrish and Knight went to new teams for less than their old clubs had offered. Horner fled to Japan, taking a job with the Yakult Swallows. Again the MLBPA filed grievances.

One player, Tiger pitcher Jack Morris, beat the system. Seeing he would receive no other offers besides Detroit's, Morris and his agent Richard Moss withdrew their bid for free agency and instead submitted to salary arbitration. Morris was awarded $1.85 million for 1987.

On September 22, 1987, Roberts finally issued his decision in the case, ruling in favor of the union. On January 22, 1988, Roberts also allowed seven players to exercise what became known as "new-look free agency." Of the seven, only Kirk Gibson signed with a new club, reaching agreement with Los Angeles on a three-year $4.5 million contract. Still unsettled was the issue of financial compensation. The MLBPA wanted anywhere between $7.2 and $15 million. The owners argued the total should be between $2.2 and $4.4 million. On August 31, 1989, Roberts awarded

$10,528,086.71 in damages to 139 players.

The decision in the second case was equally disappointing to management. After reviewing 8,346 pages of testimony, arbitrator George Nicolau found owners guilty once more of collusion, this time in the case of the free agent crop of 1986. On October 24—Nicolau had delayed his action to avoid disrupting the pennant races—new-look free agency was granted to 12 more players, including Bob Boone, Jim Clancy, and Willie Randolph, all of whom signed with new teams. Others such as Rich Gedman and Ken Dayley gained lucrative new contracts from their old clubs. The first of the damage awards involved Yankees pitcher Ron Guidry, who in June 1989 received $91,758.24 in compensation.

A third case was filed by the union in January 1989 regarding those who had become free agents after the 1987 campaign. In July 1990 Nicolau again found for labor. Seventy-six players, including such stars as Jack Clark, Gary Gaetti, Jack Morris, Dave Righetti, Mike Witt, and Paul Molitor were involved in the case, which revolved around management's creation of an "information bank" in the winter of 1986-87. This data bank reported all salary offers made to free agents. Nicolau found it a "quiet" form of cooperation between supposed rivals, endeavoring to keep tabs on what each competitor was offering on the supposedly free market. By the time damages were finally determined, they exceeded the $100 million mark.

In the midst of this series of reverses, management did win one battle. The Sixth Basic Agreement had given clubs the option of reducing rosters to 24 men. As a cost-costing measure, all clubs used the lower number in 1986 and 1987. The union again charged collusion, but in this instance Nicolau ruled in favor of management.

New Sources of Revenue

Reports of the demise of televised baseball's profitability proved premature. Toward the end of Ueberroth's tenure, a series of blockbuster broadcasting deals were negotiated. The biggest was a four-year deal with CBS in December 1988 for $1.06 billion. The network received rights to the All-Star Game, League Championship Series, World Series, and 12 regular-season weekend games. Criticism surrounded the cutback in regular-season broadcasts, but Ueberroth answered with an unprecedented deal with the cable industry. ESPN outbid such rivals as TNT and USA in January 1989 for a four-year, $400-million pact, featuring 175 regular-season games, including groundbreaking Sunday-night cablecasts. No one knew how successful the package would be, but even ESPN officials admitted they would lose money for at least the first two years. At the same time a $50-million, four-year agreement with CBS Radio for the Game of the Week, All-Star Game, and postseason contests was finalized.

While Organized Baseball as a whole was cashing in, so were individual clubs. Perhaps the best example was George Steinbrenner obtaining a $500-million, 12-year agreement with the Madison Square Garden cable network.

The Franchise Game

By 1987, 22 out of the 26 clubs either broke even or were profitable on industry-wide revenues of $910.9 million and profits of $103 million. There had always been an interest in ballclubs as rich men's toys, but when it appeared once again that money could be made at the national pastime, bidding for franchises went through the roof.

Even the most moribund franchises sold for big bucks. Somewhat understandably the New York Mets changed hands for $100 million, and Baltimore sold for $70 million, but when the woeful Seattle Mariners were peddled for $77 million (George Argyros had paid $13.1 million for these latter-day St. Louis Browns in 1981), it was clear that the economic balance had been tilted.

Back in the early 1980s, Commissioner Ueberroth announced that the majors would feature two new AL and four new NL clubs by 2000. However, by the late 1980s the game faced increased pressure from a number of sources for expansion. The Players Association wished to open up more jobs for its members. The U.S. Senate formed a 14-member panel on the subject. A new league was announced by agent Dick Moss in 1989, backed by Donald Trump's ephemeral billions.

Baseball now announced a willingness to add two more National League franchises. The NL would announce its two newest members in September 1991, who would draft entry-level minor league players in late 1991, and actually operate farm systems in 1992. During that season, they would draft college and high-school players. Major league expansion drafts occurred after the 1992 World Series. An interesting—and definitely different—aspect of this draft was that the newest senior-circuit clubs selected personnel (36 for each club) from both major leagues, and the AL and NL clubs alike divided the $95-million franchise fee from each rookie owner.

Frontrunners for the new franchises included Denver (where voters in 1990 approved a new 40,000-seat stadium); St. Petersburg (which had nearly attracted the White Sox in 1988 and the Giants in 1992); Miami; Buffalo (where the Rich family ran a big league operation at the AAA level); and Washington (a two-time loser, but a loser with political connections). The huge franchise fees plus a projected $65 million in startup costs (a figure that ultimately reached $95 million) did not dissuade prospective backers.

Major league expansion also triggered minor league expansion, as the new clubs would require new farm teams. With such franchises as Oklahoma City going for $4.5 million, the price tag at the AAA level wasn't cheap. Most observers estimated it would be $5 million per club (consider that the Mets had cost $1.8 million in 1962 and the Kansas City Royals just $5.5 million in 1969). Even applying for a minor league club required a $5,000 nonrefundable deposit, but, in September 1990, 18 groups mailed in their checks.

As minor league franchises were bought and sold for record prices, the major league clubs took notice. Claiming they no longer saw the wisdom of subsidizing such "profitable" ventures (in all too many cases the only profit came from selling to the next party willing to take operating losses), in 1990 the big leaguers started to place pressure on their farm clubs.

The Lockout of 1990

Baseball's Basic Agreement expired on December 31, 1989, and despite the prosperity both sides now enjoyed, open warfare was imminent. The Players Association was hardly blind to the marvelously round figures Ueberroth had pried out of the networks. Beyond that they were particularly irritated by the year of arbitration they had given away in the last settlement.

Club owners, on the other hand, were tired of forking over millions through the arbitration process. The problem for management was not simply the cost of losing specific arbitration cases. Winning could also be costly. In the winter of 1989-90 the 10 "losers" in the process received average raises of $477,050. Average salaries doubled

for only the second time in arbitration's 15-year history. First-year-eligible players saw paychecks skyrocket by 166 percent. While the vast majority of disputes were settled before they reached arbitration, they still involved huge increases, such as Teddy Higuera's $2,125,000 stipend and Tom Browning's pact for the same figure. Fred McGriff saw his income rise from $325,000 to $1,450,000 in a pre-arbitration settlement. A showdown had to occur.

Negotiations dragged on during the winter of 1989-90, and it was widely believed that the players would collect their checks for a few months and then strike at midseason, when the owners were gearing up for large crowds and were most vulnerable. To thwart this plan, management struck first, engaging in yet another lockout of spring-training camps.

The owners' strategy was to hold firm on the third-year threshold for arbitration. The PRC tendered a number of alternatives to the Players Association, including one granting 48 percent of club profits to players and another offering a cumbersome $4 million bonus-pool scheme to be shared by two-year players.

After 32 bitter days, the MLBPA's Donald Fehr and Charles O'Connor, the new PRC negotiator, hammered out a compromise. Seventeen percent of the second-year players would now become eligible for arbitration. The minimum salary would rise from $68,000 to $100,000, the largest percentage increase ever. Management would contribute $55 million to the players' pension fund, up from $39 million. To the casual observer this seemed a victory for labor, but the players had wanted $80 million and the settlement was a giant step back from the traditional one-third of national TV revenues that players had contended was their right. Additionally, it was written into the agreement that baseball would announce its long-stalled expansion plans within 90 days. Another change in the contract involved collusion. Henceforth, only clubs actively found guilty of the process would be fined—but they would be assessed triple damages. Although 24-man rosters were again allowed in 1990, the traditional 25-man roster would be mandated again, starting in 1991.

It was not a settlement that established any great principles, and most fans were no doubt just as puzzled as ever as to what all the shouting had been about, but it appeared that the process had cooled some tempers.

Baseball Enters the Nineties

In the 1991 season, salaries, arbitration settlements and attendance continued their seemingly inexorable climb. The average player salary soared an astonishing 42.5 percent to $851,383. The highest stipend was accorded to Los Angeles' Darryl Strawberry—$3.8 million—while the average Oakland paycheck was a handsome $1,394,119. Yet major league attendance continued to climb along with salary expenses, hitting an all-time high of 56,813,760.

Long-stalled National League expansion finally occurred in June 1991 with $95-million franchises being granted for the 1993 season to the Colorado Rockies, headed by John Antonucci, and the Florida Marlins, led by Blockbuster Video tycoon Wayne Huizenga. Commissioner Fay Vincent ruled that American League teams would receive $42 million of the franchise fees.

Issues such as disparities in television revenue still festered. Local television, cable and radio rights generated $200 million but just four teams—the Yankees, Mets, Phillies, and Dodgers—garnered more than 35 percent of the total. The Yankees' $41.5-million deal towered over the annual funding available to such small market franchises as Pittsburgh ($5.8 million), Kansas City

($5 million) and Seattle ($4 million). In September 1991, the AL voted to channel 20 percent of local broadcasting "net revenues" into a pool which would be shared equally (the NL formula, on the other hand, called for sharing 25 percent). Controversy was expected over what revenue would be considered "net."

As the 1991 season ended, another round of free-agent signings ensued with the New York Mets snagging Pittsburgh's Bobby Bonilla with a five-year, $29-million pact. This largesse was soon eclipsed by the Cubs signing 32-year old Ryne Sandberg to a four-year $28.4 million agreement. At the lower end of the spectrum, the big league minimum wage inched up to $109,000—an almost meaningless figure with the average ballplayer's salary now at $1,043,156.

Despite another 4-million-plus season in Toronto and the million-fan boost given to the Orioles by the opening of the new park at Camden Yards, major league attendance dropped by 1.6 percent in 1992. Profits plummeted from $143 million in 1990 to just $8.7 million in 1991 to virtually nothing in 1992. Nervousness increased over the coming end of the lucrative CBS television contract after the 1993 campaign. Given these alarming indicators, it was mistakenly anticipated that the extraordinarily large number of free agents testing the market after the 1992 World Series—including such stars as Barry Bonds, David Cone, Kirby Puckett, and Greg Maddux—would find few takers.

As the World Series ended, a bombshell struck Major League Baseball when ESPN announced it would not exercise its option for 1994-95 television coverage. Claiming that so far it had lost more than half of its investment in the deal, the decision makers at ESPN chose a $13-million buyout rather than further payments of $250 million for the two seasons available to them. The cable network left the door open for negotiations, but obviously at a much lower starting point. Among other factors, baseball was losing its popularity with American youth: Nielsen ratings revealed a disconcerting 24 percent drop in viewership of regular-season games by 12-to-17-year-olds from 1989 to 1992 even though overall ballpark attendance had increased during that period.

Meanwhile the saga of Bob Lurie and the San Francisco Giants went on and on. In June 1990 he had received permission to shift the club 35 miles south to Santa Clara County, California. But that November, voters in 15 Santa Clara County cities turned thumbs down on a 1 percent utility tax to pay for a new stadium—the third year in a row such a referendum had failed. In January 1992, Lurie announced plans to move to San Jose if a new $155 million, 48,000-seat stadium could be constructed. The plan foundered on the shoals of a projected 2 percent increase in the city's utility tax. On August 7, 1992, Lurie (who had paid $8 million for the franchise in 1976) announced the Giants' sale for $115 million to a group headed by Vincent J. Naimoli bent on relocating the club to St. Petersburg, Florida. That triggered a $100-million counter offer from local investors headed by Safeway magnate Peter Magowan and stockbroker Charles Schwab, who were intent on keeping the team in the Bay area. The National League, by a 9-4 vote on November 10, 1992, rejected the St. Petersburg offer, leaving the status of the Magowan offer up in the air, although the issue was ultimately settled in Magowan's favor. The maneuvering sparked new Congressional interest (particularly that of the Senate Judiciary Committee) in baseball's antitrust status.

Several other franchises changed hands in 1991 and 1992. On November 2, 1991, John Labatt Ltd. paid $67.5 million (Canadian) to acquire majority control (going from 45 percent to

90 percent ownership) of the Blue Jays. In a controversial move that sparked xenophobic responses, Jeff Smulyan turned the woeful Seattle Mariners over to Japanese interests connected to the Nintendo Corporation for $106 million. John McMullen unloaded the Astros to Texas business executive Drayton McLane, Jr., for $115 million. Finally, Domino's Pizza baron Tom Monaghan peddled the Detroit club to fellow pizza magnate Mike Ilitch (a former Tiger farmhand) for a relatively paltry $85 million. The Orioles were rumored to be on the block for $200 million.

The biggest casualty of the 1992 season was Commissioner Fay Vincent, who resigned under pressure on September 7, 1992. Brewers owner Bud Selig stepped in as Commissioner Pro Tem. The first tangible result of Vincent's departure was rescission of his controversial National League realignment plan, which would have placed the Cardinals and the Cubs in the NL West and the Reds and Braves in the NL East.

Some observers felt that Vincent's downfall was foreshadowed in December 1991 when owners hired Richard Ravitch, a one-time candidate for mayor of New York City, to the post of President of the PRC at a salary $100,000 greater than Vincent's. The owners did not want Vincent interfering in labor relations as he had when he intervened in the 1990 spring training lockout. Vincent's dismissal only fueled the rumors, already rampant if ultimately false, of an owner-generated lockout for 1993.

Sales of MLB licensed products continued to soar—from $200 million in 1987 to $1.5 billion in 1990 to $2 billion in 1992. Despite the fact that items with Mets and Yankees logos account for 20 percent of all sales, revenues were split equally among the 28 franchises. To compete with the rival NBA and NFL in an increasingly global struggle for fan dollars, MLB started to promote overseas sales and by 1991 was doing $20 million a year in foreign sales.

In 1992 even the minors got into the act with a similar centralized licensing approach (under the control of Major League Baseball Properties, which can keep up to 30 percent of the royalties). National Association licensed sales in 1992 were an estimated $12 to $15 million.

1993: A Season of Fear—and Profits

Early in 1993 it was fashionable to write baseball off as a sport that was finished. Newspapers, magazines, and even entire books purported that the game's long-awaited crash (proclaimed regularly ever since the 1860s) had finally occurred.

Attendance figures indicated otherwise. MLB set an all-time record of 70,257,938—a figure 23.7 percent above the record set in 1991. Even taking into consideration the two expansion teams, the Rockies and the Marlins, and factoring out the National League's new method of counting attendance (the same method employed by the American League, based on tickets sold, not on actual bodies in the park), attendance was estimated to be 5.2 percent above the 1991 record and 7 percent over 1992.

The Giants, on the ropes in 1992, drew 2.6 million in 1993. The lackluster Reds were estimating a $12-million profit for the season. The Rockies, who had projected a debut season attendance of 2.5 million, attracted nearly 4.5 million customers and suddenly were looking at ways to increase the size of their new Coors Field and acquire players for a run at the postseason.

A new record was set for the value of a franchise. The Orioles sold for a record $173 million at bankruptcy court auction. The club's new owners were led by Baltimore attorney Peter Angelos and Cincinnati businessman William DeWitt. Minority partners included movie director Barry Levinson, author Tom Clancy, broadcaster Jim McKay, and tennis star Pam Shriver.

The minors topped 30 million fans for the first time since 1950, when there were 446 clubs. Average 1993 per-game attendance in the National Association was 3,316—the highest in history. Eight leagues (the International, Eastern, Southern, California, Carolina, South Atlantic, Northwest, and Appalachian) posted attendance records. The International League set an all-time minor league attendance record, drawing 4.6 million customers.

In the Courts and in the halls of Congress, rumblings continued regarding removal of baseball's special legal status. On August 4, 1993, U.S. District Court Judge John Padova of Philadelphia, in a move many interpreted as a restriction of baseball's antitrust exemption, denied Organized Baseball's request to dismiss a suit brought by disgruntled St. Petersburg interests. Padova ruled that the 1922 Supreme Court decision exempted Organized Baseball from antitrust legislation only in those things that were unique to baseball, such as players' contracts. Thus, the buying and selling of clubs was not covered.

Hearings were scheduled for September 30, 1993 (but delayed until 1994) in the Senate Judiciary Committee on a measure sponsored by Howard Metzenbaum (D-Ohio) revoking baseball's antitrust exemption. Judiciary Chairman Joseph Biden (D-Del.) threatened: "Unless baseball gets its act together in a way that is monumentally different from where they are now, this committee will be back with the votes that will change the status of baseball."

A meeting took place in Kohler, Wisconsin on August 11-13, 1993, under the leadership of Richard Ravitch. While a widely anticipated agreement on revenue-sharing failed to come about, owners did pledge to refrain from a threatened lockout of players in spring training and throughout the 1994 season.

By 1993 about one-third of major league revenues was shared; in the NFL the figure was roughly 75 percent. How MLB would divide its spoils between "big market" teams and "small market" franchises was anybody's guess, but it was correctly theorized that a new revenue-sharing formula would go hand-in-hand with some sort of salary cap. Complicating the situation were threats by small-market clubs to veto televising of games from their parks by visiting clubs. The small-market clubs would have the power to do this except for games covered by the various national TV contracts.

Salaries continued to escalate in 1993, and the grossly underachieving Mets started the year with an average salary of $1,534,007. But some teams featured relatively low average salaries: the expansion Rockies ($327,000) and Marlins ($649,876) for example, and the more established Expos ($513,149) and Indians ($541,989).

The Padres angered many fans by trimming salaries and talent in the 1993 season. Star performers such as Fred McGriff, Tony Fernandez, Darrin Jackson, Gary Sheffield, and Bruce Hurst were all sent packing. General Manager Joe McIlvaine abandoned ship as owner Tom Werner successfully pursued a course of lowering the payroll from the $30 million level in 1992 to a goal of $18 million in 1993.

"They have been losing money ever since the purchase," explained Richard Ravitch. "They lost $12 million the last two years. ... And they're going to do what Milwaukee is doing, what Houston did under its prior ownership, what Pittsburgh is doing in order to be able to operate within their resources."

The most significant event of the year was the change from a two-division to a three-division league setup, a concept favored by

both the Players Association and the owners. Formal approval occurred on September 9, 1993, by a 27-1 vote, with only the Texas Rangers' managing general partner and part-owner George W. Bush dissenting. Playoffs would involve the three division winners, plus a so-called wild-card team, i.e., the non-division winner with the best won-lost record. The first round would be a best-of-five format; the second, a best of seven.

Causing controversy were fears that a team with a regular-season losing record could conceivably win a World Series. However, that possibility had already existed under the two-division system, as witnessed by the barely over-.500 Mets lasting until the seventh game of the 1973 World Series.

Meanwhile, television was becoming a problem. CBS, which claimed it had lost $500 million on its last deal, was reluctant to renew at the same rate. In May 1993 a joint venture known as The Baseball Network was created between MLB and two TV networks, NBC and ABC. Unlike prior arrangements in which MLB sold national TV rights for a fee, this new relationship gave The Baseball Network responsibility for advertising sales and production of the telecasts and established a mechanism for splitting the profits.

Signs of fiscal retrenchment were visible in scouting and the minors. A cutback in the Major League Scouting Bureau was announced in the late summer of 1993 as all 21 part-time scouts employed by the Bureau were laid off.

Facing opposition from minor league clubs and financially-strapped local communities, MLB relented on the ballpark improvement provisions of the Professional Baseball Agreement, delaying the deadline for its provisions to April 1, 1995. The minors on their part agreed to put off reopening the entire PBA until September 1994 (a reopening that would be delayed because of the 1994 strike).

The minors in 1993 also featured the creation of three independent circuits. Two of them, the Texas-Louisiana and the Frontier Leagues, were unmitigated flops, but the Northern League showed that, under the right circumstances, such entities could succeed.

1994: The Best of Times …

The 1994 season saw an explosion of offense and fan interest in the game. The initially controversial three-division structure created new races and excitement. Ken Griffey, Jr., Matt Williams, Tony Gwynn, Greg Maddux, and Jeff Bagwell were on track for monster—perhaps even historic—seasons. Minor league attendance (helped along by attractive new parks, clever marketing and promotions, and Michael Jordan's presence in the Southern League) continued its steady growth. The National Association attracted 33,355,199 fans, up 11 percent from 1993, with the Eastern, Southern, Texas, California, Midwest, Southern, New-York Penn, and Northwest leagues all setting attendance records. While the Buffalo Bisons (hampered by two rainouts) narrowly missed achieving the million fan mark for only the first time since 1988, most other clubs had no reason to complain. Totals of a million were growing commonplace at the Triple-A level, with the PCL's new Salt Lake City Buzz drawing 713,224. In independent play, both the Northern League and the newly invigorated Texas-Louisiana League did well at the gate.

On March 2, 1994, Major League Baseball, facing ever tougher competition from other sports, established a six-man committee headed by Boston's John Harrington to deal once again with the issue of expansion. The committee eventually set August 12, 1994 as the deadline for bidders for two additional expansion franchises to submit their proposals. In all, 27 groups, representing 9 cities—Buffalo, Mexico City, Monterrey, Nashville, Northern Virginia, Orlando, Phoenix, Tampa-St. Petersburg, and Vancouver—requested proposals for new franchises, which many thought would go for $150 million each. Nine groups finally sent in bids, and five groups (representing Phoenix, Orlando, St. Petersburg, and two from Northern Virginia) met with MLB's expansion committee. In Phoenix, the Maricopa County Board of Supervisors had already authorized spending up to $238 million on a new domed stadium, to be paid for in part by a one-quarter-cent increase in the local sales tax. In Tampa-St. Petersburg, 32,079 local fans left $50 deposits for season tickets. In Orlando, the Orange County Commission granted conceptual approval for a new $150 million stadium near the Florida Citrus Bowl.

… The Worst of Times

Baseball's Basic Agreement expired on December 31, 1993. Baseball beat writers certainly expected a strike, but few thought it would destroy utterly what President Bill Clinton described as "the most exciting baseball season in 40 years."

The year began with ownership initially divided on the issue of revenue sharing, but on January 18, 1994, owners agreed by a vote of 28-0 to increase it. That agreement, however, was contingent on labor accepting a salary cap. It was not until June 13 that the PRC's Richard Ravitch put forward a complicated package:

- Revenue sharing between management and labor;
- A salary cap in which no club could have a payroll of more than 110 percent of the major league average nor less than 84 percent of that average;
- Elimination of salary arbitration;
- Lowering the threshold for free agency from six years to four years, but allowing current clubs to match best offers until players reach their sixth year of service;
- An escalating (but unspecified) scale of minimum salaries for players with less than four years of service.

Ravitch proposed that this Basic Agreement extend for seven years. He estimated that if MLB revenues expanded by 7 percent, player salaries would grow from a base of $1.2 at the start of the 1994 season to $1.6 million by 2001. With a 10 percent growth, players would receive a $2-million average salary, and a revenue growth of 14 percent would yield an average player salary of a $2.6 million.

Despite a $50.3-million industry-wide operating profit in 1993, management felt compelled to press such sweeping changes. While at first glance a $50.3-million profit seemed comforting, it was a sharp drop from the peak of $214.5 million in black ink achieved in 1989. Based on club financial projections, 19 clubs reportedly faced the possibility of losing money in 1994. Later, when Bud Selig was asked how many clubs would lose money in 1994, he estimated 12 to 14.

One of the most distressed franchises was Pittsburgh. Despite drastically cutting their payroll, the Pirates had lost an estimated $40 million over the preceding five seasons. They owed $20 million to CitiBank, with $5 million of that due in August 1994. The situation grew so desperate that during the 1994 season, an emergency $8 million loan was engineered, with ownership anteing up

$4 million and the City of Pittsburgh coming up with the remainder. Still, another $8 million might prove necessary in January 1995.

Plaguing Pittsburgh was not only its small-market status but an outdated "cookie-cutter" stadium. However, the Pirates' suffering was not merely aesthetic, for they were also saddled with one of the worst leases in the majors. The club surrendered 10 percent of ticket revenues to the city, plus another 10 percent in amusement taxes. Retaining just 28 percent of concession revenues, they secured nothing from either stadium parking or advertising.

Even among still-profitable franchises there were difficulties. New Orioles owner Peter G. Angelos contended that Baltimore would suffer a $25.5 million drop in net profits in 1994. Some $10 million of that resulted from higher player salaries (including that for expensive free agents), while another $8 million came in decreases from national television revenues.

The MLBPA Response

On the other hand, players saw that MLB revenues had reached a historic high of $1.88 billion in 1993. They contended that no one was forcing ownership to pay exorbitant free-agent salaries to often overvalued players. They were not about to make concessions without receiving significant concessions in return. Basically, they were satisfied with the status quo. And even outside union ranks, political and economic conservatives likened the idea of a salary cap to such notions as wage-and-price controls.

On July 18, 1994 Donald Fehr presented this list of demands to Ravitch:

- Ending the ban on so-called repeat free agency within a five-year span if the player's club offered arbitration at contract's end;
- Reducing the threshold for arbitration from three years to two years, plus the top 17 percent of the players with between two and three years of major league service (this former threshold had existed from 1974 to 1986);
- Increasing the MLB minimum salary from $109,000 to $175,000;
- Increasing pension benefits for players who had retired before 1970.

There was no give between the two positions. The situation was further exacerbated on August 1, 1994, when management withheld a $7.8 million payment to the players' pension and benefit fund.

On August 12, 1994 (ironically, the deadline set for the delivery of expansion proposals), the players struck. They could have walked out at any point earlier in the year, but, by striking later in the season, they were able to collect a good portion (an estimated 75 percent on August 14) of their salaries and signing bonuses; at the same time, management would not yet have collected any significant portion of their $140 million due from national television contracts. Plus, with the postseason and World Series in jeopardy, Fehr and the MLBPA theorized they could force Ravitch and the PRC to a relatively quick capitulation.

It didn't happen that way.

Counteroffers and Cancellation

The costs of the strike—both direct and indirect—were immense. The average major league player lost $6,496 per day,

with the stoppage costing Bobby Bonilla, the majors' highest-paid player, $31,148 daily. The strike cost management an estimated $8.5 million in revenues per day, although this was offset by the $4.4 million they no longer had to pay each day in player salaries.

As the strike dragged on, meetings—some open, some secret—were held, but no movement occurred. On September 8, 1994, the MLBPA proposed a variant on the salary-cap and revenue-sharing ideas. Under their counterproposal, the richest 16 franchises would pay a 1.5 percent penalty on their payrolls. The sum would then be distributed among the remaining 12 clubs. In terms of revenue sharing, visiting teams in both leagues would receive 25 percent of all gate receipts. Under the present system visiting American League teams receive 20 percent of ticket sales, while in the National League visitors receive only 43 cents on each ticket, a sum equivalent to only about 4 percent of gate receipts. The union proposed no concessions on either arbitration or free agency.

Management did not consider this an answer to their problems. It also appeared that the PRC's salary-cap proposal may have been only one of a number of ways to relieve its problem of cost containment.

Also aggravating owner sensibilities was a report on MLB finances generated by Stanford University economist Roger Noll, which ownership derided as "theatrical." Some said Noll's report merely solidified ownership resolve. The MLBPA and many observers had expected management to fold quickly, but the owners (tied together by a rule mandating 75 percent approval of any settlement) held firm.

With anxieties from the networks and fans building, and difficulties in scheduling a meaningful postseason looming, a determination had to be reached on continuation of major league baseball for 1994. On September 14, Bud Selig canceled the remainder of the regular-season play, as well as the playoffs and the World Series. Only two owners, Baltimore's Peter Angelos and Cincinnati's Marge Schott, dissented from the determination. Selig's fateful announcement read:

> Due to the player strike that began on August 12, 1994, the Office of the Commissioner of Baseball, acting pursuant to a resolution of the major league clubs, reluctantly concluded today that the remainder of the 1994 season, the Division Series, the League Championship Series, and the World Series will not be played.
>
> This is a sad day. Nobody wanted this to happen, but the continuing player strike leaves us no choice but to take this action. We have reached the point where it is no longer practical to complete the remainder of the season or to preserve the integrity of postseason play.
>
> On June 14, the clubs proposed a reasonable offer to the players' union which included a guarantee of $1 billion in salary and benefits for the players—the largest players' payroll ever. Since that time the clubs have asked the players to negotiate some reasonable division of revenues between players and clubs or some other method of controlling the growth in salaries and ensuring competitive balance.
>
> The union refused to bargain with us over costs and took a hardline position that the clubs would fold as they had in past negotiations. That was a terrible mistake, one for which all of us must pay.

Resolution, Finally

On January 4, 1995, Senator Daniel Moynihan and Representative Michael Bilirakis announced plans to introduce bills to remove baseball's exemption from federal antitrust laws. A few weeks later, President Bill Clinton ordered the owners and players to resume collective bargaining and make substantial progress toward a settlement by February 6 (Clinton did not have actual jurisdiction over baseball, though the two sides did engage in a few rounds of perfunctory negotiations before the "deadline"). On February 16, spring training began, with every team but the Orioles stocking their rosters with "replacement players."

On March 14, the National Labor Relations Board announced that it would issue an unfair-labor-practices complaint against the owners, and eventually—after a variety of fruitless legal maneuverings by the owners—the owners were forced to restore the pre-strike work rules. With this, the players ended their strike, and began preparing for an abbreviated 144-game schedule that wouldn't begin until April 25. So the 1995 season was played under the old labor agreement, leaving the '96 season in doubt. Fortunately, two days before Thanksgiving, the owners voted, 26-4, to accept a new contract with the Players Association (the owners had previously failed to approve the same deal, but apparently "interim" commissioner Bud Selig changed enough votes to ensure passage), and in December the players concurred.

(One tertiary but long-lasting result of this particular labor dispute was the creation of the replacement players—or "scabs," as they were called by members of the union. Most replacement players soon disappeared from the scene, but some of them wound up playing in the major leagues. These players—including Rick Reed, Kevin Millar, Cory Lidle, and Damian Miller—were not allowed to join the Players Association, and thus did not benefit from the sale of licensed MLB items such as baseball cards and official jerseys.)

The new Collective Bargaining Agreement (CBA) ran through the 2000 season, with the union having the option to extend the agreement through 2001, which it eventually did. The highlights of the new CBA included revenue sharing among the clubs, a complex luxury-tax system (designed to discourage teams, ever so slightly, from spending more than certain amounts on player salaries), and annual increases in the minimum salaries for players.

For baseball fans, the most notable change concerned the schedule: in 1997, for the first time ever, American League and National League teams would face one another during the regular season. Officially, these "interleague" games were considered an experiment, but as a practical matter it was generally assumed that the interleague games would continue, and they've apparently become a permanent part of the game.

Expansion and Realignment

In 1995, new franchises had been awarded to ownership groups in Phoenix and Tampa-St. Petersburg, with both to begin play in 1998. This would raise the number of major league teams to 30, which presented a problem: if the Arizona Diamondbacks joined the National League and the Tampa Bay Devil Rays joined the American League—as was decided in January, 1997—then each league would contain fifteen teams, which presents serious scheduling difficulties. A committee was formed to solve the problem, and one of the preferred solutions was radical, with as many as 14 teams switching leagues, with teams in close geographical proximity—the Mets and Yankees, for example—playing in the same league.

Commissioner Selig favored "radical alignment," but not enough of his fellow owners did, and the plan was not seriously considered. Another, less radical plan that would have required "only" seven teams to switch leagues also didn't come up for a vote by the owners, because Selig knew it would not be approved (he very rarely allows the owners to vote on something that isn't a sure thing). Finally, in October 1997 the owners agreed on a modest proposal that would move the Detroit Tigers from the American League East to the AL Central and one AL Central team to the National League Central. The Kansas City Royals were given the chance to switch leagues but they declined, and instead the Brewers moved (cynics suggested that Selig orchestrated everything, because in switching to the NL the Brewers would be reviving memories of the old Milwaukee Braves' National League days and setting up more lucrative home dates against the Chicago Cubs).

These shifts left the American League with 14 teams, the National with 16. Interleague games were not "necessary" (as they would have been if both leagues had fifteen teams), but the first season of interleague play had been deemed a rousing success (at least by Selig, along with most of the baseball media), and it was incorporated into the 1998 schedule. At the time, Selig said of realignment, "This is just the first phase. There will be more to come." (We're still waiting, for the great majority of owners are loath to switch leagues, no matter how much sense it might make for some teams.)

Disaster Averted

Though the last labor dispute had been resolved eight years earlier, by 2002 that ugly affair still was fresh in the minds of many baseball fans and baseball writers, and it was widely assumed that the owners and players would once again push their every-so-often brinksmanship past the point of no return. This, despite the terrorist attacks of September 11, 2001, which at least for a while led to suggestions that in this time of national unity, the men who run baseball—the owners, yes, but the players too—certainly wouldn't threaten the national pastime with their petty squabbles.

In baseball, at least, the feelings of unity lasted somewhat less than two months. On November 6 (just a few days after the expansion Diamondbacks beat the Yankees in one of the greatest World Series), Commissioner Selig fired the opening salvo in the labor war with the announcement that the owners had voted, 28-2, to "contract" (that is, eliminate) two major league franchises, the identity of which had not yet been determined (though the Twins and especially the Expos were considered the leading candidates). Considering the impractical nature of contraction, this might reasonably have been seen as both (1) an empty threat to eliminate a few score union jobs and (2) a bargaining chip in the upcoming negotiations.

As usual, the goal on each side was, above all else, to keep as much money for themselves as possible. For ammunition, the owners had something called "The Report of the Independent Members of the Commissioner's Blue Ribbon Panel on Baseball Economics." Compiled by various friends of Commissioner Selig, the report identified a "chronic competitive imbalance" and suggested various ways of restoring balance (or "hope and faith," as Selig liked to say). With the union sure to reject any semblance of a salary cap, the panel focused on adjusting the luxury tax and revenue sharing to shift significantly more money from rich teams to less-rich teams.

The owners and players finally agreed on a new Collective

Bargaining Agreement on the morning of August 30, just a few hours before a game between the Cardinals and Cubs that would have been the first canceled by a player strike if an agreement were not reached. The new CBA was generally seen as a victory for the owners, who did get significant increases in revenue sharing, and a somewhat tougher luxury tax that some thought would at least give George Steinbrenner second thoughts about grossly outspending every other team (as it turned out, if Steinbrenner had any second thoughts, he ignored them). Meanwhile, the players successfully fought off the salary cap, and retained their rights to salary arbitration and free agency.

If You Build It, They Will Come (at least for a while)

The labor squabbles of the last 15 years were nothing new, of course; they'd been the ugliest feature of the baseball landscape since the early 1970s. What *was* new was the craze for building fancy new ballparks—almost all of them designed, superficially at least, to mimic classic buildings like Tiger Stadium and Ebbets Field—at a rate that hadn't been seen since the Dead Ball Era, when modern steel-and-concrete ballparks replaced the old wooden grandstands. Since 1989, when the Blue Jays moved into SkyDome, 13 of the 26 major league clubs that existed before 1993 had moved into new homes by 2003 (with the Phillies, Padres, and Cardinals all scheduled for new homes of their own).

The results? It's true, what all the headline writers wrote in all the towns that built the gleaming new edifices: they (the fans) did come. Those 13 teams that moved into new ballparks enjoyed an average attendance increase of 37 percent in their first full seasons in their new digs. And it's not just all those extra fannies in the seats that warm the owners' cockles; it's also the (invariably) higher ticket prices, and all those lucrative luxury suites.

Of course, teams have also discovered that a new ballpark is, all by itself, no panacea. While it's probably true that (for example) the Brewers and Pirates are better off in their new ballparks than in their old ones, they still aren't able to compete financially with most other teams because: once the novelty of the new park wears off, many fans aren't interested in paying new-ballpark prices to watch a lousy team; and anyway, a new ballpark doesn't confer a real advantage if everybody else has one, too.

Baseball in the 21st Century

For at least 40 years, various pundits have been predicting the decline and eventual demise of Major League Baseball as a popular concern. The National Football League, Marvin Miller and the combative Players Association, free agency, video games ... all these things and more were going to kill baseball.

It hasn't happened. In 2003, major league teams sold 67,630,052 tickets. Also in 2003, minor league teams sold 39 million tickets, the second-highest total ever and the highest since 1949 (when the minor leagues were comprised of 448 teams in 59 leagues; in 2003 there were 176 teams in 15 leagues). And that figure for the minors doesn't include the increasingly popular "independent" leagues.

The future? Commissioner Selig loves to talk about "internationalizing" the game, and to that end a number of regular-season games have been played in Mexico, Puerto Rico and Japan, and MLB is also serious about creating a baseball version of soccer's World Cup. It remains to be seen whether or not baseball can make significant inroads in countries that haven't traditionally played baseball. But for the foreseeable future, professional baseball is in little danger of expiring.

Chapter 28

Jackie Robinson's Signing: The Real, Untold Story

Leo Durocher and Jackie Robinson
After spending one year with the minor league Montreal Royals, Robinson earned a starring role with Durocher's Brooklyn Dodgers.

By John Thorn and Jules Tygiel

October 1945. As the Detroit Tigers and Chicago Cubs faced off in the World Series, photographer Maurice Terrell arrived at an almost deserted minor league park in San Diego, California, to carry out a top-secret assignment: to surreptitiously photograph three black baseball players.

Terrell shot hundreds of motion-picture frames of Jackie Robinson and the two other players. A few photos appeared in print but the existence of the additional images remained unknown for four decades. In April 1987, as Major League Baseball prepared a lavish commemoration of the fortieth anniversary of Robinson's debut, John Thorn unearthed a body of contact sheets and unprocessed film from a previously unopened carton donated in 1954 by *Look* magazine to the Baseball Hall of Fame in Cooperstown, New York. This discovery triggered an investigation which led to startling revelations regarding Branch Rickey, the president of the Brooklyn Dodgers, and his signing of Jackie Robinson to shatter baseball's longstanding color line; the relationship between these two historic figures; and the still controversial issue of black managers in baseball.

The popular "frontier" image of Jackie Robinson as a lone gunman facing down a hostile mob has always dominated the story

of the integration of baseball. But new information related to the Terrell photos reveals that while Robinson was the linchpin in Branch Rickey's strategy, in October 1945 Rickey intended to announce the signing of not just Jackie Robinson, but of several other Negro League stars. Political pressure, however, forced Rickey's hand, thrusting Robinson alone into the spotlight. And in 1950, after only three years in the major leagues, Robinson pressed Rickey to consider him for a position as field manager or front-office executive, raising an issue with which the baseball establishment still grapples.

The story of these revelations began with the discovery of the Terrell photographs. The photos show a youthful, muscular Robinson in a battered cap and baggy uniform fielding from his position at shortstop, batting with a black catcher crouched behind him, trapping a third black player in a rundown between third and home, and sprinting along the basepaths more like a former track star than a baseball player. All three players wore uniforms emblazoned with the name "Royals." A woman with her back to the action is the only figure visible amid the vacant stands. The contact sheets are dated October 7, 1945.

The photos were perplexing. The momentous announcement of Jackie Robinson's signing with the Montreal Royals took place on October 23, 1945. Before that date his recruitment had been a tightly guarded secret. Why, then, had a *Look* photographer taken such an

interest in Robinson two weeks earlier? Where had the pictures been taken? And why was Robinson already wearing a Royals uniform?

Thorn called Jules Tygiel, the author of *Baseball's Great Experiment: Jackie Robinson and His Legacy*, to see if he could shed some light on the photos. Tygiel knew nothing about them, but he did have in his files a 1945 manuscript by newsman Arthur Mann, who frequently wrote for *Look*. The article, drafted with Rickey's cooperation, had been intended to announce the Robinson signing but had never been published. The pictures, the researchers concluded, were to have accompanied Mann's article; they decided to find out the story behind the photo session.

The clandestine nature of the photo session did not surprise them. From the moment he had arrived in Brooklyn in 1942, determined to end baseball's Jim Crow traditions, Rickey had feared that premature disclosure of his intentions might doom his bold design. No blacks had appeared in the major leagues since 1884 when two brothers, Welday and Moses Fleetwood Walker, had played for Toledo in the American Association. Not since the 1890s had black players appeared on a minor league team. During the ensuing half-century all-black teams and leagues featuring legendary figures like pitcher Satchel Paige and catcher Josh Gibson had performed on the periphery of Organized Baseball. Baseball executives, led by Commissioner Kenesaw Mountain Landis, had strictly policed the color line, barring blacks from both major and minor leagues. Rickey therefore moved slowly and secretly to explore the issue and cover up his attempts to scout black players during his first three years in Brooklyn. He informed the Dodger owners of his plans but took few others into his confidence.

In the spring of 1945, as Rickey prepared to accelerate his scouting efforts, advocates of integration, emboldened by the impending end of World War II and the recent death of Commissioner Landis, escalated their campaign to desegregate baseball. On April 6, 1945, black sportswriter Joe Bostic appeared at the Dodgers' Bear Mountain training camp with Negro League stars Terris McDuffie and Dave "Showboat" Thomas and forced Rickey to hold tryouts for the two players. Ten days later black journalist Wendell Smith, white sportswriter Dave Egan, and Boston city councilman Isidore Muchnick engineered an unsuccessful audition with the Red Sox for Robinson and two other black athletes. In response to these events the major leagues announced the formation of a Committee on Baseball Integration. (Reflecting Organized Baseball's true intentions on the matter, the group never met.)

In the face of this heightened activity, Rickey created an elaborate smokescreen to obscure his scouting of black players. In May 1945 he announced the formation of a new franchise, the Brooklyn Brown Dodgers, and a new Negro League, the United States League. Rickey then dispatched his best talent hunters to observe black ballplayers, ostensibly for the Brown Dodgers, but in reality for the Brooklyn National League club.

A handwritten memorandum in the Rickey Papers offers a rare glimpse of Rickey's emphasis on secrecy in his instructions to Dodger scouts. The document, signed "Chas. D. Clark" and accompanied by a Negro National League schedule for April–May 1945, is headlined "Job Analysis," and defines the following "Duties: under supervision of management of club":

1. To establish contact (silent) with all clubs (local or general).
2. To gain knowledge and [sic] abilities of all players.
3. To report all possible material (players).
4. Prepare weekly reports of activities.

5. Keep composite report of outstanding players ... To travel and cover player whenever management so desire.

Clark's "Approch" [sic] was to "Visit game and loose [sic] self in stands; Keep statistical report (speed, power, agility, ability, fielding, batting, etc.) by score card"; and "Leave immediately after game."

Clark's directions, however, contain one major breach in Rickey's elaborate security precautions. According to his later accounts, Rickey had told most Dodger scouts that they were evaluating talent for a new "Brown Dodger" franchise. But Clark's first "Objective" was "To Cover Negro teams for possible major league talent." Had Rickey confided in Clark, a figure so obscure as to escape prior mention in the voluminous Robinson literature? Dodger superscout and Rickey confidante Clyde Sukeforth has no recollection of Clark, raising the possibility that Clark was not part of the Dodger family, but perhaps someone connected with black baseball. Had Clark himself interpreted his instructions in this manner?

Whatever the answer, Rickey successfully diverted attention from his true motives. Nonetheless, mounting interest in the integration issue threatened Rickey's careful planning. In the summer of 1945 Rickey constructed yet another facade. The Dodger President took into his confidence Dan Dodson, a New York University sociologist who chaired Mayor Fiorello LaGuardia's Committee on Unity, and requested that Dodson form a Committee on Baseball ostensibly to study the possibility of integration. In reality, the committee would provide the illusion of action while Rickey quietly completed his own preparations. "This was one of the toughest decisions I ever had to make while in office," Dodson later confessed. "The major purpose I could see for the committee was that it was a stall for time. ... Yet had Mr. Rickey not delivered ... I would have been totally discredited."

Thus by late August, even as Rickey's extensive scouting reports had led him to focus on Jackie Robinson as his standard bearer, few people in or out of the Dodger organization suspected that a breakthrough was imminent. On August 28, Rickey and Robinson held their historic meeting at the Dodgers' Montague Street offices in downtown Brooklyn. Robinson signed an agreement to accept a contract with the Montreal Royals, the top Dodger affiliate, by November 1.

Rickey, still concerned with secrecy, impressed upon Robinson the need to maintain silence. Robinson could tell the momentous news to his family and fiancee, but no one else. For the conspiratorial Rickey, keeping the news sheltered while continuing arrangements required further subterfuge. Rumors about Robinson's visit had already spread through the world of black baseball. To stifle speculation Rickey "leaked" an adulterated version of the incident to black sportswriter Wendell Smith. Smith, who had recommended Robinson to Rickey and advised Rickey on the integration project, doubtless knew the true story behind the meeting. On September 8, however, he reported in the *Pittsburgh Courier* that the "sensational shortstop" and "colorful major league dynamo" had met behind "closed doors. ... The nature of the conference has not been revealed," Smith continued. Rickey claimed that he and Robinson had assessed "the organization of Negro baseball," but Smith noted that "it does not seem logical [Rickey] should call in a rookie player to discuss the future organization of Negro baseball." He closed with the tantalizing thought that "it appears that the Brooklyn boss has a plan on his mind that extends further than just the future of Negro baseball as an organization." The subterfuge succeeded. Neither black nor white reporters pursued the issue.

Rickey, always sensitive to criticism by New York sports reporters and understanding the historic significance of his actions, also wanted to be sure that his version of the integration breakthrough and his role in it be accurately portrayed. To guarantee this he persuaded Arthur Mann, his close friend and later a Dodger employee, to write a 3,000-word manuscript to be published simultaneously with the announcement of the signing.

Although it was impossible to confirm this in 1987 (it has since been confirmed by Maurice Terrell himself, who was eventually located), it seemed to the researchers highly likely that Terrell's photos, commissioned by *Look,* were destined to accompany Mann's article. Clearer prints of the negatives revealed that Terrell had taken the pictures in San Diego's Lane Stadium. This fit in with Robinson's autumn itinerary. After his meeting with Rickey, Robinson had returned briefly to the Kansas City Monarchs. With the Dodger offer securing his future and the relentless bus trips of the Negro League schedule wearing him down, he had left the Monarchs before season's end and returned home to Pasadena, California. In late September he hooked up with Chet Brewer's Kansas City Royals, a postseason barnstorming team which toured the Pacific Coast, competing against other Negro League teams and major- and minor league all-star squads. Thus the word "Royals" on Robinson's uniform, which had so piqued the interest of Thorn and Tygiel, ironically turned out to relate not to Robinson's future team in Montreal, but rather to his interim employment in California.

For further information Tygiel contacted Chet Brewer, who at age 80 still lived in Los Angeles. Brewer, one of the great pitchers of the Jim Crow era, had known Robinson well. He had followed Robinson's spectacular athletic career at UCLA and in 1945 they became teammates on the Monarchs. "Jackie was major league all the way," recalled Brewer. "He had the fastest reflexes I ever saw in a player."

Robinson particularly relished facing major league all-star squads. Against Bob Feller, Robinson once slashed two doubles. "Jack was running crazy on the bases," a Royal teammate remembered. In one game he upended Gerry Priddy, Washington Senators infielder. Priddy angrily complained about the hard slide in an exhibition game. "Any time I put on a uniform," retorted Robinson, "I play to win."

Brewer recalled that Robinson and two other Royals journeyed from Los Angeles to San Diego on a day when the team was not scheduled to play. He identified the catcher in the photos as Buster Haywood and the other player as Royals third baseman Herb Souell. Souell was no longer living, but Haywood, who, like Brewer lived in Los Angeles, vaguely recalled the event, which he incorrectly remembered as occurring in Pasadena. Robinson recruited the catcher and Souell, his former Monarch teammate, to "work out" with him. All three wore their Royal uniforms. Haywood found neither Robinson's request nor the circumstances unusual. Although he was unaware that they were being photographed, Haywood described the session accurately. "We didn't know what was going on," he stated. "We'd hit and throw and run from third base to home plate."

The San Diego pictures provide a rare glimpse of the pre-Montreal Robinson. The article which they were to accompany and related correspondence in the Library of Congress offer even more rare insights into Rickey's thinking. The unpublished Mann manuscript was entitled "The Negro and Baseball: "The National Game Faces a Racial Challenge Long Ignored." As Mann doubtless based his account on conversations with Rickey and since Rickey's handwritten comments appear in the margin, it stands as the ear-

liest "official" account of the Rickey-Robinson story and reveals many of the concerns confronting Rickey in September 1945.

One of the most striking features of the article is the language used to refer to Robinson. Mann, reflecting the racism typical of postwar America, portrays Robinson as the "first Negro chattel in the so-called National pastime." At another point he writes, "Rickey felt the boy's sincerity," appropriate language perhaps for an 18-year-old prospect, but not for a 26-year-old former Army officer.

"The Negro and Baseball" consists largely of the now familiar Rickey-Robinson story. Mann recreated Rickey's haunting 1904 experience as collegiate coach when one of his black baseball players, Charlie Thomas, was denied access to a hotel. Thomas cried and rubbed his hands, chanting, "Black skin! Black skin! If I could only make 'em white." Mann described Rickey's search for the "right" man, the formation of the United States League as a cover for scouting operations, the reasons for selecting Robinson, and the fateful Rickey-Robinson confrontation. Other sections, however, graphically illustrate additional issues Rickey deemed significant. Mann repeatedly cites the costs the Dodgers incurred: $5,000 to scout Cuba, $6,000 to scout Mexico, $5,000 to establish the "Brooklyn Brown Dodgers." The final total reaches $25,000, a modest sum considering the ultimate returns, but one that Rickey felt would counter his skinflint image.

Rickey's desire to show that he was not motivated by political pressures also emerges clearly. Mann had suggested that upon arriving in Brooklyn in 1942, Rickey "was besieged by telephone calls, telegrams and letters of petition in behalf of black ball players," and that this "staggering pile of missives [was] so inspired to convince him that he and the Dodgers had been selected as a kind of guinea pig." In his marginal comments, Rickey vehemently wrote "No!" in a strong dark script. "I began all this as soon as I went to Brooklyn." Explaining why he had never attacked the subject during his two decades as general manager of the St. Louis Cardinals, Rickey referred to the segregation in that city. "St. Louis never permitted Negro patrons in the grandstand," he wrote, describing a policy he apparently had felt powerless to change.

Mann also devoted two of his twelve pages to a spirited attack on the Negro Leagues, repeating Rickey's charges that "they are the poorest excuse for the word league" and documented the prevalence of barnstorming, the uneven scheduling, absence of contracts, and dominance of booking agents. Mann revealingly traces Rickey's distaste for the Negro Leagues to the "outrageous" guarantees demanded by New York booking agent William Leuschner to place black teams in Ebbets Field while the Dodgers were on the road.

Rickey's misplaced obsession with the internal disorganization of the Negro Leagues had substantial factual basis. But Rickey had an ulterior motive. In his September 8 article, Wendell Smith addressed the issue of "player tampering," asking, "Would [Rickey] not first approach the owners of these Negro teams who have these stars under contract?" Rickey, argued Smith in what might have been an unsuccessful preemptive strike, "is obligated to do so and his record as a businessman indicated that he would." As Smith may have known, Rickey maintained that Negro League players did not sign valid contracts and so became free agents at the end of each season. Thus the Mahatma had no intention of compensating Negro League teams for the players he signed. His repeated attacks on black baseball, including the Mann article, served to justify this questionable position.

The one respect in which "The Negro and Baseball" departs radically from the common picture of the Robinson legend is in its

report of Robinson as one of a group of blacks about to be signed by the Dodgers. Mann's manuscript and subsequent correspondence from Rickey reveal that Rickey did not intend for Robinson to withstand the pressures alone. "Determined not to be charged with merely nibbling at the problem," wrote Mann, "Rickey went all out and brought in two more Negro players," and "consigned them, with Robinson, to the Dodgers' top farm club, the Montreal Royals." Mann named pitcher Don Newcombe and, surprisingly, outfielder Sam Jethroe as Robinson's future teammates. Whether the recruitment of additional blacks had always been Rickey's intention or whether he had reached his decision after meeting with Robinson in August is unclear. But by late September, when he provided information to Mann for his article, Rickey had clearly decided to bring in other Negro League stars.

During the first weekend in October, Dodger coach Chuck Dressen fielded a major league all-star team in a series of exhibition games against Negro League standouts at Ebbets Field. Rickey took the opportunity to interview at least three black pitching prospects, Newcombe, Roy Partlow and John Wright. The following week he met with catcher Roy Campanella. Campanella and Newcombe, at least, believed they had been approached to play for the "Brown Dodgers."

At the same time Rickey decided to postpone publication of Mann's manuscript. In a remarkable letter sent from the World Series in Chicago on October 7, Rickey informed Mann:

We just can't go now with the article. The thing isn't dead, not at all. It is more alive than ever and that is the reason we can't go with any publicity at this time. There is more involved in the situation than I had contemplated. Other players are in it and it may be that I can't clear these players until after the December meetings, possibly not until after the first of the year. You must simply sit in the boat. ...

There is a November 1 deadline on Robinson,—you know that. I am undertaking to extend that date until January 1st so as to give me time to sign plenty of players and make one break on the complete story. Also, quite obviously it might not be good to sign Robinson with other and possibly better players unsigned.

The revelations and tone of this letter surprised Robinson's widow, Rachel, 40 years after the event. Rickey "was such a deliberate man," she recalled, "and this letter is so urgent. He must have been very nervous as he neared his goal. Maybe he was nervous that the owners would turn him down and having five people at the door instead of just one would have been more powerful."

Events in the weeks after October 7 justified Rickey's nervousness and forced him to deviate from the course stated in the Mann letter. Candidates in New York City's upcoming November elections, most notably black Communist City Councilman Ben Davis, made baseball integration a major issue in the campaign. Mayor LaGuardia's Democratic party also sought to exploit the issue. The Committee on Baseball had prepared a report outlining a modest, long-range strategy for bringing blacks into the game and describing the New York teams, because of the favorable political and racial climate in the city, as in a "choice position to undertake this pattern of integration." LaGuardia wanted Rickey's permission to make a pre-election announcement that "baseball would shortly begin signing Negro players," as a result of the committee's work.

Rickey, a committee member, had long since subverted the panel to his own purposes. By mid-October, however, the committee had become "an election football." Again unwilling to

risk the appearance of succumbing to political pressure and thereby surrendering what he viewed as his rightful role in history, Rickey asked LaGuardia to delay his comments. Rickey hurriedly contacted Robinson, who had joined a barnstorming team in New York en route to play winter ball in Venezuela, and dispatched him to Montreal. On October 23, 1945, with Rickey's carefully laid plans scuttled, the Montreal Royals announced the signing of Robinson, and Robinson alone.

Mann's article never appeared. *Look,* having lost its exclusive, published two strips of the Terrell pictures in its November 27, 1945 issue accompanying a brief summary of the Robinson story, by then old news. The unprocessed film and contact sheets were loaded into a box and nine years later shipped to the National Baseball Hall of Fame, where they remained, along with a picture of Jethroe, unpacked until April 1987.

Newcombe, Campanella, Wright, and Partlow all joined the Dodger organization the following spring. Jethroe became a victim of the "deliberate speed" of baseball integration. Rickey did not interview Jethroe in 1945. Since few teams followed the Dodger lead, the fleet, powerful outfielder remained in the Negro Leagues until 1948, when Rickey finally bought his contract from the Cleveland Buckeyes for $5,000. Jethroe had two spectacular seasons at Montreal before Rickey, fearing a "surfeit of colored boys on the Brooklyn club," profitably sold him to the Boston Braves for $100,000. Jethroe won the Rookie of the Year Award in 1950, but his delayed entry into Organized Baseball foreshortened what should have been a stellar career. Until informed by the authors of this essay, Jethroe remained unaware of how close he had come to joining Robinson, Newcombe and Campanella in the pantheon of integration pioneers.

For Robinson, who had always occupied center stage in Rickey's thinking, the early announcement intensified the pressures and enhanced the legend. The success or failure of integration rested disproportionately on his capable shoulders. He became the lightning rod for supporter and opponent alike, attracting the responsibility, the opprobrium and ultimately the acclaim for his historic achievement.

Beyond these revelations about the Robinson signing, the Library of Congress documents add surprisingly little to the familiar story of the integration of baseball. The Rickey Papers copiously detail his post-Dodger career as general manager of the Pittsburgh Pirates, but are strangely silent about the criticial period of 1944 to 1948. Records for these years probably remained with the Dodger organization, which claims to have no knowledge of their whereabouts. National League documents for these years remain closed to the public.

In light of the controversy engendered by former Dodger general manager Al Campanis' remarks about blacks in management, however, one exchange between Rickey and Robinson becomes particularly relevant. In 1950, after his fourth season with the Dodgers, Robinson appears to have written Rickey about the possibility of employment in baseball when his playing days ended. Robinson's original letter cannot be found in either the Rickey papers or the Robinson family archives. However, Rickey's reply, dated December 31, 1950, survives. Rickey, who had recently left the Dodgers after an unsuccessful struggle to wrest control of the team from Walter O'Malley, responded to Robinson's inquiry with a long and equivocal answer.

"It is not at all because of lack of appreciation that I have not acknowledged your good letter of some time ago," began Rickey. "Neither your writing, nor sending the letter, nor its contents gave

me very much surprise." On the subject of managing, Rickey replied optimistically, "I hope that the day will soon come when it will be entirely possible, as it is entirely right, that you can be considered for administrative work in baseball, particularly in the direction of field management." Rickey claimed to have told several writers that "I do not know of any player in the game today who could, in my judgment, manage a major league team better than yourself," but that the news media had inexplicably ignored these comments.

Yet Rickey tempered his encouragement with remarks that to a reader today seem gratuitous. "As I have often expressed to you," he wrote, "I think you carry a great responsibility for your people ... and I cannot close this letter without admonishing you to prepare yourself to do a widely useful work, and, at the same time, dignified and effective in the field of public relations. A part of this preparation, and I know you are smiling, for you have already guessed my oft repeated suggestion—to finish your college course meritoriously and get your degree." This advice, according to Rachel Robinson, was a "matter of routine" between the two men ever since their first meeting. Nonetheless, to the 31-year-old Robinson, whose non-athletic academic career had been marked by indifferent success and whose endorsements and business acumen had already established the promise of a secure future, Rickey's response may have seemed to beg the question.

Rickey concluded with the promise, which seems to hinge on the completion of a college degree, that "It would be a great pleasure for me to be your agent in placing you in a big job after your playing days are finished. Believe me always." Shortly after writing this letter Rickey became the general manager of the Pittsburgh Pirates. Had Robinson ended his playing career before Rickey left the Pirates, perhaps the Mahatma would have made good on his pledge. But Rickey resigned from the Pirates at the end of the 1955 season, one year before Robinson's retirement, and never again had the power to hire a manager.

Robinson's 1950 letter to Rickey marked only the beginning of his quest to see a black manager in the major leagues. In 1952 he hoped to gain experience by managing in the Puerto Rican winter league, but, according to the *New York Post*, Commissioner Happy Chandler withheld his approval, forcing Robinson to cancel his plans. On November 30, 1952, the Dodger star raised the prospect of a black manager in a televised interview on *Youth Wants to Know*, stating that both he and Campanella had been "approached" on the subject. In 1954, after the Dodgers had fired manager Chuck Dressen, speculation arose that either Robinson or Pee Wee Reese might be named to the post. But the team bypassed both men and selected veteran minor league manager Walter Alston, who went on to hold the job for more than two decades.

Upon his retirement in 1956, Robinson, who had begun to manifest signs of the diabetes that would plague the rest of his life, had lost much of his enthusiasm for the prospect of managing, but nonetheless would probably have accepted another pioneering role. "He had wearied of the travel," states Rachel, "and no longer wanted to manage. He just wanted to be asked as a recognition of his accomplishments, his abilities as a strategist, and to show that white men could be led by a black."

Ironically, in the early years of integration Organized Baseball had bypassed a large pool of qualified and experienced black managers: former Negro League players and managers like Chet Brewer, Ray Dandridge and Quincy Trouppe. In the early 1950s Brewer and several other Negro League veterans managed all-black minor league teams, but no interracial club at any level offered a

managerial position to a black until 1961, when former Negro League and major league infielder Gene Baker assumed the reins of a low-level Pittsburgh Pirate farm team, one of only three blacks to manage a major league affiliate before 1975.

This lack of opportunity loomed as a major frustration for those who had broken the color line. "We bring dollars into club treasuries while we play," protested Larry Doby, the first black American Leaguer, in 1964, "but when we stop playing, our dollars stop. When I retired in '59 I wanted to stay in the game, to be a coach or in some other capacity, or to manage in the minors until I'd qualify for a big league job. Baseball owners are missing the boat by not considering Negroes for such jobs." Monte Irvin, who had integrated the New York Giants in 1949 and clearly possessed managerial capabilities, concurred. "Among retired and active players [there] are Negroes with backgrounds suited to these jobs," wrote Irvin. "Owning a package liquor store, bowling alley or selling insurance is hardly the vocation for an athlete who has accumulated a lifetime knowledge of the game."

Had Robinson, Doby, Irvin, or another black been offered a managerial position in the 1950s or early 1960s, and particularly if the first black manager had experienced success, it is possible that this would have opened the doors for other black candidates. As with Robinson's ascension to the major leagues, this example might ultimately have made the hiring and firing of a black manager more or less routine. Robinson dismissed the notion that a black manager might experience extraordinary difficulties. "Many people believe that white athletes will not play for a Negro manager," he argued in 1964. "A professional athlete will play with or for anyone who helps him make more money. He will respect ability, first, last, and all the time. This is something that baseball's executives must learn—that any experienced player with leadership qualities can pilot a ballclub to victory, no matter what the color of his skin."

On the other hand, the persistent biases of major league owners and their subsequent history of discriminatory hiring indicate that the solitary example of a Jackie Robinson regime would probably not have been enough to shake the complacency of the baseball establishment. Few baseball executives considered hiring blacks as managers even in the 1960s and 1970s. In 1960 Chicago White Sox owner Bill Veeck, who had hired Doby in 1947 and represented the most enlightened thinking in the game, raised the issue, but even Veeck defined special qualifications needed for a black to manage. "A man will have to have more stability to be a Negro coach or manager and be slower to anger than if he were white," stated Veeck. "The first major league manager will have to be a fellow who has been playing extremely well for a dozen years or so, so that he becomes a byword for excellence." The following year Veeck sold the White Sox; other owners ignored the issue entirely.

Robinson himself never flagged in his determination to see a black manager. In 1972 baseball commemorated the 25th anniversary of Robinson's major league debut at the World Series at Riverfront Stadium in Cincinnati. A graying, almost blind, but still defiant Robinson told a nationwide television audience, "I'd like to live to see a black manager." Nine days later he was dead.

"I would have eagerly welcomed the challenge of a managerial job before I left the game," Robinson revealed in his 1972 autobiography, *I Never Had It Made*. "I know I could have been a good manager." But despite his obvious qualifications, no one offered him a job. Thus Jackie Robinson once again had been the first—the first of many worthy black baseball players denied the chance to manage in the major leagues.

Chapter 29

Baseball and the Law

By Gary D. Hailey

Like other members of our litigation-happy society, baseball players and team owners have spent their fair share of time in the courtroom. Judges have been asked to decide lawsuits involving everything from a team's liability for fan injuries from foul balls and thrown bats to the legality of the decision to resume the infamous Yankees-Royals "Pine Tar Game" nearly a month after George Brett's home run had been ruled a game-ending out.

But the most significant baseball-related court cases were a series of mostly unsuccessful challenges to Organized Baseball's attempts to limit competition from rival leagues for players' services. That litigation has reached the United States Supreme Court three times, and all three times that Court has ruled that baseball is not governed by the antitrust laws. The reasoning behind this holding may have been perfectly logical when the first of those cases was decided in 1922, but today it seems anachronistic.

From the game's earliest days, baseball owners have struggled to keep their expenses down by maintaining control over the players, who often decide that the grass (and the money) is greener in someone else's ballpark. In 1870 the National Association of Base Ball Players tried to stop "revolving," or contract jumping, by adopting a rule requiring players to give 60 days' notice before leaving one club for another. Tougher controls were agreed to after word leaked that A. G. Spalding and three other Boston Red Stockings stars had signed contracts in the middle of the 1875 season to play for Chicago in 1876. In 1879 the National League secretly agreed to allow each team owner to "reserve" his five best players at the end of the season; other owners were prohibited from bidding for the services of the reserved players. The owners also agreed not to sign any player who refused to play for the team that reserved him.

Forty-seven National Leaguers jumped to the American Association when that rival league commenced play in 1882, but virtually none of them were reserved players. During the 1882 season, the AA induced other NL players to promise to jump leagues in 1883, but the NL fought back to prevent these impending desertions. Charles Bennett, Detroit's star catcher, accepted $100 in exchange for his written promise to sign a contract with the AA's Pittsburgh team in 1883. Before Bennett signed that contract, Detroit offered him more money to stay in the NL. Pittsburgh got wind of what was happening and immediately filed

Andy Messersmith
The free-agent era began on December 23, 1975 when Messersmith and Dave McNally won a ruling from arbitrator Peter Seitz that struck down baseball's reserve clause.

suit in Federal court, seeking an injunction ordering Bennett to sign the Pittsburgh contract.

Bennett's lawyers offered a number of legal defenses, some rather narrow and technical. The court ruled in Bennett's favor but did not issue a written opinion, so it is unclear just which of his attorneys' arguments were persuasive. But the court may have refused to enjoin Bennett's jump to Detroit simply because of the timing of the lawsuit. The Pittsburgh club would have suffered no real harm from Bennett's refusal to sign an 1883 contract until it had to play a game without him in the lineup. Its October 1882 lawsuit was, in a sense, premature because Bennett might have changed his mind and returned to Pittsburgh before the opening day of the 1883 season.

Shortstop Sam Wise followed in Bennett's footsteps, signing with the Cincinnati AA team but eventually jumping back to his NL team, the Boston Red Stockings, when they promised to increase his salary. Cincinnati persuaded an Ohio judge to order Wise not to play for Boston. But Cincinnati was unable to enforce the Ohio order in other states. Wise had to stay at home when the Red Stockings came to Cleveland, but was otherwise free to play for Boston.

The National League and American Association made peace in 1883 and signed the "National Agreement," which contained a strengthened reserve rule. The promoters of the Union Association hoped to capitalize on the players' resentment of the one-sided terms of their contracts with Organized Baseball, but the established leagues fought back hard by adopting the "Day Resolution," an agreement to blacklist any reserved player who jumped to a Union club. Star pitcher Tony Mullane, who jumped from the St. Louis Browns to the St. Louis Maroons of the new league, tried to return to the Browns after hearing about the Day Resolution. The Browns refused to welcome their prodigal son back because they knew the Maroons would haul them into court if they did. The Toledo AA club wanted Mullane, but the National Agreement did not provide for player trades or sales. The Browns simply released Mullane outright, and Toledo signed him. The Union Association failed to persuade an Ohio Federal judge to order Mullane back to the Maroons. [2] After the demise of the upstart league at the end of the 1884 season, Toledo agreed to send Mullane back to the Browns, but the Cincinnati AA club—in flagrant violation of the National Agreement—signed the 35-game winner to a lucrative bonus contract. The Association's powers-that-be ultimately awarded Mullane to Cincinnati, but ordered him to sit out the 1885 season and give back part of his bonus.

Once the Union Association was dead and buried, Organized Baseball established a maximum annual player salary of $2,000. Owners soon found ways around this provision—in 1887 Boston paid superstar Mike "King" Kelly an additional $3,000 "for use of his picture." Their reduced bargaining leverage caused the players to form the National Brotherhood of Professional Base Ball Players under the leadership of John Montgomery Ward, the New York Giants shortstop who had attended Columbia University law school in the off-season. Ward claimed that the reserve clause, the blacklist and other intimidating provisions of the standard player contract were legally unenforceable. When the owners refused to scrap the salary cap or to agree not to sell or trade players without their consent, the Brotherhood went on to form the Players League, which fielded eight teams in 1890. Over 80 National League players and almost 30 from the American Association—including future Hall of Famers Ward, Jake Beckley, Dan Brouthers, John Clarkson, Charles Comiskey, Roger Connor, Hugh Duffy, "Buck" Ewing, Tim Keefe, "King" Kelly, Connie Mack, "Orator Jim" O'Rourke, and "Old Hoss" Radbourn—signed up with the Players League.

Organized Baseball used every weapon at its disposal to strike back at this new rival. The owners told fans that the players were aligned with radical unionists. Boston reportedly gave pitcher Clarkson $10,000—five times the average 1889 salary—to desert the Brotherhood, while Spalding offered King Kelly a blank check to play for the White Stockings. When propaganda and cold, hard cash failed, the established league fielded a team of lawyers at courthouses around the country.

The reserve rule had been generally effective as a sort of gentlemen's agreement among the parties to the National Agreement not to compete for their fellow owners' players. But when the National League tried to enforce the reserve clause against the Players League, it got nowhere. A Federal court in New York City held that the Giants could not keep catcher Ewing from playing for their Brotherhood rival because the reserve provisions in his 1889 contract were "merely a contract to make a contract" for 1890 "if the parties agree." [3] The reserve clause was valuable because it gave the Giants a "prior and exclusive" right to negotiate with Ewing that was enforceable against other clubs in Organized Baseball. But as a basis for an injunction preventing a player from taking the field for a Players League team, Ewing's contract was held "wholly nugatory" because it did not set forth in detail contract terms and conditions (including salary) for 1890. A party who seeks enforcement of a contract with vague or indefinite terms is really asking the court to fill in the blank spaces in that contract, which is something that courts are reluctant to do.

Other courts objected not only to the indefiniteness of player contracts but also to their one-sidedness, which they referred to as a "lack of mutuality." Owners could release players on 10 days' notice, but the reserve clause purported to bind a player to one team for as long as the team wanted him. A New York state court judge expressed disgust at "the spectacle" of the Giants' attempt to enforce "a contract which binds [the player] for a series of years and [the team] for 10 days." [4] The National League spent $15,000 on lawyers' fees in New York alone fighting the Players League, but came away with nothing to show for it.

The Players League won the legal battles, but not the war—in fact, everyone lost money. Both sides agreed to Spalding's suggestion that some Players League teams be merged with existing NL and AA franchises and the rest be dissolved. After a bit of skirmishing over the rights to sign some of the returning Players League stars, the NL and AA merged their 16 clubs into 12 after the 1891 season, and then signed a new National Agreement with the minor leagues. Players had little choice but to accept the terms offered by the "Baseball Trust," but a few rebelled. Amos Rusie won 22 games in 1895 and led the league in strikeouts, but Giants owner Andrew Freedman rewarded him by withholding $600 in fines from his paycheck. Rusie sat out 1896 and then sued the Giants when they invoked their reserve for 1897 as well. The case was settled before trial, with all the National League owners reportedly kicking in a portion of Rusie's $5,000 claim.

As usual the next baseball war set off a spate of contract jumping and legal skirmishes. Over half of the players who suited up for the American League's first season of play were ex-National Leaguers. The senior circuit went to court to try to wrest back a number of their players, most notably Napoleon Lajoie. Lajoie signed a contract with the Phillies in 1900, but refused to be bound by the reserve clause and jumped to the Athletics before the 1901 season. The Pennsylvania Supreme Court held that the Phillies were entitled to an injunction barring the batting champ from playing for the A's. [5]

But that decision turned in part on two unusual factors. First, the Phillies' contract reserved Lajoie for only three years and stated what salary would be paid in each of those three years, so it was not simply a contract to make a contract. Second, Lajoie was a star of the very highest order. Courts are reluctant to order someone to perform a contract for personal services, although they are not at all reluctant to order the defendant to pay monetary damages equal to the harm caused by his nonperformance. Only when the harm cannot be measured in dollars or the contract involves something unique or irreplaceable are injunctions or other nonmonetary remedies granted by a court. The Phillies may have been able to find

equally talented replacements for many of their players, but Lajoie—who led the AL in hits, doubles, home runs, runs, RBIs, batting average, and slugging average in 1901—was a unique talent.

The Phillies' legal victory proved hollow. The A's quickly dealt Lajoie to Cleveland. Whenever Cleveland was scheduled to play in Philadelphia, Lajoie stayed far away. His old team's attempts to obtain an injunction from an Ohio court were not successful.

Other National League efforts to retain players also failed. Citing a Supreme Court case holding that a contract that could be abandoned on one year's notice was not enforceable, a Federal judge dismissed Brooklyn's suit against veteran catcher Deacon McGuire because the team could terminate his contract on only 10 days' notice.[6] The judge also questioned whether McGuire's talents were so "unique and peculiar" that Brooklyn could not replace him. McGuire was a fine player, but he was no Nap Lajoie. A state judge in St. Louis went further in a case involving pitcher Jack Harper. Not only was the standard NL player contract lacking in mutuality, according to the court, but it also unreasonably restrained competition in violation of the Sherman Antitrust Act.[7]

After two years of rivalry, the National League agreed to recognize the American League as an equal. The two major leagues used blacklists and boycotts to bring "outlaw" minor leagues to their knees and keep control of players who had the audacity to hold out for higher salaries. When Ty Cobb refused to accept Detroit's 1913 salary offer, the Tigers suspended him. The impasse was broken only when two Georgia congressmen called for a Federal investigation. The threat of government action got Ty Cobb a raise, but the players in general benefited much more from Organized Baseball's war with the Federal League, which no doubt had the National and American Leagues muttering "Two's company, three's a crowd" when the 1914 season opened.

The established leagues didn't even try to use the courts to stop reserve jumpers from playing for the Federal League, but they did seek injunctions against a number of players who jumped even though they had signed contracts for the upcoming season. The unscrupulous Hal Chase signed a 1914 contract with the White Sox, but then moved on to the new league. Teams could release players they didn't want on 10 days' notice, so Chase gave Chicago 10 days' warning and shuffled off to the Buffalo Federals. A New York state judge agreed with Chase's reasoning and turned down Chicago's request that he order Chase to return.[8] Not only did the contract lack mutuality, said the judge, but Organized Baseball placed so many limits on the freedom of players that they were left in a state of "quasi peonage" that was "contrary to the spirit of American institutions and ... contrary to the spirit of the Constitution of the United States." The court's opinion did contain some good news for Organized Baseball: while implying that baseball may have violated the common-law prohibition against monopolies, it ruled that baseball did not involve interstate commerce and, therefore, did not violate the Sherman Act.

The judges who heard cases involving contract jumpers occasionally showed real distaste for the whole nasty business. Phillies catcher Bill Killefer signed with the Chicago Federal League club for a substantial increase in salary, but re-signed with the Phillies only 12 days later when they topped Chicago's offer. When the Feds asked a federal judge to order Killefer not to play for Philadelphia, they were rudely received. Citing the opinions in the Ewing, Ward and McGuire cases, Judge Clarence W. Sessions noted that the right of reservation in the Phillies' 1913 contract with Killefer did not bind him for the 1914 season because it was

indefinite and lacked mutuality.[9] But he refused to enforce Chicago's contract because it came into court with "unclean hands." Killefer was under a moral, although not a legal obligation to play for Philadelphia in 1914, but Chicago persuaded him to repudiate that obligation. Both teams had "acted wrongfully and in bad faith," and the judge refused to lift a finger to help either one of them. He also let Killefer know what he thought of him, calling him "a person upon whose pledged word little or no reliance can be placed, and who, for gain to himself, neither scruples nor hesitates to disregard and violate his express engagements and agreements." Chicago appealed the decision but was unsuccessful. The Sixth Circuit Court of Appeals agreed with Judge Sessions that none of the parties to these dishonorable dealings was deserving of any assistance from the courts.[10]

Knowing that they could not outlast their better-financed rivals, the Federal League owners filed an antitrust suit against Organized Baseball in Chicago on January 5, 1915. They asked federal judge Kenesaw Mountain Landis, who had a reputation as a committed trustbuster, to declare the National Agreement's reserve and blacklisting provisions to be unreasonable and illegal restraints on competition. The trial was completed that month, but the Federal League's hopes for a quick verdict in their favor were in vain. The future baseball commissioner pondered the evidence all through the 1915 season, which resulted in another healthy dose of red ink for team owners. After waiting almost a year for Judge Landis to make up his mind, the rival leagues cut a deal. Organized Baseball bought some of the Federal League's player contracts and stadiums—in reality, they were buying peace—and the Federals dropped the antitrust suit.

The final deal satisfied everyone except AL president Ban Johnson, who preferred to fight to the death rather than pay his enemies a nickel of tribute, and the Baltimore Federal League club, which wanted to buy an existing major league franchise and move it to Baltimore. Angered by Brooklyn owner Ebbets' scornful description of their city as "one of the worst minor league towns in this country," the Baltimore owners pledged $50,000 to finance a new antitrust suit against both Organized Baseball and the Federal League owners who had sold the league out for a few pieces of silver. When the Department of Justice refused to investigate, Baltimore filed its complaint in Federal district court in Washington, D.C., in 1917.

The testimony given at the trial, which didn't begin until March 1919, left little doubt that Organized Baseball's team owners had agreed to use the reserve clause and blacklisting to maintain tight control over the supply of players and paid the Federal League to go out of business in order to protect their monopoly over professional baseball. The judge's directions to the jury virtually directed a verdict for the plaintiffs. The Baltimore club was awarded $254,000 in damages.

Organized Baseball's lawyers immediately appealed the decision. They contended that baseball was not commerce because it involved "personal effort not related to [the] production" of material goods. If baseball did not involve interstate commerce, it was not subject to the Sherman Act or any other Federal law. The court of appeals heard oral arguments on October 15, 1920, only three days after the final game of the World Series was played between the Cleveland Indians and the Brooklyn Dodgers. A few weeks later, it overturned the lower court's decision in favor of Baltimore.[11]

The appellate court first noted:

The transportation in interstate commerce of the players and the paraphernalia used by them was but an incident to the main purpose of the appellants, namely the production of the game. It was for it they were in business—not for the purpose of transferring players, balls, and uniforms ...

... So here, baseball is not commerce, though some of its incidents may be. Suppose a law firm in the city of Washington sends its members to points in different states to try lawsuits; they would travel, and probably carry briefs and records, in interstate commerce. Could it be correctly said that the firm, in the trial of the lawsuits, was engaged in trade and commerce? Or, take the case of a lecture bureau, which employs persons to deliver lectures before Chautauqua gatherings at points in different states. It would be necessary for the lecturers to travel in interstate commerce, in order that they might fulfill their engagements; but would it not be an unreasonable stretch of the ordinary meaning of the words to say that the bureau was engaged in trade or commerce?

The court of appeals then cited with approval cases holding that those who produce theatrical exhibitions, practice medicine, or launder clothes are not engaged in commerce.

The Baltimore club tried to persuade the United States Supreme Court to reinstate the original verdict in its favor. But Justice Oliver Wendell Holmes, writing for a unanimous Court, upheld the decision of the court of appeals. [12]

[E]xhibitions of base ball ... are purely state affairs. It is true that, in order to attain for the exhibitions the great popularity that they have achieved, competitions must be arranged between clubs from different cities and States. But the fact that in order to give the exhibitions the League must induce free persons to cross state lines and arrange and pay for their doing so is not enough to change the character of the business. ... [T]he transport is a mere incident, not the essential thing. That to which it is incident, the exhibition, although made for money would not be called trade or commerce in the commonly accepted use of those words. As it is put by the defendants, personal effort, not related to production, is not a subject of commerce. That which in its consummation is not commerce does not become commerce among the States because the transportation that we have mentioned takes place. To repeat the illustrations given by the Court below, a firm of lawyers sending out a member to argue a case, or the Chautauqua lecture bureau sending out lecturers, does not engage in such commerce because the lawyer or lecturer goes to another State.

The next real challenge to Organized Baseball's hegemony came a quarter century later from Don Jorge Pasqual, the millionaire organizer of the Mexican League, who lured 18 major leaguers south of the border in 1946. In August of that year, the owners amended their Rule 15 to provide that any player who jumped to the new league would be ineligible to return to Organized Baseball for five years. The Cubs' general manager, who proposed the amendment, said that the prospect of being blacklisted for five years "will do a lot more to discourage Stan Musial from going to Mexico next winter than any suits we may file on the reserve clause."

The Rule 15 blacklist stemmed the southward flow of players. Commissioner A. B. "Happy" Chandler refused to reinstate the players who returned to the states in 1947. Catcher Mickey Owen was reduced to managing a semipro club in Winner, South Dakota, while several other Mexican League refugees signed with Cuban and Canadian clubs.

When blacklisted outfielder Danny Gardella filed an antitrust complaint against Organized Baseball, a Federal district judge in New York noted the "clear trend toward a broader conception of what constitutes interstate commerce" than had existed when *Federal Baseball Club of Baltimore* was decided over 25 years earlier, but felt bound to follow the Supreme Court's decision in that case. [13] But in February 1949 a federal court of appeals voted 2-1 to reverse the district court's dismissal of Gardella's complaint. [14] Judge Learned Hand distinguished *Federal Baseball* by emphasizing the importance to modern-day baseball of interstate radio and television broadcasts of major league games. Judge Frank's separate opinion strongly condemned the reserve system.

For the "reserve clause," as has been observed, results in something resembling peonage of the baseball player. ... Although many courts have refused to enforce the "reserve" clause, yet severe and practically efficacious extra-legal penalties are imposed for violation. The most extreme of these penalties is the blacklisting of the player so that no club in Organized Baseball will hire him. ... The violator may perhaps become a ... bartender or a street-sweeper, but his chances of ever again playing baseball are exceedingly slim. [15]

Gardella's victory was not a final one; it simply allowed him the opportunity to prove his allegations in a trial. Former Cardinals Fred Martin, Max Lanier and Lou Klein filed a separate suit, and all four players asked the district court to order their immediate reinstatement pending the outcome of the trials, but the court declined to do so. [16] Faced with the prospect of spending the 1949 season in a courtroom rather than on a baseball field, the players were receptive to baseball's offer to settle the case. Commissioner Chandler later characterized his reinstatement of the four "good kids" who had "said they were sorry" for jumping their reserves as inspired by his desire to "temper justice with mercy." But the court of appeals decision—and Judge Frank's sentiments in particular—no doubt had an effect too. Gardella, who had been working as a hospital orderly after returning from Mexico, was reportedly given $60,000 to drop his case.

Subsequent litigation and congressional inquiries kept baseball's attorneys busy in the 1950s. Organized Baseball was the defendant in eight pending antitrust suits when it sought relief from Congress in 1951. At its behest three separate bills that would have granted all professional sports leagues a complete exemption from the antitrust laws were introduced in the House of Representatives that year. After lengthy hearings, Congressman Emanuel Celler's Subcommittee on the Study of Monopoly Power recommended that the bills not be passed, and none of them were. The Celler Subcommittee did not favor blanket antitrust immunity, but it did conclude that professional baseball could not operate successfully without some form of the reserve clause. [17]

After the Gardella decision, Organized Baseball's lawyers and the Subcommittee assumed that *Federal Baseball* was no longer good law. But the Supreme Court surprised them in 1953 in *Toolson v. New York Yankees*. [18] When Yankee farmhand George Toolson was placed on the ineligible list for refusing to accept a demotion to a lower-classification team, he sued the Yankees. A federal judge in California dismissed the case before trial on the

basis of *Federal Baseball.* "If [that] case is, as Judge Frank intimates [in his *Gardella* opinion], an 'impotent zombi,'" the judge wrote, "I feel that it is not my duty to so find but that the Supreme Court should so declare." [19] The Ninth Circuit Court of Appeals agreed, [20] and the Supreme Court reaffirmed *Federal Baseball* with two Justices dissenting, in a one-paragraph opinion.

In Federal Baseball ... *this Court held that ... professional baseball ... was not within the scope of the Federal antitrust laws. Congress has had the ruling under consideration but has not seen fit to bring such business under these laws by legislation having prospective effect. ... The present cases ask us to overrule the prior decision, and, with retrospective effect, hold the [antitrust laws] applicable. We think that if there are evils in this field which now warrant application to it of the antitrust laws it should be by legislation. Without re-examination of the underlying issues, the judgments below are affirmed on the authority of* Federal Baseball... [21]

The Court's conclusion that "Congress has had the ruling under consideration but has not seen fit to bring [baseball] under [the antitrust] laws by legislation" is questionable. The Celler Subcommittee report concluded that given the Gardella decision and cases subsequent to *Federal Baseball,* which took a broader view of what constituted interstate commerce, "it may be seriously doubted whether baseball should now be regarded as exempt from the antitrust laws." If Congress assumed that baseball was subject to the antitrust laws, its failure to act on bills granting an antitrust exemption was evidence that it did not intend baseball to be exempt—which was just the opposite of what the Court said in *Toolson.*

The next few years saw the Supreme Court hold that professional boxing and football did not share baseball's antitrust immunity. In *Radovich v. National Football League,* [22] the Court expressly limited the reach of the *Federal Baseball* precedent to baseball. Three justices dissented from this decision "to put baseball in a class by itself."

Another flurry of congressional activity followed. In 1957 the House Antitrust Subcommittee held fifteen days of hearings on seven different bills, some of which would have exempted all professional sports from antitrust liability. Congressman Celler introduced a bill exempting only those acts that were "reasonably necessary" to maintaining competitive balance and the integrity of sports, but the full House voted to give professional sports leagues a broader although not unlimited exemption. A Senate committee held more hearings in 1958—Casey Stengel, Mickey Mantle, Ted Williams, and Stan Musial testified the day after the All-Star Game was played in nearby Baltimore—but the full Senate never considered the bill. In a 1959 report to the membership, the Major League Baseball Players Association's lawyers said, "There does not seem any doubt that Congress will eventually pass a law concerning Baseball's right to continue its reserve clause," but Congress never came any closer to passing comprehensive sports antitrust legislation. Bills were introduced year after year—attempts to organize a third major league, franchise moves, and the CBS purchase of the Yankees inspired some of the legislative proposals—but none was enacted.

In 1972 the U.S. Supreme Court upheld *Federal Baseball* once more in *Flood v. Kuhn.* [23] When the Cardinals traded Curt Flood to the Phillies after the 1969 season, Flood refused to go. "I am [not] a piece of property to be bought and sold irrespective of my wishes," he wrote to Commissioner Bowie Kuhn. Although Flood

had not signed a contract for the 1970 season, Kuhn refused to declare him a free agent, so Flood filed suit, hiring former Supreme Court Justice and Secretary of Labor Arthur Goldberg to represent him. The lower court dismissed his case, and, by a 5-3 vote, the Supreme Court upheld its dismissal.

After opening with an overview of baseball history so effusively unjudicial that two members of the majority refused to join it, Justice Harry Blackmun's opinion recognized that, *Federal Baseball* notwithstanding, "Professional baseball is a business and it is engaged in interstate commerce," and that subsequent decisions had applied the antitrust laws to the NFL and professional boxing. Justice Blackmun referred to baseball's antitrust immunity as an "exception," an "anomaly," and an "aberration," but concluded that after 50 years, any change must come from Congress: [24]

The Court has emphasized that since 1922 baseball, with full and continuing congressional awareness, has been allowed to develop and to expand unhindered by Federal legislative action. Remedial legislation has been introduced repeatedly in Congress but none has ever been enacted. The Court, accordingly, has concluded that Congress as yet has had no intention to subject baseball's reserve system to the reach of the antitrust statutes. ... If there is any inconsistency or illogic in all this, it is an inconsistency and illogic of long standing that is to be remedied by the Congress and not by this Court.

The dissenting Justices responded that "[t]he unbroken silence of Congress should not prevent us from correcting our own mistakes," but to date neither the Court nor Congress has done so. Major League Baseball has relied upon *Federal Baseball* and *Flood* to rebuff a variety of antitrust claims, including umpires' allegations that they were illegally dismissed for union activity [25] and a minor league team's challenge to the rules governing player assignment and franchise location. [26] After *Flood,* however, baseball's antitrust status faded into the background for two decades as free agency created new legal problems.

On December 23, 1975, an arbitration panel issued a decision that shook baseball to its foundations by rejecting the owners' interpretation of the reserve clause. The reserve clause, contained in every player's contract, stated that if the player and club hadn't agreed to terms by March 1, "the Club shall have the right by written notice to the Player ... to renew this contract for one year on the same terms." [27] The owners read the reserve clause as creating another identical contract with the same right of renewal, thereby giving the club a perpetual option on the player's services. However, arbitrator Peter Seitz agreed with the players that this language created only a one-year right of renewal, after which the club had no further claim to the player. The arbitrator's decision allowed pitcher Andy Messersmith, who had played without a written contract in 1975, to sell his services to the highest bidder: Messersmith, who had earned $115,000 with the Dodgers in 1975, soon signed a three-year, $1-million contract with the Atlanta Braves.

The owners attacked the panel's decision in court but could not overcome the strong federal policy favoring arbitration of labor disputes. The courts "do not sit as an appellate tribunal to review the merits of the arbitrator's decision"; rather, they ask only whether a reasonable arbitrator could have reached that result. A century of owners' control over the labor market ended when a federal court of appeals affirmed the arbitrators' decision with the words, "We cannot say that [the reserve clause and related provisions] are not susceptible

of the construction given them by the panel. Accordingly, the award must be sustained." [28] The era of free agency had begun.

In 1976, as players and owners adjusted to the new rules, Braves owner Ted Turner ran afoul of Commissioner Kuhn by announcing he would outbid anyone for the Giants' Gary Matthews when Matthews became a free agent. Kuhn suspended Turner for one year for tampering and revoked the Braves' first-round choice in the 1977 amateur draft. A federal court upheld Turner's suspension, citing a clause in the Major League Agreement which empowered the Commissioner "to investigate ... any act ... not in the best interests of the national game of Baseball" and "to determine ... what punitive action is appropriate. ..." [29] However, the court restored the Braves' draft pick, limiting the Commissioner to those punitive sanctions expressly made available to him by the Major League Agreement. [30] Although the Commissioner had "all the attributes of a benevolent but absolute despot and all the disciplinary powers of the proverbial *pater familias*," [31] the Major League Agreement which established his authority also limited its exercise.

No team was more affected by free agency than the Oakland A's, whose talented players had won three of the previous four World Series and five straight division championships. Concluding that he couldn't afford the enormous salaries his stars would command in the open market, A's owner Charles O. Finley decided to sell them to wealthier clubs before they could leave as free agents. In June 1976, Finley sold Joe Rudi and Rollie Fingers to the Boston Red Sox for $2 million and Vida Blue to the New York Yankees for $1.5 million, but Commissioner Bowie Kuhn quickly nullified the transactions as "inconsistent with the best interests of baseball, the integrity of the game, and the maintenance of public confidence in it."

A federal judge rejected Finley's argument that Kuhn had exceeded his authority, pointing to the Commissioner's power to invalidate acts "not in the best interests of Baseball" and a provision in the Major League Agreement through which the club owners agreed to be bound by the Commissioner's decisions and to "waive such right of recourse to the courts as would otherwise have existed in their favor." [32] This decision was upheld on appeal, [33] the appeals court noting that the "waiver of recourse" provision quoted above kept Finley from going to court to challenge Kuhn's ruling unless he could show that the Major League Agreement was inconsistent with state or federal law or that the procedures followed by Kuhn "failed to follow the basic rudiments of due process of law." [34]

Pete Rose's 1989 lawsuit against Commissioner A. Bartlett Giamatti relied on just that argument—that Rose was being denied the right to a fair hearing by an unbiased decisionmaker. When Rose asked a state court judge in his home town of Cincinnati to enjoin the Commissioner from holding a hearing on charges that Rose had bet on baseball games, he claimed that Giamatti had already decided he was guilty. Giamatti's lawyers filed a motion to remove the case to federal court. In most cases, state courts have jurisdiction if one or both of the parties to the lawsuit are citizens of that state; but if the plaintiff and defendant are citizens of different states, federal courts usually have jurisdiction to hear the case. Because Rose was a citizen of Ohio and Giamatti was a citizen of New York, Giamatti was able to remove the case from the Ohio court—which might favor Ohioans over New Yorkers—to a federal court. [35] After losing that legal skirmish, Rose withdrew his lawsuit and agreed to be suspended indefinitely from baseball, so the courts never ruled on the merits of Rose's claim that the Commissioner was not treating him fairly.

Some twenty years after *Flood v. Kuhn* was decided, baseball's antitrust exemption came under attack once again. Commissioner Fay Vincent was shown the door by unhappy team owners in 1992. There was widespread speculation that the owners might lock the players out of spring training in 1993 in order to gain the upper hand in their negotiations with the MLBPA, and some owners allegedly were worried that Vincent would use the Commissioner's traditional authority to take action in the "best interests of baseball."

The mere existence of a Commissioner—in theory, an independent arbiter who could be trusted to do the right thing and keep the owners in line when they tried to go too far—had helped to deflect attacks on baseball's antitrust exemption. So when Congress held hearings on a bill to repeal the exemption in 1993, the owners promised to name a new Commissioner by the end of that year.

But baseball had no Commissioner when the 1994 season ended. With negotiations on a new collective bargaining agreement headed for a major meltdown, Senator Howard Metzenbaum of Ohio—a parking-lot tycoon who had once owned a piece of the Cleveland Indians—introduced yet another bill to repeal baseball's antitrust exemption. Despite support from Senator Connie Mack III (the grandson of the legendary owner/manager) and Congressman Jim Bunning (who won 224 major league games), the Metzenbaum bill failed to get out of committee. After the players struck on August 12, 1994, there was another attempt to repeal the antitrust exemption, but Congress adjourned without taking action on it.

Those who supported the proposals to repeal baseball's antitrust exemption touted repeal as a remedy for baseball's chronic labor-management woes. But in reality, overturning *Federal Baseball* would have done nothing of the kind.

That's because labor-management issues are never subject to the antitrust laws in the first place. As long as a collective-bargaining relationship exists, the antitrust laws do not apply—and that's true not only for baseball, but for any business. That's why you never hear about the United Auto Workers bringing an antitrust suit against General Motors, Ford or Chrysler. If a union doesn't prevail at the bargaining table, it can file an unfair-labor practice complaint with the National Labor Relations Board (NLRB), or it can go on strike—but it can't file an antitrust suit. So even if Curt Flood had been successful in persuading the Supreme Court to overrule *Federal Baseball*, the owners still would have an absolute defense to antitrust suits brought by the MLBPA (and vice versa).

On the other hand, baseball owners are not immune to charges that they are guilty of violating the federal labor laws. When employees decide to join a union, those laws provide that an employer must bargain with the union before it changes wages or terms of employment. Only if the employer and the union cannot reach an agreement—or, to use labor-law terminology, if an "impasse" is reached—can the employer unilaterally make changes.

After months of fruitless negotiations, the owners declared in late December 1994 that they and the union were at an impasse, and unilaterally imposed the salary cap that the MLBPA had refused to accept. The MLBPA promptly filed a complaint with the National Labor Relations Board, alleging that the owners acted prematurely. If anything, "impasse" seems too mild a term to describe the deadlock that then existed between owners and players, but the NLRB let it be known that they believed that the owners had acted before a legal state of impasse existed.

The owners backtracked somewhat, and negotiations resumed. Even President Bill Clinton tried to broker a deal. But the MLBPA,

led then as now by Donald Fehr, and the owners—who were planning to open the season with so-called "replacement" players—stuck to their guns. Once again, believing that they were at an impasse, the owners announced they were no longer bound by the old collective-bargaining provisions on free agency and salary arbitration.

Only a couple of days before the 1995 season was scheduled to open, Judge Sonia Sotomayor sided with the NLRB and the union and ordered the owners to restore the status quo. The owners could have locked out the players and continued to fight the MLBPA and NLRB in court, but they soon decided to throw in the towel. The replacement players were sent home, and the 1995 season belatedly got under way.

But that season and the next came and went without the owners and the players' union reaching agreement on a new collective-bargaining pact, and it began to look like Judge Sotomayor might once again be called on to decide if the impasse in fact had become an impasse for legal purposes. After the owners voted 18-12 to reject the agreement negotiated by their own negotiator, Randy Levine, it seemed likely that the 1997 season would be disrupted by labor strife. But two weeks later, the owners reversed their earlier stand and voted 26-4 in favor of accepting the very proposal they had just rejected.

The new collective-bargaining agreement contained a provision requiring Major League Baseball and the MLBPA to join forces and lobby Congress to repeal baseball's antitrust exemption in the context of labor disputes. In 1998, the strange bedfellows persuaded Congress to pass the "Curt Flood Act"—the stubborn, principled Flood had died of cancer the year before, and putting his name on this piece of special-interest legislation was a remarkably shameless and cynical act even by Washington standards. This legislation gave major league baseball players the same rights under the antitrust laws as NFL or NBA players, but did not repeal or otherwise limit baseball's antitrust exemption.

In theory, the new law gave the MLBPA another weapon to wield in future labor negotiations. If the owners declared an impasse and sought to impose a salary cap or other terms of employment on the players in the future (as they had attempted to do in 1994), the players could bring an antitrust suit against the owners if they were willing to dissolve, or "decertify" their union—when there's no union, there can be no collective-bargaining relationship, so the general labor exemption to the antitrust laws would no longer apply. That's what the NFL players did a few years ago when they were unable to persuade their league's owners to liberalize restrictive free-agency rules.

Of course, decertification would be a tactic of last resort for the MLBPA. The baseball players' union may be the most successful labor union in history, and it seems unlikely that the players would ever choose to decertify. The NFL players were in truly desperate straits when they chose to blow up their union and take their chances in court. Baseball players have a lot more to lose by decertifying than their NFL fellows.

In exchange for giving the players an antitrust remedy that they can use only if they decertify their union, the owners gained a Congressional seal of approval for baseball's unique antitrust status with respect to the amateur draft, anything to do with the minor leagues or minor league players, expansion, franchise relocation, the licensing of trademarks or other intellectual-property rights, and broadcasting agreements. In fact, major league players are the only

parties who have the legal standing to sue to enforce the new law.

Shortly after the owners announced in 2001 that they were going to "contract" MLB by eliminating two major league teams, the Florida attorney general opened an antitrust investigation, issuing subpoenas to Commissioner Selig and the owners. But the targets of the investigation, relying on baseball's judge-made antitrust exemption—which had been codified by Congress passing the Curt Flood Act—asked a federal court to put a halt to the Florida inquiry. In May 2003, a federal court of appeals agreed, holding that it had no choice but to rule in favor of MLB because the decision to contract was clearly related to the business of baseball, which had been held exempt from the antitrust laws by the Supreme Court on three separate occasions. [36] It was up to the Supreme Court or Congress to overrule those precedents, the appeals court held.

And so the exemption from the antitrust laws granted to baseball by the Supreme Court in 1922 still clings to life, despite decades of criticism by courts, politicians and assorted legal experts. That criticism may be entirely justified, but it also represents a great waste of time and energy. The fact of the matter is that baseball's antitrust exemption really has relatively little impact on the business of baseball in the 21st century. For one thing, those who have problems with baseball's owners usually have other legal remedies. In the case of MLB's ill-advised contraction decision, for example, the MLBPA argued that the owners had to negotiate with the union before eliminating any franchises, while long-term stadium leases were another legal roadblock to contraction. In addition, the antitrust laws do not tie the hands of the owners as tightly as many believe. The main benefit of MLB's antitrust exemption to the owners is that it stops antitrust challenges in their tracks so that the owners are not forced to litigate and appeal unfavorable decisions by hometown judges and juries.

1. *Allegheny Baseball Club v. Bennett*, 14 Fed. 257 (C.C.W.D. Pa., 1882).
2. *St. Louis Athletic Ass'n v. Mullane*, No. 3642 (C.C.S.D. Ohio, May 13, 1884), p.2, col.1. Reprinted in *Sporting Life*, May 21, 1884, p.2, col.1.
3. *Metropolitan Exhibition Co. v. Ewing*, 42 Fed. 198 (C.C.S.D. N.Y. 1890).
4. *Metropolitan Exhibition Co. v. Ward*, 9 N.Y.S. 779 (Sup. Ct., New York Co. 1890).
5. *Philadelphia Base Ball Club v. Lajoie*, 51 Atl. 973 (Pa. S. Ct. 1902).
6. *Brooklyn Baseball Club v. McGuire*, 116 Fed. 783 (C.C.E.D. Pa. 1902).
7. *American Base Ball & Athletic Exhibition Co. of St. Louis v. Harper*, 54 Cent. L.J. 449 (St. Louis Cir. Ct. 1902).
8. *American League Baseball Club of Chicago v. Chase*, 86 Misc. 441, 149 N.Y. Supp. 6 (Sup. Ct. 1914).
9. *Weeghman v. Killefer*, 214 Fed. 168 (W.D. Mich. 1914).
10. *Weeghman v. Killefer*, 215 Fed. 289 (6th Cir. 1914).
11. *National League of Professional Baseball Clubs v. Federal Baseball Club of Baltimore*, 269 Fed. 681 (D.C. Cir. 1921).
12. *Federal Baseball Club of Baltimore v. National League of Professional Baseball Clubs*, 259 U.S. 200 (1922).
13. *Gardella v. Chandler*, 79 F.Supp. 260 (S.D.N.Y. 1948).
14. *Gardella v. Chandler*, 172 F.2d 402 (2d Cir. 1949).
15. *Id.* at 409-10.
16. *Martin v. Chandler*, 174 F.2d 917 (2d. Cir. 1949); *Gardella v. Chandler*, 174 F.2d 919 (2d. Cir. 1949).
17. H.R. Rep. 2002, 82d Cong., 2d Sess. 228-32 (1952).
18. 346 U.S. 356 (1953).
19. *Toolson v. New York Yankees*, 101 F.Supp. 93 (S.D. Cal. 1951).
20. 200 F.2d 198 (9th Cir. 1952).
21. 346 U.S. 356 (1953).
22. 358 U.S. 445 (1957).
23. 407 U.S. 258 (1972).
24. *Id.* at 283-84.
25. *Salerno v. American League*, 429 F.2d 1003 (2d Cir. 1970).
26. *Professional Baseball Schools and Clubs, Inc. v. Kuhn*, 693 F.2d 1085 (11th Cir. 1982).
27. Player Contract, P 10(a).
28. *Kansas City Royals Baseball Corp. v. Major League Baseball Players Association*, 532 F.2d 615 (8th Cir. 1976).
29. Major League Agreement, Art. I, Sec. 2.
30. *Atlanta National League Baseball Club v. Kuhn*, 432 F. Supp. 1213 (N.D. Ga. 1977).
31. *Milwaukee American Ass'n v. Landis*, 49 F.2d 298 (N.D. Ill. 1931).
32. *Id.* at Art. VII, Sec. 2.
33. *Charles O. Finley & Co. v. Kuhn*, 569 F.2d 527 (7th Cir. 1978).
34. *Id.* at 544.
35. *Rose v. Giamatti*, 721 F. Supp. 906 (1989).
36. *Major League Baseball v. Crist*, 331 F.3d 1177 (11th Cir. 2003).

Chapter 30

Ballparks Past and Present

By Philip J. Lowry

You will find here the vital statistics for our 30 current major league parks, and more importantly for each and every one of baseball's storied shrines of the past where regular-season or post-season championship major league baseball games have been played. The saga of major league ballparks dates back to 1871, and includes an incredible variety of playing sites, from cricket grounds, polo fields, and beer taverns to racetracks, fair grounds, and cow pastures. When my book *Green Cathedrals* was published in 1993, cited were some 273 ballparks where major league baseball regular-season or championship contests had been played. After much further research, you will find here descriptions for 377 such parks. There have been several ballpark books since mine, but no one else has ever provided a complete listing of every major league park.

The focus is on ballpark geometry, the oddities in play caused by unique and crazy configurations, and what makes the game fun for fans. All dimensional changes are catalogued and dated in outfield fence distances and heights. This is crucial to understanding the statistical history of baseball. The following leagues are covered:

Yankee Stadium
The view from the upper deck of a sold-out Yankee Stadium during the 1953 World Series.

NA	National Association, 1871-75
NL	National League, 1876 to date
AA	American Association, 1882-81
UA	Union Association, 1884
PL	Players League, 1890
AL	American League, 1901 to date
FL	Federal League, 1914-15
NNL	Negro National League, 1920-31, 1933-48
ECL	Eastern Colored League, 1923-28
ANL	American Negro League, 1929
NSL	Negro Southern League, 1932
NEWL	Negro East-West League, 1932
NAL	Negro American League, 1937-60

I differ from most baseball authors by including the Negro Leagues as major leagues, rather than as a somehow different category. I was very fortunate to attend a three-day 1982 conference in Ashland, Kentucky, attended by almost all of the living Negro League veterans, and interviewed each attendee on the amazing variety of ballparks used for regular-season games by barnstorming Negro League teams. Concerning inclusion of the Negro Southern and Negro East-West Leagues in 1932, none of the three other principle Negro Leagues (NNL, ECL, NAL) were operating in 1932. Since the NSL and NEWL were the only Negro Leagues that year, they should be considered as major Negro Leagues.

Before 1900, most ballparks were simple small wooden grandstands hastily constructed around recreation fields, rarely enclosed by outfield fences. Beginning with the erection of Shibe Park and Forbes Field in 1909, however, concrete-and-steel ballparks became the rule. These big palaces signal the growing prominence of baseball and the golden era in ballpark design. Beginning in the 1950s, multipurpose stadiums were developed for use by both football and baseball, a marriage definitely not made in heaven. The result was a series of sterile concrete ashtrays. Thankfully, Baltimore's Camden Yards in 1992 presaged a return to asymmetrical, grass surface, baseball-only parks. For this we have Larry Lucchino, then of the Orioles, now of the Red Sox, to thank.

Dimensional data is difficult to interpret. There are obvious mistakes, such as typos in team guides, and incorrect measurements. Then there are other mistakes that are not so obvious, such as when team guides do not keep up-to-date as changes occur, and when

some teams listed power-alley measurements for foul lines, and vice versa. All a researcher can do in such cases is to use his best judgment.

The categories used to describe the ballparks deserve some explanation. "AKA" (also known as) gives alternate names and nicknames used for the park. "OCCUPANT" lists teams using the park in chronological order, with dates of play. "LOCATION" cites surrounding streets, with associated fields and bases, and geographical directions. Although Official Baseball Rule 1.04 states, "It is desirable that the line from home base through the pitcher's plate to second base shall run East-Northeast," you will see that this has definitely not always been the case. "DIMENSIONS" gives the distance in feet from home plate to outfield fences and the backstop, with dates denoting the first time when boundaries stood at that distance. "FENCES" lists outfield fence heights in feet, with dates for the first time fences stood at that height. "FORMER USE" describes how the site was used before park construction, while "CURRENT USE" chronicles development of the site after the park was abandoned. "CAPACITY" figures are noted only

when they change by more than 1,000, but the most recent figure is always given. "PHENOMENA" is a general category for historical data, important changes and noteworthy events.

What have I learned by immersing myself for 28 years in such details as whether North Ave. West is the south or east boundary of Recreation Park (it's the south), why the distance to center field at the Polo Grounds changed 19 times (I still don't know), and whether there was a 32-foot high wooden Marine Sergeant in play and standing against the left field wall during World War II (there was) at Forbes Field? I think what I've learned most, going through endless newspaper microfilm and historical archives, and interviewing hundreds of players, fans, umpires, and sportswriters, are two things. First, that History delights in shrouding her many precious baseball mysteries in the fog of conflicting sources, and that many facts will never be known for certain, especially concerning the Negro Leagues, whose documentation is so scarce. And second, and most importantly, that baseball research is great fun and you meet some wonderful people while doing it.

THE BALLPARKS

AKRON, OHIO
LEAGUE PARK
OCCUPANTS: NNL Akron Black Tyrites 1933; neutral site use by NEWL Pittsburgh Crawfords AM game August 8, 1932 ★ **DIMENSIONS:** Left Field 315, Center Field 385, Right Field 345 ★ **CAPACITY:** 4,500

ALBANY, NEW YORK
RIVERSIDE PARK
OCCUPANT: Neutral site use by NL Troy Trojans September 11, 1880; June 15 and September 10, 1881; May 16-18 and 30, 1882 ★ **LOCATION:** (N) Herkimer St., (W) Broadway, (S) Westerlo St., (E) Quay St.

ALTOONA, PENNSYLVANIA
COLUMBIA PARK
AKA: 4th Ave. Grounds, Waverly Field ★ **OCCUPANT:** UA Altoona Mountain Citys April 30 to May 31, 1884 ★ **LOCATION:** (N) Lower 6th Ave., (W) 3 Second St., (S) 4th Ave., (E) Mill Run Rd. ★ **CURRENT USE:** Brightly painted gasoline storage tanks and Pennsy RR tracks

PENNSYLVANIA RAILROAD PARK
OCCUPANT: Neutral site use by NNL Homestead Grays 1930s ★ **DIMENSIONS:** Right Field 150

ANAHEIM, CALIFORNIA
ANGEL STADIUM
AKA: Big A, Bigger A 1980, Anaheim Stadium 1966-97, Edison International Field of Anaheim 1998-2003 ★ **OCCUPANTS:** AL California Angels April 19, 1966 to September 25, 1996; AL Anaheim Angels April 2, 1997 to date ★ **LOCATION:** Left Field (N) Katella Ave; Third Base (W) 2000 State College Blvd. (later Gene Autry Way), then I-5; First Base (S) Orangewood Ave., then Santa Ana River; Right Field (E) Orange Freeway; Center Field (NE) Amtrak RR station ★ **DIMENSIONS:** Foul Lines 333; Bullpens 362; Power Alleys 375 (1966), 369 (1973), 374 (1974), 370 (1989), 365 (1998), 370 (2003); Deep Power Alleys 386 (1966), 396 (1998), 387 (1999), 386 (2003); Center Field 406 (1966), 402 (1973), 404 (1974), 408 (1998), 400 (1999), 404 (2003); Backstop 55 (1966), 60.5 (1973) ★ **FENCES:** Most of fence 10 (wire 1966), 7.86 (wire 1973), 7.86 (padded 1981); corners between Foul Poles and Bullpens 4.75 (steel 1966); Left Center between 386 and 404 marks 7.5 (padded 1981); padded posts at left sides of both Left and Right Field Bullpen gates 9 (padded 1981); Bullpen gates 9.95 (wire 1966); Right Center and Right Field 18 (1998) ★ **SURFACE:** Santa Ana Bermuda 1966-88, bluegrass 1989 to date ★ **FORMER USE:** Four farms: Camille Allec's 39 acres of orange and eucalyptus trees, Roland Reynolds' 70 acres of alfalfa, John Knutgen's 20 acres of corn, Bill Ross and George Lenney's 19 acres of corn ★ **CAPACITY:** 43,500 (1966), 44,500 (1967), 43,204 (1968), 64,593 (1980), 67,335 (1981), 65,158 (1984), 64,573 (1986), 33,851 (1997), 45,050 (1998)
PHENOMENA: Huge 230-foot-high letter "A" stood behind the fence in left as a scoreboard support until 1980, when it was moved to the parking lot when the stadium was enclosed for the NFL Rams. Sections 69 and 70 in center covered by green-canvas batters' background. Two thin black TV cables used to run in fair territory on the warning track from the left field corner bullpen gate to the foul pole, along the wall in foul territory about 50 feet toward third base, then into the stands. Outfield

enclosed and triple-decked in 1980. New owner Disney un-enclosed it between October 1996 and April 1998, ripped out the outfield structure and replaced it with the Outfield Extravaganza, which is supposed to look like the rocks along the Pacific Ocean, with a 90-foot high geyser.

ARLINGTON, TEXAS
ARLINGTON STADIUM
AKA: Turnpike Stadium 1965-71 ★ **OCCUPANT:** AL Texas Rangers April 21, 1972 to October 3, 1993 ★ **LOCATION:** Left Field (E) Stadium Drive East, then Six Flags Over Texas Amusement Park; Third Base (N) 1500 South Copeland Rd., then I-30; First Base (W) Stadium Drive West (later Pennant Drive), then Collins St./State Hwy 157; Right Field (S) East Randol Mill Rd. ★ **DIMENSIONS:** Foul Lines 330; Power Alleys 380 (1972), 370 (1974), 383 (1981), 380 (1982); Center Field 400; Backstop 60; Foul Territory small ★ **FENCES:** 11 (1972), 12 (1981), 11 (1986) ★ **SURFACE:** Tifway 419 Bermuda grass ★ **FORMER USE:** Minor league ballpark 1965-71 ★ **CAPACITY:** 10,500 (1965), 20,000 (1970), 35,739 (1972), 41,097 (1979), 43,508 (1985), 43,521 (1992)
PHENOMENA: Cotton Eye Joe played for the seventh-inning stretch so fans could dance in the aisles. Wind blew in directly from the outfield, but since it was the hottest park in the majors, the ball carried well. The Lone Ranger on Texas-shaped scoreboard in left center rooted for the Rangers. Largest bleachers in the majors, from foul pole to foul pole.

BALLPARK AT ARLINGTON
OCCUPANT: AL Texas Rangers April 11, 1994 to date ★ **LOCATION:** Left Field (E) 1,000 Ballpark Way, Third Base (N) Copeland Rd., then I-30, First Base (W) Pennant Drive, Right Field (S) East Randol Mill Rd. ★ **DIMENSIONS:** Left Field 334 (1994), 332 (2001); Left Center 388 (1994), 390 (2001); Center Field 400; Deepest Right Center 403 (1994), 407 (2001); Right Center 381; Right Center Corner 377; Right Field 325; Backstop 60; Foul Territory small. ★ **FENCES:** Left Field 14; Center Field and Right Field 8 ★ **CAPACITY:** 49,178 (1994), 48,100 (1996), 49,166 (1997), 49,115 (2003)
PHENOMENA: Covered pavilion porch in right features pillars reminiscent of Tiger Stadium. Wind helps carry balls hit to right center. Outfield has many nooks and crannies reminiscent of Ebbets Field. Site of first AL/NL interleague game on June 12, 1997, with Willie Mays and Nolan Ryan throwing out ceremonial first pitches.

ARLINGTON, VIRGINIA
GENTLEMEN'S DRIVING PARK
AKA: Four Mile Run Park ★ **OCCUPANTS:** AA Washington Nationals Sundays 1891; NL Washington Senators Sundays 1892-99 ★ **LOCATION:** Along Four Mile Run ★ **FORMER USE:** Horse racing track ★ **CURRENT USE:** Southern end, National Airport

ASHEVILLE, NORTH CAROLINA
McCORMICK FIELD
OCCUPANT: Neutral site use by NAL Birmingham Black Barons 1940s ★ **LOCATION:** Valley St. ★ **DIMENSIONS:** Left Field 328 (1924), 365 (1940), 325 (1985), 328 (1988), Left Center 360 (1988), Center Field 397 (1924), 410 (1940), 414 (1985), 404 (1988), Right Center 325 (1988), Right Field 301 (1924), 325 (1940), 301 (1985) ★ **CAPACITY:** 3,500 (1924), 3,000 (1940), 3,500 (1985)

ATLANTA, GEORGIA

PONCE DE LEON PARK (II)
AKA: Spiller Park 1924-32, Poncey ★ **OCCUPANTS:** NSL Atlanta Black Crackers 1932; NAL Atlanta Black Crackers 1938 ★ **LOCATION:** Left Field (N) parking lot; Third Base (W) North Blvd; First Base (S) 650 Ponce de Leon Blvd.; Right Field (E) Southern RR tracks ★ **DIMENSIONS:** Left Field 365 (1932), 330 (1951); Left Center left of scoreboard 525; Center Field 462 (1932), 448 (1938), 410 (1951); Right Field 321 (1932), 324 (1938), 321 (1951) ★ **FENCES:** Left Field 2 (hedge April 1949), 4 (cyclone fence May 1949); Left Center 25 (scoreboard); Center Field 6; Right Center 35 (magnolia tree halfway up very steep embankment, no fence; Right Field 15 ★ **CURRENT USE:** Parking lot by Sears ★ **CAPACITY:** 11,000 (1903), 15,000 (1924), 12,500 (1949)

ATLANTA-FULTON COUNTY STADIUM
AKA: Atlanta Stadium, Launching Pad ★ **OCCUPANT:** NL Atlanta Braves April 12, 1966 to October 24, 1996 ★ **LOCATION:** Left Field (NE) Georgia Ave. (later Pulman St.), then I-20; Third Base (NW) Washington St., then I-75/85; First Base (SW) 521 Eustace (later Capitol) Ave; Right Field (SE) Fulton St. ★ **DIMENSIONS:** Foul Lines 325 (1966), 330 (1967); Power Alleys 385 (1966), 375 (1974); Center Field 402 (1966), 400 (1969), 402 (1973); Backstop 59.92 (1973); Foul Territory large (1966), medium (1977) ★ **FENCES:** 6 (wire 1966), 10 (4 Plexiglas above 6 wire 1983), 10 (Plexiglas 1985) ★ **CURRENT USE:** Parking lot for Turner Field ★ **CAPACITY:** 51,500 (1966), 52,870 (1974), 52,270 (1996)
PHENOMENA: Henry Aaron's 715th home run hit here on April 8, 1974. Big Victor, a large totem-pole-styled figure, stood in the stadium in 1966. His huge head tilted and his eyes rolled whenever a Brave hit a home run. Chief Noc-A-Homa's Wigwam replaced Big Victor in 1967. From 1967 to 1971, his teepee stood on a 20-foot-square platform behind the left-field fence. In 1972, the teepee was moved to right field. From 1973 to 1977, it returned to left field. From 1978 to August 1982, the teepee was moved to left center. From August to early September 1982, it was removed in anticipation of additional revenue in the playoffs, "causing" a disastrous tailspin for the first-place Braves. Its replacement coincided with the Braves' comeback to win the 1982 division crown. Tempting fate again the next year, the teepee's removal on August 11, 1983, saw another losing streak, which could not be overcome by its return on September 16.

TURNER FIELD
AKA: Olympic Stadium 1996 ★ **OCCUPANT:** NL Atlanta Braves April 4, 1997 to date ★ **LOCATION:** Left Field (N/NW) Georgia Ave. (later Ralph Abernathy Blvd); Third Base (W/SW) Washington St. (later Pollard Ave.), then I-75/85; First Base (S/SE) Love St. (later Bill Lucas Drive); Right Field (E/NE) Capitol Ave. (later 755 Hank Aaron Drive) ★ **DIMENSIONS:** Left Field 335; Left Center 380; Center Field 401; Right Center 390 (1997), 385 (2001); Right Field 330; Backstop 53 (1997), 60 (2003); Foul Territory large ★ **FENCES:** 8 ★ **SURFACE:** Prescription Athletic Turf (PAT) grass ★ **CAPACITY:** 80,000 (1996), 50,528 (1997), 50,091 (2001)
PHENOMENA: Hosted 1996 Summer Olympics, with huge temporary bleachers out in what is now the outfield. Hand-operated scoreboard posts out-of-town scores above left-field stands. Center-field scoreboard dominated by 100-foot image of Hank Aaron hitting 715th homer. Huge Coke bottle sits in upper deck in left. Monument Grove, a large park area at the north entrance, contains statues of Ty Cobb, Hank Aaron and Phil Niekro.

ATLANTIC CITY, NEW JERSEY

BACHARACH PARK
OCCUPANTS: ECL Atlantic City Bacharach Giants 1923-27, April to May 1928; ANL Atlantic City Bacharach Giants 1929; NNL Atlantic City Bacharach Giants 1934 to September 1934; neutral site use by NNL Baltimore Black Sox August 26, 1933 ★ **LOCATION:** McKinley Ave., North New York Ave., South Carolina Ave. ★ **CURRENT USE:** Carver Hall public housing project

ATLANTIC PARK DOG TRACK
OCCUPANT: ECL Atlantic City Bacharach Giants some games 1920s ★ **LOCATION:** Absecon Blvd, by Municipal Market ★ **CURRENT USE:** Supermarket

AUSTIN, TEXAS

CLARK FIELD
OCCUPANT: Neutral site use by NAL Houston Eagles 1949-50 ★ **DIMENSIONS:** Bottom of the Cliff – Left Field 313, Left Center Scoreboard 357, Center Field 341, Right Center 303; Top of the Cliff – Left Field 350, Left Center Scoreboard 375, Deepest Center Field just left of dead center 401, Right Center 363; Right Field 300 ★ **FENCES:** Left and Right Field 10; Center Field 40; complicated measurements courtesy of March 16, 1967 Breazeale-Sims geological survey reveal that the limestone cliff height sloped from 0 at the Left Field Foul Pole to 30 in Center Field back to 0 in Right Center; majority of the cliff was 12 ★ **CAPACITY:** 5,000 (1928)
PHENOMENA: This home of the University of Texas Longhorns was the most unusual baseball field ever created. There was a 12- to 30-foot-high cliff in left center and center that forced the left and center fielders to choose whether to play on top of the cliff or in front of it. About half the outfielders chose to play on top, and about half chose to play down below. Either way, they were bound to have an adventure. The cliff could be climbed only on a goat path in left field. A typical play occurred in 1973 when the Longhorns got an inside-the-park homer to third base. Both outfielders were playing "down below," when a towering fly ball was hit to deep center.

The center fielder went back to the Cliff, but the ball landed up on the plateau. The left fielder ran up the goat path to the Plateau, but the ball hit some of the rocks on top of the Plateau and bounced down toward the left field line. The nearest fielder was the third baseman, who retrieved the ball, but his throw to the plate was nowhere near getting the batter out at home. Opened on March 24, 1928. Legend has it that Lou Gehrig hit a 611-foot homer way over the Plateau and the 40-foot-high fence in deep center in March 1929.

BALTIMORE, MARYLAND

MADISON AVENUE GROUNDS
AKA: Pastime Base Ball Grounds ★ **OCCUPANT:** Neutral site use by NA Washington Olympics July 8, 1871 ★ **LOCATION:** Center Field (E) Linden Ave., Third Base (N) Bloom St. (later Boundary Ave., later North Ave.), Home Plate (W) Madison Ave., First Base (S) an old path between what are now Roberts St. and Laurens St.

NEWINGTON PARK
OCCUPANTS: NA Lord Baltimores April 22, 1872 to October 14, 1874; NA Baltimore Marylands April 14 to June 11, 1873; AA Baltimore Orioles May 9 to September 30, 1882; neutral site use by NA Washington Olympics July 8, 1871; June 1 and 9, 1875 ★ **LOCATION:** (N) Baker St., (W) Gold St., (S) Calhoun St., (E) Pennsylvania Ave.

ORIOLE PARK (I)
AKA: Huntingdon Ave. Grounds 1887-88, American Association Park ★ **OCCUPANTS:** AA Baltimore Orioles May 1, 1883 to October 10, 1889; World Series NL Detroit Wolverines vs. AA St. Louis Browns PM game on October 21, 1887 ★ **LOCATION:** Left Field (W) Barclay St., Third Base (S) 5th (later 24th) St., First Base (E) York Rd. (later Greenmount Ave.), Right Field (N) Huntingdon Ave. (later 6th St., later 25th St.); on the SE corner of Barclay and 25th

BELAIR LOT
AKA: Union Park ★ **OCCUPANTS:** UA Baltimore Monumentals April 17 to August 8 and August 28 to September 24, 1884; neutral site use by UA Pittsburgh Stogies September 17, 1884 ★ **LOCATION:** (N) Gay St., (W) Chestnut (later Colvin) St., (S) Low St., (E) Forrest St. ★ **CURRENT USE:** Old Town Mall parking lot, just SW of Belair Market

MONUMENTAL PARK
OCCUPANT: UA Baltimore Monumentals August 25, 1884

ORIOLE PARK (II)
OCCUPANT: AA Baltimore Orioles August 27, 1890 to May 10, 1891 ★ **LOCATION:** Left Field (E) York Rd. (later Greenmount Ave.), Third Base (N) 10th (later East 29th) St., First Base (W) Barclay St., Right Field (S) 9th (later East 28th) St.; on the SW corner of Greenmount and 29th

ORIOLE PARK (III)
AKA: Baltimore Baseball and Exhibition Grounds ★ **OCCUPANTS:** AA Baltimore Orioles May 11 to October 3, 1891; NL Baltimore Orioles April 12, 1892 to October 10, 1899 ★ **LOCATION:** Left Field (E) Barclay St., Third Base (N) Huntingdon Ave. (later 6th St., later 25th St.); First Base (W) St. Paul St. (later Guilford Ave.), Right Field (S) Sumwalt (later 24th) St. and Brady's Run; on the SW corner of Barclay and 25th, just across the street from Oriole Park (I) ★ **DIMENSIONS:** Left Field 300, Right Field 350 ★ **FENCES:** 16 (wood) ★ **CAPACITY:** 30,000 (1891), 11,000 (1897)

ORIOLE PARK (IV)
AKA: American League Park ★ **OCCUPANT:** AL Baltimore Orioles April 26, 1901 to September 29, 1902 ★ **LOCATION:** Same as that for Oriole Park (II), Oriole Park (IV) was built on the same site after Oriole Park (II) was torn down, SW corner of Greenmount and 29th ★ **CURRENT USE:** Gas station

ORIOLE PARK (V)
AKA: Terrapin Park, Federal League Park ★ **OCCUPANTS:** FL Baltimore Terrapins April 13, 1914 to October 2, 1915; NAL Baltimore Elite Giants April 1938 to July 3, 1944 ★ **LOCATION:** Left Field (N) 11th (later 30th) St., Third Base (W) Vineyard Lane, First Base (S) 10th (later 29th) St., Right Field (E) York Rd. (later Greenmount Ave.); on the NW corner of Greenmount and 29th, just across the street from Oriole Parks (II) and (IV) ★ **DIMENSIONS:** Left Field 300 (1914), 305 (1944), Center Field 450 (1914), 412 (1944), Right Field 335 (1914), 310 (1944), Backstop 76 (1914) ★ **FENCES:** Left Field, Left Center 25 (wood) ★ **CAPACITY:** 16,000 (1914), 14,000 (1944)

MARYLAND BASEBALL PARK
AKA: Moore's Field ★ **OCCUPANTS:** ECL Baltimore Black Sox 1923-27, April to May 1928; ANL Baltimore Black Sox 1929; neutral site use for Negro World Series NNL Kansas City Monarchs vs. ECL Darby Hilldales games 3-4 in 1924 and NNL Chicago American Giants vs. ECL Atlantic City Bacharach Giants Game 3 in 1926

DRUID HILL
OCCUPANT: ECL Baltimore Black Sox some games 1920s ★ **LOCATION:** Madison Ave., in Druid Hill Park

BUGLE FIELD
AKA: Miss Snyder's Cow Pasture ★ **OCCUPANTS:** NEWL Baltimore Black Sox April to June 1932; NNL Baltimore Black Sox 1933, July to September 1934 ★ **LOCATION:** Biddle St., Edison Hwy

VENABLE STADIUM
AKA: Babe Ruth Stadium 1949-50, Baltimore Stadium, Metropolitan Stadium, Municipal Stadium ★ **OCCUPANTS:** NNL Baltimore Elite Giants July 4 to September 1944, 1945-48; NAL Baltimore Elite Giants 1949 ★ **LOCATION:** Same as Memorial Stadium ★ **DIMENSIONS:** Left Field 270 (1944), 291 (1949), Right Field 406 (1944), 291 (1949) ★ **CAPACITY:** 78,000 (1923), 60,000 (1940), 80,000 (1941), 30,000 (1944), 76,658 (1947), 58, 917 (1948)

MEMORIAL STADIUM
OCCUPANT: AL Baltimore Orioles April 15, 1954 to October 6, 1991 ★ **LOCATION:** Center Field (N) East 36th St.; Third Base (W) Ellerslie Ave.; Home Plate (S) 1,000 East 33rd St., section of 33rd St. near ballpark later known as Babe Ruth Plaza; First Base (E) Ednor Rd. ★ **DIMENSIONS:** Foul Lines 309; Alleys where 7-foot fence met 14-foot wall 360; Power Alleys 446 (1954), 447 (1955), 405 (1956), 380 (1958), 370 (1962), 385 (1970), 375 (1976), 378 (1977), 376 (1980), 378 (1990); Center Field 445 (1954), 450 (1955), 425 (1956), 410 (1958), 400 (1976), 405 (1977), 410 (1978), 405 (1980); Backstop 78 (1954), 58 (1961), 54 (1980), 75 (1987); Foul Territory large ★ **FENCES:** Foul Line Corners 11.33 (concrete 1954), 14 (11 concrete below 3 plywood 1959); these walls bounced balls toward center, reducing triples; Left Center to Right Center 10 (hedges April to May 1954), 8 (wire June 1954), 7 (wire 1955), 6 (wire 1958), 14 (wire 1961), 6 (wire 1963), 7 (canvas 1977) ★ **FORMER USE:** When Venable Stadium, a football stadium also used for baseball after the July 4, 1944 fire destroyed Oriole Park (III), was torn down in 1950 to make way for Memorial Stadium, home plate was moved from the north to the south ★ **CURRENT USE:** Underwater, Gale's Lump oyster reef, five miles NE of Baltimore, constructed beneath Chesapeake Bay with the concrete from the stadium ★ **CAPACITY:** 31,000 (1950), 47,855 (1953), 49,375 (1961), 52,184 (1965), 53,208 (1970), 54,076 (1986), 53,371 (1991)
PHENOMENA: Beautiful trees on an embankment beyond the fence in center. In April 1954, hedges served as the center-field fence. In June 1954, a wire fence was erected which stood right in front of the high hedges. The top six feet of this fence were covered with canvas padding in 1958 after Harvey Kuenn cut his face trying to catch a home run ball by climbing the fence. Wind helped hitters. Best crabcakes in baseball.

CAMDEN YARDS
AKA: Oriole Park at Camden Yards ★ **OCCUPANT:** AL Baltimore Orioles April 6, 1992 to date ★ **LOCATION:** Left Field (N/NW) 333 West Camden St.; Third Base (W/SW) Russell St.; First Base (S/SE) Martin Luther King Blvd, Right Field (E/NE) Howard St.; only two blocks from Babe Ruth's birthplace ★ **DIMENSIONS:** Left Field 333 (1992), 340 (2001), 333 (2002); Left Center 364 (1992), 376 (2001), 364 (2002); Deepest Left Center 410 (1992), 417 (2001), 410 (2002); Center Field 400 (1992), 407 (2001), 400 (2002); Right Center 373 (1992), 393 (2001), 373 (2002); Right Field 318 (1992), 325 (2001), 318 (2002); Backstop 57.5 (1992), 50 (2001), 57 (2002) ★ **FENCES:** Left Field to Right Center 7, Right Center to Right Field 25 ★ **FORMER USE:** Le Comte de Rochambeau, French general, camped his troops here on the way to Yorktown in 1781; Baltimore & Ohio RR Station; Ruth's Café, run by Babe Ruth's father, at 406 Conway St. in what would now be center field ★ **CAPACITY:** 48,079 (1992), 48,190 (2003)
PHENOMENA: Just behind fence in right, 432 feet from the plate, is the renovated Baltimore & Ohio (B&O) RR Warehouse, longest building on the East Coast, 1,016 feet long, only 51 feet wide, housing Orioles offices. Right field lights mounted on its roof. Each aisle seat features 1890s Orioles logo. Large Babe Ruth statue has Bambino incorrectly wearing a right-handed fielder's glove.

BATESTOWN, NEW YORK
BULL'S HEAD TAVERN
AKA: Union Grounds ★ **OCCUPANT:** Neutral site use by NA Troy Haymakers some games in 1871-72 ★ **LOCATION:** (W) Second Ave., (E) Sixth Ave; also Glenn Ave., just south of the Troy-Lansingburgh borderline, and in view of 103rd St.

BELLEVILLE, ILLINOIS
BELLEVILLE HIGH SCHOOL ATHLETIC FIELD
OCCUPANT: Neutral site use by NAL Kansas City Monarchs August 7, 1950

BIRMINGHAM, ALABAMA
RICKWOOD FIELD
OCCUPANTS: NNL Birmingham Black Barons 1924-25, 1927-30; NAL Birmingham Black Barons 1937-38, 1940-60; Negro World Series Game 6 in 1943, Games 1 and 3 in 1944 ★ **LOCATION:** Left Field (NE), Third Base (NW) East 18th St., First Base (SW) 1137 West Second Ave., Right Field (SE) RR tracks ★ **DIMENSIONS:** Left Field 405, Center Field 470, Right Field 334 ★ **FENCES:** Left Field 5, Left Center Scoreboard 35, Center to Right Field 5 ★ **CURRENT USE:** Maintained very well, used for amateur games and for one Barons minor league game every summer ★ **CAPACITY:** 9,312
PHENOMENA: Opened August 18, 1910. Patterned exactly after Forbes Field in Pittsburgh. Oldest minor league park still in use. Nobody ever won $500 by hitting a ball through the basketball net hung from the Mellow Yellow sign in right center.

BLOOMFIELD, NEW JERSEY
SPRAGUE FIELD
AKA: General Electric Field ★ **OCCUPANT:** NEWL Newark Browns 1932

★ **LOCATION:** Arlington Ave., Floyd Ave., La France Ave; First Base Bloomfield Ave.
★ **DIMENSIONS:** Left Field 330, Center Field 385, Right Field 325 ★ **FENCES:** Left Field 5, Left Center Scoreboard 35, Center to Right Field 15

BLOOMINGTON, MINNESOTA
METROPOLITAN STADIUM
AKA: The Met ★ **OCCUPANT:** AL Minnesota Twins April 21, 1961 to September 30, 1981 ★ **LOCATION:** Left Field (E) 24th Ave. South, then a cornfield; Third Base (N) West 83rd St., then Met Center and I-494; First Base (W) 8001 Cedar Ave. South/Hwy 77; Right Field (S) West 84th St. (later Killebrew Drive) ★ **DIMENSIONS:** Left Field 329 (1961), 330 (1962), 344 (1965), 346 (1967), 330 (1975), 343 (1977); Short Left Center 365 (1961), 360 (1966), 373 (1972), 350 (1975), 346 (1976), 360 (1977); Deep Left Center: 402 (1961), 435 (1965), 430 (1968), 410 (1975), 406 (1976); Deep Left Center Corner: 430 (1965), 406 (1975); Center Field 412 (1961), 430 (1965), 425 (1968), 410 (1975), 402 (1977); Deep Right Center Corner 430 (1965); Deep Right Center 402 (1961), 435 (1965), 430 (1968), 410 (1977); Short Right Center: 365 (1961), 373 (1968), 365 (1972), 370 (1977); Right Field 329 (1961), 330 (1962); Backstop 60 ★ **SURFACE:** Grass ★ **FENCES:** Left Field 8 (wire 1961), 12 (1964), 7 (1974), 12 (1977); Center Field 8 (wire 1961); Right Field 8 (wire 1961), 12 (1964), 8 (1970) ★ **FORMER USE:** Cornfield ★ **CURRENT USE:** Mall of America shopping mall, home plate is displayed there between two amusement park rides ★ **CAPACITY:** 18,200 (1956), 21,000 (1957), 30,637 (1961), 40,000 (1964), 45,921 (1973), 45,919 (1975)
PHENOMENA: 330-foot marker was curiously far from the foul pole in right, raising the distinct possibility the distance to right was actually significantly less than 330. Third major league park ever built in a cornfield. First was Walte's Pasture, home of 1875 NA Keokuk Westerns; second was South St. Park, home of 1878 NL Indianapolis Browns.

BOSTON, MASSACHUSETTS
SOUTH END GROUNDS (I)
OCCUPANTS: NA Boston Red Stockings May 16, 1871 to October 30, 1875; NL Boston Red Caps April 29, 1876 to September 10, 1887; neutral site use by NA Hartford Dark Blues August 12, 1874 ★ **LOCATION:** Center Field (NE) Railroad Roundhouse, then Gainsborough St.; Third Base (NW) New York, New Haven, and Hartford (later Boston and Providence) RR tracks, then Huntington Ave. Baseball Grounds; Home Plate (SW) Walpole St.; First Base (SE) Columbus Ave. ★ **CAPACITY:** 3,000

DARTMOUTH GROUNDS
AKA: Union Park 1884 ★ **OCCUPANTS:** UA Boston Reds April 30 to September 24, 1884; World Series NL Detroit Wolverines vs. AA St. Louis Browns October 18, 1887 ★ **LOCATION:** Huntington Ave., Dartmouth St.; near Copley Square in the Back Bay

SOUTH END GROUNDS (II)
AKA: Grand Pavilion, Walpole St. Grounds, Union Baseball Grounds, Boston Baseball Grounds ★ **OCCUPANT:** NL Boston Beaneaters May 25, 1888 to May 15, 1894 ★ **LOCATION:** same as South End Grounds (I) ★ **DIMENSIONS:** Left Field 250; Left Center 445; Center Field 500; Right Center 440; Right Field 255 ★ **CAPACITY:** 6,800 (1888)

CONGRESS STREET GROUNDS
AKA: Brotherhood Grounds ★ **OCCUPANTS:** PL Boston Reds April 19 to September 10, 1890; AA Boston Reds April 18 to October 3, 1891; NL Boston Beaneaters May 16 to June 20, 1894 ★ **LOCATION:** (NE) New York, New Haven, and Hartford RR tracks, (W) A St. and B St., (S) Congress St.; near the waterfront on Boston Harbor, adjacent to Fort Point Channel ★ **DIMENSIONS:** Left Field 250

SOUTH END GROUNDS (III)
AKA: South Side Grounds ★ **OCCUPANT:** NL Boston Braves July 20, 1894 to August 11, 1914 **LOCATION:** same as South End Grounds (I) and (II) ★ **DIMENSIONS:** Left Field 250; Left Center 445; Deepest Left Center 450, Center Field 440; Right Center 440; Right Field 255 ★ **FENCES:** Center Field 6; Right Field 20 ★ **CURRENT USE:** Ruggles MBTA Subway Station on Orange Line; cigar factory that stood behind the fence in right is still standing; twin spires from grandstand now stand on a newer building on Columbus Ave. ★ **CAPACITY:** 5,800 (1894), 7,000 (1914)

HUNTINGTON AVENUE BASEBALL GROUNDS
OCCUPANT: AL Boston Red Sox May 8, 1901 to October 7, 1911 ★ **LOCATION:** Left Field (NW) Huntington Ave; Third Base (SW) Bryant Ave. (later Rogers Ave., then Forsyth St.); First Base (SE) New York, New Haven, and Hartford RR tracks; Right Field (NE) New Gravely St., Gainsborough St.; just N of South End Grounds (II) ★ **DIMENSIONS:** Left Field 350; Left Center 440; Center Field 530 (1901), 635 (1908); Right Center 424; Right Field 280 (1901), 320 (1908); Backstop 60 ★ **FENCES:** 14 ★ **FORMER USE:** Circuses and carnivals ★ **CURRENT USE:** Cabot Cage (Godfrey Lowell Cabot Phys Ed Center) at Northeastern University, the plaque in the World Series Exhibit Room was unveiled in May 1956 to commemorate exact location of the right-field foul pole, statue of Cy Young placed in 1993 at pitcher's mound where he pitched perfect game May 5, 1904 ★ **CAPACITY:** 9,000 (1901), 11,500 (1911)

FENWAY PARK
OCCUPANTS: AL Boston Red Sox April 20, 1912 to date; NL Boston Braves April 19, May 30, 1913, August 1 and 8, September 7-29, 1914, 1914 World Series,

April 14 to July 26, 1915, April 17 and 28, 1946 ★ **LOCATION:** Left Field (N) Lansdowne St., then Boston and Albany RR tracks and Mass Turnpike/I-90; Left Field Corner (NW) Brookline Ave., Third Base (W) 24 Jersey St. (later 4 Yawkey Way), also bowling alley building attached to ballpark; First Base (S) Van Ness St. (built after ballpark); Right Field (E) Ipswich St., Fenway Garage building ★ **DIMENSIONS:** Left Field 324 (1921), 320.5 (1926), 320 (1930), 318 (1931), 320 (1933), 312 (1934), 315 (1936), 310 (1995); Left Center 379 (1934); Deep Left Center at flagpole 388 (1934); Flagpole removed from field of play in 1970; Center Field 488 (1922), 468 (1930), 388.67 (1934), 389.67 (1954); Deepest Right Center Corner (just right of dead center) 510 (1912), 550 (1922), 493 (1931) [the 593 cited in 1931-33 *Bluebooks* must be a misprint]; 420 (1934); Right Center just right of deepest corner where bullpen begins 380 (1938), 383 (1955); Right of Right Center 405 (1939), 382 (1940), 381 (1942), 380 (1943); Right Field 313.5 (1921), 358.5 (1926), 358 (1930), 325 (1931), 358 (1933), 334 (1934), 332 (1936), 322 (1938), 332 (1939), 304 (1940), 302 (1942); Backstop 68 (1912), 60 (1934); Foul Territory very small, tiniest in the majors ★ **FENCES:** Left Field 25 (wood 1912), 37.17 (tin over wooden railroad ties upper section and over concrete lower section 1934), 37.17 (hard plastic 1976); Left Field wall to bleacher wall behind flagpole 18 sloping to 17 (concrete 1934), (padding 1976) crash pad added from 18 inches to 6 feet on left and center field walls (1976); Center Field to bullpen fence 8.75 (wood 1940); Right Center bullpen fence 5.25 (wood 1940); Right Field wall and railing from bullpen 3.42 sloping to 5.37 at foul pole (steel 1940); Right Field belly low railing and wall curve out sharply from 302 marker at Right Field foul pole into deep Right Field, many a right fielder has run toward the foul line and watched helplessly as a 302-foot pop fly falls over the railing for a home run. ★ **FORMER USE:** A swamp in the Fens section of Boston ★ **CAPACITY:** 35,000 (1912), 33,368 (1961), 34,182 (1989), 33,993 (2001 evenings), 33,577 (2001 afternoons)

PHENOMENA: Duffy's Cliff was a 10-foot high incline in front of the left field wall from 1912 to 1933, extending from the foul pole to the flagpole in center, named after Sox left fielder Duffy Lewis, the acknowledged master of defensive play on the cliff. It was greatly reduced but not eliminated in 1934. The Green Monster in left completely dominates the field. A 23'7" net was placed atop the wall in 1936 to protect windows on Landsdowne St. Back in the 1930s and 1940s, tin covered the two-by-fours on the Monster. Balls hitting the tin over the two-by-fours had a live bounce, but balls hitting between the two-by-fours were dead and just dropped straight down. A ladder starts near the upper-left corner of the scoreboard, 13 feet above ground, and rises to the top. This allowed groundskeepers to remove batting practice balls from the net, before seats were added to the top of the Monster in 2003. Balls hitting uprights above the Wall that should have been homers have often been declared in play by the umpires. No ball has ever been hit over the right field roof. In 1940, to help Ted Williams hit home runs, the Red Sox added the right field bullpens, called Williamsburg, reducing the distance to the fence by 23 feet. Players have always assumed the Monster was closer than the 315 sign installed in 1936 would indicate. The foul line was measured by Art Keefe and George Sullivan in 1975 at 309 ft 5 in. On October 19, 1975, the Boston *Globe*'s aerial photography measured it at 304.779 ft. Osborn Engineering's blueprints document the distance at 308 feet. The sign was finally changed from 315 to 310 in 1995; however, the persistent 315 number still appeared in the 2003 *AL Red Book*.

BRAVES FIELD

AKA: The Wigwam, National League Field 1936-40; Bee Hive April 17, 1936 to April 29, 1941; Nickerson Field 1970s to date ★ **OCCUPANTS:** NL Boston Braves August 18, 1915 to September 29, 1935; NL Boston Bees April 17, 1936 to April 23 1941; NL Boston Braves April 29, 1941 to September 21, 1952; AL Boston Red Sox 1915-16 World Series, Sunday games April 1929 to June 1932 ★ **LOCATION:** Center Field (NW) Boston and Albany RR tracks, then Storrow Drive and Charles River; Third Base (SW) Babcock St.; Home Plate (SE) Commonwealth Ave; First Base (NE) 34 Gaffney St. (later Harry Agganis Way) ★ **DIMENSIONS:** Left Field 402.5 (April 1915), 396 (August 1915), 402.42 (1921), 404 (1922), 402.5 (1926), 320 (April 1928), 353.5 (July 1928), 340 (1930), 353.67 (1931), 359 (1933), 353.67 (1934), 368 (1936), 350 (1940), 337 (1941), 334 (1942), 340 (1943), 337 (1944); Left Center 330 (April 1928), 359 (July 1928), 365 (1942), 355 (1946); Center Field 520 (1926), 387 (April 1928), 417 (July 1928), 387.17 (1929), 394.5 (1930), 387.25 (1931), 417 (1933), 426 (1936), 407 (1937), 408 (1939), 385 (1940), 401 (1941), 375 (1942), 370 (1943), 390 (1944), 380 (1945), 370 (1946); Deepest Center Field corner just right of dead center: 550 (1915), 401 (1942), 390 (1943); Right Center 362 (1942), 355 (1943); Right Field 402 (April 1915), 375 (August 1915), 365 (1921), 364 (1928), 297.75 (1929), 297.92 (1931), 364 (1933), 297 (1936) 376 (1937), 378 (1938), 350 (1940), 340 (April 1943), 320 (July 1943), 340 (April 1944), 320 (May 1944), 340 (April 1946), 320 (May 1946), 318 (1947), 320 (1948), 319 (1948); Backstop 75 (1915), 60 (1936) ★ **FENCES:** Left Field to Right Center 10 (concrete 1915), 8 (wood 1928), 20 (wood 1946), 25 (wood 1948), 19 (wood 1953); Left Field scoreboard sides 64 (1949); middle arch 68 (1949); Left Center: 1 (gravestones July 1928); Right Center exit gate 8 (wire); Right Field 10 (6 screen above 4 wood) ★ **FORMER USE:** Allston Golf Club ★ **CURRENT USE:** Nickerson Field, home to Boston University Terriers football and WUSA soccer, using seats from down the right field line; also Myles Standish Dorms, three BU dorm towers built in what had been the seats behind third base and home plate; and the BU hockey rink where the seats down the left-field foul line had been. The Gaffney St. first-base entrance building is now the headquarters for the BU police. The concrete outer wall in right and center also still exists. The right-field foul-line bleachers, extending from first base to the right-field foul pole, still stand. Many of the seats now sit in a Rhode Island softball stadium. Plaque written by SABR to mark the site was dedicated August 6, 1988. ★ **CAPACITY:** 40,000 (1915), 46,000 (1928), 41,700 (1937), 45,000 (1939), 37,746 (1941), 36,706 (1947), 36,106 (1948), 44,500 (1952)

PHENOMENA: The Jury Box was a small bleacher section in right with very vocal fans. It got its name when a sportswriter noticed that there were only 12 people sitting in its 2,000 seats one day. In the 1940s, fir trees were planted beyond the fence in right center in an unsuccessful attempt to hide huge clouds of locomotive smoke belching from the Boston and Albany tracks. In 1984, under the old right-field bleachers, the author found an old ticket booth, turned on its side and covered with cobwebs, with a 1952 Boston Braves schedule still tacked to its wall. No matter how hard the new tries to cover up the old, the past manages to live on!

BROOKLYN, NEW YORK

UNION GROUNDS

AKA: Union Skating Rink, Union Skating Pond ★ **OCCUPANTS:** NA New York Mutuals May 25, 1871 to October 29, 1875; NA Brooklyn Eckfords May 9, 1871 to October 22, 1872; NA Brooklyn Atlantics May 7, 1873 to October 9, 1875; NL New York Mutuals April 25 to October 17, 1876; NL Hartfords of Brooklyn April 30 to September 21, 1877; AA Brooklyn Bridegrooms May 30 to June 19, 1889; neutral site use by NA Philadelphia Athletics October 30, 1871; by Elizabeth Resolutes August 4 and 7, 1873 ★ **LOCATION:** (NW) Hewes St.; (SW) Lee Ave., (SE) Rutledge St.; (NE) Harrison Ave; Marcy Ave. now runs NW-SE through the site; in Williamsburg, just across the East River from lower Manhattan ★ **DIMENSIONS:** All fences more than 500 ★ **FENCES:** 6.5 ★ **FORMER USE:** Union Skating Club's ice rink during the winter throughout the 1870s ★ **CURRENT USE:** Brownstone housing in a Hasidic neighborhood ★ **CAPACITY:** 2,000

PHENOMENA: Built by William Cammeyer. Opened May 15, 1862 for baseball, though previously used for ice skating. First enclosed baseball field ever built. One-story building in right, 350 feet from the plate, was in play.

CAPITOLINE GROUNDS

AKA: Capitoline Skating Pond, Union and Capitoline Grounds, Capitoline, Capitoline Skating Lake and Base Ball Ground ★ **OCCUPANT:** NA Brooklyn Atlantics May 6 to October 9, 1872 ★ **LOCATION:** (N/NW) Putnam Ave., (W/SW) Nostrand Ave., (S/SE) Halsey St., (E/NE) Marcy Ave; in Bedford-Stuyvesant; near the old location of 13th Regimental Armory (I), which was torn down in the late 1800s to build a railroad station; 13th Regimental Armory (II) was built ten blocks away to the NE at Sumner Ave. and Jefferson Ave. ★ **FORMER USE:** Part of a farm leased from the Lefferts family by Reuben S. Decker's father Stephen. ★ **CURRENT USE:** High school building between Nostrand and Marcy used 1888-1976 for Boys' High School, then used for alternative high school called the Street Academy

PHENOMENA: Built in 1862 by Reuben S. Decker as a skating pond. First used for baseball in 1865, three years after the Union Grounds were used for baseball. A batter hitting a home run over the top of the cone-shaped roof of a small round brick outbuilding in deep right center received a bottle of champagne. When Eddie Cuthbert stole second base here in 1865 by sliding in to evade a tag, everybody laughed at him. But when the umpires found nothing in the rule book saying it was illegal, the laughter ended, and the stolen base as we know it had been invented! The Capitoline Grounds encompassed a huge area, including several ball diamonds.

WASHINGTON PARK (I)

OCCUPANTS: AA Brooklyn Bridegrooms May 5, 1884 to May 5, 1889; neutral site use by AA New York Mets August 10, 1884 (rained out), October 8, 1887, World Series October 14 and 22, 1887 NL Detroit Wolverines vs. AA St. Louis Browns, World Series October 19, 1888 NL New York Gothams vs. AA St. Louis Browns ★ **LOCATION:** (N) Third St., (W) Fourth Ave., (S) Fifth St., (E) Fifth Ave; in the Red Hook section of south Brooklyn, near the Gowanus Canal and Bay Ridge RR tracks ★ **FORMER USE:** General George Washington used Gowanus House as his HQ during the Battle of Long Island during the Revolutionary War—the house later served as a baseball clubhouse, but eventually was reduced to rubble by the early 20th century, when it was relocated a significant distance and rebuilt. It still stands near the site of the ballpark ★ **CURRENT USE:** JJ Byrne Park

RIDGEWOOD PARK

AKA: Wallace's Grounds, Horse Market, Meyerrose's Park ★ **OCCUPANTS:** NL Brooklyn Bridegrooms Sundays May 2, 1886 to October 6, 1889; AA Brooklyn Gladiators April 17 to June 9, 1890 ★ **LOCATION:** (N) Myrtle Ave., (W) Weirfield St., (S) Wyckoff Ave., (E) Decatur St.; then in Queens, but now in Brooklyn, on the Queens-Brooklyn border, entrance was at Myrtle Ave. and Covert (now called Norman) St. ★ **CURRENT USE:** Houses

WASHINGTON PARK (II)

OCCUPANTS: AA Brooklyn Bridegrooms June 20 to October 5, 1889; NL Brooklyn Bridegrooms April 28 to October 3, 1890 ★ **LOCATION:** Same as Washington Park (I) ★ **CAPACITY:** 3,000 (1889), 8,000 (1890)

EASTERN PARK

AKA: Brotherhood Park 1890, Atlantic Park ★ **OCCUPANTS:** PL Brooklyn Wonders April 28 to September 12, 1890; NL Brooklyn Bridegrooms April 27, 1891 to October 2, 1897 ★ **LOCATION:** (N) Eastern Parkway (now Pitkin Ave.), (W) Powell St., (S) Sutter Ave., (E) Vesta Ave. (later van Sinderen St.); also Canarsie RR tracks, City Line and Brownsville Line Elevated RR tracks; in the East New York section of Brooklyn, near Jamaica Bay ★ **CAPACITY:** 12,000

WASHINGTON PARK (III)

OCCUPANT: NL Brooklyn Bridegrooms April 30, 1898 to October 5, 1912 ★ **LOCATION:** Left Field (W) Third Ave., then railyards and Gowanus Canal, Third Base (S) Third St., First Base (E) Fourth Ave., Right Field (N) First St.; also Bay Ridge RR tracks; in Red Hook, just across intersection from the location of Washington

Parks (I) and (II) ★ **DIMENSIONS:** Left Field 335 (1898), 375.95 (1908), Left Center 500 (1898), 443.5 (1908), Center Field 445 (1898), 424.7 (1908), Right Center 300 (1898), Right Field 215 (1898), 295 (1899), 301.84 (1908), Backstop 90 (1898), 15 (1908) ★ **FENCES:** Left and Center Fields 12 (brick), Right Field 42 (13 brick then 29 canvas) ★ **CAPACITY:** 18,000 (1898), 16,000 (1912)
PHENOMENA: Giants' right fielder Archie "Moonlight" Graham made his only major league appearance here on June 29, 1905 with no at bats and no defensive chances. Dr. Graham was played by Burt Lancaster in the movie *Field of Dreams*, but the movie erroneously placed his appearance in 1922 rather than in 1905. Air was putrid because of the nearby factories and canal. Fans could watch from apartments called Ginney Flats across the street from the right field wall. At the top of the 220-foot high flagpole behind the scoreboard in center was the mast of the America's Cup defender *Reliance*.

WASHINGTON PARK (IV)
OCCUPANT: FL Brooklyn Brook-Feds May 11, 1914 to September 30, 1915 ★ **LOCATION:** Same as for Washington Park (III), but orientation was different, the diamond was moved a considerable distance westward from where it had been, resulting in very different outfield distances. ★ **DIMENSIONS:** Left Field 300 (1914), Center Field 400 (1914), Right Field 275 (1914) ★ **FENCES:** 12 (brick) ★ **CURRENT USE:** 20-ft tall brick walls along Third Ave. and First St. still stand in Con Ed storage yard used for equipment, cars, and trucks at 222 First St. It is unknown whether the Third Ave. wall was part of the left-center-field wall, part of a wall behind the left-center-field wall, or part of the clubhouse in left center. The First St. wall was part of the right-center-field wall. Extensive research by Tom Gilbert and Alan Gottlieb has determined that both walls were part of Washington Park (III) that were saved and incorporated into Washington Park (IV). ★ **CAPACITY:** 18,800 (1914)

EBBETS FIELD
OCCUPANTS: NL Brooklyn Dodgers April 9, 1913 to September 24, 1957; NNL Brooklyn Eagles 1935 ★ **LOCATION:** Left Field (NE) Montgomery St.; Third Base (NW) Franklin Ave. (later Cedar Place, later McKeever Place); First Base (SW) 55 Sullivan Place; Right Field (SE) Bedford Ave; in Pigtown/Crown Heights area of Flatbush ★ **DIMENSIONS:** Left Field 419 (1913), 410 (1914), 418.75 (1921), 383.67 (1926), 382.83 (1930), 384 (1931), 353 (1932), 356.33 (1934), 365 (1938), 357 (1939), 365 (1940), 356 (1942), 357 (1947), 343 (1948), 348 (1953), 343 (1955), 348 (1957); Left Center 365 (1932), 351 (1948); Deep Left Center at bend in wall 407 (1932), 393 (1948), 395 (1954); Center Field 450 (1914), 466 (1930), 460.79 (early 1931), 447 (late 1931), 399.42 (1932), 399 (1936), 402 (1938), 400 (1939), 399 (1947), 384 (1948), 393 (1955); Right Side of Center Field grandstand 390 (1948), 376 (1948); Right Center's deepest corner 500 (1913), 476.75 (1948), 415 (1932), 403 (1948), 405 (1950), 403 (1955); right side of Right Center exit gate 399 (1932); Right Center 352 (1948); Scoreboard left side 344, right side 318; Right Field 301 (1913), 300 (1914), 296.17 (1921), 292 (1922), 301 (1926), 296.08 (1930), 295.92 (1931), 296.5 (1934), 297 (1938); Backstop 64 (1942), 70.5 (1954), 72 (1957) ★ **FENCES:** Left Field to Left Center 20 (1913), 3 (wood 1920), 9.87 (concrete 1931); Center Field 20 (1913), 393 marker 9.87 (concrete 1931) sloping upward; 376 marker 15 (concrete 1931); Right Center 9 (concrete 1913), from 376 point to screen: 15 sloping upward to 19, then down to 13; Right Center to Right Field 38 (top 19 screen, bottom 19 concave concrete wall, bent at 9.5 midpoint, vertical top half, concave angled bottom half); screen in Center Field 20 (screen above sloping concrete 1920s); Right Field before screen was built 9 (concrete 1913) ★ **FORMER USE:** Pigtown garbage dump ★ **CURRENT USE:** Ebbets Field Apartments housing development was built in 1963. IS 320 Intermediate School is across the road. Apartments were renamed Jackie Robinson Apartments at Ebbets Field in 1972. Jackie Robinson School, previously known as Crown Heights School, houses the Brooklyn Dodger Hall of Fame. ★ **CAPACITY:** 18,000 (April 9, 1913), 24,000 (June 30, 1913), 26,000 (1924), 28,000 (1926), 32,000 (1932), 35,000 (1937), 32,000 (1938), 34,219 (1940), 32,000 (1946), 31,903 (1957)
PHENOMENA: The Abe Stark sign offered a free suit at 1514 Pitkin Ave. to any batter hitting the 3'-by-30' sign. Woody English of the Dodgers was the only batter to ever hit it, on June 6, 1937. Little kids watched the game through a gap under the metal gate in right center. This was how the term "knothole gang" got started. The Rotunda was the 27-foot high domed entrance area, 80 feet in diameter, enclosed in Italian marble, with a floor tiled with stitches of a baseball, and a chandelier with 12 baseball-bat arms holding 12 globe-shaped baseballs. There were 12 turnstiles and 12 gilded ticket windows. Bama Rowell's homer for the Braves in 1946, which broke the right field scoreboard's clock, inspired Roy Hobbs' pennant-winning homer in the movie *The Natural*. Schaefer Beer sign on the top of the right-center scoreboard notified fans of official scorer's decision—the "H" in Schaefer lit up for a hit, an "E" for an error.

DEXTER PARK
AKA: Sterling Oval, Bushwick Park ★ **OCCUPANTS:** ECL Brooklyn Royal Giants 1923-27; neutral site use by NNL New York Cubans and NNL New York Black Yankees 1930s and 1940s ★ **LOCATION:** Left Field (N) Simpson St. (later 1 Park Lane South); Third Base (W) Elderts Lane (later Dexter Court), then Cypress Hills Cemetery; First Base (S) Bushwick (later Jamaica) Ave; Right Field (E) Lott Ave. (later 76th St.); overlooked by Franklin K. Lane High School; in Woodhaven area of Queens ★ **DIMENSIONS:** Left Center 418 ★ **CAPACITY:** 15,000
PHENOMENA: Most creative outfield wall billboard ever. An optician's ad read: "Don't Kill the Umpire—Maybe It's Your Eyes." First used for baseball in the 1880s. Josh Gibson hit a mammoth homer here over the 30-foot-high wall behind the left center bleachers at the 418 sign. Big incline in right field was due to a horse buried under the grass. Whether lights installed here in April 1930 were the first on the East Coast, or whether that honor goes to Dyckman Oval, is still unknown.

BUFFALO, NEW YORK
RIVERSIDE GROUNDS
OCCUPANT: NL Buffalo Bisons May 1, 1879 to September 8, 1883 ★ **LOCATION:** (N) Rhode Island St., (W) Fargo Ave., (S) Vermont St., (E) 599 West Ave. ★ **DIMENSIONS:** Foul Lines 210, Power Alleys 420, Center Field 410, Backstop 37 ★ **CURRENT USE:** Lizzie Bluett's cottage at 599 West Ave. is still standing.
PHENOMENA: A home run broke Lizzie Bluett's collarbone on May 21, 1881

OLYMPIC PARK (I)
OCCUPANT: NL Buffalo Bisons May 21, 1884 to October 7, 1885 ★ **LOCATION:** (W) Richmond Ave., (S) Summer St., (E) Howard (later Norwood) Ave.

OLYMPIC PARK (II)
AKA: Buffalo Baseball Park ★ **OCCUPANT:** PL Buffalo Bisons April 19 to October 4, 1890 ★ **LOCATION:** Left Field (E) Masten St., Third Base (N) East Ferry St., Home Plate (NW) Covenant Presbyterian Church, First Base (W) 1515 Michigan Ave., Right Field (S) Woodlawn Ave; same site was used later for Offermann Stadium.

INTERNATIONAL FAIR ASSOCIATION GROUNDS
AKA: Federal League Ball Park ★ **OCCUPANT:** FL Buffalo Buffeds May 11, 1914 to September 29, 1915 ★ **LOCATION:** (N) Puffer St. (later Northland Ave.), (W) Lonsdale Rd., (S) Boston (later Hamlin) Rd. ★ **DIMENSIONS:** Left Field 290, Center Field 400, Right Field 300 ★ **CAPACITY:** 20,000

OFFERMANN STADIUM
AKA: Robertson Park 1924, Bison Stadium 1925-34 ★ **OCCUPANT:** Neutral site use by NNL New York Black Yankees 1940s ★ **LOCATION:** same as Olympic Park (II) ★ **DIMENSIONS:** Left Field 321, Left Center 346, Center Field 400, Right Center 366, Right Field 297, Backstop 21 ★ **FENCES:** Left Field 12 (concrete 1924), 32 (concrete topped with 20 wood in two tiers to block view of spectators in bleachers across the street on Masten St.), Left Center 15, Center Field scoreboard 40 (wood 1924), 60 (wood 1934), Right Center to Right 12 (concrete 1924) ★ **CURRENT USE:** Torn down in 1960 to make way for a junior high school. Covenant Presbyterian Church still stands behind where home plate used to be.

CANTON, OHIO
MAHAFFEY PARK
OCCUPANTS: Neutral site use by NL Pittsburgh Burghers September 18, 1890; by AL Cleveland Blues June 15, 1902 and May 10 and June 21, 1903, by NEWL Pittsburgh Crawfords PM game August 8, 1932.

CHATTANOOGA, TENNESSEE
ENGEL STADIUM
OCCUPANT: Neutral site use by NNL Nashville Elite Giants in 1930s ★ **DIMENSIONS:** Left Field 368, left side of the Left Center Scoreboard 355, Center Field 471, Right Field 324 (marked), 318 (actual) ★ **FENCES:** Left Center Scoreboard 42 in the middle, 32 at the left and right side of the curving top; rest of the Outfield 22 ★ **CAPACITY:** 10,000 (1930), 8,000 (1988), 7,480 (1989)

CHICAGO, ILLINOIS
LAKE PARK (I)
AKA: White Stocking Park (I), Lakefront Park (I), Chicago Base-Ball Grounds (I), Union Base-Ball Grounds, Lake Shore Park, Lake St. Dumping Grnd, the Dump ★ **OCCUPANT:** NA Chicago White Stockings May 8 to September 29, 1871 ★ **LOCATION:** Left Field (E) Illinois Central RR tracks, then Lake Michigan, Third Base (N) Randolph St., First Base (W) Michigan Ave., Right Field (S) Madison St. ★ **DIMENSIONS:** Foul Lines 375 ★ **FENCES:** 6 (wood) ★ **FORMER USE:** Dumping ground ★ **CAPACITY:** 7,000
PHENOMENA: Burned down by Mrs. O'Leary's cow during the Great Chicago Fire of October 8-11, 1871. Back then, Lake Michigan came almost to the Illinois Central RR tracks. Much of the land has now been filled in.

23rd STREET PARK
AKA: State St. Grounds, Association Park ★ **OCCUPANTS:** NA Chicago White Stockings May 13, 1874 to October 2, 1875; NL Chicago White Stockings May 10, 1876 to October 5, 1877; neutral site use by NA Lord Baltimores May 29-30, 1872; by Philadelphia Athletics June 24, 1872; by Boston Red Stockings August 19, 1873 ★ **LOCATION:** (N) 22nd St. (later Cermak Rd.) (W) Clark St. (S) 23rd St. (E) State St. ★ **CAPACITY:** 2,500

LAKE PARK (II)
AKA: White Stocking Park (II), Lakefront Park (II), Chicago Base-Ball Grounds (II) ★ **OCCUPANT:** NL Chicago White Stockings May 14, 1878 to September 30, 1882 ★ **LOCATION:** Left Field (W) Michigan Ave., Third Base (S) Washington St., First Base (E) Illinois Central RR tracks and switchyards, Right Field (N) Randolph St.; same site as Lake Front Park (I), but oriented differently ★ **CURRENT USE:** Old Post Office ★ **CAPACITY:** 3,000

LAKE PARK (III)
AKA: White Stocking Park (III), Lakefront Park (III), Chicago Base-Ball Grounds (III) ★ **OCCUPANTS:** NL Chicago White Stockings May 5, 1883 to October 11, 1884;

UA Chicago Browns some games 1884 ★ **LOCATION:** Same as Lake Front Park (II) ★ **DIMENSIONS:** Left Field 186 (1883), 180 (1884), Left Center 280, Center Field 300, Right Center 252, Right Field 196 ★ **FENCES:** Left Field to Right Center 6 (wood), Right Field 37.5 (17.5 tarp above 20 wood) ★ **CURRENT USE:** Small city park across from Public Library, above the Grant Park underground parking garage ★ **CAPACITY:** 5,000

PHENOMENA: The First Cavalry Band played at the bandstand pagoda overlooking the main entrance. Shortest ever foul lines in the major leagues—186 to left in 1883 and only 180 in 1884, 196 to right. Hits over the fence in left were doubles in 1883, but homers in 1884, in spite of the fact that it was six feet shorter in 1884.

SOUTH SIDE PARK (I)
AKA: Chicago Cricket Club Grounds (I), 39th St. Grounds (I), Union Ball Park ★ **OCCUPANT:** UA Chicago Browns May 2 to August 1, 1884 ★ **LOCATION:** (W) Wabash Ave., (S) 39th St. (later Pershing Rd.), (E) Michigan Ave.

WEST SIDE PARK (I)
AKA: Loomis Race Track, Congress St. Grounds, Loomis St. Park ★ **OCCUPANT:** NL Chicago White Stockings June 6, 1885 to October 6, 1892 (only Mondays, Wednesdays, and Fridays 1891, only half of games 1892); neutral site use for World Series NL Detroit Wolverines vs. AA St. Louis Browns October 25, 1887; PL Chicago Pirates 1890 some games ★ **LOCATION:** Left Field (N) Congress St., Third Base (W) Loomis St., First Base (S) Harrison St., Right Field (E) Throop St. ★ **DIMENSIONS:** Foul Lines 216 ★ **FENCES:** 12 (brick) ★ **CAPACITY:** 10,300

SOUTH SIDE PARK (II)
AKA: Brotherhood Park 1890, 35th St. Grounds (I) ★ **OCCUPANTS:** PL Chicago Pirates May 5 to October 4, 1890; NL Chicago Colts May 5, 1891 to September 27, 1893 (only Tuesdays, Thursdays, Saturdays 1891, only half of games 1892), August 6 to September 30, 1894 **LOCATION:** (N) West 34th St., (W) Wentworth Ave., (S) West 35th St.; across the street from where Comiskey Park (I) was later built ★ **FENCES:** 10 (wood)

WEST SIDE PARK (II)
AKA: West Side Grounds ★ **OCCUPANTS:** NL Chicago Colts May 13, 1893 to August 5, 1894 (Sundays only 1893); May 2, 1895 to October 3, 1915; neutral site use by NL Cleveland Spiders some games 1898 ★ **LOCATION:** Left Field (E) South Wood St., Third Base (N) West Polk St., First Base (W) South Lincoln (later Wolcott) St., Right Field (S) West Taylor St. ★ **DIMENSIONS:** Left Field 340; Left Center 441; Center Field 560; Right Center 435; Right Field 316, Foul Territory large ★ **CURRENT USE:** Illinois State Hospital and Medical School ★ **CAPACITY:** 13,000 (1893), 16,000 (1915)

SOUTH SIDE PARK (III)
AKA: Chicago Cricket Club Grounds (II), 39th St. Grounds (II), White Stocking Park (IV) 1901-03, White Sox Park (I) 1904-10, Schorling's Park 1920-40, American Giants Park ★ **OCCUPANTS:** AL Chicago White Sox April 24, 1901 to June 27, 1910; NSL Chicago Cole's American Giants 1932; NNL Chicago Cole's American Giants April to May 27, 1933, 1934-35; NAL Chicago American Giants 1937-40; neutral site used by NNL Milwaukee Bears several games 1923, NNL Kansas City Monarchs in 1920s, and NNL Cuban Stars West in 1920s ★ **LOCATION:** Left Field (N) West 37th St.; Third Base (W) South Princeton Ave; First Base (S) West 39th St. (later West Pershing Rd.); Right Field (E) South Wentworth Ave. ★ **DIMENSIONS:** Left Field 355, Left Center 400, Center Field 450 ★ **FORMER USE:** Home of Wanderers cricket team ★ **CURRENT USE:** Housing project three blocks from Comiskey Park ★ **CAPACITY:** 6,600 (1904), 15,000 (1910)

COMISKEY PARK (I)
AKA: White Sox Park (II) 1910-12, Charles A. Comiskey's Baseball Palace 1910, White Sox Park (III) May 1962 to September 1975, 35th St. Grounds (II) ★ **OCCUPANTS:** AL Chicago White Sox July 1, 1910 to September 30, 1990; NL Chicago Cubs 1918 World Series; NAL Chicago American Giants 1941-52; neutral site use for 1926 Negro World Series NNL Kansas City Monarchs vs. ECL Darby Hilldales Games 8, 9, 10; for NNL Washington-Homestead Grays vs. NAL Birmingham Black Barons Game 3 1943; for NNL Newark Eagles vs. NAL Kansas City Monarchs Game 5, 1946; for NNL New York Cubans vs. NAL Cleveland Buckeyes Game 4, 1947 ★ **LOCATION:** Left Field (N) West 34th St.; Third Base (W) Portland (later South Shields') Ave., then Chicago and Western RR tracks; First Base (S) 324 West 35th St.; Right Field (E) South Wentworth Ave., then Dan Ryan Expressway/I-94 ★ **DIMENSIONS:** Foul Lines 363 (1910), 362 (1911), 365 (1927), 362 (1930), 342 (1934), 353 (1935), 340 (1936), 352 (1937), 332 (April 22, 1949), 352 (May 5, 1949), 335 (1969), 352 (marked 1971), 349 (actual 1971), 341 (1983), 347 (1986); Power Alleys 382 (1910), 375 (1927), 370 (1934), 382 (1942), 362 (April 22, 1949), 375 (May 5, 1949), 382 (1954), 375 (1955), 375 (1956), 365 (1959), 375 (1968), 370 (1969), 375 (marked 1971), 382 (actual 1971), 374 (1983), 382 (1986); Center Field 420 (1910), 450 (1926), 455 (1927), 450 (1930), 436 (1934), 422 (1936), 440 (1937), 420 (April 22, 1949), 415 (May 5, 1949), 410 (1951), 415 (1952), 400 (1969), 440 (1976), 445 (1977), 402 (marked 1981), 409 (actual 1981), 401 (1983), 409 (1986); Backstop 98 (1910), 71 (1933), 85 (1934), 86 (1975), Foul Territory large ★ **FENCES:** Foul Lines and Power Alleys 12 (concrete 1955), 9.83 (concrete 1959), 5 (wire 1969), 9.83 (concrete 1971); Center Field 15 (1927), 30 (1948), 17 (1976), 18 (1980); Left Center to Right Center Inner fences 5 (canvas 1949), 6.5 (24-foot section in front of bullpens 1969), 9 (1974), 7 (canvas 1981), 7.5 (1982), 11 (1984), 7.5 (1986) ★ **SURFACE:** Outfield grass; Infield grass (1910), carpet (1969), grass (1976) ★ **FORMER USE:** Truck garden owned by Signor Scavado and a city dump, South Side Park (II) was almost on the same site, across

Wentworth Ave. ★ **CURRENT USE:** North parking lot for Comiskey Park (II) ★ **CAPACITY:** 28,800 (1910), 52,000 (1927), 50,000 (1938), 46,550 (1942), 44,492 (1969), 43,951 (1990)

PHENOMENA: Sox shortstop Luke Appling once heard his spikes hit metal as he tried to field a bad hop. He asked for time, and the groundskeepers came out and removed a large copper kettle from the infield. From that point forward, infielders had a ready-made excuse for errors. How did the kettle get there? The site was a city dump before becoming a ballpark. Foul lines were old water hoses, painted white and squished flat. Tradition of playing the National Anthem started spontaneously when the band played it in the home seventh of the first Cubs' World Series home game here in 1918. Part of the grandstand collapsed May 17, 1913. Scene of many masterful groundskeeping tricks by Roger, Gene, and Emil Bossard. Camp Swampy in 1967 referred to the area in front of the plate, dug up and soaked with water when a White Sox sinker-baller was on the mound, but mixed with clay and gasoline and burned to provide hard soil if a sinker-baller were pitching for the visiting team. When the Sox had good bunters, more paint was added to the foul line to tilt the ball back fair. Owner Bill Veeck said all this gave the Sox an extra 12 wins a year (!).

WRIGLEY FIELD
AKA: North Side Ball Park 1914; Weeghman Park 1914-15; Whales Park 1915; Cubs' Park 1916-26; Eddie Dorr's House ★ **OCCUPANTS:** FL Chicago Whales April 23, 1914 to October 3, 1915; NL Chicago Cubs April 20, 1916 to date ★ **LOCATION:** Left Field (N/NW) West Waveland Ave; Third Base (W/SW) Seminary Ave; Home Plate (SW) North Clark St.; First Base (S/SE) 1060 West Addison St.; Right Field (E/NE) North Sheffield Ave. ★ **DIMENSIONS:** Left Field 310 (April 1914), 335 (May 1914), 327 (June 1914), 343 (1921), 325 (1923), 348 (1926), 364 (1928), 355 (1938); Deepest Left Center in the Well 357 (1938); Power Alleys 364 (1914), 368 (1938); Center Field 440 (1914), 447 (1923), 436 (1938), 400 (1938); Deepest Right Center in the Well 363 (1938); Right Field 356 (April 1914), 345 (June 1914), 321 (1915), 298 (1921), 399 (1922), 318 (1923), 321 (1928), 353 (1938); Backstop 62.42 (1930), 60.5 (1957), 62.42 (1982), 60.5 (1993); Foul Territory very small ★ **FENCES:** Left Field corner 15.92 (11.33 brick with Boston and bittersweet ivy, below 4.59 plywood), 3 wire basket in front (1985, does not change height of fence), 15 (2003); Transition between Left Field Corner and Bleachers 12.5 (screen and yellow railing on top of brick wall); Left Center to Right Center 8 (screen 1914), 11.33 (brick with ivy 1938), 11.5 (2003); 3 wire basket added in front (May 1970); Left Field Scoreboard 40 (wood July 9 to September 3, 1937); Center Field Screen 19.33 (8 wire above 11.33 brick June 18, 1963 to September 27, 1964); Right Center Triangle 17.5 in front of catwalk steps sloping down to 15.5 (screen 1928, plywood 1979, removed 1985); Right Field Corner 15.5 (11.33 brick with ivy, below 4.17 plywood), 3 wire basket in front (1985, does not change height of fence), 15 (2003) ★ **SURFACE:** grass, mixture of Merion bluegrass and clover; ivy vines on outfield walls ★ **CAPACITY:** 14,000 (1914), 18,000 (1915), 20,000 (1923), 38,396 (1927), 40,000 (1928), 36,755 (1951), 37,702 (1972), 39,600 (1989), 39,241 (2003)

PHENOMENA: The only remaining Federal League ballpark. Bill Veeck, Sr. planted 350 beautiful Japanese bittersweet ivy and 200 Boston ivy vines on the outfield wall in 1937. The center field 400 sign is actually to the right of dead center. His is the only park where it's more difficult to hit a homer down the foul line than to hit one 50 or so feet out in fair territory, because the bleachers protrude out into the outfield, creating what are called "wells." An eight-foot-high batters' background, 64 feet wide, stood on top of the wall in center from June 18, 1963 through the end of the 1964 season. Called the Whitlow Wall because Cubs' Athletic Director Robert Whitlow put it up, the screen prevented 10 homers, by Cubs and by visitors, one each by 500+ homer-hitters Ernie Banks and Willie McCovey. Ugly AstroTurf cover on seats in center, used for a second batters' background, debuted May 18, 1967, and was replaced by beautiful vines in 1990s. In 1937, six gates in the brick wall were installed as the bleachers were finished in the outfield. They were painted red, repainted blue in 1981, then green in the mid-1980s. The famous Bleacher Bums were formed in 1966 by 10 bleacher fans. On April 14, 1976, Mets' slugger Dave "King Kong" Kingman hit a homer 550 feet over Waveland and up against a frame house three doors down on the east side of Kenmore Ave.. If the ball had carried three more feet, it would have crashed through a window and smashed the TV on which Naomi Martinez was watching Kingman round the bases. Lights were inside the park, ready to be installed, but owner Phil Wrigley donated them to the war effort instead on December 8, 1941, keeping Wrigley Field in the dark until August 8, 1988.

67TH AND LANGLEY
OCCUPANT: NNL Chicago Giants 1920-21 ★ **LOCATION:** 67th St., Langley St.

NORMAL PARK
OCCUPANT: NNL Chicago American Giants 1920-21 ★ **LOCATION:** 6First St., Normal St., 63rd St., Racine Ave; on Chicago's South Side

LELAND GIANTS PARK
OCCUPANT: NNL Chicago American Giants 1922-23 ★ **LOCATION:** 69th St., 6221 Halsted St.

SOLDIER FIELD
OCCUPANT: NNL Chicago American Giants 1924 ★ **LOCATION:** Outer Drive, 425 East McFetridge Place, 14th St., Waldron Drive; in Grant Park

ASBURY BALL PARK
OCCUPANT: NNL Chicago American Giants 1925-26

PYOTT'S PARK
OCCUPANT: NNL Chicago American Giants 1928-30 ★ **LOCATION:** 48th (later

Kilpatrick) Ave., West Lake St.; on Chicago's West Side

37TH AND BUTLER
OCCUPANT: NNL Chicago American Giants 1931 ★ **LOCATION:** 37th St., Butler St.

COMISKEY PARK (II)
AKA: US Cellular Field Jan 31, 2003 to date ★ **OCCUPANT:** AL Chicago White Sox April 18, 1991 to date ★ **LOCATION:** Left Field (E) South Wentworth Ave., then Dan Ryan Expressway/I-94; Third Base (N) 333 West 35th St.; First Base (W) Portland (later South Shield's) Ave., then Chicago and Western RR tracks; Right Field (S) West 37th St.; just S of Comiskey Park (I) ★ **DIMENSIONS:** Left field 347 (1991), 330 (2001); Left Center 383 (1991), 375 (1992), 377 (2001); Center Field 400; Right Center 383 (1991), 375 (1992), 372 (2001); Right Field 347 (1991), 335 (2001); Backstop 60 ★ **FENCES:** 8 ★ **FORMER USE:** 80 privately owned residential buildings ★ **CAPACITY:** 44,702 (1991), 44,321 (1993), 45,936 (2001), 47,098 (2003)
PHENOMENA: Tied with SkyDome for the worst modern ballpark ever built. Seats in the front row of the upper deck are farther from home plate than those in last row at old Comiskey were. Twenty-two dump trucks brought 550 tons of infield dirt from old Comiskey to new Comiskey.

CINCINNATI, OHIO

LINCOLN PARK GROUNDS
AKA: Union Cricket Club Grounds, Union Grounds ★ **OCCUPANTS:** Neutral site use by NA Washington Olympics May 13, July 4, 1871; by NA Cleveland Forest Citys July 22, 1871 ★ **LOCATION:** In Lincoln Park, next to the Union Railroad Terminal

AVENUE GROUNDS
OCCUPANT: NL Cincinnati Reds April 25, 1876 to August 27, 1879 ★ **LOCATION:** (N) Monmouth St., (W) Mill Creek, (S) Alabama Ave., (E) Baltimore and Ohio RR tracks ★ **CURRENT USE:** Chester Park ★ **CAPACITY:** 3,000

BANK STREET GROUNDS
AKA: Union Athletic Park 1884 ★ **OCCUPANTS:** NL Cincinnati Reds May 1 to September 30, 1880; AA Cincinnati Reds May 21, 1882 to September 29, 1883; UA Cincinnati Outlaw Reds April 17 to October 15, 1884 ★ **LOCATION:** (N) Cross St. (W) Duck St. (S) Bank St. (E) Western Ave; three blocks N of where Crosley Field was later built ★ **CAPACITY:** 2,000

LEAGUE PARK (I)
AKA: Cincinnati Base Ball Grounds 1884-89, Western Ave. Grounds 1890, Abandoned Brickyard ★ **OCCUPANTS:** AA Cincinnati Reds May 1, 1884 to October 15, 1889; NL Cincinnati Reds April 19, 1890 to September 29, 1893; World Series NL Chicago White Stockings vs. AA St. Louis Browns October 23-24, 1885 ★ **LOCATION:** Left Field (W) McLean Ave., Third Base (S) Findlay St., First Base (E) Western Ave., Right Field (N) York St.; same site as Crosley Field but different orientation ★ **CAPACITY:** 6,000

LEAGUE PARK (II)
OCCUPANT: NL Cincinnati Reds April 20, 1894 to October 2, 1901 ★ **LOCATION:** April 20, 1894 to May 28, 1900: Left Field (W) York St., Third Base (W) McLean Ave., First Base (S) Findlay St., Right Field (E) Western Ave; same site as League Park (I) but different orientation; same site as Crosley Field with exact same orientation; May 28, 1900 to October 2, 1901: Left Field (W) McLean Ave., Third Base (S) Findlay St., First Base (E) Western Ave., Right Field (N) York St.; same site and same orientation as League Park (I) ★ **DIMENSIONS:** Left Field 253 (1894)

PALACE OF THE FANS
AKA: League Park (III) ★ **OCCUPANT:** NL Cincinnati Reds April 17, 1902 to October 12, 1911 ★ **LOCATION:** Same as League Park (II) ★ **DIMENSIONS:** Left Field 360; Power Alleys 380; Center Field 420; Right Field 450 ★ **CAPACITY:** 12,000 (1902), 25,000 (1911)

CROSLEY FIELD
AKA: Redland Field 1912-33 ★ **OCCUPANTS:** NL Cincinnati Reds April 11, 1912 to June 24, 1970; NAL Cincinnati Tigers 1937; NAL Cincinnati Buckeyes 1942; NAL Cincinnati Clowns 1943; NAL Indianapolis-Cincinnati Clowns half of the home games 1944; NAL Cincinnati Clowns 1945 ★ **LOCATION:** Same as League Parks (II) and (III); same site but different orientation from League Park (I) ★ **DIMENSIONS:** Left Field 360 (1912), 320 (1921), 352 (1926), 339 (1927), 328 (1938); Left side of scoreboard in Left Center 380; Right side of scoreboard in Left Center 383; Center Field 420 (1912), 417 (1926), 395 (1927), 393 (1930), 407 (1931), 393 (1933), 407 (1936), 387 (1938), 380 (1939), 387 (1940), 390 (1944), 387 (1955); Deepest Right Center corner 387 (1944); Right Center 383 (1955); Right Field 360 (1912), 384 (1921), 400 (1926), 383 (early 1927), 377 (late 1927), 366 (1938), 342 (1942), 366 (June 30, 1950), 342 (1953), 366 (1958); Backstop 38 (1912), 58 (1927), 66 (1943), 78 (1953) ★ **FENCES:** Center Field canvas shield above fence to protect against streetlight glare (April 16, 1935 to June 7, 1940); Left Field 18 (1938), 12 (1957), 14 (1962), 18 (1963); Clock on top of Scoreboard 58 (1957), 45 (1967); Left Center to Right Center 18 (1954), 14 (1962), 13 (1963), 23 (9.5 plywood over 13.5 concrete 1965); Right Field 7.5 (4.5 wire above 3 concrete 1938), 7.5 (4.5 wire above 3 wood 1942), 10 (7 wire above 3 concrete June 30, 1950), 10 (7 wire above 3 wood 1953), 10 (7 wire above 3 concrete 1958), 9 (6 wire above 3 concrete 1959); Flagpole in left center in play 82 ★ **FORMER USE:** Brickyard, League Parks (I), (II), and (III) ★ **CURRENT USE:** Used to impound cars 1970-72; reconstructed on farm near Union, Kentucky; replica constructed with left center scoreboard at 11540 Grooms Rd. in Blue Ash, Ohio; site is

now an industrial park; plaque placed at Findlay and Western in 1998 ★ **CAPACITY:** 25,000 (1912), 30,000 (1927), 33,000 (1938), 30,000 (1948), 29,488 (1970)
PHENOMENA: Steep embankment in front of the fence all around the outfield. In January 1937, Mill Creek flooded, covering the playing field with 21 feet of water. Pitcher Lee Grissom and Reds' traveling secretary John McDonald rowed a boat over the center-field fence. The right-field bleachers were called the Sun Deck for day games, and the Moon Deck for night games. Mislabeled as being in Cleveland in *Pride of the Yankees*, 1942 movie. To reduce noise from a new highway behind the fence in center in 1963, a 9.5-foot section of plywood was added on top of the 13.5-foot-high center field wall. The plywood was out of play; a ball hitting it was supposed to be a homer. But all during 1963-64, there were controversies about whether balls that hit near the plywood were home runs. Finally, in 1965, the plywood was made part of the wall and was put in play. Torn down in 1972.

NORTHSIDE PARK
OCCUPANT: NNL Cincinnati Cuban Stars 1921

RIVERFRONT STADIUM
AKA: Cinergy Field September 9, 1996 to December 29, 2002 ★ **OCCUPANT:** NL Cincinnati Reds June 30, 1970 to September 22, 2002 ★ **LOCATION:** Left Field (NE) Broadway, Riverfront Coliseum (later FirstStar Center), Central Bridge; Third Base (NW) 201 East Second St. (later Pete Rose Way); First Base (SW) I-71 Roebling Suspension Bridge approach ramp and Ohio River; Right Field (SE) Mehring Way, railroad tracks, Ohio River ★ **DIMENSIONS:** Foul Lines 330 (1970), 325 (2001); Left Center 375 (1970), 371 (2001), 370 (2002); Center Field 404 (1970), 393 (2001); Right Center 375 (1970), 373 (2001); Backstop 51 (1970), 41 (2001); Foul Territory small ★ **FENCES:** Foul Lines 12 (wood, 1970), 8 (wood, 1984); Power Alleys 12 (wood, 1970), 8 (wood, 1984), 14 (wood, 2001); Center Field 12 (wood, 1970), 8 (wood, 1984), 40 (wood, 2001) ★ **SURFACE:** AstroTurf-8 1970-2000 hard, balls bounced very high off it; grass 2001-02 ★ **FORMER USE:** Singing cowboy Roy Rogers grew up in a house at second base ★ **CURRENT USE:** Rose garden at Great American Ball Park commemorates Pete Rose's 4,192nd hit ★ **CAPACITY:** 51,050 (1970), 52,392 (1979), 39,000 (2001)
PHENOMENA: First to paint metric distances on outfield walls, 100.58 down the lines, 114.30 to alleys, 123.13 to center. Parking garage beneath stadium. Reds and Pirates played slowest game ever here August 30, 1978: 81 minutes per inning, called off after 3-1/2 innings and 3-1/2 hours of rain delays at 12:47 AM. Winds helped drives to left center. Bees attacked the field April 17, 1976 and delayed the game. Torn down December 29, 2002.

GREAT AMERICAN BALL PARK
OCCUPANT: NL Cincinnati Reds Mar 31, 2003 to date ★ **LOCATION:** Left Field (E/NE) Broadway; Third Base (N/NW) Pete Rose Way, then I-71; First Base (W/SW) Johnny Bench Blvd., then Riverfront Stadium; Right Field (S/SE) Mehring Way, railroad tracks, and Ohio River ★ **DIMENSIONS:** Left Field 328, Left Center 379, Center Field 404, Right Center 370, Right Field 325, Backstop 51.42, Foul Territory small ★ **FENCES:** Left Field to Left Center 12, Center Field to Right Center 8 ★ **CAPACITY:** 42,053 (2003)
PHENOMENA: Crosley Terrace features statues, benches and landscaped grass built at same incline as at old Crosley Field, whose Longines clock is on top of the scoreboard, and whose Sun/Moon Deck is recreated in right.

CLEVELAND, OHIO

NATIONAL ASSOCIATION GROUNDS
OCCUPANT: NA Cleveland Forest Citys May 11, 1871 to August 19, 1872 ★ **LOCATION:** Willson Ave. (later East 55th St.), Garden St. (later Central Ave.)

CASE COMMONS
OCCUPANT: NA Cleveland Forest Citys some games 1871-72 ★ **LOCATION:** (N) Garden St. (later Central Ave.), (S) Scovill (later Community College) Ave; also Putnam Ave. (later East 38th St.)

LEAGUE PARK (I)
AKA: Kennard St. Park ★ **OCCUPANT:** NL Cleveland Spiders May 1, 1879 to October 11, 1884 ★ **LOCATION:** (N) Silby (later Carnegie) St., (W) Kennard (later East 46th) St., (S) Cedar St.

LEAGUE PARK (II)
AKA: American Association Park 1887-88, Brookside Park ★ **OCCUPANTS:** AA Cleveland Spiders May 4, 1887 to September 15, 1888; NL Cleveland Spiders May 3, 1889 to October 4, 1890 ★ **LOCATION:** (W) East 39th St., (E) East 35th St.; also Euclid Ave., Payne Ave., Robison Trolley Line ★ **DIMENSIONS:** Foul Poles 410, Center Field 420

BROTHERHOOD PARK
AKA: Players League Park ★ **OCCUPANT:** PL Cleveland Infants April 30 to October 4, 1890 ★ **LOCATION:** First Base New York, Chicago, St. Louis RR (also called Nickel Plate RR, now used by Cleveland RTA) tracks; Willson Ave. (later East 55th St.)

LEAGUE PARK (III)
OCCUPANTS: NL Cleveland Spiders May 1, 1891 to September 24, 1899; AL Cleveland Blues April 29, 1901 to September 6, 1909 ★ **LOCATION:** Left Field (E) East 70th St.; Third Base (N) Linwood Ave; First Base (W) Dunham (later East 66th) St.; Right Field (S) Lexington Ave. Northeast; between Hough Ave. and Wade Park, on the Robison Trolley Line ★ **DIMENSIONS:** Right Field 290 ★ **FENCES:** Right Field 20 (wood) ★ **CAPACITY:** 9,000

WESTERN LEAGUE PARK
OCCUPANT: NL Cleveland Spiders, Sundays only 1890s ★ **LOCATION:** Clarke Ave., Kennard (later East 46th) St.; near Brooklyn Ave. on west side

EUCLID BEACH
OCCUPANT: NL Cleveland Spiders Sunday games on June 12 and 19, 1898 ★ **LOCATION:** The site was then nine miles outside the city limits of Cleveland in the town of Collinwood, but it is now in Cleveland

LEAGUE PARK (IV)
AKA: Dunn Field 1916-27 ★ **OCCUPANTS:** AL Cleveland Indians April 21, 1910 to July 30, 1932; April 17, 1934 to September 21, 1946; NAL Cleveland Buckeyes 1943-48, April to June 1950 ★ **LOCATION:** Same as League Park (III) ★ **DIMENSIONS:** Left Field 385 (1910), 376 (1921), 374 (1930), 373 (1934) 374 (1938), 375 (1942); Left Center 415 (1942); Deepest corner just left of dead center 505 (1916), 450 (1926), 467 (1930), 465 (1938), 460 (1939); Center Field 460 (1910), 420 (World Series 1920); Right Center 400 (1942); Right Field 290 (1921), 240 (when roped off for overflow crowds); Backstop 76 (1910), 60 (1942) ★ **FENCES:** Left Field 5 (concrete); Left Center 10 (7 screen above 3 concrete); Center Field scoreboard 35; Right Center clock 20 (left and right sides), 22 (center of clock); Right Field 45 (20 concrete topped by 25 screen 1920), 40 (20 concrete topped by 20 screen 1934) ★ **CURRENT USE:** Ticket booths and part of first-base stands remain as League Park Community Center, rest of the park was torn down in 1951, swimming pool where left field was, historical marker put here in 1979 ★ **CAPACITY:** 21,414 (1910), 22,500 (1939) **PHENOMENA:** Steel beams protruded from the wall in right, causing balls to bounce at crazy angles. Only here did left fielders handle doubles to right field. Joe DiMaggio completed his 56-game consecutive hitting streak here July 16, 1941. Teepees erected in 1946.

TATE PARK
OCCUPANTS: NNL Cleveland Tate Stars 1922; NNL Cleveland Browns 1924; NNL Cleveland Elites 1926

HOOPER FIELD
OCCUPANT: NNL Cleveland Hornets 1927

CUBS STADIUM
OCCUPANT: NNL Cleveland Cubs 1931 ★ **LOCATION:** Across the street from League Park (IV), home of the Indians

CITY PARK
OCCUPANT: NEWL Cleveland Stars April to June 1932

HARDWARE FIELD
OCCUPANT: NAL Cleveland Bears 1939-40 ★ **LOCATION:** East 79th St., Kinsman Rd.

CLEVELAND STADIUM
AKA: Lakefront Stadium 1930s, Cleveland Public Municipal Stadium 1930s, Municipal Stadium 1940s-50s, Mistake by the Lake ★ **OCCUPANT:** AL Cleveland Indians July 31, 1932 to September 24, 1933 all games; August 2, 1936; May 30 to September 6, 1937 Sundays/holidays only Memorial Day to Labor Day; April 1938 to June 1939 Sundays/holidays/selected important games only; June 27, 1939 to September 28, 1947 nights/Sundays/holidays/selected important games only (a majority of home games in 1940 and 1942-46); April 15, 1947 to October 3, 1993 all games. ★ **LOCATION:** Center Field (NE) East Ninth St.; Third Base (NW) Erieside Ave., then Donald Gray Lakefront Gardens Port Authority Dock 28 and Lake Erie; Home Plate (SW) West Third St.; First Base (SE) Cleveland Memorial Shoreway, then Amtrak/Conrail RR tracks; Boudreau Boulevard encircled the park ★ **DIMENSIONS:** Foul Lines 322 (1932), 320 (1933), 321 (1948), 320 (1953); Corners where inner fence met stadium wall 362 (1947), 370 (1980); Power Alleys 435 (1932), 365 (1947), 362 (1948), 385 (1949), 380 (1954), 400 (1965), 390 (1967), 395 (1968), 385 (1970), 395 (1991); Left Center 377 (1980); Deep Left Center 387 (1980); Grandstand Corners 435 (1932); Bleacher Corners 463 (1932); Center Field 470 (1932), 467 (1938), 450 (1939), 410 (April 27, 1947), 408 (1966), 407 (1967), 410 (1968), 400 (1970), 415 (1990), 404 (1992); Deep Right Center 395 (1980); Right Center 385 (1980); Backstop 60; Foul Territory large ★ **FENCES:** Left and Right Field 5.25 (concrete 1932), 5.5 (wire April 27, 1947), 5.25 (concrete June 6, 1947), 6 (1955), 9 (1976), 8 (1977), 8 (canvas 1984) ★ **CAPACITY:** 78,000 (1931), 73,811 (1954), 76,977 (1968), 74,208 (1982), 74,483 (1989) **PHENOMENA:** Built for Summer Olympics that were held in Los Angeles instead. Largest regular-season crowd ever was here, 86,563 (84,587 paid) for double-header vs. the Yanks on September 12, 1954. Indians forfeited to Rangers on Ten Cents Beer Night June 4, 1974, when with two Indians on base and tied in the bottom of the ninth, fans stormed the field. Before inner fence was installed April 27, 1947, there was a steep incline in front of the center-field bleacher wall, and a strange shape in the power alleys caused by the end of the double-decked grandstand, with the fence jumping abruptly deeper to the bleachers in center. The April 27 inner fence curved all the way to the foul poles. On June 6, it was moved so the inner fence just stretched across center field, hitting the permanent wall at the 362 mark. Bill Veeck buried their 1948 pennant before the September 23, 1949 game after the Tribe had been mathematically eliminated from the 1949 pennant race.

LUNA BOWL
AKA: Luna Park Stadium ★ **OCCUPANTS:** NNL Cleveland Giants August to September 1933; NNL Cleveland Red Sox 1934 ★ **LOCATION:** Woodland Ave., Woodhill Rd., Ingersoll Rd., East 110th St. ★ **CURRENT USE:** Amusement park

JACOBS FIELD
AKA: The Jake, Indians Park at Gateway 1994 ★ **OCCUPANT:** AL Cleveland Indians April 4, 1994 to date ★ **LOCATION:** Left Field (NW) East Huron Rd.; Third Base (SW) 2401 Ontario St., Broadway; First Base (SE) Carnegie Ave; Right Field (NE) East 9th St.; adjacent to Arena at Gateway, home of the NBA Cavaliers ★ **DIMENSIONS:** Foul Lines 325; Left Center 368 (1994), 370 (2001); Deepest Center Field 410; Center Field 405; Right Center 375; Backstop 59; Foul Territory small ★ **FENCES:** Left Field 19; Center and Right Field 8 (1994), 9 (2003); Right Field corner at foul line 14 ★ **CAPACITY:** 42,865 (1994), 43,863 (1997), 43,389 (2003) **PHENOMENA:** Original plan was for a downtown domed stadium, but local voters fortunately rejected it. Scoreboard in left field. Home plate from Cleveland Stadium. Hosted major league record 455 consecutive sellouts June 12, 1995 to April 2, 2001.

COLUMBUS, OHIO

RECREATION PARK (I)
OCCUPANT: AA Columbus Senators May 1, 1883 to September 22, 1884 ★ **LOCATION:** (N) Mound St., (W) Parsons Ave., (E) Meadow Lane (later Monroe St.)

RECREATION PARK (II)
OCCUPANT: AA Columbus Solons April 28, 1889 to September 22, 1891 ★ **LOCATION:** (N) Kossuth St., (W) Jaeger (later Fifth) St., (S) East Schiller St. (later East Whittier Ave.), (E) Ebner St. ★ **DIMENSIONS:** Right Field 400

NEIL PARK (I)
OCCUPANTS: Neutral site use by AL Cleveland Blues August 3, 1902; AL Cleveland Naps May 17, 1903 ★ **LOCATION:** (S) Buckingham St., (E) 551 Cleveland Ave. ★ **DIMENSIONS:** Right Field 240

NEIL PARK (II)
OCCUPANTS: NNL Columbus Buckeyes 1921; NSL Columbus Turfs August to September 1932; neutral site use by AL Detroit Tigers July 23-24, 1905 ★ **LOCATION:** same as Neil Park (I)

RED BIRD STADIUM
AKA: Jet Stadium, Franklin County Stadium, Cooper Stadium ★ **OCCUPANTS:** NNL Columbus Bluebirds April to August 1933; NNL Columbus Elite Giants 1935; neutral site use for Negro World Series NNL Washington-Homestead Grays vs. NAL Birmingham Black Barons game 4 in 1943 ★ **LOCATION:** 1155 West Mound St., Glenwood Ave. ★ **DIMENSIONS:** Left Field 415 (1938), 336 (1960), 350 (1978), 355 (1984), Center Field 450 (1938), 430 (1960), 400 (1978), Right Center 337, Right Field 315 (1938), 345 (1960), 330 (1978) ★ **FENCES:** Left Field 6, Center Field 10, Right Field 8 ★ **CURRENT USE:** Minor league baseball ★ **CAPACITY:** 17,500 (1938), 12,000 (1960), 15,000 (1978)

COVINGTON, KENTUCKY

STAR BASEBALL PARK
OCCUPANT: Neutral site use by NA Philadelphia Pearls September 21, 1875 ★ **LOCATION:** just across the river from Cincinnati, Ohio

CRAWFORDSVILLE, INDIANA

DEAN PARK
OCCUPANT: Neutral site use by NNL Indianapolis ABCs August 23, 1923

DANVILLE, VIRGINIA

PETERS' PARK
OCCUPANT: Neutral site use by NNL Homestead Grays one game in 1930s ★ **CURRENT USE:** Only the light towers and a "Peters' Park" sign remain.

DAYTON, OHIO

FAIRVIEW PARK
OCCUPANT: Neutral site use by AL Cleveland Blues June 8, 1902 ★ **LOCATION:** North Main St., Fairview St. ★ **CURRENT USE:** Brown Elementary School

DUCKS PARK
AKA: Westwood Field ★ **OCCUPANT:** NNL Dayton Marcos 1920; 1926 ★ **DIMENSIONS:** Foul Lines 360, Power Alleys 360, Center Field 360 ★ **CAPACITY:** 5,000

DENVER, COLORADO

MILE HIGH STADIUM
AKA: Bears Stadium April 1948-Dec 14, 1968 ★ **OCCUPANT:** NL Colorado Rockies April 9, 1993 to August 11, 1994 ★ **LOCATION:** Left Field (E) Clay St.; Third Base (N) West 20th Ave; First Base (W) Elliot St.; Right Field (S) West 17th Ave., I-25 ★ **DIMENSIONS:** Left Field 348 (1948), 335 (1993); Left Center 395 (1948), 375 (1993); Center Field 420 (1948), 423 (1993); Right Center 400 (1948); Right

Field 365 (1948), 370 (1993) ★ **FENCES:** 12 Left Field, 30 Center Field, 14 Right Field ★ **CAPACITY:** 19,000 (1960), 43,103 (1975), 75,123 (1985), 76,037 (1993), 76,100 (1994)

PHENOMENA: Rockies drew largest season attendance ever of 4,483,350 here in 1993. Largest NL regular season paid crowd ever, 80,227 vs. Expos April 9, 1993. Only other crowds over 80,000 include exhibition games at Melbourne Olympics in Australia (114,000, Dec 1, 1956), Berlin Olympics in Germany (108,000, August 12, 1936), and LA Coliseum honoring Roy Campanella (93,103, May 7, 1959); World Series games at LA Coliseum (92,706, October 6, 1959; 92,550, October 5, 1959; 92,294, October 4, 1959); Cleveland Stadium (86,288, October 10, 1948; 81,897, October 9, 1948); total (rather than paid) regular-season crowds at LA Coliseum (90,751, August 8, 1959; 82,794, August 31, 1959), Yankee Stadium (80,403, April 19, 1931), Cleveland Stadium (80,285, July 31, 1932); and a semipro game at Brookside Park in Cleveland (80,000 October 10, 1915).

COORS FIELD

OCCUPANT: NL Colorado Rockies April 26, 1995 to date ★ **LOCATION:** Left Field (NW) Union Pacific RR tracks, then I-25; Third Base (SW) 20th St.; First Base (SE) 2001 Blake St.; Right Field (NE) Park Ave. ★ **DIMENSIONS:** Left Field 347; Left Center 390; Deepest Left Center 420; Center Field 415; Deepest Right Center 424; Right Center 375; Right Field Corner 358; Right Field 350; Backstop 56.33 (1995), 50.33 (2003) ★ **FENCES:** Left Field to Right Center 8; Right Field (Manual Scoreboard) 14 (1995), 17 (2000), 14 (2003) ★ **FORMER USE:** Railyards ★ **CAPACITY:** 50,200 (1995), 50,449 (2003)

PHENOMENA: Originally designed for only 43,800 capacity, but increased due to huge crowds at Mile High Stadium. Upper-deck center-field bleachers known as the Rockpile. The 21st row of the upper deck is marked in purple to indicate it is 5,280 feet above sea level, or a "mile high." Features spectacular view of Rocky Mountains from first-base and right-field seats. Exceptional hitting park because of the high altitude.

DETROIT, MICHIGAN

RECREATION PARK

OCCUPANT: NL Detroit Wolverines May 2, 1881 to September 22, 1888 ★ **LOCATION:** (N) Willis St., (W) John R St., (S) Brady St., (E) Beaubien St.; current Brush St. would intersect the site; Brady St. no longer exists in this area but back then it was one block S of what is now Mack St. ★ **FENCES:** 9

BENNETT PARK

AKA: Woodbridge Grove, the Haymarket ★ **OCCUPANT:** AL Detroit Tigers April 25, 1901 to September 10, 1911 ★ **LOCATION:** Left Field (W) National (later Cochrane) Ave., Third Base (S) Michigan Ave., First Base (E) Trumbull Ave., Right Field (N) lumberyard, then Cherry St. (later Kaline Drive), same as Tiger Stadium but different orientation, in Corktown ★ **FORMER USE:** Haymarket in 1890s ★ **DIMENSIONS:** Left Field 341 (1896), 335 (1901), 321 (1908), 298 (1909 World Series); Left Center 362 (1896), 420 (1901); Center Field 467 (1896), 432 (1901), 465 (1908); Right Center 349 (1896), 348 (1901), 325 (1907 World Series), 408 (1908); Right Field 371 (1896), 345 (1901), 405 (1908) ★ **FENCES:** Left Field and Left Center 8 (1896), 12 (1901), 4 (1910); Center Field 8 (1896), 12 (1901), 16 (1910); Right Center and Right Field 8 (1896), 12 (1901), 4 (1908) ★ **CAPACITY:** 5,000 (1896), 8,500 (1901), 10,500 (1908), 14,000 (1910)

PHENOMENA: Opened in 1896. Infield was laid over a bunch of cobblestones, which worked their way up through the soil and caused many bad bounces, giving all infielders a ready excuse for any errors. The left and right field ★ **FENCES:** met in deepest left center, where there was a clubhouse. To its left was a small scoreboard, and to its right was a groundskeepers' shed, all of which were in play. The clubhouse was removed in 1908, and the small scoreboard was replaced by a larger one in 1910, just left of dead center. Temporary bleachers in right were built for the 1907 World Series. After the Tigers purchased the lumberyard behind the right field fence over the winter of 1907-08, they moved home plate 40 feet towards the outfield, added seats behind the plate, and added permanent bleachers in right. Temporary bleachers in left for the 1909 World Series were replaced in 1910 by permanent bleachers, built specifically to block the view from wildcat bleachers which sat on top of barns along National Ave. in left. Named for Charlie Bennett, Wolverines' catcher, whose legs were amputated after a train accident in 1894. He threw out the first ball every opening day from 1896 to 1927. Torn down October 1911.

BURNS PARK

AKA: West End Park ★ **OCCUPANT:** AL Detroit Tigers Sundays only April 28, 1901 to September 7, 1902 ★ **LOCATION:** (N) RR tracks, (S) Dix Ave; also Vernon St., Waterman St., Livernois Ave; near the stockyards, just outside what was then the western city limits of Detroit; today Waterman St. and Springwells St. intersect the site in Springwells Township ★ **CURRENT USE:** Shipping container storage area

TIGER STADIUM

AKA: Navin Field 1912-37, Briggs Stadium 1938-60 ★ **OCCUPANT:** AL Detroit Tigers April 20, 1912 to September 27, 1999 ★ **LOCATION:** Left Field (NW) Cherry St. (later Kaline Drive), then I-75; Third Base (SW) National (later Cochrane) Ave; First Base (SE) Michigan Ave; Right Field (NE) 2121 Trumbull Ave., same site as Bennett Park but turned around 90 degrees, in Corktown ★ **DIMENSIONS:** Left Field 345 (1921), 340.58 (1926), 339 (1930), 367 (1931), 339 (1934), 340 (1938), 342 (1939), 340 (1942); Left Center 365 (1942); Center Field 467 (1927), 455 (1930), 464 (1931), 459 (1936), 450 (1937), 440 (1938), 450 (1939), 420 (1942), 440 (1944); Right Center 370 (1942), 375 (1982); Right Field 370 (1921), 370.91 (1926), 372 (1930), 367 (1931), 325 (1936), 315 (1939), 325 (1942), 302 (1954), 325 (1955); Backstop 54.35 (1954), 66 (1955); Foul Territory small ★ **SURFACE:**

Bluegrass ★ **FENCES:** 5 concrete topped by screen; Left Field: 20 (1935), 30 (1937), 10 (1938), 12 (1940), 15 (1946), 12 (1953), 14 (1954), 12 (1955), 11 (1958), 9 (1962); Center Field 9 (1940), 15 (1946), 11 (1950), 9 (1953), 14 (1954), 9 (1955); Right of Flagpole 7 (1946); Right Field 8 (1940), 30 (1944), 10 (1945), 20 (1950), 8 (1953), 9 (1958), 30 (1961), 9 (1962); Flagpole in play 125 (5 feet in front of fence in center field, just left of dead center) ★ **FORMER USE:** Haymarket in 1890s ★ **CAPACITY:** 23,000 (1912), 29,000 (1923), 36,000 (1936), 58,000 (1938), 54,000 (1953), 52,904 (1961), 54,220 (1969), 52,687 (1981), 46,846 (1997), 52,416 (1999)

PHENOMENA: The 125-foot-high flagpole in play in deep center, just to the left of the 440 mark, was the highest outfield obstacle ever in play in baseball history. Right field second deck overhung the lower deck by 10 feet. Screen in right in 1944 and in 1961 required balls to be hit into the second deck to be home runs. Sign above entrance to visitors' clubhouse: "Visitors' Clubhouse—No Visitors Allowed." Mickey Mantle's 634-foot homer here on September 10, 1960 is the longest ever measured. Saved in 1974 when owner John Fetzer told the Pontiac Silverdome committee, "This franchise belongs to the inner city of Detroit; I'm just the caretaker." That mantle of caretaker passed on to Frank Rashid's Tiger Stadium Fan Club, which managed to stave off abandonment of the ballpark for almost a decade.

MACK PARK

OCCUPANTS: NNL Detroit Stars 1920-29; NAL Detroit Stars 1954-57; NAL Detroit Clowns 1958; NAL Detroit Stars 1959; NAL Detroit-New Orleans Stars (half of the home games) 1960 ★ **LOCATION:** Mack Ave., Fairview St. ★ **CURRENT USE:** Fairview Greens Apartments.

DEQUINDRE PARK

AKA: Linton Field, Cubs Park ★ **OCCUPANT:** NAL Detroit Stars 1937 ★ **LOCATION:** DeQuindre Ave., Modern St., Orleans St., Riopelle St., RR tracks; near Six Mile Rd.

SPORTSMAN'S PARK

OCCUPANT: NAL Detroit Stars one game 1937 ★ **LOCATION:** Livernois Ave., Burkhouse St.

COMERICA PARK

OCCUPANT: AL Detroit Tigers April 11, 2000 to date ★ **LOCATION:** Center Field (S/SE) Adams St.; Third Base (E/NE) Brush St., Home Plate (N/NW) Montcalm St.; First Base (W/SW) Whitherell St. ★ **DIMENSIONS:** Left Field 345, Left Center 398 (2000), 395 (2001), 370 (2003), Center Field 420, Right Center 380 (2000), 365 (2003), Right Field 330, Foul Territory small ★ **FENCES:** Left Field 8 (2000), 6.83 (2003), Left Center and Center Field 8 (2000), 8.5 (2003), Right Center 11 (2000), 11.5 (2003), Right Field 8 (2000), 8.5 (2003) ★ **CAPACITY:** 40,120

PHENOMENA: Center Field flagpole in play 2000-02. When the Tigers hit a home run, the fountain in center spouts and the two big tigers above the huge scoreboard in left roar. Carousel and Ferris wheel in the stands.

DOVER, DELAWARE

FAIRVIEW PARK FAIR GROUNDS

OCCUPANT: Neutral site use by NA Philadelphia Athletics June 24, 1875

DURHAM, NORTH CAROLINA

ATHLETIC PARK

OCCUPANT: Neutral site use by NAL Birmingham Black Barons 1940s ★ **LOCATION:** Left Field (N) West Geer St.; Third Base (W) Washington St.; First Base (S) West Corporation St.; Right Field (E) Foster St. ★ **DIMENSIONS:** Left Field 360 (1939), 330 (1965); Center Field 460 (1939), 410 (1965); Right Field 290 (1939), 307 (1965) ★ **FENCES:** Left Field 24 (12 wood above 12 embankment 1939), 8 (wood 1965); Center Field 27 (12 wood above 15 embankment 1939), 8 (wood 1965); Right Center 20 (8 wooden Bull above 12 Durham Technical Institute brick wall), 8 (wood 1965); Right Field 50 (35 brick above 15 embankment 1939), 16 (wood 1965)

EAST ORANGE, NEW JERSEY

GROVE STREET OVAL (II)

AKA: Grove St. Senior Ball Diamond, Monte Irvin Field, East Orange Oval ★ **OCCUPANT:** NNL New York Cubans 1941-47 ★ **LOCATION:** Left Field (E) Greenwood Ave; Third Base (N) Grove Place; First Base (W) Grove St. North; Right Field (S) Eaton Place ★ **DIMENSIONS:** Left Field 240; Center Field 360 to water fountain; Right Field 280 ★ **FENCES:** Left Field 25 (garage walls); Center Field 4 (water fountain); Right Field none ★ **CURRENT USE:** Community ball diamond

PHENOMENA: No fence in center field, but there were hedges. The four-foot high water fountain in deepest center was in play. Trees and tennis courts in right were in play, as there was no fence in right field either. Scoreboard in left, as well as poplar trees. Clubhouse down right-field line in foul territory. "Bujum" Jud Wilson hit longest ball ever hit here, over water fountain in center. Oval (I) dedicated Labor Day 1908 in New Jersey State Senate vs. New Jersey State General Assembly game. Fire destroyed that park at 4 AM on May 3, 1925. Oval (II) dedicated May 1, 1926, and renamed Monte Irvin Field June 6, 1986.

ELIZABETH, NEW JERSEY

WAVERLY FAIRGROUNDS

AKA: Domestic Field, Waverly Park, Weequahic Park ★ **OCCUPANT:** NA Elizabeth

Resolutes April 28 to July 23, 1873 ★ **LOCATION:** Frelinghuysen St., Haynes Ave., Lower Rd.; on Elizabeth side of current Elizabeth/Newark border; back then was in town of Waverly, which no longer exists ★ **CURRENT USE:** B'nai Jeshuron Cemetery, Weequahic City Park

ELMIRA, NEW YORK
MAPLE AVENUE DRIVING PARK
OCCUPANT: Neutral site use by NL Buffalo Bisons October 10, 1885

ERIE, PENNSYLVANIA
AINSWORTH FIELD
AKA: Athletic Park before 1939 ★ **OCCUPANT:** Neutral site use by NAL Kansas City Monarchs 1940s ★ **DIMENSIONS:** Left Field 390, Center Field 500, Right Field 356

EUCLID BEACH, OHIO
EUCLID BEACH
OCCUPANT: Neutral site use by NL Cleveland Spiders June 12, 1898 ★ **LOCATION:** Lakeshore Blvd, nine miles from Cleveland

FORT WAYNE, INDIANA
GRAND DUCHESS
AKA: Hamilton Field ★ **OCCUPANT:** NA Fort Wayne Kekiongas May 4 to August 29, 1871 **LOCATION:** (N) Lewis St., then subject to the "ever-present menace of the St. Mary's River (there were many floods back then), (W) Calhoun St., (S) Douglas Ave., (E) Clinton St.; between canal and West Main St. in the Nebraska neighborhood, north of Camp Allen ★ **CURRENT USE:** Catholic school
PHENOMENA: Scene of the very first major league game ever played. The Kekiongas defeated the Cleveland Forest Citys 2-0 on May 4, 1871 before 200 fans.

JAILHOUSE FLATS
AKA: League Park ★ **OCCUPANT:** Neutral site use by AL Cleveland Blues June 22 and August 31, 1902 ★ **LOCATION:** Calhoun St., North Clinton St., St. Clair St.

GEAUGA LAKE, OHIO
GEAUGA LAKE GROUNDS
OCCUPANT: Neutral site use by AA Cleveland Spiders July 22 and 29, August 26, 1888 ★ **LOCATION:** Twenty miles south of Cleveland ★ **CURRENT USE:** Geauga Lake Amusement Park

GEDDES, NEW YORK
LAKE-SIDE PARK
OCCUPANT: Neutral site use by NL Syracuse Stars Sundays 1879 ★ **LOCATION:** (NE) New York Central RR tracks; (N) Bridge St.; (SW) Delaware, Lackawanna, and Western RR tracks, called the West Shore Railroad embankment; (SE) Marsh Rd. (later Hiawatha Blvd); (E) Onondaga Lake

GLOUCESTER CITY, NEW JERSEY
GLOUCESTER POINT GROUNDS
OCCUPANT: Neutral site use by AA Philadelphia Athletics Sundays only August 5, 1888 to October 12, 1890 ★ **LOCATION:** Just behind Thompson's Hotel, along a creek

GRAND RAPIDS, MICHIGAN
RAMONA PARK
OCCUPANT: Neutral site use by AL Detroit Tigers May 24, 1903

HAMILTON, OHIO
HAMILTON GROUNDS
OCCUPANT: Neutral site use by AA Cincinnati Reds August 25, 1889
PHENOMENA: The Cincinnati Law and Order Society forced the AA Reds to abandon Sunday play at home after August 11, 1889. The Reds rescheduled their four remaining Sunday home games (August 18, 25; October 6, 13) in Ludlow, Kentucky. However, Kentucky authorities prevented them from doing so, so they moved the August 25 game against Brooklyn here, having been assured by Hamilton authorities it would be OK. But then the Hamilton Law and Order League complained. In the top of the fourth of a 2-2 game, with Joe Visner on first, and Bridegrooms' batter Rob Caruthers stepping up to the plate, Hamilton Police Chief Lindsey marched onto the diamond to arrest both teams. The players scattered to avoid arrest, but six or seven were caught and taken off to jail, where the Reds' owner had to pay Mayor Dick $149.40, or $8.30 for each of the 18 players who were in the game in the top of the fourth. The game was never finished, and the Reds played no more Sunday home games that season.

HAMPTON, VIRGINIA
HAMPTON INSTITUTE FIELD
OCCUPANT: Neutral site use by NNL Chicago American Giants 1920s

HAMTRAMCK, MICHIGAN
HAMTRAMCK STADIUM
AKA: Keyworth Stadium ★ **OCCUPANTS:** NNL Detroit Stars May 11, 1930 to September 1931; NEWL Detroit Wolves 1932; NNL Detroit Stars 1933 ★ **LOCATION:** Joseph Campau St., Berris St., Dan St., Gallagher St., Roosevelt St. ★ **DIMENSIONS:** Left Field 315, Right Field 407 ★ **FENCES:** 12 ★ **CURRENT USE:** High-school football

HARRISBURG, PENNSYLVANIA
WEST END GROUNDS
OCCUPANT: ECL Harrisburg Giants 1924-27

ISLAND STADIUM
AKA: Forsters Island Park ★ **OCCUPANT:** NNL Harrisburg-St. Louis Stars April to May 1943 (all home games in Harrisburg, none in St. Louis) ★ **LOCATION:** On Forsters Island, in the middle of the Susquehanna River

HARRISON, NEW JERSEY
HARRISON FIELD
AKA: Federal League Park 1915 ★ **OCCUPANTS:** FL Newark Peppers April 16 to October 3, 1915; NL New York Giants Sundays only 1890s, 1918; NL Brooklyn Dodgers Sundays only 1918; AL New York Yankees Sundays only 1918 ★ **LOCATION:** (N) Middlesex St., (W) Second St., then Passaic River, (S) Burlington St., (E) Third St.; between Hudson and Manhattan RR tracks and Pennsylvania RR tracks; just across the Passaic River from Newark ★ **DIMENSIONS:** Foul Lines 375, Center Field 450 ★ **CAPACITY:** 21,000 (1915) ★ **FORMER USE:** West Hudson football field

HARTFORD, CONNECTICUT
HARTFORD TROTTING PARK
OCCUPANT: Neutral use by NA Middletown Mansfields June 21, July 3, August 9, 1872

HARTFORD BALL CLUB GROUNDS
OCCUPANTS: NA Hartford Dark Blues May 1, 1874 to October 29, 1875; NL Hartford Dark Blues May 1 to September 30, 1876; neutral use by NL Hartfords of Brooklyn one game in 1877 ★ **LOCATION:** Third Base (S) Hendricksen Ave., then the Church of the Good Shepherd; (E) 230/258 Wyllys St.; also van Block Ave. ★ **CURRENT USE:** The Church of the Good Shepherd still stands on the SW corner of Wyllys and van Block.
PEHNOMENA: Three large apple trees, one in left, one in center, and one in right. The largest tree by far was the one in center, and the center fielder played right under it.

HAVANA, CUBA
ESTADIO GRAN (I)
AKA: Grand Stadium ★ **OCCUPANT:** NNL Havana Cuban Stars 1920

HOBOKEN, NEW JERSEY
ELYSIAN FIELDS
OCCUPANT: Neutral-site use by NA New York Mutuals July 4, 1873 ★ **LOCATION:** 10th St., Hudson St., Hoboken Shore Blvd; in Elysian Park, which ran along the shoreline from 6th St. to 17th St. ★ **FENCES:** None ★ **CURRENT USE:** Industrial site, public park
PHENOMENA: First baseball game between two organized teams under the Alexander Cartwright rules was played here on June 19, 1846. The New York Base Ball Club defeated the New York Knickerbockers Second Team 23-1. Two New York Knickerbocker Club teams had played earlier games here starting October 6, 1845. Earlier games had been played in New York City at Retreat in Broadway (Jones) on April 26, 1823; and at Madison Square and probably the Red House Grounds in 1832 with the First Ward Team of Lower Manhattan playing the 9th/15th Wards Teams of Upper Manhattan.

HOMESTEAD, PENNSYLVANIA
MUNICIPAL FIELD
OCCUPANT: Neutral site use by NNL Homestead Grays 1930s

HONOLULU, HAWAII
ALOHA STADIUM
AKA: Halawa Stadium 1975 ★ **OCCUPANT:** Neutral site use by NL San Diego Padres April 19-20, 1997 ★ **DIMENSIONS:** Foul Lines 325; Power Alleys 375; Center Field 400 ★ **SURFACE:** Monsanto AstroTurf ★ **CAPACITY:** 50,000

HOUSTON, TEXAS
BUFF STADIUM
AKA: Buffalo Stadium, Busch Stadium ★ **OCCUPANT:** NAL Houston Eagles 1949-50 ★ **LOCATION:** Left Field (N), Third Base (W) 4000 Harby St., First Base (S) 4001

Gulf Freeway, Right Field (E) Cullen Blvd. ★ **DIMENSIONS:** Left Field 344 (1928), 345 (1938); Center Field 430 (1928), 440 (1938); Right Field 344 (1928), 325 (1938) **FENCES:** 12 **CAPACITY:** 14,000 ★ **CURRENT USE:** Home plate's exact location is commemorated by a plaque in the Houston Sports Hall of Fame, which forms part of the Fingers Furniture Store.

COLT STADIUM

AKA: Mosquito Heaven ★ **OCCUPANT:** NL Houston Colt .45s April 10, 1962 to September 27, 1964 ★ **LOCATION:** Left Field (N) North Stadium Drive, Third Base (W) East-West Utility Rd., First Base (S) South Main St. (later Loop 610 South), Right Field (E) Kirby Drive ; just NW of the construction site for the Astrodome ★ **DIMENSIONS:** Foul Lines 360; Power Alleys 395; Center Field 420; Deepest corners in center just left and right of dead center 427; Backstop 60 ★ **FENCES:** Left and Right 8; Center Field Screen 30 ★ **CURRENT USE:** Astrodome's northwestern parking lot ★ **CAPACITY:** 25,000 (April 10, 1962), 32,601 (June 29, 1962), 33,010 (1964) **PHENOMENA:** Home of largest and peskiest mosquitoes in major league history. Park regularly sprayed by grounds crew between innings. Scoreboards in center on both sides of 30-foot-high batters' background. Lay in decay until 1970s, when moved to Torreon, Mexico's twin city of Gomez Palacio, by Mexican League Torreon Cotton Growers.

ASTRODOME

AKA: Harris County Domed Stadium 1965, 8th Wonder of the World ★ **OCCUPANT:** NL Houston Astros April 12, 1965 to October 9, 1999 ★ **LOCATION:** Center Field (E) Fannin St.; Third Base (N) Old Spanish Trail; (NW) Colt Stadium; Home Plate (W) 8400 Kirby Drive; First Base (S) Astrohall and Astroarena, then South Loop Freeway/I-610; Domed roof of 4796 Lucite panels and steel girders; just SE of Colt Stadium ★ **DIMENSIONS:** Foul Lines 340 (1965), 330 (1972), 340 (1977), 330 (1985), 325 (1992), 330 (1993), 325 (1994); Power Alleys 375 (1965), 390 (1966), 378 (1972), 390 (1977), 378 (1985), 375 (1992), 380 (1993), 375 (1994); Center Field 406 (1965), 400 (1972), 406 (1977), 400 (1985); Dome Apex 208; Backstop 60.5 (1965), 67 (1990), 52 (1993) ★ **FENCES:** Left and Right Field 16 (9 concrete below 3 wire, 2 concrete, and 2 wire plus railing, 1965), 12 (concrete, 1969), 10 (concrete, 1977), 10 (canvas, 1990), 19.5 (concrete, 1991), 10 canvas (1992); Between foul poles and scoreboards 8 (canvas, 1994), Scoreboards in left and right 16 (steel, 1994); Center Field 12 (concrete, 1965), 10 (concrete, 1977), 10 (canvas 1990) ★ **SURFACE:** Infield Grass (1965) Tifway 419 Bermuda grass specially selected for indoor play, but it died; AstroTurf on all but the part normally dirt 1966-70; on all the infield except for sliding pits 1971-99; Outfield grass April 12, 1965 to July 19, 1966, it died too; AstroTurf (July 19, 1966 to October 9, 1999) ★ **CURRENT USE:** adult league softball games ★ **CAPACITY:** 46,217 (1965), 44,500 (1968), 47,690 (1982), 54,816 (1990), 53,821 (1993), 54,370 (1999)
PHENOMENA: The second major league covered stadium, the first being the field under the Queensboro/59th St. Bridge in New York City, used by the New York Cubans of the Negro National League in the 1930s. The roof had 4,796 clear panes of glass, but they caused a glare preventing fielders from seeing the ball, so two of the eight roof sections were painted white. This killed the grass, and unfortunately introduced the world to AstroTurf. Infielders could legally catch foul flies in the dugout, either by jumping a fence or by entering the dugout through a gap in the middle of the fence. In its inaugural season of 1965, the Astrodome was the scene of a unique groundskeeping argument. The Mets claimed the groundskeepers were roof-keeping as well by manipulating the air conditioning system so air currents helped Astro long balls and hindered visitors' long balls.

MINUTE MAID PARK

AKA: Enron Field April 7, 2000-February 27, 2002, Astros Field February 27 to June 5, 2002 ★ **OCCUPANT:** NL Houston Astros April 7, 2000 to date ★ **LOCATION:** Left Field (NW/W) 501 Crawford St.; Third Base (SW/S) Texas Ave., then Union Station; First Base (SE/E) Hamilton St./US Hwy 59; Right Field (NE/N) Congress Ave; adjacent to George Brown Convention Center ★ **DIMENSIONS:** Left Field 315, Left Center 362, Center Field 435, Deepest Right Center 436, Right Center 373, Right Field 326, Backstop 49 ★ **FENCES:** Left Field 19, Left Center 25, Center Field and Right Center 10, Right Field 7 ★ **SURFACE:** Bermuda grass (April 2000), Seashore Paspalum grass (August 2001) ★ **FORMER USE:** Parking lots ★ **CAPACITY:** 40,950 (2000)
PHENOMENA: Retractable roof moves to Right Field when opened, moves back to Third Base when closed. Thirty-degree incline called Tal's Hill in deep center (named for executive Tal Smith, whose idea it was). Enron name removed after company became embroiled in controversy.

INDIANAPOLIS, INDIANA

SOUTH STREET PARK

AKA: National League Park 1878, Athletic Park ★ **OCCUPANTS:** NL Indianapolis Browns May 1 to September 14, 1878; neutral site use by AA St. Louis Browns one game in 1885 ★ **LOCATION:** (W) Delaware St., (S) South St.; also Alabama St. ★ **FORMER USE:** Cornfield

SEVENTH STREET PARK (I)

OCCUPANTS: AA Indianapolis Blues May 14 to September 20, 1884; neutral site use by NL St. Louis Maroons September 15, 1885 ★ **LOCATION:** same as Seventh St. Park (II)

BRUCE GROUNDS

OCCUPANTS: AA Indianapolis Blues Sundays only May 18 to September 21, 1884; NL Indianapolis Hoosiers Sundays only 1887-89 ★ **LOCATION:** (N) Bruce

(later 23rd) St., (W) College Ave., (S) 21st St., (E) RR tracks

SEVENTH STREET PARK (II)

OCCUPANT: NL Indianapolis Hoosiers April 28 to October 8, 1887 ★ **LOCATION:** Left Field (W) Mississippi St. (later Boulevard St., later Senate Ave.), Third Base (S) Tinker St. and 7th (later 16th) St., First Base (E) Tennessee St. (later Capitol Ave.), Right Field (N) 9th (later 18th) St. ★ **DIMENSIONS:** Left Field 286, Right Field 261

SEVENTH STREET PARK (III)

OCCUPANT: NL Indianapolis Hoosiers April 20, 1888 to October 5, 1889 ★ **LOCATION:** Left Field (N) 9th (later 18th) St., Third Base (W) Mississippi St. (later Boulevard St., later Senate Ave.), First Base (S) Tinker St. and 7th (later 16th) St., Right Field (E) Tennessee St. (later Capitol Ave.); same site as Seventh St. Park (I) and (II) but turned around so that home plate was in the SW rather than in the SE ★ **CURRENT USE:** Methodist Hospital

INDIANAPOLIS PARK

OCCUPANT: Neutral site use by NL Cleveland Spiders July 28 to August 2, 1890 ★ **LOCATION:** (N) New York St., (W) Hanna (later Oriental) St., (S) East Ohio St., (E) Arsenal Ave.

WASHINGTON PARK

AKA: Riverside Park ★ **OCCUPANT:** FL Indianapolis Hoosier-Feds April 23, 1914 **LOCATION:** Same as for Bush Stadium (Victory Field I)

GREENLAWN PARK

AKA: Federal League Park, ABCs Field, West Washington St. Park ★ **OCCUPANTS:** FL Indianapolis Hoosier-Feds April 24 to October 8, 1914; NNL Indianapolis ABCs 1920-23, April to June 1924, 1925-26 ★ **LOCATION:** (N) RR tracks, (W) White River, (S) Kentucky Ave., (E) West St.; First Base 1235 West Washington St. (later Route 40) ★ **DIMENSIONS:** Left Field 375, Center Field 400, Right Field 310 ★ **CURRENT USE:** Diamond Chain Company factory ★ **CAPACITY:** 20,000 (1914)

SPEEDWAY PARK

OCCUPANT: NNL Indianapolis ABCs some games 1920-26 ★ **LOCATION:** By Indianapolis Speedway ★ **CURRENT USE:** International Harvester plant

NORTHWESTERN AVENUE BALLPARK

OCCUPANT: NNL Indianapolis ABCs some games 1920-26 ★ **LOCATION:** Northwestern Ave., 17th St., Holton Place, 18th St.

VICTORY FIELD (I)

AKA: Perry Stadium 1931-42, Owen Bush Stadium 1968-95 ★ **OCCUPANTS:** NNL Indianapolis ABCs 1931; NSL Indianapolis ABCs 1932; NAL Indianapolis Athletics 1937; NAL Indianapolis ABCs 1938, April to May 1939; NAL Indianapolis Crawfords 1940; NAL Indianapolis-Cincinnati Clowns half of the home games 1944; NAL Indianapolis Clowns 1946-55; neutral site use by NNL Chicago Cole's American Giants May 28 to September 1933, and for Negro World Series NNL Washington-Homestead Grays vs. NAL Birmingham Black Barons game 5 in 1943 ★ **LOCATION:** 1501 West 16th St., White River, 38th St. ★ **DIMENSIONS:** Foul Lines 350 (1938), 335 (1950); Center Field 497 (1938), 500 (1947), 480 (1950), 395 (1985) ★ **CAPACITY:** 15,000 (1938), 13,254 (1947), 12,934 (1985)

IRONDEQUOIT, NEW YORK

WINDSOR BEACH

OCCUPANT: AA Rochester Hop Bitters Sundays only May 11 to July 20, 1890 ★ **LOCATION:** (N) Wabash Ave. (later Rock Beach Rd.), (W) Mouth-of-the-River Rd. (later Point Rd., then Washington Ave.), (S) railroad tracks, (E) Rock Beach Rd.; one mile SE of ballpark at Ontario Beach in Rochester ★ **CURRENT USE:** Housing development along Norcrest Drive

JACKSONVILLE, FLORIDA

RED CAP STADIUM

AKA: Jacksonville Baseball Park, Durkee Field, Barr's Field, Douglas Field ★ **OCCUPANT:** NAL Jacksonville Red Caps April to June 1938, 1941, April to July 1942 ★ **LOCATION:** Durkee Ave., 1701 Myrtle Ave., Moncrief Ave., Davis St., C (later Hopkins, later West 7th) St. ★ **DIMENSIONS:** Left Field 350, Center Field 400, Right Field 309 ★ **CAPACITY:** 4,564

JERSEY CITY, NEW JERSEY

OAKLAND PARK

AKA: Oakland Athletic Association Field, Oakdale Park ★ **OCCUPANT:** NL New York Giants April 24-25, 1889 ★ **LOCATION:** (NW) Oakland Ave., (SW) Hoboken Ave., (SE) Concord St., then a wagon works and a coal yard, (NE) Fleet St.; near Newark Ave. **PHENOMENA:** When the Giants played these two home games here, it was not neutral-site use, since they were anticipating that their entire home schedule for 1889 would be played here. But then owner John Day changed his mind, and they played the rest of the season's schedule on Staten Island at St. George Cricket Grounds.

ROOSEVELT STADIUM

OCCUPANTS: NNL New York Black Yankees some games in 1940s; NL Brooklyn Dodgers seven 1956 games and eight 1957 games April 19, 1956 to September 3, 1957 ★ **LOCATION:** Left Field (NE) Hackensack River; Third Base (NW) Newark Bay; First Base, (SW) Danforth Ave; Right Field (SE) State Hwy 440; at Droyers Point

★ **DIMENSIONS:** Foul Lines 330; Power Alleys 397; Center Field 411; Backstop 60 ★ **FENCES:** Foul Line Corners 11; Left to Center 4; Center to Right 7 ★ **CAPACITY:** 20,000 (1937), 26,000 (1938), 30,000 (1939), 25,000 (1947), 24,500 (1957) ★ **FORMER USE:** Landfill for dirt excavated from Holland Tunnel under the Hudson River

PHENOMENA: Built as WPA project in 1937 and named for FDR. Newark Bay brought mosquitoes and mist into the outfield. Willie Mays batted the only ball ever hit completely out of the park here on August 15, 1956 to beat the Dodgers 1-0. Jackie Robinson homered here for the Montreal Royals April 18, 1946, as he broke the color barrier that had racially segregated baseball since the 1800s. Torn down in 1984.

JOHNSTOWN, PENNSYLVANIA

POINT STADIUM
OCCUPANTS: Neutral site use by NNL Homestead Grays and NNL Pittsburgh Crawfords 1930s ★ **LOCATION:** Left Field (NW) John St., Third Base (SW) Route 56 Bypass and Conemaugh River, Home Plate (S) the Point, where the Little Conemaugh River and Stony Creek meet to form the Conemaugh River, First Base (SE) Little Conemaugh River, Right Field (NE) Washington St. ★ **DIMENSIONS:** Left Field 270, Center Field 475, Right Field 250 ★ **FENCES:** Left Field 70 (screen) ★ **CURRENT USE:** Community ballfield

KANSAS CITY, MISSOURI

ATHLETIC PARK
OCCUPANT: UA Kansas City Unions June 7 to October 19, 1884 ★ **LOCATION:** Summit St., Southwest Blvd.

ASSOCIATION PARK (I)
AKA: The Hole, League Park ★ **OCCUPANTS:** NL Kansas City Cowboys April 30 to September 18, 1886; AA Kansas City Blues April 18 to September 29, 1888; neutral site use by NL St. Louis Browns August 23 and October 15, 1892 ★ **LOCATION:** (W) Lydia Ave. and Tracy Ave., (S) Independence Ave., (E) Highland Ave.

EXPOSITION PARK
OCCUPANT: AA Kansas City Blues September 30, 1888 to September 30, 1889 ★ **LOCATION:** (N) 20th St., (W) Prospect Ave., (S) 15th St. (later Truman Ave.)

GORDON AND KOPPEL FIELD
AKA: Federal League Park ★ **OCCUPANT:** FL Kansas City Packers April 16, 1914 to September 28, 1915 ★ **LOCATION:** (S) Brush Creek Blvd, (E) the Paseo; also 49th St., Tracy St. ★ **CAPACITY:** 12,000 (1914)

ASSOCIATION PARK (II)
OCCUPANT: NNL Kansas City Monarchs 1920-22 ★ **LOCATION:** Center Field 2First St., Third Base RR tracks, Home Plate 19th St., First Base Olive St. ★ **FENCES:** Right Field 30 (screen) ★ **CURRENT USE:** Playground

PARADEWAY PARK
OCCUPANT: NNL Kansas City Monarchs 1923-30 ★ **LOCATION:** the Paseo, 17th St.

MUNICIPAL STADIUM
AKA: Muehlebach Field 1923-37, Ruppert Stadium 1938-42, Blues Stadium 1943-54 ★ **OCCUPANTS:** NAL Kansas City Monarchs 1937-60; AL Kansas City Athletics April 12, 1955 to September 27, 1967; AL Kansas City Royals April 8, 1969 to October 4, 1972; Negro World Series Games 5-7 in 1924, 1-4 in 1925 4 in 1942, 3-4 in 1946 ★ **LOCATION:** Left Field (N) 2 First St.; Third Base (W) Euclid Ave; First Base (S) 22nd St.; Right Field (E) 2128 Brooklyn Ave. ★ **DIMENSIONS:** Left Field 350 (1923), 312 (1955), 330 (1956), 370 (1961), 353 (1962), 331 (1963), 370 (1965), 369 (1967); Left Center 408 (1923), 382 (1955), 375 (1957), 390 (1961), 364 (1963), 392 (1964), 409 (1965), 408 (1969); Center Field 450 (1923), 432 (1950), 430 (1955), 421 (1956), 410 (1964), 421 (1965); Right Center 382 (1955), 387 (1957), 364 (1962), 360 (1963), 392 (1964), 360 (1965), 382 (1969); Right Field 350 (1923), 347 (1955), 352 (1956), 353 (1957), 338 (1963), 345 (1965), 338 (1966); Backstop 60 (1955), 70 (1963) ★ **FENCES:** Left Field 24 (screen 1956), 18.5 (concrete 1958), 38.5 (20 screen over 18.5 concrete 1959), 10 (1961), 13.5 (1962), 10 (1963), 22 (1967), 13 (1969); Center Field 12 (1958), 14 (1959), 12 (1961), 13.5 (1962), 10 (1963), 22 (screen 1966), 22 (screen 1969), 22 (screen 1970); Right Field 12 (1958), 14 (1959), 12 (1961), 13.5 (1962), 10 (1963), 4.5 (plywood 1965), 40 (screen 1966), 13 (1969), 12 (screen 1970) ★ **FORMER USE:** Swimming hole, frog pond, and ash heap ★ **CURRENT USE:** Community garden ★ **CAPACITY:** 17,476 (1923), 30,296 (1955), 32,241 (1961), 34,165 (1969), 35,561 (1971)

PHENOMENA: The right-field-embankment zoo included the mule named Charlie O (who often traveled with the team to away games), sheep, China golden pheasants, Capuchin monkeys, German checker rabbits, peafowl, and a German short-haired pointer dog, who all lived out there. Little Blowhard was a subterranean device that blew compressed air through the middle of the plate so that the umpire didn't have to brush it off. Harvey the Mechanical Rabbit rose out of the ground to the right of the plate to offer the umpire new baseballs from a basket between his ears. Charles O. Finley believed one reason the Yankees won so many pennants was their 296-foot right field porch. In April 1965, he created his own 296-foot "Pennant Porch" in right field here, but the league forced him to remove it after it was used in only two preseason games. Torn down in 1976.

KAUFFMAN STADIUM
AKA: Royals Stadium April 10, 1973 to July 2, 1993; Harry S. Truman Sports

Complex, Ewing M. Kauffman Stadium ★ **OCCUPANT:** AL Kansas City Royals April 10, 1973 to date ★ **LOCATION:** Center Field (NE) Spectacular Drive, then I-70; Third Base (NW) Lancer Lane, then Dutton Brookfield Drive ; Home Plate (SW) Royal Way, then Chiefs Way, Arrowhead Stadium, Raytown Rd., and CRI&P RR tracks; First Base (SE) Red Coat Drive, then Blue Ridge Cut-Off ★ **DIMENSIONS:** Foul Lines 330 (1973), 320 (1995), 330 (2001); Power Alleys 375 (1973), 385 (1990), 375 (1995), 385 (2004); Center Field 405 (1973), 410 (1980), 400 (1995), 410 (2004); Backstop 60; Foul Territory small ★ **FENCES:** 12 (canvas, 1973), 9 (canvas, 1995), 8 (canvas, 2004) ★ **SURFACE:** AstroTurf-8 carpet, very fast 1973-94; grass 1995 to date ★ **CAPACITY:** 40,613 (1973), 40,793 (2003)

PHENOMENA: Waterfalls and fountains run for 322 feet on embankment overlooking right center. Best visibility for hitters in the majors, but homers are few here because alleys are so deep and the fence cuts away sharply from the foul poles. During rain delays, thousands of sawed webworm moths appear. Great park for hitting triples. Kenny Pippin, in his frogman suit, cleans the pond periodically in right center. Upper-deck fans near foul poles are in relative darkness. Before 1995, when grass replaced the hated carpet, the best groundskeeper in baseball had the ironic job of maintaining an ugly plastic carpet. He kept busy maintaining the Runway and the Baja, the grassy running area and the 125-tree forest beyond the fence in left center.

KEOKUK, IOWA

WALTE'S PASTURE
OCCUPANT: NA Keokuk Westerns May 4 to June 14, 1875 ★ **LOCATION:** Center Field (E) Pleasant Lake, Third Base (N) Plane Rd., First Base (W) U.S. Routes 61 & 218, (S) Rand Park ★ **CURRENT USE:** Municipal swimming pool

PHENOMENA: Two lakes sat out in center. Outfielders often fell in while chasing fly balls.

LANSINGBURGH, NEW YORK

RENSSELAER PARK
OCCUPANT: Neutral site use by NA Troy Haymakers some games in 1871-72 ★ **LOCATION:** Left Field Oakwood Cemetery, Troy and Boston RR tracks, Third Base South (later 111th) St., First Base Hill St. (later Eighth Ave.), Right Field Middle (later 108th) St.

LAS VEGAS, NEVADA

CASHMAN FIELD
AKA: Cashman Field Center ★ **OCCUPANT:** Neutral site use by AL Oakland Athletics April 1-7, 1996 ★ **LOCATION:** 850 Las Vegas Blvd. North ★ **DIMENSIONS:** Foul Lines 328; Power Alleys 364; Center Field 433; Backstop 43 ★ **FENCES:** Left and Right Field 20, Center Field 22 ★ **CAPACITY:** 9,353 (1996), 9,500 (2004)

LEBANON, INDIANA

LEBANON FIELD
OCCUPANT: Neutral site use by NNL Indianapolis ABCs in early 1920s

LITTLE ROCK, ARKANSAS

TRAVELLERS FIELD
AKA: Ray Winder Field, Kavanaugh Field, Southern Association Park ★ **OCCUPANTS:** NSL Little Rock Grays 1932; neutral site use by NAL Birmingham Black Barons 1940s ★ **LOCATION:** (NW) Jonesboro Drive, then War Memorial Park, (W) Monroe St., (S) Eighth St. (later East-West Expressway/I-630) ★ **DIMENSIONS:** Left Field 325 (1925), 345 (1938), 320 (1983); Center Field 405 (1925), 450 (1938), 390 (1983); Right Field 300 (1925), 395 (1938), 340 (1983) ★ **CAPACITY:** 10,500 (1925), 7,000 (1938), 6,100 (1983)

LOS ANGELES, CALIFORNIA

MEMORIAL COLISEUM
AKA: O'Malley's Chinese Theatre, O'Malley's Alley ★ **OCCUPANT:** NL Los Angeles Dodgers April 18, 1958 to September 20, 1961 ★ **LOCATION:** Left Field (N) Exposition Blvd; Third Base (W) Merlo Ave., then Los Angeles Olympic Swimming Stadium; First Base (S) Santa Barbara Ave. (later Martin Luther King, Jr. Drive); Right Field (E) 3911 South Figueroa St., Los Angeles Memorial Sports Arena, then I-110 ★ **DIMENSIONS:** Left Field 250 (1958), 251.6 (1959); Left Center 320 at end of screen rectangle; Left Center where fence met wall 425 (1958), 417 (1959); Center Field 425 (1958), 420 (1959); Right Center 440 (1958), 375 (1959), 394 (1960), 380 (1961); Right Field where fence met wall 390 (1958), 333 (1959), 340 (1960); Right Field 301 (1958), 300 (1959); Backstop 60 (1958), 66 (1959); Foul Territory very strange—tremendously large area on third-base line, but almost none on first-base line ★ **FENCES:** Left Field 40 (screen 1958), 42 (screen 1959); 60 (2 support towers for screen 1958); Left Center 40 (fence 1958); from Foul Pole 140 feet into Left Center, 42 sloping to ground at 30 degree angle from 320 mark to 348 mark for distance of 24 feet (1959-60); 4 steps down from 42 to 8; first step left corner 42 sloping to 41, second step 31, third step 20, fourth step 12 (1961); Right of Screen in Left Center 8 (wire); Center to Right Field Corner 6 (wire); Right Field Corner 4 (concrete) ★ **FORMER USE:** Gravel pit; Agriculture Park in 1890s, fairs, livestock shows, amusement park booths, horse racing track and barns, saloons; Exposition Park in 1910s—armory, museum, gardens; Summer Olympics in 1932 and 1984; college and pro football ★ **CAPACITY:** 74,000 (1923), 75,000 (1928), 105,000 (1932),

103,000 (1941), 101,528 (1956), 93,000 (1958), 94,600 (1959), 70,000 (1965), 76,000 (1968), 78,000 (1972), 71,432 (1977), 73,999 (1979), 92,488 (1982)
PHENOMENA: Opened for football October 6, 1923. Cables, towers, girders, and wires above the screen in left field were in play. This directly caused the Dodgers to win the 1959 pennant. In the top of the fifth inning on September 15, 1959, Joe Adcock of the Braves hit a ball that cleared the screen but did not land in the seats because it hit a steel girder behind the screen and got caught in the mesh supporting the screen. According to the rule book, this should have been a homer. The umps gave him only a double, then changed their minds when fans shook the screen and the ball fell into the seats, then changed their minds again and pulled Adcock out of the dugout and put him back on second base. Adcock never scored, the Dodgers won in extra innings, the Dodgers and Braves ended the regular season in a tie and the Dodgers won in a playoff. Had Adcock's hit been correctly ruled a home run, the Braves would have finished alone in first place, there never would have been a playoff, and the largest World Series crowd ever, 92,706 against White Sox here on October 6, 1959, would never have happened. The 42-foot screen in left was meant to prevent 251-foot pop-ups from being homers. Commissioner Ford Frick ordered the Dodgers to construct a second screen in left, *in the seats*, 333 feet from the plate, and a ball clearing both screens would be a homer, but a ball clearing just the shorter screen would be just a double. However, after the lawyers got into the act, they found that the California Earthquake Law made construction of such a screen illegal. After 182 homers were hit to left, but only 3 to center and 8 to right in 1958, the fence in right field was shortened in 1959, resulting in more homers to right field—in 1959, 132 to left, 1 to center, 39 to right; in 1960, 155 to left, 3 to center, 28 to right; in 1961, 147 to left, 7 to center, 38 to right. A small green lightpole was in the field of play in right field.

WRIGLEY FIELD
OCCUPANT: AL Los Angeles Angels April 27 to October 1, 1961 ★ **LOCATION:** Left Field (E) Avalon Blvd; Third Base (S) 435 East 4Second Place; First Base (W) San Pedro St.; Right Field (N) East 4First Place ★ **DIMENSIONS:** Left Field 340; Power Alleys 345; Center Field 412; Right Field 338.5; Backstop 56 ★ **FENCES:** Left Field to Center Field 14.5 (concrete); Center Field to Right Field 9 (6 wire above 3 concrete) ★ **CAPACITY:** 22,000 (1925), 20,457 (1961) ★ **CURRENT USE:** Gilbert Lindsay Park, a public playground, and City Center Community Mental Health Facility
PHENOMENA: In 1961, Wrigley Field set a record for most homers (248) in one park in one season because the power alleys were only five feet farther than the foul pole in left.

DODGER STADIUM
AKA: Chavez Ravine during AL use 1962-65 by Los Angeles Angels and by California Angels, Taj O'Malley, O'Malley's Golden Gulch ★ **OCCUPANTS:** NL Los Angeles Dodgers April 10, 1962 to date; AL Los Angeles Angels April 17, 1962 to September 1, 1965; AL California Angels September 2-22, 1965 ★ **LOCATION:** Left Field (N/NW) Glendale Blvd; Third Base (W/SW) Sunset Blvd; Home Plate (S/SW) 1000 Elysian Park Ave; First Base (S/SE) Pasadena Freeway/I-10; Right Field (E/NE) Los Angeles Police Academy, Elysian Park, Golden State Freeway/I-5; in Chavez Ravine, on a hill overlooking downtown Los Angeles ★ **SURFACE:** Santa Ana Bermuda grass, Prescription Athletic Turf (PAT) ★ **DIMENSIONS:** Foul Lines 330; Power Alleys 380 (1962), 370 (1969), 385 (1983); Center Field 410 (1962), 400 (1969), NOT (see below) 395 (now); Back Stop 65 (1962), 68.19 (1963), 75 (1969); Foul Territory large ★ **FENCES:** Left Center to Right Center 10 (wood 1962), 8 (1973); Foul Poles to Bullpens in Left and Right Field Corners 3.75 (steel 1962), 3.83 (1969); the "Dip" where low corner steel wall and screen bullpen fence meet 3.42 (1962), 3.5 (1969) ★ **FORMER USE:** Used by squatters and goats ★ **CAPACITY:** 56,000 – unchanged 1962 to date; it's amazing how some numbers just never seem to change!
PHENOMENA: Although the center-field 400 sign came down in 1980, the distance is still 400 to center; the two 395 signs are to the left and right of dead center. Many references say it is 395 to center; they are incorrect. When the foul poles were installed in 1962, it was discovered that they had been positioned completely in foul territory. The next year the plate had to be moved so the poles would be in fair territory. Why must foul poles be in fair territory? That's baseball!

LOUISVILLE, KENTUCKY
ST. JAMES COURT
AKA: Louisville Baseball Park ★ **OCCUPANT:** NL Louisville Grays April 25, 1876 to September 29, 1877 ★ **LOCATION:** Left Field (W) 6th St., Third Base (S) Hill St., First Base (E) 4th St., Right Field (N) Magnolia St. ★ **CURRENT USE:** residential area of Victorian homes built in the 1890s

ECLIPSE PARK (I)
OCCUPANTS: AA Louisville Colonels May 5, 1882 to September 27, 1891; NL Louisville Colonels April 12, 1892 to September 26, 1892 ★ **LOCATION:** (N) Magazine St., (W) 29th St., (S) Elliott Ave., (E) 28th St. ★ **DIMENSIONS:** Left Field 360, Left Center 405, Center Field 495, Right Center 360, Right Field 320 ★ **FENCES:** 8 (1882), 12 (1884) ★ **FORMER USE:** Elliott Estate

ECLIPSE PARK (II)
OCCUPANT: NL Louisville Colonels September 28, 1892 to May 4, 1893 ★ **LOCATION:** same as Eclipse Park (I)

ECLIPSE PARK (III)
AKA: League Park ★ **OCCUPANT:** NL Louisville Colonels May 22, 1893 to August 2, 1899 ★ **LOCATION:** (N) Broadway, (W) 30th St., (E) 28th St.; across the street from Eclipse Parks (I) and (II) ★ **FORMER USE:** Kentucky and Indiana Company rail-

road switching yard and stockyard

ECLIPSE PARK (IV)
OCCUPANT: NL Louisville Colonels August 22 to October 7, 1899 ★ **LOCATION:** same as Eclipse Park (III)

PARKWAY FIELD
AKA: Colonels Field ★ **OCCUPANTS:** NNL Louisville White Sox 1931; NSL Louisville Black Caps April to August 1932; NAL Louisville Buckeyes 1949; NAL Louisville Black Colonels 1954 ★ **LOCATION:** Left Field (N) Eastern Parkway, Third Base (W), First Base (S) RR tracks, Right Field (E) Brook St. ★ **CAPACITY:** 13,198 (1938), 13,496 (1952) ★ **DIMENSIONS:** Left Field 331 (1923), 329 (1949), Deepest Left Center 512 (1923), 504 (1949), Center Field 467, Right Field 350 (1923), 345 (1949) ★ **CURRENT USE:** Grandstand demolished in 1961, but wall in center still has 504 marker

LUDLOW, KENTUCKY
LUDLOW BASEBALL PARK
OCCUPANT: Neutral use by NA Philadelphia Pearls September 22, 1875 ★ **LOCATION:** (S) River bluffs high on a hill; just across Ohio River from Cincinnati, Ohio

MACON, GEORGIA
LUTHER WILLIAMS FIELD
OCCUPANT: Neutral use by NAL Birmingham Black Barons 1940s ★ **DIMENSIONS:** Foul Lines 350 (1938), 330 (1983); Center Field 450 (1938), 405 (1983) ★ **CAPACITY:** 6,000 (1938), 5,000 (1960), 3,000 (1983)

McKEESPORT, PENNSYLVANIA
CYCLER PARK
OCCUPANT: Neutral site use by NEWL Homestead Grays May 30, 1932 ★ **LOCATION:** Left Field (E), Third Base (N), First Base (W), Right Field (S) ★ **DIMENSIONS:** Left Field 393, Center Field 440, Right Field 325

MEADVILLE, PENNSYLVANIA
MEADVILLE GROUNDS
OCCUPANT: Neutral site use by NA New York Mutuals July 22, 1871

MEMPHIS, TENNESSEE
MARTIN PARK
OCCUPANTS: NNL Memphis Red Sox June to September 1924, 1925, 1927, 1929-30; NSL Memphis Red Sox 1932; NAL Memphis Red Sox 1937-41, 1943-59 ★ **LOCATION:** Crump Blvd, Danny Thomas Ave. ★ **CURRENT USE:** Truck terminal

RUSSWOOD PARK
OCCUPANTS: NAL Memphis Red Sox some games 1940s ★ **LOCATION:** (N) Jefferson Ave., (W) Dunlaps St., (S) Madison Ave., (E) Edgeway St. ★ **DIMENSIONS:** Left Field 424, Center Field 366, Right Field 301 ★ **CURRENT USE:** Medical center built on site after ballpark burned down April 17, 1960.

MIAMI, FLORIDA
PRO PLAYER STADIUM
AKA: Joe Robbie Stadium 1993-96 ★ **OCCUPANT:** NL Florida Marlins April 5, 1993 to date **LOCATION:** Center Field (E) Florida Turnpike; Third Base (N) NW 20Third St., then Snake Creek Canal; Home Plate (W), Carl F. Barger Blvd, Northwest 27th (later University) Ave; First Base (S) 2267 Northwest 199th St.; also Honey Hill Rd. and 2267 Dan Marino Blvd. ★ **DIMENSIONS:** Left Field 335 (1993), 330 (1994); Power Alleys 380 (1993), 385 (1994); Deepest Left Center corner 434; Center Field 410 (1993), 404 (1994); Right Field 345; Backstop 58 (1993), 60 (2003) ★ **SURFACE:** Tifway 419 Bermuda grass ★ **FENCES:** Left Center Scoreboard 33; everywhere else 8 ★ **CAPACITY:** 75,000 (1987), 43,909 (1993), 46,238 (1995), 41,855 (1996), 42,531 (1999), 36,331 (2001)
PHENOMENA: Many nooks and crannies create crazy bounces and angles. Helipad site in the parking lot. Second-deck outfield seats covered by canvas. Thirty-three-foot high left-field wall is called the Teal Monster.

MIDDLETOWN, CONNECTICUT
MANSFIELD CLUB GROUNDS
OCCUPANT: NA Middletown Mansfields May 2 to July 4, 1872 ★ **LOCATION:** (N) River Rd., (W) Eastern Drive, (S) Silver St., (E) State Terrace; along the Connecticut River ★ **CURRENT USE:** Connecticut Valley Hospital, formerly the Connecticut Hospital for the Insane, lies just east of the site.

MILWAUKEE, WISCONSIN
MILWAUKEE BASE-BALL GROUNDS
OCCUPANT: NL Milwaukee Cream Citys May 14 to September 14, 1878 ★ **LOCATION:** (N) West Michigan Ave., (W) North 12th St., (S) West Clybourn Ave., (E) North 10th St.

WRIGHT STREET GROUNDS
AKA: Milwaukee Baseball Park (I) ★ **OCCUPANTS:** UA Milwaukee Grays September 27 to October 12, 1884; neutral site use by NL Chicago White Stockings September 4 and 25, 1885 ★ **LOCATION:** (N) West Clarke St., (W) North 12th St., (S) West Wright St., (E) North 11th St.

BORCHERT FIELD
AKA: Brewer Field, Milwaukee Athletic Park ★ **OCCUPANTS:** AA Milwaukee Brewers August 14 to October 4, 1891; NNL Milwaukee Bears July to August 1923 ★ **LOCATION:** Center Field (N) West Burleigh St., Third Base (W) 3,000 North 8th Ave., Home Plate (S) West Chambers St., First Base (E) West 7th Ave. ★ **DIMENSIONS:** Foul Lines 266, Center Field 395 ★ **CURRENT USE:** Playground ★ **CAPACITY:** 10,000 (1891), 14,000 (1941)
PHENOMENA: Pitcher Ralph Cutting's goat grazed on the grass between games. Bill Veeck moved the minor league Brewers here in 1941, and erected a 60-foot high chicken wire fence in right because he knew his team could not hit 266-foot homers, so he didn't want the other team to be able to either. The next year, he went one step further, and rigged the fence so that a hydraulic motor could move the fence along a rail on top of the right field wall into foul territory when the Brewers were up, and back into fair territory when the Brewers were in the field. He got away with this for one game, but the next day the league passed a rule against it.

LLOYD STREET GROUNDS
AKA: Milwaukee Baseball Park (II) ★ **OCCUPANT:** AL Milwaukee Brewers May 3 to September 12, 1901 ★ **LOCATION:** Center Field (N) West North St., Third Base (W) North 18th St., Home Plate (S) West Lloyd St., First Base (E) North 16th St. ★ **FENCES:** Left Field 20 (canvas screen)

COUNTY STADIUM
OCCUPANTS: NL Milwaukee Braves April 14, 1953 to September 22, 1965; AL Milwaukee Brewers April 7, 1970 to September 28, 1997, NL Milwaukee Brewers April 7, 1998 to September 28, 2000; neutral site use by AL Chicago White Sox May 15, 1968 to September 26, 1969 for nine games in 1968 and 11 in 1969 ★ **LOCATION:** Left Field (E) South 44th St. (later US-41 Stadium Freeway), then Menomonee River; Third Base (N) Story Parkway/I-94; First Base (W) General Mitchell Blvd; Right Field (S) West National Ave. ★ **DIMENSIONS:** Left Field 320 (1953), 315 (1975); Power Alleys 355 (1953), 362 (1962); Deep Alleys 397 (1953), 392 (1955); Center Field 404 (1953), 410 (1954), 402 (1955); Right Field 320 (1953), 315.37 (1954); Backstop 60 ★ **FENCES:** Left Field 4 (1953), 8 (1955), 8.33 (1959), 10 (1985); Center Field 4 (1953), 8 (1955), 8.33 (1959), 10 (1985); Right Field 4 (1953), 10 (1955) ★ **FORMER USE:** Stone quarry ★ **CAPACITY:** 36,011 (1953), 43,091 (1954), 44,091 (1965), 47,611 (1970), 54,187 (1973), 53,192 (1975)
PHENOMENA: Best bratwurst and best tailgating parties in the majors. Bernie Brewer slid into a huge beer stein in right center when a Brewer hit a homer. Cecil Fielder had the only homer ever hit over the left-field roof. Braves hosted Reds and Cards on September 24, 1954. The first game was the finish of a game two days earlier whose ending on a disputed double play was successfully protested by the Reds. The Reds tied the game after the protested game's resumption, but the Braves won 4-3 in the bottom of the ninth, and then beat the Cards 4-2. Torn down February 21, 2001.

MILLER PARK
OCCUPANT: AL Milwaukee Brewers April 6, 2001 to date ★ **LOCATION:** Left Field (E) South 44th St., then Menomonee River and Stadium Freeway/US 41; Third Base (N) Story Parkway and I-94, First Base (W) General Mitchell Blvd, Right Field (S) West National Ave., then National Soldiers Home; also One Brewers Way; in what used to be the Center Field parking lot of County Stadium ★ **DIMENSIONS:** Left Field 344 (2001), 342 (2002); Left Center 371 (2001), 374 (2002); Center Field 400; Right Center 378 (2001), 374 (2002); Right Field 355 (2001), 345 (2002); Backstop 56 ★ **FENCES:** 8 to 12 ★ **CAPACITY:** 42, 885 (2001), 41,900 (2003)
PHENOMENA: Three construction workers were killed and tons of debris were spilled over the site by a crane accident in July 1999, causing a one-year delay in its opening. Opening day was moved back to April 6, 2001.

MINNEAPOLIS, MINNESOTA
ATHLETIC PARK
OCCUPANT: Neutral site use by AA Milwaukee Brewers October 2, 1891 ★ **LOCATION:** Butler Square ★ **DIMENSIONS:** Left Field 275, Right Field 250

HUBERT H. HUMPHREY METRODOME
AKA: Minnedome, Bounce Dome, Hump Dome, Homer Dome, Hubie Dome, Thunderdome, Sweat Box (before June 28, 1983, when air conditioning arrived) ★ **OCCUPANT:** AL Minnesota Twins April 6, 1982 to date ★ **LOCATION:** Left Field (NE) Fourth St. South; Third Base (NW) 501 Chicago Ave. South (later 34 Kirby Puckett Place); First Base (SW) Sixth St. South; Right Field (SE) Tenth Ave. South ★ **DIMENSIONS:** Left Field 344 (1982), 343 (1983); Left Center 385; Center Field 407 (1982), 408 (1983); Right Center 367 (1982), 327 (1983); Right Field 327; Backstop 60; Foul Territory small; Dome Apex 186 ★ **FENCES:** Left Field 7 (canvas 1982), 13 (6 Plexiglas above 7 canvas 1983), 7 (canvas 1994); Center Field 7 (canvas 1982); Right Field 7 (canvas 1982), 13 (canvas early in 1983), 23 (canvas later in 1983) ★ **SURFACE:** SporTurf 1982-86, liveliest bounce ever on a major league turf, AstroTurf 1987 to date ★ **CAPACITY:** 54,711 (1982), 55,883 (1989), 44,457 (1996), 48,678 (1997)
PHENOMENA: More home runs are hit when the air conditioning is turned off. The curvature of the wall behind plate causes wild pitches and passed balls to bounce directly to first base rather than right back to the plate. Right-field wall called the Hefty Bag, or the Trash Bag. On May 4, 1984, in the top of the fourth, A's batter Dave Kingman hit a ball through the roof. It should have been a homer, but Kingman got only

a double. May 31, 1998 game played with temporary white 10-foot left-field foul pole after violent rainstorm snapped cable connecting the 45-foot pole to the roof, causing it to fall over.

MOBILE, ALABAMA
HARTWELL FIELD
AKA: Monroe Park, League Park ★ **OCCUPANT:** NAL Mobile Havana Cuban Giants 1957 ★ **LOCATION:** (W) Ann St., (S) Tennessee St. ★ **DIMENSIONS:** Foul Lines 335, Center Field 406
PHENOMENA: Huge scoreboard in left destroyed by lightning during a hurricane.

MONESSEN, PENNSYLVANIA
PAGE PARK
OCCUPANT: Neutral site use by NNL Homestead Grays 1930s

MONROE, LOUISIANA
CASINO PARK
AKA: Stovall Park, Ramona Park ★ **OCCUPANT:** NSL Monroe Monarchs 1932 ★ **LOCATION:** Renwick St., South 29th St., De Siard St., Missouri Pacific RR tracks ★ **DIMENSIONS:** Left Field 360, Center Field 450, Right Field 330

MONTERREY, NUEVO LEON, MEXICO
ESTADIO MONTERREY
OCCUPANT: Neutral site use by NL San Diego Padres August 16-18, 1996; April 4, 1999 ★ **DIMENSIONS:** Foul Lines 310, Center Field 400 ★ **CAPACITY:** 25,644 (1996); 26,000 (1999); 30,000 (2003) ★ **LOCATION:** Next to Monterrey's soccer stadium
PHENOMENA: Home of Monterrey Sultans of Mexican League. Harp music over P.A. after every strikeout.

MONTGOMERY, ALABAMA
CRAMTON BOWL
OCCUPANTS: NSL Montgomery Grey Sox 1932; neutral site use for Negro World Series NNL Washington-Homestead Grays vs. NAL Birmingham Black Barons, Game 7 in 1943 ★ **LOCATION:** Madison Ave., Hilliard St. ★ **DIMENSIONS:** Left Field 420, Center Field 600, Right Field 600 ★ **CAPACITY:** 10,000

COLLEGE HILL PARK
OCCUPANT: NSL Montgomery Grey Sox some games in 1932 ★ **LOCATION:** On campus of Alabama State University

MONTREAL, QUEBEC, CANADA
PARC JARRY
AKA: Jarry Park ★ **OCCUPANT:** NL Montreal Expos April 14, 1969 to September 26, 1976 ★ **LOCATION:** Left Field (NW) rue Jarry; Third Base (SW) Canadian Pacific RR tracks; First Base (SE) 285 ouest rue Faillon; Right Field (NE) rue St. Laurent, then swimming pool ★ **DIMENSIONS:** Left Field 340; Left Center 368; Center Field 415 (1969), 417 (1971), 420 (1974); Right Center 365; Right Field 340; Backstop 62 ★ **FENCES:** 8 (wire 1969), 5 (wire 1970), 8 (wire 1976) ★ **FORMER USE:** Amateur recreational ballpark ★ **CAPACITY:** 3,000 (1968), 28,000 (April 14, 1969), 28,456 (June 24, 1969)
PHENOMENA: Still under construction April to May 1969. On April 13, 1971, Opening Day fans stood on snow plowed high in mounds behind the 8.5-foot wall that stood behind the 5-foot wire screen fence in right field and viewed the game for free. Wind helped drives to left center. Homers to right landed in the swimming pool.

STADE OLYMPIQUE
AKA: Olympic Stadium, Big O, Big Owe ★ **OCCUPANT:** NL Expos de Montreal April 15, 1977 to date ★ **LOCATION:** Left Field (NW) rue Sherbrooke; Third Base (SW) boulevard Pie-IX; First Base (SE) 4545 avenue Pierre-de-Coubertin; Right Field (NE) boulevard Viau ★ **SURFACE:** AstroTurf ★ **DIMENSIONS:** Foul Lines 325 (1977), 330 (1981), 325 (1983); Power Alleys 375; Center Field 404 (1977), 405 (1979), 404 (1980), 400 (1981), 404 (1983); Dome Apex 180 above Second Base, 171 above Outfield Walls; Backstop 62 (1977), 65 (1983), 53 (1989); Foul Territory large ★ **FENCES:** 12 (wood 1977), 12 (foam 1989) ★ **CAPACITY:** 60,000 (1976), 58,838 (1977), 60,476 (1979), 58,838 (1982), 60,011 (1990), 43,739 (1992), 46,500 (1993), 43,739 (1996), 46,500 (1999)
PHENOMENA: Opened for Olympic opening ceremony July 17, 1976. Huge 623-foot-high umbrella tower in center stood half finished 1976-87. It was finally finished in 1987, but when the roof continued to cause difficulties, the decision was made to keep it closed, so the O became a fixed-dome stadium in 1989. Parts of the concrete upper section of the stadium fell down in 1991, forcing the Expos to reschedule their September home games for the road. The O became open-air again in 1998 when the dilapidated orange Kevlar roof was removed in midseason. A new blue non-retractable roof was installed in 1999.

MOUNDS, ILLINOIS
MOUNDS BALLFIELD
OCCUPANT: Neutral site use by NAL New Orleans-St. Louis Stars August to September 1939

MUNCIE, INDIANA

WALNUT PARK
OCCUPANT: Neutral site use by NNL Indianapolis ABCs September 11, 1920

NASHVILLE, TENNESSEE

SULPHUR DELL (I)
OCCUPANT: Neutral site use by NNL Memphis Red Sox 1924-25 ★ **LOCATION:** Left Field (S) Tennessee Central RR tracks; Third Base (E) Cherry St. (later Fourth Ave. North); First Base (N) Jackson St.; Right Field (W) Summer St. (later 900 Fifth Ave. North); same site as Sulphur Dell (I) and (III), but different orientation ★ **FORMER USE:** Trading post and watering hole at sulfur springs used often for picnics. First used for baseball right after the Civil War. Sulphur Dell (I) grandstand built in 1885, and torn down in the winter of 1926-27 to make way for Sulphur Dell (II). ★ **DIMENSIONS:** Left Field 334; Center Field 421; Right Field 262; Right Field Shelf when fans sat behind ropes on the bank in right 235

WILSON PARK
OCCUPANTS: NNL Nashville Elite Giants 1930; NSL Nashville Elite Giants 1932 ★ **LOCATION:** South of Meharry Medical College

SULPHUR DELL (II)
AKA: Sulphur Springs Bottom, Sulphur Dell Park, Athletic Park, the Dump, Suffer Hell ★ **OCCUPANTS:** NNL Nashville Elite Giants 1930; NSL Nashville Elite Giants 1932; NNL Nashville Elite Giants 1933-34 ★ **LOCATION:** Left Field (N) Jackson St.; Third Base (W) Summer St. (later 900 Fifth Ave. North); First Base (S) Tennessee Central RR tracks; Right Field (E) Cherry St. (later Fourth Ave. North) ★ **DIMENSIONS:** Left Field 334; Center Field 421; Right Field 262; Right Field Shelf when fans sat behind ropes on the bank in right 235 ★ **FENCES:** All Around 16 (wood 1927); Left and Center 16 (wood 1931); Right Field 16 (1927), 38.5 to 46 (16 wood below 22.5 to 30 screen from foul line to a point 186 feet from the foul line 1931) ★ **CAPACITY:** 7,000 (1927), 8,500 (1938)

NEWARK, NEW JERSEY

WIEDENMEYER'S PARK
OCCUPANT: Neutral site use by AL New York Highlanders July 17, 1904 ★ **LOCATION:** (NE) Hamburg Place (later 262 Wilson Ave.), (NW) Ave. K

NEWARK SCHOOLS STADIUM
OCCUPANT: ECL Newark Stars April to June 1926 ★ **LOCATION:** Bloomfield Ave., Roseville Ave., First Ave., North Tenth St.

MEADOWBROOK OVAL
AKA: Meadowbrook Field ★ **OCCUPANTS:** NEWL Newark Browns April to June 1932; NNL Newark Dodgers 1934-35 ★ **LOCATION:** Left Field South Orange Ave; 12th St.; adjacent to Fairmount Cemetery ★ **DIMENSIONS:** Foul Lines 300, Center Field 380 ★ **FENCES:** 12

RUPPERT STADIUM
AKA: Davids' Stadium 1926-31, Bears Stadium 1932-33, Davids' Folly ★ **OCCUPANTS:** NNL Newark Eagles 1936-48; NAL Newark Indians 1959 ★ **LOCATION:** Left Field (SE), Third Base (NE) Hamburg Place (later 262 Wilson Ave.), First Base (NW) Ave. K, Right Field (SW); on the eastern edge of Newark, in lowlands bordering the Passaic River ★ **DIMENSIONS:** Foul Lines 305 (1936), Center Field 410 (1936) ★ **FORMER USE:** Wiedenmeyer's Park 1902-14 ★ **CURRENT USE:** Industrial park ★ **CAPACITY:** 12,000 (listed), 19,000 (actual)

NEWBURGH, OHIO

BEYERLE'S PARK
OCCUPANT: Neutral site use by AA Cleveland Spiders September 2, 1888 ★ **LOCATION:** Cleveland and Canton Rd., just outside the city limits of Cleveland

NEW HAVEN, CONNECTICUT

BREWSTER RACE TRACK
AKA: Howard Ave. Grounds, Hamilton Park, Brewster Park ★ **OCCUPANTS:** NA New Haven Elm Citys April 21 to October 28, 1875; neutral site use by NL Hartford Dark Blues September 22, 1877 ★ **LOCATION:** (N) Whalley Ave., (W) West Park Ave., then West River, (S) Elm St., (E) Pendleton St.; also Howard Ave.

NEW ORLEANS, LOUISIANA

PELICAN STADIUM
AKA: Heinemann Park ★ **OCCUPANTS:** NAL New Orleans-St. Louis Stars (half of their games) 1941; NAL New Orleans Eagles 1951; neutral site use for Negro World Series NNL Washington-Homestead Grays vs. NAL Birmingham Black Barons Game 2 in 1944 ★ **LOCATION:** Left Field (NE) Tulane Ave., Third Base (NW) South Carrollton St., First Base (SW) Gravier St., Right Field (SE) Pierce St. ★ **DIMENSIONS:** Left Field 427, Center Field 405, Right Field 418 ★ **CURRENT USE:** Fountain Bay Motor Hotel

STARS FIELD
AKA: Bears Field 1957 ★ **OCCUPANTS:** NAL New Orleans Bears 1957; NAL Detroit-New Orleans Stars (half of the home games) 1960

NEW YORK, NEW YORK (see also Brooklyn)

POLO GROUNDS (I) SOUTHEAST DIAMOND
AKA: Polo Field East ★ **OCCUPANTS:** NL New York Gothams May 1, 1883 to October 13, 1888; AA New York Mets May 12-29, 1883; AA New York Mets May 31 to September 6, 1883 undetermined number of games because they preferred playing here to playing at the Southwest Diamond; AA New York Mets July 17-22, 1883; AA New York Mets July 26 to August 23, 1884 only when NL Gothams did not have a home game here that day (August 11 and 12); AA New York Mets September 24 to October 15, 1884; AA New York Mets April 24 to October 1, 1885 (when NL Gothams also had a home game that day the Mets would play earlier in the day); World Series NL Detroit Wolverines vs. AA St. Louis Browns October 15, 1887 ★ **LOCATION:** Left Field (W) Southwest Diamond, then Sixth (later Lenox) Ave., Third Base (S) West 110th St., First Base (E) Fifth Ave., Right Field (N) West 112th St.; just north of Central Park at Douglas Circle ★ **DIMENSIONS:** Foul Lines, no fences but 180 to small flags marking the foul lines ★ **FENCES:** none at first when it was the only diamond May 1-7, 1883; none for the first day when games were played at both Southeast and Southwest Diamonds on May 30, 1883; but beginning May 31 there was a short fence in front of the right-field bleachers, and a 10-foot-high canvas barrier between the two outfields (balls rolling under the canvas fence were in play, so outfielders crawled under the fence and then threw the ball over the fence back to the infield) ★ **FORMER USE:** Polo field, owned by James Gordon Bennett, publisher of the *New York Herald*, and used by the Westchester Polo Association ★ **CURRENT USE:** PS 170 ★ **CAPACITY:** 12,000
PHENOMENA: Opened for baseball use September 29, 1880. There was a large flagpole in short center field, with a flag saying "NEW YORK." There were two diamonds here. The NL Gothams and AA Mets both used the Southeast Diamond, until the Southwest Diamond was completed on May 30, 1883. However, the Southwest Diamond was so bad that the Mets always preferred playing on the Southeast Diamond, and would do so whenever they could, sometimes even playing their game there before a Gothams game just so they could avoid playing on the Southwest Diamond. Baseball ended when the city built 111th St. through center and right fields in the fall of 1888. The ballpark burned down in the spring of 1889.

POLO GROUNDS (II) SOUTHWEST DIAMOND
AKA: Polo Field West, Metropolitan Field ★ **OCCUPANT:** AA New York Mets May 30 to September 6, 1883 ★ **LOCATION:** Left Field (N) West 112th St., Third Base (W) Sixth (later Lenox) Ave., First Base (S) West 110th St., Right Field (E) Southeast Diamond, then Fifth Ave.
PHENOMENA: Raw garbage was used as landfill in making the infield, so the players hated this diamond. The Mets would play at Polo Grounds (I) Southeast Diamond whenever they could avoid playing here.

METROPOLITAN PARK
OCCUPANT: AA New York Mets May 13 to June 18, 1884; AA New York Mets July 26 to August 23, 1884 only when the NL Gothams had a home game that day at Polo Grounds Southeast Diamond (July 26 and 28, August 7 [rained out] 8, 19-23) ★ **LOCATION:** (N) West 109th St., (W) First Ave., (S) West 107th St., (E) East River
PHENOMENA: As had been the case with Polo Grounds (II) Southwest Diamond, raw garbage was used as landfill to make the infield here, so players also hated this diamond, and the Mets would again play at Polo Grounds (I) Southeast Diamond whenever they could avoid playing here. Mets' pitcher Jack Lynch said you could get malaria by just fielding a ground ball here.

ST. GEORGE CRICKET GROUNDS
AKA: Mutrie's Dump, Mutrie's Dumping Grounds ★ **OCCUPANTS:** AA New York Mets April 22, 1886 to October 7, 1887; NL New York Giants April 29 to June 14, 1889 ★ **LOCATION:** Left Field (E) Upper Bay, Third Base (N) Kill van Kull and Bedloe's (later Liberty) Island with the Statue of Liberty on it, First Base (W), Right Field (S); at St. George on Staten Island, just up the shoreline from the Staten Island Ferry dock ★ **FENCES:** none ★ **CURRENT USE:** Richmond County Bank Ballpark at St. George, home of the NY-Penn League Staten Island Yankees
PHENOMENA: First used for baseball in 1853 in a game between the Washington Club (also known as the Gotham Club) and the New York Knickerbockers. Illuminated geysers here, almost a full century before they reappeared at Kansas City's Royals Stadium. The field sloped sharply down from third base towards left field. Your ticket included free admission to the Staten Island Ferry boat ride to and from Manhattan. While watching Mets' games in 1886, fans along the first base line could watch the Statue of Liberty being erected out in the harbor behind third base.

WILD WEST GROUNDS
OCCUPANT: AA New York Mets some games in 1887 when St. George Cricket Grounds was flooded or booked with other events ★ **LOCATION:** Tomkinsville on Staten Island

POLO GROUNDS (III)
AKA: Manhattan Field, New Polo Grounds (I) 1889-90 ★ **OCCUPANTS:** NL New York Giants July 8, 1889 to September 13, 1890; AA Brooklyn Gladiators July 23 to August 3, 1890 ★ **LOCATION:** Left Field (N) West 157th St., Third Base (W) Harlem River Speedway, Coogan's Bluff, First Base (S) West 155th St., Right Field (E) 8th Ave., Harlem River; on the southern part of Coogan's Hollow ★ **CAPACITY:** 15,000
PHENOMENA: Steepest and largest embankment ever in a major league park, in

center and right fields, dwarfing even the Dodgers spring training embankment at Holman Stadium in Vero Beach. On September 14, 1889, Cap Anson got an inside-the-park homer when Giants' center fielder George Gore could not climb the muddy embankment. Separated only by a canvas fence in 1890, the NL Giants in this park and the PL Giants in Polo Grounds (IV) frequently had games underway at the same time. On May 12, 1890, Mike Tiernan hit a 13th-inning home run that fans in both parks cheered. Accounts differ as to whether Tiernan's home run landed in the outfield of the other ballpark, or whether it landed in a narrow alleyway between the two ballparks and bounced up against the other park's outfield canvas fence. If the latter, then there would have been two canvas fences separating the two ballparks.

POLO GROUNDS (IV)
AKA: Brotherhood Park 1890, New Polo Grounds (II) 1891 ★ **OCCUPANT:** PL New York Giants April 19 to September 18, 1890; NL New York Giants April 22, 1891 to April 13, 1911 ★ **LOCATION:** Center Field (SE) Eighth Ave., then IRT elevated tracks, Harlem River Drive and Harlem River; Third Base (NE) West 159th St., then IRT Railyards; Home Plate (NW) Bridge Park, then Harlem River Speedway, Coogan's Bluff, Croton Aqueduct; First Base (SW) West 157th St.; on the northern part of Coogan's Hollow, 115 feet below Coogan's Bluff; just N of Polo Grounds (III)
★ **DIMENSIONS:** Left Field 335 (April 1890), 277 (July 1890); Center Field 500 (1890), 433 (1909); Right Field 335 (April 1890), 258 (July 1890); note that the foul-pole distances in July 1890 are the exact same distances as left field at Polo Grounds (VI) when it opened (277 feet), and as right field at Polo Grounds (VI) when it closed (258 feet) ★ **FENCES:** Foul Lines 4; Bullpens 25 sloping down to 15, Power Alleys 15 sloping down to 5, Center Field 3 (rope strung between posts) ★ **FORMER USE:** Farm granted to John Lion Gardiner by King of England in 17th Century, big mystery here is that other sources indicate that Yankee Stadium also sits on land given to Mr. Gardiner—could he possibly have owned both? ★ **CAPACITY:** 16,000 (1891), 30,000 (1911)
PHENOMENA: One of the only two places where a ball could be a home run, but another ball hit higher and farther to almost the exact same point was in play; the other was League Park (IV) in Cleveland. The stands here curved about ten feet into fair territory down the left-field line, but only the corner of the stands protruded into fair territory. Behind these seats were the bullpens, which were in play. There was a sharp incline in the bullpens in front of the left field wall. One day in April 1901, Tad Dorgan, a NY *Journal* sports cartoonist, couldn't remember how to spell the word "dachshund" in describing the "red hot dachshund sausages" here, so he invented the term "hot dogs." Police estimated that 250,000 people showed up to see the Giants lose to the Cubs in the pennant playoff game October 8, 1908 necessitated by the Cubs' successful protest of the September 23, 1908 "Merkle's Boner" game, when Fred Merkle neglected to touch second base on what should have been Al Bridwell's game-winning single. Forty thousand people watched the game from Coogan's Bluff because they could not get into the ballpark. Destroyed by fire April 14-15, 1911. Only the outfield bleachers were not destroyed.

LONG ISLAND GROUNDS
AKA: Maspeth Ball Grounds, Long Island Recreation Grounds ★ **OCCUPANT:** AA Brooklyn Gladiators Sundays on July 27 and August 3, 1890 ★ **LOCATION:** Maspeth Ave., back then in the unincorporated hamlet of Maspeth which was part of Newtown on Long Island; today this is the Maspeth section of Queens.

HILLTOP PARK
AKA: Highlanders Park, American League Ballpk, the Rockpile, the Hilltop ★ **OCCUPANTS:** AL New York Yankees April 30, 1903 to October 5, 1912; NL New York Giants April 15 to May 30, 1911 ★ **LOCATION:** Left Field (N) West 168th St.; Third Base (W) Fort Washington Ave., then Hudson River; (SW) Deaf and Dumb Asylum; First Base (S) West 165th St.; Right Field (E) Broadway; on a rockpile overlooking Washington Heights, near West Side Subway ★ **DIMENSIONS:** Left Field 365; Left Center 402; Deepest Center Field 542; Center Field 432 (April 30, 1903), 390 (June 1, 1903), 395 (1904), 370 (1911); Deepest Right Center 542 (April 30, 1911), 390 (June 1, 1911), 412 (1904), 405 (1911); Right Center 492 (April 30, 1903), 346 (June 1, 1903), 412 (1904), 372 (1911); Right Field 365 (April 30, 1903), 300 (June 1, 1903), 365 (1904) ★ **FENCES:** Left Field 12 (1903), sloping from 12 to 16 (1908); Center Field 12 (1903), sloping from 12 to 20 (1904); 3 (1911); Right Field 12 (April 1903), 3 (June 1, 1903), 12 (1904) ★ **CURRENT USE:** Columbia-Presbyterian Hospital, built in the 1920s ★ **CAPACITY:** 15,000
PHENOMENA: Excellent view of Hudson River and New Jersey Palisades from upper seats behind the plate. Scoreboard in left. Large exit gate in right. Bull Durham sign shaped like a bull in right center in 1909, twice the height of the rest of the fence. Memorial dedicated at site of home plate in 1993 with cooperation of SABR, the Yankees, and Columbia Presbyterian Hospital; is located in Medical Center Garden, near Fort Washington Ave. entrance, next to Harkness Pavilion.

POLO GROUNDS (V)
AKA: Brush Stadium 1912-19, Coogan's Bluff, Coogan's Hollow, Matty Schwab's House, Harlem Meadow ★ **OCCUPANTS:** NL New York Giants June 28, 1911 to September 29, 1957; AL New York Yankees May 30, 1912; April 17, 1913 to October 7, 1922; NNL New York Cubans 1948; NAL New York Cubans 1949-50; NL New York Mets April 13, 1962 to September 18, 1963; neutral use for Negro World Series NNL Newark Eagles vs. NAL Kansas City Monarchs First game 1946 ★ **LOCATION:** same as Polo Grounds (IV) ★ **DIMENSIONS:** Left Field 277 (1912), 286.67 (1921), 279.67 (1923), 279 (1930), 280 (1943), 279 (1955); Left Field second deck 250; Left Center left of bullpen 447; Left Center right of Bullpen 455; Clubhouse front steps 460; Center Field 433 (1912), 483 (1923), 484.75 (1927), 505 (1930), 430 (1931), 480 (1934), 430 (1938), 505 (1940), 490 (1943), 505 (1944), 480 (1945), 490 (1946), 484 (1947), 505 (1949), 483 (1952), 480 (1953),

483 (1954), 480 (1955), 475 (1962), 483 (1963); Bleacher corners 425 when Center Field was 475, and 432 when Center Field was 483; Right Center left of bullpen 449; Right Center right of bullpen 440; Right Field 256.25 (1921), 257.67 (1923), 257.5 (1931), 257.67 (1942), 259 (1943), 257.67 (1944); Right Field photographers' perch 249; Backstop 65 (1942), 70 (1943), 65 (1944), 70 (1946), 74 (1949), 65 (1954), 74 (1955), 65 (1962); Foul Territory very large. Confusion reigns concerning the CF distance, and why it changed so frequently. Ron Selter's extensive research indicates that when CF was listed as 483, it was 431 feet to dead center where the center field clubhouse alcove began, and another 52 feet back to the clubhouse wall, or 483 feet to the clubhouse wall. Similarly, when CF was listed as 475, it was 423 feet to dead center where the alcove began, and 52 feet to the clubhouse wall, or 475 feet to the clubhouse wall. This would correspond with the distances of 430 to CF during 1931-33, when there were bleachers in the alcove, and during 1938-39, when there was a low fence across the alcove. One could extrapolate that when CF was listed as 505, it was 453 feet to dead center where the center field clubhouse alcove began, and 52 feet back to the clubhouse wall, which would be 505 feet to the clubhouse wall. My discussions with the ground crew reveal that the plate was definitely moved forward and backward from season to season, which would explain why the CF distance changed so frequently. Because of the unique configuration of the park, when home plate was moved forward or backward, distances to the foul poles would not change but the CF distance would change. Home-plate movements would also explain the fact that in 1934, when CF was 480, photos show that the RF foul-line seats were far from the foul line, whereas photos in 1942, when CF was 505, show that in the exact same place the RF foul line seats were right up against the foul line. During the Giants era, reading from left to right, the markers read 315, 360, 414, 447, 455, 483, 455, 449, 395, 338, 294. In the Mets years, they read 306, 405, 475, 405, 281. The foul lines were never marked. The 21-foot overhang of the second deck in left reduced the distance to the second deck from 279 to 250, not 258, because of the angle involved ★ **FENCES:** 1912-22: Left to Center 10 (concrete); Center 20 (tarp); Right Center 10 (concrete); Right Field 12 sloping down to 11 at pole (concrete); 1923-63: Left Field 16.81 (concrete); Left Center 18 (concrete); Left Center wall where it ended at bleachers 12 (concrete); Center Field bleachers wall 8.5 (4.25 wire on top of 4.25 concrete) on both sides of clubhouse runway; Center Field low wall in front of clubhouse alcove 3 (1931-33 and 1938-39); Center Field hitters background 16.5 on both sides of clubhouse runway; Center Field clubhouse 60 high and 60 wide, 50 high in 1963; Center Field top of Longines Clock 80; Center Field top of right side of scoreboard 71; Center Field top of left side of scoreboard 68; Center Field top of middle of scoreboard 64; Center Field top of 5 right scoreboard windows 57; Center Field top of 4 left scoreboard windows 55; Center Field bottom of 5 right scoreboard windows 53; Center Field bottom of 4 left scoreboard windows 48; Center Field bottom of clubhouse scoreboard 31; Center Field top of rear clubhouse wall 28; Center Field top of front clubhouse wall 19; Center Field top of 14 lower clubhouse windows 16; Center Field bottom of 14 lower clubhouse windows 11; Center Field clubhouse floor overhang 8; Center Field top of Eddie Grant Memorial 5; Center Field width of little office on top of lower clubhouse 10; Right Center 12 (concrete); Right Field 10.64 (concrete) ★ **FORMER USE:** Underneath the Harlem River, until filled in with dirt in the late 1870s. Field was raised 4.5 feet in 1949 to help with drainage. In 1874 maps, the location is shown as underneath the Harlem River. The water table was only 2-6 feet below the playing surface, and drainage was complicated by rainwater cascading off the 115-foot-high Coogan's Bluff onto the site. ★ **CURRENT USE:** Polo Grounds Towers, four 30-story apartment buildings. Willie Mays Field, an asphalt playground with six basketball backboards where center field used to be; brass historical marker. ★ **CAPACITY:** 16,000 (June 28, 1911); 30,000 (August 11, 1911), 34,000 (October 14, 1911), 39,000 (1917), 38,000 (1919), 43,000 (1923), 55,000 (1926), 56,000 (1930), 51,856 (1937), 56,000 (1940), 54,500 (1947), 56,000 (1953), 55,137 (1957), 55,000 (1962)
PHENOMENA: After the all-wooden Polo Grounds (IV) burned down April 14-15, 1911, Polo Grounds (V) was built with temporary stands for the rest of the 1911 season. The concrete double deck was not finished until 1922. This park is frequently viewed as a hitters' ballpark, but it was really a home-run ballpark. The Giants and other teams averaged .020 points less in batting average than elsewhere. Ron Selter has estimated that it was 417 feet (not 450+, as usually claimed) to where Willie Mays made "The Catch" against the Indians in the 1954 World Series; John Pastier and Bill Deane independently came to similar conclusions. There was no line on the 60-foot-high center-field clubhouse above which a ball would be a home run. There is no documentation of a ball ever hitting the clubhouse wall on the fly, much less over it. The mystery remains—what if someone *had* managed to hit one 505 feet to dead center, and 80 feet high off the Longines clock, or even 60 feet high off the top of the clubhouse wall? It definitely would have been the longest home run ever hit anywhere, anytime, probably traveling more than 700 feet were it not for the obstruction provided by the clubhouse. But it would have bounced back into center field. Would it have been a home run? Everyone would assume so, but actually nobody in the world knows, because the Polo Grounds had no ground rule to decide if a ball hitting the clubhouse wall, or the clock above the clubhouse wall, would have been in play or a home run. Only four home runs were ever hit into the bleachers in center: by Luke Easter in a Negro League game in 1948 and Joe Adcock of the Braves on April 29, 1953, and then amazingly two were hit on successive days—by Lou Brock on June 17, 1962 and Henry Aaron the next day.

DYCKMAN OVAL
OCCUPANTS: NNL Havana Cuban Stars 1920; NNL New York Cuban Stars 1922; ECL New York Cuban Stars East 1923-27, April to May 1928; ANL New York Cuban Stars East 1929; NEWL Cuban Stars 1932; NNL Cubans 1935-36 ★ **LOCATION:** Left Field (NE) West 204th St., then Henry Hudson Bridge crossing Spuyten Duyvil Creek; Third Base (NW) Nagle Ave; First Base (SW) Academy St.; Right Field (SE)

Tenth Ave., in upper Manhattan, 8 blocks E of Henry Hudson Parkway, 5 blocks E of Inwood Hill Park, S of Harlem Ship Canal, 4 blocks N of Dyckman St., in the Dyckman neighborhood ★ **CURRENT USE:** Dyckman Houses apartment buildings, along with three ball diamonds ★ **CAPACITY:** 4,500

PHENOMENA: Lights installed in April 1930 by Cuban Stars owner Alex Pompez. Still unknown whether this park or Dexter Park in Brooklyn was the first major league park in the New York area to have lights for evening games. Famous fans included Cab Calloway, Louis Armstrong, Count Basie. The Negro Leagues' nicest ballpark. Torn down in late 1930s, after Pompez lost his lease for the park during legal troubles with his numbers-racket business in 1935-37 and spent part of 1937 in a Mexico City jail, as a result of DA Thomas Dewey's campaign against Tammany Hall corruption.

CATHOLIC PROTECTORY OVAL
AKA: Capital Texture, Catholic Protection, Society for the Protection of Destitute Roman Catholic Children ★ **OCCUPANT:** NNL New York Cuban Stars West 1923-30 ★ **LOCATION:** Left Field (E) Hoguet Ave; Third Base (N) East Tremont Ave; First Base (W) White Plains Rd.; Right Field (S) McGraw Ave; also Jerome Ave., 156th St., in the Parkchester section of the East Bronx, 5 miles NE of Yankee Stadium ★ **CURRENT USE:** Parkchester Apartments, housing 45,000 people, built by Metropolitan Life Insurance in 1938; Unionport Rd. now crosses the site from home plate to center field; Metropolitan Ave. now runs from right field in to second base and then curves out to left field. ★ **CAPACITY:** 3,500 (1923)

PHENOMENA: Very tiny ballfield, with shade trees surrounding the entire field. It was said the fences were so close to the plate that the only person who could hit a triple was Cool Papa Bell. The Protectory was a Catholic home and school for impoverished boys, whose 50-piece marching band was much in demand and played before each game. One of their students was Hank Greenberg (!). No grass in the infield.

OLYMPIC FIELD
OCCUPANTS: ECL New York Lincoln Giants 1923-26, April to May 1928; ANL New York Lincoln Giants 1929 ★ **LOCATION:** (N) West 138th St., (W) 5th Ave., (S) West 135th St., (E) Madison Ave; in central Harlem ★ **CURRENT USE:** Riverton Houses (14-story apartments) built in 1947.

PHENOMENA: After the game, Lincoln Giants pitcher/manager Smokey Joe Williams would go to his "other" job, bartending nearby at Lenox Ave. and 134th St.

YANKEE STADIUM
AKA: The House That Ruth Built ★ **OCCUPANTS:** AL New York Yankees April 18, 1923 to September 30, 1973; NNL New York Black Yankees some games 1940s; neutral site use for Negro World Series NNL Washington-Homestead Grays vs. NAL Kansas City Monarchs Third game 1942, for NNL New York Cubans vs. NAL Cleveland Buckeyes Game 1, 1947; AL New York Yankees April 15, 1976 to date ★ **LOCATION:** Left Field (NE) East 161st St.; Third Base (NW) Doughty St. (later Ruppert Place); Home Plate (W) Major Deegan Expressway/I-87, then Harlem River; First Base (SW) East 157th St.; Right Field (SE) River Ave., then IRT elevated tracks; in the southwest Bronx ★ **DIMENSIONS:** Left Field 280.58 (1923), 301 (1928), 312 (1976), 318 (1988); Left Center left side of bullpen gate in short 395 (1923), 402 (1928); right side of bullpen gate 415 (1937); Left Center 387 (1976), 379 (1985); Deepest Left Center 500 (1923), 490 (1924), 457 (1937), 430 (1976), 411 (1985), 399 (1988); Center Field left side of screen 466 (1937); Center Field 487 (1923), 461 (1937), 463 (1967), 417 (1976), 410 (1985), 408 (1988); Deepest Right Center: 429 (1923), 407 (1937), 385 (1976); Right Center 353 (1976); Short Right Center left side of bullpen gate in 350 (1923), 367 (1937); right side of bullpen gate 344 (1937); Right Field 294.75 (1923), 295 (1930), 296 (1939), 310 (1976), 314 (1988); Backstop 82 (1942), 80 (1953), 84 (1976); Foul Territory large for catcher behind home plate, but small for fielders down the foul lines ★ **FENCES:** Left Field Foul Line 3.92 (3 wire above 0.92 concrete 1923), 8 (canvas 1976); Left Center left of visitors' bullpen 3.58 (3 wire above 0.58 concrete 1923); Right of Visitors' Bullpen 7.83 (3 wire above 4.83 concrete 1923), Left Center to Right Center 7 (canvas 1976); Center Field left side of screen when up for hitters' background 20 (1953), 22.25 (1959), 22.42 (1954); screen when background was down 13.83 (1953), 7 (canvas 1976); Right Center right side of screen 14.5 (3 wire above 11.5 concrete 1923); left of home bullpen 7.83 (3 wire above 4.83 concrete 1923); right side of home bullpen 3.58 (3 wire above 0.58 concrete 1923); Right Center 8 (canvas 1976), 9 (canvas 1979); Right Field Foul Line 3.75 (3 wire above 0.75 concrete 1923), 10 (canvas 1976) ★ **SURFACE:** Merion Bluegrass ★ **FORMER USE:** City plot 2106, lot 100, farm granted to John Lion Gardiner before the Revolutionary War ★ **CAPACITY:** 58,000 (1923), 62,000 (1926), 82,000 (1927), 67,113 (1928), 62,000 (1929), 71,699 (1937), 70,000 (1942), 67,000 (1948), 65,010 (1971), 54,028 (1976), 57,145 (1977), 57,478 (2003)

PHENOMENA: Fans arrive by C, D and #4 trains; subway tracks just behind the bleachers in right center. Before the 1974-75 renovations, the left-center monuments were in play—Lou Gehrig's on left, Miller Huggins' in middle, Babe Ruth's on right. Now the monuments are beyond the fence (Mickey Mantle's was added in 1996). A ball hitting the foul pole in the 1930s was ruled to be in play, not a homer. Until Rule 48 was changed by major league baseball in December 1930, with the exception of several months in 1920, balls leaving the field fair but which hooked or sliced foul before they landed were foul. This undoubtedly prevented some extra homers by Babe Ruth. Death Valley in left center has become progressively less deadly—from 500 in 1923, to 490 in 1924, to 457 in 1937, to 430 in 1976, to 411 in 1985, and finally to 399 in 1988. What most baseball executives have lost complete sight of is the fact that the most exciting play in baseball is not the home run but the triple. The Yankees played their April 15, 1998 home game at Shea after a 500-pound steel joint in the upper deck fell off.

BRONX OVAL
OCCUPANT: Neutral site use by ECL Atlantic City Bacharach Giants 1920s

LEWISOHN STADIUM
OCCUPANT: Neutral site use by ECL Atlantic City Bacharach Giants 1920s ★ **LOCATION:** Across the street from Hebrew Orphan Asylum Oval, on Amsterdam Ave. ★ **CAPACITY:** 16,000

RECREATION PARK (III)
OCCUPANT: NNL New York Cubans Monday nights in 1935 ★ **LOCATION:** Left Field 10th St., Third Base Bridge Plaza North and Queensboro/59th St. Bridge, First Base 21st St., Right Field 41st Ave., in the Long Island City area of Queens, on the east side of the Queensboro/59th St. Bridge ★ **CURRENT USE:** Queensbridge Houses, 24 six-story apartment buildings ★ **CAPACITY:** 3,000 (1927), 11,000 (1938)

HEBREW ORPHAN ASYLUM OVAL
AKA: Jasper Oval, Asylum Oval, CCNY Playground ★ **OCCUPANT:** NNL New York Black Yankees July to September 1936 ★ **LOCATION:** (N) West 138th St. and City College of New York (CCNY), (W) Convent Ave., (S) West 136th St., (E) St. Nicholas Terrace and St. Nicholas Park ★ **CURRENT USE:** CCNY Indoor Athletic Complex and paved playground for Schiff School (formerly known as PS 192)

TRIBOROUGH STADIUM
AKA: Randall's Island Stadium, JJ Downing Memorial Stadium ★ **OCCUPANT:** NNL New York Black Yankees 1937-38 ★ **LOCATION:** (N) Bronx Kills and Harlem River, Eastern Parkwy and Triborough Bridge; (W) House of Refuge, Vesta Ave; (S) Little Hell Gate, East River, and Ward's Island, Sutter Ave; (E) Sunken Meadow, Powell St., Triborough Bridge

59TH STREET BRIDGE
OCCUPANT: NNL New York Cubans 1939 ★ **LOCATION:** (N) East 60th St., (W) First Ave., (S) East 59th St., (SE) Sutton Place, (E) Queensboro/59th St. Bridge foundations and East River, overhead were the approach ramps to the bridge, in Manhattan, on the west side of the Queensboro/59th St. Bridge; on the other side of the bridge from Recreation Park (III), where Negro League games were also played

QUEENS PARK
OCCUPANT: NNL New York Cubans 1940 ★ **LOCATION:** Left Field (W) 30th Ave., Third Base (S) 58th St., First Base (E) 3First Ave., Right Field (N) 61st St.; in the Woodside area of Queens ★ **CAPACITY:** 2,500

SHEA STADIUM
AKA: Flushing Meadow Stadium 1964 ★ **OCCUPANTS:** NL New York Mets April 17, 1964 to date; AL New York Yankees April 6, 1974 to September 28, 1975; April 15, 1998 ★ **LOCATION:** Center Field (NE/E) 126th St.; Third Base (NW/N) Northern Blvd, then Whitestone Expressway/I-678, then Flushing Bay; Home Plate (SW/W) Grand Central Parkway; First Base (SE/S) 123-01 Roosevelt Ave; in Queens, near Flushing Meadow Park, site of 1939 and 1964 World's Fairs, SE of La Guardia Airport ★ **DIMENSIONS:** Foul Lines 330 (marked 1964), 341 (actual 1964), 341 (1965), 338 (1979); Power Alleys 371 (1964), 378 (2001); Center Field 410 (1964); Backstop 80 (1964), 48 (2003); Foul Territory very large ★ **FENCES:** Foul Lines 16.33 (4 wire and railing above 12.33 brick 1964), 12.33 (brick 1965), 8 (wood 1979); Power Alleys 8 (wood); Center Field small section 8.75 (wood), most 8 (wood) ★ **CAPACITY:** 55,000 (1964), 56,000 (1968), 56,521 (2001), 57,393 (2003)

PHENOMENA: Noisiest open-air ballpark in the majors by far, due to frequent La Guardia Airport aircraft noise overhead. Foul lines 1965-78 had an orange home run line painted at the top of the 12'4" brick wall. Above this was a four-foot wire screen and railing. A ball was a homer if it hit above the line. Like a similar ground rule in Crosley Field's center field, this caused so many controversies that in 1979 an inner eight-foot wooden fence was installed. Worst visibility for hitters in the majors. Christened April 16, 1964 with Dodger Holy Water from the Gowanus Canal in Brooklyn and Giant Holy Water from the Harlem River at the exact location where it passed the old Polo Grounds.

OAKLAND, CALIFORNIA
NETWORK ASSOCIATES COLISEUM
AKA: Oakland-Alameda County Coliseum April 1968 to September 1997; UMAX Coliseum September 1997 to June 1998; Oakland-Alameda County Coliseum June to September 1998; Oakland Mausoleum, the Net ★ **OCCUPANT:** AL Oakland Athletics April 17, 1968 to date ★ **LOCATION:** Center Field (NE/N) San Leandro St., then Southern Pacific RR tracks; Third Base (NW/W) 66th Ave; Home Plate (SW/S) Oakland-Alameda County Coliseum Arena (also called the Jewel Box), then Nimitz Frwy/I-880 and San Leandro Bay; First Base (SE/E) 77th Ave. (later Hegenberger Drive) ★ **DIMENSIONS:** Foul Lines 330; between Foul Lines and Power Alleys 367 (1996); Power Alleys 378 (1968), 375 (1969), 372 (1981), 362 (1996); Deep Power Alleys 388 (1996); Center Field 410 (1968), 400 (1969), 396 (1981), 397 (1982), 400 (1990); Backstop 90 (1968), 60 (1969); Foul Territory huge, largest by far in the majors ★ **FENCES:** Foul Lines 8 (plywood 1968), 10 (canvas over plywood and Plexiglas 1981), 8 (1986), Power Alleys and Center Field 8 (plywood 1968), 10 (canvas over plywood and Plexiglas 1981), 8 (1986), 18 (1996), 15 (2003) ★ **CAPACITY:** 50,000 (1968), 48,219 (1990), 42,219 (1996), 45,177 (1997), 43,662 (2001)

PHENOMENA: Referred to as the Mausoleum in the late 1970s when the scoreboard didn't work, the entire concrete stadium was depressingly gray in color, and the A's were terrible. Huge foul area reduces batting by five to seven points, making

this the best pitchers' park in the AL. Huge ugly center-field addition built for the NFL Raiders November 1995 to September 1996 is called Mount Davis.

PATERSON, NEW JERSEY

HINCHCLIFFE STADIUM
OCCUPANT: NNL New York Black Yankees 1939-48 ★ **LOCATION:** Center Field (SE) Passaic River; Third Base (NE) Redwood Ave.; Home Plate (NW) Liberty St.; First Base (SW) Maple St.; also Walnut St., Spruce St. ★ **CURRENT USE:** Community baseball park

PENDLETON, OHIO

PENDLETON PARK
AKA: East End Park, East End Grounds, Cincinnati Gym Grounds ★ **OCCUPANT:** AA Cincinnati Porkers April 25 to August 13, 1891 ★ **LOCATION:** (W) Ridgley St.; (S) Ohio River, (E) Watson St., then Tacoma Park; in the eastern suburbs of Cincinnati ★ **DIMENSIONS:** Right Field 400 ★ **CURRENT USE:** Cincinnati Gym Grounds

PETERSBURG, VIRGINIA

PETERSBURG BALLFIELD
OCCUPANT: Neutral site use by AA Richmond Virginias October 7, 1884

PHILADELPHIA, PENNSYLVANIA

JEFFERSON STREET GROUNDS (I)
AKA: Athletic Baseball Grounds (I) ★ **OCCUPANTS:** NA Philadelphia Athletics May 15, 1871 to October 28, 1875; NA Philadelphia White Stockings May 1, 1873 to October 25, 1875; NL Philadelphia Athletics April 22 to September 16, 1876 ★ **LOCATION:** (N) Jefferson Ave., (W) 27th St., (S) Master St., (E) 25th St. ★ **CAPACITY:** 3,000

CENTENNIAL PARK
OCCUPANT: NA Philadelphia Centennials April 21 to May 24, 1875

OAKDALE PARK
OCCUPANT: AA Philadelphia Athletics May 2 to September 21, 1882 ★ **LOCATION:** Huntingdon St., 11th St.

JEFFERSON STREET GROUNDS (II)
AKA: Athletic Baseball Grounds (II) ★ **OCCUPANT:** AA Philadelphia Athletics May 10, 1883 to October 11, 1890 ★ **LOCATION:** same as Jefferson St. Grounds (I) ★ **DIMENSIONS:** Center Field 500 ★ **FENCES:** 9 ★ **CAPACITY:** 3,000

RECREATION PARK
OCCUPANT: NL Philadelphia Quakers May 1, 1883 to October 9, 1886 ★ **LOCATION:** (NE) Ridge Ave., (N) Montgomery St., (W) 25th St., (S) Columbia Ave., (E) 24th St. ★ **DIMENSIONS:** Left Field 300, Right Field 247, Backstop 79 ★ **CAPACITY:** 2,000

KEYSTONE PARK
OCCUPANT: UA Philadelphia Keystones April 17 to August 7, 1884 ★ **LOCATION:** (N) Moore St., (E) Broad St., also Wharton St., 11th St.

HUNTINGDON GROUNDS (I)
AKA: Philadelphia Baseball Grounds (I) ★ **OCCUPANTS:** NL Philadelphia Phillies April 30, 1887 to August 6, 1894; World Series October 17 and 19, 1887 NL Detroit Wolverines vs. AA St. Louis Browns, World Series October 22, 1888 NL New York Gothams vs. AA St. Louis Browns ★ **LOCATION:** same as Huntingdon Grounds (II) and Baker Bowl ★ **DIMENSIONS:** Left Field 500, Right Field 310 ★ **FENCES:** 25 (brick) ★ **CAPACITY:** 12,500 (1887), 15,000 (1894)

UNIVERSITY OF PENNSYLVANIA ATHLETIC FIELD
OCCUPANT: NL Philadelphia Phillies August 11 and 14-17, 1894 ★ **LOCATION:** (W) 39th St., (E) 37th St., also Spruce St., on the Penn campus

HUNTINGDON GROUNDS (II)
AKA: Philadelphia Baseball Grounds (II) ★ **OCCUPANT:** NL Philadelphia Phillies August 18 to September 6, 1894

FOREPAUGH PARK
AKA: Brotherhood Park ★ **OCCUPANT:** PL Quakers April 30 to September 17, 1890; AA Athletics April 8 to October 5, 1891 ★ **LOCATION:** (N) York St., (W) 14th (later Broad) St., (S) Dauphin St., (E) Park Ave. ★ **DIMENSIONS:** Left Field 345, Center Field 450 (1890), 420 (1891), Right Field 380

BAKER BOWL
AKA: Huntingdon Grounds (III) 1895 to July 1913, National League Park (III) 1895-1938, the Hump, Cigar Box, Band Box, Philadelphia Baseball Grounds (III) ★ **OCCUPANTS:** NL Philadelphia Phillies May 2, 1895 to August 8, 1903; April 14, 1904 to May 14, 1927; June 24, 1927 to June 30, 1938; also neutral use by NL Cleveland Spiders July 29-30, August 5-6, 8, and 11, 1898; neutral site use for Negro World Series NNL Kansas City Monarchs vs. ECL Darby Hilldales Games 5 and 6 in 1925 ★ **LOCATION:** Left Field (N) West Lehigh Ave; Third Base (W) North 15th St.; First Base (S) West Huntingdon St.; Right Field (E) North Broad St.; field was

above Philadelphia and Reading RR tracks whose tracks ran through a tunnel beneath center field ★ **DIMENSIONS:** Left Field 335 (1921), 341.5 (1926), 341 (1930), 341.5 (1931); Center Field 408; Right Center 300; Right Field 272 (1921), 279.5 (1924), 280.5 (1925); Backstop 60 ★ **FENCES:** Left Field 4 (1895), 12 July (1929); Left Center Field to Right Center 35 (1895), 47 (with 12 screen on top 1915); Right Field 40 (tin over brick 1895), 60 (40 tin over brick, topped by 20 screen 1915) ★ **CAPACITY:** 18,000 (1895), 20,000 (1929), 18,800 (1930) ★ **CURRENT USE:** Parking lot and car wash in right center, gas station in center, bus garage from home down the right field foul line
PHENOMENA: Named the Hump because it was on an elevated piece of ground with a railroad tunnel underneath the outfield. Swimming pool in basement of the center field clubhouse prior to World War I. Ten rows of seats in right field collapsed May 14, 1927, causing the Phillies to have to play at Shibe Park from May 16-28.

COLUMBIA PARK
OCCUPANT: AL Philadelphia Athletics April 26, 1901 to October 3, 1908; NL Philadelphia Phillies August 20 to September 10, 1903 ★ **LOCATION:** (N/NE) Columbia Ave., (W/NW) 30th St., (S/SW) Oxford St., (E/SE) 29th St. ★ **CURRENT USE:** Kenny's Tires store, pizza shop, houses ★ **CAPACITY:** 9,500 (1901), 13,600 (1905)

SHIBE PARK
AKA: Connie Mack Stadium 1953-70 ★ **OCCUPANTS:** AL Philadelphia Athletics April 12, 1909 to September 19, 1954; NL Philadelphia Phillies May 16-28, 1927; July 4, 1938 to September 27, 1942; NL Philadelphia Blue Jays April 27, 1943 to October 1, 1944; NL Philadelphia Phillies April 20, 1945 to October 1, 1970; neutral site use for Negro World Series NNL Chicago American Giants vs. ECL Atlantic City Bacharach Giants, Games 1, 4 and 5 in 1926; for NNL Washington-Homestead Grays vs. NAL Kansas City Monarchs, Game 5 in 1942; for NNL Washington-Homestead Grays vs. NAL Cleveland Buckeyes, Game 4 in 1945; for NNL New York Cubans vs. NAL Cleveland Buckeyes , Game 3 in 1947 ★ **LOCATION:** Left Field (N) West Somerset St.; Third Base (W) North 2First St.; First Base (S) West Lehigh Ave; Right Field (E) North 20th St. ★ **DIMENSIONS:** Left Field 360 (1909), 378 (late 1909), 380 (1921), 334 (1922), 312 (1926), 334 (1930); Left Center 393 (1909), 387 (1922), 405 (1925), 387 (1969); Center Field 515 (1909), 502 (late 1909), 468 (1922), 448 (1950), 440 (1951), 460 (1953), 468 (1954), 447 (1960), 410 (1969); Right Center 393 (1909), 390 (1969); Right Center left of Scoreboard 400 (1942); Right Field 360 (1909), 340 (late 1909), 380 (1921), 307 (1926), 331 (1931), 331 (to lower 1934), 329 (to upper iron fence 1934); Backstop 90 (1942), 86 (1943), 78 (1956), 64 (1960) ★ **FENCES:** Left Field to Left Center 12 (4 section above 8 concrete 1949); Center Field small section 20 (1955), 8 (wood 1956), 3 (canvas 1969); Right Center Scoreboard 50 (top of black scoreboard 1956), 60 (top of Ballantine Beer sign 1956); Right Field 12 (concrete 1909), 34 (22 corrugated iron above 12 concrete 1935), 30 (1943), 50 (1949), 40 (1953), 30 (1954), 40 (1955), 32 (1956) ★ **FORMER USE:** City dog pound, also brickyard in Swampoodle neighborhood nearby ★ **CURRENT USE:** Deliverance Evangelistic Church, seating 5,100 worshippers. Top of its cross is 108 feet high, and the entrance is at first base. Several hundred of the seats were moved to Duncan Park, former home of the Sally League Phillies in Spartanburg, S.C., and to War Memorial Stadium, Greensboro, N.C. ★ **CAPACITY:** 20,000 (1909), 33,500 (1925), 27,500 (1926), 30,000 (1929), 33,000 (1930), 33,509 (1970)
PHENOMENA: First concrete-and-steel stadium in the majors. French Renaissance church-like dome on exterior roof behind the plate housed Connie Mack's office. Sod transplanted here from Columbia Park. At 20 inches, had the highest pitchers' mound. Batting cage sat behind short fence in center when measurement was only 447. Balls bounced at crazy angles off the fence in right. Dick Allen was the only batter ever to hit a homer over the 60-foot-high Ballantine Beer sign above the scoreboard in right center. Ashburn's Ridge was a specially tailored region along third base to help his bunts stay fair.

CHESSLINE PARK
OCCUPANT: ECL Philadelphia Tigers April to May 1928 ★ **LOCATION:** in the southern part of the city

PASSON FIELD
AKA: 48th and Spruce ★ **OCCUPANTS:** NNL Philadelphia Stars 1934-35; NNL Philadelphia Bacharach Giants 1934 ★ **LOCATION:** 48th St., Spruce St., 49th St., Locust St.

PENMAR PARK
AKA: 44th and Parkside, Bolden Bowl, Pennsy Railroad Park, Pennsy YMCA ★ **OCCUPANTS:** NNL Philadelphia Stars 1936-48; NAL Philadelphia Stars 1949-52 ★ **LOCATION:** 44th St., Parkside Ave., First Base Pennsylvania RR roundhouse ★ **DIMENSIONS:** Left Field 330, Center Field 410, Right Field 310
PHENOMENA: They rarely cut the grass here, so it was pitcher-friendly. Built by Pennsylvania Railroad in the mid-1920s for the company YMCA. Dense coal smoke from the locomotives going in and out of the roundhouse behind first base often interfered with fielders and delayed games. In 1947, Satchel Paige had a perfect game here through eight innings. In the ninth, he gave up three intentional walks, then he told his fielders to lie down, and struck out the side on nine pitches. Amazingly, the ballpark never fell down, despite the fact that Miss Hattie Williams used a hatchet most days to chop some wood from the grandstand. She used it for the wood fire that heated her washtub where she cooked hot dogs for her concession stand behind home plate.

VETERANS STADIUM
AKA: The Vet, Veterans Memorial Stadium ★ **OCCUPANT:** NL Philadelphia Phillies

April 10, 1971 to September 28, 2003 ★ **LOCATION:** Left Field (N/NE) Packer St., then I-76; Third Base (W/NW) Broad St., then Philadelphia Naval Hospital; First Base (S/SW) Pattison Ave., then Spectrum and John F. Kennedy Stadium (later replaced by First Union Center); Right Field (E/SE) Tenth St. ★ **DIMENSIONS:** Foul Lines 330; Power Alleys 371; Center Field 408; Backstop 60; Foul Territory large ★ **FENCES:** 8 (wood 1971); 6 (wood 1972); 12 (6 Plexiglas above 6 wood 1972) ★ **SURFACE:** AstroTurf, 1971-2000, slower since 1977; NeXturf 2001-03 ★ **CAPACITY:** 56,371 (1970), 58,651 (1977), 65,454 (1981), 66,507 (1983), 64,538 (1987), 62,382 (1990), 61,831 (2003)

PHENOMENA: Smallest hot dogs and loudest boos in baseball. Richie Hebner once said, "I stand at the plate in Philadelphia, and I don't honestly know whether I'm in Pittsburgh, Cincinnati, St. Louis, or Philly. They all look alike." This is the best description ever of the disgusting sameness of the concrete-ashtray era of 1960s-1970s ballpark architecture that threatened to destroy the soul of baseball.

CITIZENS BANK PARK

OCCUPANT: NL Philadelphia Phillies April 12, 2004 to date ★ **LOCATION:** Center Field (N) Hartranft St., Third Base (W) 11th St.; Home Plate (S) Pattison Ave; First Base (E) Darien St.; just east of Veterans Stadium, in South Philly ★ **DIMENSIONS:** Left Field 329, Power Alleys 369, Left Field deep corner 385, Left Field inner corner 381; Deepest Left Center 409, Center Field 401, Deepest Right Center 398, Right Field 330; Backstop 49.5 ★ **SURFACE:** Kentucky Bluegrass ★ **FENCES:** Left Field 9.25; Left Center 8 ft; Left Field corner 12.67; Left Field inner corner 13.33; Deepest Left Center 14.25 to 19; Center Field 6; Right Center 6 sloping up to 13.25; Right Center and Right Field 13.33 ★ **CAPACITY:** 43,000

PHENOMENA: Fifty-foot high lanterns outside the park at first, home and third. Fans arrive via Broad St. Subway.

PHOENIX, ARIZONA

BANK ONE BALLPARK

AKA: The Bob ★ **OCCUPANT:** NL Arizona Diamondbacks Mar 31, 1998 to date ★ **LOCATION:** Center Field (N) 401 East Jefferson St., Third Base (W) Fourth St., Home Plate (S) Southern Pacific RR tracks, First Base (E) Seventh St. ★ **DIMENSIONS:** Left Field 330; Power Alleys 374 (1998), 376 (2003); Deepest Corners in Power Alleys 413; Center Field 407; Right Field 334; Backstop 55; Dome Apex 200 (above Second Base), 180 (above outfield walls) ★ **FENCES:** Left and Right Field 7.5, Center Field 25 ★ **SURFACE:** Shade-tolerant DeAnza zoysia grass 1998, Kentucky Bluegrass 1999 to date ★ **CAPACITY:** 48,700 (1998), 49,033 (2001)

PHENOMENA: Dirt path between pitcher's mound and plate was first in four decades. Sun Pool Pavilion features pool and Jacuzzi holding 35 people, 415 feet from home plate, behind fence in right center field. Mark Grace was first batter to "splash" a homer here.

PIQUA, ILLINOIS

PIQUA PARK

OCCUPANT: Neutral-site use for NNL Chicago American Giants game in 1920

PITTSBURGH, PENNSYLVANIA

UNION PARK

OCCUPANT: Neutral site use by NL Indianapolis Blues August 22-24, 1878

EXPOSITION PARK (I) LOWER FIELD

OCCUPANTS: AA Pittsburgh Alleghenys May 10 to September 23, 1882; June 12 to September 6, 1883; UA Pittsburgh Stogies August 25-30, 1884 ★ **LOCATION:** (N) South Ave. (later Shore St.), (W) Grant (later Galveston) Ave., (S) Pennsylvania and Western (later Baltimore and Ohio) RR tracks, then Allegheny River, (E) School (later Scotland) St. (an extension of Bank St.); on the North Side; back then the park was in the city of Allegheny but now the site is in Pittsburgh; same site as Three Rivers Stadium.

EXPOSITION PARK (II) UPPER FIELD

OCCUPANT: AA Pittsburgh Alleghenys May 1 to June 9, 1883 ★ **LOCATION:** same as Three Rivers Stadium

RECREATION PARK

AKA: Colosseum Bike Track 1890s ★ **OCCUPANTS:** AA Pittsburgh Alleghenys May 1, 1884 to October 12, 1886; NL Pittsburgh Alleghenys April 30, 1887 to September 30, 1890; neutral site use for World Series AA St. Louis Browns vs. NL Chicago White Stockings October 22, 1885 and AA St. Louis Browns vs. NL Detroit Wolverines October 13, 1887 ★ **LOCATION:** (NE) Pittsburgh, Fort Wayne, and Chicago RR tracks and railyard, (N) Pennsylvania Ave., (W) Allegheny Ave., (S) North Ave. West, (E) Grant (later Galveston) Ave. ★ **CAPACITY:** 17,000 (1884), 9,000 (1887)

PHENOMENA: Catcher Fred Carroll's pet monkey was buried under home plate with full honors in 1887 pregame ceremony. Record low major league paid attendance of only 6 (with total crowd of only 17), with 8,483 empty seats, on April 23, 1890.

EXPOSITION PARK (III)

OCCUPANTS: PL Pittsburgh Burghers April 19 to October 4, 1890; NL Pittsburgh Pirates April 22, 1891 to June 29, 1909; FL Pittsburgh Rebels April 14, 1914 to October 2, 1915 ★ **LOCATION:** Left Field (S) Pennsylvania and Western (later Baltimore and Ohio) RR tracks, then Allegheny River; Third Base (E) School (later Scotland) St. (an extension of Bank St.); First Base (N) South Ave. (later Shore St.); Right Field (W) Grant (later Galveston) St.; on the North Side; back then the park was in the city of Allegheny but now the site is in Pittsburgh; same site as Three Rivers

Stadium ★ **DIMENSIONS:** Foul Lines 400, Power Alleys 413, Center Field 450 ★ **CAPACITY:** 6,500 (1889); 16,000 (1914)

FORBES FIELD

AKA: Oakland Orchard, Dreyfuss' Folly ★ **OCCUPANTS:** NL Pittsburgh Pirates June 30, 1909 to June 28, 1970; NNL Washington-Homestead Grays, half of the home games 1937-48 ★ **LOCATION:** Left Field (NE) Schenley Park, then Bigelow Blvd; Third Base (NW) 3940 Sennott (often misspelled "Sonnett") St., then Cathedral of Learning; First Base (SW) Boquet (often misspelled "Bouquet") St.; Right Field (SE) Joncaire St., then Pierre Ravine, Junction Hollow, Junction RR tracks ★ **DIMENSIONS:** Left Field 360 (1909), 356.5 (1921), 356 (1922), 360 (1926), 365 (1930), 335 (1947), 365 (1954); Left Center 406 (1942), 355 (1947), 406 (1954); Deepest Left Center corner left of dead center at Flagpole 462 (1909), 457 (1930); Center Field 442 (1926), 435 (1930); Right Center right side of exit gate 416 (1955); Right Center 375 (1942); Right Center left end of screen 375; Right Field 376 (1909), 376.5 (1921), 376 (1922), 300 (1925); Backstop 110 (1909), 84 (1938), 80 (1947), 84 (1953), 75 (1959) ★ **FENCES:** Left Field front fence 8 (5 screen above 3 wood 1947), 12 (9 screen on top of 3 wood 1949), 14 (screen 1950); Left Field wall 12 (1909), 12 (brick and ivy 1946); Left Field Scoreboard 25.42 (steel left and right sides), 27 (middle); Marine Sergeant at parade rest to right of Scoreboard 32 (wood June 26, 1943 to end of season); Left Center side wall angling back to meet brick wall 12 (wood, when front fence was up); Light Tower Cages just right of scoreboard and in power alleys 16.5; Center Field 12 (wood 1909), 12 (brick and ivy 1946); Right Center 9.5 (concrete 1925); Screen at left side at 375 mark 24 (14.5 wire above 9.5 concrete 1932); Screen at right side at foul pole 27.67 (18.17 wire above 9.5 concrete 1932) ★ **FORMER USE:** Schenley Farms hothouse and livery stable, cow grazing, ravine in right field, rocky football field for Carnegie Tech vs. Penn October 31, 1908 ★ **CURRENT USE:** Pitt's Mervis Hall in right, Forbes Quadrangle and Posvar Hall in infield. Center field and right center brick walls still stand, along with base of flagpole and Mazeroski Field, a Little League diamond beyond the brick wall in left center. Roberto Clemente Drive now bisects the site, running 10 feet under what used to be the playing surface. ★ **CAPACITY:** 23,000 (June 30, 1909), 24,000 (July 26, 1909), 25,000 (1915), 41,000 (1925), 40,000 (1938), 33,537 (1939), 35,000 (1960)

PHENOMENA: During World War II, from June 26 through the end of the 1943 season, a huge United States Marine made of wood stood against the left field wall, just to the right of the scoreboard. Standing at parade rest, the Marine sergeant was 32 feet high, 15 feet wide across his feet, and in play. Ivy-covered brick wall in left and left center. Greenberg Gardens, also called Kiner's Korner, was the area between the scoreboard and a chicken coop wire short fence in left put there to increase home run production 1947-53. It was called Greenberg Gardens 1947, Kiner's Korner 1948-53. A plaque today marks the spot where Bill Mazeroski's World Series-winning homer left the park in 1960 and flew above Yogi Berra's head, into the trees.

AMMON FIELD

OCCUPANT: NNL Pittsburgh Keystones 1922 ★ **LOCATION:** on the north side of the city ★ **CURRENT USE:** Ammon Playground

GRAYS FIELD

OCCUPANT: ANL Homestead Grays 1929 ★ **LOCATION:** (N) Pennsylvania RR tracks, (W) Long Ave., (E) Homewood Ave., in the Homewood section of the city

GUS GREENLEE FIELD

OCCUPANTS: NEWL Homestead Grays April to June 1932; NNL Homestead Grays 1935-36; NNL Pittsburgh Crawfords 1933-38 ★ **LOCATION:** Left Field (N) Ridgeway St.; Third Base (W) Junilia St., then Lincoln Cemetery; First Base (S) 2500 Bedford Ave; Right Field (E) Francis St., then Municipal Hospital; in the Hill District ★ **DIMENSIONS:** Left Field more than 365 ★ **FENCES:** Left and Center Fields (unknown height, made of tin); Right Field 2 (concrete) ★ **FORMER USE:** Entress Brick Company factory ★ **CURRENT USE:** Pittsburgh Housing Authority projects

PHENOMENA: Opened on April 29, 1932. Josh Gibson once hit a home run here so far out of the park that the next day, in Philadelphia, with Gibson catching, when a ball came flying out of the crowd and was caught by one of the players, the umpire said to Josh, "You're out yesterday in Pittsburgh (I)." Crawfords owner Gus Greenlee scheduled a Craws-Grays game for 12:01 AM on a Monday morning to protest the Sunday blue law that prevented Sunday night games; the game was a sellout. On July 4, 1934, Satchel Paige pitched a no-hitter here in a morning game, and then somehow got to Chicago in time to pitch a 12-inning shutout there on the same day against the American Giants. Embankment in play in front of a two-foot-high concrete wall in front of the bleachers in right, which were up on a hill.

THREE RIVERS STADIUM

AKA: The House That Clemente Built ★ **OCCUPANT:** NL Pittsburgh Pirates July 16, 1970 to October 1, 2000 ★ **LOCATION:** Left Field (E) General Robinson St., then I-279 Fort Duquesne Bridge approach ramp; Third Base (N) Lacock (later Reedsdale) St., then Ohio River Blvd; First Base (W) Manchester (later Allegheny) Ave., then Ohio River; Right Field (S) North Shore Ave., then Roberto Clemente Memorial Park, then the Point (where the Monongahela River joins the Allegheny River to form the Ohio River) ★ **SURFACE:** Tartanturf 1970-82; AstroTurf 1983-2000 ★ **DIMENSIONS:** Foul Lines 340 (1970), 335 (1975); Power Alleys 385 (1970), 375 (1975); Center Field 410 (1970), 400 (1975); Backstop 60; Foul Territory large ★ **FENCES:** 10 (wood) ★ **CAPACITY:** 50,350 (1970), 54,499 (1981), 58,727 (1988), 47,687 (2000)

PHENOMENA: Fan drove his car into the stadium and overturned a 70-gallon jug of cheese dip on December 3, 1987. Roberto Clemente statue dedicated here in 1994. Original design by Erik Sirko was for a "Stadium Over the Monongahela," with stadium above two parking-lot levels, all constructed above the Monongahela River with plenty of room for boats to pass beneath on the river.

PNC PARK
OCCUPANT: NL Pittsburgh Pirates April 9, 2001 to date ★ **LOCATION:** Left Field (E/NE) 115 Federal St., Third Base (N/NW) East General Robinson St., First Base (W/SW) Mazeroski Way (formerly East Stadium Drive), Right Field (S/SE) Allegheny River, between the Fort Duquesne and Roberto Clemente (6th St.) Bridges ★ **SURFACE:** Grass ★ **DIMENSIONS:** Left Field 325; Left Center 386 (2001), 389 (2003), Deepest Left Center 410; Center Field 399; Right Center 375, Right Field 320, Backstop 52 (2001), 51 (2003), Foul Territory small ★ **FENCES:** Left Field 6, Left Center, Center Field, and Right Center 10, Right Field 21 ★ **CAPACITY:** 38,365 (2001), 38,496 (2004)
PHENOMENA: Fans can arrive via ferryboat on the Allegheny River behind Right Field.

PROVIDENCE, RHODE ISLAND
ADELAIDE AVENUE GROUNDS
AKA: Providence Base Ball Grounds, Adelaide Park ★ **OCCUPANTS:** Neutral site use by NA New Haven Elm Citys June 12, 1875; by NA Boston Red Stockings June 22, 1875 ★ **LOCATION:** Adelaide Ave., Broad St., Hamilton St., Sackett St., Elwood Ave.

MESSER STREET GROUNDS
OCCUPANT: NL Providence Grays May 1, 1878 to September 9, 1885 ★ **LOCATION:** (N) Hudson (later Willow) St., (W) Ropes (later Ellery) St., (S) Wood St., (E) Messer St.; opposite the Messer School

ROCKY POINT PARK
OCCUPANT: Neutral site use by NL Boston Beaneaters September 6, 1903

RALEIGH, NORTH CAROLINA
DEVEREAUX MEADOW
OCCUPANTS: NAL Raleigh Tigers 1959-60; neutral site use by NAL Birmingham Black Barons 1940s ★ **LOCATION:** Downtown Blvd, West St., Peace St. ★ **DIMENSIONS:** Left Field 310, Center Field 400, Right Field 370 ★ **FENCES:** 40 everywhere ★ **CAPACITY:** 4,000

RICHMOND, VIRGINIA
VIRGINIA STATE AGRICULTURAL SOCIETY FAIR GROUNDS
OCCUPANT: Neutral site use by NA Washington Nationals April 29 and May 1, 1875 ★ **LOCATION:** Franklin St., Belvidere St., Main St., Laurel St. ★ **FENCES:** none ★ **CURRENT USE:** Union RR Station, later Science Museum of Richmond, Monroe Park

ALLEN'S PASTURE
AKA: Virginia Base-Ball Park ★ **OCCUPANT:** AA Richmond Virginias August 5 to October 15, 1884 ★ **LOCATION:** (NE) Broad St., (NW) Allen Ave., (SW) Scuffletown Rd. (later Park Ave.), (SE) Lombardy St.; opposite the RF and Pennsy RR railyards; in the Lee district near Joseph Bryan Park ★ **FENCES:** none ★ **CURRENT USE:** Monuments to Generals Robert E. Lee and Jeb Stuart at third base

RIVERHEAD, NEW YORK
RIVERHEAD STADIUM
AKA: Wivchar Stadium ★ **OCCUPANT:** Neutral site use by ECL New York Lincoln Giants 1920s ★ **LOCATION:** Harrison Ave., School St., Roanoke Ave., Old Country Rd. (later Route 58); on Long Island ★ **DIMENSIONS:** Foul Lines 325, Power Alleys 410, Center Field 500 ★ **FENCES:** 10

ROCHESTER, NEW YORK
CULVER FIELD (I)
OCCUPANT: AA Rochester Hop Bitters April 28 to October 6, 1890

JONES SQUARE
OCCUPANT: AA Rochester Hop Bitters some games 1890 ★ **LOCATION:** (N) Lorimer St., (W) Saratoga Ave., (S) Jones Ave., (E) Frank (later Plymouth) St.; also North Union St., Weld St.

CULVER FIELD (II)
OCCUPANT: Neutral site use by NL Cleveland Spiders August 27 and 29, 1898 ★ **LOCATION:** (N) University (later Atlantic) Ave., (NW) Jersey (later Russell) St., (SW) Culver Park (later 1000 University Ave.), (E) Culver Rd.; same as Culver Field (I) ★ **CURRENT USE:** Gleason Works, New York Central/Conrail RR tracks

ONTARIO BEACH
OCCUPANT: Neutral site use by NL Cleveland Spiders August 28, 1898 ★ **LOCATION:** (NW) railroad tracks; (SW) private property; (SE) Genesee River, Lake Ontario; (NE) Charlotte Beach Ave; on Genesee River, near Lake Ontario, one mile NW of Wind-sor Beach ballpark in Irondequoit, back then in town of Charlotte, but now in Rochester

RED WING STADIUM
AKA: Silver Stadium 1968 to date ★ **OCCUPANT:** Neutral site use by NNL New York Black Yankees in 1940s ★ **LOCATION:** (N) Bastian St., (W) Clinton Ave., (S) 500 Norton St., (E) Joseph Ave. ★ **DIMENSIONS:** Left Field 322, Left Center 445, Center Field 410, Right Center 360, Right Field 315 ★ **FENCES:** Left Field 6 (wire), Center to

Right 11 (wood above concrete)

ROCKFORD, ILLINOIS
AGRICULTURAL SOCIETY FAIR GROUNDS
OCCUPANT: NA Rockford Forest Citys May 5 to September 26, 1871 ★ **LOCATION:** (N) Acorn St., Cherry St., (NW) Kent Creek, (S) Mulberry St., (SW) Peach (later Jefferson) St., (E) Kilburn Ave. (later Horsman St.) ★ **DIMENSIONS:** Foul Territory almost none because trees completely surrounded the park ★ **CURRENT USE:** Fairground Park
PHENOMENA: Most interesting and strangest major league ballpark in history. Numerous trees behind the catcher and along both foul lines made catching foul pop-ups impossible. Third base was up on a hill; home plate was in a deep depression so that when tagging up from third to home, a runner was running downhill the whole way! All the way around the outfield, there was the first warning track ever. It was a deep gutter providing drainage from the adjacent quarter-mile horseracing track.

ST. LOUIS, MISSOURI
RED STOCKING BASE-BALL PARK
AKA: Compton Park 1885-98 ★ **OCCUPANT:** NL St. Louis Red Stockings May 4 to July 4, 1875 ★ **LOCATION:** Left Field (W) Theresa Ave; Third Base (S) Larned (later Atlantic) St., then Missouri Pacific RR railyards; Home Plate (SE) Gratiot St.; First Base (E) 701 South Compton Ave; Right Field (N) Scott St. ★ **CURRENT USE:** Railroad yards and Bi-State bus repair shops

SPORTSMAN'S PARK (I)
AKA: Grand Ave. Grounds ★ **OCCUPANTS:** NA St. Louis Brown Stockings May 6 to October 8, 1875; NL St. Louis Brown Stockings May 5, 1876 to October 6, 1877; neutral site use by NL Indianapolis Blues July 9, 11, and 13, 1878 ★ **LOCATION:** Left Field (W) Spring St.; Third Base (S) 3623 Dodier St.; Home Plate (SE); First Base (E) 2709 North Grand Ave. (later Blvd); Right Field (N) Sullivan Ave; same site as for Sportsman's Parks (II), (IV), and (V) but with home plate in the Southeast ★ **CAPACITY:** 3,000 (1875)

ATHLETIC PARK
OCCUPANTS: NA St. Louis Brown Stockings some games 1875; NL St. Louis Brown Stockings some games 1876-77 ★ **LOCATION:** North Market St., Garrison St., St. Louis Ave., Bacon St., Coleman St.; two blocks southeast of Sportsman's Park

VETO PARK
OCCUPANT: NA St. Louis Brown Stockings some games 1875 ★ **LOCATION:** near the Fairgrounds ★ **CURRENT USE:** Fairgrounds Park

LUCAS PARK
OCCUPANTS: NL St. Louis Brown Stockings some games 1876; UA St. Louis Maroons some games 1884 ★ **LOCATION:** Lucas St., 13th St., Locust St., 14th St. ★ **CURRENT USE:** Lucas Gardens in a tiny square block behind the Public Library

LAFAYETTE PARK
OCCUPANT: AA St. Louis Browns some games 1880s ★ **LOCATION:** Lafayette Ave., Missouri Ave., Park Ave., Mississippi Ave. ★ **CURRENT USE:** Large public park

SPORTSMAN'S PARK (II)
OCCUPANTS: AA St. Louis Browns May 2, 1882 to October 4, 1891; NL St. Louis Browns April 12 to October 13, 1892; NL St. Louis Cardinals May 5, 1901 ★ **LOCATION:** Left Field (S) 3623 Dodier St.; Third Base (E) 2907 North Grand Ave. (later Blvd); Home Plate (NE); First Base (N) Sullivan Ave; Right Field (W) Spring St.; same site as for Sportsman's Parks (I), (IV), and (V) but with home plate in the Northeast ★ **DIMENSIONS:** Left Field 350, Left Center 400, Center Field 460, Right Center 330, Right Field 285, Backstop 70 ★ **CAPACITY:** 6,000 (1882), 12,000 (1886)
PHENOMENA: Browns' owner Chris von der Ahe converted Augustus Solari's two-story house in the right-field corner into a beer garden for the 1882 season. In accordance with pre-1888 World Series rules, the beer garden was in play. Right fielders charged up into the beer gardens to retrieve balls hit there, and then relayed the ball back to the pitchers' box, after which the ball was eligible to be used to put out a runner. Imagine, a beer garden, with customers eating and drinking at their picnic tables, in play in a major league ballpark! There was also a Japanese fireworks cannon in the ballpark, made out of bamboo and wrapped with steel wire.

PALACE PARK OF AMERICA
AKA: Union Grounds ★ **OCCUPANTS:** UA St. Louis Maroons April 20 to October 19, 1884; NL St. Louis Maroons April 30, 1885 to September 23, 1886 ★ **LOCATION:** (N) Mullanphy (later Madison) St., (W) Jefferson Ave., (S) Cass Ave., (E) West 25th St. ★ **DIMENSIONS:** Foul Lines 285, Backstop 25 ★ **CAPACITY:** 10,000 (1884)

VANDEVENTER LOT (I)
OCCUPANT: NL St. Louis Maroons some games 1885-86 ★ **LOCATION:** same as Robison Field, also known as Vandeventer Lot (II)

SPORTSMAN'S PARK (III)
AKA: Robison Field, Vandeventer Lot (II), League Park 1899-1911, Cardinal Field 1918-20, Coney Island of the West, Shoot the Chutes ★ **OCCUPANTS:** NL St. Louis Cardinals April 27, 1893 to June 6, 1920; neutral site use by NL Cleveland Spiders several games in 1898 and on September 24, 1899 ★ **LOCATION:** Left Field (SE) Prairie Ave., Third Base (NE) 3852 Natural Bridge Ave., then Fairground Park; First Base (NW) Vandeventer Ave., Right Field (SW) Ashland (later Lexington) Ave; not the same

site as Sportsman's Park (I), (II), (IV), and (V) ★ **DIMENSIONS:** Left Field 470 (1893), 350 (1898), 380 (1909); Shoot the Chutes at both Left Field Foul Pole and in Right Center 625 (1896); Left Center 470 (1898); Deepest Left Center 520 (1893), 400 (1909); Center Field 500 (1893), 435 (1909); Right Center 330 (1893), 320 (1909); Right Field 290 (1893); Backstop 120 (1893); Foul Territory huge ★ **FENCES:** Shoot the Chutes at Left Field Foul Pole and in Right Field none; Left Field ropes often strung in front of fence for fans to stand behind; Center Field picket fence and bulletin board ★ **CAPACITY:** 10,300 (1893), 14,500 (1894), 15,200 (1899), 21,000 (1909) ★ **CURRENT USE:** Beaumont High School
PHENOMENA: Shoot the Chutes was the name given to two areas where the ball could roll more than 600 feet, between bleacher sections, and still be in play. One area was at the left-field foul pole, where the ball could roll to Prairie Ave., and the other area was in right field, where the ball could roll to a lake. Balls that rolled underneath the center-field scoreboard could not be reached, and were home runs.

SPORTSMAN'S PARK (IV)
OCCUPANT: AL St. Louis Browns April 23, 1902 to October 6, 1908 ★ **LOCATION:** Left Field (E) 2907 North Grand Ave. (later Blvd); Third Base (N) Sullivan Ave; Home Plate (NW); First Base (W) Spring St.; Right Field (S) 3623 Dodier St.; same site as for Sportsman's Parks (I), (II), and (V) but with home plate in the Northwest ★ **DIMENSIONS:** Left Field 330 (1902), Center Field 430 (1902), 315 (1903), Right Field 310 (1902), Backstop 60 (1902) ★ **FENCES:** Left Field 15 ★ **CAPACITY:** 8,000 (1902), 18,000 (1907)

SPORTSMAN'S PARK (V)
AKA: Busch Stadium (I) 1954-66, Bill Veeck's House ★ **OCCUPANTS:** AL St. Louis Browns April 14, 1909 to September 27, 1953; NL St. Louis Cardinals July 1, 1920 to May 8, 1966; neutral site use by NAL Kansas City Monarchs July 4, 1941; by NAL New Orleans-St. Louis Stars one game in 1941 ★ **LOCATION:** Left Field (NE) Sullivan Ave; Third Base (NW) North Spring Ave; Home Plate (W/SW); First Base (SW) 3623 Dodier St.; Right Field (SE) 2907 North Grand Ave. (later Blvd); same as earlier Sportsman's Parks, but with home plate in the West/ Southwest ★ **DIMENSIONS:** Left Field 368 (1909), 340 (1921), 356 (1923), 355 (1926), 360 (1930), 351.1 (1931); Left Center 379; Deepest corner just left of dead center 426 (1938); Center Field 430 (1926), 450 (1930), 445 (1931), 420 (1938), 422 (1939); Deepest corner just right of dead center 422 (1938); Right Center 354 (1942); Right Field 335 (1909), 295 (1912), 315 (1921), 320 (1925), 309.5 (actual 1926), 310 (marked 1926), 310 (1931), 332 (1938), 309.5 (1939); Backstop 75 (1942), 67 (1953) ★ **FENCES:** Left to Center 11.5 (concrete); 354 mark in Right Center to Right 11.5 (1909), 33 (11.5 concrete below 21.5 wire July 5, 1929), 11.5 (1955), 36.67 (11.5 concrete below 25.17 wire 1956) ★ **CURRENT USE:** Herbert Hoover Boys' Club, with baseball diamond in the same spot ★ **CAPACITY:** 17,600 (April 14, 1909), 24,040 (June 1909), 34,000 (1921), 31,250 (1947), 34,000 (1948), 30,500 (1953)
PHENOMENA: Local newspaper, the *Globe-Democrat*, had an ad on the right-center wall that showed the star of the previous game. Bill Veeck gave Satchel Paige a rocking chair to use while in the bullpen when Paige pitched for the Browns here in 1952-53. Busch eagle flapped its wings after a Cardinal home run; it sat on top of the left-center scoreboard. Flagpole in fair territory until removed in the 1950s. Bill Veeck's family lived in an apartment under the stands in the 1950s. Wire screen in front of right-field pavilion removed for entire 1955 season; it had been installed on July 5, 1929.

HANDLAN'S PARK
AKA: Federal League Park, Laclede St. Field, Grand and Market ★ **OCCUPANTS:** FL St. Louis Terriers April 16, 1914 to October 3, 1915; NNL St. Louis Giants some games 1920-21; NNL St. Louis Stars some games 1920s ★ **LOCATION:** (N) Laclede St., (W) Grand Ave., (S) Clark (later Market) St., (E) Theresa Ave; also Forest Park St. ★ **DIMENSIONS:** Left Field 325, Center Field 375, Right Field 300, Backstop 90 ★ **CAPACITY:** 12,000 (1914), 15,000 (1915)

GIANTS PARK
AKA: Tigers Park after June 15, 1922 ★ **OCCUPANT:** NNL St. Louis Giants May 9, 1920 to August 30, 1921; NNL St. Louis Stars May 30 to June 15, 1922 ★ **LOCATION:** (N) Pope Ave., (W) Prescott Ave., (S) Clarence Ave; also North Broadway, East Taylor St., Hall St., one block from Kuebler's Park, which was abandoned in 1917

STARS PARK
AKA: Dick Kent's Ballyard, Compton Park ★ **OCCUPANT:** NNL St. Louis Stars July 9, 1922 to August 11, 1931 ★ **LOCATION:** Compton St., Laclede St., Market St. ★ **DIMENSIONS:** Left Field 250, Left Center 425 ★ **CAPACITY:** 10,000 (1922)

VANDEVENTER LOT (III)
OCCUPANT: NNL St. Louis Stars some games 1920s ★ **LOCATION:** Grand Ave., Vandeventer St., Franklin St., Spring St., Belle St.

EASTON STREET PARK
OCCUPANT: NNL St. Louis Stars some games 1920s ★ **LOCATION:** Easton St., Vandeventer St., stockyards

MARKET STREET PARK
OCCUPANT: NNL St. Louis Stars some games 1920s ★ **LOCATION:** North Market St., Broadway, Elephants St.

METROPOLITAN PARK
OCCUPANT: NAL St. Louis Stars 1937 ★ **LOCATION:** same as Giants Park

SOUTH END PARK
AKA: National Nite Baseball Park ★ **OCCUPANTS:** NAL St. Louis Stars 1939; NAL New Orleans-St. Louis Stars (half of the home games) 1941 ★ **CURRENT USE:** American Can Company plant

BUSCH STADIUM (II)
AKA: Civic Center Stadium 1966, Busch Memorial Stadium 1966-83 ★ **OCCUPANT:** NL St. Louis Cardinals May 12, 1966 to date ★ **LOCATION:** Left Field (E) Broadway, then I-70, Gateway Arch, and Mississippi River; Third Base (N) Walnut St.; First Base (W) Seventh St. (later McGwire Way); Right Field (S) Spruce St. ★ **DIMENSIONS:** Foul Lines 330; Power Alleys 386 (1966), 376 (1973), 386 (1977), 383 (July 1983), 375 (1992), 372 (1996); Center Field 414 (1966), 410 (1971), 414 (1972), 404 (1973), 414 (1977), 402 (1992); Backstop 64 (Vin Scully's unofficial measurement during 1985 World Series showed this is 50 rather than 64); Foul Territory large ★ **FENCES:** Left and Right Fields 10.5 (padded concrete), 8 (padded canvas 1992); Center Field 10.5 (padded concrete 1966), 8 (wood 1973), 10.5 (padded concrete 1977), 8 (padded canvas 1992) ★ **SURFACE:** grass 1966-69; carpet (very fast) 1970-95; grass 1996 to date. From 1970 to 1976, the entire field was carpeted except for the part of the infield that is normally dirt on a grass field. In 1977 this was carpeted except for the sliding pits. This is one of only four instances where there was a full dirt infield, with an otherwise fully carpeted field, the others being Astrodome 1966-70; Candlestick 1971; Tropicana Field 1998 to date. ★ **CAPACITY:** 49,275 (1966), 53,138 (1987), 54,224 (1988), 54,727 plus 1,500 standing room = 56,227 (1990, from this time forward the Cards have included standing room in their capacity statistics, the only major league team to do so), 52,244 (1996), 49,676 (1997), 50,354 (2001)
PHENOMENA: Line-drive park, because of deep power alleys, deep center field, and quick surface. From 1966 to 1982, right-field scoreboard lights showed cardinal in flight when Cardinals homered; same show put on each time Lou Brock set a new base-stealing record. At league direction, site designated for Cubs playoffs or World Series home games from 1986 to 1988, when Wrigley Field got lights. They used to play Anheuser-Busch "King of Beers" theme song on organ during seventh inning stretch instead of "Take Me Out to the Ballgame;" now they play beer song at end of seventh.

ST. PAUL, MINNESOTA
FORT STREET GROUNDS
AKA: West Seventh St. Park ★ **OCCUPANT:** UA St. Paul Saints 1884 ★ **LOCATION:** (N) St. Clair Ave; (NW) West Seventh St.; (W) Oneida St.; (S) Chicago, Minneapolis, St. Paul, and Peoria RR tracks; (E) Duke St.; also Fort St., Jackson St., Mississippi River, on the west side of town

ST. PETERSBURG, FLORIDA
TROPICANA FIELD
AKA: Florida Suncoast Dome March 3, 1990 to August 5, 1993, Thunderdome August 5, 1993 to October 4, 1996) ★ **OCCUPANT:** AL Tampa Bay Devil Rays March 31, 1998 to date ★ **LOCATION:** Left Field (N) Central (later First) Ave. South; Third Base (W) 16th St. North; First Base (S) Dunmore (later Fourth) Ave. South; Right Field (E) 10th St. South ★ **DIMENSIONS:** Left Field 315; Power Alleys 359.5 (1998 actual), 371 (1998 marked); 370 (1999 actual and marked); Deepest Left Center 415 (1998), 410 (1999); Center Field 407 (1998), 404 (1999); Deepest Right Center 409 (1998), 404 (1999); Right Field 322; Backstop 50; Dome Apex 225 (above Second Base), 85 (above Center Field wall); Foul Territory small ★ **FENCES:** Left and Right Fields 9.5 (1998), 11.42 (1999); Center Field 9.5 (1998), 9.33 (1999) ★ **SURFACE:** AstroTurf-12 with dirt infield 1998-99, FieldTurf with dirt infield 2000 to date ★ **CAPACITY:** 45,000 (1998), 43,772 (2003)
PHENOMENA: Scene of furious rhubarbs over ground rules concerning whether balls that hit the four catwalks that hang over the outfield were homers or in play. On May 27, 1998, the league approved a ground-rule change making balls hitting the two lower catwalks automatic home runs. Restaurant windows in straightaway center field feature a specially designed dark film that gives batters an ideal background for seeing a pitch coming off the mound. Translucent roof is illuminated orange on nights when Devil Rays win.

SAN DIEGO, CALIFORNIA
QUALCOMM STADIUM
AKA: San Diego Stadium 1967-79, San Diego-Jack Murphy Stadium 1980, Jack Murphy Stadium 1981 to May 20, 1997, Qualcomm Stadium at Jack Murphy Field May 20, 1997 to date, the Murph, the Q ★ **OCCUPANT:** NL San Diego Padres April 8, 1969 to September 28, 2003 ★ **LOCATION:** Left Field (NE/N) 9449 Friars Rd.; Third Base (NW/W) Stadium Way, then a rock quarry; First Base (SW/S) San Diego River, then Camino del Rio North, and I-8; Right Field (SE/E) I-15; in Mission Valley ★ **DIMENSIONS:** Left Field 330 (1969), 327 (fence 1982), 329 (foul poles 1982); Power Alleys 375 (1969), 370 (1982); Center Field 420 (1969), 410 (1973), 420 (1978), 405 (1982); Right Field 330 (1969), 327 (fence 1982), 329 (foul poles 1982); 330 (1996); Backstop 80 (1969), 75 (1982) ★ **FENCES:** Left and Right Fields 17.5 (concrete 1969), 9 (line painted on concrete 1973), 18 (concrete 1974), 8.5 (canvas 1982); Center Field 17.5 (concrete 1969), 10 (wood 1973), 18 (concrete 1974), 8.5 (canvas 1982), one section in right center 9 (canvas 1982); Right Field 17.5 (scoreboard 1996) ★ **FORMER USE:** San Diego River and marshy swampland ★ **CAPACITY:** 50,000 (1967), 47,634 (1969), 44,790 (1973), 47,634 (1974), 51,362 (1979), 48,443 (1980), 51,362 (1981), 58,671 (1984), 59,700 (1992), 47,750 (1995), 49,639 (1996), 59,772 (1997), 57,544 (1998), 66,307 (1999), 63,890 (2003)
PHENOMENA: Hosted first-ever night to honor a Negro Leagues veteran. Chet

Brewer of the Kansas City Brewers was wheeled to home plate by his wife Tina to accept the cheers of the crowd in July 1989, shortly before he passed away at the age of 89. Named for Jack Murphy, local sports editor who campaigned to bring major league baseball to San Diego. Only park where a foul ball could be caught out of sight of all umpires and most players, in either bullpen near the foul poles.

PETCO PARK
OCCUPANT: NL San Diego Padres April 2004 to date ★ **LOCATION:** Center Field (N) K St.; Third Base (W) 7th Ave; Home Plate (S) Harbor Drive, railroad tracks, Imperial Ave; First Base (E) 10th Ave; adjacent to San Diego Convention Center ★ **SURFACE:** Grass ★ **DIMENSIONS:** Left Field 334; Left Center 367, Center Field 390; Deepest Right Center 409, Right Center 387, Right Field 322 ★ **CAPACITY:** 46,000
PHENOMENA: Lawn seating for 2,500 fans at "Park at the Park," an elevated area behind CF fence. Former iron and steel foundry, the 90-foot-high Western Metals Building, constitutes LF foul pole.

SAN FRANCISCO, CALIFORNIA
SEALS STADIUM
AKA: Home Plate Mine ★ **OCCUPANT:** NL San Francisco Giants April 15, 1958 to September 20, 1959 ★ **LOCATION:** Left Field (E) Potrero Ave; Third Base (N) Alameda St.; First Base (W) Bryant St.; Right Field (S) 16th St., then Franklin Square Park ★ **DIMENSIONS:** Left Field 340 (1931), 365 (1958), 361 (1959); Left Center 375 (1958), 364 (1959); Deepest Left Center corner just left of straightaway center 404; Center Field 400 (1931), 410 (1958), 400 (1959); Deepest Right Center corner just right of straightaway center 415; Right Center just right of 415 mark where seats jutted out 397; Right Field 385 (1931), 355 (1958), 350 (1959); Backstop 55.42 ★ **FENCES:** Left Field 15 (5 concrete below 10 wire); Center Field Scoreboard 30.5; Right Field 16 (5 concrete below 11 wire) ★ **CURRENT USE:** San Francisco Auto Center and Safeway store; seats and lights still are being used at Cheney Stadium in Tacoma, Washington ★ **CAPACITY:** 16,000 (1931), 18,600 (1932), 20,700 (1933), 25,000 (1938), 23,601 (1939), 20,700 (1941), 18,500 (1946), 22,500 (1947), 22,900 (1958), 23,750 (1959)

CANDLESTICK PARK
AKA: 3Com Park April 12, 1996 to January 1, 2002, the Stick, Maury's Lake, Cave of the Winds, Wind Tunnel, North Pole ★ **OCCUPANT:** NL San Francisco Giants April 12, 1960 to September 30, 1999 ★ **LOCATION:** Left Field (NW) Gilman Ave. (later Giants Drive); Third Base (SW) Haney Blvd. (later Jamestown Ave.), then Bay View Hill; First Base (SE) Jamestown Ave. extension, Candlestick Point and San Francisco Bay; Right Field (NE) Hunters Point, then Hunters Point Expressway/State Route 1 and San Francisco Bay; Candlestick Point's rock outcroppings were leveled to fill in water for parking lots ★ **DIMENSIONS:** Left Field 330 (1960), 335 (1968); Left Center 397 (1960), 365 (1961); Center Field 420 (1960), 410 (1961), 400 (1993); Right Center 397 (1960), 365 (1961); Right Field 330 (1965), 335 (1968), 330 (1991), 328 (1993); Backstop 73 (1960), 70 (1961), 55 (1975), 65 (1982), 66 (1985); Foul Territory very large ★ **FENCES:** 10 (wire 1960); 8 (wire 1972); 12 (6 canvas below 6 Plexiglas 1975); 9 (6 canvas below 3 Plexiglas 1982); 9 (wire 1984), 9.5 (fence posts 1984); 8 (canvas 1993) ★ **SURFACE:** grass 1960-70, carpet 1971-78, bluegrass 1979 to date ★ **CURRENT USE:** NFL 49ers football ★ **CAPACITY:** 43,765 (1960), 42,553 (1961), 58,000 (1972), 59,080 (9175), 62,000 (1989), 58,000 (1993), 63,000 (1995), 62,000 (1997), 63,000 (1999)
PHENOMENA: Named for candlestick bird, a curlew wader that was hunted almost to extinction according to ornithologist Henry Betten. Earthquake on October 17, 1989 postponed World Series game. Wind, wind, and more wind! Before stadium was enclosed, wind blew in from left center and out toward right center. By far the coldest park in the majors, resulting in fewer home runs. Croix de Candlestick pin awarded to fans at conclusion of night extra-inning games because of extreme wind-chill conditions. Beatles' last concert here August 29, 1966.

SBC PARK
AKA: Pacific Bell (Pac Bell) Park April 11, 2000 to January 1, 2004 ★ **OCCUPANT:** NL San Francisco Giants April 11, 2000 to date ★ **LOCATION:** Left Field (NE) Second St., Third Base (NW) King St., First Base (SW) Third St., Right Field (SE) McCovey Cove in China Basin, which is part of San Francisco Bay; the entire site is known as 24 Willie Mays Plaza ★ **DIMENSIONS:** Left Field 335 (2000), 339 (2003); Left Center 362 (2000), 364 (2001), Center Field 404 (2000), 399 (2003); Deepest Right Center 420 (2000), 421 (2003), Right Center ???, Right Field 307 (2000), 309 (2003), Backstop 48 ★ **FENCES:** Left Field 8, Left Center 8 sloping up to 11, Center Field 8, Right Field 25 **SURFACE:** Sports Turf hybrid bluegrass ★ **CAPACITY:** 40,930 (2000), 41,503 (2003)
PHENOMENA: Fans arrive via ferry, Muni Metro trolleys, Caltrain, and BART subway, and can watch for free from above the right-field wall. High above the left-field seats, there is a big baseball glove, 501 feet from the plate. Homers over the right-field seats splash in McCovey Cove, setting off feverish rush by boaters to recover "splash" home run balls, most of them hit by Barry Bonds.

SAN JUAN, PUERTO RICO
ESTADIO HIRAM BITHORN
OCCUPANTS: Neutral site use by AL Toronto Blue Jays April 1, 2001; by NL Montreal Expos 22 games April 11 to September 11, 2003; 22 games April 9 to July 11, 2004 ★ **DIMENSIONS:** Left Field 315, Power Alleys 360, Center Field 399, Right Field 313, Foul Territory huge ★ **FENCES:** 10 to 12 ★ **SURFACE:** Carpet ★ **CAPACITY:** 18,000

PHENOMENA: Home of Santurce Cangrejeros (Crabbers) of Puerto Rican League 1962 to date. Four flags above batters-eye background—Puerto Rico, USA, Canada, and San Juan. Three national anthems-Canada, USA, then Puerto Rico. Fans dance to salsa music. Named for first Puerto Rican to play in majors; Bithorn pitched four years for Cubs and White Sox, beginning in 1942.

SAVANNAH, GEORGIA
GRAYSON STADIUM
OCCUPANT: Neutral site use by NAL Birmingham Black Barons 1940s ★ **DIMENSIONS:** Left Field 290, Center Field 415, Right Field 320 ★ **FENCES:** Left Field Light Tower 90

SEATTLE, WASHINGTON
SICKS' STADIUM
AKA: Sicks' Select Stadium, Seattle Stadium ★ **OCCUPANT:** AL Seattle Pilots April 11 to October 2, 1969 ★ **LOCATION:** Left Field (E) Empire (later Martin Luther King Jr.) Way South; Third Base (N) South Bayview St.; First Base (W) 2700 Rainier Ave. South; Right Field (S) South McClellan St. ★ **DIMENSIONS:** Left Field 325 (1938), 305 (1969); Power Alleys 345 (1969); Corners just right and left of center 405 (1969); Center Field 400 (1938), 402 (1969); Right Field 325 (1938), 320 (1969); Backstop 54; Foul Territory very small ★ **FENCES:** Left Field and Right Field 8 (3 concrete below 5 wire); Center Field 12.55 (3 concrete below 9.55 wire) ★ **FORMER USE:** Dugdale Park, minor league ballpark from 1913 until it burned down July 4, 1932. ★ **CURRENT USE:** Loew's Home Improvement, glass display case inside the store shows Rainiers and Pilots memorabilia ★ **CAPACITY:** 15,000 (1913), 11,000 (1938), 18,000 (April 11, 1969), 25,420 (June 20, 1969), 28,500 (August 15, 1969)

KINGDOME
AKA: King County Stadium, The Tomb, Puget Puke ★ **OCCUPANT:** AL Seattle Mariners April 6, 1977 to June 27, 1999 ★ **LOCATION:** Left Field (N) 201 South King St.; Third Base (W) 589 Occidental Ave. South, then Railroad Way South; First Base (S) South Royal Brougham Way; Right Field (E) Fourth Ave. South, then Burlington Northern RR tracks, I-5 ★ **DIMENSIONS:** Left Field 315 (1977), 316 (marked 1978), 314 (actual 1978), 324 (1990), 331 (1991); Left Center: 375 (1977), 365 (1978), 357 (1981), 362 (1990), 376 (1991); Deep Left Center 385 (1990), 389 (1991); Center Field 405 (1977), 410 (1978), 405 (1981), 410 (1986), 405 (1991); Deep Right Center 375 (1990), 380 (1991); Right Center 375 (1977), 365 (1978), 357 (1981), 352 (1990); Right Field 315 (1977), 316 (1978), 314 (1990), 312 (1991); Speakers in Left (3), Left Center, and Center 110 (1977), 133.5 (1981); 11 other speakers 130; Backstop 63; Apex of Dome: 250; Foul Territory large ★ **FENCES:** Left Field 11.5 (wood 1977), 17.5 (6 Plexiglas over wood 1988), 11.5 (wood 1990), 8.5 (wood 1994); Center Field 11.5 (wood 1977); Right Field 11.5 (wood 1977), 23.25 (wood 1982), 11.5 (wood 1988) ★ **SURFACE:** AstroTurf ★ **CAPACITY:** 59,059 (1977), 57,748 (1991), 59,702 (1992), 58,100 (1996), 59,084 (1999)
PHENOMENA: Twenty-three-foot Mini-Green Monster in right and right-center called the Walla Walla. Carpet was rolled out by the Rhinoceros machine, and smoothed by the Grasshopper machine after it had been zipped together. Two foul balls went up but never came down, thus disproving the old adage of physics. U.S.S. Mariner,a huge yellow sailing ship behind the center-field fence,fired a cannon after every Mariner homer. Outfield distances marked on fences in both feet and fathoms 1977-80 (1 fathom = 6 feet). Mariners played home games on the road just before the 1994 strike after tiles fell off roof on July 19.

SAFECO FIELD
OCCUPANT: AL Seattle Mariners July 15, 1999 to date ★ **LOCATION:** Left Field (N) Royal Brougham Way, then Kingdome; Third Base (W) 1250 First Ave. South; First Base (S) South Atlantic St.; Right Field (E) Third Ave. South ★ **DIMENSIONS:** Left Field 331, Left Center 390 (1999), 388 (2003), Center Field 405, Right Center 386 (1999), 387 (2000), 385 (2003), Right Field 326 ★ **FENCES:** 8 ★ **CAPACITY:** 46,621 (1999), 47,772 (2003)
PHENOMENA: Along with the BOB in Phoenix, Minute Maid Park in Houston, Miller Park in Milwaukee, and SkyDome in Toronto, Safeco has a retractable roof. Hand-operated scoreboard in left.

SPRINGFIELD, ILLINOIS
LANPHIER PARK
AKA: Robin Roberts Stadium ★ **OCCUPANT:** Neutral site use by NAL Cincinnati Clowns one game in May 1943 ★ **LOCATION:** (N) Converse Ave., (W) Lanphier High School Football Stadium, (S) Grand Ave., (E) 15th St. ★ **DIMENSIONS:** Foul Lines 320; Center Field 410

SPRINGFIELD, MASSACHUSETTS
HAMPDEN PARK RACE TRACK
OCCUPANTS: Neutral site use by NA Troy Haymakers July 23, 1872; by NA Boston Red Stockings July 16, 1873 and May 14, 1875; Temple Cup NL Boston Beaneaters vs. NL Baltimore Orioles, one exhibition game between Temple Cup Games,October 1897 ★ **LOCATION:** South end of mile-long oval bicycle race track, running along NW-SE axis.

SPRINGFIELD, OHIO
MUNICIPAL STADIUM

OCCUPANT: Neutral site use by NNL Cincinnati Clowns May 25, 1943

SYRACUSE, NEW YORK
STAR PARK (I)
AKA: Newell Park ★ **OCCUPANTS:** NL Syracuse Stars May 28 to September 10, 1879; neutral site use by NL Buffalo Bisons June 27, 1885 ★ **LOCATION:** (N) Croton St. (later East Raynor Ave.), (W) South Salina St.

STAR PARK (II)
OCCUPANT: AA Syracuse Stars April 28 to October 6, 1890 ★ **LOCATION:** (N) Temple St., (W) Oneida St., (S) West Taylor St., (E) Delaware, Lackawanna, and Western RR tracks, (NE) South Salina St.; also South Clinton St. ★ **CURRENT USE:** Mann and Hunter Lumber Company plant, now vacant

IRON PIER
OCCUPANT: AA Syracuse Stars August 3, 1890

MC ARTHUR STADIUM
AKA: Municipal Stadium 1934-41 ★ **OCCUPANT:** Neutral site use by NNL New York Black Yankees 1940s ★ **LOCATION:** (S) East Hiawatha Blvd; also Second St. North, LeMoyne Park ★ **DIMENSIONS:** Foul Lines 335 (1934), 320 (1946), Center Field 464 (1934), 434 (1946) ★ **FENCES:** Right Center Scoreboard 24, rest of fence 8 (metal over wood) ★ **CAPACITY:** 8,000 (1975), 10,500 (1985)

THREE RIVERS, NEW YORK
THREE RIVERS PARK
OCCUPANT: Neutral site use by AA Syracuse Stars Sundays May 18 to July 20, 1890 ★ **LOCATION:** Twelve miles north of Syracuse, adjacent to the town of Phoenix; on the Rome, Ogdersburg, and Watertown Railroad; at Three Rivers Point where the Oneida and Seneca Rivers join to form the Oswego River

TOKYO, JAPAN
BIG EGG
AKA: Tokyo Dome, Tokyo Kyujyo ★ **OCCUPANTS:** Neutral-site use by NL New York Mets March 29, 2000; by NL Chicago Cubs March 30, 2000; by AL Tampa Bay Devil Rays March 30-31, 2004 ★ **LOCATION:** (N) 1-3-61 Koraku 1-chome Bunkyo-ku; (W) Tokyo Dome Hotel, JR Suidobashi; (S) Toei-Mita Line Suidobashi; (E) Marunichi Line Korakuen ★ **DIMENSIONS:** Foul Lines 328, Power Alleys 361, Center Field 400, Dome 202.34 ★ **FENCES:** 13 ★ **SURFACE:** AstroTurf ★ **CAPACITY:** 55,000
PHENOMENA: Best ballpark name. Name of this domed stadium comes from the fact that it appears from overhead and from a distance to look like, well, an egg. Crowds led by the *oendan* or cheerleaders, who wave flags, bang drums and sing songs.

TOLEDO, OHIO
LEAGUE PARK
OCCUPANT: AA Toledo Blue Stockings May 14 to September 23, 1884 ★ **LOCATION:** (NE) Jefferson Ave., (NW) 15th St., (SW) Monroe St., (SE) 13th St.

TRI-STATE FAIR GROUNDS
OCCUPANT: AA Toledo Blue Stockings September 13, 1884; neutral site use by NL Detroit October 5, 1885 ★ **LOCATION:** (N) Frazier St. (later Oakwood Ave.), (W) Woodstock Ave. (later Addington St.), (S) Dorr St., (E) Ravensburg (later Upton) Ave.

SPERANZA PARK
OCCUPANT: AA Toledo Maumees May 1 to October 2, 1890 ★ **FORMER USE:** armory **LOCATION:** (NE) Cherry St., (W) Franklin Ave., (S) Frederick St.

ARMORY PARK
OCCUPANT: Neutral site use by AL Detroit Tigers June 28 and August 16, 1903 ★ **LOCATION:** (NW) Speilbusch Ave., (SW) Jackson St., (SE) Erie St., (NE) Orange St.; also Superior St. and Maumee River ★ **FORMER USE:** armory ★ **CURRENT USE:** Federal Building

SWAYNE FIELD
AKA: Mud Hen Park ★ **OCCUPANTS:** NNL Toledo Tigers April to July 15, 1923; NAL Toledo Crawfords July to September 1939 ★ **LOCATION:** Left Field (NE) Council St., then Red Man Tobacco factory, coal piles; Third Base (NW) New York Central RR tracks; First Base (SW) Monroe St.; Right Field (SE) Detroit Ave. ★ **DIMENSIONS:** Left Field 472; Center Field 482 (1923), 448 (1938); Right Field 327; Backstop 72 ★ **CURRENT USE:** shopping center ★ **CAPACITY:** 10,000 (1923), 12,500 (1938)

TORONTO, ONTARIO, CANADA
EXHIBITION STADIUM
AKA: Prohibition Stadium April 7, 1977 to July 30, 1982, Canadian National Exhibition (CNE), CNE Stadium ★ **OCCUPANT:** AL Toronto Blue Jays April 7, 1977 to May 28, 1989 ★ **LOCATION:** Left Field (N) Ontario Drive, then Gardiner Expressway; Third Base (W) Prince's Blvd, First Base (S) Lakeshore Blvd, then Exhibition Place and Lake Ontario; Right Field (E) New Brunswick Way, then CNE Amusement Park; across the street from the Hockey Hall of Fame ★ **DIMENSIONS:** Foul Lines 330; Power Alleys 375; Center Field 400; Backstop 60 ★ **FENCES:** 12 (8 canvas below 4 wire)

★ **SURFACE:** Carpet ★ **CAPACITY:** 25,303 (1959), 38,522 (1977), 43,737 (1978)
PHENOMENA: First baseball game here, on April 7, 1977 vs. White Sox, was the only major league game ever played with snow covering the entire field, which it did for the first three innings; only the outfield was covered for the rest of the game. The zamboni, borrowed from Maple Leaf Gardens for this -10° F wind-chill game, ran over the infield between innings, but could not keep the field free from snow. Nicknamed Prohibition Stadium from opening until July 30, 1982, first day beer sales were allowed.

SKYDOME
OCCUPANT: AL Toronto Blue Jays June 5, 1989 to date ★ **LOCATION:** Center Field (N) Front St. West; Third Base (W) Spadina Ave; Home Plate (S) Gardiner Expressway; First Base (E) John St., then CN Tower ★ **DIMENSIONS:** Foul Lines 330 (1989), 328 (1990); Power Alleys 375; Center Field 400; Backstop 60; Dome Apex 310 ★ **FENCES:** 10 (canvas) ★ **FORMER USE:** Water supply pumping station at second base ★ **SURFACE:** AstroTurf-8, Toronto is the only major league city which has never hosted a major league game played the way it was intended to be played, on grass ★ **CAPACITY:** 50,516 (1989), 45,100 (2001), 50,516 (2003)
PHENOMENA: Highest dome in the majors, by far, at 310 feet. The 400-foot sign in center is actually right of dead center. Two 30-pound roof tiles fell during a game on June 22, 1995, injuring seven fans. When they open up the roof, the closed end of the stadium in center field serves as a wind scoop, causing downdrafts in the outfield that prevent home runs. April 12, 2001 game postponed when two of the three roof panels collided, sending debris into the outfield, but no visiting Royals were hurt.

TRENTON, NEW JERSEY
DUNN FIELD
OCCUPANT: Neutral site use by NNL Newark Eagles six games 1946 ★ **CURRENT USE:** Abandoned supermarket ★ **CAPACITY:** 3,500
PHENOMENA: Extremely poor lighting.

TROY, NEW YORK
HAYMAKERS' GROUNDS
OCCUPANTS: NA Troy Haymakers May 9, 1871 to June 6, 1872; NL Trojans May 18, 1880 to September 30, 1881 ★ **LOCATION:** (N) 104th St., (W) Second Ave., (S) 103rd St., (E) Fifth Ave; on Center Island, in the Hudson River near its junction with the South Branch of the Mohawk River ★ **CURRENT USE:** Twelve large pink, blue and white oil tanks

PUTNAM GROUNDS
AKA: Puts ★ **OCCUPANT:** NL Troy Trojans May 28 to September 20, 1879 ★ **LOCATION:** (N) Peoples Ave., (W) 15th St.

WASHINGTON, D.C.
OLYMPIC GROUNDS
OCCUPANTS: NA Washington Olympics May 4, 1871 to May 24, 1872; NA Washington Nationals April 15 to October 23, 1873; NA Washington Olympics April 26 to June 8, 1875 ★ **LOCATION:** (W) 17th St. Northwest, (S) S St. Northwest, (E) 16th St. Northwest ★ **CAPACITY:** 500

WHITE LOT
OCCUPANT: NA Washington Olympics some games 1871-72 ★ **LOCATION:** (NE) White House, on the Ellipse

MARYLAND AVENUE PARK
OCCUPANT: NA Washington Olympics some games 1871-72 ★ **LOCATION:** Sixth St. Northeast, Maryland Ave. Northeast, Seventh St. Northeast

NATIONAL GROUNDS
OCCUPANT: NA Washington Nationals April 20 to May 25, 1872 ★ **LOCATION:** 16th St., R St.

ATHLETIC PARK
OCCUPANT: AA Washington Nationals May 1 to August 5, 1884 ★ **LOCATION:** (N) S St. Northwest, (S) T St. Northwest, (E) Ninth St. Northwest

CAPITOL GROUNDS
OCCUPANT: UA Washington Nationals April 18 to September 25, 1884 ★ **LOCATION:** Center Field grounds of the US Capitol Building; (N) C St. Northeast; (W) Delaware Ave. Northeast; (S) B St. (later Constitution Ave.) Northeast (E) First St. Northeast ★ **CURRENT USE:** US Senate underground garage, RA Taft Memorial ★ **CAPACITY:** 6,000

SWAMPOODLE GROUNDS
OCCUPANTS: NL Washington Statesmen April 29, 1886 to September 21, 1889; World Series NL Detroit Wolverines vs. AA St. Louis Browns October 21, 1887 ★ **LOCATION:** Left Field (W) North Capitol St. Northeast, then Baltimore and Ohio RR side track; Third Base (S) F St. Northeast; First Base (E) Delaware Ave. Northeast; Right Field (N) G St. Northeast; also Massachusetts Ave; in the Swampoodle section of town ★ **CURRENT USE:** Western section of Union Station National Visitors Center used to be the infield and right field; City Post Office used to be left field ★ **CAPACITY:** 6,000

JERSEY STREET PARK
OCCUPANT: NL Washington Statesmen some games 1886-89 ★ **LOCATION:**

Jersey St. Northwest, Indiana Ave. Northwest

BOUNDARY FIELD
AKA: Beyer's Seventh St. Park ★ **OCCUPANTS:** AA Washington Nationals April 13 to October 5, 1891; NL Washington Senators April 16, 1892 to October 14, 1899 ★ **LOCATION:** (N) W St. Northwest; (W) Georgia Ave. Northwest; (S) U St. Northwest; (E) Fifth St. Northwest; also Seventh St. Northwest; Florida Ave. Northwest; the Boundary; same site as American League Park (II) and Griffith Stadium ★ **CAPACITY:** 6,500

ATLANTIC PARK
OCCUPANT: NL Washington Senators some games 1890s ★ **LOCATION:** (W) 17th St. Northwest; (E) 16th St. Northwest; U St. Northwest

RADFORD GROUNDS
OCCUPANT: NL Washington Senators some games 1890s ★ **LOCATION:** Second St. Northwest

AMERICAN LEAGUE PARK (I)
OCCUPANT: AL Washington Senators April 29, 1901 to September 29, 1903 ★ **LOCATION:** Left Field (NE) Neal St. Northeast; Third Base (NW) Trinidad Ave. Northeast; First Base (SW) Florida Ave. Northeast; Right Field (SE) Bladensburg Rd. (later H St.) Northeast; also 12th (later 13th) St. Northeast, 131/2 th St. (later 14th) St. Northeast; near the old tollgate on Bladensburg Rd.
PHENOMENA: Baseball's first public address announcer, E. Lawrence Phillips, gave the lineups by megaphone for the first time in 1902. Grandstands were literally moved to Florida Ave. and 7th for the 1904 season.

AMERICAN LEAGUE PARK (II)
OCCUPANT: AL Washington Senators April 14, 1904 to October 6, 1910 ★ **LOCATION:** same as Boundary Field and Griffith Stadium
PHENOMENA: The grounds crew had a doghouse in the outfield near the flagpole where they stored the flag between games. One day they forgot to close the doghouse door, and it just so happened that a Senator hit a ball over A's center fielder Socks Seybold's head and the ball rolled into the doghouse. Socks got his head stuck in the house trying to recover the ball. Three minutes later, the Athletics got Socks out, but the batter had long since crossed the plate with the first and only Inside-the-Dog-House-Homer in major league history.

GRIFFITH STADIUM
AKA: National Park 1911-21, Clark Griffith Park 1922 ★ **OCCUPANTS:** AL Washington Senators (first AL incarnation; now the Minnesota Twins) April 12, 1911 to October 2, 1960; NEWL Washington Pilots 1932; NNL Washington Elite Giants 1936-37; NNL Washington-Homestead Grays,half of the home games 1937-48; NNL Washington Black Senators April to August 1938; AL Washington Senators (second AL version; now the Texas Rangers) April 10 to September 21, 1961; Negro World Series Game 1 1942, Games 1 and 2 1943, Game 3 1945 ★ **LOCATION:** Left Field (E) Larch St. (later Fifth St. NW); Third Base (N) Howard University, then W St. NW; First Base (W) J. Frank Kelley Lumber and Mill Works, then Georgia Ave. (later Seventh St.) NW; Right Field (S) Spruce St. (later U St. NW); also Florida Ave. NW ★ **DIMENSIONS:** Left Field 407 (1911), 424 (1921), 358 (1926), 407 (1931), 402 (1936), 405 (1942), 375 (Opening Day 1947), 405 (remainder 1947), 402 (1948), 386 (1950), 408 (1951), 405 (1952), 388 (1954), 386 (1956), 350 (1957), 388 (1961); left of Left Center at corner 383 (1931), 366 (1954), 360 (1956); right of Left Center at bend in bleachers 409 (1942), 398 (1954), 383 (1955), 380 (1956); Left Center 391 (1911), 380 (1950); Center Field 421; Center Field corner to left of building-protection wall 423 (1926), 441 (1930), 422 (1931), 426 (1936), 420 (1942), 426 (1948), 420 (1950), 394 (1951), 420 (1952) 421 (1953), 426 (1954), 421 (1955), 426 (1961); inner tip of building-protection wall 409 (1943), 408 (1953); deepest corner at right end of building-protection wall 457 (1953), 438 (1955), 401 (1956); Right Center 378 (1954), 372 (1955), 373 (1956); Right Field 328 (1911), 326 (1921), 328 (marked 1926), 320 (actual 1926), 320 (1956); Backstop 61 ★ **FENCES:** Left Field 11.25 (foul pole to 408 mark concrete 1953), 12 (from 410 corner near left field foul pole to 408 mark just right of dead center 1954), 8 to 10 (wood in the corner in front of the bullpen at the foul pole 1955), 6.5 (wire and plywood in front of bullpen 1956); Center Field 30 (concrete 408 mark to 457 mark 1953), 31 (concrete 408 mark to 457 mark 1954), 6 (wire and plywood 1956); Right Center to left of scoreboard in front of bullpen 4 (wood from 457 mark to 435 mark 1953), 10 (wood 1955), 4 (wood 1959); Right Center Scoreboard 41 (1946); National Bohemian Beer Bottle 56 (1946); Right Field 30 (concrete 1953), 31 (concrete 1954) ★ **CURRENT USE:** Howard University Medical Center and College of Dentistry; 909 seats moved to Tinker Field in Orlando ★ **CAPACITY:** 32,000 (1921), 30,171 (1936), 31,500 (1939), 29,473 (1940), 25,048 (1948), 35,000 (1952), 28,587 (1956), 27,550 (1961)
PHENOMENA: Center-field wall detoured around five houses and a tree in center, jutting into the field of play. It was downhill from the plate to first, supposedly to help save a step for slow Washington batters. Josh Gibson (twice) and Mickey Mantle were the only batters ever to clear the left-field bleachers. In April 1953 Yankees PR Director Red Patterson promptly measured Mantle's drive as having rolled to a stop 565 feet from the plate in Perry L. Cool's backyard at 434 Oakdale St. It is often incorrectly stated that Mantle's ball traveled 565 feet in the air. Right-field clock out of play. Ball rolling between top of scoreboard and bottom of the clock was in play; if it didn't come out, it was a homer; if it did, the outfielder could throw it back into play. Presidents traditionally opened each season here by throwing out the first ball. In 1956 all distances to outfield were remeasured, and it was discovered right field had lost eight feet over the years.

STANDPIPE PARK
OCCUPANT: ECL Washington Potomacs 1924 ★ **LOCATION:** 16th St. Northwest, Euclid St. Northwest

ROBERT F. KENNEDY STADIUM
AKA: DC Stadium 1962-68; RFK Stadium ★ **OCCUPANT:** AL Washington Senators (now the Texas Rangers) April 9, 1962 to September 30, 1971 ★ **LOCATION:** Center Field (E) East Capitol St. Bridge, then Anacostia River; Third Base (N) C St. Northeast; Home Plate (W) 22nd St. Northeast; First Base (S) Independence Ave. ★ **DIMENSIONS:** Left Field 335 (1962), 260 (1982); Left Center 385 (1962), 381 (1963), 295 (1982); Center Field 410; Right Center 385 (1962), 378 (1963); Right Field 335 (1962); Backstop 60 ★ **FENCES:** 7 (wire screen); Left Field and Left Center 24 (wood, only in 1987) ★ **CAPACITY:** 43,500 (1962), 45,016 (1971)
PHENOMENA: Because of its curved dipping roof, looks like a wet straw hat or a waffle whose center stuck to the griddle. On September 30, 1971, the last game played here before the Senators moved to Texas, they led the Yankees 7-5 with two out in the ninth, but forfeited as angry fans swarmed out onto the field.

WATERVLIET, NEW YORK
TROY BALL CLUB GROUNDS
OCCUPANT: NL Troy Trojans May 20 to August 26, 1882 ★ **LOCATION:** (W) D and H Railroad tracks, (S) Genesee (later 19th) St.

WEEHAWKEN, NEW JERSEY
MONITOR PARK
OCCUPANT: Neutral site use by AA New York Mets September 11, 1887 ★ **LOCATION:** Three blocks from where Miller Stadium stands now in Hudson County

WEST NEW YORK, NEW JERSEY
WEST NEW YORK FIELD CLUB GROUNDS
AKA: Weehawken Cricket Grounds ★ **OCCUPANTS:** Neutral site use by NL Brooklyn Bridegrooms September 11 and 18 and October 2, 1898; by NL New York Giants June 4, July 16, August 13, and September 17, 1899

WESTPORT, MARYLAND
WESTPORT STADIUM
AKA: Westport Race Track, Westport Park ★ **OCCUPANT:** NAL Baltimore Elite Giants 1950-51 ★ **LOCATION:** Westport Blvd, Russell St., Bush St. ★ **CURRENT USE:** The concrete foundation for the stock-car racetrack can still be seen in a field behind a shopping center on the site

WHEELING, WEST VIRGINIA
ISLAND GROUNDS
OCCUPANT: Neutral site use by NL Pittsburgh Pirates September 22, 1890 ★ **LOCATION:** Wheeling Island, in Ohio River between Wheeling, West Virginia and Bridgeport, Ohio

WILMINGTON, DELAWARE
UNION STREET PARK
AKA: Quickstep Park ★ **OCCUPANT:** UA Wilmington Quicksteps September 2-15, 1884 ★ **LOCATION:** (N) Front St. (later Lancaster Ave.), (E) Union St.
PHENOMENA: The game on September 15, 1884 drew exactly zero fans. Faced with the prospect of a game between his last-place 2-15 Quicksteps and the next-to-last-place 16-63 Kansas City Unions (earlier in the season known as the Altoona Mountain Citys), Wilmington manager Joe Simmons called his team off the field and forfeited the game.

WORCESTER, MASSACHUSETTS
AGRICULTURAL COUNTY FAIR GROUNDS RACE TRACK
AKA: Worcester Driving Park ★ **OCCUPANTS:** Worcester NL Brown Stockings May 1, 1880 to September 29, 1882; neutral site use by NA Boston Red Stockings October 30, 1874 **LOCATION:** (N) Highland St., (W) Agricultural (later Russell) St., (S) Williams St., Cedar St., (E) Sever St.

YEADON, PENNSYLVANIA
HILLDALE PARK
AKA: Darby Catholic High School Stadium ★ **OCCUPANT:** ECL Darby Hilldales 1923-27; ANL Darby Hilldales 1929; NEWL Darby Hilldales April to June 1932 ★ **LOCATION:** Left Field (N) Bunting Lane (later MacDade Blvd); Third Base (W) Cedar Ave., then greenhouses; First Base (S) Chester Ave; Right Field (E) Darby Catholic High School (also called Yeadon School); in suburbs of Philadelphia on the Darby-Yeadon borderline, mostly in Yeadon ★ **DIMENSIONS:** Left Field 315; Right Center 400; Right Field 370 ★ **CURRENT USE:** Acme Super Saver supermarket and drive-in bank

ZANESVILLE, OHIO
MARK GREY ATHLETIC PARK
AKA: Mark Park, Farm Diamond ★ **OCCUPANT:** Neutral site use by NNL Homestead Grays one game in 1938 ★ **LOCATION:** Putnam Ave; Left Field (N), Third Base (W), First Base (S), Right Field (E) ★ **DIMENSIONS:** Left Field 304, Center Field 386, Right Center 265

Chapter 31

Baseball Commissioners

By A. D. Suehsdorf

From the beginning, Organized Baseball has been controlled by the owners of the major league clubs. Acting in concert and accountable only to themselves, they have parceled out the franchises, built the grandstands, set the ticket prices, assembled the players, written the game's rules, defined league structure and operation, dominated the minor league dependencies, and, until recent times, bound their players absolutely through the reserve clause written into every contract. Virtually the only restraint on this monopoly power has been fear of alienating the fans from whom all profit flows by actions or circumstances threatening confidence in the honesty and integrity of the game. Even this, on occasion, has been put at risk.

Owner power has been matched by owner intractability. Whatever their virtues as individuals, baseball owners in the aggregate through much of their history have been quarrelsome, devious, inclined to factional fights, and to circumventing, if not subverting, the rules of their own National Agreement under which all baseball is expected to operate. In part this has resulted from their paradoxical position as cooperative competitors, in part from the entrepreneur's traditional resistance to authority.

During the quarter century of National League supremacy (1876 to 1900), it was of little consequence that the league presidents were figureheads and the owners' squabbles flagrant. But when Ban Johnson's American League established itself as an equal in 1901—the first and only competitor ever to do so—it became imperative to create an agency empowered to arbitrate matters between the still-touchy partners and to present a facade of unity to the outside world.

The result was the National Commission of 1903: the two league presidents, Ban Johnson of the American League and Harry Pulliam of the National, and August "Garry" Herrmann, president of the Cincinnati Reds, as unsalaried chairman. The National League's edge was more apparent than real. *Gemutlich Garry* was an old friend of Ban's and had won regard in both leagues for his efforts in mediating peace between them. Further, while Herrmann and Johnson served all 17 years of the Commission's life, the National League had four presidents, breaks in continuity that diminished its role. In any event, the triumvirate was dominated by the dynamic Johnson, whose wit, energy, and administrative skill soon made him the acknowledged "Czar of Baseball."

Basically, the Commission's responsibility was interpretation and enforcement of the National Agreement, and punishment of

Kenesaw Mountain Landis
The first commissioner, shown here opening the 1923 World Series at Yankee Stadium, ruled baseball with an iron fist from 1920 to 1944.

violations by fines and suspensions. Neither the minor leagues nor the players were officially represented. The Commission assumed protection of their rights in grievances against individual clubs or the major leagues, although its concern was paternalistic at best. Intraleague matters were left to the appropriate president and his board of directors.

Overall, historians give the Commission marks of fair to good for its efforts. The first 12 years of its existence were prosperous, relatively harmonious, and progressive insofar as they consolidated baseball as the national pastime. The final five were a time of anger, turmoil, and disruption.

Strain was inherent, for the concept of the National Commission was fundamentally flawed. League presidents, by their nature, could not view intra- and interleague affairs equally. The club owners of each league expected the loyalty of their Commission representative and were infuriated when justice or

equity required a decision that went against them. It also was impossible to select a neutral chairman from among the owners themselves, yet the money men were never pleased to do the bidding of commissioners who had no financial stake in the game.

In external affairs the Commission did reasonably well. Dealings with the Base Ball Players Fraternity (1912 to 1917), while accompanied by bluster and stonewalling, were on the whole conducted fairly and brought about some improvements in player contracts. It contributed to settlement of the Federal League uprising and to keeping the game going during World War I.

Internally, it lacked the heart to confront long-range baseball problems, such as gambling, which was widespread in and around ballparks, and, in consequence, an undercurrent of crooked players, bribe offers, and thrown games. Investigations were tentative, conclusions irresolute: a coat of whitewash, or passing the buck to the league or teams concerned, while sighing with relief that no one outside baseball was the wiser.

As men of their time, the commissioners shared proprietors' beliefs in the sanctity of property and the subservience of labor, and rigorously upheld the reserve and ten-day clauses, while assiduously avoiding any legal test of their validity. Yet despite this tilt toward their employers, they showed their best side in the justice of many difficult decisions affecting the commerce in players.

Under the National Agreement players had the right to advance as far and as fast as their talents permitted. Contrarily, they were not to be "farmed" or "covered up" or otherwise hindered from pursuing this goal. The Agreement was inspired less by a regard for players than by assurance of an open market for owners, so that by offering opportunity to baseball's best prospects the clubs would enjoy a competitive balance and hold fan interest. Yet for the owners a gentleman's agreement was always more compelling than the national one. They connived with each other to diddle the draft, waiver and option processes and, incidentally, to limit salaries and rosters, hold up the pay of injured players, and burden released players with the travel costs of getting wherever they were being sent. Such sharp practice and cheese-paring economies were considered shrewd business, and the Commission, when it did not agree with them, was hard put to remedy any but the most egregious injustices.

Where it was most at risk was in settling conflicting claims to players—viz., George Sisler to the Browns instead of the Pirates, Jack Quinn to the Yankees, not the White Sox. These interclub fights were bitter and the losers nursed their grievances for years. Cumulatively, they were serious enough to topple the Commission. The last straw was President Johnson's suspension of Carl Mays in mid-1919. Having gone AWOL from the Red Sox, the pitcher was traded to New York in defiance of Ban's order that no deal be made until Mays had been disciplined. This enraged both clubs, as well as long-simmering malcontents in both leagues who had had enough of Ban, whether as president, commissioner or czar. The Yankees got the suspension overturned in court. The American League drastically reduced Ban's authority by appointing a two-owner committee to review all but the most minor fines and suspensions. And the National League, long exasperated with Herrmann for being Johnson's docile creature, forced him to resign. Johnson, having lost his customary American League backing, was powerless to keep Garry in office, although he bull-headedly blocked the election of a new Commission chairman. As rancor led to impasse, the baseball establishment drifted.

To prod the owners out of their rut, Albert D. Lasker, a promi-

nent Chicago advertising man and a substantial stockholder in the Cubs, proposed a new commission of three distinguished, disinterested public figures with "unreviewable authority" over owners, players and franchises. Wearied as they were of bosses from within the ranks, the magnates did not welcome supervision by outsiders as an improvement. While they maundered, the Black Sox scandal broke.

Horrified, if not surprised, by this corruption of their enterprise, the owners took dramatic action to restore public confidence in the game. Although splintered by in-house controversy and intrigue, they mustered a majority vote to scrap the National Agreement and create a new three-man commission. Shortly after a Grand Jury heard evidence of the 1919 World Series fix, they named Kenesaw Mountain Landis as their principal Commissioner.

Then 53, Landis had been a Federal district court judge for 15 years. He was meagerly educated, narrow in vision and simplistic in his judicial decisions, many of which were overturned on appeal. Nonetheless, with his craggy face, dramatic shock of white hair, and flamboyant manner, not to mention an easily aroused sense of outrage, he had the public image of a fierce but twinkle-eyed man of rectitude. The owners were certain he saw things their way. In 1915, he had delayed action on the Federal League's antitrust suit against the majors until a negotiated settlement could be reached and the need for a decision was past, thus avoiding once again a legal test of baseball's monopoly status. To the press and public, he had the common touch of a lifelong affection for the Cubs and, to all appearances, the backbone to clean up baseball's mess.

Commissioner Landis took office in January 1921 (although not surrendering his seat on the Federal bench for another year). His mandate was to deal as he saw fit with anything deemed "detrimental" to baseball. His powers were written into a new National Agreement and incorporated in player contracts. His decisions and penalties were to be binding. There could be no recourse to the courts and no public criticism. Even the most tentative objections were met by threats of resignation before which the owners invariably quailed.

Landis relished the free hand he had demanded and got. The appointment of associate commissioners was forgotten, and even as advisers, the two league presidents—Johnson and John A. Heydler—generally were ignored.

The eight Black Sox were first to feel the Commissioner's wrath. Whatever the courts might determine, in Judge Landis' eyes their conduct had been atrociously detrimental to baseball and he banned them all, plus Joe Gedeon, who had "guilty knowledge," for life.

Player delinquency was a continuing embarrassment. Old villainies surfaced and new ones occurred. Over the next several years six more players were expelled and many others declared ineligible for varying periods. Landis' sweeping actions often were inconsistent, arbitrary and unfair. Some rascals escaped scrutiny. Some great stars were acquitted on their own say-so. A few culprits were severely punished for trifles. Benny Kauff, indicted for, but acquitted of, auto theft, was ruled permanently ineligible because Landis decided he was probably guilty. Ray Fisher was blacklisted without explanation, hearing or appeal, evidently for negotiating with an "outlaw" club. Petitions for reinstatement of such sinners as Buck Weaver were refused or went unanswered.

Landis opposed all forms of gambling—horse racing especially—and tried to keep gamblers out of the ballparks, but with

indifferent success. He failed to act against the known gambling connections of Charles Stoneham of the Giants; the racing stables of Frank Navin of Detroit, or the betting proclivities of such dedicated horseplayers as John McGraw and Rogers Hornsby.

Still, by his vehemence and persistence he sent a clear message to baseball that crooks and cheats would not be tolerated, and he persuaded Americans that he was making their game honest again.

For all his harshness, he acted to protect the rights of players and professed sympathetic interest in them. He cracked down on cover-ups and other management maneuvering that impeded players' progress, although here, too, he was ever unpredictable. In two cover-up cases six months apart, he made the Indians turn Tommy Henrich loose, while allowing them to keep Bob Feller.

Similarly, he favored an unrestricted draft and fought a losing battle against the farm system, most prominently in skirmishes with Branch Rickey, farming's principal architect. In 1938, he made free agents of 91 Cardinal farmhands unfairly sequestered, and in 1940 another 91 young Tigers. Landis' resistance to the farm system began soon after he was installed as Commissioner and it remained a central issue of his many years in office. Whether farming killed minor league ball or kept it alive, it was an idea whose time had come, and Landis alienated many owners by his efforts to stamp it out.

The Judge loved to preside at the World Series each year. As an interleague affair, it always had been a National Commission responsibility, but Landis had his own czarist inclinations and went beyond scheduling, umpires and distribution of receipts to make the event uniquely his own. He reduced the format from nine games to seven, negotiated the first contracts for radio broadcasting, and, as he was always in attendance with his chin on the railing of a front-row box, he usurped the umpires' authority to call a game or oust a player—most notably the removal of Ducky Medwick in 1934.

It did not take the owners long to regret their hasty and comprehensive surrender of power. By the mid-1920s they were grumbling at Landis' interference in player transactions, and by 1932 voted limits on his jurisdiction in this area. The opprobrium once reserved for Ban Johnson was now applied to Landis, but stopped short of calling his bluff about quitting. Capricious, high-handed and profane as he was, he was also an unassailable national institution. Among his last acts was the legitimate but Draconian expulsion of owner William D. Cox for betting on his Philadelphia Phillies. Frail and ill as his term reached 24 years, the Judge still was the only logical candidate for Commissioner on the owners' horizon. He died at 78 in 1944 and was elected to baseball's Hall of Fame.

Rid of the tyrant at last, the magnates threw off a few of their shackles. They restricted the detrimental-to-baseball authority by exempting from it all their major league rules and any action taken in compliance with them. They wiped out the gag that prohibited criticizing a Commissioner's ruling, or going to court to block it. And they changed the margin for approval of an interleague action from a simple majority to three quarters of the clubs of each league.

They then chose 47-year-old Senator Albert B. "Happy" Chandler of Kentucky as Landis' successor. It was a surprise appointment engineered by Larry MacPhail, then a Yankee owner, who brought his colleagues, divided and squabbling as usual, to a decision.

A greater contrast to Landis would have been hard to find. Happy was the prototypical politico: shrewd, ebullient, folksy, and

smarter than he seemed. The owners obviously wanted a glad-handing goodwill ambassador for baseball and a lightweight boss for themselves. They got the first, but not the second. Although rather too exuberant and good ol' boy for the New York press, which thought him foolish and began to ride him hard, Happy was his own man. He bluntly told his new employers that they did not own baseball, that it was America's game and would remain so as long as fans did not think it "a bloody business" run by profiteers. This did not sit well in baseball's councils; nor did his efforts to improve wages and working conditions for umpires and his support of benefits for players, such as a minimum wage ($5,000!), a 25 percent limit on salary cuts, and a pension plan to be funded by a percentage of the receipts from television and radio broadcasts of the World Series.

If the owners were displeased, they knew they were in a weak position from which to object. In 1946, the upstart Mexican League was an enticing alternative to players uncertain about the level and stability of their baseball earnings.

Chandler met the Mexican League threat by suspending 18 jumpers for five years (though granting amnesty in 1949, when the insurrection failed). Several of the disgruntled jumpers thereupon filed suits challenging the sacred reserve clause, which was a profound worry to the owners until the clubs involved persuaded the plaintiffs to withdraw. Still, Chandler was seen as having invited an unnecessary risk.

The most significant event of his regime was the integration of the major leagues by Brooklyn's introduction of Jackie Robinson; the most sensational was the one-year suspension of Brooklyn's manager, Leo Durocher, both in April 1947.

While not a prime mover in Robinson's arrival, Happy was openly and genuinely supportive of Branch Rickey's stunning assault on the game's long-standing color barrier. Unlike Landis, who addressed the matter only obliquely, although his sentiments were well known, Chandler spoke forthrightly in favor of integration.

Durocher's suspension was brought on specifically by an unseemly confrontation between Leo and Larry MacPhail, but it appeared to stem from official exasperation with an accumulation of Durocher scrapes, altercations, dubious associations, on-field rows, and marital difficulties, all of which presumably added up to that convenient catchall, "conduct detrimental to baseball." It was the stiffest penalty ever levied against a manager.

Unfortunately, having pronounced judgment without citing the particulars on which it was based, Chandler enforced silence on all parties and refused to discuss it himself. In the confusion and controversy which followed, it was never made clear whether the suspension "year" was the duration of the baseball season or the calendar's twelve months, whether a suspended manager's contract was valid, and whether, at suspension's end, he could be rehired. Far from a salutary punishment, *l'affaire Durocher* made a martyr of Leo and lost face for Happy.

Throughout his term, the Commissioner was confronted by the ineradicable problems of owner manipulation of baseball rules and of inappropriate association with racing or gambling interests. In a remarkable burst of confidence, Alva Bradley of the Indians confessed blandly to generalized owner cheating, and Chandler encountered enough violations of the option process and premature signing of high-school prospects to believe him.

As always, investigations of possible wrongdoing made no friends, and adverse decisions always made enemies. Hearing

rumbles of dissatisfaction before the winter meetings of 1950, the penultimate year in which, by custom, reelection of the Commissioner would be considered, Happy asked for a vote of confidence. Nine were for, seven against—three short of the mandatory three quarters. Happy resigned, accepting one year's salary as severance. In 1982, he was elected to the Hall of Fame. He died June 15, 1991, age 92.

Ford C. Frick, 56, a one-time "gee-whiz" sportswriter and, since 1934, president of the National League, was picked to replace Happy in 1951. He was a compromise candidate maneuvered into the job by Walter O'Malley of Brooklyn, an emerging power among the magnates.

Now fully recovered from the Landis era, the owners had acquired the complacent, pliable Commissioner most to their liking. In the span of Frick's two seven-year terms, baseball underwent revolutionary changes, not one of them bearing his imprint. He busied himself with administrative detail, pursuing the struggle against gambling, punishing management infractions of baseball rules, and occasionally freeing covered-up minor leaguers. He determined that Roger Maris' 61 homers should have separate mention in the record book because they took 162 games to achieve and, like Landis and Chandler before him, he refused an appeal to reinstate old Buck Weaver of the Black Sox. Beyond that, anything the owners wanted was all right with him.

He presided over an era when commonplace air travel, widening TV markets, and beckoning tax breaks prompted the Braves, Browns, A's, Giants, and Dodgers to shift their franchises, when talk of a potential third big league was enough to hustle the majors into expanding to 10 clubs each, and when minor leagues were dying from all these invasions of their territories. The character of club ownership was changing from the rough-and-ready old-timers to big-money businessmen or corporations. Congress conducted hearings on baseball's curious exemption from the antitrust laws (though without taking action). Some prominent players were benefiting from exorbitant signing bonuses, while others were looking for greater security and considering unionization. Commissioner Frick saw these as league matters, outside his jurisdiction. In 1965, full of years, he resigned with an election to the Hall of Fame in prospect.

The choice of William D. "Spike" Eckert as Commissioner was a mistake and an embarrassment. A retired Air Force lieutenant general with a distinguished record in World War II, he had not sought the job, but was recommended by a brother officer, Curtis LeMay, bellicose boss of the Strategic Air Command, who refused to be a candidate himself. Spike, an amiable if diffident man, had become a business consultant with fair administrative skills and no knowledge of baseball. He immediately was dubbed "the Unknown Soldier." The owners supported him with four of their number to assist in his major areas of responsibility. Yet his ineptitude was obvious. He was deferential to his owners, limp with his league presidents, and had no awareness of baseball's problems or of the direction it should be headed. He aroused national indignation by failing to cancel games after the assassinations of Martin Luther King and Robert Kennedy.

In December 1968, with an organized players' strike in prospect, he was fired. As balm, he continued to receive his salary until his death in 1971. For this uncomfortable interlude, the owners had no one to blame but themselves.

When elected in 1969, Bowie Kuhn was baseball's youngest (42), tallest (six-foot-five), and biggest (240 pounds) Commissioner ever. He had worked the Griffith Stadium scoreboard as a youth, graduated Princeton, and was well acquainted with baseball through his New York law firm, which had the National League as a client.

Kuhn's first act was to get negotiations between the Major League Players Association (MLPA) and the owner's Player Relations Committee (PRC), which had stalled over the terms of a pension package, moving again. He helped bring about a successful settlement that saved the 1969 season from the disruption of a player strike.

A positive man, though in his own words a bit stiff-necked and starchy, Kuhn believed that the still-extraordinary powers of the Commissioner had been granted in order to be used. Furthermore, the owners had decided that their governance needed "restructuring," and charged him with developing a plan for more efficient administration of their business. Kuhn and an *ad hoc* committee of baseball executives and management experts proposed a further concentration of power in the Commissioner's office. The plan was utterly rejected. Many owners felt that, with more lines on the organization chart leading to the Commissioner, they would be surrendering control of their franchises.

With many important areas of baseball business excluded from his purview, Kuhn resumed his role as persuader, counselor, and positive influence. He was never more than that in the fierce negotiations with the MLPA and its zealous executive director, Marvin Miller. For the owners, negotiations were conducted by the PRC, a body of their peers. It was this group, with confirmation by the owners as a whole, which made the landmark concessions to union recognition, player agents, arbitration, free agency, the resulting destruction of the reserve clause, and skyrocketing salaries. During the 50-day player strike of 1981, cries were heard for Bowie's locking both sides in a room until they emerged with a settlement. In Landis' day, maybe, but things no longer worked that way. By 1978, the owners had made the PRC a separate corporation, distinctly separate from the Commissioner's office.

Where Kuhn acted boldly—more so than any of his predecessors—was in his dealings with owners and players. He cracked down on George Steinbrenner of the Yankees (two-year suspension), Ted Turner of the Braves (one-year suspension), and went head-to-head with Charlie Finley of the Oakland A's in what seemed unfair salary wrangles with Reggie Jackson, Vida Blue and Catfish Hunter. In 1976, believing that Finley was liquidating, not rebuilding, his club, Kuhn negated sales of three A's for $3.5 million.

He met the emerging drug problem directly, despite opposition from owners, who felt that acknowledging involvement made baseball "look bad," and from the MLPA, which resisted all disciplinary measures imposed by the Commissioner. He returned the All-Star Game voting to the fans, presided over a new and lucrative television contract, and brought the 1972 strike to a speedy conclusion.

Greater furors arose from making Willie Mays and Mickey Mantle sever their association with baseball while working for gambling casinos, and from acceding to television's demand for World Series games in prime-time hours at night.

Victims of his direct actions often became unforgiving enemies. What might be good for baseball was not necessarily good for an owner's corporate interests that underwrote his baseball venture. An insurrection that threatened his re-election in 1975 was headed off by a friendly majority. But by 1983, five National League owners were unalterably disaffected. Lingering unhappiness with

the costly 1981 strike and its aftermath was a burden. A proposal for more equitable sharing of broadcasting revenues among rich and poor clubs was a new and divisive problem. And there were renewed calls for "restructuring." Magnates now said they wanted a chief executive officer—a real corporate CEO with the business skills to guide them through the complexities of baseball in the contemporary world. Views on the powers he would have were mixed.

In the voting, the National League dissidents held firm. (There were three inconsequential "no" votes in the American League.) With 18 out of 26 owners on his side—a 69 percent approval rating—Kuhn failed to get the necessary three-quarters majority in each league.

For all the complaints, Bowie Kuhn was probably the most capable Commissioner the owners ever had, and after more years in office than anyone but Landis, it was not easy to find an equally qualified replacement. Kuhn overstayed his term by a year until Peter V. Ueberroth, 47 years old and fresh from a triumph as head of the Los Angeles Olympic Organizing Committee, was unanimously elected to a five-year term in October 1984.

In this trim, composed, and self-confident executive, the owners finally acquired the leadership they knew was needed to deal with the complexities of contemporary life that were engulfing the baseball business.

Ueberroth became the game's CEO. All departments and activities reported to him, as did the two league presidents, Dr. Bobby Brown of the American and A. Bartlett Giamatti of the National. The Commissioner's authority to discipline owners was greatly increased. He could transfer or deny any club's draft choices, and the limit on club fines was upped from $5,000 to $250,000. Reelection of the Commissioner reverted to a majority vote of the clubs, with a required minimum of five votes from each league. His salary was raised to a reported $450,000, nearly twice what Kuhn was paid.

Having concentrated power in his own hands, Ueberroth then demonstrated that his management style was to delegate responsibility. Although he took unilateral actions to tidy up baseball operations that he found "in disarray," he preferred to have problems solved by the people most closely involved. Cool and controlled in demeanor, yet insistent on high levels of performance and not afraid to make unpopular decisions—he once described himself as "shy and ruthless"—Ueberroth worked first to restore fiscal "sanity" to owners' operations. Many franchises—estimates ran as high as 21 of the 26—were losing money yet continuing to offer long-term player contracts at high wages, even to veterans headed for the inactive list. Exchanges of information to control this extravagance soon brought charges of collusion from the Players Association, which complained of a suspicious absence of bidding by clubs for free agents. Two arbitrators agreed that this was indeed the case during the 1986 and 1987 seasons. Ueberroth denied the allegation but did not dispute the judgment, insisting that baseball must find ways to improve financial stability before such looming problems as expansion could be faced. Tentatively, new franchises could be awarded by 1990 and new teams take the field by 1993.

Internally, baseball felt the impact of two pervasive social problems of the 1980s: drugs and job opportunities for minorities. Each club conducted its own rehabilitation program for drug users through its medical department. The Players Association objected to testing as an invasion of privacy and Ueberroth tended to agree, even though minor leaguers and front-office personnel were tested.

The Commissioner also was empowered to suspend relapsed players for one year without pay.

The hiring of blacks and other minorities, particularly those individuals with distinguished baseball careers, for positions of responsibility on or off the field remained a sensitive issue. Ueberroth contended that all clubs had accepted the obligation, although at his departure few, if any, highly visible jobs (such as manager, which minority groups said would prove the point of good faith) had gone to blacks or Latinos.

In assaults on gambling, Ueberroth worked principally behind the scenes to eliminate club-owner investment in racing stables or tracks. In one of his first public gestures he won approval by lifting Kuhn's rather farfetched ban on Mantle and Mays.

At his urging the Cubs chose to install lights at Wrigley Field, rather than reimburse the leagues for lost night-game revenues. While not involved in the owners' negotiations with players and umpires, he kept the parties bargaining until settlements were reached. He found a new source of income in persuading large corporations to pay for the privilege of having their products endorsed by Major League Baseball. He concluded enormous new TV contracts with CBS and ESPN. And he then announced his decision to resign as Commissioner, even if a second term were offered. Although the owners did not always welcome his assertiveness—an outsider's voice in which they heard as much coercion as persuasion—they felt he had significantly improved baseball's finances, and they accepted his resignation with regret.

National League president A. Bartlett Giamatti was chosen unanimously as Ueberroth's successor in September 1988. The seventh Commissioner signed on for five years beginning April 1, 1989, six months before the traditional October date for transfers of power.

Bart Giamatti's background was intellectually glamorous. A *magna cum laude* graduate of Yale, he taught Renaissance literature there until elected the university's president in 1978. Eight years later, after the retirement of Charles "Chub" Feeney, he became president of the National League. His first move was to hire his good friend, Francis T. "Fay" Vincent, Jr., a lawyer with high-level business experience, as baseball's first-ever deputy commissioner.

Whether as league president or Commissioner, Giamatti was first of all a fan, with the New Englander's inevitable devotion to the Red Sox. He suspended players for corking bats and scuffing balls. During the 1988 season he held firm against protests of his thirty-day suspension of Reds' Manager Pete Rose for bumping an umpire and made an unpopular decision to enforce the balk rule strictly. He supported "social justice" as the only remedy for baseball's embarrassing and persistent refusal to hire minority managers, coaches or executives at any level of the game. He also insisted that clubs improve the rowdy atmosphere of their parks. What charmed people most, however, was his unabashed love of baseball and the elegance with which he expressed his feelings—in speech or prose—for its place in American life. He was, in truth, a Commissioner not for owners, or players, or fans, but for the Game.

The major action of his 154-day term was banning Pete Rose from baseball for life. The basic question of whether Rose had engaged, as alleged, in sports gambling was never resolved, but a six-month investigation did establish his association with known gamblers and drug dealers. Rose agreed to a settlement charging him with violation of Major League Rule 21, which covers a miscellany of punishable misconduct. Rose, said Giamatti, had "engaged in a variety of acts which have stained the game, and he

must now live with the consequences of those acts." Under another Major League Rule, Rose would be free to apply for reinstatement after one year.

It was generally agreed that Commissioner Giamatti had handled an awkward and difficult problem with distinction. Nine days later, after suffering a heart attack at his summer home on Martha's Vineyard, Massachusetts, he was dead at the age of 51.

Within hours, baseball's executive council elevated Fay Vincent to Acting Commissioner, and the owners, by unanimous vote, made him their eighth Commissioner on September 13. If he lacked Giamatti's flair, he shared his friend's affection and respect for baseball. He preferred grass to turf and day games to night, liked wooden bats, disliked the designated hitter. He was a boyhood fan of the then-Philadelphia A's, but his own athletic career was cut short by a freak accident to his back while at Williams College. Damage to spinal nerves left him unable to stand comfortably for more than a few minutes at a time and forced him to walk with a cane. His qualifications for baseball's top job, however, were bona fide: Phi Beta Kappa at Williams, law degree from Yale, practicing attorney, prime mover (as president and CEO) in a turnaround of ailing Columbia Pictures, and, when the movie company was sold to Coca-Cola, vice president of a new Coke entertainment division. He had rejoined a law firm when Giamatti lured him into baseball. As Giamatti's deputy he brought the record-setting television contract to a conclusion and supervised the complex Rose investigation.

As Commissioner he moved into the spotlight when the 1989 World Series between Oakland and San Francisco was halted by a severe northern California earthquake that struck minutes before Game 3 at Candlestick Park. Vincent acted quickly and surely. "We want to be very sensitive to the state of the community," he told a candlelit press conference. "Our modest little game is not a priority." When the Series was resumed ten days later he was widely praised for his calm and tactful demeanor.

As spring training for the 1990 season was about to begin, the owners' negotiations with the players for a new collective bargaining agreement broke down and led to a lockout. Vincent brought the two sides together, and a settlement was achieved by mid-March, an effort appreciated less by the owners than by the players.

In July Vincent banned George Steinbrenner, the obstreperous owner of the New York Yankees, from the "management or day-to-day operations" of his team. Steinbrenner acknowledged that he had acted contrary to the best interests of baseball, specifically by paying a known gambler $40,000 to provide damaging information about player Dave Winfield, who had a long-standing dispute with the owner about money allegedly owed to the outfielder's charitable foundation.

Like many baseball scandals, this one had ramifications aside from the unpleasantness of seeing an owner publicly chastised by a Commissioner. It had actually come to light during Peter Ueberroth's watch. Its clues led, like a pond's ripples, in many directions; some were pursued, others not. But Steinbrenner's admission of wrongdoing seemed to satisfy the Commissioner's office, which, as it had for Rose, pronounced Steinbrenner eligible for future reinstatement.

Subsequent decisions were criticized not only for the actions taken, but for how the Commissioner reached them. In June 1992, when the owners agreed to allow the National League to expand into Colorado and Florida, Vincent ruled that the American League would be tapped for 55 percent of the players drafted to stock the new teams but would receive only $45 million of the $190 million total the new entities were paying as franchise fees. It could be argued that the AL's fourteen teams were about 55 percent of the major leagues' twenty-six, or that the NL should receive the larger reward for letting newcomers into their club.

But Vincent took heat for two departures from precedent. In five previous league expansions, franchise fees were awarded solely to the expanding league, and players were drafted only from the league in which they would be playing. Yet if the money division was unpopular, the owners had only themselves to blame. Failing to reach an agreement on their own, they had left Vincent to make the decision for them.

A few days later, when there were owner objections to sale of the Seattle Mariners to investors led by Nintendo, the Japanese video-games corporation, Vincent helped complete the deal ($125 million, the highest amount ever paid for a team) and was credited with preserving an ailing, small-market franchise.

Even so, his relations with the owners were deteriorating in an atmosphere of "disharmony and dissension." Fundamentally different views of the Commissioner's role were emerging. For Fay Vincent it meant preserving the integrity of the national pastime for all constituencies—owners, players, fans, and for America itself. Many owners felt otherwise. They owned the game and Vincent was theirs to command. Hardliners on the owners' Labor Relations Committee made this all too clear. Fearful that the Commissioner might undermine their bargaining strategy—freely predicted as union-busting—in forthcoming negotiations with the Players Association, they asked Vincent to waive the power to intervene implicit under his catch-all authority to act in "the best interests of baseball." To their great displeasure, he flatly refused.

Unrest reached crisis proportions on July 6, when the Commissioner undertook a realignment of the National League. It was ridiculous, he argued, to have the Chicago Cubs and St. Louis Cardinals in the league's eastern division while the Atlanta Braves and Cincinnati Reds were in the west. For the sake of geographic good sense, the teams should switch. Interestingly, his action was not taken unilaterally, but at the request of six NL owners who favored realignment.

Nonetheless, consternation and outrage greeted the announcement. The Tribune Company, owner of the Cubs, led the protest. It complained that traditional rivalries would be disrupted and that the Commissioner had acted arbitrarily and capriciously. It was also keenly aware that realignment would make a serious impact on its superstation operations.

Superstations have been a sore point in baseball for everybody who doesn't own one. Many teams argue that wide-ranging superstation broadcasts hurt local attendance and local television coverage. Who is going to watch the local tailender, either in the stands or on local TV, if a superstation's games involving top teams or a hot pennant race can be seen by anyone subscribing to cable? The Tribune Company, which paid handsomely to broadcast games of seven major league teams (Cubs, White Sox, Dodgers, Angels, Yankees, Phillies, Rockies) on one or another of its far-reaching TV stations, was not worrying about pennant races. Putting the Cubs on the West Coast would mean that games could not be seen in Chicago until 9 P.M., hardly prime time. Low rates for late-hour commercials could mean heavy losses of revenue. The Tribune Company went to court for an injunction to block the order.

Vincent was certain that as Commissioner he had jurisdiction in such matters as realignment. As chairman of Major League

Baseball it was his sworn duty to protect the game from encroachment and to create the best possible conditions in which it could thrive. He did not see himself as the owners' errand boy, or as the guardian of their outside interests, particularly those interests in which baseball was reduced to a subordinate role. It seemed unlikely that Bart Giamatti would have acted otherwise.

Legally, several elements of baseball's governing documents were at issue. The National League constitution, as revised in 1981, clearly states that no club can be moved without its consent. The Cubs argued that this should take precedence over anything the Commissioner is empowered to do under the Major League Agreement.

Not so, said Vincent. He acted under Article I of the Agreement, which gives what courts have previously found to be "broad and unfettered" power to act in "the best interests of baseball."

But, said the Cubs, those powers cannot be used to interfere with "intimate business decisions." Furthermore, the Commissioner's power to settle disputes between clubs (Article VII) applies only to those whose resolution is not "expressly provided" elsewhere—viz., the National League constitution. The District Court judge ruled that Article VII applied and could not be superseded by Article I's "best interest" power. A preliminary injunction was granted.

Dissident owners now pushed for a full-dress meeting of both leagues with their Commissioner to discuss his performance, perhaps to press for his resignation or, failing that, to fire him. Vincent saw no reason to oblige them. Article IX of the Agreement states that "no diminution of the compensation or powers of ... the Commissioner shall be made during his term of office."

Vincent's term ran to March 31, 1994, and, he said firmly, "I will not resign—ever."

Vincent had some support among the owners, but the movers and shakers were dead-set against him. On September 7, four days after an overwhelming vote of no confidence, he resigned. It would not serve baseball well to have its leadership endlessly involved in legal wrangling. "Owners have a duty," he said, "to take into consideration that they own a part of America's national pastime—in trust. This trust sometimes requires putting self-interest second."

Realignment pulled the trigger, but it was not the issue. It was a power struggle in which the owners prevailed. More malleable Commissioners than Vincent survived this tug-of-war, but those who clung to the eroding power the owners, with fear and trembling, once gave Judge Landis to save their game were destined for defeat. With Vincent gone, the owners were where they had wanted to be: in absolute control of their industry, with no umpire to reconcile the competing claims of players or fans.

The owners faced a prospect of an executive council of the two league presidents plus eight owners to govern the game. They—or hired or appointed delegates—would deal with such outside relationships as those with the Players Association, the radio and TV broadcasters and perhaps Congress, as well as with such internal problems as finite sources of revenue in an era of skyrocketing costs, the troublesome imbalance between large market teams (Los Angeles, New York) and small (Seattle, Pittsburgh) and, perhaps most painful, their historic inability to get along with each other.

In this uncertain environment the owners united temporarily behind one of their own, Milwaukee's Allan H. "Bud" Selig. Growing up, he had watched the minor league Milwaukee Brewers; at 35 (in 1970) he had become owner of a major league team, the

sickly Seattle Pilots, which he moved to Milwaukee and named the Brewers; and at 58 he now became overseer of every team in baseball. Selig had led the group of dissatisfied owners that forced Vincent's ouster in September 1992; now he replaced Vincent on an interim basis. After nearly six years of "searching" for a permanent commissioner, the owners unanimously elected Selig.

It seemed an unlikely climax for a former automobile executive from Wisconsin. Selig's Brewers won just one pennant in his 28 years in charge, but his fellow owners valued him nonetheless. With the collective bargaining agreement due to expire in 1994, he rallied the owners behind a proposal calling for revenue sharing and a salary cap—a concept the players union flatly rejected. On August 12, with Tony Gwynn chasing .400 and the New York Yankees and Montreal Expos having dream seasons, play was suspended. A month later, to the shock of fans worldwide, Selig announced the cancellation of the World Series.

Over eight months of ensuing negotiations, everyone from children to presidents tried and failed to move the parties toward compromise. In February the owners invited "replacement players"—the retired, the marginal and others—to fill training camps and start preparing for the season. Finally, on March 31, a federal judge issued an injunction against the owners, and the real players returned to work (with a reduced 144-game schedule). A new seven-year contract was later signed.

After the strike, baseball tried new directions: another round of playoffs, interleague play, limited revenue sharing, and more expansion. Some ideas proved popular and successful; for example, the universal retirement of Jackie Robinson's number, and regular-season games in Mexico and Japan. Other attempts, such as The Baseball Network, a cable-television venture, and Selig's failed push for radical realignment of the leagues, did not work. In 1998, however, the Brewers, under the stewardship of his daughter, Wendy Selig-Prieb, became the first team ever to switch from the American League to the National League. That same season, young fans found renewed excitement in the game after years of flagging interest; that can be attributed more to the likes of Mark McGwire and Sammy Sosa than anything that occurred in the commissioner's office. Regardless, that office became more powerful in 1999.

Baseball became centralized in the commissioner's office. Owners unanimously approved a consolidation of scheduling, discipline and umpiring in September 1999; this came just weeks after a showdown between umpires and the commissioner's office led to the loss of 22 umpires. The jobs of both league presidents—positions that predated the role of commissioner in Organized Baseball—were essentially eradicated.

In the first days of the 21st century Selig received even more power. Owners voted Selig unprecedented authority to improve the game, including the ability to fine clubs up to $2 million. Selig announced that all Internet rights for baseball's 30 franchises were to be placed under the umbrella of MLB, with all revenue shared equally.

Selig's decision to call the 2001 All-Star Game as a 7-7 tie after 11 innings provoked widespread controversy—and disgust. To make amends, in 2002 Selig, ever the tinkerer with tradition, decreed that victory in the midsummer classic would now secure home-field advantage for the winning league in the upcoming World Series.

Chapter 32

The Changing Game

By Bill Felber and Gary Gillette

In 1906, at the arguable heights of their careers, the Hall of Fame-bound trio of Joe Tinker, Johnny Evers and Frank Chance completed approximately 50 double plays. In 2000, the primary players in the last-place Tampa Bay Devil Rays infield—Fred McGriff at first base, Miguel Cairo and Bobby Smith at second, and Kevin Stocker and Felix Martinez at shortstop—turned roughly twice that number. May we infer that the finest middle infield of a bygone era would be rejected as unfit for duty on a perfectly nondescript modern team?

For the five-year period between 1921 and 1925, Rogers Hornsby batted better than .400. In the past 60 seasons, not a single major league hitter has reached that level of excellence as much as once, let alone for half a decade. May we conclude that, were he in his prime today, Hornsby would shame Tony Gwynn into anonymity?

The answers to those questions are, of course, two resounding calls of "No."

Baseball is not played in a time capsule, and neither its record book nor its archives should be read as if it were. The game played on the artificial turf of the Metrodome that you watch today on television holds the same lure as the contest your grandfather took a surrey to see at Chicago's old West Side Park. Teams contest for the same end, using fundamentally the same objects in a format governed basically by the same rules. However, technological, sociological, strategic, and cultural forces have over decades refined those elements, so that today's performances cannot easily be measured relative to yesterday's. Nor can judgment be precisely made as to the superiority of either, save subjectively in the mind's eye.

Baseball today is different from the game of the early 20th century in many ways, just as contemporary American culture is different from the horse-and-buggy era. Imagine paying a quarter for admission to the ballpark, another quarter for access to the grandstand, and a third quarter for a seat. Imagine games played before audiences of a few hundred, maybe a thousand, fans. Imagine visiting teams arriving in town on trains, bunking two to a bed, then caravaning to the ballyard in a grand parade through the streets—though never at night and never, ever on Sunday. Now imagine baseball as the only sport of widespread popularity. No professional football to speak of, no basketball, no hockey; no golf, no tennis, no track of consequence. Moreover, horse racing was only for the elite, and boxing only for the disreputable. There *was* such a time in America, and it was only a century ago.

In many ways, the game of baseball has changed precisely because America itself has changed. Whether all that change has been for the good may be argued. One might contend, for instance, that a laudable part of Americana died out when the practice of uniformed players publicly trolleying to the game (as a means of stirring fan attention) was halted in the first decade of the 20th century. However, most, if not all, aspects of baseball's growth

Elroy Face
The Pirates relief pitcher, one of baseball's first true closers, made the forkball fashionable by going 18-1 with 10 saves in 1959.

alongside society were inevitable. The 50-cent admission charge established by the National League in 1876 held for many years, but so did the rather unsavory practice of treating players as peons, to the point of doubling up sleeping arrangements. Philadelphia Athletics catcher Ossie Schreckengost once actually had it written into his contract that teammate (and bunkmate) Rube Waddell would be barred from eating animal crackers in bed because the crumbs irritated the catcher. Players today sleep in luxury hotels, and most do not even share rooms, much less beds. As the cost of

living and the cost of operating a franchise have both increased strikingly, so have the size of the grandstand and the cost of a general admission ticket, the latter by a factor of 15 or 20.

In any era and at any price, a great championship battle has always held the American populace in thrall. Tens of millions of fans watched on their living-room televisions in October 2003 as the Yankees and Marlins waged their World Series struggle long into the night. Those fans studied every decisive play from a half dozen angles on instant replay as they second-guessed managerial moves and controversial umpiring decisions. Was that excitement any greater, measure for measure, than the grip in which the cities of Boston and Baltimore were held during the final days of the 1897 National League pennant race?

The absence of television and radio then did not stay the enthusiasm of hundreds of thousands of rooters nationwide as the pulsating battle for supremacy wound to a close. The principals were the two most dominant sporting teams of their generation: The Boston Beaneaters and Baltimore Orioles had divided the previous six pennants. Now, with less than a week remaining in the 1897 season, they were locked in a virtual tie for first, each having won better than seven of every ten games played and fated by the schedule to meet for three conclusive games in Baltimore.

So all-encompassing was interest in the games that Associated Press telegraphers dispatched play-by-play accounts to every major subscribing newspaper east of the Rockies. More than three dozen correspondents—an unheard-of number for the era—covered the games. Twenty more telegraphers tapped out accounts to cities where fans had gathered in theaters or outside newspaper offices to follow the events on chalkboards. In Boston, fan interest was so great that the game reports received triple the front-page space accorded the activities of President William McKinley, who was in Boston at the same time. Throngs numbering in the thousands massed daily along Washington Street, Boston's Newspaper Row, to watch mechanical re-creations, which can be considered a distant precursor to graphical coverage of the World Series on the Internet. There was a published report of 4,000 fans jamming Boston's Music Hall to watch a similar simulation. The games at Baltimore's Union Grounds drew as many as 25,000 spectators, more than twice the previous record attendance for that facility!

The excitement of a great pennant race is a constant; only the modes of sensing that excitement change. Consider only a few of the more obvious changes: The player pool has changed, albeit at times tardily, to reflect the nation's ethnic populations. When that pool expanded to encompass Southerners, Irish, Jews, Hispanics, or African-Americans, it did so in reaction to fundamental changes such as the diminution of post-Civil War prejudice, the assimilation of immigrant populations, and the eventual willingness of white society to acknowledge blacks as equals.

Technology has worked on the grand old game in many ways. Basic improvements in the construction of the ball and glove have dramatically changed the play on the field. The field itself has changed in ways as grandiose and obvious as the abandonment of the unfenced pasture in favor of the comparative luxury of the wooden park. Intimate brick and steel stadiums of the early 20th century were followed half a century later by huge, impersonal concrete multipurpose facilities that are now being retired by atavistic retro ballparks evoking the golden years of the game.

Sociological alterations, as exemplified by population shifts from city to suburb and by the replacement of the trolley in favor of the automobile, resulted in the abandonment of many inner-city ball-parks after World War II. At the turn of the millennium, ironically, high-tech new downtown ballparks are viewed by many cities as key components in reviving sections of their aging urban cores.

Changes in national attitudes have been mirrored in the game on the field. America was a prim and proper country in 1908, and its national game was a prim and proper one, heavy on the sacrifice bunt and very light on the long ball. Americans were a profligate bunch in the late 1920s, winning and losing with abandon on Wall Street, and these restless capitalists adopted baseball heroes like Babe Ruth and Hack Wilson, who hit 'em far during the day and swigged 'em long into the night. The difference of only two decades is strikingly underscored in a baseball statistic that also speaks volumes about off-field attitudes: for the five years between 1906 and 1910, the Chicago White Sox hit a total of only 27 home runs. Ruth hit more than that by himself in every full season he played between 1919 and 1933.

Baseball's labor-management relations have also generally mirrored national patterns. The present major leagues can trace their ancestry back to the 1870s, an age when even the legality of organized labor was questioned.

The motivation behind the organizers of the National League in 1876 was to take control of a game that had been essentially run by players' cooperatives. The 1890s, the era of some of the most violent union-management conflicts (e.g., the Haymarket riot, the Pullman strike), also witnessed the last direct player challenge to the authority of ownership, the Brotherhood War, which produced the Players League. Unionization very gradually gained favor, although both nationally and in baseball that process took decades. True player free agency in the national pastime, as with worker rights in other businesses, often arrived only under the aegis of the courts.

Finally, as the educational level of America itself has changed, the strategies of baseball have evolved. The dominant function of today's late-inning reliever could hardly have been envisioned by the game's greatest minds as little as three decades ago. The stolen base, the home run and the sacrifice have all come and gone as strategic coups (and, in some cases, have come back again). It is as judgmental to speculate on whether the game of today is better than the game of 1907 as it is to posit whether Joe Tinker was a better shortstop than Nomar Garciaparra.

No one would contend that baseball has been, or is today, any more than a general mirror of its times. Neither can it seriously be suggested that the game has failed to reflect many of the historical trends that have developed during its existence. For purposes of this discussion, it is vital to recognize both of those realities. Paradoxically, only by appreciating the game's evolution can one truly begin to sense the marvelous continuum represented therein.

So, by what context does one measure Hornsby's feats of the 1920s relative to Gwynn's of the 1980s and 1990s? By the context of the technological, strategic, societal, and cultural changes that wrought both of them. Could Joe Tinker play shortstop for the Cubs of today? For that matter, could Ozzie Smith have adapted to the scrub fields, primitive travel methods, incompetent training aides, and all-but-useless gloves of Tinker's day?

These questions cannot be answered with finality. But without considering the many changing aspects of the game, attempts to even provide an answer become frivolous. What follows is an effort to examine some of the major causes of change and to provide context to a discussion of the evolving nature of baseball. It is a sport that has possessed for more than a century only one enduring and vital characteristic: it has, from the outset, been our game.

Equipment

The bat, the ball and the glove are baseball's utensils. Virtually every child old enough to root, root, root for the home team owns at least one of each. Their omnipresence serves as immutable evidence of the game's penetration into American culture. Yet today's equipment is as changed from its predecessors of generations ago as is baseball itself. Even the seemingly simple functions of each have been redefined, in part a cause and in part an effect of the changing game.

Only a few of those changes are reflected in the rulebook; to most the book has proven adaptable. Examination of the adjustments made to the game's basic tools illuminates the changes that the baseball itself has made.

For obvious reasons, rule makers have always felt the need to define how the ball shall be made. Curiously, that definition has changed very little over more than a century. Notice how similar are the two definitions that follow, the first from an 1861 convention of the National Association of Base Ball Players (NA), and the second taken from the Official Baseball Rules of 2000:

1861—The ball must weigh not less than five and one half, nor more than five and three-fourths ounces avoirdupois. It must measure not less than nine and one-half, nor more than nine and three fourths inches in circumference. It must be composed of India rubber and yarn, covered with leather.

2000—The ball shall be a sphere formed by yarn wound around a small core of cork, rubber or similar material, covered with two stripes of white horsehide or cowhide, tightly stitched together. It shall weigh not less than five nor more than five and one quarter ounces avoirdupois and measure not less than nine nor more than nine and one quarter inches in circumference.

How greatly has the ball changed in 139 years? It is about 5 percent smaller, about 9 percent lighter. Rather than an India rubber center, it may have—and in professional ball does have—a cork center. The stitching must be tight, though precisely how tight is not defined. And that's it. In every other respect, the ball put in play in the amateur games of 1861 would pass muster by modern rules.

That is not to say that the baseball of Civil War Days and the Rawlings Official model of today are virtually identical. Today's ball is far more resilient and travels greater distances. This is due to several factors.

Most obviously the modern baseball undergoes far less wear and tear. For the first half century of professional play, it was customary for a game ball—whether mushy, discolored or lopsided—to be kept in play until it was irretrievably lost. The key word here is *irretrievably*. In the 19th century, if a ball was hit into the stands, the ushers collected the ball so that play could continue. If hit out of sight, it was searched for—for as long as five minutes! Then and only then might the host team be required to furnish a second ball. The idea of going through dozens of balls per game, as is the modern custom, would have seemed frivolously wasteful to Great Grandpa.

The original policy moderated somewhat with the passing years, but it was not until 1920 that league officials stipulated the use of only clean and new baseballs. This was mandated to enhance offense as well as out of concern for player safety: worn and discolored balls frequently were hard to control or even see, as the tragic beaning death of Ray Chapman demonstrated. Those directives lent a new measure of consistency to the game, so that the ball a

batter swung at in the bottom of the ninth was not different from the one used in the first-pitch ceremonies.

The only rule change of significance affecting the ball came in 1910, and it authorized the use of a cushioned cork center as an alternative to the rubber-centered ball that had been in vogue until that time. The cork-centered ball was found to be more lively, an especially desirable trait considering the depressed (and, to the baseball-going public, depressing) league batting averages. The cork-centered ball was introduced in time for the 1910 World Series between the Philadelphia Athletics and Chicago Cubs; as a result, the two clubs batted .272, which was about 20 points higher than the regular-season league average. For the 1911 regular season, both leagues used the cork-centered ball: National League averages rose by only 4 points; however, in the American League, the climb was a heady 30 points and the league leader, Detroit's Ty Cobb, hit a stunning .420. A total of 21 American League regulars bettered .300 that season; only 8 had done so the year before. In the National League, Chicago's Frank Schulte hit 21 home runs. Schulte had tied for the home run title in 1910 with 10.

All other changes in the makeup of the ball itself—tighter winding of the yarn, introduction of different and supposedly better kinds of yarn, raised or depressed stitches—have been products of technology, not of the rule makers. About 1920, as batting averages soared and Babe Ruth began to crash home runs in unheard-of profusion, there was controversy over the substitution of Australian wool for the generic type in making baseball yarn. Surely, fans speculated, this new wool must be the reason behind the livelier ball. In fact, the explanation probably had more to do with improved methods of winding the wool than with the wool itself.

The same rulebook that has licensed virtually no change in the parameters of the baseball itself has brooked only minor adjustment with the bat, and then, generally, only by way of greater specificity. Again, compare the rules governing play in 1861 with the slightly more elaborate section from the modern rulebook:

1861—The bat must be round and must not exceed two and one half inches in diameter in the thickest part. It must be made of wood, and may be of any length to suit the striker.

2003—The bat shall be a smooth, rounded stick not more than two and three quarter inches in diameter at the thickest part and not more than 42 inches in length. The bat shall be one piece of solid wood, or formed from a block of wood consisting of two or more pieces of wood bonded together with an adhesive in such way that the grain direction in all pieces is essentially parallel to the length of the bat. Any such laminated bat shall contain only wood or adhesive.

The modern rule also contains an allowance for a small cupping of up to one inch at the bat's end, and for use of a grip-improving substance on the bat handle. But again, the stipulated differences of almost a century and a half of development are comparatively minimal.

There is a length limit where once there was none; however, at least in practice, the limit is functionally irrelevant. In today's major leagues, it is virtually unheard-of for a bat to exceed 36 inches in length, much less 42. The modern bat has gained one-quarter of an inch in girth over its ancestor, and it need no longer necessarily be of a single piece of wood, though no such laminated bats have been used in big league play to date.

Changes in the bat have tended to develop stylistically, more so than with the ball, generally under the influence of the batters themselves. Bats, of course, always have been highly personalized objects. With such a broad allowance by the rules (no weight limit, no functional length limit) hitters have tended to individualize their sticks within widely recognized norms.

Many hitters before 1920 coveted heavy "wagon-tongue" models with thick barrels capable of driving the ball over the infield, even at the expense of bat speed. Cap Anson, legendary star of the Chicago White Stockings, used just such a bat, reputedly weighing in at a manly three pounds and then some. In the 1920s Babe Ruth menaced opposing pitchers with a 48-ounce bat, though Ruth saw to it that the bat handle was tapered to accommodate his smaller-than-normal hands.

Heinie Groh, third baseman of the Cincinnati Reds and New York Giants, was no slugger of Ruthian proportion. Yet Groh's innovative "bottle" bat, with its narrow handle expanding precipitously at the hitting area to a broad surface, not only served as a personal trademark but also helped him to a .292 lifetime average and a starting role on four pennant winners.

The modern bat bears no resemblance to any of those models. It is sleeker, usually no more than 35 inches in length and no heavier than 33 ounces. The reason is simple: batting instructors, who once looked upon mass as the key factor behind a mighty poke, now focus on bat speed instead. The faster a batter can swing a bat through the strike zone, the greater the force applied to the ball. And the greater the force applied, the farther the ball travels. Presto, light bats generating greater bat speed generating more home runs.

As for gloves ... well, in the game's early days, they did not exist: Players were expected to catch the ball barehanded. For a time, they received something of an aid in that effort by a rule recording an out if a ball was caught on the first bounce. That made things a little easier.

The use of gloves was never formally barred, as were, for instance, African-American players in the old National Association rulebook; it simply was looked upon as sort of sissified. There is no clear record of who first conceived the notion of fielding with a glove, though a catcher named Delavarge of the Victory Club of Troy, New York is said to have donned a pair in 1860. Al Spalding wrote that the first to don a glove in league play was an 1875 player for the NA's St. Louis team named Charlie Waitt. In a game that year, Waitt donned a street-dress leather glove on his fielding hand. Waitt, reportedly, was ridiculed leaguewide. Despite that attitude, as more prominent players adopted Waitt's concept, the notion gradually came to be accepted.

Two points should be made about the use of early-day gloves. First, their function was utterly different from what it is today. The first gloves, lacking webbing and lacing, merely provided protection for the hands when fielding the ball. Today's larger, better-padded, webbed, laced, and pocketed gloves might more appropriately be described as fielding devices, because it is the glove, not the fielder's hands, that does much of the actual fielding work.

Second, as verification of the first point, players of the 19th century often wore gloves on both hands. For the throwing hand, they would simply snip the glove at the fingers for dexterity. Those photographs that remain of players from that era, especially the ones portraying fielding sequences, confirm that tendency.

It was not until 1895 that stipulations concerning gloves were included in the rules. Those limited the size of gloves to 10 ounces and 14 inches in circumference for all players except catchers and

first basemen, who were permitted to use any size glove. Today's rulebook, by contrast, takes a page and a half to specify dimensions, materials, lacings, and webbings for gloves. There are 13 different size limitations on the standard fielder's glove, ranging from palm width to the length of each separate finger. The transition from the glove as protection to the glove as a tightly defined fielding aid came gradually but inexorably.

The first advance was development of a pocket, an indentation in the palm of the hand where the ball was most easily and most naturally caught. As with the origination of the glove itself, there is no firm and fast date for the pocket's appearance: it simply happened, though it did not happen immediately.

To the contrary, for several years after the introduction of the glove, fielders adopted a sort of "reverse pocket" achieved by excising the leather from the palm area and leaving it bare, presumably for a better touch or feel. In all probability, the pocket was not invented by glove makers, but by players themselves, taking advantage of the natural stretching the glove's leather underwent with use. Today this is called "breaking a glove in." Today, however, pockets are made in the manufacturing process.

Credit commonly is given to a pitcher, spitballer Bill Doak of the St. Louis Cardinals, for advancing glove technology from the primordial state. In 1920 Doak approached a glove manufacturer with a plan for a new personalized glove. Many players liked personalized glove models, but Doak's was different. It envisioned a pre-formed pocket, not one that would be fashioned through constant wear. And it included a square of reinforced webbing between the thumb and finger sections as an additional aid to fielding. Previously, the fingers simply had been tied together, if they were not allowed to act independently. Doak's model remained popular for almost 30 years. Every subsequent advance in glove design, whether it was the hinged heel, short- or long-fingered design, or advanced webbing, can be traced to a concept originated by Doak.

In the 1930s rule makers mandated the use of only leather in the making of gloves—the first change in glove rules since the initial size and weight limitations were set in 1895. In 1939, acting in response to Hank Greenberg's introduction of an oversized mitt with a netted webbing, they outlawed the use of netting, limited webbing to four inches from thumb to palm (the present rule is four and one-half inches), and restricted the size of first basemen's gloves as well. Weight restrictions were dropped in 1950, and size limitations further defined.

For many years, no limitation was placed on the size of the catcher's mitt; after all, the larger the catcher's mitt, the harder it was for a catcher to dig the ball out of the glove and make a throw. In 1960, however, Baltimore manager Paul Richards knew that there was something worse than having catchers who could not evict the ball from an oversized mitt—that was having catchers who could not catch the ball at all.

The manager's problem was that his most effective pitcher was Hoyt Wilhelm, and Wilhelm's most effective pitch was a knuckleball that proved as difficult to catch as it was to hit. As Baltimore catchers soared to the top of league in passed balls, Richards devised a catcher's mitt of nearly 50 inches in circumference—perhaps twice the standard size. If Baltimore catchers could not throw out base stealers with the new mitt, they could at least have a fighting chance at preventing Wilhelm's pitches from rolling to the backstop. Shortly after the appearance of Baltimore's oversized mitt, the rule was amended to set a 38-inch circumference and 15-1/2-inch diameter limit on catchers' gloves as well.

Even after catchers' gloves were restricted in size, however, questions remained about enforcement of the 1950 size limits. So, in 1972 the rules committee drafted the present 13-point measuring system. Fortunately, there is no record of a game ever being halted while a manager challenged the legality of a fielder's glove on all 13 points.

The Playing Field

Charley "Old Hoss" Radbourn was a pitcher of considerable note in the National League of the 1880s, and a hitter of no special renown. In 1882 he won 33 games for Providence while hitting only one home run. But this story isn't about any of his 33 wins, nor even about his home run—it's about playing conditions.

On August 17, 1882, Radbourn was playing right field (as he occasionally did when not pitching) against Detroit. The Providence field was not unlike most baseball fields of the day: it was, in the literal sense, a *field.* There was little groundskeeping and often no outfield barriers; even if there were, well-heeled fans who wished to do so simply pulled their carriages onto the playing surface and watched from there.

On this particular date, John Ward of Providence and Stump Weidman of Detroit allowed no runs to cross home over 17 innings. When Radbourn advanced to the plate with one out in the 18th, the sky was growing dark. In his then-brief big league career, Hoss had never hit a home run. He was not alone in that distinction, as four-base hits were a rare sight. (That season's league leader, George Wood of Detroit, hit only seven; the league record was nine.) But Radbourn lashed at Weidman's pitch and sent it scurrying past Wood in left field. As some witnesses reported, the ball rolled close to the leg of an especially spirited black horse hitched to a wagon.

Wood raced to the spot and reached for the ball. He was prevented by, of all things, the horse's hind hoof, which swished through the air and barely missed conking him. Wood reached again; again the horse kicked. Radbourn, meanwhile, raced past second. Desperately, Wood grabbed for a handful of grass, hopeful of appeasing the critter. That did not work. Finally, Ed Hanlon obtained a stick, reached in and swatted the ball clear of danger. It was too late; as Hanlon prepared to throw, Radbourn was being carried from the field in triumph.

The mere concept of what constitutes a major league ballpark has evolved through at least five distinct transformations, each markedly different from its predecessor and each spurred by changes both in the game's strategy and in the nation's sociology. The conditions surrounding Charley Radbourn's home run in Providence in 1882 may seem bizarre to us. No more bizarre, perhaps, than artificial turf will seem three generations hence.

The parks in the first few decades of professional ball were simple open spaces with ruts worn by the players marking the baselines. At games that attracted large crowds, the fans circling the field often defined the playing area. In 1871 the National Association club in Rockford, Illinois, played on a field called by ballpark expert Phil Lowry "the strangest in major league history." The aptly-named Forest City club had a field in which trees virtually lined the baselines, so players chasing popups took their chances. Third base was on a hill, home plate in a depression, and the outfield framed by a gutter draining an adjacent horseracing track.

For several reasons, there were few of the niceties we currently associate with a ballpark. Not the least of these was that, since the game itself was new, club owners often lacked the capital necessary to develop the grounds beyond a rudimentary level. A grandstand might hold about 1,500 customers if it was expansive, but usually it held fewer. It was desirable, but by no means certain, that the playing ground be level and free of gravel, though horse droppings might literally pockmark areas of play.

Except in Rockford, trees were not much of a hazard but, even at the best of diamonds, infields were poorly sculpted and ill cared for. There were rarely such things as a scoreboard or dugout and, where outfield fences existed—first used at Brooklyn's Union Grounds—they might be as close as 180 feet from home plate or as distant as 500 feet at all points. Some fields like Brooklyn's doubled over the winter as skating rinks, when they were deliberately flooded.

Gradually, ballfields assumed a more standardized and slightly more familiar appearance. By the mid-1880s, most playing fields were at least semi-enclosed. Still, however, distances to the fences commonly were dictated as much by topography as any other consideration. When built in 1883, Chicago's Lake Front Park was considered the archetypal modern facility, seating almost 10,000. Yet its cramped site near the lake permitted only a 180-foot carry to left field, and only 300 feet to dead center! Such a field would be considered inadequate for 15-year-olds today. In contrast, at Boston's spacious Huntington Avenue Grounds a few years later, the barrier in left field was a comfortable 440 feet from home plate; it was a very long 635 feet to the fence in center. For part of the 1896 season, Robison Field in St. Louis did not even have a fence entirely circling the grounds. At one point that year, it was possible to hit a ball in play through a gap in the barrier in right field; if so, the ball could roll unimpeded for more than 600 feet ... to a lake.

If there was a single, overriding concern about ballparks in the game's first few decades, it was the danger of fire. Because wood was the common building material, facilities were susceptible to that danger, and it intruded on the game more than once, sometimes with dire results. Baltimore's Union Park was damaged by fire in 1894, while a blaze destroyed Boston's South End Grounds in the third inning of a game between the Orioles and Beaneaters that same season. A game was halted by fire at Chicago's West Side Park; several years earlier a contest actually had continued at the nearby 23rd Street Grounds while fire consumed the grandstand. Brooklyn's Washington Park fell to flames in 1889; New York's Polo Grounds was virtually destroyed in 1911.

With all of its inherent and obvious disadvantages, the wooden ballpark may seem to have been an anachronism as early as 1910; furthermore, its role in the development of the game may seem to have been quite fleeting. Was it really anachronistic? Yes. Was its role fleeting? No. The era of wood, from the opening of Brooklyn's Union Grounds in 1862 until the closing of the last wooden grandstand at Philadelphia's Baker Bowl in 1938, encompasses three quarters of a century and better than half the lifespan of the professional game to date.

The demise of the wooden park was occasioned by a number of factors, fire hazard being not the least of them. Some wooden parks were deemed to be particularly dangerous. In 1903 hundreds of fans fell (and 12 died) when a wooden rail gave way at Baker Bowl in Philadelphia. In 1907 and again in 1908, the building inspector for the city of Cincinnati submitted a detailed bill of particulars on the hazards at the Palace of the Fans. Cracked girders, decayed supports, unsafe flooring, and a defective bleacher platform were only some of the problems. Construction problems were documented in St. Louis and other cities as well. Nonetheless, the gradually widening acceptance of baseball as an important cultural event also played a part in the transition to more permanent structures.

The average attendance climbed from 100,000 per franchise in 1890 to 365,000 in 1905. Larger, stronger, and more durable venues were needed and, because of the game's growing popularity, club owners were able to provide such facilities. Motivation for the owners also came from the fact that as new parks were constructed, they could increase the numbers of more costly box seats, thus increasing potential revenues. Sound familiar?

Concrete and steel thus became the materials of choice. In 1909 Philadelphia Athletics owner Benjamin Shibe conceived and executed plans for a baseball plant upon a former brickyard at the corner of 21st and Lehigh north of Center City. The facility would be easily accessible from the city's center by trolley line and would supplant old, wooden Columbia Park, which had the added disadvantage of being located near several breweries, thus subjecting patrons to the constant odor of barley and yeast.

Shibe Park would not only smell better: it would be the grandest facility of its type ever conceived. A French Renaissance-style dome at the home plate entrance gave the stadium a distinctive, almost church-like, appearance. The concrete grandstand and bleachers followed the first- and third-base foul lines, seating 20,000. A huge scoreboard was installed in left field. The facility's price tag was a breathtaking half million dollars, yet the opening of Shibe Park set a standard that was soon widely matched.

In Pittsburgh Barney Dreyfuss already had begun construction of a replacement for old Exposition Park, the riverfront facility that had been in use since 1890. Named Forbes Field, the new ballpark opened June 30 near Schenley Park, and it included elevators, lighting in the grandstand, telephones, and even maids in the ladies rooms. Dreyfuss also conceived of providing access to the upper levels of the triple-decked grandstand by means of ramps rather than stairs, a practice in effect today. The larger capacity of Forbes paid almost immediate dividends when the Pirates celebrated the new home's inaugural season by winning a world championship.

If there is one hallmark of the concrete-and-steel stadiums raised in a dozen different cities between the years 1909 and 1923, it is their individuality. When Charles Comiskey developed plans for his new concrete-and-steel structure at 35th and Shields in Chicago in 1910, he asked his own star, pitcher Ed Walsh, to take a hand in the work. It may not be surprising, then, that Comiskey Park, both at its opening and for decades afterward, was considered one of the most tasking layouts for hitters. The original Comiskey featured 363-foot foul lines, 382-foot power alleys, and a center field of 420 feet (that, year by year, was enlarged to 455 feet). Particularly in the Dead Ball Era, the center-field fence may as well not have existed at all.

In Brooklyn's 22,000-seat Ebbets Field, which opened in 1913, the original carry to the barrier in left was 419 feet, though a street limited the distance to the fence in right field to a mere 301. (Construction of bleachers in the 1930s brought the left-field wall within a more manageable distance.)

The most unusual design of all the old parks was New York's bathtub-shaped Polo Grounds, which replaced the wooden facility of the same name after it was damaged by fire in 1911. The "new" Polo Grounds featured foul poles only about 260 feet distant from the plate, coupled with a cavernous center field that arced to distances of nearly 500 feet.

With a few exceptions, these classic-era parks served their host teams well for generations. Nevertheless, gradually at first in the 1940s and 1950s, then increasingly so in the 1960s, interior wear and exterior conditions rendered most unsatisfactory in the eyes of their tenants. Those conditions varied, but they can be summarized as follows:

Access: The classic-era parks had been dependent on trolley, subway or bus lines to deliver fans to their gates. By the 1950s, though, America was a motorized nation, and club owners felt the need for expansive parking lots as well as proximity to modern freeways. Brooklyn club owner Walter O'Malley moved his team to Los Angeles when the city failed to deliver on his demands for such a new facility. The Giants, beset at the Polo Grounds by many of the same problems, fled the same year to San Francisco.

Size: When most of the classic-era parks were constructed, crowds of 30,000 were considered exceptional. By the mid-1960s, increased costs as well as increasing attendance made such limited capacity a serious operating problem for many clubs. Neither Forbes Field in Pittsburgh, Shibe Park in Philadelphia, nor Crosley Field in Cincinnati was capable of seating much more than 35,000; when new and larger multipurpose stadiums were built in those cities, the clubs gladly moved into them.

Cost: Without exception, classic-era parks had been constructed using private capital. By the 1960s, the cost of developing the kind of 50,000-seat stadium required by a major league team was more than the club owner was able to afford or willing to spend. Fortunately, local governments, which had come to view teams as community assets, proved willing in many cases to finance or subsidize the construction. This happened as early as the 1930s in Cleveland, and again in 1954 when the city of Baltimore captured the Browns from St. Louis. Since Dodger Stadium opened in Los Angeles in 1962, more than three dozen new ballparks have opened for major league use, have been extensively renovated, or are currently under construction. Of the billions of dollars spent on these parks, only the renovation of Pro Player Stadium in Miami and the construction of Pacific Bell Park in San Francisco were not government financed. (Even the Giants' new palace, however, was subsidized by government aid in land acquisition and infrastructure development.) Oftentimes, that public involvement has taken place as one part of a larger urban-development effort, with the new park situated on once-blighted or undeveloped land near the city core and forming the centerpiece of a massive redevelopment project. This was the case earlier in cities like St. Louis as well as more recently in Baltimore, Cleveland and Denver.

Concurrent with that last trend, a new and significant factor has emerged. In the past, ballparks were forced by the exigency of private construction to conform to their surrounding, thus imbuing each park inevitably with an individual flavor. Public involvement, however, eliminated that limitation. Since the opening of Dodger Stadium, Shea Stadium and the Astrodome in the 1960s, surroundings were altered to conform to the design of the park, rather than the opposite. Freed from the constrictions of neighborhood geography, architects gave their parks a symmetry bordering on sameness in an effort to maximize utility. The result was the virtually indistinguishable trio of much-scorned 1970s "superstadiums": Riverfront in Cincinnati, Three Rivers in Pittsburgh and Veterans in Philadelphia—and each seemed best suited for the football teams in those towns, despite the success of the local baseball clubs in the years after these stadiums opened.

In truth, neither stadium designers nor club owners fell headlong into the new age of the anonymous modern multipurpose facility. The modern era of generic ballparks started with a two-decade transitional period during which these factors were gradually assimilated into the classic motif.

Cleveland's Municipal Stadium provided the introduction to this transitional period. Constructed in 1932 by the city, it was vast (potentially holding more than 80,000, it was built in a failed bid to secure the summer Olympics), virtually symmetrical, yet situated close in the central city on the lakefront. Evidence that the symbiotic relationship between a private ballclub and a public stadium had not yet taken hold is that, for 15 years after Municipal Stadium was built, the Indians occupied it only in fits and starts. Unless a large crowd was expected, Cleveland generally played its weekend games at Municipal, maintaining staid old League Park (smaller and cheaper to operate) as their weekday habitat. Not until 1947 did the Indians become full-time tenants of what became derisively known as the "Mistake by the Lake."

For the first time in 1953, then again in 1954 and 1955,, public facilities were developed with the specific aim of attracting major league teams. It worked in all three cases: luring the Braves from Boston to Milwaukee, the Browns from St. Louis to Baltimore, and the Athletics from Philadelphia to Kansas City. The moves were unprecedented in the previous half-century, yet sensible in that all three teams left cities that had proved incapable or unwilling of supporting two clubs (the perennial losing records of these three teams certainly didn't help). The stadiums in Milwaukee and Baltimore were constructed from scratch; in Kansas City, Municipal Stadium, which had served for many years as a minor league facility, was extensively renovated. None of these three parks abandoned the city for the open country, but none was reliant on mass transit, either.

The era of the modern public superstadium ironically probably dated from the opening of the last private stadium, Dodger Stadium in Los Angeles in 1962. Yet the species' zenith was achieved in 1965, when the Harris County Domed Stadium, dubbed the Astrodome, opened in Houston. The $35.5 million project broke so many traditional rules of stadium design that it literally changed the way the game was played—and not just in Houston.

The first and most obvious change, of course, was the roof that covered the facility. Baseball had come indoors; no more would rain, wind or other weather be a factor in a game's outcome. Beyond that, it changed the surface on which the game could be played. When the dome's translucent roof panels were painted to give the fielders a chance to follow flyballs, the lack of sunlight killed the grass, and artificial turf had to be installed. "AstroTurf," as it came to be called, was faster and more durable than grass but as mere carpet over concrete it was also harder on the players' legs, so it required substantial changes in strategy.

Swifter, agile fielders replaced their slow-footed but hard-hitting predecessors. Speed, whether for basestealing or cutting off basehits in the outfield gaps, supplanted brawn in the new game played on artificial turf, whether inside or outside. Within a span of little more than a decade, artificial turf became the most copied aspect of any single new ballpark built in America since the owners of the Union Grounds in Brooklyn fenced their lot. Not only did it not wear out, not only was it easier to maintain, not only did it minimize rainouts, but it also withstood far better the strain of multipurpose use for events such as football games and musical concerts. Municipalities installed the plastic stuff in most stadiums built for use by more than one team, and its widespread adoption in the NL greatly changed the character of its play.

The city of St. Louis originally built new Busch Stadium in 1966 with a grass surface, then replaced it with turf after a few years. So faddish had artificial turf become that, in 1970 when Kansas City officials developed plans for separate and individually designed football and baseball stadiums, they still installed artificial turf on the baseball field.

Thanks to the willingness of local government to subsidize new, baseball-only ballparks in the 1990s, however, baseball has seen a reversal of this trend toward artificial surfaces. Every new ballpark opened since 1989—save Tropicana Field in Tampa Bay, which quickly abandoned its traditional rug and installed a new artificial turf with simulated grass—has featured grass. Moreover, three existing parks joined the flight from AstroTurf and its derivatives since 1995, as Kauffman Stadium in Kansas City, Busch Stadium in St. Louis, and Cinergy Field in Cincinnati have reinstalled grass fields.

The design of indoor stadiums, which started the era of artificial turf, has been dramatically altered by the debut of the high-tech ballpark with a movable roof. Of the six enclosed venues, SkyDome in Toronto, BankOne Ballpark in Phoenix, and Safeco Field in Seattle all feature retractable covers, with only SkyDome, the oldest of the retractable stadiums, retaining artificial turf. Miller Park in Milwaukee, which opened in 2001, also boasted a movable roof and a grass field.

The superstadium boom of the 1960s and 1970s produced a series of parks that shared most, if not all, of the following characteristics: they altered the landscape to conform to the "ideal" of a park, rather than vice versa; they were built on large open areas that included acres of parking; they were symmetrical and predictable in design; they were proximate to interstate highways; they were built from the ground up to be multipurpose venues; they eliminated structural pillars, but in doing so sacrificed proximity of upper deck seats to the playing field; and they used artificial surfaces.

The multipurpose stadium, which a few decades ago appeared to be a fixture of the modern game, is now universally viewed as a dinosaur awaiting its doom. While only two facilities that opened after Dodger Stadium in the 1960s, 1970s or 1980s were exclusively reserved for baseball (Arlington Stadium and Royals/Kauffman Stadium), every new ballpark opened since 1990 has been baseball-only. Three others (Shea, Busch, and Anaheim/Edison International) have reverted to baseball-only status after their football tenants fled for greener pastures.

The stunning success of Baltimore's Oriole Park at Camden Yards revolutionized baseball park design as well as greatly influencing stadium and arena design in other sports. Making its debut on Opening Day 1992, the retro brick-and-steel ballpark in the shadow of an old railroad warehouse in downtown Baltimore wowed fans, players, writers, broadcasters, and politicians alike. Though Camden Yards opened only one year after the new Comiskey Park in Chicago, the difference in design between these two parks was half a century apart—even though the same architectural firm designed both. Comiskey Park was a traditional modern stadium, a drab concrete structure with blue seats, clean sight lines, and no character. Camden Yards was nothing like that.

The exterior of Baltimore's new jewel featured an arched brick facade that evoked memories of long-gone Ebbets Field. Like the famous Brooklyn park, it was built within the context of its urban environment, not built on top of an expansive concrete plain surrounded by an asphalt sea of parking lots. The color scheme of the new park, where structural steel girders were left exposed and painted green like the seats, was chosen in deliberate contrast to the dominant blues, reds, and concrete grays of existing modern stadiums. Though not really constrained by dense urban geography like the ballparks of the classic era, Camden Yards also boasted

asymmetrical dimensions in the outfield and quirky features in the outfield wall, another homage to the past. The striking differences between Camden Yards and all the other ballparks it made instantly obsolete didn't stop with the park's appearance, however.

Equally important in earning the park universal acclaim was its attention to the needs of the fans. Like historic Wrigley Field and Fenway Park, the seats in Camden Yards were closer to the field than those in multipurpose stadiums. The ballpark featured a spectacular view of the downtown Baltimore skyline through an open center field, giving the interior an airy character totally unlike the claustrophobic feeling engendered by the enclosed superstadiums, whose 360-degree, multi-tiered construction completely surrounded the field. Broad concourses, expanded concessions, plentiful restrooms, and a dozen other thoughtful touches pampered the patrons as well as thrilled management, which saw a huge increase in discretionary spending by its satisfied customers.

Perhaps the most significant moneymaking component of Baltimore's new park was the space devoted to the large number of luxury suites. Leased by corporations and wealthy individuals by the season at unheard-of prices for baseball, these suites provided a lucrative new stream of revenue for the Orioles' ownership—a revenue source that all other team owners soon wanted to tap. The popularity of the new park also guaranteed sellouts for most games, allowing the Orioles to raise ticket prices early and often and reap unforeseen windfall profits.

Proving that cloning is the sincerest form of flattery, other owners rushed to persuade their local politicians that they, too, needed such a moneymaking machine if they were going to survive and compete in baseball's brave new world. Derivative new ballparks quickly arose in downtown Cleveland and in suburban Arlington, Texas. When these also proved instantly successful, the escalation of the arms race was unstoppable, and the economic balance of the game was forever altered.

What can be said today, and what could always be said, is that in baseball more so than in any other sport, the term "home field advantage" should be taken literally. Baseball clubs spend far more time trying to tailor their teams to the home field than in any other team sport. This is true, paradoxically, despite the fact that the home-field advantage in major league baseball, in which only 53 to 54 percent of games are won by the home team, is far smaller than in football, basketball, or hockey where the home team wins approximately 60 percent of the time.

Origins of Spring Training

The precise origin of spring training, that marvelously contrived ritual that today amounts to a six-week paid vacation in the sun for athletes, media and club officials, is unknown. With few exceptions, early-day ballplayers trained privately at home. It is known that in 1870 the Chicago White Stockings organized a trip to New Orleans, but that may have been mere barnstorming rather than preparation for the coming season. The generally accepted beginning of spring training is 1886, when the White Stockings and Philadelphia Phillies traveled to Little Rock and Charleston, respectively.

The standard regimen of spring training has varied greatly from decade to decade. Today, for instance, little actual training is done in the spring, since players are expected to report in shape. Instead, the emphasis is on narrowing a roster of 40 players (plus many other spring-training invitees) to the requisite 25 by opening day. Modern spring training amounts to an extended advertisement for the season to come, with a bit of tryout camp thrown in for effect.

That was not always the case. Players in the 19th and early 20th century commonly received salaries of a few hundred or a few thousand dollars, supplementing their salaries with off-season jobs, many of questionable value to their athletic careers. These players literally required a period of a month or so to work back into shape before the start of the season. In the early 1900s the New York Giants trained in the little Texas town of Marlin, and their training was, by the strictest definition, training.

Each day began and ended with what amounted to a two-mile forced march along the railroad tracks from the hotel to the park. The routine consisted of batting and fielding practice, along with drills on the fundamentals of play. If there was a scrimmage, it usually was an intrasquad effort, or perhaps a game against a local team or minor league club. In 1906 the 16 major league teams trained in 10 different states as far north as Illinois. The notion of grouping in Florida and Arizona to make exhibition games between them more convenient would not gain full currency for the better part of another decade. In 1911 the Yankees set up their spring camp in Bermuda.

At most early camps, players oversaw their own conditioning since, as a rule, teams employed only a manager and a single coach—if that. Teams now have coaches they employ just for spring training and will occasionally even attach a coach to a player who is making a position change. Complexes are usually used to house minor league teams when spring training is over; the municipalities, which see spring training as a major source of tourism dollars, often pay for construction of these complexes.

Pitching

How prized is the pitcher? Consider that of the nine positions, candidates for eight are winnowed principally by their skill with the bat. Middle infielders can progress through the professional ranks on the strength of superior range, outfielders may prosper by dint of speed, or catchers thanks to a God-given arm. Fundamentally, however, not even an Ozzie Smith or an Ivan Rodriguez can become a regular professional player until they establish at least a minimal offensive ability. The only exception is the pitcher.

Pitchers always have been the exception, even before the designated-hitter rule legislated many of them out of that *terra incognita* known as the batter's box. In any analysis of Ty Cobb's value as a player, the first thing that comes up is his lifetime .366 batting average, yet no one would think of discussing Sandy Koufax's value to the Dodgers in terms of his .097 batting average.

In fact, the pitcher is the one and only player whose defensive contribution is so vital that the ability to hit is considered irrelevant—as is his fielding skill. Red Ruffing, the fine right-hander for the New York Yankees of the 1930s and 1940s, compiled one of the best batting records of any pitcher in the past three quarters of a century, including a .268 career average. But when he was voted into the Hall of Fame in 1967, it was on the strength of a 273-225 record, 3.80 earned run average, and on his status as the leading moundsman for seven pennant winners.

Pitching has been the staple of most successful big league franchises since batters lost the right to call for the type of pitch they liked. Connie Mack is variously quoted as having called it anywhere from 70 to 90 percent of the game. The precise figure is not important: what is important is that Mr. Mack's axiom remains generally accepted today, though logical analysis of baseball shows that pitching and fielding together comprise 50 percent of the game.

Yet, despite the constancy of the importance placed on quality

pitching, both pitching styles and the rules governing pitching have undergone more major changes than any other aspect of on-field play. This change has been so great that the best pitchers of today have virtually nothing in common with the best pitchers of a century ago. Furthermore, pitchers today bear strikingly little resemblance to their predecessors of as little as three decades earlier.

Much of this evolution took place during the game's formative years, and came via efforts by the rule makers to settle on the proper balance of batting to pitching. In the early years of professional ball in the 1860s and 1870s, pitching bore more similarity to the style employed today in fast-pitch softball than in baseball. The ball was delivered underhand and without a wrist snap from a box set at a distance of 45 feet from the plate, although pitchers fudged so much that, by 1872, wrist movement was legalized. Legalization of the wrist snap quickly spawned the development of various "trick" pitches, notably the curveball, commonly credited to William "Candy" Cummings, a much-traveled moundsman of that era who compiled a 145-94 record in the only six seasons he played as a top-level professional. Whether Cummings or any of several other pitchers of his era first perfected the art of making a ball curve, Candy generally got the credit (being elected to the Hall of Fame in 1939 for that accomplishment).

Nineteenth-century pitchers worked under virtually ever-changing conditions. For instance, the front line of the pitcher's box was moved back to 50 feet from home plate after 1880, then the box was eliminated in 1893 in favor of a "rubber" placed at 60 feet, 6 inches. The underhand delivery requirement gradually was modified to allow what in effect was a sidearm pitch in 1883, and a full overhand delivery the following year. Rules governing the ball-and-strike count—at one time nine balls were required to give the batter a walk—changed frequently until they were stabilized at four and three, respectively, in 1889. At various times, pitchers were required to deliver a high or low pitch, as requested by the batter; windups were banned, then permitted again; the size of the pitcher's box was altered almost routinely before being consigned to extinction.

It would be difficult to generalize as to whether all of those changes helped or hurt pitchers. Certainly, batting averages tended to improve as the distance between the mound and plate increased. Yet the underhand pitching style, physically much easier on the arm, enabled most teams to play an entire schedule with only one or two pitchers. And the best of them attained results that would be unthinkable today.

By way of illustration, compare the statistics that Providence's Old Hoss Radbourn compiled in 1884 with the records of the top pitchers of the following century, including the last pitcher to win 30 or more games, Detroit's Denny McLain, in 1968.

Radbourn's numbers seem even more impressive when it is noted that his Providence team played only a 112-game schedule. Of course, the comparisons are fair only as illustration of how greatly the pitching environment—the rules, conditions and strategies—changed between 1884, 1968 and the present.

At least as dynamic a force as the rulebook in the evolution of the modern pitcher has been the development of pitching strategy, notably new pitches. For while the broad regulations under which pitchers work today are not vastly different from 1893, the arsenal of pitches that have come into vogue—and occasionally passed from it—has ranged widely and sometimes wildly.

Cummings' introduction of the curveball marked the first major deviation toward finesse from what had fundamentally been a power pitcher's game to that time. Other innovators included Phonney Martin, who threw a drop or slowball, and Al Spalding and Tim Keefe, masters of the change-of-pace. However, such bolder experimentation was limited to a handful of hurlers.

While pitchers of the latter part of the 19th century occasionally dabbled in "outshoots" or "rises," the best built their reputations with speed. "Cyclone" Young in Cleveland and Amos Rusie, New York's "Hoosier Thunderbolt," were the best—and in all likelihood—the fastest of them. Young won 27 games for Cleveland in 1891, his first full season, and accumulated 511 victories over a remarkable 22-year career. The magnificence of Cy Young's record is best illustrated by the fact that the all-time runner-up, Washington's Walter Johnson, trails by almost a hundred wins. Young's 2,803 strikeouts—a record when he retired—further testify to his velocity. As for Rusie, he won 36 games in 1894 and led the league in strikeouts five times between 1890 and 1895. He also led five times in walks, initiating the popular linkage between hard throwers and control trouble.

By the mid-1890s, earned run averages rose as a reaction to the shift of the pitching distance back to 60 feet, 6 inches. The legendary Baltimore Orioles of Wee Willie Keeler had batted .343 as a team in 1894, yet did not even lead the league—Philadelphia did, at .349! In response, pitchers began to experiment more readily with changes of speed as well as with the ball itself. Chicago's Clark Griffith scraped the ball against his spikes and discovered that the scuffs added to the break of his curve, making him a 20-game winner for six consecutive seasons. Philadelphia's Al Orth, a "one-pitch wonder," mastered the art of changing speeds and won 204 games in 15 years.

Equally as significant as changes in the approach to pitching was the increase in the number of pitchers needed. In 1876 Chicago's Albert Spalding had been able to pitch in all but five of his team's 66 games. By the early 1880s, the top teams were using two pitchers. Within another decade—as the increased pitching distance, longer playing schedules and more taxing overhand motion became accepted—staffs of fewer than four to five were uncommon. The Detroit team of the 1884 National League utilized perhaps the first pitching "staff" *per se*, with four hurlers (Frank Meinke, Stump Weidman, Charley Getzien, and Dupee Shaw) each working between 147 and 289 innings. Detroit's strategy did not count for much as the club finished last but, within a decade, Baltimore rode what amounted to a four-to-six-pitcher rotation to the league championship. That staff's ace, Sadie McMahon, pitched only about one-quarter of the total number of innings worked by the sextet. In 1876, the eight National League teams basically employed a total of 13 pitchers; by 1886, that number was 24; by 1896, for 12 teams, it was 51.

By the turn of the century, the popularization of two theretofore lightly used pitches helped re-establish the pitcher as the game's dominant player. Christy Mathewson, a fresh-faced college graduate from Bucknell, brought to the New York Giants a pitch he called the "fadeaway," actually a reworked version of something known in the 1880s as an "outshoot." Today, Matty's legendary fadeaway would be called a screwball, though the popularity of that pitch has declined in recent years.

The pitch acts like a reverse curve: when thrown by a right-handed pitcher, it breaks toward a right-handed batter. Mathewson might very well have become a great pitcher even without the fadeaway, but with it he won 373 games, four times winning 30 or more, and five times helping the Giants to pennants. So difficult was the pitch to throw and control that no other major league

pitcher of the era could master it.

The other dominant pitch of the first part of the 20th century was the spitball, employed brilliantly by two men, Jack Chesbro and Ed Walsh.

Chesbro came to the major leagues with Pittsburgh in 1899 and, by 1901, had incorporated the spitball into his routine. He became a 20-game winner throwing the wet one; it would not be illegal to doctor a baseball with a foreign substance for two more decades. Chesbro won 28 games with the pennant-winning Pirates in 1902, so greatly increasing his value that he became one of a cadre of "free agents" who were recruited to the fledgling American League during the three-year interleague war. With the New York Highlanders of the young league in 1904, Chesbro's spitball took him to a 20th-century-record 41 victories, although it also set up one of the most ironic finishes to any pennant race. Because of its wild break, the spitball was one of the least predictable of pitches, yet Chesbro had walked only 88 batters that season, fewer than two every nine innings. His control of the devious delivery was impeccable.

On the final weekend of that season, Boston and New York—virtually tied for first—engaged in a five-game series, with the winner of that series becoming the champion. Chesbro's 41st victory came in the series opener, but Boston claimed the ensuing two. In the climactic fourth game, the opening contest of a last-day doubleheader, Chesbro held onto a 2–2 tie entering the ninth. An infield hit, a sacrifice and a groundout moved Boston's pennant winning run to third base. The great pitcher had been masterful to that point, walking just one and striking out five. However, in that most pivotal of situations, a Chesbro spitball bounced in the dirt and skipped toward the backstop, a wild pitch that cost New York a pennant.

Walsh, like Chesbro, perfected control of the elusive spitter and parlayed that to remarkable feats. A moundsman of modest ability prior to employing the pitch in 1906, he won 17 games that season, 24 the next, and an astonishing 40 the year after that. Irony played a central role in Walsh's career as well, for perhaps his best performance in that 40-win season of 1908 came in defeat. At the climax of a three-team race involving Cleveland, Detroit and Chicago, Walsh's White Sox came to Cleveland needing a victory to remain in contention. Walsh pitched a four-hitter and struck out 15 batters, but Cleveland's Addie Joss achieved a rare perfect game and won 1-0. The only run was unearned.

Other so-called "freak" pitches came into vogue during that era as well. Pitchers altered balls not only with spit or spikes, but also with emery paper, paraffin, mud, slippery elm, and who knows what else. But the ranks of pitchers who relied on tampering for their success still constituted a minority. Most, like Washington's Walter Johnson continued to rely on the basic fastball. Of course, most pitchers did not have a fastball the caliber of Walter Johnson's to rely on.

And on that basis, pitchers and batters lived in happy coexistence for about a decade, pausing only occasionally to admire the ascendancy of a new star like Philadelphia's Grover Cleveland Alexander. Master both of the fastball and curve, Alexander emerged in 1911 as a rookie 28-game winner and, by 1915, he was leading the Phillies to the National League pennant on the strength of a 31-victory season. With Philadelphia and later with the Chicago Cubs, he led the league in victories six times between 1911 and 1920, becoming generally acknowledged as the preeminent pitcher of the latter half of what is commonly called baseball's Dead Ball Era.

Alexander, along with Walter Johnson, continued to pitch in form beyond 1920, but that was not true of major league pitchers

as a whole. A series of factors, some mechanical, some societal, reshaped the game again following World War I and, in most instances, it was pitchers who suffered in the reshaping.

The catalyst for much of that reshaping, ironically, was a former pitcher—and a very good one. As a 20-year-old rookie in 1915, Babe Ruth won 18 games to help the Boston Red Sox to the world championship. By the following season, Ruth, a 23-game winner who added another victory in the World Series, was coming to be recognized as Boston's ace. He led the AL in earned run average (1.75), starts (41), and shutouts (9), and paced it in complete games (35) the following season as well.

By 1918, however, Ruth the pitcher was recognized as less of a hero than Ruth the slugger. He pitched in 20 games that season, winning 13 of them, but started nearly three times as often in the outfield, a response both to his hitting and to the box-office value of the fans' clamoring to see him hit. Although by no means an everyday player, the Babe tied for the league lead in home runs that season with a modest 11. More significantly, he drew crowds, both at Fenway Park and on the road. So in 1919, Boston manager Ed Barrow converted him almost exclusively to the outfield. Ruth's response was to break the all-time record for home runs—with 29—and to lead the league in runs, runs batted in, and slugging as well.

Traded to New York in 1920, Ruth almost immediately became the most celebrated player in the game's history. He slugged a then-unthinkable 54 home runs, breaking existing records for runs, RBIs, bases on balls, and slugging percentage. To the public, Ruth was "the Sultan of Swat," "the Bazoo of Bang," "the Infant Swatigy," and "the Colossus of Clout." Batting averages and home-run production rose league-wide as other players strove to imitate him. American League batters, who hit .248 with 136 home runs in 1917, raised those figures to .292 and 477 by 1921. In the National League, the increases for the same period were from .249 and 202 to .289 and 460.

Part of that 150 to 200 percent increase in the home run count could be attributed to the banning—enforced gradually as of 1920—of the spitball and other so-called "doctored" pitches, part to improved craftsmanship on the part of the baseball makers, and part to the directive by league officials to replace soiled, scuffed balls with cleaner, whiter ones. But in large measure, the change was simply a strategic one: batters swung harder and tried to drive the ball farther than ever before. Once a poke-and-run contest, baseball had become—thanks in good measure to Ruth—a slugger's game. There is no question that the fans loved it: AL attendance soared from 1.7 million in 1918 (albeit in a season shortened by the owners because of World War I) to more than 5 million in 1920.

Unfortunately for pitchers, they proved less than capable of adapting to the new and more thrilling style. The rule change barring use of the spitball, emery ball, shine ball, and other similar pitches removed a potential weapon from all arsenals, save those of 17 men who were exempted from the ban. These 17 were permitted to continue throwing the pitch, which did not actually die out until the last of them, Burleigh Grimes, retired in 1934. Effective new pitches were not developed to fill the void, though a few toyed with a knuckleball. In the late 1920s George Blaeholder, a nondescript pitcher for the St. Louis Browns, devised a pitch that eventually came to be known as the slider, but for years was derided by many as just a "nickel curve." For the most part, though, pitchers relied on the fastball, curve and a very occasional changeup. With pitchers as with batters, raw power replaced guile and cunning as their chief weapon.

The result was predictable: for the better part of two decades, batting averages, home runs and earned run averages soared. NL ERA skyrocketed from 3.13 in 1920 to 4.97 in 1930; in the AL in that period, ERA increased from 3.79 to 4.65. NL home runs more than tripled, but strikeouts increased by only 6 percent. The differences in the AL were less dramatic, but still quite large. Pitchers reasserted their competitiveness somewhat in the 1930s, though by then bat-happy baseball society had been conditioned to view a 4.00 ERA as good.

The period between 1920 and 1960 produced some exceptional pitchers, but few changes in pitching style. In the mid-1930s, a rookie right-hander in Detroit named Elden Auker bothered batters with an underhanded delivery reminiscent of the style of the 1870s. Auker's so-called submarine pitch was necessitated by an arm injury that made it difficult for him to throw overhand. He won 130 games in a 10-year career, pitching on two pennant winners and one world champion. His style would be resurrected in the modern era by relievers like Ted Abernathy, Kent Tekulve, Dan Quisenberry, and Gene Garber. In the National League, the New York Giants' Carl Hubbell also reached back in time for a cudgel. Hubbell resurrected Mathewson's fadeaway, renaming it the screwball, and mystified opponents sufficiently to record five straight 20-win seasons between 1933 and 1937, leading the Giants to three pennants.

A more conventional, and more overpowering, form belonged to Lefty Grove, who pitched for 17 years for the Philadelphia Athletics and the Boston Red Sox. Grove's trademarks were a fastball that many have called the swiftest ever and a surly disposition. Four times a league leader in victories and nine times the ERA king, Grove was the only pitcher to win 300 games in the hot-hitting 1920s and 1930s, an achievement often cited by those who point to him as the best pitcher ever. His career ERA of 3.06 is more than one full run lower than the league average for the years that he pitched (1925 to 1941).

Pitching rules, which had remained virtually untouched since 1920, underwent several adjustments between 1950 and 1969. The strike zone was tightened in 1950, the new upper limit being the armpit instead of the top of the shoulder (with the lower limit at bottom of the knees staying the same). After a decade of unprecedented home-run hitting in the 1950s, both home runs and scoring increased in 1961-62, so the old strike zone was brought back in an attempt to help the beleaguered moundsmen. The result was in the intended direction, but of a magnitude unforeseen and undesired by everyone except pitchers: scoring plunged dramatically from 1963 through 1968. American League pitchers posted a post-1920 low ERA of 2.98 in 1968 as Denny McLain won 31 games and only one AL batter (Carl Yastrzemski, at .301) could top .300. In the NL, two hard-throwing right-handers who gave enemy hitters no quarter entranced fans: Bob Gibson posted an unbelievable 1.12 ERA while Don Drysdale set a then all-time record with 58 consecutive scoreless innings. Fully 21 percent of 1968 games resulted in shutouts. Rule makers quickly responded to that offensive nadir by lowering the mound several inches and restoring the strike zone to its 1950-1962 dimensions. Scoring and home runs climbed, aided further in the American League in 1973 when the designated hitter was introduced.

It would be overly simple and wrong merely to point to the rule book as the fulcrum for all variations in pitching performance in the past five decades. Certainly, another very significant factor in the second half of the 20th century was the development of relief pitching. Beyond that, pitchers perfected pitches they had only toyed with before. The knuckleball was not new—it had been thrown since the early part of the century and, in the 1940s, the Washington Senators employed a foursome of flutter-balling starters. No pitcher employed the erratic butterfly pitch as effectively, however, as the trio of Hoyt Wilhelm and Phil Niekro—both of whom rode the knuckler to the Hall of Fame—and Phil's younger brother, Joe Niekro. Wilhelm pitched in a then-unprecedented 1,070 games over 21 years and established what at the time was the record for saves, 227. Phil Niekro won 318 games and, in tandem with Joe (who won 221), in 1987 set the record for most victories by members of one family.

A sort of variation on the knuckleball, also developed years before but resurrected recently, was the forkball or "split-fingered fastball." Credit for its development generally is given to 1940s New York Yankees pitcher Ernie Bonham, but the first famous exponent was Elroy Face, a relief pitcher for the Pittsburgh Pirates of the 1950s and 1960s. In 1959, Face compiled a sensational 18-1 record with 10 saves by the simple expedient of jamming the ball between his index and middle fingers before releasing it. This unusual grip caused the ball to have very little spin and gave it an unexpected dip as it crossed home plate; it also made it a devastating change-of-pace pitch. Face, who saved 20 games in 1958 and 24 in the Pirates' world championship year of 1960, is generally credited with ushering in the era of the modern relief ace or closer.

In the late 1970s another star reliever, Bruce Sutter of the Chicago Cubs, reinvented the same pitch with the help of his minor league pitching coach, Fred Martin, though Sutter called it his "split-fingered fastball," for he, unlike Face, threw it hard, and not as a changeup. Sutter saved 37 games for the fifth-place Cubs in 1979, and earned the Cy Young Award. In Sutter's wake, entire pitching staffs began learning what was quickly dubbed the "splitter." Roger Craig became a one-man traveling demonstration of the newly popular pitch's success. As Detroit pitching coach, he taught it to the Tigers staff in the early 1980s, and they responded by winning the world championship in 1984. Then Craig taught it to journeyman Houston right-hander Mike Scott, and he blossomed into an 18-game winner capable of recording over 300 strikeouts while leading the Astros to a divisional flag in 1986. Craig returned to managing in San Francisco, where his staff of split-finger throwers helped the Giants win the NL West title in 1987.

The most widely used new pitch, however, was the one invented by Blaeholder 50 years before—the slider. Acting much like a fastball but with a sharp, late break, the slider supplemented and frequently supplanted the slower and bigger-breaking curveball in the repertoire of most big league hurlers. Perhaps the pitch's most famous practitioner was Steve Carlton, who used it to become the second winningest left-hander of all time, behind only Warren Spahn. So disarming was Carlton's nasty slider that he became the first pitcher to win four Cy Young Awards; he also staged a dramatic contest in the mid-1980s with fastballer Nolan Ryan to see who would become the first pitcher in history to record 4,000 strikeouts.

If the evolution of pitching suggests anything, however, it is that no one style, no single delivery, no trick pitch, and no simple rule change can remain perpetually dominant. In the 1960s no two pitchers could have been more stylistically different than Juan Marichal, the high-kicking ace of the San Francisco Giants, and Sandy Koufax, the stylish left-hander of the Los Angeles Dodgers. Marichal employed seemingly every move, every trick, every pitch ever devised by professional pitchers.

He threw the fastball, the curveball, the slider, the changeup,

and the screwball; he delivered them overhanded, three-quartered, or sidearmed whenever he chose, to the great consternation of opposing hitters. Koufax relied on a fastball, a stunning curve, and (during his peak years after 1960) exemplary control. Yet in 1963, for instance, each won 25 games, each appeared among the league leaders in winning percentage, earned run average, strikeouts, complete games, and innings pitched. Between 1963 and 1966, Marichal averaged better than 23 victories; Koufax, 24.

One of the most frequently debated questions in baseball is whether modern pitchers throw harder than their predecessors. It is, of course, very difficult to answer that question. To the degree that today's pitchers are bigger and stronger than ever, to the degree that improved training and conditioning programs encourage greater speed, it is logical to assume that the fastest modern hurlers must be swifter than Cy Young or Walter Johnson or Lefty Grove. Consensus picks as to the hardest-throwing starting pitchers of the past two decades would probably be Nolan Ryan and Randy Johnson. Ryan's fastball was clocked in his prime on radar guns at about 100 miles per hour; Johnson has been routinely clocked at 100 or even higher in the late 1990s. (It is true that several relief pitchers—Rob Dibble, Roberto Hernandez, Mark Wohlers, Robb Nen, Troy Percival, and Billy Wagner—to name some of the more prominent—have been clocked as regularly throwing in the high 90s or around 100 miles per hour in recent years. However, it is like comparing apples and mangoes to talk about peak velocity for a pitcher that routinely pitches only one inning as contrasted with a starting pitcher.)

One of the biggest problems in discussing pitch velocity is changing standards. Prior to the advent of sports radar guns in the 1970s, various measures were used in an attempt to time pitches accurately. Some of the early radar guns used in the 1970s and 1980s sampled the speed of the pitch only a few times between the pitcher's release and when the ball crossed the plate. Because the pitch slows down more the farther it travels from the pitcher's hand—it can be traveling be as much as 10 miles per hour slower at the plate than when released by the pitcher—the point at which the radar gun actually "clocked" the pitch could easily make a difference of multiple miles per hour. Therefore, earlier radar guns were best used to average the velocity of many pitches, not to give a definitive reading on one pitch. Newer, digital-technology radar guns can sample the speed of a pitch hundreds of times in the split-second it takes to travel from the mound to home plate, making individual pitch readings much more accurate. There is a four-mile-per-hour difference between some of the old radar guns (which showed average big league fastballs at 85-86 m.p.h.) and the current guns (which show average velocity at 89-90 m.p.h.). The effect of this difference is that a pitcher clocked at 100 miles per hour in the late 1990s would probably have been measured as throwing in the mid-to-high 90s with some of the old guns. The best that can be said is that changing measurement standards and changing technology over the decades, plus the lack of controlled tests and systematic records, make all of these discussions about peak velocity exercises in approximation, not precision.

Old-timers, of course, did not have the advantage, or disadvantage, of pitching to radar guns, so assessments of their speed are necessarily cruder. "Rapid Robert" Feller's fastball, for instance, once was clocked against a speeding motorcycle. The finding? About 100 miles per hour. The eyewitness testimony of old-timers varies. Many picked Walter Johnson, but Johnson himself picked Smoky Joe Wood. Billy Herman selected Van Lingle Mungo.

Contemporaries like Wes Ferrell said Lefty Grove was faster than Feller, but numerous sportswriters sided with Feller as the fastest ever. Connie Mack, who played and managed across six decades, opted for Amos Rusie, the old-time "Hoosier Thunderbolt." Mack's opinion, however, could easily have been influenced by nostalgia: he batted against Rusie. Nolan Ryan was generally considered the fastest pitcher in the 1980s but, for a time, it was not universally presumed that he was the fastest on the Houston Astros! Until his crippling stroke, J.R. Richard was conceded that title by at least some that saw both.

Strategy Before 1920

There is no single "correct" way to win a pennant. If a club can hit the cover off the ball, it might have a chance. If it can field with the best, that might be enough. And if its pitchers are dominant, that, too, might do it. Then again, maybe not. If the history of major league baseball demonstrates anything, it is that the search for a single winning formula is as elusive as the search for a rainbow's end.

Since the National League of Professional Base Ball Clubs first organized for play in 1876, through the 2003 season, there have been 244 recognized major league seasons played by the two currently operating leagues plus the handful of short-lived other major leagues. It stands to reason that if, over the years, ballclubs had found one strategy to be more successful than any other, we would have witnessed consistent adoption of that strategy by winning clubs.

Why do strategies change? Why don't the modern-day Mets approach the challenge of winning in the same fashion as the White Stockings of bygone days? Many of the reasons are obvious. Plainly, changing conditions and rules dictate some of the strategic adjustments. The White Stockings and their counterparts of the 1880s would, for instance, have considered it folly to pay more than one or two pitchers and an equal number of substitutes. Rules regulated the appearances of non-regulars and, in a time of 80-game schedules and underhand deliveries, more bodies simply were not required. Night baseball and modern-day transcontinental travel place greater strains on players.

Changes in park sizes, styles and equipment contribute to strategic alterations as well. When, in the first quarter of the 20th century, improved manufacturing techniques made for a better grade of ball, managers eschewed the sacrifice in favor of swinging for the fences. The increasing popularity of artificial turf half a century later placed a renewed premium on defensive range and speed. Sociological adjustments played a part as well. The 1920 outlawing of the spitball and other pitches that defaced the ball—occasioned, at least in good measure, by "sanitary" factors as well as competitive ones—plainly contributed to generally higher batting averages throughout the 1920s and 1930s.

The *de facto* banning of the beanball and its first cousin, the knockdown pitch, in recent years resulted in some degree from public complaints about the pitch's potential danger. But another, less obvious contributor to the constant ebb and flow of baseball strategy is simple managerial practice. If a particular team employs a new—or, more often, resurrected—strategy with success, the prospect is great that competitors will emulate it. Often, these strategic adjustments are of transitory duration but, in terms of their impact on individual pennant races, they can still be important.

It is overly simplistic to equate particular strategies with specific time periods: to suggest, for instance, that because earned run averages were lower during the first decade of the 1900s, the emphasis

at that time was on pitching. Or to argue that teams stressed offense in the 1920s and 1930s because batting averages swelled, or to suggest that raw power has become the dominant force of the present-day game.

In fact, between 1900 and 1919—the commonly recognized Dead Ball Era—the league batting champion won 20 pennants, the slugging champion 19, and the earned run average champion only 16. Conversely, between 1920 and 1949—the period of unbridled hitting—32 pennants were won by clubs that led their league in ERA, only 24 by slugging leaders, and only 22 by batting average leaders.

Those numbers do not render the era labels meaningless, but they do suggest that successful managers of every generation may be following their own strategies, rather than the obvious ones. The art of strategy is as old as the game itself. When Candy Cummings discovered that he could make a baseball curve, he was developing a new strategy. So was the forgotten manager who, faced with the dilemma of none out in the ninth and the winning run at third, first brainstormed bringing both his infield and outfield in to a shallow depth, the better to cut off the run at home. When, in the 1880s, Chicago's legendarily innovative "King Kelly" apocryphally dashed from his seat on the bench, yelled "Kelly now substituting," then snagged a foul fly to save the game, he was enhancing strategy—at least until that particular practice was outlawed and substitutions permitted only during time-outs.

Perhaps the first recognized employer of what we might today consider as strategy on a prolonged basis was Ross Barnes, the second baseman of the champion Chicago White Stockings of the National League's inaugural season in 1876. The league at the time had a rule that stipulated that any ball landing in fair territory was considered a fair ball, irrespective of whether it subsequently rolled foul before passing a base. By that standard, many bunts and choppers of today would be fair balls. Barnes developed the skill of striking such "fair–foul" hits, and he did it so well that he led the league in batting that first season with a .404 average that would have been .429 if the NL hadn't counted walks as outs that year. (Barnes did not invent the fair-foul hit but he did perfect it, using it judiciously to hit for a .390 average in the five years of the league that preceded the NL, the National Association of 1871 to 1875.)

Alas for Barnes, as would be the case for some subsequent strategists of later ages, rule makers reacted to his achievement by outlawing the strategy that he had perfected. When in 1877 the requirement was established that a groundball pass first or third base in fair territory to be legitimately fair, his average plummeted to .272.

As would be expected, the development of strategy during the game's first decades occurred in very broad and general terms. There was, for instance, little thought given to the strategic advantages of relief pitchers, in-game platooning, pinch hitting, pinch running, or defensive substitution, for the simple reason that, until the late 1880s, substitutions—save for injury—were not even permitted. Naturally, the growing awareness of the value of maintaining a group of reserve players first focused on the pitcher's box.

As early as 1876, managers employed diverse approaches to pitching strategy. Four of the eight teams, including the Chicago champions, stayed fundamentally with a single hurler. In the case of Chicago manager Al Spalding, that pitcher was Spalding himself, who pitched in 61 of the team's 66 games (starting 60 of them and completing 53). But three other clubs divided the mound work roughly equally between two men of reasonably balanced skills. In the case of third-place Hartford, for instance, Tommy

Bond pitched 408 innings with a 1.68 ERA, while Candy Cummings curved his way through 216 innings with a 1.67 ERA.

Fourth-place Boston went so far as to divide the work among three pitchers, each pitching between 170 and 220 innings. Boston manager Harry Wright might have seemed very much the trend-setter had he stuck with that notion. However, the very next year, Wright jettisoned all three of his 1876 arms and signed Bond away from Hartford to pitch 58 of the club's 61 games. Boston won the 1877 flag; Cincinnati employed a three-man staff and finished last.

If we define a pitching staff as consisting of at least four pitchers, each sharing a roughly equivalent part of the responsibility, then credit for devising the first one probably belongs to Jack Chapman, who directed the fortunes of several early-day National League teams. Chapman found himself in Detroit in 1884, surrounded by little offense and even less in the way of reliable pitching. The team's earned run average in 1883 had been 3.56, second worst in the league and considerably higher than the overall 3.13 average. This was still very much an era when a single hurler could carry a team's fortunes: In Providence, Old Hoss Radbourn would win 59 games and pitch 679 innings, the equivalent of 75 complete games.

Other mound stars included Pud Galvin (46–22) in Buffalo, Larry Corcoran (35-23) in Chicago, and Mickey Welch (39-21) in New York. Chapman had no one who could hope to match such standouts day after day, so he did not try. Instead, he rotated five men, none pitching more than 30 percent of the team's innings. The result wasn't much, as Detroit still finished last. Chapman took his approach to Buffalo in 1885, where the four-man pitching rotation lasted longer than Chapman himself, as he was dismissed after a 12-19 start.

From the mid-1880s, experiments with multi-pitcher staffs became more common, but no team won a pennant utilizing such an approach until Chapman's successor in Detroit, Bill Watkins, resurrected the notion in 1887. That club, too, featured five pitchers, none of whom did very much more than a third of the work. Like Chapman, Watkins plainly was trying to mask a weakness. His everyday lineup featured some of the game's greats: outfielder Sam Thompson drove in the league's most runs, 166, and he won the walk-less version of the batting title (.372, which elevated only to .407 when the walks were added in, leaving him third behind teammate Dan Brouthers' .420 and Cap Anson's .421). The Detroit team led the league in runs, doubles, triples, batting average, slugging, and fielding percentage.

But as usual, all of the great pitchers toiled for other teams: Tim Keefe and Welch in New York, John Clarkson in Chicago, Galvin in Pittsburgh. Watkins built a five-man staff based on his only two proven arms, Lady Baldwin (42-13 in 1886) and Charles Getzien (30-11), two lightly used reserves (Pete Conway and Larry Twitchell), and Stump Weidman, signed when Kansas City's team folded after the 1886 season. Suddenly the names of Detroit pitchers began showing up in the strangest of places, like among the league leaders in key pitching categories. Getzien led in percentage and was third in wins, Conway ranked second in ERA and allowed fewer hits per nine innings pitched than anyone.

The next season, a very funny thing happened: several teams ditched their reliance on a single pitcher in favor of a staff. There remained a few holdouts: Boston's John Clarkson pitched 483 innings in 1888, 620 in 1889, and 460 as late as 1891. Within a decade of the Detroit staff's accomplishment, though, Boston's Kid Nichols could lead the league in innings pitched with a compara-

tively modest 368. The era of a team asking one man to pitch as many as 400 innings was not quite dead yet—it would surface here and there through the first decade of the 20th century—but it was dying. The change to a multiple-pitcher staff may have been hastened by Detroit's inability to snare one of the league's stronger arms, but changing conditions and rules would have made it inevitable anyway.

Occasionally, a new strategy works so well that it must be legislated against. Ross Barnes' fair-foul hit was one such. But the all-time champions, both in devising new strategies and in getting them banned, were the Baltimore Orioles teams that flourished under manager Ned Hanlon in the 1890s.

Hanlon's Orioles achieved that mastery by a singular combination of remarkable skill and superior innovative capacity. Among the strategies team members are credited with devising or popularizing:

The hit-and-run play. Stories as to the origin of the stratagem, whereby a runner breaks for the next base while the batter attempts to drive the ball through a hole vacated by the fielder covering the steal effort, are both numerous and hoary, and no definitive judgment can be rendered. Cap Anson, longtime manager of the Chicago White Stockings, is among those purported to have claimed this strategy as his own. But the best available evidence tends to support the claim of the Orioles' chief contemporary rivals, the Boston Beaneaters, and their manager, Frank Selee. John McGraw, the famous manager who played for the Orioles, insisted on the validity of Baltimore's claim. But even if Hanlon's Orioles cannot be established as the originators, they certainly brought the play to its first and lasting popularity. Typically John McGraw, leading off, would reach base, and then Willie Keeler, a superlative hitter (lifetime .341 batting average) whose principal asset was his exquisite bat control, would direct the ball to the appropriate weak spot, often resulting in runners at first and third with none out.

The Baltimore chop. There is no question as to the origin of this play, which has waned in strategic significance with the ascension of the home run. Orioles' hitters mastered it and used that mastery to advantage. The chop was deceptively simple: a hitter would employ an exaggerated downward swing to drive the pitch almost directly into the ground in front of the plate. On the hard Baltimore dirt, the result would be an infield bouncer recoiling so high off the ground that there would be no defense—infielders could merely wait in vain for the ball to descend while the batter scampered to first unchallenged.

The bunt single. The sacrifice, of course, had been around for many years prior to the emergence of the Orioles, and so had the "baby hit," or bunt single. But Baltimore players like McGraw, Hughie Jennings, and Joe Kelley were among the first to use the bunt as a steady means for reaching base. Dickey Pearce and Tom Barlow of the old Brooklyn Atlantics pioneered in this regard, and Ross Barnes followed. McGraw especially was brash in his use of the bunt, not only to reach base but also to tire out opposing hurlers, as fouls were not counted as strikes until the first decade of the 20th century.

The Orioles weren't the only innovators of the 1890s. In Boston, the Beaneaters honed their skill at the double steal, wherein the runner at first broke for second and, when the catcher attempted to retire him, the runner on third tried to score. This rather daring technique required not only nerve and teamwork but superior speed. The Beaneaters had plenty of the latter commodity with the likes of Billy Hamilton, whose 914 career stolen bases represented the all-time record before Lou Brock shattered it. The Brooklyn club of the same era is generally credited with originating the cutoff play, when an infielder intercepts an outfielder's throw to the plate in an effort to retire the batter or another runner attempting to advance an extra base.

The Orioles devised other, less gentlemanly, strategies as well. Their first baseman, "Dirty Jack" Doyle got his nickname by tripping, jostling, or holding opposing runners by the belt; Jennings at shortstop or McGraw at third were equally as likely to obstruct a runner. Baltimore outfielders were known for hiding extra balls in the tall grass to be put in play in emergencies. It was said that catcher Wilbert Robinson always kept his pockets full of pebbles, which he dropped in the shoes of batters as he squatted behind them. On offense, the Orioles were by no means above cutting bases when an umpire's back was turned.

Baltimore could do all of those things because most games of the era were officiated by a single arbiter, who could not hope to watch everything taking place on the broad expanse. Ultimately, public disgust at the Orioles' open flaunting of rules caused league officials to authorize umpiring teams. Over time, the practice grew to using four umpires. The trend started with the rule-breaking Orioles.

Possibly the most convincing evidence of the prominent role played by Hanlon's Orioles in the development of baseball strategy is the fact that the two superior minds of the subsequent generation of baseball officials were former Orioles: McGraw and Jennings. It was they who, while piloting pennant winners in the first years of the 20th century, popularized strategic innovations that would eventually assume permanent, prominent roles in the planning of every major league franchise.

Jennings took over leadership of the AL Detroit Tigers in 1907 following his retirement as an active player, and he became an immediate success. The Tigers, a 71-78 team the previous year under Bill Armour, leaped immediately to a 92-58 record and the pennant. They followed that up with pennants in 1908 and 1909 as well. Jennings' success was partially a product of being in the right place at the right time, as his managerial star ascended in almost precise concert with the development of Ty Cobb. Cobb came up as an 18-year-old rookie in 1905, winning batting titles in 12 of the 13 seasons from 1907 through 1919. Jennings deserves some credit as well, however, for analyzing his team's strengths and weaknesses and for inventing methods of overcoming the latter.

The prime example of that trait involved his handling of the Tigers' catchers. Even in their first two pennant-winning years, catching was a comparative liability for them. The regular, left-handed batting Boss Schmidt, hit just .244 and .265, and he seemed especially bedazzled by left-handed pitchers. Jennings had dealt summarily enough with other weak links by releasing them, but he did not want to dispatch Schmidt because of his still sharp defensive skills and above-average throwing arm. Instead, Jennings replaced Schmidt in the lineup against left-handers, first with right-handed Ira Thomas and then with Oscar Stanage. By splitting time at the position between two players, Jennings was following the practice of his fired predecessor.

What Jennings was using was a platoon system, and it gradually caught on. New York Highlanders manager George Stallings applied the platoon with outfielders Willie Keeler and Birdie Cree in 1909, then took the idea with him to Boston when he assumed

control of the Braves in 1914. There, his judicious mixing of a half dozen outfielders helped bring him a pennant. Although Jennings deserves the credit for popularizing platooning by demonstrating over a period of several seasons that it could work with a pennant contender, a solid case might also be made for manager Frank Bancroft as the father of platooning, way back in the 1880s.

McGraw pioneered strategy of a very different, but equally lasting, type. In 1908, 20-year-old rookie pitcher Otis "Doc" Crandall, who showed exceptional potential, came to the Giants. Crandall won 12 games, but he lacked stamina and overpowering speed, was hit hard in the later innings of games, and did his best work in relief of other pitchers. To minimize the weakness and take advantage of his strengths, McGraw in 1909 designated Crandall as the club's "relief" pitcher, chosen to enter in midgame if necessary and rescue a faltering teammate. In an era when starting pitchers were rarely removed—about two-thirds of all starts were completed that year—the concept of a pitcher actually specializing in midgame appearances seemed demeaning. Yet that is exactly what Crandall did, making two-thirds of his appearances over the next three years (1910-12) in relief, winning 20 and saving 12.

As intriguing as it was, Crandall's success did not spur an immediate flood of imitators. Managers, who found quality starting pitching difficult enough to locate, could not bring themselves to isolate one or more of their better arms for emergency duty. One of the few mimics was Patsy Donovan of the Boston Red Sox who, in 1910, converted right-hander Charley Hall from an ineffective occasional starter into a reliever of fairly consistent quality. Between 1910 and 1913, Hall made 137 pitching appearances for Boston, just 53 as a starter; in relief he won 20 of 24 decisions, saving 10 others. Fittingly, the 1912 World Series pitted Hall's Red Sox against Crandall's Giants. Hall saw more action, pitching 10-2/3 innings in two games with a 3.38 ERA. Crandall saw action in just one game as the Giants eventually lost four games to three.

While McGraw and Jennings innovated, game strategy during the Dead Ball Era stressed strong pitching, aggressive baserunning and playing for a single run. The game also featured an emphasis on standout players whose talents dwarfed their teammates. The most obvious example was Cobb, who batted .350 in 1907, .385 in 1910, .420 in 1911, and .410 in 1912. In 1910, for example, Cobb's batting average was nearly 100 points higher than any of his teammates, and his slugging average was 125 points superior. The Georgia Peach was not the only early 20th century player who could have been considered a one-man team. In Cleveland in 1911 outfielder Joe Jackson batted .408 and slugged .590 with 233 hits, 45 doubles, 19 triples, and 126 runs. The second highest totals on the team in each category were .304, .396, 142, 25, 9, and 89. In 1909 Pittsburgh's Honus Wagner led his team to the pennant with a .339 average. The second highest average among the club's regulars belonged to player-manager Fred Clarke, at .287.

With the home run not yet developed as a viable option, and with league earned run averages ranging between 2.30 and 2.70, managers often resorted to the sacrifice or the stolen base, mindful of the importance of every run. While it is not possible today to reconstruct sacrifice totals due to incomplete records, stolen base records rose higher and quicker than at any other period of the game until the 1970s. The evolution of individual and team stolen-base records clearly indicates this. In 1898 the modern standard for counting steals was developed; prior to that, any extra-base advance—whether via a pitched or hit ball—had been counted as a steal. In 1900 Brooklyn led the majors with 274 steals, while Patsy

Donovan of St. Louis and George Van Haltren of New York set the individual standard with 45. Then Frank Isbell of the American League's Chicago team set the new century's individual record in 1901 with 52 as the White Sox stole 280. In 1903 Frank Chance of the Cubs and Jimmy Sheckard of the Dodgers upped the individual mark to 67 and, in 1904, the Giants raised the team record to 283. The Giants broke their own record in 1905, stealing 291, and Cobb shattered the modern individual record in 1909 with 76 steals.

Neither record lasted one season. In 1910 Eddie Collins of the Athletics stole 81 and the Reds purloined 310. Those new standards were erased within one year, Cobb stealing 83 and the Giants 347 in 1911. Clyde Milan of Washington broke Cobb's record with 88 in 1912; then Cobb broke Milan's mark in 1915, stealing 96. The individual record was thus broken seven times and the team record five times, all in a span of 15 seasons. Cobb's record did not fall for 47 years, until Maury Wills stole 104 bases for Los Angeles in 1962. The Giants' team record of 347 steals is unsurpassed to this day.

It might seem natural for a record in a newly established category to be broken several times in quick succession, then finally reach a comparatively unattainable plateau. It might, but consider that even the original team mark of 274 set by the 1900 Dodgers would have stood into the 1970s. The first 20 years of the century were not a case of a record gradually being raised beyond reach, they were a case of teams simply stressing the running game. The very worst basestealing team in the century's first decade, the 1906 Boston Braves (who stole 93), would have won either the American or National League stolen base championship 38 times between 1925 and 1960.

Night Ball

Baseball was invented before electric lights, so it originally was a game played largely in the afternoons. Thus, extra-inning affairs or late-starting games sometimes were called on account of darkness when the opposing nines had failed to complete their contest before twilight faded. That presented a distinct problem, as the decision about when to call a game on account of darkness affected the outcome. Hall of Famer Gabby Hartnett's fabled "Home run in the gloamin'" in 1938, which helped lead the Cubs to the pennant, is probably the most famous example. Hartnett was player-manager of Chicago, which was locked in a tight race with Pittsburgh in late September. In the second game of a three-game series, the Cubs tied the game at 5-5 in the bottom of the eighth as the light faded. The umpires decided to let play continue for one more inning before calling the game; the Bucs failed to score in the top of the ninth. Hartnett, 37, led off the home half of the inning, hitting a homer on an 0-2 curveball off Pirates reliever Mace Brown to put the Cubs into first place for good.

Of course, most working people couldn't afford to take an afternoon off to attend a weekday ballgame, leading to a high proportion of businessmen—yes, they were mostly men—among the relatively sparse crowds (by today's standards) of the early 20th century. Games played on weekends and holidays consequently drew much larger attendance.

By the early 1930s, however, artificial lighting was nearing fruition for major league play. That the concept was feasible there could be no doubt: a baseball game had been played at night way back in 1880, only two years after the introduction of electric light, and the Des Moines, Iowa, club of the Western League installed lights in 1930. The idea, which caught on in a Depression era of dwindling attendance, was to stave off financial collapse by

increasing weekday attendance.

Cincinnati executive Larry MacPhail finally advanced the notion of staging big league games around the normal working fan's hours. MacPhail had good reason to lobby for the change; his Cincinnati franchise had drawn an anemic 206,000 fans in 1934, not enough to offset expenses. MacPhail and club owner Powel Crosley petitioned the National League for the right to play seven 1935 games at night; the league reluctantly agreed, taking note of the extenuating circumstance of the depressed attendance in the Queen City.

The first of those games, played May 24, pitted Cincinnati against Philadelphia, and skeptics were moved to silence when it attracted an audience of better than 20,000 to what proved to be a 2-1 Reds victory. By 1941 night ball was an accepted fact in the majority of major league parks and, by shortly after the war's end, only Wrigley Field in Chicago still lacked lighting. Today, most major league games as well as virtually all minor league games are played under the lights. Even the traditional Cubs finally capitulated to the reality of night baseball in 1988 when lights were installed at Wrigley Field, despite vigorous opposition from traditionalists as well as neighborhood residents. (Without lights, the Cubs faced the prospect of removal of any postseason home games to another ballpark.)

Attendance figures partially reflect the reason: prior to the advent of night baseball, it was considered exceptional if a ballclub drew a half million fans for the season, and the entire NL schedule of 1933 attracted only about 3.1 million fans. In the 1960s, attendance of 1 million was considered a good year at the gate for most clubs. Today, the Cleveland Indians continue a tradition of selling every seat at Jacobs Field *before* the season starts, while several clubs can anticipate drawing 3 million fans each season. Major League Baseball recorded a historic first in 1986 when all its clubs drew at least 1 million fans. The following season was the first in which MLB clubs averaged 2 million in home attendance. Seasonal attendance of less than seven figures is now considered a disgrace.

Scheduling a handful of weekday baseball games in the sunshine is still good business, as the popular "businesspersons' specials" attest, though most weekday afternoon games are mandated by the travel considerations of the modern schedule. Nevertheless, it is clear that night baseball is the normal paradigm of the national game today. Day games are a pleasant diversion, but the difference between the game as it was played before 1935 and afterward is literally a difference of night and day.

Strategy After 1920

The reasons behind the switch that occurred about 1920 from a one-run strategy based on high batting average, the sacrifice and stolen base to one focusing on power hitting are numerous and complex. Changes in rules, park design, equipment, and fan interest all played a part. The impact of those factors on the changed game is underscored in the dramatically altered statistics of the game in the 1920s and later. The numbers of runs being scored provides the clearest contrast.

Prior to the season of 1920, the major league record (in the NL-AL period since 1901) for runs scored in a season by an individual was 147, set by Ty Cobb in 1911. The highest annual total for both leagues was set in 1912, was 11,164 runs. But in 1920, New York's Babe Ruth easily broke Cobb's individual record by scoring 158. He broke it again in 1921 with 177, establishing the standard that still exists. In all, Cobb's former record was broken 13 times in the American League alone between 1920 and 1940. Meanwhile, total

runs rose to 11,935 in 1921, then broke through the 12,000 barrier the following year to 12,059. It was broken again in 1925 (12,592), again in 1929 (12,747), and again in 1930 (13,695). And that record stood for more than three decades, until it was surpassed in 1962, by which time each major league had added two teams and eight more games to the playing schedule.

Power records similarly surged. Tris Speaker's Dead Ball Era record for doubles—53, set in 1912—fell to Speaker himself in 1923 (59), and was surpassed in eight more seasons during the 1920s and 1930s; in 1936 alone five players matched or bettered that pre-1920 record. The pre-1920 record for home runs—Ruth's 29 in 1919—bears no comparison, of course, with subsequent achievements. It had been raised three times by Ruth himself in 1927, and was bettered in every single American League season until the war year of 1944, when New York's Nick Etten led the league with only 22. League slugging percentage, which ranged between .310 and .340 during the Dead Ball Era, jumped by an average of more than 20 points in both leagues in 1920 alone, and by 30 more points the following year. The increase in the American League alone was nearly 14 percent between 1919 and 1921. Slugging soared to .421 by 1930 in the American League, and to .448 in the National.

With the increase in power came a concurrent acceptance of the intentional or semi-intentional base on balls as occasionally prudent strategy. Managers, operating on the theory that discretion might be the better part of valor, instructed or allowed pitchers to "work around" certain hitters like Ruth who were capable of doing far more damage with a home run than a walk. Previously, when pitchers looked on a walk as anathema, the Chicago Cubs' Jimmy Sheckard held the record by drawing 147 of them in 1911. That lasted until Ruth walked 148 times in 1920. The Babe raised that standard to 170 in 1923. The league record of 4,282 walks issued in the NL in 1911 lasted until 1925, when American League pitchers walked 4,315 batters. The record was hiked biennially to 4,402; 4,611; 4,855; and 4,924 in the same league between 1932 and 1938.

Finally, in the 1920s and 1930s, the usage of relief pitchers first gained true prominence. In 1919 the St. Louis Cardinals' Oscar Tuero became the first relief pitcher to lead the league in appearances; he pitched in 45 games, 28 out of the bullpen. The achievement drew little notice, primarily because his team finished seventh. But in 1923 the pennant-winning Giants' Claude Jonnard and Rosy Ryan tied for the league lead in appearances, each with 45. Ryan started 15 games that season, Jonnard just one. The following season Firpo Marberry of the AL champion Washington Senators led the league with 50 appearances, only 15 of them starts. Marberry repeated as most-called upon in 1925 with 55 appearances, all in relief, in another pennant-winning year. Marberry's role was by no means yet established; he would lead the league three more times in appearances, twice as a reliever, once as a starter. Nevertheless, the idea of a specialist in quality relief pitching for first-rank teams had at last begun to gain acceptance.

When the 1927 New York Yankees blitzed the American League to win 110 games, their most frequently called upon pitcher was rookie Wilcy Moore, who won 19 games despite starting only 12. Moore pitched 38 times out of the bullpen. In 1901 National League pitchers had completed 976 games, representing nearly 90 percent of the schedule. By 1919 that figure had fallen to about 60 percent. In 1922, for the first time in history, National League pitchers completed fewer than half of all their starts. By 1930 the mark had fallen to 43 percent, and it held at roughly that level

through the 1930s and 1940s.

As the perceived importance of the complete game waned, a temporary strategic miasma settled in. Managers, less unwilling to turn to the bullpen, still had not developed effective strategies for its use. That began to change in the early 1940s when Leo Durocher developed the notion of a bullpen "ace." The Brooklyn manager used his late-inning stopper both to give his team a chance to retake the lead as well as to try to hold the lead of a tiring starter through the final innings. For the first time, a manager appeared not to expect his starter to finish—or, at least, not to mind it if he didn't. Dodger starters completed only 66 games in 1941—one of the lowest totals ever by a pennant winner—and only 67 more the following season, while Durocher used hard-throwing Hugh Casey to win 14 games and save 20 those two years.

Others emulated Durocher's strategic development. Boston's Joe Cronin won the 1946 American League pennant, thanks in good measure to the relief pitching of Bob Klinger, who appeared 27 times in relief and saved a league-high 9 games. The Yankees' Joe Page won 21 games and saved 33 in virtually exclusive bullpen action in 1947 and 1948. Slowly, the old concept of relievers merely as failed starters was eroding. As late as 1946 more than half the major league mound staffs were led in appearances by a starter, and it was still possible for Cleveland's Bob Feller to lead the league in that category. The trend was plain, however: in 1947, relievers led in appearances on 10 of the 16 staffs. By 1952, the figure was 13 of 16. In 1950 a relief pitcher, Jim Konstanty of the Phillies, won the NL's Most Valuable Player Award by pitching in a then-record 74 games, saving 22 of them and leading his team to the pennant.

Joe Black won 15 games and saved 15 more for the pennant-winning 1952 Dodgers. In 1954 Cleveland manager Al Lopez deployed a relief tandem of left-hander Don Mossi and righty Ray Narleski, who appeared in 82 games between them, saving 20. The major league save record stood at Marberry's 22, set in 1926, until Joe Page recorded 27 in 1949. Boston's Ellis Kinder matched that in 1953, and New York's Luis Arroyo topped it in 1961. Prior to 1949, only Marberry in all of baseball history had saved 20 games in a year. Between 1949 and 1961, 10 pitchers did it. All of this should be understood in the context that the concept of a "save" was unknown in the first half of the century, and the save was not adopted as an official statistic until 1969.

Player platooning, a dormant strategy after the early 1920s, was revived in the late 1940s, principally by Casey Stengel. A platoon player himself under John McGraw with the 1920s Giants, Stengel alternated left-handed hitting third basemen Bobby Brown and righty Billy Johnson in his first two years as Yankees manager. In 1951 Gil McDougald supplanted Johnson as the right-handed half of the platoon as the Yankees won the world championship all three years. By 1955 Stengel had expanded his platoon system, alternating right-handed Bill Skowron with lefty Joe Collins at first base, and subbing right-handed Elston Howard for Irv Noren in the outfield. Howard and utility man Tony Kubek both were platooned at several positions in 1957. Again, successful managers took their cues from Stengel. Fred Haney's use of the first-base platoon of Joe Adcock and Frank Torre helped the Braves to the pennant in 1957 and 1958.

The only manager to beat out Stengel for the AL pennant between 1949 and 1960, Al Lopez (who also managed Cleveland in 1954), used a platoon system to do so with the White Sox in 1959. Lopez alternated righty Bubba Phillips and lefty Billy Goodman at third base, and righty Jim McAnany and lefty Jim Rivera in right field. In 1960 Pittsburgh manager Danny Murtaugh often alternated at three positions: Hal Smith or Smoky Burgess at catcher, Dick Stuart or Rocky Nelson at first, and Gino Cimoli or Bill Virdon in center. Fred Hutchinson used platoons at three positions in 1961 (Jerry Zimmerman and John Edwards at catcher, Elio Chacon and Don Blasingame at second, Wally Post and Jerry Lynch in left), as Cincinnati took the flag. By the mid-1960s, most teams were platooning at least one position.

The other significant change in strategy during the 1950s and early 1960s was a growing acceptance of the strikeout as an acceptable price to pay for home-run power. In retrospect, that acceptance can clearly be seen as a delayed reaction, for home-run totals had begun to mount sharply in 1953. For the previous two decades, major league batters had averaged between 1,300 and 1,700 home runs annually; in 1953, they hit 2,076, a record 1,197 of them coming in the National League alone. That represented a 22 percent increase over the previous season. From 1953 through 1960, the record was raised only about 10 percent and, in fact, the raw numbers of home runs flattened and occasionally declined between 1956, the peak season for home runs in the decade, and 1960.

Strikeouts rose sharply during this period. In 1953 batters struck out 10,220 times; by 1960 that had risen steadily to more than 12,800, a climb of more than 25 percent. The strikeout explosion continued unabated through the 1960s, whether home runs rose (as they did in 1961 and 1962) or fell. In fact, between 1961 and 1966, home-run totals remained virtually level in the major leagues, despite the addition of two expansion teams. But strikeouts rose by more than 25 percent over the same period. The increase (part of which was attributable to strategic concessions and part to the enlarged strike zone), showed itself in the individual strikeout totals as well. Until 1956 the record for most strikeouts in a season was Vince DiMaggio's 134, set in 1938. Washington's Jim Lemon broke it that season with 138. In 1961 Detroit's Jake Wood broke it again, fanning 141 times. Harmon Killebrew of Minnesota raised the mark to 142 the following season; then Dave Nicholson of the Chicago White Sox increased it to 175 in 1963.

San Francisco's Bobby Bonds whiffed 187 times in 1969, then followed with 189 strikeouts in 1970, setting a record that endures. The rate of strikeouts dipped in the 1970s due to the smaller strike zone of 1969 and the designated hitter, then jumped in the 1980s. Batters' willingness to swing for the fences, of course, has only increased since then and strikeouts per game are now higher than ever. Long gone is the ingrained prejudice against striking out, as contemporary hitters have increasingly focused on taking more pitches—and, therefore, walking more often—as well as hitting for power.

The game in the 1970s and 1980s featured several other changes: the regeneration of the running game, the implementation of the designated hitter, and the further specification of the role of the relief pitcher.

Stealing bases, as well as aggressive baserunning in general, were reinvigorated in the 1960s as runs became more scarce. It was in the 1970s and 1980s, however, that baserunning reached its post-1920 height of importance. Changing playing conditions, notably the wide use of artificial surfaces, certainly played a large part, as did the talent infusion from Latin America. Many of the new players who entered the major league ranks could run well and play defense well, but not hit with power. Managerial acumen certainly had something to do with it: Whitey Herzog and others found it easier to succeed in large ballparks by emphasizing speed over

power. This two-way versatility and greater athleticism gave the Royals, Cardinals and other similar teams both an important baserunning threat and a critical defensive boost, especially in the large outfields of the modern superstadiums. The resurrection of speed also essentially banished the lumbering, one-dimensional slugger to the American League and the good hitters' parks remaining in the NL.

If the reasons behind the stolen base's surge are complex, affixing the date of its arrival as a mainstream stratagem is less so. It clearly came from Venezuela by way of Chicago in the person of Luis Aparicio in 1956. Prior to Aparicio, there had not been a genuine basestealing threat—a player capable of swiping 50 or more bases in a season—in more than a decade. Moreover, the efforts of the comparative handful of fellows who had great speed in the decade prior to that (e.g., George Case in Washington and Snuffy Stirnweiss in New York) were lost in the glare of the home run. Stolen bases plummeted from more than one per team per game in the first two decades of the century to half that in the 1920s, then continued to decline to a low point of less than one every three games for the typical team in the 1950s.

Aparicio's debut sounded the call to speed. As a rookie he led the American League in steals in 1956. His total of 21 was certainly nothing special, even for the sluggish 1950s, but the notion of a baserunner as a weapon had not yet caught on. The following season Aparicio won the title again, this time with 28 before stealing an eye-opening and crowd-pleasing 56 in 1959 (Willie Mays, the National League champion, stole 27). Aparicio would go on to win the stolen-base crown in nine successive seasons, topping 40 steals in four of the next five years.

By 1959 Aparicio was no longer the whole story. Stolen-base totals had turned upward virtually league-wide. National Leaguers stole 439 bases that season, their highest total in nearly a decade. In 1960 Los Angeles shortstop Maury Wills joined Aparicio at the 50-steal plateau, then in 1962 Wills was successful 104 times, breaking Cobb's record of 96 that had stood since 1915. The Dodgers as a team stole 198 bases, the most by any major league club since 1918.

Baserunners became a critical part of most pennant winners in the National League. Wills was a key factor in the Dodgers' NL championships in 1963, 1965 and 1966. St. Louis obtained Lou Brock in midseason 1964 and promptly took off from mediocrity to the world championship as he stole 33 bases for the Cards. Brock helped St. Louis to another World Series title in 1967, and the Cards came within one game of repeating as world champions in 1968.

By 1966 stolen bases were up almost 50 percent from the depressed levels of the 1950s, and the rate of thefts in the 1970s more than doubled the slow-footed '50s. As was the case in the Dead Ball Era, every team had its "rabbit." In 1974 Brock broke Wills' single-season record by stealing 118 bases. In 1976 Chuck Tanner's Oakland A's stole 341 bases, falling just six steals short of the all-time record established in 1911. Bill North stole 75 that season, Bert Campaneris 54, and Don Baylor 52, as nine different Oakland players stole 20 or more. Yet the A's finished second behind Kansas City, which stole "only" 218.

In the last two decades, stolen-base records were rewritten almost routinely. In 1992 Rickey Henderson, who had set the single-season mark with 130 in Oakland in 1982, broke Brock's career mark of 938; ultimately he became the first player to steal more than 1,000 bases. Henderson stole 100 or more three times in the 1980s, a feat matched by St. Louis' Vince Coleman. What's more, the list of the top 10 basestealers of all-time in terms of success percentage includes eight players from the 1980s and 1990s.

The introduction of the designated hitter in the American League in 1973 has certainly had strategic implications. The premise of the DH is that most pitchers are miserable batters and the public prefers to see more proficient batters in their place. The rule in effect allows one player to pinch hit repeatedly for the pitcher without requiring the pitcher's removal from the game.

The leagues split over the DH when it was adopted, and they have remained divided ever since. After the AL blazed the trail, the rule was also adopted by virtually every other collegiate and professional league. It became part of the World Series after a compromise between the two major leagues, used from 1976 through 1985 in alternating years. Since 1986 the DH has been employed in games played in the home ballpark of the AL champion. That compromise has also been in effect for interleague games since their inception in 1997.

The designated-hitter rule was adopted by the American League as an effort to increase offensive production and also spur fan interest. This radical move was made because AL scoring had fallen to a low of 3.41 runs per game in 1968; after a rebound in 1969-70, it then slumped again to only to 3.47 in 1972. National League scoring had fallen in the same way in the 1960s, but was almost half a run higher in 1972.

Concern about lower scoring among AL ownership was greatly heightened by the large gap in attendance between the two leagues at the time: from 1969 through 1972, the NL outdrew the AL by 36 percent. Some of this had to do with the new ballparks being occupied by NL teams; nevertheless, it is clear that the large attendance deficit spurred AL owners to action. Apparently, the move worked as a way of drumming up more business; the AL had essentially achieved parity with the NL in per-team attendance by the early 1980s and eventually surpassed the NL in 1989.

The change also accomplished its goal of injecting more offense into the AL game. In 1973 the league scoring average jumped 23 percent, one of the most dramatic one-season shifts in the game's history. Other statistics reflected the change as well: the league batting average rose from .239 to .259 and AL teams hit 32 percent more home runs.

Most teams have used the DH position as a refuge for older (and frequently slower) power hitters who are no longer capable of playing daily in the field but who are still effective offensively. Except for the common practice of using the DH to help players who are hobbled by minor injuries, or the similar stratagem of using an occasional game at DH as a rest for regulars, most designated hitters have been defensive liabilities with power bats. Teams will sometimes use high-average hitters as regular DHs (usually they must have plus speed as well), but most often a lack of real power at DH indicates lack of a better choice, not a deliberate strategy. The best DHs, epitomized by Seattle's Edgar Martinez, would certainly play regularly despite their glove if the DH rule were repealed. However, many great DHs, especially those who could no longer physically play the field due to leg or knee injuries (e.g., Chili Davis and Harold Baines), would have had to retire years earlier if not for the DH rule.

The principal points of debate concerning the effects of the DH on baseball strategy have been two: first, whether it inappropriately undermines one of baseball's appealing tenets, that all participants be complete athletes; second, whether it diminishes in-game strategic moves by managers. Detractors argue that, logically, the

DH must negatively impact on strategy by removing one of the questions a manager must repeatedly consider during the course of a game: whether to pinch hit for a reasonably effective pitcher when behind or tied. The fewer decisions the manager must make, the reasoning goes, the more muted become baseball's strategic nuances. As strategy dulls, so does the game according to this viewpoint.

Others argue, also logically, that the DH actually *enhances* strategy. The crux of this counterargument is that managers traditionally were forced into a series of very obvious pinch-hit/relief-pitcher moves that were almost always dictated by game circumstance. If the circumstances compel such moves, then they are not options at all and both brilliant and ordinary managers would make the same choices. A reasonably competent DH, by contrast, should give managers some discretion in the decision to bunt, steal, swing away, or hit and run. With the DH, a manager must decide whether to remove his pitcher based on his estimate of how well he's likely to continue to pitch, not simply that he is due to bat in an obvious pinch-hitting situation.

The use of the bullpen as a strategic factor has progressed constantly from Luis Arroyo's days in New York until the present. Again, clear evidence is found in the record book. Arroyo's 29 saves were surpassed in 1965 when Ted Abernathy of the Chicago Cubs saved 31. Kansas City's Jack Aker broke the record again the following season with 32. That record lasted only until 1970, when Cincinnati's Wayne Granger saved 35 games. The Reds' Clay Carroll raised the record to 37 in 1972, and Detroit's John Hiller saved 38 in 1973. In 1983 Kansas City's Dan Quisenberry saved 45.

Since then, nine pitchers have saved 50 or more games in one season, including Bobby Thigpen, whose 57 saves in 1990 established the current record. Discounting the strike year of 1981, Arroyo's remarkable 29 saves in 1961 would have led the major leagues in no season since 1976 (although a 1975 change liberalized how saves were to be awarded, thus making cross-era comparisons difficult).

The primary role of the bullpen has changed from rescuing incompetent starters to a carefully worked-out and often rigid strategy for victory. Modern relievers have much more clearly defined jobs. Today's ideal bullpen contains at least one left-hander whose primary job is to retire only left-handed batters, plus a right-hander who is especially tough on righty hitters, plus one or two setup pitchers, a "long man" to pitch the middle innings when necessary, and a closer. The closer's task has been narrowed so that it now is rarely more than recording the final three outs of the game if his team has a one-to-three run lead.

Specialized setup pitchers evolved from the group of undifferentiated middle relievers in the late 1980s. Their job is to bridge the gap in the seventh and eighth innings of close games between the starter or middle reliever and the closer. Only in emergencies are pitchers used in roles that differ from their specialties. Many setup pitchers who distinguish themselves graduate to the premier role of closer; indeed, most closers now serve a *de facto* apprenticeship of one or more years as setup pitchers in the majors. Other setup pitchers are veterans whose stuff is good enough to be trusted in that secondary role, but not so overpowering that it virtually guarantees success. Closers who blow more than a handful of saves are sent packing; in 2003 the Dodgers' Eric Gagne recorded 55 saves without blowing any. Many sinker-slider pitchers and breaking-ball pitchers have become good setup relievers, but few pitchers without plus fastballs have been allowed to pitch in the ninth when the game is on the line.

With these changes have come additional recognition for the very best relievers. In 1974 Mike Marshall of the Los Angeles Dodgers became the first relief pitcher to win the Cy Young Award; his credentials included 15 victories, but also a league-leading 21 saves and an incredible 106 games and 208 innings, all in relief. Three years later, New York's Sparky Lyle would win the AL award with 13 wins and 26 saves. By 1979 a reliever's victory total had become extraneous: Bruce Sutter was recognized as the National League's top pitcher that season despite winning just 6 games because he saved 37. Rollie Fingers did the same thing for Milwaukee in 1981, winning just 6 but saving 28; he was named both Cy Young Award winner and league MVP in the drastically strike-shortened season. Willie Hernandez won the 1984 Cy Young Award as well as the MVP for Detroit on the basis of only 9 victories but 32 saves.

Modern Strategy

The decade of the 1990s saw many wrenching changes in baseball, both on and off the field. Aside from the constant drumbeat of argument over economic issues, the biggest story of the final decade of the 20th century—a century of prosperity, stability, and popularity for baseball that is unparalleled among major team sports—was unquestionably the explosion of offense. In particular, the unprecedented barrage of home runs generated a huge amount of controversy, to the point where the owners were actively discussing making significant rules changes to help their shell-shocked pitchers.

On the mound, two major strategic changes helped to define the character of the 1990s. One, an increase in the size of pitching staffs, was a reaction to the dramatic increase in scoring. The other, the near-universal adoption of the Tony La Russa-style bullpen and its rigidly defined roles, was the climax of a long-running trend in relief strategy.

As scoring increased, the search by teams for pitchers who could stem the tide became almost frantic. Scouts were dispatched around the world to scour other countries for pitching talent, and many young pitchers—as well as a few veterans—came to the majors from the Dominican Republic, Venezuela, Japan, Korea, Cuba, and elsewhere. Young pitchers who were hit hard in their first few outings were quickly sent back to the minors. Veteran left-handed pitchers found they had more professional lives than cats. Typical pitching staffs ballooned from the previous standards of 9 pitchers in the American League and 10 in the National (due to the lack of the designated hitter, NL clubs pinch hit for their hurlers more often) to 11, and sometimes an even dozen! More pitchers, each pitching fewer innings, trudged to the mound to face increasingly powerful lineups in which virtually every hitter could hit a mistake over the fence.

Part of the reason for the procession of new pitchers was the decrease in workload among ace relievers and the specialization in the bullpen. Oakland's Dennis Eckersley attained the same double honor of Cy Young and MVP in 1992 as had Hernandez in 1984 and Fingers in 1981. The big difference them, however, was not in how many saves they compiled, but in how many innings each worked. Eckersley pitched just 80 innings and won just 7 games while saving 51. Eight years earlier, Hernandez pitched 140-1/3 innings while winning 9 and saving 33. In strike-shortened 1981, Fingers had logged 78 innings while posting 6 wins and 28 saves in his team's 109 games; pro-rated to a full season, his 78 innings would equate to 116.

By the time of Eckersley's ascendancy as the game's premier

reliever, the narrowly defined role of one-inning closer—a pitcher who appeared only in the ninth inning and only to protect a lead of three runs or less—had been adopted to a point of stridency. Managers almost never went to their best relievers except in ninth-inning or extrainning "save situations," even if the game might hang in the balance in an earlier inning. This managerial reluctance to use the best pitcher in the bullpen until the game was already very likely won was in stark contrast to earlier decades. The great ace relievers of the 1970s and 1980s—fearsome pitchers like Goose Gossage, Bruce Sutter, Rollie Fingers, Mike Marshall, and Sparky Lyle—could expect the bullpen phone to ring anytime after the sixth inning if the game hung in the balance. Moreover, they were expected to finish the game no matter what inning they entered. Great relievers prior to the 1990s didn't often enter the game when their team was behind, but it wasn't unheard of, either. They certainly weren't automatically held in reserve when the game was tied in the late innings, watching as their lesser bullpen compatriots tried to hold the line till their team took the lead. They frequently faced their first batter of the game with runners in scoring position, instead of almost always sauntering in from the bullpen with the bases empty.

Paradoxically, although the styles that managers have employed to wrap up victories have changed over the last five decades—and although the salaries paid to relief pitchers have changed even more—the results have not. major league teams today blow late-inning leads at almost the same frequency they did decades ago, when there was no such thing as a closer or setup man, when bullpens were commonly refuges for failed starters, and when managers signaled for relief help only at the moment of absolute peril.

That assertion will probably surprise a generation of fans brought up on the theories of Tony La Russa. His widely praised and highly structured bullpens—a lefty specialist, a righty specialist, and a setup pitcher, all setting the stage for the closer who starts the ninth inning any time his team leads by three runs or less—became the model for virtually every team in the 1990s. A manager is now frequently second-guessed if he doesn't pull a starting pitcher after seven innings, even if he may be pitching a shutout.

A detailed study of every game played in the major leagues during seasons in which managers employed distinctly different bullpen usage patterns (originally published in the fourth edition of *Total Baseball*) defies widely held perceptions. In terms of victories—and winning or losing is what matters in baseball—the eighth-inning and ninth-inning strategies of the 1990s represent little if any advance whatsoever upon those of the 1970s or the 1950s.

YEAR	1R>7I	2R>7I	3R>7I	1R>8I	2R>8I	3R>8I
1952	.805	.901	.959	.894	.955	.950
1972	.771	.866	.930	.930	.853	.978
1992	.793	.897	.944	.891	.955	.975
1999-2000	.719	.856	.922	.825	.927	.962

KEY: 1R>7I = one-run lead after seventh inning;
2R>7I = two-run lead after seventh inning, etc.

The differences do not offer evidence that one usage pattern provides better results than another, that the modern concept of a specialized bullpen contributes to winning baseball games more frequently than other, older bullpen usage patterns. Contrary to accepted wisdom, a highly structured bullpen—one in which roles are defined and adhered to in a reasonably rigid fashion—appears to provide no advantage. As a general proposition, teams with a highly structured bullpen lose late-inning leads in roughly the same

proportion as teams of previous eras. The evidence is substantial that a significant increase in the number of saves recorded in recent years is wholly reflexive and gratuitous, and provides little actual advantage in the standings.

The study was originally conducted by examining games played in 1992, 1972, and 1952, then updated in 2000 to cover the past two seasons. These seasons provide contrast both across time and in the generally accepted patterns of bullpen use. In 1992 managers assumed that their starting pitchers would not finish games and had defined clear roles for their relief staff. In 1972 bullpen roles were evolving but not yet rigid; the concept of a closer (as opposed to the earlier "fireman," who was summoned in times of trouble) was in its early stages. Several teams did not even utilize closers. In 1972 a manager hoped that his starting pitcher would finish the game, but was willing to use his bullpen if necessary. In 1952 bullpen strategies had only begun to develop. Most teams still viewed relievers as failed starters or last-resort journeymen. Complete games were reasonably common, and only a few teams—the Yankees and Phillies being examples—had developed first-rate relief specialists. In 1952 a manager hoped his starting pitcher would finish the game and turned to his bullpen only when forced to do so.

Although managers did not derive greater benefit from their bullpen in 1992 than in previous seasons, they clearly relied on it to a far greater extent. Forty years earlier, managers who led by one run after eight innings went to their bullpen only 17 percent of the time. By 1972, this figure had risen to 29 percent. In 1992, however, managers who led by one run after eight innings went to their bullpen a whopping 66 percent of the time while winning 4 percent less often. An even clearer example of this trend to reflexive bullpen use is seen in the category of games in which a team led by three runs after eight innings. In 1952 managers in that situation called for a reliever only 21.4 percent of the time; by 1972 that percentage had actually fallen fractionally, to 21.3 percent. In 1992, however, managers of teams that led by three runs after eight innings went to their bullpen 54.7 percent of the time. They could hardly have achieved a significantly greater winning percentage, since teams in that advantageous position won 95.1 percent of the time in 1952, and 95.5 percent of the time in 1972. In fact, in 1992 teams that led by three runs after eight innings also won 95.5 percent of the time.

For practical purposes, this shift in patterns of bullpen use, two generations in the making, can be compared to periodic and whimsical changes in dress hemlines: A lot of money is spent, but the gain is in the eye of the beholder.

This focus on improving pitching occurred in the context of a rapidly increasing advantage for hitters in the 1990s. Scoring had stabilized from the late 1970s through the mid-1980s at about 4.5 runs per team per game in the AL, with the DH-less NL generally about half a run per team less. Home-run rates were also relatively static over that time span. Then, in 1987, in a summer of record hot weather throughout the East and Midwest, all hell broke loose from the pitchers' viewpoint.

"The Year of the Hitter," as 1987 quickly became known, caused the same kind of consternation among fans, the media, and those in the game that "The Year of the Pitcher" had caused in 1968. While scoring rose less than 10 percent in both leagues, homers in the AL were clubbed at a pace of one per team per game, highest in AL history and only slightly below the NL record pace of 1955. In the NL homers jumped almost 20 percent to the highest rate since 1961.

As in 1968, a change in the strike-zone definition was seized upon as the means to reverse the trend. Incongruously, the *de jure* strike zone was actually *reduced* from the "batter's armpits" to the "midpoint between the top of the shoulders and the top of the uniform pants." This was an attempt to expand the *de facto* strike zone, in the context of which umpires appeared to be calling "ball" on any pitch above the waist. Even though skeptics said that the besieged men in blue weren't following the new rules, both scoring and homers plummeted in 1988 to the levels of the early 1980s.

Runs and home runs in both leagues remained relatively stable from 1988 through 1992, and the controversy was muted. Then, on April 6, 1992, without an announcement or even any plan, baseball went back to the future.

On that day, Oriole Park at Camden Yards opened its gates in Baltimore for the first time. Instantly, every other ballpark in baseball became dated, and any multipurpose stadium was living on borrowed time as a baseball venue. As the first of what came to be called the "retro ballparks," Camden Yards received universal acclaim. Its old-time feel and old-fashioned attention to detail combined with its modern amenities to thrill fans and players alike. It succeeded beyond anyone's wildest dreams and spawned a legion of imitators in other cities.

One of the essential elements in creating the fan-friendly atmosphere at Camden Yards was keeping the fans close to the field. Not having to worry about configuring the park for football games, the architects placed the seats close to the action. This seemingly innocent detail automatically boosts offense, as the ability of the fielders to catch foul popups is curtailed, resulting in more swings for the hitters. Of course, more swings means more hits and more runs.

In 1993, 16 years after the AL's expansion to 14 teams, the NL finally followed suit by placing new franchises in Colorado and Florida. The effect that playing baseball at a mile-high altitude has on the game can be seen in the statistics from Mile High Stadium, the temporary home of the Rockies for their first two seasons, and Coors Field, the Rockies' "retro" ballpark that opened in 1995. As in 1961, pumped-up offensive stats were seen in an expansion year. As in 1961, many blamed expansion for diluting the level of pitching talent, conveniently ignoring that expansion also dilutes the level of hitting talent. As in 1961, the engines fueling the offensive boom were the two new ballparks, both of which were exceedingly generous to hitters. In fact, Denver and Miami provided the two best hitters' parks in the NL in both 1993 and 1994. (Note that the calculation for ballpark effect accounts for the performance of the home team, so having a bad pitching staff doesn't affect result.)

Playing in a converted football stadium in Denver in 1993 and 1994 boosted run scoring to the level of the best hitters' parks (e.g., Wrigley and Fenway) in the most extreme years in their long history. Playing in Coors Field, a more intimate baseball-only park since 1995 (even though its dimensions are spacious by normal standards) has boosted scoring by 35 to 70 percent per year. This is a stupendous offensive inflation never seen since the advent of permanent concrete-and-steel ballparks in the early 20th century. The mile-high effect on home runs isn't quite as dramatic, but it's still huge.

After the big increase in offense and homers in 1993, the 1994 season saw another jump. All summer long, fans and the media were abuzz with speculation about whether anyone could reach the 61 home runs of Roger Maris in 1961. By then the record had stood for 33 years; Ruth's mark had stood for 34 years before it was toppled by Maris.

It was certainly not a coincidence that per-game attendance in 1994 was the highest ever seen in baseball, before or since. At the time play was stopped by the players' strike after games of August 11, two players already had hit 40 home runs: Matt Williams of the Giants (43) and Ken Griffey, Jr. of the Mariners (40). Williams was on a pace to hit 61 home runs, equal to Maris in 1961, with Griffey and others close behind.

The 1994 season—the first in major league history in which more than one home run was hit per game by each team—set the stage for the rest of the decade. As the offense steadily increased, the frequency and the importance of baserunning diminished. While the overall rate of stolen bases dropped less than 10 percent from the 1980s, it dropped more than twice as fast from 1996 to 2000 as it had from 1991 to 1995. Furthermore, the rate of stealing in 2000 (0.60 stolen bases per game) was the lowest since 1973, the first year of the DH era. Still, even at the relatively depressed rate in 2000, stolen bases were more frequent than the average for all five decades from the 1920s through the 1960s.

A little perspective on the magnitude of the offensive explosion of the 1990s is in order. As the table below shows, the past decade did not see the highest level of offense in baseball history, nor did it even see the second-highest level. Overall offense in the 1990s was below that of both the 1920s and the 1930s. Even the five-runs-plus scored by each team in each game in the last two years of the century—when the wailing and gnashing of teeth in the sports media was at its height—fail to top the list of highest-scoring seasons of all-time.

DECADE	R/G	HR	HR/G	SO/G	BA	OPS	SB/G
1901-1910	3.92	3,207	0.13	3.60	.252	.636	1.20
1911-1920	3.97	4,256	0.18	3.59	.258	.665	1.11
1921-1930	4.93	10,829	0.44	2.84	.287	.752	0.56
1931-1940	4.85	13,448	0.55	3.36	.276	.735	0.39
1941-1950	4.32	13,460	0.54	3.57	.260	.702	0.35
1951-1960	4.39	20,915	0.85	4.53	.258	.721	0.31
1961-1970	4.06	27,470	0.82	5.76	.249	.691	0.43
1971-1980	4.15	29,201	0.73	5.05	.257	.703	0.65
1981-1990	4.30	33,172	0.82	5.45	.258	.714	0.77
1991-2000	4.77	43,725	1.00	6.23	.266	.754	0.71

Stripping away all the hype in recent years about the offensive binge, the home run explosion, and the effects of repeated expansions, it's clear that the sky isn't falling in major league baseball. In 1930, generally considered to be smack in the middle of what is frequently called the "Golden Age" of baseball, fully 5.55 runs were scored by each team in the average game—8 percent more than in 2000! The golden years of 1929 and 1936 also saw runners cross the plate more frequently than in 2000. In fact, the slugger-happy 1990s saw only 4 of the top 10 scoring seasons of the century, and only 5 of the top 20.

Many trends, both intended and unintended, have combined to push scoring and homers up since the mid-1980s. The biggest reasons are the new ballparks, changes in existing ballparks, stronger hitters, and better bat selection. Putting them all together at the same time has produced the current big-offense climate in the major leagues.

Baseball fans crave intimacy, and intimacy helps hitters. The result: new baseball-only ballparks are usually better hitting venues than the parks they replace. Putting domes on ballparks in colder climates helps hitters as well. In the past two decades, teams have been constantly modifying parks to accommodate fans, and most of those modifications have directly or indirectly helped the hitters. Every time that premium seating is installed behind home plate and between the dugouts, foul pops that used to be caught fall into the stands. Outfield fences have been moved in more often than out,

and fence height has been reduced in many parks. Some of the huge new scoreboards have helped block winds blowing in at the batter.

Three factors given far more play than they deserve for increased offense are expansion, the supposed shrinking of the strike zone, and the use of performance-enhancing drugs or supplements. Evidence of abuse of steroids in baseball is scant at best; brute strength is not a requirement in baseball as it is in football or several other sports. The effects of baseball players using legal, if controversial, supplements like creatine are completely unknown. It's entirely possible that creatine might make no difference in a ballplayer's performance—think of the placebo effect.

While the strike zone has clearly been compressed at the top, it has also been expanded at the bottom and on the outside. The unhittable sinker or splitter below the knees has replaced the "high, hard one" of bygone days as the pitcher's best pitch. The downward metamorphosis of the strike zone started with the change in umpire's chest protectors, then continued as pitchers were taught to keep the ball down and to view the high fastball just as if it were a hanging breaking ball—that is, a dangerous mistake.

The relentless "keep the ball down" coaching at all levels worked until good right-handed power hitters, who used to feast on high pitches and eschew low pitches, learned to reach down and lift any pitch above the knees. Once they developed that skill, their greatly increased arm and upper-body strength, courtesy of rigorous, year-round training, allowed them to hit those pitches with power. Improved strength and conditioning has also allowed smaller players, whose game often depends on their speed or their defense, to hit more home runs (think about how rarely the term "singles hitter" is used anymore). That's also why there's been such an increase in opposite-field home runs in recent years: power hitters with incredibly strong arms now stride into pitches on the outside part of the plate and literally muscle them 400 feet to the opposite power alley. When pitchers stopped busting hitters inside with high fastballs, hitters started crowding the plate and taking advantage of the increased reach it gave them.

There's nothing mysterious about all of this; left-handed batters have been known as low-ball hitters for decades. It just took an adjustment in hitting styles for righty swingers. That takes years of practice, but professionals can and will make that kind of adjustment when their livelihood depends on it—and those hitters that can't change are quickly replaced.

Another little-appreciated improvement in hitting has come from lighter bats. Bats weighing 30 to 34 ounces have replaced the 36-to-40-ounce shillelaghs wielded by the sluggers of yesteryear. Scientists studying the physics of hitting have found that the tradeoff in distance in hitting a ball with these lighter bats is very small, but lighter bats allow hitters to hit more pitches squarely because they can swing faster and have better bat control. A 425-foot homer is no better than a 410-foot homer, but hitting more pitches harder means more long flyballs—and that means more home runs.

Finally, while expansion has most certainly diluted the pitching, particularly in the few years immediately following the addition of new teams, it has also diluted the hitting to a commensurate degree. This means that Pedro Martinez and Randy Johnson will be facing more inferior hitters, just as Alex Rodriguez and Barry Bonds will be facing more inferior pitchers. Thus, *individual* hitting and pitching records both become easier to break every time the league expands, but that doesn't mean overall offense must go up.

The upward trend in home runs has nothing to do with juicing the ball and everything to do with superb professional athletes reacting to changing circumstances. Hockey scoring has plummeted in the 1980s and 1990s, yet is anyone blaming the puck? If hockey scoring rebounds, as it surely will, will rumors spring up about the "lively puck"?

Baseball players, coaches and managers are paid large sums of money to adjust successfully when their opponents are beating them. Scoring has risen and fallen throughout baseball history for many reasons, and home-run rates have done the same. Major fluctuations can be due to seasonal variances in the weather, an especially talented crop of young players entering the league, and to the adoption of different playing, pitching, hitting and coaching strategies.

Right now, hitters have the upper hand. No doubt about it: power hitters are thriving. The beleaguered pitchers and their coaches haven't yet figured out how to counter the new generation of sluggers. But what's so bad about that? Fans *love* high-scoring games.

It's no exaggeration to say that Babe Ruth and his majestic home runs saved baseball in the 1920s. Mark McGwire and Sammy Sosa enchanted fans and non-fans with their home run heroics in 1998, lifting the game off its sickbed on the strength of their strong arms and powerful bats. Baseball can put a damper on scoring anytime it wants by changing the rules in several ways; whether it really wants to do so is another question.

One of the oldest baseball adages is that pitching and defense win games. Without assessing the validity of that old chestnut, it's plainly obvious that home runs and scoring win the hearts of fans.

Chapter 33

Baseball Families

By Larry Amman

Just as the Wright brothers were first in flight, so were Wright brothers first in baseball. In the National Association's inaugural season of 1871, the Boston team featured Harry Wright as manager and reserve outfielder, and George at shortstop. Brother Sam joined them on the bench for the 1876 season, after an apprenticeship in New Haven the year before.

Since then there have been 366 brother combinations in the majors. The only season in which there was not at least one such pair was 1899. The most recent addition is the Glavines: in 2003 first baseman Mike Glavine was a 30-year-old rookie, joining older brother and two-time Cy Young Award winner Tom on the Mets.

The first thing that strikes the eye as one reads the list is the large number who were teammates, however briefly—more than 25 percent.

Another observation one must make is how one-sided the big league performance was between so many of the combinations. For example, there are 26 members of the Hall of Fame who had brothers in the majors—plus the Negro Leagues' Foster brothers, Rube and Bill. Yet how many baseball fans have ever heard of the brothers of Bill Dickey, Christy Mathewson or Honus Wagner? How many remember the brothers of Steve Sax, Robin Yount or Eddie Murray? These big names have brothers who played in the majors briefly.

Of course, being the brother of a major leaguer never guarantees success, nor even a shot at the big leagues. The five Delahantys, the three Boyers, and the two Ferrells all had other brothers who played minor league ball only. Because the combinations in which more than one brother excelled are so rare, we can limit the focus to the more outstanding ones.

In terms of balanced, outstanding achievement no group of three or more brothers can match the DiMaggios. The enduring folk hero status of Joe DiMaggio unfortunately has not done anything to keep alive the memory of his brothers, Vince and Dom. All three were gifted outfielders, good hitters and fine all-around athletes. Vince, the oldest of these sons of a San Francisco fisherman, played for five different National League teams. In 1941 he had 21 homers and 100 RBIs for Pittsburgh. Four years later he hit four grand slams for the Phillies.

Dom DiMaggio was the youngest and smallest of the three brothers. Although lacking any of the power of the other two, he was the fastest on the bases and yielded nothing to his two brothers

Matty and Felipe Alou
Matty, left, and Felipe, along with a third brother, Jesus, played a total of 5,129 games and scored 2,213 runs over a combined 47 major league seasons.

in the grace and skill he exhibited in the outfield. His lifetime batting average was just under .300.

In the 1941 All-Star Game, Dom went to right field as a late-inning substitute to play alongside Joe in center. This was a first in the Midsummer Classic. In the eighth inning, Joe doubled and Dom singled him home. In the 1949 All-Star Game, Joe drove in Dom with what proved to be the margin of victory for the junior circuit.

Dominic, or the "Little Professor" as he was called, started four

different All-Star Games, including the 1946 contest. That year he was voted to start in center field ahead of his brother. On the season, Dom outhit Joe by 26 points (.316 to .290).

In the 1943 All-Star Game, Vince went 3-for-3, including a ninth-inning home run. While Joe and Dom were away in the military, Vince was maintaining the family tradition of excellence in All-Star Games.

The first time two brothers played against each other in an All-Star Game was in 1969. Carlos May of the White Sox came to bat as a pinch hitter with brother Lee of the Reds playing first base. In the 1990 midsummer classic, television cameras showed Sandy Alomar, Jr. at bat while Roberto Alomar set himself at second base, ready to field anything his brother might have hit his way. The Alomars have been teammates for the American League five times since then.

For the title of the best brother pitching combination (aside from the Fosters of the Negro Leagues), the competition is very close between the Niekros of Ohio and the Perrys of Williamston, North Carolina. In 1987 the ancient knuckleballing duo of Phil and Joe Niekro passed Jim and Gaylord Perry in wins. The two families remain very close in most statistical categories.

The Perry brothers had one full season as teammates—1974 with Cleveland, when the two combined for 39 victories, almost half of the team total. A year earlier, when Jim was with Detroit, the two made their only start against each other. Gaylord took the loss for Cleveland. Jim got a no-decision. In the 1970 All-Star Game the National League pitcher in the sixth and seventh innings was Gaylord Perry of the Giants. On the mound for the American League in the seventh and eighth innings was Jim Perry of the Twins. This is the only time two brothers were rival pitchers in the All-Star Game. Both have also won the Cy Young Award.

For Joe and Phil Niekro, pitching against each other was not that uncommon. It happened nine different times. The most noteworthy occasion came on September 26, 1978, in Atlanta. Before this, his last start of the season, Phil was 19–17 for the Braves; Joe was 12–14 for the Astros. Houston won, 2–0, much to the dismay of victor Joe. He loathed the idea of pitching against his brother in these circumstances.

Harry and Stan Coveleski of the coal-mining country in Pennsylvania were brother hurlers who refused to start games against each other. Stan, the younger, was in his first full season in the majors in 1916 at Cleveland while Harry was winning 20 for the third consecutive year at Detroit. Harry developed arm trouble and did not pitch another full season, but Stan went on to five 20-win seasons and a niche in the Hall of Fame.

Virtually every baseball fan has heard of the game on September 15, 1963, in which Felipe, Matty and Jesus Alou formed the San Francisco outfield for one inning. A better story about this Dominican family, however, is the race for the 1966 National League batting title.

Going into the season, Felipe, with the Atlanta Braves, had established himself as a hitter of high average and respectable power. Younger brother Matty's career so far had been disappointing. With no power, his lifetime batting average was .260. In the off-season the Giants had traded him to Pittsburgh.

With the Bucs, Matty came under the special tutelage of manager Harry Walker. "Harry the Hat" taught his pupil to chop down on the ball and to hit to left field instead of trying to pull. This, plus over 20 bunt and 30 infield singles, propelled Matty to the top of the league batting race. Second or third to him almost

all year was Atlanta leadoff man and first baseman Felipe Alou. Matty won the crown with a .342 average, while Felipe finished second at .327. The elder brother, however, led the circuit in runs, hits and total bases.

It was only fitting that Harry Walker was the cause of the enormous jump in Matty's batting average. In 1947 outfielder Harry Walker was traded from the Cardinals to the Phillies early in the season. There he won the batting title with an average 100 points higher than the year before. This was the second batting title in the family. In 1944 older brother Dixie had led the National League with a .357 mark at Brooklyn.

Brother rivalries and brother teammates come into very sharp focus under the media glare of the World Series. The Series from 1921 to 1923 featured Bob Meusel of the Yankees against older brother Emil or "Irish" of the Giants. These two outfielders were very similar in physical appearance and in capabilities.

Before the 1921 Series one writer summed up the pair:

Bob hits harder than Emil though he is not as consistent in garnering his hits. Bob also excels Emil as a thrower, but Emil is the more finished fielder. Bob is a left-field hitter, and Emil often hits to right, so the play of "Meusel flied to Meusel" may be repeated frequently during the Series.

Indeed, it was so in all three Series. In Game 3 of the 1923 World Series, each brother robbed the other of an extra-base hit. Irish emerged superior to Bob in every category—even in extra-base hits. Bob, however, had the last laugh, driving in the go-ahead run in Game 6 of the 1923 World Series to give the Yankees their first world title.

For their entire careers, the Meusels startle the observer with the closeness of all their statistics. Irish averaged .310 to Bob's .309, both for 11 seasons. Bob leads in all other categories, but not by much. If Irish's totals were increased by pro-rating them based on his 100 fewer games, the two would look like clones. Each man led his league in RBIs one time.

Two brothers whose lifetime batting averages are identical are Bob and Roy Johnson. Both of these Oklahoma Indians hit .296 as American League outfielders in the 1930s. Bob amassed 2,000 hits and almost 300 home runs, playing mostly for Connie Mack. Elder brother Roy was a speedy singles and doubles hitter. He exceeded his brother only in stolen bases in his shorter career.

The 1927 World Series featured Lloyd Waner leading off and playing center field for Pittsburgh while older brother Paul hit third and patrolled right field. In just his second season, Paul had won the batting title. Rookie Lloyd finished second in hits and third in batting average. The two combined for 460 hits during the season and were 11-for-30 in the World Series as the Yankees swept the Pirates in four games. The Waners played parts of 16 seasons together, much longer than any other pair.

In 1934 Dizzy and Paul Dean had the greatest year any pitching brothers have ever enjoyed. "Me 'n' Paul" together won 49 games during the regular season and all four of the games the Cardinals won from the Tigers in the World Series (as Dizzy had predicted). In 1935 their combined victory total was 47. These two 19-win seasons were Paul's only full years in the majors.

An even more memorable year in St. Louis Cardinals history was 1942. In the last week of August, the Cards were five games behind the defending champion Brooklyn Dodgers. Five weeks later the Cardinals clinched first place with a record September

rush. Winning five games in the last month for a total of 22 on the season was Mort Cooper. Catching him was younger brother Walker, in his first season as a regular. Mort won his September games with great flair. He was called the "fashion plate" for wearing the number on his back that equaled the victory he was seeking that day. The Cardinals beat the Yankees in a five-game World Series to shock all of baseball.

Mort also won 20 for the 1943 and 1944 pennant winners and had a victory in each of the World Series. Both brothers were named to *The Sporting News* All-Star team in 1944. Walker hit an even .300 for three Fall Classics.

The Coopers may have been the best of the 15 brother battery combinations, but Wes and Rick Ferrell have to be a close second. Rick caught his younger brother for five straight seasons. Wes won 20 their first two years together. Rick made it to the Hall of Fame but Wes has had his supporters too. Indeed, Wes and Rick Ferrell have something in common with Jesse and Lee Tannehill. In each case the pitching brother—Wes and Jesse—had a higher career batting average and more home runs than the brother who played every day.

The next great brother act in the World Series was in 1964, when Ken and Clete Boyer were the opposing third basemen. Elder brother Ken was the National League's Most Valuable Player with a league-leading 119 RBIs for St. Louis. Clete had hit an anemic .219 for the Yankees. Still, this was his chance to show the baseball world he was Ken's equal in the field.

Although neither hit for a high average in the seven games, both did well with the glove. Ken gave his team all its runs in Game 4 with a grand slam as St. Louis won the contest, 4-3. In the seventh game, Ken scored the first run and later homered. Brother Clete helped make the finish exciting as he hit one of the two solo home runs off Bob Gibson in the ninth inning. Like the Coopers, the Boyers were born and raised in the "Show Me" state. Both parents were in the stands maintaining their strict neutrality and feeling great pride.

The integrity of play when brothers square off against each other has been taken for granted for many years. This wasn't always the case. In 1933 Joe Sewell, playing third base for the Yankees, and Luke Sewell, catching for Washington, found themselves on opposite sides of a hot pennant race. They had been teammates at Cleveland for a number of years.

Reporting on a crucial game in the 1933 AL race, Shirley Povich of the *Washington Post* wrote:

> *It was brother versus brother in the seventh when Joe Sewell made a whale of a stop and throw to cut down Luke. It's things like that help prove the honesty of baseball.*

There have been five brother shortstop-second-base combinations in big league history: Granny and Garvin Hamner of the 1945 Phillies, Lou and Dino Chiozza of the 1935 Phillies, Milt and Frank Bolling of the 1958 Tigers, Eddie and Johnny O'Brien of the Pirates in the mid-1950s, and Cal and Bill Ripken of the Orioles from 1987 to 1992 and again in 1996. The O'Briens were one of seven sets of twins in the majors.

Certainly an infield comprised of only two families is something of note. The Cincinnati Reds had just that in a game at the end of the 1998 season. Newcomer Stephen Larkin was playing first. Bret Boone was stationed at the keystone. Barry Larkin was the shortstop and Aaron Boone held down the hot corner.

Josh Clarke with Louisville in the National League in 1898 and George "White Wings" Tebeau of Cleveland in 1894 and 1895 must have felt some sense of constraint in criticizing their managers. In both cases it was a brother: Fred Clarke and Patsy Tebeau. Both pilots were regular players those seasons as well. Ed Hengle, who never played in the majors, managed his brother Moxie in the Union Association for the entry that began the season in Chicago. By the end of the campaign, both Hengles were gone, and the club had moved to Pittsburgh.

No, Henry and Tommie Aaron were not the first "soul-brother" brother combination in major league baseball. The game's first black siblings were Fleet and Welday Walker, who both played for Toledo of the American Association in 1884. That circuit was then considered a major league.

Fathers and Sons

Shortly after breaking into the majors, Dale Berra was asked about similarities between himself and his famous father, Yogi. The younger Berra replied, "Our similarities are different."

Like the many malapropisms of Yogi Berra, this one by his son may appear foolish on the surface, but it contains quite a bit of underlying wisdom. In fact, it can serve as a metaphor for father-son combinations in major league baseball.

Of the 164 combinations, 58 feature both generations at the same position. There are 28 father-son pitcher combinations, six cases where both father and son caught, one where both played first, three where both played shortstop, and 20 where both father and son were outfielders. Very few fathers and sons at any position have career totals that are at all close. The only Hall of Fame father-son combination is a non-playing one, that of executives Larry and Lee MacPhail.

Another important generalization is the great increase in father-son combinations since World War II, especially in the last 40 years. The first son of a former big leaguer to break into the majors was Jack Doscher in 1903 as a pitcher for the Chicago Cubs—one of the three teams with whom his father, Herm, had toiled as a utility player years earlier. By 1945 the number of father-son combinations was 36. In 1965 the total was 66. Thus well over half of today's number has been added in the last four decades.

Is the son of a big league ballplayer more apt to develop into a major leaguer than the average boy? Some people think not. In the 1950s Hall of Famer George Sisler was asked this very question. The two-time .400 hitter shook his head over how two of his offspring had made the majors. He pointed out that baseball players are absentee fathers. They don't have much opportunity to teach their boys the fundamentals or to practice with them.

If not their fathers, perhaps other well-qualified professionals have instructed the second generation. A worthwhile study could be conducted to determine how many second-generation players who have broken in during the last two decades attended baseball camps as boys. If the number is significant, this could explain the big increase during this period.

Certainly the Sisler family deserves special attention. Father George broke into the majors just before World War I as a pitcher for the St. Louis Browns. After being switched to first base, he spent 15 years as one of the greatest performers ever at that position. Accordingly, it is only fitting that he should have one son, Dick, who was a good hitter and another son, Dave, who pitched in the majors briefly. Dick's home run on the last day of the 1950 season, which gave the Philadelphia Whiz Kids the pennant, has

given him an identity independent of his father. Also, these two men both managed in the majors for a short time. The Sislers and the Macks were the first families in which both father and son managed in the majors.

Baseball families fall into one of three categories: famous fathers only, famous sons only, and equals.

Let us consider the famous-son category first. Another way of describing these men would be to call them "fathers of ... " Two families stand out in this category. They are the Muellers and the Walkers.

Walter Mueller was a reserve outfielder for the Pirates for four seasons in the 1920s. His son, Don, hit .296 in 12 seasons as a National League outfielder. In 1954 Mueller and teammate Willie Mays battled all season for the batting title on the pennant-winning Giants. Mays finished first in hitting by three points, but Mueller led the league in hits with 212.

Dixie Walker was a pitcher for Washington from 1909 through 1912. His lifetime record was 24–30. Both his sons, Fred (or "Dixie") and Harry, won batting titles. These two are the only clear cases of a son of All-Star quality who had a father whose career in the majors was forgettable. Other families with "fathers of ... " are Coleman, Grimsley and Smalley.

In contrast, the list of "sons of ... " is a long one. There are eight playing baseball fathers in the Hall of Fame. Averill, Berra, Collins, Lindstrom, Mack, O'Rourke, and Walsh had offspring who fit this category. Four more families—Bagby, Camilli, Trosky, and Wood—had fathers of All-Star quality and sons who are footnotes to their careers. Hegan, Wills and Trout are families where the sons had respectable careers similar to those of the fathers, but the older generation was clearly superior.

We must consider first whether some of the "sons of ..." got to the majors, or second, stayed longer than they merited, because of the family name. Collins, Walsh, and Wood prove the former proposition, and Dale Berra and Marc Sullivan support the latter.

The younger Berra and Sullivan not only had the temerity to go into their father's business, but, like Bill and Cal Ripken, Jr. of Baltimore, and Moises Alou of Montreal, they had dad for their boss. The Ripkens (in 1988) and Dale Berra (in 1985) saw their fathers dismissed as managers early in the season. Moises Alou, on the other hand, voluntarily left his father Felipe's side in Montreal to sign with Florida as a free agent after the 1996 season. Cal Ripken, Sr. was not only the first father to manage two sons at once, but the first without major league playing experience to manage his sons.

Sullivan, whose father owned part of the Red Sox, traded his son to the Houston Astros before the 1988 season, where he could commiserate with the Berras on the difficulties of combining a baseball career with family obligations.

By far the most interesting category is that of the fathers and sons whose careers parallel each other.

The two Billy Sullivans caught for both the White Sox and the Tigers. Both played other positions as well as caught in one World Series. Sullivan Senior caught the older Ed Walsh; Junior caught the younger Ed Walsh—both at Chicago.

Jim and Mike Hegan were a father-son combination well known for defensive ability. Father Jim was a great handler of pitchers for Cleveland. Mike played first base and the outfield for several American League teams. Both appeared in two World Series. Mike broke into the majors just four seasons after his father's finale.

The father-son pitching combinations have few parallels. Both Thornton and Don Lee gave up home runs to Ted Williams. Only four families have had both father and son pitch in a World Series. Jim Bagby Sr. pitched for Cleveland in the 1920 Series and his son for the Red Sox in 1946. Mel Stottlemyre went 1-1 for the Yankees in the 1964 Series. Todd Stottlemyre pitched for Toronto in the 1992 and 1993 World Series. In the 1995 Fall Classic Pedro Borbon, Jr. came in for Atlanta in relief. Pedro Senior pitched for the Reds in four World Series. Jason Grimsley pitched two innings for the Yankees in 1999. His father, Ross, was 2-1 for the Reds in 1972.

Joe Schultz, Jr. received some unwanted publicity in Jim Bouton's book, *Ball Four,* for being Bouton's manager. Schultz and his father, Joe Senior, each spent almost a decade in the majors as reserve players. Senior was 46-for-170 as a pinch hitter. Junior went 43-for-160 in that same role.

It is only fitting that Buddy Bell spent a portion of his fine career with the Cincinnati Reds, the team on which his father Gus spent his best years. The two ended their careers with nearly identical batting averages and home-run totals.

Eleven father-son combinations have played in All-Star Games. Prior to 1990 only the Bell, Boone, Coleman, Law, and Hegan families could have made that boast. Then Barry Bonds, Ken Griffey Jr., both Alomar sons, Todd Hundley, and Moises Alou made their debuts in the Midsummer Classic. The Bells and Boones have similar statistics. Gus was 2-for-6, hitting a home run his first time up; Buddy was 1-for-7, hitting a triple in his first plate appearance. Ray Boone went 1-for-5 in All-Star Games with a homer; Bob was 2-for-5 in three games, and Bret made the Boones the first three-generation All-Stars, going 0-for-2 in his 2001 debut.

Both Griffeys have been Most Valuable Player in an All-Star Game: Senior in 1980 and Junior in 1992. Currently the Cincinnati center fielder is 10-for-23 as an All Star. His father was 5-for-7 in three games. Each has a home run to his credit. Barry Bonds is now 6-for-27 in All-Star competition. His father, Bobby, went 2-for-6 in three contests and was MVP in 1972.

Felipe Alou may have had some feelings of regret mixed with the great pride he felt when his son Moises drove in the winning run in the 1994 All-Star Game. Felipe appeared in two mid-summer classics, but had no at bats. In the 1996 game Mets catcher Todd Hundley went 0-for-1 to become the 10th combination. His father, Randy, went 0-for-1 in the 1969 game.

In Game 2 of the 1984 World Series, a two-run double by San Diego catcher Terry Kennedy was noted by the television announcers as something significant. This was the first time in the history of the World Series that both a father and son had an RBI. Terry's father, Bob, knocked in a run for Cleveland as an outfielder in the 1948 Series. There have been 10 families in which the father and son both played in a World Series. Six have been mentioned already; there is also Ernie and Don Johnson. The father was a substitute infielder for the Yankees in the 1923 Series. Don was the regular second baseman for the Cubs in the 1945 Series. Stan Javier appeared in the 1988 and 1989 World Series for Oakland; his father, Julian, played in four World Series. In 1962, Felipe Alou played all seven games for the Giants, hitting .269. Son Moises hit three homers for Florida in the 1997 Fall Classic. Atlanta's poor performance in the 1999 Series made it easy to overlook Bret Boone going 7-for-13 as the second baseman for the Braves. Bret's father, Bob, was 7-for-17 for Philadelphia in 1980, and grandfather

Ray was 0-for-1 for the Indians in 1948. And Bret's brother, Aaron, made his Fall Classic debut for the 2003 Yankees, going 3-for-21 with a homer, and adding to the accomplishments of the first three-generation act in the World Series.

Career statistics for the Bonds family deserve special attention. Barry Bonds has now surpassed father Bobby in every significant category. Perhaps Bobby will be remembered as "the father of..."

The Bondses are not the first African-American father-son combination in major league history. That honor goes to the Hairstons. Father Sam played in two games for the Chicago White Sox in 1951. Son Jerry was a respected pinch hitter for that team for over a decade. Grandson Jerry made his major league debut with the Baltimore Orioles in 1998.

In September 1990 Ken Griffey, Sr. took a place in the Seattle Mariners outfield next to his son. In 2001 the Tim Raineses duplicated the feat, as Senior and Junior took the field together for Baltimore. Late in the 1992 season, Bret Boone made his major league debut as the Seattle second baseman to give baseball its first three-generation family. In 1995 David Bell, son of Buddy and grandson of Gus, made his debut to give baseball its second. The Hairston family makes three. Of less significance, but of great sentimental value for Cincinnati Reds fans, was an event that occurred in September 1997. Pete Rose, Jr. played third base for a few games. More than once he threw out hitters at first base to Eduardo Perez. Pete Senior had done that many times with Tony Perez in the city's glory days in the 1970.

RELATIVES IN MAJOR LEAGUE BASEBALL

KEY
(tm) teammates
(F-S) also part of father-son combo

BROTHERS

AARON, Henry & Tommie (tm)
ACOSTA, Jose & Merito
ADAMS, Bobby & Dick (F-S)
ALLEN, Dick, Hank & Ron (tm)
ALLISON, Art & Doug (tm)
ALOMAR, Roberto & Sandy, Jr. (tm) (F-S)
ALOU, Felipe, Matty & Jesus (tm) (F-S)
ANDERSON, Kent & Mike
ANDREWS, Rob & Mike
ARMAS, Tony & Marcos (F-S)
ASPROMONTE, Bob & Ken
BAILEY, Ed & Jim (tm)
BAKER, Dave & Doug
BANDO, Chris & Sal
BANNON, Jimmy & Tom
BARNES, Jesse & Virgil (tm)
BARRETT, Marty & Tom
BAXES, Jim & Mike
BELL, Charlie & Frank
BELL, George & Juan
BELL, David & Mike (F-S)
BENES, Alan & Andy (tm)
BENNETT, Dave & Dennis (tm)
BERGEN, Bill & Marty
BIGBEE, Carson & Lyle (tm)
BLANKENSHIP, Homer & Ted (tm)
BLUEGE, Ossie & Otto
BOLLING, Frank & Milt (tm)
BOONE, Danny & Ike
BOONE, Aaron & Bret (tm) (F-S)
BOYER, Clete, Ken & Cloyd (tm)
BOYLE, Buzz & Jim
BOYLE, Eddie & Jack
BRASHEAR, Kitty & Roy
BREEDEN, Danny & Hal
BRETT, George & Ken (tm)
BREWER, Mike & Tony
BRINKMAN, Chuck & Ed
BROWN, Dick & Larry
BROWN, Jackie & Paul
BROWN, Oscar & Ollie
BROWN, Curtis & Leon
BULLINGER, Kirk & Jim
BUTLER, Rich & Bob
CAMNITZ, Harry & Howie (tm)
CAMP, Kid & Llewellan (tm)
CAMPBELL, Hugh & Mat (tm)
CANSECO, Jose & Ozzie (twins) (tm)
CANTWELL, Mike & Tom
CABRERA, Jolbert & Orlando
CARLYLE, Cleo & Roy
CASEY, Dan & Dennis (tm)
CEDENO, Andujar & Domingo
CHIOZZA, Dino & Lou (tm)
CHRISTOPHER, Lloyd & Russ
CLAPP, Aaron & John

CLARK, Jerald & Phil
CLARKE, Fred & Josh (tm)
CLARKE, Sumpter & Rufe
CLARKSON, Dad, John & Walter (tm)
CLIBURN, Stan & Stew (twins)
COFFMAN, Dick & Slick
COHEN, Andy & Syd
CONIGLIARO, Billy & Tony
CONNELL, Gene & Joe
CONNOR, Joe & Roger
CONWAY, Jim & Pete
CONWAY, Bill & Dick (tm)
COOLBAUGH, Mike & Scott
COONEY, Jimmy & Johnny (tm) (F-S)
COOPER, Mort & Walker (tm)
CORA, Joey & Jose
CORCORAN, Larry & Mike (tm)
COSCARART, Joe & Pete
COVELESKI, Harry & Stan
COVINGTON, Sam & Tex
CROMER, D.T. & Tripp
CROSS, Amos, Frank & Lave (tm)
CRUZ, Hector, Jose & Tommy (tm) (F-S)
CUCCINELLO, Al & Tony
DAILY, Con & Ed
DALY, Joe & Tom
DANNING, Harry & Ike
DARINGER, Cliff & Rolla
DARWIN, Jeff & Danny
DAVALILLO, Vic & Yo-Yo
DAVENPORT, Claude & Dave
DAVIS, Mark & Mike
DEAN, Dizzy & Paul (tm)
DEASLEY, John & Pat
DELAHANTY, Ed, Frank, Jim, Joe & Tom (tm)
DEMONTREVILLE, Gene & Lee
DICKEY, Bill & George
DILLON, Packy & John (tm)
DiMAGGIO, Vince, Joe & Dom
DONAHUE, Jiggs & Pat
DONNELLY, Pete & John
DONOVAN, Jerry & Tom
DORGAN, Jerry & Mike
DOWNS, Kelly & Dave
DOYLE, Brian & Denny
DRAKE, Sammy & Solly
DREW, Tim & J.D.
DUGAN, Bill & Ed (tm)
EDWARDS, Dave, Marshall & Mike, (twins)
ENS, Jewel & Mutz
ERAUTT, Eddie & Joe
EVERS, Joe & Johnny
EWING, Buck & John (tm)
FALK, Bibb & Chet
FARMER, Michael & Howard
FERRELL, Rick & Wes (tm)
FERRY, Cy & Jack
FINNEY, Hal & Lou
FISHER, Bob & Newt
FISHER, Chauncey & Tom
FOGARTY, Jim & Joe

FORD, Gene & Russ
FOREMAN, Brownie & Frank (tm)
FORSCH, Bob & Ken
FOUTZ, Dave & Frank
FOWLER, Art & Jesse
FREESE, Gene & George (tm)
FRIEL, Bill & Pat
FULLER, Harry & Shorty
FULMER, Chick & Washington
GAGLIANO, Phil & Ralph
GANZEL, Charlie & John (F-S)
GARBARK, Bob & Mike
GARDELLA, Al & Danny (tm)
GARRETT, Adrian & Wayne
GASTON, Alex & Milt (tm)
GEISS, Bill & Emil
GENTRY, Harvey & Rufe
GIAMBI, Jason & Jeremy (tm)
GILBERT, Harry & John (tm)
GILBERT, Charlie & Tookie (F-S)
GILES, Brian & Marcus
GLAVINE, Mike & Tom (tm)
GLEASON, Bill & Jack (tm)
GLEASON, Harry & Kid
GRABOWSKI, Al & Reggie
GRAVES, Joe & Sid
GREGG, Dave & Vean
GRIMES, Ray & Roy (twins) (F-S)
GRISSOM, Lee & Marv
GROH, Heine & Lew
GUERRERO, Vladimir & Wilton (tm)
GUMBERT, Ad & Billy
GWYNN, Chris & Tony (tm)
HACKETT, Mert & Walter (tm)
HAFEY, Bud & Tom
HAIRSTON, Jerry & John (F-S)
HAMNER, Garvin & Granny (tm)
HAMMOND, Chris & Steve
HANDLEY, Gene & Lee
HARGRAVE, Bubbles & Pinky
HATFIELD, Gil & John
HAYWORTH, Ray & Red
HEMPHILL, Charlie & Frank
HERNANDEZ, Livan & Orlando
HEVING, Joe & Johnnie
HIGH, Andy, Charlie & Hugh
HILL, Hugh & Still, Bill
HINCHMAN, Bill & Harry (tm)
HITCHCOCK, Billy & Jim
HOFFMAN, Glenn & Trevor
HOGAN, George & Happy
HOLBERT, Aaron & Ray
HOLMAN, Brian & Brad
HOVLIK, Hick & Joe
HOWARD, Del & Ivon
HUGHES, Jim & Mickey
HUGHES, Ed & Tom
HUNTER, Bill & George (twins)
IGNASIAK, Gary & Mike
IORG, Dane & Garth
IRWIN, Arthur & John
JEFFCOAT, George & Hal
JIMENEZ, Elvio & Manny

JOHNSON, Bob & Roy
JOHNSON, Chet & Earl
JOHNSTON, Doc & Jimmy
JONES, Darryl & Lynn
JONES, Gary & Steve
JONNARD, Bubber & Claude (twins)
JORGENS, Arndt & Orville
KAPPEL, Heinie & Joe
KELL, George & Skeeter
KELLER, Charlie & Hal
KELLNER, Alex & Walt (tm)
KELLY, George & Ren
KENNEDY, Jim & Junior
KEOUGH, Marty & Joe (F-S)
KIEFER, Steve & Mark
KILLEFER, Bill & Red
KILROY, Matt & Mike (tm)
KLAUS, Billy & Bobby
KLING, Bill & Johnny
KNODE, Mike & Ray
KNOTHE, Fritz & George
KOPF, Larry & Wally
KRSNICH, Mike & Rocky
LACHEMANN, Marcel & Rene
LANNING, Johnny & Tom
LANSFORD, Carney & Joe
LARKIN, Barry & Stephen (tm)
LARY, Al & Frank
LAWTON, Matt & Mareus
LEITER, Al & Mark
LELIVELT, Bill & Jack
LILLARD, Bill & Gene (tm)
LOBERT, Frank & Hans
LOOK, Bruce & Dean
LOWDERMILK, Grover & Lou (tm)
LUSH, Billy & Ernie
MACHA, Ken & Mike
MACK, Quinn & Shane
MADDUX, Greg & Mike
MAHLER, Mickey & Rick (tm)
MAISEL, Fritz & George
MANCUSO, Frank & Gus
MANGUAL, Angel & Pepe
MANSELL, John, Mike & Tom (tm)
MANUSH, Frank & Heinie
MANZANILLO, Josias & Ravelo
MARION, Marty & Red
MARTINEZ, Pedro & Ramon (tm)
MASKREY, Harry & Leech (tm)
MATHEWSON, Christy & Henry (tm)
MATTOX, Cloy & Jim
MAY, Carlos & Lee
MAYER, Erskine & Sam
McDANIEL, Lindy & Von (tm)
McFARLAN, Alex & Dan
McFARLAND, Lamont & Charles
McGEEHAN, Connie & Dan
McLAUGHLIN, Barney & Frank (tm)
MEUSEL, Bob & Irish
MILAN, Clyde & Horace (tm)
MILLER, Jake & Russ
MILLER, Bing & Ralph (tm)
MINOR, Damon & Ryan

MITCHELL, John & Charlie
MOFFETT, Joe & Sam
MOLINA, Bengie & Jose (tm)
MORIARTY, Bill & George
MORRISON, Johnny & Phil (tm)
MORRISSEY, John & Tom
MOTA, Andy & Jose (F-S)
MURRAY, Eddie & Rich
MYERS, Billy & Lynn
NETTLES, Graig & Jim
NEWKIRK, Floyd & Joel
NIEKRO, Joe & Phil (tm)
NIXON, Otis & Donell
NYMAN, Chris & Nyls
O'BRIEN, Eddie & Johnny (twins) (tm)
OGDEN, Curley & Jack
OLIVO, Chi Chi & Diomedes (F-S)
O'NEILL, Jack, Jim, Mike & Steve (tm)
ONSLOW, Eddie & Jack
O'ROURKE, Jim & John (F-S)
ORTIZ, Baby & Roberto (tm)
O'TOOLE, Denny & Jim
OWEN, Dave & Spike
PACIOREK, John, Tom & Jim
PARKER, Jay & Doc
PARROTT, Jiggs & Tom (tm)
PASCUAL, Camilo & Carlos
PATTERSON, Ham & Pat
PEITZ, Heinie & Joe (tm)
PENA, Ramon & Tony
PEPLOSKI, Henry & Pepper
PEREZ, Pascual, Melido & Carlos
PERRY, Chan & Herbert
PERRY, Gaylord & Jim (tm)
PFEFFER, Big, Jeff & Jeff
PIERSON, Dave & Dick
PIKE, Jay & Lip
PIPGRAS, Ed & George
POTTER, Dykes & Squire
RAJSICH, Dave & Gary
REACH, Al & Bob
RECCIUS, John & Phil (tm)
REUSCHEL, Paul & Rick (tm)
REYNOLDS, Harold & Don
RICKETTS, Dick & Dave
RIDDLE, Elmer & Johnny (tm)
RIPKEN, Cal & Billy (tm)
ROBINSON, Bruce & Dave
ROBINSON, Fred & Wilbert
ROENICKE, Gary & Ron
ROETTGER, Oscar & Wally
ROMO, Vicente & Enrique
ROOF, Gene & Phil
ROSENBERG, Harry & Lou
ROTH, Braggo & Frank
ROWE, Dave & Jack
ROY, Charlie & Luther
RUSSELL, Allan & Lefty
SADOWSKI, Bob, Eddie & Ted
SAUER, Ed & Hank
SAX, Dave & Steve (tm)
SAY, Jimmie & Lou (tm)
SCANLAN, Doc & Frank
SCHANG, Bobby & Wally
SCHAREIN, Art & George
SCHMIDT, Boss & Walter
SCHULTE, Herman & Leonard
SEWELL, Luke, Joe & Tommie (tm)
SHAFFER, Orator & Taylor (tm)
SHANNON, Joe & Red (twins) (tm)
SHANTZ, Billy & Bobby (tm)
SHERLOCK, Monk & Vince
SHERRY, Larry & Norm (tm)
SISLER, Dave & Dick (F-S)
SMITH, Charlie & Fred
SOWDERS, Bill, John & Len
STAFFORD, John & Jim
STANICEK, Steve & Pete
STANLEY, Buck & Joe
STOTTLEMYRE, Mel, Jr. & Todd (F-S)
STOVALL, George & Jessie
SURHOFF, B.J. & Rich
SUTHERLAND, Darrell & Gary
TANNEHILL, Jesse & Lee
TEBEAU, Patsy & White, Wings (tm)
THIELMAN, Henry & Jake

THOBE, John & Thomas
THOMAS, Bill & Roy (tm)
THOMPSON, Homer & Tommy (tm)
THRONEBERRY, Faye & Marv
TOBIN, Jim & Johnny
TORRE, Frank & Joe (tm)
TRAFFLEY, Bill & John
TREACEY, Fred & Pete (tm)
TREVINO, Alex & Bobby
TWOMBLY, Babe & George
TYLER, Fred & Lefty (tm)
TYRONE, Jim & Wayne
UNDERWOOD, Pat & Tom
UPTON, Bill & Tom
VALENTIN, Jose, Antonio & Jose, Javier
VAN, CUYK, Chris & Johnny
WADE, Ben & Jake
WAGNER, Butts & Honus
WALKER, Dixie, Sr. & Ernie (F-S)
WALKER, Dixie, Jr. & Harry (F-S)
WALKER, Gee & Hub (tm)
WALKER Fleet & Welday (tm)
WANER Lloyd & Paul (tm)
WATT, Al & Frank
WEILAND, Bob & Ed
WESTLAKE, Jim & Wally
WEYHING, Gus & John
WHEAT, Mack & Zack
WHITE, Deacon & Will (tm)
WHITNEY, Art & Frank
WILTSE, Hooks & Snake
WINGO, Al & Ivy
WOOD, Fred & Pete (tm)
WORRELL, Todd & Tim
WRIGHT, George, Harry & Sam (tm)
YOCHIM, Len & Ray
YOUNT, Larry & Robin

FATHERS & SONS

ADAMS, Bobby-Mike
ALOMAR, Sandy-Roberto & Sandy, Jr.
ALOU, Felipe-Moises
AMARO, Ruben-Ruben, Jr.
ARAGON, Angel-Jack
ARMAS, Tony-Antonio
AVERILL, Earl-Earl

BACSIK, Mike-Mike
BAGBY, Jim, Sr. & Jr.
BARNHART, Clyde-Vic
BEAMON, Charlie-Charlie
BELL, Buddy-David & Mike
BELL, Gus-Buddy
BERRA, Yogi-Dale
BERRY, Charlie-Charlie
BERRY, Joe-Joe
BONDS, Bobby-Barry
BOONE, Ray-Bob
BOONE, Bob-Bret & Aaron
BORBON, Pedro, Sr. & Jr.
BRICKELL, Fred-Fritzie
BRUCKER, Earle, Sr. & Jr.
BRUMLEY, Mike-Mike
BUFORD, Don-Damon
BURROUHS, Jeff-Sean

CAMILLI, Dolf-Doug
CAMPANIS, Alex-Jim
CARREON, Camilo-Mark
COLEMAN, Joe-Joe
COLLINS, Ed, Sr. & Jr.
CONNOLLY, Ed, Sr. & Jr.
COONEY, Jimmy-Jimmy & John
CORNEJO, Mardie-Nate
CORRIDEN, Red-John
CROUCH, Bill-Wilmer
CRUZ, Jose, Sr. & Jr.

DAVANON, Jerry-Jeffrey
DOSCHER, Herm-Jack

ELLSWORTH, Dick-Steve
ESCHEN, Jim-Larry
FLETCHER, Tom-Darrin

FRANCONA, Tito-Terry

GABRIELSON, Len-Len
GANZEL, Charlie-Babe
GILBERT, Larry-Charlie & Tookie
GRAHAM, Peaches-Jack
GREEN, Fred-Gary
GRIEVE, Tom-Ben
GRIFFEY, Ken, Sr. & Jr. (tm)
GRILLI, Steve-Jason
GRIMES, Ray-Oscar
GRIMSLEY, Ross-Ross

HAIRSTON, Sam-Jerry & John
HAIRSTON, Jerry, Sr. & Jr.
HANEY, Larry-Chris
HEGAN, Jim-Mike
HEINTZELMAN, Ken-Tom
HOOD, Wally, Sr. & Jr.
HOWARD, Bruce-David
HUNDLEY, Randy-Todd

JACQUEZ, Pat-Thomas
JAVIER, Julian-Stan
JETER, Johnny-Shawn
JOHNSON, Adam-Adam
JOHNSON, Ernie-Don

KENDALL, Fred-Jason
KENNEDY, Bob-Terry
KEOUGH, Marty-Matt
KESSINGER, Don-Keith
KRAUSSE, Lew, Sr. & Jr.
KUNKEL, Bill-Jeff

LANDRUM, Joe-Bill
LANIER, Max-Hal
LAW, Vern-Vance
LAXTON, Bill-Brett
LEE, Thornton-Don
LIEBHARDT, Glenn-Glenn
LINDSTROM, Fred-Charlie
LIVELY, Jack-Bud

MACK, Connie-Earle
MAGGERT, Harl-Harl
MALAY, Charlie-Joe
MARTIN, Barney-Jerry
MATHEWS, Nelson-T.J.
MATTHEWS, Gary, Sr. & Jr.
MATTICK, Wally-Bobby
MAY, Dave-Derrick
MAY, Pinky-Milt
McANDREW, Jim-Jamie
McKAY, Dave-Cody
McKNIGHT, Jim-Jeff
McRAE, Hal-Brian
MEINKE, Frank-Bob
MILLS, Willie-Art
MONTEAGUDO, Rene-Aurelio
MOORE, Eugene, Sr. & Jr.
MORTON, Guy, Sr. & Jr.
MOTA, Manny-Andy & Jose
MUELLER, Walter-Don

NARLESKI, Bill-Ray
NAVARRO, Julio-Jaime
NEN, Dick-Robert
NICHOLS, Chet, Sr. & Jr.
NIEKRO, Joe-Lance
NORTHEY, Ron-Scott

O'DONOGHUE, John, Sr. & Jr.
OKRIE, Frank-Len
OLIVARES, Ed-Omar
OLIVER, Bob-Darren
OLIVO, Diomedes-Gilberto, Rondon
O'ROURKE, Patsy-Joe
O'ROURKE, Jim-Queenie
OSBORNE, Tiny-Bobo

PARTENHEIMER, Steve-Stan
PEREZ, Tony-Eduardo
PILLETTE, Herman-Duane

QUEEN, Mel-Mel
RAINES, Tim, Sr. & Jr. (tm)

RATH, Fred, Sr. & Jr.
RIPLEY, Walt-Allen
ROSE, Pete, Sr. & Jr.

SAVIDGE, Ralph-Don
SCHOFIELD, Ducky-Dick
SCHULTZ, Joe, Sr. & Jr.
SEGUI, Diego-David
SHEELY, Earl-Bud
SIEBERT, Dick-Paul
SISLER, George-Dick & Dave
SKINNER, Bob-Joel
SMALLEY, Roy, Jr.-Roy, III
SPEIER, Chris-Justin
SPIEZIO, Ed-Scott
SPRAGUE, Ed, Sr. & Jr.
ST. CLAIRE, Ebba-Randy
STENHOUSE, Dave-Mike
STEPHENSON, Joe-Jerry
STILLWELL, Ron-Kurt
STOTTLEMYRE, Mel-Todd & Mel, Jr.
SULLIVAN, Billy, Sr.-Jr.
SULLIVAN, Haywood-Marc
SUSCE, George-George

TANNER, Chuck-Bruce
TARTABULL, Jose-Danny
TORREALBA, Pablo-Steve
TORRES, Ricardo-Gil
TRESH, Mike-Tom
TROSKY, Hal, Sr. & Jr.
TROUT, Paul-Steve

UNSER, Al-Del

VIRGIL, Ozzie, Sr. & Jr.

WAKEFIELD, Howard-Dick
WALKER, Dixie-Dixie & Harry
WALSH, Ed-Ed
WARD, Gary-Daryle
WATHAN, John-Dustin
WERTH, Dennis-Jayson
WHITE, JoJo-Mike
WILLS, Maury-Bump
WINE, Bobby-Robbie
WOOD, Joe-Joe
WRIGHT, Clyde-Jaret
YOUNG, Del-Del

GREAT-GRANDFATHER, AND GREAT-GRANDSON

Jim, Bluejacket & Bill, Wilkinson

GRANDFATHER AND GRANDSON

George, Rooks-Lou, Possehl
Shano, Collins-Bob, Gallagher
Bill, Brubaker-Dennis, Rasmussen
Marty & Ed, Herrmann
Ben & Jim, Spencer
Lennie & Matt, Merullo
Ray & Bret & Aaron, Boone
Bill & Roger, Salkeld
Bobby, Estalella-Robert, Estalella
Gus, David & Mike, Bell
Red & Brian, Barkley
Sam & Jerry, Hairston
Dick, Schofield & Jayson, Werth

GRANDFATHER, FATHER AND SON

BELL, Gus, Buddy, David & Mike
BOONE, Ray, Bob, Bret & Aaron
HAIRSTON, Sam, Jerry & Jerry

COLORED
BASEBALL'S
GREATEST
TREAT!

CLOWNS DIAMOND FUN SHOW!

VICTORY FIELD
— INDIANAPOLIS, IND. —

NEGRO
LEAGUE
GAME
8:30
P. M.

MON. AUG. 18

Buses Direct to Park — Music! Comedy! Fun!

BIRMINGHAM BLACK BARONS
vs

Pollock's ORIGINAL

CLOWNS

THE NEGRO AMERICAN LEAGUE EASTERN DIVISION CHAMP

Section **8**

Other Leagues

FAMOUS FIRSTS

1878: Bud Fowler becomes the first African-American in pro ball when he plays for the Lynn Live Oaks of the International Association.

1882: The Northwestern League becomes baseball's first minor league.

1946: Danny Gardella becomes the first player to quit the major leagues to play in the Mexican League.

1951: Emmett Ashford of the Southwestern International League becomes the first African-American pro umpire.

1974: The NCAA approves the use of aluminum bats for the first time.

Chapter 34

The Minor Leagues

By Bob Hoie

The International Association, founded in 1877, is frequently described as the first minor league. For two major reasons it shouldn't be so regarded. First, it was barely a league. Structurally it resembled the old National Association—there was virtually no central authority, no limitation on the number or location of member teams, no set schedule, and haphazard umpire selection. The league was so loosely assembled in fact that some member teams competed at the same time for the championships of other organizations like the New England Association and the League Alliance.

Second, the International Association was originally established as a rival to the National League and never officially recognized itself as being subordinate. It was generally acknowledged that several of its teams were as good as or better than some in the National League. Various off-the-field problems, administrative weaknesses, and a lack of solidarity and resolve on the part of the member clubs assured its subordinate status.

A strong case could be made for the 1879 Northwestern League as the first minor league—it had a preset schedule and had no pretensions of rivaling the National League, but the absence of league-appointed umpires led to frequent forfeits due to charges of biased "hometown" umpiring, and the league folded after only two months.

The Eastern Association was founded in 1881, but this was another loose alliance with no set schedule.

The first recognized minor league was another Northwestern League, this one organized on October 27, 1882. At that time they requested of the National League cooperation and reciprocity in protecting player contracts. This was necessary because independent clubs frequently lost their best players during the course of the season to the National League and later to the American Association clubs. In response to this request, the National League, American Association and Northwestern League signed a "Tripartite Agreement" in March 1883. This agreement bound the clubs to honor the contracts of players on reserve lists, assured mutual recognition of expulsions and suspensions, established territorial rights, and created an arbitration committee to settle disputes. Minimum salaries were established and pegged at a higher level in the National League and American Association than in the Northwestern League or "any other parties to the agreement," thus by implication assigning a "major" and "minor" status to the leagues.

The Interstate Association was established early in 1883 and was quickly accepted as an "alliance" league by the American Association, becoming a junior partner of the Tripartite Agreement. Both the Northwestern and the Interstate opened their seasons on May 1, 1883. Each had a formal league organization, a schedule that was preset before the season opening, and a complement of umpires appointed and paid for by the league. Both leagues recognized and accepted their status as subordinate to the two "majors." In 1884 the Interstate Association reorganized as the

Bernie Carbo
The minor league batting champ (.359) in 1969, Carbo was 1970 NL rookie of the year after batting .310 with 21 home runs for the Reds.

Eastern League and became a fourth member of what now became known as the National Agreement.

In October 1885 a new National Agreement was adopted which made the National League and American Association the principal parties and removed from minor league clubs the protection of the reserve clause. Two years later the reserve clause was reinstated for the minors, but the major-minor league distinction had been formalized. Following the collapse of the American Association in 1892, another National Agreement for the first time

established minor league classifications and gave major league clubs the right to draft minor league players at fixed prices.

While these events were taking place, Organized Baseball expanded dramatically, going from two minor leagues in 1883 to 17 by 1888. Baseball was played throughout the country, of course, but Organized Baseball was confined to the northeast quadrant of the United States in 1884; it expanded to the South in 1885, to Colorado and the upper Midwest in 1886, California in 1887, Texas in 1888, and the Pacific Northwest in 1890. So in the year that the American frontier was officially declared closed, Organized Baseball had extended to all corners of the country.

In 1887 an organization called the Negro Baseball League, fearing player raids by the still moderately integrated minors, sought and received protection under the National Agreement. The league was to play in eight cities that also had major league teams, but it folded in less than two weeks. This was unfortunately characteristic of the era. Many teams and leagues were underfinanced and were ultrasensitive to changes in the national or local economy. In addition, being unable or unwilling to pay the required fees for reserving their players, they lost their better ones at the close of the season—and those teams that even managed to finish the season could usually consider themselves lucky. During the 19th century, more than 40 percent of the leagues that started a season failed to finish it. There was, however, a solid core of support for minor league baseball. Regardless of how many leagues started each season—usually about 15 but often as many as 20—only 8 to 10 usually finished; the rest failed. The 1890s were not a period of expansion nor of stability as throughout the decade nearly half of the leagues that started a season failed to finish it. A depression in 1893 and the Spanish-American War in 1898 were significant factors, but a proliferation of "fly-by-night" operators played a role as well.

At the close of the 1900 season, the still minor American League withdrew from the National Agreement, announcing through that action its intention not to allow its players to be drafted and not to respect the reserve clause or territorial rights any longer.

In September 1901 the National League announced its intention to abrogate the National Agreement, contending that with the American League invading its cities and raiding its players the National League could not be expected to sit back and abide by restrictions which did not hinder its rival. Essentially this meant that the National, like the American, considered the players on minor league rosters "fair game."

In immediate reaction to this, the presidents of seven minor leagues met in Chicago on September 5, 1901, and in an act of self-protection they organized the National Association of Professional Baseball Leagues. On October 25 representatives of nine minor leagues met in New York and adopted a new "National Agreement." This new agreement established league classifications, roster and salary limits, and a draft system; it recognized reserve lists and created a Board of Arbitration which was given the power to suspend players, clubs or officials for violations of the agreement. By the beginning of the 1902 season, the National Association included 15 member leagues.

The American and National Leagues ratified a peace agreement early in 1903, and in late August the presidents of the two major leagues and the National Association drafted a National Agreement which was initially rejected by the minors. After some concessions were made by the majors, such as a prohibition on "farming," the plan was adopted in September. The agreement formalized relations between the majors and minors and established a National Commission to serve as a Board of Arbitration.

These agreements were necessary because the majors and minors were mutually dependent on each other. The majors needed the minors as a reliable source of talent, while the minors, many of whom relied on player sales to stay in business, needed assurances from the majors that they would recognize their property rights in players.

Despite this mutual dependence there was a basic buyer-seller conflict. The majors wanted to acquire players as cheaply as possible, while the minors wanted to sell them for as much as possible. This same conflict existed within the minors as well, with the highest-classification clubs wanting to buy cheaply from the lower minors and sell at high prices to the majors. Thus the National Agreement, the major minor agreement, and the National Association itself were uneasy alliances of clubs and leagues with competing and often conflicting objectives. Nearly annual revisions in draft rules and prices and limits on optional player assignments were required to maintain the equilibrium necessary to keep the alliance intact.

The majors favored an unlimited draft—i.e., any player on a minor league roster could be purchased for a fixed rate. As early as 1896, when Minneapolis of the Western League was decimated through what were in effect forced sales, it became clear that some limitations were necessary, so by 1905 only one player could be drafted from a club per year. The draft prices of top-classification minor leaguers went from $750 to $1,000 in 1905 and then to $2,500 in 1911. While these prices were not particularly low for average prospects in that era, they were well below the value of the best prospects in the minors; thus the draft or the threat of it served as an incentive for minor league clubs at all levels to sell their better players to major or higher-classification minor league clubs at competitive market prices. From the players' standpoint, the draft had the positive effect of allowing them eventually to advance to whatever levels their ability would take them. The lower-classification minor league clubs received lower draft prices for their players but seemed relatively satisfied with the system—after all, this was an era when the contracts of Tris Speaker, Rogers Hornsby and Ty Cobb were sold to major league clubs for $400, $500, and $700, respectively.

On the other hand, many of the higher-classification minor league clubs had never really been satisfied with the draft. As early as 1908, this dissatisfaction nearly caused the two top minor leagues at that time—the American Association and the Eastern League—to go independent. Several of the top minor league clubs drew more fans annually than some major league clubs and represented substantial investments. As a result these owners were understandably not happy with a system that forced the sale of their top players to the majors for below-market prices; in addition to the challenge to club stability and autonomy caused by the draft, the gap between the market value of the top prospects and the draft price widened throughout the 1910s.

Despite the rumblings of discontent, the establishment of the National Association ushered in a period of minor league expansion to a fairly stable core of 30 leagues. While there were still leagues that failed to finish the season, the failure rate was down to 10 to 15 percent. For some reason, in 1910 the minors reached a level never to be topped until the post-World War II boom era— 52 leagues started the season and 44 finished it. For the next five years more leagues folded, but each season generally closed with 40 leagues operating. Then, for reasons that ranged from the automo-

bile, movies, the war in Europe, and the Federal League War, the bottom started to drop out. Forty-three leagues started in the 1914 season, and by the end of the 1918 season only one was operating (ten leagues had started that year—one folded and eight suspended operations due to the war).

After the 1918 season, with most of the lower minors driven out of business, the National Association, for the first time dominated by the higher minors, adopted a resolution demanding that the majors relinquish the right of the draft and end the practice of "farming out" players. When the majors rejected these demands, the National Association withdrew from the National Agreement. Pending a new major agreement, the majors and minors reached general agreement on property rights in players and territorial rights, and the National Commission ruled that the major league draft would be suspended.

In addition, the minor leagues would not accept major league players on option, meaning that any players owned or controlled by major league clubs in excess of the active player roster limit would have to be sold or released to minor league clubs. A. R. Tierney, president of two minor leagues and a leader in the fight to end the draft, said, "This means that the minor leagues will be able to build fences for themselves instead of for the major leagues." He predicted expansion of the minors and higher sale prices for the players. He was correct on both counts. With no players on option, the majors needed to buy more players from the minors, some of whom they had been forced to sell but now had to buy back at higher prices, and without the draft the minor league clubs could virtually name their own price. The minors expanded, as the leagues that had been driven out of business during the war now reentered the fold.

A Minor Resurgence

The reappearance of the low minors again shifted the balance of power within the minors. The higher minors had never been happy with the one league, one-vote system in the National Association. Club owners were wary of having their investments affected by the vote of what they perceived as little more than "fly-by-night" operators, and on occasion they tried to change the arrangement. But just as the majors needed the minors, so the high minors needed the low minors. Thus the high minors always stopped short of enacting any measures that might drive their underlings out of the National Association.

As noted previously, many of the low minors needed the revenues they received from the draft to survive. Although the minor league draft still existed, it had ceased to be a dependable source of revenue as the combination of numerous pre-war minor league failures and returning military veterans yielded more than enough talent to fill the higher minors' rosters. In addition, many of the low minor clubs did not have the resources to scout for and sign enough players to remain competitive on the field and/or at the box office; thus they were dependent on receiving some players on option.

So while most of the higher minor leagues were prospering as never before under the new independence, by 1920 the low minors were ready to withdraw from the National Association if a new agreement with the majors restoring the draft was not adopted. In addition, some of the higher minor league clubs were upset that the "nofarming" rules were being circumvented by "gentleman's agreements." These agreements enabled the major league clubs to "sell" a player to a minor league club and "buy" him back at the end of

the season with little or no money actually changing hands.

On January 10, 1921, a new major-minor league agreement was signed. The new pact restored the major league draft with a top price of $5,000 but as a compromise gave individual minor leagues the right to be exempt from the draft; in addition major league clubs could option up to eight players for no more than two consecutive years, and a tax on player sales was instituted to help reduce the fake player transfers. Quickly the top three minors—the International League, Pacific Coast League and American Association—together with the Western and Three-I Leagues declared their exemption from the draft; this in turn prohibited them from drafting from the lower minors.

The prices the majors paid for top minor league players nearly doubled between 1919 and 1920, but they skyrocketed during the draft-exemption era. In 1921 the Giants paid $75,000 to San Francisco for Jimmy O'Connell; in 1922 the Giants paid $72,000 to Baltimore for Jack Bentley and the White Sox paid $100,000 to San Francisco for Willie Kamm. The majors clearly were not happy with this situation, and in 1922 they offered to raise the draft price to $7,500, but this failed to lure back the draft-exempt leagues. In early 1923 the majors, after considering but eventually rejecting the idea of a maximum purchase price of $25,000 for any minor league player and/or a boycott of draft-exempt leagues, declared that all players sent to the minors either by sale or option would be subject to the draft. The number of players who could be optioned was increased to 15. Western League clubs immediately began accepting players on option under these conditions.

The prices for ballplayers remained high in 1923. Baltimore of the International League was reportedly offered $100,000 by Brooklyn for Joe Boley and sold Max Bishop to the Philadelphia A's for $50,000. Salt Lake sold Paul Strand to the A's for a reported $70,000, Louisville sold Earle Combs to the Yankees for $50,000, Toronto sold Red Wingo to the Tigers for $50,000 and Rochester sold Maurice Archdeacon to the White Sox for $50,000, but these were isolated cases. Baltimore, aided by five years of draft exemption, had built a powerhouse, but many of the higher-classification minor league clubs had not been nearly as successful and found that they needed to receive players on option to fill holes and remain competitive. Therefore at the close of the 1923 season all exempt leagues but the International agreed to the modified draft which exempted only those players who had come up through the minors. In 1924, after Baltimore sold Lefty Grove to the A's for $100,000, the International League also fell into line.

The modified draft did nothing to reduce the prices paid for top minor league stars: Louisville sold Wayland Dean to the Giants for $72,000 in 1924, San Francisco sold Paul Waner and Hal Rhyne to Pittsburgh for $100,000 in 1925, and Baltimore continued selling star players to the majors for big prices—Tommy Thomas to the White Sox in 1925, Joe Boley to the A's in 1926, John Ogden to the Browns, and George Earnshaw to the A's in 1927. Also in 1927 Portland (of the PCL) sold Billy Cissel to the White Sox for a package of cash and players worth over $100,000 and Oakland sold Lyn Lary and Jimmy Reese to the Yankees for $100,000. With prices like these, clubs could afford to lose an occasional Lefty O'Doul or Hack Wilson in the modified draft.

The major-minor agreement expired at the end of the 1927 season, with the National Association members deadlocked on the issue of the draft. The majors and minors were also at an impasse, so the modified draft continued and many of the higher minor league clubs continued to prosper, both through player sales and

at the gate. The Pacific Coast League's Los Angeles franchise and ballpark were valued at $2 million, but in the lower minors all was not well through the 1920s. Leagues were operating that never should have been admitted to the National Association—for example, the West Arkansas, which operated in 1924, was comprised of six towns within a 750-square-mile area that had a combined population of 16,000 and played just a 60-game schedule.

In 1929 the rift between the high and low minors widened as the low minors, rebuffed in their efforts to nullify the modified draft agreement, now attempted to impose their own draft exemption—essentially exempting from the draft any player with fewer than two seasons of Organized Baseball.

Early in 1931 the majors and minors finally adopted a new National Agreement, including a provision which eliminated the modified draft and granted to major league clubs greater control of talent through revised option and draft rules. The higher minors had originally objected, but the majors told them to accept the universal draft or they would no longer have any relations with them. In other words, major league teams would not sell or option players to or buy players from the American Association, the International League or the Pacific Coast League. While such threats had been taken relatively lightly by the minors in the early days of the draft-exempt leagues, they were now taken seriously enough that in less than a month the three recalcitrant leagues capitulated to the majors' terms. In exchange for all this and largely to secure the support of the low minors, the majors agreed to sign only collegian amateurs, leaving all high-schoolers and sandlotters to the minors. Of course, by this time farm systems had developed to the point that most major league clubs could still sign non-collegian amateurs through their farm clubs.

Milwaukee had sold Fred Schulte to the Browns for a reported $100,000 in 1928, but this was the end of an era. There would be no more $100,000 minor leaguers; in fact there would be few if any minor leaguers sold for as much as $50,000 again. At the 1928 National Association Convention, president Mike Sexton wondered when the majors would own enough clubs to control the National Association. The farm system, an old idea now in the process of being perfected by Branch Rickey, had clearly begun to alter the way the minors operated, and despite the efforts of some—most notably Judge Landis—the trend couldn't be reversed.

The Great Depression caused a contraction of the minors in the early 1930s, but even though a near-record low of 14 leagues opened the 1933 season, none of them folded. The minors then entered an era of unprecedented growth and stability, reaching 44 leagues in 1940, with only two leagues failing to finish the season between 1933 and 1941. This can be attributed in part to the substantial involvement of the major leagues through outright ownership or regular infusions of money through working agreements, but there were obviously other factors at work. Judge Bramham, on becoming president of the National Association, instituted a number of reforms, many of which were aimed at getting rid of "fly-by-night" or "shoestring" operators. minor league baseball was better promoted—they had established a public relations department in 1934—and the advent of night baseball was of incalculable value in generating attendance, which reached 20 million in 1940. Interestingly, that year 54 percent of the minor league clubs were not affiliated with any major league clubs compared to just 37 percent that operated independently in 1936.

World War II caused the minors to drop to just 10 leagues in 1944, but in the first postwar year it was up to 43, increasing to an all-time high of 59 in 1949, and during that time no leagues folded. (In 1946 the Mexican National League, set up by Organized Baseball to compete with the outlaw Mexican League, is listed by the National Association as having folded during the season, but actually it only withdrew from the association and continued to operate independently.)

According to a general consensus, it was the coming of television that caused the minors to begin to disintegrate. Between 1949 and 1963 the number of minor leagues dropped from 59 to 18. Attendance decreased even more sharply, going from 40 million to less than 10 million over the same time period.

By 1963 the minors had become nothing more than a training ground for the majors—90 percent of the clubs were major league affiliates, and most of those that weren't affiliates were in the largely autonomous Mexican League. While television was commonly cited as the cause of the minors' contraction, some contended it was a natural response to overexpansion. Gerry Hirn, in an April 1954 *Baseball Digest* article, contended that while the number of minor leagues had dropped from 59 to 36, that was still too many and the minors would be stronger and more efficient if only 16 to 20 leagues operated. Interestingly, in 1954 three leagues failed to finish the season, the most failures in peacetime since 1932; they remain the last United States based minor leagues that failed to finish a season (the Inter-American League, which had a team in Miami but was largely based in the Caribbean, failed to finish the 1979 season—the only year it operated).

An Unexpected but Welcome Boom

For reasons that aren't entirely clear, minor league baseball exploded in popularity in the 1980s. Attendance, which had remained stuck at 10 to 11 million through the 1960s and most of the 1970s, took off in the late 1970s, topping 20 million in 1987 for the first time since 1953. Louisville, which had dropped out of Organized Ball after drawing just 116,000 in 1972, topped a million in 1983. Nashville, which dropped out in 1963 after drawing just 54,000 for the season, drew over half a million in 1980. Buffalo, which drew only 78,000 in 1969 and saw its franchise shifted to Winnipeg the following year, came back to set an all-time minor league attendance record with 1.1 million in 1988. The Louisville franchise, which didn't exist in 1981 (what became the Louisville franchise was at that time in Springfield, Illinois, drawing 120,000), sold for more than $4 million in 1987. In 1990 the far less successful Vancouver franchise sold to Japanese interests for $5.5 million. Minor league franchises that could be picked up in the early 1970s by anyone who would pay the outstanding debts were suddenly selling for several million dollars.

The high prices being paid for franchises may have precipitated the major-minor league crisis of 1990, reminiscent of the battles earlier in the century. The Professional Baseball Agreement that binds the majors and minors was set to expire at the end of 1990. The majors, who under that agreement provided substantial financial support for the minors, proposed a reduction in those subsidies. The majors believed that the now financially healthy minor league clubs should assume a greater share of operational expenses.

In addition, the majors wanted the Commissioner's office to have greater control over minor league affairs. The minors felt the majors were trying to usurp their autonomy and, to add injury to insult, charge them for the privilege. If there were no agreement, the majors threatened to place their entire farm systems in spring training complexes in Arizona and Florida. Some minor league

operators threatened to go independent and even form a third major league.

In the end, however, the majority of minor league clubs capitulated, believing that they could not afford to operate without players supplied by the major league clubs. The majors would still pick up most of the minor league operators' expenses, but the new agreement (a) eliminated the minors' share of big league TV revenue, (b) required that the minors pay a share of their ticket revenues to the majors, and (c) established minimum standards that must be met by minor league facilities by 1994 (subsequently extended to 1995).

It was generally believed that these changes, by reducing minor league clubs' profits, might stabilize or reduce the value of franchises. However in 1992 the Las Vegas franchise sold for a record $7 million and some unsuccessful Class A franchises were sold for well over $1 million each. And the fans kept coming. From 1992 to 1994 minor league attendance increased more than 6 million, going over 30 million in 1993 for the first time since 1950. In 1993 Buffalo went over a million in attendance for the sixth consecutive year, and the following year just missed a seventh million-fan season due to two rainouts. In 1998 minor league attendance went over the 35 million mark for the first time since 1949 and in 2003 it surpassed 39 million for only the second time in history.

The positive trend of the past 20 years is unprecedented, but the minors have been riding a roller-coaster of success and failure over the past century—the Newark franchise which sold for a reported $600,000 during the depths of the Depression didn't even exist 20 years later. Even today the picture is not all positive: Between 1987 and 2003 nearly 90 franchises were shifted, usually due to poor attendance. For the last decade these shifts have fueled large attendance increases as teams have moved from "dead" towns to virgin territories with spanking new state-of-the-art facilities. Nearly 90 percent of the 6 million attendance increase from 1992 to 1994 can be attributed to new ballparks (nearly all of them in new cities), expansion and other franchise shifts. Since 1994 the minor leagues' dependence on new cities and ballparks has become even more pronounced. From 1995 to 2003, while attendance in the U.S.-based minors increased each season, same-venue attendance decreased each season. For example, in 2003 attendance in the U.S.-based minor leagues increased 539,000. Four franchise shifts to cities with new ballparks—Calgary to Albuquerque; Shreveport to Frisco, Texas; Columbus, Georgia to Lake County, Ohio; and Macon to Rome, Georgia—resulted in a collective increase of 1,595,000. A new ballpark in Jacksonville contributed another 130,000 increase, and two other franchise shifts to towns without new ballparks added another 65,000, so the combined attendance of all the remaining clubs was down 1,251,000, the largest same-venue drop in attendance since 1980.

Although recent years have seen franchise shifts to what not long ago would have seemed unlikely destinations—Frisco and Round Rock, Texas, central New Jersey and suburban Cleveland, Ohio (South Atlantic League), and Brooklyn and Staten Island, New York (the short-season New York-Pennsylvania League)—all resulting in huge attendance increases, the supply of new cities with new ballparks seems to be diminishing and the big success stories of the 1980s have seen their attendance decline. In 2003 Buffalo drew 551,000, less than half their attendance in 1992. Louisville, once over a million, dropped to 311,000 in 1999, but demonstrating the value of a new ballpark, saw their attendance climb to 686,000 in 2000. But even new ballparks don't always guarantee long-term success—Ottawa, an expansion club in 1993, drew 664,000 to their new ballpark, but by 2003 their attendance had dropped to 176,000. So the current wave of success is somewhat deceptive and history tells us it won't last forever. However, regardless of fluctuations in popularity and economic viability, the minors have always been—and one may safely assume will continue to be—the primary training ground for major league players.

The Players

Great players have passed through the minors, their careers frequently going in opposite directions and occasionally teaming up or crossing in unlikely locations. In 1924 in Easton, Maryland, Jimmie Foxx broke into Organized Baseball as a catcher on a team run by player-manager Frank "Home Run" Baker in his last season as an active player. There were many others: Rube Waddell and Red Faber with Minneapolis in 1911, young Waite Hoyt and ancient Jesse Burkett with Hartford in 1916, Dazzy Vance and Roger Bresnahan with Toledo in 1917, Chief Bender and Lefty Grove with Baltimore in 1923, and more recently Enos Slaughter and Billy Williams with Houston in 1960.

Two former Negro Leaguers, their careers going in opposite directions, Ray Dandridge and Willie Mays, were teammates at Minneapolis in 1951 where another teammate was a seven-year minor league veteran, Hoyt Wilhelm. Wilhelm, a 28-year-old knuckleballer with a background that included three years in Class D ball and three more in the military service, at that time appeared to be a member of what in that era was a vast army of career minor leaguers, the best of whom held their own with the acknowledged major league greats passing through the minors, but who for a variety of reasons—some good, some not—would themselves spend the bulk of their careers in the minors.

For some of these players who were left behind, the designated-hitter rule came 50 years too late, because while they could hit both for average and power, they generally lacked speed or had defensive shortcomings. For others it is less clear what, if any, deficiencies kept them in the minors, but from these groups a few players emerged as true minor league greats whose impact on fans in minor league cities—Buzz Arlett in Oakland, Joe Hauser in Minneapolis, and Bunny Brief in Kansas City, to name a few—was as great as that of more renowned players in major league cities.

The greatest of the minor league players is generally acknowledged to be Buzz Arlett, who started his career as a right-handed spitball pitcher with the hometown Oakland Oaks in 1918 and went on to win 108 games, twice going over 25 wins in a season. The Detroit Tigers looked at him, but without the spitball, which he wouldn't be able to use in the majors, they did not consider him a prospect. After suffering arm trouble early in 1923, Buzz switched to the outfield. Although he had been nothing more than a fair-hitting pitcher, once Arlett became a regular he annually averaged nearly .360 with 30 homers and 140 RBIs through the rest of the 1920s in the minor leagues.

Early in his career as an outfielder a Cardinals scout labeled Arlett "good hit, no field," and it stuck. Finally in 1931 he was purchased by the Phillies. The 32-year-old switch-hitter batted .313 with 18 homers and 73 RBIs in a season when the National League introduced a "dead ball" in reaction to the hitting orgies of 1929 and 1930. However, at the end of the year Arlett was sent to Baltimore, where in 1932 he hit four home runs in a game twice within a five-week period and led the league with 54 homers for the season. All the same, he would never return to the majors. He spent another year

with Baltimore, when he again won the home-run title, a little over a month with Birmingham, and nearly three years with Minneapolis, where he had another home-run championship. After a few games with Syracuse in 1937, Arlett's remarkable career was over.

In addition to his 108 wins, he hit 432 homers, a minor league record that held up until Hector Espino topped it in 1977. Arlett walked a lot, didn't strike out much, ran pretty well early in his career, had a .341 lifetime batting average—.350 after he became an outfielder—and he remains the only player to finish in the top five in home runs and slugging percentage in his only season in the majors. In addition, modern statistical analysis, including range factor, suggests he was nowhere near the defensive liability he was portrayed as being. He was big (6-foot-4 , 230) and gave the appearance of being lackadaisical, which apparently irritated some of his managers, but the evidence is strong that Arlett, despite nearly two decades spent in the minors, was a major league-caliber player.

Ike Boone was another player whose hitting feats were not limited to the minors. Boone was a college teammate (at the University of Alabama) of Joe Sewell and Riggs Stephenson; his lifetime major league batting average was .321, and in his only two full seasons in the majors—1924 and 1925 with the Boston Red Sox—he hit .337 and .330. Yet due to alleged defensive deficiencies most of his career was spent in the minors.

In 1929 with the Missions of San Francisco, Boone probably had the finest season any player has had in the minors. On the all-time minor league list of single-season accomplishments, his 553 total bases that year are first, his 323 hits are second, his 195 runs scored are tied for third, and his 218 RBIs are fourth. On the all-time Pacific Coast League list, his .407 average is second, and his 55 home runs are tied for fourth.

Boone's greatness wasn't confined to a single season; in four of his first eight years in the minors he hit over .400 (he was on his way to perhaps his greatest season in 1930, batting .448 with 22 homers and 96 RBIs when he was sold to Brooklyn in late June). His .402 average with San Antonio in 1923 is the highest in 20th-century Texas League history; his .389 with New Orleans in 1921 is the fifth highest in the Southern Association; he also led the International League in batting twice. His .370 lifetime average is the minor league record for players with 10 or more seasons. He had an exceptional arm, but limited range in the outfield. Although he hit 77 home runs in a season and a half with the Missions, he was not generally regarded as a power hitter. He was, however, a great pure hitter; in 11 of his 14 seasons in the minors, he hit over .350, but while he hit very well in his two full seasons in the majors, it has been suggested he had a pronounced hitch in his swing—a weakness major league pitchers were able to exploit.

Smead Jolley was an atrocious outfielder. Stories of his defensive lapses are legion, and the statistical evidence suggests those stories are more than isolated anecdotes. Like Boone, Jolley had a powerful arm but no speed; like Arlett, he was big and awkward; and like both, he could hit—majors or minors. In the equivalent of three full major league seasons with the White Sox and Red Sox, he hit .305 and averaged 15 homers and 105 RBIs. He won six minor league batting championships—leading the Pacific Coast League in hitting three times (winning the Triple Crown with San Francisco in 1928) and the International League once. Twice he had over 300 hits in a season, and twice he drove in more than 180 runs. In the 13 minor league seasons in which he played over 100 games, he had this run: .370, .372, .346, .397, .404, .387, .360, .372, .373, .350, .309, .373, .345. Perhaps because he spent nearly

six years in the low minors, the first four as a pitcher, and had a somewhat nomadic career (he was with 13 minor league teams), he has not always been ranked in the top echelon of minor league greats, yet he may have been the finest hitter of them all.

minor league stars generally fit two stereotypes: one-dimensional players who could hit but could do nothing else well enough to stay in the majors—justly or not, Arlett, Boone and Jolley were consigned to this group. Then there are those who excelled in the minors but couldn't produce in the majors. Perhaps the classic example is Bunny Brief, who may have been the most dominant power hitter in the minor leagues. In major league trials with the Browns, White Sox and Pirates between 1912 and 1917, he was consistently unimpressive—in a combined 569 at bats, he hit .223 with 5 homers, 59 RBIs, and nearly 100 strikeouts. In the minors, however, it was a different story. Although he hit 40 or more homers only twice and never had more than 42, he had eight league home-run championships. Before going up to the majors, he led the Michigan State League twice; later he led the Pacific Coast League once and the American Association five times. He also led the Association in RBIs five times (four in succession), including a league-record 191 in 1921. He had a six-year stretch (1921 to 1926) with Kansas City and Milwaukee where he averaged 90 extra-base hits, 151 RBIs, and a .351 average per season. Brief also drew a lot of walks. Early in his career he had excellent speed, and although he played most of his career at first base, he was the best defensive outfielder of the big minor league sluggers, with good range and an excellent arm. Still, for reasons that remain unclear, Brief never played in a major league game after his 25th birthday.

Nick Cullop was another minor league great who never produced in the majors. He, like many of the great minor league sluggers, began his career as a pitcher. In trials with the Yankees, Senators, Indians, Dodgers, and Reds between 1926 and 1931 he totaled 490 at bats, hit 11 homers, drove in 67 runs, hit .249, and struck out 128 times. He was the first farm-system star, playing 1,450 games in the Cardinals chain from 1932 to 1944. In the minors, he hit 420 home runs and drove in 1,857 runs, 10 times exceeding 100 in a season.

Cullop had good speed early in his career and was a good enough outfielder to play center field into the late 1920s, but he slowed up considerably in the 1930s. While it is not clear why Brief never did well in the majors, Cullop struck out a lot even in the minors and didn't walk much—suggesting that he had holes which could be and were pitched to effectively in the majors.

Ox Eckhardt was a great football star at the University of Texas who after graduation signed with both Austin of the Texas Association and the Cleveland Indians. The resulting dispute delayed his real professional debut for three years until he was 26 years old. Ox quickly made up for lost time, hitting .376 with a league-leading 27 triples for Wichita and Amarillo in the Western League in 1928. That fall he played for the New York Giants of the NFL. His baseball contract had been acquired by the Detroit Tigers and although he was on their 40-man roster in 1929, 1930 and 1931 he never got into a game with the big club. In 1929 he was sent to Seattle, where he hit .354 and again led the league in triples. In 1930 he went to Beaumont, where he led the Texas League with a .379 average. In 1931 he was sold to the Missions, for whom he led the PCL with a .369 average. In the spring of 1932 he was with the Boston Braves—he played eight games at the start of the season as a pinch-hitter and was then sent back to the Missions, where over the next four seasons he hit .371, .414, .378, and .399, win-

ning the batting title three times. He went to the Dodgers in 1936, lasted 16, games batting just .182, and was sent to Indianapolis, where he hit .353 and .341 over the next two years. He hit .321 with Toledo and Beaumont in 1938, .361 with Memphis in 1939, and after hitting .293 with Dallas in 1940, he retired with a minor league career batting average of .367 and the highest career average in organized baseball—.365. (Ty Cobb's minor league record drops his overall average to .3630; Ike Boone's major league record drops his Organized Baseball average to .3629.) Eckhardt has the highest single-season and career batting average in the PCL, and 10 times he hit over .350.

Unlike many of the minor league stars, Eckhardt did not want for opportunities to play in the majors—counting a trial with the Indians in 1925, he had six shots, but they resulted in his playing in just 24 games. The reasons for his failure to make it in the majors are not obscure. Despite being an exceptional athlete with good speed early in his career, he was a poor fielder with a weak arm and no power. Reportedly managers tried to get him to pull the ball—an idea that should certainly have advanced his career in Detroit or Brooklyn—but it only served to foul up his swing, which he would rediscover after being returned to the minors.

A few minor league greats don't fit the stereotypes: Jigger Statz was the opposite of most—his strengths were speed and defense. Joe Hauser appeared to be on his way to a successful career in the majors, but he broke his leg, never regained his past form, and went to the minors, where he became the first (and, until Sammy Sosa in 1999, only) player to have two 60-home run seasons. Hector Espino spent virtually his entire career in Mexico, and while major league scouts believed he could hit in the majors, he apparently had no desire to leave his homeland.

Of the great minor league stars, Statz spent the most time in the majors—683 games—and the most time with one club: all of his 18 minor league seasons were with Los Angeles. His 3,473 games in Organized Baseball were a record until broken by Hank Aaron in 1976.

Statz was a great fielder; virtually all of his contemporaries considered him the best or one of the best they had seen. Playing very shallow, he reminded many of Tris Speaker. The statistics offer strong support for his claim to greatness. In four full seasons in the majors, he led the league in chances-per-game once and was second the other three years. Between 1922 and 1932 in the majors and minors he had a stretch of 10 seasons in which he played in at least 100 games and never finished lower than second in chances-per-game. He had excellent speed, but during most of his career with the Angels they were a hard-hitting club that did not feature the running game; that changed in the mid-1930s, and in the three seasons following his 36th birthday he stole 157 bases. His game was not just limited to speed and defense. A classic leadoff man of his era—a good contact hitter, small and fast—he hit .285 in the majors and .315 in the minors, collecting over 2,300 runs, 4,000 hits, 700 doubles, and 500 stolen bases in his Organized Baseball career.

On April 7, 1925, the day of Babe Ruth's "big bellyache," Joe Hauser, a 26-year-old first baseman beginning his fourth season with the Athletics, broke his leg in a non-contact play while fielding during a preseason game against the Phillies at Baker Bowl. He had a .304 average for his first three major league seasons and had hit 27 homers with 115 RBIs in 1924. The injury kept him out for the entire 1925 season. In 1926 he tried to come back but hit only .192. After an excellent season with Kansas City, he went back to the majors but didn't do much in stints with the Philadelphia A's and

Indians. Back in the minors, however, he was nothing short of remarkable. In 1930 with Baltimore he set a professional record with 63 homers; then he dropped to 31 in 1931 but still led the league. In 1932 he went to Minneapolis, where he led the American Association in homers with 49. In 1933 he broke his own home run record with 69, and he was off to a great start in 1934—33 homers, 88 RBIs in 82 games—when he broke his kneecap, knocking him out for the season. He continued to play until 1942 but never came close to achieving the success he had in the early 1930s.

Hauser did not hit for a high average, and it has been suggested that he took enormous advantage of short right-field fences in Baltimore and Minneapolis—no one would argue that point, since 50 of his 69 homers in 1933 came at home. Yet many greats played in Oriole and Nicollet Parks, and none came close to Hauser's two record-breaking seasons, which remain the two highest home-run seasons in the high minors.

Hector Espino holds the minor league career home-run record with 484, and all but three of those were hit in Mexico. At the end of the 1964 Mexican League season, the 25-year-old first baseman, who had led the league with 46 homers and a .371 batting average, was sold by Monterrey to the St. Louis Cardinals' Jacksonville farm club. He hit .300 with those three home runs in 100 at bats and was invited to spring training by the Cards for 1965, but he never reported and was eventually returned to Monterrey. In the late 1960s the California Angels coveted Espino, who had led the Mexican League in hitting from 1966 to 1968, but they were never able to consummate a deal. Espino was a legend in Mexico, but it has never been clear why he didn't try the majors—he gave conflicting answers. Possibly he enjoyed being a big fish in a small pond—it wasn't the money, since he never made more than $18,000 a year in Mexico. He was notorious for marching to his own drummer, occasionally leaving clubs for a midseason vacation, and perhaps he was unwilling to sacrifice that independence.

Espino could hit for power and average—he led the Mexican League in batting five times and home runs four times—and scouts said he could have done the same in the majors, but like many players he played too long. His power started a sharp decline after his 33rd birthday, and he was virtually helpless at the plate during his last two or three seasons. Nevertheless he ranks as perhaps the greatest minor league player who never played in the majors.

Great players do not have to be distributed evenly among all positions or across all eras, but the emphasis being on great hitters, the result is a number of outfielder-first baseman-designated hitter types, most of whom played in the high-scoring 1920s and 1930s.

Ray French was perhaps the best middle infielder in the minors. He spent 28 years in the minors, most of it in the Pacific Coast League. He played 2,740 games at shortstop and was a brilliant fielder. In the 14 seasons that he played more than 100 games at short, he led the league in chances-per-game seven times. He was not an outstanding hitter, but his fielding kept him around long enough for him to collect 3,289 hits—seventh on the all-time minor league list.

The two best 19th-century minor leaguers were first baseman Perry Werden and pitcher Willie Mains. Werden had good speed and power. He had several good years in the majors (twice leading the league in triples), won six minor league home-run titles, including two seasons when he went over 40, and his .341 lifetime average was exceptionally high for that era.

Mains was the first minor league pitcher to win 300 games, reaching that figure early in 1905. A seven-time 20-game winner,

he was also an excellent hitter in an era when pitchers were frequently expected to take a shift in the outfield. Most of his career was in the New York State League, but in an interesting example of the mobility of players even in the game's early years, in 1892 and 1893 Mains had back-to-back seasons in Portland, Oregon, and Portland, Maine.

A highly productive but not great player who deserves mention is Spencer Harris, a little left-handed-hitting outfielder who holds the minor league career records for runs, hits, doubles, total bases, and walks. He reached those levels primarily because he kept playing until he was 48 years old. He did lead the American Association in homers in 1928 while at Minneapolis, but he was aided enormously by the friendly right field fence at Nicollet Park. (He averaged 17 homers a year in 10 seasons with Minneapolis but only 6 per year in his 16 other minor league seasons.)

He was never thought of as the top player on his many minor league clubs—just as a good solid player of the type that formed the backbone of the minors for so many years.

The Pitchers

There have been few minor league pitching stars of the magnitude of the great hitters. Perhaps this is because pitching is a one-dimensional skill—no pitchers were kept in the minors because they couldn't hit or field. Many of the outstanding minor league pitchers stayed there because they didn't have great stuff. Neither Bill Thomas, who won 383 games, nor Hal Turpin, who won 271 ever got a shot at the majors, and they had the same statistical profile—they struck out few, walked even fewer, and allowed a lot of hits.

Two pitchers that didn't fit that profile, however, were Joe Martina and Dick Barrett. Martina was a power pitcher who spent most of his career with Beaumont and with his hometown New Orleans Pelicans. He held the minor league career strikeout record until ageless George Brunet broke it while toiling in the Mexican League in 1981. Martina was a workhorse, pitching over 250 innings in 13 different seasons while winning 20 games seven times. He got his first and only big league opportunity at age 35 with the world champion Washington Senators in 1924.

"Kewpie" Dick Barrett didn't really find himself until he joined Seattle of the PCL in 1935, 10 years into his professional career. A little left-hander with less than pinpoint control (he holds the minor league record for career bases on balls), he had good stuff and eight 20-win seasons.

Frank Shellenback is most frequently named as the greatest minor league pitcher. The Pacific Coast League career leader in wins with 295, Shellenback won nine games with the White Sox as a 19-year-old rookie spitballer in 1918. After a poor start the following season, he was sent to Minneapolis. In February 1920 the baseball rules committee outlawed the spitball and other trick pitches. Each major league team was allowed to designate two spitball pitchers who would be able to continue using the pitch in the majors. Unfortunately for Shellenback, he was on the Vernon roster by this time and at age 21 would be consigned forever to pitching in the minors if he couldn't get by without the spitball. Throughout much of his career, articles would be written that usually declared that Shellenback would be a major league star if he was eligible to play there. He did have a great six-year stretch with Hollywood (1928 to 1933) when he went 142-59. He was a very popular player with the Stars as well as Vernon and a fine hitter with good power, but a review of his record suggests he was never as good as everyone thought he was. He led the PCL in wins and

won-loss percentage twice each but never led in another category. He had only five 20-win seasons.

Because of the spitball ban, Shellenback was viewed as a tragic figure, but he wasn't alone. Spitballer Paul Wachtel won 203 games in the Texas League after the ban, including five 20-win seasons. Rube Robinson won 148 games in the Southern Association, including two league-leading 26-win seasons. Wheeler Fuller, who never pitched in the majors, won 156 in the Eastern League after the ban.

Perhaps the greatest minor league pitcher was Tony Freitas, a little lefty who spent all or part of 15 seasons with Sacramento. He had great control, could get the strikeout, and had nine 20-win seasons (plus two 19-win seasons). If he hadn't lost three years to the military, he probably would have won 400 games in the minors. Freitas had an impressive major league debut, going 12-5 in less than a full season with the 1932 Philadelphia A's, but that was the last success he would have in the majors.

Four other pitchers worthy of mention are Sam Gibson, George Boehler, Bill Bailey, and George Brunet.

Gibson was an underappreciated pitcher who spent most of his career in the PCL, including 12 years with San Francisco. He didn't make his Organized Baseball debut until he was 23 years old. After two promising seasons with Detroit, he never had much success in the majors, but he was extremely effective in the minors. He had six 20-win seasons (plus three 19-win seasons) and, pitching in a high-scoring era, he had eight seasons where his ERA was below 3.00.

Boehler was a hard-throwing workhorse who spent most of his career in the Western League. Twice he pitched over 400 innings, six times over 300. Unfortunately he was terribly inconsistent: with Tulsa from 1921 to 1923, when his season records were 4-20, 38-13 and 7-9. He was consistently ineffective in a number of major league trials.

Bailey had seven league-leading strikeout seasons in four different leagues (International, Texas, Southern, Western), but only three 20-win seasons. After a promising September debut with the Browns in 1907, he pitched over 200 games in the majors with five teams spread over 15 years with no success.

Brunet pitched in Organized Baseball for 33 years (1953 through 1985), and astonishingly he was a regular-rotation pitcher for all but the last year. When he was 48 years old, he had a 1.94 ERA pitching regularly in the Mexican League. He never won more than 17 games in a season, had only two 200-strikeout seasons (they were 21 years apart), but he had a credible major league career and holds the minor league career strikeout record.

The Teams

There have been a number of debates about the greatest minor league teams. The 1937 Newark Bears, the 1934 Los Angeles Angels, the 1920-1925 Ft. Worth Panthers, and the 1919-1925 Baltimore Orioles usually draw the most support. All were dominant teams with good players.

The Bears included Charlie Keller, Joe Gordon, George McQuinn, Atley Donald, and five other players who would go to the majors the following year. They won the International League pennant by 25-1/2 games with a 109-41 record. The Angels included Frank Demaree, Jigger Statz, Gene Lillard, and Fay Thomas, and they compiled an astounding 137-50 record. The Panthers (or Cats) won six straight pennants and five Dixie Series. They were led by the home run hitting of Big Boy Kraft and a fine pitching staff that included spitballer Paul Wachtel and Joe Pate.

It is doubtful that any of the three could have competed successfully in the majors. It is occasionally claimed that the 1937 Newark Bears were the Yankees' B team and could have finished second in the American League, or at least in the first division. But that ignores the talent that was in the majors. The Red Sox finished fifth in 1937 with a club that included Jimmie Foxx, Joe Cronin, Lefty Grove, Pinky Higgins, Doc Cramer, Ben Chapman, Jack Wilson, and Bobo Newsom, all of whom, it is safe to say, would have started for the Bears. The same is true of the Angels, whose pitching staff chose 1934 to have career years, and of the Cats, who played well as a team but had few players that were even considered minor league standouts.

The Orioles were a different story. Thanks to the draft exemption, Jack Dunn was able to assemble a powerhouse comprised of players ready and capable of playing in the majors. The 1922 team was probably the best minor league club ever assembled. It had Jack Bentley, Max Bishop, Fritz Maisel, and Joe Boley in the infield, and Otis Lawry, Merwyn Jacobson, and Jimmy Walsh in the outfield. The catcher was Lena Styles, and the pitchers were Lefty Grove, John Ogden, Tommy Thomas, Rube Parnham, and Harry Frank with Bentley occasionally seeing action on the mound. Grove, Ogden, and Thomas combined for 60 wins and six years later would win a combined 56 games in the majors. Parnham, a free spirit who pitched when he wanted, was around long enough to win 16 (the following year he won 33). Frank won 22, but his career would soon be cut short by illness. Bentley hit .350 and won 13 games; he went to the Giants in 1923 as a pitcher but hit .427. Bishop and Boley, who hit .261 and .343 respectively, went on to become the double-play combo with the 1929-1930 world champion Philadelphia A's. Styles was just 22 years old and hit .315, but that was his peak. Maisel (.306), Walsh (.327), Jacobson (.304), and Lawry (.333) had all played briefly and/or ineffectively in the majors but would all go on to have great careers in the International League. A 20-year-old rookie utility player on the team was Dick Porter, who hit .279 and would have seven excellent seasons with the Orioles before going on to have several good years with the Indians.

As good as the Orioles were and as good as some of their players became, it is doubtful that even they could have finished in the first division of the American or National Leagues in 1922. Yet the strongest evidence of the attraction of minor league baseball and the hold it has long held on fans who were exposed to it is that those great Oriole, Bear and Angel teams are far better known and more fondly remembered than hundreds of more talented second-division-and-higher major league clubs.

The Farm System

Farm teams are nearly as old as Organized Baseball. In 1884 the Boston Beaneaters of the National League owned a team called the Boston Reserves in the Massachusetts State Association. The Reserves, also called the Colts, were apparently intended to serve as a source of replacements for disabled members of the major league club. It has also been suggested that the farm team was a device to keep more players under contract and out of the hands of the Union Association that year. Whatever the origins of the idea, during the next decade a number of major league clubs operated such reserve teams, but they usually competed in local semipro leagues rather than in Organized Baseball and were viewed more as quick sources of replacements rather than as training grounds for players.

With John B. Day's joint ownership of the New York Gothams of the National League and the New York Metropolitans of the American Association as early as 1883 and with the proliferation of interlocking ownerships of major league clubs in the 1890s, it was only natural that some major and minor league clubs would come under joint ownership as well. The first instance of any significance, however, occurred when John T. Brush, owner of Cincinnati in the National League, entered the Indianapolis club in the newly formed Western League in 1894. While this was not the first case of joint major-minor league club ownership, Brush appears to have been the first to grasp the potential of such an arrangement. Indianapolis served as a place to develop talent that was not quite ready for the majors. The team gave Cincinnati an expanded roster as players were frequently shuffled to and from Indianapolis during the season. It also served as a source of profit because Indianapolis drew well at the gate, having become the dominant club in the Western League, with three pennants and two second-place finishes in five seasons (1895 to 1899). Indianapolis' success was aided in no small part by Brush's practice of drafting players from other Western League clubs and sending them to Indianapolis, thus simultaneously weakening the opposition and strengthening the Hoosiers. Efforts were made by the other Western League club owners to control "farming" or to modify the draft rules to stop Brush, but none were successful.

Perhaps copying Brush's strategy, in 1896 several National League clubs obtained minor league affiliates: Pittsburgh had Toronto, Boston had Wilkes-Barre, and Cleveland had Ft. Wayne. Philadelphia had a Philadelphia farm club in the Pennsylvania State League, and when that league folded, they shifted the junior club to the Atlantic Association. The New York Giants had the first farm "system," with the New York Mets in the Atlantic Association and Syracuse in the Eastern League.

When the National Agreement was adopted in 1903, it banned the "farming out" of players. Yet "farming" as defined in the agreement referred only to those efforts by major league clubs to exceed the limits on players who could be optioned through subterfuge—"fake transfers" such as loans or sell/buy-back arrangements with minor league clubs where title to a player was never surrendered.

The independent minor league operators saw farming as a curse for two reasons. First, it reduced their autonomy and potential revenue by placing more players under major league ownership, thus reducing the majors' need to buy or draft players from the minors. Second, clubs accepting players from the majors, either openly through options or secretly, might gain an unfair competitive advantage on the field. So while in 1905 the New York Giants' request to establish a working agreement with Bridgeport was validated by the National Commission, most of the legislation was focused on restricting farming, normally by limiting the number of players who could be optioned and the number of times each player could be optioned. For example, in 1904 a rule was adopted which required a player sent out on option to stay with the minor league club for the remainder of that season. In 1907 the rule was relaxed so that a major league club could option a player and recall him, but only once in a season. In 1911 a team could have no more than eight players out on option at one time.

Working agreements became quite common during this period. The major league club furnished the minor league club with its surplus players—youngsters in need of more experience or veterans past their prime who could still strengthen a minor league club—and/or cash. In return the major league club could obtain promising players from the minor league club. During this era the

formal working agreement between major and minor league clubs was usually of short duration—a year or two at most—suggesting that major league clubs targeted certain minor league clubs that had two or three players they might be interested in and established a working agreement in order to get first claim on those that developed satisfactorily. There were also informal working agreements, generally based on friendships between major and minor league club operators, and it was usually through such arrangements that the "fake transfers" banned by the National Agreement took place. In the early 1900s there was substantial traffic in players between the White Sox and Milwaukee of the American Association and between the Dodgers and Baltimore in the Eastern League. (Brewers manager Joe Cantillon was a long-time friend of Charles Comiskey, and Brooklyn manager Ned Hanlon was also a minority owner of the Orioles.)

In the early teens E.S. Barnard, vice president and general manager of the Cleveland Indians (and future American League president), developed the first true farm system. Portland (PCL) became a Cleveland affiliate in 1910. Cleveland owner Charles W. Somers acquired Toledo (American Association) in 1912 and New Orleans (Southern Association) in 1913. In 1913 Cleveland also affiliated with Waterbury (Eastern Association) and Ironton (Ohio State League). So beginning in 1913 Cleveland had two Double-A clubs, plus clubs in A, B, and D, with players moving among the various classifications. But the system quickly collapsed. Ironton folded during the 1914 season and Waterbury folded at the end of the season (and their manager Lee Fohl moved up to become Cleveland pitching coach and later manager). In 1915 Somers suffered serious financial reverses, and when bankers took over his finances in late 1915 they sold the Indians and the former Toledo club (which had relocated to Cleveland during the Federal League war), but allowed him to retain the New Orleans club. New Orleans soon fell out of the Indians orbit and Cleveland severed its affiliation with Portland at the end of the 1916 season. The short-lived farm system had produced five members of the 1920 world championship team—Stan Coveleski, Jim Bagby, Guy Morton, Joe Evans, and Ray Chapman—and although Barnard remained with Cleveland after Somers was forced to sell, there was no effort to re-establish the farm system. This suggests that rather than being a carefully considered innovation it may have been something that "just happened". But if Barnard didn't appreciate the potential of his system, Branch Rickey certainly did.

In 1921 the Cardinals, who had already acquired an interest in Ft. Smith of the Western Association and Houston of the Texas League, acquired a half interest in Syracuse of the International League. This was the beginning of Branch Rickey's farm system, but initially it attracted little attention as it didn't appear to represent anything particularly new. It was less extensive than Cleveland's had been just a few years earlier. major league clubs had been signing young talent directly off the sandlots and developing it in the minors. For example in 1910, before it had established its farm system, Cleveland signed Roger Peckinpaugh out of the Cleveland City League, gave him a brief trial, and then optioned him to New Haven and Portland in successive seasons before recalling him when he was deemed ready for the majors. This practice had developed to the point that Mike Sexton, president of the National Association, in 1921 spoke out against the fact that the majors and higher minors had preempted the low minors' traditional role of discovering and signing young talent.

As we have seen, major league clubs had occasionally owned minor league clubs, primarily to expand the number of players under their control, but these were generally higher-classification clubs, where talent was refined rather than developed. Initially Rickey's approach was much the same, but it didn't take long for the system to begin producing talent. The Cards, who had never finished higher than third in the 20th century, won the World Series in 1926 with a team that included future Hall of Famers Jim Bottomley and Chick Hafey as well as regulars Taylor Douthit, Tommy Thevenow, Les Bell, Ray Blades, Flint Rhem, and Art Reinhardt plus reserves Watty Holm, Jake Flowers, Specs Toporcer, Ernie Vick, and Bill Hallahan; virtually all of these players were by way of Syracuse and Houston, the top two clubs in what was still only a three-club farm system. Then, using money earned by the Cardinals in winning the World Series, Rickey began adding lower-classification clubs to his system—Danville in 1927, Dayton in 1928, Laurel and Scottsdale in 1929. This gave the Cardinals one Double-A, one A, two B, two C, and one D-classification club and finally enabled Rickey to sign young talent and, through a hierarchy of minor league clubs, to develop and retain continuous title to a large number of players—his theory being that out of quantity comes quality.

During the 1920s when the Cardinals were discovering, signing and developing players at little expense, the other major league clubs were essentially operating as they always had, signing some players out of the amateur ranks, optioning them out for seasoning, and buying top prospects from minor league clubs, even though the new draft rules were driving the prices of such players to unprecedented levels. For example, the Yankees team the Cardinals defeated in the 1926 World Series had just one home-grown player—Lou Gehrig, who was signed out of Columbia University in 1923 and optioned to Hartford until ready. Although this had been an inexpensive acquisition, the Yankees subsequently had purchased, for $50,000 each, Earle Combs from Louisville, Mark Koenig from St. Paul (with whom the Yankees had a working agreement) and Tony Lazzeri from Salt Lake. In 1925, the year the Pirates won the World Series, they acquired Paul Waner and Hal Rhyne from the San Francisco Seals for $100,000 and also signed Joe Cronin off the San Francisco sandlots for little more than train fare to his first assignment—Johnstown, Pennsylvania.

But the escalating prices of players and the success of the Cardinals finally encouraged other clubs to begin acquiring minor league clubs. Shortly after the Cardinals acquired the half interest in Syracuse in 1921, William Wrigley, owner of the Cubs, acquired Los Angeles of the Pacific Coast League, but he treated them virtually as separate investments. By 1927, however, major league acquisition of minor league clubs was causing concern in the minors. The first formal notice came late that year, when the American Association adopted a new constitution which effectively prohibited major league ownership of its clubs (excluding Columbus, which was already owned by Cincinnati). At the National Association meeting in December 1928, Mike Sexton wondered aloud when the majors would own enough clubs to control the National Association. Early in 1929 major league clubs owned or controlled 27 minor league clubs. At that point Commissioner Landis, who until then had been remarkably quiet on the issue of farm systems, opened fire. He began granting free agency to minor leaguers "covered up" by various major league organizations. Later in 1929, Landis denounced the farm system, and announced his intention of destroying it. In response, Sam Breadon, owner of the Cardinals, cited letters from seven minor leagues saying the farm system was beneficial to them.

Interestingly, in 1921 Landis had said, "The object of Organized Baseball is to facilitate the development of skill among ballplayers." No one could seriously argue that this wasn't the purpose of the farm system, but by 1929 Landis was accusing Rickey and Breadon of "raping the minors," robbing small-town America of its precious heritage of independent minor league baseball.

Landis tried to make good on his threat to destroy the farm system, but since it was not contrary to baseball law, he had to pick at the edges. Landis levied fines against teams having an interest in more than one team in a minor league or by granting free agency to players who were "covered up" through violations of the option rules or "secret agreements." Attracting much attention in this crusade was his granting of free agency to 74 St. Louis farmhands in 1938 and to 91 Detroit minor leaguers in 1940, but these shots were fired after the war was lost.

More important than the fireworks that erupted between Landis and Breadon at the 1929 major league meeting was Yankees owner Jacob Ruppert's declaration at the same meetings that no ballclub could afford the prices being paid for minor league players. Ruppert added that he was "going to be forced into owning minor league clubs, and so is every other major league owner in this room." At the time he spoke, the Yankees had already purchased the Chambersburg club of the Class D Blue Ridge League. In November 1931 Ruppert purchased Newark of the International League for a reported $600,000 and soon thereafter hired Baltimore general manager George Weiss to develop a farm system. Thus the farm system, a concept that had been created largely out of necessity by Branch Rickey because the Cardinals didn't have the financial resources to compete with other clubs for top minor league prospects, had in less than a decade been embraced by the wealthiest club in baseball as being the most efficient method of acquiring talent. There would still be an occasional Joe DiMaggio or Ted Williams, signed by a minor league club and sold to the majors, but the major league club that didn't establish a farm system did so at its own peril. Not coincidentally, the eight teams which were the slowest to get on the bandwagon and had the thinnest farm systems in the 1930s—the Phillies, Athletics, Senators, White Sox, Giants, Cubs, Braves, and Pirates—were, aside from the Browns, the eight least successful teams in the 1940s. (The Browns and Reds established extensive farm systems in the 1930s, and overall they were the two most improved clubs of the 1940s.)

While several clubs caught on to what St. Louis was doing, none could catch up to the Cardinals' head start. The Depression had created a large pool of young men with few career options, and Rickey signed players by the hundreds at tryout camps. Whereas during the 1920s the Cardinals system had only increased from three clubs to five, by 1936 it had expanded to 28 teams—remarkable considering that there were only 26 minor leagues that year (the Cardinals had two teams each in the Nebraska State, Georgia-Florida and Arkansas-Missouri Leagues). The Cardinal system finally topped out with 33 clubs in 1937—more than the two next-largest farm systems combined. Rickey's belief that out of quantity comes quality was proven on the field by the 1942 world champion Cardinals. Every player on the active roster, except for second-line pitchers Harry Gumbert and Whitey Moore, was a product of the St. Louis farm system, and Gumbert had been acquired in exchange for Cardinals farm graduate Bill McGee.

In addition, the sale of players developed by the Cardinals kept the coffers full—in 1940-1941 alone, Johnny Mize, Joe Medwick, and Mickey Owen were exchanged to other clubs for $240,000 and nine players.

Thus from the perspective of the majors the farm system was a success, and the minors seemed to be flourishing—going from 14 leagues in 1933 to 44 by 1940. Sam Breadon, responding to another barrage of attacks by Landis in the late 1930s, claimed that the farm system had brought stability and strength to the minors, but there were other factors at work—the proliferation of night games, better promotion, and an influx of good young talent resulted in a per-club increase in attendance of 40 percent from 1937 to 1940. During that same period the portion of minor league clubs affiliated with the majors actually dropped from 61 to 46 percent. Rickey's quantity/quality equation might have had practical merit during a depression, or again immediately following World War II when there was an influx of returning veterans. However, under normal circumstances huge farm systems were not cost-effective. While the minors were still expanding in the late 1930s, the Cardinals began pruning back their farm system of more than 30 teams. A decade later farm systems were contracting—in 1948 there were six farm systems of 20 or more teams; by 1951 there were none. The portion of minor league teams affiliated with major league teams dropped from 62 percent in 1946 to 47 percent in 1951 as major league farm systems collectively dropped from 280 to 172 clubs and outright major league ownership of minor league clubs dropped from 125 to 75.

In 1950 there were 232 minor league teams not affiliated with the majors. This was the highest number of independent teams in Organized Baseball in nearly 40 years. Nine of the 58 leagues had no teams with major league affiliations, and more than a dozen others had only one or two affiliates. These leagues operated virtually outside the player-development chain, existing much as a semipro team or league does—to provide entertainment and reflect civic pride. Their only source of revenue was through the turnstiles, and just as 40 years earlier automobiles and the movies helped drive out the marginal teams and leagues, now TV did the same. This can be clearly seen as the densely populated Northeast, the first region to be heavily penetrated by television, suffered the first wave of league failures.

Over the next few years attendance declined sharply, most of the independent clubs folded and farm systems continued to contract. In 1956 the majors established a "stabilization fund" of $500,000 to aid clubs and leagues in lower classifications, but the free-fall of leagues, clubs and attendance continued. In 1959 the majors discontinued the stabilization fund and established a fund of $1 million to finance a player-development and promotional program for the minors. In 1962 the majors and minors adopted the Player Development Plan that, by requiring each major league club to have five farm teams, would guarantee the operation of at least 100 minor league teams, which the majors felt was adequate for their player-development purposes. The plan also included the Player Development Contract, under the terms of which the parent club became responsible for all spring training costs and all or most of the salaries of players, managers and coaches.

After the AL and NL expansion in 1969, major league clubs were only required to support four farm clubs each, but their financial support of each was increased. By 1976 there were only 106 minor league teams with major league affiliations, the lowest peacetime total since 1935. American League expansion the following year created the need for additional minor league affiliates, and in subsequent years major league clubs expanded their farm systems—all of them back up to a minimum of five clubs by 1984. With the dramatic increase in minor league attendance and the resulting increase in the value of franchises in the 1980s, a new

Professional Baseball Agreement was ratified by the majors and minors in 1990. The new agreement required the minors to assume a greater share of operational expenses but the majors continued to pay the salaries and meal money of all uniformed personnel. And farm systems continued to grow—by 1994 each major league club had at least six farm clubs and the number of minor league teams with major league affiliations was up to 194, the highest total since 1950. With further major league expansion and mass signings of Latin American players necessitating rookie leagues in the Dominican Republic and Venezuela, the number of major league affiliates reached 229 in 2000.

In 1928 Mike Sexton had asked how long it would be before the majors owned enough minor league clubs to control the National Association. Other than during World War II, when the minors were severely constricted, major league clubs never have "owned" more than 28 percent of the minor league clubs. Yet possibly as early as 1934, probably by 1935, and certainly by 1936, the majors, through outright ownership, working agreements or other interlocking devices, "controlled" the National Association, and this situation was generally acknowledged throughout baseball by 1938. The majors ran the minors.

Until about 1960 there was still some room in the National Association for independent clubs and career minor leaguers. From 1961 to 1972 there were no U.S. based independent clubs (Quincy did not have a major league affiliation in 1964 but received player help from major league organizations); but from 1973 to 1992 there were three or four independent clubs per season; in 1976 and 1977 all the clubs in the Gulf States/Lone Star League were independent; and in the late 1970s the Northwest League had several independent clubs. Some of the independents were very good: Portland in the mid-1970s and Salt Lake in the late 1980s and early 1990s were both artistic and financial successes; Grays Harbor, Utica, and Helena won pennants but did not draw well at the gate. Most of the independents were very bad. In the late 1980s San Jose and Miami—initially using a number of former major leaguers, many with substance-abuse problems—were both artistic and financial disasters. In 1980 Rocky Mount had one of the worst records in the history of the game, 24-114. The one thing the independents had in common was an inability to develop talent for the majors—Tom Candiotti was one of the few successful products, Greg (the original Boomer) Wells played briefly in the majors and went on to become a star in Japan. After that it might be a tossup as to the most famous graduate—actor Kurt Russell or Atlanta pitching guru Leo Mazzone.

The minors existed almost exclusively to develop talent for the majors and the independent clubs no longer fit. While this dismayed many minor league fans and traditionalists, it should be remembered that the principal role of the minors within Organized Baseball has always been to develop talent for the majors, and to receive money in exchange. The farm system, which owed its success in no small part to the greed of some minor league operators, was merely a different device by which talent moved to the majors and money moved to the minors.

Independent Leagues

At the end of the 1992 season the Salt Lake City Trappers, in their eight seasons in the Pioneer League, had won four pennants. In 1987 they set an Organized Baseball record with 29 consecutive wins, and in the last three seasons had an average attendance of 5,700 per game—better than any club had done in the Pacific Coast League. Although they were only in a rookie league, the Trappers were arguably the most successful independent club in the minors since Baltimore and Ft. Worth in the 1920s, but they had played their last game. Shortly before the start of the 1993 season their ballpark was torn down to make way for a new stadium to house the PCL Portland Beavers, who would be moving to Salt Lake in 1994. Even before the Trappers lost their park they had lost their director of player personnel, Van Schley, and their field manager to the new independent Northern League.

In 1993 the Northern League became the first U.S. based independent league of any consequence in more than half a century. Its founder was Miles Wolff, then the publisher of *Baseball America*— a man with more than two decades of experience in the minor leagues and former owner of the Durham Bulls and several other clubs. After careful study Wolff had concluded that the upper Midwest might be a prime area for a new professional baseball league. He visited candidate cities where he generated enthusiasm and support from civic leaders for the new league, and during 1992 assembled a group of owners—most of whom had experience in minor league baseball, some with independent clubs within the context of Organized Baseball. Schley, who had owned—and supplied players for—independent clubs since 1977, was named director of baseball operations.

The Northern League began operations in 1993 with six clubs playing a 72-game schedule that began in mid-June and ended around Labor Day. Each team had a 22-man roster, of which six had to be rookies and no more than four could have more than four years playing experience. The league had a strict salary limit which would yield an average salary of about $1,000 a month; rookies would make $700 while some veterans might go as high as $2,000. The standard contract was for one year with a club option for an additional year, which enabled the clubs to sell their players to major league organizations rather than have the players simply walk away at the end of the season and make their own deals. The standard sale price was $3,000. The clubs followed the Portland/Salt Lake model of using generally unknown players who had been bypassed or jettisoned by major league organizations because they were not considered major league prospects and mixed in a few high-profile ex-major leaguers such as Pedro Guerrero and Leon Durham. In its first season the league generally drew well with St. Paul, operated by Mike Veeck, drawing near-capacity crowds every night. Rochester drew poorly and the following season the franchise was moved to Winnipeg where attendance quadrupled.

The success of the Northern League generated an explosion of independent leagues over the next few years. Most were failures. The Golden State lasted two weeks, the Atlantic Coast less than a month, the Great Central didn't finish its only season, and the Mid-American lasted a year. The Big South and North Atlantic opened with some promise but succumbed after two seasons when their best cities defected to other independent leagues. The Prairie and Heartland Leagues lasted three seasons each.

While all this was going on, the Northern League continued to thrive, expanding, shifting its weaker franchises to better markets, and in 1999 forming an alliance with the Northeast League, which had been operating for four years (in 2003 the alliance was dissolved and the Northern and Northeast Leagues went their separate ways). During the late 1990s the Northern League, or more specifically its flagship franchise in St. Paul, was the subject of numerous articles, several books and a cable-television series.

Other leagues survived. The Frontier League began operations

the same year as the Northern. It played mostly in small towns along the Ohio River, was virtually a rookie league with a lower salary scale than the Northern, and was beset with problems from the beginning—two teams folded early in the season, the league's founder was ousted in midseason, attendance was generally poor, and during the off-season there were suits and countersuits between the founder and the owners—but it survived. It has remained a league for players with limited professional experience, but it continued to upgrade its facilities, eventually moving to new parks in suburban Chicago, St. Louis, and Pittsburgh, as well as abandoned Organized Baseball cities like Evansville, Kenosha and Rockford, and in 2003 attendance went over the million mark for the first time in league history.

The Texas-Louisiana League—for much of its life a centrally owned and operated circuit—started in 1994, and the Western League in 1995. Both used slightly more experienced players than the Northern, and many of their managers had been major league players. Yet, while the Northern was a model of stability and growth, the Texas-Louisiana and Western Leagues had teams in 43 different cities. In 2002 the Texas-Louisiana loop changed its name to the Central League, brought in Miles Wolff as commissioner, upgraded its franchises, and continues to operate. On the other hand, the Western League folded after the 2002 season.

The Atlantic League, after two years of planning, made its debut in 1998. It has a much higher salary limit than the other independents and plays a longer season, which has helped to attract a number of former major leaguers, several of whom—Rickey Henderson, Jose Canseco, Carlos Baerga, Jose Lima, Tim Raines, and Ruben Sierra among the most prominent—have used the Atlantic as a stop-off en route to a return to the majors. The league operates in a number of new markets, most with brand-new ball-parks. After six years of operation the Atlantic League was drawing nearly as well as the Northern.

Just as the early success of the Northern League spawned a number of new leagues, most of which folded, the continuing success and stability of the remaining independent leagues again encouraged other leagues to start up at the turn of the new century. In 2001 the All American Association, based in the south, started operations, but it folded prior to the 2002 season. The new Southeastern League then picked up some of the pieces, but it has struggled during its two years of existence. In 2003 the Arizona-Mexico and Canadian Leagues began operations, the former lasting three weeks and the latter two months.

The independent clubs didn't fit into Organized Baseball because they weren't developing major league players. Despite the occasional Kerry Ligtenberg, Jeff Zimmerman, or Kevin Millar, they still are not effective in developing major leaguers. They have given career boosts to Jason Simontacchi and Shawn Wooten, showcased a number of retread major leaguers, and provided a haven to Cuban defectors such as Rey Ordonez, awaiting the draft, or top prospects J. D. Drew and Bobby Hill, who were unhappy with the draft. In 2003, 35 of the approximately 1,000 men who played in the majors had played in an independent league. While this sounds fairly impressive, when the 11 recycled major leaguers are excluded, it means that 50-plus independent clubs are producing about the same number of major leaguers as one typical high Class A minor league team.

But the purpose of independent leagues has never been to develop talent for the majors. When Miles Wolff started the Northern League in 1993, few expected that in ten years there would be five fairly stable independent leagues with nearly 50 clubs, drawing more than 6 million fans for the season with no let-up in sight. Miles Wolff's dream has been fulfilled.

MINOR LEAGUE ATTENDANCE (SINCE 1947)

Year	Number of Leagues	Number of Clubs	Regular Season Total Attendance	Year	Number of Leagues	Number of Clubs	Regular Season Total Attendance	Year	Number of Leagues	Number of Clubs	Regular Season Total Attendance
1947	52	388	37,815,753	1966	19	138	9,826,124	1985	17	168	18,380,000
1948	58	438	38,415,716	1967	19	141	9,940,660	1986	17	164	18,456,808
1949	59	448 (6)	39,782,717	1968	21	152	9,887,328	1987	18	176	20,215,564
1950	58 (1)	446 (14)	32,960,733	1969	21	155	9,993,615	1988	19	188	21,661,873
1951	50 (1)	371 (13)	26,135,174	1970	20	153	10,726,470	1989	19	197	23,103,593
1952	43	324 (5)	24,024,373	1971	20	155	11,134,084	1990	19	202	25,244,569
1953	38	292 (4)	21,109,565	1972	19	148	10,986,628	1991	19	207	26,590,096
1954	36 (3)	269 (22)	18,674,503	1973	18	147	10,828,828	1992	19	212	27,180,170
1955	33	243 (5)	18,203,889	1974	18	145	10,562,452	1993	19	214	30,022,761
1956	28	217 (5)	16,402,953	1975	18	137	11,021,848	1994	19	216	33,355,199
1957	28	200 (10)	14,875,346	1976	20	148 (1)	11,324,947	1995	19	216	33,126,934
1958	24	173	12,744,883	1977	19	150	13,004,297	1996	19	218	33,289,278
1959	21	150	11,622,581	1978	18	156	13,012,727	1997	21	236	34,721,716
1960	22	152	10,660,811	1979	18 (1)	155 (6)	15,304,724	1998	20	242	35,427,012
1961	22	147	9,766,505	1980	17	155 (14)	12,265,022	1999	19	241	35,179,471
1962	20	134	9,732,582	1981	17	152	16,178,790	2000	19	246	37,872,674
1963	18	130	9,749,381	1982	17	160	17,637,244	2001	19	242	38,808,339
1964	20	136	10,102,310	1983	17	162	18,599,190	2002	19	243	38,639,142
1965	19	136	10,029,518	1984	17	164	17,580,299	2003	19	242	39,069,707

INDEPENDENT LEAGUES ATTENDANCE (SINCE 1993)

Year	Number of Leagues	Number of Clubs	Regular Season Total Attendance	Year	Number of Leagues	Number of Clubs	Regular Season Total Attendance
1993	2	14 (2)	734,667				
1994	5	32	1,921,313	1999	5	45	4,871,797
1995	11 (3)	66 (14)	3,077,955	2000	5	50	5,595,073
1996	9	63 (1)	3,453,897	2001	6	53	5,995,363
1997	8	58	3,504,946	2002	6	58 (2)	6,399,523
1998	7	51 (2)	3,866,609	2003	8 (2)	66 (12)	6,376,658

( ) Did not finish season
Source: National Association of Professional Baseball Leagues

MINOR LEAGUES – STARTING AND FINISHING

Year	Leagues Started	Didn't Finish	Year	Leagues Started	Didn't Finish	Year	Leagues Started	Didn't Finish	Year	Leagues Started	Didn't Finish	Year	Leagues Started	Didn't Finish
1883	2	–	1908	39	8	1932	19	6	1958	24	–	1983	17	–
1884	7	3	1909	34	2	1933	14	–	1959	21	–	1984	17	–
1885	8	3	1910	52	8	1935	21	–	1960	22	–	1985	18	–
1886	11	3	1911	50	7	1936	26	–	1961	22	–	1986	17	–
1887	15	6	1912	45	6	1937	37	–	1962	20	–	1987	18	–
1888	17	9	1913	42	5	1938	37	–	1963	18	–	1988	19	–
1889	15	5	1914	43	7	1939	41	–	1964	20	–	1989	19	–
1890	18	9	1915	30	7	1940	44	1	1965	19	–	1990	19	–
1891	13	5	1916	25	3	1941	41	–	1966	19	–	1991	19	–
1892	14	10	1917	21	10	1942	31	5	1967	19	–	1992	19	–
1893	7	4	1918	10	9	1943	10	1	1968	21	–	1993	19	–
1894	8	2	1919	15	2	1944	10	–	1969	21	–	1994	19	–
1895	17	9	1920	22	1	1945	12	–	1970	20	–	1995	19	–
1896	15	8	1921	26	1	1946	43	1	1971	20	–	1996	19	–
1897	20	8	1922	30	2	1947	52	–	1972	19	–	1997	21	–
1898	20	11	1923	31	2	1948	58	–	1973	18	–	1998	20	–
1899	14	5	1924	29	3	1949	59	–	1974	18	–	1999	19	–
1900	15	6	1925	25	1	1950	58	1	1975	18	–	2000	19	–
1901	13	2	1926	29	4	1951	50	1	1976	20	–	2001	19	–
1902	16	2	1927	24	–	1952	43	–	1977	19	–	2002	19	–
1903	19	–	1928	30	3	1953	38	–	1978	18	–	2003	19	–
1904	23	3	1929	26	3	1954	36	3	1979	18	1			
1905	29	6	1930	23	2	1955	33	–	1980	17	–			
1906	33	5	1931	18	2	1956	28	–	1981	17	–			
1907	34	6	1934	20	1	1957	28	–	1982	17	–			

MINOR LEAGUE CLUBS/MAJOR LEAGUE AFFILIATIONS

Year	Clubs	Affiliated with Majors	Owned by Majors	Year	Clubs	Affiliated with Majors	Owned by Majors	Year	Clubs	Affiliated with Majors	Owned by Majors
1936	184	116	38	1959	150	132	30	1982	160	136	—
1937	251	154	39	1960	152	126	18	1983	162	139	—
1938	267	162	49	1961	147	129	21	1984	164	140	—
1939	292	152	48	1962	134	121	22	1985	168	140	—
1940	310	146	61	1963	130	114	22	1986	164	143	—
1941	304	147	62	1964	136	108	19	1987	176	149	—
1942	206	116	46	1965	136	110	28	1988	188	168	—
1943	66	42	23	1966	138	116	32	1989	197	179	—
1944	70	57	21	1967	141	118	36	1990	202	183	—
1945	85	68	33	1968	152	119	39	1991	207	184	—
1946	316	197	79	1969	155	128	46	1992	212	192	—
1947	388	247	103	1970	153	120	39	1993	214	193	—
1948	438	280	125	1971	155	127	45	1994	216	195	—
1949	448	243	116	1972	148	125	49	1995	216	193	—
1950	446	210	99	1973	147	117	38	1996	218	198	—
1951	371	172	75	1974	145	113	27	1997	236	214	—
1952	324	166	65	1975	137	109	26	1998	242	225	—
1953	292	152	50	1976	148	106	24	1999	241	224	—
1954	269	156	49	1977	150	113	23	2000	246	229	—
1955	243	155	40	1978	156	118	24	2001	242	226	—
1956	217	150	33	1979	155	119	—	2002	243	227	—
1957	200	153	32	1980	155	125	—	2003	242	226	—
1958	173	157	34	1981	152	133	—				

MAJOR LEAGUE FARM SYSTEMS — 1936-1969

	36	37	38	39	40	41	42	43	44	45	46	47	48	49	50	51	52	53	54	55	56	57	58	59	60	61	62	63	64	65	66	67	68	69
Boston, AL	9	10	7	8	6	7	6	3	5	4	12	13	15	11	8	8	6	6	6	6	5	7	7	6	6	6	6	5	5	5	6	6	6	6
Chicago, AL	5	4	10	8	6	5	5	0	0	0	17	12	15	9	8	8	6	8	6	6	5	6	6	6	6	6	6	5	5	5	5	5	5	5
Cleveland, AL	5	7	13	16	8	9	8	3	3	3	11	18	20	20	16	12	10	8	8	9	9	8	8	8	7	5	6	5	4	4	4	4	5	5
Detroit, AL	11	8	12	7	5	11	8	2	3	2	7	11	16	14	9	8	7	7	8	10	9	8	10	7	8	8	6	6	5	5	5	5	6	6
New York, AL	11	15	15	14		12	9	5	5	5	15	22	24	22	15	14	10	11	9	10	11	10	10	8	8	7	7	6	5	7	7	7	6	6
Phila.-K.C.-Oakland, AL	5	3	3	3	4	5	3	2	2	4	7	15	10	11	16	9	8	8	6	7	7	9	8	8	8	6	6	5	5	6	6	6	6	5
St. Louis-Baltimore, AL	3	15	16	12	11	11	6	1	3	3	11	15	20	18	13	10	12	10	12	8	9	8	9	7	7	9	6	6	6	7	6	6	6	6
Wash.-Minnesota, AL	1	5	2	8	4	6	3	1	2	2	5	7	12	9	10	6	8	7	8	7	6	8	8	7	6	7	7	7	6	8	8	8	8	8
Milwaukee-Atlanta, NL	4	6	6	6	5	4	4	1	1	2	13	15	15	11	8	8	12	11	10	10	12	15	14	12	10	9	8	7	6	5	6	7	5	4
Brooklyn.-Los Angeles, NL	5	14	14	11	18	14	10	4	7	9	21	25	26	26	22	19	17	15	15	16	14	13	12	12	12	11	9	7	8	6	6	6	6	6
Chicago, NL	5	6	8	5	5	11	11	4	6	7	18	23	19	16	15	14	10	9	9	8	8	10	8	6	6	6	5	5	5	5	6	6	5	5
Cincinnati, NL	16	10	10	10	8	8	5	2	1	3	4	8	11	10	7	4	6	7	9	9	9	11	11	8	8	6	5	5	5	4	5	5	5	5
N.Y.-S.Francisco, NL	2	11	4	5	6	7	7	3	5	8	16	19	22	19	18	14	13	9	9	10	10	10	12	9	8	9	8	7	7	6	6	6	6	5
Philadelphia, NL	1	2	3	3	8	3	2	1	3	5	9	11	15	14	12	11	11	9	9	8	8	9	9	7	10	8	7	6	6	7	7	6	6	6
Pittsburgh, NL	4	5	7	7	9	8	7	4	4	4	13	14	19	13	13	11	15	11	10	13	13	10	11	9	7	7	7	7	6	6	6	6	6	6
St. Louis, NL	28	33	32	28	29	25	22	6	7	7	18	19	22	20	21	16	15	16	22	18	15	11	14	12	9	8	6	5	5	6	6	7	7	7
L.A.-California, AL																										2	4	6	6	6	5	5	5	5
Washington, AL																										2	4	4	4	4	4	5	5	5
Houston, NL																											2	4	5	5	6	6	6	5
New York, NL																										3	4	5	4	4	5	6	6	5
Kansas City, AL																																		7
Seattle, AL																																		4
Montreal, NL																																		3
San Diego, NL																																		4

ANNUAL OVERALL MINOR LEAGUE PITCHING PERCENTAGE LEADER (20 OR MORE DECISIONS)

Year	Player	Team (League)	W-L	Pct.	Overall W-L	Overall Pct.
1900	Christy Mathewson	Norfolk (Virginia)	20-2	.909	–	–
1901	Henry Allemang	Little Rock (So. Assn.)	20-4	.833	–	–
1902	Louis Bruce	Toronto (Eastern)	18-2	.900	–	–
1903	Ernest Nichols	Spokane (Pac. Nat.)	20-4	.833	–	–
1904	Ed Craig	Springfield (Mo. Valley)	19-4	.826	–	–
1905	Bill Burns	Pittsburg (Mo. Valley)	21-3	.875	–	–
1906	Frank Dick	Marshalltown (Iowa St.)	18-3	.857	–	–
1907	Harley Young	Wichita (West. Assn.)	29-4	.879	–	–
1908	Harry Gaspar	Waterloo (Cent. Assn.)	32-4	.889	–	–
1909	Ray Fisher	Hartford (Conn.)	24-5	.828	–	–
1910	Cyrus Dahlgren	Superior (Minn.-Wis.)	22-3	.880	–	–
1911	Howard	Northrop Reading (Inter.-St.)	27-4	.871	–	–
1912	Larue Kirby	Traverse City (Mich. St.)	18-3	.857	–	–
1913	Ralph Bell	Winona (Northern)	28-6	.824	–	–
1914	Joe Chabek	Harrisburg (Tri-St.)	28-3	.903	–	–
1915	Booth Hopper	Minneapolis (A.A.)	18-3	.857	–	–
1916	Howard Ehmke	Syracuse (N.Y. St.)	31-7	.816	–	–
1917	John Verbout	Wilkes-Barre (N.Y. St.)	26-7	.788	–	–
1918	John Beckvermit	Binghamton (Int.)	17-4	.810	–	–
1919	C. A. "Chief" Bender	Richmond (Va.)	29-2	.935	–	–
1920	George Carmen	London (Mich.-Ont.)	26-2	.926	–	–
1921	Earl Keiser	Mitchell (Dakota)	20-2	–		
		Oakland (PCL)	3-0	–	23-2	.920
1922	Byrd Hodges	Joplin (West. Assn.)	26-3	.897	–	–
1923	Emil Levsen	Cedar Rapids (Miss. Val.)	19-4	.826	–	–
1924	Carl Dunagan	Dyersburg (Kitty)	19-2	.905	–	–
1925	Lloyd Brown	Ardmore-Western Assn.	17-1	.944*	–	–
1926	Frank Tubbs	Port Huron (Mich.-Ont.)	8-1	–		
		Port Huron (Mich. St.)	8-0	–		
		Oklahoma City (Western)	9-2	–	25-3	.893
1927	Ben Cantwell	Jacksonville (So'east.)	25-5	.833	–	–
1928	Paul Fittery	Carrollton (Ga.-Ala.)	21-2	.913	–	–
1929	Andrew Bednar	McCook (Neb. St.)	21-4	.840	–	–
1930	Jim Cameron	McCook (Neb. St.)	19-2	.905	–	–
1931	Lyle "Bud" Tinning	Minneapolis (A.A.)	1-2	–		
		Des Moines (West. Assn.)	24-2	–	25-4	.862
1932	Marvin Duke	Erie (Central)	23-4	.852	–	–
1933	Al Piechota	Davenport (Miss. Val.)	19-4	.826	–	–
1934	Fay Thomas	Los Angeles (PCL)	28-4	.875	–	–
1935	Lloyd Sterling	Winnipeg (Northern)	24-2	.923	–	–
1936	Bill Yocke	Akron (Mid. Atl.)	1-2	–		
		Norfolk (Piedmont)	18-1	–	19-3	.864
1937	Joe Kohlman	Salisbury (E. Shore)	25-1	.962	–	–
1938	Paige Dennis	Thomasville (N.C. St.)	28-2	.933	–	–
1939	Charles Wensloff	Joplin (West. Assn.)	26-4	.867	–	–
1940	Arthur Cyrolewski	Johnson City (App.)	20-3	.870	–	–
	J. Merwin Henley	La Crosse (Wis. St.)	20-3	.870	–	–
1941	Frank Marino	Macon (Sally)	19-1	.950	–	–
1942	Paul Minner	Elizabethton (App.)	18-2	–		
		Knoxville (So. Assn.)	1-0	–	19-2	.905
1943	Irvin Stein	Portsmouth (Piedmont)	24-6	.800	–	–
1944	Pete Naktenis	Hartford (Eastern)	18-3	.857	–	–
1945	Lewis Carpenter	Atlanta (So. Assn.)	22-2	.917	–	–
1946	Bill Kennedy	Rocky Mount (C. Plain)	28-3	.903	–	–
1947	Chris VanCuyk	Cambridge (E. Shore)	25-2	.926	–	–
1948	Albert Tefft	Blackstone (Va.)	20-1	.952	–	–
1949	Lynn Southworth	Thomasville (N.C. St.)	21-1	.955	–	–
1950	Mike Hudak	Big Stone Gap (Mt. St.)	19-2	.905	–	–
1951	Anderson Bush	Hagerstown (Int. St.)	22-3	.880	–	–
1952	Russell Harris	Ozark (Ala.-Fla.)	27-3	.900	–	–
1953	Steve Kraly	Binghamton (Eastern)	19-2	.905	–	–
1954	Don Vaughn	Merryville-Morristown (Mt. St.)	11-1	–		
		Highpoint-Thomasville (Carolina)	0-0	–		
		Vidalia (Ga. St.)	9-1	–	20-2	.909
1955	Jim Grant	Keokuk (I-I-I)	19-3	.864	–	–
1956	Francisco Ramirez	Mexico City Reds (Mex.)	20-3	.870	–	–
1957	Bob Riesner	Alexandria (Evang.)	20-0	–		
		New Orleans (So. Assn.)	0-2	–	20-2	.909
1958	Jerry Walker	Knoxville (Sally)	18-4	.818	–	–
	Art Henriksen	St. Petersburg (Fla. St.)	17-3	–		
		New Orleans (So. Assn.)	0-1	–	18-4	.818
1959	Les Bass	Boise (Pioneer)	21-3	.875	–	–
1960	Tom Haake	Grand Forks (Northern)	0-1	–		
		Dubuque (Midwest)	19-3	–	19-4	.826
1961	David Seeman	Selma (Ala.-Fla.)	17-3	–		
		Burlington (Carolina)	7-0	–	24-3	.889
1962	Bob Schmidt	Modesto (Calif.)	0-0	–		
		Jamestown (NYP)	17-3	–	17-3	.850
1963	Bob Lee	Batavia (NYP)	20-2	–		
		Asheville (Sally)	1-1	–	21-3	.875
1964	Ed Watt	Aberdeen (Northern)	14-1	–		
		Elmira (Eastern)	3-1	–	17-2	.895**
1965	Billy MacLeod	Pittsfield (Eastern)	18-0	1.000***	–	–
1966	Bob Snow	Winston-Salem (Carolina)	20-2	.909	–	–
1967	John Parker	Spartanburg (W. Car.)	17-3	.850	–	–
1968	Pablo Montes De Oca	Campeche (Mex. S.E.)	21-4	.840	–	–
1969	Don Eddy	Appleton (Midwest)	18-3	.857	–	–
1970	Jim Flynn	Albuquerque (Texas)	19-4	.826	–	–
1971	Rich Gossage	Appleton (Midwest)	18-2	.900	–	–
1972	Andres Ayon	Saltillo (Mexican)	22-3	.880	–	–
1973	Silvano Quezada	Tampico (Mexican)	22-2	.917	–	–
1974	Bob Knepper	Fresno (Calif.)	20-5	.800	–	–
1975	Jerry Garvin	Reno (Calif.)	17-5	.773	–	–
1976	Enrique Romo	Mexico City Reds (Mex.)	20-4	.833	–	–
1977	Dave Stewart	Clinton (Midwest)	17-4	–		
		Albuquerque (PCL)	1-0	–	18-4	.818
1978	Tomas Armas	Saltillo (Mexican)	22-4	.846	–	–
1979	Miguel Solis	Saltillo (Mexican)	25-5	.833	–	–
1980	Gene Nelson	Ft. Lauderdale (Fla. St.)	20-3	.870	–	–
1981	Ted Power	Albuquerque (PCL)	18-3	.857	–	–
1982	Mike Warren	Stockton-Modesto (Calif.)	19-4	.826	–	–
1983	Alfonso Pulido	Mexico City Reds (Mex.)	17-3	.850	–	–
1984	Mike Bielecki	Hawaii (PCL)	19-3	.864	–	–
1985	Eleazar Beltran	Tampico (Mexican)	18-3	.857	–	–
1986	George Ferran	Shreveport (Texas)	16-1	.941‡	–	–
1987	Bob Faron	Springfield (Midwest)	19-2	.905	–	–
1988	Jimmy Rodgers	Myrtle Beach (So. Atl.)	18-4	.818	–	–
1989	Royal Clayton	Albany (Eastern)	16-4	.800	–	–
1989	Mercedes Esquer	Yucatan (Mexican)	16-4	.800	–	–
1989	Walt Trice	Osceola (Fla. St.)	16-4	.800	–	–
1990	Randy Marshall	Fayetteville (So. Atl.)	13-0	–		
		Lakeland (Fla. St.)	7-2	–	20-2	.909
1991	Jose Martinez	Columbus (So. Atl.)	20-4	.833	–	–
1992	John Fritz	Quad Cities (Midwest)	20-4	.833	–	–
1993	John Dettmer	Charlotte (Fla. St.)	16-3	.842	–	–
	Ryan Karp	Albany (Eastern)	0-0	–		
		Prince William (Carolina)	3-2	–		
		Greensboro (So. Atl.)	13-1	–	16-3	.842+
1994	Francisco Montano	Monclova (Mexican)	19-1	.950	–	–
1995	Rich Hunter	Piedmont (Sally)	10-2	–		
		Clearwater (Fla. St.)	6-0	–		
		Reading (Eastern)	3-0	–	19-2	.905
1996	Ted Silva	Charlotte (Fla. St.)	10-2	–		
		Tulsa (Texas)	7-2	–	17-4	.810
1997	Travis Smith	El Paso (Texas)	16-3	.842	–	–
1998	John Sneed	Hagerstown (Sally)	16-2	.889···	–	–
	Narcisco Elvira	Monterrey (Mexican)	16-4	.800	–	–
1999	Jose Navarro	Mexico City Tigers (Mex.)	16-4	.800	–	–
2000	Bud Smith	Arkansas (Texas)	12-1	–		
		Memphis (PCL)	5-1	–	17-2	.895*
2000	Greg Wooten	New Haven (Eastern)	17-3	.850	–	–
2001	Matt Guerrier	Birmingham (Southern)	11-3	–		
		Charlotte (International)	7-1	–	18-4	.818
2002	Ian Ferguson	Wilmington (Carolina)	12-1	–		
		Wichita (Texas)	6-2	–	18-3	.857
2003	Travis Blackley	San Antonio (Texas)	17-3	.850	–	–

* Adding two losses to Brown's record giving him 20 decisions yields a .850 percent, better than John Schmutte, Johnstown Middle Atlantic, 19–4, .822

** Adding one loss to Watt's record, giving him 20 decisions, yields an .850 percentage, better than Dave Leonhard, Aberdeen (Northern), 16–4 .800

*** Adding two losses to MacLeod's record, giving him 20 decisions, yields a .900 percentage, better than Dave Leonhard, Elmira (Eastern), 20–5 .800

+ Adding one loss to Dettmer's and Karp's records giving them 20 decisions yields an .800 percentage, better than Urbano Lugo, Jalisco (Mexican) 17–5 .773.

‡ Adding three losses to Ferran's record, giving him 20 decisions, yields an .800 percentage, better than Kevin Armstrong, Columbia (Sally), 17–5 .773

++ Adding one loss to Smith's record, giving him 20 decisions, yields an .800 percentage, better than Brian Rose, Pawtucket (International) 17–5 .773 and Reid Cornelius combined 17–5 .773 combined with Portland (Eastern) 5–0 and Charlotte (International) 12–5

+++ Adding two losses to Sneed's record giving him 20 decisions, yields a .800 percentage

\# Adding one loss to Smith's record, giving him 20 decisions, yields an .850 percentage.

ANNUAL OVERALL MINOR LEAGUE BATTING LEADER (400 OR MORE AT BATS)

Year Player	Team (League)	G	AB	R	H	2B	3B	HR	RBI	SB	AVG.
1900 Kitty Bransfield	Worcester (Eastern)	122	501	115*	186*	30	8	17	—	40	.371*
1901 Frank Huelsman	Shreveport (So. Assn.)	121*	487	98	191*	31	10	9	—	15	.392*
1902 Emil Frisk	Denver (Western)	123	450	89	168	22	22	14*	—	20	.373*
1903 Frank Huelsman	Spokane (Pac. Int.)	98	418	89	160	35	11	6	—	14	.392*
1904 Billy Hamilton	Haverhill (New Eng.)	113	408	113*	168*	32	8	0	—	74*	.412*
1905 Charlie Hemphill	St. Paul (A. A.)	145	560	122	204*	38	12	5	—	40	.364*
1906 Mike Welday	Des Moines (Western)	129	549	93	197	—	—	—	—	31	.359
1907 Ed Householder	Aberdeen (Northwest)	127	499	64	173	30*	19	9	—	19	.347*
1908 Ward Miller	Wausau (Wis.-Ill.)	124	408	91*	156*	—	—	—	—	—	.382*
1909 Harry Welch	Omaha (Western)	151	527	81	196*	41	15	7	—	51	.372*
1910 Dave Callahan	Eau Claire (Minn.-Wis.)	126	460	92*	168*	25	17*	2	—	52	.365*
1911 Frank Huelsman	Great Falls (U.A.)	135	516	117	212	48	15	17*	125*	25	.411*
1912 Charlie Johnson	Trenton (Tri-State)	109	400	86	161	31	5	14	—	22	.403*
1913 Frank Huelsman	Salt Lake City (U.A.)	122	473	123*	200*	36*	20*	22*	126*	16	.423*
1914 Joe Harris	Bay City (So. Michigan)	139	510	135	197*	39	22*	10	—	42	.386*
1915 Big Bill Kay	Binghamton (N.Y. St.)	125	447	98*	169*	22	25*	7	—	35	.378*
1916 Hank Butcher	Denver (Western)	145	541	116	204	31	20*	15	—	32	.377*
1917 Nap Lajoie	Toronto (Int.)	151	581	83	221*	39*	4	5	—	4	.380*
1918 Polly McLarry	Shreveport (Texas)	29	84	12	24	3	1	1	—	6	.286
	Binghamton (Int.)	103	335	51	129	26	7	4	—	15	.385*
										overall	.365
1919 Joe Wilhoit	Seattle (PCL)	17	67	8	11	1	0	0	—	3	.164
	Wichita (Western)	128	526	126*	222*	41	10	7	—	13	.422*
										overall	.393
1920 Merwyn Jacobson	Baltimore (Int.)	154*	581	161*	235*	35	16*	7	—	18	.404*
1921 Jack Lelivelt	Omaha (Western)	166	659	149	274*	70*	9	14	—	24	.416*
1922 Jack Schaefer	London (Mich.-Ont.)	100	407	79	167	27	21	9	—	9	.410*
1923 Moses Solomon	Hutchinson (So'west.)	134	527	143*	222*	40*	15	49*	—	12	.421*
1924 T. P. Osborne	Mt. Pleasant (E. Tex.)	101	396	93	171*	48	3	23	—	46*	.432*[1]
1925 Paul Waner	San Francisco (PCL)	174	699	167	280	75*	7	11	130	8	.401*
1926 Bill Diester	Salina (So'west.)	106	428	110*	190*	33*	4	27	—	10	.444*
	Tulsa (Western)	11	44	5	15	4	0	0	—	0	.341
										overall	.434
1927 Elton Langford	Des Moines (Western)	149	611	132	250	47	28*	8	—	31	.409*
1928 Danny Boone	High Point (Piedmont)	128	468	123	196*	40	11	38*	131*	11	.419*
1929 Ed Kallina	Midland(W. Tex.)	94	367	126	159	28	7	44*	—	16	.433*
	Sherman (Lone Star)	17	64	22	22	—	—	6	—	1	.344
										overall	.420
1930 Tony Antista	Bisbee (Arizona St.)	109*	444	127*	191*	36	16*	17	100	18	.430*
1931 Babe Phelps	Youngstown (Mid-Atl.)	115	436	71	178	29	9	15	88	9	.408*
1932 George Puccinelli	Rochester (Int.)	133	478	102	187	34	8	28	115	2	.391*
1933 Ox Eckhardt	Mission (PCL)	189*	760	145	315*	56	16	12	143	15	.414*
1934 Frank Demaree	Los Angeles (PCL)	186	702	190*	269*	51*	4	45*	173*	41	.383*
1935 Ox Eckhardt	Mission (PCL)	172	710	149	283*	40	11	2	114	8	.399*
1936 Cal Lahman	Jamestown (Northern)	127	466	154*	182*	30	9	48*	162*	20	.391*
1937 Earl "Red" Martin	Beckley (Mt. St.)	91	360	80	144	39*	14*	8	96*	7	.400*
	Scranton (NYP)	11	41	7	10	1	0	0	4	1	.244
										overall	.384
1938 Murray Franklin	Beckley (Mt. St.)	94	385	91	169	31	13*	26*	110	13	.439*[2]
1939 Joe Schmidt	Duluth (Northern)	120	440	114*	194*	29	9	31*	133*	17	.441*
1940 Ed Schweda	Lubbock (W. Tex.-N.M.)	114	469	142	198	39	15	11	118	7	.422*
1941 Lew Flick	Elizabethton (App.)	117	502*	127*	210*	37*	13	5	116*	20	.418*
1942 Don Manno	Welch (Mt. St.)	117	457	136*	174*	32	14*	34*	122*	23	.381*
1943 George Kell	Lancaster (Inter-St.)	138	555	120*	220*	33	23*	5	79	14	.396*
1944 Roland Gladu	Hartford (Eastern)	119	417	92	155	28	14	7	102	8	.372
1945 Arden "Cotton" McCaskey	Bristol (App.)	106	437	72	164*	26*	14*	2	96	5	.375*
1946 Walt Forwood	Carbondale (N. Atl.)	111	419	98	170*	43*	7	3	101	22	.406*
1947 Jim Prince	Midland (Longhorn)	108	415	111	178	31	6	34	141	4	.429*
	Lubbock (W. Tex.-N.M.)	12	37	7	10	3	0	1	12	0	.270
										overall	.416
1948 Hershel Martin	Albuquerque (W. Tex.-N.M.)	132	447	133	190	61*	6	18	128	5	.425*
1949 Bob Montag	Pawtucket (New Eng.)	125	454	139*	192*	36	18*	21*	91	43*	.423*
1950 Oscar Sierra	Hornell (Pony)	93	358	99	151	28	2	21	114	12	.422*
	Newport News (Piedmont)	15	45	5	13	1	0	0	5	0	.289
										overall	.407
1951 D. C. "Pud" Miller	Hickory (N.C. St.)	119	426	115	181	32	1	40*	136*	2	.425*
1952 Don Stafford	Salisbury (N.C. St.)	105	392	99	160	31	3	18	90	1	.408*[3]
1953 Russ Snyder	McAlester (Sooner St.)	138	556	137	240*	32	16	2	84	74*	.432*
1954 Neal Cobb	Crestview (Ala.-Fla.)	115	435	108	188	27	8	5	124	3	.432*
1955 Tom Jordan	Artesia (Longhorn)	136	543	116	221*	69*	2	28	159*	4	.407*
1956 Len Tucker	Pampa (So'west)	140	565	181*	228	40	13	51	181	47*	.404*
1957 Fran Boniar	Reno (Calif.)	110	443	102	193	33	15	11	138*	4	.436*
	Pueblo (Western)	11	37	5	9	1	0	0	7	3	.243
										overall	.421
1958 Neb Wilson	Ft. Walton Beach-Pensacola (Ala.-Fla.)	119	409	102*	162	38*	3	24*	106*	3	.396*
1959 Tom Hamilton	St. Petersburg (Fla. St.)	125	401	109	155	20	3	20*	96	3	.387*
1960 Al Pinkston	Mexico City Reds (Mexican)	138	567	110	225*	41	11	26	144*	4	.397*
1961 Al Pinkston	Veracruz (Mexican)	109	406	79	152	26*	4	13	86	4	.374*
1962 Ramiro Caballero	Guanajuato (Mex. Center)	113	423	123	175*	25	0	59*	170	3	.414*

ANNUAL OVERALL MINOR LEAGUE BATTING LEADER (400 OR MORE AT BATS)

Year Player	Team (League)	G	AB	R	H	2B	3B	HR	RBI	SB	AVG.
1963 Vinicio Garcia	Monterrey (Mexican)	122	475	107*	175	36*	5	21	88	3	.368*
1964 Ramiro Caballero	Leon (Mex. Center)	121	460	135*	175*	29	1	35*	145*	3	.380*
1965 Alfonso Peciado	Guanajuato (Mex. Center)	130	529	103	224*	48*	14*	11	147	11	.423*
1966 Heriberto Vargas	Veracruz (Mexican)	7	14	0	3	0	0	0	0	0	.214
	Guanajuato (Mex. Center)	127	481	168*	214	33	1	55*	174*	3	.445*
										overall	.438
1967 Hilario Pena	Campeche (Mex. S.E.)	102	404	60	159	61	3	1	49	9	.394*
1968 Jim Hicks	Tulsa (PCL)	117	407	100*	149	32	7	23	85	14	.366*
1969 Bernie Carbo	Indianapolis (A.A.)	111	404	83	145	37	2	21	76	7	.359*
1970 Miguel Suarez	Tampico (Mex. Center)	126	460	105	181*	37*	4	14	101	15	.393*
1971 Teolindo Acosta	Puebla (Mexican)	133	441	75	173	22	11	7	71	17	.392*
1972 Don Anderson	Jalisco (Mexican)	130	445	76	161	31	2	8	68	0	.362*
1973 Hector Espino	Tampico (Mexican)	116	422	82	159	20	2	22	107*	3	.377*
1974 Teolindo Acosta	Puebla (Mexican)	122	464	93*	170*	17	6	2	43	20	.366*
1975 Gene Richards	Reno (Calif.)	134	501*	148*	191*	29	10	12	58	85*	.381*
1976 Pat Putnam	Asheville (W. Car.)	138	538	100	194*	33*	3	24*	142*	8	.361*
1977 Rudy Law	Lodi (California)	122	451	124	174	22	5	9	88	37	.386*
1978 Champ Summers	Indianapolis (A.A.)	132	462	98	170*	25	5	34*	124*	11	.368
1979 Jimmie Collins	Chihuahua (Mexican)	124	470	95	206*	35	10	6	60	33	.438*
1980 Jimmie Collins	Chihuahua (Mex. #1)	91	346	62	131	19	13	4	52	19	.379
	Saltillo (Mex. #2)	39	137	25	52*	8	3*	2	31*	5	.380
										overall	.379
1981 Kent Hrbek	Visalia (Calif.)	121	462	119	175	25	5	27	111	12	.379*
1982 Randy Ready	El Paso (Texas)	132	475	122*	178*	33	5	20	99	13	.375*
1983 Chris Smith	Phoenix (PCL)	123	449	88	170	31	5	21	102	4	379*
1984 Jimmie Collins	Mexico City Reds-Cordoba (Mexican)	109	403	81	166	35	4	6	59	12	.412*
1985 Oswaldo Olivares	Aguas.-Campeche (Mexican)	110	441	85	175*	22	14*	5	49	20	.397*
1986 Willie Aikens	Puebla (Mexican)	129	445	134	202*	38	3	46	154*	0	.454*
1987 Orlando Sanchez	Puebla (Mexican)	123	439	95	182	34	1	25	115	6	.415*
1988 Nelson Barrera	Mexico City Reds (Mexican)	129	460	90	171	26	0	31	124*	7	.372
1989 Willie Aikens	Leon (Mexican)	128	423	108*	167	40	1	37	131*	1	.395*
1990 Trench Davis	Saltillo (Mexican)	127	498	84	189*	33	4	5	50	20	.380
1991 Rich Renteria	Jalisco (Mexican)	104	382	90	169	30	6	24	106	17	.442*
	Indianapolis (A.A.)	20	72	6	17	5	0	1	5	0	.236
										overall	.410
1992 Raul Perez Tovar	Monclova (Mexican)	129	483	83	201	32	5	8	93	14	.416*
1993 Nelson Simmons	Jalisco (Mexican)	109	369	81	141	27	0	34	95	1	.382
	Palm Springs (California)	20	76	13	25	8	0	5	23	0	.329
										overall	.373
1994 Brian Hunter	Tucson (PCL)	128	513	113*	191*	28	9	10	51	49*	.372*
1995 Adam Riggs	San Bernardino (Calif.)	134	542	111*	196*	39*	5	24	106	31	.362*
1996 Vladimir Guerrero	West Palm Beach (Fla. St.)	20	80	16	29	8	0	5	18	2	.363
	Harrisburg (Eastern)	118	417	84	150	32	8	19	78	17	.360*
										overall	.360
1997 Mike Kinkade	El Paso (Texas)	125	468	112	180	35	12	12	109	17	.385*
1998 Miguel Flores	Monterrey (Mexican)	100	399	87	152	32	4	4	67	32	.380[4]
1999 Matias Carillo	Mexico City Tigers (Mexican)	112	421	107	175	27	2	20	98	3	.416
2000 Warren Newson	Union Laguna (Mexican)	112	417	104	161	2	1	39	121	3	.386*
2001 Julio Franco	Mexico City Tigers (Mexican)	110	407	90	178*	34	5	18	90	15	.437*
2002 Cornelio Garcia	Mexico City Reds (Mexican)	96	395	81	151	19	11*	7	54	12	.382[5]
2003 Jeremy Reed	Winston-Salem (Carolina)	65	222	37	74	18	1	4	52	27	.333
	Birmingham (Southern)	11	41	8	19	2	1	2	7	6	.463

*Led league in category

[1] If charged with 400 at bats, Osborne's average would be .428, higher than any player with 400 or more at bats.
(George Rhinehardt, Greenville (Sally) G: 120, AB: 495, R: 110*, H: 200*, 2B: 45*, 3B: 18, HR: 8, RBI: 92, SB: 32*, AVG: .404*)

[2] If charged with 400 at bats, Franklin's average would be .423, higher than any player with 400 or more at bats. (Butch Moran, Rogers (Ark.-Mo.) G: 105, AB: 406, R: 107, H: 159, 2B: 43*, 3B: 12, HR: 22*, RBI: 114, SB: 8, AVG: .392*)

[3] If charged with 400 at bats, Stafford's average would be .400, higher than any player with 400 or more at bats.
(Clint McCord, Clinton (Miss. Ohio Val.) G:119, AB: 482, R: 123, H: 189*, 2B: 40, 3B: 15, HR: 15, RBI: 109, SB: 20, AVG: .392*)

[4] If charged with 400 at bats, Flores average would be .380, higher than any player with 400 or more at bats.
(Ramon Espinosa, Mexico City Reds (Mexican) G:121, AB: 533, R: 114, H: 202, 2B: 31, 3B: 5, HR: 7, RBI: 62, SB: 16, AVG: .379)

[5] If charged with 400 at bats Garcia's average would be .378, higher than any player with 400 or more at bats {Rick Short, Salt Lake City (PCL) 105 G, 410 AB, 71 R, 146 H, 29 2B, 2 3B, 7 HR, 68 RBI, 3 SB, .3561* AVG}

Chapter 35

Black Ball

Satchel Paige and Larry Doby
The Indians went to the Negro Leagues in 1947 to sign the AL's first black player, Larry Doby, right, and added pitching legend Satchel Paige a year later.

By Jules Tygiel

More than 50 years have passed since what many have called the finest moment in the history of the national pastime—Jackie Robinson's shattering of the color barrier. Robinson's heroic triumph brought to an end six disgraceful decades of Jim Crow baseball. During that era, some of America's greatest ballplayers plied their trade on all-black teams, in Negro Leagues, on the playing fields of Latin America, and along the barnstorming frontier of the cities and towns of the United States,

but never within the major and minor league realm of "Organized Baseball." When slowly and grudgingly given their chance in the years after 1947, blacks conclusively proved their competitive abilities on the diamond, but discrimination persisted as baseball executives continued to deny them the opportunity to display their talents in both managerial and front office positions.

Scattered evidence exists of blacks playing baseball in the antebellum period: for instance, the *New York Anglo-African* of December 10, 1859, reports a game played on November 15 on Long Island, between the Henson Base Ball Club of Jamaica, New

York, and a black team called the Unknown, of Weeksville. However, the first recorded black teams surfaced in northern cities in the aftermath of the Civil War. In October 1867 the Uniques of Brooklyn hosted the Excelsiors of Philadelphia in a contest billed as the "championship of colored clubs." Before a large crowd of black and white spectators, the Excelsiors marched around the field behind a fife and drum corps before defeating the Uniques, 37-24. Two months later, a second Philadelphia squad, the Pythians, dispatched a representative to the inaugural meetings of the National Association of Base Ball Players, the first organized league. The nominating committee unanimously rejected the Pythians' application, barring "any club which may be composed of one or more colored persons." Using the impeccable logic of a racist society, the committee proclaimed, "If colored clubs were admitted there would be in all probability some division of feeling, whereas, by excluding them no injury could result to anyone." The Philadelphia Pythians, however, continued their quest for interracial competition. In 1869 they became the first black team to face an all-white squad, defeating the cross-town City Items, 27–17.

In 1876 athletic entrepreneurs in the nation's metropolitan centers established the National League, which quickly came to represent the pinnacle of the sport. The new entity had no written policy regarding blacks, but precluded them nonetheless through a "gentleman's agreement" among the owners. In the smaller cities and towns of America, however, where under-funded teams and fragile minor league coalitions quickly appeared and faded, individual blacks found scattered opportunities to pursue baseball careers. During the next decade, at least two-dozen black ballplayers sought to earn a living in this erratic professional baseball world.

Bud Fowler ranked among the best and most persistent of these trailblazers. Born John Jackson in upstate New York in 1858 and raised, ironically, in Cooperstown, Fowler first achieved recognition as a 20-year-old pitcher for a local team in Chelsea, Massachusetts. In April 1878, Fowler defeated the National League's Boston club, which included future Hall of Famers George Wright and Jim O'Rourke, 2-1, in an exhibition game, besting 40-game winner Tommy Bond. Later that season, Fowler hurled three games for the Lynn Live Oaks of the International Association, the nation's first minor league, and another for Worcester in the New England League. For the next six years, he toiled for a variety of independent and semi-professional teams in the United States and Canada. Despite a reputation as "one of the best pitchers on the continent," he failed to catch on with any major or minor league squads. In 1884, now appearing regularly as a second baseman, as well as a pitcher, Fowler joined Stillwater, Minnesota, in the Northwestern League. Over the next seven seasons, Fowler played for fourteen teams in nine leagues, seldom batting less than .300 for a season. He led the Western League in triples in 1886. "He is one of the best general players in the country," reported *Sporting Life*, "and if he had a white face he would be playing with the best of them. ... Those who know, say there is no better second baseman in the country."

In 1886, however, a better second baseman did appear in the form of Frank Grant, perhaps the greatest black player of the 19th century. The light-skinned Grant, described as a "Spaniard" in the *Buffalo Express*, batted .325 for Meridien in the Eastern League. When that squad folded he joined Buffalo in the prestigious International Association and improved his average to .340, third best in the league.

Although not as talented as Fowler and Grant, bare-handed catcher Moses Fleetwood Walker and William Edward White achieved the highest level of play of blacks of this era. White was a Brown University student who, it was recently discovered, played one game at first base for the National League Providence Grays of 1879. One quarter African American, and thus by the standards of the 1870s black, White may well have passed for white with the Grays. All the same, he becomes the major leagues' first known black player. Fleet Walker, the son of an Ohio physician, had studied at Oberlin College, where in 1881 he and his younger brother Welday helped launch a varsity baseball team. For the next two years, the elder Walker played for the University of Michigan, and in 1883 he appeared in 60 games for the pennant-winning Toledo squad in the Northwestern League. In 1884, Toledo entered the American Association, the National League's primary rival, and Walker became the first black major leaguer. In an age when many catchers caught bare-handed and lacked chest protectors, Walker suffered frequent injuries and played little after a foul tip broke his rib in mid-July. Nonetheless, he batted .263 and pitcher Tony Mullane later called him "the best catcher I ever worked with." In July, Toledo briefly signed Walker's brother, Welday, who appeared in six games, batting .182. The following year, Toledo dropped from the league, ending the Walkers' major league careers.

These early black players found limited acceptance among teammates, fans, and opponents. In Ontario in 1881, Fowler's teammates forced him off the club. Walker found that Mullane and other pitchers preferred not to pitch to him. Although he acknowledged Walker's skills, Mullane confessed, "I disliked a Negro and whenever I had to pitch to him I used anything I wanted without looking at his signals." At Louisville in 1884, insults from Kentucky fans so rattled Walker that he made five errors in a game. In Richmond, after Walker had actually left the team due to injuries, the Toledo manager received a letter from "75 determined men" threatening "to mob Walker" and cause "much bloodshed" if the black catcher appeared. On August 10, 1883, Chicago White Stockings star and manager Cap Anson had threatened to cancel an exhibition game with Toledo if Walker played. The injured catcher had not been slated to start, but Toledo manager Charlie Morton defied Anson and inserted Walker into the lineup. The game proceeded without incident.

A Hopeful Start

In 1887 Walker, Fowler, Grant, Bob Higgins, George Stovey, and three other blacks converged on the International League, a newly reorganized circuit in Canada and upstate New York, one notch below the major league level. At the same time, a new six-team entity, the League of Colored Baseball Clubs, won recognition under baseball's National Agreement, a mutual pact to honor player contracts among team owners. Thus, an air of optimism pervaded the start of the season. But 1887 would prove a fateful year for the future of blacks in baseball.

On May 6 the Colored League made its debut in Pittsburgh with "a grand street parade and a brass band concert." Twelve hundred spectators watched the hometown Keystones lose to the Gorhams of New York, 11–8. Within days, however, the new league began to flounder. The Boston franchise disbanded in Louisville on May 8, stranding its players in the Southern city. Three weeks later, league founder Walter Brown formally announced the demise of the infant circuit.

Meanwhile, in the International League, black players found their numbers growing, but their status increasingly uncertain. Six of the ten teams fielded blacks, prompting *Sporting Life* to wonder, "How far will this mania for engaging colored players go?" In Newark, fans marveled at the "colored battery" of Fleet Walker, dubbed the "coon catcher" by one Canadian newspaper, and "headstrong" pitcher Stovey. One of the greatest black pitchers of the 19th century, the left-handed Stovey won 35 games, still an International League record. Grant, in his second season as the Buffalo second baseman, led the league in batting average and home runs. Fowler, one of two blacks on the Binghamton squad, compiled a .350 average through early July and stole 23 bases.

These athletes compiled their impressive statistics under the most adverse conditions. "I could not help pitying some of the poor black fellows that played in the International League," reported a white player. "Fowler used to play second base with the lower part of his legs encased in wooden guards. He knew that about every player that came down to second base on a steal had it in for him." Both Fowler and Grant "would muff balls intentionally, so that [they] would not have to touch runners, fearing that they might injure [them]." In addition, "About half the pitchers try their best to hit these colored players when [they are] at bat." Grant, whose Buffalo teammates had refused to sit with him for a team portrait in 1886, reportedly saved himself from a "drubbing" at their hands in 1887, only by "the effective use of a club." In Toronto, fans chanted, "Kill the Nigger," at Grant, and a local newspaper headline declared, "THE COLORED PLAYERS DISTASTEFUL." In late June, Bud Fowler's Binghamton teammates refused to take the field unless the club removed him from the lineup. Soon after, on July 7, the Binghamton club submitted to the players' demands, releasing Fowler and a black teammate, a pitcher named Renfroe.

The most dramatic confrontations between black and white players occurred on the Syracuse squad, where a clique of refugees from the Southern League exacerbated racial tensions. In spring training, the club included a catcher named Dick Male, who, rumors had it, was a light-skinned black named Richard Johnson. Male charged "that the man calling him a Negro is himself a black liar," but when released after a poor preseason performance, he returned to his old club, Zanesville in the Ohio State League, and resumed his true identity as Richard Johnson. In May, Syracuse signed 19-year-old black pitcher Robert Higgins, angering the Southern clique. Higgins appeared in his first International League game in Toronto on May 25. "THE SYRACUSE PLOTTERS," as a *Sporting News* headline called his teammates, undermined his debut. According to one account, they "seemed to want the Toronto team to knock Higgins out of the box, and time and again they fielded so badly that the home team were enabled to secure many hits after the side had been retired."

"A disgusting exhibition," admonished the *Toronto World.* "They succeeded in running Male out of the club," reported a Newark paper, "and they will do the same with Higgins." One week later, two Syracuse players refused to pose for a team picture with Higgins. When manager "Ice Water" Joe Simmons suspended pitcher Doug Crothers for this incident, Crothers slugged the manager. Higgins miraculously recovered from his early travails and lack of support to post a 20-7 record.

On July 14, as the directors of the International League discussed the racial situation in Buffalo, the Newark Little Giants planned to send Stovey, their ace, to the mound in an exhibition game against

the National League Chicago White Stockings. Once again manager Anson refused to field his squad if either Stovey or Walker appeared. Unlike 1883, Anson's will prevailed. On the same day, team owners, stating that "Many of the best players in the league are anxious to leave on account of the colored element," allowed current black players to remain, but voted by a 6-4 margin to reject all future contracts with blacks. The teams with black players all voted against the measure, but Binghamton, which had just released Fowler and Renfroe, swung the vote in favor of exclusion.

Events in 1887 continued to conspire against black players. On September 11 the St. Louis Browns of the American Association refused to play a scheduled contest against the all-black Cuban Giants. "We are only doing what is right," they proclaimed. In November, the Buffalo and Syracuse teams unsuccessfully attempted to lift the International League ban on blacks. The Ohio State League, which had fielded three black players, also adopted a rule barring additional contracts with blacks, prompting Welday Walker, who had appeared in the league, to protest, "The law is a disgrace to the present age. ... There should be some broader cause—such as lack of ability, behavior and intelligence—for barring a player, rather than his color."

Only a handful of blacks appeared on integrated squads after 1887. Grant and Higgins returned to their original teams in 1888. Walker jumped from Newark to Syracuse. The following year, only Walker remained for one final season, the last black in the International League until 1946. Richard Johnson, the erstwhile Dick Male, reappeared in the Ohio State League in 1888 and in 1889 joined Springfield in the Central Interstate League, where he hit 14 triples, stole 45 bases, and scored 100 runs in 100 games. In 1890, Harrisburg in the Eastern Interstate League fielded two blacks, while Jamestown in the New York-Penn League featured another. Bud Fowler and several other black players appeared in the Nebraska State League in 1892. Three years later, Adrian in the Michigan State League signed five blacks, including Fowler and pitcher George Wilson, who posted a 29-4 record. Meanwhile Sol White, who later chronicled these events in his 1906 book, *The History of Colored Baseball,* played for Fort Wayne in the Western State League. In 1896, pitcher-outfielder Bert Jones joined Atchison in the Kansas State League where he played for three seasons before being forced out in 1898. Almost 50 years would pass before another black would appear on an interracial club in Organized Baseball.

All-Black Teams

While integrated teams grew rare, several leagues allowed entry to all-black squads. In 1889 the Middle States League included the New York Gorhams and the Cuban Giants, the most famous black team of the age. The Giants posted a 55-17 record. A year later, the alliance reorganized as the Eastern Interstate League and again included the Cuban Giants. Giants star George Williams paced the circuit with a .391 batting average, while teammate Arthur Thomas slugged 26 doubles and 10 triples, both league-leading totals. The Eastern Interstate League folded in midseason, and in 1891 the Giants made one final minor league appearance in the Connecticut State League. When this circuit also disbanded, the brief entry of the Cuban Giants in Organized Baseball came to an end.

In the 1898 season a team calling itself the Acme Colored Giants affiliated with Pennsylvania's Iron and Oil League, but won only 8 of 49 games before dropping out, marking an ignoble conclusion to these early experiments in interracial play.

Overall, at least 70 blacks appeared in Organized Baseball in the

late 19th century. About half played for all-black teams, the remainder for integrated clubs. Few lasted more than one season with the same team. By the 1890s, the pattern for black baseball that would prevail for the next half century had emerged. Blacks were relegated to "colored" teams playing most of their games on the barnstorming circuit, outside of any organized league structure. While exhibition contests allowed them to pit their skills against whites, they remained on the outskirts of baseball's mainstream, unheralded and unknown to most Americans.

As early as the 1880s and 1890s several all-black traveling squads had gained national reputations. The Cuban Giants, formed among the waiters of the Argyle Hotel to entertain guests in 1885, set the pattern and provided the recurrent nickname for these teams. Passing as Cubans, so as not to offend their white clientele, the Giants toured the East in a private railroad car playing amateur and professional opponents. In the 1890s, rivals like the Lincoln Giants from Nebraska, the Page Fence Giants from Michigan, and the Cuban X Giants in New York emerged. From the beginning these teams combined entertainment with their baseball to attract crowds. The Page Fence Giants, founded by Bud Fowler in 1895, would ride through the streets on bicycles to attract attention. In 1899, Fowler organized the All-American Black Tourists, who would arrive in full dress suits with opera hats and silk umbrellas. Their showmanship notwithstanding, the black teams of the 1890s included some of the best players in the nation. The Page Fence Giants won 118 of 154 games in 1895, with two of their losses coming against the major league Cincinnati Reds.

During the early years of the 20th century many blacks still harbored hopes of regaining access to Organized Baseball. Sol White wrote in 1906 that baseball "should be taken seriously by the colored player. An honest effort of his great ability will open the avenue in the near future wherein he may walk hand-in-hand with the opposite race in the greatest of all American games—baseball." Rube Foster, the outstanding figure in black baseball from 1910 to 1926, stressed excellence because "we have to be ready when the time comes for integration."

But even clandestine efforts to bring in blacks met a harsh fate. In 1901 Baltimore Orioles manager John McGraw attempted to pass second baseman Charlie Grant of the Columbia Giants off as an Indian named Chief Tokohama, until Chicago White Sox president Charles Comiskey exposed the ruse.

In 1911 the Cincinnati Reds raised black hopes by signing two light-skinned Cubans, Armando Marsans and Rafael Almeida, prompting the *New York Age* to speculate, "Now that the first shock is over it would not be surprising to see a Cuban a few shades darker ... breaking into the professional ranks ... it would then be easier for colored players who are citizens of this country to get into fast company." But the Reds rushed to certify that Marsans and Almeida were "genuine Caucasians," and while light-skinned Cubans became a fixture in the majors, their darker brethren remained unwelcome. Over the years, tales circulated of United States blacks passing as Indians or Cubans, but no documented cases exist.

Although most blacks lived in the South during the first two decades of the 20th century, the great black teams and players congregated in the metropolises and industrial cities of the North. Chicago emerged as the primary center of black baseball with teams like the Leland Giants and the Chicago American Giants. In New York, the Lincoln Giants, which boasted pitching stars Smokey Joe Williams and Cannonball Dick Redding, shortstop John Henry Lloyd and catcher Louis Santop, reigned supreme.

Other top clubs of the era included the Philadelphia Giants, the Hilldale Club (also of Philadelphia), the Indianapolis ABCs, and the Bacharach Giants of Atlantic City. Player contracts were non-existent or nonbinding and stars jumped frequently from team to team. "Wherever the money was," recalled John Henry Lloyd, "that's where I was."

Fans and writers often compared the great black players of this era to their white counterparts. Lloyd, one of the outstanding short-stops and hitters of that or any era, came to be known as "The Black Wagner," after his white contemporary Honus Wagner, who called it an "honor" and a "privilege" to be compared to the gangling black infielder. A St. Louis sportswriter once said when asked who was the best player in baseball history, "If you mean in Organized Baseball, the answer would be Babe Ruth; but if you mean in all baseball ... the answer would have to be a colored man named John Henry Lloyd." Pitcher "Rube" Foster earned his nickname by outpitching future Hall of Famer Rube Waddell, and Cuban Jose Mendez was called "The Black Matty" after Christy Mathewson.

The talents of Foster and Mendez notwithstanding, the greatest black pitcher of the early 20th century was 6-foot-5 "Smokey" Joe Williams. Born in 1886, Williams spent a good part of his career pitching in his native Texas, unheralded until he joined the Leland Giants in 1909 at the age of 24. From 1912 to 1923 he won renown as a strikeout artist for Harlem's Lincoln Giants. Against major league competition Williams won six games, lost four, and tied two, including a three-hit 1-0 victory over the National League champion Philadelphia Phillies in 1915. In 1925 he signed with the Homestead Grays and, although approaching his 40th birthday, starred for seven more seasons. A 1952 poll to name the outstanding black pitcher of the half-century placed Williams in first place, ahead of the legendary Satchel Paige.

Oscar Charleston ranks as the greatest outfielder of the 1910s and 1920s. With tremendous speed and a strong, accurate arm, Charleston was the quintessential center fielder. During his 15-year career starting in 1915, Charleston hit for both power and average and may have been the most popular player of the 1920s. After he retired he managed the Philadelphia Stars, Brooklyn Brown Dodgers, and other clubs.

Several major stars of this era labored outside the usual channels of black baseball. In 1914, white Kansas City promoter J. L. Wilkinson organized the All-Nations team, which included whites, blacks, Indians, Asians, and Latin Americans. Pitchers John Donaldson, Jose Mendez and Bill Drake and outfielder Cristobel Torriente played for the All-Nations team, described by one observer as "strong enough to give any major league team a nip-and-tuck battle." A black Army team from the 25th Infantry Unit in Nogales, Arizona, featured pitcher "Bullet" Joe Rogan and short-stop Dobie Moore. In 1920, when Wilkinson formed the famed Kansas City Monarchs, the players from the All-Nations and 25th Infantry teams formed the nucleus of his club. In 1921, the Monarchs challenged the minor league Kansas City Blues to a tournament for the city championship. The Blues won the series five games to three. In 1922, however, the Monarchs won five of six games to claim boasting honors in Kansas City. One week later, they swept a doubleheader from the touring Babe Ruth All-Stars.

Foster the Giant

In the years after 1910, Andrew "Rube" Foster emerged as the dominant figure in black baseball. Like many of his white contemporaries, Foster rose through the ranks of the national pastime

from star player to field manager to club owner. Born in Texas in 1879, Foster accepted an invitation to pitch for Chicago's Union Giants in 1902. "If you play the best clubs in the land, white clubs as you say," he told owner Frank Leland, "it will be a case of Greek meeting Greek. I fear nobody." By 1903 he was hurling for the Cuban X Giants against the Philadelphia Giants in a series billed as the "Colored Championship of the World." His four victories in a best-of-nine series clinched the title.

The following year, he had switched sides and registered two of three wins for the Philadelphia Giants in a similar matchup, striking out 18 batters in one game and tossing a two-hitter in another. In 1907 he rejoined the Leland Giants and, in 1910, pitched for and managed a reconstituted team of that name to a 123-6 record.

As a pitcher, Foster had ranked among the nation's best; as a manager, his skills achieved legendary proportions. A master strategist and motivator, Foster's teams specialized in the bunt, the steal and the hit-and-run, which came to characterize black baseball. Fans came to watch him sit on the bench giving signs with a wave of his ever-present pipe. He became the friend and confidant of major league managers like John McGraw. Over the years, Foster trained a generation of black managers, like Dave Malarcher, Biz Mackey, and Oscar Charleston in the subtleties of the game.

Foster entered the ownership ranks, uniting with white saloon keeper John Schorling (the son-in-law of White Sox owner Charles Comiskey) to form the Chicago American Giants in 1911. With Schorling's financial backing, Foster's managerial acumen, a regular home field in Chicago, and high salaries, the American Giants attracted the best black players in the nation. Throughout the decade, whether barnstorming or hosting opponents in Chicago, the American Giants came to represent the pinnacle of black baseball.

By World War I Foster dominated black baseball in Chicago and parts of the Midwest. In most other areas, however, white booking agents controlled access to stadiums, and as one newspaperman charged in 1917, "used circus methods to drag a bunch of our best citizens out, only to undergo humiliation ... while [they sat] back and [grew] rich off a percentage of the proceeds." In the East, Nat Strong, the part owner of the Brooklyn Royal Giants, Philadelphia Giants, Cuban Stars, Cuban Giants, New York Black Yankees, and the renowned white semi-pro team, the Bushwicks, held a stranglehold on black competition. To break this monopoly and place the game more firmly under black control, Foster created the National Association of Professional Baseball Clubs, better known as the Negro National League, in 1920.

Foster's new organization marked the third attempt of the century to meld black teams into a viable league. In 1906, the International League of Independent Baseball Clubs, which had four black and two white teams, struggled through one season characterized by shifting and collapsing franchises. Four years later, Beauregard Moseley, secretary of Chicago's Leland Giants, attempted to form a National Negro Baseball League, but the association folded before a single game had been played.

The new Negro National League of 1920, which included the top teams from Chicago, St. Louis, Detroit, and other Midwestern cities, fared far better. At Foster's insistence, all clubs, with the exception of the Kansas City Monarchs, whom Foster reluctantly accepted, were controlled by blacks. J. L. Wilkinson, who owned the Monarchs, a major drawing card, had won the respect of his fellow owners and soon overcame Foster's reservations. He became the league secretary and Foster's trusted ally. Operating under the

able guidance of Foster and Wilkinson, the league flourished during its early years. In 1923, it attracted 400,000 fans and accumulated $200,000 in gate receipts.

The success of the Negro National League inspired competitors. In 1923 booking agent Nat Strong formed an Eastern Colored League, with teams in New York, Brooklyn, Baltimore, New Jersey, and Philadelphia. With four of the six teams owned by whites, and Strong controlling an erratic schedule, the league had somewhat less legitimacy than Foster's circuit. Playing in larger population centers, however, the more affluent Eastern clubs successfully raided some of the top players of the Negro National League before the circuits negotiated an uneasy truce in 1924. Throughout the remainder of the decade, however, acrimony rather than harmony characterized interleague relations. A third association emerged in the South, where the stronger independent teams in major cities formed the Southern Negro League. While this group became a breeding ground for top players, the impoverished nature of its clientele, and the inability of clubs to bolster revenues with games against white squads, rendered them unable to prevent their best players from jumping to the higher-paying Northern teams.

At their best the Negro Leagues of the 1920s were haphazard affairs. Since most clubs continued to rely on barnstorming for their primary livelihood, scheduling proved difficult. Teams played uneven numbers of games and especially in the Eastern circuit skipped official contests for more lucrative non league matchups. Several of the stronger independent teams, like the Homestead Grays, remained unaffiliated. Umpires were often incompetent and lacked authority to control conditions. Finally, players frequently jumped from one franchise to another, peddling their services to the highest bidder. In 1926, Foster grew ill, stripping the Negro National League of his vital leadership. Two years later, the Eastern Colored League disbanded and in 1931, less than a year after Foster's death, the Negro National League departed the scene, once again leaving black baseball with no organized structure.

Two Holdovers Take Over

With the collapse of Foster's Negro National League and the onset of the Great Depression, the always borderline economics of operating a black baseball club grew more precarious. White booking agents, like Philadelphia's Eddie Gottlieb or Abe Saperstein of the Midwest, again reigned supreme. In the early 1930s, only the stronger independent clubs like the Homestead Grays or Kansas City Monarchs, novelty acts like the Cincinnati Clowns, or those teams backed by the "numbers kings" of the black ghettos could survive.

The Kansas City Monarchs emerged as the healthiest holdover from the old Negro National League. In 1929 owner Wilkinson had commissioned an Omaha, Nebraska, company to design a portable lighting system for night games. The equipment, consisting of a 250-horsepower motor and a 100-kilowatt generator, which illuminated lights atop telescoping poles 50 feet above the field, took about two hours to assemble. To pay for the innovation, Wilkinson mortgaged everything he owned and took in Kansas City businessman Tom Baird as a partner. But the gamble paid off. The novelty of night baseball allowed the Monarchs to play two and three games a day and made them the most popular touring club in the nation.

Meanwhile, in Pittsburgh, former basketball star Cumberland Posey, Jr. had forged the Homestead Grays into one of the best teams in America. Posey, the son of one of Pittsburgh's wealthiest

black businessmen, had joined the Grays, then a sandlot team, as an outfielder in 1911. By the early 1920s he owned the club and began recruiting top national players to supplement local talent. In 1925 he signed 39-year-old Smokey Joe Williams, and the following year he lured Oscar Charleston, whom many consider the top black player of that era. Over the next several seasons Posey recruited Judy Johnson, Martin Dihigo, and James "Cool Papa" Bell. In 1930 he added a catcher from the Pittsburgh sandlots named Josh Gibson, and in 1934 brought in first baseman Buck Leonard from North Carolina. Unwilling to subject himself to outside control, Posey preferred to remain free from league affiliations. Yet for two decades, the Homestead Grays reigned as one of the strongest teams in black baseball.

In the 1930s Posey faced competition from crosstown rival Gus Greenlee, "Mr. Big" of Pittsburgh's North Side numbers rackets. Greenlee took over the Pittsburgh Crawfords, a local team, in 1930. Greenlee spent $100,000 to build a new stadium, and wooed established ballplayers with lavish salary offers. In 1931 he landed the colorful Satchel Paige, the hottest young pitcher in the land, and the following year raided the Grays, outbidding Posey for the services of Charleston, Johnson, and Gibson. In 1934 Cool Papa Bell jumped the St. Louis Stars and brought his legendary speed to the Crawfords. With five future Hall of Famers, Greenlee had assembled one of the great squads of baseball history.

The emergence of Gus Greenlee marked a new era for black baseball, the reign of the numbers men. In an age of limited opportunities for blacks, many of the most talented northern black entrepreneurs turned to gambling and other illegal operations for their livelihood. Novelist Richard Wright explained, "They would have been steel tycoons, Wall Street brokers, auto moguls, had they been white." Like the political bosses of 19th-century urban America, numbers operators provided an informal assistance network for needy patrons in the impoverished black communities and represented a major source of capital for black businesses. In city after city, the numbers barons, seeking an element of respectability or an outlet to shield gambling profits from the Internal Revenue Service or merely the thrill of sports ownership, came to dominate black baseball. In Harlem second-generation Cuban immigrant Alex Pompez, a powerful figure in the Dutch Schultz mob, ran the Cuban Stars, while Ed "Soldier Boy" Semler controlled the Black Yankees. Abe Manley of the Newark Eagles, Ed Bolden of the Philadelphia Stars, and Tom Wilson of the Baltimore Elite Giants all garnered their fortunes from the numbers game. Even Cum Posey, who had no connection with the rackets, had to bring in Homestead numbers banker Rufus "Sonnyman" Jackson as a partner and financier to stave off Greenlee's challenge.

In 1933 Greenlee unified the franchises owned by the numbers kings into a rejuvenated Negro National League. Under his leadership, writes Donn Rogosin, "The Negro National League meetings were enclaves of the most powerful black gangsters in the nation." This "unholy alliance" sustained black baseball in the Northeast through depression and war. Even the collapse of the Crawfords and demolition of Greenlee Stadium in 1939 failed to weaken the league, which survived until the onset of integration. In 1937 a second circuit, the Negro American League, was formed in the Midwest and South. Dominated by Wilkinson and the Kansas City Monarchs, the Negro American League relied less on numbers brokers, but more on white ownership for their financing.

The formation of the Negro American League encouraged the rejuvenation of an annual World Series, matching the champions of the two leagues. But the Negro League World Series never achieved the prominence of its white counterpart. The fact that league standings were often determined among teams playing uneven numbers of games diluted the notion of a champion. Furthermore, impoverished urban blacks could not sustain attendance at a prolonged series. As a result, the Negro League World Series always took a back seat to the annual East-West All-Star Game played in Chicago. The East-West Game, originated by Greenlee in 1933, quickly emerged as the centerpiece of black baseball. Fans chose the players in polls conducted by black newspapers. By 1939, leading candidates received as many as 500,000 votes. Large crowds of blacks and whites watched the finest Negro League stars, and the revenues divided among the teams often spelled the difference between profit and loss at the season's end.

By the 1930s and 1940s, black baseball had become an integral part of Northern ghetto life. With hundreds of employees and millions of dollars in revenue, the Negro Leagues, as Donn Rogosin notes, "may rank among the highest achievements of black enterprise during segregation." In addition, baseball provided an economic ripple effect, boosting business in hotels, cafes, restaurants, and bars. In Kansas City and other towns, games became social events, as black citizens, recalls manager Buck O'Neil, "wore their finery." The Monarch Booster Club was a leading civic organization and the "Miss Monarch Bathing Beauty" pageant a popular event.

Black baseball also represented a source of pride for the black community. "The Monarchs was Kansas City's team," boasted bartender Jesse Fisher. "They made Kansas City the talk of the town all over the world." In several cities, white politicians routinely appeared at Opening Day games to curry favor with their often neglected black constituents. When Greenlee Field launched its operations in Pittsburgh, the mayor, city council, and county commissioners lined the field boxes. Negro League owners also played a role in the fight against segregation. In Newark, Effa Manley, who ran the Eagles with her husband Abe, served as treasurer of the New Jersey NAACP and belonged to the Citizen's League for Fair Play, which fought for black employment opportunities. Manley sponsored a "Stop Lynching" fundraiser at one Eagles home game.

The impact of the Negro Leagues, however, ranged beyond the communities whose names the teams bore. Throughout the age of Jim Crow baseball, even in those years when a substantial league structure existed, official league games accounted for a relatively small part of the black baseball experience. Black teams would typically play over 200 games a year, only a third of which counted in the league standings. The vast majority of contests occurred on the "barnstorming" circuit, pitting black athletes against a broad array of professional and semi-professional competition, white and black, throughout the nation. In the pre-television era, traveling teams brought a higher level of baseball to fans in the towns and cities of America and allowed local talent to test their skills against the professionals. While some all-white teams, like the "House of David," also trod the barnstorming trail, itinerancy was the key to survival for black squads. The capital needed to finance a Negro League team existed primarily in Northern cities, but the overwhelming majority of blacks lived in the South.

"The schedule was a rugged one," recalled catcher Roy Campanella of the Baltimore Elite Giants. "Rarely were we in the same city two days in a row. Mostly we played by day and traveled by night." After the Monarchs introduced night baseball, teams played both day and night, appearing in two and sometimes three different ballparks on the same day. Teams traveled in buses—"our

home, dressing room, dining room, and hotel"—or sandwiched into touring cars. "We had little time to waste on the road," states Quincy Trouppe, "so it was a rare treat when the cars would stop at times to let us stretch out and exercise for a few minutes." Most major hotels barred black guests, so even when the schedule allowed overnight stays, the athletes found themselves in less than comfortable accommodations. Large cities usually had better black hotels where ballplayers, entertainers, and other members of the black bourgeoisie congregated. On the road, however, Negro Leaguers more frequently were relegated to Jim Crow roadhouses, "continually under attack by bedbugs."

The black baseball experience extended beyond the confines of the United States and into Central America and the Caribbean. Negro Leaguers appeared regularly in the Cuban, Puerto Rican, Venezuelan, and Dominican winter leagues where they competed against black and white Latin stars and major leaguers as well.

Some blacks, like Willie Wells and Ray Dandridge, jumped permanently to the Mexican League, where several also became successful managers of interracial teams. As Wells explained, "I am not faced by the racial problem ... I've found freedom and democracy here, something I never found in the United States. ... In Mexico, I am a man."

Reluctant Clowns

In the United States, however, blacks often found themselves in more distasteful roles. To attract crowds throughout the nation and to keep fans interested in the frequently one-sided contests against amateur competition, some black clubs injected elements of clowning and showmanship into their pre-game and competitive performances. As early as the 1880s, comedy had characterized many barnstorming teams. Black baseball, even in its most serious form, tended to be flashier and less formal than white play. Against inferior teams, players often showboated and flaunted their superior skills. Pitcher Satchel Paige would call in his outfielders or guarantee to strike out the first six or nine batters to face him against semi-professional squads. In the late 1930s, Olympic star Jesse Owens traveled with the Monarchs, racing against horses in pre-game exhibitions.

Black teams like the Tennessee Rats and Zulu Cannibals thrived on their minstrel show reputations. The most famous of these franchises were the "Ethiopian Clowns." Originating in Miami in the 1930s, the Clowns later operated out of Cincinnati and then Indianapolis. Their antics included a "pepperball" and "shadowball" performance (later emulated by basketball's Harlem Globetrotters), and mid-game vaudeville routines by comics Spec Bebop, a dwarf, and King Tut. Players like Pepper Bassett, "the Rocking Chair Catcher," and "Goose" Tatum, a talented first baseman and natural comedian, enlivened the festivities. By the 1940s, the Clowns, through the effort of booking agent Syd Pollack, dominated the baseball comedy market. In 1943, their popularity won the Clowns entrance into the Negro Leagues, although other owners demanded they drop the demeaning "Ethiopian" nickname. Although never one of the better black teams, the Clowns greatly bolstered Negro League attendance.

Their popularity notwithstanding, the comedy teams reflected one of the worst elements of black baseball. The Clowns and Zulus perpetuated stereotypes drawn from Stepin Fetchit and Tarzan movies. "Negroes must realize the danger in insisting that ballplayers paint their faces and go through minstrel-show revues before each ballgame," protested sportswriter Wendell Smith.

Many black players resented the image that all were clowns. "Didn't nobody clown in our league but the Indianapolis Clowns," objected Piper Davis. "We played baseball."

Even without the clowning, black baseball offered a more freewheeling and, in many respects, more exciting brand of baseball than the major leagues. Since the 1920s, when Babe Ruth had revolutionized the game, the majors had pursued power strategies, emphasizing the home run above all else. Although the great sluggers of the Negro Leagues rivaled those in the National and American Leagues, they comprised but one element in the speed-dominated universe of "tricky baseball." Black teams emphasized the bunt, the stolen base and the hit-and-run. "We played by the 'coonsbury' rules," boasted second baseman Newt Allen. "That's just any way you think you can win, any kind of play you think you could get by on."

In games between white and black all-star teams, this style of play often confounded the major leaguers. Center fielder Cool Papa Bell personified this approach. Bell was so fast, marveled rival third baseman Judy Johnson, "You couldn't play back in your regular position or you'd never throw him out." In one game against a major league all-star squad, Bell scored from first base on a sacrifice bunt! In center field, his great speed allowed him to lurk in the shallow reaches of the outfield, ranging great distances to make spectacular catches.

Negro League pitching also took on a peculiar caste. "Anything went in the Negro League," reported Campanella, "Spitballs, shineballs, emery balls; pitchers used any and all of them." Since league officials could not afford to replace the balls as frequently as in Organized Baseball, scuffed and nicked baseballs remained in the game, giving pitchers great latitude for creative efforts. "I never knew what the ball would do once it left the pitcher's hand," recalled Campanella.

Since most rosters included only 14 to 18 men, Negro League players demonstrated a wide range of versatility. Each was required to fill in at a variety of positions. Star pitchers often found themselves in the outfield when not on the mound. Some won renown at more than one position. Ted "Double-Duty" Radcliffe often pitched in the first game of a doubleheader and caught in the second. Cuban Martin Dihigo, whom many rank as the greatest player of all time, excelled at every position. In 1938 he led all Mexican League pitchers with an 18-2 record and the league's hitters with a .387 average.

The manpower shortage offered opportunities for individuals to display their all-around talents, but it also limited the competitiveness of the black teams. While on a given day a Negro League franchise, featuring one of its top pitchers, might defeat a major league squad, most teams lacked the depth to compete on a regular basis. "The big leagues were strong in every position," remarks Radcliffe. "Most of the colored teams had a few stars but they weren't strong in every position."

While black teams may not have matched the top clubs in Organized Baseball, the individual stars of the 1930s and 1940s clearly ranked among the best of any age. Homestead Gray teammates Josh Gibson and Buck Leonard won renown as the Babe Ruth and Lou Gehrig of the Negro Leagues. The Grays discovered Gibson in 1929 as an 18-year-old catcher on the sandlots of Pittsburgh, where he had already earned a reputation for 500-foot home runs. For 17 years, he launched prodigious blasts off pitchers in the Negro Leagues, on the barnstorming tour, and in Latin America. As talented as any major league star, Gibson died in

January 1947 at age 35, just three months before Jackie Robinson joined the Brooklyn Dodgers. Leonard, four years older than Gibson, starred in both the Negro and Mexican Leagues as a sure-handed, power-hitting first baseman. The Newark Eagles of the early 1940s boasted the "million dollar infield" of first baseman Mule Suttles, second baseman Dick Seay, shortstop Willie Wells, and third baseman Ray Dandridge. The acrobatic fielding skills of Seay, Wells, and Dandridge led Roy Campanella to call this the greatest infield he ever saw.

Paige Stands Alone

Amidst the many talented Negro Leaguers of the 1930s and 1940s, however, one long, lean figure came to personify black baseball to blacks and whites alike. Leroy "Satchel" Paige began his prolonged athletic odyssey in his hometown in 1924 as a 17-year-old pitcher with the semi-professional Mobile Tigers. He joined the Chattanooga Black Lookouts of the Negro Southern League in 1926. Two years later the Lookouts sold his contract to the Birmingham Black Barons. By 1930 his explosive fastball, impeccable control, and eccentric mannerisms had made him a legend in the South. In 1932 Gus Greenlee brought Paige to the Pittsburgh Crawfords, with whom the colorful pitcher embellished his reputation by winning 54 games in his first two years. Greenlee also began the practice of hiring out Paige to semi-professional clubs that needed a one-day box office boost.

For seven years Paige feuded with Greenlee, jumping the club when a better offer appeared, being banished "for life," and then returning. In the mid-1930s, in addition to his stints with the Crawfords, Paige won fame by boosting Bismarck, North Dakota, to the national semi-professional championship; hurling for the Dominican Republic at the behest of dictator Rafael Trujillo; in the Mexican League; and especially on the postseason barnstorming trail, pitted against Dizzy Dean's Major League All-Stars. "That skinny old Satchel Paige with those long arms is my idea of the pitcher with the greatest stuff I ever saw," claimed the unusually immodest Dean.

Paige's appeal stemmed as much from his unusual persona as his pitching prowess. A born showman, Paige's lanky, lackadaisical presence evoked popular racial stereotypes of the age. "As undependable as a pair of second-hand suspenders," Paige often arrived late or failed to show. His names for his pitches (the "bee ball" which buzzed and would all of a sudden "be there"; the "jump ball"; and the "trouble ball") and his minstrel-show one-liners enhanced the image. But on the mound, Paige invariably rose to the occasion against top competition or challenged inferior opponents by calling in the outfield or promising to strike out the side.

In 1938 a sore arm threatened to curtail Paige's career, but the Kansas City Monarchs, hoping his reputation alone would draw fans, signed him for their traveling second team. On the road, Paige perfected a repertoire of curves and off-speed pitches, including his famous "hesitation" pitch. When his fastball returned in 1939, he became a better pitcher than ever. Promoted to the main Monarch club, Paige pitched the team to four consecutive Negro American League pennants. From 1941 through 1947, although officially still a Monarch, Paige spent far more time as an independent performer, hired out by Monarchs owner J. L. Wilkinson to semi-pro and Negro League clubs. "He kept our league going," recalls Othello Renfroe. "Anytime a team got into trouble, it sent for Satchel to pitch." Paige also continued to hurl against major league all-star teams. In the 1940s, the example of

Satchel Paige, whose legend had spread into the white community, offered the most compelling argument for the desegregation of the national pastime.

Paige's exploits against white players revealed a fundamental irony about baseball in the Jim Crow era. While Organized Baseball rigidly enforced its ban on black players within the major and minor leagues, opportunities abounded for black athletes to prove themselves against white competition along the unpoliced boundaries of the national pastime. During the 1930s, Western promoters sponsored tournaments for the best semi-professional teams in the nation. These squads often featured former and future major leaguers as well as top local talent. In 1934 the *Denver Post* tourney, "the little World Series of the West," invited the Kansas City Monarchs to compete for the $7,500 first prize. The Monarchs fought their way into the finals against the House of David team (also owned by J. L. Wilkinson) only to find themselves confronted on the mound by Paige, rented out to pitch this one game. Paige outdueled Monarchs ace Chet Brewer, 2-1. Black teams became a fixture in the *Post* series, emerging victorious for several consecutive years.

In 1935, the National Baseball Congress began an annual tournament in Wichita, Kansas. The competition attracted community squads heartily bankrolled by local business leaders. Neil Churchill, an auto dealer from Bismarck, North Dakota, recruited half a dozen black stars, including Paige and Brewer, to represent the town in the Wichita competition. Bismarck naturally swept the series, and thereafter teams that were either integrated or all black routinely appeared in the National Baseball Congress invitational each year.

In an age in which the major leagues were confined to the East and Midwest, and television had yet to bring baseball into people's homes, postseason tours by big league stars offered yet another opportunity for black players to prove their equality on the diamond. Games pitting blacks against whites were popular features of the barnstorming circuit. Until the late 1920s, when Commissioner Kenesaw Mountain Landis limited postseason play to all-star squads, black teams frequently met and defeated major league clubs in postseason competition. During the next decade, matchups between the Babe Ruth or Dizzy Dean "All-Stars" and black players became frequent. In the autumns of 1934 and 1935, Dean's team traveled the nation accompanied by the "Satchel Paige All-Stars." In one memorable 1934 game, called by baseball executive Bill Veeck "the greatest pitching battle I have ever seen," Paige bested Dean, 1-0. Surviving records of interracial contests during the 1930s reveal that blacks won two-thirds of the games. "That's when we played the hardest," asserted Judy Johnson, "to let them know, and to let the public know, that we had the same talent they did and probably a little better at times."

The rivalries proved particularly keen on the West Coast, where Monarchs co-owner Tom Baird organized the California Winter League, which included black teams, white major and minor league stars and some of Mexico's top players. In 1940, pitcher Chet Brewer formed the Kansas City Royals, which each year fielded one of the best clubs on the coast. One year the Royals defeated the Hollywood Stars, who had won the Pacific Coast League championship, six straight times. In 1945, Brewer's team, including Jackie Robinson and Satchel Paige, regularly defeated major league competition.

The most famous of the interracial barnstorming tours occurred in 1946, when Cleveland Indians pitcher Bob Feller organized a

major league All-Star Team, rented two Flying Tiger aircraft and hopped the nation accompanied by the Satchel Paige All-Stars. With Feller and Paige each pitching a few innings a day, the tour proved extremely lucrative for promoters and players alike and gave widespread publicity to the skills of the black athletes.

The World War II years marked the heyday of the Negro Leagues. With black and white workers flooding into Northern industrial centers, relatively full employment, and a scarcity of available consumer goods, attendance at all sorts of entertainment events increased dramatically. In 1942, 3 million fans saw Negro League teams play, while the East-West game in 1943 attracted over 51,000 fans. "Even the white folks was coming out big," recalled Satchel Paige.

Change in the Air

But World War II also generated forces that would challenge the foundations of Jim Crow baseball. In the armed forces, baseball teams like the Black Bluejackets of the Great Lakes Naval Station team posted outstanding records against teams featuring white major leaguers. In 1945, a well-publicized tournament of teams in the European theater featured top black players like Leon Day, Joe Green, and Willard Brown in the championship round. More significantly, the hypocrisy of blacks fighting for their country but unable to participate in the national pastime grew steadily more apparent. As wartime manpower shortages forced major league teams to rely on a 15-year-old pitcher, over-the-hill veterans, and one-armed Pete Gray, their refusal to sign black players seemed increasingly irrational. "How do you think I felt when I saw a one-armed outfielder?" moaned Chet Brewer. Pitcher Nate Moreland protested, "I can play in Mexico, but I have to fight for America where I can't play." Pickets at Yankee Stadium carried placards asking, "If we are able to stop bullets, why not balls?"

Amidst this heightened awareness, Organized Baseball repeatedly walked to the precipice of integration, but always failed to take the final leap. In 1942, Moreland and All-America football star Jackie Robinson requested a tryout at a White Sox training camp in Pasadena, California. Robinson, in particular, impressed White Sox manager Jimmy Dykes but nothing came of the event. Brooklyn Dodgers manager Leo Durocher publicly stated his willingness to sign blacks, only to receive a stinging rebuke from Commissioner Landis. Landis again short-circuited integration talk the following year. At the annual baseball meetings, black leaders led by actor Paul Robeson gained the opportunity to address major league owners on the issue, but Landis ruled all further discussion out of order.

In 1943 several minor and major league teams were rumored close to signing black players. In California, where winter league play had demonstrated the potential of black players, several clubs considered integration. The Los Angeles Angels of the Pacific Coast League announced tryouts for three black players, but pressure from other league owners doomed the plan. Oakland owner Vince DeVicenzi ordered manager Johnny Vergez to consider pitcher Chet Brewer, the most popular black player on the West Coast. Vergez refused and the issue died. Two years later, Bakersfield, a Cleveland Indians farm team in the California League, offered Brewer a position as player-coach, but the parent club vetoed the plan.

At the major league level, Washington Senators owner Clark Griffith called sluggers Josh Gibson and Buck Leonard into his office and asked if they would like to play in the major leagues. They answered affirmatively, but never heard from Griffith again.

In Pittsburgh, *Daily Worker* sports editor Nat Low pressured Pirates owner William Benswanger to arrange a tryout for catcher Roy Campanella and pitcher Dave Barnhill. At the last minute, Benswanger canceled the audition, citing "unnamed pressures."

For more than two decades, the imperial Landis had reigned over baseball as an implacable foe of integration. While hypocritically denying the existence of any "rule, formal or informal, or any understanding—unwritten, subterranean, or sub-anything—against the signing of Negro players," Landis had stringently policed the color line. His death in 1944 removed a major barrier for integration advocates.

In April 1945, with World War II entering its final months, the integration crusade gained momentum. On April 6, *People's Voice* sportswriter Joe Bostic appeared at the Brooklyn Dodger training camp at Bear Mountain, New York, with two Negro League players, Terris McDuffie and Dave "Showboat" Thomas, and demanded a tryout. Outraged, but outmaneuvered, Dodgers president Branch Rickey allowed the pair to work out with the club.

One week later, a more serious confrontation occurred in Boston. The Red Sox, under public pressure from popular columnist Dave Egan and city councilman Isidore Muchnick, agreed to audition Sam Jethroe, the Negro Leagues' leading hitter in 1944, second baseman Marvin Williams and Kansas City Monarchs shortstop Jackie Robinson, all top prospects in their mid-20s. The Fenway Park tryout, however, proved little more than a formality and the players never again heard from the Red Sox.

The publicity surrounding these events, however, forced the major leagues to address the issue at their April meetings. At the urging of black sportswriter Sam Lacy, Leslie O'Connor, Landis' interim successor, established a Major League Committee on Baseball Integration in April 1945, to review the problem. In addition, the racial views of the newly appointed commissioner, A. B. "Happy" Chandler, came under close scrutiny. A former governor of the segregated state of Kentucky, Chandler nonetheless offered at least verbal support to the entry of blacks into Organized Ball. "If a black boy can make it on Okinawa and Guadalcanal, hell, he can make it in baseball," Chandler told black reporter Rick Roberts. Whether Chandler, however, unlike Landis, would reinforce his rhetoric with positive actions remained uncertain.

Rickey Takes the First Step

Unbeknownst to the integration advocates, baseball officials and local politicians sand-dancing around the race issue, Branch Rickey, the president of the Brooklyn Dodgers, had already set in motion the events which would lead to the historic breakthrough.

Raised in rural Ohio in a strict Methodist family, Rickey, nicknamed by sportwriters "The Deacon" and "The Mahatma," had financed his way through college and law school playing and coaching baseball. His skills as a catcher merited two years in the major leagues. In 1913 he abandoned a fledgling law career to manage the St. Louis Browns, and in 1917 he began a 25-year relationship with the St. Louis Cardinals. Rickey served as the field manager of the Cardinals from 1919 to 1925, after which he became the club's vice president and business manager. In the 1920s and 1930s, Rickey perfected the farm system, whereby a major league team controlled young, undeveloped players through a chain of minor league franchises. This innovation allowed the Cardinals to compete equally with richer teams in larger cities, generating pennants for the "Gas House Gang" and allowing the team to sell off surplus talent profitably.

Although Rickey later claimed that his desire to integrate baseball dated from 1904, when an Indiana hotel had denied lodgings to a black player on his college squad, he gave no indication of any interest in the race issue during his years in St. Louis. Perhaps this stemmed from the fact that St. Louis was a Southern city with firmly entrenched segregationist traditions. Throughout Rickey's reign with the Cardinals, blacks sat in Jim Crow sections at Sportsman's Park, a policy he never openly challenged.

Nonetheless, in 1942, when Rickey left the Cardinals and assumed control of the Brooklyn Dodgers, he informed the Dodger ownership of his intentions to recruit black players in the near future. Rickey never clearly explained the motivations for this dramatic turnaround. At times Rickey cited moral considerations, stating, "I couldn't face my God much longer knowing that His black creatures are held separate and distinct from His white creatures in the game that has given me all I own." On other occasions, he eschewed the role of "crusader," proclaiming, "My selfish objective is to win baseball games. ... The Negroes will make us winners for years to come."

Some observers saw financial reasons behind Rickey's actions, citing the lure of the growing black population in Northern cities and the prospects of increased attendance. Certainly, Brooklyn offered a more congenial atmosphere for integration than St. Louis. In all probability, a combination of these factors—geographic, moral, competitive, and financial, coupled with Rickey's desire for a broader role in history—impelled him to seek black players.

From 1942 to 1945, Rickey, a conservative, cautious, and conspiratorial man, moved slowly, studying the philosophical and sociological ramifications of integration and taking few people into his confidence. During the spring and summer of 1945, under the guise of creating a new black baseball circuit, the United States League, Rickey's scouts combed the nation and the Caribbean for black players. Rickey sought one player who would spearhead the breakthrough and several other potential stars who would follow in his wake. By August 1945 scouting reports and Rickey's own investigations pointed to one man as the ideal candidate for the struggle ahead—Kansas City Monarchs shortstop Jackie Robinson.

In Robinson, Rickey had found a rare combination of athletic ability, competitive fire, intelligence, maturity, and poise. Born in Georgia and raised in Pasadena, California, Robinson had won fame at UCLA as the nation's greatest all-around athlete, earning All-America honors in football, establishing broad-jump records, and leading his basketball conference in scoring, all in addition to his baseball exploits. In 1942, he enlisted in the Army where he attended officer's candidate school and became a lieutenant. Two years later, while stationed in Texas, Robinson's refusal to move to the back of a bus resulted in a court martial and ultimate acquittal. This incident demonstrated his commitment to the cause of equal rights. After his discharge from the Army, Robinson joined the Monarchs and earned a starting spot in the 1945 East-West All-Star Game. Robinson's college education, experience in interracial athletics and military career complemented his playing talents. But his fiery pride and temper seemed a potential obstacle to his success.

On August 28, 1945, Robinson met with Rickey at the latter's Brooklyn offices. Rickey revealed his bold plan to integrate Organized Baseball and challenged Robinson to accept the primary role. Rickey flamboyantly play-acted, assuming the role of racist players, fans, and hotel clerks, impressing upon Robinson the need to "turn the other cheek" in the event of racial confrontations. By the end of the session, Robinson had signed a contract to play for the Montreal Royals in the International League, the top farm team in the Brooklyn system. Rickey promised that if Robinson's performance merited it, he would be promoted to the Dodgers.

Rickey intended to announce the Robinson signing along with that of several other black players, but political pressures stemming from the New York City fall elections forced him to abandon his original plans and, on October 23, 1945, to reveal the signing of Robinson alone. The announcement sent shock waves through the baseball establishment and placed Robinson into a spotlight that he would never relinquish. Numerous sports figures, from players to executives to reporters, predicted the ultimate failure of Rickey's "great experiment."

Robinson's first test came at spring training in Florida in 1946. Thrust into the deep South where Jim Crow reigned supreme, Robinson and black pitcher John Wright, whom Rickey had recruited to room with Robinson, were unable to room with their teammates and were barred from playing in Jacksonville and other Florida cities. In addition, a shoulder injury hindered Robinson's performance, raising doubts about his abilities.

On April 18, 1946, at Roosevelt Stadium in Jersey City, Robinson became the first black to appear in modern Organized Baseball (excepting Jimmy Claxton, who passed as white in 1916 to play in a few games for the Oakland Oaks of the Pacific Coast League). In the process he staged one of the most remarkable performances under pressure in the history of the game. In Robinson's second at bat, he hit a three-run home run. He followed this with three singles and two stolen bases, scoring a total of four runs. As *The New York Times* reported, "This would have been a big day for any man, but under the circumstances, it was a tremendous feat."

In many respects, 1946 proved a nightmare season for Robinson. Fans jeered him in Baltimore, and opposing players tormented him with insults. Pitchers made him a frequent target of brushback pitches and baserunners attempted to spike and maim him at second base. As the season drew to a close, Robinson hovered on the brink of a nervous breakdown. Through it all, however, Robinson remained a dominant force on the field. His .349 batting average and 113 runs scored led the league and paced the Royals to the International League pennant. His presence inspired new attendance records throughout the circuit. In the Little World Series, which pitted Montreal against the Louisville Colonels of the American Association, Robinson braved the hostility of Kentucky fans and stroked game-winning hits in the final two games to give the Royals the championship.

Rickey's initiative and Robinson's dramatic success failed to inspire other team owners. In August, major league executives debated a controversial report discussing the "race question" which argued that integration would "lessen the value of several major league franchises." No other clubs moved to sign black players. Only four blacks, all in the Brooklyn system, joined Robinson in Organized Baseball in 1946. At Nashua, New Hampshire, in the New England League, the Dodgers farm club fielded catcher Roy Campanella and pitcher Don Newcombe. The Nashua Dodgers won the league championship largely due to Campanella's hitting and Newcombe's hurling. In the small town of Trois Rivieres in Quebec, in the Canadian-American League, pitchers John Wright and Roy Partlow, both of whom had appeared briefly with Robinson at Montreal, led a third Dodgers farm team to a crown. Nonetheless, at the start of the 1947 season, no additional black players appeared on any major or minor league rosters.

The Big Leagues at Last

Although Robinson's performance at Montreal merited promotion to the Dodgers, Robinson remained a Royal when he reported to spring training in 1947. Rickey hoped that the Brooklyn players themselves, when exposed to Robinson's talents, would request his addition to the team. He switched Robinson to first base, a weak spot on the Dodgers, to make his case more compelling. Robinson compiled a .519 batting average against the major leaguers, but several Dodger players, instead of demanding his promotion, rebelled. Led by Fred "Dixie" Walker, a group of mostly Southern Dodgers circulated a petition against Robinson. Rickey moved quickly to short-circuit the dissension, threatening to trade any athletes who opposed Robinson. In addition, the refusal of Pete Reiser, Pee Wee Reese and other Dodgers to support the protestors effectively squelched the petition drive. Finally, on April 10, just five days before the start of the 1947 season, Rickey officially announced that Robinson would join the Dodgers.

Throughout the early months of the 1947 campaign Robinson stoically endured crises and challenges. The Philadelphia Phillies, led by manager Ben Chapman, unleashed a barrage of verbal abuse against Robinson, which horrified Dodgers players and fans. The Benjamin Franklin Hotel in Philadelphia refused lodgings for Robinson and death threats appeared among his voluminous daily mail. In early May, rumors that the St. Louis Cardinals planned to strike rather than compete against Robinson prompted National League President Ford Frick to warn the players, "If you do this you will be suspended from the league."

Opposing pitchers targeted Robinson's body at a record-setting pace and an early season 0-for-20 batting drought led many to question his qualifications as a professional baseball player. "But for the fact that he is the first acknowledged Negro in major league history," observed a Cincinnati sportswriter, "he would have been benched a week ago."

Yet, as the season unfolded, Robinson converted doubters and enemies into admirers. By the end of June, a 21-game hitting streak had raised his batting average to .315 and propelled the Dodgers into first place. Robinson's daring baserunning, typical of Negro League play, evoked images of an "Ebony Ty Cobb." In city after city, record crowds flocked to experience Robinson's charismatic dynamism as five teams set new all-time season attendance marks. While periodic controversies erupted over baserunners who used their spikes "to make a pincushion out of Robinson" at first base, Robinson won the acceptance and respect of teammates and opponents alike. In September, as the Dodgers coasted to the pennant, *The Sporting News* named Robinson the major league Rookie of the Year. To cap his triumphant season, Robinson became the first black player to appear in the World Series.

Robinson's success on the field and at the box office stimulated some movement on the part of other clubs to hire black players. In Cleveland, Bill Veeck recruited 23-year-old Larry Doby, who jumped straight from the Negro League Newark Eagles to the Indians in July. Used sparingly, Doby batted a meager .156, casting doubts upon his future. The St. Louis Browns, seeking to boost flagging attendance, signed Willard Brown and Hank Thompson of the Kansas City Monarchs. When the turnstiles failed to respond, the Browns released both Brown and Thompson, although the latter had established himself as a top prospect. In the National League, the Dodgers signed Dan Bankhead to bolster the club's pitching down the stretch. On August 25, Bankhead, the first black pitcher to appear in the major leagues, surrendered eight runs in three

innings but also slammed a home run in his initial at-bat.

In addition to the five athletes who appeared in the major leagues, a handful of blacks surfaced in the minors. Campanella succeeded Robinson at Montreal, earning accolades as "the best catcher in the business." Newcombe returned to Nashua, where he won 19 games. The independent Stamford Bombers of the Colonial League fielded six black players, and two blacks, including future major leaguer Chuck Harmon, played in the Canadian-American League. Veteran Negro League hurler Nate Moreland won 20 games in California's Class C Sunset League. For the most part, however, Organized Baseball continued to ignore the treasure trove of black talent submerged in the Negro Leagues. A full year would pass before additional major league teams would add black players to their chains.

In 1948 the integration focus shifted from the Dodgers, where Robinson now reigned at second base, to the Cleveland Indians. In spring training Larry Doby, who had performed so dismally in 1947, unexpectedly won a starting berth in the Cleveland outfield. After an erratic early-season stretch in which Doby alternated errors and strikeouts with tape-measure home runs, he batted .301 and became a key performer for the American League champion Indians. In July, Cleveland owner Bill Veeck added the legendary Satchel Paige to the team. Amidst charges that his signing had been a publicity stunt, the 42-year-old Paige won six out of seven decisions, including back-to-back shutouts, and posted a 2.47 ERA. Standing-room-only crowds greeted him in Washington, Chicago, Boston, and even in Cleveland's mammoth Municipal Stadium. The Indians, after defeating the Boston Red Sox in a pennant playoff, won the World Series in six games with Doby's .318 average leading the club.

In 1947 the Dodgers had integrated and reached the World Series; in 1948 the Indians had duplicated and surpassed this achievement. Both teams had set all-time attendance records. Remarkably, as the 1948 season drew to a close, no other franchise had followed their lead. In the minor leagues, Roy Campanella became the first black in the American Association, stopping at St. Paul before permanently joining Robinson on the Dodgers. Newcombe and Bankhead each won more than 20 games for Brooklyn affiliates. The Dodgers also added fleet-footed Sam Jethroe to the Montreal roster, where he batted .322. The Indians began to stockpile black talent as well, signing future major leaguers Al Smith, Dave Hoskins and Orestes "Minnie" Minoso to minor league contracts. Several other blacks, including San Diego catcher John Ritchey, who broke the Pacific Coast League color line, played for independent teams.

In the interregnum between the 1948 and 1949 seasons four more teams—the Giants, Yankees, Braves, and Cubs—signed blacks to play in their farm systems, and 1949 would herald the beginning of widespread integration in the minor leagues. Blacks starred in all three Triple-A leagues. In the Pacific Coast League, Luke Easter won acclaim as the "greatest natural hitter ... since Ted Williams," amassing 25 home runs and 92 RBIs in just 80 games before succumbing to a knee injury. Oakland's Artie Wilson led the league in hits, stolen bases and batting average. In the International League, Jethroe scored 151 runs and stole 89 bases while Montreal teammate Dan Bankhead won 20 games for the second straight year. At Jersey City, Monte Irvin batted .373. The outstanding performer in the American Association was Ray Dandridge. Considered by many the greatest third baseman of all time, the acrobatic Dandridge, now in his late 30s, thrilled Minneapolis fans

with his spectacular fielding, batting .364 in the process. Former Negro Leaguers turned in equally stellar performances at lower minor league levels as well.

In the major leagues, the spotlight again returned to Jackie Robinson. For three years, Robinson had honored his pledge to Branch Rickey "to turn the other cheek" and avoid confrontations. With his position in the majors firmly established, Robinson announced, "They better be prepared to be rough this year, because I'm going to be rough on them." The more combative Robinson produced his finest year, batting .342 and earning the Most Valuable Player Award. Complemented by teammates Newcombe and Campanella, Robinson led the Dodgers to another pennant.

Slow to Follow

By the end of the 1949 season, integration had achieved spectacular success at both the major and minor league levels, but most teams moved "with all deliberate speed" in signing black players. The New York Giants joined the interracial ranks in 1949 when they promoted Monte Irvin and Hank Thompson. The following year, the Boston Braves purchased Jethroe from the Dodgers for $100,000 and installed him in the starting lineup. In 1951, the Chicago White Sox acquired Minnie Minoso in a trade with Cleveland, and Bill Veeck, who had acquired the hapless St. Louis Browns, brought back Satchel Paige for another major league stint. Yet, as late as August 1953, out of sixteen major league teams only these six fielded black players. Several teams displayed an interest in signing blacks but bypassed established Negro League stars who might have jumped directly to the majors, concentrating instead on younger prospects for the minor leagues. Still others like the Red Sox, Phillies, Cardinals, and Tigers continued to pursue a whites-only policy.

This failure to hire and promote blacks occurred amidst a continuing backdrop of outstanding performances by black players. The first generation of players from the Negro Leagues proved an extraordinary group. Jackie Robinson quickly established himself as one of the dominant stars in the national pastime, compiling a .311 batting average over his 10-year career while thrilling fans with his baserunning and clutch-hitting talents. Sportswriters called him, "the most dangerous man in baseball today." Campanella won accolades as the best catcher in the National League and won the Most Valuable Player Award in 1951, 1953, and 1955. Both Campanella and Robinson later won election to the Baseball Hall of Fame. Pitcher Don Newcombe averaged better than 20 wins a season during his first five full years with the Dodgers. In addition, from 1950 to 1953 Negro League graduates Sam Jethroe, Willie Mays, Joe Black, and Jim Gilliam each won the National League Rookie of the Year Award.

In the American League, where integration proceeded at a slower pace, several players compiled outstanding records. Larry Doby, while never achieving the superstar status many expected, nonetheless became a steady producer, twice leading the league in home runs and five times driving in more than 100 runs. He was elected to the Baseball Hall of Fame in 1998. Doby's Cleveland teammate Luke Easter, who reached the majors in his mid-30s, slugged 86 home runs and drove in 300 runs in his brief three-season career. Satchel Paige, after a two-year stint with the Indians, joined the hapless St. Louis Browns from 1951 to 1953 and became one of the American League's best relief pitchers. On the Chicago White Sox, Minnie Minoso proved himself a consistent .300 hitter.

Despite their relatively small numbers, teams with black players in both major leagues regularly finished high in the standings and only in 1950 did both pennant winners field all-white squads. In addition, the more aggressive stance of National League teams in recruiting black players gave that circuit a clear superiority in World Series and All-Star contests for more than two decades.

By the end of the 1953 season, the benefits of integration had grown apparent to all but the most recalcitrant of major league owners. In September, the Chicago Cubs purchased shortstop Ernie Banks from the Kansas City Monarchs and finally elevated longtime minor league standout Gene Baker. Connie Mack's Philadelphia Athletics ended their Jim Crow era by acquiring pitcher Bob Trice. At the start of the 1954 season, the Washington Senators, St. Louis Cardinals, Pittsburgh Pirates, and Cincinnati Reds all joined the interracial ranks. The sudden integration of six more clubs left only the Yankees, Tigers, Phillies and Red Sox with all-white personnel. In addition, 1954 marked the debut of young Henry Aaron with the Braves and the return of Willie Mays, who had sparkled for the Giants in 1951, from military service.

The desegregation of Organized Baseball opened the way not only to blacks in the United States but to those in other parts of the Americas as well. Throughout the 20th century, baseball had imposed a curious double standard on Latin players, accepting those with light complexions but rejecting their darker countrymen. With the color barrier down, major league clubs found a wealth of talent in the Carribbean. Minnie Minoso, the "Cuban Comet" who integrated the Chicago White Sox, became the first of the great Latin stars. Over a 15-year career, Minoso compiled a .298 batting average. In 1954 slick-fielding Puerto Rican Vic Power launched his career with the Athletics. The following year Roberto Clemente, the greatest of the Latin stars, debuted with the Pittsburgh Pirates. The proud Puerto Rican won four batting championships and amassed 3,000 hits en route to a .317 lifetime batting average. In the late 1950s the San Francisco Giants revealed the previously ignored treasure trove that existed in the Dominican Republic. In 1958 Felipe Alou became the first of three Alou brothers to play for the Giants, and in 1960 the Giants unveiled pitcher Juan Marichal, "the Dominican Dandy," who won 243 games en route to the Hall of Fame.

Among the early Latin players were two sons of stars of the Jim Crow age. Perucho Cepeda, who had won renown as "The Bull" in his native Puerto Rico, had refused to play in the segregated Negro Leagues. His son Orlando, dubbed "The Baby Bull," went on to star for the Giants and Cardinals. Luis Tiant Sr., a standout performer in both Cuba and the Negro Leagues, lived to see Luis Jr. win over 200 major league games and excel in the 1975 World Series.

Major Changes in Minor Leagues

As the major leagues moved slowly toward complete desegregation, blacks invaded the minor leagues. In the Northern and Western states, these athletes, a combination of youthful prospects and Negro League veterans, were greeted by a storm of insults, beanballs, and discrimination. "I learned more names than I thought we had," states Piper Davis of his treatment by fans in the Pacific Coast League. At least half a dozen blacks had to be carried off the field on stretchers after being hit by pitches between 1949 and 1951. In city after city, blacks found hotels and restaurants unwilling to serve them.

"At the same time when they signed blacks and Latins," argues

John Roseboro about his Dodger employers, "they should have made sure they would be welcome." But neither the Dodgers nor other clubs provided any special assistance for their black farmhands. Despite these conditions, blacks compiled remarkable records in league after league. In the early 1950s, blacks overcame adversity and dominated the lists of batting leaders at the Triple-A level and in many of the lower circuits as well.

In 1952, blacks began to appear on minor league clubs in the Jim Crow South. The Dallas Eagles of the Texas League, hoping to boost sagging attendance, signed former Homestead Grays pitcher Dave Hoskins to become the "Jackie Robinson of the Texas League." Hoskins took the Lone Star State by storm, attracting record crowds en route to a 22-10 record. The black pitcher posted a 2.12 ERA and also finished third in the league in batting with a .328 mark. By 1955 every Texas League club except Shreveport fielded black players.

Hoskins' performance inspired other teams throughout the South to scramble for black players. In 1953 19-year-old Henry Aaron desegregated the South Atlantic League, which included clubs in Florida and Georgia, while Bill White appeared in the Carolina League. Playing for Jacksonville—a city which seven years earlier had barred Jackie Robinson—Aaron "led the league in everything but hotel accommodations." By 1954 when the United States Supreme Court issued its historic *Brown v. Board of Education* decision ordering school desegregation, blacks had appeared in most Southern minor leagues.

The integration of the South, however, did not proceed without incidents. Black players recall these years as "an ordeal" or a "sentence" and described the South as "enemy country" or a "hellhole." In 1953 the Cotton States League barred brothers Jim and Leander Tugerson from competing. The following year, Nat Peeples broke the color line in the Southern Association, but lasted only two weeks. For the remainder of the decade, the league adhered to a whites-only policy, a strategy that contributed to the collapse of the Southern Association in 1961. As resistance to the civil-rights movement mounted in the 1950s, black players found themselves in increasingly hostile territory. Even in the pioneering Texas League, teams visiting Shreveport, Louisiana, in 1956 had to leave their black players at home due to stricter segregation laws.

In the face of these obstacles, young black stars like Aaron, Curt Flood, Frank Robinson, Bill White, and Leon Wagner overcame their frustrations "by taking it out on the ball." "What had started as a chance to test my baseball ability in a professional setting," wrote Curt Flood, "had become an obligation to test myself as a man." Throughout the 1950s, blacks appeared regularly among the league leaders of the Texas, South Atlantic, Carolina, and other circuits, advancing both their own careers and the cause of integration.

As these events unfolded in the South, the major leagues completed their long overdue integration process. The Yankees, after denying charges of racism for almost a decade, finally promoted Elston Howard to the parent club in 1955. Two more years passed before the Phillies integrated, and not until 1958 did a black player don a Tiger uniform. Thus, at the start of the 1959 season, only the Boston Red Sox, who had yet to hire either black scouts or representatives in the Caribbean, retained their Jim Crow heritage. A storm of protest arose when the Red Sox cut black infielder Elijah "Pumpsie" Green just before Opening Day, but on July 21, 1959, 12 years and 107 days after Jackie Robinson's Dodger debut, Green won promotion to the Boston club, completing the cycle of major league integration.

While integration became a reality in Organized Baseball, the Negro Leagues gradually faded into oblivion. As early as 1947, Negro League attendance, especially in cities close to National League parks, dropped precipitously. "People wanted to go Brooklynites," recalls Monarchs pitcher Hilton Smith. "Even if we were playing here in Kansas City, people wanted to go over to St. Louis to see Jackie." Negro League owners hoped to offset declining attendance by selling players to Organized Baseball, but major league teams paid what Effa Manley called "bargain basement" prices for all-star talent. In 1948 the Manleys' Newark Eagles and New York Black Yankees disbanded. The Homestead Grays severed all league connections and returned to its roots as a barnstorming unit. Without these teams the Negro National League collapsed. A reorganized 10-team Negro American League, most of whose franchises were located in minor league cities, vowed to go on, but the spread of integration quickly thinned its ranks. By 1951, the league had dwindled to six teams. Two years later, only the Birmingham Black Barons, Memphis Red Sox, Kansas City Monarchs, and Indianapolis Clowns remained.

For several years in the early 1950s, the Negro Leagues remained a breeding ground for young black talent. The New York Giants plucked Willie Mays from the roster of the Birmingham Black Barons, while the Boston Braves discovered Hank Aaron on the Indianapolis Clowns. The Kansas City Monarchs produced more than two-dozen major leaguers, including Robinson, Paige, Banks, and Howard. But for most black players, the demise of the Negro Leagues had disastrous effects. "The livelihoods, the careers, the families of 400 Negro ballplayers are in jeopardy," complained Effa Manley in 1948, "because four players were successful in getting into the major leagues." The slow pace of integration left most in a state of limbo: set adrift by their former teams, but still unwelcome in Organized Baseball. Some players like Buck Leonard and Cool Papa Bell were too old to be considered, while others like Ray Dandridge and Piper Davis found themselves relegated to the minor leagues, where outstanding records failed to win them promotion.

Throughout the 1950s the Negro American League struggled to survive, recruiting teenagers and second-rate talent for the modest four-team loop. In 1963 Kansas City hosted the 30th and last East-West All-Star Game and the following year the famed Monarchs ceased touring the nation. By 1965 the Indianapolis Clowns remained as a last vestige of Jim Crow baseball. Utilizing white as well as black players, the Clowns continued for another decade. "We are all show now," explained their owner. "We clown, clown, clown."

But the legacy of the Negro Leagues remained. Robinson and other early black players introduced new elements of speed and "tricky baseball" into the major leagues, transforming and improving the quality of play. Since 1947 blacks have led the National League in stolen bases in all but two seasons. In the American League, a black or Latin baserunner has topped the league every year since 1951 with only two exceptions. Nor did this injection of speed come at the expense of power. In the 1950s and 1960s, Hank Aaron, Willie Mays and Frank Robinson reigned as the greatest power hitters in baseball. Thus, by the 1960s, the national pastime more closely resembled the well-balanced offensive structure of the Negro Leagues than the one-dimensional power-oriented attack that had typified the all-white majors.

The demise of the Negro Leagues and the decline of segregation in the majors, however, did not end discrimination. Conditions on and off the field, in spring training and in the executive suites,

repeatedly reminded the black athletes of their second-class status. In the early 1950s all-white teams taunted their black opponents with racial insults. Blacks like Jackie and Frank Robinson, Minnie Minoso and Luke Easter repeatedly appeared among the league leaders in being hit by pitches. While black superstars like Willie Mays had little difficulty ascending to the major leagues, players of only slightly above average talent found themselves buried for years in the minors. Many observers charged that teams had imposed quotas on the number of blacks they would field at one time.

In cities like St. Louis, Washington, D. C., and, later, Baltimore, black ballplayers could not stay at hotels with their teammates. In 1954 they achieved a breakthrough of sorts when the luxury Chase Hotel in St. Louis informed Jackie Robinson and other Dodger players that they could room there, but had to refrain from using the dining room or swimming pool or loitering in the lobby. Ten years later, the hotel had removed these restrictions, but still relegated black players, according to Hank Aaron, to rooms "looking out over some old building or some green pastures or a blank wall, so nobody can see us through a window."

Blacks faced even greater discrimination each year in spring training in Florida. While all spring-training sites now accepted blacks, segregation statutes and local traditions forced them to live in all-black boarding houses far from the luxury air-conditioned hotels which accommodated white players. "The whole set-up is wrong," protested Jackie Robinson. "There is no reason why we shouldn't be able to live with our teammates." When teams traveled from place to place, blacks could not join their fellow players in restaurants. Instead they had to wait on the bus until someone brought their food out to them. Some teams attempted to reduce the problems faced by blacks. Several clubs moved to Arizona, where conditions were only moderately improved. The Dodgers built a special spring-training camp at Vero Beach where players could live together. Most organizations, however, did very little to assist their black employees.

By the time that Jackie Robinson retired in 1956, conditions had barely improved. "After 10 years of traveling in the South," he charged, "I don't think advances have been fast enough. It's my belief that baseball itself hasn't done all it can to remedy the problems faced by ... players." Over the next decade, a new generation of black players militantly demanded change. Cardinals stars Bill White, Curt Flood and Bob Gibson protested against conditions in St. Petersburg, while Aaron and other black Braves demanded changes in Bradenton. In many instances, however, significant changes awaited passage of the Civil Rights Act of 1965 barring segregation in public facilities.

The Next Generation

By 1960 Robinson, Campanella, Doby, and the cadre of Negro League veterans who had formed the vanguard of baseball integration had retired. In their wake, a second generation of black players, most of whom had never appeared in the Negro Leagues, made most Americans forget that Jim Crow baseball had ever existed, as they shattered longstanding "unbreakable" records. In 1962 black shortstop Maury Wills stole 104 bases, eclipsing Ty Cobb's 47-year-old stolen-base mark. Twelve years later, outfielder Lou Brock stole 118 bases en route to breaking Cobb's career stolen-base record as well.

In 1966 Frank Robinson, who had won the National League Most Valuable Player Award in 1961, became the first player to win that honor in both leagues when he led the Baltimore Orioles to the American League pennant. By the end of his career, Robinson had slugged 586 home runs. Both Ernie Banks and Willie McCovey also amassed more than 500 home runs during this era. On the pitcher's mound, the indomitable Bob Gibson proved himself one of the greatest strikeout pitchers in the game's history. Upon retirement, Gibson had amassed more strikeouts than anyone except Walter Johnson. Brock, Frank Robinson, Banks, McCovey, and Gibson all won election to the Hall of Fame in their first year of eligibility.

The greatness of these players notwithstanding, two other black players, Willie Mays and Hank Aaron, both of whom ironically had begun their careers in the Negro Leagues, reigned as the dominant stars of baseball in the 1950s and 1960s. Originally signed by the Birmingham Black Barons of the Negro American League, Mays had joined the New York Giants in midseason 1951, sparking their triumph in the most famous pennant race in history and winning the Rookie of the Year Award. After two years in the military, he returned in 1954 to bat a league-leading .345 and hit 41 home runs. The following year, he pounded 51 homers. A spectacular center fielder, Mays won widespread acclaim as the greatest all-around player in the history of the game. In 1969 he became only the second player in major league history to hit 600 home runs and took aim at Babe Ruth's legendary lifetime total of 714. Over the next four seasons, the aging Mays added 60 more homers before retiring, still well short of Ruth's record.

Unlike Mays, who had begun his career amidst the glare of the New York media, Hank Aaron had spent his career first in Milwaukee and later in Atlanta, far distant from the center of national publicity. Nonetheless, he steadily compiled record-threatening statistics in almost every offensive category. In 1972, at age 38, he surpassed Mays' home-run total and set his sights on Ruth. Entering the 1973 season, he needed just 41 home runs to catch the Babe. Performing under tremendous pressure and fanfare, Aaron stroked 40 homers, leaving him just one shy of the record. He tied Ruth's mark with his first swing of the 1974 season. Three days later, on April 8, 1974, a nationwide television audience watched Aaron stroke home run number 715. Babe Ruth's "unreachable" record thus fell to a man whose career had started with the Indianapolis Clowns of the Negro Leagues. When Aaron retired in 1976, he boasted 755 home runs and held major league records for games played, at-bats, runs batted in, and extra-base hits. He also ranked second to Ty Cobb in hits and runs scored.

By the 1970s black players had become an accepted part of the baseball scene and regularly ranked among the most well-known symbols of the sport. Reggie Jackson, Willie Stargell and Joe Morgan had succeeded Aaron, Mays and the Robinsons as Hall of Fame caliber superstars. Yet three decades after Jackie Robinson had broken the color barrier, racism and discrimination remained a persistent problem for baseball. Several studies demonstrated that baseball management channeled blacks into positions thought to require less thinking and fewer leadership qualities. In 1968 blacks accounted for more than half of the major league outfielders, but only 20 percent of other position players. Black catchers were rare and not even one in 10 pitchers was black. The disparity had grown greater by 1986. American-born blacks comprised 70 percent of all outfield positions but only 7 percent of all pitchers, second basemen, and third basemen. There were no American-born black catchers in the major leagues at the start of the 1986 season; the 1990s, however, saw some progress with the appearance of Charles Johnson and Lenny Webster.

While superior black players had open access to the major leagues, those of average or slightly above-average skills often found their paths blocked. "The Negro player may have to be better qualified than a white player to win the same position," argued Aaron Rosenblatt in 1967. "The undistinguished Negro player is less likely to play in the major leagues than the equally undistinguished white player." Rosenblatt demonstrated that black major leaguers on the whole batted 20 points higher than whites. As batting averages dropped, so did the proportion of blacks. This trend continued into the 1980s. A 1982 study revealed that 70 percent of all black non-pitchers were everyday starters, indicating a substantial bias against blacks filling utility or pinch-hitting roles. Statistics compiled in 1986 showed a strikingly similar pattern.

The subtle nature of this on-the-field discrimination obscured it from public controversy. The failure of baseball to provide jobs for blacks in managerial and front office positions, however, became an increasing embarrassment. In the early years of integration, baseball executives bypassed the substantial pool of experienced Negro Leaguers from consideration for managerial and coaching positions. A handful of blacks, including Sam Bankhead, Nate Moreland, Marvin Williams, and Chet Brewer managed independent, predominantly all-black teams in the minor leagues. The first generation of black major leaguers fared no better. "We bring dollars into club treasuries when we play," exclaimed Larry Doby, "but when we stop playing, our dollars stop." No major league organization hired a black pilot at any level until 1961, when the Pittsburgh Pirates placed Gene Baker at the helm of their Batavia franchise. By the mid-1960s no blacks had managed in the majors and only two had held full-time major league coaching positions. The first black umpire did not appear in the majors until 1966, when Emmett Ashford appeared in the American League.

In the final years of his life, Jackie Robinson made repeated pleas for baseball to eliminate these lingering vestiges of Jim Crow. "I'd like to live to see a black manager," he stated before a national television audience at the 1972 World Series. Nine days later he died, his dream unfulfilled. In 1975 the Cleveland Indians hired Frank Robinson to be the first black major league manager. This precedent, however, opened few new doors. Robinson lasted two-and-a-half seasons with the Indians, and later managed the San Francisco Giants, the Baltimore Orioles, and the Montreal Expos. Maury Wills and Larry Doby each had brief half-season stints as managers. After four decades of integration, only these three men had received major league managerial opportunities.

A similar situation existed in major league front offices. Only one black man, Bill Lucas of the Atlanta Braves, had served as a general manager. As late as 1982, a survey of 24 clubs (the Yankees and Red Sox refused to provide information) found that of 913 available white-collar baseball jobs, blacks held just 32 positions. Among 568 full-time major league scouts, only 15 were black. While many teams hired former players as announcers, few employed blacks in these roles. Five years later, conditions had not improved. Of the top 879 administrative positions in baseball only 17 were filled by blacks and 15 by Hispanics. Four teams in California—the Dodgers, Giants, Athletics, and Angels—accounted for almost two-thirds of the minority hiring. Ten out of fourteen American League teams, and five of twelve National League franchises had no blacks in management positions.

These shortcomings came to haunt baseball in 1987. Commissioner Peter Ueberroth had dedicated the season to the commemoration of the 40th anniversary of Jackie Robinson's major league debut. As the celebration began, Los Angeles Dodgers general manager Al Campanis, who had played with Robinson at Montreal, appeared on ABC-TV's *Nightline*. When asked about the dearth of black managers, Campanis explained that blacks "may not have some of the necessities to be, let's say, a field manager or general manager." Campanis' statement, which surely reflected the thinking of many baseball executives, evoked a storm of protest and precipitated his resignation. An embarrassed Ueberroth pledged to take action to bring more blacks into leadership positions and hired University of California sociologist Harry Edwards to facilitate the process. Fifty blacks and Latins with past or present connections to baseball created their own Minority Baseball Network to apprise blacks of employment opportunities and to lobby clubs to recruit more minorities for front office jobs.

When the controversy of 1987 had subsided, few franchises had taken significant steps to increase minority hiring. Several clubs added blacks to administrative positions, but none offered field- or general-manager positions to nonwhite candidates (although Bill White was named National League president). In 1988 Frank Robinson received his third chance to manage in the major leagues, this time with the Baltimore Orioles. At midseason 1989 Cito Gaston assumed the reins of the Toronto Blue Jays. When the squads managed by Robinson and Gaston had their initial confrontation, it marked, after 40 years of integration, the first time that two teams managed by black men had competed in a major league game. Fittingly, on the final weekend of the season, the Orioles and Blue Jays met face-to-face in a series to decide the championship of the American League Eastern Division. The spectacle offered a resounding rebuke to the shortsightedness and discrimination that continue to plague the national pastime.

By the 1993 season baseball seemed to have finally made some real progress in including minorities in its managerial ranks. The season saw five black and Hispanic field managers: Gaston, who after five years at the helm of the Blue Jays ranked as one of the most successful managers in baseball history; Felipe Alou, who led the Montreal Expos to consecutive second-place finishes; Dusty Baker, who became the winningest rookie manager ever when his San Francisco Giants won 103 games; Don Baylor, who would pilot the expansion Colorado Rockies into the playoffs in only their third year of existence in 1995; and Tony Perez, who started the season as the manager of the Cincinnati Reds.

Progress extended into other areas of hiring as well. In 1994 Leonard Coleman succeeded Bill White as National League vice-president. By 1995, 27 percent of all coaches were black or Hispanic. Minority hiring in the front office expanded to 17 percent in 1992, a level that held steady through 1994. The Houston Astros named Bob Watson their general manager, making him only the second black man to assume these responsibilities. Watson assumed the same position with the New York Yankees in 1996 and under his stewardship the club won the world championship.

These undeniable gains, however, occurred against a backdrop of continuing racial controversy. The proportion of American-born black players in baseball's major leagues dropped from one in four in the late 1960s to only one in six in the late 1980s and 1990s. In minor league and college baseball, important sources of major league talent, the percentage of African-Americans was even lower. Surveys indicated that African-Americans, who had flocked to major league ballparks in the 1950s, now accounted for one out of every fourteen fans. Allegations that Cincinnati Reds owner Marge Schott had repeatedly used racial slurs (and that other owners had

ignored these offenses) led to her suspension in 1993.

There remained no American minority owners of major league clubs. All 30 chief executive officers are white. When Watson resigned after the 1997 season, there once again were no black general managers. The surge in the hiring of minority managers that had occurred in the early 1990s also seemed to have abated.

During the early 1990s baseball undertook several initiatives to improve its image among minorities. The major leagues embraced John Young's RBI (Reviving Baseball in the Inner Cities) program, an effort to entice black youth away from other sports and back to the diamond. Attempts were also made to secure health benefits for surviving Negro League players. To achieve greater recognition for players from the Jim Crow era, the Hall of Fame instructed its Veterans Committee to honor one Negro League star a year for five years. As a result, Leon Day, Willie Wells, Bill Foster, Bullet Joe Rogan, and Turkey Stearnes were selected to enter the Hall. African-American reporter Wendell Smith was named to the "writer's wing" of the Hall of Fame. Nonetheless black athletes still remain woefully underrepresented at Cooperstown.

In 1997 baseball celebrated the 50th anniversary of what most consider its "finest moment"—Jackie Robinson's Brooklyn Dodgers debut—with extraordinary and unprecedented fanfare. Major League Baseball dedicated the season to Robinson's memory. Players wore arm patches honoring his achievements. Acting Commissioner Bud Selig announced that all teams would henceforth retire his number. On April 15 President Bill Clinton appeared between innings of a game between the Los Angeles Dodgers and the New York Mets at Shea Stadium to address the nation about Robinson's legacy.

A year later the National Baseball Hall of Fame added Larry Doby, who broke the American League color line, and *Baltimore Afro-American* sportswriter Sam Lacy to its list of honorees. At times the commemorations threatened to be overwhelmed by nostalgia and commercialism. However the 1997 festivities reminded the nation once again of its past heritage—both the shameful and the heroic—and its ongoing obligations to seek greater equality in the future.

Chapter 36

Who Was the First Black Man to Play in the Major Leagues?

By W. Zachary Malinowski

Most American baseball fans know that Jackie Robinson broke the game's modern-day color barrier in 1947, when he took the field in a Brooklyn Dodgers uniform. But baseball purists have long known that several blacks played professionally as early as the 1880s. The first, it has been thought, were two brothers, Moses Fleetwood Walker and Welday Walker, who played for the Toledo Blue Stockings in 1884.

Now, baseball historians and students of the national pastime are buzzing about the significance of William Edward White's 1879 appearance in a major league game in Providence. An investigation by baseball historians and *The Providence Journal* has determined that White is the first black, and the only former slave, to have played in the major leagues. His appearance, as a first baseman for the Providence Grays, preceded the Walker brothers by five years.

The mystery of White's background and life goes back to a plantation in rural Georgia. He was the son of a white plantation owner, a captain in the Confederate Army. His mother was the captain's servant. As a young teenager, White was sent to a private boarding school in Providence and then to Brown University, where he excelled on the baseball diamond. He got the call to play in the major leagues in 1879, in a stadium on Messer Street in the West End of Providence. On documents throughout his life, White, who had light skin, declared himself white.

On June 21, 1879, the Providence Grays played the Cleveland team at the ballpark on Messer Street. It's unclear how many fans watched the Saturday afternoon game, but the Grays regularly drew 1,000 to 1,500. Manager George Wright inserted William Edward White into the lineup at first base to replace the injured starter "Old Reliable" Joe Start. White had some big shoes to fill. Start, who had a broken finger, was a 36-year-old veteran who had batted .351 in 1878 for Chicago. White was 19, and had been playing for Brown University. But on this day he was starting for the Grays, one of the top teams in the National League that would go on to win the pennant.

White had an impressive major league debut. A *Providence Journal* article about the game raved about his play at first base. "White, first baseman of the University Nine, occupied that position for Providence, and it is needless to state that he was as expert and effective, as ever, catching some widely-thrown balls with great ease. He was apparently cool and collected throughout, and will be a valuable substitute for the unfortunate [injured Joe] Start."

The *Providence Morning Star* also raved about White's major league debut and the support from his Brown teammates. "The Varsity boys lustily cheered their favorite at times, and howled with delight when he got a safe hit in the ninth inning, as they also did his magnificent steals of second in that and the fifth inning," the newspaper reported.

White had one hit in four at-bats and two stolen bases, and he scored a run. He also had 12 putouts, and Providence won, 5-3.

The end of the *Journal* article previews the Grays' upcoming series against rival Boston. The last line in the story reads, "White has been engaged to cover first in the series." But White never played again in the major leagues. The next night, Jim O'Rourke, who had played right field in White's debut, moved to first base. O'Rourke, known as Orator Jim, played 23 years in the major leagues and was posthumously elected to the Baseball Hall of Fame.

There's no mention why White was replaced in the lineup. Was it because he was black? His skin color is never mentioned in any of the newspaper articles. Rick Stattler, a baseball historian who works for the Rhode Island Historical Society Library, said the Grays may have brought in White for the day because he was the best available player in Providence. Unlike today, there was no minor league system for calling up players.

White's career ended so abruptly is anyone's guess, Stattler said. "They may have not wanted to pay White for the week," he said. "They may have decided they wanted to have one of their regular players in the lineup. He was replaced in the lineup by real players."

Buried deep inside *Total Baseball,* among the names of more than 16,000 men who have played major league baseball, is "Bill White." The entry notes that William Edward White was born in Milner, Georgia, and is "Deceased." There's no mention of the year he was born, or when and where he died. He was little more than an obscure footnote in baseball history.

Recently, a group of amateur researchers from the Society for American Baseball Research set out to find more about White. The group's goal is to learn more about all of the 16,003 men who played major league baseball. In 344 cases, including White's, there is incomplete information on their names, birth dates and deaths. Some, such as White, have such common names that it is difficult to trace their history.

Peter Morris, a biographical researcher for the Society for American Baseball Research, set his sights on White. Morris contacted a Civil War historian. A few weeks later, the historian informed Morris that White was the son of a white farmer and a mulatto woman who had lived together in Milner. Morris drove from his home in Michigan to Milner to research White's past. His journey was the subject of a front-page story in *The Wall Street Journal.* Still, Morris left Georgia with many questions. "With William White, I haven't been able to trace him at all after 20."

The Providence Journal set out to find more about the family and how White ended up in Providence. The newspaper also wanted to learn what happened to him after 1880, the last year that historians had been able to trace his whereabouts. Census, tax and historical records show that, in 1850, White's father, Andrew Jackson White, was a farmer who owned 36 slaves in Milner, a town of about 500 about 47 miles south of Atlanta. The plantation produced cotton and corn.

White, who was known as A.J. or Jack, prospered over the next decade. In the 1860 census, the number of slaves working his fields had grown to 70 and they lived on his property in 16 slave houses.

An overseer and his wife also lived on the plantation. Shanna English, director of the Old Jail Museum & Archives, in Barnesville, Georgia., said White was the local organizer for a renowned unit of Confederate soldiers known as the Holloway Grays. The next year, records show, White fought for the South as a captain in the 37th Regiment of the Georgia Infantry. He remained a soldier until the summer of 1863.

White returned to his plantation in Milner. He also served as president of the Macon & Western Railroad.

Records from the 1870 census show that White, a lifelong bachelor, had started a family. The mother of his three children was Hannah White, a mulatto "domestic servant," who had taken on his surname. The records note that Hannah White was born in 1845 in Washington, D.C. Their three children were listed as William, nine, Norah, six, and Adelett, three. Their color was noted as mulatto. Also living with them was Hannah White's mother, Sarah White, listed as a black domestic servant. At the time of William's birth in 1860, A.J. White would have been 46; Hannah White would have been about 15.

English, the local historian, said that A.J. White probably bought Hannah White in a slave market in Washington and took her back to Georgia. Her mother, who was from Maryland, may have joined her in Georgia after the slaves were emancipated in 1863. In 1870, census records show A.J. White was 55 and Hannah White was 24. They lived in a large house in the center of Milner across from the railroad depot. In 19th-century Georgia, a white man living openly with a black woman was unheard of. But White wasn't just any white man. He owned a railroad. He was a Civil War veteran. He built Milner Town Hall and Milner Baptist Church. 'He was so powerful and such a big presence in that community, he just did what he wanted to do,' English said.

Apparently, White felt that post-Civil War Georgia was not the best place for his children. In the fall of 1874, William Edward White, who was known as Eddie in Milner, and his little sister, Nora, boarded a train for Providence. They enrolled as boarders at the Friends Boarding School on Hope Street in Providence. The school would later become the Moses Brown School.

On the June 1, 1875, Rhode Island census, a list of 119 boarding students from the school were recorded. Among them were William E. White, 14, and Anna Nora White, 11, both from Georgia. The Moses Brown School has records showing that the youngest daughter, Sarah Adelaide White, followed her brother and sister to the boarding school.

On June 13, 1877, A.J. White drafted a will in Pike County, Georgia, that was extraordinary for the time. In it, he left his "trusty Servant Hannah White" $3,000 and all of his property. The will also recognizes William Edward White and his two sisters and orders the executors of the will "to support them comfortably and to Educate them." It continues, "I desire the two Eldest now at school in the North, to complete the cause so as to become thoroughly proficient in all the branches taught in that school, and I desire the youngest to be given similar advantages."

Two years later, in the spring of 1879, William E. White graduated from the Friends Boarding School. He was 18 or 19.

William E. White's skills on the baseball diamond had not gone unnoticed in Providence. White was starting at first base for the Brown University baseball team during his senior year of high school. A few weeks after graduation, White was in the lineup for the Providence Grays.

Following his major league debut, White returned to Brown and continued playing for the college team. The team played colleges such as Harvard, Amherst, Yale, and Princeton. In March of 1880, the team played three games in Washington, D.C., and Baltimore. In several accounts of the games, White's "brilliant" play or game is mentioned. Yet in the spring of 1880, the box scores show that the sure-handed White had problems fielding the ball. On May 5, 1880, he made four errors in a 16-2 loss to Princeton. In the next three games, he made six more errors. A few days later, he was moved to right field.

The 1880 Providence City Directory shows that White was living at a boarding house at 439 Benefit Street, near the corner of Wickenden Street on the city's East Side. The next year, 1881, White had moved to another boarding house nearby at 29 Benevolent Street. Records from Brown show that White was a student from 1879 through 1881: he never graduated. The last local entry for William E. White comes from the 1882 Providence City Directory. He is listed as living at 40 Broadway and working as a draftsman at 21 Butler Exchange in Providence.

A search through archives at Moses Brown School turned up an index card with the typed name, "White, William E." Beneath his name is his hometown, Milner, Georgia, crossed out in pencil. The forwarding address is 615 North Wells Street, Chicago. The entry for the new address does not include a date. In the federal censuses from 1900 and 1910, William E. White appears in Chicago with his wife and daughters. In 1900, White, 39, noted that he was born in Rhode Island in 1860. He was employed as a bookkeeper, and he lived with his wife, Hattie, and two daughters, five and three. The race of White and his family was listed as white.

In the 1910 census, White and his family were still living in Chicago. A third daughter, two, had joined the family. He was a draftsman, the same job that the William E. White in Providence had 28 years earlier. By 1920, records show William E. White had left the household. Hattie White is listed as living with her three daughters. She noted that she was married, but there was no man living in her house. There was a William White in the 1920 census living in Chicago. He was 60 years old, which would have been the same age of William E. White. He said that he was a widower and living alone, and that his parents were born in Georgia. His color? Black.

Back in Georgia, A.J. White, William's father, ran into hard times, filed for bankruptcy and died from pneumonia in 1888. He is buried in the Milner Baptist Cemetery, next door to the church he built. White's mother, Hannah White, moved to Atlanta and worked as a seamstress for the next 20 years. She then returned to Milner and worked as a maid for Dr. A.H. Huckaby. Each Sunday, she attended services at the Milner Baptist Church. She sat in the back row, the only non-white person in the church. She died on January 20, 1931.

Shanna English, the historian in Barnesville, said she has spoken to several elderly women who remembered Hannah White attending services each week at the white church. Upon her death, Hannah White was going to be buried next to A.J. White, but an elderly white "spinster" objected to the burial of a black woman in a cemetery for whites, English said. Instead, Hannah White was buried in an unmarked grave in the Old Greater Spring Hill Cemetery, the town's black cemetery.

(First appeared in The Providence Journal, *February 15, 2004. Printed with permission,* The Providence Journal, *2004)*

<table>
<tr><td>Chapter 37</td><td>Rival Leagues</td></tr>
</table>

The Chicago Feds
Chicago scored a coup when it enticed Joe Tinker (front row, center) to accept $12,000 to jump from the Cubs to the new Federal League.

By Harold Dellinger

The history of major league baseball is much more than the combined history of the National League and the American League, each of which began its existence as a "rival league." That history also includes the story of the eleven primary attempts, some successful and some not, to form leagues for whom major league status was claimed or would later be claimed. The earliest such attempt predates "the major leagues" as understood by the majority of baseball fans—that is, the 1876 founding of the National League—while the most recent such attempt triggered the expansion era that has seen the total of big league clubs expand from 16 to 30.

The National Association (1871-1875)

The "National Association of Professional Base Ball Players" was organized in New York City on March 17, 1871, by representatives of the ten leading professional clubs in the country. Among the business discussed was the adoption of a constitution similar to that of the National Association of Base Ball Players, which had ruled both professional and amateur teams and players in years prior to 1871. This new National Association is properly considered the first professional league.

The National Association (NA) elected as its first president United States Marshal James W. Kerns, the representative of the Philadelphia team. Upon payment of a $10 fee, clubs were admitted from Troy, Boston, New York, Philadelphia, Cleveland, Chicago, and Washington, plus Rockford, Illinois and Fort Wayne, Indiana. Several clubs did not join because the $10 fee, which was to be used to purchase a championship banner, seemed excessive.

League rules provided that each club was to arrange a series of five games with each other club. The club winning the most series would be declared the champion. A "championship committee" was to decide disputes between clubs. A procedure was established to decide cases involving players who signed with two or more clubs ("revolvers").

The most controversial discussions concerned the admission price. Harry Wright, the Boston representative, favored a higher rate. He said, "We must make the games worth witnessing, and there will be no fault found with the price of admission. A good game is worth 50 cents, a poor one is dear at 25 cents." In the end each club was allowed to set its own admission price, and the better clubs began demanding guarantees when playing less prosperous clubs.

The first National Association game was played at Fort Wayne on May 4, 1871, with the home team beating Cleveland 2-0. Most of the National Association teams had operated in 1870 and earlier seasons, and had nuclei of teams signed and ready to play. Most of the veteran players in the country found spots with National Association teams. Dickey Pearce, for instance, who was already a 13-year professional at age 35, played with New York. Joe Start, the premier first baseman of the day, joined the same club. Veterans

George Wright and Harry Schafer joined Harry Wright, the architect of the famous Cincinnati team of 1869-1870, on the Boston team. Chicago veterans included Mart King, James Wood, and Joe Simmons. Levi Meyerle and Al Reach played for Philadelphia.

Among the young players destined to become professional stars were pitcher Al Spalding and second baseman Roscoe Barnes. Barnes became the most adept practitioner of the fair-foul hit whereby any batted ball, not just those beyond first and third bases, that landed fair and then went foul was considered a fair hit. Adrian Anson, whose playing career would stretch to 1897, played several positions for Rockford in 1871 before moving on to Philadelphia.

The 1871 championship season was plagued by a disturbing number of cancellations, forfeits, and controversy relating to the standings. Boston had won as many games but fewer series than Philadelphia and Chicago when the "Championship Committee" decided that the winner of the October 30 Philadelphia-Chicago game would be declared the champion. The Chicago team had lost all their equipment in the great Chicago fire, which had begun on October 8, and played the game in partial uniforms and the uniforms of several other clubs. Some players wore black dress hats instead of baseball caps. Philadelphia won the game 4-1 and claimed the championship with a 22-7 record. The Philadelphia manager, Hicks Hayhurst, asked Harry Wright if he could suggest where the championship banner should be placed. The very controlled response of Wright was that perhaps it should be displayed in the Philadelphia clubhouse instead of the saloon where it usually resided.

Harry Wright's Boston club won the four National Association championships from 1872 to 1875 and so dominated the league that it became known as "Harry Wright's League." In 1875 the Boston team overwhelmed the opposition with a 71-8 record. One of the tailenders, the Brooklyn Atlantics, posted only a 2-42 record. The unequal talents of National Association teams plagued the league during its entire existence. The irregular schedule also caused many problems, and even determining how many games were won and lost by the various teams became, and has remained, almost impossible. Third baseman Robert Ferguson served as president of the National Association from 1872 through 1875.

The Boston team, of course, became the best-paid team in the league with salaries reaching levels not seen again until the mid-eighties. The players on the Boston team, however, certainly did earn their pay. Pitcher Al Spalding is credited by modern research with 204 wins in five National Association seasons, including a 54-5 mark in 1875. Only four other pitchers, including Bobby Matthews, posted as many as 100 National Association wins. Ross Barnes of Boston won the National Association batting championship for the 1872 and 1873 seasons, and his career National Association batting average is calculated at .390. Other National Association batting champions were Levi Meyerle in 1871 and 1874 and Deacon White in 1875. Batting averages were actually seldom compiled during the National Association era, and hitters were ranked by hits per game (HPG). Barnes' league-leading 1.79 HPG in 1875 made him the champion in his own day, but his average that year of .364 trailed his teammate White by three points. Barnes also became the first National League (NL) batting champion in 1876 before the fair-foul hit was abolished.

Several players, including Barnes, became so deadly with the fair-foul hit that an unusual rule change was made before the 1874 season in an attempt to balance the defense with the offense. Because of the possibility of the fair-foul hit, the first baseman and the third baseman had to play right on the foul lines, leaving huge defensive gaps in the rest of the infield. Henry Chadwick's solution, to which "there is not a reasonable objection that can be brought against it," was to add a tenth player, called the "right stop," to be stationed between first and second bases. However "reasonable" it may have been, after trial in non-championship contests Chadwick's proposal was not adopted by the National Association.

The Boston and Philadelphia teams made special schedule arrangements in 1874 to allow them to play their required games and still make a midseason trip to England. They left on the steamship *Ohio* on July 16 and arrived 11 days later. Games were played between the two teams in places like London, Liverpool, Sheffield, and Manchester, with the Boston club winning 8 of the 14 matches. The hopes of big attendance were not realized and losses of $3,000 for the trip were reported, but both clubs were successful enough at home to cover the losses. The Boston and Philadelphia teams did not return to the United States until September 9.

In the 1875 National Association season, the first "sale" of baseball players occurred, involving the two Philadelphia teams in the league that season. The Philadelphia Athletics paid the officials of the Philadelphia Centennials team to release their two best players, Bill Craver and George Bechtel, so that the Athletics might sign them and the City of Brotherly Love might thus mount a challenge to Boston for the championship. The Centennials then disbanded and the Athletics finished 15 games behind Boston's Red Stockings.

Some 23 clubs played one or more seasons in the National Association. The Philadelphia, Boston and New York clubs were charter members of the National Association and the only three clubs to play all five seasons. Chicago, a charter member, missed two seasons as a result of the great fire but played three seasons in the National Association. The other charter members—Rockford, Washington (Olympics), Troy, and Cleveland—lasted only one or two seasons. In addition to the Brooklyn Eckfords, a team that played in parts of the 1871 and 1872 campaigns, a second venerable Brooklyn team—the Atlantics, the powerhouse of the mid-1860s—participated in four National Association seasons. Besides the Athletics and Centennials, Philadelphia provided a third team—the White Stockings or "Pearls"—for the 1873 through 1875 seasons. A second Washington club played three National Association seasons, and the famous Nationals, who had won fame with a Western Tour in 1867, gave their name to an NA team for 1872. Two separate Baltimore teams—the Lord Baltimores and the Marylands—played, respectively, three and one seasons. Two St. Louis teams, neither very competent, were entered in 1875. A team from Hartford was entered in 1874 and 1875. Teams from Elizabeth, New Jersey; New Haven, Connecticut; Middletown, Connecticut; and Keokuk, Iowa, each entered unsuccessfully in one National Association season.

The National Association was easily supplanted by the newly formed National League after the 1875 season. The problems associated with scheduling and the unequal quality of opposition, because of the easy membership rules, made the stronger clubs seek a better way of doing business. Periodic problems with gamblers and rowdyism were also factors in the demise of the National Association. Even Harry Wright of Boston, whose Red Stockings had been raided of their "big four" (Spalding, Barnes, White, and Cal McVey) by the National League's godfather, William Hulbert of Chicago, entered his club in Hulbert's new league.

The remnants of the National Association met in March 1876

to organize for another season, but the attempt was unsuccessful. The National Association quietly passed from the scene.

The International Association and the National Association (1877-1880)

The International Association and its successor organization, the National Association (IA and NA, respectively), survived four years independent of the National League. The organization offered independent clubs of the era some protection against a common enemy—the National League—whose exclusiveness and aggressiveness offended and endangered the independents.

The "International Association of Professional Base Ball Players" was organized February 20, 1877, in Pittsburgh. The meeting had been called by L.C. Waite, secretary of the St. Louis Red Stockings team. Waite had circulated letters urging that the 50 or so professional clubs that were not members of the NL form an organization to promote and protect their interests. Waite believed the National League was trying to monopolize baseball to the detriment of clubs not important enough or located in cities not big enough to join the NL.

Delegates from 17 clubs attended the initial International Association meeting. A loosely formed body of outside clubs, much resembling the old National Association, was put together with features such as a $10 membership fee and a 25-cent admission price. There was no limit on the number of clubs that could enter, nor was there any standard by which the quality of the entrant could be judged. William "Candy" Cummings, a pitcher and the probable inventor of the curveball, was elected president. James A. Williams of Columbus, Ohio, became secretary-treasurer. He would hold this position for all four years that the IA/NA existed.

To compete for the championship of the International Association, teams were required to pay an extra $15 fee and schedule a set number of games against clubs similarly enrolled. Paying the extra fee were teams from London, Ontario; Columbus, Ohio; Pittsburgh, Pennsylvania; Lynn, Massachusetts; Guelph, Ontario; Manchester, New Hampshire; and Rochester, New York. Some 16 other clubs became members of the International Association but did not compete for the championship.

Only a portion of the games played each year by IA teams would count toward the championship. In practice, each club secretary would arrange games with each other club secretary to meet that year's championship requirement. There would also be other games with International Association teams that would not count toward the championship plus games versus other independent teams, National League teams, and other exhibition and "pickup" games. This was a preferred way of doing business for many professional clubs who felt they were better off playing clubs in their own vicinity more often and avoiding heavy travel expenses.

Clearly hoping to subvert a strong organization of outside clubs, the NL set up its own organization of independent clubs that came to be called the League Alliance. To member clubs of the League Alliance, the NL offered the protection of its players, plus certain other nebulous benefits. About 30 clubs were enrolled as members of the League Alliance in 1877.

The London, Ontario, team won the first International Association championship with a 14-4 record. Fred Goldsmith pitched every championship game for London and a good many of the non-championship games. IA president Candy Cummings posted only a 1-7 record for the Lynn team. The Guelph and Lynn teams failed to finish the season.

Many prominent players played in the International Association, including Mike Kelly, Joe Hornung, Lou Say, Pud Galvin, Ned Williamson, John M. Ward, and in later years Jack Glasscock, Jake Knowdell and Davey Force. Several believed the International Association was better for players than the National League. Force urged his club not to join the National League because "there is nothing in it."

J.W. Whitney of Rochester, New York, was elected president of the International Association for the 1878 season. Clubs from 13 cities enrolled for the championship—Rochester, New York; Utica, New York; London, Ontario; Pittsburgh, Pennsylvania; Manchester, New Hampshire; Lynn, Massachusetts; Buffalo, New York; Syracuse, New York; Binghamton, New York; Hornellsville, New York; New Bedford, Massachusetts; Lowell, Massachusetts; and Springfield, Massachusetts. New Bedford apparently never played a game and was replaced by New Haven, Connecticut, about May 8. On May 20 New Haven transferred to Hartford, Connecticut. On June 4 the Lynn club transferred to Worcester, Massachusetts. On June 8 the Pittsburgh club disbanded. On June 20 the Hartford club was expelled for not paying the visiting Buffalo club its share of the receipts. On July 19 the Binghamton club disbanded. On August 21 the Hornellsville and London teams disbanded. One story had the London team trying to enter the NL, but the disbandment may have been related to allegations of crooked play by some of the London players. The Rochester and Worcester teams disbanded in early October. Only six of the original thirteen International Association clubs finished the season.

Buffalo was eventually awarded the 1878 International Association championship, although not without some controversy. By one count, Syracuse had a 27-10 record and Buffalo a 32-12 record. But, as was usually done, games played against clubs that didn't finish the season were thrown out. Thus by another count Buffalo finished with a 27-10 record to 26-10 for Syracuse.

If the IA was a minor league—a very debatable proposition—then the championship Buffalo club was one of the very best minor league clubs ever put together. Every player on the team had played or would play in the major leagues, some with distinction such as Jim Galvin and Davey Force. Counting all its games, the Buffalo team compiled an 81-32 record, including a 10-7 record against National League teams. Galvin pitched 92 complete games out of 101 games started and totaled approximately 900 innings pitched. The Buffalo club was admitted into the NL for the 1879 season, where it conducted itself capably, finishing in third place. The Syracuse team was also admitted into the NL for the 1879 season.

The International Association changed its name to the "National Base-Ball Association" for the season of 1879. The name change was prompted by the fact that no Canadian clubs signed up for the new season. Nine clubs enrolled for the championship season, representing Utica, New York; Worcester, Massachusetts; Manchester, New Hampshire; Springfield, Massachusetts; New Bedford, Massachusetts; Holyoke, Massachusetts; Washington, D.C.; and two clubs from Albany, New York. L.J. Powers of Springfield served as president.

On May 21 one of the Albany clubs transferred to Rochester, New York. The Manchester club disbanded on July 5. Utica disbanded on July 12, followed very late in the season by Springfield and Rochester. If games with disbanded teams had been thrown out, as in the previous year, Holyoke with a 19-10 record would have been tied with Albany with a 19-11 record for the championship. The number of games won, not the percentage of games

won, was used to determine champions. The games against disbanded teams were not thrown out, however, and the championship was awarded to Albany with a 27-13 record over Holyoke with a 23-16 record.

For the 1880 season, the National Association enrolled clubs from only three cities—Washington, Albany, and Baltimore. Some 17 other independent clubs were affiliated with the NA but were not involved in the championship race. H.W. Garfield of Albany served as the last president of the National Association.

The Baltimore club played only two or three games before disbanding. Several of the Baltimore players were shifted to Rochester, which was admitted to membership. The Albany club disbanded about July 20 and Rochester quit in early September. The Washington club had a 27-12 record, and since it was the only team remaining, it must be considered the National Association champion.

The American Association (1882-1891)

The "American Association of Base-Ball Clubs" was formally organized November 2, 1881, in meetings at Cincinnati. The NL constitution was adopted with modifications "affording more liberal conditions to cities and players." A fixed guarantee was adopted and each club was given the right to set the admission price. H.D. McKnight of Pittsburgh was elected president and James Williams of Columbus, Ohio, was elected secretary. The secretary was to be paid a fixed salary.

Clubs were admitted to the American Association (AA) from Brooklyn, Philadelphia, Cincinnati, St. Louis, Pittsburgh, and Louisville. Applicants from Boston and New York were not admitted but were encouraged to apply again when better arrangements had been made. The Brooklyn franchise withdrew before the season began, and a team was admitted from Baltimore to fill a sixth spot. The six teams were placed in cities that did not challenge existing NL teams.

The American Association became known as the "Beer and Whiskey League" because it seemed most of the owners were involved in the production or sale of beer and other alcohols. Chris Von der Ahe, backer of the St. Louis franchise, was said to have become interested in baseball because he noticed that baseball fans drank a lot of beer. Von der Ahe owned a saloon near the St. Louis ballpark and had operated an independent team run on the cooperative plan in St. Louis during the 1881 season. The Baltimore team was backed by Harry Von der Horst, a brewer. The Louisville backers included the treasurer of the Kentucky Malting Company. In the spring of 1882, the American Association abrogated an earlier temporary rule against the sale of liquor at the ballpark.

That there was room for a new league was evident to most observers. Louisville had been without professional baseball since being removed in 1877 because of financial problems in the wake of a game-fixing scandal and expulsion of four of its players. St. Louis had been without a regular league team for the same period of time because of disputes over the sale of liquor at the ballpark. New York and Philadelphia were open because their teams had been expelled in 1876. Hulbert had "vacated" the Cincinnati franchise because of the continued sale of liquor on the grounds of the ballpark. The presence of several prime cities without professional baseball plus the greatly expanding urban population made a new league look like a promising possibility.

The NL adopted a pose of indifference toward the new league. Public statements about the AA by the NL were not inflammatory or warlike. Teams from the two leagues even played about 20 exhibition games in the spring of 1882. Unfortunately the NL chose to be indifferent about contracts signed with AA clubs. Sam Wise and John "Dasher" Troy had played for the Detroit NL club in 1881. Neither had been reserved for 1882. Wise signed with the Cincinnati AA club and Troy with the Philadelphia AA club. Then Wise and Troy signed respectively with the Boston and New York clubs of the NL and played there in 1882. The AA took the Wise case to court but failed to achieve the restraining order they sought. In retaliation the American Association, in May of 1882, decided on a strategy of "non-intercourse" with the National League. There was to be no relationship with the National League, and National League reserve lists were to be ignored.

Despite the loss of a few players, the AA managed to complete its schedule with Cincinnati winning the championship of the first season. The Cincinnati team attempted to engage in a postseason series with the NL champion but was stopped by President McKnight's orders enforcing the policy of "non-intercourse." During the season AA representatives managed to sign at least 13 NL players to options for their services in the 1883 season. The new tactic failed when most of the players failed to follow through. Detroit catcher Charlie Bennett signed such an option with Pittsburgh but then signed again with Detroit for 1883. The AA lost the case in court because an option was a preliminary agreement, not a final one.

The American Association enjoyed success in its first season. All six teams were believed to have made a profit, with Cincinnati reporting profits of $15,000. Clubs in New York and Columbus, Ohio, were added for the 1883 season. The National League dropped two of its weaker clubs, Troy and Worcester, and placed new clubs in Philadelphia and New York. NL clubs then challenged AA clubs in those two important cities.

On February 17, 1883, a joint conference or "Harmony Conference" was held in New York City with representatives of the American Association, the National League and the new Northwestern League present. The result was a "National Agreement" or "Tripartite Agreement" between the three leagues. The Tripartite Agreement provided that the three leagues would honor each other's reserve, suspension, and expulsion lists. This was the first official agreement to include provision for the reserve list. Another new feature was the creation of an arbitration committee to settle disputes between the leagues. The Northwestern League and National League endorsed the Tripartite Agreement immediately, and the American Association added its approval about a month later.

Philadelphia won the 1883 AA championship by one game over St. Louis. The eight-club format proved very successful, and most clubs reported substantial profits. Both Philadelphia and St. Louis reported profits of over $50,000. Baltimore and Cincinnati had profits in the range of $20,000 to $30,000. Two other clubs broke even, and two lost small amounts.

The "official" batting champion was Tom Mansell of the St. Louis Browns, with a .402 batting average compiled, however, in less than 30 games. Modern reference books credit Ed Swartwood of the Allegheny Club of Pittsburgh, with a .357 batting average in 94 games, as the batting champion.

In 1884 the American Association was an active participant and loser in the war with the Union Association. Probably the most ill advised move of the year was the expansion of the AA into an additional four cities, namely Toledo, Indianapolis, Washington, and

Brooklyn. With the National League operating eight teams and the Union Association with thirteen teams, there was great demand for players. *The Sporting Life* of Philadelphia remarked, "The ballplayer who fails to get employment ... had better give up all idea of ever going into the business." Two of the players who finally got their chance were the brothers Moses ("Fleet") and Welday Walker, who played part of the 1884 season with the Toledo American Association club. They were the first blacks to play in the major leagues and the last until Jackie Robinson in 1947.

Most AA clubs lost substantial amounts of money. New York reported losses of $15,000 despite winning the championship with a 75-32 record. Washington disbanded after the games of August 2, owing some $1,500 in unpaid player salaries. Richmond withdrew from the Eastern League and entered the American Association in its place. The *Spalding Guide* later assessed the 1884 AA twelve-club experiment as follows: "The Association tried the experiment of a twelve league circuit but under circumstances that insured failure from the start. ... The clubs were so unevenly matched and so badly managed that the failure of the experiment was a certainty."

For the 1885 season the American Association reduced back to eight clubs by dropping the franchises in Richmond, Toledo, Columbus, and Indianapolis. New trouble with the National League developed over the transfer of pitcher Tim Keefe from the New York AA club to the New York NL club. It had been rumored that the New York clubs were both owned by the same parties.

On December 8, 1885, the AA canceled the franchise of the New York club because of its subservient relationship to the NL. A new Washington club was admitted in its place. Unknown to the American Association owners, New York financier Erastus Wiman had just purchased the New York American Association franchise for a reported $25,000. Wiman went to court to prevent the expulsion. The New York franchise was readmitted on December 28, and the new Washington club was dropped.

The St. Louis team dominated the AA from 1885 to 1888, winning four consecutive championships. In each of those years they engaged in a World Championship Series with the National League winner, winning one series, tying one series, and losing two.

The heart of these great St. Louis teams was a cast of steady everyday players plus talented young pitchers. The regular players included Charles Comiskey, James "Tip" O'Neill, Curt Welch, Arlie Latham, A.J. "Doc" Bushong, and Tommy McCarthy. O'Neill hit an amazing "official" .492 in 1887, the only season in which a fourth strike was allowed and bases on balls were counted as hits. Modern reference works list O'Neill with a .485 average, reduced to .435 if his 50 bases on balls are discounted.

The St. Louis pitchers included Bob Caruthers, who won 40, 30 and 29 games before being traded away to Brooklyn prior to the 1888 season. Nat Hudson won 25 games one season before fading to 3 the next season. David Foutz won 114 games in four seasons, including 41 in 1886. Charles "Silver" King won 112 games in three seasons, including 45 in 1888.

Prior to the 1886 season, the owner of the New York team, Erastus Wiman, donated to the American Association a trophy to be given to the league champion each year. The "Wiman Trophy" was twenty inches high, apparently silver, and featured a ballplayer about to strike. The model for the trophy was "Chief" Roseman of the New York team. St. Louis got to keep the trophy after its string of consecutive championships.

In addition to the talented players of the St. Louis team, many

other stars of the '80s and early '90s played all or part of their careers in the AA. Pitcher Guy Hecker of Louisville, one of the early stars of the league and a 52-game winner in 1884, played eight years in the AA. Hall of Famer Tim Keefe pitched two seasons with New York in the AA, winning 41 and 37 games. Pitcher Will White of Cincinnati, the first player to wear eyeglasses, twice won more than 40 games in a season. Matt Kilroy of Baltimore struck out 513 batters in 1886 and won 46 games in 1887. Pete Browning averaged .349 for a 13-year career that included 8 spent with Louisville of the AA. Herman Long and Billy Hamilton were among those young players whose careers began in the American Association although reaching full flower in the National League.

The AA experienced successful seasons through the 1888 season, with high attendance and substantial profits. In 1886 every AA club showed a profit except the New York club. Some of the clubs reported profits approaching $100,000. Relationships with the NL were generally peaceful, although a few minor player disputes occurred. There were only three franchise shifts from 1886 to 1888. After the 1886 season the Pittsburgh club withdrew and entered the NL, citing a desire to engage in better business practices. Cleveland was admitted in Pittsburgh's place. After the 1887 season the New York franchise withdrew and a club was placed in Kansas City. The Cleveland team dropped out after the 1888 season and a Columbus team was admitted in its place.

Brooklyn won the 1889 AA championship but lost the World Series to the New York NL team. Louisville managed to lose 111 games during the season and became the first professional team to lose over 100 games in a season. Considerable tensions developed within the AA, perhaps related to schemes by Von der Ahe and others to consolidate with the NL into one 12-club circuit. On another level the tensions were related to a series of disputes relating to the treatment of the members of a "combine" within the league versus the treatment of non-combine clubs. The "combine" was said to have been composed of the owners of the St. Louis, Louisville, Columbus, and Philadelphia clubs. Particularly galling was a series of rulings on forfeits and called games that went against the non-combine clubs. Henry Chadwick stated that in 1889 the AA "saw the culmination of its career and that of its usefulness ... [as] the combine in its ranks ... gave it its death blow."

When the American Association met in New York on November 13, 1889, matters had deteriorated greatly. The dispute centered on the election of the AA president. Zach Phelps of Louisville was the "combine candidate." L.C. Krauthoff of Kansas City was the candidate of the other clubs. After two days and over forty ballots, the candidates remained deadlocked with four votes apiece. In disgust the Brooklyn and Cincinnati clubs resigned their AA memberships, followed within days by the Kansas City and Baltimore clubs. Brooklyn and Cincinnati sought and secured NL franchises for 1890 while Kansas City returned to the Western Association and Baltimore to the Eastern League.

New AA franchises were placed in Rochester, Syracuse and Toledo, and a new club was organized in Brooklyn. The first three teams brought in their players from the previous season, but the new Brooklyn team had to start from scratch. In addition, the AA lost the players from its 1889 Brooklyn, Cincinnati, Kansas City, and Baltimore teams, plus several others, to the new Players League.

Some of the AA players did not take transfer from league to league without question. One notable case involved infielder John Pickett of Kansas City. The Kansas City AA club had purchased Pickett's contract from St. Paul with his approval in May 1889 for

a reported $3,500. He signed with Kansas City for 1890 but when the club dropped out of the AA, Pickett announced that since the club was now in the minor leagues, he would break the agreement. He did so by signing with the Players League. Although he was enjoined by the courts from playing for anybody except Kansas City, he nevertheless played for Philadelphia of the Players League, where the court had no jurisdiction.

Louisville was the surprise winner of the 1890 AA championship. The tail-end Louisville club of the previous season lost fewer men to the Players League than the other AA clubs and, with the addition of several youngsters, managed to come out on top of the greatly weakened league. Payrolls were down from about $35,000 per club in 1889 to $20,000 per club in 1890. Brooklyn was plagued by poor attendance all season, and beginning with the games of August 27 it was replaced by Baltimore. Every team in the Association was thought to have lost money in 1890 except perhaps Louisville. Brooklyn of the National League engaged the Louisville team in what proved to be the last of the early World Series matches. Each team won three games before the match was called because of bad weather and public indifference. Von der Ahe and others apparently attempted a consolidation with the Players League, but the effort failed.

Negotiations throughout the fall of 1890 finally produced a settlement of the Players League war. The AA part of the agreement allowed the dropping of the Toledo, Rochester, and Syracuse franchises, replacing them with franchises in Boston and Washington. A Chicago franchise was planned but did not materialize, and a team was located in Cincinnati. All players were to return to the club that had employed them in 1889. A new National Agreement between the National League, American Association, and Western Association was signed, with provision for a National Board to rule on disputes between leagues and teams.

The peace did not last long. Louis Bierbauer and Harry Stovey had both played for Philadelphia of the AA in 1889. Both were highly regarded, and Stovey had hit as high as .404 in 1884. Bierbauer and Stovey had played for the Brooklyn and Boston Players League teams in 1890. Under terms of the peace agreement, each would have been returned to Philadelphia for the 1891 season, but that team mistakenly failed to reserve them properly. Stovey signed with the Boston National League team and Bierbauer with the Pittsburgh NL team. The latter team became known as the "Pirates" as a result of the affair. On February 14, 1891, the newly formed National Board ruled the two players could stay with the National League clubs.

Three days later, the AA withdrew from the National Agreement and a new war was on. Within days the National Board released all AA players from reservation and the National League began signing AA players. Mark Baldwin, a pitcher for Columbus in 1889, signed with Pittsburgh of the NL for 1891. He was accused by Von der Ahe of inducing St. Louis players to jump and was twice arrested on conspiracy charges. The *Spalding Guide* attributed the problems again to the American Association "combine" and stated, "The revolt ... was simply a crime, as it was a blow against the very life of the professional organizations at large—the protective compact of the National Agreement."

As a result of the American Association resignation from the National Agreement, the Western Association and a rejuvenated Eastern Association were admitted as "major leagues" for the season of 1891. The plans were that these two leagues would eventually replace the AA and stand on almost equal footing with the NL. The

NL, though, would always be superior. "That is to say, that the National League will stand forth as the leader in the matter of catering exclusively for the better class of professional club patrons."

The new Boston team won the 1891 American Association championship by 8-1/2 games over St. Louis. Several AA players jumped to the NL before the season ended, including Silver King, who ended up with Chicago. Phil Ehret and Harry Raymond of Louisville jumped to Omaha of the Western Association in late July. In early August Tom Vickery and Bill Schriver joined Anson's Chicago team. Milwaukee, one of the Western Association stalwarts, replaced Cincinnati in the American Association on August 18. The Cincinnati owners, who included Von der Ahe, retained the franchise, which was transferred to Milwaukee only for the remainder of the season. The defection of Milwaukee delayed peace negotiations, which had begun in July.

The AA met in Chicago on October 22, 1891, and admitted a new Chicago club into the league. The evidence is that Von der Ahe supplied most of the money. An attempt was made to replace Louisville with a Kansas City team, but that was not accomplished.

On December 15-18, 1891, the National League and the American Association held a joint meeting in Indianapolis. Details had been worked out earlier, and after some minor hurdles were removed, an agreement was reached. A single league, to be officially called the National League and American Association of Professional Base Ball Clubs, was formed. AA teams in Baltimore, St. Louis, Washington, and Louisville were joined with the existing eight NL clubs to form a single twelve-club league. The remaining five AA clubs, including the new Chicago club, were bought out for a total of approximately $130,000, with the debt assumed by the new league. A new split-season plan was adopted, beginning with the 1892 season. All player contracts were to be honored in full.

The *Spalding Guide* emphasized the importance of the amalgamation of the leagues as follows:

"Out of evil cometh good," says Scripture, and the saying is emphasized by the eventual outcome of the revolutionary period of 1890 and '91, in the form of the establishment of a new government for the fraternity at large, in the organization of the new twelve-club League as the successor both of the old National League and the late American Association. The compensating result ... has been the adoption of a system of professional club business on what may be regarded as true business principles, something neither of the old organizations fully enjoyed before. From this time forth we say, "Let the dead past bury its dead." Give the new era in professional baseball history a chance to show that it is an era of coming prosperity for the game at large.

The Union Association (1884)

The Union Association operated in the season of 1884 and involved itself in a spirited war with the National League and the American Association over the basic issues of the reserve rule and territorial rights.

The "Union Association of Professional Baseball Clubs" was organized in Pittsburgh on September 12, 1883. Delegates from eight cities were present, and communications from four more cities were read. H.B. Bennett of Washington, D.C., was elected president and among the most important business was the unanimous adoption of the following:

Resolved, that while we recognize the validity of all contracts made by the League and American Association, we cannot recognize any agreement whereby any number of ball-players may be reserved for any club for any time beyond the terms of their contract with such club.

The Union Association (UA) adopted, with other minor changes, the American Association constitution and chose the lively Wright and Ditson baseball for 1884 play.

"We are certain to succeed," said UA Secretary W. W. White. He added, "Our refusal to be bound by the eleven-man reserve rule assures us of the good will of every player in the country." Detractors pointed out that two major leagues were already in the field and almost no large city was without a major league team.

The UA grew out of the plans of promoter James Jackson to form a new major league in opposition to the reserve rule. "Projector" Jackson's new major league was to be called the American League. Jackson had lost control of his idea by the time of the initial Union Association meeting but was present, seeking a New York City franchise. He was not successful in that endeavor and was not further connected with the UA.

Leading directly to the events of 1884 was the prosperity of the baseball season of 1883. The reserve rule and the accompanying lack of competition for players kept salaries at a tolerable level. The American Association and National League had enjoyed high attendance and the inaugural season of the minor Northwestern League had also been successful, and expectations were that the success could be duplicated in future seasons. The Northwestern League, located in medium-sized cities of what we now call the Midwest, seemed secure in its role as the only minor league in a three-way or "Tripartite Agreement" with the two major leagues. Tripartite Agreement members enjoyed rights of reserve and protection of their territory. Baseball was suddenly good business in 1883, and challenges by those who desired a piece of the business were probably inevitable.

After consideration of the financial standing of the applicants, the UA placed franchises in Chicago, Baltimore, Philadelphia, Boston, Cincinnati, Washington, St. Louis, and Altoona, Pennsylvania. Among the substantial backers was A.W. Henderson, who owned parts of both the Baltimore and Chicago teams. George Wright owned part of the Boston team. Officials of the Pennsylvania Railroad may have sponsored the Altoona club.

Henry Lucas, a prominent young railroad man, surfaced as the backer of the St. Louis franchise and, at the UA's meeting of December 18, 1883, became its president. So important did Lucas become to Union Association affairs that he became known as "I am the Union Association Lucas."

There was heavy competition for players. Ted Sullivan was one of those who scoured the country in search of players for the UA. Increased salaries, two- and three-year contracts, and the absence of the reserve rule made Union Association offers particularly interesting. A.G. Mills, president of the National League, complained, "The Unions are making efforts to debauch our players."

The NL and the AA responded to the UA's attempted player acquisitions in several ways. Extra teams of players, called "reserve teams," were signed by several of the existing major league teams. The "reserve team" players' only obligations were to play a few exhibition games and be ready should the parent club need them. As a result the "reserve" players would not be available for a Union Association club. The Union Association owners talked of forming "preserve" clubs in retaliation.

At the NL's annual meeting, held in Washington on November 21, 1883, strict legislation was proposed by John B. Day of New York to stop players from ignoring the reserve rule. The Day Resolution read:

Resolved: That no league club shall at any time employ or enter into contract with any of its reserved players who shall, while reserved to any such club, "play with" any other club.

Although the Day Resolution would not be formally approved until the March 12, 1884, National League meeting, its policies were the operational policies of the NL from that point in time.

At its annual meeting, held in Cincinnati on December 12, 1883, the American Association surprisingly voted to expand to 12 clubs by placing new franchises in Brooklyn, Indianapolis, Toledo, and Washington. The expansion was regarded as an attempt to tie up more players and territory. Now only Altoona of the eight UA teams would exist without opposition from another team.

The American Association also adopted a modified Day Resolution, providing that deserters of the AA reserve could be accepted back any time prior to the time the player actually participated in a UA game. Once they actually played in a UA game, they would be expelled and not accepted back.

Hundreds of players received UA offers and perhaps 30 players reserved by major league clubs agreed to UA terms. Many of those eventually jumped back to their original teams. Among the most celebrated "double jumpers" were star pitchers Larry Corcoran and Tony Mullane.

Corcoran had won 34 games for Al Spalding's Chicago NL team in 1883. He agreed to, but did not sign, a contract with Spalding's club for 1884. He received a better offer from the Chicago Unions and actually signed a contract. He jumped back to the Chicago NL club with an increase in pay, after being advised by Spalding that agreeing to the original contract offer was as good as signing it. It was also said that "Spalding threatened him with everything but death."

Even more complicated was the Tony "Count" Mullane case. He had pitched for St. Louis of the AA in 1883, winning 35 games. He was reserved by them for 1884 and was offered a $1,900 salary but refused it. In November 1883 he signed with the St. Louis Unions for $2,500. Mullane was threatened with expulsion under the terms of the Day Resolution and later signed another contract with the new Toledo AA club, also for $2,500. The St. Louis AA owner, Chris Von der Ahe, agreed to the transfer to Toledo in order to keep Mullane away from the Unions. The UA obtained court orders restraining Mullane from pitching in the city of St. Louis but had no success regaining his services. Lucas announced that the Unions now would also go into the "contract-breaking business."

About 20 players opened the season with Union Association clubs after leaving behind the reserve of NL or AA clubs. David Rowe, who played for Baltimore of the AA in 1883, was among those signed by the St. Louis Unions. Hugh "One Arm" Daily had left the Cleveland NL team to pitch for the Chicago Unions. Fred Dunlap jumped from the same Cleveland team to sign with the St. Louis Unions. He resisted considerable pressure to return, including offers of increased salary. Approximately 15 other Union Association players on opening-day rosters had ignored the reserve or claims of minor league clubs.

The Union Association opened play April 17, 1884, with games in Philadelphia, Baltimore and Cincinnati. The "Grand Opening"

in St. Louis was delayed by rain until April 20, when the home team beat Chicago 7-2. The UA planned a 128-game schedule with play not ending until mid-October.

The Chicago, Baltimore, Boston, Cincinnati, and Philadelphia teams opened the season with mostly experienced, if largely unknown, players. The Washington team was composed mostly of local players, including several youngsters. Altoona opened the season with local players, only a few of whom had professional experience. Lucas, on the other hand, stocked his St. Louis team with solid major leaguers, including George "Orator" Shaffer, Lew Dickerson, and Billy Taylor, plus the previously mentioned Rowe and Dunlap.

The St. Louis team was easily the UA's best. The team won its first 20 or 21 games and did not lose a game until May 24. Baltimore and Boston were the best of the other clubs in the early portion of the season.

Altoona dropped out after the games of May 31. Poor attendance was cited as the reason. This very unremarkable major league club won only six games in its six weeks of existence.

Kansas City was admitted as the replacement for Altoona. Kansas City had been one of the original UA applicants but was not chosen because of its "far western" location. The team began play June 7 with a collection of castoffs and reserve-team players, and fared rather poorly until strengthened by the signing of several Northwestern League players. The Kansas City franchise proved one of the league's most successful at the box office if not on the field.

In early July, Billy Taylor of the St. Louis Unions, the leading pitcher in the circuit with a 25-4 record, was induced to jump back to the American Association. Lucas was angered, of course, and said, "Everything is fair in baseball as in war, and I want my share of the fun while it is going on." To replace Taylor, Lucas signed suspended Providence NL pitcher Charlie Sweeney.

The Unions planned more retaliation. In August they induced star pitcher Jim McCormick, star infielder Jack Glasscock, and journeyman catcher Charlie "Fatty" Briody to jump their Cleveland NL team to join the Cincinnati Unions. They were paid a $1,000 bonus to jump and received contracts for the rest of the season and for 1885 as well. Briody spoke for the Cleveland jumpers when he said, "It is a matter of dollars and cents." The president of the Cincinnati Unions promised that from now on, the Unions would take any player they could get. With the new players Cincinnati became one of the better teams in the UA and actually played at a level almost equal to St. Louis for the remainder of the season.

The Cleveland team was badly damaged by the defections and, with its faltering attendance, required NL subsidy to finish the season. The Cleveland team nickname became "the Remnants."

After the games of August 7, the Philadelphia Union club folded. Lucas was able to convince the owners of the Wilmington Eastern League club to enter the UA as a replacement for the Philadelphia team. Wilmington was leading the Eastern League at the time but had lost money.

There were other towns still seeking a major league franchise. Quincy, Illinois, had one of the better teams in the Northwestern League despite losing several players to the UA. The Quincy ownership applied for a franchise at or about the time the Philadelphia team folded. Receiving no immediate reply to their application, they then challenged Lucas' St. Louis Unions to a game to show their quality of play was equal to that of the Unions. The game, played on August 14, resulted in a 5-1 win for St. Louis. The

fielding of the Quincy players was much admired, but the team was not admitted.

The Chicago Unions were transferred to Pittsburgh beginning with the games of August 25. Attendance had dropped dramatically in Chicago, and competing with Al Spalding's NL team had become impossible.

It was also in August that first reports were heard that Henry Lucas might be interested in an NL franchise for St. Louis. Justus Thorner, owner of the Cincinnati Unions, was also said to be pursuing an NL franchise.

The Northwestern League ceased operations on September 7, with only four clubs still in at the end. The Northwestern League provided more players to the Union Association than any other, and suffered more than any other in the baseball war of 1884.

After the games of September 12, the Wilmington team folded. Its owners complained that they had lost almost as much money in the Union Association as in the Eastern League. Milwaukee, a remnant of the Northwestern League, was admitted in Wilmington's place. On September 18 the Pittsburgh club folded. Omaha was to replace the Pittsburgh club but then declined; St. Paul was finally admitted in its stead.

In all, thirteen cities were represented in the Union Association. Only five of the original eight teams played the entire season.

The St. Louis Unions won the championship rather easily with what is now calculated as a 94-19 record. Some 21 games back were the Cincinnati Unions with a 69-36 record. Baltimore, Boston, and short-termer Milwaukee also finished with winning records. Everybody else was a loser.

Fred Dunlap of St. Louis won the batting championship with a .412 batting average. He also led in home runs with 13. Billy Sweeney of Baltimore won 40 of the 62 games he pitched, with 374 strikeouts. "One Arm" Daily struck out 483 batters, including 19 in one game against Boston on July 7. Over 260 players appeared in one or more UA games.

Only Kansas City and Washington of the long-term Union Association clubs claimed to have made a profit during the season. Kansas City claimed profits of $6,000 and very much looked forward to another season. Washington claimed to have cleared $7,000. Every other club in the UA lost money. Although actually breaking even with his own St. Louis team, Lucas claimed losses of $17,000 overall when funds used to keep the league going were accounted for. Boston lost $5,000. Cincinnati and Chicago were thought to have lost about $15,000 apiece.

Financial losses were also the rule in the National League and the American Association. Several NL franchises had to be subsidized by the league, including Providence and Cleveland. The AA, greatly over-expanded at 12 teams, also had its troubles and even had to shift its Washington franchise to Richmond late in the season.

Only four UA teams—Milwaukee, St. Louis, Cincinnati, and Kansas City—sent delegates to the annual meeting on December 18 in St. Louis. Nevertheless plans were made for continued operation in 1885. The UA in 1885 was to be comprised of St. Louis, Kansas City, Milwaukee, Cincinnati, Columbus, Indianapolis, and possibly Detroit and Cleveland. UA teams commenced signing players, and Kansas City and Milwaukee soon had full teams signed. Henry Lucas was re-elected president.

Later in December there were "startling rumors" that Lucas was, in fact, negotiating for a National League team. Cincinnati and Washington were said to be interested in American Association franchises.

The Union Association met once more, on January 15, in Milwaukee. Lucas was not present. Only the Kansas City and Milwaukee delegates attended, and the only action taken was a vote to disband.

On April 18, 1885, the Lucas club was finally admitted into the NL. The terms of the agreement were that Lucas had to admit publicly that the reserve clause was necessary and he had to pay $6,000 in order to retain the several players he had secured from NL teams. Lucas insisted that blacklisted players be reinstated, and that was done, although several were fined up to $1,000. (As a result, the team won the nickname of "Black Diamonds" and even wore a large black diamond on its jersey fronts.) In addition, pitcher Tony Mullane was suspended for the entire 1885 season, even though he had been allowed to play in 1884.

The Players League (1890)

The "Players National League" was formed at meetings in New York City on November 4-7, 1889. The force behind the new league was the union representing most of the players in the National League: the Brotherhood of Professional Base Ball Players.

On the first day of the meeting, the Brotherhood issued its statement of why the players had found it necessary to seek the organization of a new league in opposition to the NL. The "Brotherhood Manifesto," addressed "To the Public," included the following:

> Players have been bought, sold, and exchanged as though they were sheep instead of American citizens. "Reservation" became for them another name for property right in the player. By a combination among themselves, stronger than the strongest trust, they were able to enforce the most arbitrary measures, and the player had either to submit or get out of the profession in which he had spent years in attaining a proficiency.

The Players League (PL) was conceived on an unusual theoretical basis. The plan was never for labor to completely manage its own affairs and reap all the benefits thereof. Instead the plan was to withhold labor from the capitalists of the National League but join labor with the capital of other capitalists for the greater benefit of labor. The Brotherhood proposed "to manage their managers instead of permitting their managers to manage them."

During the summer of 1889, Pittsburgh outfielder Ned Hanlon had convinced Al Johnson, a wealthy Cleveland street-car entrepreneur, of the soundness of the plan. Johnson was extremely effective in locating additional backers for the Players League. The other backers included Colonel Edwin A. McAlpin, a New York real-estate speculator, and the wealthy Wagner brothers, who were Philadelphia butchers. John Addison was a Chicago contractor. John Montgomery Ward, president of the Brotherhood of Professional Base Ball Players, was one of several players who were minority investors.

The organizers of the Players League proposed several reforms. The hated reserve clause was abolished. Two- and three-year contracts were to be offered to many players. No player would be released until the end of the season and then only by a vote of the club board of directors, which would include players. All players would receive monies at least equal to their 1889 salaries. Receipts were to be used, first, to pay club expenses. Next to be paid would be player salaries for which a guarantee fund was established.

Backers would receive the next $10,000. Additional profits would be shared by players and backers on a league-wide shared basis. The arbitrary "blacklist" was not to be tolerated. Penalties not involving blacklisting were established for drunkenness and other offenses.

In December 1889 McAlpin was elected president of the new league. Addison was elected vice president. Frank Brunnell, a former sportswriter, served as secretary-treasurer and publicist. Clubs were placed in Cleveland, New York, Brooklyn, Pittsburgh, Philadelphia, Boston, Chicago, and Buffalo.

The Brotherhood of Professional Base Ball Players had been organized in 1885 with primarily fraternal and charitable objectives. John Montgomery Ward of the New York club was chosen president and remained so through the entire history of the "Brotherhood." By 1887, 90 NL players were members and each league city had a chapter.

The Brotherhood became involved in several issues in the late '80s, including opposition to the buying and selling of players and blacklisting of players who refused to accept club salary offers. The articulate Ward offered many of the more penetrating analyses on the reserve rule. For instance, in 1887 he wrote about the hated rule, "It inaugurated a species of serfdom which gave one set of men a life-estate in the labor of another, and withheld from the latter any corresponding claim." Ward illustrated his opposition to the reserve rule with the story of what happened to outfielder Charles "Curry" Foley. When ill during the 1883 season, Foley was laid off without pay yet was reserved by the Buffalo club that fall. He was still unable to play in the spring of 1884, but the Buffalo club again refused to pay him or release him. Later in the 1884 season Foley had recovered enough to play and, in fact, received several minor league offers. Buffalo would not release him and would not pay him or reinstate him. That fall Buffalo reserved Foley again.

The Brotherhood long opposed the practice of any player being reserved at any salary less than that received the previous season. In conferences with the NL in 1888 the Brotherhood proposed that the practice be abolished. The NL postponed action on the request until most players had signed their 1889 contracts and then refused to abolish the practice. The NL also attempted to institute the Brush Classification Plan, named after Indianapolis (and, later, Cincinnati and then New York) owner John T. Brush. It provided for grouping of players by skill levels and a prescribed payment for each level. The threat of the classification plan was considered obnoxious by most NL players and led directly to the formation of the Players League in the fall of 1889. Tim Keefe, New York pitcher and secretary of the Brotherhood, remarked at the time, "The League will not classify as many as they think."

The cause of Brotherhood members Jack Rowe and Jim "Deacon" White also caused much sympathy among NL players, and there was immediate strike talk. Rowe and White had both played for the Detroit team in 1888. Each was sold to Pittsburgh prior to the 1889 season. In the meantime they had purchased part of the Buffalo minor league team, planning to play there in 1889. White became president of the Buffalo club. Frederick Stearns, president of the Pittsburgh club, said, "White may have been elected president of the Buffalo club ... but that won't allow him to play ball in Buffalo. He'll play in Pittsburgh or he'll get off the earth." Upon advice of John Ward, White and Rowe did eventually play for Pittsburgh in 1889, after becoming aware of the plans for 1890. White and Rowe became major backers of the Buffalo Players League club.

The players were enthusiastic about the prospect of the new

league. Mike "King" Kelly, when speaking of his former owners, three in number, of the Boston NL team, exuberantly proclaimed:

I'm one of the bosses now, and the triumvirate—well, to be frank, they are my understudies. The whirling of time brings ballplayers to their level. Next year they will be in command and the former presidents will have to drive horse cars for a living and borrow rain checks to see a game.

The baseball establishment never understood, or at least pretended never to understand, the Brotherhood members' desire for more control over their lives and careers. The *Spalding Guide* reported that the trouble arose "from the selfish greed of a small minority of the overpaid 'star' players of the National League of 1889, who thought they saw an opening for their becoming wealthy club magnates in the place of being fancy salaried players."

Brotherhood members were advised not to sign contracts with the NL for the 1890 season. Even after the formation of the PL, attorneys assured NL owners that the reserve clause in the contract would be enough to hold the players. Ward was personally notified that he was reserved for 1890 and would be taken to court if necessary. In January 1890 the New York NL club was denied an injunction against Ward because the reserve clause in his contract lacked fairness and mutuality. Injunctions were also sought against "Buck" Ewing of the New York club and Bill Hallman of the Philadelphia club. The NL lost those cases also. Outfielder "Orator" O'Rourke of New York, himself a lawyer, was ecstatic: "He that hath committed inequity shall not have equity."

An almost total defection of the star players from the NL followed. By March 1890 over 100 players had signed PL contracts, including virtually every star. Another 20 or so players deserted the American Association, including Pete Browning of Louisville and Silver King of St. Louis. Fewer than 40 of the 1889 NL players remained loyal to the league. Al Spalding's Chicago team retained only first baseman/manager Adrian Anson, who was a stockholder, plus pitcher Bill Hutchison and third baseman Tom Burns. The rest of the Chicago team was eventually filled out with young players, called the "colts" or "cubs" by the sportswriters. Chicago managed to finish in second place in the greatly weakened NL

The NL attempted to get several of the players to return with offers including huge salary increases, bribes, and two- and three-year contracts. The most interesting attempt involved Kelly, who was offered a $10,000 bonus and a contract to be filled in with his own figures. Kelly declined, saying, "I can't go back on the boys." PL secretary Brunnell pointed out the hypocrisy of the National League methods: "They would blacklist a man who broke a contract with them on the ground that he was unworthy of confidence, yet they brazenly offer fabulous bribes to induce our men to desert us."

Twelve players did jump PL contracts to return to the NL, but several of those, including Jake Beckley, eventually returned to the Players League. Perhaps they remembered the PL's favorite Bible quote, from 1 Peter 2:17 which advised "Honor all men. Love the Brotherhood."

PL managers included Brotherhood members and star players King Kelly at Boston, John Ward at Brooklyn, Buck Ewing at New York, Charles Comiskey at Chicago, Jack Rowe at Buffalo, and Ned Hanlon at Pittsburgh.

The Players League opened on April 19, 1890. Games were deliberately scheduled to conflict with National League games. The PL opener in New York had an attendance of 12,000 despite chilly weather. The New York rebels had a most familiar look for the New York fans as the entire opening-day lineup had played for the New York NL club in 1889. The Boston and Pittsburgh teams drew over 10,000 apiece for their openers.

By June the PL and in fact all of baseball was suffering poor attendance. In July each PL club was assessed an extra $2,500 to keep the league afloat. There was, throughout the season, widespread falsification of attendance totals by both the PL and the NL The best guess is that the former outdrew the latter by about 200,000, yet it appears certain that the totals together were less than that of the NL in 1889. Years later Al Spalding wrote in his autobiography:

If either party of this controversy ever furnished to the press one solitary truthful statement as to the progress of the war from his standpoint; if anyone at any time during the contest made true representation of conditions in his own ranks, a monument should be erected to his memory. I have no candidates to recommend for the distinction.

The NL was considerably weakened by the war, with both the New York and Pittsburgh clubs experiencing major financial problems. The New York club had to be subsidized to the extent of $80,000 and Pittsburgh required close to the same amount. Total NL losses for the 1890 season were estimated at almost $500,000.

The Players League remained reasonably solvent until bad weather in September hampered attendance and dulled a close pennant race. After the season PL secretary Brunnell reported losses of some $125,000. Boston won the PL championship with an 81-48 record but was refused its offer to play in a three-way World Series with the NL and AA winners. Chicago, Brooklyn, New York, and Philadelphia also posted winning records in the Players League. Buffalo finished last with a 36-96 mark. Pete Browning of Cleveland won the batting championship with a .391 batting average, later recomputed to .373. Chicago's Mark Baldwin won 33 games to lead the pitchers.

By the end of the 1890 season there was a general inclination by NL owners and PL backers to seek a peace. The NL was perhaps frightened into the spirit of compromise when the owner of its Cincinnati club, Aaron Stern, sold his team to a group of PL backers headed by Al Johnson. The National League declared the Cincinnati franchise forfeited and eventually awarded it to John T. Brush of Brush Classification Plan fame.

The first peace negotiations were held in early October of 1890. Al Spalding, chairman of the National League War Committee, said, "We had been playing two games all through—baseball and bluff. At this stage I put up the strongest play at the latter game I had ever presented." The PL backers "greedily accepted" the terms of surrender.

Later more formal negotiations, from which the players were excluded, produced the dismantling of the Players League. In November the New York PL backers announced that their club would be absorbed by the New York NL club. Within days, the Pittsburgh PL club was merged with the city's NL club. In December the Chicago PL team was sold to Spalding for $18,000, despite the attempt of the players to hold up the sale.

Further negotiations provided for the merging of the opposing Brooklyn teams and the entry of the Boston PL team into the American Association. The backers of the Philadelphia PL team became the owners of the Philadelphia AA franchise. The Buffalo

and Cleveland PL teams simply disappeared.

Johnson and Brunnell had been left out of the mergers. As a result they attempted to reorganize the remnants of their league into an independent eight-or ten-club circuit that would also include cities without major league baseball, such as Syracuse and Toledo, both of which had been dropped by the AA. "Wrecker" Johnson counted heavily on Brotherhood support, even though reduced salaries would be necessary. The new league was never launched, however, because the Brotherhood members had seen enough. A popular baseball poem of 1890 had a kernel of truth in it:

Backward, turn backward,
O Time, in thy rush,
Make me a slave again,
Well dressed and flush;
Bondage, come back from the shoeless shore,
And bring me the shackles I formerly wore.

John Ward attributed the defeat of the Players League to "stupidity, avarice and treachery," and it was all of that. Al Spalding speculated that the defeat of the players "settled forever the theory that professional ballplayers can at the same time direct both the business and playing ends of the game."

The Second American Association (1894)

In the fall of 1894, three years after the demise of the AA and four years after that of the PL, a new "American Association of Baseball Clubs" was proposed. At an organizational meeting in Philadelphia on October 18, 1894, franchises were granted to interests in Pittsburgh, Chicago, Milwaukee, New York, Brooklyn, Philadelphia, and Washington. Applications were also reported pending from other large cities for the proposed eight-club league. Several prominent baseball men were involved, including F.C. Richter, the influential editor of *The Sporting Life* of Philadelphia, who was elected president of the new league.

Identified as prime movers behind the new league were three men who had been active in the NL during the 1894 season: A.C. Buckenberger, who had managed the Pittsburgh team, was affiliated with the new Pittsburgh club. William Barnie, who had managed the Louisville team, was an investor in the new Brooklyn team; Fred Pfeffer, the star second baseman of the Louisville team and formerly a star with Anson's White Stockings, planned to operate the new Chicago team.

Although invading several NL cities, the organizers of the new American Association publicly stated they planned no fight if it could be avoided. They planned to adopt a schedule that did not conflict with that of the established league and vowed to honor all its player contracts.

The proposed American Association reforms included allowing play on Sunday, setting the admission price at 25 cents and prohibiting the buying and selling of player releases. The "double umpire" or two-umpire system was to be instituted. Most importantly, the oppressive reserve clause of NL contracts was to be ignored.

The American Association organizers were convinced there was ample room for two big leagues. A.W. Becannon, the backer of the New York franchise, was quoted as saying, "We only want our share of the patronage and we think we can get it." Several prominent players whose NL contracts had run out were reported considering signing with the new league.

The National League, as well as the Eastern and Western Leagues, particularly feared competition for their players and their territory. They reacted very harshly to the threat. At the NL's annual meeting on November 16, 1894, a "Manifesto" was adopted which read in part: "The obligations of contracts, the rights of reserve and the territorial rights of clubs, associations, and leagues must be upheld, and shall be, at any cost."

They also announced that the penalty for "treachery to national agreement interests" would be "ineligibility and suspension for life."

Buckenberger, Barnie and Pfeffer were suspended and given until December 31 to prove their innocence or the suspensions would be made permanent.

American Association president Richter called the threats a "tremendous bluff." Nevertheless the "bluff" worked, and little more was heard of the new organization. The new American Association died without ever adopting a schedule or signing a player.

Buckenberger was the first to ask for forgiveness. He signed an affidavit denying he had been involved in the interest of the American Association while employed by a league club. He was reinstated and later signed to manage the St. Louis team.

Barnie and Pfeffer were more of a problem. At a hearing on December 20, 1894, Barnie denied affiliating with the American Association until after his National League contract with Louisville had expired. Barnie also refused, after much "wild talk and gesticulation," to sign a letter swearing allegiance to the National Agreement. He was nevertheless reinstated because of a lack of "positive evidence" of his treachery. Barnie soon signed to manage Scranton of the Eastern League. Pfeffer forwarded his written arguments to the hearing but failed to appear personally and was blacklisted.

Pfeffer soon signed to coach the Princeton University baseball team but indicated he still desired to play. Louisville fans instituted a petition drive which collected the signatures of 10,000 persons who promised to boycott Louisville games if Pfeffer were not reinstated. Because of that pressure and the threat of a lawsuit, Pfeffer was reinstated on February 25, 1895, on the condition that he play only for Louisville, that he agree to loyalty to the National Agreement and that he pay a fine of $500. Friends paid the fine, and Pfeffer was reinstated and went on to play parts of three more seasons in the National League.

The New American Association (1900)

The "American Association of Baseball Clubs," later to be called the "New American Association," began organization at meetings in Chicago on September 17-18, 1899. The main force behind the league seems to have been George Schaefer, a St. Louis city alderman. Several prominent baseball figures were also involved, including Adrian Anson, Chris Von der Ahe, H.D. Quinn, and Al Spinks, who claimed credit for the idea for the new league. Also involved, although not initially named, were Francis Richter of *The Sporting Life* and John McGraw and Wilbert Robinson of the Baltimore NL team. H.D. Quinn was elected temporary president of the new league.

Franchises were proposed for St. Louis, Milwaukee, Detroit, Chicago, Baltimore, New York, Philadelphia, and Washington. Detroit and Milwaukee had existing Western League franchises, and the remainder of the cities had National League franchises in 1899. The intentions of the new league were announced as follow: "Honest competition, no syndicate baseball, no reserve rule, to

respect all contracts and popular prices."

The American Association organizers felt that by not recognizing the reserve rule they could compete for the best of the baseball talent. They also believed that by charging only 25 cents admission price (the NL charged 50 cents) they could capture their share of the baseball patronage. The American Association organizers "disclaimed any intention of going to war with the minor leagues, but they strongly intimated that it was war to the finish with the National organization."

The formation of the new league followed closely a confusing series of events during the summer of 1899. In June the NL had announced it would consider dropping four of its unprofitable clubs in order to increase the profits of the other eight. The Washington, Louisville, Baltimore, and Cleveland clubs were those so threatened. When rumors of the new league were first heard, Ban Johnson, president of the Western League, was identified by some as the backer of the new league. Later, when Johnson was invited to join his league with the new league, he declined, as did other Western League figures such as Charles Comiskey.

The NL had reigned as the only major league since 1892, but the 12-club format had proved unpopular with fans, and attendance dropped steadily through the decade. The existence of only one major league limited the number of cities who could offer major league baseball, and it also limited the number of would-be magnates.

The motivations of the organizers of the new league were varied. McGraw and Robinson hoped to be able to remain in Baltimore, where they were extremely popular, if the National League were to oust that city. Quinn had been unable to acquire a major league franchise for Milwaukee since his club had been dropped following the amalgamation of the NL and the original AA. Von der Ahe had been manipulated out of his NL franchise in St. Louis after the 1898 season and sought a return to his former prominence in baseball affairs. Von der Ahe even went so far as to give to the new American Association, for award to the championship team, the famous Wiman Trophy captured by his famous St. Louis Browns team for winning AA championships in 1886, 1887, and 1888.

The National League took several actions to fight the new league because "by coming into our territory the new association invites war." NL owners believed they could forbid the use of the name of the American Association because when they had absorbed the AA in 1892 they had acquired use of the name and were legally known as the National League and American Association of Baseball Clubs.

Second, the NL announced plans for their own American Association. This league, which became known as American Association II, would be organized as a minor league, would charge only 25 cents admission, and would play in National League parks when the major league teams were on the road. Third, Ban Johnson's Western League, by then with a name change to the American League, would be allowed or encouraged to move into Chicago and Cleveland.

Formal organization of the new American Association occurred in Chicago on February 13, 1900. Arrangements for the New York and Washington clubs had fallen through. Boston and Louisville clubs were admitted to join Baltimore, Milwaukee, Detroit, Chicago, and St. Louis clubs in signing the required agreements and posting a $1,200 bond. Philadelphia was still desired for the eighth club. In fact, Philadelphia was considered essential to the success of the new league. Anson was elected president of the new league and announced the new league would open play on April 16, 1900. Among other business, the name of the new league was changed to the New American Association.

McGraw traveled to Philadelphia after the Chicago meeting to finalize arrangements in that city. McGraw's conferences with W.J. Gilmore, reportedly the major backer, were unsatisfactory. Gilmore informed him he had experienced difficulty locating a place to play and would need three more weeks before he would decide if he would enter a team.

On February 16, 1900, President Anson announced the New American Association had collapsed and would not operate in 1900. Some of the backers attempted to reorganize for the 1901 season but were unsuccessful.

The Columbian Baseball League (1912)

The "Columbian Baseball League" was first proposed at a meeting in Chicago on January 13, 1912. The meeting was called by John T. Powers, an ex-president of the Wisconsin-Illinois League, and was attended by representatives of interests in cities of the Midwest.

At a meeting in St. Louis on February 12, 1912, the Columbian League was formally organized, with franchises awarded to Chicago, Kansas City, St. Louis, Louisville, Indianapolis, Detroit, Cleveland, and Milwaukee. All these cities had existing teams in the American League, National League, or the minor league American Association. Powers was elected president the new league.

The baseball public was assured that good playing grounds had been located in most of these cities and that sufficient financial resources existed to operate the new league. Powers indicated the quality of play would equal that of the high minor leagues in the first season and rival that of the major leagues in following seasons.

The Columbian League did not plan to encourage contract jumping but did announce that it would ignore the reserve clause. By late February Powers was able to display letters from 63 players interested in playing in the new league. About 40 of these had been reserved by teams within Organized Baseball. Several ex-big leaguers were announced as probable managers of Columbian League teams, including Danny Shay at Kansas City and Ed McKean at Cleveland.

Powers obviously anticipated strong opposition to the new league. He indicated that Organized Baseball would be fought under the Sherman Antitrust law if it attacked the new league. Powers added: "We are not fighting capital with capital, and do not seek a fight with any person or combination. But we have the right to exist and compete with the 'baseball trust.'"

Organized Baseball interfered very little with the new league other than labeling it an "outlaw league" and implying that it took more than just talk to operate a successful league. That opinion proved correct. When financial backing proved insufficient, the Columbian League folded before ever playing its first game. Other half-baked challengers in this period included Alfred Lawson's Union League (1908), the "Burlesquers' League" (1910) and "Daniel Fletcher's League" (1910).

The United States League (1912-1913)

The "United States League of Professional Baseball Clubs" operated briefly in both the 1912 and 1913 seasons. The United States League (USL) posed itself as the "third major league" and

attempted to exist peacefully and profitably, yet separately, from Organized Baseball.

The USL was formally organized in New York City on January 20, 1912. Its chief organizer, William Abbott Witman of Reading, Pennsylvania, was elected president of the new league. Applications for franchises were reported from twelve or thirteen cities for what was projected as an eight-club league.

The USL innovations included the absence of a reserve clause in their player contracts. However, Organized Baseball's own reserve clause was to be respected, as were existing contracts. USL contracts with players were to be made for one to three years at the option of the player. At the expiration of the contract, the player was to be a free agent. The only real conflict with Organized Baseball was over "territorial rights."

A second attempt in 1912 to form an independent league, the Columbian League (see above), proved unsuccessful, and in March several backers of that league switched allegiance and money to the USL. Most prominent and wealthy of the new backers was William C. Niesen of Chicago.

Good and solid financing for the United States League was promised, and franchises for 1912 were ultimately located in New York, Brooklyn, Cleveland, Chicago; Washington, Cincinnati; Richmond, and Reading. USL cities all had existing major league franchises except Richmond and Reading. President Witman was to operate the Reading franchise. Hall of Famer "Pop" Anson attempted to buy into both the New York and Washington franchises and tried to buy the Reading franchise and move it to Buffalo. He was rebuffed in all instances, but his interest, and the overtures of other parties, indicates a belief in the viability of the new league.

The United States League planned a 126-game schedule with play to begin on May 1. Attendance was 2,000 that day in New York, but soon it dropped to an average of 300 to 400 for most USL games. Unfortunately, much bad weather dropped attendance even further.

Several ex-major leaguers played on or managed USL teams, including Deacon Phillippe, Bert Blue, Claude Ritchey, Jack O'Connor, and Bugs Raymond. Arlie Latham umpired. Most of the players, however, were unremarkable minor leaguers and semiprofessionals, plus a significant number of promising youngsters. Among the latter was 19-year-old pitcher Al Schacht, who compiled a 5-0 record with the Cleveland team according to his autobiography.

That the USL lasted into late May amazed many. One rumor had it that the newly formed Professional Baseball Players Fraternity was secretly supporting the new league. When the Detroit Tigers of the American League staged a brief strike in support of the suspended Ty Cobb, they were reported to be jumping to the USL. At least five of the Tigers, including Cobb, did receive offers from the USL, but the strike was settled and the Tigers remained in place.

On May 20 the Cincinnati franchise owners announced that they would transfer games to an as yet undetermined site. On May 21 the Washington players quit because salaries had not been paid. The New York franchise was forfeited on May 28. Then in rapid succession the Richmond and Cincinnati franchises folded and Witman filed for personal bankruptcy with his debts including $970 owed to Reading players. Witman stated his undoing was "the combination of Organized Baseball and political forces that had been formed to trim me."

Despite Witman's accusations there is little evidence of interference with the USL by anyone in baseball. Cincinnati Reds president August Herrmann admitted, "We have no right to object to them, no right to annoy them." Most of baseball simply ignored the USL.

The last regularly scheduled games were played on June 1, although some games were played as late as June 8. Pittsburgh, with an unofficial 23-8 record, compiled easily the best record, with Richmond in second place. On June 23 Marshall Henderson of Pittsburgh succeeded Witman as president. He attempted to reorganize the USL into a six-club league to finish the season but was unsuccessful. All teams reported heavy financial losses, with the exception of the Pittsburgh club, which showed a modest profit. The *Reach Guide* summarized the 1912 United States League experience as follows:

> This organization was started, but it went the way of all "houses builded on sand," after just one month of wretched existence. The organization had neither officials, circuit, or magnates to commend themselves to the public; or players to attract or hold patronage. Furthermore, there was no baseball brain to plan and direct, no courage to combat and circumvent adverse conditions, and no capital to help the organization over the inevitable losing initial season.

The USL surfaced again on January 5, 1913, with plans for a new eight-club league based in cities in and near the East Coast. It was hoped that reduced travel costs would make the venture more profitable. Witman, his financial affairs straightened out, was again the chief organizer and was again elected president.

For 1913 franchises were awarded to Baltimore, Brooklyn, Reading, New York, Newark, Philadelphia, Washington, and Lynchburg. Plans were also announced to eventually expand into, or at least play in, foreign countries. The players were again mostly has-beens, career minor leaguers, semiprofessionals, and promising youngsters.

The 1913 USL season opened May 10 with four games. The next day New York refused to play, having not received the guarantee from the previous day. On May 12 Brooklyn refused to play Washington for the same reason. Washington and New York were dropped from the league, but reorganization failed, and the last USL game was played on May 13. Baltimore won both of its games and could be considered the unofficial league champion.

The Federal League (1913-15)

The Federal League operated in the 1913, 1914 and 1915 seasons. During the latter two seasons, it posed as severe a threat to the status quo as any league in the history of baseball.

The "Federal League of Baseball Clubs" was organized on March 8, 1913, in Indianapolis. John T. Powers, who in 1912 had tried to launch the Midwest-based Columbian League, was the chief organizer and was elected president of the new league. The Federal League (FL) was to be an independent not under the control of the National Commission. The FL did not, however, plan to tamper with players affiliated with Organized Baseball but planned to develop its own players. Each team to be entered into the Federal League had to post a bond with the new league of $5,000 and was further required to be capitalized to the extent of $100,000.

Franchises were awarded to interests in Chicago, Pittsburgh,

Cleveland, St. Louis, Indianapolis, and Cincinnati. Two more franchises were sought, but they did not materialize, possibly because of the short time remaining until the opening of the season. In addition, preparations for the Cincinnati franchise ran into trouble, and the franchise was eventually located across the Ohio River in Covington, Kentucky. FL teams challenged existing major league teams in five locations and the minor league American Association in one.

The Feds' strategy for their first season was to sign a well-known manager and as many experienced free-agent players as possible and fill out the team with promising youngsters. Burt Keeley became the manager at Chicago, Deacon Phillippe at Pittsburgh, Bill Phillips at Indianapolis, Sam Leever at Covington, Jack O'Connor at St. Louis, and Cy Young at Cleveland.

The season opened May 3 with Covington and Cleveland playing a 6-6 tie to 10 innings. The other teams opened three days later with surprisingly good attendance in some locations. On May 11, Indianapolis drew some 18,500 to a game—in part because of a new provision they had made for fans. Parking for automobiles was available, and more than 200 cars were accommodated. Unfortunately, attendance declined steadily through the remainder of the season.

Organized Baseball ignored the Federal League at first. Then in early June FL teams signed three players whom they considered were free of Organized Baseball ties but who were still claimed by their former teams. Elmer Knetzer, an ex-Brooklyn Dodger, had left that team because of illness in his family and had his salary reduced as a result. He signed with Pittsburgh, which was his hometown. Two other Pittsburgh boys, Jack Lewis and Tom Murray, felt they were unfairly assigned to St. Paul and left that team also to join the Pittsburgh Feds.

Within days, teams in Organized Baseball began raids on Federal League teams with Indianapolis losing two stars, Ben Taylor and James Scott. Several Chicago Federal League players also received offers, mostly from the NL Cubs.

The Feds also faced other difficulties. The Western Union Telegraph had refused to allow FL scores on its ticker service. In mid-June an FL representative, E.E. Gates of Indianapolis, appeared before the Interstate Commerce Commission and alleged that such refusal was a violation of the Hepburn Act. He stated that the Federal League had offered to pay for the ticker-service privilege but had been refused. The FL believed Organized Baseball was behind the Western Union refusal. Gates also conferred with U.S. Representative Thomas Gallagher (Democrat from Illinois), who had introduced a resolution in Congress asking that baseball be investigated for possible antitrust violations. Gates complained about reserve clauses, blacklists and other arbitrary actions of baseball. Gates thought the question was "Is it possible that Organized Baseball, through its years of tyrannical rule and usurpation, has secured certain privileges and immunities which do not belong to other organizations in the country?"

Indianapolis had the best team in the Federal League and by the end of June had a four-game lead over Chicago. Cleveland and Covington also had posted winning records, with Pittsburgh bringing up the rear. Despite its winning record, the Covington team was plagued by poor attendance and on June 26 was transferred to Kansas City.

On June 28 a conference of American Association and major league baseball leaders was held in Chicago to combat "the encroachments of the Federal League." Two Indianapolis American Association players, Ray Aschenfelder and Fred Link, had just signed with FL teams. That and the invasion of Kansas City was said to have "aroused all the clubs owners in the American Association to the necessity of strengthening their hold on their players and their territory." It was all-out war from that point forward.

On August 2, Powers was removed as president by the FL owners. He was replaced by James Gilmore of Chicago, who was able to stabilize matters in the Federal League and allow it to finish the season despite some talk of disbandment.

The Indianapolis Feds easily won the championship with a 75-45 record, some 10 games ahead of Cleveland. Pittsburgh finished last with a 49-71 record. "Biddy" Dolan of Indianapolis, a career minor leaguer, is usually considered the batting champion with a .346 batting average. Only one player in the league hit more than 5 home runs: Jack Kading of Chicago hit 9 to lead the league. Two pitchers, Pete Henning of Covington and Kansas City and Tom McGuire of Chicago, each pitched 18 wins to lead the hurlers. McGuire also led with 170 strikeouts.

The Federal League, instead of disbanding, expanded for the 1914 season. Clubs were added in Buffalo, Brooklyn and Baltimore, and the Cleveland club was dropped. Gilmore was extremely successful at adding men with money to the roster of FL owners. Charles Weeghman, owner of a chain of lunchrooms, took over the Chicago team. Philip Ball of St. Louis invested in the St. Louis franchise. Most important for the Fed finances, Tip-Top Bakeries owner Robert Ward became the backer of the new Brooklyn team. The Federal League declared that beginning with the 1914 season, it was a major league equal to the National and American Leagues.

FL teams challenged existing major league teams in four cities. They challenged the International League in Baltimore and Buffalo and the American Association in Indianapolis and Kansas City. St. Louis and Chicago now had three "major league" teams apiece.

The FL, at least by the beginning of the 1914 season, was organized as a single corporation with the stock divided among the owners. It is unclear whether this had also been the arrangement in 1913. The FL player contract was also different. It did not contain a reserve clause but provided for an option for the players' services for the next year. The option for the next season had to be exercised by September 15, and a minimum 5 percent increase in salary was required. A player could become a free agent after 10 FL seasons.

The Federal League jumped quickly into the fray with the signing for 1914 of three well-known major league stars as managers for their teams. George Stovall was signed to manage the Kansas City club after spending much of the 1913 season squabbling with his St. Louis American League owner. Mordecai "Three Finger" Brown joined the St. Louis club as manager after pitching for Cincinnati in 1913. Most irritating to the NL was the signing of Joe Tinker. Tinker, the long-time Chicago star of "Tinker to Evers to Chance" fame, had just been sold by the Cincinnati Reds to the Brooklyn Dodgers for a reported $15,000. Tinker at first agreed to the deal but then refused when offered a salary of only $7,500. He then signed with the Chicago Feds for $12,000 per year plus stock in the club.

Many other National and American League players used Federal League offers to seek and receive better contracts from their original clubs. The best-known case involved Bill Killefer, a catcher for the Philadelphia Phillies in 1913. Killefer promised to sign again with Philadelphia for 1914 but instead signed a three-year Fed contract for a total of $17,500. After being pressured by his

former team and threatened with the blacklist, he signed with Philadelphia again for $6,500 a season. The matter ended up in the courts with Philadelphia winning because part of Killefer's 1913 salary had been designated as payment for an option on his services for 1914. At least three other players "did a Killefer" and returned to their Organized Baseball club after signing with the FL.

National Commission rules specified a three-year suspension for reserve-rule jumpers and five-year suspensions for contract breakers.

Other notable battles were fought over the 10-day clause in the standard NL and AL contracts. This provision allowed a club to release a player on ten days' notice whereas a player was bound to a club for his whole career if the club chose. When pitcher Chief Johnson jumped his contract to sign with the Kansas City Feds, the matter ended up in court with the ruling eventually being that such a contract lacked mutuality. Then Hal Chase, first baseman of the Chicago White Sox, gave *them* a 10-day notice and jumped to the Buffalo Feds. The case ended up in court with Chase also winning.

The 1914 FL pennant winner was again Indianapolis, this time with an 88-65 record, only 1-1/2 games ahead of Chicago. Benny Kauff, "the Ty Cobb of the Federal League," was the batting champion with a .370 batting average. Dutch Zwilling of Chicago had 16 home runs to lead the league. Claude Hendrix of Chicago led the pitchers with 29 wins.

There were secret peace discussions following the 1914 season, but they proved futile because the Feds wanted too much. What was requested is not clearly indicated, but it is believed that they wished to continue operation as the third major league.

On January 5, 1915, the Federal League filed suit against Organized Baseball, charging that violations of the antitrust laws had occurred. Organized Baseball was said to have been an illegal combination and monopoly which engaged in illegal acts such as farming out of players and other actions in restraint of free trade. The suit was filed in the court of Judge Kenesaw Mountain Landis, who had a reputation as a trustbuster because of his famous antitrust decision against Standard Oil.

President Gilmore made several changes in preparation for a continuing Federal League in 1915. New money was located in the person of the fabulously rich Harry Sinclair, later to be implicated in the Teapot Dome Scandals. Sinclair wanted to operate a club in Newark as an entree into an eventual move into New York City. The FL attempted to transfer the Kansas City club to Newark, but the Kansas City investors took the matter to court. Gilmore acquiesced and allowed the club to stay in Kansas City. Eventually the Indianapolis club, pennant winner in its first two seasons, was moved to Newark. Kauff was assigned to the Brooklyn team in order to strengthen that franchise.

The player raids began again in earnest after the breakdown of the peace talks. Several members of Connie Mack's pennant-winning Philadelphia A's were known to be negotiating with the Feds, and Eddie Plank did jump. Mack sold the rest of his stars rather than lose them to the Feds, and as a result his club finished last in 1915 and in each of the next six seasons.

Most alarming to Organized Baseball was the apparent defection of Washington Senator star pitcher Walter Johnson to the Chicago FL team, Charles Weeghman's Whales. Johnson had received an offer from Washington for 1915 but found it inadequate. He then signed a three-year contract with the Whales and pocketed a $6,000 bonus. Washington owner Clark Griffith convinced Johnson to return to his fold with a contract calling for

$12,500 per season. To his credit Johnson returned the Whales' bonus, but he never adequately explained the breaking of the FL contract.

Organized Baseball also attempted its share of player raids. FL batting champion Benny Kauff signed a three-year contract with the Brooklyn Tip-Tops club after being transferred there from Indianapolis. He then signed with the New York Giants and played in exhibition games with them. The Boston Braves complained that Kauff had previously jumped his contract with Organized Baseball and was blacklisted as a contract jumper. Kauff applied for reinstatement but was refused. He then returned to the Tip-Tops.

The 1915 FL season provided the closest pennant race of all time, decided by a single percentage point. Six of the eight clubs were in the race until the last week of the season. The championship was not settled until the last day of the season when Chicago split a doubleheader with Pittsburgh to finish with an 86-66 record, just ahead of St. Louis at 87-67 and Pittsburgh at 86-67. Kauff again won the batting championship, this time with a .342 batting average. Hal Chase of Buffalo hit 17 home runs to lead in that category. George McConnell of Chicago led the pitchers with 25 wins.

By one count, that of historian Harold Seymour, 264 players appeared in one or more games in the two years the Federal League was a major league. Of that total, 43 players jumped major or minor league contracts to join the Feds, and 188 FL players had ignored the reserve clause. The remaining 33 players were free agents or had no previous professional experience.

Although aided greatly by the close pennant race, attendance was generally disappointing throughout the league in 1915. Several clubs, including Kansas City and Buffalo, were forced to seek additional financing in order to finish the season and Buffalo may have received some assistance from the league itself. The prevailing sentiment of Fed owners was to push for a settlement. That sentiment was reinforced when Brooklyn owner Robert Ward died in October.

After prolonged negotiations, a peace agreement was finally reached and signed on December 22, 1915, in Cincinnati. Terms of the agreement provided that Weeghman of the Chicago Feds would be allowed to purchase the Chicago Cubs (for a reported $500,000) and that Ball would be allowed to purchase the St. Louis Browns (for $525,000). The Ward estate was to receive $400,000, to be paid in 20 installments. The owners of the Pittsburgh Feds received $50,000 and the right to bid on several major league franchises on which prices had been established. Sinclair was given $100,000 to be paid in ten installments, as well as control of all of the Newark, Kansas City, and Buffalo players plus Benny Kauff, Lee Magee, and George Anderson of the Brooklyn team.

The Baltimore owners were offered $50,000 for their settlement but did not accept. They eventually filed suit over the agreement, with the suit dragging on until 1922 as Judge Landis deferred his verdict and propelled the case to an ultimate ruling by the Supreme Court in 1922. Other Federal League owners got left behind for the most part, although initially they were promised International League franchises. The antitrust suit pending before Judge Landis and all other suits were to be dismissed.

All Federal League players were removed from the blacklist and certified as eligible to play for Organized Baseball clubs in 1916. All FL contracts were to be paid in full, and the team that had lost them to the Feds originally could not get them back unless they purchased them.

Estimates of Federal League losses ranged from $2 million to $3 million, with the losses of the National League and American League close to $2 million. It had been a costly war, and the editor of *The Spalding Guide* mused as follows:

The war is over. It is not the intention of the editor of *The Guide* to enter into any new argument or refutation of false argument in connection with this episode in Base Ball. It is his intention, however, to call attention again to the fact that Organized Base Ball has once more proved to the world that it is the originator of the best and finest method to control a sport, which is called a nation's sport, of any method in the history of sport throughout the civilized world.

The Continental League (1959-1960)

The "Continental League" was organized on July 27, 1959, in New York City. The backers, who included several men now associated with the National League or the American League, planned an eight-club league with a very important franchise to be located in New York City. Other charter members were Denver, Houston, Toronto, and the twin cities of Minneapolis and St. Paul. The eleven other cities listed as applicants included San Juan, Puerto Rico.

New York had been abandoned after the 1957 season by both the Giants and the Dodgers. Each club cited better opportunities on the West Coast. National League president Warren Giles had even downplayed the importance of the nation's largest city by quipping, "Who needs New York?"

The founders' group of the Continental League included chairman William Shea of New York, Jack Kent Cooke of Toronto, and Craig Cullinan, Jr., of Houston. The founders hoped to operate the new league within the structure of Organized Baseball. When asked why the "third league" was being launched, one of the founders replied: "The Continental League is the result of the increasing demand of cities in this country and Canada for major league baseball. Not only New York, since losing the Giants and Dodgers, but many other cities have done everything in their power to obtain franchises in the two existing major leagues without success."

When asked what action the Continental League would take if the established major leagues opposed the new league, Shea replied, "We will go ahead anyway."

Continental League teams were to be capitalized to $2,500,000, exclusive of the cost of stadiums and other facilities. Each stadium was to have a capacity of at least 35,000. The Continental League name was one of four considered for the new league, the others being the Third League, the United States League, and the International League.

The National League and the American League were, surprisingly, not openly hostile to the new league, although several observers expressed the fear that the Continental League would weaken the minor leagues by competing in several of their best cities. Ford Frick, commissioner of baseball, announced that a committee which would include the presidents of the National and American Leagues would be appointed to meet with the representatives of the new league.

One of the motivating factors may have been the hearings being conducted by the House Judiciary Committee into possible antitrust violations by baseball. The chairman of that committee, Representative Emanuel Celler of Brooklyn, was a long-time critic of the big-business aspects of baseball. He said that if the new league

ran into any problems with which Congress could help, "it would be duty-bound to do so in the interest of the national pastime."

Pressure to accept the new league also came from Senator Estes Kefauver of Tennessee, chairman of the Senate Antitrust and Monopoly Committee. He had introduced a bill proposing to limit to 80 the number of players a major league team could control. Kefauver said of the Continental League, "I hope we can get some legislation that will help them get started."

Branch Rickey, a 76-year-old ex-major league player, manager, and executive, was appointed president of the Continental League on August 18, 1959. An hour after his appointment, Rickey met with Ford Frick's committee. Rickey's statements to the committee included, "We want your cooperation, we need your cooperation, we demand your cooperation."

After some seven hours of meeting, the committee endorsed the idea of the Continental League as a major league providing that several conditions were met. The Continental League was required to play a balanced 154-game schedule; it had to adopt the major league minimum-salary agreement, join the player pension plan and agree to admit no city smaller than the smallest currently in the major leagues. Kansas City was the smallest major league city, with a population of 460,000.

Rickey and Shea were among those who had testified in front of Senator Kefauver's committee. Their joint letter to the committee read in part:

The present major league franchise owners apparently have a total lack of loyalty to the communities which support their enterprises. The major league owner today refers to the "national pastime" with great reverence. And, when it suits him, he behaves as if he were operating a quasi-public trust. But let a better "deal" be offered in another city and he reverts instantaneously to the hundred-percent businessman whose only guide is the earnings statement.

In October 1959 Calvin Griffith, owner of the Washington Senators, was reportedly seriously considering moving his club to Minneapolis, and the Cincinnati Reds were considering relocating to New York. Both moves were apparently stymied by the pending legislation. Representative Celler said if the moves were made it would "prove that baseball is not a sport but a business."

By January 29, 1960, Buffalo, Atlanta, and Dallas-Ft. Worth had been admitted into the Continental League, thus completing an eight-club league. Branch Rickey found it significant that the Continental League completed its circuit sixty years to the day from the founding of the American League.

Indemnification of the minor leagues proved to be a major obstacle. The International League, which was to lose two cities, demanded $750,000 per city plus $100,000 relocation costs per franchise. The American Association expected $800,000 total per city lost. Although the monetary demands were later moderated, territorial issues continued to plague the Continental League with the International League proving particularly obstreperous.

The question of where the Continentals would find players was addressed in several ways. Rickey reported a number of inquiries from professional and amateur players. Second, Rickey helped form a new Class D Western Carolina League to begin operation in 1960. The Continental League was to subsidize the league with $60,000, to be divided among the eight clubs, plus paying managers' salaries, training costs, and certain transportation costs. All Western

Carolina League players were to train together and then were to be allocated to the various clubs. Frick rejected the Western Carolina League because the player pool to be operated under Continental League sponsorship violated a long-standing rule against major league teams controlling more than one team in a league.

Kefauver's bill to limit the control of Organized Baseball over players and removal of its antitrust exemption was narrowly defeated in June 1960, despite the lobbying of Senate Majority Leader Lyndon B. Johnson. With the defeat, pressure on the established major leagues was off.

On July 18, 1960, the National League voted to expand if it developed that the Continental League idea was not practical. New York was to be a part of any expansion plan, Frick assured. The American League also set up an expansion committee at about this time.

About two weeks later, on August 2, 1960, the Continental League backers submitted a formal application to Organized Baseball for recognition as the third major league. Instead, the immediate expansion of the existing major leagues by two clubs each was approved, with the eight Continental League backers concurring. With that action the Continental League formally expired.

A New York National League franchise was ultimately awarded to William Shea, with Houston joining at the same time. They began play in the 1962 season, as the Mets and the Colt .45s, respectively. The American League moved even more quickly. They allowed the Washington club to move to Minneapolis-St. Paul and admitted new clubs for 1961 in Washington (picking up the discarded Senators name) and Los Angeles (picking up the Angels name of the venerable Pacific Coast League franchise).

The rest of the Continental League cities were promised consideration when expansion occurred again. All of the Continental League cities, with the exception of Buffalo, did eventually end up with major league franchises, either through expansion or the transfer of existing clubs from other cities.

Afterword

In 1968 a Special Baseball Records Committee, appointed by the Commissioner of Baseball, considered the various claims made by and for leagues that they were or had been major leagues. Four of the "other major leagues"—the American Association (1882-1891), the Union Association (1884), the Players League (1890), and the Federal League (1914-1915)—joined the National League (1876 to present) and the American League (1901 to present) as recognized major leagues. Not recognized as part of the AL's major league history was its 1900 season; not acknowledged as part of the FL's major league history was its inaugural campaign in 1913.

The decisions of this Special Baseball Records Committee have been widely accepted by modern historians, excepting the committee's position that the National Association of 1871-1875 was somehow not major, despite its being the first professional league and the only one for five years. However, certain contemporaries of the Union Association might have expressed considerable surprise in the 1968 decision.

The claims of the other leagues that actually did operate were not accepted by the Special Baseball Records Committee and are not taken seriously by modern historians. The International Association/National Association (1877-1880) had even more erratic scheduling and procedures than the old National Association and the early years of the National League. The United States League (1912-1913) lasted only a little over a month over two seasons, and no one makes much of a case for it. None will be attempted here.

Chapter 38

College Baseball

By Beau Riffenburgh

There are a lot of similarities in the way information about football and baseball players is recorded. If you compare all-time player registers for professional football and major league baseball, for example, you will see that they both include much of the same data for any particular player: full name, height, weight, birth and death dates, and sites, years played professionally and for which teams, and the appropriate statistics. But look at the register here in *Total Baseball*. See something missing that you would see in any football listing? There is no space for college attended.

That omission says a great deal about the historic significance of college baseball. It is a game that is almost a century and a half old, but one that was neglected until relatively recently not only by most sports fans but by scouts and personnel experts of the professional leagues. Oh, it has their attention now. If you don't believe it, go to Omaha, Nebraska, at the beginning of June, and you will think that you have stumbled into a scouting combine.

But it took a long time for the college version of the national pastime to really get going. After all, the first intercollegiate baseball game was played a dozen years before the National Association became America's first major professional sports league. On July 1, 1859, Amherst and Williams played a game at Pittsfield, Massachusetts. The score, 73-32 in favor of Amherst, was as different from

Burt Hooton
As a Texas Longhorn (1969–1971), Hooton was 35-3 and pitched an NCAA record 13 shutouts before throwing a no-hitter for the Cubs in just his fourth pro start.

those of today as was the field, which included a square or diamond only 60 feet per side and a pitcher 25 feet closer to the batter than in the current game. That day, Amherst and Williams actually played a version of the "Massachusetts Game," a contest a great deal closer to rounders than the "New York Game" that developed into modern baseball.

From the very beginning of professional baseball, there were ties to the college game. In 1871, the first year of the National Association, at least two of the new professionals had previously played college ball—Rockford's Denny Mack, who had attended Villanova, and Troy's Steve Bellan, who had played for Fordham, then known as Rose Hill. In the ensuing decades there was a continual trickle of players from the colleges into the major leagues, including, around the turn of the century, Christy Mathewson from Bucknell, Eddie Plank from Gettysburg and Jack Coombs

from Colby. Connie Mack's "$100,000 infield" included two "college boys": second baseman Eddie Collins, who had played at Columbia, and shortstop Jack Barry, from Holy Cross.

Of course, college men were not warmly received into the majors. There has always been a natural reluctance by veterans to accept new players who are trying to take their jobs or those of their friends. This was perhaps even more the case in days of smaller rosters, with only 18 men on each team. And that divide was even greater between many of the long-term professionals and the youngsters from college, who were seen as being not only more highly educated, better mannered and more cultured, but from superior social and economic backgrounds.

Writing around the turn of the century, sportswriter George E. Stackhouse told the story of a catcher who became concerned when his manager began "to get the college baseball fever." The

catcher approached a local college player and asked him if he wished to turn pro. Upon receiving an answer in the negative, the catcher said, "Now that's square, old man. You know Greek, Latin and something about the world. You can make a good living anywhere. Don't interfere with us fellows, because you don't have to."

Early on, there were also many college players who simply were not interested in playing professionally. For every Lou Gehrig, who came to the Yankees from Columbia, there were numerous other college players who skipped a chance at a pro career because they could make more money in some other business, without having the unattractive travel conditions and long hours of a life in baseball. Nevertheless, by 1909 there were 57 players—approximately 14 percent of all those in the big leagues—who had college backgrounds. This figure soared to approximately one-third of the major leaguers by 1932.

Despite the obvious talent in it, the college game itself remained in the background. The colleges had to compete for attention not only with the professional leagues, but with semipro teams, town teams, and industrial league teams. In the early decades of the 20th century, the bigtime university programs were all located in the east or midwest, where weather conditions prevented an early start to the season, which was therefore necessarily short in order to conform to term dates. Limited travel opportunities due to timing and cost, a short schedule of games, and competition from others sports within the athletic department also helped to hold down the popularity of college baseball.

The College World Series

The game took a major step forward after World War II, when the NCAA began its national championship tournament. Not only did this give the sport more exposure than it previously had received, national playoffs showed that the game had expanded beyond its early strongholds. In fact, it took six years before an eastern team actually won a national title.

In 1947 four teams participated in single-elimination regionals in both the east and west, and the two winners met in the initial College World Series, at Kalamazoo, Michigan. The first national championship was won by the University of California, which defeated Yale, 8-7. The champion Bears were led by All-America outfielders Jackie Jensen and John Fiscalini. The Elis' captain was a weak-hitting first baseman named George H. W. Bush, who would ultimately become President of the United States.

Yale lost in the championship game again the next year, as the University of Southern California won the first of its record dozen national titles. The Trojans had co-coaches that year, Sam Barry and Rod Dedeaux, the latter of whom had been a three-time letterman at USC before a two-game career with the Brooklyn Dodgers. Dedeaux was just the first of numerous college coaches to win national titles after having played professionally. The next two came along almost immediately.

In 1949 the College World Series was moved from Kalamazoo to Wichita, Kansas, where it was a four-team, double-elimination tournament. Texas, coached by longtime White Sox star Bibb Falk—a career .314 hitter who had been the successor to Shoeless Joe Jackson—won the title with a 10-3 victory over Wake Forest. The Deacons, led by second baseman Charles Teague, the first three-time All-America baseball player and the tournament's most valuable player, had reached the championship game by eliminating Southern California. The next year, Texas became the first team to repeat as national champions, as the Longhorns rolled

through the newly expanded, eight-team tournament. But even more significantly, the College World Series itself, which played in a new site for the third time in four years, found a permanent home: Omaha, Nebraska. The CWS has now been in Omaha for more than half a century, and few sporting events have found venues with a local populace that has so totally embraced the event, the teams and the athletes.

Two years after Falk's second title, another former professional star coached his team to a national championship. Jack Barry had been hired as coach at Holy Cross in 1921, shortly after he retired from the major leagues. In 1952 Barry's Crusaders defeated Missouri, 8-4, to bring the east its first national title and to give Barry his first World Series title since he had played for the Boston Red Sox in the "real World Series" in 1915. Almost 40 years after Barry retired, he still holds the NCAA career record for highest winning percentage (.806).

Throughout the rest of the 1950s and the early 1960s, college baseball was dominated by a handful of universities. At USC the story was Rod Dedeaux, who had become the coach on his own when Sam Barry died in 1950. Dedeaux's Trojans won national titles in 1958, 1961, and 1963, while just missing in 1960, when they lost 2-1 in 10 innings to Minnesota. The Gophers had become a power under the leadership of Dick Siebert, the former Philadelphia Athletics first baseman. Siebert led Minnesota to its first national title in 1956 and followed that with championships in 1960 and 1964. During the early 1950s, the Gophers had perhaps their greatest pitcher ever, Paul Giel. In 1953 Giel, who had been named second-team All-America the previous season and would be again the following year, had the unusual distinction of being named first team All-America by the Baseball Coaches Association the same calendar year he was a consensus All-America in football.

Meanwhile, Big Ten rival Michigan also managed two national titles during that span, despite changing coaches. Missouri won only one title—in 1954—but the Tigers reached the championship game three other times in that period, losing to teams coached by both Dedeaux and Siebert, a dubious distinction also held by Arizona, which also lost each of its three title appearances.

The Big Three Programs

The year after Arizona lost to USC in the 1963 national championship game, a new bully showed up on the scene, just down the road from the home of the Arizona Wildcats. Coached by Bobby Winkles, who was a master at recruiting talent and making disparate personalities work well together, Arizona State became a national contender almost overnight. In 1964 the Sun Devils ended the season ranked second in the nation.

The next year, with a team loaded with talent, Arizona State stormed to its first national title. Second baseman Luis Lagunas led the nation in RBIs, center fielder Rick Monday led in triples, and pitcher Jim Merrick led in victories. Meanwhile, Luganas, Monday, and pitcher John Pavilk were named All-America, as outfielder Reggie Jackson would be the next year. Sal Bando was selected the most valuable player in the 1965 CWS, which concluded with the Sun Devils' 2-1 victory over Ohio State. Monday then became the first player chosen in the first baseball amateur draft.

The draft not only helped change the face of major league baseball, it changed the way that college programs looked at players, and the way that coaches recruited them. Initially college players were eligible to be drafted if they had attained sophomore status or

were 21 years old. Two years later the rule was changed so that players were eligible for the draft if they had attained junior status. The draft made it highly unlikely that many top-rated players would remain in a college program for four years. It also meant that players who transferred from a junior college might well leave after a single season at a major university, or, indeed, not attend a four-year college at all, since those completing junior college were also eligible for the draft.

Equally problematic for college coaches were the questions about freshman players. If drafted out of high school, a player remained eligible to be signed by the pro team until he had attended his first class. That meant a player signing a letter of intent with a university might well disregard his commitment at any moment, even once term was starting. The case of Richard Wortham, a high draft choice out of Odessa High School, who signed with the University of Texas, made many college coaches feel uncomfortable with the way major league teams interfered with their players. Before his freshman year in 1973, Wortham had to fight off the constant attentions of the professional representatives, who went so far as to walk with him to his first class, all the time attempting to sign him. Wortham attended class, however, and then stayed at Texas for four years, in the process becoming the first pitcher in NCAA history to win 50 games in his career.

Other players have not been so keen to stay in the college game. Alex Fernandez was selected in the first round of the 1988 draft, but chose rather to attend the University of Miami. His success there—he was named national Freshman of the Year in 1989 by *Baseball America*—led Fernandez to reconsider his choice. Fernandez transferred to Miami-Dade County Community College for his sophomore year. That season he went 12-2 with a 1.19 ERA and was named National Junior College Player of the Year. Fernandez was then selected by the White Sox fourth overall in the 1990 draft. By the end of the year, he was pitching in the major leagues.

A quarter of a century before Fernandez turned professional, the huge amounts of talent that Arizona State lost to the early drafts did not prevent the Sun Devils from becoming a regular national contender, in fact one of the three top teams of the mid-1960s to the mid-1970s. The Sun Devils won additional titles in 1967 and 1969, and lost in the national championship games of 1972 and 1973. Winkles' teams had such success that in 1973 the California Angels hired him as manager, making him the first college coach to manage in the majors with no previous big league experience. Winkles had not been the entire story at Arizona State, of course. In each of these appearances by the Sun Devils in the title game, they featured a pitcher who both led the nation in victories and was named All-America: Gary Gentry in 1967, Larry Gura in 1969, Craig Swan in 1972, and Eddie Bane in 1973. Gura's 19 victories were an NCAA record at the time, as were Swan's 47 career wins, Gentry's 229 strikeouts in a season, and Bane's 505 K's in a career.

Since pitching was such a key to college baseball at the time, it is not surprising that Texas, like Arizona State, was one of the three dominating powers. In 1968 Cliff Gustafson succeeded Bibb Falk as head coach, and the Longhorns immediately established the greatest pitching dynasty in the history of the college game. From 1969 to 1971 Burt Hooton of the Longhorns became the first three-time All-America pitcher and probably the most dominant ever in college. Hooton's 35-3 career mark included a 1.14 ERA and an NCAA record 13 shutouts. "Hooton is easily the best college pitcher we've ever seen," Winkles later said. "He was never

anything less than spectacular, never not at the height of his game."

Texas followed Hooton's stint with four All-America pitchers in five years, including two-timer Jim Gideon, who led the nation in victories in 1974 and 1975, tying the record of 19 the former year and setting a record with 17 without a loss the latter. At the time, only two pitchers per year were named All-America, meaning that seven times in eight years Texas had featured one of the two best pitchers in the country. Despite this, Texas won only one national title in a two-decade span, in 1975 when Gideon and Wortham combined to go 32-1. The reason the Longhorns consistently came up short was simple: Southern California.

Starting in 1968, Rod Dedeaux's Trojans put together the most successful dynasty in college baseball history. USC won the national title that year, then, after surrendering it to Arizona State, the Trojans won a record five in a row. The Trojans did not always have the best record going into the playoffs, but there was something special about them—they just knew when they came to Omaha that they were going to win—as in 1970, when, in a semifinal game against Texas, the last unbeaten team, the Trojans trailed 7-1 going into the seventh inning, yet managed to win, 8-7, in 14 innings. USC followed that up with another marathon, defeating Florida State 2-1 in 15 innings for the championship.

Nothing, however, matched the Trojans' comeback against Minnesota in 1973. Trailing the Gophers and their star pitcher Dave Winfield 7-0 going into the bottom of the ninth, USC parlayed eight singles, a stolen base, a sacrifice fly, and several Minnesota errors into a stunning 8-7 victory that eliminated Minnesota and put the Trojans into the championship game. There, they defeated Arizona State, 4-3. That team, one of the greatest in college history, included future major leaguers Fred Lynn, Roy Smalley, Steve Kemp, Rich Dauer, Randy Scarbery, Pete Redfern, Dennis Littlejohn, and Ed Putnam.

The Aluminum Bat

The 1974 season not only marked the last year of USC's reign, it signaled two major changes in college baseball. First, the NCAA adopted the designated-hitter rule. And second, it allowed the use of the aluminum bat. The new bats were a tremendous success in more ways than one. As a cost factor, they brought down bat budgets to approximately 10 percent of what they had previously been. As a weapon, they began to change the game dramatically. It was much easier to hit with the new bats. The entire surface of the bat was, more or less, a "sweet spot" and hits could be made as easily from the handle as from the meat of the bat. The ball traveled at a much greater rate coming off the bat—increasing home runs and hits to the outfield—and the "ping" sound did not help direct the fielders as did the typical crack of a bat. Runs and home runs both soared, and teams such as Arizona State, Wichita State and Oklahoma State regularly began to average more than 10 runs per game.

When the new bats were combined with increasingly longer schedules, records began to fall with alarming frequency. The individual record of 17 home runs in a season was broken in 1974, and Bob Horner of Arizona State became the first player to hit 25 in a season in 1978. In 1982 Jeff Ledbetter of Florida State shattered the record with 42 homers, and three years later Pete Incaviglia of Oklahoma State had perhaps the greatest offensive season ever, when, in a 75-game season, he set NCAA records with 48 home runs, 143 RBIs, and a slugging percentage of 1.140.

For the fan who liked to see offense, it was wonderful. For

purists, much less so. And it also began to have an effect on inter-actions with the pro game. Throughout the early 1970s, there had been a greater emphasis on taking college players in the draft. By 1977 more college players were being selected than high school players, and by 1981 five times as many college players were entering the major leagues as those drafted out of high school. But hitters were now forced to readjust to wooden bats, and quite a number struggled as they entered the minors. It was a problem that would not go away, because the universities could not return to wooden bats due to cost. The NCAA's attempts at adjusting the aluminum bats or using graphite bats have not solved the problem, and 25 years later it is still an issue. Many college players have tried to adjust to wooden bats in the summer leagues, such as the Cape Cod League, but this remains an inadequate solution.

Throughout the rest of the 1970s and during the 1980s, certain programs blossomed with the new bats, none more so than Wichita State and Oklahoma State. The Shockers—led by Joe Carter, Phil Stephenson, Jim Thomas, and Russ Morman—simply wrecked the record book between 1979 and 1983, leading the nation in hits and doubles four times each, and runs and triples five times each, as well as recording team batting averages of .384 and .378 in 1979 and 1980, respectively. At the same time, Oklahoma State's Gary Ward, one of the great hitting instructors in the history of college baseball, made the Cowboys a regular in Omaha at the end of the season. Although Ward did not guide a team to a national title, his .753 winning percentage is the sixth best of all time; he led Oklahoma State to the NCAA championship game three times; and he coached two of the most productive players in college history, Incaviglia and Robin Ventura. One of only seven three-time All-Americas (according to recognized NCAA polls), Ventura was a career .428 hitter, who set a national record when he hit safely in 58 consecutive games.

Meanwhile big numbers, and numerous records, were also put up regularly in the Rocky Mountains. The Western Athletic Conference teams tended to have small stadiums, which, in con-junction with the thin air, saw a lot of balls carry a long way. Brigham Young, Air Force and New Mexico in particular showed a great deal of power, with Deacon Winters, Wally Joyner, Cory Snyder, Jim Fregosi, Mike Willis, and Gary Daniels each having big statistical seasons undoubtedly helped by where they played most of their games.

Despite the national trends in hitting, however, certain teams continued to emphasize—and win with—pitching. Texas won one national title and made the championship game three other times in the 1980s by continuing its tradition of dominating pitching. Ten times in a dozen-year period Texas had an All-America pitcher, including the second and third ones ever to be three-time All-Americas, Greg Swindell (1984-86) and Kirk Dressendorfer (1988-90). When the Longhorns won the 1983 national champi-onship, Calvin Schiraldi was named national Pitcher of the Year, Kirk Killingsworth was honored as the nation's best relief pitcher, and Mike Capel had the best winning percentage on the team, while the other starter in the rotation was a guy named Roger Clemens.

On an individual level, the most successful pitcher was Derek Tatsuno of the University of Hawaii. Tatsuno led the nation in strikeouts three consecutive years (1977-79) and in that final year became the first pitcher to win 20 games in a season.

But, as usual, the teams that tended to win the most titles, above all, outstanding coaching. There was not a better example of

this than Jerry Kindall, who had been an All-America second baseman for Dick Siebert at Minnesota. Kindall led Arizona to three national championships—in 1976, 1980 and 1986—despite having only two All-Americas (Dave Stegman and Terry Francona) in those three years combined. Across the state Jim Brock suc-ceeded Winkles and led Arizona State to two more national titles. The California teams also continued to be hugely successful. Dedeaux won another title in 1978 before retiring with a record 1,332 victories; Mark Marquess led Stanford to a pair of national championships; and Augie Garrido turned Cal State Fullerton into a power, winning national titles in three decades: 1979, 1984 and 1995.

ESPN and Growing Popularity

The single thing that increased national interest in college base-ball more than any other happened off the field. ESPN's decisions to broadcast first the final stages of the College World Series, and then the entire series, gave national exposure to college baseball on a far-reaching level for the first time. People who didn't even know universities had baseball teams were able to watch Arizona State's 7-4 championship-game victory over Oklahoma State in 1981. And the next year the entire CWS, with teams representing all sec-tions of the country—including Miami, Wichita State, Texas, Maine, Oklahoma State, and Stanford—was broadcast nationally. Ratings were higher than many could have expected, leading the way within several years for ESPN to start showing a "game of the week" throughout the college season. Although this was later dropped, the College World Series gradually became such a pop-ular commodity that by 1989 ESPN could no longer afford the national championship game.

The growing popularity of the CWS had one unfortunate effect. The scheduling of the national championship game on net-work television required a set date for the final contest. Thus, in 1989 the format of the World Series, which had been double elim-ination for 40 years, was changed so that the eight teams were divided into two four-team divisions. The winners of each divi-sion—based on double-elimination play—met for the national title in a single-elimination game. This set up the possibility that a team with one loss could defeat a team with no losses for the title, an eventuality that actually occurred the first season of the new format.

The increased popularity of college baseball in the 1980s was also assisted by its ever-closer relationship with the major leagues. Due to ESPN, fans could now, as they had always done in football, first get to see players in college, and then follow their progress as professionals. The juxtaposition of the draft with the College World Series allowed a chance to see the play of the top selections while they were still in college. In the early 1980s, much more than previously, the colleges came to be viewed as almost a minor league, particularly as players moved quickly through the minors to the big leagues.

There have always been the unusual players who have gone straight to the majors from college, skipping the minors. In 1973 Dave Winfield was one of the first of these. Winfield, a multi-talented athlete who had major league talent as both a pitcher and a hitter, was also selected in the National Football League and National Basketball Association drafts, but instead he went imme-diately from being the CWS Most Valuable Player to the San Diego Padres. He singled off Jerry Reuss in his first at bat, hit safely in his first six games, and went on to a long and successful career,

and induction into the Hall of Fame in 2001. Five years later, after leading the nation in home runs twice and winning the Golden Spikes Award as the best amateur baseball player, Arizona State's Bob Horner went straight to the Atlanta Braves. In his first game in the pros, Horner homered off Bert Blyleven, on his way to being named National League Rookie of the Year.

Neither Winfield nor Horner, however, attained the national reputation that Pete Incaviglia had at Oklahoma State, buoyed by his two appearances in the College World Series, which gave luster to his record-setting achievements and his status as College Player of the Year. Although drafted by Montreal in 1985, Incaviglia refused to sign and was traded to the Rangers, for whom he hit 30 homers as a rookie. In 1989 two other players leapt straight from the college ranks to the major leagues after being named Player of the Year by at least one of the growing number of organizations presenting that award: John Olerud of Washington State (the only All-America baseball player who was the son of an All-America baseball player) and Jim Abbott, the amazing one-handed pitcher from Michigan. Abbott had several successful professional seasons, while Olerud is still playing in the majors.

The Game of the Sun Belt

When Wichita State won the national title in 1989, it marked the first time since 1966, when Ohio State was national champion, that the title was won by a team out of the Sun Belt. Things have returned to normal since then. But whereas the CWS used to be dominated by teams from California, Arizona, and Texas, the deep South has now become the major player.

Miami won titles in 1982 and 1985 under Ron Fraser, and in 1999 and 2001 under Jim Morris. The 6-5 victory against Florida State in 1999 marked the 17th appearance in the CWS for the Seminoles, although they have never won the national title. Georgia Tech, led by three-time All-America catcher Jason Varitek, reached the national championship game in 1994.

But for a decade beginning in 1991, one team dominated in Omaha like no one other than USC ever had, as Louisiana State won five titles. The key to this success—as Dedeaux was at USC—has been coach Skip Bertman, who was widely considered to be the top assistant in the country when he was the pitching coach for Miami under Fraser. Bertman's initial contribution was made in the development of the pitching staff, including, in 1989, Ben McDonald, who was named College Player of the Year before being the No. 1 selection in the draft.

LSU's first national championship came two years later, on the heels of Georgia's 1990 title, the first ever for a Southeastern Conference team. In that championship run, the Tigers showed the offense that they have been known for ever since, setting or tying College World Series records for home runs, runs per game and slugging percentage, as well as for fielding percentage. Two years later, LSU won again, defeating Wichita State in the title game for the second time.

In 1996 second baseman Warren Morris hit a two-out, two-run homer in the bottom of the ninth as the Tigers came from behind to defeat Miami 9-8, marking the first time that the national title was decided on a homer in the bottom of the ninth. The next year the Tigers had to outlast three other teams from the SEC—Alabama, Auburn and Mississippi State—to win the champi-

onship. Such participation makes it clear that the SEC has at least equaled the quality of baseball in the Six Pac, the southern division of the Pacific 10 Conference, which was long considered the best conference in college baseball.

Not that the Six Pac isn't still a baseball power. USC won yet another national title in 1998, this time under Mike Gillespie, after losing in the championship game to Cal State Fullerton in 1995. And since we changed centuries, Stanford has appeared in three of four championship tilts, although they have lost all three.

Meanwhile, the Big 12 has become another center of excellence after joining teams from two strong baseball conferences, the Southwest and the Big 8. In the 1990s Oklahoma and Oklahoma State both reached the national championship game. And in the past several years Nebraska has earned consecutive trips across state to Omaha. But, as it has been for so long, the best team in the region throughout the period is still Texas. From 1991 to 1993 Texas fielded its fourth three-time All-America (more than the rest of the nation combined) in Brooks Kieschnick, the only player ever to win a major award (the Dick Howser Award) as the top amateur baseball player in America more than once. In 1996 Cliff Gustafson of the Longhorns retired after having broken Dedeaux's record by recording 1,427 victories, with a .792 winning percentage, second best of any coach ever with 500 victories.

The Longhorns weren't exactly left high and dry on the coaching front, however, as they immediately hired Augie Garrido, who had led Cal State Fullerton to three titles. By 2000, when LSU won its fifth title in a decade, Garrido had Texas back at the CWS. And two years later, the Longhorns presented him with his fourth national title—one in each of four different decades—with a 12-6 victory over South Carolina, yet another Southeastern Conference team.

The 2003 season saw the first major change in the College World Series format in more than a decade. The eight teams would continue to be divided into two brackets, but the winners of the two brackets would play a best-of-three series for the title. This meant that for the first time a team with two losses could win the championship, or it might take three losses to eliminate another team.

When the series itself rolled around, a lot looked familiar, as Texas, Stanford and Fullerton all reached the final four again. However, the team that came out on top had a decidedly new look. In fact, Rice's national title was the first national championship in any sport ever for the small Houston academic powerhouse. After eliminating Texas, Rice won the first of the title series 4-3 behind All-America pitcher Jeff Niemann, who did not get a result, but did tie a 28-year-old NCAA record for most wins in a season without a loss (17-0). Stanford then tied the series with an 8-3 victory, but the final was all Rice. The Owls jumped ahead from the start and went on to record a 14-2 win that set a record for margin of victory.

Another Texas powerhouse had come onto the scene. And the newcomer promised to be back. "We're starting to think tomorrow morning about winning another one," Wayne Graham, Rice's 67-year-old head coach said after the game. In fact, Graham later added, college baseball is so much fun "that I intend to coach until I'm 80."

DIVISION I BASEBALL CHAMPIONSHIP RESULTS

Year	Champion	Coach	Score	Runner-up	Year	Champion	Coach	Score	Runner-up
1947	California	Clint Evans	8-7	Yale	1976	Arizona	Jerry Kindall	7-1	Eastern Michigan
1948	Southern California	Sam Barry	9-2	Yale	1977	Arizona State	Jim Brock	2-1	South Carolina
1949	Texas	Bibb Falk	10-3	Wake Forest	1978	Southern California	Rod Dedeaux	10-3	Arizona State
1950	Texas	Bibb Falk	3-0	Washington State	1979	Cal State Fullerton	Augie Garrido	2-1	Arkansas
1951	Oklahoma	Jack Baer	3-2	Tennessee	1980	Arizona	Jerry Kindall	5-3	Hawaii
1952	Holy Cross	Jack Barry	8-4	Missouri	1981	Arizona State	Jim Brock	7-4	Oklahoma State
1953	Michigan	Ray Fisher	7-5	Texas	1982	Miami (Florida)	Ron Fraser	9-3	Wichita State
1954	Missouri	Hi Simmons	4-1	Rollins	1983	Texas	Cliff Gustafson	4-3	Alabama
1955	Wake Forest	Taylor Sanford	7-6	Western Michigan	1984	Cal State Fullerton	Augie Garrido	3-1	Texas
1956	Minnesota	Dick Siebert	12-1	Arizona	1985	Miami (Florida)	Ron Fraser	10-6	Texas
1957	California	George Wolfman	1-0	Penn State	1986	Arizona	Jerry Kindall	10-2	Florida State
1958	Southern California	Rod Dedeaux	8-7	Missouri	1987	Stanford	Mark Marquess	9-5	Oklahoma State
1959	Oklahoma State	Toby Greene	5-3	Arizona	1988	Stanford	Mark Marquess	9-4	Arizona State
1960	Minnesota	Dick Siebert	2-1	Southern California	1989	Wichita State	Gene Stephenson	5-3	Texas
1961	Southern California	Rod Dedeaux	1-0	Oklahoma State	1990	Georgia	Steve Webber	2-1	Oklahoma State
1962	Michigan	Don Lund	5-4	Santa Clara	1991	LSU	Skip Bertman	6-3	Wichita State
1963	Southern California	Rod Dedeaux	5-2	Arizona	1992	Pepperdine	Andy Lopez	3-2	Cal State Fullerton
1964	Minnesota	Dick Siebert	5-1	Missouri	1993	LSU	Skip Bertman	8-0	Wichita State
1965	Arizona State	Bobby Winkles	2-1	Ohio State	1994	Oklahoma	Larry Cochell	13-5	Georgia Tech
1966	Ohio State	Marty Karow	8-2	Oklahoma State	1995	Cal State Fullerton	Augie Garrido	11-5	Southern California
1967	Arizona State	Bobby Winkles	11-2	Houston	1996	LSU	Skip Bertman	9-8	Miami (Florida)
1968	Southern California	Rod Dedeaux	4-3	Southern Illinois	1997	LSU	Skip Bertman	13-6	Alabama
1969	Arizona State	Bobby Winkles	10-1	Tulsa	1998	Southern California	Mike Gillespie	21-14	Arizona State
1970	Southern California	Rod Dedeaux	2-1	Florida State	1999	Miami (Florida)	Jim Morris	6-5	Florida State
1971	Southern California	Rod Dedeaux	7-2	Southern Illinois	2000	LSU	Skip Bertman	6-5	Stanford
1972	Southern California	Rod Dedeaux	1-0	Arizona State	2001	Miami (Florida)	Jim Morris	12-1	Stanford
1973	Southern California	Rod Dedeaux	4-3	Arizona State	2002	Texas	Augie Garrido	12-6	South Carolina
1974	Southern California	Rod Dedeaux	7-3	Miami (Florida)	2003	Rice	Wayne Graham	14-2	Stanford
1975	Texas	Cliff Gustafson	5-1	South Carolina					

DIVISION II BASEBALL CHAMPIONSHIP RESULTS

Year	Champion	Coach	Score	Runner-up	Year	Champion	Coach	Score	Runner-up
1968	Chapman	Paul Deese	11-0	Delta St.	1986	Troy St.	Chase Riddle	5-0	Columbus St.
1969	Illinois St.	Duffy Bass	12-0	Southwest Mo. St.	1987	Troy St.	Chase Riddle	7-5	Tampa
1970	Cal St. Northridge	Bob Hiegert	2-1	Nicholls St.	1988	Fla.Southern	Chuck Anderson	5-4	Sacramento St.
1971	Fla. Southern	Hal Smeltzly	4-0	Central Mich.	1989#	Cal Poly	Steve McFarland	9-5	New Haven
1972	Fla. Southern	Hal Smeltzly	5-1	Cal St. Northridge	1990	Jacksonville St.	Rudy Abbott	12-8	Cal St.
1973	UC Irvine	Gary Adams	9-6	Ithaca	1991	Jacksonville St.	Rudy Abbott	20-4	Mo. Southern St.
1974	UC Irvine	Gary Adams	14-1	New Orleans	1992	Tampa	Lelo Prado	11-8	Mansfield
1975	Fla. Southern	Hal Smeltzly	10-7	Marietta	1993	Tampa	Lelo Prado	7-5	Cal Poly
1976	Cal Poly Pomona	John Scolinos	17-3	SIU-Edwardsville	1994	Central Mo. St.	Dave Van Horn	14-9	Fla. Southern
1977	UC Riverside	Jack Smitheran	4-1	Eckerd	1995	Fla. Southern	Chuck Anderson	15-0	GC& SU
1978	Fla. Southern	Joe Arnold	7-2	Delta St.	1996	Kennesaw St.	Mike Sansing	4-0	St. Joseph's
1979	Valdosta St.	Tommy Thomas	3-2	Fla. Southern	1997	Cal St. Chico	Lindsay Meggs	13-12	Central Okla.
1980	Cal Poly Pomona	John Scolinos	13-6	New Haven	1998	Tampa	Terry Rupp	6-1	Kennesaw St.
1981	Fla. Southern	Joe Arnold	9-0	Eastern Ill.	1999	Cal St. Chico	Lindsay Meggs	11-5	Kennesaw St.
1982	UC Riverside	Jack Smitheran	10-1	Fla. Southern	2000	Southeastern Okla. (Tex.)	Mike Metheny	7-2	Fort Hays St.
1983	Cal Poly Pomona	John Scolinos	9-7	Jacksonville St.	2001	St. Mary's	Charlie Migl	11-3	Central Mo. St.
1984	Cal St. Northridge	Bob Hiegert	10-5	Fla. Southern	2002	Columbus St.	Greg Appleton	5-3	Cal St. Chico
1985	Fla. Southern	Chuck Anderson	15-5	Cal Poly Pomona	2003	Central Mo. St.	Brad Hill	11-4	Tampa

Participation vacated by the NCAA Committee on Infractions.

DIVISION III BASEBALL CHAMPIONSHIP RESULTS

Year	Champion	Coach	Score	Runner-up	Year	Champion	Coach	Score	Runner-up
1976	Cal St. Stanislaus	Jim Bowen	13-6	Ithaca	1990	Eastern Conn. St.	Bill Holowaty	8-1	Aurora
1977	Cal St. Stanislaus	Jim Bowen	8-5	Brandeis	1991	Southern Me.	Ed Flaherty	9-0	Col. of New Jersey
1978	Rowan	Michael Briglia	5-3	Marietta	1992	Wm. Paterson	Jeff Albies	3-1	Cal Lutheran
1979	Rowan	Michael Briglia	3-0	Cal St. Stanislaus	1993	Montclair St.	Norm Schoenig	3-1	Wis.-Oshkosh
1980	Ithaca	George Valesente	12-5	Marietta	1994	Wis.-Oshkosh	Tom Lechnir	6-2	Wesleyan (Conn.)
1981	Marietta	Don Schaly	14-12 (12)	Ithaca	1995	La Verne	Owen Wright	5-3	Methodist
1982	Eastern Conn. St.	Bill Holowaty	11-6	Cal St. Stanislaus	1996	Wm. Paterson	Jeff Albies	6-5	Cal Lutheran
1983	Marietta	Don Schaly	36-8	Otterbein	1997	Southern Me.	Ed Flaherty	15-1	Wooster
1984	Ramapo	Mickey Ennis	5-4	Marietta	1998	Eastern Conn. St.	Bill Holowaty	16-1	Montclair St.
1985	Wis.-Oshkosh	Russ Tiedemann	11-6	Marietta	1999	N.C. Wesleyan	Charle Long	1-0	St. Thomas (Minn.)
1986	Marietta	Don Schaly	11-6	Ithaca	2000	Montclair St.	Norm Schoenig	6-2	St.Thomas (Minn.)
1987	Montclair St.	Kevin Cooney	13-12 (10)	Wis.-Oshkosh	2001	St. Thomas (Minn.)	Dennis Denning	8-4	Marietta
1988	Ithaca	George Valesente	7-5	Wis.-Oshkosh	2002	Eastern Conn. St.	Bill Holowaty	8-0	Marietta
1989	N.C. Wesleyan	Mike Fox	8-7 (13)	Cal St. Stanislaus	2003	Chapman		15-2, 15-7	Christopher Newport

Chapter 39

Women in Baseball

Play Belle!
Baseball was a popular pastime among some women as early as the middle of the 19th century, as indicated by this 1869 illustration of a game at Petersboro, New York.

By Debra A. Shattuck

Women have been associated with baseball, as players or spectators, since the game's dawn in the early 19th century. Even before baseball emerged in its final form, girls and young women sometimes played precursors of the game like One Old Cat, Town Ball, and Stoolball in Colonial America. As time passed, and the boys' amusement became serious business for grown men, baseball's reputation as a masculine domain was established. In 1865, one year before Charles Peverelly observed that baseball "has now become beyond question the leading feature of the outdoor sports of the United States," Harper's Weekly proclaimed: "There is no nobler or manlier game than base-ball."

During the latter half of the 19th century, women's presence as spectators at baseball games was tolerated and sometimes encouraged. Eventually promoters of the game hosted regular "Ladies Days" to attract female fans that would bring in added gate receipts and, hopefully, have a calming effect on the sometimes unruly crowds. Many women were content with their role as spectators and moral uplifters, but others yearned for the opportunity to try their hand at the national pastime. Those who lived out their fantasy often had to endure verbal and written derision from observers anxious to preserve the baseball status quo.

For the most part, the negative attitude toward women baseball players continues to this day. Many still share the opinion of an editorialist who noted in the *St. Louis Globe-Democrat* in 1885 that "The female has no place in base ball, except to the degradation of the game." The criticisms notwithstanding, uncounted women have pursued their own field of dreams, contributing their unique chapter to baseball's rich heritage.

Many of the first women baseball players were college students. The secluded atmosphere of all-girl schools enabled women to play the game without attracting too much attention. Students at Vassar College organized two baseball clubs as early as 1866. In 1879, according to Vassar alum Sophia Foster Richardson, the Vassar girls organized at least seven baseball clubs. The private grounds of col-

lege campuses did not always protect female players from public criticism, however. In a speech to an alumni association in 1896, Richardson recalled, "The public, so far as it knew of our playing, was shocked, but in our retired grounds, and protected from observation even in these grounds by sheltering trees, we continued to play in spite of a censorious public." Within a few years, however, the "censorious public" and "disapproving mothers" had succeeded in stifling the game at Vassar. But Vassar was not the only college where women tried their hand at baseball. In a letter to her former classmates at Smith College, Minnie Stephens (class of 1883) reminisced about the baseball clubs they had organized at the school in 1880. Stephens described the enthusiasm of the players and the keen competition at games. She also related how the Victorian-style clothing of the day, generally a hindrance to sporting endeavors, had actually benefited one of the players during a heated contest: "One vicious batter drove a ball directly into the belt line of her opponent, and had it not been for the rigid steel corset clasp worn in those days, she would have been knocked out completely." Like the women at Vassar, baseball players at Smith College faced opposition that eventually forced them to give up the game for a number of years.

Women baseball players were not limited to college campuses. In Springfield, Illinois, three men organized a women's baseball club in 1875. They were confident that the novelty of women playing baseball would attract large crowds and fatten their bankroll. On September 11, 1875, the club's teams, labeled the "Blondes" and "Brunettes," played their first match. Newspapers heralded the event as the "first game of baseball ever played in public for gate money between feminine ball-tossers." The concept evidently caught on, for numerous other male entrepreneurs copied the idea and organized women's baseball teams. One group started the "Young Ladies' Baseball Club" in Philadelphia in 1883. These owners billed their team's games as entertainment spectacles, not serious competition, and they continually stressed the femininity and moral respectability of their players. A newspaper account of one of the club's first games relayed the management's claim that players were "selected with tender solicitude from 200 applicants, variety actresses and ballet girls being positively barred." Furthermore the article noted, "Only three of the lot had ever been on the stage, and they were in the strictly legitimate business."

The Young Ladies Baseball Club played its first game on August 18, 1883, at Pastime Park in Philadelphia. Despite the supposed "200 applicants," only 16 girls were mustered to form the two teams for the contest; two young men rounded out the rosters. The game was played on a regulation-size diamond, but, as one observer wrote, it was too large for the women. "A ball thrown from pitcher to second base almost invariably fell short and was stopped on the roll. The throw from first to third base was an utter impossibility." Five hundred spectators witnessed the club's debut and were caught up in "uncontrollable laughter" much of the time. From a financial standpoint, however, the venture was a success. More than 1,500 fans turned out for the club's match at the Manhattan Athletic Club on September 23, 1883, where they "laughed themselves hungry and thirsty." Though one observer conceded that "four of the girls had become expert—for girls," it is obvious that "novelty" and not "ability" was the hallmark of women's baseball at the time.

Bloomer Girls

Another novel group of women baseball players was the Bloomer Girls. Actually "Bloomer Girls" was a misnomer, since Bloomer Girls teams were composed of both men and women. Kansas City Bloomer Girls, New York Bloomer Girls, Texas Bloomer Girls, and Boston Bloomer Girls were just a few of the teams traveling from diamond to diamond in the late 19th and early 20th centuries in search of fame and fortune. Despite the number of Bloomer Girl teams, they did not play each other and no formal league was set up. Instead, they journeyed from town to town, challenging men's amateur and semi-professional teams. The Bloomer Girls teams relied on sideshow-style appeal to draw fans and, not surprisingly, the bottom line was money. The manager of the Texas Bloomer Girls wrote to one prospective promoter in 1913, assuring him that the team's seven girls and four boys, "including the one-armed boy who plays center field," would draw enough fans to ensure the backer "three hundred dollars clear money" each week. A few of the male Bloomer Girls players like "Smoky Joe" Wood and Hall of Famer Rogers Hornsby went on to become successful big league ballplayers, but the future was not as bright for the female players who could not aspire to anything higher in the baseball world.

The Bloomer Girls teams were not the only option available to baseball-playing females around the turn of the century. Women's teams and mixed teams competed occasionally in "pickup" games. One such game took place in Kearsarge, New Hampshire, on August 7, 1903. An article in the *Boston Herald* the following day noted, "The teams were made up of young ladies gowned in white and young men decked out in girls' clothes, all New Englanders, guests at the hotel." On August 31, the newspaper announced an upcoming game at Forest Hills between the "Hickey and Clover clubs," each composed of five women and four men. One year later in Flat Rock, Indiana, a group of women organized two baseball clubs: one consisting only of married players, the other only of single players.

While some women played on all-female or coed teams, others challenged social constraints of the day by playing on otherwise all-male teams. On June 12, 1903, the *Cincinnati Enquirer* printed an article about the efforts of a local woman, Miss M. E. Phelan, to get a job as center fielder with the all-male Flora Baseball Club of Indiana. Phelan wrote to the club's manager informing him, "I have played with a number of lady ball clubs and am considered the equal of the average country player." Whether the Flora club took Phelan up on her offer to play for them for "$60 per month and expenses" is unknown, but only four years later another Ohioan, Alta Weiss, became an overnight female baseball-playing sensation and, as one article put it, "perhaps the only girl in the United States to obtain [a] college education through skill as a baseball player."

Weiss, a native of Ragersville, Ohio, became a celebrity in the Cleveland area when she made her pitching debut with the all-male, semi-professional Vermilion Independents on September 2, 1907. More than 1,200 fans attended the game in which Weiss pitched five innings, giving up only four hits and one run. By the time Weiss made her second appearance on September 8, she was already being heralded as the "Girl Wonder" in the press. According to the *Vermilion News,* so many fans wanted to see Weiss play that special trains had to be run to Vermilion from Cleveland and surrounding towns.

Weiss pitched eight games for the Independents during their 1907 season. More than 13,000 fans saw the games, including a season high of 3,182, who witnessed her debut at Cleveland's League Park on October 2, 1907. At least a dozen newspapers cov-

ered her exploits. The following year her father bought a half-interest in a men's semi-professional team which was known thereafter as the Weiss All-Stars. It was based in Cleveland and, with Alta as a drawing card, played for large crowds throughout Ohio and Kentucky.

Though Weiss was far and away the best-known woman baseball player in northern Ohio at this time, she was not the only one. On June 22, 1908, the *Cleveland Press* introduced 14-year-old Carita Masteller to the public. The paper reported that she had been playing baseball for eight or nine years and was as good as Weiss. That same month Weiss pitched against another female pitcher, Irma Gribble. The two dueled again in August. In another unique game, two sisters from Bellevue, Ohio, Irene and Ruth Basford, pitched for opposing men's teams.

Another well-known woman baseball player who played on men's teams was Rhode Islander Elizabeth Murphy. "Lizzie," as she liked to be called, played amateur and semi-professional baseball from about 1915 to 1935 and was known as the "Queen of Baseball" throughout New England and eastern Canada. After playing for a number of amateur teams in Rhode Island, Murphy signed with the semi-professional Providence Independents in 1918. A few years later she joined Ed Carr's All-Stars of Boston and earned quite a reputation for her skills as a first baseman.

In 1928, while Murphy was still impressing the fans in New England, 14-year-old Margaret Gisolo helped her Blanford, Indiana, American Legion boys' baseball team win county, district, sectional, and state championships. In seven tournament games she had 9 hits in 21 at bats. She scored 10 putouts and 28 assists in the field, with no errors charged against her. A protest against her participation filed by opposing teams went all the way to the American Legion's National Americanism Commission, which referred it to the baseball commissioner, Judge Kenesaw Mountain Landis. Landis determined that American Legion rules did not specifically ban the participation of women and disallowed the protest.

Landis had to address a similar situation three years later when the "Barnum of Baseball," Chattanooga Lookouts manager Joe Engel, signed 17-year-old Jackie Mitchell to a contract with his Southern Association minor league team, thus making her the first female professional baseball player. Mitchell had been taught to pitch by major leaguer Dazzy Vance and had once struck out nine men in a row in an amateur game. She became an overnight celebrity on April 2, 1931, when she pitched in an exhibition game against the visiting New York Yankees—and struck out Babe Ruth and Lou Gehrig, back to back. Speculation continues as to whether Ruth and Gehrig were merely putting on a show or really trying to hit Mitchell's pitches. Mitchell contended that it was not a setup and that the only instructions to the players had been to try not to hit the ball straight through the pitcher's box. A number of Yankees confirmed her story. Unfortunately Mitchell never had a chance to repeat her performance as a professional baseball player. A few days after her debut, Landis informed Engel that he had disallowed Mitchell's contract on the grounds that life in baseball was too strenuous for women. Organized Baseball formalized the ban against women signing professional baseball contracts with men's teams on June 21, 1952; the ruling still stands.

A League Is Born

The restriction on women playing professional baseball on men's teams did not prevent the formation of a women's professional baseball league, however. In 1943, with wartime manpower shortages threatening major league baseball, Chicago Cubs owner Philip K. Wrigley decided to form a women's professional softball league which would play its games in the major league stadiums while the men were away at war. Within a year of its founding, the league modified its rules and the All-American Girls Baseball League (AAGBL) was born. The AAGBL made its debut in 1943, when four teams—the Rockford (Illinois) Peaches, the South Bend (Indiana) Blue Sox, the Racine (Wisconsin) Belles, and the Kenosha (Wisconsin) Comets—squared off during the league's 108-game schedule. Attendance that year was 176,000 fans, which, according to one contemporary, meant that the league was "drawing a higher percentage of the population (in league cities) than major league baseball ever did in its greatest attendance years." Attendance figures continued to rise year after year, reaching a peak in 1948, when the league's 10 teams drew almost 1,000,000 fans. That same year, AAGBL teams drew more than 100,000 fans for a series of nine games in Puerto Rico.

Unlike women's teams of the past, the AAGBL relied on players' skills, not just their gender, to draw fans to the ballpark. The more than 500 women who played in the AAGBL during its 12-year existence were top-notch athletes. Many were veterans of championship school, community or industrial softball teams, and a few had even played on boys' or men's baseball teams. In addition, many of the AAGBL managers were experienced professional baseball players—some, like Bill Wambsganss (the only player ever to achieve an unassisted triple play in a World Series), Max Carey, Jimmie Foxx, and Dave Bancroft, were legends.

The AAGBL represented one of the only times in history that women baseball players received widespread moral and financial support. Once World War II ended, however, social pressures for women to leave nontraditional jobs and return to household duties resumed. This fact, coupled with organizational problems and the rise of televised major league games, led to the demise of the AAGBL. Interest in the league all but disappeared until the 1980s, when a group of former players organized a players association and began lobbying to have the league honored in the National Baseball Hall of Fame. The popular media and serious scholars rediscovered the league and hundreds of articles about the AAGBL appeared in newspapers and magazines across the country. In October 1988 the Hall of Fame unveiled a permanent exhibit of AAGBL league memorabilia. In the summer of 1992, the AAGBL was further memorialized when it became the subject of the feature film *A League of Their Own.*

Despite the newfound popularity of the AAGBL, modern-day women baseball players still face the same obstacles and criticisms endured by 19th century players. For the most part, organized teams and leagues remain closed to women. When Commissioner Ford Frick issued his ban against women players in 1952, his purpose was to prevent teams from using women players as publicity stunts. The end result of his edict was that even highly skilled women players (like those on the all-female team that tried, unsuccessfully, to gain admission to the men's Class A Florida State League in 1984) lost an important avenue for upward mobility and legitimacy in baseball. Women who challenge baseball's "men only" reputation rarely escape the experience unscathed. Julie Croteau, who gained notoriety in the late 1980s by playing first base for the St. Mary's (Maryland) College men's baseball team, earned school and conference honors yet still had to endure derisive comments from teammates. She left school in the middle of her junior year

disillusioned with a system she believed treated women as inferior to men.

Thanks to a series of court battles in the 1970s, generations of young girls have had the opportunity to play baseball on Little League teams. The 1998 season marked the 25th season in which girls have participated in Little League baseball, and it was the first time a girl played in the championship game of the Little League World Series. A growing number of girls and women continue to find opportunities to play baseball in both female leagues and in co-educational leagues. Nearly 3 million girls and 300,000 women play amateur baseball, comprising 17.5 percent of baseball participants in the United States. Women's leagues also exist in Australia and Canada.

In 1994 the Colorado Silver Bullets began their inaugural season as the first, and only, all-female professional baseball team to be officially recognized by the National Association of Professional Baseball Leagues. Their existence was made possible by the sponsorship of the Coors Brewing Company. Competing against men's teams, the team struggled on the field during its first few seasons, but they attracted national attention. The team improved its record in 1996 to 18-34, with pitcher Pam Davis (7–7) becoming the first Bullets pitcher to avoid a losing record. The team's third season also saw its offense improve dramatically, from a .183 team batting average in 1995 to .241 in 1996. And after failing to homer in their first two seasons, the Silver Bullets delivered five in 1996.

The Bullets finished with a winning record for the first time in 1997, and their quality of play continued to improve. Three players hit above .300, and the pitching was impressive, led by Lee Anne Ketcham, who was 7–5 with a 3.35 ERA. As the season ended, though, Coors announced that they would not renew their sponsorship. Without a sponsor, the team folded after the 1997 season. "Everybody's put a lot of heart into it," founder Bob Hope said. "You've got little girls out there that had a glass ceiling in between them and the opportunity to play the game. The door's been opened, and we want to work hard to make sure it opens even wider."

Phil Niekro, a Hall of Fame pitcher and the only manager in Bullets history, said, "Women can play baseball. Someday a woman will play in the big leagues and I only hope I'm around to see it. I want to be sitting right there in the first row because I guarantee you that she will be standing in the batter's box and will be remembering the Silver Bullets. This is where we started."

The first steps towards that goal may have been taken in the past few years. Jodi Haller became the second woman to play college baseball, pitching for NAIA St. Vincent's (Pennsylvania) College in 1990. Then in the fall of 1994, Lee Anne Ketcham and Julie Croteau, both members of the Colorado Silver Bullets, played for the Maui Stingrays in the Hawaiian Winter Baseball League, a developmental winter league for players at about the Class A level.

The most promising advances were made by Ila Borders, who became the first woman to win a college baseball game in 1994. The lefthanded pitcher posted a 2–4 record with a 2.92 ERA during her freshman year for Southern California College, finishing her college career with a 4–5 record at Whittier College in 1997. Later that year, Borders became the first woman to pitch in a men's professional baseball game as a member of the St. Paul Saints of the independent Northern League. She spent parts of four seasons with four different Northern League clubs, retiring midway through the 2000 season to pursue a broadcasting career with ESPN. "I'll look back and say I did something nobody ever did," Borders said. "I'm proud of that. I wasn't out to prove women's rights or anything. I just love baseball." Scores of young girls had found a role model, but it had never been easy for Borders. "I've been spit on, had beer thrown on me and been sworn at and was hit 11 times out of 11 at bats while in college," she told the *Salt Lake Tribune*. "But the memories I have are the ovations when I would run in from the bullpen."

Borders and the Silver Bullets not only showed that women can play baseball, they also suggested that women's baseball could be economically viable. Ladies League Baseball debuted as a professional women's league in 1997 with four teams—two in Los Angeles and one each in San Jose and Phoenix. The 30-game season was a success, and the league expanded eastward in 1998. The league changed its name to Ladies League Baseball and added teams in Buffalo and New Jersey. The expanded league intended to play a 56-game schedule starting in July and ending in September. However, low attendance, and escalating costs forced LPB owners to abbreviate the first half, playing only 16 games in the first half and canceling the second half of the regular season.

Though there hasn't been as much media attention to women's baseball since the retirement of Ila Borders and the demise of the Silver Bullets, the phenomenon is still very much alive. There are women's baseball leagues and tournaments in various regions nationwide and worldwide. The International Baseball Federation announced it would sanction a Women's World Cup of Baseball in 2004 and asked Baseball Canada to host the event. Edmonton, Alberta, Canada was selected as the host city, with USA Baseball entering a national women's baseball team in the tournament, joining teams from Australia, Canada, Japan, and other nations.

If girls and women continue to enjoy opportunities to play baseball, the sport will undoubtedly lose its masculine reputation. The question is whether or not current opportunities for female players will last. If they don't, today's female baseball players may find themselves sidelined, once again, with "a league of their own," watching rather than directly experiencing the national pastime.

Awards & Honors

Frank and Barbara Robinson
The Robinsons took home a 1967 Corvette from *SPORT* magazine after
Frank was named the outstanding player of the 1966 World Series.

FAMOUS FIRSTS

1911: Baseball gives its first MVP Awards to the Cubs' Frank Schulte and the Tigers' Ty Cobb.

1933: The first major league All-Star Game is played in Chicago's Comiskey Park.

1936: Ty Cobb, Babe Ruth, Christy Mathewson, Honus Wagner, and Walter Johnson become the first players elected to the Hall of Fame.

1947: The Rookie of the Year Award is presented for the first time.

1950: The All-Star Game is broadcast on television for the first time.

1957: The Gold Glove Awards are presented for the first time.

1958: The first Cy Young Award is presented to Don Newcombe.

1962: Jackie Robinson becomes the first African-American elected to the Hall of Fame.

2002: Roger Clemens becomes the first pitcher to win six Cy Young Awards.

Chapter 40

Awards and Honors

By Bill Deane

Thisis chapter presents the history and voting results of baseball's most prestigious awards and honors, including the complete balloting and current constituency of the Baseball Hall of Fame. We have included as complete a selection of results as you'll find anywhere. Our compilation ranges from some of the oldest and best known honors, such as Most Valuable Player, to some of the newest, and some worthy but little-known prizes, such as the Fred Hutchinson Memorial Award. Included are awards for excellence in the regular season, heroics in the All-Star Game, leadership in the postseason, and character off the field. This material will be of interest to the fan who wonders how a player of the past was viewed by his contemporaries. I have ventured an additional section of "what if" awards: what if the Cy Young Award had been instituted long before its actual inception in 1956, or the Rookie of the Year before its real debut in 1947, and so on.

Balloting tables and lists of winners include each player's first initial, last name, and club city abbreviation (and point total, if applicable).

Most Valuable Player Award: History

The concept of most valuable player awards dates back more than a century. The first documented MVP-type honor in pro ball was bestowed upon James "Deacon" White of the 1875 Boston Red Stockings in the National Association. Catcher White sparked Boston to a remarkable 71-8 record that year, scoring 77 runs in 80 games and batting .355. An ardent Red Stockings' admirer presented Deacon with a silver tray, water pitcher, and loving cup inscribed with the words: won by JIM WHITE AS MOST VALUABLE PLAYER TO BOSTON TEAM, 1875.

The first official MVP honor was initiated some 35 years later. Prior to the 1910 season, baseball fan Hugh Chalmers, president and general manager of the Chalmers Motor Company, announced that he would present one of his company's automobiles—a Chalmers "30"—to the major league player who compiled the highest batting average. What appeared to be a harmless promo-

Johnny Podres
The Dodger pitcher, hugged by Roy Campanella after the final out in 1955, won the Babe Ruth Award and *SPORT* Magazine Award as the World Series MVP.

tional gimmick was soon to turn into a public-relations disaster.

The rules specified that players must accumulate a specific minimum number of times at bat, depending on position, to qualify for the award. For infielders and outfielders, it was a minimum of 350 at-bats; for catchers, 250 at-bats; and for pitchers, 100 at-bats. Interest in the award was tremendous from the outset. Ty Cobb, who already owned a Chalmers "30" roadster, wrote: "I am glad that something besides medals and trophies is offered for the championship in batting. I think the offer of a Chalmers '30'

is simply great and I hope to be lucky enough to own a new Chalmers next fall."

It developed into a two-man race, with Detroit's Cobb and Cleveland's Napoleon Lajoie, both American Leaguers, the only serious challengers for the coveted prize. Throughout the season there were charges and countercharges of favoritism by scorers in various cities. Furthermore, the general consensus of the press was that Cobb's selfish pursuit of this individual honor had cost his team the pennant. The controversy was capped by scandalous circumstances on the final day of the season.

Through games of September 16, Cobb held a solid lead over Lajoie, .368 to .357 (although, because of the era's sloppy record keeping, few actually knew the official figures at the time). From then through October 8, Cobb batted a torrid .532 (25-for-47) to seemingly lock up the crown with a .383 average. But Lajoie refused to surrender, going 30-for-54 (.556) in that same span to enter the final day, October 9, with a .376 mark. Cobb chose to sit out his final game, while Lajoie played the infamous doubleheader with the St. Louis Browns in which he went 8-for-8, including six bunt hits—remarkable for a slow-footed slugger—to edge out Cobb in the batting race … apparently. Browns' manager Jack O'Connor had instructed his rookie third baseman, Red Corriden, to play deep on Lajoie, advice with which Corriden complied. Lajoie took advantage of the strange defensive arrangement with the repeated safe bunts. Although neither Lajoie nor Corriden were implicated, there were charges of a Browns' frame-up to give the coveted batting title (and car) to the respected Lajoie over the disliked Cobb.

O'Connor lost his job due to his role in the alleged fix. Subsequently, AL president Ban Johnson announced that a "discrepancy" had been found in the official records, and that Cobb had actually won the batting crown after all (although this point was challenged by current researchers, who have evidence that Cobb was credited wrongly for a 2-for-3 game). Meanwhile, Hugh Chalmers, attempting to divorce himself from the controversy, presented autos to both Cobb and Lajoie. It was generally acknowledged that this fiasco doomed the future of individual awards of any kind.

Hoping to salvage some goodwill out of the whole idea, Chalmers came up with a new proposal for the 1911 season. This time he would award an auto to one player in each league who "should prove himself as the most important and useful player to his club and to the league at large in point of deportment and value of services rendered." The decision for this honor was to be made by a committee of baseball writers, one writer from each club city in each league. Each writer was to make eight selections, with a first-place ballot scoring eight points, on down to an eighth-place vote counting one point. Thus was born the short-lived Chalmers Award, with Ty Cobb and Frank Schulte earning recognition in 1911. Both Cobb and Schulte voluntarily withdrew from the competition in 1912, although the former received 17 points anyway.

Interest in the award diminished within a few years. By 1914 the public was distracted by baseball's battles with the new Federal League and the escalation of the World War in Europe. The timing was right for the Chalmers Award to quietly disappear; it was noted that Mr. Chalmers had agreed to present vehicles for five years and that the 1914 awards marked the fifth presentations.

On July 15, 1922, the newly formed American League Trophy Committee adopted a set of rules governing the selection of an annual award-winner. The rules specified that "the purpose of the American League Trophy is to honor the baseball player who is of greatest all-round service to his club and credit to the sport during each season; to recognize and reward uncommon skill and ability when exercised by a player for the best interests of his team, and to perpetuate his memory." The rules further instructed voters to seek out the "winning ball player," reminding them that "combined offensive and defensive ability is not always indicated by any system of records."

Eight baseball writers, one from each AL city, were enfranchised, with each required to select exactly one player from each team, for a total of eight selections. Player-managers and previous winners were to be excluded from consideration. Points were distributed the same as in the Chalmers Award: eight for first place, down to one for eighth.

The intention of Ban Johnson was to have a monument to baseball erected in East Potomac Park, Washington, D.C., engraved with the names of winners of the AL Award. This proposal was introduced as a congressional resolution in 1924, and passed in the House of Representatives before dying on the Senate Floor.

The AL voting rules led to growing criticism for several reasons, one of which was the limitation on the number of vote-getters from each team. For example, when the Browns' George Sisler won the first AL Award in 1922, he was named on all eight ballots— thus disqualifying his teammates from receiving any votes. As a result, fellow Brownie Ken Williams, who led the league in home runs (39), RBIs (155), and total bases (367) and became the first player ever to have 30 homers and 30 stolen bases in the same season, was shut out in the voting. Secondly, the rule prohibiting player-managers from eligibility drew fire. In 1925, when this rule eliminated five solid candidates from consideration, *The New York Times* wrote, "to say that it is impossible or impractical to divorce a man's managerial skill from his talents purely as a player is to reflect on the intelligence of the committee that awards the prize."

The Times further editorialized on the fallacy of assuming that no player can be the "most valuable" more than one year: "the purpose, of course, is to pass the honor around, but the effect is to pass an empty honor around." This rule became increasingly ridiculous when it eliminated Babe Ruth (and his 60 home runs) from consideration in 1927; by the following year, both Ruth and teammate Lou Gehrig, who were in the process of finishing one-two in the AL home run derby in five consecutive seasons, were ineligible for the League Award.

In 1924 the National League instituted its own award, with radical differences in the selection method: each writer voted for 10 players rather than eight (with 10 points for first place, and so on); he was not bound to vote for a certain number of players from each team; he was free to select a player-manager; and, later, he was allowed to consider previous winners of the award. Additionally, the NL offered a cash "present" of $1,000 to the award winner.

At various times between 1925 and 1951, writers were permitted to name "honorable mention" candidates, whose vote totals were listed but not counted in the balloting. Another feature of early voting reports was the listing of "cumulative vote leaders"—a forerunner to Bill James' "award shares"—over a period of years.

A number of factors led to the demise of the AL Award, including the award's loss of credibility due to the previously mentioned shortsighted voting rules. Additionally, Ban Johnson, having failed to secure the erection of his proposed monument, felt the award had fallen short of its aim. Finally, management was concerned with the efforts of award-winners to parlay their honors into

substantial pay raises. The AL Award was officially voted out at a special league meeting on May 6, 1929.

The National League followed suit with the AL's decision, but agreed to continue its award through the 1929 season. In October 1929 the Baseball Writers' Association of America (BBWAA) announced the results of an "unofficial" AL most valuable player poll, whose winner was Lew Fonseca of Cleveland.

Two months later, *The Sporting News* (*TSN*) conducted a poll of the eight writers who had previously voted on the League Award, thereby reporting Al Simmons as the "unofficial" AL Award-winner. Combining the results of these two unofficial polls gives Fonseca 77 points, followed by Heinie Manush (57), Simmons (56), Tony Lazzeri (55), and Charlie Gehringer (44).

In 1930, *TSN* chose Joe Cronin in the AL and Bill Terry in the NL. Earlier, the Associated Press also had a special committee of writers make an unofficial AL selection for 1930, while the BBWAA did the same for the NL (adding a check for $1,000 for the winner). The respective selections here were Cronin in the AL and Hack Wilson in the NL. Again combining the two sets of polls, the AL leaders were Cronin (100), Al Simmons (85), Lou Gehrig (68), Charlie Gehringer (67), and Ted Lyons (56). The NL pace-setters (with a weight adjustment and rounding) were Hack Wilson (121), Frankie Frisch (118), Bill Terry (117), Chuck Klein (63), and Floyd "Babe" Herman (56).

In an effort to standardize MVP voting, the BBWAA, in its annual winter meeting in New York on December 11, 1930, decided to appoint two committees (one in each league) to elect Most Valuable Players, with the association to "award suitable emblems to the players selected." Thus was born what is considered the modern MVP Award, with most of the flaws of its forerunners eliminated.

TSN, however, continued to make its own selections in bitter competition with the BBWAA. Finally, beginning in 1938, *TSN* agreed to unify the award by abiding with BBWAA balloting, and presenting *The Sporting News* Trophy to the winner. Among the various prizes awarded to the winners were wristwatches and shotguns.

At a meeting during the 1944 World Series, the BBWAA decided to begin issuing its own trophy, the Kenesaw Mountain Landis Award, in honor of the ailing commissioner. Landis died a month later and the official MVP Award has borne his name ever since. A plaque engraved with the names of the winners hangs in the National Baseball Library.

Two major changes in the MVP voting began in 1938. The BBWAA began polling three writers in each major league city, rather than just one, which remained in effect until it was reduced to two writers per city, starting in 1961. Also in 1938, the process was initiated to award 14 points for each first-place vote, rather than 10.

"Split votes," which have since infiltrated all the major awards, first appeared in MVP Awards in 1959. The American League MVP race that year, by consensus, was between second baseman Nellie Fox and shortstop Luis Aparicio of the champion Chicago White Sox. Late in the season, the suggestion often arose that the two ought to share the award. When the votes were in, Fox had received 14 first-place votes, Aparicio had gotten six, and four writers had split their votes between the two. Tickled with the idea of a split vote, one NL writer also resorted to this option, dividing his first-place nomination between Ernie Banks and Eddie Mathews. The "cop-out vote," having been allowed in '59, surfaced in 16 more MVP Awards, 10 Rookie of the Year, and 6 Cy Young Award elections. The ultimate folly of this practice was best exem-

plified in 1979. One NL writer split his fourth-place vote between pitching brothers Phil and Joe Niekro, evidently convinced that the two were identical twins. But the writer was still permitted to make six more selections. That meant that his fifth-, sixth-, and seventh-place selections received more points (six, five and four, respectively) than his fourth-place co-selections, who were credited with just three and a half points apiece! The 1979 NL vote, incidentally, resulted in the only actual split MVP as sentimental favorite Willie Stargell of the Pittsburgh Pirates and batting champion Keith Hernandez of the St. Louis Cardinals each received 216 votes and were declared "co-MVP." It is quite possible the tie was created by the questionable math used in the Niekro votes. In any case, split votes were outlawed sometime after 1984.

There has long been debate about the consideration of pitchers for the MVP Award, the theory (by some) that a man who plays every fourth game cannot be as valuable as a man who plays every day. The debate escalated after the inception of the Cy Young Award in 1956, giving pitchers their own exclusive honor, and the increasing practice of five-man rotations in the 1970s, giving starting pitchers even less of a chance to contribute.

As far as Jack Lang, former secretary-treasurer of the BBWAA, is concerned, there is no room for controversy. "The rules that are sent out to the voters on the [MVP] committee state: 'Keep in mind that all players are eligible. That includes pitchers, starters and relievers,'" says Lang. "Anybody on the committee that feels they cannot vote for a pitcher, we replace them. In my 24 years running the elections, only two writers have said that to me." Since 1931 pitchers have won the award 10 times in the AL and 9 times in the NL.

There have been 17 occasions in which one player received all of the available first-place MVP votes in his league. The AL players so honored are Ty Cobb (1911), Babe Ruth (1923), Hank Greenberg (1935), Al Rosen (1953), Mickey Mantle (1956), Frank Robinson (1966), Denny McLain (1968), Reggie Jackson (1973), Jose Canseco (1988), Frank Thomas (1993), and Ken Griffey Jr. (1997). The six unanimous NL selections are Carl Hubbell (1936), Orlando Cepeda (1967), Mike Schmidt (1980), Jeff Bagwell (1994), Ken Caminiti (1996), and Barry Bonds (2002). Hubbell's distinction is disputable, as two of the eight writers did not submit ballots that year and were not replaced on the selection committee.

Following are the maximum possible point totals that could have been earned by an individual receiving the first-place nomination of every writer polled:

NATIONAL LEAGUE		AMERICAN LEAGUE	
1911–14	64	1911–14	64
1924–29	80	1922–28	64
1931–37	80	1931–37	80
1938–60	336	1938–60	336
1961	224	1961–68	280
1962–68	280	1969–76	336
1969–92	336	1977–present	392
1993–97	392		
1998–present	448		

There have been numerous cases in which the MVP vote point totals did not add up to the correct figure. Reasons for this include inaccuracies in tabulation, inaccuracies in reporting, and writers who failed to vote or to complete their ballots. However, the total impact of all these errors is a small fraction of 1 percent of the total voting over the years.

Following is a complete tabulation of all the recognized MVP elections since 1911:

MVP AWARD: CHALMERS AWARD, 1911 TO 1914

1911 NATIONAL

F. Schulte, CHI	29
C. Mathewson, NY	25
L. Doyle, NY	23
H. Wagner, PIT	23
G. Alexander, PHI	23
M. Huggins, STL	21
F. Merkle, NY	19
R. Marquard, NY	19
J. Daubert, BRO	16
J. Tinker, CHI	11
C. Meyers, NY	11
J. Sheckard, CHI	9
M. Mitchell, CIN	9
M. Doolan, PHI	6
B. Harmon, STL	6
J. Archer, CHI	5
H. Lobert, PHI	4
G. Gibson, PIT	4
M. Brown, CHI	4
B. Bescher, CIN	4
B. Sweeney, BOS	3
O. Knabe, PHI	2
E. Konetchy, STL	2
D. Hoblitzell, CIN	2
J. Walsh, PHI	2
J. Devore, NY	2
F. Luderus, PHI	1
J. Kling, BOS	1
B. Adams, PIT	1
N. Rucker, BRO	1

1911 AMERICAN

T. Cobb, DET	64
E. Walsh, CHI	35
E. Collins, PHI	32
J. Jackson, CLE	28
W. Johnson, WAS	19
B. Cree, NY	16
T. Speaker, BOS	16
I. Thomas, PHI	12
C. Milan, WAS	10
V. Gregg, CLE	9
F. Baker, PHI	8
J. Coombs, PHI	6
N. Lajoie, CLE	5
J. Knight, NY	4
S. Crawford, DET	4
B. Lord, PHI	4
D. Bush, DET	4
R. Ford, NY	3
J. Barry, PHI	3
J. Austin, STL	2
F. LaPorte, STL	2
S. McInnis, PHI	1
G. McBride, WAS	1

1912 NATIONAL

L. Doyle, NY	48
H. Wagner, PIT	43
C. Meyers, NY	25
J. Tinker, CHI	22
B. Bescher, CIN	17
B. Sweeney, BOS	16
H. Zimmerman, CHI	16
R. Marquard, NY	13
O. Wilson, PIT	13
J. Daubert, BRO	13
O. Knabe, PHI	10
E. Konetchy, STL	8
C. Mathewson, NY	8
D. Paskert, PHI	6
J. Tesreau, NY	6
R. Murray, NY	5
M. Huggins, STL	5
A. Marsans, CIN	4
F. Merkle, NY	4
J. Evers, CHI	2
C. Hendrix, PIT	2
J. Archer, CHI	1
G. Alexander, PHI	1

1912 AMERICAN

T. Speaker, BOS	59
E. Walsh, CHI	30
W. Johnson, WAS	28
C. Milan, WAS	23
J. Wood, BOS	22
E. Collins, PHI	18
F. Baker, PHI	17

T. Cobb, DET	17
J. Jackson, CLE	16
H. Wagner, BOS	12
C. Gandil, WAS	7
B. Shotton, STL	6
D. Pratt, STL	5
E. Foster, WAS	4
L. Gardner, BOS	4
S. Crawford, DET	4
J. Barry, PHI	4
B. Carrigan, BOS	3
G. Moriarty, DET	3
J. Birmingham, CLE	2
D. Moeller, WAS	1
G. McBride, WAS	1
S. McInnis, PHI	1
B. Daniels, NY	1

1913 NATIONAL

J. Daubert, BRO	50
G. Cravath, PHI	40
R. Maranville, BOS	23
C. Mathewson, NY	21
C. Meyers, NY	20
V. Saier, CHI	15
L. Cheney, CHI	12
D. Miller, PIT	11
H. Wagner, PIT	11
J. Evers, CHI	10
T. Seaton, PHI	9
A. Fletcher, NY	7
J. Archer, CHI	6
M. Doolan, PHI	6
B. Sweeney, BOS	6
J. Viox, PIT	6
L. Doyle, NY	5
T. Shafer, NY	5
R. Murray, NY	4
H. Zimmerman, CHI	4
O. Knabe, PHI	4
B. Adams, PIT	3
G. Cutshaw, BRO	3
G. Burns, NY	2
A. Marsans, CIN	2
B. Humphries, CHI	2

M. Brown, CIN	1

1913 AMERICAN

W. Johnson, WAS	54
J. Jackson, CLE	43
E. Collins, PHI	30
T. Speaker, BOS	26
F. Baker, PHI	21
C. Gandil, WAS	14
S. McInnis, PHI	12
W. Schang, PHI	11
C. Milan, WAS	8
J. Barry, PHI	8
N. Lajoie, CLE	7
D. Bush, DET	6
H. Wagner, BOS	6
R. Russell, CHI	5
B. Shotton, STL	5
G. McBride, WAS	5
J. Scott, CHI	5
G. Stovall, STL	5
S. Crawford, DET	5
T. Cobb, DET	3
R. Schalk, CHI	3
C. Bender, PHI	2
T. Turner, CLE	2
S. O'Neill, CLE	1
H. Hooper, BOS	1

1914 NATIONAL

J. Evers, BOS	50
R. Maranville, BOS	44
B. James, BOS	33
G. Burns, NY	31
J. Miller, STL	18
J. Tesreau, NY	15
D. Rudolph, BOS	14
S. Magee, PHI	14
Z. Wheat, BRO	10
G. Alexander, PHI	9
R. Bresnahan, CHI	6
L. Magee, STL	6
B. Doak, STL	5
J. Viox, PIT	5
A. Fletcher, NY	5

C. Mathewson, NY	4
V. Saier, CHI	4
B. Schmidt, BOS	4
J. Daubert, BRO	4
L. McCarty, BRO	3
H. Groh, CIN	2
T. Clarke, CIN	1
G. Cravath, PHI	1

1914 AMERICAN

E. Collins, PHI	63
S. Crawford, DET	35
D. Bush, DET	17
F. Baker, PHI	17
J. Jackson, CLE	15
R. Schalk, CHI	13
E. Foster, WAS	11
B. Weaver, CHI	11
S. McInnis, PHI	11
D. Pratt, STL	10
W. Schang, PHI	10
T. Speaker, BOS	9
T. Walker, STL	9
T. Cobb, DET	7
E. Scott, BOS	7
J. Barry, PHI	6
D. Leonard, BOS	6
E. Plank, PHI	5
G. McBride, WAS	5
D. Lewis, BOS	4
H. Hooper, BOS	4
F. Maisel, NY	3
R. Peckinpaugh, NY	2
C. Milan, WAS	2
S. Agnew, STL	2
R. Hartzell, NY	2
E. Cicotte, CHI	1
G. Moriarty, DET	1

(No official awards, 1915–21)

MVP AWARD: LEAGUE AWARDS, 1922 TO 1929

1922 AMERICAN

G. Sisler, STL	59
E. Rommel, PHI	31
R. Schalk, CHI	26
L. Bush, NY	19
E. Collins, CHI	18
J. Bassler, DET	13
S. O'Neill, CLE	13
J. Judge, WAS	12
W. Pipp, NY	12
L. Blue, DET	11
C. Galloway, PHI	10
H. Heilmann, DET	8
D. Pratt, BOS	7
W. Schang, NY	7
B. Meusel, NY	6
E. Scott, NY	6
W. Johnson, WAS	5
U. Shocker, STL	5
C. Jamieson, CLE	4
J. Sewell, CLE	4
G. Burns, BOS	2
J. Dykes, PHI	2
B. Harris, WAS	2
R. Peckinpaugh, WAS	2
B. Wambsganss, CLE	2
G. Cutshaw, DET	1
C. Perkins, PHI	1

1923 AMERICAN

B. Ruth, NY	64
E. Collins, CHI	37
H. Heilmann, DET	31
W. Gerber, STL	20
J. Sewell, CLE	20

C. Jamieson, CLE	19
J. Bassler, DET	17
C. Galloway, PHI	13
G. Uhle, CLE	13
G. Burns, BOS	8
H. Ehmke, BOS	7
M. Ruel, WAS	7
R. Peckinpaugh, WAS	6
U. Shocker, STL	5
J. Judge, WAS	4
M. McManus, STL	4
K. Williams, STL	4
J. Harris, BOS	3
B. Harris, WAS	3
J. Hauser, PHI	1
W. Johnson, WAS	1
C. Perkins, PHI	1

(No National League awards, 1922–23)

1924 NATIONAL

D. Vance, BRO	74
R. Hornsby, STL	62
F. Frisch, NY	40
Z. Wheat, BRO	40
R. Youngs, NY	35
G. Kelly, NY	34
R. Maranville, PIT	33
K. Cuyler, PIT	25
J. Fournier, BRO	21
E. Roush, CIN	12
G. Wright, PIT	10
A. High, BRO	9
B. Pinelli, CIN	7

R. Bressler, CIN	6
G. Hartnett, CHI	5
B. Grimes, BRO	5
J. Bottomley, STL	4
J. Johnston, BRO	3
M. Carey, PIT	3
T. Jackson, NY	3
E. Yde, PIT	2
C. Williams, PHI	1
C. Rixey, CIN	1
G. Alexander, CHI	1
H. DeBerry, BRO	1

1924 AMERICAN

W. Johnson, WAS	55
E. Collins, CHI	49
C. Jamieson, CLE	25
H. Pennock, CHI	24
J. Bassler, DET	22
H. Severeid, STL	17
J. Hauser, PHI	13
W. Jacobson, STL	11
H. Heilmann, DET	9
J. Sewell, CLE	9
M. Ruel, WAS	7
W. Schang, NY	7
A. Simmons, PHI	7
W. Pipp, NY	6
H. Ehmke, BOS	5
I. Flagstead, BOS	5
W. Gerber, STL	4
E. Whitehill, DET	4
L. Blue, DET	3
I. Boone, BOS	2
J. Harris, BOS	2

C. Galloway, PHI	1
K. Williams, STL	1

1925 NATIONAL

R. Hornsby, STL	73
K. Cuyler, PIT	61
G. Kelly, NY	52
G. Wright, PIT	43
D. Vance, BRO	42
D. Bancroft, BOS	41
J. Bottomley, STL	28
P. Traynor, PIT	27
F. Frisch, NY	13
E. Roush, CIN	12
M. Carey, PIT	11
I. Meusel, NY	6
D. Luque, CIN	5
C. Grimm, CHI	5
Z. Wheat, BRO	4
P. Donohue, CIN	4
B. Hargrave, CIN	4
G. Harper, PHI	3
J. Sand, PHI	3
W. Gautreau, BOS	2
V. Aldridge, PIT	1

1925 AMERICAN

R. Peckinpaugh, WAS	45
A. Simmons, PHI	41
J. Sewell, CLE	21
H. Heilmann, DET	20
H. Rice, STL	18
E. Sheely, CHI	17
I. Flagstead, BOS	10
W. Jacobson, STL	10

J. Mostil, CHI	10
O. Bluege, WAS	8
M. Cochrane, PHI	8
L. Blue, DET	7
S. Coveleski, WAS	7
W. Kamm, CHI	7
E. Rommel, PHI	7
R. Schalk, CHI	7
A. Wingo, DET	7
E. Combs, NY	6
B. Meusel, NY	6
T. Lyons, CHI	5
G. Burns, CLE	4
M. McManus, STL	4
H. Pennock, NY	4
B. Bengough, NY	2
H. Ehmke, BOS	2
L. Gehrig, NY	2
I. Boone, BOS	1
J. Dugan, NY	1
P. Todt, BOS	1

1926 NATIONAL

B. O'Farrell, STL	79
H. Critz, CIN	60
R. Kremer, PIT	32
T. Thevenow, STL	30
H. Wilson, CHI	25
L. Bell, STL	24
B. Hargrave, CIN	24
F. Rhem, STL	20
F. Lindstrom, NY	17
D. Bancroft, BOS	17
H. Carlson, PHI	16
P. Waner, PIT	15

P. Traynor, PIT 14
W. Pipp, CIN 12
E. Brown, BOS 10
F. Herman, BRO 8
C. Root, CHI 8
R. Hornsby, STL 7
J. Butler, BRO 5
B. Southworth, NY-STL 5
G. Alexander, CHI-STL 5
C. Mays, CIN 4
G. Kelly, NY 2
C. Walker, CIN 1

1926 AMERICAN
G. Burns, CLE 63
J. Mostil, CHI 33
H. Pennock, NY 32
S. Rice, WAS 18
H. Heilmann, DET 16
H. Manush, DET 16
A. Simmons, PHI 16
L. Grove, PHI 12
G. Goslin, WAS 9
L. Gehrig, NY 7
T. Lazzeri, NY 7
B. Falk, CHI 6
F. Fothergill, DET 6
O. Melillo, STL 6
H. Rice, STL 6
O. Bluege, WAS 5
P. Todt, BOS 5
M. Cochrane, PHI 4
J. Judge, WAS 4
M. McManus, STL 4
B. Meusel, NY 3
E. Rigney, BOS 3
I. Flagstead, BOS 2

W. Gerber, STL 2
T. Zachary, STL 2
W. Jacobson, STL-BOS 1

1927 NATIONAL
P. Waner, PIT 72
F. Frisch, STL 66
R. Hornsby, NY 54
C. Root, CHI 46
T. Jackson, NY 42
L. Waner, PIT 25
P. Traynor, PIT 18
J. Haines, STL 16
R. Kremer, PIT 14
G. Hartnett, CHI 12
R. Lucas, CIN 10
H. Wilson, CHI 9
B. Terry, NY 6
J. Bottomley, STL 6
B. Hargrave, CIN 6
F. May, CIN 6
C. Williams, PHI 6
D. Farrell, NY-BOS 4
B. Grimes, NY 4
M. Carey, BRO 3
R. Stephenson, CHI 3
G. Alexander, STL 3
C. Hill, PIT 2
J. Petty, BRO 2
F. Ulrich, PHI 2
C. Hafey, STL 1

1927 AMERICAN
L. Gehrig, NY 56
H. Heilmann, DET 35
T. Lyons, CHI 34
M. Cochrane, PHI 18

A. Simmons, PHI 18
G. Goslin, WAS 15
M. Ruel, WAS 15
J. Dykes, PHI 14
L. Sewell, CLE 13
J. Sewell, CLE 9
T. Lazzeri, NY 8
R. Reeves, WAS 7
F. O'Rourke, STL 6
J. Tavener, DET 6
H. Lisenbee, WAS 5
E. Miller, STL 5
A. Metzler, CHI 4
I. Flagstead, BOS 3
C. Jamieson, CLE 3
W. Schang, STL 3
F. Schulte, STL 3
W. Hudlin, CLE 2
W. Regan, BOS 2
J. Rothrock, BOS 2
B. Harriss, BOS 1
P. Todt, BOS 1

1928 NATIONAL
J. Bottomley, STL 76
F. Lindstrom, NY 70
B. Grimes, PIT 53
L. Benton, NY 37
H. Critz, CIN 37
P. Traynor, PIT 28
H. Wilson, CHI 21
S. Hogan, NY 17
T. Jackson, NY 16
R. Maranville, STL 14
D. Vance, BRO 13
C. Hafey, STL 11
R. Hornsby, BOS 10

G. Hartnett, CHI 6
P. Waner, PIT 5
L. Richbourg, BOS 5
T. Douthit, STL 5
D. Bissonette, BRO 3
D. Flowers, BRO 3
J. Wilson, PHI-STL 3
A. Whitney, PHI 3
H. Ford, CIN 2
L. Thompson, PHI 1

1928 AMERICAN
M. Cochrane, PHI 53
H. Manush, STL 51
J. Judge, WAS 27
T. Lazzeri, NY 27
W. Kamm, CHI 15
G. Goslin, WAS 13
E. Combs, NY 13
C. Gehringer, DET 12
C. Myer, BOS 11
W. Hoyt, NY 8
J. Foxx, PHI 7
J. Sewell, CLE 6
L. Sewell, CLE 6
I. Flagstead, BOS 5
E. Morris, BOS 4
H. Heilmann, DET 4
C. Lind, CLE 4
W. Cissell, CHI 4
A. Thomas, CHI 4
O. Carroll, DET 3
H. Rice, DET 3
L. Fonseca, CLE 2
T. Lyons, CHI 2
J. Hodapp, CLE 2
A. Metzler, CHI 1

W. Regan, BOS 1

1929 NATIONAL
R. Hornsby, CHI 60
L. O'Doul, PHI 54
B. Terry, NY 48
B. Grimes, PIT 35
L. Waner, PIT 30
R. Lucas, CIN 29
P. Traynor, PIT 27
H. Wilson, CHI 24
F. Herman, BRO 24
G. Bush, CHI 16
C. Klein, PHI 15
M. Ott, NY 15
T. Douthit, STL 14
C. Grimm, CHI 13
T. Jackson, NY 8
R. Maranville, BOS 8
H. Critz, CIN 5
B. Friberg, PHI 4
P. Malone, CHI 3
F. Frisch, STL 2
P. Whitney, PHI 2
J. Frederick, BRO 2
R. Stephenson, CHI 1
Z. Taylor, BOS-CHI 1

(There were no official selections for the American League in 1929 or for either league in 1930.)

MVP AWARD: BASEBALL WRITERS' ASSOCIATION OF AMERICA AWARDS, 1931 TO PRESENT

1931 NATIONAL
F. Frisch, STL 65
C. Klein, PHI 55
B. Terry, NY 53
W. English, CHI 30
C. Hafey, STL 29
J. Wilson, STL 28
T. Jackson, NY 24
C. Grimm, CHI 21
E. Adams, STL 18
E. Brandt, BOS 15
R. Maranville, BOS 15
K. Cuyler, CHI 14
P. Traynor, PIT 12
R. Lucas, CIN 10
L. Waner, PIT 8
J. Bottomley, STL 8
J. Elliott, PHI 6
J. Quinn, BRO 6
N. Finn, BRO 5
W. Clark, BRO 3
P. Derringer, STL 3
C. Root, CHI 3
D. Bartell, PHI 2
J. Vergez, NY 2
F. Fitzsimmons, NY 1
L. O'Doul, BRO 1
G. Wright, BRO 1
T. Cuccinello, CIN 1
C. Gelbert, STL 1

1931 AMERICAN
L. Grove, PHI 78
L. Gehrig, NY 59
A. Simmons, PHI 51
E. Averill, CLE 43
B. Ruth, NY 40
E. Webb, BOS 22
J. Cronin, WAS 18
O. Melillo, STL 17
S. West, WAS 16
M. Cochrane, PHI 16
G. Earnshaw, PHI 12
W. Ferrell, CLE 12

F. Marberry, WAS 11
H. Rhyne, BOS 10
B. Chapman, NY 7
J. Stone, DET 6
C. Gehringer, DET 4
L. Blue, CHI 4
R. Kress, STL 3
C. Reynolds, CHI 2
W. Stewart, STL 2
G. Goslin, STL 2
D. MacFayden, BOS 2
T. Oliver, BOS 2
J. Foxx, PHI 1

1932 NATIONAL
C. Klein, PHI 78
L. Warneke, CHI 68
L. O'Doul, BRO 58
P. Waner, PIT 37
R. Stephenson, CHI 32
B. Terry, NY 25
D. Hurst, PHI 24
P. Traynor, PIT 17
B. Herman, CHI 16
M. Ott, NY 15
R. Brown, BOS 10
F. Herman, CIN 8
L. Waner, PIT 6
W. Berger, BOS 6
H. Wilson, BRO 6
E. Orsatti, STL 6
R. Maranville, BOS 5
J. Wilson, STL 5
T. Cuccinello, BRO 4
J. Dean, STL 4
F. Frisch, STL 3
R. Collins, STL 3
A. Vaughan, PIT 1
G. Bush, CHI 1

1932 AMERICAN
J. Foxx, PHI 75
L. Gehrig, NY 55
H. Manush, WAS 41

E. Averill, CLE 37
L. Gomez, NY 27
J. Cronin, WAS 26
B. Ruth, NY 26
T. Lazzeri, NY 21
A. Simmons, PHI 13
C. Gehringer, DET 13
D. Alexander, DET-BOS 10
W. Cissell, CHI-CLE 10
R. Ferrell, STL 9
L. Grove, PHI 8
J. Allen, NY 8
B. Dickey, NY 8
G. Goslin, STL 7
M. Weaver, WAS 6
H. Davis, DET 5
D. Harris, WAS 5
W. Ferrell, CLE 5
J. Levey, STL 5
T. Lyons, CHI 5
B. Sullivan, CHI 3
E. McNair, PHI 3
S. Jolley, CHI-BOS 3
G. Crowder, WAS 2
M. McManus, BOS 2
G. Walker, DET 1
J. Sewell, NY 1

1933 NATIONAL
C. Hubbell, NY 77
C. Klein, PHI 48
W. Berger, BOS 44
B. Terry, NY 35
P. Martin, STL 31
G. Mancuso, NY 24
J. Dean, STL 23
P. Traynor, PIT 20
B. Ryan, NY 19
A. Lopez, BRO 18
B. Cantwell, BOS 18
H. Schumacher, NY 11
R. Maranville, BOS 11
G. Bush, CHI 11
L. French, PIT 10

F. Frisch, STL 7
J. Bottomley, CIN 6
J. Medwick, STL 5
G. Hartnett, CHI 5
L. Warneke, CHI 4
R. Lucas, CIN 3
D. Bartell, PHI 3
A. Vaughan, PIT 2
R. Moore, BOS 2
V. Davis, PHI 1
C. Hafey, CIN 1
D. Luque, NY 1

1933 AMERICAN
J. Foxx, PHI 74
J. Cronin, WAS 62
H. Manush, WAS 54
L. Gehrig, NY 39
L. Grove, PHI 35
C. Gehringer, DET 32
G. Crowder, WAS 28
A. Simmons, CHI 19
E. Whitehill, WAS 18
O. Melillo, STL 12
S. West, STL 11
R. Ferrell, STL-BOS 9
B. Dickey, NY 9
T. Lazzeri, NY 6
J. Kuhel, WAS 5
E. Averill, CLE 5
C. Myer, WAS 5
M. Cochrane, PHI 5
B. Johnson, PHI 5
B. Chapman, NY 4
M. Bishop, PHI 1
L. Appling, CHI 1
W. Kamm, CLE 1

1934 NATIONAL
J. Dean, STL 78
P. Waner, PIT 50
J. Moore, NY 42
T. Jackson, NY 39
M. Ott, NY 37

R. Collins, STL 32
B. Terry, NY 30
C. Davis, PHI 18
P. Dean, STL 16
H. Schumacher, NY 16
C. Hubbell, NY 16
W. Berger, BOS 13
L. Warneke, CHI 10
G. Hartnett, CHI 9
G. Slade, CIN 5
K. Cuyler, CHI 4
B. Frey, CIN 4
F. Frankhouse, BOS 4
R. Boyle, BRO 4
B. Herman, CHI 4
F. Frisch, STL 4
W. Hoyt, PIT 2
A. Lopez, BRO 1
V. Mungo, BRO 1
A. Vaughan, PIT 1

1934 AMERICAN
M. Cochrane, DET 67
C. Gehringer, DET 65
L. Gomez, NY 60
S. Rowe, DET 59
L. Gehrig, NY 54
H. Greenberg, DET 29
H. Trosky, CLE 18
W. Ferrell, BOS 16
M. Owen, DET 13
J. Foxx, PHI 11
A. Simmons, CHI 9
W. Werber, BOS 8
R. Johnson, BOS 8
G. Goslin, DET 6
S. West, STL 5
M. Harder, CLE 4
F. Higgins, PHI 3
E. Averill, CLE 3
B. Knickerbocker, CLE 2

1935 NATIONAL

G. Hartnett, CHI	75
J. Dean, STL	66
A. Vaughan, PIT	45
B. Herman, CHI	38
J. Medwick, STL	37
C. Hubbell, NY	20
W. Berger, BOS	20
B. Terry, NY	20
A. Galan, CHI	18
P. Martin, STL	16
H. Leiber, NY	11
L. Warneke, CHI	9
E. Lombardi, CIN	8
F. Frisch, STL	7
C. Blanton, PIT	5
J. Moore, PHI	5
E. Allen, PHI	4
G. Mancuso, NY	4
P. Derringer, CIN	4
M. Ott, NY	3
P. Dean, STL	2
R. Collins, STL	2
C. Davis, PHI	2
P. Waner, PIT	1
B. Lee, CHI	1
T. Jackson, NY	1
D. Camilli, PHI	1

1935 AMERICAN

H. Greenberg, DET	80
W. Ferrell, BOS	62
J. Vosmik, CLE	39
C. Myer, WAS	36
L. Gehrig, NY	29
C. Gehringer, DET	26
M. Cochrane, DET	24
R. Cramer, PHI	18
M. Solters, BOS-STL	16
R. Hemsley, STL	16
J. Foxx, PHI	11
T. Bridges, DET	11
T. Lyons, CHI	10
L. Grove, BOS	8
Z. Bonura, CHI	7
L. Appling, CHI	7
L. Sewell, CHI	7
J. Allen, NY	5
J. Whitehead, CHI	4
F. Higgins, PHI	3
J. Marcum, CHI	3
E. Auker, DET	2
M. Harder, CLE	2
L. Lary, WAS-STL	1

1936 NATIONAL

C. Hubbell, NY	60
J. Dean, STL	53
B. Herman, CHI	37
J. Medwick, STL	30
P. Waner, PIT	29
M. Ott, NY	28
F. Demaree, CHI	17
G. Mancuso, NY	13
D. MacFayden, BOS	12
L. Durocher, STL	8
P. Derringer, CIN	6
G. Hartnett, CHI	6
B. Whitehead, NY	6
A. Lopez, BOS	5
V. Mungo, BRO	5
W. Berger, BOS	4
D. Camilli, PHI	4
G. Phelps, BRO	3
D. Bartell, NY	2
E. Lombardi, CIN	1
T. Moore, STL	1

1936 AMERICAN

L. Gehrig, NY	73
L. Appling, CHI	65
E. Averill, CLE	48
C. Gehringer, DET	39
B. Dickey, NY	29
V. Kennedy, CHI	27
J. Kuhel, WAS	27
J. DiMaggio, NY	26
T. Bridges, DET	25
H. Trosky, CLE	19
J. Foxx, BOS	16
G. Walker, DET	14
B. Bell, STL	10
W. Moses, PHI	7
L. Grove, BOS	5
J. Dykes, CHI	3
R. Radcliff, CHI	3
S. West, STL	2
Z. Bonura, CHI	1
E. McNair, BOS	1

1937 NATIONAL

J. Medwick, STL	70
G. Hartnett, CHI	68
C. Hubbell, NY	52
J. Turner, BOS	30
L. Fette, BOS	29
D. Bartell, NY	26
M. Ott, NY	24
P. Waner, PIT	21
B. Herman, CHI	19
J. Mize, STL	18
C. Melton, NY	17
C. Root, CHI	15
P. Whitney, PHI	13
H. Danning, NY	10
F. Demaree, CHI	9
L. Warneke, STL	6
B. Jurges, CHI	4
J. Cooney, BRO	4
B. Myers, CIN	2
L. Grissom, CIN	2
H. Manush, BRO	1

1937 AMERICAN

C. Gehringer, DET	78
J. DiMaggio, NY	74
H. Greenberg, DET	48
L. Gehrig, NY	42
L. Sewell, CHI	22
B. Dickey, NY	22
J. Cronin, BOS	19
R. Ruffing, NY	18
L. Gomez, NY	14
M. Kreevich, CHI	13
C. Travis, WAS	12
W. Moses, PHI	12
J. Allen, CLE	11
H. Clift, STL	11
R. Radcliff, CHI	10
B. Lewis, WAS	7
L. Appling, CHI	5
B. Bell, STL	5
E. Averill, CLE	4
L. Lary, CLE	4
R. Lawson, DET	4
G. Walker, DET	3
R. York, DET	1
P. Fox, DET	1

1938 NATIONAL

E. Lombardi, CIN	229
B. Lee, CHI	166
A. Vaughan, PIT	163
M. Ott, NY	132
F. McCormick, CIN	130
J. Rizzo, PIT	96
S. Hack, CHI	87
P. Derringer, CIN	70
M. Brown, PIT	62
G. Hartnett, CHI	61
J. Medwick, STL	55
J. Mize, STL	28
T. Cuccinello, BOS	23
P. Young, PIT	19
C. Bryant, CHI	16
H. Danning, NY	13
I. Goodman, CIN	11
J. VanderMeer, CIN	6
L. Durocher, BRO	6
D. Coffman, NY	6
A. Lopez, BOS	5
L. Waner, PIT	5
D. Garms, BOS	5
D. Camilli, BRO	5
C. Root, CHI	3
J. Moore, NY	3
J. Hudson, BRO	3
H. Mulcahy, PHI	3
L. Handley, PIT	2
L. Warneke, STL	1
F. Fitzsimmons, BRO	1
H. Martin, PHI	1

1938 AMERICAN

J. Foxx, BOS	305
B. Dickey, NY	196
H. Greenberg, DET	162
R. Ruffing, NY	146
B. Newsom, STL	111
J. DiMaggio, NY	106
J. Cronin, BOS	92
E. Averill, CLE	34
C. Travis, WAS	33
C. Gehringer, DET	27
J. Heath, CLE	24
J. Gordon, NY	23
H. Trosky, CLE	22
K. Keltner, CLE	16
M. Stratton, CHI	15
M. Harder, CLE	14
B. Johnson, PHI	13
H. Clift, STL	11
L. Gehrig, NY	10
P. Fox, DET	9
J. Vosmik, BOS	7
G. McQuinn, STL	7
L. Grove, BOS	7
B. Lewis, WAS	5
R. Rolfe, NY	5
C. Myer, WAS	5
E. Brucker, PHI	5
J. Allen, CLE	3
F. Crosetti, NY	2
L. Gomez, NY	1
D. Cramer, BOS	1

1939 NATIONAL

B. Walters, CIN	303
J. Mize, STL	178
P. Derringer, CIN	174
F. McCormick, CIN	159
C. Davis, STL	106
J. Brown, STL	99
J. Medwick, STL	81
L. Durocher, BRO	52
H. Danning, NY	33
L. Hamlin, BRO	32
M. Ott, NY	21
B. Jurges, NY	20
D. Camilli, BRO	20
W. Myers, CIN	18
S. Hack, CHI	17
A. Galan, CHI	15
T. Moore, STL	15
M. Arnovich, PHI	10
L. Frey, CIN	8
B. Lee, CHI	8
E. Slaughter, STL	8
W. Werber, CIN	6
M. West, BOS	5
G. Hartnett, CHI	5
I. Goodman, CIN	4
B. Hassett, BOS	4
P. Coscarart, BRO	4
E. Fletcher, BOS-PIT	4
C. Lavagetto, BRO	3
R. Bowman, STL	2
E. Miller, BOS	1
B. Herman, CHI	1

1939 AMERICAN

J. DiMaggio, NY	280
J. Foxx, BOS	170
B. Feller, CLE	155
T. Williams, BOS	126
R. Ruffing, NY	116
B. Dickey, NY	110
E. Leonard, WAS	71
B. Johnson, PHI	52
J. Gordon, NY	43
M. Kreevich, CHI	38
C. Brown, CHI	34
K. Keltner, CLE	26
G. McQuinn, STL	24
C. Gehringer, DET	21
L. Grove, BOS	17
J. Cronin, BOS	15
T. Lyons, CHI	13
H. Greenberg, DET	12
B. Newsom, STL-DET	11
J. Rigney, CHI	9
J. Kuhel, CHI	8
C. Keller, NY	7
J. Heath, CLE	7
G. Walker, CHI	7
F. Hayes, PHI	7
T. Bridges, DET	7
R. Rolfe, NY	6
B. McCosky, DET	6
E. McNair, CHI	5
H. Trosky, CLE	4
G. Case, WAS	3
M. Hoag, STL	3
R. York, DET	1
L. Appling, CHI	1

1940 NATIONAL

F. McCormick, CIN	274
J. Mize, STL	209
B. Walters, CIN	146
P. Derringer, CIN	121
F. Fitzsimmons, BRO	84
D. Walker, BRO	71
H. Danning, NY	64
S. Hack, CHI	61
E. Lombardi, CIN	38
W. Werber, CIN	36
J. Cooney, BOS	31
D. Camilli, BRO	30
E. Miller, BOS	28
D. Garms, PIT	28
A. Vaughan, PIT	27
C. Passeau, CHI	26
J. Beggs, CIN	19
T. Moore, STL	18
E. Fletcher, PIT	16
B. Nicholson, CHI	12
K. Higbe, PHI	10
C. Rowell, BOS	10
A. Lopez, BOS-PIT	9
M. Van Robays, PIT	8
R. Sewell, PIT	7
P. Reese, BRO	6
M. West, BOS	6
B. Young, NY	6
W. Wyatt, BRO	3
J. Rizzo, PHI	3
P. May, PHI	3
H. Mulcahy, PHI	3
J. Martin, STL	2
F. Gustine, PIT	1

1940 AMERICAN

H. Greenberg, DET	292
B. Feller, CLE	222
J. DiMaggio, NY	151
B. Newsom, DET	120
L. Boudreau, CLE	119
J. Foxx, BOS	110
S. Rowe, DET	62
R. York, DET	61
R. Radcliff, STL	55
L. Appling, CHI	54
R. Weatherly, CLE	34
D. Bartell, DET	26
J. Kuhel, CHI	18
S. Hudson, WAS	16
T. Williams, BOS	16
B. McCosky, DET	11
E. Bonham, NY	8
W. Judnich, STL	6
J. Babich, PHI	5
M. Tresh, CHI	4
F. Hayes, PHI	4
R. Mack, CLE	4
J. Gordon, NY	3
C. Travis, WAS	3
B. Kennedy, CHI	3
C. Gehringer, DET	3
R. Hemsley, CLE	2
T. Lyons, CHI	2
L. Finney, BOS	1
E. Auker, STL	1

1941 NATIONAL

D. Camilli, BRO	300
P. Reiser, BRO	183
W. Wyatt, BRO	151
J. Brown, STL	107
E. Riddle, CIN	98
E. White, STL	77
K. Higbe, BRO	64
J. Hopp, STL	61
J. Mize, STL	48
D. Walker, BRO	34
B. Herman, CHI-BRO	27
T. Moore, STL	26
S. Hack, CHI	26
E. Fletcher, PIT	22
J. Cooney, BOS	20
B. Nicholson, CHI	16
G. Mancuso, STL	14
F. Crespi, STL	13
M. Ott, NY	12
E. Slaughter, STL	12
B. Young, NY	10
V. DiMaggio, PIT	10
J. Tobin, BOS	10
A. Lopez, PIT	8
M. Marion, STL	8
M. Cooper, STL	8
L. Warneke, STL	7
N. Etten, PHI	6
B. Walters, CIN	6
B. Dahlgren, BOS-CHI	6
W. Werber, CIN	6
E. Crabtree, STL	5
J. Rucker, NY	4
D. Litwhiler, PHI	3
H. Danning, NY	2
C. Hubbell, NY	2
C. Lavagetto, BRO	2
A. Vaughan, PIT	2

1941 AMERICAN

J. DiMaggio, NY	291
T. Williams, BOS	254
B. Feller, CLE	174
T. Lee, CHI	144
C. Keller, NY	126
C. Travis, WAS	101
J. Gordon, NY	60
J. Heath, CLE	37
H. Newsome, BOS	32
R. Cullenbine, STL	29
J. Cronin, BOS	26
S. Chapman, PHI	25
B. Dickey, NY	18
T. Henrich, NY	16
B. McCosky, DET	12
T. Lyons, CHI	12
D. Siebert, PHI	10
L. Boudreau, CLE	10
A. Benton, DET	8
P. Rizzuto, NY	7
E. Leonard, WAS	7
B. Campbell, DET	4
R. York, DET	3
F. Hayes, PHI	3
T. Wright, CHI	2
R. Ruffing, NY	2
E. Auker, STL	1
F. Higgins, DET	1
D. DiMaggio, BOS	1

1942 NATIONAL

M. Cooper, STL	263
E. Slaughter, STL	200
M. Ott, NY	190
A. Owen, BRO	103

J. Mize, NY	97
P. Reiser, BRO	91
M. Marion, STL	81
D. Camilli, BRO	42
R. Elliott, PIT	39
C. Passeau, CHI	33
W. Cooper, STL	28
S. Musial, STL	26
E. Lombardi, BOS	24
J. Beazley, STL	24
J. Brown, STL	24
W. Wyatt, BRO	22
J. Medwick, BRO	20
T. Moore, STL	15
B. Nicholson, CHI	14
S. Hack, CHI	11
J. VanderMeer, CIN	11
T. Hughes, PHI	10
R. Starr, CIN	9
L. French, BRO	7
P. Reese, BRO	6
W. Kurowski, STL	6
R. Lamanno, CIN	4
M. West, BOS	4
L. Frey, CIN	4
F. McCormick, CIN	4
A. Javery, BOS	3
E. Miller, BOS	1

1942 AMERICAN

J. Gordon, NY	270
T. Williams, BOS	249
J. Pesky, BOS	143
V. Stephens, STL	140
E. Bonham, NY	102
T. Hughson, BOS	92
J. DiMaggio, NY	86
S. Spence, WAS	65
P. Marchildon, PHI	39
L. Boudreau, CLE	34
B. Doerr, BOS	24
T. Lyons, CHI	23
G. Case, WAS	17
K. Keltner, CLE	15
C. Keller, NY	15
W. Judnich, STL	14
B. Dickey, NY	12
D. Gutteridge, STL	12
P. Rizzuto, NY	9
C. Laabs, STL	9
F. Ferrell, STL	8
H. Borowy, NY	8
J. Bagby, CLE	6
T. Wright, CHI	6
T. Lupien BOS	4
L. Fleming, CLE	4
S. Chandler, NY	3
R. York, DET	3
B. McCosky, DET	1

1943 NATIONAL

S. Musial, STL	267
W. Cooper, STL	192
B. Nicholson, CHI	181
B. Herman, BRO	140
M. Cooper, STL	130
R. Sewell, PIT	127
E. Riddle, CIN	68
R. Elliott, PIT	52
F. McCormick, CIN	26
C. Shoun, CIN	24
E. Miller, CIN	24
M. Witek, NY	21
M. Marion, STL	20
S. Rowe, PHI	18
W. Wyatt, BRO	15
A. Vaughan, BRO	15
R. Mueller, CIN	12
A. Javery, BOS	12
S. Hack, CHI	10
M. Ott, NY	9
E. Fletcher, PIT	7
A. Adams, NY	7
L. Klein, STL	6
A. Galan, BRO	5
D. Walker, BRO	5

J. Tobin, BOS	5
D. Bartell, NY	5
P. Cavarretta, CHI	4
T. Holmes, BOS	2
R. Northey, PHI	2
B. Dahlgren, PHI	2
H. Bithorn, CHI	1
B. Walters, CIN	1
L. Frey, CIN	1

1943 AMERICAN

S. Chandler, NY	246
L. Appling, CHI	215
R. York, DET	152
W. Johnson, NY	135
B. Johnson, WAS	116
D. Wakefield, DET	72
N. Etten, NY	61
B. Dickey, NY	58
V. Stephens, STL	49
L. Boudreau, CLE	40
D. Trout, DET	38
G. Case, WAS	37
C. Keller, NY	31
B. Doerr, BOS	21
A. Smith, CLE	19
G. Priddy, WAS	17
O. Hockett, CLE	14
D. Gutteridge, STL	13
E. Wynn, WAS	13
J. Bagby, CLE	11
R. Cramer, DET	8
F. Higgins, DET	8
C. Laabs, STL	6
J. Early, WAS	6
J. Gordon, NY	4
R. Wolff, PHI	4
L. Newsome, BOS	3
J. Cronin, BOS	3
J. Flores, PHI	3
G. Maltzberger, CHI	3
F. Crosetti, NY	2
K. Keltner, CLE	2
P. Fox, BOS	1
R. Hodgin, CHI	1
J. Murphy, NY	1
D. Siebert, PHI	1
J. Tabor, BOS	1
H. Wagner, PHI	1

1944 NATIONAL

M. Marion, STL	190
B. Nicholson, CHI	189
D. Walker, BRO	145
S. Musial, STL	136
B. Walters, CIN	107
B. Voiselle, NY	107
R. Mueller, CIN	85
W. Cooper, STL	72
M. Cooper, STL	63
R. Elliott, PIT	57
R. Sewell, PIT	49
B. Dahlgren, PIT	33
F. McCormick, CIN	32
P. Cavarretta, CHI	27
R. Sanders, STL	25
M. Ott, NY	20
J. Tobin, BOS	13
J. Hopp, STL	10
R. Northey, PHI	10
J. Medwick, NY	9
J. Barrett, PIT	8
E. Miller, CIN	7
T. Holmes, BOS	6
T. Wilks, STL	4
T. Lupien, PHI	3
S. Hack, CHI	2
M. Lanier, STL	2
C. Ryan, BOS	2
A. Galan, BRO	1
W. Kurowski, STL	1
J. Russell, PIT	1

1944 AMERICAN

H. Newhouser, DET	236
D. Trout, DET	232

V. Stephens, STL	193
S. Stirnweiss, NY	129
D. Wakefield, DET	128
L. Boudreau, CLE	84
B. Doerr, BOS	75
S. Spence, WAS	56
N. Potter, STL	52
B. Johnson, BOS	51
M. Christman, STL	27
T. Hughson, BOS	22
D. Cramer, DET	14
F. Hayes, PHI	13
P. Fox, BOS	12
J. Kramer, STL	9
J. Lindell, NY	8
P. Richards, DET	8
D. Gutteridge, STL	7
F. Higgins, DET	7
G. McQuinn, STL	7
G. Kell, PHI	6
R. Cullenbine, CLE	5
N. Etten, NY	5
R. York, DET	5
R. Hemsley, NY	4
M. Kreevich, STL	4
W. Moses, CHI	4
E. Mayo, DET	3
D. Siebert, PHI	3
H. Borowy, NY	2
F. Crosetti, NY	2
R. Hodgin, CHI	2
B. Muncrief, STL	1

1945 NATIONAL

P. Cavarretta, CHI	279
T. Holmes, BOS	175
C. Barrett, BOS-STL	151
A. Pafko, CHI	131
W. Kurowski, STL	90
H. Borowy, CHI	84
H. Wyse, CHI	72
M. Marion, STL	69
D. Walker, BRO	66
G. Rosen, BRO	56
S. Hack, CHI	42
H. Brecheen, STL	31
M. Ott, NY	22
A. Galan, BRO	18
J. Hopp, STL	17
R. Elliott, PIT	15
L. Olmo, BRO	13
B. Adams, PHI-STL	12
C. Passeau, CHI	9
J. Barrett, PIT	8
E. Heusser, CIN	7
D. Johnson, CHI	7
B. Kerr, NY	7
F. McCormick, CIN	6
B. Salkeld, PIT	6
P. Lowrey, CHI	5
A. Adams, NY	4
A. Karl, PHI	4
H. Gregg, BRO	2
A. Lopez, PIT	2
P. Masi, BOS	2
E. Miller, CIN	2
V. DiMaggio, PHI	1
E. Stanky, BRO	1

1945 AMERICAN

H. Newhouser, DET.	236
E. Mayo, DET	164
S. Stirnweiss, NY	161
B. Ferriss, BOS	148
G. Myatt, WAS	98
V. Stephens, STL	94
R. Wolff, WAS	78
L. Boudreau, CLE	70
G. Case, WAS	60
P. Richards, DET	35
M. Tresh, CHI	33
J. Kuhel, WAS	29
R. Cullenbine, DET	26
H. Greenberg, DET	25
N. Etten, NY	21
T. Cuccinello, CHI	18

D. Trout, DET	17
E. Leonard, WAS	16
R. Schalk, CHI	13
J. Heath, CLE	10
G. Binks, WAS	9
B. Muncrief, STL	8
A. Benton, DET	6
R. Ferrell, WAS	6
B. Johnson, BOS	6
M. Christman, STL	5
B. Estalella, PHI	5
F. Hayes, PHI-CLE	5
D. Cramer, DET	4
W. Moses, CHI	4
E. Lake, BOS	2
R. Christopher, PHI	1
L. Newsome, BOS	1
R. York, DET	1

1946 NATIONAL

S. Musial, STL	319
D. Walker, BRO	159
E. Slaughter, STL	144
H. Pollet, STL	116
J. Sain, BOS	95
P. Reese, BRO	79
E. Stanky, BRO	67
D. Ennis, PHI	61
P. Reiser, BRO	58
P. Cavarretta, CHI	49
B. Kerr, NY	37
J. Hopp, BOS	34
E. Waitkus, CHI	21
B. Edwards, BRO	20
K. Higbe, BRO	18
H. Brecheen, STL	14
J. Mize, NY	14
G. Hatton, CIN	12
T. Holmes, BOS	11
J. Tabor, PHI	10
E. Verban, STL-PHI	10
H. Walker, STL	9
L. Rowe, PHI	8
P. Masi, BOS	7
J. VanderMeer, CIN	7
R. Schoendienst, STL	6
B. Cox, PIT	5
F. Gustine, PIT	4
M. Marion, STL	4
R. Kiner, PIT	3
W. Kurowski, STL	3
R. Mueller, CIN	3
J. Schmitz, CHI	3
P. Lowrey, CHI	2
F. McCormick, PHI	2
C. Furillo, BRO	1
O. Judd, PHI	1

1946 AMERICAN

T. Williams, BOS	224
H. Newhouser, DET	197
B. Doerr, BOS	158
J. Pesky, BOS	141
M. Vernon, WAS	134
B. Feller, CLE	105
B. Ferriss, BOS	94
H. Greenberg, DET	91
D. DiMaggio, BOS	56
L. Boudreau, CLE	37
R. York, BOS	28
L. Appling, CHI	26
T. Hughson, BOS	19
E. Caldwell, CHI	18
C. Keller, NY	17
G. Kell, PHI-DET	12
S. Chandler, NY	12
A. Robinson, NY	12
J. DiMaggio, NY	6
B. Newsom, PHI-WAS	6
V. Stephens, STL	6
P. Marchildon, PHI	5
B. Rosar, PHI	4
S. Spence, WAS	4
J. Berardino, STL	2
T. Henrich, NY	1
H. Wagner, BOS	1

1947 NATIONAL

R. Elliott, BOS	205
E. Blackwell, CIN	175
J. Mize, NY	144
B. Edwards, BRO	140
J. Robinson, BRO	106
R. Kiner, PIT	101
L. Jansen, NY	91
P. Reese, BRO	80
W. Kurowski, STL	45
H. Walker, STL-PHI	45
R. Branca, BRO	40
H. Casey, BRO	37
E. Leonard, PHI	32
E. Stanky, BRO	32
W. Spahn, BOS	26
W. Marshall, NY	20
J. Sain, BOS	20
W. Cooper, NY	19
D. Walker, BRO	14
E. Slaughter, STL	12
S. Musial, STL	12
E. Verban, PHI	9
P. Cavarretta, CHI	6
P. Lowrey, CHI	2
E. Miller, CIN	2
A. Pafko, CHI	1

1947 AMERICAN

J. DiMaggio, NY	202
T. Williams, BOS	201
L. Boudreau, CLE	168
J. Page, NY	167
G. Kell, DET	132
G. McQuinn, NY	77
J. Gordon, CLE	59
B. Feller, CLE	58
P. Marchildon, PHI	47
L. Appling, CHI	43
E. Joost, PHI	35
B. McCosky, PHI	35
T. Henrich, NY	33
F. Shea, NY	23
Y. Berra, NY	18
A. Reynolds, NY	18
B. Dillinger, STL	13
J. Pesky, BOS	11
F. Fain, PHI	9
W. Johnson, NY	9
S. Spence, WAS	9
F. Hutchison, DET	8
E. Wynn, WAS	7
B. Doerr, BOS	6
B. Rosar, PHI	6
M. Christman, WAS	4
B. McCahan, PHI	4
D. Mitchell, CLE	4
R. Cullenbine, DET	3
J. Dobson, BOS	3
J. Heath, STL	1
E. Lopat, CHI	1
V. Stephens, STL	1
T. Wright, CHI	1

1948 NATIONAL

S. Musial, STL	303
J. Sain, BOS	223
A. Dark, BOS	174
S. Gordon, NY	72
H. Brecheen, STL	61
P. Reese, BRO	60
R. Kiner, PIT	55
E. Slaughter, STL	55
D. Murtaugh, PIT	52
S. Rojek, PIT	51
R. Ashburn, PHI	48
J. Schmitz, CHI	37
R. Elliott, BOS	33
W. Spahn, BOS	31
J. Robinson, BRO	30
A. Pafko, CHI	25
J. Mize, NY	22
R. Barney, BRO	15
J. VanderMeer, CIN	13
J. Wyrostek, CIN	9
R. Branca, BRO	8

R. Campanella, BRO	8
B. Chesnes, PIT	8
P. Cavarretta, CHI	6
E. Miller, PHI	4
D. Ennis, PHI	3
G. Hatton, CIN	3
L. Jansen, NY	2
D. Walker, PIT	2
G. Hodges, BRO	1
W. Lockman, NY	1
H. Sauer, CIN	1

1948 AMERICAN

L. Boudreau, CLE	324
J. DiMaggio, NY	213
T. Williams, BOS	171
V. Stephens, BOS	121
B. Lemon, CLE	101
J. Gordon, CLE	63
T. Henrich, NY	63
G. Bearden, CLE	52
H. Newhouser, DET	48
E. Joost, PHI	39
H. Majeski, PHI	23
B. Tebbetts, BOS	23
V. Raschi, NY	23
K. Keltner, CLE	18
J. Priddy, STL	16
G. Kell, DET	14
W. Evers, DET	13
A. Zarilla, STL	11
B. Doerr, BOS	10
B. Dillinger, STL	10
J. Hegan, CLE	10
L. Appling, CHI	8
B. Feller, CLE	6
L. Brissie, PHI	5
F. Fain, PHI	5
J. Dobson, BOS	5
B. Goodman, BOS	4
B. McCosky, PHI	4
Y. Berra, NY	3
D. DiMaggio, BOS	3
L. Doby, CLE	3
C. Fannin, STL	2
P. Mullin, DET	1
P. Rizzuto, NY	1

1949 NATIONAL

J. Robinson, BRO	264
S. Musial, STL	226
E. Slaughter, STL	181
R. Kiner, PIT	133
P. Reese, BRO	118
C. Furillo, BRO	68
W. Spahn, BOS	60
D. Newcombe, BRO	55
K. Heintzelman, PHI	48
R. Schoendienst, STL	30
G. Hodges, BRO	29
H. Pollet, STL	29
D. Ennis, PHI	28
B. Thomson, NY	25
R. Campanella, BRO	22
P. Roe, BRO	21
G. Hamner, PHI	9
W. Lockman, NY	9
R. Meyer, PHI	8
K. Raffensberger, CIN	8
H. Sauer, CIN-CHI	8
T. Wilks, STL	8
R. Ashburn, PHI	6
J. Schmitz, CHI	6
A. Dark, BOS	3
M. Marion, STL	3
W. Jones, PHI	2
W. Marshall, NY	2
E. Torgeson, BOS	2
S. Gordon, NY	1
D. Sisler, PHI	1

1949 AMERICAN

T. Williams, BOS	272
P. Rizzuto, NY	175
J. Page, NY	166
M. Parnell, BOS	151

E. Kinder, BOS	122
T. Henrich, NY	121
V. Stephens, BOS	100
G. Kell, DET	80
B. Lemon, CLE	57
V. Wertz, DET	51
V. Raschi, NY	19
J. DiMaggio, NY	18
E. Joost, PHI	11
L. Boudreau, CLE	10
Y. Berra, NY	9
D. DiMaggio, BOS	7
B. Doerr, BOS	7
A. Kellner, PHI	6
E. Robinson, WAS	6
R. Sievers, STL	6
B. Tebbetts, BOS	6
L. Appling, CHI	3
A. Houtteman, DET	3
J. Priddy, STL	3
V. Trucks, DET	3
D. Mitchell, CLE	2
A. Reynolds, NY	2

1950 NATIONAL

J. Konstanty, PHI	286
S. Musial, STL	158
E. Stanky, NY	144
D. Ennis, PHI	104
R. Kiner, PIT	91
G. Hamner, PHI	79
R. Roberts, PHI	68
G. Hodges, BRO	55
D. Snider, BRO	53
S. Maglie, NY	51
E. Blackwell, CIN	41
A. Pafko, CHI	38
R. Campanella, BRO	29
A. Seminick, PHI	25
J. Robinson, BRO	23
C. Simmons, PHI	22
P. Roe, BRO	15
T. Kluszewski, CIN	14
W. Spahn, BOS	14
D. Newcombe, BRO	14
J. Sain, BOS	12
S. Gordon, BOS	11
J. Hearn, STL-NY	10
P. Reese, BRO	8
E. Waitkus, PHI	8
R. Elliott, BOS	8
E. Torgeson, BOS	6
S. Jethroe, BOS	6
H. Sauer, CHI	5
V. Bickford, BOS	4
C. Furillo, BRO	4
W. Westrum, NY	3
D. Sisler, PHI	2
H. Thompson, NY	2
L. Jansen, NY	2
W. Jones, PHI	1

1950 AMERICAN

P. Rizzuto, NY	284
B. Goodman, BOS	180
Y. Berra, NY	146
G. Kell, DET	127
B. Lemon, CLE	102
W. Dropo, BOS	75
V. Raschi, NY	63
L. Doby, CLE	57
J. DiMaggio, NY	54
V. Wertz, DET	50
W. Evers, DET	38
C. Carrasquel, CHI	21
D. Trout, DET	21
D. DiMaggio, BOS	17
I. Noren, WAS	16
B. Doerr, BOS	15
J. Mize, NY	11
J. Priddy, DET	11
A. Rosen, CLE	11
E. Yost, WAS	8
M. Parnell, BOS	7
W. Ford, NY	7
T. Williams, BOS	7

N. Garver, STL	6
V. Stephens, BOS	6
A. Houtteman, DET	6
S. Lollar, STL	4
E. Lopat, NY	3
K. Wood, STL	2
S. Dente, WAS	1
D. Philley, CHI	1

1951 NATIONAL

R. Campanella, BRO	243
S. Musial, STL	191
M. Irvin, NY	166
S. Maglie, NY	153
P. Roe, BRO	138
J. Robinson, BRO	92
R. Ashburn, PHI	69
B. Thomson, NY	62
M. Dickson, PIT	59
R. Kiner, PIT	49
W. Spahn, BOS	45
A. Dark, NY	30
R. Roberts, PHI	27
L. Jansen, NY	26
P. Reese, BRO	15
G. Hodges, BRO	10
S. Gordon, BOS	10
K. Raffensberger, CIN	8
J. Wyrostek, CIN	6
E. Blackwell, CIN	6
C. Furillo, BRO	6
D. Newcombe, BRO	3
P. Cavarretta, CHI	1
H. Sauer, CHI	1

1951 AMERICAN

Y. Berra, NY	184
N. Garver, STL	157
A. Reynolds, NY	125
M. Minoso, CLE-CHI	120
B. Feller, CLE	118
F. Fain, PHI	103
E. Kinder, BOS	66
V. Raschi, NY	64
G. McDougald, NY	63
B. Avila, CLE	49
P. Rizzuto, NY	47
E. Lopat, NY	44
T. Williams, BOS	35
E. Joost, PHI	32
G. Kell, DET	30
E. Wynn, CLE	29
N. Fox, CHI	25
B. Goodman, BOS	21
D. DiMaggio, BOS	16
G. Zernial, CHI-PHI	15
B. Shantz, PHI	14
M. Garcia, CLE	11
G. Coan, WAS	8
M. Parnell, BOS	7
E. Robinson, CHI	7
G. Woodling, NY	5
J. Pesky, BOS	5
I. Noren, WAS	4
D. Mitchell, CLE	4
V. Trucks, DET	2
E. Yost, WAS	2
J. Busby, CHI	2
J. Mize, NY	2

1952 NATIONAL

H. Sauer, CHI	226
R. Roberts, PHI	211
J. Black, BRO	208
H. Wilhelm, NY	133
S. Musial, STL	127
E. Slaughter, STL	92
J. Robinson, BRO	31
P. Reese, BRO	29
D. Snider, BRO	29
R. Campanella, BRO	25
R. Schoendienst, STL	25
A. Dark, NY	24
M. Dickson, PIT	22
D. Ennis, PHI	18
W. Lockman, NY	18

B. Thomson, NY	17
F. Baumholtz, CHI	16
T. Kluszewski, CIN	16
G. Hodges, BRO	15
R. McMillan, CIN	15
E. Mathews, BOS	13
B. Adams, CIN	9
B. Cox, BRO	8
W. Hacker, CHI	8
R. Kiner, PIT	8
S. Maglie, NY	8
K. Raffensberger, CIN	8
W. Spahn, BOS	8
P. Roe, BRO	7
S. Gordon, BOS	6
G. Hamner, PHI	5
S. Hemus, STL	5
M. Irvin, NY	5
G. Shuba, BRO	5
E. Yuhas, STL	5
A. Brazle, STL	3
J. Logan, BOS	3
T. Atwell, CHI	2
C. Metkovich, PIT	2
W. Cooper, BOS	1

1952 AMERICAN

B. Shantz, PHI	280
A. Reynolds, NY	183
M. Mantle, NY	143
Y. Berra, NY	104
E. Wynn, CLE	99
F. Fain, PHI	66
N. Fox, CHI	59
B. Lemon, CLE	58
M. Garcia, CLE	52
A. Rosen, CLE	51
E. Robinson, CHI	47
L. Doby, CLE	46
L. Easter, CLE	40
P. Rizzuto, NY	33
E. Joost, PHI	20
B. Goodman, BOS	18
J. Jensen, NY-WAS	12
S. Paige, STL	12
V. Raschi, NY	12
D. Mitchell, CLE	11
H. Bauer, NY	10
G. Woodling, NY	10
P. Runnels, WAS	8
C. Courtney, STL	7
D. Gernert, BOS	6
W. Dropo, BOS-DET	5
S. Rogovin, CHI	4
S. White, BOS	4
B. Avila, CLE	3
B. Pierce, CHI	3
J. Sain, NY	3
B. Young, STL	3
J. Collins, NY	2
C. Marrero, WAS	1
B. Porterfield, WAS	1

1953 NATIONAL

R. Campanella, BRO	297
E. Mathews, MIL	216
D. Snider, BRO	157
R. Schoendienst, STL	155
W. Spahn, MIL	120
R. Roberts, PHI	106
T. Kluszewski, CIN	69
S. Musial, STL	62
C. Erskine, BRO	54
C. Furillo, BRO	54
P. Reese, BRO	27
J. Robinson, BRO	19
D. Ennis, PHI	14
G. Hodges, BRO	13
M. Irvin, NY	11
D. O'Connell, PIT	10
H. Haddix, STL	9
F. Thomas, PIT	6
R. Ashburn, PHI	5
G. Bell, CIN	3
J. Logan, MIL	3
R. Gomez, NY	2

G. Hamner, PHI	2
D. Crandall, MIL	1
H. Thompson, NY	1

1953 AMERICAN

A. Rosen, CLE	336
Y. Berra, NY	167
M. Vernon, WAS	162
M. Minoso, CHI	100
V. Trucks, STL-CHI	81
P. Rizzuto, NY	76
B. Porterfield, WAS	64
R. Boone, CLE-DET	59
J. Piersall, BOS	56
B. Pierce, CHI	55
E. Kinder, BOS	41
H. Bauer, NY	37
A. Reynolds, NY	37
M. Parnell, BOS	27
H. Kuenn, DET	23
B. Lemon, CLE	22
E. Lopat, NY	18
G. Zernial, PHI	16
D. Philley, PHI	11
W. Ford, NY	8
B. Goodman, BOS	5
M. Mantle, NY	4
G. Woodling, NY	3
E. Yost, WAS	3
B. Martin, NY	2
C. Carrasquel, CHI	1
G. Kell, BOS	1
T. Williams, BOS	1

1954 NATIONAL

W. Mays, NY	283
T. Kluszewski, CIN	217
J. Antonelli, NY	154
D. Snider, BRO	135
A. Dark, NY	110
S. Musial, STL	97
R. Roberts, PHI	70
J. Adcock, MIL	60
P. Reese, BRO	53
G. Hodges, BRO	40
W. Spahn, MIL	38
D. Mueller, NY	30
R. Schoendienst, STL	24
F. Thomas, PIT	24
H. Wilhelm, NY	17
E. Banks, CHI	14
D. Crandall, MIL	13
J. Logan, MIL	9
E. Mathews, MIL	5
G. Hamner, PHI	5
R. Ashburn, PHI	5
S. Maglie, NY	4
G. Conley, MIL	3
M. Grissom, NY	2
R. McMillan, CIN	2
D. Rhodes, NY	1
H. Sauer, CHI	1

1954 AMERICAN

Y. Berra, NY	230
L. Doby, CLE	210
B. Avila, CLE	203
M. Minoso, CHI	186
B. Lemon, CLE	179
E. Wynn, CLE	72
T. Williams, BOS	65
H. Kuenn, DET	37
M. Vernon, WAS	30
N. Fox, CHI	30
B. Grim, NY	25
J. Finigan, PHI	19
V. Trucks, CHI	19
J. Jensen, BOS	17
M. Mantle, NY	16
I. Noren, NY	16
A. Rosen, CLE	16
J. Busby, WAS	7
J. Coleman, NY	6
B. Goodman, BOS	6
J. Garcia, CLE	6
J. Hegan, CLE	5

H. Bauer, NY	4
A. Kaline, DET	4
B. Turley, BAL	4
S. Gromek, DET	1
C. Abrams, BAL	1
R. Boone, DET	1
R. Sievers, WAS	1

1955 NATIONAL

R. Campanella, BRO	226
D. Snider, BRO	221
E. Banks, CHI	195
W. Mays, NY	165
R. Roberts, PHI	159
T. Kluszewski, CIN	111
D. Newcombe, BRO	89
S. Musial, STL	46
H. Aaron, MIL	36
P. Reese, BRO	36
J. Logan, MIL	24
W. Post, CIN	23
D. Ennis, PHI	21
R. Ashburn, PHI	17
C. Labine, BRO	11
B. Friend, PIT	10
D. Crandall, MIL	8
E. Mathews, MIL	6
D. Long, PIT	3
J. Meyer, PHI	3
G. Baker, CHI	2
C. Furillo, BRO	2
V. Law, PIT	1
F. Thomas, PIT	1

1955 AMERICAN

Y. Berra, NY	218
A. Kaline, DET	201
A. Smith, CLE	200
T. Williams, BOS	143
M. Mantle, NY	113
R. Narleski, CLE	90
N. Fox, CHI	84
H. Bauer, NY	64
V. Power, KC	53
J. Jensen, BOS	39
S. Lollar, CHI	37
G. McDougald, NY	34
B. Klaus, BOS	27
T. Byrne, NY	24
W. Ford, NY	21
R. Boone, DET	16
R. Sievers, WAS	9
H. Kuenn, DET	8
B. Pierce, CHI	8
D. Philley, CLE-BAL	6
E. Wynn, CLE	6
E. Valo, KC	5
M. Vernon, WAS	4
B. Hoeft, DET	1
D. Mossi, CLE	1
F. Sullivan, BOS	1
G. Triandos, BAL	1
J. Valdivielso, WAS	1
S. White, BOS	1

1956 NATIONAL

D. Newcombe, BRO	223
S. Maglie, BRO	183
H. Aaron, MIL	146
W. Spahn, MIL	126
J. Gilliam, BRO	103
R. McMillan, CIN	96
F. Robinson, CIN	79
P. Reese, BRO	71
S. Musial, STL	62
D. Snider, BRO	55
J. Adcock, MIL	54
B. Friend, PIT	38
H. Freeman, CIN	25
J. Antonelli, NY	18
T. Kluszewski, CIN	18
J. Robinson, BRO	17
W. Mays, NY	14
E. Bailey, CIN	13
B. Virdon, STL-PIT	13
S. Lopata, PHI	11

C. Furillo, BRO	9
L. Burdette, MIL	8
B. Buhl, MIL	7
R. Roberts, PHI	7
B. Lawrence, CIN	6
D. Long, PIT	4
W. Moon, STL	3
E. Banks, CHI	2
K. Boyer, STL	2
C. Labine, BRO	1
J. Logan, MIL	1
R. Ashburn, PHI	1

1956 AMERICAN

M. Mantle, NY	336
Y. Berra, NY	186
A. Kaline, DET	142
H. Kuenn, DET	80
B. Pierce, CHI	75
T. Williams, BOS	70
B. Nieman, CHI-BAL	55
G. McDougald, NY	55
V. Wertz, CLE	45
B. Lemon, CLE	40
H. Simpson, KC	37
W. Ford, NY	33
E. Wynn, CLE	32
J. Piersall, BOS	28
N. Fox, CHI	28
S. Lollar, CHI	27
F. Lary, DET	24
P. Runnels, WAS	24
H. Score, CLE	18
J. Jensen, BOS	15
M. Vernon, BOS	14
T. Brewer, BOS	11
H. Bauer, NY	8
C. Maxwell, DET	8
L. Aparicio, CHI	7
G. Triandos, BAL	6
F. Bolling, DET	3
M. Minoso, CHI	3
V. Power, KC	3
J. Kucks, NY	2
R. Sievers, WAS	1

1957 NATIONAL

H. Aaron, MIL	239
S. Musial, STL	230
R. Schoendienst, NY-MIL	221
W. Mays, NY	174
W. Spahn, MIL	131
E. Banks, CHI	60
G. Hodges, BRO	54
E. Mathews, MIL	45
F. Robinson, CIN	42
J. Sanford, PHI	39
D. Hoak, CIN	31
D. Blasingame, STL	26
E. Bouchee, PHI	26
B. Buhl, MIL	15
D. Ennis, STL	13
D. Groat, PIT	13
A. Dark, STL	12
D. Snider, BRO	10
F. Thomas, PIT	8
D. Drysdale, BRO	8
R. McMillan, CIN	6
D. Drott, CHI	6
G. Hamner, PHI	3
L. Burdette, MIL	2
J. Logan, MIL	1
H. Anderson, PHI	1

1957 AMERICAN

M. Mantle, NY	233
T. Williams, BOS	209
R. Sievers, WAS	205
N. Fox, CHI	193
G. McDougald, NY	165
V. Wertz, CLE	61
F. Malzone, BOS	58
M. Minoso, CHI	55
J. Bunning, DET	46
A. Kaline, DET	40
B. Pierce, CHI	35

B. Gardner, BAL	22
D. Donovan, CHI	19
Y. Berra, NY	18
G. Woodling, CLE	13
B. Grim, NY	9
B. Boyd, BAL	9
C. Maxwell, DET	5
W. Held, NY-KC	4
W. Ford, NY	4
V. Power, KC	3
J. Piersall, BOS	2
B. Skowron, NY	2
H. Kuenn, DET	2
S. Lollar, CHI	2
T. Kubek, NY	1
B. Shantz, NY	1

1958 NATIONAL

E. Banks, CHI	283
W. Mays, SF	185
H. Aaron, MIL	166
F. Thomas, PIT	143
W. Spahn, MIL	108
B. Friend, PIT	98
R. Ashburn, PHI	62
B. Mazeroski, PIT	61
O. Cepeda, SF	57
D. Crandall, MIL	48
L. Burdette, MIL	47
S. Musial, STL	39
K. Boyer, STL	31
J. Temple, CIN	26
B. Skinner, PIT	18
W. Covington, MIL	16
E. Face, PIT	8
H. Anderson, PHI	5
J. Gilliam, LA	4
B. Purkey, CIN	4
F. Robinson, CIN	4
J. Adcock, MIL	2
C. Furillo, LA	1

1958 AMERICAN

J. Jensen, BOS	233
B. Turley, NY	191
R. Colavito, CLE	181
B. Cerv, KC	164
M. Mantle, NY	127
R. Sievers, WAS	95
T. Williams, BOS	89
N. Fox, CHI	88
S. Lollar, CHI	57
P. Runnels, BOS	29
G. Triandos, BAL	27
D. Hyde, WAS	26
H. Kuenn, DET	24
C. McLish, CLE	18
V. Power, KC-CLE	15
F. Bolling, DET	10
E. Howard, NY	9
Y. Berra, NY	6
M. Minoso, CLE	6
A. Kaline, DET	5
G. McDougald, NY	5
R. Duren, NY	4
F. Lary, DET	3
J. Harshman, BAL	2
D. Donovan, CHI	1
F. Malzone, BOS	1

1959 NATIONAL

E. Banks, CHI	232.5
E. Mathews, MIL	189.5
H. Aaron, MIL	174
W. Moon, LA	161
S. Jones, SF	130
W. Mays, SF	85
E. Face, PIT	67
C. Neal, LA	64
F. Robinson, CIN	52
K. Boyer, STL	37
D. Crandall, MIL	27
L. Burdette, MIL	14
R. Craig, LA	12
J. Cunningham, STL	12
V. Pinson, CIN	11

J. Temple, CIN	8
D. Hoak, PIT	6
G. Hodges, LA	4
O. Cepeda, SF	3
V. Law, PIT	3
W. Spahn, MIL	3
G. Conley, PHI	1
W. McCovey, SF	1
D. Snider, LA	1

1959 AMERICAN

N. Fox, CHI	295
L. Aparicio, CHI	255
E. Wynn, CHI	123
R. Colavito, CLE	117
T. Francona, CLE	102
A. Kaline, DET	84
J. Landis, CHI	66
H. Kuenn, DET	64
S. Lollar, CHI	44
J. Jensen, BOS	40
C. McLish, CLE	35
Y. Berra, NY	26
M. Minoso, CLE	26
F. Malzone, BOS	24
H. Killebrew, WAS	21
G. Woodling, BAL	18
M. Mantle, NY	13
B. Richardson, NY	11
C. Pascual, WAS	9
B. Shaw, CHI	8
G. Triandos, BAL	8
B. Daley, KC	7
V. Power, CLE	5
B. Tuttle, KC	5
J. Lemon, WAS	4
P. Runnels, BOS	2
T. Williams, BOS	2
B. Allison, WAS	1
G. Staley, CHI	1

1960 NATIONAL

D. Groat, PIT	276
D. Hoak, PIT	162
W. Mays, SF	155
E. Banks, CHI	100
L. McDaniel, STL	95
K. Boyer, STL	80
V. Law, PIT	80
R. Clemente, PIT	62
E. Broglio, STL	58
E. Mathews, MIL	52
H. Aaron, MIL	49
E. Face, PIT	47
D. Crandall, MIL	31
W. Spahn, MIL	27
N. Larker, LA	21
S. Musial, STL	18
M. Wills, LA	7
V. Pinson, CIN	6
J. Adcock, MIL	5
S. Burgess, PIT	2
F. Robinson, CIN	2
L. Sherry, LA	2
P. Herrera, PHI	1

1960 AMERICAN

R. Maris, NY	225
M. Mantle, NY	222
B. Robinson, BAL	211
M. Minoso, CHI	141
R. Hansen, BAL	110
A. Smith, CHI	73
R. Sievers, CHI	58
E. Battey, CHI	57
B. Skowron, NY	56
J. Lemon, WAS	36
T. Kubek, NY	29
C. Estrada, BAL	28
T. Williams, BOS	25
V. Wertz, BOS	22
Y. Berra, NY	21
J. Gentile, BAL	21
P. Runnels, BOS	18
N. Fox, CHI	11
V. Power, CLE	11

S. Barber, BAL	7
L. Aparicio, CHI	6
J. Perry, CLE	6
G. Staley, CHI	4
J. Bunning, DET	3
G. Woodling, BAL	3
H. Kuenn, CLE	3
B. Daley, KC	3
M. Fornieles, BOS	2
C. Maxwell, DET	2
J. Piersall, CLE	2

1961 NATIONAL

F. Robinson, CIN	219
O. Cepeda, SF	117
V. Pinson, CIN	104
R. Clemente, PIT	81
J. Jay, CIN	74
W. Mays, SF	70
K. Boyer, STL	43
H. Aaron, MIL	39
M. Wills, LA	36
J. O'Toole, CIN	31
W. Spahn, MIL	31
S. Miller, SF	26
W. Moon, LA	22
G. Altman, CHI	9
J. Podres, LA	9
R. McMillan, MIL	8
E. Mathews, MIL	7
S. Koufax, LA	5
J. Roseboro, LA	4
J. Brosnan, CIN	3
J. Torre, MIL	2
L. Jackson, STL	1
J. Lynch, CIN	1
B. Malkmus, PHI	1
D. Stuart, PIT	1

1961 AMERICAN

R. Maris, NY	202
M. Mantle, NY	198
J. Gentile, BAL	157
N. Cash, DET	151
W. Ford, NY	102
L. Arroyo, NY	95
F. Lary, DET	53
R. Colavito, DET	51
A. Kaline, DET	35
E. Howard, NY	30
H. Killebrew, MIN	29
L. Aparicio, CHI	16
J. Piersall, CLE	10
S. Barber, BAL	7
D. Schwall, BOS	7
N. Siebern, KC	7
D. Donovan, WAS	5
B. Phillips, CLE	5
B. Robinson, BAL	4
C. Schilling, BOS	4
T. Morgan, LA	3
A. Smith, CHI	3
Y. Berra, NY	2
B. Richardson, NY	1
J. Romano, CLE	1
L. Thomas, NY-LA	1
H. Wilhelm, BAL	1

1962 NATIONAL

M. Wills, LA	209
W. Mays, SF	202
T. Davis, LA	175
F. Robinson, CIN	164
D. Drysdale, LA	85
H. Aaron, MIL	72
J. Sanford, SF	62
B. Purkey, CIN	33
F. Howard, LA	32
S. Musial, STL	19
J. Pagan, SF	13
D. Demeter, PHI	12
F. Alou, SF	10
B. White, STL	10
O. Cepeda, SF	9
D. Groat, PIT	7
R. Clemente, PIT	6

E. Banks, CHI — 5
K. Boyer, STL — 5
J. Callison, PHI — 5
H. Kuenn, SF — 5
J. Marichal, SF — 4
B. Skinner, PIT — 4
J. Davenport, SF — 3
S. Koufax, LA — 3
D. Crandall, MIL — 2
A. Mahaffey, PHI — 2
E. Roebuck, LA — 2
E. Kasko, CIN — 1
E. Mathews, MIL — 1

1962 AMERICAN
M. Mantle, NY — 234
B. Richardson, NY — 152
H. Killebrew, MIN — 99
L. Wagner, LA — 85
D. Donovan, CLE — 64
A. Kaline, DET — 58
N. Siebern, KC — 53
R. Rollins, MIN — 47
B. Robinson, BAL — 41
F. Robinson, CHI — 33
L. Thomas, LA — 32
T. Tresh, NY — 30
B. Moran, LA — 28
R. Terry, NY — 19
C. Pascual, MIN — 14
R. Colavito, DET — 13
H. Aguirre, DET — 10
J. Cunningham, CHI — 9
P. Runnels, BOS — 9
C. Yastrzemski, BOS — 9
V. Power, MIN — 8
D. Radatz, BOS — 8
J. Bunning, DET — 8
Z. Versalles, MIN — 8
J. Lumpe, KC — 7
E. Bressoud, BOS — 6
B. Rodgers, LA — 6
W. Ford, NY — 6
R. Herbert, CHI — 5
C. Hinton, WAS — 5
F. Malzone, BOS — 3
N. Cash, DET — 3
A. Smith, CHI — 1

1963 NATIONAL
S. Koufax, LA — 237
D. Groat, STL — 190
H. Aaron, MIL — 135
R. Perranoski, LA — 130
W. Mays, SF — 102
J. Gilliam, LA — 62
B. White, STL — 56
T. Davis, LA — 41
R. Santo, CHI — 41
V. Pinson, CIN — 32
J. Marichal, SF — 31
W. Spahn, MIL — 30
K. Boyer, STL — 19
R. Clemente, PIT — 12
J. Callison, PHI — 11
T. Taylor, PHI — 10
W. McCovey, SF — 9
M. Wills, LA — 9
D. Ellsworth, CHI — 7
J. Maloney, CIN — 7
D. Demeter, PHI — 3
D. Drysdale, LA — 3
T. Gonzalez, PHI — 2
C. Flood, STL — 1

1963 AMERICAN
E. Howard, NY — 248
A. Kaline, DET — 148
W. Ford, NY — 125
H. Killebrew, MIN — 85
D. Radatz, BOS — 84
C. Yastrzemski, BOS — 81
E. Battey, MIN — 57
G. Peters, CHI — 55
P. Ward, CHI — 52
B. Richardson, NY — 43

T. Tresh, NY — 38
C. Pascual, MIN — 29
D. Stuart, BOS — 25
A. Pearson, LA — 22
B. Allison, MIN — 15
J. Bouton, NY — 11
M. Alvis, CLE — 10
J. Pepitone, NY — 10
L. Wagner, LA — 9
S. Miller, BAL — 9
W. Causey, KC — 5
R. Rollins, MIN — 5
L. Aparicio, BAL — 3
B. Dailey, MIN — 3
J. Fregosi, LA — 3
N. Fox, CHI — 2
T. Kubek, NY — 1
F. Robinson, CHI — 1
N. Siebern, KC — 1

1964 NATIONAL
K. Boyer, STL — 243
J. Callison, PHI — 187
B. White, STL — 106.5
F. Robinson, CIN — 98
J. Torre, MIL — 85
W. Mays, SF — 66
R. Allen, PHI — 63
R. Santo, CHI — 59
R. Clemente, PIT — 56
L. Brock, CHI-STL — 40
C. Flood, STL — 38
J. Jackson, CHI — 26
J. Bunning, PHI — 23
H. Aaron, MIL — 22
J. Marichal, SF — 14
S. Ellis, CIN — 13
S. Koufax, LA — 7.5
V. Pinson, CIN — 6
J. Hart, SF — 6
B. Williams, CHI — 6
R. Amaro, PHI — 5
T. Davis, LA — 4
B. Gibson, STL — 2
C. Short, PHI — 2
R. Hunt, NY — 1
B. Schultz, STL — 1

1964 AMERICAN
B. Robinson, BAL — 269
M. Mantle, NY — 171
E. Howard, NY — 124
T. Oliva, MIN — 99
D. Chance, LA — 97
P. Ward, CHI — 67.5
B. Freehan, DET — 44
G. Peters, CHI — 44
D. Radatz, BOS — 37
H. Killebrew, MIN — 31
B. Powell, BAL — 28
W. Bunker, BAL — 23
J. Fregosi, LA — 21
A. Kaline, DET — 17
F. Robinson, CHI — 14
R. Hansen, CHI — 10
B. Richardson, NY — 9
L. Wagner, CLE — 9
J. Pizarro, CHI — 8
H. Wilhelm, CHI — 8
J. Horlen, CHI — 7
W. Ford, NY — 7
B. Allison, MIN — 5
R. Colavito, KC — 5
M. Stottlemyre, NY — 4
R. Maris, NY — 4
W. Causey, KC — 4
L. Aparicio, BAL — 3.5
D. Stuart, BOS — 3
E. Bressoud, BOS — 2
C. Osteen, WAS — 2
D. Wickersham, DET — 2
D. Lock, WAS — 1

1965 NATIONAL
W. Mays, SF — 224
S. Koufax, LA — 177

M. Wills, LA — 164
D. Johnson, CIN — 108
D. Drysdale, LA — 77
P. Rose, CIN — 67
H. Aaron, MIL — 58
R. Clemente, PIT — 56
J. Marichal, SF — 26
W. McCovey, SF — 25
J. Torre, MIL — 23
B. Williams, CHI — 21
F. Linzy, SF — 16
W. Stargell, PIT — 15
C. Flood, STL — 13
J. Hart, SF — 13
V. Law, PIT — 12
F. Robinson, CIN — 11
R. Santo, CHI — 11
E. Mathews, MIL — 8
L. Cardenas, CIN — 7
J. Maloney, CIN — 7
L. Lefebvre, LA — 7
J. Callison, PHI — 6
L. Johnson, LA — 6
C. Rojas, PHI — 5
J. Roseboro, LA — 5
R. Allen, PHI — 4
T. Cloninger, MIL — 4
J. Gilliam, LA — 3
J. Morgan, HOU — 1

1965 AMERICAN
Z. Versalles, MIN — 275
T. Oliva, MIN — 174
B. Robinson, BAL — 150
E. Fisher, CHI — 122
R. Colavito, CLE — 89
J. Grant, MIN — 74
S. Miller, BAL — 45
W. Horton, DET — 24
T. Tresh, NY — 23
E. Battey, MIN — 22
D. Wert, DET — 22
C. Yastrzemski, BOS — 22
J. Hall, MIN — 19
M. Stottlemyre, NY — 17
H. Killebrew, MIN — 15
A. Kaline, DET — 9
J. Adair, BAL — 7
R. Hansen, CHI — 7
S. McDowell, CLE — 7
B. Richardson, NY — 6
V. Davalillo, CLE — 5
J. Fregosi, CAL — 5
F. Whitfield, CLE — 5
B. Knoop, CAL — 4
D. Buford, CHI — 3
M. Mantle, NY — 3
P. Richert, WAS — 3
F. Robinson, CHI — 3
B. Campaneris, KC — 2
F. Howard, WAS — 2
R. Kline, WAS — 2
F. Mantilla, BOS — 2
N. Cash, DET — 1
T. Conigliaro, BOS — 1

1966 NATIONAL
R. Clemente, PIT — 218
S. Koufax, LA — 208
W. Mays, SF — 111
R. Allen, PHI — 107
F. Alou, ATL — 83
J. Marichal, SF — 74
P. Regan, LA — 66
H. Aaron, ATL — 57
M. Alou, PIT — 36
P. Rose, CIN — 31
G. Alley, PIT — 24
R. Santo, CHI — 23
J. Roseboro, LA — 22
O. Cepeda, SF-STL — 22
W. Stargell, PIT — 19
J. Torre, ATL — 18
W. McCovey, SF — 12
J. Lefebvre, LA — 8
G. Perry, SF — 8

C. Flood, STL — 7
M. Wills, LA — 5
R. Staub, HOU — 4
B. Mazeroski, PIT — 3
G. Beckert, CHI — 3
J. Maloney, CIN — 3
B. White, PHI — 3
L. Brock, STL — 2
B. Shaw, SF-NY — 1
C. Short, PHI — 1
W. Davis, LA — 1

1966 AMERICAN
F. Robinson, BAL — 280
B. Robinson, BAL — 153
B. Powell, BAL — 122
H. Killebrew, MIN — 96
J. Kaat, MIN — 84
T. Oliva, MIN — 71
A. Kaline, DET — 66
T. Agee, CHI — 63
L. Aparicio, BAL — 51
B. Campaneris, KC — 36
S. Miller, BAL — 27
N. Cash, DET — 23
J. Aker, KC — 22
E. Wilson, BOS-DET — 13
D. McLain, DET — 12
B. Freehan, DET — 9
A. Etchebarren, BAL — 7
B. Knoop, CAL — 6
M. Mantle, NY — 5
T. Tresh, NY — 5
J. Sanford, CAL — 4
R. Reichardt, CAL — 4
F. Valentine, WAS — 4
W. Horton, DET — 4
L. Wagner, CLE — 4
P. Richert, WAS — 3
J. Pepitone, NY — 2
T. Conigliaro, BOS — 1
S. Siebert, CLE — 1
C. Yastrzemski, BOS — 1
J. Fregosi, CAL — 1

1967 NATIONAL
O. Cepeda, STL — 280
T. McCarver, STL — 136
R. Clemente, PIT — 129
R. Santo, CHI — 103
H. Aaron, ATL — 79
M. McCormick, SF — 73
L. Brock, STL — 49
J. Perez, CIN — 43
J. Javier, STL — 41
P. Rose, CIN — 40
J. Wynn, HOU — 29
J. Jenkins, CHI — 26
C. Flood, STL — 24
E. Banks, CHI — 22
N. Briles, STL — 20
R. Staub, HOU — 12
D. Hughes, STL — 10
J. Hart, SF — 10
R. Allen, PHI — 9
T. Abernathy, CIN — 8
C. Boyer, ATL — 6
B. Gibson, STL — 5
R. Hundley, CHI — 5
J. Bunning, PHI — 5
T. Seaver, NY — 5
T. Davis, NY — 3
G. Alley, PIT — 3
T. Gonzalez, PHI — 3
W. McCovey, SF — 2

1967 AMERICAN
C. Yastrzemski, BOS — 275
H. Killebrew, MIN — 161
B. Freehan, DET — 137
J. Horlen, CHI — 91
A. Kaline, DET — 88
J. Lonborg, BOS — 82
C. Tovar, MIN — 70
J. Fregosi, CAL — 70
G. Peters, CHI — 37

G. Scott, BOS — 33
F. Robinson, BAL — 31
E. Wilson, DET — 20
D. Chance, MIN — 19
R. Hansen, CHI — 13
J. Adair, CHI-BOS — 11
P. Blair, BAL — 9
R. Petrocelli, BOS — 7
E. Howard, NY-BOS — 7
T. Oliva, MIN — 6
J. Kaat, MIN — 4
P. Casanova, WAS — 3
D. Mincher, CAL — 3
M. Lolich, DET — 2
M. Rojas, CAL — 1

1968 NATIONAL
B. Gibson, STL — 242
P. Rose, CIN — 205
W. McCovey, SF — 135
C. Flood, STL — 116
J. Marichal, SF — 93
L. Brock, STL — 73
M. Shannon, STL — 55
B. Williams, CHI — 48
G. Beckert, CHI — 40
F. Alou, ATL — 33
M. Alou, PIT — 32
H. Aaron, ATL — 19
W. Mays, SF — 14
E. Banks, CHI — 14
J. Koosman, NY — 14
J. Bench, CIN — 11
P. Regan, LA-CHI — 7
F. Jenkins, CHI — 6
T. Perez, CIN — 5
N. Briles, STL — 4
D. Maxvill, STL — 4
S. Blass, PIT — 3
T. Haller, LA — 3
R. Santo, CHI — 2
C. Carroll, ATL-CIN — 1
T. Helms, CIN — 1

1968 AMERICAN
D. McLain, DET — 280
B. Freehan, DET — 161
K. Harrelson, BOS — 103
W. Horton, DET — 102
D. McNally, BAL — 78
L. Tiant, CLE — 78
D. McAuliffe, DET — 71
F. Howard, WAS — 63
C. Yastrzemski, BOS — 50
M. Stottlemyre, NY — 43
B. Campaneris, OAK — 39
R. White, NY — 17
J. Northrup, DET — 15
L. Aparicio, CHI — 13
J. Fregosi, CAL — 11
D. Buford, BAL — 11
B. Robinson, BAL — 8
R. Jackson, OAK — 8
T. Oliva, MIN — 5
D. Cater, OAK — 5
M. Andrews, BOS — 4
B. Powell, BAL — 4
N. Cash, DET — 3
C. Tovar, MIN — 3
M. Stanley, DET — 2
W. Wood, CHI — 2
T. Uhlaender, MIN — 1

1969 NATIONAL
W. McCovey, SF — 265
T. Seaver, NY — 243
H. Aaron, ATL — 188
P. Rose, CIN — 127
R. Santo, CHI — 124
T. Agee, NY — 89
C. Jones, NY — 82
R. Clemente, PIT — 51
P. Niekro, ATL — 47
T. Perez, CIN — 28
M. Wills, MON-LA — 17
E. Banks, CHI — 15

R. Carty, ATL	12
J. Bench, CIN	12
D. Kessinger, CHI	8
T. Gonzalez, SD-ATL	8
R. Hunt, SF	8
D. Menke, HOU	8
W. Granger, CIN	8
J. Wynn, HOU	8
W. Davis, LA	7
W. Stargell, PIT	7
J. Marichal, SF	6
B. Williams, CHI	6
J. Koosman, NY	6
J. Torre, STL	6
M. Alou, PIT	6
L. Dierker, HOU	6
T. Haller, LA	3
B. Gibson, STL	2
B. Bonds, SF	2
R. Hundley, CHI	2
L. May, CIN	2
T. Sizemore, LA	2
W. Parker, LA	2
J. Edwards, HOU	1
R. Staub, MON	1
O. Cepeda, ATL	1

1969 AMERICAN

H. Killebrew, MIN	294
B. Powell, BAL	227
F. Robinson, BAL	162
F. Howard, WAS	115
R. Jackson, OAK	110
D. McLain, DET	85
R. Petrocelli, BOS	71
M. Cuellar, BAL	55
J. Perry, MIN	40
R. Carew, MIN	30
P. Blair, BAL	28
L. Cardenas, MIN	27
R. Perranoski, MIN	25
D. McNally, BAL	25
T. Oliva, MIN	21
S. Bando, OAK	18
C. Tovar, MIN	9
M. Stottlemyre, NY	8
C. Yastrzemski, BOS	8
E. Brinkman, WAS	7
J. Fregosi, CAL	7
R. Smith, BOS	6
D. Unser, WAS	5
B. Robinson, BAL	5
M. Epstein, WAS	4
M. Andrews, BOS	3
D. Bosman, WAS	3
B. Freehan, DET	3
T. Harper, SEA	2
A. Messersmith, CAL	2
R. Reese, MIN	2
K. Tatum, CAL	2
R. White, NY	2
M. Belanger, BAL	2
D. Green, OAK	1
J. Northrup, DET	1
L. Piniella, KC	1

1970 NATIONAL

J. Bench, CIN	326
B. Williams, CHI	218
T. Perez, CIN	149
B. Gibson, STL	110
W. Parker, LA	91
D. Giusti, PIT	72
P. Rose, CIN	54
J. Hickman, CHI	52
W. McCovey, SF	47
R. Carty, ATL	43
M. Sanguillen, PIT	36
R. Clemente, PIT	33
D. Clendenon, NY	26
G. Perry, SF	24
W. Stargell, PIT	20
B. Tolan, CIN	17
H. Aaron, ATL	16
J. Torre, STL	15
T. Agee, NY	13

B. Harrelson, NY	10
F. Jenkins, CHI	8
J. Merritt, CIN	8
D. Kessinger, CHI	6
C. Gaston, SD	5
D. Johnson, PHI	4
L. Walker, PIT	4
C. Morton, MON	3
B. Robertson, PIT	3
T. Seaver, NY	2
W. Granger, CIN	1

1970 AMERICAN

B. Powell, BAL	234
T. Oliva, MIN	157
H. Killebrew, MIN	152
C. Yastrzemski, BOS	136
F. Howard, WAS	91
T. Harper, MIL	78
B. Robinson, BAL	75
A. Johnson, CAL	70
J. Perry, MIN	63
F. Robinson, BAL	60
M. Cuellar, BAL	45
R. Perranoski, MIN	35
J. Fregosi, CAL	35
L. Aparicio, CHI	35
R. White, NY	25
D. McNally, BAL	22
S. McDowell, CLE	22
C. Tovar, MIN	16
T. Munson, NY	15
D. Buford, BAL	12
C. Wright, CAL	8
L. McDaniel, NY	8
R. Fosse, CLE	7
B. Campaneris, OAK	5
J. Palmer, BAL	4
R. Smith, BOS	3
S. Bando, OAK	1
T. Horton, CLE	1
B. Oliver, KC	1

1971 NATIONAL

J. Torre, STL	318
W. Stargell, PIT	222
H. Aaron, ATL	180
B. Bonds, SF	139
R. Clemente, PIT	87
M. Wills, LA	74
F. Jenkins, CHI	71
M. Sanguillen, PIT	49
T. Seaver, NY	46
A. Downing, LA	36
G. Beckert, CHI	35
L. May, CIN	28
L. Brock, STL	20
D. Giusti, PIT	16
W. McCovey, SF	15
T. Simmons, STL	13
W. Davis, LA	13
J. Johnson, SF	12
W. Mays, SF	11
R. Staub, MON	11
B. Williams, CHI	10
B. Harrelson, NY	4
B. Gibson, STL	3
R. Garr, ATL	1
D. Roberts, SD	1
P. Rose, CIN	1

1971 AMERICAN

V. Blue, OAK	268
S. Bando, OAK	182
F. Robinson, BAL	170
B. Robinson, BAL	163
M. Lolich, DET	155
F. Patek, KC	77
B. Murcer, NY	72
A. Otis, KC	67
W. Wood, CHI	54
T. Oliva, MIN	36
D. McNally, BAL	26
N. Cash, DET	21
B. Melton, CHI	18
R. Jackson, OAK	15

C. Rojas, KC	15
K. Sanders, MIL	13
P. Dobson, BAL	9
R. Smith, BOS	9
D. Johnson, BAL	9
M. Rettenmund, BAL	8
H. Killebrew, MIN	5
J. Palmer, BAL	5
L. Cardenas, MIN	5
M. Cuellar, BAL	4
C. Tovar, MIN	4
G. Scott, BOS	3
D. Buford, BAL	2
J. Hunter, OAK	1
G. Nettles, CLE	1

1972 NATIONAL

J. Bench, CIN	263
B. Williams, CHI	211
W. Stargell, PIT	201
J. Morgan, CIN	197
S. Carlton, PHI	124
C. Cedeno, HOU	112
A. Oliver, PIT	52
N. Colbert, SD	45
L. May, HOU	30
T. Simmons, STL	22
M. Marshall, MON	22
P. Rose, CIN	19
R. Clemente, PIT	16
C. Carroll, CIN	16
L. Brock, STL	13
H. Aaron, ATL	12
M. Sanguillen, PIT	12
S. Blass, PIT	9
R. Garr, ATL	7
G. Clines, PIT	6
B. Tolan, CIN	6
D. Baker, ATL	5
M. Mota, LA	4
D. Kingman, SF	3
T. McGraw, NY	2
R. Staub, NY	2
T. Seaver, NY	2
J. Cardenal, CHI	1
F. Jenkins, ChI	1
C. Speier, SF	1

1972 AMERICAN

R. Allen, CHI	321
J. Rudi, OAK	164
S. Lyle, NY	158
C. Fisk, BOS	96
B. Murcer, NY	89
G. Perry, CLE	88
W. Wood, CHI	78
L. Tiant, BOS	70.5
E. Brinkman, DET	62
M. Lolich, DET	60
J. Hunter, OAK	57
J. Mayberry, KC	27
J. Palmer, BAL	21
B. Grich, BAL	16
R. Carew, MIN	16
B. Campaneris, OAK	11
M. Epstein, OAK	11
L. Aparicio, BOS	9.5
R. Petrocelli, BOS	9
R. Jackson, OAK	9
C. May, CHI	6
G. Scott, MIL	6
D. Thompson, MIN	5
T. Harper, BOS	4
A. Kaline, DET	4
B. Freehan, DET	3
K. McMullen, CAL	3
B. Robinson, BAL	3
R. Smith, BOS	3
S. Bando, OAK	2
N. Ryan, CAL	2
A. Otis, KC	1
L. Piniella, KC	1

1973 NATIONAL

P. Rose, CIN	274
W. Stargell, PIT	250

B. Bonds, SF	174
J. Morgan, CIN	102
M. Marshall, MON	93
L. Brock, STL	65
T. Perez, CIN	59
T. Seaver, NY	57
K. Singleton, MON	52
J. Bench, CIN	41
C. Cedeno, HOU	39
H. Aaron, ATL	35
D. Johnson, ATL	34
T. Simmons, STL	20
T. McGraw, NY	17
F. Millan, NY	12
W. Davis, LA	12
D. Evans, ATL	11
L. May, HOU	9
T. Fuentes, SF	8
B. Watson, HOU	7
J. Ferguson LA	7
J. Cardenal, CHI	6
J. Billingham, CIN	6
A. Oliver, PIT	6
R. Hunt, MON	5
B. Bryant, SF	5
G. Maddox, SF	3
B. Harrelson, NY	2
B. Williams, CHI	2
G. Luzinski, PHI	2
B. Russell, LA	1

1973 AMERICAN

R. Jackson, OAK	336
J. Palmer, BAL	172
A. Otis, KC	112
R. Carew, MIN	83
J. Hiller, DET	83
S. Bando, OAK	83
J. Mayberry, KC	76
D. May, MIL	65
B. Murcer, NY	53
T. Davis, BAL	47
J. Hunter, OAK	47
T. Munson, NY	43
T. Harper, BOS	33
G. Scott, MIL	25
O. Cepeda, BOS	21
F. Robinson, CAL	21
N. Ryan, CAL	20
C. Fisk, BOS	16
B. Grich, BAL	9
C. Yastrzemski, BOS	9
D. Johnson, OAK	8
M. Belanger, BAL	8
J. Briggs, MIL	6
J. Coleman, DET	6
C. Rojas, KC	5
B. Blyleven, MIN	4
G. Perry, CLE	4
B. Campaneris, OAK	4
V. Blue, OAK	3
C. May, CHI	3
W. Horton, DET	3
B. North, OAK	3
P. Blair, BAL	2
D. Nelson, TEX	2
R. Allen, CHI	1

1974 NATIONAL

S. Garvey, LA	270
L. Brock, STL	233
M. Marshall, LA	146
J. Bench, CIN	141
J. Wynn, LA	137
M. Schmidt, PHI	136
A. Oliver, PIT	87
J. Morgan, CIN	72
R. Zisk, PIT	54
W. Stargell, PIT	43
R. Smith, STL	39
R. Garr, ATL	11
T. Simmons, STL	7
D. Cash, PHI	6
D. Concepcion, CIN	5
J. Billingham, CIN	4
C. Cedeno, HOU	4

A. Hrabosky, STL	4
A. Messersmith, LA	4
B. Capra, ATL	3
L. McGlothen, STL	2
B. McBride, STL	2
R. Hebner, PIT	2
R. Stennett, PIT	2
B. Buckner, LA	1
R. Cey, LA	1

1974 AMERICAN

J. Burroughs, TEX	248
J. Rudi, OAK	161.5
S. Bando, OAK	143.5
R. Jackson, OAK	119
F. Jenkins, TEX	118
J. Hunter, OAK	107
R. Carew, MIN	70
E. Maddox, NY	59
B. Grich, BAL	49
M. Cuellar, BAL	42
L. Tiant, BOS	41
B. Robinson, BAL	30
P. Blair, BAL	27
N. Ryan, CAL	24
B. Campaneris, OAK	23
R. Fingers, OAK	21
G. Perry, CLE	18
C. Yastrzemski, BOS	14
K. Henderson, CHI	12
J. Hiller, DET	11
L. Randle, TEX	10
B. Murcer, NY	10
L. Piniella, NY	8
R. Allen, CHI	8
S. Lyle, NY	7
T. Munson, NY	6
T. Davis, BAL	6
M. Belanger, BAL	6
D. Money, MIL	5
T. Murphy, MIL	3
H. McRae, KC	3
S. Busby, KC	3
G. Scott, MIL	2
P. Dobson, NY	1

1975 NATIONAL

J. Morgan, CIN	321.5
G. Luzinski, PHI	154
D. Parker, PIT	120
J. Bench, CIN	117
P. Rose, CIN	114
T. Simmons, STL	103
W. Stargell, PIT	69
A. Hrabosky, STL	66
T. Seaver, NY	65
R. Jones, SD	54
S. Garvey, LA	50
B. Madlock, CHI	45
D. Cash, PHI	26
R. Staub, NY	20
T. Perez, CIN	18
M. Schmidt, PHI	16
M. Sanguillen, PIT	16
R. Cey, LA	11.5
D. Kingman, NY	9
B. Watson, HOU	8
L. Brock, STL	6
L. Bowa, PHI	3
J. Reuss, PIT	2
A. Messersmith, LA	1
W. Montanez, PHI-SF	1

1975 AMERICAN

F. Lynn, BOS	326
J. Mayberry, KC	157
J. Rice, BOS	154
R. Fingers, OAK	129
R. Jackson, OAK	118
J. Palmer, BAL	82
T. Munson, NY	69
G. Scott, MIL	64.5
R. Carew, MIN	54.5
K. Singleton, BAL	44
G. Brett, KC	37.5
J. Hunter, NY	31

R. Burleson, BOS	28
C. Washington, OAK	22
T. Harrah, TEX	16
M. Torrez, BAL	12
R. Gossage, CHI	11
P. Lindblad, OAK	7
G. Tenace, OAK	7
B. Powell, CLE	6.5
D. Baylor, BAL	6
B. Campaneris, OAK	6
B. Lee, BOS	5
J. Todd, OAK	5
D. Doyle, CAL-BOS	5
R. Wise, BOS	4
J. Rudi, OAK	3
J. Kaat, CHI	2
L. May, BAL	2
B. Bonds, NY	1
C. Yastrzemski, BOS	1

1976 NATIONAL

J. Morgan, CIN	311
G. Foster, CIN	221
M. Schmidt, PHI	179
P. Rose, CIN	131
G. Maddox, PHI	98
B. Madlock, CHI	51
S. Garvey, LA	51
G. Luzinski, PHI	49
K. Griffey, CIN	49
R. Jones, SD	48
B. Watson, HOU	38
A. Oliver, PIT	30
R. Eastwick, CIN	26
J. Koosman, NY	20
S. Carlton, PHI	16
D. Cash, PHI	15
J. Richard, HOU	12
R. Monday, CHI	11
D. Kingman, NY	11
D. Parker, PIT	10
R. Robinson, PIT	9
D. Sutton, LA	7
R. Cey, LA	6
W. Montanez, SF-ATL	4
L. Brock, STL	3
C. Cedeno, HOU	3
C. Geronimo, CIN	3
R. Zisk, PIT	3
L. Bowa, PHI	1

1976 AMERICAN

T. Munson, NY	304
G. Brett, KC	217
M. Rivers, NY	179.5
H. McRae, KC	99
C. Chambliss, NY	71.5
R. Carew, MIN	71
A. Otis, KC	58
B. Campbell, MIN	56
L. May, BAL	51
J. Palmer, BAL	47
M. Fidrych, DET	41
J. Rudi, OAK	35
S. Bando, OAK	31
C. Yastrzemski, BOS	26
F. Tanana, CAL	19
R. Jackson, BAL	17
G. Nettles, NY	17
G. Tenace, OAK	13
R. Fingers, OAK	12
V. Blue, OAK	10
E. Figueroa, NY	9
S. Lyle, NY	8
R. LeFlore, DET	6
M. Littell, KC	5
R. Carty, CLE	5
R. White, NY	3
L. Tiant, BOS	3
J. Mayberry, KC	1
B. Wynegar, MIN	1

1977 NATIONAL

G. Foster, CIN	291
G. Luzinski, PHI	255
D. Parker, PIT	156

R. Smith, LA	112
S. Carlton, PHI	100
S. Garvey, LA	98
B. Sutter, CHI	68
R. Cey, LA	60
T. Simmons, STL	58
M. Schmidt, PHI	48
B. Robinson, PIT	34
T. John, LA	33
G. Templeton, STL	20
R. Fingers, SD	17
P. Rose, CIN	15
J. Burroughs, ATL	9
A. Oliver, PIT	9
J. Candelaria, PIT	8
R. Stennett, PIT	7
W. McCovey, SF	5
J. Bench, CIN	3
R. Reuschel, CHI	3
E. Valentine, MON	3
T. McGraw, PHI	2
L. Bowa, PHI	1
T. Seaver, NY-CIN	1

1977 AMERICAN

R. Carew, MIN	273
A. Cowens, KC	217
K. Singleton, BAL	200
J. Rice, BOS	163
G. Nettles, NY	112
S. Lyle, NY	79
T. Munson, NY	70
R. Jackson, NY	67
C. Fisk, BOS	67
B. Campbell, BOS	65
M. Rivers, NY	59
L. Hisle, MIN	54
G. Brett, KC	51
R. Zisk, CHI	34
J. Sundberg, TEX	30
B. Bonds, CAL	28
C. Yastrzemski, BOS	25
R. Guidry, NY	11
J. Palmer, BAL	9
R. LeFlore, DET	7
J. Thompson, DET	6
R. Burleson, BOS	5
B. Hobson, BOS	4
N. Ryan, CAL	3
G. Scott, BOS	3
H. McRae, KC	3
L. Bostock, MIN	2
T. Johnson, MIN	2
C. Chambliss, NY	1
O. Gamble, CHI	1
D. Leonard, KC	1

1978 NATIONAL

D. Parker, PIT	320
S. Garvey, LA	194
L. Bowa, PHI	189
R. Smith, LA	164
J. Clark, SF	107
G. Foster, CIN	104
G. Luzinski, PHI	48
G. Perry, SD	45
W. Stargell, PIT	39
D. Winfield, SD	37
P. Rose, CIN	35
V. Blue, SF	33
K. Tekulve, PIT	23
R. Fingers, SD	16
B. Hooton, LA	15
D. Lopes, LA	12
P. Niekro, ATL	8
B. Buckner, CHI	8
J. Burroughs, ATL	7
B. Sutter, CHI	5
G. Maddox, PHI	4
E. Cabell, HOU	2
B. Boone, PHI	1

1978 AMERICAN

J. Rice, BOS	352
R. Guidry, NY	291
L. Hisle, MIL	201

A. Otis, KC	90
R. Staub, DET	88
G. Nettles, NY	86
D. Baylor, CAL	51
E. Murray, BAL	50
C. Fisk, BOS	49
D. Porter, KC	48
R. Carew, MIN	46
M. Caldwell, MIL	41
R. Gossage, NY	39
A. Oliver, TEX	26.5
J. Sundberg, TEX	24
R. LeFlore, DET	21
R. Jackson, NY	18
C. Yastrzemski, BOS	17
G. Brett, KC	14
A. Thornton, CLE	12.5
L. Piniella, NY	11
T. Munson, NY	9
L. Bostock, CAL	8
L. Gura, KC	8
F. Lynn, BOS	6
M. Rivers, NY	6
B. Stanley, BOS	6
D. LaRoche, CAL	6
D. Money, MIL	5
W. Randolph, NY	5
D. Eckersley, BOS	4
H. McRae, KC	4
L. Roberts, SEA	3
R. Gale, KC	2
K. Singleton, BAL	2
R. Burleson, BOS	1
F. Tanana, CAL	1

1979 NATIONAL

W. Stargell, PIT	216
K. Hernandez, STL	216
D. Winfield, SD	155
L. Parrish, MON	128
R. Knight, CIN	82
J. Niekro, HOU	75.5
B. Sutter, CHI	69
K. Tekulve, PIT	64
D. Concepcion, CIN	63
D. Parker, PIT	56
D. Kingman, CHI	53
G. Foster, CIN	34
M. Schmidt, PHI	32
S. Garvey, LA	30
O. Moreno, PIT	23
P. Rose, PHI	23
G. Carter, MON	15
B. Madlock, SF-PIT	14
J. Richard, HOU	12
P. Niekro, ATL	11.5
J. Sambito, HOU	9
T. Seaver, CIN	9
J. Bench, CIN	7
A. Dawson, MON	6
G. Templeton, STL	5
G. Matthews, ATL	4
D. Collins, CIN	3
B. Horner, ATL	1

1979 AMERICAN

D. Baylor, CAL	347
K. Singleton, BAL	241
G. Brett, KC	226
F. Lynn, BOS	160.5
J. Rice, BOS	124
M. Flanagan, BAL	100
G. Thomas, MIL	87
B. Grich, CAL	58
D. Porter, KC	52
B. Bell, TEX	48
E. Murray, BAL	25.5
J. Kern, TEX	25
M. Marshall, MIN	25
B. Downing, CAL	24
S. Lezcano, MIL	18
R. Smalley, MIN	16
W. Wilson, KC	15
S. Kemp, DET	15
M. Clear, CAL	12
P. Molitor, MIL	8

R. Burleson, BOS	7
T. John, NY	5
C. Cooper, MIL	4
R. Jackson, NY	3
W. Horton, SEA	3
D. Ford, CAL	1
R. Guidry, NY	1
M. Hargrove, CLE	1

1980 NATIONAL

M. Schmidt, PHI	336
G. Carter, MON	193
J. Cruz, HOU	166
D. Baker, LA	138
S. Carlton, PHI	134
S. Garvey, LA	131
A. Dawson, MON	72
G. Hendrick, STL	50
B. Horner, ATL	42
B. McBride, PHI	32
K. Hernandez, STL	29
D. Murphy, ATL	23
C. Cedeno, HOU	14
J. Bibby, PIT	11
B. Buckner, CHI	11
T. McGraw, PHI	10
J. Bench, CIN	7
J. Clark, SF	6
J. Niekro, HOU	3
M. Easler, PIT	2
J. Reuss, LA	2
K. Griffey, CIN	1
R. LeFlore, MON	1
G. Richards, SD	1
R. Scott, MON	1

1980 AMERICAN

G. Brett, KC	335
R. Jackson, NY	234
R. Gossage, NY	218
W. Wilson, KC	169
C. Cooper, MIL	160
E. Murray, BAL	106
R. Cerone, NY	77
D. Quisenberry, KC	76.5
S. Stone, BAL	53
R. Henderson, OAK	51
A. Oliver, TEX	31.5
T. Armas, OAK	29
A. Bumbry, BAL	27
B. Oglivie, MIL	27
W. Randolph, NY	10
M. Norris, OAK	10
R. Yount, MIL	8
M. Rivers, TEX	7
B. Bell, TEX	7
A. Trammell, DET	6
K. Singleton, BAL	4
T. Perez, BOS	2
M. Dilone, CLE	2
F. Lynn, BOS	1
J. Wathan, KC	1

1981 NATIONAL

M. Schmidt, PHI	321
A. Dawson, MON	215
G. Foster, CIN	146
D. Concepcion, CIN	108
F. Valenzuela, LA	90
G. Carter, MON	77
D. Baker, LA	65
B. Sutter, STL	59
S. Carlton, PHI	41
T. Seaver, CIN	35
P. Rose, PHI	35
B. Buckner, CHI	35
G. Matthews, PHI	31
J. Cruz, HOU	25
G. Hendrick, STL	25
N. Ryan, HOU	23
B. Madlock, PIT	20
A. Howe, HOU	16
T. Raines, MON	15
R. Camp, ATL	9
K. Hernandez, STL	9
T. Herr, STL	7

G. Minton, SF	4
W. Cromartie, MON	3
S. Garvey, LA	1
M. May, SF	1

1981 AMERICAN

R. Fingers, MIL	319
R. Henderson, OAK	308
D. Evans, BOS	140
T. Armas, OAK	139
E. Murray, BAL	137
C. Lansford, BOS	109
D. Winfield, NY	98
C. Cooper, MIL	96
R. Gossage, NY	62
T. Paciorek, SEA	46
D. Murphy, OAK	45
K. Gibson, DET	40
S. McCatty, OAK	22
B. Grich, CAL	19
J. Morris, DET	17
A. Oliver, TEX	8
R. Yount, MIL	7
B. Bell, TEX	7
B. Almon, CHI	6
J. Mumphrey, NY	5
M. Hargrove, CLE	4
A. Trammell, DET	4
K. Singleton, BAL	3
S. Kemp, DET	3
D. Martinez, BAL	3
G. Luzinski, CHI	3
D. Stieb, TOR	1
G. Brett, KC	1

1982 NATIONAL

D. Murphy, ATL	283
L. Smith, STL	218
P. Guerrero, LA	175
A. Oliver, MON	175
B. Sutter, STL	134
M. Schmidt, PHI	54
J. Clark, SF	53
G. Minton, SF	44
S. Carlton, PHI	41
B. Buckner, CHI	38
B. Madlock, PIT	37
G. Carter, MON	35
O. Smith, STL	25
G. Hendrick, STL	20
T. Kennedy, SD	20
J. Morgan, SF	17
K. Hernandez, STL	12
J. Thompson, PIT	12
G. Garber, ATL	6
J. Andujar, STL	6
F. Valenzuela, LA	3
A. Dawson, MON	3
C. Chambliss, ATL	2
G. Matthews, PHI	2
R. Knight, HOU	1

1982 AMERICAN

R. Yount, MIL	385
E. Murray, BAL	228
D. DeCinces, CAL	178
H. McRae, KC	175
C. Cooper, MIL	152
R. Jackson, CAL	107
D. Evans, BOS	57
G. Thomas, MIL	44.5
D. Quisenberry, KC	39
R. Henderson, OAK	38
D. Winfield, NY	33
P. Molitor, MIL	29.5
L. Parrish, DET	26
B. Downing, CAL	22
W. Wilson, KC	16
R. Fingers, MIL	12
B. Boone, CAL	12
B. Vuckovich, MIL	11
J. Rice, BOS	10
T. Harrah, CLE	9
H. Baines, CHI	9
G. Brett, KC	9
D. Baylor, CAL	8

A. Thornton, CLE	8
B. Stanley, BOS	6
J. Palmer, BAL	5
D. Garcia, TOR	5
R. Carew, CAL	5
B. Caudill, SEA	4
B. Bell, TEX	3
C. Ripken, BAL	3
C. Lansford, BOS	1
R. Sutcliffe, CLE	1
G. Ward, MIN	1

1983 NATIONAL

D. Murphy, ATL	318
A. Dawson, MON	213
M. Schmidt, PHI	191
P. Guerrero, LA	182
T. Raines, MON	83
J. Cruz, HOU	76
D. Thon, HOU	67
B. Madlock, PIT	45
A. Holland, PHI	42
T. Kennedy, SD	37
G. Hendrick, STL	33
T. Pena, PIT	25
J. Denny, PHI	24
M. Soto, CIN	16
D. Evans, SF	16
R. Ramirez, ATL	15
J. Orosco, NY	14
L. Smith, CHI	8.5
A. Oliver, MON	3
J. Leonard, SF	2
L. Smith, STL	1.5
J. Davis, CHI	1
K. Hernandez, STL-NY	1
B. Horner, ATL	1
O. Smith, STL	1

1983 AMERICAN

C. Ripken, BAL	322
E. Murray, BAL	290
C. Fisk, CHI	209
J. Rice, BOS	150
C. Cooper, MIL	123
D. Quisenberry, KC	107.5
D. Winfield, NY	85
L. Whitaker, DET	84
L. Parrish, DET	66
H. Baines, CHI	49
W. Upshaw, TOR	41.5
W. Boggs, BOS	25
L. Hoyt, CHI	24.5
L. Moseby, TOR	21
B. Stanley, BOS	11.5
A. Trammell, DET	11
G. Luzinski, CHI	9
R. Yount, MIL	6
T. Simmons, MIL	4
R. Dotson, CHI	3.5
R. Law, CHI	2
R. Guidry, NY	2
J. Morris, DET	2
J. Cruz, SEA-CHI	1
R. Henderson, OAK	1
G. Wright, TEX	1
T. Martinez, BAL	0.5

1984 NATIONAL

R. Sandberg, CHI	326
K. Hernandez, NY	195
T. Gwynn, SD	184
R. Sutcliffe, CHI	151
G. Matthews, CHI	70
B. Sutter, STL	67
M. Schmidt, PHI	55.5
J. Cruz, HOU	53
D. Murphy, ATL	52.5
J. Davis, CHI	49
T. Raines, MON	41
L. Durham, CHI	38
R. Gossage, SD	34
G. Carter, MON	32
D. Gooden, NY	28
A. Wiggins, SD	14
R. Cey, CHI	6

K. McReynolds, SD	6
B. Dernier, CHI	6
S. Garvey, SD	5
B. Brenly, SF	1
J. Samuel, PHI	1
J. Leonard, SF	1

1984 AMERICAN

W. Hernandez, DET	306
K. Hrbek, MIN	247
D. Quisenberry, KC	235
E. Murray, BAL	197
D. Mattingly, NY	113
K. Gibson, DET	96
T. Armas, BOS	87.5
D. Winfield, NY	83
A. Trammell, DET	76.5
W. Wilson, KC	61
D. Evans, BOS	39
A. Davis, SEA	26
J. Rice, BOS	10
H. Baines, CHI	10
D. Kingman, OAK	10
L. Parrish, DET	8
W. Upshaw, TOR	8
B. Downing, CAL	6
S. Balboni, KC	5
A. Thornton, CLE	5
J. Bell, TOR	5
B. Bell, TEX	4
D. Stieb, TOR	4
L. Moseby, TOR	4
J. Beniquez, CAL	2
M. Boddicker, BAL	2
D. Alexander, TOR	1
C. Ripken, BAL	1

1985 NATIONAL

W. McGee, STL	280
D. Parker, CIN	220
P. Guerrero, LA	208
D. Gooden, NY	162
T. Herr, STL	119
G. Carter, NY	116
D. Murphy, ATL	63
K. Hernandez, NY	61
J. Tudor, STL	61
J. Clark, STL	20
V. Coleman, STL	16
T. Raines, MON	15
R. Sandberg, CHI	14
M. Marshall, LA	11
H. Brooks, MON	11
O. Hershiser, LA	9
K. Moreland, CHI	8
O. Smith, STL	5
M. Scioscia, LA	5
J. Reardon, MON	4
J. Cruz, HOU	2
B. Doran, HOU	2
M. Duncan, LA	1
T. Gwynn, SD	1
F. Valenzuela, LA	1
G. Wilson, PHI	1

1985 AMERICAN

D. Mattingly, NY	367
G. Brett, KC	274
R. Henderson, NY	174
W. Boggs, BOS	159
E. Murray, BAL	130
D. Moore, CAL	96
J. Barfield, TOR	88
J. Bell, TOR	84
H. Baines, CHI	49
B. Saberhagen, KC	45
D. Quisenberry, KC	39
D. Winfield, NY	35
C. Fisk, CHI	29
Da. Evans, DET	17
R. Guidry, NY	15
P. Bradley, SEA	12
C. Ripken, BAL	9
K. Gibson, DET	7
S. Balboni, KC	6
T. Henke, TOR	5

D. Lamp, TOR	3
K. Puckett, MIN	3
D. Alexander, TOR	3
D. Garcia, TOR	2
R. Gedman, BOS	1

1986 NATIONAL

M. Schmidt, PHI	287
G. Davis, HOU	231
G. Carter, NY	181
K. Hernandez, NY	179
D. Parker, CIN	144
T. Raines, MON	99
K. Bass, HOU	73
V. Hayes, PHI	41
T. Gwynn, SD	34
M. Scott, HOU	33
B. Doran, HOU	32
E. Davis, CIN	21
S. Sax, LA	13
R. Knight, NY	9
M. Krukow, SF	8
T. Worrell, STL	7
R. McDowell, NY	5
D. Smith, HOU	5
F. Valenzuela, LA	4
L. Dykstra, NY	4
B. Ojeda, NY	2
D. Murphy, ATL	2
C. Maldonado, SF	2

1986 AMERICAN

R. Clemens, BOS	339
D. Mattingly, NY	258
J. Rice, BOS	241
J. Bell, TOR	125
J. Barfield, TOR	107
K. Puckett, MIN	105
W. Boggs, BOS	87
W. Joyner, CAL	74
J. Carter, CLE	72
D. Righetti, NY	71
D. DeCinces, CAL	56
M. Witt, CAL	34
D. Baylor, BOS	32
T. Fernandez, TOR	17
T. Higuera, MIL	7
G. Gaetti, MIN	6
P. O'Brien, TEX	5
S. Fletcher, TEX	5
M. Barrett, BOS	5
J. Canseco, OAK	3
J. Presley, SEA	2
D. Schofield, CAL	1

1987 NATIONAL

A. Dawson, CHI	269
O. Smith, STL	193
J. Clark, STL	186
T. Wallach, MON	165
W. Clark, SF	128
D. Strawberry, NY	95
T. Raines, MON	80
T. Gwynn, SD	75
E. Davis, CIN	73
H. Johnson, NY	42
D. Murphy, ATL	34
V. Coleman, STL	20
J. Samuel, PHI	19
M. Schmidt, PHI	13
P. Guerrero, LA	12
S. Bedrosian, PHI	6
M. Thompson, PHI	4
B. Doran, HOU	1
T. Pendleton, STL	1

1987 AMERICAN

J. Bell, TOR	332
A. Trammell, DET	311
K. Puckett, MIN	201
Dw. Evans, BOS	127
P. Molitor, MIL	125
M. McGwire, OAK	109
D. Mattingly, NY	92
T. Fernandez, TOR	79
W. Boggs, BOS	64

G. Gaetti, MIN	47
J. Reardon, MIN	37
Da. Evans, DET	21
D. Alexander, DET	17
T. Henke, TOR	17
W. Joyner, CAL	17
K. Hrbek, MIN	11
D. Tartabull, KC	10
R. Yount, MIL	8
R. Clemens, BOS	7
J. Morris, DET	5
K. Seitzer, KC	5
R. Sierra, TEX	5
J. Canseco, OAK	4
M. Nokes, DET	1

1988 NATIONAL

K. Gibson, LA	272
D. Strawberry, NY	236
K. McReynolds, NY	162
A. Van Slyke, PIT	160
W. Clark, SF	135
O. Hershiser, LA	111
A. Galarraga, MON	105
G. Davis, HOU	72
D. Jackson, CIN	41
D. Cone, NY	37
T. Gwynn, SD	29
J. Franco, CIN	23
E. Davis, CIN	14
B. Bonilla, PIT	7
A. Dawson, CHI	6
R. Myers, NY	3
B. Butler, SF	2
S. Sax, LA	1

1988 AMERICAN

J. Canseco, OAK	392
M. Greenwell, BOS	242
K. Puckett, MIN	219
D. Winfield, NY	164
D. Eckersley, OAK	156
W. Boggs, BOS	107
A. Trammell, DET	62
P. Molitor, MIL	50
Dw. Evans, BOS	49
F. Viola, MIN	39
R. Yount, MIL	34
G. Brett, KC	29
D. Henderson, OAK	28
B. Hurst, BOS	15
D. Jones, CLE	11
J. Reardon, MIN	11
F. McGriff, TOR	9
R. Henderson, NY	8
M. McGwire, OAK	6
J. Carter, CLE	5
L. Smith, BOS	4
G. Gaetti, MIN	3
D. Plesac, MIL	3
D. Stewart, OAK	3
J. Franco, CLE	2
T. Fernandez, TOR	1

1989 NATIONAL

K. Mitchell, SF	314
W. Clark, SF	225
P. Guerrero, STL	190
R. Sandberg, CHI	157
H. Johnson, NY	153
M. Davis, SD	76
G. Davis, HOU	64
T. Gwynn, SD	57
E. Davis, CIN	44
M. Williams, CHI	41
L. Smith, ATL	34
J. Clark, SD	16
J. Walton, CHI	14
M. Grace, CHI	9
M. Scott, HOU	6
B. Bonilla, PIT	5
B. Butler, SF	3
T. Raines, MON	3
M. Thompson, STL	3
S. Garrelts, SF	2

1989 AMERICAN

R. Yount, MIL	256
R. Sierra, TEX	228
C. Ripken, BAL	216
J. Bell, TOR	205
D. Eckersley, OAK	116
F. McGriff, TOR	96
K. Puckett, MIN	84
B. Saberhagen, KC	82
R. Henderson, NY-OAK	67
B. Jackson, KC	46
D. Parker, OAK	44
G. Olson, BAL	35
B. Blyleven, CAL	32
D. Stewart, OAK	30
D. Mattingly, NY	25
J. Carter, CLE	23
C. Lansford, OAK	20
N. Esasky, BOS	19
T. Fernandez, TOR	9
M. Moore, OAK	6
W. Boggs, BOS	3
S. Sax, NY	3
A. Davis, SEA	2
N. Ryan, TEX	2
C. Davis, CAL	1
M. McGwire, OAK	1
M. Wilson, TOR	1

1990 NATIONAL

B. Bonds, PIT	331
B. Bonilla, PIT	212
D. Strawberry, NY	167
R. Sandberg, CHI	151
E. Murray, LA	123
M. Williams, SF	95
B. Larkin, CIN	82
D. Drabek, PIT	59
L. Dykstra, PHI	41
T. Wallach, MON	36
K. Mitchell, SF	20
E. Davis, CIN	12
C. Sabo, CIN	11
R. Gant, ATL	10
D. Gooden, NY	10
R. Martinez, LA	9
J. Carter, SD	7
R. Myers, CIN	7
P. O'Neill, CIN	6
J. Rijo, CIN	6
A. Dawson, CHI	6
D. Magadan, NY	4
B. Santiago, SD	3
B. Butler, SF	2
D. Justice, ATL	2
P. Guerrero, STL	2
K. Daniels, LA	1
A. Van Slyke, PIT	1

1990 AMERICAN

R. Henderson, OAK	317
C. Fielder, DET	286
R. Clemens, BOS	212
K. Gruber, TOR	175
B. Thigpen, CHI	170
D. Eckersley, OAK	112
G. Brett, KC	60
D. Stewart, OAK	56
B. Welch, OAK	54
F. McGriff, TOR	30
M. McGwire, OAK	29
J. Canseco, OAK	26
E. Burks, BOS	25
R. Palmeiro, TEX	22
C. Fisk, CHI	16
D. Parker, MIL	11
O. Guillen, CHI	10
J. Reed, BOS	9
K. Griffey, Jr., SEA	7
A. Trammell, DET	7
T. Pena, BOS	6
W. Boggs, BOS	5
D. Jones, CLE	3
C. Ripken, BAL	2
N. Ryan, TEX	1
D. Stieb, TOR	1

1991 NATIONAL

T. Pendleton, ATL	274
B. Bonds, PIT	259
B. Bonilla, PIT	191
W. Clark, SF	118
H. Johnson, NY	112
R. Gant, ATL	110
B. Butler, LA	103
L. Smith, STL	89
D. Strawberry, LA	76
F. McGriff, SD	23
T. Glavine, ATL	16
D. Justice, ATL	11
J. Bell, PIT	11
A. Dawson, CHI	5
J. Smiley, PIT	5
T. Gwynn, SD	4
J. Kruk, PHI	2
R. Sandberg, CHI	2
B. Larkin, CIN	2
D. Martinez, MON	1
C. Sabo, CIN	1
O. Smith, STL	1

1991 AMERICAN

C. Ripken, BAL	318
C. Fielder, DET	286
F. Thomas, CHI	181
J. Canseco, OAK	145
J. Carter, TOR	136
R. Alomar, TOR	128
K. Puckett, MIN	78
R. Sierra, TEX	63
K. Griffey, Jr., SEA	62
R. Clemens, BOS	57
P. Molitor, MIL	51
D. Tartabull, KC	32
J. Morris, MIN	29
C. Davis, MIN	21
J. Franco, TEX	17
D. White, TOR	15
S. Erickson, MIN	12
R. Aguilera, MIN	11
R. Palmeiro, TEX	6
R. Ventura, CHI	3
D. Henderson, OAK	1

1992 NATIONAL

B. Bonds, PIT	304
T. Pendleton, ATL	232
G. Sheffield, SD	204
A. Van Slyke, PIT	145
L. Walker, MON	111
D. Daulton, PHI	100
F. McGriff, SD	100
B. Roberts, CIN	64
M. Grissom, MON	54
T. Glavine, ATL	18
G. Maddux, CHI	14
R. Sandberg, CHI	12
B. Larkin, CIN	12
D. Jones, HOU	8
J. Kruk, PHI	8
M. Grace, PHI	6
D. DeShields, MON	6
R. Lankford, STL	5
J. Bagwell, HOU	4
D. Hollins, PHI	3
B. Butler, LA	2
O. Smith, STL	2
O. Nixon, ATL	1
J. Wetteland, MON	1

1992 AMERICAN

D. Eckersley, OAK	306
K. Puckett, MIN	209
J. Carter, TOR	201
M. McGwire, OAK	155
D. Winfield, TOR	141
R. Alomar, TOR	118
M. Devereaux, BAL	109
F. Thomas, CHI	108
C. Fielder, DET	83
P. Molitor, MIL	63
C. Baerga, CLE	31
E. Martinez, SEA	29

J. Morris, TOR	18
R. Clemens, BOS	16
B. Anderson, BAL	16
J. Gonzalez, TEX	15
K. Griffey, Jr., SEA	13
P. Listach, MIL	8
J. McDowell, CHI	5
J. Bell, CHI	3
M. Bordick, OAK	2
M. Mussina, BAL	2
A. Belle, CLE	1

1993 NATIONAL

B. Bonds, SF	372
L. Dykstra, PHI	267
D. Justice, ATL	183
F. McGriff, SD-ATL	177
R. Gant, ATL	176
M. Williams, SF	103
D. Daulton, PHI	79
M. Grissom, MON	66
M. Piazza, LA	49
A. Galarraga, COL	45
G. Jefferies, STL	28
R. Beck, SF	23
G. Maddux, ATL	17
B. Harvey, FLA	14
R. Thompson, SF	11
J. Blauser, ATL	9
J. Kruk, PHI	9
M. Grace, CHI	8
J. Bell, PIT	4
J. Bagwell, HOU	3
T. Gwynn, SD	2
R. Myers, CHI	2
J. Rijo, CIN	2
J. Burkett, SF	1
T. Glavine, ATL	1
J. Wetteland, MON	1

1993 AMERICAN

F. Thomas, CHI	392
P. Molitor, TOR	209
J. Olerud, TOR	198
J. Gonzalez, TEX	185
K. Griffey, Jr., SEA	182
R. Alomar, TOR	102
A. Belle, CLE	81
R. Palmeiro, TEX	52
J. McDowell, CHI	51
C. Baerga, CLE	50
J. Key, NY	29
J. Carter, TOR	25
M. Stanley, NY	15
J. Montgomery, KC	15
K. Lofton, CLE	11
T. Phillips, DET	10
C. Hoiles, BAL	10
M. Vaughn, BOS	8
D. Mattingly, NY	7
C. Ripken, BAL	7
A. Fernandez, CHI	4
D. Ward, TOR	3
G. Gagne, KC	3
K. Appier, KC	1
C. Fielder, DET	1
R. Johnson, SEA	1

1994 NATIONAL

J. Bagwell, HOU	392
M. Williams, SF	201
M. Alou, MON	183
B. Bonds, SF	144
G. Maddux, ATL	133
M. Piazza, LA	121
T. Gwynn, SD	112
F. McGriff, ATL	96
K. Mitchell, CIN	86
A. Galarraga, COL	42
L. Walker, MON	23
K. Hill, MON	22
M. Grissom, MON	22
D. Bichette, COL	19
H. Morris, CIN	18
C. Biggio, HOU	17
G. Jefferies, STL	5

J. Conine, FLA	4
T. Wallach, LA	4
J. Franco, NY	3
B. Boone, CIN	2
A. Benes, SD	1
B. Butler, LA	1
B. Saberhagen, NY	1

1994 AMERICAN

F. Thomas, CHI	372
K. Griffey, Jr., SEA	233
A. Belle, CLE	225
K. Lofton, CLE	181
P. O'Neill, NY	150
J. Key, NY	102
K. Puckett, MIN	100
J. Franco, CHI	49
D. Cone, KC	40
J. Carter, TOR	35
J. Canseco, TEX	27
C. Ripken, BAL	24
W. Boggs, NY	19
L. Smith, BAL	18
W. Clark, TEX	17
R. Palmeiro, BAL	11
M. Vaughn, BOS	10
D. Mattingly, NY	9
P. Molitor, TOR	9
C. Knoblauch, MIN	8
M. Mussina, BAL	8
C. Davis, CAL	3
J. Bere, CHI	1
R. Sierra, OAK	1

1995 NATIONAL

B. Larkin, CIN	281
D. Bichette, COL	251
G. Maddux, ATL	249
M. Piazza, LA	214
E. Karros, LA	135
R. Sanders, CIN	120
L. Walker, COL	88
S. Sosa, CHI	81
T. Gwynn, SD	72
C. Biggio, HOU	58
R. Gant, CIN	31
B. Bonds, SF	21
M. Grace, CHI	14
D. Bell, HOU	12
J. Bagwell, HOU	5
C. Hayes, PHI	4
A. Galarraga, COL	4
C. Jones, ATL	3
V. Castilla, COL	3
F. McGriff, ATL	2
P. Schourek, CIN	2
J. Conine, FLA	1
T. Henke, STL	1

1995 AMERICAN

M. Vaughn, BOS	308
A. Belle, CLE	300
E. Martinez, SEA	244
J. Mesa, CLE	130
J. Buhner, SEA	120
R. Johnson, SEA	111
T. Salmon, CAL	110
F. Thomas, CHI	86
J. Valentin, BOS	57
G. Gaetti, KC	45
R. Palmeiro, BAL	34
M. Ramirez, CLE	30
T. Wakefield, BOS	20
J. Edmonds, CAL	18
P. O'Neill, NY	14
M. McGwire, OAK	7
C. Knoblauch, MIN	5
W. Boggs, NY	5
G. DiSarcina, CAL	3
C. Ripken, BAL	3
K. Puckett, MIN	2

1996 NATIONAL

K. Caminiti, SD	392
M. Piazza, LA	237
E. Burks, COL	186

C. Jones, ATL	158
B. Bonds, SF	132
A. Galarraga, COL	112
G. Sheffield, FLA	112
B. Jordan, STL	69
J. Bagwell, HOU	59
S. Finley, SD	38
J. Smoltz, ATL	33
B. Larkin, CIN	29
M. Grissom, ATL	23
B. Gilkey, NY	13
S. Sosa, CHI	12
E. Karros, LA	10
H. Rodriguez, MON	9
T. Hundley, NY	7
L. Johnson, NY	7
D. Bichette, COL	6
T. Worrell, LA	3
K. Brown, FLA	2
T. Hoffman, SD	2
M. Alou, MON	1

1996 AMERICAN

J. Gonzalez, TEX	290
A. Rodriguez, SEA	287
A. Belle, CLE	228
K. Griffey, Jr., SEA	188
M. Vaughn, BOS	134
R. Palmeiro, BAL	104
M. McGwire, OAK	100
F. Thomas, CHI	88
B. Anderson, BAL	53
I. Rodriguez, TEX	52
K. Lofton, CLE	34
M. Duncan, NY	27
P. Molitor, MIN	19
A. Pettitte, NY	11
J. Thome, CLE	9
C. Knoblauch, MIN	8
J. Buhner, SEA	6
B. Williams, NY	6
J. Wetteland, NY	4
R. Alomar, BAL	3
T. Steinbach, OAK	1

1997 NATIONAL

L. Walker, COL	359
M. Piazza, LA	263
J. Bagwell, HOU	233
C. Biggio, HOU	157
B. Bonds, SF	123
T. Gwynn, SD	113
A. Galarraga, COL	85
J. Kent, SF	80
C. Jones, ATL	70
M. Alou, FLA	60
C. Johnson, FLA	22
G. Maddux, ATL	16
E. Alfonzo, NY	10
C. Schilling, PHI	9
R. Mondesi, LA	8
R. Lankford, STL	6
P. Martinez, MON	6
M. McGwire, STL	6
S. Sosa, CHI	5
K. Young, PIT	5
J. Blauser, ATL	4
V. Castilla, COL	3
D. Kile, HOU	3
R. Beck, SF	2
T. Womack, PIT	2
K. Lofton, ATL	1
J. Snow, SF	1

1997 AMERICAN

K. Griffey, Jr., SEA	392
T. Martinez, NY	248
F. Thomas, CHI	172
R. Myers, BAL	128
D. Justice, CLE	90
J. Thome, CLE	89
T. Salmon, ANA	84
N. Garciaparra, BOS	83
J. Gonzalez, TEX	66
R. Clemens, TOR	56
R. Johnson, SEA	42

P. O'Neill, NY	37
R. Palmeiro, BAL	36
S. Alomar, CLE	22
E. Martinez, SEA	22
I. Rodriguez, TEX	16
B. Williams, NY	14
T. Clark, DET	13
J. Buhner, SEA	12
D. Jones, MIL	5
A. Rhodes, BAL	5
R. Alomar, BAL	4
R. Greer, TEX	4
D. Jeter, NY	3
D. Cruz, DET	2
B. Radke, MIN	2
M. Rivera, NY	2
M. Vaughn, BOS	2
J. Burnitz, MIL	1

1998 NATIONAL

S. Sosa, CHI	438
M. McGwire, STL	272
M. Alou, HOU	215
G. Vaughn, SD	185
C. Biggio, HOU	163
A. Galarraga, ATL	147
T. Hoffman, SD	117
B. Bonds, SF	66
C. Jones, ATL	56
J. Kent, SF	56
V. Castilla, COL	49
J. Olerud, NY	38
V. Guerrero, MON	25
M. Piazza, LA-FLA-NY	15
T. Gwynn, SD	11
K. Brown, SD	8
L. Walker, COL	7
R. Beck, CHI	5
J. Burnitz, MIL	4
S. Rolen, PHI	3
T. Glavine, ATL	2
R. Johnson, HOU	2
D. Bichette, COL	2
J. Lopez, ATL	1
M. Morandini, CHI	1

1998 AMERICAN

J. Gonzalez, TEX	357
N. Garciaparra, BOS	232
D. Jeter, NY	180
M. Vaughn, BOS	135
K. Griffey, Jr., SEA	135
M. Ramirez, CLE	127
B. Williams, NY	103
A. Belle, CHI	98
A. Rodriguez, SEA	92
I. Rodriguez, TEX	50
R. Clemens, TOR	49
P. O'Neill, NY	36
T. Gordon, BOS	27
D. Erstad, ANA	7
T. Salmon, ANA	7
D. Wells, NY	3
J. Wetteland, TEX	3
E. Davis, BAL	2
T. Fryman, CLE	2
R. Palmeiro, BAL	2
C. Delgado, TOR	1
R. Helling, TEX	1
M. Jackson, CLE	1
P. Martinez, BOS	1
J. Thome, CLE	1

1999 NATIONAL

C. Jones, ATL	432
J. Bagwell, HOU	276
M. Williams, ARI	269
G. Vaughn, CIN	121
M. McGwire, STL	115
R. Ventura, NY	113
M. Piazza, NY	109
E. Alfonzo, NY	88
S. Sosa, CHI	87
L. Walker, COL	35
V. Guerrero, MON	34
C. Biggio, HOU	32

J. Bell, ARI	31	R. Nen, SF	12	P. LoDuca, LA	6
S. Casey, CIN	23	T. Glavine, ATL	8	F. Rodriguez, SF	4
R. Johnson, ARI	21	E. Alfonzo, NY	6	P. Nevin, SD	3
B. Wagner, HOU	19	E. Burks, SF	6	C. Floyd, FLA	2
C. Everett, HOU	15	R. Johnson, ARI	5	R. Oswalt, HOU	2
L. Gonzalez, ARI	12	D. Kile, STL	4	B. Giles, PIT	1
B. Jordan, ATL	11	B. Giles, PIT	3	V. Guerrero, MON	1
B. Giles, PIT	11	M. Alou, HOU	2	S. Kline, STL	1
M. Hampton, HOU	10	R. Hidalgo, HOU	2	S. Rolen, PHI	1
B. Larkin, CIN	7	A. Alfonseca, FLA	1	L. Walker, COL	1
B. Abreu, PHI	6				
B. Bonds, SF	3	**2000 AMERICAN**		**2001 AMERICAN**	
M. Mantei, ARI	3	Ja. Giambi, OAK	317	I. Suzuki, SEA	289
J. Kent, SF	2	F. Thomas, CHI	285	Ja. Giambi, OAK	281
K. Millwood, ATL	2	A. Rodriguez, SEA	218	B. Boone, SEA	259
T. Hoffman, SD	1	C. Delgado, TOR	206	R. Alomar, CLE	165
		P. Martinez, BOS	103	J. Gonzalez, CLE	156
1999 AMERICAN		E. Martinez, SEA	97	A. Rodriguez, TEX	141
I. Rodriguez, TEX	252	M. Ramirez, CLE	97	J. Thome, CLE	107
P. Martinez, BOS	239	D. Erstad, ANA	94	R. Clemens, NY	67
R. Alomar, CLE	226	N. Garciaparra, BOS	66	M. Ramirez, BOS	50
M. Ramirez, CLE	226	D. Jeter, NY	44	D. Jeter, NY	42
R. Palmeiro, TEX	193	M. Sweeney, KC	33	M. Rivera, NY	27
D. Jeter, NY	177	M. Ordoñez, CHI	28	T. Martinez, NY	18
N. Garciaparra, BOS	137	D. Justice, CLE-NY	23	M. Mulder, OAK	12
Ja. Giambi, OAK	49	B. Williams, NY	23	R. Palmeiro, TEX	5
S. Green, TOR	44	T. Hudson, OAK	8	D. Mientkiewicz, MIN	5
K. Griffey, Jr., SEA	42	M. Tejada, OAK	5	E. Martinez, SEA	4
B. Williams, NY	21	T. Fryman, CLE	2	C. Guzman, MIN	4
C. Delgado, TOR	16	D. Wells, TOR	2	M. Cameron, SEA	4
J. Gonzalez, TEX	10	J. Damon, KC	1	M. Tejada, OAK	3
M. Rivera, NY	9			K. Sasaki, SEA	3
A. Rodriguez, SEA	4	**2001 NATIONAL**		T. Hunter, MIN	2
O. Vizquel, CLE	3	B. Bonds, SF	438	M. Sweeney, KC	2
M. Stairs, OAK	2	S. Sosa, CHI	278	B. Zito, OAK	2
J. Jaha, OAK	1	L. Gonzalez, ARI	261	G. Anderson, ANA	2
B. Surhoff, BAL	1	A. Pujols, STL	222	C. Koskie, MIN	1
		L. Berkman, HOU	125	S. Stewart, TOR	1
2000 NATIONAL		S. Green, LA	112		
J. Kent, SF	392	J. Bagwell, HOU	109	**2002 NATIONAL**	
B. Bonds, SF	279	C. Jones, ATL	100	B. Bonds, SF	448
M. Piazza, NY	271	T. Helton, COL	90	A. Pujols, STL	276
J. Edmonds, STL	208	C. Schilling, ARI	24	L. Berkman, HOU	181
T. Helton, COL	198	R. Johnson, ARI	23	V. Guerrero, MON	168
V. Guerrero, MON	117	R. Aurilia, SF	20	S. Green, LA	146
J. Bagwell, HOU	102	M. Piazza, NY	14	J. Kent, SF	135
A. Jones, ATL	95	M. Alou, HOU	13	R. Johnson, ARI	127
G. Sheffield, LA	71	M. Morris, STL	13	J. Smoltz, ATL	124
S. Sosa, CHI	71	B. Abreu, PHI	9	S. Sosa, CHI	63
C. Jones, ATL	23	J. Rollins, PHI	8	C. Schilling, ARI	53
G. Maddux, ATL	12	B. Jordan, ATL	7	C. Jones, ATL	50

E. Gagne, LA	44	J. Bagwell, HOU	14
B. Giles, PIT	27	E. Renteria, STL	13
J. Spivey, ARI	8	P. Wilson, COL	12
P. Burrell, PHI	8	V. Guerrero, MON	10
A. Jones, ATL	7	M. Giles, ATL	9
G. Sheffield, ATL	6	R. Hidalgo, HOU	9
J. Edmonds, STL	6	J. Smoltz, ATL	9
T. Helton, COL	3	L. Castillo, FLA	8
B. Santiago, SF	2	J. Schmidt, SF	7
E. Renteria, STL	2	I. Rodriguez, FLA	5
L. Walker, COL	2	B. Wagner, HOU	5
R. Oswalt, HOU	1	L. Gonzalez, ARI	4
J. Vidro, MON	1	C. Jones, ATL	4
		B. Abreu, PHI	3
2002 AMERICAN		M. Cabrera, FLA	3
M. Tejada, OAK	356	J. Edmonds, STL	3
A. Rodriguez, TEX	254	M. Grudzielanek, CHI	3
A. Soriano, NY	234	D. Lee, FLA	3
G. Anderson, ANA	184	R. Ortiz, ATL	3
Ja. Giambi, NY	162	R. Furcal, ATL	2
T. Hunter, MIN	132	D. Willis, FLA	1
J. Thome, CLE	69		
M. Ordoñez, CHI	59	**2003 AMERICAN**	
M. Ramirez, BOS	39	A. Rodriguez, TEX	242
B. Williams, NY	32	C. Delgado, TOR	213
D. Eckstein, ANA	24	J. Posada, NY	194
N. Garciaparra, BOS	24	S. Stewart, TOR-MIN	140
B. Zito, OAK	22	D. Ortiz, BOS	130
E. Chavez, OAK	14	M. Ramirez, BOS	100
T. Percival, ANA	12	N. Garciaparra, BOS	99
E. Guardado, MIN	12	V. Wells, TOR	84
I. Suzuki, SEA	10	C. Beltran, KC	77
B. Koch, OAK	8	B. Boone, SEA	65
D. Lowe, BOS	3	M. Tejada, OAK	49
P. Martinez, BOS	1	B. Mueller, BOS	45
M. Sweeney, KC	1	Ja. Giambi, NY	36
		G. Anderson, ANA	35
2003 NATIONAL		K. Foulke, OAK	20
B. Bonds, SF	426	F. Thomas, CHI	20
A. Pujols, STL	303	E. Chavez, OAK	18
G. Sheffield, ATL	247	C. Lee, CHI	16
J. Thome, PHI	203	M. Ordoñez, CHI	16
J. Lopez, ATL	159	A. Soriano, NY	15
E. Gagne, LA	143	D. Jeter, NY	10
T. Helton, COL	75	P. Martinez, BOS	7
S. Sosa, CHI	53	I. Suzuki, SEA	6
M. Prior, CHI	44	A. Huff, TB	4
J. Pierre, FLA	39	E. Loaiza, CHI	4
M. Lowell, FLA	30	J. Varitek, BOS	4
R. Sexson, MIL	21	M. Rivera, NY	3
A. Jones, ATL	15		

Rookie of the Year Award: History

The Chicago chapter of the Baseball Writers' Association of America (BBWAA) established an award recognizing the major leagues' top rookie following the 1940 season, selecting Lou Boudreau for the honor. This procedure continued for six more years before going national. The subsequent winners of the Chicago chapter's award were Pete Reiser (1941), Johnny Beazley (1942), Bill Johnson (1943), Bill Voiselle (1944), Boo Ferriss (1945), and Eddie Waitkus (1946).

In 1947 a group of 39 baseball writers was asked to name five rookies in order of preference, with votes distributed on a 5-4-3-2-1 basis. Thus, Jackie Robinson became the first nationally recognized winner of the BBWAA Rookie of the Year Award, or the J. Louis Comiskey Memorial Award, as it was called. During the 1987 Hall of Fame induction ceremony, Commissioner Peter Ueberroth announced that, hereafter, the Rookie of the Year Award would be officially known as the Jackie Robinson Award.

In 1948 there were 48 writers taking part in the award, this time naming only a single candidate on each ballot. In 1949 the BBWAA began the process of choosing a top rookie in each league. Three writers from each league city, the same men who decided on the MVP Awards, participated in the voting. Voters were free to use their individual judgments as to the eligibility of rookie candidates, which created some problems, especially in 1950 when Al Rosen, league home-run leader with 37, was ignored by Rookie of the Year voters. Apparently they felt that Rosen's 58 previous major league at-bats were tantamount to veteran status, while winner Walt Dropo's 41 previous at-bats were not.

In 1957 formal guidelines were finally established for determining rookie status. A player could not have accumulated more than 75 at-bats, 45 innings pitched, or have been on a major league roster between May 15 and September 1 of any previous season. Shortly after, the guidelines were changed to 90 at-bats, 45 innings pitched or 45 days on a major league roster before September 1. Finally, in 1971, the at-bats and innings limits were set at 130 and 50, respectively.

There were several instances, especially in the early days of the award, in which some Rookie of the Year voters didn't bother to exercise their franchise. In 1961, as with the MVP Award, the number of voters was reduced from three to two writers from each league city.

Following two tie votes in four years (1976 NL, 1979 AL), the writers adopted the system used in Cy Young Award balloting: naming three rookies on each ballot, in order of preference, with votes distributed on a 5-3-1 basis. This system began in 1980, although it had been scheduled to start a decade earlier.

The maximum possible point total available to Rookie of the

Year Award candidates was 165 in 1947, 48 in 1948, and 24 in each league in 1949-1960. In the National League it was 16 in 1961, 20 in 1962-1968, 24 in 1969-1979, 120 in 1980-1992, 140 in 1993-97, and 160 from 1998 to the present. In the American League the maximum point total was 20 in 1961-1968, 24 in 1969-1976, 28 in 1977-1979, and 140 from 1980 to the present.

There have been 15 unanimous Rookie of the Year selections since 1947: Frank Robinson (NL, 1956), Orlando Cepeda (NL, 1958), Willie McCovey (NL, 1959), Carlton Fisk (AL, 1972), Vince Coleman (NL, 1985), Benito Santiago (NL, 1987), Mark McGwire (AL, 1987), Sandy Alomar (AL, 1990), Mike Piazza (NL, 1993), Tim Salmon (AL, 1993), Raul Mondesi (NL, 1994), Derek Jeter (AL, 1996), Scott Rolen (NL, 1997), Nomar Garciaparra (AL, 1997), and Albert Pujols (NL, 2001). Technically, Tony Kubek's 1957 AL selection was also unanimous, as the lone dissenting vote went to an ineligible player.

ROOKIE OF THE YEAR AWARD

1947
J. Robinson, BRO (NL)	129
L. Jansen, NY (NL)	105
F. Shea, NY (AL)	67
F. Fain, PHI (AL)	43
F. Baumholtz, CIN (NL)	42

(Rest of voting unknown)

1948
A. Dark, BOS (NL)	27
G. Bearden, CLE (AL)	8
R. Ashburn, PHI (NL)	7
L. Brissie, PHI (AL)	3
B. Goodman, BOS (AL)	3

1949 NATIONAL
D. Newcombe, BRO	21
D. Crandall, BOS	3

1949 AMERICAN
R. Sievers, STL	10
A. Kellner, PHI	5
G. Coleman, NY	4
B. Kuzava, CHI	1
J. Groth, DET	1
M. Garcia, CLE	1

1950 NATIONAL
S. Jethroe, BOS	11
B. Miller, PHI	5
D. O'Connell, PIT	4
E. Church, PHI	2
B. Serena, CHI	1

1950 AMERICAN
W. Dropo, BOS	15
W. Ford, NY	6
C. Carrasquel, CHI	2

1951 NATIONAL
W. Mays, NY	18
C. Nichols, BOS	4
C. Labine, BRO	2

1951 AMERICAN
G. McDougald, NY	13
M. Minoso, CLE-CHI	11

1952 NATIONAL
J. Black, BRO	19
H. Wilhelm, NY	3
D. Groat, PIT	1
E. Mathews, BOS	1

1952 AMERICAN
H. Byrd, PHI	9
C. Courtney, STL	8
S. White, BOS	7

1953 NATIONAL
J. Gilliam, BRO	11
H. Haddix, STL	4
R. Jablonski, STL	3
R. Repulski, STL	2
B. Bruton, MIL	2
F. Baczewski, CIN	1
J. Greengrass, CIN	1

1953 AMERICAN
H. Kuenn, DET	23
T. Umphlett, BOS	1

1954 NATIONAL
W. Moon, STL	17
E. Banks, CHI	4
G. Conley, MIL	2
H. Aaron, MIL	1

1954 AMERICAN
B. Grim, NY	15
J. Finigan, PHI	8
A. Kaline, DET	1

1955 NATIONAL
B. Virdon, STL	15
J. Meyer, PHI	7
D. Bessent, BRO	2

1955 AMERICAN
H. Score, CLE	18
B. Klaus, BOS	5
N. Zauchin, BOS	1

1956 NATIONAL
F. Robinson, CIN	24

1956 AMERICAN
L. Aparicio, CHI	22
T. Francona, BAL	1
R. Colavito, CLE	1

1957 NATIONAL
J. Sanford, PHI	16
E. Bouchee, PHI	4
D. Drott, CHI	3
B. Hazle, MIL	1

1957 AMERICAN
T. Kubek, NY	23
F. Malzone, BOS	1

1958 NATIONAL
O. Cepeda, SF	21

1958 AMERICAN
A. Pearson, WAS	14
R. Duren, NY	7
G. Bell, CLE	3

1959 NATIONAL
W. McCovey, SF	24

1959 AMERICAN
B. Allison, WAS	18
J. Perry, CLE	5
R. Snyder, KC	1

1960 NATIONAL
F. Howard, LA	12
P. Herrera, PHI	4
A. Mahaffey, PHI	3
R. Santo, CHI	2
T. Davis, LA	1

1960 AMERICAN
R. Hansen, BAL	22
C. Estrada, BAL	1
J. Gentile, BAL	1

1961 NATIONAL
B. Williams, CHI	10
J. Torre, MIL	5
J. Curtis, CHI	1

1961 AMERICAN
D. Schwall, BOS	7
D. Howser, KC	6
Fl. Robinson, CHI	2
C. Schilling, BOS	2
L. Thomas, LA	2
J. Wood, DET	1

1962 NATIONAL
K. Hubbs, CHI	19
D. Clendenon, PIT	1

1962 AMERICAN
T. Tresh, NY	13
B. Rodgers, LA	4
B. Allen, MIN	1
D. Chance, LA	1
D. Radatz, BOS	1

1963 NATIONAL
P. Rose, CIN	17
R. Hunt, NY	2
R. Culp, PHI	1

1963 AMERICAN
G. Peters, CHI	10
P. Ward, CHI	6
J. Hall, MIN	4

1964 NATIONAL
R. Allen, PHI	18
R. Carty, MIL	1
J. Hart, SF	1

1964 AMERICAN
T. Oliva, MIN	19
W. Bunker, BAL	1

1965 NATIONAL
J. Lefebvre, LA	13
J. Morgan, HOU	4
F. Linzy, SF	3

1965 AMERICAN
C. Blefary, BAL	12
M. Lopez, CAL	8

1966 NATIONAL
T. Helms, CIN	12
S. Jackson, HOU	3
T. Fuentes, SF	2
R. Hundley, CHI	1
C. Jones, NY	1
L. Jaster, STL	1

1966 AMERICAN
T. Agee, CHI	16
J. Nash, KC	2
D. Johnson, BAL	1
G. Scott, BOS	1

1967 NATIONAL
T. Seaver, NY	11
D. Hughes, STL	6
G. Nolan, CIN	3

1967 AMERICAN
R. Carew, MIN	19
R. Smith, BOS	1

1968 NATIONAL
J. Bench, CIN	10.5
J. Koosman, NY	9.5

1968 AMERICAN
S. Bahnsen, NY	17
D. Unser, WAS	3

1969 NATIONAL
T. Sizemore, LA	14
C. Laboy, MON	3
A. Oliver, PIT	3
B. Didier, ATL	2
L. Hisle, PHI	2

1969 AMERICAN
L. Piniella, KC	9
M. Nagy, BOS	6
C. May, CHI	5
K. Tatum, CAL	4

1970 NATIONAL
C. Morton, MON	11
B. Carbo, CIN	8
L. Bowa, PHI	3
W. Simpson, CIN	1
C. Cedeno, HOU	1

1970 AMERICAN
T. Munson, NY	23
R. Foster, CLE	1

1971 NATIONAL
E. Williams, ATL	18
W. Montanez, PHI	6

1971 AMERICAN
C. Chambliss, CLE	11
B. Parsons, MIL	5
A. Mangual, OAK	4
D. Griffin, BOS	3
P. Splittorff, KC	1

1972 NATIONAL
J. Matlack, NY	19
Dv. Rader, SF	4
J. Milner, NY	1

1972 AMERICAN
C. Fisk, BOS	24

1973 NATIONAL
G. Matthews, SF	11
S. Rogers, MON	3.5
B. Boone, PHI	2
E. Sosa, SF	2
D. Driessen, CIN	2
R. Cey, LA	1
D. Lopes, LA	1
J. Grubb, SD	1
R. Zisk, PIT	0.5

1973 AMERICAN
A. Bumbry, BAL	13.5
P. Garcia, MIL	3
D. Porter, MIL	2
S. Busby, KC	2
D. Medich, NY	2
R. Coggins, BAL	1.5

1974 NATIONAL
B. McBride, STL	16
G. Gross, HOU	7
B. Madlock CHI	1

1974 AMERICAN
M. Hargrove, TEX	16.5
B. Dent, CHI	3
G. Brett, KC	2
R. Burleson, BOS	1.5
J. Sundberg, TEX	1

1975 NATIONAL
J. Montefusco, SF	12
G. Carter, MON	9
Lr. Parrish, MON	1
R. Eastwick, CIN	1
M. Trillo, CHI	1

1975 AMERICAN
F. Lynn, BOS	23.5
J. Rice, BOS	0.5

1976 NATIONAL
B. Metzger, SD	11
P. Zachry, CIN	11
H. Cruz, STL	2

1976 AMERICAN
M. Fidrych, DET	22
B. Wynegar, MIN	2

1977 NATIONAL
A. Dawson, MON	10
S. Henderson, NY	9
G. Richards, SD	4
F. Bannister, HOU	1

1977 AMERICAN
E. Murray, BAL	12.5
M. Page, OAK	9.5
B. Wills, TEX	4
D. Rozema, DET	2

1978 NATIONAL
B. Horner, ATL	12.5
O. Smith, SD	8.5
D. Robinson, PIT	3

1978 AMERICAN
L. Whitaker, DET	21
P. Molitor, MIL	3
C. Lansford, CAL	2
R. Gale, KC	1
A. Trammell, DET	1

1979 NATIONAL
R. Sutcliffe, LA	20
J. Leonard, HOU	3
S. Thompson, CHI	1

1979 AMERICAN
J. Castino, MIN	7
A. Griffin, TOR	7
M. Clear, CAL	5
R. Davis, NY	3
R. Baumgarten, CHI	3
P. Putnam, TEX	3

1980 NATIONAL
S. Howe, LA	80
B. Gullickson, MON	53
L. Smith, PHI	49
R. Oester, CIN	16
D. Smith, HOU	13
J. Reardon, NY	2
A. Holland, SF	1

L. Durham, STL 1
B. Walk, PHI 1

1980 AMERICAN
J. Charboneau, CLE 102
D. Stapleton, BOS 40
D. Corbett, MIN 38
D. Garcia, TOR 35
B. Burns, CHI 33
R. Peters, DET 3
R. Dotson, CHI 1

1981 NATIONAL
F. Valenzuela, LA 107
T. Raines, MON 85
H. Brooks, NY 8.5
B. Berenyi, CIN 5
J. Bonilla, SD 5
T. Pena, PIT 4
M. Wilson, NY 1.5

1981 AMERICAN
D. Righetti, NY 127
R. Gedman, BOS 64
B. Ojeda, BOS 36
M. Jones, KC 8
D. Engle, MIN 4.5
M. Witt, CAL 4
S. Babitt, OAK 4
J. Bell, TOR 2
G. Ward, MIN 1.5
B. Havens, MIN 1

1982 NATIONAL
S. Sax, LA 63
J. Ray, PIT 57
W. McGee, STL 39
C. Davis, SF 32
L. DeLeon, SD 10
R. Sandberg, CHI 9
S. Bedrosian, ATL 4
D. LaPoint, STL 1
E. Show, SD 1

1982 AMERICAN
C. Ripken, BAL 132
K. Hrbek, MIN 90
W. Boggs, BOS 10.5
E. Vande Berg, SEA 9
G. Gaetti, MIN 4
D. Hostetler, TEX 3
V. Hayes, CLE 2
J. Barfield, TOR 1.5

1983 NATIONAL
D. Strawberry, NY 106
C. McMurtry, ATL 49
M. Hall, CHI 32
G. Redus, CIN 8
B. Doran, HOU 7
F. DiPino, HOU 6
G. Brock, LA 3
J. DeLeon, PIT 3
M. Thurmond, SD 1
L. Tunnell, PIT 1

1983 AMERICAN
R. Kittle, CHI 104
J. Franco, CLE 78
M. Boddicker, BAL 70

1984 NATIONAL
D. Gooden, NY 118
J. Samuel, PHI 67
O. Hershiser, LA 15
D. Gladden, SF 9
R. Darling, NY 3
C. Martinez, SD 2
J. Stone, PHI 1
T. Pendleton, STL 1

1984 AMERICAN
A. Davis, SEA 134
M. Langston, SEA 82
K. Puckett, MIN 23
T. Teufel, MIN 5
M. Young, BAL 3
R. Clemens, BOS 2

M. Gubicza, KC 1
A. Nipper, BOS 1
R. Romanick, CAL 1

1985 NATIONAL
V. Coleman, STL 120
T. Browning, CIN 72
M. Duncan, LA 9
C. Brown, SF 7
G. Davis, HOU 3
R. McDowell, NY 2
J. Orsulak, PIT 2
J. Hesketh, MON 1

1985 AMERICAN
O. Guillen, CHI 101
T. Higuera, MIL 67
E. Riles, MIL 29
O. McDowell, TEX 25
S. Cliburn, CAL 16
B. Fisher, NY 7
T. Henke, TOR 5
M. Salas, MIN 2

1986 NATIONAL
T. Worrell, STL 118
R. Thompson, SF 46
K. Mitchell, NY 22
C. Kerfeld, HOU 17
W. Clark, SF 5
B. Bonds, PIT 4
J. Deshaies, HOU 1
B. Larkin, CIN 1
B. Ruffin, PHI 1
J. Kruk, SD 1

1986 AMERICAN
J. Canseco, OAK 110
W. Joyner, CAL 98
M. Eichhorn, TOR 23
C. Snyder, CLE 16
D. Tartabull, SEA 4
R. Sierra, TEX 1

1987 NATIONAL
B. Santiago, SD 120
M. Dunne, PIT 66
J. Magrane, STL 10
C. Candaele, MON 9
G. Young, HOU 7
C. James, PHI 1
L. Lancaster, CHI 1
G. Mathews, STL 1
R. Myers, NY 1

1987 AMERICAN
M. McGwire, OAK 140
K. Seitzer, KC 64
M. Nokes, DET 32
M. Greenwell, BOS 9
D. White, CAL 5
M. Henneman, DET 1
N. Liriano, TOR 1

1988 NATIONAL
C. Sabo, CIN 79
M. Grace, CHI 61
T. Belcher, LA 35
R. Gant, ATL 22
R. Alomar, SD 11
D. Berryhill, CHI 3
G. Jefferies, NY 3
R. Jordan, PHI 2

1988 AMERICAN
W. Weiss, OAK 103
B. Harvey, CAL 49
J. Reed, BOS 48
D. August, MIL 22
D. Gallagher, CHI 18
M. Perez, CHI 9
M. Schooler, SEA 2
C. Espy, TEX 1

1989 NATIONAL
J. Walton, CHI 116
D. Smith, CHI 68
G. Jefferies, NY 18

D. Lilliquist, ATL 6
A. Benes, SD 3
C. Hayes, PHI 3
G. Harris, SD 2

1989 AMERICAN
G. Olson, BAL 136
T. Gordon, KC 67
K. Griffey, SEA 21
C. Worthington, BAL 16
J. Abbott, CAL 10
K. Brown, TEX 2

1990 NATIONAL
D. Justice, ATL 118
D. DeShields, MON 60
H. Morris, CIN 13
J. Burkett, SF 12
M. Harkey, CHI 7
T. Zeile, STL 4
M. Grissom, MON 1
L. Walker, MON 1

1990 AMERICAN
S. Alomar, CLE 140
K. Maas, NY 47
K. Appier, KC 31
J. Olerud, TOR 13
K. Tapani, MIN 9
T. Fryman, DET 5
R. Ventura, CHI 3
B. McDonald, BAL 2
A. Cole, CLE 1
S. Radinsky, CHI 1

1991 NATIONAL
J. Bagwell, HOU 118
O. Merced, PIT 53
R. Lankford, STL 28
B. Hunter, ATL 7
B. Barberie, MON 3
W. Chamberlain, PHI 3
C. McElroy, CHI 3
M. Stanton, ATL 1

1991 AMERICAN
C. Knoblauch, MIN 136
J. Guzman, TOR 68
M. Cuyler, DET 22
I. Rodriguez, TEX 10
B. DeLucia, SEA 7
M. Timlin, TOR 2
M. Whiten, TOR-CLE 2
L. Gomez, BAL 1
D. Henry, MIL 1
B. Mayne, KC 1
C. Nagy, CLE 1
P. Plantier, BOS 1

1992 NATIONAL
E. Karros, LA 116
M. Alou, MON 30
T. Wakefield, PIT 29
R. Sanders, CIN 23
D. Osborne, STL 12
M. Perez, STL 2
B. Rivera, PHI 1
F. Seminara, SD 1
B. Williams, HOU 1
M. Wohlers, ATL 1

1992 AMERICAN
P. Listach, MIL 122
K. Lofton, CLE 85
D. Fleming, SEA 23
C. Eldred, MIL 22

1993 NATIONAL
M. Piazza, LA 140
G. McMicheal, ATL 40
J. Conine, FLA 31
C. Carr, FLA 18
A. Martin, PIT 6
K. Stocker, PHI 4
W. Cordero, MON 3
K. Rueter, MON 3
C. Garcia, PIT 2
P. Martinez, LA 2

S. Cooke, PIT 1
R. Guttierez, SD 1
A. Reynoso, COL 1

1993 AMERICAN
T. Salmon, CAL 140
J. Bere, CHI 59
A. Sele, BOS 19
W. Kirby, CLE 12
R. Amaral, SEA 8
B. Gates, OAK 7
T. Neel, OAK 5
J. DiPoto, CLE 1
D. Hulse, TEX 1

1994 NATIONAL
R. Mondesi, LA 140
J. Hudek, HOU 27
R. Klesko, ATL 25
S. Trachsel, CHI 22
C. Floyd, MON 10
J. Hamilton, SD 10
W. Van Landingham, SF 9
H. Carrasco, CIN 3
B. Jones, NY 3
J. Lopez, ATL 2
S. Reynolds, HOU 1

1994 AMERICAN
B. Hamelin, KC 134
M. Ramirez, CLE 44
R. Greer, TEX 42
D. Hall, TOR 9
C. Gomez, DET 6
B. Risley, SEA 6
B. Anderson, CAL 4
J. Edmonds, CAL 2
J. Valentin, MIL 1

1995 NATIONAL
H. Nomo, LA 118
C. Jones, ATL 104
Q. Veras, FLA 14
J. Isringhausen, NY 4
J. Mabry, STL 4
C. Perez, MON 4
C. Fonville, LA 1
B. Hunter, HOU 1
C. Johnson, FLA 1
I. Valdes, LA 1

1995 AMERICAN
M. Cordova, MIN 105
G. Anderson, CAL 99
A. Pettitte, NY 16
T. Percival, CAL 13
S. Green, TOR 8
R. Durham, CHI 3
J. Tavarez, CLE 3
J. Nunnally, KC 2
T. Goodwin, KC 1
B. Radke, MIN 1
S. Sparks, MIL 1

1996 NATIONAL
T. Hollandsworth, LA 105
E. Renteria, FLA 84
J. Kendall, PIT 30
F. A. Santangelo, MON 15
R. Ordonez, NY 7
J. Dye, ATL 6
Al. Benes, STL 5

1996 AMERICAN
D. Jeter, NY 140
J. Baldwin, CHI 64
T. Clark, DET 30
R. Coppinger, BAL 6
J. Rosado, KC 6
D. Erstad, CAL 3
T. Batista, OAK 1
T. Crabtree, TOR 1
J. D'Amico, MIL 1

1997 NATIONAL
S. Rolen, PHI 140
L. Hernandez, FLA 25
M. Morris, STL 25

R. Loiselle, PIT 22
A. Jones, ATL 15
V. Guerrero, MON 9
J. Guillen, PIT 4
B. Tomko, CIN 4
J. Gonzalez, CHI 3
T. Womack, PIT 3
K. Orie, CHI 1
N. Perez, COL 1

1997 AMERICAN
N. Garciaparra, BOS 140
J. Cruz, SEA-TOR 61
J. Dickson, ANA 27
D. Cruz, DET 12
J. Wright, CLE 7
M. Cameron, CHI 5

1998 NATIONAL
K. Wood, CHI 128
T. Helton, COL 119
T. Lee, ARI 21
K. Ligtenberg, ATL 18
B. Fullmer, MON 2

1998 AMERICAN
B. Grieve, OAK 130
R. Arrojo, TB 61
M. Caruso, CHI 34
O. Hernandez, NY 25
M. Ordoñez, CHI 1
S. Ponson, BAL 1

1999 NATIONAL
S. Williamson, CIN 118
P. Wilson, FLA 88
W. Morris, PIT 69
K. Benson, PIT 5
A. Gonzalez, FLA 4
J. McEwing, STL 3
K. McGlinchy, ATL 1

1999 AMERICAN
C. Beltran, KC 133
F. Garcia, SEA 45
J. Zimmerman, TEX 27
B. Daubach, BOS 16
T. Hudson, OAK 13
C. Singleton, CHI 9
C. Lee, CHI 4
B. Koch, TOR 4
T. Nixon, BOS 1

2000 NATIONAL
R. Furcal, ATL 144
R. Ankiel, STL 87
J. Payton, NY 37
P. Burrell, PHI 10
M. Meluskey, HOU 7
L. Berkman, HOU 1
J. Pierre, COL 1
C. Smith, FLA 1

2000 AMERICAN
K. Sasaki, SEA 104
T. Long, OAK 83
M. Quinn, KC 56
B. Molina, ANA 3
K. Wunsch, CHI 2
S. Cox, TB 1
A. Kennedy, ANA 1
M. Redman, MIN 1
B. Zito, OAK 1

2001 NATIONAL
A. Pujols, STL 160
R. Oswalt, HOU 82
J. Rollins, PHI 44
B. Smith, STL 1
A. Dunn, CIN 1

2001 AMERICAN
I. Suzuki, SEA 138
C. Sabathia, CLE 73
A. Soriano, NY 35
D. Eckstein, ANA 6

2002 NATIONAL			A. Sanchez, PHI	1		J. Lackey, ANA	5		2003 NATIONAL			T. Wigginton, NY	1
J. Jennings, COL	150		J. Simontacchi, STL	1		J. Phelps, TOR	3		D. Willis, FLA	118			
B. Wilkerson, MON	57		D. Stark, COL	1		K. Mench, TEX	2		S. Podsednik, MIL	81		2003 AMERICAN		
A. Kearns, CIN	40					M. Ellis, OAK	1		B. Webb, ARI	73		A. Berroa, KC	88
K. Ishii, LA	16		2002 AMERICAN			T. Fiore, MIN	1		M. Byrd, PHI	6		H. Matsui, NY	84
D. Moss, ATL	12		E. Hinske, TOR	122		D. Mohr, MIN	1		M. Cabrera, FLA	3		R. Baldelli, TB	51
R. Jensen, SF	4		R. Lopez, BAL	97		C. Peña, DET	1		B. Lidge, HOU	3		J. Gerut, CLE	20
M. Prior, CHI	3		J. Julio, BAL	14					J. Robertson, HOU	2		M. Teixeira, TEX	9
J. Fogg, PIT	3		B. Kielty, MIN	5					J. Reyes, NY	1			

Cy Young Award: History

Commissioner Ford Frick, troubled by pitchers' lack of representation in MVP voting, spearheaded the 1956 effort to initiate a "most valuable pitcher" award. Cy Young, baseball's winningest pitcher, who had died the previous November, was the logical choice after whom to name the honor. At a special meeting on July 9, 1956, the Baseball Writers' Association of America approved, by the slim margin of 14-12, the establishment of the Cy Young Memorial Award, designed to honor the major leagues' outstanding pitcher each year beginning in 1956. Ironically, the first winner, Brooklyn's Don Newcombe, also won his league's MVP Award.

One writer from each major league city participated in the balloting. In case of a tie vote, a second balloting was to be taken between the deadlocked pitchers. Hurlers were not to be eligible to win the award more than once, a rule which was evidently scrapped within two years.

Frick was adamantly opposed to the commonly voiced idea to recognize a Cy Young winner in each league but, not long after his December 1965 retirement, the idea became a reality. On March 1, 1967, Frick's successor, William Eckert, approved the plan for dual awards, with two writers from each league city to select.

The system of having each writer make only one selection prevailed until 1969, when Detroit's Denny McLain and Baltimore's Mike Cuellar tied for the American League Cy Young Award. Thereafter, writers were instructed to name three pitchers in each

league, with five points for each first-place vote, three points for second and one point for third.

The maximum number of points available for one pitcher was 16 in 1956-60, 18 in 1961, 20 in 1962-68, 24 in 1969, 120 in 1970-76 (AL) and 1970-92 (NL), 140 in 1977-present (AL) and 1993-97 (NL), and 160 in 1998-present (NL). As with every other major award, there have been a few instances in Cy Young voting where at least one writer failed to return a ballot.

Unanimous winners of the Cy Young Award are Sandy Koufax (NL, 1963, 1965, and 1966), Bob Gibson (NL, 1968), Denny McLain (AL, 1968), Steve Carlton (NL, 1972), Ron Guidry (AL, 1978), Rick Sutcliffe (NL, 1984), Dwight Gooden (NL, 1985), Roger Clemens (AL, 1986, 1998), Orel Hershiser (NL, 1988), Greg Maddux (NL, 1994, 1995), Pedro Martinez (AL, 1999, 2000), and Randy Johnson (NL, 2002).

Relief pitchers, once overlooked in Cy Young balloting, have become strong candidates in recent years. Until 1970 only one reliever—Lindy McDaniel in 1960—had received even a single vote. The new voting system helped open opportunities for bullpen aces and in 1974 the Dodgers' Mike Marshall became the first reliever to win the Cy Young Award. He has been followed in that distinction by Sparky Lyle (AL, 1977), Bruce Sutter (NL, 1979), Rollie Fingers (AL, 1981), Willie Hernandez (AL, 1984), Steve Bedrosian (NL, 1987), Mark Davis (NL, 1989), Dennis Eckersley (AL, 1992), and Eric Gagne (NL, 2003).

CY YOUNG AWARD

1956			1963			1970 NATIONAL			D. McNally, BAL	8		N. Ryan, CAL	62
D. Newcombe, BRO (NL)	10		S. Koufax, LA (NL)	20		B. Gibson, STL	118		D. Drago, KC	1		J. Hunter, OAK	52
S. Maglie, BRO (NL)	4					G. Perry, SF	51		A. Messersmith, CAL	1		J. Hiller, DET	6
W. Spahn, MIL (NL)	1		1964			F. Jenkins CHI	16					W. Wood, CHI	3
W. Ford, NY (AL)	1		D. Chance, LA (AL)	17		D. Giusti, PIT	8		1972 NATIONAL			J. Colborn, MIL	2
			L. Jackson, CHI (NL)	2		J. Merritt, CIN	8		S. Carlton, PHI	120		V. Blue, OAK	1
1957			S. Koufax, LA (NL)	1		G. Nolan, CIN	5		S. Blass, PIT	35		B. Blyleven, MIN	1
W. Spahn, MIL (NL)	15					T. Seaver, NY	4		F. Jenkins, CHI	23		G. Perry, CLE	1
D. Donovan, CHI (AL)	1		1965			W. Granger, CIN	3		M. Marshall, MON	8			
			S. Koufax, LA (NL)	20		C. Morton, MON	2		G. Nolan, CIN	6		1974 NATIONAL		
1958						L. Walker, PIT	1		T. Seaver, NY	6		M. Marshall, LA	96
B. Turley, NY (AL)	5		1966						C. Carroll, CIN	6		A. Messersmith, LA	66
W. Spahn, MIL (NL)	4		S. Koufax, LA (NL)	20		1970 AMERICAN			D. Sutton, LA	6		P. Niekro, ATL	15
B. Friend, PIT (NL)	3					J. Perry, MIN	55		B. Gibson, STL	3		D. Sutton, LA	12
L. Burdette, MIL (NL)	3		1967 NATIONAL			D. McNally, BAL	47		M. Pappas, CHI	3		A. Hrabosky, STL	9
			M. McCormick, SF	18		S. McDowell, CLE	45					J. Billingham, CIN	8
1959			F. Jenkins, CHI	1		M. Cuellar, BAL	44		1972 AMERICAN			D. Gullett, CIN	5
E. Wynn, CHI (AL)	13		J. Bunning, PHI	1		J. Palmer, BAL	11		G. Perry, CLE	64		C. Carroll, CIN	2
S. Jones, SF (NL)	2					C. Wright, CAL	9		W. Wood, CHI	58		D. Giusti, PIT	1
B. Shaw, CHI (AL)	1		1967 AMERICAN			R. Perranoski, MIN	5		M. Lolich, DET	27		B. Capra, ATL	1
			J. Lonborg, BOS	18					J. Hunter, OAK	26		L. McGlothen, STL	1
1960			J. Horlen, CHI	2		1971 NATIONAL			J. Palmer, BAL	20			
V. Law, PIT (NL)	8					F. Jenkins, CHI	97		L. Tiant, BOS	16		1974 AMERICAN		
W. Spahn, MIL (NL)	4		1968 NATIONAL			T. Seaver, NY	61		S. Lyle, NY	3		J. Hunter, OAK	90
E. Broglio, STL (NL)	1		B. Gibson, STL	20		A. Downing, LA	40		N. Ryan, CAL	2		F. Jenkins, TEX	75
L. McDaniel, STL (NL)	1					D. Ellis, PIT	9					N. Ryan, CAL	28
			1968 AMERICAN			B. Gibson, STL	3		1973 NATIONAL			G. Perry, CLE	8
1961			D. McLain, DET	20		J. Johnson, SF	2		T. Seaver, NY	71		L. Tiant, BOS	8
W. Ford, NY (AL)	9					D. Roberts, SD	2		M. Marshall, MON	54		M. Cuellar, BAL	6
W. Spahn, MIL (NL)	6		1969 NATIONAL			J. Marichal, SF	1		R. Bryant, SF	50		J. Hiller, DET	1
F. Lary, DET (AL)	2		T. Seaver, NY	23		B. Stoneman, MON	1		J. Billingham, CIN	30			
			P. Niekro, ATL	1					D. Sutton, LA	7		1975 NATIONAL		
1962						1971 AMERICAN			F. Norman, SD-CIN	3		T. Seaver, NY	98
D. Drysdale, LA (NL)	14		1969 AMERICAN			V. Blue, OAK	98		D. Giusti, PIT	1		R. Jones, SD	80
J. Sanford, SF (NL)	4		M. Cuellar, BAL	10		M. Lolich, DET	85					A. Hrabosky, STL	33
B. Purkey, CIN (NL)	1		D. McLain, DET	10		W. Wood, CHI	23		1973 AMERICAN			J. Montefusco, SF	2
B. Pierce, SF (NL)	1		J. Perry, MIN	3					J. Palmer, BAL	88			
			D. McNally, BAL	1									

D. Gullett, CIN	1
A. Messersmith, LA	1
D. Sutton, LA	1

1975 AMERICAN

J. Palmer, BAL	98
J. Hunter, NY	74
R. Fingers, OAK	25
F. Tanana, CAL	7
J. Kaat, CHI	7
V. Blue, OAK	2
R. Gossage, CHI	2
R. Wise, BOS	1

1976 NATIONAL

R. Jones, SD	96
J. Koosman, NY	69.5
D. Sutton, LA	25.5
S. Carlton, PHI	11
R. Eastwick, CIN	6
J. Matlack, NY	5
J. Richard, HOU	2
T. Seaver, NY	1

1976 AMERICAN

J. Palmer, BAL	108
M. Fidrych, DET	51
F. Tanana, CAL	18
E. Figueroa, NY	12
L. Tiant, BOS	10
V. Blue, OAK	8
B. Campbell, MIN	7
R. Fingers, OAK	1
W. Garland, BAL	1

1977 NATIONAL

S. Carlton, PHI	104
T. John, LA	54
T. Seaver, NY-CIN	18
R. Reuschel, CHI	18
J. Candelaria, PIT	17
B. Sutter, CHI	5

1977 AMERICAN

S. Lyle, NY	56.5
J. Palmer, BAL	48
N. Ryan, CAL	46
D. Leonard, KC	45
B. Campbell, BOS	25.5
D. Goltz, MIN	19
R. Guidry, NY	5
D. Rozema, DET	4
F. Tanana, CAL	3

1978 NATIONAL

G. Perry, SD	116
B. Hooton, LA	38
V. Blue, SF	17
J. Richard, HOU	13
K. Tekulve, PIT	12
P. Niekro, ATL	10
R. Grimsley, MON	7
R. Fingers, SD	1
T. John, LA	1
D. Robinson, PIT	1

1978 AMERICAN

R. Guidry, NY	140
M. Caldwell, MIL	76
J. Palmer, BAL	14
D. Eckersley, BOS	10
R. Gossage, NY	4
F. Jenkins, TEX	2
E. Figueroa, NY	1
L. Gura, KC	1
D. Leonard, KC	1
M. Marshall, MIN	1
P. Splittorff, KC	1
B. Stanley, BOS	1

1979 NATIONAL

B. Sutter, CHI	72
J. Niekro, HOU	66
J. Richard, HOU	41
T. Seaver, CIN	20
K. Tekulve, PIT	14
P. Niekro, ATL	3

1979 AMERICAN

M. Flanagan, BAL	136

T. John, NY	51
R. Guidry, NY	26
J. Kern, TEX	25
M. Marshall, MIN	7
J. Koosman, MIN	5
D. Eckersley, BOS	1
A. Lopez, DET	1

1980 NATIONAL

S. Carlton, PHI	118
J. Reuss, LA	55
J. Bibby, PIT	28
J. Niekro, HOU	11
T. McGraw, PHI	1
S. Rogers, MON	1
J. Sambito, HOU	1
M. Soto, CIN	1

1980 AMERICAN

S. Stone, BAL	100
M. Norris, OAK	91
R. Gossage, NY	37.5
T. John, NY	14
D. Quisenberry, KC	7.5
L. Gura, KC	1
S. McGregor, BAL	1

1981 NATIONAL

F. Valenzuela, LA	70
T. Seaver, CIN	67
S. Carlton, PHI	50
N. Ryan, HOU	28
B. Sutter, STL	1

1981 AMERICAN

R. Fingers, MIL	126
S. McCatty, OAK	84.5
J. Morris, DET	21
P. Vuckovich, MIL	8.5
D. Martinez, BAL	3.5
R. Gossage, NY	3
R. Guidry, NY	2.5
B. Burns, CHI	2
L. Gura, KC	1

1982 NATIONAL

S. Carlton, PHI	112
S. Rogers, MON	29
F. Valenzuela, LA	25.5
B. Sutter, STL	25
P. Niekro, ATL	18
G. Minton, SF	4
J. Andujar, STL	1
G. Garber, ATL	1
M. Soto, CIN	0.5

1982 AMERICAN

P. Vuckovich, MIL	87
J. Palmer, BAL	59
D. Quisenberry, KC	40
D. Stieb, TOR	36
R. Sutcliffe, CLE	14
G. Zahn, CAL	7
B. Stanley, BOS	4
B. Caudill, SEA	4
D. Petry, DET	1

1983 NATIONAL

J. Denny, PHI	103
M. Soto, CIN	61
J. Orosco, NY	19
S. Rogers, MON	15
L. McWilliams, PIT	7
A. Holland, PHI	4
C. McMurtry, ATL	3
B. Welch, LA	2
N. Ryan, HOU	1
L. Smith, CHI	1

1983 AMERICAN

L. Hoyt, CHI	116
D. Quisenberry, KC	81
J. Morris, DET	38
R. Dotson, CHI	9
R. Guidry, NY	5
S. McGregor, BAL	3

1984 NATIONAL

R. Sutcliffe, CHI	120

D. Gooden, NY	45
B. Sutter, STL	33.5
J. Andujar, STL	12.5
R. Gossage, SD	3
M. Soto, CIN	2

1984 AMERICAN

W. Hernandez, DET	88
D. Quisenberry, KC	71
B. Blyleven, CLE	45
M. Boddicker, BAL	41
D. Petry, DET	3
F. Viola, MIN	2
J. Morris, DET	1
D. Stieb, TOR	1

1985 NATIONAL

D. Gooden, NY	120
J. Tudor, STL	65
O. Hershiser, LA	17
J. Andujar, STL	6
F. Valenzuela, LA	4
T. Browning, CIN	3
J. Reardon, MON	1

1985 AMERICAN

B. Saberhagen, KC	127
R. Guidry, NY	88
B. Blyleven, MIN	9
D. Quisenberry, KC	9
C. Leibrandt, KC	7
D. Alexander, TOR	5
B. Burns, CHI	2
D. Moore, CAL	2
D. Stieb, TOR	2
M. Moore, SEA	1

1986 NATIONAL

M. Scott, HOU	98
F. Valenzuela, LA	88
M. Krukow, SF	15
B. Ojeda, NY	9
R. Darling, NY	2
R. Rhoden, PIT	2
D. Gooden, NY	1
S. Fernandez, NY	1

1986 AMERICAN

R. Clemens, BOS	140
T. Higuera, MIL	42
M. Witt, CAL	35
D. Righetti, NY	20
J. Morris, DET	13
M. Eichhorn, TOR	2

1987 NATIONAL

S. Bedrosian, PHI	57
R. Sutcliffe, CHI	55
R. Reuschel, SF	54
O. Hershiser, LA	14
D. Gooden, NY	12
N. Ryan, HOU	12
M. Scott, HOU	9
B. Welch, LA	3

1987 AMERICAN

R. Clemens, BOS	124
J. Key, TOR	64
D. Stewart, OAK	32
D. Alexander, DET	8
M. Langston, SEA	7
T. Higuera, MIL	5
F. Viola, MIN	5
J. Reardon, MIN	4
J. Morris, DET	3

1988 NATIONAL

O. Hershisher, LA	120
D. Jackson, CIN	54
D. Cone, NY	42

1988 AMERICAN

F. Viola, MIN	138
D. Eckersley, OAK	52
M. Gubicza, KC	26
D. Stewart, OAK	16
B. Hurst, BOS	12
R. Clemens, BOS	8

1989 NATIONAL

M. Davis, SD	107
M. Scott, HOU	65
G. Maddux, CHI	17
O. Hershiser, LA	7
J. Magrane, STL	7
T. Belcher, LA	4
S. Garrelts, SF	4
R. Reuschel, SF	3
M. Bielecki, CHI	1
M. Williams, CHI	1

1989 AMERICAN

B. Saberhagen, KC	138
D. Stewart, OAK	80
M. Moore, OAK	10
B. Blyleven, CAL	9
N. Ryan, TEX	5
J. Ballard, BAL	3
D. Eckersley, OAK	3
G. Olson, BAL	3
J. Russell, TEX	1

1990 NATIONAL

D. Drabek, PIT	118
R. Martinez, LA	70
F. Viola, NY	19
D. Gooden, NY	8
R. Myers, CIN	1

1990 AMERICAN

B. Welch, OAK	107
R. Clemens, BOS	77
D. Stewart, OAK	43
B. Thigpen, CHI	20
D. Eckersley, OAK	2
D. Stieb, TOR	2
C. Finley, CAL	1

1991 NATIONAL

T. Glavine, ATL	110
L. Smith, STL	60
J. Smiley, PIT	26
J. Rijo, CIN	13
D. Martinez, MON	4
S. Avery, ATL	1
A. Benes, SD	1
M. Williams, PHI	1

1991 AMERICAN

R. Clemens, BOS	119
S. Erickson, MIN	56
J. Abbott, CAL	26
J. Morris, MIN	17
B. Harvey, CAL	10
M. Langston, CAL	7
K. Tapani, MIN	6
B. Gullickson, DET	5
J. McDowell, CHI	3
D. Ward, TOR	3

1992 NATIONAL

G. Maddux, CHI	112
T. Glavine, ATL	78
B. Tewksbury, STL	22
L. Smith, STL	3
D. Drabek, PIT	1

1992 AMERICAN

D. Eckersley, OAK	107
J. McDowell, CHI	51
R. Clemens, BOS	48
M. Mussina, BAL	26
J. Morris, TOR	10
K. Brown, TEX	9
C. Nagy, CLE	1

1993 NATIONAL

G. Maddux, ATL	119
B. Swift, SF	61
T. Glavine, ATL	49
J. Burkett, SF	9
J. Rijo, CIN	8
T. Greene, PHI	2
M. Portugal, HOU	2
B. Harvey, FLA	1
R. Myers, CHI	1

1993 AMERICAN

J. McDowell, CHI	124
R. Johnson SEA	75
K. Appier, KC	30
J. Key, NY	14
D. Ward, TOR	5
P. Hentgen, TOR	3
J. Guzman, TOR	1

1994 NATIONAL

G. Maddux, ATL	140
K. Hill, MON	56
B. Saberhagen, NY	42
M. Freeman, COL	4
D. Drabek, HOU	4
D. Jackson, PHI	3
J. Franco, NY	2
R. Beck, SF	1

1994 AMERICAN

D. Cone, KC	108
J. Key, NY	96
R. Johnson, SEA	24
M. Mussina, BAL	23
L. Smith, BAL	1

1995 NATIONAL

G. Maddux, ATL	140
P. Schourek, CIN	55
T. Glavine, ATL	30
H. Nomo, LA	19
R. Martinez, LA	8

1995 AMERICAN

R. Johnson, SEA	136
J. Mesa, CLE	54
T. Wakefield, BOS	29
D. Cone, TOR-NY	18
M. Mussina, BAL	14
C. Nagy, CLE	1

1996 NATIONAL

J. Smoltz, ATL	136
K. Brown, FLA	88
An. Benes, STL	9
H. Nomo, LA	5
T. Hoffman, SD	3
G. Maddux, ATL	3
T. Worrell, LA	3
D. Neagle, PIT-ATL	2
J. Fassero, MON	1
A. Leiter, FLA	1
S. Reynolds, HOU	1

1996 AMERICAN

P. Hentgen, TOR	110
A. Pettitte, NY	104
M. Rivera, NY	18
C. Nagy, CLE	12
M. Mussina, BAL	5
A. Fernandez, CHI	1
R. Fernandez, CHI	1
K. Hill, TEX	1

1997 NATIONAL

P. Martinez, MON	134
G. Maddux, ATL	75
D. Neagle, ATL	24
C. Schilling, PHI	12
D. Kile, HOU	7

1997 AMERICAN

R. Clemens, TOR	134
R. Johnson, SEA	77
B. Radke, MIN	17
R. Myers, BAL	14
A. Pettitte, NY	9
M. Mussina, BAL	1

1998 NATIONAL

T. Glavine, ATL	99
T. Hoffman, SD	88
K. Brown, SD	76
G. Maddux, ATL	10
J. Smoltz, ATL	10
A. Leiter, NY	3
R. Johnson, HOU	2

1998 AMERICAN
R. Clemens, TOR 140
P. Martinez, BOS 65
D. Wells, NY 31
D. Cone, NY 16

1999 NATIONAL
R. Johnson, ARI 134
M. Hampton, HOU 110
K. Millwood, ATL 36
J. Lima, HOU 3
B. Wagner, HOU 3
K. Brown, LA 1
T. Hoffman, SD 1

1999 AMERICAN
P. Martinez, BOS 140
M. Mussina, BAL 54

M. Rivera, NY 27
B. Colon, CLE 14
A. Sele, TEX 4
D. Cone, NY 3
J. Moyer, SEA 3
J. Wetteland, TEX 3
F. Garcia, SEA 2
K. Foulke, CHI 1
R. Hernandez, TB 1

2000 NATIONAL
R. Johnson, ARI 133
T. Glavine, ATL 64
G. Maddux, ATL 59
R. Nen, SF 20
D. Kile, STL 8
K. Brown, LA 4

2000 AMERICAN
P. Martinez, BOS 140
T. Hudson, OAK 54
D. Wells, TOR 46
A. Pettitte, NY 7
T. Jones, DET 3
R. Clemens, NY 1
M. Mussina, BAL 1

2001 NATIONAL
R. Johnson, ARI 156
C. Schilling, ARI 98
M. Morris, STL 31
J. Leiber, CHI 2
R. Oswalt, HOU 1

2001 AMERICAN
R. Clemens, NY 122

M. Mulder, OAK 60
F. Garcia, SEA 55
J. Moyer, SEA 12
M. Mussina, NY 2
T. Hudson, OAK 1

2002 NATIONAL
R. Johnson, ARI 160
C. Schilling, ARI 90
J. Smoltz, ATL 21
E. Gagne, LA 8
R. Oswalt, HOU 8
B. Colon, MON 1

2002 AMERICAN
B. Zito, OAK 114
P. Martinez, BOS 96
D. Lowe, BOS 41

J. Washburn, ANA 1

2003 NATIONAL
E. Gagne, LA 146
J. Schmidt, SF 73
M. Prior, CHI 60
R. Ortiz, ATL 9

2003 AMERICAN
R. Halladay, TOR 136
E. Loaiza, CHI 63
P. Martinez, BOS 20
T. Hudson, OAK 15
J. Moyer, SEA 12
A. Pettitte, NY 4
K. Foulke, OAK 1
J. Santana, MIN 1

Hypothetical Awards

As the "expert" in baseball award-voting, I have been asked to make a set of hypothetical award selections for the years in which no official honors were given; i.e., pre-1956 Cy Young, pre-1947 Rookie of the Year, and pre-1911 MVP Awards, along with awards for any other "missing" years.

While this assignment gave me unusual freedom, I felt a certain responsibility to make my selections consistent with the perceptions and voting trends of a particular era. For example, although there were better NL players than Cincinnati's Edd Roush in 1919, he did two things which, combined, would have virtually guaranteed him the MVP Award: he won the batting crown, which was *the* individual title in the Dead Ball Era, and he played on a pennant-winner, which has always been a key factor in MVP voting.

Besides my own opinions and intuitions, several sources were instrumental in my selection process, including:

1. Society for American Baseball Research retroactive award surveys, which have been done for pre-1949 Rookie of the Year and pre-1967 Cy Young Awards. The ballots were tremendously helpful in screening candidates and the voting results were carefully compared to my own choices.

2. Linear Weights, an overall player rating system devised by Pete Palmer, first used in *The Hidden Game of Baseball* (Doubleday, 1984, 1985), and continued in *Total Baseball*.

3. MVP voting results, for comparing Cy Young and Rookie candidates. If rookie "A" receives 75 points in the MVP election, while comparable rookie "B" receives just 10, I am forced to conclude that the on-the-spot observers discerned some important difference that we can't see in the statistics and that "A" is probably the better choice.

4. Unofficial awards, including 1940-46 Rookie and 1929-30 MVP selections.

5. Cy Young (1956-66) and Rookie of the Year (1947-48) balloting, for years in which one league had no official winner.

The resulting selections are not necessarily ones the average reader will agree with, nor even that the writer agrees with; rather, they are the ones which can be best justified with the available evidence.

In comparison with the Linear Weights system, my selections concurred 54 percent with top player selections and 59 percent with top pitcher nominations. In comparison with the SABR surveys, my selections agreed 84 percent in the Rookie of the Year Award and 79 percent in the Cy Young Award.

The big winner in the hypothetical awards is Christy Mathewson, who picks up a Rookie of the Year, two MVPs, and eight Cy Young Awards. Other pitchers capturing at least three Cy Youngs are Walter Johnson (seven); Lefty Grove (six, consecutively); Warren Spahn (four, to add to the one he actually did win); Grover Cleveland Alexander (four); Burleigh Grimes, Carl Hubbell, Bob Feller, Bucky Walters, Bob Lemon, and appropriately, Cy Young himself (three each).

Notable Rookies of the Year include Grover Cleveland Alexander, Babe Ruth, Rogers Hornsby, Dizzy Dean, Joe DiMaggio, and Ted Williams.

Honus Wagner cops six MVP Awards, including four in succession. Three-time MVPs are Nap Lajoie, Alexander, Ruth, and Hornsby. Ruth (once) and Hornsby (twice) also won official MVP Awards. Here are my hypothetical Cy Young (124), Rookie of the Year (97), and MVP (42) selections for the 20th century.

HYPOTHETICAL CY YOUNG AWARD

National League

Pitcher/Club	Year		Pitcher/Club	Year		Pitcher/Club	Year
J. McGinnity, BRO	1900		G. Alexander, CHI	1920		M. Cooper, STL	1942
N. Hahn, CIN	1901		B. Grimes, BRO	1921		M. Cooper, STL	1943
J. Taylor, CHI	1902		W. Cooper, PIT	1922		B. Walters, CIN	1944
C.Mathewson, NY	1903		D. Luque, CIN	1923		C.Barrett, BOS-STL	1945
J. McGinnity, NY	1904		D. Vance, BRO	1924		H. Pollet, STL	1946
Mathewson, NY	1905		D. Vance, BRO	1925		E.Blackwell, CIN	1947
M. Brown, CHI	1906		R. Kremer, PIT	1926		J. Sain, BOS	1948
Mathewson, NY	1907		C. Root, CHI	1927		W. Spahn, BOS	1949
Mathewson, NY	1908		B. Grimes, PIT	1928		J.Konstanty, PHI	1950
Mathewson, NY	1909		B. Grimes, PIT	1929		S. Maglie, NY	1951
Mathewson, NY	1910		P. Malone, CHI	1930		R. Roberts, PHI	1952
Mathewson, NY	1911		E. Brandt, BOS	1931		W. Spahn, MIL	1953
R. Marquard, NY	1912		L. Warneke, CHI	1932		J. Antonelli, NY	1954
Mathewson, NY	1913		C. Hubbell, NY	1933		R. Roberts, PHI	1955
B. James, BOS	1914		D. Dean, STL	1934		W. Spahn, MIL	1958
G. Alexander, PHI	1915		D. Dean, STL	1935		S. Jones, SF	1959
G. Alexander, PHI	1916		C. Hubbell, NY	1936		W. Spahn, MIL	1961
G. Alexander, PHI	1917		C. Hubbell, NY	1937		L. Jackson, CHI	1964
J. Vaughn, CHI	1918		B. Lee, CHI	1938			
J. Vaughn, CHI	1919		B. Walters, CIN	1939			
			B. Walters, CIN	1940			
			W. Wyatt, BRO	1941			

American League

Pitcher/Club	Year		Pitcher/Club	Year		Pitcher/Club	Year
C. Young, BOS	1901		R. Faber, CHI	1921		S. Chandler, NY	1943
C. Young, BOS	1902		E. Rommel, PHI	1922		D. Trout, DET	1944
C. Young, BOS	1903		G. Uhle, CLE	1923		H.Newhouser, DET	1945
J. Chesbro, NY	1904		W. Johnson, WAS	1924		H.Newhouser, DET	1946
R. Waddell, PHI	1905		S.Coveleski, WAS	1925		J. Page, NY	1947
A. Orth, NY	1906		G. Uhle, CLE	1926		B. Lemon, CLE	1948
E. Walsh, CHI	1907		W. Moore, NY	1927		M. Parnell, BOS	1949
E. Walsh, CHI	1908		L. Grove, PHI	1928		B. Lemon, CLE	1950
F. Smith, CHI	1909		L. Grove, PHI	1929		N. Garver, STL	1951
J. Coombs, PHI	1910		L. Grove, PHI	1930		B. Shantz, PHI	1952
W. Johnson, WAS	1911		L. Grove, PHI	1931		B. Pierce, CHI	1953
J. Wood, BOS	1912		L. Grove, PHI	1932		B. Lemon, CLE	1954
W. Johnson, WAS	1913		L. Grove, PHI	1933		R. Narleski, CLE	1955
W. Johnson, WAS	1914		L. Gomez, NY	1934		B. Pierce, CHI	1956
W. Johnson, WAS	1915		W. Ferrell, BOS	1935		J. Bunning, DET	1957
B. Ruth, BOS	1916		T. Bridges, DET	1936		C. Estrada, BAL	1960
E. Cicotte, CHI	1917		L. Gomez, NY	1937		D. Donovan, CLE	1962
W. Johnson, WAS	1918		R. Ruffing, NY	1938		W. Ford, NY	1963
W. Johnson, WAS	1919		B. Feller, CLE	1939		E. Fisher, CHI	1965
J. Bagby, CLE	1920		B. Feller, CLE	1940		J. Kaat, MIN	1966
			B. Feller, CLE	1941			
			T. Hughson, BOS	1942			

HYPOTHETICAL ROOKIE OF THE YEAR AWARD

National League Pitcher/Club	Year							American League Player/Club	Year				
E. Scott, CIN	1900	T. Long, STL	1915	D. Dean, STL	1932			S. Seybold, PHI	1901	J. Bagby, CLE	1916	B. Johnson, PHI	1933
C.Mathewson, NY	1901	R. Hornsby, STL	1916	F. Demaree, CHI	1933			A. Joss, CLE	1902	A. Sothoron, STL	1917	H. Trosky, CLE	1934
H. Smoot, STL	1902	L. Cadore, BRO	1917	C. Davis, PHI	1934			C. Bender, PHI	1903	S. Perry, PHI	1918	J. Powell, WAS	1935
J. Weimer, CHI	1903	C. Hollocher, CHI	1918	C. Blanton, PIT	1935			F. Glade, STL	1904	D. Kerr, CHI	1919	J. DiMaggio, NY	1936
H. Lumley, BRO	1904	O. Tuero, STL	1919	J. Mize, STL	1936			G. Stone, STL	1905	B. Meusel, NY	1920	R. York, DET	1937
E. Reulbach, CHI	1905	J. Haines, STL	1920	J. Turner, BOS	1937			C. Rossman, CLE	1906	J. Sewell, CLE	1921	K. Keltner, CLE	1938
J. Pfiester, CHI	1906	R. Grimes, CHI	1921	J. Rizzo, PIT	1938			S. Nicholls, PHI	1907	H. Pillette, DET	1922	T. Williams, BOS	1939
N. Rucker, BRO	1907	H. Miller, CHI	1922	H. Casey, BRO	1939			E. Summers, DET	1908	H. Summa, CLE	1923	W. Judnich, STL	1940
G. McQuillan, PHI	1908	G. Grantham, CHI	1923	B. Young, NY	1940			F. Baker, PHI	1909	A. Simmons, PHI	1924	P. Rizzuto, NY	1941
D. Miller, PIT	1909	K. Cuyler, PIT	1924	E. Riddle, CIN	1941			R. Ford, NY	1910	E. Combs, NY	1925	J. Pesky, BOS	1942
K. Cole, CHI	1910	J. Welsh, BOS	1925	J. Beazley, STL	1942			V. Gregg, CLE	1911	T. Lazzeri, NY	1926	B. Johnson, NY	1943
G. Alexander, PHI	1911	P. Waner, PIT	1926	L. Klein, STL	1943			D. Pratt, STL	1912	W. Moore, NY	1927	J. Berry, PHI	1944
L. Cheney, CHI	1912	L. Waner, PIT	1927	B. Voiselle, NY	1944			R. Russell, CHI	1913	E. Morris, BOS	1928	B. Ferriss, BOS	1945
J. Viox, PIT	1913	D.Bissonette,BRO	1928	K. Burkhart, STL	1945			R. Bressler, PHI	1914	D. Alexander, DET	1929	B. Lemon, CLE	1946
J. Pfeffer, BRO	1914	J. Frederick, BRO	1929	D. Ennis, PHI	1946			B. Ruth, BOS	1915	S. Jolley, CHI	1930	F. Shea, NY	1947
		W. Berger, BOS	1930							J. Vosmik, CLE	1931	G. Bearden, CLE	1948
		P. Derringer, STL	1931							J. Allen, NY	1932		

HYPOTHETICAL MOST VALUABLE PLAYER AWARD

National League Pitcher/Club	Year						American League Player/Club	Year				
H. Wagner, PIT	1900	F. Chance, CHI	1906	J. Vaughn, CHI	1918		N. Lajoie, PHI	1901	T. Cobb, DET	1907	J. Jackson, CHI	1919
H. Wagner, PIT	1901	H. Wagner, PIT	1907	E. Roush, CIN	1919		C. Young, BOS	1902	E. Walsh, CHI	1908	B. Ruth, NY	1920
H. Wagner, PIT	1902	C.Mathewson, NY	1908	R. Hornsby, STL	1920		N. Lajoie, CLE	1903	T. Cobb, DET	1909	B. Ruth, NY	1921
H. Wagner, PIT	1903	H. Wagner, PIT	1909	R. Hornsby, STL	1921		J. Chesbro, NY	1904	J. Coombs, PHI	1910	L. Fonseca, CLE	1929
J. McGinnity, NY	1904	S. Magee, PHI	1910	R. Hornsby, STL	1922		R. Waddell, PHI	1905	E. Collins, CHI	1915	J. Cronin, WAS	1930
C.Mathewson, NY	1905	G. Alexander, PHI	1915	D. Luque, CIN	1923		N. Lajoie, CLE	1906	T. Speaker, CLE	1916		
		G. Alexander, PHI	1916	H. Wilson, CHI	1930				E. Cicotte, CHI	1917		
		G. Alexander, PHI	1917						B. Ruth, BOS	1918		

HYPOTHETICAL FEDERAL LEAGUE AWARDS

	1914	1915
Most Valuable Player	B. Kauff, IND	D. Zwilling, CHI
Cy Young	C. Hendrix, CHI	G. McConnell, CHI
Rookie of the Year	B. Kauff, IND	E. Johnson, STL

Gold Glove Award: History

In a 1956 spring training survey, Elmer A. Blasco—employed by Rawlings Sporting Goods as advertising, public relations and sales manager—found that 83 percent of the active regular major league players wore Rawlings gloves or mitts. Noting that Hillerich & Bradsby (the major leagues' leading baseball bat supplier) awarded Silver Bats to the leagues' top hitters, Blasco reasoned that Rawlings ought to sponsor some sort of fielding award. After his idea was accepted by Rawlings management, Blasco contacted the Brown Shoe Company of St. Louis and obtained from them a hide of gold-lame-tanned leather used to make ladies' formal slippers. A glove was crafted from this hide, laced and stamped as a regular fielder's glove, and attached to a metal fixture on a walnut base with an appropriate engraved plate.

Thus was born the Gold Glove Award.

The October 2, 1957, edition of *The Sporting News* featured a full-page advertisement/announcement that established the fielding award: "Recognizing the importance of superior individual fielding performance to the advancement of baseball as America's national game, Rawlings [Sporting Goods Company] has established Annual Gold Glove Awards beginning with the 1957 season.

"Each of the nine major league players chosen for *The Sporting News* All-Star Fielding Team will be honored with a Rawlings Gold Glove Award. Selections will be made by a committee named by *The Sporting News*. Awards will be Rawlings custom-built gloves or mitts hand-crafted of special metallic gold-finished leather, each mounted on a suitable hardwood stand bearing an engraved plate."

TSN publisher J.G. Taylor Spink appointed 19 noted sportswriters for the selection task. They included Shirley Povich, Edgar Munzel, Hy Hurwitz, Earl Lawson, Bob Broeg, Allen Lewis, and Hal Lebowitz. A contest to predict the winners, open to baseball-playing boys, was sponsored by Rawlings.

The first Gold Glove winners were announced with great pomp and circumstance in the December 18, 1957, issue of *TSN*. "Too long neglected, the magicians of the defense have had no real recognition," the article explained, adding that the selections were made "solely on the basis of their defensive ability."

Rawlings and *TSN* also joined forces that year in the establishment of the Silver Glove Award, given to the top minor league fielder at each position—based entirely on fielding averages.

In 1958 the Gold Glove selection privilege was turned over to the major league players and an All-Star Fielding Team was selected for each league (as it still is). In 1961 the method for selecting outfielders was changed. Rather than choosing a left fielder, center fielder, and right fielder for each league, each voter was instructed to name three outfielders regardless of position (still the practice today).

In 1965 the managers and coaches of each team took over the voting responsibility, which they have retained ever since. Voters are not permitted to select players on their own teams. In 1987, 139 different managers and coaches took part in the balloting.

As with any award, the selections often draw criticism. One complaint is that too much importance is given to fielding average. Most of us realize that fielding average is not always a reliable indicator of defensive ability, but how much does it influence the Gold Glove voters?

Of the 366 fielding average leaders at the various positions between 1957 and 1987 (discounting pitchers and counting only one outfielder per league each year), 118 (32 percent) also won their respective Gold Glove Awards (see Table 1). We can say, then, that if a player leads his league in fielding average he has about a one-in-three chance of winning the Gold Glove—not an overwhelming correlation, but about four times better than random chance.

This raises some interesting questions. Since official fielding statistics are not published until months after Gold Gloves are voted on (although unofficial stats are readily available), any voter relying on fielding stats would probably have to consult (or remember) the

previous year's data. Therefore, if fielding average itself really does impress voters, we should expect to see many players winning a Gold Glove the year after they lead in fielding average. Do they? Well, no (see Table 2). The percentage here is 25 percent or one-in-four—again, considerably better than chance, but less of a factor than leading in fielding average in the current year.

And what about the influence of Gold Gloves on fielding averages? Is an official scorer less likely to charge an error against a player simply because he won a Gold Glove the previous year? Apparently not (see Table 3). The percentage of Gold Glove recipients leading in fielding average the following year is 23 percent.

"It is my belief that a lot more is considered than fielding percentage," said *TSN* editor Tom Barnidge, citing "range, throwing arm, the headiness of the ballplayer." Pete Rose, a two-time Gold Glove winner and later a voter, concurred: "There are a lot of intangibles involved in voting for the Gold Glove. Take an outfielder. The coaches and managers watch these guys all the time. How they play the hitters, how strong their arms are, how often they hit the cutoff man, and all that is taken into consideration—things that do not show up in the statistics."

Another criticism of the Gold Glove is that batting performance plays a role in the selections, contrary to the award's philosophy. As *USA Today* baseball editor Hal Bodley put it, "A player who is outstanding on defense and respectable on offense has a much better chance of getting a Gold Glove than a counterpart whose forte is fielding alone."

Other factors can be distractions to the voters: flashiness, reputations and the selection process itself. For insight on some of these and their effects, I consulted an expert on the Gold Glove: Wes Parker, a six-time winner of the award at first base. Parker, it should be noted, would seem to have no reason to gripe about the award. He grasped the honor from a seven-time winner; he won it even when he batted as low as .239; and he became one of only two non-pitchers (Roberto Clemente is the other) to win the award in his final major league season.

"I would say many, if not most, coaches and managers fail to take their voting responsibility seriously," said Parker. "They don't treat it as a vital act. They are usually much more concerned with their team and the pennant race and, as a result, tend to zip through the ballots (distributed in September). So they wind up voting for the most recognizable names."

Parker brought out another rarely discussed procedural problem: "Since players [when they were voting] and coaches are forbidden to vote for anyone on their own team, they often won't vote for the guy who is contending with their team's leading candidate for the same award. That increases their teammate's chances."

On the subject of reputation, Parker asserted that it "has a lot to do with it, absolutely. In 1966, Bill White won the award (for the seventh consecutive time), although even White admitted that I probably deserved it. It takes a couple of years for your reputation to catch up with you, but that can work to your advantage at the end of your career."

"Flashiness is a factor too," continued Parker. "It puts the player's name in the forefront of the voter's minds." Wes also concurred with the theory that a player's bat can be the difference in winning this 'fielding' award.

"[Four-time Gold Glove winner Steve] Garvey is a good example of someone who won it with his bat and notoriety, a perfect example, in fact," opines Parker. "Garvey was vastly overrated defensively ... he had no range, no arm, and no aggressiveness. He would hold the ball and allow opposing runners to take extra bases to avoid throwing errors. That's how he compiled his high [fielding] averages at first base. Remember, he was a terrible third baseman, worst I ever saw." (In 1972, Garvey's last season as a third-sacker, he led the NL with 28 errors in just 85 games, posting a woeful .902 percentage.)

"Amazingly, despite these prejudices," Parker concluded, "I think the Gold Glove choices have been excellent. At first base I think they have been perfect, with the exception of Garvey."

While the Gold Glove Award has adequately filled the need for a subjective fielding award, there is still something to be said about fielding statistics. It is fashionable to say that fielding stats are meaningless, but, as analyst Bill James said, "If a baseball statistic is meaningless to you, that is simply because you don't know what it means."

With the understanding of which fielding statistics are meaningful for each position, it is possible to make a pretty reliable judgment of a player's defensive skills based on stats alone. In recent years, several analysts have attempted to measure individual fielding performance on the basis of numbers.

One newer method is Linear Weights, Pete Palmer's translation of individual batting, pitching, and fielding statistics into runs gained and thus games won. The fielding portion of the system, Fielding or Defensive Wins, incorporates data (variously weighted according to position) on putouts, assists, errors, and double plays, comparing a player's totals against the league averages. Of the 60 players identified by the Palmer system as the best fielders in their leagues between 1957 and 1986, 28 also won their respective Gold Glove Awards.

Bill James also presented a fielding measurement system, Defensive Won/Lost Percentage (DW/L%). Of the 32 players identified by DW/L% as the best at their positions and leagues for the 1983-84 seasons, 12 (38 percent) also won their respective Gold Gloves. More recently, James unveiled an improved system in his "Win Shares" system.

The Elias Sports Bureau has demonstrated a simple and generally effective scheme for evaluating fielders: comparing the number of runs scored per nine innings while a player is on the field to the number scored when he isn't. For example, Elias calculated that the 1982-86 Cardinals averaged allowing 3.85 runs per nine innings with Ozzie Smith at shortstop, as compared to 4.04 per game with other shortstops. Now that Retrosheet has made play-by-play data universally available, this type of comparison is easier to come by; however it, too, has limitations.

So, when all is said and done about modern statistical fielding measurements, a subjective measurement—the Gold Glove—may still be the most widely acknowledged tool to rate fielders.

The following pages list the winners of the Gold Glove at each position since 1957. Complete balloting for Gold Glove elections is, unfortunately, neither available nor researchable.

GOLD GLOVE AWARD TABLES

TABLE 1. Fielding Average Leaders
Winning Gold Glove, 1957-87
(Maximum 61 Each Position).

POS.	NL	AL	TOT.	PCT.
C	7	7	14	23
1B	13	13	26	43
2B	14	5	19	31
3B	4	15	19	31
SS	14	12	26	43
OF	6	8	14	23
TOT.	58	60	118	32

TABLE 2. Fielding Average Leaders Winning
Gold Glove in Following Season, 1956-86
(Maximum 61 Each Position).

POS.	NL	AL	TOT.	PCT.
C	7	7	14	23
1B	8	11	19	31
2B	9	6	15	25
3B	3	13	16	26
SS	11	9	20	33
OF	2	5	7	11
TOT.	40	51	91	25

TABLE 3. Fielding Average Leaders Who
Won Gold Glove in Previous Season, 1958-87
(Maximum 59 Each Position).

POS.	NL	AL	TOT.	PCT.
C	3	7	10	17
1B	11	8	19	32
2B	8	2	10	17
3B	2	12	14	24
SS	10	9	19	32
OF	6	5	11	19
TOT.	40	43	83	23

GOLD GLOVE AWARD WINNERS

Pitchers

Year	National League	American League
1957	(No selection)	B. Shantz, NY
1958	H. Haddix, CIN	B. Shantz, NY
1959	H. Haddix, PIT	B. Shantz, NY
1960	H. Haddix, PIT	B. Shantz, NY
1961	B. Shantz, PIT	F. Lary, DET
1962	B. Shantz, STL	J. Kaat, MIN
1963	B. Shantz, STL	J. Kaat, MIN
1964	B. Shantz, PHI	J. Kaat, MIN
1965	B. Gibson, STL	J. Kaat, MIN
1966	B. Gibson, STL	J. Kaat, MIN
1967	B. Gibson, STL	J. Kaat, MIN
1968	B. Gibson, STL	J. Kaat, MIN
1969	B. Gibson, STL	J. Kaat, MIN
1970	B. Gibson, STL	J. Kaat, MIN
1971	B. Gibson, STL	J. Kaat, MIN
1972	B. Gibson, STL	J. Kaat, MIN
1973	B. Gibson, STL	J. Kaat, MIN
1974	A. Messersmith, LA	J. Kaat, CHI
1975	A. Messersmith, LA	J. Kaat, CHI
1976	J. Kaat, PHI	J. Palmer, BAL
1977	J. Kaat, PHI	J. Palmer, BAL
1978	P. Niekro, ATL	J. Palmer, BAL
1979	P. Niekro, ATL	J. Palmer, BAL
1980	P. Niekro, ATL	M. Norris, OAK
1981	S. Carlton, PHI	M. Norris, OAK
1982	P. Niekro, ATL	R. Guidry, NY
1983	P. Niekro, ATL	R. Guidry, NY
1984	J. Andujar, STL	R. Guidry, NY
1985	R. Reuschel, PIT	R. Guidry, NY
1986	F. Valenzuela, LA	R. Guidry, NY
1987	R. Reuschel, SF	M. Langston, SEA
1988	O. Hershiser, LA	M. Langston, SEA
1989	R. Darling, NY	B. Saberhagen, KC
1990	G. Maddux, CHI	M. Boddicker, BOS
1991	G. Maddux, CHI	M. Langston, CAL
1992	G. Maddux, CHI	M. Langston, CAL
1993	G. Maddux, ATL	M. Langston, CAL
1994	G. Maddux, ATL	M. Langston, CAL
1995	G. Maddux, ATL	M. Langston, CAL
1996	G. Maddux, ATL	M. Mussina, BAL
1997	G. Maddux, ATL	M. Mussina, BAL
1998	G. Maddux, ATL	M. Mussina, BAL
1999	G. Maddux, ATL	M. Mussina, BAL
2000	G. Maddux, ATL	K. Rogers, TEX
2001	G. Maddux, ATL	M. Mussina, BAL
2002	G. Maddux, ATL	K. Rogers, TEX
2003	M. Hampton, ATL	M. Mussina, NY

Catchers

Year	National League	American League
1957	(No selection)	S. Lollar, CHI
1958	D. Crandall, MIL	S. Lollar, CHI
1959	D. Crandall, MIL	S. Lollar, CHI
1960	D. Crandall, MIL	E. Battey, WAS
1961	J. Roseboro, LA	E. Battey, MIN
1962	D. Crandall, MIL	E. Battey, MIN
1963	J. Edwards, CIN	E. Howard, NY
1964	J. Edwards, CIN	E. Howard, NY
1965	J. Torre, MIL	B. Freehan, DET
1966	J. Roseboro, LA	B. Freehan, DET
1967	R. Hundley, CHI	B. Freehan, DET
1968	J. Bench, CIN	B. Freehan, DET
1969	J. Bench, CIN	B. Freehan, DET
1970	J. Bench, CIN	R. Fosse, CLE
1971	J. Bench, CIN	R. Fosse, CLE
1972	J. Bench, CIN	C. Fisk, BOS
1973	J. Bench, CIN	T. Munson, NY
1974	J. Bench, CIN	T. Munson, NY
1975	J. Bench, CIN	T. Munson, NY
1976	J. Bench, CIN	J. Sundberg, TEX
1977	J. Bench, CIN	J. Sundberg, TEX
1978	B. Boone, PHI	J. Sundberg, TEX
1979	B. Boone, PHI	J. Sundberg, TEX
1980	G. Carter, MON	J. Sundberg, TEX
1981	G. Carter, MON	J. Sundberg, TEX
1982	G. Carter, MON	B. Boone, CAL
1983	T. Pena, PIT	Lc. Parrish, DET
1984	T. Pena, PIT	Lc. Parrish, DET
1985	T. Pena, PIT	Lc. Parrish, DET
1986	J. Davis, CHI	B. Boone, CAL
1987	M. LaValliere, PIT	B. Boone, CAL
1988	B. Santiago, SD	B. Boone, CAL
1989	B. Santiago, SD	B. Boone, CAL
1990	B. Santiago, SD	S. Alomar, CLE
1991	T. Pagnozzi, STL	T. Pena, BOS
1992	T. Pagnozzi, STL	I. Rodriguez, TEX
1993	K. Manwaring, SF	I. Rodriguez, TEX
1994	T. Pagnozzi, STL	I. Rodriguez, TEX
1995	C. Johnson, FLA	I. Rodriguez, TEX
1996	C. Johnson, FLA	I. Rodriguez, TEX
1997	C. Johnson, FLA	I. Rodriguez, TEX
1998	C. Johnson, FLA-LA	I. Rodriguez, TEX
1999	M. Lieberthal, PHI	I. Rodriguez, TEX
2000	M. Matheny, STL	I. Rodriguez, TEX
2001	B. Ausmus, HOU	I. Rodriguez, TEX
2002	B. Ausmus, HOU	B. Molina, ANA
2003	M. Matheny, STL	B. Molina, ANA

First Basemen

Year	National League	American League
1957	G. Hodges, BRO	(No selection)
1958	G. Hodges, LA	V. Power, CLE
1959	G. Hodges, LA	V. Power, CLE
1960	B. White, STL	V. Power, CLE
1961	B. White, STL	V. Power, CLE
1962	B. White, STL	V. Power, MIN
1963	B. White, STL	V. Power, MIN
1964	B. White, STL	V. Power, LA
1965	B. White, STL	J. Pepitone, NY
1966	B. White, PHI	J. Pepitone, NY
1967	W. Parker, LA	G. Scott, BOS
1968	W. Parker, LA	G. Scott, BOS
1969	W. Parker, LA	J. Pepitone, NY
1970	W. Parker, LA	J. Spencer, CAL
1971	W. Parker, LA	G. Scott, BOS
1972	W. Parker, LA	G. Scott, MIL
1973	M. Jorgensen, MON	G. Scott, MIL
1974	S. Garvey, LA	G. Scott, MIL
1975	S. Garvey, LA	G. Scott, MIL
1976	S. Garvey, LA	G. Scott, MIL
1977	S. Garvey, LA	J. Spencer, CHI
1978	K. Hernandez, STL	C. Chambliss, NY
1979	K. Hernandez, STL	C. Cooper, MIL
1980	K. Hernandez, STL	C. Cooper, MIL
1981	K. Hernandez, STL	M. Squires, CHI
1982	K. Hernandez, STL	E. Murray, BAL
1983	K. Hernandez, STL-NY	E. Murray, BAL
1984	K. Hernandez, NY	E. Murray, BAL
1985	K. Hernandez, NY	D. Mattingly, NY
1986	K. Hernandez, NY	D. Mattingly, NY
1987	K. Hernandez, NY	D. Mattingly, NY
1988	K. Hernandez, NY	D. Mattingly, NY
1989	A. Galarraga, MON	D. Mattingly, NY
1990	A. Galarraga, MON	M. McGwire, OAK
1991	W. Clark, SF	D. Mattingly, NY
1992	M. Grace, CHI	D. Mattingly, NY
1993	M. Grace, CHI	D. Mattingly, NY
1994	J. Bagwell, HOU	D. Mattingly, NY
1995	M. Grace, CHI	J. Snow, CAL
1996	M. Grace, CHI	J. Snow, CAL
1997	J. Snow, SF	R. Palmeiro, BAL
1998	J. Snow, SF	R. Palmeiro, BAL
1999	J. Snow, SF	R. Palmeiro, TEX
2000	J. Snow, SF	J. Olerud, SEA
2001	T. Helton, COL	D.Mientkiewicz, MIN
2002	T. Helton, COL	J. Olerud, SEA
2003	D. Lee, FLA	J. Olerud, SEA

Second Basemen

Year	National League	American League
1957	(No selection)	N. Fox, CHI
1958	B. Mazeroski, PIT	F. Bolling, DET
1959	C. Neal, LA	N. Fox, CHI
1960	B. Mazeroski, PIT	N. Fox, CHI
1961	B. Mazeroski, PIT	B. Richardson, NY
1962	K. Hubbs, CHI	B. Richardson, NY
1963	B. Mazeroski, PIT	B. Richardson, NY
1964	B. Mazeroski, PIT	B. Richardson, NY
1965	B. Mazeroski, PIT	B. Richardson, NY
1966	B. Mazeroski, PIT	B. Knoop, CAL
1967	B. Mazeroski, PIT	B. Knoop, CAL
1968	G. Beckert, CHI	B. Knoop, CAL
1969	F. Millan, ATL	D. Johnson, BAL
1970	T. Helms, CIN	D. Johnson, BAL
1971	T. Helms, CIN	D. Johnson, BAL
1972	F. Millan, ATL	D. Griffin, BOS
1973	J. Morgan, CIN	B. Grich, BAL
1974	J. Morgan, CIN	B. Grich, BAL
1975	J. Morgan, CIN	B. Grich, BAL
1976	J. Morgan, CIN	B. Grich, BAL
1977	J. Morgan, CIN	F. White, KC
1978	D. Lopes, LA	F. White, KC
1979	M. Trillo, PHI	F. White, KC
1980	D. Flynn, NY	F. White, KC
1981	M. Trillo, PHI	F. White, KC
1982	M. Trillo, PHI	F. White, KC
1983	R. Sandberg, CHI	L. Whitaker, DET
1984	R. Sandberg, CHI	L. Whitaker, DET
1985	R. Sandberg, CHI	L. Whitaker, DET
1986	R. Sandberg, CHI	F. White, KC
1987	R. Sandberg, CHI	F. White, KC
1988	R. Sandberg, CHI	H. Reynolds, SEA
1989	R. Sandberg, CHI	H. Reynolds, SEA
1990	R. Sandberg, CHI	H. Reynolds, SEA
1991	R. Sandberg, CHI	R. Alomar, TOR
1992	J. Lind, PIT	R. Alomar, TOR
1993	R. Thompson, SF	R. Alomar, TOR
1994	C. Biggio, HOU	R. Alomar, TOR
1995	C. Biggio, HOU	R. Alomar, TOR
1996	C. Biggio, HOU	R. Alomar, TOR
1997	C. Biggio, HOU	C. Knoblauch, MIN
1998	B. Boone, CIN	R. Alomar, BAL
1999	P. Reese, CIN	R. Alomar, CLE
2000	P. Reese, CIN	R. Alomar, CLE
2001	F. Viña, STL	R. Alomar, CLE
2002	F. Viña, STL	B. Boone, SEA
2003	L. Castillo, FLA	B. Boone, SEA

Third Basemen

Year	National League	American League
1957	(No selection)	F. Malzone, BOS
1958	K. Boyer, STL	F. Malzone, BOS
1959	K. Boyer, STL	F. Malzone, BOS
1960	K. Boyer, STL	B. Robinson, BAL
1961	K. Boyer, STL	B. Robinson, BAL

Year	National League	American League
1962	J. Davenport, SF	B. Robinson, BAL
1963	K. Boyer, STL	B. Robinson, BAL
1964	R. Santo, CHI	B. Robinson, BAL
1965	R. Santo, CHI	B. Robinson, BAL
1966	R. Santo, CHI	B. Robinson, BAL
1967	R. Santo, CHI	B. Robinson, BAL
1968	R. Santo, CHI	B. Robinson, BAL
1969	C. Boyer, ATL	B. Robinson, BAL
1970	D. Rader, HOU	B. Robinson, BAL
1971	D. Rader, HOU	B. Robinson, BAL
1972	D. Rader, HOU	B. Robinson, BAL
1973	D. Rader, HOU	B. Robinson, BAL
1974	D. Rader, HOU	B. Robinson, BAL
1975	K. Reitz, STL	B. Robinson, BAL
1976	M. Schmidt, PHI	A. Rodriguez, DET
1977	M. Schmidt, PHI	G. Nettles, NY
1978	M. Schmidt, PHI	G. Nettles, NY
1979	M. Schmidt, PHI	B. Bell, TEX
1980	M. Schmidt, PHI	B. Bell, TEX
1981	M. Schmidt, PHI	B. Bell, TEX
1982	M. Schmidt, PHI	B. Bell, TEX
1983	M. Schmidt, PHI	B. Bell, TEX
1984	M. Schmidt, PHI	B. Bell, TEX
1985	T. Wallach, MON	G. Brett, KC
1986	M. Schmidt, PHI	G. Gaetti, MIN
1987	T. Pendleton, STL	G. Gaetti, MIN
1988	T. Wallach, MON	G. Gaetti, MIN
1989	T. Pendleton, STL	G. Gaetti, MIN
1990	T. Wallach, MON	K. Gruber, TOR
1991	M. Williams, SF	R. Ventura, CHI
1992	T. Pendleton, ATL	R. Ventura, CHI
1993	M. Williams, SF	R. Ventura, CHI
1994	M. Williams, SF	W. Boggs, NY
1995	K. Caminiti, SD	W. Boggs, NY
1996	K. Caminiti, SD	R. Ventura, CHI
1997	K. Caminiti, SD	M. Williams, CLE
1998	S. Rolen, PHI	R. Ventura, CHI
1999	R. Ventura, NY	S. Brosius, NY
2000	S. Rolen, PHI	T. Fryman, CLE
2001	S. Rolen, PHI	E. Chavez, OAK
2002	S. Rolen, STL	E. Chavez, OAK
2003	S. Rolen, STL	E. Chavez, OAK

Shortstops

Year	National League	American League
1957	R. McMillan, CIN	(No selection) L. Aparicio, CHI
1958	R. McMillan, CIN	L. Aparicio, CHI
1959	R. McMillan, CIN	L. Aparicio, CHI
1960	E. Banks, CHI	L. Aparicio, CHI
1961	M. Wills, LA	L. Aparicio, CHI
1962	M. Wills, LA	L. Aparicio, CHI
1963	B. Wine, PHI	Z. Versalles, MIN
1964	R. Amaro, PHI	L. Aparicio, BAL
1965	L. Cardenas, CIN	Z. Versalles, MIN
1966	G. Alley, PIT	L. Aparicio, BAL
1967	G. Alley, PIT	J. Fregosi, CAL
1968	D. Maxvill, STL	L. Aparicio, CHI
1969	D. Kessinger, CHI	M. Belanger, BAL
1970	D. Kessinger, CHI	L. Aparicio, CHI
1971	B. Harrelson, NY	M. Belanger, BAL
1972	L. Bowa, PHI	E. Brinkman, DET
1973	R. Metzger, HOU	M. Belanger, BAL
1974	D. Concepcion, CIN	M. Belanger, BAL
1975	D. Concepcion, CIN	M. Belanger, BAL
1976	D. Concepcion, CIN	M. Belanger, BAL
1977	D. Concepcion, CIN	M. Belanger, BAL
1978	L. Bowa, PHI	M. Belanger, BAL
1979	D. Concepcion, CIN	R. Burleson, BOS
1980	O. Smith, SD	A. Trammell, DET
1981	O. Smith, SD	A. Trammell, DET
1982	O. Smith, STL	R. Yount, MIL
1983	O. Smith, STL	A. Trammell, DET
1984	O. Smith, STL	A. Trammell, DET
1985	O. Smith, STL	A. Griffin, OAK
1986	O. Smith, STL	T. Fernandez, TOR
1987	O. Smith, STL	T. Fernandez, TOR
1988	O. Smith, STL	T. Fernandez, TOR
1989	O. Smith, STL	T. Fernandez, TOR
1990	O. Smith, STL	O. Guillen, CHI
1991	O. Smith, STL	C. Ripken, BAL
1992	O. Smith, STL	C. Ripken, BAL
1993	J. Bell, PIT	O. Vizquel, SEA
1994	B. Larkin, CIN	O. Vizquel, CLE
1995	B. Larkin, CIN	O. Vizquel, CLE
1996	B. Larkin, CIN	O. Vizquel, CLE
1997	R. Ordoñez, NY	O. Vizquel, CLE
1998	R. Ordoñez, NY	O. Vizquel, CLE
1999	R. Ordoñez, NY	O. Vizquel, CLE
2000	N. Perez, COL	O. Vizquel, CLE
2001	O. Cabrera, MON	O. Vizquel, CLE
2002	E. Renteria, STL	A. Rodriguez, TEX
2003	E. Renteria, STL	A. Rodriguez, TEX

National League Outfielders

YEAR	PLAYERS		
1957	W. Mays, NY (CF)	(No other selections)	
1958	F. Robinson, CIN (LF)	W. Mays, SF (CF)	H. Aaron, MIL (RF)
1959	J. Brandt, SF (LF)	W. Mays, SF (CF)	H. Aaron, MIL (RF)
1960	W. Moon, LA (LF)	W. Mays, SF (CF)	H. Aaron, MIL (RF)
1961	W. Mays, SF	R. Clemente, PIT	V. Pinson, CIN
1962	W. Mays, SF	R. Clemente, PIT	B. Virdon, PIT
1963	W. Mays, SF	R. Clemente, PIT	C. Flood, STL
1964	W. Mays, SF	R. Clemente, PIT	C. Flood, STL
1965	W. Mays, SF	R. Clemente, PIT	C. Flood, STL
1966	W. Mays, SF	C. Flood, STL	R. Clemente, PIT
1967	R. Clemente, PIT	C. Flood, STL	W. Mays, SF
1968	W. Mays, SF	R. Clemente, PIT	C. Flood, STL
1969	R. Clemente, PIT	C. Flood, STL	P. Rose, CIN
1970	R. Clemente, PIT	T. Agee, NY	P. Rose, CIN
1971	R. Clemente, PIT	B. Bonds, SF	W. Davis, LA
1972	R. Clemente, PIT	C. Cedeno, HOU	W. Davis, LA
1973	B. Bonds, SF	C. Cedeno, HOU	W. Davis, LA
1974	C. Cedeno, HOU	C. Geronimo, CIN	B. Bonds, SF
1975	C. Cedeno, HOU	C. Geronimo, CIN	G. Maddox, PHI
1976	C. Cedeno, HOU	C. Geronimo, CIN	G. Maddox, PHI
1977	C. Geronimo, CIN	G. Maddox, PHI	D. Parker, PIT
1978	G. Maddox, PHI	D. Parker, PIT	E. Valentine, MON
1979	G. Maddox, PHI	D. Parker, PIT	D. Winfield, SD
1980	A. Dawson, MON	G. Maddox, PHI	D. Winfield, SD
1981	A. Dawson, MON	G. Maddox, PHI	D. Baker, LA
1982	A. Dawson, MON	D. Murphy, ATL	G. Maddox, PHI
1983	A. Dawson, MON	D. Murphy, ATL	W. McGee, STL
1984	D. Murphy, ATL	B. Dernier, CHI	A. Dawson, MON
1985	W. McGee, STL	D. Murphy, ATL	A. Dawson, MON
1986	T. Gwynn, SD	D. Murphy, ATL	W. McGee, STL
1987	E. Davis, CIN	T. Gwynn, SD	A. Dawson, CHI
1988	A. Van Slyke, PIT	E. Davis, CIN	A. Dawson, CHI
1989	A. Van Slyke, PIT	E. Davis, CIN	T. Gwynn, SD
1990	A. Van Slyke, PIT	T. Gwynn, SD	B. Bonds, PIT
1991	A. Van Slyke, PIT	T. Gwynn, SD	B. Bonds, PIT
1992	A. Van Slyke, PIT	T. Gwynn, SD	B. Bonds, PIT
1993	B. Bonds, SF	L. Walker, MON	M. Grissom, MON
1994	B. Bonds, SF	L. Walker, MON	M. Grissom, MON
1995	R. Mondesi, LA	D. Lewis, SF	S. Finley, SD
1996	B. Bonds, SF	M. Grissom, ATL	S. Finley, SD
1997	B. Bonds, SF	M. Grissom, ATL	L. Walker, COL
1998	B. Bonds, SF	R. Mondesi, LA	L. Walker, COL
1999	S. Finley, ARI	A. Jones, ATL	L. Walker, COL
2000	S. Finley, ARI	A. Jones, ATL	J. Edmonds, STL
2001	L. Walker, COL	A. Jones, ATL	J. Edmonds, STL
2002	L. Walker, COL	A. Jones, ATL	J. Edmonds, STL
2003	J. Cruz, SF	A. Jones, ATL	J. Edmonds, STL

American League Outfielders

YEAR	PLAYERS		
1957	M. Minoso, CHI (LF)	A. Kaline, DET (RF)	(No other selection)
1958	N. Siebern, NY (LF)	J. Piersall, BOS (CF)	A. Kaline, DET (RF)
1959	M. Minoso, CLE (LF)	A. Kaline, DET (CF)	J. Jensen, BOS (RF)
1960	M. Minoso, CHI (LF)	J. Landis, CHI (CF)	R. Maris, NY (RF)
1961	A. Kaline, DET	J. Piersall, CLE	J. Landis, CHI
1962	J. Landis, CHI	M. Mantle, NY	A. Kaline, DET
1963	A. Kaline, DET	C. Yastrzemski, BOS	J. Landis, CHI
1964	A. Kaline, DET	J. Landis, CHI	V. Davalillo, CLE
1965	A. Kaline, DET	T. Tresh, NY	C. Yastrzemski, BOS
1966	A. Kaline, DET	T. Agee, CHI	T. Oliva, MIN
1967	C. Yastrzemski, BOS	P. Blair, BAL	A. Kaline, DET
1968	M. Stanley, DET	C. Yastrzemski, BOS	R. Smith, BOS
1969	P. Blair, BAL	M. Stanley, DET	C. Yastrzemski, BOS
1970	M. Stanley, DET	P. Blair, BAL	K. Berry, CHI
1971	P. Blair, BAL	A. Otis, KC	C. Yastrzemski, BOS
1972	P. Blair, BAL	B. Murcer, NY	K. Berry, CAL
1973	P. Blair, BAL	A. Otis, KC	M. Stanley, DET
1974	P. Blair, BAL	A. Otis, KC	J. Rudi, OAK
1975	P. Blair, BAL	J. Rudi, OAK	F. Lynn, BOS
1976	J. Rudi, OAK	Dw. Evans, BOS	R. Manning, CLE
1977	J. Beniquez, TEX	C. Yastrzemski, BOS	A. Cowens, KC
1978	F. Lynn, BOS	Dw. Evans, BOS	R. Miller, CAL
1979	Dw. Evans, BOS	S. Lezcano, MIL	F. Lynn, BOS
1980	F. Lynn, BOS	D. Murphy, OAK	W. Wilson, KC
1981	D. Murphy, OAK	Dw. Evans, BOS	R. Henderson, OAK
1982	Dw. Evans, BOS	D. Winfield, NY	D. Murphy, OAK
1983	Dw. Evans, BOS	D. Winfield, NY	D. Murphy, OAK
1984	Dw. Evans, BOS	D. Winfield, NY	D. Murphy, OAK
1985	G. Pettis, CAL	D. Winfield, NY	Dw. Evans, BOS, D. Murphy, OAK
1986	G. Pettis, CAL	J. Barfield, TOR	K. Puckett, MIN
1987	J. Barfield, TOR	K. Puckett, MIN	D. Winfield, NY
1988	K. Puckett, MIN	D. White, CAL	G. Pettis, DET
1989	D. White, CAL	G. Pettis, DET	K. Puckett, MIN
1990	G. Pettis, TEX	K. Griffey, Jr., SEA	E. Burks, BOS
1991	K. Puckett, MIN	K. Griffey, Jr., SEA	D. White, TOR
1992	K. Puckett, MIN	K. Griffey, Jr., SEA	D. White, TOR
1993	K. Griffey, Jr., SEA	D. White, TOR	K. Lofton, CLE
1994	K. Griffey, Jr., SEA	D. White, TOR	K. Lofton, CLE
1995	K. Griffey, Jr., SEA	K. Lofton, CLE	D. White, TOR
1996	K. Griffey, Jr., SEA	K. Lofton, CLE	J. Buhner, SEA
1997	J. Edmonds, ANA	K. Griffey, Jr., SEA	B. Williams, NY
1998	J. Edmonds, ANA	K. Griffey, Jr., SEA	B. Williams, NY
1999	B. Williams, NY	K. Griffey, Jr., SEA	S. Green, TOR
2000	B. Williams, NY	D. Erstad, ANA	J. Dye, KC
2001	M. Cameron, SEA	I. Suzuki, SEA	T. Hunter, MIN
2002	D. Erstad, ANA	I. Suzuki, SEA	T. Hunter, MIN
2003	M. Cameron, SEA	I. Suzuki, SEA	T. Hunter, MIN

The All-Star Game MVP Award

The All-Star Game MVP Award began in 1962, the last year in which two All-Star Games were played. It was called the Arch Ward Memorial Award, in honor of the late Chicago newspaper writer credited with conceiving the midsummer classic. Under Bowie Kuhn's regime (1970-84) the award was called the Commissioner's Trophy. Just prior to the 2002 game, it was announced that the MVP Award would hereafter be named in honor of the recently deceased Ted Williams, who had starred in several All-Star contests. In a rude irony, the Ted Williams Award was not given to

anyone that year, as the writers did not see fit to name the MVP of a tie game.

A committee of writers and executives in attendance votes on the recipient of the game's award. Only twice—Brooks Robinson in 1966 and Carl Yastrzemski in 1970—has a member of the losing team been honored. Two-time winners are Willie Mays, Steve Garvey and Gary Carter.

Following are the winners of the All-Star Game MVP Awards. Complete voting breakdowns for the award are not available.

ALL-STAR GAME MVPS

1962 Maury Wills, LA (NL) [Game 1]	1972 Joe Morgan, CIN (NL)	1982 Dave Concepcion, CIN (NL)	1993 Kirby Puckett, MIN (AL)
Leon Wagner, LA (AL) [Game 2]	1973 Bobby Bonds, SF (NL)	1983 Fred Lynn, CAL (AL)	1994 Fred McGriff, ATL (NL)
1963 Willie Mays, SF (NL)	1974 Steve Garvey, LA (NL)	1984 Gary Carter, MON (NL)	1995 Jeff Conine, FLA (NL)
1964 Johnny Callison, PHI (NL)	1975 Bill Madlock, CHI (NL),	1985 LaMarr Hoyt, SD (NL)	1996 Mike Piazza, LA (NL)
1965 Juan Marichal, SF (NL)	Jon Matlack, NY (NL)	1986 Roger Clemens, BOS (AL)	1997 Sandy Alomar, Jr., CLE (AL)
1966 Brooks Robinson, BAL (AL)	1976 George Foster, CIN (NL)	1987 Tim Raines, MON (NL)	1998 Roberto Alomar, BAL (AL)
1967 Tony Perez, CIN (NL)	1977 Don Sutton, LA (NL)	1988 Terry Steinbach, OAK (AL)	1999 Pedro Martinez, BOS (AL)
1968 Willie Mays, SF (NL)	1978 Steve Garvey, LA (NL)	1989 Bo Jackson, KC (AL)	2000 Derek Jeter, NY (AL)
1969 Willie McCovey, SF (NL)	1979 Dave Parker, PIT (NL)	1990 Julio Franco, TEX (AL)	2001 Cal Ripken, BAL (AL)
1970 Carl Yastrzemski, BOS (AL)	1980 Ken Griffey, CIN (NL)	1991 Cal Ripken, BAL (AL)	2002 (No selection)
1971 Frank Robinson, BAL (AL)	1981 Gary Carter, MON (NL)	1992 Ken Griffey, Jr., SEA (AL)	2003 Garret Anderson, ANA (AL)

League Championship Series MVP Award

MVP Awards for the League Championship Series were instituted by the National League in 1977, and in the American League three years later. A committee of writers and executives in attendance does the voting, which is announced at the conclusion of

each series. Steve Garvey, Dave Stewart, and Orel Hershiser are the only two-time winners. Winners from losing teams are Fred Lynn (1982), Mike Scott (1986), and Jeffrey Leonard (1987).

Following are the winners of LCS MVP Awards. Complete voting breakdowns are not available.

LEAGUE CHAMPIONSHIP SERIES MVPS

Year	National League	American League	Year	National League	American League
1977	Dusty Baker, LA	—	1991	Steve Avery, ATL	Kirby Puckett, MIN
1978	Steve Garvey, LA	—	1992	John Smoltz, ATL	Roberto Alomar, TOR
1979	Willie Stargell, PIT	—	1993	Curt Schilling, PHI	Dave Stewart, TOR
1980	Manny Trillo, PHI	Frank White, KC	1994	(No Series)	(No Series)
1981	Burt Hooton, LA	Graig Nettles, NY	1995	Mike Devereaux, ATL	Orel Hershiser, CLE
1982	Darrell Porter, STL	Fred Lynn, CAL	1996	Javier Lopez, ATL	Bernie Williams, NY
1983	Gary Matthews, PHI	Mike Boddicker, BAL	1997	Livan Hernandez, FLA	Marquis Grissom, CLE
1984	Steve Garvey, SD	Kirk Gibson, DET	1998	Sterling Hitchcock, SD	David Wells, NY
1985	Ozzie Smith, STL	George Brett, KC	1999	Eddie Perez, ATL	Orlando Hernandez, NY
1986	Mike Scott, HOU	Marty Barrett, BOS	2000	Mike Hampton, NY	David Justice, NY
1987	Jeffrey Leonard, SF	Gary Gaetti, MIN	2001	Craig Counsell, ARI	Andy Pettitte, NY
1988	Orel Hershiser, LA	Dennis Eckersley, OAK	2002	Benito Santiago, SF	Adam Kennedy, ANA
1989	Will Clark, SF	Rickey Henderson, OAK	2003	Ivan Rodriguez, FLA	Mariano Rivera, NY
1990	Rob Dibble, CIN,	Dave Stewart, OAK			
	Randy Myers, CIN				

World Series MVP Award

There are two major World Series MVP Awards. The New York chapter of the Baseball Writers' Association of America established one in memory of Babe Ruth in 1949, the year after the Bambino's death. Six years later, *SPORT* magazine introduced its version, presented in cooperation with the Chevrolet Motor Company (which typically presented a Corvette to the winner).

The winner of the *SPORT* award was originally chosen by the magazine's editors, but the voting process eventually went to a committee of sports reporters and officials (and, since *SPORT* folded in 2000, they are no longer involved with the award). The award is

now sanctioned by Major League Baseball, and has eclipsed the Babe Ruth Award in prestige and public recognition. It is voted on during the final game of the Series and is presented immediately following its conclusion, whereas the Ruth Award is voted on during a local chapter meeting some time after the Series has concluded.

Following are the winners of the two World Series MVP Awards. Two-time winners of the *SPORT* award are Sandy Koufax, Bob Gibson, and Reggie Jackson; double winners of the Ruth award are Koufax and Jack Morris. Winners from losing teams are Bobby Richardson (*SPORT*, 1960), and Luis Tiant (Ruth, 1975). Complete voting breakdowns on either award are not available.

WORLD SERIES MVPS

Year	Babe Ruth Award	*SPORT* Magazine Award	Year	Babe Ruth Award	*SPORT* Magazine Award
1949	Joe Page, NY (AL)	—	1955	Johnny Podres, BRO (NL)	Johnny Podres, BRO (NL)
1950	Jerry Coleman, NY (AL)	—	1956	Don Larsen, NY (AL)	Don Larsen, NY (AL)
1951	Phil Rizzuto, NY (AL)	—	1957	Lew Burdette, MIL (NL)	Lew Burdette, MIL (NL)
1952	Johnny Mize, NY (AL)	—	1958	Elston Howard, NY (AL)	Bob Turley, NY (AL)
1953	Billy Martin, NY (AL)	—	1959	Larry Sherry, LA (NL)	Larry Sherry, LA (NL)
1954	Dusty Rhodes, NY (NL)	—	1960	Bill Mazeroski, PIT (NL)	Bobby Richardson, NY (AL)

WORLD SERIES MVPS

Year	Babe Ruth Award	SPORT Magazine Award	Year	Babe Ruth Award	SPORT Magazine Award
1961	Whitey Ford, NY (AL)	Whitey Ford, NY (AL)	1982	Bruce Sutter, STL (NL)	Darrell Porter, STL (NL)
1962	Ralph Terry, NY (AL)	Ralph Terry, NY (AL)	1983	Rick Dempsey, BAL (AL)	Rick Dempsey, BAL (AL)
1963	Sandy Koufax, LA (NL)	Sandy Koufax, LA (NL)	1984	Jack Morris, DET (AL)	Alan Trammell, DET (AL)
1964	Bob Gibson, STL (NL)	Bob Gibson, STL (NL)	1985	Bret Saberhagen, KC (AL)	Bret Saberhagen, KC (AL)
1965	Sandy Koufax, LA (NL)	Sandy Koufax, LA (NL)	1986	Ray Knight, NY (NL)	Ray Knight, NY (NL)
1966	Frank Robinson, BAL (AL)	Frank Robinson, BAL (AL)	1987	Frank Viola, MIN (AL)	Frank Viola, MIN (AL)
1967	Lou Brock, STL (NL)	Bob Gibson, STL (NL)	1988	Orel Hershiser, LA (NL)	Orel Hershiser, LA (NL)
1968	Mickey Lolich, DET (AL)	Mickey Lolich, DET (AL)	1989	Dave Stewart, OAK (AL)	Dave Stewart, OAK (AL)
1969	Al Weis, NY (NL)	Donn Clendenon, NY (NL)	1990	Billy Hatcher, CIN (NL)	Jose Rijo, CIN (NL)
1970	Brooks Robinson, BAL (AL)	Brooks Robinson, BAL (AL)	1991	Jack Morris, MIN (AL)	Jack Morris, MIN (AL)
1971	Roberto Clemente, PIT (NL)	Roberto Clemente, PIT (NL)	1992	Dave Winfield, TOR (AL)	Pat Borders, TOR (AL)
1972	Gene Tenace, OAK (AL)	Gene Tenace, OAK (AL)	1993	Paul Molitor, TOR (AL)	Paul Molitor, TOR (AL)
1973	Bert Campaneris, OAK (AL)	Reggie Jackson, OAK (AL)	1994	(No Series)	(No Series)
1974	Dick Green, OAK (AL)	Rollie Fingers, OAK (AL)	1995	Tom Glavine, ATL (NL)	Tom Glavine, ATL (NL)
1975	Luis Tiant, BOS (AL)	Pete Rose, CIN (NL)	1996	Cecil Fielder, NY (AL)	John Wetteland, NY (AL)
1976	Johnny Bench, CIN (NL)	Johnny Bench, CIN (NL)	1997	Moises Alou, FLA (NL)	Livan Hernandez, FLA (NL)
1977	Reggie Jackson, NY (AL)	Reggie Jackson, NY (AL)	1998	Scott Brosius, NY (AL)	Scott Brosius, NY (AL)
1978	Bucky Dent, NY (AL)	Bucky Dent, NY (AL)	1999	Mariano Rivera, NY (AL)	Mariano Rivera, NY (AL)
1979	Willie Stargell, PIT (NL)	Willie Stargell, PIT (NL)	2000	Derek Jeter, NY (AL)	Derek Jeter, NY (AL)
1980	Tug McGraw, PHI (NL)	Mike Schmidt, PHI (NL)	2001	Randy Johnson, ARI (NL)	Randy Johnson, ARI (NL),
1981	Ron Cey, LA (NL)	Ron Cey, LA (NL),			Curt Schilling, ARI (NL)
		Pedro Guerrero, LA (NL),	2002	David Eckstein, ANA (AL)	Troy Glaus, ANA (AL)
		Steve Yeager, LA (NL)	2003	Josh Beckett, FLA (NL)	Josh Beckett, FLA (NL)

The Fireman of the Year Award

The 1950s saw the birth of a statistic called the "save." Chicago writer Jerome Holtzman has been called the inventor, or "father" of the stat, but he never felt he deserved either title. "Three people were keeping track of saves before I came along in 1957: Irving Kaze at Pittsburgh, Jim Toomey at St. Louis and Allan Roth at Brooklyn. But, by their criteria, all a pitcher had to do was finish a winning game. What I did was develop a formula."

Holtzman's original definition of a save demanded that a reliever not only preserve someone else's victory, but face the potential tying or lead run during his tenure on the mound. Holtzman proposed to compile saves on a daily basis himself, reporting the results. He wrote to *The Sporting News* publisher J.G. Taylor Spink with his proposition, and was eventually rewarded with a "100 or 200 dollar bonus" and hired to keep track of the pen men. The result was the "Fireman of the Year Award," given annually since 1960, originally to the relief pitcher in each league with the highest combined total of wins and saves. The winner is now chosen by a consensus of *TSN*'s editors, and was renamed "Reliever of the Year" in 2001.

Saves were considered "a very minor stat," said Holtzman. "Nobody paid much attention at first." But, by 1969, the save had grown in importance to the point that the Rules Committee felt obliged to make it an official statistic, the first new one in nearly a half-century.

Following are *The Sporting News*' Firemen/Relievers of the Year:

THE FIREMAN OF THE YEAR AWARD

YEAR	NATIONAL LEAGUE				YEAR	AMERICAN LEAGUE		
1960	Lindy McDaniel, STL	1983	Al Holland, PHI,		1960	Mike Fornieles, BOS	1983	Dan Quisenberry, KC
1961	Stu Miller, SF		Lee Smith, CHI		1961	Luis Arroyo, NY	1984	Dan Quisenberry, KC
1962	Elroy Face, PIT	1984	Bruce Sutter, STL		1962	Dick Radatz, BOS	1985	Dan Quisenberry, KC
1963	Lindy McDaniel, CHI	1985	Jeff Reardon, MON		1963	Stu Miller, BAL	1986	Dave Righetti, NY
1964	Al McBean, PIT	1986	Todd Worrell, STL		1964	Dick Radatz, BOS	1987	Jeff Reardon, MIN,
1965	Ted Abernathy, CHI	1987	Steve Bedrosian, PHI		1965	Eddie Fisher, CHI		Dave Righetti, NY
1966	Phil Regan, LA	1988	John Franco, CIN		1966	Jack Aker, KC	1988	Dennis Eckersley, OAK
1967	Ted Abernathy, CIN	1989	Mark Davis, SD		1967	Minnie Rojas, CAL	1989	Jeff Russell, TEX
1968	Phil Regan, LA-CHI	1990	John Franco, NY		1968	Wilbur Wood, CHI	1990	Bobby Thigpen, CHI
1969	Wayne Granger, CIN	1991	Lee Smith, STL		1969	Ron Perranoski, MIN	1991	Dennis Eckersley, OAK,
1970	Wayne Granger, CIN	1992	Doug Jones, HOU,		1970	Ron Perranoski, MIN		Bryan Harvey, CAL
1971	Dave Giusti, PIT		Lee Smith, STL		1971	Ken Sanders, MIL	1992	Dennis Eckersley, OAK
1972	Clay Carroll, CIN	1993	Randy Myers, CHI		1972	Sparky Lyle, NY	1993	Jeff Montgomery, KC
1973	Mike Marshall, MON	1994	John Franco, NY		1973	John Hiller, DET	1994	Lee Smith, BAL
1974	Mike Marshall, LA	1995	Randy Myers, CHI		1974	Terry Forster, CHI	1995	Jose Mesa, CLE
1975	Al Hrabosky, STL	1996	Trevor Hoffman, SD		1975	Goose Gossage, CHI	1996	John Wetteland, NY
1976	Rawly Eastwick, CIN	1997	Jeff Shaw, CIN		1976	Bill Campbell, MIN	1997	Mariano Rivera, NY
1977	Rollie Fingers, SD	1998	Trevor Hoffman, SD		1977	Bill Campbell, BOS	1998	Tom Gordon, BOS
1978	Rollie Fingers, SD	1999	Ugueth Urbina, MON		1978	Goose Gossage, NY	1999	Mariano Rivera, NY
1979	Bruce Sutter, CHI	2000	Antonio Alfonseca, FLA		1979	Jim Kern, TEX,	2000	Todd Jones, DET
1980	Rollie Fingers, SD,	2001	Robb Nen, SF,			Mike Marshall, MIN	2001	Mariano Rivera, NY
	Tom Hume, CIN		Armando Benitez, NY		1980	Dan Quisenberry, KC	2002	Billy Koch, OAK
1981	Bruce Sutter, STL	2002	John Smoltz, ATL		1981	Rollie Fingers, MIL	2003	Keith Foulke, OAK
1982	Bruce Sutter, STL	2003	Eric Gagne, LA		1982	Dan Quisenberry, KC		

The Rolaids Relief Man Awards

New recognition for bullpen aces came in 1976, via a product that "spells relief." The American Chicle Group of the Warner-Lambert Company began sponsoring the "Rolaids Relief Man Awards" that year, identifying the top closers in each league with an arbitrary formula: double a pitcher's number of wins, plus double his number of saves, minus his loss total (algebraically, 2W + 2S - L). The formula would be amended in 1988, with the incorporation of "blown saves" (BS): 3S + 2W - 2L - 2 BS. The current formula adds what Rolaids calls "tough saves," awarding four points for each of those. Despite the cumbersome and seemingly random formulas, the first 36 winners of this award also earned *The Sporting News* "Fireman of the Year" (still based simply on W + S) citation.

The Rolaids people continue to expand the scope of their honors. In 1979 they named Hoyt Wilhelm for their first "Career Achievement Award"; Elroy Face (1980), Kent Tekulve (1989), and Jerome Holtzman (1993) followed in that distinction. In 1981 Rolaids began sponsoring awards for the National Association leagues, and a year later they started naming monthly winners at the big league level. In 1989 they presented their first "Reliever of the Decade" nomination to Jeff Reardon; and, in 1991 they recognized Reardon, Rollie Fingers, Lee Smith, Goose Gossage, and Bruce Sutter (since joined by several others) with the creation of the "Rolaids 300-Save Club."

Perhaps Rolaids' greatest contribution, besides the increased visibility and prestige they have provided bullpen stars, has been a new statistic. Talked about for years, "blown saves" in 1988 were finally defined and tabulated on a daily basis by the Rolaids statisticians. Whenever a reliever enters a game in a save situation, and leaves with that situation no longer in effect because he has given up the lead, he is charged with a blown save.

Rolaids selections which differed from the Firemen of the Year are Rod Beck (1994), Tom Henke (1995), Jeff Brantley (1996), and Billy Wagner (1999) in the National League, and Randy Myers (1997) in the American. Also, Jim Kern (AL, 1979), Rollie Fingers (NL, 1980), Al Holland (NL, 1983), Dave Righetti (AL, 1987), Bryan Harvey (AL, 1991), Lee Smith (NL, 1992), and Armando Benitez (NL, 2001), who were co-winners of the Fireman award, were sole winners of the Rolaids version.

The Major League Executive of the Year Award

The Major League Executive of the Year Award was instituted by *The Sporting News* in 1936. With one exception, winners have been affiliated with major league teams (1966 winner Lee MacPhail was an executive in the Office of the Commissioner). George Weiss won the award four times, Branch Rickey thrice and John Hart was the last executive to win it in consecutive years. Major league executives vote for the award.

MAJOR LEAGUE EXECUTIVE OF THE YEAR AWARD

YEAR	Winner, affiliation	YEAR	Winner, affiliation	YEAR	Winner, affiliation	YEAR	Winner, affiliation
1936	Branch Rickey, STL (N)	1953	Lou Perini, MIL (N)	1970	Harry Dalton, BAL (A)	1987	Al Rosen, SF (N)
1937	Ed Barrow, NY (A)	1954	Horace Stoneham, NY (N)	1971	Cedric Tallis, KC (A)	1988	Fred Claire, LA (N)
1938	Warren Giles, CIN (N)	1955	Walter O'Malley, BKN (N)	1972	Roland Hemond, CHI (A)	1989	Roland Hemond, BAL (A)
1939	Larry MacPhail, BKN (N)	1956	Gabe Paul, CIN (N)	1973	Bob Howsam, CIN (N)	1990	Bob Quinn, CIN (N)
1940	Walter Briggs Sr., DET (A)	1957	Frank Lane, STL (N)	1974	Gabe Paul, NY (A)	1991	Andy MacPhail, MIN (A)
1941	Ed Barrow, NY (A)	1958	Joe Brown, PIT (N)	1975	Dick O'Connell, BOS (A)	1992	Dan Duquette, MON (N)
1942	Branch Rickey, STL (N)	1959	Buzzie Bavasi, LA (N)	1976	Joe Burke, KC (A)	1993	Lee Thomas, PHI (N)
1943	Clark Griffith, WAS (A)	1960	George Weiss, NY (A)	1977	Bill Veeck, CHI (A)	1994	John Hart, CLE (A)
1944	Billy DeWitt, STL (A)	1961	Dan Topping, NY (A)	1978	Spec Richardson, SF (N)	1995	John Hart, CLE (A)
1945	Phil Wrigley, CHI (N)	1962	Fred Haney, LA (N)	1979	Hank Peters, BAL (A)	1996	Doug Melvin, TEX (A)
1946	Tom Yawkey, BOS (A)	1963	Bing Devine, STL (N)	1980	Tal Smith, HOU (N)	1997	Cam Bonifay, PIT (N)
1947	Branch Rickey, BKN (N)	1964	Bing Devine, STL (N)	1981	John McHale, MON (N)	1998	Gerry Hunsicker, HOU (N)
1948	Bill Veeck, CLE (A)	1965	Calvin Griffith, MIN (A)	1982	Harry Dalton, MIL (A)	1999	Billy Beane, OAK (A)
1949	Bob Carpenter, PHI (N)	1966	Lee MacPhail	1983	Hank Peters, BAL (A)	2000	Walt Jocketty, STL (N)
1950	George Weiss, NY (A)	1967	Dick O'Connell, BOS (A)	1984	Dallas Green, CHI (A)	2001	Pat Gillick, SEA
1951	George Weiss, NY (A)	1968	Jim Campbell, DET (A)	1985	John Schuerholz, KC (A)	2002	Terry Ryan, MIN
1952	George Weiss, NY (A)	1969	John Murphy, NY (N)	1986	Frank Cashen, NY (N)	2003	Brian Sabean, SF

The Manager of the Year Award

There are at least four different versions of the Manager of the Year Award, given by the Baseball Writers Association of America, *The Sporting News*, the Associated Press, and United Press International. Although it is the newest entry of the four, the BBWAA award (instituted in 1983) has come to be regarded as the most prestigious version. Following are the winners of the BBWAA Award for each league:

MANAGER OF THE YEAR AWARD

YEAR	NATIONAL LEAGUE	YEAR		YEAR	AMERICAN LEAGUE	YEAR	
1983	Tommy Lasorda, LA	1994	Felipe Alou, MON	1983	Tony LaRussa, CHI	1994	Buck Showalter, NY
1984	Jim Frey, CHI	1995	Don Baylor, COL	1984	Sparky Anderson, DET	1995	Lou Piniella, SEA
1985	Whitey Herzog, STL	1996	Bruce Bochy, SD	1985	Bobby Cox, TOR	1996	Johnny Oates, TEX
1986	Hal Lanier, HOU	1997	Dusty Baker, SF	1986	John McNamara, BOS		Joe Torre, NY
1987	Buck Rodgers, MON	1998	Larry Dierker, HOU	1987	Sparky Anderson, DET	1997	Davey Johnson, BAL
1988	Tommy Lasorda, LA	1999	Jack McKeon, CIN	1988	Tony LaRussa, OAK	1998	Joe Torre, NY
1989	Don Zimmer, CHI	2000	Dusty Baker, SF	1989	Frank Robinson, BAL	1999	Jimy Williams, BOS
1990	Jim Leyland, PIT	2001	Larry Bowa, PHI	1990	Jeff Torborg, CHI	2000	Jerry Manuel, CHI
1991	Bobby Cox, ATL	2002	Tony LaRussa, STL	1991	Tom Kelly, MIN	2001	Lou Piniella, SEA
1992	Jim Leyland, PIT	2003	Jack McKeon, FLA	1992	Tony La Russa, OAK	2002	Mike Scioscia, ANA
1993	Dusty Baker, SF			1993	Gene Lamont, CHI	2003	Tony Peña, KC

The Player and Pitcher of the Year Awards

The Sporting News first named a Most Valuable Player in 1929, filling a void left by the discontinuation of the American League Award, and polling the same voters as had participated in the 1928 version of that honor. After the National League Award was also discontinued a year later, *TSN* announced that, thereafter, they would take it upon themselves to conduct an annual poll to replace the League Awards. They originally retained the stipulation that each voter had to select just one player on each team.

TSN continued with its polls even after the Baseball Writers Association of America started the modern version of the MVP in 1931. Competition between the two awards became acrimonious, with *TSN* at first practically ignoring the BBWAA awards, and later publishing results with condescending statements like "merely confirming the choices made earlier by *The Sporting News*." Beginning in 1938, *TSN* agreed to unify the award, abiding by the BBWAA balloting and presenting "The Sporting News Trophy" to the win-

ners. Among the various gifts awarded to the MVPs were wristwatches and shotguns.

The BBWAA and *TSN* went their separate ways again in 1944. After the 1945 elections, at the request of new Commissioner Happy Chandler, *TSN* "withdrew from the field to cooperate in making the Landis Awards, provided by the major leagues, the official designations of the year." In 1948, however, *TSN* resumed its own awards, selecting a Player of the Year and Pitcher of the Year in each league.

TSN had also been naming a Major League Player of the Year since 1936. In 1992 the NL and AL Player of the Year Awards were supplanted by this honor, though a Pitcher of the Year was still selected in each league. It should be noted that the Major League Player of the Year, since 1992, has been picked by a vote of players, whereas the leagues' Pitchers of the Year are still chosen by *TSN*'s editors. Following are the winners of *The Sporting News* awards, with asterisks denoting the Major League Players of the Year:

PLAYER AND PITCHER OF THE YEAR AWARDS

NL Player of the Year
1929 —
1930 Bill Terry, NY
1931 Chuck Klein, PHI
1932 Chuck Klein, PHI
1933 —
1934 —
1935 Arky Vaughan, PIT
1936 —
1937 Joe Medwick, STL
1938 Ernie Lombardi, CIN
1939 —
1940 Frank McCormick, CIN
1941 Dolph Camilli, BKN
1942 —
1943 Stan Musial, STL
1944 Marty Marion, STL*
1945 Tommy Holmes, BOS
1946 Stan Musial, STL*
1947 —
1948 Stan Musial, STL
1949 Enos Slaughter, STL
1950 Ralph Kiner, PIT
1951 Stan Musial, STL*
1952 Hank Sauer, CHI
1953 Roy Campanella, BKN
1954 Willie Mays, NY*
1955 Duke Snider, BKN*
1956 Hank Aaron, MIL
1957 Stan Musial, STL
1958 Ernie Banks, CHI
1959 Ernie Banks, CHI
1960 Dick Groat, PIT
1961 Frank Robinson, CIN
1962 Maury Wills, LA*
1963 Hank Aaron, MIL
1964 Ken Boyer, STL*
1965 Willie Mays, SF
1966 Roberto Clemente, PIT
1967 Orlando Cepeda, STL
1968 Pete Rose, CIN
1969 Willie McCovey, SF*
1970 Johnny Bench, CIN*
1971 Joe Torre, STL*
1972 Billy Williams, CHI*
1973 Bobby Bonds, SF
1974 Lou Brock, STL*
1975 Joe Morgan, CIN*
1976 George Foster, CIN
1977 George Foster, CIN
1978 Dave Parker, PIT
1979 Keith Hernandez, STL
1980 Mike Schmidt, PHI
1981 Andre Dawson, MON
1982 Dale Murphy, ATL
1983 Dale Murphy, ATL
1984 Ryne Sandberg, CHI*

1985 Willie McGee, STL
1986 Mike Schmidt, PHI
1987 Andre Dawson, CHI
1988 Andy Van Slyke, PIT
1989 Kevin Mitchell, SF*
1990 Barry Bonds, PIT*
1991 Barry Bonds, PIT
1992 Gary Sheffield, SD*
1993 —
1994 Jeff Bagwell, HOU*
1995 —
1996 —
1997 —
1998 Sammy Sosa, CHI*
1999 —
2000 —
2001 Barry Bonds, SF*
2002 —
2003 Albert Pujols, STL*

NL Pitcher of the Year
1929 —
1930 —
1931 —
1932 —
1933 Carl Hubbell, NY
1934 Dizzy Dean, STL
1935 —
1936 Carl Hubbell, NY*
1937 —
1938 J. Vander Meer, CIN*
1939 Bucky Walters, CIN
1940 —
1941 —
1942 Mort Cooper, STL
1943 —
1944 Bill Voiselle, NY
1945 Hank Borowy, CHI
1946 —
1947 —
1948 Johnny Sain, BOS
1949 Howie Pollet, STL
1950 Jim Konstanty, PHI
1951 Preacher Roe, BKN
1952 Robin Roberts, PHI*
1953 Warren Spahn, MIL
1954 John Antonelli, NY
1955 Robin Roberts, PHI
1956 Don Newcombe, BKN
1957 Warren Spahn, MIL
1958 Warren Spahn, MIL
1959 Sam Jones, SF
1960 Vern Law, PIT
1961 Warren Spahn, MIL
1962 Don Drysdale, LA*
1963 Sandy Koufax, LA*
1964 Sandy Koufax, LA

1965 Sandy Koufax, LA*
1966 Sandy Koufax, LA
1967 Mike McCormick, SF
1968 Bob Gibson, STL
1969 Tom Seaver, NY
1970 Bob Gibson, STL
1971 Fergie Jenkins, CHI
1972 Steve Carlton, PHI
1973 Ron Bryant, SF
1974 Mike Marshall, LA
1975 Tom Seaver, NY
1976 Randy Jones, SD
1977 Steve Carlton, PHI
1978 Vida Blue, SF
1979 Joe Niekro, HOU
1980 Steve Carlton, PHI
1981 F. Valenzuela, LA*
1982 Steve Carlton, PHI
1983 John Denny, PHI
1984 Rick Sutcliffe, CHI
1985 Dwight Gooden, NY
1986 Mike Scott, HOU
1987 Rick Sutcliffe, CHI
1988 Orel Hershiser, LA*
1989 Mark Davis, SD
1990 Doug Drabek, PIT
1991 Tom Glavine, ATL
1992 Greg Maddux, CHI
1993 Greg Maddux, ATL
1994 Greg Maddux, ATL
1995 Greg Maddux, ATL
1996 John Smoltz, ATL
1997 Pedro Martinez, MON
1998 Kevin Brown, SD
1999 Mike Hampton, HOU
2000 Tom Glavine, ATL
2001 Curt Schilling, ARI
2002 Curt Schilling, ARI
2003 Eric Gagne, LA

AL Player of the Year
1929 Al Simmons, PHI
1930 Joe Cronin, WAS
1931 Lou Gehrig, NY
1932 Jimmie Foxx, PHI
1933 Jimmie Foxx, PHI
1934 Lou Gehrig, NY
1935 Hank Greenberg, DET
1936 Lou Gehrig, NY
1937 Charlie Gehringer, DET
1938 Jimmie Foxx, BOS
1939 Joe DiMaggio, NY*
1940 Hank Greenberg, DET
1941 Joe DiMaggio, NY
1942 Joe Gordon, NY
1943 —
1944 Bobby Doerr, BOS

1945 Eddie Mayo, DET
1946 —
1947 Ted Williams, BOS*
1948 Lou Boudreau, CLE*
1949 Ted Williams, BOS*
1950 Phil Rizzuto, NY*
1951 Ferris Fain, PHI
1952 Luke Easter, CLE
1953 Al Rosen, CLE*
1954 Bobby Avila, CLE
1955 Al Kaline, DET
1956 Mickey Mantle, NY*
1957 Ted Williams, BOS*
1958 Jackie Jensen, BOS
1959 Nellie Fox, CHI
1960 Roger Maris, NY
1961 Roger Maris, NY*
1962 Mickey Mantle, NY
1963 Al Kaline, DET
1964 Brooks Robinson, BAL
1965 Tony Oliva, MIN
1966 Frank Robinson, BAL*
1967 Carl Yastrzemski, BOS*
1968 Ken Harrelson, BOS
1969 Harmon Killebrew, MIN
1970 Harmon Killebrew, MIN
1971 Tony Oliva, MIN
1972 Dick Allen, CHI
1973 Reggie Jackson, OAK*
1974 Jeff Burroughs, TEX
1975 Fred Lynn, BOS
1976 Thurmon Munson, NY
1977 Rod Carew, MIN*
1978 Jim Rice, BOS
1979 Don Baylor, CAL
1980 George Brett, KC*
1981 Tony Armas, OAK
1982 Robin Yount, MIL*
1983 Cal Ripken, BAL*
1984 Don Mattingly, NY
1985 Don Mattingly, NY*
1986 Don Mattingly, NY
1987 George Bell, TOR*
1988 Jose Canseco, OAK
1989 Ruben Sierra, TEX
1990 Cecil Fielder, DET
1991 Cal Ripken, BAL*
1992 —
1993 Frank Thomas, CHI*
1994 —
1995 Albert Belle, CLE*
1996 Alex Rodriguez, SEA*
1997 Ken Griffey, Jr., SEA*
1998 —
1999 Rafael Palmeiro, TEX*
2000 Carlos Delgado, TOR*
2001 —

2002 Alex Rodriguez, TEX*
2003 —

AL Pitcher of the Year
1929 —
1930 —
1931 —
1932 —
1933 —
1934 —
1935 —
1936 —
1937 Johnny Allen, CLE*
1938 —
1939 —
1940 Bob Feller, CLE*
1941 —
1942 —
1943 Spud Chandler, NY*
1944 Hal Newhouser, DET
1945 Hal Newhouser, DET*
1946 —
1947 —
1948 Bob Lemon, CLE
1949 Ellis Kinder, BOS
1950 Bob Lemon, CLE
1951 Bob Feller, CLE
1952 Bobby Shantz, PHI
1953 Bob Porterfield, WAS
1954 Bob Lemon, CLE
1955 Whitey Ford, NY
1956 Billy Pierce, CHI
1957 Billy Pierce, CHI
1958 Bob Turley, NY*
1959 Early Wynn, CHI*
1960 Chuck Estrada, BAL
1961 Whitey Ford, NY
1962 Dick Donovan, CLE
1963 Whitey Ford, NY
1964 Dean Chance, LA
1965 Mudcat Grant, MIN
1966 Jim Kaat, MIN
1967 Jim Lonborg, BOS
1968 Denny McLain, DET*
1969 Denny McLain, DET
1970 Sam McDowell, CLE
1971 Vida Blue, OAK
1972 Wilbur Wood, CHI
1973 Jim Palmer, BAL
1974 Catfish Hunter, OAK
1975 Jim Palmer, BAL
1976 Jim Palmer, BAL
1977 Nolan Ryan, CAL
1978 Ron Guidry, NY*
1979 Mike Flanagan, BAL
1980 Steve Stone, BAL
1981 Jack Morris, DET

1982 Dave Stieb, TOR
1983 LaMarr Hoyt, CHI
1984 Willie Hernandez, DET
1985 Bret Saberhagen, KC
1986 Roger Clemens, BOS*
1987 Jimmy Key, TOR
1988 Frank Viola, MIN

1989 Bret Saberhagen, KC
1990 Bob Welch, OAK
1991 Roger Clemens, BOS
1992 Dennis Eckersley, OAK
1993 Jack McDowell, CHI
1994 Jimmy Key, NY
1995 Randy Johnson, SEA

1996 Pat Hentgen, TOR
1997 Roger Clemens, TOR
1998 Roger Clemens, TOR
1999 Pedro Martinez, BOS
2000 Pedro Martinez, BOS
2001 Roger Clemens, NY
2002 Barry Zito, OAK

2003 Roy Halladay, TOR

Note: The following players were named Major League Player of the Year although they did not receive nomination as their league's top player: Ted Williams (1941 and 1942), Bill Mazeroski (1960), Joe Morgan (1976), and Willie Stargell (1979).

The Rookie Player and Pitcher of the Year Awards

The Sporting News instituted its Rookie of the Year Awards in 1946, a year before the BBWAA version went national. In 1949, *TSN* began recognizing a winner from each league, and in 1957 they started (sporadically, at first) selecting both a Rookie Player and a Rookie Pitcher of the Year in each league. *TSN*'s editors select the honorees. Following are the winners:

THE ROOKIE PLAYER AND PITCHER OF THE YEAR AWARDS

NL Rookie Player of the Year
1946 Del Ennis, PHI
1947 Jackie Robinson, BKN
1948 Richie Ashburn, PHI
1949 —
1950 —
1951 Willie Mays, NY
1952 —
1953 Junior Gilliam, BKN
1954 Wally Moon, STL
1955 Bill Virdon, STL
1956 Frank Robinson, CIN
1957 Ed Bouchee, PHI
1958 Orlando Cepeda, SF
1959 Willie McCovey, SF
1960 Frank Howard, LA
1961 Billy Williams, CHI
1962 Ken Hubbs, CHI
1963 Pete Rose, CIN
1964 Richie Allen, PHI
1965 Joe Morgan, HOU
1966 Tommy Helms, CIN
1967 Lee May, CIN
1968 Johnny Bench, CIN
1969 Coco Laboy, MON
1970 Bernie Carbo, CIN
1971 Earl Williams, ATL
1972 Dave Rader, SF
1973 Gary Matthews, SF
1974 Greg Gross, HOU
1975 Gary Carter, MON
1976 Larry Herndon, SF
1977 Andre Dawson, MON
1978 Bob Horner, ATL
1979 Jeff Leonard, HOU
1980 Lonnie Smith, PHI
1981 Tim Raines, MON
1982 Johnny Ray, PIT
1983 Darryl Strawberry, NY
1984 Juan Samuel, PHI
1985 Vince Coleman, STL
1986 Robby Thompson, SF
1987 Benito Santiago, SD
1988 Mark Grace, CHI
1989 Jerome Walton, CHI
1990 Dave Justice, ATL
1991 Jeff Bagwell, HOU
1992 Eric Karros, LA
1993 Mike Piazza, LA
1994 Raul Mondesi, LA
1995 Chipper Jones, ATL
1996 Jason Kendall, PIT
1997 Scott Rolen, PHI
1998 Todd Helton, COL
1999 Preston Wilson, FLA
2000 Rafael Furcal, ATL
2001 Albert Pujols, STL
2002 Brad Wilkerson, MON
2003 Scott Podsednik, MIL

NL Rookie Pitcher of the Year
1946 —
1947 —
1948 —
1949 Don Newcombe, BKN
1950 —
1951 —
1952 Joe Black, BKN
1953 —
1954 —
1955 —
1956 —
1957 Jack Sanford, PHI
1958 Carlton Willey, MIL
1959 —
1960 —
1961 Ken Hunt, CIN
1962 —
1963 Ray Culp, PHI
1964 Bill McCool, CIN
1965 Frank Linzy, SF
1966 Don Sutton, LA
1967 Dick Hughes, STL
1968 Jerry Koosman, NY
1969 Tom Griffin, HOU
1970 Carl Morton, MON
1971 Reggie Cleveland, STL
1972 Jon Matlack, NY
1973 Steve Rogers, MON
1974 John D'Acquisto, SF
1975 John Montefusco, SF
1976 Butch Metzger, SD
1977 Bob Owchinko, SD
1978 Don Robinson, PIT
1979 Rick Sutcliffe, LA
1980 Bill Gullickson, MON
1981 F. Valenzuela, LA
1982 Steve Bedrosian, ATL
1983 Craig McMurtry, ATL
1984 Dwight Gooden, NY
1985 Tom Browning, CIN
1986 Todd Worrell, STL
1987 Mike Dunne, PIT
1988 Tim Belcher, LA
1989 Andy Benes, SD
1990 Mike Harkey, CHI
1991 Al Osuna, HOU
1992 Tim Wakefield, PIT
1993 Kirk Rueter, MON
1994 Steve Trachsel, CHI
1995 Hideo Nomo, LA
1996 Alan Benes, STL
1997 Matt Morris, STL
1998 Kerry Wood, CHI
1999 Scott Williamson, CIN
2000 Rick Ankiel, STL
2001 Roy Oswalt, HOU
2002 Jason Jennings, COL
2003 Dontrelle Willis, FLA

AL Rookie Player of the Year
1946 —
1947 —
1948 —
1949 Roy Sievers, STL
1950 —
1951 Minnie Minoso, CHI
1952 Clint Courtney, STL
1953 Harvey Kuenn, DET
1954 —
1955 —
1956 Luis Aparicio, CHI
1957 Tony Kubek, NY
1958 Albie Pearson, WAS
1959 Bob Allison, WAS
1960 Ron Hansen, BAL
1961 Dick Howser, KC
1962 Tom Tresh, NY
1963 Pete Ward, CHI
1964 Tony Oliva, MIN
1965 Curt Blefary, BAL
1966 Tommie Agee, CHI
1967 Rod Carew, MIN
1968 Del Unser, WAS
1969 Carlos May, CHI
1970 Roy Foster, CLE
1971 Chris Chambliss, CLE
1972 Carlton Fisk, BOS
1973 Al Bumbry, BAL
1974 Mike Hargrove, TEX
1975 Fred Lynn, BOS
1976 Butch Wynegar, MIN
1977 Mitchell Page, OAK
1978 Paul Molitor, MIL
1979 Pat Putnam, TEX
1980 Joe Charboneau, CLE
1981 Rich Gedman, BOS
1982 Cal Ripken, BAL
1983 Ron Kittle, CHI
1984 Alvin Davis, SEA
1985 Ozzie Guillen, CHI
1986 Jose Canseco, OAK
1987 Mark McGwire, OAK
1988 Walt Weiss, OAK
1989 Craig Worthington, BAL
1990 Sandy Alomar, Jr., CLE
1991 Chuck Knoblauch, MIN
1992 Pat Listach, MIL
1993 Tim Salmon, CAL
1994 Bob Hamelin, KC
1995 Garret Anderson, CAL
1996 Derek Jeter, NY
1997 N. Garciaparra, BOS
1998 Ben Grieve, OAK
1999 Carlos Beltran, KC
2000 Mark Quinn, KC
2001 Ichiro Suzuki, SEA
2002 Eric Hinske, TOR
2003 Jody Gerut, CLE

AL Rookie Pitcher of the Year
1946 —
1947 —
1948 —
1949 —
1950 Whitey Ford, NY
1951 —
1952 —
1953 —
1954 Bob Grim, NY
1955 Herb Score, CLE
1956 —
1957 —
1958 Ryne Duren, NY
1959 —
1960 —
1961 Don Schwall, BOS
1962 —
1963 Gary Peters, CHI
1964 Wally Bunker, BAL
1965 Marcelino Lopez, CAL
1966 Jim Nash, KC
1967 Tom Phoebus, BAL
1968 Stan Bahnsen, NY
1969 Mike Nagy, BOS
1970 Bert Blyleven, MIN
1971 Bill Parsons, MIL
1972 Dick Tidrow, CLE
1973 Steve Busby, KC
1974 Frank Tanana, CAL
1975 Dennis Eckersley, CLE
1976 Mark Fidrych, DET
1977 Dave Rozema, DET
1978 Rich Gale, KC
1979 Mark Clear, CAL
1980 Britt Burns, CHI
1981 Dave Righetti, NY
1982 Ed Vande Berg, SEA
1983 Mike Boddicker, BAL
1984 Mark Langston, SEA
1985 Ted Higuera, MIL
1986 Mark Eichhorn, TOR
1987 Mike Henneman, DET
1988 Bryan Harvey, CAL
1989 Tom Gordon, KC
1990 Kevin Appier, KC
1991 Juan Guzman, TOR
1992 Cal Eldred, MIL
1993 Aaron Sele, BOS
1994 Brady Anderson, CAL
1995 Julian Tavarez, CLE
1996 James Baldwin, CHI
1997 Jason Dickson, ANA
1998 Rolando Arrojo, TB
1999 Tim Hudson, OAK
2000 Kazuhiro Sasaki, SEA
2001 C.C. Sabathia, CLE
2002 Rodrigo Lopez, BAL
2003 Rafael Soriano, SEA

Other Awards

Of the awards not listed in this book, the one people most frequently ask about is the Comeback Player of the Year Award. Why don't we include it?

We would, if it were practical. There are at least four different decades-old versions of this award, given by the Baseball Writers Association of America, *The Sporting News*, the Associated Press, and United Press International (not to mention the Players' Choice Award). None has emerged as the "official" version, and our efforts to document the various versions have been mostly unsuccessful.

The Roberto Clemente Award

Under newcomer Bowie Kuhn in 1971, the Commissioner's Office created a new annual award—simply called the Commissioner's Award—honoring the player who best exemplified baseball on and off the field. Consideration was given to a player's sportsmanship, community involvement, and contribution to his team and baseball.

On March 12, 1973, the award was renamed for Roberto Clemente, the Pittsburgh star who had died 10 weeks earlier during a mercy mission.

This award is not to be confused with a host of others bearing the Hall of Famer's name, all of which appeared soon after his death.

The Pittsburgh chapter of the BBWAA instituted the Roberto Clemente Memorial Award, given to the outstanding Pirate each year. The city of Hialeah, Florida created the Roberto Clemente Humanitarian Award, given to a private citizen in that community who best exemplified Clemente's humanitarian virtues. A third Clemente Award honored the top Latin-American player in the majors.

The Clemente Award given by the Commissioner's Office is selected by a panel of baseball executives and media personnel. It is currently sponsored by True Value, which presents some $175,000 to charities each year in conjunction with the award. Following is a list of the winners:

THE ROBERTO CLEMENTE AWARD

1971 Willie Mays	1978 Greg Luzinski	1985 Don Baylor	1992 Cal Ripken	1999 Tony Gwynn
1972 Brooks Robinson	1979 Andre Thornton	1986 Garry Maddox	1993 Barry Larkin	2000 Al Leiter
1973 Al Kaline	1980 Phil Niekro	1987 Rick Sutcliffe	1994 Dave Winfield	2001 Curt Schilling
1974 Willie Stargell	1981 Steve Garvey	1988 Dale Murphy	1995 Ozzie Smith	2002 Jim Thome
1975 Lou Brock	1982 Ken Singleton	1989 Gary Carter	1996 Kirby Puckett	2003 Jamie Moyer
1976 Pete Rose	1983 Cecil Cooper	1990 Dave Stewart	1997 Eric Davis	
1977 Rod Carew	1984 Ron Guidry	1991 Harold Reynolds	1998 Sammy Sosa	

The Ford C. Frick Award

The Ford C. Frick Award was established in 1978, and goes to a broadcaster for "major contributions to baseball." Frick, who died on April 8 of that year, had done some broadcasting early in his career, though he was better-known for his roles as NL president and baseball commissioner.

Winners of the Frick Award are selected by a panel of baseball executives and media personnel, and are honored during the annual Hall of Fame induction ceremonies. Contrary to popular belief, however, the award-winners are not members of the Baseball Hall of Fame; there is no "Broadcasters' Wing" at the Hall. As with the Spink Award, a list of the Frick honorees is displayed in the Cooperstown museum's "Scribes and Mike-Men" exhibit.

Following are the winners of the Ford C. Frick Award:

THE FORD C. FRICK AWARD

1978 Mel Allen, Red Barber	1984 Curt Gowdy	1990 By Saam	1996 Herb Carneal	2002 Harry Kalas
1979 Bob Elson	1985 Buck Canel	1991 Joe Garagiola	1997 Jimmy Dudley	2003 Bob Uecker
1980 Russ Hodges	1986 Bob Prince	1992 Milo Hamilton	1998 Jaime Jarrin	
1981 Ernie Harwell	1987 Jack Buck	1993 Chuck Thompson	1999 Arch McDonald	
1982 Vin Scully	1988 Lindsey Nelson	1994 Bob Murphy	2000 Marty Brennaman	
1983 Jack Brickhouse	1989 Harry Caray	1995 Bob Wolff	2001 Rafael "Felo" Ramirez	

The Lou Gehrig Memorial Award

The Lou Gehrig Memorial Award was established by Gehrig's college fraternity in 1955. It is administered by the fraternity's national headquarters in Oxford, Ohio. Its plaque, which resides at the Baseball Hall of Fame in Cooperstown, N.Y., describes the award as follows:

"Presented annually to the major league baseball player who both on and off the field best exemplifies the character of Lou Gehrig, Columbia University '25, who played in 2,164 games as a member of the New York American League Baseball Club. Dedicated by his brothers of Phi Delta Theta." The award is announced each spring.

Following are the winners of the Lou Gehrig Award:

THE LOU GEHRIG MEMORIAL AWARD

1955 Alvin Dark	1965 Vernon Law	1975 Johnny Bench	1985 Dale Murphy	1995 Curt Schilling
1956 Pee Wee Reese	1966 Brooks Robinson	1976 Don Sutton	1986 George Brett	1996 Brett Butler
1957 Stan Musial	1967 Ernie Banks	1977 Lou Brock	1987 Rick Sutcliffe	1997 Paul Molitor
1958 Gil McDougald	1968 Al Kaline	1978 Don Kessinger	1988 Buddy Bell	1998 Tony Gwynn
1959 Gil Hodges	1969 Pete Rose	1979 Phil Niekro	1989 Ozzie Smith	1999 Mark McGwire
1960 Dick Groat	1970 Hank Aaron	1980 Tony Perez	1990 Glenn Davis	2000 Todd Stottlemyre
1961 Warren Spahn	1971 Harmon Killebrew	1981 Tommy John	1991 Kent Hrbek	2001 John Franco
1962 Robin Roberts	1972 Wes Parker	1982 Ron Cey	1992 Cal Ripken, Jr.	2002 Danny Graves
1963 Bobby Richardson	1973 Ron Santo	1983 Mike Schmidt	1993 Don Mattingly	
1964 Ken Boyer	1974 Willie Stargell	1984 Steve Garvey	1994 Barry Larkin	

The Fred Hutchinson Memorial Award

Reds' manager Fred Hutchinson died November 12, 1964, at age 45. He had been a well-respected major league pitcher and manager for most of a quarter-century, before losing a courageous battle with cancer (diagnosed by his brother, Dr. William B. Hutchinson). Five of Fred's friends in the media—Ritter Collett, Jim Enright, Joe McGuff, Ernie Harwell, and Bob Prince—sought to keep his name alive by creating the Fred Hutchinson Memorial Award. They raised money from various celebrities, mostly baseball executives and media personnel, and incorporated the project.

The Hutch Award is presented annually to a major leaguer who "best exemplifies the character, dedication and competitive spirit" of the late manager. Consideration is given to players who overcome major physical adversity, and show dedication to their team, community and family. Winners receive a bronzed engraving of Hutchinson encased in a glass frame.

Concurrent with this presentation, a sister award is given—in the way of a scholarship—to a young medical student involved in cancer research. This selection was coordinated by Dr. Hutchinson from the Fred Hutchinson Cancer Center in Seattle (established in 1975).

Ritter Collett ran the award's business operations from his home address in Dayton, Ohio, until 1994, by which time only three of its five founders were still alive. That year, the award's administration was turned over to the Seattle Mariners in conjunction with the *Seattle Post-Intelligencer* and the Hutchinson Cancer Center.

Voting for the Hutch Award is done by a panel of baseball writers and broadcasters. Following is a list of the winners:

THE FRED HUTCHINSON MEMORIAL AWARD

1965 Mickey Mantle	1973 John Hiller	1981 Johnny Bench	1989 Dave Dravecky	1997 Eric Davis
1966 Sandy Koufax	1974 Danny Thompson	1982 Andre Thornton	1990 Sid Bream	1998 David Cone
1967 Carl Yastrzemski	1975 Gary Nolan	1983 Ray Knight	1991 Bill Wegman	1999 Sean Casey
1968 Pete Rose	1976 Tommy John	1984 Don Robinson	1992 Carney Lansford	2000 Jason Giambi
1969 Al Kaline	1977 Willie McCovey	1985 Rick Reuschel	1993 John Olerud	2001 Curt Schilling
1970 Tony Conigliaro	1978 Willie Stargell	1986 Dennis Leonard	1994 Andre Dawson	2002 Tim Salmon
1971 Joe Torre	1979 Lou Brock	1987 Paul Molitor	1995 Jim Abbott	2003 Jamie Moyer
1972 Bobby Tolan	1980 George Brett	1988 Ron Oester	1996 Omar Vizquel	

The J.G. Taylor Spink Award

As early as 1944, the Baseball Hall of Fame's administrators suggested that some sort of "Roll of Honor," distinct from actual Hall of Fame induction, be established for distinguished baseball writers. Following the December 7, 1962 death of *The Sporting News*' long-time publisher, J. G. Taylor Spink, such an award was created. Spink was the first winner of the award bearing his name.

The Spink Award is given "for meritorious contributions to baseball writing." It is voted on by a committee of BBWAA members, and presented during the following year's Hall of Fame induction ceremony. Although the winners are often erroneously said to be "inducted into the Writers' Wing of the Hall of Fame," there is no such wing and these writers are not in fact members of the Hall. The museum's library does have an exhibit, called "Scribes and Mike-Men," which—among other things—lists winners of this award.

Following are winners of the Spink Award:

THE J. G. TAYLOR SPINK AWARD

1962 J. G. Taylor Spink	1973 Warren Brown,	1979 Bob Broeg,	1988 Bob Hunter,	1999 Hal Lebovitz
1963 Ring Lardner	John Drebinger,	Tommy Holmes	Ray Kelly	2000 Ross Newhan
1964 Hugh Fullerton	John F. Kieran	1980 Joe Reichler,	1989 Jerome Holtzman	2001 Joe Falls
1965 Charles Dryden	1974 John Carmichael,	Milton Richman	1990 Phil Collier	2002 Hal McCoy
1966 Grantland Rice	James Isaminger	1981 Bob Addie,	1991 Ritter Collett	2003 Murray Chass
1967 Damon Runyon	1975 Tom Meany,	Allen Lewis	1992 Bus Saidt,	
1968 H. G. Salsinger	Shirley Povich	1982 Si Burick	Leonard Koppett	
1969 Sid Mercer	1976 Harold Kaese,	1983 Ken Smith	1993 John Wendell Smith	
1970 Heywood C. Broun	Red Smith	1984 Joe McGuff	1994 (No honoree)	
1971 Frank Graham,	1977 Gordon Cobbledick,	1985 Earl Lawson	1995 Joseph Durso	
Dan Daniel	Edgar Munzel	1986 Jack Lang	1996 Charlie Feeney	
1972 Fred Lieb,	1978 Tim Murnane,	1987 Jim Murray	1997 Sam Lacy	
J. Roy Stockton	Dick Young		1998 Bob Stevens	

The S. Rae Hickok Professional Athlete of the Year Award

The S. Rae Hickok Professional Athlete of the Year Award—better-known as the Hickok belt—was presented by the Kickik Manufacturing Company of Arlington, Texas, beginning in 1950. The trophy was a large belt of gold and jewelry, reportedly worth $30,000 in 1976, the last year the award was given.

Voting was done each month by several hundred newspaper sports editors nationwide. The 12 monthly winners then competed for the annual prize. Of the 27 annual winners, 15—including two-time winner Sandy Koufax—were from major league baseball. A list of those players follows:

THE S. RAE HICKOK PROFESSIONAL ATHLETE OF THE YEAR AWARD

1950 Phil Rizzuto	1958 Bob Turley	1965 Sandy Koufax	1969 Tom Seaver
1951 Allie Reynolds	1961 Roger Maris	1966 Frank Robinson	1972 Steve Carlton
1954 Willie Mays	1962 Maury Wills	1967 Carl Yastrzemski	1975 Pete Rose
1956 Mickey Mantle	1963 Sandy Koufax	1970 Brooks Robinson	

Chapter 41

Immortals of the Game: The National Baseball Hall of Fame

By Bill Deane

In the 1930s plans were being made to celebrate base-ball's 100th anniversary. (The year of the centennial was based on the findings of the Mills Commission three decades earlier, which erroneously concluded that the rules of the game had been devised by Abner Doubleday at Cooperstown, New York, in 1839.) A small-scale baseball museum had been established in Cooperstown to display artifacts and, as part of the centennial celebration, a pro-posal was made to establish a Hall of Fame to immortalize the game's stars. Thus, six baseball bigwigs ordered the first Hall of Fame election. On January 29, 1936, the results of this election were announced, with five immortals—Ty Cobb, Babe Ruth, Honus Wagner, Walter Johnson and Christy Mathewson—qualifying for enshrinement, although formal induction was delayed until the opening of the Hall on June 12, 1939.

Actually, there were two elections in 1936: one a poll of 226 members of the BBWAA, and the other held by a spe-cial veterans' committee of 78 designed to choose from among "old-timers." No specific guidelines were set as to who was eligible for consideration (several active players received strong support), nor to which committee would consider whom (resulting in Cy Young's split vote: 49 per-cent in the writers' election, 41 percent in the veterans'). A 75 percent majority was necessary for election by either committee, a voting feature which survives.

Elections were held by both the BBWAA and an old-timers' committee for each of the next three years, resulting in a total of 26 inductees in 1939 when The National Baseball Hall of Fame and Museum was officially dedicated. Eleven of the inductees were still living; and all of them journeyed to Cooperstown to attend the centennial cele-bration. After that, BBWAA elections were scheduled at three-year intervals, with only one player elected in 1942 and none in 1945. A decision was made to hold annual elections beginning in 1946. This continued through 1956, when it was decided to hold elections only every other year. Annual elections were resumed a decade later and continue to this day.

A nominating system was installed after the 1945 elec-tion, providing for the top 20 vote-getters in preliminary balloting to be listed alphabetically on a second and final ballot. The preliminary election's vote totals were not to be divulged until after the final balloting (so as not to influence voters), nor would they assure anyone of automatic election. However, this system proved an utter failure in 1946 and was amended in December of that year. Thereafter, anyone receiving 75 percent of the votes on the nominating ballots would be automatically elected, eliminating the runoff election.

Gary Carter and Eddie Murray
The National Baseball Hall of Fame enshrined Carter and Murray at its induction ceremonies in Cooperstown in July 2003.

No runoff was required until 1949, when Charlie Gehringer was elected on the second ballot. The nominating system was dis-continued after that year but revived in 1960-68 (providing for reconsideration of the top 30 votegetters), being put into practice in 1964 and 1967.

Currently, an eligible candidate must have played at least 10 seasons in the majors and been active at some point during a period beginning 20 years and ending 5 years before a given election (the former rule has been ignored in some recent cases). The five-year-

wait rule was first implemented in 1954 (excepting candidates who had already received 100 or more votes in a previous election); a one-year wait had been in effect from 1946 to 1953, and no wait was specified before then (due to World War II, it was sometimes unclear who was still "active"). At the other end of the span, the 20-year rule has been in effect since 1962; the cutoff was 30 years in 1956-62, and 25 years in 1946-56.

Following Roberto Clemente's tragic death, a rule was passed in 1973 providing for the immediate consideration of an eligible candidate who dies while still active, or before the five-year waiting period has elapsed. Clemente was inducted overwhelmingly (393 of 424 votes) in a special election held that March. A few months later, the new rule was amended to allow consideration at least six months after a player's death (or five years after his retirement, whichever is less).

The "Pete Rose Rule" was added to the regulations in February 1991: "Any player on baseball's ineligible list shall not be an eligible candidate." Many members of the BBWAA, in protest of the rule, cast write-in votes for Rose: 41 in 1992 and 14 in 1993. The BBWAA stopped reporting the scofflaw votes after that, but we know there were 19 in 1994 and 17 in 2000, and probably a like number in the intervening years. Of course, the votes didn't really count, since Rose was ineligible; thus, we don't list them in the charts that follow this chapter.

Ten-year active and honorary members of the BBWAA are eligible to vote in the annual election (the 10-year restriction was installed in 1947). About 500 writers submit ballots each year, voting for up to 10 eligible candidates apiece. At various times over the past three decades, it has been suggested that the enfranchisement be limited to a few dozen of the top baseball writers.

A candidate Screening Committee was first employed in 1968, limiting the ballot to 40 candidates. Standards were relaxed somewhat after former pitcher Milt Pappas vociferously objected to his elimination by this committee (Pappas was allowed on the ballot in 1979, receiving 5 of 432 votes). Nomination by two of the six members of the Screening Committee now ensures a candidate at least one try on the BBWAA ballot; however, if he receives less than 5 percent of the vote, he is eliminated from future consideration. (Fortunately for many, this rule has not always been existent; more than 70 current Hall of Famers received less than 5 percent of the vote in their first tries!)

The Baseball Hall of Fame Committee on Baseball Veterans was established in July 1953. Previously, special old-timers' committees had elected new members in 1936-39, 1944-46, and 1949.

The new committee was composed of 11 members. This number was increased to 12 in 1960, 18 in 1979, and 20 in 1987; then it was reduced to 18 in 1988 and 15 in 1996. Elections were held every other year at first, but have been held annually since 1961.

In most years the committee has been limited to naming no more than two new inductees per election. Exceptions occurred in the elections of 1953 (six), 1963 (four), 1964 (six), 1970 (three), 1971 (seven), and 1972-77 (three each). Two additional slots opened for 1995-2001, one for 19th century players, the other for Negro Leaguers. Voting details were not released to the public.

A new system was instituted following the 2001 election, and started in 2003. The Veterans' Committee is now composed of living members of the Baseball Hall of Fame, and winners of the Spink and Frick Awards. Following lengthy screening processes, the committee votes by mail, much like the BBWAA. Elections are held every other year, with non-players voted on only every four years.

Individuals considered by the Veterans Committee include managers, umpires, executives, and certain players no longer eligible through the BBWAA (except members of the committee). For eligibility under the former three groups, a person must have been retired five years, or six months if he has reached the age of 65 (a rule tailor-made for Casey Stengel's election in 1966). For players, the minimum wait is 22 years; previously, it was 25 years (1953-56, 1974-84), 30 years (1957-62), 20 years (1963-73), or 23 years (1974-2001).

On June 10, 1971, a nine-member Baseball Hall of Fame Committee on Negro Baseball Leagues was established. Candidates were to have totaled at least ten years of service in the pre-1946 Negro Leagues and/or the major leagues, without being eligible for BBWAA election. A rule specified that the "Committee shall serve until it shall dissolve itself of its own motion or until further notice from the Board of Directors" of the Hall.

At least one new member was inducted by this committee in each year between 1971 and 1977, after which the committee dissolved and was absorbed into the Veterans Committee. Only two Negro League representatives were enshrined between 1978 and 1994.

There have been a total of 258 men named to the National Baseball Hall of Fame and Museum through 2004, including 193 major league players, 23 classified as pioneers or executives, 18 Negro Leaguers, 16 managers, and 8 umpires. (Many of the latter four groups also played in the majors or minors.)

What follows is, first, a roster of the 258 members of the Hall of Fame named between 1936 and 2004; second, an index of every man who ever received so much as a single vote for the Hall of Fame, detailing each man's total for each year he received support; and third, the top ten finishers in the voting for each year of BBWAA balloting since 1936. Men named to the Hall of Fame by special committee action, such as Alexander Cartwright or Josh Gibson, may not have received votes in an election, but they are included in this index as well. (There have been four such committee groupings: the Centennial Commission of 1937-1938, the Old Timers' Committee of 1939-1949, the Veterans Committee of 1953-present, and the Negro Leagues Committee of 1971-1977.)

Of special interest are some prominent players who were not elected or named to the Hall: Gil Hodges, who received the most cumulative votes for the Hall of Fame but remains outside it; Herman Long, who finished among the top ten vote-getters in the Veterans Ballot of 1936, which during later years produced 29 future Hall of Famers; Hank Gowdy, who in the 1950s experienced a fate similar to Long's; and Marty Marion and Allie Reynolds, other long-term vote-getters who were not able to bunch their support in a given year.

The Hall of Fame itself has undergone many renovations and improvements since 1939, most notable among them being the addition of the Hall of Fame Gallery in 1958 and The National Baseball Library in 1968. In 1994 a multi-million dollar expansion linked the library to the gallery and added additional media and movie exhibits.

The Hall of Fame is open year-round and annual attendance exceeds 300,000, twice topping 400,000. Inductions are held at ceremonies during the Hall of Fame weekend, which also includes a major league game at Doubleday Field, located on the former cow pasture that, for many years, was mistakenly believed to be the site of the first game.

HALL OF FAME ROSTER

FIRST BASEMEN
Anson, Cap
Beckley, Jake
Bottomley, Jim
Brouthers, Dan
Cepeda, Orlando
Chance, Frank
Connor, Roger
Foxx, Jimmie
Gehrig, Lou
Greenberg, Hank
Kelly, George
Killebrew, Harmon
McCovey, Willie
Mize, Johnny
Murray, Eddie
Perez, Tony
Sisler, George
Terry, Bill

SECOND BASEMEN
Carew, Rod
Collins, Eddie
Doerr, Bobby
Evers, Johnny
Fox, Nellie
Frisch, Frankie
Gehringer, Charlie
Herman, Billy
Hornsby, Rogers
Lajoie, Nap
Lazzeri, Tony
McPhee, Bid
Mazeroski, Bill
Morgan, Joe
Robinson, Jackie
Schoendienst, Red

SHORTSTOPS
Aparicio, Luis
Appling, Luke
Bancroft, Dave
Banks, Ernie
Boudreau, Lou
Cronin, Joe
Davis, George
Jackson, Travis
Jennings, Hughie

Maranville, Rabbit
Reese, Pee Wee
Rizzuto, Phil
Sewell, Joe
Smith, Ozzie
Tinker, Joe
Vaughan, Arky
Wagner, Honus
Wallace, Bobby
Ward, John
Yount, Robin

THIRD BASEMEN
Baker, Frank
Brett, George
Collins, Jimmy
Kell, George
Lindstrom, Fred
Mathews, Eddie
Robinson, Brooks
Schmidt, Mike
Traynor, Pie

LEFT FIELDERS
Brock, Lou
Burkett, Jesse
Clarke, Fred
Delahanty, Ed
Goslin, Goose
Hafey, Chick
Kelley, Joe
Kiner, Ralph
Manush, Heinie
Medwick, Joe
Musial, Stan
O'Rourke, Jim
Simmons, Al
Stargell, Willie
Wheat, Zack
Williams, Billy
Williams, Ted
Yastrzemski, Carl

CENTER FIELDERS
Ashburn, Richie
Averill, Earl
Carey, Max
Cobb, Ty

Combs, Earle
DiMaggio, Joe
Doby, Larry
Duffy, Hugh
Hamilton, Billy
Mantle, Mickey
Mays, Willie
Puckett, Kirby
Roush, Edd
Snider, Duke
Speaker, Tris
Waner, Lloyd
Wilson, Hack

RIGHT FIELDERS
Aaron, Hank
Clemente, Roberto
Crawford, Sam
Cuyler, Kiki
Flick, Elmer
Heilmann, Harry
Hooper, Harry
Jackson, Reggie
Kaline, Al
Keeler, Willie
Kelly, King
Klein, Chuck
McCarthy, Tommy
Ott, Mel
Rice, Sam
Robinson, Frank
Ruth, Babe
Slaughter, Enos
Thompson, Sam
Waner, Paul
Winfield, Dave
Youngs, Ross

CATCHERS
Bench, Johnny
Berra, Yogi
Bresnahan, Roger
Campanella, Roy
Carter, Gary
Cochrane, Mickey
Dickey, Bill
Ewing, Buck
Ferrell, Rick

Fisk, Carlton
Hartnett, Gabby
Lombardi, Ernie
Schalk, Ray

PITCHERS
Alexander, Grover
Bender, Chief
Brown, Mordecai
Bunning, Jim
Carlton, Steve
Chesbro, Jack
Clarkson, John
Coveleski, Stan
Dean, Dizzy
Drysdale, Don
Eckersley, Dennis
Faber, Red
Feller, Bob
Fingers, Rollie
Ford, Whitey
Galvin, Pud
Gibson, Bob
Gomez, Lefty
Grimes, Burleigh
Grove, Lefty
Haines, Jess
Hoyt, Waite
Hubbell, Carl
Hunter, Catfish
Jenkins, Fergie
Johnson, Walter
Joss, Addie
Keefe, Tim
Koufax, Sandy
Lemon, Bob
Lyons, Ted
Marichal, Juan
Marquard, Rube
Mathewson, Christy
McGinnity, Joe
Newhouser, Hal
Nichols, Kid
Niekro, Phil
Palmer, Jim
Pennock, Herb
Perry, Gaylord
Plank, Eddie

Radbourn, Charles
Rixey, Eppa
Roberts, Robin
Ruffing, Red
Rusie, Amos
Ryan, Nolan
Seaver, Tom
Spahn, Warren
Sutton, Don
Vance, Dazzy
Waddell, Rube
Walsh, Ed
Welch, Mickey
Wilhelm, Hoyt
Willis, Vic
Wynn, Early
Young, Cy

DESIGNATED HITTERS
Molitor, Paul

FROM NEGRO LEAGUES
Bell, Cool Papa
Charleston, Oscar
Dandridge, Ray
Day, Leon
Dihigo, Martin
Foster, Willie
Foster, Rube
Gibson, Josh
Irvin, Monte
Johnson, Judy
Leonard, Buck
Lloyd, John Henry
Paige, Satchel
Rogan, Bullet Joe
Smith, Hilton
Stearnes, Turkey
Wells, Willie
Williams, Smokey Joe

MANAGERS
Alston, Walter
Anderson, Sparky
Durocher, Leo
Hanlon, Ned

Harris, Bucky
Huggins, Miller
Lasorda, Tommy
Lopez, Al
Mack, Connie
McCarthy, Joe
McGraw, John
McKechnie, Bill
Robinson, Wilbert
Selee, Frank
Stengel, Casey
Weaver, Earl

UMPIRES
Barlick, Al
Chylak, Nestor
Conlan, Jocko
Connolly, Tom
Evans, Billy
Hubbard, Cal
Klem, Bill
McGowan, Bill

PIONEERS AND EXECUTIVES
Barrow, Ed
Bulkeley, Morgan
Cartwright, Alexander
Chadwick, Henry
Chandler, Happy
Comiskey, Charles
Cummings, Candy
Frick, Ford
Giles, Warren
Griffith, Clark
Harridge, Will
Hulbert, William
Johnson, Ban
Landis, Kenesaw
MacPhail, Larry
MacPhail, Lee
Rickey, Branch
Spalding, Al
Veeck, Bill
Weiss, George
Wright, George
Wright, Harry
Yawkey, Tom

HALL OF FAME BALLOTING: TOP 10 CANDIDATES IN EACH ELECTION

1936 Veterans
Needed to Elect: 59
Cap Anson	40
Buck Ewing	40
Willie Keeler	33
Cy Young	32
Ed Delahanty	22
John McGraw	17
Herman Long	16
Charlie Radbourn	16
Mike Kelly	15
Amos Rusie	12

1936
Needed to Elect: 170
Ty Cobb	222
Babe Ruth	215
Honus Wagner	215
Christy Mathewson	205
Walter Johnson	189
Nap Lajoie	146
Tris Speaker	133
Cy Young	111
Rogers Hornsby	105
Mickey Cochrane	80

1937
Needed to Elect: 151
Nap Lajoie	168
Tris Speaker	165
Cy Young	153
Grover Alexander	125

Eddie Collins	115
Willie Keeler	115
George Sisler	106
Ed Delahanty	70
Rube Waddell	67
Jimmy Collins	66

1938
Needed to Elect: 197
Grover Alexander	212
George Sisler	179
Willie Keeler	177
Eddie Collins	175
Rube Waddell	148
Frank Chance	133
Ed Delahanty	132
Ed Walsh	110
Johnny Evers	91
Jimmy Collins	79

1939
Needed to Elect: 206
George Sisler	235
Eddie Collins	213
Willie Keeler	207
Rube Waddell	179
Rogers Hornsby	176
Frank Chance	158
Ed Delahanty	145
Ed Walsh	132
Johnny Evers	107
Miller Huggins	97

1942
Needed to Elect: 175
Rogers Hornsby	182
Frank Chance	136
Rube Waddell	126
Ed Walsh	113
Miller Huggins	111
Ed Delahanty	104
Johnny Evers	91
Wilbert Robinson	89
Mickey Cochrane	88
Frankie Frisch	84

1945
Needed to Elect: 186
Frank Chance	179
Rube Waddell	154
Ed Walsh	137
Johnny Evers	134
Roger Bresnahan	133
Miller Huggins	133
Mickey Cochrane	125
Jimmy Collins	121
Ed Delahanty	111
Clark Griffith	108

1946 Nominating
Total Voting: 202
Frank Chance	144
Johnny Evers	130
Miller Huggins	129
Rube Waddell	122

Ed Walsh	115
Frankie Frisch	104
Carl Hubbell	101
Mickey Cochrane	80
Clark Griffith	73
Lefty Grove	71

1946
Needed to Elect: 198
Frank Chance	150
Johnny Evers	110
Miller Huggins	106
Ed Walsh	106
Rube Waddell	87
Clark Griffith	82
Carl Hubbell	75
Frankie Frisch	67
Mickey Cochrane	65
Lefty Grove	61

1947
Needed to Elect: 121
Carl Hubbell	140
Frankie Frisch	136
Mickey Cochrane	128
Lefty Grove	123
Pie Traynor	119
Charlie Gehringer	105
Rabbit Maranville	91
Dizzy Dean	88
Herb Pennock	86
Chief Bender	72

1948
Needed to Elect: 91
Herb Pennock	94
Pie Traynor	93
Al Simmons	60
Charlie Gehringer	52
Bill Terry	52
Paul Waner	51
Jimmie Foxx	50
Dizzy Dean	40
Harry Heilmann	40
Bill Dickey	39

1949
Needed to Elect: 115
Charlie Gehringer	102
Mel Ott	94
Al Simmons	89
Dizzy Dean	88
Jimmie Foxx	85
Bill Terry	81
Paul Waner	73
Hank Greenberg	67
Bill Dickey	65
Harry Heilmann	59

1949 Run Off
Needed to Elect: 141
One Player Maximum
Charlie Gehringer	159
Mel Ott	128
Jimmie Foxx	89

Dizzy Dean	81
Al Simmons	76
Paul Waner	63
Harry Heilmann	52
Bill Terry	48
Hank Greenberg	44
Bill Dickey	39
Rabbit Maranville	39

1950
Needed to Elect: 126
Mel Ott	115
Bill Terry	105
Jimmie Foxx	103
Paul Waner	95
Al Simmons	90
Harry Heilmann	87
Dizzy Dean	85
Bill Dickey	78
Rabbit Maranville	66
Hank Greenberg	64

1951
Needed to Elect: 170
Mel Ott	197
Jimmie Foxx	179
Paul Waner	162
Harry Heilmann	153
Bill Terry	148
Dizzy Dean	145
Bill Dickey	118
Al Simmons	116

Rabbit Maranville	110
Ted Lyons	71

1952
Needed to Elect: 176

Harry Heilmann	203
Paul Waner	195
Bill Terry	155
Dizzy Dean	152
Al Simmons	141
Bill Dickey	139
Rabbit Maranville	133
Dazzy Vance	105
Ted Lyons	101
Gabby Hartnett	77

1953
Needed to Elect: 198

Dizzy Dean	209
Al Simmons	199
Bill Terry	191
Bill Dickey	179
Rabbit Maranville	164
Dazzy Vance	150
Ted Lyons	139
Joe DiMaggio	117
Chief Bender	104
Gabby Hartnett	104

1954
Needed to Elect: 189

Rabbit Maranville	209
Bill Dickey	202
Bill Terry	195
Joe DiMaggio	175
Ted Lyons	170
Dazzy Vance	158
Gabby Hartnett	151
Hank Greenberg	97
Joe Cronin	85
Max Carey	55

1955
Needed to Elect: 189

Joe DiMaggio	223
Ted Lyons	217
Dazzy Vance	205
Gabby Hartnett	195
Hank Greenberg	157
Joe Cronin	135
Max Carey	119
Ray Schalk	113
Edd Roush	97
Hank Gowdy	90

1956
Needed to Elect: 145

Hank Greenberg	164
Joe Cronin	152
Red Ruffing	97
Edd Roush	91
Lefty Gomez	89
Hack Wilson	74
Max Carey	65
Tony Lazzeri	64
Kiki Cuyler	55
Hank Gowdy	49

1958
Needed to Elect: 200

Max Carey	136
Edd Roush	112
Red Ruffing	99
Hack Wilson	94
Kiki Cuyler	90
Sam Rice	90
Tony Lazzeri	80
Luke Appling	77
Lefty Gomez	76
Burleigh Grimes	71

1960
Needed to Elect: 202

Edd Roush	146
Sam Rice	143
Eppa Rixey	142

Burleigh Grimes	92
Jim Bottomley	89
Red Ruffing	86
Red Faber	83
Luke Appling	72
Kiki Cuyler	72
Hack Wilson	72

1962
Needed to Elect: 120

Bob Feller	150
Jackie Robinson	124
Sam Rice	81
Red Ruffing	72
Eppa Rixey	49
Luke Appling	48
Phil Rizzuto	44
Burleigh Grimes	43
Hack Wilson	39
Ducky Medwick	34

1964
Needed to Elect: 151

Luke Appling	142
Red Ruffing	141
Roy Campanella	115
Ducky Medwick	108
Pee Wee Reese	73
Lou Boudreau	68
Al Lopez	57
Chuck Klein	56
Johnny Mize	54
Mel Harder	51
Johnny Vander Meer	51

1964 Run Off
Needed to Elect: 170
One Player Maximum

Luke Appling	189
Red Ruffing	184
Roy Campanella	138
Ducky Medwick	130
Pee Wee Reese	47
Lou Boudreau	43
Al Lopez	34
Johnny Vander Meer	20
Chuck Klein	18
Marty Marion	17

1966
Needed to Elect: 227

Ted Williams	282
Red Ruffing	208
Roy Campanella	197
Ducky Medwick	187
Lou Boudreau	115
Al Lopez	109
Enos Slaughter	100
Pee Wee Reese	95
Marty Marion	86
Johnny Mize	81

1967
Needed to Elect: 219

Ducky Medwick	212
Red Ruffing	212
Roy Campanella	204
Lou Boudreau	143
Ralph Kiner	124
Enos Slaughter	123
Al Lopez	114
Marty Marion	90
Johnny Mize	89
Pee Wee Reese	89

1967 Run Off
Needed to Elect: 230
One Player Maximum

Red Ruffing	266
Ducky Medwick	248
Roy Campanella	170
Lou Boudreau	68
Al Lopez	50
Enos Slaughter	48
Ralph Kiner	41
Johnny Vander Meer	35

Ernie Lombardi	25
Bucky Walters	24

1968
Needed to Elect: 213

Ducky Medwick	240
Roy Campanella	205
Lou Boudreau	146
Enos Slaughter	129
Ralph Kiner	118
Johnny Mize	103
Allie Reynolds	95
Marty Marion	89
Arky Vaughan	82
Pee Wee Reese	81

1969
Needed to Elect: 255

Stan Musial	317
Roy Campanella	270
Lou Boudreau	218
Ralph Kiner	137
Enos Slaughter	128
Johnny Mize	116
Marty Marion	112
Allie Reynolds	98
Joe Gordon	97
Johnny Vander Meer	95
Early Wynn	95

1970
Needed to Elect: 225

Lou Boudreau	232
Ralph Kiner	167
Gil Hodges	145
Early Wynn	140
Enos Slaughter	133
Johnny Mize	126
Marty Marion	120
Pee Wee Reese	97
Red Schoendienst	97
George Kell	90

1971
Needed to Elect: 270

Yogi Berra	242
Early Wynn	240
Ralph Kiner	212
Gil Hodges	180
Enos Slaughter	165
Johnny Mize	157
Pee Wee Reese	127
Marty Marion	123
Red Schoendienst	123
Allie Reynolds	110

1972
Needed to Elect: 297

Sandy Koufax	344
Yogi Berra	339
Early Wynn	301
Ralph Kiner	235
Gil Hodges	161
Johnny Mize	157
Enos Slaughter	149
Pee Wee Reese	129
Marty Marion	120
Bob Lemon	117

1973
Needed to Elect: 285

Warren Spahn	316
Whitey Ford	255
Ralph Kiner	235
Gil Hodges	218
Robin Roberts	213
Bob Lemon	177
Johnny Mize	157
Enos Slaughter	145
Marty Marion	127
Pee Wee Reese	126

1974
Needed to Elect: 274

Mickey Mantle	322
Whitey Ford	284

Robin Roberts	224
Ralph Kiner	215
Gil Hodges	198
Bob Lemon	190
Enos Slaughter	145
Pee Wee Reese	141
Eddie Mathews	118
Phil Rizzuto	111
Duke Snider	111

1975
Needed to Elect: 272

Ralph Kiner	273
Robin Roberts	263
Bob Lemon	233
Gil Hodges	188
Enos Slaughter	177
Hal Newhouser	155
Pee Wee Reese	154
Eddie Mathews	148
Phil Cavarretta	129
Duke Snider	129

1976
Needed to Elect: 291

Robin Roberts	337
Bob Lemon	305
Gil Hodges	233
Enos Slaughter	197
Eddie Mathews	189
Pee Wee Reese	186
Nellie Fox	174
Duke Snider	159
Phil Rizzuto	149
George Kell	129
Red Schoendienst	129

1977
Needed to Elect: 288

Ernie Banks	321
Eddie Mathews	239
Gil Hodges	224
Enos Slaughter	222
Duke Snider	212
Don Drysdale	197
Pee Wee Reese	163
Nellie Fox	152
Jim Bunning	146
George Kell	141

1978
Needed to Elect: 285

Eddie Mathews	301
Enos Slaughter	261
Duke Snider	254
Gil Hodges	226
Don Drysdale	219
Jim Bunning	181
Pee Wee Reese	169
Richie Ashburn	158
Hoyt Wilhelm	158
Nellie Fox	149

1979
Needed to Elect: 324

Willie Mays	409
Duke Snider	308
Enos Slaughter	297
Gil Hodges	242
Don Drysdale	233
Nellie Fox	174
Hoyt Wilhelm	168
Maury Wills	166
Red Schoendienst	159
Jim Bunning	147

1980
Needed to Elect: 289

Al Kaline	340
Duke Snider	333
Don Drysdale	238
Gil Hodges	230
Hoyt Wilhelm	209
Jim Bunning	177
Red Schoendienst	164
Nellie Fox	161

Maury Wills	146
Richie Ashburn	134

1981
Needed to Elect: 301

Bob Gibson	337
Don Drysdale	243
Gil Hodges	241
Harmon Killebrew	239
Hoyt Wilhelm	238
Juan Marichal	233
Nellie Fox	168
Red Schoendienst	166
Jim Bunning	164
Maury Wills	163

1982
Needed to Elect: 312

Hank Aaron	406
Frank Robinson	370
Juan Marichal	305
Harmon Killebrew	246
Hoyt Wilhelm	236
Don Drysdale	233
Gil Hodges	205
Luis Aparicio	174
Jim Bunning	138
Red Schoendienst	135

1983
Needed to Elect: 281

Brooks Robinson	344
Juan Marichal	313
Harmon Killebrew	269
Luis Aparicio	252
Hoyt Wilhelm	243
Don Drysdale	242
Gil Hodges	237
Nellie Fox	173
Billy Williams	153
Red Schoendienst	146

1984
Needed to Elect: 303

Luis Aparicio	341
Harmon Killebrew	335
Don Drysdale	316
Hoyt Wilhelm	290
Nellie Fox	246
Billy Williams	202
Jim Bunning	201
Orlando Cepeda	124
Tony Oliva	124
Roger Maris	107

1985
Needed to Elect: 297

Hoyt Wilhelm	331
Lou Brock	315
Nellie Fox	295
Billy Williams	252
Jim Bunning	214
Catfish Hunter	212
Roger Maris	128
Harvey Kuenn	125
Orlando Cepeda	114
Tony Oliva	114

1986
Needed to Elect: 319

Willie McCovey	346
Billy Williams	315
Catfish Hunter	289
Jim Bunning	279
Roger Maris	177
Tony Oliva	154
Orlando Cepeda	152
Harvey Kuenn	144
Maury Wills	124
Bill Mazeroski	100

1987
Needed to Elect: 310

Billy Williams	354
Catfish Hunter	315
Jim Bunning	289

Orlando Cepeda	179
Roger Maris	176
Tony Oliva	160
Harvey Kuenn	144
Bill Mazeroski	125
Maury Wills	113
Ken Boyer	96
Lew Burdette	96

1988
Needed to Elect: 321

Willie Stargell	352
Jim Bunning	317
Tony Oliva	202
Orlando Cepeda	199
Roger Maris	184
Harvey Kuenn	168
Bill Mazeroski	143
Luis Tiant	132
Maury Wills	127
Ken Boyer	109
Mickey Lolich	109

1989
Needed to Elect: 336

Johnny Bench	431
Carl Yastrzemski	423
Gaylord Perry	304
Jim Bunning	283
Fergie Jenkins	234
Orlando Cepeda	176
Tony Oliva	135
Bill Mazeroski	134
Harvey Kuenn	115
Maury Wills	95

1990
Needed to Elect: 333

Jim Palmer	411
Joe Morgan	363
Gaylord Perry	320
Fergie Jenkins	296
Jim Bunning	257
Orlando Cepeda	211
Tony Oliva	142
Bill Mazeroski	131
Harvey Kuenn	107
Ron Santo	96

1991
Needed to Elect: 333

Rod Carew	401
Gaylord Perry	342
Fergie Jenkins	334
Rollie Fingers	291
Jim Bunning	282
Orlando Cepeda	192
Tony Oliva	160
Bill Mazeroski	142
Ron Santo	116
Harvey Kuenn	100

1992
Needed to Elect: 323

Tom Seaver	425
Rollie Fingers	349
Orlando Cepeda	246
Tony Perez	215
Bill Mazeroski	182
Tony Oliva	175
Ron Santo	136
Jim Kaat	114
Maury Wills	110
Ken Boyer	71

1993
Needed to Elect: 318

Reggie Jackson	396
Phil Niekro	278
Orlando Cepeda	252
Tony Perez	233
Steve Garvey	176
Tony Oliva	157
Ron Santo	155
Jim Kaat	125
Dick Allen	70
Ken Boyer	69

1994
Needed to Elect: 342

Steve Carlton	436
Orlando Cepeda	335
Phil Niekro	273
Tony Perez	263
Don Sutton	259
Steve Garvey	166
Tony Oliva	158
Ron Santo	150
Bruce Sutter	109
Jim Kaat	98

1995
Needed to Elect: 345

Mike Schmidt	444
Phil Niekro	286
Don Sutton	264
Tony Perez	259
Steve Garvey	196
Tony Oliva	149
Ron Santo	139
Jim Rice	137
Bruce Sutter	137
Jim Kaat	100

1996
Needed to Elect: 353

Phil Niekro	321
Tony Perez	309
Don Sutton	300
Steve Garvey	175
Ron Santo	174
Tony Oliva	170
Jim Rice	166
Bruce Sutter	137
Tommy John	102
Jim Kaat	91

1997
Needed to Elect: 355

Phil Niekro	380
Don Sutton	346
Tony Perez	312
Ron Santo	186
Jim Rice	178
Steve Garvey	167
Bruce Sutter	130
Jim Kaat	107
Joe Torre	105
Tommy John	97

1998
Needed to Elect: 355

Don Sutton	386
Tony Perez	321
Ron Santo	204
Jim Rice	203
Gary Carter	200
Steve Garvey	195
Bruce Sutter	147
Tommy John	129
Jim Kaat	129
Dave Parker	116

1999
Needed to Elect: 373

Nolan Ryan	491
George Brett	488
Robin Yount	385
Carlton Fisk	330
Tony Perez	302
Gary Carter	168
Steve Garvey	150
Jim Rice	146
Bruce Sutter	121
Jim Kaat	100

2000
Needed to Elect: 375

Carlton Fisk	397
Tony Perez	385
Jim Rice	257
Gary Carter	248
Bruce Sutter	192
Goose Gossage	166
Steve Garvey	160
Tommy John	135
Jim Kaat	125
Dale Murphy	116

2001
Needed to Elect: 387

Dave Winfield	435
Kirby Puckett	423
Gary Carter	334
Jim Rice	298
Bruce Sutter	245
Goose Gossage	228
Steve Garvey	176
Tommy John	146
Don Mattingly	145
Jim Kaat	139

2002
Needed to Elect: 372

Ozzie Smith	433
Gary Carter	343
Jim Rice	260
Bruce Sutter	238
Andre Dawson	214
Goose Gossage	203
Steve Garvey	134
Tommy John	127
Bert Blyleven	124
Jim Kaat	109

2003
Needed to Elect: 372

Eddie Murray	423
Gary Carter	387
Bruce Sutter	266
Jim Rice	259
Andre Dawson	248
Ryne Sandberg	244
Lee Smith	210
Goose Gossage	209
Bert Blyleven	145
Steve Garvey	138

2004
Needed to Elect: 380

Paul Molitor	431
Dennis Eckersley	421
Ryne Sandberg	309
Bruce Sutter	301
Jim Rice	276
Andre Dawson	253
Goose Gossage	206
Lee Smith	185
Bert Blyleven	179
Jack Morris	133

HALL OF FAME BALLOTING: VOTE TOTALS OF ALL CANDIDATES

Hank Aaron Inducted in 1982
1982 406

Babe Adams
1937 8
1938 11
1939 11
1942 11
1945 7
1946 NOM 6
1947 22
1948 4
1949 5
1950 6
1951 12
1952 9
1953 17
1954 13
1955 24

Sparky Adams
1958 1
1960 1

Bobby Adams
1966 1

Grover Alexander Inducted in 1938
1936 55
1937 125
1938 212

Dick Allen
1983 14
1985 28
1986 41
1987 55
1988 52
1989 35
1990 58
1991 59
1992 69
1993 70
1994 66
1995 72
1996 89
1997 79

Johnny Allen
1955 1

Felipe Alou
1980 3

Jesus Alou
1985 1

Matty Alou
1980 5

Walt Alston Inducted in 1983 Manager
1983 Vet. Com.

Nick Altrock
1937 3
1938 7
1939 6
1953 1
1954 2
1958 20
1960 18

Sparky Anderson Inducted in 2000 Manager
2000 Vet. Com.

Cap Anson Inducted in 1939
1936 V 40
1939 O/T Com.

Luis Aparicio Inducted in 1984
1979 120
1980 124
1981 48
1982 174
1983 252
1984 341

Luke Appling Inducted in 1964
1953 2
1955 3
1956 14
1958 77
1960 72
1962 48
1964 142
1964 RO 189

Jimmy Archer
1937 6
1938 7
1939 3

Richie Ashburn Inducted in 1995
1968 6
1969 10
1970 11
1971 10
1972 11
1973 25
1974 56
1975 76
1976 85
1977 139
1978 158
1979 130
1980 134
1981 142
1982 126
1995 Vet. Com.

Jimmy Austin
1958 1

Earl Averill Inducted in 1975
1949 1
1952 2
1955 2
1956 3
1958 14
1960 11
1962 3
1975 Vet. Com.

Bob Bailey
1984 1

Frank Baker Inducted in 1955
1936 1
1937 13
1938 32
1939 30
1942 39
1945 26
1946 NOM 39
1946 36
1947 49
1948 4
1950 4
1951 8
1955 Vet. Com.

Dusty Baker
1992 4

Dave Bancroft Inducted in 1971
1937 3
1938 2
1939 1
1946 NOM 1
1948 4
1949 5
1950 9
1951 9
1952 11
1953 10
1954 10
1955 19
1956 15
1958 43
1960 30
1971 Vet. Com.

Sal Bando
1987 3

Ernie Banks Inducted in 1977
1977 321

Al Barlick Inducted in 1989 Umpire
1989 Vet. Com.

Ross Barnes
1936 V 3

Ed Barrow Inducted in 1953 Executive
1953 Vet. Com.

Jack Barry
1938 3
1939 1

Dick Bartell
1948 1
1951 1
1958 1
1960 1

Joe Battin
1936 V 1

Hank Bauer
1967 23
1967 RO 9

Don Baylor
1994 12
1995 12

Ginger Beaumont
1938 1
1942 1
1945 1
1946 NOM 1

Glenn Beckert
1981 1

Jake Beckley Inducted in 1971
1936 V 1
1942 1
1971 Vet. Com.

Steve Bedrosian
2001 1

Mark Belanger
1988 16

Buddy Bell
1995 8

Cool Papa Bell Inducted in 1974
1974 Neg. Com.

George Bell
1999 6

Johnny Bench Inducted in 1989
1989 431

Chief Bender Inducted in 1953
1936 2
1937 17
1938 33
1939 40
1942 55
1945 40
1946 NOM 39
1946 35
1947 72
1948 5
1949 2
1950 6
1951 35
1952 70
1953 104
1953 Vet. Com.

Charlie Bennett
1936 V 3

Larry Benton
1958 1

Moe Berg
1958 3
1960 5

Marty Bergen
1937 2
1938 1
1939 1

Wally Berger
1956 1
1958 2

Yogi Berra Inducted in 1972
1971 242
1972 339

Charlie Berry
1955 1
1958 3

Jim Bibby
1990 1

Carson Bigbee
1948 1

Jack Billingham
1986 1

Max Bishop
1955 1
1956 1
1958 4
1960 5

Ewell Blackwell
1968 5
1969 11
1970 14

Ray Blades
1958 1
1960 1

Paul Blair
1986 8

Steve Blass
1980 2

Lu Blue
1954 1

Vida Blue
1992 23
1993 37

Ossie Bluege
1948 2
1949 1
1954 1
1956 2
1958 2
1960 3

Bert Blyleven
2001 121
2002 124
2003 145
2004 179

Ping Bodie
1937 2
1949 1

Joe Boley
1942 1

Tommy Bond
1936 V 1

Bobby Bonds
1987 24
1988 27

1989	29
1990	30
1991	39
1992	40
1993	45
1994	37
1995	35
1996	24
1997	20

Bob Boone

1996	36
1997	28
1998	26
1999	27
2000	21

Jim Bottomley
Inducted in 1974

1948	4
1949	8
1950	8
1951	6
1952	7
1953	10
1954	16
1955	26
1956	42
1958	57
1960	89
1962	20
1974	Vet. Com.

Lou Boudreau
Inducted in 1970

1956	2
1958	64
1960	35
1962	12
1964	68
1964 RO	43
1966	115
1967	143
1967 RO	68
1968	146
1969	218
1970	232

Jim Bouton

| 1984 | 3 |

Larry Bowa

| 1991 | 11 |

Clete Boyer

| 1978 | 1 |
| 1979 | 3 |

Ken Boyer

1975	9
1976	15
1977	14
1978	18
1979	20
1985	68
1986	95
1987	96
1988	109
1989	62
1990	78
1991	58
1992	71
1993	69
1994	56

Bill Bradley

1936	1
1937	5
1938	2
1939	1
1942	1
1946 NOM	1

Harry Brecheen

1960	7
1968	3
1969	2
1970	3
1971	7
1972	5
1973	3

Ted Breitenstein

| 1937 | 1 |

Roger Bresnahan
Inducted in 1945

1936	47
1937	43
1938	67
1939	67
1942	57
1945	133
1945	O/T Com.

George Brett
Inducted in 1999

| 1999 | 488 |

Jim Brewer

| 1982 | 2 |

Tommy Bridges

1956	3
1958	11
1960	4
1962	1
1964	15
1964 RO	1
1966	16

Lou Brock
Inducted in 1985

| 1985 | 315 |

Dan Brouthers
Inducted in 1945

| 1936 V | 2 |
| 1945 | O/T Com. |

Gates Brown

| 1981 | 1 |

Mordecai Brown
Inducted in 1949

1936	6
1937	31
1938	54
1939	54
1942	63
1945	46
1946 NOM	56
1946	48
1949	O/T Com.

Tom Browning

| 2001 | 1 |

Bill Bruton

| 1971 | 1 |

Bill Buckner

| 1996 | 10 |

Morgan Bulkeley
Inducted in 1937
Executive

| 1937 | Cen. Com. |

Jim Bunning
Inducted in 1996

1977	146
1978	181
1979	147
1980	177
1981	164
1982	138
1983	138
1984	201
1985	214
1986	279
1987	289
1988	317
1989	283
1990	257
1991	282
1996	Vet. Com.

Lew Burdette

1973	12
1974	7
1975	11
1976	21
1977	85
1978	76

1979	53
1980	66
1981	48
1982	43
1983	43
1984	97
1985	82
1986	96
1987	96

Smoky Burgess

| 1973 | 1 |
| 1974 | 2 |

Jesse Burkett
Inducted in 1946

1936 V	1
1937	1
1938	2
1942	4
1945	2
1946 NOM	2
1946	O/T Com.

George J. Burns

1937	3
1938	3
1939	1
1949	1
1950	2

Jeff Burroughs

| 1991 | 1 |

Guy Bush

| 1956 | 2 |

Joe Bush

| 1958 | 5 |

Donie Bush

1937	1
1939	2
1942	2
1945	1
1946 NOM	2
1953	1

Brett Butler

| 2003 | 2 |

Leon Cadore

| 1948 | 1 |

Johnny Callison

| 1979 | 1 |

Dolph Camilli

1948	1
1956	1
1958	4
1960	3

Howie Camnitz

| 1945 | 1 |

Roy Campanella
Inducted in 1969

1964	115
1964 RO	138
1966	197
1967	204
1967 RO	170
1968	205
1969	270

Bert Campaneris

| 1989 | 14 |

Bill Campbell

| 1993 | 1 |

John Candelaria

| 1999 | 1 |

Jose Cardenal

| 1986 | 1 |

Leo Cardenas

| 1981 | 1 |
| 1982 | 1 |

Rod Carew
Inducted in 1991

| 1991 | 401 |

Max Carey
Inducted in 1961

1937	6
1938	6
1939	7
1945	1
1948	9
1949	12
1950	14
1951	27
1952	36
1953	55
1954	55
1955	119
1956	65
1958	136
1961	Vet. Com.

Steve Carlton
Inducted in 1994

| 1994 | 436 |

Chico Carrasquel

| 1966 | 1 |

Bill Carrigan

1937	5
1938	4
1939	2
1945	3

Clay Carroll

| 1984 | 1 |

Gary Carter
Inducted in 2003

1998	200
1999	168
2000	248
2001	334
2002	343
2003	387

Joe Carter

| 2004 | 19 |

Rico Carty

| 1985 | 1 |

Alex Cartwright
Inducted in 1938
Pioneer

| 1938 | Cen. Com. |

George Case

1958	1
1960	1
1962	1
1964	2

Dave Cash

| 1986 | 2 |

Norm Cash

| 1980 | 6 |

Phil Cavarretta

1962	2
1964	22
1964 RO	1
1966	9
1967	15
1967 RO	4
1968	23
1969	37
1970	51
1971	83
1972	61
1973	73
1974	61
1975	129

Cesar Cedeno

| 1992 | 2 |

Orlando Cepeda
Inducted in 1999

1980	48
1981	77
1982	42
1983	59
1984	124
1985	114

1986	152
1987	179
1988	199
1989	176
1990	211
1991	192
1992	246
1993	252
1994	335
1999	Vet. Com.

Ron Cey

| 1993 | 8 |

Henry Chadwick
Inducted in 1938
Pioneer

| 1938 | Cen. Com. |

Frank Chance
Inducted in 1946

1936	5
1937	49
1938	133
1939	158
1942	136
1945	179
1946 NOM	144
1946	150
1946	O/T Com.

Happy Chandler
Inducted in 1982
Executive

| 1982 | Vet. Com. |

Spud Chandler

1950	2
1951	1
1956	1
1962	2
1964	6

Ben Chapman

| 1949 | 1 |
| 1952 | 1 |

Ray Chapman

| 1938 | 1 |

Sam Chapman

| 1958 | 1 |

Oscar Charleston
Inducted in 1976

| 1976 | Neg. Com. |

Hal Chase

| 1936 | 11 |
| 1937 | 18 |

Jack Chesbro
Inducted in 1946

1937	1
1938	2
1939	6
1946 NOM	1
1946	O/T Com.

Nestor Chylak
Inducted in 1999
Umpire

| 1999 | Vet. Com. |

Bill Cissell

| 1937 | 1 |

Jack Clark

| 1998 | 7 |

Watty Clark

| 1958 | 1 |

Fred Clarke
Inducted in 1945

1936 V	9
1936	1
1937	22
1938	63
1939	59
1942	58
1945	53
1945	O/T Com.

John Clarkson
Inducted in 1963

1936 V	5
1946 NOM	1
1963	Vet. Com.

Roberto Clemente
Inducted in 1973

| 1973 | Spec. El. |

Andy Coakley

| 1938 | 1 |

Ty Cobb
Inducted in 1936

| 1936 | 222 |

Mickey Cochrane
Inducted in 1947

1936	80
1939	28
1942	88
1945	125
1946 NOM	80
1946	65
1947	128

Rocky Colavito

| 1974 | 2 |
| 1975 | 1 |

Vince Coleman

| 2003 | 3 |

Eddie Collins
Inducted in 1939

1936	60
1937	115
1938	175
1939	213

Jimmy Collins
Inducted in 1945

1936 V	8
1936	58
1937	66
1938	79
1939	72
1942	68
1945	121
1945	O/T Com.

Shano Collins

| 1937 | 1 |

Earle Combs
Inducted in 1970

1937	4
1938	7
1939	3
1945	1
1948	6
1949	6
1950	3
1952	1
1953	3
1955	1
1956	14
1958	34
1960	43
1962	6
1970	Vet. Com.

Charlie Comiskey
Inducted in 1939
Executive

| 1936 V | 6 |
| 1939 | O/T Com. |

Dave Concepcion

1994	31
1995	43
1996	63
1997	60
1998	80
1999	59
2000	67
2001	74
2002	56
2003	55
2004	57

Jocko Conlan
Inducted in 1974
Umpire
| 1974 | Vet. Com. |

Tommy Connolly
Inducted in 1953
Umpire
| 1953 | Vet. Com. |

Roger Connor
Inducted in 1976
| 1976 | Vet. Com. |

Wid Conroy
| 1945 | 1 |

Jack Coombs
1937	2
1938	2
1946 NOM	2
1948	2
1951	1

Mort Cooper
1956	2
1958	3
1960	1
1969	3

Walker Cooper
1968	8
1969	5
1970	9
1971	7
1972	8
1973	8
1974	9
1975	13
1976	56
1977	45

Wilbur Cooper
1938	1
1939	1
1948	2
1949	4
1951	1
1952	2
1953	9
1954	7
1955	11

Clint Courtney
| 1967 | 1 |

Stan Coveleski
Inducted in 1969
1938	1
1948	2
1949	3
1950	1
1958	34
1969	Vet. Com.

Billy Cox
| 1962 | 1 |

Doc Cramer
1956	4
1958	2
1960	1
1962	1
1964	12

Del Crandall
1976	15
1977	8
1978	6
1979	9

Doc Crandall
| 1938 | 1 |

Gavvy Cravath
1937	2
1938	2
1939	2
1946 NOM	1
1947	2

Sam Crawford
Inducted in 1957
1936	1
1937	5
1938	11
1939	6
1942	2
1945	4
1946 NOM	9
1957	Vet. Com.

Lou Criger
1936 V	1
1936	7
1937	16
1938	11
1939	2
1946 NOM	6

Hughie Critz
| 1956 | 2 |

Joe Cronin
Inducted in 1956
1947	6
1948	25
1949	33
1949 RO	16
1950	33
1951	44
1952	48
1953	69
1954	85
1955	135
1956	152

Frank Crosetti
1950	1
1952	1
1956	1
1958	5
1960	8
1968	15

Lave Cross
| 1939 | 1 |
| 1942 | 1 |

Al Crowder
| 1958 | 1 |
| 1960 | 1 |

Walt Cruise
| 1938 | 1 |

Jose Cruz
| 1994 | 2 |

Tony Cuccinello
| 1956 | 1 |
| 1958 | 3 |

Candy Cummings
Inducted in 1939
Pioneer
| 1939 | O/T Com. |

Kiki Cuyler
Inducted in 1968
1948	3
1949	4
1950	11
1951	8
1952	10
1953	18
1954	20
1955	35
1956	55
1958	90
1960	72
1962	31
1968	Vet. Com.

Bill Dahlen
| 1936 V | 1 |
| 1938 | 1 |

Ray Dandridge
Inducted in 1987
| 1987 | Vet. Com. |

Harry Danning
| 1958 | 1 |
| 1960 | 1 |

Alvin Dark
1966	17
1967	38
1967 RO	7
1968	36
1969	48
1970	55
1971	54
1972	55
1973	53
1974	54
1975	48
1976	62
1977	66
1978	60
1979	80
1980	43

Ron Darling
| 2001 | 1 |

Jake Daubert
1936	1
1937	2
1938	1
1939	1
1951	1
1955	1

Darren Daulton
| 2003 | 1 |

Curt Davis
| 1958 | 1 |

George Davis
Inducted in 1998
| 1998 | Vet. Com. |

Harry Davis
| 1945 | 1 |
| 1946 NOM | 2 |

Mark Davis
| 2003 | 1 |

Tommy Davis
| 1982 | 5 |

Spud Davis
| 1948 | 1 |
| 1949 | 1 |

Andre Dawson
2002	214
2003	248
2004	253

Leon Day
Inducted in 1995
| 1995 | Vet. Com. |

Dizzy Dean
Inducted in 1953
1945	17
1946 NOM	40
1946	45
1947	88
1948	40
1949	88
1949 RO	81
1950	85
1951	145
1952	152
1953	209

Doug DeCinces
| 1993 | 2 |

Ed Delahanty
Inducted in 1945
1936 V	22
1936	17
1937	70
1938	132
1939	145
1942	104
1945	111
1945	O/T Com.

Rick Dempsey
| 1998 | 1 |

Jerry Denny
| 1936 V | 6 |

Bucky Dent
| 1990 | 3 |

Paul Derringer
1948	1
1950	1
1951	1
1955	1
1956	12
1958	15
1960	8

Jim Deshaies
| 2001 | 1 |

Bill Dickey
Inducted in 1954
1945	17
1946 NOM	40
1946	32
1948	39
1949	65
1949 RO	39
1950	78
1951	118
1952	139
1953	179
1954	202

Martin Dihigo
Inducted in 1977
| 1977 | Neg. Com. |

Dom DiMaggio
1960	4
1962	2
1964	12
1968	8
1969	13
1970	15
1971	15
1972	36
1973	43

Joe DiMaggio
Inducted in 1955
1945	1
1953	117
1954	175
1955	223

Bill Dinneen
1938	4
1939	7
1942	1
1945	1
1946 NOM	1

Bill Doak
| 1958 | 3 |

Larry Doby
Inducted in 1998
1966	7
1967	10
1967 RO	1
1998	Vet. Com

Bobby Doerr
Inducted in 1986
1953	2
1956	5
1958	25
1960	15
1962	10
1964	24
1964 RO	5
1966	30
1967	35
1967 RO	15
1968	48
1969	62
1970	75
1971	78
1986	Vet. Com.

Mike Donlin
1937	6
1938	5
1939	5
1945	1

Bill Donovan
1937	3
1938	1
1939	2
1945	3
1946 NOM	4

Red Dooin
| 1937 | 1 |
| 1938 | 1 |

Brian Downing
| 1998 | 2 |

Jack Doyle
| 1936 V | 1 |

Doug Drabek
| 2004 | 2 |

Larry Doyle
1937	2
1938	4
1939	1

Walt Dropo
| 1967 | 1 |

Don Drysdale
Inducted in 1984
1975	76
1976	114
1977	197
1978	219
1979	233
1980	238
1981	243
1982	233
1983	242
1984	316

Hugh Duffy
Inducted in 1945
1936 V	4
1937	7
1938	24
1939	34
1942	77
1945	64
1945	O/T Com.

Joe Dugan
1937	1
1938	1
1948	3
1949	2
1956	1
1958	5
1960	8

Fred Dunlap
| 1936 V | 2 |

Jack Dunn
1942	1
1945	1
1946 NOM	1

Leo Durocher
Inducted in 1994
Manager
1948	1
1949	1
1952	1
1956	1
1958	28
1960	10
1962	1
1964	15
1964 RO	2

Eddie Dyer
| 1947 | 1 |

Jimmy Dykes
| 1948 | 5 |
| 1949 | 7 |

1950	2
1951	3
1952	5
1953	5
1955	1
1956	1
1958	26
1960	27
1962	6

Lenny Dykstra
| 2002 | 1 |

George Earnshaw
1948	3
1949	2
1950	2
1955	2
1956	3

Dennis Eckersley
Inducted in 2004
| 2004 | 421 |

Hank Edwards
| 1960 | 2 |

Howard Ehmke
1938	1
1949	1
1951	1
1952	1
1953	3
1954	4
1955	8
1956	8
1958	7
1960	12

Jim Eisenreich
| 2004 | 3 |

Kid Elberfeld
1936	1
1937	1
1938	2
1942	1
1945	2

Jumbo Elliott
| 1958 | 1 |

Bob Elliott
1960	2
1962	1
1964	4

Dock Ellis
| 1985 | 1 |

Del Ennis
| 1966 | 3 |
| 1967 | 2 |

Jewel Ens
| 1950 | 1 |

Carl Erskine
1966	6
1968	9
1969	4
1970	2
1971	3
1972	4
1973	4
1974	11

Billy Evans
Inducted in 1973
Umpire
| 1973 | Vet. Com. |

Darrell Evans
| 1995 | 8 |

Dwight Evans
1997	28
1998	49
1999	18

Johnny Evers
Inducted in 1946
| 1936 | 6 |
| 1937 | 44 |

1938	91
1939	107
1942	91
1945	134
1946 NOM	130
1946	110
1946	O/T Com.

Buck Ewing
Inducted in 1939

1936 V	40
1939	2
1939	O/T Com.

Red Faber
Inducted in 1964

1937	3
1938	1
1939	3
1942	1
1948	3
1949	6
1950	9
1951	8
1952	9
1953	9
1954	12
1955	27
1956	34
1958	68
1960	83
1962	30
1964	Vet. Com.

Elroy Face

1976	23
1977	33
1978	27
1979	35
1980	21
1981	23
1982	22
1983	32
1984	65
1985	62
1986	74
1987	78
1988	79
1989	47
1990	50

Ron Fairly

1985	3

Cy Falkenberg

1937	1

Bob Feller
Inducted in 1962

1962	150

Sid Fernandez

2003	2

Rick Ferrell
Inducted in 1984

1956	1
1958	1
1960	1
1984	Vet. Com.

Wes Ferrell

1948	1
1949	1
1956	7
1960	8
1962	1

Cecil Fielder

2004	1

Rollie Fingers
Inducted in 1992

1991	291
1992	349

Carlton Fisk
Inducted in 2000

1999	330
2000	397

Fred Fitzsimmons

1948	2
1949	2
1950	1
1956	3
1958	16
1960	13
1962	1

Mike Flanagan

1998	2

Art Fletcher

1937	2
1938	3
1939	1
1947	3
1948	3
1949	1
1950	1
1951	4

Elmer Flick
Inducted in 1963

1938	1
1963	Vet. Com.

Curt Flood

1977	16
1978	8
1979	14
1985	28
1986	45
1987	50
1988	48
1989	27
1990	35
1991	23
1992	42
1993	36
1994	40
1995	59
1996	71

Lew Fonseca

1948	1
1950	2
1956	2
1958	3
1960	3

Whitey Ford
Inducted in 1974

1973	255
1974	284

Bob Forsch

1995	2

Willie Foster
Inducted in 1996

1996	Vet. Com.

Eddie Foster

1938	2

George Foster

1992	24
1993	29
1994	16
1995	19

Rube Foster
Inducted in 1981
Manager

1981	Vet. Com.

Nellie Fox
Inducted in 1997

1971	39
1972	64
1973	73
1974	79
1975	76
1976	174
1977	152
1978	149
1979	174
1980	161
1981	168
1982	127
1983	173

1984	246
1985	295
1997	Vet. Com.

Jimmie Foxx
Inducted in 1951

1936	21
1946 NOM	26
1947	10
1948	50
1949	85
1949 RO	89
1950	103
1951	179

Curt Fraser

1939	1

Bill Freehan

1982	2

Jim Fregosi

1984	4

Ford Frick
Inducted in 1970
Executive

1970	Vet. Com.

Frankie Frisch
Inducted in 1947

1936	14
1939	26
1942	84
1945	101
1946 NOM	104
1946	67
1947	136

Carl Furillo

1966	2
1967	2
1970	2
1971	5
1972	2

Augie Galan

1968	2
1970	3

Pud Galvin
Inducted in 1965

1965	Vet. Com.

Phil Garner

1994	2

Ned Garver

1967	1

Steve Garvey

1993	176
1994	166
1995	196
1996	175
1997	167
1998	195
1999	150
2000	160
2001	176
2002	134
2003	138
2004	123

Lou Gehrig
Inducted in 1939

1936	51
1939	Spec. El.

Charlie Gehringer
Inducted in 1949

1945	10
1946 NOM	43
1946	23
1947	105
1948	52
1949	102
1949 RO	159

Charlie Gelbert

1947	1
1949	2
1950	1
1951	1

Bob Gibson
Inducted in 1981

1981	337

Josh Gibson
Inducted in 1972

1972	Neg. Com.

Kirk Gibson

2001	13

Warren Giles
Inducted in 1979
Executive

1979	Vet. Com.

Dave Giusti

1983	1

Jack Glasscock

1936 V	2

Kid Gleason

1937	1
1938	1
1939	1
1945	1

Lefty Gomez
Inducted in 1972

1945	7
1946 NOM	4
1947	1
1948	16
1949	17
1950	18
1951	23
1952	29
1953	35
1954	38
1955	71
1956	89
1958	76
1960	51
1962	20
1972	Vet. Com.

Mike Gonzales

1950	1
1952	1
1953	1
1958	3
1960	2

Joe Gordon

1945	1
1955	1
1956	4
1958	11
1960	11
1962	4
1964	30
1964 RO	1
1966	31
1967	66
1967 RO	13
1968	77
1969	97
1970	79

Goose Goslin
Inducted in 1968

1948	1
1949	4
1950	2
1954	1
1955	7
1956	26
1958	26
1960	30
1962	14
1968	Vet. Com.

Goose Gossage

2000	166
2001	228
2002	203
2003	209
2004	206

Hank Gowdy

1937	2
1938	8
1939	4
1942	8
1945	3
1947	1
1948	3
1949	10
1950	6
1951	26
1952	34
1953	58
1954	51
1955	90
1956	49
1958	45
1960	38

Eddie Grant

1938	1
1939	2
1942	3
1945	2
1946 NOM	1

George Grantham

1958	1

Hank Greenberg
Inducted in 1956

1945	3
1949	67
1949 RO	44
1950	64
1951	67
1952	75
1953	80
1954	97
1955	157
1956	164

Mike Greenwell

2002	2

Bobby Grich

1992	11

Ken Griffey, Sr.

1997	22

Clark Griffith
Inducted in 1946
Executive

1937	4
1938	10
1939	20
1942	71
1945	108
1946 NOM	73
1946	82
1946	O/T Com.

Burleigh Grimes
Inducted in 1964

1937	1
1938	1
1939	1
1948	7
1949	8
1950	6
1951	5
1952	9
1953	9
1955	3
1956	25
1958	71
1960	92
1962	43
1964	Vet. Com.

Charlie Grimm

1939	1
1945	1
1946 NOM	1
1948	6
1949	10
1950	13
1951	9
1952	6

1953	9
1958	26
1960	13
1962	2

Marv Grissom

1966	2

Dick Groat

1973	7
1974	4
1975	4
1976	7
1977	4
1978	3

Heinie Groh

1937	1
1938	3
1945	1
1948	1
1950	2
1954	1
1955	5
1960	1

Steve Gromek

1964	1

Orval Grove

1958	5
1960	7

Lefty Grove
Inducted in 1947

1936	12
1945	28
1946 NOM	71
1946	61
1947	123

Pedro Guerrero

1998	6

Ron Guidry

1994	24
1995	25
1996	37
1997	31
1998	37
1999	31
2000	44
2001	27
2002	23

Bill Gullickson

2000	1

Frank Gustine

1958	3

Mule Haas

1955	1
1956	1
1958	1
1960	1

Stan Hack

1948	2
1949	4
1950	8
1951	3
1956	1
1958	6
1960	6

Harvey Haddix

1971	10
1972	9
1973	1
1974	8
1975	8
1976	8
1977	7
1978	7
1979	8
1985	15

Chick Hafey
Inducted in 1971

1948	1
1949	2
1950	4

Year	Votes
1951	1
1952	1
1953	2
1954	2
1955	4
1956	16
1958	12
1960	29
1962	7
1971	Vet. Com.

Noodles Hahn

Year	Votes
1939	1

Jesse Haines
Inducted in 1970

Year	Votes
1939	1
1947	1
1948	2
1949	2
1950	11
1953	4
1954	6
1955	10
1956	14
1958	22
1960	20
1962	3
1970	Vet. Com.

Bill Hallahan

Year	Votes
1948	1
1956	1
1958	1
1960	2

Billy Hamilton
Inducted in 1961

Year	Votes
1936 V	2
1942	1
1961	Vet. Com.

Ned Hanlon
Inducted in 1996

Year	Votes
1996	Vet. Com.

Mel Harder

Year	Votes
1949	4
1950	2
1951	1
1952	10
1953	8
1958	6
1960	12
1962	7
1964	51
1964 RO	14
1966	34
1967	52
1967 RO	14

Bubbles Hargrave

Year	Votes
1947	1
1958	1
1960	1

Mike Hargrove

Year	Votes
1991	1

Toby Harrah

Year	Votes
1992	1

Bud Harrelson

Year	Votes
1986	1

Will Harridge
Inducted in 1972
Executive

Year	Votes
1972	Vet. Com.

Bucky Harris
Inducted in 1975
Manager

Year	Votes
1938	1
1939	1
1948	3
1949	11
1950	4
1951	9
1952	12
1953	21
1958	45
1960	31
1975	Vet. Com.

Gabby Hartnett
Inducted in 1955

Year	Votes
1945	2
1946 NOM	2
1947	2
1948	33
1949	35
1949 RO	7
1950	54
1951	57
1952	77
1953	104
1954	151
1955	195

Grady Hatton

Year	Votes
1966	4
1967	1

Jim Hearn

Year	Votes
1966	1
1967	1

Richie Hebner

Year	Votes
1991	1

Jim Hegan

Year	Votes
1966	5
1967	2

Harry Heilmann
Inducted in 1952

Year	Votes
1937	10
1938	14
1939	8
1942	4
1945	5
1946 NOM	23
1947	65
1948	40
1949	59
1949 RO	52
1950	87
1951	153
1952	203

Tommy Helms

Year	Votes
1983	1

Solly Hemus

Year	Votes
1966	1

Dave Henderson

Year	Votes
2000	2

Tom Henke

Year	Votes
2001	6

Tommy Henrich

Year	Votes
1952	4
1953	10
1956	2
1958	11
1960	10
1962	3
1964	13
1968	22
1969	50
1970	62

Babe Herman

Year	Votes
1942	1
1948	2
1949	5
1950	2
1951	1
1952	3
1953	2
1954	1
1955	5
1956	11
1958	13
1960	7

Billy Herman
Inducted in 1975

Year	Votes
1948	1
1956	2
1958	7
1962	4
1964	26
1964 RO	9
1966	28
1967	59
1967 RO	14
1975	Vet. Com.

Keith Hernandez

Year	Votes
1996	24
1997	45
1998	51
1999	34
2000	52
2001	41
2002	29
2003	30
2004	22

Willie Hernandez

Year	Votes
1995	2

Buck Herzog

Year	Votes
1938	1

Jim Hickman

Year	Votes
1980	1

Mike Higgins

Year	Votes
1950	2
1951	1
1958	6
1960	3

John Hiller

Year	Votes
1986	11

Bill Hinchman

Year	Votes
1937	1

Gil Hodges

Year	Votes
1969	82
1970	145
1971	180
1972	161
1973	218
1974	198
1975	188
1976	233
1977	224
1978	226
1979	242
1980	230
1981	241
1982	205
1983	237

Tommy Holmes

Year	Votes
1958	2
1960	2

Ken Holtzman

Year	Votes
1985	4
1986	5

Rick Honeycutt

Year	Votes
2003	2

Harry Hooper
Inducted in 1971

Year	Votes
1937	6
1938	4
1939	5
1948	2
1950	2
1951	3
1971	Vet. Com.

Burt Hooton

Year	Votes
1991	1

Rogers Hornsby
Inducted in 1942

Year	Votes
1936	105
1937	53
1938	46
1939	176
1942	182

Willie Horton

Year	Votes
1986	4

Art Houtteman

Year	Votes
1964	2

Charlie Hough

Year	Votes
2000	4

Elston Howard

Year	Votes
1974	19
1975	23
1976	55
1977	43
1978	41
1979	30
1980	29
1981	83
1982	40
1983	32
1984	45
1985	54
1986	51
1987	44
1988	53

Frank Howard

Year	Votes
1979	6

Waite Hoyt
Inducted in 1969

Year	Votes
1939	1
1942	1
1946 NOM	1
1948	7
1949	7
1950	11
1951	13
1952	12
1953	14
1954	14
1955	33
1956	37
1958	37
1960	29
1962	18
1969	Vet. Com.

Al Hrabosky

Year	Votes
1988	1

Kent Hrbek

Year	Votes
2000	5

Cal Hubbard
Inducted in 1976
Umpire

Year	Votes
1976	Vet. Com.

Carl Hubbell
Inducted in 1947

Year	Votes
1945	24
1946 NOM	101
1946	75
1947	140

Miller Huggins
Inducted in 1964
Manager

Year	Votes
1937	5
1938	48
1939	97
1942	111
1945	133
1946 NOM	129
1946	106
1948	4
1950	2
1964	Vet. Com.

William Hulbert
Inducted in 1995

Year	Votes
1995	Vet. Com.

Catfish Hunter
Inducted in 1987

Year	Votes
1985	212
1986	289
1987	315

Bruce Hurst

Year	Votes
2000	1

Fred Hutchinson

Year	Votes
1962	1
1964	10

Monte Irvin
Inducted in 1973

Year	Votes
1973	Neg. Com.

Charlie Irwin

Year	Votes
1938	1
1939	1

Joe Jackson

Year	Votes
1936	2
1946 NOM	2

Reggie Jackson
Inducted in 1993

Year	Votes
1993	396

Sonny Jackson

Year	Votes
1980	1

Travis Jackson
Inducted in 1982

Year	Votes
1948	5
1949	6
1950	6
1951	4
1952	1
1953	2
1954	1
1955	5
1956	14
1958	11
1960	11
1962	1
1982	Vet. Com.

Fergie Jenkins
Inducted in 1991

Year	Votes
1989	234
1990	296
1991	334

Hughie Jennings
Inducted in 1945

Year	Votes
1936 V	11
1937	4
1938	23
1939	33
1942	64
1945	92
1945	O/T Com.

Jackie Jensen

Year	Votes
1967	3
1968	3
1969	1
1970	1
1971	2
1972	1

Tommy John

Year	Votes
1995	98
1996	102
1997	97
1998	129
1999	93
2000	135
2001	146
2002	127
2003	116
2004	111

Ban Johnson
Inducted in 1937
Executive

Year	Votes
1937	Cen. Com.

Dave Johnson

Year	Votes
1984	3

Judy Johnson
Inducted in 1975

Year	Votes
1975	Neg. Com.

Bob Johnson

Year	Votes
1948	1
1956	1

Walter Johnson
Inducted in 1936

Year	Votes
1936	189

Fielder Jones

Year	Votes
1946 NOM	1

Sam P. Jones

Year	Votes
1939	1
1955	1
1956	1

Tim Jordan

Year	Votes
1951	1

Mike Jorgensen

Year	Votes
1991	1

Addie Joss
Inducted in 1978

Year	Votes
1937	11
1938	18
1939	28
1942	33
1945	23
1946 NOM	14
1960	1
1978	Vet. Com.

Joe Judge

Year	Votes
1937	1
1938	2
1949	1
1955	2
1956	2
1958	9
1960	15

Billy Jurges

Year	Votes
1949	2
1958	1

Jim Kaat

Year	Votes
1989	87
1990	79
1991	62
1992	114
1993	125
1994	98
1995	100
1996	91
1997	107
1998	129
1999	100
2000	125
2001	139
2002	109
2003	130

Al Kaline
Inducted in 1980

Year	Votes
1980	340

Willie Kamm

Year	Votes
1958	3
1960	1

Tim Keefe
Inducted in 1964

Year	Votes
1936 V	1
1964	Vet. Com.

Willie Keeler
Inducted in 1939

Year	Votes
1936 V	33
1936	40
1937	115
1938	177
1939	207

George Kell
Inducted in 1983

Year	Votes
1964	33
1964 RO	8
1966	29
1967	40
1967 RO	11
1968	47
1969	60
1970	90
1971	105
1972	115
1973	114
1974	94
1975	114
1976	129
1977	141
1983	Vet. Com.

Charlie Keller
1953	1
1956	2
1958	9
1960	7
1962	1
1964	12
1968	11
1969	14
1970	7
1971	14
1972	24

Joe Kelley
Inducted in 1971
1939	1
1942	1
1971	Vet. Com.

George Kelly
Inducted in 1973
1947	1
1948	2
1949	1
1956	2
1958	2
1960	5
1962	1
1973	Vet. Com.

King Kelly
Inducted in 1945
1936 V	15
1945	O/T Com.

Ken Keltner
1958	1
1960	1

Terry Kennedy
1997	1

Dickie Kerr
1937	1
1938	3
1939	5
1942	1
1945	1
1949	1
1951	3
1952	9
1953	13
1954	13
1955	25

Don Kessinger
1985	2

Jimmy Key
2004	3

Darryl Kile
2003	7

Harmon Killebrew
Inducted in 1984
1981	239
1982	246
1983	269
1984	335

Bill Killefer
1946 NOM	1

Matt Kilroy
1936 V	1

Ellis Kinder
1964	3

Ralph Kiner
Inducted in 1975
1962	5
1964	31
1964 RO	3
1966	74
1967	124
1967 RO	41
1968	118
1969	137
1970	167
1971	212
1972	235

1973	235
1974	215
1975	273

Dave Kingman
1992	3

Chuck Klein
Inducted in 1980
1948	3
1949	9
1950	14
1951	15
1952	19
1954	11
1955	25
1956	44
1958	36
1960	37
1962	18
1964	56
1964 RO	18
1980	Vet. Com.

Bill Klem
Inducted in 1953
Umpire
1953	Vet. Com.

Johnny Kling
1936	8
1937	20
1938	26
1939	14
1942	15
1945	12
1946 NOM	20
1948	2
1953	1

Ted Kluszewski
1967	9
1968	14
1969	11
1970	8
1971	9
1972	10
1973	14
1974	28
1975	33
1976	50
1977	55
1978	51
1979	58
1980	50
1981	56

Otto Knabe
1939	1
1946 NOM	1

Ray Knight
1994	1

Jerry Koosman
1991	4

Sandy Koufax
Inducted in 1972
1972	344

Ray Kremer
1948	1
1958	2

Red Kress
1958	1
1960	3

John Kruk
2001	1

Mike Krukow
1995	1

Harvey Kuenn
1977	57
1978	58
1979	63
1980	83
1981	93
1982	62
1983	77

1984	106
1985	125
1986	144
1987	144
1988	168
1989	115
1990	107
1991	100

Joe Kuhel
1956	1

Bob Kuzava
1964	1

Nap Lajoie
Inducted in 1937
1936 V	2
1936	146
1937	168

Kenesaw Landis
Inducted in 1944
Executive
1944	O/T Com.

Bill Lange
1936 V	6
1953	1

Hal Lanier
1979	1

Carney Lansford
1998	3

Don Larsen
1974	29
1975	23
1976	47
1977	39
1978	32
1979	53
1980	31
1981	33
1982	32
1983	22
1984	25
1985	32
1986	33
1987	30
1988	31

Tommy Lasorda
Inducted in 1997
Manager
1997	Vet. Com.

Arlie Latham
1936 V	1
1938	1
1942	1

Cookie Lavagetto
1958	4
1960	2

Vern Law
1973	9
1974	5
1975	6
1976	9
1977	5
1978	6
1979	9

Tony Lazzeri
Inducted in 1991
1945	1
1947	1
1948	21
1949	20
1949 RO	6
1950	21
1951	27
1952	29
1953	28
1954	30
1955	66
1956	64
1958	80
1960	59

1962	8
1991	Vet. Com.

Fred Leach
1958	2
1960	1

Tommy Leach
1937	1
1939	1

Bill Lee
1988	3

Sam Leever
1937	1

Bob Lemon
Inducted in 1976
1964	24
1964 RO	3
1966	21
1967	35
1967 RO	7
1968	47
1969	56
1970	70
1971	90
1972	117
1973	177
1974	190
1975	233
1976	305

Chet Lemon
1996	1

Buck Leonard
Inducted in 1972
1972	Neg. Com.

Dennis Leonard
1992	1

Emil Leonard
1960	2
1968	5
1969	4
1970	5
1971	3
1972	5
1973	6

Duffy Lewis
1937	3
1938	5
1939	6
1945	1
1951	2
1952	11
1953	20
1954	20
1955	34

Fred Lindstrom
Inducted in 1976
1949	1
1956	3
1958	5
1960	6
1962	7
1976	Vet. Com.

John Henry Lloyd
Inducted in 1977
1977	Neg. Com.

Hans Lobert
1937	2
1938	1
1939	2
1960	1

Whitey Lockman
1966	4

Mickey Lolich
1985	78
1986	86
1987	84
1988	109
1989	47
1990	27

1991	33
1992	45
1993	43
1994	23
1995	26
1996	33
1997	34
1998	39
1999	26

Ernie Lombardi
Inducted in 1986
1950	3
1951	3
1956	8
1958	4
1960	6
1962	5
1964	33
1964 RO	9
1966	34
1967	43
1967 RO	25
1986	Vet. Com.

Jim Lonborg
1985	3
1986	3

Herman Long
1936 V	16
1937	1
1938	1
1939	1
1945	1
1946 NOM	1

Ed Lopat
1968	2
1969	2
1970	1
1971	4
1972	2

Davey Lopes
1993	2

Al Lopez
Inducted in 1977
Manager
1949	1
1952	2
1953	2
1956	1
1958	34
1960	26
1962	11
1964	57
1964 RO	34
1966	109
1967	114
1967 RO	50
1977	Vet. Com.

Bobby Lowe
1936 V	2
1942	1
1945	2

John Lowenstein
1991	1

Red Lucas
1949	2
1950	1
1958	1

Dolf Luque
1937	1
1938	1
1939	1
1950	1
1952	1
1953	1
1956	1
1958	15
1960	4

Greg Luzinski
1990	1

Sparky Lyle
1988	56
1989	25
1990	25
1991	15

Fred Lynn
1996	26
1997	22

Ted Lyons
Inducted in 1955
1945	4
1946 NOM	3
1948	15
1949	29
1949 RO	14
1950	42
1951	71
1952	101
1953	139
1954	170
1955	217

Connie Mack
Inducted in 1937
Manager
1936	1
1937	Cen. Com.

Larry MacPhail
Inducted in 1978
Executive
1978	Vet. Com.

Lee MacPhail
Inducted in 1998
Executive
1998	Vet. Com.

Bill Madlock
1993	19

Sherry Magee
1937	2
1938	2
1939	1
1942	1
1945	1
1946 NOM	1
1950	1
1951	2

Sal Maglie
1964	13
1968	11

Jim Maloney
1978	2
1979	2

Gus Mancuso
1958	1

Mickey Mantle
Inducted in 1974
1974	322

Heinie Manush
Inducted in 1964
1948	1
1949	1
1956	13
1958	22
1960	20
1962	15
1964	Vet. Com.

Rabbit Maranville
Inducted in 1954
1937	25
1938	73
1939	82
1942	66
1945	51
1946 NOM	50
1947	29
1948	91
1949	38
1949 RO	39
1950	66

1951	110
1952	133
1953	164
1954	209

Firpo Marberry
1938	1
1950	1
1958	5
1960	2
1962	2

Juan Marichal
Inducted in 1983
1981	233
1982	305
1983	313

Marty Marion
1956	1
1960	37
1962	16
1964	50
1964 RO	17
1966	86
1967	90
1967 RO	22
1968	89
1969	112
1970	120
1971	123
1972	120
1973	127

Roger Maris
1974	78
1975	70
1976	87
1977	72
1978	83
1979	127
1980	111
1981	94
1982	69
1983	69
1984	107
1985	128
1986	177
1987	176
1988	184

Rube Marquard
Inducted in 1971
1936	1
1937	13
1938	10
1939	4
1946 NOM	6
1947	18
1948	6
1949	4
1951	3
1952	9
1953	19
1954	15
1955	35
1971	Vet. Com.

Mike Marshall
1987	6

Billy Martin
1967	1

Pepper Martin
1942	2
1945	1
1946 NOM	1
1948	7
1949	16
1950	7
1951	19
1952	31
1953	43
1956	7
1958	46
1960	29
1962	6
1964	19
1964 RO	5

Morrie Martin
1966	2

Dennis Martinez
2004	16

Eddie Mathews
Inducted in 1978
1974	118
1975	148
1976	189
1977	239
1978	301

Christy Mathewson
Inducted in 1936
1936	205

Don Mattingly
2001	145
2002	96
2003	68
2004	65

Lee May
1988	2

Carl Mays
1958	6

Willie Mays
Inducted in 1979
1979	409

Bill Mazeroski
Inducted in 2001
1978	23
1979	36
1980	33
1981	38
1982	28
1983	48
1984	74
1985	87
1986	100
1987	125
1988	143
1989	134
1990	131
1991	142
1992	182
2001	Vet. Com.

Jim McAleer
1936 V	1

Joe McCarthy
Inducted in 1957
Manager
1939	3
1947	2
1951	1
1953	1
1958	2
1957	Vet. Com.

Tommy McCarthy
Inducted in 1946
1936 V	1
1946	O/T Com.

Tim McCarver
1986	16

Frank McCormick
1956	3
1962	1
1964	6
1968	3

Willie McCovey
Inducted in 1986
1986	346

Lindy McDaniel
1981	1
1982	3

Gil McDougald
1966	5
1967	4
1968	4
1969	3
1970	1

1971	4
1972	4
1973	2
1974	3

Joe McGinnity
Inducted in 1946
1937	12
1938	36
1939	32
1942	59
1945	44
1946 NOM	53
1946	47
1946	O/T Com.

Bill McGowan
Inducted in 1992
Umpire
1992	Vet. Com.

John McGraw
Inducted in 1937
Manager
1936 V	17
1936	4
1937	35
1937	Cen. Com.

Tug McGraw
1990	6

Stuffy McInnis
1937	1
1938	4
1939	4
1948	5
1949	8
1950	1
1951	3

Bill McKechnie
Inducted in 1962
Manager
1945	2
1946 NOM	2
1950	1
1951	8
1962	Vet. Com.

Denny McLain
1978	1
1979	3
1985	2

Larry McLean
1937	1

Don McMahon
1980	1

Marty McManus
1958	2
1960	2

Roy McMillan
1972	9
1973	5
1974	4

Dave McNally
1981	5
1982	5
1985	7
1986	12

Bid McPhee
Inducted in 2000
2000	Vet. Com.

Cal McVey
1936 V	1

Lee Meadows
1958	2

Joe Medwick
Inducted in 1968
1948	1
1956	31
1958	50
1960	38
1962	34
1964	108

1964 RO	130
1966	187
1967	212
1967 RO	248
1968	240

Andy Messersmith
1985	3
1986	3

Bob Meusel
1937	1
1938	1
1945	1
1948	6
1949	3
1950	2
1952	1
1955	2
1956	1
1958	5
1960	10

Eddie Miksis
1964	1

Clyde Milan
1938	1
1950	1
1951	1
1952	1
1953	1
1954	3
1955	6

Felix Millan
1983	1

Bing Miller
1958	1
1960	6

Dots Miller
1948	1

Hack Miller
1937	1

Minnie Minoso
1969	6
1986	89
1987	82
1988	90
1989	59
1990	51
1991	38
1992	69
1993	67
1994	45
1995	66
1996	62
1997	84
1998	76
1999	73

Kevin Mitchell
2004	2

Johnny Mize
Inducted in 1981
1960	45
1962	14
1964	54
1964 RO	12
1966	81
1967	89
1967 RO	14
1968	103
1969	116
1970	126
1971	157
1972	157
1973	157
1981	Vet. Com.

Paul Molitor
Inducted in 2004
2004	431

Rick Monday
1990	2

Don Money
1989	1

Wally Moon
1971	2

Jo-Jo Moore
1950	1

Terry Moore
1950	1
1953	1
1958	12
1960	7
1962	1
1964	14
1967	3
1968	33

Pat Moran
1937	1
1938	1
1939	1
1945	1

Joe Morgan
Inducted in 1990
1990	363

Jack Morris
2000	111
2001	101
2002	97
2003	113
2004	133

Wally Moses
1958	1
1960	1
1968	4
1969	4
1970	5
1971	7

Johnny Mostil
1956	1
1958	1

Manny Mota
1988	18
1989	9

Hugh Mulcahy
1948	1

Van Mungo
1945	1
1948	1
1958	2
1960	2

Thurman Munson
1981	62
1982	26
1983	18
1984	29
1985	32
1986	35
1987	28
1988	32
1989	31
1990	33
1991	28
1992	32
1993	40
1994	31
1995	30

Bobby Murcer
1989	3

Dale Murphy
1999	96
2000	116
2001	93
2002	70
2003	58
2004	43

Danny Murphy
1937	1
1945	1

Eddie Murray
Inducted in 2003
2003	423

Red Murray
1937	1
1938	1

Stan Musial
Inducted in 1969
1969	317

Buddy Myer
1949	1

Randy Myers
2004	1

Art Nehf
1937	3
1938	5
1939	1
1949	1
1950	2
1951	4
1952	3
1953	4
1954	7
1955	7
1958	13

Graig Nettles
1994	38
1995	28
1996	37
1997	22

Don Newcombe
1966	7
1967	18
1967 RO	2
1968	9
1969	3
1970	5
1971	8
1972	7
1973	11
1974	7
1975	11
1976	21
1977	43
1978	48
1979	52
1980	59

Hal Newhouser
Inducted in 1992
1962	4
1964	26
1964 RO	3
1966	32
1967	62
1967 RO	13
1968	67
1969	82
1970	80
1971	94
1972	92
1973	79
1974	73
1975	155
1992	Vet. Com.

Bobo Newsom
1960	6
1962	3
1964	17
1964 RO	1
1966	25
1967	19
1967 RO	6
1968	22
1969	32
1970	12
1971	17
1972	31
1973	33

Kid Nichols
Inducted in 1949
1936 V	3

1938 3
1939 7
1942 5
1945 5
1946 NOM 1
1949 O/T Com.

Bill Nicholson
1960 1

Joe Niekro
1994 6

Phil Niekro
Inducted in 1997
1993 278
1994 273
1995 286
1996 321
1997 380

Ron Northey
1964 1

Jim Northrup
1981 1

Lefty O'Doul
1948 4
1949 4
1950 9
1951 13
1952 19
1953 11
1956 5
1958 27
1960 45
1962 13

Joe Oeschger
1948 1

Bob O'Farrell
1950 4
1958 3
1960 3

Charlie O'Leary
1953 1
1958 1
1960 1

Tony Oliva
1982 63
1983 75
1984 124
1985 114
1986 154
1987 160
1988 202
1989 135
1990 142
1991 160
1992 175
1993 157
1994 158
1995 149
1996 170

Al Oliver
1991 19

Steve O'Neill
1948 2
1949 6
1950 1
1951 3
1952 10
1953 13
1958 10

Jim O'Rourke
Inducted in 1945
1945 O/T Com.

Claude Osteen
1981 2

Mel Ott
Inducted in 1951
1949 94
1949 RO 128
1950 115
1951 197

Charlie Pabor
1936 V 1

Andy Pafko
1966 2
1967 1

Satchel Paige
Inducted in 1971
1951 1
1971 Neg. Com.

Jim Palmer
Inducted in 1990
1990 411

Milt Pappas
1979 5

Dave Parker
1997 83
1998 116
1999 80
2000 104
2001 84
2002 66
2003 51
2004 53

Lance Parrish
2001 9

Larry Parrish
1994 2

Camilo Pascual
1977 3
1978 1

Dode Paskert
1937 1

Monte Pearson
1958 1

Roger Peckinpaugh
1937 3
1938 2
1939 1
1942 2
1949 1
1952 2
1953 2
1954 1
1955 1

Heinie Peitz
1939 1

Tony Peña
2003 2

Terry Pendleton
2004 1

Herb Pennock
Inducted in 1948
1937 15
1938 37
1939 40
1942 72
1945 45
1946 NOM 41
1946 16
1947 86
1948 94

Hub Perdue
1938 1
1939 1

Tony Perez
Inducted in 2000
1992 215
1993 233
1994 263
1995 259
1996 309
1997 312
1998 321
1999 302
2000 385

Cy Perkins
1958 2

Ron Perranoski
1979 6

Gaylord Perry
Inducted in 1991
1989 304
1990 320
1991 342

Jim Perry
1981 6
1983 7

Johnny Pesky
1960 1

Rico Petrocelli
1982 3

Deacon Phillippe
1939 1
1942 1
1945 2
1946 NOM 1

Billy Pierce
1970 5
1971 7
1972 4
1973 4
1974 4

Lip Pike
1936 V 1

Lou Piniella
1990 2

Vada Pinson
1981 18
1982 6
1983 12
1985 19
1986 43
1987 48
1988 67
1989 33
1990 36
1991 30
1992 36
1993 38
1994 46
1995 32
1996 51

Wally Pipp
1958 1

Eddie Plank
Inducted in 1946
1937 23
1938 38
1939 28
1942 63
1945 33
1946 NOM 34
1946 O/T Com.

Johnny Podres
1975 3
1976 2
1977 3

Bob Porterfield
1966 1

Boog Powell
1983 5

Vic Power
1971 2
1972 3

Hub Pruett
1949 1
1950 1
1951 1
1952 1
1953 1

Kirby Puckett
Inducted in 2001
2001 423

Terry Puhl
1997 1

Jack Quinn
1948 2
1958 9
1960 2

Dan Quisenberry
1996 18

Charlie Radbourn
Inducted in 1939
1936 V 16
1939 O/T Com.

Willie Randolph
1998 5

Vic Raschi
1962 1
1964 8
1968 1
1969 3
1971 2
1972 4
1973 7
1974 3
1975 37

Bugs Raymond
1937 1

Jeff Reardon
2000 24

Pee Wee Reese
Inducted in 1984
1964 73
1964 RO 47
1966 95
1967 89
1967 RO 16
1968 81
1969 89
1970 97
1971 127
1972 129
1973 126
1974 141
1975 154
1976 186
1977 163
1978 169
1984 Vet. Com.

Pete Reiser
1958 6
1960 8

Jack Remsen
1936 V 1

Jerry Remy
1990 1

Rick Reuschel
1997 2

Jerry Reuss
1996 2

Allie Reynolds
1956 1
1960 24
1962 15
1964 35
1964 RO 6
1966 60
1967 77
1967 RO 19
1968 95
1969 98
1970 89
1971 110
1972 105
1973 93
1974 101

Del Rice
1966 2

Jim Rice
1995 137
1996 166
1997 178
1998 203
1999 146
2000 257
2001 298
2002 260
2003 259
2004 276

Sam Rice
Inducted in 1963
1938 1
1948 1
1949 3
1950 1
1951 1
1952 1
1953 3
1954 9
1955 28
1956 45
1958 90
1960 143
1962 81
1963 Vet. Com.

J.R. Richard
1986 7

Hardy Richardson
1936 V 1

Bobby Richardson
1972 8
1973 2
1974 5

Branch Rickey
Inducted in 1967
Executive
1942 3
1945 2
1967 Vet. Com.

Dave Righetti
2001 2

Jose Rijo
2001 1

Jimmy Ring
1949 1

Claude Ritchey
1945 1

Mickey Rivers
1990 2

Eppa Rixey
Inducted in 1963
1937 1
1938 2
1945 1
1947 2
1948 5
1949 4
1950 6
1951 5
1952 3
1953 3
1954 5
1955 8
1956 27
1958 32
1960 142
1962 49
1963 Vet. Com.

Phil Rizzuto
Inducted in 1994
1956 1
1962 44
1964 45
1964 RO 11
1966 54
1967 71
1967 RO 14
1968 74
1969 78
1970 79
1971 92
1972 103
1973 111
1974 111
1975 117
1976 149
1994 Vet. Com.

Robin Roberts
Inducted in 1976
1973 213
1974 224
1975 263
1976 337

Dave Robertson
1953 1

Brooks Robinson
Inducted in 1983
1983 344

Frank Robinson
Inducted in 1982
1982 370

Jackie Robinson
Inducted in 1962
1962 124

Wilbert Robinson
Inducted in 1945
Manager
1936 V 6
1937 5
1938 17
1939 46
1942 89
1945 81
1945 O/T Com.

Preacher Roe
1960 1
1962 1
1968 2
1970 1
1971 3
1972 2

Bullet Joe Rogan
Inducted in 1998
1998 Vet. Com.

Red Rolfe
1950 7
1951 6
1952 4
1953 5
1956 3
1958 13
1960 10
1962 1

Eddie Rommel
1948 3
1949 2
1950 1
1951 1
1952 2
1953 1
1958 7
1960 12

Charlie Root
1945 1
1948 3
1949 1
1950 1
1958 6
1960 2

Edd Roush
Inducted in 1962
1936 2
1937 10
1938 9
1939 8
1942 1
1945 5
1946 NOM 11
1947 25
1948 17

1949	14
1950	16
1951	21
1952	24
1953	32
1954	52
1955	97
1956	91
1958	112
1960	146
1962	Vet. Com.

Schoolboy Rowe
1958	12
1960	3
1968	6
1969	17

Nap Rucker
1936	1
1937	11
1938	12
1939	13
1942	15
1945	10
1946 NOM	13

Dick Rudolph
1937	1
1951	1

Muddy Ruel
1946 NOM	1
1950	4
1951	1
1952	1
1953	8
1954	5
1955	11
1956	16
1958	10
1960	9

Red Ruffing
Inducted in 1967
1948	4
1949	22
1949 RO	4
1950	12
1951	9
1952	10
1953	24
1954	29
1955	60
1956	97
1958	99
1960	86
1962	72
1964	141
1964 RO	184
1966	208
1967	212
1967 RO	266

Amos Rusie
Inducted in 1977
1936 V	12
1937	1
1938	8
1939	6
1942	1
1945	1
1977	Vet. Com.

Bill Russell
1992	3

Babe Ruth
Inducted in 1936
1936	215

Nolan Ryan
Inducted in 1999
1999	491

Ray Sadecki
1983	2

Johnny Sain
1962	1
1964	3

1968	7
1969	8
1970	9
1971	11
1972	21
1973	47
1974	51
1975	123

Juan Samuel
2004	2

Ryne Sandberg
2003	244
2004	309

Manny Sanguillen
1986	2

Ron Santo
1980	15
1985	53
1986	64
1987	78
1988	108
1989	75
1990	96
1991	116
1992	136
1993	155
1994	150
1995	139
1996	174
1997	186
1998	204

Hank Sauer
1966	4

Steve Sax
2000	2

Al Schacht
1939	1
1948	2
1951	4
1956	1

Germany Schaefer
1942	1
1953	1

Ray Schalk
Inducted in 1955
1936	4
1937	24
1938	45
1939	35
1942	53
1945	33
1946 NOM	36
1947	50
1948	22
1949	24
1949 RO	17
1950	16
1951	37
1952	44
1953	52
1954	54
1955	113
1955	Vet. Com.

Wally Schang
1948	1
1950	1
1956	1
1958	8
1960	11

Mike Schmidt
Inducted in 1995
1995	444

Red Schoendienst
Inducted in 1989
1969	65
1970	97
1971	123
1972	104
1973	96
1974	110

1975	94
1976	129
1977	105
1978	130
1979	159
1980	164
1981	166
1982	135
1983	146
1989	Vet. Com.

Ossie Schreckengost
1937	2
1938	2
1939	2

Frank Schulte
1937	1

Hal Schumacher
1948	1
1955	1
1956	2
1958	1
1960	11
1962	1
1964	10

Everett Scott
1937	2
1938	2
1939	1
1942	1
1947	1
1948	3
1949	3
1950	3
1951	2
1952	4
1953	5
1954	4
1955	8
1956	1

George Scott
1986	1

Jack Scott
1958	1

Mike Scott
1997	2

Tom Seaver
Inducted in 1992
1992	425

Frank Selee
Inducted in 1999
Manager
1999	Vet. Com.

George Selkirk
1948	1
1949	1
1950	1
1951	2
1952	1
1953	1

Hank Severeid
1948	1

Joe Sewell
Inducted in 1977
1937	1
1948	1
1954	1
1955	1
1956	3
1958	1
1960	23
1977	Vet. Com.

Luke Sewell
1948	1
1958	3
1960	3
1962	1

Rip Sewell
1958	1
1962	1
1964	1

Cy Seymour
1945	1

Bobby Shantz
1970	7
1971	5
1972	9
1973	5
1974	3

Jim Sheckard
1938	1
1945	1
1946 NOM	1

Bill Sherdel
1948	1
1949	1
1950	1
1951	1
1953	1
1955	1
1956	1
1958	2
1960	2

Urban Shocker
1938	1
1939	1
1948	1
1949	2
1958	4

Chris Short
1979	1

Sonny Siebert
1981	1

Roy Sievers
1971	4
1972	3

Al Simmons
Inducted in 1953
1936	4
1946 NOM	1
1947	6
1948	60
1949	89
1949 RO	76
1950	90
1951	116
1952	141
1953	199

Curt Simmons
1973	5
1974	3

Ted Simmons
1994	7

George Sisler
Inducted in 1939
1936	77
1937	106
1938	179
1939	235

Sibby Sisti
1960	1

Enos Slaughter
Inducted in 1985
1966	100
1967	123
1967 RO	48
1968	129
1969	128
1970	133
1971	165
1972	149
1973	145
1974	145
1975	177
1976	197
1977	222
1978	261
1979	297
1985	Vet. Com.

Roy Smalley
1964	1

Earl Smith
1948	1
1956	1

Hilton Smith
Inducted in 2001
2001	Vet. Com.

Lee Smith
2003	210
2004	185

Lonnie Smith
2000	1

Ozzie Smith
Inducted in 2002
2002	433

Reggie Smith
1988	3

Sherry Smith
1948	1

Duke Snider
Inducted in 1980
1970	51
1971	89
1972	84
1973	101
1974	111
1975	129
1976	159
1977	212
1978	254
1979	308
1980	333

Billy Southworth
1945	1
1946 NOM	1
1949	7
1950	1
1951	4
1952	1
1953	2
1958	18

Warren Spahn
Inducted in 1973
1973	316

Al Spalding
Inducted in 1939
Pioneer
1936 V	4
1939	O/T Com.

Tully Sparks
1946 NOM	1

Tris Speaker
Inducted in 1937
1936	133
1937	165

Chris Speier
1995	1

Jake Stahl
1938	1
1939	1

Eddie Stanky
1960	3

Mickey Stanley
1984	2

Willie Stargell
Inducted in 1988
1988	352

Rusty Staub
1991	28
1992	26
1993	32
1994	36
1995	23
1996	24
1997	18

Turkey Stearnes
Inducted in 2000
2000	Vet. Com.

Harry Steinfeldt
1937	1
1939	1
1942	1

Casey Stengel
Inducted in 1966
Manager
1938	2
1939	6
1945	2
1948	1
1949	3
1950	3
1951	8
1952	27
1953	61
1966	Vet. Com.

Riggs Stephenson
1956	2
1958	1
1960	4
1962	1

Dave Stewart
2001	38
2002	23

Dave Stieb
2004	7

Mel Stottlemyre
1980	3

Harry Stovey
1936 V	6

Gabby Street
1937	1
1938	1
1953	1

Gus Suhr
1956	1
1958	1
1960	1

Clyde Sukeforth
1958	1

Billy Sullivan
1937	1
1946 NOM	1

Jim Sundberg
1995	1

Rick Sutcliffe
2000	9

Bruce Sutter
1994	109
1995	137
1996	137
1997	130
1998	147
1999	121
2000	192
2001	245
2002	238
2003	266
2004	301

Don Sutton
Inducted in 1998
1994	259
1995	264
1996	300
1997	346
1998	386

Bill Sweeney
1945	1

Jess Tannehill
1946 NOM	1

Danny Tartabull
2003	1

Birdie Tebbetts
| 1958 | 8 |
| 1960 | 1 |

Kent Tekulve
| 1995 | 6 |

Garry Templeton
| 1997 | 2 |

Gene Tenace
| 1989 | 1 |

Fred Tenney
1936 V	1
1937	5
1938	8
1939	3
1942	1
1946 NOM	1

Bill Terry
Inducted in 1954
1936	9
1938	7
1939	16
1942	36
1945	32
1946 NOM	31
1947	46
1948	52
1949	81
1949 RO	48
1950	105
1951	148
1952	155
1953	191
1954	195

Tommy Thevenow
| 1950 | 2 |

Ira Thomas
| 1938 | 1 |

Sam Thompson
Inducted in 1974
| 1974 | Vet. Com. |

Bobby Thomson
1966	12
1967	10
1967 RO	1
1968	13
1969	6
1970	4
1971	4
1972	10
1973	3
1974	6
1975	10
1976	9
1977	10
1978	5
1979	11

Andre Thornton
| 1993 | 2 |

Luis Tiant
1988	132
1989	47
1990	42
1991	32
1992	50
1993	62
1994	42
1995	45
1996	64
1997	53
1998	62
1999	53
2000	86
2001	63
2002	85

Joe Tinker
Inducted in 1946
1937	15
1938	16
1939	12
1942	36

1945	49
1946 NOM	55
1946	45
1946	O/T Com.

Jim Tobin
| 1956 | 2 |

Fred Toney
| 1949 | 1 |

Earl Torgeson
| 1967 | 2 |

Joe Torre
1983	20
1984	45
1985	44
1986	60
1987	47
1988	60
1989	40
1990	55
1991	41
1992	62
1993	63
1994	53
1995	50
1996	50
1997	105

Mike Torrez
| 1990 | 1 |

Alan Trammell
2002	74
2003	70
2004	70

Pie Traynor
Inducted in 1948
1936	16
1938	3
1939	10
1942	45
1945	81
1946 NOM	65
1946	53
1947	119
1948	93

Dizzy Trout
| 1964 | 1 |

Virgil Trucks
| 1964 | 4 |

John Tudor
| 1996 | 2 |

Jim Turner
| 1956 | 1 |

Terry Turner
| 1947 | 2 |

George Uhle
1956	1
1958	4
1960	4

Ellis Valentine
| 1991 | 1 |

Fernando Valenzuela
| 2003 | 31 |
| 2004 | 19 |

Elmer Valo
| 1967 | 2 |

Dazzy Vance
Inducted in 1955
1936	1
1937	10
1938	10
1939	15
1942	37
1945	18
1946 NOM	31
1947	50
1948	23
1949	33
1949 RO	15

1950	52
1951	70
1952	105
1953	150
1954	158
1955	205

Johnny Vander Meer
1945	1
1956	3
1958	35
1960	31
1962	5
1964	51
1964 RO	20
1966	72
1967	87
1967 RO	35
1968	79
1969	95
1970	88
1971	98

George Van Haltren
| 1936 V | 1 |

Arky Vaughan
Inducted in 1985
1953	1
1954	2
1955	4
1956	9
1958	6
1960	10
1962	6
1964	17
1964 RO	6
1966	36
1967	46
1967 RO	19
1968	82
1985	Vet. Com.

Bobby Veach
| 1937 | 1 |

Bill Veeck
Inducted in 1991
Executive
| 1991 | Vet. Com. |

Mickey Vernon
1966	20
1967	14
1967 RO	2
1968	22
1969	21
1970	10
1971	12
1972	12
1973	23
1974	27
1975	22
1976	52
1977	52
1978	66
1979	88
1980	96

Frank Viola
| 2002 | 2 |

Bill Virdon
| 1974 | 3 |
| 1975 | 1 |

Rube Waddell
Inducted in 1946
1936	33
1937	67
1938	148
1939	179
1942	126
1945	154
1946 NOM	122
1946	87
1946	O/T Com.

Honus Wagner
Inducted in 1936
| 1936 V | 5 |
| 1936 | 215 |

Rube Walberg
| 1958 | 1 |
| 1960 | 1 |

Dixie Walker
1962	1
1964	6
1968	6
1969	9

Harry Walker
| 1958 | 1 |

Bobby Wallace
Inducted in 1953
1936 V	1
1937	1
1938	7
1939	5
1942	2
1945	3
1953	Vet. Com.

Tim Wallach
| 2002 | 1 |

Ed Walsh
Inducted in 1946
1936	20
1937	56
1938	110
1939	132
1942	113
1945	137
1946 NOM	115
1946	106
1946	O/T Com.

Bucky Walters
1950	4
1952	3
1953	10
1956	5
1958	33
1960	19
1962	5
1964	35
1964 RO	8
1966	56
1967	65
1967 RO	24
1968	67
1969	20
1970	29

Bill Wambsganss
1942	1
1950	1
1953	1
1954	4
1955	5
1956	1

Lloyd Waner
Inducted in 1967
1949	3
1950	1
1951	1
1952	2
1956	18
1958	39
1960	22
1962	5
1964	47
1964 RO	12
1967	Vet. Com.

Paul Waner
Inducted in 1952
1946 NOM	4
1948	51
1949	73
1949 RO	63
1950	95
1951	162
1952	195

John 'Monte' Ward
Inducted in 1964
| 1936 V | 3 |
| 1964 | Vet. Com. |

Lon Warneke
1949	2
1958	2
1960	4
1962	2
1964	13

Bob Watson
| 1990 | 3 |

Earl Weaver
Inducted in 1996
| 1996 | Vet. Com. |

George Weiss
Inducted in 1971
Executive
| 1971 | Vet. Com. |

Bob Welch
| 2000 | 1 |

Mickey Welch
Inducted in 1973
| 1973 | Vet. Com. |

Willie Wells
Inducted in 1997
| 1997 | Vet. Com. |

Billy Werber
1949	1
1950	1
1952	1
1958	3

Vic Wertz
1970	2
1971	2
1972	4
1973	2
1974	2
1975	5
1976	5
1977	4
1978	4

Sam West
| 1948 | 1 |

Wes Westrum
| 1964 | 2 |

Zach Wheat
Inducted in 1959
1937	5
1938	7
1939	4
1942	3
1945	2
1946 NOM	6
1947	37
1948	15
1949	15
1950	17
1951	19
1952	30
1953	32
1954	33
1955	51
1956	26
1959	Vet. Com.

Lou Whitaker
| 2001 | 15 |

Deacon White
| 1936 V | 1 |

Frank White
| 1996 | 18 |

Will White
1975	7
1976	7
1977	4

Burgess Whitehead
| 1956 | 1 |

Earl Whitehill
1956	1
1958	2
1960	3

Hoyt Wilhelm
Inducted in 1985
1978	158
1979	168
1980	209
1981	238
1982	236
1983	243
1984	290
1985	331

Billy Williams
Inducted in 1987
1982	97
1983	153
1984	202
1985	252
1986	315
1987	354

Fred Williams
1938	1
1945	1
1948	1
1949	2
1950	9
1951	7
1952	4
1953	4
1954	4
1955	3
1956	11
1958	6
1960	11

Smokey Joe Williams
Inducted in 1999
| 1999 | Vet. Com. |

Ken Williams
| 1956 | 1 |
| 1958 | 1 |

Ted Williams
Inducted in 1966
| 1966 | 282 |

Ned Williamson
| 1936 V | 2 |

Vic Willis
Inducted in 1995
| 1995 | Vet. Com. |

Maury Wills
1978	115
1979	166
1980	146
1981	163
1982	91
1983	77
1984	104
1985	93
1986	124
1987	113
1988	127
1989	95
1990	95
1991	61
1992	110

Jimmie Wilson
1948	8
1949	6
1950	4
1951	2
1952	7
1953	10
1954	8
1955	13
1956	17
1958	3
1960	6
1962	4

Jim Wilson
| 1964 | 2 |

Hack Wilson
Inducted in 1979

1937	1
1939	1
1942	1
1948	2
1949	24
1949 RO	12
1950	16
1951	21
1952	21
1953	43
1954	48
1955	81
1956	74
1958	94
1960	72
1962	39
1979	Vet. Com.

Willie Wilson

2000	10

Dave Winfield
Inducted in 2001

2001	435

Whitey Witt

1949	1

Joe Wood

1937	13
1938	6
1939	2
1942	1
1946 NOM	5
1947	29
1948	5
1950	1
1951	5

Wilbur Wood

1984	14
1985	16
1986	23
1987	26
1988	30
1989	14

Glenn Wright

1948	2
1949	1
1950	2
1951	1

1952	1
1953	3
1954	1
1955	4
1956	3
1958	8
1960	18
1962	1

George Wright
Inducted in 1937
Pioneer

1936 V	6
1937	Cen. Com.

Harry Wright
Inducted in 1953
Pioneer

1953	Vet. Com.

Whit Wyatt

1958	1

Early Wynn
Inducted in 1972

1969	95
1970	140

1971	240
1972	301

Tom Yawkey
Inducted in 1980
Executive

1980	Vet. Com.

Carl Yastrzemski
Inducted in 1989

1989	423

Steve Yeager

1992	2

Steve Yerkes

1945	1

Rudy York

1962	1
1964	10

Cy Young
Inducted in 1937

1936 V	32
1936	111
1937	153

Pep Young

1958	1

Ross Youngs
Inducted in 1972

1936	10
1937	16
1938	40
1939	34
1942	44
1945	22
1946 NOM	25
1947	36
1948	19
1949	20
1949 RO	11
1950	17
1951	34
1952	34
1953	31
1954	34
1955	48
1956	19
1972	Vet. Com.

Robin Yount
Inducted in 1999

1999	385

Tom Zachary

1958	1
1960	1

Chief Zimmer

1938	1

Chapter 42

Streaks and Feats

By Lyle Spatz

This section deals with those baseball endeavors that go beyond the daily boxscores and give the game its special appeal. They range in time from the first year of the National Association in 1871 right through the 2003 season, and in duration from such things as unassisted triple plays, which are accomplished in one at-bat, to consecutive-games-played streaks, which take years to complete. All were extraordinary in their day, and all encapsulated the drama so distinctive to baseball.

First, let's examine the streaks.

Team Winning Streaks

In 2002, the Oakland A's established a new American League record by winning 20 consecutive games between August 13 and September 4. Half were at home and half on the road. The two wins against the Kansas City Royals that tied and then broke the record came in dramatic fashion. In both, the homestanding A's scored the winning run in the last half of the ninth inning.

Oakland was in third place in the AL West, four and a half games behind Seattle when the streak started. When it ended, the A's had a three and a half game lead and were on their way to the division title.

For more than half a century before that, the 1906 Chicago White Sox and the 1947 New York Yankees had shared the American League mark for the most consecutive games won with 19. The 1906 White Sox, dubbed "the Hitless Wonders" because of a .230 team batting average, were 7-1/2 games behind and in fourth place on the second of August. Ahead of them were Philadelphia, New York and Cleveland. By the time they had won their 19th straight, on August 23, they had a 5-1/2-game lead. A week later, the Yankees started a streak of their own, a 15-gamer that carried them past Chicago, but the Sox bounced back and won the pennant by three games. In 1947, the Yanks used their 19-game win streak, 13 of which were on the road, to all but end the pennant race. They had a 3-1/2-game lead when it started, which climbed to 11-1/2 games at its conclusion.

The all-time record for consecutive games won in a season is 26, shared by the 1875 Boston Red Stockings and the 1916 New York Giants. Harry Wright's Red Stockings opened the 1875 National Association season with Al Spalding's 6-0 shutout of the New Haven Elm Citys. The victory was the first of the 26 the Red Stockings would win before suffering their first loss, a 5-4 defeat by the St. Louis Browns on June 5. Boston established a major league record that has been equaled only once in the more than a century and a quarter since it was set. However, unlike the Red Stockings who used the record to launch them to a fourth consecutive National Association title, John McGraw's 1916 New York Giants finished a mediocre fourth in the National League.

On September 7, when the New Yorkers began their record-tying streak, they were 13-1/2 games out of first place. They won

Walt Dropo
The Detroit Tigers slugger tied Pinky Higgins' major-league record by collecting 12 consecutive hits over three games in July 1952.

12 in a row, all at home, and then paused for a rain-halted 1-1 tie with Pittsburgh. The Giants then won their next 14, again all of them played at the Polo Grounds, before losing to the Boston Braves in the final home game of the season. Earlier in the 1916 season, the Giants had another significant winning streak: a 17-gamer in May, all of which, oddly enough, came on the road.

Twice National League clubs from Chicago won 21 in a row, and both were pennant-winners. When the Chicago White Stockings did it, under Cap Anson in 1880, it helped extend their

lead from 3-1/2 games to 13-1/2 games. They won the pennant by 15 games. However, when their descendants, the Chicago Cubs, won 21 in a row in September 1935, the streak capped a sensational stretch battle that allowed them to catch and then pass the St. Louis Cardinals. The Cubs were in third place, 2-1/2 games behind St. Louis, when the streak began on September 4. They took the lead with their 11th consecutive win on September 14, and by the time it ended were 6 games ahead.

Fifteen-Game Team Winning Streaks

Wins	H/A	Team	Lg.	Year	First Win	Last Win
26 (1 tie)	12/14	BOS	NA	1875	April 19*	June 3
26 (1 tie)	26/0	NY	NL	1916	September 7	September 30 (1G)
21 (1 tie)	11/10	CHI	NL	1880	June 2	July 8
21	18/3	CHI	NL	1935	September 4	September 27 (2G)
20	16/4	STL	UA	1884	April 20	May 22
20	16/4	PRO	NL	1884	August 7	September 6
20	10/10	OAK	AL	2002	August 13	September 4
19	11/8	BOS	NA	1872	May 7	July 4
19 (1 tie)	11/8	CHI	AL	1906	August 2	August 23
19	6/13	NY	AL	1947	June 29 (2G)	July 17 (2G)
18	14/4	CHI	NL	1885	June 1	June 24
18 (1 tie)	16/2	BOS	NL	1891	September 16	October 2
18	13/5	BAL	NL	1894	August 24	September 16 (1G)
18	13/5	NY	NL	1904	June 16	July 4 (2G)
18	3/15	NY	AL	1953	May 27	June 14 (2G)
17	14/3	STL	AA	1885	May 5	June 1
17	16/1	BOS	NL	1897	May 31	June 21
17	14/3	NY	NL	1907	April 25	May 18
17	1/16	WAS	AL	1912	May 30 (2G)	June 18
17	0/17	NY	NL	1916	May 9	May 29
17	5/12	PHI	AL	1931	May 5	May 25 (2G)
16	9/7	MUT	NA	1874	August 8	October 2
16	7/9	STL	UA	1884	August 26	September 17
16 (1 tie)	5/11	PHI	NL	1887	September 15	October 8**
16	14/2	PHI	NL	1890	July 8	July 26
16	11/5	PHI	NL	1892	June 11	June 28
16	12/4	PIT	NL	1909	September 9	September 27 (1G)
16	11/5	NY	NL	1912	June 19	July 3 (2G)
16	12/4	NY	AL	1926	May 10	May 26
16	13/3	NY	NL	1951	August 12 (1G)	August 27 (2G)
16	9/7	KC	AL	1977	August 31	September 15 (2G)
15	5/10	BOS	NA	1875	September 6	October 28
15	12/3	DET	NL	1886	May 8	May 29
15	15/0	STL	AA	1887	April 24	May 16
15	11/4	PIT	NL	1903	June 2	June 25 (1G)
15	12/3	NY	AL	1906	August 29	September 8
15	13/2	PHI	AL	1913	May 27 (1)	June 10
15	15/0	IND	FL	1914	June 11 (1G)	June 24
15	3/12	BRO	NL	1924	August 25	September 6 (1G)
15	11/4	CHI	NL	1936	June 4	June 21 (1G)
15	7/8	NY	NL	1936	August 11	August 28
15	11/4	BOS	AL	1946	April 25	May 10
15	9/6	NY	AL	1960	September 16	October 2**
15	10/5	MIN	AL	1991	June 1	June 16
15	9/6	ATL	NL	2000	April 16	May 2

* Beginning of season ** End of season

Consecutive Games Played

In 1989, when the late Jack Kavanagh wrote this section for the first edition of *Total Baseball*, Orioles shortstop Cal Ripken had an active streak of 1,086 consecutive games played. Nevertheless, Jack dismissed the likelihood that Ripken or anyone in the future would ever seriously challenge Lou Gehrig's record of playing in 2,130 consecutive games.

"Lou Gehrig's legacy of stamina and determination reached such a length that all historians can do about the sturdy players who came after him is measure them for the role of runner-up," wrote Jack.

At the time, with Ripken barely past the halfway mark to Gehrig, finding anyone who disagreed would have been difficult. Of course back in 1925, when Everett Scott's consecutive games played streak reached a then record 1,307, many sportswriters had also deemed it an "unbreakable" record.

Cal Ripken's rise to the top of the consecutive-games-played list

in 1995 dropped Everett Scott, the No. 2 man since 1933, down to third place. Joe Sewell, with 1,103 consecutive games played for Cleveland between 1922 and 1930, had occupied that spot for many years, but Sewell's streak is now sixth all-time.

Everett Scott

While several late 19th and early 20th century players had played in more than 500 consecutive games, Everett Scott's consecutive-games-played streak was the first to gain attention throughout baseball. While he is now mostly remembered for that streak, Scott was an excellent major league shortstop, leading all American Leaguers in fielding at that position for eight straight years (1916-23). He began his streak on June 20, 1916 as a member of the Boston Red Sox and continued it after Boston traded him to the Yankees in December 1921.

It was following the 1921 season, when Scott's consecutive game streak had reached 832, that Al Munro Elias, one of baseball's early statisticians, first took note of it. Writing in the 1922 *Baseball Bat Bag*, Elias pointed out that during the 1920 season Scott had broken the record of George Pinkney, who had played in 577 consecutive games for Brooklyn (both in the American Association and the National League) between September 21, 1885 and May 2, 1890.

Scott continued to play every game after joining the Yankees, adding another 475 games to his streak and bringing his total of consecutive games played to 1,307. Although he played at a time when the customs of pitchers throwing at hitters and runners sliding hard into infielders were much more prevalent than they are today, it was not this rougher style of play that was responsible for the streak's ending. When Yankee manager Miller Huggins benched him on May 6, 1925, it was not because of any injury Scott had suffered, but simply because he was in a batting slump.

The next day, the New York newspapers noted that Scott's streak had ended but not one reporter complained about the way it had ended. Nor was there any special ceremony to mark the streak's ending, as there had been on May 2, 1923 at Washington, when Scott played in his 1,000th consecutive game. Before that game, American League President Ban Johnson and Secretary of the Navy Edwin Denby recognized the milestone by presenting Scott with a medal.

Lou Gehrig

Lou Gehrig's consecutive-games-played streak began on June 1, 1925, when he pinch-hit for shortstop Pee Wee Wanninger. Coincidentally, it was Wanninger who was Scott's replacement at shortstop on the afternoon that Yankee manager Miller Huggins benched Scott, ending his streak. The day after pinch-hitting for Wanninger, Gehrig started at first after regular first baseman Wally Pipp complained of a headache and was given the day off. At the time, no one could have suspected that Gehrig was beginning a string of 2,130 consecutive-game appearances, a streak that would endure for fourteen years despite injuries, illnesses and accidents.

Little mention was made of the streak until June 1933, when Dan Daniel of the *New York World Telegram* wrote that Gehrig was within 60 games of breaking Scott's record. At the time, the record was only eight years old and not considered a very glamorous one. Nevertheless, as the 1933 Yankees began to look less and less like a pennant contender, Daniel and other reporters, seeking other things to write about, began occasionally to emphasize the streak in their stories.

On August 3, Lefty Grove of the A's defeated the Yankees, 7-0,

ending New York's record-streak of 308 consecutive games without being shut out. The next day, Richards Vidmer, writing in the *New York Herald Tribune*, said in his notes following the game story that "at least Lou's streak remains intact, he needs only twelve more to pass Scott." However, there were no full stories about the streak; nor was it the topic of any columns. There was no "GEHRIG WATCH," no day-by-day detailing of how close he was getting to Scott's record.

On August 14, two days before what would be the record-tying game, Gehrig played left field (Babe Ruth played first base) in an exhibition game against the Pirates at Forbes Field. It was more than a token appearance for Babe and Lou, as each player batted three times. A day later, the Yanks began a four-game series against the Browns in St. Louis. This was a time before the current "show business" mentality had permeated baseball. Therefore, the Yankees had not tried to have this series moved to New York, nor had there been any attempts by the American League to have Gehrig set the record at Yankee Stadium. Even the beat writers covering the Yankees did not make the impending record the main focus of the stories they sent back from St. Louis. As usual, the writers considered Babe Ruth the major story. Ruth was struggling at the plate and had chosen to sit out the first two games.

When Gehrig tied Scott's record by playing in his 1,307th consecutive game, his accomplishment generated no headlines. The following day, when he set the new mark, a ceremony honoring the achievement took place at home plate after Yankee pitcher Lefty Gomez retired the Browns in the first inning. Both teams gathered around American League President Will Harridge as he presented Lou with a silver statuette donated by *The Sporting News*. E. G. Brands, the editor, posed for pictures with Gehrig, as did Joe Sewell. Sewell, a Yankee teammate, had once played in 1,103 consecutive games and at the time was thought to be the man most likely to break Scott's record. Missing from the simple ceremony was Yankee manager Joe McCarthy, who was ill, and Scott, who had a business obligation in Fort Wayne, Indiana.

Although most homes had radios, there was no nationwide hookup for the ceremony. And because the Yankees did not broadcast their games, even New Yorkers heard neither the game nor the ceremony. A photograph of the presentation appeared in the *St. Louis Globe Democrat*, but not in any of the New York newspapers, nor did the New York papers headline the event. However, Gehrig did receive a congratulatory phone call that evening from Yankee owner Colonel Jacob Ruppert. He was also a guest at a dinner of the St. Louis Chamber of Commerce, where he received another statuette.

Exact attendance figures are difficult to find, but it is safe to say that the game was far from a sellout. In depression-plagued 1933, the Browns drew only 88,113 to Sportsman's Park for the entire season. Then again, there really was not much suspense involved. Everyone knew that Gehrig would show up and that he would play. Baseball was his job and he did it—every day. The fans, many of whom had lost their own jobs because of the economic situation, understood that kind of work ethic and did not consider it particularly extraordinary.

Baseball's "Iron Horse" first began to show signs of wearing out in 1938. He batted .295 that year, the first time in his career he had batted below .300. In spring training the next year it was evident that something was wrong with him, but manager McCarthy left it to Gehrig to decide when to call it quits. That day came on May 2, 1939 at Detroit. After eight feebly played games had brought his string to 2,130, Lou Gehrig advised McCarthy to replace him.

Cal Ripken

Going into the 1989 season, Cal Ripken's streak, begun on May 30, 1982, had reached a very impressive 1,068 games, the sixth longest ever; however, it was still less than half of Lou Gehrig's mark. It would take another seven seasons for Ripken to reach 2,130, a seemingly impossible task, especially for a shortstop.

But day after day and game after game, Ripken persevered, moving relentlessly toward Gehrig's place at the top. Moreover, he did it with a "grace under pressure" that brought glory to the game and stood in sharp contrast to many of the negative aspects of the national pastime. Ripken conducted his career in very much the same way Gehrig did his. He showed up every day and did his job in workmanlike fashion.

Like Gehrig, Ripken was able to shrug off those little injuries and illnesses that force most players to take an occasional day off. Yet, with the record in sight, forces beyond his control threatened to bring the streak to an end. It had reached 2,009 by August 1994 when the players' strike cost him half a season's worth of games. Moreover, the strike led the owners to propose opening the 1995 season with rosters of replacement players. Of course, if the Baltimore Orioles were to begin the season with a replacement player at shortstop, Ripken would have lost his opportunity to break Gehrig's record. Nevertheless, he stood firm with the other members of the players' union. Orioles' owner Peter Angelos added to the complications surrounding the start of the 1995 season by refusing to sign replacement players and offering to forfeit games as a result.

Fortunately for Ripken, and more so for baseball, they settled the strike, and scheduled a 144-game season. Ripken tied Gehrig's longstanding record on September 5, 1995 and then broke it the next day. Both games were against the Anaheim Angels at Baltimore's Camden Yards. Rising to the occasion, he had a combined five hits in nine at bats, with a home run in each game. But just as baseball is a different game now than it was in 1933, so is the attention the media pays to its record-breaking events. Contrary to the lack of attention when Gehrig passed Everett Scott, this was a national and even an international event, covered by newspapers, radio, and television worldwide.

When the record was his, Ripken, as he always did, accepted the plaudits modestly. He even shared the moment with the fans, circling the ballpark to shake hands with those who crowded against the railings to cheer him. After the game, he endlessly answered the same questions from reporters. Finally, when Cal had satisfied all demands, he dressed and went home to celebrate with his father, his brother Bill, and his wife and children. The next day he went to work as usual. By season's end the new record had reached 2,153 games.

Through 1996, 1997 and into 1998, Ripken continued to play every day, though now as a third baseman. Finally, on Sunday, September 20, 1998, with a week remaining in the 1998 season, Ripken without any fanfare took himself out of the lineup, ending his streak of consecutive games played at 2,632.

Cal Ripken's pursuit of Lou Gehrig's record generated a profusion of comparisons between the two "iron men." Much of what was said and written attempted to determine which player had the more difficult circumstances to overcome in recording such an amazing feat of endurance. Those who believed it was Gehrig pointed to numerous doubleheaders, long train trips, and summers without air conditioning. Ripken's defenders countered that Gehrig never had to play on artificial turf, or at night—Cleveland and Philadelphia played the first American League night game two weeks after Gehrig's streak had ended. And, they argued, playing

shortstop is a much more difficult and demanding task than playing first base.

But whatever the advantages or disadvantages each man had, the fact remains that in both Gehrig's era and in Ripken's, every other major league player performed under the same conditions. Yet no one else, in any era, has come close to playing in 2,000 consecutive games. Gehrig was among the most admired players of his time and Ripken is among the most admired of his. Deservedly so, both were quiet, decent men who preferred to let their play on the field define them, and each was probably the best American Leaguer at his position in the twentieth century.

National League Streaks

During the 1930s, Gus Suhr, a fine-fielding first baseman for the Pittsburgh Pirates, reached 822 consecutive games played. But even as he was compiling it, Suhr's streak was dwarfed by Gehrig's string in progress. Still, it far exceeded any earlier National League marks. Cardinals great Stan Musial eventually broke Suhr's National League record by playing in 895 straight games. Musial's streak, which ended in 1957 when he was 36 years old, stood as the NL mark until Billy Williams played in 1,117 games between September 1963 and September 1970.

Williams' record fell to Steve Garvey, who broke it while playing for Los Angeles and San Diego. Garvey's streak began in 1974, with the Dodgers, and ended in 1983, his first season with the Padres. A hand injury took him out of the lineup on July 29, 1983, a season after he had established the new record. Garvey's mark of 1,207 is still the National League record and is fourth all-time, exactly 100 games behind the No. 3 man, Scott.

The following table lists the 15 longest consecutive-games played streaks:

1.	2,632	Cal Ripken	May 30, 1982 to September 19, 1998
2.	2,130	Lou Gehrig	June 1, 1925 to April 30, 1939
3.	1,307	Everett Scott	June 20, 1916 to May 5, 1925
4.	1,207	Steve Garvey	September 3, 1975 to July 29, 1983
5.	1,117	Billy Williams	September 22, 1963 to September 2, 1970
6.	1,103	Joe Sewell	September 13, 1922 to April 30, 1930
7.	895	Stan Musial	April 15, 1952 to August 23, 1957
8.	829	Eddie Yost	April 30, 1949 to May 11, 1955
9.	822	Gus Suhr	September 11, 1931 to June 4, 1937
10.	798	Nellie Fox	August 8, 1955 to September 3, 1960
11.	745	Pete Rose	September 2, 1978 to August 23, 1983
12.	740	Dale Murphy	September 26, 1981 to July 8, 1986
13.	730	Richie Ashburn	June 7, 1950 to April 13, 1955
14.	717	Ernie Banks	August 28, 1956 to June 22, 1961
15.	678	Pete Rose	September 28, 1973 to May 7, 1976

Longest Hitting Streaks

Joe DiMaggio

Joe DiMaggio's 56-game hitting streak in 1941 set a record that many believe will never be equaled. Perhaps not, but unlike some other record that changes in the structure of the game have rendered unbreakable, this one is still attainable. However, the fact that no one has come within a dozen games of it in more than 60 years attests to just how great an accomplishment it was.

The winner of back-to-back American League batting championships in 1939 and 1940, DiMaggio picked right up in 1941. He batted safely in every spring-training exhibition game and continued hitting well through the first eight games of the regular season. But he slumped off after that, and by mid-May his average was barely above .300.

DiMaggio, who held the minor league record with a 61-game streak with the 1933 San Francisco Seals of the Pacific Coast

League, began his major league record streak on May 15, with a first-inning single off Ed Smith of the Chicago White Sox. It would not end until two months later, when another pitcher named Smith, Al Smith, paired with Jim Bagby, Jr. to hold him hitless in a game against the Cleveland Indians. Yet in the streak's early days, as DiMaggio's average continued to rise, the fans focused less on it than they did on Joe's battle with Ted Williams for the batting title. He would, of course, never catch Williams, who was on his way to baseball's last .400 season.

When the streak reached 19, on June 2, the death of another Yankee immortal, Lou Gehrig overshadowed it. However, when it stretched into the twenties, reporters began checking earlier consecutive-game hitting streaks, those that had been mostly unchallenged and unnoticed since 1922. That was the year first baseman George Sisler of the St. Louis Browns hit in 41 straight to break Ty Cobb's American League record, but was stopped short of Willie Keeler's major league record of 44. (Denny Lyons had a 52-game hitting streak for Philadelphia of the American Association in 1887—the year that walks were counted as hits—with walks twice keeping the streak alive.) Before DiMaggio, the only serious challenge to Sisler came in 1938, and it came from another left-handed hitting St. Louis Browns first baseman. George McQuinn ran off a string of 34 games, but McQuinn was playing in the anonymity of the second division, and his challenge drew minimal attention.

Because DiMaggio was a right-handed batter, his first target was deemed to be the record of Rogers Hornsby, who had hit in 33 straight games for the 1922 St. Louis Cardinals. On June 21, DiMaggio hit in his 34th consecutive game, passing Hornsby and putting Sisler's American League record only a week's play away. Previously noted only by baseball fans, the streak now began to capture the attention of the general public. The national media soon followed. The wire services carried stories assuring newspaper readers that Joe had extended his string with front-page bulletins, even before they gave the account of the game in which he did it. Similarly, radio newscasts often began with bulletins about the streak's progress before getting to the day's more sobering national and international events.

As they always did, rival managers juggled pitching rotations to bring their best to the mound when facing the Yankees. Despite that, and despite the growing distractions, DiMaggio continued his consistent, game-after-game pursuit of the next milestone, Sisler's league record. Even the official scorers around the league began to feel the pressure, fearful of making a scoring decision that would appear to favor DiMaggio unfairly. This was especially true for sportswriter Dan Daniel, the official scorer for games at Yankee Stadium. As the streak grew, Daniel was often besieged by fans seated nearby demanding a base hit no matter how glaring the error that allowed DiMaggio to reach base.

Years afterward, DiMaggio looked back on the 56 games and could find only one where he wished the play had not been as judgmental as it was. It came in the 30th game, the one that broke the Yankee record held jointly by Roger Peckinpaugh and Earle Combs. The White Sox came to the Stadium, and Johnny Rigney was the pitcher. He had twice been DiMaggio's victim in earlier games in the streak, but on this day had stopped the Yankee Clipper until the seventh inning. Then DiMaggio hit a routine grounder to shortstop Luke Appling. The future Hall-of-Famer moved for the ball, but it took a bad bounce, hitting him in the shoulder. In his rush to recover, Appling grabbed at the ball, dropped it, and then threw too late to first. Daniel, the official

scorer, ruled it a hit. Had he ruled it an error DiMaggio's streak would have ended that afternoon, because on his last time up, in the ninth, Taffy Wright made a leaping catch to snatch a home run out of the right-field stands.

The next day DiMaggio received another streak-extending break, in much the same way. This time the ball was hard hit and Appling could only knock it down. He could not make a throw. Daniel judged the ball too hard to handle and again scored it a hit. A few days later DiMaggio broke Hornsby's record for right-handed batters and took aim at Sisler's mark. However, it took another break for DiMaggio to get there.

The streak was at 37 when the Yanks hosted the St. Louis Browns on June 26. Going into the home eighth, Browns pitcher Elden Auker had held DiMaggio hitless, and with the Yankees ahead by two runs, it did not appear there would be a bottom of the ninth. Unless one of the first three batters kept the inning alive, Joe, due up fourth, would not bat again.

Johnny Sturm, the first man up popped out, but Red Rolfe drew a walk. Tommy Henrich, the next batter, now had a dilemma. If he hit into a double play, it would deprive DiMaggio of a chance to bat. With manager Joe McCarthy's consent, Henrich bunted and moved Rolfe to second base. Now, with first base open, it was Auker who had a dilemma. He could walk DiMaggio, or pitch to him. He chose to pitch to him, and DiMaggio promptly smashed the first pitch into left field for a double.

Sisler's American League record fell in a June 29 doubleheader at Washington's Griffith Stadium. DiMaggio tied the record in the first game and broke it in the nightcap. The record-tying hit came against Washington's best pitcher, knuckleballer Dutch Leonard, and the record breaker was a last-chance single off the relatively unknown Arnold Anderson.

Two days later, in the second game of a July 1 doubleheader against the Red Sox, DiMaggio tied Keeler's 1897 major league record. The next day, again against the Red Sox, he hit a long home run off Boston's leading winner, Dick Newsome. The blow gave him hits in 45 consecutive games and broke Keeler's longstanding mark.

Although he was no longer faced with the pressure to produce at least one hit each game, or perhaps because of it, DiMaggio continued to add to his streak. He was at 53 on July 14 when the Yanks faced Johnny Rigney at Chicago. Rigney had come close to stopping the streak at 30; now he came close to stopping it again. DiMaggio's only hit came on a dribbler down the third-base line. White Sox third baseman Bob Kennedy was playing deep, a precaution normally taken by rival third basemen when DiMaggio batted. It worked to Joe's advantage that day as he beat out the slowly hit ball; however, it would work to his disadvantage a few days later.

On July 16 the Yankees went from Chicago to Cleveland, where DiMaggio extended the streak to 56 games. The following day it finally ended, although when it did it was due more to the outstanding defense on the left side of the Indians' infield than it was to the pitching of starter Al Smith or reliever Jim Bagby, Jr. Twice Ken Keltner, playing a very deep third base, took drives down the baseline from DiMaggio and turned them into outs. Then on Joe's last at bat, he hit a ball up the middle that took an erratic hop, but shortstop Lou Boudreau grabbed it and flipped to second to start a double play. After saying "I wish it could have gone on forever," DiMaggio immediately embarked on a new streak, hitting safely in the next 16 games. Had not Keltner and Boudreau pulled off outstanding defensive plays in game 57, the streak would have reached an incredible 73 games.

During his 56-game streak, Joe DiMaggio batted .408, scored 56 runs and batted in 55. He hit 15 home runs, half his season's total, and had 35 extra-base hits. Overall, he had 91 hits in 223 at-bats, walked 21 times, was hit by a pitch twice, and struck out only 7 times.

Joe DiMaggio's 1941 Hitting Streak

Game No.	Date	Club and Pitcher(s)	AB	R	H
1	5-15	White Sox, Smith	4	0	1
2	5-16	White Sox, Lee	4	2	2
3	5-17	White Sox, Rigney	3	1	1
4	5-18	Browns, Harris, Niggeling	3	3	3
5	5-19	Browns, Galehouse	3	0	1
6	5-20	Browns, Auker	5	1	1
7	5-21	Tigers, Rowe, Benton	5	0	2
8	5-22	Tigers, McKain	4	0	1
9	5-23	Red Sox, Newsome	5	0	1
10	5-24	Red Sox, Johnson	4	2	1
11	5-25	Red Sox, Grove	4	0	1
12	5-27	Senators, Chase, Anderson, Carrasquel	5	3	4
13	5-28	Senators, Hudson	4	1	1
14	5-29	Senators, Sundra	3	1	1
15	5-30	Red Sox, Johnson	2	1	1
16	5-30	Red Sox, Harris	3	0	1
17	6-1	Indians, Milnar	4	1	1
18	6-1	Indians, Harder	4	0	1
19	6-2	Indians, Feller	4	2	2
20	6-3	Tigers, Trout	4	1	1
21	6-5	Tigers, Newhouser	5	1	1
22	6-7	Browns, Muncrief, Allen, Caster	5	2	3
23	6-8	Browns, Auker	4	3	2
24	6-8	Browns, Caster, Kramer	4	1	2
25	6-10	White Sox, Rigney	5	1	1
26	6-12	White Sox, Lee	4	1	2
27	6-14	Indians, Feller	2	0	1
28	6-15	Indians, Bagby	3	1	1
29	6-16	Indians, Milnar	5	0	1
30	6-17	White Sox, Rigney	4	1	1
31	6-18	White Sox, Lee	3	0	1
32	6-19	White Sox, Smith, Ross	3	2	3
33	6-20	Tigers, Newsom, McKain	5	3	4
34	6-21	Tigers, Trout	4	0	1
35	6-22	Tigers, Newhouser, Newsom	5	1	2
36	6-24	Browns, Muncrief	4	1	1
37	6-25	Browns, Galehouse	4	1	1
38	6-26	Browns, Auker	4	0	1
39	6-27	Athletics, Dean	3	1	2
40	6-28	Athletics, Babich, Harris	5	1	2
41	6-29	Senators, Leonard	4	1	1
42	6-29	Senators, Anderson	5	1	1
43	7-1	Red Sox, Harris, Ryba	4	0	2
44	7-1	Red Sox, Wilson	3	1	1
45	7-2	Red Sox, Newsome	5	1	1
46	7-5	Athletics, Marchildon	4	2	1
47	7-6	Athletics, Babich, Hadley	5	2	4
48	7-6	Athletics, Knott	4	0	2
49	7-10	Browns, Niggling	2	0	1
50	7-11	Browns, Harris, Kramer	5	1	4
51	7-12	Browns, Auker, Muncrief	5	1	2
52	7-13	White Sox, Lyons, Hallett	4	2	3
53	7-13	White Sox, Lee	4	0	1
54	7-14	White Sox, Rigney	3	0	1
55	7-15	White Sox, Smith	4	1	2
56	7-16	Indians, Milnar, Krakauskas	4	3	3
Totals:			**223**	**56**	**91**

Other Consecutive-Game Hitting Streaks

When Joe DiMaggio's 56-game hitting streak became a matter of national awareness in the summer of 1941, it forced baseball historians to look back at the streaks that had preceded his. Yet almost no mention was made of Bill Dahlen's 42-game streak of 1894, although it had been accomplished under the same rules as Willie Keeler's major league record set three years later. Among the things they learned was that had Dahlen not had a most peculiar "off day" on August 7, even DiMaggio's 56-game streak would be just an American League record. In the game following the end of his 42-game streak, Dahlen had put together another one of 28 games.

As it is, the 42 consecutive games in which Dahlen hit safely gives him, not Rogers Hornsby, as previously thought, the longest streak by a right-handed batter in National League history. Oddly, Dahlen was stopped by his own inability to fatten his record in a game in which almost everyone else did. While his team, the Chicago Colts, had 17 hits while winning a 10-inning game from Cincinnati, Reds' pitchers Chauncey Fisher and Tom Parrott held Dahlen hitless in 6 at bats.

The press did note the Dahlen streak when Keeler, of the Baltimore Orioles, eclipsed it in 1897, although they did not recount it in the detail they paid to subsequent streaks. Keeler's 44-game streak began on Opening Day, April 22, and continued until Frank Killen of Pittsburgh stopped him on June 19. Wee Willie's streak still stands as the National League record, tied only by Pete Rose in 1978.

Ty Cobb hit in 20 or more consecutive games seven times during his career and nearly equaled Keeler's mark in 1911, when he set an American League record with a 40-game streak. Then in 1922 two St. Louis players, George Sisler of the Browns and Rogers Hornsby of the Cardinals, created new marks for hitting safely in consecutive games. Sisler hit in 41 straight to break Cobb's AL record, and Hornsby hit in 33 straight, which was hailed as a new record for right-handed batters, at least since 1900. Dahlen's 42 was dismissed as having been made before the turn of the century, despite his having done it under much the same rules in effect in 1922.

Sisler, a popular and widely admired player, began his string on July 27 and continued to get at least one basehit per game through August and past Labor Day. He was four short of tying Cobb's record when the Detroit Tigers, managed by Cobb, came to Sportsman's Park in St. Louis for a three-game series. Hits in the first two games raised the streak to 38, and on September 11, Sisler tried for game 39, one short of Cobb's record.

Early in the game, a generous scorer had granted Sisler a streak-extending single on a fly ball that Bobby Veach had reached but could not hold. However, there were no message boards or public address systems to inform fans of scorers' decisions in 1922. So Cobb, playing center field, was too far away from the press box to see the scorer hold up one finger, the traditional sign of a safe hit. He did not know they had ruled Veach's muff a hit. As far as he knew, Sisler, coming to bat in the bottom of the ninth, with two out, a runner on first, and the score 4-3 in favor of Detroit, was hitless.

Manager Cobb had a choice. He could order Sisler, the Browns' most dangerous hitter, walked. Doing so would move the tying run into scoring position and put the winning run on base. Cobb might have been tempted to deny his rival what he thought was a last chance by ordering an intentional walk. Such a move would have been bad baseball and worse sportsmanship, and he chose not to do so. He did, however, take the precaution of removing Bob "Fatty" Fothergill, a slow-footed fielder, and replacing him in right with Ira Flagstead, a better defensive player. Then he signaled Howard Ehmke to pitch, whereupon Sisler lined a triple between Cobb and Flagstead, no doubt to the great relief of the official scorer.

Sisler had been playing the last few games with a very sore shoulder, which now ached so much he could not play the next four games against the last-place Boston Red Sox. Nevertheless, he was back in the lineup when the Yankees, a half game ahead of the Browns in a torrid pennant race's final stages, came to St. Louis for a crucial three-game series. With his shoulder and right arm bandaged, Sisler had hits in each of the first two games to tie and then break Cobb's record. Trying for number 42 in the September 18 series finale, Sisler went hitless in four plate appearances against Joe

Bush, ending the streak.

Two days later, Hornsby's streak ended at 33 when he failed to get a hit against Brooklyn's Burleigh Grimes. Hornsby's "post-1900" National League record fell in 1945 when Tommy Holmes of the Boston Braves hit in 37 consecutive games. Holmes fell seven games short of Willie Keeler's all-time NL record, and well behind Joe DiMaggio's major league high of 56.

In 1978, switch-hitting Pete Rose of the Cincinnati Reds mounted a serious challenge to both those marks. Rose had gotten his 3,000th hit on May 5, but was batting just .267 when he got two hits in a game against the Cubs on June 14. He kept adding hits, and tied Holmes in a game at Shea Stadium on July 24, and passed him the next day with a hit off Mets pitcher Craig Swan. Following the record-breaker, Holmes, who was the Mets' community relations' director and was at the game, came onto the field to shake the hand of the man who had erased him from the record books.

Rose now held the "modern" National League record and needed seven more games to break Keeler's mark of 44. He got six, tying Keeler on July 31 in Atlanta with a hit off knuckleballer Phil Niekro. The next night a rookie lefthander, Larry McWilliams, held Rose hitless through most of the game, and reliever Gene Garber struck him out in his final at-bat.

Florida Marlins second baseman Luis Castillo mounted the most recent challenge to the Rose-Keeler National League record. In 2002, the switch-hitting Castillo hit safely in 35 consecutive games before the Detroit Tigers stopped him in a June 22 interleague game. Castillo's streak is the longest ever by a foreign-born player.

Longest Hitting Streaks, NL

Player	Team	Year	G
Willie Keeler	BAL	1897	44
Pete Rose	CIN	1978	44
Bill Dahlen	CHI	1894	42
Tommy Holmes	BOS	1945	37
Billy Hamilton	PHI	1894	36
Fred Clarke	LOU	1895	35
Luis Castillo	FLA	2002	35
Benito Santiago	SD	1987	34
George Davis	NY	1893	33
Rogers Hornsby	TL	1922	33
Ed Delahanty	PHI	1899	31
Willie Davis	LA	1969	31
Rico Carty	ATL	1970	31
Vladimir Guerrero	MON	1999	31
Cal McVey	CHI	1876	30
Elmer Smith	CIN	1898	30
Stan Musial	STL	1950	30
Jerome Walton	CHI	1989	30
Luis Gonzalez	ARI	1999	30

Longest Hitting Streaks, AL

Player	Team	Year	G
Joe DiMaggio	NY	1941	56
George Sisler	STL	1922	41
Ty Cobb	DET	1911	40
Paul Molitor	MIL	1987	39
Ty Cobb	DET	1917	35
George Sisler	STL	1925	34
George McQuinn	STL	1938	34
Dom DiMaggio	BOS	1949	34
Hal Chase	NY	1907	33
Heinie Manush	WAS	1933	33
Nap Lajoie	CLE	1906	31
Sam Rice	WAS	1924	31
Ken Landreaux	MIN	1980	31
Tris Speaker	BOS	1912	30
Goose Goslin	DET	1934	30
Ron LeFlore	DET	1976	30
George Brett	KC	1980	30
Sandy Alomar, Jr.	CLE	1997	30
Nomar Garciaparra	BOS	1997	30
Eric Davis	BAL	1998	30

Consecutive Base Hits

In all the years they have played major league baseball, only two players have had 12 consecutive base hits. Pinky Higgins of the Boston Red Sox did it in 1938, and Walt Dropo of the Detroit Tigers did it in 1952. Two other American Leaguers, Tris Speaker and Johnny Pesky, had 11 straight hits, but no National Leaguer has ever exceeded 10. Nine National Leaguers have reached that mark, beginning with Ed Delahanty and Jake Gettman in 1897. Delahanty, a future Hall-of-Famer, was with Philadelphia, while Gettman, a rookie who appeared in only 36 games that season, was with Washington. In 1919, Brooklyn's Ed Konetchy joined Delahanty and Gettman with 10.

Nap Lajoie had 10 for the 1901 Philadelphia Athletics, a streak that began on April 26, the A's first American League game. After grounding out in his first at-bat against Washington, Lajoie doubled, and singled twice. He had three singles the next day against Washington, and then two singles and two triples against Boston on April 29. The streak ended when he grounded out in his first at-bat on April 30. Speaker, the Indians player/manager, was the first to exceed 10 straight, getting 11 consecutive hits in 1920.

During the 1920s five players made a run at Speaker's record but none could get beyond 10 straight hits. Four of the five were future Hall-of-Famers: American Leaguers George Sisler in 1921 and Harry Heilmann in 1922, and National Leaguers Kiki Cuyler in 1925 and Chick Hafey in 1929. The other was Harry McCurdy, a reserve catcher with the White Sox, in 1926. All got up to 10 straight, as did another Hall of Famer, Joe Medwick, in 1936.

Two years later, in 1938, Boston Red Sox third baseman Mike "Pinky" Higgins put together a string of 12 consecutive hits to break Speaker's record. Higgins did it over three games, going 4 for 4 in each. He began the streak on June 19 with three singles and a double, plus a walk, in the second game of a doubleheader against the White Sox in Chicago. Following an off day, the Red Sox were in Detroit to play a doubleheader with the Tigers. In game one, Higgins again had three singles and a double, plus a walk. After singling in his first two at-bats of the second game, public-address announcer Ty Tyson informed the crowd at Briggs Stadium that Higgins could tie Speaker's record if he got a hit the next time up. Higgins did so, and then broke Speaker's mark in his next at-bat with a single off Tigers ace Tommy Bridges. The streak ended at 12 when Higgins struck out in his final turn at the plate.

Slugging first baseman Walt Dropo of the Tigers tied Higgins' record in 1952. Dropo had begun the season with Boston, but the Red Sox had traded him to Detroit in a multiplayer deal in June. Going with Dropo was Johnny Pesky, longtime shortstop for the Red Sox, who had made his own assault on Higgins' record when he had 11 consecutive hits back in 1946. Dropo's streak began with a 5 for 5 day at Yankee Stadium on July 14. The next day, in the first game of a twi-night doubleheader at Washington's Griffith Stadium, he added four more hits. All nine hits had been singles, but in the first inning of the nightcap, Dropo tripled with the bases loaded. He had his 11th straight hit in the third inning, another single, and tied Higgins with a double off Lou Sleater in the fifth. Dropo's attempt to set a new record failed when he fouled out to catcher Mickey Grasso in the seventh.

Since Dropo tied Higgins' record 1952, only three American leaguers have gotten as many as 10 consecutive hits: Ken Singleton of Baltimore in 1981, Frank Thomas of the White Sox in 1997 and Joe Randa of Kansas City in 1999. Bip Roberts of Cincinnati had 10 in 1992, tying the National League record. Chris Stynes also had 10, getting three for the Kansas City Royals in the final games of the 1996 season, and then seven more for the 1997 Cincinnati Reds.

Most Consecutive Hits

American League

Player	Team	Year	H
Pinky Higgins	BOS	1938	12
Walt Dropo	DET	1952	12
Tris Speaker	CLE	1920	11
Johnny Pesky	BOS	1946	11
Nap Lajoie	PHI	1901	10
George Sisler	STL	1921	10
Harry Heilmann	DET	1922	10
Harry McCurdy	CHI	1926	10
Rip Radcliff	CHI	1938	10
Ken Singleton	BAL	1981	10
Frank Thomas	CHI	1997	10
Joe Randa	KC	1999	10
Frank Catalanatto	TEX	2000	10
Doc Johnston	CLE	1919	9
Ty Cobb	DET	1925	9
Sam Rice	WAS	1925	9
Hal Trosky	CLE	1936	9
Ted Williams	BOS	1939	9
Tony Oliva	MIN	1967	9
Jorge Orta	CLE	1980	9
Mickey Hatcher	MIN	1985	9
Lance Johnson	CHI	1995	9
Todd Walker	MIN	1998	9
Charles Johnson	BAL	1999	9

National League

Player	Team	Year	H
Ed Delahanty	PHI	1897	10
Jake Gettman	WAS	1897	10
Ed Konetchy	BRO	1919	10
Kiki Cuyler	PIT	1925	10
Chick Hafey	STL	1929	10
Joe Medwick	STL	1936	10
Buddy Hassett	BOS	1940	10
Woody Williams	CIN	1943	10
Bip Roberts	CIN	1992	10
Chris Stynes*	CIN	1996-97	10
Joe Kelley	BAL	1894	9
Rogers Hornsby	STL	1924	9
Taylor Douthit	STL	1926	9
Babe Herman	BRO	1926	9
Bill Jurges	NY	1941	9
Terry Moore	STL	1947	9
Dick Sisler	PHI	1950	9
Eddie Waitkus	PHI	1950	9
Dave Philley	PHI	1958-59	9
Felipe Alou	SF	1962	9
Willie Stargell	PIT	1966	9
Rennie Stennett	PIT	1975	9
Ron Cey	LA	1977	9
Andres Galarraga	COL	1993	9
Sammy Sosa	CHI	1993	9
Jose Vizcaino	NY	1996	9
Barry Bonds	SF	1998	9
John Olerud	NY	1998	9
Jim Edmonds	STL	2000	9

* The first three hits of Stynes' streak were with the 1996 Kansas City Royals.

Successive Pitching Victories

One Season

When Tim Keefe of the 1888 New York Giants set the record for consecutive victories at 19 straight, he needed only seven weeks to do it. Between June 23 and August 10, Keefe won all his 19 starts, 17 of them complete games. The two he failed to finish included one in which he was hit on the arm by a line drive while leading 8-3 in the sixth inning. Ed Crane, his replacement, held on for a 9-6 victory, credited to Keefe. The other incomplete game would not have been added to his string by today's scoring rules. On July 16, the Giants were leading Chicago 9-0 after two innings and felt confident enough to give Keefe the rest of the day off. The scoring conventions of the time gave Keefe the win.

After having lost his previous start to Boston's John Clarkson, himself a winner of 13 straight in 1885, Keefe began his great run with a 7-6 win over Philadelphia. Keefe's remarkable streak came to an end on August 14, 1888. His defense betrayed him by allowing two unearned runs that were the difference in a 4-2 loss to rookie lefthander Gus Krock of the Chicago White Stockings.

Given the winning streaks that his contemporaries had compiled, they probably thought at the time that Keefe's record was temporary. Until the 1890s, teams rarely used more than two principal pitchers. More open dates existed in the schedules, and two strong-armed men could carry the bulk of the work. A third pitcher, or a general substitute, could help in doubleheaders. Still, the regular duo met most occasions and had many more opportunities to reel off long strings of victories. In 1888, Keefe alternated on the mound with Mickey Welch, also the owner of an impressive winning streak. Welch had won 17 in a row in 1885, one less than the record set by Providence's Charles "Hoss" Radbourn in 1884. Another contemporary, Jim McCormick of Chicago, won 14 in a row in 1885 and 16 straight the next year.

Keefe's record was set when the pitching distance was 50 feet. It was equaled in 1912 by Rube Marquard, also of the New York Giants, pitching at the present distance of 60 feet, 6 inches. Marquard had been a disappointment in his first two seasons in New York, but he benefited in 1911 when manager John McGraw brought Wilbert Robinson, an expert handler of pitchers, to spring training as a coach. Marquard responded with a 24-win season, and then began his great streak on opening day of the 1912 season. The crowd at Washington Park in Brooklyn was so large the afternoon of April 11 that fans were standing 15 feet from the baselines. The Giants won this ludicrous game, 18-3, with the umpires calling a halt after six innings.

Marquard continued winning, running his record to 19-0 with a 2-1 win over Brooklyn's Nap Rucker on July 3. Five days later, the streak ended with a 7-2 loss at Chicago. But whereas present scoring rules would have subtracted a win from Keefe's streak, they would have added one to Marquard's. Under today's rules, Marquard's record would total 20 consecutive victories. In an April 20 game at the Polo Grounds, he replaced starter Jeff Tesreau in the ninth inning with the Giants trailing Brooklyn, 3-2. The Giants rallied to win the game in the bottom of the ninth, but the rules of the day gave the victory to Tesreau, the starting pitcher. Still, even at 19, the record remains unmatched within the confines of a single season.

In addition to Marquard's equaling of Tim Keefe's National League record for successive victories, the 1912 season produced a new American League record, and then an immediate challenge to it. While Marquard was engaged in his run, Washington's Walter Johnson, almost concurrently, was setting the AL record at 16. And by the time Johnson was stopped, another streak was under way, this one by Smokey Joe Wood of the Boston Red Sox.

Johnson had a 13-7 record when he began his streak with a July 5 win over the Yankees. On August 20, he defeated Cleveland for his 15th straight, breaking the former AL record of 14, set by New York's Jack Chesbro in 1904. Johnson won his 16th straight against Detroit on August 23, and had his sights on Marquard's brand-new record. However, some bad luck, and a scoring rule that today would not have cost him a loss, prevented Johnson from catching Marquard. He lost a game to St. Louis in relief after taking over in the seventh inning of a tie game. Two runners were on base, and before Johnson could get the side out one of them scored the winning run. Today they would charge the loss to the

starting pitcher, Tom Hughes, who had allowed the runner to get on base. However, in 1912 they charged the loss against whoever was pitching when the winning run scored. The press and sympathetic fans denounced the scorer's decision, but American League president Ban Johnson decreed the loss be placed against Johnson's record, and there it remains.

Meanwhile, Wood's streak, which had started on July 8, the day Marquard's ended, had grown to 13 by September 2. Although his next scheduled start, against Washington, was on September 7, the press called for it to be moved up a day so he could face Johnson. Red Sox manager Jake Stahl went along, and so on September 6, Johnson got his chance to prevent Wood from equaling or breaking his new record.

Whatever the capacity of Fenway Park was in 1912, they far exceeded it when, on a weekday, more than 30,000 baseball fans gained entrance. The crowd overflowed the stands. In fact, the players could not sit in their dugouts. Instead, they sat on chairs arranged in front of the throngs that stood just outside the baselines. Thousands more people stood in the outfield, behind ropes. The game lived up to expectations. Great defensive plays snuffed out rallies, and both pitchers stopped scoring threats with clutch strikeouts. Boston broke a scoreless tie in the sixth inning when Tris Speaker hit a fly ball that reached the roped-back crowd for a ground-rule double, and Duffy Lewis hit an opposite-field double down the right-field foul line. It just eluded the grab of Danny Moeller, scoring Speaker, and that was it. The Red Sox won, 1-0.

Wood followed with a win against Chicago and then defeated St. Louis, 2-1, on September 15 to tie Johnson's mark. However, his effort to break it failed when he lost to Detroit on September 20. The final score was 6-4, with two of the Tigers runs being unearned. It was not until 1931 that anyone again challenged Marquard's 19 consecutive pitching victories, or even the lesser American League record of 16 straight. That challenge came from Lefty Grove of the Philadelphia Athletics, a team on its way to a third consecutive pennant.

Grove tied the AL record on August 19 and everyone expected him to break it in his next start. That came four days later, Sunday, August 23 against the St. Louis Browns, a second-division team and perennial victim. Grove pitched with close to his usual brilliance, limiting the Browns to six hits, allowing only one run, and striking out six. However, the luck even the best pitchers must have to sustain a long streak deserted him. Unheralded Dick Coffman of the Browns outpitched Grove that day and shut out the Athletics, 1-0, allowing only three hits. Grove's streak ended at 16, tying him with Johnson and Wood at the top of the American League's list.

Never a gracious loser, Grove blamed the loss on the absence of Al Simmons from the lineup. Simmons was home in Milwaukee, seeing a doctor, and his replacement, Jim Moore, misjudged a fly ball, which became the game-winning hit. Grove fumed that Simmons would have caught the ball. What made the defeat even more bitter in retrospect was that Grove went on to win his next five starts.

Three years after Grove reached 16, Schoolboy Rowe of Detroit mounted another assault on the record. Rowe had started slowly in 1934, splitting his first eight decisions, but with his fifth win embarked on what would be his record-equaling streak. He won his 16th straight game on August 26 against Washington, before encountering the barrier that had blocked other American League pitchers. It was the second game of an August 29 doubleheader at Philadelphia, and Rowe was far off form. The now lowly A's

knocked him out in the seventh inning and defeated him, 13-5. Rowe had to settle for sharing the AL record with Grove, Johnson and Joe Wood.

In 2001, a fifth pitcher joined that list. The Yankees' Roger Clemens, on his way to a record sixth Cy Young Award, racked up 16 straight victories between May 26 and September 19. His record stood at 20-1 when the streak ended on September 25 with a 4-0 loss to the last-place Tampa Bay Devil Rays

Two Seasons

The record for consecutive wins beginning in one season and extending into the next belongs to Carl Hubbell of the New York Giants. Between July 17, 1936, and May 27, 1937, Hubbell won an amazing 24 games in a row. He won his last 16 decisions in 1936 and added 8 more victories in 1937 before finally losing a game.

New York had started slowly in 1936. On July 17, the day Hubbell's winning streak began with a 6-0 shutout of Pittsburgh, they were in fifth place, ten games behind the defending champion Chicago Cubs. Hubbell had lost his last start, 1-0, to the Cubs' Bill Lee on an unearned run. Three times during the streak Hubbell's mound opponent was Dizzy Dean of the St. Louis Cardinals, his great rival for National League pitching supremacy during these years. In 1936, Hubbell defeated Dean twice: 2-1 in an extra-inning game, and another 2-1 win in nine. Dean was also the victim on May 19, 1937, the day the streak reached 22.

The end of Hubbell's streak came on May 31, at the hands of the team that considered any victory over the Giants compensation for an otherwise dismal season. The Brooklyn Dodgers invaded the Polo Grounds for a doubleheader that drew the second-largest crowd that had ever crammed into the Giants' home field. Brooklyn had always been a tough team for Hubbell, yet he had beaten them five times during the streak, twice in relief. But in the opening game of the doubleheader, the Dodgers drove him out in the third inning on the way to a 10-3 victory, ending his run of consecutive wins at 24. The most serious challenge to Hubbell's record came from Pittsburgh Pirates reliever Elroy Face. After winning his final 5 decisions in 1958, Face won his first 17 in 1959, giving him 22 consecutive games won, all in relief. That, of course, also stands as the best achievement for a reliever.

Just as the 1912 season saw single-season record-setting streaks by Rube Marquard, Walter Johnson and Joe Wood, the years 1936-37 saw both leagues produce record two-season streaks. In the same two seasons that Carl Hubbell was winning 24 straight in the NL, Cleveland's Johnny Allen was running off 17 consecutive wins to establish an AL record. Allen's record, tied by Baltimore's Dave McNally during the 1969 and 1970 seasons, lasted until 1999. The year before, 1998, Roger Clemens, of the Toronto Blue Jays, took a 15-game winning streak into his final start of the season. The Blue Jays won in 13 innings, but Clemens was not involved in the decision. Thwarted in his attempt to tie the American League single-season mark, which he would do as a Yankee in 2001, he was still on track for the two-season records of Allen, McNally and Hubbell.

While it is inconceivable that the Giants would have traded Carl Hubbell after the 1936 season, the reasons for player movements are much more complex in today's game, and in February 1999 Toronto traded the Cy Young Award winner to the New York Yankees. As a Yankee, Clemens won his first 5 decisions in 1999, giving him 20 straight and establishing a new AL mark for successive victories over two seasons. After the New York Mets, an NL team, stopped the streak in an interleague game, Clemens added

another victory over an AL team. So while Clemens' two-year streak is officially 20 straight, it is actually 21 against American League opposition.

Pitchers with 12 or More Consecutive Victories in One Season

National League			American League		
Year	Pitcher	Won	Year	Pitcher	Won
1888	Tim Keefe, NY	19	1912	Walter Johnson, WAS	16
1912	Rube Marquard, NY	19	1912	Joe Wood, BOS	16
1884	Charles Radbourn, PRO	18	1931	Lefty Grove, PHI	16
1885	Mickey Welch, NY	17	1934	Schoolboy Rowe, DET	16
1890	Pat Luby, CHI	17	2001	Roger Clemens, NY	16
1959	Elroy Face, PIT	17	1932	Alvin Crowder, WAS	15
1886	Jim McCormick, CHI	16	1937	Johnny Allen, CLE	15
1936	Carl Hubbell, NY	16	1969	Dave McNally, BAL	15
1947	Ewell Blackwell, CIN	16	1974	Gaylord Perry, CLE	15
1962	Jack Sanford, SF	16	1998	Roger Clemens, TOR	15
1924	Dazzy Vance, BRO	15	2003	Roy Halladay, TOR	15
1968	Bob Gibson, STL	15	1904	Jack Chesbro, NY	14
1972	Steve Carlton, PHI	15	1913	Walter Johnson, WAS	14
1885	Jim McCormick, CHI	14	1914	Chief Bender, PHI	14
1886	John Flynn, CHI	14	1928	Lefty Grove, PHI	14
1904	Joe McGinnity, NY	14	1961	Whitey Ford, NY	14
1909	Ed Reulbach, CHI	14	1980	Steve Stone, BAL	14
1984	Rick Sutcliffe, CHI	14	1986	Roger Clemens, BOS	14
1985	Dwight Gooden, NY	14	1924	Walter Johnson, WAS	13
1996	John Smoltz, ATL	14	1925	Stan Coveleski, WAS	13
1880	Larry Corcoran, CHI	13	1930	Wes Ferrell, CLE	13
1884	Charlie Buffinton, BOS	13	1940	Bobo Newsom, DET	13
1885	John Clarkson CHI	13	1949	Ellis Kinder, BOS	13
1892	Cy Young, CLE	13	1971	Dave McNally, BAL	13
1893	Frank Killen, PIT	13	1973	Jim Hunter, OAK	13
1896	Frank Dwyer, CIN	13	1978	Ron Guidry, NY	13
1897	Fred Klobedanz, BOS	13	1983	LaMarr Hoyt, CHI	13
1898	Ted Lewis, BOS	13	1901	Cy Young, BOS	12
1909	Christy Mathewson, NY	13	1910	Russ Ford, NY	12
1910	Deacon Phillippe PIT	13	1914	H. "Dutch" Leonard, BOS	12
1927	Burleigh Grimes, NY	13	1929	Tom Zachary, NY	12
1956	Brooks Lawrence, CIN	13	1931	George Earnshaw, PHI	12
1966	Philip Regan, LA	13	1938	Johnny Allen, CLE	12
1971	Dock Ellis, PIT	13	1939	Atley Donald, NY	12
1992	Tom Glavine, Atl	13	1946	Dave Ferriss, BOS	12
1886	Charlie Ferguson, PHI	12	1961	Luis Arroyo, NY	12
1902	Jack Chesbro, PIT	12	1963	Whitey Ford, NY	12
1904	George Wiltse, NY	12	1968	Dave McNally, BAL	12
1906	Ed Reulbach, CHI	12	1971	Pat Dobson, BAL	12
1975	Burt Hooton, LA	12	1985	Ron Guidry, NY	12
1992	Mark Portugal, HOU	12	1990	Bobby Witt, TEX	12
2002	Wade Miller, HOU	12	1991	Scott Erickson, MIN	12
			1997	Brad Radke, MIN	12
			2002	Jarrod Washburn, ANA	12

Other Leagues			
Year	League	Pitcher	Won
1890	AA	Scott Stratton, LOU	15
1884	AA	Jack Lynch, NY	14
1884	UA	Jim McCormick, CIN	14
1882	AA	Will White, CIN	12

Successive Pitching Victories Against One Team

A record for successive victories by a pitcher that has lasted even longer than Carl Hubbell's 24 against the National League is one held jointly by Christy Mathewson and Carl Mays. Mathewson, an earlier New York Giants great, had an equally long win streak that came against one team, the St. Louis Cardinals. After yielding five runs and lasting just one inning in a 14-1 loss at St. Louis on May 10, 1904, Mathewson defeated the Cardinals 24 consecutive times. The streak began on June 16, 1904, with a 4-3 win at the Polo Grounds, and carried through to September 15, 1908, with a 5-4 win in relief, also at home. St. Louis ended the streak on May 24, 1909, in New York, when John Lush defeated Mathewson, 3-1.

Before Mathewson, Charles "Hoss" Radbourn of the Providence Grays held the major league record with 21 consecutive wins against the Detroit Wolverines. Radbourn had beaten Detroit 10 straight before losing to them on May 19, 1883. But he bested

them again on June 14, which started the streak of 21 straight (and 31 of 32) against the Wolverines. Win number 21 came on September 18, 1884, with the streak ending when Radbourn was charged with the loss in the game of September 20.

Carl Mays set the American League record and tied Mathewson's major league mark by defeating the Philadelphia Athletics 24 straight times between August 30, 1918 and July 24, 1923. Unlike Mathewson, who won several games in relief, all of Mays' 24 wins were as a starter, and 23 of the 24 were complete games. He launched the streak as a member of the Boston Red Sox by starting and winning both ends of an August 30, 1918 double-header. He had one more win against Philadelphia before Boston traded him to the New York Yankees on July 29, 1919. The change of uniform made no difference in Mays' effectiveness against the Athletics. He defeated them 21 consecutive times as a Yankee, before the A's ended the streak in Mays' final appearance as an American Leaguer with a 7-6 win on October 4, 1923.

Mathewson later came close to tying or breaking his own mark with 22 straight wins against Cincinnati (June 17, 1908 to August 16, 1911). And the Reds' Pete Donohue made a run with a 20-game streak against the Phillies (September 22, 1921 to July 29, 1925). However, since Donohue, only one National Leaguer has won as many as 19 straight against one team. Juan Marichal of the San Francisco Giants did so by winning his first 19 decisions against the hapless New York Mets (June 3, 1962 to June 3, 1967).

Chief Bender of the Athletics had the American League's longest streak before Mays, winning 19 straight against the St. Louis Browns from August 15, 1908 to July 23, 1913. The longest AL streak since Mays belongs to Ellis Kinder of the Boston Red Sox. Between July 22, 1948 and June 1, 1952, Kinder defeated the Chicago White Sox 18 consecutive times.

The increase in the number of teams in each league caused by expansion has led to teams playing each other far fewer times than the 22 games per season during Mathewson's and Mays' time. This has made it very difficult for modern-day pitchers to challenge those streaks.

Christy Mathewson's 24-Game Winning Streak against St. Louis

1	June 16, 1904; 4-3 @ NY	2	August 6, 1904; 8-1 @ NY
3	August 8, 1904; 4-3 @ NY (relief)	4	August 27, 1904; 9-3 @ STL
5	October 3, 1904; 3-1 @ NY	6	May 11, 1905; 4-0 @ NY
7	June 17, 1905; 7-2 @ STL	8	July 21, 1905; 14-2 @ NY
9	August 28, 1905; 8-1 @ NY	10	September 29, 1905; 6-5 @ STL (11)
11	May 26, 1906; 5-4 @ STL	12	June 15, 1906; 2-1 @ NY
13	July 14, 1906; 4-0 @ STL	14	September 28, 1906; 8-2 @ NY
15	May 17, 1907; 2-1 @ NY (12)	16	June 11, 1907; 8-7 @ STL (relief)
17	July 9, 1907; 5-3 @ NY	18	July 29, 1907; 4-3 @ STL (11)
19	August 27, 1907; 1-0 @ NY	20	June 6, 1908; 3-2 @ NY
21	July 21, 1908; 4-2 @ STL	22	July 29, 1908; 1-0 @ NY
23	August 17, 1908; 3-0 @ STL	24	September 15, 1908; 5-4 @ NY (relief)

Carl Mays' 24-Game Winning Streak against Philadelphia

1	August 30, 1918; 12-0 @ BOS (1G)	2	August 30, 1918; 4-1 @ BOS (2G)
3	May 29, 1919; 7-1 @ PHI	4	August 31, 1919; 6-0 @ NY
5	September 26, 1919; 8-2 @ NY	6	April 24, 1920; 3-2 @ NY (10)
7	June 6, 1920; 12-6 @ NY	8	July 3, 1920; 5-0 @ PHI (1G)
9	September 7, 1920; 2-0 @ NY	10	September 27, 1920; 3-0 @ PHI
11	April 13, 1921; 11-1 @ NY	12	April 21, 1921; 6-1 @ PHI
13	May 28, 1921; 5-1 @ NY (1G)	14	July 4, 1921; 14-4 @ NY
15	August 13, 1921; 7-2 @ PHI (1G)	16	September 10, 1921; 19-3 @ PHI
17	October 1, 1921; 5-3 @ NY (1G)	18	April 24, 1922; 6-4 @ NY (11)
19	May 6, 1922; 2-0 @ PHI	20	May 29, 1922; 7-4 @ NY
21	June 4, 1922; 8-3 @ NY	22	July 3, 1922; 12-1 @ PHI
23	September 2, 1922; 11-6 @ PHI (1G)	24	July 24, 1923; 9-2 @ PHI

Winning Streaks of 15 or More Against One Team (National League)

24	Christy Mathewson NY vs STL:	June 16, 1904 to September 15, 1908
22	Christy Mathewson NY vs CIN:	June 17, 1908 to August 16, 1911
21	Charles Radbourn PRO vs DET:	June 14, 1883 to September 18, 1884
20	Pete Donohue CIN vs PHI:	September 22, 1921 to July 29, 1925
19	Charles Radbourn Pro vs PHI:	May 1, 1883 to July 17, 1885
19	Juan Marichal SF vs NY:	June 3, 1962 to June 3, 1967 (1G)
18	Larry Jackson STL/CHI/PHI vs NY:	April 11, 1962 to June 20, 1967
17	John Clarkson CHI vs STL:	May 1, 1885 to August 14, 1886
17	Joe McGinnity NY vs BOS:	October 4, 1902 to May 5, 1905
17	Christy Mathewson NY vs BRO:	September 13, 1907 to June 24, 1911
17	Russ Meyer PHI/BRO vs CHI:	June 14, 1951 to April 30, 1955
16	Mickey Welch TRO vs BUF:	May 29, 1880 to July 4, 1881
16	Ed Reulbach CHI vs CIN:	July 15, 1906 to August 18, 1909
16	Ed Reulbach CHI vs BRO:	July 30, 1907 to August 10, 1910
15	Charles Buffinton BOS vs PHI:	May 4, 1883 to August 6, 1884
15	Tim Keefe NY vs IND:	May 16, 1887 to September 7, 1888
15	Kid Nichols BOS vs NY:	June 5, 1890 to May 15, 1893
15	Kid Nichols BOS vs LOU:	July 7, 1892 to June 3, 1896
15	Kid Nichols BOS vs STL:	May 6, 1895 to July 19, 1899
15	Orval Overall CHI vs STL:	June 26, 1906 to September 9, 1909
15	Christy Mathewson NY vs BOS:	June 24, 1908 to September 12, 1911
15	Robin Roberts PHI vs PIT:	May 20, 1951 to August 12, 1953

Winning Streaks of 15 or More Against One Team (American League)

24	Carl Mays BOS/NY vs PHI:	August 30, 1918 (1G) to July 24, 1923
19	Chief Bender PHI vs STL:	August 15, 1908 to July 23, 1913
18	Ellis Kinder BOS vs CHI:	July 22, 1948 (2G) to June 1, 1952
17	Mel Parnell BOS vs WAS:	July 8, 1948 to May 30, 1952 (2G)
17	Dave McNally BAL vs WAS/TEX:	July 12, 1969 to August 15, 1973
16	Jack Chesbro NY vs WAS:	April 25, 1903 to September 5, 1905
16	Walter Johnson WAS vs CHI:	June 6, 1912 to May 12, 1914
16	Bob Lemon CLE vs PHI/KC:	June 14, 1951 to August 19, 1956 (1G)
15	Walter Johnson WAS vs STL:	May 19, 1910 to August 11, 1912
15	Joe Wood BOS vs STL:	May 25, 1911 to June 15, 1914
15	Joe Bush NY vs STL:	July 11, 1922 to September 17, 1924
15	Hal Newhouser DET vs STL:	May 6, 1945 (1G) to June 29, 1947 (1G)

The Feats

Home Runs

For many fans, baseball's most glamorous record is the single-season home run mark. Babe Ruth held that distinction for 42 years, beginning with his record-breaking 29-home-run season in 1919, a record he himself broke with 54 in 1920, 59 in 1921, and 60 in 1927. Although Ruth had several challengers during those years, most notably Jimmie Foxx and Hank Greenberg, each of whom had 58, the record endured until Roger Maris hit 61 home runs in 1961. Because it came during an expansion season with an extended schedule, and because he was not a player in the Ruthian mold, Maris' achievement was not a popular one. Still, it stood for 37 years before falling in spectacular fashion.

The season-long 1998 race between massive Mark McGwire of the Cardinals and genial Sammy Sosa of the Cubs captured the nation's attention and did much to repair the damage baseball suffered after the 1994 players' strike. McGwire emerged the winner with a record-shattering 70 home runs, while Sosa finished with 66, the second highest total ever.

But while Ruth's record of 60 lasted 34 seasons, and Maris' record of 61 lasted 37, McGwire's mark was short-lived. Just three years later, in 2001, Barry Bonds of the San Francisco Giants slugged 73 home runs to establish the new single-season home-run record. Maris' 61 home runs in 1961 remains the American League record. Below are lists of the men who held the single-season home run records in the National and American Leagues, and a game-by-game listing of Barry Bonds' and Roger Maris' record-breaking seasons.

Single-Season Home-Run Record (NL)

George Hall, PHI, 1876	5	
Charley Jones, BOS, 1879	9	
Buck Ewing, NY, 1883	10	
Ned Williamson, CHI, 1887	27	
Rogers Hornsby, STL, 1922	42	
Chuck Klein, PHI, 1929	43	
Hack Wilson, CHI, 1930	56	
Mark McGwire, STL, 1998	70	
Barry Bonds, SF, 2001	73	

Single-Season Home-Run Record (AL)

Nap Lajoie, PHI, 1901	14	
Socks Seybold, PHI, 1902	16	
Babe Ruth, BOS, 1919	29	
Babe Ruth, NY, 1920	54	
Babe Ruth, NY, 1921	59	
Babe Ruth, NY, 1927	60	
Roger Maris, NY, 1961	61	

Barry Bonds' 73-Home Run Season (2001)

HR	Date	Opposing Pitcher, Club	Place	On Base
1	April 2	Woody Williams, San Diego	H	0
2	April 12	Adam Eaton, San Diego	A	0
3	April 13	Jamey Wright, Milwaukee	A	1
4	April 14	Jimmy Haynes, Milwaukee	A	2
5	April 15	David Weathers, Milwaukee	A	0
6	April 17	Terry Adams, Los Angeles	H	1
7	April 18	Chan Ho Park, Los Angeles	H	0
8	April 20	Jimmy Haynes, Milwaukee	H	1
9	April 24	Jim Brower, Cincinnati	H	1
10	April 26	Scott Sullivan, Cincinnati	H	1
11	April 29	Manny Aybar, Chicago	H	0
12	May 2	Todd Ritchie, Pittsburgh	A	1
13	May 3	Jimmy Anderson, Pittsburgh	A	1
14	May 4	Bruce Chen, Philadelphia	A	1
15	May 11	Steve Trachsel, New York	H	0
16	May 17	Chuck Smith, Florida	A	1
17	May 18	Mike Remlinger, Atlanta	A	0
18	May 19	Odalis Perez, Atlanta	A	0
19	May 19	Jose Cabrera, Atlanta	A	0
20	May 19	Jason Marquis, Atlanta	A	0
21	May 20	John Burkett, Atlanta	A	0
22	May 20	Mike Remlinger, Atlanta	A	0
23	May 21	Curt Schilling, Arizona	A	0
24	May 22	Russ Springer, Arizona	A	1
25	May 24	John Thomson, Colorado	H	0
26	May 27	Denny Neagle, Colorado	H	1
27	May 30	Robert Ellis, Arizona	H	0
28	May 30	Robert Ellis, Arizona	H	1
29	June 1	Shawn Chacon, Colorado	A	1
30	June 4	Bobby Jones, San Diego	H	0
31	June 5	Wascar Serrano, San Diego	H	1
32	June 7	Brian Lawrence, San Diego	H	1
33	June 12	Pat Rapp, Anaheim (AL)	H	0
34	June 14	Lou Pote, Anaheim (AL)	H	0
35	June 15	Mark Mulder, Oakland (AL)	H	0
36	June 15	Mark Mulder, Oakland (AL)	H	0
37	June 19	Adam Eaton, San Diego	A	0
38	June 20	Rodney Myers, San Diego	A	1
39	June 23	Darryl Kile, St. Louis	A	1
40	July 12	Paul Abbott, Seattle (AL)	A	0
41	July 18	Mike Hampton, Colorado	H	0
42	July 18	Mike Hampton, Colorado	H	1
43	July 26	Curt Schilling, Arizona	A	0
44	July 26	Curt Schilling, Arizona	A	3
45	July 27	Brian Anderson, Arizona	A	0
46	August 1	Joe Beimel, Pittsburgh	H	0
47	August 4	Nelson Figueroa, Philadelphia	H	1
48	August 7	Danny Graves, Cincinnati	A	0
49	August 9	Scott Winchester, Cincinnati	A	0
50	August 11	Joe Borowski, Chicago	A	2
51	August 14	Ricky Bones, Florida	H	3
52	August 16	A. J. Burnett, Florida	H	0
53	August 16	Vic Darensbourg, Florida	H	2
54	August 18	Jason Marquis, Atlanta	H	0
55	August 23	Graeme Lloyd, Montreal	A	0
56	August 27	Kevin Appier, New York	A	0
57	August 31	John Thomson, Colorado	H	1
58	September 3	Jason Jennings, Colorado	H	0
59	September 4	Miguel Batista, Arizona	H	0
60	September 6	Albie Lopez, Arizona	H	0
61	September 9	Scott Elarton, Colorado	A	0
62	September 9	Scott Elarton, Colorado	A	0
63	September 9	Todd Belitz, Colorado	A	2
64	September 20	Wade Miller, Houston	H	1
65	September 23	Jason Middlebrook, San Diego	A	0
66	September 23	Jason Middlebrook, San Diego	A	0
67	September 24	James Baldwin, Los Angeles	A	0
68	September 28	Jason Middlebrook, San Diego	H	0
69	September 29	Chuck McElroy, San Diego	H	0
70	October 4	Wilfredo Rodriguez, Houston	A	0
71	October 5	Chan Ho Park, Los Angeles	H	0
72	October 5	Chan Ho Park, Los Angeles	H	0
73	October 7	Dennis Springer, Los Angeles	H	0

San Francisco played 162 games in 2001. Bonds played in 153 games.

Roger Maris' 61-Home Run Season (1961)

HR	Date	Opposing Pitcher, Club	Place	On Base
1	April 26	Paul Foytack, Detroit	A	0
2	May 3	Pedro Ramos, Minnesota	A	2
3	May 6	Eli Grba, Los Angeles	A	0
4	May 17	Pete Burnside, Washington	H	1
5	May 19	Jim Perry, Cleveland	A	1
6	May 20	Gary Bell, Cleveland	A	0
7	May 21	Chuck Estrada, Baltimore	H	0
8	May 24	ene Conley, Boston	H	1
9	May 28	Cal McLish, Chicago	H	1
10	May 30	Gene Conley, Boston	A	0
11	May 30	Mike Fornieles, Boston	A	2
12	May 31	Billy Muffett, Boston	A	0
13	June 2	Cal McLish, Chicago	A	2
14	June 3	Bob Shaw, Chicago	A	2
15	June 4	Russ Kemmerer, Chicago	A	0
16	June 6	Ed Palmquist, Minnesota	H	2
17	June 7	Pedro Ramos, Minnesota	H	0
18	June 9	Ray Herbert, Kansas City	H	1
19	June 11 +	Eli Grba, Los Angeles	H	0
20	June 11 +	Johnny James, Los Angeles	H	0
21	June 13	Jim Perry, Cleveland	A	0
22	June 14	Gary Bell, Cleveland	A	1
23	June 17	Don Mossi, Detroit	A	0
24	June 18	Jerry Casale, Detroit	A	1
25	June 19	Jim Archer, Kansas City	A	0
26	June 20	Joe Nuxhall, Kansas City	A	0
27	June 22	Norm Bass, Kansas City	A	1
28	July 1	Dave Sisler, Washington	H	1
29	July 2	Pete Burnside, Washington	H	2
30	July 2	Johnny Klippstein, Washington	H	1
31	July 4	Frank Lary, Detroit	H	1
32	July 5	Frank Funk, Cleveland	H	0
33	July 9 *	Bill Monbouquette, Boston	H	0
34	July 13	Early Wynn, Chicago	A	1
35	July 15	Ray Herbert, Chicago	A	0
36	July 21	Bill Monbouquette, Boston	H	0
37	July 25 *	Frank Baumann, Chicago	H	1
38	July 25	Don Larsen, Chicago	H	0
39	July 25 +	Russ Kemmerer, Chicago	H	0
40	July 25 +	Warren Hacker, Chicago	H	2
41	August 4	Camilo Pascual, Minnesota	H	2
42	August 11	Pete Burnside, Washington	A	0
43	August 12	Dick Donovan, Washington	A	0
44	August 13 *	Bennie Daniels, Washington	A	0
45	August 13 +	Marty Kutyna, Washington	A	1
46	August 15	Juan Pizarro, Chicago	H	0
47	August 16	Billy Pierce, Chicago	H	1
48	August 16	Billy Pierce, Chicago	H	0
49	August 20	Jim Perry, Cleveland	A	1
50	August 22	Ken McBride, Los Angeles	A	1
51	August 26	Jerry Walker, Kansas City	A	0
52	September 2	Frank Lary, Detroit	H	0
53	September 2	Hank Aguirre, Detroit	H	1
54	September 6	Tom Cheney, Washington	H	0
55	September 7	Dick Stigman, Cleveland	H	0
56	September 9	Mudcat Grant, Cleveland	H	0
57	September 16	Frank Lary, Detroit	A	1
58	September 17	Terry Fox, Detroit	A	1
59	September 20	Milt Pappas, Baltimore	A	0
60	September 26	Jack Fisher, Baltimore	H	0
61	October 1	Tracy Stallard, Boston	H	0

* First game of doubleheader.
+Second game of doubleheader.
New York played 163 games in 1961 (one tie on April 22). Maris played in 161 games.

Four Home Runs in a Game

It is a rare feat for a batter to hit four home runs in a game—so rare that before Mike Cameron and Shawn Green did it in 2002 it had never happened twice in the same season. And when Carlos Delgado joined the list in 2003, it was the first time four home-run games had occurred in consecutive seasons.

Batters with four home runs in one game

Bobby Lowe, Boston, May 30, 1894, vs Cincinnati (second game)
Ed Delahanty, Philadelphia, July 13, 1896, vs Chicago (NL)
Lou Gehrig, New York (AL), June 3, 1932, at Philadelphia (AL)
Chuck Klein, Philadelphia (NL), July 10, 1936, at Pittsburgh (10 inning game)
Pat Seerey, Chicago (AL), July 18, 1948, at Philadelphia (AL) (11 inning game)
Gil Hodges, Brooklyn, August 31, 1950, vs Boston (NL)
Joe Adcock, Milwaukee, July 31, 1954, at Brooklyn
Rocky Colavito, Cleveland, June 10, 1959, at Baltimore
Willie Mays, San Francisco, April 30, 1961, at Milwaukee
Mike Schmidt, Philadelphia, April 17, 1976, at Chicago (NL) (10 inning game)
Bob Horner, Atlanta, July 6, 1986, vs Montreal
Mark Whiten, St Louis, September 7, 1993, at Cincinnati
Mike Cameron, Seattle, May 2, 2002, at Chicago (AL)
Shawn Green, Los Angeles, May 23, 2002, at Milwaukee
Carlos Delgado, Toronto, September 25, 2003, vs Tampa Bay

Grand Slam Home Runs

Their frequency has increased dramatically in recent seasons; still, few feats electrify a crowd like the grand-slam home run. Nap Lajoie hit two grand slams in 1901 and added one in 1902 and one in 1907 to hold the American League record in the league's early years. That mark held until 1922 when Babe Ruth hit his fifth grand slam. Ruth kept adding to his total, holding the record until 1934 when Lou Gehrig passed him by hitting his 17th. Gehrig retired with 23 grand slams, the major league record. However, in contrast to the American League, which has had only three lifetime record holders, the National League has had twelve, including several players who have held it twice. The current NL leader is Willie McCovey, with 18 grand slams. Although he holds neither league record, Eddie Murray, with 19, is second only to Gehrig in total grand slams. Murray had 16 in the American League and 3 in the National.

Lou Gehrig's 23 Grand-Slam Home Runs

HR#	Date	Pitcher/Team
11	July 23, 1925	Frederick Marberry WAS
44	May 7, 1927	Ted Lyons CHI
65	July 4, 1927	Bobby Burke WAS
88	May 11, 1928	Joe Shaute CLE
142	September 10, 1929	Phil Page DET
145	September 18, 1929	Milt Shoffner CLE
154	May 22, 1930	Bill Shores PHI
179	July 31, 1930	Ed Durham BOS
223	August 29, 1931	Lefty Grove PHI
225	August 31, 1931	Lloyd Brown WAS
227	September 1, 1931	Ed Morris BOS
240	May 26, 1932	General Crowder WAS
265	September 9, 1932	Earl Whitehill DET
305	May 10, 1934	Lee Stine CHI
307	May 13, 1934	Lloyd Brown CLE
314	June 10, 1934	Bill Dietrich PHI
321	July 5, 1934	Lefty Stewart WAS
359	July 7, 1935	Bobo Newsom WAS
368	August 21, 1935	Jim Walkup STL
414	August 15, 1936	Randy Gumpert PHI
422	September 9, 1936	Oral Hildebrand CLE
458	August 31, 1937	Mel Harder CLE
488	August 20, 1938	Buck Ross PHI

Eddie Murray's 19 Grand-Slam Home Runs

HR#	Date	Pitcher/Team
30	April 28, 1978	Lerrin LaGrow CHI (AL)
68	July 31, 1979	Reggie Cleveland MIL (AL)
122	August 16, 1981	Ross Baumgarten CHI (AL)
126	September 7, 1981	Wayne Garland CLE (AL)
134	April 5, 1982	Dennis Leonard KC (AL)
155	August 26, 1982	Ken Schrom TOR (AL)
193	September 18, 1983	Pete Ladd MIL (AL)
212	June 19, 1984	Bob Stanley BOS (AL)
215	July 7, 1984	Larry Gura KC (AL)
240	July 9, 1985	Curt Wardle MIN (AL)
243	July 25, 1985	Floyd Bannister CHI (AL)
251	August 26, 1985	Alan Fowlkes CAL (AL)
260	April 19, 1986	Dave Rozema TEX (AL)
265	May 18, 1986	Jose Rijo OAK (AL)
334	April 10, 1989	Mike LaCoss SF (NL)
404	June 2, 1992	Trevor Wilson SF (NL)
412	September 4, 1992	Tim Belcher CIN (NL)
495	August 10, 1996	Jeff Darwin CHI (AL)
501	September 21, 1996	Scott Brow TOR (AL)

Willie McCovey's 18 Grand-Slam Home Runs

HR#	Date	Pitcher/Team
24	June 12, 1960	Carl Willey MIL
119	June 22, 1964	John Tsitouris CIN
160	September 10, 1965	Ted Abernathy CHI
166	April 27, 1966	Milt Pappas CIN
205	April 22, 1967	Ramon Hernandez ATL
229	September 23, 1967	Juan Pizarro PIT
231	September 27, 1967	Tug McGraw NY
238	May 4, 1968	Larry Jaster STL
292	June 28, 1969	Jack Fisher CIN
308	August 26, 1969	Jerry Johnson PHI
318	April 4, 1970	Bill Stoneman MON
322	May 10, 1970	Tug McGraw NY
364	July 21, 1971	Dave Giusti PIT
374	July 2, 1972	Don Sutton LA
416	May 19, 1974	Tom Bradley SF
440	May 30, 1975	Bob Apodaca NY
478	June 27, 1977	Joe Hoerner CIN
483	August 8, 1977	Wayne Twitchell MON

Ultimate Grand-Slam Home Runs

The most spectacular of all grand slam home runs is the "ultimate grand slam," the one that comes in the home team's final at bat and carries them to a one run victory. A relatively rare occurrence, only 23 ultimate grand slams have been hit in major league history. Jason Giambi of the Yankees had the most recent one, on May 17, 2002. The Yanks were trailing the Twins, 12-9, but had the bases loaded in the home half of the 14th inning. Giambi drove Mike Trombley's first pitch into the seats to give New York a dramatic 13-12 victory.

Date	Batter	Team	Pitcher	Team	Score
Sep. 10, 1881	Roger Connor*	TRO-NL	Lee Richmond	WOR	8-7
Sep. 24, 1925	Babe Ruth	NY-AL	Sarge Connally	CHI	6-5 (10)
May 23, 1936	Sam Byrd	CIN-NL	Cy Blanton	PIT	4-3
July 8, 1950	Jack Phillips	PIT-NL	Harry Brecheen	STL	7-6
June 16, 1952	Bobby Thomson	NY-NL	Willard Schmidt	STL	8-7
July 15, 1952	Eddie Joost	PHI-AL	Satchel Paige	STL	7-6
Sep. 11, 1955	Del Crandall*	MIL-NL	Herm Wehmeier	PHI	5-4
May 11, 1956	Danny Kravitz	PIT-NL	Jack Meyer	PHI	6-5
July 25, 1956	Roberto Clemente	PIT-NL	Jim Brosnan	CHI	9-8
Aug. 31, 1963	Ellis Burton*	CHI-NL	Hal Woodeshick	HOU	6-5
Aug. 2, 1970	Tony Taylor	PHI-NL	Mike Davison	SF	7-6
Aug. 1, 1971	Carl Taylor*	STL-NL	Ron Herbel	SD	11-10
April 22, 1973	Ron Lolich*	CLE-AL	Sonny Siebert	BOS	8-7 (11)
May 1, 1979	Roger Freed*	STL-NL	Joe Sambito	HOU	7-6
April 13, 1983	Bo Diaz*	PHI-NL	Neil Allen	NY	10-9
Aug. 31, 1984	Buddy Bell*	TEX-AL	Pete Ladd	MIL	7-6
Apr. 13, 1985	Phil Bradley*	SEA-AL	Ron Davis	MIN	8-7
Aug. 29, 1986	Dick Schofield*	CAL-AL	Willie Hernandez	DET	13-12
June 21, 1988	Alan Trammell*	DET-AL	Cecilio Guante	NY	7-6
May 17, 1996	Chris Hoiles*	BAL-AL	Norm Charlton	SEA	14-13
July 28, 2001	Brian Giles*	PIT-NL	Billy Wagner	HOU	9-8 (1G)
May 17, 2002	Jason Giambi	NY-AL	Mike Trombley	MIN	13-12 (14)

* Home run came with two men out.
(Chart courtesy of Herman Krabbenhoft, Baseball Quarterly Review)

Two Grand Slams in One Game

In 2003 Bill Mueller of the Boston Red Sox became the 10th American Leaguer and 12th player overall to hit two bases-loaded home runs in the same game. In 1999 Fernando Tatis hit his two in the same *inning*.

Date	Player	Innings
May 24, 1936	Tony Lazzeri NY (AL)	2nd and 5th
July 4, 1939	Jim Tabor BOS (AL)	3rd and 6th (2nd Game)
July 27, 1946	Rudy York BOS (AL)	2nd and 5th
May 9, 1961	Jim Gentile BAL (AL)	1st and 2nd
July 3, 1966	Tony Cloninger ATL (NL)	1st and 4th
June 24, 1968	Jim Northrup DET (AL)	5th and 6th
June 26, 1970	Frank Robinson BAL (AL)	5th and 6th
September 4, 1995	Robin Ventura CHI (AL)	4th and 5th
August 14, 1998	Chris Hoiles BAL (AL)	3rd and 8th
April 23, 1999	Fernando Tatis STL (NL)	3rd and 3rd
May 10, 1999	Nomar Garciaparra BOS (AL)	1st and 8th
July 29, 2003	Bill Mueller BOS (AL)	7th and 8th

Triple Crown Winners—Batting

For a batter to win the Triple Crown, he must be his league's season leader in batting average, home runs and runs batted in. Back in 1878, Paul Hines of the Providence Grays led the National League in home runs and runs batted in, but finished second to Abner Dalrymple in batting. However, researchers later uncovered two tie games played by Hines and one by Dalrymple. Adding the stats from those games revealed that Hines' batting average was now higher than Dalrymple's, .358 to .356.

In 1968, a special Baseball Records Committee approved this new information and retroactively awarded a Triple Crown to Paul Hines. Hines enjoyed the distinction of being the first Triple Crown winner from 1969, when Macmillan published the first edition of *The Baseball Encyclopedia*, through 1994, when Major League Baseball and *Total Baseball* adopted a new stance. Because the National League of 1878 did not count individual marks amassed in tie games, the ruling was that the championship should return to Dalrymple, despite his lower average under modern reconstruction.

Hines' ouster makes Tip O'Neill baseball's first Triple Crown winner. O'Neill, playing for the 1887 St. Louis Browns, led the American Association, then a major league, in batting (.485) home runs (14), and RBIs (123). O'Neill's .485 average reflects the one-year rule that counted walks as hits. However, even without the boost that his 50 walks gave him, O'Neill's .435 average would have remained the league's highest.

Because runs batted in, while known as a baseball statistic as early as 1879, did not become an official measure until 1920, they had to be reconstructed for earlier seasons. This allowed baseball historians to award Triple Crowns retroactively not only to O'Neill, but also to Napoleon Lajoie and Ty Cobb. At one time, Hugh Duffy was also included among the retroactive Triple Crown winners. In addition to his 18 home runs and 145 runs batted in, Duffy batted .440 for the 1894 Boston Beaneaters, the major leagues' highest batting average ever (excluding 1887). However, the addition of individual statistics from protested games (in keeping with the National League practice of 1894) raised the RBI total of Philadelphia's Sam Thompson to 147, making him the leader.

Lajoie, who had jumped from the Philadelphia Phillies to the Philadelphia Athletics of the new American League, won his crown in 1901. The great second baseman's most sensational season ever—a .426 batting average, 14 home runs and 145 runs batted in—brought instant respect to the new league. Lajoie would again win the batting and RBI titles with Cleveland in 1904, but fall short in the home-run race.

Detroit's Cobb succeeded Lajoie as the American League's superstar, but despite ten batting championships and four RBI titles, won only one Triple Crown, in 1909. He did come close two other times, in 1907 and 1911, finishing second in home runs in each of those years. Cobb's great rival was Honus Wagner of the National League's Pittsburgh Pirates. Wagner won eight batting titles, and combined them with RBI crowns in 1908 and 1909, but lost out on home runs (he was second in 1908).

Finishing with eight home runs, only one behind his Cincinnati teammate Fred Odwell, cost Cy Seymour a Triple Crown in 1905. The home-run title was the most difficult for the stars of the dead-ball era to achieve, although it was a second place finish to Jake Daubert in the batting race that kept the Phillies' Gavvy Cravath from a Triple Crown in 1913. Rogers Hornsby of the St. Louis Cardinals just missed winning a Triple Crown in 1921, when his 21 home runs were two behind the Giants' George Kelly. But a year later Hornsby did lead in all three departments to become the first National Leaguer to win a Triple Crown. He repeated in 1925.

Babe Ruth got two legs of the Triple Crown seven times without ever winning one. Although he had many home-run titles, and he frequently topped the league in RBIs, the competition for batting championships in the 1920s was intense. Cobb, George Sisler and Harry Heilmann often topped .400, and Heilmann alone accounted for four batting titles. Ruth's second place finishes to Heilmann and to Heinie Manush in the 1923 and 1926 batting races, and to Goose Goslin in the 1924 RBI race cost him Triple Crown honors in each of those three years.

In the 1930s, the American League's two great first basemen, Jimmie Foxx and Lou Gehrig, were each a threat to claim the Crown every year. Gehrig won in 1934, but when Foxx narrowly failed in two different seasons, it was not the Yankee great who stymied him. In 1932, Dale Alexander, who split the season between Detroit and Boston, edged Foxx out for the batting title. Alexander, the first player to win while appearing with two teams, barely qualified for the championship, but his .367 topped the .364 by Foxx. The following year, 1933, Foxx won his lone Triple Crown.

Foxx had moved from the Athletics to the Red Sox by 1938, when he had his second near miss of the Triple Crown. This time it was the home-run lead that eluded him. Foxx hit 50 home runs while also winning batting and RBI honors. However, 1938 was the season Hank Greenberg hit 58 homers in his dramatic chase to equal Babe Ruth's record.

The National League also produced two Triple Crown winners in the 1930s: Chuck Klein and Joe Medwick. Klein won as a member of the Phillies in 1933, the same season Foxx was doing likewise for the A's. It was the only year that each league produced a Triple Crown winner, and they played for the same city. Medwick was with the St. Louis Cardinals in 1937, when he became the National League's last Triple Crown winner. Stan Musial, another Cardinal great, narrowly missed his bid for a Triple Crown in 1948. Musial led the NL in batting and RBIs, and just about every other hitting category, but finished one home run behind Johnny Mize and Ralph Kiner, who tied for the title with 40.

Ted Williams added the home-run title to his league-leading .406 batting average in 1941, but fell one leg short of the Triple Crown when Joe DiMaggio topped the RBI column. The next year Williams won all three titles for the first of his two Triple Crowns.

Several wartime players won two legs of the Triple Crown: Rudy York, with the Detroit Tigers in 1943, and Bill Nicholson, a

Chicago Cubs outfielder in 1943 and 1944. Both led in home runs and runs batted in but were far outdistanced in batting average.

Williams had gone off to serve in World War II after winning the Triple Crown in 1942. He returned in 1946 to finish second in each of the Triple Crown categories. Washington's Mickey Vernon beat him out for the batting title, and Hank Greenberg, who had blocked Foxx in 1938, had his last hurrah with the Tigers, topping Williams in both home runs and runs batted in. With Greenberg gone to the National League in 1947, Williams easily claimed his second Triple Crown. No one was close to him in any of the three prize categories, and despite three prime seasons lost to wartime service, the Red Sox star seemed most likely to be the first to win the Triple Crown three times. He would come agonizingly close in 1949. DiMaggio, winner of the home-run and RBI titles in 1948, was injured much of the season and did not compete for individual honors. Williams' chief 1949 rival in those two categories was his Red Sox teammate, Vern Stephens. He would edge Stephens in home runs, and tie him for the RBI lead, but lose the batting race to the Tigers' George Kell on the season's final day. By going hitless as the Sox lost the pennant-deciding game in New York, Williams finished at .3427. Kell, meanwhile, had two hits to finish at. 3429. It was the closest any player ever came to a Triple Crown without actually winning it and the closest anyone has come to earning the honor three times.

Cleveland's Al Rosen had a similar near miss in 1953. Rosen won the home-run and RBI titles, but Mickey Vernon edged him for the batting championship, .337 to .336. Mickey Mantle was at his peak in 1956 when he won the Triple Crown. Mantle won his only batting title with a .353 average, while leading the league with 52 home runs and 130 runs batted in. In 1966, Frank Robinson of Baltimore won a Triple Crown in his first season in the American League. The former Cincinnati star won the home run and RBI titles comfortably, and while his .316 batting average would not have made the top five in the National League in 1966, it was one of only two above .300 in the American League. One year later, Carl Yastrzemski of the Red Sox used the second of his three batting titles to win the major leagues' most recent Triple Crown. Yastrzemski's RBI and home run titles (he tied Harmon Killebrew in home runs) were the only ones of his career.

Since Yaz won the last Triple Crown, many players have won two legs, but failed on the third. Three National Leaguers—Joe Torre in 1971, Al Oliver in 1982, and Todd Helton in 2000—have won batting titles and the RBI championship, but not the home-run race. Torre and Oliver were not serious threats to lead in home runs, but Helton's total of 42 was only eight behind the leader.

Most of those who have won two titles in their Triple Crown quests have led the home run and RBI races, but lagged far behind in the batting race. Among the players who have won home-run and RBI titles in the same season (including several who have done it multiple times), are Frank Howard, Johnny Bench, Willie Stargell, George Foster, Andre Dawson, Eddie Murray, Tony Armas, Jose Canseco, Mike Schmidt, and Willie McCovey. Of all these sluggers, only McCovey came close to a batting title. His .320 mark in 1969 was fifth in the league behind Pete Rose's .348.

Barry Bonds lost the Triple Crown in 1993, his first year in San Francisco, because his excellent .336 batting average was only good for fourth place behind Colorado's Andres Galarraga's .370. Galarraga was on the other side in 1996. He won the home run and RBI crowns, but batted only .304. Dante Bichette, another Colorado slugger, lost out in 1995 because his .340 average was 28

points behind Tony Gwynn's winning mark of .368. Gwynn also won batting titles in 1987, 1989 and 1996, years when Andre Dawson, Kevin Mitchell and Galarraga won the other two legs of the Triple Crown.

Rod Carew was Gwynn's counterpart in the American League. Carew's batting championships helped block five potential Triple Crown seasons: Harmon Killebrew in 1969, Dick Allen in 1972, Reggie Jackson in 1973, George Scott in 1975, and Jim Rice in 1978. In reality, only Rice, who hit .315 to finish 15 points behind Carew, was a serious Triple Crown contender.

In the past few seasons, Mark McGwire of the 1999 Cardinals and Juan Gonzalez of the 2002 Texas Rangers captured the home-run and RBI titles, but missed out on the batting title. Therefore, 66 years have now elapsed since the last Triple Crown winner in the National League, and 36 in the American League. Obviously, the proliferation of teams has made winning the Triple Crown much more difficult. The previous winners all played in an eight-team league except for Hugh Duffy (12 teams) and Carl Yastrzemski (10 teams), while current American Leaguers compete in a 14-team league and National Leaguers in a 16-team league. Yet players continue to come close to achieving this lofty feat, and so the hope remains that we will again see it accomplished.

Triple Crown Batters
American League

Player	Team	Year	HR	RBI	BA
Nap Lajoie	PHI	1901	14	125	.422
Ty Cobb	DET	1909	9	107	.377
Jimmie Foxx	PHI	1933	48	163	.356
Lou Gehrig	NY	1934	49	165	.363
Ted Williams	BOS	1942	36	137	.356
Ted Williams	BOS	1947	32	114	.343
Mickey Mantle	NY	1956	52	130	.353
Frank Robinson	BAL	1966	49	122	.316
Carl Yastrzemski	BOS	1967	44	121	.326

National League

Player	Team	Year	HR	RBI	BA
Rogers Hornsby	STL	1922	42	152	.401
Rogers Hornsby	STL	1925	39	143	.403
Chuck Klein	PHI	1933	28	120	.368
Joe Medwick	STL	1937	31	154	.374

American Association

Player	Team	Year	HR	RBI	BA
Tip O'Neill	STL	1887	14	123	.485

Triple Crown Winners—Pitching

The pitcher's equivalent of the Triple Crown requires that the pitcher lead the league in wins, strikeouts and earned run average. But as with runs batted in for hitters, earned run average for pitchers was not an official statistic in the game's early years. It did not become so in the National League until 1912 and in the American League until 1913. When historians began reconstructing earned run averages for those early years, they discovered that Tommy Bond of Boston was the first pitcher to win a Triple Crown. Bond, the only 19th-century pitcher on the list of Triple Crown winners who is not in the Hall of Fame, led the National League in the three categories in 1877, the second year of the league's existence.

The next pitcher to claim the Triple Crown retroactively was Charles "Hoss" Radbourn in 1884. Radbourn pitched the Providence Grays to the National League pennant almost single-handedly that season, after Charlie Sweeney's departure had left

him as the team's only pitcher. Along with his 59 victories, the most ever won by a pitcher in a season, and 441 strikeouts, Radbourn had a 1.38 ERA at a time when the league mark was 2.98. Tim Keefe of the New York Giants achieved his Triple Crown in 1888 when his 35 victories edged out Boston's John Clarkson who had 33. A year later, Clarkson raised his win total to a league-leading 49 that, along with his 284 strikeouts and 2.73 ERA, earned him the Triple Crown.

Amos Rusie was the most dominant pitcher of the 1890s, and his overwhelming fastball may have been the principal reason the distance of the pitcher's box was pushed back in 1893. But even at the new distance of 60 feet, 6 inches, Rusie continued to dominate. In 1894, along with again leading the league in strikeouts, he topped all pitchers with 36 wins and an ERA of 2.78. Rusie's earned run average was nearly a run lower than the second-place finisher, Jouett Meekin, and close to two and a half runs below the league ERA.

Boston's Cy Young brought prestige to the new American League by winning a Triple Crown in 1901, just as Nap Lajoie, another established star, had done by winning the batters' version. Christy Mathewson of the New York Giants won two Triple Crowns, one in 1905 and one in 1908. In 1905 Matty won 31 games, struck out 206 and had an ERA of 1.28. That same year Rube Waddell, in his last great year with the Philadelphia Athletics, also won a Triple Crown. Waddell produced 27 wins, 287 strikeouts and an ERA of 1.48 to become the first left-hander to join the ranks of Triple Crown winners.

The World Series, inaugurated in 1903 but boycotted by the Giants in 1904, was resumed in 1905. The Giants and A's had won their respective pennants, but the unpredictable Waddell injured his arm while wrestling with a teammate and could not pitch in the Series. A confrontation between Waddell and Mathewson would have been the only one of its kind. Never since have both pennant winners also had a Triple-Crown-winning pitcher.

Walter Johnson won three Triple Crowns in his long career, winning them at widely spaced intervals. The first came in 1913, the next in 1918, and the last in 1924, when he helped pitch the Senators to their first American League pennant.

Grover Cleveland Alexander of the Philadelphia Phillies produced the most impressive reign ever enjoyed by a Triple Crown winner. A year after winning two legs of the crown in 1914—he missed on ERA—Alexander had three successive seasons with 30 or more victories. Starting with the pennant-winning 1915 season, he won 31, 33 and 30 games, while each time also leading the NL in ERA and strikeouts. (Fred Anderson of the Giants had a lower ERA than Alexander in 1917, but he had only 8 complete games. To be eligible for the title under the rules of the time, a pitcher had to have at least 10 complete games.)

Alexander was in the Army in 1918; nevertheless, Jim "Hippo" Vaughn of the Chicago Cubs gave the National League its fourth straight season with a Triple Crown winner. Oddly, Alexander had been a member of the Cubs when he served his time in the Army. Despite his three consecutive Triple Crowns, the Phillies sold him and his battery mate Bill Killefer to Chicago following the 1917 season. Alexander got into only three games in 1918 while Vaughn was in the star's role, but the two teammates competed for the Triple Crown in 1919. Alexander led the league in ERA and Vaughn in strikeouts; however, neither came close to topping the league in wins. The following year Alexander won another Triple Crown. It was his fourth, still the most ever won by a pitcher.

Brooklyn's Dazzy Vance led the National League in wins twice, in earned run average three times, and in strikeouts seven times. Yet only in 1924 did he lead in all three, a feat that won him not only a Triple Crown, but also earned him the Chalmers Award as the National League's Most Valuable Player.

Lefty Grove won back-to-back Triple Crowns for the pennant-winning Philadelphia Athletics in 1930 and 1931, adding the first Baseball Writers Association's Most Valuable Player Award in '31. They were Grove's only two crowns, surprising for a pitcher who with the Athletics and later with the Boston Red Sox led the American League in individual Triple Crown categories a total of 20 times.

Another southpaw ace, the Yankees' Lefty Gomez, also won two Triple Crowns, although not consecutively. Gomez won in 1934, a season when the Yankees did not win the pennant, and in 1937, when they did.

Bucky Walters, a converted third baseman, led Cincinnati to a pennant in 1939 by winning the National League's first Triple Crown in 15 years. The Reds repeated in 1940, but Walters missed doing so when he lost the strikeout title to Philadelphia's Kirby Higbe.

Cleveland's Bob Feller led the league in victories six times and in strikeouts seven, and in five seasons he led in both. But only in 1940 did Feller add the ERA title necessary to give him the Triple Crown. (Ernie Bonham had a lower ERA, 1.90 to Feller's 2.62, but the Yankee rookie pitched only 99 innings.)

Hal Newhouser came close to winning back-to-back Triple Crowns in the last two years of World War II. He won two legs in 1944, but came in second to Detroit Tiger teammate Dizzy Trout for ERA honors. Newhouser won the crown in 1945, as the Tigers won the pennant, then won two legs again in 1946, this time against peacetime competition. However his 275 strikeouts, an amount good enough to lead the league in most seasons, fell far below Bob Feller's record 348. Eighteen years passed between Newhouser's Triple Crown in 1945 and 1963, when Sandy Koufax won the first of his three. During that period, the honor eluded even Warren Spahn. The great Boston and Milwaukee lefthander topped the National League in victories eight times, led in strikeouts four times, and took the ERA title three times, but he could never achieve all three in a single season.

Koufax, who reached stardom after the Dodgers moved from Brooklyn to Los Angeles, won Triple Crowns again in 1965 and 1966. Unlike any previous winner, Koufax left the game following a Triple Crown season. An arthritic left arm caused his early retirement after a 1966 season of 27 victories, 317 strikeouts and an ERA of 1.73.

Not surprisingly, all three of Koufax's Triple Crowns were achieved in pennant-winning years for the Dodgers. A Triple Crown-winning pitcher has not always meant a pennant for his team, but the two have gone together more often than not. However, never has there been such a contrast in the success of a team's best pitcher and the rest of its staff as there was in 1972, when Steve Carlton took the honor despite pitching for a last-place team. The Phillies won 59 games, and Carlton won 27 of them. He struck out 310 and, for the only time in his career, led in ERA, at 1.97.

Another drought followed Carlton's success, despite the presence of such future Hall of Fame pitchers as Tom Seaver, Ferguson Jenkins, Jim Palmer, Gaylord Perry, Nolan Ryan, Phil Niekro, Don Sutton, and Catfish Hunter. Yankee southpaw Ron Guidry came the closest in 1978, when he had the most wins (25) and the lowest

ERA (1.74), but he had 12 fewer strikeouts than Ryan.

The post-Carlton drought ended in 1985, when 20-year-old Dwight Gooden of the New York Mets won the Triple Crown with a remarkable 24-4 record, a 1.53 earned run average, and 268 strikeouts. A year later, Roger Clemens, Gooden's American League contemporary, matched his 24-4 record and also won the ERA title, but his 238 strikeouts were 7 behind Seattle's Mark Langston.

Clemens would win two legs again in 1991, failing this time to lead the league in wins. Then, after 13 seasons with the Red Sox, Clemens signed as a free agent with Toronto in 1997 and won the American League's first Triple Crown in 52 years. Clemens repeated the feat in 1998, although he had to win his final 15 games to do it. (Clemens, Rick Helling, and David Cone all finished with 20 victories.)

In 1999 Pedro Martinez notched the American League's third consecutive Triple Crown with one of the greatest pitching seasons in baseball history. Martinez, who succeeded Clemens as the ace of the Red Sox staff, won 23 of 27 decisions, struck out 313 batters, and compiled an ERA that was less than half the league average (2.07 to 4.86). Martinez missed repeating in 2000, despite winning the ERA and strikeout titles by large margins, when his 18 wins were two short of the league high.

After failing to lead in wins cost him the honor with Seattle in 1995 and Arizona in 1999, Randy Johnson became the newest addition to the ranks of Triple Crown winners in 2002. Johnson won 24 games for the Diamondbacks, struck out 334, and had a 2.32 earned run average.

Triple Crown Pitchers
American League

Player	Team	Year	W	L	SO	ERA
Cy Young	BOS	1901	33	10	158	1.62
Rube Waddell	PHI	1905	27	10	287	1.48
Walter Johnson	WAS	1913	36	7	243	1.14
Walter Johnson	WAS	1918	23	13	162	1.27
Walter Johnson	WAS	1924	23	7	158	2.72
Lefty Grove	PHI	1930	28	5	209	2.54
Lefty Grove	PHI	1931	31	4	175	2.06
Lefty Gomez	NY	1934	26	5	158	2.33
Lefty Gomez	NY	1937	21	11	194	2.33
Bob Feller	CLE	1940	27	11	261	2.61
Hal Newhouser	DET	1945	25	9	212	1.81
Roger Clemens	TOR	1997	21	7	292	2.05
Roger Clemens	TOR	1998	20	6	271	2.65
Pedro Martinez	BOS	1999	23	4	313	2.07

National League

Player	Team	Year	W	L	SO	ERA
Tommy Bond	BOS	1877	40	17	170	2.11
Charles Radbourn	PRO	1884	59	12	441	1.38
Tim Keefe	NY	1888	35	12	333	1.74
John Clarkson	BOS	1889	49	19	284	2.73
Amos Rusie	NY	1894	36	13	195	2.78
Christy Mathewson	NY	1905	31	9	206	1.28
Christy Mathewson	NY	1908	37	11	259	1.43
Grover Alexander	PHI	1915	31	10	241	1.22
Grover Alexander	PHI	1916	33	12	167	1.55
Grover Alexander	PHI	1917	30	13	200	1.83
Hippo Vaughn	CHI	1918	22	10	148	1.74
Grover Alexander	CHI	1920	27	14	173	1.91
Dazzy Vance	BRO	1924	28	6	262	2.16
Bucky Walters	CIN	1939	27	11	137	2.29
Sandy Koufax	LA	1963	25	5	306	1.88
Sandy Koufax	LA	1965	26	8	382	2.04
Sandy Koufax	LA	1966	27	9	317	1.73
Steve Carlton	PHI	1972	27	10	310	1.97
Dwight Gooden	NY	1985	24	4	268	1.53
Randy Johnson	ARI	2002	24	5	334	2.32

Most Strikeouts by Pitchers in a Game

The 1884 season, the first in which overhand pitching was allowed, saw a great increase in the number of strikeouts per game. Four pitchers had one-game totals of 18 or more strikeouts. Charles Sweeney of Providence did it in the National League, while Chicago's Hugh Daily, Boston's Dupee Shaw, and Milwaukee's Henry Porter accomplished the feat in the Union Association. Sweeney and Daily had 19, while Shaw and Porter had 18.

Cleveland's Bob Feller was the first pitcher working at the modern distance to strike out 18 batters in a regulation game. Feller, still a month shy of his 20th birthday, did it at home against Detroit on the last day of the 1938 season, breaking the major league record of 17 that he shared with Dizzy Dean of the Cardinals. Sandy Koufax of the Dodgers tied Feller's mark in 1959 and again in 1962, as did Houston's Don Wilson in 1968.

A year later, another National League lefthander, Steve Carlton, became the first to fan 19 batters in a game. Despite his record achievement, Carlton yielded two two-run homers to Ron Swoboda and his Cardinals lost the game to the New York Mets, 4-3.

Carlton's record, later tied by Tom Seaver and Nolan Ryan, fell to Boston's Roger Clemens in 1986. In a late April game against the Seattle Mariners, the Red Sox fireballer struck out 20 batters, and then, astoundingly, duplicated the feat ten years later at Detroit.

In May 1998, Chicago Cubs rookie Kerry Wood, making only his fifth big league start, tied Clemens' major league mark and set the National League record by striking out 20 Houston Astros.

Arizona's Randy Johnson joined the list of pitchers with a 20-strikeout game in 2001. On May 8, Johnson fanned 20 Cincinnati batters in nine innings, but left with the score tied in a game that lasted two more innings.

Tom Cheney, a journeyman pitcher for the expansion Washington Senators, struck out 21 Baltimore Orioles in a 16-inning game in 1962. Cheney is the only major league pitcher to exceed twenty strikeouts in a single game of any length.

18 or More Strikeouts, Post-1893
Nine Inning Game

20: Kerry Wood, Chicago (NL), May 6, 1998, vs Houston
20: Roger Clemens, Boston, September 18, 1996 at Detroit
20: Roger Clemens, Boston, April 29, 1986 vs Seattle
19: Randy Johnson, Seattle, June 24, 1997 vs Oakland
19: Randy Johnson, Seattle, August 8, 1997 vs Chicago
19: David Cone, New York (NL), October 6, 1991 at Philadelphia
19: Nolan Ryan, California, August 12, 1974 vs Boston
19: Tom Seaver, New York (NL), April 22, 1970 vs San Diego
19: Steve Carlton, St. Louis, September 15, 1969 vs New York (NL)
18: Roger Clemens, Toronto, August 25, 1998 vs Kansas City
18: Randy Johnson, Seattle, September 27, 1992 at Texas (8 innings)
18: Ramon Martinez, Los Angeles, June 4, 1990 vs Atlanta
18: Bill Gullickson, Montreal, September 10, 1980 vs Chicago
18: Ron Guidry, New York (AL), June 17, 1978 vs California
18: Nolan Ryan, California, September 10, 1976 at Chicago
18: Don Wilson, Houston, July 14, 1968 at Cincinnati
18: Sandy Koufax, Los Angeles, April 24, 1962 at Chicago
18: Sandy Koufax, Los Angeles, August 31, 1959 vs San Francisco
18: Bob Feller, Cleveland, October 2, 1938 vs Detroit

Extra-Inning Game

21: Tom Cheney, Washington, September 12, 1962 at Baltimore, 16 innings
20: Randy Johnson Arizona (NL), May 8, 2001 vs Cincinnati (pitched nine innings of an 11-inning game.)
19: Luis Tiant, Cleveland, July 3, 1968 vs Minnesota, 10 innings
19: Nolan Ryan, California, June 14, 1974 vs Boston, 12 innings
19: Nolan Ryan, California, August 20, 1974 at Detroit, 11 innings
19: Nolan Ryan, California, June 8, 1977 vs Toronto, 10 innings
18: Jack Coombs, Philadelphia, September 1, 1906 at Boston (AL), 24 innings
18: Warren Spahn, Boston, June 14, 1952 vs Chicago (NL), 15 innings
18: Jim Maloney, Cincinnati, June 14, 1965 vs New York (NL), 11 innings
18: Chris Short, Philadelphia, October 2, 1965 at New York, 15 innings

No-Hitters

Of the more than 200 major league pitchers who have thrown no hitters, two deserve special mention: Johnny Vander Meer and Nolan Ryan.

In 1938, Vander Meer became the first pitcher in major league history to have two no hitters in one season, and he is still the only one to have thrown back-to-back no hitters. The Cincinnati left-hander no-hit the Boston Braves, 3-0, at Crosley Field on June 11, 1938, and in his next start, on June 15, he no-hit Brooklyn, 6-0, in the first night game ever played at Ebbets Field.

Nolan Ryan pitched the first four of his record seven no-hitters as a member of the California Angels. The first was on May 15, 1973 when he defeated the Kansas City Royals, 3-0, in Kansas City. Exactly two months later, on July 15, he got No. 2 in a 6-0 win at Detroit. Ryan tossed his third no-hitter, a 4-0 home victory against the Twins, on September 28, 1974 in his final start of the season. No-hitter number four, Ryan's 100th major league victory, was also at home, a gritty 1-0 win against Baltimore on June 1, 1975.

Ryan was with the National League's Houston Astros when he threw his fifth no-hitter, defeating Los Angeles 5-0 in the Astrodome on September 26, 1981. That one broke the record that he had shared previously with Sandy Koufax for the most lifetime no-hitters.

Back in the American League with the Texas Rangers, Ryan tossed a 5-0 no-hitter at Oakland on June 11, 1990. His sixth no-hitter allowed the 43-year-old Ryan to replace Cy Young, who was 41 when he no-hit the Yankees 8-0 on June 30, 1908, as the oldest man ever to pitch a no-hitter. On May 1, 1991, in Texas, Ryan no-hit the Toronto Blue Jays, 3-0, for the seventh and final no-hitter of his illustrious career. In doing so, he established a new record for being the oldest pitcher to have a no-hitter, but now it was as a 44-year-old.

Also worthy of special mention are those who pitched complete perfect games of nine innings or more:

Lee Richmond, Wor vs Cle NL, 1-0; June 12, 1880
John Ward, Pro vs Buf NL, 5-0; June 17, 1880
Cy Young, Bos vs Phi AL, 3-0; May 5, 1904
Addie Joss, Cle at Chi AL, 1-0; October 2, 1908
Charlie Robertson, Chi at Det AL, 2-0; April 30, 1922
Don Larsen, NY AL vs Bro NL, 2-0; October 8, 1956 (World Series)
Jim Bunning, Phi at NY NL, 6-0; June 21, 1964 (1st game)
Sandy Koufax, LA vs Chi NL, 1-0; September 9, 1965
Catfish Hunter, Oak vs Min AL, 4-0; May 8, 1968
Len Barker, Cle vs Tor AL, 3-0; May 15, 1981
Mike Witt, Cal at Tex AL, 1-0; September 30, 1984
Tom Browning, Cin vs LA NL, 1-0; September 16, 1988
Dennis Martinez, Mon at LA NL, 2-0; July 28, 1991
Kenny Rogers, Tex vs Cal AL, 4-0; July 29, 1994
David Wells, NY vs Min AL, 4-0; May 17, 1998
David Cone, NY (AL) vs Mon (NL), 5-0; July 18, 1999 (interleague game)

No-hit games, nine or more innings

(Number to left is career total if greater than one)

Joe Borden, Phi vs Chi NA, 4-0; July 28, 1875
George Bradley, StL vs Har NL, 2-0; July 15, 1876
Lee Richmond, Wor vs Cle NL, 1-0; June 12, 1880 (perfect game)
John Ward, Pro vs Buf NL, 5-0; June 17, 1880 (perfect game)
Larry Corcoran, Chi vs Bos NL, 6-0; August 19, 1880
Jim Galvin, Buf at Wor NL, 1-0; August 20, 1880
Tony Mullane, Lou at Cin AA, 2-0; September 11, 1882
Guy Hecker, Lou at Pit AA, 3-1; September 19, 1882
2 Larry Corcoran, Chi vs Wor NL, 5-0; September 20, 1882
Hoss Radbourn, Pro vs Cle NL, 8-0; July 25, 1883
Hugh Daily, Cle at Phi NL, 1-0; September 13, 1883
Al Atkinson, Phi vs Pit AA, 10-1; May 24, 1884
Ed Morris, Col at Pit AA, 5-0; May 29, 1884
Frank Mountain, Col at Was AA, 12-0; June 5, 1884

3 Larry Corcoran, Chi vs Pro NL, 6-0; June 27, 1884
2 Jim Galvin, Buf at Det NL, 18-0; August 4, 1884
Dick Burns, Cin at KC UA, 3-1; August 26, 1884
Ed Cushman, Mil vs Was UA, 5-0; September 28, 1884
Sam Kimber Bro vs Tol AA, 0-0; October 4, 1884 (10 innings, tie)
John Clarkson, Chi at Pro NL, 4-0; July 27, 1885
Charlie Ferguson, Phi vs Pro NL, 1-0; August 29, 1885
2 Al Atkinson, Phi vs NY AA, 3-2; May 1, 1886
Adonis Terry, Bro vs StL AA, 1-0; July 24, 1886
Matt Kilroy, Bal at Pit AA, 6-0; October 6, 1886
2 Adonis Terry, Bro vs Lou AA, 4-0; May 27, 1888
Henry Porter, KC at Bal AA, 4-0; June 6, 1888
Ed Seward, Phi vs Cin AA, 12-2; July 26, 1888
Gus Weyhing, Phi vs KC AA, 4-0; July 31, 1888
Cannonball Titcomb, Roc at Syr AA, 7-0; September 15, 1890
Tom Lovett, Bro vs NY NL, 4-0; June 22, 1891
Amos Rusie, NY vs Bro NL, 6-0; July 31, 1891
Ted Breitenstein, StL vs Lou AA, 8-0; October 4, 1891 (1st game) (first start in the major leagues)
Jack Stivetts, Bos vs Bro NL, 11-0; August 6, 1892
Ben Sanders, Lou vs Bal NL, 6-2; August 22, 1892
Bumpus Jones, Cin vs Pit NL, 7-1; October 15, 1892 (first game in the major leagues)
Bill Hawke, Bal vs Was NL, 5-0; August 16, 1893
Cy Young, Cle vs Cin NL, 6-0; September 18, 1897 (1st game)
2 Ted Breitenstein, Cin vs Pit NL, 11-0; April 22, 1898
Jim Hughes, Bal vs Bos NL, 8-0; April 22, 1898
Red Donahue, Phi vs Bos NL, 5-0; July 8, 1898
Walter Thornton, Chi vs Bro NL, 2-0; August 21, 1898 (2nd game)
Deacon Phillippe, Lou vs NY NL, 7-0; May 25, 1899
Noodles Hahn, Cin vs Phi NL, 4-0; July 12, 1900
Christy Mathewson, NY at StL NL, 5-0; July 15, 1901
Jim Callahan, Chi vs Det AL, 3-0; September 20, 1902 (1st game)
Chick Fraser, Phi at Chi NL, 10-0; September 18, 1903 (2nd game)
2 Cy Young, Bos vs Phi AL, 3-0; May 5, 1904 (perfect game)
Jesse Tannehill, Bos at Chi AL, 6-0; August 17, 1904
2 Christy Mathewson, NY at Chi NL, 1-0; June 13, 1905
Weldon Henley, Phi at StL AL, 6-0; July 22, 1905 (1st game)
Frank Smith, Chi at Det AL, 15-0; September 6, 1905 (2nd game)
Bill Dinneen, Bos vs Chi AL, 2-0; September 27, 1905 (1st game)
Johnny Lush, Phi at Bro NL, 6-0; May 1, 1906
Mal Eason, Bro at StL NL, 2-0; July 20, 1906
Jeff Pfeffer, Bos vs Cin NL, 6-0; May 8, 1907
Nick Maddox, Pit vs Bro NL, 2-1; September 20, 1907
3 Cy Young, Bos at NY AL, 8-0; June 30, 1908
Hooks Wiltse, NY vs Phi NL, 1-0; July 4, 1908 (1st game, ten innings)
Nap Rucker, Bro vs Bos NL, 6-0; September 5, 1908 (2nd game)
Dusty Rhoades, Cle vs Bos AL, 2-1; September 18, 1908
2 Frank Smith, Chi vs Phi AL, 1-0; September 20, 1908
Addie Joss, Cle vs Chi AL, 1-0; October 2, 1908 (perfect game)
2 Addie Joss, Cle vs Chi AL, 1-0; April 20, 1910
Chief Bender, Phi vs Cle AL, 4-0; May 12, 1910
Joe Wood, Bos vs StL AL, 5-0; July 29, 1911 (1st game)
Ed Walsh, Chi vs Bos AL, 5-0; August 27, 1911
George Mullin, Det vs StL AL, 7-0; July 4, 1912 (2nd game)
Earl Hamilton, StL at Det AL, 5-1; August 30, 1912
Jeff Tesreau, NY at Phi AL, 3-0; September 6, 1912 (1st game)
Joe Benz, Chi vs Cle AL, 6-1; May 31, 1914
George Davis, Bos vs Phi NL, 7-0; September 9, 1914 (2nd game)
Ed Lafitte, Bro vs KC FL, 6-2; September 19, 1914
Rube Marquard, NY vs Bro NL, 2-0; April 15, 1915
Frank Allen, Pit at StL FL, 2-0; April 24, 1915
Claude Hendrix, Chi at Pit FL, 10-0; May 15, 1915
Alex Main, KC at Buf FL, 5-0; August 16, 1915
Jimmy Lavender, Chi at NY NL, 2-0; August 31, 1915 (1st game)
Dave Davenport, StL vs Chi FL, 3-0; September 7, 1915
2 Tom L. Hughes, Bos vs Pit NL, 2-0; June 16, 1916
Rube Foster, Bos vs NY AL, 2-0; June 16, 1916
Joe Bush, Phi vs Cle AL, 5-0; August 26, 1916
Hubert (Dutch) Leonard, Bos vs StL AL, 4-0; August 30, 1916
Eddie Cicotte, Chi at StL AL, 11-0; April 14, 1917
George Mogridge, NY at Bos AL, 2-1; April 24, 1917
Fred Toney, Cin at Chi NL, 1-0; May 2, 1917 (10 innings)
Ernie Koob, StL vs Chi AL, 1-0; May 5, 1917
Bob Groom, StL vs Chi AL, 3-0; May 6, 1917 (2nd game)
Babe Ruth (0 innings) and Ernie Shore (9 innings), Bos vs Was AL, 4-0; June 23, 1917 (1st game) (Shore relieved Ruth after Ruth had been thrown out of the game for protesting a walk to the first batter. The runner was caught stealing and Shore retired the remaining 26 batters in order.)
2 Hubert (Dutch) Leonard, Bos at Det AL, 5-0; June 3, 1918
Hod Eller, Cin vs StL NL, 6-0; May 11, 1919
Ray Caldwell, Cle at NY AL, 3-0; September 10, 1919 (1st game)
Walter Johnson, Was at Bos AL, 1-0; July 1, 1920
Charlie Robertson, Chi at Det AL, 2-0; April 30, 1922 (perfect game)
Jesse Barnes, NY vs Phi NL, 6-0; May 7, 1922
Sam Jones, NY at Phi AL, 2-0; September 4, 1923

Howard Ehmke, Bos at Phi AL, 4-0; September 7, 1923
Jesse Haines, StL vs Bos NL, 5-0; July 17, 1924
Dazzy Vance, Bro vs Phi NL, 10-1; September 13, 1925 (1st game)
Ted Lyons, Chi at Bos AL, 6-0; August 21, 1926
Carl Hubbell, NY vs Pit NL, 11-0; May 8, 1929
Wes Ferrell, Cle vs StL AL, 9-0; April 29, 1931
Bobby Burke, Was vs Bos AL, 5-0; August 8, 1931
Paul Dean, StL at Bro NL, 3-0; September 21, 1934 (2nd game)
Vern Kennedy, Chi vs Cle AL, 5-0; August 31, 1935
Bill Dietrich, Chi vs StL AL, 8-0; June 1, 1937
Johnny Vander Meer, Cin vs Bos NL, 3-0; June 11, 1938
2   Johnny Vander Meer, Cin at Bro NL, 6-0; June 15, 1938 (next start after June 11)
Monte Pearson, NY vs Cle AL, 13-0; August 27, 1938 (2nd game)
Bob Feller, Cle at Chi AL, 1-0; April 16, 1940 (opening day)
Tex Carleton, Bro at Cin NL, 3-0; April 30, 1940
Lon Warneke, StL at Cin NL, 2-0; August 30, 1941
Jim Tobin, Bos vs Bro NL, 2-0; April 27, 1944
Clyde Shoun, Cin vs Bos NL, 1-0; May 15, 1944
Dick Fowler, Phi vs StL AL, 1-0; September 9, 1945 (2nd game)
Ed Head, Bro vs Bos NL, 5-0; April 23, 1946
2   Bob Feller, Cle at NY AL, 1-0; April 30, 1946
Ewell Blackwell, Cin vs Bos NL, 6-0; June 18, 1947
Don Black, KC vs Phi AL, 3-0; July 10, 1947 (1st game)
Bill McCahan, Phi vs Was AL, 3-0; September 3, 1947
Bob Lemon, Cle at Det AL, 2-0; June 30, 1948
Rex Barney, Bro at NY NL, 2-0; September 9, 1948
Vern Bickford, Bos vs Bro NL, 7-0; August 11, 1950
Cliff Chambers, Pit at Bos NL, 3-0; May 6, 1951 (2nd game)
3   Bob Feller, Cle vs Det AL, 2-1; July 1, 1951 (1st game)
Allie Reynolds, NY at Cle AL, 1-0; July 12, 1951
2   Allie Reynolds, NY at Bos AL, 8-0; September 28, 1951 (1st game)
Virgil Trucks, Det vs Was AL, 1-0; May 15, 1952
Carl Erskine, Bro vs Chi NL, 5-0; June 19, 1952
2   Virgil Trucks, Det at NY AL, 1-0; August 25, 1952
Bobo Holloman, StL vs Phi AL, 6-0; May 6, 1953 (first start in the major leagues)
Jim Wilson, Mil vs Phi NL, 2-0; June 12, 1954
Sam Jones, Chi vs Pit NL, 4-0; May 12, 1955
2   Carl Erskine, Bro vs NY NL, 3-0; May 12, 1956
Mel Parnell, Bos vs Chi AL, 4-0; July 14, 1956
Sal Maglie, Bro vs Phi NL, 5-0; September 25, 1956
Don Larsen, NY AL vs Bro NL, 2-0; October 8, 1956 (World Series) (perfect game)
Bob Keegan, Chi vs Was AL, 6-0; August 20, 1957 (2nd game)
Jim Bunning, Det at Bos AL, 3-0; July 20, 1958 (1st game)
Hoyt Wilhelm, Bal vs NY AL, 1-0; September 20, 1958
Don Cardwell, Chi vs StL NL, 4-0; May 15, 1960 (2nd game)
Lew Burdette, Mil vs Phi NL, 1-0; August 18, 1960
Warren Spahn, Mil vs Phi NL, 4-0; September 16, 1960
2   Warren Spahn, Mil vs SF NL, 1-0; April 28, 1961
Bo Belinsky, LA vs Bal AL, 2-0; May 5, 1962
Earl Wilson, Bos vs LA AI, 2-0; June 26, 1962
Sandy Koufax, LA vs NY NL, 5-0; June 30, 1962
Bill Monbouquette, Bos at Chi AL, 1-0; August 1, 1962
Jack Kralick, Min vs KC AL, 1-0; August 26, 1962
2   Sandy Koufax, LA vs SF NL, 8-0; May 11, 1963
Don Nottebart, Hou vs Phi NL, 4-1; May 17, 1963
Juan Marichal, SF vs Hou NL, 1-0; June 15, 1963
Ken T. Johnson, Hou vs Cin NL, 0-1; April 23, 1964 (lost game)
3   Sandy Koufax, LA at Phi NL, 3-0; June 4, 1964
2   Jim Bunning, Phi at NY NL, 6-0; June 21, 1964 (1st game; perfect game)
Jim Maloney, Cin at Chi NL, 1-0; August 19, 1965 (1st game; 10 innings)
4   Sandy Koufax, LA vs Chi NL, 1-0; September 9, 1965 (perfect game)
Dave Morehead, Bos vs Cle AL, 2-0; September 16, 1965
Sonny Siebert, Cle vs Was AL, 2-0; June 10, 1966
Steve Barber (8 2/3 innings). and Stu Miller (1/3 inning) Bal vs Det AL, 1-2; April 30, 1967 (1st game; lost game)
Don Wilson, Hou vs Atl NL, 2-0; June 18, 1967
Dean Chance, Min at Cle AL, 2-1; August 25, 1967 (2nd game)
Joe Horlen, Chi vs Det AL, 6-0; September 10, 1967 (1st game)
Tom Phoebus, Bal vs Bos AL, 6-0; April 27, 1968
Catfish Hunter, Oak vs Min AL, 4-0; May 8, 1968 (perfect game)
George Culver, Cin at Phi NL, 6-1; July 29, 1968 (2nd game)
Gaylord Perry, SF vs StL NL, 1-0; September 17, 1968
Ray Washburn, StL at SF NL, 2-0; September 18, 1968
Bill Stoneman, Mon at Phi NL, 7-0; April 17, 1969
2   Jim Maloney, Cin vs Hou NL, 10-0; April 30, 1969
2   Don Wilson, Hou at Cin NL, 4-0; May 1, 1969
Jim Palmer, Bal vs Oak AL, 8-0; August 13, 1969
Ken Holtzman, Chi vs Atl NL, 3-0; August 19, 1969
Bob Moose, Pit at NY NL, 4-0; September 20, 1969
Dock Ellis, Pit at SD NL, 2-0; June 12, 1970 (1st game)
Clyde Wright, Cal vs Oak AL, 4-0; July 3, 1970
Bill Singer, LA vs Phi NL, 5-0; July 20, 1970
Vida Blue, Oak vs Min AL, 6-0; September 21, 1970

2   Ken Holtzman, Chi at Cin NL, 1-0; June 3, 1971
Rick Wise, Phi at Cin NL, 4-0; June 23, 1971
Bob Gibson, StL at Pit NL, 11-0; August 14, 1971
Burt Hooton, Chi vs Phi NL, 4-0; April 16, 1972
Milt Pappas, Chi vs SD NL, 8-0; September 2, 1972
2   Bill Stoneman, Mon vs NY NL, 7-0; October 2, 1972 (1st game)
Steve Busby, KC at Det AL, 3-0; April 27, 1973
Nolan Ryan, Cal at KC AL, 3-0; May 15, 1973
2   Nolan Ryan, Cal at Det AL, 6-0; July 15, 1973
Jim Bibby, Tex at Oak AL, 6-0; July 20, 1973
Phil Niekro, Atl vs SD NL, 9-0; August 5, 1973
2   Steve Busby, KC at Mil AL, 2-0; June 19, 1974
Dick Bosman, Cle vs Oak AL, 4-0; July 19, 1974
3   Nolan Ryan, Cal vs Min AL, 4-0; September 28, 1974
4   Nolan Ryan, Cal vs Bal AL, 1-0; June 1, 1975
Ed Halicki, SF vs NY NL, 6-0; August 24, 1975 (2nd game)
Vida Blue (5 innings), Glenn Abbott (1 inning), Paul Lindblad (1 inning), and Rollie Fingers (2 innings), Oak vs Cal AL, 5-0; September 28, 1975
Larry Dierker, Hou vs Mon NL, 5-0; July 9, 1976
Blue Moon Odom (5 innings) and Francisco Barrios (4 innings), Chi at Oak AL, 6-0; July 28, 1976
John Candelaria, Pit vs LA NL, 2-0; August 9, 1976
John Montefusco, SF at Atl NL, 9-0; September 29, 1976
Jim Colborn, KC vs Tex AL, 6-0; May 14, 1977
Dennis Eckersley, Cle vs Cal AL, 1-0; May 30, 1977
Bert Blyleven, Tex at Cal AL, 6-0; September 22, 1977
Bob Forsch, StL vs Phi NL, 5-0; April 16, 1978
Tom Seaver, Cin vs StL NL, 4-0; June 16, 1978
Ken Forsch, Hou vs Atl NL, 6-0; April 7, 1979
Jerry Reuss, LA at SF NL, 8-0; June 27, 1980
Charlie Lea, Mon vs SF NL, 4-0; May 10, 1981 (2nd game)
Len Barker, Cle vs Tor AL, 3-0; May 15, 1981 (perfect game)
5   Nolan Ryan, Hou vs LA NL, 5-0; September 26, 1981
Dave Righetti, NY vs Bos AL, 4-0; July 4, 1983
2   Bob Forsch, StL vs Mon NL, 3-0; September 26, 1983
Mike Warren, Oak vs Chi AL, 3-0; September 29, 1983
Jack Morris, Det at Chi AL, 4-0; April 7, 1984
Mike Witt, Cal at Tex AL, 1-0; September 30, 1984 (perfect game)
Joe Cowley, Chi at Cal AL, 7-1; September 19, 1986
Mike Scott, Hou vs SF NL, 2-0; September 25, 1986
Juan Nieves, Mil vs Bal AL, 7-0; April 15, 1987
Tom Browning, Cin vs LA NL, 1-0; September 16, 1988 (perfect game)
Mark Langston (7 innings) and Mike Witt (2 innings), Cal vs Sea AL, 1-0; April 11, 1990
Randy Johnson, Sea vs Det AL, 2-0; June 2, 1990
6   Nolan Ryan, Tex at Oak AL, 5-0; June 11, 1990
Dave Stewart, Oak at Tor AL, 5-0; June 29, 1990
Fernando Valenzuela, LA vs StL NL, 6-0; June 29, 1990
Terry Mulholland, Phi vs SF NL, 6-0; August 15, 1990
Dave Stieb, Tor at Det AL, 3-0; September 2, 1990
7   Nolan Ryan, Tex vs Tor AL. 3-0; May 1, 1991
Tommy Greene, Phi at Mon NL, 2-0; May 23, 1991
Bob Milacki (6 innings), Mike Flanagan (1 inning), Mark Williamson (1 inning), Gregg Olson (1 inning) Bal at Oak AL, 2-0; July 13, 1991
Dennis Martinez, Mon at LA NL, 2-0; July 28, 1991 (perfect game)
Wilson Alvarez, Chi at Bal AL. 7-0; August 11, 1991
Bret Saberhagen, KC vs Chi AL, 7-0; August 26, 1991
Kent Mercker (6 innings), Mark Wohlers (2 innings), Alejandro Pena (1 inning), Atl at SD NL. 1-0; September 11, 1991
Kevin Gross, LA vs SF NL, 2-0; August 17, 1992
Chris Bosio, Sea vs Bos AL, 7-0; April 22, 1993
Jim Abbott, NY vs Cle AL, 4-0; September 4, 1993
Darryl Kile, Hou vs NY NL, 7-1; September 8, 1993
Kent Mercker, Atl at LA NL, 6-0; April 8, 1994
Scott Erickson, Min vs Mil AL, 6-0; April 27, 1994
Kenny Rogers, Tex vs Cal AL, 4-0; July 29, 1994 (perfect game)
Ramon Martinez, L.A. at Fla. NL, 7-0; July 14, 1995
Al Leiter, Fla vs Col NL, 11-0; May 11, 1996
Dwight Gooden, NY vs Sea AL, 2-0; May 14, 1996
Hideo Nomo, LA at Col NL, 9-0; September 17, 1996
Kevin Brown, Fla at SF NL, 9-0; June 10, 1997
Francisco Cordova (10 innings) and Ricardo Rincon (1 inning), Pit vs Hou NL, 3-0; July 12, 1997
David Wells, NY vs Min AL, 4-0; May 17, 1998 (perfect game)
Jose Jiminez, StL at Ari NL, 1-0; June 25, 1999
David Cone, NY (AL) vs Mon (NL), 5-0; July 18, 1999 (interleague game) (perfect game)
Eric Milton, Min at Ana AL, 7-0; September 11, 1999
2   Hideo Nomo, Bos at Bal AL, 3-0; April 4, 2001
A. J. Burnett, Fla at SD NL, 3-0; May 12, 2001
Bud Smith, StL at SD NL, 4-0; September 3, 2001
Derek Lowe Bos vs TB AL, 10-0, April 27, 2002
Kevin Millwood Phi vs SF NL, 1-0 April 27, 2003
Roy Oswalt (1 inning), Pete Munro (2.2 innings), Kirk Saarloos (1.1 innings), Brad Lidge (2 innings), Octavio Dotel (1 inning), Billy Wagner (1 inning) Hou at NY (AL) 8-0; June 11, 2003 (interleague game)

No-hit games broken up in extra innings

Earl Moore, Cle vs Chi AL, 2-4; May 9, 1901 (allowed first hit in 10th and lost in 10th)

Bob Wicker, Chi at NY NL, 1-0; June 11, 1904 (won in 12th after allowing first hit in 10th)

Harry McIntyre, Bro vs Pit NL, 0-1; August 1, 1906 (lost in 13th after allowing first hit in 11th)

Red Ames, NY vs Bro NL, 0-3; April 15, 1909 (lost in 13th after allowing first hit in 10th)

Tom Hughes, NY vs Cle AL, 0-5; August 30, 1910 (2nd game) (lost in 11th after allowing first hit in 10th)

Jim Scott, Chi at Was AL, 0-1; May 14, 1914 (allowed first hit in 10th and lost in 10th)

Hippo Vaughn, Chi vs Cin NL, 0-1; May 2, 1917 (allowed first hit in 10th and lost in 10th)

Bobo Newsom, StL vs Bos AL, 1-2; September 18, 1934 (allowed first hit in 10th and lost in 10th)

Johnny Klippstein (7 innings), Hershell Freeman (1 inning) and Joe Black (3 innings), Cin at Mil NL, 1-2; May 26, 1956 (lost in 11 innings after allowing first hit in 10th)

Harvey Haddix, Pit at Mil NL, 0-1; May 26, 1959 (allowed first hit in 13th, after pitching 12 perfect innings, and lost in 13th)

Jim Maloney, Cin vs NY NL, 0-1; June 14, 1965 (allowed first hit in 11th and lost in 11th)

Mark Gardner, Mon at LA NL, 0-1; July 26, 1991 (allowed first hit in 10th and lost in 10th)

Pedro Martinez (9 innings) and Mel Rojas (1 inning), Mon vs SD NL; 1-0; June 3, 1995 (Martinez pitched 9 perfect innings, but allowed a hit in the tenth, Rojas relieved and finished the game)

The Unassisted Triple Play

In a night game at St. Louis on August 10, 2003, Rafael Furcal of Atlanta completed the major leagues' 12th unassisted triple play.* As with the previous eleven, it occurred with runners on first and second and was made by an infielder. In the fifth inning, the Cardinals had Mike Metheny at second and Orlando Palmiero at first. Both were running when the batter, pitcher Woody Williams, lined out to Furcal. Furcal tagged second base, retiring Metheny, and then tagged Palmiero, who was trying to get back to first.

The Cleveland Indians have been involved in 5 of the major leagues' 12 unassisted triple plays. Indians shortstop Neal Ball executed the first one during the first game of a July 19, 1909 doubleheader against the Red Sox at Cleveland's League Park. In the second inning, Ball caught a liner hit by Boston's Amby McConnell, stepped on second base to retire Heinie Wagner before he could get back safely, and then tagged out Jake Stahl before he could return to first.

The most celebrated unassisted triple play, and the only one made in a World Series, was turned in by Cleveland Indians second baseman Bill Wambsganss against Brooklyn in Game 5 of the 1920 Series. The Dodgers were trailing, 7-0, but their first two batters in the top of the fifth inning, Pete Kilduff and Otto Miller, reached base safely. When Clarence Mitchell, a very good-hitting pitcher, cracked a line drive that appeared to be heading to center field, both took off running. But Wambsganss had been playing Mitchell perfectly. He made the catch, ran over and doubled Kilduff off second, then turned to find Miller standing in the baseline and tagged him out.

Cleveland players had executed the American League's first two

unassisted triple plays, but George Burns, playing for the Boston Red Sox (between stints as a member of the Indians), made Cleveland the victim in 1923. On September 14 at Fenway Park, first baseman Burns caught Frank Brower's second-inning liner, tagged Rube Lutzke off first, and ran to second to get Riggs Stephenson before he could return.

Three weeks later, on October 6, shortstop Ernie Padgett of the Boston Braves turned in the National League's first unassisted triple play. It came at Braves Field in the fourth inning of the second game of a season-ending doubleheader. Padgett, playing in only his fourth major league game, speared a liner by Philadelphia's Walter Holke, tagged second base to retire Cotton Tierney, then ran after and tagged Cliff Lee, the baserunner from first.

Pittsburgh shortstop Glenn Wright, playing at home, started his unassisted triple play in the usual manner, by catching a line drive. On May 7, 1925, Wright snared a ninth-inning liner off the bat of the Cardinals' Jim Bottomley, whereupon he doubled Jimmy Cooney off second and tagged out Rogers Hornsby coming from first.

Jimmy Cooney went from victim to perpetrator in 1927. Playing shortstop for the Cubs in a game at Pittsburgh on May 30, he became the only player to be involved in two unassisted triple plays. In the fourth inning, with Clyde Barnhart on first and Lloyd Waner on second, both running on the pitch, Cooney caught Paul Waner's line drive. He stepped on second to retire Lloyd Waner and tagged out Barnhart when he reached the bag.

A day later, first baseman Johnny Neun of the Detroit Tigers duplicated the feat, executing the only game-ending unassisted triple play. Neun caught a line drive hit by Cleveland's Homer Summa in the top of the ninth, tagged Charlie Jamieson before he could get back to first, and ran to step on second to retire Glenn Myatt.

Following these back-to-back occurrences, the major leagues did not have another unassisted triple play for 41 years. On July 30, 1968, in the bottom of the first inning of a game at Cleveland, the Indians had Dave Nelson on second and Russ Snyder on first. Joe Azcue lined one at Washington Senators shortstop Ron Hansen, who stepped on second to retire Nelson and tagged Snyder coming from first.

Philadelphia Phillies second baseman Mickey Morandini's unassisted triple play at Pittsburgh on September 20, 1992 was the first one in the National League in 65 years. In the home sixth, Morandini made a diving catch of a line drive off the bat of Jeff King. He hustled to second base to double off Andy Van Slyke, and then tagged Barry Bonds, who was running from first base.

On July 8, 1994, Red Sox shortstop John Valentin became the first American Leaguer to make an unassisted triple play since Ron Hansen in 1968. Seattle was batting in the top of the sixth inning, with Keith Mitchell at first base and Mike Blowers at second. With the runners moving, Valentin caught Marc Newfield's line drive, stepped on second to erase Blowers, then tagged Mitchell, who was about to run past him.

Randy Velarde's unassisted triple play, in the sixth inning of a

---

*Total Baseball has eliminated the unassisted triple play purportedly made by Providence's Paul Hines and carried in some earlier editions. In the eighth inning of that May 8, 1878 game, Boston had Ezra Sutton at second and Jack Manning at third, when Jack Burdock hit a looping fly ball to short left-center field. Both runners took off, but Hines, the center fielder, caught the ball and stepped on third, retiring Manning and, presumably, Sutton. However, further research has indicated that Sutton, the runner from second, may not have passed third base when Hines made the catch. If Sutton had done so, stepping on that base would have put him out. However, it is known that Hines threw the ball to Providence second baseman Charlie Sweasy, who stepped on that base either to record the third out or to make "double certain" of the out. Either way, Hines' exploit is too ambiguous to be resolved with satisfaction.

May 29, 2000 game at Yankee Stadium, was the first ever to involve either the Athletics or the Yankees. With Jorge Posada of the Yanks running from first (he got there on Velarde's error) and Tino Martinez running from second, second baseman Velarde caught a line drive hit by Shane Spencer. He tagged Posada and then ran over and stepped on second to retire Martinez.

Unassisted Triple Plays

Player	Team	Pos	Date	Opp	At	Inn	Batter
Neal Ball	CLE (AL)	SS	July 19, 1909	BOS	CLE	2 (1G)	Amby McConnell
Bill Wambsganss	CLE (AL)	2B	October 10, 1920	BRO	CLE	5	Clarence Mitchell
George Burns	BOS (AL)	1B	September 14, 1923	CLE	BOS	2	Frank Brower
Ernie Padgett	BOS (NL)	SS	October 6, 1923	PHI	BOS	4 (2G)	Walter Holke
Glenn Wright	PIT (NL)	SS	May 7, 1925	STL	PIT	9	Jim Bottomley
Jimmy Cooney	CHI (NL)	SS	May 30, 1927	PIT	PIT	4	Paul Waner
Johnny Neun	DET (AL)	1B	May 31, 1927	CLE	DET	9	Homer Summa
Ron Hansen	WAS (AL)	SS	July 30, 1968	CLE	CLE	1	Joe Azcue
Mickey Morandini	PHI (NL)	2B	September 20, 199	PIT	PIT	6	Jeff King
John Valentin	BOS (AL)	SS	July 8, 1994	SEA	BOS	6	Marc Newfield
Randy Velarde	OAK (AL)	2B	May 29, 2000	NY	NY	6	Shane Spencer
Rafael Furcal	ATL (NL)	SS	August 10, 2003	STL	STL	5	Woody Williams

Chapter 43

The All-Star Game: Rise and Fall of a Rich Tradition

By Frederick Ivor-Campbell and Bill Deane

Although the tradition of All-Star Games in baseball dates back to an 1858 series between teams of stars from Brooklyn and New York (they were called "picked nines" in those days), the current All-Star series began when Arch Ward, sports editor of the Chicago *Tribune*, persuaded hesitant league owners to go along with his proposal for a game between stars from the American League and National League, to be played in Chicago during that city's Century of Progress Exposition in 1933.

All-Star managers (who, except for the first game, have been the pilots of the previous year's pennant winners) shared with fans the selection of players for the first two games. From 1935 through 1946 the manager selected his whole squad. Since 1947, he has chosen his pitchers and all other players except the eight members of the starting lineup. The fans chose the starters from 1947 to 1957; after an incident of ballot-box stuffing by Cincinnati partisans in 1957, the major league players, coaches and managers made the choice from 1958 to 1969; in 1970 the selection of starting lineups was returned to the fans.

In 1959, it was decided to play two All-Star Games, raising extra money for the players' pension fund, for old-timers who played before the pension plan was started and for youth baseball. The two-game format was scrapped after the 1962 season, due to scheduling difficulties and diminished interest in the event.

Gradually over the last quarter of the 20th century, the All-Star Game became a sideshow, with few players or fans taking it seriously. Many players selected for the teams would refuse to go, preferring a three-day vacation to nurse real or imagined injuries, or just out of umbrage at not having been chosen as a starter. Certain pitchers were deemed unavailable because their teams didn't want their rotations thrown out of whack. In 1985, new "Fan Fest" events, including a home-run derby, began adding to the carnival atmosphere of the game. Roster sizes were increased to 30, and managers became more concerned with getting everybody in the game than playing to win. It all came to a head in 2002, when both teams ran out of pitchers by the 11th inning, and Commissioner Bud Selig was forced to stop the game with a 7-7 score. To appease the outraged public, Selig announced that such a thing would never recur, and that, in a two-year experiment starting in 2003, new incentive would be added for the teams and players to take the game seriously: the winning league would secure home-field advantage for that year's World Series.

The American League dominated the early years of the series, winning the first three games, and extending their winning margin

Connie Mack and John McGraw
Longtime rivals, Mack (left) and McGraw squared off as managers in major league baseball's first All-Star Game, played in Chicago in 1933.

to eight games (12–4) by 1949. The National League cut the lead in half with four straight wins, and by 1964 had drawn even in the series as the two leagues stood at 17 wins apiece, plus one tie. The National Leaguers continued their drive, winning 25 All-Star Games between 1960-85, including 19 of 20 between 1963-82, to build a commanding 36–19 lead in the series. In recent years, though, the American Leaguers have battled back, winning six in a row from 1988 to 1993 and again from 1997 to 2003, discounting the '02 tie.

The overall record now stands at 40 wins for the National League and 32 for the American, with two ties.

GAME 1

Comiskey Park, Chicago
July 6, 1933
AL, 4–2
NL 000 002 000   2   8   0
AL 012 001 00X   4   9   1
Pitchers: HALLAHAN, Warneke (3), Hubbell (7) vs
  GOMEZ, Crowder (4), Grove (7)
Home Runs: Ruth-A, Frisch-N
Attendance: 49,200

Baseball's two grand old managers—Connie Mack and John McGraw—were chosen to lead the American and National League squads in the first All-Star Game, and American League starting pitcher Lefty Gomez of the Yankees took home honors both as the first All-Star winning pitcher and as the first player to drive in an All-Star run (singling in Jimmie Dykes in the second inning). But it was another "grand old man"—Babe Ruth—who made the game's headlines. At 38, in his next-to-last season as a Yankee, he lined a two-run homer in the third to make the score 3–0. In right field he robbed Chick Hafey of a hit with a remarkable running catch of Hafey's line drive in the eighth inning.

Frank Frisch homered for the Nationals, following up Pepper Martin's RBI with a solo shot in the National League's two-run sixth. But the American stars countered with an insurance run in the bottom of the sixth, as Earl Averill singled in Joe Cronin to end the scoring. Carl Hubbell for the Nationals and Lefty Grove for the Americans blanked the opposition through the final innings.

GAME 2

Polo Grounds, New York
July 10, 1934
AL, 9–7
AL 000 261 000   9   14   1
NL 103 030 000   7   8   1
Pitchers: Gomez, Ruffing (4), HARDER (5) vs
  Hubbell, Warneke (4), MUNGO (5), J.Dean (6),
  Frankhouse (9)
Home Runs: Frisch-N, Medwick-N
Attendance: 48,363

This was the game in which Carl Hubbell struck out Babe Ruth, Lou Gehrig, Jimmie Foxx, Al Simmons, and Joe Cronin in order in the first two innings. Hubbell also walked two and gave up two hits in his three innings of work, but allowed no run to score as his Nationals took a 4–0 lead on homers by Frank Frisch in the first and Joe Medwick (for three runs) in the third off American starter (and first-game winner) Lefty Gomez.

But with Hubbell gone, the Americans pounced on Lon Warneke and Van Lingle Mungo for four runs each in the fourth and fifth innings. The Nationals battled back for three off Red Ruffing in their half of the fifth, to come within a run of tying the game. But Mel Harder relieved Ruffing with none out and put out the fire, one-hitting the National stars over the final five innings. The Americans picked up an insurance run in the sixth off Dizzy Dean before Dean and Fred Frankhouse shut them down, too, through the final three frames.

GAME 3

Municipal Stadium, Cleveland
July 8, 1935
AL, 4–1
NL 000 100 000   1   4   1
AL 210 010 00X   4   8   0
Pitchers: WALKER, Schumacher (3), Derringer (7),
  J.Dean (8) vs GOMEZ, Harder (7)
Home Runs: Foxx-A
Attendance: 69,812

Lefty Gomez started his third All-Star Game, and pitched a record six innings to pick up his second All-Star win. For three innings he shut out the Nationals as the Americans built a lead behind him on Jimmie Foxx's two-run homer in the first, and Rollie Hemsley's triple and Joe Cronin's run-scoring fly in the second. The National Leaguers tried to catch up in the

fourth, when they put together two of their three hits off Gomez—a double by Arky Vaughan and a single by Bill Terry—and scored a run. But an inning later Foxx nullified the National run, singling Joe Vosmik home for his third RBI.

Gomez blanked the National stars through two more innings before yielding to Mel Harder, who came in to close his second All-Star Game. Harder had created an All-Star record the previous year with his five consecutive scoreless innings pitched, and extended the record to eight, with three more shutout innings to end the game.

GAME 4

Braves Field, Boston
July 7, 1936
NL, 4–3
AL 000 000 300   3   7   1
NL 020 020 00X   4   9   0
Pitchers: GROVE, Rowe (4), Harder (7) vs J.DEAN,
  Hubbell (4), C.Davis (7), Warneke (7)
Home Runs: Galan-N, Gehrig-A
Attendance: 25,534

The National League, which had not yet won an All-Star Game, scored first in the second when Gabby Hartnett tripled in a run off Lefty Grove—rookie Joe DiMaggio missing his try for a shoe-top catch of Hartnett's drive to right field. Pinky Whitney then singled in Hartnett. Augie Galan homered off Schoolboy Rowe (and the right field foul pole) in the fifth, and DiMaggio's bobble of Billy Herman's single a batter later put Herman in position to score an unearned fourth run, on Joe Medwick's single, that proved to be the margin of victory.

The Americans, shut out through six by Dizzy Dean and Carl Hubbell, nearly tied the game in the seventh off Curt Davis as Lou Gehrig homered and Luke Appling singled in two more. But Lon Warneke took over and, after loading the bases with a walk, escaped disaster as shortstop Leo Durocher snared DiMaggio's vicious line drive to his right for the third out. Warneke shut the Americans out over the final two innings to preserve the one-run lead and the National League's first All-Star win.

GAME 5

Griffith Stadium, Washington
July 7, 1937
AL, 8–3
NL 000 111 000   3   13   0
AL 002 312 00X   8   13   2
Pitchers: J.DEAN, Hubbell (4), Blanton (4),
  Grissom (5), Mungo (6), Walters (8) vs GOMEZ,
  Bridges (4), Harder (7)
Home Runs: Gehrig-A
Attendance: 31,391

President Franklin Roosevelt attended the game and saw the AL capture its fourth win in five tries. Lou Gehrig homered and doubled to drive in half the American League's eight runs in an easy American win. Lefty Gomez started his fourth All-Star Game in five years and earned his third win. And AL reliever Mel Harder pitched the final innings for his third All-Star Game in a row, pushing his record for consecutive All-Star shutout innings to 13. Yet the game is remembered not for any of these things, but for Earl Averill's line drive in the third inning which fractured Dizzy Dean's toe and led to the premature end of his spectacular career. (Dean recovered from the broken toe, but tried to resume his pitching too soon. In favoring the toe, he changed his delivery and irreparably injured his pitching arm.)

The Americans began their scoring when Gehrig, who preceded Averill in the batting order, homered off Dean in the third, with one aboard. They added to their score in each of the next three innings, so that although the Nationals countered with single runs in the three middle innings, they only fell farther behind.

GAME 6

Crosley Field, Cincinnati
July 6, 1938
NL, 4–1
AL 000 000 001   1   7   4
NL 100 100 20X   4   8   0
Pitchers: GOMEZ, Allen (4), Grove (7) vs
  VANDER MEER, Lee (4), Brown (7)
Attendance: 27,607

For the fifth (and final) time, Lefty Gomez started for the American League, and although he gave up only two hits and no earned runs in his three innings, he was saddled with the loss when an error by shortstop Joe Cronin paved the way for a National League run in the first.

The Nationals scored their only earned run in the fourth when Mel Ott tripled and Ernie Lombardi singled him home. But in the seventh they recorded two more unearned runs when Leo Durocher bunted to move Frank McCormick to second. Both McCormick and Durocher scored as third baseman Jimmie Foxx threw wildly to first and right fielder Joe DiMaggio (who chased the ball down) missed home plate with his throw from the outfield.

In the ninth DiMaggio singled and Cronin doubled him home in partial atonement for their errors. But as Johnny Vander Meer and "Big Bill" Lee had each blanked the American stars on one hit in their fine three-inning one-run stints, the Americans' errors cost them the game.

GAME 7

Yankee Stadium, New York
July 11, 1939
AL, 3–1
NL 001 000 000   1   7   1
AL 000 210 00X   3   6   1
Pitchers: Derringer, LEE (4), Fette (7) vs Ruffing,
  BRIDGES (4), Feller (6)
Home Runs: J.DiMaggio-A
Attendance: 62,892

Six Yankees started for the American League, and one of them—Joe DiMaggio—hit the game's only home run. But it was a young Cleveland pitcher—28-year-old Bob Feller, playing in his first All-Star Game—who turned in the most memorable performance.

The Nationals scored first, with a run in the third on three hits off the American League starter, Red Ruffing. But the Americans came back with two runs in the fourth on a walk, two singles, and a bobbled grounder by shortstop Arky Vaughan. DiMaggio hit his insurance homer an inning later.

In the top of the sixth, after two singles and an error had loaded the bases with National stars, with only one out, Feller replaced Tommy Bridges to face Vaughan (who had earlier singled and scored his team's only run). One pitch got Feller out of the inning as Vaughan grounded into a 4–6–3 double play. Feller shut out the National stars over the final three innings, striking out Johnny Mize and Stan Hack in the ninth to end the game and give the Americans their fifth All-Star victory.

GAME 8

Sportsman's Park, St. Louis
July 9, 1940
NL, 4–0
AL 000 000 000   0   3   1
NL 300 000 01X   4   7   0
Pitchers: RUFFING, Newsom (4), Feller (7) vs
  DERRINGER, Walters (3), Wyatt (5), French (7),
  Hubbell (9)
Home Runs: West-N
Attendance: 32,373

The National Leaguers made short work of the Americans, scoring three times in the first inning and holding the opposing stars to three hits for the All-Star Game's first shutout. Before American League starter Red Ruffing retired a single National batter in the bottom of the first inning, three of the game's four runs had been scored, on singles by Arky Vaughan and Billy Herman and Max West's home run to right

center.

Ruffing then settled down, and he and Buck Newsom held the Nationals to just three additional hits through the seventh. Bob Feller gave up the Nationals' fourth run in the eighth, on a walk, a sacrifice, and Harry Danning's single.

Five National League pitchers combined for the shutout, permitting only five batters to reach base while striking out seven. Starter Paul Derringer, who struck out three men in his two innings, was awarded the win.

GAME 9

Briggs Stadium, Detroit
July 8, 1941
AL, 7–5
NL 000 001 220   5 10 2
AL 000 101 014   7 11 3
Pitchers: Wyatt, Derringer (3), Walters (5), PASSEAU (7) vs Feller, Lee (4), Hudson (7), SMITH (8)
Home Runs: Vaughan-N (2), Williams-A
Attendance: 54,674

The National Leaguers entered the last of the ninth with a 5–3 lead and hopes of nailing down their first back-to-back All-Star victories. The American stars had scored their first run in the fourth. The Nationals tied the score in the top of the sixth, but the Americans countered with a run later in the inning. The Nationals' Arky Vaughan then made a bid to be the game's hero, homering in the seventh off Sid Hudson with a man aboard to restore the National lead, and homering again an inning later off Edgar Smith for two more runs.

A double and single by the DiMaggio brothers Joe and Dom brought the Americans a run closer in the eighth, but they still needed two to tie as they faced Claude Passeau in the bottom of the ninth. Two one-out singles and a walk loaded the bases, and a force play at second (that just missed being a game-ending double play) scored Ken Keltner from third. With two men now out and the Americans still down a run, Ted Williams homered on a letter-high fastball against the upper parapet in right for three more runs and another American League victory.

GAME 10

Polo Grounds, New York
July 6, 1942
AL, 3–1
AL 300 000 000   3 7 0
NL 000 000 010   1 6 1
Pitchers: CHANDLER, Benton (5) vs M.COOPER, Vander Meer (4), Passeau (7), Walters (9)
Home Runs: Boudreau-A, York-A, Owen-N
Attendance: 33,694

Home runs accounted for all the scoring as the American League, in something of a reverse of the 1940 game, scored three times in the top of the first to defeat the Nationals. Lou Boudreau, leading off, hit the game winner off Mort Cooper's second pitch, into the upper deck in left field. A double and two outs later, Rudy York put one over the fence near the short right field foul line for two more runs.

The Americans hit safely only four more times, and scored no more runs, but they already had more than enough, as Spud Chandler and Al Benton combined to shut out the National League stars for seven innings, until Mickey Owen, pinch-hitting for pitcher Claude Passeau in the eighth, hit his only home run of the summer.

This was the second All-Star Game played in the Polo Grounds. It had been Brooklyn's turn to host the game at Ebbets Field, but because the proceeds were destined for the war effort, the site was shifted to the larger stadium. The game might as well have been held in Brooklyn, though, as a pregame rain held attendance to well below the Polo Grounds' capacity.

GAME 11

Shibe Park, Philadelphia
July 13, 1943
AL, 5–3
NL 100 000 101   3 10 3
AL 031 010 00X   5 8 1
Pitchers: M.COOPER, Vander Meer (3), Sewell (6), Javery (7) vs LEONARD, Newhouser (4), Hughson (7)
Home Runs: Doerr-A, V.DiMaggio-N
Attendance: 31,938

For the first time, the All-Star Game was played at night. And for the only time in All-Star history, no Yankee played—although six had been named to the American League squad. But Yankee Joe McCarthy (serving for the sixth time as American manager) was piqued by criticism that he favored his own players, and retaliated by keeping them all on the bench.

The only DiMaggio in this wartime game was Pittsburgh's Vince, and he provided most of the National League power—going 3-for-3 with eight total bases and two of his team's three runs. But after the Nationals had jumped to a one-run lead in the first, Bobby Doerr of the Americans homered off Mort Cooper with two aboard in the second to put the American stars ahead. They added to their lead with a run in the third and another in the fifth. DiMaggio scored in the seventh after tripling off Tex Hughson and added a homer against Hughson in the ninth, but his heroics were not enough to overcome the American League's march to its third win in a row, and its eighth in 11 tries.

GAME 12

Forbes Field, Pittsburgh
July 11, 1944
NL, 7–1
AL 010 000 000   1 6 3
NL 000 040 21X   7 12 1
Pitchers: Borowy, HUGHSON (4), Muncrief (5), Newhouser (7), Newsom (8) vs Walters, RAFFENSBERGER (4), Sewell (6), Tobin (9)
Attendance: 29,589

For the second time the game was played at night, and for the seventh time Joe McCarthy managed the American team. But this time—unlike Game 11—he let his Yankees play. He started Yankees pitcher Hank Borowy, who not only shut out the Nationals in his three innings, but drove in a run in the second to give his team the lead.

That was all the American stars got. For the first four innings it was enough, but in the fifth a double, four singles, a walk, an error, and a stolen base brought in four National League runs. In the seventh, Whitey Kurowski doubled in two more National runs, and in the eighth a missed third strike, two walks, and a flyball produced a seventh and final tally.

No home runs were hit in the game, only the second time that had happened in All-Star play. But Phil Cavarretta of the Nationals tripled—and reached base four additional times on a single and three walks for a new All-Star on-base record.

GAME 13

Fenway Park, Boston
July 9, 1946
AL, 12–0
NL 000 000 000   0 3 0
AL 200 130 24X   12 14 1
Pitchers: PASSEAU, Higbe (4), Blackwell (5), Sewell (8) vs FELLER, Newhouser (4), Kramer (7)
Home Runs: Keller-A, Williams-A (2)
Attendance: 34,906

No All-Star Game was played in 1945 because of restrictions on wartime travel, but when the classic resumed in 1946 the American stars avenged their 1944 loss with the most decisive All-Star victory to date: 12–0. American pitchers Bob Feller, Hal Newhouser, and Jack Kramer combined to hold the National stars to three singles and a walk, as their teammates pounded National pitching for 14 hits, including two doubles and three home runs.

But the game belonged to Ted Williams. Back after three years at war, and playing before his home-town fans, he equaled Phil Cavarretta's 1944 on-base record in spectacular fashion, with one walk, two singles, and two Home Runs: one a drive into the center field bleachers and the other the first homer ever hit off Rip Sewell's looping "eephus" pitch. He scored the game's first run in the first inning as Charlie Keller followed his walk with a homer, and went on to break an All-Star record by scoring three more times, while driving in a record five runs.

GAME 14

Wrigley Field, Chicago
July 8, 1947
AL, 2–1
AL 000 001 100   2 8 0
NL 000 100 000   1 5 1
Pitchers: Newhouser, SHEA (4), Masterson (7), Page (8) vs Blackwell, Brecheen (4), SAIN (7), Spahn (8)
Home Runs: Mize-N
Attendance: 41,123

Johnny Mize homered for the National League off rookie Spec Shea in the fourth inning for the game's first run, following three one-hit innings by the two lanky starters, Ewell Blackwell of the Nationals and Hal Newhouser of the Americans. Mize's run remained the only score until the sixth inning, when the American Leaguers tied the game on two singles and a double-play grounder.

Sharp baserunning by Bobby Doerr—plus a little luck—led to the Americans' second run an inning later. Doerr singled, then stole second. He took third when pitcher Johnny Sain's pickoff throw bounced off Doerr's back into the outfield. Pinch hitter Stan Spence then singled Doerr home with what proved to be the game's final—and winning—run. The Nationals put men on first and third in the eighth, but shortstop Lou Boudreau's spectacular stop of a hot grounder and sharp throw to first retired the side and ended the threat.

GAME 15

Sportsman's Park, St. Louis
July 13, 1948
AL, 5–2
NL 200 000 000   2 8 0
AL 011 300 00X   5 6 0
Pitchers: Branca, SCHMITZ (4), Sain (4), Blackwell (6) vs Masterson, RASCHI (4), Coleman (7)
Home Runs: Musial-N, Evers-A
Attendance: 34,009

Vic Raschi pitched three shutout innings for the American stars and drove in two go-ahead runs with a fourth-inning single. The 5-2 win marked the third time since the All-Star Game originated in 1933—won its third classic in a row that the American League had three straight wins.

The Nationals scored first on Stan Musial's two-run homer in the top of the first. But that was all they got, as starter Walt Masterson settled down and shut out the Nationals through the second and third innings. Raschi then came on for his shutout stint, and Joe Coleman stopped the Nationals without even a hit over the final three innings.

Meanwhile, the Americans scored a run in the second on Hoot Evers' homer, and tied the game with another run in the third on two walks, a double steal, and an outfield fly. Then in the fourth, when two walks and a single had loaded the bases, pitcher Raschi singled in the third and fourth American runs. Joe DiMaggio's pinch-hit sacrifice fly scored a fifth run. Johnny Sain and Ewell Blackwell shut out the Americans the rest of the way, but the damage had been done.

GAME 16

Ebbets Field, Brooklyn
July 12, 1949
AL, 11–7

AL 4 0 0 2 0 2 3 0 0   11 13 1
NL 2 1 2 0 0 2 0 0 0   7   12 5

Pitchers: Parnell, TRUCKS (2), Brissie (4), Raschi (7)
vs Spahn, NEWCOMBE (2), Munger (5),
Bickford (6), Pollet (7), Blackwell (8), Roe (9)
Home Runs: Musial-N, Kiner-N
Attendance: 32,577

Each team scored seven earned runs in this game which saw a total of 25 hits, including seven doubles and two home runs. But two first-inning National League errors let in four unearned American runs to provide the margin for the American League's fourth consecutive All-Star win. Stan Musial and Ralph Kiner each drove in two National runs with homers, but Eddie Joost singled in two runs for the Americans and Joe DiMaggio singled and doubled in three more to lead the American attack. For the second year in a row, Vic Raschi shut out the National stars for three innings, this time holding the American lead over the final third of the game.

The game was notable as the first to include black players: three Dodgers (Jackie Robinson, Roy Campanella, and Don Newcombe) for the National League, and Larry Doby for the American. With the Americans now ahead 12-4 in the series, it also marked the farthest extent of American League domination of the midsummer classic.

GAME 17

Comiskey Park, Chicago
July 11, 1950
NL, 4–3

NL 0 2 0 0 0 0 0 0 1 0 0 0 0 1   4 10 0
AL 0 0 1 0 2 0 0 0 0 0 0 0 0 0   3   8 1

Pitchers: Roberts, Newcombe (4), Konstanty (6),
Jansen (7), BLACKWELL (12) vs Raschi,
Lemon (4), Houtteman (7), Reynolds (10),
GRAY (13), Feller (14)
Home Runs: Kiner-N, Schoendienst-N
Attendance: 46,127

For the first time, the All-Star Game went into extra innings, and for the first time the National League won a game as the visiting team. Three pitchers each hurled three innings of shutout ball: Bob Lemon and Allie Reynolds for the American League and Ewell Blackwell (who finished the game and got the win) for the Nationals. But top pitching honors were earned by National Leaguer Larry Jansen, who struck out six and gave up only one hit over five shutout innings.

The National stars scored first with two runs in the second. The Americans came back with one in the third, and tied and took the lead in the fifth on George Kell's run-scoring fly and an RBI single by Ted Williams (who, it was later learned, had broken his left elbow making an off-the-wall catch in the first inning). But in the top of the ninth, Ralph Kiner of the Nationals hit a game-tying homer, and 4-1/2 scoreless innings later Red Schoendienst—on the first pitch of the 14th inning—homered off American Leaguer Ted Gray with what proved to be the game winner.

GAME 18

Briggs Stadium, Detroit
July 10, 1951
NL, 8–3

NL 1 0 0 3 0 2 1 1 0   8 12 1
AL 0 1 0 1 1 0 0 0 0   3 10 2

Pitchers: Roberts, MAGLIE (3), Newcombe (6),
Blackwell (9) vs Garver, LOPAT (4), Hutchinson (5),
Parnell (8), Lemon (9)
Home Runs: Musial-N, Elliott-N, Wertz-A, Kell-A,
Hodges-N, Kiner-N
Attendance: 52,075

In a game moved from Philadelphia to help Detroit celebrate its 250th birthday, hometowners Vic Wertz and George Kell of the Tigers hit solo homers in the fourth and fifth innings to bring the American stars

within a run of the Nationals. But they came no closer, as the National Leaguers pulled away for a convincing 8-3 victory.

The Nationals, aided by six innings of shutout pitching (including three by Don Newcombe), produced four home runs of their own to drive in six of their eight runs. With the score tied 1-1 going into the fourth inning, Stan Musial greeted Ed Lopat's first pitch with a shot to the right field upper deck. Bob Elliott added two more runs later in the inning with a homer to left. Gil Hodges increased the National League lead to 6–3 with a two-run homer in the sixth, and Ralph Kiner concluded the Nationals' scoring with a solo upper-deck shot to left center in the eighth. For the first time in All-Star play, the National League had won two games in a row.

GAME 19

Shibe Park, Philadelphia
July 8, 1952
NL, 3–2

AL 0 0 0 2 0   2 5 0
NL 1 0 0 2 0   3 3 0

Pitchers: Raschi, LEMON (3), Shantz (5) vs
Simmons, RUSH (4)
Home Runs: J.Robinson-N, Sauer-N
Attendance: 32,785

No sun shone for this rain-shortened game, but two hometown pitchers did. Curt Simmons of the Phillies held the American stars to one hit as he shut them out over the first three innings. And the Athletics' Bobby Shantz—in the midst of an MVP season—struck out the side in the fifth for the Americans.

But home runs and rain determined the final outcome. Jackie Robinson opened the scoring with a homer off Vic Raschi in the bottom of the first to give the Nationals a 1–0 lead. In the fourth the Americans came back to take the lead briefly with two runs on a double, a walk, and two singles off eventual winner Bob Rush. In the bottom of the inning, Hank Sauer's home run off Bob Lemon with one aboard returned the lead to the National League. And there it stayed through a scoreless fifth, when the rain, which had fallen throughout the game, at last brought the soggy festivities to the All-Star series' first premature conclusion.

GAME 20

Crosley Field, Cincinnati
July 14, 1953
NL, 5–1

AL 0 0 0 0 0 0 0 0 1   1 5 0
NL 0 0 0 0 2 0 1 2 X   5 10 0

Pitchers: Pierce, REYNOLDS (4), Garcia (6) Paige (8)
vs Roberts, SPAHN (4), Simmons (6), Dickson (8)
Attendance: 30,846

For the first 4-1/2 innings, pitchers for both sides held the opposition scoreless, with one hit each. Then the National Leaguers got to Allie Reynolds for two runs in the bottom of the fifth on a hit batsman, a walk, and two singles.

This proved margin enough for the National League's fourth consecutive victory, as four National pitchers held the Americans to just two hits through eight innings before three singles in the ninth gave the American Leaguers their only run. For good measure, though, the National stars added a run in the seventh, and two more in the eighth (with three singles and a walk off Satchel Paige in his only All-Star appearance).

Enos Slaughter of the Nationals provided much of the game's excitement. With two singles, a walk, and a stolen base, he drove in one run and scored two others, and defensively made a spectacular diving catch in right field. Pee Wee Reese's double in the seventh (scoring Slaughter) was the game's only extra-base hit.

GAME 21

Municipal Stadium, Cleveland
July 13, 1954
AL, 11–9

NL 0 0 0 5 2 0 0 2 0   9 14 0
AL 0 0 4 1 2 1 0 3 X   11 17 1

Pitchers: Roberts, Antonelli (4), Spahn (6),
Grissom (6), CONLEY (8), Erskine (8) vs Ford,
Consuegra (4), Lemon (4), Porterfield (5),
Keegan (8), STONE (8), Trucks (9)
Home Runs: Rosen-A (2), Boone-A, Kluszewski-N,
Bell-N, Doby-A
Attendance: 68,751

American starter Whitey Ford gave up only one hit in three shutout innings, and National starter Robin Roberts shut out the American stars through two. But in the bottom of the third Al Rosen tagged Roberts for a three-run homer, and Ray Boone followed with a solo shot. By the end of the game new All-Star records had been set for hits (31), runs (20), and pitchers used (13), and the record of six home runs had been equaled.

The Nationals topped the American four-run third with five straight hits off Sandy Consuegra in the fourth, for five runs. The Americans tied the game with a run in their half of the fourth, but Ted Kluszewski homered in the fifth for two more National League runs. In the bottom of the fifth, Rosen homered again, for two, to bring the Americans even again.

A run in the sixth put the Americans ahead, but Gus Bell's two-run blast in the eighth returned the Nationals to the top by one. They were threatening to lengthen that lead when Dean Stone entered the contest in relief of Bob Keegan with two out and Red Schoendienst on third. As Stone delivered on a 1-1 count, Schoendienst broke for home and was tagged out, setting the stage for Stone to become the winning pitcher without retiring a batter. Larry Doby tied it up for the American League later in the eighth with a home run, and Nellie Fox drove in the American's final two runs a few batters later with a bases-loaded single.

In the ninth, the Nationals' Stan Musial blasted two over the fence—both foul—with a man aboard. But Virgil Trucks retired him and Gil Hodges to preserve the American League's first victory in five games.

GAME 22

County Stadium, Milwaukee
July 12, 1955
NL, 6–5

AL 4 0 0 0 0 1 0 0 0 0 0 0   5 10 2
NL 0 0 0 0 0 0 2 3 0 0 0 1   6 13 1

Pitchers: Pierce, Wynn (4), Ford (7), SULLIVAN (8)
vs Roberts, Haddix (4), Newcombe (7), Jones (8),
Nuxhall (8), CONLEY (12)
Home Runs: Mantle-A, Musial-N
Attendance: 45,314

Down 5–0 in the seventh inning, the National Leaguers came back to tie the game and send it into extra innings. The Americans attacked early, scoring four runs off Robin Roberts (three of them on Mickey Mantle's home run to center) before the game's first out had been recorded. They added a fifth run in the sixth inning. Meanwhile, pitchers Billy Pierce and Early Wynn were shutting the Nationals down on four hits.

In the seventh, though, two singles, a walk, and an American error gave the Nationals two runs. In the eighth, four two-out singles and another error tied the game. Joe Nuxhall for the Nationals and the Americans' Frank Sullivan prevented further scoring through the 11th. In the top of the 12th, Gene Conley replaced Nuxhall and struck out the side: Al Kaline, Mickey Vernon, and Al Rosen. Sullivan returned for the Americans to face Stan Musial in the bottom of the 12th. Musial hit the first pitch—a fastball—over the screen in right and the game was over.

GAME 23

Griffith Stadium, Washington
July 10, 1956
NL, 7–3
NL 001 211 200   7 11 0
AL 000 003 000   3 11 0
Pitchers: FRIEND, Spahn (4), Antonelli (6) vs
PIERCE, Ford (4), Wilson (5), Brewer (6), Score (8),
Wynn (9)
Home Runs: Mays-N, Williams-A, Mantle-A,
Musial-N
Attendance: 28,843

Four of the game's greatest sluggers—Willie Mays, Stan Musial, Ted Williams, and Mickey Mantle—hit home runs, three of them off two of the game's greatest pitchers—Whitey Ford and Warren Spahn. But the star of the game was National League third baseman Ken Boyer, who went 3-for-5, scoring one run and driving in another, while making three spectacular diving and leaping plays in the field.

The National stars scored five times—including twice in the fourth on Mays' homer off Ford—before the Americans put a run on the board. But in the bottom of the sixth, Williams homered for two runs off Spahn, and Mantle followed him with another homer to bring the Americans within two. But that was the end of their scoring, as Johnny Antonelli relieved Spahn to stop the American stars the rest of the way. The Nationals scored twice more in the seventh—one of the runs coming on Musial's homer—ensuring them a comfortable 7–3 victory.

GAME 24

Sportsman's Park, St. Louis
July 9, 1957
AL, 6–5
AL 020 001 003   6 10 0
NL 000 000 203   5 9 1
Pitchers: BUNNING, Loes (4), Wynn (7), Pierce (7),
Mossi (9), Grim (9) vs SIMMONS, Burdette (2),
Sanford (6), Jackson (7), Labine (9)
Attendance: 30,693

Cincinnati fans stuffed the ballot boxes and elected Reds to start everywhere but first base. Commissioner Ford Frick removed two elected starters, but left five Reds in the lineup. They could not bring the National League the victory, though.

The Americans scored twice in the second on singles and walks to take a lead they held to the finish. Although reliever Lew Burdette—after walking in the second run—stopped the American stars through the fifth, Jim Bunning and Billy Loes were combining to keep the Nationals from scoring through the first six innings. The Americans, meanwhile, added a third run in the top of the sixth on a double, a wild pitch, and a single.

The Nationals scored their first two in the seventh, on two singles and a double, to draw within a run of a tie. But in the top of the ninth the Americans combined two singles, an error, a sacrifice bunt, and Minnie Minoso's pinch double for three more runs. They needed them all because the Nationals responded in their half of the ninth with three runs of their own on a blend of walks, hits (including Willie Mays' triple), and a wild pitch. With two out and a runner at second, Gil Hodges lined one deep to left-center. But Minoso, now in left field, snared the drive on the run to end the game.

GAME 25

Memorial Stadium, Baltimore
July 8, 1958
AL, 4–3
NL 210 000 000   3 4 2
AL 110 011 00X   4 9 2
Pitchers: Spahn, FRIEND (4), Jackson (6), Farrell (7)
vs Turley, Narleski (2), WYNN (6), O'Dell (7)
Attendance: 48,829

Although American League pitchers held the National Leaguers to only four hits (all singles), the Nationals took a quick lead, and held it for half the game before they were overtaken. Willie Mays and

Stan Musial singled in the top of the first, both scoring as American starter Bob Turley proceeded to give up a sacrifice fly, hit a batter, walk a man, and unload a wild pitch.

The Americans came back with one run in their half of the first, but the Nationals drove Turley out with their third run as Mays (who had reached on a fielder's choice) worked his way around the bases on a steal, an error, and Bob Skinner's single. Once again the Americans answered with a run, but they didn't tie the game until Mickey Vernon scored on a bases-loaded ground out in the fifth. An inning later they took the lead when pinch hitter Gil McDougald singled home Frank Malzone.

Billy O'Dell set down the Nationals in order over the final three innings to preserve the lead and give the American Leaguers their second consecutive victory. It would take more than 30 years before the American League could again claim consecutive All-Star victories.

GAME 26

Forbes Field, Pittsburgh
July 7, 1959
NL, 5–4
AL 000 100 030   4 8 0
NL 100 000 22X   5 9 1
Pitchers: Wynn, Duren (4), Bunning (7), FORD (8),
Daley (8) vs Drysdale, Burdette (4), Face (7),
ANTONELLI (8), Elston (9)
Home Runs: Mathews-N, Kaline-A
Attendance: 35,277

For the third year in a row, the game was decided by one run, with the National League celebrating the city of Pittsburgh's bicentennial by breaking the American League's win streak at two.

Eddie Mathews homered for the Nationals in the bottom of the first for the only run in the first three innings, as Don Drysdale stopped the Americans without a hit or walk, fanning four. Al Kaline tied the game in the top of the fourth with an American home run for the only score of the middle three innings, as Ryne Duren one-hit the Nationals. Like Drysdale, Duren fanned four.

In the last of the seventh, though, a double and two singles off Jim Bunning put the Nationals ahead by two runs. The NL lead lasted only briefly, however, as the Americans moved back into the lead with three runs in the eighth off Roy Face, with two singles, a walk, and a double after Face had retired the first two men. But in their half of the eighth the Nationals hit Whitey Ford, tying the game with a single-sacrifice-single, and scoring the game winner on Willie Mays' triple to center.

GAME 27

Memorial Coliseum, Los Angeles
August 3, 1959
AL, 5–3
AL 012 000 110   5 6 0
NL 100 010 100   3 6 3
Pitchers: WALKER, Wynn (4), Wilhelm, (6),
O'Dell, (7), McLish (8) vs DRYSDALE, Conley (4),
Jones (6), Face (8)
Home Runs: Malzone-A, Berra-A, F. Robinson-N,
Gilliam-N, Colavito-A
Attendance: 55,105

To raise extra money for the players' pension fund and other causes, a second All-Star Game was scheduled for 1959, the first ever to be played in August, and the first on the West Coast. The American stars avenged their earlier defeat with a 5–3 win, out-homering the Nationals three to two.

The National Leaguers scored first on a first-inning double and sacrifice fly, but Frank Malzone tied the score with the game's first home run. Yogi Berra homered an inning later with one on for a 3–1 American lead, but Frank Robinson brought the Nationals back to within one with his homer in the fifth. The Americans replaced that run in the top of the seventh on a walk, two errors, and a single, but Junior Gilliam countered with a home run in the last of the inning. Rocky Colavito scored the game's final run for the Americans in the eighth with the game's final

homer.

Don Drysdale, the pitching standout of the July game, struck out five this time, but also walked three and gave up three runs on homers to take the loss.

GAME 28

Municipal Stadium, Kansas City
July 11, 1960
NL, 5–3
NL 311 000 000   5 12 4
AL 000 001 020   3 6 1
Pitchers: FRIEND, McCormick (4), Face (6), Buhl (8),
Law (9) vs MONBOUQUETTE, Estrada (3),
Coates (4), Bell (6), Lary (8), Daley (9)
Home Runs: Banks-N, Crandall-N, Kaline-A
Attendance: 30,619

The day was hot—the temperature broke 100—and so were the National League bats. Willie Mays had three hits, including a leadoff triple and a double; Ernie Banks homered and doubled; Del Crandall homered and singled; and Joe Adcock doubled and singled for three-fourths of the Nationals' 12 hits. The National League scored five unanswered runs in the first three innings to take an unbeatable lead. Starter Bob Friend, meanwhile, blanked the Americans on one hit through three innings and Mike McCormick held them scoreless for two more before yielding the first American run in the sixth on Nellie Fox's bases-loaded single. Roy Face then came on to douse the fire, getting Luis Aparicio to ground into a double play.

Four American League pitchers stopped the National stars after the third inning, and Al Kaline homered for two more American runs in the eighth. In the ninth the Americans put men on first and second with one away. But their comeback fell short, as Vern Law came on to retire Brooks Robinson and Harvey Kuenn and preserve the National victory.

GAME 29

Yankee Stadium, New York
July 13, 1960
NL, 6–0
NL 021 000 102   6 10 0
AL 000 000 000   0 8 0
Pitchers: LAW, Podres (3), S.Williams (5),
Jackson (7), Henry (8), McDaniel (9) vs FORD,
Wynn (4), Staley (6), Lary (8), Bell (9)
Home Runs: Mathews-N, Mays-N, Musial-N,
Boyer-N
Attendance: 38,362

Only two days after the first All-Star Game, the squads met a second time before fewer than 39,000 fans in capacious Yankee Stadium. It was no contest. Vern Law, who had completed and saved the first game, started and won this one. His two shutout innings set the pace for the five National pitchers who followed him to fashion the first National League shutout in 20 years. The American stars got only two fewer hits than the Nationals, but only one was for extra bases, whereas four of the National League hits were home runs.

Eddie Mathews began the scoring with a two-run homer in the second, and Willie Mays (on his way to a second straight 3-for-4 game) homered for the third National run an inning later. No one scored through the three middle innings, but in the seventh Stan Musial broke his own record with his sixth All-Star homer—a mighty shot three tiers up in right—and in the ninth Ken Boyer completed the rout with a two-run shot to left.

GAME 30

Candlestick Park, San Francisco
July 11, 1961
NL, 5–4
AL 000 001 002 1   4 4 2
NL 010 100 010 2   5 11 5
Pitchers: Ford, Lary (4), Donovan (4), Bunning (6),
Fornieles (8), WILHELM (8) vs Spahn, Purkey (4),
McCormick (6), Face (9), Koufax (9), MILLER (9)
Home Runs: Killebrew-A, Altman-N
Attendance: 44,115

National League pitchers began the game where

they had left off the year before. For five innings Warren Spahn and Bob Purkey shut out the American stars without a hit or base on balls. In the sixth, Harmon Killebrew homered off Mike McCormick to end the American drought, but it was the only hit McCormick yielded through the eighth.

Meanwhile, the Nationals had taken a 3–1 lead with runs in the second and fourth innings and George Altman's homer in the eighth. In the top of the ninth, Candlestick's notorious winds helped put the Americans back in the game. Their second and third hits of the game brought in one run, and their fourth (and last) hit put another man on base. The tying run came in when the wind blew pitcher Stu Miller off the mound for a balk to advance the runners, and then twisted a grounder out of third baseman Ken Boyer's grasp for a run-scoring error. In the 10th, the wind may have contributed to the Americans' go-ahead run as Boyer's throw to first sailed into the outfield, allowing Nellie Fox (who had walked) to score from first.

But in the last of the 10th the wind finally came to the aid of the Nationals, rendering useless the famous knuckleball of American reliever Hoyt Wilhelm, who gave up the tying run on hits by Hank Aaron and Willie Mays and lost the game when Roberto Clemente singled in Mays from second.

GAME 31

Fenway Park, Boston
July 31, 1961
Tie, 1–1
NL 000 001 000   1   5   1
AL 100 000 000   1   4   0
Pitchers: Purkey, Mahaffey (3), Koufax (5), Miller (7) vs Bunning, Schwall (4), Pascual (7)
Home Runs: Colavito-A
Attendance: 31,851

In the second All-Star Game of 1961, the weather again played a crucial role, as heavy rain at the end of the ninth inning forced the first All-Star tie.

Rocky Colavito's home run for the Americans in the first inning turned out to be his squad's only run, as four National League pitchers combined to shut out the American stars on only three singles the rest of the way. The American League pitching was just as effective, with starter Jim Bunning and finisher Camilo Pascual each pitching three no-hit innings. Don Schwall, who pitched the middle three innings, gave up all five National League hits and the Nationals' one run. But even that might have been prevented.

In the sixth, with two on and two out, American League shortstop Luis Aparicio waited for a slow grounder, failing to get the ball in time to throw the batter out and end the inning. The Nationals scored when Bill White followed with a hot ground single up the middle. Aparicio made a brilliant stop on White's ball to prevent more than one run from scoring, but it did drive in the game's tying—and final—run.

GAME 32

D.C. Stadium, Washington
July 10, 1962
NL, 3–1
NL 000 002 010   3   8   0
AL 000 001 000   1   4   0
MVP: Willis-N
Pitchers: Drysdale, MARICHAL (4), Purkey (6), Shaw (8) vs Bunning, PASCUAL (4), Donovan (7), Pappas (9)
Attendance: 45,480

The stadium was new, President John F. Kennedy threw out the first ball, and starters Don Drysdale of the Nationals and Jim Bunning of the Americans both pitched three innings of one-hit shutout ball. But Maury Wills stole the show. Entering the game in the sixth inning to run for 41-year-old Stan Musial, who had singled, Wills stole second, then scored on Dick Groat's single up the middle for the game's first run. Another single, a long fly out, and a ground out scored Groat with the second (and, as it turned out, winning) run.

Two singles and a fly out by Roger Maris brought in an American run in the bottom of the sixth off Bob

Purkey. But that was all they got, as Purkey and Bob Shaw one-hit the American stars through the final three innings.

In the eighth inning Wills manufactured an insurance run for the Nationals. On first with a leadoff single, he somehow reached third on Jim Davenport's single to short left, racing from second to third as left fielder Rocky Colavito threw in to second. He scored after tagging on a foul out to right. Wills earned All-Star Most Valuable Player honors in the first year it was awarded.

GAME 33

Wrigley Field, Chicago
July 30, 1962
AL, 9–4
AL 001 201 302   9   10   0
NL 010 000 111   4   10   4
MVP: Wagner-A
Pitchers: Stenhouse, HERBERT (3), Aguirre (6), Pappas (9) vs Podres, MAHAFFEY (3), Gibson (5), Farrell (7), Marichal (8)
Home Runs: Runnels-A, Wagner-A. Colavito-A, Roseboro-N
Attendance: 38,359

With this second game of 1962, the leagues ended their four-year experiment of playing two All-Star games a year. The Americans out-homered the Nationals to spoil the National League's attempt to even the series at 16 wins apiece. But no matter—the American stars would win only once again in the next 20 years.

The National stars scored first on a double and single in the second, but Pete Runnels evened the score in the third with a solo homer, and Leon Wagner put the Americans ahead with a two-run shot an inning later. After Tom Tresh doubled home a fourth American run in the sixth, Rocky Colavito put the game out of reach with a three-run blast in the seventh.

The Nationals tried to come back with runs in the seventh and eighth, but the Americans neutralized them with two more of their own in the ninth (on two errors, two Juan Marichal wild pitches, a double, and a long fly out). With the score now 9-3, John Roseboro's solo homer in the last of the ninth put the Nationals in the home-run column, but that was all.

GAME 34

Municipal Stadium, Cleveland
July 9, 1963
NL, 5–3
NL 012 010 010   5   6   0
AL 012 000 000   3   11   1
MVP: Mays-N
Pitchers: O'Toole, JACKSON (3), Culp (5), Woodeshick (6), Drysdale (8) vs McBride, BUNNING (4), Bouton (6), Pizarro (7), Radatz (8)
Attendance: 44,160

Willie Mays sparked the National League to victory with his baserunning and timely hitting. Although he had only one hit—a single—he scored two runs and drove in two others in the Nationals' 5–3 win.

The National stars scored first when Mays walked in the second inning, stole second, and came in on a single by Dick Groat. The Americans tied the game in the last of the second, but in the top of the third Mays singled in one run, stole second again, and scored his second run on Ed Bailey's single.

Once again the Americans came back in the bottom of the third to tie the game on Albie Pearson's double, followed by two singles sandwiched around an infield out. But these were their last runs, as four National pitchers shut them out on four singles the rest of the way. Meanwhile, Mays drove in what proved to be the winning run with a ground out in the fifth. In the eighth the Nationals scored a final run when Ron Santo singled home Bill White, who had singled and stolen second.

GAME 35

Shea Stadium, New York
July 7, 1964
NL, 7–4
AL 100 002 100   4   9   1
NL 000 210 004   7   8   0
MVP: Callison-N
Pitchers: Chance, Wyatt (4), Pascual (5), RADATZ (7) vs Drysdale, Bunning (4), Short (6), Farrell (7), MARICHAL (9)
Home Runs: B.Williams-N, Boyer-N, Callison-N
Attendance: 50,850

A new stadium in the midst of a World's Fair was the venue for this game in which the National League at last drew even with the American at 17 wins apiece.

The American stars jumped into the lead with an unearned run in the first, but the Nationals (after Dean Chance had shut them out through three innings) overtook the Americans in the fourth, on home runs by Billy Williams and Ken Boyer, and Dick Groat doubled in a third run in the fifth. In the top of the sixth the Americans tied the score when Brooks Robinson tripled in a pair, and took the lead again an inning later on a sacrifice fly that barely scored Elston Howard ahead of Willie Mays' throw from center.

The Americans held their slim lead into the bottom of the ninth. But Mays walked (after fouling off five third strikes), stole second, and scored the tying run on a single to short right and an errant throw home. One intentional walk and two outs later, Johnny Callison hit Dick Radatz's fastball over the fence in right to win the game.

GAME 36

Metropolitan Stadium, Bloomington, Minnesota
July 13, 1965
NL, 6–5
NL 320 000 100   6   11   0
AL 010 140 000   5   8   0
MVP: Marichal-N
Pitchers: Marichal, Maloney (4), Drysdale (5), KOUFAX (6), Farrell (7), Gibson (8) vs Pappas, Grant (2), Richert (4), McDOWELL (6), Fisher (8)
Home Runs: Mays-N, Torre-N, Stargell-N, McAuliffe-A, Killebrew-A
Attendance: 46,706

For a while it looked as though the Nationals would run away with the game. Willie Mays led off with a home run in the first, and Joe Torre added two runs with a homer later in the inning. In the second Willie Stargell homered for two more runs to make the score 5-0. National starter Juan Marichal stopped the Americans on one hit through three innings.

But the American stars battled back. A single, a walk, and another single off Marichal's replacement, Jim Maloney, brought in one run in the fourth. Maloney retired the first two men in the fifth, but then he gave up a walk followed by a home run to Dick McAuliffe, and a scratch single followed by a Harmon Killebrew homer—and the score was tied at 5-5.

Only one more run was scored. In the seventh, Willie Mays, who had walked and gone to third on Hank Aaron's single, scored on Ron Santo's infield hit to short. The Nationals held off American threats in the eighth and ninth to take the All-Star series lead for the first time.

GAME 37

Busch Memorial Stadium, St. Louis
July 12, 1966
NL, 2–1
AL 010 000 000   1   6   0
NL 000 100 0001   2   6   0
MVP: B. Robinson-A
Pitchers: McLain, Kaat (4), Stottlemyre (6), Siebert (8), RICHERT (10) vs Koufax, Bunning (4), Marichal (6), G.PERRY (9)
Attendance: 49,936

The celebration of another new stadium and the city's bicentennial—and a temperature of 106 degrees Fahrenheit—greeted participants in the

1966 classic. Pitching dominated: seven pitchers hurled two innings or more each of shutout ball. American starter Denny McLain threw three perfect innings, but the National League's Sandy Koufax gave the Americans a run in the second when he let loose a wild pitch after Brooks Robinson had tripled.

The Nationals tied the score in the fourth with three singles off Jim Kaat, but that ended the scoring for both sides through the regulation nine innings. Gaylord Perry stopped the American stars in the top of the 10th, but in the last half of the inning, National Leaguer Tim McCarver singled off Pete Richert, was sacrificed to second, and came across with the winning run on Maury Wills' single to right.

GAME 38

Anaheim Stadium, Anaheim
July 11, 1967
NL, 2–1
NL 010 000 000 000 001   2   9   0
AL 000 001 000 000 000   1   8   0
MVP: Perez-N
Pitchers: Marichal, Jenkins (4), Gibson (7), Short (9), Cuellar (11), DRYSDALE (13), Seaver (15) vs Chance, McGlothlin (4), Peters (6), Downing (9), HUNTER (11)
Home Runs: Allen-N, B.Robinson-A, Perez-N
Attendance: 46,309

This was a game of strikeouts, home runs, and extra innings. Every one of the dozen pitchers used in the game struck out at least one batter. American Leaguers Gary Peters (who pitched three perfect middle innings) and Catfish Hunter struck out four apiece, while Ferguson Jenkins of the Nationals tied the All-Star record with six. The game total of 30 strikeouts shattered the previous record of 20 set in 1955.

Apart from the splendid pitching, three home runs provided the only excitement—and the only scoring—in this longest All-Star Game. Richie Allen of the Nationals scored first, homering to center off Dean Chance in the second inning. The Americans' Brooks Robinson tied the score in the sixth with a shot off Jenkins. And 8-1/2 innings later, in the top of the 15th, National Leaguer Tony Perez homered off Hunter for the game's third and final run. Tom Seaver set down the Americans in the bottom of the inning, and the game—after a record three hours and 41 minutes—was history.

GAME 39

Astrodome, Houston
July 9, 1968
NL, 1–0
AL 000 000 000   0   3   1
NL 100 000 00X   1   5   0
MVP: Mays-N
Pitchers: TIANT, Odom (3), McLain (5), McDowell (7), Stottlemyre (8), John (8) vs DRYSDALE, Marichal (4), Carlton (6), Seaver (7), Reed (9), Koosman (9)
Attendance: 48,321

This game could be described by what was missing: fresh air and real grass (it was the first All-Star Game held indoors), hitting (the eight hits were a new low for a nine-inning All-Star Game), and earned runs (the game's only run came with the help of an error). In fact, if it weren't for 37-year-old Willie Mays, the game might not have had any runs at all. Starting only because of an injury to Pete Rose, National Leaguer Mays led off the bottom of the first with a single, and took second when first baseman Harmon Killebrew mishandled pitcher Luis Tiant's pickoff throw for an error. Mays took third as the rattled Tiant threw a wild pitch to walk Curt Flood, and scored when Willie McCovey grounded into a double play. Mays became the first two-time All-Star MVP, having also won the award in 1963.

The pitching on both sides was superb, but the National Leaguers shone especially bright. Tom Seaver gave up two of the Americans' three hits (all of which were doubles), but struck out five in his two innings. Juan Marichal hurled two perfect innings, fanning three. And none of the six National pitchers

walked a man. One American, Killebrew, couldn't walk. Stretching for a throw at first, the slugger tore a hamstring and missed the next two months, the most serious All-Star Game casualty since Ted Williams' broken elbow 18 years earlier.

GAME 40

R.F.K. Memorial Stadium, Washington, D.C.
July 23, 1969
NL, 9–3
NL 125 100 000   9   11   0
AL 011 100 000   3   6   2
MVP: McCovey-N
Pitchers: CARLTON, Gibson (4), Singer (5), Koosman (7), Dierker (8), P.Niekro (9) vs STOTTLEMYRE, Odom (3), Knowles (3), McLain (4), McNally (5), McDowell (7), Culp (9)
Home Runs: Bench-N, Howard-A, McCovey-N (2), Freehan-A
Attendance: 45,259

After four one-run victories in a row, the National Leaguers finally broke loose, massing 10 of their 11 hits in the first four innings for nine runs and a crushing win. Scoring an unearned run in the first on a dropped outfield fly, and two in the second on Johnny Bench's home run, the Nationals erupted in the third for five runs off Blue Moon Odom before two outs had been recorded. Willie McCovey's two-run homer began the third-inning scoring, and an error, single, and two doubles added three more runs before Odom was mercifully relieved. McCovey homered again in the fourth for the Nationals' final tally.

The American bats were not wholly silent, but the solo homers by Frank Howard and Bill Freehan in the second and third, and a third run in the fourth, couldn't counter the Nationals' attack.

The final five innings of the game were as quiet as the opening four had been noisy. No runs scored, and the two teams together managed only three hits.

GAME 41

Riverfront Stadium, Cincinnati
July 14, 1970
NL, 5–4
AL 000 001 120 000   4   12   0
NL 000 000 103 001   5   10   0
MVP: Yastrzemski-A
Pitchers: Palmer, McDowell (4), J.Perry (7), Hunter (9), Peterson (9), Stottlemyre (9), WRIGHT (11) vs Seaver, Merritt (4), G.Perry (6), Gibson (8), OSTEEN (10)
Home Runs: Dietz-N
Attendance: 51,838

In a new stadium opened only two weeks earlier, no one scored for the first five innings, as Jim Palmer and Sam McDowell of the Americans and Tom Seaver and Jim Merritt of the Nationals held the opposition to two hits per team. The Americans finally scored a run in the sixth, and another in the seventh. The Nationals got one back in the last of the seventh, but the Americans increased their lead to 4–1 in the eighth when Brooks Robinson tripled home two baserunners.

Fans had already begun to leave the park when the Nationals' Dick Dietz homered off Catfish Hunter to lead off the last of the ninth. Two pitchers, three singles, and a sacrifice fly later, the game was tied and headed for extra innings. Claude Osteen held the Americans scoreless from the 10th through the 12th, and the Nationals also failed to score in the 10th and 11th. But in the last of the 12th, with two out, Pete Rose, Billy Grabarkewitz, and Jim Hickman singled. Hometowner Rose, racing home from second on Hickman's hit, crashed into catcher Ray Fosse with a force that injured both players and still provokes controversy—but which also gave the National League its eighth straight victory.

GAME 42

Tiger Stadium, Detroit
July 13, 1971
AL, 6–4
NL 021 000 010   4   5   0
AL 004 002 00X   6   7   0
MVP: F. Robinson-A
Pitchers: ELLIS, Marichal (4), Jenkins (6), Wilson (7) vs BLUE, Palmer (4), Cuellar (6), Lolich (8)
Home Runs: Bench-N, Aaron-N, Jackson-A, F. Robinson-A, Killebrew-A, Clemente-N
Attendance: 53,559

With an assist from a favorable wind, six all-time greats homered to account for all the scoring as the American League broke its eight-game All-Star drought with a 6-4 victory. Johnny Bench put the Nationals in front with a two-run homer in the second inning off Vida Blue, and Hank Aaron—with his first All-Star home run—added a third run off Blue an inning later. But the Americans, shut out by Dock Ellis through the first two innings, rocked back in the bottom of the third as Reggie Jackson and Frank Robinson wrested the lead from the Nationals with a pair of two-run homers. Robinson's blast made him the first player to hit an All-Star home run for both leagues, and Jackson's memorable homer hit the light tower atop the second deck of the stadium in right-center.

Ferguson Jenkins yielded the game's fifth homer, Harmon Killebrew's two-run shot for the Americans in the sixth. Roberto Clemente brought the Nationals a run closer with his solo homer off Mickey Lolich in the eighth, but that ended the team's scoring, and (for a year, anyway) the National League's All-Star stranglehold.

GAME 43

Atlanta-Fulton County Stadium, Atlanta
July 25, 1972
NL, 4–3
AL 001 000 020 0   3   6   0
NL 000 002 001 1   4   8   0
MVP: Morgan-N
Pitchers: Palmer, Lolich (4), G.Perry (6), Wood (8), McNALLY (10) vs Gibson, Blass (3), Sutton (4), Carlton (6), Stoneman (7), McGRAW (9)
Home Runs: Aaron-N, Rojas-A
Attendance: 53,107

The American Leaguers tried to extend their All-Star win streak to two games, and for a time it looked as though they might do it. In the third, they scored the only run of the first half of the game as Jim Palmer and Mickey Lolich held the Nationals to two hits through the first five innings. In the sixth Hank Aaron thrilled the hometown crowd with a two-run homer deep to left to shift the lead to the National League. But Cookie Rojas restored the American lead with his own two-run shot in the eighth.

The Americans held their lead into the bottom of the ninth, but after two singles and a force out, the score was tied. Tug McGraw set down the American stars in order in the 10th, but American reliever Dave McNally was not so fortunate. He walked leadoff batter Nate Colbert, who was sacrificed to second. Joe Morgan then sent the American Leaguers back into the ranks of losers with a sharp RBI single to right center. His single also gave the Nationals their seventh win in seven extra-inning games.

GAME 44

Royals Stadium, Kansas City
July 24, 1973
NL, 7–1
NL 002 122 000   7   10   0
AL 010 000 000   1   5   0
MVP: Bonds-N
Pitchers: WISE, Osteen (3), Sutton (5), Twitchell (6), Giusti (7), Seaver (8), Brewer (9) vs Hunter, Holtzman (2), BLYLEVEN (3), Singer (4), Ryan (6), Lyle (8), Fingers (9)
Home Runs: Bench-N, Bonds-N, W.Davis-N
Attendance: 40,849

Once again a new stadium was chosen to host

the All-Star Game, and once again the National League emerged victorious. The Americans scored first, with a run in the second when Reggie Jackson scored from second on a single after doubling off the center field wall. But that was the beginning and end of their offense, as six National pitchers shut them out on three hits the rest of the way.

Meanwhile the National League hitters came to life, producing seven runs in four innings. Two walks and two singles in the third brought in two runs, and Johnny Bench's homer in the fourth made the score 3–1. In the fifth, Bobby Bonds—in the midst of his finest season—homered for two more National runs. And in the sixth, Willie Davis' home run completed the game's scoring, bringing in the Nationals' sixth and seventh runs.

The final third of the game was anticlimactic, as only two hits were made after the sixth inning. But Bonds brought the crowd to life briefly in the seventh, stretching one of those hits into a double with some audacious baserunning (ensuring his selection as the game's MVP).

GAME 45

Three Rivers Stadium, Pittsburgh
July 23, 1974
NL, 7–2
AL 002 000 000   2   4   1
NL 010 210 12X   7   10   1
MVP: Garvey-N
Pitchers: G.Perry, TIANT (4), Hunter (6), Fingers (8) vs Messersmith, BRETT (4), Matlack (6), McGlothen (7), Marshall (8)
Home Runs: R.Smith-N
Attendance: 50,706

Steve Garvey, who was elected to the National League starting lineup on write-in votes (his name was omitted from the fans' All-Star ballot), sparked the Nationals to yet another convincing win over the hapless American stars. After singling in the second inning, Garvey scored the game's first run on Ron Cey's double.

The Americans took the lead with two runs in the top of the third, capitalizing on two walks and an error sandwiched between Thurman Munson's leadoff double and Dick Allen's single. They might have scored more had not Garvey snared Bobby Murcer's hot grounder for an assist on the third out.

Garvey doubled in the tying run in the fourth, and Cey's RBI groundout restored the Nationals' lead. Lou Brock added a run in the fifth with a single and some inspired baserunning, and Reggie Smith homered in the seventh. Don Kessinger's triple and a wild pitch by Rollie Fingers in the eighth contributed to two final National League runs.

GAME 46

County Stadium, Milwaukee
July 15, 1975
NL, 6–3
NL 021 000 003   6   13   1
AL 000 003 000   3   10   1
MVP: Matlack-N, Madlock-N
Pitchers: Reuss, Sutton (4), Seaver (6), MATLACK (7), R.Jones (9) vs Blue, Busby (3), Kaat (5), HUNTER (7), Gossage (9)
Home Runs: Garvey-N, Wynn-N, Yastrzemski-A
Attendance: 51,480

When National stars Steve Garvey and Jim Wynn led off the second with back-to-back homers and their teammates added another run in the third, it looked as if the National League might be on its way to another easy win. But the American pitchers shut down the National League offense for the next five innings, and Carl Yastrzemski made a contest of it with a three-run homer in the sixth off Tom Seaver to tie the score.

In the top of the ninth, though, the Americans all but gave the game away. Left fielder Claudell Washington dropped a fly on the run (it was scored a hit) and misplayed a line drive that went for a double. Goose Gossage came in to relieve Catfish Hunter on the mound and hit the next batter to load the bases. Bill Madlock then drove in two of the baserunners

with a single through the drawn-in infield, and Pete Rose knocked in the third run of the inning with a sacrifice fly.

Randy Jones set the Americans down in order in the bottom of the ninth, and—voila!—the National League had won again.

GAME 47

Veterans Stadium, Philadelphia
July 13, 1976
NL, 7–1
AL 000 100 000   1   5   0
NL 202 000 03X   7   10   0
MVP: Foster-N
Pitchers: FIDRYCH, Hunter (3), Tiant (5), Tanana (7) vs R.JONES, Seaver (4), Montefusco (6), Rhoden (8), K.Forsch (9)
Home Runs: Foster-N, Lynn-A, Cedeno-N
Attendance: 63,974

Tom Seaver gave up a home run to Fred Lynn in the fourth inning, but that was the Americans' only score as the Nationals held the American stars to five hits while celebrating the nation's bicentennial with 10 hits and seven runs.

Rookie standout Mark Fidrych was chosen to start for the Americans and was promptly rapped for two runs. Pete Rose led off with a single and was tripled home by Steve Garvey, who scored himself on a groundout. The Nationals doubled their score in the third inning as George Foster tagged Catfish Hunter for two runs with a mighty home run to left center, and capped their assault with three more in the eighth off Frank Tanana, including a two-run homer by Cesar Cedeno.

The fans had elected five members of Cincinnati's "Big Red Machine" to the National League starting lineup, and Sparky Anderson, the Reds' and National squad's manager, added two more. They provided the bulk of the Nationals' offense, with seven hits, four RBIs, and four runs scored.

GAME 48

Yankee Stadium, New York
July 19, 1977
NL, 7–5
NL 401 000 020   7   9   1
AL 000 002 102   5   8   0
MVP: Sutton-N
Pitchers: SUTTON, Lavelle (4), Seaver (6), R.Reuschel (9) vs PALMER, Kern (3), Eckersley (4), LaRoche (6), Campbell (7), Lyle (8)
Home Runs: Morgan-N, Luzinski-N, Garvey-N, Scott-A
Attendance: 56,683

The Nationals' Joe Morgan homered off Jim Palmer to open the game, and before Palmer escaped the first inning three more National Leaguers had crossed the plate on a single, double, and Greg Luzinski's homer. Palmer got through the second inning without further damage, but before he was relieved in the third, Steve Garvey had homered to give the Nationals a 5–0 lead.

The Americans fought back against Tom Seaver in the sixth and seventh. Seaver retired two in the sixth, but then gave up two singles, and two runs as Richie Zisk doubled the runners home. Two more singles in the seventh produced a third American run.

But the Nationals—assisted by pitcher Sparky Lyle's wild pitch and hit batsman—put a sixth and seventh run on the board in the eighth with a double and single. The Americans added two final runs of their own in the bottom of the ninth on George Scott's homer off Goose Gossage, but fell short of victory once again.

GAME 49

San Diego Stadium, San Diego
July 11, 1978
NL, 7–3
AL 201 000 000   3   8   1
NL 003 000 04X   7   10   0
MVP: Garvey-N
Pitchers: Palmer, Keough (3), Sorensen (4), Kern (7), Guidry (7), GOSSAGE (8) vs Blue, Rogers (4), Fingers (6), SUTTER (8), P. Niekro (9)
Attendance: 51,549

Rod Carew led off both the first and third innings with triples—an All-Star record—scoring both times as the Americans took a 3–0 lead into the bottom of the third. But then Jim Palmer, who had shut the Nationals out on one hit through the first two innings, lost his touch. After yielding a leadoff single, he retired two batters, but then issued three walks to force in a run, and when Steve Garvey singled past the short-stop two more runs scored to tie the game.

No one scored through the next 4-1/2 innings, with Larry Sorensen turning in the game's top pitching performance as he shut the Nationals out on one hit through the three middle innings. But in the last of the eighth, Goose Gossage (the National League's closer the previous year) took the mound this year for the Americans. Garvey greeted him with a leadoff triple and scored what proved to be the winning run on a wild pitch. A walk and three singles added three insurance runs before the inning ended. Bruce Sutter and Phil Niekro blanked the Americans in the ninth, and the Nationals had extended their current win streak to seven.

GAME 50

Kingdome, Seattle
July 17, 1979
NL, 7–6
NL 211 001 011   7   10   0
AL 302 001 000   6   10   0
MVP: Parker-N
Pitchers: Carlton, Andujar (2), Rogers (4), G. Perry (6), Sambito (6), LaCoss (6), SUTTER (8) vs Ryan, Stanley (3), Clear (5), KERN (7), Guidry (9)
Home Runs: Lynn-A, Mazzilli-N
Attendance: 58,905

Mike Schmidt tripled and George Foster doubled to drive in the game's first runs as the Nationals began their scoring in the top of the first. The Americans fought back to take the lead later in the inning as Don Baylor doubled home one run and Fred Lynn homered for two more. The Nationals tied the score with a run in the second and went ahead again in the third when Schmidt scored after doubling. But the Americans recaptured the lead in the bottom of the third, scoring twice on a single, wild pitch, ground out, hit batsman, single, and error.

Three innings later the Nationals again tied the game, but the Americans went ahead for the third time with a run in their half of the sixth. Outstanding throws by right fielder Dave Parker, who notched two assists, helped to keep the Americans from pulling away. In the eighth the Nationals' Lee Mazzilli homered for yet another tie, and an inning later Ron Guidry walked Mazzilli with the bases loaded to force in the Nationals' go-ahead seventh run. When Bruce Sutter kept the Americans from scoring in the bottom of the ninth, the National Leaguers had for the second time defeated the Americans eight years in a row.

GAME 51

Dodger Stadium, Los Angeles
July 8, 1980
NL, 4–2

AL	000 020 000	2 7 1
NL	000 012 10X	4 7 0

MVP: Griffey-N
Pitchers: Stone, JOHN (4), Farmer (6), Stieb (7), Gossage (8) vs Richard, Welch (3), REUSS (6), Bibby (7), Sutter (8)
Home Runs: Lynn-A, Griffey-N
Attendance: 56,088

For 4-2/3 innings J.R. Richard and Bob Welch held the American stars scoreless. But then Rod Carew singled and Fred Lynn drove in the game's first runs with his third All-Star homer.

The Americans' Steve Stone and Tommy John pitched even better, setting the Nationals down in order through four innings. John continued the perfect streak through the first two outs of the fifth, but then Ken Griffey homered, and the Americans' spell on the National Leaguers was broken.

While three National pitchers limited the Americans to a single and a walk over the final four innings, three singles and an error sent the Nationals into the lead in the sixth. A passed ball surrounded by two wild pitches moved Dave Concepcion around the bases in the seventh (he had reached on a fielder's choice) for the Nationals' fourth run. They didn't really need it, though, as Bruce Sutter—the winning pitcher in the two previous All-Star games—saved this one with two final innings of no-hit ball for the Nationals' ninth successive win.

GAME 52

Municipal Stadium, Cleveland
August 9, 1981
NL, 5–4

NL	000 011 120	5 9 1
AL	010 003 000	4 11 1

MVP: Carter-N
Pitchers: Valenzuela, Seaver (2), Knepper (3), Hooton (5), Ruthven (6), BLUE (7), Ryan (8), Sutter (9) vs Morris, Barker (3), K.Forsch (5), Norris (6), Davis (7), FINGERS (8), Stieb (8)
Home Runs: Singleton-A, Carter-N (2), Parker-N, Schmidt-N
Attendance: 72,086

The game, delayed until August by the mid-season players' strike, drew an All-Star record crowd of more than 72,000 fans, and the managers set a new record by using 56 players. But the game itself followed a familiar pattern.

The Americans scored first in the second inning on Ken Singleton's home run off Tom Seaver, and held their slim lead into the fifth on Len Barker's two innings of perfect pitching. But Ken Forsch replaced Barker in the fifth and Gary Carter homered off his first pitch to tie the score. Dave Parker's homer off Mike Norris an inning later put the Nationals ahead for the first time, but the Americans came right back in the bottom of the inning, putting together four singles and a sacrifice fly for three runs and a two-run advantage.

Gary Carter's second home run of the game—this time off Ron Davis' first pitch—brought the Nationals within one in the seventh, and Mike Schmidt's two-run blast off Rollie Fingers in the eighth restored their lead. Three National pitchers shut out the Americans without a hit over the final three innings as closer Bruce Sutter picked up his second consecutive All-Star save and the National Leaguers had their 10th consecutive victory.

GAME 53

Olympic Stadium, Montreal
July 13, 1982
NL, 4–1

AL	100 000 000	1 8 2
NL	021 001 00X	4 8 1

MVP: Concepcion-N
Pitchers: ECKERSLEY, Clancy (4), Bannister (5), Quisenberry (6), Fingers (8) vs ROGERS, Carlton (4), Soto (6), Valenzuela (8), Minton (8), Howe (9), Hume (9)
Home Runs: Concepcion-N
Attendance: 59,057

In the first All-Star Game held outside the United States, the American League for the third year in a row put the first run on the board, but for the 11th year in a row the final score showed the National League the winner. Two singles, a wild pitch, and a sacrifice fly gave the Americans a run in the top of the first. But starter Steve Rogers of the host Expos held the Americans scoreless for the remainder of his three innings while the Nationals struck back for two runs in the second on Dave Concepcion's home run, and added another in the third when Ruppert Jones—who had tripled to open the inning—scored on a sacrifice fly.

Six National League pitchers (and shortstop Ozzie Smith's spectacular stop and throw to first with two on in the eighth) joined Rogers in holding the American stars scoreless after the first inning. Two hometowners put together the Nationals' final run in the sixth. Al Oliver, leading off, doubled down the line in left and took third as the ball got by left fielder Rickey Henderson. Two outs later Gary Carter lined a pitch to center, scoring Oliver as Willie Wilson's dive for the ball came up short.

GAME 54

Comiskey Park, Chicago
July 6, 1983
AL, 13–3

NL	100 110 000	3 8 3
AL	117 000 22X	13 15 2

MVP: Lynn-A
Pitchers: SOTO, Hammaker (3), Dawley (3), Dravecky (5), Perez (7), Orosco (7), L.Smith (8) vs STIEB, Honeycutt (4), Stanley (6), Young (8), Quisenberry (9)
Home Runs: Rice-A, Lynn-A
Attendance: 43,801

The game returned to the park where it had originated 50 years earlier, and the American League, after 11 years of All-Star losses, unleashed its pent-up fury to produce the greatest margin of victory in 37 years. The game began, though, as an embarrassment of errors. American starter Dave Stieb struck out the side in the first, but along the way two errors (one of them Stieb's) let in a run. An unearned run in the bottom of the first tied the score and another in the second put the American League ahead for good (making a loser out of the unfortunate National starter Mario Soto).

The hitting began in earnest in the last of the third as the Americans scored seven times for a new one-inning record. Among their six hits (also a record for an All-Star inning) were a homer by Jim Rice, a triple by George Brett, and a bases-loaded blast by Fred Lynn—his fourth All-Star home run and the first grand slam in All-Star history. With the score now 9–1, the National League's single runs in the fourth and fifth were exercises in futility, and the Americans' two each in the seventh and eighth served chiefly to boost the winning total to 13—another All-Star high.

GAME 55

Candlestick Park, San Francisco
July 10, 1984
NL, 3–1

AL	010 000 000	1 7 2
NL	110 000 01X	3 8 0

MVP: Carter-N
Pitchers: STIEB, Morris (3), Dotson (5), Caudill (7), Hernandez (8) vs LEA, Valenzuela (3), Gooden (5), Soto (7), Gossage (9)
Home Runs: Brett-A, Carter-N, Murphy-N
Attendance: 57,756

Only four times in the previous 54 All-Star Games had a pitcher struck out the side in order. In this game, three more pitchers did it. And, on this 50th anniversary of Carl Hubbell's five consecutive strike-outs, two of those pitchers combined to break Hubbell's record with six back-to-back whiffs. Hubbell, who threw out the first ball, also saw an All-Star nine-inning record set with 21 total Ks (11 by National League pitchers, 10 by American).

In the fourth inning, National star Fernando Valenzuela mowed down three of the game's premier sluggers: Dave Winfield, Reggie Jackson, and George Brett. The three men Dwight Gooden retired on strikes an inning later (Lance Parrish, Chet Lemon, and rookie Alvin Davis) were slightly less formidable, still, it was an impressive performance for a 19-year-old rookie (the youngest player in All-Star history). The three that American Leaguer Bill Caudill struck out in the seventh were no slouches either: Tim Raines, Ryne Sandberg (in the midst of an MVP season), and Keith Hernandez.

Three of the four runs scored in the game were homers. The National League's run in the first was unearned, but the Americans' George Brett homered to center to tie the game in the second, and the Nationals' go-ahead run later in the inning came on Gary Carter's blast to left. In the eighth, National Leaguer Dale Murphy also put one over the left field fence to end the scoring.

GAME 56

H. Humphrey Metrodome, Minneapolis
July 16, 1985
NL, 6–1

NL	011 020 002	6 9 1
AL	100 000 000	1 5 0

MVP: Hoyt-N
Pitchers: HOYT, Ryan (4), Valenzuela (7), Reardon (8), Gossage (9) vs MORRIS, Key (3), Blyleven (4), Stieb (6), Moore (7), Petry (9), W.Hernandez (9)
Attendance: 54,960

The American Leaguers scored first, as Rickey Henderson led off the bottom of the first with a single and circled the bases on a steal, error, and sacrifice fly. But the five National pitchers blanked the Americans the rest of the way on only four more singles.

Meanwhile, the National stars methodically dismantled the Americans for their 36th All-Star victory. In the top of the second, after Darryl Strawberry singled and stole second, Terry Kennedy, whose error had led to the American League run, redeemed himself by singling Strawberry home. An inning later, with two out, Tom Herr doubled and scored the go-ahead (and winning) run on Steve Garvey's single.

In the fifth the Nationals scored two more runs on a hit batsman, Tim Wallach's ground-rule double, and Ozzie Virgil's single, and finished their scoring in the ninth with another pair on three walks and Willie McGee's double—another ground-rule bounce out of play off the lively Metrodome surface. Goose Gossage struck out the final two American batters in the bottom of the ninth, and the Nationals had increased their winning margin in the series to a new high of 17 games.

GAME 57

Astrodome, Houston
July 15, 1986
AL, 3–2

AL	020 000 100	3	5	0
NL	000 000 020	2	5	1

MVP: Clemens-A
Pitchers: CLEMENS, Higuera (4), Hough (7),
Righetti (8), Aase (9) vs GOODEN, Valenzuela (4),
Scott (7), Fernandez (8), Krukow (9)
Home Runs: Whitaker-A, White-A
Attendance: 45,774

National League pitchers struck out 12 Americans, led by Fernando Valenzuela's five in a row, which matched the mark set by Carl Hubbell in 1934. (Two years earlier Valenzuela had helped set a multipitcher All-Star record of six consecutive strikeouts.) In the eighth inning Sid Fernandez, after walking two, struck out the next three.

Though the American Leaguers struck out fewer men, their pitching was more effective on the whole. Starter Roger Clemens hurled three perfect innings (three balls and 21 strikes), and Teddy Higuera one-hit the Nationals over the next three. Charlie Hough struck out three in the eighth after yielding the Nationals' only extra-base hit (a double) to Chris Brown. But catcher Rich Gedman couldn't handle Hough's knuckleball, and Brown advanced to third on the first strikeout (ruled a wild pitch) and scored on the second, a passed ball which also enabled batter Hubie Brooks to reach first safely. Brooks moved up on a balk and scored the Nationals' second run on Steve Sax's single.

But home runs had already undone the Nationals. With two gone in the second, Dave Winfield doubled off starter Dwight Gooden, and Lou Whitaker clubbed an 0–2 pitch over the fence in right. And in the seventh, Frank White (hitting for Whitaker) knocked Mike Scott's 0–2 pitch over the fence in left-center for what proved the margin of American League victory.

GAME 58

Oakland-Alameda County Coliseum, Oakland
July 14, 1987
NL, 2–0

NL	000 000 000 000 2	2	8	2
AL	000 000 000 000 0	0	6	1

MVP: Raines-N
Pitchers: Scott, Sutcliffe (3), Hershiser (5),
R.Reuschel (7), Jo.Franco (8), Bedrosian (9),
L.SMITH (10), S. Fernandez (13) vs Saberhagen,
Morris (4), Langston (6), Plesac (8), Righetti (9),
Henke (9), J.HOWELL (12)
Attendance: 49,671

None of the previous 57 All-Star Games had gone more than eleven innings without at least one run crossing the plate. But this game went more than twice that before National Leaguer Tim Raines tripled in two runs in the top of the 13th for the game's only scoring. It was the National League's eighth win in eight extra-inning All-Star games.

Both teams missed scoring opportunities in the ninth inning. Raines singled for the Nationals with only one out, and became the game's first runner to reach third when a throw from first on his attempted steal went into center field. But a fly to short right and a foul out left him stranded. In the bottom of the ninth, the Americans came close to winning the game as Dave Winfield headed for home from second on a missed 4-6-1 double play. But National pitcher Steve Bedrosian, covering first, snared the off-center throw from short and fired it home to catch Winfield for the third out.

The Americans again reached third in the 11th as Larry Parrish singled and moved around on a sacrifice and ground out. But pitcher Lee Smith (whose three shutout innings earned him the win) struck out Tony Fernandez to end the threat.

GAME 59

Riverfront Stadium, Cincinnati
July 12, 1988
AL, 2–1

AL	001 100 000	2	6	2
NL	000 100 000	1	5	0

MVP: Steinbach-A
Pitchers: VIOLA, Clemens (3), Gubicza (4), Stieb (6),
Russell (7), Jones (8), Plesac (8), Eckersley (9) vs
GOODEN, Knepper (4), Cone (5), Gross (6),
Davis (7), Walk (7), Hershiser (8), Worrell (9)
Home Run: Steinbach-A
Attendance: 55,837

Oakland's Terry Steinbach was not among the 10 top American League catchers in batting; because of time lost to injuries, he was not even his club's leading catcher in games played. But the fans voted him to start in the All-Star Game, and he won it for the American Leaguers with a home run in his first trip to the plate and a sacrifice fly his next time up. Steinbach's homer—a drive off Dwight Gooden that led off the third inning—caromed off the glove of a leaping Darryl Strawberry over the wall in right for the game's first score. His sacrifice fly—high and deep to left in the fourth inning—scored Dave Winfield (aboard with his record seventh All-Star double) to give the American League a 2–0 lead.

Steinbach also contributed to the National League run later in the fourth. His throwing error on Vince Coleman's steal of second enabled Coleman to advance to third, whence he scored on a wild pitch by Mark Gubicza.

American starter Frank Viola, the midseason league leader in wins, was awarded the victory for his two perfect innings pitched. Dennis Eckersley, the majors' top reliever, preserved the win for the Americans with a perfect ninth inning.

GAME 60

Anaheim Stadium, Anaheim
July 11, 1989
AL, 5–3

NL	200 000 010	3	9	1
AL	212 000 00X	5	12	0

MVP: Jackson-A
Pitchers: Reuschel, SMOLTZ (2), Sutcliffe (3),
Burke (4), M. Davis (6), Howell (7), Williams (8) vs
Stewart, RYAN (2), Gubicza (4), Moore (5),
Swindell (6), Russell (7), Plesac (8), Jones (8)
Home Runs: Jackson-A, Boggs-A
Attendance: 64,036

The National stars struck early with a pair of two-out runs in the top of the first inning, and a double steal put two more runners in scoring position. But left fielder Bo Jackson stifled the assault with a fine running catch, then opened the American half of the first with a massive home run to center field off Rick Reuschel. Wade Boggs, the next man up, added insult to the 40-year-old Reuschel's first All-Star start, tying the game with another homer.

In the second inning Jackson drove in the American League's go-ahead run with a slow grounder off young John Smoltz, and an inning later four American singles produced two more runs. A quartet of National League pitchers held the Americans scoreless on just three hits over the final six innings, and their teammates rallied for a third National run in the eighth. But Doug Jones (the majors' top reliever in 1989) came on to get the final out of the eighth, and in the ninth preserved the American lead to give the American Leaguers their first repeat All-Star victory in 31 years.

National League hurler Smoltz, at age 22 the youngest player in the lineup, took the loss. Nolan Ryan, back in the American League after nine National League seasons, earned the win with two shutout innings. Not only was he the oldest player on either side, he was the oldest All-Star winning pitcher ever at age 42.

GAME 61

Wrigley Field, Chicago
July 10, 1990
AL, 2–0

AL	000 000 200	2	7	0
NL	000 000 000	0	2	1

MVP: Ju. Franco-A
Pitchers: Welch, Stieb (3), SABERHAGEN (5),
Thigpen (7), Finley (8), Eckersley (9) vs Armstrong,
R. Martinez (3), D. Martinez (4), Viola (5),
D. Smith (6), BRANTLEY (6), Dibble (7), Myers (8),
Jo. Franco (9)
Attendance: 39,071

Back-to-back American League singles off Jeff Brantley had put men on third and first and brought Julio Franco to the plate in the seventh inning, when heavy rain halted the game for more than an hour. During the delay Brantley's side stiffened, so when Franco finally got his turn at bat he faced a new National pitcher, Rob Dibble. Franco lined Dibble's third pitch into the gap in right center for a double—the only extra-base hit of the game—driving in what proved to be the game's only runs.

Damp air and a stiff breeze in from left field helped tame the offense. American League batters managed to accumulate seven hits, but the Nationals were held to two—an All-Star all-time low. No runner advanced as far as third base until the sixth inning, when American stars Kelly Gruber and Jose Canseco pulled off a double steal. No National Leaguer reached that far, and if it weren't for Barry Larkin's third-inning steal, no National runner would even have stood on second base.

American League hurler Bret Saberhagen's two perfect middle innings earned him the win, and Dennis Eckersley, after yielding a leadoff hit in the ninth, retired the final three batters to record his second All-Star save in three years. The victory was the third in a row for the American Leaguers, the first time they had put together such a string of triumphs in 41 years.

GAME 62

SkyDome, Toronto
July 9, 1991
AL, 4–2

NL	100 100 000	2	10	1
AL	003 000 10X	4	8	0

MVP: Ripken-A
Pitchers: Glavine, MARTINEZ (3), Viola (5),
Harnisch (6), Smiley (7), Dibble (7), Morgan (8) vs
Morris, KEY (3), Clemens (4), McDowell (5),
Reardon (7), Aguilera (7), Eckersley (9)
Home Runs: Ripken-A, Dawson-N
Attendance: 52,383

The National League took an early 1–0 lead on singles by Tony Gwynn, Will Clark, and Bobby Bonilla in the top of the first, and held it for two innings on Tom Glavine's strong pitching, which included three strikeouts. But Dennis Martinez yielded successive singles to Rickey Henderson and Wade Boggs in the third inning, and the next batter, Cal Ripken Jr., homered to center to give the Americans all the runs they would need for victory.

National Leaguer Andre Dawson led off the fourth inning with a massive home run to center off Roger Clemens. This brought the Nationals to within a run of tying the game, but they scored no more, as a succession of American League pitchers shut them down on a walk and four singles the rest of the way. In the seventh inning the Americans added an insurance run when Joe Carter singled and moved around the bases on a call of catcher interference (the first in All-Star history), a sacrifice bunt, and Harold Baines' sacrifice fly to right.

Jimmy Key, the pitcher of record when Ripken's three-run homer put the American League ahead, was awarded the win. Dennis Eckersley, who pitched a perfect ninth, earned a record third All-Star save.

It was only the second time in All-Star history that the American League had won four games in a row.

GAME 63

Jack Murphy Stadium, San Diego
July 14, 1992
AL, 13–6
AL 411 004 030   13 19 1
NL 000 001 032   6 12 1
MVP: Griffey-A
Pitchers: BROWN, McDowell (2), Guzman (3), Clemens (4), Mussina (5), Langston (6), Nagy (7), Montgomery (8), Aguilera (8), Eckersley (9) vs GLAVINE, Maddux (2), Cone (4), Tewksbury (5), Smoltz (6), Martinez (7), Jones (8), Charlton (9)
Home Runs: Sierra-A, Griffey-A, Clark-N
Attendance: 59,372

By the time the National Leaguers pushed across their first run in the sixth inning, the Americans had already scored 10 times, and although American bats caught fire for five more runs in the eighth and ninth, they were powerless to prevent the American League from stretching its All-Star win streak to five games. National League starting pitcher Tom Glavine could not repeat his strong 1991 start: before his relief after 1-2/3 innings in 1992, he was tagged for nine singles and five runs. In the third inning, Ken Griffey Jr., who had driven in one of the first-inning runs, added the sixth American score with a homer off Greg Maddux. When he came up again to lead off the sixth inning, Griffey doubled to initiate a new American scoring spree, which included two-out doubles by Carlos Baerga and Robin Ventura, capped by Ruben Sierra's home run—all off Bob Tewksbury, who had set down the Americans 1–2–3 an inning earlier. Travis Fryman's RBI single and Roberto Kelly's two-run double in the eighth closed out the American League scoring.

Will Clark's two-out blast off Rick Aguilera in the last of the eighth was the National League's first three-run homer since 1964, but it was too little to make more than a dent in the American lead. With two men out in the ninth, a pair of singles off Dennis Eckersley loaded the bases, and Bip Roberts' single drove in two of the baserunners to bring the NL run total to six (enough to have defeated the AL in the seven previous All-Star Games).

Starter Kevin Brown was awarded the win; Glavine took the loss.

GAME 64

Oriole Park at Camden Yards, Baltimore
July 13, 1993
AL, 9–3
AL 011 033 10X   9 11 0
NL 200 001 000   3   7 2
MVP: Puckett-A
Pitchers: Mulholland, Benes (3), BURKETT (5), Avery (5), Smoltz (6), Beck (7), Harvey (8) vs Langston, Johnson (3), McDOWELL (5), Key (6), Montgomery (7), Aguilera (8), Ward (9)
Home Runs: Sheffield-N, Alomar-A, Puckett-A
Attendance: 48,147

Barry Bonds doubled off Mark Langston with one out in the first inning and Gary Sheffield followed with a home run to left that gave the National League two runs before the American Leaguers came to bat. In the bottom of the second inning, though, Kirby Puckett's solo shot over the center field wall off Terry Mulholland narrowed the gap, and an inning later Roberto Alomar led off with a homer to right off Andy Benes that evened the score.

The Americans pushed ahead in the last of the fifth when, with John Burkett pitching, Ivan Rodriguez lined a ground rule double to left and Albert Belle singled him home. Belle took second on an error, and scored on Ken Griffey Jr.'s single; Griffey scored on Puckett's double into the gap at left center. A half inning later, Barry Larkin drove Bonds home with a sacrifice fly to narrow the score to 5–3, but the Americans blew the game open in the sixth with a trio of unearned runs. After shortstop Jeff Blauser failed to field a grounder by Carlos Baerga—depriving pitcher Steve Avery of a 1–2–3 inning—Avery walked Belle and Devon White doubled, sending Baerga home and Bell to third. John Smoltz, who relieved Avery,

unloaded a pair of wild pitches that enabled Belle and White to score.

In the bottom of the seventh inning, Terry Steinbach tagged Rod Beck for a double high off the wall in right to drive in the ninth—and final—AL run. The Nationals got runners to second and third in the eighth with just one out, but failed to score. Duane Ward retired the National Leaguers in order in the ninth to give the American League its sixth straight All-Star victory.

GAME 65

Three Rivers Stadium, Pittsburgh
July 12, 1994
NL, 8–7
AL 100 003 3000   7 15 0
NL 103 001 0021   8 12 1
MVP: McGriff-N
Pitchers: Key, Cone (3), Mussina (5), Johnson (6) Hentgen (7), Alvarez (8), L.Smith (9), BERE (10) vs Maddux, Hill (4), Drabek (6), Hudek (6), Jackson (7), Beck (7), Myers (8), JONES (10)
Home Runs: Grissom-N, McGriff-N
Attendance: 59,568

A blend of youth and experience enabled the National League to snap the American Leaguers' six-game winning streak with one of the tightest finishes in All-Star history. In the bottom of the 10th inning, with the score tied, 7–7, Tony Gwynn, a veteran of 10 All-Star games, led off by chopping a single to center off novice All-Star Jason Bere. He took off when novice All-Star Moises Alou drove Bere's second pitch to the base of the wall in left center. AL catcher Ivan Rodriguez received the ball—relayed sharply from the outfield—just as Gwynn slipped between the catcher's legs with the winning run.

It was a close game all the way. The teams traded single runs in the first inning. In the third, the National Leaguers grabbed the biggest lead of the evening when they sandwiched a hit batsman and Gwynn's double between a pair of singles to knock David Cone for three runs. In the top of the sixth the Americans evened the score again with a trio of runs off Doug Drabek. Then Marquis Grissom hit a home run off Randy Johnson a half inning later.

Once again the Americans knotted the game when Scott Cooper doubled home Ivan Rodriguez in the seventh and took their first (and, as it turned out, only) lead when Ken Lofton singled to score Chuck Knoblauch and Cooper. A fourth run would have scored in the seventh, however, if shortstop Ozzie Smith—39 years old and playing in his 13th All-Star contest—had not made a spectacular diving stop of Knoblauch's drive and recovered to force Mickey Tettleton at second.

The Americans maintained their 7–5 advantage into the last of the ninth. Pinch hitter Fred McGriff, after fouling off a third strike, brought National League fans to their feet with a game-tying home run. Doug Jones held the Americans scoreless in the top of the 10th, and the stage was set for the Gwynn–Alou finish.

GAME 66

The Ballpark at Arlington
July 11, 1995
NL, 3–2
NL 000 001 110   3   3 0
AL 000 200 000   2   8 0
MVP: Conine-N
Pitchers: Nomo, Smiley (3), Green (5), Neagle (6), Perez (7), SLOCUMB (7), Henke (8), Myers (9) vs Johnson, Appier (3), Martinez (5), Rogers (7), ONTIVEROS (8), Wells (8), Mesa (9)
Home Runs: Thomas-A, Biggio-N, Piazza-N, Conine-N
Attendance: 50,920

On a 96-degree evening at The Ballpark in Arlington, Texas, the National League made the most of just three hits (the lowest for a winning squad since 1952) in defeating the AL, 3-2. The key: all three hits were home runs.

After 5-2/3 innings it certainly didn't appear the NL would triumph. AL pitchers Randy Johnson, Kevin Appier, and Dennis Martinez combined to no-hit

senior circuit batters. Not until Craig Biggio homered off Martinez did the National Leaguers collect their first hit. That cut the AL's margin to 2-1, since Frank Thomas had delivered a monster two-run homer off John Smiley in the fourth. The ball landed in a left field luxury box and was eventually retrieved by Donald Fehr's 9-year-old nephew.

Mike Piazza tied the game an inning later by homering off Kenny Rogers. In the eighth inning Jeff Conine pinch-hit for Ron Gant. Facing Steve Ontiveros, who had also just entered the game, the 29-year-old Conine delivered a 410-foot homer to the lower deck in left. That was all the National League needed to win—and it earned Conine All-Star MVP honors.

Pregame excitement centered about the figure of Dodgers rookie Hideo Nomo. Nomo, the first Japanese national to appear in an All-Star Game, was also the first rookie to start since Fernando Valenzuela in 1981. Much of his native land stopped work (it was 9 a.m. in Japan) to watch—and cheer—Nomo's performance as he allowed just one hit in two innings and struck out Kenny Lofton, Edgar Martinez, and Albert Belle.

GAME 67

Veterans Stadium, Philadelphia
July 9, 1996
NL, 6–0
AL 000 000 000   0   7 0
NL 121 002 00X   6 12 1
MVP: Piazza-N
Pitchers: NAGY, Finley (3), Pavlik (5), Percival (7), Hernandez (8) vs SMOLTZ, Brown (3), Glavine (4), Bottalico (5), Martinez (6), Trachsel (7), Worrell (8), Wohlers (9), Leiter (9)
Home Runs: Piazza-N, Caminiti-N
Attendance: 62,670

Mike Piazza, a native of nearby Norristown, Pa., homered his first time up, doubled in his next at bat, and called the signals behind the plate as nine pitchers combined to shut down the potent AL lineup. Indians manager Mike Hargrove's powerpacked AL lineup, which had Baltimore's Brady Anderson (who finished the year with 50 homers) batting eighth, managed only seven singles against the NL's parade of pitchers.

John Smoltz, like his counterpart Charles Nagy, was making his first All-Star start. Smoltz allowed only two hits and a walk in two innings to get the win. Nagy, on the other hand, was touched for four hits and three runs, including a 445-foot home run by Piazza leading off the second.

Center fielder Lance Johnson, who started and played the entire game in place of injured Tony Gwynn, had three hits and a stolen base. He set the tone for the game by legging out a double on the first pitch from Nagy, taking third on a groundout by Barry Larkin and scoring on a groundout by Barry Bonds. Following Piazza's homer, Chipper Jones singled and went to second on a groundout by Craig Biggio. Jones scored on a single by Henry Rodriguez. Piazza brought home the NL's fourth run with a double off Chuck Finley to score Larkin. Ken Caminiti homered to right off Roger Pavlik in the sixth and Craig Biggio delivered the final run later in the inning.

Ozzie Smith, playing his 15th and final All-Star Game, stole the show in the latter innings. Smith, who earlier announced that 1996 was his final season, received a long standing ovation when he came to bat in the seventh. He also started a double play at shortstop in the ninth.

GAME 68

Jacobs Field, Cleveland
July 8, 1997
AL, 3-1

```
NL 000 000 100    1  3  0
AL 010 000 20X    3  7  0
```

MVP: S. Alomar-A
Pitchers: Maddux, Schilling (3), Brown (5), Martinez (6), ESTES (7), B.Jones (8) vs Johnson, Clemens (3), Cone (4), Thompson (5), Hentgen (6), ROSADO (7), Myers (8), Rivera (9)
Home Runs: E. Martinez-A, Lopez-N, S. Alomar-A
Attendance: 44,945

Sandy Alomar Jr. broke a seventh-inning tie and sent the Cleveland crowd into a frenzy with a two-out, two-run home run off Shawn Estes. Although there were three home runs hit at Jacobs Field, pitching was the name of the game. Eight American League pitchers limited the National League to just three hits to halt a three-year losing streak.

The most lasting image of game occurred in the top of the second inning with the long-awaited showdown between Randy Johnson and Larry Walker. The lefty-lefty matchup began with Johnson's first pitch sailing over the head of Walker—reminiscent of Johnson's memorable meeting with John Kruk in the 1993 All-Star Game—but Walker surprised everyone, by turning his helmet around and then stepping across the plate to bat right-handed. He took a pitch (another ball) before returning to bat from the left side and drawing a walk without taking the bat off his shoulder.

Edgar Martinez, the first designated hitter ever voted by the fans to start at the position in the All-Star Game, drilled a line drive over the fence in left field for a 1-0 American League lead in the second inning off Greg Maddux. Outstanding defensive plays by Roberto Alomar, Joey Cora, and Cal Ripken, who made his 14th consecutive All-Star start, but his first at third base, helped four American League pitchers nurse the 1-0 lead until the seventh inning. Javier Lopez, in his first All-Star at bat, pulled a pitch from Luis Rosado off the foul pole in left field to tie the game at 1-1. In the bottom of the seventh inning, Shawn Estes issued the only NL walk of the evening to Bernie Williams and Sandy Alomar, who entered the game having hit in his last 30 games of the first half of the season, homered to make it a 3-1 game. Randy Myers and Mariano Rivera each pitched perfect innings to give the AL its first win since 1993.

GAME 69

Coors Field, Denver
July 7, 1998
AL, 13-8

```
AL 000 413 113   13  19  2
NL 002 130 020    8  12  1
```

MVP: R. Alomar-A
Pitchers: Wells, Clemens (3), Radke (4), COLON (5), Arrojo (6), Wetteland (7), Gordon (8), Percival (9) vs Maddux, Glavine, Brown (4), Ashby (5), URBINA (6), Hoffman (7), Shaw (8), Nen (9)
Home Runs: A. Rodriguez-A, Bonds-N, R. Alomar-A
Attendance: 51,267

This Rocky Mountain version of the All-Star Game featured the most runs (21), but it was a defensive play that was the pivotal play of the game. With the National League having closed the gap to 10-8 with runners on first and second and none out in the eighth, Devon White singled to left and Fernando Vina was thrown out at the plate by Paul O'Neill. Had Vina held up, the bases would have been loaded with nobody out for Andres Galarraga, the NL RBI leader the past two years who had 72 RBI at the All-Star break, but his smash up the middle was turned into an inning-ending double play by Omar Vizquel.

Roberto Alomar was one of seven All-Stars to have a multiple-hit game, but the second baseman, who also had a walk, a stolen base, and a home run, was chosen as the game's Most Valuable Player a year after his brother, Sandy, was named MVP in the 1997 game. Roberto Alomar was one of just three players to homer in a game where longballs were

expected to be plentiful in the thin air of Denver's high elevation. (The expectations were further heightened when 83 home runs were hit in the previous day's annual Home Run Derby, which was won by reluctant participant Ken Griffey, Jr.) The furthest ball hit in the All-Star Game came off the bat of Barry Bonds, a three-run shot that gave the NL a short-lived 6-5 lead after five innings.

A rocky sixth inning by both pitcher Ugueth Urbina and catcher Javier Lopez included three stolen bases, a wild pitch, a passed ball, and a run-scoring single by Ivan Rodriguez that gave the AL a lead it did not relinquish. The AL scored at least one run in every inning after the fourth. One of those runs came off Jeff Shaw, who spent the first half of the season pitching for the Reds, but he was traded to the Dodgers shortly before the All-Star break and became the first player to debut in a new uniform in the All-Star Game.

GAME 70

Fenway Park, Boston
July 13, 1999
AL, 4-1

```
NL 001 000 000    1  7  1
AL 200 200 00X    4  6  2
```

MVP: Martinez-A
Pitchers: SCHILLING, Johnson (3), Bottenfield (4), Lima (5), Millwood (6), Ashby (7), Hampton (7), Hoffman (8), Wagner (8) vs MARTINEZ, Cone (3), Mussina (5), Rosado (6), Zimmerman (7), Hernandez (8), Wetteland (9)
Attendance: 34,187

The 70th All-Star Game was a thoroughly Boston affair. The 20th century's greatest players were honored prior to the game at Fenway Park, but Ted Williams, who threw out the first pitch, stole the show. The Red Sox Hall of Famer found himself surrounded by admiring All-Stars of both past and present. When Williams left the field, Pedro Martinez took over the show at his home ballpark.

Martinez struck out the first four batters he faced, the first time that had happened in All-Star competition; his feat called to mind Carl Hubbell's five straight strikeouts of American League sluggers in the 1934 game. Martinez retired all six batters he faced, striking out five of them. He set the tone for the American League's 4-1 win and walked away with Most Valuable Player honors. (The extra effort that night, however, briefly landed the Red Sox star on the disabled list.)

In all, the National League struck out 12 times and managed just seven hits and one run. The American League, on the other hand, scored twice in the first inning against Curt Schilling on two-out hits by Jim Thome and Cal Ripken. The National League scored its run in the third inning off David Cone as Barry Larkin singled home Jeromy Burnitz. The American League added two runs the following inning against Kent Bottenfield. Nine National League pitchers fanned 10 batters, setting an All-Star record with 22 strikeouts between the two squads.

GAME 71

Turner Field, Atlanta
July 11, 2000
AL, 6-3

```
AL 001 200 003    6  10  2
NL 001 010 001    3   9  2
```

MVP: Jeter-A
Pitchers: Wells, BALDWIN (3), Sele (4), Isringhausen (5), Lowe (6), T. Jones (7), Hudson (8), Rivera (9) vs Johnson, Graves (2), Brown (3), LEITER (4), Glavine (5), Kile (6), Wickman (8), Hoffman (9)
Home Runs: C. Jones-N
Attendance: 51,323

The list of players who weren't at the 71st All-Star Game was practically a lineup of its own. Mark McGwire, Alex Rodriguez, Cal Ripken, Barry Bonds, Ken Griffey, Manny Ramirez, Mike Piazza, Pedro Martinez, and Greg Maddux were unavailable because of injuries, although Griffey did participate in the previous night's Home Run Derby. The game

itself, however, was a tight, well-pitched 6-3 victory for the American League, with almost half the game's runs scored in the ninth inning.

Starters Randy Johnson and David Wells led a procession of eight pitchers for each All-Star squad. Kevin Brown surrendered the game's first run when he walked Carl Everett with the bases loaded in the third inning. Chipper Jones, who had three hits on the night, tied the game in the bottom of the inning with a home run off winning pitcher James Baldwin. Jones was heartily embraced by the hometown crowd at Turner Field, but the loudest ovation of the night was reserved for Andres Galarraga, who earned a trip to the All-Star Game after sitting out a season because of cancer.

Derek Jeter, the American League's starting shortstop in place of Alex Rodriguez, singled in the go-ahead runs in the fourth inning to earn Most Valuable Player honors. The American League put the game away with three runs in the ninth on RBIs by Matt Lawton and Magglio Ordonez, aided by an infield error. Manager Joe Torre, whose Yankees had beaten Bobby Cox's Braves in eight consecutive World Series games, won his second All-Star Game while paired against the Atlanta skipper. Of the American League's four straight All-Star wins, Torre was manager in three of the games.

GAME 72

Safeco Field, Seattle
July 10, 2001
AL, 4-1

```
NL 000 001 000    1  3  1
AL 001 012 00X    4  8  0
```

MVP: Ripken-A
Pitchers: R. Johnson, PARK (3), Burkett (4), Hampton (5), Lieber (6), Morris (7), Shaw (8), Wagner (8), Sheets (8) vs Clemens, GARCIA (3), Pettitte (4), Mays (5), Quantrill (6), Stanton (6), Nelson (7), Percival (8), Sasaki (9)
Home Runs: Ripken-A, Jeter-A, Ordonez-A
Attendance: 47,364

The 72nd All-Star Game turned into the Cal Ripken show. The Orioles' future Hall of Famer, who had announced his retirement effective at the end of the season, was chosen as the AL's starting third baseman. As the game was about to start, shortstop Alex Rodriguez—as a gesture of respect—switched positions with Ripken for an inning, putting Cal at the position at which he had starred for most of his 21-year career. Then, in his first at bat of the game, Ripken homered to start the AL to a 4-1 victory. In the sixth inning, the game was delayed so that Ripken and Tony Gwynn, also retiring at the end of the season, could receive the Commissioner's Historic Achievement Award. To cap off the night, Ripken was named the game's MVP.

In winning their fifth straight game, American League pitchers held the NL to just three hits. The senior circuit's only run scored on a sixth-inning double by Jeff Kent, a single by Lance Berkman and a sacrifice fly by Ryan Klesko. The AL tallied on solo homers by Ripken in the third, and Derek Jeter and Magglio Ordonez in the sixth, sandwiched around an unearned run in the fifth. "I've been able to go to a whole lot of them," said Ripken about his 18th and final All-Star Game, "but this is by far the most special."

GAME 73

Miller Park, Milwaukee
July 9, 2002
Tie, 7-7

```
AL 000 110 410 00    7  12  0
NL 013 010 200 00    7  13  0
```

Pitchers: Lowe, Halladay (3), Buehrle (4), Zito (6), Guardado (8), Sasaki (8), Urbina (8), Rivera (9), Garcia (10) vs Schilling, Williams (3), Perez (4), Gagne (5), Hoffman (6), Remlinger (7), Kim (7), Nen (8), Smoltz (9), Padilla (10)
Home Runs: Bonds-N, Soriano-A
Attendance: 41,871

It was supposed to be a glorious day in Milwaukee, as new Miller Park hosted the midsummer classic in Commissioner Bud Selig's home-

town. Instead, it became a fiasco, with Selig jeered by a disgusted crowd.

The National League came out swinging. Barry Bonds, who had earlier been robbed of a homer by Torii Hunter, launched a three-run blast off the second deck of the right-field stands, giving the NL a 4-0 lead. But the junior circuit scored runs in the fourth and fifth, and then exploded for four in the seventh to take a 6-5 lead. The Nationals regained the advantage with two in the bottom of the frame, but the AL tied the score in the top of the eighth.

And there things stood for the next three innings. By the 11th frame, both teams were using their final pitchers, and both hurlers—Freddy Garcia (AL) and Vicente Padilla (NL)—were in their second inning of work. Managers Joe Torre and Bob Brenly conferred with Selig, saying they were uncomfortable with using their pitchers any longer. Selig was left with little option but to announce that the game would end after the 11th inning—win, lose or draw. Amid ruthless booing from the sellout crowd, the game ended in a 7-7 tie. To add insult to injury, the writers—having announced that the All-Star MVP Award would hereafter be named after Ted Williams, who had died four days earlier—chose not to select an honoree for this game.

GAME 74

U.S. Cellular Field, Chicago
July 15, 2003
AL, 7-6

NL	000 050 100	6	11	1
AL	001 002 13X	7	9	0

MVP: Anderson-A
Pitchers: Schmidt, Wolf (3), Wood (4), Ortiz (5), W. Williams (6), Wagner (7), GAGNE (8) vs Loaiza, Clemens (3), Moyer (4), Hasegawa (5), Guardado (5), Mulder (6), DONNELLY (8), Foulke (9)
Home Runs: Helton-N, Anderson-A, A. Jones-N, Giambi-A, Blalock-A
Attendance: 47,609

The theme for the 74th All-Star Game was "This Time It Counts." Responding to criticism about the 2002 result, and the evidence that the players and managers didn't really care who won, Commissioner Bud Selig announced that, in a two-year experiment starting in 2003, the winning league would gain home-field advantage in the following World Series—a significant edge, since 15 of the last 17 teams with home-field advantage had won it all. The AL cashed in, coming from behind to win this game on a

dramatic home run.

The NL seemingly had things in hand after a five-run fifth. A two-run homer by Todd Helton, a two-run double by Andruw Jones and an RBI-single by Albert Pujols gave the senior circuit a 5-1 lead. They still led, 6-4, going into the bottom of the eighth, with relief aces Eric Gagne and John Smoltz poised to close the door. Gagne was on his way to the NL Cy Young Award, for a regular-season performance in which he would convert all 55 save opportunities presented to him.

But not this one. With one out, Garret Anderson—who had homered earlier—lashed a double. Gagne got the second out, but Vernon Wells followed with another double, cutting the lead in half. Then, Hank Blalock, making his All-Star debut as a pinch-hitter, unloaded a two-run homer to give the AL their margin of victory. And this time it counted.

The International Game

Doug Mientkiewicz
A dramatic home run by Mientkiewicz in the ninth inning propelled the United States over Korea in the semi-finals of the Olympic baseball competition in Sydney in 2000. The U.S. then beat Cuba for the gold medal.

Section **10**

FAMOUS FIRSTS

1888: The Chicago White Stockings and all-star squad embark on baseball's first "around the world" tour.

1920: The first Japanese pro team, the Nihon Undo Kyokai, is formed.

1936: A professional baseball league is launched in Japan for the first time.

1953: Phil Paine becomes the first ex-major leaguer to play in Japan.

1963: An All-Hispanic All Star game is held for the first (and last) time.

1964: Masanori Murakami becomes the first major league player from Japan.

1984: Baseball was added for the first time as a "demonstration" sport at the Olympics.

1992: Baseball becomes an Olympic medal sport for the first time and Cuba wins the first gold medal.

1994: Chan Ho Park of the Dodgers becomes the major league's first Korean born player.

Chapter 44

Baseball in Japan

By Yoichi Nagata and John B. Holway

This may be the golden age of Japanese baseball. An explosion of great young players is filling the rosters of the 12 professional teams. Japanese feel a new pride in the exploits of Hideki Matsui, Ichiro Suzuki, Hideo Nomo, and others in America. And yet the future has never looked so problematic.

The Major League Invasion

After Nomo opened America for Japanese players in 1995, 15 players—mostly pitchers—had arrived there through 2003. In the winter of 2003, Japan shipped another quality player, Kazuo "Little" Matsui, to the Mets. He is athletically superior to Ichiro, and hits from both sides with power. Like Hideki "Big" Matsui (no relation), Kaz never missed a game in eight seasons. Born in 1975, he had 33 homers with a .305 average but a career-high 124 strikeouts in 2003. He signed with the Mets for $23 million for three years, about twice as much as Ichiro's original $13-million, three-year contract with the Mariners (Ichiro has since signed a contract with Seattle for $44 million for four years). Another export, closer Akinori Otsuka (pronounced Oats-ka), who amassed 137 saves in seven years, joined the Padres.

Nomo not only opened America to Japanese players, he opened Japan to American teams. In 2000 two season-opening games were played at the Tokyo Dome between the Chicago Cubs and the New York Mets. Scheduled Seattle-Oakland season-opening games in 2003 were canceled due to the war in Iraq, disappointing many Japanese.

In 2004 the major leagues scheduled another season-opening series, between the Yankees and Devil Rays. The Yankees are almost "Japan's team," because Hideki Matsui plays for them. The series will also be Matsui's homecoming celebration.

U.S.-Japan Series

Japanese baseball was born in the 1870s. Professor Horace Wilson is among those credited with being Nippon's Abner Doubleday. By 1908 Japanese teams beat the visiting University of Washington four games out of ten. The Chicago White Sox and New York Giants visited in 1913. The nation's first pro team formed in 1920. Casey Stengel's All-Stars arrived in 1922, and Ty Cobb followed in 1928 to teach his batting secrets. Three years later a team featuring Lou Gehrig, Lefty Grove, Al Simmons, Frankie Frisch, and Lefty O'Doul toured Japan.

In 1934 Babe Ruth, Gehrig, Simmons, O'Doul, Jimmie Foxx, Charlie Gehringer, Earl Averill, and Lefty Gomez arrived. They won all their games handily—except one. Eighteen-year-old high schooler Eiji Sawamura whiffed Gehringer, Ruth, Gehrig, and Foxx in succession but lost, 1-0.

Sawamura starred on the Tokyo Giants when Japan's first professional league formed in 1936. Killed in World War II, he was later honored when Japan's equivalent of the Cy Young Award was

Sadaharu Oh
Oh became a national hero in Japan by smashing 868 home runs for the Yomiuri Giants to become professional baseball's all-time leader.

named after him. The league lasted until the bombing of 1945. After World War II, General Douglas MacArthur encouraged Japan's major leagues to resume.

Lefty O'Doul brought his Pacific Coast League San Francisco Seals to Japan in 1949. The legendary Russian emigre, Vic Starffin, held them to one hit in eight innings before losing, 1-0. In 1951 O'Doul and Joe DiMaggio led a U.S. squad to Tokyo. The Japanese captured their first victory over the Americans, beating Bobby Shantz, 3-1. DiMaggio hit his last homer during the tour.

American teams continued the tradition every other year. In the spring of 1953 the Tokyo Giants visited Florida, winning just one of five against big league clubs, beating the New York Giants, 9-7. That fall an All-Star team including Bob Lemon, Robin Roberts, Yogi Berra, Enos Slaughter, Eddie Mathews, Hank Sauer, and Harvey Kuenn lost their first game, 5-4, to the fifth-place Japanese Orions but won their next 11.

That same year the New York Giants also visited Japan, winning twelve and losing one, with one tie. They came from behind to beat Masaichi Kaneda, 5-3. Then a little submarine-baller, Takumi Otomo, defeated knuckleballer Hoyt Wilhelm, 1-0, on an eighth-inning home run.

By 1956 the champion Dodgers dropped four games in Japan. It was not until 1989 that Japan, for the first time, came out ahead of the Americans, beating the Dodgers, nine games to eight. The following year they did it again, whipping an All-Star team including Roger Clemens, Barry Bonds, Cecil Fielder, Roberto Alomar, and Dave Stewart, four games to three. The games built much goodwill, and without them Japanese baseball would not have reached its present stage. After many one-sided victories in the first half of the century, the Americans discovered they had to work harder to beat the bigger and improved Japanese. They still usually win but now have to send their best talent and play seriously. Over the last 18 years, this is how the series has gone:

Year	USA	Japan	Notable Players
1986	6	1	Ripken, Canseco, Sandberg, Murphy
1988	3	2	Hershiser, Puckett, Larkin, Molitor
1990	3	4	Bonds, Fielder, R. Johnson, Alomar, Dibble, Thigpen
1992	7	3	Clemens, R.Johnson, Griffey Jr., Franco, Dykstra, O. Smith, Hershiser, Butler, Piazza, Offerman
1996	4	2	Nomo, Gonzalez, Galarraga, Piazza, Bonds, Sheffield, Franco, Percival
1998	6	2	Sosa, Garciaparra, Ramirez, Delgado, Hoffman
2000	5	2	Bonds, Sasaki, R. Johnson, Delgado, Sheffield
2002	4	3	Giambi, Bonds, T. Hunter, Suzuki, Ohka, Colon
Total	**38**	**19 (6 ties)**	

In 1990 Japan's Hideo Nomo defeated Rob Dibble, 2-1, then lost 5-0 on a combined no-hitter by Randy Johnson and Chuck Finley. The 1996 series was another exciting one, played before crowds of 45,000. Japanese fans, who could see all Nomo's games with the Dodgers on post-midnight TV, knew all the U.S. stars intimately.

The 1998 series was televised to the States. Sosa batted .500 with two home runs; Japan's Ichiro Suzuki hit .364 with six steals in seven attempts. The teams used the American Rawlings ball, which is slightly larger and heavier than the Japanese version. Sosa, acclaimed MVP both on and off the field, exchanged bats with Ichiro before the first game.

In 2002 the hottest player was Kazuo Matsui, now with the New York Mets. He hit two home runs, one from each side of the plate, in the same game. Norihiro Nakamura also hit two home runs, and it almost led to his joining the Mets.

The Olympics

Ever since baseball became an Olympic sport, Japan has been tough on the Americans, often beating some of its top future stars out of gold and silver medals. The record:

Year	Gold	Silver	Notable U.S. players
1984	Japan	USA	W. Clark, McGwire, Mack, B. Larkin, Swift, B. Witt
1988	USA	Japan	J. Abbott, An. Benes, T. Martinez, Nagy, Ventura
1992	Cuba	Taiwan	Ja. Giambi, Tucker
1996	Cuba	Japan	T. Lee, Kotsay
2000	USA	Cuba	Franklin, Oswalt, Sheets, Mientkiewicz

In 1996 the United States thrashed Japan in their first meeting, 15-5, in a game called under the "mercy" rule. The semi-final rematch figured to be another easy triumph as the Americans eyed the final round against Cuba for the gold. Instead, Japan shocked America, 11-2. Japan smashed five homers and knocked out Kris Benson, top pick in the major league draft. The loss forced America to settle for bronze.

For the 2000 Games, Japan's combined team of Pacific League and amateur players came home empty, the first time Japan had struck out in the baseball medals. The Central League wouldn't let its players participate in the middle of the pennant season, but these results made it reconsider. For the 2003 qualifying round Japan sent an all-professional team managed by legendary hero Shigeo Nagashima, home-run king Sadaharu Oh's old teammate. They thoroughly beat China, 13-1, Taiwan, 9-0, and Korea, 2-0. The United States did not qualify in its division.

The 2003 Season

In the Pacific League, Oh managed the Daiei Hawks to the Japan championship. This was the first time a PL team had won since Oh's 1999 Hawks. Daiei used to boast power hitters but had weak pitching. In 2003 it lost cleanup hitter Hiroki Kokubo due to injuries. But it still had four men who batted in over 100 runs each, and the Hawks posted the highest single-season team batting average in Japanese history, .296. Oh's long-time headache was cured by new pitching arms: left-handed Rookie of the Year Tsuyoshi Wada and Kazumi Saito, who shared the PL's Sawamura Award.

In the Central League, the darlings of the Osaka fans, the Hanshin Tigers, won the pennant for the first time in 18 years. During that span they were in the cellar 10 times. The night they clinched the pennant, 5,000 fans jumped with joy into the polluted Dotonbori River. The nearby Kentucky Fried Chicken restaurant locked its Colonel Sanders statue in the store. On Hanshin's previous victory night in 1985, a similar statue had been dumped into the river and never found (like Babe Ruth's piano). The ensuing 18-year pennant drought was blamed on the Curse of Colonel Sanders.

With fiery Senichi Hoshino in the manager's seat, the Tigers acquired Tomoaki Kanemoto, who changed his style from one-dimensional slugger to a hitter with flexibility, depending on the situation. The Tigers' closer, Australian Jeff Williams, a former Atlanta Brave, was another newcomer. He changed from overhand to sidearm, and it made his slider more effective. His ERA was 1.54. Former major leaguer Hideki Irabu also joined the Tigers and recovered most of his old fastball, overcoming two injury-plagued seasons in America. Kei Igawa won 20 games for the CL's Sawamura Award and MVP.

Just as the 2003 U.S. postseason generated incredible excitement, so did the Japan Series. It went to the seventh game, with three walk-off (sayonara) games and two extra-inning contests. The home team won every game.

Game 1: *Hawks 5, Tigers 4.* Sayonara in the ninth inning. Both teams started their 20-game winners: Kazumi Saito for the Hawks and Kei Igawa for the Tigers. The seesaw game went into the bottom of the ninth with the score tied. The Hawks had men on first and second with two outs. DH Julio Zuleta, a former Boston Red Sox player, hit a long fly to center, where the 5-foot-7 Norihiro Akaboshi jumped but couldn't reach it. Akaboshi injured his hand when he landed on the artificial turf. A .312-batter with 61 steals,

he was sub-par the rest of the series.

Game 2: *Hawks 13, Tigers 0.* Irabu was knocked out in the second. Young Munenori Kawasaki hit two triples, a Japan Series record.

Game 3: *Tigers 2, Hawks 1 (10 innings).* The Tigers' Tomoaki Kanemoto hit a game-tying homer off Tsuyoshi Wada. In the bottom of the 10th, with the bases loaded, the Tigers' Atsushi Fujimoto hit a sacrifice fly to win.

Game 4: *Tigers 6, Hawks 5 (10 innings).* Kanemoto hit a sayonara home run.

Game 5: *Tigers 3, Hawks 2.* Kanemoto hit a solo shot in the first. The Hawks came back with a two-run homer by former Texas Ranger Pedro Valdes. The Tigers' cleanup hitter, Shinjiro Hiyama, hit a bases-loaded single to win it.

Game 6: *Hawks 5, Tigers 1.* The Hawks knocked Irabu out again, this time in the third. Lefty Toshiya Sugiuchi won his second game en route to being named Series MVP.

Game 7: *Hawks 6, Tigers 2.* Wada started for the Hawks. Wada has a 90-mph fastball, but his strong point is a delivery that hides the ball until the last instant, plus a mental toughness that's rare for a rookie. Catcher Kenji Jojima hit two home runs, and Oh got his second Japan Series ring, joining the list of "*maestro* managers."

The Baseball Landscape

In a Japanese newspaper poll in early 2003, 59 percent of respondents named baseball their favorite spectator sport. Japan's pro soccer league, the J League, received 28 percent, but it is steadily growing, especially after the fever of the 2002 World Cup in Japan and Korea. Fans under 30 like soccer almost as much as baseball. Young people, especially women, say J League players dress better off the field or on TV than baseball players. At the annual awards ceremony all the recipients wear black ties. Unlike European soccer, the J League plays in the summer, in direct competition with baseball. The 28 professional soccer teams are scattered all over Japan, while the 12 pro baseball teams are concentrated in the big cities. Major league baseball in the U.S. received 17 percent in the poll, but this was before Godzilla Matsui's debut with the Yankees.

In 2003, three factors supported enthusiasm for baseball. First, the long-time pennant-starved Hanshin Tigers of Osaka, a favorite of the fans, won the CL championship. It caused fever not only in the Osaka area, but also all over Japan. Second, Ichiro's and Matsui's superb performances in the States gave a boost to baseball in Japan. Third, an influx of young quality players stepped onto the main stage. They are called "The Matsuzaka Generation" after Daisuke Matsuzaka of the Seibu Lions. Now players from his generation, who went to college, are joining the pro leagues. The top of the list is the Daiei Hawks' southpaw, Tsuyoshi Wada, the 2003 PL Rookie of the Year with a 14-5 record. Two others are young Hawk rookie Nagisa Arakaki and sophomore Toshiya Sugiuchi, the 2003 Japan Series MVP. Another pitcher in The Matsuzaka Generation: the Yomiuri Giants' Hiroshi Kisanuki, a hard thrower with a good forkball, who was the CL Rookie of the Year in 2003.

The Tokyo Giants

The Tokyo Giants, who play in the Tokyo Dome, are the Yankees of Japan. Led by Sadaharu Oh and "Golden Boy" Shigeo Nagashima, they won 30 pennants in 54 years. From 1965 through 1973, the heyday of Oh and Nagashima, they won nine straight Japan Series. Only one pro team in any country in any sport, Josh

Gibson's 1937-1945 Negro League Homestead Grays, has equaled that mark. Thanks to immense publicity from their parent company, the Yomiuri newspaper and TV empire, the Giants are by far the nation's favorite team. In a newspaper poll, 38 percent chose the Giants first. Next were the Hanshin Tigers (11 percent); last were the Nippon Ham Fighters (0.1 percent.).

Naturally, the Giants have a special working agreement with the Yankees. Like the Yanks, the Giants found that money can't always win the World Series ring, but they try nonetheless. Yomiuri got two-time home-run champ Roberto Petagine of Venezuela to fill the spot Hideki Matsui vacated, and they topped both leagues in homers with 204 in 2003. After the season, they acquired former home-run leader Hiroki Kokubo from the Daiei Hawks in a mysterious fashion (the Hawks traded Kokubo to the Giants for nothing). The Giants also added outfielder Tuffy Rhodes, a two-time home run king, to their 2004 lineup. Giants' ace pitcher Koji Uehara wondered, "Why are they collecting clean-up hitters?" The Giants payroll increased to $50 million in 2004.

Thanks to the Giants, their league, the Central, attracted 32,100 fans per game in 2003, far above the rival Pacific League's 24,200 (the U.S. major leagues averaged about 26,000). In the southern city of Fukuoka, the Hawks, managed by the immortal Oh, drew 46,100 a game in their retractable Fukuoka Dome.

The PL has long proposed interleague play, to cash in on the drawing power of the Giants, but the CL teams refuse; they don't want to share their lucrative games against Tokyo. Each league now plays a 140-game schedule (up from 130), a move demanded by the Giants to increase profits.

Gaijin (Foreigners)

Foreign players have starred in Japan for many years. The most successful in recent years is outfielder Tuffy Rhodes, a former Chicago Cub now with the Yomiuri Giants. With Kintetsu, he led the PL three times in home runs (1999, 2001 and 2003). He loves Osaka and speaks the dialect fluently. But he will play his ninth year in Japan for the Yomiuri Giants. He wanted a multi-year contract, but money-short Kintetsu offered only a one-year pact.

Alex Ramirez of the Yakult Swallows learned to hit breaking balls and won the CL home run and RBI titles in 2003, and was second in batting average with .333. In five years, 1999-2003, *gaijin* won 12 of 20 homer and RBI titles, while Japanese won 9 of 10 batting titles.

In 1990 the Hiroshima Carp opened a baseball academy in the Dominican Republic, scouting low-priced teenage talent to replace often over-priced former big leaguers. Unfortunately, their biggest catch, Alfonso Soriano, wound up playing for the Yankees.

In 2003, 62 *gaijin* played in Japan, including 44 from the U.S. and 13 from Latin America. Among these, 51 were former big leaguers, including some cup-of-coffee guys, but no big shots.

The Japanese leagues are turning their eyes to neighboring Asian countries. Sadaharu Oh, whose father is Chinese, brought the Fukuoka Daiei Hawks to Taiwan for regular-season games in 2002. Korean and Japanese All-Star series were held in 1991, 1995 and 1999, when no major leaguers visited Japan. Japan won eight games and lost three. In the past ten years Japanese teams brought in players who had made good in the Taiwan and Korean leagues. They enjoy much higher salaries in Japan than at home.

For 2004, Asia's home run king, Seung-yeop Lee—who broke Oh's single-season Asian record of 55 in the final game of 2003— has signed with Bobby Valentine's Lotte Marines for $4.6 million

for two years. Lee wants to play in the U.S. majors, and tried the American market, but he didn't receive a satisfactory offer.

Six non-Asians joined Japanese teams through Taiwan and Korea. Former Diamondbacks' player Alex Cabrera, from Venezuela but an import from Taiwan, continued his power-hitting. The right-handed slugger's three-year home run production is 49, 55 and 50. His 55 in 2002 tied Japan's record, held by Oh and Rhodes. In 2003 Cabrera was walked so many times, he once stepped up to the plate left-handed.

The 2003 CL home run co-champ with 40, Tyrone Woods, joined the Yokohama Bay Stars after slugging 174 in five seasons in Korea. Woods (.273) also led the CL in strikeouts.

New Land for Pro Baseball

For the first time the northern island of Hokkaido will have a franchise in Sapporo, host to the 1972 Winter Olympic Games and the largest city (1.8 million) north of Tokyo. It will be the transplanted Nippon Ham Fighters of the Pacific League, who shared the Tokyo Dome with the Yomiuri Giants. But while the Giants drew 53,757 fans per game in 2003, the Fighters drew a mere 18,800. The shift of the long-suffering team is expected to cultivate new baseball fans in the north of Japan. Sapporo hosted several regular-season games every year, but this is the first time that a pro team will call it home. Nippon Ham wants to follow the example of the Fukuoka Daiei Hawks, who fill their domed stadium almost every game on the southern island Kyushu, after huge efforts to woo the fans.

Unfortunately Fighters' manager Trey Hillman, a former Texas Rangers Triple A skipper, can boast few stars. Third baseman Michihiro Ogasawara is the franchise player. The slugging Samurai look-alike won batting titles in 2002 and '03 (.340 and .360) and led both leagues with a .473 OBP. He also won the equivalent of a Gold Glove at his new position, third base, after converting from first base. To back him up, the Fighters signed former Met outfielder Tsuyoshi Shinjo. A .247-lifetime hitter in Japan, Shinjo batted .245 in the United States. The flashy Shinjo's first press conference in Sapporo drew large media and fan attention. He showed up wearing a white leather jacket, white shirt, and blue jeans, and said he wants to drive all around Hokkaido in his red Ferrari. Nippon Ham definitely sold a "hot dog" at the Sapporo Dome.

Home from America

Of the Japanese who followed Nomo across the Pacific, not all were stars at home. Several, such as Shinjo, were journeyman players, who nevertheless were good enough to win spots on U.S. major league rosters for a short time.

Hideki Irabu returned to the CL Hanshin Tigers and showed solid pitching (13-8, 3.85). He helped lift them from the second division to the CL pennant, their first in 18 years. He regained much of his old form after two injury-plagued seasons in America. After 2003, he tried in vain to go back to the U.S. majors, as his family is still in California.

Masato Yoshii and Mac Suzuki together were expected to propel the Kobe Orix BlueWave in 2003, but both had injuries. Yoshii was 2-7, 6.51, Suzuki, 4-9, 7.06.

Former Met Satoru Komiyama couldn't find a team to play for, so he worked for TV as a commentator, mostly for televised games from the United States. He decided to put on a uniform again for his old manager, Bobby Valentine, and the Chiba Lotte Marines in 2004.

The first Japanese in the U.S. majors, Mashi Murakami, was a hard-throwing reliever for the San Francisco Giants in 1964-1965. He struck out 100 men in 89 innings, won five, lost one, and saved nine. After his parent club, the Nankai Hawks, demanded his return, his stats in Japan for the next 18 years were a disappointing 103-82, 3.64.

Stadiums

At a time when older, smaller parks are being torn down, Japan boasts six domed stadiums. While nostalgic parks boom in the United States, roofs and AstroTurf are Japan's wave of the future. Most domes boast U.S.-sized playing fields, replacing shorter fences in the older parks. Fukuoka Dome in southern Japan, which opened in 1997, has a retractable roof that folds up like a giant fan. The first Japanese dome, Tokyo Dome, nicknamed "The Big Egg," has an inflatable roof similar to Minnesota's Metrodome. All the domes are centerpieces of huge downtown entertainment-shopping complexes, and they host events such as concerts, wrestling matches and auto shows.

Outfielder Arihito Muramatsu left the Hawks for the Orix Blue Wave, choosing grass over money because, he said, concrete is no good for his knees. Blue Wave's home, Yahoo! BB Stadium, is the only one with both infield and outfield grass like an America park.

Central League

Team	Stadium	Seats	LF/RF	CF
Tigers	Koshien	53,000	315	394
Swallows	Meiji	49,000	300	396
Giants	Tokyo Dome	55,000	328	400
Dragons	Nagoya Dome	40,500	328	400
Carp	Hiroshima	32,000	302	381
Bay Stars	Yokohama	29,000	310	389

Pacific League

Team	Stadium	Seats	LF/RF	CF
Hawks	Fukuoka Dome	48,000	328	400
Buffalo	Osaka Dome	48,000	328	400
Fighters	Sapporo Dome	42,000	328	400
Blue Wave	Yahoo! BB	35,000	325	400
Lions	Seibu Dome	31,000	328	400
Marines	Chiba Marine	30,000	326	400

Although many of these capacities are considered inflated by 20 percent, most teams are drawing very well. Japan's economy keeps current attendance at the '90s level of 23.6 million (13.5 in the CL, 10.1 in the PL).

Attendance

Three clubs went over the 3-million mark in 2003. Hanshin increased attendance by 23 percent over 2002.

Team	Total	Average
Yomiuri Giants	3,763,000	53,757
Hanshin Tigers	3,300,000	47,143
Daiei Hawks	3,228,000	46,100

Average Attendance per Game

1950	4,350
1960	10,300
1970	12,300
1980	20,700
1990	26,300
2000	27,600
2003	28,800
(1992 was 29,900, a record)	

Salaries

Despite the nation's economic problems, the average Japanese player earned $550,000 in 2003, a 43 percent increase in 10 years, and about one-fourth of the average U.S. player's pay. The highest-

paid Japanese players in 2004:

1. Roberto Petagine, the Giants' Venezuelan star, $6.3 million
2. Tuffy Rhodes, new Giants' outfielder, $5.5 million
3. Hironori Nakamura, Kintetsu Buffaloes' third baseman, $4.5 million
4. Kazuhiro Kiyohara, Giants' veteran slugger, $4.1 million
5. Michihiro Ogasawara, Nippon Ham Fighters' third baseman, $3.6 million
Kenji Jojima, Japan champion Hawks' MVP catcher, $3.6 million
Alex Cabrera, ex-Diamondback who hit 55 homers in '02, $3.6 million

Yomiuri had the largest payroll, an estimated $50 million, which exceeds that of several U.S. big league teams. That is one reason Japanese players hope to play for the Giants or a U.S. team. They also get the best endorsement contracts and highest autograph prices and, after retiring, the best jobs as TV color commentators. Even a second-level player makes more than Triple A U.S. minor leaguers.

The Future

Few authorities see a bright future for the Japanese pro leagues. Like it or not, Japan clubs will probably function as farm teams for the big leagues. So far there have been two types of Japanese major leaguers: *One,* top players, who have proved they can play in the majors—Nomo, Ichiro, Matsui, Sasaki, and Ishii. They are highly valued in America, which led to Little Matsui signing a huge contract with the Mets. *Two,* the so-so players, such as Komiyama, Yoshii, Shinjo, and Kashiwada, who want to taste the majors to top off their careers.

It may be concluded that only top players can make long-time major leaguers. So the Japanese leagues will survive with second-tier players and younger players waiting for free agency. It's a nine-year wait in Japan for free agency, compared to six in the U.S. majors. This will be a big help to Japanese baseball.

One of the goals throughout the history of Japanese baseball has been a real World Series. Some journalists have proposed a playoff, in which the top teams of Japan, Korea and Taiwan would play for the Asian championship, and the winner would play in the U.S. Division series. However, there is little reason for the majors to agree. Even if it doesn't come true, most Japanese are satisfied to see their countrymen playing on the world's top stage, the U.S. major leagues. In an informal poll of 53 college students, 51 said the departure of Japan's stars to America is a good thing. Younger people seem to favor Japanese athletes, businesspersons, musicians, and artists doing well abroad.

Since Ichiro joined Seattle in 2001, Japanese have adopted a daily routine. In the morning, they watch Ichiro or Godzilla Matsui play on television. At night they watch Japanese games, mostly the Yomiuri Giants, on TV. Office workers, who cannot watch at work, read about Ichiro and Matsui in evening tabloids on the train going home.

SINGLE-SEASON LEADERS

Batting

YEAR	CENTRAL LEAGUE	PACIFIC LEAGUE
1950	Fumio Fujimura .362	Hiroshi Oshita .339
1951	Tetsuharu Kawakami .377	Hiroshi Oshita .383
1952	Michio Nishizawa .353	Shigeya Iijima .336
1953	Tetsuharu Kawakami .347	Isami Okamoto .318
1954	Wally Yonamine .361	Larry Raines .337
1955	Tetsuharu Kawakami .338	Futoshi Nakanishi .332
1956	Wally Yonamine .338	Yasumitsu Toyoda .325
1957	Wally Yonamine .343	Kazuhiro Yamauchi .331
1958	Kenjiro Tamiya .320	Futoshi Nakanishi .314
1959	Shigeo Nagashima .334	Kohei Sugiyama .323
1960	Shigeo Nagashima .334	Kihachi Enomoto .344
1961	Shigeo Nagashima .353	Isao Harimoto .336
1962	Katsuya Morinaga .307	Jack Bloomfield .374
1963	Shigeo Nagashima .341	Jack Bloomfield .335
1964	Shinichi Eto .323	Yoshinori Hirose .366
1965	Shinichi Eto .336	Katsuya Nomura .320
1966	Shigeo Nagashima .344	Kihachi Enomoto .351
1967	Toshio Naka .343	Isao Harimoto .336
1968	Sadaharu Oh .326	Isao Harimoto .336
1969	Sadaharu Oh .345	Isao Harimoto .333
		Yozo Nagafuchi .333
1970	Sadaharu Oh .325	Isao Harimoto 383
1971	Shigeo Nagashima .320	Shinichi Eto .337
1972	Tsutomu Wakamatsu .329	Isao Harimoto .353
1973	Sadaharu Oh .355	Hideji Kato .337
1974	Sadaharu Oh .332	Isao Harimoto .340
1975	Koji Yamamoto .319	Jinten Haku .319
1976	Kenichi Yazawa .354	Satoru Yoshioka .309
1977	Tsutomu Wakamatsu .358	Michiyo Arito .329
1978	Jitsuo Mizutani .348	Kyosuke Sasaki .354
1979	Felix Millan .346	Hideo Kato .354
1980	Kenichi Yazawa .369	Leron Lee .358
1981	Taira Fujita .358	Hiromitsu Ochiai .326
1982	Keiji Nagasaki .351	Hiromitsu Ochiai .325
1983	Akinobu Mayumi .353	Hiromitsu Ochiai .332
1984	Toshio Shinozuka .334	Boomer Wells .355
1985	Randy Bass .350	Hiromitsu Ochiai .367
1986	Randy Bass .389*	Hiromitsu Ochiai .360
1987	Toshio Shinozuka .333	Hiromasa Arai .366
	Kozo Shoda .333	
1988	Kozo Shoda .340	Hideaki Takazawa .327
1989	Warren Cromartie .378	Boomer Wells .322
1990	Jim Paciorek .326	Norifumi Nishimura .338
1991	Atsuya Furuta .339	Mitsuchika Hirai .314

YEAR	CENTRAL LEAGUE	PACIFIC LEAGUE
1992	Jack Howell .331	Makoto Sasaki 322
1993	Tom O'Malley .329	Hatsuhiko Tsuji .319
1994	Alonzo Powell .324	Ichiro Suzuki .385
1995	Alonzo Powell .355	Ichiro Suzuki .342
1996	Alonzo Powell .340	Ichiro Suzuki .356
1997	Takanori Suzuki .335	Ichiro Suzuki .345
1998	Takanori Suzuki .337	Ichiro Suzuki .358
1999	Robert Rose .369	Ichiro Suzuki .343
2000	Tatsuhiko Kinjo .346	Ichiro Suzuki .387*
2001	Hideki Matsui .333	Kazuya Fukuura .346
2002	Kosuke Fukudome .343	Michihiro Ogasawara .340
2003	Makoto Imaoka .340	Michihiro Ogasawara .360

Home Runs

YEAR	CENTRAL LEAGUE	PACIFIC LEAGUE
1950	Makoto Kozuru 51	Kaoru Betto 43
1951	Noboru Aota 32	Hiroshi Oshita 26
1952	Satoru Sugiyama 27	Yasuhiro Fukami 25
1953	Fumio Fujimura 27	Futoshi Nakanishi 36
1954	Noboru Aota 31	Futoshi Nakanishi 31
1955	Yukihiko Machida 31	Futoshi Nakanishi 35
1956	Noboru Aota 25	Futoshi Nakanishi 29
1957	Takao Sato 22	Katsuya Nomura 30
	Noboru Aota 22	
1958	Shigeo Nagashima 29	Futoshi Nakanishi 23
1959	Takeshi Kuwata 31	Kazuhiro Yamauchi 25
	Toru Mori 31	
1960	Katsumi Fujimoto 22	Kazuhiro Yamauchi 32
1961	Shigeo Nagashima 28	Katsuya Nomura 29
		Masahiro Nakada 29
1962	Sadaharu Oh 38	Katsuya Nomura 44
1963	Sadaharu Oh 40	Katsuya Nomura 52
1964	Sadaharu Oh 55*	Katsuya Nomura 41
1965	Sadaharu Oh 42	Katsuya Nomura 42
1966	Sadaharu Oh 48	Katsuya Nomura 34
1967	Sadaharu Oh 47	Katsuya Nomura 35
1968	Sadaharu Oh 49	Katsuya Nomura 38
1969	Sadaharu Oh 44	Tokuji Nagaike 41
1970	Sadaharu Oh 47	Katsuo Osugi 44
1971	Sadaharu Oh 39	Katsuo Osugi 44
1972	Sadaharu Oh 48	Tokuji Nagaike 41
1973	Sadaharu Oh 51	Tokuji Nagaike 43
1974	Sadaharu Oh 49	Clarence Jones 38
1975	Koichi Tabuchi 43	Masahiro Doi 34
1976	Sadaharu Oh 49	Clarence Jones 36
1977	Sadaharu Oh 50	Leron Lee 34

*League record

YEAR	CENTRAL LEAGUE	PACIFIC LEAGUE
1978	Koji Yamamoto 44	Bobby Mitchell 36
1979	Masayuki Kakefu 48	Charlie Manuel 37
1980	Koji Yamamoto 44	Charlie Manuel 48
1981	Koji Yamamoto 43	Hiromitsu Kadota 44
		Tony Solaita 44
1982	Masayuki Kakefu 35	Hiromitsu Ochiai 32
1983	Yasunori Oshima 36	Hiromitsu Kadota 40
	Koji Yamamoto 36	
1984	Masaru Uno 37	Boomer Wells 37
	Masayuki Kakefu 37	
1985	Randy Bass 54	Hiromitsu Ochiai 50
1986	Randy Bass 47	Hiromitsu Ochiai 52
1987	Rick Lancellotti 39	Koji Akiyama 43
1988	Carlos Ponce 33	Hiromitsu Kadota 44
1989	Larry Parrish 42	Ralph Bryant 49
1990	Hiromitsu Ochiai 34	Orestes Destrade 42
1991	Hiromitsu Ochiai 37	Orestes Destrade 39
1992	Jack Howell 38	Orestes Destrade 41
1993	Akira Eto 34	Ralph Bryant 42
1994	Yasuaki Taihoh 38	Ralph Bryant 35
1995	Akira Eto 39	Hiroki Kokubo 28
1996	Takeshi Yamasaki 39	Troy Neel 32
1997	Dwayne Hosey 38	Nigel Wilson 37
1998	Hideki Matsui 34	Nigel Wilson 33
1999	Roberto Petagine 44	Tuffy Rhodes 40
2000	Hideki Matsui 42	Norihiro Nakamura 39
2001	Roberto Petagine 39	Tuffy Rhodes 55*
2002	Hideki Matsui 50	Alex Cabrera 55*
2003	Alex Ramirez 40	Tuffy Rhodes 51
	Tyrone Woods 40	

Pitching Wins

YEAR	CENTRAL LEAGUE	PACIFIC LEAGUE
1950	Shigeo Sanada 39*	Jun Aramaki 26
1951	Shigeru Sugishita 28	Masaru Eto 24
1952	Takehiko Bessho 33	Masaaki Noguchi 23
1953	Takumi Otomo 27	Tokuji Kawasaki 24
1954	Shigeru Sugishita 32	Motoji Taku 26
		Fumio Tanaka 26
1955	Ryohei Hasegawa 30	Motoji Taku 24
	Takumi Otomo 30	
1956	Takehiko Bessho 27	Masayoshi Miura 29
1957	Masaichi Kaneda 28	Kazuhisa Inao 35
1958	Masaichi Kaneda 31	Kazuhisa Inao 33
1959	Motoshi Fujita 27	Tadashi Sugiura 38
1960	Ritsuo Horimoto 29	Shoichi Ono 33
1961	Hiroshi Gondo 35	Kazuhisa Inao 42*
1962	Hiroshi Gondo 30	Masahiro Kubo 28
1963	Masaichi Kaneda 30	Kazuhisa Inao 28
1964	Gene Bacqu 29	Masaaki Koyama 30
1965	Minoru Murayama 25	Yukio Ozaki 27
1966	Minoru Murayama 24	Tetsuya Yoneda 25
1967	Kenjiro Ogawa 29	Masaaki Ikenaga 24
1968	Yutaka Enatsu 25	Mutsuo Minagawa 31
1969	Kazumi Takahashi 22	Keishi Suzuki 24
1970	Masaji Hiramatsu 25	Fumio Narita 25
1971	Masaji Hiramatsu 17	Masaaki Kitaru 24
1972	Tsuneo Horiuchi 26	Hisashi Yamada 20
		Tomehiro Kaneda 20
1973	Yutaka Enatsu 24	Fumio Narita 21
1974	Yukitsura Matsumoto 20	Tomehiro Kaneda 16
	Motoyasu Kaneshige 20	
1975	Yoshiro Sotokoba 20	Osamu Higashio 23
1976	Kojiro Ikegaya 20	Hisashi Yamada 26
1977	Satoshi Takahashi 20	Keishi Suzuki 20
1978	Osamu Nomura 17	Keishi Suzuki 25
1979	Shigeru Kobayashi 22	Hisashi Yamada 21
1980	Suguru Egawa 16	Isamu Kida 22
1981	Suguru Egawa 20	Yutaro Imai 19
		Choji Murata 19
1982	Manabu Kitabeppu 20	Mikio Kudo 20
1983	Kazuhiko Endo 18	Osamu Higashio 18
		Kazuhiro Yamauchi 18
1984	Kazuhiko Endo 17	Yutaro Imai 21
1985	Tatsuo Komatsu 17	Yoshinori Sato 21
1986	Manabu Kitabeppu 18	Hisanobu Watanabe 16
1987	Tatsuo Komatsu 17	Yukihiko Yamaoki 19
1988	Kazuyuki Ono 18	Hisanobu Watanabe 15
	Akimitsu Ito 18	Yukihiro Nishizaki 15
		Hiroaki Matsuura 15
1989	Masaki Saito 20	Hideyuki Awano 19
	Takashi Nishimoto 20	
1990	Masaki Saito 20	Hideo Nomo 18
		Hisanobu Watanabe 18
1991	Shinji Sasaoka 17	Hideo Nomo 17
1992	Masaki Saito 17	Hideo Nomo 18
1993	Shinji Imanaka 17	Hideo Nomo 17
	Masahiro Yamamoto 17	Koji Noda 17
	Hiroki Nomura 17	
1994	Masahiro Yamamoto 19	Hideki Irabu 15
1995	Masaki Saito 18	Kip Gross 16
1996	Masaki Saito 16	Kip Gross 17
	Balvino Galvez 16	
1997	Masahiro Yamamoto 18	Fumiya Nishiguchi 15
1998	Kenjiro Kawasaki 17	Fumiya Nishiguchi 13
		Kazuhiro Takeda 13
		Tomohiro Kuroki 13
1999	Koji Uehara 20	Daisuke Matsuzaka 16
2000	Melvin Bunch 14	Daisuke Matsuzaka 14
2001	Shugo Fujii 14	Daisuke Matsuzaka 15
2002	Koji Uehara 17	Jeremy Powell 17
	Kevin Hodges 17	
2003	Kei Igawa 20	Kazumi Saito 20

*League record

Earned Run Average

YEAR	CENTRAL LEAGUE	PACIFIC LEAGUE
1950	Nobuo Oshima 2.03	Jun Aramaki 2.06
1951	Kiyoshi Matsuda 2.01	Susumu Yuki 2.08
1952	Tadashi Kajioka 1.71	Susumu Yuki 1.91
1953	Takumi Otomo 1.85	Tokuji Kawasaki 1.98
1954	Shigeru Sugishita 1.39	Motoji Takuwa 1.58
1955	Takehiko Bessho 1.33	Takashi Nakagawa 2.08
1956	Shozo Watanabe 1.45	Kazuhisa Inao 1.06*
1957	Masaichi Kaneda 1.63	Kazuhisa Inao 1.37
1958	Masaichi Kaneda 1.30	Kazuhisa Inao 1.42
1959	Minoru Murayama 1.19	Tadashi Sugiura 1.40
1960	Noboru Akiyama 1.75	Shoichi Ono 1.98
1961	Hiroshi Gondo 1.70	Kazuhisa Inao 1.69
1962	Minoru Murayama 1.20	Osamu Kubota 2.21
1963	Minoru Kakimoto 1.70	Masahiro Kubo 2.36
1964	Gene Bacque 1.89	Yoshiro Tsumajima 2.15
1965	Masaichi Kaneda 1.84	Kiyohiro Miura 1.57
1966	Tsuneo Horiuchi 1.39	Kazuhisa Inao 1.79
1967	Masatoshi Gondo 1.40	Mitsuhiro Adachi 1.75
1968	Yoshiro Sotokoba 1.94	Mutsuo Minagawa 1.61
1969	Yutaka Enatsu 1.81	Masaaki Kitaru 1.72
1970	Minoru Murayama 0.98*	Michio Sato 2.05
1971	Kazuhiro Fujimoto 1.71	Hisashi Yamada 2.37
1972	Takeshi Yasuda 2.08	Toshihiko Sei 2.36
1973	Takeshi Yasuda 2.02	Tetsuya Yoneda 2.47
1974	Shitoshi Sekimoto 2.28	Michio Sato 1.91
1975	Sohachi Aniya 1.91	Choji Murata 2.20
1976	Takamasa Suzuki 2.98	Choji Murata 1.82
1977	Hisao Niura 2.32	Hisashi Yamada 2.28
1978	Hisao Niura 2.81	Keishi Suzuki 2.02
1979	Masaji Hiramatsu 2.39	Tetsuji Yamaguchi 2.49
1980	Hiromu Matsuoka 2.35	Isamu Kida 2.28
1981	Suguru Egawa 2.29	Noriaki Okabe 2.70
1982	Akio Saito 2.07	Satoshi Takahashi 1.84
1983	Osamu Fukuma 2.62	Osamu Higashio 2.92
1984	Seiji Kobayashi 2.20	Yutaro Imai 2.93
1985	Tatsuo Komatsu 2.65	Kimiyasu Kudo 2.76
1986	Manabu Kitabeppu 2.43	Yoshinori Sato 2.83
1987	Masumi Kuwata 2.17	Kimiyasu Kudo 2.41
1988	Yutaka Ono 1.70	Hirofumi Kono 2.38
1989	Masaki Saito 1.62	Choji Murata 2.50
1990	Masaki Saito 2.17	Hideo Nomo 2.91
1991	Shinji Sasaoka 2.44	Tomio Watanabe 2.35
1992	Koki Morita 2.05	Motoyuki Akahori 1.80
1993	Masahiro Yamamoto 2.05	Kimiyasu Kudo 2.06
1994	Genji Kaku 2.45	Hiroshi Shintani 2.91
1995	Terry Bross 2.33	Hideki Irabu 2.53
1996	Masaki Saito 2.36	Hideki Irabu 2.40
1997	Yutaka Ohno 2.85	Satoru Komiyama 2.49
1998	Shigeki Noguchi 2.34	Satoru Kanemura 2.73
1999	Koji Uehara 2.09	Kimiyasu Kudo 2.38
2000	Kazuhisa Ishii 2.61	Nobuyuki Ebisu 3.27
2001	Shigeki Noguchi 2.46	Nathan Minchey 3.26
2002	Masumi Kuwata 2.22	Masahiko Kaneda 2.50
2003	Kei Igawa 2.80	Kazumi Saito 2.83
		Daisuke Matsuzaka 2.83

Most Valuable Players

YEAR	CENTRAL LEAGUE	PACIFIC LEAGUE
1950	Makoto Kozuru, OF	Kaoru Betto, OF
1951	Tetsuharu Kawakami, 1B	Kazuto Tsuoka, 2B
1952	Takehiko Bessho, P	Susumu Yuki, P
1953	Takumi Otomo, P	Isami Okamoto, 2B
1954	Shigeru Sugishita, P	Hiroshi Oshita, OF

1955	Tetsuharu Kawakami, 1B	Tokuji Iida, OF
1956	Takehiko Bessho, P	Futoshi Nakanishi, 3B
1957	Wally Yonamine, OF	Kazuhisa Inao, P
1958	Motoshi Fujita, P	Kazuhisa Inao, P
1959	Motoshi Fujita, P	Tadashi Sugiura, P
1960	Noboru Akiyama, P	Kazuhiro Yamauchi, OF
1961	Shigeo Nagashima, 3B	Katsuya Nomura, C
1962	Minoru Murayama, P	Isao Harimoto, OF
1963	Shigeo Nagashima, 3B	Katsuya Nomura, C
1964	Sadaharu Oh, 1B	Joe Stanka, P
1965	Sadaharu Oh, 1B	Katsuya Nomura, C
1966	Shigeo Nagashima, 3B	Katsuya Nomura, C
1967	Sadaharu Oh, 1B	Mitsuhiro Adachi, P
1968	Shigeo Nagashima, 3B	Tetsuya Yoneda, p
1969	Sadaharu Oh, 1B	Tokuji Nagaike, OF
1970	Sadaharu Oh, 1B	Masaaki Kitaru, P
1971	Shigeo Nagashima, 3B	Tokuji Nagaike, OF
1972	Tsuneo Horiuchi, P	Yutaka Fukumoto, OF
1973	Sadaharu Oh, 1B	Katsuya Nomura, C
1974	Sadaharu Oh, 1B	Tomehiro Kaneda, P
1975	Koji Yamamoto, OF	Hideji Kato, 1B
1976	Sadaharu Oh, 1B	Hisashi Yamada, P
1977	Sadaharu Oh, 1B	Hisashi Yamada, P
1978	Tsutomu Wakamatsu, OF	Hisashi Yamada, P
1979	Yutaka Enatsu, P	Charlie Manuel, OF

1980	Koji Yamamoto, OF	Isamu Kida, P
1981	Suguru Egawa, P	Yutaka Enatsu, p
1982	Takayoshi Nakao, C	Hiromitsu Ochiai, 2B
1983	Tatsunori Hara, 3B	Osamu Higashio, P
1984	Sachio Kinugasa, 3B	Boomer Wells, 1B
1985	Randy Bass, 1B	Hiromitsu Ochiai, 3B
1986	Manabu Kitabeppu, P	Hiromichi Ishige, SS
1987	Kazuhiro Yamakura, C	Osamu Higashio, P
1988	Genji Kaku, P	Hiromitsu Kadota, OF
1989	Warren Cromartie, OF	Ralph Bryant, OF
1990	Masaki Saito, P	Hideo Nomo, P
1991	Shinji Sasaoka, P	Taigen Kaku, P
1992	Jack Howell, 3B	Takehiro Ishii, P
1993	Atsuya Furuta, C	Kimiyasu Kudo, P
1994	Masumi Kuwata, P	Ichiro Suzuki, OF
1995	Tom O'Malley, OF	Ichiro Suzuki, OF
1996	Hideki Matsui, OF	Ichiro Suzuki, OF
1997	Atsuya Furuta, C	Fumiya Nishiguchi, P
1998	Kazuhiro Sasaki, P	Kazuo Matsui, SS
1999	Shigeki Noguchi, P	Kimiyasu Kudo, P
2000	Hideki Matsui, OF	Nobuhiko Matsunaka, 1B
2001	Roberto Petagine, 1B	Tuffy Rhodes, OF
2002	Hideki Matsui, OF	Alex Cabrera, 1B
2003	Kei Igawa, P	Kenji Jojima, C

LIFETIME LEADERS

Home Runs

1. Sadaharu Oh	868
2. Katsuya Nomura	657
3. Hiromitsu Kadota	567
4. Koji Yamamoto	536
5. Hiromitsu Ochiai	510
6. Isao Harimoto	504
6. Sachio Kinugasa	504
8. Katsuo Osugi	486
9. Kazuhiro Kiyohara	480
10. Koichi Tabuchi	474

Batting (4,000 AB)

1. Leron Lee	.320
2. Tsutomu Wakamatsu	.319
3. Isao Harimoto	.319
4. Boomer Wells	.317
5. Tetsuharu Kawakami	.313

6. Wally Yonamine	.311
7. Hiromitsu Ochiai	.311
8. Takanori Suzuki	.310
9. Kazuo Matsui	.309
10. Leon Lee	.308

Notes: Ichiro Suzuki's career average is .353 with 3,619 at-bats.

Other leaders:

Hits: Isao Harimoto	3,085
RBIs: Sadaharu Oh	2,170
SB: Yutaka Fukumoto	1,065
BB: Sadaharu Oh	2,504

Wins

1. Masaichi Kaneda	400-298
2. Tetsuya Yoneda	350-285
3. Masaaki Koyama	320-232
4. Keishi Suzuki	317-238

5. Takehiko Bessho	310-178
6. Victor Starffin	303-176
7. Hisashi Yamada	284-166
8. Kazuhisa Inao	276-137
9. Takao Kajimoto	254-255
10. Osamu Higashio	251-247

Strikeouts

1. Masaichi Kaneda	4490
2. Tetsuya Yoneda	3388
3. Masaaki Koyama	3159
4. Keishi Suzuki	3061
5. Yutaka Enatsu	2987
6. Takao Kajimoto	2945
7. Kazahisa Inao	2574
8. Kimiyasu Kudo	2438
9. Choji Murata	2363
10. Minoru Murayama	2271

POSTSEASON AND PLAYOFFS

Pennant Winners

Nippon Pro-Baseball League

1936	Tokyo Giants
1937-Spring	Tokyo Giants
-Fall	Osaka Tigers
1938-Spring	Osaka Tigers
-Fall	Tokyo Giants
1940	Tokyo Giants
1941	Tokyo Giants
1942	Tokyo Giants
1943	Tokyo Giants
1944	Hanshin Tigers
1945	(Play Suspended)
1946	Kinki Greatring
1947	Osaka Tigers
1948	Nankai Hawks
1949	Yomiuri Giants

Japan Series

1950 Mainichi Orions, PL 4, Shochiku Robins, CL 2
1951 Yomiuri Giants, CL 4, Nankai Hawks, PL 1
1952 Yomiuri Giants, CL 4, Nankai Hawks, PL 2
1953 Yomiuri Giants, CL 4, Nankai Hawks, PL 3
1954 Chunichi Dragons, CL 4, Nishitetsu Lions, PL 3
1955 Yomiuri Giants, CL 4, Nankai Hawks, PL 3
1956 Nishitetsu Lions, PL 4, Yomiuri Giants, CL 2
1957 Nishitetsu Lions, PL 4, Yomiuri Giants, CL 0
1958 Nishitetsu Lions, PL 4, Yomiuri Giants, CL 3
1959 Nankai Hawks, PL 4, Yomiuri Giants, CL 0
1960 Taiyo Whales, CL 4, Daimai Orions, PL 0
1961 Yomiuri Giants, CL 4, Nankai Hawks, PL 2
1962 Toei Flyers, PL 4, Hanshin Tigers, CL 2

1963 Yomiuri Giants, CL 4, Nishitetsu Lions, PL 3
1964 Nankai Hawks, PL 4, Hanshin Tigers, CL 3
1965 Yomiuri Giants, CL 4, Nankai Hawks, PL 1
1966 Yomiuri Giants, CL 4, Nankai Hawks, PL 1
1967 Yomiuri Giants, CL 4, Hankyu Braves, PL 2
1968 Yomiuri Giants, CL 4, Hankyu Braves, PL 2
1969 Yomiuri Giants, CL 4, Hankyu Braves, PL 2
1970 Yomiuri Giants, CL 4, Lotte Orions, PL 1
1971 Yomiuri Giants, CL 4, Hankyu Braves, PL 1
1972 Yomiuri Giants, CL 4, Hankyu Braves, PL 1
1973 Yomiuri Giants, CL 4, Nankai Hawks, PL 1
1974 Lotte Orions, PL 4, Chunichi Dragons, CL 2
1975 Hankyu Braves, PL 4, Hiroshima Carp, CL 0
1976 Hankyu Braves, PL 4, Yomiuri Giants, CL 3
1977 Hankyu Braves, PL 4, Yomiuri Giants, CL 1
1978 Yakult Swallows, CL 4, Hankyu Braves, PL 3
1979 Hiroshima Carp, CL 4, Kintetsu Buffaloes, PL 3
1980 Hiroshima Carp, CL 4, Kintetsu Buffaloes, PL 3
1981 Yomiuri Giants, CL 4,
    Nippon Ham Fighters, PL 2
1982 Seibu Lions, PL 4, Chunichi Dragons, CL 2
1983 Seibu Lions, PL 4, Yomiuri Giants, CL 3
1984 Hiroshima Carp, CL 4, Hankyu Braves, PL 3
1985 Hanshin Tigers, CL 4, Seibu Lions, PL 2
1986 Seibu Lions, PL 4, Hiroshima Carp, CL 3
1987 Seibu Lions, PL 4, Yomiuri Giants, CL 2
1988 Seibu Lions, PL 4, Chunichi Dragons, CL 1
1989 Yomiuri Giants, CL 4, Kintetsu Buffaloes, PL 3
1990 Seibu Lions, PL 4, Yomiuri Giants, CL 0
1991 Seibu Lions, PL 4, Hiroshima Carp, CL 3
1992 Seibu Lions, PL 4, Yakult Swallows, CL 3
1993 Yakult Swallows, CL 4, Seibu Lions, PL 3
1994 Yomiuri Giants, CL 4, Seibu Lions, PL 2

1995 Yakult Swallows, CL 4, Orix Blue Wave, PL 1
1996 Orix Blue Wave, PL 4, Yomiuri Giants, CL 1
1997 Yakult Swallows, CL 4, Seibu Lions, PL 1
1998 Yokohama Bay Stars, CL 4, Seibu Lions, PL 2
1999 Daiei Hawks, PL 4, Chunichi Dragons, CL 1
2000 Youmiuri Giants, CL 4, Daiei Hawks, PL 2
2001 Yakulta Sawallows, CL 4,
    Kintetsu Buffaloes, PL 1
2002 Youmiuri Goiants, CL 4, Seibu Lions, PL 0
2003 Daiei Hawks, PL 4, Hanshin Tigers, CL 3

Pacific League Play-off

Year	Winner	Loser
1973	Nankai Hawks	Hankyu Braves
1974	Lotte Orions	Hankyu Braves
1975	Hankyu Braves	Kintetsu Buffaloes
1976	Hankyu Braves (won both halves)	
1977	Hankyu Braves	Lotte Orions
1978	Hankyu Braves (won both halves)	
1979	Kintetsu Buffaloes	Hankyu Braves
1980	Kintetsu Buffaloes	Hankyu Braves
1981	Nippon Ham Fighters	Lotte Orions
1982	Seibu Lions	Nippon Ham Fighters

Notes on pronunciation: Vowels are the same as Spanish: A = ah, I = ee, U = oo, E = ay, O = oh. Y is a consonant or "ee," thus "kyo" and "ryo" are pronounced something like "keo" and "reo." U is usually not emphasized and sometimes almost dropped entirely. Some combinations change a bit in actual speech. "Shita" comes out "sh'ta," and "hito" and "hiko" sound like "sh'to" and "sh'ko." G is always hard, as in "gh."

Chapter 45

Baseball in the Caribbean

By Rob Ruck

Soon after the World Series marks the season's end in the United States, baseball springs back to life in and around the Caribbean. There, to the beat of salsa and merengue and against a backdrop of palm trees and seasonal labor, some of the best baseball in the world is played each winter. While most of South America follows football and the British West Indies follows cricket, the rest of the Caribbean basin plays baseball—and has for more than a century.

Since baseball fever first infected Cuba in the 1870s, the game has infiltrated the sporting psyches of Mexico, Nicaragua, the Dominican Republic, Venezuela, Puerto Rico, Panama, and Colombia. Although tied to major league baseball in four of these countries through a set of winter leagues and as a source of fresh talent, Caribbean baseball is not simply an appendage of the game as it is played in the U.S. Rather, baseball has acquired an autonomous persona as the peoples of the region have made the game into their own national pastimes.

More than simply recreation or a display of grace and competence, baseball has catalyzed national consciousness and cohesion in the Caribbean basin. A critical part of the fabric of everyday life, the sport has also influenced how these societies have come to define themselves, their relations with each other, and their ties to the United States. "It's more than a game," Dominican winter league general manager Winston Llenas once remarked. "It's our passion. It's almost our way of life."

Pedro Julio Santana stands at his office window in what was once the colonial zone of Santo Domingo. A sportsman at the center of Dominican baseball's evolution during the 20th century, he searches for words to describe how the game penetrated his country and the rest of the basin. Glancing below to the hulking walls of the first Catholic cathedral in the western hemisphere, Santana finds his metaphor. "It is much the same as that which happened with Christianity. Jesus could be compared to the North Americans, but the apostles were the ones that spread the faith, and the apostles of baseball were Cubans. Even though the Dominican Republic and Puerto Rico were occupied by the North Americans, the Cubans first brought baseball here, and to Mexico and Venezuela, too."

Caribbean baseball's first epicenter was Cuba. Baseball arrived

Minnie Minoso
Among the most exciting players to come out of Cuba, Minoso made his major league debut in 1949 and became a five-decade player by playing one game in 1980.

there in the 19th century, brought by sailors, students, and businessmen from the United States as well as by Cubans who had traveled north. The U.S. military occupations that followed the 1898 conflict with Spain stimulated baseball's expansion there and across the basin. By the time the Good Neighbor Policy had supplanted the Big Stick in the 1930s, baseball was entrenched. Moreover, Cuban baseball had become the focal point of an international network that stretched from the Caribbean basin through the Negro Leagues.

What was likely the first ballgame in Cuba with local participation occurred in June 1866, when sailors of a U.S. ship taking on sugar invited Cuban longshoremen to play. *El Club Habana* (Havana) began two years later, crushing a team from Matanzas in the first organized contest of two Cuban teams.

Havana's victory over Matanzas featured two of Cuba's sporting pioneers, Esteban Bellan and Emilio Sabourin. Bellan became the first Latino in U.S. organized baseball, playing three seasons in the National Association (1871-1873). Sabourin, the A. G. Spalding of Cuban baseball, was the motivating force behind the *Liga de Beisbol Profesional Cubana,* whose inaugural tournament was won by Sabourin's reconstituted Havana club in 1878. Sabourin proselytized for his sport as well as for the cause of Cuban independence from Spain until his contribution of baseball revenues to the independence movement incurred the wrath of Spanish officials. They imprisoned Sabourin until his death and banned baseball in parts of their colony.

While initially a game of the more affluent and those with contact with the U.S., baseball soon spread to all classes of Cuban society, both urban and rural. U.S. military occupations, support by companies and businessmen, and close ties to political elites would shape its subsequent development, much as these forces would do so elsewhere in the basin.

The game was organized on three overlapping levels in its early years. The first was an *ad hoc* player-organized, self-directed network of teams. The second involved clubs sponsored by businessmen, companies and politicians who sought the promotional advantages of such patronage. The third level was that of professional (sometimes semi-professional) baseball, which organized championships from 1878 until 1961, with a changing cast of teams and format. In some years, no tournaments were held, while in others both a summer and winter season took place. Havana, Almendares, Santa Clara, Cienfuegos, and Marianao were the league's mainstays.

Until the 1959 Cuban Revolution and the ensuing U.S. blockade, Cuba set the standard for Caribbean baseball. It sent the most players to the major and Negro leagues while its winter and summer tournaments featured the highest caliber of Latin ball and attracted players from both the States and the basin. Cuban players, radio broadcasts and emigrants, in turn, became baseball's emissaries to the rest of the region.

In the Dominican Republic, Cubans who had migrated to escape the turmoil of the Ten Years' War (1868-1878) were the first to form teams. Young Dominicans emulated them and joined with compatriots who had studied in the United States to establish a self-organized matrix of teams and tournaments well in place before the U.S. Marines arrived in 1916 for their eight-year occupation. Santo Domingo's *Licey*, the oldest of the six professional Dominican clubs, formed in 1907, while the forerunners of San Pedro de Macoris' *Estrellas Orientales,* Santiago's *Aguilas Cibaenas,* and Santo Domingo's other club, *Escogido,* took to the field soon afterward.

While Dominicans refer to these early decades as the romantic epoch of baseball, commercial forces were already at work there and across the basin. Teams occasionally recruited players with the lure of financial reward and soon began importing Cubans and Puerto Ricans for championship tournaments. Moreover, local clubs often induced talented players with payment in cash or work. North American oil companies in Venezuela, rum distilleries and tobacco manufacturers in Cuba, and sugar cane companies in Nicaragua, Puerto Rico, Cuba, and the Dominican Republic sponsored or assisted workplace teams for recreation and community entertainment, but with an industrial agenda, too—winning their workers' hearts and minds.

During these "Yankee years," between 1898 and 1933, when the Marines hit the beaches 34 times in 10 different basin countries, they found baseball already implanted in Cuba, Puerto Rico, Nicaragua, Mexico, and the Dominican Republic. They never made it to Venezuela, but would have found baseball there, too, as early as the organization of the Caracas club in 1895. The occupations, though, helped to push the sport along. While Nicaraguans had played on their Atlantic coast since 1888, the nation's longest-running pro team, *Boer,* was founded by the U.S. consul in Managua. In the Dominican Republic, U.S. marines and sailors played ball to bolster morale; they were frequently challenged by Dominican teams, for whom these contests were both a test of sporting abilities and national character. Far more baseball was in evidence by the end of the U.S. stay on the island.

Professional Imports

While Cubans and some other basin natives had broken into baseball in the States during the first half of the century, the center of gravity for Caribbean baseball remained a regional one. A "Have Glove—Will Travel" mentality soon took hold of basin baseball and its ablest practitioners made the rounds of national tournaments. A core of the finest black players from the States—then barred from major league play by the color line, as were most Latinos—joined them in Cuba, the Dominican Republic, Puerto Rico, Venezuela, and Mexico.

Caribbean baseball's apogee was probably reached in the summer of 1937 in the Dominican Republic during a national championship dedicated to the re-election of the then state-of-the-art dictator Rafael Trujillo. Top Dominican players were joined by the best Cuban, Puerto Rican and Negro League talent that the Dominican peso could buy to form a three-team league. Santiago boasted the services of Martin Dihigo, Luis Tiant, Sr. and Horacio Martinez; San Pedro de Macoris countered with Tetelo Vargas, Ramon Bragana and Cocaina Garcia, while the eventual victor, *Ciudad Trujillo* (a merger of *Licey* and *Escogido* that represented the city Trujillo had renamed in his own honor) relied on future Hall of Famers Josh Gibson, Cool Papa Bell, and Satchel Paige, as well as Silvio Garcia, Perucho Cepeda and Sam Bankhead. Baseball on the island was the equal of that played anywhere that summer. These players barnstormed year-round, and many of them later played together as *Santa Clara* in Cuba and as *La Concordia* in Venezuela.

The proprietary interest taken by caudillos such as Trujillo or Nicaragua's Anastasio Somoza ensured baseball of its most-favored-sport status and contributed to the growth of strong regional rivalries. Caribbean participation in the *Mundiales*, the world amateur baseball championships that began in 1938, and later the Caribbean Series of pro circuits, which started in 1949, reinforced the game's hegemony.

Latin ball was an opportunity for North American players to supplement their income and hone their skills in encounters that sometimes surpassed the caliber of major league play. However, it was also a threat to Organized Baseball in the States. Major league teams had played in Cuba before the turn of the century, and afterward Negro League squads as well as individual black and white pros journeyed south. The 1937 raids on the Negro Leagues by

Dominican teams destroyed the Pittsburgh Crawfords, and other Negro League squads frequently lost their best players and gate attractions to basin teams. From 1939 until the demise of independent black baseball a decade later, Venezuelan and Mexican franchises vied for Negro Leaguers during the summer months, enticing Josh Gibson, Ray Dandridge, and other stars to jump their teams. They offered better pay and a different atmosphere. "Not only do I get more money playing here, but I live like a king," Willie Wells wrote to *Pittsburgh Courier* sportswriter Wendell Smith in 1939 to explain his switch from the Newark Eagles to Vera Cruz. "I am not faced with the racial problem. ... I've found freedom and democracy here, something I never found in the United States. ... Here, in Mexico, I am a man."

The major leagues were less vulnerable to such competition, but even they blanched when Mexican liquor mogul Jorge Pasquel sought major leaguers in addition to Negro Leaguers to bolster the six-team summer Mexican League in 1946. Railroad workers from the States had taught the game to their Mexican colleagues as early as the 1880s and a strong semi-pro league formed in the 1920s. In Sonora and Mexico City, the game felt the pull of baseball across the northern border, which Mexican and black teams frequently crossed. In the Yucatan, baseball pointed more toward the Caribbean, especially Cuba. Pasquel, pumping new capital into the league, persuaded Mickey Owen, Sal Maglie and Max Lanier to desert their major league teams, prompting the latter to ban them. Pasquel also pursued Stan Musial, reportedly placing $50,000 on the bed in his spring-training hotel room at a time when the Cardinals' outfielder was making but $13,000 a season. Other basin leagues also lost top players in the Mexican effort to upgrade. Pasquel's challenge, however, was blunted by Organized Baseball in the States, which tried to limit any competition for its players, and by the Mexican League's own logistical and financial difficulties. The challenge faded after the 1948 season. In the aftermath of the Mexican raids and with integration imminent, major league baseball began to sign accords with professional leagues throughout the basin, formalizing player movement and institutionalizing winter play.

That was especially important, for with the end of the color line in 1947 Latinos soon renewed their assault on major league ball. By the 1970s, the basin would constitute the freshest source of talent in the majors, especially important as the black community turned away from baseball as part of a general shift toward other sports in the United States. But Latin players—black and white— had played pro ball in the United States long before Jackie Robinson's historic debut.

Colombia's Luis Castro broke ground in baseball's modern era, after the creation of the National and American Leagues, but Cubans for the most part led the way. While Castro played only part of the 1902 season, Rafael Almeida and Armando Marsans spearheaded a Cuban invasion in 1911 that left its imprimatur on the game and numbered over 30 players before integration. Another 90 or so Cubans played major league ball after that divide.

The crucial factor controlling the entry of Cubans and other basin players into the major leagues was skin color. Barnstorming their way through black communities from the early century on, Cuban teams had become a mainstay of the Negro leagues that began in 1920. Popular draws, the Cuban Stars and the New York Cubans featured Latinos too dark to pass the color line into the majors. Playing most of their contests on the road, these Caribbean squads injected talent and a tropical allure to the game. Cubans Martin Dihigo, Alejandro Oms, Luis Tiant, Sr., Orestes "Minnie"

Minoso, and Silvio Garcia were joined on these pan-Caribbean aggregations by Dominicans Horacio Martinez and Tetelo Vargas, Puerto Rican Peruchin Cepeda, Panamanian Pat Scantlebury, and sometimes several black North Americans who passed for Cubans. A few Cubans, such as Cristobal Torriente, a powerful outfielder, and Jose de la Caridad Mendez, *"El Diamante Negro,"* who took a no-hitter into the ninth inning the first time he faced the barnstorming Cincinnati Reds, became mainstays of other Negro League franchises.

Lighter-skinned Cubans from that predominantly mixed island played on the other side of sport's racial boundary in the States, in the major leagues. Perhaps the greatest pre-Jackie Robinson Cuban major leaguer was Adolfo Luque, a pitcher whose 20 big league seasons were capped by a brilliant 27-8 record in 1923 and a winning relief stint of shutout ball in the seventh game of the 1933 World Series. Following that game, Clark Griffith, whose Washington Senators had lost the Series, decided to back a scouting expedition to Cuba. He sent Joe Cambria.

"Papa Joe," as many still refer to Cambria, stocked the Senators with Cubans. Among his first signees was Roberto Estalella, from the sugarcane milltown that Hershey Chocolate operated in Cardenas. The *Cincinnati Enquirer* had greeted the signings of Almeida and Marsans in 1911 with relief, introducing them as "two of the purest bars of Castilian soap to ever wash upon our shores," but the darker-hued Estalella was more controversial. No one challenged this indirect breaching of the color line, although it prompted Red Smith to write his classic column in which he suspected that "there was a Senegambian somewhere in the Cuban batpile where Senatorial lumber was seasoned."

The player regarded in the Caribbean as the best Cuban ever, and arguably the finest ballplayer of all time, never played major league ball. Martin Dihigo displayed his talents in Cuba, the United States, Mexico, Venezuela, and the Dominican Republic, and is enshrined in the Halls of Fame of three of these nations. Dihigo excelled at the plate, on the mound, and as a manager, but integration came too late for him. His bust at Havana's *Estadio Latinoamericano* reads simply, *El Immortal.*

The contradiction that some Cubans played in the majors and others in the Negro Leagues was not lost upon blacks in the States or on Latin ballplayers. As early as Almeida's and Marsans' 1911 debut, the African-American press began to hope that black ballplayers would soon follow them into baseball's most exclusive league. And while Negro Leaguers went south to adulation and greater pay, dark-skinned Latinos who came north encountered prejudice based on both skin color and nationality. As major leaguers such as Ty Cobb, Tris Speaker and Carl Hubbell traveled south to play in winter ball, black North Americans and Latinos found that they could more than hold their own. These symbolic victories were appreciated both in the States and throughout the basin. North American blacks and the peoples of the region shared each other's athletes and appropriated each other's sporting heroes and symbols. If a proving ground was necessary to show that blacks could compete with whites, that the two could coexist on the same squad, or to dispel any other racial shibboleth, Caribbean baseball was just that.

Following integration, the more farsighted owners began scouring the islands for prospects. Soon a fresh wave of Latinos arrived in the majors, including three future Hall of Famers: Venezuela's Luis Aparicio, Puerto Rico's Roberto Clemente and the Dominican Republic's Juan Marichal. They signaled, moreover, a

shift away from Cuba as the primary spawning waters for Caribbean players.

With the 1959 Cuban Revolution and the subsequent deterioration of relations with the U.S., Cuba fell out of Organized Baseball's system. The Havana Sugar Kings, an International League franchise affiliated with the Reds since 1954, were on their way to winning the Little World Series of the Triple A minor leagues in 1959, just months after Fidel Castro came to power. The revolutionary government offered to underwrite the Sugar Kings' debts, and Castro sought to keep the franchise there, "even if I have to pitch," but the International League shipped the club to Jersey City during the 1960 season. Baseball in Cuba was cut off completely from baseball in the United States, and the movement of players and equipment halted. Cuba developed its own sporting-goods industry and relied on the repatriated Dihigo, a political exile during the 1950s who had given money to Che Guevara and who now returned to help teach the game. Cuban baseball soon shed its commercial skin and sought instead to advance the social and political aims of the revolution. Cuba has remained the powerhouse in world amateur baseball ever since, but the island stopped producing new major leaguers. After the Zoilo Versalles-Tony Oliva-Tony Perez generation passed out of baseball, the next set of Cubans to reach the majors were those who, while born on the island, had grown up in the United States.

Dominican Dominance

The fulcrum of baseball power, meanwhile, shifted one island to the east, where the Dominican Republic shared Hispaniola with French-speaking, soccer-playing Haiti. After the star-studded 1937 season, pro ball in the Dominican Republic entered a 14-year hiatus. While an occasional tournament celebrated an event such as the nation's centennial, Dominican pros Horacio Martinez and Tetelo Vargas plied their trade in Cuba, Venezuela or the United States. But several forces revitalized Dominican baseball in the 1940s, and after the reappearance of a professional league in 1951, these dynamics propelled over 100 players to the major leagues.

The first catalyst was the birth of the *Mundial,* an international championship tournament for amateur baseball. After its inauguration in England in 1938, the *Mundial* moved to the Caribbean. Held in the basin throughout the 1940s, with Cuba hosting five consecutive tournaments, the *Mundial* had a decidedly Latin flavor and became the most important sporting competition in which these nations competed on something approximating equal footing, both with each other and with the United States. Basin nations won every championship from 1940 through 1972, with Cuba winning 11 out of 18 times.

National aspirations and international rivalries sometimes were injected into the *Mundial.* An irate Anastasio Somoza fired the Nicaraguan manager and took to the dugout to direct the team himself. Nicaraguan national honor was restored by a victory over Cuba in the final game of the 1972 series, an event still celebrated as one of the Central American nation's greatest sporting exploits. The Dominican victory in 1948, coming just months after virtually the entire national championship team perished in a plane crash by the Rio Verde, captivated the Republic and lent impetus to pro ball's rebirth there.

A second factor in Dominican baseball's rejuvenation was the creation of the *Direccion General de Deportes.* Modeled in part after the comparable Cuban agency, this government body organized regional and then national tournaments for amateur baseball (often with semi-professional overtones) that gave further purpose to local, company, and armed forces support. Many of the Dominicans that entered the majors from the late 1950s on, including Marichal, Manuel Mota, and the three Rojas Alou brothers, played on these squads.

The final catalysts to Dominican ascendancy were bananas and sugarcane, and the concentrations of baseball fervor and expertise that they fostered. While the sugarcane milltowns of the southeast produce the most prospects today, the banana region along the northwest border with Haiti was instrumental in cultivating the first contingent of pros in the late 1950s. There the Grenada Company, a United Fruit Company subsidiary, began two teams for its workers and their sons in the 1940s. The squad won three national championships, and Juan Marichal and Guayubin Olivo passed through its ranks to the majors.

Dominican sugarcane milltowns, like those in Cuba, had long given rise to ballclubs. The six-month long *tiempo muerto,* or dead season, when the cane required minimal attention and most workers were unemployed, contributed to an intense sporting environment, first for cricket and ultimately for baseball. In the 1920s and 1930s, *Central La Romana's Papagayo* team was an amateur powerhouse, and in the 1940s the milltowns in and around San Pedro de Macoris made their play. There the descendants of cricket-playing migrants from the British West Indies brought to cut cane and work in the mills displayed an aptitude for playing baseball and an approach to organizing the game that made San Pedro baseball's Mecca. Since Rico Carty's breakthrough in the 1960s, San Pedro has contributed about one-third of the Dominicans to play in the big leagues. The town currently sends more of its native sons to the majors on a per-capita basis than any town ever has. There is probably no other place on earth where the game is played as well and as widely.

Since the end of the color line, ballplayers from Cuba, the Dominican Republic, Venezuela, Puerto Rico, Panama, Nicaragua, Mexico, Colombia, and even the Bahamas have played major league ball. Although the Dominican Republic leads this basin contingent, substantial numbers of Puerto Ricans and Venezuelans are present, too. Mexico, despite a population that dwarfs the rest of the region combined and its well-developed pro leagues, sends few players to the majors. Unlike the other basin leagues, Mexican teams retain first rights to sign any native amateur. A major league club, therefore, must buy the contract from a player's Mexican club, usually for more than it costs to sign a prospect elsewhere in the region. This relationship, the summer Mexican league, and perhaps cultural factors, too, persuade native ballplayers to remain in Mexico.

Cuba opted out of this network after its revolution, and Nicaragua, whose 11-year fling with the pro winter leagues ended in 1967, followed suit after its 1979 revolution. Panama and Colombia have also tried winter ball, but financial pressures made play sporadic.

The flow of players continues to run both north and south. Minor and major leaguers from the U.S. still play in the winter leagues, which currently operate in Venezuela, Puerto Rico, the Dominican Republic, and Mexico. In their heyday during the 1950s and 1960s, these winter leagues featured major leaguers like Tommy Lasorda, Whitey Ford and Willie Stargell. But as major league salaries soared in the 1970s and unfavorable rates of exchanges weakened basin economies, the winter leagues restricted the number of North American imports. Minor leaguers and inex-

perienced major leaguers have replaced them. For them, these leagues provide the chance to play in the winter months, developing the potential that might allow them to crack a big league roster. They also earn higher pay than they do in the minors, encounter competition from top Latino players, and are treated as demigods by the impassioned *fanaticos* of the winter game.

The winners of the winter leagues have met in a *Serie del Caribe* since 1949. Between 1949 and 1960, the pennant-winning squads of Cuba, Panama, Puerto Rico, and Venezuela played in early February to determine a champion of the Caribbean. Cuba won over half of these tournaments, but after the revolution, the series was discontinued. When it resumed in 1970, Mexico and the Dominican Republic replaced Cuba and Panama. The current round-robin format sends the teams that win their postseason tournaments to the *Serie del Caribe* along with a number of reinforcements, including North Americans, from their defeated opponents. Willie Mays, Monte Irvin, Camilo Pasqual, Rico Carty, and Vic Pellot Power are among those who have starred in these postseason celebrations.

Winter ball has descended from its zenith of the 1950s and 1960s largely due to economic dynamics beyond the control of the Caribbean franchises. Rising player and fuel costs, devalued currencies, and underdevelopment pushed many into deficits, with government subsidies often vital to their continuation. Government support, long a feature of basin baseball, helps to keep current the Dominican saying that there will never be political trouble during the baseball season, only afterward. But by the middle of the 1980s, fewer of the established Latin major leaguers suited up for the October-through-January campaign. The demands of the regular season, the threat of injury, and the relatively inconsequential pay of winter ball suggest that this trend will continue. The pattern, however, has given younger Latin ballplayers the chance to play before knowledgeable fans and against competition that is often at a major league level.

Major Accomplishments

Early in the 21st century, the impact of players from the Caribbean basin on major league ball has never been greater. Major league baseball, meanwhile, currently exerts an unprecedented influence on the region's sporting culture and economy. These twin dynamics reflect how much the sport's center of gravity has shifted northward throughout the Western Hemisphere.

The 1997 major league playoffs, which featured a pan-Caribbean array of talent, concluded with the surprising World Series triumph of a team based in Miami, the city often dubbed Latin America's capital. The Florida Marlins won again in 2003. They and the other teams in the playoffs featured an astounding cast of Latin players. These postseason showcases of Latin players reflected a more fundamental shift in the game's demographics. At the start of the 2003 season, Latin players comprised a quarter of all major leaguers, almost three times the proportion of 15 years ago. Latin ballplayers now outnumber African-Americans in the majors. Nor are these players simply filling out rosters. Latin ballplayers are at the forefront of the game's efforts to reinvigorate itself after a decade in which baseball has been subject to ridicule more often than enthusiasm. At recent All-Star games, one third of the players were from Latin America, including Pedro Martinez, Javy Lopez, Sammy Sosa, Ivan Rodriguez, Alex Rodriguez, Vladimir Guerrero, and Albert Pujols.

Major league baseball's demographic transformation is even more advanced at its grassroots, where a greater proportion of

minor leaguers is from the Caribbean basin, about 36 percent in 1998. Given these numbers, the continuing growth of baseball in the Caribbean, and the relative waning of interest in the game among youth in the United States, the size of the Latin cohort will undoubtedly swell during the foreseeable future. If the trickle of Cuban ballplayers fleeing their island to seek their fortunes in the majors becomes a mass exodus, Latins could soon make up one-third or more of major league rosters.

But if ballplayers from the Caribbean basin are recasting the professional game in the United States and Canada, reciprocal influences have been just as profound in the region. Where once the winter leagues mattered most in their respective societies, now major league baseball has become the focal point of fan interest and player development. Major league ball injects substantially more revenue, employs more people and captures much more of the fans' attention than the now diminished winter leagues.

Major leaguers from the Dominican Republic, which spearheads the current Latin contingent to the majors, collectively earn between $200 and $300 million a year, a figure large enough to be included in the country's estimation of its balance of payments. About one-tenth of all major leaguers comes from this nation of 8.5 million people. Only California, with over four times the population, sends more of its sons to the majors. On a per-capita basis, the Dominican Republic is clearly preeminent. Several dozen other Dominicans play professionally in Japan, Korea and Taiwan while over 1,000 labor in the minor leagues, and hundreds more work in non-playing positions for the 30 major league clubs.

Major league baseball penetration, which once took the form of a network of scouts and bird dogs who periodically scoured the region for talent, has acquired a year-round presence, especially in the Dominican Republic and Venezuela. Virtually every major league club maintains a full-time base of operations in these two countries. That presence includes a 32-team Dominican Summer League (DSL) with 35 players on each roster and an eight-team Venezuelan Summer League (VSL) as well as an infrastructure of baseball academies. The DSL and VSL were begun in 1985 and 1997 to circumvent the limit placed on the number of visas granted to major league organizations to bring their foreign-born minor league players to work in the United States. The 30 clubs divide a total of only 865 visas, but those boys signed to contracts who remain outside the United States do not require visas. Most of them, who range in age from 17 to 19, never make it to a minor league camp.

The academies, meanwhile, offer major league organizations a network of training camps for their young Latin players. Since Epy Guerrero developed the first academy, in Villa Mella outside Santo Domingo, in the mid-1980s for the Toronto Blue Jays, and the Los Angeles Dodgers built a state-of-the-art facility in 1987 in Las Palmas, other organizations have followed suit in the Dominican Republic and in Venezuela.

Caribbean baseball's integration into an industry built around major league ball has reached the point where agents from the U.S. are intervening with talented youngsters before they sign their first professional contracts. For decades, major league clubs have been able to sign Latin prospects for signing bonuses of only $3,000 to $5,000. Though often a windfall to the player's family, such a bonus was and remains a pittance compared to those received by youth in the United States, Canada and Puerto Rico, where players are subject to the annual amateur draft. The disparity in signing bonuses allowed major league clubs to adopt a different strategy in

the region, signing far more players for far less money in anticipation that their investment would pay off if only a few emerged from the pack. But as some Latin players and their families have become more sophisticated about the market, they have retained agents. Such representation often greatly boosts a legitimate prospect's signing bonus, although it can cause a club to lose interest in a marginal player. Major league clubs, now sometimes forced to spend a great deal more to acquire players, are understandably appalled at their loss of leverage over boys vulnerable because of naivete, poverty and lack of bargaining clout.

Winter league play, meanwhile, has lost some of its luster. As salaries for major league players skyrocketed, from an average of $51,500 in 1976 to $2.3 million in 2003, the incentive to play winter ball waned. Though the crisis in winter ball has abated somewhat, the caliber of play is not what it once was. Older fans still recall winter baseball's golden ages when it was an important source of income for ballplayers during the off-season and the route that most aspiring North American minor leaguers took to prove they were good enough to play major league ball. Now, young North Americans seeking to break into the majors are more likely to play in the Arizona Fall League than in the Caribbean.

Winter ball, as a result, means less to the people of the region than it once did, while the fate of their countrymen in the majors means more. The national baseball cultures of the Dominican Republic, Mexico, Puerto Rico, Venezuela, Nicaragua, Colombia, and Panama have been overwhelmed by the pull of major league baseball. Even Cuba, which lost its minor league team after the 1959 revolution and subsequently developed its own "amateur" league, one which has dominated international competition ever since, has begun to lose players and the attention of its *fanaticos* to the major league game. The goal of young boys throughout the region is first and foremost to become a major leaguer in the U.S. or Canada. What happens there matters more than what takes place in the Caribbean's respective baseball cultures.

While winter ball will not reprise its golden age in the foreseeable future, and other sports, especially basketball, are making inroads, baseball remains *el rey de deportes* throughout the basin. From the rocky hillsides and arid plains of northern Mexico through the canefields of the islands to the basin's southernmost flank in the Andes, baseball commands a fascination approaching reverence.

Baseball's significance derives from the role that it played in the coming together of these societies in the twentieth century. Knitting a common cultural fabric, serving as a vent to social and political tensions, and offering a vehicle not only for individual mobility but collective social affirmation, baseball indeed has been more than a game. It has offered the citizens of the basin a chance to enter a ritual kinship embracing all fans and players. And while reflecting the progressive penetration of the United States in the region, baseball has been more than a cultural transmission belt for North American values. Beating each other and excelling in the major leagues and international competitions at a time when the Caribbean basin has encountered difficulties in asserting either its political or economic autonomy have been tremendous sources of pride. And that symbolic recognition has become a catalyst to national cohesion and consciousness for the region in its evolution over the past century.

FIRST MAJOR LEAGUERS FROM CARIBBEAN BASIN COUNTRIES

Country	Player	Year	Team
Cuba	Esteban Bellan	1871	Troy Haymakers
	Rafael Almeida	1911	Cincinnati Reds
	Armando Marsans	1911	Cincinnati Reds
Colombia	Luis "Jud" Castro	1902	Philadelphia Athletics
Mexico	Baldomero "Mel" Almada	1933	Boston Red Sox
Venezuela	Alejandro Carrasquel	1939	Washington Senators
Puerto Rico	Hiram Bithorn	1942	Chicago Cubs
Panama	Hector Lopez	1955	Kansas City Athletics
	Humberto Robinson	1955	Milwaukee Braves
Dominican Republic	Osvaldo Virgil	1956	New York Giants
Virgin Islands	Joe Christopher	1959	Pittsburgh Pirates
Nicaragua	Dennis Martinez	1976	Baltimore Orioles
Honduras	Gerald Young	1987	Houston Astros
Curacao	Hensley Meulens	1990	New York Yankees
Belize	Chito Martinez	1991	Baltimore Orioles
Aruba	Gene Kingsale	1996	Baltimore Orioles

SERIE DEL CARIBE

Series	Year	Site	Winning Team/Country
I	1949	Cuba	Almendares/Cuba
II	1950	Puerto Rico	Carta Vieja/Panama
III	1951	Venezuela	Santurce/Puerto Rico
IV	1952	Panama	La Habana/Cuba
V	1953	Cuba	Santurce/Puerto Rico
VI	1954	Puerto Rico	Caguas/Puerto Rico
VII	1955	Venezuela	Santurce/Puerto Rico
VIII	1956	Panama	Cienfuegos/Cuba
IX	1957	Cuba	Marianao/Cuba
X	1958	Puerto Rico	Marianao/Cuba
XI	1959	Venezuela	Almendares/Cuba
XII	1960	Panama	Cienfuegos/Cuba
	1961-69	Not Held	
XIII	1970	Venezuela	Magallanes/Venezuela
XIV	1971	Puerto Rico	Licey/Dominican Republic
XV	1972	Dominican Republic	Ponce/Puerto Rico
XVI	1973	Venezuela	Licey/Dominican Republic
XVII	1974	Mexico	Caguas/Puerto Rico
XVIII	1975	Puerto Rico	Bayamon/Puerto Rico
XIX	1976	Dominican Republic	Hermosillo/Mexico
XX	1977	Venezuela	Licey/Dominican Republic
XXI	1978	Mexico	Mayaguez/Puerto Rico
XXII	1979	Puerto Rico	Magallanes/Venezuela
XXIII	1980	Dominican Republic	Licey/Dominican Republic
	1981	Not Held	
XXIV	1982	Mexico	Caracas/Venezuela
XXV	1983	Venezuela	Arecibo/Puerto Rico
XXVI	1984	Puerto Rico	Zulia/Venezuela
XXVII	1985	Mexico	Licey/Dominican Republic
XXVIII	1986	Venezuela	Mexicali/Mexico
XXIX	1987	Mexico	Caguas/Venezuela
XXX	1988	Dominican Republic	Escogido/Dominican Republic
XXXI	1989	Mazatlan	Zulia/Venezuela
XXXII	1990	Miami	Escogido/Dominican Republic
XXXIII	1991	Miami	Licey/Dominican Republic
XXXIV	1992	Mexico	Mayaguez/Puerto Rico
XXXV	1993	Mexico	Mayaguez/Puerto Rico
XXXVI	1994	Mexico	Licey/Dominican Republic
XXXVII	1995	Puerto Rico	San Juan/Puerto Rico
XXXVIII	1996	Dominican Republic	Culiacan/Mexico
XXXIX	1997	Mexico	Aguilas/Dominican Republic
XL	1998	Venezuela	Aguilas/Dominican Republic
XLI	1999	Puerto Rico	Licey/Dominican Republic
XLII	2000	Dominican Republic	Santurce/Puerto Rico
XLIII	2001	Mexico	Aguilas/Dominican Republic
XLIV	2002	Venezuela	Culiacan/Mexico
XLV	2003	Puerto Rico	Aguilas/Dominican Republic

Chapter 46

Baseball and the Olympics

By David Osinski

Even though it became the 25th sport in the Summer Olympiad as recently as October 13, 1986, Olympic baseball is increasingly facing the kind of hardball that has been played in international political circles for years. After its inclusion in the 1992 Barcelona Olympics, baseball seemed ready to take a prominent position in the Games. At the same time, within the Olympic movement century-old barriers to professionals participating in the Olympics were crumbling, signaling the need for adjustment in all sports.

The International Baseball Association (IBA), a scant eleven years old as of 1986, had been the driving force in achieving Olympic medal status for its 50 million players from some 90 baseball-playing countries. (Only 36 countries were playing baseball when the IBA was formed in 1975 as an amalgamation of two separate international baseball organizations.) In 1995 the IBA member countries find themselves enjoying the warmth of the Olympic family, yet at the same time chafing at some of the family's demands, most particularly the inclusion of professional athletes in the Summer Olympiads. To understand the challenges posed to the international baseball community by this mandate requires a review of Olympic baseball history.

Baseball Competition in the 20th Century

Ever since the very early 1900s, baseball enthusiasts and administrators had lobbied for the sport's inclusion in the Olympics. But it was not until 1984, at the final press conference following the 1984 Summer Olympiad in Los Angeles, that their labors were rewarded, as Juan Antonio Samaranch, International Olympic Committee president, proclaimed his belief that baseball deserved to be the next sport added to the Olympics.

Although there is little corroborative documentation, the report of James E. Sullivan, Olympic Director of the 1904 Olympics held in St. Louis, notes that a baseball competition among amateurs was held in June of that year. Because many other local or regional events were also part of the Olympiad, the competition most probably did not include athletes from any of the other 12 countries that came to the Midwest, and thus did not further international baseball's growth.

The morning of Monday, July 15, 1912, witnessed the first "international" baseball game, under aegis of the Games of the Fifth Olympiad as a team of host Swedes locked horns with members of the U.S. track and field delegation to play the exhibition sport. The six-inning affair ended with the hosts, whose nation had begun to play baseball only two summers before the Stockholm Olympics, on the short end of a 13-3 score.

The following day, an all-U.S. exhibition was held as the U.S. delegation members from the western part of the country bowed to their eastern counterparts by a score of 6-3. Jim Thorpe, the celebrated U.S. amateur athlete and future major leaguer, played right field for the eastern team.

Despite being passed over as a possible exhibition sport during the Olympiads held in Europe during the 1920s, baseball had acquired an international champion by 1936 (it was part of the Central American Championships of 1926). In the 1932 Los Angeles Olympics, baseball lost out to football and lacrosse, but American Leslie Mann, a former major league outfielder, lobbied successfully to stage an exhibition baseball game during the 1936 Berlin Olympics.

While the original intent was to have a U.S. team face a team from Japan, both teams were formed from the Americans who had tried out for the team in Baltimore. The nighttime affair, staged in front of over 90,000 German fans in the principal Olympic venue, saw the "World Champions" edge the "Olympics" by virtue of a seventh-inning blast by Les McNeese breaking a 5-5 tie. Mann had sealed his name in Olympic history as the manager of the teams.

Two years after the Berlin Olympics, the first "World Championship" was held in Great Britain between a team from the U.S. and one from the host country, but the Olympics and baseball parted ways with the world at war, precluding the inclusion of baseball in the scheduled Games in Tokyo for 1940 and London for 1944, neither of which took place.

The U.S. soccer team provided the manpower in the first exhibition baseball game in the 1950s as the U.S. defeated host Finland before some 4,000 enthusiasts in Helsinki. The fact that Finnish baseball, a traditional bat and ball game with the name of *pesapallo,* possesses a pitcher who merely tosses the ball to the batter figured largely in the first inning as the North Americans scored 7 runs, on their way to a 19-1 verdict.

By 1956, when the Melbourne Olympiad was held during the start of Southern Hemisphere summer, baseball was over 60 years old in several parts of Australia, although it was usually played at local clubs only by adults. An exhibition started before track-and-field events on December 1. A team made up of U.S. military men brought to Australia for the exhibition managed an 11-5 spanking of the hosts as more than 114,000 people filled the stands at the Melbourne Cricket Ground for the track-and-field meet. The attendance stands as the record to the present (although it was a hybrid doubleheader, with racing rather than another ballgame concluding the twin bill).

In the winter of 1964, for the first time in Olympic baseball history, representative teams were recruited and prepared to compete. For the U.S., Rod Dedeaux of the University of Southern California, the all-time winningest college coach, created a team of college stars from as far away as Florida, eight of whom eventually played in the majors. On October 11, more than 50,000 baseball fans cheered the host Japanese team. Shawn Fitzmaurice of the University of Notre Dame homered on the first pitch of the game, and the U.S. prevailed, 6-2.

The success in 1964 died aborning after the IOC voted in 1972 to discontinue demonstration sports during the Summer

Olympiad. However, once the 1984 Games were awarded to Los Angeles, the international baseball community rallied with leadership from Dodgers owner Peter O'Malley and future commissioner Peter Ueberroth. With the Dodgers agreeing to host baseball in their stadium and international baseball unified under Dr. Robert E. Smith, who also headed the U.S. Baseball Federation, baseball managed to become a demonstration sport and proved to the IOC members that its contribution was significant.

Ironically the first real baseball series proved disappointing to American fans primed for an easy victory. Although the U.S. had by far the most formidable amateur team ever assembled for an Olympic event and its leader, Rod Dedeaux, once again tutored such future stars such as Will Clark, Mark McGwire and Barry Larkin, Japan's first baseman, Katsumi Hirosawa, broke open a 3-1 game with a three-run home run that insured a 6-3 victory and the gold medal for his team.

Cuba, defending Pan American champion and winner of eight of eleven Pan American titles dating to 1951, boycotted the Games, leaving the Republic of Korea, Italy, Nicaragua, Chinese Taipei, the Dominican Republic, and Canada to round out the two-group competition. For the first time, the Olympic baseball event reflected the sport's essence of daily competition, allowing the best teams to surface and compete for medal-round rewards.

Four years later, real baseball competition returned to the Olympics in Seoul, South Korea, as Smith and the Korean baseball leader Jong Nak Kim lobbied successfully to have the sport played at Chamsil Stadium, directly across the quad from the Olympic track-and-field venue. Defending champion Japan returned to face the U.S., Puerto Rico, the Netherlands, Chinese Taipei, Canada, and Australia. (Cuba repeated its boycott.)

The U.S.'s Jim Abbott turned back the Japanese as he pitched his team to a 5-3 win and the gold medal. Korean fans responded to the competition, but, because of baseball's status as a demonstration sport, ticket sales and national media coverage lagged behind those of the medal sports.

Realization of the Goal

Official status in the Summer Olympiad brings designation of the International Olympics Committee as the sole world governing body for the sport; a seat in ASOIF, the 25-member organization of the summer Olympic sports; and revenues from the Olympiad. Baseball's official inclusion in 1986 allowed the sport to point toward the first tournament that would bring gold medals at the end of the competition.

Host to the Summer Olympics in 1992, Barcelona built a cozy stadium seating 7,000 fans in a country with 6,000 registered baseball players, and Cuba couldn't find a reason not to visit the *madre patria* and compete. The islanders blitzed the competition to capture the gold and remained undefeated in the field made up of host Spain, Puerto Rico, Italy, the Dominican Republic, U.S., Japan, and Chinese Taipei. All activity in Cuba ceased as the population stopped to watch their heroes turn back Chinese Taipei, 13-3, in the final game. The U.S. came home without a medal.

Playing before its countrymen in 1996 at the Atlanta Games, the U.S. baseball team rebounded from a semi-final loss to Japan to win its first official Olympic medal. The U.S. team defeated Nicaragua, 10-3, for the bronze medal. But the real action was in the supercharged finale, as Cuba belted eight home runs—three by Omar Linares—to defeat Japan.

The 27th Summer Olympiad took place in the millennium year of 2000 in Sydney, Australia, just "up the track" from the 1956 version held in Melbourne.

The newest version of Olympic baseball featured continental champions and vice-champions from Europe (the Netherlands and Italy), the Americas (U.S., Cuba), Africa (South Africa), and Asia (Japan and Korea), as well as host Australia, representing Oceania. The seven-game round-robin ended with Cuba and the U.S. at 6-1, Korea and Japan at 4-3, the Netherlands at 3-4, Italy and Australia at 2-5, and South Africa at 1-6. Cuba and the U.S. topped the Asian semi-final opponents, Japan and Korea respectively, and the U.S. shut out the defending Olympic champion Cubans for the gold medal, the first time in the three official Olympic baseball competitions that the Cubans had to settle for silver.

The United States' victorious path resulted from timely pitching performances and miraculous power surges that electrified the average attendance of 14,000 fans at the Sydney Olympic Park. In the opening round-robin game, the first charge sprung off the bat of Mike Neil, who belted a walk-off home run in the 13th inning off Japanese reliever Toshiya Sugiuchi for a 4-2 U.S. win. Neil's drive over the right-field fence capped a close game in which the Nippon team had scored single runs in the eighth and ninth innings to send the game into extra innings.

The U.S. then easily handled the first South African nine to compete in Olympic competition with an 11-1 rout. Although the Springboks won just one game during the competition, their 3-2 victory over the Netherlands kept the Dutch from finishing in a three-way tie for third place in the round-robin.

After defeating the Dutch by a 6-2 score in which the U.S. team led from the outset, the Americans met their match in the Korean national team. Battling through seven scoreless innings, U.S. fireworks erupted as future major league batting star Doug Mientkiewicz jolted the Korean medal hopes with a two-out grand slam homer in the eighth that stood for a 4-0 U.S. win. Mientkiewicz later reminisced, "That was the greatest thrill of my life, something you dream about. To walk up there late in the game, bases loaded, full count, and hit one out of the yard, that's what me and my dad dreamed about when I was a little kid."

The Olympus Gods provided the spark that allowed the Yanks to defeat a determined Italian team 4-2 in the next first-round game. With the score tied in the eighth inning, walks to Neil and to Ernie Young were followed by a throwing error by Italian pitcher Jason Simontacchi, plating the wining runs.

Archrival Cuba shut out the Americans until the ninth inning when two hits resulted in the only run, tarnishing a 6-1 win for the defending Olympic champions. After the Yanks handed host Australia a 12-1 beating the next night, both Cuba and the U.S. finished the round-robin with 6-1 won-lost records.

On a stormy night that interrupted play for two hours, Korea attempted to avenge its heart-wrenching loss to the U.S. in the first round. The semi-final game was tied 2-2 in the seventh when Mientkiewicz managed to shoot a single into right field, setting the stage for a game-tying sacrifice fly. Nothing, however, could prepare the Korean players for Mientkiewicz's sonic blast in the bottom of the ninth inning to break the tie, 3-2, ending the Korean gold-medal hopes and sending the U.S. into the title game against Cuba.

In the bronze-medal game, the Koreans showed great resiliency by rebounding from the two losses to the U.S. and edging their Japanese counterparts, 3-1. The bronze was the first-ever Olympic

baseball medal for the Koreans.

In the gold-medal game Team U.S. coasted to a 4-0 shutout victory over Cuba, the reigning Olympic champion and world champion for the last eight tournaments, dating back to 1982. Future major league pitcher Ben Sheets scattered three hits over nine innings, sealing the gold.

The lineup for the 2004 Summer Olympiad in Greece includes entries from Europe (host Greece, The Netherlands, and Italy), Asia (Japan and Chinese Taipei), the Americas (Cuba and Canada), and Oceania/Africa (the winner of South Africa vs. Australia). That's right, no U.S.—the defending champions were ousted during a huge upset in the qualifying competition.

After finishing 3-0 in its pool in the Americas' qualifying tournament held in Panama City, Panama (October 30 to November 10, 2003), Team U.S. met the Mexican National Team—0-3 in its pool—in a quarterfinal game. Held in check by ex-MLB starter Rigo Beltran, the U.S. players watched as Luis A. Garcia belted a home run in the top of the ninth to give Mexico a 2-1 lead. A U.S. rally in the last half-inning fell short with runners at second and third, thus eliminating the defending Olympic champion from that

tournament, and from advancing to the 28th Summer Olympiad.

Baseball's continuation in the Olympic movement had been challenged during the latter half of 2002, resulting in a vote among International Olympic Committee members in Mexico City that delayed any action regarding the sport's Olympic future until after the 2004 Olympiad. This will be the first Olympiad in which the national team of the United States, the largest consumer of sports television, will not be participating, possibly affecting revenue and IOC members' perceptions related to the viability of Olympic baseball.

International baseball, with 108 playing countries around the world, and professional leagues dotting Asia, the Americas, and Oceania, is healthy. It is greatly reinforced by being part of the Olympic movement, one that nurtures sport during the four years between Summer Olympiads. National sports budgets are allocated depending on results and programs with the Olympics in mind. Coaching courses and athletic scholarships are available through the Olympic Solidarity arm; new baseball countries go first to their National Olympic Committee for start-up funding. Baseball belongs among its peer sports in the Olympic movement.

OLYMPIC BASEBALL RESULTS

1896-1988 not held

1992 Barcelona, Spain
Medal-game results:
Final: Cuba 11, Taiwan 1
Consolation: Japan 8, USA 3
Gold: Cuba
Luis Ulacia Álvarez, Alberto Hernández Pérez, Lazaro Vargas Álvarez, Omar Linares Izquierdo, Germán Mesa Fresneda, Juan Padilla Alfonso, Lourdes Gurriel Delgado, José Estrada González, Osvaldo Fernández Rodríguez, Orlando Hernández Pedroso, Giorge Díaz Loren, Omar Ajete Iglesias, Victor Mesa Martínez, Jorge Valdés Berriel, José Delgado Díez, Rolando Arrojo Ávila, Orestes Kindelan Olivares, Antonio Pacheco Masso, Juan Pérez Rondón, Ermidelio Urrutia Quiroga
Silver: Taiwan
Lin Chao-Huang, Lin Kun-Han, Wang Kuang-Shih, Chen Wei-Chen, Huang Wen-Po, Wu Shih-Hsih, Chang Yaw-Teing, Liao Ming-Hsiung, Lo Kuo-Chong, Huang Chung-Yi, Lo Chen-Jung, Chen Chi-Hsin, Chiang Tai-Chuan, Pai Kun-Hong, Kuo Lee Chien-Fu, Ku Kuo-Chian, Tsai Ming-Hung, Chang Cheng-Hsien, Chang Wen-Chung, Jong Yeu-Jeng
Bronze: Japan
Koichi Oshima, Shigeki Wakaayashi, Masafumi Nishi, Koji Tokunaga, Akihiro Togo, Hirotami Kojima, Hiroki Kokubo, Hiroyuki Sakaguchi, Yasunori Takami, Yasuhiro Sato, Kento Sugiyama, Katsumi Watanabe, Kazutaka Nishiyama, Masahito Kohiyama, Tomohito Ito, Masonori Sugiura, Takashi Miwa, Shinichi Sato, Hiroshi Nakamoto, Shinichiro Kawabata
Also: 4th - USA; 5th - Puerto Rico; 6th - Dominican Republic; 7th - Italy; 8th - Spain

1996 Atlanta, USA
Medal-game results:
Final: Cuba 13, Japan 9
Consolation: USA 10, Nicaragua 3
Gold: Cuba
Luis Ulacia Álvarez, Alberto Hernández Pérez, Eduardo Paret Pérez, Omar Linares Izquierdo, Rey Isaac Vaillant, Juan Padilla Alfonso, Miguel Caldés Luis, Osmani Romero Turcas, Lázaro Vargas Álvarez, Omar Luis Martínez, José Estrada González, Antonio Scull Hernández, Omar Ajete Iglesias, Pedro Luis Lazo Iglesias, Eliecer Montes de Oca Fleites, Juan Manrique García, Orestes Kindelán Olivares, Antonio Pacheco Massó, José Antonio Contreras Camejo, Jorge Fumero

Silver : Japan
Kosuke Fukudome, Masahiro Nojima, Nobuhiko Matsunaka, Makoto Imaoka, Takao Kuwamoto, Tadahito Iguchi, Yasuyuki Saigo, Hideaki Okubo, Daishin Nakamura, Koichi Misawa, Masao Morinaka, Jutaro Kimura, Takeo Kawamura, Hitoshi Ono, Masahiko Mori, Masanori Sugiura, Takashi Kurosu, Takayuki Takabayashi, Tomoaki Sato, Yoshitomo Tani
Bronze: USA
Robert "R. A." Dickey, Warren Morris, Octavio "Augie" Ojeda, Mark Kotsay, Jason Williams, J. Chad Allen, Chad Green, Kiplan Harkrider, Braden Looper, Travis Lee, Andrew "A. J." Hinch, Jacque Jones, Brian Loyd, Troy Glaus, Seth Greisinger, Matthew LeCroy, Kristin Benson, Jim Parque, Jeff Weaver, Billy Koch
Also: 4th – Nicaragua; 5th – Holland; 6th – Italy; 7th – Australia; 8th - Korea

2000 Sydney, Australia
Medal-game results:
Final: USA 4, Cuba 0
Consolation: Korea 3, Japan 1
Gold: USA
Bret Abernathy, Kurt Ainsworth, Pat Borders, Sean Burroughs, John Cotton, Travis Dawkins, Adam Everett, Ryan Franklin, Chris George, Shane Heams, Marcus Jensen, Mike Kinkade, Rick Krivida, Doug Mientkiewicz, Mike Neil, Roy Oswalt, Jon Rauch, Anthony Sanders, Bobby Seay, Ben Sheets, Brad Wilkerson, Todd Williams, Ernie Young, Tim Young
Silver: Cuba
Omar Ajete Iglesia, Yovany Aragon Rodríguez, Miguel Caldés Luis, Danel Castro Muñagorri, José Antonio Contreras Camejo, Yobal Dueñas Martínez, Yasser Gómez Soto, José Ibar Medina, Orestes Kindelán Olivares, Pedro Luis Lazo Iglesias, Omar Linares Izquierdo, Oscar Macías Hernández, Juan Manrique García, Javier Méndez González, Rolando Meriño Betancourt, Germán Mesa Fresneda, Antonio Pacheco Massó, Ariel Pestano Valdes, Gabriel Pierre Rojas, Maels Rodriguez Corrales, Antonio Scull Hernández, Luis Ulacia Álvarez, Lázaro Valle Martell, Norge Luis Vera Peralta
Bronze: Korea
Chong Tae-hyon, Chung Min-tae, Hong Sung-heon, Jang Sung-ho, Jin Pil-jung, Jung Soo-keun, Kim Dong-joo, Kim Han-soo, Kim Ki-tai, Kim Soo-kyung, Kim Tae-gyun, Koo Dae-sung, Lee Byung-kyu, Lee Sung-ho, Lee Seung-ho, Lim Chang-yong, Lim Sun-dong, Park Jae-hong, Park Jin-man, Park Jong-ho, Park Kyung-oan, Park Seok-jin, Son Min-han, Song Jin-woo)
Also: 4th – Japan; 5th – Holland; 6th – Italy; 7th – Australia; 8th – South Africa

Biographies and Team Histories

Luis Aparicio
A nine-time Gold Glove winner, the slick-fielding shortstop led the AL in stolen bases from 1956 through 1964.

FAMOUS FIRSTS

1888: The Washington Nationals become the first major league club to train in Florida.

1920: The New York Yankees become the first baseball team to draw 1 million fans.

1923: Babe Ruth becomes the first player to earn $50,000 in a season.

1947: Cleveland's Larry Doby becomes the first African-American player in the AL.

1953: After 70 years in Boston, the Braves move and play their first game in Milwaukee.

1964: Clete and Ken Boyer become the first brothers to hit home runs in the same World Series game.

1969: Kansas City, Seattle, Montreal and San Diego play their first seasons in the major leagues.

1975: Cleveland hires Frank Robinson as the major leagues' first African-American manager.

1978: The Los Angeles Dodgers become the first team to draw 3 million fans.

1991: The Toronto Blue Jays become the first team to draw 4 million fans.

1991: Roger Clemens becomes the first player to earn $5 million in a season.

1997: Albert Belle earns the first $10 million salary.

Chapter 47

From Babe to Mel ... The Top 100 People in Baseball History

By Alan Schwarz and John Thorn

Picking the 100 Most Important People in baseball history is an inherently personal—and incendiary—enterprise. "Important" can mean so many things to so many people that 10,000 monkeys at 10,000 typewriters might have an easier time of it, though you can bet even they wouldn't finish without a good argument over No. 72.

Importance, of course, is in the eye of the beholder. In the realm of baseball history, it can be found in the sheer skill of a player, in the number of home runs he hit and pennant races he influenced. It can lie in the game's pioneers, the men whose decisions and actions determined how the sport would evolve in its embryonic stages, as well as the more modern executives and innovators who shaped the sport ever since. It can be seen in men like Jackie Robinson and Roberto Clemente, who pried open rosters to new sources of talent but, more enduringly, to an entire nation's reluctant eyes. The candidates go on and on. Heck, to many people, the most important ballplayer ever might be the distant uncle who made the majors—or the hero from their first-ever big league game, the afternoon when they fell in love with baseball forever.

Any list like this is better for the bouillabaisse. But in panning back and examining more than 150 years of baseball, from the day that Alexander Cartwright scribbled out the first rules to the Florida Marlins' 2003 World Series championship, we had to set for ourselves some guidelines. They were:

1. Importance derives from how much baseball, mainly from the fans' perspective, would have evolved differently had that person not existed. Therefore, executives will often rank much higher than many legendary players. Walter O'Malley couldn't hit Bob Feller to save his life, but he had more influence on the game.

2. That influence indeed can come from many directions. While the players serve as the game's pillars, they would topple without the buttresses of people who make the game possible and accessible. This Top 100 tips our cap to several announcers, one ballpark architect, and the mastermind behind the grandfather of the book you're holding now, *The Baseball Encyclopedia*.

3. Though they are increasingly forgotten by each subsequent generation, 19th-century figures had a tremendous role in shaping the game. There was more at stake in 1870 than 1970; an early nudge in one direction or the other, for good or ill, could have sent baseball on a drastically different course.

4. The list attempts to sum up what we believe to be educated opinion, but nonetheless represents our own. We made the choices, while an army of other writers penned the biographies.

Now, a word about No. 1. It came down to two people—Babe Ruth and Jackie Robinson—who ascended above everyone else for reasons about which you soon will read. But choosing between them for the top spot was an excruciating decision, extending beyond baseball to the United States at large. In fact, it was only after recognizing the breadth of the argument that we finally chose Ruth.

Babe Ruth, by virtue of his talent and charisma, carried baseball from the depths of the Black Sox scandal into modern eminence; who changed the mindset of the sport from speed to slugging; and who was, lest we forget, baseball's best all-around talent ever. Jackie Robinson too holds a monumental place in the game's history, a spectacular player who, by virtue of breaking baseball's longstanding color barrier and carrying himself with unwavering mettle afterward, receives credit for helping spark the modern civil-rights movement. Robinson was undoubtedly baseball's most *admirable* person. We see no shame in his being the second-most important ballplayer to baseball; he remains the most important ballplayer to the United States.

We are loath to allow all this talk of No. 1, No. 2 and all the way down to No. 100 to take away from the accomplishments of each and every person on the list—and the nearly 16,000 others that didn't make it, too. They all deserve their place in our memory, which is of course what *Total Baseball* is all about.

Without further ado, here are our picks, followed by fairly full profiles of the top 20 and snapshots of the rest.

THE 100 MOST IMPORTANT PEOPLE IN BASEBALL HISTORY

1. Babe Ruth
2. Jackie Robinson
3. Alexander Cartwright
4. Marvin Miller
5. Branch Rickey
6. Roberto Clemente
7. Henry Chadwick
8. Jim Creighton
9. Kenesaw Mountain Landis
10. George Steinbrenner
11. Joe DiMaggio
12. Hank Aaron
13. John McGraw
14. Connie Mack
15. Walter O'Malley
16. John Montgomery Ward
17. Cal Ripken
18. Mickey Mantle
19. Christy Mathewson
20. Curt Flood

21. Bud Selig
22. Jim Bouton
23. Candy Cummings
24. Satchel Paige
25. Willie Mays
26. Nap Lajoie
27. Barry Bonds
28. Harry & George Wright
29. Ty Cobb
30. Ted Williams
31. Walter Johnson
32. Bruce Sutter
33. Earl Weaver
34. Joe Jackson
35. Judge Bramham
36. Ray Chapman
37. Nolan Ryan
38. Honus Wagner
39. Alex Rodriguez
40. Bill James

41. Sandy Alderson
42. Sol White
43. Red Barber
44. Pete Rose
45. Larry MacPhail
46. Rickey Henderson
47. Greg Maddux
48. Cy Young
49. Peter V. Ueberroth
50. Tony La Russa
51. William Hulbert
52. Ban Johnson
53. Mark McGwire
54. Sammy Sosa
55. Albert Spalding
56. Ichiro Suzuki
57. Reggie Jackson
58. Dan Okrent
59. Rube Foster
60. Luis Aparicio

61. The Spink Family
62. Ozzie Smith
63. Jacob Ruppert
64. Cap Anson
65. Bill Veeck
66. Dizzy Dean
67. Joe Spear
68. Frank Robinson
69. Donald Fehr
70. George Weiss
71. Sadaharu Oh
72. Abner Doubleday
73. Lou Gehrig
74. John Dewan
75. Bill Doak
76. Casey Stengel
77. Rube Waddell
78. Hank Greenberg
79. Miles Wolff
80. King Kelly

81. Livan Hernandez
82. Hal Richman
83. Peter Seitz
84. Ken Griffey Jr.
85. Bob Feller
86. David Neft
87. John Schuerholz
88. Minnie Minoso
89. Harry Caray
90. Dick Young
91. Scott Boras
92. Frank Bancroft
93. Arch Ward
94. Martin Dihigo
95. Roger Kahn
96. Lefty O'Doul
97. Ned Hanlon
98. Whitey Herzog
99. Carl Hubbell
100. Mel Allen

1. BABE RUTH

Babe Ruth was not only the greatest baseball player who ever lived, but the most flamboyant. His gargantuan appetites and prodigious talents, ensconced in an oversized body with a face like that of a bloated Cupid, made him one of the most recognizable figures in American history. In the 1920s his name appeared in print more often than anyone's except the president of the United States. In World War II, when American soldiers shouted "To hell with the Emperor!" at their Japanese counterparts, the Japanese hollered back, "To hell with Babe Ruth!"

Ruth revolutionized the game with his unprecedented slugging. At his death in 1948 he owned 56 major league batting records, plus 10 American League marks. His record of 60 home runs in a single season was not surpassed until Roger Maris hit 61 in 1961. Ruth's lifetime tally of 714 home runs was not bested until 1974, when Henry Aaron hit No. 715 after nearly 3,000 more at bats than Ruth had needed to accomplish the feat. Ruth's average of one home run for every 11.76 at bats was for long the best in major league history.

In addition to his remarkable batting feats, Ruth was the best left-handed pitcher of his era, and might have finished up as one of the best hurlers ever had his hitting not necessitated his change to a position player. Pitching for the Boston Red Sox, he won more than 20 games in both 1917 and 1918; lifetime he was 94–46 for a winning percentage of .671. He led the AL with a 1.75 ERA in 1916; nine of his victories were shutouts, and opponents managed to bat only .201 against him. Over the five-year period from 1915 to 1919 Ruth had a 2.16 ERA. He threw 29-2/3 consecutive scoreless innings in World Series play, another of his records that lasted until 1961.

His legacy went beyond baseball statistics. Because Ruth was well paid by the end of his career, he helped increase salaries for all players. In 1914, as a rookie with Baltimore in the Eastern League, he earned $600, and by 1930 he was up to $80,000. When someone pointed out to Ruth that he was earning $5,000 more than President Herbert Hoover's annual salary, the Babe supposedly replied, "So what? I had a better year than he did."

The Babe Ruth who was merely one of baseball's finest pitchers and the Babe Ruth who would soon become fabled as the game's greatest slugger began to diverge from one another in 1918. That was the season that Ruth's teammate Harry Hooper advised Red Sox manager Ed Barrow to move the Babe to the outfield full time. Barrow's compromise was to have Ruth pitch in 20 games, and play either the outfield or first base in 72 more. Ruth won 13 games, recorded a 2 22 ERA and tied for the AL's home-run crown with 11. The experiment was ruled a success. Ruth moved to the outfield for 111 games in 1919 and made only 17 pitching appearances. That year he exploded for 29 home runs, setting a new major league record. He also led the league in runs, RBIs, on-base percentage, and slugging average.

But the Red Sox finished sixth, and owner Harry Frazee, needing money to invest in a Broadway show, sold Ruth to the Yankees for $125,000 and a $300,000 loan, collateralized by Fenway Park. It's been known ever since as the "Curse of the Bambino." Boston, which had won the World Series with Ruth pitching in 1918 (the franchise's fifth title since 1903), would not claim another world championship for the rest of the century; the Yankees, who had never captured a pennant prior to Ruth's arrival, would become the most successful franchise in baseball history.

In 1920 Ruth hit a mind-boggling 54 home runs, scored 158 runs, and drove in 137. He batted .376, and slugged an incredible .847, a single-season record until Barry Bonds topped it in 2001. The Polo Grounds, which the Yankees shared with the New York Giants, was much friendlier to left-handed long-ball hitters than Fenway Park, and Ruth fell in love with the place. In 1921 he ripped 59 homers, drove in 171 runs, and scored 177 times. The Yankees won the pennant for the first of three straight seasons. Still only 26 years old, Ruth hit his 137th career homer, surpassing Roger Connor's previous lifetime record.

Ruth ushered in a new era of power in baseball, winning back the fans that had been soured by the Black Sox Scandal. But when the Babe tried to capitalize on his fame by organizing an all-star team for a postseason barnstorming tour, Commissioner Kenesaw Mountain Landis, who wanted to establish the World Series as the definitive postseason event, suspended Ruth and teammate Bob Meusel for the first six weeks of the 1922 season. It would prove the first season since 1917 that Ruth did not lead the league in homers; it would happen only once more in the next nine years.

In 1923 Yankee Stadium opened, and sportswriter Fred Lieb dubbed it "The House that Ruth Built." On Opening Day, before 74,200 fans, Ruth provided the Yankees' margin of victory with a three-run homer. That season he led the league in runs, homers, RBIs, walks, slugging, and on-base percentage, just as he had in 1920 and 1921. More importantly, in 1923 the Yankees claimed their first world championship, beating the Giants in the Series after losing the two previous years.

After missing much of the 1925 season due to what was diagnosed as an "intestinal abscess" and a suspension for carousing, the Bambino bounced back in 1926. Ruth and Lou Gehrig set off on a seven-year tear the likes of which the sport had never seen. During that span the duo averaged 84 homers and 303 RBIs a year. In 1927, when Ruth slugged his record 60 home runs, Gehrig added 47; the big first baseman finished second to the Babe in home runs each season from 1927 to 1931.

The Yanks won pennants in 1926, 1927, 1928, and 1932. They swept the World Series in three of those seasons, with Ruth batting .400, .625, and .333 and slugging .800, 1.375, and .733. Game 3 of the 1932 World Series witnessed what has become the Babe's most legendary home run. With the Yankees down, 4-3, in the fifth inning, Ruth came to bat against Cubs pitcher Charlie Root. When Ruth took strike one, he held up one finger to indicate he knew the count. He repeated the gesture on the second strike. With one strike to go, Ruth held up his bat to indicate he had a single strike left—or, depending upon one's interpretation, he pointed to center field to signal where he would send Root's next offering. He then proceeded to slam the ball into the bleachers. The allegedly "called shot" has become an indelible part of baseball lore.

The Yankees did not sign Ruth for 1935. Instead, he was offered a contract with the Boston Braves as player, assistant manager and vice president. The last two were a sham: Boston was only trying to beef up attendance by having the overweight, aging legend around. But Ruth's bat held one more round of fireworks on May 25, 1935, when he homered three times against the Pirates in Pittsburgh. The third blast, over the right-field roof of Forbes Field, was his final major league home run, and it was, typically, a monster shot.

Ruth was one of the five charter members inducted into the Hall of Fame in 1936. He spent the final years of his life waiting for some club to offer him a managerial position; the closest he got was a coaching position with the Brooklyn Dodgers in 1938. When Ruth died of throat cancer in 1948, thousands paid their respects to the great slugger as his body lay in state at Yankee Stadium.

2. JACKIE ROBINSON

One of baseball's most historic moments came in 1947 when Brooklyn's Jackie Robinson became the first African-American player to compete in modern major league baseball. Instead of fanfare, Robinson was greeted with unprecedented hostility, pressure and publicity, but he was buoyed by the knowledge that every one of his fellow African-Americans was counting on him to succeed. The stakes were a lot higher than a pennant race or a batting title. "To do what he did has got to be the most tremendous thing I've ever seen in sports," said Brooklyn teammate Pee Wee Reese, whose gesture of acceptance turned the tide for Robinson the rookie.

Robinson had starred in baseball, football, track, and basketball at Pasadena Junior College and later at UCLA. Alongside Kenny Washington, he nearly took UCLA to the Rose Bowl. He was also All-America in basketball, and he broke a national record for the long jump previously set by his brother, Mack. When his athletic eligibility ended, Robinson left UCLA, got a job with the National Youth Administration, and played briefly with the Honolulu Bears football club.

After World War II broke out, Robinson was accepted at the Army's Officers Candidate School and was commissioned as a second lieutenant. At Fort Riley, Kansas, he was not allowed to play on either the football or baseball team. When the football team was being formed, Robinson was ordered to go home on leave. When the baseball team held tryouts, he was told to audition for the non-white team, only to discover that the team didn't exist. Later, after being sent to Fort Hood, Texas, Robinson was court-martialed for violating Jim Crow statutes. Found innocent, in November 1944 he was given an honorable discharge.

In April 1945 Robinson signed a $450-a-month contract with the Negro American League's Kansas City Monarchs. But he didn't enjoy the barnstorming life and segregated facilities and didn't fit in with his less-educated teammates. Unknown to Robinson, Brooklyn general manager Branch Rickey was hatching a scheme to integrate the major leagues.

The first step of Rickey's master plan was the formation of the six-team United States Baseball League, an ostensibly new Negro League circuit that was to include a franchise called the Brooklyn Brown Dodgers. This enabled Rickey to dispatch scouts to survey black talent without arousing suspicion.

In April 1945, before Robinson heard from Rickey, he was given a tryout by the Boston Red Sox, who ironically were to become the last major league club to integrate. Robinson and fellow Negro Leaguers Sam Jethroe and Marvin Williams were each given a perfunctory trial and a quick brush-off.

On August 27, 1945, Rickey brought Robinson to the Dodgers' offices at 215 Montague Street in Brooklyn. Robinson, who thought Rickey wanted him for the Brown Dodgers, was shocked to learn that the Brooklyn general manager wanted him to sign with the minor league Montreal Royals. But before any deal could be completed, Rickey needed to evaluate Robinson's ability to handle the pressure and abuse that, as a pioneer, he was certain to encounter.

To test Robinson, Rickey observed the ballplayer's responses to a series of hypothetical scenarios, including one in which a white player hurls offensive racial epithets at Robinson and then punches him in the face. Rickey took a mock swing at Robinson, and hollered, "What do you do now, Jackie? What do you do now?" Robinson replied, "I get it, Mr. Rickey. I've got another cheek. I turn the other cheek." That was the answer Rickey wanted to hear.

On October 23 he announced that Robinson had signed a contract with Montreal. (Rickey had intended for others to join Robinson as Brooklyn farmhands but his plan went awry; see "Jackie Robinson's Signing: The Real, Untold Story" by John Thorn and Jules Tygiel on page 569 in this volume.)

Robinson's first appearance in Organized Baseball took place at Jersey City's Roosevelt Stadium on April 18, 1946. In front of a packed house, Robinson went 4-for-5 with a homer, four RBIs, four runs, and two stolen bases. In what was to become his trademark, he defiantly danced away from the base, unnerving Jersey City pitchers into committing two balks.

It was a good start, but the resistance that Rickey had feared soon followed. Syracuse fans taunted Robinson, there was a rumored protest by Baltimore players, and Robinson's two black teammates that year washed out. By the end of the season the exhausted Robinson was a nervous wreck. He was also the International League's batting champion at .349.

Robinson was clearly ready for the big leagues, but Rickey was still playing his cards close to his vest. He sent Robinson to Havana for Dodgers spring training in 1947, at the same time keeping him on the Montreal roster. Rickey was like a chess master, plotting every move and trying to anticipate every countermove.

One countermove he may not have anticipated was a revolt by some of the Dodgers. A number of players, including Dixie Walker, began circulating a petition to present to Rickey stating their opposition to playing with a black man. But Manager Leo Durocher woke the players up late one night for a team meeting and told them to take their petition and stuff it. Rickey arrived the next day and repeated the message. The mutiny was over before it started.

Rickey was not content, however, to have Robinson's teammates merely accept him; he wanted them to want Robinson. In an effort to win the players over, he scheduled seven exhibition games between Montreal and Brooklyn, during which Robinson's .625 batting performance opened a few eyes, to say the least. Still, Robinson's spot in the Dodgers lineup was not announced until five days before Opening Day. Ironically, the news was overshadowed by Durocher's year-long suspension for consorting with gamblers.

On April 15, 1947, before 26,623 Ebbets Field fans, the majority of whom were African-Americans, Robinson played his first major league game. The 28-year-old went hitless that day and struggled for the first weeks of the season. The behavior of several other National League teams didn't help.

The Phillies, under manager Ben Chapman, were so hostile and vicious that they drove Eddie Stanky, a one-time opponent of Robinson, to defend his teammate publicly. In Cincinnati locals made death threats not only against Robinson but also against Reese, his teammate and supporter. A hush fell over the Cincinnati crowd as Reese walked over to Robinson and signaled his support by putting his arm around him. In May, St. Louis management and National League president Ford Frick quashed a threatened strike by Cardinals players.

In June Rickey brought up pitcher Dan Bankhead to room with Robinson. Meanwhile, Robinson had not only started hitting but also began to shake up the entire league with his brash baserunning, daring pitchers to pick him off. With Robinson leading the charge, the Dodgers won the pennant, and he captured both *The Sporting News* and the Baseball Writers Association Rookie of the Year honors. Even Walker, an early opponent of Robinson's signing, admitted, "He is everything Branch Rickey said he was when he came up from Montreal."

Robinson was the sparkplug of the great Dodgers teams of the era. He batted .300 or better six straight years and led the league in 1949 with a .342 average, winning the Most Valuable Player Award in the process.

Robinson had been an "old" rookie—28 in 1947—and for the last few years of his career he was bothered by knee trouble and had problems with Dodgers management. In late 1956 his playing days ended in a swirl of confusion and controversy. He sold a story to *Look* magazine for $50,000 in which he announced his intention to retire. He did not, however, officially inform the Dodgers, and in December they traded him to the New York Giants for journeyman pitcher Dick Littlefield and $30,000.

The Giants offered Robinson $60,000 to stay on, and he considered the offer. But when Dodgers general manager Buzzie Bavasi claimed that the *Look* article had only been a ploy by Robinson to get a bigger contract, Robinson stubbornly decided to prove him wrong. He retired at age 37.

Out of baseball, Robinson busied himself with a variety of interests, including a position with a coffee company and the board chairmanship of Freedom National Bank. In 1962 he was elected to the Hall of Fame in his first year of eligibility.

Robinson grew increasingly ill with diabetes, suffered two heart attacks, and died from the second one at his Stamford, Connecticut, home in 1972. In 1987 the National League Rookie of the Year Award was renamed for him. In 1997, in an unprecedented move, Acting Commissioner Bud Selig ordered that his No. 42 be retired by every major league team.

3. ALEXANDER CARTWRIGHT

His Hall of Fame plaque reads: "Alexander Joy Cartwright Jr. 'Father of Modern Base Ball.' Set bases 90 feet apart. Established nine innings a game and 9 players a team. Organized the Knickerbocker Baseball Club of N.Y. in 1845. Carried baseball to Pacific Coast and Hawaii in pioneer days." Although the three specific accomplishments credited to him on the plaque cannot be attributed to him alone, he was a powerful influence on the game's primal years and represents all the indispensable work of his Knickerbocker club.

According to legend, Abner Doubleday invented baseball in 1839 at Cooperstown, New York, but this story has since been thoroughly disproved. Baseball was never really "invented"; it evolved. Young Americans had played the old English games of base and ball and several American variants since the 1700s. Those games gradually metamorphosed into baseball as we know it today, and Cartwright stood tall in making baseball a "manly" and "scientific" game worthy of adult attention.

Born in New York on April 17, 1820, Cartwright left school at age 16 and entered the business world, as was common in those days. Bright and ambitious, he started as a clerk and soon advanced to a position of responsibility.

After work, Cartwright joined other young New Yorkers to play ball. The group included merchants, lawyers and clerks whose professional status allowed them to leave work in mid-afternoon to enjoy healthy recreation. Common laborers usually had to work until dusk.

According to one early Knickerbocker, Dr. Daniel Lucius Adams, the group's game was called "base ball" rather than rounders or town ball, which in later years were said to have been the direct antecedents of the Knickerbocker, or "New York Game"

of ball. Adams began playing after 1839, when he set up his medical practice in New York. His group was preceded by an earlier association, "the New York Base Ball Club," but according to Adams it had "no definite organization" and did not last long.

Several members of the New York Base Ball Club joined other young men in a new assembly that included Cartwright. In his diary, Cartwright claims to be one of the group's better players. The jovial and gregarious clerk was a leader of the group when it wrote a formal constitution that named it "the Knickerbocker Base Ball Club of September 23, 1845." Cartwright served as secretary and vice president.

Cartwright may have been the first to suggest to his fellow Knickerbockers that they write down the rules of baseball, thereby codifying the regulations members had been following for years. He and three other members defined 14 playing rules, only three of which differed markedly from the rules of rounders.

They laid out the field in a diamond shape rather than a square, introduced the concept of foul territory, and discarded the practice of retiring a runner by hitting him with a thrown ball ("plunking"). These rules were created out of necessity: the diamond and foul territory were suggested by the dimensions of Madison Square, where the Knickerbockers played until 1846, and plunking was eliminated as ungentlemanly and potentially hazardous.

Perhaps more interesting is what the new rules did not include. The bases were not set at 90 feet apart. The length of the game was not set at nine innings, nor were the number of players mandated as nine. Other equally important rules that led to the modern game were also not included by the Knickerbockers. The distance from the pitcher's mound to the plate was not mentioned; the rules did not state that a ball had to be caught on the fly to record an out (the first bounce was good enough); and there was no system of balls and strikes. The only fixed dimension was the 42 paces from home to second base and from third base to first. (For many years this was interpreted as placing the bases very nearly 90 feet apart. However, the size of a "pace" in 1845 was 2-1/2 to 3 feet depending on which authority was consulted. The Knickerbocker bases were only about 75 feet apart if the smaller measurement is used.)

After five or more years of intramural play on Manhattan Island, with their rules in hand and their new playground at the Elysian Fields in Hoboken, the Knickerbockers sought an opponent. On June 19, 1846, they met the New York Nine at the Elysian Fields in what is often called the first modern baseball game. The Nine won, 23-1. The score indicates that the game followed the rules of early ball games, ending after a specific number of runs rather than innings. Although Cartwright was supposedly one of the best Knickerbocker players, he umpired the game and enforced a six-cent fine, payable on the spot, for swearing.

Over the next few years the Knickerbockers rarely played with nine men on a side. More often they had eight men—three outfielders, three infielders, the pitcher, and the catcher—although ten and sometimes as many as twelve players were also used.

Cartwright went to California during the great gold rush of 1849. As he made his way across the Great Plains, he brought a Knickerbocker baseball with him and is said to have taught baseball to anyone willing to play. By August he arrived in San Francisco, too late to strike gold; after only six weeks he gave up and booked passage for New York on a boat taking the Pacific route.

Cartwright became ill and put ashore on the Sandwich Islands, now known as Hawaii. He fell in love with the tropical islands and sent for his family, who joined him in 1851. His interest in baseball

continued, and he established leagues throughout the islands. He prospered in business and died wealthy on September 9, 1892.

The game continued to evolve in New York. In 1849 and 1850 the position of shortstop was created to facilitate relaying outfield throws. D.L. Adams was the first to play at that position. Initially, the position was set between the outfield and the infield, for at that time the ball was so light that few outfielders could throw it all the way to the infield.

Alexander Cartwright's contributions to the game's development might have been forgotten had it not been for Abner Doubleday. In 1938 the Hall of Fame in Cooperstown, New York, was nearly ready to open, and a great deal of the publicity named Doubleday as the game's inventor, following upon a three-year study by the Mills Commission that culminated in "findings" reported in the Spalding Guide of 1908.

This grated on the Cartwright family. Cartwright's grandson Bruce presented the Hall with his grandfather's diaries, clippings, and other paraphernalia that showed how Cartwright and the Knickerbockers had codified the transformation of rounders into baseball, thus rendering the Doubleday tale a fairy tale. But by that time publicity surrounding the Doubleday legend was too widespread for the founders of the Hall to reverse their course. After all, the general's supposed brainstorm was the reason for building the Hall of Fame in Cooperstown in the first place.

Fortunately, no one had to call the Civil War hero a liar. He never claimed to have invented baseball and had been dead for a decade before anyone else asserted that he had. The Hall of Fame wisely chose to downplay the myth, and Doubleday was never elected as Cartwright was in 1939—a de facto rejection of the Doubleday claim.

Cartwright's role in developing the early game in New York and in spreading it across the continent to Hawaii is certainly important. But it is more accurate to view him as a symbol of all those who helped to change the game from an old English diversion and favorite of American schoolboys into our national pastime.

4. MARVIN MILLER

Few men have affected baseball's history more than Marvin Miller. The Players Association executive director for 18 years, Miller led his union in a revolution that forever changed the balance of power between players and owners. "The players have so much power that they should get one more thing done," Manager Paul Richards, Miller's bitter adversary, once said. "They should get Marvin Miller inducted into Cooperstown. That man has taken over." Richards, of course, was being sarcastic. But the irony is that Miller might well be inducted into the Hall of Fame one day. Baseball's establishment failed to see the players' perspective—that Miller only taught the players how to fight and how to win.

Miller was born in Brooklyn on April 14, 1917 and grew up a staunch Dodgers fan. During World War II he served with the War Labor Board and after the war he worked for the U.S. Reconciliation Service of the Labor Department, the International Association of Machinists, and the United Auto Workers before joining the United Steelworkers of America as a staff economist in 1950. Eventually he became their chief economist and a confidant of union presidents Philip Murray and I.W. Abel.

In 1965 Miller weighed job offers from Harvard and the Carnegie Endowment for World Peace. He also considered staying with the union and ultimately running for its presidency. While he was considering his options, representatives from the Players Association, seeking to replace Judge Robert Cannon, asked to meet with him.

Originally major league owners had seen the Players Association as a harmless company union. They even offered to fund its operation. But once Miller took over, all bets were off. After almost 100 years of absolute power the owners were not prepared to cede control. But the shrewd Miller was to turn the owners' arrogance back upon them to devastating effect.

Quickly he took a traditionally anti-union work force and rallied it behind him. "He was able to do it because he was honest and everything he said was the actual truth," Brooks Robinson contended. Miller was also among the smartest men in baseball. He combined a brilliant mind with an uncanny ability to lay out his position in such a logical manner that it seemed impossible to disagree with him.

In 1969 a strike threatened, but it was averted when management conceded to Miller by increasing the pension fund and the minimum major league salary and recognizing the right of players to employ agents. But in 1972 the Players Association staged the first general work stoppage in baseball history, delaying the start of the season for 13 days and forcing the cancellation of 86 regular-season games. The players wanted a 17-percent raise in pension benefits to keep pace with the cost of living since enactment of the last Basic Agreement in 1969 and $500,000 to cover increased health-care benefits. The negotiations stalled.

On March 9 the White Sox became the first club to authorize the union's Executive Board to strike. Through mid-March a strike was unanimously supported. Not until four negative votes were cast by the Red Sox on March 16 did anyone break rank. The final vote was 663-10 in favor of strike authorization, with two abstentions.

Dick Young of the *New York Daily News*, the most influential sports columnist in the country, led the anti-union movement among the media, a movement that split along generational lines. "Ballplayers are no match for him," Young wrote of Miller. "He has a steel trap mind wrapped in a melting butter voice. He runs the players through a high-pressure spray the way an auto goes through a car wash, and that's how they come out, brainwashed. With few exceptions, they follow him blindly, like zombies."

The way the players saw it, Young was as blind as the owners. He refused to acknowledge that times were changing. Miller played devil's advocate with his union whenever a strike was near. He wanted to make sure union members understood the consequences of their actions. Finally a strike was authorized by an Executive Board vote of 47-0 with only the Dodgers' Wes Parker abstaining. Rick Reichardt, the player representative for the White Sox, characterized Miller's behavior during the vote as "very conservative," adding, "the whole tone of the meeting was very professional. He wasn't an instigator."

The strike began on April 1, five days before the start of the regular season. A storm of fan protest greeted the move. The players eventually won an increased management contribution of $490,000 to their benefits plan, plus a transfer of $400,000 in surplus pension funds to improve retirement benefits and maintain their health benefits.

"The real issues were never a question of pension or money," Miller said. "They were more of a question of human dignity." Lost amid the dollar figures in the newspaper stories was a very important concession that had been granted to labor—the right to arbitrate grievances. In just a few years that right would turn baseball on its head.

Coming hard on the heels of baseball's first strike was the U.S. Supreme Court's June 19 ruling in the Curt Flood case. Flood had challenged the reserve clause, which effectively bound a player to his team in perpetuity. By a 5-3 majority, the high court reaffirmed the game's antitrust exemption that kept the reserve clause intact. Yet changes definitely were coming. In 1973 the players won the right to salary arbitration, a huge step for the union.

Then in December of that year arbitrator Peter Seitz voided Catfish Hunter's Oakland contract due to owner Charles Finley's failure to comply with its terms. By itself the decision hardly affected free agency, but the frenzied bidding war that erupted for Hunter's services presaged what would soon come.

The Yankees signed Hunter, one of baseball's best pitchers, to a multi-year deal worth more than $3 million. That opened a lot of eyes, especially on the players' side. They began to understand what they would be worth on the open market.

In December 1975 Seitz let the other shoe drop when he overturned the reserve clause in the Dave McNally and Andy Messersmith cases. The way the owners had always interpreted it, the reserve clause allowed them to renew a contract in perpetuity and thus bind a player to a team for as long as the team wished. In effect, the players contended, they were slaves no matter how high their wages were.

Seitz ruled that the option year in every contract was just that: one option year that could not be renewed unilaterally. Miller was not entirely surprised. In one of Seitz's rulings involving the National Basketball Association, the arbitrator had cited a 1969 California Court of Appeals decision. It had given Rick Barry the right to sign with an American Basketball Association team after playing out his option year with the San Francisco Warriors. The NBA's option clause was an exact duplicate of Organized Baseball's. After Seitz's ruling, the players and owners worked out a new Basic Agreement that gave players the right to free agency after six years, a requirement still in effect.

Miller faced one more great battle. In 1980 owners wanted to institute compensation for teams losing free agents. Players adamantly opposed the owners' plan since it would severely damage the players' negotiating leverage. The first midseason strike in baseball history was barely averted. But a year later on June 11, 1981, with the issue still unresolved, the players struck.

Again public sympathy was hardly with the players, who were now earning a minimum salary of $32,000 a year and an average wage of $193,000. The strike cost the players $28 million in lost wages, and the clubs each lost anywhere from $1.6 million to $7.6 million in revenues. In many cases the losses were offset by the owners' $50 million in strike insurance, which had been purchased at a cost of $2.2 million. Miller, who was making $160,000 a year, did not accept his salary for the duration of the strike.

The strike was settled on July 31, with one-third of the season lost, in a settlement that included complex compensation formulas. Eventually the owners scrapped the formulas because the union had insisted that all teams, not just those signing free agents, had to submit players to the compensation pool. This did not sit well with teams that opted out of the market but still lost a player.

Throughout the years, Miller's chief antagonist was Bowie Kuhn, the game's commissioner from 1969 to 1984. He considered Miller an "old-fashioned, 19th- century trade unionist who hated management generally, and the management of baseball specifically." For his part Miller said of Kuhn, "To paraphrase Voltaire on God, if Bowie Kuhn had never existed, we would have had to invent him."

When Miller retired in 1984 Reggie Jackson said, "Marvin Miller took on the establishment and whipped them. We never would have been free agents without him."

5. BRANCH RICKEY

Branch Rickey was a baseball genius, the greatest front-office man the game has ever known. He was also a sanctimonious, hypocritical cheapskate, a man who would play fast and loose with the rules and go back on his word when it suited him. That he was a successful general manager for 42 consecutive years, for the Browns, Cardinals, Dodgers, and Pirates, becomes almost irrelevant when compared to how much he did to shape the modern baseball landscape.

First, he literally invented the farm system in the early 1920s when he was with the Cardinals. Before that the minor leagues were composed of independent teams that survived by developing and then selling players to the majors.

Second, he integrated baseball. What Rickey did transcended the game and became a significant event in the history of the United States.

Finally, his plans to form a third major league in 1959 convinced the leaders of Major League Baseball that they had to expand. That was the beginning of a sports explosion in this country that continues to this day.

Raised on an Ohio farm, Wesley Branch Rickey coached and played semipro baseball and football to pay his way through Ohio Wesleyan College. A devout Methodist, he kept a promise to his mother that he would not play or work on Sundays. He wouldn't even travel on the Sabbath. Of course, later in his career his teams played on Sundays and he always called the ballpark to check on the day's receipts.

While at Ohio Wesleyan he also coached the baseball team. He had a black first baseman, Charles Thomas, who was refused admission to a South Bend hotel on a trip to play Notre Dame. Rickey finally persuaded hotel management to allow Thomas to share his room. In the room, according to Rickey, Thomas rubbed his hands together and cried to his 21-year-old coach, "Black skin, black skin. If only I could make it white." Years later, Rickey tearfully retold the story and said it was the genesis of his crusade to break the color barrier in the major leagues.

A catcher with a strong arm, Rickey began his professional career in 1903, and after impressing scouts while playing for Dallas he was purchased by the Reds late in the 1904 season. But Reds manager Joe Kelley released him when he learned that Rickey wouldn't play on Sundays. Rickey kicked around with other clubs through 1907 (not counting two cameo at bats with the Browns in 1914).

He began taking law classes at Michigan and in 1911 became the school's baseball coach. After he got his degree and went into practice he also agreed to do some scouting for the Browns. In 1913 Rickey became a full-time employee of the Browns as an executive assistant, and soon after that became their general manager. In the final weeks of the season Bob Hedges gave him the manager's job as well, which Rickey kept through the 1915 season. True to his oath, he stayed home on Sundays, letting a coach handle the team.

His on-field acumen didn't help the Brownies, but his legal background and Michigan connection did. George Sisler had signed a professional contract as an underage high schooler without parental consent, but he had not accepted any money. He then decided to enroll at Michigan. When the pro contract threatened his eligibility, Rickey advised the family to move to invalidate the agreement.

Rickey was thus able to keep the star of his team, and the grateful young Sisler signed with Rickey's Browns when he graduated in 1915—after Rickey convinced club owner Bob Hedges to break a gentlemen's agreement that had earmarked Sisler for the Pirates.

By the time Sisler had become a star for the Browns, Hedges had sold the team to Phil Ball, and Rickey had moved across town to the bankrupt Cardinals as club president. After serving as a major in a World War I chemical warfare unit with Ty Cobb, Christy Mathewson, and Sisler, Rickey returned to the Cardinals as president and, saving a $10,000 salary, as field manager. After the club finished seventh in 1919 while teetering on the verge of bankruptcy, Sam Breadon bought 72 percent of the stock. Rickey owned the rest.

Breadon demoted Rickey to vice president but allowed him to continue as field manager. About that time Rickey developed his farm system plan—out of necessity. The Cardinals could not afford to compete with other teams to purchase top talent from independent minor league teams. Rickey had to devise a method of acquiring teams. He had to establish a system of tracking and evaluating players in every organization in the majors. He had to hire a network of scouts and organize tryout camps. He also had to develop an organization-wide teaching system. It was a task perfectly suited to Rickey's energy and intellect, and one he was able to carry out even though he was still the field manager. When he was done, the Cardinals farm system included 33 teams. In contrast, each major league franchise today operates only five or six minor league teams.

By 1942 Rickey's contract was up in St. Louis. He was fed up with Breadon, and vice versa. No one really knows if he was fired or if he quit, but he moved over to the Dodgers without missing a beat. Rickey protégé Larry MacPhail was leaving the Dodgers club after building it into a contender, so Brooklyn hired Rickey as president and general manager. He also bought 25 percent of the team.

Rickey could now move ahead with his plans to integrate baseball. By the end of World War II Rickey sensed the timing was right. He also knew it was a smart move. More and more teams were starting to copy his farm system, and he wanted, as always, to stay a step ahead of the competition. And unlike Bill Veeck, who integrated the American League when he signed Larry Doby in 1947, Rickey never paid a Negro League team for a player, knowing Negro League owners would not want to be blamed for delaying the end of the color barrier.

Rickey's expansion machinations began in the spring of 1945, when he announced the formation of the Brooklyn Brown Dodgers to play in a new United States Baseball League and dispatched scouts to search the Negro Leagues for talent. However, the Brown Dodgers and USBL were a scam designed to hide Rickey's real purpose—the integration of the established major leagues.

On October 23, 1945, with the approval of his Dodgers partners, Rickey signed Jackie Robinson. After a brilliant 1946 season in Montreal, Robinson joined the Dodgers in 1947 and was an immediate star. Rickey's Dodgers thus got the jump on the rest of baseball, signing such black stars as pitcher Don Newcombe, catcher Roy Campanella, pitcher Joe Black, and second baseman Jim "Junior" Gilliam. As a result, between 1947 and 1956 the Dodgers won seven pennants in 10 years.

Rickey, however, did not last long enough in Brooklyn to enjoy all the fruits of his labors. Walter O'Malley, one of Rickey's partners, wanted control of the team and after the 1950 season led a boardroom coup that forced Rickey out. Rickey, however, cried all the way to the bank because a clause in his contract forced the Dodgers to match the highest bid for his stock if he was not rehired. Rickey produced a $1.25-million offer, more than double O'Malley's estimate of the stock's value. O'Malley went to his grave believing the offer was a phony.

Rickey moved on to Pittsburgh, laying the foundation for the 1960 Pirates team that won the World Series. His greatest coup with the Pirates was drafting Roberto Clemente from the Dodgers, who were trying to hide him in the minors by not playing him regularly.

Rickey's last venture was the Continental League, his response to the majors' repeated refusal to expand beyond 16 teams. One of his fellow "owners" was Joan Payson, who eventually acquired the expansion New York Mets franchise. Rickey was 77 by then, but his involvement in the proposed new league, which presaged the American Football League, the American Basketball Association, and the World Hockey League, was enough to put the fear of God into the major leagues. By 1961 Organized Baseball initiated an expansion program that has since nearly doubled the number of major league teams.

Rickey died in 1965, less than two weeks before his 84th birthday. He was inducted into the Hall of Fame in 1967.

6. ROBERTO CLEMENTE

Roberto Clemente Walker played the game as if it were his and his alone. His haughty stance at the plate, the way he snared flyballs, and the way he slung the ball from right field to third base were all unique. He won four batting titles and a dozen Gold Gloves. But it is not his on-field exploits that place him this high among our Top 100. As Jackie Robinson broke a barrier for African-Americans, Clemente was and remains a beacon for generations of Latin American boys who dream of playing baseball on the big stage. (Fernando Valenzuela may likewise inspire future generations of Mexican lads.)

As a youth in Puerto Rico, Clemente sneaked peeks at his favorite player, Monte Irvin, through the outfield fence. As a teenager he played in the same Puerto Rico winter league outfield with Willie Mays, and the scouts took notice. The Dodgers signed him for $10,000, although he received offers nearly three times that after agreeing to the contract. A rule at the time stated that Clemente could be drafted by any team for $4,000 if he wasn't brought up to the majors. Yet the Dodgers sent him to their Triple A farm club in Montreal, where Clemente felt he was treated oddly. The Dodgers were trying to hide him from the Giants, but this was never explained to him, and he was so hurt and confused by the way he was handled that he thought of quitting. He recalled, "If I struck out I stayed in the lineup. If I played well I was benched. One day I hit three triples and was benched the next day. Another game I was taken out for a pinch hitter in the first inning with the bases loaded."

After this disappointing first season Clemente returned to Puerto Rico. While he was visiting his brother, who was dying of a brain tumor, a drunk driver plowed into his car. The crash damaged three spinal discs, an injury that would plague Clemente for the rest of his career.

When the last-place Pirates met after the 1954 season to discuss who they should draft first, Clyde Sukeforth said to Pittsburgh general manager Branch Rickey, who had also been his boss in Brooklyn, "You will never live long enough to draft a boy with this kind of ability for $4,000 again."

During his first two seasons as the Pirates' right fielder Roberto Clemente gunned down 18 and 20 runners, respectively, on the

bases. In his second year he hit .311. Clemente, and all of Pittsburgh, had a terrific year in 1960. He hit 16 homers and batted .314, and his 94 RBIs led the team as they shocked baseball by upsetting the powerful Yankees in the World Series.

Always a proud man, Clemente took it hard when he got the news that he had only finished eighth in the 1960 Most Valuable Player voting. It pushed him to try even harder. The next season Clemente changed his bat. To avoid over-swinging on bad balls he began to use heavier lumber and went on to enjoy 11 .300-plus seasons in the next 12 years. He won his first batting title in 1961, hitting .351 with 23 homers, 10 triples, and 89 RBIs.

That year Clemente missed the last five games of the season because a Don Drysdale fastball had chipped a bone in his right elbow, requiring off-season surgery. Because of the aggressive way he played, he suffered numerous other injuries. Unlike other players who declined to speak about their physical problems, Clemente discussed his aches and pains with anyone who asked. ("My bad shoulder feels good, but my good shoulder feels bad," he once said.) His constant complaining about aches and pains didn't sit well with Pittsburgh sportswriters, who accused him of being a hypochondriac, overlooking the fact that Clemente played more than 140 games for eight seasons in a row.

In 1964 and 1965 he won batting titles again, but the Pirates felt he wasn't providing as much power as he could. Manager Harry "the Hat" Walker asked him to swing for the fences more often. Clemente responded by belting 29 homers and driving in 119 runs in 1966, although his batting average fell a dozen points to .317.

His defensive abilities never suffered. In one game, in a bases-loaded situation, a batter lined an apparent single to right. The runner on third didn't see any need to hustle home; Clemente fired a strike to the catcher for a stunning force-out. Clemente won the league's Most Valuable Player Award in 1966, and he felt that the injustice of 1960 had been rectified.

He suddenly became more open, eagerly taking the reins of leadership in the clubhouse. If a young Pirate had a problem, Clemente discussed it quietly. Manager Walker failed to get new Pirate Matty Alou to quit pulling every pitch and use a heavier bat, but Clemente spoke to Alou. The newcomer responded with a 111-point increase in his batting average and won the league batting title.

With the arrival of rookies Manny Sanguillen, Richie Hebner, and Al Oliver in 1969, Clemente's role as a leader became even more valuable. From 1969 through 1971 Clemente hit .345, .352, and .341. The Pirates honored him in 1970 at their new Three Rivers Stadium. Puerto Rican fans, who by now viewed him as a demigod, delivered a scroll signed by 300,000 people in Puerto Rico (roughly 10 percent of the island's population).

More than 43,000 fans showed up for the festivities and game, which the Bucs won, 11-0. Clemente obligingly had two hits and made a great catch of a Joe Morgan line drive. He also made a running, diving grab of a foul popup by Denis Menke that meant absolutely nothing to the outcome of the game and tore his knee open in the process. "It's the only way I know how to play baseball," he explained.

His intensity and skill received their finest showcase in 1971. The Pirates knocked off the Giants in the 1971 National League Championship Series, with Clemente hitting .333 and driving in four runs. In the World Series against the favored Baltimore Orioles, Clemente hit in all seven games, batting .414 and slugging .759. Writer Roger Angell said, "Clemente played a kind of baseball that none of us had ever seen before—throwing and running

and hitting at something close to the level of absolute perfection."

Clemente would never scale such heights again. Injuries allowed him to play in only 102 games in 1972, but he still hit .312. His double off the Mets' Jon Matlack on September 30 was his 3,000th hit. The Pirates again made it to the NLCS but lost on Bob Moose's wild pitch in the ninth inning of the final game.

In late December of that year a devastating earthquake struck Nicaragua. More than 6,000 people were killed, 20,000 injured, and tens of thousands left homeless. Clemente raised money and other contributions to help the survivors. As always, he was tireless, pleading for donations personally, negotiating discounts with airlines for transporting the materials, and packing and loading boxes for shipment. While Puerto Rico celebrated the holidays, Clemente was working 16-hour days to see that earthquake victims received what they needed.

After hearing that some of the supplies sent to Nicaragua were not getting to the right people, Clemente decided to take matters into his own hands. He decided to fly to Nicaragua in a cargo plane and make sure that distribution was carried out properly. On New Year's Eve he boarded an overloaded DC-7 that he had rented for $4,000 to fly to Nicaragua. The plane crashed into the ocean shortly after takeoff.

New Year's Day was to have been a day of great celebration in Puerto Rico, with a new governor being inaugurated. Instead, the inaugural festivities were canceled, and the entire Pirates team flew to Puerto Rico for the funeral.

The Hall of Fame waived the five-year wait between last playing appearance and eligibility for Clemente, as it had done earlier for Lou Gehrig. The first Latin player so honored, he was inducted into the Hall of Fame on the same day as his boyhood idol, Monte Irvin. In 1971 the Commissioner's Office had started an annual award to the player who best exemplified baseball on and off the field; in 1973 it was renamed the Roberto Clemente Award.

More than 20 years after his death, a video about Clemente on the Three Rivers Stadium scoreboard produced instant, awestruck silence, followed by respectful applause and cheers touched with sadness. A statue of him was unveiled at Three Rivers Stadium at the 1994 All-Star Game. He had said in the late 1960s, "If you have an opportunity to make things better and you don't, then you are wasting your time on this earth."

7. HENRY CHADWICK

Having played cricket and rounders in his native England, Chadwick came to America with his family in 1837 at age 13. He first played baseball in 1847 and pronounced it a descendant of the earlier English games. When nearly a decade later he first saw games between skilled players, he recognized baseball's potential to become America's national game. His writings and influence helped make that potential a fact.

Chadwick began his reporting career with the *Long Island Star* in 1844. In the late 1850s, he began covering baseball games as a reporter for several newspapers, most notably the *New York Clipper* and the *Brooklyn Eagle*. In connection with this, he developed the box score and devised a system of scoring that is little changed today, although he borrowed many aspects of the system from fellow sportswriter M.J. Kelly. In his devotion to making baseball a "scientific" game, he devised new measures of player performance, championed those invented by others, and created the statistical underpinnings that bind the game's present to its past while providing a roadmap for understanding how teams succeed or fail.

Chadwick influenced the development of playing rules, game strategies, scoring practices, and even the moral tone of the game. Most important, though, was his relentless promotion of baseball as the national pastime, a game that would be a tonic for America as cricket surely was Great Britain.

Chadwick continued to write and comment on baseball for more than 50 years. He originated the first guide, *Beadle's Dime Baseball Player*, in 1860, and edited *DeWitt's Guide* through the 1870s and *Spalding's Base Ball Guide* from 1881 to 1908. His *The Game of Base Ball* (1868) was the first hardcover book published on the subject.

Widely influential for his writings, he also had a direct influence in shaping the game by serving on various rules committees, beginning in 1858. He opposed gambling, drunkenness, and rowdiness among players, sometimes to no avail. Chadwick considered himself one of "the intelligent majority" who preferred scientific hitting over slugging, and fielding prowess above all.

Chadwick did not win all his battles. He opposed professionalism among players, and chastised the National Association when it decided to pay umpires. He opposed creation of the National League, writing that the latter was "a sad blunder." But he took on owners and players with equal gusto. In his most enduring squabble, he traced baseball's origins to the English game of rounders, rejecting the jingoistic notion that it sprang into life fully formed on native soil. He gave credit to the Knickerbockers as the game's true pioneers, but held fast to his belief that the game migrated to America from England. A long-standing friendly argument with nativist Albert G. Spalding over baseball's origins prompted Spalding to form a commission to look into the matter. Headed by former NL president Abraham G. Mills, it concluded in the *Spalding Guide* of 1908 that the game had been invented in Cooperstown by Civil War hero Abner Doubleday.

Chadwick—more the "Father of Baseball" than Doubleday and as much as any man—died from pneumonia in 1908 after attending Opening Day in Brooklyn. Flags around the league flew at half-staff in his honor. In 1938 he was named to the Hall of Fame; he remains the only writer honored not in a separate exhibit but with his own plaque.

8. JIM CREIGHTON

Jim Creighton was baseball's first national star, probably its first professional, and its first martyr. He was the greatest hitter of his time, and his pitching revolutionized the game. Remarkably, he accomplished all this by the age of 21.

In 1857, at the age of 16, Creighton helped to organize a neighborhood team, the Young America Base Ball Club. The next year, he and his friend George Flanley founded the Niagara Club. Creighton played both second and third base. In the ninth inning of a game between the Niagaras and the Brooklyn Stars, perhaps the best junior team in the area, he took over the pitching duties with his team well behind. From that moment on, baseball was never the same.

According to the existing rules, the ball was supposed to be "pitched"—that is, delivered with a stiff-armed, locked-wrist, underhand motion, much like a bowler's delivery. Throwing the ball was illegal, the calling of balls and strikes was still in the future, and the pitcher's task was simply to deliver the ball to the batter so that he could hit it. A kind of partnership developed between the pitcher and the batter. As the game grew more competitive, pitchers tried to make batters hit the ball to a location where it

would produce an out. But the rules of the day, which limited pitchers to pitching underhanded, left them with few options. Most pitchers tried to keep the ball away from the batter, hoping that frustration would lead to a swing at a "bad" pitch. Consequently, with no bases on balls awarded to limit an at bat, some batters stayed at the plate for up to 15 minutes.

That changed when Creighton became a pitcher. According to an eyewitness account, "When Creighton got to work something new was seen in base ball—a low, swift delivery, the ball rising from the ground past the shoulder to the catcher. The Stars soon saw they could not cope with such pitching." Creighton was responsible for several important innovations. He threw much faster than other pitchers did, and because there was no mound the ball's trajectory was nearly horizontal, as opposed to the arcing lobs batters expected. Also, he put spin on the ball in such a way that his fast pitches hopped or darted as they approached the plate. These inventions changed the face of baseball.

As Creighton's reputation grew, some claimed that he could make the ball dip, rise, or sail at will. A few historians have even suggested that he was the first man to throw a curveball, but if he did it was probably not intentional.

How did Creighton come up with such a revolutionary pitching style? He cheated. As he brought his long right arm around he imparted an almost imperceptible, and completely illegal, wrist snap. Although the ball was still being hurled underhand, Creighton was throwing it instead of pitching it like a horseshoe.

The new style sparked a great deal of controversy. Purists correctly insisted that Creighton's tosses were illegal. Other pitchers studied Creighton, trying to imitate him. Fans were excited by the way he threw. The game moved faster and was more interesting. Umpires maintained that they saw nothing illegal. When Henry Chadwick, the era's most influential baseball writer, commended Creighton for his "head work," the battle was over and the groundwork laid for the game as we know it today: a mortal struggle between pitcher and batter.

After his pitching performance against the Stars, Creighton was recruited for their team. In 1859 he jumped to the top-flight Brooklyn Excelsiors (almost certainly in exchange for under-the-table "emoluments") and traveled with them throughout the East in 1860 and 1861. With Creighton as their star they regularly won games by such inflated margins as 51-6 and 45-16. Not only did Creighton pitch and usually win every game, he went the entire 1860 season with an unparalleled average of zero in the outs-per-game category (which in those rudimentary days of statistical accounting meant that his number of games played exceeded the times he hit into outs). He was also an excellent fielder; and on top of all his baseball accomplishments, he was America's top young cricket player.

Batters eventually learned how to hit Creighton's offerings, and it soon became clear that mere speed on the pitch was not enough. Even though the balls were delivered from only 45 feet away, the best batters managed to get around on the pitches. To counter this Creighton developed the ability to change speeds, just as other pitchers of his day were learning to do.

No one knows how much the Excelsiors secretly paid their "amateur" pitching star, but today Creighton is generally considered to have been the first professional ballplayer. He became famous, and large crowds turned out to see him perform. Young players tried to duplicate his style. Teams even adopted his name. Decades later, fans who had seen him pitch would remark that while stars such as Charley Radbourn and Tim Keefe were good

pitchers, they weren't Creightons.

In late 1862, in a game between the Excelsiors and the Unions of Morrisania, a Westchester County team (Morrisania is today a neighborhood in the Bronx, and thus part of New York City), Creighton smashed a home run. As he swung, he heard something pop. Circling the bases, he remarked to George Flanley as he crossed the plate, "I must have snapped my belt." Then he collapsed. After several days of internal hemorrhaging he died on October 18, 1862, five months shy of his 22nd birthday.

Creighton's grief-stricken teammates erected a tall granite monument over his grave in Brooklyn's Greenwood Cemetery. Carved on it are crossed bats, a base, a cap, a shoe, and a scorebook. A large stone baseball rests on top. The baseball has worn away over time, but the memorial to baseball's first star remains a shrine for baseball antiquarians. (For more about Creighton, see "The First Great Pitcher," by John Thorn on page 51 in this volume.)

9. KENESAW MOUNTAIN LANDIS

Baseball's first commissioner, the flinty, colorful, and often arbitrary Judge Kenesaw Mountain Landis took control of the game when its integrity was in question. When he died nearly a quarter of a century later, baseball's name had long since been restored.

Landis was the son of Dr. Abraham Landis, who had lost the use of his leg in the Civil War battle of Kennesaw Mountain in northwest Georgia. At his son's birth on November 20, 1866, Dr. Landis suggested they call him "Kenesaw Mountain." The name and the misspelling stuck.

His early career gave little indication of the heights Landis would later reach. A high-school dropout, his first ambition was to be a brakeman on the Vandalia and Southern Railroad, but the company's officials rejected his application. The diminutive Landis won some fame as a bicycle racer at various Indiana fairgrounds and operated a roller-skating rink before moving to journalism. While covering court cases for Indiana's *Logansport Journal*, he decided to become a lawyer and enrolled in the YMCA Law School of Cincinnati. In 1891 Landis obtained his degree from Chicago's Union Law School.

Two of his brothers, Charles and Frederick, were Indiana congressmen. In part through their auspices, while still in his 20s Landis sat in on cabinet meetings representing the State Department. Appointed to the federal judiciary by Theodore Roosevelt, Landis quickly earned a reputation for quirky and newsworthy justice.

He fined Standard Oil $29,240,000, a record penalty at that time. He jailed Industrial Workers of the World members and Socialist Congressman Victor Berger for antiwar activities during World War I. Those cases and others placed him squarely in the public eye, even though his decisions were often overturned.

In one fiery wartime speech Landis demanded that Kaiser Wilhelm II, his six sons, and 5,000 German militarists be "lined up against a wall and shot down in justice to the world and to Germany." Many thought him a mere grandstander. "His career typifies the heights to which dramatic talent may carry a man in America if only he has the foresight not to go on the stage," said Heywood Broun.

But Organized Baseball had a high opinion of Landis. During the Federal League war he had done the baseball establishment a great service. The existing major leagues had faced a stiff challenge from the Federal League, both on the field and in the courts, as the upstart circuit sought to overturn baseball's reserve clause. Landis heard the case within a month, and the owners of the established leagues held their breath.

But then Landis firmly sat on the case. Months passed and he issued no decision. It was obvious he didn't want to issue one, because he knew what a flimsy legal structure baseball was built upon. "Both sides must understand that any blows at this thing called baseball would be regarded by this court as a blow to a national institution," Landis had warned from the bench.

Finally, the Federal League threw in the towel, getting the best deal they could from Organized Baseball. Landis' inaction had been the key. "Many persons felt that Landis had saved baseball in 1915," wrote J.G. Taylor Spink of *The Sporting News*. "Had he ruled Organized Baseball to be a gigantic trust, the Federal League contention, he could have thrown the whole game into chaos. There would have been no sanctity of baseball territory. Had he decided against the legality of the reserve and 10-day clauses, the effect would have been free agencies for all the great players of the time."

Landis had saved the owners' hides and they knew it. When the 1919 World Series fix became public knowledge in September 1920, they needed someone to restore confidence in the badly shaken institution. Game fixing and gambling had been pervasive in the game since the 1860s, with only an occasional scandal becoming public record (such as the 1877 "Louisville Crooks" swindle that nearly tore apart the National League, or Hal Chase's all-too-open collusion with gamblers in the 1910s). Landis was an obvious choice. He demanded absolute power and got it.

Will Rogers once remarked, "The game needed a touch of class and distinction, and somebody said, 'Get that old guy who sits behind first base all the time. He's out here every day anyway.' So they offered him a season pass and he grabbed it."

In the summer of 1921 the accused "Black Sox" were acquitted under highly questionable circumstances. Long used to having his decisions overturned by higher courts, Landis, as commissioner of baseball, returned the favor and reversed the jury's decision. "Regardless of the outcome of juries," he said, "no player that throws a ball game, no player that entertains proposals or promises to throw a game, no player that sits in a conference with a bunch of crooked players where the ways and means of throwing games are discussed, and does not promptly tell his club about it, will ever again play professional baseball."

Old and new scandals continued to plague baseball for the first few years of Landis' tenure. Youthful Giants outfielder Jimmy O'Connell and Giants coach Cozy Dolan were banned from the game following a failed bribe attempt. Frankie Frisch, Ross Youngs, and George Kelly were implicated but cleared by Landis. Phil Douglas was also banned after offering to throw a game. Outfielder Benny Kauff was blacklisted for implication in an auto-theft ring; as in the Black Sox scandal, Landis ignored the verdict of a jury, this time with what many critics felt was far less justification.

Landis was a headstrong, autocratic czar. *Current Biography* termed him "the only successful dictator in United States history." But Organized Baseball already had a dictator in American League president Ban Johnson. Johnson was by no means ready to relinquish the hold he had on the game. Throughout the early 1920s Landis consolidated power at the expense of his rival. The proud Johnson was left humiliated and stripped of real authority.

The last great scandal of Landis' tenure involved the biggest names in baseball—Ty Cobb and Tris Speaker. In 1926 pitcher Dutch Leonard accused the two stars of conspiring to fix the last game of the 1919 season. Leonard also accused Smokey Joe Wood of placing bets on the contest for Cobb and Speaker. Landis' ver-

dict exonerating the accused trio has come under heavy criticism from some historians.

Landis was a staunch opponent of Branch Rickey's minor league farm system and fought it tooth and nail. "It will be the ruination of the individual minor league club owners," he declared. He liberated numerous minor league players during his term in office. In one 1938 case, the commissioner freed 91 Cardinals farmhands, including Pete Reiser and Skeeter Webb. In January 1940 he hit the Detroit system, freeing scores of players and costing the Tigers an estimated $500,000.

One of Landis' most important personnel decisions came on December 10, 1936, when he awarded young Bob Feller's contract to Cleveland. Another significant decision involved the freeing of Tommy Henrich from the Indians' system in April 1937. Henrich was able to sign with the Yankees for a $25,000 bonus.

Landis' assumption of control over all World Series decisions, his well-publicized disciplining and suspension of Babe Ruth after the 1921 Series, and his removal of Cardinals outfielder Joe Medwick from the field in the riotous seventh game of the 1934 World Series all created headlines.

World War II threatened to interrupt Major League Baseball, but Landis indirectly obtained President Franklin Roosevelt's green light to continue the national pastime. His last major move was in 1943 when he banned Phillies owner William D. Cox from the game for gambling.

It was not until Landis died that Major League Baseball club owners finally integrated their teams. Many have contended that this was no coincidence. One oft-told tale contended that Landis scuttled Bill Veeck's plan to buy and integrate the Phillies. Recent scholarship has largely debunked that story.

Just before Landis died on November 25, 1944, his contract was extended to January 1953, when he would have been 86 years old. Such was the hold of Judge Landis on baseball that, even as frail as he was, no one dared oppose him.

Shortly after he died, Landis was voted into the Hall of Fame. Despite his faults, he was passionately devoted to baseball and to preserving its integrity. "Baseball is something more than a game to an American boy," he declared. "It is his training field for life work. Destroy his faith in its squareness and honesty and you have destroyed something more; you have planted suspicion of all things in his heart."

10. GEORGE STEINBRENNER

Since 1973 George Steinbrenner, the brash, bullying owner of the Yankees, has sided firmly with the long tradition of meddling management who can't keep their hands off the baseball team. And, true to his character, he has meddled more than anyone else. Everything Steinbrenner does he does to excess. He is truly a Yankee Doodle Dandy, born on the Fourth of July in 1930.

Love him or hate him, his influence on the game has been pervasive and undeniable. The first owner to grasp not only the perils but also the opportunities of free agency, Steinbrenner stands first among owners in driving up player salaries as he restored the Yankees to their accustomed perch atop the baseball world after the dismal CBS years. He spent millions more than other owners on free agents (beginning with Catfish Hunter in 1975 and Reggie Jackson in 1977) because he made more millions—not at the gate, necessarily, but through lucrative, smartly negotiated media alliances.

Steinbrenner put together a money-generating empire that begins and ends with the Yankees' coveted logo. His tactics, however

unnerving, have borne fruit. His Yanks of the late 1970s and early 1980s won five division titles in a six-year span. The juggernaut clubs of the late 1990s were not dissimilar from the other Yankees teams that dominated baseball throughout the 20th century.

During his incorrigible and irrepressible tenure in baseball, Steinbrenner has hired some of the savviest players around, and sooner or later humiliated them off the payroll (usually followed by an acerbic exchange in the papers). One of the first owners to take full advantage of the free-agent system, he built a team that won back-to-back world titles in 1977 and 1978. Then he threw good money after bad on unproductive, expensive free agents, and his team fell into chaos. The once-proud Yankees became known as the "Bronx Zoo." The 1980s marked the first decade the Yankees hadn't won a World Series since the 1910s, but the franchise rebounded in the 1990s, culminating in an American League-record 114 regular-season wins in 1998 season and a repeat World Series sweep in 1999.

Steinbrenner was the leader of 15 limited partners who bought the Yankees from CBS for $10 million, $3.2 million less than the network had paid nine years earlier. "I won't be active in day-to-day club operations at all," he said at the time. It wasn't long before one partner commented, "Nothing is more limited than being a limited partner of George's."

When Don Baylor was asked why he said he would reject an offer by Steinbrenner to manage the Yanks, he replied, "I came into this game sane, and I want to leave it sane." No Steinbrenner relationship was ever more typical than his mercurial connection with the scrappy Billy Martin, a man he hired five times and fired five times. It was Martin who said of Reggie Jackson and Steinbrenner, "They deserve each other. One's a born liar, the other's convicted."

In 1974, Steinbrenner pleaded guilty to charges of making illegal campaign contributions to Richard Nixon. Commissioner Bowie Kuhn suspended him for two years, then reinstated him after 15 months. In 1990, investigations by the commissioner's office indicated that Steinbrenner had paid a small-time gambler $40,000 to "dig up dirt" on Dave Winfield so that Steinbrenner could back out of his contractual agreement to contribute to Winfield's educational foundation. Commissioner Fay Vincent banned Steinbrenner from the game. Less than three years later, in one of his last acts as commissioner before he got fired, Vincent reinstated the man they called "The Boss."

Back in baseball again in 1993, Steinbrenner lectured the press at spring training with predictions on the season and then made headlines during the regular schedule by threatening to move the Yankees to New Jersey unless the city built him a new stadium in a better part of town. The Yankees remained in the Bronx, but he brought the Garden State a little closer to Yankee Stadium when he created the YankeeNets in 1999, a venture that broke apart in 2004 as the Nets were sold. From 1996-2000, the Yankees won four World Series—and the payroll soared. By the start of the 2004 season, following the acquisition of Alex Rodriguez, it was approaching $200-million.

11. JOE DiMAGGIO

Of the great players in baseball history, only a handful have possessed a unique, inimitable style. Joe DiMaggio was one of those players. His grace, almost princely elegance, and a diffidence born of painful shyness truly set him apart … and made him, oddly, a hero for his age: the more distant he was, the closer his fans felt to him.

His 1941 record of hitting safely in 56 consecutive games might be called a freak statistic, but in some ways it is the perfect

Joe DiMaggio stat. DiMaggio was both "the Yankee Clipper," a quiet, effortless batter who moved like a graceful sailing ship, and "Joltin' Joe," the potent slugger. Gifted with an incredible batting eye, DiMaggio struck out only 369 times in his career. His rookie year was his worst for whiffs, with 39. In his sensational 1941 season he hit 30 homers and struck out only 13 times. But it was as a fielder and baserunner that his intelligent style of play was most obvious. Manager Joe McCarthy said simply, "He was the best baserunner I ever saw."

In 1932 Joe's older brother Vince was playing for the minor league San Francisco Seals in the DiMaggios' hometown, and the team needed a new shortstop. "Why don't you try my brother, Joe?" Vince suggested. "He's pretty good." The 17-year-old Joe played just three games for the Seals that year, but in 1933 he tore up the Pacific Coast League, hitting .340 with 28 homers and a league-leading 169 RBIs. He also hit safely in 61 consecutive games, foreshadowing his 1941 feat.

His strong season sparked the interest of scouts. But the Seals stalled. The team needed cash, like so many others during the Great Depression, and management figured DiMaggio would be worth even more, perhaps as much as $100,000, if he played another season for the Seals.

After DiMaggio broke his knee getting out of a cab in 1934, the scouts stopped calling for a while. But prior to the 1935 season the Yankees offered the Seals $25,000 and five minor leaguers for DiMaggio. San Francisco agreed, on condition that DiMaggio play one more season on the coast. Joe's performance indicated that the Yanks had gotten a bargain: he batted .398 and led the league in RBIs and outfield assists.

DiMaggio's big league debut with the Yankees came on May 3, 1936. He set American League rookie records that season with 132 runs scored and 15 triples. He hit .323, belted 29 homers, and drove in 125 runs. His 22 assists led all AL outfielders. He had 21 assists the next season and had managed another 20 in 1938 before runners wised up.

Like many Americans, DiMaggio served during World War II. He missed three full seasons, from age 28 to 31. Before the war he had been the model of consistency—from 1936 through 1942 batting over .300 every year, bettering .350 three times. He had more than 100 RBIs each season, including 167 in 1937. He was the AL's Most Valuable Player in 1939 and in 1941. For the first seven years of DiMaggio's career, his Yankees only once failed to make the World Series—and they won the world championship five times.

After his stellar 1937 season DiMaggio made what was probably the only public-relations gaffe of his career. After reminding team management that his 151 runs scored, 46 homers, and .673 slugging percentage led the league, he asked for a substantial raise, from $15,000 to $45,000. When his bosses told him that all-time great Lou Gehrig was making only $41,000, DiMaggio's answer was terse and to the point: "Gehrig is underpaid."

DiMaggio held out for more money until late that April, but the fans didn't like it. He got nasty letters and was booed when he returned to play after signing for $25,000. But he earned his raise. DiMaggio won back-to-back batting championships in 1939 and 1940, and he hit more than 30 home runs and drove in more than 125 runs both years.

On May 15, 1941, DiMaggio started his streak of hitting safely in 56 consecutive games, during which he batted .408. The streak came to an end in Cleveland on July 17 in front of 67,468 fans, when Ken Keltner made two great plays and Lou Boudreau made

another to keep DiMaggio off the bases. DiMaggio's streak had lasted 12 games longer than Willie Keeler's 19th-century effort (subsequently tied by Pete Rose).

The next day DiMaggio hit safely again, and continued for 16 more games. His record-breaking hitting streak helped him win his second MVP Award. He finished the season with a .357 average and 125 RBIs. Ted Williams' outstanding .406 average that year earned him a mere second place in MVP balloting.

DiMaggio batted "only" .305 in 1942, and was out for the next three seasons because of the war. After he returned to play, a series of injuries hampered his effectiveness. He never won another batting title and only twice reached the 30-homer, 100-RBI level that he had topped in five of his first seven years.

Prior to the 1947 season DiMaggio underwent surgery on his left heel and on his right elbow to remove bone chips. Despite the surgery, he won the American League MVP that year. In November 1948 he once again underwent surgery to remove a bone spur on his right heel. This time DiMaggio's comeback was slow and painful, and he missed the first 65 games of the 1949 season. Reports came in that fans were praying for him all across the country, and one day in June the pain suddenly and miraculously disappeared. He began an intense period of rehabilitation.

He rejoined the lineup for a series in Fenway Park. The Yanks were locked in a tight battle for first place with the Red Sox after Boston had won nine of its last ten games. Back to his old tricks, DiMaggio belted four homers and drove in nine runs in the three-game Yankee sweep. He finished the season with a .346 batting average with 14 homers and 67 RBIs in only 76 games. The Yankees went on to take the 1949 world championship.

In 1950 DiMaggio's average fell to .301, second-lowest in his career, but he still swatted 32 homers, drove in 122 runs, and led the league in slugging average. That year he became the first player ever to homer three times in one game in Washington's mammoth Griffith Stadium.

With the new decade, DiMaggio's physical problems returned; his body was wearing out. He struggled to play 116 games and batted only .263 in 1951. He decided to retire. The Yankees offered him a full $100,000 salary if he would play in only home games during the 1952 season, but the great DiMaggio declined.

Joe never left the American consciousness, even in retirement. In 1954 he married movie star Marilyn Monroe. Their marriage didn't last long, but the couple remained close friends for the rest of Monroe's life. For decades after her death, fresh flowers appeared at her grave each day—many speculated that they came from DiMaggio.

The man who had been celebrated in song throughout his career was once again honored in songwriter Paul Simon's song, "Mrs. Robinson," in the late '60s. And in the 1970s and '80s Joe DiMaggio showed up on TV screens across the country as a spokesman for a coffeemaker in ads.

DiMaggio worked as a coach and front office executive for Charlie Finley's Oakland A's in 1968 and 1969. In 1969 he was honored during baseball's centennial celebration as the greatest living ballplayer. He died March 8, 1999.

12. HANK AARON

Henry Aaron combined exceptional natural physical ability and lightning-quick reflexes with a professorial study of opposing pitchers to break Babe Ruth's "unbreakable" record of 714 home runs. In fact, he surpassed Ruth's record by 41. The African-

American Aaron made waves well beyond baseball. That he moved almost overnight from a segregated environment into the white major league baseball world had a deep impact on Aaron. When he realized he could use his talents as a springboard to speak out effectively against racial intolerance and inequality, he became more than just a highly skilled athlete. He became a man with a mission.

His approach to hitting was scientific but not technical. As Aaron described it, "Ted Williams concentrated on the things he had to do himself. I concentrated on the pitcher. I didn't stay up nights worrying about my weight distribution or the location of my hands or the turn of my hips; I stayed up thinking about the pitcher I was going to face the next day."

The success of his relaxed style confounded many observers. Pitcher Robin Roberts once said, "Aaron is the only batter who could fall asleep between pitches and still wake up in time to hit the next one." Some misjudged him as lazy. An article on Aaron in *Time* magazine was titled "The Talented Shuffler." According to *Time*, "Thinking, Aaron likes to imply, is dangerous. But by now everyone knows that Aaron is not as dumb as he looks when he shuffles around the field." As Lonnie Wheeler, Aaron's collaborator on his autobiography, *I Had a Hammer*, reflected, "It was odd that Joe DiMaggio was also quiet and deliberate, and yet in DiMaggio's case these traits were perceived as dignity and grace, which translated into American heroism. In Aaron's case, the same qualities translated into comparative invisibility."

Aaron's rise from Alabama teenager to major league star happened quickly. He signed with the Negro League Indianapolis Clowns in 1952 for $200 a month. A shortstop, he batted cross-handed, but on the Clowns of that time no one bothered with his style, probably thinking it was part of the show. The truly competitive era of the Negro Leagues had ended with the integration of the majors. The Clowns were barnstormers like their basketball counterparts, the Harlem Globetrotters, and featured players with names such as King Tut and Spec Bebop. Why they were called the Indianapolis Clowns was a mystery to Aaron. "We never made it to Indiana the whole time I was with the team."

It was with the Clowns that the young Aaron got a bitter taste of racial hatred. On a northern trip, the team was rained out of a Sunday doubleheader at Griffith Stadium in Washington, D.C. "We had breakfast while we were waiting for the rain to stop, and I can still envision sitting with the Clowns in a restaurant behind Griffith Stadium and hearing them break all the plates in the kitchen after we were finished eating. What a horrible sound. Even as a kid, the irony of it hit me: here we were in the capital in the land of freedom and equality, and they had to destroy the plates that had touched the forks that had been in the mouths of black men. If dogs had eaten off those plates, they'd have washed them."

Signed by the Boston Braves for $7,500, Aaron played 87 games for Eau Claire in 1952, hitting .336 with nine home runs and 61 RBIs. The following year Aaron, outfielder Horace Garner, and infielder Felix Mantilla were sent to Class A Jacksonville to break the color line in the South Atlantic League.

Aaron was expected to play the 1954 season at either Class AAA Toledo or AA Atlanta. He was hoping he would not have to help integrate another Southern league when his hero, Bobby Thomson, broke a leg in spring training. The next day Aaron started for the Braves in Thomson's place in left field against the Red Sox in Sarasota, Fla. He came to the plate against pitcher Ike Delock, who had given up a prodigious minor league homer to Aaron the year before. Aaron said, "I cracked one over a row of trailers that bor-

dered that outfield fence—hit it so hard that Ted Williams came running out from the clubhouse wanting to know who it was that could make a bat sound that way when it hit a baseball."

Aaron's major league debut was typically understated. The Braves' highlight film of their 1954 season featured only one shot of Aaron, hitting a foul ball. But the next year marked the first of 20 years in which he would hit 20 or more home runs, and the year after that he led the league in batting average. But 1957 was the real breakout year for Aaron and the Braves as he delivered a league-leading 44 homers and 132 RBIs, and the Braves became world champions.

With St. Louis challenging in a wintry late September, Aaron hit an 11th-inning homer that clinched the pennant for the Braves. "I galloped around the bases, and when I touched home plate the whole team was there to pick me up and carry me off the field…. I had always dreamed about a moment like Bobby Thomson had in '51, and this was it." After Aaron's career ended he said that this had been his most satisfying homer. Milwaukee set a league season attendance record, and Aaron was elected MVP.

Although Aaron maintained his standard of excellence over the next ten years, Milwaukee's fortunes plummeted. When the team moved to Atlanta in 1966 things changed forever for Aaron. He found the southern air to his liking, slugging 44 and 39 homers, respectively, in his first two years there. He was 34 years old and had 481 lifetime home runs, and neither he nor anyone else was thinking about Babe Ruth's mark.

In spring training of 1969 the Braves invited Satchel Paige along as a goodwill gesture. Aaron looked around at all the youngsters and felt "as old as Satchel." He began to think of retirement. Then legendary baseball historian Lee Allen pulled him aside. Allen explained the place Aaron was about to create for himself in baseball history. With his second home run that season he would pass Mel Ott. He had a good chance to get more at bats than anyone else in history, and with 2,792 lifetime hits he had an excellent chance to reach the 3,000 level attained by only eight players. Aaron listened.

Thirty-one years later, it is hard to comprehend the enmity that Hank Aaron inspired as he entered the 1973 season 41 home runs behind Ruth. Atlanta police had to assign a bodyguard to him. It was rumored that Aaron's daughter had been kidnapped from her college dorm, and Aaron told sportswriters about the hate mail he'd received. It became big news, and before long Aaron was receiving more supportive letters than threatening ones. At the end of the year he received a plaque from the U.S. Post Office for having received the most mail of any nonpolitician during the year—930,000 letters. Aaron finished 1973 with 40 homers, leaving him at 713.

The next year began with a minor brouhaha. The Braves wanted to hold Aaron out of the lineup for their first three road games so he could tie and break Ruth's record in Atlanta. The commissioner's office and many sportswriters felt that such maneuvering was a travesty. Ordered to play at least two of the games, Aaron hit homer No. 714 off Jack Billingham in his first at bat of the season. He sat out the second game, and in the third he struck out twice and grounded out once against Clay Kirby.

Aaron's tie-breaking home run came at home against Al Downing of the Dodgers. In Aaron's first at bat, Downing had walked him. When Aaron finally came around to score, he broke Mays' NL record for runs. But no one noticed. The Dodgers were ahead, 3-1, in the fourth and Aaron was again at bat. With a man on first, Downing didn't want to walk him again. Aaron deposited a low slider into the Braves' bullpen in left field for home run No.

715. Teammates, fans, and Aaron's mother met him at the plate. The game was halted for a brief ceremony, and the next time Aaron batted the stands had nearly emptied.

Aaron ended the season with 733 homers. He was traded to the American League Milwaukee Brewers, where he added 22 more for a career total of 755. Aaron once said, "I believed, and I still do, that there was a reason why I was chosen to break the record. It's my task to carry on where Jackie Robinson left off."

The last player from the Negro Leagues to play in the white majors, he left a legacy much greater than his remarkable playing record.

13. JOHN McGRAW

"There has been only one manager and his name is John McGraw," Connie Mack once observed. That quote alone gives baseball fans a good indication of McGraw's place in baseball history. But not only was he one of the national pastime's most respected and feared tacticians, McGraw was also a scrappy infielder with a lifetime .334 average on one of baseball's greatest teams. Another accomplishment not noted in his lifetime was his lifetime on-base percentage of .466, surpassed in baseball history only by Babe Ruth and Ted Williams.

John Joseph McGraw's mother and four of his siblings died in a diphtheria epidemic, and he was sent to live with relatives. He still came under his father's supervision, however, which was no help to his baseball career. His father hated the game and walloped young McGraw once for breaking some church windows beyond right-center field. To protect his hide, McGraw became skilled at hitting to the opposite field.

McGraw pitched for local teams before signing a $40-a-month contract with Olean, New York, of the New York and Pennsylvania League in 1890. Converted into a third baseman by manager Albert Kenney, McGraw then bounced around the minor leagues before impressing Billy Barnie of the American Association Orioles in August 1891.

That Baltimore team was perhaps the toughest squad of all time, and the young McGraw soon emerged as the toughest and meanest Oriole. In those days rookies were as welcome on a club as a case of typhoid, and McGraw's arrival wasn't greeted with huzzahs. The diminutive 120-pound rookie was jeered as a "batboy," and one day found himself literally shoved off the Oriole bench. The brash McGraw proceeded to punch out his tormentors in full view of the Orioles' bewildered fans.

That incident gained him acceptance from his teammates. Soon McGraw was trying out new tricks. In those days only one umpire called each game, and McGraw developed such tactics as grabbing an opponent's belt as the player rounded third, causing runners to play with their belts loosened, or just physically blocking a runner from the base.

He also was a master at fouling off balls, waiting until he got just the right pitch to hit and tiring out the pitcher, for in the nineteenth century a foul ball was not a strike. "There wasn't any of them that could foul 'em off harder than McGraw," teammate "Wee Willie" Keeler said. "He could slam 'em out on a line so fast that even the umpire couldn't tell he was doing it on purpose." In spring training of 1930, a rapidly aging McGraw purposely fouled off 26 straight pitches.

If McGraw couldn't get on base that way, he had other options. He might, for example, just lean over the pitch and allow himself to be hit by it. Years later on seeing the introduction of batting hel-

mets, Casey Stengel would remark, "If we'd had them when I was playing, John McGraw would have insisted that we go up to the plate and get hit in the head."

The Orioles captured three straight National League pennants from 1894 through 1896. Manager Ned Hanlon pioneered a tricky style of play that emphasized the hit-and-run, the delayed steal, the Baltimore chop, and anything any of his players could think of that might lead to scoring a run or saving one. McGraw may have learned the ropes from "Foxy Ned," but he extended the science of baseball into a managerial dynasty that descended directly to Casey Stengel, Billy Martin and Whitey Herzog.

In 1899 McGraw became the Orioles' player-manager, but when that franchise was lopped off from the National League in 1900 he was sold along with two other players to St. Louis for $15,000. He hated the idea of playing in that city and refused to report until the reserve clause was stricken from his contract. He played in only 99 games, but still hit .344.

In 1901 he became manager of Ban Johnson's American League entry in Baltimore. McGraw and Johnson were an odd combination. Johnson had pledged that one of the main tenets of the new league would be respect for umpires. McGraw was the premier umpire-baiter in the land. Throughout 1901 and 1902 McGraw and Johnson clashed. Finally in July 1902 McGraw was suspended indefinitely.

In retaliation, McGraw conspired to deliver the Baltimore franchise to the forces of the National League. As part of the bargain he was named manager of the New York Giants. "McGraw was one of the hardest men in the league to control and now that he has left I cannot see how the American League has lost anything," Ban Johnson said at the time.

McGraw immediately began a house-cleaning of the New York franchise. One of his first moves was to return promising young Christy Mathewson to full-time pitching duty. A McGraw predecessor, Horace Fogel, had attempted to shift Mathewson to first base.

The Giants were a last-place club when McGraw arrived in 1902. By 1904 they were league champions. Although peace had been declared between the National and American leagues, and a World Series had been played in 1903, McGraw and Giants owner John T. Brush so hated Ban Johnson and his upstart circuit that they refused to take part in any postseason play that year.

In 1905, however, they relented, and it was a wise choice. Christy Mathewson pitched three shutouts against the A's, and the Giants became world champions. McGraw won pennants again in 1911, 1912, 1913, and 1917, but lost the World Series each year. "Not that this record reflects upon the system I have maintained as a manager, for frankly, I am not willing to concede that it does," McGraw wrote in *Baseball Magazine* in 1919.

McGraw's teams played "scientific" baseball, manufacturing runs instead of swinging for the fences. He was a teacher first and a manager second. "The Little Napoleon," said spitballer Burleigh Grimes, who pitched for McGraw's Giants in 1927, "taught me more about pitching in the first 15 minutes than I had learned in 11 previous seasons."

One of McGraw's methods was to sign as many college players as possible. McGraw, who had attended St. Bonaventure University, once said, "The difference is simply this—the college boy, or anyone else with even a partially trained mind, immediately tries to find his faults; the unschooled fellow usually tries to hide his. The moment a man locates his faults he can quickly correct them. The man who thinks he is keeping his mistakes under cover

will never advance a single step until he sees the light."

McGraw had his share of disappointments in the game. His club lost the 1908 pennant in heartbreaking fashion on the famed "Merkle Boner," in which Fred Merkle forgot to touch second base. In the 1912 World Series he had victory snatched away from him on Fred Snodgrass' "$30,000 Muff." He saw his young favorites, pitcher Christy Mathewson and outfielder Ross Youngs, die early.

McGraw truly relished his role of Little Napoleon, the baseball genius who directed each move and countermove on the diamond. One of his favorite activities was to call every pitch thrown by Giants hurlers. "I signaled for every ball that was pitched to Ruth during the last World Series," he said in 1923.

McGraw was at his cockiest in a crucial 1921 series against the Pirates. With the bases loaded, George "Highpockets" Kelly came to the plate for New York. Kelly worked the count to three balls and no strikes, and traditionally McGraw never allowed batters to hit on 3-0. Now determined to outflank the opposition, he flashed a sign for Kelly to swing away. Kelly did a double take but followed orders and delivered a grand slam. "McGraw comes strutting in [saying] if my brains hold out, we'll win it," Kelly recalled. The Giants swept the five-game series from Pittsburgh and won the pennant by four games.

McGraw captured world championships in 1921 and 1922, but lost the World Series in both 1923 and 1924. In the late 1920s and early 1930s he became increasingly irascible. "He could be very unfair at times," said long-time Giants third baseman Freddy Lindstrom. Often McGraw would not even bother to show up at the ballpark. Finally in 1932 he called first baseman Bill Terry into his office to turn over the manager's responsibilities to him. McGraw resigned on June 4, taking the headline from Yankees legend Lou Gehrig, who hit hit four home runs in that day's game.

McGraw died of cancer and uremia on February 25, 1934, and was elected to the Hall of Fame posthumously.

14. CONNIE MACK

It is often said that baseball managers are hired to be fired. Many managers have even been dismissed from a first-place team or one that had just earned a pennant. But for 50 years Philadelphia Athletics manager Connie Mack didn't have to worry about where he would work the next season. Whether he won a pennant, as he did nine times, or finished last, as he did on 17 occasions, he knew the boss would have him back, because Mack also owned the team.

In later years many believed Cornelius Alexander McGillicuddy had adopted the name "Mack" as a kindness to newspaper typesetters, but Mack himself told writer Fred Lieb, "Except when we voted, our people always called themselves Mack." Mack's father, a Civil War veteran, worked in the cotton mills and shoe factories around Brookfield, Massachusetts. When he died, his son left school and worked in a shoe factory to help support the family. He also played ball with some local teams.

Mack's career as a major league catcher is often described as undistinguished, but this perception stems largely from his mediocre batting average. The 6-foot 1-inch, 150-pound stringbean was never a strong hitter, compiling a .245 average in 11 seasons. But the most important part of a catcher's grueling and dangerous job was not hitting but calling the pitches and throwing out base stealers.

While Mack wasn't a Buck Ewing or a King Kelly with a bat in his hands, he was generally considered a strong defensive player, very smart and very tricky. He learned to brush players' bats with his glove, and he apologized with such sincerity that the batters often believed the interference was accidental. A caught foul tip was an out, and on swinging strikes Mack often mimicked the sound of a foul tip, thereby retiring many batters who never touched the ball.

After catching for Washington through 1889, Mack joined Buffalo of the Players League. He invested some of his own money in the team, which may explain his appearance in a career-high 123 games. When the Players League folded after one season, Mack joined Pittsburgh in 1891, the same year the team became known as the "Pirates" for its tricky maneuvers to acquire players.

Pittsburgh made a strong run for the pennant in 1893, finishing second as Mack fractured his ankle in a collision at home plate that reduced him to part-time work for the rest of his playing days. When the Pirates tumbled in the standings in 1894, Mack was named manager late in the season. The team had few good hitters, so one of his first moves was to freeze the baseballs in the clubhouse icebox before each game, thereby deadening them. Mack posted a winning record as the Pirates skipper in 1895 and 1896 but was fired after a dispute with an interfering owner.

Mack became manager of the Milwaukee team of the Western League in 1897 through his friendship with league president Ban Johnson. In 1900 the league changed its name to the American League, and in 1901 Johnson proclaimed that it would compete directly with the National League. Sporting goods manufacturer Ben Shibe was granted a franchise in Philadelphia. Mack became manager and owner of 25 percent of the club. He called the team the Athletics, after a Philadelphia team of the old American Association during the 1880s and a celebrated amateur nine that went back to 1860. When John McGraw said that a team in Philadelphia would be "a white elephant," or heavy money loser, a confident Mack took the white elephant as the team's symbol.

Known as "the Tall Tactician," Mack always managed in his street clothes. Another of his idiosyncrasies was his practice of moving his players around on the field by waving his scorecard. To the public he seemed like a fatherly, and later grandfatherly, figure. But Mack could make hard decisions. His players most admired his honesty.

Mack led the A's to their first pennant in 1902, largely behind pitchers Rube Waddell and Eddie Plank. Pitching, Mack often said, was 75 percent of baseball. Strong pitching always marked his winning teams, and Mack developed a reputation for turning young pitchers into stars. Both Plank and Chief Bender went directly from the college campus to the majors under Mack's guidance, and his patience with the talented but highly eccentric Waddell made possible the pitcher's greatest seasons.

In 1905 Mack won another pennant, but in the World Series, the second between the American and National Leagues, the Athletics were the victims of pitching. Although Bender shut out McGraw's Giants in one game, New York's Christy Mathewson threw three shutouts against Philadelphia and Joe McGinnity tossed a fourth to give the Giants the Series. Waddell was unable to pitch in the Series due to an injury.

Mack rebuilt the Athletics during the next few years. In 1910 he developed his best team to date and won pennants in 1910, 1911, 1913, and 1914. Plank and Bender were still outstanding. Jack Coombs, another former college star, was the staff ace until an illness derailed his career in 1913. The team also featured the "$100,000 Infield" of Stuffy McInnis, Eddie Collins, Jack Barry, and Frank Baker. The Athletics won the World Series in 1910, 1911, and 1913, twice defeating McGraw's Giants. Although the A's were heavily favored in 1914, the lightly regarded "Miracle" Boston Braves swept them in four games.

Despite being a success in the standings, the Athletics struggled financially. Attendance dropped dramatically in 1914 as Philadelphia fans took the club's success for granted. Meanwhile, the outlaw Federal League was offering huge contracts to NL and AL stars and Mack could not compete. Before the 1914 World Series he told Plank and Bender, both of whom had been loyal to Mack for years, to accept the more lucrative Federal League offers for the following season. The outbreak of war in Europe also cast the future of Organized Baseball in doubt. Many believed the United States would become involved and that baseball would be suspended.

Mack decided to sell off most of his stars, maintaining that the A's nucleus of young, inexpensive players could keep the team in contention. He was wrong. In 1915 Philadelphia nosedived to last and stayed there for seven seasons.

Beginning in 1922 Mack slowly brought the team back into contention. One player at a time, he added future Hall of Famers Mickey Cochrane, Lefty Grove, Al Simmons, and Jimmie Foxx to his existing stable of stars that included Jimmy Dykes, Bing Miller, George Earnshaw, Mule Haas, Rube Walberg, and Max Bishop. After finishing second in both 1927 and 1928, the Athletics won the pennant in 1929.

Mack surprised the Chicago Cubs in the World Series by starting veteran righthanded sidearm pitcher Howard Ehmke. Once a star hurler, by 1929 Ehmke was thought to be washed up and appeared infrequently for the A's. But Mack believed that Ehmke's sidearm deliveries coming out of the white-shirted background at Wrigley Field would baffle the Cubs.

Ehmke won the game, 3-1, striking out 14, a Series record that lasted 23 years. The A's trailed, 8-0, in the bottom of the seventh inning of Game 4, then rallied for 10 runs to win. They won the Series in Game 5 when, behind 2-0, they scored three runs in the bottom of the ninth. After the season Mack received the Edward W. Bok Award as the individual who had rendered the greatest service to Philadelphia.

Mack's star-studded A's won a second world championship in 1930 and a pennant in 1931, but the St. Louis Cardinals upset them in the World Series. By then the Depression held America in its grip. With the highest-paid team in baseball, Mack had no choice but to sell his stars once again. By 1935 the Athletics were back in the cellar.

During the next dozen years the team finished last nine times and never got out of the second division. Mack was still able to find and develop some good young players, but he was often forced to sell them before they reached stardom.

In 1948 Mack managed his last first-division team, a veteran crew that edged into fourth place. By then he was 85 years old, and subordinates did most of the real managing. After the 1950 season, when the A's again finished last, Mack stepped down. In 53 seasons he had won 3,731 games and lost 3,948, both all-time records. Mack died in 1956 at age 93. By then, Shibe Park had been rechristened in his name, but his beloved A's had moved to Kansas City under new ownership.

15. WALTER O'MALLEY

Probably no man in baseball history has ever been so hated in a community as Walter O'Malley, who hijacked Brooklyn's beloved Dodgers and moved them to Los Angeles. When Brooklyn-born writers Jack Newfield and Pete Hamill once decided to list the three most despicable villains of the century, each wrote down Hitler,

Stalin and O'Malley. But a less villainous view of O'Malley has taken hold in recent years, and there are even those who proclaim him a Johnny Appleseed of baseball, taking it West from New York as Alexander Cartwright had in 1849.

Walter O'Malley was born in the Bronx, attended Culver Military Academy, and earned an engineering degree from the University of Pennsylvania and a law degree from Fordham. He began to practice law in New York City in 1931, and in 1941 George McLaughlin, president of the Brooklyn Trust Company, which held the Dodgers' substantial loans, appointed O'Malley as the club's attorney.

Under club president Larry MacPhail, the once-pathetic Dodgers had become a competitive team, but their finances were still a mess. O'Malley stepped in to straighten them out and did a marvelous job. By 1944 the franchise was in the black. When stock held by the Ebbets and McKeever families was made available in 1945, O'Malley, general manager Branch Rickey, and John L. Smith, president of Pfizer Chemical Corporation, each ended up with 25 percent of the franchise.

Both Rickey and O'Malley were strong-willed men, and it is not surprising that they clashed on virtually every issue. Rickey had an encyclopedic knowledge of baseball on his side, but O'Malley had Smith. When Smith died, however, his widow decided to sell out. By prior agreement the stock had to be offered to both O'Malley and Rickey before it could go to any outsider.

Only O'Malley had the money to acquire the shares, but before Rickey left for the Pirates he rigged a scheme that jacked the price up to $1.05 million. O'Malley grudgingly paid because it gave him control of the franchise. He was able to purchase the Smith stock because the Dodgers were not his only financial undertaking. He owned the New York Subway Advertising Company, which had an estimated value of $7 million, and he was a partner in the Brooklyn Borough Gas Company. O'Malley's other holdings were part ownership of a $5-million building materials manufacturing company, partial ownership of a building block company, and 6 percent ownership of the Long Island Railroad.

Once O'Malley had control of the club, the "Rickey people" were pushed out. This didn't affect the Dodgers' team, which continued to dominate the National League. O'Malley was making good money, but he wasn't making enough to be satisfied. Ebbets Field may have been cozy and lovable, but it could only hold 31,902 fans. O'Malley also felt that the neighborhood surrounding Ebbets Field was declining, a legacy of the middle-class exodus to the suburbs.

By 1956 O'Malley was working overtime on a plan to leave Ebbets Field, and he was planning on more than one level. First there was the local angle. He had the engineering firm of Clarke and Rapuano develop plans for a new ballpark on Atlantic Avenue near the Long Island Railroad Terminal. Wherever the Dodgers ended up, O'Malley was intent on building the first privately owned stadium in 30 years. The city fathers, not aware of how serious O'Malley was about moving the franchise, made two counterproposals. The first involved a site at Brooklyn's Parade Grounds. The second was at Flushing Meadow in Queens, where Shea Stadium was later built. O'Malley wasn't interested.

At a banquet in 1956 Cubs owner P.K. Wrigley made a rare public appearance, and O'Malley took advantage of the opportunity to offer Wrigley a swap: the Cubs' Los Angeles Angels franchise for the Dodgers' Fort Worth Cats. The deal was consummated in February 1957, paving the way for the Dodgers' shift to

Los Angeles.

In the mean time, O'Malley had been in contact with Los Angeles officials. Early in the 1956 season Los Angeles County supervisor Kenneth Hahn had visited New York in an attempt to secure a team for Los Angeles. He had no thought whatsoever of cajoling the defending world champs into moving west. His real target was Calvin Griffith's Washington Senators. Instead O'Malley contacted Hahn and stunned him with the news that he intended to move the Dodgers to Los Angeles.

After the season O'Malley secretly visited Los Angeles and toured the city in a sheriff's department helicopter, looking for an acceptable stadium site. He found it in a place called Chavez Ravine a few minutes' drive from the downtown area. O'Malley was understandably tight-lipped about his plans, but word eventually leaked out. On May 29, 1957, the National League gave approval for both the Dodgers and the Giants to move to the West Coast. Giants' owner Horace Stoneham was also eager to leave New York. The Polo Grounds was crumbling and the neighborhood around it was in seemingly irreversible decline. New York baseball fans were devastated, but calamity provided opportunity as O'Malley's nemesis Branch Rickey combined with such folks as Bill Shea and Joan Payson to announce a rival Continental League as a stalking horse for MLB expansion.

On October 7 the Los Angeles City Council voted to swap Chavez Ravine for nearby Wrigley Field, which O'Malley had acquired in the franchise transaction with the Cubs. The city agreed to spend $2 million to upgrade the area, and the county to sink $2.4 million into access roads. The next day O'Malley announced that the Brooklyn Dodgers were no more. His team took temporary quarters at the huge Los Angeles Coliseum until Dodger Stadium, built with a $10-million advance from Union Oil of California, was completed in 1962. O'Malley made sure his franchise was as profitable as possible. There were no water fountains in Dodger Stadium until loud protests were made. Likewise there was no free television coverage of Dodgers home games at first. O'Malley hated to give away anything. But even with water fountains and free TV, the Dodgers prospered beyond his wildest dreams.

Because of his wealth, success, and brains he became Organized Baseball's most powerful owner. "It's just a lot of bunk to say I run baseball and am more powerful than the commissioner," O'Malley once argued. Yet it was an open secret that O'Malley had installed Bowie Kuhn as commissioner in 1969, and had then prevented Kuhn's unseating in 1975 during an owners' revolt. And it was also O'Malley who had Kuhn call off the owners' spring training lockout in 1976.

O'Malley died of cancer at the Mayo Clinic in Minnesota in 1979. His son Peter owned the Dodgers franchise until it was sold in 1997.

16. JOHN MONTGOMERY WARD

If Ward wasn't the most important person in baseball during the late 19th century, he certainly was the most interesting. His career as a star player, winning manager, labor organizer, and club owner placed him at the center of many of the most significant events of the period, both on and off the field.

Ward was born in Bellefonte, Pennsylvania, in 1860. A gifted student athlete, he attended Pennsylvania State College and won acclaim as a pitcher on the baseball team. He pitched an exhibition game for the independent Philadelphia Athletics in 1877, and although he lost, 5-0, he accepted a professional contract from a team in Janesville, Wisconsin for $20 a week and a $75 bonus. The Bellefonte newspaper editorialized, "There is no reason why a baseball pitcher should not become eventually a great man, but the chances for Monte's sake, we are sorry to say, are against it, and trust he will pause and reconsider."

Ward proved the critics wrong. In 1878, his rookie season in the National League, he was the star right-handed pitcher for Providence, winning 22 games and leading the league with a 1.51 ERA. On August 9 he pitched and won two games in one day.

The great George Wright and "Orator" Jim O'Rourke joined the Providence team in 1879. With a better defense behind him and a stronger offense, Ward pitched the Grays to the pennant. He won a league-leading 47 games and lost only 17. His .734 winning percentage and 239 strikeouts also led the NL. In 1880 he won 40 games and threw a league-leading 9 shutouts. On June 17 of that year, he threw the second perfect game and third no-hitter in league history, a 5-0 win over Buffalo.

But Ward was only 20 years old, and the strain on his arm proved too great. After pitching 587 innings in 1879 and 595 in 1880, he battled a sore arm during the next three seasons, pitching fewer innings each year. Yet when he was able to throw, he continued to be successful. On August 17, 1882, he won an 18-inning game, 1-0. But by 1884 his arm was shot, and he appeared in his final nine games as a hurler. In seven seasons Ward won 161 games against 101 losses.

Although finished as a hurler, Ward was hardly washed up as a player. Even as early as 1879, when he was at his best as a hurler, Ward played outfield or third base on the days he wasn't on the mound. A right-handed thrower, he was a fair left-handed batter, particularly adept at bunting and hitting behind a runner. Ward was an excellent baserunner and fast in the field. Furthermore, he was an exceptional leader. In 1880, though younger than most of his teammates, he even filled in as manager for part of the season.

After his arm went bad, Ward spent more time as a position player. In 1883 the New York Gothams acquired his contract, and during most of the 1884 season he was New York's regular center fielder. He hit .253 and scored 98 runs. According to some reports, he threw left-handed to rest his ailing right arm. Although he never returned to the mound, his arm recovered enough to allow him to become the Gothams' regular shortstop in 1885. He was instantly one of the top players at the position.

In both 1888 and 1889 the Giants won the NL pennant, and much of the credit went to their dashing shortstop. In 1889 the Giants trailed in the Series three games to two going into the sixth game. Hank O'Day had shut out New York for eight innings and St. Louis led, 1-0, but in the bottom of the ninth Ward singled and then stole second and third. He scored to tie the game on Connor's single. Then, in the eleventh inning, he drove in the winning run. The Giants went on to win the next three games and the Series.

While enjoying a full career on the field, Ward also remained busy off the field, earning a law degree from Columbia University. In 1885 the Brotherhood of Professional Base Ball Players was formed to protect and benefit the players collectively and individually, to promote a high standard of conduct, and to foster and encourage the interests of baseball. Ward was elected president. Some team owners feared any sort of player organization, but most at least paid lip service to the aims of the Brotherhood.

After the 1888 season Albert Spalding led a group of stars on a round-the-world trip to introduce baseball and open new markets for his sporting goods. While Ward and other stars were out of the

country, the owners pushed through a rule to categorize the players and pay them according to rank. Since the owners determined the categories, the new system first lowered, then froze, player salaries.

For more than a year Ward tried to negotiate, but the owners refused to recognize the Brotherhood. Finally, the situation reached an impasse. In 1890 the players, under Ward, revolted, solicited financial backers, and formed the Players League. Most of the star players in both the National League and the American Association jumped to the new league.

During the 1890 season the three major leagues competed in many of the same cities. All three lost money, and the backers of the Players League lost heart, even though their attendance was the best of the three. After only one year the new league collapsed. A year later the mortally wounded American Association also went under, and four of its teams were absorbed by the NL.

Ward was shortstop and manager of the PL's Brooklyn team, which finished second. In the settlement after the season, Brooklyn's Players League backer and Ward each gained stock in the Brooklyn NL club. Ward assumed the player-manager position with Brooklyn, a team that soon became popularly known as "Ward's Wonders." He moved the club up to third in the standings in 1892, when he led the league with 80 stolen bases.

That same year Ward won 20 shares of New York Giants stock on a bet with one of their stockholders on where the Giants would finish. Such a conflict of interest and betting on standings would be prohibited by Organized Baseball today. It was common in the 1890s for owners to own shares in other teams ("syndicate baseball," it came to be called), and occasionally players and managers did the same. In fact, half the owners in the league held Giants stock.

The team, however, was going rapidly downhill. Because the National League needed a strong draw in New York, both to protect its stock holdings and to ensure a large visitor's share of the take, the other clubowners worked out a deal. Ward resigned as Brooklyn manager and became the Giants' skipper. In 1893 New York finished fifth in the 12-team NL, and in 1894 he pushed them to second.

In an effort to establish a profitable postseason series similar to the prototypical World Series of the 1880s, the NL instituted the Temple Cup in 1894, with the division winner playing the second-place finisher in a best-of-seven series. The Baltimore Orioles won the pennant that year but didn't take the Temple Cup very seriously. Ward's Giants ambushed the Orioles and swept them in four straight games. Ward himself hit .294 and led his team in RBIs.

At age 34 Ward was at the pinnacle of the baseball world, a successful player-manager of a championship team. He chose that moment to retire. His successful law practice was growing, but he resigned primarily due to his inability to get along with Andrew Freedman, the Tammany Hall politician who had taken over the Giants. Ward was hardly alone; few men could work for Freedman for long. By the time he sold his control of the Giants in 1903, Freedman had fired or otherwise lost a dozen managers and driven the Giants to the lowest point in their history.

Ward became a leading corporate lawyer in New York but continued to be involved in baseball. He represented Amos Rusie when the famous pitcher sued Freedman for money he was owed. The case was eventually settled out of court to Rusie's benefit. In 1909 Ward was a leading, though eventually unsuccessful, candidate to become NL president. In 1911 and 1912 he was president and part owner of the Boston Braves, and in 1913 he was business manager of the Brooklyn team in the Federal League. He was also the founder and first president of the Long Island Golf Association. He wrote several books and numerous magazine articles on baseball.

Ward died in 1925. Nearly 40 years later, in 1964, he was named to the Hall of Fame.

17. CAL RIPKEN

Cal Ripken will be forever remembered for "the streak." He became the most durable player to ever put on a major league uniform on September 6, 1995, when he appeared in his 2,131st consecutive game. He surpassed Lou Gehrig's "unbreakable record" (according to Gehrig's plaque at Yankee Stadium) at a time when baseball was still suffering the repercussions of the 1994 strike. The national Ripken watch, as he approached the magic number, helped heal some of the wounds felt by many fans. The ovation at Camden Yards on that historic night lasted more than 20 minutes.

The following season Ripken would also break the world record of 2,216 consecutive games, a number reached by Sachio Kinugasa, third baseman for the Hiroshima Carp of Japan's Central League. Ripken's streak would end at 2,632 on September 19, 1998 with no one in the ballpark aware of the game's significance. The next night, 30 minutes before the final Orioles home game of the year, Ripken unexpectedly asked Baltimore manager Ray Miller to take him out of the lineup. He wasn't hurt; he could have played; it was simply time to put an end to a personal accomplishment that had begun to overshadow team goals. Ryan Minor was his replacement.

Ripken was an Oriole practically from birth. He was born and raised in Maryland, the son of an Orioles minor league manager, Cal Sr., the taciturn founder of "the Oriole Way." Baltimore drafted the young Ripken out of high school in the second round of the 1978 amateur draft. He broke into the major leagues shortly after the close of the 1981 players strike, debuting as a pinch runner on August 10 against Kansas City. Like Gehrig, once he stepped on the field, it was nearly impossible to get him off it.

In 1982 he was named American League Rookie of the Year after leading rookies in nearly every offensive category. He started the season at third base, but soon shifted to shortstop where he would play every game, and practically every inning, for the next 14 seasons before returning to third base in 1997. He wouldn't miss a game at third for almost two seasons.

In that span, Ripken became one of the game's best shortstops with both the bat and glove. Ripken won the AL MVP in 1983 as the leader of an Orioles team that won the World Series; in 1991 he won the award again because of his outstanding achievements (34 homers, 114 RBIs, .556 slugging average) on a sixth-place team. In between MVPs, his father was hired to manage the club, but Cal Sr. was dismissed in the midst of a 21-game losing streak to start the 1988 season.

Cal Jr. became one of baseball's most popular players: through 1999 he had appeared in 17 straight All-Star Games. He set a major league record (since broken) with 95 consecutive errorless games in 1990, and followed that with back-to-back Gold Glove Awards in 1991 and 1992. He also earned numerous honors for his work off the field as well, including the Bart Giamatti Caring Award (1989), Roberto Clemente Award (1992), and Lou Gehrig Award (1992).

In 1993 Ripken passed Ernie Banks as the all-time home run leader for shortstops. The following year he hit his 300th home run. On September 2, 1999 he became the 29th player to hit 400 home runs, but his season ended prematurely—with him just nine hits shy of 3,000—because of surgery to relieve pressure in his

lower back. Despite the death of his father in midyear, his .340 average in 332 at bats was the highest of his career, even if it was the first time in 19 years that he failed to play in at least 99 percent of his team's games. The highlights of the season were his 400th home run and a six-hit game on June 13 during an interleague visit to Atlanta.

Ripken returned for two more seasons of diminishing productivity, but he did cross the 3,000-hit divide. In a particularly satisfying and sentimental farewell appearance at the 2001 All-Star Game, Cal, who had been voted in as the AL's starting third baseman, accepted the offer of starting shortstop Alex Rodriguez to switch positions to open the game. Cal then proceeded to hit a home run in his first time at bat. He was named the All-Star Game MVP in his league's 4-1 victory.

18. MICKEY MANTLE

Mickey Charles Mantle was the son of Oklahoma lead and zinc miner Mutt Mantle. "I always wished my dad could be somebody else than a miner," Mantle once said. "I knew it was killing him. He was underground eight hours a day. Every time he took a breath, the dust and dampness went into his lungs."

Mutt Mantle named his boy after legendary catcher Gordon "Mickey" Cochrane and started him switch-hitting at age 5. "He believed that any kid could develop into a switch hitter if you taught him early enough," recalled Mantle. Mutt would pitch to young Mantle from one side, and Mickey's grandfather would lob the ball to him from the other.

Mantle played football and baseball for Commerce High School, earning the nickname "the Commerce Comet." During one football practice he was kicked in the left shin, and not only did his ankle swell to twice its normal size, but he also developed a 104-degree fever. He eventually developed osteomyelitis (inflammation of the bone marrow) and was threatened with amputation. But at Oklahoma City's Crippled Children's Hospital, Mantle received penicillin injections every three hours around the clock, and his condition improved almost immediately.

When he recovered, New York Yankees scout Tom Greenwade signed him to a $400-a-month contract. When Mutt Mantle hinted his son could make as much working in the mines and playing ball on Sundays, Greenwade threw in a $1,100 bonus. Greenwade knew at the time he was getting someone special. "The first time I saw Mantle I knew how Paul Krichell felt when he first saw Lou Gehrig. He knew that as a scout he'd never have another moment like it."

Mantle was sent to Independence of the Class D K-O-M League, where he batted .313. He played shortstop and committed 47 errors in only 89 games. His next destination was Joplin in the Class C Western Association, where he hit a league-leading .383 with 26 homers and 136 runs batted in.

"He should lead the league in everything," Yankees manager Casey Stengel said of Mantle before the 1951 season. "With his combination of speed and power he should win the triple batting crown every year. In fact, he should do everything he wants to do."

One thing Mantle couldn't do, however, was play shortstop. He had made 55 errors at Joplin. With Phil Rizzuto still firmly in control of the position in New York, Mantle needed to find another role. He had the speed and range to play center field, but an aging Joe DiMaggio still owned the position, and any attempt to move New York's hero could cause a riot. Stengel tried Mantle in right field.

Mantle went north with the Yankees in 1951 and started on Opening Day. He impressed observers with a 450-foot homer off Randy Gumpert on May 1, but, overall, he had trouble adjusting to big league pitching. The Yankees finally realized that Mantle required more seasoning and shipped him down to Kansas City.

Mantle's hitting slump continued. He called home and told his father, "I don't think I can play baseball any more." The next day Mutt Mantle arrived in Kansas City and started packing his son's belongings into a suitcase.

That was enough to jolt Mantle out of his slump. During his 40-game stay at Kansas City, he batted .361, hit 11 homers, drove in 50 runs, and was back in Yankee Stadium by the close of August.

In Game 2 of that year's World Series, Mantle tripped over an exposed drainpipe in Yankee Stadium's right-center field. He tore cartilage in his knee and missed the rest of the Series. The day after the injury, Mutt Mantle, a spectator at the World Series, was taken ill. By the next summer he was dead of Hodgkin's Disease, the same malady that had killed Mutt's father.

Mickey Mantle soon developed into a star, but he was still a small-town boy in the big city. He shared an apartment above the Stage Delicatessen with Hank Bauer and Johnny Hopp, and in his first year gained 25 pounds from eating corned beef, cheesecake, and matzo ball soup. He eventually became fast friends with Whitey Ford and Billy Martin—and with that duo, his diet was often more liquid than solid.

In 1957, a fight broke out at New York's Copacabana nightclub involving Mantle and Martin. In an effort to protect Mantle from further trouble the Yankees traded Martin to the Athletics. The two remained friends, however. "We used to tease each other about whose liver was going to go first," said Mantle.

Part of the reason for Mantle's high living was his suspicion that he would follow his father and grandfather to an early grave. At age 46 Mantle lamented, "If I knew I was going to live this long, I would have taken better care of myself."

Mantle specialized in monster home runs. One of his most famous was a 565-foot blast at Washington's Griffith Stadium in 1953. "I never saw a ball hit so far. You could have cut it up into 15 singles," marveled Yankees pitcher Bob Kuzava. On May 13, 1955, Mantle hit three homers into the distant Yankee Stadium bleachers. Each cleared the 461-foot sign. On May 23, 1963, he struck the park's right-field facade. It was estimated that—had it kept sailing—the ball would have traveled 602 feet.

Mantle was perhaps at his finest in the mid-1950s. In 1956 he won the American League Triple Crown with 52 homers, 130 RBIs, and a .353 batting average. He hit three more home runs in the World Series and won the AL Most Valuable Player Award. In 1957 Mantle again won the MVP Award. In the 1957 World Series, Milwaukee second baseman Red Schoendienst came down on Mantle's right shoulder. The injury would hamper him for years, although he would win another MVP Award in 1962, along with a Gold Glove.

In 1961 Mantle and teammate Roger Maris were both in pursuit of Babe Ruth's 60-home run single-season record. In September, Mantle developed a cold he couldn't shake and announcer Mel Allen recommended an East Side physician who could fix him right up—"the best there is." The doctor, garbed in a bloodstained smock, injected Mantle with some mysterious substance that immediately put him into a dizzied, feverish state.

Mantle missed several crucial games and had to have the area where he had been injected cut open and lanced. In the end he played eight fewer games and had 76 fewer at bats than Maris, who

had eclipsed Ruth's record by a single homer. The doctor even had the nerve to send Mantle a bill. "I never did pay it," said Mantle. "I wanted to sue. A few years later he stopped practicing."

Even though that malady went away, injuries continued to haunt Mantle. Playing in Baltimore in June 1963, he broke his ankle and was out of the lineup for two months. His first at bat after returning to active duty was a pinch-hit, game-tying homer with two outs in the ninth inning.

But Mantle's best days were over. His damaged shoulder caused him great pain, and in the mid-1960s he had difficulty throwing and even batting from the left side. He played first base the final two years of his career.

During spring training in 1969 Mantle announced his retirement. "I can't play any more," he stated. "I can't hit the ball when I need to. I can't steal second when I need to. I can't go from first to third when I need to. I can't score from second when I need to. I have to quit."

After his retirement Mantle became involved in a number of ventures including a popular restaurant on New York's Park Avenue South. He also announced for a while on NBC's *Saturday Game of the Week*. He was inducted into the Hall of Fame in 1974, his first year of eligibility.

In later years the once-shy Mantle emerged as a raconteur and may, in fact, have been even more popular than he was while playing. In one of his stories St. Peter met him at the Pearly Gates. "Sorry, Mickey," St. Peter said, "because of the way you lived on earth, you can't come in. But, before you leave, would you please autograph these baseballs for Him?"

After a 1993 stay in the Betty Ford Center in California, Mantle also emerged in the unlikely role of clean-living spokesman. He appeared on TV programs to talk about his experiences and to warn kids about drug and alcohol abuse. The transformation was apparently too late for Mantle himself. In 1994 he received a liver transplant at Baylor University Hospital in Dallas. Around the same time, he formed the Mickey Mantle Foundation to raise awareness of the importance of becoming an organ donor.

Ironically, it was during the successful transplant surgery that doctors discovered an inoperable cancer lesion. Mickey Mantle died August 13, 1995 at the age of 63.

19. CHRISTY MATHEWSON

In a sport dominated by ruffians, Christy Mathewson exuded a sense of nobility. Not only was he a great pitcher—the co-holder of the National League record for career victories, with 373, and the league record holder for most victories in a season, with 37—but also he was a gentleman, a man of moral convictions who inspired an entire generation of fans. Mothers could contemplate their sons growing up to become baseball players if the game welcomed men like Matty.

"Mathewson was the greatest pitcher who ever lived," said Connie Mack, who managed the Philadelphia Athletics through a half-century of baseball. "He had knowledge, judgment, perfect control, and form. It was wonderful to watch him pitch … when he wasn't pitching against you."

In the 1905 World Series against the Athletics Mathewson pitched three complete-game shutouts. In 1908 he walked an average of less than one player per game while winning 37 games (he won 30 or more games four time). From June 13 through July 18, 1913, he pitched 68 consecutive innings without surrendering a single base on balls. For 12 consecutive years he captured a minimum of 22 victories.

Christopher Mathewson began pitching at age 13 for his hometown team in Honesdale, Pennsylvania. It was there that Mathewson later added a new pitch to his arsenal, learning the delivery from a left-handed teammate. "Williams [Dave Williams, who went on to pitch briefly for the Boston Red Sox] pitched this ball with the same motion that he threw his out-curve," noted Mathewson, "but turned his hand over and snapped his wrist as he let the ball go. He never could tell where it was going, so it was of no use to him in a game. It was a freak delivery. It fascinated me."

At Bucknell College Mathewson continued to star as a pitcher but also made a name for himself in football. He was known as "Gun Boots" because of his skill in dropkicking. Signed to a professional baseball contract with Taunton, Massachusetts, of the New England League, he made his professional debut came on July 21, 1899, in a 6-5 loss to Manchester.

The next year Mathewson signed with Norfolk of the Virginia League. He was 20-2 by late July, when he was sold to the Giants for $2,000. Manager John "Phenomenal" Smith, a one-time big league pitcher himself, had offers for Mathewson from both the Phillies and the Giants and gave the pitcher his choice. Mathewson, believing the Giants were more in need of pitching, opted for New York.

In New York, manager George Davis christened Mathewson's trick pitch the "fadeaway." Despite his innovation, Mathewson proved ineffective in 1900, going 0-3 with a 5.08 ERA, and returned to Norfolk at season's end. The Cincinnati Reds proceeded to draft Mathewson off the Norfolk roster, but the Giants had second thoughts about handing the talented righthander back. They traded washed-up fireballer Amos Rusie for him on December 15, 1900. Rusie, who had already accumulated 245 big league victories, would not win another game. The deal turned out to be baseball's greatest steal.

Mathewson had a wide variety of pitches, including a fastball, curve, and the aforementioned fadeaway. Although the fadeaway was his most famous pitch, he never would say which of his offerings was the best. "Anybody's best pitch is the one the batters ain't hitting that day," he observed. "And it doesn't take long to find out. If they start hitting my fastball, they don't see it anymore that afternoon. If they start getting a hold of my curveball, I just put it away for the day. When they start hitting both of them on the same day, that's when they put me away."

As successful as he was, Mathewson was, to some extent, a hard-luck pitcher. Bad things often happened to the Giants when Mathewson took the mound in big games. It was Mathewson who was pitching against the Cubs on September 23, 1908, when first baseman Fred Merkle pulled his famed "Merkle Boner" play, forgetting to touch second base when Al Bridwell drove in what appeared to be the winning run from third base. Merkle headed into the clubhouse to join the celebration but was called out by umpire Hank O'Day. The game ended in a deadlock.

That tie had to be replayed on October 8, 1908. With the pennant at stake, "Big Six" Mathewson was once again on the mound. He sailed along until the third inning, when center fielder Cy Seymour, stubbornly ignoring Mathewson's entreaties to play deeper, saw a Joe Tinker fly ball sail over his head for a triple. Four runs scored that inning, and the Giants lost the game, 4-2, as well as the flag.

Mathewson was the victim again in the the final inning of the final game of the 1912 World Series when Fred Snodgrass committed his "$30,000 Muff" in center field and catcher Chief Meyers

and Merkle let an easy foul pop drop between them. Mathewson lost another heartbreaker as the Red Sox won the game and the Series.

If Mathewson had one flaw, it was his lack of concentration when he had a big lead. "Matty was a great one for loafing when the pressure was off, when we were way ahead," teammate Larry Doyle said. "He was only great when he had to be. In tight ball games, he was darn near impossible to hit. But when the score was lopsided, Matty didn't seem to care a whit about his reputation and he'd toss in plenty of fat ones."

In 1914 Mathewson started to wear out. He finished with a record of 24-13, but in the second half of the season he began to complain of pains in his left side. In 1915 Mathewson suffered his first losing season since 1902, and by 1916 he was being used out of the bullpen. On July 20, 1916, McGraw traded Mathewson to the Reds along with two other future Hall of Famers, Edd Roush and Bill McKechnie, for Reds manager Buck Herzog and outfielder Red Killefer.

Although the deal was made to allow Mathewson to manage Cincinnati, Reds fans were probably relieved to get him off the Giants' mound. With New York, Mathewson's record against the Reds was 64-18, with 22 wins in a row at one point.

Mathewson's last pitching performance, his only one for the Reds, was a specially contrived matchup against another aging hurler and Matty's longtime rival, the Cubs' Mordecai "Three Finger" Brown. In the second game of a Labor Day doubleheader, Mathewson outlasted Brown, 10-8.

After several decades the significance of this game became apparent. The annals showed that when Mathewson retired he had accumulated 372 victories, a National League record. Grover Cleveland Alexander subsequently won 373, consigning Mathewson's mark to second place. But a statistician later discovered that a May 1902 Mathewson 4-2 victory over Pittsburgh had been erroneously entered in the record books as a loss. Matty's crown had been restored, even if it had to be shared.

Mathewson managed Cincinnati until midseason 1918, when he joined the armed services and served as a captain on the Western Front, where he was hit by a whiff of poison gas. In 1919 he returned to baseball as a coach for the Giants, but two years later was diagnosed as having tuberculosis in both lungs.

He was sent to Saranac Lake, N.Y., for treatment, where one of his lungs collapsed. Baseball was his medicine. "When a fellow cannot read, or write, or talk, and can only move his fingers and forearms, it requires some resourcefulness to keep his mind off his troubles. I started working out a baseball game, figuring every chance and studying how it should be played mechanically so as to offer the same chances as are offered on a ballfield. It interested me and kept my mind engaged."

In 1922 Mathewson returned home, and his spirit was too strong to merely survive. In 1923 he accepted the post of general manager of Judge Emil Fuchs' Boston Braves. It was a challenge Mathewson never should have taken. In 1925 the strain caused him to collapse. He returned to Saranac Lake and died there on October 7, as the World Series opened. Players on both squads wore black armbands in tribute.

In 1936 Christy Mathewson was among the first five players to be enshrined in the Hall of Fame.

20. CURT FLOOD

Every time a major leaguer collects a paycheck, he should thank Curt Flood. In 1970 the St. Louis Cardinals' center fielder sued Major League Baseball in an effort to eliminate the reserve clause that had, since 1879, bound a player to his team forever. Although Flood lost the battle, the players ultimately won the war. Flood's suit paved the way for arbitration, free agency, and million-dollar salaries.

After two short trials with Cincinnati, Flood was traded to St. Louis. He came to the majors to stay in 1958 at age 20. Flood played sparingly until the middle of 1961, when Johnny Keane replaced Solly Hemus as the Cardinals' skipper. In 1961 he batted .322, up 85 points from the previous year. It was the first of six .300-plus seasons in his remaining nine years with the Cardinals.

Flood's real gift was playing outfield. He won the first of seven straight Gold Glove Awards in 1963. By the middle of the decade it was widely acknowledged that he'd surpassed Willie Mays as baseball's best center fielder. A 1968 *Sports Illustrated* cover featured a self-portrait by Flood the painter.

From September 3, 1965, through June 2, 1967, Flood played 226 errorless games in the outfield for a National League record and handled 568 consecutive chances, a record in the majors. On June 19, 1967, two weeks after he muffed a ball to end the streak, Flood completed the first unassisted double play by an NL outfielder in 34 years, the first in the majors since 1945.

Surprisingly, Flood's most memorable moment in three World Series appearances occurred when he misjudged a fly ball in the 1968 classic. With two out in the seventh inning of a scoreless Game 7, Jim Northrup drove a Bob Gibson pitch deep into center field. Flood took a step in and then could not catch up to the drive, which fell for a triple, scoring both runners. Northrup later scored, and Detroit held on to win the Series.

Flood was a co-captain, with Tim McCarver, of those St. Louis pennant winners. When the Cards failed to win a third straight flag in 1969, the front office set about remaking the squad. Late in the season Flood complained publicly about management throwing in the towel while the team still had a chance to win in 1970. He was among the first to go.

On October 7, 1969, the Cardinals traded Flood, McCarver, pitcher Joe Hoerner, and outfielder Byron Browne to Philadelphia for first baseman Dick Allen, second baseman Cookie Rojas, and pitcher Jerry Johnson. Flood found out about the trade from a reporter who called to ask for a comment. After 12 years with the Cardinals, he felt he had earned more consideration. "If I had been a foot-shuffling porter, they might have at least given me a pocket watch," Flood wrote. Moreover, he said, the trade "violated the logic and integrity of my existence. I was not a consignment of goods."

He declared he would retire rather than report to Philadelphia, a standard ploy for a traded veteran player. He disliked the Philadelphia organization's reputation and the city's treatment of black players. But as the hurt of the trade faded, its injustice remained. Flood began to think about suing baseball over the reserve clause, which bound him either to play for Philadelphia or retire. He consulted a local attorney, who endorsed the possibility of a successful lawsuit.

Flood met with Marvin Miller, executive director of the Major League Baseball Players Association (MLBPA), who had been trying to reform the game's archaic labor-relations policies ever since he had taken over as head of the union in 1966. Miller warned that the suit could end Flood's career and cost him hundreds of thousands of dollars in lost salary as well as legal fees. Flood declared, "I want to go out like a man instead of disappearing like a bottle cap."

Still, Flood took Miller's advice to think the suit through care-

fully. He dined with Philadelphia general manager John Quinn, who thought at the time that he'd convinced Flood to join the Phillies. Flood decided to proceed with the suit anyway, and in mid-December he met with MLBPA representatives, who voted unanimously to pay legal fees and other expenses related to Flood's suit.

On December 24, 1969, Flood, with help from Miller and former U.S. Supreme Court Justice Arthur Goldberg, drafted the following letter to baseball Commissioner Bowie Kuhn:

"After twelve years in the major leagues, I do not feel I am a piece of property to be bought and sold irrespective of my wishes. I believe that any system which produces that result violates my basic rights as a citizen and is inconsistent with the laws of the United States and of the several States.

"It is my desire to play baseball in 1970, and I am capable of playing. I have received a contract offer from the Philadelphia club, but I believe I have the right to consider offers from other clubs before making any decision. I, therefore, request that you make known to all Major League clubs my feelings in this matter, and advise them of my availability for the 1970 season."

Kuhn's reply reaffirmed Organized Baseball's intention to hold Flood to the provisions of his 1969 contract, which included the right of the Cardinals to assign it wherever they pleased. In April, Philadelphia acquired first baseman Willie Montanez and minor league pitcher Bob Browning from St. Louis as substitutes for Flood. In January 1970, the case of *Flood v. Kuhn* was filed in U.S. District Court in New York. Judge Irving Ben Cooper denied Flood's request for an injunction voiding the trade and recommended the issue be settled in a trial, which began in May.

Hall of Famers Jackie Robinson and Hank Greenberg testified for Flood, along with former club owner Bill Veeck and former pitcher and author Jim Brosnan. No active players testified for Flood, nor did any show up to give moral support. Despite the MLBPA representatives' vote, rank-and-file players were divided, some believing Organized Baseball's dire predictions that eliminating the reserve clause would destroy the game.

Sitting out the 1970 season to avoid prejudicing his case, Flood went to Copenhagen after the trial to paint and to pursue plans to open a restaurant. In August, Judge Cooper decided against Flood without touching on the merits of the reserve clause. His ruling simply upheld the 1922 U.S. Supreme Court decision exempting Organized Baseball from antitrust laws because it was not interstate commerce. A federal appeals court upheld Cooper's ruling, but the U.S. Supreme Court agreed to hear Flood's appeal.

On June 12, 1972, the Supreme Court ruled in a 5-3 decision against Flood, with Justice Lewis Powell abstaining because he held stock in Anheuser-Busch, which owned the Cardinals. However, the majority opinion hoisted a warning flag for baseball, calling its antitrust exemption an "aberration" and an "anomaly." Flood's suit had exposed the vulnerability of Organized Baseball's legal position, as well as its immorality, and had begun the march toward the modification of the reserve rules, which culminated in arbitrator Peter Seitz's 1976 ruling establishing free agency.

Flood reaped little from shaking the game to its roots. With his U.S. business interests going sour, he accepted owner Bob Short's offer to play for the Washington Senators for the 1971 season, after securing an agreement that Major League Baseball's attorneys would not use it against him in court. Short had to send Philadelphia a player for the right to negotiate with Flood and two more after signing him. But after batting .200 in 13 games, Flood left the team, saying that age and rust had robbed him of his skills.

Flood went back to Europe, landing in Spain, but ultimately returned to the Bay Area, where he worked as a broadcaster for the Oakland Athletics in 1978, painted, and headed Oakland's Little League. And in one final irony, the man who had sued a commissioner of Organized Baseball ultimately became one himself. Flood headed the short-lived Senior League, which played its single season in the winter of 1989-90. He died January 20, 1997.

21. BUD SELIG

Allan H. Selig grew up watching the minor league Milwaukee Brewers; at 35 he became owner of a major league team and named it the Brewers; and at 58 he became overseer of every team in baseball. Selig led a group of dissatisfied owners that forced the ouster of baseball commissioner Fay Vincent in September 1992, then replaced Vincent on an *interim* basis. Six years later, the owners unanimously elected Selig and he has emerged as the most powerful commissioner since Kenesaw Mountain Landis.

With the collective bargaining agreement due to expire in 1994, Selig rallied the owners behind a proposal calling for revenue sharing and a salary cap—a concept the players union flatly rejected. On August 12, with Tony Gwynn chasing .400, play was suspended. A month later Selig announced the cancellation of the World Series.

After the strike, baseball tried new directions: another round of playoffs, interleague play, limited revenue sharing, and more expansion. As the game slowly returned to 1994 levels of popularity, the governance of baseball became centralized in the commissioner's office. The jobs of both league presidents—positions that predated the role of commissioner in Organized Baseball—were essentially eradicated.

In the first days of the 21st century the owners gave Selig even more control. He was criticized in 2001 when he ended the All-Star Game with the scored tied 7-7 in the 11th inning. A year later he oversaw the successful negotiation of a new collective bargaining agreement, the first time the owners and players reached agreement without a work stoppage.

22. JIM BOUTON

With the exception of two years with the New York Yankees in 1963 and 1964, Jim Bouton's career as a pitcher consisted primarily of comeback tries. His greatest success actually came when he wrote *Ball Four*, a revealing book about what players in the national pastime said, did, and thought.

Bouton's sometimes hilarious, often disturbing, stories of the sexism and childish high jinks typical of major leaguers shocked the baseball establishment. Commissioner Bowie Kuhn said that the book was "detrimental to baseball." Mickey Mantle vowed he would never appear in an Old Timers game with Bouton. (The Yankees did not invite Bouton to one until 1998.)

In a sense, Bouton's book was a sequel to the two books written in the 1960s by another bullpen habitué, Jim Brosnan: *The Long Season* and *Pennant Race*. Those books certainly upset the baseball establishment, but *Ball Four* leapt well beyond that. Tales of players taking amphetamines (greenies, in the parlance of the day), taking the field while hung over, and ogling young women were scattered throughout Bouton's reminiscences of the 1969 season, as he tried to mount a comeback as a knuckleballer with the expansion Seattle Pilots.

Bouton's irreverence was disarming: "I've been tempted to say into a microphone that I feel I won tonight because I don't believe

in God." Or, "Lots of people look up to Billy Martin. That's because he just knocked them down." The close of the book became his most famous quote: "You spend a good part of your life gripping a baseball, and in the end it turns out it was the other way all the time."

23. CANDY CUMMINGS

William "Candy" Cummings is the probable inventor of the curveball, and thus the chief nemesis of every man who has ever picked up a bat. His place on this list is secured not only through his own real accomplishments but also in praise of other, not-so-famous men: Elmer Stricklett, spitball; Russ Ford, emery ball; George Blaeholder, slider, and so on.

Thirty years after his retirement, Cummings described how the Big Idea came to him. "It was in the 1860s that I discovered the curve ball, and strange to say, it was the idle throwing of half a clam shell that gave birth to such an idea. As I watched the shells sail through their irregular course, the theory developed in my mind that I might apply it in baseball…. I was laughed at by scientific men and experts, but I finally proved to them that the stunt could be done, and for a long time I was known as the 'boy wonder.'"

While it may never be proven conclusively that Cummings invented the curve, his claim was backed by such 19th-century notables as George Wright, Albert Spalding and Cap Anson.

The 5-foot 9, 120-pound stringbean used his newly invented pitch to work his way up from semipro teams in Brooklyn to five ballclubs in the National Association and the National League from 1872 to 1877. He led the NA in ERA, shutouts, and innings pitched in 1873, and he won 35 games in 1875.

If only his NL totals of 21-22 are counted, he is, along with Rollie Fingers and Leroy "Satchel" Paige, one of only three Hall of Fame pitchers with losing major league won-lost records. But for all three, the story is greater than the stats.

24. SATCHEL PAIGE

Baseball historians may debate whether Satchel Paige was the finest pitcher of all time. There is certainly no question that he was the most quoted. With observations such as "Never look back; something may be gaining on you" he has made his mark on *Bartlett's* as well as *Total Baseball*.

Paige was born in Mobile, Alabama, the seventh of 11 children. The official date is 1906, but 1903 and 1908 have also been suggested. He got his nickname from toting bags at the Mobile railroad station at the age of seven.

He signed on with a local black semipro team, the Mobile Tigers, in 1924, then moved onto Chatanooga. Soon he was a celebrity in the world of southern black baseball. He had his own roadster, played guitar with Louis Armstrong's orchestra, and supped with Jelly Roll Morton.

In 1931 Paige went north to one of the finest black teams around, Gus Greenlee's Pittsburgh Crawfords. With the Crawfords, Paige teamed with Josh Gibson to form one of baseball's most impressive batteries. His Kansas City Monarchs of 1939 to 1942 may be mentioned alongside the Yankees of 1936-39 for greatest team ever.

In 1946 Branch Rickey broke baseball's color barrier when he signed Jackie Robinson. "Somehow I'd always figured it would be me," said Paige. When the 1948 season opened he was still on the Monarchs' roster. Then Cleveland Indians owner Bill Veeck decided to give the 42-year-old a chance. "Everybody told me he was through," said Veeck. "That was understandable. They thought he

was human." Satch pitched a shutout in his second start, drew 200,000 fans to his first three starts, and compiled a 6-1 record.

In 1952 Paige was 12-10 for the Browns. He barnstormed in 1954 and rejoined the Monarchs in 1955. In 1956 he signed up again with Veeck, who was operating the Miami Marlins in the International League. He finished the year 11-4 with a 1.86 ERA.

In 1965 Charles Finley brought him back to the big leagues for one more game in Kansas City, and at the presumed age of 59 he pitched three shutout innings against the Boston Red Sox.

25. WILLIE MAYS

The most exciting and best player of the 1960s, Mays raced around the bases or into deepest center field, his hat flying off behind him. "The only man who could have caught that ball," one announcer said, "just hit it." Willie Mays embodied The Joy of Baseball. In the history of the game, there may have been better outfielders, players with better arms, batters with higher averages and more homers, and faster runners who stole more bases. But no one could do all those things at his skill level, and so any discussion of "baseball's greatest player" must include Willie Mays.

Mays signed his first professional contract at age 17, with the Birmingham Black Barons of the Negro National League. Sold to the New York Giants in 1950, he reached the big club and became Rookie of the Year in the mad pennant rush of the following year. Called into the service after only 34 games in 1952, he did not return until 1954. When he did come back, he lit up New York like a Roman candle. He led all National League hitters that year with a .345 average and 13 triples. He tied for third in home runs, with 41, drove in 110 runs, and scored 119. The Giants won the pennant by five games and swept the Indians in the World Series, thanks in part to "the Catch," perhaps the game's most famous highlight clip. Harry Hooper, who played next to Tris Speaker in the Red Sox outfield for six years, said that Mays was the best outfielder ever … and Speaker had been *everyone's* choice for greatest outfielder till Mays came along.

And did we mention that he hit 660 home runs? That he won MVP Awards eleven years apart, one in New York, the other in San Francisco? That upon his return to New York in 1973 he hit a home run to win his first game as a Met?

One testimony to Mays' legacy is the number of today's superstars who wear his uniform No. 24 as a tribute. They have included Willie's godson Barry Bonds (while at Pittsburgh), Ken Griffey Jr., and Rickey Henderson.

26. NAP LAJOIE

When fans debate the question of who was baseball's best player in the first decade of the 20th century, the names most often mentioned are Honus Wagner, Ty Cobb and Nap Lajoie. Fellow Hall of Famer Kid Nichols called Lajoie "the hardest hitter I ever pitched to."

One of the best second basemen of all time and, by all accounts, the most graceful, Lajoie was also one of the most successful right-handed hitters. An established star with the NL Phillies, where he'd hit .378 in 1899, he jumped to Connie Mack's AL Philadelphia A's in 1901. The presence of Lajoie, Cy Young, and a few others helped legitimize the AL as a major league. Lajoie's .426 is still the highest batting average achieved since the 19th century.

The following year an injunction by the Phillies, who claimed that Lajoie had breached a contract with them, prevented him from playing in the state of Pennsylvania. This forced A's manager

Connie Mack and AL president Ban Johnson to shift Lajoie to the struggling Cleveland franchise, where he spent the bulk of his career. (When the team played the A's in Philadelphia in 1902, Lajoie did not accompany them.)

Lajoie was an instant sensation with Cleveland, so much so that the team was named after him—the Cleveland Naps—when he commenced to manage the club in 1905. Lajoie hit over .300 in 16 of his 21 seasons and finished with 3,242 hits for a .338 average. The controversy over the 1910 race to the batting championship—during which he trailed Ty Cobb going into the final day of the season, then overtook him through some dubious collusion, then saw the AL award the title to Cobb, then have two of Cobb's hits removed after both Cobb and Lajoie were long dead—is detailed in "The History of Major League Baseball Statistics," by John Thorn and Pete Palmer, in Section 13 of this volume.

It's difficult to argue Nap Lajoie's place among baseball's greats: his records speak volumes, and he was immensely popular. As Tommy Leach said, "Even when the son of a gun was blocking you off the base, he was smiling and kidding with you." Lajoie was elected into the Hall of Fame in 1937.

27. BARRY BONDS

Barry Bonds was one of the best players in the 1990s both defensively and offensively. He captured a Gold Glove in every season of the 1990s except two. He missed winning four consecutive MVPs in 1990-93 by the slimmest of margins. *The Sporting News* named him the player of the decade. But Bonds was only beginning.

After finishing second to teammate Jeff Kent in the 2000 MVP race, he took the next three while shattering the game's elite batting records: home runs (73 in 2001), slugging (.863, also that year), on-base average (.582 in 2002), walks, (177 in 2001, 198 in 2003), and OPS (1.381 in 2002), and park-adjusted OPS (275 in 2002). Oh, and he hit .370 in 2002 to lead the league at the age of 38. When naming the greatest player of all time, he may be mentioned with Babe Ruth, Ted Williams, and his godfather, Willie Mays.

San Francisco drafted Bonds out of high school in San Mateo, California, but when the Giants offered $70,000 instead of the $75,000 he wanted, Bonds wound up at Arizona State University. The Pittsburgh Pirates made him the sixth overall pick in the 1985 draft and they installed him in their outfield a year later.

He did not develop quickly with the Pirates. From 1986 to 1989 he did not exceed 59 RBIs and batted higher than .261 only once. The Pirates tried to trade Bonds when his contract demands exceeded his production, but other teams shied away because of his moodiness. The Bucs held on to Bonds; in 1990 they were glad they did.

In 1993 Bonds returned to his hometown San Francisco. He batted .336 with 46 home runs, and he became the first player to lead the league in on-base percentage and slugging percentage since Mike Schmidt in 1981.

Seemingly driven to become better and better, Bonds took on an intensive workout schedule after 1996. The result was another 40 home runs and his seventh Silver Slugger Award in 1997. Like Hank Aaron in his later years, not only did Bonds show no sign of slipping, but his power, bat speed, and mental approach to the game reached new zeniths. He is the Babe Ruth of our era, and the story of his enduring legacy to the game is yet to be written.

28. HARRY & GEORGE WRIGHT

Baseball's Wright Brothers are as illustrious in their chosen field as Orville and Wilbur were in theirs. Harry Wright, born in

England, was saluted on his death in 1895 by legendary baseball writer and promoter Henry Chadwick as "the father of professional base ball playing." George, twelve years younger, was born in New York, to which the family, led by their cricket-professional father, had emigrated in the late 1830s. He was simply the greatest player of his day, a national hero with the Cincinnati Red Stockings of 1869-70, managed by brother Harry.

Harry Wright instituted dozens of innovations, including the backup system, whereby fielders back up each other and pitchers back up bases; pregame batting practice; hand signals; the double steal and the hidden-ball trick, and more. The *Cincinnati Enquirer* said of Wright, "He is a baseball Edison. He eats base ball, breathes base ball, thinks base ball, and incorporates base ball in his prayers." All his life he fought to make the occupation of professional baseball player a respectable trade for grown men.

While serving as a cricket professional in Cincinnati, Harry was invited to form a baseball club that would reflect glory on the Queen City. He recruited outstanding players from the east, principal among these—and the highest paid—being his brother George, who led the Red Stockings on their undefeated national tour of 1869 by hitting over .600 with 57 home runs. His talents at the plate, however, were secondary to his fielding. In 1911, when Honus Wagner was at the height of his career playing the same position as Wright, the *New York Journal's* Sam Crane called Wright "the best shortstop ever."

But George was equally important to the development of the game off the field, starting a sporting-goods house in Boston with teammate Charlie Gould that evolved into the great Wright & Ditson firm, which in turn consolidated with that of fellow pioneer ballplayers Al Reach and Albert Spalding.

Though Harry's contribution may be more important than that of George, the younger brother made it to the Hall of Fame in 1937, sixteen years ahead of the elder.

29. TY COBB

In 1936 Cobb was the first man elected to Cooperstown, mostly by voters who grew up in his era. Babe Ruth was second. The majority of today's critics would reverse the order and maybe drop Cobb a few more pegs besides. The reason, of course, is that the modern game, with its emphasis on home runs, has evolved in a Ruthian rather than a Cobbian direction.

After all these years, he's still first in batting average (.366). He collected 12 AL batting titles in 13 years, hit over .400 three times, led in steals six times, and in runs five times. In other words, he was the best at the things he tried to be best at. Cobb epitomized the dead-ball era, which is to say, baseball before the sluggers took over.

He was no home run hitter, managing only 118 in 24 seasons. But for most of those seasons, going for homers against a misshapen, sodden ball was a losing proposition. Still, in 1925 he hit three homers in one game, and two in the next, just showing off.

Considering all that, it's a bit disconcerting to find a few modernists working overtime to chisel Cobb down to a so-so level. Essentially, the argument is that modern players are bigger, faster, better trained, and face more difficult challenges. None of the old-timers could make it big today, they say. Cobb might hit .260.

We believe a "modern" Cobb would have the same advantages in diet, training, and baseball experiences the other moderns have. He'd be bigger, faster, and better trained. He might not hit .366—though we shouldn't bet against it—but he'd be right up there showing other moderns his heels.

Now, if the critics want to stomp on Cobb, they can attack his personality. "The Georgia Peach" was mean, vindictive, selfish, vain, a bully, a racist, paranoid, cruel, and hot-tempered. But it was just because of those nasty attributes that Cobb would have found a way to win in any age.

30. TED WILLIAMS

Until Barry Bonds' most recent years, either Williams or Babe Ruth was the greatest hitter of all time, and you could probably cover the difference with an ant's umbrella. Despite losing nearly five seasons in two wars, Williams put together a statistical record that would stand against anyone's.

Here are the career figures: .344 batting average, 521 home runs, 1,798 runs, 1,839 RBIs, 2,019 walks, and a .634 slugging average. His on-base percentage is the highest all-time (Ruth is next) and his slugging percentage is second, to Ruth. And there is the .406 batting average in 1941, two MVP awards, six batting titles, two batting Triple Crowns, the All-Star Game home runs, and the home run in his final at bat.

Williams, perhaps the most patient and precise hitter ever, defined hitting in his era. In his book *The Science of Hitting* he preached plate discipline, pitch recognition and command of the strike zone. He was a disciple of slugging percentage and on-base percentage as key indicators of performance. He set standards that would be studied by future generations of players and would be credited by the likes of Wade Boggs and Jason Giambi as keys to their success.

"You want to teach hitting right," Giambi once said. "Buy every kid in this country a copy of Ted's book."

Williams, who once said his goal in life was "to walk down the street and have people say, 'There goes the greatest hitter who ever lived,'" was elected to the Hall of Fame in 1966. He died in 2002.

31. WALTER JOHNSON

Johnson is high up on everyone's list of nominees as the greatest pitcher of all time. His statistics alone are staggering. Working for a Washington team that finished in the second division in 10 of his 21 seasons, he nevertheless won 417 games (second only to Cy Young), threw an all-time record 110 shutouts, and compiled a 2.17 ERA, the seventh-best career mark. He won more 1-0 games—and lost more—than any other man. Simply to state his 1913 numbers is enough to give you a shiver: 36-7, 11 shoutouts, 1.14 ERA, and, in 346 innings, 243 strikeouts against 38 walks.

He did nearly all of this with a fabled fastball, thrown with an easy sidearm motion. It came in straight as string, but the hitters couldn't get around on it. Only late in his career did Johnson bother to develop a curve. For years his 3,509 strikeouts was considered an unbreakable record, but a more free-swinging age has changed that; even though he has been surpassed by several latter-day pitchers, with more surely to come, Johnson still may be the greatest strikeout artist ever.

Johnson finally made it to the World Series in 1924 at the age of 36. The old man was 23-7 and led the league in his usual categories: wins, ERA, strikeouts, and shutouts. He lost his first two starts, despite having an entire nation wishing for "Old Barney" to make up for all the tough years with a World Series win. (The sweetly conflated nickname linked his speed with that of auto-race king Barney Oldfield.) And then in Game 7, he came on in relief to pitch the final four frames of a miraculous 12th-inning Senators victory.

If he wasn't the greatest pitcher ever, you'd want him to be. In 1936 he was one of the first five players elected to the Hall of Fame.

32. BRUCE SUTTER

The first practitioner of what came to be called "the pitch of the 1980s," the split-finger fastball, Bruce Sutter was for nine years the dominant closer in the National League. He was a Cy Young Award winner—only the second reliever to be so honored—a four-time winner of the Fireman of the Year Award, the pitcher who set the current trend of one-inning closers, and the man who won baseball's pivotal arbitration decision.

Sutter was blessed with exceptionally large hands—his fingers were "a full joint longer than normal," according to historian Martin Quigley—and a limber wrist that enabled him to throw the pitch harder. Sutter's splitter was much more deceiving to batters because it spun quickly enough to look like a fastball.

Sutter notched 27 saves in 1978 for the fifth-place Cubs, and in 1979 he won the Cy Young Award when he spun a 2.23 ERA to accompany his 37 saves. After the season he applied for salary arbitration, one of the first stars to do so. Sutter asked for $700,000; the Cubs offered half that. The arbitrator, required to choose one figure or the other, went with Sutter. The decision sent shock waves throughout major league baseball. As a result a player with a handful of experience could compare his stats to someone with a proven portfolio, even someone who had signed a rich free-agent contract. Richard Wagner, conservative owner of the Reds, called the Sutter decision "an atom bomb for our industry."

After he led the league in saves again in 1980 and was chosen for the All-Star Game for the fourth straight year, Whitey Herzog and the Cardinals went after him. Sutter won Game 2 and saved Games 3 and 7 of the 1982 World Series against the Brewers to give St. Louis its first world championship since 1967.

Sutter finished up with the Braves, finally succumbing to the long series of injuries that had marked his career even before he hit the majors.

33. EARL WEAVER

Earl Weaver presided over the Orioles' dynasty of the 1970s, leading them to six division titles, four pennants and a world championship. His winning percentage of .583 ranks in the top 10 all-time. Although it was said his teams relied on "pitching and the three-run homer" to win, Weaver was actually a highly innovative manager. He schooled his players in fundamentals, pioneered the use of computer charts, extended the use of platooning, and even wrote a training manual used by the entire Orioles organization. Always open to new ideas, his motto became the title of his autobiography: *It's What You Learn After You Know It All That Counts.*

He never got past Double A as a minor league second baseman, but once he moved to managing he found his way to major leagues in 1968. Although Jim Palmer cracked, "The only thing Earl knows about pitching is that he couldn't hit it," he and coach George Bamberger produced 20-game winners 22 times, with six Cy Young Awards mixed in. Several pitchers, including Mike Cuellar, Steve Stone and Mike Torrez came from other organizations to achieve their best seasons with the Orioles.

Weaver was known for his rages against umpires. He was ejected from 91 games during his career. Once he was booted from both ends of a doubleheader.

However, Weaver was so respected as a psychologist that some believe his tantrums were staged to arouse his team. Weaver was elected to the Hall of Fame in 1996.

34. JOE JACKSON

One of the great natural hitters, Shoeless Joe averaged .356 for his career, the third best ever, using his favorite bat, "Black Betsy," and a sweet swing that Babe Ruth even copied. Ironically it was Ruth's popularity that helped fans forget the infamy that Jackson and his co-conspirators on the 1919 Chicago White Sox brought to baseball. Yet Jackson remains an important figure in baseball lore, linked in Baseball's Hall of Shame with such names as Jim Devlin, Hal Chase and Pete Rose.

An illiterate millhand, Joe hit .408 as a Cleveland rookie in 1911. He finished second to Ty Cobb's .420. The next year Joe hit .395 and finished second again to Cobb (.410). Except for 10 games in 1908-1909, Joe always hit .300. But a trade to the White Sox in 1915 threw him in with the proverbial bad company.

The White Sox were building a great team, but it was a team divided. Joe resented the club's college-educated second baseman Eddie Collins and his cadre of followers. The other side, the ones who griped about the a low salaries owner Charles Comiskey paid, the ones who hung with the sharpies who looked for an edge, that side accepted Joe. They didn't snicker at his lack of sophistication, or make fun of his Southern drawl.

Despite the division on the team, it won the 1917 pennant and World Series. In 1919 the Sox paraded to another pennant and were installed as heavy favorites over Cincinnati in the World Series. But eight men on the team had a different idea, including Jackson and even Buck Weaver, who knew of the fix but kept his knowledge to himself.

The story broke late in the 1920 season, while Jackson was hitting .382. The Black Sox were indicted in Chicago. Jackson admitted his guilt, but none of the players was convicted in court. There was no doubt of what they'd done, but the evidence, including confessions, mysteriously disappeared. No matter, Judge Kenesaw Mountain Landis, the baseball commissioner, banned the "Black Sox" from the game for life.

Jackson, as well as others in the group of "eight men out," played outlaw ball under an assumed name.

35. WILLIAM G. BRAMHAM

Judge William G. Bramham, a lawyer from Durham, NC, was the third President of the National Association of Professional Baseball Leagues, the parent organization of minor league baseball. He served from 1932 through 1946. Bramham had been active in baseball for many years, having been president of the Piedmont, the Sally, the Virginia, and the Eastern North Carolina Leagues. When he was elected head of the NA during the depths of the Depression, the minors were reeling and in need of strong leadership.

At the 1932 convention when Judge Bramham was elected, only five leagues stated their intention to operate the following season. Fourteen eventually operated in 1933, as Bramham brought to minor league baseball the stability and strength it needed. He made certain that the fly-by-night operators were not allowed in the minors, and his strong positions and enforcement gave minor league baseball credibility.

By 1940, 44 leagues were operating, and minor league baseball was thriving across the country. World War II brought a necessary reversal as players were called into national service, and in 1943 only 13 leagues were in operation. But Bramham continued to give the leadership that was necessary, and in 1946, less than a year

after the war had ended, 41 leagues were back in operation. Bramham retired that winter and died the following summer but the policies he instituted helped shape the minors' postwar boom that saw 59 leagues and 438 teams in 1949 with over 41 million in attendance.

In the 1930's and 1940's baseball was truly the "national pastime," even with major league baseball confined to 10 cities and played mostly in the Northeast quadrant of the United States. Minor league baseball made the sport a national game, with teams in small towns in the South, in growing cities in the Midwest, and in major markets on the West Coast. Before radio, before television, bush league baseball gave the sport its national identity. Men like Judge Bramham, Frank Shaughnessy of the International League, Joe Engel in Chattanooga and hundreds of forgotten local baseball operators showcased the sport and forged its imprint on the nation's consciousness.

36. RAY CHAPMAN

On August 17, 1920, popular Cleveland shortstop Ray Chapman stepped to the plate at New York's Polo Grounds against the Yankees' Carl Mays. As was his custom, Chapman crouched toward the plate. Catcher Muddy Ruel had trouble seeing the ball, which was headed straight at Chapman. One witness said Chapman seemed "hypnotized." There was an "explosive sound" and the ball came bounding back at Mays, who fielded it and flipped it to first baseman Wally Pipp for what he thought was the inning's first out. Pipp caught the ball and started to toss it around the infield, when suddenly he became aware something was wrong with Chapman.

"We need a doctor," home plate umpire Tom Connolly shouted. "Is there a doctor in the house?" The Indians gathered around Chapman, who at first could not speak, as the Yankees team physician applied ice to his injury. After a few minutes Chapman was able to stand, to the immense relief of the crowd. With the assistance of two teammates Chapman began walking off the field toward the center field clubhouse. At second base he crumpled to the ground; he died 12 hours later at St. Lawrence Hospital.

Chapman's unfortunate death eventually had far-reaching implications for baseball. Some baseball scholars feel that this incident had perhaps as much influence in sparking the batting revolution of the 1920s as did Babe Ruth and the introduction of the "lively ball."

The spitball, shineball, and all other dubious pitches had been outlawed on February 9, 1920, six months before Chapman's death. After Chapman died, balls hit into the stands stayed there, and umpires tossed out nicked or scuffed balls with greater frequency. In 1919 the National League went through 22,095 baseballs; in 1924 that figure had grown to 54,030. Batters now got to swing at baseballs that were more visible and less apt to "sail." Batting averages rose accordingly.

37. NOLAN RYAN

The all-time strikeout leader, with 5,714, Nolan Ryan hurled a record seven no-hitters during his remarkable 27-year career. A physical marvel, he was still throwing fastballs more than 90 miles per hour in his final year, at age 46.

Ryan made two appearances with the Mets in 1966, and despite his great promise he was only 29-38 through the 1971 season. Then he was traded to the California Angels along with three other players for Jim Fregosi.

In eight years with the Angels, Ryan led the league in strikeouts seven times, five times recording more than 300. In 1973 he fanned a major league record 383 and pitched two no-hitters. He went on to throw two more as an Angel, tying Sandy Koufax for the career record … but Ryan's career was barely at the halfway point. In November 1979 the Astros signed the free agent to a $4.5 million, four-year contract, making him the game's first million-dollar man.

In his first six years with Houston he harnessed his stuff, reducing his strikeouts and walks, and suddenly became a winning pitcher. He pitched a record fifth no-hitter against the Dodgers.

Ryan led the league in strikeouts again in 1988 despite missing the last two weeks of the season because of a hamstring injury. After the season the Astros offered him a contract with a 20-percent salary cut. On December 7, 1988, Ryan signed as a free agent with the Texas Rangers. In Arlington Ryan went from great pitcher to baseball legend.

In his first season with the Rangers, the 42-year-old Ryan led the majors in strikeouts and ranked among AL leaders in innings, ERA, and wins. He pitched a pair of one-hit complete games and carried five different no-hitters into the eighth inning or later, losing two in the ninth. On August 22 Ryan fanned Oakland's Rickey Henderson for his 5,000th strikeout.

Ryan's adherence to a grueling physical-fitness routine paid off in a career longer than any other power pitcher's. In 1990, at age 43, he became the oldest pitcher to throw a no-hitter by beating Oakland, 5-0, on June 11. The following year, as the major leagues' oldest player at age 44, Ryan pitched his seventh no-hitter.

He retired in 1993, and was elected to the Hall of Fame in 1999.

38. HONUS WAGNER

If a knowledgeable baseball fan in 1920 had been asked to name Major League Baseball's all-time All-Star team, the shortstop would undoubtedly have been Honus Wagner. Ask a knowledgeable fan today the same question and the shortstop would be the same (although Alex Rodriguez may yet supplant him if, after his trade to the Yankees, he resumes playing shortstop).

The reason for Wagner's longevity as baseball's best shortstop is simple. No other shortstop has ever combined offensive and defensive excellence the way he did; only Cal Ripken came close, and these two bookends of the 20th century cast the mold for the shortstop of the future.

Wagner broke into the big leagues in 1897. Primarily an outfielder and third baseman for the Louisville Colonels of the 12-team NL, Wagner came to the Pittsburgh Pirates in 1900 in the largest trade in baseball history up to that time. Louisville owner Barney Dreyfuss, learning that his team was about to be dropped from the NL, sent fourteen players to Pittsburgh for $25,000 and four Pittsburgh players. Dreyfuss then purchased the Pittsburgh team. Traded to Pittsburgh along with Wagner were future Hall of Famers Fred Clarke and Rube Waddell.

Playing right field, third base, second base, first base, and even pitching (he hurled three scoreless innings) during the 1900 season, Wagner won his first batting title and led the league in triples, doubles, and slugging average. Not until 1901, at age 27, did he become Pittsburgh's regular shortstop. From 1900 through 1909 5-foot-11, 200-pound barrel of a man led the NL in hitting seven times and even led in stolen bases five times. He drove in six runs in the 1909 World Series against the Tigers of Ty Cobb, the first time two batting champions faced each other in a Series. Wagner hit .333, Cobb .231, and the Pirates sent Detroit down to their third straight Series defeat.

Among the legendary baseball names who called Wagner the greatest player ever were Ed Barrow, Sam Crawford, Bill Klem, John McGraw, and Branch Rickey.

39. ALEX RODRIGUEZ

If Ernie Banks spoke the first word on what a power-hitting shortstop might accomplish, Alex Rodriguez may have the final say. Banks hit 40-plus home runs in four consecutive seasons, from 1957 to 1960, between the ages of 26 and 29. At this writing, Rodriguez has reached the 40-mark in six consecutive seasons between ages 22 and 27, twice crossing the 50 barrier to go where no shortstop had gone before.

In a golden age of big, mobile, powerful shortstops who could flat-out hit, much of the talk in the mid-1990s centered on Nomar Garciaparra and Derek Jeter in the Northeast. However, Rodriguez was making a case for himself in the Northwest as the best of the lot. Having reached the majors with the Seattle Mariners at age 18 in 1993, he broke out in a big way in his first full season as a starter in 1996, scoring 141 runs, knocking in 123, and belting 54 doubles and 36 homers. He also led the league in batting with a .358 mark.

A six-year man and thus a free agent at the remarkably tender age of 25, Rodriguez signed a 10-year, $252-million deal with the Texas Rangers in 2001, making him the highest-paid player in the history of the game. And if any ballplayer was worth that much money, Alex Rodriguez proved he was that player, averaging over 50 home runs in his first three seasons as a Ranger and winning the 2003 AL MVP despite playing for a last-place club.

Following upon his stunning February 2004 trade to the New York Yankees, Rodriguez was slated to open the season at third base, with Derek Jeter staying in place at shortstop.

40. BILL JAMES

For the past 25 years, baseball has been in the throes of a statistics revolution. No one person was more responsible for this than Bill James, the most influential baseball writer of the 20th century.

His annual *Baseball Abstract* series, self-published out of his Kansas home from 1977-81 and by Ballantine from 1982-88, introduced hundreds of thousands of fans to the power of statistical analysis. From the Runs Created metric (which boiled down batters' accomplishments into a far more meaningful number than RBIs) to his Pythagorean Method (which helped predict teams' won-lost records from their runs scored and allowed) to whimsical devices like the Favorite Toy (which estimated the chances of young players reaching milestones such as 3,000 hits), James's analysis pierced through baseball's conventional wisdom and mapped out a new understanding of the sport. He also was a fantastic writer, funny and always irreverent.

A native Kansan, James wrote his first baseball articles for *Baseball Digest* in the mid-1970s but had so much to say that he decided to publish his own annual guide to the game. The project immediately consumed his every waking hour, particularly his minimum-wage shift as night watchman at the Stokely-Van Camp factory in Lawrence. "I'd spend five minutes an hour making sure the furnaces didn't blow up," he later recalled, "and 55 minutes working on my numbers." The result was the *1977 Baseball Abstract – Featuring 18 Categories of Statistical Information That You Just Can't Find Anywhere Else.* The 68-page compendium sold 70 copies through mail order for $3.50 apiece.

Word of James' brilliance spread, however, and after a 1981 *Sports Illustrated* profile launched him into prominence, Ballantine

began publishing the *Abstract* nationally. It became a New York Times bestseller, at its peak selling 150,000 copies.

James had his largest influence after he stopped writing his *Abstracts* and moved on to more traditional books. Many kids who read him grew up to work in baseball, including general managers Jim Duquette (Mets), Billy Beane (A's), Danny Evans (Dodgers), and Theo Epstein (Red Sox). It's no coincidence that Epstein's Red Sox hired James before the 2003 season as a Senior Advisor.

41. SANDY ALDERSON

Bill James changed baseball from the outside. Alderson did it from the inside.

A California attorney before joining the A's in 1981 and becoming GM in 1982, Alderson didn't enter the game with a traditional outlook. Specifically, he had read Bill James and appreciated his scientific approach to the game. Alderson analyzed player-performance numbers as much as any GM to that point and built the A's around power and the ability to draw a walk, launching the "on-base revolution" long before Billy Beane was celebrated for this in Michael Lewis' *Moneyball*.

He worked only in Oakland through 1997, but Alderson's effect went far beyond that city. After working in the A's system, young executives there routinely moved on to top-notch big league jobs: Walt Jocketty (St. Louis), Ron Schueler (White Sox), and Billy Beane (A's, as Alderson's successor) all went on to win division titles as general managers of other clubs. Bob Watson, an A's hitting coach, was GM of the 1996 World Series-champion Yankees team. Dusty Baker, Don Baylor, and Dave Stewart all played for Oakland in the late 1980s before graduating to management roles elsewhere.

Alderson moved on to MLB as executive vice president of baseball operations and proceeded to bring some order to rules that had been skirted for years (rule-book enforcement of the strike zone and delaying tactics, notably) and to an umpiring fiefdom that had frustrated players, owners and fans. The most influential baseball executive of the past 25 years, Alderson will be tremendously important in implementing such proposed innovations as the worldwide draft, world cup, and inner-city academies.

42. SOL WHITE

One of black baseball's true founding fathers, Sol White's life spanned the time between the segregation of professional baseball in the 1880s and its re-integration in 1947.

White played for integrated minor league teams from 1887 through 1895, was a star second baseman (and played every position but pitcher) for several Negro League powerhouses, and helped found and manage one of the top black teams of the first decade of the century. In 1907 he wrote the only history of the early years of African-American ball, *Sol White's Official Base Ball Guide*.

Born only three years after the end of the Civil War in Bellaire, Ohio, a small town across the Ohio River from Wheeling, West Virginia, White grew up to be a fast runner and a feared hitter. He played for the integrated Ohio State League team in Wheeling in 1887 and batted .381, but was cut when the league drew the color line in 1888.

He later played for integrated teams in Trenton, New Jersey; York, Pennsylvania; and Fort Wayne, Indiana. He never batted less than .333, and his lifetime average in the integrated minors was an impressive .360. But by 1895 integration in professional baseball was a thing of the past.

In 1902 White paired up with Philadelphia sportswriter H.

Walter Schlichter to found the Philadelphia Giants, which White managed from 1904 through 1907. The Giants attracted the best black players in the game and became the dominant force in black baseball. The records indicate that from 1902 through 1906 they played 680 games and won 507 of them. In 1906 the Giants went 108-31. They offered to play the winner of the Cubs-White Sox World Series, "and thus decide who can play baseball best, the white or black Americans," but received no answer to their invitation.

In his book, White paints an honest picture of the difficulty of life as a black ballplayer, pointing out that the average white major leaguer made $2,000 in 1906, while the average black professional player netted only $466.

But White added, "Baseball is a legitimate profession. It should be taken seriously by the colored player. An honest effort of his great ability will open the avenue in the near future wherein he may walk hand in hand with the opposite race in the greatest of all American games—baseball."

43. RED BARBER

Red Barber was working at college radio station WRUF in Gainesville, Florida, in 1934 when Larry MacPhail invited him to Cincinnati to broadcast the Reds' games. "The Old Redhead" announced the Reds' games when they were at home and did re-creations from the teletype when they were out of town. When MacPhail joined the Dodgers in 1938, he lifted the ban of radio broadcasts that the Yankees, Giants and Dodgers had agreed to impose. He understood that, contrary to popular belief, "giving the games away for free" would boost attendance, not hurt it. Just as dramatically, he proclaimed that the Dodgers would broadcast both home and away games live, with Barber as the announcer.

The soft, friendly rhythms of Barber's voice were just what Brooklyn fans wanted on lazy summer afternoons. Barber began to plumb his southern heritage for catch phrases that became his signatures: "the bases are FOB" (full of Brooklyns); "oh, doctor!"; "hold the phone"; and "tearin' up the pea patch."

During World War II, Barber took pride in using the power of radio for good—he solicited war bond sales and promoted Red Cross blood drives. But then he had his integrity tested in a visceral way. In 1945, when Dodger boss Branch Rickey told Barber he was going to hire a black player, Barber was upset by the news. A Southerner, he contemplated resigning but finally concluded that he was a reporter first; nothing else mattered.

Barber left the Dodgers in a salary dispute and joined the Yankees in 1954. For 10 years Barber and Mel Allen, who was already on the scene, were the voices of the Yankees, but ownership unceremoniously canned Allen in 1964 and Barber two years later.

After leaving the Yankees, Barber began a new career as a writer and published six books. His study of baseball on the air, *The Broadcasters*, is still the finest book on how life in the booth really works. His story of the signing of Jackie Robinson, *1947: The Year All Hell Broke Loose in Baseball*, is a masterpiece of American history.

In 1978 Barber was chosen as the first recipient of the Ford C. Frick Award with, appropriately, Mel Allen.

44. PETE ROSE

Once the most exciting player of his age, Charlie Hustle committed baseball's cardinal sin and bet on baseball games; banished from any official contact with the game, he was sadly reduced to Charlie Hustler, making a living at the periphery of the game he

loved while promoting his case for a restoration to grace. Once he monopolized center stage with his unsuccessful pursuit of Joe DiMaggio's hit streak in 1978 and his surpassing Ty Cobb's lifetime hit record in 1985; two decades later, he regained center stage by finally confessing the full extent of his gambling.

As with Cobb, the same traits that drove Rose to the heights of competitive sport ultimately brought him down. In the end, he makes the list of baseball's most important people for his heroism and for his clay feet; the story is indivisible.

In addition to the lifetime hits record, Rose played more games than any other man (3,562), won three batting titles, and made the NL All-Star team seventeen times at five positions. He was Rookie of the Year in 1963, MVP ten years later, and played in his last World Series ten years later still, at age 42. He never wanted to leave baseball.

No one can take from Pete Rose his four pennants with the Reds or his two with the Phillies. No one can take from him the fundamental affection of the American people, who still want everything to come out all right for Pete, to see his plaque in the Baseball Hall of Fame alongside the records and artifacts of his greatness. You could look it up.

45. LARRY MacPHAIL

Night ball, radio broadcasts, batting helmets, air travel, old-timers' day, fireworks, three championship dynasties, loud feuds with his managers—the chances are that anything that Bill Veeck, Charles Finley, or George Steinbrenner thought up, Larry MacPhail had already done.

Wounded and gassed in World War I, MacPhail had even tried to kidnap the Kaiser in a daring adventure. (All he got was the Kaiser's ashtray.) General John Pershing, commander of the American forces in Europe, called the stunt crazy but added, "I'd have given a year's pay to have been with those boys."

Back home Larry took over the Cardinals' Columbus farm team and pioneered night games and air travel by baseball clubs. The fiery redhead also was fired by St. Louis, a pattern that would become standard.

As general manager of Cincinnati in 1935, MacPhail brought the first lights to a major league park ("Every night will be a Sunday"). President Franklin D. Roosevelt flipped a switch at the White House to turn on the lights for Major League Baseball's first night game on May 24, 1935. MacPhail also laid the groundwork for the Reds' champs of 1939-1940.

Moving to the moribund Dodgers in 1938, Larry brought Red Barber from Cincinnati to broadcast home games at a time when all three New York City clubs were scared that radio would decimate their attendance, hired manager Leo Durocher, and built a winner in 1941.

After another tour in the Army as a colonel, MacPhail engineered a one-third interest in the Yankees, with partners Del Webb and Dan Topping being the capital providers. He installed lights in Yankee Stadium and brought the Yanks to a pennant and world championship in 1947. During the victory celebration, he engaged in a loud public brawl. The next day his partners terminated his contract as club administrator and bought him out.

He was elected to the Hall of Fame in 1978.

46. RICKEY HENDERSON

It has become commonplace to say that Rickey Henderson is the greatest leadoff hitter who ever lived. Indeed, Henderson's leadoff ability is the key to assessing his career. He set the table with walks and hits, he advanced with stolen bases, he scored runs, and he was better at doing this than any player in the history of the game. Maybe he followed Bobby Bonds and Willie Mays as a model for the power-speed combination that has inspired so many players of today, but in truth Rickey Henderson is beyond comparison; he is unique.

When he set the career mark for stolen bases in 1991, he declared to the crowd: "Today, I am the greatest of all time." As Dizzy Dean used to say, "It ain't braggin' if you can do it." This accomplishment came nine years after he had surpassed Lou Brock's single-season record. Also in that year he won the AL steals title for the 11th time in 12 seasons.

After a productive but not altogether harmonious four years with the Yankees, Henderson came back to the A's in June 1989 and led them to the postseason. He was devastating throughout October, especially against Toronto. In five games he hit two homers, knocked in five runs, and stole eight bases while batting .400 in one of the most dominant playoff performances ever. He batted .474 in the earthquake-interrupted World Series, including a leadoff home run in Game 4 in San Francisco.

Rickey played for Toronto, another World Series winner, in 1993, and then his vagabond years commenced in earnest, with nine stops over the next ten years, culminating in a 30-game stint with the Dodgers in 2003, at age 44, in which he added two home runs to make his lifetime total 297. Although his batting average had been slipping for some years, Henderson continued to draw walks, steal bases, and score runs. In each of these categories he is the all-time leader.

47. GREG MADDUX

After posting four solid seasons with the Cubs, recognition finally came to Maddux in 1992, when he pitched in the All-Star Game, led the league in wins with 20, and earned his first Cy Young award. His timing could not have been better, as he became a highly coveted free agent that winter. Maddux spurned the New York Yankees and their extra $6 million to come to Atlanta, where the Braves had appeared in back-to-back World Series.

Maddux won his second straight Cy Young Award with a 20-10 record, 267 strikeouts, and 2.36 ERA in his first year as a Brave. He was on pace to better those numbers in 1994 when the baseball strike ended his season with 16 wins and a miniscule 1.56 ERA. He bettered that the following year with a 19-2 season, 1.63 ERA, and 10 complete games to lead the league in each category. He then pitched a two-hitter against the Cleveland Indians in his first-ever World Series start. "He doesn't seem dominating," Cleveland's Jim Thome said, "then you look up on the scoreboard and you've got one hit and it's the eighth inning."

Indeed, Maddux has never had an overpowering fastball, but his combination of pinpoint control with exceptional movement has baffled hitters for more than a decade. He's also been a model of efficiency, throwing a lot of innings with remarkably low pitch counts. "There are no secrets," Maddux said. "To pitch, you have to do two things. You have to locate your fastball and change speeds. That's all you have to do. If you can do those two things, you can pitch."

The Cy Young streak ended at four in 1996, but Maddux kept on winning. Through the 2003 season, his last with the Braves, before he returned to Chicago, he had won 15 games or more for 16 straight seasons, a feat unmatched in the annals.

48. CY YOUNG

How important is Cy Young in the history of baseball? Well, they named that award after him for some good reason. And if the Cy Young Award had been around in his day he would have picked up at least four himself (1892 and 1901-03).

They called him Cy either because he threw baseballs against a fence until it looked like a cyclone had hit it or because he showed up at the Cleveland Spiders' park in 1890 carrying a cardboard suitcase, wearing a cheap, too-small suit, and looking like what you'd get if you mail-ordered for a hick. (Farmboys in the big city were then called, invariably, either Rube or Cyrus).

But from his first pitch, he was the Spiders' best pitcher, and he continued as the staff ace for whatever team he played for during the next 20 years. Young's career record looks like a misprint: 511-313. He tops the lists in both wins *and* losses! Even when he retired in 1911, after 22 seasons, his arm was still up to the task; fat and 40, he just couldn't bend down to field bunts anymore. He never had a sore arm, even though he pitched over 400 innings five times and over 300 in 11 other seasons.

He was elected to the Hall of Fame in 1937. The award named in his honor was first given out in 1956, one year after his death at age 88.

49. PETER UEBERROTH

Peter Ueberroth was hired as Organized Baseball's sixth commissioner in 1984 to restore financial sanity to the game. Through clever marketing, improved licensing agreements, large television contracts, and corporate sponsorships he made great strides in that direction. Unfortunately, he misread the ability of the players' union and, in a series of rulings that management had colluded to cripple free agency, the owners had to turn over all the profits they had reaped under Ueberroth's regime—and more. And when he left the job after five years in office, Ueberroth handed his successor, Bart Giamatti, one of the hottest potatoes baseball had ever fielded—the Pete Rose gambling controversy.

As head of the 1984 Olympic Games in Los Angeles, he used slick marketing, bent the arms of corporate sponsors, and turned $215 million in profit. Then he turned his attention to baseball, coming on board in after the close of the Games though he had been hired in March.

During his first week on the job, Ueberroth had to deal with an umpire strike. Then the players went on strike, but he helped settle the issue in only two days. One of the players' largest concerns was that owners would collude to hold down free-agent signings, so they requested and received contract language to prevent such actions. During his term, corporate sponsorships and broadcast deals kicked in millions to the sport's coffers. During the first three years of Ueberroth's tenure Organized Baseball realized a $206 million profit.

Then the MLBPA filed a grievance, claiming that the owners had done exactly what they had promised not to—they had colluded in the signing of free agents. Three times the union filed collusion charges; three times it won its case. In total, Organized Baseball had to return $280 million to the free agents who had been victimized.

Ueberroth decided not to run for a second term. His legacy turned out to be not prosperity but distrust, as the seeds of 1994 were planted during his tenure.

50. TONY LA RUSSA

By general acclaim the smartest manager in the game today, Tony La Russa has won through preparedness, game control, and an us-against-them mentality that has won him the enduring allegiance of players and staff from Chicago to Oakland to St. Louis.

In 1977, his final season as an indifferent player in the major and minor leagues, La Russa was a player-coach in the Cardinals organization. Paul Richards, who had met him when they were in the Atlanta Braves' chain, was working for the White Sox and gave La Russa a chance to manage their Class AA Knoxville farm team in 1978. La Russa joined the White Sox as a coach later that year, went back to manage their Class AAA Iowa affiliate at the start of 1979, and took over the 46-60 White Sox from Don Kessinger on August 2. He hasn't spent a year away from a major league helm since.

With coach Dave Duncan, who has accompanied him in his travels, La Russa developed the concept of clearly defined roles for all pitchers, an approach they readily admitted works best for pitchers of average talent, who perform better when they know exactly what is expected of them. Critics say that La Russa's method is over-managing—designed to prevent second-guessing by creating the match-up that looks best on paper while slowing the game to a crawl.

He pushed the frontiers of computerizing reports and charts. He occasionally played a hunch, but many of his less obvious moves resulted from careful research.

When Jose Canseco left Oakland he drew chuckles by saying he preferred Texas because in Oakland, "All they cared about is winning." At the end of the 2003 season, La Russa had won the most games of any active manager.

51. WILLIAM HULBERT

Following the 1875 season, marked by the fourth consecutive pennant won by the Boston Red Stockings, the National Association was in ruin, brought down by a combination of non-competitive play, rampant gambling, and drunkenness—on the field and off. But most of all, the death of the NA was caused by the birth of a bigger idea. That great notion was the National League of Professional Base Ball Clubs—a capitalist consortium of stock companies dreamed up by William A. Hulbert, owner of the Chicago White Stockings.

In addition to creating professional baseball as we know it today, his accomplishments include the institution of league-scheduled play; the hiring of a staff of professional umpires; the protection of the new league's principles in its very first year, when he boldly expelled two clubs rather than compromise his vision; and the rescue of the game's reputation after the scandal of the "Louisville Four," who conspired to toss away the 1877 pennant.

After the 1879 season Hulbert expelled the Cincinnati franchise from the NL for selling "spirituous and malt liquors" on the grounds, which violated his sensibilities though not, in truth, league statute. In so doing, Hulbert sparked an insurrection of his own: a rival league, the American Association, centered in the fun-loving, hard-drinking city of Cincinnati, started play in 1882.

Hulbert was not around to observe its debut. On April 10, 1882, at the age of 49, baseball's great architect died of a heart attack.

52. BAN JOHNSON

A former sportswriter, Johnson built the American League from the old Western League, a minor loop that he and Charles Comiskey took over in 1893. In 1900 they changed its name and in 1901 proclaimed it a major league. They raided the NL for star players and managers and built the league into what they claimed it to be. From the perspective of a century later, Johnson not only thrust his own league into prominence, he saved the National League from itself and major league baseball for all of us.

Johnson ran his league with tunnel vision. A humorless workaholic, his word was law among the original AL team owners. He banned liquor from his ballparks and fined for profanity and rowdyism. He backed his umpires, raising their status. Although nominally the president of the AL, he was called the "Czar of Baseball" because he dominated the three-man commission that governed the game until 1920.

But his power slipped as new owners who resented his dictatorial ways entered the AL. Even his old ally, Comiskey, turned against him. When the Black Sox scandal broke in 1920, Johnson demanded a full investigation, causing a final break with Comiskey, who owned the Sox. One result was that the commission was replaced by a czar, Judge Landis. Ban fought his loss of power for six years before resigning. He was elected to the Hall of Fame in 1937.

53. MARK McGWIRE

Mark McGwire hit a rookie record 49 homers in 1987, then hit more than 30 home runs in each of the next three seasons with the A's. But in 1991, McGwire struggled, hitting only .201 with 22 home runs. Writers warmed up that old term, "flash in the pan."

McGwire bounced back to post 42 home runs but painful heel and back injuries scuttled most of the 1993 and 1994 seasons. A strike-shortened season and two separate stints on the disabled list limited him to just 104 games in 1995, but in his 317 at bats he put on one of the most prodigious power displays in major league history. He had more home runs than singles (39 to 35), and hit the most homers of anyone in history with so few at bats. This gave a taste of what was to come.

In 1997 McGwire hit 34 home runs through the first four months of the season. Despite his success on the field, it was clear that his days in Oakland were numbered. He would be a free-agent at the end of the 1997 season, and the rebuilding Athletics were unlikely to pay a 34-year-old slugger the kind of money he could earn elsewhere.

The Athletics worked out a trade with the St. Louis Cardinals in July 1997. He finished the season with 58 home runs; only Ruth and Maris had hit more in a single season.

Both fell in September 1998 not only to McGwire but also to the Cubs' Sammy Sosa. On September 5 McGwire hit his 60th to tie Ruth; two days later he tied Maris. The next night, against Cubs pitcher Steve Trachsel, he hit Number 62 for the record. Sosa and McGwire embraced on the field as a national television audience applauded. But there was still a lot of season—and a lot of Sosa—left.

On September 25, the season's final Friday, Sosa hit number 66 to move ahead of McGwire. "Big Mac" responded 45 minutes later with number 66 of his own. Then he poured it on in the last two games—67, 68, 69, 70.

The record didn't last long, as Barry Bonds surpassed it only three years later. But McGwire's hold on the nation's attention remains unparalleled. He retired after the 2001 season.

54. SAMMY SOSA

Until the 1998 season many baseball fans outside of Chicago would have had trouble identifying Sammy Sosa. But after his historic duel with Mark McGwire in pursuit of the single-season home run record, the personable outfielder became a celebrity in the U.S. and a folk hero in his native Dominican Republic.

"Slammin' Sammy" was already a very good player, hitting 30 homers and batting in over 100 runs each year from 1995 to 1997. He exhibited a cannon arm and good speed. On the other hand, he struck out too often, walked too seldom, ran bases erratically, and made mistakes in the field. The Cubs hoped for more. In 1998 they got it. Sosa became a more patient hitter, raising his batting average and power numbers. Sosa exploded for 20 home runs in June, the most ever hit in a month. As he battled all season with Mark McGwire for the most coveted record in baseball, Sosa seemed to delight in his rival's accomplishments.

By season's end, Sosa became the second player to surpass Roger Maris' single season record, but his 66 home runs still left him just shy of McGwire's 70. He did, however, lead the majors with 158 RBIs, and led the Cubs into the postseason. McGwire had the record, but Sosa had the MVP.

In 1999 he again shadowed McGwire in the home-run derby, this time slugging 63 to McGwire's 65. But as injury drove McGwire to an early retirement, Sosa continued to star; in 2001 he had his greatest season, with 64 homers and his highest on-base and slugging percentages ever. In 2002, he hit 'just' 49 homers, and in 2003, he led the Cubs to within one win of a return to the World Series. However, he was labeled a cheater by many after being caught, and suspended, for using a corked bat in May 2003.

55. ALBERT SPALDING

In 1899 a *New York Times* reporter described Al Spalding in the following manner: "His face is that of a Greek hero, his manner that of a Church of England Bishop … and he is the father of the greatest sport the world has ever known." Baseball has more than enough "fathers," but Spalding was a star player, a pennant-winning manager, the president of the most successful club of his era, a proselytizer for the religion of baseball worldwide, and through his sporting-goods company, the largest in the world, his name was on the baseball itself. At a time when every American who read Horatio Alger harbored the dream of becoming a captain of industry, Spalding was proof that it was indeed possible to rise from humble beginnings to become wealthy, honored and influential. That he made his ascent by means of America's national game was icing on the cake.

Born in Byron, Illinois, Spalding grew up in nearby Rockford and became the star pitcher for the Forest City nine. In 1871 Harry Wright offered him $1,500 to join the Boston Red Stockings, for whom he compiled a 54-5 mark in 1875. For the 1876 season he was lured to William Hulbert's Chicago White Stockings and collaborated with him in the founding of the National League.

In 1877 he formed the A.G. Spalding & Bros. Company to manufacture and sell sporting goods. He led two baseball teams on a round-the-world tour in 1888-89. And to cap his fabulous career in baseball, he launched a commission which erroneously concluded that baseball was invented by Abner Doubleday in Cooperstown in 1939.

56. ICHIRO SUZUKI

Ichiro Suzuki (who goes by his first name) burst on the U.S. scene in 2001 at age 27, leading the American League in batting average (.350), hits (242) and stolen bases (56) while winning both Rookie of the Year and Most Valuable Player awards. He added Gold Gloves in the following two seasons.

American fans were astounded, but Japanese fans glowed knowingly, for they had seen Ichiro win the Pacific League batting championship for the past seven years in a row. Despite his youth, he had been the highest-paid player in Japan's history. But Ichiro felt he had nothing more to prove to his fans back home; he wanted to play on the game's biggest stage. As his nation's first position player to come to the U.S. at the height of his career—as pitcher Hideo Nomo had done in 1995—Ichiro proved that while East is East and West is West, in baseball at least the twain may meet.

Ichiro set the stage for other Japanese stars to follow in his steps and, in turn, to set the stage for the international competition that Al Spalding had promoted more than a century before. Indeed, the demographics of baseball have shifted dramatically in the last generation, to the extent that U.S. nationals make for an ever decreasing portion of major league rosters. For the health of the game, that's a good thing, and Ichiro's pioneering role will grow in importance in the coming years.

57. REGGIE JACKSON

Any athlete who is recognized by his first name alone is in select company. In the minds of baseball fans, the name Reggie require no more additional information than those of, say, Babe, Ted, Joe, Mickey, Willie, or Ichiro.

Reggie came to the big leagues with Oakland in 1968 and immediately signaled his hallmark style with 29 home runs and a new record 171 strikeouts. His swing was Ruthian and he was willing to walk back from the plate as often as it took to exert his power in each and every game. Purists groaned, pointing to his batting average, which settled in at .262 at the end of his 21-year career. But Reggie led his A's to five straight divisional titles in 1971-75, including three straight World Series victories; his style fit the times, and his team.

After a single season in Baltimore in 1976 Reggie came to New York, where with the Yankees he earned the name Mr. October. In the deciding game of the 1977 World Series against the Dodgers he hit three home runs on three pitches off three different pitchers, making for a record total of five in the Series.

Reggie left New York in 1982 to spend five productive years with the Angels and a swan song with the A's. He was elected to the Hall of Fame in 1993.

58. DAN OKRENT

Dan Okrent was the writer who introduced Bill James to the nation in *Sports Illustrated,* and he was the creator of *The Ultimate Baseball Book.* But nothing compares to what he did in 1980.

It was then that he unleashed fantasy baseball upon the sports world. The idea of friends keeping their own rosters and having them rated by players' stats was not totally new; faculties at Harvard University and the University of Michigan had done it in the 1960s, and city newspapers ran boiled-down games periodically. But Okrent made his game alarmingly realistic: 23-man rosters, a salary cap, trading deadlines and more. Eight statistics were used to rank the teams: batting average, home runs, RBIs, and steals for position players; wins, ERA, saves, and ratio (hits plus walks per nine innings) for pitchers.

The game began among only Okrent and his friends, who met over lunch at a restaurant called La Rotisserie Française. They called their league the Rotisserie League, and after Okrent wrote an article about the game in *Inside Sports,* it caught on like wildfire. Leagues sprouted up in boardrooms and classrooms throughout the country. One original member of that Rotisserie League, Glen Waggoner, wrote an annual guide to the game that spread the gospel far and wide.

In many ways, fantasy league baseball protected the popularity of baseball through the strike-ridden '80s and '90s. By 2003, according to the Fantasy Sports Trade Association, 15 million adults were playing in some fantasy sports league, whether in baseball, football, basketball, even NASCAR auto racing.

59. RUBE FOSTER

In 1903, pitching for the Cuban X-Giants, Andrew Foster won four games in the best-of-seven championship series against Sol White's Philadelphia Giants. Describing his style in later years he said, "I have often smiled with the bases full and two strikes and three balls on the hitter. This seems to unnerve them." When he bested Rube Waddell of the Philadelphia Athletics in an exhibition that year, fans called him "the Black Rube," and the nickname stuck as he moved from Philadelphia to Chicago.

Before the 1911 season started, Foster formed a partnership with Chicago tavern-owner (and son-in-law of Charles Comiskey) John C. Schorling and created the Chicago American Giants, one of the greatest black clubs of all time. They played their home games in old South Side Park, which Schorling had purchased and renovated to seat 9,000 fans.

In 1919, he joined a number of club owners and started the Negro National League (NNL). Not surprisingly, Foster was elected president and secretary, but in truth he took total control of the fragile league. He handled all bookings, was responsible for settling all disputes, and hired the umpires, while continuing as manager of the Giants. The NNL grew stronger by the mid-1920s and spawned imitators. A Southern Negro League soon formed, as did the Eastern Colored League. The first real Negro World Series took place from 1924 through 1927. But the herculean effort of building black baseball took its toll on Foster. Committed to the Kankakee State Hospital following a nervous breakdown in 1926, he died there in 1930.

60. LUIS APARICIO

A pioneering combination of defense and speed, Luis Aparicio led AL shortstops in fielding percentage each year from 1959 to 1966 and each year from 1956 to 1964 he led the league in stolen bases, with yearly totals unseen for a generation. Maury Wills and Lou Brock would pilfer more bases than Luis in the era, and Rickey Henderson later sped past by all of them, but Little Looey was the man who revived a lost art.

Aparicio seemed born to play baseball. His father, Luis Sr., had been an excellent shortstop in Venezuela, playing until he was 41 and running the Maracaibo Gavilanes Winter League club. Soon Luis was playing better than his father ever did, signing a contract with Frank Lane of the Chicago White Sox in 1953.

Rookie of the Year in 1956, three years later he led the "Go-Go Sox" to their first World Series appearance since 1919. Repeating

the pattern, he moved to the Orioles in 1963, and three years later helped them to their first World Series.

Aparicio went on to own an insurance agency in Venezuela; he also handled television commentary of baseball in his homeland. In 1984 he became the first Venezuelan elected to the Baseball Hall of Fame.

61. THE SPINK FAMILY

Viewed from the perspective of today's role of journalists in the baseball world, it is hard to grasp the prestige the Spinks enjoyed—and the power they wielded—as publishers and editors of *The Sporting News* for nearly a century. Today an all-sports weekly, TSN was once regarded as the Bible of Baseball, and J.G. Taylor Spink, particularly, was the self-appointed guardian of the sport.

His uncle, Alfred H. Spink, founded *The Sporting News* in 1886, but he got his start in baseball as sports editor of the *St. Louis Post* and then as press agent for Chris von der Ahe's St. Louis Browns. He brought his brother Charles (Taylor's father) into *The Sporting News* as business manager and soon Charles controlled the company, championing challenges to the baseball establishment. Al went on to write *The National Game* in 1910, a valuable history.

When Charles died in 1914, Taylor took over the editorial reins. He expanded his weekly's coverage to include the box scores of all major and minor league games—all the way down to D Class ball. He created a network of more than 300 stringers to make certain that every tidbit of baseball news in the whole country would be available to his readers. When World War I reduced subscriptions, Spink conjured up a scheme to get the publication into the soldiers' hands free of charge; a generation of American men became avid *Sporting News* readers.

After Taylor passed away in 1962, his son, C.C. Johnson Spink (named for AL president Ban Johnson), guided the publication for 15 years until it was sold to Times-Mirror.

62. OZZIE SMITH

Ozzie Smith was in a class by himself at shortstop. Thomas Boswell of the *Washington Post* once wrote of him, "Instead of '1' his number should be '8,' but turned sideways because the possibilities he brings to his position are almost infinite."

The National League's career leader in Gold Gloves and by general acclaim the best-fielding shortstop of all time, Smith also made himself into an above-average hitter and fine base-stealer. It was Smith's glove, however, that made him a legend. He not only got to balls that other players could not even reach, he turned them into double plays; in fact, Smith retired having taken part in more twin-killings than any shortstop in history. He also rarely missed games. Only Luis Aparicio played more games at the position than Smith.

After winning two Gold Gloves in San Diego and setting a record for assists with 621 in 1980, Smith was traded to the Cardinals for shortstop Garry Templeton after the 1981 season. He spent the rest of his career in St. Louis, learning to fit his talents to the spacious dimensions and artificial turf at Busch Stadium. In 1985 the switch-hitter improved his batting average to .276 and uncharacteristically won the deciding game of the NLCS with a ninth-inning home run, the only left-handed home run of his 19-year career.

Although he piled up 2,460 hits and 580 stolen bases, it was his glove that won him his plaque in Cooperstown in 2002.

63. JACOB RUPPERT

Yankee Stadium may be known figuratively as The House That Ruth Built, but in point of fact it was owner Jacob Ruppert who built not only the palace in the Bronx but also the Yankees' tradition of excellence.

A high-living, big-spending son of a brewery magnate, Jacob Ruppert was no stranger to the elite of New York society. In fact, he had served as a four-term U.S. congressman from the "silk stocking" district of Manhattan. He went from silk stockings to sweat socks courtesy of Giants manager John McGraw. In 1915 McGraw introduced Ruppert to millionaire engineer and contractor Colonel Tillinghast L'Hommedieu Huston and suggested that the two of them buy the downtrodden New York Yankees.

Having paid $460,000 for the Yanks (back then everyone thought he had been taken for a ride, as the lowly Highlanders had previously been purchased for $18,000), Ruppert chose people to run his team and didn't interfere with them. Behind Huston's back, he hired Miller Huggins to manage the team. Huston's dislike of Huggins eventually caused the dissolution of the partnership with Ruppert.

Ruppert obtained Babe Ruth from the Red Sox in the final days of 1919 and shortly thereafter hired Red Sox manager Ed Barrow as the team's business manager. With the Huggins-Ruth-Barrow threesome in place, the Yankees won a rash of pennants and became the dominant team in the American League.

He was called Colonel Ruppert because of his rank in the seventh regiment of the National Guard. He looked after his own interests, building Yankee Stadium to house his star Babe Ruth. It cost $2.5 million but was well worth the investment.

64. CAP ANSON

Adrian Constantine Anson was a great hitter, manager, and innovator, one of the men who popularized baseball, and a star whose playing career ran so long (27 years at the major league level) that his nickname went from "Baby" to "Cap" to "Pop." When he finally left the team in 1897, the press called the young White Stockings he had managed the "Orphans."

A big man (6-feet, 227 pounds) who used his fists to enforce his rules, the least popular being his no-drinking edict, Anson was a martinet. Whether the players liked his style or not, he led his club to five pennants between 1880 and 1886.

He also helped segregate the national pastime. In 1883 the White Stockings showed up for an exhibition game in Toledo, Ohio. The presence of Moses Fleetwood Walker, an African-American ballplayer, in the opposing lineup so upset Anson that he cursed and raged from the dugout and threatened to withdraw his team from the game. Toledo countered with the possibility of withholding Chicago's financial guarantee, and Anson backed down. Both he and Walker took the field. Anson's threat did work on other occasions, however, and for later historians looking to ascribe blame for baseball's segregation he became the lightning rod.

Following a brief stint in 1898 as manager of the New York Giants, Anson returned to in Chicago to run his poolroom. Elected city clerk in 1905, he came under official investigation and was turned out of office in 1907. To make ends meet he managed a semipro team and turned to the vaudeville stage, this time with his two daughters. But all his efforts failed, and Anson declared bank-

ruptcy. The National League attempted to come to his aid, but the proud old first baseman refused all charity. When he died the next year, the league paid for his funeral.

65. BILL VEECK

Bill Veeck was baseball's promotional genius, raconteur, bon vivant and patron saint of fun at the ballpark. His many memorable innovations included planting the ivy at Wrigley Field in Chicago, inventing the exploding scoreboard, letting fans manage his teams, using a midget as pinch hitter, and putting a shower in the bleachers. Veeck also brought pennants to two teams that had gone a combined 68 years without any and he integrated the American League by signing Larry Doby and Satchel Paige.

During his stints as owner of the Cleveland Indians, the Chicago White Sox (twice), the St. Louis Browns, and two minor league teams, Veeck was part shaman, part sham. He believed that any team that relied solely on true baseball fans for its patronage would "go out of business by Mother's Day." With this in mind, Veeck the baseball purist became the game's P. T. Barnum, a characterization he hated. He preferred to be called a hustler … and literally wrote the book on the art: *The Hustler's Handbook.*

The Indians' 1948 world championship, the Tribe's first since 1920, was Veeck's finest moment. That year the team drew an unprecedented 2,620,627 fans—a record that stood for three decades—and won their one-game pennant playoff against the Boston Red Sox. Pitching for Cleveland was Gene Bearden, a rookie knuckleballer acquired from the hated Yankees on the recommendation of Casey Stengel, formerly one of Veeck's managers in Milwaukee. Bearden also won his only World Series start and saved the finale of the Tribe's six-game Series win over the Boston Braves. "Lost in a lot of the showmanship was a tremendously sound baseball mind," said son Mike Veeck.

66. DIZZY DEAN

Dizzy Dean was a man of many accomplishments and even more words, some of which were standard English. The National League's last 30-game winner and a card-carrying member of St. Louis' "Gas House Gang," Dean often made good on his outrageous boasts. As he put it, "It ain't bragging if you can do it."

In 1934 the Cardinals won the pennant as rookie Paul Dean contributed 19 wins on top of his brother's 30. The Deans were even better in the postseason. As the Cardinals prepared for the World Series against the Detroit Tigers, Dizzy predicted, "Me and Paul'll win two games apiece." That's exactly what happened.

Dizzy Dean's career began to unravel in July 1937. In the All-Star Game Earl Averill lined a ball off Dean's left little toe, fracturing it. Coming back to the mound after only two weeks, with "splints on my foot, and a shoe two sizes too big," he compensated by altering his motion. He hurt his arm and was never the same again.

During the off-season Branch Rickey traded Dean to the Cubs, with whom he lasted as both a player and a coach until June 1941, when he started broadcasting Cardinals and Browns games for Falstaff beer. Dean's disregard for correct grammar caught the attention of the St. Louis Board of Education, which demanded that he be taken off the air. Dean stood his ground. "Let the teachers teach English, and I will teach baseball." As for his use of "ain't," he said, "There is a lot of people in the United States who say isn't, and they ain't eatin'."

67. JOE SPEAR

Joe Spear may be the most important person on this list whose name you don't recognize. He is the national pastime's Christopher Wren, the head baseball architect for Hellmuth, Obata & Kassabaum—the Kansas City firm whose designs revolutionized the 21st century ballpark experience. He led the design of Oriole Park at Camden Yards and Jacobs Field in Cleveland, the only two ballparks ever awarded National AIA Awards for Architecture. He and his firm also designed the new ballparks in Cincinnati, San Francisco, Detroit, Denver, San Diego, and Philadelphia.

Spear helped pioneer the practice of building the stadium in deference to its neighborhood, as Camden Yards preserved the now-famous warehouse and Pac Bell lets home runs splash into San Francisco Bay. The former paradigm of concrete ashtrays moated by parking lots seems a distant memory.

The big story is that thanks to HOK, major league baseball played in multipurpose stadiums is largely a thing of the past. Intimacy and human scale have returned to the old ball game.

68. FRANK ROBINSON

Few ballplayers have had as much impact on the game as Frank Robinson. He won the Rookie of the Year Award in 1956 and Most Valuable Player Award in both leagues, with the Cincinnati Reds in 1961 and the Baltimore Orioles in 1966. He collected 586 home runs. In 1975 he became the game's first African-American manager (hitting a home run in his first at bat to help register his first managerial victory). After becoming an influential major league executive in the 1990s, at age 66 he returned to the field to manage the Montreal Expos. And at every stop along the way, he was an outspoken advocate of equal opportunity for African-Americans in baseball.

Although Robinson played for five teams during his 21-year career, his main achievements came with the Cincinnati Reds from 1956 through 1965 and with the Baltimore Orioles from 1966 through 1972. In 1961 Robinson was voted league MVP as the Reds won their first pennant since 1940.

At the end of the 1965 season Cincinnati general manager William DeWitt traded Robinson to the Orioles for pitchers Milt Pappas and Jack Baldschun and outfielder Joe Simpson. DeWitt branded Robinson "an old 30," a phrase that would ultimately cost him his job. In Robinson's first season in Baltimore he led the Orioles to a pennant and a World Series sweep of the Los Angeles Dodgers, winning the Triple Crown and MVP. Finishing his playing career with the Dodgers, Angels and Indians, he remained a part-time DH in his two full years at the Cleveland helm.

69. DONALD FEHR

As executive director of the Major League Baseball Players Association, Donald Fehr guided the players' union through some of baseball's most turbulent times. His first involvement with baseball came when he worked on the Andy Messersmith case. The MLBPA had just won the right to free agency in arbitration, and Fehr successfully represented the players in the owners' federal-court appeal.

Fehr became the union's executive director in 1984, two years after Marvin Miller retired. Where Miller was a fiery union leader, Fehr was more stoical but no less effective in defending and extending the players' gains. His main successes have been proving collusion in the 1986-88 off-seasons and fighting off implementa-

tion of a salary cap in 1994-95. Fearing that the owners would implement their own plan unilaterally, Fehr led the players in a walkout on August 12, 1994.

Despite the fact that many serious financial issues remained unresolved after play resumed in 1995, Fehr felt that a much better rapport came to exist between the Players Association and the Commissioner's office. "We don't always agree, we don't always get it done," Fehr said, "but there is a much higher level of joint commitment to trying to avoid difficulties.... I would like to think that everybody will remember what we went through in '94 and do their level best to avoid it."

In August 2002, Fehr and Commissioner Bud Selig agreed to a four-year deal on the collective bargaining agreement—the first deal without a work stoppage since 1969.

70. GEORGE WEISS

"The last of the empire builders," Weiss, more than any other man, was responsible for the unprecedented success of the New York Yankees from the mid-1930s until the mid-1960s: 22 pennants and 17 world championships.

He began with the Eastern League New Haven franchise in 1919 and advanced to become general manager of Baltimore of the International League in 1929. In 1932 Jacob Ruppert, admiring the farm system Branch Rickey had built for the St. Louis Cardinals, appointed Weiss farm director of the Yankees, a position he continued to hold under the new ownership of Del Webb, Dan Topping, and Larry MacPhail. The torrent of talent that flowed into the Yankee system was the envy of every other team in baseball, and it wasn't just about money.

In 1948, after MacPhail was cast aside by his partners, Weiss became general manager of the Yankees. One of his first moves was to hire Casey Stengel as manager, despite Stengel's reputation as a clown and a loser. With Weiss supplying the players and Stengel managing them, the Yankees won 10 pennants between 1949 and 1960.

Both he and Stengel were let go as "too old" after the 1960 season. Weiss became president of the expansion Mets in 1961, again hired Stengel as manager, and together they laid the groundwork for the future success of that team. In the meantime, the Yankees that Weiss had built continued to win pennants through 1964, and then collapsed into the poorest Yankees' decade since before World War I.

71. SADAHARU OH

Sadaharu Oh, the most prolific home run hitter of all time, played his entire career for the Yomiuri (Tokyo) Giants in Japan. Oh combined an unorthodox, one-footed batting stance and a uniquely Eastern hitting philosophy to help him slam 868 home runs during a 22-year career. As a product of the publicity surrounding Hank Aaron's pursuit and capture of Babe Ruth's home-run record, the two men became friends and U.S. fans became more attuned to Japanese baseball.

Oh signed with the Giants in 1959, and his early struggles at the plate gave no indication of the heroics to come. "My big weakness was that I had a 'hitch' in my swing," Oh said. "The hitch grew more, not less, pronounced with time, so that at the beginning of my first year as a pro it was very deeply ingrained."

In 1962 the Giants' batting coach, a distinguished swordsman named Hiroshi Arakawa, taught Oh to hit the way master swordsmen learn to battle. According to Arakawa there were seven steps to proper hitting form—fighting spirit, stance, grip, backswing, forward stride, downswing, and impact. As a result of this training Oh strung together 19 straight 30-plus home run seasons, despite a yearly schedule of only 140 games. He hit four homers in a single game in 1963, set the Japanese single-season home run record with 55 in 1964, and was named Most Valuable Player nine times. After retiring in 1980 Oh has managed the Tokyo Giants and the Fukuoka Daiei Hawks.

72. ABNER DOUBLEDAY

In the words of historian Harold Peterson, "Abner Doubleday didn't invent baseball. Baseball invented Abner Doubleday." So what explains his presence on this list? He is important because, despite the efforts of generations of scholars, he remains the popular answer to the question, "Who is the father of baseball?" He is important because without him the Baseball Hall of Fame would be somewhere other than Cooperstown, New York. And he is important in the way that Casey of "Casey at the Bat" is important: he makes for a heck of a good story, full of twists and turns too convoluted to go into here (see "The True Father of Baseball" on page 44 in this volume).

The real Abner Doubleday was a formidable person but the fraudulent one is whom we celebrate here. In 1861 he was at Fort Sumter, South Carolina, and commanded the first Union gun to answer the Confederate shelling that began the Civil War. Later he fought at Gettysburg and eventually rose to the rank of major general. When he died in 1893 no one who knew him could recall his ever mentioning his great invention.

In the 1905 *Guide*, Albert Spalding called for a blue-ribbon commission to investigate the origin of the game. The commission threw its support behind a letter from Abner Graves, a seventyish mining engineer in Denver who claimed Doubleday had "outlined with a stick in the dirt the present diamond-shaped Base Ball field, indicating the location of the players in the field, and [I] afterward saw him make a diagram of the field on paper, with a crude pencil memorandum of the rules for his new game, which he named 'Base Ball.'"

73. LOU GEHRIG

His accomplishments on the field made him an authentic American hero, but Lou Gehrig's tragic early death made him a legend. Sportswriter Jim Murray described the tall, strong Gehrig as "Gibraltar in cleats."

Signed by Yankees scout Paul Krichell in 1923, Gehrig got into a few games as September callup that year, then became a Yankee for good in 1925, commencing his streak of 2,130 straight games on June 1. The streak nearly obscured Gehrig's power-hitting exploits, especially as Babe Ruth began to decline in the 1930s. As only one example of his countless feats, on full display in his statistical entry, in his 13 full seasons Gehrig averaged 147 RBIs; no player was to gather so many *in a single season* for four decades.

Gehrig played the first eight games of the 1939 season, but he managed only four hits. On a ball hit back to pitcher Johnny Murphy, Gehrig had trouble getting to first in time for the throw. When he returned to the dugout, his teammates complimented him on the "good play." Gehrig knew it was time to leave.

The next day, as Yankee captain, he took the lineup card to the umpires, as usual. But his name was not on the card. Babe Dahlgren was stationed at first. Later in the month, doctors at the Mayo Clinic diagnosed Gehrig as having a very rare degenerative disease: amyotrophic lateral sclerosis. There was no chance he would ever play baseball again. He died in 1941 at age 38.

74. JOHN DEWAN

Statistics have been described as baseball fans' narcotic. If so, for most of the computer age, Dewan has been the main dealer.

A Chicago actuary who grew up playing Strat-O-Matic baseball and loving statistics, Dewan helped relaunch a failing company called STATS Inc. in 1985. (Before that, STATS had been a software company that helped three major league teams keep their own numbers.) Dewan envisioned the company as a direct data provider to media, teams and fans. He aimed to deliver statistics instantly and electronically—in real time, as it was later called--years before that concept hit the mainstream. His vision brought billions of statistics to fans and made him a multimillionaire.

Dewan's STATS Inc. broke the Elias Sports Bureau monopoly in the late 1980s by providing statistics to companies left and right, from *Sports Illustrated* to ESPN to *USA Today*. Dewan and partner Dick Cramer designed a new, bulked-up box score that presented far more information than the ones of old, with new categories such as pitch counts, ground balls and fly balls, blown save opportunities, runners moved up, and holds for middle relievers.

STATS aligned early with America Online, and in the mid-'90s brought fans an innovation they had only dreamt of before: the real-time box score. Fans with a phone line could "watch" every game unfold on their computers, through the statistics, live.

Rotisserie fans rejoiced. Sports leagues did not, however, claiming that real-time statistics delivery violated their property rights. Dewan and STATS fought the leagues in federal court and won the case in 1996, ushering in even more innovation in real-time data delivery.

Dewan and his partners sold STATS Inc. to NewsCorp in 2000 for $45 million. He later started a new company called Baseball Info Solutions.

75. BILL DOAK

"Spittin' Bill" Doak may have been responsible for causing more batters to be retired than any other pitcher in the history of baseball. He did so not with his pitching, fine though it was (NL leader in ERA in 1914 and 1921), but by inventing a baseball glove so superior to any used earlier that he earned royalties from it for nearly 35 years.

Before Doak came along, fielders' mitts were nothing but small leather pillows. They helped protect the hand but did not help the fielder make a catch, particularly before they were broken in. Players often spent several seasons pounding out a satisfactory pocket; some even cut the palm out of the glove to form a pocket.

Around 1920 Doak sketched a glove with a pocket already formed. He inserted a lace of leather strips between the thumb and first finger, which were previously connected with a single slab of leather. He took his sketches to the Rawlings Sporting Goods Company, and within a few years the Doak Glove was the most popular mitt on the market. It still protected the hand but for the first time helped the player snag the ball. Fielding improved dramatically in the 1920s, and, with continued improvement in glove design based on Doak's breakthrough, new records continue to be set today.

76. CASEY STENGEL

Casey Stengel, who knew how to tell a story, sometimes started one like this: "Now take Ty Cobb, who is dead at the present time." Or he sometimes said, "There comes a time in everyone's life, and

I've had plenty of them." Stengel left behind too many stories, too many laughs, too many outrageous stunts, and too many run-on sentences that started at Point A and meandered through the rest of the alphabet. His version of the English language even developed a name—Stengelese. He is the James Joyce of baseball and a national treasure.

His record with the Yankees is one of unparalleled success—10 pennants in 12 years, 7 World Series wins, 5 of them in a row. That he was the least likely candidate to manage the Barons of the Bronx only adds to the charm of his life story.

After posting rotten records as manager of the Brooklyn Dodgers and then the Boston Braves, Stengel was thought to be washed up. But he bounced back with championship clubs in the minors and in 1948 his old friend George Weiss confounded the press and brought him to the Yankees. After losing the 1960 World Series to Pittsburgh in the final inning of the final game, both Weiss and Stengel were bounced.

But there was a final act for each, with the engagingly awful New York Mets. Stengel managed his last game on July 24, 1965, though he didn't bow out quietly. That night at Toots Shor's restaurant he attended a party to honor the invitees for the next day's Old Timer's Game. He fell, breaking his left hip.

The next year, Stengel was elected to the Hall of Fame, and both the Mets and Yankees retired his uniform No. 37.

77. RUBE WADDELL

Historian Lee Allen described Waddell's 1903 season: "He began that year sleeping in a firehouse in Camden, New Jersey, and ended it tending bar in a saloon in Wheeling, West Virginia. In between those events he won 22 games for the Philadelphia Athletics, played left end for the Business Men's Rugby Football Club of Grand Rapids, Michigan, toured the nation in a melodrama called *The Stain of Guilt,* courted, married and became separated from May Wynne Skinner of Lynn, Massachusetts, saved a woman from drowning, accidentally shot a friend through the hand, and was bitten by a lion."

A muscular 6-footer with a wicked overhand delivery of a blazing fastball and an excellent curve, George Edward Waddell was a strikeout pitcher in an era when most batters choked up and slapped at the ball. He led his league in strikeouts seven times, six consecutively. Waddell's 349 strikeouts in 1904 was baseball's all-time record until Sandy Koufax broke it 61 years later.

As tough as he was on the mound, Waddell was even tougher to deal with personally; he was a low-intellect, high-spirited country boy who came by his nickname honestly. In a way he was a vestige of baseball's past; college-boy Christy Mathewson pointed to the future. When Mark "The Bird" Fidrych came along in the 1970s, there was barely a man alive who could make the connection. (For more about Rube's place in baseball history, see John Thorn's essay on page 150 in this volume.)

78. HANK GREENBERG

Giants manager John McGraw had his eyes out for a Jewish player to entice New York's large Jewish community to the ballpark. But his scouts saw Hank Greenberg play high school baseball and reported that he was too clumsy. The Yankees and Senators made offers, but each had an entrenched star at his position. Greenberg signed with the Tigers and by June 1933 he was a fixture at first base. Two years later he drove in 170 runs and was named the league's MVP.

Throughout his early playing days Greenberg was subjected to ethnic taunts, even by the Cubs in the 1935 World Series. He never retaliated, claiming that the slurs only motivated him to play better. He lent his support to Jackie Robinson when the invective came his way in 1947.

Greenberg's lifetime rate of .92 RBIs per game is matched only by Lou Gehrig and Sam Crawford, and when he retired in 1947, his 331 homers were the fifth-best total. Yet Greenberg's career numbers could have been even better had he not missed four and a half seasons in the armed services. The second baseball player to join the military during World War II (Hugh Mulcahy was the first), Greenberg received his discharge on December 5, 1941. Two days later the Japanese attacked Pearl Harbor, and he re-enlisted. He had barely swung a bat in more than four years when he returned to his team in front of nearly 50,000 delirious Detroit fans on July 1, 1945. He slugged a homer to lead the Tigers to a win.

79. MILES WOLFF

More than anyone, Miles Wolff is responsible for the modern renaissance of minor league baseball, as it emerged from the lean years of the 1960s and '70s to the boom of the 1980s and '90s. Wolff bought the Carolina League's Durham Bulls for just $2,666 in 1979, nurtured it into a local success, and owned the franchise as it became a national symbol of the minor leagues after the release of the film *Bull Durham* in 1988. He sold the team in 1990 for $4 million just as the minors began to flourish again.

A baseball purist at heart, Wolff grew frustrated at the money- and marketing-driven approach exhibited by the regular minor leagues, whose clubs were beholden to the major league organizations to which they fed players. (Communities rarely got to know the best players, because they were promoted to the next level within three or sixth months.) So in 1993, Wolff re-established the Northern League, a circuit in the upper Midwest made up of teams that operated outside the sphere of Organized Baseball. The Northern League's six clubs signed players—often minor league veterans on their way down or overlooked collegians—to stock their rosters. The Northern League was an instant success and spawned imitators across the country.

Wolff's first baseball job came in 1971 as the general manager of the Double-A Savannah (Georgia) Braves, and he subsequently was a GM in Anderson, South Carolina., and Jacksonville, Florida.

Wolff also owned *Baseball America*, the Durham-based magazine of the minor leagues, for most of its lifetime. He bought the magazine from founder Allan Simpson in 1982 and served as president and publisher until selling the company in 2000.

80. KING KELLY

Michael Joseph Kelly is regarded today as a lovable scamp, a legendary figure who played the archetypes of knave, fool, and jester at will. What has been lost along the way to the 21st century is that in his day he was the greatest player in the game and the hero of his age.

In 1880 Chicago manager Cap Anson induced Kelly to join the White Stockings and he soon became the darling of Chicago, the quintessential "man about town." The only thing he consumed faster and in greater quantity than alcohol was Anson's patience.

Kelly's baserunning alone was worth the price of admission. The fans yelled, "Slide, Kelly, slide!" as soon as he reached base. An enterprising songwriter eventually turned the cheer into a song that enjoyed great popularity, particularly in Chicago.

After hitting .388 in 1886 and leading the White Sox to another pennant, Kelly was sold to Boston. The city of Chicago was stunned. Anson was certainly fed up with Kelly's drinking, and player contracts had often been peddled before, but no player of Kelly's stature had ever been sold and the $10,000 price tag was unprecedented.

By the 1890s Kelly's indulgent lifestyle was beginning to catch up with him. His body, which once looked like that of a Greek god, began to look like a Grecian vase. In November 1894, his baseball days behind him, he was on his way to Boston to appear at the Palace Theater when he was stricken with pneumonia. As they carried his stretcher into the hospital, the attendants tripped and dumped Kelly on the floor. "That's me last slide," he said. A few days later he died.

81. LIVAN HERNANDEZ

Livan Hernandez, a star member of the world-renowned Cuban National team, defected to the U.S. in 1995. He was not the first Cuban to do so—Rene Arocha and Rey Ordonez had preceded him in the 1990s and Barbaro Garbey had come over in 1980. And he was not the last—his brother Orlando, for example, fled in a ramshackle boat in 1997.

But Livan was the most important. He signed with Florida as a free agent, whereas Arocha and Ordonez had been signed through a lottery, much as Tom Seaver came to the Mets after Atlanta bungled his initial signing. Ariel Prieto was the last notable Cuban defector to expose himself to the amateur draft, back in 1995; ever since Hernandez, the sponsors or agents of defectors from the Cuban National squad have made certain that these top-rank players jumped to a country other than the U.S. before offering their services to U.S. major league clubs. This made defecting more lucrative and spawned even more defections.

Hernandez cost the Florida Marlins a $2.5 million signing bonus in 1996, when the club was determined to expand its Latin American fan base, but he was worth every penny. After only 30 minor league games, the durable right-hander established himself as a major leaguer with a nine-game winning streak in 1997. He became an overnight sensation by virtue of his performance in October 1997. He was chosen the MVP of the Championship Series after beating Atlanta twice, including an NLCS-record 15 strikeouts in Game 5. Then, in the Marlins' World Series victory over the Cleveland Indians, Hernandez won two more games and the WS MVP. Since then, he has played for the Giants and Expos.

82. HAL RICHMAN

Strat-O-Matic baseball has amused 11-year-old boys for more than 40 years. Few of those know that the game was invented by an 11-year-old boy himself.

Hal Richman, who grew up in New York in the early 1950s, loved playing Ethan Allen's All-Star Baseball—a simulation game in which players' performances were determined by spinning discs—but grew frustrated by that game's not having pitchers involved. Richman invented his own game, which first used a deck of playing cards to randomize the outcome of at-bats. He played the game with friends in summer camp, added strategies such as stolen bases and sacrifice bunts, and later made the probabilities more realistic by using two dice to determine outcomes. After earning an accounting degree at Bucknell University, Richman decided on a nifty name for his game—Strat-O-Matic—and borrowed $3,500 from friends in 1961 to launch the game commercially.

Within three years, the game was a hit. It wound up selling millions of editions and still is in production today with, of course, the inevitable computer edition. For generations of young fans, Strat-O-Matic was one of the favorite connections to the sport, and their main lens into strategy and team-building. The impact of Richman's game and others like it (APBA, Pursue the Pennant and so on) goes far beyond kids' basements: In a 2002 *Baseball America* survey of major league teams' front-office executives, 50 percent of them said they played Strat-O-Matic or a similar game as a kid.

83. PETER SEITZ

Peter Seitz never swung a bat or pitched an inning during a major league game, yet his impact on Organized Baseball was enormous. As an arbitrator for MLB and the MLBPA, he laid the groundwork for baseball's current system of free agency.

Andy Messersmith of the Los Angeles Dodgers and Dave McNally of the Montreal Expos requested free-agent status after pitching in the 1975 season without signing new contracts. Thus the two challenged the legality of the automatic-renewal clause in the standard contract.

Their appeal was heard by three officials: John Gaherin, who represented the owners; Marvin Miller, the economist who was executive director of the MLBPA; and Seitz, a professional arbitrator from New York who served as an impartial judge.

In a 70-page opinion, Seitz cast the deciding vote that ruled Messersmith and McNally free agents. "It was represented to me," Seitz said, "that any decision sustaining Messersmith and McNally would have dire results, wreak great harm to the reserve system and do serious damage to the sport of baseball and would encourage many other players to elect and become free agents.

"The panel's sole duty is to interpret and apply agreements and understandings of the parties. If any of the expressed apprehensions and fears are soundly based, I am confident that the dislocations and damage to the reserve system can be avoided or minimized through good-faith collective bargaining between the parties."

Following his decision, Seitz was immediately fired by baseball's owners, who called his action detrimental to the game.

Seitz held other important positions as a labor-management arbitrator, including work with the National Basketball Association, New York City and the Defense Department.

84. KEN GRIFFEY, JR.

Those too young to have seen Willie Mays in his prime could see in Ken Griffey, Jr. the player nearest to Mays in ability. Just 30 years old, and finishing the 1999 season with 398 career home runs, Griffey had already placed himself in elite company. He had led the AL in homers four times, including back-to-back seasons in 1997-98 with 56 homers. He also won 10 consecutive Gold Gloves and made numerous leaping catches in center field to rob opponents of home runs. Elected by experts to the "All Century Team" announced in July 1999, he was then voted by fans as one of the top 25 players of the 20th Century.

Griffey, Jr. was also baseball's most marketable star, despite playing in a medium-sized market in Seattle. He was the consensus pick to challenge Hank Aaron's home-run record, and he more than anyone may have saved major league baseball in the Northwest. And yet, when the opportunity came to exercise his free agency and go home to Cincinnati, where he had grown up watching his father star for the Reds, Junior pulled up stakes. (Griffey, Sr. had finished with the Mariners in 1991, playing 51 games over his last two seasons alongside his son.)

After a 40-home run, 118-RBI debut in the National League, Griffey ran into an incredible string of injuries that reduced him to part-time duty and left many wondering whether he would ever again display the form he had exhibited with Seattle.

85. BOB FELLER

He grew up on a farm just west of Des Moines, Iowa, in the small town of Van Meter. Farm chores made him strong, and his father made him a pitcher. According to Feller, his father "made a home plate in the yard, and I'd throw to him over it. He even built me a pitching rubber. When I was 12, we built a ballfield on our farm. We fenced the pasture, put up the chicken wire and the benches and even a little grandstand behind first base. We formed our own team and played other teams from around the community on weekends." That was the way it was, not so long ago, and Bob Feller stands as a proud symbol of what made baseball America's game.

In July 1936 the 17-year-old Feller made his debut for Cleveland in an exhibition game, striking out eight St. Louis Cardinals in three innings. From that moment on, he was major league news. After several relief appearances, he made his first start in mid-August and struck out 15 St. Louis Browns in a 4-1 victory. In September he struck out 17 Philadelphia Athletics, tying the major league mark and setting a new AL record. Then he went home to finish high school.

In 1941 Feller went 25-13 with 260 strikeouts but missed more than a month of the season. The day after Japan bombed Pearl Harbor he enlisted in the Navy. While some baseball stars spent the war playing exhibition baseball games to build the troops' morale, Feller served as a chief specialist on the battleship *Alabama*, winning five campaign ribbons and eight battle stars.

Feller came back from the war better than ever. He won 26 games for the sixth-place Indians, 10 of them shutouts, while striking out 346. He finished his career at 266-162 and a 3.25 ERA.

Named to the Hall of Fame in 1962, his first year of eligibility, Feller was bothered by his Hall of Fame plaque, which lists his baseball career as spanning "1936 to 1941" and "1945 to 1956" with no explanation. He once suggested to Commissioner Peter Ueberroth that the plaque might be changed to reflect the facts. The commissioner answered that such a change would be "inconvenient."

"Well," said Feller, "it was inconvenient to get shot at."

86. DAVID NEFT

It's hard to believe today, with books such as *Total Baseball* in every baseball fan's library, but for most of baseball's first 100 years there was no such thing as a comprehensive book of historical statistics. Then David Neft came along.

The closest thing baseball had was *The Official Encyclopedia of Baseball*, first published in 1951, but that listed only a few statistics per player. Neft, a New York formal statistician working for Information Concepts Incorporated in the 1960s, sold his bosses—and the Macmillan publishing company—on a book that listed more than a dozen statistics for every player, all the way back to 1876. It was a mammoth undertaking, and it changed the course of baseball fandom.

The business of building a credible baseball encyclopedia was amazingly complicated in the 1960s. Computers were only beginning to handle the type of data entry, storage and checking required. Second, baseball's records, particularly before 1920, were in complete disarray. Players were missing or identified incorrectly.

Sources such as old *Spalding Guides* were notoriously shoddy, and even the official statistics put out by the leagues back then had hundreds of errors. Neft's team of researchers criss-crossed the country, from library microfilm rooms to long-lost graveyards, to look up old box scores and recreate statistics from 1876-20 virtually from scratch, and to resolve other conflicts.

Finally published in 1969, *The Baseball Encyclopedia* ran 2,338 pages and weighed six and a half pounds. One *New York Times* reviewer raved that it was "the book I'd take with me to prison." It flew through its first printing of 50,000 books and ultimately sold more than 100,000 copies. The book began a new era of fanaticism for baseball statistics and history.

Neft went on to create encyclopedias in other sports, and his *Sports Encyclopedia: Baseball* has been issued annually for three decades.

87. JOHN SCHUERHOLZ

No modern general manager has been able to win more often, and in more places, than John Schuerholz. He has been a master at juggling batting lines with bottom lines, and has been able to keep his teams in contention every season for 20 years.

Schuerholz's job is barely recognizable compared to the one that former GMs such as George Weiss held, before arbitration and free agency, before the media and ownership demands, before the draft and international market, before 29 other clubs and three rounds of playoffs. With that in consideration, some might consider Schuerholz the best general manager in baseball history.

His Braves have won one World Series, five pennants and 12 straight division championships (a professional sports record). In doing so, Schuerholz did have the advantage of a large payroll, but he never lost sight of the player-development aspects of running a club, deftly weaving in top prospects while acquiring established veterans through trades and free agency. As other large-revenue teams such as the Orioles and Dodgers floundered, the Braves kept winning season after season.

Before heading to Atlanta in 1990, Schuerholz ran the Royals, with whom he won the 1985 World Series. He helped build Kansas City into baseball's model expansion club throughout the '70s while serving in player development, presiding over a minor league system that produced the likes of George Brett, Frank White, Dennis Leonard, Bret Saberhagen, Danny Jackson and Bo Jackson, feeding teams that finished first or second every year from 1975 to 1985.

88. MINNIE MINOSO

Saturnino Orestes Armas "Minnie" Minoso was the first dark-skinned Latin to play in the U.S. major leagues and an inspiration to generations of Caribbean youth. It is not too much to say that he was the Jackie Robinson for Latin America.

Minoso, who grew up in Cuba's Matanzas Province, left school at age 14 to work in the sugar fields. In 1946 he signed with Alex Pompez's New York Cubans for $150 a month plus a boat ticket to Key West and train fare to New York. Cleveland's Bill Veeck purchased the 25-year old Minoso in 1948 and assigned him to Dayton in the Class A Central League. He made it to Cleveland the next year, but he lasted only nine games.

He returned to the majors as a 28-year-old rookie in 1951, but after eight games with the Indians he was traded to the White Sox. He hit .326 that season and led the league in stolen bases and triples.

In December 1957, after hitting .310 with 103 RBIs, Minoso was traded to Cleveland but in 1960 Veeck reacquired Minoso for the White Sox in a seven-player trade. Minoso responded in 1960 by leading the AL in hits, with 184, and by finishing second to Roger Maris in RBIs. He was 37.

Father Time was catching up with Minoso. He retired in 1964—sort of. On September 11, 1976, Veeck, who was again running the White Sox, reactivated the 53-year-old Minoso so he could become a four-decade major leaguer. For once in his baseball career Minoso was nervous.

"It's been many years since I face pitching like this," he said. "I hope [the fans] forgive me." That day he went hitless against the Angels' Frank Tanana. But the next afternoon he faced 25-year-old Sid Monge, who had been only 20 days old when Minoso first appeared in the American League. Minnie singled to left.

89. HARRY CARAY

When young Harry Carabina decided he wanted to be a baseball announcer, he conned his way into an audition with Merle Jones, owner of KMOX, St. Louis' largest radio station. After the audition Jones commented, "Your voice has an exciting timbre." He helped Carabina land his first broadcasting job, in Joliet, Illinois, and the voice of the renamed Harry Caray went on to excite fans for well over half a century.

Caray's first major league job was with his hometown Cardinals, and he stayed there for 25 years, from 1945 to 1969, working with four different owners—Sam Breadon, Fred Saigh, Bob Hannegan, and August Busch, who fired him.

He went on to work for Charlie Finley in Oakland, but after one season with the A's he returned to the Midwest. The Chicago White Sox hired him in 1971 and he stayed on when the team was sold to Bill Veeck in 1976. On Opening Day that year, when the crowd began singing "Take Me out to the Ball Game" during the seventh-inning stretch, Veeck noticed that Caray was singing along in the broadcasters' booth.

Without the announcer's knowledge Veeck had a microphone set up in the booth, and Caray's raspy singing voice was soon booming throughout the stadium. Confronted by Caray, Veeck explained, "Anybody in the ballpark hearing you sing that song knows he can sing as well as you can. Probably better than you can. So he or she sings along." From that day on Caray's enthusiastic rendering of the song was a Chicago tradition, especially on the North Side when he moved to the Cubs for the final years of his career.

90. DICK YOUNG

Dick Young began his career with the *New York Daily News* as a messenger boy in 1937. After 45 years there he moved to the *Post*, but he had already changed the style of covering a baseball game forever. In the age of day baseball, the writers for afternoon papers had the players all to themselves after a game. Young, working for a morning paper with multiple editions, hung around the clubhouse to pick up quotes, "like a chipmunk looking for nuts," in the uncomplimentary phrase that stuck. With these he would not only flesh out his game stories but also pepper his popular and, to the targets of his gibes, enfuriating column, "Young Ideas."

No beat reporter today would dream of filing a game story without a quote. No baseball writer has ever dipped his pen in vitriol to greater effect. And no baseball writer prior to him would risk utter alienation from the source of future stories, as he did on a habitual basis.

Love him, hate him, you couldn't ignore him. Even as his

readers came increasingly to resent his testiness and his tendency to expound on the decline of society in general, he remained influential to the last. He died in 1987.

91. SCOTT BORAS

No player agents has been more hated by management and vilified by the media than Scott Boras, and no agent has been more effective for his clients, and contributed more to the escalation of player salaries over the past decade.

Boras, born in Elk Grove, CA in 1952, began his involvement in professional baseball as an infielder/outfielder in the St. Louis organization during the mid-1970s. He never advanced past Class AA, retiring in 1977. In the off-season he pursued a law degree, becoming convinced of the inequity of minor league contracts. "The deals were unilaterally imposed and the team could get out of them at any time," he said later. "There was never any negotiation."

In his new career as an agent, Boras looked to challenge the system. After drawn-out, confrontational negotiations, he secured ever-larger amounts for top picks Andy Benes, Ben McDonald and Brien Taylor, the New York Yankees' first selection in 1991 who signed for $1.55 million—and never reached the major leagues. Although Boras continually added to his major league client roster (he won for Kevin Brown baseball's first nine-figure contract) it was another amateur, Florida State outfielder J.D. Drew, who gained him his greatest notoriety.

In 1996 amateurs Travis Lee and Matt White had escaped the draft through a loophole and commanded deals for over $10 million each; Boras envisioned even bigger numbers for Drew. The Philadelphia Phillies drafted Drew second overall, but refused to meet Drew's $11-million salary demand. After a season in the independent Northern League, Drew went back into the draft, was selected by St. Louis and signed for $8-million.

Boras reached the pinnacle of his fame when, following the 1999 season, he negotiated a 10-year, $252-million contract that sent free agent Alex Rodriguez to Texas. Three years later, that contract prevented a trade to Boston before the Yankees finally obtained Rodriguez early in 2004.

92. FRANK BANCROFT

He never played professional baseball, he managed his last game over a century ago, he won only one pennant, and he's not in the Hall of Fame. So how does this gent make the list?

In a baseball career that spanned more than 40 years, he led the first professional U.S. team to visit the Caribbean. The one pennant he won was capped by victory in the very first World Series (1884, not 1903). He was talented enough as a manager to be hired by six big league clubs—and contentious enough to wear out his welcome mat with seven, a record unequaled unless you count Billy Martin playing Judy to George Steinbrenner's Punch.

Oh, and one last thing. He was the pioneer of platooning, with his 1884 Providence Grays of 1884, and perhaps earlier, with his Detroit Wolverines.

Bancroft first managed during the Civil War, arranging baseball games between Union Army regiments. Later he settled in New Bedford, Massachusetts, ran several successful businesses, and in 1878 became manager of New Bedford's entry in the International Association, the first minor league. After the season he took his team barnstorming to Cuba. Two years later he was at the helm of Worcester when it entered the National League.

His other managerial stops were (in sequence) Detroit, Cleveland, Providence, Philadelphia, Indianapolis, and Cincinnati. In 1892 he became business manager of the Reds, a post he held until his death in 1921.

93. ARCH WARD

Notre Dame graduate Arch Ward's first job was as the first sports publicity director his alma mater ever had. After one year there he moved to the *Rockford Star* to write sports. Five years later he was in the big leagues of sports journalism: sportswriter and, later, sports editor of the *Chicago Tribune.*

In 1933, Ward hit upon the idea of having a baseball game between stars from both leagues, as a sporting way to tie in to the "Century of Progress" Exposition in Chicago that year. He saw that July 6 was an open date for all major league clubs, so he began to push the idea in his columns. In addition to promoting the city and the fair, Ward felt it could serve a charitable cause as well: raising funds for the "Professional Ball Players of America." (He was surely connecting baseball officials to their memory of the 1911 All-Star benefit game on behalf of the family of Cleveland's Addie Joss.) This was during the cold heart of the Depression, and Ward figured some former players who were financially strapped would benefit. Many owners disliked the idea, and when they finally agreed to it, they firmly stipulated it would be a one-time event.

As history has demonstrated, the concept was a smash from the very beginning. John McGraw came out of retirement to manage the National League. Babe Ruth, even though he was 38 years old, was the star, with both a two-run homer and a critical running catch. Seventeen future Hall of Famers played for the 47,595 fans that came to Comiskey Park. Of the $52,000 raised, $45,000 was donated to former players in need of financial assistance.

In 1934, Ward conjured up another all-star idea: the College All-Stars against the champions of the NFL, an event that ran annually through 1976.

94. MARTIN DIHIGO

Only Martin Dihigo has been elected to the Cuban, Mexican, and United States Baseball Halls of Fame. His speed, size, and strong throwing arm made him one of the most versatile players in baseball history. During his 30-year career Dihigo played every position on the field—sometimes more than one in the same game—and played each of them exceptionally well.

Dihigo was arguably the greatest Cuban ballplayer of all time. Among Cuban-born players, only Cristobal Torriente was considered his peer at the plate. Johnny Mize, who played for a team Dihigo managed in the Dominican Republic winter league in 1943, said Dihigo was the greatest player he'd ever seen. Buck Leonard shared Mize's opinion: "He could run, hit, throw, think, pitch, and manage."

Known as "El Maestro" in Mexico and "El Immortal" in Cuba, Dihigo began his U.S. career as an 18-year-old second baseman for the Cuban Stars. After five years he moved on to the Homestead Grays, and had short stints with the Philadelphia Hilldales, the Baltimore Black Sox, and the New York Cubans. Dihigo won three Negro League home run crowns and tied Josh Gibson for another. As a pitcher, he racked up more than 200 wins in American and Mexican ball.

He played sparingly as player-manager for the New York Cubans in 1945 and continued to play and manage in Cuba and Mexico until the early 1950s, when he returned to Cuba to stay. Dihigo served as Cuba's minister of sports until his death in 1971.

In 1977 he became the first Cuban to be elected to the National Baseball Hall of Fame.

95. ROGER KAHN

Brooklyn-born Roger Kahn began covering the Dodgers for the *New York Herald Tribune* as a kid out of college. Ebbets Field was his graduate school, where he learned about baseball and baseball players, and most enduringly, the boys of summer in their ruin.

In his prolific career as an author of notable sports books, none of his titles stands above *The Boys of Summer*. Indeed, when *Sports Illustrated* selected its 100 Greatest Sports Books in 2002, Kahn's masterpiece ranked #2; only a boxing book stood above it.

Kahn showed a generation of writers that even if they start their careers in the toy department of a newspaper, to use Red Smith's phrase for the sports department, they can aspire to literature. He showed a generation of fans that as their boyhood heroes grow frail, as they themselves soon will, the road to heroism remains open and wide.

Within half a decade, 1966 to 1972, baseball books grew up, with other monumental accomplishments such as Larry Ritter's *The Glory of Their Times* (1966), Harold Seymour's *Baseball: The Golden Age* (1971), Roger Angell's *The Summer Game* (1972), and, in an altogether different vein, Jim Bouton and Leonard Shecter's *Ball Four* (1970). Roger Kahn was in the thick of this golden age and, in a personal golden age that extended into the current century, went on to write such fine books as *A Flame of Pure Fire* and *October Men*.

96. LEFTY O'DOUL

They called Lefty O'Doul "The Man in the Green Suit" because he was given to wearing a bright green sport jacket day in and day out. They might have also called him the American father of Japanese baseball, the NL batting champion of 1929 (with a .398 average), and "Mr. Pacific Coast League," because, in his lengthy and varied career, he was all of these things.

O'Doul started out as a pitcher. He was signed by the San Francisco Seals of the PCL in 1917, and pitched a handful of games with the Yankees in 1919 through 1922. Traded to the Red Sox, he ended his pitching career in a blaze of ineptitude, surrendering 13 runs in one inning of work in a 27-3 loss.

Returning to the majors as a 31-year-old outfielder, he hit .319 for the Giants in 1928 but John McGraw didn't like his fielding and traded him. With the Phillies O'Doul banged out a league-leading .398 average, 32 home run and, in what remains an NL record, 254 hits. He won another batting title in 1932 with the Dodgers.

He is famous as the answer to the trivia question, "Who has the highest batting batting average of any man eligible for the Hall of Fame who isn't in it?" (He hit .349 over 11 seasons; only Joe Jackson's .356 is higher.) How good a hitter was he? With Vancouver, at age 59, O'Doul sent himself up as a pinch hitter and walloped a triple. How did he do it? There were two reasons, he said: "The first is clean living, and the second is to bat against a pitcher who's laughing so hard he can hardly throw the ball."

Starting with the Seals in 1935 O'Doul began a long career of managing in the Pacific Coast League. He remained with San Francisco until 1951 (serving as vice president of the club from 1948 to 1951), and also managed San Diego ,Oakland, Vancouver, and Seattle.

Starting in the early 1930s O'Doul made the first of more than 20 trips to Japan. There he assisted Matsutoro Shoriki in founding the first professional team, which he dubbed the Giants in honor of his last major league club. After Japan's defeat in World War II, O'Doul returned to the country to help restore baseball and the defeated nation's morale.

On leaving baseball in 1958, O'Doul founded a popular San Francisco restaurant. It remains a landmark on Geary Street just off Union Square, and they make a heck of a corned-beef sandwich.

97. NED HANLON

Though never a strong hitter, Edward Hugh Hanlon was a fine outfielder and, more importantly, a leader. At age 24 he was named captain and found himself leading a team of luminaries when the Detroit Wolverines roared to the world championship in 1887. In 1892 he received an offer to manage the Baltimore Orioles, a team that had been absorbed into the NL when the American Association disbanded after the 1891 season.

The Orioles were awful. They finished 1892 dead last, 54-1/2 games out of first. Hanlon built a new team by gambling on young, unproven players. In 1893 he acquired third baseman John McGraw, outfielder Joe Kelley, and catcher Wilbert Robinson. The next year he added outfielder Willie Keeler, shortstop Hughie Jennings, and veteran first baseman Dan Brouthers. All six were eventually named to the Hall of Fame. By 1894 Hanlon's club was fully established, and the Orioles won the pennant for three years running.

Attendance fell off as the Orioles finished second in 1897 and 1898. In 1899 the team merged with Brooklyn, and Hanlon received 10 percent of Brooklyn's stock. He was now both president of the Orioles and manager of Brooklyn. He shifted most of Baltimore's best players to Brooklyn, creating a powerhouse that was christened "Hanlon's Superbas," after a vaudeville act of the same name. (Hanlon himself had been nicknamed "Ned" after a famous contemporary oarsman named Ned Hanlan.) The Superbas won pennants in 1899 and 1900, giving Hanlon five flags and two second-place finishes in his seven years as a manager.

Hanlon's greatest legacy is not his string of pennants but the success of the managers he influenced: Joe Kelley, Hughie Jennings, Wilbert Robinson, and John McGraw. Hanlon joined his disciples in the Hall of Fame in 1996.

98. WHITEY HERZOG

Dorrel Norman Elvert "Whitey" Herzog changed the face of managerial strategy in the 1970s and 1980s as he transformed lackluster franchises in Kansas City and St. Louis into AstroTurf-exploiting, speed-dominated division champions and pennant winners. Stolen bases, defense and relief pitching were at the heart of "WhiteyBall."

His career as a ballplayer was undistinguished and marred by injuries. Having been traded to Baltimore at the start of the 1961 season, he missed Opening Day after being hit in the nose by a ball coming through the back of a batting cage. Herzog was dealt to Detroit in 1962, and in early 1963 he was beset by an ear infection that hastened his retirement.

In 1965 he became a Kansas City coach and lasted until getting into a shouting match with Charlie Finley regarding traveling expenses. The next year he was named a coach for the New York Mets, and later became director of player personnel for the team.

In 1973 Herzog replaced Ted Williams as the Texas Rangers' manager but couldn't turn their fortunes around. In July 1975, however, Jack McKeon was fired at Kansas City, and Herzog was offered the managerial post. It was with the Royals that WhiteyBall first took shape, and it paid off with three successive AL West titles,

but each time the Royals lost to the Yankees in the Championship Series. After Herzog finished second in 1979, he was gone.

"I thought I did my greatest job of managing that year, and yet I got fired," said Herzog. "It's amazing how fast you can get dumb in this game."

Yet as one door closed, another opened. In June 1980 Herzog was got a job across the state with the Cardinals. The results were a world championship in 1982 and pennants in 1985 and 1987.

99. CARL HUBBELL

Carl Hubbell was nicknamed "the Meal Ticket" because that's what he was to the New York Giants and manager John McGraw during his career. Hubbell earned two Most Valuable Player Awards and over two seasons won 24 games in a row. He is best remembered for the 1934 All-Star Game during which he struck out future Hall of Fame sluggers Babe Ruth, Lou Gehrig, Jimmie Foxx, Al Simmons, and Joe Cronin in succession. But what made him important (as opposed to merely a great player) was that with his trademark screwball he showed the baseball world that—even after the 1920 ban on spitballs, emery balls, and other trick pitches that had been dead-ball era staples—a pitcher without much of fastball or curve could still be a star.

Hubbell didn't throw a screwball in high school, and the rest of his arsenal didn't interest baseball scouts, but Hubbell refused to give up. Persistence paid off, and he caught on with the Class D Oklahoma State League's Cushing Refiners. In June 1924 the circuit collapsed, and by season's end Hubbell was with the Class A Western League's Oklahoma City Indians. There Hubbell met an older pitcher named Lefty Thomas who worked with him on developing a sinker. As Hubbell tinkered with the new delivery he kept turning his wrist farther and farther over, and as he did he developed an entirely new pitch—the screwball. Christy Mathewson had thrown a "fadeaway," a changeup with a reverse break, but Hubbell threw his pitch hard—so hard and so often that when his career was done, his left arm turned inward.

The Tigers purchased him at the close of the 1925 season but told him not to throw that crazy pitch. He never threw a pitch of any sort for Detroit despite three years in their system.

Hubbell was about ready to quit baseball when scout Dick Kinsella routed him to John McGraw's Giants. There he registered five consecutive 20-game seasons, amid a myriad of other feats. He was elected to the Hall of Fame in 1947, and lived to the age of 85.

100. MEL ALLEN

The single most recognizable—and likable—voice in the history of baseball broadcasting may well have been that of Mel Allen. Although his broadcasting career included stints covering football and other sports, his many years of broadcasting the Yankees, the World Series, and the All-Star Game have forever linked his comfortable style with the Golden Age of Baseball on the air. His easy drawl and signature "How 'bout that, sports fans?" were inextricably connected with the pleasure of baseball.

In 1937 Allen obtained his law degree from the University of Alabama, where he had broadcast Crimson Tide football games for the CBS affiliate in Birmingham and, with the recommendation of pioneer broadcaster Ted Husing, he was hired as a CBS staff announcer for $45 a week. When Larry MacPhail broke the New York baseball radio blackout, Allen was hired as the Yankees' broadcaster for the 1940 season. He and Red Barber, voice of the Dodgers, did the first of their World Series broadcasts together the following year. Allen proved to be an immediate hit with New York fans. He nicknamed Joe DiMaggio "The Yankee Clipper" and christened Phil Rizzuto "Scooter." In 1948 Allen introduced his famous home run call: "It's going, going, gone!"

In a move that devastated Allen for years to come, he was fired after the 1964 season. For a decade he was essentially gone from the national scene. But when Major League Baseball introduced its first syndicated series, *This Week In Baseball*, in 1977, Allen was back for a victory lap. When the Yankees hired him to work their cablecasts in 1985, *Sports Illustrated* waxed eloquent. "The Voice is back where it belongs…. When you hear it, it's summer again, a lazy July or August afternoon with sunlight creeping across the infield."

Chapter 48

Team Histories

The Washington Senators
Despite deep political connections, the Washington Senators couldn't make a go of it in two tries in the nation's capitol. Here, President Eisenhower throws out the first pitch to start the AL season April 18, 1960. Watching are Bob Allison of the Sens, and vice-president Richard Nixon, seated, left.

By Frederick Ivor-Campbell, Matthew Silverman and Bill Deane

When the Tampa Bay Devil Rays and Arizona Diamondbacks began play in 1998 they brought to 112 the number of clubs (plus those of the Negro major leagues) that have played major league ball at one time or another since baseball's first professional league—the National Association—was organized in 1871. Some of the early teams dropped out after only a few games, but several have played for more than a century, and one—the present Atlanta Braves—has played every season from 1871 to the present. The only existing franchise older than Atlanta's (which originated as the Boston Red Stockings, then became the Boston and Milwaukee Braves before moving to Atlanta) is the Chicago Cubs, which organized in 1870, a year before league play began. The White Stockings (as they were first known) missed two seasons (1872 and 1873) in the aftermath of the great Chicago fire, but have since then continuously represented the same city longer than any other club in baseball history.

Here are brief histories of 30 current big league clubs, arranged alphabetically by city or state. These are followed by summary histo-

ries of the 82 other clubs—now defunct—that at one time also represented their cities in the major leagues. The story of an older franchise that preceded the current one in a direct line of descent is contained within the current team's entry. For example, the St. Louis Browns of 1902-53 will be found within the Baltimore Orioles section, but the Providence Grays, who departed from the National League after the 1885 season, scattering its players to the winds, will bear mention only in the final, "graveyard" section of this essay.

Anaheim Angels (aka Los Angeles Angels, California Angels)

Of the 10 teams added to the major leagues in the 1960s and '70s, the Angels were quickest to put together a winning season, finishing third in the American League in only their second year of play.

Former cowboy actor and singer Gene Autry brought the club into being as the Los Angeles Angels in December 1960. They played their first season, 1961, in Los Angeles' Wrigley Field, a former minor league park with power alleys only five feet deeper than the foul poles; five Angels hit 20 or more home runs that year. Though the team finished seventh in the standings, they were second in homers only to the mighty Yankees.

What the Angels lost in home runs in 1962 (when they moved

out of Wrigley Field into the Dodgers' new stadium), they more than made up in pitching. Paced by rookie Dean Chance, the Angels nearly doubled their wins on the road, and, as late as mid-August, stood in second place, within striking distance of New York. Though they tailed off in September, they finished a respectable third, 10 games back.

The team collapsed to ninth the next year, but in 1964 Chance's pitching and splendid relief by rookie Bob Lee helped lift the team back into the first division. Among Chance's league-leading 11 shutouts were six 1-0 victories.

Los Angeles became the California Angels in 1965 in anticipation of their move south to a new stadium in Anaheim the following year, but neither the name change nor the new location stirred them out of the second division. In 1967 with below-average run production but the league's third-best pitching, the Angels shot up from ninth to third in midseason before leveling off to fifth. After dismal seasons in 1968 and 1969, career years in 1970 by pitcher Clyde Wright (22 wins, including a no-hitter) and newly acquired left fielder Alex Johnson (202 hits and a league-high .329 batting average) helped the Angels snap back with an 86-76 record that matched their previous best (1962).

The seven losing seasons that followed 1970 were somewhat redeemed by the arrival in 1972 of pitcher Nolan Ryan, who burst into superstardom as an Angel, setting a modern record of 383 strikeouts in 1973 and hurling four no-hitters in three years (1973 to 1975). Ryan's effectiveness dipped in 1978, but the club as a whole came to life, contending closely for the Western Division title all season until Kansas City shot ahead in September.

In 1979 Don Baylor became the first (and only) DH to be named league Most Valuable Player, as a renewed offense powered California to its first division title. Baltimore stopped the Angels in the ALCS, though. The team's run production dropped off dramatically the next year, and the club followed up its best season with its worst.

After another losing season in 1981 (during which Jim Fregosi was replaced as manager by 20-year veteran Gene Mauch), California lured free agent Reggie Jackson from the Yankees. With Jackson leading a resurgent offense and Geoff Zahn headlining the league's second-best pitching staff, the Angels rebounded to 93 wins in 1982 and their second division title. They defeated Milwaukee in the first two games of the ALCS, but lost the next three. A disappointed Mauch retired.

Again, in 1983, the Angels followed a championship with a poor season—not quite as bad as 1980, but still their third worst to that point. In 1984 they rebounded to .500, good enough for second in a weak division. Pitcher Mike Witt concluded his rise to staff ace with a perfect game on the season's last day.

Gene Mauch came out of retirement to manage the Angels again in 1985. With pitching that featured splendid relief from newly acquired Donnie Moore (31 saves; 1.92 ERA), the team led the division much of the season, but lost three of four to Kansas City in the final week to fall a game behind the Royals into second.

With Witt's 18 wins and 2.84 ERA pacing the staff and rookie first baseman Wally Joyner leading the offense, California won the 1986 division crown with ease. In the ALCS against Boston, the Angels took three of the first four games, and were within one pitch of capturing their first pennant in Game 5, but the Sox rallied to win.

For the third time the Angels followed up their division championship with a losing season, this time dropping the 1987 season finale to tie for last place in the AL West. Manager Mauch retired again, this time for good. After another losing season brought them

home a distant fourth in 1988, the Angels signed Doug Rader to manage the club. They also acquired a veteran pitcher—Bert Blyleven—who led a resurgence that lifted the club to its third best won-lost record ever. Since the West was now the stronger AL division, the team's 91 wins carried them only into third place. In 1990 they dropped just one place in the standings, but plummeted below .500, 23 games out of first.

The Angels began strong in 1991, and moved into the division lead on July 3, but seven straight losses plunged them to fifth; although they finished at .500 for the season, just 14 games out of first, they wound up in the division cellar. After four sub-.500 seasons the Angels (paced by Jim Edmonds' 107 RBIs and Mark Langston's 15-7 mark) led the newly-configured AL West for most of the 1995 season, only to fade and finish in a tie in the division race with the upstart Seattle. The AL West title was decided by a one-game playoff in which the Mariners' Randy Johnson made the difference. California's improvement made it one of only three major league clubs to register an increase in per-game attendance over 1994.

The Angels fell to last in 1996, resulting in manager Marcel Lachemann's firing. He was replaced by John McNamara on an interim basis, and former Astros pilot Terry Collins took over the post later. At the end of 1996 the Angels changed their name (to Anaheim Angels), owners (the Walt Disney Company purchased the team), and manager (Collins arrived from Houston). In 1998 they changed their stadium (a reconstructed ballpark was renamed Edison Field), but they could not change their luck. In 1997 the Angels had chased both the Mariners for the AL West title and the Yankees for the AL Wild Card before coming up short of both. Injuries, which hurt the team's chances in 1997, caught up to them again in '98. The Texas Rangers supplanted the Angels atop the standings in the final week of the season to win the AL West title.

The Angels fell apart in 1999. Dissension between Collins and the players, especially new first baseman Mo Vaughn, resulted in the manager getting axed at season's end. Rookie skipper Mike Scioscia led the Angels to 82 wins in 2000 despite the fact that no one on the inexperienced starting staff won in double figures. Troy Glaus emerged as one of the league's best third baseman, and his AL-best 47 home runs helped Anaheim set a club mark with 236 homers. Left fielder Darin Erstad set team records with a .355 average and 240 hits, the highest hit total in the major leagues in 15 years.

After dropping to 75-87, 41 games out of first place, in 2001, the Angels shocked the baseball world in '02. Led by the offense of Garret Anderson (123 RBIs, .306), Glaus (30 homers, 111 RBIs), and unlikely heroes like keystone combination Adam Kennedy and David Eckstein, plus the pitching of Jarrod Washburn (18-6) and Ramon Ortiz (15-9), Anaheim won a club-record 99 games to earn the AL Wild Card berth. They then defeated the heavily favored Yankees with a .376 team batting average in the ALDS, three games to one. After that, the Angels dismantled the Twins, four games to one, in the ALCS. The dream appeared over in the World Series when the Giants won three of the first five games and led Game 6, 5-0, in the seventh inning. But the Angels staged a miracle rally to win the game, then finished off the Giants the next day to claim the world championship.

But it was back to reality in 2003. The Angels nosedived back to 75-87, finishing next-to-last in the West.

Arizona Diamondbacks
Along with the Tampa Bay Devil Rays, the Arizona Diamond-backs were granted a $130 million NL expansion franchise on

March 9, 1995. Jerry Colangelo, owner of the National Basketball Association's Phoenix Suns, headed the Diamondbacks ownership group. Joe Garagiola, Jr., a former player agent, was named the team's first general manager. In November 1994, more than three years before the first scheduled game, the Diamondbacks named former Yankees pilot Buck Showalter as the franchise's first field manager.

In Bank One Ballpark, a $335 million retractable-roofed, natural-grass facility in downtown Phoenix, the Diamondbacks drew 3,602,856 fans their first season. After getting off to a rocky start—they lost their first five games—the Diamondbacks finished strong and posted key victories in the closing weeks of the season against the Chicago Cubs, San Francisco Giants, and New York Mets, who were locked in a fight-to-the-finish struggle for the final playoff berth. Mound ace Andy Benes came within two outs of a September no-hitter and Travis Lee, who had the first hit and home run in club history, was one of the year's top rookies. Devon White was the team's first All-Star.

Arizona became the first team to reach the postseason in just its second year of existence. The Diamondbacks won 100 games, including 17 wins by National League Cy Young Award winner Randy Johnson. He also led the NL in complete games and innings and his 364 strikeouts were the fourth most in the 20th century. Jay Bell, Matt Williams and Steve Finley each hit 30 home runs and drove in 100 runs, and Luis Gonzalez batted .336 with 111 RBIs. Arizona, however, fell to the Mets in the 1999 Division Series.

The Diamondbacks seemed poised to repeat as NL West champion for the first two months of the 2000 season, but the Giants took over first place. Despite the midseason acquisition of Curt Schilling, who, along with Johnson, gave Arizona one of baseball's best righty-lefty combinations, the Diamondbacks finished third. Showalter was fired the day after the season ended and was replaced by Bob Brenly, who had been a broadcaster for the team.

Brenly could do no wrong in 2001. Led by Johnson (21-6) and Schilling (22-6), and the surprising power surge of Gonzalez (57 homers, nearly double his previous high), the D'backs regained the AL West title. They then knocked off the Cardinals, three games to two, in the Divisional Series, and the Braves, four games to one, in the Championship Series. Arizona at last ran up against the mighty Yankees, winners of four of the previous five world championships. Behind their aces, the Diamondbacks easily won the first two games at home. New York was a different story. The Yankees reeled off three straight one-run victories, the last two following blown saves by Arizona closer Byung-Hyun Kim. But the D'backs regrouped to win Game 6, then gave the Yanks a taste of their own medicine in the clincher. A ninth-inning bloop hit by Gonzalez off seemingly invincible closer Mariano Rivera gave Arizona the world championship in only their sixth year of existence.

The dynamic duo was no less effective in 2002, as Johnson won his fourth-straight Cy Young Award with a 24-5 log, while Schilling again finished second on the strength of a 23-7 season. The Diamondbacks won the West again with a 98-64 record, but were stopped cold by the Cardinals, losing the NLDS in three straight. Physical woes held Johnson and Schilling to a combined 14-17 record in 2003, and Arizona was lucky to escape with a third-place, 84-78 season, their worst showing since their debut year.

Atlanta Braves (aka Boston Red Stockings, Boston Beaneaters, Boston Braves, Boston Bees, Milwaukee Braves)

The Atlanta Braves, who first played in 1871 as Boston's Red Stockings, are the only club to field a team every season of professional league baseball.

When the game's first openly professional club, the Cincinnati Red Stockings, decided to revert to amateur status, manager/outfielder Harry Wright and three of his teammates (including brother George, the greatest player of the 1860s) took their talents and club nickname to Boston where, with infielders Ross Barnes and Harry Schafer and pitcher Al Spalding, they formed the nucleus of a team that would dominate the five-year history of the first professional league, the National Association. After a close second-place finish in their first year, the Red Stockings won four pennants in convincing fashion, including a 71-8 record in 1875 with an .899 winning percentage that has never since been approached in major league ball.

When the National League replaced the NA in 1876, four of Boston's best players, including Spalding and Barnes, deserted the club for Chicago. After a fourth-place finish in 1876, the Red Stockings lured pitcher Tommy Bond from Hartford and finished at the top in 1877 and '78. Bond dominated NL pitching, winning 80 games (40 each year), 22 more than his nearest rival. Although he won 43 more in 1879, Boston slipped to second, behind the Providence Grays, managed by brother George.

In 1880 the Red Stockings suffered their first losing season. After a second consecutive sixth-place finish the next year, Harry Wright left to manage Providence, but Boston rebounded to third in 1882 and surprised everyone in 1883 by outplaying favored Chicago and Providence to capture their seventh pennant.

Providence knocked them out of the race late in 1884, and Boston remained out of contention the next four seasons. In 1889, though, with several players signed from the defunct Detroit Wolverines (including batting champ Dan Brouthers), and 49 wins from pitcher John Clarkson, the Beaneaters (as they were now more commonly known) waged a two-team race for the championship with the New York Giants. Boston won as many games as the Giants, but lost two more and finished a game behind their New York rivals.

Frank Selee, who had managed two straight minor league pennant winners, was hired from Omaha along with his star pitcher, Charles "Kid" Nichols. Their arrival in 1890 ushered in Boston's second golden era. When they left the club twelve years later, the Beaneaters had won five more NL pennants. Nichols won 27 games in his rookie season, but Boston—decimated by defections to the outlaw Players League—finished only fifth. With the return of some of the defectors in 1891, Clarkson won 33 games, Nichols recorded the first of seven 30-win seasons, and the Beaneaters returned to the top.

When the NL expanded in 1892 from eight teams to twelve, in the wake of the collapse of the rival American Association, the schedule was also expanded and the season divided into two halves. Boston won the first half and the Cleveland Spiders the second. In a World Series to determine the league champion, the Beaneaters (102-48) defeated the Spiders.

The split season was abandoned and the schedule reduced in 1893—and Boston captured its third straight pennant. Center fielder Hugh Duffy hit .363. The next year Duffy led the way with .440, which is still the major league record. His Beaneaters didn't win the pennant, but they became the first club in a decade (and the last until 1920) to hit over 100 home runs. Five Beaneaters drove in 100 runs or more, and the team set a big league record for runs scored (1,220).

Boston dropped out of contention for a couple of years, but bounced back in 1897 to edge Baltimore for the pennant. In the Temple Cup series, though, played between the first- and second-

place teams for the world title, the Orioles overwhelmed the Beaneaters, four games to one. The next year Boston won 102 games to lead the league, but the league had abandoned the four-year-old Temple Cup.

After coming in second in 1899, the Boston club dropped out of pennant contention for 14 years, finishing as far back as 66-1/2 games (in 1906) and losing as many as 108 (in 1909). The Braves (as they were now known) rose to fifth in 1913 under new manager George Stallings. Through the first half of 1914, however, the Braves seemed to be destined for another cellar finish.

In mid-July they stood a last-place eighth in a tight field. Six days and six wins later they were third. By mid-August they had climbed to second; on August 26 they replaced the New York Giants in first. For two weeks they alternated between first and second, then broke out of the pack to win the pennant by 10-1/2 games.

Boston's heroes were pitchers Dick Rudolph and Bill James, both in only their second full big league seasons. Rudolph won 26 games in 1914 and James won 26; then they added two more each in the "Miracle" Braves' World Series sweep of the heavily favored Philadelphia Athletics.

A seven-game losing streak in early September dropped them out of a tie for first in 1916. They rallied, but finished third. It was the Braves' last close race for 32 years.

From 1917 through 1945 the Braves finished as high as fourth in only three seasons and only once did they come as close as nine games from the top. With four years in the cellar and eleven in seventh place, the team finished near the bottom of the league more than half the time.

In 1946, with dynamic new ownership headed by contractor Lou Perini; a new manager, Billy Southworth, who had led the Cardinals to three pennants and two world championships; and the return of war veterans like pitchers Warren Spahn and Johnny Sain, the Braves had their first winning season in eight years. At the end of the season Boston acquired third baseman Bob Elliott from Pittsburgh. He enjoyed a career year in 1947, powering the Braves to third place. Spahn and Sain won 21 games each.

Spahn dropped to 15 wins in 1948, but Sain won 24. Four veterans—plus rookie shortstop Alvin Dark—hit over .300. With the league's best pitching and hitting, the Braves moved out in front in June and shook off their last challengers with a September spurt. From there on, the Braves' path in Boston was downhill. Cleveland beat them in the World Series, and the club dropped to fourth for the next three years. Southworth resigned partway through the 1951 season. In 1952 the team fell to seventh; home attendance was less than one-fifth what it had been four years earlier. The next spring Perini moved the franchise to Milwaukee in the league's first realignment since 1900.

The move was a spectacular success. Not only did the Braves rebound to second place, but attendance jumped 649 percent over their previous year in Boston to set an NL record of more than 1.8 million. The league's best pitching staff was led by the trio that would anchor Milwaukee's years of greatness: veteran Warren Spahn, sophomore Lew Burdette, and rookie Bob Buhl. In 1953 Eddie Mathews led the league in home runs, a category the Braves would own in the coming years as Hank Aaron joined the team the following year.

The Braves were slightly ahead through much of the 1956 season until five straight losses in early September brought them even with the surging Dodgers. The issue was not settled until the final day, when a Dodger victory over Pittsburgh left Milwaukee a game back in second.

The acquisition of veteran second baseman Red Schoendienst from St. Louis in June 1957 steadied the infield and gave the team a baserunner for Mathews and Aaron to drive home. In August the Braves drew away from the pack, then recovered from a September slump to win the pennant by eight games over St. Louis. The Yankees took them to seven games in the World Series, but Burdette's shutout in the finale brought the Braves their first world championship since 1914.

Milwaukee repeated as league champions in 1958, but in the Fall Classic, after taking three of the first four games from the Yankees, they lost the Series in seven. The race was much tighter in 1959 until the Giants broke away from the Dodgers and Braves in August. But in September the Giants faltered as the others surged past them, and the season ended with the Braves and Dodgers tied. In a best-of-three playoff, the Dodgers took the pennant in two games—both by only one run and the second only after 12 innings.

A portent for the Braves' future could be seen in the crowd of under 20,000 that attended the first playoff game in Milwaukee. After setting a third NL record in 1957, Milwaukee attendance had gradually declined, dropping below 2 million in 1958, the club's second pennant year, and even further in this year of the tight pennant race. When attendance dropped in 1965 to a new Milwaukee low of just over half a million, the club pulled up stakes again and moved to Atlanta.

The Braves' won-lost records in Milwaukee in 1965 and Atlanta in 1966 were nearly identical—but in Atlanta attendance improved by almost a million. Aaron was still at the height of his powers, and younger players were beginning to make their mark. Reliever Phil Niekro was converted to a starter in 1967 and responded with the league's best ERA.

After finishing no higher than fifth in their first three seasons in Atlanta, the Braves celebrated 1969, the first year of divisional play, with a late-season drive that carried them to the championship of the West. Veteran Orlando Cepeda, newly acquired from St. Louis, joined Aaron in supplying power, and Niekro won 23 games as the Braves won 10 in a row to clinch the title in their next-to-last game. In the league's first Championship Series, though, the "Miracle" Mets of New York swept Atlanta in three games.

From there it was mostly downhill for the next decade. After breaking Babe Ruth's career home-run record in the 1974 home opener, Aaron returned to Milwaukee (to the AL Brewers) in 1975. Attendance in Atlanta dwindled without Aaron. Yachtsman Ted Turner bought the club in 1976 and attendance rose, but the team sank to the bottom of the division for four years.

In 1982, though, with power from outfielder Dale Murphy and third baseman Bob Horner, and exceptional pitching from Niekro (17-4) and reliever Gene Garber (30 saves), Atlanta grabbed the division lead with a season-opening 13-game winning streak and recovered from a midsummer collapse to edge Los Angeles by one game for their second divisional crown. But they were swept by St. Louis in the NLCS.

For the next two seasons Murphy's league-leading slugging carried the Braves to second place. By 1986, though, they had sunk into the division cellar. Murphy boosted them up a notch in 1987 with the most productive season of his career, but as his power at the plate dropped the next year, the Braves sunk to their worst finish in 53 years.

With the first bottom-to-top comeback in NL history, the Braves captured the West in 1991. As Atlanta's home attendance zoomed back above 2 million for the first time since 1983, the Braves won a

battle with Los Angeles that saw 11 ties or lead changes in the season's final weeks. The Braves captured the city's first pennant with a victory over Pittsburgh in seven games. Free agent Terry Pendleton (the NL MVP) joined David Justice and Ron Gant to power Atlanta's offense, while a trio of young pitchers—Tom Glavine, Steve Avery, and John Smoltz—anchored one of the league's best staffs.

In the World Series the Braves overcame a two-game deficit to take a Series lead before falling short by one extra-inning run in each of the final two games. The following season was very similar. Once again the Braves won the NL West and edged Pittsburgh for the pennant, although this time it took a come-from-behind win in the final at-bat of Game 7 to beat the Pirates. Once again they faltered in the World Series, this time succumbing to Toronto in six games.

For the third season in a row, in 1993 the Braves topped the NL West, this time charging from ten games back in July to a four-game lead in mid-September, then holding off resurgent San Francisco to clinch the crown on the season's final day. After building a 2-1 lead in the NLCS, though, they fell to the Phillies in six games.

When the players' strike ended the 1994 season in August, pitcher Greg Maddux, en route to a record third consecutive Cy Young Award, was fashioning one of the greatest seasons in years. Atlanta's 68-46 record ranked second in the NL only to Montreal's 74-40. But a new divisional alignment had moved the Braves from the NL West to the East—Montreal's division—so they finished second, six games behind the Expos.

Behind Maddux (19-2, 1.63 ERA), who won his fourth straight Cy Young, and rookie star Chipper Jones, the Braves bounced back in 1995, romping to the NL East title. Atlanta also charged past wild-card Colorado in the first round of the new postseason format and swept the Reds in the NLCS. In the World Series the Braves met the Indians in a rematch of the 1948 Fall Classic. This time the results were far different as Atlanta triumphed in six games.

The Braves won the NL East again in 1996. Atlanta's staff was paced this time by Cy Young winner John Smoltz (24-8, 276 strikeouts), Tom Glavine (15-10), and Mark Wohlers (39 saves); its offense was led by Chipper Jones (.309, 30 HRs, 110 RBIs), Ryan Klesko (34 HRs, 93 RBIs), and Fred McGriff (28 HRs, 107 RBIs). In the first round of the postseason Atlanta rolled over Los Angeles. In the NLCS, the club had its back to the wall. Down three games to one, it rallied with 12-1, 3-1, and 15-0 wins over Tony LaRussa's Cards. The Braves kept it up in the first two games of the World Series, stomping Joe Torre's Yankees 12-1 and 4-0. The pundits were about to anoint the Braves as one of history's greatest teams. Then, suddenly, they ran out of gas, losing the next four straight to New York.

That seemed to set the pattern for the years that followed: "America's Team" continued to win the NL East each year, only to fall short in the postseason. The Braves lost the Divisional Series to the Cardinals in 2000, the Giants in 2002, and the Cubs in 2003. They lost the Championship Series to the Marlins in 1997, the Padres in 1998, and the Diamondbacks in 2001. And they lost the World Series to the Yankees in 1999. Fans and the media painted the team as autumn underachievers, unmindful of the fact that only one of eight postseason teams each year can win it all.

The Braves did have many highlights during those years, nonetheless. They won a club-record 106 games in 1998, and topped 100 wins in 1997, 1999, 2002, and 2003 as well. Tom Glavine won his second Cy Young Award in 1998, Chipper Jones copped the NL MVP Award in 1999, and Rafael Furcal was the league's Rookie of the Year in 2000, the year Turner Field hosted the All-Star Game.

Baltimore Orioles (aka St. Louis Browns)

The history of professional league baseball in Baltimore dates back to 1872, to the Lord Baltimores of the National Association, and includes the great National League Orioles of the 1890s. The city was also represented in the American League's first big league seasons, 1901 and 1902. But when those Orioles moved to New York in 1903 and became the Highlanders (later Yankees), Baltimore was without a big league club for more than half a century, until the transfer of the Browns from St. Louis in 1954.

The current Orioles didn't get their start in St. Louis, though. Their first home was Milwaukee, where they finished in the AL cellar in 1901. When they moved to St. Louis the next year, they lured several valuable players from the city's NL Cardinals—including 1901 batting champ Jesse Burkett, star shortstop Bobby Wallace, and the Cards' three best pitchers. They also took on the Cardinals' discarded nickname, becoming the new St. Louis Browns.

The Browns finished a strong second to the Philadelphia Athletics in their first St. Louis season, but fell to sixth the next year and, except for a fourth-place finish in 1908 (thanks to the pitching of newly acquired veteran Rube Waddell), remained mired in the second division until 1920. Late in the 1913 season a young Branch Rickey was hired to manage the Browns. In his two full seasons he was unable to lift the club out of the second division, but he did sign college star George Sisler (whom he had coached at the University of Michigan)

In 1916, his first full season, Sisler led the Browns in hitting as they caught fire in August to record their first winning season in eight years. Pitcher Urban Shocker was obtained from the Yankees two years later and by 1920 had developed into a 20-game winner. Also in 1920, Sisler connected for what is still a major league record 257 hits and batted .407 to help move the Browns up to fourth, their first finish that high since 1908. The next year Shocker's 27 victories brought them a winning season and third place. And in 1922 the team recorded its finest record ever in St. Louis: 93 wins and a .604 winning percentage.

The 1922 Browns, led by Sisler's sizzling .420 average, hit .313 as a team to lead the league. Left fielder Ken Williams ran away with the RBI title and beat out Babe Ruth and Tilly Walker for the home run crown. (Ruth, to be honest, did miss nearly a third of the season that year.) Sisler and Williams even finished one-two in stolen bases. And though Shocker slipped a bit to 24 wins, he led a pitching staff that recorded the league's lowest ERA. The team led the league in the standings throughout July and into August before the Yankees nudged ahead of them. The Browns never regained the lead, remaining second, a heartbreaking single game back, at season's end.

Falling back to fifth the next year, as Sisler missed the whole season with a sinus infection, the Browns remained out of contention for the next 21 years, dropping to their lowest point in 1939 with 111 losses. They had three winning seasons in the war years of 1942 to 1945. The Browns captured their only pennant in 1944, edging the Detroit Tigers on the final day after trailing them through most of September. The World Series—an all-St. Louis affair—proved anticlimactic as the Browns lost in six games.

The Browns finished third in 1945 before sinking back into the second division. Even the club's purchase by the dynamic Bill Veeck in July 1951 couldn't rouse them. A month after buying the Browns, Veeck made his best-remembered move; bringing in midget Eddie Gaedel for one plate appearance (he walked).

Unable to earn either victories or money in St. Louis, Veeck sold the club in September 1953 to a Baltimore group, who relocated

and renamed them the Orioles. The new owners hired the brilliant Paul Richards to rebuild the team as manager. It took him (and Lee MacPhail, who became general manager and president in 1958) several years to move the Orioles above .500. In 1960 young third baseman Brooks Robinson and rookie Jim Gentile led the team as it made its first run for the pennant since 1944. In first place in early September, they finished second when the Yanks won 15 straight.

The next year the Orioles did even better, winning six more games than they had in 1960. Gentile hit 46 home runs and drove in 141. But the Yankees and Tigers had even better years and the Orioles finished a distant third.

When Hank Bauer was brought in to manage the Orioles in 1964, the team entered its golden decades—twenty years which saw them win seven division titles, six pennants, and three world championships, with only two finishes below third. With Robinson driving in runs and left fielder Boog Powell slugging at a league-leading pace, the Orioles finished with wins in seven of their final eight games. But the White Sox won their last nine and the Yankees put together an eleven-game streak near the end to take the pennant and leave Baltimore in third, two games back.

After another third-place finish in 1965, the Orioles acquired slugger Frank Robinson from Cincinnati and moved second-year pitcher Jim Palmer into the starting rotation. Palmer won 15 to lead a balanced staff, and Frank Robinson captured the Triple Crown. With both Robinsons and Powell driving in 100 runs or more, the Orioles romped to their first pennant. They continued the romp in the World Series, holding Los Angeles to a total of just two runs as they swept to their first world title.

A drop in offensive production and the loss of Palmer to injuries for most of the season plunged Baltimore into a tie for sixth in 1967. Palmer was out the next year, too, but pitchers Dave McNally and Jim Hardin burst to the forefront with fine seasons to lift the club back to second.

Baltimore coach Earl Weaver, a pennant-winning manager in the Orioles farm system, replaced Hank Bauer at the Orioles' helm in mid-1968 to begin what became one of the longest and most successful managerial tenures of recent times. In 14 full seasons Weaver led his club to six Eastern Division titles and six second-place finishes, with one season each in third and fourth. In seven of the 14 years the Orioles compiled the league's lowest ERA, including five consecutive seasons (1969-1973). Baltimore pitchers put together 21 different 20-game seasons in those seasons (eight of them by Jim Palmer), and garnered six Cy Young Awards.

In the first three years of divisional play Baltimore ran away with the East championship and swept the American League Championship Series to capture the pennant each time. The 1969 team (despite an embarrassingly easy loss to the New York Mets in the World Series) is often ranked among the greatest clubs of all time. With overwhelming pitching and fielding, the Orioles took the division crown by 19 games, winning a club-record 109. The Orioles also were tops in fielding and their pitchers gave up nearly a run less per game than the league average.

Baltimore's performance in 1970 was nearly as impressive. Mike Cuellar and Dave McNally won 24 games each, and Jim Palmer contributed 20 more wins to the Orioles total of 108. This time they won the World Series as well, rolling over Cincinnati in five games behind an unforgettable performance by MVP Brooks Robinson.

In the 1971 World Series, though, Pittsburgh came back from losses in the first two games to defeat the Orioles by a run in Game 7. The Orioles captured divisional titles in 1973 and '74,

but it was 1979 before they triumphed in the ALCS. Once again, however, they faced the Pirates in the World Series and once again took the Series lead, only to fall again in the seventh game.

The 1979 pennant was Weaver's last, as late-season Oriole surges in 1980 and '82 fell just short. But in 1983 the Orioles—paced by the pitching of veteran Scott McGregor and rookie Mike Boddicker and the hitting and fielding of Cal Ripken, Jr. at short and Eddie Murray at first—made new manager Joe Altobelli look good. After a comfortable divisional win, they trounced the Chicago White Sox in the ALCS and the Philadelphia Phillies in the World Series.

Despite the return of Earl Weaver in 1985, the Orioles fell to last in the East in 1986. Though they rose to sixth in 1987, their .414 winning percentage was their lowest in 32 years. Then in 1988 they hit rock bottom, not only finishing last but also beginning the season with an AL record-setting 21 consecutive defeats.

Yet Baltimore's rebound was even more startling than its plummet. Under manager Frank Robinson (who had been handed the hapless Orioles early in the 1988 season) the 1989 Orioles held first place for most of the season before finishing second, two games behind Toronto. The O's reverted to sub-.500 seasons in 1990 and 1991, despite an MVP season by Cal Ripken in the latter year, as Robinson was fired in favor of coach Johnny Oates.

The Orioles returned to respectability at festive new Orioles Park at Camden Yards, finishing a solid third in 1992 and '93. At a bankruptcy auction in August 1993, a group led by Peter Angelos agreed to purchase the club for a record $173 million. The O's improved to second in 1994, then dropped to third under Phil Regan in '95. Cal Ripken, Jr. had twice won AL MVP honors and was a fixture on the All-Star team, but none of these accomplishments could compare to the spectacle at Camden Yards in 1995. He finally broke Lou Gehrig's consecutive-game playing streak on September 6 in an uplifting ceremony that highlighted an otherwise disappointing season.

Under new manager Davey Johnson, the Orioles (88-74) underperformed until midseason. Owner Angelos resisted temptations to break up the team and instead acquired veteran Eddie Murray, who hit his 500th home run and helped spark a successful stretch run for a wild-card berth. Offense was the name of the game for this team as it slammed a major league record 257 homers. Standouts included Brady Anderson (50 HRs), Rafael Palmeiro (39 HRs, 142 RBIs), Roberto Alomar, Ripken, and pitcher Mike Mussina.

Baltimore's 1996 postseason appearance (its first since 1983) was overshadowed, however, by Alomar's spitting on umpire John Hirschbeck. Baltimore upset the favored Indians in the Division Series, but in the ALCS (aided by a controversial Game 1 home run that should have been ruled fan interference) the Orioles fell to Joe Torre's Yankees in five games.

The Orioles won the AL East in 1997 and knocked off the Seattle Mariners in the Division Series with surprising ease, but nothing proved easy in the ALCS. Mussina's dominating performance—25 strikeouts in 15 innings and a 0.60 ERA—was wasted as the Orioles lost both his starts to Cleveland in extra innings. On the day that Davey Johnson was named AL Manager of the Year he resigned as the result of a dispute with Angelos.

Six straight fourth-place, sub-.500 seasons followed under Ray Miller and Mike Hargrove, and attendance in 2002 dipped below 3 million for the first time since the strike-shortened 1994 season. Ripken provided most of the team's few highlights during this period, voluntarily ending his consecutive-game streak at 2,632 in Baltimore's final home game of 1998, reaching his 3,000th career

hit early in 2000, and winning the All-Star Game MVP in 2001, his final season. Hargrove was fired after the 2003 season and was replaced by Lee Mazzilli.

Boston Red Sox (aka Americans, Pilgrims, Puritans, Plymouth Rocks, Somersets)

Since the end of World War II, the Red Sox have won the American League pennant four times, only to lose the World Series each time in the seventh game. It was not always thus. In their first two decades they were the league's most successful club, winners of six pennants and five world championships. (No World Series was played in the year of their second pennant.)

Organized in 1901 as one of four new eastern clubs in Ban Johnson's newly formed American League, Boston's Americans (or Pilgrims, Puritans, Plymouth Rocks, or Somersets, as they were variously called) quickly established themselves as one of the game's strongest teams. Star third baseman Jimmy Collins was lured from Boston's National League club to manage the new Americans, and he assembled a team that included such former NL standouts as slugger Buck Freeman and pitcher Cy Young. Finishing a strong second in the AL's inaugural major league season, the Pilgrims quickly supplanted their mediocre NL counterparts in the hearts and wallets of Boston fans.

After a third-place finish in 1902, the Pilgrims ran away from the rest of the league in 1903 to take their first pennant by 14-1/2 games over Philadelphia. Young led the league in victories for the third straight season, Freeman took titles in home runs, total bases and RBIs and second-year outfielder Patsy Dougherty finished first in hits and runs scored. In the first modern World Series, Boston overcame Pittsburgh's favored Pirates, thereby confirming the AL's claim to major league status in the public mind.

Boston repeated as pennant winners in 1904, but by a much narrower margin, after a struggle with the New York Highlanders that wasn't settled until the last day of the season. The NL Giants refused to play Boston in a World Series that year.

Over the next few years, as the Pilgrims dropped into the league cellar, new owner John I. Taylor (whose father, *Boston Globe* publisher Charles Taylor, was said to have bought the club for his son to give him something useful to do) rid the team of many of the players who had brought it glory. Eventually Taylor was himself maneuvered out of the club presidency, but it turned out he had not been a wanton destroyer. In driving out the old guard he had been making room for new young players: pitcher Joe Wood, for example, and a sprightly outfield of Tris Speaker, Harry Hooper and Duffy Lewis. The club—now known as the Red Sox—rose out of its depths in the final years of Taylor's presidency, even challenging the league leaders through much of 1909 before dropping away in late August. In 1911, in one of the last acts of his presidency, Taylor had, with his father, purchased land in Boston's Fenway section and built a new ballpark.

Sparked by the spectacular pitching of Wood and Speaker's play at the bat and in center field, the Red Sox of 1912 took the league lead in early June and were never headed, finishing with a club-record 105 victories. In the October they edged John McGraw's Giants and Christy Mathewson in one of the most exciting World Series ever, four games to three, with one tie. Three years later, with a staff that boasted the AL's four top pitchers in winning percentage (including rookie Babe Ruth), the Sox captured their fourth pennant. After a first-game loss to the Phillies in the World Series, Boston recovered to sweep the next four by one run apiece.

Joe Wood's ailing arm finally gave out, and Tris Speaker was traded to Cleveland at the start of the 1916 season following a salary dispute. But with Ruth winning 23 games to lead the team, the Sox slid past the White Sox and Tigers in mid-September to take their fifth pennant and waltzed over Brooklyn in the Series.

Incipient disaster struck the Red Sox that December when New York theatrical entrepreneurs Hugh Ward and Harry Frazee bought the club. They put little cash into the deal, counting on future profits to pay the bulk of the purchase price. Ward sailed for Australia, leaving Frazee to run the club. For a while the future looked bright. After a second-place finish in 1917, Frazee hired minor league executive Ed Barrow as manager, and when many of the team's regulars left for military service in World War I, Frazee bought and traded for worthy replacements. In a season shortened a month because of the war, the Sox edged Cleveland for their sixth pennant and defeated the Chicago Cubs for their fifth world championship.

Frazee's theater losses put him in a financial bind and gradually forced him to sell off the best of his players—mostly to the Yankees, who had plenty of money, and an office just a short hop from Frazee's New York theater. Though the Sox fell to sixth place in 1919, Babe Ruth kept attention fixed on the team as he went to the outfield and startled the baseball world with a record 29 home runs. But that winter Frazee sold Ruth to the Yankees for $100,000 and a $300,000 mortgage on Fenway Park.

The Red Sox were on a 15-year sojourn in the second division that even a 1923 change in ownership was powerless to end. From 1922 through 1932 the Sox emerged from last place only twice. In 1932 they reached their nadir, losing 111 games and finishing 64 games out of first.

Young and wealthy Tom Yawkey bought the club in 1933 and promptly began what would be a lifetime effort to restore Boston to its former glory. His first effort to pull the club out of the cellar was to buy success ready-made with such established stars as Lefty Grove, Jimmie Foxx and Joe Cronin; however, this failed to lift the Red Sox into pennant contention. But as general manager Eddie Collins began turning up young players to join the veterans, the club's fortune rose. The emergence between 1938 and 1942 of players like Bobby Doerr, Ted Williams and pitcher Tex Hughson brought Boston a level of success not seen since 1918. In four of the five years they finished second to the Yankees, achieving in 1942 their highest winning percentage since 1915.

The loss of most of these newcomers to military service in World War II delayed further progress. But with the arrival of rookie pitching sensation Dave Ferriss in 1945, and the acquisition of slugging first baseman Rudy York that winter, the club was prepared for its returning war veterans to join in bringing Boston its greatest season since 1912. With 104 victories, the 1946 Sox won their long-delayed seventh pennant by 12 games over second-place Detroit. In the World Series the favored Sox bowed to the Cardinals in Game 7 by one run.

The Yankees ran away from the pack in 1947, but the three years that followed saw the Red Sox three times in the throes of pennant fever. In 1948, after falling back a bit in late September, the Sox won four at the very end to tie Cleveland for first—but lost the one-game playoff. The next year they were 12 games behind the Yankees on July 4 but pulled up gradually to take a one-game lead into the final two-game series in New York. One Sox victory would win the pennant, but the Yankees took both games. In 1950 Boston played the league's best ball through July and August to pull within a game of the Yankees on September 18, but then lost four

in a row and all hope of the pennant.

In 1951 the Sox collapsed at season's end to finish third, 11 games back. They came no closer the next 15 years, finishing with eight consecutive losing seasons from 1959 through 1966.

In 1967 the Sox awakened from their long slumber. A ten-game win streak in mid-July shot them out of mediocrity into the midst of a four-team race for the pennant that was not settled until Boston beat Minnesota and Detroit split a doubleheader on the final day, leaving the Sox on top. Carl Yastrzemski, who had replaced Ted Williams in left field six years earlier, clinched the Triple Crown with a game-winning home run and six other hits in the final two must-win games. But Boston lost the World Series to St. Louis in seven games.

It was eight years before the Red Sox won another pennant, but they came close in 1972, losing the AL East crown by half a game to Detroit in the season's final series. They led the division two years later from mid-July through early September, then fell apart and finished third. But the next year, 1975, they maintained to the end the lead they first took in May, and swept Oakland in the ALCS for their ninth pennant. Television viewers will long remember Carlton Fisk's home run that won Game 6 of the World Series from Cincinnati, but their fans also remember that the Sox lost Game 7 the next night, 4-3. Owner Tom Yawkey died the following July without winning the world championship he had sought for more than 40 years.

Boston contended seriously in 1977 in a tight three-way race, pulling ahead for a time in June and again in August, but ultimately falling 2-1/2 games short. The next year, though, the Sox pulled off another amazing finish. After blowing a 7-1/2-game late-August lead, they won their final eight scheduled games to tie the Yankees. But in the one-game playoff, Yankees shortstop Bucky Dent's three-run pop-fly homer over Fenway's cozy left-field wall proved Boston's ruin. The Sox rallied in the eighth to draw within a run, but with two out and a man on third in the ninth, Yastrzemski popped up and the season was history.

Yaz retired in 1983, but outfielders Jim Rice and Dwight Evans remained from the 1975 champions. In Wade Boggs, the Red Sox had their most consistent hitter since Ted Williams, and, in Roger Clemens, Boston had its most exciting pitcher since Joe Wood. In 1986 the Red Sox won their 10th pennant, with an amazing comeback over California from a 3-1 deficit in the ALCS. Against the New York Mets in the World Series, the Red Sox were within one pitch of capturing their first world title in 68 years, but they lost that sixth game, and again lost Game 7.

When a pitching decline dropped the Sox to fifth place in 1987, and the All-Star break the next year found them barely above .500, manager John McNamara was replaced by coach Joe Morgan. The Sox responded with 19 wins in their next 20 games and, despite a slump at season's end, took the title in the AL East by one game. In the ALCS, though, Oakland swept to the pennant in four games.

In 1990, with Clemens back in peak form after a season and a half below par, the Sox arrived at midseason in first place. After trading the lead back and forth with Toronto, they captured the crown of the East on the season's final day. But in the ALCS Oakland again swept past them to the pennant.

Despite Roger Clemens' third Cy Young Award, the Sox dropped to a second-place tie with Detroit in 1991, and three straight sub-.500 seasons under Butch Hobson thereafter. His replacement, Kevin Kennedy, constantly juggled lineups to give the Sox the 1995 AL East by the surprisingly comfortable margin of

seven games over the Yankees. Key to the club's victory was AL RBI king Mo Vaughn, who captured MVP honors. Boston, however, was no match for the powerful Indians, falling to them, 3-0, in the first round of the postseason.

After two mediocre seasons, the Sox embarked on a string of six consecutive second-place finishes beginning in 1998, trailing the Yankees each time. Newcomers Nomar Garciaparra (the 1997 AL Rookie of the Year) and Pedro Martinez (acquired from Montreal after winning the NL Cy Young Award) led the retooled Boston club over this period. Martinez won the AL Cy Young Award in 1999 and 2000, while Garciaparra took the batting title the same two years.

The Sox were able win the AL Wild Card in three of these six seasons, but the "Curse of the Bambino" lived on. Boston lost the 1998 Division Series to Cleveland in four games, and dropped the 1999 and 2003 LCS to the archrival Yankees.

Theo Epstein took over as Red Sox General Manager after the 2002 season, at 28 the youngest GM in the majors. One of his first moves was to hire baseball analyst Bill James as a consultant, but there was little evidence of James's influence in 2003. His bullpen-by-committee idea was scrapped well before the season was over, and the Sox batted their two regulars with the lowest on-base percentages at the top of the order all season.

The 2003 season was particularly heartbreaking to Boston fans. The potent offense set records for most extra-base hits, most total bases, and highest slugging percentage (.491) in a season. The Sox knocked off the A's in the ALDS, advancing to a showdown with the Yankees. Boston was five outs away from winning the pennant, with a 5-2 lead and Martinez on the mound in Game 7. But the Yanks tied the game in the eighth inning, then won it in the 11th on Aaron Boone's home run. The second-guessers in the media and the fandom blamed manager Grady Little for leaving Martinez in too long, and Little was dismissed just days later. Terry Francona became the team's fifth manager in 2-1/2 years, succeeding Jimy Williams, Joe Kerrigan, interim skipper Mike Cubbage, and Little.

Chicago Cubs (aka White Stockings, Colts, Orphans)

The Cubs have represented the same city in the major leagues longer than any other club. Organized in 1870 to provide a professional challenge to Cincinnati's Red Stockings, the next year the White Stockings (as they were originally known) were one of the founding members of the game's first professional league—the National Association.

Despite the great Chicago fire, which destroyed their ballpark, uniforms and club business records late in the 1871 season, the White Stockings completed their schedule, finishing third to the Athletics of Philadelphia. But they dropped out of the NA for the next two years because of the fire's devastation. In 1875, in the midst of a second losing season following their return, the club arranged for four of champion Boston's best players to jump to Chicago for the 1876 season. That winter, White Stockings president William A. Hulbert and pitcher/manager Al Spalding (one of the jumpers) led in forming a new league to replace the NA.

Sparked by its Boston players and infielder Adrian "Cap" Anson (lured from the Athletics), the 1876 White Stockings outscored their opponents by more than five runs per game and handily won the first championship of the new National League. The next year, when Spalding (whose pitching had brought Chicago 47 of its 52 victories in 1876) switched over to first base, the club fell to fifth. Spalding retired from the field in 1878 to attend to his young sporting goods firm (though he returned as club president from

1882 through 1891).

In 1879 Anson was named to manage the team. For the next 12 years the White Stockings ranked among baseball's best, garnering five pennants (1880-1882, 1885, 1886) and four second-place finishes. Anson's strict discipline did not make him popular with his often rowdy teammates, but his consistency as a player set an example, and his innovative management made the most of his players' abilities. Anson's forcefulness, however, contributed to baseball's most grievous setback: His adamant refusal in the mid-1880s to take the field against black players prevented the racial integration of the major leagues.

After a close finish behind Boston in 1891, the White Stockings' first era as an NL power ended. In each of the next 11 seasons they fell at least 15 games short of the top. The team's youthful ineptitude was reflected in the nicknames that succeeded "White Stockings": the "Colts," the "Orphans" (in 1898, after Anson—by then known as "Pop"—was fired after 19 years at the helm), and finally, the "Cubs."

When Frank Selee (who had led Boston to greatness in the 1890s) was hired to manage the Cubs in 1902, he inherited a team that had ended the 1901 season 37 games out. By 1903 he had turned catcher/outfielder Frank Chance into a first baseman, moved Joe Tinker from third to short and brought Johnny Evers up from Troy to play second. The new double-play combination flourished not only in the field but also at the bat. The Cubs finished third in 1903 with their best record since 1898.

That winter Selee traded for pitcher Mordecai "Three Finger" Brown. After leading the Cubs to second place in 1904, Selee signed rookie hurler Ed Reulbach, but, ill with tuberculosis, he took a leave of absence in the middle of the 1905 season. Chance took his place and brought the team to third; Selee never returned, but he had gone a long way toward building a championship team.

Trades for outfielder Jimmy Sheckard and third baseman Harry Steinfeldt, the signing of rookie pitcher Jack Pfiester and the acquisition during the 1906 season of pitchers Orval Overall and Jack Taylor completed one of the greatest teams of all time. The Cubs passed the Giants to take the lead early in May and kept on rising. New York and Pittsburgh made a race of it through July, but the Cubs won 55 of their final 65 games to finish with a record 116 victories against only 36 defeats, 20 games ahead of second-place New York.

Brown's 1.04 ERA was the league's best, with Pfiester and Reulbach second and third. The team ERA was a remarkably low 1.76. Chicago scored 80 more runs than its nearest rival, and yielded 89 fewer. But in the World Series, the crosstown "Hitless Wonder" White Sox matched the Cubs' hitting and pitched twice as effectively to take the crown in six games.

The Cubs' hitting and run production fell off in 1907, but their pitching did not (ERA: 1.73). With 107 wins, they captured their second straight pennant, by "only" 17 games. This time, however, their dominance carried over into the World Series as they swept Detroit after an opening-game tie.

The pennant race of 1908 was one of the tightest in baseball history. On September 22 the Cubs won two from the Giants to pull into a virtual tie for first (with Pittsburgh third, 1-1/2 games back). The next day the Giants appeared to have beaten the Cubs with an RBI single in the last of the ninth. But young Fred Merkle, on first when the hit was made, failed to continue on to second and was forced out by alert Cubs second baseman Johnny Evers for the third out, which negated the Giant run. Because of increasing

darkness and the mob of excited fans on the field, the game was called and ruled a tie.

After another week and a half in which all three teams took turns in front, Chicago defeated Pittsburgh to pull ahead by half a game, leaving the Pirates and Giants tied for second. But New York had one more game—and defeated the Boston Braves to pull into a tie with the Cubs. The "Merkle boner" game thus had to be replayed and, this time, the Cubs won to take their third straight pennant. In the World Series they again beat Detroit in five games. Their second straight world title was also, to date, their last.

The Cubs won 104 games in 1909 as their pitching staff recorded an ERA under 2.00 for the third time in four years. Still, Chicago finished second to the powerful Pirates, who won 110 and captured the World Series.

In 1910 their 104 wins carried them to another pennant, by a comfortable 13 games. After a World Series loss to the Philadelphia Athletics, and seasons in second and third place, Chance resigned, protesting the unwillingness of owner Charles Murphy to spend money for top players.

The Cubs got a new owner in 1916, and with him a new ballpark. Charles Weeghman, who had owned the Chicago Whales in the short-lived Federal League, purchased the Cubs when the rival circuit went under, and moved them into the park he had built for the Whales.

The team that next carried Chicago to the pennant, in the war-shortened season of 1918, featured only one name familiar to Cubs fans from earlier championship seasons—Fred Merkle. The man whose boner as a Giant rookie had made possible their pennant in 1908 was now their leading run producer. As in earlier pennant-winning seasons, fine pitching predominated, with veteran Jim "Hippo" Vaughn the league's best pitcher on the league's top staff.

Several years of decline followed the Cubs' World Series loss to the Boston Red Sox. The club hit bottom in 1925 with its first cellar finish in 53 years of league play, but a new era of greatness was at hand. In 1921 wealthy chewing-gum manufacturer William Wrigley had purchased control of the Cubs, with a determination to spend what was needed to produce a winner.

The seeds Wrigley planted eventually bore fruit. In 1926 he hired Joe McCarthy—a successful minor league manager—to lead the club and drafted outfielder Lewis "Hack" Wilson from Toledo. Wilson immediately became one of the league's leading offensive threats, and the Cubs rebounded to the first division. In 1927 they even led the league through August before dropping back to fourth. A postseason trade brought them outfielder Hazen "Kiki" Cuyler and a close third-place finish in 1928. Then the Cubs traded with the Braves for second baseman Rogers Hornsby and in 1929 returned to the top. Led by Wilson's 159 RBIs and Hornsby's 149, five Cubs drove in more than 90 runs each. After battling Pittsburgh for the lead through mid-July, the Cubs hurtled ahead to take the pennant by 10-1/2 games, despite a late-season slump. The slump continued through the World Series, though, as the Athletics humbled the Cubs in five games.

Just four games from the end of the hot pennant race in 1930 (the year Wilson set the major league RBI record with 191), McCarthy—still smarting from criticism arising from the World Series loss—quit as manager. With Hornsby at the helm, the Cubs preserved a second-place finish. They dropped to third the next year, but returned to the top in 1932. Hornsby, near the end of his playing days, was dropped as manager in August, with the Cubs in second, and replaced by first baseman Charlie Grimm. Pitcher Lon Warneke,

in his first full season as a starter, led the league in wins and ERA. The club enjoyed a hot streak in August to move out in front of slumping Pittsburgh and hung on to take the flag by four games. The Yankees provided the World Series humiliation this time, a four-game sweep that afforded McCarthy (now the Yankees manager) with sweet revenge for the Chicago fans' criticism three years earlier.

It had become a pattern: three years, another pennant. In 1935 a balanced offense (led by catcher Gabby Hartnett and second baseman Billy Herman) and the league's best pitching brought the Cubs up from fourth in late June to first in September. They clinched the pennant with three games to go, with their 20th win of a 21-game streak. In the World Series, Detroit stopped the Cubs in six games.

After two seasons in second, it was time for another pennant. Bill Lee, the club's top pitcher in 1935, was now the league's finest, as was the Cubs' staff. With the club languishing six and a half games back in midseason, Grimm quit as manager and was replaced by catcher Hartnett. In September the Cubs came to life, rising to second early in the month. They overtook Pittsburgh with their ninth consecutive win on Hartnett's homer against the Pirates in the growing darkness with two away in the bottom of the ninth, which became known as the "Homer in the Gloaming." The Cubs clinched the pennant four games later, on the next-to-last day of the season. The Yankees swept Chicago to hand the Cubs their sixth straight World Series loss.

In 1940, after 14 straight winning seasons, the Cubs began a five-year stretch below .500. Jimmie Wilson replaced Hartnett as manager in 1941; then Grimm returned near the start of the 1944 season. The club finished a distant fourth that year, but in 1945, after a middling start, they won 26 of 30 midseason games to take a lead they never relinquished. Balanced pitching (sparked by Hank Borowy, who went 11-2 after coming over from the Yankees in July) and the hitting of veteran first baseman Phil Cavarretta (.355) and center fielder Andy Pafko (110 RBIs) held off the pressing St. Louis Cardinals to preserve a 16th Cubs pennant. Although they battled Detroit through a full seven games in the World Series, they ended up losing again.

For the next 23 years the Cubs remained out of pennant contention. But in 1969, the first year of divisional play, under the lively management of Leo Durocher they took an early lead in the NL East. With a potent offense led by veteran sluggers Ron Santo, Ernie Banks and Billy Williams, the team continued rising through early August. But the New York Mets rose even faster and farther; they didn't pause when Chicago leveled off in late August, and while the Cubs were losing eight straight in September the Mets were winning ten in a row. The Cubs wound up eight games back.

The 1970s were a disappointing decade, with several division leads melting away in the summertime sun at Wrigley. In 1981 the Wrigley family sold the club to the Chicago Tribune Company. Three years later, with a new manager, Jim Frey, and an almost wholly different roster, the new management capped its rebuilding program with the acquisition of pitcher Rick Sutcliffe from Cleveland in mid-June 1984. As Sutcliffe fashioned a 16-1 record for his new club, the Cubs went on to capture their first division title. After winning the first two games of the NLCS against San Diego, the pennant was swept out from under them in the final three.

In 1989 the team, now managed by Don Zimmer, bounced back to duplicate its 1984 success. With a balanced offense and pitching vastly improved over the previous season, the Cubs took the NL East lead for good on August 7. Once again, though, they

were unable to persevere to the pennant, losing the best-of-seven NLCS to San Francisco in five games.

It took nearly a decade for the Cubs to contend again. Between 1990 and 1997, Chicago finished between third and fifth each year, only once winning as many as 80 games. Zimmer, Joe Altobelli, Jim Essian, Jim Lefebvre, and Tom Trebelhorn were managerial casualties during this dry spell. One of the team's few bright lights, Greg Maddux, left as a free agent after winning the 1992 Cy Young Award, and Chicago icon Ryne Sandberg retired—twice. Ownership snarled when baseball commissioner Fay Vincent proposed transferring the club from the NL East to the West in 1993, but the threat passed when Vincent, under pressure from owners dissatisfied with his leadership, resigned before the end of the 1992 season.

Things turned around suddenly in 1998. Sammy Sosa blossomed from a solid player to a superstar, and 20-year-old Kerry Wood tied the all-time record with 20 strikeouts in just his fifth big league game, on his way to the NL Rookie of the Year Award. Under Jim Riggleman, the Cubs won 90 games and the NL Wild Card in a one-game playoff with the Giants, before being swept by the Braves in the NLDS.

Sosa had set a major league record that year with 20 home runs in June and his long-ball exploits had challenged even those of Mark McGwire. Sosa was at Busch Stadium when McGwire hit his record-breaking 62nd home run, and a few days later Sosa also hit number 62. Sammy finished the season with 66 homers to McGwire's 70, but won the NL MVP Award over Big Mac.

Despite 63 and 50 more homers by Sosa, the Cubs finished last in 1999 and 2000, with Don Baylor taking over the reins in the latter year. Chicago leaped to third in 2001, as Sammy slammed 64 more, then dropped to fifth, and Baylor was gone, replaced briefly by Bruce Kimm.

The Cubs made another rags-to-riches rise in 2003 under new manager Dusty Baker. Despite Sosa's suspension for a bat-corking incident, Chicago won 88 games, edging Houston by a game for the NL Central title. They then knocked off the Braves in the NLDS, and seemed about to reach their first World Series since 1945. The Cubs had a three-games-to-one lead over the Marlins in the NLCS, giving Chicago three chances to get the clincher. It looked as if they had it in Game 6, with ace Mark Prior (18-6 in the regular season) holding a 3-0 lead with one out in the eighth inning, but the Marlins mauled the Cubs with an eight-run inning, then put them out of their misery the next day, en route to the world championship.

Chicago White Sox (White Stockings)

When minor league owner Charlie Comiskey transferred his club from St. Paul to Chicago as part of the move to upgrade the American League to major league status, he called it the White Stockings, after the Chicago team that had dominated the National League in its early years. The new Chicago team revived memories of the old White Stockings, winning the AL championship in 1900 and repeating the triumph in 1901, the circuit's first major league season. Manager Clark Griffith (who had jumped to the White Stockings from Chicago's NL Cubs) was the team's star pitcher in 1901, winning 24 of 31 decisions as his team took the lead in May and held off the threatening Boston Somersets the rest of the way.

Griffith's effectiveness fell off in 1902, as did the team, (now called the White Sox) which took a sizable lead in July, only to slide back to fourth in August. Griffith left the next year and the White Sox sank to seventh. It would take 18 years and baseball's biggest

scandal for the Sox to finish that low again.

In 1904, after center fielder Fielder Jones replaced left fielder Nixey Callahan as manager, the Sox rose into first place for a moment in August before settling back to third. The next year they made up a seven-game deficit in September to catch the Philadelphia Athletics, but the loss of two games to the A's stalled their drive and left them in second.

Nothing stalled the White Sox drive in 1906. Although they ranked at the very bottom of the league in hitting and entered June five games below .500, their pitching and hustle pulled them through. "Big Ed" Walsh, who had finally mastered the spitball after two years of trying, won 17 games, including a league-high 10 shutouts. Doc White contributed 18 wins with a league-best 1.52 ERA, and Frank Owen and Nick Altrock won 22 and 20, respectively. The Sox shot to the top in August with a 19-game win streak (including eight shutouts). Early in September, New York's Highlanders passed them but, after the two teams traded the lead back and forth for a couple of weeks, the Sox spurted to take the pennant by three games. If the race was close, so were the individual games: the Sox achieved nearly one-third of their victories by the margin of a single run. The "Hitless Wonders" carried their momentum through the World Series, shocking the mighty crosstown Cubs (who had won a record 116 games that year) in six games.

In 1907, after leading the league much of the first half, the Sox slipped to third. The next year Walsh pitched in the final seven games on his way to a career-high 40 wins. In a tight finish he pulled the Sox to within a half game of first-place Detroit before they dropped back to third with a loss to the Tigers on the final day.

It was 1915 before the Sox (piloted by rookie manager Clarence H. "Pants" Rowland) next finished that high, and 1916 before they again challenged seriously for the pennant. Comiskey, though accused of pinching pennies in his payment of players, was willing to spend what was needed to acquire them. After the 1914 season he purchased star second baseman Eddie Collins from the A's and promising young Oscar "Happy" Felsch from minor league Milwaukee. The following August he acquired the great "Shoeless" Joe Jackson from Cleveland. Together with the league's best pitching staff, they carried the Sox into the thick of a three-way race and a close second-place finish in 1916. A year later the Sox took the pennant with the best winning percentage the club has ever compiled. Ten-year-veteran pitcher Eddie Cicotte enjoyed his first 20-win season with a league-high 28, and a league-and career-best 1.53 ERA. After dueling the Boston Red Sox most of the season, Chicago streaked out of reach in late August to finish with 100 wins. In the World Series against the New York Giants they captured their second (and, to date, their last) world title, in six games.

With several key players out much of 1918 for military or civilian war service, the White Sox finished out of the running, a dismal sixth. But in 1919, with the team back at full strength, the race once again went to Chicago. If their pitching didn't have quite the depth of the 1917 squad, its best hurlers were in peak form. Cicotte, after an off-year in 1918, attained a career high with 29 wins, as did Lefty Williams with 23 victories. Collins and Jackson enjoyed their best seasons in several years, and Buck Weaver had never been better. Old-time pitcher and second baseman Kid Gleason was a rookie as a big league manager, but his Sox began strong and, after slipping briefly into second in midseason, pulled ahead in July to stay.

When the Sox lost the World Series to underdog Cincinnati,

there were rumors of a fix, but nothing came to light for nearly a year. The White Sox looked better than ever in 1920. Though they fell back in May after a hot April, by mid-August they were embroiled in the thick of a tight three-team race. Felsch, Collins and Weaver had never played better, Jackson was enjoying one of his very best seasons, and four pitchers were on their way to more than 20 wins. Chicago might not have caught Cleveland's rampaging Indians, but it didn't help that talk of a White Sox scandal revived late in the season, or that the grand jury convened only eight games from the end, or that eight Sox players were indicted and suspended with just three games to play. The team finished two games back, in second place.

The indicted players—infielders Chick Gandil, Swede Risberg and Fred McMullin, plus Cicotte, Felsch, Jackson, Weaver, and Williams—were acquitted in court when three crucial confessions disappeared, but they were banned for life from Organized Baseball by Commissioner Kenesaw Mountain Landis. The White Sox did not soon recover from the loss. In 1921 they began 15 years of wandering in the second division. The Sox finished last three times in that span, plus a seventh-place finish in 1932 that left the Sox a club-worst 56-1/2 games out of first.

Two of the club's greatest and most durable players arrived during these years: pitcher Ted Lyons (who won 260 games for the Sox in 21 years) in 1923, and in 1930 shortstop Luke Appling (who averaged .310 in his 20 years with the club). Owner Comiskey died in 1931, in the midst of his club's most dismal era. Lyons and Appling were around long enough to enjoy a few fourth- and third-place seasons but neither saw the Sox contend seriously for the pennant. After his playing career was over, Lyons managed the team for a few years—until 1948, when the Sox lost 101 games and finished last.

That year Frank Lane was lured from the presidency of the American Association to take charge as Chicago's general manager. When Lane hired Paul Richards to manage the club in 1951, the Sox began what became a 17-year string of winning seasons.

In 1951, Richards' first season, the Sox spent a month in first place before drifting down to fourth, and the next year began a five-year run in third place. In 1954 they won 94 games but were out of the race by August—that was the year Cleveland won 111 and the second-place Yankees 103. Richards moved on to Baltimore, but Marty Marion, who replaced him, kept the Sox in third place.

After the Sox fell from first place in early September, Frank Lane left at the end of the 1955 season. Young Chuck Comiskey (one of the grandchildren of Charlie Comiskey who now owned the club) took over the front office. A year later Comiskey replaced Marion with Al Lopez, who had piloted the great Cleveland club of 1954 and whose teams, in his six seasons of managing, had never finished below second. Lopez continued his success in Chicago: the Sox moved up to second (though well behind the Yankees) in 1957 and '58. In March 1959 Bill Veeck (who had in previous years owned the Cleveland Indians and the St. Louis Browns) bought a controlling interest in the White Sox from the Comiskey family and stepped into instant success.

With the Yankees suffering an off-year in 1959, Chicago and Cleveland battled for the lead throughout the summer, until the White Sox pulled away in late August. The same 94-60 record that had given them only a distant third in 1954 now carried them to their first pennant in 40 years. The close and successful pennant race, and the club's dynamic new ownership, pushed Sox home attendance up more than 78 percent to a new club record.

As they had in 1906, pitching and hustle won the Sox their 1959 pennant. The league's best staff was led by veteran Early Wynn (enjoying his last big season with a league high of 22 wins) and young Bob Shaw (with a career high of 18), and featured the league's top relievers in Gerry Staley and Turk Lown. Shortstop Luis Aparicio, in the midst of a nine-year reign as stolen-base leader, set a personal high in runs scored as the club went 35-15 in one-run games. But in the World Series, Los Angeles stopped Chicago in six games.

The next year the Sox remained competitive until September, but finished third. After dropping to fourth and fifth the next two years (in a league now expanded to 10 teams), they returned to second in 1963. The next year the Sox finished a season-long three-way race with nine straight wins, enough to pull them past Baltimore, but a game short of catching the Yankees, whose 11-game streak a week earlier had put them out in front. After a third straight second-place finish in 1965, manager Lopez resigned for health reasons.

Under Eddie Stanky—and with the AL's stingiest pitching staff in 49 years—the Sox competed into the final week of a hot 1967 race, when five straight losses at the end dropped them to fourth. They would rise above .500 only twice in the next 13 years. In 1970 they lost a club-record 106 games to finish at the bottom of the AL West. Two years later they took the division lead briefly in late August before dropping back to second, and in 1977 they held the lead through much of the summer before tailing off to third.

Bill Veeck had sold the club and repurchased it in 1976. But in January 1981, after three losing seasons and troubled by poor health and skyrocketing player salaries, he sold the Sox once again, to a group headed by Jerry Reinsdorf and Eddie Einhorn. With Reinsdorf heading the club's baseball operations and Tony LaRussa piloting the team on the field, the Sox briefly became one of the best teams in baseball. With their best record since 1920, the 1983 Sox carried the AL West by 20 games. Rookie slugger Ron Kittle led the attack, backed up by fourth-year outfielder Harold Baines and resurgent old-timers Greg Luzinski and Carlton Fisk. Pitchers LaMarr Hoyt and Rich Dotson attained personal bests to lead the majors in wins (with 24 and 22), and White Sox home attendance for the first time topped 2 million. In the ALCS, though, after a close win over Baltimore in the opener, Chicago lost the next three games and the pennant. Chicago's pitching and offense (except for Baines) collapsed the next season, and the team remained out of serious contention for six years.

The Sox enjoyed a surprising renaissance in the 1990s, with the emergence of young stars such as Frank Thomas, Jack McDowell, Bobby Thigpen, and Robin Ventura. The team battled for first place for much of 1990 before finishing a solid second, as Thigpen shattered the major league saves record with 57. The White Sox continued to contend in a new venue starting in 1991, having vacated the old Comiskey Park in favor of a new stadium by the same name next door (the park would be renamed U.S. Cellular Field in 2003). Chicago came within ten games of first in three straight seasons, before winning the AL West under Gene Lamont in 1993, as Thomas won the MVP and McDowell the Cy Young Award. The Sox lost the ALCS to the eventual world champion Toronto Blue Jays in six games.

In 1994 Frank Thomas was rising to even greater heights and became the first American Leaguer since Roger Maris in 1960 and 1961 to be named MVP in back-to-back seasons. The Sox were hanging on to a slim first-place lead over Cleveland in the new Central division when the players struck to end the season.

Despite more strong seasons by Thomas, the club dropped to

third in 1995 and second in 1996, well behind the Indians each year. After the season they shocked the baseball world by signing Cleveland slugger Albert Belle to a $10 million-per-year contract, and pundits were predicting the Thomas-Belle tandem would rival Ruth and Gehrig of the Murderers' Row Yankees. But Belle had an off-year in 1997, Thomas did the same in '98, and Belle was sent packing to Baltimore. The highlight of the 1997 season was the first-ever Cubs-Sox interleague series.

Following four straight second-place finishes, the Sox finally rose back to the top of the weak AL Central under Jerry Manuel in 2000, before bowing to the Mariners in three straight games in the AL Divisional Series. Thereafter, the team reverted to mediocrity, barely reaching .500 in the early years of the new century, and finishing second behind Minnesota in 2002 and 2003. Once again, the White Sox front office was unable to make the acquisitions necessary to build a consistent winner. Manuel was fired after the 2003 season and replaced by former Sox shortstop Ozzie Guillen.

Cincinnati Reds (aka Red Stockings, Red Legs)

Red Stockings was the nickname of two pioneering Cincinnati ballclubs—the first avowedly professional team, which was undefeated in 1869, and the charter member club in the National League of 1876-1880. After a year on the sidelines, the reformed Reds joined the new American Association and captured the 1882 pennant by 11-1/2 games, with a .688 winning percentage that is still the club record. Seven Reds enjoyed career highs in batting, pitcher Will White led the association with 40 wins and rookie second baseman John "Bid" McPhee proved himself one of the game's classiest fielders.

McPhee remained 18 years with the Reds and established himself as the finest second baseman of the 19th century. But the club would go 37 years before it won another pennant. Twice in their seven remaining years in the AA the Reds finished second, and they enjoyed six winning seasons. Transferring from the AA to the NL in 1890, they finished fourth; at 10-1/2 games out of first it was their closest finish between 1884 and their next pennant-winning season, 1919.

In 1902 club owner John T. Brush sold out to a group of Cincinnati's political bosses, who in mid-August named August "Garry" Herrmann (formerly head of the water-works commission) to run it. Herrmann not only remained president of the Reds for 25 years, but he also chaired the three-man National Commission that oversaw Organized Baseball, from its establishment in 1903 until 1920 (when his resignation brought about the commission's demise).

A midseason trade in 1916 brought the Reds Christy Mathewson (at the end of his pitching career) to manage the team, plus outfielder Edd Roush. The next year, with Roush leading the league in batting, the Reds edged above .500 and into fourth place. In 1918 an August spurt boosted the Reds into third place, in a season shortened by a month because of World War I. Roush enjoyed another banner year, but Mathewson left for the Army just before the season ended.

First baseman Hal Chase—suspected of throwing games—was traded away after the season and replaced by veteran Jake Daubert. Southpaw Slim Sallee was purchased from the Giants and right-hander Ray Fisher from the Yankees. Pat Moran (who had led the Phillies to a pennant in 1915) was hired to replace Mathewson at the Cincinnati helm. Thus fortified, the Reds in 1919 won their second pennant. Three pitchers—Sallee (21-7), Hod Eller (20-9)

and Dutch Ruether (19-7, 1.82 ERA)—reached career peaks; Fisher (14-5) enjoyed one of his best years; Roush won another batting title and finished second in NL RBIs; and three Reds finished in the league's top four in runs scored. The Reds drove quickly from the gate, but faltered in May and didn't pass the Giants for first place until July. They finished nine games in front. Rumors of a White Sox fix to throw the World Series clouded the Reds' Series triumph—and spoiled it entirely when, a year later, the scandal became public and the truth of the rumors was confirmed.

In 1920 Cincinnati led the league entering September, but Brooklyn spurted and the Reds slumped to a third-place finish, 10-1/2 games out. They dropped to sixth in 1921, but recovered for five years in the first division, including three second-place finishes.

The Reds finished in the second division for 11 years, hitting bottom with four straight cellar finishes from 1931 through 1934. President Herrmann retired after the 1927 season, and within two years a controlling interest in the Reds was sold to a wealthy Cincinnatian, Sidney Weil. But Weil lost his fortune in the stock market crash of 1929. While he continued to run the Reds for four years, his stock in the club was actually held by the Central Trust Company. In his efforts to turn the club around, Weil acquired catcher Ernie Lombardi from Brooklyn in March 1932 and pitcher Paul Derringer from the St. Louis Cardinals the following May. Derringer lost 25 games in his first season in Cincinnati and 21 the next, but both remained with the club long enough to star in its return to glory. Owner Weil, however, relinquished his control to the bank in 1933, at the depth of the Depression and of the team's fortunes.

The bank hired Larry MacPhail (who had rescued minor league Columbus by introducing night baseball there) to run the Reds. MacPhail in turn hired Frank Lane to develop a minor league farm system, and persuaded Cincinnati industrialist Powel Crosley, Jr., to invest in the club. On May 24, 1935, Crosley and MacPhail brought night ball to the major leagues (the Reds, with Derringer pitching, beat the Phillies, 2-1), and with it a sharp upswing in attendance at Crosley Field. By June 1936, Crosley's increased investment in the Reds had made him the majority owner. The temperamental MacPhail quit suddenly in mid-September 1936, but the Reds replaced him with another successful minor league executive, Warren Giles, who ran the club until his selection in 1952 as president of the NL.

After rising to sixth place in 1935 and fifth the next year, the Reds dropped back into the cellar in 1937. But the following year, under new manager Bill McKechnie, they rose into the first division once again—even holding second place briefly in September before slipping to fourth. Derringer enjoyed the first of three peak seasons, young Johnny Vander Meer contributed 15 wins (including two consecutive no-hitters) and Bucky Walters, after his acquisition from the Phillies in June, compiled his first winning season since converting from third baseman to pitcher in 1935. Lombardi led the NL in batting, and first baseman Frank McCormick, in his first full season, led the league in hits. The stage was set for the club's first back-to-back pennants.

Several Reds reached the apex of their careers in 1939, among them Walters (27-11) and Derringer (25-7), who between them topped most of the league's pitching stats, and McCormick, who led the league in RBIs and hits and finished second in batting. The club pulled out of the pack to the front before the end of May and held the lead to the end, although St. Louis closed the gap with a late-season surge.

Cincinnati's sweep by the Yankees in the World Series was something of a shock, but the club had recovered its poise by the next spring. Starting strong and—except for a small dip in August—pushing steadily upward throughout the season, the Reds shook off the persistent Dodgers in midseason and finished 12 games in front with their first 100-win season. McCormick and Lombardi powered the offense, and Walters for the second year in a row took NL crowns in wins and ERA. This time the team's triumph carried through the World Series as Walters and Derringer won two games apiece to edge the Tigers in seven games to win their second world championship.

The Reds' pitching remained strong in 1941, but their hitting and run production fell off and the team struggled to finish third. They remained in the upper division through 1944, but then dropped into an 11-year trough of losing seasons.

Ted Kluszewski was in his ninth season as the Reds' slugging first baseman when Cincinnati next offered a serious run for the pennant in 1956 under manager Birdie Tebbetts. Kluszewski led the club in hitting and RBIs, but his 35 home runs were good enough only for third behind rookie Frank Robinson's 38 and Wally Post's 36 on a team that hammered 221 during the season to tie the then-major league record set nine years earlier by the Giants. The Reds' offense led the league in runs scored and kept them in the thick of a three-team race throughout the season. That same year, for the first time ever they drew more than a million fans at home.

The Reds dropped out of a tight race in August 1957, and suffered losing seasons the next three years. Gabe Paul, who had succeeded Warren Giles as club president and general manager, left to help organize the new Houston club after the 1960 season. Owner Crosley died the following spring. Bill DeWitt, who replaced Paul as president (and ultimately purchased control of the club), acquired pitcher Joey Jay from the Milwaukee Braves and third baseman Gene Freese from the White Sox. Jay in 1961 tied for the league lead with 21 wins, and Freese homered 26 times and drove in 87 runs—both career highs. Most of the team improved on their 1960 stats, and despite a poor start that saw them enter May in last place, the Reds had risen to the top by mid-June. The streaking Dodgers caught them briefly in August, but then fell away. In the World Series, though, it was the Yankees winning in five games.

The Reds next threatened in 1964 when, in a wild three-way finish, they won nine straight in late September to take first place for a day before slipping into a tie for second, one game behind St. Louis. In 1965 a young Pete Rose recorded the first of his 10 seasons with 200 hits as the Reds battled among the leaders much of the summer before dropping off to fourth.

That December, after a decade of standout offense in Cincinnati, Frank Robinson was traded to Baltimore. The next year, while Robinson won the Triple Crown in assisting his new team to the world championship, the Reds suffered their first losing season in six years and sank to seventh place. That winter, owner DeWitt completed the sale of the team to a group led by Cincinnati newspaper publisher Francis Dale and brothers James and William Williams, who later acquired a controlling interest in the club.

In 1969, the first year of divisional play, the Reds rose into the thick of a five-way race in the NL West before stumbling as Atlanta and San Francisco surged in the final three weeks. But the season provided a foretaste of the decade to come as the team captured league crowns in slugging and home runs.

At midseason in 1970 the Reds moved out of Crosley Field—their home for 58 years—into the new Riverfront Stadium.

Catcher Johnny Bench and third baseman Tony Perez, with the finest seasons of their long careers, paced an overwhelming offense as the team hammered out a new club-high 102 wins to reward rookie manager Sparky Anderson with victory in the NL West by 14-1/2 games, and gain the name "Big Red Machine." In the National League Championship Series the Reds continued their triumph with a three-game sweep of East winner Pittsburgh. But mighty Baltimore humbled the Reds in the World Series, 4-1.

Cincinnati's hitting and run production fell off sharply the next year, and the club dropped to fourth with their only losing season of the decade. But in 1972—spurred on after a slow start by Johnny Bench's recovery of power, Gary Nolan's finest season on the mound, and the all-around mastery of newly acquired second baseman Joe Morgan—the Reds cruised to a division title. Victory in the NLCS came harder, as powerful Pittsburgh carried the series to the full five games before handing the Reds the pennant with a wild pitch in the last inning of the final game. Cincinnati's defeat in the World Series was also close: the Reds won three, and Oakland's four wins were each achieved by a margin of just one run.

The Reds repeated in the NL West in 1973 with a second-half surge from fourth place that carried them past front-runner Los Angeles in September. But the much weaker New York Mets ended Cincinnati's pennant hopes in a five-game loss in the NLCS best remembered for Rose's brawl with Bud Harrelson.

In 1974 the Reds finished four games behind the Dodgers in second place. But over the next two years the Big Red Machine flattened all opposition. In 1975, after hovering around .500 through mid-May, the Reds began an ascent that carried them to what are still club records: 108 victories and a winning margin of 20 games. The team featured balanced pitching (six starters won in double figures), an offense in which every regular drove in more than 45 runs (averaging nearly 77 apiece), the best fielding in the majors, and a big NL lead in stolen bases. After a three-game sweep of Pittsburgh in the NLCS, the Reds subdued the stubborn Boston Red Sox in seven games for their first world title in 35 years, and their third overall.

They won their fourth the next year. Joe Morgan, at the peak of his career, led the NL in slugging, finished second to teammate George Foster in RBIs, and stole 60 bases as he won his second consecutive MVP award. Balanced pitching and offense again put the Reds in front to stay in June, carrying the team to 102 wins and a 10-game lead over Los Angeles at the finish. The NLCS produced another sweep—of Philadelphia this time. The World Series was also a sweep as the Reds dispatched the Yankee, thus becoming the first team to go through the Championship Series and World Series without losing a game.

Two years of second-place finishes followed, and the Reds replaced Sparky Anderson at the helm with John McNamara, who led the club back to the top of the NL West in 1979. Pete Rose, after 16 years in Cincinnati, had signed with the Phillies as a free agent, but Ray Knight (who replaced Rose at third base) minimized the loss with a team-high .318 batting average. Houston led the division much of the summer, but a sustained Reds' surge in August brought them even, then pulled them ahead in early September, where they hung on to take the title by just 1-1/2 games. But that was the end of the Reds' decade of splendor; Pittsburgh swept past them to the pennant in the NLCS.

Joe Morgan left the club after the season, returning as a free agent to Houston, whence he had come eight years earlier. In 1980 the Reds dipped in midseason, recovering to make a race of it in August, only to fade a bit and finish third. The next year, in a season shortened and split in two by a players' strike, the Reds compiled the best overall record in the majors. But they came away empty-handed by finishing half a game behind Los Angeles in the first half-season and 1-1/2 games back of Houston in the second half, losing a chance at postseason play when the owners decided to pit the half-season winners against each other.

As a penurious front office continued to trade away its stars or lose them to free agency, the dispirited Reds dropped to the bottom of the NL West in 1982 with a club-worst 101 losses. Manager McNamara yielded in midseason to coach Russ Nixon, who was himself replaced by Vern Rapp after another last-place finish in 1983. Robert Howsam, Sr., whose shrewd trading as general manager had been instrumental in building the mighty Reds of the 1970s, was called out of semi-retirement to restore the club to respectability. Howsam signed free-agent slugger Dave Parker from Pittsburgh, and late in the 1984 season brought Pete Rose back as player-manager. Early in 1985 the NL approved the sale of the Reds to Marge Schott, a Cincinnati automobile dealer. With Parker enjoying his most productive seasons in several years, and the emergence of outfielder Eric Davis and reliever John Franco, owner Schott's public enthusiasm for her team was rewarded with four straight second-place finishes. The highlight of that period came in 1985 when Rose broke Ty Cobb's record for most career hits.

Turmoil ruled the Reds in 1989. Disabling injuries to a dozen players, including such 1988 standouts as pitcher Danny Jackson and infielders Barry Larkin and Chris Sabo, contributed most to the team's drop to fifth place. Baseball's investigation of manager Pete Rose on charges of gambling on baseball games and other offenses—an investigation which resulted in Rose's banishment from the game in August—did nothing to bolster Cincinnati's play on the field. The team had its lowest win total in five years.

Yet the distress of 1989 was all but forgotten in 1990 as the Reds, under new manager Lou Piniella, leaped to a 9-0 start and held on to first place through the entire season. Larkin and Sabo—whole again—anchored a balanced offense, while pitchers Randy Myers, Rob Dibble and Norm Charlton (nicknamed "The Nasty Boys") provided All-Star relief to a solid core of starters. In the NLCS, the Reds captured the pennant from Pittsburgh in six games, then startled Oakland's heavily favored Athletics with a four-game sweep.

The club slipped to fifth, second and fifth the next three years, and Piniella was replaced by Cincinnati hero—but managing novice—Tony Perez for 1993. Perez lasted only until May 24, when veteran manager Davey Johnson took his place. Meanwhile, Marge Schott's fellow NL owners imposed a one-year ban on her participation in club affairs for making racial slurs.

The Reds turned their fortunes around in 1994 and were atop the new Central division when the strike ended the season. When play resumed in 1995 the Reds showed they had indeed been for real, winning the division by nine games as Larkin earned the MVP Award. The Reds swept LA in the first round of playoffs but in turn were swept by the Braves in the NLCS. At season's end Johnson left the team for Baltimore and was replaced by Ray Knight, who himself was replaced by Jack McKeon in 1997, as the team suffered through three straight mediocre seasons.

Cincinnati became the surprise team of the National League in 1999, thanks to some shrewd front-office moves and unexpected individual performances. The Reds seemed to have a firm grasp on the National League wild card when the Mets lost eight of nine games going into the final weekend of the season. The Reds, how-

ever, lost consecutive games in Milwaukee while the Mets swept the Pirates. Cincinnati won its last scheduled game of the season, following a rain delay of more than eight hours, to force a one-game playoff. The Reds fell to the Mets at Cinergy Field to bring a sour end to a successful year.

Cincinnati's failure in the final days of the season turned into triumph in the off-season when GM Jim Bowden landed Ken Griffey, Jr. in a historic trade. Expectations faded, however, when the Cardinals started off 2000 hot and never let the Reds get within striking distance. McKeon, the NL Manager of the Year a season before, was fired after an 85-win season and replaced with Bob Boone, the father of Reds' third baseman Aaron Boone. Three losing seasons followed, with Griffey suffering major injuries each year and missing more than 250 games between 2001 and 2003. About the only highlight during this period was the opening of Cincinnati's Great American Ball Park in 2003. Boone was fired in July of that year, and Class-A manager Dave Miley was promoted to the job.

Cleveland Indians (aka Blues, Broncos, Naps)

The Indians finished in the top half of the league nearly 70 percent of the time through their first 68 years, and wound up in the cellar only once (in 1914). Cleveland then experienced only five winning seasons from 1969 through 1993. The team's greatest period of success has come since 1995.

The Indians (who were at first called the Blues because of the color of their uniforms) succeeded Cleveland's National League Spiders, who in 1899, their final season, lost a major league record 134 games. When the NL dropped the Spiders at the end of the season, Ban Johnson, president of the emerging American League, grasped the opportunity to move into this major market. In 1901, when Johnson proclaimed the AL a major league, Cleveland lured several players from NL clubs and played much better than the Spiders had, but still finished next-to-last in their first big league season. The next year the Bronchos (as they decided to call themselves) languished in last place through June. But during the season they acquired several players through trade and purchase—most notably star second baseman Napoleon "Nap" Lajoie and pitcher Bill Bernhard—who turned the Bronchos around in midseason and lifted them above .500 (and into fifth place) by season's end.

With Lajoie sparkling in the field and dominating the league at the plate, the fans soon settled on another nickname for the club—the Naps—that lasted as long as Lajoie remained in Cleveland. Late in the 1904 season, Lajoie was named manager. After enjoying moderate success in two of the next three seasons, the 1908 Naps experienced their best year and one of the team's most exciting finishes ever.

With a 10-game winning streak near the end of the season, they moved from fourth to first, only to be surpassed by Detroit's 10-game streak. Each team won its season finale, but the Tigers, because they had not made up an earlier rainout, took the pennant by half a game. Cleveland protested that if Detroit had played the missed game and lost, Cleveland would have gained a tie, forcing a playoff that might have brought them the championship. The dispute eventually led to a rules change requiring ties or washouts to be replayed if their outcome could determine the pennant winner.

Poor seasons alternated with good the next few years. Lajoie quit as manager but remained as player. Pitching ace Addie Joss pitched a second no-hitter (he had hurled a perfect game at the height of the 1908 race), but before the start of the 1911 season, he was dead of tubercular meningitis. Outfielder Joe Jackson—acquired from the Athletics—hit .408 in his first full big league

season. The club reached bottom in 1914 with a last-place finish that found them 48-1/2 games out of first place … and 18-1/2 out of seventh. After the season Lajoie went to Philadelphia (the fans then voted to rename the club the Indians), and the next August Jackson was sold to the Chicago White Sox as attendance dropped to its lowest level since 1901.

By the time the 1916 season began, though, new ownership had acquired the great Tris Speaker from Boston and brought up from the minors a pair of promising pitchers, Jim Bagby (Sr.) and Stan Coveleski. Sparked by the three newcomers, the Indians rose to third in 1917, and to close second-place finishes the next two years. In 1920 everything came together. Speaker, who had taken over as manager the previous July, hit .388. Coveleski also had one of his best years with 24 wins. Bagby, in the finest season of his career, led the league with 31 victories, and veteran pitcher Ray Caldwell (picked up from the Boston Red Sox the previous summer) added another 20. Six regulars hit over .300; the club as a whole hit .303.

The team rebounded from the devastating loss of Ray Chapman, who was killed by a pitch from Carl Mays in August. The Yankees dropped back a bit in mid-September, but the White Sox hung close until the final week, when eight of their players were indicted and suspended as suspects in the Black Sox scandal of 1919. The Sox lost two of their final three games and all hope of catching up. The Indians defeated the Dodgers in a World Series that is best remembered for second baseman Bill Wambsganss' unassisted triple play in Game 5.

Cleveland led much of the way in 1921 before a late slump and a New York surge gave the Yankees their first pennant. Through the next quarter century the Indians came close to a pennant only twice. In 1926, with two veteran Georges—pitcher Uhle and first baseman Burns—enjoying their finest seasons, the Indians came to life in midseason and drew within three games of the Yankees by season's end. Fourteen years later, in 1940, behind the 27 wins of 21-year-old Bob Feller and the inspired play (in the field and at the bat) of second-year shortstop Lou Boudreau, Cleveland made an even closer run for the flag. Throughout the summer the Indians were in or near first place, but six losses in nine games with a resurgent Detroit in late August and September left them a game back at the finish.

Two years later Boudreau, at age 24, was named to manage the Tribe. His team stirred little interest through the war years but in 1946, with Feller back from military service, Cleveland fans boosted home attendance above a million for the first time. The next year, their first full season under new president Bill Veeck, the Indians climbed to fourth. More significantly, Veeck hired the league's first black player, Larry Doby, who became a mainstay of the Indians for the next eight years.

In 1948 the Indians began an era of excellence with a victory in one of the closest pennant races ever. Through June they ran a three-way race with the Yankees and the surprisingly lively Philadelphia Athletics; in July the Red Sox rose out of nowhere to make it a four-way struggle. In September the A's fell behind, but the three remaining clubs stayed close, and on September 24 found themselves in a three-way tie. Cleveland moved ahead with a four-game win streak, but Boston, after a pair of losses, won their final four (including two to eliminate New York). Cleveland's final-day loss to Detroit left them tied with Boston. In a one-game playoff in Boston the next day (the first playoff in AL history), manager-shortstop Boudreau capped his MVP season with two home runs to help give rookie Gene Bearden his 20th win. The exciting race drew more than 2.6 million Cleveland fans to Municipal Stadium,

a new major league record. The World Series against the Boston Braves was anticlimactic—a Cleveland triumph in six games.

By 1951 both owner Veeck and manager Boudreau had moved on, but under new manager Al Lopez the Indians fashioned a six-year stretch in which they finished second to the Yankees five times, and in 1954, with 111 victories, they won their third pennant The Lopez years, 1951 to 1956, were punctuated by the power of players like Doby, Luke Easter, Al Rosen, and Vic Wertz. But it was pitching that gave the team its consistency. Bob Lemon and Early Wynn won between 17 and 23 games in every one of the six years, as did Mike Garcia through 1954. As Garcia and Feller (who won 22 in 1951) faded, Art Houtteman was acquired from Detroit for a couple of good years, and Herb Score came along for his two explosive seasons.

The 1954 season was the Yankees' best season in 18 years from 1943 through 1960, a period in which they won 12 pennants, but it turned out to be the best year in Cleveland history. The Yankees kept the race close until the end of July and finished with 103 victories. But the Indians became the first American League team to win 111. Wynn and Lemon tied for the league lead with 23 wins apiece, and Garcia captured the ERA crown. Doby led the league in homers and RBIs, and second baseman Bobby Avila took the batting title. Heavily favored to defeat the Giants in the World Series, the Tribe and their fans were shocked when the NL champs swept them in four games.

After Lopez left to manage the White Sox in 1957, the Indians slipped below .500 for the first time in a decade. Rocky Colavito's power and Cal McLish's pitching brought them back in 1959, when they finished second to Lopez's White Sox. Their next highest post-Lopez finish came nine years later, in 1968, when Luis Tiant and Sam McDowell pitched them into third.

From 1969 through 1993, the final 25 years at Cleveland Stadium, Indians' fans had little to cheer about. The team completed practically every season in the bottom half of the AL East, rising above .500 in only four seasons while finishing eight years in the division cellar. The period of disappointment ended with tragedy, with the 1993 preseason deaths of relievers Tim Crews and Steve Olin and severe injury to starter Bob Ojeda in a boating accident. But it also ended with hope, with the emergence of new stars such as Albert Belle and Kenny Lofton.

The Indians—playing in brand-new Jacobs Field—were up for 1994. Belle, who ranked among AL leaders in almost every offensive category, and Lofton, who added the league lead in hits to another stolen-base title, paced a powerful offense that kept the team in the thick of a tight race with Chicago in the league's new Central division. With their best chance in decades to bring Cleveland a winner, the Indians trailed the White Sox by just one game when the season ended prematurely due to a player strike.

The Indians dominated the AL in 1995, rolling to a 100-44 record and capturing the AL Central title by a phenomenal 30 games. Paced by Albert Belle (who despite the shortened season led the AL with 50 homers, 121 runs, 377 total bases, 52 doubles, and a .690 slugging percentage), the club batted .291 and slugged 207 homers. Meanwhile, Tribe pitchers posted a league-best 3.83 ERA. The Indians swept the Red Sox in the first round of the postseason and then edged the upstart Mariners in the ALCS before falling to Atlanta, 4-2, in the World Series. The fans appreciated their team's superb effort, however, and in the off-season the club became the first to sell out every seat for the entire upcoming campaign.

The 1996 Indians repeated as AL Central champions. Team standouts included Albert Belle (48 home runs and an AL-best 148 RBIs), Kenny Lofton (.317 and a league-leading 75 stolen bases), Jim Thome (38 HRs), Jose Mesa (39 saves), and Charles Nagy (17-5, 3.41). The Tribe fell, however, to wild-card Baltimore in the first round of the postseason.

Despite losing Belle to the rival White Sox, the Indians returned to the World Series in 1997, surprising both the Yankees and the Orioles along the way. Sandy Alomar, Jr., who had been the MVP at the All-Star Game at Jacobs Field in July, continued his heroics in October. His home run off New York's Mariano Rivera in the eighth inning of Game 4 of the Division Series tied the game as the Indians rallied to win the series. The Indians beat the favored Orioles in the ALCS on a series-deciding home run by Tony Fernandez in the top of the 11th inning of Game 6. The World Series went seven games and was also decided in the 11th inning, but the Florida Marlins were the winners.

The 1998 Indians won the AL Central Division for the fourth consecutive season. Manny Ramirez led the offense with 45 home runs and 145 RBIs and shortstop Omar Vizquel won his sixth consecutive Gold Glove. The Indians lost the first game of the Division Series to the Red Sox, but won the next three games to take the series. Next came the Yankees, who had bettered Cleveland's AL record with 114 wins in 1998; the Indians briefly held a 2-1 series lead before succumbing in six games. Still, the Indians were the only team to win any postseason games against the eventual world champions.

The 1999 Indians, led by Ramirez's 165 RBIs, won the Central title for the fifth consecutive year, but it was not enough. Cleveland won the first two games of the Division Series before losing three straight to the Red Sox. Mike Hargrove, winner of 721 games for Cleveland since 1991, was replaced by Charlie Manuel, who brought the team home in second place in 2000.

The Indians reclaimed the divisional crown in 2001, but as in 1998, they were matched up against a team that had set a league record for victories—this time the Seattle Mariners, with 116. Cleveland took Seattle to the deciding fifth game of the Divisional Series before bowing.

Cleveland's stock plunged in 2002. The team suffered through its worst record (74-88) since 1991 and its lowest attendance since the strike year of 1994. Joel Skinner replaced Manuel, then Eric Wedge replaced Skinner, but it didn't help, as the team skidded even further, to 68-94 and next-to-last place in 2003.

Colorado Rockies

Denver was one of two cities awarded a National League franchise in June 1991 (Miami was the other), in the league's first expansion since Montreal and San Diego were added in 1969. The new teams took the field for the first time in 1993, their rosters stocked primarily with players selected from the other major league clubs in a special expansion draft. Denver, which chose to call itself the Colorado Rockies, drew nearly 4.5 million fans to cavernous Mile High Stadium, the largest season attendance in the history of sport.

Though their 5.41 ERA was by far the worst in the majors, the Rockies, under rookie manager Don Baylor, not only avoided the NL West cellar, but they also set a new league record for most wins by an expansion team, with 67. Retreads Andres Galarraga, Charlie Hayes and Dante Bichette headed an impressive offense, with Galarraga rebounding from a .219 average to lead the league in batting at .370.

This proved to be the Rockies' theme: hitters with modest or even puny credentials would thrive in the thin air of Denver, while

pitchers—even those with previous success—would be driven out of town with bloated ERAs and self-doubts.

Despite a 53-64 record in 1994, the Rockies finished third, just 6-1/2 games out of first place in the weak NL West. In 1995 the team moved into Coors Field (drawing 3.3 million fans), and Baylor won NL Manager of the Year honors as the team finished just one game behind LA in the NL West and earned a wild-card playoff slot in the process. Key Rockies included Galarraga, Bichette, Vinny Castilla, and Larry Walker, each of whom topped 30 homers. The dream ended in the first round of the playoffs, however, as Colorado fell to Atlanta, three games to one.

Ever since, the team has hovered around .500, finishing between third and fifth each year, and engaging in a lot of high-scoring games. Even the 1998 All-Star Game at Coors Field was a typical Mile High slugfest, a 13-8 AL win. Impressive numbers were carved out during this period by Galarraga (leading the NL with 47 homers and 150 RBIs in 1996), Walker (winning the 1997 NL MVP with 49 homers and a .366 average in 1997, then taking three of the next four batting titles), and Todd Helton (topping the circuit with 147 RBIs and a .372 average in 2000).

But all that offense couldn't save the job of the team's first manager, Don Baylor. Jim Leyland, who won the 1997 World Series with the other team born in 1993, the Florida Marlins, was hired to manage the Rockies but lasted just one year before retiring. Neither Buddy Bell nor Clint Hurdle fared any better, and team attendance sunk below three million for the first time in 2002.

After a decade of similar results, Rockies' management must wonder what it takes to win in Denver. A team which scores five-and-a-half runs a game can't compete if the pitching allows six but, as mentioned, even previously successful hurlers, like Darryl Kile and Mike Hampton, tend to self-destruct in Colorado. It could well be that, despite the gaudy batting stats, the Rockies have not yet had enough bona fide hitters to take the pressure off the pitchers.

Detroit Tigers

One of the more successful clubs in the American League, the Tigers have enjoyed winning seasons nearly 70 percent of the time. In 18 of their 61 winning seasons, they have remained in contention into the final days, 11 times emerging triumphant as league or division champions.

Detroit was one of the clubs from Ban Johnson's Western League, renamed the American League, that raised itself to major league status in 1901 with a talent raid on the long-established National League. In their first six big league seasons, the Tigers displayed little bite, finishing in the second division four times and never threatening for the league lead.

In 1907 all that changed. Sparked by a young right fielder, Ty Cobb (who in his first full big league season led the league in batting, slugging, hits, RBIs, and stolen bases) and led by a dynamic new manager, Hugh "Eeyah" Jennings (who knew enough not to try to tell Cobb how to play the game), the Tigers clawed their way to the pennant in a four-way race. The outcome might have been different if two late-season games with second-place Philadelphia had not been rained out. (Today's rules would require that the games be made up.)

The 1908 race was even closer, with four teams contending into late September. The race wasn't settled until the final day, when Detroit beat Chicago to edge Cleveland by half a game. Once again the pennant hinged on a rainout that had not been made up. And once again Cobb dominated the league's hitters (though he slipped

to fourth in stolen bases).

The Tigers had a slightly easier time of it the next year. It was a three-way race into September, but Detroit then pulled away to finish three and a half games ahead of Philadelphia. Cobb, in his best season yet, took the Triple Crown and returned to the top in stolen bases. But the Tigers were again unable to win a World Series. In 1907, after an opening-game tie, the Chicago Cubs had swept the next four. The Cubs lost Game 3 the next year, but won the other four. And in 1909 Pittsburgh and Detroit alternated victories, with the Pirates emerging world champions in seven games.

Jennings managed Detroit for eleven more seasons; then Cobb took the reins for six years before leaving for Philadelphia. But the Tigers won no more pennants in the Cobb era. Cobb himself continued to dominate the league offensively through 1919. In 1911 he achieved career highs in most offensive categories, including a batting average of .420, but the Tigers managed no better than a distant second to the Athletics. In 1915 they started strong and remained in the race throughout the season. Cobb stole what was for 47 years a modern-record 96 bases, and the team's 100 wins proved to be the highest total in their first 33 years. But after running neck and neck with the Red Sox through most of August, the Tigers slumped a bit in early September—just enough for the Sox to take the flag by two and a half games. A close third-place finish the next year marked the Tigers' last serious challenge for 18 years.

In 1934, after six straight years in the second division, and only three years after their most distant finish ever (47 games out), the Tigers turned themselves around to win the pennant with a 101-53 record and a .656 winning percentage, the highest in club history. Two newly acquired veterans—manager/catcher Mickey Cochrane and outfielder Goose Goslin—enjoyed fine seasons at the bat, as did first baseman Hank Greenberg (.339, 139 RBIs), in his first full season, and second baseman Charlie Gehringer (.356, 127 RBIs). The two other infielders, third baseman Marv Owen and shortstop Billy Rogell, enjoyed their finest seasons at the plate for a club whose batting average led the league at .300. It took the Tigers a month to get going, but by mid-July they had shot ahead of the Yankees to win by seven games. But once again, victory in the World Series eluded them as the St. Louis Cardinals blew them away, 11-0, in Game 7.

Paced by Greenberg's 170 RBIs in 1935, Detroit—after another slow start—moved up so sharply in July and August that even a September slump gave the Yankees no opportunity to catch them. And finally, in their fifth try, the Tigers won a world championship, overcoming Chicago in six games despite the loss of Greenberg, who broke his wrist in Game 2. Part-owner Frank Navin, who had run the club for three decades, had finally seen his Tigers reach the very top. A month later, after falling from a horse, he suffered a heart attack and died.

Del Baker had replaced Cochrane as manager when Detroit next made a run for the pennant in 1940. In a tight race the Tigers caught up with Cleveland in early September and traded the lead with them for two weeks before pulling ahead to stay with two wins in a three-game series. In the pennant clincher, Detroit's Floyd Giebell outdueled Cleveland great Bob Feller 2-0 for his third—and last—big league victory. In the World Series the Tigers lost once again, as Cincinnati came from behind in Game 7 for a 2-1 win.

Two losing seasons followed, and Steve O'Neill replaced Baker at the helm. In 1944 the wartime Tigers, behind the splendid pitching of workhorses Dizzy Trout and Hal Newhouser (one-two in ERA and innings pitched, and winners of 27 and 29 games, respectively),

joined the race in late August and found themselves tied with the St. Louis Browns for first going into the last game of the season. But the Browns beat the Yankees, and Detroit lost to Washington.

Hank Greenberg's release from military service in mid-1945 sparked another run for the pennant. The Tigers held the lead from mid-June through August, but in September the surging Senators caught up with them. The race once again went down to the final day, and the final inning, when Greenberg's grand slam overcame a St. Louis lead to give Detroit the flag. Newhouser, with 25 wins and a 1.81 ERA, was named AL MVP for the second straight year. In the World Series his ERA shot up to 6.10, but he still managed to win two games (including the finale) as the Tigers took the Cubs in seven for their second world title.

In the 23 years that passed before their next pennant, the Tigers came close only twice. In 1950 they led the race through the middle of the season, but were caught by the Yankees late in August. After retaking the lead in early September, the two clubs ran neck-and-neck for a while before Detroit fell away to second.

Two years later the Tigers reached their nadir: their first cellar finish. After a decade in which they finished no higher than fourth, they rebounded in 1961 as first baseman Norm Cash and left fielder Rocky Colavito both enjoyed the most explosive seasons of their careers. Compiling their best season record since 1934, Detroit led the league through parts of June and July. But this was the year of Maris and Mantle and 109 Yankee victories; when the season ended, the Tigers' 101 wins had earned them only second place.

They came much closer six years later in the great four-way race of 1967 that saw three clubs still contending on the final day, when the Tigers split a doubleheader to tie with Minnesota for second. If 1967 was a scramble, 1968 belonged to Detroit. Denny McLain won 31 games (the last major leaguer to win 30) to lead the team to a 103-win finish, 12 games ahead of Baltimore. Down three games to one in the World Series, the pitching of McLain in Game 6 and Mickey Lolich in Games 5 and 7 brought the Tigers back against the Cardinals and gave them their third world championship.

A strike at the start of 1972 contributed to the Tigers' first divisional title, which culminated a four-way race in the AL East. Detroit defeated Boston two games out of three at season's end, to edge the Sox by half a game. But if the strike had not wiped out an unequal number of games, the end of the season could have seen the two clubs tied.

The Tigers lost the pennant to Oakland with a 2-1 loss in the finale of a close American League Championship Series, and dropped out of contention for a decade. In 1974 they finished at the bottom of the division and the next year lost 102 games to post the worst record in the majors.

Finally, after seven seasons in the second division, Detroit put together a strong second half in strike-divided 1981, fading only at the end to tie for second. Three years later the Tigers were back on top with one of their best years. Opening the season 9-0, they ended April at 18-2, stretched their mark to 35-5 by late May, and were never headed, finishing a team-record 15 games in front with 104 wins, their most ever. Their balanced pitching staff led the league in ERA, even though none of their starters finished among the top ten. Willie Hernandez (who with Aurelio Lopez compiled a 19-4 record from the bullpen, with 46 saves) earned both Cy Young and MVP awards. After sweeping Kansas City in the ALCS, the Tigers took the world championship—their fourth—from San Diego in five games.

In 1987 the Tigers caught the Blue Jays in the season's final series, tying them for the lead in the first game, moving to the front

with a 12-inning win in the second game, and clinching the division crown in the finale, 1-0. In the ALCS, though, Minnesota stopped the favored Tigers, four games to one.

Injuries sidelined veteran keystoners Alan Trammell and Lou Whitaker more than a month each in 1988. All the same, the Tigers led the AL East much of the season before falling back and rallied at season's end to finish second, one game behind Boston.

The next year, though, as new waves of injury broke over an aging lineup, the Tigers dropped into the division cellar in June and kept sinking, finishing with 103 losses and the worst record in the majors. But in 1990, newly acquired first baseman Cecil Fielder sparked a recovery to third place. Fielder, back in the U.S. after a season in Japan, topped the majors in home runs (with 51, the most in the AL since 1961), slugging percentage and runs batted in.

The 1991 Tigers clawed their way back from an eight-game deficit in mid-July into a tie with first-place Toronto seven weeks later; they finished tied for second with Boston. In 1992, for the third year in a row, Detroit led the AL in home runs, but this time their big bats couldn't lift the club above sixth place. Texas edged the Tigers for the home run crown in 1993, but Detroit challenged for their division lead through August and, after a dip in September, surged to tie Baltimore for third place.

The Tigers wouldn't see the good side of .500 for a long time thereafter. After finishes of last and next-to-last in the strike-shortened seasons of 1994 and '95, Sparky Anderson retired as manager. Whitaker also called it a career, and Trammell followed a year later; it was the end of an era in Detroit.

The Buddy Bell-led 1996 Tigers compiled baseball's worst record (53-109) but improved by 26 games the next year. After the Tigers shifted to the AL Central in 1998, the team foundered. Bell was dismissed late in the campaign and replaced by Larry Parrish, who lasted just one full season.

After 88 seasons in historic Tiger Stadium, the team—headed by new skipper Phil Garner—moved to spacious new Comerica Park in 2000. The club improved to 79-83, and attendance was the highest since the 1984 world-championship season.

It was all downhill from there. The Tigers' loss total increased to 96 in 2001, 106 in '02, and an unthinkable 119 in '03. Garner and Luis Pujols lost managerial jobs, and Alan Trammell took over just in time to see the team set a league record for losses in a season. Only a final-week surge enabled the '03 Tigers to avoid breaking the 1962 Mets' modern major league mark of 120 losses.

Florida Marlins

One of two new clubs to join the National League in 1993, the Florida Marlins were formed after the selection, in June 1991, of Miami and Denver as cities for the league's first expansion teams since 1969. Headed by entertainment magnate H. Wayne Huizenga, the Marlins played in Joe Robbie Stadium (which Huizenga partially owned). In their first season the Marlins featured one of the game's premier relievers in Bryan Harvey, whose 45 saves ranked third in the NL and contributed to 70 percent of the club's 64 victories. Though the Marlins lost their final six games, they finished ahead of the New York Mets for sixth place in the NL East.

In the strike-shortened seasons of 1994 and 1995 they finished in the division cellar. In 1995, however, Pat Rapp showed signs of promise with a 14-7 mark and rookie second baseman Quilvio Veras led the NL with 56 stolen bases. Even though the Marlins fired manager Rene Lachemann in midseason of 1996 (replacing him with interim manager John Boles), they moved up to third

place (80-82) with help from Gary Sheffield (42 HRs, 120 RBIs, 118 runs scored), Al Leiter (200 strikeouts), Kevin Brown (league-leading 1.89 ERA), and Robb Nen (35 saves).

In the offseason, the Marlins signed manager Jim Leyland and within a few months they had practically a whole new team. In less than three weeks the Marlins signed six free agents—Bobby Bonilla, Moises Alou, Alex Fernandez, Jim Eisenreich, John Cangelosi, and Dennis Cook—and suddenly they were one of the best teams in baseball. The Marlins battled Atlanta for the NL East title (they went 8-4 against the Braves during the season), but failing that, they still managed to hold off the Mets for the wild card. The Marlins swept the Giants in the Division Series and then shocked the Braves in six games to win the pennant.

Rookie Livan Hernandez, who was Most Valuable Player of the NLCS, earned MVP honors for the World Series as well. It was second-year shortstop Edgar Renteria, however, who won the World Series with a single in the bottom of the 11th inning of Game 7 to score Craig Counsell, whose sacrifice fly had tied the game in the ninth. Their victory over Cleveland not only made the Marlins the first wild-card team to win the World Series, but in only their fifth season of existence, they were also the earliest expansion franchise to win a world championship.

As quickly as success had come, it disappeared. Quoting huge financial losses on the championship team, owner Huizenga looked to sell the Marlins, and in the meantime, traded away the nucleus of the champions before they ever got a chance to defend the title. By the end of the year, only everyday players Renteria and Counsell remained (and Renteria was traded to St. Louis during the winter meetings). The Marlins were finally sold to commodities trader John Henry and John Boles was named manager of the team for the second time, replacing Jim Leyland, who resigned after the 1998 season. General manager Dave Dombrowski, who, in Huizenga's "house cleaning" had secured several top prospects from other organizations, signed a five-year contract to remain with the club.

The Marlins finished last for the second straight year in 1999. The team received solid seasons from shortstop Alex Gonzalez and rookie center fielder Preston Wilson—between them they led the Marlins in a dozen offensive categories. Florida's 15-game improvement in 2000, however, was mainly due to pitching. All-Star Ryan Dempster led the staff with 14 wins, including a one-hit shutout of the Mets. Antonio Alfonseca led the major leagues in saves as the Marlins developed one of baseball's best young bullpens. Luis Castillo led the majors in stolen bases and batted .334 atop a lineup that included Cliff Floyd and Mike Lowell, who both enjoyed solid comeback seasons.

Two fourth-place finishes and a slow start in 2002 followed, as managers Boles, Tony Perez and Jeff Torborg were sent packing. Attendance dropped to just 813,111 in 2002, and there were talks that the Marlins would be moved or even eliminated.

All that changed in 2003. With the Marlins floundering at 16-22, veteran catcher Ivan Rodriguez was signed as a free agent, 21-year-old pitcher Dontrelle Willis debuted on May 9 and 72-year-old skipper Jack McKeon took over the team the next day. McKeon provided paternal leadership, while Rodriguez steadied a youthful pitching staff. The electrifying Willis went 9-1 before the All-Star break and went on to capture the Rookie of the Year Award. The Marlins had the best record in baseball over the last four months of the season, finishing with 91 wins and the NL wild-card spot.

The Marlins went on to upset the Giants, winners of 100 games, in the NL Divisional Series. The Cubs seemed to have them licked in the Championship Series when they took a three-games-to-one lead. Josh Beckett, 23, kept Florida's hopes alive with a two-hit shutout in Game 5—the first complete game of his pro career. It was Beckett who had said, before the postseason even started, that "I think with youth, there's a little bit of stupidity. I think we just might be stupid enough to pull this off."

The Cubs had a 3-0 lead in the eighth inning of Game 6, with ace Mark Prior on the mound. But the Marlins erupted for an eight-run inning, then finished off the Cubs the next day, with Beckett pitching four scoreless innings of relief. Rodriguez, who drove in ten runs in the seven games, was named MVP of the Series.

It was on to the World Series against the heavily favored Yankees. The Yanks won two of the first three, outscoring their opponents, 14-5. But the plucky Marlins refused to roll over, and eked out the next two. When Series MVP Beckett shut out the Bronx Bombers in Game 6, the Marlins were world champions for the second time in their 11-year existence—even though they had never won a divisional title, and only twice finished above .500.

Houston Astros (aka Colt .45s)

The Colt .45s (as the Astros were originally known) had hoped to begin their history in the Harris County Domed Stadium. When the start of the vast project was delayed, a temporary outdoor park was built for them next door in time for their 1962 inaugural. Heat, humidity and giant mosquitoes held Colt home attendance below a million in each of their three outdoor seasons. In 1965, they brought big league baseball indoors for the first time, and the fans arrived—more than 2 million the first year. The original grass under the dome was real, but when the skylight panels were coated over so fielders wouldn't lose sight of high flies, the grass died. In 1966 the club (now known as the Astros) and the stadium (now called the Astrodome) brought to baseball yet another innovation—AstroTurf.

The Houston franchise, conceived as an entry in the abortive Continental League, first took the field instead in the National League. Houston and the New York Mets were part of the league's first expansion since shrinking from 12 teams to eight in 1900. Shrewd player selection by general manager Paul Richards kept the new team from being as bad as the Mets. Although they suffered just as long playing below .500 (seven years), they finished below New York in the standings only once.

When the NL added two more teams in 1969 and split into two divisions, the Astros for the first time made a serious title run. Though they wound up fifth in the West (ahead of only the expansion San Diego Padres), they rose to within two games of the top in August, and again in September before a six-game losing streak dropped them out of contention. With an 81-81 record, they finished out of the ranks of losers for the first time.

After dropping below .500 again in 1970 and '71, the Astros made their second run for the division title in 1972. At the end of June they were battling with Cincinnati for the lead, but the Reds pulled away over the rest of the season while Houston leveled off for an eventual second-place finish 10-1/2 games back. With a record of 84-69, the Astros had fashioned their first winning season.

In 1975 they endured their worst year ever, losing 97 games to finish at the bottom of the West, 43-1/2 games behind the Reds. But the next year pitcher J.R. Richard, with the first of several fine seasons, brought the club up to third with his 20 wins. By 1979 Richard was the NL's most overwhelming pitcher, leading the league with 313 strikeouts and a 2.71 ERA. His 18 wins and team-

mate Joe Niekro's 21 sparked a team that spent much of the summer in first place before falling to a game and a half behind Cincinnati at the end.

Houston and Los Angeles battled back and forth for the division lead throughout 1980. Richard began strong and seemed headed for his finest year. With a 10-4 record, he was the starting pitcher in the All-Star Game. But shortly after midseason he suffered a stroke that ended his big league career. Led by Joe Niekro, Nolan Ryan and Vern Ruhle (who replaced Richard in the rotation and finished 12-4), the best pitching staff in baseball kept the Astros in the race to season's end, although three straight losses to the Dodgers had left the clubs tied for first. In a one-game playoff, Houston rebounded with a 7-1 win (Niekro's 20th) to capture the division title. In the National League Championship Series, the Astros took the Phillies to the 10th inning of the final game before bowing three games to two.

When a player strike cut the middle out of the 1981 season, intradivisional playoffs were scheduled between the winners of the two halves. Houston, the second-half champion, defeated first-half victor Los Angeles in the first two games, but lost the next three, and the division title.

After four years in the middle of the division, the Astros stormed back in 1986 with their best season ever, winning 15 of their last 19 games to conquer the West. Pitcher Mike Scott, who had developed a deceptive split-finger fastball, won 18 and led the NL in strikeouts, innings and ERA. On September 25 he clinched the division crown with a no-hitter. In the NLCS the Astros lost to the Mets in six games, but three of New York's wins came in its final at bat, including a 16-inning victory in Game 6.

In each of the next three seasons the Astros drew within a game and a half of first place in August, only to tumble out of the race in the season's final weeks. Rookie first baseman Jeff Bagwell's strong performance at the plate gave Astros fans one of their few reasons to cheer in 1991 as their team plummeted to last place.

The offense set club records in batting average and home runs in 1993, and the pitching staff compiled the second lowest ERA in the majors, as ace Mark Portugal concluded his brilliant 18-4 season with 12 straight wins. But the Astros couldn't approach powerful Atlanta and San Francisco and finished third in their division, 19 games out.

Free-agent Portugal departed for San Francisco in 1994, but pitcher Doug Drabek rebounded after an off-year, and MVP Bagwell's slugging dominated the NL. Playing in the Central Division under new manager Terry Collins, the Astros struggled to catch division leader Cincinnati, and had drawn within half a game of the Reds when the season ended. The following year was almost a replay of 1994, as the Astros again finished second to Cincinnati. And in 1996 the Astros were bridesmaids again, this time finishing second, six games behind St. Louis.

At season's end Astros broadcaster Larry Dierker replaced Collins as manager. Dierker, the ace of the Astros pitching staff more than two decades earlier, let developing pitchers like Shane Reynolds, Mike Hampton and Jose Lima stay in games longer and they quickly learned from their mistakes and gained confidence. After three years of finishing second, the Astros finally won the NL Central in Dierker's rookie season as manager. They were quickly swept by Atlanta in the playoffs.

Even though 1997 ace Darryl Kile (19-7, 2.57 ERA) left for Colorado as a free agent, the Astros repeated as division champs in 1998. A last-minute trade for Randy Johnson of Seattle fortified an already solid pitching staff and helped Houston to a club-record 102 wins. The hot Astros ran into an even hotter Padres team and lost in the Division Series, three games to one.

The Astros won their third consecutive division title in 1999 behind 20-game winners Hampton and Lima and a solid batting order that featured Craig Biggio, Carl Everett and Bagwell, yet the team lost in the Division Series for the third year running. After several offseason changes—including Everett to Boston plus Hampton and Derek Bell to the Mets—the Astros fell flat in their new home. Enron Field proved to be popular with both fans and hitters, but Houston's vaunted pitching staff took a beating, and the team slumped to fourth. While the Astros placed third in batting and led the league in home runs, including 47 by Bagwell and 44 by Richard Hidalgo, the club allowed the most homers and had the worst ERA. This proved to be more a reflection of the new park than either the hitters' prowess or the pitchers' lack thereof. Enron Field—which was renamed Astros Field, then Minute Maid Park, after Enron went bust in 2002—ranks behind only Coors Field as a hitters' haven.

The Astros rebounded to a first-place tie with the Cardinals in 2001. Since both teams qualified for the postseason, no playoff was necessary; Houston was declared divisional champion based on head-to-head record. But the Astros were swept by the Braves in the NLDS.

Jimy Williams took over the reigns as Houston finished second in both 2002 and '03. The Cardinals topped them by 13 games in the former season, and the Cubs edged them by one in the final days of the latter.

Kansas City Royals

Two years after the Athletics abandoned Kansas City for the West Coast, patent medicine millionaire Ewing Kauffman bankrolled an expansion club for the city. Where the A's had been unable in 13 years to fashion even one winning season, the Royals did it in 1971, their third year. One of the most successful of all expansion clubs, the Royals finished either first or second in their division in 14 of their first 20 years.

In their fifth season, 1973, the year they moved into new Royals Stadium, the Royals also made their first serious run for the division title. A midsummer spurt carried them into first place in August before they leveled off to another second-place finish behind Oakland.

After a third second-place race with Oakland in 1975 (during which manager Jack McKeon was replaced by Whitey Herzog), the Royals won the division crown in 1976, taking the lead two months into the season and holding it to the end. Third baseman George Brett won his first AL batting championship by one point over teammate Hal McRae. The Royals and New York were tied after four games in the American League Championship Series, but the Yankees snatched the pennant on Chris Chambliss' home run in the bottom of the ninth inning of the final game.

For two more years the Royals dominated the AL West but failed to stop the Yankees in the ALCS. In 1977, with a pitching staff that led the league in ERA and a balanced offense that included four players with more than 20 home runs and 80 RBIs, the Royals compiled a record of 102-60—their finest to date. Though they didn't move into the division lead until mid-August, they were nearly unstoppable the rest of the way. In the ALCS they once again battled New York all the way, only to lose the Series and pennant for the second time in the final inning of Game 5.

The American League West divisional race was a bit tighter in

1978, as California hung close to Kansas City through much of August and into September, before the Royals finally pulled away. In the ALCS, the Royals tied the series with a big win in Game 2, but the Yankees came back to take the next two by one run each for their third straight flag.

The Royals slipped to second place in 1979, but the next year (led now by rookie manager Jim Frey) they overwhelmed the rest of a weak division. Despite a month-long decline in September, Kansas City finished the season 14 games ahead of Oakland for their fourth divisional title. This was the year Brett chased .400 (ending at .390, at that time the highest major league average since Ted Williams hit .406 in 1941), reliever Dan Quisenberry enjoyed his first big season (12 wins, 33 saves), and starter Dennis Leonard came back from an off-year to record his third 20-win season in four years. It was also the year the Royals finally beat the Yankees to capture their first pennant—with a three-game sweep in the ALCS. In the World Series, though, Philadelphia emerged on top in six games.

The player strike of 1981 divided the season into two halves. In the first half the Royals finished fifth, but part way through the second half Dick Howser (who had managed the Yankees to the East title the previous year) replaced Frey as Royals manager. The Royals rallied to finish first, a game ahead of Oakland. But in the special playoffs, the A's (who had won the first-half race) beat Kansas City for the division title with a three-game sweep.

Two more second-place finishes in 1982 (a close race with California) and 1983 (20 games behind the Chicago White Sox) were followed in 1984 by a fifth division championship in a three-way race with California and Minnesota. But Detroit swept away the Royals' pennant hopes in the ALCS, in the minimum three games.

For Kansas City, 1985 was a season of catching up. Few picked the Royals to win the West, but with starters Charlie Leibrandt (17-9) and Bret Saberhagen (20-6) finishing two-three in the league ERA race, reliever Quisenberry leading the league in saves for the fourth straight year, and veteran George Brett healthy and enjoying one of his best seasons ever, the Royals chased California throughout the summer and caught them in the final week to take their sixth division crown, by a single game.

In the ALCS against Toronto, the Royals fell behind three games to one, which would have eliminated them in earlier years. Saved by the expansion of the series from five games to seven, they came back with three straight wins for their second pennant. Repeating the suspense in the World Series, the Royals again fell behind 3-1 to St. Louis, before rallying once again to win three straight for their first world championship.

During the 1986 season, manager Howser left the club because of a brain tumor. The Royals dropped below .500 and finished third, their lowest rank in a dozen years. Howser was unable to return to the helm in 1987 as he had hoped and died during the summer.

In 1989 Bret Saberhagen, with his most sparkling season yet (23-6, 2.16 ERA), hurled the Royals to their best record since 1980, but their 92 wins earned them only a ninth second-place finish—although Saberhagen earned his second Cy Young Award. Confounding predictions of another strong season, following free-agent acquisitions Mark Davis and Storm Davis, the Royals in 1990 floundered in the division cellar much of the summer. They wound up in sixth place, 27-1/2 games out. George Brett, now 37, rallied from the worst start of his career (a .200 batting average in early May) to hit .329 and capture his third AL batting title.

Slugging outfielder Danny Tartabull enjoyed a peak season in 1991, and helped lift Kansas City back above .500. But in the strong AL West no club suffered a losing season, so the Royals again had to settle for sixth. When Tartabull left for the Yankees in 1992, the Royals faltered again. But as the West was now the weaker division, the club's 72-90 record was good enough for a fifth-place tie.

In the final season of his playing career at Kansas City, George Brett led his team in RBIs in 1993, and Kevin Appier led AL pitchers in ERA, as the Royals returned above .500 to finish third. Ewing Kauffman, the club's founder and owner, died in August, and Royals Stadium was renamed in his honor.

In 1994, after a sluggish first half, the Royals picked up the pace to challenge Chicago and Cleveland in the new American League Central division. At season's end, the Royals were still third but—thanks largely to Cy Young Award winner David Cone's 16-5 season—only four games behind first-place Chicago. Manager Bob Boone's Royals finished second again in 1995—but this time 30 games back of Cleveland.

Playing on natural turf for the first time in Kauffman Stadium's history, the Royals finished last in both 1996 and '97, as Boone gave way to Tony Muser. The team continued to flounder the next five seasons, losing between 85 and 100 games each year.

Under Tony Pena, who took over during the 2002 season, the Royals had a resurgence in '03. After a torrid start, the club finished third, just seven games behind the division-leading Twins, and posted their first winning season (83-79) since 1994. Pena earned Manager of the Year honors, and shortstop Angel Berroa was named the league's top rookie.

Los Angeles Dodgers (aka Brooklyn Bridegrooms, Superbas, Dodgers, Robins)

When the Dodgers left Brooklyn for Los Angeles, an era ended. From baseball's earliest days Brooklyn had been prominent; the city's Atlantics were the nation's best team in the mid-1860s, and since 1884 Brooklyn had been home to major league ball. But before the start of the 1958 season, its link to the big time was severed by an owner who saw greener fields to the west.

The club's origins were modest. After winning the championship of the minor Inter-State Association in 1883, Brooklyn moved up to the major league American Association in 1884 and endured three losing seasons in its first four years. But in 1888, after signing three regulars from New York's newly defunct Mets and buying pitching/hitting stars Bob Caruthers and Dave Foutz from the AA champion St. Louis Browns, Brooklyn finished second to St. Louis, and the next year dethroned the Browns for their first big league pennant. In a World Series against the National League champion New York Giants, the Bridegrooms (as the Brooklyns had been nicknamed) won three of the first four games, but lost the next five.

Before the start of the 1890 season, Brooklyn transferred from the AA to the more prestigious NL. Many NL clubs performed below par that year, weakened by the loss of players to the outlaw Players League. But Brooklyn held on to most of its players and swept to its second straight pennant. In postseason play, poor weather and lack of fan support caused the World Series against AA winner Louisville to be called off after each team had won three games and tied one. The next year, with other NL teams renewed by players from the failed PL, Brooklyn finished sixth.

When the AA folded after the 1891 season, Brooklyn picked up slugger Dan Brouthers and pitcher George Haddock from pennant-winning Boston, and rebounded in 1892 to finish second and third in the two halves of a divided season. But for the next five

years they finished no higher than fifth, and in 1898 sank to tenth in what was then a twelve-team league.

Help was on the way, however. The owners of the Baltimore Orioles—Harry Von der Horst and Ned Hanlon—seeing an opportunity to move into the more lucrative Brooklyn market, purchased a half interest in the Bridegrooms. Hanlon retained his Baltimore presidency, but took over as manager in Brooklyn, bringing along with him the core of the Orioles—shortstop Hughie Jennings and outfielders Joe Kelley and Willie Keeler—plus his two best pitchers, Jim Hughes and Doc McJames.

The infusion of new talent worked wonders, as Brooklyn in 1899 (with a new nickname, the Superbas) took the NL lead in late May, during a 22-game winning streak, and held it the rest of the way. That winter, when Baltimore was dropped as the NL cut back from 12 teams to 8, Hanlon moved more Orioles to Brooklyn (including pitcher Joe "Iron Man" McGinnity), and once again led the Superbas to the pennant. That year they also won their first world championship in a series played with second-place Pittsburgh for the elegant Chronicle-Telegraph Cup.

Charley Ebbets, who had risen from ticket seller to president, took over majority ownership with the purchase of Von der Horst's stock, thereby quashing Hanlon's proposed move back to Baltimore. Ebbets' clashes with Hanlon hastened the club's decline. In 1903 the team began a 12-year sojourn in the second division, including a last-place finish in 1905 with their worst record ever (48-104, 56-1/2 games out). Perhaps the most memorable events of these years were the change in nickname to Dodgers and their move to brand-new Ebbets Field in 1913.

Hanlon was fired as manager after the disastrous 1905 season, but it was not until Wilbert Robinson took over in 1914 that the team began to pull out of its doldrums. Pitcher Jack Pfeffer, in his first full big league season, won 23 games for the fifth-place Dodgers that year, and two years later led them to the pennant with 25 wins and a sparkling 1.92 ERA.

But the Dodgers lost the 1916 World Series to the Boston Red Sox, and in 1917 fell all the way to seventh. After three years in the second division, they bounced back in 1920, turning a three-way race into a rout with 16 wins in their final 18 games. After another World Series loss, to Cleveland, the Dodgers returned to the second division for another three years. In 1924 they began slowly, but leaped from 12 games back to an early-September lead, only to slip 1-1/2 games behind the Giants at the finish.

Charley Ebbets died the following April, and Robinson was named to replace him. In his five years as president the club suffered on the field, finishing sixth each year. Fired as president but retained as manager, "Uncle Robby" saw his Robins (as the Dodgers were now known) lead the league in 1930 most of the time from mid-May to a mid-August decline, then retake the lead for a day in mid-September before tailing off once more to finish fourth. That was Uncle Robby's last hurrah. When the Robins provided no serious challenge in their fourth-place run the next year, he resigned after 18 years at the wheel.

A succession of managers followed, but it was not until the Dodgers brought in the free-spending Larry MacPhail as general manager in 1938 that the club began to pull itself back into contention. The highlight of MacPhail's first year with the Dodgers was not the team's finish (seventh) but the introduction of night baseball to Ebbets Field (on June 15, when Cincinnati's Johnny Vander Meer defeated Brooklyn with his second consecutive no-hitter).

MacPhail's most brilliant move may have been his conversion of shortstop Leo Durocher into manager Leo Durocher. The loud, driven Durocher alienated many (including MacPhail himself), but provided inspired leadership and a will to win that overcame complaints against him. After a third-place finish in 1939 and second place in 1940, the Dodgers battled the St. Louis Cardinals through all of 1941 before pulling ahead to clinch the pennant with just two games remaining. Veteran first baseman Dolf Camilli led the league in home runs and RBIs; sophomore outfielder Pete Reiser led the league in batting, slugging and runs scored; and pitchers Kirby Higbe and Whitlow Wyatt tied for the league lead with 22 wins apiece, as the Dodgers won 100 games. Only their loss to the Yankees in the World Series marred their finest season in 42 years.

In 1942 they played even better, winning 104 games. But a late-season five-game slump dropped them behind the surging Cardinals. MacPhail and many of his players left for the war, and though the club finished third in 1943 and 1945, it was not until 1946 that the Dodgers again presented a serious challenge. Once again the Cards and Dodgers made a two-team race of it, but this time the race ended in a tie, forcing the first league playoff ever. The Cardinals won the pennant with wins in the first two games.

When MacPhail left for the Army, Branch Rickey was hired to run the club. MacPhail had left the club financially sound; Rickey set about to make it a consistent winner. Famed as the developer of the Cardinals farm system, he was determined at Brooklyn to tap the one source of talent that the major leagues had willfully neglected: black players. He signed Jackie Robinson to Montreal (Brooklyn's leading farm team), and after a year there promoted him to the Dodgers for the 1947 season. Thus began the club's golden Brooklyn decade: 10 years in which they won six pennants and—in 1955—a World Series. Two other races went right to the wire; only once did they finish as low as third.

With manager Durocher suspended from baseball for a year for consorting with gamblers, the Dodgers in 1947 were led by grandfatherly Burt Shotton, brought out of his Florida retirement. Robinson's hustle put him at the top of the league in stolen bases and second in runs scored. The team pulled up from fourth in June to first in July, and held the lead to the end. In the World Series they lost to the Yankees in an exciting seven games.

Durocher returned to the helm in 1948, but was replaced by Shotton in midsummer, with the Dodgers in fifth place. Shotton saw the team rise to third that season, then battle back and forth with the Cardinals throughout 1949 before edging them by a game on the final day. Robinson, in an MVP season, led the NL in hitting and stolen bases and finished among the leaders in most other offensive categories. Rookie pitcher Don Newcombe led the team in victories with 17, and Preacher Roe led the league in winning percentage. Again the World Series was a loss to the Yankees, this time in only five games.

In 1950 the Dodgers nearly caught the staggering Phillies, losing out only in the 10th inning of the final game. President Rickey left the club for Pittsburgh and was replaced by Walter O'Malley, who replaced manager Shotton with Charlie Dressen. The slugging of catcher Roy Campanella and first baseman Gil Hodges and 20-win seasons by Roe (22-3) and Newcombe (20-9) kept the Dodgers in front through most of 1951, but New York's surging Giants closed from 13 games back in August to tie for the lead at the finish. The teams split the first two playoff games. In Game 3 the Dodgers were leading by two runs in the last of the ninth when Bobby Thomson's three-run homer gave New York the flag.

The next year, though, the Giants fell short and Brooklyn took

the pennant with relative ease. But not the World Series. Although Brooklyn held a 3-2 lead after five games, the Yankees came back to take the final two.

The Dodgers repeated as NL champions in 1953 with their best season ever. The Dodgers overwhelmed the league, hitting 19 points and slugging 63 points above the league average, as the team outscored its nearest rival by more than a run per game. With a club-record 105 wins, the Dodgers cruised to the pennant by 13 games. But again the Yankees took the World Series, in six games.

Dressen wanted a three-year deal and was let go when he turned down one for only a year. Minor league manager Walter Alston wasn't so demanding, and signed for 1954 the first of a historic string of 23 one-year Dodger contracts that would see him into the Hall of Fame. After a second-place finish in Alston's rookie year, the Dodgers in 1955 took the lead from the start and—never challenged—walked away with their 11th pennant. Outfielder Duke Snider, with one of his most productive seasons, led the league's most powerful squad; Newcombe (20-5) paced the league's best pitching staff.

Once more in the World Series, Brooklyn faced the Yankees, and once more the Series went seven games. But this time there was joy in Brooklyn—Johnny Podres shut out New York in the finale! In an exciting three-way fight in 1956, the Dodgers repeated as pennant-winners, taking their final three games to edge the Milwaukee Braves. Newcombe, in his greatest year, clinched the flag on the final day with his 27th win. In the World Series, though, it was *deja vu*—a sixth Yankee triumph, in seven games. The golden decade was over.

The Dodgers, despite the league's best pitching, vacated the 1957 race in August, finishing third. Before the start of the next season, they had vacated Brooklyn as well, for Los Angeles. Playing in Memorial Coliseum (a converted football stadium) the L.A. Dodgers sank to seventh place in 1958. But the next year the reawakened bats of aging Duke Snider and Gil Hodges, the fiery pitching of young Don Drysdale, and the late-season pitching heroics of Roger Craig (recalled from Spokane) kept the team in the thick of a tight race that found them tied with the Braves at season's end. The Dodgers won the first playoff game in Milwaukee, and captured big league baseball's first West Coast pennant at home the next day, in the 12th inning. Then they defeated the Chicago White Sox to give the West its first World Series winner.

After finishes of fourth and second, the Dodgers produced record-breaking excitement in 1962 as they moved into brand-new Dodger Stadium in the hills above Los Angeles. Between the new ballpark and the excitement generated on the field, more than 2.75 million fans passed through the turnstiles—a new attendance record that would last until the Dodgers themselves broke it 15 years later. As pitcher Don Drysdale and left fielder Tommy Davis ignited the league with career-high seasons, and shortstop Maury Wills became the first major leaguer of the century to steal 100 bases, the team locked into a season-long struggle for first place with archrival San Francisco. But after holding a narrow lead much of the season, the Dodgers dropped their last four games to finish in yet another tie. The playoff must have reminded fans of 1951. As they had then, the Giants and Dodgers split the first two games, and the Dodgers once again held a 4-2 lead in the ninth inning of the third game. This time, though, it was not a home run that undid them, but a bases-loaded walk.

Sandy Koufax—who had won 14 games in 1962 (and the first of five straight ERA crowns) despite losing half the year with circulation problems in his fingers—rose to dominate the world of pitching the next four years. For three of those years his Dodgers

dominated the NL. In 1963 Koufax's 25-5 season carried Los Angeles into the World Series against the Yankees, where two more wins helped put the New Yorkers away in the minimum four games. The next year Koufax slipped to 19 wins, but the Dodgers fell all the way to a tie for sixth.

They rebounded to the top in 1965. Koufax won 26 and Drysdale 23 in a tight four-team race that saw them fall behind the Giants in early September, only to retake the lead for good later in the month with 13 straight wins. The World Series against Minnesota went to the seventh game before Koufax nailed down another world title with his second shutout in three days.

The race in 1966 was just as close as in '65, with three teams switching leads throughout the season. But the Dodgers, third at the end of August, put together streaks of five and seven wins in September to move to the top, where Koufax clinched the pennant on the final day with his 27th victory. And then it was all over. After a losing effort in Game 2 of the World Series (a Baltimore sweep), Koufax, at age 30, retired because of arthritis in his pitching elbow. The Dodgers sank to eighth the next year, and seventh in 1968.

In 1969, the first season of divisional play, Los Angeles found itself in the thick of a five-team race in the West until eight straight losses in late September dropped them to fourth. No one challenged Cincinnati in 1970, but the next year the Dodgers closed to within a game of the front-running Giants in September before their drive stalled.

A late-season slump let Cincinnati get to the top in 1973, but the Dodgers held their lead to the end in 1974. Newly acquired veteran outfielder Jimmy Wynn and first baseman Steve Garvey, in his first full season, led the club offensively; pitcher Mike Marshall set a modern major league record with 106 appearances in relief of a staff that was the league's best (which earned him the Cy Young Award). The Dodgers beat Pittsburgh handily in the NLCS for their fifth Los Angeles pennant, but lost the World Series to Oakland in five games.

Cincinnati proved untouchable in 1975 and '76, but in 1977 the Dodgers—under new manager Tom Lasorda, who moved up from the coaching staff when Alston retired—jumped to an early lead and held it all the way. Garvey's 33 home runs led a balanced offense in which four players hit 30 or more homers. Again the Dodgers won the NLCS (in four games, against Philadelphia), and again they lost the World Series (to the Yankees, in six games).

Although the divisional race was closer—and the Dodgers broke baseball's 3-million attendance barrier for the first time—1978 was in most respects a replay of 1977. Garvey again led the club offensively, the Dodgers again beat out Cincinnati in the West and Philadelphia in a four-game NLCS, and the Yankees again defeated the Dodgers in a six-game World Series.

A season-long back-and-forth battle with Houston in 1980 ended in a tie for first—the fifth tie for the Dodgers, three more than any other club. In the playoff (reduced from three games to one to bring the NL into line with AL practice), Houston won easily.

When the players went out on strike partway through 1981, the Dodgers, paced by the spectacular pitching of rookie Fernando Valenzuela, found themselves half a game in front of Cincinnati. In a special playoff with Houston, the winner of the NL West second half of the split season, the Dodgers defeated the Astros in five games for the division title, and also went the distance in beating Montreal for the pennant. Facing the Yankees for the 11th time in World Series play, they lost the first two games, but swept the next four to capture their sixth world title.

In 1982, after a poor start, the Dodgers fought back to take the lead in August and again in September before dropping back to second, a game out. More successful drives in 1983 and '85 led to their fifth and sixth division titles, but culminated in defeat in the NLCS—to Philadelphia in 1983 and St. Louis two years later.

In 1988, with an infusion of talent from the American League—most notably slugger Kirk Gibson and relief ace Jay Howell—and a spectacular season from starter Orel Hershiser (who concluded his 23-8 year with a major league record 59 consecutive scoreless innings), the Dodgers bounced back to the top of the NL West. It took them the full seven games to down the favored Mets in the NLCS, but in the World Series they humbled Oakland's powerful Athletics in just five games for their seventh world crown. Kirk Gibson's pinch-hit two-run homer in the bottom of the ninth off Dennis Eckersley in Game 1 was the turning point of the series. A panel of local experts later selected the home run by the gimpy Gibson as the greatest moment in Los Angeles sports history.

Led by Hershiser (whose 15-15 record belied another strong season) the Dodgers yielded the fewest runs in the NL in 1989. A lack of offense, however, left the team no better than fourth. Hershiser underwent shoulder surgery in April 1991, but young Ramon Martinez picked up the slack and won 20 games for the second-place Dodgers.

From early May to late August 1991, the Dodgers occupied first place in their division, paced by the majors' stingiest pitching staff and the hot bats of free agent signees Brett Butler and Darryl Strawberry. Seven straight losses after the All-Star break began the team's descent into a great struggle with ascendant Atlanta. From August 21 through season's end the two clubs stayed within two games of each other. With four games to go, Los Angeles held a one-game lead. But they lost their next three games, and all hope of the division crown.

In 1992 everything fell apart. Unable to parry the twin blows of injury and inexperience, the Dodgers stumbled to the worst record in the majors, and finished last for only the second time in their 109 years of major league play. Rookie catcher Mike Piazza burst upon the scene in 1993 to rank among NL leaders in batting, slugging, home runs, and RBIs, as the Dodgers recovered to finish in fourth place. A final-game victory over San Francisco brought their season record to .500, and deprived the Giants of a tie for the division title.

Japanese rookie sensation Hideo Nomo paced the NL with 236 strikeouts in 1995 and led the Dodgers to the NL West title—by just one game over the power-hitting Colorado Rockies. But in the first round of the postseason, Los Angeles fell to Cincinnati in three straight.

In mid-1996 a heart attack felled Lasorda, and he handed over the club's reins to Bill Russell. Piazza (.344, 36 HRs, 105 RBIs), Eric Karros and Raul Mondesi led the offense, and outfielder Todd Hollandsworth became the fifth consecutive Dodger to win NL Rookie of the Year honors. Martinez, Nomo, Ismael Valdes, and Todd Worrell paced a staff that led the majors with a 3.46 ERA. Los Angeles lost the West Division title to San Diego on the final day of the season but achieved a postseason berth via the wild-card route. The 1996 Dodgers faced Atlanta in the playoffs and met the same fate as the 1995 team had at the hands of the Reds: a humiliating three-game sweep.

The model of stability in baseball for decades, the Dodgers underwent huge changes over the next two years. First, major league owners grudgingly approved Rupert Murdoch and the Fox Corporation as the new owners of the team. Then, the Dodgers traded their biggest star, Mike Piazza, after he turned down a sizable contract offer. The trade, which brought Bobby Bonilla, Gary Sheffield and Charles Johnson from the Marlins, was made by Fox executives and didn't go through general manager Fred Claire. Russell and Claire were both dismissed soon after and were replaced by minor league manager Glenn Hoffman and Tommy Lasorda, who returned as interim GM. The Dodgers ended the season in third place, their lowest finish since 1993. Kevin Malone was hired as full-time general manager late in 1998 and Davey Johnson became the team's third manager in six months after the franchise had had just two managers from 1954 to 1996. To cap off the changes, they signed pitcher Kevin Brown to a seven-year, $105 million contract.

The new-look Dodgers were a disappointment in 1999. Los Angeles won just 77 games, the fewest wins ever by one of Johnson's clubs over a full season, and, after Brown the club's vaunted pitching looked ordinary. The Dodgers finished the 20th century behind only the Yankees and Giants for overall wins, but they began the 21st a distant second in both the NL West and wild-card standings. The pitching staff returned to form—including an ERA title by Brown and an outstanding year by Chan Ho Park—but the Dodgers batted just .257 and left more runners on base than any other club in the league. Despite a strong finish, aided by Gary Sheffield's .325 average and 43 home runs, manager Johnson was replaced by coach Jim Tracy at season's end.

The Dodgers finished third, just six games out, in both 2001 and '02. Shawn Green led the offense both years, hitting a club-record 49 homers in '01 and 42 more—including four in one game—in '02. Los Angeles improved to second in 2003, though they had fewer wins (85) and were farther behind first place than in any of the previous three seasons. Reliever Eric Gagne converted each of his 55 save opportunities, posting a 1.20 ERA and taking home the NL Cy Young Award.

Real estate developer Frank McCourt purchased the Dodgers in early 2004.

Milwaukee Brewers (aka Seattle Pilots)

When in 1969 the new Seattle Pilots played their home opener in the refurbished minor league Sick's Stadium, 7,000 seats and the left-field fence were still unfinished. The Pilots may not have needed the seats. Fewer than 700,000 fans came to see them play—the third-worst attendance in the league—as they drifted into the cellar of the American League West with 98 losses. (In fact the most memorable thing about that season was a controversial book, *Ball Four*, by Pilots pitcher Jim Bouton.) That winter the Pilots—renamed the Brewers—moved to Milwaukee, where a genuine big league stadium (vacated by the Braves five years earlier) awaited them.

Attendance improved nearly 38 percent in Milwaukee, although the Brewers of 1970 won only one game more than the Pilots had in Seattle. It would be eight more years before they experienced their first winning season. Meanwhile, in 1972, they switched divisions from West to East, trading places with the Washington Senators, who moved West to become the Texas Rangers. Hank Aaron came to the Brewers in 1975 to finish his career where it had started in 1954 (with the Milwaukee Braves), but Aaron's presence helped the club at the gate more than in the standings.

The Brewers broke their losing pattern in 1978. One key front-office move leading to the turnaround was the signing of free agent Larry Hisle (who the previous year with Minnesota had led the league in RBIs). Hisle proved his worth in 1978, leading an offense that sprang to life under rookie manager George Bamberger to top

the league in hitting, slugging, homers, and runs scored. On the mound Mike Caldwell won 22 games in the best season of his career. Although the Brewers never threatened the Red Sox or the Yankees for the lead, they did rise from below .500 in early June to finish a solid third, 24 games above .500.

A shoulder injury the next April marked the beginning of the end of Hisle's career and perhaps cost Milwaukee the division title. Even without him the team compiled what is still their best winning percentage (.590), as outfielder Gorman Thomas (45 home runs, 123 RBIs) and several other hitters attained new career peaks of productivity. While they never seriously threatened front-running Baltimore, they rose past Boston in late August to finish second.

Most of the Milwaukee bats remained hot in 1980, but injuries, ragged pitching and Bamberger's heart attack (which caused him to miss the first part of the season and retire in early September) contributed to a distant third-place finish. In strike-divided 1981, league-leading performances by two newly acquired pitchers—starter Pete Vuckovich (14-4) and reliever Rollie Fingers (28 saves)—helped give the Brewers the best overall record in the AL East, and the second-half championship. But in the special intradivisional playoffs with first-half winner New York, the Yankees captured the division crown three games to two.

The Brewers started slowly in 1982; at the end of May they were two games below .500, near the bottom of the division. A day later Buck Rodgers, the Milwaukee coach who had replaced Bamberger as manager two years earlier, was himself replaced by coach Harvey Kuenn. By mid-July the team had risen to first place, and they led the West by more than six games as September neared. Baltimore had cut the lead to three games by the time Milwaukee arrived for the season's final four games. One win would give the Brewers their first division championship, but they lost the first three games by five, six, and eight runs. Don Sutton, who had been acquired from Houston a month earlier, faced Oriole Jim Palmer in the season finale: the Brewers took the division title with a 10-2 win.

Milwaukee's offense—"Harvey's Wallbangers"—had been awesome, scoring more than a run per game above the league average. Just about every offensive category featured one or two Brewers among the league's top three: in hits they took all three top spots. Shortstop Robin Yount, who finished first in slugging, hits, total bases and doubles, was named major league player of the year.

In postseason play California took a 2-0 lead in the ALCS, but Milwaukee came back to take the final three games and the pennant. In the World Series against St. Louis, the Brewers twice took the lead in games, but the Cardinals scored the last five runs of Game 7 to win the Series.

Milwaukee dropped to fifth in 1983, then to last place the next year, 36-1/2 games back. It was not until 1987 that they returned to the winning track, finishing third with 91 victories. As veterans Robin Yount and Paul Molitor continued to spark the team's offense, and starter Ted Higuera and reliever Dan Plesac headlined the AL East's best pitching staff, the Brewers in 1988 rose above .500 to stay at the end of August, and finished in a tie for third, just two games behind champion Boston. With Yount and Molitor enjoying even more productive seasons in 1989, and reliever Plesac on a club-record pace for saves, the Brewers drew within half a game of first place in August. But injuries and league-worst fielding took their toll, and the club faded to fourth, right at .500. In 1990, as poor fielding led to more than 100 unearned runs, the Brewers dropped to sixth.

Paul Molitor enjoyed a banner season in 1991, and, from the first week in August to the finish, the Brewers played at a torrid

.750 clip. But they had begun their comeback 15 games behind, and too late to raise themselves more than one place in the standings. With another sterling season from Molitor in 1992, plus Robin Yount's milestone 3,000th hit and another strong finish (after a better first half), Milwaukee drew within two games of ultimately victorious Toronto in the season's final week. Still, the Brewers' 92-70 record and second-place finish were their best since their pennant-winning season a decade earlier.

That was their last hurrah for a while. The Brewers suffered through one sub-.500 season after another throughout the rest of the 1990s and into the next century. With three-division realignment in 1994, the team became one of five clubs inserted into the AL's new Central Division, thus becoming the only club to play in three different divisions. Then, because of the addition of a new team to each league in 1998, it was decided that one existing team had to switch leagues to give both leagues an even number of teams for scheduling purposes. Milwaukee, which had been home to the Braves from 1953 to 1965, returned to the National League with a game between the Brewers and, fittingly, the Braves in Atlanta on March 31. Bud Selig, who had been acting commissioner since 1992, put his shares of the Brewers in a trust and handed ownership of the club to his daughter when he was officially named commissioner in 1998.

Garner was followed in the managerial reigns by Jim Lefebvre, Davey Lopes, Jerry Royster, and Ned Yost between 1999-2003, and Dean Taylor succeeded Sal Bando as general manager. County Stadium, which remained open a year longer than planned because of a fatal crane accident at the new ballpark site, hosted its final game in 2000.

The Brewers moved to Miller Park in 2001, but the new surroundings couldn't distract from the team's poor performance. The Brewers sunk below 70 wins in each of the next three years, bottoming out at 56-106 in 2002.

Minnesota Twins (aka Washington Senators, Nationals)

The Twins' beginnings as the Washington Senators were inauspicious. When American League president Ban Johnson established the Senators as part of his move in 1901 to raise the league to major league status, he staffed it with the manager and many of the players from his disbanded Kansas City franchise. Within a decade, four of the eight teams in the new major league had won two or more pennants, and three others had enjoyed at least one season in second place. But the Senators, after sixth-place finishes in their first two seasons, spent the next nine years in seventh or eighth.

Even the arrival of promising young fireballer Walter Johnson didn't seem to help. By 1909 he was the league's second-best strikeout artist, but he lost 25 games and the Senators finished farther back than ever—56 games from the top. Johnson turned his record around the next two years, winning 25 games in 1910 and in 1911, but the team rose only to seventh.

When Clark Griffith—a 42-year-old former pitching great and one of the founders of the American League—was hired to manage the Senators after the 1911 season, the club's fortunes took an immediate turn for the better. Griffith revamped the lineup—most strikingly in the acquisition of first baseman Chick Gandil from minor league Montreal. The Senators in 1912 won 17 straight games after Gandil was put into the lineup, and found themselves in the midst of a pennant race. The Boston Red Sox eventually ran away from the field, but the Senators held off Philadelphia for second place. Johnson won 33 games, and his 1.39 ERA led the league.

The next season was Johnson's finest. His league-leading 36

wins, 11 shutouts, and 1.14 ERA were also career bests and enabled Washington to overtake Cleveland late in the season for another second-place finish. But while Johnson continued to top 20 wins per season for several years before beginning to fade, his team was unable to stay competitive.

Griffith wanted the Senators to spend more to attract good players; when his demands were rejected, he bought a controlling interest in the club and named himself president. A year later, in 1921, he retired as field manager. Under a succession of veteran player-managers the team showed some improvement over the next three years, but Griffith's surprise appointment of 27-year-old second baseman Bucky Harris to manage the team in 1924 worked wonders. Left fielder Goose Goslin drove in more runs than Babe Ruth, and Walter Johnson put together his best season in years to head the league's best pitching staff. A hot streak in June shot the team from fifth to first, and a strong stretch drive in August and September brought home their first pennant. In the World Series a ground ball's lucky bounce over the head of the Giants' third baseman brought the Senators victory in the last of the 12th inning of the seventh game.

Though the Senators, aided by the acquisition of veteran pitcher Stan Coveleski from Cleveland, fought off the A's to repeat as pennant winners in 1925, they were less successful in postseason play. Once again the Series went the full seven games, but this time Pittsburgh won the title.

The Senators enjoyed winning seasons in five of the next seven years, as Johnson retired from the mound and replaced Harris as manager. But it was not until 1933, when Johnson was replaced by 26-year-old shortstop Joe Cronin, that the team again pursued the pennant beyond midseason. Two veteran pitchers at the top of their form—Alvin "General" Crowder and Earl Whitehill—and a balanced offense led by Cronin and first baseman Joe Kuhel kept the Senators close to New York through July, and then, as the Yankees leveled off in August, shot the team up out of reach. Although they tailed off a bit at the end, the Senators won the pennant handily, compiling a .651 winning percentage that is still the club record. The New York Giants, though, took Washington's measure in the World Series and overcame them in five games.

The following October a drop from third place in June to a distant seventh at season's end had plunged home attendance nearly 25 percent below the previous year. With finances always a problem in Washington, Griffith traded Joe Cronin, his manager, star shortstop and (since September) son-in-law, to the Boston Red Sox for a lesser shortstop and $225,000.

Only twice in their remaining quarter century in Washington did the Senators rise higher than fourth or finish closer than 17 games from the top. In 1943 they placed second, 13-1/2 games behind the runaway Yankees. And two years later, after a poor start, they caught up with frontrunner Detroit in September, only to stall and finish one and a half games out. The Senators finished in the cellar in four of their last six seasons in Washington.

Calvin Griffith, Clark's adopted son, assumed the club presidency when his father died in 1955. Within three years he was making plans to move the club to Minneapolis. There were threats from Congress and a plea from President Eisenhower not to move the Senators—and at first the league itself opposed the move. But Washington was not a good baseball town even when the Senators were playing well, and in October 1960 a solution was reached. The league would let Griffith move his club to Minnesota, and Washington would be granted a new expansion team.

Players like outfielders Bob Allison and Harmon Killebrew, and pitcher Camilo Pascual, who had enjoyed productive seasons before the move, were even more productive at Metropolitan Stadium in Minnesota. Other standouts became regulars or joined the club after the move—Zoilo Versalles at shortstop, Rich Rollins at third, Jim Kaat on the mound, and (arriving in 1964) outfielder Tony Oliva and pitcher Jim "Mudcat" Grant. Infielder Rod Carew began a remarkable 12-year stint with the Twins in 1967.

Former outfielder Sam Mele made his major league managerial debut during 1961, and in 1962 saw his Twins come close to catching the Yankees in mid-September, finishing second. The next year they didn't catch fire until August and wound up third. In 1964 they dropped below .500 into a tie for sixth. But after the end of June 1965 no one challenged them as they breezed to their first Minnesota pennant. Oliva led the league in batting for the second straight year, and Versalles (in what was far and away his finest season) led the league in total bases and runs scored. Mudcat Grant led the league with 21 victories (his only 20-win season) and six shutouts, and Kaat's 18 wins were the league's third best. In the World Series it took a three-hitter by Los Angeles' Sandy Koufax to stop the Twins in the seventh game.

After a poor start in 1966 that saw them enter July deep in fifth place, the Twins played better than anyone else the rest of the season to sneak ahead of Detroit into second. Killebrew, who had been injured much of the previous year, returned with his old power in '66, and Kaat posted a career-high 25 wins.

The Twins began 1967 with another poor start. With the team in disarray and in sixth place, the easygoing Mele was replaced in June by hard-driving Cal Ermer, a longtime minor league manager. By mid-July the team had risen to second, and a month later (after dropping back to fourth) moved to the top in one of the greatest pennant races ever. Four clubs battled for the title, with three still in the running on the final day. But Boston defeated Minnesota to win the pennant, and Detroit split a doubleheader to tie the Twins for second. The next year Minnesota finished seventh.

Fiery rookie manager Billy Martin replaced Ermer in 1969 and, in this first season of divisional play, piloted the Twins to the championship of the West. Killebrew exploded for the best season of his career (49 home runs, 140 RBIs), and Carew won the first of his seven batting titles. The first American League Championship Series, though, was a disaster for the Twins as Baltimore swept to the pennant in three games. Veteran manager Bill Rigney replaced the difficult Martin at the helm, and piloted Minnesota to an almost identical division crown in 1970, again by a nine-game margin. Pitcher Jim Perry, with 24 victories, enjoyed his second straight 20-win season, and the best of his career. The ALCS, though, was another repeat performance—a Baltimore sweep.

For the next 13 years the Twins remained out of contention; it was not until the flowering of a new generation of young players in 1984 that a Minnesota title threat could be taken seriously.

The Twins' decline on the field was matched by a decline in attendance, which even their move indoors to the Hubert H. Humphrey Metrodome in 1982 did not significantly redress. The Griffith family, unwilling to risk the high cost of luring proven talent, decided to give up the club after more than 60 years of family ownership. Early in 1984 a buyer was found in Carl Pohlad, a wealthy Minneapolis banker. By the time Pohlad's purchase was completed at the end of July, the Twins' young team had blossomed into the West's front-runner, paced by pitcher Frank Viola's sudden development into a winner, and by the arrival in May of rookie

center-field sparkplug Kirby Puckett. Although the Twins leveled off in August and lost their final six games, to fall to .500 and a tie for second, they had brought the crowds back to the ballpark. The 1984 team drew more than 1.5 million fans for the first time ever and remained well above a million the next two years despite a pair of losing seasons.

In 1987, under manager Tom Kelly, the Minnesota fans were rewarded for their faithfulness. Although the Twins lost their last five games to finish only eight above .500, their winning record at home was the best in the league and their title in the West was never in doubt. More surprising was their decisive triumph over favored Detroit in the ALCS, four games to one. In the first World Series to feature indoor play, the Twins won the four games played in their Metrodome to capture Minnesota's first baseball world championship in seven games.

Although the Twins in 1988 improved on their 1987 won-lost record—and Frank Viola, Kirby Puckett and relief ace Jeff Reardon enjoyed career peaks—they finished well back of Oakland in the race for the division crown. But their home attendance, which had jumped 66 percent in 1987 to top 2 million for the first time, bounded another 45 percent in 1988 to make the Twins the first AL club ever to attract more than 3 million fans in a season.

As the team suffered a general decline in pitching and hitting in 1989, Viola—in the middle of a disappointing season—was traded to the Mets and the Twins finished fifth. Reardon, a free agent, left for Boston after the season. The Twins continued their downhill slide in 1990, slipping from fifth place at midseason to their first cellar finish in eight years.

On May 27, 1991, the Twins stood sixth in the AL West. Three weeks later, after winning 18 of 19 games, they were first. There they finished, becoming (like Atlanta in the NL) the first AL team to rise from last place to first in successive seasons. Minnesota's attack featured a balanced offense in which seven players drove in 50 runs or more, and a pitching revival that starred veteran free agent Jack Morris and a pair of young hurlers with their first big seasons, Scott Erickson (who won 12 in a row before the end of June) and Kevin Tapani (16-9, 2.99 ERA). In the ALCS, the Twins overcame Toronto in five games, then came back from a 3-2 World Series deficit to defeat Atlanta with a pair of extra-inning victories, including a 10-inning win in Game 7 as Morris pitched a shutout and Gene Larkin drove in the only run.

After his single starring season in Minnesota, Morris moved on to Toronto to hurl the Blue Jays into the championship. The Twins, meanwhile, arrived at midseason of 1992 first in the AL West, where they remained into early August before drifting back into a second-place finish behind Oakland. Veteran superstar Dave Winfield left Toronto for Minnesota in 1993, where in September he passed the 3,000-hit mark. But the Twins slid out of contention early, and finished tied for fifth.

It was the start of an eight-year drought. The Twins never rose above 78 wins or fourth place between 1993 and 2000, posting the worst record in the AL in the last two of those years. Attendance sunk to 1.06 million, barely one-third of their 1988 peak. As Major League Baseball threatened contraction of two teams, the Twins were high on the list of candidates for extinction.

But the Twins rose from the dead, as exciting young players like Cristian Guzman and Torii Hunter helped turned the franchise around. Minnesota soared to an 85-77, second-place finish in Tom Kelly's last season, then won the AL Central Division championship under Ron Gardenhire in each of the next two years. The Twins toppled Oakland in the 2002 ALDS before bowing to the eventual world champion Angels in the ALCS. In 2003, Minnesota was unable to get past the Yankees in the Divisional Series.

Montreal Expos

In the spring of 1969, in an unfinished "temporary" ballpark that would be the Expos' home for eight years, major league baseball came to Canada. One of two clubs added to the National League in this first year of divisional play—Montreal in the East and San Diego in the West—the Expos finished 48 games out of first. Although they matched San Diego's 52-110 record and last-place divisional finish, they outdrew the Padres by better than two to one, with a home attendance of more than 1.2 million fans.

After a second last-place season (but much improved at 73-89) in 1970, the Expos moved a notch out of the cellar to fifth in 1971 and '72, and into pennant contention in 1973. Outfielder Ken Singleton became the first Expo to drive in 100 or more runs, rookie pitcher Steve Rogers compiled a sparkling 1.54 ERA, and reliever Mike Marshall set a new major league record with 92 pitching appearances (winning 14 games and saving a league-high 31). In the tightest race of the century, all six clubs remained in contention into September, when Philadelphia dropped away. In mid-September Montreal won six straight to catch front-running Pittsburgh, but the Expos finished the season in fourth place, three and a half games behind the champion New York Mets.

Center fielder Willie Davis (acquired from Los Angeles in a trade for Mike Marshall) led the Expos' offense in another fourth-place season in 1974. The club sank back to a tie for last in 1975 and sole possession of the cellar a year later, with a 55-107 record nearly as bad as their first season (and a home attendance little more than half that of 1969).

But with the acquisition of heavy-hitting Tony Perez from Cincinnati, a new manager—the controversial Dick Williams—and strong seasons from catcher Gary Carter, sophomore outfielder Ellis Valentine and rookie Andre Dawson, the club snapped back in 1977 to win 20 more games than the previous year and rise to fifth. And with their move into the new Olympic Stadium (built for the 1976 Olympics), attendance rebounded from a club low to a new high.

After climbing another notch to fourth in 1978 (as the newly acquired Ross Grimsley became their first—and, to date, only—20-game winner), the Expos put on a run for the title that drove attendance in 1979 to over 2 million. Third baseman Larry Parrish, with a career-high season, led the club in batting and home runs in a balanced attack that saw five players drive in more than 70 runs. The pitching too was balanced, with six pitchers winning 10 games or more on a staff that compiled the league's lowest ERA. With a fast start in April, the Expos led the East through much of June and into July, when a surging Pittsburgh caught up with them. Both clubs climbed away from the pack to the end of the season. Montreal fell back a bit in August but caught up with the Pirates in September and carried the race to the final day before dropping off to second.

The 1980 race was just as exciting. A three-way struggle with Philadelphia and Pittsburgh through most of the summer narrowed to two teams in September as the Pirates fell away. In a crucial late-September series, the Expos beat the Phillies two games of three to take a half-game lead, but in the final series a week later Philadelphia won two games to clinch the crown.

In a 1981 season divided by a players' strike, Montreal finished the first part of the season in third place, but held off St. Louis to win the second part by half a game. The Expos then won the divi-

sion championship in a special playoff with first-half winner Philadelphia—their first title—but lost the National League Championship Series to Los Angeles.

As the Expos declined gradually over the next five years, most of the regulars left through trade, free agency or retirement. But in 1987, two 1981 rookies who had remained in Montreal—outfielder Tim Raines and third baseman Tim Wallach—helped lead the Expos to third place, just four games back, with 91 wins.

Strong midsummer surges in 1988 and 1989 propelled the Expos into the thick of the race in the NL East, in 1989 lifting them into the lead for six straight weeks following the acquisition from Seattle of mound ace Mark Langston. But in both years, late-season slumps dropped the club to identical 81-81 finishes. In 1990 strong pitching (despite the loss of free agents Langston, Bryn Smith and Pascual Perez) kept the Expos competitive well into September before they fell out of the race.

The collapse of a huge cement beam at Olympic Stadium in September 1991—which forced the Expos to play all their remaining games on the road—was emblematic of the team's collapse into the cellar with their worst record in 15 years. But the club revived in 1992 under new manager Felipe Alou, who was promoted from coach in late May. The Expos rose from fifth place to second behind the pitching of Ken Hill and veteran ace Dennis Martinez, and the batting leadership of right fielder Larry Walker. The Expos finished an even closer second in 1993, just three games behind Philadelphia, with a record of 94-68. On August 7, 1994, pitcher Hill moved into the NL lead with his 16th win of the season. Walker and Moises Alou—manager Felipe's son—dueled for the club's offensive leadership. Montreal stood atop the mountain with the best record in the majors. Five days later, the season was over when the players went on strike.

Even though the club fell to last (66-78) in 1995, the club turned a $40,000 profit—a dramatic turnaround from 1994 when, due to the strike, the club lost an estimated $15.9 million. Helping the balance sheet was the modesty of the payroll—just $10 million. The Expos (88-74) challenged for a postseason berth in 1996 but fell short in the final week despite the efforts of Henry Rodriguez (36 HRs, 103 RBIs), Mark Grudzielanek (.306, 201 hits), Jeff Fassero (15-11, 222 strikeouts), and Mel Rojas (36 saves).

Pedro Martinez became the first Expos pitcher to win the NL Cy Young Award, in 1997. He was the first pitcher to combine 300 strikeouts and an ERA below 2.00 since Steve Carlton in 1972, but it was a bittersweet year for Montreal. Escalating salaries forced the Expos to trade Martinez as well as second baseman Mike Lansing and to allow first baseman David Segui, catcher Darrin Fletcher and outfielder Rodriguez to leave as free agents.

The stripped-down 1998-2001 Expos suffered through four straight seasons with between 94 and 97 losses each year, as attendance dropped from 1.5 million to 609,473. Jeffrey Loria took over as chairman of the franchise in 1999, and Felipe Alou finally departed two years later, replaced by Jeff Torborg. Young outfielder Vladimir Guerrero was about the only thing Montreal had to cheer about during this period, emerging into a superstar with an average of 40 homers, 118 RBIs, and a .324 BA each year.

It looked like the Expos would be eliminated by contraction, or at least relocated. In 2002, Major League Baseball took control of the orphaned team and appointed Frank Robinson to manage it. Robby brought the Expos home with a shocking second-place, 83-79 finish, their best since 1996. To prove it was no fluke, the team duplicated that record in 2003, while playing 22 "home" games in San Juan,

Puerto Rico. With the loss of Guerrero and star pitcher Javier Vazquez to free agency, however, prospects for the future look bleak.

New York Mets

Branch Rickey's projected Continental League never materialized, but its New York and Houston franchises were admitted to the National League, expanding the league to 10 clubs in 1962. Few major league teams have been as inept as the New York Mets were in their first season. Despite the presence of such New York favorites as manager Casey Stengel, pitcher Roger Craig and first baseman Gil Hodges, and of one-time-star players like outfielders Richie Ashburn and Frank Thomas who were still near peak form, the Mets finished at the bottom of the league in batting, fielding and pitching. They won only one game in four and suffered a 20th-century record 120 losses.

New York fans—deprived of National League baseball since the defection of the Dodgers and Giants to the West Coast four years earlier—found their ineptitude lovable. By their third season, having moved out of the old Polo Grounds into brand-new Shea Stadium, the last-place Mets were regularly outdrawing the pennant-bound Yankees.

Former New York Giants catcher Wes Westrum replaced the aging Stengel as manager part way through the 1965 season, and the next year saw the club rise out of the cellar for the first time. They fell back to 10th in 1967 (despite rookie Tom Seaver's 16 wins), and Westrum was replaced at the helm by Gil Hodges. With Jerry Koosman joining Seaver in the starting rotation and setting a new club record with 19 victories, Hodges led the Mets in 1968 back up to ninth place with their first season of more than 70 victories.

In 1969 the majors inaugurated divisional play, but the Mets got off to their usual indifferent start. At the end of May, however, they began to win consistently. By early June they were second in the NL East, though well back of the explosive Chicago Cubs. By September, though, the Cubs were faltering. The "Miracle Mets" caught and passed them with a 10-game winning streak and continued on to take the division title. In Tom Seaver's Hall of Fame career, it was probably his finest season. He won his last 10 starts, sparking the team's final push to triumph, and finished with a league-high 25 wins that still stands as the club record. After a three-game sweep of West champion Atlanta in the league's first Championship Series, the Mets faced the mighty Baltimore Orioles—regarded by many as one of baseball's all-time greatest teams—for the world championship. The Met miracle continued; after an opening-game loss, the New Yorkers humbled the Orioles with four straight wins.

The Mets of 1970 remained competitive into mid-September as they sought to repeat their '69 triumph. But they fell back at the end while Pittsburgh spurted, and finished third. Just before the start of the 1972 season, coach Yogi Berra moved up to manage the club after Hodges suffered a fatal heart attack two days before his 48th birthday.

In 1973 the NL East experienced the tightest major league race of the century. Chicago moved out in front of the pack early in the season, but folded in July and August. So did the Mets, who fell from third to a last-place sixth. Although the Mets were last in late August, they were less than seven games out of first. A series of bursts in September, culminating in a seven-game winning streak, shot the Mets through the division into first place by September 21. Although they finished the season only three games above .500, they topped the division by a game and a half. In the NLCS they

held off the favored Cincinnati Reds to take the pennant in the maximum five games, but they lost the World Series in seven when Oakland won the final two games.

The Mets then entered a decade-long decline. Though they won as often in 1975 and '76 as they had in 1973, they didn't come close to capturing the East, and dropped into a seven-year trough in 1977 which included five seasons in last place. Seaver was traded to Cincinnati in 1977 and Koosman (after two disastrous seasons) was sent to Minnesota in the fall of 1978 (where he won 20 the next year). The heirs of original owner Joan Whitney Payson sold the club to Nelson Doubleday (of the publishing company) and Fred Wilpon in January 1980. In February the new owners hired Frank Cashen as general manager, hoping he could rebuild the Mets as he had the Baltimore Orioles in the late 1960s.

It took a few years to achieve the right blend, but when outfielder Darryl Strawberry was brought up from the minors early in 1983 and first baseman Keith Hernandez was acquired from St. Louis in June, the mix had nearly all the needed ingredients. In 1984, under new manager Davey Johnson, and with rookie pitchers Dwight Gooden and Ron Darling combining for 29 wins, the Mets rebounded to second place with their second-best season record up till then.

The rise continued in 1985. With catcher Gary Carter (newly acquired from Montreal) leading the club in homers and RBIs, and Gooden cementing his superstardom at age 20 with a phenomenal 24-4, 1.53 ERA season, the Mets won 98 games—eight more than the year before—and came within a game of tying St. Louis late in September before slipping three games back at the finish.

When the Mets acquired pitcher Bob Ojeda from the Boston Red Sox after the season, many predicted an easy division title for them in 1986. For once, the pundits were right. With Carter, Strawberry and Hernandez powering the offense, and Ojeda, Darling and Gooden all placing among the league's top five pitchers in ERA, the Mets won two of every three games (108 in all) to capture the division title by 21-1/2 games.

The postseason battles were tougher. The Mets won the pennant from Houston with a 16-inning victory in Game 6 of the NLCS, but came within a strike of elimination by the Red Sox in Game 6 of the World Series before rallying to take that game and the next for their second world crown.

Strawberry enjoyed his finest season yet in 1987, and pitchers Terry Leach and Rick Aguilera put together a combined won-lost record of 22-4. But Ojeda was lost to injury early in the season and the Mets, though they hung close and posted 92 wins, lost out— as in 1985—to St. Louis by three games.

David Cone (20-3, 2.22 ERA) emerged in 1988 as the ace of the league's best pitching staff, which, with the power of Darryl Strawberry and Kevin McReynolds behind it, carried the Mets back to the top of the NL East, 15 games ahead of runner-up Pittsburgh. But the favored Mets lost the pennant to underdog Los Angeles in seven games.

With co-captains Carter and Hernandez injured and in decline, the Mets floundered through 1989, salvaging a narrow second-place finish with four wins in the season's final three days. The two captains were released after the season. Early the following year, with the Mets mired almost 10 games out, manager Davey Johnson was replaced by coach Bud Harrelson. In June the team took off, ignited by Strawberry's suddenly hot bat and propelled themselves into first place before the end of the month. Through July and August the Mets and Pittsburgh lobbed the division lead back and forth, until the Pirates consigned the New Yorkers to second place

for good with a three-game sweep in early September.

Free-agent Strawberry signed with Los Angeles for 1991, but the Mets competed strongly into July before tumbling to fifth place with their first losing season in eight years. It was the beginning of a six-year swoon for New York, during which the team never finished above .500. The period saw the flop of high-priced free agent Bobby Bonilla, the losingest (103 in 1993) Mets' team since the Stengel era, and the dismissal of four managers.

Bobby Valentine took over the team in 1996, and a year later had it back to respectability, as the Mets finished 88-74. They had the most come-from-behind victories in baseball (47) and they won the first-ever regular season game against the Yankees. The Mets were full of surprises, but the biggest was Rick Reed, a former replacement player who finished sixth in the league with a 2.89 ERA. In 1998 the Mets had the same record as the year before, but the club remained in the hunt for the wild card until the final day of the season. Two players acquired from the Marlins, pitcher Al Leiter (17-6, 2.47 ERA) and catcher Mike Piazza, who batted .328 with 32 home runs and 111 RBIs while playing for three teams during the season, teamed with John Olerud (.353) to help put the Mets in a position to reach the postseason for the first time in a decade. The year ended in agonizing fashion as New York lost its last five games of the season and finished one game shy of the Giants and Cubs in what would have been the first three-way playoff in major league history.

The Mets finished second in each of the next two years, but the team reached the playoffs on both occasions—the first repeat post-season performance in franchise history. In 1999 the Mets crumbled in late September by losing eight of nine games. New York rallied in the closing days of the season, however, to force a tie for the wild card, and then won a one-game playoff in Cincinnati on Leiter's two-hit shutout. Backup catcher Todd Pratt beat the Diamondbacks with a series-ending home run in the bottom of the 10th inning of Game 4 of the Division Series. The Mets eventually lost to rival Atlanta in six games in the NLCS, with each of the last three games decided in the home team's final at bat.

Edgardo Alfonzo and Piazza each batted .324 while Leiter and fellow southpaw Mike Hampton combined for 31 wins—each member of the starting staff won at least 10 games—to lead the Mets to the wild card again in 2000. Against the favored Giants, the Mets won twice in extra innings and Bobby Jones pitched a one-hitter to clinch the Division Series. The Mets flew past the Cardinals to claim their first league championship since 1986. Under the glare of the Subway Series, though, the Mets fell to the crosstown Yankees in a taut five-game World Series.

The Mets slipped to third in 2001 and last in 2002, and Valentine was fired in favor of Art Howe. But Howe, who had enjoyed a successful seven-year run in Oakland, had a rude awakening in New York. The '03 Mets finished last, losing 95 games.

New York Yankees (aka Baltimore Orioles, New York Highlanders)

In its first 20 seasons, the club that became the New York Yankees won no league championships and finished second only twice. But for the next 44 years the Yankees dominated the American League, winning nearly two of every three pennants and 20 World Series. After another pennant drought of 12 years, the club in six years won five division titles, four pennants, and two world championships. Their next pennant drought, which ended in 1996, lasted 14 years, and was the second longest in their history. That year the Yankees started yet another streak, with four

World Series titles in five years—including three in a row.

The Yankees began as the Baltimore Orioles in 1901. But AL president Ban Johnson really wanted a club in New York and, after outmaneuvering the politically influential Giants (who didn't want a competing big league team in their city), Johnson moved the Orioles to the northern end of Manhattan in 1903.

In 1904 the Highlanders (as they were known during their first years in New York because of the high land on which their park was built) chased the Boston Pilgrims through midsummer, catching them in August and trading first place back and forth into October. After Jack Chesbro defeated Boston on October 7 to give New York a half-game lead (his 41st win, a 20th-century major league record), the Pilgrims came back to win the next two. In the fourth game of the series, with Chesbro again pitching and the score tied, 2-2, in the top of the ninth, a wild pitch over the New York catcher's head let in Boston's pennant-clinching run.

The Highlanders again led the league in late September two years later, before tailing off to finish three games behind Chicago. But that was the last time they contended seriously for the title for 14 years. In that span they finished last twice: in 1908 they lost 103 games, and in 1912 the team suffered through its most distant finish ever—55 games behind the Red Sox.

In 1914 Jacob Ruppert and Tillinghast L'Hommedieu Huston bought the Yankees, and the next year they purchased pitcher Bob Shawkey from the Philadelphia A's. Shawkey's 24 victories in 1916 led the Yankees to their first winning season in six years, and in 1919, on returning from military service, his 20 wins (plus nine by Carl Mays, who came to the club in a controversial midseason deal with the Red Sox) brought the Yankees to third—their closest finish in 13 years.

That winter, on the recommendation of manager Miller Huggins, the Yankees paid a then-record $125,000 (plus a $300,000 loan) to the Red Sox for Babe Ruth. Ruth, with 54 home runs in 1920, obliterated the record of 29 he had set the year before, and Mays and Shawkey won 46 games in a three-way pennant race that ended with New York a close third.

At season's end Ruppert hired Ed Barrow as general manager. While managing the Red Sox, Barrow had converted Ruth from a pitcher to outfielder. His trade with Boston that gave the Yankees pitcher Waite Hoyt and catcher Wally Schang was just the improvement needed to bring the Yankees their first pennant in 1921. Ruth's 59 homers and his career-high 171 RBIs didn't hurt, either.

The prickly Carl Mays, staff ace in 1921 with a 27-9 record, slipped to 13-14 the next year. But the Yankees continued to decimate the Red Sox roster with trades that brought them pitchers "Bullet Joe" Bush and "Sad Sam" Jones and infielders Everett Scott and Joe Dugan. Bush's 26 wins in 1922 made up for Mays' decline, and the Yankees captured their second straight league championship.

Both races had been tight two-way struggles—with Cleveland in 1921 and the St. Louis Browns in 1922—and both pennants had been followed by a World Series loss to the Giants. But in 1923 the Yankees at last put everything together. After sharing the Giants' Polo Grounds since 1913, they were at home in brand-new Yankee Stadium just across the Harlem River in the Bronx. With the addition of yet another pitcher from the Red Sox—Herb Pennock—and a .393 year from Ruth, they took the lead from the start and built it over the summer to a 16-game margin by the end. For the third time the Yankees faced the Giants in the World Series; this time they beat them, in six games, for their first world championship.

The Yankees lost a close race to Washington in 1924 and col-lapsed into seventh place in 1925—a year in which Ruth was lost much of the season to surgery and suspension. And yet, it wasn't all bad. Center fielder Earle Combs, in his first full season, hit .342 to lead Yankee regulars. Left fielder Bob Meusel filled Ruth's shoes as AL home run and RBI leader, and first baseman Lou Gehrig arrived to stay. With Ruth's return to full strength in 1926 and the establishment of a new middle infield of Tony Lazzeri and Mark Koenig, the Yankees took their fourth pennant. They lost a close World Series to the Cardinals.

Many observers rank the 1927 Yankees as baseball's greatest team ever. Ruth hit his landmark 60 home runs and Gehrig drove in 175 as the Yankees fashioned a remarkable 110-44 mark. Waite Hoyt led the league in ERA and rookie Wilcy Moore proved the league's premier reliever. As a team the Yankees led the league in hitting (.307) and slugging (.489); their pitchers compiled a 3.20 ERA (the next best team, the White Sox, had an ERA of 3.91). In the World Series they swept the Pittsburgh Pirates.

The resurgent Athletics made the 1928 race much closer, but New York won three in a row from the A's in mid-September to pull ahead, and held on for their sixth pennant. Another Series sweep (this time against the Cardinals) gave them their third world title.

An ill Huggins yielded the club's reins in September 1929 and died before the season ended. By the time the Yankees returned to the top in 1932, their manager was Joe McCarthy. He had led the Chicago Cubs to the NL pennant in 1929; in fifteen seasons at New York he would lead his club to eight more pennants and seven world championships.

A New York pennant and World Series triumph over the Cubs in 1932 was followed by three second-place finishes to Washington (in 1933) and Detroit (in 1934 and 1935). Ruth had retired by the time the Bronx Bombers returned to the top in 1936, but Gehrig was still in top form, catcher Bill Dickey and outfielder George Selkirk developed into formidable sluggers, and Joe DiMaggio arrived to take over center field. New York finished 19-1/2 games in front and buried the Giants in the World Series.

Three more pennants and three more world titles followed in 1937 to 1939. Lefty Gomez emerged as the league's premier pitcher in 1937 and DiMaggio picked up the home run and slug-ging crowns. Again the Giants were vanquished in the World Series. Rookie second baseman Joe Gordon and sophomore out-fielder Tommy Henrich joined Dickey, DiMaggio and a declining Gehrig in leading the slugging Yankees to the 1938 crown and a Series sweep of the Cubs. A balanced attack in 1939 saw seven of the eight starters (including Babe Dahlgren, who replaced the dying Gehrig at first) drive in 80 runs or more as the Yankees won 106 to run away with their 11th pennant—and eighth World Series, another sweep, with Cincinnati the victim. For the fourth straight year the offense topped the league in slugging and over-shadowed the steady—if unspectacular—pitching staff, which compiled the league's stingiest ERA for the sixth consecutive year.

After catching the Tigers with a 19-4 spurt in late summer, the 1940 Yankees fell away to finish a close third. But then came another three convincing pennant wins and a pair of Series triumphs as the nation moved into World War II. Outfielders DiMaggio and Charlie Keller dominated the offense in 1941, which included a 56-game hit streak for the former, and rookie shortstop Phil Rizzuto hit .307. Brooklyn was the loser in a five-game World Series.

Keller, DiMaggio and Gordon provided the power, and Tiny Bonham (with 21 wins), Spud Chandler and rookie Hank Borowy

headed the league-leading pitching staff that propelled the Yankees to 103 wins and another easy pennant in 1942. But after winning their previous eight World Series, the Yankees were finally stopped, in five games, by the St. Louis Cardinals.

By 1943 many Yankees were in military service. But pitchers Chandler, Bonham, Borowy, and Murphy were not, and they led the charge to the team's seventh pennant in eight years. In the Series the Yankees reversed the results of the previous year, turning back St. Louis in five.

In January 1945, Dan Topping and Del Webb bought the club and installed Larry MacPhail as president, giving him a third of the club and a 10-year contract to run it. The volatile, innovative MacPhail had previously brought life to Cincinnati and Brooklyn. But manager McCarthy, who couldn't get along with MacPhail, quit early in the 1946 season, and the team finished a distant third.

DiMaggio and the others were back from the war by 1946, but it was not until 1947—under new manager Bucky Harris, and with sparkling pitching from Allie Reynolds (acquired from Cleveland), rookie Frank "Spec" Shea and reliever Joe Page—that the Yankees returned to the top of the heap with an easy pennant win and a narrow World Series triumph over Brooklyn. On the day the Yankees won the Series, though, president MacPhail embarrassed the club and undid himself by brawling in public. Topping and Webb bought out his contract and share of the ownership. Topping took over the presidency, promoting farm director George Weiss to run the club as general manager.

After the Yankees dropped a pair of season-ending games to the Red Sox to finish third in a tight 1948 race, Weiss replaced manager Harris with Casey Stengel, who in nine years of managing the Braves and Dodgers had only twice seen his club finish as high as fifth. But with Weiss providing a steady stream of talented players via the farm system and canny trades, the Yankees under Stengel proved all but invincible into the '60s.

Stengel's Yankees began by putting together a record string of five world championships. No major league club had ever won five pennants in a row, let alone five World Series, and the Yankees didn't accomplish the feat easily. In 1949 they saw the Red Sox come from 12 games back in midseason to pass them with a three-game series sweep in late September, only to rescue the title with two close must-win victories over the Sox in the season's final games. In the World Series, Brooklyn was again the victim, in five games.

After losing much of 1949 to injury, DiMaggio returned with power in 1950, shortstop Rizzuto and catcher Yogi Berra enjoyed the finest seasons of their careers, and pitcher Whitey Ford broke into the majors, winning all nine of his decisions as a starter (he lost once in relief). Though three of the games in the World Series were decided by just one run, New York took Philadelphia's "Whiz Kids" in four straight.

No Yankee drove in as many as 90 runs in 1951, and Ford was drafted for two years of military service. But the remaining pitchers doubled their shutout production and lowered the team ERA by more than half a run per game, enough to propel the club ahead of Cleveland in mid-September. In the World Series the Yankees shook the Giants, four games to two. Cleveland challenged once again in 1952, and again fell just short, as did Brooklyn in carrying the World Series to seven games.

Finally, in 1953, Stengel's Yankees won with relative ease. Ford, back from the Army, won 18 to lead the club to a finish eight and a half games in front. Once again it was Brooklyn in the World Series, and once again the Yankees beat them. In 1954 New York won 103 games—the most in Stengel's 12-year tenure. But Cleveland won an AL-record 111 to take the flag by eight games.

In 1955, though, it was back to second place for Cleveland as New York, with Mickey Mantle now established as one of the game's most productive hitters, settled in for another four pennants. As August passed into September, three teams were within a game of each other at the top. But the Chicago White Sox faltered, leaving the Yankees and Indians to fight it out. With two weeks left, New York won eight straight to pass Cleveland for good. Facing the Dodgers in the World Series for the sixth time, the Yankees finally lost, as Johnny Podres shut them out in Game 7.

From 1956 through 1958 the Yankees seldom found themselves out of first place. In postseason play, they went the full seven games all three years, winning twice—from the Dodgers for the sixth time in 1956, which included Larsen's perfect game performance, and from the Milwaukee Braves in 1958, after losing to the Braves the year before.

In 1959 the Yankees started poorly and never did rise much above .500, finishing a distant third with their worst won-lost record in 34 years. After the season, George Weiss sent an aging Hank Bauer to Kansas City in a trade that brought Roger Maris to New York. In 1960 Maris, with AL titles in slugging and RBIs, won the MVP award. He and Mantle dominated the power stats and led the charge back to the top as the Yankees won their final 15 games to bury the faltering Orioles.

New York's 1960 pennant was the first in another five-flag streak, but it was the last for Stengel. After Pittsburgh toppled the Yankees in the World Series on Bill Mazeroski's famous home run, president Topping retired both the 70-year-old Stengel and general manager Weiss, 65, who had been with the club for 28 years.

With the season lengthened by eight games in 1961, Maris broke Ruth's home-run record and rookie manager Ralph Houk led the club to 109 wins. Ford enjoyed a splendid 25-4 season and celebrated with two more wins in the World Series as the Yankees humbled Cincinnati in five games.

Pitcher Ralph Terry moved out of Ford's shadow in 1962 with 23 wins. Though the Yankees finished just five games ahead of Minnesota, there was little doubt about the outcome from midseason on. In a close World Series with San Francisco, Terry won two, including Game 7 with a 1-0 shutout.

Though New York won pennants the next two years, the 1962 world title was to be their last until the George Steinbrenner era 15 years later. Despite the loss to injury of Mantle and Maris for much of 1963, New York dominated the AL, winning by 10-1/2 games with 104 wins. But in postseason play the Yankees were themselves dominated by the Dodgers (now in Los Angeles), who held them to just four runs in a Series sweep.

Yogi Berra replaced Houk as manager for 1964. In a season-long three-way race with the White Sox and Orioles that found the clubs virtually tied in mid-September, only an 11-game win streak gave the Yankees the space they needed for their final one-game margin of victory. Pitcher Jim Bouton won a pair in the World Series, but the Cardinals took the crown in seven. Berra was fired and replaced by Cardinals manager Johnny Keane.

During the 1964 season Topping had sold the Yankees to CBS. The next year the club, which had gone 40 years without a losing season, dropped to sixth place, and in 1966 fell to their first cellar finish in more than half a century. Even Houk's return as manager in 1967—though it led to some winning seasons—failed to restore the once-proud club to pennant contention, except once, in 1972,

when it was mid-September before they fell out of a tight race to finish fourth.

In January 1973 a syndicate headed by Cleveland shipping magnate George Steinbrenner purchased the Yankees from CBS. Although he had vowed not to take a prominent role in running the club, Steinbrenner soon emerged as one of baseball's most active owners. Through a series of shrewd trades, offers of big contracts to free agents —like Catfish Hunter in 1975—and what became a round-robin of managerial changes, Steinbrenner's Yankees became competitive again, finishing a close second to Baltimore in 1974, and returning to the top with three successive pennants and a pair of world championships.

Manager Billy Martin (a former Yankees second baseman) led the renewed club to a runaway division title in 1976. First baseman Chris Chambliss homered in the last of the ninth of the final game of the ALCS to give the Yankees the pennant over the Kansas City Royals. Cincinnati swept New York in the World Series, but the Yankees came back the next year to edge Baltimore and Boston in a three-way race that saw the teams shift back and forth in the standings throughout the season. Slugger Reggie Jackson, signed as a free agent the previous autumn, turned the club's power trio of Chambliss, Graig Nettles and Thurman Munson into a quartet as the Yankees recorded their first 100-win season in 14 years. After another ninth-inning win over Kansas City in the ALCS finale, New York won the World Series in six games over Los Angeles. Jackson became "Mr. October" with five home runs—three of them in successive at-bats in the final game.

The 1978 season provided as exciting a race as baseball is likely to see. In mid-July it looked like a Red Sox romp, but the fourth-place Yankees put on a great surge, catching the faltering Sox with a four-game series sweep in early September. Boston dropped three and a half games back, but won their final eight games to catch New York on the final day. In the one-game tiebreaker, shortstop Bucky Dent lofted a wind-blown three-run homer over Boston's close left-field wall in the seventh, and Jackson homered an inning later for New York's final run in the 5-4 win. Again the Royals were the victims in the ALCS, as were the Dodgers in the World Series.

After dropping to fourth in 1979, the Yankees held off Baltimore in 1980 to win their fourth division title—but this time Kansas City swept to the pennant in three games. In 1981 the Yankees found themselves in first place when the players struck in June and were thus admitted to an intradivisional playoff with the season's second-half winner, Milwaukee. Narrowly defeating the Brewers for the division title, New York swept Oakland for the pennant in the ALCS. But after taking the first two games from Los Angeles in the World Series, they were stopped cold as the Dodgers won the next four.

The Yankees fell below .500 the next year, and although they revived to win 91 games in 1983, they failed to frighten the division leaders until 1985. First baseman Don Mattingly drove in more runs than any other American Leaguer since 1953 and newcomer (from Oakland) Rickey Henderson scored more often than any major leaguer since 1949 to keep the Yankees in the running until Toronto eliminated them with just one game to go.

But constant roster manipulation and managerial rotation (Billy Martin alone was hired and fired five times) at last set in motion a steady drop in effectiveness. While the team remained in the thick of a tight 1988 divisional race until three season-ending losses set them back into fifth place, their won-lost record showed a third straight season of decline. In 1989 the Yankees sank to their worst finish in 22 years and in 1990 they dropped to the floor of the AL East with the club's worst record since 1913.

Before the 1990 season ended, Steinbrenner was gone. As penalty for his dealings with a gambler named Howard Spira in an attempt to gain information damaging to Yankees outfielder Dave Winfield, Steinbrenner relinquished his controlling interest in the club in August. When fans at Yankee Stadium heard the news, they stood and applauded for 90 seconds.

Their string of consecutive losing seasons stretched to four, something that hadn't happened to the Yankees in 76 years. In 1993 the Yankees bounced back and—bolstered by the league's best hitting and a strong season from newly acquired pitcher Jimmy Key—contended seriously into September, finishing second to Toronto.

They were even better in 1994. With Key in the midst of one of his best seasons ever, and a solid offense paced by right fielder Paul O'Neill (whose .603 slugging average stood 99 points above his previous career high), the Yankees were enjoying the league's best won-lost record and a 6-1/2 game lead in the AL East when the players' strike cut the season short in August.

The 1995 Yankees earned the first-ever AL wild-card slot. Standouts included Wade Boggs (.324), Paul O'Neill (24 HRs), Bernie Williams (.307), David Cone (9-2 with New York after coming over from Toronto), and Jack McDowell (15-10). After taking a tough loss to Seattle in the Division Series, the Yankees saw the departure of McDowell, veteran Don Mattingly and manager Buck Showalter (who became manager of the new Arizona Diamondbacks). Joe Torre replaced Showalter, continuing a tradition of managers—Casey Stengel, Yogi Berra, and Dallas Green—who have managed both the Mets and the Yankees.

In 1996, despite a late season swoon, Torre's Yankees (92-70) captured the AL East championship. Standout Yankees included Bernie Williams (.305, 29 HRs, 102 RBIs), Paul O'Neill (.302, 19 HRs, 91 RBIs), Tino Martinez (.292, 25 HRs, 117 RBIs), AL Rookie of the Year Derek Jeter (.314), Andy Pettitte (21-8), and John Wetteland (43 saves). In the first round of the postseason, New York overcame Texas in four games.

In the ALCS, the Yanks rolled over Baltimore in five games. Assisting the Bombers was the "Angel in the Outfield," a 12-year-old boy who caught Jeter's fly ball by reaching over the rightfield wall in Game 1. Instead of a fan interference call, Jeter was credited with a pivotal homer.

In the first two games of the World Series against Atlanta the Yankees looked outclassed, losing 12-1 and 4-0. But New York rebounded to win the next four, including a 10-inning Game 4 comeback from a 6-0 deficit. The victory was particularly sweet for manager Torre, whose brother Frank received a long-awaited heart transplant the day before Game 6.

In 1997 the Yankees reached the postseason as a wild-card team and seemed to have the easier assignment in facing Cleveland, but the Indians had the Yankees' number. Cleveland rallied to take the last two games to end New York's season.

The Yankees dominated baseball in 1998. They eclipsed the AL record with 114 wins as they rolled through the regular season. They allowed Texas just one run in three Division Series games, but ran into trouble again with the Indians. A controversial Game 2 loss in the ALCS was followed by another loss in Cleveland as the Yankees trailed 2-1 in the series. From there, New York ran the table, winning the last three games in the ALCS and winning four straight against the Padres in the WS. It marked the Yankees' seventh sweep and 24th world championship.

Two more world championships followed: one seemingly easy

and the other as the team with the worst record of any postseason participant. The 1999 Yankees won 16 fewer games than the previous season, and still won 98 times. The Yankees lost just once during the postseason and swept the World Series for the second straight year—this time against Atlanta. The following year the Yankees lost 15 of their final 18 games, but won 11 of 16 postseason games to become the third Yankees club—and fourth team in history—to capture three or more world championships in succession. Making it sweeter was the first Subway Series since 1956. The Yankees won a memorable five-game Series from the Mets.

As the new century dawned, the Yankees continued to dominate during the regular season, but seemed to lose their aura of invincibility in October. New York averaged 100 wins a year between 2001 and 2003, handily winning all three AL East titles, but fell short of the big prize each time.

Everything seemed normal when the Yankees beat the A's in the 2001 ALDS, then trounced the Mariners—who had broken New York's three-year-old AL record with 116 wins—in the ALCS. After losing the first two World Series games at Arizona, the Yankees reeled off three straight one-run victories at home, the last two heart-stopping, come-from-behind wins. After a Game 6 loss, New York had everything in place for yet another world championship: a 2-1 lead in the bottom of the ninth inning of Game 7, with dominant closer Mariano Rivera on the mound. But Arizona clawed back to tie the game, then win it on a bloop single by Luis Gonzalez, and the Yanks' run was over.

The Yankees didn't get past the first round in 2002, losing the ALDS in an upset to the eventual world champion Anaheim Angels. But New York was back in the World Series the next year, after knocking off Minnesota and Boston. The Red Sox gave them a tough fight in the ALCS, but blew a three-run lead in the eighth inning of Game 7, and Aaron Boone's 11th-inning homer gave New York the pennant. The Yanks had only to beat the upstart Florida Marlins to win it all, and took two of the first three World Series games in commanding fashion. But the Marlins refused to roll over, and won the next three games, including a clinching Game 6 shutout by Florida's Josh Beckett.

Yankees' individual highlights during these years were provided by Alfonso Soriano, Jason Giambi, Hideki Matsui, and Roger Clemens, among others. After a decent rookie season in 2001, Soriano emerged as a star with 39 homers and 41 steals in 2002, and 38-35 in '03. Giambi joined the Yankees as a free agent after the 2001 season, and smashed 41 homers in each of his first two years with the club, before being traded before the '04 season, and. Matsui, a superstar slugger in Japan, knocked in 106 runs as an AL rookie in 2003. Clemens won his record sixth Cy Young Award with a 20-3 record in 2001, then notched his 300th career win and 4000th career strikeout in 2003, before briefly retiring, then signing with Houston for 2004.

Oakland Athletics (aka Philadelphia Athletics, Kansas City Athletics)

The history of the Athletics is a tale of three cities—a story of the best of teams and of the worst of teams. With a 13-year sojourn in Kansas City between residence in Philadelphia and Oakland, the A's are the only club to include a stop in Middle America in their trek from East to West. While the A's are second only to the Yankees in AL championships (with 15), they have also finished last in the league or division 27 times, and in 16 seasons have lost 100 games or more—both AL worsts, by far. A club of extremes, they have been

either at the top or at the bottom in nearly one season out of two.

When Ban Johnson established four eastern clubs for his American League in 1901, he chose Connie Mack to manage the new Philadelphia Athletics and gave him a quarter ownership of the club. Mack, who had been managing the league's Milwaukee franchise, settled in at Philadelphia and set a record for managerial longevity—50 years—that is unlikely ever to be surpassed.

In his first 14 years the A's dominated the league with six pennants and two close second-place finishes. After finishing fourth in 1901, the club won its first pennant the next year, pulling away from the field with spurts in August and September. Rube Waddell led the team with 24 wins and six regulars hit over .300. The next two years saw the A's fade in August, but in 1905, after forging ahead in early August and hanging onto the lead with two crucial wins over Chicago's surging White Sox in late September, the A's opened October with a five-game winning streak to clinch their second flag. Waddell, with 26 wins, once again led the club (followed closely by Eddie Plank's 25) and compiled a league-leading 1.48 ERA. In the Athletics' first World Series appearance, though, New York's Christy Mathewson provided most of the pitching heroics, shutting out the A's three times in the Giants' 4-1 Series triumph.

Another August decline in 1906 was followed in 1907 by a comeback struggle from fifth place in late May to a 2-1/2-game lead in mid-September. But the loss of a crucial game to Detroit several days later, and the failure to make up a rainout and a tie, left the A's 1-1/2 games behind the Tigers at the finish.

In 1908 the A's suffered their first losing season, but they rebounded in 1909 to chase the Tigers throughout the summer before tailing off to second. In 1910, with a pitching staff that compiled a stunning 1.79 ERA (paced by Jack Coombs, whose 31 wins included 13 shutouts) and with league-leading fielding and hitting, the A's pulled ahead for good in June, increasing their lead through the rest of the season to finish 14-1/2 games in front. In the World Series they continued to dominate, outscoring the Chicago Cubs 35-15 as they took their first world title, in five games. The A's repeated just as convincingly in 1911. With their "$100,000 infield" of Stuffy McInnis, Eddie Collins, Jack Barry, and Frank "Home Run" Baker averaging .323 at the bat, and Jack Coombs winning 28 games to lead the club (and the league), the A's overtook Detroit in August to win by 13-1/2 games. In the World Series, Baker homered against the Giants, and the A's defeated Mathewson twice, avenging their 1905 humiliation with a victory in six games.

A third-place finish in 1912 broke the pennant streak, but the Athletics came back for two more in 1913 and '14, in both seasons pulling away in early June for easy wins. In the 1913 World Series the A's again felled the Giants, this time in just five games, but the next year they were in turn humiliated by the upstart Boston Braves, who stunned Philadelphia with the first sweep since the renewal of World Series play in 1903.

That winter, Mack began to dismantle his championship club, selling second baseman Collins to the White Sox and watching Chief Bender go to the Federal League. Third baseman Baker, unable to work out a contract, sat out the 1915 season before moving on to the Yankees.

The A's sank immediately to last place, where they remained for seven years. In 1915 they lost 109 games and finished 58-1/2 games out. The next year they lost 117 games to set a league record for ineptitude that was surpassed only in the next century.

It was a decade before Mack was able to restore the club to respectability. In 1924 he brought up Al Simmons, and the next

year Jimmie Foxx and pitcher Lefty Grove. Thus renewed, the A's in 1925 battled Washington to the end of August before backing off to second. In 1927 they won 91 games, though their second-place finish was 19 games back of the overwhelming Yankees. In 1928 the A's battled from well back of New York in midseason to overtake them briefly in September, only to lose three of four games in a critical head-to-head series and slip back to second.

From 1929 through 1931, though, the A's interrupted New York's domination of the AL with three spectacular seasons. In 1929 sophomore pitcher George Earnshaw blossomed into the league's big winner with 24 victories and Grove led the league's stingiest staff with a league-low 2.81 ERA. Six players drove in 79 runs or more (led by Simmons' league-high 157) in powering the A's to 104 wins and an impressive finish 18 games ahead of the Yankees.

After swamping the Cubs in the World Series (including a record-setting 10-run eighth inning at Shibe Park that wiped out an 8-0 deficit in Game 4), the A's repeated as pennant winners in 1930. Simmons led the league in batting (.381) and Grove led its pitchers in just about everything: wins (28), ERA, strikeouts—even saves. Again the World Series was no contest as the A's downed the Cardinals in six.

Earnshaw won more than 20 games for his third successive season in 1931, Simmons repeated as batting leader (.390), and Grove enjoyed what would be the finest season of his career (31-4, 2.06 ERA) in carrying the A's to 107 wins—their best record ever. But in Game 7 the Cardinals ended Philadelphia's championship run.

Following a second-place finish in 1932, Mack began selling off his stars again. This time the reason was primarily economic. Home attendance—never robust—fell off sharply after 1931, as the Great Depression and the A's decline made their impact felt. By 1935 the Athletics were back in the cellar, where they finished in 10 of Mack's final 16 seasons as manager in Philadelphia.

In 1946 Mack, who had been the A's majority stockholder since 1940, divided his shares among his three sons, provoking a family squabble over control of the club. In 1950 the two eldest, Roy and Earle, bought out Connie Jr. and pressured their 87-year-old father to retire. But with Connie Sr. gone, attendance (which had risen to new highs in the baseball boom that followed World War II) dropped off again. When the A's finished 60 games behind champion Cleveland and attendance dropped to an 18-year low in 1954, the Macks sold the club to Chicagoan Arnold Johnson, who moved it to Kansas City.

Attendance increased by more than a million the first season in Kansas City and the team rose a couple of places to sixth. But 1955 was the high point of their 13-year stay in the Midwest; the Kansas City A's never again rose above seventh, and they finished last six times.

Owner Johnson died in March 1960, and that December his heirs sold the club to the enterprising but abrasive Charles O. Finley. Finley brought in a succession of new managers over the next few years, and in 1965 outfitted his players in new bright green-and-yellow uniforms. But with the league's expansion to 10 teams in 1961, the A's had two places lower to sink—and did. After finishing 10th in 1967 for the third time in four years, Finley moved the club to California.

In 1968, their first year on the West Coast, they put together their first winning season in 16 years. The next year, with the start of divisional play, the A's took second in the AL West. Reggie Jackson, in only his second full big league season, enjoyed his finest year, with 47 home runs, 118 RBIs and AL highs in slugging (.608)

and runs scored (123).

After another second-place finish in 1970, the A's were ready for a return to glory. In the next five years they won five division titles, winning both the AL pennant and the World Series from 1972 to 1974. In 1971, with a new manager, Dick Williams, and three pitchers who reached their prime all at once (Vida Blue, Catfish Hunter and reliever Rollie Fingers), the A's enjoyed their best season in 40 years and won the West by a whopping 16 games. Baltimore swept them in the American League Championship Series, but they came back to take the West again the next year. Detroit took them to the limit in the ALCS, as did Cincinnati in the World Series, but in both series the A's prevailed in the deciding game by the margin of a single run.

The next year, 1973, Jackson led the league in slugging, homers and RBIs; Ken Holtzman joined Blue and Hunter in the 20-win column; and home attendance crept over a million for the first time in Oakland as the A's ran their string of Western Division titles to three. Once again they were pushed to the limit in the post-season—by Baltimore in the ALCS and the New York Mets in the World Series—and once again they emerged as world champions.

Manager Williams quit in a dispute with Finley and was replaced by Alvin Dark, but the outcome in 1974 (except for a drop in attendance to under a million) was the same. Hunter bore more of the pitching load and wound up tied for the AL lead with 25 wins. His 2.49 ERA also led the league, as the staff ended Baltimore's five-year hold on the ERA title. The A's toppled the Orioles in the ALCS and (in the first World Series held entirely on the West Coast) won their third consecutive world title in five closely fought games with Los Angeles.

Catfish Hunter moved to the Yankees as a free agent, and Baltimore regained the ERA crown in 1975, but pitchers Paul Lindblad and newcomer Dick Bosman combined for a 20-5 record to supplement the efforts of Blue, Holtzman and Fingers and carry Oakland to an unprecedented fifth straight division title. But there the magic stopped, as Boston swept to the pennant in the ALCS.

Finley, with moves reminiscent of Connie Mack, tried to sell off his star players: Blue, Jackson, Fingers, Holtzman, and out-fielder/first baseman Joe Rudi, one of the team's steadiest hitters. The proposed sales made some sense: the players planned to leave the club at the end of their 1976 option year, and by disposing of them before they played out their option Finley could at least be compensated for his loss. The Jackson and Holtzman deals were approved, but baseball commissioner Bowie Kuhn blocked the sale of the others, citing the "best interests of baseball."

The weakened A's came back from a poor start to close within two and a half games of the Kansas City Royals in 1976, but they dropped to last place the next year. After another last-place finish in 1979, Finley hired fiery Billy Martin to manage the club. Martin brought the A's in second in 1980 (and his propensity for leaving starters in resulted in an astounding 94 complete games, almost twice as many as Milwaukee's second-best total). The A's finished first in the first half of strike-divided 1981. They won the Western Division championship by sweeping Kansas City in the special intradivisional playoffs but were swept by the Yankees in the ALCS.

Finley's sale of the club in 1981 to the Levi's jeans company signaled a turn toward normalcy and popularity. Despite a losing season in 1982, the club set a home attendance record as over 1.7 million fans came to watch Rickey Henderson's successful assault on the stolen-base record (130). In 1987 the A's finished right at .500—for the first time in their history a perfectly average team.

The next season they inaugurated a new multiyear reign as the league's best. Starter Dave Stewart and closer Dennis Eckersley anchored the league's strongest pitching staff and "Bash Brothers" Jose Canseco and Mark McGwire headlined an awesome offense. From 1988 through 1990 the team had its second run of three straight pennants since moving to Oakland (and the third three-pennant run in franchise history). In 1988 they built a 13-game margin of victory over runner-up Minnesota, winning 104 games and drawing more than 2 million fans to their home games for the first time. They swept Boston in the ALCS but faltered in the World Series, losing to underdog Los Angeles in five games.

Injuries to several key players—especially Canseco, who missed the first half of the season with a broken wrist—kept the A's from dominating AL play through most of 1989. But the preseason signing of free agent starter Mike Moore had strengthened the pitching, and a June trade that brought Rickey Henderson back after more than four years with the Yankees gave the A's the push they needed to prevail.

At full strength by season's end, the A's overwhelmed Toronto in five games for their 14th pennant, then swept San Francisco for their ninth world title as a franchise. Only the surprising White Sox challenged Oakland in 1990, and they too fell away in the latter half of the season as the A's walked to the division title with 103 wins. The potent offense was made even more formidable by the late-season acquisition of Harold Baines from Texas and Willie McGee from St. Louis. But the key to Oakland's dominance was its pitchers, who for the third year in a row compiled the league's lowest earned run average. Bob Welch led the majors with 27 wins, Dave Stewart put together his fourth straight 20-win season, and Dennis Eckersley rebounded from an injury-hampered 1989 with his finest relief year yet. The A's swept Boston to take their third straight pennant, but—shades of 1988!—floundered in the World Series, succumbing in just four games to Cincinnati's aroused Reds.

In 1991 the A's stayed at or near the top into late June before slipping to fourth. Eckersley remained in top form, however, and in 1992 proved almost invincible, with 51 saves to earn the Cy Young Award. Jose Canseco's trade to Texas during the season severed the Bash Brothers' tandem offense, but Mark McGwire enjoyed a banner season at the bat. Despite a wave of injuries that would have sunk most teams, the A's stayed afloat near the front through the first half season and held steady in the second half to win their fourth division title in five years. In the ALCS the A's fell to Toronto in six games.

With an injury to McGwire that sidelined him more than four months, plus a general decline on the mound and at the bat that saw the team finish with the league's worst batting and earned run averages, the 1993 A's did what only two major league clubs before them (the 1915 Athletics and 1885 St. Louis Maroons) had ever done before: tumble into the cellar after a first-place finish the year before.

The A's weren't winning much more often in 1994 when the players' strike halted play in August, but in the weak AL West their 51-63 record was good enough to land them in second place, just a game out of first. In 1995 their 67-77 mark earned them last place in the AL West. More significant, though, was the sale of the club by the Haas family to Bay Area businessmen Steve Schott and Ken Hofmann and the departure of manager Tony LaRussa.

The power-hitting 1996 A's (78-84) edged up to third place, largely on the basis of McGwire's 52 homers. The 1997 season was a disappointment all around: the A's failed to have a pitcher win 10 games for the second straight year, third baseman Scott Brosius batted 101 points lower than in 1996, and the team was forced to trade McGwire rather than lose him to free agency. Pitcher Kenny Rogers, who came from the Yankees in a trade for Brosius, was the team's top winner in 1998, and Ben Grieve (the AL Rookie of the Year) gave the A's a young power bat to go along with sluggers Matt Stairs and Jason Giambi.

Oakland became a contender in 1999 as general manager Billy Beane acquired several solid players—Randy Velarde, Jason Isringhausen, Kevin Appier, and Omar Olivares—at the July 30 trading deadline. Oakland immediately won nine of its next 10 and remained in the hunt for the wild card until the closing weeks of the season. The A's exceeded all expectations the following year. Jason Giambi hit 43 home runs with 137 RBIs and batted .333 to earn the MVP Award and lead one of the league's most explosive offenses. Second-year starter Tim Hudson flourished as the staff ace, winning his 20th game on the last day of the season to clinch Oakland's first postseason berth since 1992. The A's forced the Yankees to five games in the Division Series, but New York held on to win Game 5 to end the season for the AL West champs.

Oakland's pitching staff became the envy of the majors, as young guns Hudson, Mark Mulder and Barry Zito combined for 56 wins in 2001 and 57 in '02. Though Oakland won 11 more games in 2001 than they had in 2000, they slipped to second place: their mere 102 wins were no match for Seattle's AL record 116. The A's earned the wild card spot, but were again edged by the Yankees, three games to two, in the ALDS. Giambi, following another outstanding season, left the team as a free agent and signed with those same Yanks.

The Athletics didn't miss a beat, winning 103 games and the divisional title in 2002. Included was an AL-record 20-game winning streak. Shortstop Miguel Tejada (34, 131, .308) won the MVP, while Zito (23-5, 2.75) took the Cy Young Award. But, for the third straight year, Oakland lost a five-game Divisional Series, this time in an upset to the Twins. After seven seasons at the helm, Howe left the A's to take over the Mets.

The A's continued to win, in 2003, under Ken Macha, notching 96 victories to top the West once again, then taking the first two ALDS games. But incredibly, for the fourth consecutive year, Oakland's season ended in Game 5 of the Divisional Series. This time, the wild-card Red Sox were responsible for the death blow, after winning the last three games by a total of four runs.

Philadelphia Phillies (aka Blue Jays)

It took the Phillies 32 years to win their first pennant, and 97 years to win their first world championship. They have finished last in their league or division 30 times—one season in four. In the nine years from 1975 through 1983, though, they were one of the most formidable teams in baseball.

Alfred J. Reach, a sporting goods entrepreneur and former player, and Colonel John Rogers, a Philadelphia lawyer and politician, organized the Phillies in 1883 to bring Philadelphia back into the National League after a six-year absence. In their first season, the Phillies won only 17 of 98 decisions to finish last, as far out of seventh as the seventh-place team was from first.

Reach hired the respected Harry Wright to manage the Phillies in 1884, and while Wright failed to lead them to a pennant in a decade at the helm, he did make them respectable. His fourth-place 1886 team, in fact, compiled a winning percentage of .623 that remained the club's best for 90 years. In 1887 the Phillies, with three pitchers winning more than 20 games, finished second, just three and a half games behind Detroit—their closest finish until

their first pennant 28 years later.

The Phillies remained in the upper division 12 of the next 14 years. For five years—1891 to 1895—they fielded an outfield of Ed Delahanty, Billy Hamilton and Sam Thompson—Hall of Famers who rank among the top hitters of all time. In the three heavy-hitting seasons that followed the lengthening of the pitching distance to its present 60 feet, 6 inches in 1893, Delahanty, Hamilton and Thompson—with help from players like catcher Jack Clements (.394 in 1895) and utility outfielder Tuck Turner (.416 in 1894)—sparked the Phillies to three team batting titles with batting averages of over .300. In 1894 the big three joined Turner in batting over .400 and the team hit .349—still the major league club record.

In 1899, with Delahanty's .410 leading the way, the Phillies once again topped .300 to lead the league. Though the team finished third, they won 94 games, a club high they would not surpass for 77 years. President Reach sold his interest in the club after a dispute with co-owner Rogers, and Rogers lost star second baseman Nap Lajoie in a salary dispute to the Athletics (Philadelphia's new entry in the rival American League). But the Phillies chased frontrunner Pittsburgh through much of 1901. Though they slumped in August, they recovered to finish second.

It was the end of an era. Delahanty deserted to the AL the next season, and the Phillies dropped to seventh. Rogers sold the club to a syndicate. By 1904 the team was in last place, losing 100 games for the first time. They rose into the first division the next season, but didn't mount a serious pennant run until 1911, when the pitching of rookie Grover Cleveland Alexander kept them in the thick of the race into midseason. Two years later the Phillies enjoyed first place through most of June until they faded to a distant second.

In 1915 Alexander brought his ERA down more than a run per game to a league-low and career-best 1.22, with 12 shutouts among his 31 wins. Right fielder Gavvy Cravath and first baseman Fred Luderus finished one-two among NL sluggers, and Cravath won home-run and RBI crowns. For half a season all eight clubs were in the thick of a tight race, with the Cubs and Phillies at the top of the heap. But in July the Cubs folded, and in August and September the Phillies took off to outdistance the late-surging Boston Braves for their first pennant.

The World Series was a Phillies' heartbreak. Four of the five games were decided by a single run—but the runs belonged to the Boston Red Sox, who swept four after the Phillies had won the opener.

Alexander shut out a record-tying 16 opponents the following year, winning a career-high 33, and teammate Eppa Rixey had his first big year with 22 wins. The club trailed the Dodgers through most of the season but caught them in September, only to fall away again in the final week.

After Alexander's 30 wins had brought the Phillies another second-place finish in 1917, the club dealt him to Chicago and embarked on 31 years of wandering in the desert. After 14 losing seasons (eight of them in last place), Philadelphia climbed to fourth, two games above .500, in 1932, but dropped back the next year into the second division (including nine last-place finishes) for 16 more years.

Several outstanding players spent time in Philadelphia during these years: Dave Bancroft (a rookie in their pennant season), Cy Williams, Freddy Leach, Chuck Klein, Lefty O'Doul, and Dick Bartell. Of these, only Williams and Klein retired as Phillies. The financially strapped management traded away the others at the height of their careers in deals that included cash as well as players. Even Klein—perhaps the greatest of them all—was sold twice before returning a third time to Philly to end his career.

The Phillies in 1930 produced a season that ranks among the most extraordinary of all time. With Klein and O'Doul leading the way at .386 and .383, every regular hit at least .280, to give the Phillies a team batting average of .315. But Phillies pitchers yielded a record 1199 runs while compiling the worst big league ERA ever—6.71. The club lost 102 games and finished last.

The Phillies' move in 1938 out of tiny, antiquated Baker Bowl into the Athletics' Shibe Park did nothing for attendance—or for performance. The team strung together a club-record five consecutive last-place finishes from 1938 to 1942, in which they averaged 107 losses per season and finished between 43 and 62-1/2 games out of first.

In February 1943 the league took control of the debtridden club and sold it to a group headed by New York sportsman William D. Cox. Cox didn't last long; before the year was out he was barred from baseball for betting on the Phillies. His controlling interest was sold to Robert M. Carpenter, who installed his son, Robert Jr., as president. The younger Carpenter hired former pitcher Herb Pennock as general manager with instructions to build a farm system, and a new era began in the club's history.

Outfielder Del Ennis had come up to hit .313 in 1946, but Pennock died (in January 1948) before he could see the full fruits of his labor. First baseman Dick Sisler would be purchased in March and rookie outfielder Richie Ashburn would lead Philadelphia hitters with a .333 average. Willie Jones wouldn't nail down third base for another year, and rookie pitchers Robin Roberts and Curt Simmons wouldn't overawe the opposition for a couple of seasons yet. But the team that would be dubbed the "Whiz Kids" was gathering. Triple-A manager Eddie Sawyer was brought up in late July.

The loss of first baseman Eddie Waitkus (shot in the chest by a crazed young woman) and midseason complacency threatened to strand the Phillies in the second division in 1949. Sawyer fired up his players in a special team meeting, and the Phillies rallied to finish third with the club's best record in 32 years.

With new red-pinstripe uniforms and a recovered Eddie Waitkus, the 1950 Phillies pulled away from a tightly bunched first division in July and August, but late in September they fell to within two games of onrushing Brooklyn. The Dodgers took the first game of a season-ending two-game series to narrow the gap to one. In the finale Ashburn threw out a Dodger at the plate in the ninth to preserve a tie and Sisler gave the Phillies the lead with a three-run homer the next inning. When Brooklyn failed to score in the bottom of the tenth, the Whiz Kids had their pennant.

Curt Simmons, who was called up for military service in September after winning 17 games, missed the World Series. As in 1915, the result for Philadelphia was frustration and heartbreak, as the Phillies were swept by the Yankees—losing each of the first three games by a single run.

Roberts' pitching kept the Phillies in the first division for four of the next five years, but the team made no serious run at another pennant. And when Roberts began to lose his effectiveness the team kept sinking, to fifth for two years, then to the cellar for four more, culminating in 1961 with the longest big league losing streak of the century—23 games.

The club stuck with new manager Gene Mauch, and the 1962 Phillies edged above .500 for the first time in nine years (finishing seventh in a league newly expanded to 10 teams). In 1963 they moved up to fourth with a strong second half. In 1964, with the acquisition of pitcher Jim Bunning from Detroit and infielder

Richie (later Dick) Allen's productive rookie season, Mauch's Phillies moved way out in front in August. But they blew their lead with 10 straight losses in late September while Cincinnati was winning nine in a row and St. Louis eight. Only victories in their final two games salvaged a second-place tie.

Pitcher Steve Carlton, acquired from St. Louis in an off-season trade, accounted for nearly half the Phillies' 59 wins in 1972. His 27 victories for the league's worst team gave the club a ray of hope for the future and earned Carlton the Cy Young Award. Carlton lost a league-high 20 games the next year. He regained his form over the next three seasons, and the Phillies gradually rose to the top of the division.

In 1974 sophomore third baseman Mike Schmidt burst to the forefront of the league's power hitters. The Phillies dropped out of contention in August but wound up third, their best finish since the league split into divisions in 1969. The next year outfielder Greg Luzinski joined Schmidt among the league's top sluggers and the club rose to second, with their first winning season since 1967.

In 1976 they enjoyed their finest regular season ever. With Schmidt and Luzinski providing the power, Carlton returning to the ranks of 20-game winners and Jim Lonborg climaxing a long comeback with 18 wins, the Phillies took the division lead in May and pulled away, recovering from a late-season dive to finish well ahead of Pittsburgh. Their 101 wins, .624 winning percentage, and nine-game margin of victory remain club records.

The Phillies were swept by Cincinnati in the National League Championship Series, but they came back the next year to duplicate their record 101 wins for another comfortable first-place finish. Carlton won 23 (and his second Cy Young Award), and Luzinski enjoyed the best season of his career, driving in 130 runs. After defeating Los Angeles in the NLCS opener, though, the Phillies lost the pennant with three straight defeats.

In 1978, even though Schmidt and Carlton had off-years, the Phillies led much of the season and captured the division title a third straight time. But it was a tight race, and they barely survived a late-season Pittsburgh surge to finish a game and a half in front. For the third time, their triumph in the East was followed by defeat in the NLCS—for the second time at the hands of Los Angeles in four games.

Danny Ozark, in his seventh year as Phillies manager, was replaced by Dallas Green late in a disappointing 1979 season that saw the club stumble after a strong start. The club rallied in September to finish fourth. But Schmidt was back in top form, and Pete Rose had arrived via free agency to add his bat and hustle.

In a three-way race in 1980 that remained close through August, the Phillies hung tight without being able to move into the lead. But as Pittsburgh folded in late August and early September, the Phillies edged in front briefly, then battled back and forth with Montreal. Tied with the Expos as the clubs met in Montreal for the season's final three games, Philadelphia took the first, 2-1, then—in 11 innings—the second, to clinch their fourth division title in five years. Schmidt, with perhaps his finest season, drove in 121 runs and was named NL MVP; Carlton, with 24 wins, won his third Cy Young Award; and veteran reliever Tug McGraw enjoyed his best season in years. In an NLCS in which four of the five games went into extra innings, the Phillies prevailed over Houston, capturing their first pennant since the Whiz Kids 30 years earlier. And in the World Series, fortune finally smiled on the team as they overcame Kansas City in six games.

The Phillies won the first half of the strike-divided 1981 season.

In the special intradivisional playoff against Montreal, Philadelphia fought back to tie the series after losing the first two games—only to lose the finale. The Carpenter family, citing the prohibitive cost of running a major league club, sold the team. Manager Dallas Green also left and was replaced by Pat Corrales, who kept the club in the thick of the 1982 race until the final month, when the Phillies slipped 3-1/2 games back, to second. And Carlton did it again: his 23 wins earned him the Cy Young trophy, making him the first pitcher to win the award four times.

Mike Schmidt again dominated the Phillies' offense in 1983, but Carlton yielded to John Denny as the team's pitching ace. Newly acquired reliever Al Holland emerged as one of the league's best. After general manager Paul Owens took over for Corrales as manager in midseason, the Phillies came alive and took the division title by six games. Carlton dominated the NLCS with an ERA of 0.66 and two wins as the Phillies won their fourth pennant.

But their golden age ended in the World Series, when Baltimore triumphed in five games. The Phillies dropped to .500 and fourth place in 1984, and suffered a losing fifth-place season in 1985. They rebounded to second in 1986 (but 21-1/2 games behind New York), then dropped back below .500 in 1987. Mike Schmidt, the only remaining member of the 1980 world champions, continued to power the offense. Despite an impressive lineup of everyday players in 1988, the Phils collapsed, finishing in the division cellar for the first time in 15 years. Unable to recover from a shoulder injury, Schmidt retired in May 1989, and despite several midseason trades the Phillies again finished last in the NL East. The Phillies followed that with a tie for fourth in 1990, a distant third in 1991 and, in 1992, their third last-place finish in five years.

Strengthened by the signing of several free agents and sustained by solid performances throughout the roster, the Phillies reversed course in 1993. Led by Len Dykstra's peak season at the plate, the team grabbed the division lead at the start of the year and never let go, fending off Montreal's late-season surge to take the NL East title by three games. In the NLCS they won their fifth NL pennant, defeating Atlanta in six games, but in the World Series they blew a pair of late-inning leads and fell in six games to repeat champion Toronto.

The Phillies didn't contend for the next seven years, finishing under .500 each time. Fregosi was fired after the 1996 season, but Terry Francona fared no better in his four years at the helm. Phillies' ace Curt Schilling went to Arizona in a trade in 2000. Still, there was reason for hope, with the developments of youngsters Scott Rolen and Bobby Abreu.

Former fiery Phillies shortstop Larry Bowa took over the team in 2001 and had instant success: the Phils improved by 21 games and finished second, just two games behind the perennial champion Braves. Two third-place finishes followed in Philly, with the '03 club—led by home-run champ Jim Thome, a free-agent acquisition—contending for the wild card. With a respectable team, and a new stadium (Citizens Bank Park) ready to open, Phillies' fans had reason for excitement about the 2004 season.

Pittsburgh Pirates (aka Alleghenys, Innocents)

Pittsburgh became a big league city in 1882, when its Allegheny baseball club joined with five other teams to form the American Association. Allegheny president H.D. McKnight was named president of the new league, but the club made little stir until it hired Horace Phillips as manager and replaced its personnel in 1885 with players from the defunct Columbus club, which had finished

second in the AA the year before. The new Alleghenys finished a distant third in 1885, but after purchasing Pud Galvin from Buffalo they improved in 1886 to finish a respectable second behind the invincible St. Louis Browns.

Flushed with success, Allegheny in 1887 became the first club to desert the AA for the older and more highly regarded National League. There they found the competition stiffer and sank back into the second division. In 1890, when most of the team jumped to the rival Pittsburgh Players' League club, Allegheny (known that year as the Innocents) suffered the worst season in Pittsburgh major league history, finishing last, 66-1/2 games out of first place (and 23 out of seventh), with a won-lost record of 23-113.

When the Players League folded after just one season, Allegheny merged with its PL counterpart to form the Pittsburgh Athletic Company, thereby retrieving many of its old regulars. The club also hired a second baseman—Lou Bierbauer—whose signing (or theft, as his old club saw it) gave the Innocents a new and more enduring nickname: the Pirates. The renewed club still finished last in 1891, but 36 games closer to the top than the year before, and only fractionally out of seventh place.

In 1893 a rules change moved the pitcher 5-1/2 feet farther back from home plate. Of all the NL clubs, the Pirates benefited most from the change: their batting average jumped 63 points—28 more than that of the league as a whole—while their pitchers suffered less than most. The club finished second, with a .628 winning percentage that was their best of the century. Lefty Frank Killen, acquired from Washington, led the club's resurgence with a league-leading 34 wins.

Although catcher Connie Mack was called upon to manage the club toward the end of the 1894 season and led them to winning seasons the next two years, the Pirates did not make another serious run for the pennant until 1900. With a team transformed yet again by players from a defunct club—this time the Louisville Colonels—the Pirates battled Brooklyn's Superbas almost to the end of the season before dropping four and a half games back, a solid second. Although they lost the postseason Chronicle-Telegraph Cup games (that year's World Series) to the Superbas, the Pirates were embarked on an era of greatness.

In the merger that brought the Louisville players to Pittsburgh, the Colonels' owner Barney Dreyfuss acquired half ownership of the Pirates. A year later he bought the other half. His perennial hope for the club was a first-division finish; the Pirates reached that goal in 26 of his 32 years as owner.

Four of the former Louisville players—outfielder-turned-short-stop Honus Wagner, outfielder/manager Fred Clarke, third baseman/outfielder Tommy Leach, and pitcher Deacon Phillippe (and one carryover from the old Pirates, pitcher Sam Leever)—remained with Pittsburgh long enough to help lead them to four pennants and, in 1909, their first world championship. In the 16 years Clarke managed the Pirates, they also finished second five times and slipped out of the first division only in Clarke's final two seasons at the helm.

In contrast to the club's devastation by the Players League raid of 1890, the Pirates were unaffected in 1901 by raiders from the American League (which that year turned itself into a major league largely by drawing off talent from National League clubs). Only third baseman Jimmy Williams defected to the Americans, and he was ably replaced by Tommy Leach. The Pirates, with the league's best pitching (Jesse Tannehill and Deacon Phillippe finished one-two in ERA, and Jack Chesbro at 21-10 led in winning per-

centage), captured their first pennant by a comfortable seven and a half games over the Philadelphia Phillies.

The Pirates repeated as pennant winners in 1902 and 1903. The 1902 team was overwhelming. One Pirate or another led the league in nearly every offensive category: Ginger Beaumont in hits and batting; Tommy Leach in home runs; and Honus Wagner in slugging, RBIs, runs scored, doubles, and stolen bases. Pitcher Jack Chesbro's 28 wins led the league, and the top five NL pitchers in winning percentage were all Pirates. The club held the lead the whole season, finishing 27-1/2 games ahead of second-place Brooklyn, still a major league record.

Pitchers Chesbro and Tannehill deserted to the AL's New York Highlanders the next season, but their loss merely made Pittsburgh's pennant-winning margin (6-1/2 games) smaller than it might have been. Wagner beat out teammate Fred Clarke for the NL batting crown and finished second to Clarke in slugging. Beaumont took the titles in hits, runs, and total bases. Pitcher Sam Leever, with his finest season, led the club with 25 wins and the league in ERA and winning percentage. Owner Dreyfuss arranged with the AL champion Boston Pilgrims for a best-of-nine World Series—the first between NL and AL champions—but the Pirates lost it in eight games as their tired pitchers at last succumbed to overwork.

Although the Pirates twice finished second over the next four years, they didn't come close to capturing another pennant until 1908, when, in one of the tightest NL races ever, they were edged out by the Chicago Cubs and finished one game back, tied with the New York Giants for second.

The following year, though, they moved in June into the new concrete-and-steel Forbes Field and celebrated by returning to the top of the league with a club record 110 wins—holding off the dogged Cubs throughout the season to win the pennant by six and a half games. And this time they won the World Series, too, although they needed the full seven games to subdue the Detroit Tigers.

Wagner remained the league's dominant offensive force. Aging pitchers Leever and Phillippe were overshadowed by a new crop of standouts: Vic Willis, Howie Camnitz, Nick Maddox, and Lefty Leifield—and the astonishing rookie Babe Adams, who after going 12-3 (with a 1.11 ERA) during the season, won three more games in the World Series.

The Series triumph ended an era. Wagner was past his prime and wound down his long career over the next several seasons as the Pirates dropped out of contention for a dozen years. Only Babe Adams remained of the world championship team when Pittsburgh next made a contest of the pennant race in 1921. That season saw the Pirates take an early lead and hold it most of the summer until a late-season decline dropped them to second place.

Former Pittsburgh infielder Bill McKechnie replaced George Gibson as manager during the following season with the club in fifth place, and saw the Pirates spurt to second before fading to third at the finish. Two more third-place seasons—with the Pirates finishing just three games out of first in 1924—paved the way for another pennant in 1925.

The 1925 Pirates fielded several stars: shortstop Glenn Wright, who led the club with 121 RBIs; sophomore right fielder Kiki Cuyler, who led the team in hitting (.357) and the league in runs scored; third baseman Pie Traynor, who shone on the field and at the bat; and Max Carey, who beat out Cuyler for the league stolen-base title and enjoyed his finest season (.343) at the plate. The team as a whole hit .307 to lead the league and ran away with the pennant, spurting to catch the front-running Giants in midseason and

pushing ahead to an eight-and-a-half-game lead by season's end.

The World Series was tougher, but the Pirates prevailed over the Washington Senators, defeating veteran Walter Johnson in a seventh-game slugfest, 9-7. Babe Adams, hero of the 1909 Series and now, at 43, nearing the end of his long career, pitched one shutout inning in Game 4.

Rookie outfielder Paul Waner arrived the next season and hit .336, but the team, which had led the race going into August, fell into decline late in the month and finished third. Max Carey sparked an unsuccessful player uprising against the management and was sold to Brooklyn just before the Pirates collapsed in August, and manager McKechnie was replaced after the season by former Washington manager Donie Bush.

In 1927, his first season at the helm, Bush won the pennant, even though Kiki Cuyler was benched for half the season for refusing to bat second in the order. But Paul Waner's younger brother Lloyd arrived to join Paul in the outfield, and the pair tore up the league, finishing one-two in hits (237 and 223) as Paul also took crowns in batting (.380; Lloyd was third at .355), RBIs, and total bases, while Lloyd led in runs scored. In and out of first place throughout the season, the Pirates moved into the lead a final time at the start of September and held on to edge the St. Louis Cardinals by a game and a half. In the World Series, though (played with Cuyler on the bench), the Pirates were swept by the imposing '27 Yankees.

Barney Dreyfuss died in February 1932. Ownership of the Pirates passed to his widow, who named their son-in-law Bill Benswanger president. The team finished a competitive second in 1932 and 1933, but then fell back until 1938. With Pie Traynor now manager, they moved out in front in midseason and held their lead comfortably until late September, when 10 straight Chicago victories (including three against Pittsburgh) dropped the Pirates to second place, where they finished, two games back.

The Pirates showcased some great players in their lean years, like shortstop Arky Vaughan in the 1930s and early '40s, and slugger Ralph Kiner, who won or shared the league home-run title all seven of his seasons with Pittsburgh in the 1940s and '50s. But after 1938 the club finished no closer than eight games from the top for 21 years.

The Pirates were purchased in 1946 by a four-man syndicate that included singer Bing Crosby and real estate tycoon John W. Galbreath. Galbreath later bought a majority interest in the club and, as president, hired Branch Rickey to rebuild the Pirates into contenders.

Barney Dreyfuss had resisted the development of minor league systems and preferred to scour unaffiliated minor league teams himself in search of young talent. Rickey, who pioneered the farm system in St. Louis and Brooklyn, laid the foundation for Pittsburgh's resurgence. Six of the eight regulars who would lead the Pirates to their next championship in 1960 were already in the 1958 lineup, including Dick Groat, Bill Mazeroski and Roberto Clemente; the leading pitchers of 1958—Bob Friend, Vern Law and reliever Roy Face—topped the 1960 staff, too.

They began strong in 1960 and, shaking off their last challenger in late July, built up a seven-game margin of victory by season's end. Batting champion Groat paced a balanced offense that led the league in hitting, and pitcher Law, with 20 wins, enjoyed the finest season of his career. Facing the Yankees in the World Series, the Pirates were overwhelmed in the three games they lost, but they won the world title with four close wins, capped by Mazeroski's famous home run in the bottom of the ninth inning of the final game.

Pittsburgh again led the league in batting in 1961, with Clemente (whose .351 batting average led the league) and first baseman Dick Stuart (35 home runs, 117 RBIs) enjoying especially fine seasons. But the pitching fell apart, and the club dropped to sixth place.

When the Pirates next made a serious run for the pennant, in 1966, Harry Walker managed the team and center fielder Matty Alou (newly acquired from San Francisco) won the batting crown. (His brother Felipe of Atlanta was runner-up—the only one-two brother finish ever.) In a season-long three-way race, the Pirates took a lead in August but lost it early in September and finished third, three games out. They dropped to sixth again the next season and remained out of the pennant race for three years.

In 1970 John Galbreath's son Daniel was named Pirates' president, and Danny Murtaugh returned a third time to pilot the Pirates. (His second stint was for half a season in 1967.) The team began slowly and entered June with a record under .500. But they were already on their way up, and they moved out of aging Forbes Field into the brand-new Three Rivers Stadium in mid-July. They slipped into a three-way tangle for first in the NL East in mid-September, but shot ahead later in the month to take the division title. The power was now supplied by first baseman Bob Robertson and outfielder Willie Stargell, but Roberto Clemente was still in top form and Bill Mazeroski was still at second base, though nearing the end of his career.

In the 1970 National League Championship Series, the Pirates were swept by Cincinnati. But they came back the next season to overwhelm the East in a race that was no race after June, then defeated San Francisco for their eighth pennant, three games to one. Their slugging—paced by Stargell's 48 home runs—was tops in the NL, and reliever Dave Giusti saved a league-leading 30 games in support of a balanced pitching staff. Clemente hit .414 in the World Series (with half his hits going for extra bases) as the Pirates overcame a 2-0 deficit to edge Baltimore in seven games for their fourth world title.

In 1972, after a slow start, Pittsburgh (now managed by their former center fielder Bill Virdon) rocketed to their third straight division championship—by 11 games over Chicago. The club lost, narrowly, to Cincinnati in the NLCS, then suffered an even greater loss when Clemente was killed that winter in a plane crash. Clemente, who had collected exactly 3,000 hits with the Pirates, had the usual five-year waiting period waived by the Hall of Fame and was enshrined in Cooperstown in 1973.

The Pirates played poorly the next season, yet even with a losing record finished third in a five-way divisional race. Murtaugh returned as manager a fourth (and final) time late in the season and piloted the club to two more NL East titles the next two years.

The 1974 championship drive featured a comeback from last place in early July to first by late August, followed by a nip-and-tuck race in September with St. Louis that was settled by a 10th-inning Pittsburgh victory over Chicago in the season's final game. Stargell's bat was joined by those of Al Oliver and Richie Zisk as the Pirates outhit the rest of the league. In the NLCS, though, the Los Angeles Dodgers overcame Pittsburgh handily, three games to one.

The Pirates won the 1975 race more easily, holding the lead from early June as right fielder Dave Parker, in his first full big league season, led the club in home runs and RBIs, and the league in slugging. Rennie Stennett, now the second baseman, tied Wilbert Robinson's 1892 record by going 7-for-7 in a nine-inning game at Wrigley Field. Their regular season-success failed to carry over to the postseason as Pittsburgh fell in the NLCS for the fourth

time in five tries.

A distant second-place finish in 1976 was followed that December by manager Murtaugh's untimely death. His successor, Chuck Tanner (acquired in a trade with Oakland), kept the Pirates competitive in his first two seasons, steering them to within five games of the champion Phillies in 1977, then—with an amazing August-September spurt from way below .500—to within a game and a half of the Phillies in 1978.

In 1979 the Pirates again started slowly but began to move up in May and pushed to the front, ahead of Montreal, in late July. By mid-September, though, the Expos had caught up, and it was not until the final day that Pittsburgh had its sixth NL East title. Parker and the aging Stargell (now called "Pops") were still the club's big bats. Submariner Kent Tekulve had emerged as the bullpen ace and was one of six Pittsburgh pitchers to win 10 games or more.

In the NLCS the Pirates repaid Cincinnati for their 1975 humiliation, sweeping to the pennant in three games. In the World Series they seemed to have met their match in Baltimore, falling behind, three games to one. But Pops rallied his "family" to victory in the final three must-win contests, and Pittsburgh for a fifth time reigned at the top of the baseball world. Stargell was a three-time MVP that season—the NLCS, the World Series, and sharing the regular season MVP trophy with Keith Hernandez of St. Louis.

For seven years the Pirates drifted downhill. The club's family spirit disintegrated, fans deserted the team, and it seemed for a time that the Pirates would leave Pittsburgh. But in 1985 a group of local corporations and individuals purchased the club from the Galbreaths, determined (with the assistance of a loan from the city of Pittsburgh) to keep the Pirates in town. Syd Thrift, a trader of consummate skill, was named general manager, and Chicago White Sox coach Jim Leyland was hired to his first job as a big league pilot. Under the new regime the club improved gradually, until in 1988 it once again proved itself a serious contender in the NL East. Thrift had built a team second only to New York's mighty Mets, one that drew more than 1.8 million fans in Pittsburgh—a club record. Thrift, however, clashed with the team's directors and he was fired at season's end.

Plagued all season by injuries, Pittsburgh plunged to fifth in 1989. But in 1990, as Doug Drabek put together a career season on the mound and the bats of Barry Bonds and Bobby Bonilla boomed, the Pirates arrived at the All-Star break in first place by half a game over New York. With Drabek and Zane Smith (newly acquired from Montreal) all but unbeatable down the stretch, the Pirates, after exchanging the lead with New York several times, swept a series against the Mets in early September to extend a narrow lead. The Bucs clinched the NL East title at the end of the month with eight straight wins.

The Pirates repeated as division champions in 1991 and 1992. Bonds and Bonilla again led the offense in 1991, and pitcher John Smiley won 20 games as the team built an early lead and enlarged it to 14 games by season's end. In 1992, even the departure of Bonilla (who signed with the Mets as a free agent) and Smiley (dealt to Minnesota) didn't hamper the Pirates. Center fielder Andy Van Slyke took up the offensive slack with one of his best seasons, and pitcher Tim Wakefield rose from the minors at the end of July to compile an 8-1 record as the Pirates breezed to the title by nine games. But the three-time division champions could not win a pennant. In the 1990 NLCS they fell to Cincinnati in six games. The next year they built a 3-2 lead over Atlanta, but lost the final two games. And in 1992, down three games to two, the Bucs fought back to within one out of victory in Game 7 before an Atlanta pinch hit cut them down once again.

The departure of free agent Barry Bonds to San Francisco was the most crucial of many roster changes for 1993, which saw more than half the 1992 NL East championship squad replaced. The revamped Pirates fielded near the top of the league and batted near the middle, but their pitching fell apart and the team finished fifth.

Things didn't get much better over the next decade, and as of 2004 Pittsburgh hadn't had a winning season since the '92 campaign. Financial problems continued to haunt the team, and the payroll was slashed to the bone in 1995, resulting in the Pirates posting the NL's worst record (58-86). Attendance plunged from over 2 million in 1991 to under a million in '95. In February 1996 Sacramento newspaper heir Kevin McClatchy, 32, moved to purchase the club for $90 million. Leyland resigned after the 1996 season, just in time to lead the Florida Marlins to a world championship.

Several of Pittsburgh's best players followed Leyland out of town in cost-cutting trades, but the Pirates turned out to be one of baseball's biggest surprises in 1997. New manager Gene Lamont kept the Pirates alive in the NL Central chase until the final week of the season, and they finished second despite a 79-83 record. But Pittsburgh didn't come within 18 games of first during the next three seasons, and Lamont was replaced by Lloyd McClendon.

The Pirates moved into PNC Park in 2001, but it didn't help the team's performance. Despite unheralded stars like Brian Giles and Jason Kendall, the Bucs lost 100 games. They were slightly better in '02 and '03, but with attendance decreasing by nearly 700,000 in the second year at PNC, the team was mentioned as a contraction candidate.

St. Louis Cardinals (aka Brown Stockings, Browns, Perfectos)

The club that is now the Cardinals first fielded a team in 1881, and the next season became a charter member of the American Association, a new major league formed in part to offer fans the beer and Sunday baseball forbidden by the older National League. Chris Von der Ahe, one of the club's founders and its first president, at first saw in baseball simply a source of customers for his St. Louis saloon and beer garden, but he developed a love for the game itself as his Brown Stockings—or Browns—developed into one of the era's greatest teams.

After a losing season in 1882, Von der Ahe hired Ted Sullivan, a noted judge of baseball talent, to manage the Browns. Sullivan brought in third baseman Arlie Latham and pitcher Tony Mullane to strengthen a team that already boasted a fine pitcher in Jumbo McGinnis (25-18 in 1882) and one of the game's premier first baseman in Charlie Comiskey. Although Sullivan quit before the end of his first season because of the continued interference of the volatile Von der Ahe, the Browns finished second in the AA, just a game behind champion Philadelphia.

When Mullane bolted the Browns in 1884, the club slipped to fourth. But help was on the way. In July Von der Ahe purchased the Bay City, Michigan, club to acquire its heavy-hitting pitcher Dave Foutz, and in September added another hitting pitcher, "Parisian Bob" Caruthers, to the roster. In 1885—with Comiskey now the manager, left fielder Tip O'Neill blossoming into one of baseball's best hitters and Caruthers and Foutz winning 40 and 33 games— the Browns rose to the top, 16 games ahead of second-place Cincinnati. They finished on top four years in a row, tying Chicago's White Stockings (3-3-1) in the 1885 World Series and defeating them, four games to two, the next year for the AA's only

Series triumph over their NL rivals.

Pitcher Silver King joined the club in 1887, and outfielder Tommy McCarthy arrived the following year. They helped keep the Browns at the top of the AA through 1888 (although the team lost the World Series both years). But Von der Ahe's sale of Foutz and Caruthers to Brooklyn following the 1887 season boosted Brooklyn to second place in 1888. The next year Brooklyn edged the Browns for the pennant, and the club's first era of greatness was over.

When the AA folded after the 1891 season, the Browns were taken into the NL, but fared poorly there, finishing ninth and then 11th in the divided season of 1892. They rose no higher than ninth in the remaining years of Von der Ahe's ownership, dropping into the cellar (63-1/2 games out) in 1897 and returning to the bottom with a club-worst 111 losses the next season.

New owners Frank and Stanley Robison (who also controlled the Cleveland club) transferred the best Cleveland players and their manager to St. Louis in 1899. Dubbed the Perfectos, the revitalized St. Louis club fell short of perfection, but did rise to a first-division fifth place that year and (now known as the Cardinals) rose to fourth in 1901 before sinking back into the second division for a dozen years.

After Stanley Robison died in 1911 (his brother Frank had died in 1905), the club passed into the possession of Frank's daughter Helene Britton, who ran it behind the scenes until, in 1916, she sold it to a syndicate headed by her attorney James C. Jones. Jones hired Branch Rickey away from the AL St. Louis Browns to run the club.

Rickey took over a team with two chief assets: manager Miller Huggins and a promising young infielder, Rogers Hornsby. Huggins had managed the Cards to third place in 1914, before Hornsby arrived, and, after a pair of losing seasons he brought them up to third again in 1917. Huggins was lost to the New York Yankees the next year, and Rickey left the club temporarily for military service in the Great War. When Rickey returned in 1919, he took over as manager himself. In 1921 and 1922 the team finished third, closer to the leaders than the club had finished since joining the NL in 1891. Led by Hornsby's .397 and .401 batting, the team hit over .300 both seasons.

Sam Breadon increased his investment in the Cardinals until he was majority stockholder and club president in 1920, with Rickey as vice president and general manager. Breadon moved the Cards out of the inadequate wooden Cardinal Park during the 1920 season into the more modern Sportsman's Park, owned by the Browns and built on the site of Von der Ahe's original ground.

Early in the 1925 season, with the Cards in last place, Breadon replaced Rickey as field manager with second baseman Hornsby. The switch worked. In 1925 the Cards rebounded to fourth, and in 1926 they captured their first pennant since the glory days of the old Browns four decades earlier—edging Cincinnati in the final week of the season. The season was made perfect by victory in the World Series over Miller Huggins' Yankees as midseason pickup Grover Cleveland Alexander won Game 6 and saved Game 7 for the Cardinals.

But Breadon and his irascible player-manager had a falling out, and Hornsby was traded that winter to the New York Giants for second baseman Frank Frisch and pitcher Jimmy Ring. The trade enraged fans, but the team finished a close second in 1927, and returned to the top (under new manager Bill McKechnie) in a tight race the following season.

McKechnie, fired after the Yankees swept the Cards in the 1928 World Series and rehired in the midst of a St. Louis slump the next season, left to manage the Boston Braves in 1930. Former catcher

Gabby Street, who replaced him, led the Cards back to the top again for successive pennants in 1930 and 1931, and in 1931 to a World Series victory over the Philadelphia Athletics. The 1930 race saw the club shoot from below .500 in mid-June to 30 games over .500 by season's end, overtaking three other teams to clinch the flag just three games from the finish. The 1931 team ran away with the pennant, leading all the way and finishing 13 games in front. Outfielder Chick Hafey and first baseman Jim Bottomley finished first and third in NL batting, and pitcher Bill Hallahan led the league in strikeouts (for the second year in a row) and tied for the lead in wins, with 19. Four of the league's top five base stealers— led by Frisch and including outfielder Pepper Martin in his first full season—were Cardinals.

When the Cards dropped to sixth place in 1932 and showed little improvement the following year, Breadon replaced manager Street with Frisch. Breadon's move paid immediate dividends. Though the club finished fifth that season, their record improved after Frisch took over, and the next year, in a season-long uphill struggle, the Cards won 13 of their final 15 games to pass the front-running New York Giants in the final week.

Writers labeled the 1934 Cardinals the "Gashouse Gang" for their rowdy and daring play. In addition to team veterans Frisch and Martin (who had been shifted from the outfield to third base), the gang included shortstop Leo Durocher, left fielder Joe "Ducky" Medwick and the team's leading hitter and slugger, first baseman Rip Collins, who in a career-best season led the league in slugging average and tied for first in home runs.

The pitching staff was headed by the league-leading Jerome "Dizzy" Dean (30-7) and his rookie brother Paul (19-11). Of the team's final nine wins, Diz and Paul accounted for seven. Each won another pair in the Cards' World Series triumph over Detroit.

The next two seasons the Cardinals moved into the lead late in the season only to wind up second. After the team slipped into the second division in 1938, Breadon replaced Frisch as manager with Ray Blades, who led a late-season run for the flag in 1939 but finished second. When the Cards failed to contend in 1940, Breadon brought up Rochester manager Billy Southworth for a second time. Southworth had failed as McKechnie's replacement in 1929, but this time he stuck, becoming one of the club's greatest skippers.

Through all these years Rickey was revolutionizing baseball as he built the game's first and most extensive "farm system" of minor league clubs. The Cardinals' farm teams would—until the other major league clubs caught on and caught up—provide St. Louis with a competitive advantage in recruitment and development.

In the closing days of the 1941 season, perhaps that system's greatest product arrived at the big club: Stan Musial. Southworth brought the club in a close second that year after a season-long back-and-forth struggle with Brooklyn. The next year—Musial's first full season—the Cardinals enjoyed their winningest season ever: 106 victories.

They needed them all, too, for Brooklyn won 104 games, leading the race until mid-September, when the Cardinals passed them and held on to a narrow lead by winning 12 of their final 13 games. St. Louis pitchers Mort Cooper and Johnny Beazley finished one-two in National League wins and ERA, while Enos Slaughter and Musial paced the offense. The club maintained its momentum in the World Series, taking the Yankees in five games.

St. Louis retained its preeminence for two more years as baseball gradually lost players to military service in World War II. Slaughter and Beazley were gone by 1943. But Cooper remained to compile

two more 20-plus winning seasons, and Musial was not called until after the 1944 season. With 105 wins in both 1943 and 1944, the Cards ran away with two more pennants, losing to the Yankees in the 1943 World Series, but taking their sixth world title the next year from their St. Louis landlords, the AL champion Browns.

Owner Breadon had fired Rickey in 1942 (objecting to the personal profit Rickey made from selling the club's unneeded farm players) and Southworth left to manage the Boston Braves after the 1945 season. Rickey went on to head the Brooklyn Dodgers, building for them a farm system and tapping the large reservoir of black players. In 1946, the last year of all-white major league ball, the Cards (managed now by Eddie Dyer) and the Dodgers waged a two-team pennant race, ending the season in the first major league tie for first place. St. Louis won the first two games in a best-of-three playoff against Brooklyn and went on to surprise the favored Boston Red Sox in the World Series in seven games.

St. Louis was slow to integrate and the Cards lost ground to teams like Brooklyn, whose black players brought an immediate upswing in the club's success. After the 1947 season Breadon sold the club to Fred Saigh and Robert Hannegan (the U.S. Postmaster General). Musial enjoyed his finest season in 1948, but the club finished second again in a lackluster race. The next year, though, the Cards and Dodgers tangled in a season-long struggle for first place that was not resolved until the season's last day—with Brooklyn on top.

The Cardinals threatened to move to Milwaukee, but beer magnate August Busch, Jr., purchased the club early in 1953 and the same year bought Sportsman's Park from the Browns (who were moving to Baltimore). With Busch's infusion of money and enthusiasm, the club slowly revived. They made runs for the pennant in 1957, 1960, and 1963, but each time tailed off sharply in the final week of the season.

The Cards were playing below .500, in seventh place, in mid-June 1964 when the arrival (via trade with the Cubs) of speedy young Lou Brock sparked a revival of both the team and player. Brock, who had been hitting .251 in Chicago, with 10 stolen bases, hit .348 the rest of the season and stole 33 more bases as the Cards hurtled into the midst of a four-way race for the pennant that was settled in their favor with an 11-5 win on the final day. After surprising the Yankees in seven games in the World Series, the Cardinals were themselves surprised when manager Johnny Keane left to take the helm of the Yankees. The club slipped into the second division for a couple of years under the management of their great former second baseman Red Schoendienst.

Busch built them a striking new stadium in 1966, and the next season the team rebounded to the top again, running away from the field in the last half of the season behind the heavy hitting of Orlando Cepeda, the bat and speed of Brock, and a pitching staff of remarkable breadth and balance. Bob Gibson's three World Series wins over Boston edged the Cards to a ninth world title and set the stage for Gibson's astonishing season the following year.

With his 22 wins leading the Cards to another pennant in 1968, Gibson hurled 13 shutouts and compiled an ERA of just 1.12—both feats the best in more than half a century, both ranking among the top five big league performances ever. After winning two World Series games, Gibson lost Game 7 as Detroit took the crown.

Schoendienst continued as manager through 1976—a club record 12 years—but led the team to no more championships. When divisional play was inaugurated in 1969, geography was ignored as the Cards were installed in the East to add strength to what seemed the weaker division. But it was 14 years before they won their first divisional championship. Four times they finished second, losing twice by only a game and a half in the back-to-back tight races of 1973 and 1974.

In the strike-shortened divided season of 1981, manager Dorrel "Whitey" Herzog's Cards compiled the best overall record in the NL East, but because they had finished the two halves of the season second to Philadelphia and Montreal they were ineligible for postseason play.

With the defensive wizard shortstop Ozzie Smith (acquired from San Diego) and rookie speedster Willie McGee bolstering an already strong team, the Cardinals of 1982 prevailed against the Phillies in the race for the East. St. Louis then swept West champion Atlanta for the pennant and captured their 10th World Series crown in a seven-game struggle with Milwaukee.

After two seasons out of the running, the Cards in 1985 gained the power of veteran Jack Clark (acquired from San Francisco) and the speed of rookie Vince Coleman. With career-best seasons from Willie McGee and newly acquired pitcher John Tudor, the team edged the New York Mets for the division title and defeated Los Angeles for the pennant but lost the World Series in seven games to Kansas City.

Clark missed two-thirds of the 1986 season to injury, and the Cards finished below .500, but they rebounded to edge the Mets again for the championship of the East in 1987 as Clark and Coleman enjoyed their finest seasons at the bat. The reinjured Clark made only a token appearance as the Cards edged San Francisco for the league championship, and he missed the World Series entirely as St. Louis bowed to Minnesota in seven games. That winter Clark signed as a free agent with the Yankees, and, in 1988, the Cardinals dropped to fifth place, 25 games out.

With solid pitching and hitting, and the league's best fielding, the 1989 Cardinals drew within half a game of the division lead on September 8, then fell out of the race with six straight losses, finishing third. As the season drew to a close, long-time owner August Busch, Jr., died at age 90. The next July, with the club uncharacteristically mired at the bottom of the NL East, manager Herzog resigned. Under new manager Joe Torre (a former NL MVP in St. Louis) the Cards revived briefly, but then dropped their final seven games to insure their first basement finish in 72 years.

Reliever Lee Smith provided the key to St. Louis' 1991 rebound to second place: his 47 saves—a NL record—preserved more than half the wins of a team that won 37 games by a single run. Smith saved another 43 games in 1992 and the Cards won nearly as often as they had the previous year, but this time finished third. The defense developed a leak in 1993, and the pitching faltered, but four regulars—Bernard Gilkey, Todd Zeile, and newcomers Gregg Jefferies and Mark Whiten (who became the 12th player to hit four home runs in a game)—scaled new heights offensively to keep the Cardinals competitive through much of the season and give them another third-place finish. In 1994 the team—now playing in the NL's new Central Division—performed below .500 for the first time since 1990.

The weak-hitting Cards slipped to fourth in 1995. Torre was fired as the season wound down and was replaced by interim manager Mike Jorgensen and ultimately by former A's pilot Tony LaRussa. The big news of the year, however, came in December when Anheuser-Busch sold the club for $150 million to an investment group headed by St. Louis banker Andrew Baur and William DeWitt Jr., whose father had once owned the Browns and the Reds.

In 1996, Ozzie Smith's last season, the LaRussa-led Cards (88-

74) outpaced Houston and Cincinnati for the NL Central championship. Aiding St. Louis's effort were Ron Gant (30 HRs, 82 RBIs), Brian Jordan (17 HRs, 104 RBIs), Andy Benes (18-10), and Dennis Eckersley (30 saves). In the first round of the postseason the Cards rolled over San Diego in three straight but in the NLCS ran into the Atlanta buzzsaw. Ahead three games to one, the Cards couldn't put away the pennant as the Braves rolled to 12-1, 3-1, and 15-0 victories in the last three games.

The 1997 and 1998 seasons were disappointing in the standings, but the Cardinals nonetheless became a top drawing card at home and on the road. A 1997 trading deadline deal with Oakland for Mark McGwire was worth its weight in gold. McGwire's combined total of 58 homers in 1997 was the most since Roger Maris broke Babe Ruth's mark with 61 home runs in 1961. In 1998 McGwire obliterated that record. As fans packed the left-field stands across the country just to see McGwire take batting practice, "Big Mac" became the first player to hit 50 home runs in three straight seasons. Before a national television audience, McGwire hit his record-breaking 62nd home run on September 8. He finished with an astounding 70 home runs, beating out Sammy Sosa, who blasted 66 homers for the Cubs.

McGwire followed his epic 1998 season with 65 home runs the next year, and also collected his 500th career blast, but little else went right for the Cardinals. General manager Walt Jocketty made several key moves in the offseason, acquiring Darryl Kile from Colorado and Jim Edmonds from Anaheim. Kile won 20 games and Edmonds hit 40 home runs, marking the first time in history that two acquisitions both reached those plateaus in their first season with a new club. McGwire, however, was lost to regular duty for the second half as a knee injury limited him to a pinch-hitting role. So Jocketty made another key deal by bringing 36-year-old first baseman Will Clark to St. Louis. Clark, who would announce his retirement at the end of the season, batted .345 in 51 games for the division champs. Clark and Edmonds keyed a shocking sweep of the Braves in the Division Series, but St. Louis succumbed to the Mets in five games in the NLCS.

Led by Rookie of the Year Albert Pujols, the Cardinals finished the 2001 season in a tie with Houston for first place. Since both teams qualified for the postseason, no playoff was necessary; Houston was declared divisional champion based on head-to-head record, and St. Louis got the wild-card spot. The Cards gave the eventual-world champion Diamondbacks a fight, but lost, three games to two.

The Cards won the divisional crown by 13 games in 2002, then gained revenge over Arizona with a three-game sweep, before dropping the NLCS to the Giants in just five games. Despite a monster season by Pujols, who led the NL in runs (137), hits (212), doubles (51), total bases (394), and batting (.359), the Cards lost a three-team dogfight for the NL Central in 2003, finishing three games behind the Cubs and two behind the Astros.

San Diego Padres

In their first 15 years the Padres put together only one winning season. In their 16th, they won the National League pennant. Founded in the 1969 expansion that saw the two major leagues divide into East and West divisions, the Padres finished last in the six-team NL West their first six seasons, ending each year from 28-1/2 to 42 games behind the division champion.

Their first season was their worst. With 110 losses, the Padres finished not only 41 games out of first but 29 games out of fifth.

First baseman Nate Colbert, with 24 home runs, provided San Diego's brightest ray of hope. He proved to be one of the Padres' standout performers through their last-place years, and in 1972 became the first Padre to drive in more than 100 runs. Colbert also had the greatest day in club history with five home runs and 13 RBIs in a doubleheader against Atlanta on August 1, 1972.

Big league baseball was not an instant hit in San Diego. Home attendance barely topped half a million in the Padres' first year, and, though it rose a little over the next few seasons, the increase was not enough to make the club viable. Owner C. Arnholt Smith decided early in 1974 to sell the franchise to a buyer who planned to move the team to Washington, D.C. New uniforms had been manufactured and the club's files were packed for the move, when the builder of the McDonald's fast-food empire, longtime baseball fan Ray Kroc, stepped in with an offer to buy the Padres for cash and keep them in San Diego.

Though Kroc's 1974 Padres finished last with the same 60-102 record they had posted the year before, his sense of showmanship drew spectators. Home attendance shot up 76 percent, rising above a million for the first time. The Padres then began to draw fans on their own merits as they finally pulled themselves out of the cellar. Pitcher Randy Jones, who in 1974 had led the league with 22 losses, turned his record around and for two years shone as one of the game's finest pitchers. He halved his 1974 ERA to a league-leading 2.24, winning 20 games as the Padres rose to fourth place in 1975 and posted a winning percentage over .400 for the first time. The next year Jones won a league-high 22 games and earned the Cy Young Award—the first major award to come to a San Diego player.

Outfielder Dave Winfield came up as a rookie in 1973, and the following year became the team RBI leader, a position he held in six of his seven full seasons with the Padres. Reliever Rollie Fingers signed as a free agent. In each of his four seasons in San Diego (1977-1980) he led the team in saves, twice also leading the league. In 1978 the Padres acquired veteran pitcher Gaylord Perry from Texas and installed rookie Ozzie Smith at shortstop. Perry's sparkling 21-6 season gave San Diego its second Cy Young winner, and together with Smith's play in the field, Winfield's bat (.308, 97 RBIs) and Fingers' 37 saves, brought the Padres their first winning season.

All these stars had gone—and owner Kroc had recently died—by the time the Padres recorded a second winning season six years later, and won the division title and NL pennant with a new blend of experience and youth. Sparked by recently acquired veterans Steve Garvey at first, Graig Nettles at third, Goose Gossage in the bullpen, and a bevy of younger stars like batting champ Tony Gwynn and hard-hitting outfielder Kevin McReynolds, the Padres moved into first place to stay in early June. From August 3 to the end of the season, they played only .500 ball but still won the championship of the weak Western Division by 12 games. Underdogs in the National League Championship Series, the Padres lost the first two games in Chicago, but pulled themselves together to take the pennant with three come-from-behind wins at home.

Their decline began with their World Series loss to Detroit. The end of 1985 saw them tied for third, and in 1986 they slipped below .500 and into fourth place. In 1987 Gwynn won his second batting title and rookie catcher Benito Santiago capped the season with a 34-game hitting streak to cop Rookie of the Year honors. But with most of the 1984 standouts faded or traded, the Padres' decline was complete: the club for the ninth time in its 19 years finished last.

In late May 1988, with the team at 16-30, general manager Jack McKeon took over as field manager from Larry Bowa. Under

McKeon the Padres went 67-48, with nine wins in their final 10 games, and shot from sixth place to third in the NL West.

In 1989 a trio of veteran pitchers—starters Bruce Hurst (lured from Boston as a free agent) and Ed Whitson and closer Mark Davis—attained new peaks of performance. Slugger Jack Clark (newly acquired from the Yankees) turned on the power after a slow start to complement Tony Gwynn's fourth season as NL batting leader. The Padres stumbled through the first half, arriving at the All-Star break four games below .500, but climbed steadily through the final two months to a second-place finish with their second-best winning percentage ever.

With the loss of free agent Davis in 1990, plus injuries to Clark and catcher Santiago, even the new power of Joe Carter (acquired from Cleveland) could not lift the club above a tie for fourth. New owners, headed by TV producer Tom Werner, took control of the Padres from Ray Kroc's widow Joan in mid-June. McKeon resigned his managerial position, which went to coach Greg Riddoch a month later, and was fired as general manager in September.

Slugger Fred McGriff arrived for 1991 (in a trade that sent Carter and young Roberto Alomar to Toronto) and helped power the Padres into third place. In 1992 he was joined by Gary Sheffield, who revived after an injury-ridden season at Milwaukee to lead the NL in batting and rank with McGriff among the league leaders in home runs and RBIs. The Padres again finished third, but Sheffield and McGriff were traded away during the 1993 season in cost-cutting moves that, combined with poor team pitching and fielding, dumped the Padres into the NL West cellar, a club record 43 games out of first.

Although the Padres had improved their winning percentage somewhat over 1993 by the time the 1994 season was cut short in August by the strike, their 47-70 record was the worst in the majors. One of San Diego's few reasons to cheer in 1994 was the hitting of Gwynn, whose .394 batting average was the best in the NL since Bill Terry's .401 in 1930.

In December 1994 a group led by Larry Lucchino and John Moores acquired the club. GM Randy Smith resigned in mid-season 1995, but the club rebounded slightly to a third place finish (70-74) as Gwynn (.368) won his sixth batting title.

The 1996 Padres (91-71) surprised virtually everyone by catching the Dodgers and capturing the NL West title on the last day of the season. Standout Padres included Gwynn (with a league-leading .353 average), NL MVP Ken Caminiti (40 HRs, 130 RBIs), Steve Finley (30 HRs, 95 RBIs), Rickey Henderson (37 stolen bases), and Trevor Hoffman (42 saves). Their Cinderella season, however, came to an end in the first round of the postseason as they lost in three straight to St. Louis.

Other than Gwynn winning his eighth batting crown (tying Honus Wagner for the most in NL history), the 1997 season was a disappointment in San Diego. The Padres rebounded for a franchise-best 98 wins in 1998. New acquisition Kevin Brown anchored the rotation (18-7, 2.38 ERA, 257 strikeouts), Trevor Hoffman shattered the Padres record with 53 saves, and Greg Vaughn exploded for a club-record 50 home runs. The Padres surprised the favored Astros in the Division Series and then won the pennant in six games against Atlanta. They were tied or held a lead late in three of the four World Series games, but they could not stop the Yankees' march to a sweep. The Padres' biggest victory of the year, however, came on November 3, when voters approved a new stadium. PETCO Park was slated to open in 2004.

Much as the Padres quickly sank in the standings after their 1984 pennant, San Diego plummeted again after the 1998 National League championship. The team finished last or next-to-last in each of the next five seasons, never reaching .500 and at last dipping below .400 in 2003. Gwynn retired after the 2001 season, having collected 3,141 hits for the Padres.

San Francisco Giants (aka New York Gothams, New York Giants)

The expulsion of Troy and Worcester from the National League after the 1882 season cleared the way for the league to reestablish clubs in the major markets of Philadelphia and New York. Manufacturer John B. Day was awarded the New York franchise. Purchasing the defunct Troy club, he divided their players between the new NL Gothams and his other club, the Metropolitans of the American Association, and set them up on adjoining grounds north of Central Park, on a field once used for polo.

The Mets fared better than the Gothams, finishing fourth in 1883 to the Gothams' sixth, and winning the AA pennant the next year while the Gothams rose only to fifth in the NL. Since the NL, with greater prestige and higher ticket prices, offered potentially greater profit, Day switched some of his Mets to the Gothams in 1885, including ace hurler Tim Keefe and manager Jim Mutrie. The results were immediate: the Mets sank to seventh place while the Gothams (dubbed "my Giants" by an enthusiastic Mutrie) rose to the thick of a pennant race with Chicago. At the finish Chicago was on top by two games, but the Giants had won more than three games out of four for a .759 winning percentage that is not only the club's best ever, but one of the highest in major league history. Pitchers Keefe and Mickey Welch together won 76 of the team's 85 victories, and first baseman Roger Connor led the league in batting.

The Giants won their first pennant in 1888 and their second the next year in a one-game squeaker over Boston. Keefe and Welch, still going strong, combined for 61 wins in '88 and 55 in '89. Continuing their winning ways in the World Series, the Giants triumphed easily over St. Louis in 1888 and overcame a three-games-to-one deficit to vanquish Brooklyn the next year.

In 1890, ravaged by the loss of players to the rival Players League, the Giants finished sixth, but they recovered several players when the PL folded at the end of the season. (They also moved into the PL ballpark, named it after their original Polo Grounds, and played there for 67 years). They rose to third in 1891, but Day could no longer afford to maintain the team and sold out to financier Edward Talcott. Talcott brought back former Giants star John M. Ward to manage the club and in 1894 saw the team rise to a close second-place finish behind Baltimore. Pitchers Amos Rusie and Jouett Meekin tied for the league lead with 36 wins apiece. In postseason Temple Cup play, the Giants swept Baltimore in four games for their third world championship.

That winter Talcott sold control of the club to Tammany Hall politician Andrew Freedman. The club's fortunes sank under Freedman's abrasive and heavy-handed rule. In 1902, his final year of ownership, the Giants suffered their lowest winning percentage—.353—and most distant finish ever—53-1/2 games behind champion Pittsburgh.

In the midst of the 1902 season, though, a skirmish in the war between the NL and the upstart American League led to a Giants turnaround. John T. Brush, owner of the NL Cincinnati Reds, bought the AL Baltimore Orioles, then released Orioles manager John McGraw and several key players to sign with NL clubs. Five joined the Giants, including McGraw, catcher Roger Bresnahan,

and pitcher Joe "Iron Man" McGinnity. That winter, Brush sold the Reds and Orioles and bought the Giants.

In 1903, with Bresnahan hitting .350 and McGinnity winning a league-high 31 games (closely followed by third-year phenom Christy Mathewson's 30 wins), manager McGraw saw his Giants win 36 more games than they had in 1902 and finish a solid second in the standings. In McGraw's 29 full seasons at the helm, the team won 10 pennants and finished second 11 times.

Just two years after their worst season ever, McGraw in 1904 led the Giants to one of their best. Their 106 wins and 13-game winning margin remain franchise records. The club led the NL in pitching, hitting, fielding, and base stealing. McGinnity led league pitchers in several categories with a career-best 35-8, 1.61 ERA season. Mathewson, right behind with 33 wins, led the league in strikeouts.

The only disappointment of 1904 was McGraw's refusal to face Boston in a World Series. His rejection of the AL champions as worthy opponents was the last shot fired in a war between the two leagues. By the time the Giants had repeated as NL pennant winners a year later, the World Series was an official and permanent feature of the baseball landscape.

Mathewson led NL pitchers in 1905 with 31 wins and an ERA of 1.27, and outfielder "Turkey Mike" Donlin, acquired from Cincinnati the previous July, erupted with the best season of his career, batting a team-high .356 and scoring a league-high 124 runs. The Giants won only one game less than the year before and held a comfortable lead throughout the season. Matty's three shutouts against the Philadelphia Athletics in the World Series secured the club's fourth world crown.

It was 1911 before the Giants won their next pennant. Despite 96 wins in 1906 they finished a distant second to the Chicago Cubs, who won a record 116 games. In 1908 the Giants came within a disputed play of the pennant. On September 23, playing Chicago (with whom they were tied at the top of a three-way race), Giants baserunner Fred Merkle failed to run to second on a single by Al Bridwell that would have driven in the winning run from third. Merkle was forced at second after the ball (or a second ball—the argument still rages) was recovered amid the horde of fans who overran the field. The force-out at second negated the run, and the game was ruled a tie. At season's end, when the two clubs found themselves again tied at the top, the "Merkle boner" game was replayed. The Cubs won the game and the flag, leaving the Giants in a second-place tie with Pittsburgh.

In 1911 the Giants pulled away from the Cubs in September for the first of three straight pennants. (Early in the season most of the Polo Grounds was rebuilt in concrete after fire destroyed the wooden stands.) The following year the Giants took the lead in May and held it comfortably the rest of the way. In 1913 they didn't move into first until late June, but then they quickly put the flag out of reach and finished 12-1/2 games ahead of the faltering Phillies. Mathewson led the team in victories over the three years, with 74, followed closely by Rube Marquard, who enjoyed the three best seasons of his career with 73 wins. Matty led the NL in ERA in 1911 and 1913, and rookie Jeff Tesreau took the honors in 1912 (winning 17 games that season and 22 the next). Giants pitching led the league all three seasons, as did their hitting, which featured a balanced offense paced by infielders Larry Doyle and Art Fletcher and catcher John "Chief" Myers.

In the World Series, though, the Giants fell short of the title three times. The Philadelphia Athletics defeated them handily in 1911 and 1913, but the Giants carried the 1912 Series against the Boston Red Sox to the 10th inning of the final game before a pair of fielding lapses by the Giants enabled Boston to rally for the win.

Boston's "Miracle" Braves, in their 1914 surge from last place to the pennant, passed the front-running Giants for good in early September. The next year, five of the eight NL clubs found themselves bunched within three and a half games of one another at the lower end of the standings as the season ended—with the Giants at the very bottom. The 1916 season was characterized by dips and surges, but even a 26-game winning streak in September couldn't raise the team higher than fourth. In 1917 a balanced pitching staff—paced by Ferdie Schupp's one big season (21-7, 1.95 ERA)—hurled the Giants to the front early in June and kept them there to the finish. Once more, though, the World Series proved to be a disappointment, with a loss to the Chicago White Sox in six games.

Three years of second-place finishes followed, in the midst of which the Giants changed owners. Brush had died in 1912 and was succeeded as president by his son-in-law Harry Hempstead. But in January 1919 Brush's heirs sold the club to financier and racehorse fancier Charles A. Stoneham, with manager McGraw becoming a minority stockholder.

In 1921 McGraw brought home the first of four straight winners for Stoneham. Seven regulars hit over .300 (led by third baseman Frank Frisch's .341); first baseman George Kelly's 23 home runs topped the NL. The club hung close to Pittsburgh through August, then broke into a lead which the fading Pirates could not challenge. In postseason play the Giants lost the first two games to the Yankees, but charged back to win their fifth world title. The next year outfielder Emil "Irish" Meusel celebrated his first full season in New York with a team-high 132 RBIs, as the Giants fended off a mid-season challenge from St. Louis to pull away to a comfortable margin at the end. The World Series was especially sweet: a four-game sweep of the Yankees (another game ended in a tie).

Cincinnati and Pittsburgh hung just behind the Giants through much of 1923, but never quite caught up. The Giants' league-leading offense was led by individual NL highs in RBIs (Meusel), runs scored (outfielder Ross Youngs), and hits and total bases (Frisch). But the Yankees finally caught the Giants in the World Series, 4-2.

George Kelly took the NL RBI title in 1924. The club's hitting remained the league's best, and by early August the Giants had taken a 10-game lead. But they then leveled off while Brooklyn and Pittsburgh surged. Brooklyn, in fact, took over the lead for a day in early September, but the Giants emerged triumphant at the end by 1-1/2 games. The World Series, though, was as heartbreaking as the pennant race had been heartstopping: the Giants lost to Washington in the last of the 12th inning of the seventh game when a grounder bounced over the head of Giants rookie third baseman Fred Lindstrom to drive in the Series-ending run.

Close finishes in 1927 and 1928 were the nearest McGraw's Giants came to another pennant. Ill and tired, he quit early in the 1932 season with the team in last place, naming first baseman Bill Terry to replace him. Under Terry the Giants rose only to sixth that season, but McGraw had built a squad fit for a new era of greatness. He had persuaded Terry to leave a career with Standard Oil for one with the Giants; he had saved Mel Ott's unique but effective batting stance from revision by well-meaning minor league managers by keeping Ott out of the minors; and he had rescued pitcher Carl Hubbell from mediocrity by encouraging the screwball pitch other managers had tried to suppress in the minors.

Hubbell and Ott formed the heart of the club that would win a

trio of pennants under Terry's management. In 1933 the Giants moved to the front in June and, despite a late-September slump, finished well ahead of runner-up Pittsburgh. Ott, with what was for him an off-year, powered the offense with 23 homers and 103 RBIs, while Hubbell led the league in wins, shutouts and ERA. Hubbell also hurled two wins against Washington in the World Series, and Ott won it all for New York with a 10th-inning home run in Game 5. McGraw, still the club's vice president, threw a party for "his" Giants after the Series. The following February he died, at age 60.

As they had the previous season, the Giants of 1934 emerged from the crowd to take and hold first place into late September. They rose higher than they had in 1933 and didn't slump as far at the end. But their five end-of-season losses were enough to drop them two games behind the surging Cardinals at the finish. Again in 1935 they led the league much of the season. But they had begun to level off in mid-July and finished the season well back in third. Charles Stoneham died in January 1936, and his son Horace—who at age 33 had already run the club for a year— assumed the club presidency.

In 1936, and again in 1937, the Giants came from behind to take the flag. Hubbell sparked their second-half resurgence in 1936, winning his final 16 decisions of the season as the Giants rose from fourth to first. In the World Series, though, Hubbell, after one win, was stopped by the Yankees in his try for a second. The Yankees took the Series in six games.

Again the next year the Giants hid behind the leaders most of the season until a surge in late August coincided with a Chicago decline and shot the Giants to the front. The Cubs recovered, but New York continued its winning ways and finished ahead by three games. But again the Yankees dominated the World Series, winning in five games.

Hubbell's years of greatness were now over, and while the Giants led the NL through the first half of 1938, they finished five games out in third place. It would be 12 years before they again finished that close to the top. Ott replaced Terry as manager in 1942, but the Giants sank to the cellar in 1943 with their second-worst season ever, and finished last again three years later.

Halfway through the 1948 season the baseball world was startled to learn that Leo Durocher, the fiery manager of the Brooklyn Dodgers, had switched his allegiance to their arch foes, the Giants. Durocher discarded the club's top three home-run hitters of 1947 and added agile infielders Alvin Dark and Eddie Stanky to the roster. By 1950, with the blossoming of Sal Maglie into a first-rank pitcher and the timely midseason purchase of hurler Jim Hearn, the Giants were once more a challenger, spurting in the second half from below .500 to within five games of the top.

After losing their first 11 games the next year, the Giants began a long climb. A sixteen-game August winning streak and a seven-game streak at season's end tied them with Brooklyn and forced a three-game playoff. After a win and a loss, the Giants entered the last of the ninth inning of Game 3 trailing by a 4-1 score. Two singles and a double cut the deficit by a run and brought on Ralph Branca to face Bobby Thomson. Thomson homered to left and the Giants won the pennant. Their defeat by the Yankees in the World Series dimmed the miracle a bit, but it couldn't detract from the career bests of pitchers Maglie and Larry Jansen, who tied for the NL lead with 23 wins apiece, and of former Negro League great Monte Irvin, who hit .312 and led the league in RBIs.

The next year Irvin was lost until August with a broken ankle, Jansen (with a back problem) fell off to 11-11, and Willie Mays—

a promising rookie in 1951—left early in the season for a hitch in the Army. Still, the Giants hung close to Brooklyn for much of the summer and finished second. In 1953, though, they fell apart in midseason and wound up in fifth, 35 games out.

Mays returned in 1954 to enjoy one of his strongest seasons, and pitchers Johnny Antonelli (newly acquired from Milwaukee), sophomore Ruben Gomez, and reliever Marv Grissom all burst forth with the best seasons of their careers. The Giants pulled away from Brooklyn in July and held on with a late-season rush to win by five games. Underdogs to powerful Cleveland in the World Series, they stunned the Indians (and the rest of the baseball world) with a four-game sweep. It was their eighth world title—and, so far, their last.

Manager Durocher retired after a distant third-place finish in 1955, and Bill Rigney, who replaced him (the first of seven straight rookie managers to be hired by the Giants over the next 20 years), presided over a pair of sixth-place seasons in the club's final years in New York. Persuaded by the Dodgers' Walter O'Malley that California was the land of baseball opportunity, Giants owner Stoneham announced in August 1957 his decision to move the club to San Francisco before the next season.

The move succeeded. Home attendance doubled, even though the team had to play in a former minor league park that seated fewer than 23,000 fans. When new Candlestick Park opened in 1960 attendance climbed to nearly 1.8 million, a new club high. Better still, rookie sensations like Orlando Cepeda in 1958 and Willie McCovey in 1959, plus the continuing mastery of Willie Mays, made the Giants competitive once again. In their first 14 San Francisco seasons, they compiled winning records—a longer string than they had ever known in New York.

Candlestick Park, though, proved a cold and windy place to watch baseball, and after its inaugural season fans began to drift away. Attendance picked up some in 1962, however, as the Giants battled for first all summer with the Los Angeles Dodgers. Mays, Cepeda and Felipe Alou headlined the league's best offense, and a pair of veteran pitchers—Jack Sanford and Billy O'Dell—garnered the most wins of their careers (24 and 19, respectively) as part of a balanced staff that also got 16 wins from veteran Billy Pierce and 18 from the emerging great Juan Marichal. Still, the Giants trailed the Dodgers most of the season until the Giants won and the Dodgers lost on the final day to force another playoff. As in 1951, the Giants won the first game and lost the second, and overcame a ninth-inning deficit in the finale to win the pennant. Also as in 1951, they lost the World Series to the Yankees, although this time they held on until the final out of Game 7 before losing their grip on the crown.

The 1963 Giants offered little challenge to the leaders after June, but the next three years found them locked to the end in tight struggles for the flag. Although they finished fourth in 1964, they were still in contention with just two games to play, in one of the closest four-way races ever. The next year they took the lead from the Dodgers early in September, only to lose it in the final week. And in 1966, in a season-long three-way race with the Dodgers and Pirates, the Giants weren't eliminated until the final day.

The turbulence of these races was reflected in the team itself. Cepeda (until traded to St. Louis in 1966) continually railed against his managers and his low pay. Alvin Dark, after four winning seasons as manager, was fired in 1964 when some of his racist comments ended up in print. And Marichal was fined and suspended for nine days in 1965 for hitting Dodgers catcher John Roseboro over the head with his bat.

After a pair of distant second-place finishes, the Giants in 1969

(with the fine work of Marichal and McCovey augmented by the speed and power of young outfielder Bobby Bonds) found themselves in the thick of a five-way race for the championship of the newly created NL West. The race wasn't settled until the final week, when Atlanta's 10-game winning streak knocked the Giants out of first. Two years later, with Bonds the chief source of offensive power and fine pitching from starters Marichal and Gaylord Perry and reliever Jerry Johnson, the Giants moved out in front at the start of the season and held their lead all the way. In the National League Championship Series, though, they succumbed to Pittsburgh with three losses after an opening-game win.

The NLCS loss signaled the end of an era. McCovey was past his prime and Marichal had enjoyed his last big year. Mays, after 20 seasons as a Giant, was sent to the Mets in 1972 so he could close out his career in New York, where it had begun. That year the Giants suffered their first losing season in San Francisco, and attendance for the first time dropped below what it had been in their final New York season.

Attendance had reached such a low point by the mid1970s that Stoneham negotiated the club's sale to a Canadian brewery which planned to move it to Toronto. But San Francisco's mayor George Moscone delayed the sale until a buyer could be found who would keep the Giants in the city. San Francisco realtor Robert Lurie stepped forth with half the purchase price, and Arizona cattleman Arthur "Bud" Herseth provided the rest. (Toronto settled for an expansion club, the Blue Jays.)

After six years out of the running, the Giants in 1978 played at the top of the NL West through much of the summer before dropping to third (and home attendance jumped more than a million above the previous year). But they fell below .500 the next two years—making seven losing seasons in the nine that followed their division title of 1971.

In 1982 the Giants—paced by the slugging of Jack Clark and Greg Minton's sparkling relief pitching—made one of the most impressive comebacks since divisional play was instituted in 1969, driving from 10 games below .500 to within two games of champion Atlanta at season's end. But they dropped to fifth the following year, and to a last-place sixth in 1984 and 1985.

When Roger Craig was called on to manage the final weeks of the 1985 season, there was no stopping the Giants' slide to a club-record 100 losses. But the next year, inspiring a "can-do" spirit among the players, Craig turned the club around. Veteran hurler Mike Krukow won a career-high 20 games, eight players contributed more than 40 RBIs each, and the team captured 26 of their 83 wins in their final at bat. In first place at midseason, the Giants slipped (in part because of injuries) to third by season's end, but the fans were back—over 700,000 more than a year earlier.

The club set a new home attendance record of more than 1.9 million in 1987 as it returned to the top of the NL West for the first time in 16 years. Sophomore first baseman Will Clark led a balanced offense, and several shrewd in-season acquisitions by the front office spurred a second-half drive from five games back to a six-game lead at the finish. But after taking a three-games-to-two advantage over St. Louis in the NLCS, the Giants failed to score in the final two games and the Cardinals captured the flag.

Injuries contributed to the Giants' decline to fourth place the next year, but in 1989 Clark enjoyed his strongest season yet, and left fielder Kevin Mitchell erupted with league-high power, pacing the NL in homers (47), RBIs (125), and slugging percentage (.635) to lead a San Francisco assault on the division title. For the first

time, the Giants passed the 2-million mark in home attendance. After holding first place from mid-June to the finish, they pushed past the stubborn Cubs in the NLCS to win the first Giants pennant in 27 years and the 19th in franchise history. But the earthquake that delayed Game 3 of the World Series only postponed a sweep by mighty Oakland.

The Giants' downward slide over the next three years—to third place in 1990, fourth in 1991, and fifth in 1992—coincided with futile efforts to persuade Bay area voters to approve public funding for a new stadium to replace unpopular Candlestick Park. In August 1992, owner Bob Lurie arranged to sell the club to a group of investors who planned to move it to St. Petersburg, Florida. In November, though, the sale and move were blocked by the other major league owners.

The signing of free agent Barry Bonds ignited a turnaround in 1993. As Bonds put together another Ruthian season, and Matt Williams rebounded from his worst season to his best, starting pitchers John Burkett and Bill Swift developed into 20-game winners and closer Rod Beck saved the second most games (48) in NL history. The Giants lost their once-big lead to surging Atlanta in September, but revived to tie the Braves with three games to go. Although a final-game loss to Los Angeles cost them the division title, their 103 wins tied for third best in club history.

On August 11, 1994, the Giants stood five games below .500, but only 3-1/2 games out of first place in the weak NL West. Bonds was enjoying another fine season at the bat, but Williams' 43 home runs (within legitimate striking distance of Roger Maris' record of 61) stole the headlines. When the players went out on strike the next day, one of the most exciting offensive seasons ever went down the drain.

In 1995 manager Dusty Baker's Giants fell to last (67-77) despite Bonds' 33 homers and 104 RBIs. The Giants (68-94) remained in the NL basement in 1996 as Bonds (.308, 42 HRs, 129 RBIs) again compiled superstar numbers.

The Giants were transformed from "worst to first" in 1997. The additions of second baseman Jeff Kent (28 HRs, 118 RBIs) and three pitchers from the White Sox (Wilson Alvarez, Roberto Hernandez and Danny Darwin) plus the emergence of starter Shawn Estes (19-5, 3.48 ERA) helped push the Giants to the division title. The eventual world champion Florida Marlins beat the Giants twice in their last at bat on the way to a sweep in the Division Series. In 1998 the Giants put together a 10-game winning streak in the final week of the season to come from four games behind to tie the Cubs and force a one-game playoff for the NL Wild Card. Despite a late rally by the Giants in the playoff game, the Cubs held on to win at Wrigley Field.

The 1999 season, the club's last at Candlestick, yielded 86 wins yet left the team a distant second to division champ Arizona. The franchise finished the 20th century with the most wins of any National League team. The new century brought a new ballpark and success.

The club christened beautiful Pacific Bell Park and sold out every game. After winning just once in the park's first month, the Giants were unstoppable at home and finished the season with the best record of any team in baseball. Bonds hit 49 home runs and scored 129 times, while Kent drove in 125 and won the MVP Award; Ellis Burks battled through injuries to bat .344. San Francisco's starting staff was good, but its bullpen was even better with Felix Rodriguez and Robb Nen providing one of baseball's best setup-closer tandems. The Giants won the division by 11 games over Los Angeles. Game 1 of the Division Series was San

Francisco's first postseason win in 11 years, but the Mets won the next three to bring an abrupt end to the season.

The story of the 2001 season was Bonds. From the beginning of the campaign, though he got few pitches to hit, Bonds was hitting homers at a record pace. He cracked Number 500 in April, and passed Mel Ott, Eddie Mathews, Ernie Banks, Ted Williams, and Willie McCovey on the all-time list over the next two months. Bonds hit nine home runs in six games in May, and had 39 by the All-Star break, another record. He continued to move up the all-time ladder, passing Jimmie Foxx, Mickey Mantle, Mike Schmidt, and Reggie Jackson in the second half. By the end of the season Bonds had amassed 73 homers, breaking Mark McGwire's three-year-old record. Bonds also established new single-season marks for walks (177) and slugging percentage (.863). However, it wasn't enough to lift the Giants above second place; they finished two games behind the Diamondbacks.

Bonds was just as good in 2002. He broke his own record for walks (198) and set new marks for intentional passes (68) and on-base percentage (.582). His home-run total dropped to 46, but he batted a whopping .370 to lead the league, and also topped it with a .799 slugging percentage. Though the Giants again finished second, this time they earned the league's wild-card spot, and made it pay off. Bonds, shaking his past postseason failures, shined as the Giants knocked off the Braves, three games to two, and the Cardinals, four games to one. After winning three of the first five World Series games against Anaheim, and taking a 5-0 lead in Game 6, the Giants were eight outs away from a world championship. But, in a stunning reversal, they blew the lead, losing 6-5, then lost Game 7 the next day.

After ten years, Baker left San Francisco and joined the Cubs for the 2003 season; Felipe Alou took over the Giants. Despite missing part of the season while attending to his dying father, Bonds rung up his third straight MVP campaign in 2003, leading San Francisco to 100 wins and the division title. But after the Giants won the first game of the NLDS, the Marlins shocked them with three straight wins on their way to the world championship.

Seattle Mariners

The Mariners began play in 1977, returning major league baseball to the Pacific Northwest eight years after the Seattle Pilots had moved to Milwaukee after only one season. With a 64-98 inaugural season, the Mariners avoided last place in the American League West only because the Oakland A's had plummeted faster and farther. The hitting of first baseman Dan Meyer, outfielder Leroy Stanton and rookie center fielder Ruppert Jones—who combined for 73 home runs—and the relief pitching of rookie Enrique Romo, who contributed 16 saves and eight wins, provided most of the highpoints of that first season.

There was less to cheer about the next year as the production of the first-season heroes fell off and the Mariners took early possession of the cellar and lost a club-record 104 games. They finished 12 games out of sixth place, 35 out of first. Much of the offense that was generated came from outfielder Leon Roberts. Acquired from Houston over the winter, Roberts became the Mariners' first .300 hitter.

The club moved up a notch in 1979, to sixth place (and Seattle also hosted that year's All-Star Game). Meyer and Jones regained much of their earlier power, first baseman Bruce Bochte hit .316 and drove in 100 runs, and DH Willie Horton, near the end of a long career, enjoyed one of his finest seasons, driving in 106 runs

and leading the club with 29 homers.

As the Mariners, with the league's weakest hitting, dropped back into the cellar the next season, attendance fell to a new low, and some of the original owners decided to sell out. In January 1981 California real-estate magnate George Argyros purchased control of the club, and later bought out the remaining partners to take sole ownership.

Pitching finally arrived in 1982 in the form of Bill Caudill and rookie Ed Vande Berg. The pair, working in relief, combined for 21 wins and 31 saves. Starter Floyd Bannister led the league in strikeouts while winning 12 games (tying Caudill for the team lead), and veteran Gaylord Perry added 10 victories, including his 300th career win in May. The team finished above .450 for the first time, fourth in the AL West, a new high.

Caudill's 26 saves in 1983 couldn't prevent a slide back into last place. But the club's farm system was beginning to produce quality talent, and 1984 saw the arrival of two standouts: first baseman Alvin Davis, whose 27 homers and 116 RBIs earned him AL Rookie of the Year honors, and pitcher Mark Langston, a 17-game winner in 1984 and AL strikeout leader in three of his first four seasons. Rookie third baseman Jim Presley hit 10 home runs in 70 games and proceeded to blossom into one of the club's leading power hitters the next year.

After sixth-place finishes in 1984 and '85, the Mariners fell off to last again in 1986. Langston's 19 wins led the team's 1987 rebound to fourth. Infielder Harold Reynolds stole his 60th base in the final game to give the Mariners their first league leader in an offensive category.

After dropping back into the cellar in 1988 and rising a notch to sixth in 1989, the Mariners revived under new ownership in 1990 to challenge the .500 barrier. Center fielder Ken Griffey, Jr. began to fulfill the promise he had shown as a 19-year-old rookie the previous summer. Sophomore hurler Erik Hanson—with 18 wins and an ERA among the league's best—replaced the traded Mark Langston as ace of a young pitching staff that compiled the league's third lowest ERA. The Mariners entered August third in the strong AL West, with a winning record that they maintained through mid-month before stumbling to fifth place with their 14th straight losing season.

At last, in 1991, Seattle produced its first winning season, rising from an even .500 with six wins in the final eight games. Griffey overcame a lackluster first half to reach new Mariner heights in batting (.327) and slugging (.527), but the club still finished fifth, and manager Jim Lefebvre was fired. It also continued to lose money, so in June 1992, as the Mariners sailed for the sixth time to the bottom of the AL West, the club was sold. The new ownership group included (for the first time) substantial local representation, but as major financing came from Hiroshi Yamauchi, the Japanese president of computer-game giant Nintendo, and his son-in-law, a Washington State resident but Japanese national, the sale was delayed until jingoistic opposition to it subsided—and the deal was restructured to insure American control of the club. On the field Griffey enjoyed another strong season, and third baseman Edgar Martinez hit .343 to give Seattle its first league batting champion.

A torn hamstring sidelined Martinez much of 1993, but Griffey shone brighter than ever at the bat, and pitcher Randy Johnson finished with nine straight wins (for a 19-8 season record) and 308 strikeouts (a 15-year AL high). Their exploits lifted the Mariners into third place for a day in late September before they settled into fourth, with their second winning season ever.

In 1994 the Mariners again enjoyed stellar performances from Griffey and Johnson, but despite six straight wins before the season ended in August, they wound up 14 games below .500. In the weak AL West, though, their mini-streak brought them within two games of division leader Texas—and a third-place finish, their highest ever.

After a long climb during the 1995 season, the Mariners (paced by Edgar Martinez's league-leading .356 average and Randy Johnson's league-leading 294 strikeouts and 2.48 ERA) caught the Angels in the AL West division race and forced a one-game playoff. Behind Johnson, Seattle took the game and went on to nip the New York Yankees in the first round of the postseason in one of the most exciting series in baseball history. But in the ALCS the powerhouse Indians proved too much for Seattle, defeating them in six games.

Injuries to Johnson and Martinez hampered the 1996 Mariners and they slipped to second (85-76) despite shortstop Alex Rodriguez's major league-best .358 average and 54 doubles. In 1997 the Mariners survived a rocky bullpen to stave off the Angels for the AL West title. Griffey earned AL MVP honors and led the league with 56 home runs, 147 RBIs, 125 runs, .646 slugging, and 393 total bases. Attendance, which had topped 1 million just twice in the team's first eight seasons, reached 3 million in 1997. The Mariners faltered in the Division Series, however, falling to the Orioles in four games.

Poor pitching buried the Mariners early in 1998 and not even another 56 home runs from Griffey could save the Mariners from a distant third-place finish. The club moved into its new ballpark in midseason 1999, and the pitchers learned it was to their liking. Rookie Freddy Garcia won 17 games and Jamie Moyer added 14. Griffey learned, however, that he did not like spacious Safeco Field and asked to be traded at season's end. Griffey, with the power to veto any trade, left new general manager Pat Gillick little choice but to send him to Cincinnati.

Free-agent first baseman John Olerud and new center fielder Mike Cameron anchored the defense, and the pitching continued to blossom in 2000. American League Rookie of the Year Kazuhiro Sasaki brought stability to a traditionally porous bullpen, and free agent Aaron Sele won 17 games. The Mariners had the league's best home record, yet the AL's worst home batting average. Alex Rodriguez and Edgar Martinez combined for 79 home runs and drove in 277 runs, including a league-best 145 RBIs by Martinez. The M's clinched a wild-card berth on the final day of the season and shocked the White Sox with a three-game sweep in the Division Series. Seattle blanked the Yankees for the first 16 innings of the ALCS, but then New York rallied to take the series in six games.

After the season, Rodriguez left the team as a free agent, signing a $252 million deal with the Texas Rangers. Fans wondered how a team could lose three future Hall of Famers in three years and still compete. But the 2001 Mariners not only competed, they enjoyed a record-setting season: an astonishing 116-46 record, breaking the AL record for wins set by the 1998 Yankees, and matching the major league mark set by the 1906 Cubs.

A big reason for Seattle's success was a 27-year-old rookie. After nine seasons as a superstar in the Japanese Pacific League, Ichiro Suzuki came to America and signed with the Mariners. Dispelling doubts that he could adapt to the U.S. majors, Suzuki led the AL in hits (242), stolen bases (56) and batting (.350); won the Gold Glove; and became only the second man to earn Rookie of the Year and MVP honors in the same season. With Bret Boone also having a huge year, the M's won the AL West handily, then squeaked past the Indians in the ALDS. But the Yankees put an end to a glorious season, beating Seattle in five games in the ALCS.

The Mariners came back to earth after that, dropping to 93 wins in each of the next two seasons, good for finishes of only third and second. After the 2002 season, Piniella was released so he could take the helm of the Tampa Bay Devil Rays, and Bob Melvin took over the M's.

Tampa Bay Devil Rays

Along with the Arizona Diamondbacks, the Tampa Bay Devil Rays were granted a $130 million major league expansion franchise on March 9, 1995. The Devil Rays played their first game at the newly renovated (and renamed) Tropicana Field in St. Petersburg on March 31, 1998. The first pitch in franchise history, by Wilson Alvarez, was a long time in coming to finally bring baseball to the Tampa area.

The White Sox had planned to move to St. Petersburg in the late 1980s and only remained in the Windy City when funding was approved for a new Comiskey Park. The Mariners had considered moving to St. Petersburg in 1991. And in late 1992 a Tampa Bay group led by businessman Vince Naimoli thought it had purchased the San Francisco Giants from Bob Lurie for $115 million, but NL owners voted against moving the club from one Bay Area to another. Naimoli was eventually awarded the Devil Rays franchise and he named Chuck LaMar as the club's first general manager. Shortly after the Florida Marlins won the 1997 World Series, Tampa Bay scooped up Marlins pitching coach Larry Rothschild and made him the team's first manager.

Rookie Rolando Arrojo, the team's first All-Star, won 14 games to break the single-season expansion record. By contrast, the rest of the starters won just 25 games between them. There were plenty of whiffs at Tropicana Field: Tampa Bay pitchers fanned 1,003 batters and their hitters struck out 1,101 times. Highlights of their first season included Tampa native Wade Boggs hitting the first home run in club history; Quinton McCracken setting the expansion record for hits and outfield assists; and the Devil Rays becoming the first expansion team to be four wins over .500 in their first season at 10-6. Their fast start was all that kept the Devil Rays from hitting the century mark in losses as the team finished its inaugural season with the AL's worst record at 63-99.

After three years the Devil Rays had still not reached 100 losses in a season, but they had not escaped the cellar either. Tampa Bay had difficulty drawing crowds and even more trouble earning wins. The 1999 team won just 33 of 81 games at Tropicana Field. Their highlights were memorable but brief: Wade Boggs achieved his 3,000th hit, becoming the first to do so with a home run; Jim Morris, 35, made the impressive jump from high-school teacher to major league pitcher in one year; Jose Canseco hit 32 home runs in half a season before having back surgery; and Roberto Hernandez won or saved 45 games—unfortunately the team won just 24 other times.

In 2000 they avoided the league's worst record by going 8-2 to close out the season, including their first-ever sweep of the Yankees. It was hardly the season that the team had envisioned, however. The Devil Rays had fashioned a powerful new look: acquisitions Greg Vaughn and Vinny Castilla, plus holdovers Fred McGriff and Jose Canseco. Vaughn battled through injuries to hit 28 home runs, one more than Fred McGriff, who hit his 400th career homer during the season. Castilla, however, hit just six homers and Canseco homered nine times before the club placed him on waivers.

Things only got worse for Tampa Bay. The team lost 100 games in 2001 and 106 in '02, as attendance dropped from 2.5 million in

their debut season to barely over a million in '02. In 2001 Rothschild was replaced by Hal McRae, who in turn gave way to Lou Piniella after the 2002 season.

Piniella brought a fiery personality and an impressive résumé, but his results in Tampa Bay were little better than those of his predecessors. The D-Rays barely avoided another 100-loss season, finishing 63-99 in 2003. Giving some hope for the future were exciting 21-year-old rookie Rocco Baldelli, who batted .289 and excelled in center field, and the development of 26-year-old right fielder Aubrey Huff (34, 107, .311) into a star.

Texas Rangers (aka Washington Senators)

As part of the first American League expansion, a new Washington club was added to the league in November 1960, to replace the old Senators, who were moving to Minnesota to become the Twins. The old Senators had languished in the second division their final 14 years in Washington, and the new Senators scarcely improved on that record. In each of their first four seasons they lost 100 games or more, tying for last place in 1961 and holding down the bottom all by themselves for two years before rising to ninth in 1964.

Although as an expansion team the new Senators had to make do at first with expendable players from the established clubs, they were not devoid of talent. In their first season, pitcher Dick Donovan led the league with a 2.40 earned run average, though injuries and the lack of offensive support held his won-lost record to 10-10. Their most valuable player, he was nonetheless traded with two teammates to Cleveland for outfielder Jimmy Piersall. Piersall proved a major disappointment in Washington, batting only .244 while Donovan was winning 20 games for his new club.

Not all the Senators' trades proved disastrous. In late 1964 they sent another promising pitcher—Claude Osteen—to the Dodgers in a deal that brought them five players, including third baseman Ken McMullen and outfielder Frank Howard. Osteen blossomed into a consistent winner in Los Angeles, but at the same time, McMullen brought strength to the Washington infield and Howard became one of the league's offensive stars.

The Senators' blend of youth and experience jelled in 1969 under rookie manager Ted Williams, as several key players—including McMullen and Howard—enjoyed career-best seasons. The club finished above .500 for the first time, driving with a late-season spurt to within a game of third-place Boston in the league's Eastern Division.

But 1969 was a one-year phenomenon. After losing seasons in 1970 and '71 (and the loss of much of their fan support), owner Bob Short pulled up stakes and moved the club to Arlington, Texas (midway between Fort Worth and Dallas), where, as the Texas Rangers, they have been ever since. Their first summer in Texas resembled their first in Washington: they lost 100 games (despite a strike-shortened season) and finished last. Williams was replaced by a new rookie manager—Whitey Herzog—but the club did no better in 1973.

Before the season's end Herzog gave way to Billy Martin. Martin came too late to save the Rangers from another lost season, but the next year he spurred the team to the kind of turnaround Williams had managed five years earlier. Behind the 25-12 pitching of Ferguson Jenkins (acquired in the off-season from the Cubs) and the hitting of league MVP Jeff Burroughs and AL Rookie of the Year Mike Hargrove, the Rangers spurted in the second half of 1974 from a sub-.500 record to second place in the AL West, only five games behind Oakland.

The Rangers rebounded from two losing seasons to their finest season yet in 1977 (94-68, .580) and second place, behind strong pitching and the blooming of Jim Sundberg as a hitter to go along with his league-leading catching. The return of Fergie Jenkins (after two years in Boston), the sparkling 11-5 season of rookie Steve Comer, and a September surge kept the club competitive in 1978. Jim Kern's brilliant relief work the next season helped the club recover from a nosedive in July and August to edge Minnesota for a strong third-place finish.

After a losing season in 1980, the Rangers bounced back in 1981 to record their second-best winning percentage ever (.543)—and finishes of second and third in the two halves of the strike-divided season. Then they slipped below .500 again for four more years. Pitcher Charlie Hough's knuckleball, and strong seasons at the bat from Pete O'Brien, Larry Parrish, Scott Fletcher, and rookie Pete Incaviglia helped new manager Bobby Valentine guide the Rangers to a second-place finish after last-place seasons in 1984 and '85.

Once more, though, the turnaround was brief: in 1987 losses in their final games of the season dropped the Rangers into a tie at the bottom of the division, and in 1988 they finished only two games out of the cellar, in sixth place.

A group of investors headed by George W. Bush—then the President's son, later to become President himself—purchased control of the Rangers in March 1989, and strikeout king Nolan Ryan returned to the American League as a Ranger after nine years in Houston. The strong arms of starter Ryan (who recorded his 5,000th career strikeout during the season) and reliever Jeff Russell, the potent bats of outfielder Ruben Sierra and second baseman Julio Franco (newly acquired from Cleveland), and a 10-1 start that put the club in first place for a month (before they settled back to fourth) highlighted a return to the winning side of the ledger. In 1990 Ryan hurled his 300th win and sixth no-hitter, first baseman Rafael Palmeiro peaked at the plate, and pitcher Bobby Witt enjoyed his finest season, with 17 wins. After a slow first half, the Rangers rose from sixth place to third, compiling an 83-79 record identical to that of the year before.

A 14-game win streak in May 1991 boosted the Rangers into first place for several days, although they again finished third. Jose Guzman joined Ryan (who fashioned a seventh no-hitter) among the league's top pitchers, and young slugger Juan Gonzalez formed with Franco, Palmeiro, and Sierra a powerful quartet that made the Rangers the top scoring team in the majors. In 1992 pitcher Kevin Brown won 21 games and Gonzalez topped the majors in home runs. But an overall decline in offense, and disastrous fielding and relief pitching, dropped the team below .500 after a competitive first half as manager Valentine was fired in July. In the year's biggest in-season trade, the club acquired Jose Canseco from Oakland for Sierra, Witt and Russell.

The Rangers surged to within a game of first place in mid-July 1993 and remained competitive into September, finishing second. Canseco injured his elbow in a relief pitching stint in June and was lost for the season, but Gonzalez again led the league in home runs (with 46), while also leading his team in batting and RBIs. Nolan Ryan retired after an injury-shortened season, and as the Rangers ended their tenure at Texas Stadium, their new home arose on the other side of the parking lot.

In the weak AL West of 1994, it didn't matter that the Rangers played losing ball in the new Ballpark in Arlington. Despite their worst record in six years—a .456 winning percentage that would have consigned them to the cellar of the East or Central divisions—the Rangers were a game ahead of Oakland, in first place,

when the strike ended the season. Texas' won-lost percentage improved to .538 in 1995 but that was only good enough for third.

In 1996 the Rangers (90-72) won their first division title on the heavy hitting of MVP Juan Gonzalez (47 HRs, 144 RBIs), Dean Palmer (38 HRs, 107 RBIs), Rusty Greer (.321, 100 RBIs), and Kevin Elster (24 HRs, 99 RBIs). The Rangers boasted an unusually well-balanced rotation—Ken Hill (16-10), Roger Pavlik (15-8), Bobby Witt (16-12), and Darren Oliver (14-6)—along with reliever Mike Henneman (31 saves) and late-season addition John Burkett (5-2). The Yankees, however, rolled over Texas in the first round of the postseason despite five home runs by Gonzalez.

Johnny Oates, who shared AL Manager of the Year honors in 1996, could do little with the Rangers in 1997. The most significant thing that happened in Texas was the first-ever interleague game on June 12; later in the month, Texas starter Bobby Witt became the first AL pitcher to homer in the regular season in 25 years. The Rangers jousted with the Angels for first place in the AL West for much of 1998 before they swept Anaheim in the final week of the season to capture the title. Trades for Royce Clayton and Todd Zeile revitalized the left side of the infield while new acquisition Todd Stottlemyre won several big games down the stretch. Gonzalez, who had 100 RBIs at the All-Star break, drove in 157 runs and won his second AL MVP. Rick Helling became the third 20-game winner in Rangers history and John Wetteland set the club record with 42 saves. All the same, just as in 1996, they ran into the Yankees in the Division Series and were quickly dispatched.

The 1999 campaign ended with a club-record 95 wins, another MVP Award (this time for Ivan Rodriguez), and a smashing return to Texas by Rafael Palmeiro, but for the third time in four years the Yankees knocked off the Rangers in the Division Series. The club tried a new direction, trading Gonzalez to the Tigers for several young players, of whom Gabe Kapler had the biggest impact. He had a 28-game hitting streak, while his .302 average and 32 doubles were better numbers than Gonzalez put together in Detroit. Palmeiro followed up a 47-homer, 140-RBI output with 39 homers and 120 RBIs in 2000. But it was pitching and defense that was the team's undoing. Texas was last in the league in ERA and had the lowest fielding percentage as well. Part of that certainly had to do with the absence of nine-time Gold Glove catcher Rodriguez, who missed the second half of the year with a broken thumb.

The Rangers hoped to fix all their problems by acquiring another Rodriguez, at a record price. On December 11, 2000, Texas signed free agent Alex Rodriguez to a 10-year, $252 million contract. The All-Star shortstop did everything that could have been expected. Over the next three years, Rodriguez played every Rangers' game but one, led the AL in homers each season (52, 57, 47), won two Gold Glove Awards, and earned the league's 2003 MVP Award.

Unfortunately, A-Rod couldn't pitch, and neither could anybody else on the team. Texas finished last each year, with respective loss totals of 89, 90 and 91. Oates gave way to Jerry Narron in 2001, and to Buck Showalter after the 2002 season.

Rodriguez was traded in early '04, to the Yankees, ostensibly for second baseman Alfonso Soriano.

Toronto Blue Jays

For a while, in February 1976, it looked as if the National League's San Francisco Giants would move to Toronto, where there were buyers eager for the club. But when the Giants were sold in March to new owners determined to keep them in San Francisco, the American League jumped in to establish Toronto as an American League city, setting up an expansion club, the Blue Jays, who began play the next year in Exhibition Stadium.

It took seven years for the Jays to lift themselves out of last place in the seven-team American League East. For five years they had the cellar all to themselves, never finishing closer than 11 games behind the sixth-place club.

In their first season, the Jays' 107 losses left them 45-1/2 games out of first, as the team performed at the bottom of the division in hitting, fielding and pitching. In 1978 their fielding improved dramatically, but the Jays still lost over 100 games, and there was little doubt after April who would finish last.

The next year was the team's worst ever. While every other Eastern Division club was compiling a winning record, Toronto plunged relentlessly downward and, despite a brief rally in September, finished 28-1/2 games out of sixth place (50-1/2 out of first), with 109 losses.

The club's turnaround began in 1980. It was late June before the Jays began their drop away from the rest of the division, and for the first time they finished with fewer than 100 losses. Pitchers Jim Clancy and Dave Stieb each had an ERA below 4.00 for the first time, and newly acquired second baseman Damaso Garcia combined with shortstop Alfredo Griffin to form the league's best double-play combination. There were still two more seasons in the cellar, but in strike-divided 1981 the Jays played a creditable second half for the first time, and in 1982 they spurted in September to tie the Indians for sixth at season's end. Garcia in 1982 became a .300 hitter and a leading base stealer, Clancy put together his first winning season and Stieb his second, and Stieb's five shutouts led the league.

In 1983, with seven of the team's eight principal pitchers enjoying winning seasons, and the Jays' hitters leading the league in team batting and slugging, they recorded their first winning season—in fourth place, only nine games out of first. Their balanced pitching and offense carried them to a repeat 89-73 record in 1984—this time for second place (though they finished a distant 15 games behind Detroit).

In 1985 the Blue Jays topped their division with 99 victories, edging the Yankees by two games. Their pitching was better than ever. Doyle Alexander won 17 games, Jimmy Key and Dave Stieb contributed 14 each, and reliever Dennis Lamp compiled an impressive 11-0 record. Stieb led the league in ERA, with Key fourth. Tony Fernandez, in his first full big league season, sparkled as expected at short, but also proved unexpectedly solid at the bat. Eight Jays drove in more than 50 runs, with outfielders George Bell (95), Jesse Barfield (84) and Lloyd Moseby (71) pacing the club's balanced attack.

In the ALCS the Jays won three of their first four games against Kansas City but lost the next three, and the pennant. Equally discouraging was their drop to fourth place in 1986. Barfield, Bell and Fernandez all improved at the plate, but the league-leading pitchers of 1985 dropped back to the middle of the pack in '86 (though rookie Mark Eichorn sparkled in long relief).

Toronto sprang back stronger than ever in 1987. Jim Clancy (15-11, 3.54 ERA) enjoyed his best season yet, as did Jimmy Key (17-8), whose 2.76 ERA led the league. Once again, as in 1985, the team ERA was the league's lowest. And the offense remained strong. (George Bell, league RBI leader with 134, was named the American League MVP at season's end.) The Jays led their division going into the season's final series against second-place Detroit, though four straight losses had reduced the lead to just one game. Needing to

win two of the three games to take the AL East title, or one to tie the Tigers and force a playoff, Toronto lost the first two games. In the season finale, Jimmy Key hurled a three-hitter, striking out eight. But one of the hits was a home run—the only run of the game, as it turned out. Toronto's seven-game losing streak had cost them what would have been their second title in three years.

In 1988, a rocky season made worse by Bell's feud with manager Jimy Williams (who wanted the unwilling outfielder to serve as designated hitter), the Jays surged at the end—with six straight wins—into a tie for third place. Dave Stieb pitched two one-hitters in September, both of which were no-hitters through 8-2/3 innings.

When Toronto's front office replaced manager Williams with batting coach Cito Gaston in mid-May 1989, the Jays were drowning near the bottom of the AL East with a record of 12-24. By mid-August they had bobbed above .500 to stay, and on September 1 replaced Baltimore in first place. With a pair of one-run victories over the Orioles at the end of the month, the Jays preserved their narrow lead and clinched the division title. But Oakland outplayed them in the ALCS, taking the pennant in five games.

From mid-June 1990 to the final day of the season, the Blue Jays battled Boston for the division lead before settling for second. Stieb (after two more one-hitters in 1989) at last hurled a no-hitter, and third baseman Kelly Gruber earned a place with Bell and McGriff among Toronto's power elite. But the brightest Toronto star of 1989-90 was the new SkyDome, with its 11,000-ton retractable roof and its restaurants and hotel rooms above the outfield wall. After the Jays moved into the Dome on June 5, 1989, attendance zoomed, and by season's end the club set a new American League home attendance record of nearly 3.4 million. In 1990, with a full season in the Dome, the Jays attracted a new major league record of 3,885,284. Attendance surpassed 4 million in 1991 and 1992.

McGriff and Bell had departed by 1991, but an improved Devon White, plus newly acquired slugger Joe Carter and second baseman Roberto Alomar, led an offense that—together with the league's stingiest pitching staff—brought the Jays through a tight race to their third divisional title. For the third time, though, they crashed in the ALCS, this time trampled by Minnesota in five games. With the addition of a pair of free-agent veterans—pitcher Jack Morris (who went 21-6) and Dave Winfield (108 RBIs)—Toronto in 1992 finally completed the puzzle. The Jays sported a balanced offense (six players drove in 60 runs or more) and outstanding pitching from starter Juan Guzman (16-5; 2.64 ERA) and relievers Tom Henke and Duane Ward. In the ALCS the Jays defeated Oakland in six games to bring Canada its first major league pennant, and then they stopped stubborn Atlanta in six games to carry home the championship of the world.

Nearly half the team was new in 1993, but after a tight battle with several clubs through most of the season, the Jays pulled away to capture their fourth divisional title in five years, by a comfortable seven-game margin. John Olerud hit over .400 through the first half of the season and finished with a league-high .363. Paul Molitor, signed from Milwaukee as a free agent, hit better than anyone else in the league from midseason on, and finished second in the AL. Together with Roberto Alomar, Olerud and Molitor became the first teammates since 1893 to take the top three spots in a major league batting race. In the ALCS the Blue Jays bowled over the Chicago White Sox for the AL pennant in six games. The

World Series wasn't necessarily pretty (Toronto beat the Philadelphia Phillies in Game 4 by a dizzying 15-14 score), but it was memorable. Joe Carter's two-out, three-run home run off Mitch Williams in climactic Game 6 made this World Series just the second to end on a home run.

The glory faded fast in 1994. At the July All-Star break the Blue Jays lay at the bottom of the AL East. While they pulled themselves up to third before the players' strike ended the season in August, they remained 16 games out of first, their first losing season in a dozen years. The losing continued in 1995 as the Jays stripped their roster of most of the veterans of its world championship squad. Toronto tied Minnesota for the dubious honor of worst won-lost record (56-88).

Toronto edged up slightly in 1996, to fourth (74-88) in the AL East. Pat Hentgen (20-10, 181 strikeouts) won the 1996 AL Cy Young Award and Roger Clemens—with a league-leading 21 wins, 2.05 ERA, and 292 strikeouts—kept the award in Toronto in 1997. Clemens won it again in 1998 (his record fifth Cy Young), in a season in which he earned his 3,000th strikeout, ended the year with 15 consecutive wins, and copped his second consecutive Triple Crown. Offensively, Jose Canseco socked 46 home runs and Tony Fernandez batted .321 in his third tour of duty with the Blue Jays. Led by new manager Tim Johnson, who replaced Cito Gaston, Toronto made a late run at the Red Sox for the AL Wild Card. The Blue Jays won 11 straight games and 14 of 16 in the closing weeks of the season, but Toronto finished four games back.

The 1999 season looked gloomy while the team was still in spring training. An unhappy Clemens was traded to the division rival Yankees for David Wells, Homer Bush and Graeme Lloyd. Johnson, meanwhile, was fired as manager because his untrue comments regarding his military career had caused dissention on the team. With a new ace and a new manager, Jim Fregosi, the Blue Jays took the lead in the wild-card race in August. A nine-game SkyDome losing streak, however, doomed Toronto to a third-place finish.

For the second year in a row, a star player asked to be traded and was sent to a large U.S. market. Many, including Wells, wondered if the Blue Jays got equal value from Los Angeles in the Shawn Green-Raul Mondesi deal. Mondesi had 24 homers and 67 RBIs in 96 games, and provided ample protection in the lineup for red-hot Carlos Delgado (.344, 41 homers, 137 RBIs, 99 extra-base hits), but Mondesi missed the final two months with an injury. The Jays became the second team in history to have seven 20-homer players (Tony Batista, Brad Fullmer, Jose Cruz, Jr., Shannon Stewart, Darrin Fletcher, Mondesi, and Delgado), and led the AL in home runs. Toronto finished third again despite a 20-win season by Wells and 10 wins each from Frank Castillo, Esteban Loaizia, Chris Carpenter, and Kelvim Escobar. After the season Fregosi was replaced by Buck Martinez, a broadcaster with the club.

The Jays continued their gradual slide, dipping to 80 wins in 2001 and starting 20-33 in '02. Martinez was fired and replaced by Carlos Tosca, who led the team to a 58-51 record the rest of the season and an 86-76 mark in '03. In the tough AL East, this was good enough only for the Jays' fifth- and sixth-straight third-place finishes, behind the Yankees and Red Sox each year.

Nevertheless, Carlos Delgado and Roy Halladay gave Blue Jays' fans something to cheer about in 2003. Delgado smashed 42 homers, including four in one late-season game, and knocked in 145 runs to lead the league. Halladay won 15 straight decisions en route to a 22-7 record and the AL Cy Young Award.

Defunct Clubs

In addition to the many Negro League teams, some 112 ballclubs have played in the major leagues since the first professional association was formed in 1871. The 30 that still do (including their lineal ancestors from earlier cities) are described above; here are the other 82, listed according to the league and year in which they first played major league ball. Official club names precede the name of the city; nicknames follow.

National Association, 1871-1875

Two of the 23 clubs that played at one time or another in baseball's first professional league still play in the majors: the Atlanta Braves (then the Boston Red Stockings) and the Chicago Cubs (then the White Stockings). The other 21 are:

Athletic of Philadelphia: NA 1871-1875, NL 1876. Organized in 1860 as an amateur club, the Athletics became one of the dominant teams of the decade. As professionals they won the first NA pennant in 1871. After one year in the NL, they were expelled for failing to make the final western trip of the season.

Forest City of Cleveland, NA 1871-1872. In the midst of a second losing season, the club disbanded in August 1872.

Forest City of Rockford, Illinois, NA 1871. As an amateur club, Forest City (with its 16-year-old pitcher Al Spalding) was the only team to defeat the famous Washington Nationals on their pioneering midwestern tour of 1867. As professionals, Forest City finished seventh of the nine NA teams in 1871.

Kekionga of Fort Wayne, NA 1871. The Kekiongas won the first NA game ever played but dropped out of the association before the end of the season.

Mutual of New York, NA 1871-1875, NL 1876. Organized as an amateur club in 1857, the Mutuals were said to be backed financially by New York's notorious William Marcy "Boss" Tweed. Frequently accused of corrupt practices, the club was one of the leading eastern teams of the late 1860s. They were declared national champions of 1868 and proclaimed themselves national champions of 1870. On the demise of the NA the Mutuals entered the NL, but they were expelled after one season (along with the Athletics) for failing to play their final games in the West.

Olympic of Washington, D.C., NA 1871-1872. Unsuccessful in 1872 after playing well the year before, the Olympics disbanded about midseason.

Union of Troy, New York, NA 1871-1872. The Haymakers, as they were popularly known, dropped out of the NA halfway through the 1872 season.

Atlantic of Brooklyn, NA 1872-1875. One of the greatest clubs of the amateur era, the Atlantics (organized in 1855) went undefeated in 1864 and 1865 and won three successive national championships, 1864 to 1866. But in four NA seasons their combined won-lost record was only 49-139, including a dismal 2-42 in 1875.

Eckford of Brooklyn, NA 1872. Another great early amateur club—like the Atlantics, organized in 1855—they won the national championship in 1862 and again (with an undefeated season of 10 games) the next year. The Eckfords actually joined the NA in August 1871, replacing Kekionga, but their 1871 games were later erased from the record because they had failed to enter the association at the start of the season.

Lord Baltimore of Baltimore, NA 1872-1874. After twice finishing third, the Lord Baltimores (or "Canaries," for their yellow silk jerseys) disbanded two games before the end of the 1874 season, while in last place.

Mansfield of Middletown, Connecticut, NA 1872. Disbanded in late August.

National of Washington, D.C., NA 1872-1873, 1875. Organized as amateurs in 1859, the Nationals were the first eastern club to tour as far west as Chicago and St. Louis. After skipping the 1874 race, the Nationals reentered the NA in 1875, but dropped out in July.

Maryland of Baltimore, NA 1873. Dropped out after six games.

Philadelphia, NA 1873-1875. Known successively as the "White Stockings," "Pearls," and "Phillies," the team finished a strong second to Boston in their first season, but slipped to fourth and fifth the next two years.

Resolute of Elizabeth, New Jersey, NA 1873. Disbanded in August with a 2-21 record.

Hartford Dark Blues, NA 1874-1875, NL 1876-1877. After a weak first season, the Dark Blues finished third in its next three seasons, as standings are today reckoned. But by the 1876 guidelines (which used the number of games won rather than winning percentage), Hartford that year placed second. In 1877 the club played its home games in Brooklyn.

Centennial of Philadelphia, NA 1875. Dropped out in late May.

New Haven Elm Citys, NA 1875. Failed to play out their schedule.

St. Louis Brown Stockings, NA 1875, NL 1876-1877. George Bradley pitched all but five of the Browns' 39 wins in 1875, when they finished fourth, and all 45 victories in 1876, when they finished a strong third in number of victories; they were second in winning percentage. With Bradley lost to Chicago the next year, St. Louis dropped below .500—and out of the league.

St. Louis Red Stockings, NA 1875. A successful amateur club that decided to take a fling at pro ball, the Red Stockings played only a few games in the NA.

Western of Keokuk, Iowa, NA 1875. Disbanded in mid-June.

National League, 1876

When the National League was founded to replace the ill-organized National Association, it included six of the stronger NA clubs plus independent clubs in Cincinnati and Louisville. The league's composition was in continual flux to the end of the century as clubs were dropped and added, shrinking the league to as few as six teams and expanding it to as many as twelve. Two clubs that first played major league ball in the NL still do: the Philadelphia Phillies and the San Francisco (originally New York) Giants, both organized in 1883. (The Boston and Chicago franchises that continue to this day as the Atlanta Braves and Chicago Cubs had their starts in the National Association.) Those that have not survived:

Cincinnati Red Stockings, NL 1876-1880. From last place in 1876 (and 1877, when their games were not counted because of the club's reorganization and failure to pay its dues), the Reds—with seven new regulars—rose to second in 1878, only to fall back to fifth in 1879 and last again in 1880. That fall, when they refused to accept a new rule abolishing liquor sales and Sunday baseball on club grounds, they were dropped from league membership.

Louisville Grays, NL 1876-1877. The strong Louisville team led the league in mid-August 1877, but seven suspicious losses to chief rivals Boston and Hartford dropped the Grays out of first place. After Boston clinched the pennant, Louisville revived to secure second place, but four players—including pitching ace Jim Devlin—were expelled from baseball for throwing games. Their expulsion showed the NL's determination to wipe out corruption, but it also caused the St. Louis Browns, who had planned to sign three of the four Louisville players for 1878, to resign from the

league. Louisville, too, dropped out of the league before the next season, unable to find adequate replacements for the four.

Indianapolis Browns, NL 1878. Finished fifth of six teams.

Milwaukee Grays (or Cream Cities), NL 1878. Finished a last-place sixth, 26 games back of Boston.

Providence Grays, NL 1878-1885. One of the great teams in the NL's early years, Providence won pennants in 1879 and 1884, finishing no lower than third in seven of their eight seasons. In 1884, pitcher Charley "Old Hoss" Radbourn won a record 59 games, then pitched the Grays to victory in baseball's first World Series with a three-game sweep of the American Association champion New York Mets. But as they dropped to fourth place the next year, finishing for the first time below .500, their fans deserted them. Late that autumn the club was dissolved.

Buffalo Bisons, NL 1879-1885. Buffalo moved up to the majors after winning the International Association pennant in 1878. Jim "Pud" Galvin pitched nearly 70 percent of Buffalo's victories as he led them to four first-division finishes in seven big league seasons. First baseman Dan Brouthers, in his five years with Buffalo, twice won the batting title and led NL sluggers five times.

Cleveland Blues, NL 1879-1884. Cleveland's fortunes rested in large measure with pitcher Jim McCormick (who also managed the club their first two seasons). In 1880, their best season, McCormick won a career-high 45 games to bring the Blues in third. In 1883 Cleveland was in first place when McCormick's injured arm put him out for the season after he had won 23 games. The Blues dropped to fourth. The club folded after a seventh-place finish in 1884, a season that saw McCormick and two other Blues jump to the Union Association.

Stars of Syracuse, NL 1879. After finishing a close second to Buffalo in the International League in 1878, the Stars moved with the Bisons to the NL, but disbanded after a single unsuccessful season.

Troy, New York, Trojans, NL 1879-1882. After four losing seasons the franchise was expelled to make room for a club in New York City.

Worcester, Massachusetts, Brown Stockings, NL 1880-1882. After a pair of losing minor league seasons, Worcester was admitted to the NL to replace the defunct Stars of Syracuse. After finishing a respectable fifth in 1880, Worcester dropped into the cellar for two seasons before being ousted in 1883 for a new Philadelphia club.

Detroit Wolverines, NL 1881-1888. Buffalo's sale of its "big four" (Dan Brouthers, Hardy Richardson, Jack Rowe, and Deacon White) to Detroit late in 1885 transformed a perennial also-ran into a contender. The club finished second in 1886 and won the pennant in 1887. In a World Series played in 10 different cities, the Wolverines trounced St. Louis 10 games to 5. In 1888, after finishing fifth, they expired.

Kansas City Cowboys, NL 1886. They finished seventh, 58-1/2 games out.

Washington Senators, NL 1886-1889. In their four seasons, the Senators finished out of the cellar only once: next to last in 1887.

Indianapolis Hoosiers, NL 1887-1889. After dropping below Washington into the cellar in 1887, the Hoosiers and Senators traded places for their final two years.

American Association, 1882-1891

Three of the six clubs that formed the AA in 1882 still represent their cities in the majors today: Allegheny (Pittsburgh), Cincinnati, and St. Louis. Brooklyn, which entered the AA two years later, today represents Los Angeles. The others:

Athletic of Philadelphia, AA 1882-1890. After finishing a distant second in the AA's first season, the Athletics in 1883 took the pennant from St. Louis by a single game. First baseman Harry Stovey, who led AA batters in most offensive categories that year, was even more productive in 1884. The A's dropped to seventh and never challenged for the crown again. Expelled from the AA after the 1890 season for financial reasons, they were replaced by the Philadelphia club from the defunct Players League.

Baltimore Orioles, AA 1882-1889, 1890-1891, NL 1892-1899. After eight seasons out of pennant contention (including four in last place), the Orioles dropped out of the AA to play minor league ball in 1890. Toward the end of the season, when Brooklyn's new franchise went under, the Orioles returned to complete Brooklyn's season (finishing a combined last). After rising to third in 1891, the AA's final year, the Orioles were invited into the expanding NL, where they dropped to a 12th-place last (54-1/2 games out) in 1892.

Ned Hanlon, hired to manage Baltimore early in the 1892 season, set about building a championship club. By 1894, with a lineup that included six future Hall of Famers, Hanlon led his club to a narrow pennant victory over New York, though the Giants swept the Orioles in the first Temple Cup Series, 4-0.

For five years Hanlon's brand of scrappy, hustling play made the Orioles the terror of the NL. Led by shortstop Hughie Jennings and outfielders Willie Keeler and Joe Kelley, the club repeated as NL champions in 1895 and 1896, and finished second to Boston the next two years. They lost the Temple Cup to Cleveland (4 games to 1) in 1895, but swept the Spiders the next year, 4-0, and took the cup again in 1897, defeating Boston, 4-1, in what turned out to be the Temple Cup swan song.

Baltimore owners Hanlon and Harry Von der Horst purchased a half-interest in the Brooklyn club in 1899 (retaining a half-interest in Baltimore), and switched Jennings, Kelley and Keeler to Brooklyn. Hanlon also went over as manager, leaving third baseman John McGraw in charge of the Orioles. McGraw hit .391 and rookie pitcher Joe McGinnity won 28 games to bring the team in fourth. But Hanlon's Superbas won the pennant, and, when the NL cut back to eight teams after the season, Baltimore got the ax.

Eclipse of Louisville/Louisville Colonels (or Cyclones), AA 1882-1891, NL 1892-1899. The club, which changed its official name from Eclipse to Louisville after the 1883 season, was one of only two teams to play all 10 seasons of the major league AA. (St. Louis—the present Cardinals—was the other.) Louisville finished above .500 in five of its first six years, but only once in that time closed within 10 games of the top—in 1884, when Guy Hecker's 52 wins brought the team in third. Slugger Pete Browning paced the offense in their early years, winning batting titles in 1882 (his rookie season), 1885, and 1886, and hammering a second-best .457 in 1887 (.402 if adjusted to eliminate walks, which were counted as hits that year). A bat made for Browning by woodworker John Hillerich inspired the creation of the Louisville Slugger line of bats.

By 1889, though, the club had sunk to last place, finishing 66-1/2 games out of first, with 111 losses. The next year, although Hecker and Browning defected to the outlaw PL, the club was less affected by deserters than other AA teams. The Colonels (paced by the league's best hitter, William "Chicken" Wolf, and its best pitcher, Scott Stratton) made one of the greatest turnarounds in big league history, winning the pennant by 10 games over second-place Columbus. In the World Series against Brooklyn, poor weather and small crowds ended play after the teams had tied once and won three apiece.

Even though the Colonels finished next to last in 1891, they

were one of four clubs taken into the NL after the AA folded. They never finished higher than ninth in the NL, and for three straight years (1894-1896) they occupied the cellar. When the league cut back from twelve teams to eight after the 1899 season, Louisville merged with the Pittsburgh Pirates.

Columbus Colts (or Senators), AA 1883-1884. From sixth place in 1883, Columbus climbed to second in 1884 behind the 34-13 pitching of rookie Ed Morris. But when the AA dropped back from twelve clubs to eight in 1885, Columbus was out.

Metropolitan of New York, AA 1883-1887. After success in minor league and independent play since 1880, the Mets entered the AA in 1883 as the association expanded from six clubs to eight. With 41 victories from pitcher Tim Keefe (who was picked up from disbanded Troy), the Mets finished fourth. The next season, with first baseman Dave Orr hitting .354 in his first full major league season and pitcher Jack Lynch matching Keefe with 37 wins apiece, the Mets won the AA pennant handily. But they lost baseball's first World Series to the Providence Grays. When manager Jim Mutrie, third baseman Dude Esterbrook and pitcher Keefe were transferred in 1885 to the New York Giants (the two clubs had the same owner), the Mets sank to seventh place, where they finished in their final three seasons.

Indianapolis Blues, AA 1884. Finished 11th of 12 clubs, 46 games behind.

Toledo Blue Stockings, AA 1884. Catcher Fleet Walker (who played in 42 games) and his brother Welday (five games) were the major leagues' first openly black players and the last blacks until Jackie Robinson broke the color bar for good in 1947.

Washington, D.C., AA 1884. The popularity of the city's Union Association Nationals proved too much for this inept AA club, which went under in early August.

Virginia of Richmond, AA 1884. When Washington disbanded in August, the Wilmington club of the Eastern League was invited to join the AA as its replacement. Wilmington declined (and later jumped to the UA), but Virginia—also a member of the EL—accepted the invitation and took over Washington's remaining games. Washington-Virginia finished a combined 24-81, in last place.

Cleveland Spiders, AA 1887-1888, NL 1889-1899. After two losing seasons in the AA, the Spiders moved to the NL, where they continued below .500 for three more years. But in 1892 Cy Young's league-leading pitching brought them the second-half championship of the league's experimental split season. Cleveland lost the World Series to first-half winner Boston, losing five after tying the first game.

Second-place finishes in 1895 and 1896 qualified the Spiders for the Temple Cup series against champion Baltimore. In 1895 they beat the Orioles for the world title 4 games to 1, but were swept the next year.

In 1899, when owner Frank Robison transferred all the team's best players to St. Louis (which he also owned), Cleveland suffered the worst season in major league history, winning only 20 games while losing a record 134. They finished 35 games behind 11th-place Washington and 84 games out of first. After the season the Spiders died, as the NL cut back from twelve teams to eight.

Kansas City Blues, AA 1888-1889. Finished last in 1888, next to last in 1889.

Columbus Colts (or Solons), AA 1889-1891. In 1890, with the AA weakened by the replacement of half its franchises with new clubs and by defections to the outlaw PL, Columbus (which retained several of its regulars) rose from its 1889 sixth-place finish

to second behind Louisville. When the PL folded and the defectors returned in 1891, Columbus dropped back to sixth.

Brooklyn Gladiators, AA 1890. Formed as a replacement for the Brooklyn club that forsook the AA for the NL in 1890, the Gladiators floundered and were replaced by Baltimore late in the season.

Rochesters, AA 1890. Played .500 ball, finishing fifth.

Syracuse Stars, AA 1890. Finished sixth.

Toledo Maumees, AA 1890. Finished fourth.

Cincinnati Porkers, AA 1891. Also known as "Kelly's Killers" for their manager Mike "King" Kelly, the club went bankrupt in August and was replaced by Milwaukee.

Milwaukee Brewers, AA 1891. This Western League club moved up to the AA in August. Taking five players and the 43-57 record from the defunct Cincinnati club, Milwaukee went 21-15 the rest of the way to lift the Cincinnati-Milwaukee combination from seventh to fifth by season's end.

Washington Senators, AA 1891, NL 1892-1899. Despite a cellar finish in the AA's final year, the Senators were taken into the expanding NL. Of its nine losing seasons, the best was a tie for sixth in the twelve-team NL of 1897.

Union Association, 1884

Formed in opposition to the reserve rule that governed players in the National League and American Association, the Union Association struggled through one season. The first eight clubs listed here began the season. The other five are listed according to the month they entered the UA as replacement teams. All 13—like the Union Association itself—are long extinct:

Altoona, Pennsylvania, Unions, UA 1884. The first of several Union Association clubs to drop out of competition during the season, Altoona disbanded on May 31, but reorganized as an independent club two days later with many of the same players taking the field.

Baltimore Unions, UA 1884. Bill Sweeney's league-leading 40 wins accounted for 70 percent of third-place Baltimore's victories.

Boston Unions, UA 1884. Outfielder Tom McCarthy, the UA's only Hall of Famer, hit .215 in this, his rookie big league season. Boston finished fourth.

Chicago Browns/Pittsburgh Stogies, UA 1884. Financial woes caused the Chicago Browns to relocate in Pittsburgh in late August, but the club quit altogether less than a month later.

Cincinnati Outlaw Reds, UA 1884. With three 20-game winners—including Jim McCormick, who won 21 after defecting from the NL in midseason—Cincinnati compiled a strong 69-36 record, but still finished 21 games behind champion St. Louis.

Keystone of Philadelphia, UA 1884. In early August Keystone dropped out of the league and reorganized as an independent semipro club.

National of Washington, D.C., UA 1884. Finished sixth, 46-1/2 games back.

St. Louis Maroons, UA 1884, NL 1885-1886. Batting 47 points above the league average, the Maroons scored 184 runs more than the next-best club to run away with the pennant. They were the only UA club to survive 1884 as a major league team. In the NL, where they were dubbed "the black diamonds," because of their previously expelled players, they were unable to fashion a winning season or finish higher than sixth.

Kansas City Unions, UA 1884. Formed to replace Altoona, Kansas City went 16-63 in its partial season.

Wilmington, Delaware Quicksteps, UA 1884. After Wilmington had gone 51-12 to sew up the Eastern League title, they jumped to the UA in August to replace Philadelphia's Keystones. But as several players failed to make the jump with them, the move was a disaster on the field (2-16) and financially. They failed in mid-September.

Milwaukee Grays, UA 1884. One of only two teams left in the deteriorating Northwestern League, Milwaukee moved up to the UA in September to complete the schedule of dropout Pittsburgh.

St. Paul White Caps, UA 1884. With the disbanding of the Northwestern League in September, St. Paul joined the UA to take over Wilmington's remaining games.

Players League, 1890

Formed in rebellion against the NL owner John T. Brush's classification plan, a scheme to limit players' pay, the PL drew many of the finest players from the NL and AA, and proved the most popular league with the fans. But when only one club turned a profit, the clubs' financial backers deserted and the league died. Two clubs were admitted to the AA, and many of the rest merged with their National League counterparts:

Boston Red Stockings, PL 1890, AA 1891. Boston won the PL pennant with such stars as Dan Brouthers, Charley Radbourn, Hardy Richardson, and manager Michael "King" Kelly. The only PL club to make money, Boston joined the AA the next year and won another pennant. But when the popular Kelly defected to Boston's NL Beaneaters (who also won a pennant for the city in 1891), the fans defected too, and the Red Stockings died along with the AA at the end of the season.

Brooklyn Wonders, PL 1890. At the end of a season in which they edged New York for second place, the Wonders merged with Brooklyn's NL pennant-winners.

Buffalo Bisons, PL 1890. After a last-place finish 20 games back of their nearest competitor, the Bisons simply went out of business.

Chicago Pirates, PL 1890. Mark Baldwin, with a league-high 34 wins, and Charles "Silver" King, with 30, pitched Chicago into fourth place. Both went to Pittsburgh the next year, although the franchise was absorbed by Chicago's NL Colts.

Cleveland Infants, PL 1890. Like Cleveland's NL Spiders of 1890, the Infants finished next to last. But one of their three managers, infielder Oliver Wendell "Patsy" Tebeau, would go on to lead the Spiders to their finest seasons.

Philadelphia Quakers, PL 1890, *Philadelphia Athletic,* AA 1891. Although they finished sixth in their PL season, the Quakers compiled a winning record. When the Athletics of the AA were expelled following the 1890 season, the Quakers were admitted in their place and awarded the name "Athletic." The team finished fourth in 1891, but was not among the four clubs taken into the NL when the AA folded, because Philadelphia already had an NL team (the Phillies).

New York Giants, PL 1890. Paced by the hitting of first baseman Roger Connor and outfielder Jim O'Rourke, New York's PL Giants finished third. In November the club merged with the city's NL Giants.

Pittsburgh Burghers, PL 1890. After a sixth-place finish, the Pittsburgh PL club and the NL Allegheny Club combined to form the new Pittsburgh Athletic Club, which still represents Pittsburgh in the NL.

American League, 1901

When Western League president Ban Johnson renamed the circuit in 1900 and proclaimed it a major league the next year, he little knew how stable it would be. For over half a century (1903-1953) the same eight clubs represented the same eight cities. Even today, although the league has expanded and several clubs have moved to new cities, not one franchise has perished.

Federal League, 1914-1915

After an inaugural season as a six-team minor league in 1913, the FL expanded to eight teams and declared war on the NL and AL for their players. After two big league seasons, and despite two of the game's most exciting pennant races ever, the league died for lack of patronage, and with it went its eight franchises:

Baltimore Terrapins, FL 1914-1915. Jack Quinn and George Suggs, with 26 and 25 wins, pitched Baltimore to third place in 1914. But when Quinn and Suggs lost their stuff the next year, the club sank out of sight, 24 games behind seventh-place Brooklyn.

Brooklyn Tip-Tops (or Brookfeds), FL 1914-1915. The Brookfeds finished fifth in 1915 and not even the acquisition of batting and base-stealing champ Benny Kauff could stop Brooklyn from slipping to seventh the next year.

Buffalo Buffeds, FL 1914-1915. Finished fourth in 1914, sixth the next year.

Chicago Chifeds (or Whales), FL 1914-1915. After leading the league through July and much of August in 1914, only to lose out after a late-season struggle with Indianapolis, the Whales came back in 1915 to triumph in an even tighter race that saw the three top teams separated at the finish by only half a game. Owner Charles Weeghman was permitted to buy the NL Cubs in 1916, and many Whales joined the Cubs to play at what was then Weeghman Park and is now known as Wrigley Field.

Indianapolis Federals (or Hoosiers), FL 1914; *Newark Peps,* FL 1915. Five regulars hit over .300 (paced by Benny Kauff's league-leading .370) in 1914, and the team as a whole hit 22 points above the league average. From fourth place in August the Hoosiers fought back to capture the flag from Chicago by 1-1/2 games, with seven consecutive wins at the end. The only major league pennant winner to move to a new city the next year, the Hoosiers became the Peps in 1915. Though they remained competitive into September, an eight-game losing streak dropped them out of the race and they finished fifth.

Kansas City Packers, FL 1914-1915. After a sixth-place finish in 1914, the Packers competed in a five-way race through much of 1915. But from first place on August 21 they dropped to fifth a week later and finished fourth.

Pittsburgh Rebels, FL 1914-1915. After avoiding last place in 1914 only by St. Louis' late-season nosedive, Pittsburgh turned itself around the next year, luring first baseman Ed Konetchy from their NL rival Pirates, and pitcher Frank Allen from the NL Brooklyn Robins. Both enjoyed the best season of their careers to lead the Rebels into first place in late August, where they remained until they were dropped to third by losing three out of four at the end to the champion Whales.

St. Louis Terriers, FL 1914-1915. After finishing last in 1914, St. Louis added veteran pitcher Eddie Plank to its roster. From a club with two 20-game losers, the Terriers became in 1915 a team with three 20-game winners (including Plank), pulling up from fifth late in August to catch the leaders with a nine-game winning streak. At the finish, though, they ranked second—by less than one percentage point, the narrowest big league pennant margin ever. In 1916 Terriers owner Phil Ball took over the AL St. Louis Browns.

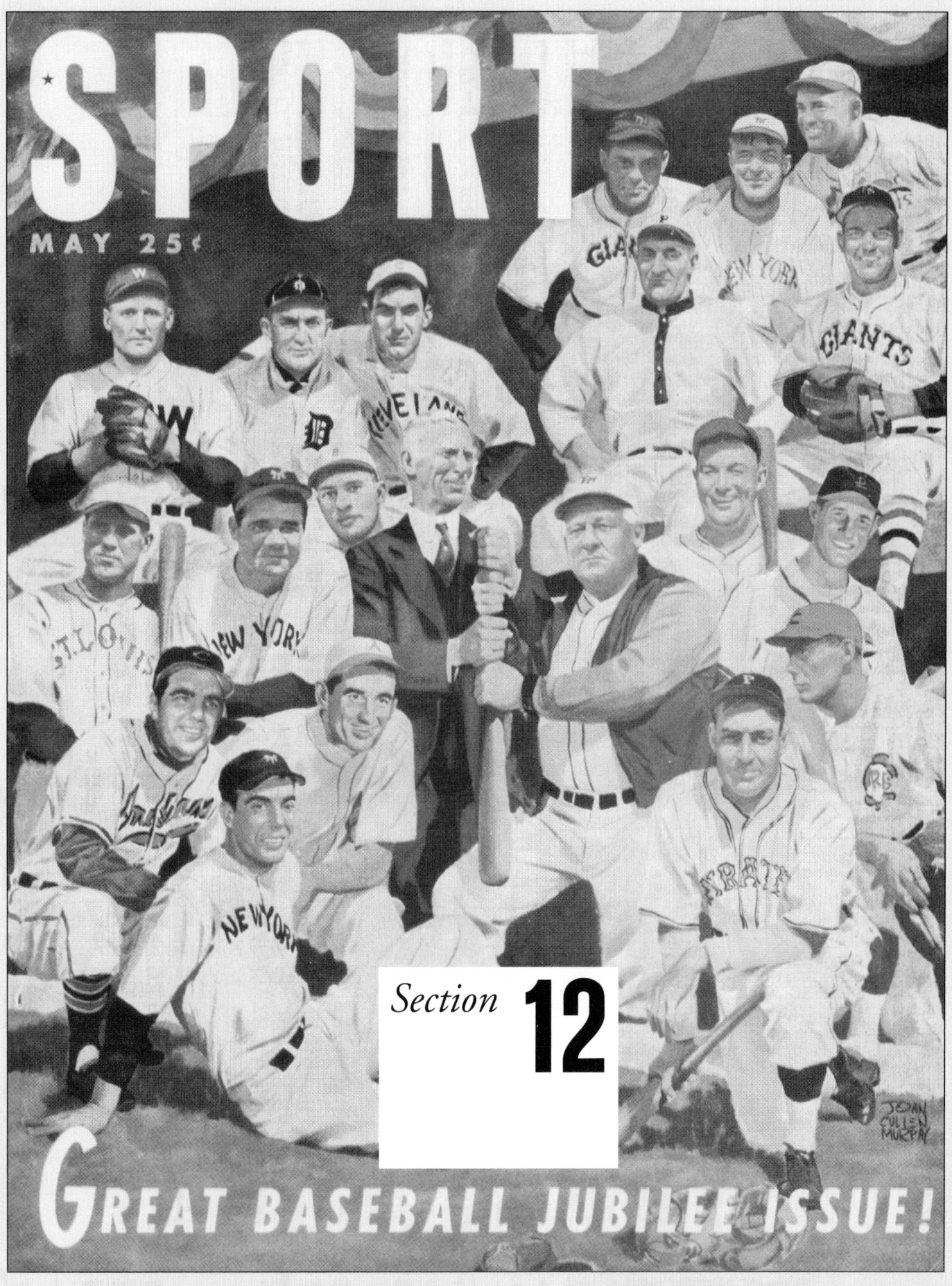

SPORT

MAY 25¢

Section **12**

GREAT BASEBALL JUBILEE ISSUE!

SPORT Heroes of Baseball

For the May 1951 issue of *SPORT* magazine the editors commissioned an illustration by John Cullen Murphy that featured the 20 baseball immortals pictured on the previous page. Here is the key to the illustration.

1. Rogers Hornsby
2. Christy Mathewson
3. Bill Terry
4. Mel Ott
5. Honus Wagner
6. Nap Lajoie
7. Ty Cobb
8. Walter Johnson
9. George Sisler
10. Babe Ruth
11. Jim Collins
12. Connie Mack
13. John McGraw
14. Gabby Hartnett
15. Stan Musial
16. Edd Roush
17. Pie Traynor
18. Mickey Cochrane
19. Joe DiMaggio
20. Lou Boudreau

FAMOUS FIRSTS

1914: Honus Wagner becomes the first player in the 20th century to record 3,000 hits.

1920: New York newcomer Babe Ruth hits his first home run for the Yankees.

1924: In leading the American League with six shutouts, Walter Johnson became the first major leaguer in history to pass the 100 shutout mark.

1927: Ty Cobb becomes the first player in major league history to record 4,000 career hits.

1931: After leading the AL with 31 wins, Lefty Grove becomes the first winner of the new MVP Award.

1939: For the first time after 2,130 games, Lou Gehrig does not appear in the Yankees lineup.

Chapter 49

Honus Wagner, The Flying Dutchman

Barrel-chested and bow-legged, Honus Wagner cut a strange figure at shortstop. But from 1897-1917 his talents set a standard that has not been surpassed to this day.

By Frank Graham
SPORT Magazine, January 1960

Honus Wagner was five feet, 11 inches tall and, at his playing peak, weighed 200 pounds. He was broad-shouldered, barrel-chested and bow-legged, and his tremendous hands hung almost to his knees. An anonymous writer in Pittsburgh once wrote of him that his legs took off at the ankles in a curving sweep to meet in surprise at his waistline. Lefty Gomez said he was the only man he had ever seen who could tie his shoestrings without bending.

He was the greatest shortstop by so wide a margin that his selection for that post on anybody's all-time, all-star team is unchallenged. He entered the National League with Louisville in 1897 and retired as a Pittsburgh Pirate in 1917, at the age of 43. He played in more games (2,794), made more hits (3,420), more doubles (643), and more triples (252) than any other player in the history of the league, and eight times he led it in batting. Impressive as they are, these figures only dimly reflect the glories of this gentle, craggy-faced giant who was called "The Flying Dutchman." He was a hero not only to the fans but to his mates and to those who played against him. A statue to his memory stands near Forbes Field for present-day fans to gaze upon, but the old ones need no reminder of how he looked. His likeness, in repose and in action, long ago was etched in their minds and hearts and is unforgettable.

To many of his contemporaries Hans was more than the greatest shortstop of all time. He was the greatest player of all time. Among these were Edward Grant Barrow, who found him in the minor leagues and sold him to the majors; Fred Clarke, who managed him in Louisville and Pittsburgh; and John McGraw, whose Giants he tormented through all the years he was in the league. It was Clarke who took him from the outfield and posted him at short at a time when he was regarded as the best outfielder in the league. Not, as Fred pointed out, because he thought Hans would play better in the infield, but because he needed a shortstop. At one time or another, in emergencies, he played every position except catcher, and no one doubted that if he had gone back of the bat he would have been the greatest catcher, too.

As a hitter he had no weakness upon which the pitchers could prey. Year after year he faced the likes of Cy Young, Christy Mathewson, Mordecai Brown, and Grover Cleveland Alexander, and hammered them as hard as he did the lesser lights. Just when they, or any of the others, thought they had him figured, he would blast the very kind of pitches that had stopped him. The only pitcher who ever bothered him consistently was an obscure toiler with the Chicago Cubs.

"His name was Jack Taylor," Hans once recalled, "and he started games only now and then. It looked like I ought to knock his pitches seven miles, but for five years I couldn't do anything with him. Finally I got so disgusted I turned around and batted left-handed against him. It worked. I got a three-bagger and my luck against Taylor changed."

John Peter Wagner, whose father was a Bavarian immigrant coal miner, was born in Carnegie (then called Mansfield) in Pennsylvania on February 24, 1874. There were nine children in the family but three of them died before John Peter was born or when he was too young to remember. Four of the survivors were

boys—Al, Luke, Charlie and, as he then was called, Honus—and they all liked to play ball. But even to them, mining came first, and, one by one, they followed their father into the pits. Hans was 12 when it was his turn to join the others in digging coal to keep their home together. His was a boy's job, loading cars at a boy's pay—79 cents a ton. By 14, he was doing a man's work. In all he spent five years in the mines. "Too long," he would say, whenever he talked of those years. "The dampness got into my legs and stayed there. All during my time as a player there were days when my legs ached something awful."

The boys played ball on their lunch hour and on Sundays, and developed such skills that the game became, in time, their profession. For all except Charlie, but he got out of the mines, too, opening a barber shop and, later, a pool hall. Al, the most proficient player in the beginning, went off to play with Steubenville in the Tri-State League, while Luke and Hans played semi-pro ball on Saturdays and Sundays and worked in the steel mills or at odd jobs between times.

Hans was 20 years old when, on Al's recommendation, he was signed by the Steubenville club at a salary of $35 a month. Al had urged him, as he was growing up, to learn to play all positions. Hans had learned, and he played them all for Steubenville, even pitching, and he hit .402 in 44 games. Then he began to roam, for it was an era in which contracts were loosely regarded in the minor leagues and a player felt free to move whenever he received a better offer. Before the year 1895, was out, Hans played with Mansfield in the Ohio State League and Adrian in the Michigan State League, and wound up with Warren in the Iron-Oil League.

In the fall of that year, the Atlantic League was organized and Ed Barrow, destined to become one of the greatest of all baseball executives but then a struggling young man with high hopes but a slender bankroll, bought the Paterson, N.J., franchise for $800 in partnership with Charles I. McKee, the proprietor of a lunch room in Pittsburgh. It was there in February of 1896, Barrow wrote in his book, *My Fifty Years in Baseball*, that a casual conversation with one Shad Gwilliam, a semi-pro baseball promoter in Pittsburgh, resulted in a break for Wagner that sped his progress to the National League.

Shad asked Ed how he was fixed for players, and Ed said he was doing okay but could use a couple more.

"Why don't you get Wagner?" Shad said.

"Which Wagner?" Ed asked.

"Honus," Shad said. "Al's already signed with Toronto."

Ed knew the brothers. He had seen them at Steubenville when he had the Wheeling club in the Tri-State League. He knew that, at the time, Al was the better ballplayer, but he had been impressed with Hans' terrific strength and smashing power at the plate. Sure, the boy was awkward but he could be developed. The next day Ed went to Mansfield.

The only one in Charlie Wagner's pool hall was a big kid dozing in a chair in front of a pot-bellied stove. "They're all down at the railroad yards, having a throwing match," the boy said.

Ed found Hans and eight or ten other young fellows walking up the railroad tracks. Hans was wearing a derby hat with a chicken feather stuck in the band. Ed didn't waste any time. He asked Hans how he'd like to play for him in Paterson. Hans pretended indifference. Ed kept talking and every once in a while Hans, as though he were bored, would pick up a stone or a hunk of coal and throw it a couple of hundred yards up the track in a great, sweeping, effortless motion. Ed knew now that he had to have this ungainly,

but gifted young man for his ball club. The salary limit at Paterson was $100 a month. Ed offered $125 and Hans accepted.

With Paterson that first season, Wagner played in the outfield and at first and third bases. Barrow had a notion that he belonged at shortstop, but didn't use him there because he had Charlie Bastian, a former big leaguer, in that position. and there were other spots where Hans could, and did, help him. The fans were quick to respond to this glorious Dutchman. They not only went to see him play but followed him in the streets. A cigar manufacturer came out with a Honus Wagner perfecto. A brewer, not to be outdone, named a brand of beer for him. A raft of babies born in the town that year were christened John Peter in his honor.

His appeal was as strong to his teammates as to his public, and not only because, day after day, he won or saved ballgames for them as he shattered the enemy pitchers or, regardless of where he was playing, always seemed to come up with the big play in the critical moments. That most of the stories written about the games featured him and that his name constantly was in the headlines could not shake his simple modest ways. He took no bows for his successes and he still was the butt of harmless practical jokes played on him in the clubhouse or the taverns where the players gathered in the evening for a few beers.

It was inevitable, of course, that he should play the stellar role on the Fourth of July when one of the first night baseball games ever played was put on by the Paterson and Wilmington clubs at Wilmington. It was a stunt to revive interest in the home club, which had attracted very little attention on its merits up to that time. The arc lights, set up on wooden poles around the field, sputtered horribly and more than once went out. Even when they glowed at their brightest, the visibility was poor, the outfielders barely could be seen from the stands and the indoor baseball that was used was of little help to the hitters. The fans, about 2,000 of them at a dollar a head, felt they had been cheated, and they howled. The players agreed with them that the game was a joke, there was a lot of clowning on the field, and the Wilmington pitcher, Doc Amole, provided, with Wagner's unwitting help, a socko finish.

On the first pitch to him in the sixth inning, Hans swung mightily and connected with a huge, white, paper-covered "torpedo" that Amole had smuggled into the park. There was a frightening explosion and the players ran for the clubhouse, followed by the fans, who wanted their money back.

Wagner hit .348, kept the club high in the race and wound up the year in glory as Paterson defeated Hartford in a postseason series, four games to two.

It was obvious that the minor leagues couldn't hold him very much longer. Before midseason of 1897, he was being looked at closely by National League managers or their agents—in that time the clubs did not have the elaborate scouting systems they have today, and a manager either went in person to see a prospect or he sent one of his players. Curiously, of those who saw Hans, only one was impressed. Connie Mack, who managed the Pirates, and Bill Joyce, manager of the Giants, looked at him hopefully and came away in bleak silence. Frank Selee, of Boston, one of the truly great pilots of the era, was outspoken in his disappointment. "I wouldn't give you a dime for him," he told Barrow.

The only one who, having carefully scouted Wagner for five days, saw in him all that Barrow had seen, was Harry Pulliam, who was to become president of the National League but in those days was secretary of the Louisville club, owned by Barney Dreyfuss. He

offered $2,000 for the Dutchman and Barrow told him a story.

"When I signed Wagner last year," Ed said, "Captain Kerr wanted to buy him from me." (Captain William W. Kerr was the owner of the Pittsburgh club.) "I told him that he couldn't have Wagner but that if I ever was of a mind to sell him, I would give Kerr the first chance to buy him. And that I must do."

Barrow wired Kerr about the $2,000 offer and Kerr wired back that he would meet it. Pulliam then raised his bid to $2,100 and Kerr backed off. So Wagner, who was hitting .379 in Paterson, went to the big league, where he hit .344 for the balance of the season.

It was a rugged time in baseball, especially for bushers, and Wagner was cussed and tossed around, just like the rest of them. But not for long. First his own teammates, and finally even the tough Orioles, learned that words alone couldn't hurt him or even make him mad. And it didn't pay to match muscles with him.

"Get outa my way, kid, or I'll spit in your eye!" a Louisville regular bellowed as Wagner tried to edge into the batter's box for some pre-game licks. The rookie, a regular himself for five days with Louisville, obligingly retreated to the dugout, where manager Fred Clarke, the aggressive leader who was to become one of the Dutchman's closest friends, blasted him.

"You don't have to take that kind of stuff from any player on this club," he said. "Now get back in that box or get off this ball club!"

His duty now clear, Wagner marched back to the plate, where the regular glared at him and then spat tobacco juice on his shoes. Taking a hitting position on the other side of the plate, Honus leveled his bat on the other man's head and announced, "I'm up here to hit at something, and I don't much care what it is."

And with that, he took a solid swing that missed the chin of the other player by an inch or so. Wagner got his cuts and very little trouble thereafter.

It was easy to be deceived by Wagner's amiable temper. In an era of physically bruising baseball, it was sometimes mistaken for a sign of timidness. Even Clarke was disturbed when Honus refused to fight back when belted on the basepaths.

He would say, "Don't let those Baltimore rowdies like McGraw maul you. You want to stay in the big leagues, don't you? Then fight back!"

In his very first major league game, Wagner learned a little bit about how the Orioles operated, and they got a hint of what Honus could do. "On my first time up," Honus used to love to recall, "I got a single. The next time I might have had a triple but Jack Doyle gave me the hip at first, Hughie Jennings chased me wide around second, and McGraw blocked me off at third, and knocked the wind out of me putting the ball into my belly.

"You should have heard Clarke cuss me out. He was ready to send me back to the minors then and there. But I got another chance late in the game. I sent one deep into center that was good for extra bases. I dumped Doyle on his behind at first, left Jennings in the dirt at second and tramped all over McGraw's feet coming into third. Clarke was so tickled to see McGraw fuming and cussing that he came over to the coach's box and said, 'Nice day, ain't it, Muggsy?'"

In 1900 he reached Pittsburgh, where he had always wanted to be. This came about when, with the paring of the National League from 12 clubs to eight, Louisville was dropped and Dreyfuss shifted his interests and his ballplayers to the Smoky City, retaining Clarke as his manager.

Hans felt that that was where he belonged. Mansfield—or Carnegie—was only a short ride from Pittsburgh on the steam cars. That part of Pennsylvania was his country. He loved every coal-blackened corner of it, and as long as he lived he never would leave it, save to play ball. It was there that he knew his greatest glory and, as though inspired by him, the Pirates won the pennant in 1901, 1902, 1903, and 1909. They played the Boston American League club in the World Series in 1903 and lost, largely because Hans, being human, had slumps, too. He had one in that Series, hitting only .214. But in 1909, when they met the Detroit Tigers, Pittsburgh won, four games to two. The star of the series was not Ty Cobb but John Peter Wagner.

The first meeting of the two absolutely fearless competitors was a memorable one. Cobb had reached first base and shouted over to Wagner, "Hey, Krauthead, I'm comin' down on the next pitch!"

As good as his word, Cobb set sail with the next pitch. The ball and Ty's feared spikes arrived almost simultaneously. But before the steel could dig into Wagner's shins, Honus smashed the ball into Cobb's mouth. The bleeding Tiger ace had to leave the game to have three stitches in his torn lip.

Cobb never tried to tangle with Wagner after that, and he even admitted grudgingly, "That damned Dutchman is the only man in the game I can't scare."

He was truly great in the pennant-winning years and for a number of years thereafter as the Pirates, winning or always in contention, almost literally fought McGraw's Giants and Frank Chance's Cubs in a three-cornered rivalry seldom equaled for fierceness in the history of the game. Ranging wide between second and third, he played shortstop as it never had been played before and never has been played since. As Johnny Evers, who, as a Cub, fought him bitterly yet had a warm admiration for him, once said: "His big hands were like shovels. When he came up with a ground ball, like as not he'd have both hands full of dirt, for he dug deep. And when he let go with that powerful arm of his, the first baseman or whomever he threw to had to be careful not to get hit in the eye with a clod or a stone."

On the bases Hans was incredibly fast and crafty. The old Pirates used to say: "Whenever he wants to steal a base, there is nobody going to stop him."

He led the league five times, reaching his high point in 1907, when he stole 61 bases. He never was reckless on the paths nor ran helter-skelter. He picked his spots and although he was no model of grace as he set out for second or third or home, he covered the ground and arrived in a swirl of dust. It is not on record that he ever spiked an opposing player.

Off the field he was a plain man. He dressed quietly and a bit on the rumpled side, and an old slouch hat was his trademark. He made little money, getting no more than $10,000 a year at most, but if ever there was among the professionals, an amateur at heart, it was Hans. He must have known that if he had played for the Giants or the Cubs he would have earned thrice what Dreyfuss paid him, but he never envied the New York or Chicago players. When Ban Johnson was expanding the new American League to major proportions at the turn of the century, he offered the young Wagner the almost unheard of sum of $21,000 to sign with him. Hans went straight to Dreyfuss.

"They want me to go to that other league," he said. "I would like to stay with you. Give me a contract."

Dreyfuss gave him a contract and he signed it. Whether or not he got a raise nobody but he and Dreyfuss ever knew. Whatever he

got obviously satisfied him. Barney was his friend and knew what was good for him.

The Dutchman's indifference to money was so pronounced that it sometimes irritated his friends. One winter, for instance, Cobb wanted Hans to join him and Nap Lajoie in a vaudeville tour for which he would be paid $1,000 a week. He turned Ty down, protesting that he was no actor, although all that would have been demanded of him was to put on a Pirate uniform, get out on the stage and swing a bat.

When he genuinely wished to retire after the 1909 season because his legs were bothering him, Dreyfuss persuaded him to remain simply by saying: "But we need you."

"Then I'll stay," he said.

"Wait till I get a contract!" Barney said. "How much do you want?"

"Oh," Hans said, "the usual amount."

Slowing down, naturally, as the years moved on but still a great player, he struggled through until 1916. In 1915 Clarke had retired and Jimmy Callahan was the new manager. Callahan was a nice fellow and Hans liked him, but things were different. Besides, his legs were bothering him again and after the 1916 campaign, he once more said he was through ... and once more Dreyfuss persuaded him to take another fling. Moreover, Barney fired Callahan on July 1 and appointed Hans manager.

Few, even among the old-timers, remember that Wagner ever was a manager. This isn't strange. He took the job unwillingly on July 1 and gave it up on July 4, because he was not suited for it and he knew it. His one weakness in baseball was that he couldn't tell anyone else how to play the game. No one ever had told him and he thought it would be kind of silly for him to tell anyone else or to give orders to the men with whom he had played.

His replacement was Hugo Bezdek, who had been baseball and football coach at Penn State but was a raw hand in the professional game. Hans promised to help him as much as possible, and he chided the other players when they grumbled about their "amateur manager."

Before the season was over, Hans was through. He played his last game on September 17, 1917, and went home to his wife, whom he'd married only the year before. He didn't know what he was going to do and, in the lean years that followed, he tried many things. He had a brief, unhappy whirl as baseball and basketball coach at Carnegie Tech. He organized the Honus Wagner All-Star basketball team and the Honus Wagner All-Star baseball team, and he played with both for ten years, For a short time, he was sergeant-at-arms in the state legislature. He and Pie Traynor opened a sporting goods store in Pittsburgh and they went broke in the Depression.

In 1933, he finally returned to major league baseball as a coach with the Pirates and spent 19 years going around the circuit again. It was the pleasant twilight of his career, going to spring training, being in the clubhouse and in the dugout, riding the rails again, reliving the old days in the stories—some of them outlandish—that he told the players. Frank Frisch, one of the managers under whom he nominally served as coach, says of him: "He really had nothing to do, but it was great for all of us just to have him around. Once in a while, sitting next to me in the dugout when one of our guys would make an error, he'd say softly to me: 'He didn't start the play right, Frank.'"

But he'd never say anything in criticism to the players. They loved him for his gentle ways, and they laughed at his stories, and they had the greatest respect for him as a ballplayer, sensing that no matter how good they became they could never be as great as he was. And they even believed his tall tales.

There was the one about an outfielder who backed up to the fence to make a catch but as he drew back to throw out a runner trying to score after the catch, his arm punched a hole in the boards and there he was, hung up on the fence as the runner scored.

Then there was the train. The way he told it was: "Nothing like this ever happened before or since. There was a railroad running by the ball park and one day I hit a ball over the center-field fence just as a train was going by. The ball went right down the smokestack but the engine went 'puff, puff' and blew the ball right back over the fence—and the center fielder caught it."

Hans was retired on a pension by the Pirates in February of 1952, just eight days before his 78th birthday.

In October of 1955, following a fall in his home, he was bedridden and, in the last week of November, he slipped into a coma. Death came to him with his wife, two daughters and other members of his family at his side.

"He just slept away," one of them said.

Chapter 50

Ty Cobb, The Georgia Peach

With bat, spikes and fists, Ty Cobb always played to win but never aimed to please. He had extraordinary talent, but is remembered as a terrible person and a great player.

By Josh Greenfeld
SPORT Magazine, November 1958

Baseball players as a breed are enormously popular. The better ballplayers are more than popular, they are idolized. And the few great stars of the game are venerated with a genuine love. Yet it is an historic irony of our national sport that the very best baseball player who ever lived was widely and passionately hated.

On a spring afternoon in 1912 the stands of the old Highlander Park were packed. The fans had turned out not so much to cheer for the last-place New York club, but rather to jeer at the colorful Tigers of Hughie Jennings. And there was one Tiger in particular whom they chose to ride unmercifully. He was the Detroit center fielder, the original angry man of baseball, Ty Cobb.

For seven seasons, the tight-lipped, jut-jawed Georgia Peach had been the scourge of the American League as he played the game with an original brand of arrogance, aggressiveness and bull-headed brilliance. Baseball to him was neither a gentlemanly contest of athletic skills nor simply a way of earning a living in the fresh and open air. It was, instead, a compulsive, knock 'em down, kick 'em in the face, stamp 'em out, never-ending, relentless war. He approached it with the energy of a Henry Armstrong, the art of a Willie Pep, the fury of a Jack Dempsey.

Cobb was an exciting, electric ballplayer, and he was utterly fearless. Once he participated in a series with each of his legs a mass of raw flesh. "He had a temperature of 103," the great sportswriter Grantland Rice later recalled. "The doctor had ordered him to bed for a three-day rest. That afternoon he got three hits and stole three bases, sliding into second and third on sore and battered flesh."

A healthy Cobb was all the more daring and remarkable. Early in the 1912 season, a stunned Philadelphia writer reported to his readers that he had witnessed a once-in-a-lifetime feat on the baseball diamond: "Tyrus Cobb beat out a single down the first-base line, stole second, then shouted in warning that he would steal third and proceeded to do so. Then, with two strikes on the batter, Cobb broke for the plate. The pitch was a little high, and before the catcher could pull it down, Cobb slid home. The man at the plate hadn't swung at the ball, but Cobb had gone all the way around the bases!"

The Philadelphia reporter had erred in one trifling detail. It was not the first time Cobb had gone around the bases in such a manner. Nor was it to be the last time.

Yet Cobb's miraculous deeds failed to earn for him the adulation of the fans. Just as they were impressed and excited by his prowess, the people were antagonized and repelled by his self-centered, hot-tempered manner. And they came to view each successive Cobb triumph with the sullen disdain a vanquished people accords a hated conqueror.

Sometimes their hatred flared openly. In 1910, after being charged with deliberately spiking Home Run Baker, Cobb received 13 letters from the Black Hand Society threatening him with death. The next season some irate fans tried to hijack him off a Chicago-bound train "in order to teach him a lesson." Nor was the intense dislike of Cobb reserved to the fans alone. In one of the most shameful episodes in baseball history, some of his fellow ballplayers actually tried to push him out of the American League

batting championship that same year.

Sparks always flew when Cobb was around. Take, for example, the mild May afternoon in 1912 when an angry brigade of anti-Cobb fans congregated in the left-field stands at the New York ballpark. The foremost heckler among them was a lusty-lunged, booming-voiced man named Lueker. Lueker's razzing went beyond the limits of decency. He was violently abusive in his insults, shamelessly vulgar in his epithets.

Cobb was angered by the cascade of invective, but he did his best to control his hasty temper. However, at the end of the fourth inning, Sam Crawford, his fellow outfielder, nudged him. "You don't have to take that kind of stuff from anyone," Sam said indignantly.

"He better simmer down," Cobb said, casting a burning glance into the stands.

"If he don't," Crawford volunteered, "we're all behind you."

Cobb wasn't due to bat the next inning, and rather than tempt fate by passing the left-field stands, he sat out the Detroit half of the inning in the bullpen. But the next inning, he had to come in for his turn at bat. As he ran in from his center-field position, the heckler cut loose with an especially vile volley.

Cobb was fuming. The skin on his face tightened into a violent red. His fists clenched and unclenched nervously. Even after he was seated in the dugout, the taunts continued to rain down on him. His eyes turned cold and hard, narrowing into a fierce glint. When the inning was over, he left the dugout slowly and deliberately. "Oh oh," manager Hughie Jennings said excitedly to the men on the Tiger bench, "he's going to do it. You see that look in his eyes? When Ty gets that look, there's nothing can stop him."

Cobb trotted mechanically down the left-field foul line toward his position. Suddenly, he stopped, veered and charged toward the grandstand like an angry bull, vaulting the rail and pushing and slashing his way through the mass of stunned spectators until he got to Lueker.

The crowd watched dumbfoundedly as the furious ballplayer punched the offending fan savagely. The people could scarcely believe what they were seeing. No ballplayer had ever before dared to venture into the stands.

Disgustedly, Cobb pushed the limp figure of Lueker aside. Now the crowd awoke into a mob and moved menacingly toward Cobb. Ty chopped and fought his way through them and back to the playing field. Several fans yelled out, "Let's get him and finish him!"

But the Detroit players had sprung into action. Armed with bats, they stood at the foot of the stands challenging the belligerent crowd. "Just try and get him!" Wahoo Sam Crawford shouted.

For a tense moment it seemed as if the fans would storm the field. They seethed with the fury of a lynch mob. The park became frighteningly silent. Nerves tightened, muscles quivered. The fuse was burning.

But the moment passed. The rage of the crowd subsided. Cobb was ejected and the ballgame continued.

The incident, however, had repercussions. In fact, it was only the beginning of one of the most bizarre chapters in baseball history. After receiving the umpire's report of the fight, league president Ban Johnson suspended Ty indefinitely. The Tigers held a meeting and voted to go on strike until he was reinstated. They did so not out of any great sympathy or affection for Cobb but because they were in the midst of a difficult pennant race and they knew all too well that his .400 bat was indispensable.

The Tigers were scheduled to play the Athletics in Philadelphia the next day. Manager Jennings telegraphed Detroit owner Frank Navin the news that "the boys will not play without Cobb. And it'll cost us $5,000 for every game in which we can't field a team."

Navin, stung by the threat to his pocketbook, wired Jennings to dig up a team, any team. And the "Tigers" that took the field the following day were a choice assortment of local semi-pros, sandlotters and college boys. A circus-loving hometown crowd of 20,000 watched the Athletics maul the pick-up Tigers by a score of 24-2.

When Ban Johnson heard about the farce, he was infuriated. He cancelled the remainder of the Philadelphia series, called in the striking Tigers and laid down an ultimatum: "Unless this team reports in Washington for its next scheduled game," he threatned, "I'll banish every one of you from Organized Baseball."

The stubborn Tigers held another meeting. Cobb, playing the rare role of peacemaker, prevailed upon his teammates to quit their strike. And they did so while Cobb sat out a 10-day suspension. The disgruntled Tigers finished sixth that year, well behind Boston.

But the fans were still out to get Cobb. They wanted vengeance for the beating inflicted upon the heckler. Later that season, while Cobb and his wife were driving to the train station in Detroit, three thugs jumped the car at a red light and attacked him with a knife. Ty successfully fought them off, but not before he had been badly cut.

Still, Cobb didn't stop fighting with the fans. One day he exploded at a waiter in Cleveland. Another day he matched blows with a Detroit butcher. These fights were in addition to the day-in, day-out altercations he had with his fellow ballplayers on the field and in the locker room.

There wasn't a man on the Detroit team Cobb could call a friend, and many of them despised him as cordially as he hated opposing ballplayers and umpires. Ty knew it and seethed, but did nothing until Charles "Dutch" Schmidt joined the club in 1906. Schmidt was a huge 25-year-old rookie catcher and one of the strongest men in baseball. He had been a boxer and had actually fought the great Jack Johnson. Cobb took one look at the easy-going giant who liked to give locker-room demonstrations of his strength, and instantly found an outlet for the rage he could not release against his other teammates.

"Why, you big baboon," he berated the newcomer, "where in hell did they ever get a pair of shoes for those feet? Why, I bet you never even wore shoes back in Arkansas."

"They sure is kinda tight at that," the unsuspecting rookie said, grinning. "Sure wish I could wear a pair like yours, Ty. I hear you keep them spikes real sharp." With that the fun-loving Schmidt grabbed one of Cobb's shoes and, swinging his ham-like fist like a sledge, hammered the spikes into the wooden floor of the locker room. The other players roared as Cobb strained to tug the shoe loose. "You lousy busher!" he screamed, his face turning tomato red. "I'll get you for that! I'm gonna beat hell out of you! I'm gonna cut you into little pieces!"

If Cobb had a sadistic streak in him, as many of his contemporaries have claimed, it showed at its worst in his treatment of Schmidt from that day on. He took special delight in tormenting and harassing the confused rookie. He doused him with water, put sand in his food, berated him in the dugout and humiliated him in public. Every man on the Detroit club and most of the town's baseball writers knew what was happening and waited breathlessly for Schmidt to blow his top. The fact that he could easily have killed Cobb with his bare hands seemed to bother no one. They actually wanted to see him try. And Cobb himself was driven by the same insane desire. Every failure to get a substantial rise out of Schmidt

galled him to a fresh outburst of fury.

"You're yellow!" he screamed at the giant one afternoon. "You're a skunk with a yellow stripe and you stink! You're just a big, muscle-bound ape and you haven't got an ounce of guts in your belly!"

"You shouldn't talk like that to me, Ty," Schmidt said, with a deep frown. "I don't take that kinda stuff from folks. If you wasn't on the same team, I think I'd make you put up your dukes."

It was more than Cobb could take. Like a David without a slingshot, he hurled himself into the amazed Goliath. His fists, elbows and knees all sought vulnerable parts of Schmidt's hard body. The big fellow had his hands full simply holding him off. He looked around at the silent ring of players for some word of advice.

"Give it to him good, Dutch," one of them said. "It's the only language he knows."

Outweighed by more than 50 pounds, Cobb didn't just lose that fight; he was massacred. The big man aimed all his punches at Ty's body, sending him bouncing repeatedly off the lockers and walls. But Ty kept coming back for more. Even when Schmidt begged him to give up, Cobb groggily kept coming at him. Finally the other players, satisfied that Ty had learned his lesson, stepped in and stopped it.

The most amazing part of the story was that they were mistaken. Cobb not only didn't let up his torrent of abuse, but actually went after Schmidt again a few weeks later, with the same results. Even though Schmidt later sided with Cobb in another fight and Ty showed his gratitude by simply ignoring him thereafter, the giant was always nervous and ill at ease when Cobb was around.

Cobb's extramural brawls are just too numerous to catalog, but one other tussle is worthy of mention. According to impartial street-fight observers, it rates even higher than the famous Mickey Walker-Harry Greb aftermath. This was the run-in Ty had with umpire Billy Evans. It took place under the Detroit grandstand after a ballgame. For a full hour, fists flew. Cobb took a terrible beating, but finally gained the upper hand by resorting to roughhouse tactics.

Ty Cobb simply could never acknowledge defeat. His emotional public face was made up in equal parts of flaming anger and icy superiority. He scoffed openly at sentimentality; he rejected sympathy of any kind; he had few, if any, close friends. Both within and without the fraternity of baseball, he was a very lonely man.

His nature regarded any indication of sentiment or friendliness as a sign of weakness and he played the lone wolf role to the hilt. He ate alone, roomed alone, and even demanded the same absolute privacy when he was home with his family. In his later years, when he should have mellowed as the need for a competitive edge vanished, he remained the same. After 39 years of marriage, in which she had stood faithfully by him as he progressed from a nickel-nursing ballplayer to a multi-millionaire soft-drink stockholder, his wife, Shirley Lombard Cobb, divorced Ty in 1947.

Ty tried another marriage, to a woman much younger than himself, only to see that, too, dissolve in a divorce court two years later. Even a deeper personal tragedy was the loss of two of his three sons in the prime of life. Herschel Cobb died suddenly in 1951 at the age of 33, and Ty, Jr., died in 1952 at the age of 42. One son, Jimmie, and two daughters survive, but today Cobb's only real solace lies in his memories of his baseball achievements.

His achievements, of course, were exceptional. A quick glance at his record reveals that Cobb is the sole member of the ultra-exclusive 4,000-hit club. And 96 stolen bases in one season is a record that stands even more impregnable than Ruth's 60 home runs in a season. But what is most amazing about Ty's records is the fact that he was neither a natural hitter in the Ruthian sense nor a speed merchant of the stopwatch variety.

The triumph of Ty Cobb was one of sheer drive, a drive impelled by an anger that would have destroyed a lesser man. But fortunately, in baseball, Cobb found an outlet for his fury. And instead of being destroyed, he successfully created for himself a legendary career in the socially sanctioned world of sports.

One would surely suppose that Cobb's anger was spawned in some jungle-like community—the fierce squalor of a city slum or the barefoot poverty of a backwoods town. But Tyrus Raymond Cobb was the eldest son of a well-to-do and respected family of the Old South. His father, W. H. Cobb, was a distinguished educator who served as a Georgia State Senator. His mother was a quiet, aristocratic lady of considerable charm. The social standing of the family was above question.

Ty was born on December 18, 1886, in the town of Narrows, Georgia, near the Carolina border, and he grew up in the nearby community of Royston. There he worked in the corn fields and played Town Ball with the other boys. Town Ball was a simplified variant of baseball; the runner was declared out if the fielder hit him with the ball while he was rounding the bases. Ty developed astonishing agility in dodging these throws, but more important, he discovered at an early age that running the basepaths was an exciting sport. In Town Ball too, Ty learned how to place his hits. For since there was no set number of players to a side, different fielding situations confronted the hitter each time he came up to bat.

From Town Ball young Tyrus graduated into sandlot baseball, and by the time he was a lean 13 he was the regular shortstop of the Royston Rompers. But baseball as a career was at this point far from his ambition. He hoped some day to attend the University of Georgia and study medicine.

His father, the Senator, had other ideas about Tyrus' future. He wanted his son to become a lawyer. Often he forced young Ty to go down to the local judge's office to read among the musty law papers of Blackstone. Ty would go there, but, obstinate and bitter, he would merely thumb through the pages and stare out the window.

As Ty grew older, the arguments with his father over his choice of a career grew in frequency and intensity. "I can still see him," Cobb has recalled, "standing tall and stern, his hands behind his back, telling me I didn't know what I wanted to be. It made me feel that something was wrong with me."

Ty found that nothing was wrong with him on the baseball field. There he could assert himself and still come out on top. An intelligent youngster, he studied the rules and the tactics of the game. Diligently, he practiced the fundamentals.

Without his father's knowledge, Ty wrote to the Augusta team of the old Sally League for a tryout. They agreed to give him one at his own expense. Now Ty's troubles came to a head at home. Senator Cobb was shocked by the idea. Professional baseball, in those days, was scarcely considered a proper occupation for a respectable young man.

In a bitter all-night session, father and son squared away at each other. Tempers flared, but neither would give ground. Finally, in the early hours of the morning, the outraged father, realizing that

nothing could stop his strong-willed son, begrudgingly gave faint consent.

Still, it was under a dark cloud of protest that Tyrus set out for Augusta. He carried more than the usual burdens of the young athlete heading for his first important trial. For he felt that he had to show them. And he swore to himself that he would not return home to his family until he had made good. And he did, too, after being sent down briefly.

In 1905, the Detroit Tigers conducted their spring training in Augusta and Ty relished the practice games with the major leaguers. He hustled, he ran his pants off, he razzed the famous ballplayers in the big league lineup, he argued violently with the umpires. But the major leaguers, far from being nonplussed by the brash youngster, merely dismissed him as a fresh kid busher.

Ty watched enviously as the Tigers headed north and Augusta opened its season in the Sally League. His roommate was a pitcher from Atlanta named Nap Rucker, later to become a hero in Brooklyn. Rucker once told an anecdote which is immensely revealing of the young Cobb.

In those days the Augusta players dressed and showered in their hotel rooms. Rucker, easy-going, and Cobb were getting along fine until one afternoon when Nap, knocked out of the box, went straight to their hotel room. When Cobb returned from the ballpark, Rucker was already in the shower. For several minutes Ty waited outside the bathroom door. Then, when Rucker emerged, Cobb went at him savagely. "I take my shower first," Ty ordered coldly.

"What's the matter?" the astonished Rucker asked, backing away. "You gone crazy? Just 'cause I got to the shower first today?"

"Nap, please try to understand," Cobb said, now somewhat subdued. "I've got to be first, no matter what it is."

In his compulsion to be first, Ty became his own press agent. Grantland Rice, then writing sports for the *Atlanta Journal,* suddenly was besieged with telegrams from readers named "Smith" and "Johnson" and "Brown" calling attention to "the sensational play of Augusta's new rookie phenomenon." Granny tersely replied to one of the telegrams, "The mails should be fast enough for Cobb," then decided he had better take a look at the "new boy wonder."

Fortunately, Cobb was leading the league in batting and living up to his self-inspired press notices. He sold Granny, and subsequently, through Granny's widely read stories, news of his exploits began to reach the major leagues.

The Detroit club, hard hit by injuries at the time, dispatched Hennie Youngman to scout "that wild, crazy kid we saw last spring." And upon Youngman's recommendation, manager Bill Armour decided to buy Cobb's contract for $750. The only mention made of the transition in the Detroit newspapers was a simple one-line report that "Cyrus Cobb, Augusta outfielder, was signed today to play for the Tigers." Upon his arrival in the Motor City, Cobb promptly informed the reporters that his name was Tyrus, with a T. But, bored and uninterested, they walked away.

It would be nice to report that from the moment in 1905 that he first put on a uniform, 18-year-old Ty Cobb was established as a major league ballplayer. But the facts won't hold for it. He did get a hit in his first big league time at bat, a solid double off spitballer Jack Chesbro. But he finished his brief rookie year in the majors hitting a quiet .240.

Cobb reported to spring training in 1906 determined to stick with the Tigers.

To say that Cobb succeeded is an understatement. Within two weeks he didn't have a friend on the ballclub. Within a month no one was even speaking to him. But by the end of the season he was installed as the regular center fielder.

In 1907, with the rookie stigma removed and a hard shell developing to cover his thin-skinned sensitivity, the terror of Cobb began to show itself at the plate and on the basepaths. Leading the league in batting, RBIs, total hits and stolen bases, Ty spearheaded the Tigers to the first of three straight pennants. He even achieved the status of a hero.

But Ty's popularity didn't last very long. The following spring the 21-year-old batting champion was a holdout. He wanted a salary of $5,000. The sportswriters of the day regarded the request as unreasonable—ballplayers in those days weren't supposed to like money—and when holdout Cobb missed spring training, they rapped him hard.

Only when owner Frank Navin finally offered a compromise contract of $4,500 did Cobb report to camp. Each subsequent season, too, he was a perennial holdout, forcing the Detroit management to raise the ante steadily, until he was getting a salary of $40,000 a year, the high-water mark in major league pay until Babe Ruth came along in more plush days.

Cobb was always shrewd about what he did with his hard-earned money. Playing for Detroit in the early days of automobile expansion, he invested wisely in the growing industry. Coming from Georgia, he was naturally attracted to the cotton market, into which he ventured with great discernment. His biggest financial coup, the one that was to cushion him for life, also came about because of his Georgia upbringing. In 1921 he bought a large block of stock in Coca Cola at $1.18 per share and watched the decimal point slide over until the stocks were worth $181 per share. When he retired from baseball, Cobb was one of the few professional athletes ever to end his career in the graceful role of a millionaire in his own right.

In his approach to baseball, Cobb was a realist, too, always cultivating his investment in himself. During the winter he would walk and hunt endlessly to build up his legs. During spring training he wore weighted shoes that caused him to work harder and paid off later by making his feet seem to fly when he switched to ordinary playing shoes. Following the same principle, he was the first hitter to swing three bats as he approached the plate.

Probably the most scientific ballplayer of all time, the mentally alert Cobb studied both himself and the other players continuously. He compiled his own book on pitchers. And he discovered for himself a way to snap out of a slump. He simply tried to meet the ball and hit it right back to the pitcher's box. Only when he had regained his confidence would he try swinging freely again.

Cobb gripped his bat in a unique way, almost a choke, his right hand three inches from the knob, his left hand three inches higher. He explained his reasoning this way: "If you had a long pole and wanted to touch something with it, how would you do it? By holding it down on the end with both hands? Or by putting one hand down here and the other up here to give you better leverage? Well, that's what I do with my bat. That's how I get around on the ball."

With his sliding grip, and his feet planted close together, Ty could lean into the pitch and place a hit anywhere. Defensive shifts such as those set up against Ted Williams would have been meaningless against him. Ty called his shots to left, right, or center field. He bunted down either baseline, applying a "reverse English" that

made the ball roll dead. If he had any weakness or blind spot, two generations of American League pitchers never discovered it.

Ring Lardner, in a short story, succinctly records the greatest tribute to Cobb's batting ability. A rookie pitcher asks his manager, "How do you get Cobb out?" "That's easy," the manager answers snidely. "You just get a gun and shoot him."

The more traditional recourse held open to a pitcher in dealing with a difficult hitter is the base on balls. But to walk Cobb deliberately was to invite disaster. He could, and often did, score from first on a single. A sacrifice bunt was often sufficient for him to get from first to third. He could score from second on an infield out. And, of course, he was always a threat to steal any base at any time.

So respected was Cobb's base-stealing talent that once during a pre-game skull session, manager Connie Mack of the Athletics posed this question to his catcher, Wally Schang: "Now, suppose Cobb was on second and you knew he was going to steal third? What would you do?"

Schang shot back his answer unhesitatingly. "Why, that's easy, Mr. Mack. I'd call for a pitchout, fake a throw to third, hold on to the ball, and try to tag the bum as he slid home."

In addition to his other abilities, Cobb was a superlative fielder. He would try for any ball regardless of personal risk. He could take a backward somersault dive into the bleachers, land on his neck, and still come up with the catch. His throwing arm was accurate. One afternoon, shifting from his customary center-field position to right field, he threw out three runners at first base.

Legend has it that Cobb would sit on the steps of the dugout before a game nonchalantly sharpening his spikes. That, of course, is only legend. But a legend, it should be remembered, is a believable untruth. Ty Cobb carefully converted his reputation for violence and volatility into base hits and stolen bases by purposely creating the kind of charged atmosphere of high tension in which he thrived best. Opposing players became nervous and edgy, pulling bonehead plays, as they tried to anticipate the unpredictable Cobb. At the same time many players actually lived in physical fear of him. The word passed around the league was "Don't get Cobb mad." For one never knew what the Georgian might do next. An old-timer said recently, "I used to feel he'd just as soon chase me out of the park with his spikes as look at me."

To Cobb, victory was the only consideration. Just as he would strike fear into the hearts of his opponents in order to gain it, so too could he willingly cast doubts into the minds of his friends. On Shoeless Joe Jackson, he used the subtler and more devious form of psychology. Jackson considered himself a friend of Cobb's. They bore a mutual respect for each other's skills and shared the same common origin as southerners. But in a contest, no one was a friend of Cobb's.

In 1911, while Cobb and Jackson were vying for the league batting title, Detroit came into Cleveland for a six-game series. And Cobb tendered Jackson a special treatment he had devised for the occasion. On the first day of the series he arranged to pass Joe as the clubs exchanged the field during batting practice. Jackson good naturedly walked up to Cobb. "Hello, Ty," he said smiling.

Cobb's face turned red. "Stay *away* from me!" he growled.

"What's the matter?" Jackson asked, surprised.

"Just keep out of my way," Cobb sneered.

Each inning as they passed each other when the teams changed sides, Jackson would ask, plaintively, "What did I do, Ty? What's the matter?" Cobb, in turn, just glared silently.

Jackson suffered the confusion of the innocent. With his mind distracted as he tried to figure out how he had irritated Cobb, he went hitless in the first three games of the series. Meanwhile actor Cobb's average swelled into a commanding lead.

"I stole that title from Jackson," Cobb boasts with a loud laugh. "If I waited for nature to take its course, he would have beaten me. I had to come up with something." Cobb hit .420 that year, Jackson .408.

That Cobb succeeded in "stealing" the title was almost poetic justice, for in the previous season his fellow ballplayers had conspired to cheat him out of a batting crown that was rightfully his. In 1910, Cobb and Nap Lajoie, the affable Cleveland second baseman, were locked in a close battle for the championship. That year, the Chalmers Auto Company offered the added incentive of a new car to the league leader. Detroit finished its season with Ty the apparent batting champ. The Indians had a doubleheader with the St. Louis Browns on that last day of the season. The games could have no bearing on the standings. The Browns, among themselves, agreed to let the popular Lajoie know that hits were his for the asking. They played far back on the infield grass and feebly waved their gloves as Lajoie bunted eight for eight, apparently gaining enough points to edge out Cobb for the title.

Hugh Fullerton, a resolute and fair-minded sportswriter, was indignant at the travesty. He went back over an early-season game, in which he had been the official scorer, and, unbeknown to anyone, changed from an error to a hit the scoring of a questionable play on which Cobb had reached first base. When the official figures were announced it was Cobb .385, Lajoie .384.

Winning batting championships was a compulsive habit with Cobb. In his first 14 full seasons in the league he won 12 of them. In his 15th season he broke the pattern of the obsession. And in his 16th season he changed the focus of his energies in what many consider to have been his worst move in baseball. He became a manager.

The Tigers, whose leadership Ty assumed in 1921, were far from championship caliber. They had finished seventh the previous season. But Ty quickly molded them into the hittingest club of all time; the team batting average was a lusty .316. Harry Heilmann, who had been a .309 hitter in 1920, became a .394 hitter in '21. Cobb himself hit .389. Still the club could do no better than finish sixth.

By 1923, however, the Tigers were a driving second-place club, with Cobb pushing his players unstintingly. By and large, though, Ty was unhappy as a manager. The game of baseball as he relished it—the carefully placed hit, the adroit bunt, the skillful steal, the niggardly pursuit of a single run and the zealous guarding of it—was a thing of the past. A new power game had arrived, and Ty was out of step and skill with it.

Cobb sadly summed up the transformation that had taken place. "I guess more fans would rather watch Ruth clout one over the fence than watch me steal a base."

After the 1926 season, at the age of 40, Cobb gave up the helm of the Tigers, and announced his retirement as a player. But Connie Mack lured him to the A's as a player with a $60,000 offer. Even at 41, the efficiency of the battle-scarred Georgia Peach was unimpaired as he hit an astonishing .357, stole 22 bases, and earned a suspension for himself by unceremoniously pushing umpire Red Ormsby around. However, after one more season—hitting .323 at the age of 42—Cobb called it quits for good.

Since leaving baseball, Ty has often seen fit to defend his good name. He stoutly denies any allegation that he ever played dirty ball. "Aggressive, yes, but dirty, no! But I guess if they ever make a

movie out of my life the first scene will show me crashing into third base, cutting somebody's leg off."

Cobb also becomes infuriated when he is said to have been lucky. He believes he made his own luck. "I was alert. I'd notice things and I'd store them away. And then when I applied them it might seem like luck, but it wasn't. I had planned it."

Of late, Cobb's name has been appearing on the news pages with a quiet but consistent frequency. At the age of 71 he has returned to his home state of Georgia. He has established in his hometown of Royston a medical center in honor of his father. He has set up an educational foundation to help young students through college. And he is now building for himself a dream house on top of a mountain.

"There is a quality about the people where a fellow is born that makes him feel like he belongs," a comparatively mellow Cobb told Atlanta sportswriter Furman Bisher recently. "This is the country where I belong. I don't want to be set aside from the rest of the people. I just want to ease into life here without any fanfare."

Perhaps Cobb has gone full circle and found peace. Perhaps his anger has abated and the fire that seemed unquenchable has finally been banked. But some years ago another famous Georgian,

Grantland Rice, visited the retired Cobb. They were joined by Nig Clarke, the old Cleveland catcher, and the three old-timers fell to reminiscing. Granny reminded Clarke of the knack he had of tossing his mitt away after a two-out tag as if the call couldn't even be considered close.

Clarke laughed. "I fooled a lot of umps that way. Many's the time I missed the runner but the umps still called him out."

Clarke turned to Cobb. "I missed the tag on you at least five times when you were called out."

Cobb put down his drink. His face was flushed. Suddenly he leaped across the table at Clarke and began to pound him. "Five runs!" he shouted, "You cost me five runs!"

That was more like Cobb.

Epilogue

An early stockholder in Coca-Cola and General Motors, Ty Cobb enjoyed a millionaire's retirement in his native Georgia. But he was afflicted with poor health in his final years, suffering from prostate cancer, diabetes and chronic heart disease until his death in 1961 at age 74.

<table>
<tr><td></td></tr>
</table>

Chapter 51

Walter Johnson, The Big Train

The great power pitcher of the 20th century, Walter Johnson led the AL in strikeouts 12 times while winning 417 games and posting a remarkable 110 shutouts.

By Jack Zanger
SPORT Magazine, November 1961

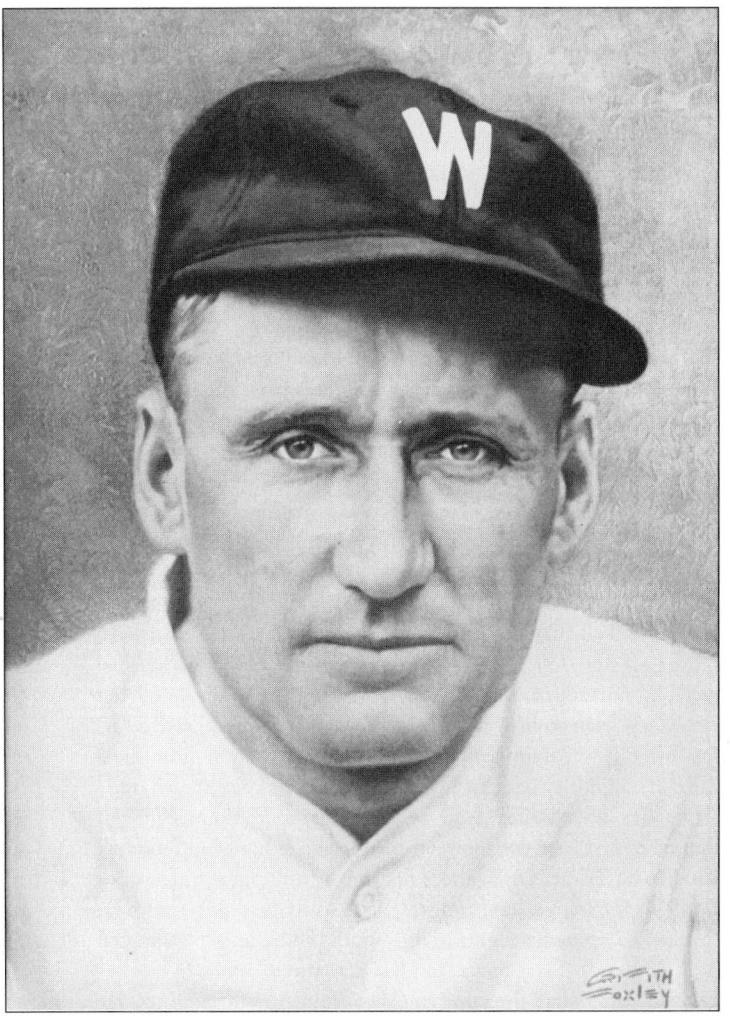

They called him "The Big Train," and "Barney," and "The Coffeyville Express." But of all Walter Johnson's nicknames the most appropriate seems to be "Sir Walter." It so perfectly mirrors the kind of man he was—popular, confident, full of pride, and still authentically humble.

The best illustration of the respect and love Walter commanded from baseball fans everywhere can be seen in the bittersweet aftermath of his final World Series appearance. It was the seventh game of the 1925 Series between the Washington Senators and the Pittsburgh Pirates. A steady, day-long rain had churned the Pittsburgh playing field into a sea of mud. Going into the bottom of the eighth, the Senators led, 7-6.

Johnson had won the first and fourth games for Washington, 4-1 and 4-0. Now he was just four outs from his third win of the Series—and from becoming the first pitcher to win four consecutive World Series games. But Johnson was a tired man. He was one month short of his 38th birthday and his magnificent right arm, which had fashioned 396 victories in 19 big league seasons, had reached the limit of endurance.

Pittsburgh catcher Earl Smith doubled with one down and Skeeter Bigbee's pinch-hit double sent him home with the tying run. After Eddie Moore walked, Max Carey reached first on an error of a potential double-play ball. Kiki Cuyler hoisted a foul-line double that scored two runs—and that was the game.

The Pittsburgh fans went wild in their heroes' finest hour. Yet they still showered their sympathies on the weary Johnson. "Tough luck, Walter," they said as the beaten pitcher trudged in his ploughboy gait from the mucky field. "Sorry it had to be you." There were other outpourings of regret from Pirate fans who had hated to see the great pitcher fail. It is unlikely that such ungrudging compassion would be piled upon an enemy today.

But a full generation has passed since Walter Johnson threw his last big league pitch. The times have faded and memories are short. Now there are only the greybeards and musty records to testify to his greatness. He had everything to go with his tireless arm—strength, stamina, speed. No pitcher in history could throw faster over the nine-inning route—and then come back and do it again the next day. Don Drysdale's swift one still snaps hitters' heads back, and Ryne Duren can be untouchable for an inning or two, but when you talk of fastball pitchers you have to start with Johnson.

How fast was he? There was the day in 1923, Johnson's 17th season in the American League, when Lu Blue, who played first base for the Detroit Tigers, struck out on a Johnson fastball and walked disgustedly back to the bench. "How can you hit 'em when you can't see 'em," he growled. In time Lu's line became synonymous with Johnson.

Ray Chapman of the Cleveland Indians, who became baseball's only beanball fatality years later, once dropped his bat at the plate and walked away after taking two Johnson darts for called strikes. "That's only strike two," shouted Billy Evans, umpiring behind the plate.

"You can have the next one," Chapman shouted without turning around. "It won't do me any good."

Gabby Street, who caught Johnson's early years at Washington, described Walter's blinding speed this way: "When the right arm

started around, my big glove was up and ready. It was too late to wait another tenth of a second."

Perhaps Johnson himself reluctantly put the clincher on any arguments about his speed. Shortly before World War II Johnson, living quietly in retirement on his farm at Germantown, Maryland, was invited to Washington by sportswriter Shirley Povich to watch Bob Feller pitch. Feller was then at his blazing best. During the first couple of innings, Johnson turned to his host and murmured things like, "Mighty fast" and "He smokes that ball, goodness gracious." Finally Povich popped the jackpot question. "Tell me, Walter, does Feller throw that ball as fast as you did?"

Johnson, who had a reputation for always speaking the simple truth, hesitated a long, thoughtful moment. Then he turned and said, "No."

Ironically, Johnson's lightning fastball always terrified him even more than it did the batters. He feared he might hit and seriously injure someone. Unbelievable as it sounds in this day when the brushback is part of almost every pitcher's repertoire, Johnson only once intentionally aimed a pitch at a hitter. He was goaded into doing it. Before a game with the Philadelphia Athletics in 1912, Mike Martin, the Senators' trainer, got on Walter to teach Frank (Home Run) Baker a lesson.

"He's been ruining us all season," Martin said in exasperation. Johnson shook his head.

"Well, Walter, you must be yellow," Martin said with a sneer.

That did it. When Baker stepped in against him, Johnson reared back in his classic windup and sent a high hard one directly at the batter's head. The pitch missed its mark as Baker went sprawling in the dirt. A white-faced Johnson, who later said, "I'd give a thousand dollars if I could take back that pitch," raced to the fallen man. But Baker simply motioned him back to the mound and dug in again.

On another occasion Johnson nicked Eddie Collins on the leg with a fastball. Collins hit the ground as if his knees had been blown off and rolled over groaning in pain. Through clenched teeth he murmured, "I think my leg's broken." Johnson, all but trembling, bent to help him up. "Believe me, Eddie," he said sorrowfully, "it was unintentional. It must have got away from me a little. It's a hot day and the perspiration ..." His voice trailed off.

Collins waved him away with an agonized expression and limped to first base. Johnson returned to the mound still brooding about poor Eddie. On Walter's first pitch to the next hitter, poor Eddie lit for second base and stole it so easily he didn't even have to slide. Cupping his hands to his mouth, Eddie impishly shouted to the mound, "I was lucky. You just grazed me."

"Sir Walter" had the same courtly attitude toward umpires. He never allowed an umpire's decision to upset him, nor was he ever known to protest a call.

Billy Evans once called one of Johnson's pitches a ball and later admitted it should have been a strike. The call almost cost Walter a 1-0 victory. The game over, Evans hastily headed for the umpire's dressing room, hoping to avoid Johnson. But the big pitcher caught up to him under the stands.

"Bill, what was wrong with that next-to-last pitch?" Johnson asked, referring to the critical call.

"What did you think was wrong with it, Walter?" Evans hedged.

"Might have been a little low," Johnson replied dryly. There was a silent pause, then the two men burst out laughing.

Johnson didn't laugh so hard at his teammates who constantly kicked away ballgames on him. Yet he never lost his temper, never

reprimanded them. A writer, reflecting on the poor teams Walter played with most of his 21 Senator seasons, once asked him how he would have liked playing for contending clubs all those years. Johnson shrugged. "Washington is home to me," he said. "If I had a chance to go to a pennant-winning team and play in a World's Series, I'd rather stay here with my home team."

From the day he first reported to the Senators, a long, lean farmboy with a whipsaw arm, until the day he hung up his uniform for good, Walter Johnson remained his same guileless self. Despite his quixotic philosophy about baseball and life, though, he was far from being a fatuous rube. His own candid appraisal of the way he pitched bears a trace of his earthy wit: "I just try to throw as hard as I can when I think I've got to throw as hard as I can. And sometimes I guess I don't throw quite hard enough."

He was a sandy-haired man, 6-foot-1, 195 pounds, with blue eyes and a ruddy complexion. His arms dangled almost to his knees. Those long arms, many contended, powered his incredible speed. He was a paradox in motion: a gangling, herky-jerk farmer walking to the mound; a picture of rhythm and coordination on the mound. One writer described his pitching grace as follows: "There is an ease and freedom and a smoothness in the long, loose swing that shows no sign of strain." Johnson also had excellent poise and concentration and he never, in season or out, allowed himself to get out of condition.

With the sports pages having kept us posted throughout the 1961 season on Warren Spahn's and Early Wynn's steady advance toward victory 300, it seems almost unbelievable that any pitcher could have won more than 400 games. Walter Johnson did. Toiling 21 seasons, made longer by the fact that he spent them with the generally hapless Senators, he hung up 417 victories. Only Cy Young topped him, with 511.

Attempting to reel off all Johnson's pitching records would take on the monotony of a railroad announcer calling off the milk run between New York and Los Angeles. But Walter's major records should be noted: he pitched the most American League games, 802; led the league in strikeouts the most years, 12; pitched the most complete games, 531; struck out the most batters in the majors, 3,509; pitched the most innings 5,914; pitched the most shutouts, 110; pitched the most consecutive shutout innings, 56; recorded the lowest earned-run average for 300 or more innings in one season, 1.14.

Walter Perry Johnson was the second of six children born to Frank and Minnie Johnson.

"I was born November 6, 1887, on a farm four miles out of Humboldt, Kansas," he said. "We had no near neighbors, there weren't any kids to play with, so up to the time I was 14 years old, I had never heard of baseball. Then my family moved to Fullerton, California, in the oil fields, and I started in high school. All the boys played baseball there, so I took it up and I liked it—I always have."

The high-school team had pitchers to spare, so Walter became a catcher. Halfway through his first game, the coach noticed Walter was pegging the ball back harder than the pitcher was throwing it in, so he was sent to the mound. "I got beat 21-0," he said later. However, the reason for the lopsided defeat had nothing to do with Walter's inexperience; the Fullerton catcher was unable to hang onto his hopping fastballs, and batter after batter who struck out reached first as the pitches tore through the unhappy receiver. "The next Saturday our club imported a catcher who could corral the balls and we played the opposing team on its home grounds," Johnson said. "In 15 innings the score stood 0 to 0. I was 16 then,

and I guess that's the greatest game I ever played."

After that young Walter divided his time between working in the oil fields and pitching semi-pro ball. A friend persuaded him to join Tacoma in the Northwestern League, but Walter was not seasoned enough for such fast company. Cut loose, Walter migrated to Weiser, Idaho, where he pitched the last two months of the 1906 season.

The following year he returned to Weiser and immediately stood the league on its ear. He ran up a string of 86 straight score-less innings and by mid-season he had won 13 and lost two, racking up 210 strikeouts and yielding an average of less than three hits a game.

About this time Senator manager Joe Cantillon was being flooded by persistent letters from a voluntary scout—a Washingtonian on the road for the U.S. Geological Society who raved about the fire-balling wizard of Weiser. Cantillon finally dispatched his western representative, Cliff Blankenship, to look at Johnson, though he was certain it would be a waste of time. Actually, it was only a side trip for Blankenship, who was on his way to Kansas to see a promising young outfielder, Clyde Milan.

After signing Milan for the Senators, Blankenship arrived in Weiser just in time to watch Johnson pitch 12 innings of scoreless ball before losing 1-0 when his infield booted a couple. It turned out to be a prophetic game, because Johnson was to be involved in 60 1-0 decisions in Washington, and he was to lose 20 of them. Blankenship made an outright offer to take Walter back to Washington with him, but the wary 19-year-old wasn't going on any train ride all the way east without some guarantee. "I can pitch baseball," he said, "but not if I am worried. I'll go with you only under the condition that I have a return ticket in my pocket when I start." The scout readily agreed, thus completing what must be the biggest bargain in baseball history. For a $250 investment the Washington Senators had acquired Walter Johnson.

The Big Train wound up his first season in the majors with a 5-9 record. The year was 1907.

The following year Johnson pulled his famed iron-man stunt, pitching three consecutive shutouts against the New York Yankees, then the Highlanders, in four days. Starting on Friday, September 4, he blanked the New Yorkers in their ballpark on four hits, 3-0. The next day he tossed a three-hit, 6-0 win. There was no game the day after because Sunday ball was then outlawed in New York. But on Monday he went out again and beat them in the opener of a doubleheader, 4-0, pitching a two-hitter.

All sorts of stories are attached to this feat. One of the more credible versions is that Johnson had once claimed he might some day get around to pitching three shutouts in a row and had asked Cantillon for the assignment. "He was faster in the third game than he was in the first," wrote Grantland Rice, who witnessed the games.

It was Rice, incidentally, who nicknamed Johnson "The Big Train" when he wrote, "The Big Train comes to town today," heralding a big series. Walter's teammates dubbed him "Barney," after Barney Oldfield, because he liked to drive his car at speeds up to 40 miles an hour. "The Coffeyville Express" nickname started when Johnson made Coffeyville, Kansas, his off-season home, where he staged his only serious holdout in 1911 before compromising to sign for $7,000.

He became a 20-game winner for the first time (Johnson was to win 20 or more games 12 seasons) in 1910, when he turned in 25 victories for the seventh-place Senators. He also struck out 313 batters, tops in the league. Since Washington won only 66 games that year, Johnson had the distinction of winning more than a

third of them.

Two events marked 1912 as an important year for Johnson. The Senators hired a new manager, Clark Griffith, with whom he soon cemented a close friendship. It was Griffith's skillful maneuvering that prevented Walter from jumping to the Federal League in 1914. Johnson won 16 games in a row in 1912, beginning on July 3 and ending August 23 at St. Louis—on a fluke call.

Johnson had relieved Tom Hughes in the eighth inning with the score tied, 2-2, and two men on base. Walter gave up the hit that drove in the runners and he was charged with the defeat. A great howl went up protesting the decision, but it wasn't until years later that the American League established the present rule which charges the pitcher who puts the winning runs on with the loss.

The 33-12 record he posted in 1912 was diminished by the 36-7 mark he achieved the following season. What's more, 1913 was the year Johnson strung together 56 consecutive scoreless innings, a record that has become a sort of Holy Grail to pitchers ever since. This was the year, too, that Walter, the shy bachelor who never drank or took part in the clubhouse card games, met Hazel Lee Roberts, daughter of Nevada Congressman Edward Roberts, and began a slow, formal courtship that finally resulted in their marriage in 1914. Walter and Hazel bought a farm near Bethesda, Maryland, and had five children. The greatest tragedy in Johnson's life was Hazel's death in 1930, at the age of 36, after a brief bout with pleurisy. It left a lonely gap in his life.

In the decade from 1914 to 1923, Johnson became the most invincible pitcher baseball had ever seen, turning in six successive 20-game-plus seasons. The best the Senators could finish was third. Then, just as it was beginning to seem that Johnson would never get his crack at winning a World Series game, the Senators won their first pennant.

It was 1924 and the New York Giants under John McGraw were the National League champions. This was to be McGraw's last pennant. Washington's Bucky Harris, then a stripling manager of 27, had made good in his first year on the job. The opener was in Washington, and who else but Walter Johnson, whose 23-7 mark had more to do with the pennant's hanging in the capital than any other single factor, would be nominated to start? A crowd of 35,760, including President Calvin Coolidge, had squeezed into the tiny ballpark to see Johnson throw back the swaggering Giants.

But the fans had little to cheer about as the Giants, behind their dandy little left-hander, Art Nehf, beat Johnson in 12 innings, 4-3. He had fanned 12 men and pitched his heart out, but the Washington support, or lack of it, finally led to his undoing. He was a used-up pitcher when Bucky Harris asked him to start the fifth game, with the Series tied at two games apiece, and the Giants laced 13 hits to beat him a second time, 6-2. When news of the game reached the city on the Potomac, you could cut the gloom with a knife.

That should have been it. But fate owed one to the valiant Big Train, and he got another chance when Harris sent him in to pitch the ninth inning of the seventh game. The Senators had tied the score, 3-3, in the bottom of the eighth and nobody wanted the chance to hold the Giants back more than Johnson. He was magnificent. Though the Giants got men on base, Johnson reached back each time and slammed the door, fanning the dangerous Frank Frisch with a man on in the 11th, striking out Hack Wilson with trouble brewing in the 12th.

Then the ball took the right bounce for Johnson. With one out in the Senators' 12th, Giant catcher Hank Gowdy dropped Muddy

Ruel's pop foul, giving him another swing. Ruel then doubled to left. Johnson hit for himself and grounded to short, but Travis Jackson fumbled the ball and all hands were safe. The next batter was center fielder Earl McNeely, and it was his ground ball that became the famed "pebble hit," taking a weird bounce over third baseman Freddy Lindstrom's head and driving Ruel around from second with the winning run.

The Washington Senators were the world champions of baseball! Pandemonium broke loose. There was Cal Coolidge waiting at the dugout to clasp Johnson's hand as he came off the field the winning pitcher. For an hour the fans stood in the darkening ballpark and shouted themselves hoarse. The old sing-song line, "Washington—first in war, first in peace and last in the American League," was passé.

Coolidge paid tribute to Johnson's performance after the game, saying, "It has to be remembered that though he was not successful in the two previous games he pitched, it was his skill that won the pennant and put Washington in the World's Series. Everyone was pleased to see him come back at the close of the last game."

High above the field in the press box, Johnson's old umpire friend Billy Evans dried his eyes with a handkerchief and whispered, "This is the biggest kick I've ever gotten out of baseball."

That was the summit of Johnson's career. Though there was enough power left in his arm to win 20 games in 1925 and lead the Senators to their second pennant in a row, there was heartbreak to follow in the Series with the Pirates and ugly recriminations between Harris and Ban Johnson, the American League president.

Johnson started and won the Series opener, 4-1. He shut out Pittsburgh in the fourth game, 4-0, to win his third consecutive World Series game. But again the Series went to seven games and Harris asked the grizzled, now leg-sore veteran to try again. Try he did, in the rain and mud of Forbes Field that grey October afternoon before the years finally came tumbling down on him in that bitter eighth inning. He lost the game and the Series for the Senators. If it was an hour for Johnson to grieve it was an embattled one for Harris. He was vilified for stretching Johnson to the breaking point.

"You put up a game fight," Ban Johnson wired Harris. "This I admire. You lost the Series for sentimental reasons. This should never occur in a World Series."

Harris saw the wire and knew the last two sentences indicted him. He angrily replied to the league president: "Sentimental reasons played absolutely no part in my desire to pitch Johnson and my decision to use him. Walter Johnson pitched wonderful ball."

Johnson began his 20th big league season by pitching a 15-inning shutout against the Athletics, beating Ed Rommel, 1-0. It was his 14th opening-day start, of which he won nine, and during which he had pitched before five different Presidents of the United States. His last active season was 1927, when he posted a 5-6 mark.

Clark Griffith, who told Walter there would always be a place for him in baseball, got Johnson a job managing Newark in 1928. The following year he brought him back home to manage Washington, which, unfortunately, he did with little success for four years. Then Billy Evans, by that time general manager of the Indians, talked Alva Bradley into appointing Walter the Cleveland manager. This proved to be an even sadder experience than his Washington managerial tenure and after a couple of seasons he went back to his farm.

He entered politics for a brief period, but his main joy was his early loves: working the land, hunting with his dogs and raising chickens, ducks and turkeys. In 1936 he was voted into Baseball's Hall of Fame. He lived the life of a retired country squire until that day in April, 1946, when he walked into Georgetown University Hospital to undergo treatment for a brain tumor. With an entire nation alerted to the tragic final hours, Johnson died on the night of December 10, 1946.

Eulogies for the great pitcher who had lived an exemplary life poured in from everywhere, including one from President Harry Truman. But the words that seem best to sum up the man are the ones he uttered after losing the final game of the 1925 World Series. "I tried my best to give everything I had," he said, "but it wasn't good enough. I had plenty of stuff, my leg felt all right and my arm all right also, but it was certainly no day for pitching. It was far too cold and rainy. It's tough, but they had the better ball team out there, and they won. And that's all there is to that."

No one could have spoken a more fitting valedictory for The Big Train.

Chapter 52

"Tell Me About Babe Ruth..."

Babe Ruth was a larger-than-life character, and six years after he died his life and times were celebrated in a tribute by one of America's most respected sportswriters.

By Frank Graham
SPORT Magazine, October 1954

He is young. No child, mind you, but not old enough to vote. Eighteen, probably. He remembers Babe Ruth but the Babe he remembers was aging and sickened. He remembers when Babe died, the lying-in-state at Yankee Stadium and the funeral from St. Patrick's Cathedral, the flags at half staff and the great crowd on Fifth Avenue that steamy August day in 1948. All this he remembers, yet in his mind, as in the minds of so many other Americans of his generation, the Babe dwelt not as a man but as a legend.

Now he met one who had known the Babe, who had seen him from the very beginning of his major league career and through all the years of his greatness, who had traveled many a mile with him and been with him day and night, and he said:

"Tell me about Babe Ruth. Tell me all about him."

"There is no man who can tell you all about him," the other said, "But I'll tell you what I can."

He was a very simple man and, in some ways, a primitive man. He had little education and little need for what he had, for it was as if his life had been ordered for him, so that he did not have to turn a page in a book or do sums in arithmetic to gain the knowledge he needed to become rich and famous. He traveled the world over, yet when his travels were done, he could tell you nothing about the places he had been save the places where he had had fun. He literally walked with kings, yet he couldn't remember their names. He couldn't even tell you the names of all his teammates, although he had names of his own for them, such as Chicken Neck, Flop Ears, Duck Eye, Horse Nose and Rubber Belly.

His appetites were prodigious, and as long as he was in robust health ... and he was for almost all of his life ... he made no effort to restrain them. The jug and the platter were as much a part of his existence as the bat and the ball. He had a fondness for automobiles which he drove at such terrific speeds as to wear them out or, in reckless moments, wrap them around stone walls and telegraph poles. Although he was not a consistently heavy gambler and won or lost comparatively modest golf, bridge and poker bets, he had streaks in which he lost thousands of dollars on the horses, the dice and the wheel.

He was warm-hearted, fabulously generous, genuinely fond of children, greatly moved by the ills and trials of others, devoted to his family and his friends—and would not have known how to deal with an enemy for the simple reason that he never had one.

His true name was George Herman Ruth and he was of German descent. Born in Baltimore, he was a product of a broken home. He had a sister, younger than he, but they were separated when, at the age of seven, he was committed to St. Mary's Industrial School, there to remain, according to the law, until he was 21. Brother and sister lost track of each other so completely that they did not meet again until Babe had reached his peak with the Yankees in 1927. His mother died while he still was a small boy but his father lived to see him wear the uniform of the Boston Red Sox. However, in the years of the Babe's confinement, he and his father had become estranged and they saw little of one another in the time between his release and his father's death.

There should be a reminder here that St. Mary's was not a corral

for incorrigibles, but a haven for boys such as the Babe was, free of home control, running the streets at all hours and exposed to the dangers of a kind of life no boy ever should know. In the school he received religious training, bumbled his way through the classrooms and, as he grew older, was set to the task of learning the trade of tailoring.

Meanwhile, he was playing baseball ... and now it was the spring of 1913 and one who was to be his friend through all the remaining years of his life saw him for the first time: Brother Gilbert, teacher and baseball coach at St. Joseph's College.

"We had a great kid pitcher named Ford Meadows on our team," the Brother was to say much later, "and scouts from five major league clubs were on his trail. Then Jack Dunn sent Fritz Maisel down to look him over for the Baltimore club and I was so afraid Dunnie would sign him—because I knew Maisel would recommend him—that I said to Dunn:

"'Jack if you let this fellow alone, I'll give you the best young left-hander you ever saw.'

"Now, the truth is that I never had seen this young fellow pitch. But I had seen him play ball and while I do not profess to be one of those who can look down the years and see greatness in line for any individual, I had reason to believe that, with proper handling, this boy would become a great pitcher some day.

"I was at St. Mary's one day early in 1913 and I saw this boy who, so far as I was concerned, was just a big kid in blue overalls. He was catching for one of the teams in a league they had at St. Mary's and if you ever wanted to see a bone out of joint or one of nature's misfits, you should have seen him, a left-handed catcher, squatting back of the plate. All he had was a mask and a glove, made for a righthander, which he wore on his left hand. When he had to make a throw to second, he would take off his glove, tuck it under his right arm—and throw. And how he could throw! The ball was three feet off the ground going through the box and three feet off the ground when it got to second base. I knew that, with an arm like that, he could be made into a pitcher.

"Then I saw him go to bat. The pitcher for the other side was a tall, lean boy by the name of Tom Padget. As he wound up, he turned his back to the hitter before he let the ball go. I looked at him winding up and then I looked at Ruth. There he stood, just as you saw him standing at the plate when he was at the very top of his career. There was determination in his attitude—he had the will to do. Padget pitched the ball and Ruth hit it against the right-field fence. The next time up, he hit it over the center-field fence. The third time, he hit it over the left-field fence. Ah, but the fourth time, he delightfully, deliciously, delectably, struck out! And he looked better striking out than he did hitting home runs."

The Babe became a pitcher, and although Brother Gilbert had not seen him in the box when he talked to Dunn, he had heard such high praise of the boy from Brother Albert, the coach at St. Mary's, that it was with confidence he virtually handed him to the manager of the Orioles. Dunn went to see the Babe and immediately made up his mind to take him, although he didn't see him pitch, either. It was in the winter of 1913-1914 and the boy, now 19 years old, over six feet tall, weighing 170 and towering above his playmates, was sliding on a strip of ice on the frozen playing field.

Brother Paul, the head of the school, convinced that the Babe never would become either a scholar or a tailor, believing that whatever future he had was in baseball, and with complete trust in Dunn, gained the consent of the authorities to release him in Jack's custody. Under the terms of the release the Orioles' manager would

be responsible for him until he had attained his majority.

Dunn signed him to a contract calling for a salary of $600 for the season of 1914 and in March, he went straight from the school to the Orioles' training camp at Fayetteville, North Carolina. During the training season he received no pay, but Dunn had outfitted him with clothing on the eve of his departure from the school and now gave him a small allowance each week.

After 12 years behind the gates of St. Mary's, he was living in a sort of Never-Never land. He'd worn overalls and denim shirts most of the time at St. Mary's. His "best" suit was the poor best the struggling Brothers could afford on their skimpy budget. Now he was as well dressed as any other ballplayer in the camp, and better dressed than many. A nickel in his pocket at St. Mary's must have been heaven sent, for, on the outside, there was neither kith nor kin to send money to him. Now he had dollar bills, even an occasional five-dollar bill, in his pocket. Of necessity, he had been regimented at St. Mary's. Now he was an individual. Off the ball field, his time was his own. He even could stay up until 11 o'clock at night if he wanted to. At St. Mary's, he had been a boy among boys. Now he was a man among men. He could smoke cigars and shoot pool and have a glass of beer.

Dunnie was looking after him, of course, but Dunnie held him on a long leash, wanting him to make a place for himself in a world he'd scarcely known since he was seven years old. But pulling him up short now and then, lecturing him sometimes, treating him as a father would a son who, you might say, had grown up overnight.

"Dunn's baby," the other players called him, and soon they were calling him "Babe" and that's how he got his name, for at St. Mary's he'd been "George" to the Brothers and to the other boys as well. At first, he resented being called Babe but he was to know the day, not far distant from his time at Fayetteville, when he would glory in it.

A man among men, he was a pitcher among pitchers—and for all his absolute lack of experience beyond the playing field at St. Mary's, there was no better pitcher in the camp. In July, he was sold to the Red Sox. In August, he was optioned to the Providence club, which Joe Lannin, owner of the Red Sox, also owned and which had a chance to win the International League pennant. By his pitching he converted that chance into the pennant itself (all told, between Baltimore and Providence, he won 22 games), and in 1915 he was back in Boston and won 18 games as the Red Sox captured the pennant. Thus, within the short span of a year, he went from St. Mary's to the major leagues on a permanent basis and, on the way, was the major factor in the winning of the championship in what then was the strongest minor league in the country.

By 1916 he was fastening a strangle hold on fame. In that season he was one of the American League's top winners with 23 victories and 12 defeats. He led the league in earned-run average with 1.75. In the World Series, he won a 14-inning pitching duel with Sherrod Smith of Brooklyn in the longest Series game ever played. Yet, in many respects, he still was the big kid with only two years between him and St. Mary's. His natural disposition was childlike and he wanted to be friends with everybody but now and then the crude, cruel humor of the other players was too much for him and, when they taunted him, he flew into quick rages. Once, when prodded to anger, he said to his tormentor: "If you don't let me alone, I'll kill you!"

Frightened, the other backed off. "I figured he might have a knife or a gun," he explained.

A rumor started and spread through the league. Ruth was dangerous. He carried a knife or, sometimes, a gun. Lay off him. He

might kill you. When, as had to happen, Babe heard of it, he laughed. But his threat, however empty, and the rumor that grew out of it had cooled off the jesters. Besides, he had become too big a man on the ballclub to be treated as an ignorant kid so lately sprung from a shelter for waifs. He was a hero to the Boston public now, along with Duffy Lewis, Harry Hooper (Tris Speaker, third member of that great outfield, had gone to Cleveland after the 1915 season), Everett Scott, Jack Barry, Carl Mays, Sam Jones, Dutch Leonard, Ernie Shore and the manager and catcher, Bill Carrigan. That was a good and colorful team.

He was 21 years old in 1916 and Dunn no longer was his guardian. He was legally a man and free to do as he pleased and by now he was doing it. Not yet used to his new freedom, he began to live it up after hours but, fortunately for him, a new check was placed upon him. Carrigan, a college graduate and a Maine banker between seasons, was a tough one to cross and not only was respected by the players but feared by them, too, for he was capable of enforcing discipline with his fists, if necessary. He brought the Babe sharply into line and after that, there was no cause for complaint about his behavior.

Carrigan resigned following the 1916 Series triumph and Barry was appointed as his successor. The Babe hadn't the awe of Barry that he'd had of Carrigan and was off and rolling again. But in 1918, when Barry had gone into the World War I Navy and Ed Barrow had become the manager, he found himself once more under a strict drill master with a well-earned reputation as a rough-and-tumble fighter. Barrow had a story about his first brush with the Babe.

"He had stayed out all night," Ed said, "and in the morning, I went up to his room. I could hear him talking to his roommate and, without knocking, I opened the door and went in. His roommate was dressing but the Babe, still fully dressed, was reclining on his bed, smoking his pipe and reading a paper.

"'When you finish dressing,' I said to his roommate, 'get out. I want to talk to this fellow privately.'

"The Babe jumped to his feet and up yelled: 'You got nerve, busting in here! I ought to punch you in the nose!'

"Then he said to the other player: 'This is your room as much as it is mine. You stay here as long as you please.'

"'Not me!' the fellow said, and he grabbed his coat and ducked out. I locked the door and turned to Ruth and said:

"'No one has punched me in the nose for a long time and I advise you not to try it. Sit down.'

"I talked to him like a Dutch uncle for about 15 minutes," Ed said. "I told him he was the best left-handed pitcher in baseball—which he was—and that he had a chance to be the greatest of all time. I told him he was the only one who could ruin his career, which he was bound to do if he kept on the way he was going. By the time I got through, he was bawling. When I saw he was really repentant, I said to him:

"'I'm not trying to spoil your fun, Babe. I was young once, too, and I liked to get out and around in the evening. But you've got to take care of yourself and you've got to be back at the hotel at a reasonable hour. Now, I'm going to put you on your honor. No matter what time you get back, I want you to leave a note in my box telling me what time it was.'

"He promised he would," Ed said, "and he did, and it was seldom that he was later than 11 o'clock."

That season was marked by another notable continuation of his already glittering record. Because of his growing power as a hitter,

Barrow made full use of him and between turns in the box, he played first base and in the outfield. As a pitcher, he won 13 games, lost seven and had an earned-run average of only 2.22. All told, he was in 95 games, hit an even .300 and, with 11 home runs, tied Tilly Walker for the league lead.

The Red Sox won the pennant again and hooked up with the Chicago Cubs in the World Series. In the opening game, Ruth shut the Cubs out. In the fourth game, he did not allow a run until the eighth inning. As the run he had yielded to the Dodgers in 1916 had been a homer by Hy Myers in the first inning, he now had pitched 29 consecutive scoreless innings in World Series play, a record that still stands and of which he was as proud, in later years, as he was of his home-run record.

The years 1919 and 1920 were fateful years in his life. In 1919, Barrow switched him to the outfield and he rocked the little world of baseball by hitting 29 home runs, thereby becoming the greatest drawing card in the sport. In January, 1920, he was sold to the Yankees and so set forth on a new era, an era in which he was to become famous all over the world and to cause men to say that here was the greatest ballplayer who ever lived.

Records sometimes make dull reading, save for those who have a passion for statistics, but there is nothing dull about the record of Babe Ruth as a Yankee from 1920 through 1934. Read it or, if you've read it, read it again. The home runs, the total bases, the runs scored, the runs driven in through 15 championship seasons and seven World Series.

But look now to the man himself as greatness beyond the wildest dream of any ballplayer enveloped him; as he lifted the Yankees to a point where they dominated the game; and as he revolutionized it.

He tied his own home-run mark on July 15, 1920, and broke it by hitting two more homers the following day. The nation was thrilled and crowds stormed the Polo Grounds, which the Yankees then shared with the Giants, and all the other ballparks where he played. Crowds swirled about him wherever he went for an evening ... and now he was going anywhere his boundless energy and equally boundless capacity for fun led him. The wraps were off him at last and never, bar one historic occasion, would be placed upon him again.

The situation for fun-making for him, and for the other players as well, was perfect on the club owned by Col. Jacob Ruppert, multimillionaire brewer, and Col. Tillinghast L'Hommedieu Huston, who had made at least one million dollars and possibly two as an engineer. Ruppert had affronted Huston by appointing Huggins as manager of the club in 1918 while his partner, whose own choice had been Wilbert Robinson, was serving in France. Til never forgave Jake for it. Most of his displeasure, however, was vented on Huggins, whom he ignored when they chanced to meet and openly ridiculed before the players and the newspapermen. As a result, the Little Miller's attempts to control the players off the field and sometimes on it ... were futile, and the players, knowing that any shackles placed upon them by the manager would be struck off by Huston, thumbed their noses at the manager.

There being no night ball in that time, the Babe had all the hours between dusk and dawn in which to amuse himself and he used up most of them in that fashion as he went swinging from town to town. On the hotel registers when the Yankees were on the road, Ping Bodie was listed as his roommate but when someone asked Ping one day whom he roomed with, he said: "A suit case."

In Washington, Joe Judge, the Senators' first baseman, met the

Babe coming out of the Hotel Willard.

"Your ballclub here?" Joe asked.

"No," the Babe said. "They're over at the Whatsis, down the street. But I'm staying here."

"It must be nice to be rich," Joe said. "How much do they soak you here?"

"A hundred bucks a day for a suite."

"A hundred bucks a day!"

"Well," the Babe growled, "a fellow's got to entertain, don't he?"

His salary of $10,000 a year in Boston in 1919 had been doubled. What was all that money for if not to be spent?

The Yanks finished third in 1920 as Ruth hit the astounding number of 54 home runs. In 1921, they believed from the beginning they would win the pennant and there was no holding them, especially the Babe. In 1921, too, Ed Barrow had been brought down from Boston the fall before to take the post of busness manager of the Yankees. He sought earnestly to bolster Huggins' status as boss of the players but without much success and he had no control over Ruth, as he had had in Boston.

When the club was in the East, the players were permitted to travel from town to town in their own cars, if they chose to do so and, naturally, the Babe so chose. His car was a 12-cylinder job with a cruising speed of 90 miles an hour and, the Babe had discovered to his delight, capable of doing 110 when he put his foot down on the floor. And so, with his penchant for scorching the highways, there was a summer night when he came very close to a horrible death.

The Yanks had played Washington that day. The Babe had hit two home runs and was in a gay and jubilant mood when he set off for Philadelphia, next stop on the schedule, with Lefty O'Doul, Freddy Hofmann and Charlie O'Leary, the coach, in his car. Thirty miles out of Philadelphia, they whirled through a town, dark now because the hour was late.

"Kennett Square," O'Leary said, clutching his straw hat. "This is where Herb Pennock lives."

A half mile farther on, the Babe saw, too late, a sharp curve, faced with a stone embankment. As he jammed on the brakes, the car swerved, skidded and turned over twice. O'Leary had been flung clear of the car but the others were pinned under it. Miraculously unhurt, except for minor bruises and abrasions, they crawled out, and Ruth rushed to O'Leary, lying face down and unconscious on the road. Thinking Charlie had been mortally hurt, he cried:

"Oh, God! Bring him back! God! Take me instead!"

As Charlie stirred the Babe implored: "Speak to me, Charlie! Speak to me!"

Charlie suddenly sat up. Looking about him, he yelled: "Hey! What the hell happened to my straw hat?"

The battered car was hauled away and the party completed the journey to Philadelphia by taxicab. News of the accident had traveled fast and, in at least one channel, had been distorted. The paper that was on Babe's breakfast tray screamed:

"BABE RUTH KILLED IN AUTO ACCIDENT!"

Huggins tried, in the light of the Babe's near miss, to forbid the players thenceforth to travel by car, but Huston rejected his plea.

"Let them do as they please," he said coldly. "They're winning, aren't they?"

They were winning. They won the pennant, as they had said they would. Won it as the Babe hit .378—and made 59 home runs. They couldn't beat the Giants in the World Series. The Babe hit

.313 in the Series but made only one home run and an arm injury kept him out of two of the games.

When the Series was over, he announced that he and his pal, Bob Meusel, who played left field for the Yankees when the Babe played in right, and right field when the Babe played in left, were going to tour the country with a barnstorming ballclub made up of major league players. Kenesaw Mountain Landis, who had become Commissioner of Baseball the year before, sternly warned him there was a rule forbidding World Series players to make such tours. The Commissioner's word was law in baseball and club owners shivered and shook when he scowled at them. But not the Babe.

"Tell the Judge," he said, in effect, "that he can go jump in the lake."

"That goes for me, too," his pal Meusel said.

So they left on their tour and the Judge promptly slapped them down, ruling that while they might train with the club in the spring of 1922, they would be suspended without pay from the opening day of the season in mid-April until the 20th of May. The Babe laughed when he heard the Judge's verdict. What did a couple of weeks' pay mean to him? Just a few thousand dollars— and he'd pick that much up hitting home runs in the tank towns. Moreover, Ruppert and Huston had agreed to pay him $54,000 for the 1922 season.

"Babe," Huston said when he signed the contract, "this is a lot of money. We're paying it to you because we believe you are worth it. Now let me ask you a question: How much of the money we've already paid you have you saved?"

"Not much," the Babe admitted. "You know ..."

"Yes," Huston said. "I think I do. Now, here's what I want you to do this year: take only half your pay, minus the money Landis has docked you, and let me bank the other half for you. Surely, you can live—and have a lot of fun—on $27,000. Well, go ahead. Spend all of it—and at the end of the season, you'll have the other $27,000 in the bank."

The Babe thought that was a good idea.

"Sure," he said. "Go ahead."

So he took down only half his pay and had $27,000 stashed away by late September—and in November—he dropped into the club offices and told Huston he wanted it.

"All of it?" Huston asked.

"Yep," the Babe said. "I'm going to start a chicken farm near Sudbury, Massachusetts."

In vain did Huston argue with him about the foolhardiness of his plan. In vain, when he remained obdurate, did Huston tell him he wouldn't give him the money, The Babe had a simple answer for his objections and his threat.

"It's my money," he said, "and I want it now."

So he got it and sunk it in the chicken farm. He might as well have used it to make a down payment on the purchase of the Brooklyn Bridge for, inevitably, he lost it all.

Meanwhile, the Yankees opened the season without the Babe and Meusel. When the culprits returned there was a second and, the fans seemed to think, really official opening on May 21. Even the fact that the St. Louis Browns beat them that day and that neither Babe nor Bob got a base hit had little effect on the crowd. The Big Guy was back and that was all that mattered.

Five days later there was a tubulent scene at the Polo Grounds when the Babe tried to invade the grandstand during the ballgame with the intention of throttling a loud-mouth who had been

abusing him from a spot just back of the Yankees' dugout. Cops, ushers and teammates checked his rush for an aisle leading from the field and umpire Tommy Connolly ordered him to the clubhouse. Connolly, who was very fond of the Babe and secretly sympathized with him in his righteous anger, never forgot the incident.

"It was the last time I ever put a player out of a game," he once said, "and the last time any umpire ever put the Babe out."

It was a sort of omen, that flareup of the Babe's, for this was to be a year of turbulence for the Yankees all along the line. Before the month of May was over, notice of eviction from the Polo Grounds was served on Ruppert and Huston by Charles A. Stoneham, an action for which the Babe indirectly was responsible, since it was he who had made it possible for the Yankees to take the popular play away from the Giants. The situation so irked Stoneham that he was willing to forfeit the rent the Yankees paid in order to get them out of the ballpark. This was why the Yankee Stadium came into being, ready for occupancy in the spring of 1923 and why it was so aptly called "The House That Ruth Built."

Ruppert, Huston and Barrow, disturbed by reports of the nightly goings-on of some of the players on the road, as the season wore on, planted among them a private detective who passed himself off as a Good Time Charlie with money, liquor and race-track information.

His report, highlighted by details having to do with parties, horse playing and high-jinks in a Joliet, Illinois, brewery, trapped the Babe, along with a half dozen or more of the others. They had no inkling of what was going on until, on their return from the West for a series in Boston, they were met by Landis, who read the report aloud and then blistered their ears.

Curiously enough, the Babe, not ordinarily a suspicious person, had been the only one to suspect their new-found "friend."

"I'll bet you a hundred bucks," he said to Mays one day, "the guy is a detective."

"You're nuts," Mays said. "But you got a bet."

When, in Boston, Landis had completed his lecture, laced with warnings as to what would happen if the offenses were repeated, the Babe turned to Mays.

"All right, sucker," he said. "I'll take cash or a check."

On the second Western trip, fist fights in the dugout became the order of the day. Even the Babe, who couldn't fight at all but thought he could, got into one with the usually mild-mannered Wally Pipp, the first baseman, in St. Louis. They were pried apart by the other players as they rolled on the dugout floor, but Ruth challenged Pipp to resume the fight in the clubhouse after the game and the challenge was accepted. However, no punches were thrown in the clubhouse. Wally and the Babe hit successive home runs in the eighth inning to defeat the Browns and the battle on the bench was forgotten.

There were other fights along the way but the Yanks, taking them in stride, swept on to the pennant again. It wasn't, over all, one of the Babe's typical seasons. He hit a meager .315 and his home run output fell off to 35, while in the World Series, which they lost to the Giants in four straight games, barring one tie, he made only two hits in 17 times at bat.

On April 18, 1923, the Stadium was opened in a game with the Red Sox. It was a perfect opening. Bob Shawkey, dean of the staff in point of service and, as such, selected for the starting assignment, defeated Howard Ehmke, 4-1, and the Babe hit his first homer into the right-field bleachers.

In May, following months of bickering between them, Huston sold his stock to Ruppert. The Yankees were playing in Chicago and Ruppert sent a wire to Huggins which he ordered read to the players: "I now am the sole owner of the Yankees. Miller Huggins is my manager."

It had a salutary effect on the players. They knew that from then on Huggins would have complete control of them and that back of him Ruppert and Barrow would stand firmly. The only one who was to forget it was the Babe, but that didn't come about until two years later.

The day after this citation of Ruppert's affirmation of Huggins' authority, the Babe gave a dramatic demonstration of his extraordinary talent for rising dramatically in an emergency. The Yankees and the White Sox were tied, 1-1, going into the 15th inning and, in a box next to the dugout, Mark Roth, the road secretary, was sweating it out because the club had been booked on an early train for New York and the railroad had warned him the train could not be held much longer. Joe Dugan opened the inning with a single and Ruth was on his way to the plate when he noticed the anguish in Mark's face.

"What's the matter with you?" he asked. "Sick?"

"Yes," Mark said. "If you bums don't win this game in a hurry, we'll blow the train."

"Take it easy," the Babe said. "I'll get us out of here."

Whereupon he hit the first ball pitched to him by Mike Cvengros, a little left-hander, into the right-field stand. In the home half, the Yanks quickly retired the Sox and, after a quick change in the clubhouse, were whirled to the train in a fleet of taxis. As they were getting aboard, the Babe boomed at Mark:

"Why the hell didn't you tell me about that before?"

Nobody could stop the Yanks that year. They won the pennant by 17 games and beat the Giants, four out of six, in the World Series. The man out in front all the way? The Babe. During the season, he hit .393 and made 41 home runs. In the World Series, he shelled the Giant pitchers with three home runs—two of them in succession in the second game—a triple, a double and two singles, for an average of .368.

Nineteen-twenty-four was one of his finest years. So great a force was he, so consistent and thunderous his hitting, that because of him the Yankees almost won the pennant again as, coming up behind the league-leading Senators, they won 18 out of 22 games. But injuries and pitching lapses had retarded them earlier and they finished second. The Babe hit .378 to lead the league and walloped 46 home runs.

He was riding high now—and riding to a fall, though no one could have guessed it—and as he fell, the Yankees crashed with him. The club, on the way north from St. Petersburg, Florida, in the spring of 1925, had reached Asheville, North Carolina, when he suffered an attack of acute indigestion, the climax of a months-long spin around the groaning board so weird at times it is doubtful if anyone else could have survived it. He was rushed to New York where, at St. Vincent's Hospital, physicians found him to be gravely ill. It was weeks before he got back into the lineup and by that time the Yanks had, astonishingly, begun to come apart and Huggins and Barrow were trying desperately to rebuild them as they disintegrated. To no avail, however.

So badly off were they that, even when he had regained his health, the Babe could not help them and, more shocking than the collapse of the team itself was his surrender to the listless, bewildered atmosphere in which he found himself. No longer was it a pleasure for him to go to the ballpark, no longer did he attack the

enemy pitchers with gusto. His batting average sank to, for him, a new low of .246.

Once he left the ballpark, however, his spirits brightened. He was well again and, forgetful of the miseries through which he had so lately passed, he not only was up to his old tricks but managed to think up a few new ones in his quest for diversions that would take his mind off the daily horrors on the field to which he was a witness and in which he had a part. Huggins was patient with him for a time, even as he dawdled by day and romped by night but now, harried by his indifference and the descent of the club to seventh place, the Little Miller's patience was worn thin.

The break between them, long expected by the other players, in whose presence they had quarreled almost daily, came in St. Louis. The Babe was late reaching Sportsman's Park. The Yanks were at batting practice and the clubhouse was deserted save for Huggins and Waite Hoyt, who was to pitch that afternoon. As the Babe began to undress, Huggins said:

"Don't bother to uniform today."

"What did you say?" the Babe demanded.

"I said for you not to bother."

"Now what's the matter?" the Babe asked.

"You know very well what's the matter," Hug said. "And I'll tell you something else: I'm sorry, but this is the finish. You're fined $5,000 and suspended indefinitely."

"You'll never get away with this!" the Babe roared. "I'll never play another game for you, you little ———. I'll go to New York and see Jake! You don't think he'll stand for this, do you?"

"Do as you please," Huggins said, and walked from the room.

What the Babe didn't know was that Huggins already had been assured of the support of Ruppert and Barrow. When he reached New York, he said to reporters who met him at the Grand Central and, at his invitation, followed him to his hotel:

"I'll never play for the Yankees again as long as Huggins is the manager. He's trying to alibi himself at my expense and I'm not going to let him get away with it. If Jake still wants him to manage his club, he can get somebody else to play right field."

Within an hour, he was summoned to Ruppert's office in the brewery. There he was closeted with the Colonel and Barrow. After 15 minutes, the reporters were admitted by Barrow. Ruppert was grim, tight lipped. The Babe, looking very forlorn, sat slumped in his chair.

"Ruth has changed his mind," the Colonel said. "He will continue to play for Mr. Huggins. Is that right, Ruth?"

"Yes," the Babe said.

"Ruth is sorry about the whole thing," Ruppert said. "We are all sorry, but it had to be."

One of the reporters asked when the Babe would be allowed to play.

"That's up to Huggins," Ruppert said. "Ruth will report to him when the team returns."

"And the fine?"

"The fine goes."

The Babe, genuinely contrite by now, apologized to Huggins and was reinstated immediately. Only one month of the season remained. The Yankees were locked in seventh place and the Babe couldn't get them out of it but he tried so hard that he raised his batting average to .290.

It also was in 1925 that Lou Gehrig, out of Columbia University and seasoned on the Yankees' farm club in Hartford, returned to the Stadium to stay and, on June 2, replaced Pipp at first base and went on to his almost incredible run of 2,130 consecutive games. It was in 1926 that the Babe and Lou first really teamed up to give the Yankees the greatest one-two punch in baseball history. Ruth, of course, always was the dominant member of this mauling combination. Lou never resented this. He was as great an admirer of the Babe as any kid in the bleachers and was content to walk in his shadow. The time would come when relations between them would be strained almost to the breaking point but that would not be until years later.

Rebuilt now after the debacle of 1925, the Yankees crashed to the pennant again as Ruth hit .372 and hammered out 47 home runs, but they could not prevail against the Cardinals in the World Series although the Babe made four home runs.

So pleased were Ruppert, Barrow and Huggins by the Babe's earnest efforts and solid results that his salary, which had remained static at $52,000, was jumped to $70,000 for 1927.

That was the year, 1927. The year in which the Babe reached his greatest heights, and in which the Yankees, with Gehrig, Tony Lazzeri, Meusel, Earle Combs, Joe Dugan, Mark Koenig, Pat Collins and Johnny Grabowski swinging behind him, and Hoyt, Herb Pennock, George Pipgras and Wilcey Moore pitching superbly, they set an American League record by winning 110 games, and the pennant by 19. Officially, the flag was theirs when they won a doubleheader from the Red Sox in Boston on Labor Day. To the rest of the league, however, the race was over as early as the Fourth of July when, at the Stadium, they repulsed the Senators, who had moved up on them in June. The Yankees not only beat them in a doubleheader but the scores—12-1 and 21-1—terrified all the other clubs.

The Babe hit .356 that year and reached the still unmatched total of 60 home runs. Gehrig, hitting .378, made 47 homers. Many of these came with Ruth, just ahead of him in the batting order, on base. Pictures in the newspapers of Ruth having scored, shaking hands with Gehrig crossing the plate, or Gehrig, waiting his turn to hit, shaking hands with Ruth crossing the plate, became commonplace.

So great was the demand in the minor league cities within the orbit of the Yankees' travel to see them in action that exhibition games in St. Paul, Dayton, Buffalo, Toronto, and Indianapolis were arranged and even Cincinnati and Pittsburgh, having no American League teams, got into the act. The Babe, naturally, was the one the fans wanted most to see.

He never failed them, on or off the field. He took bows and exchanged greetings with his idolators from train windows or platforms. He hit home runs the like of which they'd never seen. In Toronto, boys swarming out of the bleachers in the eighth inning so hemmed him in and so steadfastly refused to disperse that it was necessary to call the game. In Indianapolis, an overflow crowd good naturedly razzed him when he failed to hit a ball out of the infield in three times at bat. On his fourth try, his towering smash cleared the right-field fence and the street beyond and, when last seen by those in the roof-top press box, was bouncing from box car to box car in the adjacent freight yards.

"I guess I didn't show those people something!" he exulted on his return to the dugout. "Make fun of me, will they?"

At Sing Sing Prison, where the Yankees also played, he hit two home runs, one over the right-field wall, the other over the wall in center field, where the yard is deepest. No one ever had hit a ball over that wall and the delight of the prisoners was equaled only by that of the Babe. The thrill he got from hitting a home run, even

in an exhibition game, had its part in his tremendous success. Once, when he was in retirement and he and Frank Frisch were cutting up old touches, he said:

"The way the other teams used to shift to right field for me, I could have hit .600 just by lobbing the ball into short left field."

"Why didn't you?" Frisch asked.

And the Babe said: "Because the people wanted to see me hit home runs and I got a kick out of hitting them."

As the 1927 pennant race had been a cake walk for the Yankees, so was the World Series with the Pirates. It was over in four games. Ruth hit .400 and his two homers helped to wreck the hapless foes.

Lost in the clamor over the Babe's home-run accumulation was the fact that nine years after he had been truly rated as the best left-handed pitcher in either league, he had become the best outfielder. Although he made some spectacular catches, his book on the hitters was so complete that he was able to make plays easily that lesser outfielders could have made only with a great flourish—or not at all. Much was said at the time about the velocity of Meusel's throws from the outfield. Babe didn't have Bob's power but his accuracy exceeded Bob's to a point where it bordered on perfection.

Nineteen-twenty-eight, and the big offensive rolled again. Ruth wasn't getting quite as many singles, doubles and triples as he did the year before but his home-run pace again was terrific. Pennant bound once more, Ruth—and some others—also were picking up speed once more on the candle-light circuit.

The Yankees had a long lead in August when they were hamstrung by injuries. Among the walking wounded was the Babe, who had a bad charley-horse in his right leg and aggravated it daily by his insistence on playing when he should have been on the bench. They were overtaken by the Athletics but belted the A's back to second place in a Sunday doubleheader at the Stadium in September and two days later, the Babe virtually clinched the flag for them when he beat the A's with a home run. His batting average that season was a mere .323—but he had racked up 54 home runs. He and Gehrig combined to destroy the Cardinals in the World Series, which was wrapped up in four games. Lou hit .545 and made four home runs, the Babe hit .625 and, in the final game, hit homers in three successive times at bat.

The Series ended in St. Louis and the train ride of the Yankees back to New York was a wild one. At the height of the celebration, the Babe ripped the shirts off the backs of the other players, Huggins, the club officials, the newspapermen and, finally, Ruppert fell into his clutches. As the Babe stripped him to the waist, the Colonel, who never before had been manhandled, murmured:

"Is this usual, Ruth?"

Shortly after the opening of the 1929 season, the Babe was married to Mrs. Claire Hodgson, a widow with a teen-age daughter. He had been married once before, to a girl named Helen Woodford in his early years with the Red Sox, but she had died in a fire, leaving him with an eight-year-old daughter. The Babe, unable to care for the child himself, had placed her with her mother's relatives but now that he was married again and had a home of his own after years living in one hotel after another, he sent for her.

"I got a wife and a family all in one day," he said, with a big grin.

The second Mrs. Ruth was to exert a tremendous influence in his life. It was she who put an end to his wild spending and, with the help of Christy Walsh, his business manager, saw to it that a substantial part of his earnings was salted away in annuities that, in the shadowed years ahead, served his needs so well.

That year, despite Ruth's consistent thumping at the plate—a .345 average and 46 homers—the Yankees fell off the pace, finishing second as the Athletics were first under the wire and, as the season waned, Huggins, who had been in poor health for some time, died within five days after a carbuncle spread poison through his weakened system. The Babe, who had come to love the little man who once had so sharply slapped him down, was deeply affected and followed him to his grave in Cincinnati.

There was a rumor that Ruth would be Huggins' successor and he made no secret of his willingness to accept the post but Barrow, whose province it was to select the new manager, settled on Bob Shawkey after futile attempts to sign Donie Bush, Eddie Collins and Arthur Fletcher, then a coach with the Yankees. As to the Babe, Barrow said:

"No one admires him more than I do—as a player. As a manager, I never even considered him."

And so for the first time, but not the last, the Babe was passed over, but in recognition of his continuing great contributions to the team even in a losing season, he was rewarded with a two-year contract calling for $80,000 a year.

Shawkey did well in 1930, considering that the Yankee regulars, Ruth and Gehrig excepted, were wearing out (Babe's final marks were .359 and 49 home runs; Lou's .379 and 41) and finished third. But some of the players with whom Bob had served in the ranks had not been too responsive to his leadership and Ruppert and Barrow decided to make a change. This time they chose Joe McCarthy, who had just been released by the Cubs, and the Babe seriously was upset.

So were some of the other players, who felt that he deserved the elevation, and it was a divided camp into which McCarthy moved at St. Petersburg in 1931. Joe, hardboiled, a disciplinarian and a perfectionist, whipped the malcontents quickly into line. He knew that the Babe regarded him as an interloper but he knew also that when the season opened, the Babe would put his personal feelings aside and play for him as whole-heartedly as he had for Huggins. Relations between them were not friendly, however, and never would be.

Ruth raised his batting average to .373 and unloaded 46 homers as the Yanks finished second, but that winter his salary was cut to $75,000. Much as he grumbled about that, he was back swinging as hard as ever in 1932 as, for the first time, McCarthy drove the club to a pennant. In the third game of the World Series with the Cubs, Babe brought off one of his most amazing feats.

When the Series began, the Cubs rode him hard and never let up and now it was the third game, played in Chicago and, in the third inning, Charlie Root, pitching for the Cubs, blazed a fastball over the plate. The Babe grinned at the yapping Cub bench-warmers and held up one finger. He took a second strike and repeated the gesture. Then, with his right arm, he waved toward the wall in right center—and on the next pitch, hammered the ball over the wall in right center.

As an indication of his faculty of thinking like a champion, there was his reply to a remark made at nine o'clock that night by columnist Joe Williams.

"If you'd missed that ball, you sure would have looked like a sucker," Joe said.

"By God!" Babe exclaimed. "I sure would have, wouldn't I?"

The Yankees closed out the Series in the fourth game and Ruth, with his great show against Root and another homer besides, once more was the big hero, but time was running out on him. McCarthy was rebuilding the team about him and he was hard pressed now to keep up with the younger fellows and with Gehrig,

too, and for the 1933 season, the Yankees proposed to slash his salary to $50,000.

"No," the Babe said.

He had held out before but never had he been as determined about it as he was this time. While Barrow handled the signing of all the other players, Ruppert claimed for himself the distinction, each year, of signing the Babe. There were several meetings between them in New York during the winter but the Babe was adamant about not taking the $50,000.

He didn't either. He signed for $52,000.

It was about that time that Ruth and Gehrig broke over what Lou considered an overbearing, paternalistic attitude on the Babe's part, Lou's final words being, roughly: "You mind your business and I'll mind mine."

The reconciliation did not come until six years later, although they were frigidly polite to each other during the brief remainder of the Babe's career with the Yankees and when, occasionally, they met thereafter. It was on "Gehrig Appreciation Day" at the Stadium in 1939 that the Babe came out of the stands and threw his arms around Lou and there were tears in the eyes of both of them.

The Babe slowed down rapidly through the 1933 season, his average dropping to .301 and his home runs to 34 as the Yanks wheeled home in second place. In 1934, it was plain that he was woefully near the end. But McCarthy wisely made no move to bench him.

In view of the Babe's managerial aspirations and his growing criticism of McCarthy, he obviously was no longer of service to the Yankees. When Judge Emil Fuchs, owner of the Boston Braves, expressed an interest in him they gracefully gave the Babe his unconditional release. Fuchs was willing to pay but Ruppert would take no money for his greatest star.

And so, on February 25, 1935, the Babe passed from New York, leaving behind a thousand memories of his greatness. His experience with the Braves was short-lived and unhappy, for all he succeeded in doing was to confuse the players by his presence on the bench, since they didn't know exactly what his status was, and to disrupt McKechnie's operations because Bill didn't know, either. He served briefly with the Dodgers as a coach. But that association was an unhappy one, too. At the end of the 1938 season he retired from baseball for good.

Thereafter his time was given over mainly to playing golf in the North in the summer and in Florida in the winter until, late in 1946, he became ill. He spent nearly three months in the French Hospital in New York, where he underwent an operation on his neck to alleviate the condition. It merely prolonged his life for a little while, for he had a cancer and there was no hope of his recovery.

One day Frank Stevens, head of the catering firm and an old friend of the Babe's, went to see him in the hospital.

"I'm not going to die in this room, Frank," the Babe said. "I'm going to get out in the sun again and have some fun."

So, in the spring of 1947, he was in Florida again, where he had spent so many happy and exciting days and nights. He visited the Yankees and the other ballclubs training in that state and, though enfeebled and wasted, he enjoyed himself. One day, seated in a box at Al Lang Field in St. Petersburg, he pointed to a hotel across the street from the right-field fence.

"I hit that hotel with a ball once," he said. "I really hit the tar out of that ball!"

Among those in the box was a young reporter who wasn't impressed.

"That wasn't much of a drive for you," he said.

"Hell!" the Babe said. "This park wasn't here then. We played in the old one, back there where the parking space is!"

The young reporter's eyes popped. "Oh!" he said, and there was awe in his voice.

The Babe hung on gamely that summer, even making several appearances at the Stadium where, as in the old days, the fans rose to greet him with cheers. But with the coming of another spring he was bed-ridden and, on August 16, 1948, he died.

Every once in a while since then, when a big hitter in the majors gets into a hot home-run streak, the sports pages start comparing his record with that of Ruth's at a comparable date. Someday, probably, a hitter will get 60 or more homers and, thus, go down in the record book along with the Babe. It is extremely doubtful that anyone will ever exceed or duplicate his records as a hitter and pitcher. And no matter what the record books of the future show there certainly will never be another Babe Ruth.

We were lucky there was one.

Chapter 53

Rogers Hornsby, The Rajah

He was the greatest right-handed hitter of his time—and he knew it. Proud, aloof and outspoken, Rogers Hornsby stood alone as a hitter and set benchmarks that still endure.

By Frank Graham
SPORT Magazine, May 1959

When Rogers Hornsby was a little boy, his mother admonished him never to be afraid to stand alone or to tell the truth. He never forgot her words and, largely because of his uncompromising candor, he lost one job after another in baseball. This could have embittered a lesser man but it has left no scars on Hornsby. He doesn't say so today in so many words, but it must be important to him that he never has taken back his words and never has failed to say exactly what has been on his mind.

He's a strange man, they say; he's hard to figure. But he isn't, really. Let's say he's a self-sufficient man, who can walk a lonely road without ever feeling lonely. As far back as his early playing days with the Cardinals, the other players didn't know quite what to make of him. They were a gregarious crew, but he paid little heed to them, as though they didn't exist.

"He comes into the clubhouse," one of them said, "suits up and goes out on the field. After the game he takes his shower, dresses and leaves, and we don't see him again until the next day. He hardly ever talks to anybody, except during the ballgame. Nobody knows where he lives or who his friends are."

"I don't know any more about him than the players do," said Miller Huggins, the manager of the St. Louis club at the time. "I know this much, though. He'll show up every day in shape to play, which is more than I can say for some of the others."

This was still true of him 10 years later, in 1927, when he was traded to the Giants. By that time he had achieved greatness both as a player and as manager of the Cardinals. He had won the first pennant in St. Louis history and had beaten the Yankees in the World Series. He had hit over .400 in three different seasons. And yet, as many times as he had played against the Giants, he had no more than a nodding acquaintance with any of them. The only men whose companionship he sought in New York that year were the baseball writers. This was not because he wanted anything from them, for he never courted publicity, and the wealth of it he received was wasted on him because he rarely read it. But he had got to know some of them when, on their stays in St. Louis with the Giants, they had visited him in the dugout. Hornsby liked to talk to them.

His attitude toward club owners and officials ran the gamut from affection to scorn. Branch Rickey, John McGraw and Judge Emil Fuchs came closer to being heroes to him than any men he has ever known. He despised Sam Breadon and Charles A. Stoneham. He enjoyed the rough give-and-take of his all-too-short association with Phil Ball. He fought with two generations of Veecks. He had no regard whatever for Kenesaw Mountain Landis from the start, believing the first commissioner was nothing but a stuffed shirt.

As a manager, he demanded unquestioning obedience and an all-out effort from his players, which was no more than he had given to the managers under whom he served. Whenever their ideas as to how the game should be played hadn't coincided with his own, he had remained silent, and now he insisted his players do the same. As a dedicated professional, he had never sought or expected praise from a manager for a job well done. So it was perfectly natural that, as a manager, he did not reward a player with so

much as a pat on the back for a hit or a play that had won a game. Hornsby was baffled by the resentment aroused in some of his players by his lack of warmth toward them. It was simply beyond his understanding. To the Rajah, baseball was a battle won by the fittest. There was no time or place in that battle for friendship.

His very nickname, The Rajah, seemed to fit him perfectly. He was proud, aloof and, in his own way, majestic. These characteristics might have seemed presumptuous in a lesser player, but Hornsby measured up to them on the field.

Hornsby played 23 seasons of major league baseball, many of them burdened by the dual responsibilities of player-manager, but his lifetime average of .358 stands today like a monument. In six consecutive seasons, from 1920 to 1925, he led the National League in hitting, and he added a seventh title in 1928. He had back-to-back seasons of .424 and .403 at the height of his prowess. He won the coveted triple crown of hitting—batting average, home runs and runs batted in—twice. He was twice named the league's Most Valuable Player. He led the National League in slugging for nine seasons and still holds the all-time slugging percentage record. He was one of the first immortals enshrined in the Baseball Hall of Fame at Cooperstown.

Huggins was the manager who did the most to shape his career, for Hornsby was a skinny 19-year-old boy when he came up from the Denison, Texas, club of the Western Association to the Cardinals late in the season of 1915 with batting averages of .232 and .277 to show for his two years in the minors. Huggins, a small, slight, intense man who later became the manager of the greatest of all Yankee teams, was the playing manager of the Cardinals when Hornsby arrived on the scene. For 11 years in Cincinnati and St. Louis, despite his stunted growth and slowness of foot, Huggins had been one of the best second basemen in the major leagues.

Rog was a shortstop then. He was sure-handed in the field, he had a strong arm and he could run. He was a line-drive hitter but a spotty one, mainly because he would swing at almost anything. He was 5-foot-11 and weighed just under 140 pounds. In 18 games, through August and September, he hit .246.

Huggins was concerned about Hornsby's stringy build and thought he might have to turn him back to the minors for a year or so until he got the weight and strength he needed, and he told Rog so. But when the boy reported to training camp the following spring, Huggins was pleased to see that over the winter he had gained nearly 25 pounds of muscle, built up and toughened by farm work. The summer before, Hug had told him to choke up on his bat and crowd the plate. Now he told him to take a grip on the end of the bat and stand back. He looked big and strong enough to hit the long ball.

"With those eyes," Hug said, "all you have to do is take your time. Don't swing until the ball's where you want it."

Rog hadn't yet settled into the stride that was to take him to enduring fame when Huggins left St. Louis for New York after the 1917 season. But he was steadily reaching it. It was his own effort thereafter that made him the great hitter he ultimately became, but Huggins had been the first to point the way for him, and he was always grateful to the little man. He still speaks of him with respect. In Hornsby's book, only McGraw was superior to Hug, and none of the others was close to him.

Branch Rickey, who took command of the Cardinals in 1919, became one of the best friends Rog ever had, but Branch wasn't his cup of tea as a manager. Branch had a school-masterish approach and explained his theories to the players with the aid of a black-

board, on which he drew diagrams after the manner of a football coach. Sometimes he expressed himself in language that was beyond the comprehension of his players, yet he drew no criticism from Hornsby, openly or by implication. But when, in June of 1925, Sam Breadon kicked Rickey upstairs to the front office and appointed Rog as his successor, it is significant that the first thing Hornsby did was literally to throw the blackboard out of the clubhouse window as a sign to the players that the old order had changed.

"You're supposed to be big league ballplayers," he said to them. "If you are, you don't need anybody to draw pictures to show you what you should do with the ball when it's hit to you. If you aren't, you won't be around much longer."

This must have been a welcome switch for the players. In last place at the time, they put on a tremendous push and finished fourth. It also is significant that not then, or in the following year, were there any players who showed the slightest sign of discontent with his handling of them. He was still no more one of them, socially, than he had been as a player. Nor was he any more effusive in their moments of triumph than he had been in years past. Yet they won the pennant in 1926 and beat the Yankees in the World Series.

Hornsby behaved the same with his superiors as he did with his players. He even took on Judge Landis at a meeting in the Judge's office in Chicago attended by representatives of the Cardinals and the Yankees, to discuss arrangements for the 1926 World Series. At its conclusion, Landis said, "I've selected the New York Central Railroad as the official route for the two clubs."

"The Cardinals," Hornsby said, "will ride the Pennsylvania."

Everyone in the room, including the Judge, was shocked at the brash words.

"Did I not make myself plain, young man?" he asked sternly.

"Yes," Hornsby said. "I heard you right. But we've used the Pennsylvania between St. Louis and New York for a long time and I'm not going to take the business away from them now."

And, having made himself equally plain, Rog walked from the room. Landis knew that he had been defeated, for although the powers granted to him by the club owners in his contract were virtually limitless, no clause gave him the right to tell a ballclub that it must favor one railroad over another. How he explained his defeat to the New York Central no one ever knew, but it must have been embarrassing. And he never forgot it.

That was, you might say, the preliminary bout between them. The main event took place seven years later. Landis summoned Hornsby to his office and asked him if it were true that he bet on the horses.

"Sure," Rog said.

"Then I must order you to stop doing so."

"No," Hornsby said.

"I've ordered you to stop!" the Judge thundered.

"Look," Rog said, "I don't drink or smoke or go to the races, or read hardly anything but the box scores and the averages. I've got to have some relaxation and this is how I get it. I get a kick out of studying the form and trying to beat a race. I like the horses because they give me fast action."

Then, his voice cold and hard, he added, "It's no different than buying stock in the market, except that I use my own money."

Again he walked out on the Judge. This time he had hit him with a crippling punch: the stock he referred to had been bought by Landis as an investment for the baseball treasury, administered by the commissioner's office. In the crash of 1929, it was wiped off the boards. Rog always will believe that his reminding the Judge of

his poor judgment resulted in his virtual exile from the majors after his release as manager of the Browns in 1937.

Another of Hornsby's sparring partners was Sam Breadon, who was a boy off the West Side of New York when, in 1904, he went to St. Louis to find work on the World's Fair grounds. Liking the city, he remained there, prospered in the growing automobile business and, in time, bought the controlling interest in the Cardinals. Away from his desk at the ballpark or in his automobile agency, he could be a stimulating companion and an expansive host.

Rog had had very little contact with Breadon before he was elevated to the management of the Cardinals. He didn't believe then, nor does he now, that a ballplayer should spend much time in the front office, nor an owner in the clubhouse. It was an attitude that the fun-loving Breadon couldn't understand, and resented.

Even during the 1926 World Series, Hornsby had no time for his employer, remaining away from the parties Sam gave in St. Louis and New York and even on the trains between the two cities. It was on the return trip from New York to St. Louis, after the final game of the Series, that he heard that Breadon had offered the manager's job to Bill Killefer, one of Hornsby's coaches. He heard it not from Breadon but from Killefer himself, who added that he had told Sam he could go to hell. The coolness Rog had previously felt toward the owner now turned to ice.

He had learned earlier that the open-handed host was, in his natural setting as a businessman, shrewd, tough and tight. He hadn't raised Rog's salary when he put him on double duty as player-manager the year before. He hadn't renewed his contract after the winning of the pennant and the World Series. And when Breadon traded him to the Giants for second baseman Frank Frisch, pitcher Jimmy Ring and an undisclosed amount of money, he violently denied that the sudden ascendancy of the Cardinals under Hornsby had increased the value of the stock in the club that Rog shrewdly had bought. Rog would take what was offered him for the stock, or else.

Hornsby laughed grimly when he heard that.

"Breadon's got it wrong," he said. "I'll get what I have been informed by an accounting firm in St. Louis is a fair price for the stock—or else."

When the deal that sent Hornsby from St. Louis to New York was made, it didn't occur to anybody that Rog couldn't play for the Giants while he was a stockholder in the Cardinals. But he refused to sell cheap, even when he reported for training with the Giants at Sarasota, Fla. His situation there was a doubly difficult one. Manager of the world champions the year before, he had been reduced to an ordinary player on a strange club.

McGraw said to him, "You just go your own way around here, watch yourself and hold your tongue. You never can tell what might happen. I'm not going to go on managing this ballclub forever."

If that was a veiled promise, Hornsby didn't take it as such. He had been hired as a player for the Giants, not as a possible future manager. He took orders from McGraw. He hit, he ran, he played second base. But he ate alone in a dining room where, all about him, the other players were grouped at tables for two, four or six. He roomed alone, where the others were paired off. His only companions in the evening were the writers.

Then, suddenly, there were complications. McGraw was involved in a real estate deal that collapsed. Threatened with suits by enraged investors, he frequently had to leave camp for a day or two at a time to consult with lawyers. He appointed Hornsby captain of the team and told the players: "When I'm not here,

Hornsby will be in charge of you."

Other captains of the Giants had worn the title loosely. But not Hornsby. He accepted it as a responsibility. One day, when McGraw was away, he sharply criticized Freddy Lindstrom for the manner in which he had made a play at third base during an exhibition game.

"That's the way the Old Man wants us to make it," Lindstrom said.

"Then, when he's here, make it that way," Hornsby said. "When he's not here, make it the way I tell you to."

"Who the hell do you think you are?" Lindstrom snapped. "When you put that bat down, you're no bargain."

The pitcher, the catcher and the other infielders listened in silence.

Hornsby said, "You do as I tell you and keep your mouth shut."

He looked at the others. "That goes for the rest of you," he said.

One night when the club was in Tampa, and Eddie Roush, the center fielder, was holding out at his home in Oakland City, Ind., one of the writers said to Rog, "Not for publication, but what do you think of the outfield situation with Roush missing?" At the time, McGraw was saying he didn't need Roush and he could hold out all year if he wanted to.

"Before I tell you," Rog said, "I want to say this. I don't talk 'not for publication.' Anything I say you can put in the paper and if anybody doesn't like it, he can lump it. Now I'll tell you what I think of the outfield. I think it stinks. They got to get Roush in there to keep those clowns from knocking their heads together under fly balls, and if they don't get him, no matter how much they have to pay him, they're crazy. McGraw hasn't asked me for any advice, but if he does, I'll tell him what I just told you."

In St. Augustine, when McGraw secretly left the club to go to New York to confer with club owner Charlie Stoneham on the Roush case, the writers were grousing about it when Hornsby joined them on the veranda of the hotel.

"What's everybody mad about?" he asked.

"McGraw's gone to New York," one of them said.

"What difference does it make?" Rog asked. "Who the hell cares where he is?"

"I do, for one," the writer said. "I'm responsible to my paper for news out of this camp and I like to know where the manager is. And as for you, my friend, you'd better quit popping off like that. Somebody may run to McGraw and tell him about it."

"Nuts!" Hornsby said. "I never said anything behind his back I wouldn't say to his face. They can run and tell him all they want."

As the club journeyed north for the opening of the season in Philadelphia, there was increasing tension throughout the league over Hornsby's stock situation. Breadon refused to increase his offer and league president John Heydler said Hornsby couldn't play with the Giants until he had disposed of his Cardinal holdings. McGraw issued an unprecedented statement, blasting Heydler and threatening to get an injunction to restrain the president from barring the player. But McGraw, secretly worried for all the bold front he had assumed, attempted to soften Hornsby's resistance.

"Don't talk to me, Mr. McGraw," Rog said. "Talk to Breadon. He's the one that's holding this thing up."

McGraw called Leo Bondy, Stoneham's lawyer and counsel for the Giants. Bondy met the club in Washington early one morning in April and went to Hornsby's room. Rog was sitting up in bed, reading the box scores in a morning paper.

"I'm Mr. Bondy," Leo said.

"I know," Rog said. "What can I do for you?"

"I came to talk to you about your stock in the Cardinals."

Hornsby looked at him in silence for a moment, then said, "Why don't you mind your own business, Mr. Bondy?"

Leo beat a hasty retreat. Later he said, "I've never met such a cold, hard man."

Single-handed, Hornsby successfully stood off the entire league. The owners of the other clubs, viewing with horror the possibility that they would lose a great drawing card if Hornsby were to be ruled ineligible, finally chipped in to make up the difference between Breadon's offer and Hornsby's demands.

So Hornsby played with the Giants that year, and he hit .361. In the frequent absences of McGraw from the club because of illness, he was the acting manager. In spite of him, the Giants couldn't win, although on the last western trip of the year, he got them up to second place, only to see them fall back to third as the season ended.

On January 10, 1928, Hornsby abruptly was traded to the Boston Braves for Frank Hogan, a young catcher, and Jimmy Welsh, an outfielder. Such a deal seemed incredible. Questioned by reporters, Stoneham and secretary Jim Tierney denied there were any ulterior reasons for the dismissal of the great ballplayer.

Naturally, the newspapers had a field day trying to guess why Stoneham had pulled the rug from under Hornsby. Casual remarks dropped by him during the season had indicated he did not share in the general admiration for the player, which wasn't surprising since Hornsby had ignored him to the point of rudeness. But there had to be more to it than that.

A writer who traveled with the Giants said, at the time, "Rog swore at Stoneham. I heard him. Stoneham got excited about the Giants' pennant chances when they were on the last western trip and he went to Pittsburgh for the series there. After they'd lost a game, he met Rog in the lobby of the Schenley Hotel and asked him why he hadn't used Jack Cummings as a pinch-hitter in the ninth inning. Rog was burning, anyway, although I don't suppose that made any difference. Well, he glared at Stoneham and said, 'Are you trying to tell me how to manage the club?'

"Stoneham said, 'Why, no. I just thought ...'

"And Rog said, 'I don't care what you thought, you ——. If you don't like the way I'm running this club, get somebody else to do it.'"

Emil Fuchs, lawyer, former New York City magistrate, fan, and friend of McGraw's, owned the Boston Braves. They were a pretty bad ballclub. They had finished seventh in 1926 and again in 1927, and Dave Bancroft, the manager and also a close friend of Judge Fuchs, had grown weary of struggling with them. Fuchs, at Bancroft's request, released him so that he might join the Brooklyn club as a coach. To replace him, the Judge engaged Jack Slattery, who, following a scant major league career that had ended nearly 20 years before, had been very successful as a local college coach at Tufts, Boston College and Harvard. This, of course, was before the Judge had any idea the Giants were going to drop Hornsby in his lap.

Again Hornsby was cast in an arduous role. Slattery, although little known elsewhere in the league, was something of a hero in Boston, where he had been born and reared. He was extremely well liked by the Boston newspapermen and had been hired, Fuchs said, on their recommendation. When the inevitable happened, it was Rog who, inevitably, had to take the rap. Hornsby, under a contract Fuchs had to assume when he got the player, drew a salary of $40,000. Slattery's pay was $10,000. At the training camp,

reporters from other cities irked the Boston writers by looking to Hornsby for their stories and giving Slattery a polite brush. None of this was Hornsby's fault, yet the Boston writers, in their loyalty to Slattery, gave him a bad press.

The impression that the readers back in Boston gathered was that Rog deliberately was undermining Jack. This was heightened when, shortly after the season opened, Slattery resigned and Fuchs announced that Hornsby was the manager. Thus he entered upon his new duties in an atmosphere of hostility in which even the players joined, for, characteristically, he had made no move to seek either their companionship or their favor.

"I understand," a New York writer said to him one day in the dugout at Braves Field, "that your players think you are a —— and a ——. Did you know that?"

"Oh, sure," Rog said, laughing. "Listen, I'm not conducting a popularity contest. I'm running a ballclub. I don't care what they think of me, just as long as they play ball for me the best they can. I told some of them the other day that if they lived as clean as I do, and tried as hard, they could be great ballplayers, too. I guess they didn't believe me. They haven't improved any."

Hornsby hit .387 but the Braves finished a miserable seventh, losing 103 games (only the Phillies of that vintage could have contrived to do worse), and everybody in Boston was happy when the season ended. Meanwhile, the Cubs had been third, behind the Cardinals and the Giants, and manager Joe McCarthy said to William Wrigley, owner of the club, and William L. Veeck, its president, "Get Hornsby for me and I'll win the pennant next year."

They were agreeable and the deal was not long in the making, for Wrigley had money and Fuchs had none. Yet the parting of Fuchs and Hornsby was a sad one. Between these two men, so utterly different in their backgrounds, their thoughts and their manner of living, a warm friendship had formed. Fuchs was so reluctant to accept Wrigley's gold that he yielded only when Hornsby angrily demanded, "What's the matter with you? Have you lost your mind? I can't help this ballclub. Take the money and get some ballplayers."

The Cubs won the pennant in 1929, and Hornsby hit .380. On September 23, 1930, McCarthy was fired and Hornsby was appointed in his stead. The "I-told-you-so's" echoed through the concrete canyons of the Loop. Joe was bitter. His trouble hadn't been with Wrigley but with Veeck, and he believed that Veeck's attitude toward him had been inspired by Hornsby. Apparently, no one thought to ask Hornsby about it, and he said nothing.

Rog lasted through the 1931 season and deep into 1932 when, once more, he ran into an open switch and was derailed. It seems that Veeck, who under the nom de plume of "Bill Bailey," had been a first-rate baseball writer on a Chicago newspaper, still was exporting from his box seat at Wrigley Field, and Rog's strategy frequently didn't meet with his approval. Besides, he had been irked by reports about Rog's horse playing, and he lent an ear to the complaints of some of the players who had been tongue-lashed by the manager. As August came on, there had to be a blow-up. And there was. Rog was out and Charley Grimm took over the dugout.

There was a short, peaceful and reasonably quiet interlude for Hornsby in 1933. Branch Rickey had persuaded Sam Breadon to sign him on as a Cardinals' pinch-hitter and utility infielder. But the respite ended in July. Rickey told him that Phil Ball, owner of the Browns, wanted him as a manager, and advised him to accept the post, which he did.

Ball, who had made a fortune in the ice business, had got into

baseball through his purchase of the St. Louis franchise in the "outlaw" Federal League in 1914, and when the Feds collapsed after the 1915 season, he was permitted to buy the Browns. Short but powerfully built, tough minded and tough talking, he terrorized his managers, his players, most of the umpires, some of the St. Louis newspapermen and a few of his colleagues.

When he heard that Landis had grudgingly approved his hiring of Hornsby, he snorted, "That pipsqueak! I'll hire anybody I please and to hell with him."

His association with Hornsby was a match made in heaven, for their ideas were identical and they spoke the same language.

"Ball's giving a party tonight," Rog said to the newspapermen covering the Yankees when they reached St. Louis shortly after his appointment. "I'd like very much to have you all there."

"From what I've heard of him," one of them said, "I have no desire to go to any party he gives."

"Never mind him," Rog said. "He's only picking up the tab. But it's for me, and you're my friends, so come ahead. All of you. He's not a bad guy but I don't like some of his friends and I want him to meet some of mine."

So they went to the party and, on meeting Ball, liked him. Tough, blunt, honest, he was much like Rog.

"Do you know what this guy said to me when I signed him?" Ball asked over cocktails. "He said: 'You know, you have a lousy ballclub.'"

"You have, too," Hornsby said. "You tried to argue with me but I wouldn't let you. You have a lousy ballclub, like I told you, and it's still lousy and you can't make it good just by hiring a new manager. You ought to know that by now. You've had enough managers. Why don't you get some ballplayers?"

"How do you like this guy?" Ball asked, turning to one of the newspapermen.

"I like him very much," the other said.

Ball grinned. "So do I," he said. "I'll get him some ballplayers."

Had Ball lived longer, the course of Hornsby's life almost surely would have been different, and the Browns still might be in St. Louis. For Ball was determined to give the city the best ballclub money could buy, and he had precisely the right man to run it. But before the coming of another season Ball was stricken and died—and Hornsby was on the merry-go-round again.

He didn't leave St. Louis immediately. Indeed, he was there until August of 1937. But with the sale of the club following Ball's death, matters worsened steadily. The quality of the players, low as it had been, deteriorated. There were frequent jangles between Rog and the new owner, Donald Barnes, a small-loan tycoon, and his business manager, Bill DeWitt. Rog bought some stock in Barnes' company and the break came when he made his final payment of $4,000 on it with a check he had just received from a bookmaker.

"So you're still playing the horses!" Barnes said.

"That's right," Rog said.

"Stop it!" Barnes snapped.

"Why?"

"Because it's bad for baseball."

"It's no worse," Rog said, "than taking interest from widows and orphans on loans. Or selling them stock in this stinking ballclub."

The next stop for Rog was the minor leagues: Baltimore, then Chattanooga, Oklahoma City, Fort Worth as coach, manager or general manager. Then the trail led to Beaumont and Seattle.

He was beckoned back to the majors in 1952 by Bill Veeck, son of the man who had fired him from the Cubs long years before. Young Bill, who had made a great success of the Cleveland Indians, now had the Browns. Clever, energetic, brash, awed by no one and equaling Hornsby himself in candor, it seemed to Rog, as it did to many others, that they would get along famously. It was instead a short, unhappy union. Veeck tried his hand at telling Rog how to run the club. The break came in Boston as early as June 10. Rog said he wasn't sore at any one, especially Veeck. He shouldn't have been. He had worked only a few months on a three-year contract and Bill paid him off roughly $100,000. Still, he was upset by the sudden smashing of what he had thought would become a permanent engagement in St. Louis, a town he had always liked and where, in turn, he had always been liked and appreciated.

But it had to be that way with him, for he still couldn't compromise with himself and he had to speak up where a prudent man would have sought a more amicable solution. So, with the $100,000 in the bank, he went job-hunting once more.

He didn't have to look very long. Gabe Paul tapped him as successor to Luke Sewell as manager of the Cincinnati Reds. Luke was an easy-going man and, apparently, unappreciated by his players. Gabe thought the strictness of a Hornsby regime was just what they needed. The job, which extended only until the closing days of the 1953 season, was an anticlimax in Rog's tumultuous career. He moved the club up from sixth place to fifth. He unquestionably helped some of the young players. But there came a day when he wasn't wanted any more and he walked out, puzzled as always.

At 63, the Rajah still hasn't changed much. When he climbs into his uniform as batting coach of the Cubs, the pot belly is quite noticeable and his round red face and gleaming eyes give him the look of a beardless Santa Claus in flannels. But as he glares at the Cub hitters from behind the batting cage in pre-game practice and comments on their efforts, you can tell it's the same old Hornsby. When he sees something he doesn't like, his correction is short and biting. When Ernie Banks whiplashes a drive into the seats, he stands silent and offers no congratulations.

And when the batting practice is over, and Hornsby walks back to the dugout, he's almost always alone.

Epilogue

Hornsby ended his baseball career with the New York Mets, joining the fledgling expansion franchise as a scout in 1961 and then joining the coaching staff in 1962 for the Mets inaugural season. Before the 1963 season he underwent cataract surgery and, while in hospital, died from heart failure. He was 66.

Chapter 54

Lou Gehrig, The Iron Horse

The Lou Gehrig legend was forged out of his rich human qualities—courage, humility, sincerity—as he overcame every obstacle he faced except the one that killed him.

By Tom Meany
SPORT Magazine, Septermber, 1958

What kind of a guy was Lou Gehrig?' That's a question those who knew Lou find themselves being asked with increasing frequency, even though it is 17 years since the great Yankee first baseman died, nearly 20 since he wore the flannels of the club he helped to make the Bronx Bombers the scourge of the American League. And it's a good question, too, for the Iron Horse was quite a man and only those who knew him can attempt to separate the facts from the legend.

Gehrig was not the automaton, the robot his record of 2,130 consecutive games might lead folks to believe he was. He was flesh and blood, he lived, loved, yes and died, in the personal pattern each man must follow according to his own lights. The record he left behind him in the baseball books is one of endurance but the record he left with those who knew him is a far more human one, the memory of a man who was both great and humble, strong and generous, simple and sincere.

Truly great ballplayers have worn the Yankee uniform, worn it proudly and with distinction. The list is a long one and it spans several generations, as baseball generations go. It is necessary to name only a few—Babe Ruth, Joe DiMaggio, Mickey Mantle. Yet none of the greats, past or present, was more representative of the true Yankee spirit than Lou Gehrig, the kid from the sidewalks of New York. He was a Yankee in the great tradition.

In this day and age, it may seem unnecessary to go into detail about Gehrig's record of consecutive games, yet an explanation of sorts is vital to any true concept of Gehrig the man. In a sense, the man was the record. Lou's record is one that will stand the test of time. It is a record made of stamina and physical endurance and courage. Neither trick fences nor an injection of rabbit juice into the baseball can threaten this record or remove it from the books. It will take a man—not a change in equipment or a specially-designed ballpark—to challenge this record. That it will endure seems self-evident. I personally doubt whether any of the modern ballplayers ever will put together 1,000 consecutive games, due to the complexities of the schedule, with night games, twi-nighters, day games and doubleheaders all being tossed haphazardly into the melange now called a schedule.

That Gehrig's record was made before night games became prevalent is, of course, true. It is no blemish on the record for, had there been scads of night games in Lou's era, he still would have played in all of them, for he was that kind of a guy. Except in its very late stages, the consecutive-game record was not an obsession with Gehrig. Indeed, Lou was close to the best previous consecutive-game record—Everett (Deacon) Scott's 1,307—before he even realized that he was on his way to a record. He was just doing what he was being paid to do—playing first base every day.

Frank Graham relates in his book, *Lou Gehrig—A Quiet Hero,* how Dan Daniel, the dean of Yankee writers, discovered that Lou was on his way to break Scottie's record. This was in July of 1933 when Gehrig had played in the neighborhood of 1,250 games. Daniel asked Lou when he had last missed a game.

"I never missed one," Lou said simply. "Not since the day I replaced Wally Pipp at first base."

"Do you realize how many consecutive games you've played?"

Dan persisted.

"Well, that was in 1925, in June," Lou replied, doing a bit of mental arithmetic, "and this is 1933, so it must be up in the hundreds."

"It sure is," Dan laughed. "You're up to about 1,250, which means you'll break Scott's record this year. I'm trying to check to see whether you played the day before you replaced Pipp."

Gehrig had been in some games earlier in the 1925 season, but he couldn't recall whether he had played the day before. Daniel tracked down the story, stopped by Gehrig's table at dinner after the game and informed him that he now had played 1,250 consecutive games. Gehrig's only surprise was that the string was so long. In playing every game, he merely felt he was doing his duty. As a kid in grammar school, he never missed a day, once sneaking out after his mother's departure for work when she had left him bedded down for the day with an attack of grippe.

Gehrig had pinch-hit for Pee Wee Wanninger on June 1, 1925 at Yankee Stadium, so the day he replaced Pipp at first base actually was game No. 2 in the string, a string that was to endure until the morning of May 2, 1939, when he met manager Joe McCarthy in Detroit and requested to be benched for the best interests of the team. The last game of the streak was played in New York on April 30.

Pipp, Gehrig's predecessor at first base, asked Doc Woods, the Yankee trainer, for a couple of aspirin on that fateful June 2, 1925. One story has it that Wally had been hit in batting practice by a young college pitcher, who later was to become one of America's top football coaches, Charley Caldwell of Princeton. Another version is that Wally's headache stemmed from an old eye injury.

Whatever the reason for Pipp's headache, manager Miller Huggins sympathetically advised Wally to take the day off and let "the kid from Columbia" take over. In later years, Pipp was to make quite a joke of the headache. "Some day off," Wally chuckled. "I never got back to first base for another season and then in another league—with Cincinnati in the National."

This was the start of the legend of indestructible Lou, a record taken so matter of factly by teammates and the public that the very nonchalance with which it was accepted was in itself a tribute to Gehrig. It was taken for granted mainly because Lou himself took it for granted.

Gehrig had the reputation of being a plodder, which didn't come close to doing him justice. The truth of the matter is that Lou, with his great and powerful physique, was not, in fact, an athlete. He had to master the tricks of his trade patiently. When he mastered them, and supplemented his ability, with his great physical skills, he was truly a star. It was in much the same manner that Rocky Marciano became the heavyweight champion of the world. Like Gehrig, all Rocky brought with him when he started was his physical prowess. By patiently adapting himself to the lessons of Charley Goldman, Rocky became the best heavyweight of his time. The simile is not entirely accurate, for Marciano, even when he had conquered everybody in sight, still lacked the finesse of many who had held the crown before him. Gehrig, until his declining season, was a fine first baseman, not fancy, to be sure, but considerably more than adequate. If working hard to master first the fundamentals and then the niceties of his trade means being a plodder, then Lou was a plodder.

Gehrig had a theory, whether he knew it or not, that almost any obstacle in this world could be overcome by hard work. When Lou was playing at the High School of Commerce, his coach, Harry Kane, worked with him so he could hit left-handed pitchers. Lou's

coach at Columbia, Andy Coakley, worked with him so he could overcome a weakness against curveballs and change-of-pace pitches. Pipp, although as soon as he saw the muscular Gehrig for the first time he realized that his own days as a Yankee first baseman were numbered, worked patiently with him around the bag.

With Kane, with Coakley, with Pipp, with anybody who could teach him anything about baseball, Gehrig worked. As Pipp said of him, "He didn't learn quickly but he learned thoroughly. He sweated out each detail, step by step until he had mastered it."

Characteristic of Lou was the conquering of his last fault as a defensive first baseman. He had had an almost incurable habit of going too far to his right for ground balls, taking grounders which should have been fielded by the second baseman and on which the pitcher, assuming the second baseman would take the ball, would not break from the mound to cover first. The fault in itself is an insight into Lou's nature—he wanted to do as much work as he could. Gehrig set about methodically to overcome this flaw in his technique. He practiced daily the number of strides he safely could go to his right without poaching on the second baseman's territory. In his mind's eye there was an invisible line, varying with the batter and with his defensive position, a boundary which kept his fielding ambition within reason.

If Lou was methodical in his practice at first base, he was to prove it in another way in the World Series of 1927, which opened at Pittsburgh's Forbes Field. Additional temporary field boxes had been built in front of the stands on the first-base side. The day before the Series opened, the Yankees put on the most awesome exhibition of batting practice ever seen in any ballpark. Bob Meusel and Gehrig belted the ball out of sight, to the amazement of the Pirates who were in the stands watching them. Lou even cleared the center-field fence, something no National Leaguer ever had been able to do.

Yet Gehrig didn't devote all of his attention to slugging that afternoon. He found time to pace the distance *in foul territory* between first base and the temporary field seats. Then, in the two games at Forbes Field, he was able to make a couple of astonishing catches of foul pops, on one occasion draping himself over the railing to make the grab.

For all his Teuton thoroughness, Gehrig was a man of great sentiment and greater humility. Consider him on Gehrig Appreciation Day at Yankee Stadium, July 4, 1939. Lou was through now, although it wasn't as readily apparent as it was to become some few weeks later. Here assembled to wish Lou well were members of the 1927 club, still considered the greatest team in the Yankee dynasty. There were rafts of gifts, scores of messages from notables.

There have been "appreciation days" before and since, but this was one which thoroughly deserved the appellation. For the fans, as well as the players and the press, appreciated Gehrig's position, his fate to be struck down at the height of his career. Lou's words of thanks that day were a masterpiece of sincerity. His prepared speech had been thrown away and he spoke from his heart, concluding thusly: "I may have been given a bad break, but I have an awful lot to live for. With all this, I consider myself the luckiest man on the face of this earth."

Coming from anyone else, that could have been mawkish, but those who knew Lou knew its sincerity, just as did those personal friends who, on Christmas Eve, 1940, received a telegram from Lou and his wife, Eleanor, in which was stressed the gratefulness of this wonderful pair for their friends, their appreciation of God's kindness in making this friendship possible. In less than six months, Lou was dead.

"What kind of a guy was Lou Gehrig?"

For one thing, he was tremendously honest with himself. This is a trait possessed by all too few and almost never found in those who bask in the spotlight and find themselves surrounded by adulant sycophants. Gehrig never made the mistake of kidding himself. I can recall a rainy day in Chicago's Hotel Del Prado, late in the season of 1934. The afternoon had been devoted to a bridge game, which had recently broken up, and I lingered for a last cigarette and a chat with Lou, who was policing up the room so that Bill Dickey wouldn't find it untidy when he returned from the movies. Detroit was well on its way to its first pennant in 25 years and there wasn't much the Yankees could do about it. The subject was baseball but the conversation was hardly cheerful.

This was Ruth's last year with the Yankees. The great man had tailed off perceptibly, so much so that there was talk among some of the younger and brasher Yankees of getting up a petition requesting that Ruth bench himself for the good of the team. Relations between Ruth and his manager, Joe McCarthy, never cordial at best, had worsened considerably.

"I don't suppose the Babe will be with us next year?" I remarked, really more an observation than a question.

"No," Lou said, "and it's a shame. The big fellow did a lot for this ballclub and for all baseball. He'll be missed all over."

This conversation came at a time when Babe and Lou weren't on the best of terms, either. There was no open break between them, but a definite coolness existed, nevertheless.

"With Ruth gone, you should be getting your share of the headlines," I said.

Gehrig laughed. "I'm not a headline guy and we may as well face it," he said. "I'm just the guy who's in there every day, the fellow who follows Babe in the batting order. When Babe's turn at bat is over, whether he strikes out or belts a home run, the fans are still talking about him when I come up to bat. If I stood on my head at the plate, nobody'd pay any attention."

When Lou said he wasn't a "headline guy," he was exactly right. In 1932, he hit four home runs in a game against the Athletics in Philadelphia, the first player in modern times to accomplish this feat. News of it should have rocked the baseball world, but John McGraw chose that very afternoon to suddenly resign after having managed the Giants for three decades. Mac got the headlines and Lou's four homers were relegated to the second sports page.

It was ever thus with Gehrig, and it wasn't entirely because he operated in the shadow of the great Ruth. Lou's very reliability and dependability negated his chances of true and total appreciation. This was evident in 1935, the first year that Gehrig played without Ruth.

The late Christy Walsh, who had served as business manager for both Ruth and Gehrig, and served them well, too, tried to capitalize on the fact that Lou was now the unchallenged big gun in the Yankee arsenal. In this promotion, the Yankee organization cooperated whole-heartedly, even to the extent of naming Gehrig team captain, a post which had been vacant on the Yankees for a decade. Ruth had held it until his rebellion in 1925, the year Lou joined the club.

It was a boom that fizzled. Gehrig was the same sturdy, steady, conscientious performer without Ruth that he had been with him. As a matter of fact, it could have been that he didn't care for the spotlight, for his batting average and run production both fell off markedly that season, only to pick up again the next year when Joe DiMaggio joined the club. Highly ballyhooed long before his arrival from the Pacific Coast, Joe lived up to his billing and copped

the headlines. Gehrig, with someone else front and center on the stage, again was the same booming hitter that he had been when Ruth was in his glory.

Not until he became fatally stricken and stepped out of the Yankee lineup was Gehrig considered Page One news. As a cynical writer remarked at the time, "Poor Lou! He has to practically die to get on the front page." The fellow wasn't so far wrong at that.

"What kind of a guy was Lou Gehrig?"

Well, Joe McCarthy, his manager for the last nine years of his career, could tell you, but he won't because Joe isn't a pop-off guy, any more than Lou was. For a long time, McCarthy considered Gehrig the best ballplayer he ever managed, although he took pains never to say so while Lou played for him.

McCarthy and Gehrig were genuinely close friends, particularly in later years when Joe felt at home with the Yankees and Lou learned to respect his tremendous managerial talents. One of Joe's top assets as a manager was that the ballplayer who could fool him hadn't been born. But this had no bearing on his relations with Gehrig, for Lou never tried to fool him.

It is doubtful if Gehrig felt toward McCarthy as he felt toward Miller Huggins, his first manager. The reasons are almost self-explanatory. When McCarthy's path crossed that of Gehrig, Lou was a mature man, an established star. When Lou first met Hug, he was "the kid from Columbia," uncertain of his reception with the Yankees, who were already beginning their dominance of the American League, and unsure of his ability to remain with the club, let alone become a regular or a star.

The tiny Huggins was a kindly, understanding man and basically shy. He sensed the bewilderment in young Gehrig and set to work to eliminate it. Because Gehrig's father had become an invalid when Lou was only a boy, and his mother, Christina, had had to assume the burdens of the family breadwinner until Lou was old enough to contribute his share, his life had revolved around the strong character of his mother. Today's headshrinkers probably would say that Huggins became a "father image" to Gehrig.

It is true that, aside from his previous coaches, Kane at the High School of Commerce and Coakley at Columbia, Huggins was the first male adult to supervise Gehrig's life. Gehrig had a great admiration for the tiny Miller, and Hug's sudden death in the closing days of the 1929 season was a great personal shock to Gehrig, as though a member of his immediate family had died.

Funeral services were held for Huggins in Manhattan, before the body was taken to his native Cincinnati for burial. The Yankees, looking strangely abashed in their street attire, filed by his bier respectfully. A writer, covering by telephone, called back to his city desk to report that Gehrig was seen to wipe tears from his eyes as he passed the casket.

"Just give us the facts, old boy," said the hard-boiled rewrite man. "Don't try to make 'East Lynne' out of this."

The reporter was right. I was there and I saw Gehrig wiping the tears from his eyes; and Lou was one of the Yankees who accompanied the body to Woodlawn Cemetery in Cincinnati for the final ceremonies. It was fortunate for Gehrig that there weren't many games remaining for the Yankees to play after Hug's death, because, for the first and only time in his career, Lou lost his zest for baseball. It no longer was a pleasure for him to go to Yankee Stadium.

"What kind of a guy was Lou Gehrig?"

Well, he had a rough boyhood, rough because of economic conditions. By today's standards, Lou could have been called underprivileged, although he never regarded his status as such and probably

never even heard the term. He thought he had a dandy boyhood.

Lou was the only surviving child of German emigrants. Four children had been born in all, one before Lou and two later, but none lived long enough for Lou to have any memory of them. His father, Henry, an iron worker, fell into ill health when Lou was in grammar school, and his condition permitted only spasmodic work for a time, and then none at all. In the brief period when the senior Gehrig enjoyed sound health, he was an enthusiastic gymnast who used to take his son to the gym with him.

Gehrig was an outsize kid, strong, healthy and agile. He played all the neighborhood games on the corner lot—and there were such things as vacant lots in Manhattan in those days when Lou was growing up. When he entered the High School of Commerce, he had the physique of a promising athlete and, moreover, the desire and the ambition to become an athlete. He was to star there in baseball, football and soccer, and it was his athletic prowess which made it possible for him to get to Columbia University.

Columbia already had entered Lou's life when he was in high school, but not as the college on which he had set his sights. In those days before unemployment insurance and social security, it was a tragedy for the head of the family to be idle because of ill health, or indeed for any reason. Lou's mother stepped into the breach. She did what was euphemistically known as "odd chores," which could mean anything from washing to sewing, from cooking to house cleaning. Lou helped her before and after school, pitching in whenever and wherever he could. It was while he was at Commerce that his parents obtained what amounted to steady employment at Columbia's Sigma Nu fraternity house. Mrs. Gehrig did the cooking, the father acted as handy man, and Lou, when he had the free time from school, waited on tables.

It was a tough schedule for a high school boy. Lou had to go to school from home, then uptown to practice or play, and then back down again to help his mother at the Sigma Nu house. His homework and studying often were done while making these trolley car trips all over Manhattan.

It was while handling these back-breaking chores that Gehrig achieved his first national fame. The High School of Commerce won the New York City PSAL championship and was chosen to play the Chicago city champions, Lane Tech, at Wrigley Field in Chicago. In this game, with the score tied at 8-8 in the ninth inning, Gehrig stepped up with the bases filled and belted the ball clean out of Wrigley Field, a schoolboy grand slam in a major league ballpark. Even if Gehrig had been imaginative, which he wasn't, he couldn't possibly have foreseen that a dozen years later, in that same ballpark, he would team up with the fabulous Babe Ruth to hit back-to-back World Series homers. And, as a footnote, it might be noted that there was an air of prophecy about that schoolboy grand-slammer. As a Yankee, Lou was to hit 23 home runs with the bases loaded, still the major league record for grand-slam homers. Gehrig, born in 1903, had just turned 17 when he hit that schoolboy home run in Wrigley Field.

When Lou went to Columbia, oddly enough, it was on the strength of his football skills—not baseball—that he was offered a scholarship. About two-dozen colleges had offered him the customary room, board, books and tuition, but he picked Columbia on the strength of his and his parents' association with the Sigma Nu house and his friendship with Bobby Watt. Watt had been manager of the chapter house, but by the time Gehrig was ready for college, he was serving as Columbia's graduate manager of athletics. A Columbia quarterback of distinction, George Pease, was just breaking into Columbia's varsity lineups in football and baseball as Gehrig was concluding his athletic career. Years later I asked Pease, a long-time friend, how he had found Lou during his college days. George answered very much on the positive side, citing all the attributes of Gehrig as a person and as an athlete, and then made an unusual, thoughtful observation. "Every once in a while, when things weren't going too well with the teams," Pease remarked, "Lou seemed to be cranky with us."

Pease was an intelligent boy, in high school at Manual Training in Brooklyn and later at Columbia, and his choice of the word "cranky" seemed peculiar. Yet, it was revealing. Gehrig, the perfectionist, was head and shoulders over most of his Lion teammates, and when their slips threatened to undo the whole team, Lou became impatient—not surly, not lording it over them, but just, as George said, cranky.

It was while he was a student at Columbia that Gehrig committed his only fall from grace. Approached by a scout from the New York Giants, Lou agreed to play with Hartford, in the Eastern League, during the summer months under a false name. He didn't show a great deal of imagination in the selection of his alias, however, since he made up the name Lewis.

Gehrig had graduated from Commerce in February of 1921 and had to take an extension course which would give him sufficient credits to permit him to enter Columbia in September. He was told that the practice of collegians playing summer ball under assumed names was standard operating procedure and he believed it. Or, maybe he didn't quite believe it, but the money he was promised looked to be a big lift to the family exchequer, never robust at any time.

Lou played only a dozen games at Hartford before the Columbia authorities learned about it. Watt, his sponsor, went to Hartford to explain his error to Lou. What Bobby found was a disillusioned kid, homesick and sick of baseball, too. He was away from home for the first time and he missed his parents terribly. And his hitting at Hartford was nothing sensational, .261—with one extra-base hit, a double.

Watt explained the facts of life to him, and Lou promptly renounced Hartford and returned home, forlorn and penitent. Watt's intelligence and diplomacy saved his athletic career. Letters were dispatched to all of Columbia's future opponents. The Lions agreed that Lou would serve a sentence of ineligibility until the fall of 1922, when he would pick up with the football team. When Watt explained the extenuating circumstances, the straitened finances of the Gehrig family, the disbelief on Lou's part that he was doing anything dishonorable, all of Columbia's opponents agreed that Lou could represent the Light Blue in varsity sports from September of 1922 until he graduated.

"What kind of a guy was Lou Gehrig?"

Well, there are those who will tell you that he was cheap, that he was a nickel-nurser. Don't believe them, because these stories and insinuations have their foundation in the early poverty of the Gehrigs, when every penny had to be watched. They offer no insight into the true nature of the man himself.

Gehrig received neither a whopping bonus nor a huge salary when he signed with the Yankees after Columbia completed its 1923 baseball season. Aside from the few dollars he picked up playing under the name of Lewis at Hartford in 1921, Lou had been unable to make any real contribution to the family income. The finances were complicated by medical and doctor bills for Henry Gehrig's chronic illness. Practically all the money Lou

received from the Yankees in 1923 had been used to meet current expenses and to pay overdue obligations. Lou was stone broke when he went south for his first Yankee spring training in 1924.

Ballplayers do not receive any salary until the season opens, but in recent years they have been getting $25 a week for expenses while in spring training. This is to cover tips, laundry and other incidentals. The ballclub pays the hotel bill, including meals, and, of course, the transportation from the player's home town to the training camp. When Gehrig joined the Yankees in New Orleans in 1924, the $25 a week allowance was still years away. He had to pay for all incidentals, including tips.

Lou started out with a little more than ten bucks, which had to last him through six weeks of training. Obviously, he couldn't tip very lavishly, and the chances are that he did some of his own laundry in his room on the quiet. If so, he was neither the first ballplayer nor the last to use the tub in his room as a launderette. When you have to stretch money as Lou did in that New Orleans camp, you learn to count the pennies. It isn't so much that a penny saved is a penny earned as it is that a penny spent is a penny gone forever.

Later on, when Gehrig was one of baseball's greatest stars, there were many tales about his first spring training camp, most of them appealing, all of them apocryphal. The best was that Lou took a job as a dishwasher working nights and that Miller Huggins was unable to understand why a young man of Gehrig's exemplary living habits appeared for practice looking so haggard. Hug, according to the yarn, investigated, learned the facts, obtained a salary advance for Lou and had him quit the pearl-diving job in the restaurant. Another was that Gehrig worked nights as a waiter and quit the job only when Babe Ruth led a party of Yankees into the dining room, causing Lou to flee to the kitchen and out the back way before his teammates could have a chance to recognize him.

Neither story is true. Frank Graham, whose biography of Gehrig is the most authoritative of the several printed, reveals that Lou went only so far as to apply for a job as a waiter. The way Graham tells it, which is probably the way it happened, is that Gehrig and his roommate, Benny Bengough, had entered a restaurant to apply for waiters' jobs and then beat it when Benny spotted four Yankee stars—Herb Pennock, Joe Dugan, Waite Hoyt and Bob Meusel—dining at a nearby table. That was as close as Lou came to working his way through spring training camp.

Although Gehrig had an appreciation of all the finer things in life, his boyhood conditioned him for the simpler pleasures. One of them was billiards. Back in the early '30s, several of the writers traveling with the Yankees were bitten with the billiard bug, probably as the result of many pleasant evenings spent in St. Louis in the company of Charley Peterson, the master trick shot artist. Among those afflicted were John Drebinger, Marshall Hunt, Arthur Mann and myself. One afternoon Gehrig overheard us talking about the previous night's game and said, "Why don't you fellows invite me along next time? I'm pretty handy with a cue." He joined us occasionally after that and was more deft than you would imagine. It was quite a sight to see Lou's huge bulk hefted over the table, delicately nursing the balls for a balkline or straight rail run.

The point of this anecdote is not Gehrig's cue-handling ability but his financial approach. We played only when the Yankees were on the road—this was in that delightful era of all day games—and the custom was to grab a cab after dinner and head for the nearest reputable billiard academy; no pool halls for us. On arrival, one of us would pay the cabdriver and then pro-rate the cost among the bunch, whether it was three, four or five of us. I don't recall ever

having Gehrig along when it was a party of five, since that would have been a pretty tight squeeze in any cab and a five-handed billiard match would be fairly awkward. When the game ended, we divided the time charges among the players.

Gehrig always chipped in his share of the cab going to the billiard room and his share of the time charges, but on the return trip he frequently jockeyed so as to be the last one in the cab and therefore the first one out. Then, when the cab reached the hotel, Lou would fling the fare to the driver and race into the lobby of the hotel. The point is that Lou would gladly have shouldered the cost of the entire evening's entertainment, which usually ran around $5 and certainly never as high as $10. To do that, however, would have been an insult to us, and Gehrig had the graciousness and decency to understand it. Paying the final cab bill, however, was just a gesture to let us know that he had enjoyed the evening. It certainly wasn't the gesture of a tightwad.

"What kind of a guy was Lou Gehrig?"

It is doubtful if any prominent athlete ever was as closely associated with his mother as Gehrig was with Mom Gehrig. She accompanied him to spring training, while Pop remained at home. She went to games at Yankee Stadium daily, along with Pop. Lou took her to all the hit shows on Broadway, to all the top restaurants. He never had many dates, even in high school or college. Gehrig, now a high-salaried ballplayer, sharer in several World Series purses, was perhaps baseball's most eligible bachelor. Yet there were no romances, even in the gossip columns. Gehrig laughed it off by saying Mom still was his best girl. Many who knew him well doubted that he would ever marry while his mother lived.

Yet Lou finally met the girl he wanted to marry, met her in Chicago when the Yankees were in the process of sweeping the Cubs four straight in the 1932 World Series. She was Eleanor Twitchell, a pert, attractive blond. After the Bombers had won the first two games in Yankee Stadium, the team arrived in Chicago around noon on a Friday, with the third game scheduled for Saturday at Wrigley Field, site of Gehrig's first publicized home run. There was a small dinner party in somebody's home in Chicago that evening and Gehrig was one of the guests. So was Eleanor. And, for the first time in his life, Gehrig, now 29, was seriously attracted to a girl. He wrote to her during the winter, visited her during the following summer when the Yankees played in Chicago. Lou, like the proper gentleman, met her family and Eleanor visited the East to meet his parents.

It was characteristic that Gehrig should tell his mother of his plans to marry Eleanor, almost as if he were asking parental permission. He wondered if Mom would be jealous. When Mrs. Gehrig gave her blessing to the future Mrs. Gehrig, Lou beamed. In slightly less than a year after Lou and Eleanor had met, they were married in New Rochelle. Gehrig's marriage, which was to be a tremendously happy one, even though cut short so tragically, came as a complete surprise to his fellow Yankees. The average ballplayer marries quite young, younger, in fact, than the average American, and Lou had been regarded by his teammates as a confirmed bachelor.

Eleanor was the perfect counterpart to the still shy Gehrig. Poised and intelligent, she brought out all the best in Lou, even to the point of supervising his reading, reading that Lou had neglected because of his devotion to baseball. There were those close to the newlyweds who thought perhaps Mom Gehrig stayed too close to her beloved son and her newly acquired daughter-in-law. If this was the case, Eleanor had the good sense to keep it to herself, but it must have been something of a task to convince as dutiful a son as Lou that his wife now, rather than his mother, had first claim.

The new bride did nothing to bridge the gulf between Lou and the Ruths, a separation of friendship which simply had deteriorated, rather than come as the result of any sharp rupture. Apparently it was Eleanor's idea that Lou could choose his own friends, that he was big enough and old enough to stand on his own feet. When Gehrig was stricken, Babe was at his side at Gehrig Appreciation Day in Yankee Stadium and the manner in which he flung his arms about Lou left no doubt about the high regard he had for the baseball hero whom he had once called "Buster." The nickname was an affectionate one, bestowed by Ruth whose memory was lamentable when it came to proper names. Gehrig was "Buster" to Babe because he was only a kid when he first joined the Yankees and because he could bust the ball a mile.

"What kind of a guy was Lou Gehrig?"

Well, he was the kind of guy sportswriters began to worry about when he showed signs of mysteriously slipping during the 1938 season. Baseball writers, despite occasional stories which seem to drip vitriol, are sentimentalists at heart, but not so blindly sentimental that their tear ducts go to work automatically, like a sprinkler alarm system, when a star begins to set. Most of them have seen the lights go out too often. But it was different with Gehrig, as it was with Ruth or as it will be with Stan Musial, when The Man begins to blur around the edges.

The sympathy manifested for Gehrig during the 1938 season, which was intensified in spring training at St. Petersburg in 1939, had no overtones of tragedy. None of the writers, none of Gehrig's teammates, including Bill Dickey, his roommate, had any idea that there was anything organically wrong with Lou. Their concern was simply that for a great ballplayer who had suddenly lost his touch.

Jim Kahn, a top-flight baseball writer on the late lamented *New York Sun*, was the first to have an inkling that there was something about Gehrig's slump which made it different from all others. Kahn, who had been writing baseball for as long as Lou had been playing it, had seen other good hitters fade, but there was something different about Lou's case. He wasn't hitting the ball into the dirt, popping it up or missing it entirely. "I've been watching Lou closely," Kahn said, "and there's something wrong with him. I don't mean his batting average, I mean something physically wrong. What it is, I haven't the faintest idea. There's nothing wrong with his swing or with his timing. He's meeting the ball cleanly but he isn't hitting it anywhere. Whatever has happened, he's lost all his power."

Gehrig finished up the season with a .295 average and 29 home runs. It was the first time he had gone below .300 since his first year as a regular, 1925, and his homer output was his lowest in 10 years. And even these figures are deceptive, for Gehrig had done well in the early part of the season. The Yankees romped through the World Series with Chicago in four straight, but Lou contributed only four singles and didn't bat in a run. It was his seventh Series and the first in which he didn't make an extra-base hit.

Lou had played well enough in the early part of 1938 to be named first baseman on the American League All-Star team, an honor which had been his ever since the game was devised by the *Chicago Tribune's* Arch Ward in 1933. The slump, which began somewhere in August, was rapid, and by the spring of 1939, when the Yankees had assembled in St. Petersburg for training, Gehrig's condition was truly alarming. It wasn't simply that he wasn't hitting—he wasn't doing anything. He was pitifully slow in his reactions, as awkward as he had been when he first came out of Columbia to join the Yankees.

The observation that Jim Kahn had made the year before was now plain to all—something was radically physically wrong with Gehrig. Lou was pitiful in spring training, although he did hit two home runs in Norfolk, Va., on the last stop of the barnstorming trip home with the Dodgers. The homers, to be honest about it, were pop flies over a short right-field fence, and they were the last the Iron Man was ever to hit.

Then came the day in Detroit in May when Gehrig told McCarthy he was benching himself for the good of the team. He had played eight games that season, batting .143, and his four base hits had all been singles. On the final play of Lou's final game at Yankee Stadium, April 30, Johnny Murphy fielded a ball hit to the left of the pitcher's mound and Gehrig barely got to first in time to take the throw.

"Nice play, Lou," Murphy said.

"That was it," Gehrig said grimly to McCarthy two days later. "I should have been on first waiting for Johnny's throw. When the players start feeling sorry for you, it's time to quit."

Lou's deterioration seemed to increase even more rapidly after his visit to the Mayo Clinic in Rochester, Minnesota. The report, which he delivered to general manager Ed Barrow in mid-June, was a shock to the nation, as it was to those who knew Lou. Barrow, who had a greater affection for Gehrig than he had entertained for any ballplayer since the days when he had discovered Honus Wagner, was visibly shaken every time he mentioned Gehrig's case. Stripped of medical terminology, Gehrig was suffering from a paralysis which made it impossible to play baseball and essential for him to conserve his energy. Two years later he was dead.

In the spring of 1939 and for the first half of the season, I had been covering the New York Giants for the *World-Telegram*. All I knew about Gehrig was what I read in the papers. I hadn't seen him on a ballfield since the last game of the 1938 World Series until I saw him walk feebly to the plate at the 1939 All Star game and deliver the American League lineup to the umpires in his post as honorary captain of the team. For the balance of 1939, I covered the Yankees as they rolled to their fourth straight pennant and fourth straight World Series triumph, a record at the time. Lou seemed to fade before your eyes. For instance, Gehrig, his roommate Dickey and Red Rolfe were devoted bridge players. Usually a newspaperman filled in as the fourth. I did so on a couple of occasions. In a two-week span, Gehrig's hands lost so much articulation that he couldn't deal the cards and he held the cards so tightly that they curved like row boats and a new deck was necessary after every few deals.

Here was a man dying before you, dying and joking about the hands he held, the plays he made or should have made, the boners made by his partner or his opponents, joking and laughing with death just around the corner.

That's the kind of guy Lou Gehrig was.

Chapter 55

Charlie Gehringer: The Mechanical Man

Charlie Gehringer performed without fanfare, but with the skillful day-to-day consistency that made him one of baseball's all-time great second basemen.

By Lawrence S. Ritter
SPORT Magazine, April 1969

Denny McLain won 31 games last year for the Detroit Tigers, sparked his team to the American League pennant and was the toast of baseball.

Joe Namath led the New York Jets to an American Football League championship, then—almost single handedly—slew the terrible NFL dragon, the Baltimore Colts, and was the toast of football.

There are further similarities between the two foremost athletes of our day.

One played the organ, was a cut-up off the field, and always said whatever was in his mind.

The other grew a Fu-Manchu moustache, wore a mink coat, was a cut-up off the field, and always said whatever was in his mind.

McLain and Namath are examples of the jet-age superstar—the athlete who commands attention not just by his skills on the field, but also by his flamboyance, his candor, his braggadocio, his colorful adventures off the field.

He is a product of our times, all right, but he is not yet the typical professional athlete. The other type still abounds—the type who accomplishes perhaps as much as a McLain or Namath, but is never heard from, on or off the field.

In another day, there was a supreme example of this type athlete. His name was Charlie Gehringer.

Charlie who?

Charlie Gehringer, one of the three or four best second basemen in the history of baseball.

Charlie Gehringer who, from 1926 through 1942—a distinguished 16-year career—was by all odds the most outstanding second baseman in the American League.

Charlie Gehringer who, in the field and at bat, was brilliant, effortless, consistent—the man who could be counted on time after time to start Tiger rallies with his bat and end opposition rallies with his glove. Charlie Gehringer, who hit .356 in 1934, and followed that in the three succeeding years with .330, .354 and .371. Who was the backbone of the Detroit pennant winners of 1934, 1935, and 1940. Who was named the American League's Most Valuable Player in 1937. Who was the American League's second baseman in six straight All-Star games. Who was so versatile that he even led the league in stolen bases one year.

Charlie Gehringer. Who accomplished all this with so little fuss and such a minimum of bother that he came to be known on the field as the "Mechanical Man" and off the field as ... "The Silent Marvel."

"Greatly exaggerated," Charlie Gehringer says today, "greatly exaggerated." He is 66 years old but looks at least 20 years younger. He still has that slightly crooked, wry smile, the one that is seen in most of the still photographs taken of him in the 1930s. His hair is hardly gray and his figure is trim, and he protests gently his image as a "Mechanical Man," as a "Silent Marvel."

"I *always* used to talk," he says, "especially if somebody asked me something. Gave about 50 skillion 'Father-and-Son' night speeches during the off-season. And, by gosh, Chief Hogsett and I talked every day. He was my best friend. Heck, we talked all the time. What do they want, anyway?"

Chief Elon Hogsett, a strapping Cherokee from Kansas, pitched for the Tigers from 1929 through 1936. Invariably, he and

Gehringer roomed together on the road. Lee Allen, historian at the Hall of Fame, has recorded their verbosity as follows: "One morning Hal Walker, a writer for the *Toronto Globe and Mail,* had breakfast with them. Hogsett turned to Gehringer and said, 'Pass the salt, please.' Gehringer obliged, but said in reproach, 'You might have pointed.' "

Goose Goslin was Gehringer's teammate on the 1934 and 1935 Detroit pennant winners. "Talkative!" roars the Goose. "Of course he was talkative. Both of them were. Every morning at breakfast Gehringer would nod and the Chief would say 'Ugh' and that's the last you'd hear from either of them till the next morning."

Bucky Harris was Charlie's manager for four years, from 1929 through 1932. "What stands out in my mind," recalls Bucky, "is that he was so very shy and very modest. After I got to know him better, I discovered something: when he got mad, which wasn't very often, the veins in his neck would swell up. If somebody wasn't paying attention to the game, or something like that, and they pulled a boner and blew it, then you could see those veins stand out. Charlie was angry. That's the only way you could tell, though. He never raised his voice or gave any other sign of being annoyed. Nor did he ever say much of anything else, either. He'd be around, you know, listening and taking everything in, but he never said very much himself."

He really didn't have to. Longtime Detroit sports columnist H.G. Salsinger once wrote about the Mechanical Man, "Only Nap Lajoie ever matched Gehringer for sheer grace. He had poetry of motion and, like Lajoie, made every chance look easy."

Indeed, he made everything look so easy that everyone took his feats for granted. Won the game with a double? Got three for four? Turned a sure single into an unbelievable double play? Who—Gehringer? Well, so what, doesn't he always?

The glory years for the Detroit Tigers were the mid-thirties, especially 1934 and '35, when Detroit put pennants together back-to-back. It was a team that featured the slugging of Hank Greenberg, the inspiration of the player-manager, catcher Mickey Cochrane, the fine pitching from Schoolboy Rowe and Tommy Bridges. And the quiet, all-round, exceptional skill of the second baseman, Charlie Gehringer.

In 1934, Gehringer batted .356 and was one of the Tigers' heroes in the losing World Series with the St. Louis Cardinals, one of the most tumultuous Series of all times.

The Cardinals won the first game easily, 8-3, though Gehringer, batting third in the order, between Cochrane and Greenberg, got two hits. The Tigers won the second game in the 12th inning when Gehringer walked, took second on a walk to Greenberg and sped home with the winning run on a single by Goose Goslin. Charlie also got a single in that game.

The Cardinals came back to take the third game, despite Gehringer's single and double. But then the Tigers exploded for a 10-4 victory in the fourth game. That one was typical in that Gehringer figured as the silent partner in a moment of high drama.

In the fourth inning, the game still close, Dizzy Dean, the pitcher, came in as a pinch-runner. Cardinal manager Frankie Frisch felt that Dean's presence in the game would be a tonic to his team. It proved instead to be a near disaster.

With Leo Durocher on second and Dean on first, Pepper Martin hit a hard groundball to Gehringer's right. Charlie skimmed over ground as he always did, backhanding the ball flawlessly and flipping underhand to shortstop Billy Rogell for the force on Dean. But then Rogell, trying to make the double play, hit

Dizzy in the back of the head, and the big pitcher went out cold. The ball caromed away and Durocher scored the tying run and, when Dean recovered consciousness in the clubhouse, he said, "Well, I guess I broke up that double play." Newspaper accounts that followed ignored Gehringer's role in the drama, and his two more hits.

But Charlie could not be ignored in the fifth game. Dizzy Dean, having recovered amazingly from the bump on his head, was the Cardinals' starting pitcher, and he was in rare form. The Tigers scored one run in the second inning but Dean held the Tigers to the sixth. The Tigers' first batter that inning was Gehringer.

The Mechanical Man wasted no time. With that picture-book swing of his, that fluid swing from an alert half-crouch, Gehringer connected with a Dean fastball and hit a home run to the roof of the right-field pavilion. That blow so shook Dean (Gehringer, after all, had hit only 11 home runs in the 1934 season) that he allowed one more run that inning. But Charlie Gehringer's was the difference in the Tigers' 3-1 victory.

The Cardinals came back to win the World Series from Detroit, but Gehringer had done his job. He led all Tiger batters with 11 hits and a .379 average.

In 1935 the Tigers went all the way again. Gehringer batted .330, drove in 108 runs, got 201 hits, including 19 home runs, and led the league's second basemen in assists. And, this time, the Tigers beat the Cubs in the World Series. And this time Gehringer hit .374. In 20 World Series games and six All-Star games, Gehringer's batting average was .356, which gives you a pretty good idea of his grace under pressure.

And grace was his game in the field, too. "It wasn't that he was so fast out there," recalls Hank Greenberg, "rather it was that he had this terrific ability to play the hitters just right. Of course, he wasn't slow by any means. But the main thing was the way he'd be where the ball was hit—practically before the batter even swung at the pitch. He made everything look so simple it used to make me mad."

When you arrive in Detroit, where Gehringer still lives, you immediately come to grips with the Gehringers. You are barely out of the Detroit Metropolitan Airport parking lot, 21 miles west of downtown, before you find yourself driving along the William G. Rogell Freeway. When you spin off the William G. Rogell Freeway onto the Edsel Ford Expressway (why Edsel Ford and not the Charles Leonard Gehringer Expressway?) you have a choice. You can turn left and head via Ann Arbor for Lansing, 74 miles away, or you can turn right toward downtown Detroit, Cadillac Square, the tunnel to Canada, and the ballpark.

If it's left you choose, 27 miles before you reach the State Capitol Building in Lansing, you will pass by Fowlerville (pop. 1,674 in 1965). Here—or, more precisely, on the 80-acre family farm two miles south of town—Charles Leonard Gehringer was born on May 11, 1903. Charlie was the next-to-youngest of four children, two sons and two daughters. At an early age baseball became a passion, and he still remembers with obvious delight the many hours spent at the kitchen table—getting in his mother's way as she tried to prepare supper. He would be compiling a scrapbook of newspaper and magazine photos of the Tiger stars of his youth—Cobb, of course, who won the American League batting title every year but one from 1907 through 1919; Sam Crawford, perennial leader in triples; Donie Bush, scrappy Detroit shortstop from 1909 through 1921; Bobby Veach, star Tiger outfielder from 1913 through 1923. All these and many more were painstakingly cut out

and pasted in the treasured scrapbook. Just about everyone except a Tiger second baseman. Detroit never seemed to be able to fill that spot with the right man before Gehringer took it over in 1926, and they haven't had much better luck since he retired in 1942.

By the time he was nine or ten, Charlie was spending all his spare time either playing or thinking about baseball. Detroit won the pennant in 1907, '08 and '09, and in succeeding years the youngster went about his farm chores dreaming of the day it would happen again. He milked the cows and with each squirt into the pail he dreamed of a Crawford triple or a Cobb double—a line shot over the infield or a crackling grass-cutter down the first-base line. *Ping, pang! Ping, pang!* By the time the milking had been finished the Tigers would have scored at least 15 runs and the opposing team would have been whitewashed again!

He took care of the horses, fed the pigs and chickens, and plowed the fields. He did everything millions of farm boys have done since the dawn of time, with but one exception. Surprisingly, he did no hunting. Not even for rabbits or quail. He recalls that there never was a rifle or gun of any sort in the Gehringer home. And later, when the Gehringer children grew up and established their own households, either on their own farmsteads or elsewhere, none of them ever had a firearm in any of their homes either. Once or twice, in later years, he went hunting with teammates, but soon stopped.

"I wasn't a bad shot," he says, "but I really didn't enjoy it. After a while I started to aim to *miss* the animal. Felt better that way."

At Fowlerville High, Gehringer pitched and played the infield, and played on the basketball team as well. He was a good pitcher—he lost only one game in three years—but he was equally good at bat, so that when he wasn't pitching he was at second base or short-stop. He also played on the Fowlerville town team. In those days most American communities, even those as small as Fowlerville, had a local baseball team: a game against neighboring Howell or Williamston inspired excitement rivaled only by the approach of the annual County Fair.

As the best ballplayer in all of Fowlerville—the best pitcher, the best hitter, and the best fielder—Charles Leonard Gehringer became something of a local celebrity by the time he was only a sophomore at Fowlerville High. His parents, however, never let it go to his head: baseball was fine for a boy's spare time, but first came the farm chores and second the schoolwork. Only after those were done, and done well, was Charlie to play baseball. He was a good student, though, and schoolwork was never something he tried to avoid. Nor his farm work. He did his chores regularly, and his homework faithfully, in the thorough Gehringer style, and then he was off for town on his bike—with his Louisville Slugger bat, his taped-up ball, and his all-purpose glove.

After graduation from high school, Charlie left the farm to enroll at the University of Michigan at Ann Arbor, a freshman undecided as to whether he'd rather major in Physical Education or English Literature. But one thing he did know: the University of Michigan had a varsity baseball team, and Charlie Gehringer wanted to play on it.

In 1923, during his freshman year at Ann Arbor, Gehringer continued, whenever possible, to play second base for the home-town Fowlerville nine. Because of this, his life took a new although not entirely unpredictable direction. A Fowlerville resident, Floyd Smith, had a hunting date with Tiger outfielder Bobby Veach. Smith spent most of the afternoon raving about Fowlerville's mir-acle second baseman. By the time the afternoon was over, Veach

didn't have any rabbits but he did have an earful, and he lost no time in relaying the information to manager Cobb, who in turn passed it on to Tiger President Frank Navin.

The result was that young Gehringer was asked to come to Detroit for closer inspection. For the better part of a morning, Charlie worked out under the scrutiny of the most demanding baseball man who ever lived, Tyrus Raymond Cobb. After about two hours, Cobb sent word to Navin to join him on the field and the workout continued, now with both watching his every move.

"I guess I should have been nervous," says Charlie today, thinking back to that morning, "but I really wasn't. Everywhere I'd played, all my life, I'd been as good as anybody on the field. I didn't see why things should suddenly be any different than they'd always been."

And they weren't. Cobb and Navin were impressed enough to offer him a contract on the spot—$3600, plus a $300 bonus for signing. But much to their astonishment they did not receive an immediate acceptance. Charlie Gehringer wanted to go home first and check with his parents.

Dad thought it was a pretty good idea but Mom couldn't see that it made any sense at all. Both Gehringers had emigrated to the United States from southern Germany and neither was too familiar with this baseball business. What was it all about, anyway? What kind of way was that to make a living? Wasn't the farm good enough? Finally, after no little persuasion, Mother Gehringer, without enthusiasm, gave her consent. (Ironically, Charlie's father died shortly thereafter and never did see his son play professionally, but his mother became a devoted fan as the years passed by and frequently came to the park to see him play.)

Charlie returned to Ann Arbor, withdrew from school and proceeded on to Detroit to sign the contract. However, he insisted on one additional stipulation: if he were farmed out to the minor leagues it must be to some place not too far from Fowlerville. Navin agreed, and the signatures were duly affixed.

During the two following years, 1924 and 1925, Gehringer per-fected the skills that were to bring him to Detroit in 1926. And he did it not far from home—in 1924 with London, Ontario in the Michigan-Ontario League, and in 1925 with Toronto in the Triple-A International League. At Toronto he proved he was ready: he hammered out 206 hits, batted .325, drove in 108 runs, and led the league's second basemen in fielding.

Ty Cobb was still the Tiger manager when Gehringer came up to stay in 1926. It was the last of Ty's 22 years in Detroit, his sixth as a not overly successful manager. Gehringer remembers being treated very well by Cobb at the beginning of the season, almost fawned over, but as time went on matters deteriorated.

"I don't know exactly what happened," Gehringer recalls. "At first he was so nice to me I really couldn't believe the stories other players told about his moods and his temper and the way he treated some of his men. He seemed like a great guy to me. But then he gradually changed. I still can't figure out why. I know I wasn't any ball of fire that year. But I don't think that was it. By the end of the season, though, he wasn't talking to me anymore. If he had any-thing to say, he'd have one of the coaches or some other player tell me."

Cobb was gone from the scene in 1927 and it was much better for Gehringer. He batted .317 that year, the first of a string of .300 or better averages that extended through 14 seasons with but one interruption, 1932, when he slipped to .298. (He led the American League in batting in 1937 with a .371 mark and was named the

league's Most Valuable Player.) He drove in over 100 runs for seven consecutive seasons except for one, when he slipped to 96. And his fielding was just as consistent. Someone, in 1927, called him The Mechanical Man and it stuck, the nickname remaining with him throughout his playing days. And it was appropriate.

By the time he was through he had broken just about all Tiger batting records except those held by Ty Cobb himself. Aside from Cobb, Charlie had played in more Tiger games, gotten more hits, scored more runs, hit more doubles and hit for more total bases than anyone in the history of the club. In addition, he is third among all-time Detroit players in triples (behind Crawford and Cobb) and in runs batted in (behind Cobb and Heilmann). He is even fifth in home runs (behind Greenberg, York, Kaline and Cash), although he never considered himself a home-run hitter.

Gehringer rarely swung at the first pitch. Many experts still regard him as the greatest two-strike hitter in the history of the game, and he rarely struck out. In 1936 he struck out only 13 times in 641 official times at hat. To Satchel Paige, who has seen just about all of them, Josh Gibson—the late home-run king of the Negro leagues—was the best hitter he ever saw. The next best was Charles Leonard Gehringer. "Gehringer was real tough for me," says Paige. "The toughest of all those stickers. You couldn't fool him. When they hit flatfooted they're the best hitters, and he sure stood there flat-footed. DiMaggio was good, but that Gehringer—he was *real* good."

Gehringer now lives and works about 20 miles north of Tiger Stadium, where he is associated with the firm of Gehringer and Forsythe, manufacturers' representatives for automobile interior upholstery. Except for a brief period as Detroit general manager, from 1951 to 1953, he has been out of baseball since his retirement as an active player in 1942. He does not look back upon his two years as a front-office executive with particular fondness.

"It wasn't near as much fun as playing," he frowns. But then his eyes brighten: "One thing I did enjoy about that job, though, was the phone calls from Bill Veeck. He was running the St. Louis Browns then, and at least twice a day he'd phone me and want to make some crazy trade or arrange some outlandish promotion. It got so I used to wake up in the morning looking forward to those calls from Veeck. They were the highlights of my day."

He stared out the window and watched the cars doing 60 along Route 10, 30 yards away. He twirled a pencil idly between thumb and forefinger of both hands. His mind was a thousand miles away. He tapped the pencil against the edge of his desk, lightly, and continued to look out at Route 10. A Volkswagen went by, followed closely by a Dodge Coronet.

"You know something?" he said, finally. "If I were a kid again I'd still want to be a ballplayer. I'd like to do it all over again, the same way. It was a wonderful life."

A trailer truck loaded with new Fords rumbled past. "Of course," he went on, "being a youngster today is a lot rougher, I think, than when I grew up. We had problems, too, in our day, but things were less complicated then. We knew right from wrong, good from bad, or thought we did, anyway. Today everything is so confused it's hard to tell up from down. Like Vietnam. I wish we weren't there. I can't blame the youngsters for being upset and protesting the situation. It's a rough deal. All I hope is they don't go too far and mess up their lives in the process. You only come by this way once, you know, and if you boot one too many ... well ... that's the old ballgame ..."

He suddenly tossed the pencil on the desk and swiveled his big chair away from the window: "Hey, you must be starved. How about some lunch?"

Epilogue
Gehringer lived out a quiet retirement near Detroit and died following a stroke in 1993. He was 89.

Chapter 56

The Ol' Diz, Dizzy Dean

Dizzy Dean was the genuine article, a mighty character who bragged that he'd win, and then went out and did so during a colorful 17-year career.

By Jack Newcombe
SPORT Magazine, October 1959

The sun and shadow of early October cut pleasant patterns on a field rimmed with the jostling and excited movement of the crowd, the flutter of flags and bunting. Across the scarred grass behind home plate a ballplayer in the clean white and red of the St. Louis Cardinals walked between two policemen. He was big and loose-gaited, and from the perch of his cap and the smile on his face it was apparent, that he was as pleased as a schoolboy with the escort. A band shambled behind them brassily playing *Happy Days Are Here Again*. As the group neared the first-base grandstand, the discordant noises of the crowd swelled into a giant roar of welcome.

Dizzy Dean tipped his cap and stepped up to a field box to be introduced to and photographed with the assembled governors of Missouri, Kansas and Oklahoma. The governors, and nearly everyone else in Sportsman's Park that World Series afternoon, knew that the Cardinals' president, Sam Breadon, had ordered police protection for Dean. Breadon was not concerned with outside threats against his 30-game winner. He wanted to make sure Dean would not lead himself astray before the Detroit Tigers were beaten and the Series was won. The day before, Breadon had watched with disbelief as Dizzy accepted the beckoning wave of two strangers in a car and rode off with them toward downtown St. Louis. "They was just two fans wanted to give me a lift," Dizzy later explained to his shaken employer. Breadon solemnly lectured Dean on the desperate ways of gamblers who might want to safeguard a bet on Detroit. Then, to Dizzy's delight, he clamped a police watch on him. (Three days later, in Detroit, Dizzy *was* missing for more than an hour before game time. When he finally showed up, he told his unsympathetic manager, Frankie Frisch, that he had been talking with Henry Ford and had lost track of the time.)

Dean's entrance under guard for the third game of the Series was no more dramatic than his exit. He left the field draped helplessly in the arms of four teammates while approximately 38,000 prayerful St. Louis fans watched in shocked silence. Put into the game as a pinch-runner, Dean had tried to break up a double play with both his feet and his head. He succeeded spectacularly. The relay throw by shortstop Billy Rogell caromed off his forehead, felling him like a sawed pine. He was carried off dazed but not seriously damaged.

Dizzy's mishap gave rise to a flock of bad jokes about the content and consistency of ballplayers' heads. One of them is firmly imbedded in baseball history, along with other rich Dizzy Dean lore. Reporters questioned Dizzy's pitching brother, Paul, or

"Daffy" as he was unsuccessfully nicknamed, after the game. The much-repeated interview runs something like this:

Question: "How's Diz?"

Answer: "He wasn't hurt much. He just got a glancin' blow. He wasn't even unconscious. He was talkin' all the time."

Question: "What was he saying?"

Answer: "Oh, nuthin'. He was just talkin'."

All this was 25 years ago. A new generation of baseball fans has since grown up to cheer new heroes and new teams. But the image of Dizzy Dean is clear. He was the mighty pitcher who won and boasted about it; the uninhibited, sometimes naive and eccentric character who got in jams with his boss, needed bodyguards and got hit on the head running bases. Dean's enduring status as one of

baseball's most colorful figures has been enhanced over the years by Dean himself. Unlike most ballplayers, who drop out of sight and sound when they leave the game, Dean has remained within earshot of millions of people who watch baseball on television and listen to it on radio. For over 15 years now, announcer Dean's distinctive brand of baseball rhetoric, with its heavy concentration of cornpone and reverse-English expressions, has helped fans draw an imaginative picture of Dean the brash country boy and star ballplayer. It doesn't matter much that there is little resemblance between the well-practiced commercial performance of Dizzy today and the genuine, cotton-country wit of the uninhibited young Cardinal pitcher of the 1930s.

The Dean legend will flourish as long as there are records to re-examine and World Series games to reminisce over. The figures will show that for six years, which is all there really was to his injury-shortened career, Dizzy was as good as any pitcher is ever likely to be. He won 18, 20, 30, 28, 24 and 13 games from 1932 to 1937. He was in only one World Series while he was in his prime, but he and brother Paul helped make it one of the most eventful in baseball history. The Deans beat the Tigers four times in 1934. It would be known as the Dean World Series if Ducky Medwick, a brash junior member of the famous St. Louis Gas House Gang, hadn't detonated a riot among Detroit bleacher fans in the seventh game. Dizzy's pitching through those six seasons was good enough to boost him into the Hall of Fame. Probably no one else in the Baseball Museum at Cooperstown compressed his feats into such a brief span.

There are, of course, other reasons why Dizzy Dean will continue to be the subject of nostalgic stories, anecdotes and jokes that are part of the language of baseball. He was fortunate enough to come to the game when men showed an earthy zest for playing baseball for a living. Ballplayers were less cultured then, less controlled and far more colorful. Winning games was serious business but there was some free-wheeling fun to be had, too.

Born 20 years later, Dean might have been even more successful as a pitcher but he would have been far less a character. He would have made a lot more money but he would have had a lot less fun doing it. Dizzy got wound up on this subject not long ago at his home in Phoenix, Ariz. "Sure, they got good players now," he said. "But as far as color goes and things like that, they just don't do things as far as gags. We'd do anything. We'd give a kid from the bushes a key and tell him to open the pitcher's box. And we'd start a rhubarb just by walking down the base and saying something. If it rained, we'd put up an umbrella to show the umpire. Now you can't even open your mouth to the umpires. You never read anything in the paper about ballplayers having fun. You see the same thing in the paper every day. Baseball is strictly a business."

In Dean's day a ballplayer didn't have to search far to find an accomplice in a little after-game skylarking. The Gas House Gang of 1934 was loaded with fun-seekers. Actually, some of the famous diversions that have been charged to Dizzy over the years were originated by others. For example, it wasn't Dean who dropped the water bag out the fourth-floor window of the Hotel Kenmore in Boston, barely missing manager Frankie Frisch and a St. Louis sportswriter. But the bag *was* dropped from Dizzy's room. And Dizzy was in on, but not the instigator of, the sneezing-powder prank that scattered a women's club gathering from a hotel patio.

In the historic Bellevue-Stratford Hotel hoax, Dizzy just went along with the gag and ended up as the surprised hero of the operation. Dizzy, Paul, Pepper Martin, Heinie Schuble, and Rip Collins

had picked up coveralls and some carpenters' equipment in a pawn shop. Collins, who along with Martin served as recreation directors of the Gas House Gang, suggested they might have some fun around the hotel in their rigs. They put on the coveralls and invaded the barbershop, from which they were promptly chased. Suddenly they found themselves on the edge of a banquet room with a luncheon in progress. They up-ended an empty table and began measuring, pointing, pounding and otherwise making clumsy construction noises. The luncheon speaker ground uncertainly to a halt. Everyone turned to the bedlam in the corner of the hall.

"We're redecorating," Collins announced. "But you go right ahead. You're not bothering us a bit."

The hoax collapsed moments later when one of the luncheon guests recognized Dean. There was a burst of happy applause from the crowd. And Dizzy was steered triumphantly to the speakers' table to address the luncheon.

Dizzy was justly famous for his absenteeism, but he played in an era when going AWOL was no more unusual than going four-for-four. Once when he jumped the club in Philadelphia, he gave four sportswriters four different reasons for his disappearance. He felt that each writer deserved an exclusive story. When he and Paul skipped an exhibition game in Detroit in 1934—for which they drew a seven-day suspension—their explanation to manager Frankie Frisch was classically simple: "We got tired from pitchin' in the hot sun."

Dizzy's personality, so well suited to that rollicking baseball period and that St. Louis team, was also shaped by his boyhood and his early exposure to the game. His background explains much of the good-humored boasting, undisciplined capering and occasional rebelling that made Dizzy such a famous—and such a fond—figure. And it also helps explain why in later years, after the money rolled in and Dizzy became a character for business reasons, he was sometimes resentful of the old stories and went out of his way to discount them.

As a boy Dizzy was deprived of most of the material pleasures of growing up and many of the necessities. He was born in Lucas, Arkansas, in 1911. (Dizzy gave his early biographers fits by naming two or three other birthplaces.) He was one of five children of sharecropping parents who moved from cotton field to cotton field. Dizzy was named Jay Hanna but later was called Jerome Herman, which was the name of a neighborhood playmate who died. Dizzy took the name, he said, because he felt sorry for the dead child's father. Dizzy's mother died when he was three. Pa, or Albert, Dean drove the others from job to job in Arkansas, Oklahoma and Texas in a sputtering jalopy.

The inevitable jokes have sprung up about Dizzy's boyhood. He occasionally uses one on a radio-TV audience: "I only got as far as the second grade—and I didn't do too well in the first," or "I was a 'cockeye' (left-handed pitcher) once. When I was a kid I used to pitch rocks at squirrels. I threw so hard with my right arm that I squashed them squirrels up somethin' terrible so they ain't fit for eatin'. So when I was rustlin' grub, I'd throw left-handed."

In truth his boyhood held few jokes for Jerome Herman Jay Hanna Dean. At the age of ten, he was getting up at five in the morning and picking as much as 400 pounds of cotton a day. When there was time and daylight left, Pa Dean played ball with Dizzy, Paul and older brother Elmer. He taught them to "chunk outdrops, slow balls and fastballs." In the dusty pickup games outside the work fields, the Deans were hard to beat.

When Dizzy was 16 he did something a lot of poor kids

without schooling or an apparent career turned to in the 1920s. He joined the Army. For Dizzy the Army offered new shoes, clothes, three meals a day—and a chance to play baseball. He put on his first baseball uniform (with the letters of the 12th Field Artillery) and when he was pitching and the officers and men were watching, he was, for the first time in his life, "a somebody."

With his father's encouragement and $120 of his small savings, Dizzy bought his way out of the Army a few months before his three-year hitch ended. He took a public service job in San Antonio just so he could pitch for the company baseball team. There he was "discovered," observed and signed by a St. Louis Cardinal scout and sent off to make his heavy mark on Organized Baseball.

Dizzy played first with St. Joseph, Misouri, in the Western League. It is unlikely that the citizens of that quiet, riverbank town had ever encountered anyone quite like him, in or out of a baseball uniform. Dizzy accumulated victories and I.O.U.'s at a whirring pace. He roomed at three different addresses. He apologized to his manager for allowing insignificant hits and runs. He learned opposing batters' favorite pitches and then struck them out with them. Once he spotted a bike underneath the stands and he spent his time between innings riding it. Dizzy won 17 games for St. Joe in 1930 and had everyone in town talking about his pitching and his eccentricities.

The Cardinals were so impressed with their hard-throwing ex-Army pitcher that they sent him to Houston late in the summer where he struck out 95 blinking Texas League batters in 85 innings. St. Louis general manager Branch Rickey yielded to one more curiosity about Dean. He brought him to Sportsman's Park to see what he could do against major league hitters. Dizzy, who had swaggered his way around St. Joseph and Houston, wasn't inclined to stop swaggering just because he was in the big city. The Cardinals were on their way to the pennant. When Dizzy walked in, he gave every appearance of having pitched them there all by himself. The Cards' crusty manager, Gabby Street, decided to work Dizzy against Pittsburgh on the last day of the season. He and his champions sat back and waited for the 19-year-old braggart to get his ears pinned. Dizzy won, 3-1, allowing only three hits.

Gabby Street and the Cardinals heard a lot more from Dizzy at their 1931 spring training base in Bradenton, Fla. And what Gabby saw and heard was enough to bring the old World War I sergeant to the frothing point. Dizzy began his training like a rheumatic veteran on a convalescence program. Before the first week was up, he was reporting even later than the hung-over sportswriters. Street snapped at him in his sharpest drill-field tongue. In exhibition games Dizzy tormented his manager with comments like "I jest wished I was throwin'." Street sent him up against the world champion Philadelphia Athletics, hoping they would provide the humiliation he could not. In one inning Dizzy struck out Simmons, Foxx and Cochrane.

Street finally blew up at Dean and ordered him out of uniform. Dizzy got himself reinstated. But when the season began, he was back in Houston, far from Gabby Street's view.

Dizzy had sensational success that summer in Texas. He won 26 games and struck out 303 batters. But, even more important to his baseball future, he got married. Like everything else Dizzy did, the courtship and marriage were feverishly conducted. He pursued the girl, Patricia Nash, in borrowed cars, proposed that they get married at the ballpark (they did not) and had to touch a friend for $2 to pay for the marriage license.

Marriage helped stabilize the erratic, irresponsible young athlete. Pat Dean saw that he got to the ballpark on time, most of the time. And she showed him that it was possible to keep money as well as to spend it. Dizzy earned $3,000 the first year they were married and they banked a third of it. Pat became his unofficial business manager. Over the years, she helped negotiate many of his non-baseball contracts. And frequently, when Dizzy wasn't available, she spoke for him to agents, newspapermen or whoever was demanding his time. Mrs. Dean didn't reform or remake Dizzy but she helped to moderate him.

Dizzy made the St. Louis varsity in 1932, and if he wasn't exactly the picture of deportment he was at least improved over his last visit with the club. On the pitching mound he was a little crude, sometimes wild, but nearly always exciting. He had the carriage and outline of a ballplayer Ring Lardner might have described. He was bony, often uncombed. He was all strength and enthusiasm. You had the idea he was going to kick up the left leg and let go with everything he had. And that's what he did.

He was not at the peak of his power in 1932 but he was fast approaching it. Leo Durocher, who played shortstop for Cincinnati in Dean's rookie year, was already acquiring respect for the young man's pitching. A year later Leo joined the Cardinals and became an admiring business partner of Dean's.

"Dizzy had everything," Leo said. "Fastball, curve and, later, control. He gave it to them sidearm, overhand, three-quarters. The ball was always alive. He had a high hard ball that came in around the shoulders, and just as the batter would swing at it, it would be up around his ears. He didn't need it but we sometimes doctored the ball for him. I kept the prong on my belt sharp and I'd scratch it and take the ball to Diz, saying 'It's on top.' No one needed help less. He could tell the batters what was coming and strike them out.

"The day he struck out 17 to set the National League record (July 30, 1933 in Chicago), there was a hot sun and the white shirts in the center-field bleachers made a tough background for the hitters. James Mosolf was up for the last out. Bill Klem was behind the plate. Dizzy's fast one blew in and Klem called it a ball. But Mosolf had had enough. He walked away, saying, 'It was a strike, Bill.'"

Even after he had fine control of his curve and could throw the change in the right spot, Dizzy enjoyed laying back and drilling the ball past the hitters, good and bad.

Frankie Frisch, who had the considerable burden of playing second base and managing Dean and the other free-spirited Cardinals of the mid-'30s, still gets a rise out of banquet audiences with this example of Dean's strikeout prowess. "There was an actor fellow named Johnny Perkins who was such a great Cardinal fan he traveled around with us. On the way up to Boston once—I don't hear of it until later—Dizzy and Perkins got to talking about Vince DiMaggio. You know, the one who struck out so much.

"Well, Diz bets Perkins a quarter he can strike him out four times the next day.

"First time up, he gets DiMaggio on strikes easy. He strikes him out again, and then a third time. He was really pouring it on and I'm enjoying it 'cause I don't know of any bet. When Vince comes up for the fourth time, Diz busts two big strikes past him. Vince nicks the next pitch and sends a pop-up near the kid catcher I'm using, Bruce Ogrodowski. Diz races off the mound screamin' as Ogrodowski circles under it. 'Drop it! Drop it!' he hollers. The kid is so rattled he drops it. Diz takes a deep breath and strolls back to the mound. You'd think he'd just pitched a no-hitter. I walk over and start bawlin' him out for interfering. But he says nothing and

heaves a third strike past DiMaggio he never saw or heard. And he wins his lousy quarter bet."

In 1934, Dizzy was joined on the Cardinal staff by brother Paul, two and a half years younger. Dizzy had been plugging his kid brother from the time he first reported to the Cards. Paul was signed right off a cotton farm in 1931. Much more docile and withdrawn than his famous brother, Paul made a slower start in the minors. He wasn't an effective pitcher for very long—he developed arm trouble—but he was very good in 1934. And he was made to appear even better by Dizzy's constant boasts and compliments. "Why, I'm just a busher compared to Paul," Dizzy would say. "If you think I'm fast, wait'll you see my brother Paul." It was pleasant, effective propaganda. And it built a relationship between the Deans that did both them and the Cardinals a lot of good. Paul undoubtedly pitched better with Dizzy's verbal support. Certainly the batters respected him more because he was Dizzy's brother—and Dizzy said he was a winner.

Paul had a crackling overhand fastball and a big, easy motion that was much like Dizzy's. From the bleachers it was hard to tell which Dean was pitching.

In the pre-season bantering about "Me and Paul," Dizzy was quoted as predicting that the two of them were a cinch to win 45 games in the 1934 season. Dizzy had denied he ever made such a heady prophecy. But since the boys won 49 together (Dizzy 30, Paul 19), there is no point in worrying about the denial.

Dizzy made another startlingly accurate prediction, or more accurately a boast, that summer. Late in the season, when he and Paul were piling up three and four victories a week, he told a sportswriter in New York, "Tomorrow Zachary and Benge (Dodger pitchers) will be pitching against one-hit Dean and no-hit Dean."

Dizzy pitched the first half of the doubleheader at Ebbets Field and taunted the Dodgers in a 13-0 win. He gave up three hits, slightly over his estimate, but he got a couple of hits himself and pushed his strikeouts for the year to 176. In the second game Paul did his best to make an honest prophet out of Dizzy. He threw a no-hitter at the Dodgers, barely missing a perfect game. His only slip was walking Len Koenecke in the first inning. During the noisy back-slapping in the Cardinal clubhouse after the game, Dizzy said: "If I'd knowed Paul was going to pitch a no-hitter, I'd a pitched one myself."

The summer of '34 was the Deans' to gloat, boast, clown and laugh. They were nearly invincible on the pitching mound. Dizzy might have won ten more games if he had been serious enough about it. Off the field, Paul usually went Dizzy's way, which was not always the way the Cardinals were going at the moment.

The Deans started a rebellion in mid-season that temporarily detracted from their won-lost records. Following a doubleheader, which they pitched and won, Paul and Dizzy failed to show up at the St. Louis railroad station to catch a train for Detroit, where a benefit exhibition game was scheduled. While Dizzy enjoyed a leisurely dinner at the home of friends, an angry Frisch announced that the Deans would be suspended and fined. The loss of the two pitchers appeared crucial. It was mid-August and the Cardinals were a half-dozen games behind the Giants.

When Dizzy confronted Frisch after they had ducked the Detroit game, he said: "You can't drop us, Frank. You won't win no pennant without us."

"The hell I won't," Frisch replied. "I'll pitch Hallahan, Haines, Carleton and Walker, and we'll win." (They won seven of their next eight.)

Frisch lifted the suspensions after a week but he refused to cancel the fines. Dizzy and Paul said they wouldn't play if they had to pay. In a rage Dizzy ripped his uniform shirt. The torn shirt became a symbol of his and Paul's defiance, so he ripped up another for the benefit of photographers. The rebellion was settled only within the office of Judge Landis. In a "closed" hearing that grew so noisy waiting newspapermen heard most of the wrangling, the Deans were reinstated. The costs to Dizzy were: $100 fine for missing the exhibition game, $350 for seven days' wages, $36 for two torn uniforms. Paul was fined $100.

The episode temporarily cooled relations between Frisch, Dizzy and Paul, but it didn't noticeably disturb their work, once they returned to it. The Cardinals moved into first place on the next-to-the-last day of the season, beating Cincinnati behind Paul. Dizzy took care of the formal clinching the next afternoon, shutting out the Reds, 9-0.

The Cardinals and Tigers were an exciting World Series match. Detroit had taken over the American League race in August and had beaten the Yankees by seven games. The club's new manager, Mickey Cochrane, had had fine hitting from the veteran, Charlie Gehringer, young slugger Hank Greenberg, Goose Goslin and Marv Owen. A kid from Waco, Texas, Lynwood (Schoolboy) Rowe, had won 24 games and Tommy Bridges 22. The Gas House Gang was an appealing mixture of class and daring, drive and ability. Martin at third, Durocher at short and Frisch at second supplied all the aggressiveness a team could use. Rip Collins was a graceful first-baseman and the best percentage hitter on the team. Second to Collins in batting was the young outfielder from Carteret, New Jersey, Ducky Medwick. The Cardinals were not a long-hitting team but they ran hard and fought hard. And they had the Deans.

Dizzy won the opener in Detroit, 8-3, and was full of apologies for it. "I just couldn't get my fast one to act up. It just hung up there. Why, that Greenberg hit a curve (for a home run) a kid could a hit. That's a ballclub! I could bring four National League teams over here and win the American League."

Detroit vibrated with talk about the Deans and the World Series, the first in that city in 25 years. News of the games filled front pages, crowding the arrest of Bruno Richard Hauptmann in the Lindbergh kidnapping case and the threat of revolutionary war in Spain. The city's enthusiasm became feverish the next day when young Rowe outpitched Hallahan, 3-2.

Dizzy relaxed, warned the Tigers to beware of Paul in the next game, and sent a collect wire to Branch Rickey, who was awaiting the team's arrival in St. Louis: "Breezed through that game with nothing but my glove. Tell everybody hello. Cook everyone a good meal, sandwiches and everything." (Dizzy's kitchen tastes in those days ran to quantity, not quality. Today he enjoys both. When President Eisenhower met him in a golf game, he said, "Dizzy, for a man who plays golf so well, how can you permit yourself to get so overweight?" Dizzy replied: "Well, Mr. President, I was on a diet for 25 years. Now that I'm makin' some money, I'm going to eat good.")

In St. Louis for the third game, the crowd brought Dizzy Dean Hats (straw bonnets with red ribbons), then sat back in the sun and watched Paul stop Detroit, 4-1. He pitched shutout ball until the ninth.

Before the fourth game, Pepper Martin ate a plate of apples for good luck (as he had done successfully in the 1931 World Series). But nothing but misfortune struck the Gas House Gang. Dizzy at first had a ball, parading around the field with his police escort. Martin made three errors. Then Dizzy made his ill-fated dash from first to second as a pinch-runner. Detroit won, 10-4.

Dizzy was given a protective helmet by a fan before the fifth game. He posed and clowned in it and promised to wear it when he got on base. But Dizzy had his hands full on the pitching mound. The Gas House Gang couldn't get to Tommy Bridges. And the Tigers pecked Dizzy for three runs. There were rumblings of revolt against the umpiring of Brick Owens. Dean slammed the ball into the dirt after a disputed call and catcher Bill DeLancey fumed so loudly he was later fined $200. Detroit won, 3-1. Dizzy was quiet as the team packed and entrained for Detroit.

If the Deans' faith in themselves was shaken by Dizzy's setback, it wasn't apparent before the sixth game in Detroit. Dizzy had an audience with Henry Ford and stayed so long he was nearly the last man to arrive at Navin Field. It never occurred to him that Paul might fail and the Cards might lose the Series. Paul was indeed superb through a very tense afternoon. He outpitched Schoolboy Rowe and drove in the tie-breaking run that won the game, 4-3. Afterwards, weary and grinning in the clubhouse, he took on the unaccustomed role as confident spokesman for the Deans: "Dizzy will take care of those guys," he said.

Dizzy did. But before Dean and the Gashouse Gang had their lopsided triumph (11-0) and the world championship, there was an afternoon filled with comedy, melodrama and brutality. The World Series had seen nothing like it. Dizzy humiliated the Tigers even before they took the field by yelling at manager Cochrane as he warmed up starting pitcher Elden Auker: "He just won't do, Mickey. He won't do."

The Tigers collapsed in the third inning as the Cards ran up seven runs. Dizzy toyed with the Detroit batters, alternately fogging the ball past them and then easing up charitably. They couldn't hit him. In the sixth Ducky Medwick cracked a triple off the right-field bleachers and dove into third in a sweep of dust. Suddenly he took a swipe at third-baseman Marvin Owen with his spikes and the two players piled into each other. After the fight Medwick took his position in left only to be met by a booing, fist-waving crowd in the wooden stands. Angry and frustrated, the fans started to heave bottles, chairs and cushions at Medwick, who left the game.

Dizzy ended the season and the Series as he had started—by horsing around. Pitching to Greenberg, who had already struck out twice, Dizzy began grooving fastballs. Frisch leaped in from second base and said: "Look, you fool around any more and I'll yank you!"

"You can't do that," Dizzy replied. "I just wanted to see if this guy could hit *anything*."

Diz then struck Hank out again.

The Deans had other successes ahead of them—they won 47 together the following season—but they never reached the artistic and spiritual peak of 1934. No one could ride that high for long. Paul had only one more winning year before he pulled up lame.

Dizzy kept the hop on his high hard one and his penchant for getting into trouble for a few more seasons. If he was "hard to handle," he was worth it to the Cardinals. Their advertisements and game announcements carried the line: "Dizzy Dean in Person."

Of course, he wasn't always there. He was occasionally being interviewed by the commissioner or league president or threatening to go on strike until somebody raised brother Paul's salary. A long feud with National League president Ford Frick culminated in 1937 with Frick suspending Dean indefinitely for a slur printed in a newspaper. The Belleville (Ill.) *Daily Advocate* quoted Dean as saying at a church smoker: "Umpire Barr and Ford Frick are the two biggest crooks in baseball."

Dizzy denied it. "I was in a church, and am I like to pop off like that in a church?" he said.

In April, 1938, Dizzy was sold to the Chicago Cubs for $185,000 and three front-line players. It was one of baseball's biggest business deals. There was much controversy about it, and about whether or not the Cubs had a bargain or a problem. No one, including Dizzy, knew it, but they had a lemon.

The summer before, in the All-Star game at Washington, Dizzy had been injured on the left foot by a batted ball. He had won 13 and lost one going into the game and was on his way to another 20-plus season. "I tried to pitch in Boston ten days later, wearing a splint on my left big toe," Dizzy said. "I couldn't pitch natural and I was off balance. I cut loose once and my arm went kinda numb. It was never the same."

Dizzy won only 16 major league games after that. He experimented with a new motion, new pitches. He went back to the Texas League "to learn to throw sidearm." He consulted "about 100 doctors." He tried as hard as he could to keep doing the thing he enjoyed most in life.

For some time after he quit the majors in 1941, Dizzy kept on playing baseball. He took a job as a broadcaster of games and spent most of his spare time making guest appearances as a pitcher in sandlot and semi-pro games around Missouri. As an announcer, Dean acquired a popularity and fame that even exceeded his pitching reputation. He started out announcing with a delivery that shocked grammarians and mothers and delighted his rural Midwest following. He made honest blunders and apologized for them, used expressions he had heard around the farm and clubhouse, and otherwise acted very unlike a paid announcer. Letters of complaint and delighted approval poured in. Sponsors began to take Dean seriously. And Dizzy, who had acquired much sound business sense when he was pitching for and bargaining with Branch Rickey, made the most of his malapropisms.

Today, on the CBS-TV "Games of the Week," Dizzy is somewhat more refined but he still leans heavily on his baseball lexicon. He doesn't often sing "The Wabash Cannonball" between innings but he consistently messes up the lineups, pronouncing Aparicio *Aparachee* and Skowron *Skarn*. He tells viewers that his sponsor is watching the game on a "closed circus." And he can still be refreshingly blunt on the air. Complaining about a decision by umpire Bill McKinley, he once exclaimed: "Why, they shot the wrong McKinley!"

Now 25 years after he clowned, boasted and pitched his way to the summit in sports, Dizzy is plump and prosperous. He weighs over 260 and nobody knows what his oil and real estate holdings in the Southwest are worth. He no longer gets his pleasure from dropping water bags out of hotel windows or from baiting umpires. He would rather play golf than go to the ballpark. He is a "character" only during business hours, when the microphone is open. But occasionally he reverts to the Ol' Diz, or young Dizzy, and strikes very close to the truth, as he did not long ago.

"I may not have been the greatest pitcher," he said, "but I was amongst them."

Epilogue

Dizzy Dean became one of the most entertaining sportscasters in American history. His malapropisms, one-liners, serenades and overall charm made the Game of the Week, *broadcast Saturday and Sunday afternoons, a national hit. But when CBS got out of the baseball broadcasting business in the mid 1960s, NBC brought in Curt Gowdy and Dean was out of a job. He lived to the age of 83, dying from a heart attack in Reno, Nevada, in 1974.*

The Golden Oldies

Left: Nap Lajoie, a catalyst in the successful establishment of the American League and the only man to hit as high as .426 since the 19th century (he did it in 1901)

Right: Cap Anson, the foremost player of the 19th century and the first man to gather 3,000 hits

The Golden Oldies

Opposite page: Walter Johnson, the Big Train, whose 417 wins rank second all-time and whose 3,509 strikeouts stood as the record for 62 years until Steve Carlton (and then seven more) slipped by

Top left: Cy Young, whose 511 wins, along with so many other records, will not be surpassed

Top middle: Grover Cleveland Alexander, the only four-time winner of pitching's Triple Crown and tied with Mathewson for third in career wins, with 373

Top right: Christy Mathewson, baseball's first truly national hero but ultimately a tragic figure, dying of tuberculosis at 45

Below: Honus Wagner, consummate hitter, baserunner and shortstop, and none other than John McGraw's choice (he saw Babe Ruth too) as the greatest player ever

The Greatest

Top left: Ted Williams, arguably the game's greatest hitter, owner of the highest on-base percentage in history (.483), one of just two double winners of batting's Triple Crown—and the last man to hit .400

Lower left: Barry Bonds, the Pirate-cum-Giant, who set the single-season home run record of 73 in 2001 and will likely own the career mark before he's done

Lower right: Ty Cobb, a loud-cussing, sweet-hitting, base-thieving original whose all-time hit record stood for 62 years and whose record .366 career batting average has now lasted 31 years longer

Opposite page: Babe Ruth, whose pitching exploits—before he became the game's greatest power hitter—render him, in many minds, as the greatest of the great

Alton S. Tobey

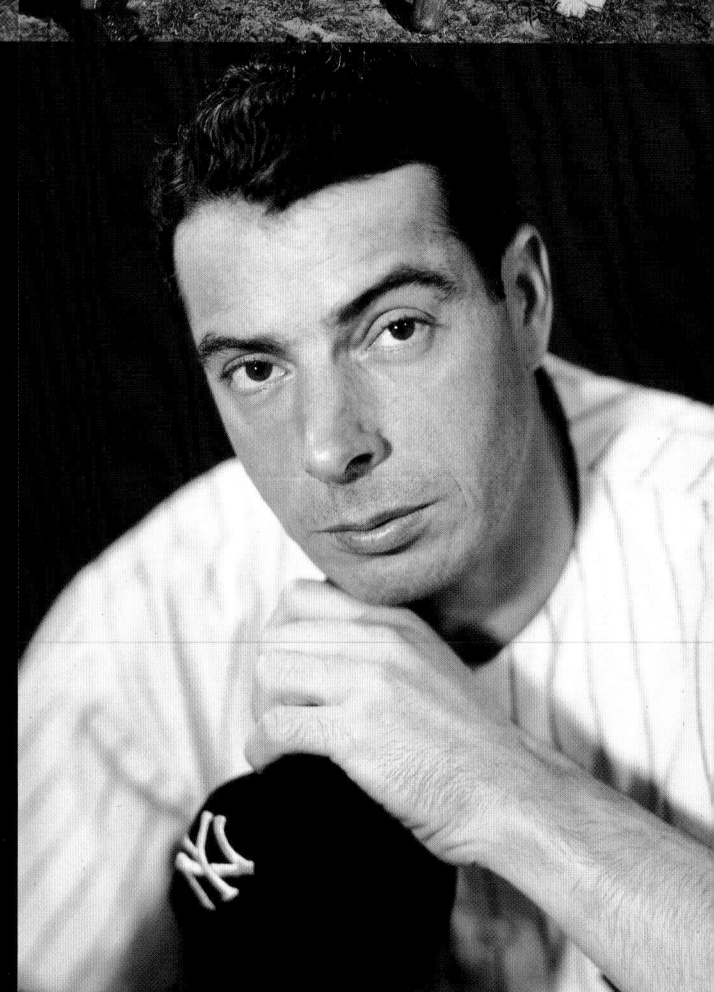

The MVPs

All seven men on these pages are tied for second best with three MVP awards apiece, precisely half Barry Bonds' haul

Top left: Jimmie Foxx, the Red Sox slugger who prevailed as AL MVP in '32, '33 and '38

Top right: Stan Musial (and friends), the ultimate Cardinal and National League MVP in '43, '46 and '48

Lower right: Joe DiMaggio, the Yankee Clipper, author of a record 56-game hitting streak in 1941 and AL MVP in '39, '41 and '47

Opposite page, clockwise from top left: Roy Campanella, the great Dodger backstop and NL MVP in '51, '53 and '55; Yogi Berra, Campy's AL alter-ego and MVP in '51, '54 and '55; Mike Schmidt, the slugging Phillie third baseman voted NL MVP in '80, '81 and '86; Mickey Mantle, Yankee legend and AL MVP in '56, '57 and '62

The Brains

Opposite page: Connie Mack, whose record 3,731 managerial wins are unassailable

Top left: Branch Rickey, baseball's greatest visionary, father of the modern farm system and co-conspirator, with Jackie Robinson, in the wildly successful 1947 plot to integrate the sport

Top right: Casey Stengel, who appeared in a record 10 World Series (winning a record seven, tying him with Joe McCarthy) and Walter Alston, who signed 23 one-year contracts en route to winning 2,040 games, second to Sparky Anderson among the moderns

Lower right: John McGraw, whose swaggering, tough-guy act netted him 2,763 wins, second only to Mack

The Brains

The Big Bangers

Opposite page: Willie Mays, perhaps the game's greatest all-round talent, whose 660 home runs ranked him No. 3 on the career list (with godson Barry Bonds closing fast) entering the 2004 season

Top left: Roger Maris, whose 61-homer season in—yep, '61—carried an asterisk for 28 years, then stood on its own for just nine before Mark McGwire slugged 70 in 1998

Top right: Henry Aaron, who eclipsed the cherished Babe's career record of 714 homers, finishing with 755, and who also stands atop the all-time list in total bases and RBIs

Lower left: Frank Robinson, No. 5 in career homers with 586 and the only man to be named MVP in both leagues

Lower right: Sammy Sosa and Mark McGwire, whose epic home run battle in '98—McGwire prevailed, 70 to 66—ushered in the new big banger era

The Big Bangers

The Hit Men

Opposite page: Rogers Hornsby, the only man besides Ted Williams to twice win batting's Triple Crown and No. 2 to Cobb in career batting average, at .358

Top left: Shoeless Joe Jackson, third in career average at .356 but never able to erase the stain of the 1919 World Series, thrown by his Chicago White Sox

Top right: Pete Rose, No. 1 in games played (3,562) and hits registered (4,256) but, like Jackson, a man whose off-field peccadillos have left him on the outside of Cooperstown looking in

Middle right: Tris Speaker, a maestro with the bat and No. 5 on the career hit list with 3,514, including a record 792 doubles

Lower right: Carl Yastrzemski, No. 7 in career hits, No. 2 in games played and plate appearances, No. 1 in the hearts of Red Sox Nation and the last man to win batting's Triple Crown, way back in 1967

The Hit Men

The Pioneers

Opposite page: Jackie Robinson, whose busting of the color barrier on April 15, 1947 changed the course, not to mention entire tenor, of the game

Top right: Roberto Clemente, the first Hispanic superstar and a committed humanitarian who died in a plane crash on New Year's Eve, 1972, bringing relief supplies to victims of a Nicaraguan earthquake

Lower left: Larry Doby, the American League's first African American player, who followed Robinson by just 81 days but in his quiet, steadfast way left an indelible mark of his own

Lower right: Ichiro Suzuki, the first MVP and batting champion to hail from another continent

The Pioneers

The Lethal Lefties

Opposite page: Sandy Koufax, brilliant, enigmatic, twice a World Series MVP, thrice winner of both the Cy Young Award (when there was only one handed out) and pitching's Triple Crown and probably the greatest lefthander of all time

Left: Lefty Grove, 300 career wins, a record nine times the AL ERA champ and twice a Triple Crown champ

Lower left: Steve Carlton, four-time Cy Young Award winner, No. 2 in career strikeouts with 4,136, and a Triple Crown winner, in 1972

Lower middle: Warren Spahn, who won 20 games a record 13 times and led the NL in victories a record eight times en route to becoming the winningest lefty of all time, with 363 Ws

Lower right: Randy Johnson, five Cy Young Awards and counting, and an all-time leading average of 11.16 strikeouts per nine-inning game

The Lethal Lefties

The Rapid Righties

The Rapid Righties

Opposite page, clockwise from top left:
Roger Clemens, a record six-time Cy
Young Award winner, No. 3 in career
strikeouts with 4,099 and twice winner
of pitching's Triple Crown; Bob Gibson,
owner of the lowest modern single-
season ERA (1.12 in 1968) and twice
World Series MVP; Tom Seaver, owner of
three Cy Young Awards, 311 wins and
3,640 Ks, good for No. 6 on the all-time
list; Bob Feller, who tied with Walter
Johnson for the most seasons leading
the AL in wins (six) and was the league's

Top left: Nolan Ryan, he of the record 100.9
mile-per-hour fastball, 324 wins and career
major league standards for no-hitters
(seven) and strikeouts (5,714), the latter
leaving him an absurd 40% ahead of the
No. 2 man, Steve Carlton

Top right: Greg Maddux, the once-and-
future Cub and winner of a record four
consecutive Cy Young Awards

Lower left: Jim Palmer, architect of eight
20-win seasons—the most by a righty since
Walter Johnson—and three Cy Young Awards

Lower right: Don Sutton, a winner 324 times
and No. 7 on the career strikeout list

The Iron Men

The Iron Men

Top left: Lou Gehrig, the classy Yankee whose 2,130 consecutive game streak began on June 1, 1925 and ended on May 2, 1939, when he yanked himself from the Yankee lineup due to a deteriorating physical state later diagnosed as amyotrophic lateral sclerosis, also known as ALS and, ever after, Lou Gehrig's Disease; he never played again and passed away on June 2, 1941

Lower left: Cal Ripken, the superb Orioles shortstop who broke Gehrig's record on September 6, 1995 and went on to play 2,632 games in a row, before pulling himself from the lineup on September 20, 1998

The Robber Barons

Top left: Lou Brock, whose 118 steals in 1974 at age 35 eclipsed Maury Wills' record and who still ranks No. 2 on the career list with 938 thefts

Top right: Maury Wills, who led the NL in steals six years in a row and whose 104 in 1962 toppled Ty Cobb's 47-year-old record

Below: Rickey Henderson, whose all-time record 1,406 stolen bases may never be caught, even if his record 2,295 runs and 2,190 walks are

The Robber Barons

October Heroes

Top left: Reggie Jackson, who won his first World Series MVP award with the Oakland A's in 1973 but truly earned his nickname on October 18, 1977, when he slugged three consecutive home runs as the Yankees eliminated the Dodgers in six games

Lower left: Bobby Thomson, whose shot-heard-'round-the-world on October 3, 1951 won the Giants the pennant over the Brooklyn Dodgers

Below right: Bill Mazeroski, whose home run in the bottom of the ninth inning on October 13, 1960 earned the Pirates a wild, seventh-game World Series title over the Yankees

Lower right: Don Larsen, whose perfect game on October 8, 1956 helped the Yankees to a seven-game triumph over the Dodgers

The Modern Warriors

Below: Pedro Martinez, three-time Cy Young Award winner, who ranks No. 2 all-time with an average 10.5 strikeouts per game and No. 1 with a career winning percentage of .712

Lower left: Albert Pujols, the first player in major league history to hit .300 with at least 30 home runs, 100 RBIs and 100 runs scored in each of his first three seasons

Lower right: Alex Rodriguez, the reigning AL MVP, the game's best-compensated player and, now, an employee of George Steinbrenner—could a guy lead a more charmed existence?

The Modern Warriors

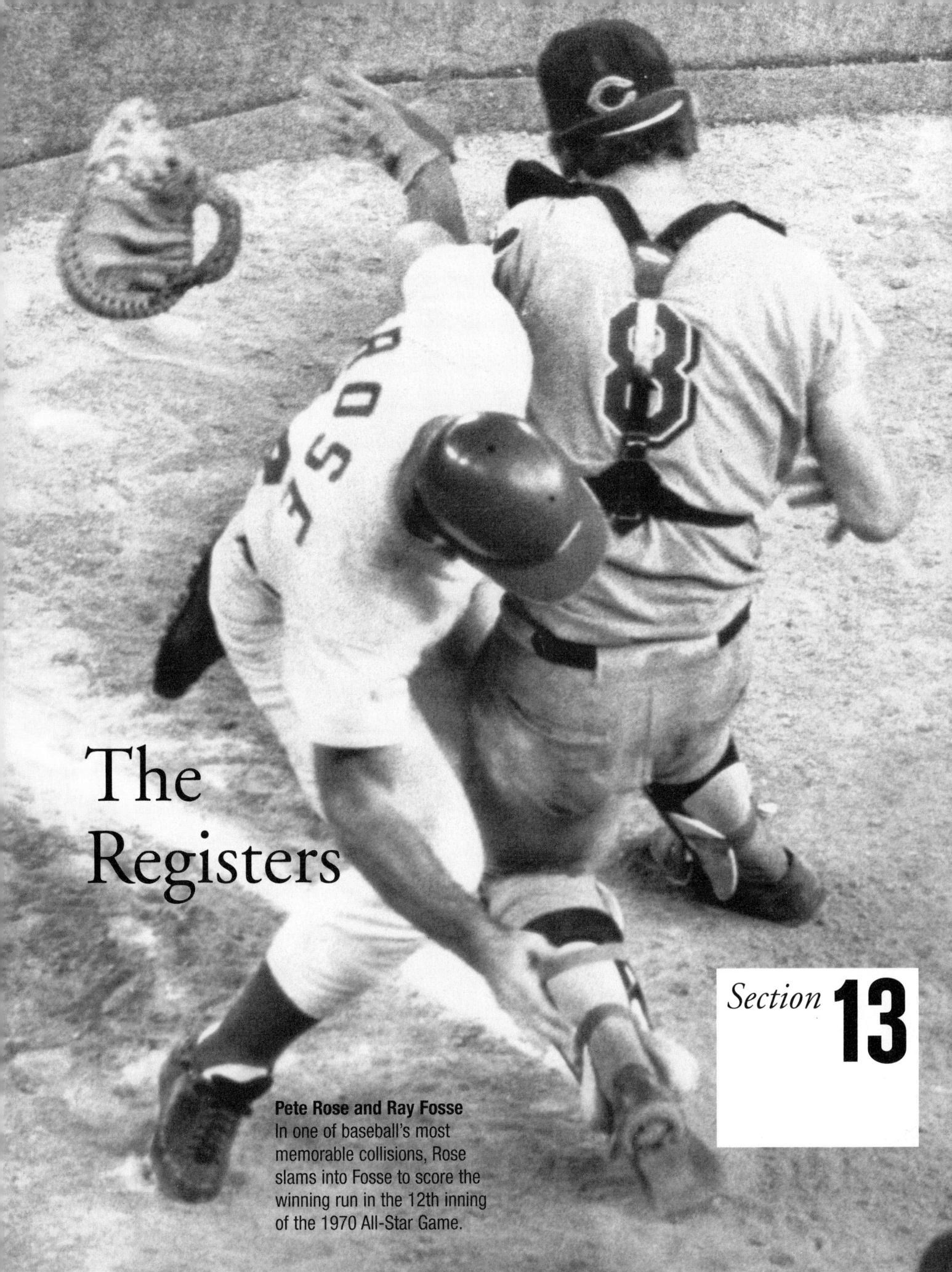

The Registers

Section 13

Pete Rose and Ray Fosse
In one of baseball's most
memorable collisions, Rose
slams into Fosse to score the
winning run in the 12th inning
of the 1970 All-Star Game.

FAMOUS FIRSTS

1961: Roger Maris becomes the first major leaguer to hit 61 home runs in a season.

1965: Emmett Ashford becomes the first African-American to umpire a major league game.

1969: The first official major league save is recorded by the Dodgers' Bill Singer.

1972: Bernice Gera becomes the first female professional umpire.

Chapter 57

The History of Major League Baseball Statistics

By John Thorn, Pete Palmer and Joseph M. Wayman

The statistical section of *Total Baseball*, presents the record of major league contests played from 1871 through 2003, through 2,445 team seasons. The Player and Pitcher Registers include all 16,003 players who ever set foot on a major league field for even a fraction of an inning.

In its debut edition in 1989, *Total Baseball* won critical acclaim and a devoted following not only for its breadth and depth of information but also for its pioneering "sabermetric" stats that offered alternative, unofficial measures of player performance. Yet for all its innovation, *Total Baseball* has stood squarely in the tradition of baseball record keeping; it is—like each new spring of our national pastime—a link in a long, long chain. As the New York Knickerbockers' game of 150 years ago lives on in the game of today, so is this volume enriched by the labors of statisticians from Henry Chadwick to Ernie Lanigan, from S.C. Thompson and Seymour Siwoff and the Hirdt brothers to David Neft and Bill James.

How we came from the Knickerbockers' primitive accounting of outs and runs to the vast array of statistics available today is an interesting process, in which Major League Baseball's role has been central. Through its evolving scoring rules and procedures, its judicious (if, for some tastes, slow) endorsement of new measures, and its continuing mission to set the record straight, the Commissioner's Office and its official scorers have provided fans with a wealth of statistical data unmatched by any other sport—perhaps any other human activity—on Earth.

Here is how we who love baseball came to this fortunate estate.

The Origins, 1845-1875

Baseball and stats were a tandem from the very Eden of the game. The first box score appeared in the *New York Morning News* on October 22, 1845, less than a month after Alexander Cartwright and his Knickerbocker teammates codified the first set of rules. Why did these early players and scribes measure individual performance rather than simply count the score? In part to imitate the custom of cricket; yet the larger explanation is that the numbers served to legitimize men's concern with a boys' pastime. The pioneers of baseball reporting—William Cauldwell of the *Sunday Mercury*, William Porter of *Spirit of the Times,* an unknown annalist at the *News,* and later Henry Chadwick—may indeed have reflected that if they did not cloak the game in the "importance" of statistics, it might not seem worthwhile for adults to read about, let alone play. Statistics elevated baseball from other boys' field games of the 1840s and '50s to make it somehow systematic and serious, like business; despite baseball's essential simplicity, it was laced with intricate detail that suited it perfectly to quantification.

In the development of baseball statistics, no man is more important than Father Chadwick. Born in England in 1824, he came to these shores at age 13 steeped in the tradition of cricket. In his teens he played the English game and in his twenties he reported

Henry Chadwick
The journalist and baseball pioneer introduced statistics to the game by perfecting the box score and endorsing the first batting averages.

on it for a variety of newspapers, including the *Long Island Star* and *The New York Times*. In the early 1840s, before the Knickerbocker rules eliminated the practice of retiring a baserunner by throwing the ball at him rather than to the base, Chadwick occasionally played baseball too, but he was not favorably impressed, having received "some hard hits in the ribs." Not until 1856, by which time he had been a cricket reporter for a decade, were Chadwick's eyes opened to the possibilities in the American game, which had improved dramatically since his youth.

In 1868 he recalled, "On returning from the early close of a cricket match on Fox Hill, I chanced to go through the Elysian Fields during the progress of a contest between the noted Eagle and Gotham clubs. The game was being sharply played on both sides, and I watched it with deeper interest than any previous ball game between clubs that I had seen. It was not long before I was struck with the idea that base ball was just the game for a national sport for Americans ... as much so as cricket in England. At the time I refer to I had been reporting cricket for years, and, in my method of taking notes of contests, I had a plan peculiarly my own. It was not long, therefore, after I had become interested in baseball, before I began to invent a method of giving detailed reports of leading contests at baseball...."

Thus Chadwick's cricket background was largely the impetus to his method of scoring a baseball game, the format of his early box scores, and the copious if primitive statistics that appeared in his year-end summaries in the *New York Clipper,* Beadle's *Dime Base-Ball Player,* and other publications.

Actually, cricket had begun to shape baseball statistics even before Chadwick's conversion. The first box score reported on two categories, outs and runs: outs, or "hands out," counted both unsuccessful times at bat and outs run into on the basepaths; "runs" were runs scored, not those driven in. The reason for not recording hits in the early years, when coverage of baseball matches appeared alongside reports of cricket matches, was that, unlike baseball, cricket had no such category as the successful hit which did not produce a run. To reach "base" in cricket is to run to the opposite wicket, which tallies a run; to hit the ball, commence to run, yet not score a run is to have been put out.

Cricket box scores were virtual play-by-plays, a fact made possible by the lesser number of possible events. This play-by-play aspect was applied to a baseball box score as early as 1856; interestingly, despite the abundance of detail, hits were not accounted, nor did they appear in Chadwick's own box scores until 1867. The batting champion as declared by Chadwick, whose computations were immediately and universally accepted as "official," was the man with the highest average of runs per game. An inverse though imprecise measure of batting quality was outs per game. After 1863, when a fair ball caught on one bounce was no longer an out, fielding leaders were those with the greatest total of fly catches, assists, and "foul bounds" (fouls caught on one bounce). Pitching effectiveness was based purely on control, with the leader recognized as the one whose delivery offered the most opportunities for outs at first base and led to the fewest passed balls.

In a sense, Chadwick's measuring of baseball as if it were cricket can be viewed as correct: when you strip the game to its basic elements, those that determine victory or defeat, outs and runs are indeed all that count in the end. No individual statistic is meaningful to the team unless it relates directly to the scoring of runs or their prevention.

Early player stats were of the most primitive kind, the counting kind. They'd tell you how many runs, or outs, or fly catches had occurred—later, how many hits or total bases. Counting is the most basic of all statistical processes; the next step up is averaging, and Chadwick was the first to put this into practice.

As professionalism infiltrated the game, teams began to bid for star-caliber players. Stars were known not by their stats but by their style until 1865, when Chadwick began to record in the *Clipper* a form of batting average taken from the cricket pages—runs per game. Two years later, in his newly founded baseball weekly, *The Ball Players' Chronicle,* he began to record not only average runs and outs per game, but also home runs, total bases, total bases per game—and hits per game. The averages were expressed not with decimal places but in the standard cricket format of the "average and over." Thus a batter with 23 hits in six games would have an average expressed not as 3.83 but as "3-5"—an average of 3 with an overage, or remainder, of 5. Another innovation was to remove from the individual accounting all bases gained through errors. Runs scored by a team, beginning in 1867, were divided between those scored after a man reached base on a clean hit and those arising from a runner's having reached base on an error. This was a clear precursor of the modern earned run average.

By the end of the decade Chadwick was recording total bases and home runs, but he placed little stock in either, as conscious attempts at slugging violated his cricket-bred image of "form." Just as cricket aficionados watch the game for the many opportunities for fine fielding it affords, so was baseball from its inception perceived as a fielders' sport. The original Knickerbocker rules of 1845, in fact, specified that a ball hit out of the field of the fly—in fair territory or foul—was a foul ball! "Long hits are showy," Chadwick wrote in the *Clipper* in 1868, "but they do not pay in the long run. Sharp grounders insuring the first base certain, and sometimes the second base easily, are worth all the hits made for home-runs which players strive for."

Chadwick prevailed, and the batting average used from that year on is the same as that used today except in its denominator, where at bats replaced games in 1876. Moreover, Chadwick created a measure in the 1860s that divided total bases by games played; change that denominator to at bats and you have today's slugging average—which, incidentally, was not accepted by the National League as an official statistic until 1923 and by the American until 1946.

Chadwick's "total bases average" represents the game's first attempt at a weighted average—an average in which the elements collected together in the numerator or the denominator are recognized numerically as being unequal. In this instance, a single is the unweighted unit, the double is weighted by a factor of two, the triple by three, and the home run by four. Statistically, this is a distinct leap forward from, first, counting, and next, averaging. The weighted average is in fact the cornerstone of today's statistical innovations, or sabermetrics.

The 1870s gave rise to some new batting stats and to the first attempt to quantify thoroughly the other principal facets of the game, pitching and fielding. Although the *Clipper* recorded base hits and total bases as early as 1868, a significant wrinkle was added in 1870 when at bats were listed as well. This was a critical introduction because it permitted the improvement of the batting average, first introduced in its current form by H.A. Dobson of Washington, D.C., in the *Dime Base-Ball Player* of 1872, and first computed "officially"—that is, for the newly created National League—in 1876, the lone year in which bases on balls were figured as outs. Since then the batting average has not changed, except for 1887, when bases on balls were counted as *hits*.

The objections to the batting average are well known, but to date have not disturbed its place as the most popular measure of hitting ability. First of all, the batting average makes no distinction between the single, the double, the triple, and the home run, treating all as the same unit. This objection had been addressed in 1868 by Chadwick's total bases average. Second, the batting average gives no indication of the effect of that base hit—that is, its value to the team. Third, the batting average does not take into account those occasions when first

base is reached via a walk, hit batsman, or error. This last point was addressed at a surprisingly early date, too: in 1879 the National League adopted as an official statistic a forerunner of the on base percentage; it was called "reached first base," which included times reached by error as well as base on balls and base hits. (Being hit by a pitch did not give the batter first base until the ensuing decade.)

The Flowering, 1876-1920

Ever since the Civil War, serial guides like *Beadle* and *DeWitt* and sporting columns like those in the *Clipper* had carried year-end tabulations of batting, fielding, and pitching exploits, varying from year to year with the brainstorms of Chadwick or other demon compilers like New York's M.J. Kelly or Philadelphia's Al Wright. But the year 1876 was special. It was significant not only for the founding of the National League and the official debut of the batting average in its current form, it was also the Centennial of the United States, which was marked by a giant exposition in Philadelphia celebrating the mechanical marvels of the day. American ingenuity reigned, and technology was seen as the new handmaiden of democracy. Baseball, that mirror of American life, reflected the fervor for things scientific with an explosion of statistics far more complex than those seen before, particularly in the previously neglected areas of pitching and fielding. The increasingly minute statistical examination of the game met a responsive audience, one primed to view complexity as a measure of worth.

In 1876 the number of "official" offensive stats tabulated at season's end—i.e., in any of the publications inspired by Chadwick or Albert Spalding—was six: games, at bats, runs, hits, runs per game, and batting average. (And as with all the various guides until 1941, the stats of men who played in fewer than a specified minimum number of games were not noted.) Of these six, only runs and runs per game were common in the 1860s, while that decade's tabulation of total bases vanished. The number of official offensive stats a hundred years later? Twenty. (Today the number is 21, with the addition of on base percentage.)

The number of "official" pitching categories in 1876 was 11, and there were some modernistic surprises, such as earned run average, hits allowed, hits per game, and opponents' batting average. Strikeouts were not recorded, for Chadwick saw them strictly as a sign of poor batting rather than good pitching. (His view had such an impact that pitcher strikeouts were not kept officially until 1889.) The number of official pitching stats today? Twenty-four.

The number of fielding categories in 1876 was six. One hundred years later it was still six (with the exception of the catcher, who gets a seventh: passed balls), dramatizing how the game, which originated as a showcase for fielders, had changed. The fielding stats of 1876 lumped "battery errors" with fielding errors, so that wild pitches and passed balls—in some years, even walks—diminished one's fielding percentage. This practice continued until 1887, but in *Total Baseball* battery errors are not included in fielding stats. Battery-mates' fielding stats were boosted by the awarding of an assist to the pitcher on strikeouts. This practice lasted until 1889, but is not reflected in *Total Baseball*.

The custom in 1876, as it is now, was to combine putouts, assists, and errors to form a "percentage of chances accepted," or what is today known as fielding average or fielding percentage. A "missing link" variant, devised by Al Wright in 1875, was to form averages by dividing the putouts by the number of games to yield a "putout average"; dividing the assists similarly to arrive at an "assist average"; and dividing putouts plus assists by games to get "fielding average."

These averages took no account of errors. (Wright's "fielding average" was reborn a century later as Bill James' "range factor.")

The public's appetite for new statistics was not sated by the outburst of 1876. New measures were introduced in dizzying profusion in the remaining years of the century. Some of these did not catch on and were soon dropped for all time, like the meaningless "total bases run," while others fizzled only to reappear with new vigor in the twentieth century. These include (a) the above-mentioned "reached first base," which resurfaced in the early 1950s in an unofficial, improved form called on base percentage and became an official stat more than thirty years later, and (b) an 1860s stat, earned run average, which was periodically revived before dropping from sight in the 1880s, only to return triumphant to the National League in 1912 and the American League in 1913. (In 1913 Ban Johnson not only proclaimed the ERA official, he became so enamored with it that he also instructed AL scorers to compile no official won-lost records. This state of affairs lasted for seven years, 1913-1919, but *Total Baseball* does record wins and losses by pitchers in those years, in accordance with the understood scoring practices of the time.)

Another stat that was "sent back to the minors" before its eventual adoption as an official stat in 1920 was the run batted in. Introduced by a Buffalo newspaper in 1879, the stat was picked up the following year by the *Chicago Tribune* and even became an official NL stat for the opening months of 1891. By season's end it had faded as most NL scorers declined to account for it in their summaries. (The American Association, however, recorded it all year long.) Ernie Lanigan picked up the RBI baton with his reports to the *New York Press* from 1907 through 1919, but he did not figure RBIs for men who played in fewer than ten games, or club totals for traded players.

For *Total Baseball* we have placed much reliance upon the source material donated by Information Concepts, Inc. (ICI) to the National Baseball Library in Cooperstown following publication of *The Baseball Encyclopedia,* which it developed for publication by Macmillan in 1969. David Neft also kindly supplied us with his unpublished RBI data for the previously missing National League seasons of 1880-1885. The John Tattersall collection of nineteenth century game accounts and box scores was valuable for uncovering RBIs as well. (For a detailed accounting of the sources employed for the statistical portion of *Total Baseball,* see the conclusion of the essay.)

Other statistics introduced officially before the turn of the century were stolen bases (though not caught stealing); doubles, triples, and homers; and sacrifice bunts (though an at-bat was charged from 1889 through 1893). Pitcher strikeouts, bases on balls, and the hit-by-pitch also appeared before 1900, but hit-by-pitch stats were not kept for batters on a systematic basis until 1917 in the NL and 1920 in the AL. Through newspaper research, we have filled in HBP data from 1884 through 1916 in the National League; the Players League of 1890; the American Association of 1882-1891; from 1901 through 1919 in the American League, and the 1914-1915 Federal League.

Hit into double play—including line outs as well as an groundouts—was an erratically recorded stat in the 19th century, but separate stats for groundouts into double plays have been kept by the leagues only since 1933 in the NL and 1939 in the AL. Batters' strikeouts were reported unofficially in 1891, but not as a league stat until 1910 in the NL and 1913 in the AL. Innings pitched were not kept until 1908 in the AL and 1903 in the NL. You can see what a patchwork quilt the records of Major League Baseball

were in its early years.

Stolen bases were awarded not only for clean steals but also for extra bases taken through daring, from the first year in which totals were kept, 1886, until 1898. Because the figures reported in the guides were grossly inflated (such as Harry Stovey's ostensible 156 steals in 1888), the figures in *Total Baseball* reflect game-by-game research and refiguring. Caught-stealing (CS) figures are available on a very sketchy basis in some of the later years of the century, as some newspapers carried the data in the box scores of hometown games. From 1912 on, Lanigan recorded CS in box scores of the *New York Press,* but the leagues did not keep the figure officially until 1920. The AL has tabulated CS from that year to the present, excepting 1927, which members of the Society for American Baseball Research reconstructed from newspaper box scores. National League caught-stealing data exists for 1920-1925, and for 1951 to the present.

The new century added little in the way of new official statistics—ERA, RBI, and slugging average are better regarded as revivals despite their respective adoption dates of 1912, 1920, and 1923. But back in 1908 there was a classic case of a statistic rushing in to fill a void, as Phillies' manager Billy Murray observed that his outfielder Sherry Magee had the happy facility of providing a long fly ball whenever presented with a situation of a man on third and fewer than two outs. Taking up the cudgel on his player's behalf, Murray protested to the NL office that it was unfair to charge Magee with an unsuccessful time at bat when he was in fact succeeding, doing precisely what the situation demanded. (More recent stats—the save and the short-lived game-winning run batted in, or GWRBI—have followed from this sort of perception that something important was occurring on the field yet had no verifiable reality because it was not being measured.)

A signal event took place in 1912: the publication by *Baseball Magazine* editor John Lawres of *Who's Who in Baseball,* a small book that became the first to provide career statistics and personal facts for a group of players. Although thoroughly inadequate by today's standards—its only tabulations were games, batting average, and fielding average (even for pitchers, who were given no pitching records!)—*Who's Who* was a groundbreaking work. It gave rise to a much-expanded format in 1916 and inspired two other significant encyclopedic works: in 1914, George Moreland's self-published opus called *Balldom* (grandiosely subtitled "The Britannica of Baseball,") and Ernest J. Lanigan's *Baseball Cyclopedia,* also sponsored by *Baseball Magazine,* which debuted in 1922 and was updated annually through 1933.

The Golden Age, 1920-1968

There have been other new statistical tabulations in this century, but generally of the counting sort: complete games (NL 1910, AL 1922), games started (AL 1926, NL 1938), games finished (NL 1920, AL 1926). And there were sacrifice bunts allowed (NL 1913, AL 1921), intentional bases on balls (only since 1955), and, in the next period, saves (1969) and game-winning RBIs (1980). The only new average since slugging average was adopted in 1923 has been the on base percentage, adopted in 1984.

The ICI group computed saves for years prior to 1969. Another such stat that failed to survive, alas, was stolen bases off pitchers, which the American League recorded only in 1920-1924; it has been recorded on an unofficial basis since the 1980s by the Elias Sports Bureau and Baseball Workshop. The only new fielding measure was team double plays, added to the AL list in 1912 and the NL in 1919. Other new and more interesting stats appeared in

the 1940s and '50s but failed to gain the official stamp of approval, such as Ted Oliver's Weighted Rating System, Alfred P. Berry's Average Bases Allowed (opponents' slugging average), and Branch Rickey and Allan Roth's Isolated Power. (See the ensuing essay, "Sabermetrics" for more about other unorthodox measures, some of which have gained wide acceptance and may, like the on base percentage, one day be officially embraced.)

This period of baseball's history may have fielded its most dazzling array of stars, but strategically and statistically it was rather dim. There was some excitement, however, in baseball record keeping. First came *Daguerreotypes,* issued by *The Sporting News* in 1934, featuring the playing records of many retired players both celebrated and obscure; most if not all of these statistical and biographical profiles originally appeared in the pages of TSN. Although its number of statistical categories was fewer than one might have wished, *Daguerreotypes* was very useful and, through its several editions ably edited by Paul MacFarlane, long-lived.

In 1940 came *The Sporting News Baseball Register,* which supplied full records for active players, managers, coaches, and umpires, plus a grab-bag of former stars. Since the expansion of the major leagues from 16 teams to 30, the *Register* has only accommodated contemporary players and managers, but it remains a valuable source.

Then in 1951 came the first true encyclopedia of baseball, the claims of Moreland and Lanigan notwithstanding. Compiled by Hy Turkin and S.C. Thompson, *The Official Encyclopedia of Baseball* was published by the A.S. Barnes Company. Its 620 pages contained a wealth of features such as manager and umpire rosters, historical essays, playing tips, a bibliography, and much more. But the heart of the volume and the key to its subsequent success was a register of nearly nine thousand men who had played one or more games at the major league level from 1871 through 1949 (the 1950 record of players appearing in ten games or more was tacked on to the end). In this register, Turkin/Thompson also offered birth and death data and what today seems fairly limited statistical information but by previous standards was a veritable cornucopia: year, club, league, position, games, and batting average or won-lost record. A landmark volume that did much to inspire this one, the Barnes encyclopedia endured through ten revised editions, the last being published in 1979, 10 years after the initial appearance of Macmillan's *The Baseball Encyclopedia.*

The Barnes encyclopedia went a long way toward making the study of baseball history and records a respectable pursuit, just as a century earlier the statistical accounting of a boys' game had helped to make baseball a sport for grown men. The researchers' ranks expanded to include such men as Bob Davids, who in 1971, aided by other experts like Cliff Kachline, Bill Haber, Ray Nemec, John Pardon, and Joe Simenic, would create SABR, the Society for American Baseball Research (pronounced "saber"). Formerly the lonely pursuit of a handful of "nuts" like S.C. Thompson, baseball research and sabermetrics—a neologism that Bill James coined in honor of SABR, signifying the statistical analysis of the game's records—would become the pastime of thousands.

An article in *Life* magazine by Branch Rickey on August 2, 1954, gave further impetus to the study of baseball statistics, but not just to set the historical record straight. Indeed, this article may be viewed as the opening shot of the sabermetric assault of the 1980s. In "Goodby to Some Old Baseball Ideas," Rickey, with the aid of some new mathematical tools supplied by Dodger statistician Allan Roth, sought to puncture some long-held conceptions about how the game was divided among its elements (batting,

baserunning, pitching, fielding), who was best at playing it, and what caused one team to win and another to lose. This is a pretty fair statement of what sabermetrics is about.

Rickey attacked the batting average and proposed in its place the on base percentage, but the most important thing he did for baseball statistics was to strip the game and its stats to their pre-1876 essentials and start again, this time remembering that individual stats came into being as an attempt to apportion the players' contributions to achieving a team victory.

Rickey and Roth devised a formula to measure a team's efficiency in turning its offensive and defensive statistics into runs, and thus wins. They realized, and had confirmed for them by mathematicians at the Massachusetts Institute of Technology, that just as the team which scores more runs in a game gets the win, so a team which over the course of a season scores more runs than it allows should win more games than it loses—and by an extent correlated to its run differential.

From this startlingly simple (or rather, seemingly simple) observation of 1954 flowed: first, the trailblazing but little noted work of George Lindsey in the 1950s and early 1960s, when he developed a model for run-scoring probability from the 24 combinations of outs and bases occupied; the development of "percentage baseball" stats and strategies by Earnshaw Cook in the 1960s; the play-by-play analysis of complete seasons by the Mills brothers, Eldon and Harlan, in 1969-1970; the recording and analysis of situational statistics by the Elias Sports Bureau for use by Major League Baseball and its clubs; and, over the next two decades, the statistical and historical works of many sabermetricians.

The Computer Age, 1969-

Despite the death of Turkin in 1957 and Thompson 10 years later, their encyclopedia remained the dominant book of baseball statistics, although many fans were frustrated with the fragmentary records it presented. As Frank V. Phelps wrote in the 1987 edition of *The National Pastime*, "Gaps and obvious errors in official averages, the lack of many early records, difficulty in securing the records of players who appeared in only a few games, and frustrating discrepancies among existing guides and registers had long since created a desire for an ultimate, complete, correct set of major league records. But it wasn't until the mid-1960s that the development of sophisticated computers which could absorb, retain, order, and output huge amounts of data finally made a project feasible."

Beginning in 1967, a battalion of researchers commanded by David Neft foraged through the official records and newspaper box scores to provide freshly compiled figures for those who had no ERAs, RBIs, slugging averages, saves, and all manner of wonderful things. The material which finally appeared in the tome was entered into a data bank, and the book was the first to be typeset entirely by computer, now a common practice. Published in 1969, *The Baseball Encyclopedia* was a milestone in computer technology, but as indispensable as the computer were the old-fashioned scrapbooks and files of Lee Allen and John Tattersall. The result was a mammoth ledger book of the major leagues more thorough than any that had ever appeared before.

The ICI group not only found new data to correct old inaccuracies but also applied new yardsticks to men who had gone to their graves never having heard of an RBI or a save. The ICI research that went into *The Baseball Encyclopedia* of 1969 created new stars, launching several previously underappreciated heroes of old into the Hall of Fame, such as Sam Thompson, Addie Joss, Roger Connor,

and Amos Rusie. Their phenomenal level of play was hidden simply because statisticians back then were not recording the particular numbers which would show them off to best advantage. If sabermetrics consists of finding things in the existing data that were not seen before, or in collecting that data which makes possible the application of new statistics to old performances, the first edition of *The Baseball Encyclopedia* was a monument in the course of sabermetrics.

However, its subsequent editions declined from that standard, dropping valuable data, altering figures for star players in a misguided homage to tradition, and making a shambles of individual/team balance in the totals. The seventh edition was issued in 1988 and, like the five that preceded it, was less accurate than the classic first issue. The eighth edition, published in 1990, corrected many of the errors in the seventh but retained many once-contested errors that historians had long since expunged from the record, while changing other statistics in a manner at variance with Major League Baseball's standards and with a rationale that remains unclear. For the ninth edition, Major League Baseball distanced itself from the both the product and its database.

Even when *The Baseball Encyclopedia* was being readied back in 1968-1969, the ICI findings raised the hackles of traditionalists, prompting the formation by Major League Baseball of a Special Baseball Records Committee. Its members ruled upon such matters as whether, for the historical record, bases on balls should be counted as hits (as they were in 1887), outs (as they were in 1876), or neither (as has been the practice in all other years); or whether "sudden-death" home runs—37 game-winning blows with men on base that they identified as having occurred in the bottom half of the ninth or an extra inning—would be credited as homers or, in the practice before 1920, would count for only as many bases as were needed to push across the winning run. In the latter controversy, committee members first decided to count the disputed blows as homers, but then, when complaints arose that Babe Ruth's famous total of 714 would change to 715, they reversed themselves. They also decided that the National Association of 1871-1875 was not a major league, while the Federal League, Union Association, and Players League were; and they ruled on several other issues, all of which were published in the Appendix to *The Baseball Encyclopedia*.

Because in its first three editions *Total Baseball* enjoyed neither the privilege nor the responsibility of official Major League Baseball status, the editors committed themselves to the *process* of history—its research, reporting, and interpretation—rather than to its product. History is not static and unchanging. The editors' course then as now seemed unexceptionable: publish the best-documented data and remain humbly amenable to subsequent revision in the light of new evidence. (This is not very different from the placard in the Baseball Hall of Fame, which elegantly sidesteps a problem by stating that although later studies have called into question the accuracy of information on the plaques, the facts as engraved were believed to be accurate at the time.)

However, it must be acknowledged that we paid little mind to the consequences of our findings and reasoned judgments, such as the stripping of a batting championship from Ty Cobb in 1910 or Bobby Avila in 1954. For the fourth, landmark edition of *Total Baseball*, our challenge was to devise a more historically sensitive framework that would permit us to incorporate the best modern research while continuing to honor the judgments of the past.

Total Baseball abided by the Special Baseball Records Committee's decision on game-ending homers—not to preserve Ruth's total, but because there were many more such homers before

1920 than the 37 the committee identified, and the disputes surrounding some of them are now beyond settling. Like Turkin/Thompson and all previous record books, and in accordance with the view of most historians, we rejected the committee's position that the National Association was not a major league. We committed fully to the creation of a full statistical record of that trailblazing circuit, and hoped one day to integrate the NA and NL records of such players as Al Spalding, Cap Anson, George Wright, and all the others who played in the professional league between 1871 and 1875. For now, we provide NA stats within the Player and Pitcher Registers, but total them separately from those of the NL (or, in the rare case of a prodigiously extended playing career, the American Association, a major league from 1882 through 1891).

We also differed from the committee's ruling on awarding pitchers' wins and losses in the years before 1920. Not finding any official scoring rule or practice for that time, its members chose to apply 1950 guidelines to decisions awarded in 1876-1920. This well-intentioned decision produced substantial alterations in the records of such hurlers as Cy Young, Christy Mathewson, Grover Alexander, and others. In the ensuing years, the notable research of Frank Williams (reported in "All the Record Books Are Wrong," *The National Pastime,* 1982) revealed that there was indeed a pattern and a rationale for the way decisions were awarded in those days; the data in *Total Baseball* conforms with his meticulously substantiated findings.

More involved, and perhaps of most direct interest to fans and media, are the subjects of (a) statistical discrepancies between the record presented in *Total Baseball* and the figures published in other reference works, or memorialized on Hall of Fame plaques, and (b) the implications of corrected data for the awarding of batting championships. We will address those questions, as well as the larger ones of transcription accuracy and ledger balance, in the "Issues and Answers" section of this essay.

Let's resume our chronicle of how Major League Baseball and others have kept the record of the game. Besides the debut of *The Baseball Encyclopedia* (and the Miracle Mets and the centennial of professional baseball), there were two other interesting baseball developments in 1969. The first and less celebrated was a research project launched by Eldon and Harlan Mills that, like the ICI effort, could not have been contemplated without the computer. The Mills brothers tracked the entire major league seasons of 1969 and 1970 on a play-by-play basis. Then they applied to that record the probabilities of winning that derived from each possible outcome of a plate appearance, as determined by a computer simulation incorporating nearly eight thousand possibilities. What, for example, was the visiting team's chance of winning the game before the first pitch was thrown? Fifty percent, if we are pitting two theoretical teams of equal or unknown ability on a neutral site. If the first man fails to get on base, the chances of the visiting team winning are reduced to 49.8 percent; should he hit a double, the visiting team's chance of victory is raised to 55.9 percent, as determined by the simulation. Every possible situation—combining half-inning, score, men on base, and men out—was tested by the simulator to arrive at "Win Points."

The Millses' purpose was to determine the clutch value of, say, hitting a homer with two men on and one man out in the bottom of the ninth, with the team trailing by two runs, the situation Bobby Thomson faced in the climactic National League game of 1951— oddly, the rookie year of the first modern computer. (That home run gained for him 1,472 Win Points; had it come with no one on in the eighth inning of a game in which his team led 4-0, the homer would have been worth only 12 Win Points.) What the Mills brothers were attempting to do was to evaluate not only the *what* of a performance, which traditional statistics indicate, but the *when,* or clutch factor, which no measure to that time could provide.

This project, detailed in a small book issued in 1970 called *Player Win Averages,* proceeded from the same impulse that led to other measures of clutch performance: the game-winning RBI, introduced as an official Major League Baseball stat in 1980 and scrapped in 1989; the measures of batting performance in late-inning and men-on-base situations first published by Seymour Siwoff, Steve Hirdt, and Peter Hirdt of the Elias Sports Bureau in 1985; and the historically complete indexes of clutch hitting and clutch pitching developed for the first edition of this book.

The other noteworthy baseball event of 1969 was the official adoption by the major leagues of the save, the stat associated with relief pitching, the game's most significant strategic development since the advent of the gopher ball. Now shown in the papers on a daily basis, saves were not officially recorded at all until 1960. It was at the instigation of Jerome Holtzman of the *Chicago Sun-Times,* with the cooperation of *The Sporting News,* that this statistic was finally accepted (although Pat McDonough, a founding member of SABR, had developed a similar stat in 1924 which he called "games finished by relief hurlers"; its first appearance in print came in the *New York Telegram* three years later). The need for the save arose because relievers operated at a disadvantage when it came to picking up wins. The bullpen specialists were a new breed, and as their role increased, the need emerged to identify excellence, as it had long ago for batters, starting pitchers, and fielders.

The save's prime statistical drawback was that there was no negative to counteract the positive, no stat for saves blown (except, all too often, a victory for the "fireman"); unofficial attempts to develop such a stat have accelerated in recent years, and now are part of the formula for the Fireman of the Year award.

August 10, 1971, marked another milestone, the founding in Cooperstown of SABR, the group in whose annual publications most of today's sabermetricians cut their analytical teeth. Its statistical analysis research committee, headed for more than a decade by Pete Palmer and most recently by Clem Comly, has served as a sounding board for the inventive approaches of such men as Dallas Adams, Dick Cramer, Steve Mann, Craig Wright, Gary Gillette, and Bill James.

Developments of the ensuing decade include the previously mentioned adoption of the GWRBI in 1980; it rewarded the batter who drove in a run to give his club a lead that it would never relinquish. This stat was pilloried in the press from its introduction; Major League Baseball finally gave up on it before the 1989 season. In 1984 on base percentage was made official, thirty years after its introduction to the general baseball public by Rickey and Roth.

Situational stats, unofficial but widely reported and employed, have been the specialty of the Elias Sports Bureau, the Baseball Workshop, and STATS, Inc.—performance in day games vs. night, grass vs. artificial turf, lefty vs. righty, day game following night, bases-loaded situations, and so on. When the data is drawn from a large enough sample, these stats can be provocative and meaningful; they represent the wave of the future in baseball, and are fast becoming useful analytical tools for review of the past. Elias has recorded situational data systematically since 1975, Baseball Workshop since 1984.

Total Baseball

The next major event in the history of baseball record keeping was *Total Baseball*. Founded upon a unique historical database that Pete Palmer had cultivated for decades—in the tradition of baseball archivists like S.C. Thompson, Bradshaw Swales, Leonard Gettelson, and John Tattersall—*Total Baseball* is the third-generation encyclopedia of the game. Just as the advent of the Macmillan/ICI encyclopedia supplanted Turkin/Thompson, the standard for two decades, *Total Baseball* has taken advantage of new technology and new research. The work of members of the Society for American Baseball Research has helped to make the data more accurate than ever before. A cast of volunteers working on the Baseball Archive website have enlarged, updated and made free to researchers the data used in this book, based on Pete Palmer's research.

There are, of course, the traditional stats one would expect in a baseball reference work; there are many of the more revealing sabermetric stats (discussed in detail in the essay that follows this); there are stats never published before their appearance in this book.

Issues and Answers: Sources of Baseball Statistics

There are six major sources for baseball statistical research, and thus for the statistics that comprise *Total Baseball*. By far the most significant one is the official Major League Baseball records kept by the leagues, published in the baseball guides, and maintained on microfilm at the Baseball Hall of Fame in Cooperstown and in the league offices. These records cover the years since 1903 for the National League and 1905 for the American League. Any official source data before these years were lost.

The second major source is the computer printouts prepared by ICI for *The Baseball Encyclopedia* in 1969. These cover the NL for 1891-1902, the AL for 1901-04, the Federal League for 1914-15, plus all the 19th-century major leagues (1882-91 American Association, 1884 Union Association, and the 1890 Players League). These records, obtained from newspaper box scores, were turned over to the Baseball Hall of Fame and made public by agreement with its resident historian Lee Allen, who permitted ICI to use his voluminous player demographic files.

The third source is John Tattersall's newspaper box score research for the NL of 1876 through 1890. Since Tattersall had done such careful work, day-by-day computer printouts were never generated for this period. Any day-by-day records created by Tattersall have been lost, but what has survived is a batting and fielding summary and a pitching summary for each club each year listing many categories. This collection, now owned by SABR, also includes the home run log, which lists every home run ever hit from 1871 to date, the date, teams, game location, batter, pitcher, inning, men on base, and other notes.

The fourth source for baseball statistics is a box score collection accumulated by Michael Stagno, covering the National Association of 1871-1875, which was also purchased by SABR. Preliminary basic data was calculated by Stagno. Bob Richardson of Boston and Bob Tiemann of St. Louis have accumulated complete totals in all categories from this data with the exception of caught stealing data.

The fifth source is additional work done by the ICI researchers for the 1969 edition, covering data that were not kept officially during the years since 1903 for the NL and 1905 for the AL. Examples of this data are runs batted in before 1920; extra base hits in the AL for 1905 and 1906, double plays by fielders before 1920 in the NL and 1923 in the AL; pitching data except wins and losses for the AL for 1905-07, earned runs for pitchers before 1912 NL and 1913 AL; complete games before 1913 NL and 1926 AL; games started before 1926 AL and 1938 NL; and saves before 1969. Any day-by-day records from this source have been lost, but the season totals have survived.

The sixth source is newspaper box score research to pick up additional categories not covered by the first five sources. Examples of this are hit by pitch for batters before 1917 NL and 1920 AL (by Alex Haas, Tattersall, Palmer, and many others), triple plays by fielders before 1928 AL and 1930 NL (mainly by Jim Smith), home runs allowed by pitchers before 1950 AL and 1952 NL (again by Tattersall). Frank Williams carefully researched AL pitching records for 1901 through 1919, when the league records were particularly sloppy. Retrosheet has contitnued and expanded this work.

Issues and Answers: Discrepancies

The original data for record books and Hall of Fame plaques, before the 1969 ICI research, were mostly obtained from two sources, the Spalding and Reach annual guides and two *Sporting News* publications: the *Baseball Register* (published yearly 1940 to date), which often contained records of oldtimers, and *Daguerreotypes* (published every so often from 1934 to date), which had records of all Hall of Famers and many other notable players. This research was done from guides and newspapers by Paul Rickart, Leonard Gettelson and Paul MacFarlane.

When the 1969 encyclopedia came out, there were many small differences in player stats when compared to the traditional data. However, since any records used to generate guide data in the early years were lost, the new data appeared to be more reliable. In addition, many more categories were given, like extra-base hits, runs batted in, pitcher innings, hits and earned runs allowed, and fielder double plays. Also included in the new data were club splits for traded players and information on those who played in fewer than 15 games.

In addition to the previously mentioned retroactive scoring decisions of the Special Records Committee, it ruled to include in the averages many games that were thrown out before, particularly in 1877, 1879, and 1899. Also included were the NL's tie games of five or more innings in 1878 through 1884 (38 of them), previously uncounted. Before 1912 in the NL pinch hitters and defensive replacements were included in the official game sheets, but the players were not credited with a game played. The committee decided to add these in, too.

Our research has uncovered a great many small errors and a few major ones in the official statistics. This was done by comparing individual totals to team totals, and by rechecking the addition on the player sheets. Most of these errors were in the American League, particularly before 1920, for which the record keeping was very sloppy. The NL has been much better over the years. For example, from 1910 to date, the NL took the sum of all the batter and fielder stats for each team, compared them to the sum of the team stats, and resolved almost all the differences. The AL did not start doing this until 1973 when the record keeping was first computerized. The NL went to computers in 1981.

For example, up through 1935, most AL clubs are not in agreement in player sums and team figures for at bats and hits. The differences are usually small, fewer than 10. (We have corrected the larger discrepancies of those years, but the smaller ones are yet to be resolved.) For 1905 to 1920, the team totals are further removed from the sum of the players, so that *The Baseball Encyclopedia* and *Total*

Baseball have replaced the team totals with the sum of the players. We corrected all the post-1935 cases of team at-bat and hit totals not agreeing, but have not yet begun work on the previous years.

An interesting quirk in the way records are kept—and another reminder, as if one needed it, that baseball record keeping remains subject to error and controversy—occurred as recently as the strike-shortened season of 1981. The American League rule was to round off the innings pitched at the end of the season, although the weekly reports showed thirds of innings. Baltimore's Sammy Stewart had 29 earned runs in 112-1/3 innings, while Oakland's Steve McCatty had 48 in 185-2/3 innings. This gave Stewart the ERA title, 2.323 to 2.327. But when the innings were rounded off, McCatty won, 2.32 to 2.33. McCatty got the title, but the next year both leagues decided to count thirds of innings.

Issues and Answers: Hall of Famers

The data reported by the ICI group in the first edition of *The Baseball Encyclopedia* upset many people in baseball, for their numbers were different from those traditionally accepted; in subsequent editions, many of the prominent players' statistics were fudged back to their traditional values. Yet 1969 had hardly been the first time corrections had been made to official data. In 1929 Grover Cleveland Alexander won his 373rd game, breaking Christy Mathewson's National League record, then thought to be 372. He never won another game. A number of years later, Joseph Reichler found a game in which, by the rules of that time, Matty should have gotten the win, this game taking place on May 21, 1902. The official record was changed and Matty pulled into a tie with Alex. The problem was that no one checked all of Mathewson's other games to see how many times he received a win under the old rules that wouldn't have been credited that way today. When ICI did its original research in 1968, it found Matty had only 367 wins by today's rules, while Alexander had 374. (Further research, notably by Frank Williams, has restored Alexander and Mathewson to a tie at 373 wins.)

In another celebrated example of record-book flip-flops, when the American League was formed in 1901, Nap Lajoie was credited with a .422 average, with 220 hits in 543 at bats. After a number of years, someone noticed that if you take these at bats and hits, the average comes out only to .405, so his average was changed. (Turkin/Thompson gave Nap a mark of .409 in its first edition.) Later in the 1950s, John Tattersall had his doubts and decided to go through his newspaper collection of box scores. He found 229 hits for Lajoie, not 220—the error had been in the figure for hits, not in the figure for batting average. Thus his average was restored to .422, which happened to be the highest in American League history. Then ICI research in this area came up with a .426 mark (232 for 544, based on newspaper accounts), which was published in the first edition, then trimmed back to .422 in subsequent editions. The .426 figure is the one this book uses, because the day-by-day source data for the American League of 1901 has been lost, and the newspaper reconstruction is more credible.

Lajoie seemed to be involved in a number of controversies. ICI research found four more hits for him in 1902, raising his average from .369 to .378. Later editions of *The Baseball Encyclopedia* changed Lajoie's stats back to the old values; we have not.

In 1910 there was a very close batting race between Cobb and Lajoie. At the end of the season, most people thought Nap had won, based on his getting eight hits in a doubleheader on the final day of the season (six of them bunts). There was talk that the opposing Browns had let him get the bunts by playing back, so that

the hated Cobb would lose. However, the AL office went over their figures and gave Cobb the title, .385 to .384. Nearly 80 years later, Palmer discovered a critical error: a game in which Cobb had two hits in three at bats had been entered twice. This was found because Sam Crawford had 14 games on his official sheet for the homestand yet the Tigers had only played 13. It turned out that Detroit played a doubleheader on September 24, but the second game inadvertently was inserted in the official sheets as being played on September 25. Later, this second game of the 24th, which appeared to be missing, was put in the scoresheets again. The League Office discovered this mistake soon after its official announcement that Cobb had won the batting title, because the double entry was corrected for all the other Detroit players. However, Ban Johnson had made a big deal out of how carefully his people had checked the figures in order to settle the controversy, so the AL kept quiet about the gaffe, leaving Cobb the winner.

Appeals to Commissioner Kuhn in 1981 to set the matter straight officially were to no avail, because that would not only have changed the outcome of the 1910 batting race, it would also have altered Cobb's lifetime hit total, then being pursued to massive media attention by Pete Rose. Kuhn's statement read, in part, "The passage of seventy years, in our judgment ... constitutes a certain statute of limitation as to recognizing any changes in the records with confidence of the accuracy of such changes. ... Since a variety of questions have been raised through the years about the accuracy of the statistics of that period, the only way to make changes with confidence would be for a complete and thorough review of all team and individual statistics. That is not practical." It may not have not been practical, but we have embarked upon such a course and dedicate ourselves to that ongoing process.

Asked at the time how we would have resolved the dispute over the 1910 batting race, we responded in this way: remove Cobb's two redundant hits and alter his batting average accordingly, effectively dropping it beneath Lajoie's, and correct his lifetime hit total as well; however, retain Cobb's batting championship, for two reasons—one, because Lajoie's flurry of bunt hits were highly suspect, and two, because Cobb was awarded the title *in his day,* and awards should be permanent, not contingent. Furthermore, a reasonable case can be made that Ban Johnson, if he had believed that Lajoie's tainted hits would have been sufficient to produce a batting championship, would have nullified them; after all, he did banish from baseball the Browns' manager who had instructed his rookie third baseman to play exceptionally deep.

It is this singular event in baseball history that supplied a model for how *Total Baseball* and Major League Baseball together developed a policy for incorporating new research finds into the historical record without revoking long-held personal championships. Player records may be changed upon the evidence of historical error, but league awards and titles are forever.

Here is what happened in the now celebrated Honus Wagner case in the 1990 edition of *The Baseball Encyclopedia,* over which Major League Baseball and the Macmillan publishing firm became estranged. The Macmillan editor noticed that previous-edition figures for Wagner did not agree with the data presented in the first edition in 1969. He assumed that the data had been corrupted over the years, and thus returned the 1897-1900 data to the original figures, costing Wagner 12 hits. However, the editor did not restore the 1901-02 data, which would have resulted in Wagner losing three more hits. The outcome was that Wagner had a total of 3415 hits in the 1969 edition, 3430 in the 1988 edition (the traditional

figure) and 3418 in the 1990 edition (and again in 1993). One of the problems with the Macmillan newspaper research was that it did not count protested games in the player data. Although the games were thrown out of the standings, the player stats *did* count in the league compilations at the time, which should be the criterion for inclusion. (Protested games were included in the official records through 1909, then omitted 1910-1919, and were made once again part of the official records in 1920. When our review of these protested games prior to 1909 is completed, the individual stats will be added to our figures.)

Wagner was involved in three of these protested games. There were about twenty-five of them altogether in the nineteenth century. However, the newspaper research did show up additional differences in player stats beyond those from the protested games.

When checking the plaques for the Hall of Fame players, we found about 40 players with differences from the *Total Baseball* data. Most were nineteenth century players with small differences due to discrepancies between the old guide figures and the later newspaper research. Some had to do with rule changes growing out of the 1969 Special Records Committee. For the 20th century, there were a number of differences due to official errors, mostly in the area of pitcher won-lost marks in the 1901-1919 American League period. There were only a few outright errors on the plaques. Exact differences can be found by comparing *Daguerreotypes* (which often agrees with the plaques) with *Total Baseball*.

In four previous editions of *Total Baseball* we offered a detailed guide to variances between the plaques and the record embodied in *Total Baseball* (TB) for every Hall of Famer. This painstaking effort, of interest only to specialists perhaps, was the bridge between Major League Baseball, wary of changes to the traditional records, and the vanguard of historical research and reconstruction. Here is a lone example of the record comparisons of those earlier editions:

Cap Anson *Plaque, four batting titles; TB, four**

In 1879, Anson appears to have been the beneficiary of 20 extra hits, either by error or, as is commonly believed, a civic-minded Chicago official scorer. This error was found by John Tattersall in his review of newspaper box scores. In addition he (and we) incorporated the player records of four Chicago tie games, of which Anson played in two. His traditional mark of .407 was really only .317, and is so recorded in this volume; however, although a modern accounting would result in an 1879 batting title for Paul Hines, with .357, we credit the championship that year to Anson, as an instance of the Major League Baseball policy cited above (i.e., records may change to reflect new findings, but awards and titles are historical events, not to be retracted).

*The singular season of 1887 presents a different case. Following the long-standing directive of the Special Baseball Records Committee, we did not, until the seventh edition of *Total Baseball*, count walks as hits for this season, the practice which had been the sole basis of Anson's fourth batting championship. The modern computation revealed Sam Thompson to have had the highest batting average, with a mark of .372, and had prompted us to withdraw the fourth batting title from Anson; now, with this [seventh] edition, the 1887 championship is restored to him with a mark of .421.

Issues and Answers: League Batting Leaders

Until the fourth edition of *Total Baseball*, Major League Baseball had established no official historical record, despite its product endorsement of several statistical compendiums over the years. As a result, writers, historians, statisticians, and fans were offered a choice amongst differing annual league batting leaders, depending on the major record book favored. Those most favored by recent chroniclers have been *Total Baseball* and *The Baseball Encyclopedia* because they contained all player and club records.

There are two recognized record summary tomes which feature leaders in various statistical categories, lifetime or single-season: *The Book of Baseball Records* (Elias Sports Bureau Inc.) and *The Complete Baseball Record Book* (The Sporting News). Though both are respected works, and both organizations have had long and often official relationships with Organized Baseball, neither record book enjoys official status, and discrepancies exist between the two.

There was *no* official batting championship rule until 1950. *Total Baseball* and *The Baseball Encyclopedia* remedied this oversight by formulating—independently—their own guidelines for the many years of omission, each based on their own concepts of fairness and equality. In previous editions, *Total Baseball* established the following criteria for batting championships: 1876 through 1956, qualification by having plate appearances equal to 3.1 per game times the number of scheduled games, thus conforming to the Major League Baseball practice since 1957. The batting championship criteria for *The Baseball Encyclopedia* over the years have been: 1876 through 1919, games played equal to at least 60 percent of games the team scheduled; 1920 through 1949, at least 100 games played, based on acceptance of the unofficial but universally assumed rule requiring appearance in at least 100 games; and 1950 to the present, the various changing official rule definitions.

In a policy shift endorsed by Major League Baseball, *Total Baseball* identifies league batting champions according to the practice of the time, in each league, and each champion will have his seasonal batting average recorded in boldface in his entry in the Player Register. However, as noted above in the discussion of the 1910 AL batting race, in the Annual Record section of this volume, we record the highest batting averages in each league season as correctly calculated, although not necessarily in descending order.

The history of the official batting championship rule is as follows: (1) 1950 and 1951, 400 official times at bat; (2) 1952 through 1954, 400 official times at bat or, if less than 400 times at bat and by adding enough imaginary hitless at bats so as to total 400, "he still would have the highest batting average in his league, he shall be the champion batter"; (3) 1955 and 1956, 400 official times at bat; (4) 1957 through 1966, 3.1 plate appearances per game times number of scheduled games, equaling 477 in a 154-game schedule and 502 in a 162-game schedule; and (5) 1967 to the present, 3.1 plate appearances per scheduled game, except that "if there is any player whose average would be the highest if he were charged with the required number of plate appearances or official at bats, then that player shall be awarded the batting championship."

In the strike-shortened season of 1972, a 156-game standard prevailed instead of the 162 scheduled games. In the strike seasons of 1981 and 1994, the rule of 3.1 plate appearances per game was applied to the number of games played by each team, rather than to those scheduled.

The early record tomes, the *Spalding Record Book* and *The Sporting News Record Book*, placed Jake Stenzel (NL) in the lead for 1893 and Nap Lajoie (AL) on top in 1905. Both Stenzel and Lajoie were the leaders during the life of the Spalding volumes, 1908-1924, and in the *Sporting News* volume from its debut in 1921 until 1929, when Hugh Duffy replaced Stenzel and 1930, when Elmer Flick supplanted Lajoie. The reasoning behind the *Sporting*

News switches was that both Stenzel and Lajoie failed to meet the unwritten criterion of a representative number of games—Stenzel had played in only 60 games and Lajoie in 65, not even half of their club's scheduled games. Otherwise the early record books' leaders were those endorsed by the leagues.

The Spalding Record Book in its 1917 edition made two important batting championship changes, both on the basis of mathematical errors which their editors had noted. To that time, Dan Brouthers had been tied with Cupid Childs for the highest batting average in 1892, but had been awarded the title based on his having played in more games, which was the tie-breaking guideline of the day. In 1917, however, Childs went to the front on the basis of extended batting average (calculating to extra decimal places beyond the thousandths that comprise conventional reporting of batting averages).

Next, Lajoie's average of .422 in 1901 was reduced in 1917 because of a *Reach Guide* typo in the hit column to a .405 figure. The Spalding management (the once independent Reach company had long since been acquired by Spalding) should have known that in 1892, the criterion for awarding a batting championship was indeed games played, not extended batting average, and that in 1901 they would have found Lajoie's correct (as then calculated) average in any number of newspapers. Lajoie's .422 average was restored in 1954 in response to John Tattersall's research, but Childs remained, until this writing, ahead of Brouthers in the NL's *Green Book.* (Since the fifth edition of *Total Baseball*, Brouthers has been credited as the champion because he played in more games, which was the criterion of the time—not because modern research has lowered Childs' batting average from .335 to .317.)

During its formative years, 1876 through 1919, the National League omitted any mention of batting championship criteria in its published rules. Certainly, this should have been addressed before 1920. Still, batting championships were tacitly acknowledged by the league, with guidelines drawn primarily from the comments of Henry Chadwick.

From 1876 to ca. 1888, the criterion was understood to be the best seasonal performance; as expressed by Chadwick in the *Spalding Guide* of 1887, "an average rating of a player should be on a season's work." Seasonal leadership may be deduced when the league's recognized champion was not listed first in the official averages. His preeminence was based on a representative number of games played over the season in which he excelled, as opposed to the nominal leader's handful of games.

The yardstick between 1889 and 1919 was playing in at least 100 games. In the 1890 *Spalding Guide* Chadwick wrote: "With the object in view of equalizing the averages and placing the names of the batsmen who have played in 100 games or over, are given the front rank, while those who have played in 50 games and over occupy second place, and those in 25 games and over third place, and so on."

The American League rules in its early years, 1901 through 1919, omitted any batting championship language. In honoring Cobb as its 1914 bat champ, the AL was undoubtedly proceeding from the guideline of best seasonal performance.

As discussed in the "Sources of Baseball Statistics" section of this essay, *Total Baseball* relies upon newspaper research and other data for the years before 1903 in the NL and 1905 in the AL. For subsequent seasons, the official league day-by-day sheets are available for study. The record summary books issued by Elias and *Sporting News* accept all the batting leaders recognized in the yearly Guides (*Spalding, Reach,* etc.). These champions are also accepted in today's league publications (AL *Red Book* and NL *Green Book*).

Henceforward, *Total Baseball* recognizes the same champions, with the exception of 1892, discussed above.

For students of the game, Joe Wayman documented the variances among the record books and encyclopedias and highlighted particularly those traditional batting champions whom previous editions of *Total Baseball* had toppled from the pinnacle. Even though most of these champions have been rethroned, the following thumbnail account of the debatable batting leaders will serve to explain the seeming anomaly of a batting champion whose average is lower than that of a rival.

OFFICIAL					TB (eds. 1-5)				
	G	AB	H	BA		G	AB	H	BA
1878 NL Dalrymple	60	267	95	.356	Hines	62	257	92	.358
1879 NL Anson	49	221	90	.407	Hines	85	409	146	.357
1884 NL O'Rourke	104	448	197	.350	Kelly	108	452	160	.354
1887 NL Anson*	122	532	224	.421	Thompson	127	545	203	.372
1892 NL Brouthers	152	588	197	.335	Brouthers	152	588	197	.335
1892 NL Childs	144	552	185	.335					
1893 NL Duffy	131	537	203	.378	Hamilton	82	355	135	.380
1902 AL Delahanty	123	473	178	.376	Lajoie	87	352	133	.378
1910 AL Cobb	140	509	196	.385	Lajoie	159	591	227	.384
1914 AL Cobb	97	345	127	.368	Collins	152	526	181	.344
1926 NL Hargrave	105	326	115	.353	Waner, P.	144	536	180	.336
1932 AL Alexander	124	392	144	.367	Foxx	154	585	213	.364
1938 AL Foxx	149	565	197	.349	Foxx	149	565	197	.349
1940 NL Garms	103	358	127	.355	Hack	149	603	191	.317
1942 NL Lombardi	105	309	102	.330	Slaughter	152	591	188	.318
1954 AL Avila	143	555	189	.341	Williams	117	386	133	.345
1981 NL Madlock	83	279	95	.341	Rose	107	431	140	.325

*Anson would be a .347 hitter without the benefit of his walks, which count as hits for only that year and make the difference in his winning the batting championship over Thompson.

1878: Abner Dalrymple captured the NL's batting title. Modern record tomes *(The Baseball Encyclopedia* and *Total Baseball)* list Paul Hines in the top spot. The NL in 1878 did not include tie games in its official averages, while today's record tomes count them. Thus, by counting tie games, Hines emerges with the higher average, but does not take away Dalrymple's championship.

1879: Cap Anson, the day's recognized batting champion, has been challenged by the moderns *(The Baseball Encyclopedia, Total Baseball, The Sports Encyclopedia: Baseball,* and *The National League Story,* Lee Allen) as to whether his .407 average is legitimate. In fact, the average was disputed as early as the 1880 DeWitt Guide, the averages for which were compiled by William Stevens of the *Boston Herald,* and *Balldom* (1914), compiled by George Moreland. *Total Baseball* keeps the title with Anson in recognition of the league action at the time, but reports his batting average correctly in the Player Register and in the Annual Record's listing of top batting averages in the 1879 NL.

1884: The official batting champion remains Orator Jim O'Rourke. Newspaper box scores, game accounts, and the results of tie games elevate King Kelly to a higher average. Tie games were not included in the official averages at the time, and how to handle them today remains a matter of controversy. No matter how we treat Kelly's 2-for-4 in his only tie-game appearance (August 11), his average is higher than O'Rourke's.

1887: In only this season, bases on balls counted as hits. One month into the season, the American Association wanted to scrap the rule, but the NL would not consent. *Total Baseball* now honors the rules of the day and thus recognizes Anson as the batting champion.

1892: Brouthers and Childs were honored as co-champions at .335, as discussed above. Childs had the higher extended average, .3351, against Brouthers' .3350 mark. By the day's reasoning, however, Brouthers is the leader. As Chadwick noted in the *Spalding*

Guide, "the lead in all cases of tie scores in base hits belongs by right to the batsman who has played in the greatest number of games, and in this case Brouthers batted in 152 games to Childs' 144." Childs' statistics, as compiled by ICI from newspapers, yield a batting average of .317, placing him third.

1893: Billy Hamilton's average was higher than Duffy's, and he would have met modern criteria for plate appearances. The NL, however, honored Duffy because he appeared in at least 100 games, which was expected of the leading players of that day. The title is thus accorded to him.

1902: The ICI sheets gave Lajoie four more hits than the guides had credited him with originally.

1910: Cobb is the champion, for reasons discussed amply above.

1914: Cobb, due to his proven hitting excellence, was awarded the championship because, in all reasoned probability, he would have been the leader over the full season. Consider also that the batting championship for the Chalmers car in 1910 for position players was based on 350 at bats. Cobb would have easily captured the crown based on a mythical 100 game requirement, even though he was three games shy.

1926: Bubbles Hargrave topped three other questionable contenders—those not credited with at least 400 at bats. All qualified for the title, though, based on the period's acceptance of appearance in at least 100 games. In Hargrave's favor was his position—catcher. Over the years, catchers were considered somewhat differently when it came to handing out awards, because of the demands of their position. In fact, in order for a catcher to qualify for the fielding championship at his position, he need only have appeared in at least 77 games. Hargrave caught in 93 games.

1932: Dale Alexander had the games and at bats to satisfy the AL as to his claim. If the 400-at-bat rule had been on the books, Alexander no doubt would have been inserted into the lineup until he secured eight additional at bats. If Jimmie Foxx were recognized as champion today, he would have the first of two consecutive Triple Crowns.

1938: Foxx was the AL leader—no ifs, ands, or buts about it. The AL had a rule in 1938 requiring the batting " ... winner to be at least 400 times at bat." *(Reach Guide,* 1939) Taffy Wright is the trivia-question champion, batting .350 in 100 games.

1940: Debs Garms raised a few eyebrows as a come-from-nowhere champion. If enough imaginary at bats to reach 400 were to be added to Garms' total, his adjusted average would still be one point higher than that of Stan Hack, the runner-up.

1942: Ernie Lombardi was the recognized NL batting king. As a *Sporting News* headline advised, "Ernie's 105 contests suffice to qualify him for a second title." The announcement called attention to the "inquiries" which had been made regarding a Lombardi award since the AL had put in place a 400 at bat requirement. Bill James noted that the NL announced a "meritorious 400 at bat" requirement after the problematic Garms award two years earlier. NL President Frick, however, contended there was no specific bat rule and catchers, because of their demanding position, deserved special consideration. The catcher's fielding championship by this time was based on 100 games, lessening the Frick contention. Frick may have had in mind the prior, 77-game catching requirement for fielding leadership. Thus, Frick's reasoning could have been to create a proportion: 77 games for catchers is to 100 games for position players what 77 percent of 400 at bats (308) for catchers is to 400 at bats for position players.

1954: Ted Williams, the batter with the highest average in the AL, did not meet the official qualifications to claim the title. The 1954 official Rule 10.17 spelled out the champion as one who, with at least 400 at bats, or with fewer than 400 at bats plus enough imaginary ones to equal 400, has the higher average. Under the official rules definition, Bobby Avila is the batting leader. During the closing weeks of the campaign, Williams was aware of the rule but continued to be selective of pitches, rather than swing at those outside the strike zone simply in order to reach the required 400 at bats. Williams' extended average based on adding imaginary at bats to his 386 is a .331 figure.

1981: Bill Madlock is the official batting champion by the rules of the day. Due to the strike-shortened season, the games a team played, rather than the scheduled games, were the basis for individual championships. Pittsburgh, Madlock's club, played 103 games. Thus, 103 X 3.1 = 319 plate appearances to qualify for the batting championship. Madlock topped the required 319 PA's by one, with 279 at bats, four sacrifice flies, 34 bases on balls, three hit by pitch, and no sacrifice hits or interference calls. *Total Baseball* awarded the title to Pete Rose in editions 1 and 2, based on average games played per team, then corrected the procedure in its third edition.

The records of the four defunct major leagues show only the American Association had batting champions not agreeing with *Total Baseball* champions. This happened twice: in the 1884 AA, the official winner was Dude Esterbrook though his teammate Dave Orr actually batted 50 points higher; and in the 1886 AA, the champ was officially Orr though Guy Hecker's recomputed average nips him by a point. (Pete Browning also surpassed Orr and was listed as champion in earlier editions of *Total Baseball*, for which a guideline of 3.1 plate appearances per game was employed throughout.)

A Little Help from Our Friends

The computer has made possible the rapid analysis of mountains of raw baseball data. But as invaluable as the computer has been in producing and cross-checking the statistical data for *Total Baseball*, the editors owe more to the people who have contributed their time, their expertise, their love of the game, and their passion for getting things right. These individuals are listed below, or in the Acknowledgements, or in the table at the end of the book that enumerates those readers of the earlier editions who helped us improve the accuracy of *Total Baseball* this time around. A collective debt is owed to the Society for American Baseball Research and the National Baseball Library.

The six principal sources of the statistics herein were discussed earlier. Supplemental sources were:

● For work on the Stagno Collection of NA data, 1871-75, SABR's 19th-century research committee, headed successively by John Thorn and Mark Rucker, Bob Tiemann, Bob Richardson, Fred Ivor-Campbell, John Husman, and Paul Wendt.

● For batters hit by pitch, 1884-1896 AA/NL/PL, 1909-1916 NL, 1909-1919 AL, research from newspapers by Alex Haas, Pete Palmer, John Schwartz, Bob Davids, John Tattersall, Lyle Spatz, Herb Goldman, Keith Carlson, Tom Chase, Ed Luteran, Frank Phelps, and others. (Note: research continues for the 1897-1908 period, but the data is, at this writing, about 95 percent complete.)

● For home runs allowed by pitchers, 1876-1950 AL/NL, the Tattersall Collection, aided by Bob McConnell.

● For runs batted in, 1903-1919 NL, 1905-1919 AL, ICI research.

● For runs batted in, 1880-1885 NL and 1882-87, 1890 AA, David Neft.

- For pitcher saves (except 1901-1919 AL) 1876-1968 NL/AA/UA/PL/AL, ICI research.
- For stolen bases, 1886 NL, Spalding *Baseball Guide.*
- For wins and losses for pitchers, 1876-1900 NL/AA/PL, and for wins, losses, games started, complete games, shutouts, saves, 1901-1919 AL, and complete pitching data, 1892, research from newspapers and official sheets by Frank Williams.
- For shutouts, 1876-1939, Joe Wayman.
- For biographical data, the biographical research committee of SABR, notably Richard Topp and Bill Carle.
- For caught-stealing data, 1914-1916 AL, 1915-1916 NL, Ernie Lanigan, courtesy of Bob Davids.
- For home/away data, 1876-1891 NL/AA/UA/PL, Bob McConnell.
- For game scores, 1876-1884 NL/AA/UA, Bob Tiemann.
- For game scores, 1885-1891 NL/AA/PL, Richard Topp.
- For runs and homers home/away, 1980s NL/AL, Bill Carr.

Missing data includes:

- Hit batters: 1897-1908, scattered data, especially for New York and Cincinnati.
- Caught stealing: 1886-1914, 1916 (players with fewer than 20 steals), 1917-1919, 1926-1950 NL; 1886-1891 AA; 1890 PL; 1901-1913, 1916 (players with fewer than 20 steals), 1917-1919, 1914-15 FL.
- Sacrifice hits: 1927-1930 (fly balls advancing runners to any base counted as sacrifice hits).
- Sacrifice flies: 1908-1930, 1939 (sacrifice flies are counted as sacrifice hits for these years).
- Runs batted in, 1882-1884 AA; 1884 UA. Partial data is shown for 1882-84. For 1885-87 and 1890, about 10 percent of the data is estimated.
- Strikeouts for batters: 1882-1888, 1890 AA; 1884 UA; 1897-1909 NL; 1901-1912 AL. (Team batting strikeouts are presented for 1897-1902 NL and 1901-1904 AL.)

Incomplete data for those years up to 1903 NL and 1905 AL are available from the ICI computer printouts at the National Baseball Library. Additional research could turn up more data. If your research or sharp eye should detect errors or gaps in *Total Baseball,* please write us in care of the publisher (or alternatively, simply e-mail us at stats@sportmediagroup.com) and we'll be delighted to improve our data and credit your catch in the next edition.

Chapter 58

Sabermetrics

By Phil Birnbaum

Are power pitchers better in the cold than finesse pitchers? Baltimore Orioles manager Joe Altobelli thought so. In 1985, he decided to arrange his rotation so Storm Davis would have as many starts as possible in April. Altobelli thought that Davis, the hardest thrower on his staff, would perform better than his finesse pitchers. The move was not a success; Davis finished April with an ERA of 7.23.

This series of events led Bill James to wonder about Altobelli's hypothesis. Do hard throwers indeed outperform finesse pitchers in April? He turned to his library of *Sporting News* guides. He found 30 pairs of starters with identical season won-lost records but where one of the pair was a power pitcher, and the other was a finesse pitcher.

How did the groups compare in April? Almost the exact opposite of how Altobelli thought.

	Finesse Pitchers	Power Pitchers
April	63-37, .630	49-51, .490
Overall	539-345, .610	539-345, .610

The power pitchers not only performed significantly worse than the finesse pitchers—they didn't even break .500.

Sabermetrics

That study, in a nutshell, is sabermetrics—the science of answering questions about baseball through the analysis of the statistical evidence. Sabermetrics is a science, and has at its core the scientific method: conclusions must be based on evidence and logic, and any principle of sabermetrics can be modified, or even overturned, by new or better evidence.

And, like other sciences, conclusions are not always clear-cut. While Bill James found that power pitchers don't outperform in April, they *did* outperform in the colder months of May and September (.642 and .654, respectively). Perhaps, James suggested, Altobelli was right that power pitchers can handle the cold. Maybe it's the not the weather but rather the vagaries of the irregular April rotations that throw off their rhythm. That's a reasonable hypothesis, and someday someone will take a look at the evidence—perhaps comparing power pitchers who started every fifth day in April to power pitchers who started irregularly.

Sabermetrics was still in its earliest stages of acceptance when Bill James wrote up that study in his 1986 *Baseball Abstract*. There had been occasional, pioneering statistical works published in the 1950s and '60s (and one as early as 1917), but sabermetrics truly began to reach avid baseball fans starting in 1982, with the publication of the first of James' commercially published annual *Abstract*s (he had begun self-publishing them in 1977). Also, 1984 saw Pete Palmer and John Thorn publish their book *The Hidden Game of Baseball*, which remains relevant even 20 years later.

The years since have seen an explosion of interest in statistical analysis of baseball. This is due in large part to the rise of Rotisserie and Fantasy Baseball, but also to increasing fan interest in baseball knowledge for its own sake.

These days, a search for "sabermetrics" on the internet yields thousands of web pages. Much original, high-quality research is published on the web, and the Society for American Baseball Research (SABR) issues a quarterly sabermetric journal. Several baseball annuals, aimed mainly at fantasy-baseball aficionados, have developed solid and important methods for evaluating and predicting player performance.

Academia, too, is beginning to take notice of sabermetrics, albeit slowly. Papers about baseball have made it to various journals in fields such as statistics and game theory. However, many of those researchers are not always up to date on the past two decades of progress in the field—which, having been published outside their academic journals, don't make it to the scientific indexes—and some of their studies wind up reinventing the wheel.

Most importantly, the past several years have seen major league teams embrace sabermetrics as part of the knowledge base from which to manage a baseball team. Although the Texas Rangers had employed sabermetrician Craig Wright for a few years in the '80s, there was little further interest until the late 1990s, when the Oakland A's, under the stewardship of general manager Billy Beane, made sabermetrics the foundation of their talent evaluation. A few years later, the Blue Jays joined the club, hiring away Beane's assistant J.P. Ricciardi as their GM. And, in late 2002, the Boston Red Sox made headlines when they hired the 28-year-old, sabermetrically literate Theo Epstein as the youngest GM in major league history. Almost immediately, Epstein made further headlines by signing Bill James as a consultant.

These hirings made sabermetrics respectable, but only a few months later Michael Lewis would make it notorious. His bestselling book, *Moneyball*, released in May 2003, documented the A's rise to the top of the standings on a second-division budget. Lewis was given full access to Billy Beane and the Oakland front office. The result is an entertaining account, in full and sometimes unflattering detail, of how Beane disdained the advice of his bewildered old-school scouts, relying on assistant Paul Depodesta and his laptop computer to implement sabermetric ideas on how to draft players. A chapter of Lewis' book is devoted exclusively to those ideas; it quotes Bill James so extensively that one reviewer said it was like reading an old *Baseball Abstract*. A few months after the book came out, the Dodgers made Depodesta their new General Manager.

If baseball executives could have safely ignored sabermetric principles before, it is safe to say they can do so no more. It is a good bet that if Joe Altobelli were considering his April strategy today, he'd have a sabermetrician on-staff to consult with first.

Sabermetric Statistics

Studies like the Altobelli one notwithstanding, most baseball fans' awareness of sabermetrics is through its new statistics. And with good reason; formulas like Runs Created and Linear Weights are among the most significant and useful results the field has pro-

duced. They answer important questions about how baseball teams win. The sabermetric statistics can be divided into four basic types: batting, pitching, fielding, and all three combined. Let's start by examining some batting statistics.

Batting Statistics: Linear Weights

The Linear Weights formula answers the question, "if a batter with these stats replaced an average batter on an average team, how many more (or fewer) runs would it score?" The answer, as we will see, is expressed in runs above or below average. To understand Linear Weights, let's start with this famous table from Pete Palmer. Given the baserunners and number of outs, the table gives the number of runs expected to score in the remainder of the current inning.

Men On	Number of Outs		
FST	0	1	2
---	.454	.249	.095
x--	.783	.478	.209
-x-	1.068	.699	.348
xx-	1.380	.888	.457
--x	1.277	.897	.382
x-x	1.639	1.088	.494
-xx	1.946	1.371	.661
xxx	2.254	1.546	.798

FST=First, Second, Third bases
Table 1: Number of runs scoring in remainder of inning given Base/Out situation

For instance, with the leadoff batter up—that is, no outs and nobody on—you can expect .454 runs to score before the third out. But if there's a runner on first, and none out, an average .783 runs will score.

How did we get these numbers? By simply looking at actual records of baseball games. If we go through a bunch of seasons' worth of play-by-play game descriptions, we can find every situation where a team had a runner on first and nobody out. Sometimes, we'll see that the pitcher struck out the next three batters and nobody scored. Other times, the runner will have been doubled home with two outs, and one run will have scored. Still other times, there will be a series of hits, and maybe four or five runs will have scored. But if we average them all out, we'll get .783 runs.

Of course, the number depends on which games we analyze. The table we're using is based on 1961-1973; these days, with the explosion of home runs, all the numbers in the table will be higher. But the conclusions we draw will be much the same. (Actually, Palmer employed a simulation, as play-by-play data weren't available at the time of his study. But the results are nonetheless quite accurate.)

From this chart, we can already discover a few things about a baseball offense. For instance, we know a leadoff single changes the situation from .454 runs to .783 runs; so a leadoff single is worth the difference between the two values, or .329 runs. What if the leadoff batter makes out? That reduces the team's run potential from .454 to .249 runs, so the leadoff out is negative .205 runs.

The difference to the team between the leadoff hitter getting on base or making an out is astonishingly high. It scores .783 runs after a leadoff single (or walk), but only .249 runs after an out. And so the average team will score *three times as many runs* if the leadoff hitter reaches first base than if he doesn't. It is for this reason that sabermetricians rate the ability to get on base as one of the most crucial skills a leadoff hitter, or indeed the entire team, can have.

Of course, not all singles are leadoff singles. Take, for instance, a single that comes with one out and a runner on third base. Before the single, the run potential was .897. After the single, the run potential is .478, with one run having scored. The difference

(.478 − .897 + 1 run) equals .581 runs. So a single with one out and a man on third is worth .581 runs.

Every situation will lead to a different value of a single—singles with one out, with two outs, where runners advance one base, where runners advance two bases, where the batter takes second on an attempt to throw a runner out at home. We can again look at play-by-play baseball records, see how often each situation happens, and average them all out. The result is how much a single is worth, on average. If we carry out this result, as Palmer did, we wind up with a number around .46. In other words, an average single is worth an extra .46 runs to an average team.

There's nothing stopping us from doing the same calculation for doubles, or home runs, or outs. Combining all these results together gives us Palmer's original Linear Weights formula:

Batting Runs = (0.46) 1B + (0.80) 2B + (1.02) 3B + (1.40) HR − .33 (BB+HBP) + .3(SB) − .6(CS) − .25 (AB-H)

Palmer called this statistic Batting Runs rather than Linear Weights, saving the latter designation for his entire system (including pitching and fielding). In practice, however, Linear Weights is used more often. In this chapter, we will use the two interchangeably.

If a single is worth .46 runs, and a double is worth .8 runs, and an out is worth a negative .25 runs, then it makes sense that if we add up the values of all a player's events, we get how many runs above average he is responsible for. An average player will have zero batting runs; a good player will have positive batting runs; and a below-average player will have negative batting runs.

Take, for instance, Mark McGwire and Sammy Sosa in 1998:

	AB	H	2B	3B	HR	BB	Avg	BR
McGwire	509	152	21	0	70	162	.299	+107
Sosa	643	198	20	0	66	73	.308	+ 73

The Linear Weights formula tells us that McGwire produced 107 more runs for his team than an average player would have; Sosa produced only 73 more runs than average. As you can imagine, both these figures will appear high on the all-time list. The rule of thumb is that +50 batting runs is an MVP candidate, and +25 is a very solid regular. Indeed, there are some pretty good players at zero—remember, zero is league average.

It's important to emphasize that Batting Runs is a measurement, not a player rating. Linear Weights does not say that McGwire is a better player than Sosa because he had more batting runs. It simply lays out the result that, as well as can be measured, McGwire would have added 107 runs to an average team, and Sosa would have added 73. Naturally, most sabermetricians do agree, for this and other reasons, that McGwire had a much better year than Sosa. But it's a human being making that evaluation, not a measure. The measure lays out an objective result, measured in runs. Sabermetrics provides evidence to inform a decision on which player is "better," but does not make the decision for us.

You will find Batting Runs included in offensive stat lines in the Player Register section of this book. For register purposes, the standard formula has been adjusted for accuracy in certain ways; these are described in the Glossary, and in the next chapter, "Linear Weights."

Runs Created

Runs Created is another statistic that evaluates offenses. It answers a similar question to Linear Weights: If this were a team's batting line, how many runs would the team score?

In its simplest form, the statistic is:

$$\text{Runs} = \frac{(H + BB)\ (\text{Total Bases})}{AB + BB}$$

The formula, discovered by Bill James, is one of the most elegant in sabermetrics. It expresses the idea that to score runs, you need to get men on base (H+BB); advance them home (multiply by total bases); and do that in as few opportunities as possible (divide by AB+BB).

The Runs Created formula works well. Run on a team's statistics, it usually predicts the team's number of runs quite accurately. Run on a player's batting line, Runs Created can be used to estimate the number of runs the player contributed to his team. Here, again, are Sosa and McGwire:

	AB	H	2B	3B	HR	BB	Avg	RC
McGwire	509	152	21	0	70	162	.299	179
Sosa	643	198	20	0	66	73	.308	157

McGwire had 179 runs created; Sosa had 157. This is generally in line with the results we obtained with Linear Weights. Again, these are extremely high values belonging to two extremely talented hitters. Runs Created for a player figures along the same scale as runs scored or RBI—100 runs created is a typical milestone for a fine season.

You'll notice that the simplified version of Runs Created we're using here doesn't include such events as stolen bases, sacrifice hits and hit by pitch. But there are other, more detailed versions that do. A full list of the various Runs Created formulas can be found in the Glossary.

Runs Created Per Game

Runs Created and Linear Weights are both estimates of how much bulk offense a player contributed. The more playing time a player receives, the more runs he will create, and the more Batting Runs he will put on the board (both positive and negative).

And that's important information to have. But if you want to find out how "good" a performance is, it's not enough. If Player A had 70 runs last year, and Player B had 55 runs created, which will earn more as a free agent? We can't tell. If they each played a full season, Player A probably ranks higher; but if Player B played only half the year because of injury, he's creating runs at the rate of 110 per season, and is probably a much better hitter than Player A.

To evaluate Players A and B properly, we want to know not just *how many* runs they created, but the *rate* at which they created runs. To measure that rate, Bill James created a stat called "Runs Created per Game" (RC/G), or sometimes, "Runs Created per 27 outs" (RC/27). The idea is this: Mark McGwire created 179 runs. How many is that per game? Well, there are 27 outs in a game; and approximately 25.5 outs per game on which a batter receives one at-bat. (The other 1.5 outs are outs on bases, like caught stealing or the back end of a double play.) McGwire made 357 outs at bat (509 AB − 152 H). And so, that's exactly 14 games (357 divided by 25.5). McGwire created 179 runs in 14 games, which is 12.8 runs per game.

In formula form, this is:

$$RC/G = \frac{RC}{(AB - H)\ /\ 25.5}$$

If we took nine McGwires, and had them play baseball against an average team, we'd expect them to score an average 12.8 runs per game. The pitchers that faced him would give up 12.8 runs per game; factoring in maybe one unearned run per game, their ERAs would be in the 11.80 range. Running the same calculation for Sosa's 1998 yields 9.0 runs per game. If the McGwires played the Sosas, a typical score would be 13 to 9.

Again, keep in mind that a player with more RC/G isn't necessarily "better" or "more valuable" than a player with a lower RC/G. A September call-up who goes 4-for-10 may have a very high RC/G, but that should be taken with the same grain of salt with which you evaluate his .400 batting average.

Still, RC/G is one of the most informative ways to summarize a player's rate of offensive productivity, and with this edition of *Total Baseball*, we have included it in the Player Register for the first time.

OPS

It was 1982 when you could first read about Runs Created on your bookstore shelf; Batting Runs followed in 1984. Twenty years later, they are still largely ignored by the baseball mainstream.

But one sabermetric statistic has started to make some impact over the last few years—OPS, which stands for "on-base plus slugging," and which, like Linear Weights, is a Palmer creation. It's just the sum of a player's on-base percentage plus his slugging percentage:

$$OPS = OBP + SLG$$

While it's not the most accurate way to evaluate an offense—Runs Created per game, for instance, is more precise—OPS does have the virtue of being easy to compute and explain. It's probably for that reason that it's the first sabermetrically accepted offensive stat to penetrate the gates of baseball officialdom. The official Major League Baseball website, for instance, includes OPS in its player batting stats, and many other stats sources do, too.

For sabermetricians, OPS is an easy, quick-and-dirty way to roughly evaluate an offense without resorting to a calculator. But when accuracy is important, the other statistics will take precedence. Not only are they more accurate, but the results they provide are denominated in runs, which makes them meaningful and testable. OPS just provides a number.

If OPS doesn't give us a number of runs, how can we say that it "works" in any sense? Well, OPS's advantage is that it correlates with run scoring and RC/G very well. If one player has a higher OPS than another, he'll probably have a higher RC/G as well. Of course, that's also true for many other statistics, but to a much lesser extent. It's easy to find players with 10 home runs who have more RC/G than a player with 30 home runs—but it's very difficult to find a player with an OPS of .700 who has more RC/G than a player with an OPS of .800.

Batting Statistics: Accuracy

As we have noted, the crucial thing about a statistic is that it works—that it accurately estimates or measures what it claims to estimate or measure. If we're going to accept Batting Runs, or Runs Created, or OPS, we are entitled—even required—to demand evidence that it works.

One way to verify the accuracy of offensive statistics is to test them on teams. For teams, we know their exact offensive statistics, and how many runs they scored; and so we can compare the predictions to the actual results.

For each National League team, let's compare the actual runs to the estimates. In the table below, the "BR + League Avg" column is

batting runs plus the league-average 746 runs scored that season— Linear Weights' prediction of actual runs scored. The "Dif" column is the number of runs by which the estimate exceeded or fell short of the "real" value.

Team	Actual Runs	Raw BR	BR+Lg. AVG	Dif	RC	RC Dif	OPS
Atlanta	907	152	899	–8	934	27	.824
St. Louis	876	120	867	–9	889	13	.804
Colorado	853	80	827	–26	837	–16	.790
Houston	805	36	782	–23	793	–12	.767
Philadelphia	791	38	784	7	788	–3	.762
San Francisco	755	26	772	17	779	24	.763
Pittsburgh	753	23	770	17	776	23	.758
Florida	751	10	756	5	759	8	.754
Chicago Cubs	724	–26	720	–4	735	11	.739
Arizona	717	–8	738	19	760	43	.746
Milwaukee	714	–1	745	29	751	37	.748
Montreal	711	–40	706	–5	705	–6	.727
Cincinnati	694	–77	670	–24	676	–18	.713
San Diego	678	–47	699	21	707	29	.721
NY Mets	642	–119	627	–15	619	–23	.688
Los Angeles	574	–165	581	7	595	21	.671

Batting Runs accurately predicted the top six offensive teams and the bottom five, albeit slightly out of order. It was off by roughly 30 runs in some cases, and single digits in others. Runs Created was a bit more accurate still. It predicted the top six in exact order, and bottom five with only one misplaced team. Its estimates were off by 30 runs only twice. Finally, though OPS doesn't actually estimate a number of runs, its rankings were also very close to the rankings of actual runs scored. It got the top four in order; just missed on 5th and 6th; and got the bottom five with only one miss.

It seems fair to say that all three of these statistics can be considered to do what they claim. To be accepted, any new statistic would have to show itself capable of at least this level of accuracy.

Pitching Statistics

Baseball offense and defense are both measured in runs—the object of the game is to score as many as possible, and allow the opponent to score as few as possible. The complexity of offensive statistical formulas comes, in large part, from a need to convert traditional offensive stats, such as walks and hits, into runs. But when it comes to pitching, there are already traditional statistics measured in runs—ERA and runs allowed. And so, as we will see, sabermetric pitching stats will be much simpler than their offensive counterparts.

Linear Weights Pitching Runs

ERA represents how many earned runs a pitcher allowed. The Linear Weights system tries to measure runs above average. And so, "pitching runs," the pitching statistic that forms part of Pete Palmer's trio of Linear Weights stats, is simply the number of runs by which the pitcher's ERA beats the league average:

$$\text{Pitching Runs} = \frac{IP}{9} \times (\text{League ERA} - \text{Pitcher ERA})$$

While this statistic does accurately measure the number of runs the pitcher gives up compared to the league average, the pitcher's stats are very much influenced by the defense behind him. If his fielders are better than average, saving the team, say, 10 runs, those saved runs are reflected in ERA, even though they were saved by the fielders rather than the pitcher.

To isolate the pitcher's contribution, this edition of *Total Baseball* has adjusted Pitching Runs to subtract out the effects of the fielders, as measured by Fielding Runs (described in the next

section). The formula therefore becomes:

$$\text{Pitching Runs} = \frac{IP}{9} \times (\text{League ERA} - \text{Pitcher ERA}) - \frac{\text{pitcher IP}}{\text{team IP}} (\text{Team Fielding Runs})$$

A total of +50 runs is an MVP-caliber year, the same as for batters. And, again as for batters, any positive total is above average, so even a pitcher with zero pitching runs should have no problem finding a job in the major leagues.

Component ERA

Linear Weights counts the number of runs the pitcher actually gave up. An alternative is to count the number of runs the pitcher would be *estimated* to have given up. That is, we take the composite batting line of all the batters facing that pitcher, and use Runs Created to estimate how many runs that batting line should have scored. When we estimate a pitcher's ERA that way, the result, a Bill James creation, is called *Component ERA*.

Why would we do this? Why estimate the number of runs when we have the actual number of runs right there in ERA? Because it might be a more accurate reflection of the pitcher's talent.

When a Runs Created estimate is different from the number of runs that actually score, the discrepancy comes from the timing of the hits. For instance, suppose a pitcher pitches a 10-hit complete game. Runs Created might predict that three runs will score. But if all ten hits come in the first inning, the pitcher would probably give up seven or eight runs. On the other hand, if he scatters those 10 hits about one per inning, he'll probably only give up a run or two. The Runs Created prediction remains three runs, but the actual number can vary from a shutout to a blowout, depending on the extent to which the hits are bunched together.

So, if the timing of hits is a characteristic of the pitcher, ERA will be a more accurate indication of a pitcher's ability. But if it's not—if hit timing is essentially random—then the Runs Created estimate will be better, since it takes the luck out of the equation.

The evidence shows that, indeed, hit timing is essentially a matter of luck. You could refer to favorable hit timing as "clutch pitching," since a pitcher who scatters his hits allowed is essentially pitching better with runners on base, when it's more important. And since a large body of research suggests that clutch hitting is not an actual skill (see "Clutch Hitting," later), it's not surprising to find that clutch pitching isn't, either.

The full formula appears in the Glossary, but the basic idea is:

$$\text{Component ERA} = \text{Estimated Runs Created} \times \frac{9}{IP} - .56$$

The .56 term in the formula is an estimate of unearned runs.

Component ERA is important because it may turn out to be a better predictor of future pitcher performance than ERA itself. Since discrepancies between actual and component ERA are largely a matter of luck, a pitcher with an ERA of 5.00 but a Component ERA of 4.50 will probably have a better season next year than a pitcher who's the other way around. Rotisserie players, take note.

Fielding Statistics

The job of a fielder is to convert batted balls into outs; how well a fielder does that is the standard by which his defense should be measured. Conventional fielding statistics, however, don't do a very good job of tracking that vital information.

Traditionally, fielders are ranked by fielding percentage—how frequently (or infrequently) they make errors. This information has

value, certainly. The fielder's job is to turn a playable ball into an out, and errors identify instances when the player failed to do that. But when an infielder fails to get to a ball in the hole, it's certainly as much a failure as when he reaches it and then bobbles the throw. Indeed, the error might be better—at least on a bobble, baserunners will advance only one base. But if the ball makes it through to the outfield, the runners might advance two bases, or even more.

The shortstop with the steadiest hands might make ten fewer errors a year than average. But a shortstop with the best range may make *fifty* more plays. Traditional fielding statistics ignore those fifty, and count only the ten. So while errors are important, they form a very small part of the fielder's performance record; which is why sabermetricians have concluded that the usual fielding stats do a poor job of separating the better fielders from the lesser ones.

Zone Rating

Why is it that we can tell good pitchers and good hitters from the statistics, but not good fielders? Because for pitching and hitting, we have a context for the statistics—the *opportunities* that the player had. We count both successes and failures. A batter with 150 hits—successes—may be a mediocre hitter or a good hitter, depending on how many opportunities he had. With 450 failures, his batting average is .250 and we can declare him about average. With only 300 failures, he's a league-leading .333 hitter.

Fielding percentage does count successes and failures, but its problem is that it considers only *one type* of failure—the one called "errors." If we were able to count the other type—the balls the player didn't get to—we'd have a much better statistic. To do that, though, we need play-by-play game data, so we could know how many balls were hit in the vicinity of the player. Some of that data came available in the early '90s, and a Philadelphia writer named Pete DeCoursey used it to create a statistic called "Defensive Average." Later, STATS, Inc., which tabulates even more detailed play-by-play data, built on DeCoursey's work, coming up with a statistic they called "Zone Rating."

STATS took a diagram of a baseball field and divided it into "zones." Certain zones were then assigned to different positions. The zone closest to third base, of course, is assigned to the third baseman. Outfielders are assigned certain zones for flyballs, and certain other zones for line drives. And some zones are assigned to nobody, on the grounds that no fielder can be expected to field a ball there.

Roughly speaking, Zone Rating is the percentage of balls hit into the zone that the fielder turned into outs. It's approximately the reverse of batting average. If batters hit .150 on balls hit to shortstop Rich Aurilia, he would have a zone rating of .850.

There are two special cases. First, a fielded ball that's turned into a double play counts as two outs (but only one opportunity); and, second, if a fielder gets to a ball outside his zone, it nonetheless counts as if it were in his zone. Here's the full formula:

$$\text{Zone Rating} = \frac{\text{Number Of Balls Turned Into Outs} + \text{Balls Turned Into Double Plays}}{\text{Balls In Zone} + \text{Balls Outside Zone That Were Turned Into Outs}}$$

Since Zone Rating counts exactly what it's supposed to, it has the potential to be a very reliable fielding stat. However, the accuracy of the stat depends on the reliability of those collecting the data. Are they accurately recording where the batted balls were hit? Are they consistent in how they distinguish a flyball from a line drive? And are the zones assigned to the fielders realistic? If the answers to all three questions are "yes," Zone Rating could be the

ideal defensive stat. Its drawback is that it can't be calculated based on publicly available data.

Here are the best and worst for each position in 2003 (full-time players):

Position	Best	Worst
SP	1.000, Many	.867, Randy Wolf
C	1.000, Many	.500, Greg Myers
1B	.900, Doug Mientkiewicz	.792, Paul Konerko
2B	.889, Mark Ellis	.763, Roberto Alomar
3B	.810, Chris Stynes	.697, Eric Hinske
SS	.896, David Eckstein	.791, Derek Jeter
LF	.915, Garret Anderson	.789, Manny Ramirez
CF	.927, Carlos Beltran	.834, Preston Wilson
RF	.918, Juan Encarnacion	.802, Larry Walker

You'll note that the standards for Zone Rating vary with position; .800 is excellent for a third baseman but poor for a shortstop. If you use Zone Rating to compare players, be sure they play the same position.

Defensive Efficiency Record

To compute Zone Rating, we need to know the number of balls hit in a fielder's zone. But what if we consider the entire field to be one big zone? Since we *do* know the number of balls hit in the field—it's just the number of balls in play—we can get a zone rating for the team as a whole.

This statistic—invented by Bill James many years before Zone Rating—is called "Defensive Efficiency Record," or DER. It's just the percentage of balls in play turned into outs:

$$\text{DER} = \frac{\text{Plays Made}}{\text{Plays Made} + \text{Plays Not Made}}$$

DERs range around .695. A mark of .720 is exceptional, and .680 is poor.

Obviously, pitchers on a team with a high DER will appear better than they are, as sinking line drives and grounders deep in the hole are turned into outs. The reverse is true for low-DER teams, as balls fall in for hits that would otherwise be caught.

Range Factor

We are able to calculate Zone Rating for players only if we have both the number of plays made and the number of opportunities. We can't retroactively calculate the Zone Rating of, say, Phil Rizzuto in 1948, because STATS, Inc. wasn't around then, and so we don't know how many balls were hit into his zone. But let's make a simplifying assumption: that over the course of the season, the number of opportunities evens out, and every shortstop will have roughly the same number of balls hit to him.

In that case, we can just count the number of plays a fielder makes per game. That statistic, originated in the 1870s by Al Wright but reintroduced by James, is called "range factor."

$$\text{Range Factor} = \frac{\text{Putouts} + \text{Assists}}{\text{Games}}$$

It's a simple statistic, but it does roughly work. Players with great range like Brooks Robinson and Ozzie Smith do score a high Range Factor, and players with a reputation for fielding mediocrity score low. Range Factor correlates reasonably well with Zone Rating: there are exceptions, but generally the same players consistently score high on both.

Range Factor does have its problems, though. One is the assumption that all players at a position will have roughly the same

number of opportunities. This is not correct, especially for the corner infielders; third basemen, for instance, will have fewer balls hit to them on a team with lots of right-handed pitching. That's because their opponents will load up on left-handed batters, who tend to hit more balls to the right side of the diamond.

More significantly, the "games" column of a fielder's statistical line isn't necessarily an accurate indication of how much he played. A starting shortstop may play 160 games and 1,280 innings—eight innings per game—while his late-inning defensive replacement might have 40 "games" but 160 innings—four innings per game. In that case, even if the regular is no better than the replacement, his range factor will be twice as high. For that reason, the statistic is best not used on utility players. But even starters might differ from each other in innings played per game, so use Range Factor with caution. For the modern era, where a player's defensive innings played is available, the problem is eliminated by computing games as innings played over nine. But then you still can't compare Phil Rizzuto to Alex Rodriguez.

Standards for Range Factor vary by position, since positions vary in how many balls are hit to that part of the field. It is meaningless to compare an outfielder's raw range factor to a shortstop's.

Fielding Runs

Fielding Runs is the third member of the Linear Weights trio (joining Batting Runs and Pitching Runs). It takes a fielder's range, compares it to the rest of the league, and expresses the difference as the number of runs the player saves (or costs) his team compared to the league average.

The formula varies by position. For second base, shortstop and third base, the calculation works like this:

For every assist the player had above average, score .4 fielding runs;
For every putout or double play the player had above average, score .2 fielding runs;
For every error the player had fewer than average, score .2 fielding runs.

Note that assists are worth double; according to Palmer, that's because "more fielding skill is generally required to get one than to record a putout." And, of course, if the player is worse than average, he scores negative runs.

Both the player's stats and league average are adjusted for the number of strikeouts that occurred while the player was in the field. That's obviously because strikeouts reduce the number of fielding opportunities available.

That is how the number was produced that appeared in previous editions of *Total Baseball*. However, for this edition, we have improved the accuracy of Fielding Runs by making several adjustments to the formula. These adjustments are based on Bill James' groundbreaking work on fielding in his 2002 book *Win Shares* (of which more soon). The adjustments are:

● *Innings Played:* The number of defensive innings for each player is known for recent years, but must be estimated for the rest of baseball history. Previously, innings were estimated by using the player's plate appearances. Now, they are estimated using James' new procedure that uses the player's fielding stats instead of plate appearances. We describe that procedure in more detail in the Glossary.
● *Team Defense:* The worse the team's defense, the more plays each player will have the opportunity to make. That's because every ball the left fielder can't get to is an out not made; every out not made means another batter will reach the plate that

otherwise wouldn't. More batters means more balls to field. A shortstop who plays 5 percent of the league's innings might (for instance) play 5.1 percent of the league's balls in play if he plays on a poor-fielding team, or 4.9 percent of the league's balls in play on a good fielding team. And so, instead of using innings played (outs minus strikeouts), we use *balls in play* (at-bats minus strikeouts) as the basis of a player's expectation. Thus, players whose teammates are better or worse than average are no longer under- or over-rated.
● *Groundball/Flyball Staffs:* If a team has a predominantly groundball staff, the infielders will have more opportunities to make plays; the reverse is true on a flyball staff. And so, we adjust each fielder's expected plays based on the proportion of groundballs given up by the pitchers on his team. Since we don't know that number explicitly—it's available only through play-by-play data, which is unavailable for most of major league history—we have to estimate it.

The estimate, as devised by James, is based on assists. The more groundballs a team fields, the more assists its fielders will record. And so if a team makes more assists than the league average, we assume more groundballs than average, and adjust both infielders' and outfielders' fielding runs accordingly. In effect, we are now comparing a player to the league average in *plays made per estimated groundball* for infielders, and *plays made per estimated flyball* for outfielders.

Full explanations of the Fielding Runs formulas are in the Glossary.

Overall Statistics

This edition of *Total Baseball* presents two statistics that combine players' contributions in hitting, pitching, and fielding, in an attempt to measure total performance. These are "Total Player Wins" and "Win Shares."

Total Player Wins

Total Player Wins, or TPW, is an estimate of the number of wins, positive or negative, that a player contributed to his team as compared to an average player—whether those wins were contributed by hitting, pitching, or fielding. We start by adjusting batting runs for the player's position. It's easy to find a first baseman who's 20 batting runs above average, but much harder to find a +20 shortstop. The skills required for certain positions limit the pool of players who can play adequate defense, and so the available hitting talent pool is smaller for some positions than for others. What we do, then, is adjust the player's batting runs so that instead of reflecting runs above (or below) average for all players in the *league*, they represent the number of runs above average *for that position*.

We take the position-adjusted batting runs figure and add the other two Linear Weights measures—Fielding Runs and Pitching Runs. The result is the number of runs, positive or negative, that a player contributed above or below a hypothetical average player at his position. We then convert that number to wins. Roughly speaking, each ten runs makes a difference of one win, although the exact number changes from year to year (see "Runs Per Win," below). A player with a total of +50 runs, then, would receive about +5 wins—or a TPW of +5.

$$TPW = \frac{\text{Batting Runs Adjusted For Position} + \text{Pitching Runs} + \text{Fielding Runs}}{\text{Runs Per Win}}$$

Readers of previous editions of *Total Baseball* will notice that this is the same statistic, invented by Palmer, that has been called

"Total Baseball Ranking"; and it's also similar to the former "Total Player Rating." The change stems from the idea that TPW, strictly speaking, is not actually a "rating" or a "ranking," but an empirical measure of the number of wins the player contributed.

In theory, adding every player's TPW for a team should give us roughly the number of games above .500 the team won. In the "Annual Record" section of this book, the differential between TPW and actual wins is shown in the "DIF" column.

Win Shares

As we just saw, TPW attempts to isolate each individual player's contribution to team victory. So does Win Shares. But Win Shares does it in reverse.

TPW starts from the players' records, and tries to measure the theoretical contribution in wins. Win Shares does the opposite. Win Shares starts with the team's wins, and works backwards, figuring out a way to apportion those wins among the team's players. Figuring Win Shares for a player absolutely requires that you know how many games his team won; and it also requires that you have the complete stats of all his teammates. Win Shares does not and cannot work in isolation.

TPW answers the question, "how many wins would player X contribute to an average team?" Win Shares answers the question, "how many of his teams actual wins should we apportion to player X?"

The details of the method by which wins are apportioned to players are very complex and intricate. As Bill James, who introduced Win Shares in his 2002 book of that name, wrote:

> *In its execution, the Win Shares method is almost incomprehensively complicated. ... We decided, in making Win Shares, to worry about everything; we decided that there was no factor too small that it wasn't worrying about.*

While the particulars are complicated, the general idea is easy to grasp. James starts by dividing the team's wins into two: offensive and defensive. A team with great hitting and bad pitching might see most of its wins allocated to hitters; and vice-versa. Then, the defensive wins are allocated between pitchers and fielders. Finally, the three stacks of wins—batting, pitching and fielding—are apportioned among the individual players.

What comes out at the end is a number of Win Shares that is three times the number of wins the player contributed. Honus Wagner's 1908 is the highest single season mark of the 20th century; Wagner had 59 win shares, which means he is personally credited with 19 and two-thirds of the Pirates' 98 wins.

While TPW is denominated in "wins above average," Win Shares is denominated in actual wins (or, thirds of actual wins). The players on an 81-81 team *should* have a TPW of something near zero; but they *must* have 243 Win Shares among them.

Despite the fact that individual Win Shares are limited by the performance of the team, similar players will have similar Win Shares even if they labor for teams of wildly differing ability. The 1972 Phillies won only 59 games, which means they have just 177 Win Shares to divide among the players. Even so, Steve Carlton, who went 27-10 for that miserable team, led both leagues that year with 40 Win Shares.

In addition to the method itself, there is also great value in some of the issues James had to research to get the formulas to work. His revolutionary treatment of fielding statistics forms the basis of changes we have made to Fielding Runs, as well as his method for estimating defensive innings for part-time players. In the long run, *Win Shares* will be remembered not just for the new statistic itself, but for the new knowledge revealed in those side issues. We are pleased to be able to include Win Shares in the Player and Pitcher Registers of this edition of *Total Baseball*.

What Sabermetrics Has Taught Us About Baseball

Numbers and formulas are all very well and good—but many of the most interesting questions about baseball don't explicitly involve numbers. Do some catchers handle pitchers better than others? Why is there a home-field advantage? Which hitters are good in the clutch? Every serious baseball fan has wondered about these things. And the statistical record of baseball, combined with some of the new statistics that accurately measure performance, can shed light on these issues.

What are A-Rod's chances of getting to 3,000 hits? Which kinds of players are the best draft choices? Who should bat cleanup and who should bat leadoff? Here's what sabermetrics has to say about some of these questions.

Catcher ERA

The statistical record of baseball tells us certain things about a catcher's defensive performance. We know how good an arm he has by his record throwing out basestealers. And we can estimate his fielding by his adjusted range, or by his zone rating. But what we don't know is how well he handles the pitchers, how adeptly he calls the game, or how effectively he frames pitches in the strike zone.

The reason we don't know this is because there aren't any objective statistics that count it. We might see, during a game, that Ivan Rodriguez placed his glove in exactly the right position to fool the umpire into calling a strike on that outside pitch. But that's a subjective judgment—can you count how many times that happens with any degree of accuracy?

And perhaps we see Mike Piazza head to the mound to talk to his struggling starter, who immediately starts throwing strikes and gets out of the inning. How do we know how much of that credit actually belongs to Piazza? Perhaps the pitcher was just lucky, or he was able to adjust his delivery independent of Piazza's advice.

In a celebrated 1989 study, Craig Wright investigated whether he could look at ERA to nail down the catcher's contribution. He looked at situations where two different catchers caught the same pitchers. If one catcher was better at game-calling than the other, the pitchers should have had a better ERA with that catcher—in other words, his "Catcher ERA" should be lower.

Wright cited a few examples. Between 1977 and 1982, Rangers' catcher Jim Sundberg had a catcher ERA worse than that of his backups by about 20 points a year. In 1983, as Wright watched, Sundberg embarked on a plan, with coach Glen Ezell, to work on his handling of pitchers. From 1983 to 1988, his aggregate Catcher ERA improved by about 30 points.

And Wright told about the best pitcher-handler of all: the legendary (to sabermetricians, anyway) Doug Gwosdz. Appearing in only 69 career major league games, all for the San Diego Padres, Gwosdz had a Catcher ERA an astounding 1.20 runs better than expected. Gwosdz started only 23 games behind the plate in his career; in those 23 games, the San Diego starters went 16-3, with six shutouts and a 2.05 ERA.

Wright's observations put forth a strong argument that a

catcher's game-calling skills can save his team a lot of runs. That hypothesis won some confirmation from a later study by Tom Hanrahan, whose results showed that experienced catchers have better Catcher ERAs than young catchers, supporting the idea that pitch-calling is a skill that can be learned.

But in 2000, a more comprehensive analysis of the issue appeared. Keith Woolner's study plotted the distribution of Catcher ERA over a large group of catchers. The distribution was virtually identical to the chance distribution that would theoretically arise if there were no differences among the catchers. This was an unexpected result. Can catchers really be so similar in pitch-handling skills that it doesn't matter who's behind the plate? It seems implausible, and, given the conflict between the results of the various studies, we look to future research to cast more light on this question.

Clutch Hitting

Do certain players have the ability to hit better in the clutch? With the pressure on, in the late innings and the game on the line, are some players able to lift their game to a higher level, so that their performance under pressure is better than usual?

The 1985 *Elias Baseball Analyst* reported that the previous year, Bill Buckner was the major leagues' leading clutch hitter, batting .403 in "pressure" situations but only .272 overall, a difference of 131 points. (The Elias definition of a pressure situation is an at-bat in the seventh inning or later, with the score tied or the batting team down by one, two, or three runs—four runs if the bases are loaded. Various studies use different definitions, but they all preserve our intuitive notion of "clutchness.") Was Buckner's 131-point increase in performance due to random luck, or did it show a real ability on his part to concentrate when the game was on the line?

The hypothesis is fairly hard to test, because "clutch" at-bats come in such small numbers. Only 10 percent of a player's at-bats might qualify as clutch, and in only 60 at-bats performance variation may be inherent in the sample size. Just as an average player might hit .350 on Tuesdays by plain dumb luck, he might hit .350 in the clutch for the same reason. So various statistical tests were needed.

In 1977, Dick Cramer, one of sabermetrics' enduring practitioners, noted that if clutch hitting were truly a skill, clutch players this year would tend to be clutch players next year. So Cramer compared players' clutch performance in 1969 to their performance in 1970. There was no correlation, and Cramer concluded that the evidence indicated clutch hitting is random luck.

In 1989, Palmer approached the problem a different way. Palmer observed that even if clutch-hitting skill didn't exist—that is, if batters hit the same in the clutch as in pressure-free situations—you would still expect some batters to have good clutch stats, just as a fair coin will occasionally land heads 8 times out of 10. But the range of clutch stats can then be predicted statistically—a normal curve with a certain average and a certain spread. On the other hand, if clutch hitting were real, the distribution would be a different normal curve, with a much wider spread.

So he plotted the clutch stats of 330 players over the period 1979 to 1989. The result was expressed by the curve that would be expected if there were no clutch ability. Of 330 players, one player would be expected to exceed three standard deviations from the mean (about a 50- to 60-point difference between clutch and nonclutch batting average). And exactly one did (Tim Raines, who hit 56 points better in the clutch). Outside 2 SDs, or 40-50 points, there should have been 5 percent, or 16 players; there were 14— almost an exact correspondence with the "random chance" model.

Other studies since have repeatedly confirmed Cramer and Palmer, in finding no evidence for clutch hitting as a skill. That conclusion remains the strong sabermetric consensus today.

The Favorite Toy

The Favorite Toy is a formula that attempts to answer the question, "what is this player's chance of reaching 3,000 hits (or any other difficult career goal)?" Another Bill James creation that's been around since the early 1980s, it's called a "toy" instead of a "principle" because Bill didn't test it too seriously. Also, Bill wrote that it works only for an exceptional player pursuing a difficult goal, and it remains a bit fuzzy deciding who and what qualify.

Having said that, a recent study by Shane Holmes shows that the Toy does, in fact, work pretty well. Holmes found every player who ever made it halfway to 3,000 hits. He then figured the Toy's estimate of the player's chance of making it the rest of the way, and checked whether the player was eventually successful. He found the probabilities pretty much matched the actual proportions. The Toy predicted that of the 506 players who reached 1,500 hits, 30 of them would eventually reach 3,000. The actual count was 25— with active players likely to provide about five more.

The calculation is easier to understand if presented in three steps. First, calculate the player's established hits per season:

$$\text{Established Hits} = \frac{1}{2}\,\text{Last Year's Hits} + \frac{1}{3}\,\text{Two Years Ago Hits} + \frac{1}{6}\,\text{Three Years Ago Hits}$$

Second, use his age to estimate how many years he's got left to play:

$$\text{Years Remaining} = 24 - .6\,(\text{age})$$

Finally, use those two results to calculate the player's chance:

$$\text{Chance} = \frac{\text{Established Hits x Years Remaining}}{\text{Hits Needed To Reach Goal}} - 0.5$$

Of course, if you're predicting 500 home runs instead of 3,000 hits, just substitute "home runs" for "hits."

(Technical notes for readers who want to try this at home: If Years Remaining is less than 1.5, use 1.5; a chance of less than zero should be considered zero; the chance cannot be higher than .97 to the power of years remaining; and if the player is below average, the chance cannot be higher than .75 to the power of years remaining.)

Outfielder Arms

In the previous section, we emphasized that a fielder's job is to turn balls into outs, and the sabermetric fielding statistics concentrate on that skill. But for outfielders, there's a secondary skill that can help the team—a strong and accurate arm. An outfielder skilled in this respect can keep runners from advancing, or throw runners out who are trying to advance on a base hit or flyball.

Both traditional and sabermetric fielding stats give at least a bit of credit for outfielder assists (or "baserunner kills," as Bill James calls them). But an outfielder's arm can save runs by reputation alone, if fear of being put out keeps a runner from trying to take the extra base. And that factor isn't measured at all.

A few years ago, Clem Comly addressed that omission in his study of outfielder arms. Suppose that there's one out with a runner on first base, and the batter hits a single. Employing the base/out chart (Table 1, previous section), he observed that if the runner holds at second base, the runners on first and second (with one out) would be worth .888 runs. But if the runner takes third, the

situation is worth 1.088 runs. If the outfielder's arm can hold the runner to second, he's saved the team the difference between those two values, or exactly .2 runs.

Of course, we don't know if the runner held up because of the outfielder's skill—maybe the hit was so shallow that the runner wouldn't even beat a three-hopper to third base. But over a long period of time, we should see outfielders with strong arms limiting baserunner advancement much more than outfielders with weak arms. That is, over a hundred opportunities, the average outfielder might save those .2 runs 50 times. If Harry Limpnoodle saved those runs only 30 times, but Joe Howitzer held the runner 70 times, we'd be able to say that Harry cost his team 4 runs (20 times .2) compared to the average, but Joe saved his team 4 runs.

And that's what Comly did. For every outfielder from 1959 to 1987, he calculated how many advancement runs above or below average his arm allowed runners to take on singles (including runners on first, runners on second, and runs saved on baserunner kills). The resulting statistic he called ARM—for "Average Run Equivalent." While his results were not park-adjusted—Carl Yastrzemski's all-time best career ARM is likely at least partly due to Fenway's unusual left-field dimensions—the results are both interesting and informative.

Aside from Yaz, who has the best ARM record of all time (with 56 runs saved), the list is dominated by the usual strong-armed suspects—Valentine, Clemente, Barfield, etc. Notable, however, is the unexpected all-time single season leader—Juan Beniquez in 1976 (12.4 runs saved), and the 1978 Expos, who had all three of their outfielders in the all-time top 4 for their respective outfield position.

Batting Orders

There are 362,880 ways to form a batting order by arranging nine players. Which way is best? This question is one of the most asked, and most researched, of sabermetric questions. The evidence to date can be summarized in two points: (1) conventional wisdom is pretty good; and (2) it doesn't matter much anyway.

The traditional batting order appears to be roughly correct. The better hitters should be weighted towards the top of the order—specifically, men who can get on base should bat at the top, and power hitters who can drive them home should bat in the middle of the order.

If there's anything upon which conventional wisdom can be improved, it's the traditional idea that your second-place hitter should be a contact man who doesn't strike out much, the better to advance the leadoff man who (hopefully) reached base ahead of him. This theory doesn't hold up—it turns out that it's much more important for the second-place hitter to reach base than to advance the runner. The most important attribute of the top two hitters is an ability to reach base.

But even the worst batting orders aren't *that* bad. Various researchers have come to similar conclusions—that even the worst batting order is only twenty to thirty runs per season worse than the best. In the subset of batting orders that managers would consider—that is, if you leave out the obviously horrid orders where the pitcher leads off and Barry Bonds bats eighth—the differences are even smaller.

Palmer ran a simulation of a traditional batting order, which he designated "123456789." He then ran the same simulation on a second batting order, where the power hitters bat first: 345612789. The result: the traditional order proved better, but only by 0.011 runs per game: 1.6 runs per season. (The very worst order was

987216543, but even that one cost only 22.3 runs per year.)

Simulation is the easiest way to evaluate a batting order, but there is another way—using a mathematical technique involving what is called a "Markov Chain." A sabermetrician named Mark Pankin has authored numerous studies using Markov chains. In one such study, he looked at actual 1990 lineups for each major league team, and figured out the difference between that batting order and the best order his model could find. The typical result: the best order beat the manager by only about 7 runs per season, or less than one win.

These are only two of a myriad of studies that reach roughly the same conclusion—about a win a season, tops, for any improvement on the traditional batting order. With so little on the line, batting-order selection is considered a minor issue to most sabermetricians. The consensus: managers would be better off spending their time deciding *who* to play, rather than where in the lineup to insert them.

Voros

"Major league pitchers don't appear to have the ability to prevent hits on balls in play."

This famous conclusion from Voros McCracken is one of the most discussed and most controversial sabermetric findings of the last decade.

Our mental image is that if you manage to get wood on the bat against Pedro Martinez, it's likely to be a slow roller to short or a pop-up to the infield. But against a AAA-caliber pitcher, you'd see lots of line drives and booming doubles into the gap.

McCracken argued that's not true. He found that, with the exception of home runs, a ball in play has roughly the same chance of becoming a hit regardless of who the pitcher was. While some pitchers will have many of their balls in play fall in for hits, and some pitchers will have fewer, the differences are due mostly to the quality of the fielders, and to random luck.

A flood of incredulity greeted Voros' original article—could it really be true that once the ball is in play, the pitcher doesn't matter? Within a year, a flurry of studies weakened Voros' hypothesis a bit. It's not true that pitchers have *no* effect—but it is true that they have *very little* effect. The pitcher does matter, these studies found, but not much.

What does "not much" mean? One study found that higher-strikeout pitchers did indeed have lower opposition batting averages on balls in play (this statistic is called "IPavg"), but that a difference of about 150 strikeouts over a season is only about 7 points in IPavg (that is, .007). Another study found that pitcher skill represented only 9 percent of the statistical year-to-year variation in IPavg. Another finding was that at most, only one-seventh of a pitcher's difference above or below average was due to the pitcher's characteristics, with the rest due to other factors (such as the defense behind him).

Also, several studies showed that knuckleball pitchers consistently outperform in IPavg. Clifford Blau checked a sample of knuckleballers with over 30,000 combined career innings, and found a group IPavg 13 points better than normal. And there does seem to be a small difference between groundball and flyball pitchers.

The largest study of specific pitchers came from Tom Tippett. He found 351 pitchers with long careers, and compared their IPavg with what would be expected if IPavg were entirely random. (This is the approach we have seen before, in testing for effects on

Catcher ERA and clutch hitting.) He found that 12 percent of pitchers were outside the 99 percent confidence interval—twelve times as many as expected. His conclusion: the ability to control IPavg is a real skill.

Here are Tippett's all-time career leaders:

Pitcher	IPavg vs Tm
Charlie Hough	−.026
Don Wilson	−.023
Andy Messersmith	−.021
Ned Garver	−.020
Tim Wakefield	−.019
Catfish Hunter	−.017
Bud Black	−.017
Oral Hildebrand	−.017
Walter Johnson	−.016
Dave Stieb	−.016

(Tippett used IPavg compared to the rest of the pitchers on his team, in order to control for park effects and the skill of the defense.)

While these results are probably statistically significant, in that they measure a real skill of the pitcher, the effect does seem quite small. The 10th best pitcher of all time is only 16 points better than average. But the 10th best *hitter* of all time is much more than 16 points above average.

These findings have substantial implications for forecasting future pitcher performance. A pitcher whose IPavg is much worse than his teammates' is likely to improve next year, and one much better is likely to fall back.

Here are the major league bests and worsts in IPavg in 2002, along with their ERAs for 2003:

Name	IPavg, 2002	ERA, 2002	ERA, 2003
Esteban Loaiza	.322	5.71	2.90
Steve Sparks	.314	5.52	4.88
Julian Tavarez	.312	5.39	3.66
Ben Sheets	.310	4.15	4.44
Brian Lawrence	.308	3.69	4.19
Average (equal weight)		4.89	4.01
Damian Moss	.220	3.42	6.21
Derek Lowe	.224	2.58	4.47
Ramon Ortiz	.232	3.88	5.20
Jamie Moyer	.238	3.32	3.27
Barry Zito	.238	2.75	3.30
Average (equal weight)		3.19	4.49

Who would have expected the top group, with an average 2002 ERA of 4.89, to outperform the bottom group, with an ERA of 3.19? But in 2003, that's exactly what happened.

Voros' finding is probably one of the most important in any forecaster's toolkit. The difference between Loaiza's .322 and an average pitcher is about 50 hits a season. That's about 35 runs, or an ERA difference of more than 1.00. If you were a major league general manager, wouldn't you want to have a list of free-agent pitchers who were likely to improve or decline by a run per game this year?

Pythagorean Projection

Bill James' Pythagorean Projection is a formula that converts a team's offense and defense to a winning percentage. It says that a team's winning percentage can be estimated by:

$$\text{Winning PCT} = \frac{\text{Runs Scored}^2}{\text{Runs Scored}^2 + \text{Runs Allowed}^2}$$

Testing has shown that the Pythagorean Projection is quite accurate—plug in a team's run scored and runs allowed, and you'll find that most teams finished with a winning percentage very close

to their estimates. Differences are caused by the timing of runs—more runs than usual scored in blowouts, for instance.

But it has also been shown that timing of runs is largely random. And so when a team's winning percentage varies from their Pythagorean estimate, the difference is usually just caused by luck, and won't tend to repeat next year. This is called the "Johnson Effect," named after Bryan Johnson, a sportswriter with the (Toronto) *Globe and Mail*, who came up with the luck hypothesis back in the '80s. The Johnson effect suggests that the Pythagorean estimate for a team is a better predictor of its subsequent success than its actual record. The 2003 Minnesota Twins won the AL Central with a record of 90-72. But Pythagoras suggests that with 805 Runs Scored and 758 Runs Allowed, they should have won only 85.6 games. We conclude that luck played a part in the Twins unexpected success, to the tune of 4.4 games.

Conversely, Pythagoras says the Mariners should have won 97.5 games, but they fell short of that by 4.5 wins. The A's, on the other hand, were projected to win 94.3, but won 95. Again, the implication is that based only on runs scored and allowed, the two teams "should have" finished in the opposite order in the standings.

In this edition of *Total Baseball*, we include an estimate of "Pythagorean Wins" in the Annual Record section.

Runs Per Win

If a batter contributes 30 runs above average to his team, how many more games will the team win? One way to figure that out is to use the Pythagorean formula. If an average team scores 750 runs and gives up 750 runs, it will play .500 ball and win 81 games. But with our +30 player, it will now score 780, while still giving up 750. That means it will play at about a .520 clip:

$$\frac{780^2}{780^2 + 750^2} = .520$$

That means it will win about 84 games—the +30 runs has led to an extra +3 wins. That's one win for every ten extra runs, which is the sabermetric rule of thumb:

$$\text{Extra Wins} = \frac{\text{Extra Runs}}{10}$$

A slightly more accurate conversion, and the one we use in our calculation of the TPW statistic, is based on Palmer's observation that the number of runs per win can be estimated by the formula:

$$\text{Runs Per Win} = 10\sqrt{\text{League Runs Per Inning}}$$

For many major league seasons, both teams combined to score an average of nine runs per game, or one run per inning. For those years, one win is created for every 10 runs. But if the league scores fewer than one run per inning (as in 1968), it takes fewer runs to create a win; and vice-versa in years where the league scores more than one run per inning. So the formula we use is:

$$\text{Extra Wins} = \frac{\text{Extra Runs}}{10\sqrt{\text{League Runs Per Inning}}}$$

Still, the simple "10 runs per win" is accurate enough for casual use.

Home Field Advantage

The home field advantage is consistent and universal. Throughout baseball history, home teams have won about 54% of their games—about a 44-37 home record in a 162-game season.

Why does this happen?

The answer is elusive, and evidence is scarce. For all the research that's been done, we have very little idea why home teams are so good. There are various theories, though, and various ways to test them.

The stress of travel makes visiting teams worse. If that were the case, we should find that the advantage disappears for the first couple of games of a home stand. After all, if both the home team and visiting teams just flew in, they should be equally affected.

The home crowd lifts the home team to a better performance. If this were true, we should find a larger home-field advantage with larger crowds. Or, we should find a larger advantage for more important games, where presumably the fans will be more eager and enthusiastic. Or, we should find that the advantage is smaller in games where the visiting team has lots of fans in the crowd—Chicago at Milwaukee, say, or Mets vs. Yankees.

The home team gains its advantage from batting last. In this case, simulations should be able to replicate a home-field advantage. We should also be able to find that the advantage is much lower if we consider only the first five innings—since the source of the advantage is late-inning strategy. And, back in the 19th century and the early part of the 20th, there were many games where the home team batted first; did the visiting team have the advantage in those games?

Familiarity with the park. Perhaps home teams play better because they know the park better. If that's the case, we should find less advantage in the first year a team plays in its new park.

Tailoring the team to the park. If Fenway park is tough on left-handed pitchers, the Red Sox will stack their rotation with righties. As a result, they should have more success at Fenway than their opponents, who won't have the stacked lineup. If that's true, we should find that parks like Fenway that have a strong tendency to favor certain types of players should feature higher home-field advantages.

Umpires. Do umpires subconsciously favor the home team? It's not that farfetched—a call in favor of the home team is cheered; one that goes against it is booed. Umpires are only human, and prefer cheers to boos. Replays show that umpires don't blow safe/out calls very often. But what about strike-zone calls? Calling a ball a strike helps the pitching team by about .15 runs (and vice-versa). Four of those a game—two for each team—will help the home team by .6 runs, which is more than enough for a .550 winning percentage. But to test this theory, we need to find some way of identifying miscalled pitches.

Physical and Psychological Benefits. Players are more comfortable in their home city; being with their families, eating their own food, having their preferred day-to-day routine. That might simply translate into better performance. If that's the case, we might find that recently traded players don't perform better at home; that players whose families live elsewhere aren't as productive at home; and that players who grew up in a different city might play better there.

So we have seven different theories, and the potential to uncover evidence for or against any of the seven. What do we know so far?

In *The Diamond Appraised*, Craig Wright addresses the "crowd" theory. He found that even when teams saw a dramatic increase in their attendance, their home-field advantage stayed roughly the same. He checked the "new park" theory, and found that the advantage stayed roughly constant in the new park. And he demonstrated that the "batting last" effect is minimal at best. And a later academic study found no evidence that travel days influence the road team's performance, casting some doubt on the "stress of travel" theory.

On the other hand, an academic study by Richard Pollard did find a small "new park" effect—home teams went from .547 to .537 after moving to a new park in the same city. The numbers were based on only seven teams. But when combined with a similar effect in hockey and basketball, the result attained statistical significance. Still, that study is only barely statistically significant, and does contradict Wright's research.

As Charlie Pavitt, who reviewed both those studies, put it, "the moral of the story seems to be that … we still have no good idea what causes home field advantage." It is one of the largest unresolved issues in sabermetric research.

Minor League Statistics

In 1985, Bill James called this "the most important research that I have ever done." Three years later, he called it the most important sabermetric discovery ever.

What is it? Simply the finding that a hitter's minor league statistics can be made meaningful in predicting future performance—as meaningful as major league statistics.

It's hard to believe now, but managers once mistrusted minor league statistics. Wrote James in his 1985 *Baseball Abstract:* "That minor league statistics are not valid as an indicator of major league hitting ability is a belief which is virtually universally accepted both by American sportswriters and professional baseball men."

James proceeded to demolish this belief. He found that the higher quality of play makes runs in the majors 18 percent harder to come by than in AAA or AA ball. So to get a batting line that's just as reliable an indicator of the player's ability as a major league line, you take a hitter's minor league stats and (a) adjust them for the level of offense in the minor league park; (b) adjust them in a certain way that reflects an 18 percent reduction; and (c) adjust them for the major league park to which the player will be moving. The adjusted batting line is called an "MLE," for "major league equivalent."

To take one of James' examples: Although Greg Brock hit .310 with 44 home runs in Albuquerque in 1982, he hit only .224 with 20 homers for the Dodgers one year later. But, as James showed, offense in Albuquerque, a hitter's park in a hitter's league, is 40 percent higher than in Los Angeles. Compound that with the standard 18 percent reduction, and Brock's .310/44 turns into an MLE of .247/24: a very close match for his actual 1983 performance.

Revolutionary at the time, the MLE method has now become mainstream. The better baseball annuals routinely include MLEs for hundreds of prospects. The concept has proven so useful that the Oakland A's, under Billy Beane and Paul Depodesta, produced a similar (unpublished) method for college players.

These days, MLEs form the basis of thousands of Fantasy Baseball decisions … and, we would hope, major league front-office decisions too.

Drafting

There's a scene in *Moneyball* from the 2001 draft. It's the first round, and the A's GM Billy Beane has watched as their best picks are snapped up by other teams. The A's haven't expected this, and their plan is in a bit of disarray. With their next pick, head scout Grady Fuson impulsively takes pitcher Jeremy Bonderman, at that time a high-schooler out of Washington State.

Then, Michael Lewis writes, "Billy, in a single motion, erupted from his chair, grabbed it, and hurled it right through the wall."

Why? Because to Beane, the A's had just wasted a first-round draft choice. Beane knew what his head of scouting did not: that both pitchers and high-school draft choices, on average, prove to be much less valuable than position-player and college picks.

We know that because of a monumental study from Bill James. In 36 pages, sent to a small newsletter readership in 1984, James analyzed every top-50 draft pick since 1965. He found that when you take draft position into account, high-school players were generally mediocre picks. Comparing high-school choices to college choices *taken with roughly the same pick*, he found that the college choices returned 84 percent more value—a huge, huge difference.

As for pitchers, Bill found that they produced 18 percent less value than expected, which doesn't sound too bad. But that value was mainly bulk, concentrated in unexceptional workaday pitchers. As of the year of James' study, only one pitcher drafted in the top 50 had won a Cy Young award (Vida Blue). Pitchers, James wrote, were unpredictable; pitchers drafted 41-50 still are some 60 percent as valuable as pitchers drafted 1-10. But batters drafted 41-50 have only about 20 percent as much value as their top-ten counterparts. So not only did Grady Fuson squander a first-round pick on a high-school player—he lowered his odds even further by selecting a pitcher.

The results of James' study do *not* necessarily mean that pitchers don't develop as well as hitters, or college players are better players. Rather, it could just be (and probably is) that these classes of players are simply overestimated because they're hard to project. Scouts might be impressed by, say, a hard throwing high-schooler—and it might just be that for a 17-year-old, there's more time for something to go wrong with his development, or for him to get injured. Also, pitchers' performances are harder to project into the future, even at the major league level—their performance fluctuates much more than batters'. If scouts don't take these considerations into account, they'll pay a higher price for these types of players than the investment returns indicate.

Or, look at it this way—if you're in a fantasy league that uses a draft, are you going to pick Johnny Damon in the first round? Of course not—Damon is a fine player, but the first round is for the likes of Barry Bonds and Pedro Martinez. If you waste a first round pick on Johnny Damon, you're going to lose. And if you use a first round pick on a high-school pitcher, you're probably going to lose too. You might get lucky, of course, but the odds are against you. You should be grabbing a fine college hitter now, and saving the high-school pitcher for the later rounds.

By the way, Beane might also have known that his team was perhaps taking a third, regional whammy—historically, draft picks from the Pacific Northwest had produced a third less value than expected. The South was even worse, at 38 percent below average. The North, on the other hand, was better than expected, by 21 percent. Why do the regions vary? Probably just overscouting. As James wrote, "the scouts spend a lot of time in the South because it gets warm down there while the North is still freezing … they see more of the players [there], see the ones they like more often, and wind up falling in love with them."

And so Beane and his scouts now know that to get the odds in their favor (and reduce the number of chair-shaped holes in their walls), they should choose college players over high-school players; choose position players over pitchers; and choose players from the underscouted North.

Having said all that, what was true in 1984 may be true no longer. What James discovered were not rules of nature, but rules of human nature. Players from the North aren't really better than players from the South—it's just that fewer scouts knew about them, so they could be had with lower picks. Now that James' study has been public for twenty years, that might no longer be true. Just as undervalued stocks jump in value when suddenly discovered by the financial gurus, it could be that northern players, or college players, or position players started getting more attention, and perhaps they are now fully valued.

James' original study covered the first 20 drafts. It is now 20 drafts since then, and time for another study to tell us if the findings still hold.

Sacrifices and Steals

Is the sacrifice bunt a good play? One way to answer that question is to look at how many runs score with the bunt, versus how many runs will score without it. Let's take the situation with the runner on first and none out. Before the bunt, that situation is worth .783 runs, as we have seen. After a successful bunt, there's a runner on second with one out, which is worth .699 runs. So, from the standpoint of runs scoring, the sacrifice looks like a bad play: it costs .084 of a run. And this makes sense; if the sac bunt generated runs, managers would do it all the time, not just in critical situations.

But consider the bottom of the 9th with the score tied. In that situation, we don't care that, on average, fewer runs score after the bunt, so long as the winning run has a better chance of scoring. That is, we're willing to accept a smaller chance of the second, third, and fourth runs, in return for a greater chance of the one run.

In a 1999 study, Tom Ruane analyzed play-by-play data to find the chance of scoring at least one run in the inning in the different base-out situations. Here's his chart:

Men On FST	Number of Outs		
	0	1	2
---	.261	.148	.061
x--	.424	.267	.124
-x-	.608	.400	.216
xx-	.617	.413	.219
--x	.819	.651	.269
x-x	.843	.646	.275
-xx	.841	.667	.274
xxx	.855	.664	.316

Table 2: Probability of scoring at least one run before the end of the inning, given the current base/out situation

With a runner on first and nobody out, there's a 42.4 percent chance of scoring. With a runner on second and one out, the chance is only 40 percent. Again, it looks like the sacrifice is a bad idea, reducing the chance of winning the game by 2.4 percent.

But not necessarily. Ruane's numbers are averages, over every inning of every game played in the 1980s. There might be special, specific situations where the sacrifice actually *increases* the chance of winning. For instance, suppose the runner on second is very fast. His chance of scoring on a single is much higher than average. Rather than a 40 percent chance of scoring, the team may have, for instance, a 45 percent chance—and if that's the case, the bunt is good strategy. Still, these would be special cases, and the record seems to show that the bunt is not a good idea in most situations. Judging by how often they bunt, it seems that most modern managers, other than Gene Mauch, agree.

We can repeat the same analysis for the stolen base. As we saw, with a runner on first and nobody out, the inning is worth .783 runs. If the runner steals second, we have a runner on second with nobody out, which is worth 1.068 runs. But if the runner is caught

stealing, we have nobody on with one out, which is worth only .249 runs. So a successful steal gains the team .285 runs (the difference between 1.068 and .783). A caught stealing costs the team .534 runs (the difference between .249 and .783).

The numbers are slightly different with one out, and with a runner on third base—but the results are fairly similar. In general, it takes two stolen bases to make up for one caught stealing, and the rule of thumb is that a two-thirds success rate is necessary for the steal strategy to be worth the attempt.

Of course, this doesn't take into account the fact that the batter has a bigger hole to hit into with the first baseman holding the runner; nor does it take into account the pitcher's distraction, or the batter taking pitches to give the runner an opportunity to go. Research continues into these factors.

Again, just as for the sacrifice, in certain situations the steal might make more sense—if you're going for just the one run. Again turning to Tom Ruane's chart, we see that a successful steal increases the chance of scoring one run by .184 (from .424 to .608). The caught stealing, however, reduces the chance by .276 (from .424 to .148). The CS is now only about 50 percent worse than the SB, which means that the breakeven rate is 60 percent, rather than 66 percent—still rather high.

But, again, if the runner is particularly fast, might getting him in scoring position make the steal worth it even with a lower success rate? Tom's study says the opposite—the faster the runner, the worse the steal strategy! Why? Because there are other advantages to fast runners on first—with their speed, they reduce the number of force-outs, reduce the chance of a double play, and are more likely to take third on a subsequent single. Speed increases the value of the runner on first more than it increases the value of the same runner on second—and, therefore, the cost of a CS is higher.

Both steals and sacrifices are commonly called "one-run strategies," as they attempt to increase the probability of scoring one run, at the expense of the chance of a big inning. And sabermetric research supports the consensus that, except in the case of a very proficient base thief or an exceptional sacrifice situation, one-run strategies will cost the team runs—and wins.

Streaks

Often, when a batter is at the plate, announcers like to tell you about his recent performance. "Joe is 11 for 25 in his last six games, for a .440 average," they'll say. The implication, of course, is that Joe is on a hot streak, at the top of his game, and he's likely to keep running hot for a while.

But is that true? Is a player on a hot streak more likely to continue it? And is a player on a cold streak a weaker offensive threat because of it?

Statisticians seem to love this question—it's easily the most researched in the statistical journals, even by researchers who have never heard of sabermetrics. The consensus there, as well as in the sabermetric community, is that the evidence shows no "streakiness" effect. In general, in baseball and other sports, there is no tendency for player performance to be dependent on how "hot" or "cold" the player has been lately. Streaks, it seems, are nothing more than luck. What follows is a list of a few of the sabermetric studies on the question.

In the 1986 *Bill James Baseball Abstract*, the author quotes a study in which Steven Copley charted the performance of Astros' batters the day after they had a good game (2 hits or better), and

after they had a bad game (0-for-3 or worse). He found no difference between the two groups in their next day's performance.

A larger study in the 1987 *Elias Baseball Analyst* looked at over 100 players in the 1986 season. They found that as a group, the players hit about the same following a 5-game (good) streak as following a 5-game slump. About half of the players performed better after a streak, and about half were better after a slump. But a significantly higher number of players hit better after a 3-day slump than after a 3-day streak—and the same was true for 10-day periods. In this one study, players hit better when they were cold than when they were hot—an unexpected result.

Even if it's not a general rule that players are better after a hot streak, maybe it's nonetheless true for certain players. Perhaps some individual players exhibit a tendency to be streaky—that is, have long hot streaks followed by long cold-streaks—while other players are consistent (fewer and shorter streaks of either type). In 2000, Charlie Pavitt examined that issue. He noted, for each week of a season, whether a player was above or below average, and wrote the weeks as a string. For instance, a player with a string "AAB-BABABBABABABBAAABAB" seems very consistent—no long streaks of above-average play, and no long streaks of below-average play. On the other hand, a player with a string of "AAAABBBBB-BAABBBBBAAABBB" has several long strings of As and Bs, and can be said to have had a streaky season.

Charlie figured these strings for 11 years worth of major league data, and compared his sample of several hundred players to what would be expected by chance. Again, the actual results were nearly indistinguishable from what you'd see if the strings were generated by coin flips. The evidence suggests that players are intrinsically neither streaky nor consistent—no matter what the TV announcer implies.

The Count

"The best pitch in baseball is strike one," goes the adage. And strike one is indeed very, very important. A study by Pete Palmer, in *The Hidden Game of Baseball*, showed that after an 0-1 count, batters hit much worse than after a 1-0 count. Palmer didn't include a full batting line, but a subsequent study on my part [P.B.] did:

	AB	H	2B	3B	HR	BB	SO	AVG	SLG	OBP
0 and 1	33524	7780	1295	157	633	1627	8001	.232	.337	.268
1 and 0	31011	8279	1546	194	896	5076	4210	.267	.416	.370

After a first-pitch ball, the pitcher is more than three times as likely to walk the batter as after a first-pitch strike. He's also more likely to give up a home run, and about half as likely to strike the batter out. By combined application of the Runs Created formula and the Pythagorean Projection, my study showed that if every batter started with a 1-0 count, his team would go 98-64 for the season. But if every batter started with a strike against him, his team's record would be 52-110.

In terms of raw runs, Palmer's study showed that the first-pitch strike is worth a savings of .033 runs to the pitching team. If you average out *all* strikes, not just first pitch strikes, the average strike is worth about .082 runs. An average ball, on the other hand, costs a team .056 runs.

The average strike is worth .082 runs—but some strikes are worth more than others. It turns out that the most valuable strike is the one that turns the 3-2 count into a strikeout. That single pitch is worth almost a third of a run.

Technically speaking, the best pitch in baseball is strike three.

Chapter 59

Linear Weights

By Pete Palmer and John Thorn

In 1982 Milwaukee's Robin Yount had the year of his life, batting .331 with 29 homers, 114 RBIs and 129 runs scored; he led the American League in hits, doubles, total bases and slugging percentage, while finishing just one point behind the league leader in batting average; for the first of two times in his career, he was voted the Most Valuable Player in the American League, being named first on all but one of the 28 ballots cast by the baseball writers.

Over in the other league, Mike Schmidt of the Phillies was having an off year, batting only .280 with 35 homers and 87 RBIs; the previous year, when he had been awarded the MVP, in only 102 games played he had totaled 31 homers and 91 RBIs. He did lead the league once again in 1982 in slugging percentage, and he did win the Gold Glove at third base for the seventh straight year, yet in the MVP balloting none of the ballots listed him higher than fourth; 10 ballots were cast without listing him at all.

For Yount, 1982 was a crowning achievement; for Schmidt, a disappointment: that was the verdict reached by the baseball writers and conventional baseball statistics. Yet in terms of actual performance, as determined by the Linear Weights measure of runs contributed, Schmidt's "off year" was scarcely different from Yount's. With the bat, Yount accounted for 59 park-adjusted runs beyond what an average batter might have contributed; Schmidt, 46. Through base stealing, Yount added 2; Schmidt none. With the glove, Yount was 1 run below league average at his position, shortstop; Schmidt was 14 above average at third base. Total runs contributed: Yount 60, Schmidt 60. (Because Yount's batting so far exceeded that of other shortstops, while third base provided several heavy hitters, Yount contributed 7.6 extra wins to his Brewers; Schmidt contributed 6.1 to the Phillies.) Both men had outstanding seasons, the best in their respective leagues, and both outstripped the second-best player by about the same margin.

Viewing player (and team) performance through this sort of prism frequently produces such illuminating results. Cecil Fielder had a wonderful year in 1990, with his 51 homers, 132 RBIs, and league-leading figures in slugging average and extra-base hits. But how did he convince any writer voting for MVP that he had a better year than Rickey Henderson? In *Total Baseball,* you could look it up: Fielder contributed 3.8 extra wins to his team (wins that an average player would not), which was the fourth-best figure in the American League that year; Henderson was responsible for a whopping 7.2, the top mark in 1990.

This is the kind of analysis of player performance possible with a variety of sabermetric measures, not just the Linear Weights System. The common ingredient of most of the new, as yet unofficial, statistics is their creators' recognition of the relationship between runs and wins. These newly calculated measures are not official statistics of Major League Baseball, but they are constructed from the raw data of the official record. Some of the new measures may one day be officially embraced, as the on-base percentage

became an official stat three decades after its introduction. Because of fan interest, we include them in the Player and Pitcher Registers that follow, alongside the officially tabulated numbers.

But it is the Linear Weights method that forms *Total Baseball's* "bottom line" statistic of Total Player Wins. As we do not expect the reader to take our method on faith, a full description of the statistic and its merits is in order.

Runs and Wins

George Lindsey, in an article in *Operations Research* in 1963, was the first to assign run values to the various offensive events which lead to runs: Runs = $(.41)1B + (.82)2B + (1.06)3B + (1.42)HR$. He based these values on recorded play-by-play data and basic probability theory. Unlike Earnshaw Cook, who in the following year assigned run values on the basis of the sum of the individual scoring probabilities—that is, the *direct* run potential of the hit or walk plus those of the baserunners set in motion—Lindsey recognized that a substantial part of the run value of any non-out is that it *brings another man to the plate*. This additional batter has a one-in-three chance of reaching base and thus of bringing another man to the plate with the same chance, as do the batters to follow. The *indirect* run potential of these batters cannot be ignored.

Steve Mann's Run Productivity Average (RPA) assigned these values based on observation of some 12,000 plate appearances: RPA = $(.51)1B + (.82)2B + (1.38)3B + (2.63)HR + (.25)BB + (.15)SB - (.25)CS$, all divided by plate appearances, then plus .016. His values were denominated in terms of the number of runs and RBIs each event produced. Bill James, at about the same time, came up with a similar formula, since shunned, with values based on runs plus RBIs *minus home runs*. The drawbacks to the approaches of Mann and James were the drawbacks of the RBI and of the run scored; these statistics are peripheral to the main point, which is team runs, and they should therefore be considered philosophically inferior to the formula Lindsey proposed, despite his failure to account for walks, steals and other events.

The run values in the Linear Weights formula for identifying batters' real contributions are derived from Pete Palmer's 1978 computer simulation of all major league games played since 1901. All the data available concerning the frequencies of the various events was collected; following a test run, these were tabulated. Unmeasured quantities, such as the probability of a man going from first to third on a single vs. that of his advancing only one base, were assigned values based on play-by-play analysis of over 100 World Series contests. The goal was to get all the measured quantities very nearly equal to the league statistics; then the simulation would provide run values of each event in terms of net runs produced above average. Expressing the values in those terms would give a meaningful baseline to individual performances, because if you are told that a player contributed 87 runs you don't know what that signifies unless you know the average

level of run contribution in that year: 87 may sound like a lot, but if the norm was 80, then you know the player contributed only 7 runs beyond average.

The values obtained from the simulation are remarkably similar from one era to the next, confounding expectations that the home run would prove more valuable today than in the dead-ball era, or that the steal was once a primary offensive weapon. These values are expressed in beyond-average runs.

Run Values of Various Events, by Periods

Event	Period			
	1901-20	1921-40	1941-60	1961-77
Home Run	1.36	1.40	1.42	1.42
Triple	1.02	1.05	1.03	1.00
Double	.82	.83	.80	.77
Single	.46	.50	.47	.45
Walk/HBP	.32	.35	.35	.33
Stolen Base	.20	.22	.19	.19
Caught Stealing	−.33	−.39	−.36	−.32
Out*	−.24	−.30	−.27	−.25

*An out is considered to be a hitless at bat and its value is set so that the sum of all events times their frequency is zero, thus establishing zero as the baseline, or norm, for performance.

Just as these run values change marginally with changing conditions of play, they differ slightly up and down the batting order (a homer is not worth as much to the leadoff hitter as it is to the fifth-place batter; a walk is worth more for the man batting second than for the man batting eighth); however, these differences have been averaged out in the figures above. For evaluating runs contributed by any batter at any time, there may be no better method than Batting Runs, the Linear Weights formula derived from the computer simulation which is the basis of the table above.

The Formula

Batting Runs = (.47) 1B + (.78) 2B + (1.09) 3B + (1.40) HR + (.33) (BB + HB) + (.22) SB − (.45) CS − (.25) (AB − H)

The Linear Weights formula for batters may be long, but it calls for only addition, subtraction and multiplication and thus is as simple as the slugging average, whose incorrect weights (1, 2, 3, and 4) it revises and expands upon. Each event has a value and a frequency, just as in slugging average, yet—as in no batting statistic previously seen—outs are treated as offensive events with a run value of their own (albeit a negative one), a truth so obvious it somehow escaped notice. Just as the run potential for a team in a given half inning is boosted by a man reaching base, it is diminished by a man being retired; not only has he failed to change the situation on the bases but he has deprived his team of the services of a man further down the order who might have come up in this half inning, either with men on base and/or with scores already in.

What Batting Runs does is to take every offensive event and to treat it in terms of its impact upon the team—an average team, so that a man does not benefit in his individual record for having the good fortune to bat cleanup with the Giants or suffer for batting seventh with the Brewers. The relationship of individual performance to team play is stated poorly or not at all in conventional baseball statistics. In Batting Runs it is crystal clear: the linear progression, the sum of the various offensive events, when weighted by their accurately predicted run values, will total the runs contributed by that batter or that team beyond the league average.

The negative value of the batting out (AB−H) in the formula,

shown as −.25, is recalculated each year for each league, to a value that brings the league's composite batting line to zero batting runs. In seasons in which run scoring is high, the negative value of the out will increase, to as high as −.30 in recent times. When run scoring is low, the out value will be as low as −.22 or −.23.

Batting Runs

Just as runs are proportional to the events that form them, so are they proportional to wins and losses. This statement, a truism today, was a novelty in 1954 when, in *Life Magazine* of all places, Branch Rickey and Allan Roth first stated the correlation between run differentials and team standings. But they did not take the next step, to recognize that not only a team's standing but even its won-lost record could be predicted from the run totals.

It turns out there is a predictable relationship between batting runs and wins. The number of batting runs it takes to turn a loss into a win, Palmer wrote in the 1982 issue of the SABR annual *The National Pastime,* is "10 times the square root of the average number of runs scored per inning by both teams. Thus in normal play, when 4.5 runs per game are scored by each club, each team scores .5 runs per inning—totaling one run, the square root of which is one, times 10."

Note that when we refer to the need for approximately 10 additional runs scored (or 10 fewer allowed) to provide a team with an additional win, we do not mean that it takes 10 runs to win any given game. Obviously, in a specific game, a one-run margin is all that is required; but statistics are designed for the long haul, not the short.

So the conversion from a batter's Linear Weights runs to wins is a snap: simply divide Batting Runs by the number of runs it takes to gain an extra win in a given year. Taking the exploits of Babe Ruth in 1927, we see that through batting alone he contributed 107 runs, or 10.1 wins, since in the American League in 1927 it took 10.53 runs to produce an additional win. If every other player on the Yankees had performed at the league average, the New York record should have been 87-67 (10 wins above the league average 77-77 in the 154-game season).

Fielding Runs

When Rickey and Roth came up with their "efficiency formula" for run scoring and run prevention, the defensive half of the equation was divided into five segments, the last of which was fielding, to which they assigned a mathematical value of zero. "There is nothing on earth," Rickey declared, "anyone can do with fielding."

Since then many have tried, with mixed results, to improve upon the mere toting up of raw data—putouts, assists, errors, double plays. Our own effort, called "fielding runs," rates each player based on plays he made compared to the league average. For infielders, an extra assist is worth 0.4 runs; an extra putout or double play is worth 0.2 runs; and, similarly, one error fewer committed, compared to the league, is also worth 0.2 runs.

In 2002, Bill James revolutionized the evaluation of defense in his book "Win Shares." He developed new ways to estimate innings fielded for players for whom actual data is not available. He came up with formulas to estimate the tendency of a staff to throw groundballs, and to estimate the number of unassisted putouts at first base. And he explained that players on poor-fielding teams will have more fielding opportunities—since a play not made brings another batter to the plate, and another opportunity for the defense to field a ball.

For this edition of *Total Baseball*, the editors have enhanced Fielding Runs to take these factors into account. Fuller details on this complex subject can be found in the Glossary.

Pitching Runs

Determining the run contributions of pitchers is much easier than determining those of fielders or batters. Actual runs allowed are known, as are innings pitched. Through Pitching Runs, we seek to determine the number of beyond-average runs a pitcher saved—the number he prevented from scoring that an average pitcher would have allowed. The formula is simply:

$$\text{Pitcher's Runs} = \text{Innings Pitched} \times (\text{League ERA}/9) - \text{ER}$$

If the league ERA is 4.21 (as the National League's was in 1994) and a pitcher's ERA is also 4.21, he will by definition have held batters in check at the league average no matter how many innings he pitched. If, however, his ERA was 1.56 and he hurled 202 innings (as Greg Maddux did for the Braves in '94), he will have saved a certain number of runs that an average pitcher might have allowed in his place—according to the formula, 59.6 runs.

But that 59.6 runs includes the contributions of the fielders behind him. Starting with this edition of *Total Baseball*, the editors adjust pitching runs to reflect the contribution of the team's total fielding runs. In 1994, the Braves were worse than average in the field. Therefore, Maddux's Pitching Runs increase from 59.6 to 61.7—he actually saved 61.7 runs, but his fielders gave back 2.1 of those by not making the plays an average defense would have.

Linear Weights in Practice

Having formulas for pitching, fielding and batting (which includes baserunning, figured on the basis of a stolen base being worth .22 runs and a caught stealing −.45) we can assess the run-scoring contribution of every individual who has ever played the game, and thus the number of wins that he has contributed in a given season or over his career. The number of runs required to produce an additional win has varied over the years between 9 and 11 runs, with a very few league seasons outside those parameters.

Limited by conventional baseball statistics, one might, in 1990, have uttered something like, "The White Sox are only one pitcher away from winning the division." With Linear Weights, these kinds of statements, or rather the concerns they reflect, can be approached with some data and with some degree of objectivity. The White Sox finished 94-68 in 1990, while their Linear Weights projected them to finish at 81-81. To win next season, the Sox might reasonably need 96 wins. Could one pitcher—like Bob Welch, for whom they bid in the free-agent bazaar—make the difference? To do so, he would have to contribute about 150 Pitching Runs, a feat no pitcher has ever accomplished. In 1990, pitching for Oakland—and remember, the Linear Weights formula is divorced from considerations of batter support—Welch contributed 15 park-adjusted Pitching Runs. So presuming that he pitched as well for the White Sox as he did for the Athletics, or even slightly better, he would not be enough to "win" the flag on paper; Chicago would need help from other quarters.

Park Factor

A central issue for sabermetricians is the network of illusion created by home-park dimensions, atmospheric conditions, and visibility for batters. How many home runs would Troy Glaus hit if he played half his games in Fenway Park? Will the Boston Red Sox and Colorado Rockies keep "failing" to put together solid pitching staffs—or has their pitching been adequate all along? Why have the American League leaders in triples so often worn a Royals uniform? One's home park has a powerful effect on a player's record, elevating some good players to greatness and denying the spotlight to some outstanding performers.

If we desire to remove the silver spoon or the millstone that a home park can be, and measure individual ability alone, we must create a statistical balancer that diminishes the individual batting marks created in parks like Coors and augments those created in Oakland. Pete Palmer developed an adjustment that enabled us, for the first time, to measure a player's accomplishments apart from the influence of his home park. He looked to the single measure in which all these variables are reflected—runs. If a stadium is a "hitters' park," it stands to reason that more runs would be scored there than in a park perceived as neutral, just as a "pitchers' park" could be expected to depress scoring.

The full and lengthy explanation for the computation of the Park Factor is left to the Glossary, where hardy readers might consider taking a peek right now. For most of us, though, it will be enough to understand a simplified calculation. Suppose teams (home and road combined) score 10 percent more runs in Fenway than on the road. Since Red Sox players play only half their games at Fenway, we divide that in half, to a 5 percent increase. Compared against a league average of 1.00, we would say that Fenway has a "batter park factor" of 1.05.

Relativity

Sabermetric statistics can be marvelous tools for cross-era comparisons, enabling us to determine if baseball's history is truly a seamless web or if its seams are real enough, but are camouflaged by traditional statistics. If Batter A presented himself to you for approval with these statistics—.330 batting average, 16 home runs, 107 RBIs—what would your reaction be? You'd like to have him on your team, right? And what to make of Batter B, who presents these numbers—.257 batting average, 14 home runs, 53 RBIs? Not bad for a middle infielder with a good glove, you say, but otherwise undistinguished? In fact, the "impressive" figures of Batter A represent the average performance of a National League outfielder in 1930, while the "blah" figures of Batter B are those of the average American League outfielder of 1968: the former has more than twice the RBIs of the latter, along with a batting average 73 points higher, yet the two performed at identical levels, and an argument could be made that Batter B was superior because he played in an era with a higher level of average skill. A cross-era adjustment would show that both players were at the league average—an adjusted" statistic of 100, or 100 percent of the norm.

Why do we need relative measures? Basically, for the same reason we need statistics altogether, to compare, to interpret, and to comprehend, but in a more reasonable and accurate manner when the disparity of the data sources makes the use of absolute, unadjusted numbers illogical.

Total Player Wins

Total Player Wins (previously called "Total Baseball Ranking") is the most important statistic for evaluating player performance in *Total Baseball*. Each formula distills the detailed analysis of the different components of the game—batting, baserunning, fielding, and pitching—into a single number that describes how a particular player compares to the average major league player.

The standard chosen for this comparison is wins—the ultimate currency in the national pastime. TPW takes each player's performance into account, places that performance in the proper context of the ballpark, the league, and the way the game is being played, and then translates it into how many games he won or lost for his team. For more detail, see the discussions of how TPW is computed in the introductions to the Player Register and the Pitcher Register, respectively, as well as in the Glossary.

The translation from the various performance statistics into the wins or losses of TPW is accomplished by comparing each player to an average player at his position for that season in that league. A player who is exactly average will have 0 TPW. A mark of +5 wins or higher—enough to turn an average team into an 86-76 team—is an MVP-quality season. Players with substantial negative TPWs will soon find themselves out of a job.

Refinements to the Eighth Edition

The changes made to the Linear Weights statistics in this edition of *Total Baseball* are the most substantial yet. We outline those changes here; full details can be found in the Glossary.

The Batting Runs figures, as calculated for each player, are now measured against the league average hitter; in previous editions, they were measured against the league average, but omitting pitchers. This change ensures that the player figures sum to the team total, and that the league correctly sums to zero.

The Batting Runs weighting for a caught stealing has changed to –0.45 (from the previous figure of –0.35). Analysis has shown that this is a more accurate figure.

Batting Runs now include the contribution of the player's stolen bases and caught stealing. Previously, the SB/CS values were in a separate statistic, "Stolen Base Runs." They are now rolled into Batting Runs, as per Palmer's standard Linear Weights formula (and for easier comparison to statistics like Runs Created and RC/G, which have always included baserunning). We do, however, list leaders in Stolen Base Runs in the Annual Record and All-Time Leaders sections of the book.

The basic Fielding Runs formula remains the same, based on the differences between the player's record and his expected record. However, we have added several adjustments to the calculation for that expected record—including, for instance, adjustments for a groundball staff, or poor-fielding teammates. Also, we have adjusted first basemen's assists to account for estimated unassisted putouts, and we no longer adjust the catcher's Fielding Runs for the proficiency of the pitching staff.

As noted, we have changed the name of the statistic "Total Baseball Ranking" to "Total Player Wins" (TPW). Both the Player and Pitcher Registers now display each player's total of this statistic. For both pitchers and hitters, TPW is based on the sum of a player's batting (which includes SB/CS), pitching, and fielding. Previously, we used the similar "Total Player Rating" for batters (which did not include pitching), and "Total Pitcher Index" for pitchers (which did not include batting at positions other than pitcher). For batters who do not pitch, and pitchers who did not play any other position, TPW is the same as TPR or TPI. But for Babe Ruth, both the Player and Pitcher Registers registers will now list an identical TPW; the Player Register TPW will also include pitching, and the Pitcher Register TPW will also include Ruth's batting record as an outfielder.

We now separate defense into pitching and fielding. Previously, if a pitcher allowed 20 earned runs fewer than the league average, he would receive +20 pitching runs. Now, if the team had +2 fielding runs (after prorating to the pitcher's innings) in the games he pitched, the pitcher would receive only +18 pitching runs.

We have discontinued the practice from previous editions of *Total Baseball* where, in calculating pitcher wins, the season Runs per Win figure was adjusted for the run environment as created by each pitcher's own performance. (For instance, in games started by a talented pitcher, the two teams might combine for 8 runs, on average, instead of 9. That would result in a different Runs per Win figure for that pitcher, and his TPW would increase.) Now, we use the league's Runs Per Win figure without adjusting for the specific pitcher.

Finally, we no longer use "Relief Ranking Runs" adjustment in the calculation of a pitcher's TPW. Previously, pitchers with a large percentage of saves (or wins, or losses) per inning pitched were assumed to be pitching in more important situations, and the calculation of TPW amplified their pitching runs to account for this. We no longer do this.

That's all for now, but the quest for more complete information is certainly ongoing, as is research that will result in refinements to the Linear Weights Method and its statistics.

Chapter 60

The Player Register

The Player Register consists of the central batting, baserunning and fielding statistics of every man who has batted in major-league play since 1871, excepting those men who were primarily pitchers. A pitcher's complete batting record, however, is included for those pitchers who also, over the course of their careers, played in 100 or more games at another position, or played in more than half of their total major-league games at a position other than pitcher, or played more games at a position other than pitcher in at least one year.

The players are listed alphabetically by surname and, when more than one player bears the name, alphabetically by common name—either his first name or nickname. On the whole, we have been conservative in ascribing nicknames, doing so only when the player was in fact known by that name during his playing days.

We have used boldface numerals to indicate a league-leading total in those categories in which a player is truly attempting to excel (no boldface is given to the "leaders" in batter strikeouts, times caught stealing, at bats, or games played). An asterisk appears alongside the team for which a player appeared in postseason competition. For players selected to the All-Star Game, a star will appear to the right of the team/league column.

The record for each man who played in more than one season is given in a line for each season, plus a career total line. If he played for more than one team in a given year, his totals for each team are stated on separate lines. And if the teams for which he played in his "traded year" are in the same league, then his full record is stated in both separate and combined fashion. (In the odd case of a man playing for three or more clubs in one year, with some of these clubs being in the same league, the combined total line will reflect only his play in that one league.) We include position data in the "Yr" line for traded players. A man who played in only one year will have no additional career total line, since it would be identical to his seasonal listing.

Batting records for the National Association are included in The Player Register because the editors, like most baseball historians, regard it as a major league, inasmuch as it was the only professional league of its day and supplied the National League of 1876 with most of its players.

They benefit from the SABR research project which to date has produced extra-base hits, corrected averages, walks, and some stolen bases, strikeouts, and other data heretofore unavailable for the National Association.

Gaps remain elsewhere in the official record of baseball and in the ongoing process of historical reconstruction. The reader will note an ellipsis ("....") for some single-season entries; this is not a typographical lapse but a sign that the information does not exist or has not yet been found.

For a discussion of which data is missing for particular years, see "The History of Major League Baseball Statistics." Here is a quick summation of the missing data:

Hit batters, 1897-1908 NL/AL, 5 percent missing;

Caught stealing, 1886-1914, 1916 for players with fewer than 20 stolen bases, 1917–1919, 1926–1950 NL; 1886-1891 AA; 1890 PL; 1901-1913, 1916 for players with fewer than 20 stolen bases, 1917–1919 AL; 1914-1915 FL;

Sacrifice hit, 1908-1930, 1939 (in these years fly balls scoring runners counted as sacrifice hits, and in 1927-1930 fly balls advancing runners to any base counted as sacrifices);

Sacrifice fly, 1908-1930, 1939 (counted but inseparable from sacrifice hits), 1940–1953 (not counted);

Runs batted in, 1882-1884 AA;

Strikeouts for batters, 1882-1888, 1890 AA; 1884 UA; 1897-1909 NL; 1901-1912 AL.

For a key to the team and league abbreviations used in the Player Register, flip to the last page of this volume.

Looking at the biographical line for any player, we see first his last and common name in bold, followed by his full given name and nickname (and any other name he may have used or been born with, such as the matronymic of a Latin American player). His date and place of birth follow "b" and his date and place of death follow "d." Then comes his manner of batting and throwing, abbreviated for a left-handed batter who throws right as BL/TR (a switch hitter would be shown as BB for "bats both" and a switch thrower as TB for "throws both"). Next is height and weight information; then, and for most players last, is his debut date.

Some pitchers continue in major league baseball after their pitching days are through, as managers, coaches, or even umpires. A player whose biographical line concludes with an M can also be located in the Manager Roster; and one with a U occupies a place in the Umpire Roster. The select few who have been enshrined in the Baseball Hall of Fame are noted with a "HOF 19xx" identifier. They are also listed in the Hall of Fame Roster in Chapter 41.

The explanations for the statistical column heads follow; for more technical information about formulas and calculations, see the Glossary.

The vertical rules in the column header line separate the stats into six logical groupings: year, team, league, fundamental counting stats for batters; hits and plate appearances broken out into their component counting stats, along with baserunning stats; basic calculated averages; sabermetric figures of more complex calculation; fielding stats; and overall sabermetric stats.

For this edition of *Total Baseball,* there are several changes to the statistical categories found in the Player Register.

First, the calculation of Batting Runs now includes the contribution of the player's stolen bases and caught stealing; previously, these were calculated separately as "Stolen Base Runs." However, we continue to present the top-100 SBR performances in the "Leaders" section.

Second, the column for "Total Player Rating" has been changed to "Total Player Wins." TPW is basically the same as the old TPR, but includes the contributions of a player's pitching record, if he

pitched. Babe Ruth is the player most prominently affected by the change. (Readers of those older editions will recognize that TPW is the new name for what was previously called "Total Baseball Ranking.")

Third, the formula for "ratio" has been changed to (hits plus walks) per inning; with the advent of fantasy baseball, this has become the customary definition.

Fourth, we have added a column for Runs Created, the Bill James measure of how many total runs were produced by the player's batting and baserunning.

Fifth, we have added a column for "Runs Created per Game."

This statistic is an estimate of the number of runs a team would score if this player batted in each of the nine lineup spots, and complements Batting Runs by providing an estimate of the rate of the player's offensive contribution.

Sixth, we have revamped the "Fielding Runs" statistic; details can be found in the Glossary.

Seventh, we no longer downgrade TPW for the Federal League and Union Association; we present the results as is, and leave league and era comparisons to the reader.

And, finally, we have added a column for each player's Win Shares.

PLAYER REGISTER KEYS

YEAR — Year of play (When a space in the column is blank, this indicates that the man has played for two or more clubs in the last year stated in the column; if those clubs were in the same league, then the man will also have a combined total line, beginning with the abbreviation "Yr" placed in the TM-L column.)

Yr — Year's totals for play with two or more clubs in same league. (See comments for YEAR)

* — Denotes postseason play: World Series, League Championship Series, or Division Series

TM-L — Team and League (See comments for YEAR.)

★ — Named to All-Star Game

G — Games

AB — At bats (Bases on balls were counted as at-bats by scorers in 1876 and 1887, and are included in the total for those years.)

R — Runs

H — Hits (Bases on balls were counted as hits by scorers in 1887, and are included in the total for that year.)

2B — Doubles

3B — Triples

HR — Home Runs

RBI — Runs Batted In

BB — Bases on Balls (Bases on balls were counted as hitless at-bats by scorers in 1876.)

SO — Strikeouts

SB — Stolen Bases

CS — Caught Stealing

AVG — Batting Average (Figured as hits over at bats; mathematically meaningless averages created through a division by zero are rendered as dashes. League leaders in this category, as in others in the Player Register, are noted by bold type. However, some boldface leaders in batting average will have lower marks than other batters who are not credited with having won a championship; for a full explanation of the reasoning for this anomaly, see "The History of Major League Baseball Statistics.")

OBP — On Base Percentage (See comments for AVG.)

SLG — Slugging Average (See comments for AVG.)

OPS — On Base Plus Slugging

OPS+ — Adjusted On Base Plus Slugging (On Base Percentage plus Slugging Average, normalized to league average and adjusted for home-park factor. Higher is better; a mark of 100 is a league-average performance.)

BR/A — Batting Runs (Linear Weights measure of runs contributed beyond what a league-average batter (not including pitchers) might have contributed, defined as zero. Occasionally the curious figure of -0 will appear in this column, or in the columns of other Linear Weights measures of batting, baserunning, fielding, and the TPW. This "negative zero" figure signifies a run contribution that falls below the league average, but to so small a degree that it cannot be said to have cost the team a run. The measure has been adjusted for home-park factor as described in the Glossary (see "park factor"). Non-pitchers' BR is normalized to league batting statistics for non-pitchers; pitchers' BR is normalized to league batting for pitchers only, and so a pitcher's BR cannot be directly compared to a non-pitcher's. Batting Runs now includes runs resulting from stolen bases and times caught stealing; in previous editions of *Total Baseball*, this was calculated separately and called "stolen base runs.")

RC — Runs Created (The Bill James measure of bulk batting contribution, measured in runs. See Glossary for formulas.)

RC/G   Runs Created per Game (An estimate of how many runs a team would score per game if its lineup were composed of nine identical batters with this player's stats.)

FR   Fielding Runs (The Linear Weights measure of runs saved beyond what a league-average player at that position might have saved, defined as zero; this stat is calculated to take account of the particular demands of the different positions; see Glossary for formulas, and for the major changes made to FR for this edition of *Total Baseball*.)

G/POS   Positions played (This is a ranking from left to right by frequency of the positions played in the field or at designated hitter. An asterisk to the left of the position indicates, generally, that in a given year the man played about two-thirds of his team's scheduled games at that position; more precisely, it is figured at 20 games in 1871, 30 in 1872, 35 in 1873, 40 in 1874, and 50 in 1875; two-thirds of the scheduled games in 1876-1900, and 100 or more games since. When a slash separates positions, the man played those positions listed to the left of the bar in 10 or more games and the positions to the right of the bar in fewer than 10 games. If there is no slash, he played all positions listed in 10 or more games. For the lifetime line, the asterisk signifies 1,000 games and the slash marks a dividing point of 100 games. We have included the total number of games. at each position for each player's primary positions, as well as other positions where space allows. The career totals for outfielders do not provide a per-position breakdown, but games played at each outfield position are listed in the biographical line at the top of each listing.) The position abbreviations are:

1: First base	LF: Left Field
2: Second base	RF: Right Field
S: Shortstop	P: Pitcher
3: Third base	D: Designated hitter
O: Outfield	C: Catcher
CF: Center Field	

WS   Win Shares (The Bill James estimate of how many of his team's wins this player was individually responsible for, multiplied by 3.)

TPW   Total Player Wins (This is the sum of a player's Adjusted Batting Runs, Fielding Runs, and Pitching Runs, minus his positional adjustment, all divided by the Runs Per Win factor for that year—generally around 10, historically in the 9 to 11 range. For more information on the formula and the Runs Per Win concept, see the Glossary. In the lifetime line, the TPW is the sum of the seasonal TPWs. For men who also pitched, TPW will include the contributions made by their pitching stats; Babe Ruth is the player most prominently affected. TPW is the new name for what was previously called "Total Baseball Ranking." It is also similar to the former "Total Player Rating," with the exception that TPW also includes the player's pitching contribution, if any.)

Total   For players whose careers include play in the National Association as well as other major leagues, two totals are given, where the record of his years in the National Association is shown alongside the notation "Total 2 n," where 2 stands for the number of years totaled and n stands for National Association. For players whose careers began in 1876 or later, the lifetime record is shown alongside the notation "Total x," where x stands for the number of post-1875 years totaled.

• AARON, Hank Henry Louis "Hammer, Hammerin' Hank" Aaron b: 2/5/1934, Mobile, AL BR/TR, 6', 180 lbs. Deb: 4/13/1954 HOF: 1982 Career OF: 313-293-2184

YEAR TM-L	G	AB	R	H	2B	3B	HR	RBI	BB	SO	SB	CS	AVG	OBP	SLG	OPS	OPS+	BR/A	RC	RC/G	FR	G/POS	WS	TPW
1954 Mil-N	122	468	58	131	27	6	13	69	28	39	2	2	.280	.325	.447	.771	105	1	64	4.81	-2	*O-116(105-0-11)	13	-0.8
1955 Mil-N★	153	602	105	189	37	9	27	106	49	61	3	1	.314	.369	.540	.908	144	37	114	6.92	3	*O-126(26-0-105),2-27	29	3.7
1956 Mil-N★	153	609	106	200	34	14	26	92	37	54	2	4	.328	.369	.558	.927	154	42	115	6.99	8	*O-152(0-0-152)	30	4.5
1957*Mil-N★	151	615	118	198	27	6	44	132	57	58	1	1	.322	.379	.600	.979	170	58	136	8.48	1	*O-150(1-69-83)	35	5.3
1958*Mil-N★	153	601	109	196	34	4	30	95	59	49	4	1	.326	.387	.546	.933	157	48	121	7.59	2	*O-153(0-39-120)	32	4.5
1959 Mil-N★	154	629	116	223	46	7	39	123	51	54	8	0	.355	.406	.636	1.042	188	77	156	9.74	-1	*O-152(0-13-144)/3-5	38	7.2
1960 Mil-N★	153	590	102	172	20	11	40	126	60	63	16	7	.292	.359	.566	.925	160	47	119	7.23	3	*O-153(0-3-151)/2-2	35	4.6
1961 Mil-N★	155	603	115	197	39	10	34	120	56	64	21	9	.327	.386	.594	.979	165	55	132	8.06	6	*O-154(0-71-88)/3-2	35	5.2
1962 Mil-N★	156	592	127	191	28	6	45	128	66	73	15	7	.323	.393	.618	1.012	171	58	140	8.84	-1	*O-153(0-83-71)/1-1	34	5.0
1963 Mil-N★	161	631	121	201	29	4	44	130	78	94	31	5	.319	.394	.586	.980	180	70	149	8.92	-3	*O-161(0-0-161)	41	6.1
1964 Mil-N★	145	570	103	187	30	2	24	95	62	46	22	4	.328	.394	.514	.908	152	44	112	7.38	9	*O-139(0-0-139),2-11	33	4.6
1965 Mil-N★	150	570	109	181	40	1	32	89	60	81	24	4	.318	.384	.560	.943	161	49	122	7.90	5	*O-148(0-0-148)	31	4.6
1966 Atl-N★	158	603	117	168	23	1	44	127	76	96	21	3	.279	.360	.539	.899	144	39	118	6.93	5	*O-158(0-4-158)/2-2	27	3.6
1967 Atl-N★	155	600	113	184	37	3	39	109	63	97	17	6	.307	.373	.573	.946	169	54	126	7.77	4	*O-152(0-11-141)/2-1	34	5.1
1968 Atl-N★	160	606	84	174	33	4	29	86	64	62	28	5	.287	.356	.498	.855	154	43	104	6.07	6	*O-151(0-0-151),1-14	32	4.3
1969*Atl-N★	147	547	100	164	30	3	44	97	87	47	9	10	.300	.398	.607	1.005	177	55	128	8.41	-1	*O-144(0-0-144)/1-4	38	4.8
1970 Atl-N★	150	516	103	154	26	1	38	118	74	63	9	0	.298	.389	.574	.962	146	35	116	8.22	0	*O-125(0-0-125),1-11	25	2.8
1971 Atl-N★	139	495	95	162	22	3	47	118	71	58	1	1	.327	.414	.669	1.082	190	59	137	10.59	-5	1-71,O-60(1-0-59)	33	4.9
1972 Atl-N★	129	449	75	119	10	0	34	77	92	55	4	0	.265	.391	.514	.906	142	29	91	7.05	3	*1-109,O-15(0-0-15)	21	2.4
1973 Atl-N★	120	392	84	118	12	1	40	96	68	51	1	1	.301	.406	.643	1.048	173	40	104	9.78	-1	*O-105(87-0-18)	20	3.4
1974 Atl-N★	112	340	47	91	16	0	20	69	39	29	1	0	.268	.343	.491	.834	126	11	58	6.04	-2	O-89(89-0-0)	13	0.5
1975 Mil-A★	137	465	45	109	16	2	12	60	70	51	0	1	.234	.336	.355	.691	95	-1	56	4.01	0	*D-128/O-3(3-0-0)	9	-0.6
1976 Mil-A	85	271	22	62	8	0	10	35	35	38	0	1	.229	.317	.369	.686	102	1	31	3.85	-0	D-74/O-1	5	-0.2
Total 23	3298	12364	2174	3771	624	98	755	2297	1402	1383	240	73	.305	.377	.555	.932	156	951	2550	7.54	38	*O-2760,1-210,D-202/2-43,3	643	85.4

• AARON, Tommie Tommie Lee Aaron b: 8/5/1939, Mobile, AL d: 8/16/1984, Atlanta, GA BR/TR, 6'3", 200 lbs. Deb: 4/10/1962 C Career OF: 136-1-2

YEAR TM-L	G	AB	R	H	2B	3B	HR	RBI	BB	SO	SB	CS	AVG	OBP	SLG	OPS	OPS+	BR/A	RC	RC/G	FR	G/POS	WS	TPW
1962 Mil-N	141	334	54	77	20	2	8	38	41	58	6	0	.231	.315	.374	.689	86	-5	40	3.97	3	*1-110,O-42(42-0-0)/2-1,3	7	-0.7
1963 Mil-N	72	135	6	27	6	1	1	15	11	27	0	3	.200	.260	.281	.542	57	-9	8	1.76	-3	1-45,O-14(14-1-0)/2-6,3-1	1	-1.4
1965 Mil-N	8	16	1	3	0	0	0	1	1	2	0	0	.188	.235	.188	.423	21	-2	1	1.11	0	/1-6	0	-0.2
1968 Atl-N	98	283	21	69	10	3	1	25	21	37	3	4	.244	.296	.311	.607	82	-7	24	2.84	1	O-62(62-0-0),1-28/3-1	4	-1.2
1969*Atl-N	49	60	13	15	2	0	1	5	6	6	0	1	.250	.318	.333	.652	82	-2	6	3.57	0	1-16/O-8(8-0-0)	1	-0.3
1970 Atl-N	44	63	3	13	2	0	2	7	3	10	0	0	.206	.242	.333	.576	50	-5	4	1.78	-1	1-16,O-12(10-0-2)	0	-0.6
1971 Atl-N	25	53	4	12	2	0	0	3	3	5	0	0	.226	.268	.264	.532	48	-4	3	1.91	1	1-11/3-7	0	-0.3
Total 7	437	944	102	216	42	6	13	94	86	145	9	8	.229	.293	.327	.621	75	-33	86	2.95	1	1-232,O-138/3-10,2-7	13	-4.8

• ABAD, Andy Fausto Andres Abad b: 8/25/1972, Palm Beach, FL BL/TL, 6'1", 184 lbs. Deb: 9/10/2001

YEAR TM-L	G	AB	R	H	2B	3B	HR	RBI	BB	SO	SB	CS	AVG	OBP	SLG	OPS	OPS+	BR/A	RC	RC/G	FR	G/POS	WS	TPW
2001 Oak-A	1	1	0	0	0	0	0	0	0	0	0	0	.000	.000	.000	.000	-100	-0	0	.00	-0	/1-1	0	0.0
2003 Bos-A	9	17	1	2	0	0	0	0	2	5	0	1	.118	.211	.118	.328	-10	-3	0	.42	-1	/1-7,O-1	0	-0.5
Total 2	10	18	1	2	0	0	0	0	2	5	0	1	.111	.200	.111	.311	-14	-3	0	.40	-1	/1-8,O-1	0	-0.5

• ABADIE, John John Abadie b: 11/4/1854, Philadelphia, PA d: 5/17/1905, Pemberton, NJ BR/TR, 6', 192 lbs. Deb: 4/26/1875

YEAR TM-L	G	AB	R	H	2B	3B	HR	RBI	BB	SO	SB	CS	AVG	OBP	SLG	OPS	OPS+	BR/A	RC	RC/G	FR	G/POS	WS	TPW
1875 Cen-n	11	45	3	10	0	0	0	4	0	3	1	0	.222	.222	.222	.444	60	-1	3	2.11	0	1-11	....	-0.1
Atl-n	1	4	1	1	0	0	0	1	0	0	0	0	.250	.250	.250	.500	85	-0	0	2.52	0	/1-1	....	0.0
Yr.	12	49	4	11	0	0	0	5	0	3	1	0	.224	.224	.224	.449	62	-1	3	2.14	0	1-12	....	-0.1

• ABBATICCHIO, Ed Edward James "Batty" Abbaticchio b: 4/15/1877, Latrobe, PA d: 1/6/1957, Fort Lauderdale, FL BR/TR, 5'11", 170 lbs. Deb: 9/4/1897 Career OF: 0-2-1

YEAR TM-L	G	AB	R	H	2B	3B	HR	RBI	BB	SO	SB	CS	AVG	OBP	SLG	OPS	OPS+	BR/A	RC	RC/G	FR	G/POS	WS	TPW
1897 Phi-N	3	10	0	3	0	0	0	0	1	....	0	....	.300	.364	.300	.664	78	-0	1	4.23	0	/2-3	0	0.0
1898 Phi-N	25	92	9	21	4	0	0	14	7	....	4	....	.228	.290	.272	.562	64	-4	9	3.22	-6	3-20/2-4,O-1	1	-0.9
1903 Bos-N	136	489	61	111	18	5	1	46	52	....	23	....	.227	.306	.290	.597	73	-16	54	3.63	1	*2-116,S-17	10	-1.2
1904 Bos-N	154	579	76	148	18	10	3	54	40	....	24	....	.256	.309	.337	.646	103	2	71	4.16	-15	*S-154	18	-0.9
1905 Bos-N	153	610	70	170	25	12	3	41	35	....	30	....	.279	.326	.374	.700	111	7	87	5.07	-23	*S-152/O-1	16	-1.1
1907 Pit-N	147	496	63	130	14	7	2	82	65	....	35	....	.262	.357	.331	.687	114	11	76	5.07	-15	*2-147	20	-0.3
1908 Pit-N	146	500	43	125	16	7	1	61	58	....	22	....	.250	.336	.316	.652	108	7	62	4.03	6	*2-144	22	1.7
1909*Pit-N	36	87	13	20	0	0	1	16	19	....	2	....	.230	.368	.264	.632	92	0	9	3.51	1	S-18/2-4,O-1	4	0.3
1910 Pit-N	3	3	0	0	0	0	0	0	0	0	0	....	.000	.000	.000	.000	-94	-1	0	.00	0	/S-1	0	-0.1
Bos-N	52	178	20	44	4	2	0	10	12	16	2	....	.247	.295	.292	.587	68	-8	16	2.98	-6	S-46/2-1	1	-1.3
Yr.	55	181	20	44	4	2	0	10	12	16	2	....	.243	.290	.287	.577	66	-8	16	2.91	-7	S-47/2-1	1	-1.4
Total 9	855	3044	355	772	99	43	11	324	289	16	142	....	.254	.325	.325	.650	99	-2	385	4.25	-57	2-419,S-388/3-20,O-3	92	-4.0

• ABBEY, Charlie Charles S. Abbey b: 10/14/1866, Falls City, NE d: 4/27/1926, San Francisco, CA BL/TL, 5'8.5", 169 lbs. Deb: 8/16/1893 U Career OF: 92-184-173

YEAR TM-L	G	AB	R	H	2B	3B	HR	RBI	BB	SO	SB	CS	AVG	OBP	SLG	OPS	OPS+	BR/A	RC	RC/G	FR	G/POS	WS	TPW
1893 Was-N	31	116	11	30	1	4	0	12	12	6	9	....	.259	.333	.336	.670	80	-3	16	5.05	2	O-31(31-0-0)	2	-0.3
1894 Was-N	129	523	95	164	26	18	7	101	58	38	31	....	.314	.389	.472	.862	111	9	111	8.04	5	*O-129(54-74-0)	13	0.3
1895 Was-N	133	516	102	142	14	10	8	84	43	43	28	....	.275	.339	.388	.727	88	-10	80	5.69	1	*O-132(3-98-31)	7	-1.4
1896 Was-N	79	301	47	79	12	6	1	49	27	20	16	....	.262	.331	.352	.683	80	-9	43	4.87	-3	O-78(2-11-65)/P-1	5	-1.3
1897 Was-N	80	300	52	78	14	8	3	34	27	....	9	....	.260	.329	.390	.719	90	-5	43	5.05	2	O-80(2-1-77)	5	-0.6
Total 5	452	1756	307	493	67	46	19	280	167	107	93	....	.281	.351	.404	.755	93	-18	293	6.04	7	O-450/P-1	32	-3.4

• ABBOTT, Fred Harry Frederick Abbott b: 10/22/1874, Versailles, OH d: 6/11/1935, Los Angeles, CA BR/TR, 5'10", 180 lbs. Deb: 4/25/1903 U

YEAR TM-L	G	AB	R	H	2B	3B	HR	RBI	BB	SO	SB	CS	AVG	OBP	SLG	OPS	OPS+	BR/A	RC	RC/G	FR	G/POS	WS	TPW
1903 Cle-A	77	255	25	60	11	3	1	25	7	....	8	....	.235	.270	.314	.583	76	-8	25	3.29	2	C-71/1-3	6	0.1
1904 Cle-A	41	130	14	22	4	2	0	12	6	....	2	....	.169	.206	.231	.437	38	-9	7	1.70	-2	C-33/1-7	1	-0.9
1905 Phi-N	42	128	9	25	6	1	0	12	6	....	4	....	.195	.248	.258	.506	53	-8	10	2.41	0	C-34/1-5	2	-0.4
Total 3	160	513	48	107	21	6	1	49	19	....	14	....	.209	.248	.279	.527	60	-25	43	2.64	0	C-138/1-15	9	-1.2

• ABBOTT, Jeff Jeffrey William Abbott b: 8/17/1972, Atlanta, GA BR/TL, 6'2", 190 lbs. Deb: 6/10/1997 Career OF: 63-81-55

YEAR TM-L	G	AB	R	H	2B	3B	HR	RBI	BB	SO	SB	CS	AVG	OBP	SLG	OPS	OPS+	BR/A	RC	RC/G	FR	G/POS	WS	TPW
1997 Chi-A	19	38	8	10	1	0	1	2	0	6	0	0	.263	.263	.368	.632	65	-2	3	2.25	0	O-10(5-1-4)/D-3	0	-0.3
1998 Chi-A	89	244	33	68	14	1	12	41	9	28	3	3	.279	.304	.492	.796	105	-0	35	5.06	-4	O-76(20-38-27)/D-2	7	-0.5
1999 Chi-A	17	57	5	9	0	0	2	6	5	12	1	1	.158	.226	.263	.489	24	-7	3	1.23	-1	O-17(17-0-0)	0	-0.8
2000*Chi-A	80	215	31	59	15	1	3	29	21	38	2	1	.274	.345	.395	.740	85	-5	31	5.10	-4	O-65(20-33-16)/D-7	4	-0.9
2001 Fla-N	28	42	5	11	3	0	0	5	3	7	0	0	.262	.326	.333	.659	74	-2	5	3.86	0	O-17(1-9-8)	1	-0.2
Total 5	233	596	82	157	33	2	18	83	38	91	6	5	.263	.311	.416	.727	85	-16	76	4.36	-9	O-185/D-12	12	-2.7

• ABBOTT, Kurt Kurt Thomas Abbott b: 6/2/1969, Zanesville, OH BR/TR, 5'11", 185 lbs. Deb: 9/7/1993 Career OF: 32-4-8

YEAR TM-L	G	AB	R	H	2B	3B	HR	RBI	BB	SO	SB	CS	AVG	OBP	SLG	OPS	OPS+	BR/A	RC	RC/G	FR	G/POS	WS	TPW
1993 Oak-A	20	61	11	15	1	0	3	9	3	20	2	0	.246	.281	.410	.691	89	-1	6	3.30	-1	O-13(13-0-0)/S-6,2-2	2	-0.2
1994 Fla-N	101	345	41	86	17	3	9	33	16	98	3	0	.249	.292	.394	.687	75	-13	40	4.01	-7	S-99	6	-1.2
1995 Fla-N	120	420	60	107	18	7	17	60	36	110	4	3	.255	.321	.452	.773	101	-2	61	5.01	-9	*S-115	11	-0.1
1996 Fla-N	109	320	37	81	18	7	8	33	22	99	3	3	.253	.307	.428	.735	94	-5	40	4.31	1	S-44,3-33,2-20	8	0.1
1997*Fla-N	94	252	35	69	18	2	6	30	14	68	3	1	.274	.315	.433	.747	98	-2	33	4.62	0	2-54,O-10(10-0-0)/S-7,3-4,D	8	0.0
1998 Oak-A	35	123	17	33	7	1	2	9	10	34	2	1	.268	.328	.390	.719	88	-2	16	4.38	-3	S-28/O-5(5-0-1),D-3,3-1	2	-0.4
Col-N	42	71	9	18	6	0	3	15	2	19	0	0	.254	.284	.465	.749	76	-3	9	4.12	-1	O-9(4-0-5),2-7,S-7,3-3,D-1	1	-0.4
1999 Col-N	96	286	41	78	17	2	8	41	16	69	3	2	.273	.311	.430	.741	67	-16	38	4.68	-3	2-66/1-8,O-4(0-2-2),S-3	7	-1.6
2000*NY-N	79	157	22	34	7	1	6	12	14	51	1	1	.217	.285	.389	.673	71	-8	17	3.70	-4	S-39,2-23/3-2,O-2(0-2-0)	2	-0.8
2001 Atl-N	6	9	0	2	0	0	0	0	0	3	1	0	.222	.222	.222	.444	15	-1	1	2.16	0	/2-1,S-1	0	0.1
Total 9	702	2044	273	523	109	23	62	242	133	571	22	11	.256	.307	.423	.729	86	-52	261	4.40	-25	S-349,2-173/3-43,O-43,1-8,D	47	-4.5

• ABBOTT, Ody Ody Cleon Abbott b: 9/5/1888, New Eagle, PA d: 4/13/1933, Washington, DC BR/TR, 6'2", 180 lbs. Deb: 9/10/1910

YEAR TM-L	G	AB	R	H	2B	3B	HR	RBI	BB	SO	SB	CS	AVG	OBP	SLG	OPS	OPS+	BR/A	RC	RC/G	FR	G/POS	WS	TPW
1910 StL-N	22	70	2	13	2	1	0	6	6	20	3	....	.186	.250	.243	.493	46	-5	5	2.21	0	O-21(0-21-0)	0	-0.6

• ABERCROMBIE, Frank Francis Patterson Abercrombie b: 1851, Fort Towson, OK d: 11/11/1939, Philadelphia, PA Deb: 10/21/1871

YEAR TM-L	G	AB	R	H	2B	3B	HR	RBI	BB	SO	SB	CS	AVG	OBP	SLG	OPS	OPS+	BR/A	RC	RC/G	FR	G/POS	WS	TPW
1871 Tro-n	1	4	0	0	0	0	0	0	0	0	0	0	.000	.000	.000	.000	-99	-1	0	.00	-1	/S-1	....	-0.1

YEAR	TM-L	G	AB	R	H	2B	3B	HR	RBI	BB	SO	SB	CS	AVG	OBP	SLG	OPS	OPS+	BR/A	RC	RC/G	FR	G/POS	WS	TPW
• ABERNATHY, Brent		Michael Brent Abernathy b: 9/23/1977, Atlanta, GA BR/TR, 6'1", 185 lbs. Deb: 6/25/2001																							
2001	TB-A	79	304	43	82	17	1	5	33	27	35	8	3	.270	.329	.382	.711	88	-5	40	4.62	2	2-79	10	0.1
2002	TB-A	117	463	46	112	18	4	2	40	25	46	10	4	.242	.289	.311	.600	61	-26	42	3.06	4	*2-116/D-1	7	-1.5
2003	TB-A	2	7	1	0	0	0	0	0	0	0	1	0	.000	.000	.000	.000	-102	-2	0	.00	0	/2-2	0	-0.1
	KC-A	10	27	2	2	0	0	0	0	1	3	0	0	.074	.107	.074	.181	-45	-6	0	.10	-1	/2-9	0	-0.6
	Yr.	12	34	3	2	0	0	0	0	1	3	1	0	.059	.086	.059	.145	-56	-8	0	.08	0	2-11	0	-0.7
Total	**3**	**208**	**801**	**92**	**196**	**35**	**5**	**7**	**73**	**53**	**84**	**19**	**7**	**.245**	**.297**	**.327**	**.624**	**66**	**-38**	**82**	**3.45**	**6**	**2-206/D-1**	**17**	**-2.2**
• ABERSON, Cliff		Clifford Alexander "Kif" Aberson b: 8/28/1921, Chicago, IL d: 6/23/1973, Vallejo, CA BR/TR, 6', 200 lbs. Deb: 7/18/1947 Career OF: 48-0-1																							
1947	Chi-N	47	140	24	39	6	3	4	20	20	32	0	....	.279	.369	.450	.819	121	4	23	5.86	1	0-40(40-0-0)	4	0.3
1948	Chi-N	12	32	1	6	1	0	1	6	5	10	0	....	.188	.297	.313	.610	68	-1	3	3.49	0	/0-8(8-0-0)	0	-0.2
1949	Chi-N	4	7	0	0	0	0	0	0	0	2	0	....	.000	.000	.000	.000	-103	-2	0	.00	0	/0-1	0	-0.2
Total	**3**	**63**	**179**	**25**	**45**	**7**	**3**	**5**	**26**	**25**	**44**	**0**	**....**	**.251**	**.343**	**.408**	**.751**	**104**	**1**	**26**	**5.09**	**1**	**/0-49**	**4**	**-0.1**
• ABNER, Shawn		Shawn Wesley Abner b: 6/17/1966, Hamilton, OH BR/TR, 6'1", 190 lbs. Deb: 9/8/1987 Career OF: 74-152-120																							
1987	SD-N	16	47	5	13	3	1	2	7	2	8	1	0	.277	.306	.511	.817	116	1	8	6.09	1	0-14(6-2-6)	1	0.1
1988	SD-N	37	83	6	15	3	0	2	5	4	19	0	1	.181	.227	.289	.516	48	-6	5	1.97	0	0-35(10-11-17)	0	-0.8
1989	SD-N	57	102	13	18	4	0	2	14	5	20	1	0	.176	.215	.275	.489	39	-8	6	1.91	-1	0-51(23-23-6)	1	-1.1
1990	SD-N	91	184	17	45	9	0	1	15	9	28	2	3	.245	.287	.310	.597	64	-10	16	2.87	-1	0-62(23-35-6)	3	-1.3
1991	SD-N	53	115	15	19	4	1	1	5	7	25	0	0	.165	.220	.243	.463	29	-11	6	1.54	1	0-39(0-36-3)	1	-1.1
	Cal-A	41	101	12	23	6	1	2	9	4	18	1	2	.228	.257	.366	.623	70	-5	8	2.63	1	0-38(0-31-7)/D-3	2	-0.5
1992	Chi-A	97	208	21	58	10	1	1	16	12	35	1	2	.279	.327	.351	.678	91	-3	24	4.00	0	0-94(12-14-75)/D-1	5	-0.5
Total	**6**	**392**	**840**	**89**	**191**	**39**	**4**	**11**	**71**	**43**	**153**	**6**	**8**	**.227**	**.271**	**.323**	**.593**	**65**	**-44**	**72**	**2.85**	**-0**	**0-333/D-4**	**13**	**-5.2**
• ABRAMS, Cal		Calvin Ross "Abie" Abrams b: 3/2/1924, Philadelphia, PA d: 2/25/1997, Fort Lauderdale, FL BL/TL, 6', 185 lbs. Deb: 4/20/1949 Career OF: 101-94-270																							
1949	Bro-N	8	24	6	2	1	0	0	0	7	6	1	....	.083	.290	.125	.415	15	-3	1	1.46	-1	/0-7(7-0-0)	0	-0.4
1950	Bro-N	38	44	5	9	1	0	0	4	9	13	0	....	.205	.340	.227	.567	51	-3	4	3.22	-0	0-15(9-1-5)	0	-0.3
1951	Bro-N	67	150	27	42	8	0	3	19	36	26	3	2	.280	.419	.393	.813	118	6	27	6.40	-1	0-34(34-0-0)	6	0.2
1952	Bro-N	10	10	1	2	0	0	0	0	2	4	0	0	.200	.333	.200	.533	51	-1	1	2.89	0	/0-1	0	-0.1
	Cin-N	71	158	23	44	9	2	2	13	19	25	1	0	.278	.356	.399	.755	109	3	25	5.76	-1	0-46(31-18-0)	5	0.0
	Yr.	81	168	24	46	9	2	2	13	21	29	1	0	.274	.354	.387	.741	105	2	25	5.57	-1	0-47(32-18-0)	5	-0.1
1953	Pit-N	119	448	66	128	10	6	15	43	58	70	4	4	.286	.368	.435	.803	109	6	77	6.29	3	*0-112(0-0-112)	13	0.6
1954	Pit-N	17	42	6	6	1	1	0	2	10	9	0	0	.143	.308	.214	.522	39	-3	3	2.22	1	0-13(5-3-5)	0	-0.3
	Bal-A	115	423	67	124	22	7	6	25	72	67	1	4	.293	.401	.421	.822	135	22	76	6.53	0	*0-115(0-14-101)	16	1.9
1955	Bal-A	118	309	56	75	12	3	6	32	89	69	2	8	.243	.416	.359	.776	118	12	52	5.54	0	0-96(13-58-46)/1-4	13	0.9
1956	Chi-A	4	3	0	1	0	0	0	0	2	1	0	0	.333	.600	.333	.933	150	1	1	12.31	-0	/0-2(1-0-1)	0	0.0
Total	**8**	**567**	**1611**	**257**	**433**	**64**	**19**	**32**	**138**	**304**	**290**	**12**	**18**	**.269**	**.387**	**.392**	**.779**	**113**	**40**	**268**	**5.84**	**2**	**0-441/1-4**	**53**	**2.5**
• ABREU, Bobby		Bob Kelly Abreu b: 3/11/1974, Aragua, Venezuela BL/TR, 6', 160 lbs. Deb: 9/1/1996 Career OF: 16-19-956																							
1996	Hou-N	15	22	1	5	1	0	0	1	2	3	0	0	.227	.292	.273	.564	54	-1	2	2.45	0	/0-7(6-0-1)	0	-0.2
1997*	Hou-N	59	188	22	47	10	2	3	26	21	48	7	2	.250	.329	.372	.701	86	-3	25	4.78	1	0-53(10-1-43)	6	-0.4
1998	Phi-N	151	497	68	155	29	6	17	74	84	133	19	10	.312	.411	.497	.908	135	29	106	7.80	8	*0-146(0-0-146)	26	2.9
1999	Phi-N	152	546	118	183	35	**11**	20	93	109	113	27	9	.335	.448	.549	.998	146	46	142	9.82	-12	*0-146(0-0-146)/D-5	26	2.4
2000	Phi-N	154	576	103	182	42	10	25	79	100	116	28	8	.316	.418	.554	.972	142	42	139	8.99	3	*0-152(0-0-152)	23	3.5
2001	Phi-N	162	588	118	170	48	4	31	110	106	137	36	14	.289	.399	.543	.941	144	43	130	7.76	-6	*0-162(0-0-162)	26	2.8
2002	Phi-N	157	572	102	176	**50**	6	20	85	104	117	31	12	.308	.417	.521	.938	152	49	130	8.26	-5	*0-154(0-18-148)	29	3.6
2003	Phi-N	158	577	99	173	35	1	20	101	109	126	22	9	.300	.413	.468	.881	138	38	117	7.30	-5	*0-158(0-0-158)	28	2.3
Total	**8**	**1008**	**3566**	**631**	**1091**	**250**	**40**	**136**	**569**	**635**	**793**	**170**	**64**	**.306**	**.412**	**.513**	**.925**	**140**	**242**	**791**	**8.07**	**-17**	**0-978/D-5**	**164**	**16.8**
• ABREU, Joe		Joseph Lawrence Abreu b: 5/24/1913, Oakland, CA d: 3/17/1993, Hayward, CA BR/TR, 5'8", 160 lbs. Deb: 4/23/1942																							
1942	Cin-N	9	28	4	6	1	0	1	3	4	4	0	....	.214	.313	.357	.670	96	-0	3	3.65	-1	/3-6,2-2	1	-0.1
• ABSTEIN, Bill		William Henry "Big Bill" Abstein b: 2/2/1883, St. Louis, MO d: 4/8/1940, St. Louis, MO BR/TR, 6', 185 lbs. Deb: 9/25/1906																							
1906	Pit-N	8	20	2	4	0	0	0	3	0	....	2	....	.200	.200	.200	.400	24	-2	1	2.01	-1	/2-3,0-2(0-0-2)	0	-0.3
1909*	Pit-N	137	512	51	133	20	10	1	70	27	....	16	....	.260	.302	.344	.646	96	-5	59	3.75	-3	*1-135	13	-1.1
1910	StL-A	25	87	1	13	2	0	0	3	2	....	3	....	.149	.169	.172	.341	7	-9	3	.98	0	1-23	0	-1.1
Total	**3**	**170**	**619**	**54**	**150**	**22**	**10**	**1**	**76**	**29**	**....**	**21**	**....**	**.242**	**.281**	**.315**	**.596**	**82**	**-16**	**63**	**3.27**	**-3**	**1-158/2-3,0-2**	**13**	**-2.4**
• ACOSTA, Merito		Baldomero Pedro (Fernandez) Acosta b: 5/19/1896, Bauta, Cuba d: 11/17/1963, Miami, FL BL/TL, 5'7", 140 lbs. Deb: 6/15/1913 Career OF: 51-27-56																							
1913	Was-A	12	20	3	6	0	1	0	1	4	2	2	....	.300	.417	.400	.817	136	1	4	7.07	-1	/0-9(5-1-1)	1	0.0
1914	Was-A	39	74	10	19	2	2	0	4	11	18	3	4	.257	.353	.338	.691	104	-0	8	3.79	1	0-25(15-4-5)	2	0.0
1915	Was-A	72	163	20	34	4	1	0	18	28	15	8	4	.209	.338	.245	.584	73	-4	17	3.09	-1	0-53(22-2-29)	3	-0.8
1916	Was-A	5	8	0	1	0	0	0	0	2	0	0	....	.125	.300	.125	.425	28	-1	0	1.11	1	/0-4(4-0-0)	0	0.0
1918	Was-A	3	2	0	0	0	0	0	0	0	1	0	....	.000	.000	.000	.000	-102	-0	0	.00	0	....	0	-0.1
	Phi-A	49	169	23	51	3	3	0	14	18	10	4	....	.302	.369	.355	.724	117	4	24	4.77	-1	0-45(5-20-21)	6	0.1
	Yr.	52	171	23	51	3	3	0	14	18	11	4	....	.298	.365	.351	.716	115	3	24	4.70	-1	0-45(5-20-21)	6	0.0
Total	**5**	**180**	**436**	**56**	**111**	**9**	**7**	**0**	**37**	**63**	**46**	**17**	**8**	**.255**	**.354**	**.307**	**.661**	**96**	**-0**	**53**	**3.92**	**-2**	**0-136**	**12**	**-0.8**
• ADAIR, Jerry		Kenneth Jerry Adair b: 12/17/1936, Sand Springs, OK d: 5/31/1987, Tulsa, OK BR/TR, 6', 175 lbs. Deb: 9/2/1958 C																							
1958	Bal-A	11	19	1	2	0	0	0	0	1	7	0	0	.105	.150	.105	.255	-30	-3	0	.54	0	S-10/2-1	0	-0.2
1959	Bal-A	12	35	3	11	0	1	0	2	1	5	0	0	.314	.333	.371	.705	95	-0	4	4.97	-2	2-11/S-1	1	-0.1
1960	Bal-A	3	5	1	1	0	0	1	1	0	0	0	0	.200	.200	.800	1.000	159	0	1	5.40	0	/2-3	0	0.1
1961	Bal-A	133	386	41	102	21	1	9	37	35	51	5	2	.264	.329	.394	.722	94	-4	51	4.61	6	*2-107,S-27/3-2	14	1.2
1962	Bal-A	139	538	67	153	29	4	11	48	27	77	7	7	.284	.321	.414	.735	101	-3	66	4.32	-1	*S-113,2-34/3-1	16	0.8
1963	Bal-A	109	382	34	87	21	3	6	30	9	51	3	3	.228	.249	.346	.595	66	-19	27	2.28	-2	*2-103	6	-1.3
1964	Bal-A	155	569	56	141	20	3	9	47	28	72	3	2	.248	.284	.341	.625	73	-22	50	2.95	10	*2-153	14	0.2
1965	Bal-A	157	582	51	151	26	3	7	66	35	65	6	4	.259	.304	.351	.654	84	-14	55	3.19	16	*2-157	18	1.8
1966	Bal-A	17	52	3	15	1	0	0	3	4	8	0	0	.288	.339	.308	.647	89	-1	6	3.79	-1	2-13	2	0.0
	Chi-A	105	370	27	90	18	2	4	36	17	44	3	2	.243	.278	.335	.613	81	-10	31	2.74	-2	S-75,2-50	8	-0.4
	Yr.	122	422	30	105	19	2	4	39	21	52	3	2	.249	.286	.332	.618	82	-11	37	2.86	-3	S-75,2-63	10	-0.4
1967	Chi-A	28	98	6	20	4	0	0	9	4	17	0	1	.204	.243	.245	.488	46	-7	5	1.49	-2	2-27	1	-0.7
	*Bos-A	89	316	41	92	13	1	3	26	13	35	1	4	.291	.323	.367	.690	96	-3	34	3.77	4	3-35,S-30,2-23	8	0.4
	Yr.	117	414	47	112	17	1	3	35	17	52	1	5	.271	.304	.338	.642	84	-10	39	3.17	2	2-50,3-35,S-30	9	-0.3
1968	Bos-A	74	208	18	45	1	0	2	12	9	28	0	0	.216	.252	.250	.502	49	-13	11	1.73	-3	S-46,2-12/3-7,1-1	2	-1.3
1969	KC-A	126	432	29	108	9	1	5	48	20	36	1	3	.250	.288	.310	.598	67	-21	32	2.43	-16	*2-109/S-8,3-1	3	-3.0
1970	KC-A	7	27	0	4	0	0	0	1	5	3	0	1	.148	.281	.148	.429	22	-3	1	1.22	2	/2-7	0	-0.1
Total	**13**	**1165**	**4019**	**378**	**1022**	**163**	**19**	**57**	**366**	**208**	**499**	**29**	**29**	**.254**	**.294**	**.347**	**.641**	**79**	**-123**	**376**	**3.12**	**10**	**2-810,S-310/3-46,1-1**	**93**	**-2.8**
• ADAIR, Jimmy		James Aubrey "Choppy" Adair b: 1/25/1907, Waxahachie, TX d: 12/9/1982, Dallas, TX BR/TR, 5'10.5", 154 lbs. Deb: 8/24/1931 C																							
1931	Chi-N	18	76	9	21	3	1	0	3	1	8	1	....	.276	.286	.342	.628	67	-4	7	3.37	-1	S-18	1	-0.4
• ADAMS, Bert		John Bertram Adams b: 6/21/1891, Wharton, TX d: 6/24/1940, Los Angeles, CA BB/TR, 6'1", 185 lbs. Deb: 8/30/1910																							
1910	Cle-A	5	13	1	3	0	0	0	0	0	....	0	....	.231	.231	.231	.462	44	-1	1	1.69	2	/C-5	0	0.1
1911	Cle-A	2	5	0	1	0	0	0	0	1	....	0	....	.200	.333	.200	.533	49	-0	0	2.51	0	/C-2	0	0.0
1912	Cle-A	20	54	5	11	2	1	0	6	4	....	0	....	.204	.259	.278	.536	52	-4	4	2.28	0	C-20	1	-0.2
1915	Phi-N	24	27	1	3	0	0	0	2	2	3	0	....	.111	.172	.111	.284	-13	-4	1	.77	-4	C-23/1-1	0	-0.8
1916	Phi-N	11	13	2	3	0	0	0	1	0	3	0	....	.231	.231	.231	.462	40	-1	1	1.80	-1	C-11	0	-0.2
1917	Phi-N	43	107	4	22	4	1	1	7	0	20	0	....	.206	.206	.290	.495	49	-7	6	1.80	2	C-38/1-1	2	-0.3
1918	Phi-N	84	227	10	40	4	0	0	12	10	26	5	....	.176	.214	.194	.408	23	-21	11	1.39	-4	C-76	3	-2.1

YEAR TM-L	G	AB	R	H	2B	3B	HR	RBI	BB	SO	SB	CS	AVG	OBP	SLG	OPS	OPS+	BR/A	RC	RC/G	FR	G/POS	WS	TPW
1919 Phi-N	78	232	14	54	7	2	1	17	6	27	4	....	.233	.252	.293	.545	59	-12	17	2.44	1	C-73/1-1	3	-0.7
Total 8	267	678	37	137	17	4	2	45	23	79	9	....	.202	.229	.248	.477	41	-49	40	1.86	-4	C-248/1-3	9	-4.0
• ADAMS, Bob	Robert Melvin Adams b: 1/6/1952, Pittsburgh, PA BR/TR, 6'2", 200 lbs. Deb: 7/10/1977																							
1977 Det-A	15	24	2	6	1	0	2	2	0	5	0	0	.250	.250	.542	.792	103	-0	3	4.88	0	/1-2,C-1	1	0.0
• ADAMS, Bobby	Robert Henry Adams b: 12/14/1921, Tuolumne, CA d: 2/13/1997, Gig Harbor, WA BR/TR, 5'10.5", 170 lbs. Deb: 4/16/1946 C Career OF: 0-0-3																							
1946 Cin-N	94	311	35	76	13	3	4	24	18	32	16	....	.244	.292	.344	.636	83	-8	31	3.28	21	2-74/O-2(0-0-2),3-1	8	1.8
1947 Cin-N	81	217	39	59	11	2	4	20	25	23	9	....	.272	.358	.396	.754	101	1	33	5.34	-1	2-69	8	0.3
1948 Cin-N	87	262	33	78	20	3	1	21	25	23	6	....	.298	.361	.408	.770	112	4	39	5.43	-6	2-64/3-7	9	0.1
1949 Cin-N	107	277	32	70	16	2	0	25	26	36	4	....	.253	.317	.325	.642	72	-11	29	3.60	-5	2-63,3-14	5	-1.3
1950 Cin-N	115	348	57	98	21	8	3	25	43	29	7	....	.282	.361	.414	.774	103	2	55	5.85	4	2-53,3-42	12	0.8
1951 Cin-N	125	403	57	107	12	5	5	24	43	40	4	10	.266	.338	.357	.695	86	-11	49	4.18	0	3-60,2-42/O-1	10	-0.9
1952 Cin-N	154	637	85	180	25	4	6	48	49	67	11	9	.283	.334	.363	.696	93	-7	77	4.23	12	*3-154	17	0.5
1953 Cin-N	150	607	99	167	14	6	8	49	58	67	3	2	.275	.338	.357	.696	81	-16	78	4.58	12	*3-150	14	-0.5
1954 Cin-N	110	390	69	105	25	6	3	23	55	46	2	5	.269	.364	.387	.751	93	-4	58	5.20	6	3-93/2-2	12	0.2
1955 Cin-N	64	150	23	41	11	2	2	20	20	21	2	0	.273	.370	.413	.783	101	2	24	5.72	4	3-42/2-5	5	0.6
Chi-A	28	21	8	2	0	1	0	3	4	4	0	0	.095	.240	.190	.430	16	-2	1	1.72	-1	/3-9,2-1	0	-0.3
1956 Bal-A	41	111	19	25	6	1	0	7	25	15	1	1	.225	.368	.297	.665	84	-1	15	4.17	-5	3-24,2-18	3	-0.5
1957 Chi-N	60	187	21	47	10	2	1	10	17	28	0	3	.251	.320	.342	.663	79	-6	21	3.72	-6	3-47/2-1	3	-1.3
1958 Chi-N	62	96	14	27	4	4	0	4	6	15	2	0	.281	.324	.406	.730	93	-1	13	4.65	0	1-11/3-9,2-7	2	0.0
1959 Chi-N	3	2	0	0	0	0	0	0	0	1	0	0	.000	.000	.000	.000	-101	-1	0	.00	0	/1-1	0	-0.1
Total 14	1281	4019	591	1082	188	49	37	303	414	447	67	30	.269	.340	.368	.708	90	-60	523	4.54	34	3-652,2-399/1-12,O-3	108	-0.7
• ADAMS, Buster	Elvin Clark Adams b: 6/24/1915, Trinidad, CO d: 9/1/1990, Rancho Mirage, CA BR/TR, 6', 180 lbs. Deb: 4/27/1939 Career OF: 58-426-44																							
1939 StL-N	2	1	1	0	0	0	0	0	0	0	0	....	.000	.000	.000	.000	-94	-0	0	.00	0	....	0	0.0
1943 StL-N	8	11	1	1	1	0	0	1	4	4	0	....	.091	.333	.182	.515	48	-1	1	2.65	0	/O-6(0-6-0)	0	-0.1
Phi-N	111	418	48	107	14	7	4	38	39	67	2	....	.256	.319	.352	.671	98	-2	48	3.94	-6	*O-107(1-107-0)	11	-1.2
Yr.	119	429	49	108	15	7	4	39	43	71	2	....	.252	.320	.347	.667	96	-2	49	3.90	-7	*O-113(1-113-0)	11	-1.3
1944 Phi-N	151	584	86	165	35	3	17	64	74	74	2	....	.283	.370	.440	.810	132	26	99	5.97	6	*O-151(0-151-0)	22	2.9
1945 Phi-N	14	56	6	13	3	1	2	8	5	5	0	....	.232	.295	.429	.724	103	-0	7	3.98	0	O-14(13-0-0)	1	-0.1
StL-N	140	578	98	169	26	0	20	101	57	75	3	....	.292	.359	.441	.800	119	14	94	5.97	-8	*O-140(14-126-0)	23	0.2
Yr.	154	634	104	182	29	1	22	109	62	80	3	....	.287	.353	.440	.793	117	13	101	5.78	-8	*O-154(27-126-0)	24	0.1
1946 StL-N	81	173	21	32	6	0	5	22	29	27	3	....	.185	.312	.306	.619	73	-6	19	3.38	-1	O-58(24-35-0)	3	-0.9
1947 Phi-N	69	182	21	45	11	1	2	15	26	29	2	....	.247	.341	.352	.693	87	-3	23	4.44	0	O-51(6-1-44)	3	-0.4
Total 6	576	2003	282	532	96	12	50	249	234	281	12	....	.266	.346	.400	.747	110	28	290	5.06	-9	O-527	63	0.3
• ADAMS, Dick	Richard Leroy Adams b: 4/8/1920, Tuolumne, CA BR/TL, 6', 185 lbs. Deb: 5/20/1947																							
1947 Phi-A	37	89	9	18	2	3	2	11	2	18	0	0	.202	.220	.360	.579	58	-6	7	2.73	1	1-24/O-3(1-0-2)	1	-0.5
• ADAMS, Doug	Harold Douglas Adams b: 1/27/1943, Blue River, WI BL/TR, 6'3", 185 lbs. Deb: 9/8/1969																							
1969 Chi-A	8	14	1	3	0	0	0	1	1	3	0	0	.214	.267	.214	.481	34	-1	1	1.47	0	/C-4	0	-0.1
• ADAMS, George	George Adams b: Grafton, MA BR/TR, 5'6", 175 lbs. Deb: 6/14/1879																							
1879 Syr-N	4	13	0	3	0	0	0	0	1	1	....	....	.231	.286	.231	.516	82	-0	1	2.46	-1	/1-2,O-2(0-2-0)	0	-0.1
• ADAMS, Glenn	Glenn Charles Adams b: 10/4/1947, Northbridge, MA BL/TR, 6'1", 185 lbs. Deb: 5/4/1975 Career OF: 95-0-50																							
1975 SF-N	61	90	10	27	2	1	4	15	11	25	1	0	.300	.382	.478	.860	132	4	17	7.23	-1	O-25(16-0-9)	4	0.2
1976 SF-N	69	74	2	18	4	0	0	3	1	12	1	0	.243	.253	.297	.551	54	-4	5	2.05	0	/O-6(4-0-2)	0	-0.5
1977 Min-A	95	269	32	91	17	0	6	49	18	30	0	2	.338	.380	.468	.848	132	11	46	6.64	0	D-47,O-44(16-0-28)	9	0.8
1978 Min-A	116	310	27	80	18	1	7	35	17	32	0	1	.258	.297	.390	.687	90	-5	33	3.67	0	*D-101/O-5(2-0-3)	4	-0.8
1979 Min-A	119	326	34	98	13	1	8	50	25	27	2	2	.301	.356	.420	.776	104	2	50	5.62	-1	D-55,O-53(45-0-8)	8	-0.2
1980 Min-A	99	262	32	75	11	2	6	38	15	26	2	4	.286	.325	.412	.737	94	-4	31	3.92	-1	D-81,O-12(12-0-0)	4	-0.7
1981 Min-A	72	220	13	46	10	0	2	24	20	26	0	1	.209	.275	.282	.557	57	-12	15	2.21	0	D-62	0	-1.5
1982 Tor-A	30	66	2	17	4	0	1	11	4	5	0	0	.258	.300	.364	.664	74	-2	7	3.22	0	D-27	0	-0.3
Total 8	661	1617	152	452	79	5	34	225	111	183	6	10	.280	.327	.398	.725	96	-12	204	4.40	-2	D-373,O-145	29	-3.0
• ADAMS, Herb	Herbert Loren Adams b: 4/14/1928, Hollywood, CA BL/TL, 5'9", 160 lbs. Deb: 9/17/1948 Career OF: 14-68-3																							
1948 Chi-A	5	11	1	3	1	0	0	0	1	1	0	0	.273	.333	.364	.697	88	-0	2	4.50	1	/O-4(0-2-2)	0	0.1
1949 Chi-A	56	208	26	61	5	3	0	16	9	16	1	2	.293	.323	.346	.669	79	-8	23	4.06	0	O-48(14-33-1)	4	-0.9
1950 Chi-A	34	118	12	24	2	3	0	2	12	7	3	0	.203	.288	.271	.559	45	-9	10	2.90	-1	O-33(O-33-0)	1	-1.0
Total 3	95	337	39	88	8	6	0	18	22	24	4	2	.261	.310	.320	.631	67	-17	35	3.64	0	/O-85	5	-1.8
• ADAMS, Jim	James J. Adams b: 1868, East St. Louis, IL TR Deb: 4/21/1890																							
1890 StL-a	1	4	0	1	0	0	0	0	0	....	0	....	.250	.250	.250	.500	41	-0	0	2.26	0	/C-1	0	0.0
• ADAMS, Mike	Robert Michael Adams b: 7/24/1948, Cincinnati, OH BR/TR, 5'9", 180 lbs. Deb: 9/10/1972 Career OF: 27-2-2																							
1972 Min-A	3	6	0	2	0	0	0	0	0	1	0	0	.333	.333	.333	.667	94	-0	1	4.50	0	/O-1	0	0.0
1973 Min-A	55	66	21	14	2	0	3	6	17	18	2	1	.212	.381	.379	.760	110	2	11	5.21	-1	O-24(23-1-0)/D-2	2	0.0
1976 Chi-N	25	29	1	4	2	0	0	2	8	7	0	0	.138	.342	.207	.549	54	-1	3	3.08	-1	/O-4(2-0-2),3-3,2-1	0	-0.2
1977 Chi-N	2	2	0	0	0	0	0	0	0	1	0	0	.000	.000	.000	.000	-90	-1	0	.00	0	/O-2(1-1-0)	0	-0.1
1978 Oak-A	15	15	5	3	1	0	0	1	7	2	0	0	.200	.455	.267	.721	113	1	3	5.95	0	/2-6,3-3,D-3	1	0.1
Total 5	100	118	27	23	5	0	3	9	32	29	2	1	.195	.375	.314	.689	93	1	17	4.62	-2	/O-31,2-7,3-6,D-5	3	-0.3
• ADAMS, Ricky	Ricky Lee Adams b: 1/21/1959, Upland, CA BR/TR, 6'2", 180 lbs. Deb: 9/15/1982																							
1982 Cal-A	8	14	1	2	0	0	0	0	0	2	1	0	.143	.200	.143	.343	-4	-2	0	.80	0	/S-8	0	-0.1
1983 Cal-A	58	112	22	28	2	0	2	6	5	12	1	1	.250	.300	.321	.621	72	-5	11	3.23	3	S-38,3-16/2-4	2	0.1
1985 SF-N	54	121	12	23	3	1	2	10	5	23	1	1	.190	.228	.281	.509	44	-10	7	1.91	2	S-25,3-16/2-6	1	-0.7
Total 3	120	247	35	53	5	1	4	16	10	37	3	2	.215	.260	.291	.551	54	-16	19	2.41	4	/S-71,3-32,2-10	3	-0.7
• ADAMS, Sparky	Earl John Adams b: 8/26/1894, Zerbe, PA d: 2/24/1989, Pottsville, PA BR/TR, 5'5.5", 151 lbs. Deb: 9/18/1922 Career OF: 2-0-2																							
1922 Chi-N	11	44	5	11	0	1	0	3	4	3	1	2	.250	.313	.295	.608	56	-3	4	2.82	0	2-11	0	-0.3
1923 Chi-N	95	311	40	90	12	0	4	35	26	10	20	19	.289	.346	.367	.713	88	-8	37	3.86	-6	S-79/O-1	7	-0.6
1924 Chi-N	117	418	66	117	11	5	1	27	40	20	15	17	.280	.344	.337	.682	83	-12	48	3.80	1	S-88,2-19	12	-0.1
1925 Chi-N	149	627	95	180	29	8	2	48	44	15	26	12	.287	.341	.368	.709	80	-17	80	4.54	19	*2-144/S-5	17	0.6
1926 Chi-N	154	624	95	193	35	3	0	39	52	27	27	....	.309	.367	.375	.742	99	1	86	4.94	19	*2-136,3-19/S-2	21	2.4
1927 Chi-N	146	647	100	189	17	7	0	49	42	26	26	....	.292	.335	.340	.675	81	-17	73	3.98	8	2-60,3-53,S-40	16	0.1
1928 Pit-N	135	539	91	149	14	6	0	38	64	18	8	....	.276	.357	.325	.682	76	-16	65	4.11	7	*2-107,S-27/O-1	12	-0.3
1929 Pit-N	74	196	37	51	8	1	0	11	15	5	3	....	.260	.316	.311	.627	55	-14	19	3.36	-5	S-30,2-20,3-15/O-2(2-0-0)	3	-1.4
1930*StL-N	137	570	98	179	36	9	0	55	45	27	7	....	.314	.365	.409	.774	84	-14	84	5.35	-10	*3-104,2-25/S-7	15	-1.4
1931*StL-N	143	608	97	178	**46**	5	1	40	42	24	16	....	.293	.340	.390	.730	92	-7	83	4.92	-14	*3-138/S-6	20	-1.5
1932 StL-N	31	127	22	35	3	1	0	13	14	5	0	....	.276	.352	.315	.667	79	-3	15	4.24	-2	3-30	3	-0.4
1933 StL-N	8	30	1	5	1	0	0	0	1	3	0	....	.167	.219	.200	.419	19	-3	1	1.04	0	/S-5,3-3	0	-0.2
Cin-N	137	538	59	141	21	1	1	22	44	30	3	....	.262	.320	.310	.631	82	-11	56	3.61	0	*3-132/S-8	14	-0.7
Yr.	145	568	60	146	22	1	1	22	45	33	3	....	.257	.315	.305	.620	79	-15	57	3.46	1	*3-135,S-13	14	-0.9
1934 Cin-N	87	278	38	70	16	1	0	14	20	10	2	....	.252	.307	.317	.623	69	-12	29	3.69	-2	3-38,2-29	4	-1.1
Total 13	1424	5557	844	1588	249	48	9	394	453	223	154	50	.286	.343	.353	.695	82	-137	679	4.27	16	2-551,3-532,S-297/O-4	144	-4.9
• ADAMS, Spencer	Spencer Dewey Adams b: 6/21/1898, Layton, UT d: 11/24/1970, Salt Lake City, UT BL/TR, 5'9", 158 lbs. Deb: 5/8/1923																							
1923 Pit-N	25	56	11	14	0	1	0	4	6	6	2	1	.250	.323	.286	.608	60	-3	5	3.37	-4	2-11/S-6	1	-0.6
1925*Was-A	39	55	11	15	4	1	0	4	5	4	1	1	.273	.333	.382	.715	83	-2	7	4.24	-3	2-15/S-8,3-3	1	-0.4

YEAR TM-L	G	AB	R	H	2B	3B	HR	RBI	BB	SO	SB	CS	AVG	OBP	SLG	OPS	OPS+	BR/A	RC	RC/G	FR	G/POS	WS	TPW
1926*NY-A	28	25	7	3	1	0	0	1	3	7	1	0	.120	.214	.160	.374	-1	-3	1	1.31	0	/2-4,3-1	0	-0.3
1927 StL-A	88	259	32	69	11	3	0	29	24	33	1	8	.266	.333	.332	.665	71	-14	28	3.56	-4	2-54,3-28	4	-1.4
Total 4	180	395	61	101	16	5	0	38	38	50	5	10	.256	.324	.322	.646	66	-22	41	3.47	-11	/2-84,3-32,S-14	6	-2.8

• ADCOCK, Joe Joseph Wilbur Adcock b: 10/30/1927, Coushatta, LA d: 5/3/1999, Coushatta, LA BR/TR, 6'4", 220 lbs. Deb: 4/23/1950 M Career OF: 310-0-0

YEAR TM-L	G	AB	R	H	2B	3B	HR	RBI	BB	SO	SB	CS	AVG	OBP	SLG	OPS	OPS+	BR/A	RC	RC/G	FR	G/POS	WS	TPW
1950 Cin-N	102	372	46	109	16	1	8	55	24	24	2	....	.293	.336	.406	.742	94	-4	48	4.68	1	0-75(75-0-0),1-24	9	-0.9
1951 Cin-N	113	395	40	96	16	4	10	47	24	29	1	2	.243	.288	.380	.668	77	-15	36	2.97	3	*0-107(107-0-0)	5	-1.9
1952 Cin-N	117	378	43	105	22	4	13	52	23	38	1	4	.278	.321	.460	.781	115	4	53	4.97	1	0-85(85-0-0),1-17	12	-0.1
1953 Mil-N	157	590	71	168	33	6	18	80	42	82	3	2	.285	.334	.453	.787	110	6	85	5.09	-3	*1-157	17	-0.5
1954 Mil-N	133	500	73	154	27	5	23	87	44	58	1	4	.308	.367	.520	.887	137	24	95	6.88	-7	*1-133	21	0.9
1955 Mil-N	84	288	40	76	14	0	15	45	31	44	0	2	.264	.340	.469	.808	118	6	42	4.92	-8	1-78	9	-0.7
1956 Mil-N	137	454	76	132	23	1	38	103	32	86	1	0	.291	.339	.597	.936	**154**	32	88	6.86	-2	*1-129	22	2.4
1957*Mil-N	65	209	31	60	13	2	12	38	20	51	0	0	.287	.352	.541	.893	146	13	38	6.51	-3	1-56	9	0.6
1958*Mil-N	105	320	40	88	15	1	19	54	21	63	0	0	.275	.322	.506	.828	125	10	47	5.02	1	1-71,0-22(22-0-0)	11	0.6
1959 Mil-N	115	404	53	118	19	2	25	76	32	77	0	0	.292	.344	.535	.879	141	22	73	6.49	11	1-89,0-21(21-0-0)	17	2.7
1960 Mil-N★	138	514	55	153	21	4	25	91	46	86	2	2	.298	.357	.500	.857	142	28	89	6.22	10	*1-136	25	3.0
1961 Mil-N	152	562	77	160	20	0	35	108	59	94	2	1	.285	.355	.507	.862	133	26	96	5.99	6	*1-148	22	2.3
1962 Mil-N	121	391	48	97	12	1	29	78	50	91	2	0	.248	.335	.506	.841	126	13	62	5.27	0	*1-112	13	0.8
1963 Cle-A	97	283	28	71	7	1	13	49	30	53	1	2	.251	.323	.420	.743	107	2	37	4.47	-2	1-78	8	-0.5
1964 LA-A	118	366	39	98	13	0	21	64	48	61	0	2	.268	.353	.475	.828	142	20	59	5.58	-4	*1-105	15	1.0
1965 Cal-A	122	349	30	84	14	0	14	47	37	74	2	2	.241	.315	.401	.716	104	1	43	4.16	-3	1-97	9	-0.7
1966 Cal-A	83	231	33	63	10	3	18	48	31	48	2	2	.273	.359	.576	.935	168	20	43	6.37	0	1-71	12	1.7
Total 17	1959	6606	823	1832	295	35	336	1122	594	1059	20	25	.277	.339	.485	.824	126	208	1033	5.46	-2	*1-1501,0-310	236	10.5

• ADDIS, Bob Robert Gordon Addis b: 11/6/1925, Mineral, OH BL/TR, 6', 175 lbs. Deb: 9/1/1950 Career OF: 36-54-48

YEAR TM-L	G	AB	R	H	2B	3B	HR	RBI	BB	SO	SB	CS	AVG	OBP	SLG	OPS	OPS+	BR/A	RC	RC/G	FR	G/POS	WS	TPW
1950 Bos-N	16	28	7	7	1	0	0	2	3	5	1	....	.250	.323	.286	.608	66	-1	3	3.64	0	/0-7(2-1-4)	0	-0.2
1951 Bos-N	85	199	23	55	7	0	1	24	9	10	3	2	.276	.308	.327	.634	76	-7	20	3.50	-3	0-46(31-10-5)	3	-1.3
1952 Chi-N	93	292	38	86	13	2	1	20	23	30	4	4	.295	.346	.363	.709	96	-2	37	4.62	4	0-79(3-42-37)	9	0.0
1953 Chi-N	10	12	2	2	1	0	0	1	2	0	0	0	.167	.286	.250	.536	40	-1	1	2.77	1	/0-3(0-1-2)	0	0.0
Pit-N	4	3	0	0	0	0	0	0	0	2	0	0	.000	.000	.000	.000	-101	-1	0	.00	0	....	0	-0.1
Yr.	14	15	2	2	1	0	0	1	2	2	0	0	.133	.235	.200	.435	15	-2	1	2.13	1	/0-3(0-1-2)	0	-0.1
Total 4	208	534	70	150	22	2	2	47	37	47	8	6	.281	.327	.341	.668	84	-13	61	4.06	2	0-135	12	-1.5

• ADDUCI, Jim James David Adduci b: 8/9/1959, Chicago, IL BL/TL, 6'5", 200 lbs. Deb: 9/12/1983 Career OF: 18-0-9

YEAR TM-L	G	AB	R	H	2B	3B	HR	RBI	BB	SO	SB	CS	AVG	OBP	SLG	OPS	OPS+	BR/A	RC	RC/G	FR	G/POS	WS	TPW
1983 StL-N	10	20	0	1	0	0	0	0	1	6	0	0	.050	.095	.050	.145	-59	-4	0	.17	0	/1-6,0-1	0	-0.5
1986 Mil-A	3	11	2	1	1	0	0	0	1	2	0	0	.091	.167	.182	.348	-5	-2	0	1.05	0	/1-3	0	-0.1
1988 Mil-A	44	94	8	25	6	1	1	15	0	15	0	1	.266	.266	.383	.649	79	-4	9	3.25	0	0-24(16-0-9),D-10/1-3	2	-0.4
1989 Phi-N	13	19	1	7	1	0	0	0	0	4	0	0	.368	.368	.421	.789	125	1	3	6.63	0	/1-4,0-1	0	0.1
Total 4	70	144	11	34	8	1	1	15	2	27	0	1	.236	.247	.326	.573	58	-9	12	2.89	1	/0-26,1-16,D-10	2	-1.0

• ADDY, Bob Robert Edward "Magnet" Addy
b: 2/1845, Rochester, NY d: 4/9/1910, Pocatello, ID BL/TR, 5'8", 160 lbs. Deb: 5/6/1871 M/U NA OF: 0-1-98 Career OF: 3-1-85

YEAR TM-L	G	AB	R	H	2B	3B	HR	RBI	BB	SO	SB	CS	AVG	OBP	SLG	OPS	OPS+	BR/A	RC	RC/G	FR	G/POS	WS	TPW
1871 Rok-n	25	118	30	32	6	0	0	13	4	0	8	1	.271	.295	.322	.617	81	-1	14	5.04	-1	*2-22/S-3	....	-0.2
1873 Phi-n	10	51	12	16	1	0	0	10	2	0	0	1	.314	.340	.333	.673	97	-1	6	5.01	-3	2-10	....	-0.3
Bos-n	31	152	37	54	5	2	1	36	1	0	2	3	.355	.359	.434	.794	124	3	25	7.57	-1	0-31(0-0-31)	....	0.3
Yr.	41	203	49	70	6	2	1	46	3	0	2	4	.345	.354	.409	.763	117	2	31	6.90	-3	0-31(0-0-31),2-10	....	0.0
1874 Har-n	50	213	25	51	9	2	0	23	1	1	4	2	.239	.243	.300	.543	70	-8	17	3.10	6	*2-45/3-5,S-1	....	-0.4
1875 Phi-n	69	310	60	80	8	4	0	43	0	2	16	8	.258	.258	.310	.568	93	-3	30	3.67	-2	*0-68(0-1-67)/2-2	....	-0.1
1876 Chi-N	32	147	36	40	4	1	0	16	5	0	....	....	.272	.306	.324	.630	98	-1	14	3.96	0	0-32(3-0-29)	3	-0.1
1877 Cin-N	57	245	27	68	2	3	0	31	6	5	....	....	.278	.295	.310	.605	102	2	23	3.57	3	*0-57(0-1-56)	4	0.4
Total 4 n	185	844	164	233	29	8	1	125	8	3	30	15	.276	.283	.333	.616	91	-11	91	4.42	0	/0-99,2-79,3-5,S-4	....	-0.7
Total 2	89	392	63	108	6	4	0	47	11	5	....	....	.276	.299	.315	.614	101	1	37	3.71	2	/0-89	7	0.3

• ADERHOLT, Morrie Morris Woodroe Aderholt b: 9/13/1915, Mount Olive, NC d: 3/18/1955, Sarasota, FL BL/TR, 6'1", 188 lbs. Deb: 9/13/1939 Career OF: 42-0-3

YEAR TM-L	G	AB	R	H	2B	3B	HR	RBI	BB	SO	SB	CS	AVG	OBP	SLG	OPS	OPS+	BR/A	RC	RC/G	FR	G/POS	WS	TPW
1939 Was-A	7	25	5	5	0	0	1	4	2	6	0	1	.200	.259	.320	.579	51	-2	2	2.43	-2	/2-7	0	-0.3
1940 Was-A	1	2	0	0	0	0	0	0	0	0	0	0	.000	.000	.000	.000	-107	-1	0	.00	0	/2-1	0	-0.1
1941 Was-A	11	14	3	2	0	0	0	1	1	3	0	0	.143	.200	.143	.343	-8	-2	0	1.04	-2	/2-2,3-1	0	-0.4
1944 Bro-N	17	59	9	16	2	3	0	10	4	4	0	....	.271	.317	.407	.724	105	0	8	4.99	-2	0-13(11-0-2)	2	-0.3
1945 Bro-N	39	60	4	13	1	0	0	6	3	10	0	....	.217	.254	.233	.487	36	-5	4	2.16	0	/0-8(7-0-1)	0	-0.6
Bos-N	31	102	15	34	4	0	2	11	9	6	3	....	.333	.387	.431	.819	127	4	18	6.86	-1	0-24(24-0-0)/2-1	3	0.1
Yr.	70	162	19	47	5	0	2	17	12	16	3	....	.290	.339	.358	.697	94	-2	21	4.95	-1	0-32(31-0-1)/2-1	3	-0.4
Total 5	106	262	36	70	7	3	3	32	19	29	3	1	.267	.317	.351	.668	85	-7	32	4.40	-7	/0-45,2-11,3-1	5	-1.5

• ADKINS, Dick Richard Earl Adkins b: 3/3/1920, Electra, TX d: 9/12/1955, Electra, TX BR/TR, 5'10", 165 lbs. Deb: 9/19/1942

YEAR TM-L	G	AB	R	H	2B	3B	HR	RBI	BB	SO	SB	CS	AVG	OBP	SLG	OPS	OPS+	BR/A	RC	RC/G	FR	G/POS	WS	TPW
1942 Phi-A	3	7	2	1	0	0	0	0	2	2	0	0	.143	.333	.143	.476	37	-0	1	2.32	0	/S-3	0	-0.1

• ADKINSON, Henry Henry Magee Adkinson b: 9/1/1874, Chicago, IL d: 5/1/1923, Salt Lake City, UT Deb: 9/25/1895

YEAR TM-L	G	AB	R	H	2B	3B	HR	RBI	BB	SO	SB	CS	AVG	OBP	SLG	OPS	OPS+	BR/A	RC	RC/G	FR	G/POS	WS	TPW
1895 StL-N	1	5	1	2	0	0	0	0	0	2	0	....	.400	.400	.400	.800	108	0	1	7.38	0	/0-1	0	0.0

• ADLESH, Dave David George Adlesh b: 7/15/1943, Long Beach, CA BR/TR, 6', 187 lbs. Deb: 5/12/1963

YEAR TM-L	G	AB	R	H	2B	3B	HR	RBI	BB	SO	SB	CS	AVG	OBP	SLG	OPS	OPS+	BR/A	RC	RC/G	FR	G/POS	WS	TPW
1963 Hou-N	6	8	0	0	0	0	0	0	0	4	0	0	.000	.000	.000	.000	-107	-2	0	.00	-2	/C-6	0	-0.4
1964 Hou-N	3	10	0	2	0	0	0	0	0	5	0	0	.200	.200	.200	.400	14	-1	0	1.35	0	/C-3	0	-0.1
1965 Hou-N	15	34	2	5	1	0	0	3	2	12	0	0	.147	.216	.176	.393	13	-4	1	1.15	0	C-13	0	-0.3
1966 Hou-N	3	6	0	0	0	0	0	0	0	4	0	0	.000	.000	.000	.000	-107	-2	0	.00	1	/C-1	0	-0.1
1967 Hou-N	39	94	4	17	1	0	1	4	11	28	0	0	.181	.267	.223	.490	43	-7	5	1.57	-1	C-31	1	-0.6
1968 Hou-N	40	104	3	19	1	1	0	4	5	27	0	0	.183	.227	.212	.439	33	-8	5	1.58	-1	C-36	1	-0.9
Total 6	106	256	9	43	3	1	1	11	18	80	0	0	.168	.228	.199	.427	26	-24	12	1.41	-2	/C-90	2	-2.4

• AFENIR, Troy Michael Troy Afenir b: 9/21/1963, Escondido, CA BR/TR, 6'4", 185 lbs. Deb: 9/14/1987

YEAR TM-L	G	AB	R	H	2B	3B	HR	RBI	BB	SO	SB	CS	AVG	OBP	SLG	OPS	OPS+	BR/A	RC	RC/G	FR	G/POS	WS	TPW
1987 Hou-N	10	20	1	6	1	0	0	1	0	12	0	0	.300	.300	.350	.650	74	-1	2	4.05	-1	C-10	0	-0.1
1990 Oak-A	14	14	0	2	0	0	0	2	0	6	0	0	.143	.143	.143	.286	-21	-2	0	.70	-3	C-12/D-1	0	-0.5
1991 Oak-A	5	11	0	1	0	0	0	0	0	2	0	0	.091	.091	.091	.182	-53	-2	0	.00	0	/C-4,D-1	0	-0.2
1992 Cin-N	16	34	3	6	1	2	0	4	5	12	0	0	.176	.282	.324	.606	69	-1	4	3.28	0	C-15	1	-0.1
Total 4	45	79	4	15	2	2	0	7	5	32	0	0	.190	.238	.266	.504	39	-7	6	2.40	-3	/C-41,D-2	1	-0.9

• AGBAYANI, Benny Benny Peter Agbayani, Jr. b: 12/28/1971, Honolulu, HI BR/TR, 6', 225 lbs. Deb: 6/17/1998 Career OF: 282-10-66

YEAR TM-L	G	AB	R	H	2B	3B	HR	RBI	BB	SO	SB	CS	AVG	OBP	SLG	OPS	OPS+	BR/A	RC	RC/G	FR	G/POS	WS	TPW
1998 NY-N	11	15	1	2	0	0	0	0	1	5	0	2	.133	.188	.133	.321	-14	-3	0	.00	0	/0-9(1-2-6)	0	-0.4
1999*NY-N	101	276	42	79	18	3	14	42	32	60	6	4	.286	.367	.525	.892	126	10	51	6.53	-1	0-80(47-4-45)/D-2	9	0.5
2000*NY-N	119	350	59	101	19	1	15	60	54	68	5	5	.289	.394	.477	.871	124	13	68	6.98	-3	*0-110(102-3-12)/D-1	14	0.6
2001 NY-N	91	296	28	82	14	2	6	27	36	73	4	5	.277	.365	.399	.764	103	1	42	4.84	-5	0-84(84-0-0)	8	-0.7
2002 Col-N	48	117	10	24	5	0	4	19	10	35	1	0	.205	.268	.350	.618	53	-8	10	2.88	0	0-37(37-0-0)/D-1	2	-1.0
Bos-A	13	37	5	11	1	0	0	8	6	5	0	0	.297	.395	.324	.720	93	-0	5	4.95	1	0-13(11-1-3)	2	0.0
Total 5	383	1091	145	299	57	6	39	156	139	246	16	16	.274	.364	.445	.808	109	12	176	5.61	-9	0-333/D-4	35	-0.9

• AGEE, Tommie Tommie Lee Agee b: 8/9/1942, Magnolia, AL d: 1/22/2001, New York, NY BR/TR, 5'11", 195 lbs. Deb: 9/14/1962 Career OF: 64-934-124

YEAR TM-L	G	AB	R	H	2B	3B	HR	RBI	BB	SO	SB	CS	AVG	OBP	SLG	OPS	OPS+	BR/A	RC	RC/G	FR	G/POS	WS	TPW
1962 Cle-A	5	14	0	3	0	0	0	2	0	4	0	0	.214	.214	.214	.429	16	-2	1	1.58	0	/0-3(2-1-0)	0	-0.2
1963 Cle-A	13	27	3	4	1	0	1	3	2	9	0	0	.148	.207	.296	.503	39	-2	1	1.65	1	0-13(4-3-6)	0	-0.1
1964 Cle-A	13	12	0	2	0	0	0	0	0	3	0	0	.167	.167	.167	.333	-7	-2	0	.90	-1	0-12(0-3-10)	0	-0.3
1965 Chi-A	10	19	2	3	1	0	0	3	2	6	0	1	.158	.238	.211	.449	30	-2	1	.91	0	/0-9(0-5-6)	0	-0.3
1966 Chi-A★	160	629	98	172	27	8	22	86	41	127	44	18	.273	.328	.447	.775	129	24	88	4.72	9	*0-159(8-156-0)	28	2.9

YEAR TM-L	G	AB	R	H	2B	3B	HR	RBI	BB	SO	SB	CS	AVG	OBP	SLG	OPS	OPS+	BR/A	RC	RC/G	FR	G/POS	WS	TPW
1967 Chi-A★	158	529	73	124	26	2	14	52	44	129	28	10	.234	.303	.371	.673	102	3	58	3.65	0	*O-152(10-136-9)	20	-0.3
1968 NY-N	132	368	30	80	12	3	5	17	15	103	13	8	.217	.256	.307	.563	68	-15	27	2.34	0	*O-127(0-116-13)	5	-2.2
1969*NY-N	149	565	97	153	23	4	26	76	59	137	12	9	.271	.343	.464	.807	121	14	91	5.67	-2	*O-146(0-143-7)	28	0.9
1970 NY-N	153	636	107	182	30	7	24	75	55	156	31	15	.286	.345	.469	.813	115	12	101	5.64	-1	*O-150(0-149-2)	23	0.7
1971 NY-N	113	425	58	121	19	0	14	50	50	84	28	6	.285	.363	.428	.791	125	18	68	5.63	0	*O-107(0-94-32)	19	1.5
1972 NY-N	114	422	52	96	23	0	13	47	53	92	8	9	.227	.319	.374	.694	99	-2	46	3.50	-3	*O-109(6-91-20)	11	-0.9
1973 Hou-N	83	204	30	48	5	2	8	15	16	55	2	5	.235	.294	.397	.691	90	-5	22	3.57	0	O-67(34-18-17)	4	-0.8
StL-N	26	62	8	11	3	1	3	7	5	13	1	0	.177	.239	.403	.642	75	-2	3	1.47	0	O-19(0-19-2)	1	-0.3
Yr.	109	266	38	59	8	3	11	22	21	68	3	5	.222	.281	.398	.680	87	-7	25	3.02	0	O-86(34-37-19)	5	-1.1
Total 12	1129	3912	558	999	170	27	130	433	342	918	167	81	.255	.321	.412	.733	108	38	507	4.38	4	*O-1073	139	0.6

• AGGANIS, Harry Harry "The Golden Greek" Agganis b: 4/20/1929, Lynn, MA d: 6/27/1955, Cambridge, MA BL/TL, 6'2", 200 lbs. Deb: 4/13/1954

YEAR TM-L	G	AB	R	H	2B	3B	HR	RBI	BB	SO	SB	CS	AVG	OBP	SLG	OPS	OPS+	BR/A	RC	RC/G	FR	G/POS	WS	TPW
1954 Bos-A	132	434	54	109	13	8	11	57	47	57	6	3	.251	.324	.394	.718	86	-8	57	4.48	3	*1-119	9	-1.3
1955 Bos-A	25	83	11	26	10	1	0	10	10	10	2	0	.313	.387	.458	.845	116	2	15	6.55	0	1-20	3	0.2
Total 2	157	517	65	135	23	9	11	67	57	67	8	3	.261	.334	.404	.739	91	-6	72	4.79	3	1-139	12	-1.1

• AGLER, Joe Joseph Abram Agler b: 6/12/1887, Coshocton, OH d: 4/26/1971, Massillon, OH BL/TL, 5'11", 165 lbs. Deb: 10/1/1912 Career OF: 52-9-18

YEAR TM-L	G	AB	R	H	2B	3B	HR	RBI	BB	SO	SB	CS	AVG	OBP	SLG	OPS	OPS+	BR/A	RC	RC/G	FR	G/POS	WS	TPW
1912 Was-A	2	1	0	0	0	0	0	0	0	....	0	....	.000	.000	.000	.000	-99	-0	0	.00	0	/1-1	0	0.0
1914 Buf-F	135	463	82	126	17	6	0	20	77	78	21	....	.272	.376	.335	.711	99	3	65	4.69	5	1-76,O-54(44-5-6)	17	0.4
1915 Buf-F	25	73	11	13	1	2	0	2	20	14	2	....	.178	.355	.247	.601	78	-1	7	2.94	-2	O-20(6-3-11)/1-1	2	-0.4
Bal-F	72	214	28	46	4	2	0	14	34	38	15	....	.215	.325	.252	.578	66	-8	22	3.23	2	1-58/O-4(2-1-1),2-3	3	-0.7
Yr.	97	287	39	59	5	4	0	16	54	52	17	....	.206	.333	.251	.584	69	-8	29	3.15	1	1-59,O-24(8-4-12)/2-3	5	-1.0
Total 3	234	751	121	185	22	10	0	36	131	130	38	....	.246	.359	.302	.661	87	-5	93	4.07	6	1-136/O-78,2-3	22	-0.6

• AGNEW, Sam Samuel Lester "Slam" Agnew b: 4/12/1887, Farmington, MO d: 7/19/1951, Sonoma, CA BR/TR, 5'11", 185 lbs. Deb: 4/10/1913

YEAR TM-L	G	AB	R	H	2B	3B	HR	RBI	BB	SO	SB	CS	AVG	OBP	SLG	OPS	OPS+	BR/A	RC	RC/G	FR	G/POS	WS	TPW
1913 StL-A	105	307	27	64	9	5	2	24	20	49	11	....	.208	.272	.290	.562	66	-14	26	2.66	7	*C-103	5	0.1
1914 StL-A	115	311	22	66	5	4	0	16	24	63	10	8	.212	.279	.254	.533	63	-16	23	2.38	1	*C-115	6	-0.6
1915 StL-A	104	295	18	60	4	2	0	19	12	36	5	2	.203	.247	.231	.477	45	-21	18	2.00	-2	*C-102	2	-1.6
1916 Bos-A	40	67	4	14	2	1	0	7	6	4	0	....	.209	.293	.269	.562	69	-3	6	2.69	-1	C-38	2	-0.1
1917 Bos-A	85	260	17	54	6	2	0	16	19	30	2	....	.208	.267	.246	.513	57	-14	17	2.11	-6	C-85	4	-1.5
1918*Bos-A	72	199	11	33	8	0	0	6	11	26	0	....	.166	.221	.206	.427	29	-18	9	1.34	1	C-72	3	-1.2
1919 Was-A	42	98	6	23	7	0	0	10	10	8	1	....	.235	.312	.306	.618	74	-3	10	3.24	5	C-36	3	0.4
Total 7	563	1537	105	314	41	14	2	98	102	216	29	10	.204	.265	.253	.518	56	-87	111	2.25	6	C-551	25	-4.5

• AGUAYO, Luis Luis (Muriel) Aguayo b: 3/13/1959, Vega Baja, Puerto Rico BR/TR, 5'9", 185 lbs. Deb: 4/19/1980

YEAR TM-L	G	AB	R	H	2B	3B	HR	RBI	BB	SO	SB	CS	AVG	OBP	SLG	OPS	OPS+	BR/A	RC	RC/G	FR	G/POS	WS	TPW
1980 Phi-N	20	47	7	13	1	2	1	8	2	3	1	1	.277	.306	.447	.753	102	-0	6	4.74	-1	2-14/S-5	2	0.0
1981*Phi-N	45	84	11	18	4	0	1	7	6	15	1	0	.214	.283	.298	.580	62	-4	8	3.15	-3	2-21,S-21/3-3	2	-0.6
1982 Phi-N	50	56	11	15	1	2	3	7	5	7	1	1	.268	.339	.518	.857	133	2	9	5.80	-5	2-21,S-15/3-5	3	-0.2
1983 Phi-N	2	4	1	1	0	0	0	0	1	2	0	0	.250	.400	.250	.650	85	-0	1	4.54	-1	/S-2	0	0.0
1984 Phi-N	58	72	15	20	4	0	3	11	8	16	0	0	.278	.350	.458	.808	123	2	12	5.94	1	3-14,2-12,S-10	3	0.4
1985 Phi-N	91	165	27	46	7	3	6	21	22	26	1	0	.279	.383	.467	.850	133	8	29	5.93	-3	S-60,2-17/3-7	8	1.1
1986 Phi-N	62	133	17	28	6	1	4	13	8	26	1	1	.211	.271	.361	.632	70	-6	13	3.06	-1	2-31,S-20/3-1	2	-0.5
1987 Phi-N	94	209	25	43	9	1	12	21	15	56	0	0	.206	.275	.431	.706	81	-7	24	3.71	5	S-78/2-6,3-2	5	0.4
1988 Phi-N	49	97	9	24	3	0	3	5	13	17	2	0	.247	.336	.371	.707	101	1	13	4.53	0	S-27,3-13/2-2	3	0.2
NY-A	50	140	12	35	4	0	3	8	7	33	0	2	.250	.291	.343	.633	77	-5	13	3.01	1	3-33,2-13/S-6	1	-0.4
1989 Cle-A	47	97	7	17	4	1	1	8	7	19	0	0	.175	.245	.268	.513	44	-7	6	1.85	-1	3-19,S-15,2-10/D-2	1	-0.8
Total 10	568	1104	142	260	43	10	37	109	94	220	7	5	.236	.307	.393	.700	91	-17	133	3.99	-7	S-259,2-147/3-97,D-2	30	-0.4

• AHEARN, Charlie Charles Ahearn b: Troy, NY Deb: 6/19/1880

YEAR TM-L	G	AB	R	H	2B	3B	HR	RBI	BB	SO	SB	CS	AVG	OBP	SLG	OPS	OPS+	BR/A	RC	RC/G	FR	G/POS	WS	TPW
1880 Tro-N	1	4	1	1	0	0	0	0	0	0	....	....	.250	.250	.250	.500	66	-0	0	2.35	0	/C-1	0	0.0

• AIKENS, Willie Willie Mays Aikens b: 10/14/1954, Seneca, SC BL/TR, 6'3", 220 lbs. Deb: 5/17/1977

YEAR TM-L	G	AB	R	H	2B	3B	HR	RBI	BB	SO	SB	CS	AVG	OBP	SLG	OPS	OPS+	BR/A	RC	RC/G	FR	G/POS	WS	TPW
1977 Cal-A	42	91	5	18	4	0	0	6	10	23	1	2	.198	.277	.242	.519	45	-7	6	2.16	-1	1-13,D-13	0	-0.9
1979 Cal-A	116	379	59	106	18	0	21	81	61	79	1	3	.280	.381	.493	.874	138	21	71	6.56	-3	1-55,D-51	15	1.3
1980*KC-A	151	543	70	151	24	0	20	98	64	88	1	0	.278	.362	.433	.794	116	13	82	5.25	-5	*1-138,D-13	16	0.0
1981*KC-A	101	349	45	93	16	0	17	53	62	47	0	0	.266	.382	.458	.840	142	22	62	6.14	0	1-99	13	1.7
1982 KC-A	134	466	50	131	29	1	17	74	45	70	0	1	.281	.348	.457	.805	119	12	69	5.20	-2	*1-128	14	0.3
1983 KC-A	125	410	49	124	26	1	23	72	45	75	0	0	.302	.374	.539	.913	147	26	78	6.98	-4	*1-112/D-6	17	1.6
1984 Tor-A	93	234	21	48	7	0	11	26	29	56	0	0	.205	.298	.376	.674	82	-6	26	3.71	0	D-81/1-2	2	-0.8
1985 Tor-A	12	20	2	4	1	0	1	5	3	6	0	0	.200	.304	.400	.704	89	-0	2	3.49	0	D-11	0	0.0
Total 8	774	2492	301	675	125	2	110	415	319	444	3	6	.271	.358	.455	.813	123	81	398	5.54	-15	1-547,D-175	77	3.1

• AINGE, Danny Daniel Ray Ainge b: 3/17/1959, Eugene, OR BR/TR, 6'4", 175 lbs. Deb: 5/21/1979 Career OF: 6-25-2

YEAR TM-L	G	AB	R	H	2B	3B	HR	RBI	BB	SO	SB	CS	AVG	OBP	SLG	OPS	OPS+	BR/A	RC	RC/G	FR	G/POS	WS	TPW
1979 Tor-A	87	308	26	73	7	1	2	19	12	58	1	0	.237	.270	.286	.556	50	-22	23	2.47	1	2-86/D-1	3	-1.6
1980 Tor-A	38	111	11	27	6	1	0	4	2	29	3	0	.243	.263	.315	.578	55	-6	9	2.73	1	O-29(6-22-1)/3-3,D-2,2-1	1	-0.6
1981 Tor-A	86	246	20	46	6	2	0	14	23	41	8	5	.187	.259	.228	.487	39	-19	15	1.88	1	3-77/S-6,O-4(0-3-1),2-2,D	3	-2.0
Total 3	211	665	57	146	19	4	2	37	37	128	12	5	.220	.265	.269	.534	46	-47	47	2.28	3	/2-89,3-80,O-33,S-6,D-4	7	-4.1

• AINSMITH, Eddie Edward Wilbur "Dorf" Ainsmith b: 2/4/1892, Cambridge, MA d: 9/6/1981, Fort Lauderdale, FL BR/TR, 5'11", 180 lbs. Deb: 8/9/1910

YEAR TM-L	G	AB	R	H	2B	3B	HR	RBI	BB	SO	SB	CS	AVG	OBP	SLG	OPS	OPS+	BR/A	RC	RC/G	FR	G/POS	WS	TPW
1910 Was-A	33	104	4	20	1	2	0	9	6	....	0	....	.192	.236	.240	.477	52	-6	6	1.74	1	C-30	1	-0.3
1911 Was-A	61	149	12	33	2	3	0	14	10	....	5	....	.221	.275	.275	.550	55	-9	12	2.72	2	C-47	2	-0.4
1912 Was-A	61	186	22	42	7	2	0	22	14	....	4	....	.226	.280	.285	.565	61	-10	17	2.77	1	C-59	5	-0.4
1913 Was-A	84	229	26	49	4	4	2	20	12	41	17	....	.214	.262	.293	.555	61	-12	20	2.81	-5	C-79/P-1	5	-1.5
1914 Was-A	62	151	11	34	7	0	0	13	9	28	8	5	.225	.273	.272	.545	61	-8	12	2.52	-3	C-51	3	-0.8
1915 Was-A	47	120	13	24	4	2	0	6	10	18	7	4	.200	.267	.267	.534	59	-7	9	2.42	2	C-42	3	-0.2
1916 Was-A	51	100	11	17	4	0	0	8	8	14	3	....	.170	.231	.210	.441	33	-8	7	1.87	-2	C-46	2	-0.8
1917 Was-A	125	350	38	67	17	4	0	42	40	48	16	....	.191	.280	.263	.543	66	-14	30	2.61	12	*C-119	9	0.8
1918 Was-A	96	292	22	62	10	9	0	20	29	44	6	....	.212	.283	.308	.592	80	-8	27	2.83	2	C-89	8	0.2
1919 Det-A	114	364	42	99	17	12	3	32	45	30	9	....	.272	.354	.409	.763	117	8	54	5.11	-7	*C-106	15	1.0
1920 Det-A	69	186	19	43	5	3	1	19	14	19	4	3	.231	.285	.306	.591	58	-11	17	2.87	-5	C-61/1-1	1	-1.1
1921 Det-A	35	98	6	27	5	2	0	12	13	7	1	0	.276	.360	.367	.728	87	-1	14	4.95	-3	C-34	2	-0.2
StL-N	27	62	5	18	0	1	0	5	3	4	0	0	.290	.323	.323	.646	73	-2	7	3.83	-2	C-23/1-1	2	-0.3
1922 StL-N	119	379	46	111	14	4	13	59	28	43	2	3	.293	.343	.454	.797	109	4	58	5.51	2	*C-116	16	1.2
1923 StL-N	82	263	22	56	11	6	3	34	22	19	4	0	.213	.276	.335	.611	62	-13	26	3.16	-4	C-80	4	-1.2
Bro-N	2	10	0	2	0	0	0	2	0	0	0	1	.200	.200	.200	.400	6	-2	0	.57	1	/C-2	0	0.0
Yr.	84	273	22	58	11	6	3	36	22	19	4	1	.212	.274	.330	.603	60	-15	26	3.06	-3	C-82	4	-1.3
1924 NY-N	10	5	0	3	0	0	0	0	0	0	0	0	.600	.600	.600	1.200	229	1	2	22.90	-2	/C-9	0	-0.1
Total 15	1078	3048	299	707	108	54	22	317	263	315	86	16	.232	.296	.324	.620	76	-99	317	3.37	-10	C-993/1-2,P-1	78	-4.0

• AITON, George George Wilson Aiton b: 12/29/1890, Kingman, KS d: 8/16/1976, Van Nuys, CA BB/TR, 5'11.5", 175 lbs. Deb: 6/29/1912

YEAR TM-L	G	AB	R	H	2B	3B	HR	RBI	BB	SO	SB	CS	AVG	OBP	SLG	OPS	OPS+	BR/A	RC	RC/G	FR	G/POS	WS	TPW
1912 StL-A	10	17	1	4	0	0	0	1	4	....	0	....	.235	.381	.235	.616	80	-0	1	2.99	0	/O-7(4-2-0)	0	0.0

• AKE, John John Leckie Ake b: 8/29/1861, Altoona, PA d: 5/11/1887, La Crosse, WI BR/TR, 6'1", 180 lbs. Deb: 5/12/1884

YEAR TM-L	G	AB	R	H	2B	3B	HR	RBI	BB	SO	SB	CS	AVG	OBP	SLG	OPS	OPS+	BR/A	RC	RC/G	FR	G/POS	WS	TPW
1884 Bal-a	13	52	1	10	0	1	0	2	0	....	....	....	.192	.208	.231	.438	41	-3	3	1.67	-3	/3-9,O-3(2-0-1),S-1	0	-0.5

• AKERS, Bill William G. "Bump" Akers b: 12/25/1904, Chattanooga, TN d: 4/13/1962, Chattanooga, TN BR/TR, 5'11", 178 lbs. Deb: 9/8/1929

YEAR TM-L	G	AB	R	H	2B	3B	HR	RBI	BB	SO	SB	CS	AVG	OBP	SLG	OPS	OPS+	BR/A	RC	RC/G	FR	G/POS	WS	TPW
1929 Det-A	24	83	15	22	4	1	1	9	10	9	2	0	.265	.351	.373	.725	86	-1	12	4.87	-3	S-24	2	-0.1
1930 Det-A	85	233	36	65	8	5	9	40	36	34	5	5	.279	.375	.472	.848	111	4	42	6.14	6	S-49,3-26	10	1.5
1931 Det-A	29	66	5	13	2	2	0	3	7	6	0	1	.197	.274	.288	.562	46	-5	5	2.55	-7	S-21/2-2	1	-1.0

YEAR TM-L	G	AB	R	H	2B	3B	HR	RBI	BB	SO	SB	CS	AVG	OBP	SLG	OPS	OPS+	BR/A	RC	RC/G	FR	G/POS	WS	TPW
1932 Bos-N	36	93	8	24	3	1	1	17	10	15	0	....	.258	.330	.344	.674	85	-2	11	4.10	-8	3-20/2-5,S-5	2	-0.9
Total 4	174	475	64	124	17	9	11	69	63	64	7	6	.261	.349	.404	.753	93	-4	70	5.00	-12	/S-99,3-46,2-7	15	-0.6
• ALBERTS, Butch	Francis Burt Alberts b: 5/4/1950, Williamsport, PA BR/TR, 6'2", 205 lbs. Deb: 9/7/1978																							
1978 Tor-A	6	18	1	5	1	0	0	0	0	2	0	0	.278	.278	.333	.611	70	-1	2	3.46	0	/D-4	0	-0.1
• ALBERTS, Gus	Augustus Peter Alberts b: 1861, Reading, PA d: 5/7/1912, Idaho Springs, CO BR/TR, 5'6.5", 180 lbs. Deb: 5/1/1884																							
1884 Pit-a	2	5	1	1	0	0	0	0	0	....	....	....	.200	.200	.200	.400	30	-0	0	1.41	-1	/S-2	0	-0.1
Was-U	4	16	4	4	0	0	0	....	4	....	....	....	.250	.400	.250	.650	128	1	2	3.83	2	/S-4	1	0.2
1888 Cle-a	102	364	51	75	10	6	1	48	41	....	26	....	.206	.299	.275	.573	87	-3	39	3.60	-0	S-53,3-49	10	0.0
1891 Mil-a	12	41	6	4	0	0	0	2	7	5	1	....	.098	.260	.098	.358	2	-6	1	.95	-3	3-12	0	-0.7
Total 3	120	426	62	84	10	6	1	50	52	5	27	....	.197	.298	.256	.554	79	-8	42	3.30	-3	/3-61,S-59	11	-0.7
• ALBRIGHT, Jack	Harold John Albright b: 6/30/1921, St. Petersburg, FL d: 7/22/1991, San Diego, CA BR/TR, 5'9", 175 lbs. Deb: 5/19/1947																							
1947 Phi-N	41	99	9	23	4	0	2	5	10	11	1	....	.232	.303	.333	.636	71	-4	10	3.43	-3	S-33	2	-0.5
• ALCANTARA, Israel	Israel (Cristosomo) Alcantara b: 5/6/1973, Bani, Dominican Republic BR/TR, 6'2", 180 lbs. Deb: 6/25/2000 Career OF: 9-0-14																							
2000 Bos-A	21	45	9	13	1	0	4	7	3	7	0	0	.289	.333	.578	.911	121	1	9	7.53	-1	/D-8,0-7(1-0-7),1-5	2	0.0
2001 Bos-A	14	38	3	10	1	0	0	3	3	13	1	0	.263	.317	.289	.607	61	-2	3	2.61	0	/0-8(6-0-2),1-4,D-1	1	-0.3
2002 Mil-N	16	32	3	8	1	0	2	5	0	6	0	1	.250	.250	.469	.719	85	-1	3	3.54	-1	/0-7(2-0-5),1-2	0	-0.3
Total 3	51	115	15	31	3	0	6	15	6	26	1	1	.270	.306	.452	.758	91	-2	15	4.67	-2	/0-22,1-11,D-9	3	-0.6
• ALCARAZ, Luis	Angel Luis (Acosta) Alcaraz b: 6/20/1941, Humacao, Puerto Rico BR/TR, 5'9", 165 lbs. Deb: 9/13/1967																							
1967 LA-N	17	60	1	14	1	0	0	3	1	13	1	1	.233	.246	.250	.496	46	-4	3	1.87	2	2-17	1	-0.1
1968 LA-N	41	106	4	16	1	0	2	5	9	23	1	1	.151	.217	.217	.434	33	-9	5	1.41	-4	2-20,3-13/S-1	1	-1.3
1969 KC-A	22	79	15	20	2	1	1	7	7	9	0	0	.253	.314	.342	.656	83	-2	8	3.71	-3	2-19/3-2,S-1	2	-0.4
1970 KC-A	35	120	10	20	5	1	1	14	4	13	0	0	.167	.194	.250	.444	21	-13	6	1.45	-1	2-31	1	-1.3
Total 4	115	365	30	70	9	2	4	29	21	58	2	2	.192	.236	.260	.496	42	-28	22	1.95	-7	/2-87,3-15,S-2	5	-3.1
• ALCOCK, Scotty	John Forbes Alcock b: 11/29/1885, Wooster, OH d: 1/30/1973, Wooster, OH BR/TR, 5'9.5", 160 lbs. Deb: 4/19/1914																							
1914 Chi-A	54	156	12	27	4	2	0	7	7	14	4	2	.173	.213	.224	.438	32	-14	8	1.62	-5	3-48/2-1	1	-1.9
• ALDRETE, Mike	Michael Peter Aldrete b: 1/29/1961, Carmel, CA BL/TL, 5'11", 185 lbs. Deb: 5/28/1986 Career OF: 278-24-135																							
1986 SF-N	84	216	27	54	18	3	2	25	33	34	1	3	.250	.355	.389	.743	110	3	31	4.82	6	1-37,0-31(30-0-2)	7	0.6
1987*SF-N	126	357	50	116	18	2	9	51	43	50	6	0	.325	.398	.462	.860	133	19	68	7.28	0	0-79(43-13-30),1-33	16	1.4
1988 SF-N	139	389	44	104	15	0	3	50	56	65	6	5	.267	.360	.329	.689	103	3	47	4.14	-1	*0-115(83-7-40),1-10	13	-0.3
1989 Mon-N	76	136	12	30	8	1	1	12	19	30	1	3	.221	.321	.316	.637	81	-4	14	3.16	2	0-37(16-3-19),1-10	1	-0.4
1990 Mon-N	96	161	22	39	7	1	1	18	37	31	1	2	.242	.387	.317	.704	100	2	22	4.76	2	0-38(26-0-14),1-18	3	0.1
1991 SD-N	12	15	2	0	0	0	0	1	3	4	0	1	.000	.167	.000	.167	-48	-3	0	.07	1	/0-5(5-0-0)	0	-0.3
Cle-A	85	183	22	48	6	1	1	19	36	37	1	2	.262	.384	.322	.706	97	1	26	5.00	-2	1-47,0-16(16-0-0)/D-7	6	-0.4
1993 Oak-A	95	255	40	68	13	1	10	33	34	45	1	1	.267	.353	.443	.796	120	7	40	5.42	-1	1-59,0-20(17-0-3)/D-6	11	0.1
1994 Oak-A	76	178	23	43	5	0	4	18	20	35	2	0	.242	.318	.337	.655	76	-6	20	3.95	1	0-35(21-0-15),1-27/D-1	3	-0.7
1995 Oak-A	60	125	18	34	8	0	4	21	19	23	0	0	.272	.372	.432	.804	116	3	21	5.85	-2	1-35,0-16(9-1-6)	4	-0.1
Cal-A	18	24	1	6	0	0	0	3	0	8	0	0	.250	.250	.250	.500	31	-2	1	1.76	0	/D-2,0-2(2-0-0),1-1	0	-0.2
Yr.	78	149	19	40	8	0	4	24	19	31	0	0	.268	.355	.403	.758	103	1	22	5.15	-2	1-36,0-18(11-1-6)/D-2	4	-0.3
1996 Cal-A	31	40	5	6	1	0	3	8	5	4	0	0	.150	.244	.400	.644	60	-3	3	2.20	-1	/D-6,0-6(4-0-2),1-1	0	-0.3
*NY-A	32	68	11	17	5	0	3	12	9	15	0	1	.250	.338	.456	.794	98	-1	10	5.29	-1	/D-9,0-9(6-0-4),1-8,P-1	2	-0.2
Yr.	63	108	16	23	6	0	6	20	14	19	0	1	.213	.303	.435	.738	84	-4	13	4.00	-2	D-15,0-15(10-0-6)/1-9,P-1	2	-0.6
Total 10	930	2147	277	565	104	9	41	271	314	381	19	18	.263	.358	.377	.736	104	18	304	4.89	2	0-409,1-286/D-31,P-1	66	-0.8
• ALDRIDGE, Cory	Cory Jerome Aldridge b: 6/13/1979, San Angelo, TX BL/TR, 6', 210 lbs. Deb: 9/5/2001																							
2001 Atl-N	8	5	1	0	0	0	0	0	0	4	0	0	.000	.000	.000	.000	-98	-1	0	.00	0	/0-4(1-1-2)	0	-0.2
• ALENO, Chuck	Charles Aleno b: 2/19/1917, St. Louis, MO d: 2/10/2003, Deland, FL BR/TR, 6'1.5", 215 lbs. Deb: 5/15/1941																							
1941 Cin-N	54	169	23	41	7	3	1	18	11	16	3	....	.243	.289	.337	.626	76	-6	16	3.27	-3	3-40/1-2	5	-0.8
1942 Cin-N	7	14	1	2	1	0	0	0	3	3	0	....	.143	.294	.214	.508	50	-1	1	2.50	1	/3-2,2-1	0	0.1
1943 Cin-N	7	10	0	3	0	0	0	1	2	1	0	....	.300	.417	.300	.717	110	0	1	5.66	-0	/0-2(2-0-0)	1	0.0
1944 Cin-N	50	127	10	21	3	0	1	15	15	15	0	....	.165	.259	.213	.471	35	-11	8	1.84	-4	3-42/1-3,S-3	1	-1.5
Total 4	118	320	34	67	11	3	2	34	31	35	3	....	.209	.281	.281	.563	59	-17	26	2.68	-6	/3-84,1-5,S-3,0-2,2-1	7	-2.1
• ALEXANDER, Dale	David Dale "Moose" Alexander b: 4/26/1903, Greeneville, TN d: 3/2/1979, Greeneville, TN BR/TR, 6'3", 210 lbs. Deb: 4/16/1929																							
1929 Det-A	155	626	110	**215**	43	15	25	137	56	63	5	9	.343	.397	.580	.977	148	40	140	8.46	-5	*1-155	24	2.4
1930 Det-A	154	602	86	196	33	8	20	135	42	56	6	5	.326	.372	.507	.878	118	15	112	6.96	-6	*1-154	19	-0.1
1931 Det-A	135	517	75	168	47	3	3	87	64	35	5	8	.325	.401	.445	.846	118	16	93	6.90	-7	*1-126/0-4(4-0-0)	13	-0.3
1932 Det-A	23	16	0	4	0	0	0	4	6	2	0	0	.250	.455	.250	.705	84	0	2	5.36	0	/1-2	1	0.0
Bos-A	101	376	58	140	27	3	8	56	55	19	4	5	.372	.454	.524	.978	157	34	91	9.97	1	*1-101	14	2.3
Yr.	124	392	58	144	27	3	8	60	61	21	4	5	**.367**	.454	.513	.966	153	34	93	9.75	1	*1-103	15	2.3
1933 Bos-A	94	313	40	88	14	1	5	40	25	22	0	1	.281	.336	.380	.716	90	-5	40	4.72	4	1-79	6	-0.7
Total 5	662	2450	369	811	164	30	61	459	248	197	20	28	.331	.394	.497	.891	128	100	478	7.45	-12	1-617/0-4	77	3.6
• ALEXANDER, Gary	Gary Wayne Alexander b: 3/27/1953, Los Angeles, CA BR/TR, 6'2", 200 lbs. Deb: 9/12/1975 Career OF: 12-0-8																							
1975 SF-N	3	3	1	0	0	0	0	0	1	2	0	0	.000	.250	.000	.250	-25	-0	0	.59	-1	/C-2	0	-0.1
1976 SF-N	23	73	12	13	1	1	2	7	10	16	1	0	.178	.277	.301	.578	62	-3	7	2.89	-1	C-23	1	-0.3
1977 SF-N	51	119	17	36	4	2	5	20	20	33	3	1	.303	.411	.496	.907	143	8	24	7.21	-4	C-33/0-1	5	0.6
1978 Oak-A	58	174	18	36	6	1	10	22	22	66	0	3	.207	.299	.425	.725	107	0	19	3.38	0	D-45/0-6(3-0-3),1-1,C-1	3	-0.2
Cle-A	90	324	39	76	14	3	17	62	35	100	0	2	.235	.311	.454	.765	114	4	47	4.93	-4	C-66,D-25	10	0.3
Yr.	148	498	57	112	20	4	27	84	57	166	0	5	.225	.307	.444	.751	111	4	66	4.35	-4	D-70,C-67/0-6(3-0-3),1-1	13	0.1
1979 Cle-A	110	358	54	82	9	2	15	54	46	100	4	2	.229	.319	.391	.710	90	-5	46	4.20	-6	C-91,D-13/0-2(1-0-1)	9	-0.7
1980 Cle-A	76	178	22	40	7	1	5	31	17	52	0	4	.225	.292	.360	.652	77	-8	15	2.72	0	D-40,C-13/0-2(1-0-1)	1	-0.9
1981 Pit-N	21	47	6	10	4	1	1	6	3	12	0	0	.213	.260	.404	.664	84	-1	5	3.31	1	/1-9,0-8(7-0-2)	1	-0.2
Total 7	432	1276	169	293	45	11	55	202	154	381	8	12	.230	.315	.411	.726	100	-5	163	4.18	-15	C-229,D-123/0-19,1-10	30	-1.4
• ALEXANDER, Hugh	Hugh Alexander b: 7/10/1917, Buffalo, MO d: 11/25/2000, Oklahoma City, OK BR/TR, 6', 190 lbs. Deb: 8/15/1937																							
1937 Cle-A	7	11	0	1	0	0	0	0	0	5	1	0	.091	.091	.091	.182	-54	-2	0	.35	-1	/0-3(1-0-3)	0	-0.3
• ALEXANDER, Manny	Manuel De Jesus Alexander b: 3/20/1971, San Pedro de Macoris, Dominican Republic BR/TR, 5'10", 165 lbs. Deb: 9/18/1992 Career OF: 4-0-2																							
1992 Bal-A	4	5	1	1	0	0	0	0	0	3	0	0	.200	.200	.200	.400	12	-1	0	1.35	0	/S-3	0	-0.1
1993 Bal-A	3	0	1	0	0	0	0	0	0	0	0	0	....	....	....	....	-96	0	0	....	0	....	0	0.0
1995 Bal-A	94	242	35	57	9	1	3	23	20	30	11	4	.236	.299	.318	.617	60	-14	25	3.41	-3	2-81/S-7,3-2,D-1	3	-1.3
1996*Bal-A	54	68	6	7	0	0	0	4	3	27	3	3	.103	.141	.103	.244	-37	-15	1	.28	-3	S-21/2-7,3-7,0-3(3-0-0),D,P	1	-2.0
1997 NY-N	54	149	26	37	9	3	2	15	9	38	11	0	.248	.296	.389	.685	80	-2	18	4.23	3	2-31,S-26/3-1	4	0.4
Chi-N	33	99	11	29	3	1	1	7	8	16	2	1	.293	.358	.374	.732	90	-1	13	4.61	-1	S-28/2-4	2	0.0
Yr.	87	248	37	66	12	4	3	22	17	54	13	1	.266	.321	.383	.704	84	-4	31	4.38	2	S-54,2-35/3-1	6	0.4
1998*Chi-N	108	264	34	60	10	1	5	25	18	66	4	1	.227	.279	.330	.609	57	-16	24	3.00	-6	S-50,2-27,3-19/D-2,0-1	3	-1.9
1999 Chi-N	90	177	17	48	11	2	0	15	10	38	4	0	.271	.310	.356	.666	69	-8	21	4.24	-3	S-30,3-22,2-17/0-2(0-0-2)	4	-0.8
2000 Bos-A	101	194	30	41	4	3	4	19	13	41	2	0	.211	.261	.325	.586	46	-16	18	3.08	1	3-63,S-20/2-7,D-3	3	-1.3
Total 8	541	1198	161	280	46	11	15	108	81	259	37	9	.234	.286	.328	.614	58	-74	119	3.35	-11	S-185,2-174,3-114/D-7,0-6,P	20	-6.9
• ALEXANDER, Matt	Matthew Alexander b: 1/30/1947, Shreveport, LA BB/TR, 5'11", 169 lbs. Deb: 8/23/1973 Career OF: 25-40-31																							
1973 Chi-N	12	5	4	1	0	0	0	1	1	1	2	0	.200	.333	.200	.533	48	0	1	5.18	0	/0-3(0-3-0)	0	0.0
1974 Chi-N	45	54	15	11	2	1	0	0	12	12	8	4	.204	.358	.278	.636	76	-1	6	3.04	-4	3-19/0-4(0-2-1),2-2	1	-0.5

YEAR TM-L	G	AB	R	H	2B	3B	HR	RBI	BB	SO	SB	CS	AVG	OBP	SLG	OPS	OPS+	BR/A	RC	RC/G	FR	G/POS	WS	TPW
1975 Oak-A	63	10	16	1	0	0	0	0	1	1	17	10	.100	.182	.100	.282	-19	-2	0	.00	-2	D-17,0-11(1-3-7)/2-3,3-2	0	-0.5
1976 Oak-A	61	30	16	1	0	0	0	0	0	5	20	7	.033	.033	.033	.067	-84	-5	0	.00	-1	0-23(7-7-11),D-19	0	-0.7
1977 Oak-A	90	42	24	10	1	0	0	2	4	6	26	14	.238	.304	.262	.566	57	-3	0	.00	-10	0-31(7-17-8),S-12/2-4,3-1,D	0	-1.3
1978 Pit-N	7	0	2	0	0	0	0	0	0	0	4	1	....	....	....	....	-96	0	0	.00	0	....	0	0.0
1979*Pit-N	44	13	16	7	0	1	0	1	0	0	13	1	.538	.538	.692	1.231	223	4	7	28.06	-2	0-11(6-3-3)/S-1	2	0.3
1980 Pit-N	37	3	13	1	1	0	0	0	0	0	10	3	.333	.333	.667	1.000	170	1	0	.00	-1	/0-4(2-2-0),2-1	0	0.0
1981 Pit-N	15	11	5	4	0	0	0	0	0	1	3	2	.364	.364	.364	.727	103	-0	1	3.03	0	/0-6(2-3-1)	0	0.0
Total 9	**374**	**168**	**111**	**36**	**4**	**2**	**0**	**4**	**18**	**26**	**103**	**42**	**.214**	**.294**	**.262**	**.556**	**54**	**-6**	**15**	**2.25**	**-19**	**/0-93,D-37,3-22,S-13,2-10**	**3**	**-2.7**

• ALEXANDER, Nin William Henry Alexander b: 11/24/1858, Pana, IL d: 12/22/1933, Pana, IL BR/TR, 5'4.5", 163 lbs. Deb: 6/7/1884

YEAR TM-L	G	AB	R	H	2B	3B	HR	RBI	BB	SO	SB	CS	AVG	OBP	SLG	OPS	OPS+	BR/A	RC	RC/G	FR	G/POS	WS	TPW
1884 KC-U	19	65	2	9	0	0	0	....	1	....	....	....	.138	.152	.138	.290	-2	-6	1	.70	2	C-17/0-2(0-2-0),S-2	0	-0.2
StL-a	1	4	0	0	0	0	0	0	0	....	....	....	.000	.000	.000	.000	-97	-1	0	.00	0	/C-1,0-1	0	-0.1

• ALEXANDER, Walt Walter Ernest Alexander b: 3/5/1891, Atlanta, GA d: 12/29/1978, Fort Worth, TX BR/TR, 5'10.5", 165 lbs. Deb: 6/21/1912

YEAR TM-L	G	AB	R	H	2B	3B	HR	RBI	BB	SO	SB	CS	AVG	OBP	SLG	OPS	OPS+	BR/A	RC	RC/G	FR	G/POS	WS	TPW
1912 StL-A	37	97	5	17	4	0	0	5	8	....	1	....	.175	.245	.216	.462	34	-8	6	1.74	1	C-37	1	-0.5
1913 StL-A	43	110	5	15	2	1	0	7	4	36	1	....	.136	.174	.173	.347	2	-14	3	.88	4	C-43	1	-0.8
1915 StL-A	1	1	0	0	0	0	0	0	0	0	0	....	.000	.000	.000	.000	-104	-0	0	.00	0	/C-1	0	-0.1
NY-A	25	68	7	17	4	0	1	5	13	16	2	1	.250	.370	.353	.723	117	2	10	4.70	7	C-24	4	1.2
Yr.	26	69	7	17	4	0	1	5	13	16	2	1	.246	.366	.348	.714	114	2	10	4.62	7	C-25	4	1.1
1916 NY-A	36	78	8	20	6	1	0	3	13	20	0	....	.256	.376	.359	.735	118	2	11	4.72	1	C-27	4	0.6
1917 NY-A	20	51	1	7	2	1	0	4	4	11	1	....	.137	.200	.216	.416	27	-5	3	1.40	-1	C-20	1	-0.5
Total 5	**162**	**405**	**26**	**76**	**18**	**3**	**1**	**24**	**42**	**83**	**5**	**1**	**.188**	**.271**	**.254**	**.525**	**56**	**-23**	**32**	**2.42**	**11**	**C-152**	**11**	**-0.1**

• ALFONZO, Edgardo Edgardo Antonio Alfonzo b: 8/11/1973, Santa Teresa, Venezuela BR/TR, 5'11", 185 lbs. Deb: 4/26/1995

YEAR TM-L	G	AB	R	H	2B	3B	HR	RBI	BB	SO	SB	CS	AVG	OBP	SLG	OPS	OPS+	BR/A	RC	RC/G	FR	G/POS	WS	TPW
1995 NY-N	101	335	26	93	13	5	4	41	12	37	1	1	.278	.305	.382	.687	82	-10	37	3.91	1	3-58,2-29/S-6	8	-0.7
1996 NY-N	123	368	36	96	15	2	4	40	25	56	2	0	.261	.308	.345	.653	75	-13	39	3.60	3	2-66,3-36,S-15	6	-0.6
1997 NY-N	151	518	84	163	27	2	10	72	63	56	11	6	.315	.394	.432	.827	121	17	94	6.70	9	*3-143,S-12/2-3	28	2.9
1998 NY-N	144	557	94	155	28	2	17	78	65	77	8	3	.278	.357	.427	.784	107	6	87	5.58	-4	*3-144/S-1	22	0.4
1999*NY-N	158	628	123	191	41	1	27	108	85	85	9	2	.304	.390	.502	.891	127	28	126	7.34	-6	*2-158	29	2.8
2000*NY-N★	150	544	109	176	40	2	25	94	95	70	3	2	.324	.429	.542	.971	149	45	131	9.13	4	*2-146/D-2	36	5.2
2001 NY-N	124	457	64	111	22	0	17	49	51	62	5	0	.243	.326	.403	.728	91	-5	63	4.74	-6	*2-122	15	-0.4
2002 NY-N	135	490	78	151	26	0	16	56	62	55	6	0	.308	.394	.459	.853	129	24	94	7.31	13	*3-134	25	3.9
2003*SF-N	142	514	56	133	25	2	13	81	58	41	5	2	.259	.339	.391	.730	92	-5	68	4.54	-10	*3-133/2-6	17	-1.3
Total 9	**1228**	**4411**	**670**	**1269**	**237**	**16**	**133**	**619**	**516**	**539**	**50**	**16**	**.288**	**.367**	**.439**	**.806**	**112**	**86**	**740**	**6.02**	**4**	**3-648,2-530/S-34,D-2**	**186**	**12.0**

• ALICEA, Luis Luis Rene (De Jesus) Alicea b: 7/29/1965, Santurce, Puerto Rico BB/TR, 5'9", 177 lbs. Deb: 4/23/1988 Career OF: 10-0-1

YEAR TM-L	G	AB	R	H	2B	3B	HR	RBI	BB	SO	SB	CS	AVG	OBP	SLG	OPS	OPS+	BR/A	RC	RC/G	FR	G/POS	WS	TPW
1988 StL-N	93	297	20	63	10	4	1	24	25	32	1	1	.212	.278	.283	.561	61	-16	22	2.33	-7	2-91	3	-2.2
1991 StL-N	56	68	5	13	3	0	0	0	8	19	0	1	.191	.276	.235	.512	45	-5	5	2.29	1	2-11/3-2,S-1	0	-0.4
1992 StL-N	85	265	26	65	9	11	2	32	27	40	2	5	.245	.324	.385	.709	103	-1	32	4.06	9	2-75/S-4	8	1.1
1993 StL-N	115	362	50	101	19	3	3	46	47	54	11	1	.279	.368	.373	.741	101	4	53	5.14	0	2-96/0-4(4-0-0),3-1	15	0.9
1994 StL-N	88	205	32	57	12	5	5	29	30	38	4	5	.278	.378	.459	.837	119	5	37	6.27	1	2-53/0-2(2-0-0)	8	0.9
1995*Bos-A	132	419	64	113	20	3	6	44	63	61	13	10	.270	.374	.375	.749	93	-4	62	4.79	6	*2-132	13	0.8
1996*StL-N	129	380	54	98	26	3	5	42	52	78	11	3	.258	.355	.382	.736	95	-0	56	5.03	0	*2-125	11	0.4
1997 Ana-A	128	388	59	98	16	7	5	37	69	65	22	8	.253	.376	.369	.745	94	1	61	5.36	-3	*2-105,3-12/D-6	14	0.3
1998*Tex-A	101	259	51	71	15	3	6	33	37	40	4	3	.274	.375	.425	.800	103	2	45	6.08	1	2-45,3-26,D-17/0-2(2-0-0)	9	0.4
1999 Tex-A	68	164	33	33	10	0	3	17	28	32	2	1	.201	.318	.317	.635	60	-10	18	3.44	-2	2-37,3-10/D-7,0-1	1	-0.9
2000 Tex-A	139	540	85	159	25	8	6	63	59	75	1	3	.294	.369	.404	.773	94	-4	81	5.33	-14	*2-128/3-8,D-4,S-2	12	-1.2
2001 KC-A	113	387	44	106	16	4	4	32	23	56	8	6	.274	.321	.367	.688	75	-15	45	4.09	-2	2-67,D-22,3-18	5	-1.5
2002 KC-A	94	237	28	54	8	2	1	23	32	34	2	3	.228	.322	.291	.613	58	-14	23	3.22	6	2-32,3-32,D-16/1-2,0-1,S-1	3	-0.7
Total 13	**1341**	**3971**	**551**	**1031**	**189**	**53**	**47**	**422**	**500**	**624**	**81**	**50**	**.260**	**.349**	**.369**	**.719**	**89**	**-57**	**539**	**4.61**	**-5**	**2-997,3-109/D-72,0-10,S-8,1**	**102**	**-2.2**

• ALLANSON, Andy Andrew Neal Allanson b: 12/22/1961, Richmond, VA BR/TR, 6'5", 225 lbs. Deb: 4/7/1986

YEAR TM-L	G	AB	R	H	2B	3B	HR	RBI	BB	SO	SB	CS	AVG	OBP	SLG	OPS	OPS+	BR/A	RC	RC/G	FR	G/POS	WS	TPW
1986 Cle-A	101	293	30	66	7	3	1	29	14	36	10	1	.225	.263	.280	.543	49	-19	22	2.41	-8	C-99	0	-2.2
1987 Cle-A	50	154	17	41	6	0	3	16	9	30	1	1	.266	.307	.364	.670	76	-6	17	3.75	1	C-50	4	-0.2
1988 Cle-A	133	434	44	114	11	0	5	50	25	63	5	9	.263	.307	.323	.630	75	-18	42	3.24	4	*C-133	14	-0.5
1989 Cle-A	111	323	30	75	9	1	3	17	23	47	4	4	.232	.291	.294	.586	64	-16	27	2.76	-1	*C-111	4	-1.0
1991 Det-A	60	151	10	35	10	0	1	16	7	31	0	1	.232	.266	.318	.584	60	-9	12	2.67	-1	C-56/1-2,D-1	3	-0.7
1992 Mil-A	9	25	6	8	1	0	0	0	1	2	3	1	.320	.346	.360	.706	100	0	3	3.81	-1	/C-9	0	0.0
1993 SF-N	13	24	3	4	1	0	0	2	1	2	0	0	.167	.200	.208	.408	10	-3	1	1.09	-1	/C-8,1-2	0	-0.4
1995 Cal-A	35	82	5	14	3	0	3	10	7	12	0	1	.171	.244	.317	.562	45	-7	7	2.55	1	C-35	2	-0.4
Total 8	**512**	**1486**	**145**	**357**	**48**	**4**	**16**	**140**	**87**	**223**	**23**	**18**	**.240**	**.286**	**.310**	**.597**	**64**	**-78**	**131**	**2.90**	**-4**	**C-501/1-4,D-1**	**27**	**-5.4**

• ALLEN, Bernie Bernard Keith Allen b: 4/16/1939, East Liverpool, OH BL/TR, 6', 185 lbs. Deb: 4/10/1962

YEAR TM-L	G	AB	R	H	2B	3B	HR	RBI	BB	SO	SB	CS	AVG	OBP	SLG	OPS	OPS+	BR/A	RC	RC/G	FR	G/POS	WS	TPW
1962 Min-A	159	573	79	154	27	7	12	64	62	82	0	1	.269	.340	.403	.743	95	-4	80	4.90	-24	*2-158	19	-1.3
1963 Min-A	139	421	52	101	20	1	9	43	38	52	0	0	.240	.304	.356	.661	83	-10	46	3.77	-16	*2-128	8	-1.7
1964 Min-A	74	243	28	52	8	1	6	20	33	30	1	2	.214	.310	.329	.640	77	-7	25	3.37	-3	2-71	4	-0.4
1965 Min-A	19	39	2	9	2	0	0	6	6	8	0	0	.231	.333	.282	.615	73	-1	4	3.57	1	2-10/3-1	1	0.1
1966 Min-A	101	319	34	76	18	1	5	30	26	40	2	3	.238	.300	.348	.648	80	-9	31	3.24	-1	2-89/3-2	7	-0.2
1967 Was-A	87	254	13	49	5	1	3	18	18	43	1	2	.193	.246	.256	.502	50	-16	17	2.08	6	2-75	3	-0.5
1968 Was-A	120	373	31	90	12	4	6	40	28	35	2	0	.241	.301	.343	.644	98	-1	38	3.55	2	*2-110/3-2	13	1.1
1969 Was-A	122	365	33	90	17	4	9	45	50	35	5	4	.247	.337	.389	.726	108	4	48	4.48	5	*2-110/3-6	13	1.6
1970 Was-A	104	261	31	61	7	1	8	29	43	21	0	2	.234	.342	.360	.702	99	-0	34	4.39	0	2-80,3-12	8	0.4
1971 Was-A	97	229	18	61	11	1	4	22	33	27	2	1	.266	.359	.376	.734	115	5	33	5.23	-4	2-41,3-34	9	0.3
1972 NY-A	84	220	26	50	9	0	9	21	23	42	0	1	.227	.300	.391	.691	108	1	26	3.85	-1	3-44,2-20	7	0.1
1973 NY-A	17	57	5	13	3	0	0	4	5	5	0	0	.228	.290	.281	.571	64	-3	5	2.80	0	2-13/D-2	1	-0.2
Mon-N	16	50	5	9	1	0	2	9	5	4	0	0	.180	.255	.320	.575	56	-3	4	2.82	-2	/2-9,3-8	1	-0.5
Total 12	**1139**	**3404**	**357**	**815**	**140**	**21**	**73**	**351**	**370**	**424**	**13**	**16**	**.239**	**.315**	**.357**	**.673**	**91**	**-43**	**391**	**3.90**	**-37**	**2-914,3-109/D-2**	**94**	**-1.3**

• ALLEN, Bob Robert Gilman Allen b: 7/10/1867, Marion, OH d: 5/4/1943, Little Rock, AR BR/TR, 5'11", 175 lbs. Deb: 4/19/1890 M

YEAR TM-L	G	AB	R	H	2B	3B	HR	RBI	BB	SO	SB	CS	AVG	OBP	SLG	OPS	OPS+	BR/A	RC	RC/G	FR	G/POS	WS	TPW
1890 Phi-N	133	456	69	103	15	11	2	57	87	54	13	....	.226	.356	.320	.676	95	1	58	4.35	38	*S-133	21	3.9
1891 Phi-N	118	438	46	97	7	4	1	51	43	44	12	....	.221	.291	.263	.554	60	-22	38	3.00	12	*S-118	10	-0.6
1892 Phi-N	152	563	77	128	20	14	2	64	61	60	15	....	.227	.304	.323	.627	90	-7	61	3.81	27	*S-152	18	2.6
1893 Phi-N	124	471	86	126	19	12	8	90	71	40	8	....	.268	.369	.410	.779	107	5	76	5.84	15	*S-124	17	2.2
1894 Phi-N	41	154	27	40	10	4	0	19	17	11	4	....	.260	.337	.377	.714	74	-7	21	4.89	-1	S-40	3	-0.4
1897 Bos-N	34	119	33	38	5	0	1	24	18	....	1	....	.319	.409	.387	.795	104	1	20	6.36	7	S-32/2-1,0-1	5	0.9
1900 Cin-N	5	15	0	2	1	0	0	1	0	....	0	....	.133	.188	.200	.388	7	-2	1	1.18	-1	/S-5	0	-0.2
Total 7	**607**	**2216**	**338**	**534**	**77**	**45**	**14**	**306**	**297**	**209**	**53**	**....**	**.241**	**.334**	**.335**	**.669**	**88**	**-31**	**276**	**4.36**	**97**	**S-604/2-1,0-1**	**74**	**8.2**

• ALLEN, Bob Robert Allen b: 10/13/1894, Muscoda, WI d: 12/18/1975, Naperville, IL BR/TR, 5'10", 180 lbs. Deb: 8/20/1919

YEAR TM-L	G	AB	R	H	2B	3B	HR	RBI	BB	SO	SB	CS	AVG	OBP	SLG	OPS	OPS+	BR/A	RC	RC/G	FR	G/POS	WS	TPW
1919 Phi-A	9	22	3	3	1	0	0	0	3	7	0	....	.136	.269	.182	.451	27	-2	1	1.38	-1	/0-6(0-6-0)	0	-0.3

• ALLEN, Chad John Chad Allen b: 2/6/1975, Dallas, TX BR/TR, 6'1", 195 lbs. Deb: 4/6/1999 Career OF: 160-1-32

YEAR TM-L	G	AB	R	H	2B	3B	HR	RBI	BB	SO	SB	CS	AVG	OBP	SLG	OPS	OPS+	BR/A	RC	RC/G	FR	G/POS	WS	TPW
1999 Min-A	137	481	69	133	21	3	10	46	37	89	14	7	.277	.331	.395	.726	81	-14	62	4.58	-3	*0-133(133-0-1)/D-2	7	-2.2
2000 Min-A	15	50	2	15	3	0	0	7	3	14	0	2	.300	.352	.360	.712	78	-2	6	3.94	0	0-15(2-0-13)	1	-0.3
2001 Min-A	57	175	20	46	13	2	4	20	19	37	1	2	.263	.335	.429	.764	97	-2	23	4.50	1	0-27(16-0-15),D-22	2	-0.3
2002 Cle-A	5	10	0	1	1	0	0	0	0	2	0	0	.100	.100	.200	.300	-23	-2	0	.00	-1	/0-4(3-0-1)	0	-0.2
2003 Fla-N	12	24	2	5	1	1	0	0	0	5	0	0	.208	.240	.333	.573	49	-2	2	2.23	1	/0-8(6-1-2),D-1	0	-0.1
Total 5	**226**	**740**	**93**	**200**	**39**	**6**	**14**	**73**	**59**	**147**	**15**	**11**	**.270**	**.328**	**.396**	**.723**	**82**	**-22**	**93**	**4.35**	**-2**	**0-187/D-25**	**10**	**-3.1**

• ALLEN, Dick Richard Anthony Allen b: 3/8/1942, Wampum, PA BR/TR, 5'11", 190 lbs. Deb: 9/3/1963 Career OF: 256-1-0

YEAR TM-L	G	AB	R	H	2B	3B	HR	RBI	BB	SO	SB	CS	AVG	OBP	SLG	OPS	OPS+	BR/A	RC	RC/G	FR	G/POS	WS	TPW
1963 Phi-N	10	24	6	7	2	1	0	2	0	5	0	0	.292	.292	.458	.750	114	0	2	3.11	-1	/0-7(7-0-0),3-1	0	-0.1

YEAR	TM-L	G	AB	R	H	2B	3B	HR	RBI	BB	SO	SB	CS	AVG	OBP	SLG	OPS	OPS+	BR/A	RC	RC/G	FR	G/POS	WS	TPW
1964	Phi-N	162	632	**125**	201	38	**13**	29	91	67	138	3	4	.318	.383	.557	.940	163	52	135	8.04	15	*3-162	**41**	**7.1**
1965	Phi-N★	161	619	93	187	31	14	20	85	74	150	15	2	.302	.378	.494	.873	146	41	119	6.98	-6	*3-160/S-2	33	3.7
1966	Phi-N★	141	524	112	166	25	10	40	110	68	136	10	6	.317	.398	**.632**	**1.030**	**181**	**57**	131	**9.38**	-1	3-91,O-47(47-0-0)	35	5.6
1967	Phi-N★	122	463	89	142	31	10	23	77	75	117	20	5	.307	**.404**	.566	**.970**	**173**	48	109	**8.74**	-8	*3-121/2-1,S-1	29	4.3
1968	Phi-N	152	521	87	137	17	9	33	90	74	161	7	7	.263	.356	.520	.876	160	37	97	6.40	-3	*O-139(139-1-0),3-10	32	3.1
1969	Phi-N	118	438	79	126	23	3	32	89	64	144	9	3	.288	.378	.573	.952	168	40	95	7.80	-15	*1-117	22	1.7
1970	StL-N★	122	459	88	128	17	5	34	101	71	118	5	4	.279	.378	.560	.938	145	28	97	7.59	-14	1-79,3-38/O-3(3-0-0)	19	0.8
1971	LA-N	155	549	82	162	24	1	23	90	93	113	8	1	.295	.398	.468	.866	154	43	102	6.60	3	3-67,O-60(60-0-0),1-28	29	4.4
1972	Chi-A★	148	506	90	156	28	5	**37**	**113**	**99**	126	19	8	.308	**.422**	**.603**	**1.025**	**198**	**66**	131	**9.42**	0	*1-143/3-2	**40**	**6.3**
1973	Chi-A★	72	250	39	79	20	3	16	41	33	51	7	2	.316	.398	.612	1.010	175	25	59	8.57	2	1-67/2-2,D-1	15	2.3
1974	Chi-A★	128	462	84	139	23	1	**32**	88	57	89	7	1	.301	.379	**.563**	**.942**	164	39	96	7.49	-7	*1-125/2-1,D-1	24	2.4
1975	Phi-N	119	416	54	97	21	3	12	62	58	109	11	2	.233	.330	.385	.714	94	-2	52	4.05	-6	*1-113	8	-1.7
1976*	Phi-N	85	298	52	80	16	1	15	49	37	63	11	4	.268	.349	.480	.829	130	12	47	5.33	-5	1-85	11	0.0
1977	Oak-A	54	171	19	41	4	0	5	31	24	36	1	3	.240	.337	.351	.688	89	-3	20	3.90	2	1-50/D-1	4	-0.3
Total	**15**	**1749**	**6332**	**1099**	**1848**	**320**	**79**	**351**	**1119**	**894**	**1556**	**133**	**52**	**.292**	**.381**	**.534**	**.914**	**157**	**485**	**1290**	**7.30**	**-43**	**1-807,3-652,O-256/2-4,D-3,S**	**342**	**39.5**

• ALLEN, Dusty Dustin R. Allen b: 8/9/1972, Oklahoma City, OK BR/TR, 6'4", 235 lbs. Deb: 7/1/2000

YEAR	TM-L	G	AB	R	H	2B	3B	HR	RBI	BB	SO	SB	CS	AVG	OBP	SLG	OPS	OPS+	BR/A	RC	RC/G	FR	G/POS	WS	TPW
2000	SD-N	9	12	0	0	0	0	0	0	2	5	0	0	.000	.143	.000	.143	-64	-3	0	.08	0	/O-2(2-0-0),1-1,D-1	0	-0.3
	Det-A	18	16	5	7	2	0	2	2	2	7	0	0	.438	.500	.938	1.438	260	4	8	23.28	-1	1-17/3-1,O-1	0	0.2

• ALLEN, Ethan Ethan Nathan Allen b: 1/1/1904, Cincinnati, OH d: 9/15/1993, Brookings, OR BR/TR, 6'1", 180 lbs. Deb: 6/21/1926 Career OF: 301-757-107

YEAR	TM-L	G	AB	R	H	2B	3B	HR	RBI	BB	SO	SB	CS	AVG	OBP	SLG	OPS	OPS+	BR/A	RC	RC/G	FR	G/POS	WS	TPW
1926	Cin-N	18	13	3	4	1	0	0	0	0	3	0	....	.308	.308	.385	.692	88	-0	1	4.13	0	/O-9(5-0-4)	0	-0.1
1927	Cin-N	111	359	54	106	26	4	2	20	14	23	12	....	.295	.325	.407	.732	98	-2	46	4.46	-4	O-98(14-72-13)	10	-1.2
1928	Cin-N	129	485	55	148	30	7	1	62	27	29	6	....	.305	.343	.402	.745	96	-4	65	4.80	-2	*O-129(1-128-0)	15	-1.1
1929	Cin-N	143	538	69	157	27	11	6	64	20	21	21	....	.292	.317	.416	.734	84	-16	68	4.51	3	*O-137(24-134-10)	13	-1.8
1930	Cin-N	21	46	10	10	1	0	3	7	5	2	1	....	.217	.294	.435	.729	77	-2	6	4.00	-1	O-15(1-13-1)	1	-0.3
	NY-N	76	238	48	73	9	2	7	31	12	23	5	....	.307	.340	.450	.790	91	-4	35	5.24	0	O-62(1-54-7)	6	-0.6
	Yr.	97	284	58	83	10	2	10	38	17	25	6	....	.292	.332	.447	.779	88	-6	41	5.02	-1	O-77(2-67-8)	7	-0.9
1931	NY-N	94	298	58	98	18	2	5	43	15	15	6	....	.329	.363	.453	.816	121	8	49	6.19	-3	O-77(40-23-14)	10	0.2
1932	NY-N	54	103	13	18	6	2	1	7	1	12	0	....	.175	.198	.301	.499	33	-10	6	1.86	-1	O-24(11-13-0)	0	-1.2
1933	StL-N	91	261	25	63	7	3	0	36	13	22	3	....	.241	.280	.291	.571	60	-13	22	2.85	4	O-67(0-46-21)	4	-1.3
1934	Phi-N	145	581	87	192	**42**	4	10	85	33	47	6	....	.330	.370	.468	.838	108	7	99	6.37	7	*O-145(87-47-16)	16	0.7
1935	Phi-N	156	645	90	198	46	1	8	63	43	54	5	....	.307	.351	.419	.770	96	-3	100	5.80	11	*O-156(19-136-1)	20	0.3
1936	Phi-N	30	125	21	37	3	1	1	9	4	8	4	....	.296	.318	.360	.678	75	-5	14	3.88	-2	O-30(11-16-6)	2	-0.8
	Chi-N	91	373	47	110	18	6	3	39	13	30	12	....	.295	.322	.399	.722	91	-6	47	4.50	-3	O-89(73-16-0)	8	-1.3
	Yr.	121	498	68	147	21	7	4	48	17	38	16	....	.295	.321	.390	.711	87	-10	61	4.35	-5	*O-119(84-32-6)	10	-2.1
1937	StL-A	103	320	39	101	18	1	0	31	21	17	3	4	.316	.360	.378	.738	85	-8	43	4.98	2	O-78(12-54-14)	4	-0.8
1938	StL-A	19	33	4	10	3	1	0	4	2	4	0	0	.303	.343	.455	.797	98	-0	5	5.67	0	/O-7(2-5-0)	1	-0.1
Total	**13**	**1281**	**4418**	**623**	**1325**	**255**	**45**	**47**	**501**	**223**	**310**	**84**	**4**	**.300**	**.336**	**.410**	**.745**	**92**	**-59**	**606**	**4.95**	**10**	***O-1123**	**110**	**-9.2**

• ALLEN, Ham Frank Erwin Allen b: 4/20/1846, Augusta, ME d: 2/6/1881, Natick, MA Deb: 4/27/1872

YEAR	TM-L	G	AB	R	H	2B	3B	HR	RBI	BB	SO	SB	CS	AVG	OBP	SLG	OPS	OPS+	BR/A	RC	RC/G	FR	G/POS	WS	TPW
1872	Man-n	17	70	9	19	1	0	0	7	0	1	0	0	.271	.271	.271	.543	76	-1	6	3.38	2	/O-9(4-3-2),S-8	....	0.0

• ALLEN, Hank Harold Andrew Allen b: 7/23/1940, Wampum, PA BR/TR, 6', 190 lbs. Deb: 9/9/1966 Career OF: 137-95-72

YEAR	TM-L	G	AB	R	H	2B	3B	HR	RBI	BB	SO	SB	CS	AVG	OBP	SLG	OPS	OPS+	BR/A	RC	RC/G	FR	G/POS	WS	TPW
1966	Was-A	9	31	2	12	0	0	1	6	3	6	0	0	.387	.441	.484	.925	167	3	7	9.43	-1	/O-9(8-0-3)	2	0.2
1967	Was-A	116	292	34	68	8	4	3	17	13	53	3	4	.233	.266	.318	.584	75	-11	22	2.51	-4	O-99(59-65-1)	3	-2.0
1968	Was-A	68	128	16	28	2	2	1	9	7	16	0	0	.219	.265	.289	.554	70	-5	9	2.36	-3	O-25(12-0-13),3-16,2-11	2	-0.9
1969	Was-A	109	271	42	75	9	3	1	17	13	28	12	3	.277	.312	.343	.655	88	-4	26	3.34	-3	O-91(48-16-42)/3-6,2-3	5	-1.1
1970	Was-A	22	38	3	8	2	0	0	4	5	9	0	0	.211	.302	.263	.565	60	-2	3	2.97	0	O-17(5-3-10)	0	-0.2
	Mil-A	28	61	4	14	4	0	0	4	7	5	0	1	.230	.309	.295	.604	67	-3	5	2.83	1	O-14(1-11-2)/2-5,1-4	1	-0.3
	Yr.	50	99	7	22	6	0	0	8	12	14	0	1	.222	.306	.283	.589	64	-5	9	2.89	1	O-31(6-14-12)/2-5,1-4	1	-0.5
1972	Chi-A	9	21	1	3	0	0	0	0	0	2	0	0	.143	.143	.143	.286	-15	-3	0	.41	1	/3-6	0	-0.2
1973	Chi-A	28	39	2	4	2	0	0	0	1	9	0	1	.103	.125	.154	.279	-21	-7	0	.22	0	/3-9,1-8,O-5(4-0-1),2-1,C-1	0	-0.8
Total	**7**	**389**	**881**	**104**	**212**	**27**	**9**	**6**	**57**	**49**	**128**	**15**	**9**	**.241**	**.282**	**.312**	**.594**	**74**	**-32**	**74**	**2.79**	**-9**	**O-260/3-37,2-20,1-12,C-1**	**13**	**-5.3**

• ALLEN, Hezekiah Hezekiah "Ki" Allen b: 2/25/1863, Westport, CT d: 9/21/1916, Saugatuck, CT, 5'11", 160 lbs. Deb: 5/16/1884

YEAR	TM-L	G	AB	R	H	2B	3B	HR	RBI	BB	SO	SB	CS	AVG	OBP	SLG	OPS	OPS+	BR/A	RC	RC/G	FR	G/POS	WS	TPW
1884	Phi-N	1	3	0	2	0	0	0	0	0	0	....	....	.667	.667	.667	1.333	336	1	1	37.58	0	/C-1	0	0.0

• ALLEN, Horace Horace Tanner "Pug" Allen b: 6/11/1899, Deland, FL d: 7/5/1981, Canton, NC BL/TR, 6', 187 lbs. Deb: 6/15/1919

YEAR	TM-L	G	AB	R	H	2B	3B	HR	RBI	BB	SO	SB	CS	AVG	OBP	SLG	OPS	OPS+	BR/A	RC	RC/G	FR	G/POS	WS	TPW
1919	Bro-N	4	7	0	0	0	0	0	0	0	2	0	....	.000	.000	.000	.000	-98	-2	0	.00	0	/O-2(1-1-0)	0	-0.2

• ALLEN, Jack Cyrus Alban Allen b: 10/2/1855, Woodstock, IL d: 4/21/1915, Girard, PA BR/TR, 160 lbs. Deb: 5/1/1879

YEAR	TM-L	G	AB	R	H	2B	3B	HR	RBI	BB	SO	SB	CS	AVG	OBP	SLG	OPS	OPS+	BR/A	RC	RC/G	FR	G/POS	WS	TPW
1879	Syr-N	11	48	7	9	2	1	0	3	1	5	....	....	.188	.204	.271	.475	62	-2	3	1.95	-4	/3-8,O-3(0-0-3)	0	-0.5
	Cle-N	16	60	7	7	1	1	0	4	1	9	....	....	.117	.131	.167	.298	-3	-6	1	.71	3	3-14/O-2(0-2-0)	1	-0.3
	Yr.	27	108	14	16	3	2	0	7	2	14	....	....	.148	.164	.213	.377	26	-8	4	1.24	-1	3-22/O-5(0-2-3)	1	-0.8

• ALLEN, Jamie James Bradley Allen b: 5/29/1958, Yakima, WA BR/TR, 6', 205 lbs. Deb: 5/1/1983

YEAR	TM-L	G	AB	R	H	2B	3B	HR	RBI	BB	SO	SB	CS	AVG	OBP	SLG	OPS	OPS+	BR/A	RC	RC/G	FR	G/POS	WS	TPW
1983	Sea-A	86	273	23	61	10	0	4	21	33	52	6	5	.223	.309	.304	.613	67	-12	26	3.00	-10	3-82/D-2	3	-2.3

• ALLEN, Kim Kim Bryant Allen b: 4/5/1953, Fontana, CA BR/TR, 5'11", 175 lbs. Deb: 9/2/1980 Career OF: 3-2-2

YEAR	TM-L	G	AB	R	H	2B	3B	HR	RBI	BB	SO	SB	CS	AVG	OBP	SLG	OPS	OPS+	BR/A	RC	RC/G	FR	G/POS	WS	TPW
1980	Sea-A	23	51	9	12	3	0	0	3	8	3	10	3	.235	.350	.294	.644	78	-0	6	3.79	-1	2-15/O-4(3-0-2),S-1	1	-0.1
1981	Sea-A	19	3	1	0	0	0	0	0	0	2	2	1	.000	.000	.000	.000	-96	-1	0	.00	-2	/2-2,D-2,O-2(0-2-0)	0	-0.2
Total	**2**	**42**	**54**	**10**	**12**	**3**	**0**	**0**	**3**	**8**	**5**	**12**	**4**	**.222**	**.333**	**.278**	**.611**	**70**	**-1**	**6**	**3.48**	**-2**	**/2-17,O-6,D-2,S-1**	**1**	**-0.3**

• ALLEN, Luke Lucas G. Allen b: 8/4/1978, Covington, GA BL/TR, 6'2", 208 lbs. Deb: 9/10/2002

YEAR	TM-L	G	AB	R	H	2B	3B	HR	RBI	BB	SO	SB	CS	AVG	OBP	SLG	OPS	OPS+	BR/A	RC	RC/G	FR	G/POS	WS	TPW
2002	LA-N	6	7	2	1	1	0	0	0	2	3	0	0	.143	.333	.286	.619	70	-0	1	3.78	0	/O-3(0-0-3)	0	0.0
2003	Col-N	2	2	0	0	0	0	0	0	0	0	0	0	.000	.000	.000	.000	-88	-1	0	.00	0	....	0	-0.1
Total	**2**	**8**	**9**	**2**	**1**	**1**	**0**	**0**	**0**	**2**	**3**	**0**	**0**	**.111**	**.273**	**.222**	**.495**	**41**	**-1**	**1**	**2.52**	**0**	**/O-3**	**0**	**-0.1**

• ALLEN, Myron Myron Smith "Zeke" Allen b: 3/22/1854, Kingston, NY d: 3/8/1924, Kingston, NY BR/TR, 5'8", 150 lbs. Deb: 7/19/1883 Career OF: 106-3-41

YEAR	TM-L	G	AB	R	H	2B	3B	HR	RBI	BB	SO	SB	CS	AVG	OBP	SLG	OPS	OPS+	BR/A	RC	RC/G	FR	G/POS	WS	TPW
1883	NY-N	1	4	0	0	0	0	0	1	0	2	....	....	.000	.000	.000	.000	-101	-1	0	.00	0	/P-1	1	0.1
1886	Bos-N	1	3	0	0	0	0	0	0	0	1	0	....	.000	.000	.000	.000	-104	-1	0	.00	0	/2-1	0	0.0
1887	Cle-a	117	499	66	164	22	10	4	77	36	....	26	....	.329	.335	.393	.728	106	4	71	5.76	1	*O-115(73-1-41)/3-3,P-2,S	11	0.5
1888	KC-a	37	136	23	29	6	4	0	10	9	....	4	....	.213	.267	.316	.583	81	-3	13	3.25	8	O-35(33-2-0)/P-2	4	0.5
Total	**4**	**156**	**642**	**89**	**193**	**28**	**14**	**4**	**88**	**45**	**3**	**30**		**.301**	**.317**	**.371**	**.688**	**98**	**-1**	**84**	**5.07**	**10**	**O-150/P-5,3-3,S-2,2-1**	**16**	**1.0**

• ALLEN, Nick Artemus Ward Allen b: 9/14/1888, Norton, KS d: 10/16/1939, Hines, IL BR/TR, 6', 180 lbs. Deb: 5/1/1914

YEAR	TM-L	G	AB	R	H	2B	3B	HR	RBI	BB	SO	SB	CS	AVG	OBP	SLG	OPS	OPS+	BR/A	RC	RC/G	FR	G/POS	WS	TPW
1914	Buf-F	32	63	3	15	1	0	0	4	3	12	4	....	.238	.273	.254	.527	48	-4	5	2.63	1	C-26	1	-0.2
1915	Buf-F	84	215	14	44	7	1	0	17	18	34	4	....	.205	.269	.247	.516	52	-13	15	2.19	0	C-80	4	-0.8
1916	Chi-N	5	16	1	1	0	0	0	1	0	3	0	....	.063	.063	.063	.125	-56	-3	0	.11	-1	/C-4	0	-0.4
1918	Cin-N	37	96	6	25	2	2	0	5	4	7	0	....	.260	.297	.323	.620	91	-1	9	3.16	2	C-31	3	0.3
1919	Cin-N	15	25	7	8	0	1	0	5	2	6	0	....	.320	.393	.400	.793	142	1	4	5.74	0	C-12	2	0.2
1920	Cin-N	43	85	10	23	3	1	0	4	6	11	0	0	.271	.340	.329	.670	94	0	10	4.04	0	C-36	4	0.2
Total	**6**	**216**	**500**	**41**	**116**	**13**	**5**	**0**	**36**	**33**	**73**	**8**	**0**	**.232**	**.288**	**.278**	**.566**	**68**	**-20**	**42**	**2.81**	**1**	**C-189**	**14**	**-0.6**

• ALLEN, Pete Jesse Hall Allen b: 5/1/1868, Columbiana, OH d: 4/16/1946, Philadelphia, PA BR/TR, 5'8.5", 185 lbs. Deb: 8/4/1893

YEAR	TM-L	G	AB	R	H	2B	3B	HR	RBI	BB	SO	SB	CS	AVG	OBP	SLG	OPS	OPS+	BR/A	RC	RC/G	FR	G/POS	WS	TPW
1893	Cle-N	1	4	0	0	0	0	0	0	0	0	0	....	.000	.000	.000	.000	-94	-1	0	.00	0	/C-1	0	-0.1

• ALLEN, Rod Roderick Bernet Allen b: 10/5/1959, Los Angeles, CA BR/TR, 6'1", 185 lbs. Deb: 4/7/1983 Career OF: 2-0-2

YEAR	TM-L	G	AB	R	H	2B	3B	HR	RBI	BB	SO	SB	CS	AVG	OBP	SLG	OPS	OPS+	BR/A	RC	RC/G	FR	G/POS	WS	TPW
1983	Sea-A	11	12	1	2	0	0	0	0	0	1	0	0	.167	.167	.167	.333	-8	-2	0	.90	0	/D-3,O-2(0-0-2)	0	-0.2
1984	Det-A	15	27	6	8	1	0	0	3	2	8	1	0	.296	.367	.333	.700	96	0	4	5.18	-0	D-11/O-2(2-0-0)	1	0.0

YEAR	TM-L	G	AB	R	H	2B	3B	HR	RBI	BB	SO	SB	CS	AVG	OBP	SLG	OPS	OPS+	BR/A	RC	RC/G	FR	G/POS	WS	TPW
1988	Cle-A	5	11	1	1	1	0	0	0	0	2	0	0	.091	.091	.182	.273	-25	-2	0	.49	0	/D-4	0	-0.2
Total	3	31	50	8	11	2	0	0	3	2	11	1	0	.220	.264	.260	.524	48	-3	4	2.94	0	/D-18,0-4	1	-0.4
• ALLEN, Ron	Ronald Frederick Allen b: 12/23/1943, Wampum, PA BB/TR, 6'3", 205 lbs. Deb: 8/11/1972																								
1972	StL-N	7	11	2	1	0	0	1	1	3	5	0	0	.091	.286	.364	.649	84	-0	1	2.51	-1	/1-5	0	-0.1
• ALLEN, Sled	Fletcher Manson Allen b: 8/23/1886, West Plains, MO d: 10/16/1959, Lubbock, TX BR/TR, 6'1", 180 lbs. Deb: 5/4/1910																								
1910	StL-A	14	23	3	3	1	0	0	1	1	....	0	....	.130	.231	.174	.405	29	-2	1	1.23	-1	C-12/1-1	0	-0.3
• ALLENSON, Gary	Gary Martin Allenson b: 2/4/1955, Culver City, CA BR/TR, 5'11", 185 lbs. Deb: 4/8/1979 C																								
1979	Bos-A	108	241	27	49	10	2	3	22	20	42	1	1	.203	.267	.299	.566	50	-17	19	2.39	-5	*C-104/3-3	2	-1.8
1980	Bos-A	36	70	9	25	6	0	0	10	13	11	2	2	.357	.458	.443	.901	141	5	15	8.11	-1	C-24/D-6,3-5	4	0.4
1981	Bos-A	47	139	23	31	8	0	5	25	23	33	0	0	.223	.337	.388	.726	102	1	18	4.26	-4	C-47	4	-0.1
1982	Bos-A	92	264	25	54	11	0	6	33	38	39	0	3	.205	.307	.314	.621	67	-12	26	3.15	0	C-91	6	-0.8
1983	Bos-A	84	230	19	53	11	0	3	30	27	43	0	1	.230	.317	.317	.634	70	-9	23	3.21	0	C-84	5	-0.5
1984	Bos-A	35	83	9	19	2	0	2	8	9	14	0	0	.229	.304	.325	.630	71	-3	7	2.82	0	C-35	1	-0.2
1985	Tor-A	14	34	2	4	1	0	0	3	0	10	0	0	.118	.118	.147	.265	-27	-6	0	.38	0	C-14	0	-0.6
Total	7	416	1061	114	235	49	2	19	131	130	192	3	7	.221	.309	.325	.635	71	-42	109	3.28	-10	C-399/3-8,D-6	22	-3.4
• ALLENSWORTH, Jermaine	Jermaine Lamont Allensworth b: 1/11/1972, Anderson, IN BR/TR, 6', 189 lbs. Deb: 7/23/1996 Career OF: 15-273-42																								
1996	Pit-N	61	229	32	60	9	3	4	31	23	50	11	6	.262	.340	.380	.720	87	-4	31	4.62	0	0-61(0-61-0)	6	-0.4
1997	Pit-N	108	369	55	94	18	2	3	43	44	79	14	7	.255	.345	.339	.684	79	-10	47	4.18	-3	*0-104(0-104-0)	7	-1.2
1998	Pit-N	69	233	30	72	13	3	3	24	17	43	8	4	.309	.374	.429	.803	109	3	39	6.23	-1	0-66(0-66-0)	8	0.3
	KC-A	30	73	15	15	5	0	0	3	9	17	7	0	.205	.326	.274	.600	57	-3	9	3.91	-1	0-27(1-24-2)	1	-0.4
	NY-N	34	54	9	11	2	0	2	4	2	16	0	2	.204	.246	.352	.597	56	-5	4	2.50	-2	0-31(4-4-25)	0	-0.7
	Yr.	103	287	39	83	15	3	5	28	19	59	8	6	.289	.350	.415	.765	100	-1	43	5.45	-3	0-97(4-70-25)	8	-0.4
1999	NY-N	40	73	14	16	2	0	3	9	9	23	2	1	.219	.313	.370	.683	74	-3	9	3.91	0	0-33(10-14-15)	1	-0.4
Total	4	342	1031	155	268	49	8	15	114	104	228	42	20	.260	.342	.367	.708	84	-22	139	4.57	-8	0-322	23	-2.8
• ALLEY, Gene	Leonard Eugene Alley b: 7/10/1940, Richmond, VA BR/TR, 5'10", 165 lbs. Deb: 9/4/1963																								
1963	Pit-N	17	51	3	11	1	0	0	0	2	12	0	1	.216	.245	.235	.481	39	-4	3	1.66	1	/3-7,2-4,S-4	1	-0.3
1964	Pit-N	81	209	30	44	3	1	6	13	21	56	0	1	.211	.289	.321	.609	72	-8	20	3.12	3	S-61/3-3,2-1	5	0.0
1965	Pit-N	153	500	47	126	21	6	5	47	32	82	7	2	.252	.302	.348	.650	82	-11	52	3.56	15	*S-110,2-40/3-1	15	1.7
1966	Pit-N	147	579	88	173	28	10	7	43	27	83	8	8	.299	.336	.418	.753	108	4	79	4.82	9	*S-143	22	2.6
1967	Pit-N★	152	550	59	158	25	7	6	55	36	70	10	5	.287	.339	.391	.730	108	6	70	4.47	-7	*S-146	19	1.2
1968	Pit-N★	133	474	48	116	20	2	4	39	39	78	13	5	.245	.309	.321	.630	90	-4	45	3.04	11	*S-109,2-24	13	2.1
1969	Pit-N	82	285	28	70	3	2	8	32	19	48	4	0	.246	.295	.354	.649	83	-6	29	3.36	3	2-53,S-25/3-5	7	0.3
1970*	Pit-N	121	426	46	104	16	5	8	41	31	70	7	3	.244	.300	.362	.662	79	-14	46	3.71	14	*S-108/2-8,3-2	12	1.3
1971*	Pit-N	114	348	38	79	8	7	6	28	35	43	9	2	.227	.298	.342	.640	80	-8	36	3.44	-6	*S-108/3-1	8	-0.2
1972*	Pit-N	119	347	30	86	12	2	3	36	38	52	4	3	.248	.322	.320	.642	85	-7	36	3.57	15	*S-114/3-4	11	2.2
1973	Pit-N	76	158	25	32	3	2	2	8	20	28	1	0	.203	.292	.285	.577	62	-8	12	2.43	1	S-49/3-8	2	-0.2
Total	11	1195	3927	442	999	140	44	55	342	300	622	63	30	.254	.312	.354	.666	88	-60	428	3.69	59	S-977,2-130/3-31	115	10.8
• ALLIE, Gair	Gair Roosevelt Allie b: 10/28/1931, Statesville, NC BR/TR, 6'1", 190 lbs. Deb: 4/13/1954																								
1954	Pit-N	121	418	38	83	8	6	3	30	56	84	1	1	.199	.296	.268	.564	49	-30	37	2.91	-24	S-95,3-19	2	-4.7
• ALLIETTA, Bob	Robert George Allietta b: 5/1/1952, New Bedford, MA BR/TR, 6', 190 lbs. Deb: 5/6/1975																								
1975	Cal-A	21	45	4	8	1	0	1	2	1	6	0	0	.178	.196	.267	.462	32	-4	2	1.48	0	C-21	0	-0.4
• ALLISON, Andy	Andrew K. Allison b: 1848, New York, NY, 5'10", 150 lbs. Deb: 5/7/1872 U																								
1872	Eck-n	24	93	11	15	3	0	0	9	0	3	0	0	.161	.161	.194	.355	10	-7	3	1.18	-2	1-22/0-1	....	-0.6
• ALLISON, Art	Arthur Algernon Allison b: 1/29/1849, Philadelphia, PA d: 2/25/1916, Washington, DC, 5'8", 150 lbs. Deb: 5/4/1871 U NA OF: 8-56-45																								
1871	Cle-n	29	137	28	40	4	5	0	19	2	5	3	1	.292	.302	.394	.696	104	1	18	5.67	0	*0-29(0-29-0)/2-2	....	0.1
1872	Cle-n	19	87	13	23	4	0	0	8	0	2	0	0	.264	.264	.310	.575	81	-1	7	3.54	-1	0-19(0-17-2)	....	-0.2
1873	Res-n	23	99	12	32	2	0	0	11	0	0	0	0	.323	.323	.343	.667	106	1	11	5.13	-2	0-21(8-9-4)/1-3,C-1	....	0.0
1875	Was-n	26	112	18	24	3	1	0	3	1	2	6	0	.214	.221	.259	.480	69	-2	8	2.66	-3	1-23/0-3(0-1-2),C-1	....	-0.3
	Har-n	40	175	26	42	4	1	1	19	0	3	1	2	.240	.240	.291	.531	80	-5	13	2.80	3	0-37(0-0-37)/2-2,1-1,C-1	....	0.0
	Yr.	66	287	44	66	7	2	1	22	1	5	7	2	.230	.233	.279	.511	75	-6	21	2.74	0	0-40(0-1-39),1-24/2-2,C-2	....	-0.3
1876	Lou-N	31	132	9	27	2	1	0	10	2	6	....	....	.205	.220	.238	.458	44	-9	7	1.90	7	0-23(0-0-23)/1-8	1	-0.2
Total	4 n	137	610	97	161	17	7	1	60	3	12	10	3	.264	.268	.320	.587	87	-5	57	3.85	-2	0-109/1-27,2-4,C-3	....	-0.4
• ALLISON, Bill	William Andrew Allison b: 9/17/1848, d: 6/12/1923, Deb: 5/21/1872																								
1872	Eck-n	5	19	5	3	0	0	0	1	0	1	0	0	.158	.158	.158	.316	-3	-2	0	.94	-1	/1-2,0-2(0-1-1),2-1	....	-0.2
• ALLISON, Bob	William Robert Allison b: 7/11/1934, Raytown, MO d: 4/9/1995, Rio Verde, AZ BR/TR, 6'3", 220 lbs. Deb: 9/16/1958 Career OF: 527-187-631																								
1958	Was-A	11	35	1	7	1	0	0	0	2	5	0	2	.200	.243	.229	.472	31	-4	1	1.20	0	0-11(1-10-0)	0	-0.5
1959	Was-A★	150	570	83	149	18	**9**	30	85	60	92	13	8	.261	.334	.482	.816	122	15	85	5.03	-7	*0-149(7-134-9)	18	0.0
1960	Was-A	144	501	79	126	30	3	15	69	92	94	11	9	.251	.370	.413	.783	110	9	79	5.21	8	*0-140(0-4-139)/1-4	16	1.2
1961	Min-A	159	556	83	136	21	3	29	105	103	100	2	7	.245	.367	.450	.817	111	8	93	5.48	0	*0-150(0-0-150),1-18	17	-0.3
1962	Min-A	149	519	102	138	24	8	29	102	84	115	8	5	.266	.372	.511	.883	130	23	102	6.87	6	*0-147(2-0-146)	23	1.8
1963	Min-A★	148	527	**99**	143	25	4	35	91	90	109	6	1	.271	.381	.533	**.914**	**150**	38	113	7.68	4	*0-147(0-8-146)	28	3.3
1964	Min-A★	149	492	90	141	27	4	32	86	92	99	10	1	.287	.406	.553	.959	162	47	119	8.84	-1	1-93,0-61(27-28-16)	25	4.0
1965*	Min-A	135	438	71	102	14	5	23	78	73	114	10	2	.233	.345	.445	.790	118	13	73	5.62	8	*0-122(122-0-0)/1-3	22	1.4
1966	Min-A	70	168	34	37	6	1	8	19	30	34	6	0	.220	.348	.411	.759	110	5	27	5.44	-1	0-56(44-1-11)	7	0.1
1967	Min-A	153	496	73	128	21	6	24	75	74	114	6	4	.258	.357	.470	.826	132	21	87	6.18	-7	*0-145(138-0-9)	24	0.7
1968	Min-A	145	469	63	116	16	8	22	52	52	98	9	7	.247	.325	.456	.781	128	15	65	4.64	-2	*0-117(116-1-1),1-17	16	0.7
1969*	Min-A	81	189	18	43	8	2	8	27	29	39	2	4	.228	.333	.418	.751	107	1	24	4.10	2	0-58(58-0-0)/1-3	5	0.0
1970*	Min-A	47	72	15	15	5	0	1	7	14	20	1	0	.208	.345	.319	.664	83	-1	9	4.04	0	0-17(12-1-4)/1-7	2	-0.2
Total	13	1541	5032	811	1281	216	53	256	796	795	1033	84	50	.255	.360	.471	.831	126	189	877	5.96	9	*0-1320,1-145	203	12.2
• ALLISON, Doug	Douglas L. Allison b: 7/1845, Philadelphia, PA d: 12/19/1916, Washington, DC BR/TR, 5'10.5", 160 lbs. Deb: 5/5/1871 U NA OF: 0-4-49 Career OF: 0-2-5																								
1871	Oly-n	27	133	28	44	10	2	2	27	0	2	1	1	.331	.331	.481	.812	137	6	22	7.71	-1	*C-27	....	0.3
1872	Tro-n	23	115	23	35	4	2	0	20	1	3	1	1	.304	.310	.374	.684	108	1	14	5.36	2	C-22/S-1	....	0.2
	Eck-n	18	79	18	27	2	1	0	5	1	2	0	0	.342	.350	.392	.742	151	6	11	6.63	-3	C-18	....	0.2
	Yr.	41	194	41	62	6	3	0	25	2	5	1	1	.320	.327	.381	.708	125	6	25	5.85	-1	*C-40/S-1	....	0.4
1873	Res-n	19	83	11	24	5	0	0	8	0	0	0	0	.289	.289	.349	.639	96	0	9	4.44	1	C-18/0-3(0-1-2)	....	0.1
	Mut-n	11	48	6	10	0	0	0	3	1	0	0	0	.208	.224	.208	.433	30	-4	2	1.85	1	C-11/0-1	....	-0.2
	Yr.	30	131	17	34	5	0	0	11	1	0	0	0	.260	.265	.298	.563	71	-4	11	3.43	1	C-29/0-4(0-1-3)	....	-0.1
1874	Mut-n	65	318	68	90	7	5	0	28	6	5	1	0	.283	.296	.336	.633	99	-1	33	4.32	-5	*0-47(0-3-44),C-34/2-1	....	-0.2
1875	Har-n	61	269	38	67	7	0	0	21	6	3	2	0	.249	.265	.275	.541	84	-4	21	3.02	3	*C-59/1-2,0-2(0-0-2)	....	0.0
1876	Har-N	44	166	19	43	4	0	0	15	3	9	....	....	.259	.277	.288	.565	82	-4	13	3.11	6	C-40/0-6(0-1-5)	5	0.3
1877	Har-N	29	115	14	17	2	0	0	6	3	7	....	....	.148	.169	.165	.335	6	-11	3	.93	2	C-29	1	-0.7
1878	Pro-N	19	76	9	22	2	0	0	7	1	8	....	....	.289	.299	.316	.614	102	0	7	3.74	1	C-19/P-1	3	0.2
1879	Pro-N	1	5	0	0	0	0	0	0	0	1	....	....	.000	.000	.000	.000	-102	-1	0	.00	0	/C-1	0	-0.1
1883	Bal-a	1	3	2	2	0	0	0	0	0	....	....	....	.667	.667	.667	1.333	321	1	1	38.27	0	/C-1,0-1	0	0.1
Total	5 n	224	1045	192	297	35	10	2	112	15	15	5	2	.284	.294	.343	.637	101	3	112	4.53	-3	C-189/0-53,1-2,2-1,S-1	....	0.4
Total	5	94	365	44	84	8	0	0	28	7	25	....	....	.230	.247	.254	.501	61	-15	25	2.54	9	/C-90,0-7,P-1	9	-0.2

YEAR TM-L	G	AB	R	H	2B	3B	HR	RBI	BB	SO	SB	CS	AVG	OBP	SLG	OPS	OPS+	BR/A	RC	RC/G	FR	G/POS	WS	TPW
• ALLISON, Milo	Milo Henry Allison b: 10/16/1890, Elk Rapids, MI d: 6/18/1957, Kenosha, WI BL/TR, 6', 155 lbs. Deb: 9/26/1913 Career OF: 5-6-6																							
1913 Chi-N	2	6	1	2	0	0	0	0	0	1	1	....	.333	.333	.333	.667	90	-0	1	5.69	0	/0-1	0	0.0
1914 Chi-N	1	1	0	1	0	0	0	0	0	0	0	....	1.000	1.000	1.000	2.000	497	0	1	∞	0	....	0	0.1
1916 Cle-A	14	18	10	5	0	0	0	0	6	1	0	....	.278	.458	.278	.736	115	1	3	4.78	0	/0-5(1-0-4)	1	0.1
1917 Cle-A	32	35	4	5	0	0	0	0	9	7	3	....	.143	.318	.143	.461	38	-2	3	2.17	-2	0-11(4-5-2)	0	-0.5
Total 4	49	60	15	13	0	0	0	0	15	9	4	....	.217	.373	.217	.590	73	-1	7	3.18	-2	/0-17	1	-0.4
• ALLRED, Beau	Dale Le Beau Allred b: 6/4/1965, Mesa, AZ BL/TL, 6', 190 lbs. Deb: 9/7/1989 Career OF: 23-3-30																							
1989 Cle-A	13	24	0	6	3	0	0	1	2	10	0	0	.250	.308	.375	.683	90	-0	3	4.39	1	/0-5(3-0-2),D-2	1	0.1
1990 Cle-A	4	16	2	3	1	0	1	2	2	3	0	0	.188	.278	.438	.715	97	-0	2	4.34	0	/0-4(0-3-1)	0	-0.1
1991 Cle-A	48	125	17	29	3	0	3	12	25	35	2	2	.232	.364	.328	.692	92	-0	17	4.40	-1	0-42(20-0-27)/D-1	2	-0.3
Total 3	65	165	19	38	7	0	4	15	29	48	2	2	.230	.349	.345	.694	93	-1	22	4.40	0	/0-51,D-3	3	-0.3
• ALMADA, Mel	Baldomero Melo (Quiros) Almada b: 2/7/1913, Huatabampo, Mexico d: 8/13/1988, Caborca, Mexico BL/TL, 6', 170 lbs. Deb: 9/8/1933 Career OF: 25-461-125																							
1933 Bos-A	14	44	11	15	0	0	1	3	11	3	3	1	.341	.473	.409	.882	137	4	10	8.40	0	0-13(7-6-0)	2	0.3
1934 Bos-A	23	90	7	21	2	1	0	10	6	8	3	2	.233	.281	.278	.559	42	-8	7	2.59	2	0-23(0-16-7)	1	-0.6
1935 Bos-A	151	607	85	176	27	9	3	59	55	34	20	9	.290	.350	.379	.729	83	-15	83	4.85	0	*0-149(0-126-25)/1-3	14	-1.8
1936 Bos-A	96	320	40	81	16	4	1	21	24	15	2	4	.253	.305	.338	.643	55	-25	33	3.52	-1	0-81(11-3-69)	3	-2.7
1937 Bos-A	32	110	17	26	6	2	1	9	15	6	0	1	.236	.328	.355	.683	69	-6	13	4.05	-3	0-27(4-2-21)/1-4	2	-1.0
Was-A	100	433	74	134	21	4	4	33	38	21	12	4	.309	.365	.404	.769	98	-0	66	5.63	8	*0-100(0-97-3)	14	0.5
Yr.	132	543	91	160	27	6	5	42	53	27	12	5	.295	.357	.394	.751	92	-6	79	5.28	5	*0-127(4-99-24)/1-4	16	-0.4
1938 Was-A	47	197	24	48	7	4	1	15	8	16	4	1	.244	.277	.335	.612	56	-13	19	3.18	3	0-47(0-47-0)	3	-1.0
StL-A	102	436	77	149	22	2	3	37	38	22	9	5	.342	.398	.422	.820	106	5	74	6.72	-9	*0-101(0-101-0)	10	-0.6
Yr.	149	633	101	197	29	6	4	52	46	38	13	6	.311	.362	.395	.757	91	-8	93	5.49	-6	*0-148(0-148-0)	13	-1.6
1939 StL-A	42	134	17	32	2	1	1	7	10	8	1	0	.239	.292	.291	.583	48	-10	12	3.01	-1	0-34(3-31-0)	1	-1.1
Bro-N	39	112	11	24	4	0	0	3	9	17	2	....	.214	.273	.250	.523	40	-9	8	2.33	0	0-32(0-32-0)	2	-1.0
Total 7	646	2483	363	706	107	27	15	197	214	150	56	27	.284	.342	.367	.710	79	-78	324	4.66	1	0-607/1-7	52	-8.9
• ALMEIDA, Rafael	Rafael D. "Mike" Almeida b: 6/30/1887, Havana, Cuba d: 3/18/1969, Havana, Cuba BR/TR, 5'9", 164 lbs. Deb: 7/4/1911																							
1911 Cin-N	36	96	9	30	5	1	0	15	9	16	3	....	.313	.383	.385	.769	120	3	16	5.61	-3	3-27/2-1,S-1	3	0.0
1912 Cin-N	16	59	9	13	4	3	0	10	5	8	0	....	.220	.281	.390	.671	85	-2	6	3.42	0	3-15	1	-0.2
1913 Cin-N	50	130	14	34	4	2	3	21	11	16	4	....	.262	.324	.392	.716	104	0	17	4.40	-1	3-37/0-3(0-3-0),S-2,2-1	4	0.0
Total 3	102	285	32	77	13	6	3	46	25	40	7	....	.270	.335	.389	.725	106	2	39	4.60	-5	/3-79,0-3,S-3,2-2	8	-0.1
• ALMON, Bill	William Francis Almon b: 11/21/1952, Providence, RI BR/TR, 6'3", 190 lbs. Deb: 9/2/1974 Career OF: 123-8-35																							
1974 SD-N	16	38	4	12	1	0	0	3	2	9	1	0	.316	.350	.342	.692	98	0	5	5.10	-2	S-14	2	0.0
1975 SD-N	6	10	0	4	0	0	0	0	0	1	0	0	.400	.400	.400	.800	130	0	2	7.20	0	/S-2	1	0.0
1976 SD-N	14	57	6	14	3	0	1	6	2	9	3	1	.246	.271	.351	.622	82	-1	6	3.39	1	S-14	2	0.1
1977 SD-N	155	613	75	160	18	11	2	43	37	114	20	9	.261	.303	.336	.639	79	-18	61	3.34	16	*S-155	15	1.4
1978 SD-N	138	405	39	102	19	2	0	21	33	74	17	5	.252	.308	.309	.617	79	-10	40	3.38	-7	*3-114,S-15/2-7	8	-1.8
1979 SD-N	100	198	20	45	3	0	1	8	21	48	6	5	.227	.301	.258	.559	57	-12	16	2.65	-3	2-61,S-25/0-1	3	-1.2
1980 Mon-N	18	38	2	10	1	1	0	3	1	5	0	0	.263	.282	.342	.624	73	-2	3	2.70	-3	S-12/2-1	1	-0.3
NY-N	48	112	13	19	3	2	0	4	8	27	2	0	.170	.225	.232	.457	29	-10	6	1.89	-2	S-22,2-18/3-9	1	-1.0
Yr.	66	150	15	29	4	3	0	7	9	32	2	0	.193	.239	.260	.499	40	-12	10	2.09	-4	S-34,2-19/3-9	2	-1.3
1981 Chi-A	103	349	46	105	10	2	4	41	21	60	16	6	.301	.344	.375	.719	109	5	46	4.83	10	*S-103	13	2.7
1982 Chi-A	111	308	40	79	10	4	4	26	25	49	10	8	.256	.314	.354	.668	83	-8	34	3.75	2	*S-108/D-1	8	0.4
1983 Oak-A	143	451	45	120	29	1	4	63	26	67	26	8	.266	.309	.361	.670	89	-5	51	3.80	-1	S-52,3-40,1-38,0-23(9-0-15)/2,D	10	-0.5
1984 Oak-A	106	211	24	47	11	0	7	16	10	42	5	7	.223	.258	.374	.632	78	-9	18	2.73	-3	0-48(33-1-17),1-44,D-12/3-4,C,S	2	-1.5
1985 Pit-N	88	244	33	66	17	0	6	29	22	61	10	7	.270	.333	.414	.747	109	1	32	4.38	4	S-43,0-32(26-6-0)/1-7,3-7	6	0.8
1986 Pit-N	102	196	29	43	7	2	7	27	30	38	11	4	.219	.323	.383	.706	92	-1	25	4.08	-5	0-54(53-0-2),3-28,S-19/1-4	4	-0.8
1987 Pit-N	19	20	5	4	1	0	0	1	1	5	0	0	.200	.238	.250	.488	29	-2	1	2.11	-1	/S-4,0-2(2-0-0),3-1	0	-0.3
NY-N	49	54	8	13	3	0	0	4	8	16	1	0	.241	.339	.296	.635	74	-2	6	4.15	-2	S-22,2-10/1-2,0-1	1	-0.2
Yr.	68	74	13	17	4	0	0	5	9	21	1	0	.230	.313	.284	.597	63	-4	8	3.58	-3	S-26,2-10/0-3(2-0-1),1-2,3	1	-0.6
1988 Phi-N	20	26	1	3	2	0	0	1	3	11	0	0	.115	.207	.192	.399	15	-3	1	1.43	-1	/3-9,S-5,1-1	0	-0.4
Total 15	1236	3330	390	846	138	25	36	296	250	636	128	60	.254	.307	.343	.650	83	-78	354	3.58	2	S-616,3-212,0-161,2-102/1,D,C	77	-2.7
• ALMONTE, Erick	Erick R. Almonte b: 2/1/1978, Santo Domingo, Dominican Republic BR/TR, 6'2", 180 lbs. Deb: 9/4/2001																							
2001 NY-A	8	4	0	2	1	0	0	0	0	1	2	0	.500	.500	.750	1.250	220	1	2	27.27	0	/S-4,D-3	1	0.1
2003 NY-A	31	100	17	26	6	0	1	11	8	24	1	0	.260	.321	.350	.671	79	-3	11	3.83	-6	S-31	1	-0.6
Total 2	39	104	17	28	7	0	1	11	8	25	3	0	.269	.327	.365	.693	83	-2	13	4.41	-6	/S-35,D-3	2	-0.5
• ALOMAR, Roberto	Roberto (Velazquez) Alomar b: 2/5/1968, Ponce, Puerto Rico BB/TR, 6', 185 lbs. Deb: 4/22/1988																							
1988 SD-N	143	545	84	145	24	6	9	41	47	83	24	6	.266	.328	.382	.709	105	5	68	4.23	18	*2-143	22	3.0
1989 SD-N	158	623	82	184	27	1	7	56	53	76	42	17	.295	.352	.376	.727	108	8	85	4.66	-4	*2-157	23	0.9
1990 SD-N★	147	586	80	168	27	5	6	60	48	72	24	7	.287	.343	.381	.723	98	0	76	4.58	10	*2-137/S-5	19	1.5
1991*Tor-A★	161	637	88	188	41	11	9	69	57	86	53	11	.295	.357	.436	.793	114	19	107	5.97	-6	*2-160	25	1.7
1992*Tor-A★	152	571	105	177	27	8	8	76	87	52	49	9	.310	.406	.427	.833	128	32	111	7.17	-6	*2-150/D-1	**34**	3.1
1993*Tor-A★	153	589	109	192	35	6	17	93	80	67	55	15	.326	.411	.492	.903	141	42	125	7.80	5	*2-150	30	5.3
1994 Tor-A★	107	392	78	120	25	4	8	38	51	41	19	8	.306	.389	.452	.840	116	11	68	6.05	5	*2-106	13	1.9
1995 Tor-A★	130	517	71	155	24	7	13	66	47	45	30	3	.300	.358	.449	.807	109	12	84	5.78	9	*2-128	16	2.5
1996*Bal-A★	153	588	132	193	43	4	22	94	90	65	17	6	.328	.418	.527	.945	138	38	132	8.21	12	*2-141,D-10	31	5.1
1997*Bal-A★	112	412	64	137	23	2	14	60	40	43	9	3	.333	.396	.500	.896	136	23	81	7.28	5	*2-109/D-2	21	3.1
1998 Bal-A★	147	588	86	166	36	1	14	56	59	70	18	5	.282	.350	.418	.768	100	2	88	5.34	1	*2-144/D-3	19	0.9
1999*Cle-A★	159	563	**138**	182	40	3	24	120	99	96	37	6	.323	.430	.533	.963	138	42	139	8.84	0	*2-156/D-3	**35**	4.5
2000 Cle-A★	155	610	111	189	40	2	19	89	64	82	39	4	.310	.381	.475	.856	113	19	114	6.67	-1	*2-155	20	2.4
2001*Cle-A★	157	575	113	193	34	12	20	100	80	71	30	6	.336	.420	.541	.961	149	47	138	8.98	-5	*2-157	37	4.8
2002 NY-N	149	590	73	157	24	4	11	53	57	83	16	4	.266	.332	.376	.708	90	-7	75	4.46	-19	*2-147	16	-2.0
2003 NY-N	73	263	34	69	17	1	2	22	29	40	6	0	.262	.340	.357	.698	85	-4	33	4.26	-10	2-72	7	-1.1
Chi-A	67	253	42	64	11	1	3	17	30	37	6	2	.253	.335	.340	.674	79	-7	29	3.73	-2	2-67	5	-0.5
Total 16	2323	8902	1490	2679	498	78	206	1110	1018	1109	474	112	.301	.376	.444	.820	117	282	1557	6.20	12	*2-2279/D-19,S-5	373	37.1
• ALOMAR, Sandy	Santos (Velazquez) Alomar b: 6/18/1966, Salinas, Puerto Rico BR/TR, 6'5", 215 lbs. Deb: 9/30/1988																							
1988 SD-N	1	1	0	0	0	0	0	0	0	1	0	0	.000	.000	.000	.000	-102	-0	0	.00	0	....	0	0.0
1989 SD-N	7	19	1	4	1	0	1	6	3	3	0	0	.211	.318	.421	.739	109	0	2	3.92	0	/C-6	1	0.1
1990 Cle-A★	132	445	60	129	26	2	9	66	25	46	4	1	.290	.331	.418	.748	108	4	60	4.80	-7	*C-129	15	0.6
1991 Cle-A★	51	184	10	40	9	0	0	7	8	24	0	4	.217	.265	.266	.532	47	-15	12	2.06	2	C-46/D-4	2	-1.0
1992 Cle-A★	89	299	22	75	16	0	2	26	13	32	3	3	.251	.293	.324	.618	74	-12	27	3.07	0	C-88/D-1	9	-0.6
1993 Cle-A	64	215	24	58	7	1	6	32	11	28	3	1	.270	.323	.395	.719	92	-2	28	4.56	0	C-64	6	0.2
1994 Cle-A	80	292	44	84	15	1	14	43	25	31	8	4	.288	.348	.490	.838	113	5	48	5.91	1	C-78	12	1.0
1995*Cle-A	66	203	32	61	6	0	10	35	7	26	3	1	.300	.333	.478	.811	106	1	30	5.11	0	C-61	7	0.5
1996*Cle-A★	127	418	53	110	23	0	11	50	19	42	1	0	.263	.300	.397	.697	75	-18	44	3.58	0	*C-124/1-1	8	-0.9
1997*Cle-A★	125	451	63	146	37	0	21	83	19	48	0	2	.324	.355	.545	.901	126	14	80	6.52	-6	*C-119/D-1	18	1.6
1998*Cle-A★	117	409	45	96	26	2	6	44	18	45	0	3	.235	.272	.352	.624	59	-27	35	2.77	1	*C-111/D-3	6	-1.7
1999*Cle-A	37	137	19	42	13	0	6	25	4	23	0	1	.307	.326	.533	.859	109	1	23	6.24	-3	C-35/D-1	4	0.0
2000 Cle-A	97	356	44	103	16	2	7	42	16	41	2	2	.289	.327	.404	.732	82	-11	45	4.46	-9	C-95/D-1	8	-1.2
2001 Chi-A	70	220	17	54	8	1	4	21	12	17	1	2	.245	.291	.345	.636	65	-12	21	3.12	-4	C-69	4	-1.1
2002 Chi-A	51	167	21	48	10	1	7	25	5	14	0	0	.287	.312	.485	.797	105	0	23	4.98	0	C-50	4	0.4
Col-N	38	116	8	31	4	0	0	12	4	19	0	0	.267	.292	.302	.593	49	-9	9	2.58	-2	C-38	1	-0.8

YEAR TM-L	G	AB	R	H	2B	3B	HR	RBI	BB	SO	SB	CS	AVG	OBP	SLG	OPS	OPS+	BR/A	RC	RC/G	FR	G/POS	WS	TPW
2003 Chi-A	75	194	22	52	12	0	5	26	4	17	0	0	.268	.283	.407	.690	79	-7	21	3.77	-7	C-75	4	-0.9
Total 16	1227	4126	485	1133	229	10	109	543	193	457	25	24	.275	.313	.414	.727	88	-87	507	4.27	-32	*C-1188/D-11,1-1	109	-3.9

• ALOMAR, Sandy Santos (Conde) Alomar b: 10/19/1943, Salinas, Puerto Rico BB/TR, 5'9", 155 lbs. Deb: 9/15/1964 C Career OF: 5-0-3

YEAR TM-L	G	AB	R	H	2B	3B	HR	RBI	BB	SO	SB	CS	AVG	OBP	SLG	OPS	OPS+	BR/A	RC	RC/G	FR	G/POS	WS	TPW
1964 Mil-N	19	53	3	13	1	0	0	6	0	11	1	0	.245	.245	.264	.509	43	-4	3	2.16	3	S-19	1	0.1
1965 Mil-N	67	108	16	26	1	1	0	8	4	12	12	5	.241	.268	.269	.536	51	-7	7	1.85	0	S-39,2-19	2	-0.4
1966 Atl-N	31	44	4	4	1	0	0	2	1	10	0	0	.091	.111	.114	.225	-37	-8	1	.38	1	2-21/S-5	0	-0.7
1967 NY-N	15	22	1	0	0	0	0	0	0	6	0	0	.000	.000	.000	.000	-102	-6	0	.00	-1	S-10/3-3,2-2	0	-0.7
Chi-A	12	15	4	3	0	0	0	0	2	0	2	0	.200	.294	.200	.494	50	-0	1	2.18	0	/S-8,2-2	0	0.0
1968 Chi-A	133	363	41	92	8	2	0	12	20	42	21	8	.253	.294	.287	.581	76	-10	32	2.88	-25	2-99,3-27/S-9,0-1	6	-3.0
1969 Chi-A	22	58	8	13	2	0	0	4	4	6	2	0	.224	.274	.259	.533	47	-4	5	2.76	-1	2-22	1	-0.3
Cal-A	134	559	60	140	10	2	1	30	36	48	18	3	.250	.296	.281	.577	65	-23	50	3.12	-3	*2-134	11	-1.9
Yr.	156	617	68	153	12	2	1	34	40	54	20	3	.248	.294	.279	.573	63	-27	54	3.08	-4	*2-156	12	-2.2
1970 Cal-A★	162	672	82	169	18	2	2	36	49	65	35	12	.251	.303	.293	.596	68	-27	64	3.22	17	*2-153,S-10/3-1	17	0.2
1971 Cal-A	162	689	77	179	24	3	4	42	41	60	39	10	.260	.301	.321	.622	82	-13	70	3.54	20	*2-137,S-28	21	2.1
1972 Cal-A	155	610	65	146	20	3	1	25	47	55	20	12	.239	.294	.287	.581	78	-18	52	2.86	5	*2-154/S-4	15	-0.3
1973 Cal-A	136	470	45	112	7	1	0	28	34	44	25	10	.238	.290	.257	.547	60	-23	39	2.72	2	*2-110,S-31	9	-1.1
1974 Cal-A	46	54	12	12	0	1	0	1	2	8	2	0	.222	.250	.259	.509	49	-3	4	2.25	0	S-19,2-15/3-5,D-1,0-1	0	-0.2
NY-A	76	279	35	75	8	0	1	27	14	25	6	4	.269	.304	.308	.612	79	-8	25	3.11	-6	2-76	6	-1.0
Yr.	122	333	47	87	8	1	1	28	16	33	8	4	.261	.295	.300	.595	74	-11	29	2.97	-6	2-91,S-19/3-5,D-1,0-1	6	-1.2
1975 NY-A	151	489	61	117	18	4	2	39	26	58	28	6	.239	.278	.305	.582	66	-19	44	2.99	4	*2-150/S-1	10	-0.5
1976*NY-A	67	163	20	39	4	0	1	10	13	12	12	7	.239	.295	.282	.578	70	-6	14	2.74	0	2-38/S-6,3-3,1-1,0-1	3	-0.5
1977 Tex-A	69	83	21	22	3	0	1	11	8	13	4	3	.265	.337	.337	.674	84	-2	10	3.96	0	D-26,2-18/S-6,0-5(4-0-1),1,3	2	-0.2
1978 Tex-A	24	29	3	6	1	0	0	1	1	7	0	0	.207	.233	.241	.475	34	-3	2	1.98	0	/1-9,2-6,3-3,D-3,S-2	0	-0.3
Total 15	1481	4760	558	1168	126	19	13	282	302	482	227	80	.245	.291	.288	.579	68	-183	421	2.97	14	*2-1156,S-197/3-43,D-30,1,0	104	-8.6

• ALOU, Felipe Felipe Rojas Alou b: 5/12/1935, Haina, Dominican Republic BR/TR, 6', 195 lbs. Deb: 6/8/1958 M/C Career OF: 434-484-736

YEAR TM-L	G	AB	R	H	2B	3B	HR	RBI	BB	SO	SB	CS	AVG	OBP	SLG	OPS	OPS+	BR/A	RC	RC/G	FR	G/POS	WS	TPW
1958 SF-N	75	182	21	46	9	2	4	16	19	34	4	2	.253	.327	.390	.717	91	-2	24	4.66	-2	0-70(28-3-44)	5	-0.7
1959 SF-N	95	247	38	68	13	2	10	33	17	38	5	3	.275	.322	.466	.788	109	2	36	5.03	-1	0-69(0-10-64)	7	-0.1
1960 SF-N	106	322	48	85	17	3	8	44	16	42	10	2	.264	.303	.410	.713	99	-0	39	4.08	-3	0-95(68-7-24)	9	-0.8
1961 SF-N	132	415	59	120	19	0	18	52	26	41	11	4	.289	.334	.465	.799	113	7	62	5.31	-5	*0-122(42-6-87)	14	-0.5
1962*SF-N★	154	561	96	177	30	3	25	98	33	66	10	7	.316	.359	.513	.872	133	23	103	6.92	-8	*0-150(11-2-141)	25	0.5
1963 SF-N	157	565	75	159	31	9	20	82	27	87	11	2	.281	.321	.474	.795	127	19	83	5.24	-7	*0-153(6-13-144)	21	0.2
1964 Mil-N	121	415	60	105	26	3	9	51	30	41	5	2	.253	.310	.395	.705	96	-2	51	4.30	-2	0-92(14-60-27),1-18	12	-0.9
1965 Mil-N	143	555	80	165	29	2	23	78	31	63	8	4	.297	.340	.481	.821	128	19	90	5.99	-1	0-91(66-24-9),1-69/3-2,S-1	21	1.1
1966 Atl-N★	154	666	**122**	**218**	32	6	31	74	24	51	5	7	.327	.362	.533	.895	143	35	123	7.06	1	1-90,0-79(47-40-4)/3-3,S-1	28	2.8
1967 Atl-N	140	574	76	157	26	3	15	43	32	50	6	5	.274	.320	.408	.727	108	4	73	4.50	-7	1-85,0-56(24-30-5)	15	-1.1
1968 Atl-N★	160	662	72	**210**	37	5	11	57	48	56	12	11	.317	.367	.438	.805	140	30	103	5.86	-3	*0-158(0-158-0)	31	2.5
1969*Atl-N	123	476	54	134	13	1	5	32	23	23	4	6	.282	.320	.345	.665	86	-11	51	3.81	-7	*0-116(3-102-13)	13	-2.3
1970 Oak-A	154	575	70	156	25	3	8	55	32	31	10	5	.271	.311	.367	.678	89	-10	63	3.82	2	*0-145(101-5-81)/1-1	13	-1.7
1971 Oak-A	2	8	0	2	1	0	0	0	0	1	0	0	.250	.250	.375	.625	76	-0	1	3.02	1	/0-2(2-0-0)	0	0.0
NY-A	131	461	52	133	20	6	8	69	32	24	5	5	.289	.337	.410	.747	118	8	59	4.54	-4	0-80(7-20-56),1-42	14	-0.2
Yr.	133	469	52	135	21	6	8	69	32	25	5	5	.288	.336	.409	.745	117	8	60	4.51	-4	0-82(9-20-56),1-42	14	-0.2
1972 NY-A	120	324	33	90	18	1	6	37	22	27	1	0	.278	.328	.395	.723	118	7	41	4.53	2	1-95,0-15(0-0-15)	10	0.3
1973 NY-A	93	280	25	66	12	0	4	27	9	25	0	1	.236	.260	.321	.581	65	-14	22	2.69	-3	1-67,0-22(1-1-21)	2	-2.3
Mon-N	19	48	4	10	1	0	1	4	2	4	0	1	.208	.240	.292	.532	45	-4	2	1.47	2	0-15(14-3-0)/1-1	1	-0.3
1974 Mil-A	3	3	0	0	0	0	0	0	0	2	0	0	.000	.000	.000	.000	-101	-1	0	.00	0	/0-1	0	-0.1
Total 17	2082	7339	985	2101	359	49	206	852	423	706	107	67	.286	.330	.433	.763	114	110	1028	5.02	-46	*0-1531,1-468/3-5,S-2	241	-3.5

• ALOU, Jesus Jesus Maria Rojas "Jay" Alou b: 3/24/1942, Haina, Dominican Republic BR/TR, 6'2", 195 lbs. Deb: 9/10/1963 C Career OF: 445-5-655

YEAR TM-L	G	AB	R	H	2B	3B	HR	RBI	BB	SO	SB	CS	AVG	OBP	SLG	OPS	OPS+	BR/A	RC	RC/G	FR	G/POS	WS	TPW
1963 SF-N	16	24	3	6	1	0	0	5	0	3	0	1	.250	.280	.292	.572	66	-2	1	1.96	-1	0-12(11-0-3)	0	-0.3
1964 SF-N	115	376	42	103	11	0	3	28	13	35	6	6	.274	.305	.327	.632	77	-13	35	3.22	-3	*0-108(9-4-99)	6	-2.4
1965 SF-N	143	543	76	162	19	4	9	52	13	40	8	5	.298	.318	.398	.716	98	-3	61	3.98	-5	*0-136(6-0-133)	14	-2.0
1966 SF-N	110	370	41	96	13	1	1	20	9	22	5	5	.259	.281	.308	.589	62	-20	28	2.51	-4	*0-100(59-0-42)	3	-3.2
1967 SF-N	129	510	55	149	15	4	5	30	14	39	1	7	.292	.316	.367	.683	96	-6	55	3.85	-5	*0-123(79-0-50)	12	-2.1
1968 SF-N	120	419	26	110	15	4	0	39	9	23	1	4	.263	.280	.317	.597	79	-13	31	2.43	0	*0-105(49-0-65)	6	-2.3
1969 Hou-N	115	452	49	112	19	4	5	34	15	30	4	6	.248	.278	.341	.619	74	-19	38	2.83	-5	*0-112(65-0-58)	5	-3.2
1970 Hou-N	117	458	59	140	27	3	1	44	21	15	3	2	.306	.338	.384	.722	97	-3	55	4.37	-3	*0-108(30-0-88)	10	-1.2
1971 Hou-N	122	433	41	121	21	4	2	40	13	17	3	7	.279	.307	.360	.667	91	-9	43	3.48	1	*0-109(52-0-63)	9	-1.6
1972 Hou-N	52	93	8	29	4	1	0	11	7	5	0	2	.312	.366	.376	.743	114	1	11	4.42	-2	0-23(10-0-14)	2	-0.3
1973 Hou-N	28	55	7	13	2	0	1	8	1	6	0	0	.236	.276	.327	.603	67	-3	4	2.49	-1	0-14(1-0-13)	0	-0.4
*Oak-A	36	108	10	33	3	0	1	11	2	6	0	0	.306	.318	.361	.679	96	-1	12	4.09	0	0-21(18-1-4)/D-6	3	-0.2
1974*Oak-A	96	220	13	59	8	0	2	15	5	9	0	0	.268	.291	.332	.623	84	-5	19	2.92	2	D-41,0-25(9-0-16)	2	-0.5
1975 NY-N	62	102	8	27	3	0	0	11	4	5	0	1	.265	.299	.294	.593	68	-5	8	2.61	1	0-20(15-0-5)	1	-0.5
1978 Hou-N	77	139	7	45	5	1	2	19	6	5	0	0	.324	.352	.417	.769	123	4	19	5.00	-1	0-28(27-0-1)	4	0.2
1979 Hou-N	42	43	3	11	4	0	0	10	6	7	0	0	.256	.347	.349	.696	96	-0	4	3.24	0	/0-6(5-0-1),1-1	1	0.0
Total 15	1380	4345	448	1216	170	26	32	377	138	267	31	46	.280	.307	.353	.660	87	-98	426	3.40	-26	*0-1050/D-47,1-1	78	-19.9

• ALOU, Matty Mateo Rojas Alou b: 12/22/1938, Haina, Dominican Republic BL/TL, 5'9", 160 lbs. Deb: 9/26/1960 Career OF: 197-844-282

YEAR TM-L	G	AB	R	H	2B	3B	HR	RBI	BB	SO	SB	CS	AVG	OBP	SLG	OPS	OPS+	BR/A	RC	RC/G	FR	G/POS	WS	TPW
1960 SF-N	4	3	1	1	0	0	0	0	0	0	0	0	.333	.333	.333	.667	88	-0	0	4.50	-0	/0-1	0	0.0
1961 SF-N	81	200	38	62	7	2	6	24	15	18	3	2	.310	.358	.455	.813	118	5	32	5.87	-4	0-58(16-3-40)	7	-0.3
1962*SF-N	78	195	28	57	8	1	3	14	14	17	3	1	.292	.349	.390	.739	100	0	27	5.12	-1	0-57(35-9-21)	6	-0.4
1963 SF-N	63	76	4	11	1	0	0	2	2	13	0	1	.145	.177	.158	.335	-3	-10	2	.79	0	0-20(13-2-7)	0	-1.2
1964 SF-N	110	250	28	66	4	2	1	14	11	25	5	3	.264	.303	.308	.611	71	-10	23	3.26	-3	0-80(42-18-35)	4	-1.7
1965 SF-N	117	324	37	75	12	2	2	18	17	28	10	2	.231	.274	.299	.573	60	-16	24	2.39	2	*0-103(72-11-3)/P-1	4	-1.9
1966 Pit-N	141	535	86	183	18	9	2	27	24	44	23	15	**.342**	.375	.421	.795	120	13	84	5.88	0	*0-136(1-135-0)	20	1.0
1967 Pit-N	139	550	87	186	21	7	2	28	24	42	16	10	.338	.372	.413	.785	124	16	85	6.03	-1	*0-134(0-134-0)/1-1	23	1.2
1968 Pit-N★	146	558	59	185	28	4	0	52	27	26	18	10	.332	.365	.396	.761	130	19	79	5.25	-2	*0-144(0-144-0)	23	1.5
1969 Pit-N★	162	698	105	**231**	**41**	6	1	48	42	35	22	8	.331	.371	.411	.782	121	21	109	6.07	2	*0-162(1-162-0)	27	2.0
1970*Pit-N	155	677	97	201	21	8	1	47	30	18	19	11	.297	.331	.356	.687	87	-15	79	4.22	3	*0-153(0-152-1)	16	-1.5
1971 StL-N	149	609	85	192	28	6	7	74	34	27	19	10	.315	.355	.415	.771	113	10	89	5.36	-4	0-94(0-73-21),1-57	23	-0.1
1972 StL-N	108	404	46	127	17	2	3	31	24	23	11	4	.314	.354	.389	.743	112	7	54	4.90	3	1-66,0-39(1-0-38)	11	0.4
*Oak-A	32	121	11	34	5	0	1	16	11	12	2	1	.281	.346	.347	.693	112	2	15	4.51	1	0-32(2-0-31)/1-1	5	0.2
1973 NY-A	123	497	59	147	22	1	2	28	30	43	5	2	.296	.340	.356	.696	100	-0	57	4.09	-5	0-85(0-0-85),1-40/D-1	10	-1.3
StL-N	11	11	1	3	0	0	0	1	1	0	0	0	.273	.333	.273	.606	70	-0	1	1.35	1	/1-1,0-1	0	0.0
1974 SD-N	48	81	8	16	3	0	0	3	5	6	0	0	.198	.244	.235	.479	36	-7	4	1.66	-1	0-13(13-0-0)/1-2	0	-0.9
Total 15	1667	5789	780	1777	236	50	31	427	311	377	156	80	.307	.346	.381	.727	105	35	764	4.82	-8	*0-1312,1-168/D-1,P-1	179	-3.0

• ALOU, Moises Moises Rojas Alou b: 7/3/1966, Atlanta, GA BR/TR, 6'3", 190 lbs. Deb: 7/26/1990 Career OF: 907-99-469

YEAR TM-L	G	AB	R	H	2B	3B	HR	RBI	BB	SO	SB	CS	AVG	OBP	SLG	OPS	OPS+	BR/A	RC	RC/G	FR	G/POS	WS	TPW
1990 Pit-N	2	5	0	1	0	0	0	0	0	0	0	0	.200	.200	.200	.400	11	-1	0	.00	0	/0-2(2-0-0)	0	-0.1
Mon-N	14	15	4	3	0	1	0	0	0	3	0	0	.200	.200	.333	.533	46	-1	1	2.15	0	/0-5(1-2-2)	0	-0.1
Yr.	16	20	4	4	0	1	0	0	0	3	0	0	.200	.200	.300	.500	37	-2	1	1.55	1	/0-7(3-2-2)	0	-0.1
1992 Mon-N	115	341	53	96	28	2	9	56	25	46	16	2	.282	.332	.455	.787	122	11	53	5.51	1	*0-100(79-13-15)	15	1.0
1993 Mon-N	136	482	70	138	29	6	18	85	38	53	17	6	.286	.345	.483	.828	114	9	79	5.81	1	*0-136(102-12-34)	21	0.4
1994 Mon-N★	107	422	81	143	31	5	22	78	42	63	7	6	.339	.401	.592	.994	153	31	98	8.90	-2	*0-106(63-0-45)	22	2.4
1995 Mon-N	93	344	48	94	22	0	14	58	29	56	4	3	.273	.346	.459	.805	106	2	53	5.38	-1	0-92(61-4-30)	11	-0.2
1996 Mon-N	143	540	87	152	28	2	21	96	49	83	9	4	.281	.343	.457	.801	106	4	82	5.35	2	*0-142(33-7-123)	20	-0.2
1997*Fla-N★	150	538	88	157	29	5	23	115	70	85	9	5	.292	.377	.493	.870	131	25	100	6.64	-5	*0-150(91-54-22)	23	1.6
1998*Hou-N★	159	584	104	182	34	5	38	124	84	87	11	3	.312	.403	.582	.985	159	52	138	8.77	-2	*0-154(152-6-0)/D-1	29	4.3
2000 Hou-N	126	454	82	161	28	2	30	114	52	45	3	3	.355	.423	.623	1.047	152	36	112	9.25	-13	*0-121(59-0-64)/D-1	17	1.6

YEAR TM-L	G	AB	R	H	2B	3B	HR	RBI	BB	SO	SB	CS	AVG	OBP	SLG	OPS	OPS+	BR/A	RC	RC/G	FR	G/POS	WS	TPW
2001*Hou-N★	136	513	79	170	31	1	27	108	57	57	5	1	.331	.401	.554	.955	136	29	110	8.02	-4	*O-130(0-0-130)/D-4	21	1.8
2002 Chi-N	132	484	50	133	23	1	15	61	47	61	8	0	.275	.339	.419	.758	100	1	68	4.97	-2	*O-124(122-1-4)/D-2	9	-0.6
2003*Chi-N	151	565	83	158	35	1	22	91	63	67	3	1	.280	.359	.462	.821	114	12	93	5.87	-3	*O-142(142-0-0)/D-9	20	0.2
Total 12	1464	5287	829	1588	318	31	239	986	556	706	92	34	.300	.371	.508	.879	127	211	987	6.75	-27	*O-1404/D-17	208	12.3

• ALPERMAN, Whitey Charles Augustus Alperman b: 11/11/1879, Etna, PA d: 12/25/1942, Pittsburgh, PA BR/TR, 5'10", 180 lbs. Deb: 4/13/1906

YEAR TM-L	G	AB	R	H	2B	3B	HR	RBI	BB	SO	SB	CS	AVG	OBP	SLG	OPS	OPS+	BR/A	RC	RC/G	FR	G/POS	WS	TPW
1906 Bro-N	128	441	38	111	15	7	3	46	6	....	13	....	.252	.284	.338	.622	102	-2	50	3.65	5	*2-103,S-24/3-1	11	0.5
1907 Bro-N	141	558	44	130	23	**16**	2	39	13	....	5	....	.233	.266	.342	.608	98	-5	54	3.24	18	*2-115,3-14,S-12	15	1.7
1908 Bro-N	70	213	17	42	3	1	1	15	9	....	2	....	.197	.253	.235	.488	58	-10	14	1.96	-3	2-42/3-9,O-5(0-0-5),S-2	1	-1.4
1909 Bro-N	111	420	35	104	19	12	1	41	2	....	7	....	.248	.262	.357	.619	95	-6	40	3.17	6	*2-108	9	0.0
Total 4	450	1632	134	387	60	36	7	141	30	....	27	....	.237	.268	.331	.599	93	-23	158	3.15	27	2-368/S-38,3-24,O-5	36	0.9

• ALSTON, Dell Wendell Alston b: 9/22/1952, Valhalla, NY BL/TR, 6', 180 lbs. Deb: 5/17/1977 Career OF: 52-4-54

YEAR TM-L	G	AB	R	H	2B	3B	HR	RBI	BB	SO	SB	CS	AVG	OBP	SLG	OPS	OPS+	BR/A	RC	RC/G	FR	G/POS	WS	TPW
1977 NY-A	22	40	10	13	4	0	1	4	3	4	3	3	.325	.372	.500	.872	137	1	6	4.54	1	D-10/O-2(0-0-2)	1	0.2
1978 NY-A	3	3	0	0	0	0	0	0	0	2	0	0	.000	.000	.000	.000	-102	-1	0	.00	0	....	0	-0.1
Oak-A	58	173	17	36	2	0	1	10	10	21	11	10	.208	.251	.237	.488	40	-16	10	1.71	-3	O-50(22-0-29)/1-9,D-3	1	-2.1
Yr.	61	176	17	36	2	0	1	10	10	23	11	10	.205	.247	.233	.480	38	-17	10	1.67	-3	O-50(22-0-29)/1-9,D-3	1	-2.2
1979 Cle-A	54	62	10	18	0	2	1	12	10	10	4	4	.290	.389	.403	.792	114	1	10	5.33	0	O-30(18-0-12)/D-7	2	0.0
1980 Cle-A	52	54	11	12	1	2	0	9	5	7	2	4	.222	.311	.315	.626	72	-3	5	2.47	-1	O-26(12-4-11)/D-6	0	-0.5
Total 4	189	332	48	79	7	4	3	35	28	44	20	21	.238	.301	.310	.611	71	-18	30	2.78	-3	O-108/D-26,1-9	4	-2.5

• ALSTON, Tom Thomas Edison Alston b: 1/31/1926, Greensboro, NC d: 12/30/1993, Winston-Salem, NC BL/TR, 6'5", 210 lbs. Deb: 4/13/1954

YEAR TM-L	G	AB	R	H	2B	3B	HR	RBI	BB	SO	SB	CS	AVG	OBP	SLG	OPS	OPS+	BR/A	RC	RC/G	FR	G/POS	WS	TPW
1954 StL-N	66	244	28	60	14	2	4	34	24	41	3	5	.246	.319	.369	.687	78	-9	27	3.77	5	1-65	3	-0.8
1955 StL-N	13	8	0	1	0	0	0	0	0	0	0	0	.125	.125	.125	.250	-33	-2	0	.48	0	/1-7	0	-0.2
1956 StL-N	3	2	0	0	0	0	0	0	0	0	0	0	.000	.000	.000	.000	-100	-1	0	.00	0	/1-3	0	-0.1
1957 StL-N	9	17	2	5	1	0	0	2	1	5	0	0	.294	.333	.353	.686	83	-0	2	4.70	-1	/1-6	0	-0.2
Total 4	91	271	30	66	15	2	4	36	25	46	3	5	.244	.312	.358	.670	74	-12	30	3.68	4	/1-81	3	-1.2

• ALSTON, Walter Walter Emmons "Smokey" Alston b: 12/1/1911, Venice, OH d: 10/1/1984, Oxford, OH BR/TR, 6'2", 195 lbs. Deb: 9/27/1936 M HOF: 1983

YEAR TM-L	G	AB	R	H	2B	3B	HR	RBI	BB	SO	SB	CS	AVG	OBP	SLG	OPS	OPS+	BR/A	RC	RC/G	FR	G/POS	WS	TPW
1936 StL-N	1	1	0	0	0	0	0	0	0	1	0	....	.000	.000	.000	.000	-100	-0	0	.00	0	/1-1	0	-0.1

• ALTENBURG, Jesse Jesse Howard Altenburg b: 1/2/1893, Ashley, MI d: 3/12/1973, Lansing, MI BL/TR, 5'9", 158 lbs. Deb: 9/19/1916 Career OF: 5-2-3

YEAR TM-L	G	AB	R	H	2B	3B	HR	RBI	BB	SO	SB	CS	AVG	OBP	SLG	OPS	OPS+	BR/A	RC	RC/G	FR	G/POS	WS	TPW
1916 Pit-N	8	14	2	6	1	1	0	0	1	1	0	....	.429	.467	.643	1.110	237	2	4	13.65	-1	/O-8(4-2-0)	1	0.2
1917 Pit-N	11	17	1	3	0	0	0	3	0	4	0	....	.176	.176	.176	.353	8	-2	1	.99	0	/O-4(1-0-3)	0	-0.2
Total 2	19	31	3	9	1	1	0	3	1	5	0	....	.290	.313	.387	.700	112	0	5	5.39	-1	/O-12	1	-0.1

• ALTIZER, Dave David Tilden "Filipino" Altizer b: 11/6/1876, Pearl, IL d: 5/14/1964, Pleasant Hill, IL BL/TR, 5'10.5", 160 lbs. Deb: 5/29/1906 Career OF: 4-53-52

YEAR TM-L	G	AB	R	H	2B	3B	HR	RBI	BB	SO	SB	CS	AVG	OBP	SLG	OPS	OPS+	BR/A	RC	RC/G	FR	G/POS	WS	TPW
1906 Was-A	115	433	56	111	9	5	1	27	35	....	37	....	.256	.324	.307	.631	103	3	58	4.57	-19	*S-113/O-2(0-0-2)	15	-1.4
1907 Was-A	147	540	60	145	15	5	2	42	34	....	38	....	.269	.319	.326	.645	115	9	72	4.61	-7	S-80,1-50,O-17(0-19-0)	15	0.3
1908 Was-A	67	205	19	46	1	1	0	18	13	....	8	....	.224	.274	.239	.513	73	-6	16	2.48	-5	2-38,3-16/1-4,S-1	3	-1.2
Cle-A	29	89	11	19	1	2	0	5	7	....	7	....	.213	.278	.270	.548	78	-2	9	2.99	3	O-24(0-20-4)/S-3	4	0.0
Yr.	96	294	30	65	2	3	0	23	20	....	15	....	.221	.275	.248	.524	75	-8	26	2.65	-2	2-38,O-24(0-20-4),3-16/1-4,S	7	-1.2
1909 Chi-A	116	382	47	89	6	7	1	20	39	....	27	....	.233	.330	.293	.623	101	3	47	3.90	11	O-61(4-14-45),1-46	14	1.2
1910 Cin-N	3	10	3	6	0	0	0	0	3	0	0	....	.600	.692	.600	1.292	290	3	4	27.06	0	/S-3	2	0.3
1911 Cin-N	37	75	8	17	4	1	0	4	9	5	2	....	.227	.318	.307	.624	78	-2	8	3.45	0	S-23/1-1,2-1,O-1	2	-0.1
Total 6	514	1734	204	433	36	21	4	116	140	5	119	....	.250	.318	.302	.619	101	7	216	4.10	-17	S-223,O-105,1-101/2-39,3-16	55	-0.9

• ALTMAN, George George Lee "Big George" Altman b: 3/20/1933, Goldsboro, NC BL/TR, 6'4", 200 lbs. Deb: 4/11/1959 Career OF: 222-184-396

YEAR TM-L	G	AB	R	H	2B	3B	HR	RBI	BB	SO	SB	CS	AVG	OBP	SLG	OPS	OPS+	BR/A	RC	RC/G	FR	G/POS	WS	TPW
1959 Chi-N	135	420	54	103	14	4	12	47	34	80	1	0	.245	.312	.383	.696	85	-9	51	4.13	3	*O-121(0-121-0)	11	-1.2
1960 Chi-N	119	334	50	89	16	4	13	51	32	67	4	3	.266	.332	.455	.788	114	6	51	5.32	-1	O-79(26-32-23),1-21	11	0.1
1961 Chi-N★	138	518	77	157	28	**12**	27	96	40	92	6	2	.303	.358	.560	.917	137	26	105	7.52	-2	*O-130(1-25-115)/1-3	20	1.5
1962 Chi-N★	147	534	74	170	27	5	22	74	62	89	19	7	.318	.394	.511	.906	136	29	110	7.77	-1	*O-129(0-6-125),1-16	20	1.8
1963 StL-N	135	464	62	127	18	7	9	47	47	93	13	4	.274	.343	.401	.744	104	5	66	5.02	-3	*O-124(12-0-116)	15	-0.8
1964 NY-N	124	422	48	97	14	1	9	47	18	70	4	2	.230	.263	.332	.595	68	-19	35	2.81	12	*O-109(95-0-14)	5	-1.3
1965 Chi-N	90	196	24	46	7	1	4	23	19	36	3	2	.235	.302	.342	.644	79	-5	21	3.70	-1	O-45(44-0-1)/1-2	3	-1.0
1966 Chi-N	88	185	19	41	6	0	5	17	14	37	2	2	.222	.276	.335	.612	68	-8	17	2.98	0	O-42(41-0-1)/1-4	1	-1.1
1967 Chi-N	15	18	1	2	2	0	0	1	2	8	0	0	.111	.200	.222	.422	20	-2	1	1.53	0	/O-4(3-0-1),1-1	0	-0.2
Total 9	991	3091	409	832	132	34	101	403	268	572	52	22	.269	.331	.432	.763	105	23	456	5.21	7	O-783/1-47	86	-2.0

• ALTOBELLI, Joe Joseph Salvatore Altobelli b: 5/26/1932, Detroit, MI BL/TL, 6', 185 lbs. Deb: 4/14/1955 M/C Career OF: 26-4-2

YEAR TM-L	G	AB	R	H	2B	3B	HR	RBI	BB	SO	SB	CS	AVG	OBP	SLG	OPS	OPS+	BR/A	RC	RC/G	FR	G/POS	WS	TPW
1955 Cle-A	42	75	8	15	3	0	2	5	5	14	0	1	.200	.259	.320	.579	53	-6	6	2.72	-2	1-40	1	-0.9
1957 Cle-A	83	87	9	18	3	2	0	9	5	14	3	2	.207	.258	.287	.545	49	-6	7	2.32	-2	1-56/O-7(1-4-2)	0	-1.0
1961 Min-A	41	95	10	21	2	1	3	14	13	14	0	0	.221	.315	.358	.673	75	-3	11	3.90	0	O-25(25-0-0)/1-2	1	-0.5
Total 3	166	257	27	54	8	3	5	28	23	42	3	3	.210	.280	.323	.603	60	-15	24	3.00	-5	/1-98,O-32	2	-2.4

• ALUSIK, George George Joseph Alusik b: 2/11/1935, Ashley, PA BR/TR, 6'3.5", 175 lbs. Deb: 9/11/1958 Career OF: 109-1-62

YEAR TM-L	G	AB	R	H	2B	3B	HR	RBI	BB	SO	SB	CS	AVG	OBP	SLG	OPS	OPS+	BR/A	RC	RC/G	FR	G/POS	WS	TPW
1958 Det-A	2	2	0	0	0	0	0	0	0	1	0	0	.000	.000	.000	.000	-93	-1	0	.00	-0	/O-1	0	-0.1
1961 Det-A	15	14	0	2	0	0	0	2	1	4	0	0	.143	.200	.143	.343	-6	-2	1	1.08	0	/O-1	0	-0.2
1962 Det-A	2	2	0	0	0	0	0	0	0	0	0	0	.000	.000	.000	.000	-97	-1	0	.00	0	....	0	-0.1
KC-A	90	209	29	57	10	1	11	35	16	29	1	1	.273	.327	.488	.815	112	3	33	5.54	-1	O-50(35-0-22)/1-1	6	-0.2
Yr.	92	211	29	57	10	1	11	35	16	29	1	1	.270	.325	.483	.808	111	2	33	5.47	-1	O-50(35-0-22)/1-1	6	-0.2
1963 KC-A	87	221	28	59	11	0	9	37	26	33	0	1	.267	.347	.439	.786	114	4	33	5.19	2	O-63(30-1-36)	7	0.3
1964 KC-A	102	204	18	49	10	1	3	19	30	36	0	0	.240	.343	.343	.686	89	-2	25	4.13	-2	O-44(43-0-3),1-12	4	-0.6
Total 5	298	652	75	167	31	2	23	93	73	103	1	2	.256	.335	.416	.750	102	2	91	4.82	-1	O-159/1-13	17	-0.9

• ALVARADO, Luis Luis Cesar (Martinez) "Pimba" Alvarado b: 1/15/1949, Lajas, Puerto Rico d: 3/20/2001, Lajas, Puerto Rico BR/TR, 5'9", 162 lbs. Deb: 9/13/1968

YEAR TM-L	G	AB	R	H	2B	3B	HR	RBI	BB	SO	SB	CS	AVG	OBP	SLG	OPS	OPS+	BR/A	RC	RC/G	FR	G/POS	WS	TPW
1968 Bos-A	11	46	3	6	2	0	0	1	1	11	0	0	.130	.167	.174	.341	3	-5	1	.83	0	S-11	1	-0.5
1969 Bos-A	6	5	0	0	0	0	0	0	0	2	0	1	.000	.000	.000	.000	-95	-2	0	.00	0	/S-5	0	-0.1
1970 Bos-A	59	183	19	41	11	0	1	10	9	30	1	2	.224	.260	.301	.561	51	-13	13	2.30	4	3-29,S-27	2	-0.7
1971 Chi-A	99	264	22	57	14	1	0	8	11	34	1	2	.216	.247	.277	.524	47	-20	18	2.25	-1	S-71,2-16	2	-1.4
1972 Chi-A	103	254	30	54	4	1	4	29	13	36	2	2	.213	.254	.283	.537	58	-14	15	1.91	-7	S-81,2-16/3-2	3	-1.5
1973 Chi-A	80	203	21	47	7	2	0	20	4	20	6	2	.232	.250	.286	.536	49	-14	14	2.35	-12	2-45,S-18,3-10/D-1	1	-2.2
1974 Chi-A	8	10	1	1	0	0	0	0	0	1	0	0	.100	.100	.100	.200	-41	-2	0	.30	-2	/S-4,2-1,3-1	0	-0.3
StL-N	17	36	3	5	2	0	0	1	2	6	0	0	.139	.184	.194	.379	6	-5	1	1.02	2	S-17	1	-0.2
Cle-A	61	114	12	25	2	0	0	12	6	14	1	1	.219	.258	.237	.495	44	-8	7	1.89	0	2-46/S-7,D-3	1	-0.6
Yr.	69	124	13	26	2	0	0	12	6	15	1	1	.210	.246	.226	.472	37	-10	7	1.75	-2	2-47,S-11/D-3,3-1	1	-0.9
1976 StL-N	16	42	5	12	1	0	0	3	3	6	0	0	.286	.333	.310	.643	82	-1	5	4.06	-2	2-16	1	-0.2
1977 NY-N	1	2	0	0	0	0	0	0	0	0	0	0	.000	.000	.000	.000	-105	-1	0	.00	0	/2-1	0	0.0
Det-A	2	1	0	0	0	0	0	0	0	0	0	0	.000	.000	.000	.000	-95	-0	0	.00	-1	/3-2	0	-0.1
Total 9	463	1160	116	248	43	4	5	84	49	160	11	10	.214	.248	.271	.518	47	-84	74	2.07	-18	S-241,2-141/3-44,D-4	12	-7.9

• ALVAREZ, Clemente Clemente Rafael Alvarez b: 5/18/1968, Anzoategui, Venezuela BR/TR, 5'11", 180 lbs. Deb: 9/19/2000

YEAR TM-L	G	AB	R	H	2B	3B	HR	RBI	BB	SO	SB	CS	AVG	OBP	SLG	OPS	OPS+	BR/A	RC	RC/G	FR	G/POS	WS	TPW
2000 Phi-N	2	5	1	1	0	0	0	0	0	1	0	0	.200	.200	.200	.400	1	-1	0	1.35	1	/C-2	0	0.0

• ALVAREZ, Gabe Gabriel DeJesus Alvarez b: 3/6/1974, Navojoa, Mexico BR/TR, 6'1", 205 lbs. Deb: 6/22/1998 Career OF: 2-0-5

YEAR TM-L	G	AB	R	H	2B	3B	HR	RBI	BB	SO	SB	CS	AVG	OBP	SLG	OPS	OPS+	BR/A	RC	RC/G	FR	G/POS	WS	TPW
1998 Det-A	58	199	16	46	11	0	5	29	18	65	1	3	.231	.301	.362	.663	71	-10	22	3.66	-8	3-55/D-2	3	-1.6
1999 Det-A	22	53	5	11	3	0	2	4	3	9	0	0	.208	.250	.377	.627	57	-4	5	3.34	0	D-12/O-5(0-0-5),3-2	0	-0.4
2000 Det-A	1	1	0	0	0	0	0	0	2	1	0	1	.000	.667	.000	.667	92	-0	0	2.34	0	/D-1	0	0.0
SD-N	11	13	1	2	1	0	0	0	1	1	0	0	.154	.214	.231	.445	13	-2	1	1.71	-1	/3-3,O-2(2-0-0)	0	-0.2
Total 3	92	266	22	59	15	0	7	33	24	76	1	4	.222	.291	.357	.648	66	-15	28	3.48	-9	/3-60,D-15,O-7	3	-2.3

YEAR	TM-L	G	AB	R	H	2B	3B	HR	RBI	BB	SO	SB	CS	AVG	OBP	SLG	OPS	OPS+	BR/A	RC	RC/G	FR	G/POS	WS	TPW
• ALVAREZ, Orlando	Jesus Manuel Orlando (Monge) Alvarez b: 2/28/1952, Rio Grande, Puerto Rico BR/TR, 6', 165 lbs. Deb: 9/1/1973 Career OF: 11-1-0																								
1973	LA-N	4	4	0	1	1	0	0	0	0	1	0	0	.250	.250	.500	.750	108	0	1	4.50	0	....	0	0.0
1974	LA-N	2	1	0	0	0	0	0	0	0	0	0	0	.000	.000	.000	.000	-104	-0	0	.00	-0	/0-1	0	0.0
1975	LA-N	4	4	0	0	0	0	0	0	0	1	0	0	.000	.000	.000	.000	-105	-1	0	.00	0	....	0	-0.1
1976	Cal-A	15	42	4	7	1	0	2	8	0	3	0	0	.167	.167	.333	.500	47	-3	2	1.80	1	0-11(10-1-0)/D-2	0	-0.3
Total	**4**	**25**	**51**	**4**	**8**	**2**	**0**	**2**	**8**	**0**	**5**	**0**	**0**	**.157**	**.157**	**.314**	**.471**	**37**	**-4**	**3**	**1.78**	**1**	**/0-12,D-2**	**0**	**-0.4**
• ALVAREZ, Ossie	Oswaldo (Gonzalez) Alvarez b: 10/19/1933, Bolondron, Cuba BR/TR, 5'10", 165 lbs. Deb: 4/19/1958																								
1958	Was-A	87	196	20	41	3	0	0	5	16	26	1	1	.209	.269	.224	.493	38	-16	13	2.17	-1	S-64,2-14/3-3	3	-1.3
1959	Det-A	8	2	0	1	0	0	0	0	0	1	0	0	.500	.500	.500	1.000	166	0	1	13.50	0	....	0	0.0
Total	**2**	**95**	**198**	**20**	**42**	**3**	**0**	**0**	**5**	**16**	**27**	**1**	**1**	**.212**	**.271**	**.227**	**.498**	**39**	**-16**	**13**	**2.24**	**-1**	**/S-64,2-14,3-3**	**3**	**-1.3**
• ALVAREZ, Rogelio	Rogelio (Hernandez) Alvarez b: 4/18/1938, Pinar del Rio, Cuba BR/TR, 5'11", 183 lbs. Deb: 9/18/1960																								
1960	Cin-N	3	9	1	1	0	0	0	0	0	3	0	0	.111	.111	.111	.222	-38	-2	0	.38	-1	/1-2	0	-0.2
1962	Cin-N	14	28	1	6	0	0	0	2	1	10	0	0	.214	.241	.214	.456	23	-3	2	1.85	-1	1-13	0	-0.4
Total	**2**	**17**	**37**	**2**	**7**	**0**	**0**	**0**	**2**	**1**	**13**	**0**	**0**	**.189**	**.211**	**.189**	**.400**	**8**	**-5**	**2**	**1.46**	**-1**	**/1-15**	**0**	**-0.7**
• ALVAREZ, Tony	Antonio Enrique Alvarez b: 5/10/1979, Caracas, Venezuela BR/TR, 6'1", 200 lbs. Deb: 9/4/2002																								
2002	Pit-N	14	26	6	8	2	0	1	2	3	5	1	0	.308	.379	.500	.879	128	1	5	7.72	-1	/0-8(2-6-1)	1	0.0
• ALVIS, Max	Roy Maxwell Alvis b: 2/2/1938, Jasper, TX BR/TR, 5'11", 187 lbs. Deb: 9/11/1962																								
1962	Cle-A	12	51	1	11	2	0	0	3	2	13	3	1	.216	.245	.255	.500	36	-4	3	2.25	-2	3-12	0	-0.6
1963	Cle-A	158	602	81	165	32	7	22	67	36	109	9	7	.274	.326	.460	.786	118	12	90	5.25	0	*3-158	25	1.2
1964	Cle-A	107	381	51	96	14	3	18	53	29	77	5	5	.252	.315	.446	.761	110	3	53	4.76	-5	*3-105	13	-0.2
1965	Cle-A★	159	604	88	149	24	2	21	61	47	121	12	8	.247	.311	.397	.708	99	-3	74	4.16	-14	*3-156	15	-1.8
1966	Cle-A	157	596	67	146	22	3	17	55	50	98	4	7	.245	.306	.378	.683	95	-6	66	3.76	-1	*3-157	16	-0.7
1967	Cle-A★	161	637	66	163	23	4	21	70	38	107	3	10	.256	.302	.403	.705	106	-1	73	3.81	-5	*3-161	17	-0.6
1968	Cle-A	131	452	38	101	17	3	8	37	41	91	5	5	.223	.294	.327	.621	89	-7	42	3.07	-5	*3-128	10	-1.3
1969	Cle-A	66	191	13	43	6	0	1	15	14	26	1	1	.225	.278	.272	.550	53	-12	13	2.18	-1	3-58/S-1	1	-1.5
1970	Mil-A	62	115	16	21	2	0	3	12	5	20	1	2	.183	.217	.278	.495	35	-11	5	1.42	1	3-36	1	-1.0
Total	**9**	**1013**	**3629**	**421**	**895**	**142**	**22**	**111**	**373**	**262**	**662**	**43**	**46**	**.247**	**.304**	**.390**	**.693**	**97**	**-30**	**420**	**3.90**	**-32**	**3-971/S-1**	**98**	**-6.7**
• ALVORD, Billy	William Charles "Uncle Bill" Alvord b: 8/1863, St. Louis, MO, 5'10", 187 lbs. Deb: 4/30/1885																								
1885	StL-N	2	5	0	0	0	0	0	0	1	2	....	....	.000	.167	.000	.167	-45	-1	0	.00	-1	/3-2	0	-0.2
1889	KC-a	50	186	23	43	8	9	0	18	10	35	3	....	.231	.270	.371	.641	77	-7	20	3.70	0	3-34/2-8,S-8	3	-0.5
1890	Tol-a	116	495	69	135	13	16	2	52	22	....	21	....	.273	.304	.376	.679	97	-6	64	4.74	6	*3-116	13	0.2
1891	Cle-N	13	59	7	17	2	2	1	7	0	7	0	....	.288	.300	.441	.741	110	0	8	5.14	-2	3-13	2	-0.1
	Was-a	81	312	28	73	8	3	0	30	11	38	3	....	.234	.260	.279	.539	57	-19	24	2.66	7	3-81	2	-0.8
1893	Cle-N	3	12	2	2	0	0	0	2	0	1	0	....	.167	.167	.167	.333	-11	-2	0	.91	-1	/3-3	0	-0.2
Total	**5**	**265**	**1069**	**129**	**270**	**31**	**30**	**3**	**109**	**44**	**83**	**27**	**....**	**.253**	**.283**	**.346**	**.629**	**81**	**-35**	**117**	**3.88**	**10**	**3-249/2-8,S-8**	**20**	**-1.6**
• ALYEA, Brant	Garrabrant Ryerson Alyea b: 12/8/1940, Passaic, NJ BR/TR, 6'3", 215 lbs. Deb: 9/11/1965 Career OF: 176-0-71																								
1965	Was-A	8	13	3	3	0	0	2	6	1	4	0	0	.231	.286	.692	.978	171	1	2	4.87	-1	/1-3,0-1	0	0.0
1968	Was-A	53	150	18	40	11	1	6	23	10	39	0	0	.267	.317	.473	.790	141	7	21	4.81	-1	0-39(16-0-24)	7	0.3
1969	Was-A	104	237	29	59	4	0	11	40	34	67	1	3	.249	.346	.405	.751	115	4	32	4.41	-1	0-69(36-0-36)/1-3	7	0.0
1970*	Min-A	94	258	34	75	12	1	16	61	28	51	3	3	.291	.367	.531	.898	143	14	46	6.26	1	0-75(73-0-2)	12	1.3
1971	Min-A	79	158	13	28	4	0	2	15	24	38	1	1	.177	.290	.241	.530	50	-10	11	2.12	0	0-48(47-0-1)	1	-1.3
1972	Oak-A	20	31	3	6	1	0	1	2	3	5	0	0	.194	.265	.323	.587	78	-1	3	2.63	3	/0-8(2-0-6)	1	0.2
	StL-N	13	19	0	3	1	0	0	1	0	6	0	0	.158	.158	.211	.368	4	-2	1	1.07	1	/0-3(1-0-2)	0	-0.2
Total	**6**	**371**	**866**	**100**	**214**	**33**	**2**	**38**	**148**	**100**	**210**	**5**	**7**	**.247**	**.329**	**.421**	**.751**	**112**	**13**	**115**	**4.40**	**1**	**0-243/1-6**	**28**	**0.3**
• AMALFITANO, Joey	John Joseph Amalfitano b: 1/23/1934, San Pedro, CA BR/TR, 5'11", 180 lbs. Deb: 5/2/1954 M/C																								
1954	NY-N	9	5	2	0	0	0	0	0	0	4	0	0	.000	.000	.000	.000	-99	-1	0	.00	0	/3-4,2-1	0	-0.2
1955	NY-N	36	22	8	5	1	1	0	1	2	2	0	0	.227	.292	.364	.655	72	-1	2	3.95	-0	/S-5,3-2	0	-0.1
1960	SF-N	106	328	47	91	15	3	1	27	26	31	2	3	.277	.336	.351	.687	94	-3	39	4.22	3	3-63,2-33/S-3,0-1	10	0.2
1961	SF-N	109	384	64	98	11	4	2	23	44	59	7	4	.255	.332	.320	.652	77	-12	44	4.00	-6	2-95/3-6	9	-1.0
1962	Hou-N	117	380	44	90	12	5	1	27	45	43	4	4	.237	.319	.303	.622	73	-14	36	3.10	-13	*2-110/3-5	6	-1.8
1963	SF-N	54	137	11	24	3	0	1	7	12	18	2	6	.175	.247	.219	.466	36	-13	6	1.30	2	2-37/3-7	1	-0.9
1964	Chi-N	100	324	51	78	19	6	4	27	40	42	2	7	.241	.333	.373	.707	95	-3	38	3.91	-8	2-86/1-1,S-1	8	-0.5
1965	Chi-N	67	96	13	26	4	0	0	8	12	14	2	2	.271	.364	.313	.676	90	-1	12	4.31	0	2-24/S-4	3	0.1
1966	Chi-N	41	38	8	6	2	0	0	3	4	10	0	0	.158	.238	.211	.449	26	-4	2	1.59	-4	2-12/3-3,S-2	0	-0.7
1967	Chi-N	4	1	0	0	0	0	0	0	0	1	0	0	.000	.000	.000	.000	-96	-0	0	.00	0	....	0	0.0
Total	**10**	**643**	**1715**	**248**	**418**	**67**	**19**	**9**	**123**	**185**	**224**	**19**	**26**	**.244**	**.322**	**.321**	**.642**	**78**	**-53**	**180**	**3.51**	**-26**	**2-398/3-90,S-15,1-1,0-1**	**37**	**-4.9**
• AMARAL, Rich	Richard Louis Amaral b: 4/1/1962, Visalia, CA BR/TR, 6', 175 lbs. Deb: 5/27/1991 Career OF: 232-101-52																								
1991	Sea-A	14	16	2	1	0	0	0	0	1	5	0	0	.063	.167	.063	.229	-34	-3	0	.29	0	/2-5,3-2,D-2,S-2,1-1	0	-0.3
1992	Sea-A	35	100	9	24	3	0	1	7	5	16	4	2	.240	.276	.300	.576	61	-5	7	2.35	1	3-17,S-17/0-3(3-1-1),1-2,2	1	-0.4
1993	Sea-A	110	373	53	108	24	1	1	44	33	54	19	11	.290	.352	.367	.719	92	-4	49	4.55	-3	2-77,3-19,S-14/D-9,1-3	12	-0.2
1994	Sea-A	77	228	37	60	10	2	4	18	24	28	5	1	.263	.336	.377	.713	82	-5	31	4.59	-8	2-42,0-16(14-2-0)/S-7,D-6,1	4	-1.1
1995*	Sea-A	90	238	45	67	14	2	2	19	21	33	21	2	.282	.342	.382	.725	87	-1	35	5.31	1	0-73(53-29-8)/D-1	6	-0.2
1996	Sea-A	118	312	69	91	11	3	1	29	47	55	25	6	.292	.393	.356	.749	91	1	50	5.64	0	0-91(63-26-5),2-15,1-10/D-6,3	7	0.0
1997*	Sea-A	89	190	34	54	5	0	1	21	10	34	12	8	.284	.330	.326	.656	73	-8	19	3.18	-3	0-52(39-9-6),1-14,2-11/D-3,3,S	1	-1.2
1998	Sea-A	73	134	25	37	6	0	1	4	13	24	11	1	.276	.345	.343	.688	80	-2	18	4.96	-3	0-52(43-4-9),2-11/1-7,D-5,3	2	-0.5
1999	Bal-A	91	137	21	38	8	1	0	11	15	20	9	6	.277	.353	.350	.703	83	-4	18	4.36	-2	0-50(14-18-19),D-18/1-2,2,3	2	-0.7
2000	Bal-A	30	60	10	13	1	1	0	6	7	8	6	2	.217	.299	.267	.565	47	-4	4	1.84	3	0-19(3-12-4)/D-5,1-1	1	-0.1
Total	**10**	**727**	**1788**	**305**	**493**	**82**	**10**	**11**	**159**	**176**	**277**	**112**	**39**	**.276**	**.346**	**.351**	**.697**	**82**	**-35**	**231**	**4.41**	**-14**	**0-356,2-164/D-55,1-42,3-42,S**	**36**	**-4.8**
• AMARO, Ruben	Ruben (Mora) Amaro b: 1/6/1936, Veracruz, Mexico BR/TR, 5'11", 170 lbs. Deb: 6/29/1958 C																								
1958	StL-N	40	76	8	17	2	1	0	0	5	8	0	1	.224	.272	.276	.548	44	-7	5	2.09	-5	S-36/2-1	0	-0.9
1960	Phi-N	92	264	25	61	9	1	0	16	21	32	0	1	.231	.293	.273	.565	56	-16	21	2.70	-5	S-92	4	-1.4
1961	Phi-N	135	381	34	98	14	9	1	32	53	59	1	0	.257	.351	.349	.700	88	-4	49	4.39	6	*S-132/1-3,2-1	10	1.2
1962	Phi-N	79	226	24	55	10	0	0	19	30	28	5	2	.243	.335	.288	.622	71	-8	23	3.35	5	S-78/1-1	7	0.4
1963	Phi-N	115	217	25	47	9	2	2	19	19	31	0	1	.217	.280	.304	.584	69	-9	18	2.71	-2	S-63,3-45/1-5	4	-0.8
1964	Phi-N	129	299	31	79	11	0	4	34	16	37	1	6	.264	.308	.341	.649	84	-9	30	3.38	-1	S-79,1-58/2-3,3-3,0-1	9	-0.5
1965	Phi-N	118	184	26	39	7	0	0	15	27	22	1	1	.212	.316	.250	.566	63	-8	15	2.64	-4	1-60,S-60/2-6	3	-1.0
1966	NY-A	14	23	0	5	0	0	0	3	0	2	0	0	.217	.217	.217	.435	26	-2	1	.88	-1	S-14	0	-0.2
1967	NY-A	130	417	31	93	12	0	1	17	43	49	3	2	.223	.297	.259	.556	68	-15	32	2.51	-7	*S-123/3-3,1-2	7	-1.3
1968	NY-A	47	41	3	5	1	0	0	0	9	6	0	0	.122	.280	.146	.426	33	-3	2	1.75	-1	S-23,1-22	0	-0.4
1969	Cal-A	41	27	4	6	0	0	0	1	4	6	0	0	.222	.323	.222	.545	58	-1	3	2.78	-3	1-18/2-9,S-5,3-2	1	-0.4
Total	**11**	**940**	**2155**	**211**	**505**	**75**	**13**	**8**	**156**	**227**	**280**	**11**	**14**	**.234**	**.310**	**.292**	**.603**	**70**	**-82**	**200**	**3.04**	**-16**	**S-705,1-169/3-53,2-20,0-1**	**45**	**-5.4**
• AMARO, Ruben	Ruben Amaro, Jr. b: 2/12/1965, Philadelphia, PA BB/TR, 5'10", 175 lbs. Deb: 6/8/1991 Career OF: 108-106-132																								
1991	Cal-A	10	23	0	5	1	0	0	2	3	3	0	0	.217	.308	.261	.569	59	-1	2	2.49	0	/0-5(3-0-2),2-4,D-1	1	-0.2
1992	Phi-N	126	374	43	82	15	6	7	34	37	54	11	5	.219	.305	.348	.652	85	-7	40	3.40	-4	*0-113(27-27-68)	4	-1.5
1993	Phi-N	25	48	7	16	2	2	1	6	6	5	0	0	.333	.407	.521	.928	149	3	10	7.57	0	0-16(3-8-6)	3	0.4
1994	Cle-A	26	23	5	5	1	0	2	5	2	3	2	1	.217	.280	.522	.802	101	-0	3	4.62	-1	0-12(1-10-1)/D-3	0	-0.1
1995*	Cle-A	28	60	5	12	3	0	1	7	4	6	1	3	.200	.273	.300	.573	48	-6	4	2.17	0	0-22(5-14-6)/D-3	2	-0.6
1996	Phi-N	61	117	14	37	10	0	2	15	9	18	0	0	.316	.380	.453	.833	117	3	20	6.44	0	0-35(0-7-28)/1-1	4	0.2
1997	Phi-N	117	175	18	41	6	1	2	21	21	24	1	1	.234	.323	.314	.638	68	-8	18	3.53	0	0-72(26-37-15)/1-1	1	-0.9

YEAR TM-L	G	AB	R	H	2B	3B	HR	RBI	BB	SO	SB	CS	AVG	OBP	SLG	OPS	OPS+	BR/A	RC	RC/G	FR	G/POS	WS	TPW
1998 Phi-N	92	107	7	20	5	0	1	10	6	15	0	0	.187	.230	.262	.492	29	-11	7	1.98	-0	0-51(43-3-6)	1	-1.2
Total 8	**485**	**927**	**99**	**218**	**43**	**9**	**16**	**100**	**88**	**128**	**15**	**10**	**.235**	**.312**	**.353**	**.665**	**80**	**-28**	**105**	**3.71**	**-5**	**0-326/D-7,2-4,1-2**	**16**	**-3.9**

• AMBLER, Wayne Wayne Harper Ambler b: 11/8/1915, Abington, PA d: 1/3/1998, Ponte Vedra Beach, FL BR/TR, 5'8.5", 165 lbs. Deb: 6/4/1937

YEAR TM-L	G	AB	R	H	2B	3B	HR	RBI	BB	SO	SB	CS	AVG	OBP	SLG	OPS	OPS+	BR/A	RC	RC/G	FR	G/POS	WS	TPW
1937 Phi-A	56	162	3	35	5	0	0	11	13	8	1	0	.216	.274	.247	.521	33	-16	12	2.41	0	2-56	1	-1.2
1938 Phi-A	120	393	42	92	21	2	0	38	48	31	2	1	.234	.317	.298	.615	56	-26	40	3.41	-13	*S-116/2-4	4	-2.8
1939 Phi-A	95	227	15	48	13	0	0	24	22	25	1	0	.211	.281	.269	.550	42	-20	17	2.26	-1	S-77,2-19	2	-1.5
Total 3	**271**	**782**	**60**	**175**	**39**	**2**	**0**	**73**	**83**	**64**	**4**	**1**	**.224**	**.298**	**.279**	**.577**	**48**	**-62**	**69**	**2.85**	**-14**	**S-193/2-79**	**7**	**-5.4**

• AMELUNG, Ed Edward Allen Amelung b: 4/13/1959, Fullerton, CA BL/TL, 5'11", 180 lbs. Deb: 7/28/1984 Career OF: 9-6-13

YEAR TM-L	G	AB	R	H	2B	3B	HR	RBI	BB	SO	SB	CS	AVG	OBP	SLG	OPS	OPS+	BR/A	RC	RC/G	FR	G/POS	WS	TPW
1984 LA-N	34	46	7	10	0	0	0	4	2	4	3	2	.217	.250	.217	.467	33	-4	2	1.56	0	0-23(9-4-11)	0	-0.6
1986 LA-N	8	11	0	1	0	0	0	0	0	4	0	0	.091	.091	.091	.182	-53	-2	0	.00	0	/0-4(0-2-2)	0	-0.3
Total 2	**42**	**57**	**7**	**11**	**0**	**0**	**0**	**4**	**2**	**8**	**3**	**2**	**.193**	**.220**	**.193**	**.413**	**17**	**-7**	**2**	**1.23**	**0**	**/0-27**	**0**	**-0.8**

• AMEZAGA, Alfredo Alfredo (Delgado) Amezaga b: 1/16/1978, Obregon, Mexico BB/TR, 5'10", 165 lbs. Deb: 5/24/2002

YEAR TM-L	G	AB	R	H	2B	3B	HR	RBI	BB	SO	SB	CS	AVG	OBP	SLG	OPS	OPS+	BR/A	RC	RC/G	FR	G/POS	WS	TPW
2002 Ana-A	12	13	3	7	2	0	0	2	0	1	1	0	.538	.538	.692	1.231	224	2	4	16.95	0	/S-5,D-1	2	0.3
2003 Ana-A	37	105	15	22	3	2	2	7	9	23	2	2	.210	.278	.333	.612	63	-6	10	2.82	2	S-24,3-13/D-1	1	-0.3
Total 2	**49**	**118**	**18**	**29**	**5**	**2**	**2**	**9**	**9**	**24**	**3**	**2**	**.246**	**.305**	**.373**	**.678**	**79**	**-4**	**14**	**3.82**	**2**	**/S-29,3-13,D-2**	**3**	**0.0**

• AMOROS, Sandy Edmundo (Isasi) Amoros b: 1/30/1930, Havana, Cuba d: 6/27/1992, Miami, FL BL/TL, 5'7.5", 170 lbs. Deb: 8/22/1952 Career OF: 318-29-29

YEAR TM-L	G	AB	R	H	2B	3B	HR	RBI	BB	SO	SB	CS	AVG	OBP	SLG	OPS	OPS+	BR/A	RC	RC/G	FR	G/POS	WS	TPW
1952*Bro-N	20	44	10	11	3	1	0	3	5	14	1	0	.250	.327	.364	.690	90	-0	6	4.76	-1	0-10(3-4-7)	1	-0.1
1954 Bro-N	79	263	44	72	18	6	9	34	31	24	1	4	.274	.353	.490	.843	113	3	45	6.00	2	0-70(68-1-2)	10	0.1
1955*Bro-N	119	388	59	96	16	7	10	51	55	45	10	5	.247	.350	.402	.752	96	-1	57	4.91	-1	*0-109(102-8-5)	12	-0.8
1956*Bro-N	114	292	53	76	11	8	16	58	59	51	3	4	.260	.386	.517	.903	130	13	61	7.04	-2	0-86(79-5-10)	14	0.7
1957 Bro-N	106	238	40	66	7	1	7	26	46	42	3	2	.277	.401	.403	.804	107	5	41	6.00	0	0-66(65-1-2)	9	0.0
1959 LA-N	5	5	1	1	0	0	0	1	0	1	0	0	.200	.200	.200	.400	6	-1	0	1.35	0	....	0	-0.1
1960 LA-N	9	14	1	2	0	0	0	0	3	2	0	0	.143	.294	.143	.437	23	-1	1	1.67	0	/0-3(0-1-3)	0	-0.1
Det-A	65	67	7	10	0	0	1	7	12	10	0	0	.149	.278	.194	.473	28	-7	4	1.97	-1	0-10(1-9-0)	0	-0.8
Total 7	**517**	**1311**	**215**	**334**	**55**	**23**	**43**	**180**	**211**	**189**	**18**	**15**	**.255**	**.363**	**.430**	**.793**	**104**	**12**	**215**	**5.57**	**-2**	**0-354**	**46**	**-1.0**

• ANDERSON, Alf Alfred Walton Anderson b: 1/28/1914, Gainesville, GA d: 6/23/1985, Albany, GA BR/TR, 5'11", 165 lbs. Deb: 4/20/1941

YEAR TM-L	G	AB	R	H	2B	3B	HR	RBI	BB	SO	SB	CS	AVG	OBP	SLG	OPS	OPS+	BR/A	RC	RC/G	FR	G/POS	WS	TPW
1941 Pit-N	70	223	32	48	7	2	1	10	14	30	2	....	.215	.265	.278	.543	53	-14	17	2.51	-8	S-58	2	-1.8
1942 Pit-N	54	166	24	45	4	1	0	7	18	19	4	....	.271	.342	.307	.650	89	-2	18	3.90	-7	S-48	4	-0.7
1946 Pit-N	2	1	0	0	0	0	0	0	1	0	0	....	.000	.500	.000	.500	47	0	0	.00	0	....	0	0.0
Total 3	**126**	**390**	**56**	**93**	**11**	**3**	**1**	**17**	**33**	**49**	**6**	**....**	**.238**	**.300**	**.290**	**.589**	**69**	**-16**	**35**	**3.07**	**-15**	**S-106**	**6**	**-2.5**

• ANDERSON, Andy Andy Holm Anderson b: 11/13/1922, Bremerton, WA d: 7/18/1982, Seattle, WA BR/TR, 5'11", 172 lbs. Deb: 5/10/1948

YEAR TM-L	G	AB	R	H	2B	3B	HR	RBI	BB	SO	SB	CS	AVG	OBP	SLG	OPS	OPS+	BR/A	RC	RC/G	FR	G/POS	WS	TPW
1948 StL-A	51	87	13	24	5	1	1	12	8	15	0	0	.276	.337	.391	.728	91	-1	10	3.71	-1	2-21,S-10/1-2	1	-0.1
1949 StL-A	71	136	10	17	3	0	1	5	14	21	0	1	.125	.207	.169	.376		-21	5	1.04	0	S-44/2-8,3-8	1	-1.9
Total 2	**122**	**223**	**23**	**41**	**8**	**1**	**2**	**17**	**22**	**36**	**0**	**1**	**.184**	**.257**	**.256**	**.513**	**35**	**-22**	**15**	**2.00**	**-2**	**/S-54,2-29,3-8,1-2**	**2**	**-2.0**

• ANDERSON, Brady Brady Kevin Anderson b: 1/18/1964, Silver Spring, MD BL/TL, 6'1", 185 lbs. Deb: 4/4/1988 Career OF: 698-927-139

YEAR TM-L	G	AB	R	H	2B	3B	HR	RBI	BB	SO	SB	CS	AVG	OBP	SLG	OPS	OPS+	BR/A	RC	RC/G	FR	G/POS	WS	TPW
1988 Bos-A	41	148	14	34	5	3	0	12	15	35	4	2	.230	.317	.304	.621	72	-5	16	3.42	0	0-41(0-17-25)	2	-0.6
Bal-A	53	177	17	35	8	1	1	9	8	40	6	4	.198	.232	.271	.504	42	-15	11	1.97	0	0-49(0-49-0)	1	-1.6
Yr.	94	325	31	69	13	4	1	21	23	75	10	6	.212	.273	.286	.559	56	-20	27	2.61	0	0-90(0-66-25)	3	-2.2
1989 Bal-A	94	266	44	55	12	2	4	16	43	45	16	4	.207	.324	.312	.636	82	-3	31	3.69	-3	0-79(3-75-1)/D-8	7	-0.7
1990 Bal-A	89	234	24	54	5	2	3	24	31	46	15	2	.231	.333	.308	.641	83	-2	28	3.89	1	0-63(44-21-1),D-11	7	-0.2
1991 Bal-A	113	256	40	59	12	3	2	27	38	44	12	5	.230	.341	.324	.665	89	-2	33	4.11	-1	*0-101(75-26-9)/D-2	6	-0.5
1992 Bal-A★	159	623	100	169	28	10	21	80	98	98	53	16	.271	.378	.449	.828	128	31	118	6.47	4	*0-158(148-7-3)	29	3.0
1993 Bal-A	142	560	87	147	36	8	13	66	82	99	24	12	.263	.367	.425	.792	108	8	94	5.75	0	*0-140(126-18-3)/D-2	18	0.3
1994 Bal-A	111	453	78	119	25	5	12	48	57	75	31	1	.263	.358	.419	.777	95	3	76	5.95	-3	*0-109(76-38-5)	12	-0.3
1995 Bal-A	143	554	108	145	33	10	16	64	87	111	26	7	.262	.372	.444	.816	109	12	101	6.43	-8	*0-142(131-40-0)	19	0.0
1996*Bal-A★	149	579	117	172	37	5	50	110	76	106	21	8	.297	.399	.637	1.036	157	51	150	9.28	-1	*0-143(0-143-0)/D-2	28	4.7
1997*Bal-A★	151	590	97	170	39	7	18	73	84	105	18	12	.288	.394	.469	.863	128	26	117	7.24	-6	*0-124(0-124-0),D-25	26	1.8
1998 Bal-A	133	479	84	113	28	3	18	51	75	78	21	7	.236	.357	.420	.776	103	5	78	5.49	-9	*0-130(0-130-0)	13	-0.2
1999 Bal-A	150	564	109	159	28	5	24	81	96	105	36	7	.282	.408	.477	.885	129	35	123	7.83	-5	*0-136(9-129-0),D-10	23	2.8
2000 Bal-A	141	506	89	130	26	0	19	50	92	103	16	9	.257	.380	.421	.800	108	9	89	5.96	-7	*0-127(16-88-24),D-11	15	0.0
2001 Bal-A	131	430	50	87	12	3	8	45	60	77	12	4	.202	.311	.300	.611	66	-19	45	3.47	2	*0-121(56-6-66)/D-3	8	-2.2
2002 Cle-A	34	80	4	13	4	0	1	5	18	23	4	0	.163	.330	.250	.580	59	-3	8	2.80	-1	0-29(14-16-2)/D-1	0	-0.5
Total 15	**1834**	**6499**	**1062**	**1661**	**338**	**67**	**210**	**761**	**960**	**1190**	**315**	**100**	**.256**	**.365**	**.425**	**.790**	**108**	**133**	**1118**	**5.89**	**-36**	***0-1692/D-75**	**214**	**5.8**

• ANDERSON, Dave David Carter Anderson b: 8/1/1960, Louisville, KY BR/TR, 6'2", 185 lbs. Deb: 5/8/1983

YEAR TM-L	G	AB	R	H	2B	3B	HR	RBI	BB	SO	SB	CS	AVG	OBP	SLG	OPS	OPS+	BR/A	RC	RC/G	FR	G/POS	WS	TPW
1983 LA-N	61	115	12	19	4	2	1	2	12	15	6	3	.165	.244	.261	.505	40	-10	8	2.04	1	S-53/3-1	2	-0.5
1984 LA-N	121	374	51	94	16	2	3	34	45	55	15	5	.251	.335	.329	.664	88	-4	44	3.88	-2	*S-111,3-11	12	0.6
1985*LA-N	77	221	24	44	6	0	4	18	35	42	5	4	.199	.311	.281	.592	69	-9	21	2.96	9	3-51,S-25/2-2	5	0.2
1986 LA-N	92	216	31	53	9	0	1	15	22	39	5	1	.245	.315	.301	.616	76	-6	20	2.96	0	3-51,S-34/2-5	4	-0.3
1987 LA-N	108	265	32	62	12	3	1	13	24	43	9	5	.234	.300	.313	.613	64	-14	26	3.27	3	S-65,3-35/2-5	5	-0.5
1988*LA-N	116	285	31	71	10	2	2	20	32	45	4	2	.249	.327	.319	.646	89	-4	30	3.47	8	S-82,3-12,2-11	8	1.2
1989 LA-N	87	140	15	32	2	0	1	14	17	26	2	0	.229	.312	.264	.576	67	-5	13	3.13	-1	S-33,3-18/2-7	4	-0.5
1990 SF-N	60	100	14	35	5	1	1	6	3	20	1	2	.350	.369	.450	.819	129	3	15	5.90	1	S-29,2-13/1-3,3-2	3	0.5
1991 SF-N	100	226	24	56	5	2	2	13	12	35	2	4	.248	.286	.314	.600	71	-11	18	2.59	-2	S-63,1-16,3-11/2-6	2	-1.1
1992 LA-N	51	84	10	24	4	0	3	8	4	11	0	4	.286	.318	.440	.759	115	-1	9	3.52	-3	3-26/S-7	1	-0.3
Total 10	**873**	**2026**	**244**	**490**	**73**	**12**	**19**	**143**	**206**	**331**	**49**	**30**	**.242**	**.313**	**.318**	**.631**	**79**	**-60**	**204**	**3.30**	**15**	**S-502,3-218/2-49,1-19**	**46**	**-0.8**

• ANDERSON, Dwain Dwain Cleaven Anderson b: 11/23/1947, Oakland, CA BR/TR, 5'11", 165 lbs. Deb: 9/3/1971

YEAR TM-L	G	AB	R	H	2B	3B	HR	RBI	BB	SO	SB	CS	AVG	OBP	SLG	OPS	OPS+	BR/A	RC	RC/G	FR	G/POS	WS	TPW
1971 Oak-A	16	37	3	10	2	1	0	3	5	9	0	1	.270	.372	.378	.750	115	1	5	5.15	0	S-10/2-5,3-1	2	0.1
1972 Oak-A	3	7	2	0	0	0	0	0	1	4	0	0	.000	.125	.000	.125	-64	-1	0	.13	0	/3-1,S-1	0	-0.1
StL-N	57	135	12	36	4	1	1	8	8	23	0	1	.267	.313	.333	.646	85	-3	13	3.40	-4	S-43,3-13/2-1	3	-0.4
1973 StL-N	18	17	5	2	0	0	0	0	4	4	0	0	.118	.286	.118	.403	16	-2	1	1.56	-2	/S-3,0-2(0-2-0)	0	-0.3
SD-N	53	107	11	13	0	0	0	3	14	29	2	0	.121	.223	.121	.345	-2	-14	4	1.05	-2	S-39/3-6	1	-1.3
Yr.	71	124	16	15	0	0	0	3	18	33	2	0	.121	.232	.121	.353		-16	5	1.12	-4	S-42/3-6,0-2(0-2-0)	1	-1.7
1974 Cle-A	2	3	0	1	0	0	0	0	0	1	0	0	.333	.333	.333	.667	93	-0	0	4.50	0	/2-1	0	0.0
Total 4	**149**	**306**	**33**	**62**	**6**	**2**	**1**	**14**	**32**	**70**	**2**	**2**	**.203**	**.282**	**.245**	**.527**	**50**	**-20**	**23**	**2.49**	**-8**	**/S-96,3-21,2-7,0-2**	**6**	**-2.1**

• ANDERSON, Ferrell Ferrell Jack "Andy" Anderson b: 1/9/1918, Maple City, KS d: 3/12/1978, Joplin, MO BR/TR, 6'1", 200 lbs. Deb: 4/16/1946

YEAR TM-L	G	AB	R	H	2B	3B	HR	RBI	BB	SO	SB	CS	AVG	OBP	SLG	OPS	OPS+	BR/A	RC	RC/G	FR	G/POS	WS	TPW
1946 Bro-N	79	199	19	51	10	0	2	14	18	21	1	....	.256	.330	.337	.667	88	-3	22	3.76	-1	C-70	6	-0.1
1953 StL-N	18	35	1	10	2	0	0	1	0	4	0	0	.286	.286	.343	.629	63	-2	4	3.80	0	C-12	1	-0.2
Total 2	**97**	**234**	**20**	**61**	**12**	**0**	**2**	**15**	**18**	**25**	**1**	**0**	**.261**	**.324**	**.338**	**.662**	**85**	**-5**	**26**	**3.77**	**-1**	**/C-82**	**7**	**-0.3**

• ANDERSON, Garret Garret Joseph Anderson b: 6/30/1972, Los Angeles, CA BL/TL, 6'3", 190 lbs. Deb: 7/27/1994 Career OF: 869-310-154

YEAR TM-L	G	AB	R	H	2B	3B	HR	RBI	BB	SO	SB	CS	AVG	OBP	SLG	OPS	OPS+	BR/A	RC	RC/G	FR	G/POS	WS	TPW
1994 Cal-A	5	13	0	5	0	0	0	1	0	2	0	0	.385	.385	.385	.769	98	-0	2	6.49	0	/0-4(4-0-0)	0	0.0
1995 Cal-A	106	374	50	120	19	1	16	69	19	65	6	2	.321	.355	.505	.861	122	11	65	6.48	1	*0-100(99-1-1)/D-1	11	0.7
1996 Cal-A	150	607	79	173	33	2	12	72	27	84	7	9	.285	.315	.405	.721	82	-21	68	3.90	1	*0-146(140-3-6)/D-1	6	-2.4
1997 Ana-A	154	624	76	189	36	3	8	92	30	70	10	4	.303	.337	.409	.746	92	-8	80	4.67	5	*0-148(130-27-4)/D-4	16	-0.8
1998 Ana-A	156	622	62	183	41	7	15	79	29	80	8	3	.294	.327	.455	.782	100	-2	89	5.19	5	*0-155(39-0-122)	18	-0.5
1999 Ana-A	157	620	88	188	36	2	21	80	34	81	3	4	.303	.339	.469	.809	104	0	93	5.50	3	*0-153(32-116-6)/D-4	16	0.3
2000 Ana-A	159	647	92	185	40	3	35	117	24	87	7	6	.286	.311	.519	.831	103	-3	93	5.06	-6	*0-148(0-137-15),D-10/1-1	15	-0.9
2001 Ana-A	161	672	83	194	39	2	28	123	27	100	13	6	.289	.316	.478	.794	103	-0	97	5.23	2	*0-149(144-12-0),D-12	17	-0.5
2002*Ana-A★	158	638	93	195	**56**	3	29	123	30	80	6	4	.306	.337	.539	.876	128	22	111	6.38	-1	*0-147(137-14-0),D-10	24	1.3

YEAR TM-L	G	AB	R	H	2B	3B	HR	RBI	BB	SO	SB	CS	AVG	OBP	SLG	OPS	OPS+	BR/A	RC	RC/G	FR	G/POS	WS	TPW
2003 Ana-A★	159	638	80	201	**49**	4	29	116	31	83	6	3	.315	.347	.541	.888	134	28	113	6.65	9	*O-144(144-0-0),D-15	26	2.8
Total 10	1365	5455	703	1633	349	27	193	872	251	732	66	41	.299	.331	.479	.810	107	27	811	5.39	19	*O-1294/D-57,1-1	149	0.0

• ANDERSON, George
George Jendrus "Andy" Anderson
b: 9/26/1889, Cleveland, OH d: 5/28/1962, Cleveland, OH BL/TR, 5'8.5", 160 lbs. Deb: 5/26/1914 Career OF: 110-33-118

YEAR TM-L	G	AB	R	H	2B	3B	HR	RBI	BB	SO	SB	CS	AVG	OBP	SLG	OPS	OPS+	BR/A	RC	RC/G	FR	G/POS	WS	TPW
1914 Bro-F	98	364	58	115	13	3	3	24	31	50	16	....	.316	.376	.393	.769	118	9	57	5.70	-1	O-92(70-21-1)	13	0.4
1915 Bro-F	136	511	70	135	23	9	2	39	52	54	20	....	.264	.342	.356	.698	108	6	66	4.45	-4	*O-134(40-12-82)	14	-0.5
1918 StL-N	35	132	20	39	4	5	0	6	15	7	0	....	.295	.380	.402	.782	143	7	20	5.34	-1	O-35(0-0-35)	6	0.5
Total 3	269	1007	148	289	40	17	5	69	98	111	36	....	.287	.359	.375	.734	116	22	143	5.00	-6	O-261	33	0.4

• ANDERSON, Goat
Edward John Anderson b: 1/13/1880, Cleveland, OH d: 3/15/1923, South Bend, IN BL/TR Deb: 4/11/1907

YEAR TM-L	G	AB	R	H	2B	3B	HR	RBI	BB	SO	SB	CS	AVG	OBP	SLG	OPS	OPS+	BR/A	RC	RC/G	FR	G/POS	WS	TPW
1907 Pit-N	127	413	73	85	3	1	1	12	80	....	27	....	.206	.343	.225	.568	77	-5	44	3.38	-4	*O-117(2-24-91)/2-5	12	-1.6

• ANDERSON, Hal
Harold Anderson b: 2/10/1904, St. Louis, MO d: 5/1/1974, St. Louis, MO BR/TR, 5'11", 160 lbs. Deb: 4/12/1932

YEAR TM-L	G	AB	R	H	2B	3B	HR	RBI	BB	SO	SB	CS	AVG	OBP	SLG	OPS	OPS+	BR/A	RC	RC/G	FR	G/POS	WS	TPW
1932 Chi-A	9	32	4	8	0	0	0	2	0	1	0	1	.250	.250	.250	.500	32	-4	2	1.77	1	/O-9(0-9-0)	0	-0.3

• ANDERSON, Harry
Harry Walter "Harry the Horse" Anderson
b: 9/10/1931, North East, MD d: 6/11/1998, Greenville, DE BL/TR, 6'3", 210 lbs. Deb: 4/18/1957 Career OF: 349-0-4

YEAR TM-L	G	AB	R	H	2B	3B	HR	RBI	BB	SO	SB	CS	AVG	OBP	SLG	OPS	OPS+	BR/A	RC	RC/G	FR	G/POS	WS	TPW
1957 Phi-N	118	400	53	107	15	4	17	61	36	61	2	3	.268	.337	.453	.790	113	6	61	5.28	0	*O-109(107-0-2)	14	0.0
1958 Phi-N	140	515	80	155	34	6	23	97	59	95	0	2	.301	.376	.524	.900	137	27	100	7.06	-10	O-87(87-0-0),1-49	19	0.9
1959 Phi-N	142	508	50	122	28	6	14	63	43	95	1	1	.240	.306	.402	.707	85	-12	62	4.15	7	*O-137(137-0-0)	12	-1.3
1960 Phi-N	38	93	10	23	2	0	5	12	10	19	0	0	.247	.333	.430	.763	107	1	13	5.05	-1	O-16(16-0-0),1-12	2	-0.1
Cin-N	42	66	6	11	3	0	1	9	11	20	0	0	.167	.286	.258	.543	49	-4	6	2.76	0	1-15/O-4(2-0-2)	0	-0.6
Yr.	80	159	16	34	5	0	6	21	21	39	0	0	.214	.313	.358	.672	82	-3	19	4.04	-1	1-27,O-20(18-0-2)	2	-0.7
1961 Cin-N	4	4	0	1	0	0	0	0	0	1	0	0	.250	.250	.250	.500	33	-0	0	2.25	0	....	0	0.0
Total 5	484	1586	199	419	82	16	60	242	159	291	3	6	.264	.337	.450	.787	109	17	242	5.32	-4	O-353/1-76	47	-1.1

• ANDERSON, Jim
James Lea Anderson b: 2/23/1957, Los Angeles, CA BR/TR, 6', 170 lbs. Deb: 7/2/1978

YEAR TM-L	G	AB	R	H	2B	3B	HR	RBI	BB	SO	SB	CS	AVG	OBP	SLG	OPS	OPS+	BR/A	RC	RC/G	FR	G/POS	WS	TPW
1978 Cal-A	48	108	6	21	7	0	0	7	11	16	0	0	.194	.269	.259	.528	51	-7	7	2.00	-1	S-47/2-1	2	-0.4
1979*Cal-A	96	234	33	58	13	1	3	23	17	31	3	2	.248	.302	.350	.652	78	-8	24	3.35	6	S-82,3-10/2-6,C-3	6	0.5
1980 Sea-A	116	317	46	72	7	0	8	30	27	39	2	4	.227	.294	.325	.619	69	-15	30	3.12	-5	S-65,3-33/D-5,2-2,C-1	5	-1.4
1981 Sea-A	70	162	12	33	7	0	2	19	17	29	3	5	.204	.283	.284	.567	61	-9	12	2.38	-2	S-68/3-2	2	-0.6
1983 Tex-A	50	102	8	22	1	1	0	6	5	8	1	2	.216	.252	.245	.497	38	-9	6	1.74	-4	S-27,2-17/3-3,O-3(2-0-1),D,C	1	-1.1
1984 Tex-A	39	47	2	5	0	0	0	1	4	7	0	0	.106	.176	.106	.283	-19	-8	1	.74	1	S-31/3-6,2-1	1	-0.4
Total 6	419	970	107	211	35	2	13	86	81	130	9	13	.218	.281	.298	.579	60	-55	81	2.64	-5	S-320/3-54,2-27,D-7,C-5,O-3	17	-3.4

• ANDERSON, John
John Joseph "Honest John" Anderson
b: 12/14/1873, Sarpsborg, Norway d: 7/23/1949, Worcester, MA BB/TR, 6'2", 180 lbs. Deb: 9/8/1894 Career OF: 560-229-219

YEAR TM-L	G	AB	R	H	2B	3B	HR	RBI	BB	SO	SB	CS	AVG	OBP	SLG	OPS	OPS+	BR/A	RC	RC/G	FR	G/POS	WS	TPW
1894 Bro-N	17	63	14	19	1	3	1	19	3	3	7	....	.302	.333	.460	.794	97	-1	12	7.27	-2	O-16(15-1-0)/3-1	2	-0.3
1895 Bro-N	103	423	77	122	11	14	10	87	12	29	24	....	.288	.316	.452	.767	105	1	70	6.23	-8	*O-101(89-0-12)	12	-1.3
1896 Bro-N	108	430	70	135	23	17	1	55	18	23	37	....	.314	.344	.453	.798	116	7	82	7.34	1	O-68(33-9-26),1-42	14	0.3
1897 Bro-N	117	492	93	160	28	12	4	85	17	....	29	....	.325	.357	.455	.812	120	12	93	7.22	-4	*O-115(115-0-0)/1-3	16	-0.2
1898 Bro-N	19	69	11	19	3	4	0	8	5	....	2	....	.275	.333	.435	.768	120	1	11	5.79	0	/O-5(2-1-2)	0	0.1
Was-N	110	430	70	131	28	18	9	71	23	....	18	....	.305	.357	.516	.873	150	24	88	7.67	2	O-93(13-78-2),1-17	15	1.8
Bro-N	6	21	1	3	2	0	0	2	1	....	0	....	.143	.217	.238	.455	31	-2	1	1.64	0	O-17(17-0-0)/1-2	2	-0.3
Yr.	135	520	82	153	33	**22**	9	81	29	....	20	....	.294	.348	**.494**	.842	141	24	100	7.13	2	*O-115(32-79-4),1-19	17	1.7
1899 Bro-N	117	439	65	118	18	7	4	92	27	....	25	....	.269	.317	.369	.686	86	-10	61	5.00	-1	O-76(7-61-8),1-41	12	-1.5
1901 Mil-A	138	576	90	190	46	7	8	99	24	....	35	....	.330	.360	.476	.836	137	26	114	7.77	4	*1-125,O-13(12-0-1)	20	2.5
1902 StL-A	126	524	60	149	29	6	4	85	21	....	15	....	.284	.316	.385	.701	95	-5	71	4.95	-3	*1-126/O-3(2-0-1)	12	-1.0
1903 StL-A	138	550	65	156	34	8	2	78	23	....	16	....	.284	.312	.385	.698	111	6	73	4.89	10	*1-133/O-7(2-3-2)	19	1.4
1904 NY-A	143	558	62	155	27	12	3	82	23	....	20	....	.278	.313	.385	.699	115	8	77	4.91	4	*O-112(46-52-13),1-33	19	0.6
1905 NY-A	32	99	12	23	3	1	0	14	8	....	9	....	.232	.296	.283	.579	75	-3	11	3.92	-2	O-22(1-19-2)/1-3	3	-0.6
Was-A	101	400	50	116	21	6	1	38	22	....	22	....	.290	.330	.380	.710	130	12	59	5.46	0	O-97(16-3-78)/1-4	17	0.8
Yr.	133	499	62	139	24	7	1	52	30	....	31	....	.279	.323	.361	.684	119	10	71	5.14	-2	*O-119(17-22-80)/1-7	20	0.2
1906 Was-A	151	583	62	158	25	4	3	70	19	....	**39**	....	.271	.296	.343	.639	105	1	73	4.51	1	*O-151(151-0-0)	18	-0.8
1907 Was-A	87	333	33	96	12	4	0	44	34	....	19	....	.288	.359	.348	.708	137	15	50	5.55	-2	1-61,O-26(26-0-0)	13	1.1
1908 Chi-A	123	355	36	93	17	1	0	47	30	....	21	....	.262	.321	.315	.637	109	4	43	4.05	2	O-87(13-2-72)/1-9	15	0.2
Total 14	1636	6345	871	1843	328	124	50	976	310	55	338	....	.290	.329	.405	.734	115	97	990	5.75	2	*O-1009,1-599/3-1	209	2.9

• ANDERSON, Kent
Kent McKay Anderson b: 8/12/1963, Florence, SC BR/TR, 6'1", 180 lbs. Deb: 4/15/1989

YEAR TM-L	G	AB	R	H	2B	3B	HR	RBI	BB	SO	SB	CS	AVG	OBP	SLG	OPS	OPS+	BR/A	RC	RC/G	FR	G/POS	WS	TPW
1989 Cal-A	86	223	27	51	6	1	0	17	17	42	1	2	.229	.286	.265	.551	57	-13	17	2.52	-3	S-70/2-7,3-5,O-2(0-0-2),D	5	-1.1
1990 Cal-A	49	143	16	44	6	1	1	5	13	19	0	2	.308	.369	.385	.754	113	2	20	4.84	-2	S-28,3-16/2-5	3	0.3
Total 2	135	366	43	95	12	2	1	22	30	61	1	4	.260	.319	.311	.631	79	-11	37	3.38	-5	/S-98,3-21,2-12,O-2,D-1	8	-0.9

• ANDERSON, Marlon
Marlon Ordell Anderson b: 1/6/1974, Montgomery, AL BL/TR, 5'10", 198 lbs. Deb: 9/8/1998

YEAR TM-L	G	AB	R	H	2B	3B	HR	RBI	BB	SO	SB	CS	AVG	OBP	SLG	OPS	OPS+	BR/A	RC	RC/G	FR	G/POS	WS	TPW
1998 Phi-N	17	43	4	14	3	0	1	4	1	6	2	0	.326	.341	.465	.806	108	1	7	6.55	1	/2-9	2	0.2
1999 Phi-N	129	452	48	114	26	4	5	54	24	61	13	2	.252	.293	.361	.654	62	-26	49	3.75	8	*2-121	8	-1.2
2000 Phi-N	41	162	10	37	8	1	1	15	12	22	2	2	.228	.282	.309	.590	49	-14	13	2.67	1	2-41	2	-1.0
2001 Phi-N	147	522	69	153	30	2	11	61	35	74	8	5	.293	.340	.421	.761	98	-3	72	4.88	8	*2-140	16	1.1
2002 Phi-N	145	539	64	139	30	6	8	48	42	71	5	1	.258	.317	.380	.698	87	-11	63	4.00	-2	*2-143	10	-0.6
2003 TB-A	145	482	59	130	27	3	6	67	41	60	19	3	.270	.331	.376	.706	87	-6	63	4.63	-1	*2-134/D-4,O-3(3-0-0)	12	-0.1
Total 6	624	2200	254	587	124	16	32	249	155	294	49	13	.267	.319	.381	.700	82	-58	268	4.23	15	2-588/D-4,O-3	50	-1.6

• ANDERSON, Mike
Michael Allen Anderson b: 6/22/1951, Florence, SC BR/TR, 6'2", 200 lbs. Deb: 9/2/1971 Career OF: 115-78-443

YEAR TM-L	G	AB	R	H	2B	3B	HR	RBI	BB	SO	SB	CS	AVG	OBP	SLG	OPS	OPS+	BR/A	RC	RC/G	FR	G/POS	WS	TPW
1971 Phi-N	26	89	11	22	5	1	2	5	13	28	0	0	.247	.343	.393	.736	108	1	13	5.25	1	O-26(0-26-0)	3	0.1
1972 Phi-N	36	103	8	20	5	1	2	5	19	36	1	0	.194	.320	.320	.640	80	-2	12	3.89	4	O-35(0-3-34)	2	0.1
1973 Phi-N	87	193	32	49	9	1	9	28	19	53	0	3	.254	.324	.451	.775	110	1	27	4.91	0	O-67(0-12-57)	5	-0.1
1974 Phi-N	145	395	35	99	22	2	5	34	37	75	2	1	.251	.315	.354	.669	83	-9	41	3.56	6	*O-133(1-2-131)/1-1	8	-1.0
1975 Phi-N	115	247	24	64	10	3	4	28	17	66	1	2	.259	.312	.372	.685	86	-6	27	3.78	2	*O-105(0-24-88)/1-3	5	-0.8
1976 StL-N	86	199	17	58	8	1	1	12	26	30	1	1	.291	.376	.357	.733	108	3	27	4.89	1	O-58(24-2-33)/1-5	6	0.1
1977 StL-N	94	154	18	34	4	1	4	17	14	31	2	3	.221	.286	.338	.623	68	-8	14	3.02	-1	O-77(2-1-74)	3	-1.2
1978 Bal-A	53	32	2	3	0	1	0	3	3	10	0	0	.094	.171	.156	.328	-8	-5	1	.95	-3	O-47(41-2-6)	0	-0.8
1979 Phi-N	79	78	12	18	4	0	1	2	13	14	1	2	.231	.341	.321	.661	79	-2	9	3.62	0	O-70(47-6-20)/P-1	2	-0.4
Total 9	721	1490	159	367	67	11	28	134	161	343	8	12	.246	.321	.362	.684	88	-27	173	3.94	9	O-618/1-9,P-1	34	-4.1

• ANDERSON, Sparky
George Lee Anderson b: 2/22/1934, Bridgewater, SD BR/TR, 5'9", 170 lbs. Deb: 4/10/1959 M/C HOF: 2000

YEAR TM-L	G	AB	R	H	2B	3B	HR	RBI	BB	SO	SB	CS	AVG	OBP	SLG	OPS	OPS+	BR/A	RC	RC/G	FR	G/POS	WS	TPW
1959 Phi-N	152	477	42	104	9	3	0	34	42	53	6	9	.218	.283	.249	.532	42	-41	32	2.13	8	*2-152	7	-2.2

• ANDRES, Ernie
Ernest Henry "Junie" Andres b: 1/11/1918, Jeffersonville, IN BR/TR, 6'1", 200 lbs. Deb: 4/16/1946

YEAR TM-L	G	AB	R	H	2B	3B	HR	RBI	BB	SO	SB	CS	AVG	OBP	SLG	OPS	OPS+	BR/A	RC	RC/G	FR	G/POS	WS	TPW
1946 Bos-A	15	41	0	4	2	0	0	1	3	5	0	0	.098	.159	.146	.305	-14	-6	1	.67	1	3-15	1	-0.6

• ANDREW, Kim
Kim Darrell Andrew b: 11/14/1953, Glendale, CA BR/TR, 5'10", 160 lbs. Deb: 4/16/1975

YEAR TM-L	G	AB	R	H	2B	3B	HR	RBI	BB	SO	SB	CS	AVG	OBP	SLG	OPS	OPS+	BR/A	RC	RC/G	FR	G/POS	WS	TPW
1975 Bos-A	2	2	0	1	0	0	0	0	0	0	0	0	.500	.500	.500	1.000	169	0	1	13.50	-1	/2-2	0	0.0

• ANDREWS, Ed
George Edward Andrews
b: 4/5/1859, Painesville, OH d: 8/12/1934, West Palm Beach, FL BR/TR, 5'8", 160 lbs. Deb: 5/1/1884 U Career OF: 192-455-5

YEAR TM-L	G	AB	R	H	2B	3B	HR	RBI	BB	SO	SB	CS	AVG	OBP	SLG	OPS	OPS+	BR/A	RC	RC/G	FR	G/POS	WS	TPW
1884 Phi-N	109	420	74	93	21	2	0	23	9	42	....	....	.221	.238	.281	.519	65	-16	29	2.42	-17	*2-109	6	-2.6
1885 Phi-N	103	421	77	112	15	3	0	23	32	25	....	....	.266	.318	.316	.634	108	5	43	3.79	-1	*O-99(99-0-0)/2-5	14	0.1
1886 Phi-N	107	437	93	109	15	4	2	28	31	35	**56**	....	.249	.299	.316	.615	86	-7	59	4.90	1	*O-104(1-103-0)/2-3	17	-0.8
1887 Phi-N	104	485	110	172	19	7	4	67	21	21	57	....	.355	.359	.422	.781	110	5	93	7.87	-8	*O-99(0-99-0)/2-7,1-1	18	-0.6
1888 Phi-N	124	528	75	126	14	4	3	44	21	41	35	....	.239	.272	.297	.569	77	-15	53	3.59	-6	*O-124(0-124-0)	12	-2.4

YEAR TM-L	G	AB	R	H	2B	3B	HR	RBI	BB	SO	SB	CS	AVG	OBP	SLG	OPS	OPS+	BR/A	RC	RC/G	FR	G/POS	WS	TPW
1889 Phi-N	10	39	10	11	1	0	0	7	2	4	7	....	.282	.317	.308	.625	69	-2	6	5.84	-1	/0-9(8-0-1),2-1	1	-0.3
Ind-N	40	173	32	53	11	0	0	22	5	10	7	....	.306	.330	.370	.700	93	-2	24	5.30	-2	0-40(0-40-0)/2-1	3	-0.5
Yr.	50	212	42	64	12	0	0	29	7	14	14	....	.302	.327	.358	.686	89	-4	30	5.40	-3	0-49(8-40-1)/2-2	4	-0.7
1890 Bro-P	94	395	84	100	14	2	3	38	40	32	21	....	.253	.323	.322	.645	68	-19	49	4.49	-3	*0-94(1-89-4)	9	-2.1
1891 Cin-a	83	356	47	75	7	4	0	26	33	35	22	....	.211	.279	.253	.532	48	-26	32	3.03	16	0-83(83-0-0)	5	-1.1
Total 8	774	3254	602	851	117	26	12	278	194	245	205	....	.262	.301	.320	.621	82	-78	389	4.35	-21	0-652,2-126/1-1	85	-10.4

• ANDREWS, Fred Fred Andrews b: 5/4/1952, Lafayette, LA BR/TR, 5'8", 163 lbs. Deb: 9/26/1976

YEAR TM-L	G	AB	R	H	2B	3B	HR	RBI	BB	SO	SB	CS	AVG	OBP	SLG	OPS	OPS+	BR/A	RC	RC/G	FR	G/POS	WS	TPW
1976 Phi-N	4	6	1	4	0	0	0	0	2	0	1	1	.667	.778	.667	1.444	303	2	4	31.80	0	/2-4	1	0.2
1977 Phi-N	12	23	3	4	0	1	0	2	1	5	1	0	.174	.208	.261	.469	24	-2	1	1.50	1	/2-7	0	-0.1
Total 2	16	29	4	8	0	1	0	2	3	5	2	1	.276	.364	.345	.708	98	-0	5	5.29	0	/2-11	1	0.0

• ANDREWS, Jim James Pratt Andrews b: 6/5/1865, Shelburne Falls, MA d: 12/27/1907, Chicago, IL Deb: 4/19/1890

YEAR TM-L	G	AB	R	H	2B	3B	HR	RBI	BB	SO	SB	CS	AVG	OBP	SLG	OPS	OPS+	BR/A	RC	RC/G	FR	G/POS	WS	TPW
1890 Chi-N	53	202	32	38	4	2	3	17	23	41	11	....	.188	.278	.272	.550	58	-11	19	3.03	1	0-53(0-0-54)	3	-1.0

• ANDREWS, Mike Michael Jay Andrews b: 7/9/1943, Los Angeles, CA BR/TR, 6'3", 195 lbs. Deb: 9/18/1966

YEAR TM-L	G	AB	R	H	2B	3B	HR	RBI	BB	SO	SB	CS	AVG	OBP	SLG	OPS	OPS+	BR/A	RC	RC/G	FR	G/POS	WS	TPW
1966 Bos-A	5	18	1	3	0	0	0	0	0	2	0	0	.167	.167	.167	.333	-4	-2	1	.94	1	/2-5	0	-0.1
1967*Bos-A	142	494	79	130	20	0	8	40	62	72	7	7	.263	.348	.352	.700	99	1	63	4.23	-1	*2-139/S-6	16	1.4
1968 Bos-A	147	536	77	145	22	1	7	45	81	57	3	8	.271	.369	.354	.724	113	10	75	4.82	-2	*2-139/S-4,3-1	24	2.4
1969 Bos-A★	121	464	79	136	26	2	15	59	71	53	1	1	.293	.393	.455	.847	129	21	88	6.78	1	*2-120	24	3.1
1970 Bos-A	151	589	91	149	28	1	17	65	81	63	2	1	.253	.346	.390	.737	96	-1	84	4.93	-21	*2-148	16	-1.2
1971 Chi-A	109	330	45	93	16	0	12	47	67	36	3	5	.282	.405	.439	.844	135	17	62	6.51	-15	2-76,1-25	13	0.6
1972 Chi-A	148	505	58	111	18	0	7	50	70	78	2	2	.220	.317	.297	.614	82	-9	54	3.40	-18	*2-145/1-5	15	-2.1
1973 Chi-A	52	159	10	32	9	0	0	10	23	28	0	1	.201	.302	.258	.560	57	-9	12	2.37	-2	D-30/1-9,2-6,3-5	0	-1.2
*Oak-A	18	21	1	4	1	0	0	0	3	1	0	0	.190	.292	.238	.530	53	-1	1	2.17	-1	/2-9,D-2	0	-0.2
Yr.	70	180	11	36	10	0	0	10	26	29	0	1	.200	.301	.256	.557	57	-10	14	2.35	-3	D-32,2-15/1-9,3-5	0	-1.4
Total 8	893	3116	441	803	140	4	66	316	458	390	18	25	.258	.356	.369	.724	104	26	439	4.77	-58	2-787/1-39,D-32,S-10,3-6	108	2.7

• ANDREWS, Rob Robert Patrick Andrews b: 12/11/1952, Santa Monica, CA BR/TR, 6', 185 lbs. Deb: 4/7/1975

YEAR TM-L	G	AB	R	H	2B	3B	HR	RBI	BB	SO	SB	CS	AVG	OBP	SLG	OPS	OPS+	BR/A	RC	RC/G	FR	G/POS	WS	TPW
1975 Hou-N	103	277	29	66	5	4	0	19	31	34	12	5	.238	.315	.285	.600	73	-9	27	3.05	-3	2-94/S-6	5	-0.6
1976 Hou-N	109	410	42	105	8	5	0	23	33	27	7	3	.256	.312	.300	.612	81	-10	37	3.00	13	*2-107/S-3	10	1.1
1977 SF-N	127	436	60	115	11	3	0	25	56	33	5	6	.264	.348	.303	.650	76	-14	49	3.86	-8	*2-115	8	-1.5
1978 SF-N	79	177	21	39	3	3	1	11	20	18	5	1	.220	.299	.288	.588	67	-7	17	3.13	-2	2-62/S-1	4	-0.6
1979 SF-N	75	154	22	40	3	0	2	13	8	9	4	1	.260	.296	.318	.614	73	-6	14	2.99	-8	2-53/3-3	2	-1.2
Total 5	493	1454	174	365	30	15	3	91	148	121	33	16	.251	.320	.298	.619	76	-45	143	3.27	-8	2-431/S-10,3-3	29	-2.9

• ANDREWS, Shane Darrell Shane Andrews b: 8/28/1971, Dallas, TX BR/TR, 6'1", 215 lbs. Deb: 4/26/1995

YEAR TM-L	G	AB	R	H	2B	3B	HR	RBI	BB	SO	SB	CS	AVG	OBP	SLG	OPS	OPS+	BR/A	RC	RC/G	FR	G/POS	WS	TPW
1995 Mon-N	84	220	27	47	10	1	8	31	17	68	1	1	.214	.273	.377	.650	67	-12	22	3.31	3	3-51,1-29	4	-1.0
1996 Mon-N	127	375	43	85	15	2	19	64	35	119	3	1	.227	.296	.429	.725	86	-9	49	4.50	16	*3-123	11	0.9
1997 Mon-N	18	64	10	13	3	0	4	9	3	20	0	0	.203	.239	.438	.676	73	-3	7	3.52	2	3-18	1	-0.1
1998 Mon-N	150	492	48	117	30	1	25	69	58	137	1	6	.238	.318	.455	.773	102	-3	69	4.68	16	*3-147	13	1.5
1999 Mon-N	98	281	28	51	8	0	11	37	43	88	1	0	.181	.290	.327	.618	57	-19	27	2.98	-4	3-82,1-18/D-1	2	-2.2
Chi-N	19	67	13	17	4	0	5	14	7	21	0	1	.254	.333	.537	.871	117	1	12	6.29	1	3-19/1-1	2	0.2
Yr.	117	348	41	68	12	0	16	51	50	109	1	1	.195	.298	.368	.666	69	-18	39	3.56	-3	*3-101,1-19/D-1	4	-2.0
2000 Chi-N	66	192	25	44	5	0	14	39	27	59	1	1	.229	.330	.474	.804	102	-0	28	4.79	5	3-58/1-6	5	0.5
2002 Bos-A	7	13	2	1	1	0	0	0	1	3	0	0	.077	.200	.154	.354	-4	-2	1	1.13	1	/3-4,1-2,0-1	0	-0.1
Total 7	569	1704	196	375	76	4	86	263	191	515	7	10	.220	.301	.421	.722	85	-46	215	4.16	40	3-502/1-56,D-1,0-1	38	-0.3

• ANDREWS, Stan Stanley Joseph "Polo" Andrews b: 4/17/1917, Lynn, MA d: 6/10/1995, Bradenton, FL BR/TR, 5'11", 178 lbs. Deb: 6/11/1939

YEAR TM-L	G	AB	R	H	2B	3B	HR	RBI	BB	SO	SB	CS	AVG	OBP	SLG	OPS	OPS+	BR/A	RC	RC/G	FR	G/POS	WS	TPW
1939 Bos-N	13	26	1	6	0	0	0	1	1	2	0	....	.231	.259	.231	.490	35	-2	1	1.79	-2	C-10	0	-0.4
1940 Bos-N	19	33	1	6	0	0	0	2	0	3	1	....	.182	.182	.182	.364	1	-4	1	1.09	0	C-14	0	-0.4
1944 Bro-N	4	8	1	1	0	0	0	1	1	2	0	....	.125	.222	.125	.347	-1	-1	0	1.08	0	/C-4	0	-0.1
1945 Bro-N	21	49	5	8	0	1	0	2	5	4	0	....	.163	.255	.204	.459	29	-5	3	1.58	0	C-21	1	-0.3
Phi-N	13	33	3	11	2	0	1	6	1	5	1	....	.333	.353	.485	.838	135	1	6	7.04	-1	C-12	2	0.1
Yr.	34	82	8	19	2	1	1	8	6	9	1	....	.232	.292	.317	.609	69	-3	8	3.43	0	C-33	3	-0.2
Total 4	70	149	11	32	2	1	1	12	8	16	2	....	.215	.259	.262	.521	45	-11	11	2.48	-2	/C-61	3	-1.1

• ANDREWS, Wally William Walter Andrews b: 9/18/1859, Philadelphia, PA d: 1/20/1940, Indianapolis, IN BR/TR, 6'3", 170 lbs. Deb: 5/22/1884

YEAR TM-L	G	AB	R	H	2B	3B	HR	RBI	BB	SO	SB	CS	AVG	OBP	SLG	OPS	OPS+	BR/A	RC	RC/G	FR	G/POS	WS	TPW
1884 Lou-a	14	49	10	10	5	1	0	8	4	....	....	....	.204	.264	.347	.611	102	0	5	3.25	-1	/1-9,3-3,0-1,S-1	1	-0.1
1888 Lou-a	26	93	12	18	6	3	0	6	13	....	5	....	.194	.292	.323	.615	99	0	10	3.78	1	1-26	2	-0.1
Total 2	40	142	22	28	11	4	0	14	17	....	5	....	.197	.283	.331	.614	100	1	15	3.60	0	/1-35,3-3,0-1,S-1	3	-0.2

• ANDRUS, Bill William Morgan "Andy" Andrus b: 7/25/1907, Beaumont, TX d: 3/12/1982, Washington, DC BR/TR, 6', 185 lbs. Deb: 9/19/1931

YEAR TM-L	G	AB	R	H	2B	3B	HR	RBI	BB	SO	SB	CS	AVG	OBP	SLG	OPS	OPS+	BR/A	RC	RC/G	FR	G/POS	WS	TPW
1931 Was-A	3	7	0	0	0	0	0	1	0	1	0	0	.000	.000	.000	.000	-100	-2	0	.00	0	/3-2	0	-0.2
1937 Phi-N	3	2	0	0	0	0	0	0	0	2	0	....	.000	.000	.000	.000	-92	-1	0	.00	0	/3-1	0	-0.1
Total 2	6	9	0	0	0	0	0	1	0	3	0	0	.000	.000	.000	.000	-98	-3	0	.00	-1	/3-3	0	-0.3

• ANDRUS, Fred Frederick Hotham Andrus b: 8/23/1850, Washington, MI d: 11/10/1937, Detroit, MI BR/TR, 6'2", 185 lbs. Deb: 7/25/1876 ♦

YEAR TM-L	G	AB	R	H	2B	3B	HR	RBI	BB	SO	SB	CS	AVG	OBP	SLG	OPS	OPS+	BR/A	RC	RC/G	FR	G/POS	WS	TPW
1876 Chi-N	8	36	6	11	3	0	0	2	0	5	....	....	.306	.306	.389	.694	116	0	4	4.91	-2	/0-8(1-3-5)	1	-0.2
1884 Chi-N	1	5	3	1	0	0	0	0	1	0	....	....	.200	.333	.200	.533	66	0	0	2.35	0	/P-1	1	0.1
Total 2	9	41	9	12	3	0	0	2	1	5	....	....	.293	.310	.366	.675	109	0	5	4.56	-2	/0-8,P-1	2	-0.1

• ANDRUS, Wiman William Wiman Andrus b: 10/14/1858, Orono, Canada d: 6/17/1935, Miles City, MT, 5'6.5", 155 lbs. Deb: 9/15/1885

YEAR TM-L	G	AB	R	H	2B	3B	HR	RBI	BB	SO	SB	CS	AVG	OBP	SLG	OPS	OPS+	BR/A	RC	RC/G	FR	G/POS	WS	TPW
1885 Pro-N	1	4	0	0	0	0	0	0	0	1	....	....	.000	.000	.000	.000	-104	-1	0	.00	1	/3-1	0	0.0

• ANGLEY, Tom Thomas Samuel Angley b: 10/2/1904, Baltimore, MD d: 10/26/1952, Wichita, KS BL/TR, 5'8", 190 lbs. Deb: 4/23/1929

YEAR TM-L	G	AB	R	H	2B	3B	HR	RBI	BB	SO	SB	CS	AVG	OBP	SLG	OPS	OPS+	BR/A	RC	RC/G	FR	G/POS	WS	TPW
1929 Chi-N	5	16	1	4	1	0	0	6	2	2	0	....	.250	.333	.313	.646	61	-1	2	3.18	1	/C-5	0	0.1

• ANKENMAN, Pat Frederick Norman Ankenman b: 12/23/1912, Houston, TX d: 1/13/1989, Houston, TX BR/TR, 5'4", 125 lbs. Deb: 4/16/1936

YEAR TM-L	G	AB	R	H	2B	3B	HR	RBI	BB	SO	SB	CS	AVG	OBP	SLG	OPS	OPS+	BR/A	RC	RC/G	FR	G/POS	WS	TPW
1936 StL-N	1	3	0	0	0	0	0	0	0	3	0	....	.000	.000	.000	.000	-100	-1	0	.00	-1	/S-1	0	-0.2
1943 Bro-N	1	2	1	1	0	0	0	0	0	0	0	....	.500	.500	.500	1.000	189	0	1	13.50	0	/S-1	0	0.0
1944 Bro-N	13	24	1	6	1	0	0	3	0	2	0	....	.250	.250	.292	.542	53	-2	2	2.03	0	2-11/S-2	0	-0.1
Total 3	15	29	2	7	1	0	0	3	0	5	0	....	.241	.241	.276	.517	42	-2	2	2.16	-1	/2-11,S-4	0	-0.3

• ANNIS, Bill William Perley Annis b: 5/24/1857, Stoneham, MA d: 6/10/1923, Kennebunkport, ME BR, 5'7", 150 lbs. Deb: 5/1/1884

YEAR TM-L	G	AB	R	H	2B	3B	HR	RBI	BB	SO	SB	CS	AVG	OBP	SLG	OPS	OPS+	BR/A	RC	RC/G	FR	G/POS	WS	TPW
1884 Bos-N	27	96	17	17	2	0	0	3	0	8	....	....	.177	.177	.198	.375	18	-9	3	1.20	-1	0-27(4-15-8)	0	-1.0

• ANSON, Cap Adrian Constantine "Pop" Anson
b: 4/17/1852, Marshalltown, IA d: 4/14/1922, Chicago, IL BR/TR, 6', 227 lbs. Deb: 5/6/1871 M HOF: 1939 NA OF: 1-5-31 Career OF: 45-3-1

YEAR TM-L	G	AB	R	H	2B	3B	HR	RBI	BB	SO	SB	CS	AVG	OBP	SLG	OPS	OPS+	BR/A	RC	RC/G	FR	G/POS	WS	TPW
1871 Rok-n	25	120	29	39	**11**	3	0	16	2	1	6	2	.325	.336	.467	.803	134	5	21	8.11	1	*3-20/C-5,2-2,1-1,0-1	....	0.4
1872 Ath-n	46	217	60	90	10	7	0	50	16	3	6	6	.415	**.455**	.525	.980	200	25	56	13.04	-8	*3-46	....	1.1
1873 Ath-n	52	254	53	101	9	2	0	36	5	1	0	2	.398	.409	.449	.858	144	12	48	9.41	-2	*1-36,3-11/2-3,C-3,0-3(0-3-0)	....	0.7
1874 Ath-n	55	260	51	87	8	3	0	37	4	1	6	0	.335	.345	.388	.733	125	7	38	6.62	-3	1-24,3-20/0-8(0-0-8),S-6,C	....	0.4
1875 Ath-n	69	326	84	106	15	3	0	58	4	2	11	6	.325	.333	.390	.723	135	9	47	6.15	8	1-32,0-25(0-2-23),C-13/3-5	....	1.6
1876 Chi-N	66	321	63	110	9	7	2	59	12	8	....	....	.343	.380	.450	.830	157	17	54	7.62	16	*3-66/C-2	14	3.1
1877 Chi-N	59	255	52	86	**19**	1	0	32	9	3	....	....	.337	.360	.420	.779	129	8	39	6.42	5	3-40,C-31	11	1.3
1878 Chi-N	60	261	55	89	12	2	0	40	13	1	....	....	.341	.372	.402	.775	145	12	40	6.41	-8	*0-48(45-3-0)/2-9,3-3,C-3	9	0.3
1879 Chi-N	51	227	40	72	20	1	0	34	2	2	....	....	**.317**	.323	.414	.737	133	7	31	5.62	3	1-51	9	0.7
1880 Chi-N	86	356	54	120	24	1	1	**74**	14	12	....	....	.337	.362	.419	.781	154	19	55	6.45	11	*1-81/3-9,2-1,S-1	20	2.6
1881 Chi-N	84	343	67	**137**	21	7	1	**82**	26	4	....	....	**.399**	**.442**	.510	**.952**	**186**	**34**	79	**10.39**	8	*1-84/C-2,S-1	22	3.5
1882 Chi-N	82	348	69	126	29	8	1	**83**	20	7	....	....	.362	.397	.500	.897	183	32	71	8.77	-5	*1-82/C-1	18	1.8

YEAR TM-L	G	AB	R	H	2B	3B	HR	RBI	BB	SO	SB	CS	AVG	OBP	SLG	OPS	OPS+	BR/A	RC	RC/G	FR	G/POS	WS	TPW
1883 Chi-N	98	413	70	127	36	5	0	68	18	9	....	....	.308	.336	.419	.755	118	8	60	5.74	-3	*1-98/P-2,C-1,O-1	15	-0.2
1884 Chi-N	112	475	108	159	30	3	21	**102**	29	13	....	....	.335	.373	.543	.916	170	36	99	8.58	-4	*1-112/C-3,P-1,S-1	19	1.8
1885*Chi-N	112	464	100	144	**35**	7	7	**108**	34	13	....	....	.310	.357	.461	.819	142	20	78	6.62	-7	*1-112/C-1	23	0.3
1886*Chi-N	125	504	117	187	35	11	10	**147**	55	19	29	....	.371	.433	.544	.977	169	42	134	11.45	8	*1-125,C-12	30	3.7
1887 Chi-N	122	532	107	224	33	13	7	102	60	18	27	....	**.421**	.422	.517	.939	141	27	117	10.09	10	*1-122/C-1	19	2.2
1888 Chi-N	134	515	101	177	20	12	12	**84**	47	24	28	....	**.344**	**.400**	.499	**.899**	172	42	117	9.33	1	*1-134	29	3.1
1889 Chi-N	134	518	100	161	32	7	7	117	86	19	27	....	.311	.414	.440	.854	132	25	108	8.03	10	*1-134	21	2.1
1890 Chi-N	139	504	95	157	14	5	7	107	**113**	23	29	....	.312	**.443**	.401	.844	141	34	105	8.01	2	*1-135/C-3,2-2	24	2.2
1891 Chi-N	136	540	81	157	24	8	8	**120**	75	29	17	....	.291	.378	.409	.788	129	22	92	6.50	2	*1-136/C-2	21	1.1
1892 Chi-N	146	559	62	152	25	9	1	74	67	30	13	....	.272	.354	.354	.708	113	10	77	5.08	-1	*1-146	19	0.7
1893 Chi-N	103	398	70	125	24	2	0	91	68	12	13	....	.314	.415	.384	.800	115	12	71	6.86	-4	*1-101	11	0.7
1894 Chi-N	84	343	85	133	29	4	5	100	41	15	17	....	.388	.457	.539	.997	133	19	95	11.72	0	1-82/2-1	11	1.5
1895 Chi-N	122	474	87	159	23	6	2	91	55	23	12	....	.335	.408	.422	.830	107	6	90	7.44	-2	*1-122	14	0.3
1896 Chi-N	108	402	72	133	18	2	2	90	49	10	24	....	.331	.407	.400	.808	109	7	78	7.54	-5	*1-98,C-10	12	0.2
1897 Chi-N	114	424	67	121	17	3	3	75	60	....	11	....	.285	.379	.361	.740	92	-3	65	5.53	-4	*1-103,C-11	10	-0.5
Total 5 n	247	1177	277	423	53	18	0	197	31	8	29	16	.359	.376	.435	.811	147	57	210	8.32	-4	3-102/1-93,O-37,C-22,S-6,2	....	4.2
Total 22	2277	9176	1722	3056	529	124	97	1880	953	294	247	....	.333	.395	.446	.841	138	439	1756	7.71	34	*1-2058,3-118/C-83,O-49,2,P,S	381	32.3

• ANTHONY, Eric

Eric Todd Anthony b: 11/8/1967, San Diego, CA BL/TL, 6'2", 195 lbs. Deb: 7/29/1989 Career OF: 114-40-416

YEAR TM-L	G	AB	R	H	2B	3B	HR	RBI	BB	SO	SB	CS	AVG	OBP	SLG	OPS	OPS+	BR/A	RC	RC/G	FR	G/POS	WS	TPW
1989 Hou-N	25	61	7	11	2	0	4	7	9	16	0	0	.180	.286	.410	.696	100	-0	7	3.85	0	O-21(3-0-18)	1	-0.1
1990 Hou-N	84	239	26	46	8	0	10	29	29	78	5	0	.192	.285	.351	.637	76	-7	26	3.40	1	O-71(13-0-59)	3	-0.8
1991 Hou-N	39	118	11	18	6	0	1	7	12	41	1	0	.153	.231	.229	.460	31	-11	7	1.73	3	O-37(0-0-37)	1	-0.9
1992 Hou-N	137	440	45	105	15	1	19	80	38	98	5	4	.239	.301	.407	.707	103	-1	53	4.09	-5	*O-115(1-2-113)	15	-0.8
1993 Hou-N	145	486	70	121	19	4	15	66	49	88	3	5	.249	.320	.397	.717	94	-6	61	4.33	-7	*O-131(0-23-121)	11	-1.9
1994 Sea-A	79	262	31	62	14	1	10	30	23	66	6	2	.237	.298	.412	.710	79	-9	31	3.95	-2	O-71(62-5-10)/D-4	3	-1.3
1995*Cin-N	47	134	19	36	6	0	5	23	13	30	2	1	.269	.333	.425	.759	99	-1	20	5.13	0	O-24(4-1-20),1-17	3	-0.2
1996 Cin-N	47	123	22	30	6	0	8	13	22	36	0	1	.244	.359	.488	.846	122	4	22	6.20	-1	O-37(13-0-24)	3	0.1
Col-N	32	62	10	15	2	0	4	9	10	20	0	1	.242	.347	.468	.815	91	-1	10	5.46	1	O-19(1-9-10)	1	-0.1
Yr.	79	185	32	45	8	0	12	22	32	56	0	2	.243	.355	.481	.836	111	2	32	5.95	-1	O-56(14-9-34)	4	0.0
1997 LA-N	47	74	8	18	3	2	2	5	12	18	2	0	.243	.349	.419	.768	108	2	12	5.87	1	O-21(17-0-4)	2	0.2
Total 9	682	1999	249	462	81	8	78	269	217	491	24	14	.231	.308	.397	.705	91	-30	249	4.18	-9	O-547/1-17,D-4	43	-5.8

• ANTOLICK, Joe

Joseph Antolick b: 4/11/1916, Hokendauqua, PA d: 6/25/2002, Catasauqua, PA BR/TR, 6', 185 lbs. Deb: 9/20/1944

YEAR TM-L	G	AB	R	H	2B	3B	HR	RBI	BB	SO	SB	CS	AVG	OBP	SLG	OPS	OPS+	BR/A	RC	RC/G	FR	G/POS	WS	TPW
1944 Phi-N	4	6	1	2	0	0	0	0	1	0	0	....	.333	.429	.333	.762	120	0	1	6.54	0	/C-3	0	0.1

• ANTONELLI, John

John Lawrence Antonelli b: 7/15/1915, Memphis, TN d: 4/18/1990, Memphis, TN BR/TR, 5'10.5", 165 lbs. Deb: 9/16/1944

YEAR TM-L	G	AB	R	H	2B	3B	HR	RBI	BB	SO	SB	CS	AVG	OBP	SLG	OPS	OPS+	BR/A	RC	RC/G	FR	G/POS	WS	TPW
1944 StL-N	8	21	0	4	1	0	0	1	0	4	0	....	.190	.190	.238	.429	20	-2	1	1.51	1	/1-3,3-3,2-2	0	-0.1
1945 StL-N	2	3	0	0	0	0	0	0	0	1	0	....	.000	.000	.000	.000	-98	-1	0	.00	-1	/3-1	0	-0.1
Phi-N	125	504	50	129	27	2	1	28	24	24	1	....	.256	.292	.323	.616	73	-20	45	3.11	-12	*3-108,2-23/1-1,S-1	7	-3.0
Yr.	127	507	50	129	27	2	1	28	24	25	1	....	.254	.291	.321	.612	72	-21	45	3.09	-13	*3-109,2-23/1-1,S-1	7	-3.1
Total 2	135	528	50	133	28	2	1	29	24	29	1	....	.252	.287	.318	.605	70	-23	46	3.02	-12	3-112/2-25,1-4,S-1	7	-3.3

• ANTONELLO, Bill

William James Antonello b: 5/19/1927, Brooklyn, NY d: 3/4/1993, Fridley, MN BR/TR, 5'11", 185 lbs. Deb: 4/30/1953

YEAR TM-L	G	AB	R	H	2B	3B	HR	RBI	BB	SO	SB	CS	AVG	OBP	SLG	OPS	OPS+	BR/A	RC	RC/G	FR	G/POS	WS	TPW
1953 Bro-N	40	43	9	7	1	1	1	4	2	11	0	0	.163	.200	.302	.502	28	-5	2	1.80	-1	O-25(20-2-4)	0	-0.6

• APARICIO, Luis

Luis Ernesto (Montiel) "Little Louie" Aparicio b: 4/29/1934, Maracaibo, Venezuela BR/TR, 5'9", 160 lbs. Deb: 4/17/1956 HOF: 1984

YEAR TM-L	G	AB	R	H	2B	3B	HR	RBI	BB	SO	SB	CS	AVG	OBP	SLG	OPS	OPS+	BR/A	RC	RC/G	FR	G/POS	WS	TPW
1956 Chi-A	152	533	69	142	19	6	3	56	34	63	**21**	4	.266	.312	.341	.653	71	-20	59	3.79	11	*S-152	14	0.3
1957 Chi-A	143	575	82	148	22	6	3	41	52	55	**28**	8	.257	.319	.332	.651	78	-14	65	3.87	-4	*S-142	16	-0.7
1958 Chi-A★	145	557	76	148	20	9	2	40	35	38	**29**	6	.266	.310	.345	.655	82	-10	62	3.88	18	*S-145	19	2.1
1959*Chi-A★	152	612	98	157	18	5	6	51	53	40	**56**	13	.257	.319	.332	.651	80	-10	70	3.83	5	*S-152	19	0.8
1960 Chi-A★	153	600	86	166	20	7	2	61	43	39	**51**	8	.277	.326	.343	.669	82	-7	73	4.09	25	*S-153	20	3.0
1961 Chi-A★	156	625	90	170	24	4	6	45	38	33	**53**	13	.272	.315	.352	.667	79	-14	72	3.97	2	*S-156	17	0.2
1962 Chi-A★	153	581	72	140	23	5	7	40	32	36	**31**	12	.241	.282	.334	.616	65	-28	54	3.07	10	*S-152	13	-0.5
1963 Bal-A★	146	601	73	150	18	8	5	45	36	35	**40**	6	.250	.294	.331	.625	77	-13	62	3.51	-2	*S-145	18	-0.3
1964 Bal-A★	146	578	93	154	20	3	10	37	49	51	**57**	17	.266	.327	.363	.690	92	-1	71	4.12	7	*S-145	21	2.0
1965 Bal-A	144	564	67	127	20	10	8	40	46	56	26	7	.225	.287	.339	.626	76	-16	57	3.25	10	*S-141	17	0.7
1966*Bal-A	151	659	97	182	25	8	6	41	33	42	25	11	.276	.312	.366	.677	95	-4	74	3.92	18	*S-151	22	2.9
1967 Bal-A	134	546	55	127	22	5	4	31	29	44	18	5	.233	.273	.313	.586	73	-17	47	2.89	-12	*S-131	8	-1.9
1968 Chi-A	157	622	55	164	24	4	4	36	33	43	17	11	.264	.303	.334	.637	92	-8	61	3.41	13	*S-156	19	2.1
1969 Chi-A	156	599	77	168	24	5	5	51	66	29	24	4	.280	.354	.362	.716	96	2	81	4.74	1	*S-154	20	2.1
1970 Chi-A★	146	552	86	173	29	3	5	43	53	34	8	3	.313	.375	.404	.779	110	10	85	5.70	-15	*S-146	18	1.2
1971 Bos-A★	125	491	56	114	23	0	4	45	35	43	6	4	.232	.286	.303	.589	63	-24	44	2.94	-14	*S-121	8	-2.6
1972 Bos-A★	110	436	47	112	26	3	3	39	26	28	3	3	.257	.302	.351	.653	89	-7	45	3.56	-12	*S-109	11	-0.7
1973 Bos-A	132	499	56	135	17	1	0	49	43	33	13	1	.271	.328	.309	.637	76	-12	53	3.64	0	*S-132	13	0.2
Total 18	2601	10230	1335	2677	394	92	83	791	736	742	506	136	.262	.313	.343	.655	82	-195	1137	3.79	60	*S-2583	293	10.9

• APPLING, Luke

Lucius Benjamin "Old Aches and Pains,Luscious Luke" Appling
b: 4/2/1907, High Point, NC d: 1/3/1991, Cumming, GA BR/TR, 5'10", 183 lbs. Deb: 9/10/1930 M/C HOF: 1964

YEAR TM-L	G	AB	R	H	2B	3B	HR	RBI	BB	SO	SB	CS	AVG	OBP	SLG	OPS	OPS+	BR/A	RC	RC/G	FR	G/POS	WS	TPW
1930 Chi-A	6	26	2	8	2	0	0	2	0	0	2	0	.308	.308	.385	.692	77	-1	3	4.79	-2	/S-6	0	-0.2
1931 Chi-A	96	297	36	69	13	4	1	28	29	27	9	2	.232	.303	.313	.616	66	-12	30	3.44	-10	S-76/2-1	5	-1.5
1932 Chi-A	139	489	66	134	20	10	3	63	40	36	9	8	.274	.329	.374	.703	87	-10	60	4.33	2	S-85,2-30,3-14	12	0.0
1933 Chi-A	151	612	90	197	36	10	6	85	56	29	6	11	.322	.379	.443	.822	122	16	100	6.22	4	*S-151	25	3.0
1934 Chi-A	118	452	75	137	28	6	2	61	59	27	3	1	.303	.384	.405	.788	100	2	73	6.06	-10	*S-110/2-8	14	0.1
1935 Chi-A	153	525	94	161	28	6	1	71	122	40	12	6	.307	.437	.389	.826	112	19	100	7.02	17	*S-153	24	4.5
1936 Chi-A★	138	526	111	204	31	7	6	128	85	25	10	6	**.388**	.474	.508	.981	137	37	131	10.42	2	*S-137	29	4.3
1937 Chi-A	154	574	98	182	42	8	4	77	86	28	18	10	.317	.407	.439	.846	113	15	107	6.98	10	*S-154	28	3.3
1938 Chi-A	81	294	41	89	14	0	0	44	42	17	1	3	.303	.392	.350	.742	85	-6	42	5.35	3	S-78	9	0.3
1939 Chi-A★	148	516	82	162	16	6	0	56	105	37	16	9	.314	.430	.368	.798	103	10	90	6.37	6	*S-148	24	2.4
1940 Chi-A★	150	566	96	197	27	13	0	79	69	35	3	5	.348	.420	.442	.862	122	21	109	7.59	19	*S-150	28	4.8
1941 Chi-A★	154	592	93	186	26	8	1	57	82	32	12	8	.314	.399	.390	.789	111	12	98	6.24	10	*S-154	29	3.3
1942 Chi-A	142	543	78	142	26	4	3	53	63	23	17	5	.262	.342	.341	.682	94	-1	70	4.51	-1	*S-141	20	0.8
1943 Chi-A★	155	585	63	192	33	2	3	80	90	29	27	8	**.328**	**.419**	.407	.825	142	39	109	7.10	6	*S-155	**40**	6.2
1945 Chi-A	18	57	12	21	2	2	1	10	12	7	1	0	.368	.478	.526	1.005	197	8	16	12.01	-2	S-17	6	0.9
1946 Chi-A★	149	582	59	180	27	5	1	55	71	41	6	4	.309	.384	.378	.762	118	17	88	5.57	6	*S-149	26	3.3
1947 Chi-A★	139	503	67	154	29	0	8	49	64	28	8	6	.306	.386	.412	.797	126	19	81	5.88	-12	*S-129/3-2	22	1.6
1948 Chi-A	139	497	63	156	16	2	0	47	94	35	10	4	.314	.423	.354	.777	112	16	82	6.03	-2	3-72,S-64	17	1.8
1949 Chi-A	142	492	82	148	21	5	5	58	121	24	7	12	.301	.439	.394	.833	125	23	90	6.28	-10	*S-141	19	2.1
1950 Chi-A	50	128	11	30	3	4	0	13	12	8	2	0	.234	.300	.320	.620	61	-7	12	2.91	1	S-20,1-13/2-1	1	-0.5
Total 20	2422	8856	1319	2749	440	102	45	1116	1302	528	179	108	.310	.399	.398	.798	113	218	1493	6.23	35	*S-2218/3-88,2-40,1-13	378	40.3

• ARAGON, Angel

Angel (Valdes) "Pete" Aragon b: 8/2/1890, Havana, Cuba d: 1/24/1952, New York, NY BR/TR, 5'5", 150 lbs. Deb: 8/20/1914 Career OF: 5-3-1

YEAR TM-L	G	AB	R	H	2B	3B	HR	RBI	BB	SO	SB	CS	AVG	OBP	SLG	OPS	OPS+	BR/A	RC	RC/G	FR	G/POS	WS	TPW
1914 NY-A	6	7	1	1	0	0	0	0	1	2	0	....	.143	.333	.143	.476	44	-0	1	2.10	0	/O-1	0	-0.1
1916 NY-A	12	24	1	5	0	0	0	3	2	2	2	....	.208	.269	.208	.478	43	-2	2	2.54	0	/3-8,O-2(1-0-1)	0	-0.1
1917 NY-A	14	45	2	3	1	0	0	2	2	2	0	....	.067	.106	.089	.195	-40	-8	1	.31	-1	/O-6(4-2-0),3-4,S-2	0	-0.9
Total 3	32	76	4	9	1	0	0	5	5	6	2	....	.118	.183	.132	.315	-5	-10	3	1.11	0	/3-12,O-9,S-2	0	-1.1

• ARAGON, Jack

Angel Valdes (Reyes) Aragon b: 11/20/1915, Havana, Cuba d: 4/4/1988, Clearwater, FL BR/TR, 5'10", 176 lbs. Deb: 8/13/1941

YEAR TM-L	G	AB	R	H	2B	3B	HR	RBI	BB	SO	SB	CS	AVG	OBP	SLG	OPS	OPS+	BR/A	RC	RC/G	FR	G/POS	WS	TPW
1941 NY-N	1	0	0	0	0	0	0	0	0	0	0	....	....	....	....	....	-98	0	0	....	0	....	0	0.0

YEAR TM-L	G	AB	R	H	2B	3B	HR	RBI	BB	SO	SB	CS	AVG	OBP	SLG	OPS	OPS+	BR/A	RC	RC/G	FR	G/POS	WS	TPW
• ARCHDEACON, Maurice	Maurice John "Flash,Comet" Archdeacon b: 12/14/1898, St. Louis, MO d: 9/5/1954, St. Louis, MO BL/TL, 5'8", 153 lbs. Deb: 9/17/1923 Career OF: 1-95-2																							
1923 Chi-A	22	87	23	35	5	1	0	4	6	8	2	3	.402	.441	.483	.924	145	5	17	8.28	-1	O-20(0-18-2)	3	0.3
1924 Chi-A	95	288	59	92	9	3	0	25	40	30	11	7	.319	.410	.372	.781	106	5	47	5.80	1	O-77(0-77-0)	9	0.3
1925 Chi-A	10	9	2	1	0	0	0	0	2	1	0	0	.111	.273	.111	.384		-1	0	1.43	0	/O-1	0	-0.1
Total 3	127	384	84	128	14	4	0	29	48	39	13	10	.333	.413	.391	.803	111	9	65	6.15	0	/O-98	12	0.5
• ARCHER, Jimmy	James Patrick Archer b: 5/13/1883, Dublin, Ireland d: 3/29/1958, Milwaukee, WI BR/TR, 5'10", 168 lbs. Deb: 9/6/1904																							
1904 Pit-N	7	20	1	3	0	0	0	1	0	....	0	....	.150	.150	.150	.300	-7	-3	0	.71	-1	/C-7,O-1	0	-0.3
1907*Det-A	18	42	6	5	0	0	0	0	4	....	0	....	.119	.196	.119	.315	1	-5	1	.84	1	C-17/2-1	1	-0.3
1909 Chi-N	80	261	31	60	9	2	1	30	12	....	5	....	.230	.266	.291	.558	71	-10	22	2.66	-11	C-80	7	-1.4
1910*Chi-N	98	313	36	81	17	6	2	41	14	49	6	....	.259	.293	.371	.663	94	-5	36	3.75	-2	C-49,1-40	10	-0.2
1911 Chi-N	116	387	41	98	18	5	4	41	18	43	5	....	.253	.288	.357	.645	80	-13	41	3.51	-2	*C-102,1-10/2-1	11	-0.7
1912 Chi-N	120	385	35	109	20	2	5	58	22	36	7	....	.283	.330	.384	.715	95	-4	51	4.49	-5	*C-118	13	0.0
1913 Chi-N	111	368	38	98	14	7	2	44	19	27	4	....	.266	.311	.359	.670	91	-5	41	3.74	-4	*C-103/1-8	12	-0.1
1914 Chi-N	79	248	17	64	9	2	0	19	9	9	1	....	.258	.284	.310	.595	77	-8	21	2.93	-3	C-76	7	-0.5
1915 Chi-N	97	309	21	75	11	5	1	27	11	38	5	6	.243	.273	.320	.594	79	-10	27	2.92	1	C-88/1-4	8	-0.3
1916 Chi-N	77	205	11	45	6	2	1	30	12	24	3	....	.220	.269	.283	.552	63	-9	18	2.72	1	C-61/3-1	2	-0.4
1917 Chi-N	2	2	0	0	0	0	0	0	0	1	0	....	.000	.000	.000	.000	-93	-0	0	.00	0	....	0	0.0
1918 Pit-N	24	58	4	9	1	2	0	3	1	6	0	....	.155	.197	.241	.438	32	-5	3	1.38	3	C-21/1-1	1	0.0
Bro-N	9	22	3	6	0	1	0	0	1	5	0	....	.273	.304	.364	.668	104	0	2	3.71	1	/C-7	1	0.2
Cin-N	9	26	2	7	1	0	0	2	1	3	0	....	.269	.296	.308	.604	86	-1	2	3.03	1	/C-7,1-1	1	0.1
Yr.	42	106	9	22	2	3	0	5	3	14	0	....	.208	.243	.283	.526	60	-5	7	2.18	5	C-35/1-2	3	0.3
Total 12	847	2646	246	660	106	34	16	296	124	241	36	6	.249	.288	.333	.621	80	-77	266	3.30	-19	C-736/1-64,2-2,3-1,O-1	74	-4.0
• ARCHIE, George	George Albert Archie b: 4/27/1914, Nashville, TN d: 9/20/2001, Nashville, TN BR/TR, 6', 170 lbs. Deb: 9/14/1938																							
1938 Det-A	3	2	1	0	0	0	0	0	0	1	0	0	.000	.000	.000	.000	-95	-1	0	.00	0	....	0	-0.1
1941 Was-A	105	379	45	102	20	4	3	48	30	42	8	4	.269	.324	.367	.691	86	-8	45	4.15	-7	3-73,1-23	8	-1.4
StL-A	9	29	3	11	3	0	0	5	7	3	2	0	.379	.500	.483	.983	156	3	8	10.33	0	/1-8	1	0.3
Yr.	114	408	48	113	23	4	3	53	37	45	10	4	.277	.339	.375	.714	92	-4	53	4.54	-7	3-73,1-31	9	-1.1
1946 StL-A	4	11	1	2	1	0	0	0	0	1	0	0	.182	.182	.273	.455	25	-1	1	1.68	2	/1-3	0	0.0
Total 3	121	421	50	115	24	4	3	53	37	47	10	4	.273	.333	.371	.704	90	-6	53	4.43	-5	/3-73,1-34	9	-1.1
• ARCIA, Jose	Jose Raimundo (Orta) Arcia b: 8/22/1943, Havana, Cuba BR/TR, 6'3", 170 lbs. Deb: 4/10/1968 Career OF: 16-13-0																							
1968 Chi-N	59	84	15	16	4	0	1	8	3	24	0	0	.190	.218	.274	.492	44	-6	5	2.04	-2	O-17(5-13-0),2-10/S-7,3-1	1	-0.8
1969 SD-N	120	302	35	65	11	3	0	10	14	47	14	7	.215	.255	.272	.526	49	-21	20	2.11	-9	2-68,S-37/3-8,O-4(4-0-0),1	2	-2.5
1970 SD-N	114	229	28	51	9	3	0	17	12	36	3	6	.223	.282	.288	.570	55	-17	18	2.54	0	S-67,2-20/3-9,O-7(7-0-0)	3	-1.1
Total 3	293	615	78	132	24	6	1	35	29	107	17	13	.215	.260	.278	.538	51	-43	43	2.26	-12	S-111/2-98,O-28,3-18,1-1	6	-4.4
• ARDELL, Dan	Daniel Miers Ardell b: 5/27/1941, Seattle, WA BL/TL, 6'2", 190 lbs. Deb: 9/14/1961																							
1961 LA-A	7	4	1	1	0	0	0	0	1	2	0	0	.250	.400	.250	.650	70	-0	1	4.01	0	/1-1	0	0.0
• ARDNER, Joe	Joseph A. "Old Hoss" Ardner b: 2/27/1858, Mount Vernon, OH d: 9/15/1935, Cleveland, OH BR/TR, 160 lbs. Deb: 5/1/1884																							
1884 Cle-N	26	92	6	16	1	1	0	4	1	24	....	....	.174	.183	.207	.389	21	-8	4	1.29	-10	2-25/3-1	0	-1.5
1890 Cle-N	84	323	28	72	13	1	0	35	17	40	9	....	.223	.266	.269	.535	57	-18	26	2.76	-15	2-84	3	-2.7
Total 2	110	415	34	88	14	2	0	39	18	64	9	....	.212	.248	.255	.504	50	-27	30	2.42	-24	2-109/3-1	3	-4.2
• ARDOIN, Danny	Daniel Wayne Ardoin b: 7/8/1974, Mamou, LA BR/TR, 6', 218 lbs. Deb: 8/2/2000																							
2000 Min-A	15	32	4	4	1	0	1	5	8	10	0	0	.125	.300	.250	.550	40	-3	3	2.92	2	C-15	0	0.0
• ARFT, Hank	Henry Irven "Bow Wow" Arft b: 1/28/1922, Manchester, MO d: 12/14/2002, St. Louis, MO BL/TL, 5'10.5", 190 lbs. Deb: 7/27/1948																							
1948 StL-A	69	248	25	59	10	3	5	38	45	43	1	2	.238	.355	.363	.718	89	-4	34	4.57	-2	1-69	4	-0.8
1949 StL-A	6	5	1	1	1	0	0	2	0	1	0	0	.200	.200	.400	.600	55	-0	0	2.77	0	....	0	0.0
1950 StL-A	98	280	45	75	16	4	1	32	46	48	3	2	.268	.375	.364	.739	87	-4	43	5.41	0	1-84	7	-0.7
1951 StL-A	112	345	44	90	16	5	7	42	41	34	4	6	.261	.339	.397	.736	96	-4	48	4.78	5	1-97	8	-0.2
1952 StL-A	15	28	1	4	3	1	0	4	5	7	0	0	.143	.273	.321	.594	63	-1	3	2.76	-1	1-10	0	-0.2
Total 5	300	906	116	229	46	13	13	118	137	133	8	10	.253	.352	.375	.727	90	-13	128	4.83	2	1-260	19	-1.9
• ARIAS, Alex	Alejandro Arias b: 11/20/1967, New York, NY BR/TR, 6'3", 185 lbs. Deb: 5/12/1992																							
1992 Chi-N	32	99	14	29	6	0	0	7	11	13	0	0	.293	.375	.354	.729	105	1	13	4.71	-2	S-30	3	0.1
1993 Fla-N	96	249	27	67	5	1	2	20	27	18	1	1	.269	.348	.321	.669	76	-8	29	4.09	-1	2-30,3-22,S-18	4	-0.6
1994 Fla-N	59	113	4	27	5	0	0	15	9	19	0	1	.239	.301	.283	.584	52	-8	9	2.54	-2	S-20,3-15	1	-0.9
1995 Fla-N	94	216	22	58	9	2	3	26	22	20	1	0	.269	.342	.370	.712	87	-4	27	4.23	-1	S-36,3-21/2-6	5	-0.2
1996 Fla-N	100	224	27	62	11	2	3	26	17	28	2	0	.277	.336	.384	.720	92	-2	30	4.92	3	3-59,S-20/1-1,2-1	6	0.3
1997*Fla-N	74	93	13	23	2	0	1	11	12	12	0	1	.247	.352	.301	.653	76	-3	9	3.14	-1	3-37,S-11	1	-0.3
1998 Phi-N	56	133	17	39	8	0	1	16	13	18	2	0	.293	.361	.376	.736	93	-1	19	5.34	-4	S-38/3-5,2-1	3	-0.2
1999 Phi-N	118	347	43	105	20	1	4	48	36	31	2	2	.303	.375	.401	.775	94	-3	51	5.27	-7	S-95/3-2,2-1	10	-0.3
2000 Phi-N	70	155	17	29	9	0	2	15	16	28	1	0	.187	.276	.284	.560	41	-14	14	2.76	-3	S-39,3-10/2-1	2	-1.3
2001 SD-N	70	137	19	31	9	0	2	12	17	22	1	0	.226	.316	.336	.652	75	-5	15	3.68	-3	3-18,1-17,2-13,S-13	3	-0.7
2002 NY-A	6	7	0	0	0	0	0	0	1	2	0	0	.000	.125	.000	.125	-63	-2	0	.13	0	/3-4,S-1	0	-0.2
Total 11	775	1773	203	470	84	6	18	196	181	211	10	5	.265	.341	.350	.691	80	-47	216	4.21	-22	S-321,3-193/2-53,1-18	38	-4.3
• ARIAS, George	George Alberto Arias b: 3/12/1972, Tucson, AZ BR/TR, 5'11", 190 lbs. Deb: 4/2/1996																							
1996 Cal-A	84	252	19	60	8	1	6	28	16	50	2	0	.238	.284	.349	.633	60	-16	24	3.24	16	3-83/D-1	4	0.1
1997 Ana-A	3	6	1	2	0	0	0	1	0	0	0	0	.333	.333	.333	.667	74	-0	1	4.50	0	/3-1,D-1	0	0.0
SD-N	11	22	2	5	1	0	0	2	0	1	0	0	.227	.227	.273	.500	33	-2	1	1.16	0	/3-8	0	-0.2
1998*SD-N	20	36	4	7	1	1	1	4	3	16	0	0	.194	.293	.361	.654	76	-1	4	3.90	0	3-14/1-1	1	-0.2
1999 SD-N	55	164	20	40	8	0	7	20	6	54	0	0	.244	.271	.421	.691	77	-7	17	3.45	0	3-50	3	-0.6
Total 4	173	480	46	114	18	2	14	55	25	121	2	0	.238	.278	.371	.649	66	-26	47	3.27	16	3-156/D-2,1-1	8	-0.8
• ARLETT, Buzz	Russell Loris Arlett b: 1/3/1899, Elmhurst, CA d: 5/16/1964, Minneapolis, MN BB/TR, 6'3.5", 210 lbs. Deb: 4/14/1931																							
1931 Phi-N	121	418	65	131	26	7	18	72	45	39	3	....	.313	.387	.538	.925	135	21	90	8.08	-2	O-94(0-0-94),1-13	16	1.2
• ARMAS, Marcos	Marcos Rafael (Ruiz) Armas b: 8/5/1969, Puerto Piritu, Venezuela BR/TR, 6'5", 195 lbs. Deb: 5/25/1993																							
1993 Oak-A	15	31	7	6	2	0	1	1	1	12	1	0	.194	.242	.355	.597	62	-2	3	3.15	-1	1-12/D-2,O-1	0	-0.3
• ARMAS, Tony	Antonio Rafael (Machado) Armas b: 7/2/1953, Anzoategui, Venezuela BR/TR, 5'11", 200 lbs. Deb: 9/6/1976 Career OF: 124-615-623																							
1976 Pit-N	4	6	0	2	0	0	0	1	0	2	0	0	.333	.333	.333	.667	89	-0	1	4.50	0	/O-2(1-1-0)	0	0.0
1977 Oak-A	118	363	26	87	8	2	13	53	20	99	1	2	.240	.279	.380	.660	79	-12	37	3.35	3	*O-112(3-84-30)/S-1	8	-1.2
1978 Oak-A	91	239	17	51	6	1	2	13	10	62	1	2	.213	.251	.272	.523	50	-17	16	2.08	-3	O-85(2-40-47)/D-3	2	-2.4
1979 Oak-A	80	278	29	69	9	3	11	34	16	67	1	0	.248	.292	.421	.712	95	-3	33	4.10	0	O-80(12-17-53)	7	-0.6
1980 Oak-A	158	628	87	175	18	8	35	109	29	128	5	3	.279	.313	.500	.813	128	19	89	4.95	5	*O-158(0-10-152)	22	1.6
1981*Oak-A★	109	440	51	115	24	3	**22**	76	19	115	5	1	.261	.295	.480	.775	126	12	61	4.94	-2	*O-109(0-2-108)	18	0.5
1982 Oak-A	138	536	58	125	19	2	28	89	33	128	2	2	.233	.279	.433	.712	96	-5	61	3.76	-2	*O-135(0-5-133)/D-1	13	-1.5
1983 Bos-A	145	574	77	125	23	2	36	107	29	131	0	1	.218	.258	.453	.711	85	-16	55	3.04	-6	*O-116(0-116-0),D-27	7	-2.4
1984 Bos-A★	157	639	107	171	29	5	**43**	**123**	32	156	1	3	.268	.304	.531	.834	120	13	97	5.32	-9	*O-126(0-126-1),D-31	20	0.1
1985 Bos-A	103	385	50	102	17	5	23	64	18	90	0	0	.265	.301	.514	.816	114	5	54	4.82	-2	O-79(16-69-2),D-19	9	0.0
1986*Bos-A	121	425	40	112	21	4	11	58	24	77	0	3	.264	.306	.409	.715	92	-7	49	4.03	-5	*O-117(9-108-19)/D-1	9	-1.4
1987 Cal-A	28	81	8	16	3	1	3	9	1	11	1	0	.198	.207	.370	.578	51	-6	5	2.05	0	O-27(2-0-26)	0	-0.7
1988 Cal-A	120	368	42	100	20	2	13	49	22	87	1	3	.272	.313	.443	.756	112	3	46	4.33	4	*O-113(74-36-10)/D-5	9	0.4

YEAR TM-L	G	AB	R	H	2B	3B	HR	RBI	BB	SO	SB	CS	AVG	OBP	SLG	OPS	OPS+	BR/A	RC	RC/G	FR	G/POS	WS	TPW
1989 Cal-A	60	202	22	52	7	1	11	30	7	48	0	0	.257	.282	.465	.748	109	1	26	4.56	1	0-47(5-1-42)/D-6,1-2	7	0.0
Total 14	**1432**	**5164**	**614**	**1302**	**204**	**39**	**251**	**815**	**260**	**1201**	**18**	**20**	**.252**	**.290**	**.453**	**.742**	**103**	**-13**	**629**	**4.15**	**-19**	*0-1306/D-93,1-2,S-1	**131**	**-7.6**
• ARMBRISTER, Ed	Edison Rosanda Armbrister b: 7/4/1948, Nassau, Bahamas BR/TR, 5'11", 160 lbs. Deb: 8/31/1973 Career OF: 55-8-36																							
1973*Cin-N	18	37	5	8	3	1	1	5	2	8	0	0	.216	.256	.432	.689	92	-1	4	3.73	-1	0-14(3-4-7)	1	-0.2
1974 Cin-N	9	7	0	2	0	0	0	0	1	1	0	0	.286	.375	.286	.661	88	-0	1	4.58	0	/0-4(2-0-2)	0	-0.1
1975*Cin-N	59	65	9	12	1	0	0	2	5	19	3	1	.185	.254	.200	.454	27	-6	4	1.78	-1	0-19(10-4-7)	0	-0.8
1976*Cin-N	73	78	20	23	3	2	2	7	6	22	7	3	.295	.345	.462	.807	124	2	13	5.40	1	0-32(20-0-13)	3	0.2
1977 Cin-N	65	78	12	20	4	3	1	5	10	21	5	6	.256	.341	.423	.764	102	-1	9	3.54	0	0-27(20-0-7)	1	-0.2
Total 5	**224**	**265**	**46**	**65**	**11**	**6**	**4**	**19**	**24**	**71**	**15**	**10**	**.245**	**.310**	**.377**	**.688**	**89**	**-6**	**31**	**3.68**	**-1**	/0-96	**5**	**-1.0**
• ARMBRUSTER, Charlie	Charles A. Armbruster b: 8/30/1880, Cincinnati, OH d: 10/7/1964, Grants Pass, OR BR/TR, 5'9", 180 lbs. Deb: 7/17/1905																							
1905 Bos-A	35	91	13	18	4	0	0	6	18	....	3	....	.198	.336	.242	.578	83	-0	9	3.15	-4	C-35	3	-0.1
1906 Bos-A	72	201	9	29	6	1	0	6	25	....	2	....	.144	.242	.184	.426	34	-14	10	1.54	5	C-66/1-1	2	-0.3
1907 Bos-A	23	60	2	6	1	0	0	0	8	....	1	....	.100	.206	.117	.323	3	-6	2	.96	1	C-21	1	-0.3
Chi-A	1	3	0	0	0	0	0	0	1	....	0	....	.000	.250	.000	.250	-20	-0	0	.00	1	/C-1	0	0.1
Yr.	24	63	2	6	1	0	0	0	9	....	1	....	.095	.208	.111	.319	2	-7	2	.91	2	C-22	1	-0.3
Total 3	**131**	**355**	**24**	**53**	**11**	**1**	**0**	**12**	**52**	....	**6**	....	**.149**	**.262**	**.186**	**.448**	**41**	**-21**	**21**	**1.80**	**4**	C-123/1-1	**6**	**-0.7**
• ARMBRUSTER, Harry	Henry "Army" Armbruster b: 3/2/1882, Cincinnati, OH d: 12/10/1953, Cincinnati, OH BL/TL, 5'10", 190 lbs. Deb: 4/30/1906																							
1906 Phi-A	91	265	40	63	6	3	2	24	43	....	13	....	.238	.353	.306	.658	103	4	37	4.41	-1	0-74(0-40-34)	10	0.0
• ARMSTRONG, Bob	Robert Armstrong b: 1850, Baltimore, MD, 6'2", 160 lbs. Deb: 6/26/1871																							
1871 Kek-n	12	49	9	11	2	1	0	5	0	1	0	1	.224	.224	.306	.531	50	-4	3	2.79	0	0-12(0-11-1)	....	-0.3
• ARMSTRONG, George	Noble George "Dodo" Armstrong b: 6/3/1924, Orange, NJ d: 7/24/1993, Orange, NJ BR/TR, 5'10", 190 lbs. Deb: 4/26/1946																							
1946 Phi-A	8	6	0	1	1	0	0	0	1	1	0	0	.167	.286	.333	.619	73	-0	1	3.56	0	/C-4	0	0.0
• ARNDT, Harry	Harry J. Arndt b: 2/12/1879, South Bend, IN d: 3/25/1921, South Bend, IN BR/TR Deb: 7/2/1902 Career OF: 8-0-74																							
1902 Det-A	10	34	4	5	0	1	0	7	6	....	0	....	.147	.275	.206	.481	34	-3	2	1.88	0	0-10(7-0-3)/1-1	0	-0.3
Bal-A	68	248	41	63	7	4	2	28	35	....	9	....	.254	.355	.339	.694	89	-2	34	4.83	-3	0-62(1-0-61)/2-4,3-2,S-1	5	-0.8
Yr.	78	282	45	68	7	5	2	35	41	....	9	....	.241	.346	.323	.668	82	-5	37	4.43	-3	0-72(8-0-64)/2-4,3-2,1-1,S	5	-1.1
1905 StL-N	113	415	40	101	11	6	2	36	24	....	13	....	.243	.290	.313	.603	82	-10	44	3.50	-8	2-90/0-9(0-0-9),3-7,S-5	8	-1.8
1906 StL-N	69	256	30	69	7	9	2	26	19	....	5	....	.270	.320	.391	.711	127	7	35	4.75	8	3-65/1-1,0-1	10	1.9
1907 StL-N	11	32	3	6	1	0	0	2	1	....	0	....	.188	.212	.219	.431	36	-2	2	1.52	1	/1-4,3-3	0	-0.2
Total 4	**271**	**985**	**118**	**244**	**26**	**20**	**6**	**99**	**85**	....	**27**	....	**.248**	**.312**	**.333**	**.645**	**92**	**-11**	**117**	**4.02**	**-2**	/2-94,0-82,3-77,1-6,S-6	**23**	**-1.2**
• ARNDT, Larry	Larry Wayne Arndt b: 2/25/1963, Fremont, OH BR/TR, 6'1", 195 lbs. Deb: 6/6/1989																							
1989 Oak-A	2	6	1	1	0	0	0	0	0	1	0	0	.167	.167	.167	.333	-6	-1	0	.98	0	/1-1,3-1	0	-0.1
• ARNOLD, Billy	Willis S. Arnold b: 3/2/1851, Middletown, CT d: 1/17/1899, Albany, NY Deb: 4/26/1872 U																							
1872 Man-n	2	7	2	1	0	0	0	0	0	0	0	0	.143	.143	.143	.286	-13	-1	0	.76	0	/0-2(0-0-2)	....	-0.1
• ARNOLD, Chris	Christopher Paul Arnold b: 11/6/1947, Long Beach, CA BR/TR, 5'10", 160 lbs. Deb: 9/7/1971																							
1971 SF-N	6	13	2	3	0	0	1	3	1	2	0	0	.231	.286	.462	.747	110	0	2	4.83	0	/2-3	1	0.0
1972 SF-N	51	84	8	19	3	1	1	4	8	12	0	1	.226	.293	.321	.615	73	-3	7	2.80	1	3-17/2-7,S-4	1	-0.2
1973 SF-N	49	54	7	16	2	0	1	13	8	11	0	0	.296	.387	.389	.776	111	1	8	5.31	-1	/C-9,2-1,3-1	2	0.0
1974 SF-N	78	174	22	42	7	3	1	26	15	27	1	1	.241	.305	.333	.639	75	-6	19	3.67	-1	2-31/3-7,S-1	3	-0.6
1975 SF-N	29	41	4	8	0	0	0	0	4	8	0	0	.195	.267	.195	.462	28	-4	2	1.36	1	/2-4,0-4(3-0-1)	0	-0.3
1976 SF-N	60	69	4	15	0	1	0	5	6	16	0	0	.217	.280	.246	.526	49	-5	4	1.93	0	/2-8,3-4,1-1,S-1	0	-0.4
Total 6	**273**	**435**	**47**	**103**	**12**	**5**	**4**	**51**	**42**	**76**	**1**	**2**	**.237**	**.305**	**.315**	**.620**	**72**	**-17**	**42**	**3.19**	**0**	/2-54,3-29,C-9,S-6,0-4,1-1	**7**	**-1.5**
• ARNOVICH, Morrie	Morris "Snooker" Arnovich b: 11/16/1910, Superior, WI d: 7/20/1959, Superior, WI BR/TR, 5'10", 168 lbs. Deb: 9/14/1936 Career OF: 526-12-8																							
1936 Phi-N	13	48	4	15	3	0	1	7	1	3	0	....	.313	.353	.438	.790	102	0	7	5.27	2	0-13(13-0-0)	1	0.1
1937 Phi-N	117	410	60	119	27	4	10	60	34	32	5	....	.290	.349	.449	.798	107	3	63	5.54	5	*0-107(97-9-1)	10	0.3
1938 Phi-N	139	502	47	138	29	0	4	72	42	37	2	....	.275	.333	.357	.690	89	-7	60	4.25	10	*0-133(130-1-3)	10	-0.5
1939 Phi-N★	134	491	68	159	25	2	5	67	58	28	7	....	.324	.397	.413	.811	124	18	83	6.41	7	*0-132(131-2-0)	17	1.8
1940 Phi-N	39	141	13	28	2	1	0	12	14	15	0	....	.199	.276	.227	.503	42	-11	9	2.00	2	0-37(36-0-1)	1	-1.1
*Cin-N	62	211	17	60	10	2	0	21	13	10	1	....	.284	.326	.351	.677	86	-4	23	3.78	2	0-60(57-0-3)	5	-0.5
Yr.	101	352	30	88	12	3	0	33	27	25	1	....	.250	.305	.301	.606	68	-15	31	3.02	4	0-97(93-0-4)	6	-1.6
1941 NY-N	85	207	25	58	8	3	2	22	23	14	2	....	.280	.352	.377	.729	103	1	27	4.56	0	0-61(61-0-0)	5	-0.1
1946 NY-N	1	3	0	0	0	0	0	0	0	0	0	....	.000	.000	.000	.000	-99	-1	0	.00	-0	/0-1	0	-0.1
Total 7	**590**	**2013**	**234**	**577**	**104**	**12**	**22**	**261**	**185**	**139**	**17**	....	**.287**	**.350**	**.383**	**.733**	**99**	**0**	**272**	**4.83**	**29**	0-544	**49**	**-0.2**
• ARUNDEL, Tug	John Thomas Arundel b: 6/30/1862, Auburn, NY d: 9/5/1912, Romulus, NY Deb: 5/23/1882 U																							
1882 Phi-a	1	5	0	0	0	0	0	....	0	....	....	....	.000	.000	.000	.000	-90	-1	0	.00	0	/C-1	0	-0.1
1884 Tol-a	15	47	6	4	0	0	0	0	3	....	....	....	.085	.140	.085	.225	-24	-6	1	.37	2	C-15	1	-0.3
1887 Ind-N	43	165	13	39	4	0	0	13	8	12	8	....	.236	.241	.223	.464	31	-14	11	2.23	-3	C-42/0-2(0-0-2),1-1	1	-1.2
1888 Was-N	17	51	2	10	0	1	0	3	5	10	1	....	.196	.268	.235	.503	65	-2	4	2.35	-4	C-17	1	-0.5
Total 4	**76**	**268**	**21**	**53**	**4**	**1**	**0**	**16**	**16**	**22**	**9**	....	**.198**	**.224**	**.196**	**.420**	**26**	**-23**	**15**	**1.83**	**-6**	/C-75,0-2,1-1	**3**	**-2.0**
• ASADOOR, Randy	Randall Carl Asadoor b: 10/20/1962, Fresno, CA BR/TR, 6'1", 185 lbs. Deb: 9/14/1986																							
1986 SD-N	15	55	9	20	5	0	0	7	3	13	1	2	.364	.397	.455	.851	137	2	9	6.56	0	3-15/2-2	2	0.2
• ASBELL, Jim	James Marion "Big Train" Asbell b: 6/22/1914, Dallas, TX d: 7/6/1967, San Mateo, CA BR/TR, 6', 195 lbs. Deb: 5/8/1938																							
1938 Chi-N	17	33	6	6	2	0	0	3	3	9	0	....	.182	.250	.242	.492	35	-3	2	2.25	1	0-10(7-0-3)	0	-0.2
• ASBJORNSON, Casper	Robert Anthony Asbjornson b: 6/19/1909, Concord, MA d: 1/21/1970, Williamsport, PA BR/TR, 6'1", 196 lbs. Deb: 9/17/1928																							
1928 Bos-A	6	16	0	3	1	0	0	1	1	1	0	0	.188	.235	.250	.485	28	-2	1	1.96	0	/C-6	0	-0.2
1929 Bos-A	17	29	1	3	0	0	0	0	1	6	0	0	.103	.133	.103	.237	-39	-6	0	.43	-1	C-15	0	-0.6
1931 Cin-N	45	118	13	36	7	1	0	22	7	23	0	....	.305	.349	.381	.731	102	0	16	5.07	1	C-31	3	0.3
1932 Cin-N	29	58	5	10	2	0	1	4	0	15	0	....	.172	.186	.259	.445	19	-7	3	1.49	-1	C-16	0	-0.7
Total 4	**97**	**221**	**19**	**52**	**10**	**1**	**1**	**27**	**9**	**45**	**0**	**0**	**.235**	**.272**	**.303**	**.575**	**57**	**-14**	**20**	**3.08**	**-1**	/C-68	**3**	**-1.1**
• ASHBURN, Richie	Don Richard "Whitey,Put Put" Ashburn b: 3/19/1927, Tilden, NE d: 9/9/1997, New York, NY BL/TR, 5'10", 170 lbs. Deb: 4/20/1948 HOF: 1995 Career OF: 84-1995-43																							
1948 Phi-N★	117	463	78	154	17	4	2	40	60	22	**32**	....	.333	.410	.400	.810	122	17	82	7.04	5	*0-116(15-102-0)	21	1.8
1949 Phi-N	154	662	84	188	18	11	1	37	58	38	9	....	.284	.343	.349	.692	88	-10	82	4.56	6	*0-154(0-154-0)	19	-0.8
1950*Phi-N	151	594	84	180	25	**14**	2	41	63	32	14	....	.303	.372	.402	.774	105	6	91	5.66	-3	*0-147(0-147-0)	23	-0.1
1951 Phi-N★	154	643	92	**221**	31	5	4	63	50	37	29	6	.344	.393	.426	.819	122	25	118	7.07	16	*0-154(0-154-0)	28	3.7
1952 Phi-N	154	613	93	173	31	6	1	42	75	30	16	11	.282	.362	.357	.720	101	3	86	4.93	9	*0-154(0-154-0)	21	0.8
1953 Phi-N★	156	622	110	**205**	25	9	2	57	61	35	14	6	.330	.394	.408	.802	110	13	109	6.69	10	*0-156(0-156-0)	26	1.5
1954 Phi-N	153	559	111	175	16	8	1	41	**125**	46	11	8	.313	**.442**	.376	.818	116	23	107	7.06	7	*0-153(0-153-0)	26	2.1
1955 Phi-N	140	533	91	180	32	9	3	42	105	36	12	10	**.338**	**.449**	.448	.898	142	38	117	8.55	-4	*0-140(0-140-0)	29	2.7
1956 Phi-N	154	628	94	190	26	8	3	50	79	45	10	1	.303	.385	.384	.769	110	14	101	6.08	10	*0-154(0-154-0)	28	1.7
1957 Phi-N	156	626	93	186	26	8	0	33	**94**	44	13	10	.297	.392	.364	.756	108	11	95	5.52	16	*0-156(0-156-1)	26	2.0
1958 Phi-N★	152	615	98	**215**	24	**13**	2	33	**97**	48	30	12	**.350**	**.441**	.441	.882	136	40	129	8.11	3	*0-152(0-152-0)	28	3.6
1959 Phi-N	153	564	86	150	16	2	1	20	79	42	9	11	.266	.362	.307	.669	79	-15	66	4.01	-8	*0-149(0-149-0)	14	-3.1
1960 Chi-N	151	547	99	159	16	5	0	40	**116**	50	16	4	.291	**.416**	.338	.754	110	19	91	6.07	1	*0-146(45-106-0)	22	1.3
1961 Chi-N	109	307	49	79	7	4	0	19	55	27	7	6	.257	.375	.306	.682	82	-5	39	4.40	0	0-76(14-62-0)	6	-0.8

YEAR TM-L	G	AB	R	H	2B	3B	HR	RBI	BB	SO	SB	CS	AVG	OBP	SLG	OPS	OPS+	BR/A	RC	RC/G	FR	G/POS	WS	TPW
1962 NY-N★	135	389	60	119	7	3	7	28	81	39	12	7	.306	.426	.393	.819	119	16	72	6.89	-1	0-97(10-56-42)/2-2	12	1.1
Total 15	2189	8365	1322	2574	317	109	29	586	1198	571	234	92	.308	.397	.382	.779	111	194	1386	6.14	68	*0-2104/2-2	329	17.5

• ASHBY, Alan Alan Dean Ashby b: 7/8/1951, Long Beach, CA BB/TR, 6'2", 190 lbs. Deb: 7/3/1973 C

YEAR TM-L	G	AB	R	H	2B	3B	HR	RBI	BB	SO	SB	CS	AVG	OBP	SLG	OPS	OPS+	BR/A	RC	RC/G	FR	G/POS	WS	TPW
1973 Cle-A	11	29	4	5	1	0	1	3	2	11	0	0	.172	.226	.310	.536	49	-2	2	2.42	-2	C-11	0	-0.4
1974 Cle-A	10	7	1	1	0	0	0	0	1	2	0	0	.143	.250	.143	.393	15	-1	0	1.42	-1	/C-9	0	-0.2
1975 Cle-A	90	254	32	57	10	1	5	32	30	42	3	2	.224	.309	.331	.639	81	-6	26	3.08	-2	C-87/1-2,3-1,D-1	6	-0.4
1976 Cle-A	89	247	26	59	5	1	4	32	27	49	0	2	.239	.314	.316	.630	86	-5	24	3.22	3	C-86/1-2,3-1	8	0.2
1977 Tor-A	124	396	25	83	16	3	2	29	50	51	0	2	.210	.301	.280	.582	59	-22	34	2.67	0	*C-124	6	-1.6
1978 Tor-A	81	264	27	69	15	0	9	29	28	32	1	1	.261	.334	.420	.755	109	3	35	4.51	-1	C-81	9	0.6
1979 Hou-N	108	336	25	68	15	2	2	35	26	70	0	0	.202	.264	.277	.541	50	-23	24	2.30	-4	*C-105	5	-2.2
1980★Hou-N	116	352	30	90	19	2	3	48	35	40	0	0	.256	.323	.347	.670	94	-3	38	3.67	-4	*C-114	11	-0.1
1981★Hou-N	83	255	20	69	13	0	4	33	35	33	0	2	.271	.359	.369	.727	112	4	34	4.60	1	C-81	11	0.9
1982 Hou-N	100	339	40	87	14	2	12	49	27	53	2	0	.257	.313	.416	.729	111	4	44	4.48	-4	C-95	11	0.5
1983 Hou-N	87	275	31	63	18	1	8	34	31	38	0	0	.229	.307	.389	.696	98	-1	31	3.63	-4	C-85	6	-0.2
1984 Hou-N	66	191	16	50	7	0	4	27	20	22	0	0	.262	.335	.361	.696	103	1	24	4.22	1	C-63	6	0.4
1985 Hou-N	65	189	20	53	8	0	8	25	24	27	0	0	.280	.364	.450	.814	130	8	29	5.40	-1	C-60	8	1.0
1986★Hou-N	120	315	24	81	15	0	7	38	39	56	1	0	.257	.339	.371	.710	99	-0	40	4.39	-5	*C-103	11	-0.1
1987 Hou-N	125	386	53	111	16	0	14	63	50	52	0	1	.288	.371	.438	.809	118	10	61	5.63	-2	*C-110	13	1.3
1988 Hou-N	73	227	19	54	10	0	7	33	29	36	0	0	.238	.324	.374	.699	104	1	28	4.16	-1	C-66	7	0.5
1989 Hou-N	22	61	4	10	1	1	0	3	7	8	0	0	.164	.261	.213	.474	38	-5	4	1.78	-1	C-19	0	-0.5
Total 17	1370	4123	397	1010	183	13	90	513	461	622	7	10	.245	.323	.361	.684	93	-37	478	3.86	-27	*C-1299/1-4,3-2,D-1	118	-0.2

• ASHFORD, Tucker Thomas Steven Ashford b: 12/4/1954, Memphis, TN BR/TR, 6'1", 195 lbs. Deb: 9/21/1976

YEAR TM-L	G	AB	R	H	2B	3B	HR	RBI	BB	SO	SB	CS	AVG	OBP	SLG	OPS	OPS+	BR/A	RC	RC/G	FR	G/POS	WS	TPW
1976 SD-N	4	5	0	3	1	0	0	0	1	0	2	0	.600	.667	.800	1.467	342	2	4	47.70	0	/3-1	1	0.2
1977 SD-N	81	249	25	54	18	0	3	24	21	35	2	3	.217	.280	.325	.606	69	-12	22	2.85	0	3-74,S-10/2-4	3	-1.2
1978 SD-N	75	155	11	38	11	0	3	26	14	31	1	0	.245	.308	.374	.682	97	-1	18	3.92	-4	3-32,2-18,1-14	4	-0.5
1980 Tex-A	15	32	2	4	0	0	0	3	3	3	0	0	.125	.200	.125	.325	-9	-5	1	.76	-1	3-12/S-2	0	-0.6
1981 NY-A	3	0	0	0	0	0	0	0	0	0	0	0	....	....	....	....	-101	0	0	....	-1	/2-2	0	-0.1
1983 NY-N	35	56	3	10	0	1	0	2	7	4	0	0	.179	.270	.214	.484	36	-5	3	1.98	0	3-15,2-13/C-1	1	-0.4
1984 KC-A	9	13	1	2	1	0	0	0	1	2	0	0	.154	.214	.231	.445	23	-1	0	1.05	0	/3-9	0	-0.1
Total 7	222	510	42	111	31	1	6	55	47	75	5	3	.218	.285	.318	.603	71	-22	48	3.09	-6	3-143/2-37,1-14,S-12,C-1	9	-2.8

• ASHLEY, Billy Billy Manual Ashley b: 7/11/1970, Trenton, MI BR/TR, 6'7", 227 lbs. Deb: 9/1/1992 Career OF: 158-0-26

YEAR TM-L	G	AB	R	H	2B	3B	HR	RBI	BB	SO	SB	CS	AVG	OBP	SLG	OPS	OPS+	BR/A	RC	RC/G	FR	G/POS	WS	TPW
1992 LA-N	29	95	6	21	5	0	2	6	5	34	0	0	.221	.260	.337	.597	69	-4	8	2.84	-2	0-27(1-0-26)	1	-0.7
1993 LA-N	14	37	0	9	0	0	0	0	2	11	0	0	.243	.282	.243	.525	45	-3	3	2.59	2	0-11(11-0-0)	0	-0.1
1994 LA-N	2	6	0	2	1	0	0	0	0	2	0	0	.333	.333	.500	.833	121	0	1	6.75	-0	/0-2(2-0-0)	0	0.0
1995★LA-N	81	215	17	51	5	0	8	27	25	88	0	0	.237	.322	.372	.694	90	-3	25	3.87	2	0-69(69-0-0)	3	-0.4
1996★LA-N	71	110	18	22	2	1	9	25	21	44	0	0	.200	.333	.482	.815	121	3	18	5.34	0	0-38(38-0-0)	4	0.2
1997 LA-N	71	131	12	32	7	0	6	19	8	46	0	0	.244	.293	.435	.728	95	-2	17	4.42	0	0-35(35-0-0)	2	-0.3
1998 Bos-A	13	24	3	7	3	0	3	7	2	11	0	0	.292	.346	.792	1.138	180	3	7	10.73	0	/D-5,1-2,0-2(2-0-0)	1	0.2
Total 7	281	618	56	144	23	1	28	84	63	236	0	0	.233	.308	.409	.717	95	-6	78	4.29	1	0-184/D-5,1-2	11	-1.1

• ASMUSSEN, Tom Thomas William Asmussen b: 9/26/1876, Chicago, IL d: 8/21/1963, Arlington Heights, IL TR Deb: 8/10/1907

YEAR TM-L	G	AB	R	H	2B	3B	HR	RBI	BB	SO	SB	CS	AVG	OBP	SLG	OPS	OPS+	BR/A	RC	RC/G	FR	G/POS	WS	TPW
1907 Bos-N	2	5	0	0	0	0	0	0	0	....	0	....	.000	.000	.000	.000	-100	-1	0	.00	0	/C-2	0	-0.1

• ASPROMONTE, Bob Robert Thomas Aspromonte b: 6/19/1938, Brooklyn, NY BR/TR, 6'2", 185 lbs. Deb: 9/19/1956 Career OF: 60-0-2

YEAR TM-L	G	AB	R	H	2B	3B	HR	RBI	BB	SO	SB	CS	AVG	OBP	SLG	OPS	OPS+	BR/A	RC	RC/G	FR	G/POS	WS	TPW
1956 Bro-N	1	1	0	0	0	0	0	0	0	1	0	0	.000	.000	.000	.000	-93	-0	0	.00	0	....	0	0.0
1960 LA-N	21	55	1	10	1	0	1	6	0	6	1	0	.182	.196	.255	.451	21	-6	3	1.55	1	S-15/3-4	0	-0.5
1961 LA-N	47	58	7	14	3	0	0	2	4	12	0	0	.241	.290	.293	.583	51	-4	5	2.73	-1	/3-9,S-4,2-2	0	-0.5
1962 Hou-N	149	534	59	142	18	4	11	59	46	54	4	5	.266	.333	.376	.710	97	-3	67	4.35	-3	*3-142,S-11/2-1	14	-0.6
1963 Hou-N	136	468	42	100	9	5	8	49	40	57	3	1	.214	.277	.306	.583	72	-16	38	2.65	-9	*3-131/1-1	7	-2.7
1964 Hou-N	157	553	51	155	20	3	12	69	35	54	6	7	.280	.332	.392	.725	109	5	69	4.30	-15	*3-155	19	-1.1
1965 Hou-N	152	578	53	152	15	2	5	52	38	54	2	2	.263	.312	.322	.634	85	-12	57	3.39	2	*3-146/1-6,S-4	14	-1.1
1966 Hou-N	152	560	55	141	16	3	8	52	35	63	0	4	.252	.298	.334	.632	81	-16	50	2.99	-4	*3-149/1-2,S-2	8	-2.1
1967 Hou-N	137	486	51	143	24	5	6	58	45	44	2	2	.294	.356	.401	.758	120	13	67	4.93	-5	*3-133	18	0.9
1968 Hou-N	124	409	25	92	9	2	1	46	35	57	1	0	.225	.289	.264	.553	68	-14	30	2.39	1	3-75,0-36(35-0-2)/1-1,S-1	5	-1.8
1969★Atl-N	82	198	16	50	8	1	3	24	13	19	0	1	.253	.305	.348	.654	82	-5	21	3.58	-7	0-24(24-0-0),3-23,S-18/2-2	4	-1.3
1970 Atl-N	62	127	5	27	3	0	0	7	13	13	0	0	.213	.286	.236	.522	39	-11	9	2.22	0	3-30/S-4,1-1,0-1	1	-1.0
1971 NY-N	104	342	21	77	9	1	5	33	29	25	0	2	.225	.286	.301	.587	67	-16	27	2.49	2	3-97	4	-1.5
Total 13	1324	4369	386	1103	135	26	60	457	333	459	19	24	.252	.310	.336	.646	86	-86	441	3.41	-38	*3-1094/0-61,S-59,1-11,2-5	94	-13.4

• ASPROMONTE, Ken Kenneth Joseph Aspromonte b: 9/22/1931, Brooklyn, NY BR/TR, 6', 180 lbs. Deb: 9/2/1957 M

YEAR TM-L	G	AB	R	H	2B	3B	HR	RBI	BB	SO	SB	CS	AVG	OBP	SLG	OPS	OPS+	BR/A	RC	RC/G	FR	G/POS	WS	TPW
1957 Bos-A	24	78	9	21	5	0	0	4	17	10	0	1	.269	.400	.333	.733	97	0	11	4.77	-4	2-24	2	-0.2
1958 Bos-A	6	16	0	2	0	0	0	0	3	1	0	0	.125	.263	.125	.388	10	-2	1	1.05	-1	/2-6	0	-0.3
Was-A	92	253	15	57	9	1	5	27	25	28	1	1	.225	.297	.328	.626	73	-9	23	3.01	-3	2-72,3-11/S-1	4	-0.8
Yr.	98	269	15	59	9	1	5	27	28	29	1	1	.219	.295	.316	.611	69	-11	24	2.88	-5	2-78,3-11/S-1	4	-1.1
1959 Was-A	70	225	31	55	12	0	2	14	26	39	2	1	.244	.323	.324	.647	79	-6	23	3.39	-9	2-52,S-12/1-1,0-1	4	-1.1
1960 Was-A	4	3	0	0	0	0	0	0	0	1	0	0	.000	.000	.000	.000	-99	-1	0	.00	0	....	0	-0.1
Cle-A	117	459	65	133	20	1	10	48	53	32	4	1	.290	.366	.403	.769	111	9	69	5.42	-7	2-80,3-36	16	0.8
Yr.	121	462	65	133	20	1	10	48	53	33	4	1	.288	.364	.400	.764	110	8	69	5.37	-7	2-80,3-36	16	0.7
1961 LA-A	66	238	29	53	10	0	2	14	33	21	0	0	.223	.322	.290	.612	58	-13	24	3.34	11	2-62	4	0.3
Cle-A	22	70	5	16	6	1	0	5	6	3	0	0	.229	.289	.343	.632	70	-3	6	2.97	-2	2-21	1	-0.3
Yr.	88	308	34	69	16	1	2	19	39	24	0	0	.224	.315	.302	.617	61	-16	30	3.25	9	2-83	5	0.0
1962 Cle-A	20	28	4	4	2	0	0	1	6	5	0	0	.143	.294	.214	.508	41	-2	2	2.41	-1	/2-6,3-3	0	-0.2
Mil-N	34	79	11	23	2	0	0	7	6	5	0	1	.291	.349	.316	.665	82	-2	7	3.02	0	2-12/3-6	1	-0.1
1963 Chi-N	20	34	2	5	3	0	0	4	4	4	0	0	.147	.237	.235	.472	35	-3	2	1.66	1	/2-7,1-2	0	-0.2
Total 7	475	1483	171	369	69	3	19	124	179	149	7	5	.249	.332	.338	.670	82	-33	169	3.83	-15	2-342/3-56,S-13,1-3,0-1	32	-2.2

• ASSELSTINE, Brian Brian Hanly Asselstine b: 9/23/1953, Santa Barbara, CA BL/TR, 6'1", 175 lbs. Deb: 9/14/1976 Career OF: 43-63-60

YEAR TM-L	G	AB	R	H	2B	3B	HR	RBI	BB	SO	SB	CS	AVG	OBP	SLG	OPS	OPS+	BR/A	RC	RC/G	FR	G/POS	WS	TPW
1976 Atl-N	11	33	2	7	0	0	1	3	1	2	0	0	.212	.235	.303	.538	49	-2	3	2.42	-1	/0-9(0-7-2)	0	-0.3
1977 Atl-N	83	124	12	26	6	0	4	17	9	10	1	0	.210	.263	.355	.618	57	-8	12	3.10	-2	0-35(9-13-13)	1	-1.0
1978 Atl-N	39	103	11	28	3	3	2	13	11	16	2	1	.272	.353	.417	.771	103	1	16	5.23	-2	0-35(0-11-31)	4	-0.2
1979 Atl-N	8	10	1	1	0	0	0	0	1	2	0	0	.100	.182	.100	.282	-20	-2	0	.25	-0	/0-1	0	-0.2
1980 Atl-N	87	218	18	62	13	1	3	25	11	37	1	3	.284	.322	.394	.716	96	-3	24	3.77	-5	0-61(29-32-2)	4	-1.0
1981 Atl-N	56	86	8	22	5	0	2	10	5	7	1	0	.256	.297	.384	.680	89	-1	9	3.49	0	0-16(4-0-12)	1	-0.2
Total 6	284	574	52	146	27	4	12	68	38	74	5	4	.254	.304	.378	.682	83	-15	63	3.69	-9	0-157	10	-3.0

• ASTROTH, Joe Joseph Henry Astroth b: 9/1/1922, East Alton, IL BR/TR, 5'9", 187 lbs. Deb: 8/13/1945

YEAR TM-L	G	AB	R	H	2B	3B	HR	RBI	BB	SO	SB	CS	AVG	OBP	SLG	OPS	OPS+	BR/A	RC	RC/G	FR	G/POS	WS	TPW
1945 Phi-A	10	17	1	1	0	0	0	1	0	1	0	0	.059	.111	.059	.170	-50	-3	0	.24	-1	/C-8	0	-0.5
1946 Phi-A	4	7	0	1	0	0	0	0	0	2	0	0	.143	.143	.143	.286	-20	-1	0	.00	0	/C-4	0	-0.1
1949 Phi-A	55	148	18	36	4	1	0	12	21	13	1	0	.243	.337	.284	.621	67	-6	15	3.37	0	C-44	4	-0.3
1950 Phi-A	39	110	11	36	3	1	1	18	18	3	0	0	.327	.422	.400	.822	113	3	18	6.09	-1	C-38	4	0.3
1951 Phi-A	64	187	30	46	10	2	2	19	18	13	0	1	.246	.312	.353	.665	78	-6	21	3.85	-1	C-57	4	-0.4
1952 Phi-A	104	337	24	84	7	2	1	36	25	27	2	2	.249	.305	.291	.596	62	-17	27	2.66	-1	*C-102	6	-1.3
1953 Phi-A	82	260	28	77	15	2	3	24	27	12	1	0	.296	.367	.404	.771	104	2	38	5.29	9	C-79	10	1.5
1954 Phi-A	77	226	22	50	8	1	1	23	21	19	0	0	.221	.296	.279	.575	58	-13	20	3.01	3	C-71	4	-0.6
1955 KC-A	101	274	29	69	4	1	5	23	47	33	2	3	.252	.373	.328	.702	89	-3	35	4.09	3	*C-100	9	0.5
1956 KC-A	8	13	0	1	0	0	0	0	0	1	0	0	.077	.077	.077	.154	-59	-3	0	.23	1	/C-8	0	-0.2
Total 10	544	1579	163	401	51	10	13	156	177	124	6	6	.254	.334	.324	.658	77	-46	175	3.73	12	C-511	41	-1.0

YEAR TM-L	G	AB	R	H	2B	3B	HR	RBI	BB	SO	SB	CS	AVG	OBP	SLG	OPS	OPS+	BR/A	RC	RC/G	FR	G/POS	WS	TPW
• ATHERTON, Charlie	Charles Morgan Herbert "Prexy" Atherton b: 11/19/1874, New Brunswick, NJ d: 12/19/1935, Vienna, Austria BR/TR, 5'10", 160 lbs. Deb: 5/30/1899																							
1899 Was-N	65	242	28	60	5	6	0	23	21	....	2	....	.248	.313	.318	.631	74	-9	26	3.69	-8	3-63/0-1	3	-1.4
• ATKINS, Garrett	Garrett Bernard Atkins b: 12/12/1979, Orange, CA BR/TR, 6'2", 210 lbs. Deb: 8/3/2003																							
2003 Col-N	25	69	6	11	2	0	0	4	3	14	0	0	.159	.205	.188	.394	3	-10	3	1.23	-5	3-19	0	-1.5
• ATKINSON, Ed	Edward Atkinson b: 1851, Baltimore, MD Deb: 10/22/1873																							
1873 Was-n	2	8	2	0	0	0	0	0	0	0	0	0	.000	.000	.000	.000	-103	-2	0	.00	0	/0-2(0-0-2)	....	-0.1
• ATKINSON, Lefty	Hubert Burley Atkinson b: 6/4/1904, Chicago, IL d: 2/12/1961, Chicago, IL BL/TL, 5'6.5", 149 lbs. Deb: 8/5/1927																							
1927 Was-A	1	1	1	0	0	0	0	0	0	0	0	0	.000	.000	.000	.000	-101	-0	0	.00	0	....	0	0.0
• ATTREAU, Dick	Richard Gilbert Attreau b: 4/8/1897, Chicago, IL d: 7/5/1964, Chicago, IL BL/TL, 6', 160 lbs. Deb: 9/14/1926																							
1926 Phi-N	17	61	9	14	1	1	0	5	6	5	0	....	.230	.299	.279	.577	53	-4	5	2.79	-3	1-17	0	-0.8
1927 Phi-N	44	83	17	17	1	1	1	11	14	18	1	....	.205	.320	.277	.597	60	-4	8	3.04	-2	1-26	1	-0.8
Total 2	**61**	**144**	**26**	**31**	**2**	**2**	**1**	**16**	**20**	**23**	**1**	**....**	**.215**	**.311**	**.278**	**.589**	**57**	**-8**	**13**	**2.94**	**-5**	**/1-43**	**1**	**-1.5**
• ATWELL, Toby	Maurice Dailey Atwell b: 3/8/1924, Leesburg, VA d: 1/25/2003, Purcellville, VA BL/TR, 5'9.5", 185 lbs. Deb: 4/15/1952																							
1952 Chi-N★	107	362	36	105	16	3	2	31	40	22	2	1	.290	.362	.367	.730	102	2	49	4.91	-5	*C-101	11	0.2
1953 Chi-N	24	74	10	17	2	0	1	8	13	7	0	0	.230	.345	.297	.642	68	-3	9	4.20	-1	C-24	2	-0.2
Pit-N	53	139	11	34	6	0	0	17	20	12	0	0	.245	.352	.288	.640	70	-5	14	3.37	0	C-45	2	-0.3
Yr.	77	213	21	51	8	0	1	25	33	19	0	0	.239	.349	.291	.640	69	-8	23	3.65	-1	C-69	4	-0.6
1954 Pit-N	96	287	36	83	8	4	3	26	43	21	2	3	.289	.387	.376	.764	101	2	42	5.06	5	C-88	11	1.1
1955 Pit-N	71	207	21	44	8	0	1	18	40	16	0	1	.213	.343	.266	.608	65	-9	21	3.25	1	C-67	5	-0.4
1956 Pit-N	12	18	0	2	0	0	0	3	1	5	0	0	.111	.158	.111	.269	-27	-3	0	.20	-0	/C-9	0	-0.3
Mil-N	15	30	2	5	1	0	2	7	4	1	0	0	.167	.265	.400	.665	80	-1	3	3.65	0	C-10	1	0.0
Yr.	27	48	2	7	1	0	2	10	5	6	0	0	.146	.226	.292	.518	41	-4	4	2.16	0	C-19	1	-0.3
Total 5	**378**	**1117**	**116**	**290**	**41**	**7**	**9**	**110**	**161**	**84**	**4**	**5**	**.260**	**.357**	**.333**	**.690**	**86**	**-17**	**139**	**4.24**	**0**	**C-344**	**32**	**0.0**
• ATWOOD, Bill	William Franklin Atwood b: 9/25/1911, Rome, GA d: 9/14/1993, Snyder, TX BR/TR, 5'11.5", 190 lbs. Deb: 4/15/1936																							
1936 Phi-N	71	192	21	58	9	2	2	29	11	15	0	....	.302	.346	.401	.747	92	-2	27	5.03	-3	C-53	3	-0.2
1937 Phi-N	87	279	27	68	15	1	2	32	30	27	3	....	.244	.317	.326	.643	69	-12	32	4.00	-4	C-80	5	-1.1
1938 Phi-N	102	281	27	55	8	1	3	28	25	26	0	....	.196	.261	.263	.525	44	-21	19	2.18	1	C-94	2	-1.5
1939 Phi-N	4	6	0	0	0	0	0	1	2	3	1	....	.000	.250	.000	.250	-29	-1	0	.59	0	/C-2	0	-0.1
1940 Phi-N	78	203	7	39	9	0	0	22	25	18	0	....	.192	.284	.236	.520	47	-14	14	2.29	4	C-69	2	-0.7
Total 5	**342**	**961**	**82**	**220**	**41**	**4**	**7**	**112**	**93**	**89**	**4**	**....**	**.229**	**.299**	**.302**	**.601**	**61**	**-50**	**92**	**3.23**	**-1**	**C-298**	**12**	**-3.5**
• ATZ, Jake	John Jacob Atz b: 7/1/1879, Washington, DC d: 5/22/1945, New Orleans, LA BR/TR, 5'9.5", 150 lbs. Deb: 9/24/1902 Career OF: 0-1-3																							
1902 Was-A	3	10	1	1	0	0	0	0	0	....	0	....	.100	.100	.100	.200	-44	-2	0	.51	1	/2-3	0	-0.1
1907 Chi-A	4	8	0	1	0	0	0	0	0	....	0	....	.125	.125	.125	.250	-21	-1	0	.49	1	/3-2,0-1	0	0.0
1908 Chi-A	83	206	24	40	3	0	0	27	31	....	9	....	.194	.311	.209	.520	71	-4	17	2.55	-7	2-46,S-18/3-1	6	-1.2
1909 Chi-A	119	381	39	90	18	3	0	22	38	....	14	....	.236	.309	.299	.608	96	-1	40	3.39	-8	*2-114/O-3(0-0-3),S-1	13	-0.9
Total 4	**209**	**605**	**64**	**132**	**21**	**3**	**0**	**49**	**69**	**....**	**23**	**....**	**.218**	**.304**	**.263**	**.567**	**83**	**-8**	**58**	**2.99**	**-13**	**2-163/S-19,O-4,3-3**	**19**	**-2.2**
• AUBREY, Harry	Harry Herbert "Chub" Aubrey b: 7/5/1880, St. Joseph, MO d: 9/18/1953, Baltimore, MD BR/TR Deb: 4/22/1903																							
1903 Bos-N	96	325	26	69	8	2	0	27	18	....	7	....	.212	.264	.249	.514	49	-22	25	2.50	-16	S-94/2-1,O-1	1	-3.3
• AUDE, Rich	Richard Thomas Aude b: 7/13/1971, Van Nuys, CA BR/TR, 6'5", 180 lbs. Deb: 9/9/1993																							
1993 Pit-N	13	26	1	3	1	0	0	4	1	7	0	0	.115	.148	.154	.302	-19	-4	1	.74	-1	/1-7,O-1	0	-0.6
1995 Pit-N	42	109	10	27	8	0	2	19	6	20	1	2	.248	.287	.376	.663	72	-6	10	3.10	-4	1-32	1	-1.1
1996 Pit-N	7	16	0	4	0	0	0	1	0	8	0	0	.250	.250	.250	.500	32	-2	1	1.25	0	/1-4	0	-0.2
Total 3	**62**	**151**	**11**	**34**	**9**	**0**	**2**	**24**	**7**	**35**	**1**	**2**	**.225**	**.259**	**.325**	**.584**	**52**	**-12**	**12**	**2.58**	**-4**	**/1-43,O-1**	**1**	**-1.9**
• AUERBACH, Rick	Frederick Steven Auerbach b: 2/15/1950, Woodland Hills, CA BR/TR, 6', 165 lbs. Deb: 4/13/1971																							
1971 Mil-A	79	236	22	48	10	0	1	9	20	40	3	2	.203	.271	.258	.530	51	-15	17	2.38	-2	S-78	3	-1.0
1972 Mil-A	153	554	50	121	16	3	2	30	43	62	24	8	.218	.277	.269	.546	64	-22	42	2.44	-4	*S-153	9	-1.0
1973 Mil-A	6	10	2	1	1	0	0	0	0	1	0	1	.100	.100	.200	.300	-18	-2	0	.00	-1	/S-2	0	-0.3
1974*LA-N	45	73	12	25	0	0	1	4	8	9	4	2	.342	.407	.384	.791	127	3	11	5.28	-3	S-19,2-16/3-3	3	0.2
1975 LA-N	85	170	18	38	9	0	0	12	18	22	3	2	.224	.298	.276	.574	63	-9	13	2.44	-4	S-81/2-1,3-1	2	-0.7
1976 LA-N	36	47	7	6	0	0	0	1	6	6	0	1	.128	.226	.128	.354	2	-6	1	.68	-2	S-12/3-8,2-7	1	-0.7
1977 Cin-N	33	45	5	7	2	0	0	3	4	7	0	0	.156	.224	.200	.424	15	-5	2	1.43	-1	2-19,S-12	1	-0.5
1978 Cin-N	63	55	17	18	6	0	2	5	7	12	1	0	.327	.413	.545	.958	166	5	13	8.73	-3	S-26,2-10/3-3	4	0.4
1979*Cin-N	62	100	17	21	8	1	1	12	14	19	0	1	.210	.307	.340	.647	76	-4	11	3.56	-2	3-18,S-16/2-3	2	-0.4
1980 Cin-N	24	33	5	11	1	1	1	4	3	5	0	3	.333	.389	.515	.904	150	1	5	5.65	0	/3-3,S-3,2-1	1	0.1
1981 Sea-A	38	84	12	13	3	0	1	6	4	15	1	1	.155	.202	.226	.428	22	-9	4	1.38	2	S-38	1	-0.4
Total 11	**624**	**1407**	**167**	**309**	**56**	**5**	**9**	**86**	**127**	**198**	**36**	**21**	**.220**	**.287**	**.286**	**.573**	**65**	**-63**	**119**	**2.73**	**-19**	**S-440/2-57,3-36**	**27**	**-4.2**
• AUGUSTINE, Dave	David Ralph Augustine b: 11/28/1949, Follansbee, WV BR/TR, 6'2", 174 lbs. Deb: 9/3/1973 Career OF: 5-10-5																							
1973 Pit-N	11	7	1	2	1	0	0	0	0	1	0	0	.286	.286	.429	.714	98	-0	0	1.93	0	/O-9(4-4-1)	0	0.0
1974 Pit-N	18	22	3	4	0	0	0	0	0	5	0	1	.182	.182	.182	.364	2	-3	0	.49	1	O-11(1-6-4)	0	-0.2
Total 2	**29**	**29**	**4**	**6**	**1**	**0**	**0**	**0**	**0**	**6**	**0**	**1**	**.207**	**.207**	**.241**	**.448**	**25**	**-3**	**1**	**.82**	**2**	**/O-20**	**0**	**-0.2**
• AULDS, Leslie	Leycester Doyle "Tex" Aulds b: 12/28/1920, Farmerville, LA d: 10/13/1999, Hondo, TX BR/TR, 6'2", 185 lbs. Deb: 5/25/1947																							
1947 Bos-A	3	4	0	1	0	0	0	0	0	1	0	0	.250	.250	.250	.500	36	-0	0	2.31	0	/C-3	0	0.0
• AULT, Doug	Douglas Reagan Ault b: 3/9/1950, Beaumont, TX BR/TL, 6'3", 200 lbs. Deb: 9/9/1976 Career OF: 7-0-1																							
1976 Tex-A	9	20	0	6	1	0	0	0	1	3	0	0	.300	.333	.350	.683	98	-0	2	4.67	-1	/1-4,D-3	0	-0.1
1977 Tor-A	129	445	44	109	22	3	11	64	39	68	4	4	.245	.311	.382	.693	87	-9	48	3.54	8	*1-122/D-4	6	-0.9
1978 Tor-A	54	104	10	25	1	1	3	7	17	14	0	0	.240	.352	.356	.708	98	0	13	3.93	-3	1-25/O-7(6-0-1),D-5	2	-0.5
1980 Tor-A	64	144	12	28	5	1	3	15	14	23	0	1	.194	.275	.306	.581	56	-9	12	2.70	2	1-32,D-21/O-1	0	-0.9
Total 4	**256**	**713**	**66**	**168**	**29**	**5**	**17**	**86**	**71**	**108**	**4**	**5**	**.236**	**.311**	**.362**	**.673**	**83**	**-18**	**75**	**3.45**	**6**	**1-183/D-33,O-8**	**8**	**-2.3**
• AURILIA, Rich	Richard Santo Aurilia b: 9/2/1971, Brooklyn, NY BR/TR, 6', 170 lbs. Deb: 9/6/1995																							
1995 SF-N	9	19	4	9	3	0	2	4	1	2	1	0	.474	.500	.947	1.447	280	5	8	16.84	1	/S-6	2	0.6
1996 SF-N	105	318	27	76	7	1	3	26	25	52	4	1	.239	.297	.296	.592	59	-18	30	3.24	5	S-93,2-11	5	-0.6
1997 SF-N	46	102	16	28	8	0	5	19	8	15	1	1	.275	.327	.500	.827	117	2	16	5.21	2	S-36	5	0.6
1998 SF-N	122	413	54	110	27	2	9	49	31	62	3	3	.266	.321	.407	.727	95	-5	55	4.68	9	*S-120	13	1.3
1999 SF-N	152	558	68	157	23	1	22	80	43	71	2	3	.281	.338	.444	.783	103	-0	80	5.06	8	*S-150	18	1.9
2000*SF-N	141	509	67	138	24	2	20	79	54	90	1	2	.271	.341	.444	.785	104	1	75	5.10	13	*S-140	20	2.4
2001 SF-N★	156	636	114	**206**	37	5	37	97	47	83	1	3	.324	.370	.572	.943	149	42	130	7.74	7	*S-149	33	6.0
2002*SF-N	133	538	76	138	35	2	15	61	37	90	1	2	.257	.309	.413	.722	92	-9	66	4.15	-2	*S-131	14	0.0
2003*SF-N	129	505	65	140	26	1	13	58	36	82	2	2	.277	.327	.410	.736	93	-7	63	4.39	-10	*S-123/D-1	13	-0.7
Total 9	**993**	**3598**	**491**	**1002**	**190**	**14**	**126**	**473**	**282**	**547**	**16**	**17**	**.278**	**.333**	**.444**	**.777**	**105**	**12**	**522**	**5.12**	**32**	**S-948/2-11,D-1**	**123**	**11.4**
• AUSMUS, Brad	Bradley David Ausmus b: 4/14/1969, New Haven, CT BR/TR, 5'11", 195 lbs. Deb: 7/28/1993																							
1993 SD-N	49	160	18	41	8	1	5	12	6	28	2	0	.256	.283	.413	.696	82	-4	19	4.15	2	C-49	3	0.1
1994 SD-N	101	327	45	82	12	1	7	24	30	63	5	1	.251	.316	.358	.673	77	-10	37	3.77	2	C-99/1-1	5	-0.2
1995 SD-N	103	328	44	96	16	4	5	34	31	56	16	5	.293	.357	.412	.769	106	4	50	5.34	3	*C-100/1-1	13	1.4
1996 SD-N	50	149	16	27	4	0	1	13	13	27	1	4	.181	.261	.228	.489	32	-16	8	1.70	-3	C-46	1	-1.5
Det-A	75	226	30	56	12	0	4	22	26	45	3	4	.248	.331	.354	.685	73	-10	27	3.92	1	C-73	7	-0.3
1997*Hou-N	130	425	45	113	25	1	4	44	38	78	14	6	.266	.330	.358	.688	83	-10	51	4.10	2	*C-129	13	0.1

YEAR TM-L	G	AB	R	H	2B	3B	HR	RBI	BB	SO	SB	CS	AVG	OBP	SLG	OPS	OPS+	BR/A	RC	RC/G	FR	G/POS	WS	TPW
1998*Hou-N	128	412	62	111	10	4	6	45	53	60	10	3	.269	.357	.357	.714	91	-3	51	4.25	-1	*C-124	14	0.5
1999 Det-A★	127	458	62	126	25	6	9	54	51	71	12	9	.275	.365	.415	.780	98	-1	70	5.30	-3	*C-127	17	0.4
2000 Det-A	150	523	75	139	25	3	7	51	69	79	11	5	.266	.358	.365	.723	86	-9	69	4.50	10	*C-150/1-1,2-1,3-1	16	1.0
2001*Hou-N	128	422	45	98	23	4	5	34	30	64	4	1	.232	.285	.341	.626	58	-27	39	3.05	8	*C-127	10	-0.9
2002 Hou-N	130	447	57	115	19	3	6	50	38	71	2	3	.257	.324	.353	.677	75	-17	44	3.19	3	*C-129	9	-0.5
2003 Hou-N	143	450	43	103	12	2	4	47	46	66	5	3	.229	.306	.291	.597	54	-30	42	3.10	18	*C-143	12	-0.2
Total 11	1314	4327	542	1107	191	29	63	430	431	708	85	44	.256	.330	.357	.687	79	-133	506	3.94	43	*C-1296/1-3,2-1,3-1	120	-0.3

• AUSTIN, Henry Henry C. Austin b: 1844, Brooklyn, NY d: 9/3/1895, Amityville, NY Deb: 4/28/1873

YEAR TM-L	G	AB	R	H	2B	3B	HR	RBI	BB	SO	SB	CS	AVG	OBP	SLG	OPS	OPS+	BR/A	RC	RC/G	FR	G/POS	WS	TPW
1873 Res-n	23	101	10	25	3	3	0	11	0	4	0	0	.248	.248	.337	.584	78	-2	9	3.46	-1	0-23(0-14-9)	....	-0.2

• AUSTIN, Jimmy James Philip "Pepper" Austin b: 12/8/1879, Swansea, Wales d: 3/6/1965, Laguna Beach, CA BB/TR, 5'7.5", 155 lbs. Deb: 4/19/1909 M/C

YEAR TM-L	G	AB	R	H	2B	3B	HR	RBI	BB	SO	SB	CS	AVG	OBP	SLG	OPS	OPS+	BR/A	RC	RC/G	FR	G/POS	WS	TPW
1909 NY-A	136	437	37	101	11	5	1	39	32	....	30	....	.231	.285	.286	.571	80	-10	45	3.23	7	*3-111,S-23/2-1	13	0.1
1910 NY-A	133	432	46	94	11	4	2	36	47	....	22	....	.218	.305	.275	.580	77	-10	45	3.19	7	*3-133	12	0.1
1911 StL-A	148	541	84	141	25	11	2	45	69	....	26	....	.261	.351	.359	.709	102	3	79	4.75	17	*3-148	17	2.4
1912 StL-A	149	536	57	135	14	8	2	44	38	....	28	....	.252	.306	.319	.625	82	-14	62	3.75	3	*3-149	10	-0.6
1913 StL-A	142	489	56	130	18	6	2	42	45	51	37	....	.266	.338	.339	.677	101	1	66	4.45	7	*3-142	15	1.3
1914 StL-A	130	466	55	111	16	4	0	30	40	59	20	23	.238	.300	.290	.590	80	-18	41	2.75	2	*3-127	10	-1.3
1915 StL-A	141	477	61	127	6	6	1	30	64	60	18	15	.266	.355	.310	.666	103	1	59	3.94	9	*3-141	15	1.5
1916 StL-A	129	411	55	85	15	6	1	28	74	59	19	....	.207	.333	.280	.613	89	-2	47	3.56	-4	*3-124	11	-0.3
1917 StL-A	127	455	61	109	18	8	0	19	50	46	13	....	.240	.319	.314	.633	97	-1	50	3.53	3	*3-121/S-6	14	0.6
1918 StL-A	110	367	42	97	14	4	0	20	53	32	18	....	.264	.359	.324	.683	109	6	49	4.33	-16	S-57,3-48	11	-0.4
1919 StL-A	106	396	54	94	9	9	1	21	42	31	8	....	.237	.314	.313	.627	74	-13	40	3.36	7	3-98	8	-0.4
1920 StL-A	83	280	38	76	11	3	1	32	31	15	2	4	.271	.352	.343	.695	82	-6	35	4.21	3	3-75	5	-0.1
1921 StL-A	27	66	8	18	2	1	0	2	4	7	2	1	.273	.324	.333	.657	64	-3	7	3.71	-1	S-14/2-6,3-2	1	-0.3
1922 StL-A	15	31	6	9	3	1	0	1	3	2	0	0	.290	.353	.452	.805	105	0	5	6.03	-3	/3-9,2-2	1	-0.2
1923 StL-A	1	0	0	0	0	0	0	0	0	0	0	0	....	....	....	....	-95	0	0	....	0	/C-1	0	0.0
1925 StL-A	1	1	0	0	0	0	0	0	0	0	0	0	.000	.000	.000	.000	-95	-0	0	.00	0	/3-1	0	0.0
1926 StL-A	1	2	1	1	1	0	0	1	0	0	1	0	.500	.500	1.000	1.500	272	1	1	31.93	0	/3-1	0	0.1
1929 StL-A	1	1	0	0	0	0	0	0	0	0	0	0	.000	.000	.000	.000	-96	-0	0	.00	0	/3-1	0	0.0
Total 18	1580	5388	661	1328	174	76	13	390	592	363	244	43	.246	.326	.314	.640	90	-67	633	3.76	40	*3-1431,S-100/2-9,C-1	143	2.3

• AUTRY, Chick Martin Gordon Autry b: 3/5/1903, Martindale, TX d: 1/26/1950, Savannah, GA BR/TR, 6', 180 lbs. Deb: 4/20/1924

YEAR TM-L	G	AB	R	H	2B	3B	HR	RBI	BB	SO	SB	CS	AVG	OBP	SLG	OPS	OPS+	BR/A	RC	RC/G	FR	G/POS	WS	TPW
1924 NY-A	2	0	1	0	0	0	0	0	0	0	0	0	....	1.000	....	1.000	172	0	0	∞	-1	/C-2	0	0.0
1926 Cle-A	3	7	1	1	0	0	0	0	1	0	0	0	.143	.250	.143	.393	4	-1	0	1.34	0	/C-3	0	-0.1
1927 Cle-A	16	43	5	11	4	1	0	7	0	6	0	0	.256	.256	.395	.651	66	-2	4	3.22	0	C-14	1	-0.2
1928 Cle-A	22	60	6	18	6	1	1	9	1	7	0	0	.300	.311	.483	.795	105	0	9	5.28	0	C-18	2	0.1
1929 Chi-A	43	96	7	20	6	0	1	12	1	8	0	0	.208	.224	.302	.527	35	-10	6	2.19	-2	C-30	1	-0.9
1930 Chi-A	34	71	1	18	1	1	0	5	4	8	0	0	.254	.293	.296	.589	52	-5	6	3.02	1	C-29	1	-0.3
Total 6	120	277	21	68	17	3	2	33	7	29	0	0	.245	.269	.350	.619	59	-18	26	3.16	-2	/C-96	5	-1.4

• AUTRY, Chick William Askew Autry b: 1/2/1885, Humboldt, TN d: 1/16/1976, Santa Rosa, CA BL/TL, 5'11", 168 lbs. Deb: 9/18/1907 Career OF: 8-4-0

YEAR TM-L	G	AB	R	H	2B	3B	HR	RBI	BB	SO	SB	CS	AVG	OBP	SLG	OPS	OPS+	BR/A	RC	RC/G	FR	G/POS	WS	TPW
1907 Cin-N	7	25	3	5	0	0	0	0	1	....	0	....	.200	.231	.200	.431	34	-2	1	1.62	-1	/0-7(4-3-0)	0	-0.4
1909 Cin-N	9	33	3	6	2	0	0	4	2	....	1	....	.182	.229	.242	.471	46	-2	2	1.86	0	/1-9	0	-0.2
Bos-N	65	199	16	39	4	0	0	13	21	....	5	....	.196	.279	.216	.495	51	-11	15	2.19	1	1-61/0-4(4-1-0)	1	-1.2
Yr.	74	232	19	45	6	0	0	17	23	....	6	....	.194	.272	.220	.492	51	-13	17	2.15	2	1-70/0-4(4-1-0)	1	-1.4
Total 2	81	257	22	50	6	0	0	17	24	....	6	....	.195	.269	.218	.486	49	-15	18	2.10	1	/1-70,0-11	1	-1.8

• AVEN, Bruce David Bruce Aven b: 3/4/1972, Orange, TX BR/TR, 5'9", 180 lbs. Deb: 8/27/1997 Career OF: 124-19-51

YEAR TM-L	G	AB	R	H	2B	3B	HR	RBI	BB	SO	SB	CS	AVG	OBP	SLG	OPS	OPS+	BR/A	RC	RC/G	FR	G/POS	WS	TPW
1997 Cle-A	13	19	4	4	1	0	0	2	1	5	0	1	.211	.250	.263	.513	33	-2	1	1.78	1	0-13(10-1-2)	0	-0.2
1999 Fla-N	137	381	57	110	19	2	12	70	44	82	3	0	.289	.376	.444	.819	112	8	67	6.37	3	*0-102(78-9-24)/D-6	14	0.7
2000 Pit-N	72	148	18	37	11	0	5	25	5	31	2	3	.250	.275	.426	.700	74	-8	15	3.42	-2	0-41(17-8-20)	1	-1.0
LA-N	9	20	2	5	0	0	2	4	3	8	0	0	.250	.348	.550	.898	130	1	4	7.38	0	/0-9(9-0-0)	1	0.0
Yr.	81	168	20	42	11	0	7	29	8	39	2	3	.250	.284	.440	.725	81	-7	19	3.87	-2	0-50(26-8-20)	2	-1.0
2001 LA-N	21	24	3	8	2	0	1	2	0	5	0	0	.333	.385	.542	.926	147	2	5	8.78	0	/0-9(5-0-4)	1	0.1
2002 Cle-A	7	17	1	2	0	0	0	0	4	4	1	0	.118	.286	.118	.403	13	-2	1	1.08	0	/0-7(5-1-1)	0	-0.2
Total 5	259	609	85	166	33	2	20	103	57	135	6	4	.273	.346	.432	.777	100	-1	93	5.39	1	0-181/D-6	17	-0.5

• AVERILL, Earl Howard Earl "Rock" Averill
b: 5/21/1902, Snohomish, WA d: 8/16/1983, Everett, WA BL/TR, 5'9.5", 172 lbs. Deb: 4/16/1929 HOF: 1975 Career OF: 83-1476-31

YEAR TM-L	G	AB	R	H	2B	3B	HR	RBI	BB	SO	SB	CS	AVG	OBP	SLG	OPS	OPS+	BR/A	RC	RC/G	FR	G/POS	WS	TPW
1929 Cle-A	151	597	110	198	43	13	18	96	63	53	13	13	.332	.398	.538	.936	134	28	125	7.74	-6	*0-151(0-151-0)	26	1.5
1930 Cle-A	139	534	102	181	33	8	19	119	56	48	10	7	.339	.404	.537	.941	131	25	116	8.21	0	*0-134(0-132-2)	24	1.8
1931 Cle-A	155	627	140	209	36	10	32	143	68	38	9	9	.333	.404	.576	.979	147	42	144	8.96	-1	*0-155(0-155-0)	30	3.5
1932 Cle-A	153	631	116	198	37	14	32	124	75	40	5	8	.314	.392	.569	.961	137	32	140	8.40	-7	*0-153(0-153-0)	30	1.9
1933 Cle-A★	151	599	83	180	39	16	11	92	54	29	3	1	.301	.363	.474	.837	115	13	104	6.59	1	*0-149(0-149-0)	26	1.0
1934 Cle-A★	154	598	128	187	48	6	31	113	99	44	5	3	.313	.414	.569	.982	149	44	145	9.27	6	*0-154(0-154-0)	33	4.4
1935 Cle-A★	140	563	109	162	34	13	19	79	70	58	8	4	.288	.368	.496	.863	119	15	105	6.78	-3	*0-139(0-139-0)	22	0.8
1936 Cle-A★	152	614	136	**232**	39	**15**	28	126	65	35	3	3	.378	.438	.627	1.065	159	55	168	11.51	-6	*0-150(0-150-0)	27	4.0
1937 Cle-A★	156	609	121	182	33	11	21	92	88	65	5	4	.299	.387	.493	.880	120	18	119	7.25	-8	*0-156(0-156-0)	24	0.6
1938 Cle-A★	134	482	101	159	27	15	14	93	81	48	5	2	.330	.429	.535	.965	143	35	115	9.39	0	*0-131(0-118-13)	26	2.8
1939 Cle-A	24	55	8	15	8	0	1	7	6	12	0	1	.273	.344	.473	.817	111	0	9	5.95	0	0-11(0-0-11)	2	-0.1
Det-A	87	309	58	81	20	6	10	58	43	30	4	2	.262	.354	.463	.817	100	-1	53	5.85	-3	0-80(75-5-0)	9	-0.7
Yr.	111	364	66	96	28	6	11	65	49	42	4	3	.264	.353	.464	.817	101	-0	62	5.86	-3	0-91(75-5-11)	11	-0.7
1940*Det-A	64	118	10	33	4	1	2	20	5	14	0	0	.280	.309	.381	.690	71	-5	14	4.11	1	0-22(7-11-5)	1	-0.5
1941 Bos-N	8	17	2	2	0	0	0	2	1	4	0	....	.118	.211	.118	.328	-6	-2	1	.95	1	/0-4(1-3-0)	0	-0.1
Total 13	1668	6353	1224	2019	401	128	238	1164	774	518	70	57	.318	.395	.534	.928	132	300	1358	8.09	-25	*0-1589	280	20.9

• AVERILL, Earl Earl Douglas Averill b: 9/9/1931, Cleveland, OH BR/TR, 5'10", 190 lbs. Deb: 4/19/1956 Career OF: 72-0-0

YEAR TM-L	G	AB	R	H	2B	3B	HR	RBI	BB	SO	SB	CS	AVG	OBP	SLG	OPS	OPS+	BR/A	RC	RC/G	FR	G/POS	WS	TPW
1956 Cle-A	42	93	12	22	6	0	3	14	14	25	0	1	.237	.343	.398	.740	93	-1	13	4.58	1	C-34	3	0.1
1958 Cle-A	17	55	2	10	1	0	2	7	4	7	1	0	.182	.250	.309	.559	54	-3	4	2.34	-1	3-17	0	-0.4
1959 Chi-N	74	186	22	44	10	0	10	34	15	39	0	1	.237	.300	.452	.752	98	-2	25	4.64	-1	C-32,3-13/0-5(5-0-0),2-2	4	-0.1
1960 Chi-N	52	102	14	24	4	0	1	13	11	16	1	1	.235	.316	.304	.620	71	-4	10	3.12	-1	C-34/3-1,0-1	2	-0.4
Chi-A	10	14	2	3	0	0	0	2	4	2	0	0	.214	.389	.214	.603	68	-0	2	3.86	0	/C-5	1	0.0
1961 LA-A	115	323	56	86	9	0	21	59	62	70	1	0	.266	.388	.489	.877	119	11	64	6.87	-1	C-88/0-9(9-0-0),2-1	13	1.3
1962 LA-A	92	187	21	41	9	0	4	22	43	47	0	0	.219	.368	.332	.700	93	0	26	4.74	0	0-49(49-0-0)/C-6	6	-0.2
1963 Phi-N	47	71	8	19	2	0	3	8	9	14	0	0	.268	.350	.423	.773	123	2	11	4.99	0	C-20/0-8(8-0-0),1-1,3-1	3	0.3
Total 7	449	1031	137	249	41	0	44	159	162	220	3	3	.242	.349	.409	.758	100	3	154	5.06	-4	C-219/0-72,3-32,2-3,1-1	32	0.5

• AVILA, Bobby Roberto Francisco (Gonzales) Avila b: 4/2/1924, Veracruz, Mexico BR/TR, 5'10", 175 lbs. Deb: 4/30/1949

YEAR TM-L	G	AB	R	H	2B	3B	HR	RBI	BB	SO	SB	CS	AVG	OBP	SLG	OPS	OPS+	BR/A	RC	RC/G	FR	G/POS	WS	TPW
1949 Cle-A	31	14	3	3	0	0	0	3	1	3	0	0	.214	.267	.214	.481	29	-1	1	1.50	0	/2-5	0	-0.2
1950 Cle-A	80	201	39	60	10	2	1	21	29	17	5	0	.299	.390	.383	.773	102	3	32	5.52	-4	2-62/S-2	7	0.2
1951 Cle-A	141	542	76	165	21	3	10	58	60	31	14	8	.304	.374	.410	.783	118	14	84	5.48	11	*2-136	24	3.2
1952 Cle-A★	150	597	102	179	26	**11**	7	45	67	36	12	10	.300	.371	.415	.787	127	21	93	5.43	-11	*2-149	24	1.9
1953 Cle-A	141	559	85	160	22	3	8	55	58	27	10	8	.286	.355	.379	.735	101	1	75	4.63	11	*2-140	22	2.3
1954*Cle-A★	143	555	112	189	27	2	15	67	59	31	9	7	**.341**	.405	.477	.882	138	29	109	7.24	32	*2-141/S-7	34	**7.5**
1955 Cle-A★	141	537	83	146	22	4	13	61	82	47	1	4	.272	.370	.400	.771	103	3	81	5.03	5	*2-141	20	1.9
1956 Cle-A	138	513	74	115	14	2	10	54	70	68	17	4	.224	.323	.318	.641	68	-20	57	3.65	17	*2-135	14	0.6
1957 Cle-A	129	463	60	124	19	3	5	48	46	47	2	4	.268	.335	.354	.690	89	-7	55	4.03	0	*2-107,3-16	13	0.1
1958 Cle-A	113	375	54	95	21	3	5	30	55	45	5	7	.253	.350	.365	.716	100	-0	50	4.45	6	2-82,3-33	12	1.1
1959 Bal-A	20	47	1	8	0	0	0	0	4	5	0	0	.170	.235	.170	.406	14	-5	1	.76	0	0-10(1-0-9)/2-8,3-1	0	-0.6

YEAR TM-L	G	AB	R	H	2B	3B	HR	RBI	BB	SO	SB	CS	AVG	OBP	SLG	OPS	OPS+	BR/A	RC	RC/G	FR	G/POS	WS	TPW
Bos-A	22	45	7	11	0	0	3	6	6	11	0	0	.244	.333	.444	.778	107	0	6	4.32	0	2-11	1	0.1
Yr.	42	92	8	19	0	0	3	6	10	16	0	0	.207	.284	.304	.589	60	-5	7	2.39	0	2-19,0-10(1-0-9)/3-1	1	-0.4
Mil-N	51	172	29	41	3	2	3	19	24	31	3	0	.238	.332	.331	.663	84	-2	22	4.17	-6	2-51	4	-0.5
Total 11	1300	4620	725	1296	185	35	80	467	561	399	78	52	.281	.360	.388	.748	105	34	666	4.93	60	*2-1168/3-50,0-10,S-9	175	17.7
• AVILES, Ramon	Ramon Antonio (Miranda) Aviles b: 1/22/1952, Manati, Puerto Rico BR/TR, 5'9", 155 lbs. Deb: 7/10/1977																							
1977 Bos-A	1	0	0	0	0	0	0	0	0	0	0	0	....	....	....	....	-89	0	0	.00	0	/2-1	0	0.0
1979 Phi-N	27	61	7	17	2	0	0	12	8	8	0	0	.279	.371	.311	.683	85	-1	8	4.36	-1	2-27	2	-0.1
1980*Phi-N	51	101	12	28	6	0	2	9	10	9	0	0	.277	.342	.396	.738	100	0	13	4.54	-5	S-29,2-15	3	-0.3
1981*Phi-N	38	28	2	6	1	0	0	3	3	5	0	0	.214	.290	.250	.540	52	-2	2	2.67	-5	2-20,3-13/S-5	0	-0.6
Total 4	117	190	21	51	9	0	2	24	21	22	0	0	.268	.344	.347	.692	87	-2	24	4.15	-11	/2-63,S-34,3-13	5	-1.0
• AYALA, Benny	Benigno (Felix) Ayala b: 2/7/1951, Yauco, Puerto Rico BR/TR, 6'1", 185 lbs. Deb: 8/27/1974 Career OF: 140-2-16																							
1974 NY-N	23	68	9	16	1	0	2	8	7	17	0	0	.235	.316	.338	.654	84	-1	7	3.33	0	0-20(18-0-2)	1	-0.3
1976 NY-N	22	26	2	3	0	0	1	2	2	6	0	1	.115	.179	.231	.409	16	-3	1	1.05	0	/0-7(4-0-3)	0	-0.4
1977 StL-N	1	3	0	1	0	0	0	0	0	1	0	0	.333	.333	.333	.667	81	-0	0	4.50	2	/0-1	0	0.2
1979*Bal-A	42	86	15	22	5	0	6	13	6	9	0	0	.256	.304	.523	.828	123	2	13	5.20	-1	0-24(23-1-1),D-10	3	0.0
1980 Bal-A	76	170	28	45	8	1	10	33	19	21	0	0	.265	.339	.500	.839	128	6	28	5.84	1	D-41,0-19(16-1-2)	6	0.6
1981 Bal-A	44	86	12	24	2	0	3	13	11	9	0	1	.279	.367	.407	.774	123	3	13	5.21	1	D-27/0-4(4-0-0)	3	0.3
1982 Bal-A	64	128	17	39	6	0	6	24	5	14	1	1	.305	.331	.492	.823	123	3	19	5.61	-1	0-25(25-0-0),D-17/1-3	4	0.1
1983*Bal-A	47	104	12	23	7	0	4	13	9	18	0	0	.221	.283	.404	.687	88	-2	12	3.76	-1	0-24(19-0-5),D-11	2	-0.5
1984 Bal-A	60	118	9	25	6	0	4	24	8	24	1	1	.212	.262	.364	.626	73	-5	10	2.75	0	D-34,0-13(11-0-2)	1	-0.6
1985 Cle-A	46	76	10	19	7	0	2	15	4	17	0	0	.250	.288	.421	.709	92	-1	9	3.89	-1	0-20(20-0-0)/D-3	1	-0.3
Total 10	425	865	114	217	42	1	38	145	71	136	2	4	.251	.309	.434	.743	104	1	113	4.43	-1	0-157,D-143/1-3	21	-0.8
• AYLWARD, Dick	Richard John "Dandy" Aylward b: 6/4/1925, Baltimore, MD d: 6/11/1983, Spring Valley, CA BR/TR, 6', 190 lbs. Deb: 5/1/1953																							
1953 Cle-A	4	3	0	0	0	0	0	0	0	1	0	0	.000	.000	.000	.000	-103	-1	0	.00	-1	/C-4	0	-0.1
• AYRAULT, Joe	Joseph Allen Ayrault b: 10/8/1971, Rochester, MI BR/TR, 6'3", 190 lbs. Deb: 9/1/1996																							
1996 Atl-N	7	5	0	1	0	0	0	0	0	1	0	0	.200	.333	.200	.533	43	-0	0	1.13	-1	/C-7	0	-0.1
• AZCUE, Joe	Jose Joaquin (Lopez) "The Immortal Azcue" Azcue b: 8/18/1939, Cienfuegos, Cuba BR/TR, 6', 200 lbs. Deb: 8/3/1960																							
1960 Cin-N	14	31	1	3	0	0	0	3	2	6	0	1	.097	.152	.097	.248	-30	-6	0	.40	0	C-14	1	-0.5
1962 KC-A	72	223	18	51	9	1	2	25	17	27	1	0	.229	.292	.305	.597	59	-13	20	3.06	4	C-70	3	-0.5
1963 KC-A	2	4	0	0	0	0	0	0	0	1	0	0	.000	.000	.000	.000	-96	-1	0	.00	0	/C-1	0	-0.1
Cle-A	94	320	26	91	16	0	14	46	15	46	1	1	.284	.316	.466	.782	117	5	42	4.61	2	C-91	14	1.3
Yr.	96	324	26	91	16	0	14	46	15	47	1	1	.281	.313	.460	.773	114	4	42	4.53	2	C-92	14	1.2
1964 Cle-A	83	271	20	74	9	1	4	34	16	38	0	2	.273	.318	.358	.676	88	-5	30	3.94	-1	C-76	8	-0.3
1965 Cle-A	111	335	16	77	7	0	2	35	27	54	2	1	.230	.293	.269	.562	60	-17	24	2.36	2	*C-108	6	-1.0
1966 Cle-A	98	302	22	83	10	1	9	37	20	22	0	2	.275	.324	.404	.728	108	2	38	4.41	-2	C-97	10	0.4
1967 Cle-A	86	295	33	74	12	5	11	34	22	35	0	3	.251	.309	.437	.747	117	4	37	4.28	2	C-86	13	1.2
1968 Cle-A★	115	357	23	100	10	0	4	42	28	33	1	1	.280	.332	.342	.674	106	2	40	3.95	6	C-97	15	1.5
1969 Cle-A	7	24	1	7	0	0	1	1	4	3	0	0	.292	.393	.417	.810	122	1	4	6.89	2	/C-6	1	0.3
Bos-A	19	51	7	11	2	0	0	3	4	5	0	0	.216	.273	.255	.528	46	-4	3	1.89	1	C-19	0	-0.2
Cal-A	80	248	15	54	6	0	1	19	27	28	0	1	.218	.300	.254	.554	59	-13	17	2.14	6	C-80	5	-0.4
Yr.	106	323	23	72	8	0	2	23	35	36	0	1	.223	.303	.266	.569	62	-16	24	2.39	8	*C-105	6	-0.3
1970 Cal-A	114	351	19	85	13	1	2	25	24	40	0	0	.242	.294	.302	.596	67	-16	30	2.83	-4	*C-112	7	-1.5
1972 Cal-A	3	2	0	0	0	0	0	0	0	1	0	0	.000	.000	.000	.000	-106	-0	0	.00	0	/C-2	0	-0.1
Mil-A	11	14	0	2	0	0	0	0	1	5	0	0	.143	.200	.143	.343	3	-2	0	.90	1	/C-9	0	-0.1
Yr.	14	16	0	2	0	0	0	0	1	6	0	0	.125	.176	.125	.301	-10	-2	0	.77	0	C-11	0	-0.2
Total 11	909	2828	201	712	94	9	50	304	207	344	5	12	.252	.307	.344	.651	85	-62	287	3.43	17	C-868	83	-0.2
• AZOCAR, Oscar	Oscar Gregorio (Azocar) Azocar b: 2/21/1965, Soro, Venezuela BL/TL, 6'1", 170 lbs. Deb: 7/17/1990 Career OF: 90-0-19																							
1990 NY-A	65	214	18	53	8	0	5	19	2	15	7	0	.248	.258	.355	.613	69	-8	20	3.38	0	0-57(47-0-12)/D-1	3	-1.0
1991 SD-N	38	57	5	14	2	0	0	9	1	9	2	0	.246	.271	.281	.552	54	-3	4	2.67	-1	0-13(12-0-1)/1-1	1	-0.5
1992 SD-N	99	168	15	32	6	0	0	8	9	12	1	0	.190	.232	.226	.458	30	-15	9	1.69	-1	0-37(31-0-6)	0	-1.9
Total 3	202	439	38	99	16	0	5	36	12	36	10	0	.226	.249	.296	.546	52	-27	34	2.60	-2	0-107/1-1,D-1	4	-3.4
• BABB, Charlie	Charles Amos Babb b: 2/20/1873, Milwaukie, OR d: 3/20/1954, Portland, OR BB/TR, 5'10.5", 165 lbs. Deb: 4/17/1903																							
1903 NY-N	121	424	68	105	15	8	0	46	45	....	22	....	.248	.350	.321	.671	88	-4	58	4.68	5	*S-113/3-8	16	0.5
1904 Bro-N	151	521	49	138	18	3	0	53	53	....	34	....	.265	.345	.311	.656	106	6	71	4.68	6	*S-151	18	1.8
1905 Bro-N	75	235	27	44	8	2	0	17	27	....	10	....	.187	.303	.238	.541	67	-7	21	2.82	-8	S-36,1-31/3-5,2-2	3	-1.5
Total 3	347	1180	144	287	41	13	0	116	125	....	66	....	.243	.339	.300	.639	91	-5	150	4.28	4	S-300/1-31,3-13,2-2	37	0.8
• BABE, Loren	Loren Rolland "Bee Bee" Babe b: 1/11/1928, Pisgah, IA d: 2/14/1984, Omaha, NE BL/TR, 5'10", 180 lbs. Deb: 8/19/1952 C																							
1952 NY-A	12	21	1	2	1	0	0	0	4	4	1	0	.095	.240	.143	.383	9	-2	1	1.58	1	/3-9	0	-0.2
1953 NY-A	5	18	2	6	1	0	2	6	0	2	0	0	.333	.333	.722	1.056	185	2	4	9.99	2	/3-5	1	0.4
Phi-A	103	343	34	77	16	2	0	20	35	20	0	1	.224	.300	.283	.583	56	-21	30	2.91	5	3-93/S-1	3	-1.6
Yr.	108	361	36	83	17	2	2	26	35	22	0	1	.230	.302	.305	.606	62	-19	34	3.20	7	3-98/S-1	4	-1.2
Total 2	120	382	37	85	18	2	2	26	39	26	1	1	.223	.298	.296	.594	59	-21	36	3.10	8	3-107/S-1	4	-1.4
• BABINGTON, Charlie	Charles Percy Babington b: 5/4/1895, Cranston, RI d: 3/22/1957, Providence, RI BR/TR, 6', 170 lbs. Deb: 7/20/1915																							
1915 NY-N	28	33	5	8	3	1	0	2	0	4	1	....	.242	.265	.394	.659	104	-0	4	3.85	-1	0-12(2-11-1)/1-1	1	-0.1
• BABITT, Shooty	Mack Neal Babitt b: 3/9/1959, Oakland, CA BR/TR, 5'8", 174 lbs. Deb: 4/9/1981																							
1981 Oak-A	54	156	10	40	1	3	0	14	13	13	5	4	.256	.314	.301	.615	82	-4	14	2.85	2	2-52	3	0.0
• BACKMAN, Wally	Walter Wayne Backman b: 9/22/1959, Hillsboro, OR BB/TR, 5'9", 160 lbs. Deb: 9/2/1980																							
1980 NY-N	27	93	12	30	1	1	0	9	11	14	2	3	.323	.400	.355	.755	115	2	13	4.72	-1	2-20/S-8	3	0.2
1981 NY-N	26	36	5	10	2	0	0	0	4	7	1	0	.278	.350	.333	.683	96	0	5	4.69	-1	2-11/3-1	1	0.0
1982 NY-N	96	261	37	71	13	2	3	22	49	47	8	7	.272	.387	.372	.759	114	6	39	5.18	-5	2-88/3-6,S-1	10	0.5
1983 NY-N	26	42	6	7	0	1	0	3	2	8	0	0	.167	.205	.214	.419	16	-5	2	1.11	-1	2-14/3-2	0	-0.6
1984 NY-N	128	436	68	122	19	2	1	26	56	63	32	9	.280	.362	.339	.701	99	5	57	4.49	3	*2-115/S-8	17	1.4
1985 NY-N	145	520	77	142	24	5	1	38	36	72	30	12	.273	.321	.344	.666	88	-8	61	4.00	4	*2-140/S-1	17	0.3
1986*NY-N	124	387	67	124	18	2	1	27	36	32	13	7	.320	.378	.385	.763	114	8	59	5.51	-9	*2-113	16	0.5
1987 NY-N	94	300	43	75	6	1	1	23	25	43	11	3	.250	.308	.287	.594	62	-15	28	3.16	-7	2-87	4	-1.8
1988*NY-N	99	294	44	89	12	0	0	17	41	49	9	5	.303	.390	.344	.733	118	9	42	5.02	4	2-92	12	1.6
1989 Min-A	87	299	33	69	9	2	1	26	32	45	1	1	.231	.307	.284	.592	63	-14	28	3.13	-14	2-84/D-1	4	-2.6
1990*Pit-N	104	315	62	92	21	3	2	28	42	53	6	3	.292	.377	.397	.774	118	9	49	5.71	1	3-71,2-15	12	1.0
1991 Phi-N	94	185	20	45	12	0	0	15	30	30	3	2	.243	.349	.308	.657	87	-2	22	4.03	1	2-36,3-20	5	-0.1
1992 Phi-N	42	48	6	13	1	0	0	6	6	9	1	0	.271	.352	.292	.644	84	-0	5	3.29	0	2-10/3-2	1	0.0
1993 Sea-A	10	29	2	4	0	0	0	0	1	8	0	0	.138	.167	.138	.305	-17	-5	1	.80	-1	/3-9,2-1	0	-0.6
Total 14	1102	3245	482	893	138	19	10	240	371	480	117	52	.275	.350	.339	.689	95	-11	411	4.36	-28	2-826,3-111/S-18,D-1	102	-0.3
• BADER, Art	Arthur Herman Bader b: 9/21/1886, St. Louis, MO d: 4/5/1957, St. Louis, MO BR/TR, 5'10", 160 lbs. Deb: 8/2/1904																							
1904 StL-A	2	3	0	0	0	0	0	0	1	....	0	....	.000	.250	.000	.250	-19	-0	0	.00	1	/0-1	0	0.0
• BADGRO, Red	Morris Hiram Badgro b: 12/1/1902, Orillia, WA d: 7/13/1998, Kent, WA BL/TR, 6', 190 lbs. Deb: 6/20/1929 Career OF: 4-14-80																							
1929 StL-A	54	148	27	42	12	0	1	18	11	15	1	0	.284	.342	.385	.727	83	-3	20	4.75	-2	0-37(0-0-37)	3	-0.8
1930 StL-A	89	234	30	56	18	3	1	27	13	27	3	5	.239	.285	.355	.640	59	-17	23	3.20	1	0-61(4-14-43)	2	-1.8
Total 2	143	382	57	98	30	3	2	45	24	42	4	5	.257	.307	.366	.674	69	-20	43	3.78	-2	/0-98	5	-2.6

YEAR TM-L	G	AB	R	H	2B	3B	HR	RBI	BB	SO	SB	CS	AVG	OBP	SLG	OPS	OPS+	BR/A	RC	RC/G	FR	G/POS	WS	TPW
• BAERGA, Carlos	Carlos Obed (Ortiz) Baerga b: 11/4/1968, Santurce, Puerto Rico BB/TR, 5'11", 200 lbs. Deb: 4/14/1990																							
1990 Cle-A	108	312	46	81	17	2	7	47	16	57	0	2	.260	.304	.394	.698	94	-4	37	4.08	-4	3-50,S-48/2-8	8	-0.7
1991 Cle-A	158	593	80	171	28	2	11	69	48	74	3	2	.288	.348	.398	.746	105	4	82	4.99	4	3-89,2-75/S-2	18	1.1
1992 Cle-A★	161	657	92	205	32	1	20	105	35	76	10	2	.312	.359	.455	.814	129	25	105	5.93	11	*2-160/D-1	28	4.1
1993 Cle-A★	154	624	105	200	28	6	21	114	34	68	15	4	.321	.361	.486	.847	126	22	106	6.18	14	*2-150/D-4	28	4.2
1994 Cle-A	103	442	81	139	32	2	19	80	10	45	8	2	.314	.338	.525	.863	118	10	75	6.21	5	*2-102/D-1	13	1.8
1995*Cle-A★	135	557	87	175	28	2	15	90	35	31	11	2	.314	.358	.452	.810	108	7	88	5.86	8	*2-134/D-1	23	2.0
1996 Cle-A	100	424	54	113	25	0	10	55	16	25	1	1	.267	.304	.396	.700	76	-18	47	3.82	-5	*2-100	6	-1.6
NY-N	26	83	5	16	3	0	2	11	5	2	0	0	.193	.256	.301	.557	48	-6	5	1.60	-2	1-16/3-6,2-1	0	-1.0
1997 NY-N	133	467	53	131	25	1	9	52	20	54	2	6	.281	.314	.396	.710	88	-12	53	3.95	1	*2-131	11	-0.5
1998 NY-N	147	511	46	136	27	1	7	53	24	55	0	1	.266	.307	.364	.671	77	-19	52	3.42	2	*2-144	10	-1.0
1999 SD-N	33	80	6	20	1	0	2	5	6	14	1	0	.250	.318	.338	.656	72	-3	9	3.77	1	2-13,3-13/1-2,D-1	1	-0.2
Cle-A	22	57	4	13	0	0	1	5	4	10	1	1	.228	.279	.281	.559	41	-5	4	2.04	-1	3-15/2-6,D-1	1	-0.6
2002 Bos-A	73	182	17	52	11	0	2	19	7	20	6	0	.286	.319	.379	.698	83	-3	21	4.17	2	D-32,2-17/3-1	2	-0.2
2003 Ari-N	105	207	31	71	13	0	4	39	18	20	1	1	.343	.401	.464	.865	113	5	38	6.92	1	1-19,2-15/D-6,3-5	7	0.4
Total 12	1458	5196	707	1523	270	17	130	744	278	551	59	24	.293	.337	.427	.763	102	1	720	4.94	37	*2-1056,3-179/S-50,D-47,1-37	156	8.0
• BAEZ, Jose	Jose Antonio Baez b: 12/31/1953, San Cristobal, Dominican Republic BR/TR, 5'8", 160 lbs. Deb: 4/6/1977																							
1977 Sea-A	91	305	39	79	14	1	1	17	19	20	6	1	.259	.305	.321	.626	72	-11	30	3.41	8	2-77/D-3,3-1	6	0.1
1978 Sea-A	23	50	8	8	0	1	0	2	6	7	1	0	.160	.250	.200	.450	28	-4	3	1.90	3	2-14/3-3,D-1	1	0.0
Total 2	114	355	47	87	14	2	1	19	25	27	7	1	.245	.297	.304	.601	65	-15	34	3.18	11	/2-91,3-4,D-4	7	0.1
• BAEZ, Kevin	Kevin Richard Baez b: 1/10/1967, Brooklyn, NY BR/TR, 6', 160 lbs. Deb: 9/3/1990																							
1990 NY-N	5	12	0	2	1	0	0	0	0	0	0	0	.167	.167	.250	.417	13	-1	0	.00	0	/S-4	0	-0.1
1992 NY-N	6	13	0	2	0	0	0	0	0	0	0	0	.154	.154	.154	.308	-13	-2	0	.35	-1	/S-5	0	-0.2
1993 NY-N	52	126	10	23	9	0	0	7	13	17	0	0	.183	.259	.254	.513	38	-11	9	2.28	2	S-52	2	-0.6
Total 3	63	151	10	27	10	0	0	7	13	17	0	0	.179	.244	.245	.489	33	-14	9	1.89	2	/S-61	2	-0.9
• BAGWELL, Bill	William Mallory "Big Bill" Bagwell b: 2/24/1896, Choudrant, LA d: 10/5/1976, Choudrant, LA BL/TL, 6'1", 175 lbs. Deb: 4/17/1923 Career OF: 26-0-0																							
1923 Bos-N	56	93	8	27	4	2	2	10	6	12	0	0	.290	.333	.441	.774	107	1	14	5.33	1	0-22(22-0-0)	2	0.0
1925 Phi-A	36	50	4	15	2	1	0	10	2	2	0	0	.300	.327	.380	.707	74	-2	6	4.45	-1	/0-4(4-0-0)	1	-0.3
Total 2	92	143	12	42	6	3	2	20	8	14	0	0	.294	.331	.420	.751	96	-1	20	5.02	0	/0-26	3	-0.2
• BAGWELL, Jeff	Jeffrey Robert Bagwell b: 5/27/1968, Boston, MA BR/TR, 6', 195 lbs. Deb: 4/8/1991																							
1991 Hou-N	156	554	79	163	26	4	15	82	75	116	7	4	.294	.391	.437	.828	141	33	98	6.38	1	*1-155	23	2.4
1992 Hou-N	162	586	87	160	34	6	18	96	84	97	10	6	.273	.375	.444	.819	137	31	98	5.73	11	*1-159	29	3.3
1993 Hou-N	142	535	76	171	37	4	20	88	62	73	13	4	.320	.393	.516	.909	146	37	105	7.17	8	*1-140	22	3.2
1994 Hou-N★	110	400	**104**	147	32	2	39	**116**	65	65	15	4	.368	**.461**	**.750**	**1.211**	**220**	**73**	137	**13.23**	12	*1-109/0-1	**30**	**7.4**
1995 Hou-N	114	448	88	130	29	0	21	87	79	102	12	5	.290	.403	.496	.899	145	33	93	7.46	12	*1-114	20	3.4
1996 Hou-N★	162	568	111	179	**48**	2	31	120	135	114	21	7	.315	.454	.570	1.025	182	78	156	10.08	3	*1-162	**41**	6.5
1997*Hou-N★	162	566	109	162	40	2	43	135	127	122	31	10	.286	.430	.592	1.022	171	67	153	9.58	0	*1-159/D-1	32	5.1
1998*Hou-N	147	540	124	164	33	1	34	111	109	90	19	7	.304	.427	.557	.984	161	54	134	8.99	2	*1-147	29	4.2
1999*Hou-N★	162	562	**143**	171	35	0	42	126	**149**	127	30	11	.304	.458	.591	1.049	165	67	161	10.18	-7	*1-161/D-2	**37**	4.3
2000 Hou-N	159	590	**152**	183	37	1	47	132	107	116	9	6	.310	.428	.615	1.044	151	49	156	9.58	4	*1-158/D-1	25	3.7
2001*Hou-N	161	600	126	173	43	4	39	130	106	135	11	3	.288	.400	.568	.969	139	39	138	8.18	8	*1-160	30	3.2
2002 Hou-N	158	571	94	166	33	2	31	98	101	130	7	3	.291	.406	.518	.925	135	33	124	7.71	3	*1-153/D-4	22	2.3
2003 Hou-N	160	605	109	168	28	2	39	100	88	119	11	4	.278	.375	.524	.899	125	24	115	6.65	-1	*1-158	22	0.9
Total 13	1955	7125	1402	2137	455	30	419	1421	1287	1406	196	74	.300	.415	.549	.964	154	617	1668	8.39	56	*1-1935/D-8,0-1	362	49.7
• BAHRET, Frank	Frank F. Bahret b: 1858, Poughkeepsie, NY d: 3/30/1888, Poughkeepsie, NY, 6'1", 184 lbs. Deb: 4/17/1884																							
1884 Bal-U	2	8	0	0	0	0	0	....	0	....	....	....	.000	.000	.000	.000	-91	-2	0	.00	0	/0-2(0-1-1)	0	-0.1
• BAILEY, Bill	Harry Lewis Bailey b: 11/19/1881, Shawnee, OH d: 10/27/1967, Seattle, WA BL/TR, 5'10.5", 170 lbs. Deb: 4/21/1911																							
1911 NY-A	5	9	1	1	0	0	0	0	0	....	0	....	.111	.111	.111	.222	-36	-2	0	.30	0	/0-2(0-0-0),3-1	0	-0.2
• BAILEY, Bob	Robert Sherwood Bailey b: 10/13/1942, Long Beach, CA BR/TR, 6'1", 188 lbs. Deb: 9/14/1962 Career OF: 399-2-3																							
1962 Pit-N	14	42	6	7	2	1	0	6	6	10	1	1	.167	.271	.262	.533	44	-4	3	2.41	-1	3-12	0	-0.4
1963 Pit-N	154	570	60	130	15	3	12	45	58	98	10	9	.228	.305	.328	.633	82	-14	58	3.36	-8	*3-153/S-3	12	-2.3
1964 Pit-N	143	530	73	149	26	3	11	51	44	78	10	8	.281	.337	.404	.741	108	5	68	4.48	-6	*3-105,0-35(34-2-2)/S-2	15	-0.3
1965 Pit-N	159	626	87	160	28	3	11	49	70	93	10	14	.256	.330	.363	.693	95	-7	72	3.88	-13	*3-142,0-28(28-0-0)	14	-2.2
1966 Pit-N	126	380	51	106	19	3	13	46	47	65	5	3	.279	.361	.447	.809	123	13	60	5.55	-1	3-96,0-20(20-0-0)	14	1.2
1967 LA-N	116	322	21	73	8	2	4	28	40	50	5	5	.227	.314	.301	.615	84	-7	29	2.84	-2	3-65,0-27(27-0-0)/1-4,S-1	6	-1.1
1968 LA-N	105	322	24	73	9	3	8	39	38	69	1	2	.227	.310	.348	.658	105	2	35	3.55	-1	3-90/0-1,S-1	9	0.1
1969 Mon-N	111	358	46	95	16	6	9	53	40	76	3	3	.265	.341	.419	.760	111	5	49	4.67	2	1-85,0-12(12-0-0)/3-1	8	0.0
1970 Mon-N	131	352	77	101	19	3	28	84	72	70	5	3	.287	.409	.597	1.006	166	34	86	8.58	-1	3-48,0-44(44-0-0),1-18	21	3.1
1971 Mon-N	157	545	65	137	21	4	14	83	97	105	13	7	.251	.364	.382	.746	111	12	78	4.70	-3	*3-120,0-51(51-0-1)/1-9	21	0.6
1972 Mon-N	143	489	55	114	10	4	16	57	59	112	6	7	.233	.317	.368	.685	92	-6	56	3.71	-8	*3-134/0-5(5-0-0),1-3	12	-1.6
1973 Mon-N	151	513	77	140	25	4	26	86	88	99	5	8	.273	.380	.489	.870	134	24	90	5.96	-3	*3-146/0-2(2-0-0)	21	2.1
1974 Mon-N	152	507	69	142	20	2	20	73	100	107	4	7	.280	.400	.446	.845	129	22	89	6.00	-6	0-78(78-0-0),3-68	20	1.2
1975 Mon-N	106	227	23	62	5	0	5	30	46	38	4	4	.273	.398	.361	.759	107	4	34	5.06	2	0-61(61-0-0)/3-3	7	0.4
1976 Cin-N	69	124	17	37	6	1	6	23	16	26	0	0	.298	.379	.508	.887	146	8	22	6.25	-1	0-31(31-0-0),3-10	5	0.6
1977 Cin-N	49	79	9	20	2	1	2	11	12	10	1	1	.253	.352	.380	.731	94	-0	11	4.54	0	1-19/0-3(4-0-0)	2	-0.1
Bos-A	2	2	0	0	0	0	0	0	0	1	0	0	.000	.000	.000	.000	-89	-1	0	.00	0	....	0	-0.1
1978 Bos-A	43	94	12	18	3	0	4	9	19	19	2	1	.191	.333	.351	.684	84	-1	12	4.05	0	D-34/3-1,0-1	2	-0.2
Total 17	1931	6082	772	1564	234	43	189	773	852	1126	85	83	.257	.350	.403	.753	110	89	852	4.71	-49	*3-1194,0-399,1-138/D-34,S	189	0.9
• BAILEY, Ed	Lonas Edgar Bailey b: 4/15/1931, Strawberry Plains, TN BL/TR, 6'2", 205 lbs. Deb: 9/26/1953																							
1953 Cin-N	2	8	1	3	1	0	0	1	1	3	0	0	.375	.444	.500	.944	145	1	2	10.46	0	/C-2	0	0.1
1954 Cin-N	73	183	21	36	2	3	9	20	35	34	1	0	.197	.326	.388	.714	83	-4	26	4.54	-2	C-61	5	-0.4
1955 Cin-N	21	39	3	8	1	1	1	4	4	10	0	0	.205	.326	.359	.685	77	-1	4	3.66	0	C-11	1	0.0
1956 Cin-N★	118	383	59	115	8	2	28	75	52	50	2	0	.300	.388	.551	.939	140	23	83	7.94	1	*C-106	23	3.0
1957 Cin-N★	122	391	54	102	15	2	20	48	73	69	5	3	.261	.380	.463	.843	117	12	72	6.33	-5	*C-115	17	1.3
1958 Cin-N	112	360	39	90	23	1	11	59	47	61	2	2	.250	.338	.411	.749	92	-4	51	4.89	0	C-99	11	0.0
1959 Cin-N	121	379	43	100	13	0	12	40	62	53	2	0	.264	.370	.393	.763	100	3	58	5.31	6	*C-117	15	1.5
1960 Cin-N★	133	441	52	115	19	3	13	67	59	70	1	0	.261	.351	.406	.756	104	5	65	5.08	-1	*C-129	14	1.0
1961 Cin-N	12	43	4	13	4	0	0	2	3	5	0	0	.302	.348	.395	.743	95	-0	6	5.48	0	C-12	2	0.0
SF-N★	107	340	39	81	9	1	13	51	42	41	1	5	.238	.329	.385	.714	92	-5	42	4.09	-1	*C-103/0-1	11	-0.1
Yr.	119	383	43	94	13	1	13	53	45	46	1	5	.245	.331	.386	.717	92	-5	48	4.22	-1	*C-115/0-1	13	-0.1
1962*SF-N	96	254	32	59	9	1	17	45	42	42	1	1	.232	.354	.476	.831	123	9	44	5.80	-4	C-75	12	0.8
1963 SF-N★	105	308	41	81	8	0	21	68	50	64	0	6	.263	.368	.494	.861	147	18	54	6.09	-2	C-88	17	2.2
1964 Mil-N	95	271	30	71	10	1	5	34	34	39	2	0	.262	.346	.362	.708	99	1	35	4.50	-7	C-80	10	-0.2
1965 SF-N	24	28	1	3	0	0	0	3	6	7	0	0	.107	.265	.107	.372	9	-3	1	.83	1	C-12/1-2	1	-0.2
Chi-N	66	150	13	38	6	0	5	23	34	28	0	1	.253	.391	.393	.785	119	5	23	4.98	-1	C-54/1-3	6	0.7
Yr.	90	178	14	41	6	0	5	26	40	35	0	1	.230	.372	.348	.720	101	2	24	4.15	0	C-66/1-5	7	0.5
1966 Cal-A	5	3	0	0	0	0	0	0	1	1	0	0	.000	.250	.000	.250	-22	-0	0	.59	0	....	0	0.0
Total 14	1212	3581	432	915	128	15	155	540	545	577	17	18	.256	.358	.429	.787	110	58	566	5.42	-15	*C-1064/1-5,0-1	145	9.7
• BAILEY, Fred	Frederick Middleton "Penny" Bailey b: 8/16/1895, Mount Hope, WV d: 8/16/1972, Huntington, WV BL/TL, 5'11", 150 lbs. Deb: 8/19/1916 Career OF: 10-15-4																							
1916 Bos-N	6	10	0	1	0	0	0	1	0	3	0	....	.100	.100	.100	.200	-41	-2	0	.29	0	/0-2(1-0-0)	0	-0.2

YEAR TM-L	G	AB	R	H	2B	3B	HR	RBI	BB	SO	SB	CS	AVG	OBP	SLG	OPS	OPS+	BR/A	RC	RC/G	FR	G/POS	WS	TPW
1917 Bos-N	50	110	9	21	2	1	1	5	9	25	3	....	.191	.270	.255	.525	65	-4	8	2.29	0	0-27(9-15-4)	1	-0.7
1918 Bos-N	4	4	1	1	0	0	0	0	0	1	0	....	.250	.250	.250	.500	55	-0	0	1.99	0	....	0	0.0
Total 3	60	124	10	23	2	1	1	6	9	29	3	....	.185	.257	.242	.499	57	-6	8	2.11	-1	/0-29	1	-0.9
• BAILEY, Gene	Arthur Eugene Bailey b: 11/25/1893, Pearsall, TX d: 11/14/1973, Houston, TX BR/TR, 5'8", 160 lbs. Deb: 9/10/1917 Career OF: 43-91-42																							
1917 Phi-A	5	12	1	1	0	0	0	0	1	1	0	....	.083	.154	.083	.237	-28	-2	0	.50	-1	/0-4(4-0-0)	0	-0.3
1919 Bos-N	4	6	0	2	0	0	0	1	0	2	1	....	.333	.333	.333	.667	105	0	1	5.80	0	/0-3(0-1-1)	0	0.0
1920 Bos-N	13	24	2	2	0	0	0	0	3	3	0	1	.083	.185	.083	.269	-22	-4	1	.53	-0	/0-8(5-4-1)	0	-0.5
Bos-A	46	135	14	31	2	0	0	5	9	15	2	7	.230	.283	.244	.527	42	-13	9	1.95	-2	0-40(9-16-15)	1	-1.6
1923 Bro-N	127	411	71	109	11	7	1	42	43	34	9	7	.265	.343	.333	.677	81	-9	49	4.08	2	*0-100(25-60-17)/1-5	9	-1.3
1924 Bro-N	18	46	7	11	3	0	1	4	7	6	1	0	.239	.340	.370	.709	93	0	6	4.40	0	0-17(0-10-8)	1	-0.1
Total 5	213	634	95	156	16	7	2	52	63	61	13	15	.246	.321	.303	.624	68	-28	66	3.38	0	0-172/1-5	11	-3.8
• BAILEY, Mark	John Mark Bailey b: 11/4/1961, Springfield, MO BB/TR, 6'5", 195 lbs. Deb: 4/27/1984 C																							
1984 Hou-N	108	344	38	73	16	1	9	34	53	71	0	1	.212	.321	.343	.664	93	-3	40	3.79	-4	*C-108	9	-0.1
1985 Hou-N	114	332	47	88	14	0	10	45	67	70	0	2	.265	.390	.398	.788	124	13	51	5.17	-2	*C-110/1-2	14	1.7
1986 Hou-N	57	153	9	27	5	0	4	15	28	45	1	1	.176	.304	.288	.591	66	-7	13	2.62	1	C-53/1-1	3	-0.4
1987 Hou-N	35	64	5	13	1	0	0	3	10	21	1	0	.203	.311	.219	.530	45	-5	5	2.31	-1	C-27	0	-0.5
1988 Hou-N	8	23	1	3	0	0	0	0	5	6	0	1	.130	.286	.130	.416	24	-2	1	1.13	0	/C-8	0	-0.3
1990 SF-N	5	7	1	1	0	0	1	3	0	2	0	0	.143	.143	.571	.714	90	-0	1	2.57	0	/C-1	1	0.0
1992 SF-N	13	26	0	4	1	0	0	1	3	7	0	0	.154	.241	.192	.434	26	-3	1	1.71	0	/C-7	0	-0.3
Total 7	340	949	101	209	37	1	24	101	166	222	2	5	.220	.338	.337	.675	93	-6	111	3.81	-7	C-314/1-3	27	0.1
• BAILOR, Bob	Robert Michael Bailor b: 7/10/1951, Connellsville, PA BR/TR, 5'11", 170 lbs. Deb: 9/6/1975 C Career OF: 79-105-254																							
1975 Bal-A	5	7	0	1	0	0	0	0	1	0	0	0	.143	.250	.143	.393	14	-1	0	1.42	1	/S-2,2-1	0	0.0
1976 Bal-A	9	6	2	2	0	1	0	0	0	0	0	1	.333	.333	.667	1.000	200	0	1	2.91	-1	/D-1,S-1	0	0.0
1977 Tor-A	122	496	62	154	21	5	5	32	17	26	15	6	.310	.336	.403	.739	99	-0	66	4.93	-3	0-63(15-47-2),S-53/D-7	12	0.0
1978 Tor-A	154	621	74	164	29	7	1	52	38	21	5	6	.264	.312	.338	.650	81	-17	66	3.67	8	*0-125(3-25-102),3-28/S-4	12	-1.5
1979 Tor-A	130	414	50	95	11	5	1	38	36	27	14	8	.229	.300	.287	.588	59	-24	37	2.95	2	*0-118(4-4-113)/3-9,D-1	4	-2.6
1980 Tor-A	117	347	44	82	14	2	1	16	36	33	12	8	.236	.312	.297	.609	65	-17	33	3.18	8	0-98(41-28-33),S-12,3-11/P,2,D	6	-1.2
1981 NY-N	51	81	11	23	3	1	0	8	8	11	2	0	.284	.356	.346	.701	101	1	10	4.24	-1	S-22,2-13,0-13(10-0-3)/3-1	2	0.1
1982 NY-N	110	376	44	104	14	1	0	31	20	17	20	3	.277	.317	.319	.636	79	-8	41	3.84	5	S-60,2-56,3-21/0-4(3-1-0)	10	0.3
1983 NY-N	118	340	33	85	8	0	1	30	20	23	18	3	.250	.294	.282	.576	61	-15	28	2.79	6	S-75,2-50,3-11/0-3(2-0-1)	6	-0.2
1984 LA-N	65	131	11	36	4	0	0	8	8	1	3	1	.275	.317	.305	.622	76	-4	13	3.35	0	2-23,3-17,S-16	3	-0.2
1985*LA-N	74	118	8	29	3	1	0	7	3	5	1	0	.246	.270	.288	.559	58	-7	9	2.47	6	3-45,2-16/S-5,0-1	2	0.0
Total 11	955	2937	339	775	107	23	9	222	187	164	90	36	.264	.312	.325	.638	76	-91	305	3.56	31	0-425,S-250,2-160,3-143/D,P	57	-5.4
• BAINES, Harold	Harold Douglas Baines b: 3/15/1959, Easton, MD BL/TL, 6'2", 195 lbs. Deb: 4/10/1980 Career OF: 9-30-1039																							
1980 Chi-A	141	491	55	125	23	6	13	49	19	65	2	4	.255	.284	.405	.689	87	-12	50	3.47	-5	*0-137(0-0-137)/D-1	8	-2.4
1981 Chi-A	82	280	42	80	11	7	10	41	12	41	6	2	.286	.320	.482	.802	131	10	41	5.30	1	0-80(0-0-80)/D-1	10	0.7
1982 Chi-A	161	608	89	165	29	8	25	105	49	95	10	3	.271	.326	.469	.794	115	12	91	5.25	-1	*0-161(1-3-160)	19	0.2
1983*Chi-A	156	596	76	167	33	2	20	99	49	85	7	5	.280	.336	.443	.779	108	5	85	5.00	-1	*0-155(1-20-142)	20	-0.3
1984 Chi-A	147	569	72	173	28	10	29	94	54	75	1	2	.304	.364	**.541**	.906	141	30	109	7.11	1	*0-147(0-7-147)	24	2.3
1985 Chi-A★	160	640	86	198	29	3	22	113	42	89	1	1	.309	.353	.467	.820	118	14	98	5.57	2	*0-159(0-0-159)/D-1	25	0.9
1986 Chi-A★	145	570	72	169	29	2	21	88	38	89	2	1	.296	.343	.465	.808	114	10	87	5.56	9	*0-141(0-0-141)/D-3	20	1.1
1987 Chi-A★	132	505	59	148	26	4	20	93	46	82	0	0	.293	.353	.479	.832	115	10	84	6.12	0	*D-117/0-8(0-0-8)	13	0.5
1988 Chi-A	158	599	55	166	39	1	13	81	67	109	0	0	.277	.351	.411	.762	113	11	83	4.88	0	*D-147/0-9(0-0-10)	18	0.5
1989 Chi-A★	96	333	55	107	20	1	13	56	60	52	0	1	.321	.426	.505	.931	165	31	72	8.01	-1	D-70,0-25(0-0-24)	16	2.8
Tex-A	50	172	18	49	9	0	3	16	13	27	0	2	.285	.335	.390	.725	102	-1	21	4.43	0	D-46/0-1	2	-0.3
Yr.	146	505	73	156	29	1	16	72	73	79	0	3	.309	.397	.465	.863	145	31	93	6.76	-1	*D-116,0-26(0-0-25)	18	2.5
1990 Tex-A	103	321	41	93	10	1	13	44	47	63	0	1	.290	.380	.449	.829	131	14	53	5.82	0	D-95/0-2(0-0-2)	8	1.1
*Oak-A	32	94	11	25	5	0	3	21	20	17	0	2	.266	.395	.415	.810	132	4	15	5.20	0	D-30	3	0.3
Yr.	135	415	52	118	15	1	16	65	67	80	0	3	.284	.384	.441	.825	131	18	68	5.67	0	*D-125/0-2(0-0-2)	11	1.4
1991 Oak-A★	141	488	76	144	25	1	20	90	72	67	0	1	.295	.387	.473	.860	145	31	89	6.64	0	*D-125,0-12(1-0-10)	22	2.6
1992*Oak-A	140	478	58	121	18	0	16	76	59	61	1	3	.253	.335	.391	.726	109	5	62	4.48	-1	*D-116,0-23(6-0-17)	15	-0.1
1993 Bal-A	118	416	64	130	22	0	20	78	57	52	0	0	.313	.395	.510	.905	136	22	82	7.23	0	*D-116	15	1.4
1994 Bal-A	94	326	44	96	12	1	16	54	30	49	0	0	.294	.356	.485	.840	108	4	54	6.14	0	D-91	6	-0.2
1995 Bal-A	127	385	60	115	19	1	24	63	70	45	0	2	.299	.407	.540	.947	141	24	81	7.50	0	*D-122	11	1.7
1996 Chi-A	143	495	80	154	29	0	22	95	73	62	3	1	.311	.401	.503	.904	133	27	98	7.22	0	*D-141	13	1.6
1997 Chi-A	93	318	40	97	18	0	12	52	41	47	0	1	.305	.384	.475	.859	128	13	57	6.58	0	D-86	10	0.8
*Bal-A	44	134	15	39	5	0	4	15	14	15	0	0	.291	.358	.418	.776	105	1	20	5.48	0	D-35/0-1	2	-0.1
Yr.	137	452	55	136	23	0	16	67	55	62	0	1	.301	.377	.458	.835	121	14	77	6.25	0	*D-121/0-1	12	0.7
1998 Bal-A	104	293	40	88	17	0	9	57	32	40	0	0	.300	.371	.451	.822	114	7	45	5.37	0	D-80	8	0.2
1999 Bal-A★	107	345	57	111	16	1	24	81	43	38	1	2	.322	.397	.583	.980	151	26	75	8.07	0	D-96	13	1.9
*Cle-A	28	85	5	23	2	0	1	22	11	10	0	0	.271	.354	.329	.684	73	-3	10	4.34	0	D-25	2	-0.4
Yr.	135	430	62	134	18	1	25	103	54	48	1	2	.312	.388	.533	.921	136	23	86	7.32	0	*D-121	15	1.5
2000 Bal-A	72	222	24	59	8	0	10	30	29	39	0	0	.266	.351	.437	.788	103	1	34	5.35	0	D-62	3	-0.2
*Chi-A	24	61	2	13	5	0	1	9	7	11	0	0	.213	.294	.344	.638	60	-4	7	3.73	0	D-16	1	-0.4
Yr.	96	283	26	72	13	0	11	39	36	50	0	0	.254	.339	.417	.756	94	-3	40	4.99	0	D-78	4	-0.6
2001 Chi-A	32	84	3	11	1	0	0	6	8	16	0	0	.131	.207	.143	.349	-5	-13	3	.96	0	D-22	0	-1.3
Total 22	2830	9908	1299	2866	488	49	384	1628	1062	1441	34	34	.289	.359	.465	.824	121	280	1608	5.80	3	*D-1644,0-1061	307	15.1
• BAIRD, Al	Albert Wells Baird b: 6/2/1895, Cleburne, TX d: 11/27/1976, Shreveport, LA BR/TR, 5'9", 160 lbs. Deb: 9/10/1917																							
1917 NY-N	10	24	1	7	0	0	0	4	2	2	2	....	.292	.346	.292	.638	100	0	3	4.36	-1	/2-7,S-3	1	0.0
1919 NY-N	38	83	8	20	1	0	0	5	5	9	3	....	.241	.284	.253	.537	63	-4	6	2.60	2	2-24/S-9,3-5	2	-0.2
Total 2	48	107	9	27	1	0	0	9	7	11	5	....	.252	.298	.262	.560	71	-4	9	2.97	1	/2-31,S-12,3-5	3	-0.2
• BAIRD, Doug	Howard Douglas Baird b: 9/27/1891, St. Charles, MO d: 6/13/1967, Thomasville, GA BR/TR, 5'9.5", 148 lbs. Deb: 4/18/1915 Career OF: 10-27-3																							
1915 Pit-N	145	512	49	112	26	12	1	53	37	88	29	12	.219	.277	.322	.599	82	-11	51	3.12	0	*3-120,0-20(0-20-0)/2-3	11	-0.9
1916 Pit-N	128	430	41	93	10	7	1	28	24	49	20	16	.216	.263	.279	.542	66	-21	32	2.31	-5	3-80,2-29,0-16(10-5-1)	4	-2.7
1917 Pit-N	43	135	17	35	6	1	0	18	20	19	8	....	.259	.355	.319	.673	104	2	18	4.37	-1	3-41/2-2	4	0.2
StL-N	104	364	38	92	19	12	0	24	23	52	18	....	.253	.301	.371	.672	108	3	45	4.00	8	*3-103/0-2(0-2-0)	14	1.5
Yr.	147	499	55	127	25	13	0	42	43	71	26	....	.255	.316	.357	.673	107	4	62	4.10	6	*3-144/2-2,0-2(0-2-0)	18	1.7
1918 StL-N	82	316	41	78	12	8	2	25	25	42	25	....	.247	.304	.354	.659	104	1	40	4.12	10	3-81/0-1,S-1	9	1.5
1919 StL-N	16	33	4	7	0	1	0	4	2	3	2	....	.212	.257	.273	.530	63	-2	3	2.60	-3	/3-8,2-1,0-1	0	-0.5
Phi-N	66	242	33	61	13	3	2	30	22	28	13	....	.252	.317	.355	.672	95	-1	30	4.15	6	3-66	7	0.8
Bro-N	20	60	6	11	0	1	0	8	1	10	3	....	.183	.197	.217	.413	24	-6	3	1.59	1	3-17	1	-0.5
Yr.	102	335	43	79	13	5	2	42	25	41	18	....	.236	.291	.322	.613	79	-8	36	3.46	3	3-91/2-1,0-1	8	-0.2
1920 Bro-N	6	6	1	2	0	0	0	1	2	1	0	0	.333	.556	.333	.889	154	1	2	8.37	-1	/3-2	1	0.0
NY-N	7	8	0	1	0	0	0	0	1	3	0	0	.125	.222	.125	.347	1	-1	0	1.02	0	/3-4	0	-0.1
Yr.	13	14	1	3	0	0	0	1	3	4	0	0	.214	.389	.214	.603	82	-0	2	4.08	-1	/3-6	1	0.0
Total 6	617	2106	230	492	86	45	6	191	157	295	118	28	.234	.291	.326	.616	88	-35	223	3.38	15	3-522/0-40,2-35,S-1	51	-0.7
• BAKER, Bill	William Presley Baker b: 2/22/1911, Paw Creek, NC BR/TR, 6', 200 lbs. Deb: 5/4/1940 C/U																							
1940*Cin-N	27	69	5	15	1	1	0	7	4	8	2	....	.217	.260	.261	.521	44	-5	4	1.82	-2	C-24	1	-0.6
1941 Cin-N	2	1	0	0	0	0	0	0	1	1	0	....	.000	.500	.000	.500	49	0	0	3.51	0	/C-1	0	0.0
Pit-N	35	67	5	15	3	0	0	6	11	0	0	....	.224	.333	.269	.602	71	-2	7	3.17	-1	C-33	2	-0.1
Yr.	37	68	5	15	3	0	0	6	12	1	0	....	.221	.338	.265	.602	71	-2	7	3.17	-1	C-34	2	-0.1
1942 Pit-N	18	17	1	2	0	0	0	2	1	0	0	....	.118	.167	.118	.284	-16	-2	0	.68	-0	C-11	0	-0.2
1943 Pit-N	63	172	12	47	6	3	1	26	22	6	3	....	.273	.365	.360	.726	106	2	23	4.71	1	C-56	7	0.7

YEAR TM-L	G	AB	R	H	2B	3B	HR	RBI	BB	SO	SB	CS	AVG	OBP	SLG	OPS	OPS+	BR/A	RC	RC/G	FR	G/POS	WS	TPW
1946 Pit-N	53	113	7	27	4	0	1	8	12	6	0	....	.239	.312	.301	.613	72	-4	11	3.21	-1	C-41/1-1	2	-0.3
1948 StL-N	45	119	13	35	10	1	0	15	15	7	1	....	.294	.373	.395	.768	102	1	17	5.36	0	C-36	5	0.3
1949 StL-N	20	30	2	4	1	0	0	4	2	2	0	....	.133	.188	.167	.354	-4	-4	1	1.07	-0	C-10	0	-0.4
Total 7	**263**	**588**	**45**	**145**	**25**	**5**	**2**	**68**	**68**	**30**	**6**	**....**	**.247**	**.328**	**.316**	**.644**	**79**	**-15**	**63**	**3.66**	**-1**	**C-212/1-1**	**17**	**-0.8**

• BAKER, Charlie Charles A. Baker b: 1/15/1856, West Boylston, MA d: 1/15/1937, Manchester, NH BR, 5'4", 140 lbs. Deb: 8/1/1884

YEAR TM-L	G	AB	R	H	2B	3B	HR	RBI	BB	SO	SB	CS	AVG	OBP	SLG	OPS	OPS+	BR/A	RC	RC/G	FR	G/POS	WS	TPW
1884 CP-U	15	57	5	8	2	0	1	....	0	....	....	....	.140	.140	.228	.368	24	-4	2	1.07	0	0-11(0-0-11)/S-3,2-1	0	-0.4

• BAKER, Chuck Charles Joseph Baker b: 12/6/1952, Seattle, WA BR/TR, 5'11", 180 lbs. Deb: 4/7/1978

YEAR TM-L	G	AB	R	H	2B	3B	HR	RBI	BB	SO	SB	CS	AVG	OBP	SLG	OPS	OPS+	BR/A	RC	RC/G	FR	G/POS	WS	TPW
1978 SD-N	44	58	8	12	1	0	0	3	2	15	0	0	.207	.233	.224	.457	31	-5	3	1.67	-0	2-24,S-12	1	-0.4
1980 SD-N	9	22	0	3	1	0	0	0	0	4	0	0	.136	.136	.182	.318	-13	-3	1	.78	2	/S-8	0	-0.1
1981 Min-A	40	66	6	12	0	3	0	6	1	8	0	0	.182	.194	.273	.467	31	-6	3	1.27	-4	S-31/2-3,3-1,D-1	1	-0.8
Total 3	**93**	**146**	**14**	**27**	**2**	**3**	**0**	**9**	**3**	**27**	**0**	**0**	**.185**	**.201**	**.240**	**.441**	**25**	**-15**	**7**	**1.36**	**-2**	**/S-51,2-27,3-1,D-1**	**2**	**-1.4**

• BAKER, Dave David Glenn Baker b: 11/25/1956, Lacona, IA BL/TR, 6', 185 lbs. Deb: 9/12/1982

YEAR TM-L	G	AB	R	H	2B	3B	HR	RBI	BB	SO	SB	CS	AVG	OBP	SLG	OPS	OPS+	BR/A	RC	RC/G	FR	G/POS	WS	TPW
1982 Tor-A	9	20	3	5	1	0	0	2	3	3	0	0	.250	.400	.300	.700	88	0	3	5.08	-2	/3-8	1	-0.2

• BAKER, Del Delmer David Baker b: 5/3/1892, Sherwood, OR d: 9/11/1973, San Antonio, TX BR/TR, 5'11.5", 176 lbs. Deb: 4/16/1914 M/C

YEAR TM-L	G	AB	R	H	2B	3B	HR	RBI	BB	SO	SB	CS	AVG	OBP	SLG	OPS	OPS+	BR/A	RC	RC/G	FR	G/POS	WS	TPW
1914 Det-A	44	70	4	15	2	1	0	1	6	9	0	2	.214	.276	.271	.548	63	-4	5	2.26	-4	C-38	1	-0.7
1915 Det-A	68	134	16	33	3	3	0	15	15	15	3	1	.246	.327	.313	.640	87	-2	16	3.77	-6	C-61	4	-0.5
1916 Det-A	61	98	7	15	4	0	0	6	11	8	2	....	.153	.245	.194	.439	31	-8	6	1.73	-6	C-59	1	-1.3
Total 3	**173**	**302**	**27**	**63**	**9**	**4**	**0**	**22**	**32**	**32**	**5**	**3**	**.209**	**.289**	**.265**	**.554**	**64**	**-14**	**27**	**2.74**	**-16**	**C-158**	**6**	**-2.4**

• BAKER, Doug Douglas Lee Baker b: 4/3/1961, Fullerton, CA BB/TR, 5'9", 165 lbs. Deb: 7/2/1984

YEAR TM-L	G	AB	R	H	2B	3B	HR	RBI	BB	SO	SB	CS	AVG	OBP	SLG	OPS	OPS+	BR/A	RC	RC/G	FR	G/POS	WS	TPW
1984*Det-A	43	108	15	20	4	1	0	12	7	22	3	0	.185	.241	.241	.482	34	-9	7	2.08	0	S-39/2-5,D-1	2	-0.5
1985 Det-A	15	27	4	5	1	0	0	1	0	9	0	0	.185	.185	.222	.407	11	-3	1	1.36	-2	S-12/2-1	0	-0.5
1986 Det-A	13	24	1	3	1	0	0	0	2	7	0	0	.125	.192	.167	.359	-1	-3	1	1.19	-0	S-10/2-2,D-1	0	-0.3
1987 Det-A	8	1	0	0	0	0	0	0	0	1	0	0	.000	.000	.000	.000	-105	-0	0	.00	-1	/S-6,2-1,3-1	0	-0.1
1988 Min-A	11	7	1	0	0	0	0	0	0	5	0	0	.000	.000	.000	.000	-97	-2	0	.00	-1	/S-9,2-1,3-1	0	-0.3
1989 Min-A	43	78	17	23	5	1	0	9	9	18	0	0	.295	.382	.385	.767	109	1	13	5.92	-2	2-25,S-19/D-1	3	0.0
1990 Min-A	3	1	0	0	0	0	0	0	0	0	0	0	.000	.000	.000	.000	-94	-0	0	.00	-1	/2-3	0	-0.1
Total 7	**136**	**246**	**38**	**51**	**11**	**2**	**0**	**22**	**18**	**62**	**3**	**0**	**.207**	**.270**	**.268**	**.538**	**49**	**-17**	**22**	**2.89**	**-6**	**/S-95,2-38,D-3,3-2**	**5**	**-1.6**

• BAKER, Dusty Johnnie B. Baker b: 6/15/1949, Riverside, CA BR/TR, 6'2", 187 lbs. Deb: 9/7/1968 M/C Career OF: 1117-490-348

YEAR TM-L	G	AB	R	H	2B	3B	HR	RBI	BB	SO	SB	CS	AVG	OBP	SLG	OPS	OPS+	BR/A	RC	RC/G	FR	G/POS	WS	TPW
1968 Atl-N	6	5	0	2	0	0	0	0	0	1	0	0	.400	.400	.400	.800	140	0	1	7.20	-1	/0-3(0-3-0)	0	0.0
1969 Atl-N	3	7	0	0	0	0	0	0	0	3	0	0	.000	.000	.000	.000	-100	-2	0	.00	0	/0-3(0-3-0)	0	-0.2
1970 Atl-N	13	24	3	7	0	0	0	4	2	4	0	0	.292	.346	.292	.638	69	-1	2	3.39	-1	0-11(5-4-2)	0	-0.2
1971 Atl-N	29	62	2	14	2	0	0	4	1	14	0	1	.226	.238	.258	.496	38	-6	3	1.78	0	0-18(1-4-16)	0	-0.6
1972 Atl-N	127	446	62	143	27	2	17	76	45	68	4	7	.321	.388	.504	.892	139	22	85	7.03	-6	*0-123(30-121-3)	23	1.2
1973 Atl-N	159	604	101	174	29	4	21	99	67	72	24	3	.288	.364	.454	.818	116	18	103	6.08	-3	*0-156(0-156-0)	20	1.2
1974 Atl-N	149	574	80	147	35	0	20	69	71	87	18	7	.256	.339	.422	.761	107	6	83	4.93	-3	*0-148(0-102-112)	20	-0.4
1975 Atl-N	142	494	63	129	18	2	19	72	67	57	12	7	.261	.349	.421	.770	109	6	74	5.12	2	*0-136(0-12-129)	17	0.1
1976 LA-N	112	384	36	93	13	0	4	39	31	54	2	4	.242	.300	.307	.608	74	-15	33	2.79	-6	*0-106(0-83-24)	6	-2.5
1977*LA-N	153	533	86	155	26	1	30	86	58	89	2	6	.291	.367	.512	.879	134	23	99	6.67	-5	*0-152(150-1-2)	21	1.0
1978*LA-N	149	522	62	137	24	1	11	66	47	66	12	3	.262	.327	.375	.702	96	-2	66	4.37	1	*0-145(145-0-0)	13	-0.7
1979 LA-N	151	554	86	152	29	1	23	88	56	70	11	4	.274	.342	.455	.797	117	13	84	5.34	1	*0-150(150-0-0)	18	0.7
1980 LA-N	153	579	80	170	26	4	29	97	43	66	12	10	.294	.346	.503	.848	137	24	96	5.87	-1	*0-151(151-1-1)	24	1.6
1981*LA-N★	103	400	48	128	17	3	9	49	29	43	10	7	.320	.367	.445	.812	134	16	63	5.76	-1	*0-101(101-0-0)	16	1.1
1982 LA-N★	147	570	80	171	19	1	23	88	56	62	17	10	.300	.366	.458	.824	132	23	96	6.09	-10	*0-144(144-0-1)	22	0.7
1983*LA-N	149	531	71	138	25	1	15	73	72	59	7	1	.260	.350	.395	.746	107	7	78	5.09	-2	*0-143(143-0-0)	19	-0.1
1984 SF-N	100	243	31	71	7	2	3	32	40	27	4	1	.292	.392	.374	.767	120	9	39	5.72	-3	0-62(29-0-33)	9	0.3
1985 Oak-A	111	343	48	92	15	1	14	52	50	47	2	1	.268	.361	.440	.802	128	14	54	5.49	0	1-58,0-35(32-0-5),D-13	13	0.9
1986 Oak-A	83	242	25	58	8	0	4	19	27	37	0	1	.240	.316	.322	.638	80	-7	24	3.33	1	0-55(36-0-20),D-15/1-3	4	-0.8
Total 19	**2039**	**7117**	**964**	**1981**	**320**	**23**	**242**	**1013**	**762**	**926**	**137**	**73**	**.278**	**.351**	**.432**	**.782**	**116**	**149**	**1084**	**5.34**	**-36**	***0-1842/1-61,D-28**	**245**	**3.2**

• BAKER, Floyd Floyd Wilson Baker b: 10/10/1916, Luray, VA BL/TR, 5'9", 160 lbs. Deb: 5/4/1943 C

YEAR TM-L	G	AB	R	H	2B	3B	HR	RBI	BB	SO	SB	CS	AVG	OBP	SLG	OPS	OPS+	BR/A	RC	RC/G	FR	G/POS	WS	TPW
1943 StL-A	22	46	5	8	2	0	0	4	6	4	0	1	.174	.269	.217	.487	42	-4	3	1.84	-1	S-10/3-1	0	-0.4
1944*StL-A	44	97	10	17	3	0	0	5	11	5	2	0	.175	.259	.206	.465	32	-8	6	2.03	-1	2-17,S-16	1	-0.7
1945 Chi-A	82	208	22	52	8	0	0	19	23	12	3	2	.250	.325	.288	.613	81	-4	22	3.62	-1	3-58,2-11	6	-0.5
1946 Chi-A	9	24	2	6	1	0	0	3	2	3	0	0	.250	.308	.292	.599	71	-1	2	3.37	1	/3-6	0	0.0
1947 Chi-A	105	371	61	98	12	3	0	22	66	28	9	7	.264	.375	.313	.688	96	1	49	4.62	14	*3-101/2-1,S-1	14	1.5
1948 Chi-A	104	335	47	72	8	3	0	18	73	26	4	10	.215	.359	.257	.615	67	-15	35	3.42	10	3-71,2-18/S-1	6	-0.4
1949 Chi-A	125	388	38	101	15	4	1	40	84	32	3	1	.260	.392	.327	.719	94	2	59	5.44	8	*3-122/S-3,2-1	13	1.0
1950 Chi-A	83	186	26	59	7	0	0	11	32	10	1	1	.317	.417	.355	.772	102	3	30	5.90	4	3-53/2-3,0-2(2-0-0)	6	0.6
1951 Chi-A	82	133	24	35	6	1	0	14	25	12	0	1	.263	.380	.323	.703	93	-0	18	4.59	-2	3-44/2-5,S-3	3	-0.2
1952 Was-A	79	263	27	69	8	0	0	33	30	17	1	0	.262	.342	.293	.635	81	-5	30	4.09	1	2-68/S-7,3-1	8	0.0
1953 Was-A	9	7	0	0	0	0	0	0	1	0	0	0	.000	.222	.000	.222	-37	-1	0	.45	-1	/3-1	0	-0.2
Bos-A	81	172	22	47	4	2	0	24	24	10	0	2	.273	.365	.320	.685	82	-4	21	4.21	-1	3-37,2-16	4	-0.4
Yr.	90	179	22	47	4	2	0	24	25	10	0	2	.263	.359	.307	.666	77	-5	21	4.02	-2	3-38,2-16	4	-0.6
1954 Bos-A	21	20	1	4	2	0	0	3	0	1	0	0	.200	.200	.300	.500	32	-2	1	2.03	-1	/3-7,2-1	0	-0.3
Phi-N	23	22	0	5	0	0	0	0	5	4	0	0	.227	.370	.227	.598	60	-1	2	3.65	1	/3-7,2-2	0	0.0
1955 Phi-N	5	8	0	0	0	0	0	0	0	1	0	0	.000	.000	.000	.000	-102	-2	0	.00	1	/3-1	0	-0.1
Total 13	**874**	**2280**	**285**	**573**	**76**	**13**	**1**	**196**	**382**	**165**	**23**	**25**	**.251**	**.360**	**.297**	**.658**	**82**	**-42**	**279**	**4.21**	**33**	**3-510,2-143/S-41,0-2**	**61**	**0.0**

• BAKER, Frank Frank Watts Baker b: 10/29/1946, Meridian, MS BL/TR, 6'2", 178 lbs. Deb: 8/9/1970

YEAR TM-L	G	AB	R	H	2B	3B	HR	RBI	BB	SO	SB	CS	AVG	OBP	SLG	OPS	OPS+	BR/A	RC	RC/G	FR	G/POS	WS	TPW
1970 NY-A	35	117	6	27	4	1	0	11	14	26	1	2	.231	.323	.282	.605	72	-5	11	3.29	2	S-35	3	0.2
1971 NY-A	43	79	9	11	2	0	0	2	16	22	3	0	.139	.284	.165	.449	32	-6	5	1.84	2	S-38	1	-0.1
1973*Bal-A	44	63	10	12	1	2	1	11	7	7	0	0	.190	.271	.317	.589	66	-3	6	3.10	0	S-32/2-7,1-1,3-1	2	-0.1
1974*Bal-A	24	29	3	5	1	0	0	0	3	5	0	0	.172	.250	.207	.457	34	-2	1	1.60	-4	S-17/2-3,3-1	0	-0.5
Total 4	**146**	**288**	**28**	**55**	**8**	**3**	**1**	**24**	**40**	**60**	**4**	**2**	**.191**	**.294**	**.250**	**.544**	**55**	**-15**	**24**	**2.64**	**0**	**S-122/2-10,3-2,1-1**	**6**	**-0.5**

• BAKER, Frank John Franklin "Home Run" Baker b: 3/13/1886, Trappe, MD d: 6/28/1963, Trappe, MD BL/TR, 5'11", 173 lbs. Deb: 9/21/1908 HOF: 1955

YEAR TM-L	G	AB	R	H	2B	3B	HR	RBI	BB	SO	SB	CS	AVG	OBP	SLG	OPS	OPS+	BR/A	RC	RC/G	FR	G/POS	WS	TPW
1908 Phi-A	9	31	5	9	3	0	0	2	0	....	0	....	.290	.290	.387	.677	112	0	4	3.80	3	/3-9	2	0.3
1909 Phi-A	148	541	73	165	27	**19**	4	85	26	....	20	....	.305	.343	.447	.790	146	25	90	5.70	2	*3-146	27	3.6
1910*Phi-A	146	561	83	159	25	15	2	74	34	....	21	....	.283	.329	.392	.721	127	15	79	4.84	16	*3-146	25	3.9
1911*Phi-A	148	592	96	198	42	14	**11**	115	40	....	38	....	.334	.379	.508	.887	149	35	127	7.87	7	*3-148	35	4.6
1912 Phi-A	149	577	116	200	40	21	**10**	**130**	50	....	40	....	.347	.404	.541	.945	176	54	140	9.39	12	*3-149	39	7.0
1913*Phi-A	149	564	116	190	34	9	**12**	**117**	63	31	34	....	.337	.413	.493	.906	169	49	122	8.18	12	*3-149	38	6.9
1914*Phi-A	150	570	84	182	23	10	**9**	89	53	37	19	20	.319	.380	.442	.822	153	30	95	6.02	12	*3-149	35	5.2
1916 NY-A	100	360	46	97	23	2	10	52	36	30	15	....	.269	.344	.428	.772	129	12	58	5.67	6	3-96	17	2.2
1917 NY-A	146	553	57	156	24	2	6	71	48	27	18	....	.282	.345	.365	.710	116	10	72	4.64	8	*3-146	21	2.4
1918 NY-A	126	504	65	154	24	5	6	62	38	13	8	....	.306	.357	.409	.765	128	15	74	5.20	12	*3-126	23	3.4
1919 NY-A	141	567	70	166	22	1	10	83	44	18	13	....	.293	.346	.388	.734	105	3	77	4.88	-3	*3-141	20	0.4
1921*NY-A	94	330	46	97	16	2	9	71	26	12	8	5	.294	.353	.436	.789	98	-1	51	5.46	9	3-83	12	1.1
1922*NY-A	69	234	30	65	12	3	7	36	15	14	1	3	.278	.327	.444	.771	97	-3	33	4.90	-10	3-60	7	-0.8
Total 13	**1575**	**5984**	**887**	**1838**	**315**	**103**	**96**	**987**	**473**	**182**	**235**	**28**	**.307**	**.363**	**.442**	**.805**	**136**	**243**	**1020**	**6.13**	**85**	***3-1548**	**301**	**40.3**

• BAKER, Frank Frank Baker b: 1/11/1944, Bartow, FL BL/TR, 5'10", 180 lbs. Deb: 7/27/1969 Career OF: 63-6-30

YEAR TM-L	G	AB	R	H	2B	3B	HR	RBI	BB	SO	SB	CS	AVG	OBP	SLG	OPS	OPS+	BR/A	RC	RC/G	FR	G/POS	WS	TPW
1969 Cle-A	52	172	21	44	5	3	3	15	14	34	2	1	.256	.316	.372	.688	89	-3	20	4.00	-1	0-46(46-0-0)	4	-0.7

YEAR TM-L	G	AB	R	H	2B	3B	HR	RBI	BB	SO	SB	CS	AVG	OBP	SLG	OPS	OPS+	BR/A	RC	RC/G	FR	G/POS	WS	TPW
1971 Cle-A	73	181	18	38	12	1	1	23	12	34	1	3	.210	.263	.304	.567	55	-12	13	2.37	0	0-51(17-6-30)	1	-1.5
Total 2	125	353	39	82	17	4	4	38	26	68	3	4	.232	.289	.337	.626	72	-15	33	3.14	-2	/0-97	5	-2.2
• BAKER, Gene	Eugene Walter Baker b: 6/15/1925, Davenport, IA d: 12/1/1999, Davenport, IA BR/TR, 6'1", 170 lbs. Deb: 9/20/1953 C																							
1953 Chi-N	7	22	1	5	1	0	0	0	1	4	1	0	.227	.261	.273	.534	38	-2	2	2.21	-1	/2-6	0	-0.3
1954 Chi-N	135	541	68	149	32	5	13	61	47	55	4	5	.275	.336	.425	.761	96	-5	76	4.83	-4	*2-134	14	0.1
1955 Chi-N★	154	609	82	163	29	7	11	52	49	57	9	7	.268	.324	.392	.717	89	-10	76	4.20	6	*2-154	16	0.8
1956 Chi-N	140	546	65	141	23	3	12	57	39	54	4	3	.258	.311	.377	.689	85	-12	62	3.80	20	*2-140	11	2.0
1957 Chi-N	12	44	4	11	3	1	1	10	6	3	0	0	.250	.353	.432	.785	111	1	7	5.04	-3	3-12	1	-0.2
Pit-N	111	365	36	97	19	4	2	36	29	29	3	2	.266	.322	.356	.678	84	-8	41	3.86	-3	3-60,S-28,2-13	7	-0.8
Yr.	123	409	40	108	22	5	3	46	35	32	3	2	.264	.325	.364	.689	87	-7	48	3.99	-6	3-72,S-28,2-13	8	-1.0
1958 Pit-N	29	56	3	14	2	1	0	7	8	6	0	0	.250	.344	.321	.665	80	-1	6	3.76	-1	3-11/2-3	1	-0.2
1960*Pit-N	33	37	5	9	0	0	0	4	2	9	0	0	.243	.282	.243	.525	45	-3	3	2.26	0	/3-7,2-1	0	-0.3
1961 Pit-N	9	10	1	1	0	0	0	0	3	2	0	0	.100	.308	.100	.408	15	-1	0	1.40	0	/3-3	0	-0.1
Total 8	630	2230	265	590	109	21	39	227	184	219	21	17	.265	.323	.385	.708	88	-42	272	4.13	15	2-451/3-93,S-28	50	1.0
• BAKER, George	George F. Baker b: 1859, St. Louis, MO Deb: 5/24/1883 Career OF: 3-2-3																							
1883 Bal-a	7	22	0	5	0	0	0	0	0	....	....	....	.227	.227	.227	.455	45	-1	1	1.92	-3	/S-4,C-3,0-1	0	-0.3
1884 StL-U	80	317	39	52	6	0	0	....	5	....	....	....	.164	.177	.183	.360	21	-26	11	1.11	-1	C-68/2-4,0-4(2-1-2),3-3,S	6	-1.8
1885 StL-N	38	131	5	16	0	0	0	5	9	28	....	....	.122	.179	.122	.301	-1	-14	3	.69	-9	C-32/3-3,0-2(1-1-0),2-1	0	-1.9
1886 KC-N	1	4	1	1	0	0	0	0	0	1	0	....	.250	.250	.250	.500	49	-0	0	2.31	0	/C-1	0	0.0
Total 4	126	474	45	74	6	0	0	5	14	29	0	....	.156	.180	.169	.349	16	-42	15	1.03	-13	C-104/0-7,3-6,S-6,2-5	6	-4.1
• BAKER, Howard	Howard Francis Baker b: 3/1/1888, Bridgeport, CT d: 1/16/1964, Bridgeport, CT BR/TR, 5'11", 175 lbs. Deb: 8/11/1912																							
1912 Cle-A	11	30	1	5	0	0	0	2	5	....	0	....	.167	.286	.167	.452	29	-3	1	1.43	-1	3-10	0	-0.3
1914 Chi-A	15	47	4	13	1	1	0	5	3	8	2	1	.277	.320	.340	.660	100	-0	5	4.02	-1	3-15	1	-0.1
1915 Chi-A	2	2	0	0	0	0	0	0	0	2	0	....	.000	.000	.000	.000	-97	-0	0	.00	0	....	0	0.0
NY-N	1	3	0	0	0	0	0	0	0	0	0	....	.000	.000	.000	.000	-106	-1	0	.00	-0	/3-1	0	-0.1
Total 3	29	82	5	18	1	1	0	7	8	10	2	1	.220	.289	.256	.545	62	-4	7	2.73	-2	/3-26	1	-0.5
• BAKER, Jack	Jack Edward Baker b: 5/4/1950, Birmingham, AL BR/TR, 6'5", 225 lbs. Deb: 9/11/1976																							
1976 Bos-A	12	23	1	3	0	0	1	2	1	5	0	0	.130	.167	.261	.428	21	-2	1	1.00	0	/1-8,D-1	0	-0.3
1977 Bos-A	2	3	0	0	0	0	0	0	0	1	0	0	.000	.000	.000	.000	-89	-1	0	.00	0	/1-1	0	-0.1
Total 2	14	26	1	3	0	0	1	2	1	6	0	0	.115	.148	.231	.379	9	-3	1	.88	0	/1-9,D-1	0	-0.4
• BAKER, Jesse	Jesse Baker b: 3/4/1895, Cleveland, OH d: 7/29/1976, West Los Angeles, CA BR/TR, 5'4", 140 lbs. Deb: 9/14/1919																							
1919 Was-A	1	0	0	0	0	0	0	1	0	0	0	....	....	....	....	....	-101	0	0	.00	0	/S-1	0	0.0
• BAKER, Phil	Philip Baker b: 9/19/1856, Philadelphia, PA d: 6/4/1940, Washington, DC BL/TL, 5'8", 152 lbs. Deb: 5/1/1883 U Career OF: 2-40-26																							
1883 Bal-a	28	121	22	33	2	1	1	0	8	....	....	....	.273	.318	.331	.648	106	1	13	4.15	-7	C-19,0-14(1-1-12)/S-1	2	-0.4
1884 Was-U	86	371	75	107	12	5	1	....	11	....	....	....	.288	.309	.356	.665	128	11	42	4.43	-1	1-39,0-32(0-32-0),C-27	13	0.7
1886 Was-N	81	325	37	72	6	5	1	34	20	32	16	....	.222	.267	.280	.547	70	-11	29	3.12	-6	1-56,0-21(1-7-14)/C-4	3	-1.9
Total 3	195	817	134	212	20	11	3	34	39	32	16	....	.259	.293	.322	.615	102	1	84	3.84	-14	/1-95,0-67,C-50,S-1	18	-1.6
• BAKER, Tracy	Tracy Lee Baker b: 11/7/1891, Pendleton, OR d: 3/14/1975, Placerville, CA BR/TR, 6'1", 180 lbs. Deb: 6/19/1911																							
1911 Bos-A	1	0	0	0	0	0	0	0	0	....	0	....	....	....	....	....	-101	0	0	.00	0	/1-1	0	0.0
• BAKO, Paul	Gabor Paul II Bako b: 6/20/1972, Lafayette, LA BL/TR, 6'2", 205 lbs. Deb: 4/30/1998																							
1998 Det-A	96	305	23	83	12	1	3	30	23	82	1	1	.272	.323	.348	.671	74	-12	35	4.08	3	C-94	5	-0.3
1999 Hou-N	73	215	16	55	14	1	2	17	26	57	1	1	.256	.336	.358	.694	77	-8	27	4.21	-0	C-71	5	-0.3
2000 Hou-N	1	2	0	0	0	0	0	0	0	1	0	0	.000	.000	.000	.000	-95	-1	0	.00	0	/C-1	0	0.0
Fla-N	56	161	10	39	6	1	0	14	22	48	0	0	.242	.337	.292	.629	64	-8	16	3.43	-2	C-56	4	-0.6
*Atl-N	24	58	8	11	4	0	2	6	5	15	0	0	.190	.254	.362	.616	53	-5	5	2.64	-1	C-23/1-1	1	-0.4
Yr.	81	221	18	50	10	1	2	20	27	64	0	0	.226	.313	.308	.621	60	-13	21	3.18	-3	C-80/1-1	5	-1.1
2001*Atl-N	61	137	19	29	10	1	2	15	20	34	1	0	.212	.312	.343	.655	68	-6	15	3.72	2	C-60	3	-0.1
2002 Mil-N	87	234	24	55	8	1	4	20	20	46	0	2	.235	.295	.329	.624	65	-13	22	3.20	-5	C-76	3	-1.3
2003*Chi-N	70	188	19	43	13	3	0	17	22	47	0	1	.229	.313	.330	.643	69	-9	20	3.63	-11	C-69	5	-1.5
Total 6	468	1300	119	315	67	8	13	119	138	330	3	5	.242	.316	.336	.652	69	-61	140	3.68	-14	C-450/1-1	26	-4.6
• BALAZ, John	John Lawrence Balaz b: 11/24/1950, Toronto, Canada BR/TR, 6'3", 180 lbs. Deb: 9/10/1974 Career OF: 31-0-8																							
1974 Cal-A	14	42	4	10	0	0	1	5	2	10	0	0	.238	.289	.310	.598	76	-1	4	3.31	0	0-12(12-0-0)	1	-0.2
1975 Cal-A	45	120	10	29	8	1	1	10	5	25	0	0	.242	.272	.350	.622	80	-4	12	3.31	2	0-27(19-0-8),D-11	2	-0.3
Total 2	59	162	14	39	8	1	2	15	7	35	0	0	.241	.276	.340	.616	79	-5	16	3.31	2	/0-39,D-11	3	-0.5
• BALBONI, Steve	Stephen Charles Balboni b: 1/16/1957, Brockton, MA BR/TR, 6'3", 225 lbs. Deb: 4/22/1981																							
1981 NY-A	4	7	2	2	1	1	0	2	1	4	0	0	.286	.375	.714	1.089	211	1	2	10.65	0	/1-3,D-1	1	0.1
1982 NY-A	33	107	8	20	2	1	2	4	6	34	0	0	.187	.230	.280	.510	40	-9	7	2.13	-1	1-26/D-5	0	-1.2
1983 NY-A	32	86	8	20	2	0	5	17	8	23	0	0	.233	.298	.430	.728	101	-0	11	4.24	-2	1-23/D-4	2	-0.4
1984*KC-A	126	438	58	107	23	2	28	77	45	139	0	0	.244	.320	.498	.818	122	12	69	5.48	-5	*1-125/D-1	14	-0.1
1985*KC-A	160	600	74	146	28	2	36	88	52	166	1	1	.243	.309	.477	.786	111	7	86	4.90	-9	*1-160	16	-1.2
1986 KC-A	138	512	54	117	25	1	29	88	43	146	0	0	.229	.290	.451	.741	96	-5	67	4.40	-2	*1-137	10	-1.5
1987 KC-A	121	386	44	80	11	1	24	60	34	97	0	0	.207	.275	.427	.702	80	-13	43	3.66	0	1-55,D-52	4	-1.6
1988 KC-A	21	63	2	9	2	0	2	5	1	20	0	0	.143	.156	.270	.426	17	-7	3	1.35	-1	1-13/D-6	0	-0.9
Sea-A	97	350	44	88	15	1	21	61	23	67	0	1	.251	.299	.480	.779	110	2	48	4.73	1	D-56,1-40	8	-0.2
Yr.	118	413	46	97	17	1	23	66	24	87	0	1	.235	.279	.448	.726	96	-5	51	4.18	0	D-62,1-53	8	-1.1
1989 NY-A	110	300	33	71	12	2	17	59	25	67	0	0	.237	.302	.460	.762	113	4	39	4.32	-2	D-82,1-20	7	-0.1
1990 NY-A	116	266	24	51	6	0	17	34	35	91	0	0	.192	.293	.406	.699	93	-3	33	4.00	-3	D-72,1-28	4	-0.9
1993 Tex-A	2	5	0	3	0	0	0	0	0	2	0	0	.600	.600	.600	1.200	233	1	2	24.30	0	/D-2	1	0.1
Total 11	960	3120	351	714	127	11	181	495	273	856	1	2	.229	.295	.451	.745	101	-11	410	4.42	-24	1-630,D-281	67	-8.0
• BALCENA, Bobby	Robert Rudolph Balcena b: 8/1/1925, San Pedro, CA d: 1/5/1990, San Pedro, CA BR/TL, 5'7", 160 lbs. Deb: 9/16/1956																							
1956 Cin-N	7	2	2	0	0	0	0	0	0	1	0	0	.000	.000	.000	.000	-94	-1	0	.00	0	/0-2(2-0-0)	0	-0.1
• BALDELLI, Rocco	Rocco Daniel Baldelli b: 9/25/1981, Woonsocket, RI BR/TR, 6'4", 190 lbs. Deb: 3/31/2003																							
2003 TB-A	156	637	89	184	32	8	11	78	30	128	27	10	.289	.329	.416	.745	96	-3	86	4.84	8	*0-154(0-154-0)/D-2	14	0.6
• BALDWIN, Billy	Robert Harvey Baldwin b: 6/9/1951, Tazewell, VA BL/TL, 6', 175 lbs. Deb: 7/29/1975 Career OF: 3-13-15																							
1975 Det-A	30	95	8	21	3	0	4	8	5	14	2	1	.221	.260	.379	.639	75	-4	10	3.42	1	0-25(0-13-13)/D-1	2	-0.3
1976 NY-N	9	22	4	6	1	1	1	5	1	2	0	0	.273	.304	.545	.850	146	1	4	5.92	1	/0-5(3-0-2)	1	0.2
Total 2	39	117	12	27	4	1	5	13	6	16	2	1	.231	.268	.410	.679	89	-2	13	3.87	3	/0-30,D-1	3	-0.1
• BALDWIN, Frank	Frank De Witt Baldwin b: 12/25/1928, High Bridge, NJ BR/TR, 5'11", 195 lbs. Deb: 4/22/1953																							
1953 Cin-N	16	20	0	2	0	0	0	0	1	9	0	0	.100	.143	.100	.243	-35	-4	0	.31	0	/C-6	0	-0.4
• BALDWIN, Henry	Henry Clay "Ted" Baldwin b: 6/13/1894, Chadds Ford, PA d: 2/24/1964, West Chester, PA BR/TR, 5'11", 180 lbs. Deb: 5/22/1927																							
1927 Phi-N	6	16	1	5	0	0	0	1	1	2	0	....	.313	.353	.313	.665	78	-0	2	4.08	0	/S-3,3-2	0	-0.1
• BALDWIN, Jeff	Jeffrey Allen Baldwin b: 9/5/1965, Milford, DE BL/TL, 6'1", 180 lbs. Deb: 5/22/1990																							
1990 Hou-N	7	8	1	0	0	0	0	0	1	2	0	0	.000	.111	.000	.111	-69	-2	0	.10	0	/0-3(2-0-1)	0	-0.2
• BALDWIN, Kid	Clarence Geoghan Baldwin b: 11/1/1864, Newport, KY d: 7/10/1897, Cincinnati, OH BR/TR, 5'6", 147 lbs. Deb: 7/27/1884 U Career OF: 11-13-8																							
1884 KC-U	50	191	19	37	6	3	0	....	4	....	....	....	.194	.210	.257	.467	66	-5	11	1.92	7	C-44,0-10(8-2-0)/2-1,3-1	2	0.5

YEAR TM-L	G	AB	R	H	2B	3B	HR	RBI	BB	SO	SB	CS	AVG	OBP	SLG	OPS	OPS+	BR/A	RC	RC/G	FR	G/POS	WS	TPW
CP-U	1	1	0	1	0	0	0	....	0	....	....	....	1.000	1.000	1.000	2.000	616	1	1	∞	0	/C-1	0	0.0
Yr.	51	192	19	38	6	3	0	....	4	....	....	....	.198	.214	.260	.475	68	-4	12	1.92	7	C-45,0-10(8-2-0)/2-1,3-1	2	0.5
1885 Cin-a	34	126	9	17	1	0	1	8	3	....	....	....	.135	.155	.167	.322	2	-14	3	.83	-5	C-25/0-6(0-5-1),2-2,P-2,3	2	-1.8
1886 Cin-a	87	315	41	72	8	7	3	32	8	....	12	....	.229	.252	.327	.579	78	-10	30	3.30	-7	C-71,3-13/0-6(0-5-1)	7	-1.0
1887 Cin-a	96	394	46	104	15	10	1	57	6	....	13	....	.264	.271	.351	.622	71	-18	41	3.86	-3	*C-96/0-2(2-0-0)	8	-1.0
1888 Cin-a	67	271	27	59	11	3	1	25	3	....	4	....	.218	.235	.292	.526	65	-12	20	2.54	-1	C-65/0-2(0-0-2),1-1	6	-0.7
1889 Cin-a	60	223	34	55	14	2	1	34	5	32	7	....	.247	.273	.341	.614	72	-10	23	3.66	-2	C-55/0-4(1-1-2),1-1,3-1	4	-0.6
1890 Cin-N	22	72	5	11	0	0	0	10	3	6	2	....	.153	.187	.153	.339	-1	-9	2	1.08	1	C-20/0-2(0-0-2)	1	-0.6
Phi-a	24	90	5	21	1	2	0	12	4	....	2	....	.233	.274	.289	.563	67	-4	8	3.02	0	C-19/3-5	2	-0.2
Total 7	441	1683	186	377	56	27	7	178	36	38	40	....	.224	.243	.299	.543	63	-82	140	2.86	-12	C-396/0-32,3-21,2-3,1-2,P-2	32	-5.5

• BALDWIN, Lady Charles Busted Baldwin b: 4/8/1859, Oramel, NY d: 3/7/1937, Hastings, MI BL/TL, 5'11", 160 lbs. Deb: 9/30/1884 Career OF: 13-5-2 ♦

YEAR TM-L	G	AB	R	H	2B	3B	HR	RBI	BB	SO	SB	CS	AVG	OBP	SLG	OPS	OPS+	BR/A	RC	RC/G	FR	G/POS	WS	TPW
1884 Mil-U	7	27	6	6	3	0	0	....	0	....	....	....	.222	.222	.333	.556	85	-0	2	2.73	0	/0-5(0-5-0),P-2	3	-0.1
1885 Det-N	31	124	12	30	6	3	0	18	6	22	....	....	.242	.277	.339	.616	98	3	12	3.42	1	P-21,0-12(10-0-2)	14	2.3
1886 Det-N	57	204	25	41	6	3	0	25	18	44	3	....	.201	.266	.260	.526	59	2	15	2.53	4	P-56/0-2(2-0-0)	53	4.9
1887*Det-N	24	95	15	33	0	1	0	7	10	6	4	....	.347	.354	.294	.648	79	3	11	4.50	1	P-24	14	0.5
1888 Det-N	6	23	5	6	0	0	0	3	3	3	0	....	.261	.346	.261	.607	96	1	2	3.38	0	/P-6,0-1	0	-1.2
1890 Bro-N	2	3	1	0	0	0	0	0	1	1	0	....	.000	.250	.000	.250	-25	-0	0	.00	0	/P-2	0	-0.3
Buf-P	7	28	4	8	1	0	0	2	2	1	0	....	.286	.333	.321	.655	82	1	3	4.15	-1	/P-7	1	0.0
Total 6	134	504	68	124	16	7	0	55	40	77	7	....	.246	.290	.291	.581	76	10	45	3.19	6	P-118/0-20	85	6.2

• BALDWIN, Reggie Reginald Conrad Baldwin b: 8/19/1954, River Rouge, MI BR/TR, 6'1", 195 lbs. Deb: 5/25/1978

YEAR TM-L	G	AB	R	H	2B	3B	HR	RBI	BB	SO	SB	CS	AVG	OBP	SLG	OPS	OPS+	BR/A	RC	RC/G	FR	G/POS	WS	TPW
1978 Hou-N	38	67	5	17	5	0	1	11	3	3	0	0	.254	.286	.373	.659	89	-1	6	3.19	-1	C-17	1	-0.2
1979 Hou-N	14	20	0	4	1	0	0	1	0	1	0	0	.200	.200	.250	.450	23	-2	1	.75	0	/C-3,1-1	0	-0.3
Total 2	52	87	5	21	6	0	1	12	3	4	0	0	.241	.267	.345	.611	75	-3	7	2.57	-1	/C-20,1-1	1	-0.4

• BALENTI, Mike Michael Richard Balenti b: 7/3/1886, Calumet, OK d: 8/4/1955, Altus, OK BR/TR, 5'11", 175 lbs. Deb: 7/19/1911 Career OF: 8-1-0

YEAR TM-L	G	AB	R	H	2B	3B	HR	RBI	BB	SO	SB	CS	AVG	OBP	SLG	OPS	OPS+	BR/A	RC	RC/G	FR	G/POS	WS	TPW
1911 Cin-N	8	8	2	2	0	0	0	0	0	1	3	....	.250	.250	.250	.500	42	-1	1	5.11	0	/S-2,0-1	0	-0.1
1913 StL-A	70	211	17	38	2	4	0	11	6	32	3	....	.180	.206	.227	.434	28	-20	10	1.46	-5	S-56/0-8(8-0-0)	2	-2.3
Total 2	78	219	19	40	2	4	0	11	6	33	6	....	.183	.208	.228	.436	28	-21	12	1.58	-5	/S-58,0-9	2	-2.4

• BALES, Lee Wesley Owen Bales b: 12/4/1944, Los Angeles, CA BB/TR, 5'10.5", 165 lbs. Deb: 8/7/1966

YEAR TM-L	G	AB	R	H	2B	3B	HR	RBI	BB	SO	SB	CS	AVG	OBP	SLG	OPS	OPS+	BR/A	RC	RC/G	FR	G/POS	WS	TPW
1966 Atl-N	12	16	4	1	0	0	0	0	0	5	0	0	.063	.063	.063	.125	-64	-3	0	.11	0	/2-7,3-3	0	-0.3
1967 Hou-N	19	27	4	3	0	0	0	2	8	7	1	1	.111	.314	.111	.425	28	-2	2	1.56	0	/2-6,S-1	0	-0.2
Total 2	31	43	8	4	0	0	0	2	8	12	1	1	.093	.235	.093	.328		-6	2	1.05	-1	/2-13,3-3,S-1	0	-0.6

• BALL, Art Arthur Clark Ball b: 4/1876, KY d: 12/26/1915, Chicago, IL TR, 168 lbs. Deb: 8/1/1894

YEAR TM-L	G	AB	R	H	2B	3B	HR	RBI	BB	SO	SB	CS	AVG	OBP	SLG	OPS	OPS+	BR/A	RC	RC/G	FR	G/POS	WS	TPW
1894 StL-N	1	3	0	1	0	0	0	0	0	1	0	....	.333	.333	.333	.667	61	-0	0	4.44	-1	/2-1	0	-0.1
1898 Bal-N	32	81	7	15	2	0	0	8	7	....	2	....	.185	.258	.210	.468	34	-7	5	2.07	4	3-15,S-14/2-2,0-1	1	-0.2
Total 2	33	84	7	16	2	0	0	8	7	1	2	....	.190	.261	.214	.475	35	-7	6	2.13	3	/3-15,S-14,2-3,0-1	1	-0.3

• BALL, Jeff Jeffery D. Ball b: 4/17/1969, Merced, CA BR/TR, 5'10" Deb: 6/10/1998

YEAR TM-L	G	AB	R	H	2B	3B	HR	RBI	BB	SO	SB	CS	AVG	OBP	SLG	OPS	OPS+	BR/A	RC	RC/G	FR	G/POS	WS	TPW
1998 SF-N	2	4	0	1	0	0	0	0	0	0	0	0	.250	.250	.250	.500	34	-0	0	2.25	0	/1-1	0	-0.1

• BALL, Jim James Chandler Ball b: 2/22/1884, Harford County, MD d: 4/7/1963, Glendale, CA BR/TR, 5'11", 175 lbs. Deb: 9/21/1907

YEAR TM-L	G	AB	R	H	2B	3B	HR	RBI	BB	SO	SB	CS	AVG	OBP	SLG	OPS	OPS+	BR/A	RC	RC/G	FR	G/POS	WS	TPW
1907 Bos-N	10	36	3	6	2	0	0	3	2	....	0	....	.167	.211	.222	.433	36	-3	2	1.50	0	C-10	0	-0.2
1908 Bos-N	6	15	1	1	0	0	0	0	1	....	0	....	.067	.125	.067	.192	-39	-2	0	.31	0	/C-6	0	-0.2
Total 2	16	51	4	7	2	0	0	3	3	....	0	....	.137	.185	.176	.362	13	-5	2	1.10	0	/C-16	0	-0.4

• BALL, Neal Cornelius Ball b: 4/22/1881, Grand Haven, MI d: 10/15/1957, Bridgeport, CT BR/TR, 5'7", 145 lbs. Deb: 9/12/1907

YEAR TM-L	G	AB	R	H	2B	3B	HR	RBI	BB	SO	SB	CS	AVG	OBP	SLG	OPS	OPS+	BR/A	RC	RC/G	FR	G/POS	WS	TPW
1907 NY-A	15	44	5	9	1	1	0	4	1	....	1	....	.205	.222	.273	.495	53	-3	3	2.26	-3	S-11/2-5	0	-0.6
1908 NY-A	132	446	35	110	16	2	0	38	21	....	32	....	.247	.284	.291	.575	86	-8	45	3.37	-10	*S-130/2-1	12	-1.5
1909 NY-A	8	29	5	6	1	1	0	3	3	....	2	....	.207	.281	.310	.592	86	-0	3	3.29	-3	/2-8	0	-0.4
Cle-A	96	324	29	83	13	2	1	25	17	....	17	....	.256	.295	.318	.613	90	-5	36	3.61	-11	S-95	8	-1.4
Yr.	104	353	34	89	14	3	1	28	20	....	19	....	.252	.294	.317	.611	90	-5	39	3.58	-14	S-95/2-8	8	-1.8
1910 Cle-A	54	123	13	25	3	1	0	12	9	....	4	....	.203	.258	.244	.501	56	-6	9	2.25	-10	S-27/2-7,0-6(0-5-1),3-3	2	-1.7
1911 Cle-A	116	412	45	122	14	9	3	45	27	....	21	....	.296	.339	.396	.735	104	0	62	5.30	5	2-94,3-17/S-1	12	0.8
1912 Cle-A	40	132	12	30	4	1	0	14	9	....	7	....	.227	.277	.273	.549	55	-8	12	2.90	-0	2-37	2	-0.7
*Bos-A	18	45	10	9	2	0	0	6	3	....	5	....	.200	.250	.244	.494	40	-4	4	2.73	0	2-17	0	-0.4
Yr.	58	177	22	39	6	1	0	20	12	....	12	....	.220	.270	.266	.535	51	-12	16	2.85	0	2-54	2	-1.1
1913 Bos-A	23	58	9	10	2	0	0	4	9	13	3	....	.172	.294	.207	.501	46	-4	4	2.23	-2	2-10/S-7,3-1	0	-0.6
Total 7	502	1613	163	404	56	17	4	151	99	13	92	....	.250	.295	.314	.609	83	-36	178	3.65	-35	S-271,2-179/3-21,0-6	36	-6.6

• BALLENGER, Pelham Pelham Ashby Ballenger b: 2/6/1894, Gilreath Mill, SC d: 12/8/1948, Greenville County, SC BR/TR, 5'11", 160 lbs. Deb: 5/7/1928

YEAR TM-L	G	AB	R	H	2B	3B	HR	RBI	BB	SO	SB	CS	AVG	OBP	SLG	OPS	OPS+	BR/A	RC	RC/G	FR	G/POS	WS	TPW
1928 Was-A	3	9	0	1	0	0	0	0	0	1	0	0	.111	.111	.111	.222	-42	-2	0	.35	1	/3-3	0	-0.1

• BAMBERGER, Hal Harold Earl "Dutch" Bamberger b: 10/29/1924, Lebanon, PA BL/TR, 6', 173 lbs. Deb: 9/15/1948

YEAR TM-L	G	AB	R	H	2B	3B	HR	RBI	BB	SO	SB	CS	AVG	OBP	SLG	OPS	OPS+	BR/A	RC	RC/G	FR	G/POS	WS	TPW
1948 NY-N	7	12	0	1	0	0	0	0	1	2	0		.083	.154	.083	.237	-34	-2	0	.48	0	/0-3(0-1-2)	0	-0.2

• BANCKER, Stud John Bancker b: Philadelphia, PA Deb: 4/19/1875

YEAR TM-L	G	AB	R	H	2B	3B	HR	RBI	BB	SO	SB	CS	AVG	OBP	SLG	OPS	OPS+	BR/A	RC	RC/G	FR	G/POS	WS	TPW
1875 NH-n	19	72	3	11	0	0	0	2	0	3	1	0	.153	.153	.153	.306	7	-5	2	.91	0	C-14/2-4,3-3,1-1,S-1	....	-0.5

• BANCROFT, Dave David James "Beauty" Bancroft b: 4/20/1891, Sioux City, IA d: 10/9/1972, Superior, WI BB/TR, 5'9.5", 160 lbs. Deb: 4/14/1915 M/C HOF: 1971

YEAR TM-L	G	AB	R	H	2B	3B	HR	RBI	BB	SO	SB	CS	AVG	OBP	SLG	OPS	OPS+	BR/A	RC	RC/G	FR	G/POS	WS	TPW
1915*Phi-N	153	563	85	143	18	2	7	30	77	62	15	27	.254	.346	.330	.676	104	-3	64	3.61	7	*S-153	21	1.6
1916 Phi-N	142	477	53	101	10	0	3	33	74	57	15	....	.212	.323	.252	.574	75	-10	46	3.04	23	*S-142	20	2.7
1917 Phi-N	127	478	56	116	22	5	4	43	44	42	14	....	.243	.307	.335	.641	93	-4	52	3.57	20	*S-120/2-3,0-2(2-0-0)	18	2.8
1918 Phi-N	125	499	69	132	19	4	0	26	54	36	11	....	.265	.338	.319	.656	94	-2	55	3.82	19	*S-125	17	3.0
1919 Phi-N	92	335	45	91	13	7	0	25	31	30	8	....	.272	.333	.352	.686	99	0	41	4.19	1	S-88	11	0.9
1920 Phi-N	42	171	23	51	7	2	0	5	9	12	1	7	.298	.337	.363	.700	96	-3	19	3.81	7	S-42	5	0.7
NY-N	108	442	79	132	29	7	0	31	33	32	7	5	.299	.349	.396	.745	115	9	61	4.97	29	*S-108	21	5.0
Yr.	150	613	102	183	36	9	0	36	42	44	8	12	.299	.346	.387	.732	110	7	80	4.64	36	*S-150	26	5.7
1921*NY-N	153	606	121	193	26	15	6	67	66	23	17	10	.318	.389	.441	.830	119	20	106	6.32	21	*S-153	31	5.7
1922*NY-N	156	651	117	209	41	5	4	60	79	27	16	11	.321	.397	.418	.815	109	13	111	6.32	25	*S-156	27	5.2
1923*NY-N	107	444	80	135	33	3	1	31	62	23	8	7	.304	.391	.399	.789	110	9	72	5.90	24	S-96,2-11	20	4.2
1924 Bos-N	79	319	49	89	11	1	2	21	37	24	4	4	.279	.356	.339	.694	91	-2	40	4.43	-3	S-79	10	0.3
1925 Bos-N	128	479	75	153	29	8	2	49	64	22	7	4	.319	.400	.426	.826	122	19	85	6.49	22	*S-125	22	5.1
1926 Bos-N	127	453	70	141	18	6	1	44	64	29	3	....	.311	.399	.384	.783	122	18	72	5.58	-4	*S-123/3-2	20	2.7
1927 Bos-N	111	375	44	91	13	4	1	31	43	36	5	....	.243	.322	.307	.629	75	-12	38	3.41	6	*S-104/3-1	9	0.6
1928 Bro-N	149	515	47	127	19	5	0	51	59	20	7	....	.247	.326	.303	.629	66	-24	53	3.41	10	*S-149	11	0.2
1929 Bro-N	104	358	35	99	11	3	1	44	29	11	7	....	.277	.331	.332	.663	66	-19	40	3.74	-4	*S-102	6	-1.1
1930 NY-N	10	17	0	1	1	0	0	0	2	1	0	....	.059	.158	.118	.276	-33	-4	0	.60	-1	/S-8	0	-0.4
Total 16	1913	7182	1048	2004	320	77	32	591	827	487	145	75	.279	.355	.358	.714	98	7	954	4.59	204	*S-1873/2-14,3-3,0-2	269	39.4

• BANDO, Chris Christopher Michael Bando b: 2/4/1956, Cleveland, OH BB/TR, 6', 195 lbs. Deb: 8/13/1981 C

YEAR TM-L	G	AB	R	H	2B	3B	HR	RBI	BB	SO	SB	CS	AVG	OBP	SLG	OPS	OPS+	BR/A	RC	RC/G	FR	G/POS	WS	TPW
1981 Cle-A	21	47	3	10	3	0	0	6	2	2	0	0	.213	.245	.277	.521	51	-3	3	2.12	0	C-15/D-2	0	-0.3
1982 Cle-A	66	184	13	39	6	1	3	16	24	30	0	0	.212	.303	.304	.607	68	-8	17	3.00	-1	C-63/3-2	4	-0.7
1983 Cle-A	48	121	15	31	3	0	4	15	15	19	0	1	.256	.338	.380	.718	94	-1	15	4.07	1	C-43	4	0.1
1984 Cle-A	75	220	38	64	11	0	12	41	33	35	1	2	.291	.383	.505	.888	141	12	41	6.39	-2	C-63/1-1,3-1,D-1	10	1.4
1985 Cle-A	73	173	11	24	4	1	0	13	22	21	0	1	.139	.236	.173	.409	14	-21	7	1.25	2	C-67	2	-1.6
1986 Cle-A	92	254	28	68	9	0	2	26	22	49	0	1	.268	.329	.327	.655	81	-7	27	3.51	0	C-86	3	-0.4
1987 Cle-A	89	211	20	46	9	0	5	16	12	28	0	0	.218	.260	.332	.592	55	-14	17	2.64	3	C-86	3	-0.8

YEAR TM-L	G	AB	R	H	2B	3B	HR	RBI	BB	SO	SB	CS	AVG	OBP	SLG	OPS	OPS+	BR/A	RC	RC/G	FR	G/POS	WS	TPW
1988 Cle-A	32	72	6	9	1	0	1	8	8	12	0	0	.125	.222	.181	.403	14	-8	3	1.10	1	C-32	1	-0.6
Det-A	1	0	0	0	0	0	0	0	0	0	0	0	....	....	....	....	-104	0	0	....	0	/C-1	0	0.0
Yr.	33	72	6	9	1	0	1	8	8	12	0	0	.125	.222	.181	.403	14	-8	3	1.10	0	C-33	1	-0.6
1989 Oak-A	1	2	0	1	0	0	0	1	0	1	0	0	.500	.500	.500	1.000	189	0	1	13.50	0	/C-1	0	0.1
Total 9	498	1284	134	292	46	2	27	142	138	197	1	5	.227	.303	.329	.633	73	-49	131	3.27	2	C-457/3-3,D-3,1-1	27	-2.8
• BANDO, Sal	Salvatore Leonard Bando b: 2/13/1944, Cleveland, OH BR/TR, 6', 205 lbs. Deb: 9/3/1966 C																							
1966 KC-A	11	24	1	7	1	1	0	1	1	3	0	0	.292	.320	.417	.737	113	0	3	4.98	3	/3-7	1	0.3
1967 KC-A	47	130	11	25	3	2	0	6	16	24	1	0	.192	.295	.246	.541	63	-5	11	2.82	3	3-44	2	-0.2
1968 Oak-A	162	605	67	152	25	5	9	67	51	78	13	4	.251	.317	.354	.670	108	7	69	3.89	-7	*3-162/0-1	21	0.0
1969 Oak-A★	162	609	106	171	25	3	31	113	111	82	1	4	.281	.401	.484	.885	153	46	124	7.30	-9	*3-162	36	3.8
1970 Oak-A	155	502	93	132	20	2	20	75	118	88	6	10	.263	.409	.430	.839	136	29	94	6.31	-10	*3-152	24	1.9
1971*Oak-A	153	538	75	146	23	1	24	94	86	55	3	7	.271	.380	.452	.831	137	27	93	5.90	-8	*3-153	29	1.9
1972*Oak-A★	152	535	64	126	20	3	15	77	78	55	3	1	.236	.342	.368	.711	117	15	70	4.36	11	*3-151/2-1	23	2.8
1973*Oak-A★	162	592	97	170	**32**	3	29	98	82	84	4	2	.287	.378	.498	.876	153	42	113	6.83	-6	*3-159/D-3	31	3.7
1974*Oak-A★	146	498	84	121	21	2	22	103	86	79	2	3	.243	.360	.426	.786	134	24	80	5.36	3	*3-141/D-3	21	2.7
1975*Oak-A	160	562	64	129	24	1	15	78	87	80	7	1	.230	.338	.356	.694	98	3	73	4.41	5	*3-160	19	0.8
1976 Oak-A	158	550	75	132	18	2	27	84	76	74	20	6	.240	.337	.427	.764	128	22	84	5.16	0	*3-155/S-5,D-2	24	2.2
1977 Mil-A	159	580	65	145	27	3	17	82	75	89	4	2	.250	.339	.395	.734	99	1	81	4.79	-1	*3-135,D-24/2-1,S-1	17	-0.2
1978 Mil-A	152	540	85	154	20	6	17	78	72	52	3	2	.285	.375	.439	.814	128	22	92	6.04	7	*3-134,D-12/1-5	23	2.8
1979 Mil-A	130	476	57	117	14	3	9	43	57	42	2	0	.246	.330	.345	.675	82	-10	54	3.81	-6	*3-109,D-19/1-4,2-1,P-1	9	-1.7
1980 Mil-A	78	254	28	50	12	1	5	31	29	35	5	3	.197	.282	.311	.593	64	-13	22	2.72	-1	3-57,D-15/1-7	2	-1.5
1981*Mil-A	32	65	10	13	4	0	2	9	6	3	1	1	.200	.268	.354	.621	82	-2	6	2.90	-2	3-15/1-9,D-2	1	-0.4
Total 16	2019	7060	982	1790	289	38	242	1039	1031	923	75	46	.254	.355	.408	.763	120	210	1069	5.17	-18	*3-1896/D-80,1-25,S-6,2-3,0,P	283	19.0
• BANISTER, Jeff	Jeffery Todd Banister b: 1/15/1965, Weatherford, OK BR/TR, 6'2", 200 lbs. Deb: 7/23/1991																							
1991 Pit-N	1	1	0	1	0	0	0	0	0	0	0	0	1.000	1.000	1.000	2.000	472	0	1	∞	0	....	0	0.0
• BANKS, Brian	Brian Glen Banks b: 9/28/1970, Mesa, AZ BB/TR, 6'3", 200 lbs. Deb: 9/9/1996 Career OF: 49-0-17																							
1996 Mil-A	4	7	2	4	2	0	1	2	1	2	0	0	.571	.625	1.286	1.911	353	3	6	52.09	0	/0-3(3-0-0),1-1	1	0.2
1997 Mil-A	28	68	9	14	1	0	1	8	6	17	0	1	.206	.270	.265	.535	40	-6	5	2.28	1	0-15(15-0-1)/1-5,3-1,D-1	0	-0.6
1998 Mil-N	24	24	3	7	2	0	1	5	4	7	0	0	.292	.393	.500	.893	133	1	5	8.14	-2	/C-5,1-2,3-1,0-1	1	-0.1
1999 Mil-N	105	219	34	53	7	1	5	22	25	59	6	1	.242	.320	.352	.671	70	-9	26	4.11	0	1-44,C-40/0-5(4-0-1)	3	-0.9
2002 Fla-N	20	28	3	9	1	0	1	4	1	6	0	0	.321	.345	.464	.809	115	0	5	6.50	0	/0-8(3-0-5),1-1,3-1	1	0.0
2003*Fla-N	92	149	14	35	6	2	4	23	25	38	2	1	.235	.352	.383	.735	96	-0	21	4.65	-3	0-33(23-0-10),1-12/D-1	3	-0.5
Total 6	273	495	65	122	19	3	13	64	62	129	8	3	.246	.333	.376	.708	84	-11	68	4.67	-4	/1-65,0-65,C-45,3-3,D-2	9	-1.9
• BANKS, Ernie	Ernest "Mr. Cub" Banks b: 1/31/1931, Dallas, TX BR/TR, 6'1", 180 lbs. Deb: 9/17/1953 C HOF: 1977																							
1953 Chi-N	10	35	3	11	1	1	2	6	4	5	0	0	.314	.385	.571	.956	142	2	8	9.32	2	S-10	2	0.4
1954 Chi-N	154	593	70	163	19	7	19	79	40	50	6	10	.275	.328	.427	.755	94	-10	80	4.67	-6	*S-154	15	-0.3
1955 Chi-N★	154	596	98	176	29	9	44	117	45	72	9	3	.295	.347	.596	.942	144	36	117	7.17	5	*S-154	32	5.3
1956 Chi-N★	139	538	82	160	25	8	28	85	52	62	6	9	.297	.359	.530	.889	137	25	99	6.71	-8	*S-139	22	2.9
1957 Chi-N★	156	594	113	169	34	6	43	102	70	85	8	4	.285	.363	.579	.942	150	41	123	7.44	-13	*S-100,3-58	28	3.7
1958 Chi-N★	154	617	119	193	23	11	**47**	**129**	52	87	4	4	.313	.370	**.614**	.984	157	47	135	8.05	-7	*S-154	31	5.3
1959 Chi-N★	155	589	97	179	25	6	45	**143**	64	72	2	4	.304	.379	.596	.975	156	45	126	7.68	5	*S-154	33	6.3
1960 Chi-N★	156	597	94	162	32	7	**41**	117	71	69	1	3	.271	.353	.554	.907	145	35	113	6.64	6	*S-156	29	**5.6**
1961 Chi-N★	138	511	75	142	22	4	29	80	54	75	1	2	.278	.349	.507	.856	122	15	88	6.11	8	*S-104,0-23(23-0-0)/1-7	19	3.0
1962 Chi-N★	154	610	87	164	20	6	37	104	30	71	5	1	.269	.311	.503	.814	110	6	89	5.06	2	*1-149/3-3	14	-0.1
1963 Chi-N	130	432	41	98	20	1	18	64	39	73	0	3	.227	.297	.403	.700	94	-4	50	3.84	1	*1-125	9	-1.1
1964 Chi-N	157	591	67	156	29	6	23	95	36	84	1	2	.264	.310	.450	.760	107	3	77	4.52	8	*1-157	15	0.2
1965 Chi-N★	163	612	79	162	25	3	28	106	55	64	3	5	.265	.331	.453	.784	116	11	87	4.92	-3	*1-162	18	-0.2
1966 Chi-N	141	511	52	139	23	7	15	75	29	59	0	1	.272	.317	.432	.750	105	2	66	4.47	0	*1-130/3-8	11	-0.6
1967 Chi-N★	151	573	68	158	26	4	23	95	27	93	2	2	.276	.312	.455	.767	112	7	74	4.45	-1	*1-147	17	-0.4
1968 Chi-N	150	552	71	136	27	0	32	83	27	67	2	0	.246	.288	.469	.757	116	9	72	4.40	-1	*1-147	18	0.0
1969 Chi-N★	155	565	60	143	19	2	23	106	42	101	0	0	.253	.313	.416	.729	91	-8	71	4.26	-1	*1-153	14	-2.1
1970 Chi-N	72	222	25	56	6	2	12	44	20	33	0	0	.252	.317	.459	.776	94	-3	32	4.89	-3	1-62	5	-1.1
1971 Chi-N	39	83	4	16	2	0	3	6	6	14	0	0	.193	.247	.325	.572	53	-5	7	2.59	0	1-20	0	-0.7
Total 19	2528	9421	1305	2583	407	90	512	1636	763	1236	50	53	.274	.333	.500	.833	122	254	1513	5.63	-7	*1-1259,S-1125/3-69,0-23	332	26.1
• BANKS, George	George Edward Banks b: 9/24/1938, Pacolet Mills, SC d: 3/1/1985, Spartanburg, SC BR/TR, 5'11", 185 lbs. Deb: 4/15/1962 Career OF: 10-0-12																							
1962 Min-A	63	103	22	26	0	2	4	15	21	27	0	0	.252	.384	.408	.792	109	2	16	4.99	0	0-17(7-0-11)/3-6	3	0.1
1963 Min-A	25	71	5	11	4	0	3	8	9	21	0	0	.155	.259	.338	.597	65	-3	6	2.69	0	3-21	1	-0.4
1964 Min-A	1	1	0	0	0	0	0	0	0	1	0	0	.000	.000	.000	.000	-99	-0	0	.00	0	....	0	0.0
Cle-A	9	17	6	5	1	0	2	3	6	6	0	0	.294	.478	.706	1.184	226	3	6	14.59	0	/0-3(3-0-1),2-1,3-1	2	0.3
Yr.	10	18	6	5	1	0	2	3	6	7	0	0	.278	.458	.667	1.125	212	3	6	13.47	0	/0-3(3-0-1),2-1,3-1	2	0.3
1965 Cle-A	4	5	0	1	1	0	0	0	1	3	0	1	.200	.333	.400	.733	107	-0	0	2.03	0	/3-1	0	0.0
1966 Cle-A	4	4	0	1	0	0	0	1	0	1	0	0	.250	.250	.250	.500	44	-0	0	2.25	0	....	0	0.0
Total 5	106	201	33	44	6	2	9	27	37	59	0	1	.219	.346	.403	.749	103	1	30	4.67	-1	/3-29,0-20,2-1	6	-0.1
• BANKSTON, Everett	Wilborn Everett Bankston b: 5/25/1893, Barnesville, GA d: 2/26/1970, Griffin, GA BL/TR, 5'11", 180 lbs. Deb: 8/15/1915																							
1915 Phi-A	11	36	6	5	1	1	1	2	2	5	1	....	.139	.205	.306	.511	55	-2	2	2.08	0	/0-8(4-4-0)	0	-0.3
• BANNING, Jim	James M. Banning b: 6/11/1865, New York, NY d: 10/14/1952, St. Paul, MN BL/TR, 5'6", 150 lbs. Deb: 9/27/1888																							
1888 Was-N	1	0	0	0	0	0	0	0	0	0	0	....	....	....	....	....	-106	0	0	....	0	/C-1	0	0.0
1889 Was-N	2	1	0	0	0	0	0	0	0	0	0	....	.000	.000	.000	.000	-106	-0	0	.00	1	/C-2	0	0.0
Total 2	3	1	0	0	0	0	0	0	0	0	0	....	.000	.000	.000	.000	-106	-0	0	.00	1	/C-3	0	0.0
• BANNISTER, Alan	Alan Bannister b: 9/3/1951, Montebello, CA BR/TR, 5'11", 175 lbs. Deb: 7/13/1974 Career OF: 254-72-100																							
1974 Phi-N	26	25	4	3	0	0	0	1	3	7	0	0	.120	.241	.120	.361	3	-3	1	1.20	-1	/0-8(0-8-0),S-2	0	-0.5
1975 Phi-N	24	61	10	16	3	1	0	0	1	9	2	2	.262	.274	.344	.618	68	-3	5	2.79	0	0-18(4-14-1)/2-1,S-1	1	-0.4
1976 Chi-A	73	145	19	36	6	2	0	8	14	21	12	4	.248	.319	.317	.636	86	-1	17	3.81	-2	0-43(29-13-4),S-14/2-4,D-4,3	3	-0.5
1977 Chi-A	139	560	87	154	20	3	3	57	54	49	4	3	.275	.341	.338	.678	86	-9	66	4.12	-21	*S-133/2-3,0-3(2-2-0)	11	-1.6
1978 Chi-A	49	107	16	24	3	2	0	8	11	12	3	3	.224	.303	.290	.592	67	-5	9	2.83	-2	D-19,0-15(8-7-0)/S-8,2-2	1	-0.7
1979 Chi-A	136	506	71	144	28	8	2	55	43	40	22	6	.285	.344	.383	.728	96	-0	69	4.85	-17	2-65,0-47(47-0-2),3-12/D-9,1	13	-1.5
1980 Chi-A	45	130	16	25	6	0	0	9	12	16	5	2	.192	.261	.238	.499	38	-11	8	1.95	0	0-23(22-0-1),3-17	1	-1.2
Cle-A	81	262	41	86	17	4	1	32	28	25	9	2	.328	.393	.435	.828	126	11	46	6.53	-7	2-41,0-40(9-9-26)/3-3,S-2	11	0.6
Yr.	126	392	57	111	23	4	1	41	40	41	14	4	.283	.350	.370	.719	97	1	54	4.81	-7	0-63(31-9-27),2-41,3-20/S-2	12	-0.6
1981 Cle-A	68	232	36	61	11	1	1	17	16	19	16	2	.263	.310	.332	.642	86	-1	27	4.17	-5	0-35(18-6-17),2-30/1-2,S-1	7	-0.7
1982 Cle-A	101	348	40	93	16	1	4	41	42	41	18	5	.267	.348	.353	.701	94	0	47	4.67	-3	0-55(46-4-9),2-48/S-2,3-1,D	9	-0.3
1983 Cle-A	117	377	51	100	25	4	5	45	31	43	6	6	.265	.326	.393	.719	93	-5	48	4.26	3	0-91(58-8-34),2-27/1-3,D-3	9	-0.4
1984 Hou-N	9	20	2	4	2	0	0	0	2	2	0	0	.200	.273	.300	.573	65	-1	2	3.00	-1	/S-4,0-1	0	-0.2
Tex-A	47	112	20	33	2	1	2	9	21	17	3	0	.295	.410	.384	.794	117	5	20	6.77	-7	2-25/D-9,0-3(1-1-1),1-1,3	5	-0.1
1985 Tex-A	57	122	17	32	4	1	1	6	14	17	8	2	.262	.338	.336	.674	84	-1	15	4.45	-4	D-21,0-14(9-0-5),2-10/3-5,1	2	-0.6
Total 12	972	3007	430	811	143	28	19	288	292	318	108	37	.270	.337	.355	.692	90	-25	381	4.39	-67	0-396,2-256,S-167/D-66,3-40,1	73	-8.1
• BANNON, Jimmy	James Henry "Foxy Grandpa" Bannon b: 5/5/1871, Amesbury, MA d: 3/24/1948, Glen Rock, NJ BR/TR, 5'5", 160 lbs. Deb: 6/15/1893 U Career OF: 4-1-345																							
1893 StL-N	26	107	9	36	3	4	0	15	4	5	8	....	.336	.366	.439	.805	113	1	21	7.70	-5	0-24(1-0-23)/S-2,P-1	3	-1.0
1894 Bos-N	128	494	130	166	29	10	13	114	62	42	47	....	.336	.414	.514	.928	109	5	128	10.13	16	*0-128(0-0-128)/P-1	18	1.2
1895 Bos-N	124	493	101	171	35	5	6	74	54	31	28	....	.347	.417	.475	.891	123	17	113	9.15	9	*0-122(1-0-121)/P-1	19	1.6

YEAR TM-L	G	AB	R	H	2B	3B	HR	RBI	BB	SO	SB	CS	AVG	OBP	SLG	OPS	OPS+	BR/A	RC	RC/G	FR	G/POS	WS	TPW
1896 Bos-N	89	344	53	87	9	5	0	50	32	23	16	....	.253	.318	.308	.626	62	-19	41	4.11	1	0-76(2-1-73)/2-6,S-5,3-3	5	-1.8
Total 4	367	1438	293	460	76	24	19	253	152	101	99	....	.320	.389	.446	.835	103	4	303	8.04	21	0-350/S-7,2-6,3-3,P-3	45	-0.1

• BANNON, Tom Thomas Edward "Ward Six,Uncle Tom" Bannon
b: 5/8/1869, Amesbury, MA d: 1/26/1950, Lynn, MA BR/TR, 5'8", 175 lbs. Deb: 5/10/1895 Career OF: 14-1-8

YEAR TM-L	G	AB	R	H	2B	3B	HR	RBI	BB	SO	SB	CS	AVG	OBP	SLG	OPS	OPS+	BR/A	RC	RC/G	FR	G/POS	WS	TPW
1895 NY-N	37	159	33	43	6	2	0	8	7	8	20	....	.270	.301	.333	.635	65	-9	23	5.17	2	0-21(13-0-8),1-16	3	-0.7
1896 NY-N	2	7	1	1	1	0	0	0	1	1	0	....	.143	.250	.286	.536	42	-1	1	2.26	-1	/0-2(1-1-0)	0	-0.1
Total 2	39	166	34	44	7	2	0	8	8	9	20	....	.265	.299	.331	.630	64	-9	23	5.03	1	/0-23,1-16	3	-0.8

• BARAJAS, Rod Rodrigo Richard Barajas b: 9/5/1975, Ontario, CA BR/TR, 6'2", 229 lbs. Deb: 9/25/1999

YEAR TM-L	G	AB	R	H	2B	3B	HR	RBI	BB	SO	SB	CS	AVG	OBP	SLG	OPS	OPS+	BR/A	RC	RC/G	FR	G/POS	WS	TPW
1999 Ari-N	5	16	3	4	1	0	1	3	1	1	0	0	.250	.294	.500	.794	95	-0	2	5.07	0	/C-5	1	0.0
2000 Ari-N	5	13	1	3	0	0	1	3	0	4	0	0	.231	.231	.462	.692	67	-1	1	3.74	-1	/C-5	0	-0.1
2001*Ari-N	51	106	9	17	3	0	3	9	4	26	0	0	.160	.191	.274	.464	17	-14	6	1.74	-16	C-50	1	-2.7
2002*Ari-N	70	154	12	36	10	0	3	23	10	25	1	0	.234	.293	.357	.651	64	-8	16	3.36	-19	C-69/1-1	3	-2.4
2003 Ari-N	80	220	19	48	15	0	3	28	14	43	0	0	.218	.268	.327	.595	49	-17	18	2.69	5	C-79	5	-0.7
Total 5	211	509	44	108	29	0	11	66	29	99	1	0	.212	.260	.334	.594	50	-39	44	2.79	-32	C-208/1-1	10	-6.0

• BARBARE, Walter Walter Lawrence "Dinty" Barbare b: 8/11/1891, Greenville, SC d: 10/28/1965, Greenville, SC BR/TR, 6', 162 lbs. Deb: 9/17/1914

YEAR TM-L	G	AB	R	H	2B	3B	HR	RBI	BB	SO	SB	CS	AVG	OBP	SLG	OPS	OPS+	BR/A	RC	RC/G	FR	G/POS	WS	TPW
1914 Cle-A	15	52	6	16	2	2	0	5	2	5	1	4	.308	.345	.423	.769	126	-0	7	4.05	1	3-14/S-1	2	0.2
1915 Cle-A	77	246	15	47	3	1	0	11	10	27	6	5	.191	.235	.211	.446	33	-22	14	1.71	6	3-68/1-1	3	-1.4
1916 Cle-A	13	48	3	11	1	0	0	3	4	9	0	....	.229	.288	.250	.538	58	-2	4	2.54	1	3-12	1	-0.1
1918 Bos-A	13	29	2	5	3	0	0	2	0	1	1	....	.172	.172	.276	.448	36	-3	2	1.49	-3	3-11/S-1	0	-0.6
1919 Pit-N	85	293	34	80	11	5	1	34	18	18	11	....	.273	.317	.355	.672	98	-1	36	4.09	2	3-80/2-1	9	0.3
1920 Pit-N	57	186	9	51	5	2	0	12	9	11	5	3	.274	.308	.323	.630	79	-5	18	3.43	-1	S-34,2-12/3-5	4	-0.3
1921 Bos-N	134	550	66	166	22	7	0	49	24	28	11	4	.302	.331	.367	.698	89	-6	68	4.33	-5	*S-121/2-8,3-2	15	0.3
1922 Bos-N	106	373	38	86	5	4	0	40	21	22	2	0	.231	.272	.265	.537	41	-31	28	2.50	2	2-45,3-38,1-14	2	-2.4
Total 8	500	1777	173	462	52	21	1	156	88	121	37	16	.260	.297	.315	.612	71	-69	177	3.29	4	3-230,S-157/2-66,1-15	36	-4.0

• BARBARY, Red Donald Odell Barbary b: 6/20/1920, Simpsonville, SC d: 9/27/2003, Simpsonville, SC BR/TR, 6'3", 195 lbs. Deb: 5/22/1943

YEAR TM-L	G	AB	R	H	2B	3B	HR	RBI	BB	SO	SB	CS	AVG	OBP	SLG	OPS	OPS+	BR/A	RC	RC/G	FR	G/POS	WS	TPW
1943 Was-A	1	1	0	0	0	0	0	0	0	0	0	0	.000	.000	.000	.000	-104	-0	0	.00	0	....	0	0.0

• BARBEAU, Jap William Joseph Barbeau b: 6/10/1882, New York, NY d: 9/10/1969, Milwaukee, WI BR/TR, 5'5", 140 lbs. Deb: 9/27/1905

YEAR TM-L	G	AB	R	H	2B	3B	HR	RBI	BB	SO	SB	CS	AVG	OBP	SLG	OPS	OPS+	BR/A	RC	RC/G	FR	G/POS	WS	TPW
1905 Cle-A	11	37	1	10	1	1	0	2	1	....	1	....	.270	.289	.351	.641	101	-0	4	3.98	0	2-11	1	0.0
1906 Cle-A	42	129	8	25	5	3	0	12	9	....	5	....	.194	.257	.279	.536	69	-5	11	2.76	-10	3-32/S-6	1	-1.5
1909 Pit-N	91	350	60	77	16	3	0	25	37	....	19	....	.220	.302	.283	.585	78	-9	35	3.27	-13	3-85	8	-2.1
StL-N	48	175	23	44	3	0	0	5	28	....	14	....	.251	.370	.269	.639	105	4	23	4.38	-9	3-47	6	-0.5
Yr.	139	525	83	121	19	3	0	30	65	....	33	....	.230	.326	.278	.604	87	-5	58	3.63	-22	*3-132	14	-2.6
1910 StL-N	7	21	4	4	0	1	0	2	3	3	0	....	.190	.292	.286	.577	71	-1	2	2.62	1	/3-6,2-1	1	0.1
Total 4	199	712	96	160	25	8	0	46	78	3	39	....	.225	.311	.282	.593	84	-11	75	3.45	-30	3-170/2-12,S-6	17	-3.9

• BARBEE, Dave David Monroe Barbee b: 5/7/1905, Greensboro, NC d: 7/1/1968, Albermarle, NC BR/TR, 5'11.5", 178 lbs. Deb: 7/29/1926 Career OF: 77-1-10

YEAR TM-L	G	AB	R	H	2B	3B	HR	RBI	BB	SO	SB	CS	AVG	OBP	SLG	OPS	OPS+	BR/A	RC	RC/G	FR	G/POS	WS	TPW
1926 Phi-A	19	47	7	8	1	1	1	5	2	4	0	0	.170	.220	.298	.518	32	-5	3	2.12	0	0-10(0-0-10)	0	-0.5
1932 Pit-N	97	327	37	84	22	6	5	55	18	38	1	....	.257	.300	.407	.706	89	-6	40	4.25	0	0-78(77-1-0)	7	-1.0
Total 2	116	374	44	92	23	7	6	60	20	42	1	0	.246	.290	.393	.683	82	-11	44	3.96	0	/0-88	7	-1.5

• BARBER, Charlie Charles D. Barber b: 1854, Philadelphia, PA d: 11/23/1910, Philadelphia, PA BR/TR Deb: 4/17/1884

YEAR TM-L	G	AB	R	H	2B	3B	HR	RBI	BB	SO	SB	CS	AVG	OBP	SLG	OPS	OPS+	BR/A	RC	RC/G	FR	G/POS	WS	TPW
1884 Cin-U	55	204	38	41	1	4	0	....	11	....	....	....	.201	.242	.245	.487	60	-9	12	2.13	9	3-55	5	0.1

• BARBER, Turner Tyrus Turner Barber b: 7/9/1893, Lavinia, TN d: 10/20/1968, Milan, TN BL/TR, 5'11", 170 lbs. Deb: 8/19/1915 Career OF: 194-76-70

YEAR TM-L	G	AB	R	H	2B	3B	HR	RBI	BB	SO	SB	CS	AVG	OBP	SLG	OPS	OPS+	BR/A	RC	RC/G	FR	G/POS	WS	TPW
1915 Was-A	20	53	9	16	1	1	0	6	6	7	0	3	.302	.383	.358	.742	120	0	7	4.22	1	0-19(3-0-16)	2	0.0
1916 Was-A	15	33	3	7	0	1	1	5	2	3	0	....	.212	.257	.364	.621	87	-1	3	3.09	-1	0-10(6-0-4)	0	-0.3
1917 Chi-N	7	28	2	6	1	0	0	2	2	8	1	....	.214	.267	.250	.517	55	-1	2	2.30	1	/0-7(1-6-0)	0	-0.1
1918*Chi-N	55	123	11	29	3	2	0	10	9	16	3	....	.236	.293	.293	.586	77	-3	11	2.95	-3	0-27(4-17-15)/1-4	2	-0.9
1919 Chi-N	76	230	26	72	9	4	0	21	14	17	7	....	.313	.355	.387	.742	122	6	33	5.17	-1	0-68(53-13-2)	8	0.3
1920 Chi-N	94	340	27	90	10	5	0	50	9	26	5	6	.265	.290	.324	.613	74	-12	31	3.01	-7	1-69,0-17(6-8-3)/2-2	5	-2.2
1921 Chi-N	127	452	73	142	14	4	1	54	41	24	5	9	.314	.379	.369	.748	99	0	64	5.06	3	*0-123(90-20-14)	12	-0.5
1922 Chi-N	84	226	35	70	7	4	0	29	30	9	7	4	.310	.391	.376	.767	97	1	35	5.58	-3	0-47(31-0-16),1-16	7	-0.6
1923 Bro-N	13	46	3	10	2	0	0	8	2	2	0	1	.217	.250	.261	.511	36	-5	3	1.96	1	0-12(0-12-0)	0	-0.4
Total 9	491	1531	189	442	47	21	2	185	115	112	28	23	.289	.343	.351	.694	93	-15	189	4.27	-9	0-330/1-89,2-2	36	-4.6

• BARBERIE, Bret Bret Edward Barberie b: 8/16/1967, Long Beach, CA BB/TR, 5'11", 180 lbs. Deb: 6/16/1991

YEAR TM-L	G	AB	R	H	2B	3B	HR	RBI	BB	SO	SB	CS	AVG	OBP	SLG	OPS	OPS+	BR/A	RC	RC/G	FR	G/POS	WS	TPW
1991 Mon-N	57	136	16	48	12	2	2	18	20	22	0	0	.353	.443	.515	.958	171	14	31	8.86	-2	S-19,2-10,3-10/1-1	8	1.4
1992 Mon-N	111	285	26	66	11	0	1	24	47	62	9	5	.232	.356	.281	.637	83	-4	33	3.81	4	3-63,2-26/S-1	8	0.1
1993 Fla-N	99	375	45	104	16	2	5	33	33	58	2	4	.277	.347	.371	.718	87	-7	48	4.51	6	2-97	10	0.4
1994 Fla-N	107	372	40	112	20	2	5	31	23	65	2	0	.301	.356	.406	.762	95	-2	55	5.62	12	*2-106	9	1.5
1995 Bal-A	90	237	32	57	14	0	2	25	36	50	3	3	.241	.355	.325	.680	77	-7	29	4.01	3	2-74/D-5,3-3	5	-0.1
1996 Chi-N	15	29	4	1	0	0	1	2	5	11	0	1	.034	.176	.138	.314	-15	-5	1	.78	0	/2-6,3-2,S-1	0	-0.5
Total 6	479	1434	163	388	73	6	16	133	164	268	16	13	.271	.358	.363	.722	93	-11	198	4.81	23	2-319/3-78,S-21,D-5,1-1	40	2.8

• BARBIERI, Jim James Patrick Barbieri b: 9/15/1941, Schenectady, NY BL/TR, 5'7", 155 lbs. Deb: 7/5/1966

YEAR TM-L	G	AB	R	H	2B	3B	HR	RBI	BB	SO	SB	CS	AVG	OBP	SLG	OPS	OPS+	BR/A	RC	RC/G	FR	G/POS	WS	TPW
1966*LA-N	39	82	9	23	5	0	0	3	9	7	2	0	.280	.352	.341	.693	102	1	11	4.95	0	0-20(9-0-11)	3	0.0

• BARCLAY, George George Oliver "Deerfoot" Barclay b: 5/16/1876, Millville, PA d: 4/3/1909, Philadelphia, PA BR/TR, 5'10", 162 lbs. Deb: 4/17/1902 Career OF: 381-1-17

YEAR TM-L	G	AB	R	H	2B	3B	HR	RBI	BB	SO	SB	CS	AVG	OBP	SLG	OPS	OPS+	BR/A	RC	RC/G	FR	G/POS	WS	TPW
1902 StL-N	137	543	79	163	14	2	3	53	31	....	30	....	.300	.345	.350	.695	119	12	79	5.38	-6	*0-137(137-0-0)	20	-0.2
1903 StL-N	108	419	37	104	10	8	0	42	15	....	12	....	.248	.278	.310	.588	70	-18	41	3.39	-4	*0-107(107-0-0)	4	-2.7
1904 StL-N	103	375	41	75	7	4	1	28	12	....	14	....	.200	.237	.248	.485	52	-22	27	2.27	-7	*0-103(103-0-0)	2	-3.7
Bos-N	24	93	5	21	3	1	0	10	2	....	3	....	.226	.258	.280	.537	68	-4	8	2.77	-1	0-24(6-1-17)	1	-0.6
Yr.	127	468	46	96	10	5	1	38	14	....	17	....	.205	.241	.254	.495	55	-25	35	2.37	-8	*0-127(109-1-17)	3	-4.3
1905 Bos-N	29	108	5	19	1	0	0	7	2	....	2	....	.176	.205	.185	.391	17	-11	5	1.35	-4	0-28(28-0-0)	0	-1.8
Total 4	401	1538	167	382	35	15	4	140	62	....	61	....	.248	.286	.298	.584	79	-42	159	3.56	-22	0-399	27	-9.0

• BARD, Josh Joshua David Bard b: 3/30/1978, Ithaca, NY BB/TR, 6'3", 215 lbs. Deb: 8/23/2002

YEAR TM-L	G	AB	R	H	2B	3B	HR	RBI	BB	SO	SB	CS	AVG	OBP	SLG	OPS	OPS+	BR/A	RC	RC/G	FR	G/POS	WS	TPW
2002 Cle-A	24	90	9	20	5	0	3	12	4	13	0	0	.222	.255	.378	.633	66	-5	7	2.36	0	C-24	1	-0.3
2003 Cle-A	91	303	25	74	13	1	8	36	22	53	0	2	.244	.295	.373	.668	77	-12	31	3.45	9	C-87/D-1	7	0.3
Total 2	115	393	34	94	18	1	11	48	26	66	0	2	.239	.286	.374	.660	75	-16	38	3.19	9	C-111/D-1	8	0.0

• BARFIELD, Jesse Jesse Lee Barfield b: 10/29/1959, Joliet, IL BR/TR, 6'1", 205 lbs. Deb: 9/3/1981 C Career OF: 3-87-1340

YEAR TM-L	G	AB	R	H	2B	3B	HR	RBI	BB	SO	SB	CS	AVG	OBP	SLG	OPS	OPS+	BR/A	RC	RC/G	FR	G/POS	WS	TPW
1981 Tor-A	25	95	7	22	3	2	2	9	4	19	4	3	.232	.270	.368	.638	77	-3	8	2.59	3	0-25(0-0-25)	2	-0.2
1982 Tor-A	139	394	54	97	13	2	18	58	42	79	1	4	.246	.323	.426	.750	95	-4	54	4.61	2	*0-137(1-3-136)/D-1	11	-0.8
1983 Tor-A	128	388	58	98	13	3	27	68	22	110	2	5	.253	.300	.510	.810	111	2	55	4.82	5	*0-120(0-1-120)/D-5	11	0.2
1984 Tor-A	110	320	51	91	14	1	14	49	35	81	8	2	.284	.359	.466	.824	122	11	55	6.19	2	0-88(0-9-79)/D-9	11	0.9
1985*Tor-A	155	539	94	156	34	9	27	84	66	143	22	8	.289	.371	.536	.907	141	32	106	7.03	16	*0-154(0-8-147)	26	4.0
1986 Tor-A★	158	589	107	170	35	2	**40**	108	69	146	8	8	.289	.371	.559	.929	145	35	122	7.44	14	*0-157(0-18-147)	28	4.1
1987 Tor-A	159	590	89	155	25	3	28	84	58	141	3	5	.263	.332	.458	.789	104	1	87	5.15	14	*0-158(0-13-152)	19	0.7
1988 Tor-A	137	468	62	114	21	5	18	56	41	108	7	3	.244	.306	.425	.731	102	0	60	4.28	11	*0-136(0-13-132)/D-1	12	0.7
1989 Tor-A	21	80	8	16	4	0	5	11	5	28	0	2	.200	.256	.438	.693	98	-2	9	3.48	2	0-21(1-0-20)	1	-0.1
NY-A	129	441	71	106	19	1	18	56	82	122	5	3	.240	.362	.410	.772	119	13	70	5.38	3	*0-129(0-18-120)	15	1.3
Yr.	150	521	79	122	23	1	23	67	87	150	5	5	.234	.347	.415	.762	116	12	78	5.08	5	*0-150(1-18-140)	16	1.3
1990 NY-A	153	476	69	117	21	2	25	78	82	150	4	3	.246	.362	.456	.818	127	19	84	6.02	9	*0-151(0-4-151)	22	2.4
1991 NY-A	84	284	37	64	12	0	17	48	36	80	1	0	.225	.313	.447	.760	107	2	38	4.38	5	0-81(1-0-81)	8	0.5

YEAR TM-L	G	AB	R	H	2B	3B	HR	RBI	BB	SO	SB	CS	AVG	OBP	SLG	OPS	OPS+	BR/A	RC	RC/G	FR	G/POS	WS	TPW
1992 NY-A	30	95	8	13	2	0	2	7	9	27	1	1	.137	.212	.221	.433	21	-10	4	1.10	0	0-30(0-0-30)	0	-1.1
Total 12	**1428**	**4759**	**715**	**1219**	**216**	**30**	**241**	**716**	**551**	**1234**	**66**	**47**	**.256**	**.338**	**.466**	**.804**	**116**	**96**	**749**	**5.41**	**86**	***0-1387/D-16**	**166**	**12.6**
• BARKER, Al	Alfred L Barker b: 1/18/1839, Rockford, IL d: 9/15/1912, Rockford, IL Deb: 6/1/1871																							
1871 Rok-n	1	4	0	1	0	0	0	2	1	0	0	0	.250	.400	.250	.650	96	0	0	4.31	-0	/0-1	....	0.0
• BARKER, Glen	Glen F. Barker b: 5/10/1971, Albany, NY BB/TR, 5'10", 180 lbs. Deb: 4/7/1999 Career OF: 6-169-12																							
1999*Hou-N	81	73	23	21	2	0	1	11	11	19	17	6	.288	.388	.356	.744	92	1	12	5.21	0	0-57(4-46-8)/D-1	3	0.0
2000 Hou-N	84	67	18	15	2	1	2	6	7	23	9	6	.224	.307	.373	.680	67	-4	7	3.26	0	0-69(2-63-4)	1	-0.4
2001 Hou-N	70	24	12	2	0	0	0	1	3	6	4	6	.083	.241	.083	.325	-10	-6	0	.18	0	0-60(0-60-0)	1	-0.5
Total 3	**235**	**164**	**53**	**38**	**4**	**1**	**3**	**18**	**21**	**48**	**30**	**18**	**.232**	**.333**	**.323**	**.657**	**66**	**-9**	**20**	**3.48**	**0**	**0-186/D-1**	**5**	**-0.9**
• BARKER, Kevin	Kevin Stewart Barker b: 7/26/1975, Bristol, VA BL/TL, 6'3", 205 lbs. Deb: 8/19/1999																							
1999 Mil-N	38	117	13	33	3	0	3	23	9	19	1	0	.282	.333	.385	.718	82	-3	16	5.05	0	1-31	4	-0.6
2000 Mil-N	40	100	14	22	5	0	2	9	20	21	1	0	.220	.355	.330	.685	76	-3	14	4.59	-2	1-32	2	-0.7
2002 SD-N	7	19	0	3	0	0	0	0	1	6	1	0	.158	.200	.158	.358	-5	-3	1	.90	-1	/1-6	0	-0.4
Total 3	**85**	**236**	**27**	**58**	**8**	**0**	**5**	**32**	**30**	**46**	**3**	**0**	**.246**	**.333**	**.343**	**.677**	**73**	**-9**	**30**	**4.46**	**-4**	**/1-69**	**6**	**-1.7**
• BARKER, Ray	Raymond Herrell "Buddy" Barker b: 3/12/1936, Martinsburg, WV BL/TR, 6', 192 lbs. Deb: 9/13/1960																							
1960 Bal-A	5	6	0	0	0	0	0	0	0	3	0	0	.000	.000	.000	.000	-101	-2	0	.00	0	/0-1	0	-0.2
1965 Cle-A	11	6	0	0	0	0	0	0	2	2	0	0	.000	.250	.000	.250	-22	-1	0	.29	0	/1-3	0	-0.1
NY-A	98	205	21	52	11	0	7	31	20	46	1	0	.254	.329	.410	.739	109	3	28	4.71	5	1-61/3-3	6	0.5
Yr.	109	211	21	52	11	0	7	31	22	48	1	0	.246	.326	.398	.724	105	2	28	4.55	5	1-64/3-3	6	0.4
1966 NY-A	61	75	11	14	5	0	3	13	4	20	0	0	.187	.228	.373	.601	72	-3	7	2.83	3	1-47	1	-0.1
1967 NY-A	17	26	2	2	0	0	0	0	3	5	0	0	.077	.172	.077	.249	-25	-4	0	.54	0	1-13	0	-0.5
Total 4	**192**	**318**	**34**	**68**	**16**	**0**	**10**	**44**	**29**	**76**	**1**	**0**	**.214**	**.286**	**.358**	**.644**	**83**	**-7**	**35**	**3.65**	**8**	**1-124/3-3,0-1**	**7**	**-0.4**
• BARKETT, Andy	Andrew Jon Barkett b: 9/5/1974, Miami, FL BL/TL, 6'1", 205 lbs. Deb: 5/28/2001																							
2001 Pit-N	17	46	5	14	2	0	1	3	4	7	1	0	.304	.373	.413	.786	101	0	7	5.44	1	0-10(9-0-2)/1-4,D-1	1	0.1
• BARKLEY, Red	John Duncan Barkley b: 9/19/1913, Childress, TX d: 12/12/2000, Waco, TX BR/TR, 5'11", 160 lbs. Deb: 9/2/1937																							
1937 StL-A	31	101	9	27	6	0	0	14	14	17	1	0	.267	.357	.327	.683	73	-3	13	4.48	-7	2-31	1	-0.8
1939 Bos-N	12	11	1	0	0	0	0	0	1	2	0	....	.000	.083	.000	.083	-82	-3	0	.05	0	/S-7,3-4	0	-0.3
1943 Bro-N	20	51	6	16	3	0	0	7	4	7	1	....	.314	.364	.373	.736	113	1	7	5.40	-2	S-18	2	0.0
Total 3	**63**	**163**	**16**	**43**	**9**	**0**	**0**	**21**	**19**	**26**	**2**	**0**	**.264**	**.341**	**.319**	**.660**	**75**	**-5**	**20**	**4.36**	**-9**	**/2-31,S-25,3-4**	**3**	**-1.1**
• BARKLEY, Sam	Samuel E. Barkley b: 5/24/1858, Wheeling, WV d: 4/20/1912, Wheeling, WV BR/TR, 5'11.5", 180 lbs. Deb: 5/1/1884 M																							
1884 Tol-a	104	435	71	133	**39**	9	1	0	22	....	....	....	.306	.342	.444	.786	149	22	68	6.16	18	*2-103/C-2	21	4.0
1885*StL-a	106	418	67	112	18	10	3	53	25	....	....	....	.268	.312	.380	.693	113	5	51	4.49	19	*2-96,1-11	21	2.4
1886 Pit-a	122	478	77	127	31	8	1	69	58	....	22	....	.266	.345	.370	.715	125	15	70	5.42	8	*2-112/0-8(8-0-0),1-2	20	2.3
1887 Pit-N	89	370	44	106	10	4	1	35	30	24	6	....	.286	.294	.285	.579	65	-14	31	3.12	-2	1-53,2-36	3	-1.6
1888 KC-a	116	482	67	104	21	6	4	51	26	....	15	....	.216	.262	.309	.571	78	-14	44	3.14	-33	*2-116	8	-4.0
1889 KC-a	45	176	36	50	6	2	0	23	15	20	8	....	.284	.340	.341	.681	89	-3	24	4.99	-12	2-41/1-4	4	-1.2
Total 6	**582**	**2359**	**362**	**632**	**125**	**39**	**10**	**231**	**176**	**44**	**51**	**....**	**.268**	**.314**	**.359**	**.672**	**106**	**11**	**288**	**4.50**	**-2**	**2-504/1-70,0-8,C-2**	**77**	**1.9**
• BARLOW, Tom	Thomas H. Barlow b: 1852, NY Deb: 5/2/1872 U																							
1872 Atl-n	37	171	34	53	1	0	0	10	3	2	7	5	.310	.322	.316	.638	83	-7	20	5.07	3	*C-36/S-4,3-1	....	-0.2
1873 Atl-n	55	271	48	74	0	2	1	14	4	0	3	3	.273	.284	.299	.583	82	-3	24	3.72	-2	*C-55/2-1,S-1	....	-0.3
1874 Har-n	32	155	37	46	5	1	0	12	2	2	**17**	4	.297	.306	.335	.641	102	1	22	5.82	12	S-32	....	1.0
1875 NH-n	1	5	1	1	0	0	0	0	0	0	0	0	.200	.200	.200	.400	45	-0	0	1.51	1	/S-1	....	0.0
Atl-n	1	4	0	0	0	0	0	0	0	0	0	0	.000	.000	.000	.000	-115	-1	0	.00	-1	/2-1	....	-0.2
Yr.	2	9	1	1	0	0	0	0	0	0	0	0	.111	.111	.111	.222	-26	-1	0	.76	0	/2-1,S-1	....	-0.1
Total 4 n	**126**	**606**	**120**	**174**	**6**	**3**	**1**	**36**	**9**	**4**	**27**	**12**	**.287**	**.298**	**.310**	**.608**	**86**	**-9**	**67**	**4.58**	**13**	**/C-91,S-38,2-2,3-1**	**....**	**0.4**
• BARMES, Bruce	Bruce Raymond "Squeaky" Barmes b: 10/23/1929, Vincennes, IN BL/TR, 5'8", 165 lbs. Deb: 9/13/1953																							
1953 Was-A	5	5	1	1	0	0	0	0	0	0	0	0	.200	.200	.200	.400	8	-1	0	1.38	0	/0-1	0	-0.1
• BARMES, Clint	Clint Harold Barmes b: 3/6/1979, Vincennes, IN BR/TR, 6', 175 lbs. Deb: 9/5/2003																							
2003 Col-N	12	25	2	8	2	0	0	2	0	10	0	0	.320	.370	.400	.770	89	-0	4	5.91	1	S-12	1	0.1
• BARNA, Babe	Herbert Paul Barna b: 3/2/1915, Clarksburg, WV d: 5/18/1972, Charleston, WV BL/TR, 6'2", 210 lbs. Deb: 9/16/1937 Career OF: 163-0-12																							
1937 Phi-A	14	36	10	14	2	0	2	9	2	6	1	0	.389	.421	.611	1.032	159	3	9	11.22	0	/0-9(9-0-0),1-1	1	0.3
1938 Phi-A	9	30	4	4	0	0	0	2	3	5	0	0	.133	.212	.133	.345	-12	-5	1	.99	-0	/0-7(4-0-3)	0	-0.5
1941 NY-N	10	42	5	9	3	0	1	5	2	6	0	....	.214	.250	.357	.607	68	-2	4	3.11	1	0-10(2-0-8)	0	-0.2
1942 NY-N	104	331	39	85	8	7	6	58	38	48	3	....	.257	.333	.378	.711	107	3	44	4.68	-4	0-89(88-0-1)	11	-0.7
1943 NY-N	40	113	11	23	5	1	1	12	16	9	3	....	.204	.302	.292	.594	72	-4	11	3.23	-2	0-31(31-0-0)	1	-0.8
Bos-A	30	112	19	19	4	1	2	10	15	24	2	1	.170	.268	.277	.545	58	-6	9	2.63	0	0-29(29-0-0)	1	-0.8
Total 5	**207**	**664**	**88**	**154**	**22**	**9**	**12**	**96**	**76**	**98**	**9**	**1**	**.232**	**.311**	**.346**	**.657**	**88**	**-11**	**78**	**4.04**	**-5**	**0-175/1-1**	**14**	**-2.7**
• BARNES, Bill	William H. Barnes b: Indianapolis, IN Deb: 9/27/1884																							
1884 StP-U	8	30	2	6	1	0	0	....	0	....	....	....	.200	.200	.233	.433	46	-2	1	1.67	-2	/0-8(0-8-0)	0	-0.4
• BARNES, Eppie	Everett Duane Barnes b: 12/1/1900, Ossining, NY d: 11/17/1980, Mineola, NY BL/TL, 5'9", 175 lbs. Deb: 9/25/1923																							
1923 Pit-N	2	2	0	1	0	0	0	0	0	1	0	0	.500	.500	.500	1.000	161	0	0	12.72	0	/1-1	0	0.0
1924 Pit-N	2	5	0	0	0	0	0	0	0	1	0	0	.000	.000	.000	.000	-98	-1	0	.00	0	/1-1	0	-0.1
Total 2	**4**	**7**	**0**	**1**	**0**	**0**	**0**	**0**	**0**	**2**	**0**	**0**	**.143**	**.143**	**.143**	**.286**	**-24**	**-1**	**0**	**2.12**	**1**	**/1-2**	**0**	**-0.1**
• BARNES, Honey	John Francis Barnes b: 1/31/1900, Fulton, NY d: 6/18/1981, Lockport, NY BL/TR, 5'10", 175 lbs. Deb: 4/20/1926																							
1926 NY-A	1	0	0	0	0	0	0	0	1	0	0	0	....	1.000		1.000	180	0	0	∞	0	/C-1	0	0.0
• BARNES, John	John Delbert Barnes b: 4/24/1976, San Diego, CA BR/TR, 6'2", 205 lbs. Deb: 9/16/2000 Career OF: 5-2-14																							
2000 Min-A	11	37	5	13	4	0	0	2	2	6	0	1	.351	.415	.459	.874	116	1	6	5.52	2	0-11(2-2-8)	1	0.2
2001 Min-A	9	21	1	1	0	0	0	0	1	3	0	0	.048	.130	.048	.178	-49	-5	0	.27	0	/0-9(3-0-6)	0	-0.4
Total 2	**20**	**58**	**6**	**14**	**4**	**0**	**0**	**2**	**3**	**9**	**0**	**1**	**.241**	**.313**	**.310**	**.623**	**57**	**-4**	**6**	**3.33**	**3**	**/0-20**	**1**	**-0.2**
• BARNES, Larry	Larry Richard Barnes b: 7/23/1974, Bakersfield, CA BL/TL, 6'1", 195 lbs. Deb: 4/11/2001 Career OF: 3-0-0																							
2001 Ana-A	16	40	2	4	0	0	1	2	1	9	0	0	.100	.122	.175	.297	-22	-7	1	.52	-0	1-16/0-1	0	-0.8
2003 LA-N	30	38	2	8	2	0	0	2	1	9	0	0	.211	.231	.263	.494	30	-4	2	2.13	0	/1-8,0-2(2-0-0)	1	-0.5
Total 2	**46**	**78**	**4**	**12**	**2**	**0**	**1**	**4**	**2**	**18**	**0**	**0**	**.154**	**.175**	**.218**	**.393**	**3**	**-11**	**3**	**1.24**	**0**	**/1-24,0-3**	**1**	**-1.3**
• BARNES, Lute	Luther Owens Barnes b: 4/28/1947, Forest City, IA BR/TR, 5'10", 160 lbs. Deb: 8/6/1972																							
1972 NY-N	24	72	5	17	2	2	0	6	6	4	0	1	.236	.295	.319	.614	76	-3	6	2.88	1	2-14/S-6	2	0.0
1973 NY-N	3	2	2	1	0	0	0	1	0	1	0	0	.500	.500	.500	1.000	181	0	1	13.50	0	....	0	0.0
Total 2	**27**	**74**	**7**	**18**	**2**	**2**	**0**	**7**	**6**	**5**	**0**	**1**	**.243**	**.300**	**.324**	**.624**	**79**	**-2**	**7**	**3.05**	**1**	**/2-14,S-6**	**2**	**0.0**
• BARNES, Red	Emile Deering Barnes b: 12/25/1903, Suggsville, AL d: 7/3/1959, Mobile, AL BL/TR, 5'10.5", 158 lbs. Deb: 9/29/1927 Career OF: 17-182-12																							
1927 Was-A	3	11	5	4	1	0	0	0	1	3	0	0	.364	.417	.455	.871	127	0	2	7.97	1	/0-3(0-1-2)	0	0.1
1928 Was-A	114	417	82	127	22	15	6	51	55	38	7	3	.305	.391	.472	.863	127	18	80	7.01	2	*0-104(8-96-1)	17	1.5
1929 Was-A	72	130	16	26	5	2	1	15	13	12	1	0	.200	.273	.292	.565	45	-10	11	2.79	-2	0-30(8-14-9)	0	-1.3
1930 Was-A	12	12	1	2	1	0	0	0	0	3	0	0	.167	.167	.250	.417	4	-2	0	1.27	0	....	0	-0.2
Chi-A	85	266	48	66	12	7	1	31	26	20	4	2	.248	.317	.357	.675	73	-10	31	3.97	-1	0-72(1-71-0)	4	-1.3

YEAR TM-L	G	AB	R	H	2B	3B	HR	RBI	BB	SO	SB	CS	AVG	OBP	SLG	OPS	OPS+	BR/A	RC	RC/G	FR	G/POS	WS	TPW
Yr.	97	278	49	68	13	7	1	31	26	23	4	2	.245	.311	.353	.664	71	-12	32	3.85	-1	0-72(1-71-0)	4	-1.4
Total 4	286	836	152	225	41	24	8	97	95	76	12	5	.269	.347	.404	.752	96	-4	125	5.23	0	0-209	21	-1.1
• BARNES, Ross	Roscoe Charles Barnes b: 5/8/1850, Mount Morris, NY d: 2/5/1915, Chicago, IL BR/TR, 5'8.5", 145 lbs. Deb: 5/5/1871 U NA OF: 1-0-0																							
1871 Bos-n	31	157	**66**	63	10	9	0	34	13	1	11	6	.401	.447	.580	1.027	186	17	47	14.72	10	2-16,S-15	....	1.6
1872 Bos-n	45	229	81	**99**	**28**	2	1	44	9	4	12	2	**.432**	.454	**.585**	**1.039**	**206**	**29**	68	**15.95**	20	*2-45	....	3.2
1873 Bos-n	60	322	**125**	**137**	**29**	8	2	62	**18**	2	**13**	4	**.425**	**.456**	**.584**	**1.040**	**191**	**36**	94	**15.16**	15	*2-47,3-13	....	3.4
1874 Bos-n	51	259	72	88	12	4	0	41	8	2	8	7	.340	.360	.417	.777	140	9	43	7.21	13	*2-51/0-1	....	1.5
1875 Bos-n	78	393	**115**	**143**	20	4	1	58	7	3	29	6	.364	**.375**	.443	.818	177	32	78	**8.99**	20	*2-76/0-3(0-0-0),S-2	....	**4.1**
1876 Chi-N	66	342	**126**	**138**	**21**	**14**	1	59	**20**	8	....	....	**.404**	**.462**	**.590**	**1.052**	**222**	**41**	90	**13.69**	11	*2-66/P-1	20	4.6
1877 Chi-N	22	92	16	25	1	0	0	5	7	4	....	....	.272	.323	.283	.606	82	-2	9	3.54	-8	2-22	2	-0.7
1879 Cin-N	77	323	55	86	9	2	1	30	16	25	....	....	.266	.301	.316	.617	109	4	31	3.72	-0	*S-61,2-16	10	0.7
1881 Bos-N	69	295	42	80	14	1	0	17	16	16	....	....	.271	.309	.325	.634	104	2	30	3.81	0	*S-63/2-7	9	0.5
Total 5 n	265	1360	**459**	**530**	**99**	27	4	239	**55**	12	**73**	25	**.390**	**.413**	.511	.924	**179**	**122**	329	**11.73**	78	2-235/S-17,3-13,0-4	....	13.8
Total 4	234	1052	239	329	45	17	2	111	59	53	....	....	.313	.356	.401	.757	141	46	160	6.34	3	S-124,2-111/P-1	41	5.0
• BARNES, Sam	Samuel Thomas Barnes b: 12/18/1899, Suggsville, AL d: 2/19/1981, Montgomery, AL BL/TR, 5'8", 150 lbs. Deb: 9/14/1921																							
1921 Det-A	7	11	2	2	1	0	0	0	2	1	0	0	.182	.357	.273	.630	63	-0	1	3.82	2	/2-2	0	0.1
• BARNES, Skeeter	William Henry Barnes b: 3/3/1957, Cincinnati, OH BR/TR, 5'11", 180 lbs. Deb: 9/6/1983 Career OF: 37-11-30																							
1983 Cin-N	15	34	5	7	0	0	1	4	7	3	2	2	.206	.372	.294	.666	84	-1	4	4.06	1	/1-7,3-7	1	0.0
1984 Cin-N	32	42	5	5	0	0	1	3	4	6	0	0	.119	.196	.190	.386	8	-5	2	1.08	0	3-11/0-3(3-0-0)	0	-0.5
1985 Mon-N	19	26	0	4	1	0	0	0	0	2	0	1	.154	.154	.192	.346	-4	-4	0	.43	1	/3-4,0-3(1-0-2),1-1	0	-0.4
1987 StL-N	4	4	1	1	0	0	1	3	0	0	0	0	.250	.250	1.000	1.250	208	1	1	9.00	0	/3-1	0	0.0
1989 Cin-N	5	3	1	0	0	0	0	0	0	0	0	1	.000	.000	.000	.000	-97	-1	0	.00	0	....	0	-0.1
1991 Det-A	75	159	28	46	13	2	5	17	9	24	10	7	.289	.327	.491	.818	121	3	24	5.20	0	0-33(13-5-17),3-17/1-9,2-7,D	5	0.2
1992 Det-A	95	165	27	45	8	1	3	25	10	18	3	1	.273	.322	.388	.710	97	-1	20	4.24	-7	3-39,1-17,0-15(4-6-5)/2-7,D	6	-0.8
1993 Det-A	84	160	24	45	8	1	2	27	11	19	5	5	.281	.327	.381	.709	90	-3	19	3.99	-4	1-27,0-18(12-0-6),3-13,D-13,2/S	3	-0.9
1994 Det-A	24	21	4	6	0	0	1	4	0	2	0	1	.286	.286	.429	.714	81	-1	2	2.72	-1	1-15/0-4(4-0-0),D-1	0	-0.2
Total 9	353	614	95	159	30	4	14	83	41	74	20	18	.259	.310	.389	.699	90	-13	72	3.92	-10	/3-92,1-76,0-76,2-24,D-24,S	15	-2.8
• BARNEY, Ed	Edmund J. Barney b: 1/23/1890, Amery, WI d: 10/4/1967, Rice Lake, WI BL/TR, 5'10.5", 178 lbs. Deb: 7/22/1915 Career OF: 26-49-1																							
1915 NY-A	11	36	1	7	0	0	0	8	3	6	2	1	.194	.256	.194	.451	35	-3	2	1.84	0	0-10(3-7-0)	0	-0.4
Pit-N	32	99	16	27	1	2	0	5	11	12	7	3	.273	.363	.323	.686	110	2	13	4.50	0	0-26(3-22-1)	4	0.1
1916 Pit-N	45	137	16	27	4	0	0	9	23	15	8	....	.197	.313	.226	.539	66	-4	13	2.90	2	0-40(20-20-0)	3	-0.5
Total 2	88	272	33	61	5	2	0	22	37	33	17	4	.224	.324	.257	.581	78	-5	29	3.31	2	/0-76	7	-0.8
• BARNHART, Clyde	Clyde Lee "Pooch" Barnhart b: 12/29/1895, Buck Valley, PA d: 1/21/1980, Hagerstown, MD BR/TR, 5'10", 155 lbs. Deb: 9/22/1920 Career OF: 336-0-213																							
1920 Pit-N	12	46	5	15	4	2	0	5	1	2	1	0	.326	.340	.500	.840	135	2	8	6.64	1	3-12	2	0.4
1921 Pit-N	124	449	66	116	15	13	3	62	32	36	3	3	.258	.312	.370	.682	78	-13	53	3.91	-4	*3-118	10	-1.0
1922 Pit-N	75	209	30	69	7	5	1	38	25	7	3	2	.330	.402	.426	.828	112	5	37	6.63	-8	3-30,0-26(5-0-21)	7	-0.2
1923 Pit-N	114	327	60	106	25	13	9	72	47	21	5	7	.324	.409	.563	.972	151	23	74	8.21	5	0-92(0-0-92)	18	2.1
1924 Pit-N	102	344	49	95	6	11	3	51	30	17	8	4	.276	.338	.384	.721	91	-3	46	4.55	3	0-88(0-0-88)	9	-0.7
1925*Pit-N	142	539	85	175	32	11	4	114	59	25	9	5	.325	.391	.447	.838	106	8	96	6.59	-2	*0-138(138-0-0)	19	-0.4
1926 Pit-N	76	203	26	39	3	0	0	10	23	13	1	....	.192	.278	.207	.484	30	-19	13	1.96	-1	0-61(54-0-8)	2	-2.4
1927*Pit-N	108	360	65	115	23	4	3	54	37	19	2	....	.319	.384	.431	.815	110	6	59	5.79	1	0-94(94-0-0)	14	0.1
1928 Pit-N	61	196	18	58	6	2	4	30	11	9	3	....	.296	.333	.408	.741	89	-4	26	4.72	0	0-48(45-0-4)/3-1	5	-0.7
Total 9	814	2673	404	788	121	61	27	436	265	149	35	21	.295	.360	.416	.776	100	5	412	5.41	-4	0-547,3-161	86	-2.8
• BARNHART, Vic	Victor Dee Barnhart b: 9/1/1922, Hagerstown, MD BR/TR, 6', 188 lbs. Deb: 10/1/1944																							
1944 Pit-N	1	2	0	1	0	0	0	0	1	1	0	....	.500	.667	.500	1.167	222	1	1	22.68	1	/S-1	0	0.1
1945 Pit-N	71	201	21	54	7	0	0	19	9	11	2	....	.269	.300	.303	.603	65	-10	17	2.78	-8	S-60/3-4	2	-1.3
1946 Pit-N	2	1	0	0	0	0	0	0	0	0	0	....	.000	.000	.000	.000	-98	-0	0	.00	0	....	0	0.0
Total 3	74	204	21	55	7	0	0	19	10	12	2	....	.270	.304	.304	.608	67	-9	17	2.88	-7	/S-61,3-4	2	-1.2
• BARNIE, Billy	William Harrison "Baid Billy" Barnie b: 1/26/1853, New York, NY d: 7/15/1900, Hartford, CT, 5'7", 157 lbs. Deb: 5/7/1874 M/U NA OF: 0-8-31 Career OF: 0-1-6																							
1874 Har-n	45	190	21	35	4	2	0	19	1	13	2	2	.184	.188	.226	.415	31	-16	9	1.66	-9	C-30,0-29(0-4-25)/S-1	....	-1.8
1875 Wes-n	10	36	3	4	1	0	0	2	0	3	0	0	.111	.111	.139	.250	-13	-4	1	.52	1	/0-7(0-3-4),C-3	....	-0.3
Mut-n	9	34	1	5	0	0	0	1	1	0	0	0	.147	.171	.147	.318	11	-3	1	.89	-1	/C-6,0-3(0-1-2)	....	-0.3
Yr.	19	70	4	9	1	0	0	3	1	3	0	0	.129	.141	.143	.284	-1	-7	1	.70	0	0-10(0-4-6)/C-9	....	-0.6
1883 Bal-a	17	55	7	11	0	0	0	0	2	....	....	....	.200	.228	.200	.428	38	-4	3	1.64	-2	C-13/0-6(0-0-6),S-1	0	-0.4
1886 Bal-a	2	6	0	0	0	0	0	0	1	....	0	....	.000	.143	.000	.143	-55	-1	0	.00	0	/C-1,0-1	0	-0.1
Total 2 n	64	260	25	44	5	2	0	22	2	16	2	2	.169	.176	.204	.379	22	-23	10	1.39	-9	/C-39,0-39,S-1	....	-2.3
Total 2	19	61	7	11	0	0	0	0	3	....	0	....	.180	.219	.180	.399	28	-5	3	1.44	-2	/C-14,0-7,S-1	0	-0.5
• BARONE, Dick	Richard Anthony Barone b: 10/13/1932, San Jose, CA BR/TR, 5'9", 165 lbs. Deb: 9/22/1960																							
1960 Pit-N	3	6	0	0	0	0	0	0	0	1	0	0	.000	.000	.000	.000	-99	-2	0	.00	-1	/S-2	0	-0.2
• BARR, Scotty	Hyder Edward Barr b: 10/6/1886, Bristol, TN d: 12/2/1934, Fort Worth, TX BR/TR, 6', 175 lbs. Deb: 8/22/1908 Career OF: 2-15-0																							
1908 Phi-A	19	56	4	8	2	0	0	1	3	....	0	....	.143	.200	.179	.379	22	-5	2	1.04	-4	2-11/3-4,1-2,0-2(1-1-0)	0	-0.9
1909 Phi-A	22	51	5	4	1	0	0	1	11	....	2	....	.078	.254	.098	.352	12	-5	2	1.11	-2	0-15(1-14-0)/1-7	1	-0.9
Total 2	41	107	9	12	3	0	0	2	14	....	2	....	.112	.228	.140	.368	16	-9	4	1.08	-6	/0-17,2-11,1-9,3-4	1	-1.8
• BARRAGAN, Cuno	Facundo Anthony Barragan b: 6/20/1932, Sacramento, CA BR/TR, 5'11", 180 lbs. Deb: 9/1/1961																							
1961 Chi-N	10	28	3	6	0	0	1	2	2	7	0	0	.214	.267	.321	.588	54	-2	2	2.55	0	C-10	0	-0.1
1962 Chi-N	58	134	11	27	6	1	0	12	21	28	0	2	.201	.310	.261	.571	53	-9	11	2.42	-1	C-55	1	-0.8
1963 Chi-N	1	1	0	0	0	0	0	0	0	1	0	0	.000	.000	.000	.000	-95	-0	0	.00	0	/C-1	0	-0.1
Total 3	69	163	14	33	6	1	1	14	23	36	0	2	.202	.301	.270	.571	52	-11	13	2.42	-1	/C-66	1	-1.0
• BARRANCA, German	German (Costales) Barranca b: 10/19/1956, Veracruz, Mexico BL/TR, 6', 160 lbs. Deb: 9/2/1979																							
1979 KC-A	5	5	3	3	1	0	0	0	0	0	3	1	.600	.600	.800	1.400	269	1	2	20.02	2	/2-1,3-1,D-1	1	0.3
1980 KC-A	7	0	3	0	0	0	0	0	0	0	0	0	....	....	....	....	-99	0	0	....	0	....	0	0.0
1981 Cin-N	9	6	2	2	0	0	0	1	0	0	0	0	.333	.333	.333	.667	88	-0	1	4.50	0	....	0	0.0
1982 Cin-N	46	51	11	13	1	3	0	2	2	9	2	0	.255	.283	.392	.675	85	-1	6	3.86	-1	/2-6	1	-0.2
Total 4	67	62	19	18	2	3	0	3	2	9	5	1	.290	.313	.419	.732	100	0	9	4.95	1	/2-7,3-1,D-1	2	0.1
• BARRETT, Bill	William Joseph "Whispering Bill" Barrett b: 5/28/1900, Cambridge, MA d: 1/26/1951, Cambridge, MA BR/TR, 6', 175 lbs. Deb: 5/13/1921 Career OF: 74-28-400																							
1921 Phi-A	14	30	3	7	2	1	0	3	0	5	0	0	.233	.233	.367	.600	51	-2	2	2.84	-1	/S-8,P-4,3-2,1-1	0	-0.4
1923 Chi-A	44	162	17	44	7	2	2	23	9	24	12	3	.272	.310	.377	.686	81	-3	20	4.13	0	0-40(40-1-0)/3-1	3	-0.6
1924 Chi-A	119	406	52	110	18	5	2	56	30	38	15	10	.271	.326	.355	.680	78	-14	47	3.96	-18	S-77,0-28(25-3-0)/3-8	6	-2.4
1925 Chi-A	81	245	44	89	23	3	3	40	24	27	5	6	.363	.420	.518	.938	145	15	52	8.09	-5	2-41,0-27(3-1-23)/3-4,S-4	11	0.9
1926 Chi-A	111	368	46	113	31	4	6	61	25	26	9	7	.307	.353	.462	.815	115	6	59	5.55	-5	*0-102(1-0-102)/1-2	11	-0.7
1927 Chi-A	147	556	62	159	35	9	4	83	52	46	20	13	.286	.347	.403	.750	96	-4	78	4.76	5	*0-147(0-12-136)	13	-0.9
1928 Chi-A	76	235	34	65	11	2	3	26	14	30	8	3	.277	.320	.379	.699	84	-5	29	4.35	-1	0-37(4-1-32),2-25	6	-0.9
1929 Chi-A	3	1	0	0	0	0	0	0	2	0	0	0	.000	.667	.000	.667	87	0	0	8.82	0	....	0	0.0
Bos-A	111	370	57	100	23	4	3	35	51	38	11	8	.270	.363	.378	.742	93	-3	53	4.87	6	*0-109(1-10-101)/3-1	9	-0.4
Yr.	114	371	57	100	23	4	3	35	53	38	11	8	.270	.365	.377	.743	93	-2	54	4.88	6	*0-109(1-10-101)/3-1	9	-0.4

YEAR TM-L	G	AB	R	H	2B	3B	HR	RBI	BB	SO	SB	CS	AVG	OBP	SLG	OPS	OPS+	BR/A	RC	RC/G	FR	G/POS	WS	TPW
1930 Bos-A	6	18	3	3	1	0	0	1	1	3	0	0	.167	.211	.222	.433	10	-2	1	1.51	0	/0-5(0-0-5)	0	-0.3
Was-A	6	4	0	0	0	0	0	0	1	2	0	0	.000	.200	.000	.200	-44	-1	0	.33	0	/0-1	0	-0.1
Yr.	12	22	3	3	1	0	0	1	2	5	0	0	.136	.208	.182	.390		-3	1	1.28	0	/0-6(0-0-6)	0	-0.3
Total 9	718	2395	318	690	151	30	23	328	209	239	80	50	.288	.347	.405	.752	97	-14	341	4.92	-20	0-496/S-89,2-66,3-16,P-4,1	59	-5.7
• BARRETT, Bill	William Barrett b: Baltimore, MD Deb: 7/8/1871 U																							
1871 Kek-n	1	5	1	1	1	0	0	1	0	0	0	0	.200	.200	.400	.600	66	-0	0	3.23	0	/3-1,C-1	....	0.0
1872 Oly-n	1	4	0	0	0	0	0	0	0	0	0	0	.000	.000	.000	.000	-106	-1	0	.00	-1	/C-1	....	-0.1
1873 Bal-n	1	4	0	1	0	0	0	0	0	0	0	1	.250	.250	.250	.500	49	-1	0	1.95	-1	/0-1,S-1	....	-0.1
Total 3 n	3	13	1	2	1	0	0	1	0	0	0	1	.154	.154	.231	.385	8	-2	1	1.73	-2	/C-2,3-1,0-1,S-1	....	-0.2
• BARRETT, Bob	Robert Schley "Jumbo" Barrett b: 1/27/1899, Atlanta, GA d: 1/18/1982, Atlanta, GA BR/TR, 5'11", 175 lbs. Deb: 4/30/1923																							
1923 Chi-N	3	3	0	1	0	0	0	0	0	0	0	0	.333	.333	.333	.667	76	-0	0	4.24	0	....	0	0.0
1924 Chi-N	54	133	12	32	2	3	5	21	7	29	1	0	.241	.279	.414	.692	82	-3	15	3.90	-1	2-25,1-10/3-8	3	-0.4
1925 Chi-N	14	32	1	10	1	0	0	7	1	4	1	2	.313	.333	.344	.677	72	-2	3	3.22	0	/3-6,2-4	0	-0.2
Bro-N	1	1	0	0	0	0	0	1	0	0	0	0	.000	.000	.000	.000	-103	-0	0	.00	0	....	0	0.0
Yr.	15	33	1	10	1	0	0	8	1	4	1	2	.303	.324	.333	.657	67	-2	3	3.10	0	/3-6,2-4	0	-0.2
1927 Bro-N	99	355	29	92	10	2	5	38	14	22	1	....	.259	.289	.341	.630	68	-17	34	3.21	-3	3-96	5	-1.4
1929 Bos-A	68	126	15	34	10	0	0	19	10	6	3	1	.270	.324	.349	.673	75	-4	15	4.04	2	3-34/1-4,2-2,0-1	3	-0.1
Total 5	239	650	57	169	23	5	10	86	32	61	6	3	.260	.296	.357	.653	72	-27	68	3.51	-2	3-144/2-31,1-14,0-1	11	-2.1
• BARRETT, Jimmy	James Erigena Barrett b: 3/28/1875, Athol, MA d: 10/24/1921, Detroit, MI BL/TR, 5'9", 170 lbs. Deb: 9/13/1899 Career OF: 99-707-49																							
1899 Cin-N	26	92	30	34	2	4	0	10	18	....	4	....	.370	.477	.478	.956	159	9	24	10.39	-1	0-26(3-0-23)	5	0.6
1900 Cin-N	137	545	114	172	11	7	5	42	72	....	44	....	.316	.400	.389	.789	121	20	106	7.36	6	*0-137(0-115-22)	23	1.6
1901 Det-A	135	542	110	159	16	9	4	65	76	....	26	....	.293	.385	.378	.763	107	9	92	6.26	18	*0-135(0-135-0)	23	1.8
1902 Det-A	136	509	93	154	19	6	4	44	74	....	24	....	.303	.397	.387	.784	116	15	91	6.68	6	*0-136(0-136-0)	22	1.4
1903 Det-A	136	517	95	163	13	10	2	31	**74**	....	27	....	.315	**.407**	.391	.798	144	33	98	6.99	5	*0-136(0-136-0)	26	3.3
1904 Det-A	162	624	83	167	10	5	0	31	**79**	....	15	....	.268	.353	.300	.652	111	12	74	4.23	8	*0-162(0-162-0)	26	1.5
1905 Det-A	20	67	2	17	1	0	0	3	6	....	0	....	.254	.324	.269	.593	88	-1	6	3.19	-1	0-18(0-18-0)	1	-0.2
1906 Cin-N	5	12	1	0	0	0	0	0	2	....	0	....	.000	.143	.000	.143	-53	-2	0	.00	1	/0-4(0-0-4)	0	-0.2
1907 Bos-A	106	390	52	95	11	6	1	28	38	....	3	....	.244	.314	.310	.624	100	1	41	3.59	6	0-99(96-3-0)	9	0.0
1908 Bos-A	3	8	0	1	0	0	0	1	1	....	0	....	.125	.222	.125	.347	13	-1	0	.78	0	/0-2(0-2-0)	0	-0.1
Total 10	866	3306	580	962	83	47	16	255	440	....	143	....	.291	.379	.359	.738	117	96	533	5.87	48	0-855	135	9.7
• BARRETT, John	John Barrett b: Brooklyn, NY Deb: 9/18/1872																							
1872 Atl-n	8	34	7	7	1	0	0	2	0	1	1	0	.206	.206	.235	.441	30	-3	2	2.18	0	/0-8(8-0-0)	....	-0.2
• BARRETT, Johnny	John Joseph "Jack" Barrett b: 12/18/1915, Lowell, MA d: 8/17/1974, Seabrook Beach, NH BL/TL, 5'10.5", 170 lbs. Deb: 4/14/1942 Career OF: 22-173-328																							
1942 Pit-N	111	332	56	82	11	6	0	26	48	42	10	....	.247	.347	.316	.664	92	-1	40	4.17	2	0-94(15-5-74)	10	-0.5
1943 Pit-N	130	290	41	67	12	3	1	32	32	23	5	....	.231	.316	.303	.619	77	-8	30	3.55	-2	0-99(4-3-92)	6	-1.6
1944 Pit-N	149	568	99	153	24	**19**	7	83	86	56	**28**	....	.269	.366	.415	.782	115	13	93	5.86	-3	*0-147(1-67-92)	25	0.3
1945 Pit-N	142	507	97	130	29	4	15	67	79	68	25	....	.256	.357	.418	.775	111	8	81	5.63	-5	*0-132(0-75-57)	18	-0.3
1946 Pit-N	32	71	7	12	3	0	0	6	8	11	1	....	.169	.253	.211	.464	32	-6	4	1.98	-1	0-21(0-12-9)	0	-0.8
Bos-N	24	43	3	10	3	0	0	6	12	1	0	....	.233	.400	.302	.702	99	1	6	4.89	0	0-17(2-11-4)	2	0.0
Yr.	56	114	10	22	6	0	0	12	20	12	1	....	.193	.313	.246	.559	59	-6	10	3.04	-1	0-38(2-23-13)	2	-0.8
Total 5	588	1811	303	454	82	32	23	220	265	201	69	....	.251	.349	.369	.718	100	7	255	4.91	-10	0-510	61	-3.0
• BARRETT, Marty	Martin F. Barrett b: 11/1860, Port Henry, NY d: 1/29/1910, Holyoke, MA BR/TR, 5'9", 170 lbs. Deb: 6/24/1884																							
1884 Bos-N	3	6	0	0	0	0	0	0	0	4	....	....	.000	.000	.000	.000	-101	-1	0	.00	0	/C-3	0	-0.1
Ind-a	5	13	1	1	1	0	0	0	1		....	....	.077	.143	.154	.297	-3	-1	0	.67	-1	/C-4,0-1	0	-0.2
• BARRETT, Marty	Martin Glenn Barrett b: 6/23/1958, Arcadia, CA BR/TR, 5'10", 176 lbs. Deb: 9/6/1982																							
1982 Bos-A	8	18	0	1	0	0	0	0	0	1	0	0	.056	.056	.056	.111	-66	-4	0	.00	0	/2-7	0	-0.4
1983 Bos-A	33	44	7	10	1	1	0	2	3	1	0	0	.227	.277	.295	.572	54	-3	4	2.68	-3	2-23/D-5	0	-0.5
1984 Bos-A	139	475	56	144	23	3	3	45	42	25	5	3	.303	.361	.383	.744	101	2	66	5.10	-13	*2-136	16	-0.3
1985 Bos-A	156	534	59	142	26	0	5	56	56	50	7	5	.266	.338	.343	.681	84	-11	62	3.94	-2	*2-155	13	-0.5
1986*Bos-A	158	625	94	179	39	4	4	60	65	31	15	7	.286	.355	.381	.735	100	2	87	4.79	-4	*2-158	22	0.6
1987 Bos-A	137	559	72	164	23	0	3	43	51	38	15	2	.293	.354	.351	.704	85	-8	74	4.57	26	*2-137	16	2.4
1988*Bos-A	150	612	83	173	28	1	1	65	40	35	7	3	.283	.334	.337	.670	85	-12	69	3.84	3	*2-150	14	-0.5
1989 Bos-A	86	336	31	86	18	0	1	27	32	12	4	1	.256	.324	.318	.643	77	-9	35	3.36	8	2-80/D-4	6	0.1
1990*Bos-A	62	159	15	36	4	0	0	13	15	13	4	0	.226	.297	.252	.549	52	-9	13	2.60	1	2-60/3-1,D-1	4	-0.7
1991 SD-N	12	16	1	3	1	0	1	3	0	3	0	0	.188	.235	.438	.673	83	-0	2	3.55	0	/2-2,3-2	1	0.0
Total 10	941	3378	418	938	163	9	18	314	304	209	57	21	.278	.340	.347	.687	86	-53	412	4.15	15	2-908/D-10,3-3	92	0.1
• BARRETT, Michael	Michael Patrick Barrett b: 10/22/1976, Atlanta, GA BR/TR, 6'3", 200 lbs. Deb: 9/19/1998																							
1998 Mon-N	8	23	3	7	2	0	1	2	3	6	0	0	.304	.407	.522	.929	144	2	5	8.97	1	/3-3,C-3	1	0.3
1999 Mon-N	126	433	53	127	32	3	8	52	32	39	0	2	.293	.346	.436	.783	99	-3	60	4.94	-6	3-66,C-59/S-2	11	-0.4
2000 Mon-N	89	271	28	58	15	1	1	22	23	35	0	1	.214	.278	.288	.566	42	-25	21	2.53	-8	3-55,C-28	1	-2.9
2001 Mon-N	132	472	42	118	33	2	6	38	25	54	2	1	.250	.291	.367	.657	67	-24	47	3.40	-9	*C-131	2	-2.3
2002 Mon-N	117	376	41	99	20	1	12	49	40	65	6	3	.263	.336	.418	.753	94	-4	50	4.44	5	*C-110/1-6	12	0.9
2003 Mon-N	70	226	33	47	9	2	10	30	21	37	0	0	.208	.281	.398	.679	63	-13	24	3.49	-8	C-68	6	-1.6
Total 6	542	1801	200	456	111	9	38	193	144	236	8	7	.253	.312	.388	.700	77	-67	208	3.91	-26	C-399,3-124/1-6,S-2	33	-6.1
• BARRETT, Tom	Thomas Loren Barrett b: 4/2/1960, San Fernando, CA BB/TR, 5'9", 157 lbs. Deb: 7/2/1988																							
1988 Phi-N	36	54	5	11	1	0	0	3	7	8	0	0	.204	.306	.222	.529	53	-3	4	2.50	0	2-10	1	-0.3
1989 Phi-N	14	27	3	6	0	0	0	1	1	7	0	0	.222	.250	.222	.472	36	-2	2	1.99	-1	/2-9	0	-0.4
1992 Bos-A	4	3	1	0	0	0	0	0	2	0	0	0	.000	.400	.000	.400	19	-0	0	2.34	0	/2-2	0	0.0
Total 3	54	84	9	17	1	0	0	4	10	15	0	0	.202	.295	.214	.509	46	-5	6	2.32	-2	/2-21	1	-0.7
• BARRIOS, Jose	Jose Manuel Barrios b: 6/26/1957, New York, NY BR/TR, 6'4", 195 lbs. Deb: 4/23/1982																							
1982 SF-N	10	19	2	3	0	0	0	0	1	4	0	0	.158	.200	.158	.358	1	-3	0	.78	-1	/1-7	0	-0.4
• BARRON, Red	David Irenus Barron b: 6/21/1900, Clarksville, GA d: 10/4/1982, Atlanta, GA BR/TR, 5'11.5", 185 lbs. Deb: 6/10/1929																							
1929 Bos-N	10	21	3	4	1	0	0	1	1	4	2	....	.190	.227	.238	.465	16	-3	1	1.70	1	/0-6(6-0-0)	0	-0.2
• BARRON, Tony	Anthony Dirk Barron b: 8/17/1966, Portland, OR BR/TR, 6', 185 lbs. Deb: 6/2/1996																							
1996 Mon-N	1	1	0	0	0	0	0	0	0	1	0	0	.000	.000	.000	.000	-98	-0	0	.00	0	....	0	0.0
1997 Phi-N	57	189	22	54	12	1	4	24	12	38	0	1	.286	.335	.423	.758	97	-2	27	5.09	1	0-53(0-0-53)	4	-0.4
Total 2	58	190	22	54	12	1	4	24	12	39	0	1	.284	.333	.421	.754	96	-2	27	5.05	1	/0-53	4	-0.4
• BARROWS, Cuke	Roland Barrows b: 10/20/1883, Gray, ME d: 2/10/1955, Gorham, ME BL/TR, 5'8", 158 lbs. Deb: 9/18/1909 Career OF: 11-0-16																							
1909 Chi-A	5	20	1	3	0	0	0	2	0	....	0	....	.150	.190	.150	.340	8	-2	1	.81	2	/0-5(5-0-0)	0	-0.1
1910 Chi-A	6	20	0	4	0	0	0	1	3	....	0	....	.200	.304	.200	.504	61	-1	1	1.91	-1	/0-6(6-0-0)	0	-0.2
1911 Chi-A	13	46	5	9	2	0	0	4	7	....	2	....	.196	.315	.239	.554	57	-2	4	2.84	0	0-13(0-0-13)	1	-0.3
1912 Chi-A	8	13	0	3	0	0	0	2	2	....	1	....	.231	.333	.231	.564	64	-0	2	3.34	1	/0-3(0-0-3)	0	0.0
Total 4	32	99	6	19	2	0	0	9	12	....	3	....	.192	.292	.212	.504	50	-6	8	2.33	1	/0-27	1	-0.6
• BARROWS, Frank	Franklin L. Barrows b: 10/22/1846, Hudson, OH d: 2/6/1922, Fitchburg, MA Deb: 5/20/1871 U																							
1871 Bos-n	18	86	13	13	2	1	0	11	0	0	1	0	.151	.151	.198	.349	-1	-12	3	1.20	-2	0-17(13-0-4)/2-1	....	-0.9

• BARRY, Jack John Joseph Barry b: 4/26/1887, Meriden, CT d: 4/23/1961, Shrewsbury, MA BR/TR, 5'9", 158 lbs. Deb: 7/13/1908 M

YEAR TM-L	G	AB	R	H	2B	3B	HR	RBI	BB	SO	SB	CS	AVG	OBP	SLG	OPS	OPS+	BR/A	RC	RC/G	FR	G/POS	WS	TPW
1908 Phi-A	40	135	13	30	4	3	0	8	10	....	5	....	.222	.291	.296	.587	85	-2	13	3.11	-6	2-20,S-14/3-3	3	-0.9
1909 Phi-A	124	409	56	88	11	2	1	23	44	....	17	....	.215	.307	.259	.566	77	-9	40	2.99	-11	*S-124	11	-1.8
1910*Phi-A	145	487	64	126	19	5	3	60	52	....	14	....	.259	.336	.337	.673	112	8	61	4.13	-10	*S-145	19	0.3
1911*Phi-A	127	442	73	117	18	7	1	63	38	....	30	....	.265	.333	.344	.677	90	-6	62	4.55	1	*S-127	16	0.5
1912 Phi-A	140	483	75	126	19	9	0	55	47	....	22	....	.261	.335	.337	.673	96	-2	63	4.30	1	*S-139	16	0.9
1913*Phi-A	134	455	62	125	20	6	3	85	44	32	15	....	.275	.349	.365	.714	111	7	64	4.53	-2	*S-134	20	1.5
1914*Phi-A	140	467	57	113	12	0	0	42	53	34	22	13	.242	.324	.268	.592	81	-10	48	3.20	9	*S-140	18	1.1
1915 Phi-A	54	194	16	43	6	2	0	15	15	9	6	5	.222	.284	.273	.558	69	-9	16	2.62	-7	S-54	2	-1.3
*Bos-A	78	248	30	65	13	2	0	26	24	11	0	....	.262	.342	.331	.672	104	2	32	4.12	2	2-78	10	0.6
Yr.	132	442	46	108	19	4	0	41	39	20	6	5	.244	.317	.305	.622	90	-7	48	3.46	-5	2-78,S-54	12	-0.7
1916 Bos-A	94	330	28	67	6	1	0	20	17	24	8	....	.203	.277	.227	.505	52	-19	27	2.43	5	2-94	6	-1.4
1917 Bos-A	116	388	45	83	9	0	2	30	47	27	12	....	.214	.305	.253	.558	71	-12	39	2.86	-3	*2-116	9	-1.5
1919 Bos-A	31	108	13	26	5	1	0	2	5	5	2	....	.241	.293	.306	.599	72	-4	11	3.08	-5	2-31	2	-0.9
Total 11	1223	4146	532	1009	142	38	10	429	396	142	153	18	.243	.321	.303	.624	88	-55	476	3.60	-26	S-877,2-339/3-3	132	-2.9

• BARRY, Jeff Jeffrey Finas Barry b: 9/22/1969, Medford, OR BB/TR, 6'1", 190 lbs. Deb: 6/9/1995 Career OF: 16-40-21

YEAR TM-L	G	AB	R	H	2B	3B	HR	RBI	BB	SO	SB	CS	AVG	OBP	SLG	OPS	OPS+	BR/A	RC	RC/G	FR	G/POS	WS	TPW
1995 NY-N	15	15	2	2	1	0	0	0	1	8	0	0	.133	.188	.200	.388	2	-2	1	1.27	-0	/0-2(1-0-1)	0	-0.2
1998 Col-N	15	34	4	6	1	0	0	2	2	11	0	0	.176	.222	.206	.428	11	-4	2	1.62	0	0-10(1-8-5)	0	-0.5
1999 Col-N	74	168	19	45	16	0	5	26	19	29	0	4	.268	.349	.452	.802	79	-7	25	5.04	1	0-56(14-32-15)	3	-0.6
Total 3	104	217	25	53	18	0	5	28	22	48	0	4	.244	.320	.396	.716	64	-14	27	4.20	1	/0-68	3	-1.3

• BARRY, Rich Richard Donovan Barry b: 9/12/1940, Berkeley, CA BR/TR, 6'4", 205 lbs. Deb: 7/4/1969

YEAR TM-L	G	AB	R	H	2B	3B	HR	RBI	BB	SO	SB	CS	AVG	OBP	SLG	OPS	OPS+	BR/A	RC	RC/G	FR	G/POS	WS	TPW
1969 Phi-N	20	32	4	6	1	0	0	0	5	6	0	0	.188	.316	.219	.535	54	-2	2	2.17	-1	/0-9(9-0-0)	0	-0.3

• BARRY, Shad John C. Barry b: 10/27/1878, Newburgh, NY d: 11/27/1936, Los Angeles, CA BR/TR Deb: 5/30/1899 Career OF: 214-39-371

YEAR TM-L	G	AB	R	H	2B	3B	HR	RBI	BB	SO	SB	CS	AVG	OBP	SLG	OPS	OPS+	BR/A	RC	RC/G	FR	G/POS	WS	TPW
1899 Was-N	78	247	31	71	7	5	1	33	12	....	11	....	.287	.328	.368	.697	92	-3	35	5.12	-7	0-23(20-0-3),1-22,3-13,S-13/2	5	-1.0
1900 Bos-N	81	254	40	66	10	7	1	37	13	....	9	....	.260	.301	.366	.667	74	-11	32	4.37	-6	0-24(22-1-1),S-18,2-16,1-10/3	4	-1.6
1901 Bos-N	11	40	3	7	2	0	0	6	2	....	1	....	.175	.233	.225	.458	30	-4	2	1.91	0	0-11(11-0-0)	0	-0.5
Phi-N	67	252	35	62	10	0	1	22	15	....	13	....	.246	.294	.298	.591	70	-10	28	3.66	-9	2-35,3-16,0-13(3-9-1)/S-1	4	-1.8
Yr.	78	292	38	69	12	0	1	28	17	....	14	....	.236	.285	.288	.573	65	-13	30	3.41	-10	2-35,0-24(14-9-1),3-16/S-1	4	-2.3
1902 Phi-N	138	543	65	156	20	6	3	58	44	....	14	....	.287	.343	.363	.706	118	11	76	5.01	-8	*0-137(7-0-130)/1-1	17	-0.3
1903 Phi-N	138	550	75	152	24	5	1	60	30	....	26	....	.276	.321	.344	.664	92	-6	72	4.65	-6	*0-107(105-2-0),1-30/3-1	12	-1.8
1904 Phi-N	35	122	15	25	2	0	0	3	11	....	2	....	.205	.281	.221	.503	58	-5	9	2.29	13	0-32(11-6-15)/3-1	1	0.6
Chi-N	73	263	29	69	7	2	1	26	17	....	12	....	.262	.310	.316	.625	93	-2	31	4.00	-3	0-30(0-13-17),1-18,3-16/S-8,2	8	-0.7
Yr.	108	385	44	94	9	2	1	29	28	....	14	....	.244	.300	.286	.586	82	-8	40	3.44	9	0-62(11-19-32),1-18,3-17/S,2	9	-0.1
1905 Chi-N	27	104	10	22	2	0	0	10	5	....	5	....	.212	.255	.231	.485	43	-7	8	2.41	0	1-26	1	-0.8
Cin-N	125	494	90	160	11	12	1	56	33	....	16	....	.324	.372	.401	.773	117	11	85	6.14	-15	*1-124/0-2(1-1-0)	18	-0.6
Yr.	152	598	100	182	13	12	1	66	38	....	21	....	.304	.352	.371	.723	105	3	92	5.44	-14	*1-150/0-2(1-1-0)	19	-1.4
1906 Cin-N	73	279	38	80	10	5	1	33	26	....	11	....	.287	.354	.369	.723	120	7	43	5.29	-1	1-43,0-30(14-7-9)	8	0.4
StL-N	62	237	26	59	9	1	0	12	15	....	6	....	.249	.299	.295	.595	89	-3	24	3.40	-2	0-35(0-0-35),1-21/3-6	4	-0.7
Yr.	135	516	64	139	19	6	1	45	41	....	17	....	.269	.329	.335	.664	106	3	67	4.41	-3	0-65(14-7-44),1-64/3-6	12	-0.4
1907 StL-N	81	294	30	73	5	2	0	19	28	....	4	....	.248	.320	.279	.599	91	-2	30	3.35	-4	0-81(0-0-81)	6	-1.2
1908 StL-N	74	268	24	61	8	1	0	11	19	....	9	....	.228	.286	.265	.551	80	-6	23	2.77	1	0-69(0-0-69)/S-2	4	-0.9
NY-N	37	67	5	10	1	1	0	5	9	....	1	....	.149	.260	.194	.454	43	-4	4	1.70	-2	0-31(20-0-10)	0	-0.8
Yr.	111	335	29	71	9	2	0	16	28	....	10	....	.212	.281	.251	.531	72	-10	27	2.54	-1	*0-100(20-0-79)/S-2	4	-1.7
Total 10	1100	4014	516	1073	128	47	10	391	279	....	140	....	.267	.321	.330	.651	93	-36	502	4.29	-49	0-625,1-295/2-60,3-54,S-42	92	-11.8

• BARTEE, Kimera Kimera Anotchi Bartee b: 7/21/1972, Omaha, NE BR/TR, 6', 175 lbs. Deb: 4/3/1996 Career OF: 29-157-3

YEAR TM-L	G	AB	R	H	2B	3B	HR	RBI	BB	SO	SB	CS	AVG	OBP	SLG	OPS	OPS+	BR/A	RC	RC/G	FR	G/POS	WS	TPW
1996 Det-A	110	217	32	55	6	1	1	14	17	77	20	10	.253	.308	.304	.612	56	-15	22	3.14	0	0-99(4-95-2)/D-2	1	-1.3
1997 Det-A	12	5	4	1	0	0	0	0	2	2	3	1	.200	.500	.200	.700	93	1	1	6.76	0	/0-6(3-3-0),D-3	0	0.0
1998 Det-A	57	98	20	19	5	1	3	15	6	35	9	5	.194	.240	.357	.598	52	-8	8	2.37	0	0-29(11-18-1),D-10	1	-0.7
1999 Det-A	41	77	11	15	1	3	0	3	9	20	3	3	.195	.279	.286	.565	44	-7	6	2.26	-1	0-38(0-38-0)/D-1	1	-0.8
2000 Cin-N	11	4	2	0	0	0	0	0	0	2	1	0	.000	.200	.000	.200	-43	-1	0	1.05	0	/0-3(2-1-0)	0	-0.1
2001 Col-N	12	15	0	0	0	0	0	1	2	5	0	0	.000	.167	.000	.167	-42	-3	0	.28	-1	0-10(9-2-0)	0	-0.4
Total 6	243	416	69	90	12	5	4	33	36	141	36	19	.216	.284	.298	.582	48	-33	37	2.69	-3	0-185/D-16	3	-3.3

• BARTELL, Dick Richard William "Rowdy Richard,Shortwave" Bartell b: 11/22/1907, Chicago, IL d: 8/4/1995, Alameda, CA BR/TR, 5'9", 160 lbs. Deb: 10/2/1927 C

YEAR TM-L	G	AB	R	H	2B	3B	HR	RBI	BB	SO	SB	CS	AVG	OBP	SLG	OPS	OPS+	BR/A	RC	RC/G	FR	G/POS	WS	TPW
1927 Pit-N	1	2	0	0	0	0	0	0	2	0	0	....	.000	.500	.000	.500	41	0	0	3.14	0	/S-1	0	0.0
1928 Pit-N	72	233	27	71	8	4	1	36	21	18	4	....	.305	.377	.386	.763	96	-0	34	5.16	-2	2-39,S-27/3-1	7	0.1
1929 Pit-N	143	610	101	184	40	13	2	57	40	29	11	....	.302	.347	.420	.766	87	-14	86	5.01	14	S-74,2-70	16	1.0
1930 Pit-N	129	475	69	152	32	13	4	75	39	34	8	....	.320	.378	.467	.845	102	2	82	6.18	8	*S-126	18	2.2
1931 Phi-N	135	554	88	160	43	7	0	34	27	38	6	....	.289	.325	.392	.717	85	-12	72	4.43	-5	*S-133/2-3	11	-0.7
1932 Phi-N	154	614	118	189	48	7	1	53	64	47	8	....	.308	.379	.414	.792	101	4	102	5.74	16	*S-154	21	3.0
1933 Phi-N★	152	587	78	159	25	5	1	37	56	46	6	....	.271	.340	.336	.675	83	-11	73	4.19	-1	*S-152	13	-0.1
1934 Phi-N	146	604	102	187	30	4	0	37	64	59	13	....	.310	.384	.373	.757	91	-4	92	5.70	22	*S-146	18	2.9
1935 NY-N	137	539	60	141	28	4	14	53	37	52	5	....	.262	.316	.406	.722	94	-5	72	4.51	9	*S-137	18	1.4
1936*NY-N	145	510	71	152	31	3	8	42	40	36	6	....	.298	.355	.418	.773	108	6	79	5.51	23	*S-144	24	3.8
1937*NY-N★	128	516	91	158	38	2	14	62	40	38	5	....	.306	.367	.469	.836	124	17	92	6.52	23	*S-128	28	4.9
1938 NY-N	127	481	67	126	26	1	9	49	55	60	4	....	.262	.347	.376	.724	98	0	67	4.83	14	*S-127	17	2.4
1939 Chi-N	105	336	37	80	24	2	3	34	42	25	6	....	.238	.335	.348	.683	82	-7	41	3.98	-5	*S-101/3-1	10	-0.5
1940*Det-A	139	528	76	123	24	3	7	53	76	53	12	2	.233	.335	.330	.665	67	-23	65	4.10	6	*S-139	11	-0.6
1941 Det-A	5	12	0	2	1	0	0	1	2	2	0	1	.167	.333	.250	.583	51	-1	1	2.46	-1	/S-5	0	-0.2
NY-N	104	373	44	113	20	0	5	35	52	29	6	....	.303	.394	.397	.791	121	13	60	5.82	0	3-84,S-21	15	1.7
1942 NY-N	90	316	53	77	10	3	5	24	44	34	4	....	.244	.351	.342	.692	102	3	41	4.42	2	3-52,S-31	12	0.9
1943 NY-N	99	337	48	91	14	0	5	28	47	27	5	....	.270	.371	.356	.727	110	6	47	4.93	11	3-54,S-33	13	2.3
1946 NY-N	5	2	0	0	0	0	0	0	0	0	0	....	.000	.000	.000	.000	-99	-1	0	.00	-1	/3-4,2-2	0	-0.2
Total 18	2016	7629	1130	2165	442	71	79	710	748	627	109	3	.284	.355	.391	.747	96	-27	1107	5.05	134	*S-1679,3-196,2-114	252	24.3

• BARTIROME, Tony Anthony Joseph Bartirome b: 5/9/1932, Pittsburgh, PA BL/TL, 5'10", 155 lbs. Deb: 4/19/1952 C

YEAR TM-L	G	AB	R	H	2B	3B	HR	RBI	BB	SO	SB	CS	AVG	OBP	SLG	OPS	OPS+	BR/A	RC	RC/G	FR	G/POS	WS	TPW
1952 Pit-N	124	355	32	78	10	3	0	16	26	37	3	3	.220	.273	.265	.538	48	-25	28	2.66	0	*1-118	2	-2.9

• BARTLEY, Boyd Boyd Owen Bartley b: 2/11/1920, Chicago, IL BR/TR, 5'8.5", 165 lbs. Deb: 5/30/1943

YEAR TM-L	G	AB	R	H	2B	3B	HR	RBI	BB	SO	SB	CS	AVG	OBP	SLG	OPS	OPS+	BR/A	RC	RC/G	FR	G/POS	WS	TPW
1943 Bro-N	9	21	0	1	0	0	0	1	1	3	0	....	.048	.091	.048	.139	-59	-4	0	.20	-2	/S-9	0	-0.6

• BARTLING, Irv Henry Irving Bartling b: 6/27/1914, Bay City, MI d: 6/12/1973, Westland, MI BR/TR, 6', 175 lbs. Deb: 9/8/1938

YEAR TM-L	G	AB	R	H	2B	3B	HR	RBI	BB	SO	SB	CS	AVG	OBP	SLG	OPS	OPS+	BR/A	RC	RC/G	FR	G/POS	WS	TPW
1938 Phi-A	14	46	5	8	1	1	0	5	3	7	0	0	.174	.224	.239	.464	17	-6	3	1.76	-3	S-13/3-1	0	-0.7

• BARTON, Bob Robert Wilbur Barton b: 7/30/1941, Norwood, OH BR/TR, 6', 175 lbs. Deb: 9/17/1965

YEAR TM-L	G	AB	R	H	2B	3B	HR	RBI	BB	SO	SB	CS	AVG	OBP	SLG	OPS	OPS+	BR/A	RC	RC/G	FR	G/POS	WS	TPW
1965 SF-N	4	7	1	4	0	0	0	1	0	0	0	0	.571	.571	.571	1.143	217	1	2	20.57	0	/C-2	1	0.1
1966 SF-N	43	91	1	16	2	1	0	3	5	5	0	0	.176	.219	.220	.439	22	-10	4	1.44	1	C-39	2	-0.7
1967 SF-N	7	19	0	4	0	0	0	1	0	2	0	0	.211	.250	.211	.461	33	-2	1	1.44	-0	/C-7	0	-0.1
1968 SF-N	46	92	4	24	2	0	0	5	7	18	0	0	.261	.313	.283	.596	80	-2	9	3.21	2	C-45	3	0.2
1969 SF-N	49	106	5	18	2	0	0	1	9	19	0	0	.170	.241	.189	.430	22	-11	5	1.37	-2	C-49	1	-1.2
1970 SD-N	61	188	15	41	6	0	4	16	15	37	1	1	.218	.279	.314	.593	61	-11	16	2.84	2	C-59	3	-0.6
1971 SD-N	121	376	23	94	17	2	5	23	35	49	0	5	.250	.317	.346	.663	94	-5	36	3.25	7	*C-119	10	0.8
1972 SD-N	29	88	1	17	1	0	0	9	2	19	2	0	.193	.211	.205	.416	20	-9	4	1.27	0	C-29	1	-0.8
1973 Cin-N	3	1	0	0	0	0	0	0	1	0	0	0	.000	.500	.000	.500	53	0	0	3.51	0	/C-2	0	0.0
1974 SD-N	30	81	4	19	1	0	0	7	13	19	0	0	.235	.340	.247	.587	69	-3	8	3.09	5	C-29	2	0.4
Total 10	393	1049	54	237	31	3	9	66	87	168	3	6	.226	.288	.287	.575	65	-51	85	2.64	15	C-380	23	-2.0

YEAR TM-L	G	AB	R	H	2B	3B	HR	RBI	BB	SO	SB	CS	AVG	OBP	SLG	OPS	OPS+	BR/A	RC	RC/G	FR	G/POS	WS	TPW
• BARTON, Harry	Harry Lamb Barton b: 1/20/1875, Chester, PA d: 1/25/1955, Upland, PA BB/TR, 5'6.5", 155 lbs. Deb: 4/15/1905																							
1905 Phi-A	29	60	5	10	2	1	0	3	3	....	2	....	.167	.206	.233	.440	39	-4	4	1.82	-2	C-13/1-2,3-2,O-1	1	-0.6
• BARTON, Vince	Vincent David Barton b: 2/1/1908, Edmonton, Canada d: 9/13/1973, Toronto, Canada BL/TR, 6', 180 lbs. Deb: 7/17/1931 Career OF: 0-0-95																							
1931 Chi-N	66	239	45	57	10	1	13	50	21	40	1	....	.238	.323	.452	.775	104	1	36	5.18	-5	O-61(0-0-61)	7	-0.8
1932 Chi-N	36	134	19	30	2	3	3	15	8	22	0	....	.224	.273	.351	.623	67	-6	13	3.25	-1	O-34(0-0-34)	2	-1.0
Total 2	**102**	**373**	**64**	**87**	**12**	**4**	**16**	**65**	**29**	**62**	**1**	**....**	**.233**	**.306**	**.416**	**.721**	**91**	**-6**	**50**	**4.47**	**-6**	**/O-95**	**9**	**-1.7**
• BARTOSCH, Dave	David Robert Bartosch b: 3/24/1917, St. Louis, MO BR/TR, 6'1", 190 lbs. Deb: 4/28/1945																							
1945 StL-N	24	47	9	12	1	0	0	1	6	3	0	....	.255	.340	.277	.616	71	-2	5	3.81	0	O-11(4-0-7)	1	-0.2
• BASGALL, Monty	Romanus Basgall b: 2/8/1922, Pfeifer, KS BR/TR, 5'10.5", 175 lbs. Deb: 4/19/1948 C																							
1948 Pit-N	38	51	12	11	1	0	2	6	3	5	0	....	.216	.259	.353	.612	63	-3	5	2.98	0	2-22	1	-0.2
1949 Pit-N	107	308	25	67	9	1	2	26	31	32	1	....	.218	.291	.273	.564	51	-21	25	2.70	-6	2-98/3-3	3	-2.2
1951 Pit-N	55	153	15	32	5	2	0	9	12	14	0	0	.209	.271	.268	.539	44	-12	10	2.03	-4	2-55	2	-1.3
Total 3	**200**	**512**	**52**	**110**	**15**	**3**	**4**	**41**	**46**	**51**	**1**	**0**	**.215**	**.282**	**.279**	**.561**	**50**	**-36**	**40**	**2.52**	**-10**	**2-175/3-3**	**6**	**-3.8**
• BASHANG, Al	Albert C. Bashang b: 8/22/1888, Cincinnati, OH d: 6/23/1967, Cincinnati, OH BB/TR, 5'8", 150 lbs. Deb: 7/30/1912 Career OF: 5-0-0																							
1912 Det-A	6	12	3	1	0	0	0	0	3	....	0	....	.083	.267	.083	.350	1	-1	0	.61	0	/O-6(5-0-0)	0	-0.2
1918 Bro-N	2	5	0	1	0	0	0	0	0	0	0	....	.200	.200	.200	.400	22	-0	0	1.17	1	/O-1	0	0.0
Total 2	**8**	**17**	**3**	**2**	**0**	**0**	**0**	**0**	**3**	**0**	**0**	**....**	**.118**	**.250**	**.118**	**.368**	**7**	**-2**	**0**	**.76**	**0**	**/O-7**	**0**	**-0.2**
• BASHORE, Walt	Walter Franklin Bashore b: 10/6/1909, Harrisburg, PA d: 9/26/1984, Sebring, FL BR/TR, 6', 170 lbs. Deb: 7/14/1936																							
1936 Phi-N	10	10	1	2	0	0	0	0	1	3	0	....	.200	.273	.200	.473	26	-1	1	2.13	-1	/O-6(0-6-0),3-1	0	-0.2
• BASINSKI, Eddie	Edwin Frank "Bazooka,Fiddler" Basinski b: 11/4/1922, Buffalo, NY BR/TR, 6'1", 172 lbs. Deb: 5/20/1944																							
1944 Bro-N	39	105	13	27	4	1	0	9	6	10	1	....	.257	.310	.314	.624	77	-3	11	3.44	-2	2-37/S-3	2	-0.4
1945 Bro-N	108	336	30	88	9	4	0	33	11	33	0	....	.262	.293	.313	.606	69	-15	29	2.91	-1	*S-101/2-6	6	-0.9
1947 Pit-N	56	161	15	32	6	2	4	17	18	27	0	....	.199	.279	.335	.615	61	-10	15	2.94	-5	2-56	1	-1.2
Total 3	**203**	**602**	**58**	**147**	**19**	**7**	**4**	**59**	**35**	**70**	**1**	**....**	**.244**	**.292**	**.319**	**.611**	**68**	**-28**	**55**	**3.01**	**-9**	**S-104/2-99**	**9**	**-2.4**
• BASS, Doc	William Capers Bass b: 12/4/1899, Macon, GA d: 1/12/1970, Macon, GA BL/TL, 5'10", 165 lbs. Deb: 7/29/1918																							
1918 Bos-N	2	1	1	1	0	0	0	0	0	0	1	....	1.000	1.000	1.000	2.000	532	0	2	∞	0	....	0	0.1
• BASS, John	John E. Bass b: 1850, Baltimore, MD, 5'6", 150 lbs. Deb: 5/4/1871																							
1871 Cle-n	22	89	18	27	1	**10**	3	18	3	4	0	1	.303	.326	.640	.967	179	8	19	9.53	-4	*S-22/C-1	....	0.3
1872 Atl-n	2	7	0	1	1	0	0	1	0	0	0	0	.143	.143	.286	.429	25	-1	0	1.51	0	/O-2(0-0-2)	....	-0.1
1877 Har-N	1	4	1	1	0	0	0	0	0	0	....	....	.250	.250	.250	.500	65	-0	0	2.35	0	/O-1	0	-0.1
Total 2 n	**24**	**96**	**18**	**28**	**2**	**10**	**3**	**19**	**3**	**4**	**0**	**1**	**.292**	**.313**	**.615**	**.928**	**168**	**8**	**19**	**8.83**	**-4**	**/S-22,O-2,C-1**	**....**	**0.2**
• BASS, Kevin	Kevin Charles Bass b: 5/12/1959, Redwood City, CA BB/TR, 6', 183 lbs. Deb: 4/9/1982 Career OF: 209-194-953																							
1982 Mil-A	18	9	4	0	0	0	0	0	1	1	0	0	.000	.100	.000	.100	-74	-2	0	.19	-1	O-14(0-6-8)/D-2	0	-0.4
Hou-N	12	24	2	1	0	0	0	1	0	8	0	0	.042	.042	.042	.083	-83	-6	0	.00	0	/O-7(4-4-0)	0	-0.7
1983 Hou-N	88	195	25	46	7	3	2	18	6	27	2	2	.236	.259	.333	.592	67	-10	16	2.78	-2	O-52(0-5-47)	2	-1.5
1984 Hou-N	121	331	33	86	17	5	2	29	6	57	5	5	.260	.279	.360	.639	84	-10	32	3.41	-2	O-81(0-31-52)	6	-1.5
1985 Hou-N	150	539	72	145	27	5	16	68	31	63	19	8	.269	.316	.427	.743	109	5	71	4.59	1	*O-141(10-105-39)	19	0.2
1986*Hou-N★	157	591	83	184	33	5	20	79	38	72	22	13	.311	.359	.486	.845	135	24	97	5.94	-3	*O-155(2-41-133)	27	1.5
1987 Hou-N	157	592	83	168	31	5	19	85	53	77	21	8	.284	.347	.449	.796	113	11	90	5.37	1	*O-155(0-0-155)	18	0.4
1988 Hou-N	157	541	57	138	27	2	14	72	42	65	31	6	.255	.316	.390	.706	106	7	66	4.15	2	*O-147(0-0-147)	19	0.5
1989 Hou-N	87	313	42	94	19	4	5	44	29	44	11	4	.300	.362	.435	.796	131	13	51	6.02	1	O-84(31-0-53)	17	1.2
1990 SF-N	61	214	25	54	9	1	7	32	14	26	2	2	.252	.304	.402	.706	96	-3	25	3.95	-3	O-55(0-0-55)	7	-0.7
1991 SF-N	124	361	43	84	10	4	10	40	36	56	7	4	.233	.309	.366	.675	92	-4	39	3.53	1	*O-101(23-0-79)	5	-0.7
1992 SF-N	89	265	25	71	11	3	7	30	16	53	7	7	.268	.312	.411	.723	109	0	31	4.00	-1	O-72(56-0-21)	5	-0.3
NY-N	46	137	15	37	12	2	2	9	7	17	7	2	.270	.306	.431	.736	108	1	18	4.57	-1	O-39(28-0-13)	3	-0.1
Yr.	135	402	40	108	23	5	9	39	23	70	14	9	.269	.310	.418	.728	109	2	49	4.19	-1	*O-111(84-0-34)	8	-0.3
1993 Hou-N	111	229	31	65	18	0	3	37	26	31	7	1	.284	.359	.402	.761	107	4	35	5.48	-1	O-64(12-2-51)	9	0.0
1994 Hou-N	82	203	37	63	15	1	6	35	28	24	2	3	.310	.397	.483	.879	135	10	38	6.81	0	O-57(11-0-47)	9	0.8
1995 Bal-A	111	295	32	72	12	0	5	32	24	47	8	8	.244	.305	.336	.641	66	-17	26	2.78	0	O-77(32-0-53),D-19	2	-2.0
Total 14	**1571**	**4839**	**609**	**1308**	**248**	**40**	**118**	**611**	**357**	**668**	**151**	**73**	**.270**	**.325**	**.411**	**.736**	**106**	**23**	**635**	**4.54**	**-6**	***O-1301/D-21**	**148**	**-2.9**
• BASS, Randy	Randy William Bass b: 3/13/1954, Lawton, OK BL/TR, 6'1", 210 lbs. Deb: 9/3/1977																							
1977 Min-A	9	19	0	2	0	0	0	0	0	5	0	0	.105	.105	.105	.211	-43	-4	0	.33	0	/D-6	0	-0.4
1978 KC-A	2	2	0	0	0	0	0	0	0	0	0	0	.000	.000	.000	.000	-97	-1	0	.00	0	....	0	-0.1
1979 Mon-N	2	1	0	0	0	0	0	0	0	0	0	0	.000	.000	.000	.000	-101	-0	0	.00	0	/1-1	0	0.0
1980 SD-N	19	49	5	14	0	1	3	8	7	7	0	0	.286	.386	.510	.896	157	4	10	7.99	-2	1-15	3	0.1
1981 SD-N	69	176	13	37	4	1	4	20	20	28	0	1	.210	.294	.313	.607	78	-6	15	2.77	0	1-50	2	-0.8
1982 SD-N	13	30	1	6	0	0	1	8	2	4	0	0	.200	.273	.300	.573	63	-2	3	2.94	0	/1-9	1	-0.2
Tex-A	16	48	5	10	2	0	1	6	1	7	0	0	.208	.240	.313	.553	53	-3	4	2.31	0	/D-7,1-6	0	-0.4
Total 6	**130**	**325**	**24**	**69**	**6**	**2**	**9**	**42**	**30**	**51**	**0**	**1**	**.212**	**.287**	**.326**	**.613**	**78**	**-11**	**32**	**3.20**	**-2**	**/1-81,D-13**	**6**	**-1.8**
• BASSETT, Charley	Charles Edwin Bassett b: 2/9/1863, Central Falls, RI d: 5/28/1942, Pawtucket, RI BR/TR, 5'10", 150 lbs. Deb: 7/22/1884																							
1884 Pro-N	27	79	10	11	2	1	0	6	4	15	....	....	.139	.181	.190	.371	17	-7	3	1.12	1	3-13/S-7,O-2(1-1-0),2-1	1	-0.5
1885 Pro-N	82	285	21	41	8	2	0	16	19	60	....	....	.144	.197	.186	.383	25	-22	11	1.19	3	2-39,S-23,3-20/C-1	3	-1.6
1886 KC-N	90	342	41	89	19	8	2	32	36	43	6	....	.260	.331	.380	.711	109	3	46	4.92	-2	S-82/3-8	9	0.4
1887 Ind-N	119	477	41	129	14	6	1	47	25	31	25	....	.270	.278	.294	.572	61	-23	45	3.43	0	*2-119	5	-1.6
1888 Ind-N	128	481	58	116	20	3	2	60	32	41	24	....	.241	.297	.308	.604	91	-4	52	3.87	-16	*2-128	12	-1.6
1889 Ind-N	127	477	64	117	12	5	4	68	37	38	15	....	.245	.304	.317	.620	72	-19	52	3.80	0	*2-127	8	-1.2
1890 NY-N	100	410	52	98	13	8	0	54	29	25	14	....	.239	.300	.310	.610	78	-12	43	3.69	9	*2-100	9	0.0
1891 NY-N	130	524	60	136	19	8	4	68	36	29	16	....	.260	.312	.349	.661	96	-3	64	4.43	1	*3-121/2-9	14	0.1
1892 NY-N	35	130	9	27	2	3	0	16	6	11	0	....	.208	.254	.269	.523	59	-7	9	2.39	5	2-30/3-5	1	-0.1
Lou-N	79	313	36	67	5	5	2	35	15	19	16	....	.214	.250	.281	.531	66	-13	27	2.93	-2	3-73/2-6	5	-1.3
Yr.	114	443	45	94	7	8	2	51	21	30	16	....	.212	.251	.278	.529	64	-20	36	2.77	2	3-78,2-36	6	-1.4
Total 9	**917**	**3518**	**392**	**831**	**114**	**49**	**15**	**402**	**239**	**312**	**116**	**....**	**.236**	**.285**	**.304**	**.590**	**75**	**-108**	**351**	**3.51**	**-1**	**2-559,3-240,S-112/O-2,C-1**	**67**	**-7.4**
• BASSLER, Johnny	John Landis Bassler b: 6/3/1895, Lancaster, PA d: 6/29/1979, Santa Monica, CA BL/TR, 5'9", 170 lbs. Deb: 7/11/1913 C																							
1913 Cle-A	1	2	0	0	0	0	0	0	0	0	0	....	.000	.000	.000	.000	-97	-0	0	.00	-1	/C-1	0	-0.1
1914 Cle-A	43	77	5	14	1	1	0	6	15	8	3	2	.182	.323	.221	.543	61	-3	6	2.40	1	C-25/3-1,O-1	1	-0.1
1921 Det-A	119	388	37	119	18	5	0	56	58	16	2	1	.307	.401	.379	.780	101	5	63	5.92	-2	*C-114	13	0.9
1922 Det-A	121	372	41	120	14	0	0	41	62	12	2	1	.323	.422	.360	.782	109	10	62	6.10	-1	*C-118	15	1.6
1923 Det-A	135	383	45	114	12	3	0	49	76	13	2	2	.298	.414	.345	.759	103	8	61	5.62	10	*C-128	19	2.5
1924 Det-A	124	379	43	131	20	3	1	68	62	11	2	1	.346	.441	.422	.864	125	20	76	7.67	-2	*C-122	21	2.4
1925 Det-A	121	344	40	96	19	3	0	52	74	6	1	1	.279	.408	.352	.760	96	3	56	5.63	-6	*C-118	13	0.4
1926 Det-A	66	174	20	53	8	1	0	22	45	6	0	0	.305	.447	.362	.810	111	7	33	6.71	5	C-63	10	1.5
1927 Det-A	81	200	19	57	7	0	0	24	45	9	1	0	.285	.416	.320	.736	92	2	31	5.43	1	C-67	8	0.6
Total 9	**811**	**2319**	**250**	**704**	**99**	**16**	**1**	**318**	**437**	**81**	**13**	**8**	**.304**	**.416**	**.361**	**.777**	**104**	**51**	**388**	**6.00**	**5**	**C-756/3-1,O-1**	**100**	**9.8**
• BASTIAN, Charlie	Charles J. Bastian b: 7/4/1860, Philadelphia, PA d: 1/18/1932, Pennsauken, NJ BR/TR, 5'6.5", 145 lbs. Deb: 8/18/1884																							
1884 Wil-U	17	60	6	12	1	3	2	....	3	....	....	....	.200	.238	.417	.655	114	1	6	3.56	7	2-16/P-1,S-1	1	0.7
KC-U	11	46	6	9	3	0	1	....	4	....	....	....	.196	.260	.326	.586	112	1	4	3.03	0	2-11	1	0.2
Yr.	28	106	12	21	4	3	3	....	7	....	....	....	.198	.248	.377	.625	113	2	10	3.33	7	2-27/P-1,S-1	2	0.9
1885 Phi-N	103	389	63	65	11	5	4	29	35	82	....	....	.167	.236	.252	.488	59	-16	24	1.97	15	*S-103	8	0.2

YEAR	TM-L	G	AB	R	H	2B	3B	HR	RBI	BB	SO	SB	CS	AVG	OBP	SLG	OPS	OPS+	BR/A	RC	RC/G	FR	G/POS	WS	TPW
1886	Phi-N	105	373	46	81	9	11	2	38	33	73	29	....	.217	.281	.316	.597	80	-9	42	3.91	3	*2-87,S-10/3-8	12	-0.2
1887	Phi-N	60	240	33	66	11	1	1	21	19	29	11	....	.275	.284	.285	.569	55	-14	22	3.28	-4	2-39,S-18/3-4	3	-1.4
1888	Phi-N	80	275	30	53	4	1	1	17	27	41	12	....	.193	.282	.225	.507	60	-11	21	2.60	12	2-65,3-14/S-1	6	0.3
1889	Chi-N	46	155	19	21	0	0	0	10	25	46	1	....	.135	.256	.135	.391	10	-18	6	1.14	3	S-45/2-1	2	-1.2
1890	Chi-P	80	283	38	54	10	5	0	29	33	37	4	....	.191	.287	.261	.548	45	-23	23	2.70	-8	S-64,2-12/3-4	3	-2.3
1891	Cin-a	1	4	0	0	0	0	0	0	0	0	0	....	.000	.000	.000	.000	-92	-1	0	.00	1	/2-1	0	0.0
	Phi-N	1	0	0	0	0	0	0	0	0	0	0	....	....	....	....	....	-98	0	0	....	0	/S-1	0	0.0
Total	**8**	**504**	**1825**	**241**	**361**	**49**	**26**	**11**	**144**	**179**	**308**	**57**	**....**	**.198**	**.268**	**.264**	**.532**	**59**	**-91**	**148**	**2.72**	**28**	**S-243,2-232/3-30,P-1**	**36**	**-3.7**

• BATCH, Emil — Emil "Heinie,Ace" Batch b: 1/21/1880, Brooklyn, NY d: 8/23/1926, Brooklyn, NY BR/TR, 5'7", 170 lbs. Deb: 9/13/1904 Career OF: 128-1-23

YEAR	TM-L	G	AB	R	H	2B	3B	HR	RBI	BB	SO	SB	CS	AVG	OBP	SLG	OPS	OPS+	BR/A	RC	RC/G	FR	G/POS	WS	TPW
1904	Bro-N	28	94	9	24	1	2	2	7	1	....	6	....	.255	.271	.372	.643	100	-1	12	4.17	0	3-28	2	0.0
1905	Bro-N	145	568	64	143	20	11	5	49	26	....	21	....	.252	.285	.352	.637	96	-5	65	3.92	-12	*3-145	11	-1.4
1906	Bro-N	59	203	23	52	7	6	0	11	15	....	3	....	.256	.311	.350	.660	115	3	24	4.02	-1	0-50(47-0-3)/3-2	7	-0.1
1907	Bro-N	116	388	38	96	10	3	0	31	23	....	7	....	.247	.291	.289	.580	89	-6	38	3.17	-4	*0-102(81-1-20)/3-2,2-1,S	7	-1.8
Total	**4**	**348**	**1253**	**134**	**315**	**38**	**22**	**7**	**98**	**65**	**....**	**37**	**....**	**.251**	**.290**	**.334**	**.624**	**97**	**-9**	**140**	**3.71**	**-17**	**3-177,0-152/2-1,S-1**	**27**	**-3.3**

• BATEMAN, John — John Alvin Bateman b: 7/21/1940, Killeen, TX d: 12/3/1996, Sand Springs, OK BR/TR, 6'3", 220 lbs. Deb: 4/19/1963

YEAR	TM-L	G	AB	R	H	2B	3B	HR	RBI	BB	SO	SB	CS	AVG	OBP	SLG	OPS	OPS+	BR/A	RC	RC/G	FR	G/POS	WS	TPW
1963	Hou-N	128	404	23	85	8	6	10	59	13	103	0	0	.210	.251	.334	.585	71	-16	33	2.62	1	*C-115	6	-1.0
1964	Hou-N	74	221	18	42	8	0	5	19	17	48	0	1	.190	.251	.294	.545	56	-13	14	2.04	3	C-72	3	-0.7
1965	Hou-N	45	142	15	28	3	1	7	14	12	37	0	1	.197	.260	.380	.640	83	-4	11	2.35	1	C-39	2	-0.1
1966	Hou-N	131	433	39	121	24	3	17	70	20	74	0	0	.279	.319	.467	.785	123	12	58	4.64	2	*C-121	15	2.1
1967	Hou-N	76	252	16	48	9	0	2	17	17	53	0	0	.190	.247	.250	.497	44	-18	14	1.76	2	C-71	3	-1.4
1968	Hou-N	111	350	28	87	19	0	4	33	23	46	1	1	.249	.301	.337	.638	93	-3	31	2.94	-1	*C-108	8	0.1
1969	Mon-N	74	235	16	49	4	0	8	19	12	44	0	2	.209	.250	.328	.578	60	-14	17	2.33	-1	C-66	2	-1.3
1970	Mon-N	139	520	51	123	21	5	15	68	28	75	8	4	.237	.277	.383	.660	75	-21	51	3.23	5	*C-137	11	-1.0
1971	Mon-N	139	492	34	119	17	3	10	56	19	87	1	0	.242	.276	.350	.625	76	-17	40	2.63	1	*C-137	9	-1.1
1972	Mon-N	18	29	0	7	1	0	0	3	3	4	0	0	.241	.313	.276	.588	67	-1	2	2.90	0	/C-7	0	-0.1
	Phi-N	82	252	10	56	9	0	3	17	8	39	0	1	.222	.249	.294	.543	52	-17	17	2.29	-2	C-80	1	-1.6
	Yr.	100	281	10	63	10	0	3	20	11	43	0	1	.224	.256	.292	.548	54	-18	20	2.35	-2	C-87	1	-1.8
Total	**10**	**1017**	**3330**	**250**	**765**	**123**	**18**	**81**	**375**	**172**	**610**	**10**	**10**	**.230**	**.273**	**.350**	**.624**	**77**	**-112**	**289**	**2.84**	**9**	**C-953**	**60**	**-6.0**

• BATES, Billy — William Derrick Bates b: 12/7/1963, Houston, TX BL/TR, 5'7", 155 lbs. Deb: 8/17/1989

YEAR	TM-L	G	AB	R	H	2B	3B	HR	RBI	BB	SO	SB	CS	AVG	OBP	SLG	OPS	OPS+	BR/A	RC	RC/G	FR	G/POS	WS	TPW
1989	Mil-A	7	14	3	3	0	0	0	0	0	1	2	0	.214	.214	.214	.429	21	-1	0	.60	0	/2-7	0	-0.1
1990	Mil-A	14	29	6	3	1	0	0	2	4	7	4	0	.103	.212	.138	.350		-3	2	1.57	0	2-14	1	-0.3
	*Cin-N	8	5	2	0	0	0	0	0	0	2	2	1	.000	.000	.000	.000	-96	-1	0	.00	0	/2-1	0	-0.2
Total	**2**	**29**	**48**	**11**	**6**	**1**	**0**	**0**	**2**	**4**	**10**	**8**	**1**	**.125**	**.192**	**.146**	**.338**	**-3**	**-5**	**2**	**1.10**	**-1**	**/2-22**	**1**	**-0.6**

• BATES, Bud — Hubert Edgar Bates b: 3/16/1912, Los Angeles, CA d: 4/29/1987, Long Beach, CA BR/TR, 6', 165 lbs. Deb: 9/16/1939

YEAR	TM-L	G	AB	R	H	2B	3B	HR	RBI	BB	SO	SB	CS	AVG	OBP	SLG	OPS	OPS+	BR/A	RC	RC/G	FR	G/POS	WS	TPW
1939	Phi-N	15	58	8	15	2	0	1	2	2	8	1	....	.259	.283	.345	.628	71	-3	5	2.74	1	0-14(1-13-0)	1	-0.2

• BATES, Charlie — Charles William Bates b: 9/17/1907, Philadelphia, PA d: 1/29/1980, Topeka, KS BR/TR, 5'10", 165 lbs. Deb: 9/22/1927

YEAR	TM-L	G	AB	R	H	2B	3B	HR	RBI	BB	SO	SB	CS	AVG	OBP	SLG	OPS	OPS+	BR/A	RC	RC/G	FR	G/POS	WS	TPW
1927	Phi-A	9	38	5	9	2	2	0	2	3	5	3	1	.237	.293	.395	.687	73	-2	4	3.94	0	/0-9(0-1-8)	1	-0.3

• BATES, Del — Delbert Oakley Bates b: 6/12/1940, Seattle, WA BL/TR, 6'2", 195 lbs. Deb: 5/6/1970

YEAR	TM-L	G	AB	R	H	2B	3B	HR	RBI	BB	SO	SB	CS	AVG	OBP	SLG	OPS	OPS+	BR/A	RC	RC/G	FR	G/POS	WS	TPW
1970	Phi-N	22	60	1	8	2	0	0	1	6	15	0	1	.133	.257	.167	.424	16	-7	3	1.30	0	C-20	1	-0.7

• BATES, Jason — Jason Charles Bates b: 1/5/1971, Downey, CA BB/TR, 5'11", 170 lbs. Deb: 4/26/1995

YEAR	TM-L	G	AB	R	H	2B	3B	HR	RBI	BB	SO	SB	CS	AVG	OBP	SLG	OPS	OPS+	BR/A	RC	RC/G	FR	G/POS	WS	TPW
1995*	Col-N	116	322	42	86	17	4	8	46	42	70	3	6	.267	.355	.419	.774	80	-10	48	5.26	-4	2-82,S-20,3-15	10	-0.9
1996	Col-N	88	160	19	33	8	1	1	9	23	34	2	1	.206	.314	.288	.601	48	-12	15	2.86	-2	2-37,S-18,3-12	1	-1.2
1997	Col-N	62	121	17	29	10	0	3	11	15	27	0	1	.240	.338	.397	.735	74	-5	16	4.56	1	2-22,S-16/3-6	2	-0.2
1998	Col-N	53	74	10	14	3	0	0	3	8	21	0	0	.189	.268	.230	.498	27	-8	4	1.74	-1	2-17/3-3,S-3	0	-0.9
Total	**4**	**319**	**677**	**88**	**162**	**38**	**5**	**12**	**69**	**88**	**152**	**5**	**8**	**.239**	**.333**	**.363**	**.696**	**66**	**-35**	**83**	**4.12**	**-6**	**2-158/S-57,3-36**	**13**	**-3.2**

• BATES, Johnny — John William Bates b: 8/21/1882, Steubenville, OH d: 2/10/1949, Steubenville, OH BL/TL, 5'7", 168 lbs. Deb: 4/12/1906 Career OF: 218-644-220

YEAR	TM-L	G	AB	R	H	2B	3B	HR	RBI	BB	SO	SB	CS	AVG	OBP	SLG	OPS	OPS+	BR/A	RC	RC/G	FR	G/POS	WS	TPW
1906	Bos-N	140	504	52	127	21	5	6	54	36	....	9	....	.252	.315	.349	.664	110	5	61	4.09	-9	*0-140(7-133-0)	12	-1.2
1907	Bos-N	126	447	52	116	18	12	2	49	39	....	11	....	.260	.329	.367	.695	118	9	60	4.58	-1	*0-120(1-1-118)	14	0.2
1908	Bos-N	127	445	48	115	14	6	1	29	35	....	25	....	.258	.315	.324	.639	106	3	53	4.01	-2	*0-117(101-8-8)	13	-0.7
1909	Bos-N	63	236	27	68	15	3	1	23	20	....	15	....	.288	.354	.390	.744	125	7	37	5.60	4	0-60(60-0-0)	9	0.7
	Phi-N	77	266	43	78	11	1	1	15	28	....	22	....	.293	.365	.353	.718	122	8	43	5.46	-1	0-73(11-62-0)	10	0.3
	Yr.	140	502	70	146	26	4	2	38	48	....	37	....	.291	.360	.371	.730	123	14	81	5.53	3	*0-133(71-62-0)	19	1.1
1910	Phi-N	135	498	91	152	26	11	3	61	61	49	31	....	.305	.385	.420	.805	131	20	93	6.59	8	*0-131(25-103-3)	24	2.3
1911	Cin-N	148	518	89	151	24	13	1	61	103	59	33	....	.292	.415	.394	.808	131	28	99	6.69	-2	*0-147(0-145-2)	23	1.8
1912	Cin-N	81	239	45	69	12	7	1	29	47	16	10	....	.289	.406	.410	.816	127	11	45	6.28	2	0-65(1-64-0)	12	0.9
1913	Cin-N	131	407	63	113	13	7	6	51	67	30	21	....	.278	.388	.388	.776	122	15	67	5.60	3	*0-111(0-24-88)	15	1.3
1914	Cin-N	58	155	29	39	7	5	2	15	28	17	4	....	.252	.380	.400	.780	128	7	25	5.29	-6	0-54(0-54-0)	6	-0.3
	Chi-N	9	8	2	1	0	0	0	1	1	1	0	....	.125	.300	.125	.425	28	-1	0	1.05	0	/0-3(0-2-1)	0	-0.1
	Yr.	67	163	31	40	7	5	2	16	29	18	4	....	.245	.376	.387	.762	123	6	25	5.06	-6	0-57(0-56-1)	6	-0.3
	Bal-F	59	190	24	58	6	3	1	29	38	18	6	....	.305	.429	.384	.813	133	11	34	6.16	-1	0-59(12-48-0)	9	0.8
Total	**9**	**1154**	**3913**	**565**	**1087**	**167**	**73**	**25**	**417**	**503**	**190**	**187**	**....**	**.278**	**.367**	**.377**	**.744**	**122**	**124**	**617**	**5.40**	**-4**	***0-1080**	**147**	**6.2**

• BATES, Ray — Raymond Bates b: 2/8/1890, Paterson, NJ d: 8/15/1970, Tucson, AZ BR/TR, 6', 165 lbs. Deb: 5/31/1913

YEAR	TM-L	G	AB	R	H	2B	3B	HR	RBI	BB	SO	SB	CS	AVG	OBP	SLG	OPS	OPS+	BR/A	RC	RC/G	FR	G/POS	WS	TPW
1913	Cle-A	27	30	4	5	0	2	0	4	3	9	3	....	.167	.265	.300	.565	63	-1	3	2.92	0	3-12/0-2(0-2-0)	1	-0.2
1917	Phi-A	127	485	47	115	20	7	2	66	21	39	12	....	.237	.277	.320	.597	83	-12	45	3.02	-3	*3-124	9	-1.3
Total	**2**	**154**	**515**	**51**	**120**	**20**	**9**	**2**	**70**	**24**	**48**	**15**	**....**	**.233**	**.277**	**.318**	**.595**	**82**	**-14**	**48**	**3.01**	**-3**	**3-136/0-2**	**10**	**-1.4**

• BATHE, Bill — William David Bathe b: 10/14/1960, Downey, CA BR/TR, 6'2", 200 lbs. Deb: 4/12/1986

YEAR	TM-L	G	AB	R	H	2B	3B	HR	RBI	BB	SO	SB	CS	AVG	OBP	SLG	OPS	OPS+	BR/A	RC	RC/G	FR	G/POS	WS	TPW
1986	Oak-A	39	103	9	19	3	0	5	11	2	20	0	0	.184	.208	.359	.567	55	-7	7	2.14	-1	C-39	1	-0.7
1989*	SF-N	30	32	3	9	1	0	0	6	0	7	0	0	.281	.281	.313	.594	72	-1	3	3.23	0	/C-7	0	-0.2
1990	SF-N	52	48	3	11	0	1	3	12	7	12	0	0	.229	.327	.458	.786	118	1	7	4.59	-1	/C-8	2	0.1
Total	**3**	**121**	**183**	**15**	**39**	**4**	**1**	**8**	**29**	**9**	**39**	**0**	**0**	**.213**	**.254**	**.377**	**.631**	**75**	**-7**	**17**	**2.94**	**-3**	**/C-54**	**3**	**-0.8**

• BATISTA, Rafael — Rafael (Sanchez) Batista b: 10/20/1947, San Pedro de Macoris, Dominican Republic BL/TL, 6'1", 195 lbs. Deb: 6/17/1973

YEAR	TM-L	G	AB	R	H	2B	3B	HR	RBI	BB	SO	SB	CS	AVG	OBP	SLG	OPS	OPS+	BR/A	RC	RC/G	FR	G/POS	WS	TPW
1973	Hou-N	12	15	2	4	0	0	0	2	1	6	0	0	.267	.313	.267	.579	62	-1	1	3.07	0	/1-8	0	-0.1
1975	Hou-N	10	10	0	3	1	0	0	0	0	4	0	0	.300	.300	.400	.700	100	0	1	2.70	0	....	0	0.0
Total	**2**	**22**	**25**	**2**	**7**	**1**	**0**	**0**	**2**	**1**	**10**	**0**	**0**	**.280**	**.308**	**.320**	**.628**	**77**	**-1**	**2**	**2.91**	**0**	**/1-8**	**0**	**-0.1**

• BATISTA, Tony — Leocadio Batista b: 12/9/1973, Puerto Plata, Dominican Republic BR/TR, 6', 180 lbs. Deb: 6/3/1996

YEAR	TM-L	G	AB	R	H	2B	3B	HR	RBI	BB	SO	SB	CS	AVG	OBP	SLG	OPS	OPS+	BR/A	RC	RC/G	FR	G/POS	WS	TPW
1996	Oak-A	74	238	38	71	10	2	6	25	19	49	7	3	.298	.353	.433	.785	100	-0	37	5.79	5	2-52,3-18/D-4,S-4	9	0.7
1997	Oak-A	68	188	22	38	10	1	4	18	14	31	2	2	.202	.265	.330	.594	55	-13	15	2.42	-3	S-61/3-4,2-1,D-1	2	-1.2
1998	Ari-N	106	293	46	80	16	1	18	41	18	52	1	1	.273	.322	.519	.840	117	5	47	5.62	-2	2-41,S-34,3-15	10	0.8
1999	Ari-N	44	144	16	37	5	0	5	21	16	17	2	0	.257	.340	.396	.735	85	-3	21	5.09	6	S-43	6	0.7
	Tor-A	98	375	61	107	25	1	26	79	22	79	2	0	.285	.332	.565	.897	121	10	67	6.28	9	S-98	15	2.5
2000	Tor-A★	154	620	96	163	32	2	41	114	35	121	5	4	.263	.309	.519	.828	101	-4	94	5.29	11	*3-154	18	0.8
2001	Tor-A	72	271	29	56	11	1	13	45	13	66	0	1	.207	.253	.399	.652	67	-15	27	3.34	1	3-72	4	-1.3
	Bal-A	84	308	41	82	16	5	12	42	19	47	5	1	.266	.309	.468	.776	106	2	43	4.89	3	D-33,3-29,S-20	8	0.4
	Yr.	156	579	70	138	27	6	25	87	32	113	5	2	.238	.283	.435	.718	88	-13	70	4.14	3	*3-101,D-33,S-20	12	-0.8
2002	Bal-A★	161	615	90	150	36	1	31	87	50	107	5	4	.244	.312	.457	.769	106	3	85	4.73	-4	*3-154/D-7	16	0.1
2003	Bal-A	161	631	76	148	20	1	26	99	28	102	4	3	.235	.273	.393	.666	75	-25	61	3.24	-6	*3-154/D-7	11	-2.9
Total	**8**	**1022**	**3683**	**515**	**932**	**181**	**15**	**182**	**571**	**234**	**671**	**33**	**19**	**.253**	**.304**	**.459**	**.763**	**96**	**-40**	**497**	**4.64**	**19**	**3-600,S-260/2-94,D-52**	**99**	**0.7**

YEAR TM-L	G	AB	R	H	2B	3B	HR	RBI	BB	SO	SB	CS	AVG	OBP	SLG	OPS	OPS+	BR/A	RC	RC/G	FR	G/POS	WS	TPW
• BATISTE, Kevin	Kevin Wade Batiste b: 10/21/1966, Galveston, TX BR/TR, 6'2", 175 lbs. Deb: 6/13/1989																							
1989 Tor-A	6	8	1	2	0	0	0	0	0	5	0	0	.250	.250	.250	.500	44	-1	1	2.25	0	/0-5(2-0-3)	0	-0.1
• BATISTE, Kim	Kimothy Emil Batiste b: 3/15/1968, New Orleans, LA BR/TR, 6', 193 lbs. Deb: 9/8/1991																							
1991 Phi-N	10	27	2	6	0	0	0	1	1	8	0	1	.222	.250	.222	.472	34	-3	1	1.58	1	/S-7	0	-0.1
1992 Phi-N	44	136	9	28	4	0	1	10	4	18	0	0	.206	.229	.257	.486	37	-12	7	1.49	-3	S-41	1	-1.3
1993*Phi-N	79	156	14	44	7	1	5	29	3	29	0	1	.282	.300	.436	.736	95	-2	19	4.35	1	3-58,S-24	5	0.1
1994 Phi-N	64	209	17	49	6	0	1	13	1	32	1	1	.234	.242	.278	.519	34	-21	11	1.70	-2	3-42,S-17	1	-2.0
1996 SF-N	54	130	17	27	6	0	3	11	5	33	3	3	.208	.237	.323	.560	48	-11	8	2.02	-3	3-25/S-7	0	-1.4
Total 5	251	658	59	154	23	1	10	64	14	120	4	6	.234	.252	.318	.570	52	-49	46	2.28	-7	3-125/S-96	7	-4.7
• BATSCH, Bill	William McKinley Batsch b: 5/18/1892, Mingo Junction, OH d: 12/31/1963, Canton, OH BR/TR, 5'10.5" Deb: 9/9/1916																							
1916 Pit-N	1	0	0	0	0	0	0	0	1	0	0	....	....	1.000	....	1.000	218	0	0	....	0	....	0	0.0
• BATTAM, Larry	Lawrence J. Battam b: 5/1/1878, Brooklyn, NY d: 1/27/1938, Brooklyn, NY, 5'11" Deb: 9/28/1895																							
1895 NY-N	2	4	0	1	0	0	0	0	2	1	0	....	.250	.500	.250	.750	99	0	1	4.61	0	/3-2	0	0.0
• BATTEN, George	George Burnett Batten b: 10/7/1891, Haddonfield, NJ d: 8/4/1972, New Port Richey, FL BR/TR, 5'11", 165 lbs. Deb: 9/28/1912																							
1912 NY-A	1	3	0	0	0	0	0	0	0	....	0	....	.000	.000	.000	.000	-94	-1	0	.00	0	/2-1	0	-0.1
• BATTEY, Earl	Earl Jesse Battey b: 1/5/1935, Los Angeles, CA d: 11/15/2003, Ocala, FL BR/TR, 6'1", 205 lbs. Deb: 9/10/1955																							
1955 Chi-A	5	7	1	2	0	0	0	0	1	1	0	0	.286	.444	.286	.730	97	0	1	3.78	0	/C-5	0	0.0
1956 Chi-A	4	4	1	1	0	0	0	0	1	1	0	0	.250	.400	.250	.650	74	-0	0	.00	-1	/C-3	0	-0.1
1957 Chi-A	48	115	12	20	2	3	3	6	11	38	0	2	.174	.246	.322	.568	54	-9	8	2.17	-1	C-43	2	-0.8
1958 Chi-A	68	168	24	38	8	0	8	26	24	34	1	0	.226	.330	.417	.747	106	2	24	4.80	2	C-49	7	0.6
1959 Chi-A	26	64	9	14	1	2	2	7	8	13	0	0	.219	.306	.391	.696	91	-1	8	4.47	1	C-20	3	0.1
1960 Was-A	137	466	49	126	24	2	15	60	48	68	4	5	.270	.349	.427	.776	108	4	67	4.90	0	*C-136	16	1.1
1961 Min-A	133	460	70	139	24	1	17	55	53	66	3	3	.302	.378	.470	.847	118	12	78	6.06	0	*C-131	20	1.9
1962 Min-A★	148	522	58	146	20	3	11	57	57	48	0	0	.280	.351	.393	.743	96	-2	70	4.62	5	*C-147	19	1.0
1963 Min-A★	147	508	64	145	17	1	26	84	61	75	0	0	.285	.371	.476	.847	133	24	89	6.17	2	*C-146	26	3.5
1964 Min-A	131	405	33	110	17	1	12	52	51	49	1	1	.272	.354	.407	.762	110	7	54	4.39	-2	*C-125	12	1.1
1965*Min-A★	131	394	36	117	22	2	6	60	50	23	0	0	.297	.379	.409	.788	118	11	63	5.80	0	*C-128	22	1.8
1966 Min-A★	115	364	30	93	12	1	4	34	43	30	4	1	.255	.339	.327	.666	87	-4	39	3.69	3	*C-113	13	0.5
1967 Min-A	48	109	6	18	3	1	0	8	13	24	0	0	.165	.254	.211	.465	36	-8	6	1.64	-1	C-41	2	-0.9
Total 13	1141	3586	393	969	150	17	104	449	421	470	13	12	.270	.351	.409	.760	106	36	508	4.85	8	*C-1087	142	9.9
• BATTIN, Joe	Joseph V. Battin b: 11/11/1851, Philadelphia, PA d: 12/10/1937, Akron, OH BR/TR Deb: 8/11/1871 M/U NA OF: 0-4-6																							
1871 Cle-n	1	3	0	0	0	0	0	0	1	0	0	0	.000	.250	.000	.250	-21	-0	0	.00	0	/0-1	....	0.0
1873 Ath-n	1	5	4	3	0	0	0	2	1	0	0	0	.600	.667	.600	1.267	260	1	2	31.26	0	/0-1	....	0.1
1874 Ath-n	51	226	40	52	11	1	0	27	1	7	3	2	.230	.233	.288	.521	61	-12	16	2.77	6	*2-41/0-7(0-2-5),S-5	....	-0.6
1875 StL-n	67	284	31	71	6	3	0	33	0	6	15	3	.250	.250	.292	.542	96	3	25	3.43	8	*2-62/3-6,C-2,0-1	....	0.6
1876 StL-N	64	289	34	85	11	4	0	46	6	6	....	....	.294	.315	.367	.682	134	10	34	4.75	18	*3-63/2-1	15	2.7
1877 StL-N	57	226	28	45	3	7	1	22	6	17	....	....	.199	.220	.288	.507	62	-9	15	2.23	0	3-32,2-21/0-5(0-5-0),P-1	3	-0.7
1882 Pit-a	34	133	13	28	5	1	1	....	3	....	....	....	.211	.228	.286	.514	76	-3	9	2.37	17	3-34	4	1.3
1883 Pit-a	98	388	42	83	9	6	1	0	11	....	....	....	.214	.236	.276	.511	67	-13	26	2.37	17	*3-98/P-2	7	0.6
1884 Pit-a	43	158	10	28	1	2	0	0	3	....	....	....	.177	.198	.209	.406	32	-12	7	1.41	6	3-43	2	-0.4
CP-U	18	69	8	13	2	0	0	....	0	....	....	....	.188	.188	.217	.406	39	-4	3	1.45	10	3-18	0	0.6
Bal-U	17	59	3	6	1	0	0	....	0	....	....	....	.102	.102	.119	.220	-23	-8	1	.39	1	3-17	1	-0.6
Yr.	35	128	11	19	3	0	0	....	0	....	....	....	.148	.148	.172	.320	10	-12	4	.93	11	3-35	1	0.0
1890 Syr-a	29	119	15	25	2	1	0	13	8	....	8	....	.210	.260	.244	.504	54	-6	10	2.78	-5	3-29	1	-0.9
Total 4 n	120	518	75	126	17	4	0	62	3	13	18	5	.243	.248	.292	.539	82	-8	43	3.25	15	2-103/0-10,3-6,S-5,C-2	....	0.1
Total 6	360	1441	153	313	34	21	3	81	37	23	8	....	.217	.238	.277	.516	70	-44	103	2.55	64	3-334/2-22,0-5,P-3	33	2.6
• BATTLE, Allen	Allen Zelmo Battle b: 11/29/1968, Grantham, NC BR/TR, 6', 170 lbs. Deb: 4/26/1995 Career OF: 39-34-14																							
1995 StL-N	61	118	13	32	5	0	0	2	15	26	3	3	.271	.358	.314	.672	79	-4	15	4.27	-1	0-32(15-7-14)	3	-0.5
1996 Oak-A	47	130	20	25	3	0	1	5	17	26	10	2	.192	.295	.238	.534	38	-11	11	2.61	1	0-47(24-27-0)	1	-1.0
Total 2	108	248	33	57	8	0	1	7	32	52	13	5	.230	.325	.274	.599	58	-14	25	3.36	0	/0-79	4	-1.5
• BATTLE, Howard	Howard Dion Battle b: 3/25/1972, Biloxi, MS BR/TR, 6', 210 lbs. Deb: 9/5/1995																							
1995 Tor-A	9	15	3	3	0	0	0	0	4	8	1	0	.200	.368	.200	.568	53	-1	2	3.78	1	/3-6,D-1	0	0.0
1996 Phi-N	5	5	0	0	0	0	0	0	0	2	0	0	.000	.000	.000	.000	-99	-1	0	.00	0	/3-1	0	-0.2
1999*Atl-N	15	17	2	6	0	0	1	5	2	3	0	0	.353	.421	.529	.950	138	1	4	7.89	0	/3-6	1	0.1
Total 3	29	37	5	9	0	0	1	5	6	13	1	0	.243	.349	.324	.673	73	-1	5	4.83	0	/3-13,D-1	1	-0.1
• BATTLE, Jim	James Milton Battle b: 3/26/1901, Bailey, TX d: 9/30/1965, Chico, CA BR/TR, 6'1", 170 lbs. Deb: 9/9/1927																							
1927 Chi-A	6	8	1	3	0	1	0	0	0	1	0	0	.375	.375	.625	1.000	160	1	2	7.79	-1	/3-4,S-2	1	0.0
• BATTS, Matt	Matthew Daniel Batts b: 10/16/1921, San Antonio, TX BR/TR, 5'11", 200 lbs. Deb: 9/10/1947																							
1947 Bos-A	7	16	3	8	1	0	1	5	1	1	0	0	.500	.529	.750	1.279	236	3	7	22.44	0	/C-6	2	0.3
1948 Bos-A	46	118	13	37	12	0	1	24	15	9	0	0	.314	.391	.441	.832	115	3	21	6.30	-1	C-41	5	0.3
1949 Bos-A	60	157	23	38	9	1	3	31	25	22	1	0	.242	.350	.369	.719	84	-3	22	4.80	-3	C-50	4	-0.4
1950 Bos-A	75	238	27	65	15	3	4	34	18	19	0	0	.273	.327	.412	.739	80	-8	31	4.63	-3	C-73	7	-0.7
1951 Bos-A	11	29	1	4	1	0	0	2	1	2	0	0	.138	.167	.172	.339	-8	-4	1	.75	0	C-11	0	-0.4
StL-A	79	248	26	75	17	1	5	31	21	21	2	0	.302	.357	.440	.796	111	4	38	5.54	-3	C-64	8	0.4
Yr.	90	277	27	79	18	1	5	33	22	23	2	0	.285	.338	.412	.749	99	-1	39	4.95	-3	C-75	8	0.0
1952 Det-A	56	173	11	41	4	1	3	13	14	22	1	0	.237	.298	.324	.622	72	-6	17	3.28	2	C-55	3	-0.2
1953 Det-A	116	374	38	104	24	3	6	43	24	36	2	3	.278	.322	.406	.728	97	-4	48	4.54	-1	*C-103	11	0.1
1954 Det-A	12	21	1	6	1	0	0	5	2	4	0	0	.286	.348	.333	.681	89	-0	3	4.52	0	/C-8	1	0.0
Chi-A	55	158	16	36	7	1	3	19	17	15	0	1	.228	.303	.342	.645	74	-6	15	2.89	0	C-42	4	-0.4
Yr.	67	179	17	42	8	1	3	24	19	19	0	1	.235	.308	.341	.649	76	-6	17	3.06	0	C-50	5	-0.4
1955 Cin-N	26	71	4	18	4	1	0	13	4	11	0	0	.254	.293	.338	.631	63	-4	6	2.97	-0	C-21	1	-0.3
1956 Cin-N	3	2	0	0	0	0	0	0	1	1	0	0	.000	.333	.000	.333		-0	0	1.17	0	....	0	0.0
Total 10	546	1605	163	432	95	11	26	220	143	163	6	4	.269	.330	.391	.721	90	-26	208	4.49	-9	C-474	46	-1.2
• BAUER, Hank	Henry Albert Bauer b: 7/31/1922, East St. Louis, IL BR/TR, 6', 192 lbs. Deb: 9/6/1948 M/C Career OF: 177-29-1292																							
1948 NY-A	19	50	6	9	1	1	1	9	6	13	1	0	.180	.268	.300	.568	51	-3	5	3.08	-1	0-14(8-0-7)	1	-0.5
1949*NY-A	103	301	56	82	6	6	10	45	37	42	2	2	.272	.354	.432	.786	107	2	47	5.34	2	0-95(21-25-60)	11	0.1
1950*NY-A	113	415	72	133	16	2	13	70	35	41	2	3	.320	.380	.463	.843	118	10	75	6.83	1	*0-110(36-0-82)	16	0.6
1951*NY-A	118	348	53	103	19	3	10	54	42	39	5	2	.296	.373	.454	.827	128	14	60	6.26	0	*0-107(51-1-62)	15	0.9
1952*NY-A★	141	553	86	162	31	6	17	74	50	61	6	7	.293	.355	.463	.818	134	22	91	5.92	5	*0-139(18-0-122)	21	2.3
1953*NY-A★	133	437	77	133	20	6	10	57	59	45	2	3	.304	.394	.446	.841	131	20	81	6.94	7	*0-126(3-1-124)	20	2.4
1954 NY-A★	114	377	73	111	16	5	12	54	40	42	4	4	.294	.362	.459	.821	128	13	63	6.08	0	*0-108(8-0-104)	16	1.0
1955*NY-A	139	492	97	137	20	5	20	53	56	65	8	4	.278	.362	.461	.823	122	15	86	6.28	8	*0-133(5-0-131)/C-1	21	1.8
1956*NY-A	147	539	96	130	18	7	26	84	59	72	4	2	.241	.318	.445	.764	103	-0	77	4.77	-3	*0-146(7-0-143)	16	-0.7
1957*NY-A	137	479	70	124	22	**9**	18	65	42	64	7	2	.259	.324	.455	.779	112	8	71	5.12	0	*0-135(3-0-134)	17	0.3
1958*NY-A	128	452	62	121	22	6	12	50	32	56	3	2	.268	.318	.423	.740	106	2	60	4.71	-3	*0-123(2-0-121)	13	-0.5
1959 NY-A	114	341	44	81	20	0	9	39	33	54	4	2	.238	.309	.375	.684	90	-5	41	4.08	-5	*0-111(4-0-108)	7	-1.3
1960 KC-A	95	255	30	70	15	0	3	31	21	36	1	0	.275	.332	.369	.701	89	-4	30	3.92	-4	0-67(0-0-67)	4	-1.0
1961 KC-A	43	106	11	28	3	1	3	18	9	8	1	0	.264	.322	.396	.718	90	-1	14	4.66	-1	0-35(11-2-27)	2	-0.4
Total 14	1544	5145	833	1424	229	57	164	703	521	638	50	33	.277	.347	.439	.786	114	92	801	5.51	7	*0-1449/C-1	180	5.0

YEAR TM-L	G	AB	R	H	2B	3B	HR	RBI	BB	SO	SB	CS	AVG	OBP	SLG	OPS	OPS+	BR/A	RC	RC/G	FR	G/POS	WS	TPW
• BAUGHMAN, Justin	Justin Reis Baughman b: 8/1/1974, Mountain View, CA BR/TR, 5'11", 175 lbs. Deb: 5/17/1998																							
1998 Ana-A	63	196	24	50	9	1	1	20	6	36	10	4	.255	.281	.327	.607	57	-12	17	2.91	-2	2-59/S-3,D-1	3	-1.1
2000 Ana-A	16	22	4	5	2	0	0	0	1	2	3	0	.227	.261	.318	.579	44	-1	2	3.65	0	/2-5,S-5,D-4	0	-0.1
Total 2	79	218	28	55	11	1	1	20	7	38	13	4	.252	.279	.326	.604	56	-14	20	2.98	-2	/2-64,S-8,D-5	3	-1.2
• BAUMANN, Paddy	Charles John Baumann b: 12/20/1885, Indianapolis, IN d: 11/20/1969, Indianapolis, IN BR/TR, 5'9", 160 lbs. Deb: 8/10/1911 Career OF: 16-4-20																							
1911 Det-A	26	94	8	24	2	4	0	11	6	....	1	....	.255	.307	.362	.669	82	-3	11	3.79	3	2-23/0-3(0-0-3)	2	0.0
1912 Det-A	16	42	3	11	1	0	0	7	6	....	4	....	.262	.354	.286	.640	86	-0	6	4.63	-2	/3-6,2-5,0-2(0-1-0)	1	-0.2
1913 Det-A	50	191	31	57	7	4	1	22	16	18	4	....	.298	.353	.393	.745	120	4	28	4.91	-6	2-49	6	-0.1
1914 Det-A	3	11	1	0	0	0	0	0	2	1	0	....	.000	.154	.000	.154	-52	-2	0	.27	0	/2-3	0	-0.2
1915 NY-A	76	219	30	64	13	1	2	28	28	32	9	10	.292	.380	.388	.768	130	6	33	5.01	5	2-43,3-19/0-1	10	1.4
1916 NY-A	79	237	35	68	5	3	1	25	19	16	10	....	.287	.352	.346	.698	108	2	33	4.90	-3	0-28(12-1-15),3-26/2-9	8	-0.1
1917 NY-A	49	110	10	24	2	1	0	8	4	9	2	....	.218	.246	.255	.500	52	-7	7	2.05	-6	2-18/0-7(4-1-2),3-1	1	-1.5
Total 7	299	904	118	248	30	13	4	101	81	76	30	10	.274	.340	.350	.690	104	1	117	4.36	-9	2-150/3-52,0-41	28	-0.7
• BAUMER, Jim	James Sloan Baumer b: 1/29/1931, Tulsa, OK d: 7/8/1996, Paoli, PA BR/TR, 6'2", 185 lbs. Deb: 9/14/1949																							
1949 Chi-A	8	10	2	4	1	1	0	2	2	1	0	0	.400	.571	.700	1.271	243	3	5	21.12	0	/S-7	1	0.3
1961 Cin-N	10	24	0	3	0	0	0	0	0	9	0	0	.125	.125	.125	.250	-33	-5	0	.52	0	/2-9	0	-0.4
Total 2	18	34	2	7	1	1	0	2	2	10	0	0	.206	.289	.294	.584	66	-2	5	4.93	0	/2-9,S-7	1	-0.1
• BAUMGARTNER, John	John Edward Baumgartner b: 5/29/1931, Birmingham, AL BR/TR, 6'1", 190 lbs. Deb: 4/14/1953																							
1953 Det-A	7	27	3	5	0	0	0	2	0	5	0	0	.185	.185	.185	.370		-4	1	1.16	-1	/3-7	0	-0.5
• BAUMHOLTZ, Frank	Frank Conrad Baumholtz b: 10/7/1918, Midvale, OH d: 12/14/1997, Winter Springs, FL BL/TL, 5'10.5", 175 lbs. Deb: 4/15/1947 Career OF: 100-301-487																							
1947 Cin-N	151	643	96	182	32	9	5	45	56	53	6	....	.283	.341	.384	.726	93	-7	88	4.95	-3	*0-150(0-29-136)	17	-1.5
1948 Cin-N	128	415	57	123	19	5	4	30	27	32	8	....	.296	.344	.395	.739	103	1	57	5.09	2	*0-110(20-23-67)	11	-0.1
1949 Cin-N	27	81	12	19	5	3	1	8	6	8	0	....	.235	.295	.407	.703	86	-2	10	3.87	1	0-20(13-0-7)	1	-0.3
Chi-N	58	164	15	37	4	2	1	15	9	21	2	....	.226	.270	.293	.563	52	-11	14	2.87	0	0-43(0-7-38)	1	-1.2
Yr.	85	245	27	56	9	5	2	23	15	29	2	....	.229	.279	.331	.609	64	-13	24	3.21	1	0-63(13-7-45)	2	-1.5
1951 Chi-N	146	560	62	159	28	10	2	50	49	36	5	4	.284	.346	.380	.726	93	-5	74	4.70	-6	*0-140(17-64-60)	14	-1.5
1952 Chi-N	103	409	59	133	17	4	4	35	27	27	5	7	.325	.371	.416	.787	116	7	64	5.83	3	*0-101(0-47-65)	16	0.8
1953 Chi-N	133	520	75	159	36	7	3	25	42	36	3	3	.306	.359	.419	.778	100	-0	82	5.90	-7	*0-130(0-69-64)	15	-1.2
1954 Chi-N	90	303	38	90	12	6	4	28	20	15	1	3	.297	.343	.416	.758	95	-3	42	5.07	-3	0-71(10-61-13)	8	-1.0
1955 Chi-N	105	280	23	81	12	5	1	27	16	24	0	1	.289	.330	.379	.709	88	-5	33	4.04	1	0-63(40-0-23)	6	-0.7
1956 Phi-N	76	100	13	27	0	0	0	9	6	6	0	2	.270	.318	.270	.588	61	-6	8	2.65	0	0-15(0-1-14)	1	-0.7
1957 Phi-N	2	2	0	0	0	0	0	0	0	0	0	0	.000	.000	.000	.000	-103	-1	0	.00	0	....	0	-0.1
Total 10	1019	3477	450	1010	165	51	25	272	258	258	30	20	.290	.342	.389	.731	95	-33	470	4.89	-12	0-843	90	-7.4
• BAUTISTA, Danny	Daniel (Alcantara) Bautista b: 5/24/1972, Santo Domingo, Dominican Republic BR/TR, 5'11", 170 lbs. Deb: 9/15/1993 Career OF: 172-122-388																							
1993 Det-A	17	61	6	19	3	0	1	9	1	10	3	1	.311	.323	.410	.732	96	-0	8	4.69	1	0-16(0-9-8)/D-1	1	0.0
1994 Det-A	31	99	12	23	4	1	4	15	3	18	1	2	.232	.255	.414	.669	68	-6	9	2.90	-2	0-30(0-14-16)/D-1	1	-0.8
1995 Det-A	89	271	28	55	9	0	7	27	12	68	4	1	.203	.237	.314	.550	42	-24	19	2.28	-1	0-86(2-0-84)/D-1	1	-2.7
1996 Det-A	25	64	12	16	2	0	2	8	9	15	1	2	.250	.342	.375	.717	81	-2	8	4.29	-1	0-22(12-0-12)/D-1	1	-0.4
Atl-N	17	20	1	3	0	0	0	1	2	5	0	0	.150	.261	.150	.411	11	-3	0	.67	0	0-14(2-2-10)	0	-0.3
1997*Atl-N	64	103	14	25	3	2	3	9	5	24	2	0	.243	.284	.398	.682	75	-4	11	3.61	-1	0-57(48-1-10)	2	-0.6
1998*Atl-N	82	144	17	36	11	0	3	17	7	21	1	0	.250	.285	.389	.674	75	-6	15	3.52	-3	0-58(53-1-4)/D-1	2	-1.0
1999 Fla-N	70	205	32	59	10	1	5	24	4	30	3	0	.288	.305	.420	.724	85	-5	25	4.44	0	0-60(22-18-31)	3	-0.7
2000 Fla-N	44	89	9	17	4	0	4	12	5	20	1	0	.191	.234	.371	.605	52	-7	8	2.88	2	0-38(25-5-17)	1	-0.6
Ari-N	87	262	45	83	16	7	7	47	20	30	5	2	.317	.372	.511	.883	117	6	47	6.31	1	0-82(2-21-67)	9	0.4
Yr.	131	351	54	100	20	7	11	59	25	50	6	2	.285	.338	.476	.814	101	-1	55	5.39	3	*0-120(27-26-84)	10	-0.2
2001*Ari-N	100	222	26	67	11	2	5	26	14	31	3	2	.302	.346	.437	.783	95	-2	32	5.13	2	0-61(3-28-33)	6	-0.1
2002 Ari-N	40	154	22	50	5	2	6	23	11	21	4	2	.325	.370	.500	.870	116	3	27	6.60	-4	0-39(0-5-37)	5	-0.2
2003 Ari-N	88	284	29	78	16	3	4	36	21	50	3	2	.275	.333	.394	.728	81	-8	37	4.49	-5	0-79(3-18-59)	5	-1.6
Total 11	754	1978	253	531	94	18	51	254	114	343	31	14	.268	.312	.412	.723	82	-57	246	4.28	-10	0-642/D-5	37	-8.4
• BAXES, Jim	Dimitrios Speros Baxes b: 7/5/1928, San Francisco, CA d: 11/14/1996, Garden Grove, CA BR/TR, 6'1", 190 lbs. Deb: 4/11/1959																							
1959 LA-N	11	33	4	10	1	0	2	5	4	7	1	0	.303	.395	.515	.910	130	2	6	6.17	4	3-10	2	0.6
Cle-A	77	247	35	59	11	0	15	34	21	47	0	1	.239	.299	.466	.764	111	2	30	4.01	-7	2-48,3-22	7	-0.1
• BAXES, Mike	Michael Baxes b: 12/18/1930, San Francisco, CA BR/TR, 5'10", 175 lbs. Deb: 4/17/1956																							
1956 KC-A	73	106	9	24	3	1	1	5	18	15	0	1	.226	.339	.302	.641	70	-4	12	3.56	-3	S-62/2-1	2	-0.5
1958 KC-A	73	231	31	49	10	1	0	8	21	24	1	6	.212	.286	.264	.550	52	-17	17	2.35	1	2-61/S-4	2	-1.3
Total 2	146	337	40	73	13	2	1	13	39	39	1	7	.217	.303	.276	.579	58	-22	29	2.73	-2	/S-66,2-62	4	-1.7
• BAXTER, Moose	John Morris Baxter b: 7/27/1876, Chippewa Falls, WI d: 8/7/1926, Portland, OR BL/TR, 6'2", 200 lbs. Deb: 4/19/1907																							
1907 StL-N	6	21	1	4	0	0	0	0	0	....	0	....	.190	.190	.190	.381	20	-2	1	1.19	-1	/1-6	0	-0.3
• BAY, Harry	Harry Elbert "Deer Foot" Bay b: 1/17/1878, Pontiac, IL d: 3/20/1952, Peoria, IL BL/TL, 5'8", 138 lbs. Deb: 7/23/1901 Career OF: 65-580-20																							
1901 Cin-N	41	157	25	33	1	2	1	3	13	....	4	....	.210	.275	.261	.536	60	-8	13	2.73	-1	0-40(0-25-15)	1	-1.1
1902 Cin-N	6	16	3	6	0	0	0	1	2	....	0	....	.375	.474	.375	.849	148	1	3	7.48	0	/0-3(3-0-0)	1	0.1
Cle-A	108	455	71	132	10	5	0	23	36	....	22	....	.290	.343	.334	.678	92	-4	64	4.94	4	*0-107(24-79-4)	12	-0.5
1903 Cle-A	140	579	94	169	15	12	1	35	29	....	**45**	....	.292	.329	.364	.693	110	6	89	5.41	0	*0-140(26-114-0)	21	0.0
1904 Cle-A	132	506	69	122	12	9	3	36	43	....	**38**	....	.241	.307	.318	.625	99	0	64	4.29	4	*0-132(5-127-0)	17	-0.3
1905 Cle-A	144	552	90	166	18	10	0	22	36	....	36	....	.301	.349	.370	.719	126	16	89	5.68	-3	*0-144(0-144-0)	23	0.6
1906 Cle-A	68	280	47	77	8	3	0	14	26	....	17	....	.275	.337	.325	.662	109	3	39	4.76	-3	0-68(0-68-0)	9	-0.4
1907 Cle-A	34	95	14	17	1	1	0	7	10	....	7	....	.179	.271	.211	.482	53	-4	8	2.60	2	0-31(7-23-1)	2	-0.5
1908 Cle-A	2	0	0	0	0	0	0	0	0	....	0	....	....	....	....	....	-100	0	0	....	0	....	0	0.0
Total 8	675	2640	413	722	65	42	5	141	195	....	169	....	.273	.328	.336	.663	103	11	369	4.83	2	0-665	86	-2.0
• BAY, Jason	Jason Raymond Bay b: 9/20/1978, Trail, Canada BR/TR, 6'2", 200 lbs. Deb: 5/23/2003																							
2003 SD-N	3	8	2	2	1	0	1	2	1	1	0	0	.250	.400	.750	1.150	210	1	3	11.74	0	/0-3(0-3-0)	1	0.2
Pit-N	27	79	13	23	6	1	3	12	18	28	3	1	.291	.423	.506	.929	138	6	19	9.03	-1	0-26(24-2-1)	4	0.3
Yr.	30	87	15	25	7	1	4	14	19	29	3	1	.287	.421	.529	.949	145	7	22	9.29	-1	0-29(24-5-1)	5	0.5
• BAYLESS, Dick	Harry Owen Bayless b: 9/6/1883, Joplin, MO d: 12/16/1920, Santa Rita, NM BL/TR, 5'9", 178 lbs. Deb: 9/9/1908																							
1908 Cin-N	19	71	7	16	1	0	1	3	6	....	0	....	.225	.304	.282	.585	90	-1	6	2.78	2	0-19(0-2-17)	2	0.0
• BAYLOR, Don	Don Edward Baylor b: 6/28/1949, Austin, TX BR/TR, 6'1", 195 lbs. Deb: 9/18/1970 M/C Career OF: 623-37-195																							
1970 Bal-A	8	17	4	4	0	0	0	4	2	3	1	1	.235	.316	.235	.551	54	-1	1	2.50	0	/0-6(3-4-0)	0	-0.2
1971 Bal-A	1	2	0	0	0	0	0	1	2	1	0	0	.000	.600	.000	.600	83	0	0	6.32	0	/0-1	0	0.1
1972 Bal-A	102	320	33	81	13	3	11	38	29	50	24	2	.253	.332	.416	.748	118	12	47	4.98	-5	0-84(35-13-48)/1-9	13	0.2
1973*Bal-A	118	405	64	116	20	4	11	51	35	48	32	9	.286	.362	.437	.799	125	17	65	5.61	-1	*0-110(110-0-0)/1-6,D-1	16	0.9
1974*Bal-A	137	489	66	133	22	1	10	59	43	56	29	12	.272	.343	.382	.726	112	10	65	4.57	-8	*0-129(112-2-26)/1-8,D-1	16	-0.6
1975 Bal-A	145	524	79	148	21	6	25	76	53	64	32	17	.282	.363	.489	.851	148	32	90	5.90	-3	*0-135(127-5-6)/D-7,1-2	24	2.1
1976 Oak-A	157	595	85	147	25	1	15	68	58	72	52	12	.247	.334	.368	.702	110	15	80	4.48	-2	0-76(27-2-50),1-69,D-23	19	0.3
1977 Cal-A	154	561	87	141	27	0	25	75	62	76	26	12	.251	.339	.433	.772	113	12	81	4.77	-2	0-77(48-11-19),D-61,1-18	16	0.4
1978 Cal-A	158	591	103	151	26	0	34	99	56	71	22	9	.255	.338	.472	.810	130	24	93	5.28	-3	*D-102,0-39(39-0-0),1-17	23	1.6
1979*Cal-A★	162	628	**120**	186	33	3	36	**139**	71	51	22	12	.296	.377	.530	.908	147	41	126	7.16	-5	0-97(78-0-19),D-65/1-1	29	2.8
1980 Cal-A	90	340	39	85	12	2	5	51	24	32	6	6	.250	.320	.341	.661	83	-9	36	3.52	-1	0-54(37-0-18),D-36	5	-1.4
1981 Cal-A	103	377	52	90	18	1	17	66	42	51	3	3	.239	.326	.427	.753	116	7	51	4.43	1	D-97/1-4,0-1	9	0.5

YEAR TM-L	G	AB	R	H	2B	3B	HR	RBI	BB	SO	SB	CS	AVG	OBP	SLG	OPS	OPS+	BR/A	RC	RC/G	FR	G/POS	WS	TPW
1982*Cal-A	157	608	80	160	24	1	24	93	57	69	10	4	.263	.333	.424	.758	106	6	84	4.73	0	*D-155	13	0.0
1983 NY-A	144	534	82	162	33	3	21	85	40	53	17	7	.303	.366	.494	.861	139	29	96	6.49	0	*D-136/O-5(2-0-4),1-1	21	2.4
1984 NY-A	134	493	84	129	29	1	27	89	38	68	1	1	.262	.343	.489	.832	132	21	83	5.89	0	*D-127/O-5(1-0-4)	16	1.6
1985 NY-A	142	477	70	110	24	1	23	91	52	90	0	4	.231	.336	.430	.766	111	6	70	4.81	0	*D-140	12	0.2
1986*Bos-A	160	585	93	139	23	1	31	94	62	111	3	5	.238	.346	.439	.785	112	10	91	5.23	-1	*D-143,1-13/O-3(3-0-0)	16	0.3
1987 Bos-A	108	339	64	81	8	0	16	57	40	47	5	2	.239	.360	.404	.764	99	2	52	5.04	0	D-97	7	-0.1
*Min-A	20	49	3	14	1	0	0	6	5	12	0	1	.286	.397	.306	.703	87	-1	6	3.93	0	D-14	1	-0.1
Yr.	128	388	67	95	9	0	16	63	45	59	5	3	.245	.364	.392	.756	98	1	57	4.91	0	*D-111	8	-0.2
1988*Oak-A	92	264	28	58	7	0	7	34	34	44	0	1	.220	.335	.326	.661	89	-3	30	3.78	0	D-80	6	-0.5
Total 19	**2292**	**8198**	**1236**	**2135**	**366**	**28**	**338**	**1276**	**805**	**1069**	**285**	**120**	**.260**	**.346**	**.436**	**.782**	**119**	**231**	**1247**	**5.17**	**-31**	***D-1285,O-822,1-148**	**262**	**10.5**
• BEACH, Jack	Stonewall Jackson Beach b: 1862, Alexandria, VA d: 7/23/1896, Alexandria, VA Deb: 5/1/1884																							
1884 Was-a	8	31	3	3	2	0	0	0	0	....	....	....	.097	.097	.161	.258	-20	-4	0	.49	-1	/O-8(1-0-7)	0	-0.5
• BEADLE, Dave	David A. Beadle b: 1/1864, New York, NY d: 9/22/1925, New York, NY BL, 6'2", 200 lbs. Deb: 6/17/1884																							
1884 Det-N	1	3	0	0	0	0	0	0	0	2	....	....	.000	.000	.000	.000	-106	-1	0	.00	-1	/C-1,O-1	0	-0.1
• BEALL, Bob	Robert Brooks Beall b: 4/24/1948, Portland, OR BB/TL, 5'11", 180 lbs. Deb: 5/12/1975																							
1975 Atl-N	20	31	2	7	2	0	0	1	6	9	0	0	.226	.351	.290	.642	77	-1	4	4.09	-0	/1-8	1	-0.1
1978 Atl-N	108	185	29	45	8	0	1	16	36	27	4	5	.243	.369	.303	.672	81	-4	22	3.99	2	1-40/O-8(6-2-0)	3	-0.5
1979 Atl-N	17	15	1	2	2	0	0	1	3	4	0	0	.133	.278	.267	.544	46	-1	1	2.69	0	/1-3	0	-0.1
1980 Pit-N	3	3	0	0	0	0	0	0	0	1	0	0	.000	.000	.000	.000	-98	-1	0	.00	0	....	0	-0.1
Total 4	**148**	**234**	**32**	**54**	**12**	**0**	**1**	**18**	**45**	**41**	**4**	**5**	**.231**	**.357**	**.295**	**.652**	**76**	**-7**	**28**	**3.85**	**2**	**/1-51,O-8**	**4**	**-0.8**
• BEALL, Johnny	John Woolf Beall b: 3/12/1882, Beltsville, MD d: 6/13/1926, Beltsville, MD BL/TR, 6', 180 lbs. Deb: 4/17/1913 Career OF: 14-18-18																							
1913 Cle-A	6	6	0	1	0	0	0	1	0	2	0	....	.167	.167	.167	.333	-2	-1	0	.75	0	....	0	-0.1
Chi-A	17	60	10	16	0	1	2	3	0	0	1	....	.267	.279	.400	.679	99	-1	6	3.73	0	O-17(0-17-0)	2	-0.2
Yr.	23	66	10	17	0	1	2	4	0	2	1	....	.258	.269	.379	.647	90	-1	7	3.43	0	O-17(0-17-0)	2	-0.2
1915 Cin-N	10	34	3	8	1	0	0	3	5	10	0	1	.235	.350	.265	.615	86	-1	3	2.96	1	O-10(9-1-0)	1	0.0
1916 Cin-N	6	21	3	7	2	0	1	4	3	7	1	....	.333	.417	.571	.988	207	3	5	9.50	1	/O-6(5-0-0)	1	0.4
1918 StL-N	19	49	2	11	1	0	0	6	3	6	0	....	.224	.269	.245	.514	59	-2	4	2.22	-1	O-18(0-0-18)	0	-0.4
Total 4	**58**	**170**	**18**	**43**	**4**	**1**	**3**	**17**	**11**	**25**	**2**	**1**	**.253**	**.306**	**.341**	**.647**	**95**	**-2**	**19**	**3.63**	**2**	**/O-51**	**4**	**-0.3**
• BEALS, Tommy	Thomas L. Beals b: 8/1850, NY d: 10/2/1915, San Francisco, CA BR, 5'5", 144 lbs. Deb: 7/27/1871 U NA OF: 9-23-18																							
1871 Oly-n	10	36	6	7	0	0	0	1	2	0	2	0	.194	.237	.194	.431	27	-3	2	2.37	2	/O-8(4-0-4),2-2	....	0.0
1872 Oly-n	9	36	6	11	1	1	0	5	1	1	0	0	.306	.324	.389	.713	125	1	5	5.77	-1	/2-5,O-2(0-2-0),S-2	....	0.0
1873 Was-n	37	169	35	46	9	5	0	24	1	1	1	0	.272	.276	.385	.661	97	0	19	4.64	7	2-26,C-13/O-1	....	0.4
1874 Bos-n	19	97	20	19	3	4	0	17	0	2	0	1	.196	.196	.309	.505	56	-6	6	2.29	2	2-12/O-9(1-2-6)	....	-0.3
1875 Bos-n	35	155	38	41	2	6	0	16	3	1	1	0	.265	.278	.355	.633	114	2	16	4.14	-1	O-30(3-19-8)/2-8	....	0.2
1880 Chi-N	13	46	4	7	0	0	0	3	1	6	....	....	.152	.170	.152	.322	10	-4	1	.86	-3	O-10(0-0-10)/2-3	0	-0.7
Total 5 n	**110**	**493**	**105**	**124**	**15**	**16**	**0**	**63**	**7**	**5**	**4**	**1**	**.252**	**.262**	**.347**	**.609**	**91**	**-5**	**48**	**3.88**	**9**	**/2-53,O-50,C-13,S-2**	**....**	**0.2**
• BEAMON, Charlie	Charles Alfonzo Beamon, Jr. b: 12/4/1953, Oakland, CA BL/TL, 6'1", 183 lbs. Deb: 9/11/1978																							
1978 Sea-A	10	11	2	2	0	0	0	0	1	1	0	0	.182	.250	.182	.432	23	-1	1	1.70	1	/D-6,1-2	0	0.0
1979 Sea-A	27	25	5	5	1	0	0	0	0	5	1	0	.200	.200	.240	.440	18	-3	1	1.34	-0	/1-7,D-5,O-2(2-0-0)	0	-0.3
1981 Tor-A	8	15	1	3	1	0	0	0	2	2	0	0	.200	.294	.267	.561	59	-1	1	2.99	0	/D-4,1-1	0	-0.1
Total 3	**45**	**51**	**8**	**10**	**2**	**0**	**0**	**0**	**3**	**8**	**1**	**0**	**.196**	**.241**	**.235**	**.476**	**32**	**-5**	**3**	**1.89**	**1**	**/D-15,1-10,O-2**	**0**	**-0.4**
• BEAMON, Trey	Clifford Beamon b: 2/11/1974, Dallas, TX BL/TR, 6'3", 195 lbs. Deb: 8/4/1996 Career OF: 22-0-18																							
1996 Pit-N	24	51	7	11	2	0	0	6	4	6	1	1	.216	.273	.255	.528	39	-5	4	2.42	-1	O-15(5-0-11)	1	-0.6
1997 SD-N	43	65	5	18	3	0	0	7	2	17	1	2	.277	.309	.323	.632	72	-4	6	3.19	0	O-20(15-0-5)	1	-0.3
1998 Det-A	28	42	4	11	4	0	0	2	5	13	1	0	.262	.340	.357	.698	81	-1	5	3.62	0	D-11/O-4(2-0-2)	0	-0.1
Total 3	**95**	**158**	**16**	**40**	**9**	**0**	**0**	**15**	**11**	**36**	**3**	**3**	**.253**	**.306**	**.310**	**.616**	**64**	**-9**	**14**	**3.05**	**0**	**/O-39,D-11**	**2**	**-1.0**
• BEAN, Bill	William Daro Bean b: 5/11/1964, Santa Ana, CA BL/TL, 6', 185 lbs. Deb: 4/25/1987 Career OF: 69-55-62																							
1987 Det-A	26	66	6	17	2	0	0	4	5	11	1	1	.258	.310	.288	.598	63	-4	6	3.10	1	O-24(5-17-3)	1	-0.4
1988 Det-A	10	11	2	2	0	1	0	0	0	2	0	0	.182	.182	.364	.545	51	-1	1	2.03	0	/O-4(0-2-3),1-2,D-1	0	-0.1
1989 Det-A	9	11	0	0	0	0	0	0	2	3	0	0	.000	.214	.000	.214	-36	-2	0	.41	-1	/O-6(4-1-2),1-2	0	-0.3
LA-N	51	71	7	14	4	0	0	3	4	10	0	2	.197	.250	.254	.504	45	-6	4	1.98	0	O-44(28-11-7)	0	-0.8
1993 SD-N	88	177	19	46	9	0	5	32	6	29	2	4	.260	.292	.395	.687	80	-7	18	3.39	2	O-54(11-17-32),1-12	4	-0.7
1994 SD-N	84	135	7	29	5	1	0	14	7	25	0	1	.215	.254	.267	.520	37	-13	8	1.98	0	O-39(17-7-15),1-16	1	-1.4
1995 SD-N	4	7	1	0	0	0	0	0	1	4	0	0	.000	.125	.000	.125	-66	-2	0	.13	0	/O-4(4-0-0)	0	-0.2
Total 6	**272**	**478**	**42**	**108**	**20**	**2**	**5**	**53**	**25**	**84**	**3**	**8**	**.226**	**.270**	**.308**	**.578**	**55**	**-34**	**38**	**2.56**	**1**	**O-175/1-32,D-1**	**6**	**-3.8**
• BEAN, Joe	Joseph William Bean b: 3/18/1874, Boston, MA d: 2/15/1961, Atlanta, GA BR/TR, 5'8", 138 lbs. Deb: 4/28/1902																							
1902 NY-N	50	182	13	40	2	1	0	5	5	....	9	....	.220	.245	.242	.486	51	-11	14	2.50	-8	S-48	1	-1.8
• BEANE, Billy	William Lamar Beane b: 3/29/1962, Orlando, FL BR/TR, 6'4", 195 lbs. Deb: 9/13/1984 Career OF: 75-7-33																							
1984 NY-N	5	10	0	1	0	0	0	0	0	2	0	1	.100	.100	.100	.200	-44	-2	0	.00	0	/O-5(2-1-2)	0	-0.3
1985 NY-N	8	8	0	2	1	0	0	1	0	3	0	0	.250	.250	.375	.625	74	-0	1	3.38	0	/O-2(1-0-1)	0	-0.1
1986 Min-A	80	183	20	39	6	0	3	15	11	54	2	3	.213	.258	.295	.553	49	-14	12	2.16	-3	O-67(64-5-1)/D-5	1	-1.9
1987 Min-A	12	15	1	4	2	0	0	1	0	6	0	0	.267	.267	.400	.667	71	-1	2	3.93	0	/O-7(0-0-7)	0	-0.1
1988 Det-A	6	6	1	1	0	0	0	1	0	2	0	0	.167	.167	.167	.333	-7	-1	0	.90	0	/O-6(4-1-1)	0	-0.1
1989 Oak-A	37	79	8	19	5	0	0	11	0	13	3	1	.241	.241	.304	.544	54	-5	5	2.16	-1	O-25(4-0-21)/1-4,D-4,3-1,C	2	-0.6
Total 6	**148**	**301**	**30**	**66**	**14**	**0**	**3**	**29**	**11**	**80**	**5**	**5**	**.219**	**.247**	**.296**	**.542**	**48**	**-23**	**20**	**2.16**	**-4**	**O-112/D-9,1-4,3-1,C-1**	**3**	**-3.1**
• BEARD, Ollie	Oliver Perry Beard b: 5/2/1862, Lexington, KY d: 5/28/1929, Cincinnati, OH BR/TR, 5'11", 180 lbs. Deb: 4/17/1889 U																							
1889 Cin-a	141	558	96	159	13	14	1	77	35	39	36	....	.285	.328	.364	.692	94	-7	80	5.34	21	*S-141	21	1.6
1890 Cin-N	122	492	64	132	17	15	3	72	44	13	30	....	.268	.331	.382	.713	108	4	74	5.44	2	*S-113/3-9	17	0.8
1891 Lou-a	68	257	35	62	4	5	0	24	33	9	7	....	.241	.330	.296	.626	80	-6	28	3.81	4	3-61/S-7	6	0.0
Total 3	**331**	**1307**	**195**	**353**	**34**	**34**	**4**	**173**	**112**	**61**	**73**	**....**	**.270**	**.330**	**.357**	**.687**	**97**	**-9**	**182**	**5.07**	**27**	**S-261/3-70**	**44**	**2.4**
• BEARD, Ted	Cramer Theodore Beard b: 1/7/1921, Woodsboro, MD BL/TL, 5'8", 165 lbs. Deb: 9/5/1948 Career OF: 23-59-73																							
1948 Pit-N	25	81	15	16	1	3	0	7	12	18	5	....	.198	.316	.284	.600	62	-4	8	3.49	0	O-22(0-22-0)	2	-0.5
1949 Pit-N	14	24	1	2	0	0	0	1	2	2	0	....	.083	.154	.083	.237	-34	-5	0	.48	-1	O-10(0-0-10)	0	-0.5
1950 Pit-N	61	177	32	41	6	2	4	12	27	45	3	....	.232	.333	.356	.689	79	-5	22	4.14	1	O-49(1-21-27)	3	-0.5
1951 Pit-N	22	48	7	9	1	0	1	3	6	14	0	0	.188	.291	.271	.562	51	-3	4	3.05	0	O-15(12-4-0)	0	-0.4
1952 Pit-N	15	44	5	8	2	1	0	3	7	9	2	0	.182	.294	.273	.567	56	-2	4	3.00	0	O-13(0-3-10)	0	-0.3
1957 Chi-A	38	78	15	16	1	0	0	7	18	14	3	2	.205	.354	.218	.572	59	-3	7	3.04	2	O-28(0-3-25)	1	-0.2
1958 Chi-A	19	22	5	2	0	0	1	2	6	5	3	0	.091	.286	.227	.513	44	-1	2	3.13	0	O-15(10-6-1)	0	-0.1
Total 7	**194**	**474**	**80**	**94**	**11**	**6**	**6**	**35**	**78**	**107**	**16**	**2**	**.198**	**.315**	**.285**	**.600**	**61**	**-23**	**49**	**3.38**	**2**	**O-152**	**6**	**-2.5**
• BEASLEY, Lew	Lewis Paige Beasley b: 8/27/1948, Sparta, VA BL/TR, 5'10", 172 lbs. Deb: 5/21/1977																							
1977 Tex-A	25	32	5	7	1	0	0	3	2	2	1	1	.219	.265	.250	.515	41	-3	2	2.13	-2	O-18(14-0-4)/D-1,S-1	0	-0.5
• BEATTY, Desmond	Aloysius Desmond "Desperate" Beatty b: 4/7/1893, Baltimore, MD d: 10/6/1969, Norway, ME BR/TR, 5'8.5", 158 lbs. Deb: 9/28/1914																							
1914 NY-N	2	3	0	0	0	0	0	1	0	0	0	....	.000	.000	.000	.000	-104	-1	0	.00	-1	/3-1,S-1	0	-0.2
• BEAUCHAMP, Jim	James Edward Beauchamp b: 8/21/1939, Vinita, OK BR/TR, 6'2", 205 lbs. Deb: 9/22/1963 C Career OF: 47-28-3																							
1963 StL-N	4	3	0	0	0	0	0	0	0	2	0	0	.000	.000	.000	.000	-91	-1	0	.00	0	....	0	-0.1
1964 Hou-N	23	55	6	9	2	0	2	4	5	16	0	0	.164	.246	.309	.555	59	-3	4	2.45	-1	O-15(11-4-0)/1-2	0	-0.5

YEAR TM-L	G	AB	R	H	2B	3B	HR	RBI	BB	SO	SB	CS	AVG	OBP	SLG	OPS	OPS+	BR/A	RC	RC/G	FR	G/POS	WS	TPW
1965 Hou-N	24	53	5	10	1	0	0	4	5	11	0	2	.189	.259	.208	.466	36	-5	3	1.49	2	/O-9(9-0-0),1-3	0	-0.4
Mil-N	4	3	0	0	0	0	0	0	1	1	0	1	.000	.250	.000	.250	-23	-1	0	.00	0	/1-2	0	-0.1
Yr.	28	56	5	10	1	0	0	4	6	12	0	3	.179	.258	.196	.454	32	-6	3	1.37	1	/O-9(9-0-0),1-5	0	-0.6
1967 Atl-N	4	3	0	0	0	0	0	1	0	0	0	0	.000	.000	.000	.000	-101	-1	0	.00	0	....	0	-0.1
1968 Cin-N	31	57	10	15	2	0	2	14	4	19	0	0	.263	.311	.404	.715	106	0	7	4.33	-1	O-13(1-11-1)/1-1	2	-0.1
1969 Cin-N	43	60	8	15	1	0	1	8	5	13	0	0	.250	.308	.317	.624	71	-2	6	3.65	-1	/O-9(5-4-0),1-3	1	-0.3
1970 Hou-N	31	26	3	5	0	0	1	4	3	7	0	1	.192	.276	.308	.584	59	-2	2	2.13	-1	O-16(13-3-0)	0	-0.3
StL-N	44	58	8	15	2	0	1	6	8	11	2	0	.259	.348	.345	.693	85	-1	8	4.90	1	O-10(2-6-2)/1-5	1	-0.1
Yr.	75	84	11	20	2	0	2	10	11	18	2	1	.238	.326	.333	.660	77	-3	10	3.97	0	O-26(15-9-2)/1-5	1	-0.4
1971 StL-N	77	162	24	38	8	3	2	16	9	26	3	1	.235	.279	.358	.637	76	-5	16	3.19	-3	1-44/O-1	2	-1.1
1972 NY-N	58	120	10	29	1	0	5	19	7	33	0	0	.242	.289	.375	.664	90	-2	13	3.64	-2	1-35/O-5(5-0-0)	3	-0.7
1973*NY-N	50	61	5	17	1	1	0	14	7	11	1	0	.279	.353	.328	.681	91	-0	8	4.36	-1	1-11	2	-0.2
Total 10	**393**	**661**	**79**	**153**	**18**	**4**	**14**	**90**	**54**	**150**	**6**	**5**	**.231**	**.292**	**.334**	**.627**	**75**	**-23**	**66**	**3.33**	**-7**	**1-106/O-78**	**11**	**-4.1**

• BEAUMONT, Ginger Clarence Howeth Beaumont b: 7/23/1876, Rochester, WI d: 4/10/1956, Burlington, WI BL/TR, 5'8", 190 lbs. Deb: 4/21/1899 Career OF: 18-1380-8

YEAR TM-L	G	AB	R	H	2B	3B	HR	RBI	BB	SO	SB	CS	AVG	OBP	SLG	OPS	OPS+	BR/A	RC	RC/G	FR	G/POS	WS	TPW
1899 Pit-N	111	437	90	154	15	8	3	38	41	....	31	....	.352	.416	.444	.860	137	23	97	8.91	4	*O-100(3-96-1)/1-2	20	1.8
1900*Pit-N	138	567	105	158	14	9	5	50	40	....	27	....	.279	.331	.362	.692	90	-8	81	4.99	-15	*O-138(0-138-0)	14	-3.0
1901 Pit-N	133	558	120	185	14	5	8	72	44	....	36	....	.332	.382	.418	.800	128	20	107	7.35	-9	*O-133(0-133-0)	25	0.5
1902 Pit-N	130	541	100	**193**	21	6	0	67	39	....	33	....	**.357**	.404	.418	.822	148	31	109	7.96	-1	*O-130(0-130-0)	31	2.5
1903*Pit-N	141	613	**137**	**209**	30	6	7	68	44	....	23	....	.341	.390	.444	.833	133	26	119	7.59	-3	*O-141(0-141-0)	28	1.5
1904 Pit-N	153	615	97	**185**	12	12	3	54	34	....	28	....	.301	.338	.374	.712	117	11	92	5.29	-6	*O-153(0-153-0)	24	-0.2
1905 Pit-N	103	384	60	126	12	8	3	40	22	....	21	....	.328	.365	.424	.789	131	14	70	6.71	0	O-97(0-96-0)	19	0.9
1906 Pit-N	80	310	48	82	9	3	2	32	19	....	1	....	.265	.311	.332	.643	96	-2	35	3.75	-7	O-78(0-78-0)	7	-1.4
1907 Bos-N	150	580	67	**187**	19	14	4	62	37	....	25	....	.322	.366	.424	.790	148	30	103	6.61	8	*O-149(0-149-0)	28	3.5
1908 Bos-N	125	476	66	127	20	6	2	52	42	....	13	....	.267	.328	.347	.674	117	9	58	4.16	-1	*O-121(0-121-0)	17	0.3
1909 Bos-N	123	407	35	107	11	4	0	60	35	....	12	....	.263	.321	.310	.631	92	-4	45	3.69	0	*O-111(0-111-0)	9	-1.0
1910*Chi-N	76	172	30	46	5	1	2	22	28	14	4	....	.267	.373	.343	.716	110	3	24	4.69	-3	O-56(15-34-7)	7	-0.2
Total 12	**1463**	**5660**	**955**	**1759**	**182**	**82**	**39**	**617**	**425**	**14**	**254**	**....**	**.311**	**.362**	**.393**	**.755**	**122**	**152**	**940**	**6.07**	**-33**	***O-1407/1-2**	**229**	**5.1**

• BEAVENS, Ed Edward P. Beavens b: 1848, Troy, NY TR, 5'8", 138 lbs. Deb: 5/9/1871

YEAR TM-L	G	AB	R	H	2B	3B	HR	RBI	BB	SO	SB	CS	AVG	OBP	SLG	OPS	OPS+	BR/A	RC	RC/G	FR	G/POS	WS	TPW
1871 Tro-n	3	15	7	6	0	0	0	5	0	0	2	0	.400	.400	.400	.800	129	1	3	11.48	0	/2-3	....	0.1
1872 Atl-n	10	43	6	9	2	0	0	2	1	0	0	0	.209	.227	.256	.483	41	-4	3	2.34	-9	2-10/O-1,S-1	....	-0.9
Total 2 n	**13**	**58**	**13**	**15**	**2**	**0**	**0**	**7**	**1**	**0**	**2**	**0**	**.259**	**.271**	**.293**	**.564**	**64**	**-3**	**6**	**4.25**	**-9**	**/2-13,O-1,S-1**	**....**	**-0.9**

• BECANNON, Buck James Melvin Becannon b: 8/22/1859, New York, NY d: 11/5/1923, New York, NY, 5'10", 165 lbs. Deb: 10/15/1884 U ♦

YEAR TM-L	G	AB	R	H	2B	3B	HR	RBI	BB	SO	SB	CS	AVG	OBP	SLG	OPS	OPS+	BR/A	RC	RC/G	FR	G/POS	WS	TPW
1884*NY-a	1	3	0	0	0	0	0	0	0	....	....	....	.000	.000	.000	.000	-102	-0	0	.00	0	/P-1	1	0.0
1885 NY-a	10	33	3	10	0	0	0	2	1	....	....	....	.303	.343	.303	.646	114	2	4	4.13	0	P-10	1	-2.5
1887 NY-N	1	5	0	0	0	0	0	0	0	2	0	....	.000	.000	.000	.000	-105	-1	0	.00	0	/3-1	0	-0.1
Total 3	**12**	**41**	**3**	**10**	**0**	**0**	**0**	**2**	**1**	**2**	**0**	**....**	**.244**	**.279**	**.244**	**.523**	**74**	**0**	**4**	**3.06**	**-0**	**/P-11,3-1**	**2**	**-2.6**

• BECHTEL, George George A. Bechtel b: 9/2/1848, Philadelphia, PA, 5'11", 165 lbs. Deb: 5/20/1871 U NA OF: 15-7-156 ♦

YEAR TM-L	G	AB	R	H	2B	3B	HR	RBI	BB	SO	SB	CS	AVG	OBP	SLG	OPS	OPS+	BR/A	RC	RC/G	FR	G/POS	WS	TPW
1871 Ath-n	20	94	24	33	9	1	1	21	2	2	4	0	.351	.365	.500	.865	147	6	19	9.84	1	O-15(1-3-11)/3-3,P-3	....	-0.3
1872 Mut-n	51	248	60	74	11	2	0	41	6	3	9	1	.298	.315	.359	.674	114	7	32	5.60	-2	*O-50(13-0-37)/1-1	....	0.6
1873 Phi-n	53	258	53	63	12	1	1	40	9	1	2	1	.244	.270	.310	.580	69	-10	23	3.53	7	*O-52(0-1-51)/P-3	....	-0.1
1874 Phi-n	32	151	29	42	4	5	1	34	2	1	0	0	.278	.288	.391	.678	111	2	17	4.79	-5	O-28(1-0-28)/P-6	....	-0.3
1875 Cen-n	14	61	12	17	5	0	0	7	1	1	0	0	.279	.290	.361	.651	136	4	7	4.39	-1	P-14	....	-0.2
Ath-n	35	164	33	46	6	2	0	20	1	3	2	0	.280	.285	.341	.626	105	1	17	4.23	0	O-31(0-3-29)/P-4	....	0.3
Yr.	49	225	45	63	11	2	0	27	2	4	2	0	.280	.286	.347	.633	113	4	23	4.28	-1	O-31(0-3-29),P-18	....	0.1
1876 Lou-N	14	55	2	10	1	0	0	2	0	1	....	....	.182	.182	.200	.382	23	-5	2	1.28	-1	O-14(0-0-14)	0	-0.6
NY-N	2	10	2	3	0	0	0	0	0	0	....	....	.300	.300	.300	.600	115	0	1	3.69	-1	/O-2(0-2-0)	0	-0.1
Yr.	16	65	4	13	1	0	0	2	0	1	....	....	.200	.200	.215	.415	37	-5	3	1.60	-3	O-16(0-2-14)	0	-0.7
Total 5 n	**205**	**976**	**211**	**275**	**47**	**11**	**3**	**163**	**21**	**11**	**17**	**2**	**.282**	**.297**	**.362**	**.659**	**105**	**10**	**114**	**4.96**	**0**	**O-176/P-30,3-3,1-1**	**....**	**-0.1**

• BECK, Clyde Clyde Eugene "Jersey" Beck b: 1/6/1900, Bassett, CA d: 7/15/1988, Temple City, CA BR/TR, 5'10", 176 lbs. Deb: 5/19/1926

YEAR TM-L	G	AB	R	H	2B	3B	HR	RBI	BB	SO	SB	CS	AVG	OBP	SLG	OPS	OPS+	BR/A	RC	RC/G	FR	G/POS	WS	TPW
1926 Chi-N	30	81	10	16	0	0	1	4	7	15	0	....	.198	.261	.235	.496	34	-8	5	2.00	4	2-30	1	-0.3
1927 Chi-N	117	391	44	101	20	5	2	44	43	37	0	....	.258	.332	.350	.682	83	-9	46	3.93	8	2-99,3-17/S-1	10	0.3
1928 Chi-N	131	483	72	124	18	4	3	52	58	58	3	....	.257	.341	.329	.670	77	-15	56	3.97	2	3-87,S-47/2-1	12	-0.3
1929 Chi-N	54	190	28	40	7	0	0	9	19	24	3	....	.211	.282	.247	.530	32	-20	14	2.34	8	3-33,S-14	2	-0.8
1930 Chi-N	83	244	32	52	7	0	6	34	36	32	2	....	.213	.314	.316	.630	53	-19	26	3.32	-1	S-57,2-24/3-2	3	-1.3
1931 Cin-N	53	136	17	21	4	2	0	19	21	14	1	....	.154	.272	.213	.485	34	-12	10	2.07	0	3-38/S-6	1	-1.1
Total 6	**468**	**1525**	**203**	**354**	**56**	**11**	**12**	**162**	**184**	**180**	**9**	**....**	**.232**	**.317**	**.307**	**.624**	**63**	**-82**	**156**	**3.35**	**20**	**3-177,2-154,S-125**	**29**	**-3.4**

• BECK, Erve Ervin Thomas "Dutch" Beck b: 7/19/1878, Toledo, OH d: 12/23/1916, Toledo, OH BR/TR, 5'10", 168 lbs. Deb: 9/19/1899 U

YEAR TM-L	G	AB	R	H	2B	3B	HR	RBI	BB	SO	SB	CS	AVG	OBP	SLG	OPS	OPS+	BR/A	RC	RC/G	FR	G/POS	WS	TPW
1899 Bro-N	8	24	2	4	2	0	0	2	0	....	0	....	.167	.167	.250	.417	13	-3	1	1.36	1	/2-6,S-2	0	-0.2
1901 Cle-A	135	539	78	156	26	8	6	79	23	....	7	....	.289	.320	.401	.720	103	1	74	5.03	-12	*2-132	14	-0.9
1902 Cin-N	48	187	19	57	10	3	1	20	3	....	2	....	.305	.319	.406	.726	113	2	26	5.19	-1	2-32/1-6,O-6(3-0-3)	5	0.0
Det-A	41	162	23	48	4	0	2	22	4	....	3	....	.296	.313	.358	.671	84	-4	20	4.50	0	1-36/O-5(0-0-5)	3	-0.5
Total 3	**232**	**912**	**122**	**265**	**42**	**11**	**9**	**123**	**30**	**....**	**12**	**....**	**.291**	**.315**	**.390**	**.705**	**99**	**-5**	**120**	**4.86**	**-13**	**2-170/1-42,O-11,S-2**	**22**	**-1.6**

• BECK, Frank Frank J. Beck b: 11/1858, Poughkeepsie, NY d: 2/8/1941, Detroit, MI TR, 5'9", 141 lbs. Deb: 5/2/1884 ♦

YEAR TM-L	G	AB	R	H	2B	3B	HR	RBI	BB	SO	SB	CS	AVG	OBP	SLG	OPS	OPS+	BR/A	RC	RC/G	FR	G/POS	WS	TPW
1884 Pit-a	3	12	1	4	1	0	0	0	0	....	....	....	.333	.333	.417	.750	141	1	2	5.87	-0	/P-3	0	-0.5
Bal-U	5	20	1	2	1	0	0	....	0	....	....	....	.100	.100	.150	.250	-15	-2	0	.48	-1	/O-4(0-0-4),P-2	0	-0.7

• BECK, Fred Frederick Thomas Beck b: 11/17/1886, Havana, IL d: 3/12/1962, Havana, IL BL/TL, 6'1", 180 lbs. Deb: 4/14/1909 Career OF: 29-173-66

YEAR TM-L	G	AB	R	H	2B	3B	HR	RBI	BB	SO	SB	CS	AVG	OBP	SLG	OPS	OPS+	BR/A	RC	RC/G	FR	G/POS	WS	TPW
1909 Bos-N	96	334	20	66	5	6	2	27	17	....	5	....	.198	.245	.266	.512	56	-18	23	2.14	2	O-57(12-42-2),1-33	2	-2.2
1910 Bos-N	154	571	52	157	32	9	**10**	64	19	55	8	....	.275	.307	.415	.722	105	-1	73	4.48	5	*O-134(2-125-7),1-19	13	-0.3
1911 Cin-N	41	87	7	16	1	2	2	20	1	13	2	....	.184	.193	.310	.504	41	-8	5	1.89	0	O-16(4-5-7)/1-6	0	-0.9
Phi-N	66	210	26	59	8	3	3	25	17	21	3	....	.281	.346	.390	.737	105	1	29	4.84	-2	O-61(11-1-50)	6	-0.4
Yr.	107	297	33	75	9	5	5	45	18	34	5	....	.253	.304	.367	.671	87	-7	35	3.92	-2	O-77(15-6-57)/1-6	6	-1.2
1914 Chi-F	157	555	51	155	23	4	11	77	44	66	9	....	.279	.341	.395	.736	116	11	75	4.64	-6	*1-157	17	0.2
1915 Chi-F	121	373	35	83	9	3	5	38	24	38	4	....	.223	.277	.303	.580	75	-13	31	2.72	-2	*1-117	5	-1.8
Total 5	**635**	**2130**	**191**	**536**	**78**	**27**	**33**	**251**	**122**	**193**	**31**	**....**	**.252**	**.301**	**.360**	**.661**	**93**	**-28**	**237**	**3.73**	**-3**	**1-332,O-268**	**43**	**-5.3**

• BECK, Zinn Zinn Bertram Beck b: 9/30/1885, Steubenville, OH d: 3/19/1981, West Palm Beach, FL BR/TR, 5'10.5", 160 lbs. Deb: 9/14/1913

YEAR TM-L	G	AB	R	H	2B	3B	HR	RBI	BB	SO	SB	CS	AVG	OBP	SLG	OPS	OPS+	BR/A	RC	RC/G	FR	G/POS	WS	TPW
1913 StL-N	10	30	4	5	1	0	0	2	4	10	1	....	.167	.265	.200	.465	34	-2	2	1.88	0	/3-5,S-5	0	-0.2
1914 StL-N	137	457	42	106	15	11	3	45	28	32	14	....	.232	.282	.333	.615	83	-11	45	3.21	12	*3-122,S-16	12	0.6
1915 StL-N	70	223	21	52	9	4	0	15	12	31	3	10	.233	.282	.309	.591	79	-10	18	2.54	2	3-62/S-4,2-2	4	-0.7
1916 StL-N	62	184	8	41	7	1	0	10	14	21	3	....	.223	.281	.272	.553	71	-6	15	2.71	-3	3-52/1-1,2-1	3	-0.9
1918 NY-A	11	8	0	0	0	0	0	0	1	0	1	0	.000	.000	.000	.000	-98	-2	0	.00	-1	/1-5,3-1	0	-0.3
Total 5	**290**	**902**	**75**	**204**	**32**	**16**	**3**	**73**	**58**	**95**	**21**	**10**	**.226**	**.279**	**.307**	**.586**	**76**	**-32**	**80**	**2.84**	**9**	**3-242/S-25,1-6,2-3**	**19**	**-1.6**

• BECKENDORF, Heinie Henry Ward Beckendorf b: 6/15/1884, New York, NY d: 9/15/1949, Jackson Heights, NY BR/TR, 5'9", 174 lbs. Deb: 4/16/1909

YEAR TM-L	G	AB	R	H	2B	3B	HR	RBI	BB	SO	SB	CS	AVG	OBP	SLG	OPS	OPS+	BR/A	RC	RC/G	FR	G/POS	WS	TPW
1909 Det-A	15	27	1	7	1	0	0	1	2	....	0	....	.259	.310	.296	.607	88	-0	3	3.12	0	C-15	1	0.0
1910 Det-A	3	7	0	3	0	0	0	2	1	....	0	....	.429	.500	.429	.929	179	1	1	9.64	0	/C-2	1	0.1
Was-A	37	103	8	15	1	0	0	10	5	....	0	....	.146	.207	.155	.363	14	-10	4	1.00	-3	C-36	2	-1.0
Yr.	40	110	8	18	1	0	0	12	6	....	0	....	.164	.227	.173	.400	25	-9	5	1.36	-3	C-38	3	-0.9
Total 2	**55**	**137**	**9**	**25**	**2**	**0**	**0**	**13**	**8**	**....**	**0**	**....**	**.182**	**.243**	**.197**	**.440**	**37**	**-10**	**8**	**1.68**	**-3**	**/C-53**	**4**	**-0.9**

• BECKER, Beals David Beals Becker b: 7/5/1886, El Dorado, KS d: 8/16/1943, Huntington Park, CA BL/TL, 5'9", 170 lbs. Deb: 4/19/1908 Career OF: 252-199-313

YEAR TM-L	G	AB	R	H	2B	3B	HR	RBI	BB	SO	SB	CS	AVG	OBP	SLG	OPS	OPS+	BR/A	RC	RC/G	FR	G/POS	WS	TPW
1908 Pit-N	20	65	4	10	0	1	0	0	2	....	2	....	.154	.191	.185	.376	20	-6	2	1.17	-1	O-17(0-0-17)	0	-0.9

YEAR TM-L	G	AB	R	H	2B	3B	HR	RBI	BB	SO	SB	CS	AVG	OBP	SLG	OPS	OPS+	BR/A	RC	RC/G	FR	G/POS	WS	TPW
Bos-N	43	171	13	47	3	1	0	7	7	....	7	....	.275	.303	.304	.607	96	-1	17	3.59	-1	0-43(0-1-42)	4	-0.4
Yr.	63	236	17	57	3	2	0	7	9	....	9	....	.242	.272	.271	.544	75	-7	20	2.86	-2	0-60(0-1-59)	4	-1.4
1909 Bos-N	152	562	60	138	15	6	6	24	47	....	21	....	.246	.305	.326	.631	91	-7	64	3.61	-1	*0-152(0-0-152)	11	-1.6
1910 NY-N	80	126	18	36	2	4	3	24	14	25	11	....	.286	.357	.437	.794	131	5	23	6.49	1	0-45(6-23-14)/1-1	5	0.4
1911*NY-N	88	172	28	45	11	1	1	20	26	22	19	....	.262	.359	.355	.713	97	0	28	5.68	1	0-55(17-6-33)	5	-0.2
1912*NY-N	125	402	66	106	18	8	6	58	54	35	30	....	.264	.354	.393	.747	101	1	66	5.48	2	*0-117(1-93-26)	15	-0.3
1913 Cin-N	30	108	11	32	5	3	0	14	6	12	0	....	.296	.333	.398	.731	109	1	14	4.53	2	0-28(9-8-11)	3	0.1
Phi-N	88	306	53	99	19	10	9	44	22	30	11	....	.324	.369	.539	.908	151	18	62	7.39	0	0-77(42-36-2)/1-1	14	1.5
Yr.	118	414	64	131	24	13	9	58	28	42	11	....	.316	.360	.502	.862	140	19	75	6.63	2	*0-105(51-44-13)/1-1	17	1.6
1914 Phi-N	138	514	76	167	25	5	9	66	37	59	16	....	.325	.370	.446	.816	133	20	87	6.31	5	*0-126(87-32-8)	22	2.0
1915*Phi-N	112	338	38	83	16	4	11	35	26	48	12	15	.246	.301	.414	.716	114	0	40	3.80	-4	0-98(90-0-8)	10	-0.9
Total 8	876	2764	367	763	114	43	45	292	241	231	129	15	.276	.335	.397	.732	111	31	403	4.98	4	0-758/1-2	89	-0.2

• BECKER, Heinz Heinz Reinhard "Dutch,Bunions" Becker b: 8/26/1915, Berlin, Germany d: 11/11/1991, Dallas, TX BB/TR, 6'2", 200 lbs. Deb: 4/21/1943

YEAR TM-L	G	AB	R	H	2B	3B	HR	RBI	BB	SO	SB	CS	AVG	OBP	SLG	OPS	OPS+	BR/A	RC	RC/G	FR	G/POS	WS	TPW
1943 Chi-N	24	69	5	10	0	0	0	2	9	6	0	....	.145	.244	.145	.389	14	-7	3	1.10	1	1-18	0	-0.8
1945*Chi-N	67	133	25	38	8	2	2	27	17	16	0	....	.286	.375	.421	.796	124	5	22	5.96	-1	1-28	5	0.2
1946 Chi-N	9	7	0	2	0	0	0	1	1	1	0	....	.286	.375	.286	.661	91	0	1	4.58	0	....	0	0.0
Cle-A	50	147	15	44	10	1	0	17	23	18	1	0	.299	.401	.381	.782	128	7	25	6.45	-1	1-44	6	0.5
1947 Cle-A	2	2	0	0	0	0	0	0	0	1	0	0	.000	.000	.000	.000	-103	-1	0	.00	0	....	0	-0.1
Total 4	152	358	45	94	18	3	2	47	50	42	1	0	.263	.359	.346	.706	103	4	50	4.98	-1	/1-90	11	-0.1

• BECKER, Joe Joseph Edward Becker b: 6/25/1908, St. Louis, MO d: 1/11/1998, Sunset Hills, MO BR/TR, 6'1", 180 lbs. Deb: 5/10/1936 C

YEAR TM-L	G	AB	R	H	2B	3B	HR	RBI	BB	SO	SB	CS	AVG	OBP	SLG	OPS	OPS+	BR/A	RC	RC/G	FR	G/POS	WS	TPW
1936 Cle-A	22	50	5	9	3	1	1	11	5	4	0	0	.180	.255	.340	.595	45	-5	4	2.89	-2	C-15	0	-0.5
1937 Cle-A	18	33	3	11	2	1	0	2	3	4	0	0	.333	.405	.455	.860	116	1	6	7.52	0	C-12	1	0.1
Total 2	40	83	8	20	5	2	1	13	8	8	0	0	.241	.315	.386	.701	74	-4	11	4.51	-2	/C-27	1	-0.4

• BECKER, Marty Martin Henry Becker b: 12/22/1893, Tiffin, OH d: 9/25/1957, Cincinnati, OH BB/TL, 5'8.5", 155 lbs. Deb: 9/8/1915

YEAR TM-L	G	AB	R	H	2B	3B	HR	RBI	BB	SO	SB	CS	AVG	OBP	SLG	OPS	OPS+	BR/A	RC	RC/G	FR	G/POS	WS	TPW
1915 NY-N	17	52	5	13	2	0	0	3	2	9	3	....	.250	.278	.288	.566	76	-2	6	3.34	1	0-16(0-16-1)	0	-0.2

• BECKER, Rich Richard Godhard Becker b: 2/1/1972, Aurora, IL BL/TL, 5'10", 199 lbs. Deb: 9/10/1993 Career OF: 104-477-159

YEAR TM-L	G	AB	R	H	2B	3B	HR	RBI	BB	SO	SB	CS	AVG	OBP	SLG	OPS	OPS+	BR/A	RC	RC/G	FR	G/POS	WS	TPW
1993 Min-A	3	7	3	2	2	0	0	0	5	4	1	1	.286	.583	.571	1.155	211	2	3	13.10	-1	/0-3(0-3-0)	0	0.1
1994 Min-A	28	98	12	26	3	0	1	8	13	25	6	1	.265	.351	.327	.678	76	-2	13	4.46	3	0-26(1-23-2)/D-1	1	0.0
1995 Min-A	106	392	45	93	15	1	2	33	34	95	8	9	.237	.305	.296	.601	57	-27	35	2.88	5	*0-105(2-99-5)	3	-2.0
1996 Min-A	148	525	92	153	31	4	12	71	68	118	19	5	.291	.375	.434	.809	102	5	88	5.94	10	*0-146(15-121-10)	20	1.4
1997 Min-A	132	443	61	117	22	3	10	45	62	130	17	5	.264	.356	.395	.751	94	-1	68	5.40	-2	*0-128(9-115-13)	12	-0.2
1998 NY-N	49	100	15	19	4	2	3	10	21	42	3	1	.190	.331	.360	.691	83	-2	13	4.34	1	0-41(17-14-13)	3	-0.2
Bal-A	79	113	22	23	1	0	3	11	22	34	2	0	.204	.343	.292	.635	69	-4	12	3.36	-1	0-61(5-13-43)/D-1	2	-0.5
1999 Mil-N	89	139	15	35	5	2	5	16	33	38	5	0	.252	.395	.424	.820	109	4	26	6.43	-2	0-50(16-19-17)/D-2	4	0.2
Oak-A	40	125	21	33	3	0	1	10	25	43	3	2	.264	.395	.312	.707	87	-1	17	4.76	1	0-39(17-32-8)	3	-0.1
2000 Oak-A	23	47	11	11	2	0	1	5	11	17	1	0	.234	.390	.340	.730	89	0	7	5.34	2	0-19(8-14-1)/D-2	2	0.2
Det-A	92	238	48	58	12	0	7	34	56	70	1	2	.244	.388	.382	.770	99	1	41	5.90	-2	0-80(14-24-47)/D-4	7	-0.2
Yr.	115	285	59	69	14	0	8	39	67	87	2	2	.242	.388	.375	.764	97	1	48	5.81	1	0-99(22-38-48)/D-6	9	0.0
Total 8	789	2227	345	570	100	12	45	243	350	616	66	26	.256	.360	.372	.732	89	-25	323	4.96	16	0-698/D-10	57	-1.4

• BECKERT, Glenn Glenn Alfred Beckert b: 10/12/1940, Pittsburgh, PA BR/TR, 6'1", 190 lbs. Deb: 4/12/1965

YEAR TM-L	G	AB	R	H	2B	3B	HR	RBI	BB	SO	SB	CS	AVG	OBP	SLG	OPS	OPS+	BR/A	RC	RC/G	FR	G/POS	WS	TPW
1965 Chi-N	154	614	73	147	21	3	3	30	28	52	6	8	.239	.276	.298	.574	60	-35	47	2.57	-5	*2-153	8	-2.8
1966 Chi-N	153	656	73	188	23	7	1	59	26	36	10	4	.287	.318	.348	.665	84	-14	73	4.03	-29	*2-152/S-1	11	-3.0
1967 Chi-N	146	597	91	167	32	3	5	40	30	25	10	3	.280	.314	.369	.683	90	-7	68	4.07	2	*2-144	18	0.9
1968 Chi-N	155	643	**98**	189	28	4	4	37	31	20	8	4	.294	.328	.369	.697	102	2	79	4.49	-1	*2-155	23	1.7
1969 Chi-N★	131	543	69	158	22	1	1	37	24	24	6	0	.291	.328	.341	.669	77	-14	60	3.97	-5	*2-129	14	-1.0
1970 Chi-N★	143	591	99	170	15	6	3	36	32	22	4	1	.288	.324	.349	.673	72	-23	66	4.00	0	*2-138/0-1	11	-1.4
1971 Chi-N★	131	530	80	181	18	5	2	42	24	24	3	2	.342	.370	.406	.776	104	4	76	5.35	-9	*2-129	20	0.3
1972 Chi-N★	120	474	51	128	22	2	3	43	23	17	2	1	.270	.307	.344	.650	76	-15	47	3.39	6	*2-118	11	-0.1
1973 Chi-N	114	372	38	95	13	0	0	29	30	15	0	2	.255	.314	.290	.605	64	-18	32	2.88	-4	2-88	6	-1.7
1974 SD-N	64	172	11	44	1	0	0	7	11	8	0	0	.256	.301	.262	.562	61	-9	14	2.95	-6	2-36/3-1	2	-1.3
1975 SD-N	9	16	2	6	1	0	0	0	1	0	0	0	.375	.412	.438	.849	145	1	3	8.07	0	/3-4	1	0.1
Total 11	1320	5208	685	1473	196	31	22	360	260	243	49	25	.283	.319	.345	.664	81	-128	565	3.85	-49	*2-1242/3-5,0-1,S-1	125	-8.3

• BECKLEY, Jake Jacob Peter "Eagle Eye" Beckley
b: 8/4/1867, Hannibal, MO d: 6/25/1918, Kansas City, MO BL/TL, 5'10", 200 lbs. Deb: 6/20/1888 U HOF: 1971 Career OF: 2-3-1

YEAR TM-L	G	AB	R	H	2B	3B	HR	RBI	BB	SO	SB	CS	AVG	OBP	SLG	OPS	OPS+	BR/A	RC	RC/G	FR	G/POS	WS	TPW
1888 Pit-N	71	283	35	97	15	3	0	27	7	22	20	....	.343	.363	.417	.780	160	18	51	7.45	-2	1-71	14	1.0
1889 Pit-N	123	522	91	157	24	10	9	97	29	29	11	....	.301	.345	.437	.781	130	20	84	6.13	7	*1-122/0-1	19	1.4
1890 Pit-P	121	516	109	167	38	**22**	9	120	42	32	18	....	.324	.381	.535	.916	156	39	115	8.89	5	*1-121	21	2.7
1891 Pit-N	133	554	94	162	20	19	4	73	44	46	13	....	.292	.353	.419	.772	128	18	89	6.11	6	*1-133	16	1.2
1892 Pit-N	151	614	102	145	21	19	10	96	31	44	30	....	.236	.288	.381	.669	102	-3	78	4.49	9	*1-151	19	0.5
1893 Pit-N	131	542	108	164	32	19	5	106	54	26	15	....	.303	.386	.459	.846	127	21	105	7.33	10	*1-131	17	2.4
1894 Pit-N	132	537	123	185	36	19	7	122	43	16	21	....	.345	.412	.521	.934	125	22	127	9.40	3	*1-131	17	1.9
1895 Pit-N	130	534	104	175	31	19	5	110	24	20	20	....	.328	.380	.485	.865	130	22	110	8.00	3	*1-129	18	2.0
1896 Pit-N	59	217	44	55	7	5	3	32	22	28	8	....	.253	.349	.373	.723	94	-1	33	5.12	1	1-56/0-3(0-3-0),2-1	5	-0.1
NY-N	46	182	37	55	8	4	6	38	9	7	11	....	.302	.352	.489	.841	124	5	36	7.49	0	1-45/0-2(2-0-0)	5	0.4
Yr.	105	399	81	110	15	9	9	70	31	35	19	....	.276	.351	.426	.777	107	4	69	6.13	0	*1-101/0-5(2-3-0),2-1	10	0.3
1897 NY-N	17	68	8	17	2	3	1	11	2	....	2	....	.250	.301	.412	.713	90	-1	9	4.82	2	1-17	1	0.1
Cin-N	97	365	76	126	17	9	7	76	18	....	23	....	.345	.395	.499	.894	127	12	83	9.09	-6	*1-97	14	0.5
Yr.	114	433	84	143	19	12	8	87	20	....	25	....	.330	.380	.485	.865	121	11	93	8.35	-3	*1-114	15	0.6
1898 Cin-N	118	459	86	135	20	12	4	72	28	....	6	....	.294	.348	.416	.764	111	4	71	5.68	-3	*1-118	14	0.1
1899 Cin-N	135	517	87	172	27	16	3	99	40	....	20	....	.333	.392	.464	.856	132	22	106	7.78	4	*1-134	20	2.3
1900 Cin-N	141	558	98	190	26	10	2	94	40	....	23	....	.341	.389	.434	.822	130	23	107	7.46	7	*1-140	21	2.6
1901 Cin-N	140	580	78	178	36	13	3	79	28	....	4	....	.307	.346	.429	.776	133	22	92	5.78	0	*1-140	18	1.9
1902 Cin-N	129	531	82	175	23	7	5	69	34	....	15	....	.330	.377	.427	.804	135	21	94	6.87	-4	*1-129/P-1	18	1.4
1903 Cin-N	120	459	85	150	29	10	2	81	42	....	23	....	.327	.384	.447	.831	123	13	91	7.55	3	*1-119	17	1.3
1904 StL-N	142	551	72	179	22	9	1	67	35	....	17	....	.325	.375	.403	.778	147	30	94	6.29	-3	*1-142	23	2.5
1905 StL-N	134	514	48	147	20	10	1	57	30	....	12	....	.286	.333	.370	.702	113	7	70	4.84	3	*1-134	16	0.8
1906 StL-N	87	320	29	79	16	6	0	44	13	....	3	....	.247	.283	.334	.617	96	-3	33	3.41	-1	1-85	5	-0.6
1907 StL-N	32	115	6	24	3	0	0	7	1	....	0	....	.209	.222	.235	.457	45	-8	7	1.81	-3	1-32	0	-1.2
Total 20	2389	9538	1602	2934	473	244	87	1577	616	270	315	....	.308	.361	.436	.797	126	303	1686	6.63	42	*1-2377/0-6,2-1,P-1	318	25.0

• BECQUER, Julio Julio (Villegas) Becquer b: 12/20/1931, Havana, Cuba BL/TL, 5'11.5", 178 lbs. Deb: 9/13/1955 Career OF: 6-0-0

YEAR TM-L	G	AB	R	H	2B	3B	HR	RBI	BB	SO	SB	CS	AVG	OBP	SLG	OPS	OPS+	BR/A	RC	RC/G	FR	G/POS	WS	TPW
1955 Was-A	10	14	1	3	0	0	0	1	0	1	0	0	.214	.214	.214	.429	16	-2	1	1.58	0	/1-2	0	-0.1
1957 Was-A	105	186	14	42	6	2	2	22	10	29	3	3	.226	.269	.312	.581	59	-11	13	2.22	0	1-43	0	-1.4
1958 Was-A	86	164	10	39	3	0	0	12	8	21	1	2	.238	.273	.256	.529	47	-12	10	2.00	5	1-42/0-1	1	-1.0
1959 Was-A	108	220	20	59	12	5	1	26	8	17	3	2	.268	.297	.382	.679	85	-5	22	3.40	2	1-53	3	-0.6
1960 Was-A	110	298	41	75	15	7	4	35	12	35	1	3	.252	.283	.389	.672	79	-11	27	2.98	-2	1-77/P-1	3	-1.8
1961 LA-A	11	8	0	0	0	0	0	0	1	5	0	0	.000	.111	.000	.111	-61	-2	0	.10	0	/1-5	0	-0.2
Min-A	57	84	13	20	1	2	5	18	2	12	0	1	.238	.256	.476	.732	86	-3	9	3.78	0	1-18/0-5(5-0-0),P-1	1	-0.5
Yr.	68	92	13	20	1	2	5	18	3	17	0	1	.217	.242	.435	.677	72	-5	9	3.39	0	1-23/0-5(5-0-0),P-1	1	-0.7
1963 Min-A	1	0	1	0	0	0	0	0	0	0	0	0	....	....	....	....	-98	0	0	....	0	....	0	0.0
Total 7	488	974	100	238	37	16	12	114	41	120	8	11	.244	.277	.352	.629	70	-47	82	2.77	5	1-240/0-6,P-2	8	-5.7

• BEDELL, Howie Howard William Bedell b: 9/29/1935, Clearfield, PA BL/TR, 6'1", 185 lbs. Deb: 4/10/1962 C

YEAR TM-L	G	AB	R	H	2B	3B	HR	RBI	BB	SO	SB	CS	AVG	OBP	SLG	OPS	OPS+	BR/A	RC	RC/G	FR	G/POS	WS	TPW
1962 Mil-N	58	138	15	27	1	2	0	2	11	22	1	0	.196	.255	.232	.487	33	-13	9	2.12	-1	0-45(44-2-0)	0	-1.6

YEAR TM-L	G	AB	R	H	2B	3B	HR	RBI	BB	SO	SB	CS	AVG	OBP	SLG	OPS	OPS+	BR/A	RC	RC/G	FR	G/POS	WS	TPW
1968 Phi-N	9	7	0	1	0	0	0	1	1	0	0	0	.143	.250	.143	.393	20	-1	0	1.53	0	....	0	-0.1
Total 2	**67**	**145**	**15**	**28**	**1**	**2**	**0**	**3**	**12**	**22**	**1**	**0**	**.193**	**.255**	**.228**	**.482**	**32**	**-13**	**9**	**2.08**	**-1**	**/O-45**	**0**	**-1.7**

• BEDFORD, Gene William Eugene Bedford b: 12/2/1896, Dallas, TX d: 10/6/1977, San Antonio, TX BB/TR, 5'8", 170 lbs. Deb: 6/25/1925

YEAR TM-L	G	AB	R	H	2B	3B	HR	RBI	BB	SO	SB	CS	AVG	OBP	SLG	OPS	OPS+	BR/A	RC	RC/G	FR	G/POS	WS	TPW
1925 Cle-A	2	3	1	0	0	0	0	0	0	1	0	0	.000	.000	.000	.000	-99	-1	0	.00	-1	/2-2	0	-0.2

• BEECHER, Ed Edward Harry Beecher b: 7/2/1860, Guilford, CT d: 9/12/1935, Hartford, CT BL/TL, 5'10", 185 lbs. Deb: 6/28/1887 Career OF: 190-28-62

YEAR TM-L	G	AB	R	H	2B	3B	HR	RBI	BB	SO	SB	CS	AVG	OBP	SLG	OPS	OPS+	BR/A	RC	RC/G	FR	G/POS	WS	TPW
1887 Pit-N	41	176	15	48	8	0	2	22	7	8	8	....	.273	.281	.325	.606	72	-6	18	3.76	5	O-41(18-22-1)	2	-0.2
1889 Was-N	42	179	20	53	9	0	0	30	5	4	3	....	.296	.319	.346	.665	91	-2	21	4.47	-3	O-39(1-0-38)/1-3	3	-0.5
1890 Buf-P	126	536	69	159	22	10	3	90	29	23	14	....	.297	.341	.392	.733	104	3	78	5.61	-7	*O-126(119-0-7)/P-1	10	-1.0
1891 Was-a	58	235	35	57	11	3	2	28	27	9	17	....	.243	.333	.340	.674	97	-0	33	4.93	0	O-58(52-6-0)	5	-0.2
Phi-a	16	71	9	15	2	4	0	7	3	4	7	....	.211	.243	.352	.595	68	-4	8	3.78	0	O-16(0-0-16)	1	-0.4
Yr.	74	306	44	72	13	7	2	35	30	13	24	....	.235	.314	.343	.657	91	-4	41	4.66	0	O-74(52-6-16)	6	-0.6
Total 4	**283**	**1197**	**148**	**332**	**52**	**17**	**7**	**177**	**71**	**48**	**49**	**....**	**.277**	**.322**	**.363**	**.685**	**94**	**-9**	**159**	**4.91**	**-5**	**O-280/1-3,P-1**	**21**	**-2.3**

• BEELER, Jodie Joseph Sam Beeler b: 11/26/1921, Dallas, TX d: 10/8/2002, Mesquite, TX BR/TR, 6', 170 lbs. Deb: 9/21/1944

YEAR TM-L	G	AB	R	H	2B	3B	HR	RBI	BB	SO	SB	CS	AVG	OBP	SLG	OPS	OPS+	BR/A	RC	RC/G	FR	G/POS	WS	TPW
1944 Cin-N	3	3	0	0	0	0	0	0	0	2	0	....	.000	.000	.000	.000	-104	-1	0	.00	-1	/2-1,3-1	0	-0.2

• BEGLEY, Gene Eugene T. Begley b: 6/7/1861, Brooklyn, NY Deb: 9/11/1886

YEAR TM-L	G	AB	R	H	2B	3B	HR	RBI	BB	SO	SB	CS	AVG	OBP	SLG	OPS	OPS+	BR/A	RC	RC/G	FR	G/POS	WS	TPW
1886 NY-N	5	16	1	2	0	0	0	1	1	3	1	....	.125	.176	.125	.301	-7	-2	1	1.05	0	/C-3,O-2(0-0-2)	0	-0.1

• BEGLEY, Jim James Lawrence "Imp" Begley b: 9/19/1902, San Francisco, CA d: 2/22/1957, San Francisco, CA BR/TR, 5'6", 145 lbs. Deb: 5/28/1924

YEAR TM-L	G	AB	R	H	2B	3B	HR	RBI	BB	SO	SB	CS	AVG	OBP	SLG	OPS	OPS+	BR/A	RC	RC/G	FR	G/POS	WS	TPW
1924 Cin-N	2	5	1	1	0	0	0	0	2	0	0	0	.200	.429	.200	.629	75	0	1	4.14	0	/2-2	0	0.0

• BEHEL, Steve Stephen Arnold Douglas Behel b: 11/6/1860, Earlville, IL d: 2/15/1945, Los Angeles, CA Deb: 9/27/1884 Career OF: 35-33-0

YEAR TM-L	G	AB	R	H	2B	3B	HR	RBI	BB	SO	SB	CS	AVG	OBP	SLG	OPS	OPS+	BR/A	RC	RC/G	FR	G/POS	WS	TPW
1884 Mil-U	9	33	5	8	1	0	0	....	3	....	....	....	.242	.306	.273	.578	97	0	3	3.16	0	/O-9(9-0-0)	1	0.0
1886 NY-a	59	224	32	46	5	2	0	17	22	....	16	....	.205	.279	.246	.525	68	-7	20	3.08	-2	O-59(26-33-0)	3	-1.0
Total 2	**68**	**257**	**37**	**54**	**6**	**2**	**0**	**17**	**25**	**....**	**16**	**....**	**.210**	**.283**	**.249**	**.532**	**72**	**-7**	**23**	**3.09**	**-2**	**/O-68**	**4**	**-1.0**

• BEJMA, Ollie Alojzy Frank Bejma b: 9/12/1907, South Bend, IN d: 1/3/1995, South Bend, IN BR/TR, 5'10", 165 lbs. Deb: 4/24/1934 U

YEAR TM-L	G	AB	R	H	2B	3B	HR	RBI	BB	SO	SB	CS	AVG	OBP	SLG	OPS	OPS+	BR/A	RC	RC/G	FR	G/POS	WS	TPW
1934 StL-A	95	262	39	71	16	3	2	29	40	36	3	2	.271	.376	.378	.754	88	-4	40	5.31	-1	S-32,2-14,3-13/O-9(0-0-9)	7	-0.2
1935 StL-A	64	198	18	38	8	2	2	26	27	21	1	0	.192	.289	.283	.572	46	-16	18	2.88	-4	2-47/S-8,3-2	1	-1.5
1936 StL-A	67	139	19	36	2	3	2	18	27	21	0	0	.259	.380	.360	.739	81	-3	21	5.31	-6	2-32/3-7,S-1	3	-0.7
1939 Chi-A	90	307	52	77	9	3	8	44	36	27	1	3	.251	.331	.378	.709	79	-11	39	4.28	0	2-81/3-1,S-1	8	-0.6
Total 4	**316**	**906**	**128**	**222**	**35**	**11**	**14**	**117**	**130**	**105**	**5**	**5**	**.245**	**.343**	**.354**	**.697**	**75**	**-34**	**118**	**4.40**	**-11**	**2-174/S-42,3-23,O-9**	**19**	**-2.9**

• BELANGER, Mark Mark Henry Belanger b: 6/8/1944, Pittsfield, MA d: 10/6/1998, New York, NY BR/TR, 6'1", 170 lbs. Deb: 8/7/1965

YEAR TM-L	G	AB	R	H	2B	3B	HR	RBI	BB	SO	SB	CS	AVG	OBP	SLG	OPS	OPS+	BR/A	RC	RC/G	FR	G/POS	WS	TPW
1965 Bal-A	11	3	1	1	0	0	0	0	0	0	0	1	.333	.333	.333	.667	88	-0	0	.00	-1	/S-4	0	-0.2
1966 Bal-A	8	19	2	3	1	0	0	0	0	3	0	0	.158	.158	.211	.368	5	-2	1	1.08	1	/S-6	0	-0.1
1967 Bal-A	69	184	19	32	5	0	1	10	12	46	6	1	.174	.224	.217	.442	31	-15	10	1.62	-4	S-38,2-26/3-2	1	-1.5
1968 Bal-A	145	472	40	98	13	0	2	21	40	114	10	1	.208	.275	.248	.523	59	-20	35	2.37	15	*S-145	10	0.8
1969*Bal-A	150	530	76	152	17	4	2	50	53	54	14	6	.287	.354	.345	.699	95	-1	66	4.38	12	*S-148	18	3.0
1970*Bal-A	145	459	53	100	6	5	1	36	52	65	13	2	.218	.304	.259	.564	56	-24	42	2.99	15	*S-143	12	0.7
1971*Bal-A	150	500	67	133	19	4	0	35	73	48	10	8	.266	.367	.320	.687	97	1	63	4.32	13	*S-149	21	3.3
1972 Bal-A	113	285	36	53	9	1	2	16	18	53	6	3	.186	.239	.246	.485	43	-20	18	1.93	8	*S-105	5	-0.1
1973*Bal-A	154	470	60	106	15	1	0	27	49	54	13	6	.226	.305	.262	.567	61	-22	41	2.78	12	*S-154	10	0.8
1974*Bal-A	155	493	54	111	14	4	5	36	51	69	17	7	.225	.300	.300	.601	76	-14	49	3.18	10	*S-155	16	1.6
1975 Bal-A	152	442	44	100	11	1	3	27	36	53	16	4	.226	.286	.276	.562	63	-19	40	2.88	27	*S-152	14	2.6
1976 Bal-A★	153	522	66	141	22	2	1	40	51	64	27	17	.270	.337	.326	.663	101	0	60	3.85	21	*S-153	23	4.1
1977 Bal-A	144	402	39	83	13	4	2	30	43	68	15	8	.206	.288	.274	.562	58	-22	34	2.63	30	*S-142	11	2.0
1978 Bal-A	135	348	39	74	13	0	0	16	40	55	6	6	.213	.305	.250	.555	61	-17	29	2.67	25	*S-134	9	2.0
1979*Bal-A	101	198	28	33	6	2	0	9	29	33	5	1	.167	.276	.217	.493	36	-16	15	2.18	5	S-98	3	-0.4
1980 Bal-A	113	268	37	61	7	3	0	22	12	25	6	3	.228	.261	.276	.537	48	-19	20	2.48	2	*S-109	5	-0.9
1981 Bal-A	64	139	9	23	3	2	1	10	12	25	2	1	.165	.242	.237	.479	39	-11	8	1.75	-1	S-63	3	-0.7
1982 LA-N	54	50	6	12	1	0	0	4	5	10	1	0	.240	.309	.260	.569	62	-2	4	2.64	-1	S-44/2-1	1	-0.1
Total 18	**2016**	**5784**	**676**	**1316**	**175**	**33**	**20**	**389**	**576**	**839**	**167**	**75**	**.228**	**.302**	**.280**	**.582**	**68**	**-225**	**533**	**2.98**	**188**	***S-1942/2-27,3-2**	**162**	**16.9**

• BELARDI, Wayne Carroll Wayne Belardi b: 9/5/1930, St. Helena, CA d: 10/21/1993, Santa Cruz, CA BL/TL, 6'1", 185 lbs. Deb: 4/18/1950

YEAR TM-L	G	AB	R	H	2B	3B	HR	RBI	BB	SO	SB	CS	AVG	OBP	SLG	OPS	OPS+	BR/A	RC	RC/G	FR	G/POS	WS	TPW
1950 Bro-N	10	10	0	0	0	0	0	0	0	4	0	....	.000	.000	.000	.000	-98	-3	0	.00	0	/1-1	0	-0.3
1951 Bro-N	3	3	1	1	0	1	0	0	0	2	0	0	.333	.333	1.000	1.333	240	1	1	13.84	0	....	0	0.1
1953*Bro-N	69	163	19	39	3	2	11	34	16	40	0	0	.239	.311	.485	.796	101	-0	26	5.49	0	1-38	4	-0.2
1954 Bro-N	11	9	0	2	0	0	0	1	2	3	0	0	.222	.364	.222	.586	55	-0	1	3.53	0	....	0	0.0
Det-A	88	250	27	58	7	1	11	24	33	34	1	0	.232	.333	.400	.733	102	1	35	4.60	0	1-79	7	-0.3
1955 Det-A	3	3	0	0	0	0	0	0	0	1	0	0	.000	.000	.000	.000	-102	-1	0	.00	0	....	0	-0.1
1956 Det-A	79	154	24	43	3	1	6	15	15	13	0	0	.279	.373	.429	.801	111	3	25	5.82	-1	1-31/O-2(2-0-1)	5	0.0
Total 6	**263**	**592**	**71**	**143**	**13**	**5**	**28**	**74**	**66**	**97**	**1**	**0**	**.242**	**.332**	**.422**	**.754**	**100**	**0**	**88**	**5.03**	**0**	**1-149/O-2**	**16**	**-0.8**

• BELCHER, Kevin Kevin Donnell Belcher b: 8/8/1967, Waco, TX BR/TR, 6', 170 lbs. Deb: 9/3/1990

YEAR TM-L	G	AB	R	H	2B	3B	HR	RBI	BB	SO	SB	CS	AVG	OBP	SLG	OPS	OPS+	BR/A	RC	RC/G	FR	G/POS	WS	TPW
1990 Tex-A	16	15	4	2	1	0	0	0	2	6	0	0	.133	.235	.200	.435	23	-2	1	1.72	0	/O-9(2-5-2)	0	-0.2

• BELDEN, Ira Ira Allison Belden b: 4/16/1874, Cleveland, OH d: 7/15/1916, Lakewood, OH BL/TR, 5'11", 175 lbs. Deb: 9/17/1897

YEAR TM-L	G	AB	R	H	2B	3B	HR	RBI	BB	SO	SB	CS	AVG	OBP	SLG	OPS	OPS+	BR/A	RC	RC/G	FR	G/POS	WS	TPW
1897 Cle-N	8	30	5	8	0	2	0	4	2		0	....	.267	.333	.400	.733	88	-1	4	4.79	2	/O-8(0-0-8)	1	0.1

• BELK, Tim Timothy William Belk b: 4/6/1970, Cincinnati, OH BR/TR, 6'3", 200 lbs. Deb: 6/25/1996

YEAR TM-L	G	AB	R	H	2B	3B	HR	RBI	BB	SO	SB	CS	AVG	OBP	SLG	OPS	OPS+	BR/A	RC	RC/G	FR	G/POS	WS	TPW
1996 Cin-N	7	15	2	3	0	0	0	0	1	2	0	0	.200	.250	.200	.450	21	-2	1	1.83	-1	/1-6	0	-0.3

• BELL, Beau Roy Chester Bell b: 8/20/1907, Bellville, TX d: 9/14/1977, College Station, TX BR/TR, 6'2", 185 lbs. Deb: 4/16/1935 Career OF: 68-0-534

YEAR TM-L	G	AB	R	H	2B	3B	HR	RBI	BB	SO	SB	CS	AVG	OBP	SLG	OPS	OPS+	BR/A	RC	RC/G	FR	G/POS	WS	TPW
1935 StL-A	76	220	20	55	8	2	3	17	16	16	1	1	.250	.304	.345	.649	65	-12	23	3.72	-7	O-37(10-0-27),1-15/3-3	2	-2.1
1936 StL-A	155	616	100	212	40	12	11	123	60	55	4	1	.344	.403	.502	.905	119	19	126	8.14	-5	*O-142(12-0-133),1-17	18	0.3
1937 StL-A★	156	642	82	**218**	**51**	8	14	117	53	54	2	2	.340	.391	.509	.900	124	22	127	7.87	1	*O-131(0-0-131),1-26/3-2	16	1.2
1938 StL-A	147	526	91	138	35	3	13	84	71	46	1	3	.262	.350	.414	.765	91	-9	79	5.30	-4	*O-132(0-0-132)/1-4	9	-1.9
1939 StL-A	11	32	4	7	1	0	1	5	4	3	0	0	.219	.324	.344	.668	69	-1	4	3.71	0	/O-9(0-0)	0	-0.2
Det-A	54	134	14	32	4	2	0	24	24	16	0	1	.239	.358	.299	.657	65	-7	15	3.50	1	O-37(37-0-0)	2	-0.7
Yr.	65	166	18	39	5	2	1	29	28	19	0	1	.235	.352	.307	.659	66	-8	19	3.54	1	O-46(46-0-0)	2	-0.9
1940 Cle-A	120	444	55	124	22	2	4	58	34	41	2	2	.279	.332	.365	.697	83	-11	55	4.46	0	O-97(0-0-97),1-14	10	-1.7
1941 Cle-A	48	104	12	20	4	3	0	9	10	8	1	2	.192	.270	.288	.558	50	-8	8	2.31	-2	O-14(0-0-14),1-10	0	-1.1
Total 7	**767**	**2718**	**378**	**806**	**165**	**32**	**46**	**437**	**272**	**239**	**11**	**12**	**.297**	**.362**	**.432**	**.794**	**98**	**-8**	**437**	**5.91**	**-16**	**O-599/1-86,3-5**	**57**	**-6.3**

• BELL, Buddy David Gus Bell b: 8/27/1951, Pittsburgh, PA BR/TR, 6'1", 185 lbs. Deb: 4/15/1972 M/C Career OF: 11-64-66

YEAR TM-L	G	AB	R	H	2B	3B	HR	RBI	BB	SO	SB	CS	AVG	OBP	SLG	OPS	OPS+	BR/A	RC	RC/G	FR	G/POS	WS	TPW
1972 Cle-A	132	466	49	119	21	1	9	36	34	29	5	6	.255	.310	.363	.673	96	-4	52	3.88	4	*O-123(0-63-65)/3-6	13	-0.6
1973 Cle-A★	156	631	86	169	23	7	14	59	49	47	7	15	.268	.327	.393	.720	100	-5	76	4.16	15	*3-154/O-2(0-1-1)	21	0.9
1974 Cle-A	116	423	51	111	15	1	7	46	35	29	1	3	.262	.323	.352	.675	95	-3	46	3.67	6	*3-115/D-1	13	0.2
1975 Cle-A	153	553	66	150	20	4	10	59	51	72	6	5	.271	.334	.376	.710	100	-0	69	4.32	1	*3-153	16	0.0
1976 Cle-A	159	604	75	170	26	2	7	60	44	49	3	8	.281	.332	.366	.698	105	1	71	4.12	4	*3-158/1-2	20	0.4
1977 Cle-A	129	479	64	140	23	4	11	64	45	63	1	8	.292	.354	.426	.780	115	7	68	4.88	13	*3-118,O-11(11-0-0)	15	1.8
1978 Cle-A	142	556	71	157	27	8	6	62	39	43	1	3	.282	.329	.392	.721	103	1	65	4.03	24	*3-139/D-1	16	2.4
1979 Tex-A	162	670	89	200	42	3	18	101	30	45	5	4	.299	.331	.451	.782	110	6	95	5.06	18	*3-147,S-33	22	2.4
1980 Tex-A★	129	490	76	161	24	4	17	83	40	39	3	1	.329	.379	.498	.877	142	28	88	6.78	12	*3-120/S-3	21	3.8
1981 Tex-A★	97	360	44	106	16	1	10	64	42	30	3	3	.294	.373	.428	.801	137	18	58	5.75	21	3-96/S-1	18	4.0
1982 Tex-A★	148	537	62	159	27	2	13	67	70	50	5	4	.296	.379	.426	.806	127	22	87	5.90	23	*3-145/S-4	25	4.3
1983 Tex-A	156	618	75	171	35	3	14	66	50	48	3	5	.277	.335	.411	.746	106	3	78	4.40	11	*3-154	17	1.2
1984 Tex-A★	148	553	88	174	36	5	11	83	63	54	2	1	.315	.388	.458	.845	129	24	95	6.23	23	*3-147	26	4.5

YEAR TM-L	G	AB	R	H	2B	3B	HR	RBI	BB	SO	SB	CS	AVG	OBP	SLG	OPS	OPS+	BR/A	RC	RC/G	FR	G/POS	WS	TPW
1985 Tex-A	84	313	33	74	13	3	4	32	33	21	3	2	.236	.311	.335	.647	76	-10	31	3.20	8	3-83	5	-0.3
Cin-N	67	247	28	54	15	2	6	36	34	27	0	1	.219	.313	.368	.682	86	-5	27	3.57	-3	3-67	5	-0.9
1986 Cin-N	155	568	89	158	29	3	20	75	73	49	2	8	.278	.365	.445	.811	117	12	91	5.56	2	*3-151/2-1	23	1.2
1987 Cin-N	143	522	74	148	19	2	17	70	71	39	4	1	.284	.370	.425	.796	105	6	84	5.76	-6	*3-142	17	-0.2
1988 Cin-N	21	54	3	10	0	0	0	3	7	3	0	0	.185	.279	.185	.464	34	-4	3	1.69	2	3-13/1-2	0	-0.3
Hou-N	74	269	24	68	10	1	7	37	19	29	1	1	.253	.302	.375	.678	97	-2	29	3.69	-2	3-66/1-7	8	-0.4
Yr.	95	323	27	78	10	1	7	40	26	32	1	1	.241	.298	.344	.642	86	-7	32	3.32	0	3-79/1-9	8	-0.7
1989 Tex-A	34	82	4	15	4	0	0	3	7	10	0	0	.183	.247	.232	.479	35	-7	4	1.60	1	D-22/3-9,1-1	0	-0.7
Total 18	**2405**	**8995**	**1151**	**2514**	**425**	**56**	**201**	**1106**	**836**	**776**	**55**	**79**	**.279**	**.343**	**.406**	**.750**	**109**	**85**	**1218**	**4.73**	**176**	***3-2183,0-136/S-41,D-24,1,2**	**301**	**23.8**

• BELL, David

David Michael Bell b: 9/14/1972, Cincinnati, OH BR/TR, 5'10", 170 lbs. Deb: 5/3/1995

YEAR TM-L	G	AB	R	H	2B	3B	HR	RBI	BB	SO	SB	CS	AVG	OBP	SLG	OPS	OPS+	BR/A	RC	RC/G	FR	G/POS	WS	TPW
1995 Cle-A	2	2	0	0	0	0	0	0	0	0	0	0	.000	.000	.000	.000	-99	-1	0	.00	0	/3-2	0	0.0
StL-N	39	144	13	36	7	2	2	19	4	25	1	2	.250	.280	.368	.648	69	-8	15	3.58	-2	2-37/3-3	2	-0.8
1996 StL-N	62	145	12	31	6	0	1	9	10	22	1	1	.214	.269	.276	.545	45	-12	10	2.38	0	3-45,2-20/S-1	1	-1.0
1997 StL-N	66	142	9	30	7	2	1	12	10	28	1	0	.211	.263	.310	.573	50	-11	12	2.72	-4	3-35,2-23,S-13	2	-1.3
1998 StL-N	4	9	0	2	1	0	0	0	0	3	0	0	.222	.222	.333	.556	44	-1	1	2.57	-0	/3-4,2-1	0	-0.1
Cle-A	107	340	37	89	21	2	10	41	22	54	0	4	.262	.310	.424	.734	86	-10	42	4.17	3	*2-101/3-6,1-1,S-1	8	-0.2
Sea-A	21	80	11	26	8	0	0	8	5	8	0	0	.325	.365	.425	.790	105	1	12	5.51	-1	2-14/1-5,3-5,0-1	2	0.0
Yr.	128	420	48	115	29	2	10	49	27	62	0	4	.274	.321	.424	.745	89	-10	53	4.41	2	*2-115,3-11/1-6,0-1,S-1	10	-0.2
1999 Sea-A	157	597	92	160	31	2	21	78	58	90	7	4	.268	.335	.432	.767	92	-9	89	5.22	-9	*2-154/1-4,S-1	16	-1.0
2000*Sea-A	133	454	57	112	24	2	11	47	42	66	2	3	.247	.319	.381	.700	81	-15	55	4.03	-4	3-93,2-48/1-2,D-1,S-1	8	-1.4
2001*Sea-A	135	470	62	122	28	0	15	64	28	59	2	1	.260	.305	.415	.720	93	-7	59	4.34	18	*3-134/1-2	14	1.2
2002*SF-N	154	552	82	144	29	2	20	73	54	80	1	2	.261	.337	.429	.766	105	2	77	4.74	0	*3-139,2-12/S-3,1-2	19	0.5
2003 Phi-N	85	297	32	58	14	0	4	37	41	40	0	0	.195	.301	.283	.584	57	-18	27	2.91	7	3-85/2-3	4	-0.9
Total 9	**965**	**3232**	**407**	**810**	**176**	**12**	**85**	**388**	**274**	**475**	**15**	**17**	**.251**	**.315**	**.391**	**.706**	**84**	**-87**	**398**	**4.19**	**8**	**3-551,2-413/S-20,1-16,D-1,0**	**76**	**-5.1**

• BELL, Derek

Derek Nathaniel Bell b: 12/11/1968, Tampa, FL BR/TR, 6'2", 215 lbs. Deb: 6/28/1991 Career OF: 37-325-814

YEAR TM-L	G	AB	R	H	2B	3B	HR	RBI	BB	SO	SB	CS	AVG	OBP	SLG	OPS	OPS+	BR/A	RC	RC/G	FR	G/POS	WS	TPW
1991 Tor-A	18	28	5	4	0	0	0	1	6	5	3	2	.143	.314	.143	.457	30	-3	2	1.97	-1	0-13(7-6-0)	0	-0.4
1992*Tor-A	61	161	23	39	6	3	2	15	15	34	7	2	.242	.326	.354	.680	86	-2	19	3.78	1	0-56(24-18-15)/D-1	4	-0.3
1993 SD-N	150	542	73	142	19	1	21	72	23	122	26	5	.262	.307	.417	.724	90	-6	71	4.56	-4	*0-125(1-119-6),3-19	12	-0.9
1994 SD-N	108	434	54	135	20	0	14	54	29	88	24	8	.311	.356	.454	.810	112	9	67	5.57	-5	*0-108(0-108-0)	11	0.5
1995 Hou-N	112	452	63	151	21	2	8	86	33	71	27	9	.334	.389	.442	.832	128	20	79	6.53	-1	*0-110(0-30-82)	16	1.5
1996 Hou-N	158	627	84	165	40	3	17	113	40	123	29	3	.263	.316	.418	.733	99	2	82	4.50	1	*0-157(0-2-157)	14	-0.6
1997*Hou-N	129	493	67	136	29	3	15	71	40	94	15	7	.276	.345	.438	.783	107	5	72	5.07	-1	*0-125(0-36-89)/D-1	11	-0.1
1998*Hou-N	156	630	111	198	41	2	22	108	51	126	13	3	.314	.369	.490	.860	127	25	114	6.70	-1	*0-154(0-0-154)	22	1.6
1999*Hou-N	128	509	61	120	22	0	12	66	50	129	18	6	.236	.309	.350	.659	67	-25	53	3.41	-8	*0-126(0-0-126)	4	-3.7
2000*NY-N	144	546	87	145	31	1	18	69	65	125	8	4	.266	.350	.425	.775	99	-1	82	5.21	-9	*0-143(0-5-142)/P-1	16	-2.0
2001 Pit-N	46	156	14	27	3	0	5	13	25	38	0	2	.173	.287	.288	.576	49	-13	13	2.54	-1	0-46(5-1-43)	1	-1.6
Total 11	**1210**	**4578**	**642**	**1262**	**232**	**15**	**134**	**668**	**377**	**955**	**170**	**51**	**.276**	**.339**	**.421**	**.760**	**100**	**11**	**652**	**4.97**	**-29**	***0-1163/3-19,D-2,P-1**	**111**	**-5.9**

• BELL, Fern

Fernando Jerome Lee "Danny" Bell b: 1/21/1913, Ada, OK d: 8/29/2000, Rancho Mirage, CA BR/TR, 6', 180 lbs. Deb: 4/17/1939

YEAR TM-L	G	AB	R	H	2B	3B	HR	RBI	BB	SO	SB	CS	AVG	OBP	SLG	OPS	OPS+	BR/A	RC	RC/G	FR	G/POS	WS	TPW
1939 Pit-N	83	262	44	75	5	8	2	34	42	18	2	....	.286	.385	.389	.774	110	6	42	5.82	-1	0-67(15-46-7)/3-1	9	0.3
1940 Pit-N	6	3	0	0	0	0	0	1	1	1	0	....	.000	.250	.000	.250	-26	-0	0	.59	0	....	0	0.0
Total 2	**89**	**265**	**44**	**75**	**5**	**8**	**2**	**35**	**43**	**19**	**2**	**....**	**.283**	**.383**	**.385**	**.768**	**109**	**5**	**42**	**5.74**	**-1**	**/0-67,3-1**	**9**	**0.2**

• BELL, Frank

Frank Gustav Bell b: 1863, Cincinnati, OH d: 4/14/1891, Cincinnati, OH, 6' Deb: 7/7/1885

YEAR TM-L	G	AB	R	H	2B	3B	HR	RBI	BB	SO	SB	CS	AVG	OBP	SLG	OPS	OPS+	BR/A	RC	RC/G	FR	G/POS	WS	TPW
1885 Bro-a	10	29	5	5	0	1	0	2	0	....	....	....	.172	.200	.241	.441	39	-2	1	1.61	-4	/C-5,0-4(0-3-1),3-2	0	-0.5

• BELL, George

George Antonio (Mathey) "Liberty" Bell
b: 10/21/1959, San Pedro de Macoris, Dominican Republic BR/TR, 6'1", 190 lbs. Deb: 4/9/1981 Career OF: 1123-0-114

YEAR TM-L	G	AB	R	H	2B	3B	HR	RBI	BB	SO	SB	CS	AVG	OBP	SLG	OPS	OPS+	BR/A	RC	RC/G	FR	G/POS	WS	TPW
1981 Tor-A	60	163	19	38	2	1	5	12	5	27	3	2	.233	.256	.350	.606	69	-7	14	2.99	0	0-44(26-0-18)/D-8	2	-1.0
1983 Tor-A	39	112	5	30	5	4	2	17	4	17	1	1	.268	.305	.438	.743	96	-1	13	4.14	-1	0-34(28-0-6)/D-2	2	-0.4
1984 Tor-A	159	606	85	177	39	4	26	87	24	86	11	2	.292	.328	.498	.826	121	16	95	5.75	-3	*0-147(66-0-90)/D-7,3-3	19	0.6
1985*Tor-A	157	607	87	167	28	6	28	95	43	90	21	6	.275	.331	.479	.811	116	14	97	5.69	1	*0-157(157-0-0)/3-2	21	0.7
1986 Tor-A	159	641	101	198	38	6	31	108	41	62	7	8	.309	.352	.532	.884	133	25	113	6.47	-5	*0-147(147-0-0),D-11/3-2	23	1.2
1987 Tor-A★	156	610	111	188	32	4	47	**134**	39	75	5	1	.308	.357	.605	.962	146	37	125	7.54	0	*0-148(149-0-0)/D-7,2-1.3	26	2.9
1988 Tor-A	156	614	78	165	27	5	24	97	34	66	4	2	.269	.308	.446	.754	108	4	78	4.36	-4	*0-149(149-0-0)/D-7	16	-0.6
1989*Tor-A	153	613	88	182	41	2	18	104	33	60	4	3	.297	.337	.458	.795	130	20	89	5.17	-5	*0-134(134-0-0),D-19	22	1.0
1990 Tor-A★	142	562	67	149	25	0	21	86	32	80	3	2	.265	.308	.422	.730	97	-5	70	4.27	-1	*0-106(106-0-0),D-36	12	-1.1
1991 Chi-N★	149	558	63	159	27	0	25	86	32	62	2	6	.285	.328	.468	.796	116	7	81	5.19	-1	*0-146(146-0-0)	14	0.2
1992 Chi-A	155	627	74	160	27	0	25	112	31	97	5	2	.255	.297	.418	.715	99	-3	68	3.65	0	*D-140,0-15(15-0-0)	13	-1.0
1993 Chi-A	102	410	36	89	17	2	13	64	13	49	1	1	.217	.248	.363	.612	64	-23	33	2.58	0	*D-102	1	-3.0
Total 12	**1587**	**6123**	**814**	**1702**	**308**	**34**	**265**	**1002**	**331**	**771**	**67**	**36**	**.278**	**.320**	**.469**	**.789**	**113**	**84**	**878**	**5.04**	**-18**	***0-1227,D-339/3-8,2-1**	**171**	**-0.4**

• BELL, Gus

David Russell Bell b: 11/15/1928, Louisville, KY d: 5/7/1995, Montgomery, OH BL/TR, 6'1.5", 196 lbs. Deb: 5/30/1950 Career OF: 162-811-683

YEAR TM-L	G	AB	R	H	2B	3B	HR	RBI	BB	SO	SB	CS	AVG	OBP	SLG	OPS	OPS+	BR/A	RC	RC/G	FR	G/POS	WS	TPW
1950 Pit-N	111	422	62	119	22	11	8	53	28	46	4	....	.282	.333	.443	.776	99	-2	63	5.53	6	*0-104(0-0-104)	9	0.1
1951 Pit-N	149	600	80	167	27	**12**	16	89	42	41	1	4	.278	.330	.443	.773	103	-1	88	5.33	3	*0-145(0-0-145)	16	-0.2
1952 Pit-N	131	468	53	117	21	5	16	59	36	72	1	4	.250	.306	.419	.725	97	-5	61	4.49	-7	*0-123(0-0-123)	8	-1.6
1953 Cin-N★	151	610	102	183	37	5	30	105	48	72	0	2	.300	.354	.525	.879	124	19	113	6.80	3	*0-151(0-145-6)	24	1.4
1954 Cin-N★	153	619	104	185	38	7	17	101	48	58	5	3	.299	.353	.465	.818	108	6	100	5.86	-8	*0-153(0-153-0)	20	-0.9
1955 Cin-N	154	610	88	188	30	6	27	104	54	57	4	4	.308	.364	.510	.874	122	18	114	7.01	-16	*0-154(0-154-0)	21	-0.5
1956 Cin-N★	150	603	82	176	31	4	29	84	50	66	6	2	.292	.349	.501	.850	117	15	105	6.33	-11	*0-149(0-149-0)	22	-0.3
1957 Cin-N★	121	510	65	149	20	3	13	61	30	54	0	1	.292	.335	.420	.755	95	-4	70	4.93	-11	*0-121(0-121-0)	13	-2.1
1958 Cin-N	112	385	42	97	16	2	10	46	36	40	2	3	.252	.318	.382	.699	80	-12	46	4.04	-9	*0-107(20-87-0)	7	-2.7
1959 Cin-N	148	580	59	170	27	2	19	115	29	44	2	3	.293	.329	.445	.774	101	-2	81	5.03	-2	*0-145(6-0-141)	15	-0.9
1960 Cin-N	143	515	65	135	19	5	12	62	29	40	4	3	.262	.303	.388	.691	86	-11	60	4.05	-3	*0-131(41-0-97)	9	-2.0
1961*Cin-N	103	235	27	60	10	1	3	33	18	21	1	1	.255	.308	.345	.653	72	-10	25	3.59	-3	0-75(43-1-33)	4	-1.6
1962 NY-N	30	101	8	15	2	0	1	6	10	7	0	1	.149	.225	.198	.423	14	-13	5	1.37	4	0-26(0-0-26)	1	-1.1
Mil-N	79	214	28	61	11	3	5	24	12	17	0	0	.285	.323	.435	.758	104	0	30	5.07	1	0-58(52-1-8)	6	-0.1
Yr.	109	315	36	76	13	3	6	30	22	24	0	1	.241	.291	.359	.650	74	-12	34	3.70	4	0-84(52-1-34)	7	-1.2
1963 Mil-N	3	3	0	1	0	0	0	0	0	0	0	0	.333	.333	.333	.667	94	-0	0	4.50	0	....	0	0.0
1964 Mil-N	3	3	0	0	0	0	0	0	0	1	0	0	.000	.000	.000	.000	-99	-1	0	.00	0	....	0	-0.1
Total 15	**1741**	**6478**	**865**	**1823**	**311**	**66**	**206**	**942**	**470**	**636**	**30**	**31**	**.281**	**.333**	**.445**	**.778**	**102**	**-1**	**962**	**5.31**	**-54**	***0-1642**	**175**	**-12.6**

• BELL, Jay

Jay Stuart Bell b: 12/11/1965, Pensacola, FL BR/TR, 6'1", 185 lbs. Deb: 9/29/1986

YEAR TM-L	G	AB	R	H	2B	3B	HR	RBI	BB	SO	SB	CS	AVG	OBP	SLG	OPS	OPS+	BR/A	RC	RC/G	FR	G/POS	WS	TPW
1986 Cle-A	5	14	3	5	2	0	1	4	2	3	0	0	.357	.438	.714	1.152	211	2	5	13.81	0	/2-2,D-2	1	0.2
1987 Cle-A	38	125	14	27	9	1	2	13	8	31	2	0	.216	.269	.352	.621	62	-7	13	3.44	-6	S-38	1	-0.8
1988 Cle-A	73	211	23	46	5	1	2	21	21	53	4	2	.218	.292	.280	.571	59	-11	18	2.85	-10	S-72/D-1	2	-1.6
1989 Pit-N	78	271	33	70	13	3	2	27	19	47	5	3	.258	.309	.351	.660	91	-4	28	3.37	-3	S-78	8	-0.1
1990*Pit-N	159	583	93	148	28	7	7	52	65	109	10	6	.254	.332	.362	.694	94	-5	72	3.91	1	*S-159	17	0.9
1991*Pit-N	157	608	96	164	32	8	16	67	52	99	10	6	.270	.331	.428	.759	114	9	85	4.59	1	*S-156	22	2.3
1992*Pit-N	159	632	87	167	36	6	9	55	55	103	7	5	.264	.327	.383	.710	101	0	80	4.28	9	*S-159	24	2.3
1993 Pit-N★	154	604	102	187	32	9	9	51	77	122	16	10	.310	.393	.437	.830	122	21	104	6.16	26	*S-154	26	5.9
1994 Pit-N	110	424	68	117	35	4	9	45	49	82	2	0	.276	.355	.441	.796	105	4	65	5.31	8	*S-110	19	2.0
1995 Pit-N	138	530	79	139	28	4	13	55	55	110	2	5	.262	.336	.404	.740	92	-8	70	4.61	2	*S-136/3-3	13	0.5
1996 Pit-N	151	527	65	132	29	3	13	71	54	108	6	4	.250	.326	.391	.717	86	-12	68	4.35	-7	*S-151	15	-0.6
1997 KC-A	153	573	89	167	28	3	21	92	71	101	10	6	.291	.373	.461	.834	113	12	99	6.15	15	*S-149/3-4	21	3.8
1998 Ari-N	155	549	79	138	29	5	20	67	81	129	3	5	.251	.355	.432	.786	106	4	85	5.24	2	*S-138,2-15	20	1.8
1999*Ari-N★	151	589	132	170	32	6	38	112	82	132	7	4	.289	.379	.557	.936	132	28	127	7.72	-17	*2-148/D-2,S-1	23	1.7
2000 Ari-N	149	565	87	151	30	6	18	68	70	88	7	3	.267	.351	.437	.788	95	-4	91	5.64	-6	*2-145/D-1	19	-0.3

YEAR TM-L	G	AB	R	H	2B	3B	HR	RBI	BB	SO	SB	CS	AVG	OBP	SLG	OPS	OPS+	BR/A	RC	RC/G	FR	G/POS	WS	TPW
2001*Ari-N	129	428	59	106	24	1	13	46	65	79	0	1	.248	.352	.400	.752	88	-6	63	4.95	-7	2-80,3-40/D-3	12	-0.9
2002 Ari-N	32	49	3	8	1	0	2	11	5	9	0	0	.163	.255	.306	.561	43	-4	4	2.25	1	/3-6,1-5,2-2,S-2	1	-0.4
2003 NY-N	72	116	11	21	1	0	0	3	22	38	0	0	.181	.321	.190	.511	39	-9	8	2.24	-3	2-14,3-14,1-13,S-12/D-1	1	-1.2
Total 18	**2063**	**7398**	**1123**	**1963**	**394**	**67**	**195**	**860**	**853**	**1443**	**91**	**60**	**.265**	**.346**	**.416**	**.762**	**101**	**9**	**1086**	**4.99**	**7**	***S-1515,2-406/3-67,1-18,D-10**	**245**	**15.6**
• BELL, Juan	Juan (Mathey) Bell b: 3/29/1968, San Pedro de Macoris, Dominican Republic BR/TR, 5'11", 176 lbs. Deb: 9/6/1989 Career OF: 1-1-2																							
1989 Bal-A	8	4	2	0	0	0	0	0	0	1	1	0	.000	.000	.000	.000	-103	-1	0	.00	0	/D-4,2-2,S-2	0	0.0
1990 Bal-A	5	2	1	0	0	0	0	0	0	1	0	0	.000	.000	.000	.000	-103	-1	0	.00	0	/D-1,S-1	0	-0.1
1991 Bal-A	100	209	26	36	9	2	1	15	8	51	0	0	.172	.203	.249	.452	25	-22	11	1.65	-7	2-77,S-15/D-4,0-1	2	-2.6
1992 Phi-N	46	147	12	30	3	1	1	8	18	29	5	0	.204	.295	.259	.554	58	-7	13	2.91	4	S-46	2	0.1
1993 Phi-N	24	65	5	13	6	1	0	7	5	12	0	1	.200	.268	.323	.591	58	-4	6	2.86	0	S-22	1	-0.3
Mil-A	91	286	42	67	6	2	5	29	36	64	6	6	.234	.322	.322	.644	75	-11	31	3.56	-4	2-47,S-40/0-3(0-1-2),D-2	6	-0.9
1994 Mon-N	38	97	12	27	4	0	2	10	15	21	4	0	.278	.375	.381	.756	97	1	16	5.86	1	2-25/3-3,S-1	4	0.3
1995 Bos-A	17	26	7	4	2	0	1	2	2	10	0	0	.154	.214	.346	.560	41	-2	2	2.44	-1	/S-6,2-5,3-1	0	-0.3
Total 7	**329**	**836**	**107**	**177**	**30**	**6**	**10**	**71**	**84**	**189**	**16**	**7**	**.212**	**.286**	**.298**	**.584**	**59**	**-46**	**78**	**3.07**	**-6**	**2-156,S-133/D-11,3-4,0-4**	**15**	**-3.8**
• BELL, Kevin	Kevin Robert Bell b: 7/13/1955, Los Angeles, CA BR/TR, 6', 195 lbs. Deb: 6/16/1976																							
1976 Chi-A	68	230	24	57	7	6	5	20	18	56	2	1	.248	.305	.396	.701	103	0	28	4.12	-3	3-67/D-1	6	-0.3
1977 Chi-A	9	28	4	5	1	0	1	6	3	8	0	0	.179	.258	.321	.579	57	-2	3	2.90	1	/S-5,3-4,0-1	0	-0.1
1978 Chi-A	54	68	9	13	0	0	2	5	5	19	1	0	.191	.257	.279	.536	50	-4	5	2.10	4	3-52/D-1	1	-0.1
1979 Chi-A	70	200	20	49	8	1	4	22	15	43	2	4	.245	.298	.355	.653	75	-8	20	3.38	9	3-68/S-2	4	0.0
1980 Chi-A	92	191	16	34	5	2	1	11	29	37	0	0	.178	.286	.241	.527	46	-13	15	2.44	0	3-83/D-3,S-3	1	-1.4
1982 Oak-A	4	9	1	3	1	0	0	0	0	2	0	0	.333	.333	.444	.778	117	0	1	6.00	0	/3-3,D-1	0	0.0
Total 6	**297**	**726**	**74**	**161**	**22**	**9**	**13**	**64**	**70**	**165**	**5**	**5**	**.222**	**.292**	**.331**	**.623**	**74**	**-27**	**72**	**3.23**	**10**	**3-277/S-10,D-6,0-1**	**12**	**-1.9**
• BELL, Les	Lester Rowland Bell b: 12/14/1901, Harrisburg, PA d: 12/26/1985, Hershey, PA BR/TR, 5'11", 165 lbs. Deb: 9/18/1923																							
1923 StL-N	15	51	5	19	2	1	0	9	9	7	1	0	.373	.467	.451	.918	146	5	12	9.59	1	S-15	3	0.7
1924 StL-N	17	57	5	14	3	2	1	5	3	7	0	0	.246	.295	.421	.716	91	-1	7	4.29	-4	S-17	1	-0.3
1925 StL-N	153	586	80	167	29	9	11	88	43	47	4	5	.285	.334	.422	.755	90	-11	82	4.99	6	*3-153/S-1	15	0.4
1926*StL-N	155	581	85	189	33	14	17	100	54	62	9	....	.325	.383	.518	.901	135	28	112	6.87	-11	*3-155	25	2.6
1927 StL-N	115	390	48	101	26	6	9	65	34	63	5	....	.259	.320	.426	.746	95	-4	52	4.50	-15	*3-100,S-10	11	-1.2
1928 Bos-N	153	591	58	164	36	7	10	91	40	45	1	....	.277	.323	.413	.736	96	-6	77	4.42	4	*3-153	16	0.8
1929 Bos-N	139	483	58	144	23	5	9	72	50	42	4	....	.298	.364	.422	.786	98	-1	74	5.34	-23	*3-127/2-1,S-1	11	-1.5
1930 Chi-N	74	248	35	69	15	4	5	47	24	27	1	....	.278	.342	.431	.773	85	-6	36	5.00	-4	3-70/1-2	6	-0.5
1931 Chi-N	75	252	30	71	17	1	4	32	19	22	0	....	.282	.332	.405	.737	95	-2	35	4.94	4	3-70	8	0.4
Total 9	**896**	**3239**	**404**	**938**	**184**	**49**	**66**	**509**	**276**	**322**	**25**	**5**	**.290**	**.346**	**.438**	**.784**	**102**	**2**	**486**	**5.25**	**-43**	**3-828/S-44,1-2,2-1**	**96**	**1.4**
• BELL, Mike	Michael John Bell b: 12/7/1974, Cincinnati, OH BR/TR, 6'2", 210 lbs. Deb: 7/20/2000																							
2000 Cin-N	19	27	5	6	0	0	2	4	4	7	0	0	.222	.323	.444	.767	89	-1	4	5.41	2	3-13	1	0.1
• BELL, Mike	Michael Allen Bell b: 4/22/1968, Lewiston, NY BL/TL, 6'1", 175 lbs. Deb: 5/2/1990																							
1990 Atl-N	36	45	8	11	5	1	1	5	2	9	0	1	.244	.292	.467	.758	99	-1	4	2.83	-1	1-24	1	-0.2
1991 Atl-N	17	30	4	4	0	0	1	1	2	7	1	0	.133	.188	.233	.421	17	-3	1	.97	-1	1-14	0	-0.5
Total 2	**53**	**75**	**12**	**15**	**5**	**1**	**2**	**6**	**4**	**16**	**1**	**1**	**.200**	**.250**	**.373**	**.623**	**66**	**-4**	**5**	**2.05**	**-1**	**/1-38**	**1**	**-0.7**
• BELL, Rudy	John Bell b: 1/1/1881, Wausau, WI d: 7/28/1955, Albuquerque, NM BR/TR, 5'8.5", 158 lbs. Deb: 9/16/1907																							
1907 NY-A	17	52	4	11	2	1	0	3	3	....	4		.212	.268	.288	.556	72	-2	6	3.33	-2	0-17(12-0-5)	1	-0.5
• BELL, Terry	Terence William Bell b: 10/27/1962, Dayton, OH BR/TR, 6', 195 lbs. Deb: 9/3/1986																							
1986 KC-A	8	3	0	0	0	0	0	0	2	1	0	0	.000	.400	.000	.400	20	-0	0	1.87	-2	/C-8	0	-0.2
1987 Atl-N	1	1	0	0	0	0	0	0	0	1	0	0	.000	.000	.000	.000	-95	-0	0	.00	0	....	0	0.0
Total 2	**9**	**4**	**0**	**0**	**0**	**0**	**0**	**0**	**2**	**2**	**0**	**0**	**.000**	**.333**	**.000**	**.333**	**1**	**-0**	**0**	**1.40**	**-2**	**/C-8**	**0**	**-0.3**
• BELLA, Zeke	John Bella b: 8/23/1930, Greenwich, CT BR/TL, 5'11", 185 lbs. Deb: 9/11/1957 Career OF: 12-0-17																							
1957 NY-A	5	10	0	1	0	0	0	0	1	2	0	0	.100	.182	.100	.282	-21	-2	0	.69	1	/0-4(1-0-3)	0	-0.1
1959 KC-A	47	82	10	17	2	1	1	9	9	14	0	0	.207	.293	.293	.586	60	-4	6	2.44	1	0-25(11-0-14)/1-1	0	-0.4
Total 2	**52**	**92**	**10**	**18**	**2**	**1**	**1**	**9**	**10**	**16**	**0**	**0**	**.196**	**.282**	**.272**	**.553**	**52**	**-6**	**7**	**2.24**	**2**	**/0-29,1-1**	**0**	**-0.5**
• BELLAN, Steve	Esteban Enrique Bellan b: 1850, Havana, Cuba d: 8/8/1932, Havana, Cuba, 5'6", 154 lbs. Deb: 5/9/1871																							
1871 Tro-n	29	128	26	32	3	3	0	23	9	2	4	4	.250	.299	.320	.620	77	-5	14	4.35	-5	*3-28/S-1	....	-0.7
1872 Tro-n	23	114	22	30	4	0	0	16	0	0	1	0	.263	.263	.298	.561	71	-4	9	3.48	-4	/S-9,3-8,0-6(0-6-0)	....	-0.6
1873 Mut-n	8	32	4	7	2	0	0	3	2	0	0	0	.219	.265	.281	.546	63	-1	2	2.98	-6	/3-7,2-3	....	-0.5
Total 3 n	**60**	**274**	**52**	**69**	**9**	**3**	**0**	**42**	**11**	**2**	**5**	**4**	**.252**	**.281**	**.307**	**.587**	**73**	**-10**	**26**	**3.84**	**-15**	**/3-43,S-10,0-6,2-3**	**....**	**-1.7**
• BELLE, Albert	Albert Jojuan "Joey" Belle b: 8/25/1966, Shreveport, LA BR/TR, 6'1", 210 lbs. Deb: 7/15/1989 Career OF: 1017-0-297																							
1989 Cle-A	62	218	22	49	8	4	7	37	12	55	2	2	.225	.272	.394	.666	84	-6	22	3.41	0	0-44(15-0-31),D-17	6	-0.8
1990 Cle-A	9	23	1	4	0	0	1	3	1	6	0	0	.174	.208	.304	.513	42	-2	1	1.60	0	/D-6,0-1	0	-0.2
1991 Cle-A	123	461	60	130	31	2	28	95	25	99	3	1	.282	.326	.540	.866	134	19	71	5.30	2	0-89(88-0-2),D-32	15	1.7
1992 Cle-A	153	585	81	152	23	1	34	112	52	128	8	2	.260	.324	.477	.801	124	17	87	5.09	-4	*D-100,0-52(52-0-0)	16	0.8
1993 Cle-A★	159	594	93	172	36	3	38	**129**	76	96	23	12	.290	.378	.552	.930	147	39	119	6.91	9	*0-150(150-0-0)/D-9	27	3.9
1994 Cle-A★	106	412	90	147	35	2	36	101	58	71	9	6	.357	.442	.714	1.156	191	56	131	12.56	0	*0-104(104-0-0)/D-2	24	4.7
1995*Cle-A★	143	546	**121**	173	**52**	1	**50**	**126**	73	80	5	2	.317	.403	**.690**	1.094	175	59	144	9.65	6	*0-142(142-0-0)/D-1	30	5.5
1996*Cle-A★	158	602	124	187	38	3	48	**148**	99	87	11	0	.311	.414	.623	1.037	158	57	156	9.52	3	*0-152(152-0-0)/D-6	31	4.9
1997 Chi-A★	161	634	90	174	45	1	30	116	53	105	4	4	.274	.336	.491	.827	117	13	96	5.20	-7	*0-154(154-0-0)/D-7	18	-0.2
1998 Chi-A	163	609	113	200	48	2	49	152	81	84	6	4	.328	.408	**.655**	**1.063**	**175**	**66**	158	**9.61**	1	*0-159(159-0-0)/D-4	**37**	**5.7**
1999 Bal-A	161	610	108	181	36	1	37	117	101	82	17	3	.297	.403	.541	.943	143	45	135	8.01	1	*0-154(0-0-154)/D-7	24	3.5
2000 Bal-A	141	559	71	157	37	1	23	103	52	68	0	5	.281	.346	.474	.820	110	5	86	5.39	-4	*0-110(0-0-110),D-31	15	-0.6
Total 12	**1539**	**5853**	**974**	**1726**	**389**	**21**	**381**	**1239**	**683**	**961**	**88**	**41**	**.295**	**.374**	**.564**	**.938**	**144**	**368**	**1207**	**7.33**	**7**	***0-1311,D-222**	**243**	**28.8**
• BELLHORN, Mark	Mark Christian Bellhorn b: 8/23/1974, Boston, MA BB/TR, 6'1", 195 lbs. Deb: 6/10/1997 Career OF: 1-3-3																							
1997 Oak-A	68	224	33	51	9	1	6	19	32	70	7	1	.228	.324	.357	.681	79	-5	29	4.40	2	3-40,2-17/D-3,S-1	5	-0.2
1998 Oak-A	11	12	1	1	1	0	0	1	3	4	2	0	.083	.313	.167	.479	30	-1	1	3.13	-1	/3-5,D-2,S-2,2-1	0	-0.2
2000 Oak-A	9	13	2	2	0	0	0	0	2	6	0	0	.154	.267	.154	.421	11	-2	1	1.65	-1	/2-2,3-2,S-1	0	-0.2
2001 Oak-A	38	74	11	10	1	2	1	4	7	37	0	0	.135	.210	.243	.453	19	-9	4	1.62	-3	2-12/3-9,S-5,D-3,0-1	1	-1.1
2002 Chi-N	146	445	86	115	24	4	27	56	76	144	7	5	.258	.374	.512	.886	133	22	89	7.01	-5	2-77,3-36,1-22,S-12/0-1	19	2.0
2003 Chi-N	51	139	15	29	7	1	2	22	29	46	3	3	.209	.349	.317	.666	77	-4	17	3.91	-4	3-42	3	-0.7
Col-N	48	110	12	26	3	0	0	4	21	32	2	3	.236	.368	.264	.632	60	-6	12	3.72	-2	2-20,3-15/S-6,0-5(0-3-2),1	1	-0.7
Yr.	99	249	27	55	10	1	2	26	50	78	5	6	.221	.358	.293	.651	70	-11	29	3.83	-6	3-57,2-20/S-6,0-5(0-3-2),1	4	-1.5
Total 6	**371**	**1017**	**160**	**234**	**45**	**8**	**36**	**106**	**170**	**339**	**21**	**12**	**.230**	**.346**	**.396**	**.742**	**95**	**-5**	**154**	**5.07**	**-14**	**3-149,2-129/S-27,1-23,D-8,0**	**29**	**-1.1**
• BELLIARD, Rafael	Rafael Leonidas (Matias) Belliard b: 10/24/1961, Puerto Nuevo Mao, Dominican Republic BR/TR, 5'6", 150 lbs. Deb: 9/6/1982																							
1982 Pit-N	9	2	3	1	0	0	0	0	0	0	1	0	.500	.500	.500	1.000	175	0	1	20.52	-1	/S-4	0	-0.1
1983 Pit-N	4	1	1	0	0	0	0	0	0	1	0	0	.000	.000	.000	.000	-98	-0	0	.00	-0	/S-3	0	0.0
1984 Pit-N	20	22	3	5	0	0	0	0	0	1	4	1	.227	.227	.227	.455	28	-2	1	1.93	-2	S-12/2-1	0	-0.3
1985 Pit-N	17	20	1	4	0	0	0	1	0	5	0	0	.200	.200	.200	.400	12	-2	1	1.35	0	S-12	0	-0.2
1986 Pit-N	117	309	33	72	5	2	0	31	26	54	12	2	.233	.299	.262	.561	55	-17	26	2.70	3	S-96,2-23	4	-0.5
1987 Pit-N	81	203	26	42	4	3	1	15	20	25	5	1	.207	.288	.271	.559	49	-14	17	2.66	-3	S-71/2-7	2	-1.0
1988 Pit-N	122	286	28	61	0	4	0	11	26	47	7	1	.213	.288	.241	.529	54	-15	21	2.30	-3	*S-117/2-3	4	-1.2
1989 Pit-N	67	154	10	33	4	0	0	8	8	22	5	2	.214	.253	.240	.493	43	-11	10	2.09	-0	S-40,2-20/3-6	2	-0.9
1990 Pit-N	47	54	10	11	3	0	0	6	5	13	1	2	.204	.283	.259	.543	52	-4	4	1.99	-1	2-21,S-10/3-5	1	-0.5
1991*Atl-N	149	353	36	88	9	2	0	27	22	63	3	1	.249	.297	.286	.583	61	-18	31	3.04	-1	*S-145	7	-1.0

YEAR TM-L	G	AB	R	H	2B	3B	HR	RBI	BB	SO	SB	CS	AVG	OBP	SLG	OPS	OPS+	BR/A	RC	RC/G	FR	G/POS	WS	TPW
1992*Atl-N	144	285	20	60	6	1	0	14	14	43	0	1	.211	.255	.239	.494	38	-24	17	1.91	-1	*S-139/2-1	5	-1.7
1993*Atl-N	91	79	6	18	5	0	0	6	4	13	0	0	.228	.291	.291	.582	56	-5	7	2.95	-1	S-58,2-24	2	-0.4
1994 Atl-N	46	120	9	29	7	1	0	9	2	29	0	2	.242	.266	.317	.583	50	-10	9	2.32	-3	S-26,2-18	2	-1.1
1995*Atl-N	75	180	12	40	2	1	0	7	6	28	2	2	.222	.255	.244	.500	32	-18	11	1.92	1	S-40,2-32	4	-1.4
1996*Atl-N	87	142	9	24	7	0	0	3	2	22	3	1	.169	.181	.218	.399	4	-20	5	.94	-2	S-63,2-15	2	-1.8
1997 Atl-N	72	71	9	15	3	0	1	3	1	17	0	1	.211	.222	.296	.518	33	-8	4	1.86	-2	S-53/2-7	1	-0.7
1998 Atl-N	7	20	1	5	0	0	0	1	0	1	0	0	.250	.250	.250	.500	32	-2	1	1.19	0	/S-7	0	-0.2
Total 17	1155	2301	217	508	55	14	2	142	136	384	43	17	.221	.271	.259	.531	46	-170	164	2.30	-16	S-896,2-172/3-11	36	-12.9
• BELLIARD, Ron	Ronald Belliard b: 4/7/1975, New York, NY BR/TR, 5'8", 180 lbs. Deb: 9/12/1998																							
1998 Mil-N	8	5	1	1	0	0	0	0	0	0	0	0	.200	.200	.200	.400	6	-1	0	1.35	-1	/2-1	0	-0.1
1999 Mil-N	124	457	60	135	29	4	8	58	64	59	4	5	.295	.382	.429	.811	106	4	74	5.64	0	*2-119/3-1,S-1	15	1.0
2000 Mil-N	152	571	83	150	30	9	8	54	82	84	7	5	.263	.358	.389	.747	90	-7	83	4.96	9	*2-151	17	0.9
2001 Mil-N	101	364	69	96	30	3	11	36	35	65	5	2	.264	.337	.453	.790	104	2	57	5.46	12	2-96	13	1.8
2002 Mil-N	104	289	30	61	13	0	3	26	18	46	2	3	.211	.260	.287	.547	44	-25	20	2.18	-7	2-49,3-42	1	-3.0
2003 Col-N	116	447	73	124	31	2	8	50	49	71	7	2	.277	.351	.409	.761	86	-8	67	5.33	-10	*2-113	12	-1.3
Total 6	605	2133	316	567	133	18	38	224	248	325	25	17	.266	.345	.399	.744	89	-35	300	4.84	4	2-529/3-43,S-1	58	-0.7
• BELLINGER, Clay	Clayton Daniel Bellinger b: 11/18/1968, Oneonta, NY BR/TR, 6'3", 215 lbs. Deb: 4/9/1999 Career OF: 32-36-7																							
1999*NY-A	32	45	12	9	2	0	1	2	1	10	1	0	.200	.217	.311	.529	33	-5	3	2.11	-1	3-16/1-8,D-4,0-2(2-0-0),2,S	1	-0.5
2000*NY-A	98	184	33	38	8	2	6	21	17	48	5	0	.207	.291	.370	.661	66	-9	22	3.94	1	0-46(17-26-5),2-21,3-18,1-10/S	3	-0.6
2001*NY-A	51	81	12	13	1	1	5	12	4	23	1	2	.160	.209	.383	.592	51	-7	5	1.97	3	0-25(13-10-2),3-17/1-6,S-2,D	1	-0.4
2002 Ana-A	2	1	0	0	0	0	0	0	0	1	0	0	.000	.000	.000	.000	-100	-0	0	.00	0	/1-2	0	0.0
Total 4	183	311	57	60	11	3	12	35	22	82	7	2	.193	.260	.363	.623	57	-21	30	3.11	4	/0-73,3-51,1-26,2-22,S-9,D-5	5	-1.5
• BELLMAN, Jack	John Hutchins "Happy Jack" Bellman b: 3/4/1864, Louisville, KY d: 12/8/1931, Louisville, KY Deb: 4/23/1889																							
1889 StL-a	1	2	1	1	0	0	0	0	1	0	0	....	.500	.667	.500	1.167	207	0	1	18.11	0	/C-1	0	0.1
• BELLOIR, Rob	Robert Edward Belloir b: 7/13/1948, Heidelberg, West Germany BR/TR, 5'10", 155 lbs. Deb: 8/2/1975																							
1975 Atl-N	43	105	11	23	2	1	0	9	7	8	0	0	.219	.268	.257	.525	44	-8	7	1.96	-6	S-38/2-1	1	-1.1
1976 Atl-N	30	60	5	12	2	0	0	4	5	7	0	0	.200	.262	.233	.495	39	-5	4	2.19	-1	S-12,3-10/2-5	1	-0.5
1977 Atl-N	6	1	2	0	0	0	0	0	0	0	0	0	.000	.000	.000	.000	-89	-0	0	.00	-1	/S-3	0	-0.1
1978 Atl-N	2	1	0	1	1	0	0	0	0	0	0	0	1.000	1.000	2.000	3.000	647	1	2	∞	0	/3-1,S-1	0	0.0
Total 4	81	167	18	36	5	1	0	13	12	15	0	0	.216	.268	.257	.526	45	-12	13	2.03	-8	/S-54,3-11,2-6	2	-1.7
• BELTRAN, Carlos	Carlos Ivan Beltran b: 4/24/1977, Manati, Puerto Rico BB/TR, 6', 190 lbs. Deb: 9/14/1998 Career OF: 2-682-3																							
1998 KC-A	14	58	12	16	5	3	0	7	3	12	3	0	.276	.323	.466	.788	99	0	9	5.16	1	0-14(0-14-0)	2	0.1
1999 KC-A	156	663	112	194	27	7	22	108	46	123	27	8	.293	.342	.454	.796	99	-1	101	5.40	-4	*0-154(0-154-0)/D-2	18	-0.3
2000 KC-A	98	372	49	92	15	4	7	44	35	69	13	0	.247	.312	.366	.678	68	-16	43	3.90	2	0-88(2-83-3)/D-7	5	-1.3
2001 KC-A	155	617	106	189	32	12	24	101	52	120	31	1	.306	.365	.514	.879	118	22	123	7.49	12	*0-152(0-152-0)/D-3	27	3.3
2002 KC-A	162	637	114	174	44	7	29	105	71	135	35	7	.273	.350	.501	.851	110	13	115	6.32	1	*0-149(0-149-0),D-12	21	1.3
2003 KC-A	141	521	102	160	14	10	26	100	72	81	41	4	.307	.393	.522	.915	122	25	116	8.26	7	*0-130(0-130-0)/D-8	28	3.2
Total 6	726	2868	495	825	137	43	108	465	279	540	150	20	.288	.354	.478	.832	106	44	507	6.33	18	0-687/D-32	101	6.3
• BELTRE, Adrian	Adrian (Perez) Beltre b: 4/7/1979, Santo Domingo, Dominican Republic BR/TR, 5'11", 170 lbs. Deb: 6/24/1998																							
1998 LA-N	77	195	18	42	9	0	7	22	14	37	3	1	.215	.278	.369	.648	73	-8	20	3.36	-4	3-74/S-2	4	-1.1
1999 LA-N	152	538	84	148	27	5	15	67	61	105	18	7	.275	.355	.428	.783	103	3	86	5.65	-8	*3-152	15	-0.3
2000 LA-N	138	510	71	148	30	2	20	85	56	80	12	5	.290	.363	.475	.837	116	12	87	6.08	8	*3-138/S-1	22	2.2
2001 LA-N	126	475	59	126	22	4	13	60	28	82	13	4	.265	.313	.411	.724	92	-6	61	4.43	4	*3-124/S-2	12	0.0
2002 LA-N	159	587	70	151	26	5	21	75	37	96	7	5	.257	.306	.426	.732	97	-7	71	4.15	1	*3-157	16	-0.3
2003 LA-N	158	559	50	134	30	2	23	80	37	103	2	2	.240	.293	.424	.717	89	-12	67	4.02	3	*3-157/S-1	14	-0.7
Total 6	810	2864	352	749	144	18	99	389	233	503	55	24	.262	.323	.428	.751	97	-17	392	4.72	2	3-802/S-6	83	-0.4
• BELTRE, Esteban	Esteban (Valera) Beltre b: 12/26/1967, Ingenio Quisqueya, Dominican Republic BR/TR, 5'10", 172 lbs. Deb: 9/3/1991																							
1991 Chi-A	8	6	0	1	0	0	0	0	1	1	1	0	.167	.286	.167	.452	29	-0	1	2.75	-2	/S-8	0	-0.2
1992 Chi-A	49	110	21	21	2	0	1	10	3	18	1	0	.191	.212	.236	.449	26	-11	5	1.48	-8	S-43/D-4	1	-1.7
1994 Tex-A	48	131	12	37	5	0	0	12	16	25	2	5	.282	.361	.321	.681	78	-6	15	3.70	1	S-41/3-5,2-1	2	-0.1
1995 Tex-A	54	92	7	20	8	0	0	7	4	15	0	0	.217	.250	.304	.554	42	-8	7	2.53	-1	S-36,2-15/3-1	1	-0.7
1996 Bos-A	27	62	6	16	2	0	0	6	4	14	1	0	.258	.303	.290	.593	50	-5	6	3.17	-3	3-13/2-8,S-6,D-1	1	-0.6
Total 5	186	401	46	95	17	0	1	35	28	73	5	5	.237	.287	.287	.573	51	-29	33	2.71	-13	S-134/2-24,3-19,D-5	5	-3.3
• BEMIS, Harry	Harry Parker Bemis b: 2/1/1874, Farmington, NH d: 5/23/1947, Cleveland, OH BR/TR, 5'6.5", 175 lbs. Deb: 4/23/1902																							
1902 Cle-A	93	317	42	99	12	7	1	29	19	....	3	....	.312	.366	.404	.770	118	8	50	5.88	1	C-87/0-2(0-0-2),2-1	11	1.7
1903 Cle-A	92	314	31	82	20	3	1	41	8	....	5	....	.261	.295	.354	.648	95	-2	35	3.99	-2	C-74,1-10/2-1	9	0.2
1904 Cle-A	97	336	35	76	11	6	0	25	8	....	6	....	.226	.259	.295	.554	75	-10	29	2.85	-7	C-79,1-13/2-1	5	-1.0
1905 Cle-A	70	226	27	66	13	3	0	28	13	....	3	....	.292	.344	.376	.720	126	7	32	5.09	-2	C-58/2-4,3-2,1-1	9	1.1
1906 Cle-A	93	297	28	82	13	5	2	30	12	....	8	....	.276	.311	.374	.685	115	4	39	4.63	-9	C-81	9	0.3
1907 Cle-A	65	172	12	43	7	0	0	19	7	....	5	....	.250	.283	.291	.574	82	-4	17	3.27	-6	C-51/1-2	3	-0.6
1908 Cle-A	91	277	23	62	9	1	0	33	7	....	14	....	.224	.253	.264	.517	68	-10	22	2.53	-10	C-76/1-2	5	-1.5
1909 Cle-A	42	123	4	23	2	3	0	13	0	....	2	....	.187	.194	.252	.446	39	-9	6	1.54	-2	C-36	1	-0.9
1910 Cle-A	61	167	12	36	5	1	1	16	5	....	3	....	.216	.238	.275	.514	60	-8	12	2.20	-1	C-46	2	-0.6
Total 9	704	2229	214	569	92	29	5	234	79	....	49	....	.255	.292	.329	.621	92	-25	242	3.71	-38	C-588/1-28,2-7,3-2,0-2	54	-1.2
• BENARD, Marvin	Marvin Larry Benard b: 1/20/1971, Bluefields, Nicaragua BL/TL, 5'10", 180 lbs. Deb: 9/5/1995 Career OF: 102-456-239																							
1995 SF-N	13	34	5	13	2	0	1	4	1	7	1	0	.382	.400	.529	.929	147	2	7	8.56	0	/0-7(0-7-0)	2	0.2
1996 SF-N	135	488	89	121	17	4	5	27	59	84	25	11	.248	.334	.330	.664	79	-13	57	3.93	-1	*0-132(5-102-38)	8	-1.4
1997*SF-N	84	114	13	26	4	0	1	13	13	29	3	1	.228	.318	.289	.607	63	-6	11	3.34	0	0-36(14-6-18)/D-1	2	-0.6
1998 SF-N	121	286	41	92	21	1	3	36	34	39	11	4	.322	.398	.434	.831	126	12	52	6.86	-3	0-79(12-9-64)/D-2	10	0.6
1999 SF-N	149	562	100	163	36	5	16	64	55	97	27	14	.290	.360	.457	.817	113	10	94	6.06	-6	*0-142(4-123-20)	20	0.4
2000*SF-N	149	560	102	147	27	6	12	55	63	97	22	7	.263	.343	.396	.740	93	-4	82	5.18	3	*0-141(21-128-38)	14	-0.1
2001 SF-N	129	392	70	104	19	2	15	44	29	66	10	5	.265	.322	.439	.761	101	-0	56	5.07	-2	*0-109(15-75-37)	11	-0.3
2002 SF-N	65	123	16	34	9	2	1	13	7	26	5	1	.276	.321	.407	.727	94	-1	16	4.60	2	0-38(14-6-20)	3	0.0
2003 SF-N	46	71	5	14	3	1	0	4	4	9	1	0	.197	.240	.268	.508	33	-7	4	1.83	3	0-21(17-0-4)	1	-0.4
Total 9	891	2630	441	714	138	21	54	260	265	454	105	43	.271	.344	.402	.745	97	-6	381	5.10	-4	0-705/D-3	71	-1.6
• BENAVIDES, Freddie	Alfredo Benavides b: 4/7/1966, Laredo, TX BR/TR, 6'2", 180 lbs. Deb: 5/14/1991																							
1991 Cin-N	24	63	11	18	1	0	0	3	1	15	1	0	.286	.308	.302	.609	69	-2	6	3.32	2	S-20/2-3	1	0.1
1992 Cin-N	74	173	14	40	10	1	1	17	10	34	0	1	.231	.277	.318	.595	66	-8	15	2.84	-1	2-37,S-34/3-1	4	-0.7
1993 Col-N	74	213	20	61	10	3	3	26	6	27	3	2	.286	.306	.404	.710	76	-8	25	4.15	-11	S-48,2-19/3-5,1-1	5	-1.5
1994 Mon-N	47	85	8	16	5	1	0	6	3	15	0	0	.188	.225	.271	.495	28	-9	5	1.82	-3	2-36/3-5,1-3,S-3	1	-1.1
Total 4	219	534	53	135	26	5	4	52	20	91	4	3	.253	.284	.343	.626	64	-28	50	3.22	-13	S-105/2-95,3-11,1-4	11	-3.2
• BENCH, Johnny	Johnny Lee Bench b: 12/7/1947, Oklahoma City, OK BR/TR, 6'1", 208 lbs. Deb: 8/28/1967 HOF: 1989 Career OF: 55-2-54																							
1967 Cin-N	26	86	7	14	3	1	1	6	5	19	0	1	.163	.209	.256	.465	29	-8	4	1.25	1	C-26	2	-0.7
1968 Cin-N★	154	564	67	155	40	2	15	82	31	96	1	5	.275	.315	.433	.748	115	8	71	4.40	11	*C-154	24	3.1
1969 Cin-N★	148	532	83	156	23	1	26	90	49	86	6	6	.293	.357	.487	.844	128	18	92	6.27	8	*C-147	28	3.5
1970*Cin-N★	158	605	97	177	35	4	**45**	**148**	54	102	5	2	.293	.351	.587	.937	140	31	121	7.22	6	*C-139,0-24(15-2-6),1-12/3	**34**	4.2
1971 Cin-N★	149	562	80	134	19	2	27	61	49	83	2	1	.238	.300	.423	.723	108	4	66	3.97	3	*C-141,1-12,0-12(10-0-3)/3	19	1.3
1972*Cin-N★	147	538	87	145	22	2	**40**	**125**	100	84	6	6	.270	.386	.541	.927	**171**	51	110	6.91	-2	*C-129,0-17(0-0-17)/1-7,3	37	5.8
1973*Cin-N★	152	557	83	141	17	3	25	104	83	83	4	1	.253	.350	.429	.779	121	18	82	4.90	1	*C-134,0-23(0-0-23)/1-4,3	26	2.4

YEAR TM-L	G	AB	R	H	2B	3B	HR	RBI	BB	SO	SB	CS	AVG	OBP	SLG	OPS	OPS+	BR/A	RC	RC/G	FR	G/POS	WS	TPW
1974 Cin-N★	160	621	108	174	38	2	33	**129**	80	90	5	4	.280	.365	.507	.872	144	35	114	6.60	6	*C-137,3-36/1-5	34	4.8
1975*Cin-N★	142	530	83	150	39	1	28	110	65	108	11	0	.283	.363	.519	.882	140	30	101	6.84	-1	*C-121,0-19(16-0-3)/1-9	30	3.5
1976*Cin-N★	135	465	62	109	24	1	16	74	81	95	13	2	.234	.350	.394	.744	108	9	69	5.06	5	*C-128/0-5(5-0-0),1-1	19	2.1
1977 Cin-N★	142	494	67	136	34	2	31	109	58	95	2	4	.275	.353	.540	.893	133	21	92	6.56	-5	*C-135/0-8(7-0-1),1-4,3-1	22	2.2
1978 Cin-N★	120	393	52	102	17	1	23	73	50	83	4	2	.260	.345	.483	.828	129	15	65	5.68	0	*C-107,1-11/0-2(1-0-1)	20	2.0
1979*Cin-N★	130	464	73	128	19	0	22	80	67	73	4	2	.276	.367	.459	.826	123	16	79	6.01	0	*C-126/1-2	22	2.2
1980 Cin-N★	114	360	52	90	12	0	24	68	41	64	4	2	.250	.330	.483	.813	124	11	57	5.36	-4	*C-105	15	1.2
1981 Cin-N	52	178	14	55	8	0	8	25	17	21	0	2	.309	.369	.489	.858	139	8	31	6.38	-1	1-38/C-7	9	0.5
1982 Cin-N	119	399	44	103	16	0	13	38	37	58	1	2	.258	.321	.396	.717	98	-3	48	4.10	-8	*3-107/1-8,C-1	7	-1.3
1983 Cin-N★	110	310	32	79	15	2	12	54	24	38	0	1	.255	.308	.432	.741	100	-2	37	4.11	-5	3-42,1-32/C-5,0-1	8	-0.9
Total 17	2158	7658	1091	2048	381	24	389	1376	891	1278	68	43	.267	.345	.476	.821	127	259	1240	5.62	12	*C-1742,3-195,1-145,0-111	356	35.9

• BENEDICT, Art Arthur Melville Benedict b: 3/31/1862, Cornwall, IL d: 1/20/1948, Blue Rapids, KS BR/TR Deb: 5/14/1883

YEAR TM-L	G	AB	R	H	2B	3B	HR	RBI	BB	SO	SB	CS	AVG	OBP	SLG	OPS	OPS+	BR/A	RC	RC/G	FR	G/POS	WS	TPW
1883 Phi-N	3	15	3	4	1	0	0	4	0	4	....	....	.267	.267	.333	.600	89	-0	1	3.42	-3	/2-3	0	-0.2

• BENEDICT, Bruce Bruce Edwin Benedict b: 8/18/1955, Birmingham, AL BR/TR, 6'1", 190 lbs. Deb: 8/18/1978 C

YEAR TM-L	G	AB	R	H	2B	3B	HR	RBI	BB	SO	SB	CS	AVG	OBP	SLG	OPS	OPS+	BR/A	RC	RC/G	FR	G/POS	WS	TPW
1978 Atl-N	22	52	3	13	2	0	0	1	6	6	0	0	.250	.328	.288	.616	66	-2	5	3.64	1	C-22	1	0.0
1979 Atl-N	76	204	14	46	11	0	0	15	33	18	1	3	.225	.333	.279	.613	64	-10	20	3.22	-2	C-76	3	-0.9
1980 Atl-N	120	359	18	91	14	1	2	34	28	36	3	3	.253	.309	.315	.624	72	-14	34	3.06	0	*C-120	9	-0.9
1981 Atl-N★	90	295	26	78	12	1	5	35	33	21	1	1	.264	.344	.363	.707	98	-0	37	4.29	8	C-90	12	1.3
1982*Atl-N	118	386	34	95	11	1	3	44	37	40	4	4	.246	.317	.303	.620	71	-15	37	3.15	2	*C-118	12	-0.8
1983 Atl-N★	134	423	43	126	13	1	2	43	61	24	1	3	.298	.388	.348	.735	98	1	57	4.85	7	*C-134	18	1.5
1984 Atl-N	95	300	26	67	8	1	4	25	34	25	1	2	.223	.304	.297	.601	65	-14	27	2.91	-2	C-95	7	-1.2
1985 Atl-N	70	208	12	42	6	0	0	20	22	12	0	1	.202	.281	.231	.512	42	-16	13	2.00	0	C-70	2	-1.3
1986 Atl-N	64	160	11	36	10	1	0	13	15	10	1	0	.225	.299	.300	.599	62	-8	13	2.61	1	C-57	2	-0.5
1987 Atl-N	37	95	4	14	1	0	1	5	17	15	0	1	.147	.277	.189	.466	25	-11	6	1.81	1	C-35	1	-0.8
1988 Atl-N	90	236	11	57	7	0	0	19	19	26	0	2	.242	.298	.271	.569	61	-12	20	2.82	4	C-89	5	-0.4
1989 Atl-N	66	160	12	31	3	0	1	6	23	18	0	0	.194	.299	.231	.530	52	-9	13	2.57	3	C-65	4	-0.3
Total 12	982	2878	214	696	98	6	18	260	328	251	12	20	.242	.322	.299	.621	71	-110	282	3.24	23	C-971	76	-4.2

• BENES, Joe Joseph Anthony "Bananas" Benes b: 1/8/1901, Long Island City, NY d: 3/7/1975, Elmhurst, NY BR/TR, 5'8.5", 158 lbs. Deb: 5/9/1931

YEAR TM-L	G	AB	R	H	2B	3B	HR	RBI	BB	SO	SB	CS	AVG	OBP	SLG	OPS	OPS+	BR/A	RC	RC/G	FR	G/POS	WS	TPW
1931 StL-N	10	12	1	2	0	0	0	0	2	1	0	....	.167	.333	.167	.500	37	-1	1	2.33	-1	/S-6,2-2,3-1	0	-0.1

• BENGOUGH, Benny Bernard Oliver Bengough b: 7/27/1898, Niagara Falls, NY d: 12/22/1968, Philadelphia, PA BR/TR, 5'7.5", 168 lbs. Deb: 5/18/1923 C

YEAR TM-L	G	AB	R	H	2B	3B	HR	RBI	BB	SO	SB	CS	AVG	OBP	SLG	OPS	OPS+	BR/A	RC	RC/G	FR	G/POS	WS	TPW
1923 NY-A	19	53	1	7	2	0	0	3	4	2	0	0	.132	.193	.170	.363	-4	-8	2	1.08	-1	C-19	1	-0.7
1924 NY-A	11	16	4	5	1	1	0	3	2	0	0	0	.313	.389	.500	.889	128	1	3	7.05	-0	C-11	1	0.1
1925 NY-A	95	283	17	73	14	2	0	23	19	9	0	2	.258	.305	.322	.626	60	-18	28	3.38	8	C-94	7	-0.5
1926 NY-A	36	84	9	32	6	0	0	14	7	4	1	0	.381	.435	.452	.887	134	5	17	8.20	3	C-35	5	0.9
1927*NY-A	31	85	6	21	3	3	0	10	4	4	0	3	.247	.281	.353	.634	66	-6	7	2.89	2	C-30	2	-0.2
1928*NY-A	58	161	12	43	3	1	0	9	7	8	0	0	.267	.302	.298	.600	60	-9	15	3.24	3	C-58	5	-0.3
1929 NY-A	23	62	5	12	2	1	0	7	0	2	0	0	.194	.194	.258	.452	16	-8	3	1.58	0	C-23	1	-0.7
1930 NY-A	44	102	10	24	4	2	0	12	3	8	1	0	.235	.257	.314	.571	46	-8	8	2.72	0	C-44	1	-0.5
1931 StL-A	40	140	6	35	4	1	0	12	4	4	0	3	.250	.271	.293	.564	46	-12	10	2.48	3	C-37	2	-0.6
1932 StL-A	54	139	13	35	7	1	0	15	12	4	0	1	.252	.311	.317	.628	60	-9	14	3.48	3	C-47	3	-0.3
Total 10	411	1125	83	287	46	12	0	108	62	45	2	9	.255	.295	.317	.613	59	-72	107	3.29	21	C-398	28	-2.7

• BENIQUEZ, Juan Juan Jose (Torres) Beniquez b: 5/13/1950, San Sebastian, Puerto Rico BR/TR, 5'11", 165 lbs. Deb: 9/4/1971 Career OF: 295-735-184

YEAR TM-L	G	AB	R	H	2B	3B	HR	RBI	BB	SO	SB	CS	AVG	OBP	SLG	OPS	OPS+	BR/A	RC	RC/G	FR	G/POS	WS	TPW
1971 Bos-A	16	57	8	17	2	0	0	4	3	4	3	1	.298	.333	.333	.667	83	-1	6	3.34	-5	S-15	1	-0.5
1972 Bos-A	33	99	10	24	4	1	1	8	7	11	2	0	.242	.292	.333	.626	81	-2	10	3.39	-3	S-27	2	-0.2
1974 Bos-A	106	389	60	104	14	3	5	33	25	61	19	11	.267	.313	.357	.671	86	-8	41	3.57	-6	0-97(7-91-0)/D-4	8	-1.8
1975*Bos-A	78	254	43	74	14	4	2	17	25	26	7	10	.291	.359	.402	.761	106	-0	34	4.48	0	0-44(31-13-2),D-20,3-14	7	-0.3
1976 Tex-A	145	478	49	122	14	4	0	33	39	56	17	6	.255	.315	.301	.617	79	-11	47	3.35	7	*0-141(0-141-0)/2-1	12	-0.8
1977 Tex-A	123	424	56	114	19	6	10	50	43	43	26	18	.269	.338	.413	.750	102	-0	55	4.19	2	*0-123(0-123-0)	13	0.0
1978 Tex-A	127	473	61	123	17	3	11	50	20	59	10	12	.260	.294	.378	.673	88	-12	48	3.35	-1	*0-126(0-126-0)	9	-1.5
1979 NY-A	62	142	19	36	6	1	4	17	9	17	3	3	.254	.307	.394	.702	90	-3	16	3.53	3	0-60(18-38-4)/3-3	3	-0.1
1980 Sea-A	70	237	26	54	10	0	6	21	17	25	2	3	.228	.280	.346	.626	70	-11	20	2.72	-3	0-65(2-63-0)/D-1	2	-1.6
1981 Cal-A	58	166	18	30	5	0	3	13	15	16	2	1	.181	.253	.265	.518	49	-11	11	1.97	-5	0-55(15-36-7)/D-1	1	-1.8
1982*Cal-A	112	196	25	52	11	2	3	24	15	21	3	0	.265	.321	.388	.709	93	-1	25	4.15	-2	*0-107(37-25-51)	4	-0.5
1983 Cal-A	92	315	44	96	15	0	3	34	15	29	4	2	.305	.344	.381	.725	100	-0	39	4.48	-1	0-84(38-30-31)/D-6	7	-0.4
1984 Cal-A	110	354	60	119	17	0	8	39	18	43	0	3	.336	.373	.452	.825	128	12	55	5.81	-2	0-98(64-8-50)	13	0.5
1985 Cal-A	132	411	54	125	13	5	8	42	34	46	4	3	.304	.364	.418	.783	114	8	59	5.10	-2	0-71(18-36-22),1-46,D-14/3,S	13	0.2
1986 Bal-A	113	343	48	103	15	0	6	36	40	49	2	3	.300	.378	.397	.775	113	7	51	5.19	-2	0-54(44-3-9),3-25,D-16,1-14	10	0.1
1987 KC-A	57	174	14	41	7	0	3	26	11	26	0	0	.236	.285	.328	.613	60	-10	14	2.65	-3	0-22(17-2-4),D-15/1-6,3-6	1	-1.4
Tor-A	39	81	6	23	5	1	5	21	5	13	0	0	.284	.333	.556	.889	127	3	14	6.06	-1	D-15/0-7(3-0-4),1-2	2	0.2
Yr.	96	255	20	64	12	1	8	47	16	39	0	0	.251	.300	.400	.700	82	-7	28	3.67	-3	D-30,0-29(20-2-8)/1-8,3-6	3	-1.2
1988 Tor-A	27	58	9	17	2	0	1	8	8	6	0	0	.293	.379	.379	.758	113	1	8	4.46	0	D-19/0-1	1	0.1
Total 17	1500	4651	610	1274	190	30	79	476	349	551	104	76	.274	.329	.379	.707	95	-39	553	4.02	-24	*0-1155,D-111/1-68,3-49,S,2	109	-9.8

• BENITEZ, Yamil Yamil Antonio Benitez b: 10/5/1972, San Juan, Puerto Rico BR/TR, 6'2", 180 lbs. Deb: 9/15/1995 Career OF: 86-4-44

YEAR TM-L	G	AB	R	H	2B	3B	HR	RBI	BB	SO	SB	CS	AVG	OBP	SLG	OPS	OPS+	BR/A	RC	RC/G	FR	G/POS	WS	TPW
1995 Mon-N	14	39	8	15	2	1	2	7	1	7	0	2	.385	.400	.641	1.041	163	2	8	8.21	0	0-14(3-4-8)	2	0.2
1996 Mon-N	11	12	0	2	0	0	0	2	0	4	0	0	.167	.167	.167	.333	-11	-2	0	.90	-1	/0-4(3-0-1)	0	-0.3
1997 KC-A	53	191	22	51	7	1	8	21	10	49	2	2	.267	.307	.440	.747	90	-4	25	4.68	-2	0-52(31-0-22)	3	-0.8
1998 Ari-N	91	206	17	41	7	1	9	30	14	46	2	2	.199	.263	.374	.637	65	-12	19	2.92	1	0-62(49-0-13)/D-2	1	-1.3
Total 4	169	448	47	109	16	3	19	60	25	106	4	6	.243	.291	.420	.710	82	-15	53	3.98	-2	0-132/D-2	6	-2.2

• BENJAMIN, Mike Michael Paul Benjamin b: 11/22/1965, Euclid, OH BR/TR, 6'3", 169 lbs. Deb: 7/7/1989

YEAR TM-L	G	AB	R	H	2B	3B	HR	RBI	BB	SO	SB	CS	AVG	OBP	SLG	OPS	OPS+	BR/A	RC	RC/G	FR	G/POS	WS	TPW
1989 SF-N	14	6	6	1	0	0	0	0	0	1	0	0	.167	.167	.167	.333	-5	-1	0	.90	-2	/S-8	0	-0.2
1990 SF-N	22	56	7	12	3	1	2	3	3	10	1	0	.214	.254	.411	.665	83	-2	5	3.11	1	S-21	1	0.1
1991 SF-N	54	106	12	13	3	0	2	8	7	26	3	0	.123	.191	.208	.399	12	-12	5	1.34	3	S-51/3-1	2	-0.6
1992 SF-N	40	75	4	13	2	1	1	3	4	15	1	0	.173	.215	.267	.482	38	-6	4	1.82	1	S-33/3-2	1	-0.4
1993 SF-N	63	146	22	29	7	0	4	16	9	23	0	0	.199	.264	.329	.593	59	-9	13	2.73	8	2-23,S-23,3-16	5	0.1
1994 SF-N	38	62	9	16	5	1	1	9	5	16	5	0	.258	.343	.419	.762	102	1	10	5.26	3	S-18,2-10/3-5	3	0.6
1995 SF-N	68	186	19	41	6	0	3	12	8	51	11	1	.220	.256	.301	.557	48	-13	15	2.64	4	3-43,S-16/2-8	2	-0.7
1996 Phi-N	35	103	13	23	5	1	4	13	12	21	3	1	.223	.316	.408	.724	88	-2	13	4.30	2	S-31/2-1	3	0.2
1997 Bos-A	49	116	12	27	9	1	0	7	4	27	2	3	.233	.264	.328	.592	52	-9	9	2.55	0	3-19,S-16/2-5,1-4,D-1,P-1	1	-0.7
1998*Bos-A	124	349	46	95	23	0	4	39	15	73	3	0	.272	.314	.372	.686	76	-12	39	3.80	4	2-87,S-20,3-11,1-10/D-2	8	-0.4
1999 Pit-N	110	368	42	91	26	7	1	37	20	90	10	1	.247	.290	.364	.654	64	-20	41	3.74	20	S-93,2-12/3-6	10	0.8
2000 Pit-N	93	233	28	63	18	2	2	19	12	45	5	4	.270	.315	.391	.705	77	-9	28	4.05	17	3-34,S-30,2-27/1-1	5	1.0
2002 Pit-N	108	120	7	18	2	1	0	3	7	31	0	4	.150	.203	.183	.386	3	-19	3	.78	-1	3-62,S-15,2-11/1-1,0-1	2	-1.8
Total 13	818	1926	227	442	109	15	24	169	106	429	44	14	.229	.279	.339	.618	61	-112	187	3.15	59	S-375,3-199,2-184/1-16,D,0,P	43	-2.1

• BENJAMIN, Stan Alfred Stanley Benjamin b: 5/20/1914, Framingham, MA BR/TR, 6'2", 194 lbs. Deb: 9/16/1939 Career OF: 9-53-112

YEAR TM-L	G	AB	R	H	2B	3B	HR	RBI	BB	SO	SB	CS	AVG	OBP	SLG	OPS	OPS+	BR/A	RC	RC/G	FR	G/POS	WS	TPW
1939 Phi-N	12	50	4	7	2	1	0	2	1	6	1	....	.140	.157	.220	.377		-7	1	.37	0	/0-7(4-2-2),3-5	0	-0.7
1940 Phi-N	8	9	1	2	0	0	0	1	1	1	0	....	.222	.300	.222	.522	48	-1	1	2.62	1	/0-2(0-0-2)	0	0.0
1941 Phi-N	129	480	47	113	20	7	3	27	20	81	17	....	.235	.266	.325	.591	68	-22	39	2.69	-2	*0-110(2-26-86)/1-8,2-2,3	2	-3.0
1942 Phi-N	78	210	24	47	8	3	2	8	10	27	5	....	.224	.262	.319	.581	73	-8	18	2.85	1	0-45(0-25-21),1-15	1	-1.0
1945 Cle-A	14	21	1	7	2	0	0	3	0	0	0	1	.333	.333	.429	.762	126	0	3	4.74	1	/0-4(3-0-1)	1	0.1
Total 5	241	770	77	176	32	11	5	41	32	115	23	1	.229	.260	.318	.578	67	-38	61	2.60	1	0-168/1-23,3-6,2-2	4	-4.7

• BENNERS, Ike Isaac B. Benners b: 6/7/1856, Philadelphia, PA d: 4/18/1932, Philadelphia, PA BL, 175 lbs. Deb: 5/1/1884

YEAR TM-L	G	AB	R	H	2B	3B	HR	RBI	BB	SO	SB	CS	AVG	OBP	SLG	OPS	OPS+	BR/A	RC	RC/G	FR	G/POS	WS	TPW
1884 Bro-a	49	189	25	38	11	5	1	0	7	....	....	....	.201	.237	.328	.565	82	-4	15	2.75	-6	0-49(49-0-0)	3	-1.1

YEAR TM-L	G	AB	R	H	2B	3B	HR	RBI	BB	SO	SB	CS	AVG	OBP	SLG	OPS	OPS+	BR/A	RC	RC/G	FR	G/POS	WS	TPW
Wil-U	6	22	0	1	0	0	0	....	1	....	....	....	.045	.087	.045	.132	-53	-3	0	.12	0	/0-6(0-3-3)	0	-0.3
• BENNETT, Charlie	Charles Wesley Bennett b: 11/21/1854, New Castle, PA d: 2/24/1927, Detroit, MI BR/TR, 5'11", 180 lbs. Deb: 5/1/1878 Career OF: 24-25-21																							
1878 Mil-N	49	184	16	45	9	0	1	12	10	26	....	....	.245	.284	.310	.593	89	-2	17	3.28	-13	C-35,0-20(0-16-4)	2	-1.4
1880 Wor-N	51	193	20	44	9	3	0	18	10	30	....	....	.228	.266	.306	.572	86	-3	16	2.97	-1	C-46/0-6(0-3-3)	6	-0.2
1881 Det-N	76	299	44	90	18	7	7	64	18	37	....	....	.301	.341	.478	.819	148	16	50	6.45	14	*C-70/3-5,0-3(1-2-0)	15	3.0
1882 Det-N	84	342	43	103	16	10	5	51	20	33	....	....	.301	.340	.450	.790	151	20	54	6.17	8	*C-65,3-11/2-7,1-1,S-1	19	3.0
1883 Det-N	92	371	56	113	34	7	5	55	26	59	....	....	.305	.350	.474	.825	155	25	63	6.73	0	*C-72,2-15,0-12(1-4-7)	18	2.8
1884 Det-N	90	341	37	90	18	6	3	40	36	40	....	....	.264	.334	.378	.713	131	14	44	4.84	-3	*C-80/0-5(1-0-4),S-4,1-1,2,3	11	1.6
1885 Det-N	91	349	49	94	24	13	5	60	47	37	....	....	.269	.356	.456	.812	161	25	58	6.14	1	C-62,0-19(17-0-2),3-10	15	3.0
1886 Det-N	72	235	37	57	13	5	4	34	48	29	4	....	.243	.371	.391	.763	128	10	37	5.54	1	C-69/0-4(3-0-1),S-1	13	1.5
1887*Det-N	46	190	26	69	6	5	3	20	30	22	7	....	.363	.363	.400	.763	108	3	26	5.79	3	C-45/1-1,0-1	8	0.8
1888 Det-N	74	258	32	68	12	4	5	29	31	40	4	....	.264	.347	.399	.746	137	12	38	5.41	2	C-73/1-1	12	2.0
1889 Bos-N	82	247	42	57	8	2	4	28	21	43	7	....	.231	.296	.328	.624	70	-11	27	3.73	-8	C-82	8	-1.1
1890 Bos-N	85	281	59	60	17	2	3	40	72	56	6	....	.214	.377	.320	.698	96	2	37	4.45	1	C-85	11	0.9
1891 Bos-N	75	256	35	55	9	3	5	39	42	61	3	....	.215	.332	.332	.664	84	-6	30	4.03	1	C-75	9	0.1
1892*Bos-N	35	114	19	23	4	0	1	16	27	23	6	....	.202	.355	.263	.618	80	-2	13	3.88	-3	C-35	4	-0.1
1893 Bos-N	60	191	34	40	6	0	4	27	40	36	5	....	.209	.352	.304	.656	69	-8	23	3.99	-7	C-60	6	-0.8
Total 15	1062	3851	549	1008	203	67	55	533	478	572	42	....	.262	.340	.387	.728	119	95	532	5.07	-4	C-954/0-70,3-27,2-23,S-6,1	157	15.0
• BENNETT, Fred	James Fred "Red" Bennett b: 3/15/1902, Atkins, AR d: 5/12/1957, Atkins, AR BR/TR, 5'9", 185 lbs. Deb: 4/13/1928 Career OF: 3-0-19																							
1928 StL-A	7	8	0	2	1	0	0	0	0	2	0	0	.250	.250	.375	.625	60	-0	1	3.18	-0	/0-1	0	-0.1
1931 Pit-N	32	89	6	25	5	0	1	7	7	4	0	....	.281	.333	.371	.704	90	-1	11	4.53	-1	0-21(3-0-18)	2	-0.3
Total 2	39	97	6	27	6	0	1	7	7	6	0	0	.278	.327	.371	.698	88	-2	12	4.42	-1	/0-22	2	-0.4
• BENNETT, Gary	Gary David Bennett b: 4/17/1972, Waukegan, IL BR/TR, 6', 190 lbs. Deb: 9/24/1995																							
1995 Phi-N	1	1	0	0	0	0	0	0	0	1	0	0	.000	.000	.000	.000	-99	-0	0	.00	0	....	0	0.0
1996 Phi-N	6	16	0	4	0	0	0	1	2	6	0	0	.250	.333	.250	.583	56	-1	1	3.20	1	/C-5	0	0.0
1998 Phi-N	9	31	4	9	0	0	0	3	5	5	0	0	.290	.389	.290	.679	81	-1	4	4.28	0	/C-9	1	-0.1
1999 Phi-N	36	88	7	24	4	0	1	21	4	11	0	0	.273	.304	.352	.657	64	-5	7	2.73	-3	C-32	2	-0.6
2000 Phi-N	31	74	8	18	5	0	2	5	13	15	0	0	.243	.371	.392	.763	92	-0	12	5.88	1	C-31	3	0.2
2001 Phi-N	26	75	8	16	3	1	1	6	9	19	0	0	.213	.298	.320	.618	61	-4	8	3.30	-3	C-24	1	-0.5
NY-N	1	1	0	1	0	0	0	0	0	0	0	0	1.000	1.000	1.000	2.000	442	0	1	∞	0	....	0	0.0
Col-N	19	55	7	15	3	0	1	4	3	5	0	0	.273	.322	.382	.704	66	-3	7	4.47	-3	C-19	0	-0.4
Yr.	46	131	15	32	6	1	2	10	12	24	0	0	.244	.313	.351	.664	66	-6	16	3.77	-5	C-43	1	-0.9
2002 Col-N	90	291	26	77	10	2	4	26	15	45	1	3	.265	.314	.354	.668	65	-16	30	3.49	-11	C-90	4	-2.1
2003 SD-N	96	307	26	73	15	0	2	42	24	48	3	0	.238	.297	.306	.603	64	-16	28	3.06	-16	C-91	6	-2.5
Total 8	315	939	86	237	40	3	11	108	75	155	4	3	.252	.315	.337	.652	67	-45	98	3.51	-33	C-301	17	-5.9
• BENNETT, Herschel	Herschel Emmett Bennett b: 9/21/1896, Elwood, MO d: 9/9/1964, Springfield, MO BL/TR, 5'9.5", 160 lbs. Deb: 4/19/1923 Career OF: 101-21-81																							
1923 StL-A	5	4	0	0	0	0	0	0	1	1	0	0	.000	.200	.000	.200	-42	-1	0	.33	-0	/0-1	0	-0.1
1924 StL-A	41	94	16	31	4	3	1	11	3	6	1	0	.330	.364	.468	.832	107	1	16	6.53	-1	0-21(12-0-9)	3	-0.1
1925 StL-A	93	298	46	83	11	6	2	37	18	16	4	10	.279	.324	.376	.700	73	-16	34	3.85	-2	0-73(41-12-21)	4	-2.2
1926 StL-A	80	225	33	60	14	2	1	26	22	21	2	1	.267	.337	.360	.697	78	-7	28	4.41	4	0-50(36-6-9)	4	-0.7
1927 StL-A	93	256	40	68	12	2	3	30	14	21	6	2	.266	.311	.363	.675	72	-11	30	3.94	1	0-55(12-2-42)	4	-1.3
Total 5	312	877	135	242	41	13	7	104	58	65	13	13	.276	.327	.376	.704	77	-33	108	4.26	1	0-200	15	-4.4
• BENNETT, Joe	Joseph Rosenblum Bennett b: 7/2/1900, New York, NY d: 7/11/1987, Morro Bay, CA BR/TR, 5'9", 168 lbs. Deb: 7/5/1923																							
1923 Phi-N	1	0	0	0	0	0	0	0	0	0	0	0	....	....	....	....	-90	0	0	....	0	/3-1	0	0.0
• BENNETT, Pug	Justin Titus Bennett b: 2/20/1874, Ponca, NE d: 9/12/1935, Kirkland, WA BR/TR, 5'11", 165 lbs. Deb: 4/12/1906																							
1906 StL-N	153	595	66	156	16	7	1	34	56	....	20	....	.262	.334	.318	.651	108	6	74	4.21	-16	*2-153	15	-0.9
1907 StL-N	87	324	20	72	8	2	0	21	21	....	7	....	.222	.272	.259	.531	69	-12	26	2.64	-14	2-83/3-3	4	-2.9
Total 2	240	919	86	228	24	9	1	55	77	....	27	....	.248	.312	.297	.610	94	-6	101	3.64	-30	2-236/3-3	19	-3.9
• BENSON, Vern	Vernon Adair Benson b: 9/19/1924, Granite Quarry, NC BL/TR, 5'10", 180 lbs. Deb: 7/31/1943 M/C Career OF: 6-0-0																							
1943 Phi-A	2	2	0	0	0	0	0	0	0	1	0	0	.000	.000	.000	.000	-101	-0	0	.00	0	....	0	-0.1
1946 Phi-A	7	5	1	0	0	0	0	0	1	3	0	0	.000	.167	.000	.167	-51	-1	0	.23	-0	/0-2(2-0-0)	0	-0.1
1951 StL-N	13	46	8	12	3	1	1	7	6	8	0	0	.261	.346	.435	.781	108	1	8	6.06	1	/3-9,0-4(4-0-0)	2	0.2
1952 StL-N	20	47	6	9	2	0	2	5	5	9	0	0	.191	.269	.362	.631	73	-2	5	3.52	0	3-15	1	-0.2
1953 StL-N	13	4	2	0	0	0	0	0	1	2	0	0	.000	.200	.000	.200	-42	-1	0	.35	0	....	0	-0.1
Total 5	55	104	17	21	5	1	3	12	13	22	0	0	.202	.291	.356	.646	74	-3	13	4.12	1	/3-24,0-6	3	-0.3
• BENTLEY, Jack	Jack Needles Bentley b: 3/8/1895, Sandy Spring, MD d: 10/24/1969, Olney, MD BL/TL, 5'11.5", 200 lbs. Deb: 9/6/1913 ♦																							
1913 Was-A	3	3	0	0	0	0	0	0	0	0	0	....	.000	.000	.000	.000	-98	-0	0	.00	0	/P-3	2	0.3
1914 Was-A	30	40	7	11	2	0	0	4	0	5	0	....	.275	.275	.325	.600	77	2	4	3.27	-1	P-30	9	0.8
1915 Was-A	4	2	0	0	0	0	0	0	0	1	0	....	.000	.000	.000	.000	-98	-0	0	.00	0	/P-4	1	0.2
1916 Was-A	2	0	0	0	0	0	0	0	0	0	0	0	....	....	....	....	-101	0	0	....	0	/P-2	0	0.0
1923*NY-N	52	89	9	38	6	2	1	14	3	4	0	0	.427	.446	.573	1.019	169	15	22	11.05	-1	P-31	15	-0.1
1924*NY-N	46	98	12	26	5	1	0	6	3	13	0	0	.265	.287	.337	.624	69	4	9	3.40	-1	P-28	12	0.0
1925 NY-N	64	99	10	30	5	2	3	18	9	11	0	0	.303	.361	.485	.846	119	11	17	6.61	-1	P-28/0-3(0-0-3),1-1	12	-0.6
1926 Phi-N	75	240	19	62	12	3	2	27	5	4	0	....	.258	.273	.358	.632	66	-12	22	3.15	-5	1-56/P-7	1	-3.0
NY-N	3	4	0	1	0	0	0	0	0	0	0	....	.250	.250	.250	.500	35	-0	0	2.02	0	/P-1	0	0.1
Yr.	78	244	19	63	12	3	2	27	5	4	0	....	.258	.273	.357	.630	65	-12	23	3.13	-5	1-56/P-8	1	-2.9
1927 NY-N	8	9	1	2	0	0	1	2	1	1	0	....	.222	.300	.556	.856	125	1	1	5.45	0	/P-4,1-2	1	0.2
Total 9	287	584	58	170	30	8	7	71	21	39	0	0	.291	.316	.406	.722	91	20	77	4.75	-8	P-138/1-59,0-3	53	-1.9
• BENTON, Butch	Alfred Lee Benton b: 8/24/1957, Tampa, FL BR/TR, 6'1", 190 lbs. Deb: 9/14/1978																							
1978 NY-N	4	4	1	2	0	0	0	2	0	0	0	0	.500	.600	.500	1.100	218	1	1	18.31	-0	/C-1	0	0.1
1980 NY-N	12	21	0	1	0	0	0	0	2	4	0	0	.048	.167	.048	.214	-39	-4	0	.29	-1	/C-8	0	-0.5
1982 Chi-N	4	7	0	1	0	0	0	1	0	1	0	0	.143	.143	.143	.286	-19	-1	0	.64	-0	/C-4	0	-0.1
1985 Cle-A	31	67	5	12	4	0	0	7	3	9	0	0	.179	.214	.239	.453	24	-7	3	1.56	0	C-26	0	-0.6
Total 4	51	99	6	16	4	0	0	10	5	14	0	0	.162	.217	.202	.419	16	-11	5	1.58	-1	/C-39	0	-1.1
• BENTON, Rabbit	Stanley W. "Stan" Benton b: 9/29/1901, Cannel City, KY d: 6/7/1984, Mesquite, TX BR/TR, 5'7", 150 lbs. Deb: 9/13/1922																							
1922 Phi-N	6	19	1	4	1	0	0	3	2	1	0	0	.211	.286	.263	.549	39	-2	2	2.67	-1	/2-5	0	-0.3
• BENZINGER, Todd	Todd Eric Benzinger b: 2/11/1963, Dayton, KY BB/TR, 6'1", 190 lbs. Deb: 6/21/1987 Career OF: 69-5-123																							
1987 Bos-A	73	223	36	62	11	1	8	43	22	41	5	4	.278	.348	.444	.792	105	1	34	5.14	4	0-61(14-5-47)/1-2	6	0.1
1988*Bos-A	120	405	47	103	28	1	13	70	22	80	2	3	.254	.294	.425	.719	95	-5	48	4.04	-6	1-85,0-48(5-0-43)/D-1	6	-1.7
1989 Cin-N	161	628	79	154	28	3	17	76	44	120	3	7	.245	.297	.381	.677	89	-13	70	3.79	-10	*1-158	10	-3.6
1990*Cin-N	118	376	35	95	14	2	5	46	19	69	3	4	.253	.296	.340	.636	71	-17	38	3.44	-6	1-95,0-10(10-0-0)	5	-3.0
1991 Cin-N	51	123	7	23	3	2	1	11	10	20	2	0	.187	.248	.268	.516	43	-9	9	2.21	0	1-21,0-15(15-0-0)	0	-1.1
KC-A	78	293	29	86	15	3	2	40	17	46	2	6	.294	.339	.386	.724	99	-3	36	4.43	-3	1-75/D-1	8	-1.2
1992 LA-N	121	293	24	70	16	2	4	31	15	54	2	4	.239	.276	.348	.624	77	-11	26	2.97	-1	0-51(18-0-33),1-42	4	-1.7
1993 SF-N	86	177	25	51	7	2	6	26	13	35	0	0	.288	.337	.452	.789	112	2	27	5.57	-3	1-40/0-7(7-0-0),3-1	5	-0.4
1994 SF-N	107	328	32	87	13	2	9	31	17	84	2	1	.265	.305	.399	.705	86	-8	40	4.34	-6	1-99	4	-2.2
1995 SF-N	9	10	2	2	0	0	1	2	2	3	0	0	.200	.333	.500	.833	120	0	2	5.34	0	/1-5	0	0.0
Total 9	924	2856	316	733	135	18	66	376	181	552	21	29	.257	.304	.386	.690	88	-62	329	3.96	-32	1-622,0-192/D-2,3-1	48	-14.7

YEAR TM-L	G	AB	R	H	2B	3B	HR	RBI	BB	SO	SB	CS	AVG	OBP	SLG	OPS	OPS+	BR/A	RC	RC/G	FR	G/POS	WS	TPW
• BERARDINO, Johnny	John "Bernie" Berardino b: 5/1/1917, Los Angeles, CA d: 5/19/1996, Los Angeles, CA BR/TR, 5'11.5", 180 lbs. Deb: 4/22/1939 C																							
1939 StL-A	126	468	42	120	24	5	5	58	37	36	6	2	.256	.314	.361	.675	71	-21	53	3.90	-17	*2-114/3-8,S-2	5	-2.8
1940 StL-A	142	523	71	135	31	4	16	85	32	46	6	8	.258	.301	.424	.725	84	-17	64	4.19	-3	*S-112,2-13/3-9	12	-1.0
1941 StL-A	128	469	48	127	30	4	5	89	41	27	3	5	.271	.332	.384	.716	86	-11	57	4.20	-10	*S-123/3-1	8	-1.2
1942 StL-A	29	74	11	21	6	0	1	10	4	2	3	1	.284	.329	.405	.735	104	0	11	5.32	-1	/3-6,S-6,1-5,2-4	2	0.0
1946 StL-A	144	582	70	154	29	5	5	68	34	58	2	4	.265	.306	.357	.664	81	-17	61	3.66	-6	*2-143	13	-1.5
1947 StL-A	90	306	29	80	22	1	1	20	44	26	6	5	.261	.358	.350	.708	95	-1	40	4.40	0	2-86	8	0.3
1948 Cle-A	66	147	19	28	5	1	2	10	27	16	0	1	.190	.328	.279	.607	64	-7	14	3.06	2	2-20,1-18,S-12/3-3	2	-0.5
1949 Cle-A	50	116	11	23	6	1	0	13	14	14	0	1	.198	.295	.267	.563	50	-9	10	2.84	-4	3-25/2-8,S-3	1	-1.2
1950 Cle-A	4	5	1	2	0	0	0	3	1	0	0	0	.400	.500	.400	.900	137	0	1	10.40	1	/2-1,3-1	0	0.1
Pit-N	40	131	12	27	3	1	1	12	19	11	0	....	.206	.307	.267	.574	51	-9	11	2.60	1	2-36/3-3	1	-0.6
1951 StL-A	39	119	13	27	7	1	0	13	17	18	1	1	.227	.324	.303	.626	68	-5	12	3.44	-4	3-31/2-2,1-1,0-1	2	-0.9
1952 Cle-A	35	32	5	3	0	0	0	2	10	8	0	1	.094	.310	.094	.403	17	-3	2	1.46	-3	/2-8,S-8,3-4,1-2	0	-0.6
Pit-N	19	56	2	8	4	0	0	4	4	6	0	0	.143	.200	.214	.414	14	-7	2	1.35	0	2-18	1	-0.5
Total 11	912	3028	334	755	167	23	36	387	284	268	27	29	.249	.316	.355	.672	77	-106	339	3.79	-43	2-453,S-266/3-91,1-26,0-1	55	-10.3
• BERBERET, Lou	Louis Joseph Berberet b: 11/20/1929, Long Beach, CA d: 4/6/2004, Las Vegas, NV BL/TR, 5'11", 212 lbs. Deb: 9/17/1954																							
1954 NY-A	5	5	1	2	0	0	0	3	1	1	0	0	.400	.500	.400	.900	154	0	1	10.17	0	/C-3	0	0.1
1955 NY-A	2	5	1	2	0	0	0	2	1	0	0	0	.400	.500	.400	.900	146	0	1	10.17	1	/C-1	0	0.1
1956 Was-A	95	207	25	54	6	3	4	27	46	33	0	0	.261	.402	.377	.779	107	5	33	5.59	2	C-59	8	1.0
1957 Was-A	99	264	24	69	11	2	7	36	41	38	0	1	.261	.365	.398	.763	109	5	37	4.71	4	C-77	10	1.2
1958 Was-A	5	6	0	1	0	0	0	0	4	1	0	0	.167	.500	.167	.667	94	0	1	5.51	0	/C-2	0	0.1
Bos-A	57	167	11	35	5	3	2	18	31	32	0	2	.210	.337	.311	.648	74	-5	18	3.50	-3	C-49	3	-0.6
Yr.	62	173	11	36	5	3	2	18	35	33	0	2	.208	.344	.306	.651	75	-5	19	3.57	-3	C-51	3	-0.5
1959 Det-A	100	338	38	73	8	2	13	44	35	59	0	0	.216	.290	.367	.656	75	-12	36	3.42	-4	C-95	6	-1.2
1960 Det-A	85	232	18	45	4	0	5	23	41	31	2	0	.194	.318	.276	.593	58	-12	22	3.07	1	C-81	5	-0.8
Total 7	448	1224	118	281	34	10	31	153	200	195	2	3	.230	.341	.350	.691	86	-19	150	4.04	0	C-367	32	-0.2
• BERBLINGER, Jeff	Jeffrey James Berblinger b: 11/19/1970, Wichita, KS BR/TR, 6', 190 lbs. Deb: 9/7/1997																							
1997 StL-N	7	5	1	0	0	0	0	0	0	1	0	0	.000	.000	.000	.000	-101	-1	0	.00	0	/2-4	0	-0.1
• BERG, Dave	David Scott Berg b: 9/3/1970, Roseville, CA BR/TR, 5'11", 185 lbs. Deb: 4/2/1998 Career OF: 7-0-15																							
1998 Fla-N	81	182	18	57	11	0	2	21	26	46	3	0	.313	.399	.407	.806	117	6	33	6.64	-5	2-27,3-25,S-17	9	0.4
1999 Fla-N	109	304	42	87	18	1	3	25	27	59	2	2	.286	.348	.382	.730	89	-5	40	4.74	-2	S-37,2-29,3-19/0-3(3-0-0)	6	-0.3
2000 Fla-N	82	210	23	53	14	1	1	21	25	46	3	0	.252	.346	.343	.689	78	-6	27	4.32	-8	S-49,3-13,2-11	5	-0.9
2001 Fla-N	82	215	26	52	12	1	4	16	14	39	0	1	.242	.294	.363	.657	71	-10	23	3.62	-8	2-34,S-19,3-16	3	-1.5
2002 Tor-A	109	374	42	101	26	2	4	39	26	57	0	2	.270	.326	.382	.708	84	-9	47	4.34	-3	2-52,3-20,0-13(3-0-10),S-13,1/D	8	-1.0
2003 Tor-A	61	161	26	41	6	1	4	18	11	34	0	1	.255	.302	.379	.681	77	-6	16	3.41	-9	2-24,3-17/D-6,0-6(1-0-5),1,S	1	-1.4
Total 6	524	1446	177	391	87	6	18	140	129	281	8	6	.270	.336	.376	.712	86	-30	186	4.47	-34	2-177,S-136,3-110/0-22,D-14,1	32	-4.7
• BERG, Moe	Morris Berg b: 3/2/1902, New York, NY d: 5/29/1972, Belleville, NJ BR/TR, 6'1", 185 lbs. Deb: 6/27/1923 C																							
1923 Bro-N	49	129	9	24	3	2	0	6	2	5	1	0	.186	.198	.240	.439	16	-15	6	1.52	-10	S-47/2-1	1	-2.0
1926 Chi-A	41	113	4	25	6	0	0	7	6	9	0	2	.221	.261	.274	.535	41	-11	8	2.20	3	S-31/2-2,3-1	1	-0.4
1927 Chi-A	35	69	4	17	4	0	0	4	4	10	0	0	.246	.288	.304	.592	55	-5	6	2.98	-3	2-11,C-10/S-6,3-3	1	-0.6
1928 Chi-A	76	224	25	55	16	0	0	29	14	25	2	1	.246	.302	.317	.619	63	-12	23	3.27	2	C-73	5	-0.5
1929 Chi-A	107	352	32	101	7	0	0	47	17	16	5	1	.287	.323	.307	.630	64	-17	36	3.64	4	*C-106	7	-0.7
1930 Chi-A	20	61	4	7	3	0	0	7	1	5	0	0	.115	.129	.164	.293	-27	-12	1	.62	0	C-20	1	-0.9
1931 Cle-A	10	13	1	1	1	0	0	0	1	1	0	0	.077	.143	.154	.297	-21	-2	0	.68	-1	/C-8	0	-0.3
1932 Was-A	75	195	16	46	8	1	1	26	8	13	1	1	.236	.266	.303	.569	48	-16	16	2.68	1	C-75	4	-0.9
1933 Was-A	40	65	8	12	3	0	2	9	4	5	0	0	.185	.232	.323	.555	46	-5	5	2.38	-1	C-35	1	-0.4
1934 Was-A	33	86	5	21	4	0	0	6	6	4	2	0	.244	.301	.291	.592	55	-5	8	3.23	-2	C-31	1	-0.5
Cle-A	29	97	4	25	3	1	0	9	1	7	0	0	.258	.265	.309	.575	47	-8	8	2.80	0	C-28	2	-0.6
Yr.	62	183	9	46	7	1	0	15	7	11	2	0	.251	.283	.301	.583	51	-13	16	3.01	-2	C-59	3	-1.1
1935 Bos-A	38	98	13	28	5	0	2	12	5	3	0	0	.286	.320	.398	.718	79	-3	12	4.59	1	C-37	3	-0.1
1936 Bos-A	39	125	9	30	4	1	0	19	2	6	0	0	.240	.264	.288	.552	34	-13	10	2.57	3	C-39	2	-0.7
1937 Bos-A	47	141	13	36	3	1	0	20	5	4	0	0	.255	.281	.291	.572	43	-13	12	2.85	-1	C-47	2	-1.0
1938 Bos-A	10	12	0	4	0	0	0	0	0	1	0	0	.333	.333	.333	.667	64	-1	1	4.24	-0	/C-7,1-1	0	-0.1
1939 Bos-A	14	33	3	9	1	0	1	5	2	3	0	0	.273	.314	.394	.708	77	-1	4	4.17	0	C-13	1	0.0
Total 15	663	1813	150	441	71	6	6	206	78	117	11	5	.243	.278	.299	.577	49	-139	157	2.88	-2	C-529/S-84,2-14,3-4,1-1	32	-9.7
• BERGAMO, Augie	August Samuel Bergamo b: 2/14/1917, Detroit, MI d: 8/19/1974 Grosse Pointe, MI BL/TL, 5'9", 165 lbs. Deb: 4/25/1944 Career OF: 38-1-89																							
1944*StL-N	80	192	35	55	6	3	2	19	35	23	0	....	.286	.399	.380	.779	118	7	32	6.15	-2	0-50(31-1-19)/1-2	8	0.2
1945 StL-N	94	304	51	96	17	2	3	44	43	21	0	....	.316	.401	.414	.815	124	11	55	6.84	3	0-77(7-0-70)/1-2	14	1.0
Total 2	174	496	86	151	23	5	5	63	78	44	0	....	.304	.400	.401	.801	121	18	88	6.57	1	0-127/1-4	22	1.2
• BERGEN, Bill	William Aloysius Bergen b: 6/13/1878, North Brookfield, MA d: 12/19/1943, Worcester, MA BR/TR, 6', 184 lbs. Deb: 5/6/1901																							
1901 Cin-N	87	308	15	55	6	4	1	17	8	....	2	....	.179	.199	.234	.433	27	-29	16	1.62	5	C-87	4	-1.5
1902 Cin-N	89	322	19	58	8	3	0	36	14	....	2	....	.180	.214	.224	.438	32	-27	17	1.66	9	C-89	5	-0.9
1903 Cin-N	58	207	21	47	4	2	0	19	7	....	2	....	.227	.252	.266	.518	43	-16	15	2.46	-2	C-58	2	-1.2
1904 Bro-N	96	329	17	60	4	2	0	12	9	....	3	....	.182	.204	.207	.411	28	-28	16	1.48	13	C-93/1-1	5	-0.6
1905 Bro-N	79	247	12	47	3	2	0	22	7	....	4	....	.190	.213	.219	.431	31	-21	14	1.70	8	C-76	3	-0.6
1906 Bro-N	103	353	9	56	3	3	0	19	7	....	2	....	.159	.175	.184	.359	13	-36	13	1.11	10	*C-103	5	-1.8
1907 Bro-N	51	138	2	22	3	0	0	14	1	....	1	....	.159	.165	.181	.347	9	-15	5	1.03	2	C-51	2	-1.0
1908 Bro-N	99	302	8	53	8	2	0	15	5	....	1	....	.175	.189	.215	.404	30	-25	13	1.25	14	C-99	6	-0.1
1909 Bro-N	112	346	16	48	1	1	1	15	10	....	4	....	.139	.163	.156	.319	-1	-41	10	.81	19	*C-112	8	-1.2
1910 Bro-N	89	249	11	40	2	1	0	14	6	39	0	....	.161	.180	.177	.357	4	-31	9	1.01	17	C-89	6	-0.6
1911 Bro-N	84	227	8	30	3	1	0	10	14	42	2	....	.132	.183	.154	.337	-6	-32	7	.89	7	C-84	5	-2.0
Total 11	947	3028	138	516	45	21	2	193	88	81	23	....	.170	.194	.201	.395	19	-302	134	1.34	102	C-941/1-1	51	-11.4
• BERGEN, Marty	Martin Bergen b: 10/25/1871, North Brookfield, MA d: 1/19/1900, North Brookfield, MA TR, 5'10", 170 lbs. Deb: 4/17/1896																							
1896 Bos-N	65	245	39	66	6	4	4	37	11	22	6	....	.269	.309	.376	.684	75	-10	31	4.56	0	C-63/1-1	6	-0.4
1897*Bos-N	87	327	47	81	11	3	2	45	18	....	5	....	.248	.295	.318	.613	58	-21	33	3.55	-9	*C-85/0-1	6	-1.9
1898 Bos-N	120	446	62	125	16	5	3	60	13	....	9	....	.280	.302	.359	.661	85	-12	53	4.28	-9	*C-117/1-2	12	-0.9
1899 Bos-N	72	260	32	67	11	3	1	34	10	....	4	....	.258	.290	.335	.625	65	-14	27	3.72	0	C-72	5	-0.7
Total 4	344	1278	180	339	44	15	10	176	52	22	24	....	.265	.299	.347	.646	72	-58	145	4.03	-17	C-337/1-3,0-1	29	-3.8
• BERGER, Boze	Louis William Berger b: 5/13/1910, Baltimore, MD d: 11/3/1992, Bethesda, MD BR/TR, 6'2", 180 lbs. Deb: 8/17/1932																							
1932 Cle-A	1	1	0	0	0	0	0	0	0	1	0	0	.000	.000	.000	.000	-94	-0	0	.00	0	/S-1	0	0.0
1935 Cle-A	124	461	62	119	27	5	5	43	34	97	7	5	.258	.310	.371	.681	74	-19	53	3.98	3	*2-120/S-3,1-2,3-1	10	-0.8
1936 Cle-A	28	52	1	9	2	0	0	3	1	14	0	0	.173	.189	.212	.400	-1	-9	2	1.26	-2	/1-8,2-8,3-7,S-2	1	-0.9
1937 Chi-A	52	130	19	31	5	0	5	13	15	24	1	1	.238	.322	.392	.714	79	-5	17	4.27	-3	3-40/2-1,S-1	3	-0.6
1938 Chi-A	118	470	60	102	15	3	3	36	43	80	4	1	.217	.284	.281	.565	41	-43	40	2.80	-6	S-67,2-42/3-9	5	-3.7
1939 Bos-A	20	30	4	9	2	0	0	2	1	10	0	0	.300	.323	.367	.689	73	-1	4	4.38	-1	S-10/3-5,2-2	1	-0.2
Total 6	343	1144	146	270	51	8	13	97	94	226	12	7	.236	.296	.329	.624	58	-77	116	3.40	-9	2-173/S-84,3-62,1-10	20	-6.3
• BERGER, Brandon	Brandon Charles Berger b: 2/21/1975, Covington, KY BR/TR, 5'11", 200 lbs. Deb: 9/9/2001 Career OF: 19-4-32																							
2001 KC-A	6	16	4	5	1	1	2	2	2	2	0	0	.313	.389	.875	1.264	202	2	6	13.86	-1	/0-5(5-0-0),D-1	1	0.1
2002 KC-A	51	134	16	27	5	1	6	17	8	32	1	0	.201	.257	.388	.645	61	-8	13	3.27	2	0-36(14-4-21),D-10/1-1	2	-0.7
2003 KC-A	13	32	3	7	0	0	0	3	5	4	0	0	.219	.324	.219	.543	42	-3	3	2.89	0	0-11(0-0-11)/D-1	1	-0.3
Total 3	70	182	23	39	6	2	8	22	15	38	1	0	.214	.281	.401	.683	70	-8	22	3.99	2	/0-52,D-12,1-1	4	-0.8

YEAR TM-L	G	AB	R	H	2B	3B	HR	RBI	BB	SO	SB	CS	AVG	OBP	SLG	OPS	OPS+	BR/A	RC	RC/G	FR	G/POS	WS	TPW
• BERGER, Clarence	Clarence Edward Berger b: 11/1/1894, East Cleveland, OH d: 6/30/1959, Washington, DC BL/TR, 6', 185 lbs. Deb: 9/23/1914																							
1914 Pit-N	6	13	2	1	0	0	0	0	1	4	0	....	.077	.143	.077	.220	-36	-2	0	.27	-1	/O-5(0-0-5)	0	-0.3
• BERGER, Joe	Joseph August "Fats" Berger b: 12/20/1886, St. Louis, MO d: 3/6/1956, Rock Island, IL BR/TR, 5'10.5", 170 lbs. Deb: 4/11/1913																							
1913 Chi-A	79	223	27	48	6	2	2	20	36	28	5	....	.215	.330	.287	.616	81	-4	23	3.19	2	2-71/S-4,3-1	7	-0.1
1914 Chi-A	48	148	11	23	3	1	0	3	13	9	2	8	.155	.224	.189	.413	25	-17	6	1.10	-2	S-28,2-12/3-7	1	-1.9
Total 2	127	371	38	71	9	3	2	23	49	37	7	8	.191	.289	.248	.537	60	-21	29	2.30	0	/2-83,S-32,3-8	8	-2.0
• BERGER, Johnny	John Henne Berger b: 8/27/1901, Philadelphia, PA d: 5/7/1979, Lake Charles, LA BR/TR, 5'9", 165 lbs. Deb: 4/20/1922																							
1922 Phi-A	2	1	0	1	0	0	0	0	0	0	1	0	1.000	1.000	1.000	2.000	411	1	1	∞	0	/C-2	0	0.1
1927 Was-A	9	15	1	4	0	0	0	1	2	3	0	0	.267	.353	.267	.620	63	-1	2	3.69	-1	/C-9	1	-0.2
Total 2	11	16	1	5	0	0	0	1	2	3	1	0	.313	.389	.313	.701	83	-0	3	3.69	-2	/C-11	1	-0.1
• BERGER, Tun	John Henry Berger b: 12/6/1867, Pittsburgh, PA d: 6/10/1907, Pittsburgh, PA TR, 204 lbs. Deb: 5/9/1890 U Career OF: 4-4-37																							
1890 Pit-N	104	391	64	104	18	4	0	40	35	23	11	....	.266	.337	.332	.670	108	6	49	4.50	-7	O-41(4-3-36),S-33,C-21/2-6,3	7	0.1
1891 Pit-N	43	134	15	32	2	1	1	14	12	10	4	....	.239	.315	.291	.606	79	-3	14	3.68	-8	C-18,2-17/S-6,O-2(0-1-1)	2	-0.8
1892 Was-N	26	97	9	14	2	1	0	3	7	9	3	....	.144	.210	.186	.395	20	-9	5	1.47	-2	S-18/C-9	1	-1.0
Total 3	173	622	88	150	22	6	1	57	54	42	18	....	.241	.313	.301	.614	88	-7	67	3.79	-17	/S-57,C-48,O-43,2-23,3-1	10	-1.6
• BERGER, Wally	Walter Anton Berger b: 10/10/1905, Chicago, IL d: 11/30/1988, Redondo Beach, CA BR/TR, 6'2", 198 lbs. Deb: 4/15/1930 Career OF: 344-943-9																							
1930 Bos-N	151	555	98	172	27	14	38	119	54	69	3	....	.310	.375	.614	.990	138	32	124	8.15	0	*O-145(145-0-0)	26	1.8
1931 Bos-N	156	617	94	199	44	8	19	84	55	70	13	....	.323	.380	.512	.892	143	36	122	7.53	7	*O-156(0-156-0)/1-1	**31**	**3.8**
1932 Bos-N	145	602	90	185	34	6	17	73	33	66	5	....	.307	.346	.468	.815	121	16	98	6.11	1	*O-134(0-134-0),1-11	26	1.3
1933 Bos-N★	137	528	84	165	37	8	27	106	41	77	2	....	.313	.365	.566	.932	**177**	50	113	8.21	0	*O-136(0-136-0)	**36**	4.9
1934 Bos-N★	150	615	92	183	35	8	34	121	49	65	2	....	.298	.352	.546	.899	148	38	119	7.16	-5	*O-150(0-150-0)	33	2.8
1935 Bos-N★	150	589	91	174	39	4	**34**	**130**	50	80	3	....	.295	.355	.548	.903	151	40	115	7.21	4	*O-149(0-149-0)	21	3.9
1936 Bos-N★	138	534	88	154	23	3	25	91	53	84	1	....	.288	.361	.483	.844	134	25	95	6.54	3	*O-133(0-133-0)	23	2.4
1937 Bos-N	30	113	14	31	9	1	5	22	11	33	0	....	.274	.344	.504	.848	140	6	21	6.65	0	O-28(28-0-0)	6	0.5
*NY-N	59	199	40	58	11	2	12	43	18	30	3	....	.291	.359	.548	.907	141	11	39	7.24	-1	O-52(3-46-3)	10	0.8
Yr.	89	312	54	89	20	3	17	65	29	63	3	....	.285	.354	532	.886	141	16	60	7.02	-1	O-80(31-46-3)	16	1.3
1938 NY-N	16	32	5	6	0	0	0	4	2	4	0	....	.188	.235	.188	.423	17	-4	2	1.63	1	/O-9(0-8-1)	0	-0.3
Cin-N	99	407	74	125	23	4	16	56	29	44	2	....	.307	.356	.501	.857	137	19	73	6.76	-3	O-98(98-0-0)	17	1.1
Yr.	115	439	79	131	23	4	16	60	31	48	2	....	.298	.347	.478	.826	129	15	74	6.34	-2	*O-107(98-8-1)	17	0.8
1939*Cin-N	97	329	36	85	15	1	14	44	36	63	1	....	.258	.341	.438	.778	107	3	50	5.35	-5	O-95(66-29-0)	11	-0.7
1940 Cin-N	2	2	0	0	0	0	0	0	0	1	0	....	.000	.000	.000	.000	-99	-1	0	.00	0	....	0	-0.1
Phi-N	20	41	3	13	2	0	1	5	4	8	1	....	.317	.378	.439	.817	130	2	7	6.30	-1	O-11(4-2-5)/1-1	1	0.0
Yr.	22	43	3	13	2	0	1	5	4	9	1	....	.302	.362	.419	.780	120	1	7	5.90	-1	O-11(4-2-5)/1-1	1	0.0
Total 11	1350	5163	809	1550	299	59	242	898	435	694	36	....	.300	.359	.522	.881	140	272	977	7.02	-0	*O-1296/1-13	241	22.2
• BERGERON, Peter	Peter Francis Bergeron b: 11/9/1977, Greenfield, MA BL/TR, 6'2", 185 lbs. Deb: 9/7/1999 Career OF: 45-252-0																							
1999 Mon-N	16	45	12	11	2	0	0	1	9	5	0	0	.244	.370	.289	.659	72	-2	6	4.45	1	O-13(13-3-0)	1	-0.1
2000 Mon-N	148	518	80	127	25	7	5	31	58	100	11	13	.245	.321	.349	.671	68	-29	60	3.80	5	*O-146(32-117-0)	6	-2.3
2001 Mon-N	102	375	53	79	11	4	3	16	28	87	10	7	.211	.275	.285	.560	44	-32	30	2.56	-4	*O-101(0-101-0)	3	-3.5
2002 Mon-N	31	123	24	23	3	2	0	7	22	44	10	3	.187	.310	.244	.554	47	-8	12	3.07	-1	O-31(0-31-0)	2	-0.9
Total 4	297	1061	169	240	41	13	8	55	117	236	31	23	.226	.306	.312	.618	57	-71	107	3.29	1	O-291	12	-6.8
• BERGH, John	John Baptist Bergh b: 10/8/1857, Boston, MA d: 4/17/1883, Boston, MA Deb: 8/5/1876																							
1876 Phi-N	1	4	0	0	0	0	0	0	0	2	....	....	.000	.000	.000	.000	-101	-1	0	.00	0	/C-1,O-1	0	-0.1
1880 Bos-N	11	40	2	8	3	0	0	0	2	5	....	....	.200	.238	.275	.513	76	-1	3	2.31	-1	C-11	1	-0.2
Total 2	12	44	2	8	3	0	0	0	2	7	....	....	.182	.217	.250	.467	60	-2	3	2.05	-2	/C-12,O-1	1	-0.3
• BERGHAMMER, Marty	Martin Andrew "Pepper" Berghammer b: 6/18/1888, Elliott, PA d: 12/21/1957, Pittsburgh, PA BL/TR, 5'9", 172 lbs. Deb: 9/8/1911																							
1911 Chi-A	2	5	0	0	0	0	0	0	0	....	0	....	.000	.167	.000	.167	-53	-1	0	.00	0	/2-2	0	-0.1
1913 Cin-N	74	188	25	41	4	1	1	13	10	29	16	....	.218	.269	.266	.535	53	-12	17	2.79	-2	S-54,2-13	2	-1.1
1914 Cin-N	77	112	15	25	2	0	0	6	10	18	4	....	.223	.287	.241	.528	56	-6	8	2.46	3	S-33,2-13	2	-0.1
1915 Pit-F	132	469	96	114	10	6	0	33	83	44	26	....	.243	.371	.290	.661	92	1	59	4.14	-6	*S-132	16	0.5
Total 4	285	774	136	180	16	7	1	52	103	91	46	....	.233	.335	.275	.610	77	-18	85	3.53	-5	S-219/2-28	20	-0.9
• BERGMAN, Al	Alfred Henry "Dutch" Bergman b: 9/27/1890, Peru, IN d: 6/20/1961, Fort Wayne, IN BR/TR, 5'7", 155 lbs. Deb: 8/29/1916																							
1916 Cle-A	8	14	2	3	0	1	0	0	2	4	0	....	.214	.313	.357	.670	95	-0	2	3.69	0	/2-3	0	0.0
• BERGMAN, Dave	David Bruce Bergman b: 6/6/1953, Evanston, IL BL/TL, 6'1.5", 185 lbs. Deb: 8/26/1975 Career OF: 88-1-18																							
1975 NY-A	7	17	0	0	0	0	0	0	2	4	0	0	.000	.105	.000	.105	-70	-4	0	.09	0	/O-6(0-0-6)	0	-0.4
1977 NY-A	5	4	1	1	0	0	0	1	0	0	0	0	.250	.250	.250	.500	37	-0	0	2.05	0	/O-3(1-1-1),1-2	0	-0.1
1978 Hou-N	104	186	15	43	5	1	0	12	39	32	2	0	.231	.364	.269	.633	86	-1	20	3.65	-2	1-66,O-29(29-0-0)	4	-0.6
1979 Hou-N	13	15	4	6	0	0	1	2	0	3	0	0	.400	.400	.600	1.000	179	1	4	10.80	0	/1-4	1	0.1
1980*Hou-N	90	78	12	20	6	1	0	3	10	10	1	0	.256	.341	.359	.700	104	1	10	4.46	2	1-59/O-5(3-0-2)	2	0.1
1981 Hou-N	6	6	1	1	0	0	1	1	0	0	0	0	.167	.167	.667	.833	134	0	1	3.60	0	/1-1	0	0.0
SF-N	63	145	16	37	9	0	3	13	19	18	2	0	.255	.341	.379	.721	106	2	19	4.52	1	1-33,O-15(15-0-0)	4	0.1
Yr.	69	151	17	38	9	0	4	14	19	18	2	0	.252	.335	.391	.726	107	2	20	4.48	2	1-34,O-15(15-0-0)	4	0.2
1982 SF-N	100	121	22	33	3	1	4	14	18	11	3	0	.273	.367	.413	.780	118	4	20	6.00	-2	1-69/O-6(4-0-3)	5	-0.1
1983 SF-N	90	140	16	40	4	1	6	24	24	21	2	1	.286	.394	.457	.851	139	8	25	6.36	2	1-50/O-6(6-0-0)	7	0.9
1984*Det-A	120	271	42	74	8	5	7	44	33	40	3	4	.273	.358	.417	.775	114	5	41	5.22	6	*1-114/O-2(1-0-1)	9	0.7
1985 Det-A	69	140	8	25	2	0	3	7	14	15	0	0	.179	.253	.257	.510	41	-11	9	1.89	-1	1-44/D-5,O-1	0	-1.5
1986 Det-A	65	130	14	30	6	1	1	9	21	16	0	0	.231	.338	.315	.653	79	-3	15	3.87	0	1-41/D-8,O-2(1-0-1)	2	-0.5
1987*Det-A	91	172	25	47	7	3	6	22	30	23	0	1	.273	.384	.453	.838	126	7	32	6.59	-2	1-65/D-7,O-7(3-0-4)	7	0.3
1988 Det-A	116	289	37	85	14	0	5	35	38	34	0	2	.294	.376	.394	.771	121	8	43	5.34	1	1-64,D-30,O-13(13-0-0)	11	0.5
1989 Det-A	137	385	38	103	13	1	7	37	44	44	1	3	.268	.346	.361	.707	102	1	50	4.54	1	*1-123/D-7,O-1	10	-0.6
1990 Det-A	100	205	21	57	10	1	2	26	33	17	3	2	.278	.378	.366	.744	108	4	29	4.87	-3	D-51,1-27/O-5(5-0-0)	5	-0.2
1991 Det-A	86	194	23	46	10	1	7	29	35	40	1	1	.237	.354	.407	.761	108	3	30	5.31	-1	1-49,D-13/O-4(4-0-0)	7	-0.1
1992 Det-A	87	181	17	42	3	0	1	10	20	19	1	0	.232	.308	.265	.574	62	-8	16	2.89	-3	1-55,D-12/O-1	0	-1.5
Total 17	1349	2679	312	690	100	16	54	289	380	347	19	14	.258	.351	.367	.719	102	17	364	4.67	-1	1-866,D-133,O-106	74	-2.9
• BERKELBACH, Frank	Francis P. Berkelbach b: 7/27/1853, Philadelphia, PA d: 6/10/1932, Merchantville, NJ, 6', 182 lbs. Deb: 7/4/1884																							
1884 Cin-a	6	25	3	6	0	1	0	3	0	....	....	....	.240	.296	.320	.616	96	-0	2	3.52	-1	/O-6(6-0-0)	1	-0.1
• BERKENSTOCK, Nate	Nathan Berkenstock b: 1831, PA d: 2/23/1900, Philadelphia, PA Deb: 10/30/1871																							
1871 Ath-n	1	4	0	0	0	0	0	0	0	3	0	0	.000	.000	.000	.000	-101	-1	0	.00	0	/O-1	....	0.0
• BERKMAN, Lance	William Lance Berkman b: 2/10/1976, Waco, TX BB/TL, 6'1", 205 lbs. Deb: 7/16/1999 Career OF: 419-163-90																							
1999 Hou-N	34	93	10	22	2	0	4	15	12	21	5	1	.237	.324	.387	.711	80	-2	12	4.45	-1	O-27(22-0-8)/1-1	1	-0.4
2000 Hou-N	114	353	76	105	28	1	21	67	56	73	6	2	.297	.395	.561	.956	131	18	81	8.32	-4	O-96(40-0-63)/1-2	10	0.9
2001*Hou-N★	156	577	110	191	**55**	5	34	126	92	121	7	9	.331	.434	.620	1.054	160	53	158	10.46	2	*O-155(128-40-7)	32	4.9
2002 Hou-N★	158	578	106	169	35	2	42	**128**	107	118	8	4	.292	.406	.578	.984	149	44	140	8.85	-11	*O-156(76-122-12)	30	3.2
2003 Hou-N	153	538	110	155	35	6	25	93	107	108	5	3	.288	.414	.515	.929	134	32	121	8.16	-1	*O-153(153-1-0)	25	2.4
Total 5	615	2139	412	642	155	14	126	429	374	441	31	19	.300	.411	.562	.973	142	144	512	8.80	-14	O-587/1-3	98	11.0
• BERMAN, Bob	Robert Leon Berman b: 1/24/1899, New York, NY d: 8/2/1988, Bridgeport, CT BR/TR, 5'8", 158 lbs. Deb: 6/4/1918																							
1918 Was-A	2	0	0	0	0	0	0	0	0	0	0	....	....	....	....	....	-102	0	0	....	0	/C-1	0	0.0

YEAR TM-L	G	AB	R	H	2B	3B	HR	RBI	BB	SO	SB	CS	AVG	OBP	SLG	OPS	OPS+	BR/A	RC	RC/G	FR	G/POS	WS	TPW
• BERNARD, Curt	Curtis Henry Bernard b: 2/18/1878, Parkersburg, WV d: 4/10/1955, Culver City, CA BL/TR, 5'10", 150 lbs. Deb: 9/17/1900 Career OF: 0-8-26																							
1900 NY-N	20	71	9	18	2	0	0	8	6	....	1	....	.254	.329	.282	.611	73	-2	7	3.55	-2	0-19(0-0-19)/S-1	1	-0.5
1901 NY-N	23	76	11	17	0	2	0	6	7	....	2	....	.224	.289	.276	.565	67	-3	7	3.06	-2	0-15(0-8-7)/2-4,S-2,3-1	1	-0.6
Total 2	43	147	20	35	2	2	0	14	13	....	3	....	.238	.309	.279	.588	70	-5	14	3.30	-4	/0-34,2-4,S-3,3-1	2	-1.1
• BERNAZARD, Tony	Antonio (Garcia) Bernazard b: 8/24/1956, Caguas, Puerto Rico BB/TR, 5'9", 160 lbs. Deb: 7/13/1979																							
1979 Mon-N	22	40	11	12	2	0	1	8	15	12	1	2	.300	.500	.425	.925	156	4	9	7.47	1	2-14	3	0.6
1980 Mon-N	82	183	26	41	7	1	5	18	17	41	9	2	.224	.290	.355	.645	79	-4	19	3.52	1	2-39,S-22	4	0.0
1981 Chi-A	106	384	53	106	14	4	6	34	54	66	4	4	.276	.368	.380	.748	118	11	56	5.04	-3	*2-104/S-1	16	1.4
1982 Chi-A	137	540	90	138	25	9	11	56	67	88	11	0	.256	.340	.396	.736	101	5	78	4.88	13	*2-137	20	2.5
1983 Chi-A	59	233	30	61	16	2	2	26	17	45	2	1	.262	.312	.373	.685	85	-5	27	3.90	4	2-59	6	0.2
Sea-A	80	300	35	80	18	1	6	30	38	52	21	8	.267	.353	.393	.746	101	3	44	5.00	-11	2-79	9	-0.4
Yr.	139	533	65	141	34	3	8	56	55	97	23	9	.265	.336	.385	.720	94	-3	71	4.52	-6	*2-138	15	-0.2
1984 Cle-A	140	439	44	97	15	4	2	38	43	70	20	13	.221	.293	.287	.580	60	-24	37	2.65	13	*2-136/D-1	6	-0.4
1985 Cle-A	153	500	73	137	26	3	11	59	69	72	17	9	.274	.363	.404	.767	111	9	75	5.19	-9	*2-147/S-1	17	0.7
1986 Cle-A	146	562	88	169	28	4	17	73	53	77	17	8	.301	.367	.456	.823	125	20	96	6.17	11	*2-146	25	3.8
1987 Cle-A	79	293	39	70	12	1	11	30	25	49	7	4	.239	.301	.399	.700	83	-8	35	4.02	-7	2-78	5	-1.1
Oak-A	61	214	34	57	14	1	3	19	30	30	4	4	.266	.357	.383	.740	103	1	29	4.59	-4	2-59/D-3	6	0.0
Yr.	140	507	73	127	26	2	14	49	55	79	11	8	.250	.325	.393	.718	92	-7	64	4.26	-11	*2-137/D-3	11	-1.1
1991 Det-A	6	12	0	2	0	0	0	0	0	4	0	0	.167	.167	.167	.333	-7	-2	0	.90	0	/2-2,D-2	0	-0.2
Total 10	1071	3700	523	970	177	30	75	391	428	606	113	55	.262	.341	.387	.728	100	8	508	4.65	9	*2-1000/S-24,D-6	117	7.0
• BERNHARDT, Juan	Juan Ramon (Coradin) Bernhardt b: 8/31/1953, San Pedro de Macoris, Dominican Republic BR/TR, 5'11", 160 lbs. Deb: 7/10/1976																							
1976 NY-A	10	21	1	4	1	0	0	1	0	4	0	0	.190	.190	.238	.429	25	-2	1	1.51	-1	/0-4(1-0-3),D-2,3-1	0	-0.3
1977 Sea-A	89	305	32	74	9	2	7	30	5	26	2	3	.243	.260	.354	.614	66	-16	25	2.69	-1	D-54,3-21/1-8	1	-1.9
1978 Sea-A	54	165	13	38	9	0	2	12	9	10	1	1	.230	.274	.321	.595	67	-8	14	2.81	0	1-25,3-22/D-2	1	-1.0
1979 Sea-A	1	1	0	1	0	0	0	0	0	0	0	0	1.000	1.000	1.000	2.000	434	0	1	∞	0	....	0	0.0
Total 4	154	492	46	117	19	2	9	43	14	40	3	4	.238	.263	.339	.603	66	-25	41	2.68	-2	/D-58,3-44,1-33,0-4	2	-3.2
• BERNIER, Carlos	Carlos (Rodriguez) Bernier b: 1/28/1927, Juana Diaz, Puerto Rico d: 4/6/1989, Juana Diaz, Puerto Rico BR/TR, 5'9", 180 lbs. Deb: 4/22/1953																							
1953 Pit-N	105	310	48	66	7	8	3	31	51	53	15	14	.213	.332	.316	.648	70	-15	32	3.23	3	0-86(11-57-18)	4	-1.6
• BERO, Johnny	John George Bero b: 12/22/1922, Gary, WV d: 5/11/1985, Gardena, CA BL/TR, 6', 170 lbs. Deb: 9/26/1948																							
1948 Det-A	4	9	2	0	0	0	0	0	1	1	0	0	.000	.100	.000	.100	-70	-2	0	.08	0	/2-2	0	-0.3
1951 StL-A	61	160	24	34	5	0	5	17	26	30	1	1	.213	.323	.338	.660	76	-5	19	3.86	-5	S-55/2-1	3	-0.7
Total 2	65	169	26	34	5	0	5	17	27	31	1	1	.201	.311	.320	.631	69	-7	19	3.62	-6	/S-55,2-3	3	-1.0
• BERRA, Dale	Dale Anthony Berra b: 12/13/1956, Ridgewood, NJ BR/TR, 6', 190 lbs. Deb: 8/22/1977																							
1977 Pit-N	17	40	0	7	1	0	0	3	1	8	0	0	.175	.195	.200	.395	6	-5	2	1.32	1	3-14	0	-0.5
1978 Pit-N	56	135	16	28	2	0	6	14	13	20	3	1	.207	.287	.356	.642	75	-5	14	3.43	1	3-55/S-2	3	-0.4
1979 Pit-N	44	123	11	26	5	0	3	15	11	17	0	0	.211	.276	.325	.601	61	-7	10	2.62	-4	3-22,S-22	2	-0.9
1980 Pit-N	93	245	21	54	8	2	6	31	16	52	2	0	.220	.271	.343	.614	69	-10	22	2.94	-4	3-48,S-45/2-4	4	-1.2
1981 Pit-N	81	232	21	56	12	0	2	27	17	34	11	1	.241	.302	.319	.621	74	-6	24	3.57	-1	3-42,S-30,2-18	5	-0.4
1982 Pit-N	156	529	64	139	25	5	10	61	33	83	6	6	.263	.311	.386	.697	91	-9	59	3.73	5	*S-153/3-6	14	1.2
1983 Pit-N	161	537	51	135	25	1	10	52	61	84	8	5	.251	.328	.358	.685	87	-9	63	4.00	18	*S-161	19	2.7
1984 Pit-N	136	450	31	100	16	0	9	52	34	78	1	3	.222	.278	.318	.596	67	-22	38	2.73	6	*S-135/3-1	8	-0.2
1985 NY-A	48	109	8	25	5	1	1	8	7	20	1	1	.229	.276	.321	.597	64	-6	9	2.86	-2	3-41/S-6	1	-0.7
1986 NY-A	42	108	10	25	7	0	2	13	9	14	0	0	.231	.297	.352	.648	76	-4	12	3.83	1	S-19,3-18/D-4	2	-0.1
1987 Hou-N	19	45	3	8	3	0	0	2	8	12	0	0	.178	.302	.244	.546	49	-3	4	2.70	-1	S-18/2-3	1	-0.3
Total 11	853	2553	236	603	109	9	49	278	210	422	32	17	.236	.297	.344	.641	76	-85	258	3.35	19	S-591,3-247/2-25,D-4	59	-0.9
• BERRA, Yogi	Lawrence Peter Berra b: 5/12/1925, St. Louis, MO BL/TR, 5'7.5", 194 lbs. Deb: 9/22/1946 M/C HOF: 1972 Career OF: 148-0-115																							
1946 NY-A	7	22	3	8	1	0	2	4	1	1	0	0	.364	.391	.682	1.073	193	2	6	11.80	1	/C-6	2	0.4
1947*NY-A	83	293	41	82	15	3	11	54	13	12	0	1	.280	.310	.464	.775	115	3	41	5.00	-6	C-51,0-24(12-0-12)	11	-0.1
1948 NY-A★	125	469	70	143	24	10	14	98	25	24	3	3	.305	.341	.488	.830	120	9	77	6.12	1	C-71,0-50(0-0-50)	18	1.1
1949*NY-A★	116	415	59	115	20	2	20	91	22	25	2	1	.277	.323	.480	.802	111	2	65	5.73	9	*C-109	21	1.6
1950*NY-A★	151	597	116	192	30	6	28	124	55	12	4	2	.322	.383	.533	.915	136	30	125	8.05	2	*C-148	32	3.7
1951*NY-A★	141	547	92	161	19	4	27	88	44	20	5	4	.294	.350	.492	.842	131	20	92	6.12	3	*C-141	31	3.0
1952*NY-A★	142	534	97	146	17	1	30	98	66	24	2	3	.273	.358	.478	.835	139	26	95	6.43	-2	*C-140	29	3.3
1953*NY-A★	137	503	80	149	23	5	27	108	50	32	0	3	.296	.363	.523	.886	142	26	98	7.24	2	*C-133	28	3.5
1954 NY-A★	151	584	88	179	28	6	22	125	56	29	0	1	.307	.371	.488	.859	139	29	107	6.83	5	*C-149/3-1	34	4.2
1955*NY-A★	147	541	84	147	20	3	27	108	60	20	1	0	.272	.352	.470	.821	121	15	90	5.84	-6	*C-145	24	1.6
1956*NY-A★	140	521	93	155	29	2	30	105	65	29	3	2	.298	.381	.534	.914	144	32	108	7.61	2	*C-135/0-1	31	4.0
1957*NY-A★	134	482	74	121	14	2	24	82	57	24	1	2	.251	.331	.438	.769	110	6	69	4.92	6	*C-121/0-6(5-0-1)	23	1.9
1958*NY-A★	122	433	60	115	17	3	22	90	35	35	3	0	.266	.323	.471	.795	120	11	67	5.45	1	C-88,0-21(0-0-21)/1-2	21	1.7
1959 NY-A★	131	472	64	134	25	1	19	69	43	38	1	2	.284	.349	.462	.811	125	15	77	5.94	5	*C-116/0-7(1-0-6)	23	2.6
1960*NY-A★	120	359	46	99	14	1	15	62	38	23	2	1	.276	.350	.446	.796	120	10	55	5.34	3	C-63,0-36(20-0-17)	16	1.4
1961*NY-A★	119	395	62	107	11	0	22	61	35	28	2	0	.271	.333	.466	.799	117	9	62	5.54	4	0-87(81-0-8),C-15	16	0.9
1962*NY-A★	86	232	25	52	8	0	10	35	24	18	0	1	.224	.302	.388	.690	87	-5	26	3.66	2	C-31,0-28(28-0-0)	6	-0.4
1963*NY-A	64	147	20	43	6	0	8	28	15	17	1	0	.293	.362	.497	.859	139	8	26	6.45	3	C-35	9	1.3
1965 NY-N	4	9	1	2	0	0	0	0	0	3	0	0	.222	.222	.222	.444	27	-1	0	1.71	1	/C-2	0	0.0
Total 19	2120	7555	1175	2150	321	49	358	1430	704	414	30	26	.285	.350	.482	.832	126	247	1284	6.16	36	*C-1699,0-260/1-2,3-1	375	35.8
• BERRAN, Dennis	Dennis Martin Berran b: 10/8/1887, Merrimac, MA d: 4/28/1943, Boston, MA BL/TL Deb: 8/11/1912																							
1912 Chi-A	2	4	1	1	0	0	0	0	0	....	0	....	.250	.250	.250	.500	44	-0	0	2.04	0	/0-2(2-0-0)	0	0.0
• BERRES, Ray	Raymond Frederick Berres b: 8/31/1907, Kenosha, WI BR/TR, 5'9", 170 lbs. Deb: 4/24/1934 C																							
1934 Bro-N	39	79	7	17	4	0	0	3	1	16	0	....	.215	.225	.266	.491	32	-8	5	1.97	0	C-37	1	-0.7
1936 Bro-N	105	267	16	64	10	1	1	13	14	35	1	....	.240	.280	.296	.576	55	-17	21	2.73	2	*C-105	5	-0.9
1937 Pit-N	2	6	0	1	0	0	0	0	0	0	0	....	.167	.167	.167	.333	-9	-1	0	.92	0	/C-2	0	-0.1
1938 Pit-N	40	100	7	23	2	0	0	6	8	10	0	....	.230	.287	.250	.537	48	-7	7	2.18	2	C-40	2	-0.3
1939 Pit-N	81	231	22	53	6	1	0	16	11	25	1	....	.229	.267	.264	.532	44	-18	15	2.11	2	C-80	3	-1.2
1940 Pit-N	21	32	2	6	0	0	0	2	1	1	0	....	.188	.212	.188	.400	11	-4	1	1.14	1	C-21	0	-0.2
Bos-N	85	229	12	44	4	1	0	14	18	19	0	....	.192	.251	.218	.469	32	-21	13	1.75	6	C-85	3	-1.1
Yr.	106	261	14	50	4	1	0	16	19	20	0	....	.192	.246	.215	.461	30	-25	14	1.68	7	*C-106	3	-1.3
1941 Bos-N	120	279	21	56	10	0	1	19	17	20	2	....	.201	.247	.247	.494	41	-22	15	1.73	6	*C-120	5	-1.1
1942 NY-N	12	32	0	6	0	0	0	1	2	3	0	....	.188	.235	.188	.423	24	-3	1	1.36	-1	C-12	0	-0.3
1943 NY-N	20	28	1	4	1	0	0	0	1	2	0	....	.143	.172	.179	.351	1	-4	1	.81	1	C-17	0	-0.3
1944 NY-N	16	17	4	8	0	0	1	2	1	0	0	....	.471	.526	.647	1.173	230	3	5	14.73	0	C-12	2	0.4
1945 NY-N	20	30	4	5	0	0	0	2	2	3	0	....	.167	.219	.167	.385	8	-4	1	1.07	0	C-20	0	-0.4
Total 11	561	1330	96	287	37	3	3	78	76	134	4	....	.216	.260	.255	.515	42	-105	87	2.09	18	C-551	21	-6.2
• BERROA, Angel	Angel Maria (Selmo) Berroa b: 1/27/1980, Santo Domingo, Dominican Republic BR/TR, 6', 175 lbs. Deb: 9/18/2001																							
2001 KC-A	15	53	8	16	2	0	0	4	3	10	2	0	.302	.339	.340	.679	74	-2	6	4.17	0	S-14	1	0.0
2002 KC-A	20	75	8	17	7	1	0	5	7	10	3	0	.227	.301	.347	.648	64	-3	8	3.89	3	S-20	1	0.1
2003 KC-A	158	567	92	163	28	7	17	73	29	100	21	5	.287	.342	.451	.794	94	-3	87	5.33	2	*S-158	16	1.2
Total 3	193	695	108	196	37	8	17	82	39	120	26	5	.282	.337	.432	.769	90	-8	102	5.09	5	S-192	18	1.3
• BERROA, Geronimo	Geronimo Emiliano Berroa b: 3/18/1965, Santo Domingo, Dominican Republic BR/TR, 6', 195 lbs. Deb: 4/5/1989 Career OF: 100-0-243																							
1989 Atl-N	81	136	7	36	4	0	2	9	7	32	0	1	.265	.301	.338	.639	80	-4	13	3.49	-1	0-34(1-0-33)	2	-0.7

YEAR	TM-L	G	AB	R	H	2B	3B	HR	RBI	BB	SO	SB	CS	AVG	OBP	SLG	OPS	OPS+	BR/A	RC	RC/G	FR	G/POS	WS	TPW
1990	Atl-N	7	4	0	0	0	0	0	0	1	1	0	0	.000	.200	.000	.200	-38	-1	0	.00	0	/O-3(3-0-0)	0	-0.1
1992	Cin-N	13	15	2	4	1	0	0	0	2	1	0	1	.267	.389	.333	.722	103	-0	2	3.33	1	/O-3(3-0-0)	0	0.0
1993	Fla-N	14	34	3	4	1	0	0	0	2	7	0	0	.118	.167	.147	.314	-14	-6	1	.52	-1	/O-9(1-0-8)	0	-0.6
1994	Oak-A	96	340	55	104	18	2	13	65	41	62	7	2	.306	.385	.485	.871	134	18	66	7.16	2	D-44,O-42(36-0-7)/1-9	14	1.4
1995	Oak-A	141	546	87	152	22	3	22	88	63	98	7	4	.278	.354	.451	.805	115	11	87	5.67	-1	D-72,O-71(17-0-54)	16	0.1
1996	Oak-A	153	586	101	170	32	1	36	106	47	122	0	3	.290	.347	.532	.879	121	15	103	6.32	1	D-91,O-61(17-0-54)	16	0.6
1997	Oak-A	73	261	40	81	12	0	16	42	36	58	3	2	.310	.396	.540	.936	145	17	53	7.33	-4	O-43(0-0-43),D-32	7	0.9
	*Bal-A	83	300	48	78	13	0	10	48	40	62	1	2	.260	.353	.403	.756	100	-0	44	5.01	-1	D-42,O-40(0-0-40)	7	-0.6
	Yr.	156	561	88	159	25	0	26	90	76	120	4	4	.283	.373	.467	.840	120	17	97	6.06	-5	O-83(0-0-83),D-74	14	0.3
1998	Cle-A	20	65	6	13	3	1	0	3	7	17	1	0	.200	.278	.277	.555	44	-5	5	2.54	1	O-14(14-0-0)/D-5	1	-0.5
	Det-A	52	126	17	30	4	1	1	10	17	27	0	1	.238	.338	.310	.647	70	-6	14	3.66	0	D-37/O-4(2-0-2)	1	-0.7
	Yr.	72	191	23	43	7	2	1	13	24	44	1	1	.225	.318	.298	.616	61	-11	19	3.27	1	D-42,O-18(16-0-2)	2	-1.2
1999	Tor-A	22	62	11	12	3	0	1	6	9	15	0	0	.194	.315	.290	.605	55	-4	5	2.53	0	D-17/O-2(2-0-0)	0	-0.5
2000	LA-N	24	31	2	8	0	1	0	5	4	8	0	0	.258	.343	.323	.665	74	-1	3	3.33	1	/O-6(4-0-2),1-2	1	-0.1
Total	**11**	**779**	**2506**	**379**	**692**	**113**	**9**	**101**	**382**	**276**	**510**	**19**	**16**	**.276**	**.352**	**.449**	**.801**	**110**	**35**	**396**	**5.55**	**-2**	**D-340,O-332/1-11**	**65**	**-0.6**

• BERRY, Charlie Charles Francis Berry b: 10/18/1902, Phillipsburg, NJ d: 9/6/1972, Evanston, IL BR/TR, 6', 185 lbs. Deb: 6/15/1925 C/U

YEAR	TM-L	G	AB	R	H	2B	3B	HR	RBI	BB	SO	SB	CS	AVG	OBP	SLG	OPS	OPS+	BR/A	RC	RC/G	FR	G/POS	WS	TPW
1925	Phi-A	10	14	1	3	1	0	0	3	0	2	0	0	.214	.214	.286	.500	24	-2	1	1.98	-1	/C-4	0	-0.2
1928	Bos-A	80	177	18	46	7	3	1	19	21	19	1	1	.260	.342	.350	.692	84	-4	22	4.36	-2	C-63	4	-0.3
1929	Bos-A	77	207	19	50	11	4	1	21	15	29	2	4	.242	.302	.348	.650	68	-11	21	3.44	3	C-72	5	-0.3
1930	Bos-A	88	256	31	74	9	6	6	35	16	22	2	0	.289	.331	.441	.772	98	-1	38	5.21	3	C-85	8	0.7
1931	Bos-A	111	357	41	101	16	2	6	49	29	38	4	0	.283	.337	.389	.726	96	0	48	4.96	4	*C-102	11	1.0
1932	Bos-A	10	32	0	6	3	0	0	6	3	2	0	0	.188	.257	.281	.538	40	-3	2	2.46	1	C-10	0	-0.2
	Chi-A	72	226	33	69	15	6	4	31	21	23	3	0	.305	.364	.478	.842	124	9	40	6.67	5	C-70	8	1.6
	Yr.	82	258	33	75	18	6	4	37	24	25	3	0	.291	.351	.453	.805	114	6	43	6.08	6	C-80	8	1.5
1933	Chi-A	86	271	25	69	8	3	2	28	17	16	0	0	.255	.301	.328	.629	70	-12	27	3.53	-6	C-83	3	-1.3
1934	Phi-A	99	269	14	72	10	2	0	34	22	23	1	0	.268	.323	.320	.643	69	-12	29	3.75	3	C-99	5	-0.4
1935	Phi-A	62	190	14	48	7	3	3	29	10	20	0	0	.253	.290	.368	.658	70	-9	20	3.74	4	C-56	3	-0.2
1936	Phi-A	13	17	0	1	1	0	0	1	6	2	0	0	.059	.304	.118	.422	8	-2	1	1.72	0	C-12	0	-0.2
1938	Phi-A	1	2	0	0	0	0	0	0	0	0	0	0	.000	.000	.000	.000	-103	-1	0	.00	0	/C-1	0	0.0
Total	**11**	**709**	**2018**	**196**	**539**	**88**	**29**	**23**	**256**	**160**	**196**	**13**	**5**	**.267**	**.322**	**.374**	**.696**	**83**	**-47**	**251**	**4.38**	**13**	**C-657**	**47**	**0.2**

• BERRY, Charlie Charles Joseph Berry b: 9/6/1860, Elizabeth, NJ d: 2/16/1940, Phillipsburg, NJ BR/TR, 5'11", 175 lbs. Deb: 4/30/1884

YEAR	TM-L	G	AB	R	H	2B	3B	HR	RBI	BB	SO	SB	CS	AVG	OBP	SLG	OPS	OPS+	BR/A	RC	RC/G	FR	G/POS	WS	TPW
1884	Alt-U	7	25	2	6	0	0	0	....	0	....	....	....	.240	.240	.240	.480	62	-1	1	2.18	-4	/2-7	0	-0.4
	KC-U	29	118	15	29	6	1	1	....	1	....	....	....	.246	.252	.339	.591	113	2	10	3.25	-3	2-22/O-8(1-7-0),3-1	3	0.0
	CP-U	7	27	4	3	2	0	0	....	0	....	....	....	.111	.111	.185	.296	-2	-3	1	.66	1	/2-7	0	-0.2
	Yr.	43	170	21	38	8	1	1	....	1	....	....	....	.224	.228	.300	.528	87	-1	12	2.63	-7	2-36/O-8(1-7-0),3-1	3	-0.6

• BERRY, Claude Claude Elzy "Admiral" Berry b: 2/14/1880, Losantville, IN d: 2/1/1974, Richmond, IN BR/TR, 5'7", 165 lbs. Deb: 4/22/1904

YEAR	TM-L	G	AB	R	H	2B	3B	HR	RBI	BB	SO	SB	CS	AVG	OBP	SLG	OPS	OPS+	BR/A	RC	RC/G	FR	G/POS	WS	TPW
1904	Chi-A	3	1	1	0	0	0	0	0	1	....	0	....	.000	.500	.000	.500	68	0	0	.00	-0	/C-3	0	0.0
1906	Phi-A	10	30	2	7	0	0	0	2	2	....	1	....	.233	.281	.233	.515	60	-1	2	2.66	2	C-10	1	0.2
1907	Phi-A	8	19	2	4	2	0	0	1	2	....	0	....	.211	.286	.316	.602	90	-0	2	3.10	-1	/C-8	1	0.0
1914	Pit-F	124	411	35	98	18	9	2	36	26	50	6	....	.238	.284	.341	.624	82	-11	41	3.14	7	*C-122	8	0.6
1915	Pit-F	100	292	32	56	11	1	1	26	29	42	7	....	.192	.269	.247	.516	50	-18	21	2.24	1	C-99	7	-1.0
Total	**5**	**245**	**753**	**72**	**165**	**31**	**10**	**3**	**65**	**60**	**92**	**14**	**....**	**.219**	**.279**	**.299**	**.577**	**68**	**-31**	**66**	**2.76**	**9**	**C-242**	**17**	**-0.3**

• BERRY, Joe Joseph Howard "Hodge" Berry, Sr. b: 9/10/1872, Wheeling, WV d: 3/13/1961, Allenwood, NJ BB/TR, 5'9", 172 lbs. Deb: 9/4/1902

YEAR	TM-L	G	AB	R	H	2B	3B	HR	RBI	BB	SO	SB	CS	AVG	OBP	SLG	OPS	OPS+	BR/A	RC	RC/G	FR	G/POS	WS	TPW
1902	Phi-N	1	4	0	1	0	0	0	1	1	....	1	....	.250	.400	.250	.650	101	0	1	7.24	0	/C-1	0	0.0

• BERRY, Joe Joseph Howard "Nig" Berry, Jr. b: 12/31/1894, Philadelphia, PA d: 4/29/1976, Philadelphia, PA BB/TR, 5'10.5", 159 lbs. Deb: 7/18/1921

YEAR	TM-L	G	AB	R	H	2B	3B	HR	RBI	BB	SO	SB	CS	AVG	OBP	SLG	OPS	OPS+	BR/A	RC	RC/G	FR	G/POS	WS	TPW
1921	NY-N	9	6	0	2	0	1	0	2	1	1	0	0	.333	.429	.667	1.095	185	1	2	11.61	-2	/2-7	1	-0.1
1922	NY-N	6	0	0	0	0	0	0	0	0	0	0	0	....	....	....	....	-99	0	0		0	....	0	0.0
Total	**2**	**15**	**6**	**0**	**2**	**0**	**1**	**0**	**2**	**1**	**1**	**0**	**0**	**.333**	**.429**	**.667**	**1.095**	**185**	**1**	**2**	**11.61**	**-2**	**/2-7**	**1**	**-0.1**

• BERRY, Ken Allen Kent Berry b: 5/10/1941, Kansas City, MO BR/TR, 6', 180 lbs. Deb: 9/9/1962 Career OF: 202-1018-141

YEAR	TM-L	G	AB	R	H	2B	3B	HR	RBI	BB	SO	SB	CS	AVG	OBP	SLG	OPS	OPS+	BR/A	RC	RC/G	FR	G/POS	WS	TPW
1962	Chi-A	3	6	2	2	0	0	0	0	0	0	0	0	.333	.333	.333	.667	80	-0	1	4.50	1	/O-2(1-1-1)	0	0.1
1963	Chi-A	4	5	2	1	0	0	0	0	1	1	0	0	.200	.333	.200	.533	55	-0	0	2.84	0	/O-2(2-0-0),2-1	0	-0.1
1964	Chi-A	12	32	4	12	1	0	1	4	5	3	0	1	.375	.459	.500	.959	171	3	7	7.94	0	O-12(0-12-0)	2	0.3
1965	Chi-A	157	472	51	103	17	4	12	42	28	96	4	2	.218	.269	.347	.617	79	-15	45	3.08	10	*O-156(0-156-0)	12	-1.0
1966	Chi-A	147	443	50	120	20	2	8	34	28	63	7	10	.271	.317	.379	.696	106	-0	51	3.92	4	*O-141(101-13-41)	14	-0.4
1967	Chi-A★	147	485	49	117	14	4	7	41	46	68	9	8	.241	.311	.330	.641	93	-5	49	3.37	3	*O-143(50-38-86)	14	-1.1
1968	Chi-A	153	504	49	127	21	2	7	32	25	64	6	6	.252	.289	.343	.632	90	-9	46	3.03	2	*O-151(0-149-2)	11	-1.3
1969	Chi-A	130	297	25	69	12	2	4	18	24	50	1	2	.232	.296	.327	.623	71	-13	27	3.04	2	*O-120(2-116-2)	4	-1.4
1970	Chi-A	141	463	45	128	12	2	7	50	43	61	6	4	.276	.346	.356	.702	90	-5	54	4.02	7	*O-138(0-138-0)	10	-0.2
1971	Cal-A	111	298	29	66	17	0	3	22	18	33	3	2	.221	.273	.309	.581	69	-13	23	2.45	3	*O-101(8-94-0)	6	-1.3
1972	Cal-A	119	409	41	118	15	3	5	39	35	47	5	3	.289	.348	.377	.724	122	11	56	4.83	10	*O-116(0-116-0)	22	2.0
1973	Cal-A	136	415	48	118	11	2	3	36	26	50	1	6	.284	.328	.342	.670	96	-5	41	3.34	-2	*O-129(15-111-4)	10	-1.1
1974	Mil-A	98	267	21	64	9	2	1	24	18	26	3	1	.240	.295	.300	.595	72	-9	24	3.07	2	O-82(5-74-5),D-13	5	-1.0
1975	Cle-A	25	40	6	8	1	0	0	1	1	7	0	1	.200	.238	.225	.463	31	-4	2	1.44	-1	O-18(18-0-0)/D-5	0	-0.6
Total	**14**	**1383**	**4136**	**422**	**1053**	**150**	**23**	**58**	**343**	**298**	**569**	**45**	**46**	**.255**	**.309**	**.344**	**.653**	**91**	**-64**	**425**	**3.46**	**41**	***O-1311/D-18,2-1**	**110**	**-7.0**

• BERRY, Neil Cornelius John Berry b: 1/11/1922, Kalamazoo, MI BR/TR, 5'10", 170 lbs. Deb: 4/20/1948

YEAR	TM-L	G	AB	R	H	2B	3B	HR	RBI	BB	SO	SB	CS	AVG	OBP	SLG	OPS	OPS+	BR/A	RC	RC/G	FR	G/POS	WS	TPW
1948	Det-A	87	256	46	68	8	1	0	16	37	23	1	3	.266	.358	.305	.663	75	-9	31	4.08	-1	S-41,2-26	6	-0.6
1949	Det-A	109	329	38	78	9	1	0	18	27	24	4	2	.237	.299	.271	.569	51	-23	27	2.68	-12	2-95/S-4	3	-2.9
1950	Det-A	39	40	9	10	1	0	0	7	6	11	0	0	.250	.348	.275	.623	59	-2	5	3.96	1	S-12/2-2,3-1	1	-0.1
1951	Det-A	67	157	17	36	5	2	0	9	10	15	4	2	.229	.275	.287	.562	52	-11	13	2.81	-6	S-38,2-10/3-7	1	-1.4
1952	Det-A	73	189	22	43	4	3	0	13	22	19	1	3	.228	.311	.280	.592	65	-9	17	3.02	-3	S-66/3-2	2	-0.9
1953	StL-A	57	99	14	28	1	2	0	11	9	10	1	2	.283	.343	.333	.676	82	-3	11	3.60	-4	3-18,2-15/S-6	1	-0.6
	Chi-A	5	8	1	1	0	0	0	0	1	1	0	0	.125	.222	.125	.347	-4	-1	0	.48	1	/2-3	0	0.0
	Yr.	62	107	15	29	1	2	0	11	10	11	1	2	.271	.333	.318	.651	75	-4	11	3.32	-4	2-18,3-18/S-6	1	-0.6
1954	Bal-A	5	9	1	1	0	0	0	0	1	2	0	0	.111	.200	.111	.311	-14	-1	0	.85	0	/S-5	0	-0.1
Total	**7**	**442**	**1087**	**148**	**265**	**28**	**9**	**0**	**74**	**113**	**105**	**11**	**12**	**.244**	**.317**	**.286**	**.603**	**62**	**-60**	**104**	**3.17**	**-24**	**S-172,2-151/3-28**	**14**	**-6.6**

• BERRY, Sean Sean Robert Berry b: 3/22/1966, Santa Monica, CA BR/TR, 5'11", 210 lbs. Deb: 9/17/1990

YEAR	TM-L	G	AB	R	H	2B	3B	HR	RBI	BB	SO	SB	CS	AVG	OBP	SLG	OPS	OPS+	BR/A	RC	RC/G	FR	G/POS	WS	TPW
1990	KC-A	8	23	2	5	1	1	0	4	2	5	0	0	.217	.280	.348	.628	76	-1	2	3.58	0	/3-8	1	-0.1
1991	KC-A	31	60	5	8	3	0	0	1	5	23	0	0	.133	.212	.183	.395	10	-7	2	1.26	2	3-30	1	-0.5
1992	Mon-N	24	57	5	19	1	0	1	4	1	11	2	1	.333	.345	.404	.748	112	1	8	5.09	-1	3-20	1	0.0
1993	Mon-N	122	299	50	78	15	2	14	49	41	70	12	2	.261	.354	.465	.819	112	7	52	5.98	4	3-96	12	1.2
1994	Mon-N	103	320	43	89	19	2	11	41	32	50	14	0	.278	.349	.453	.802	106	6	53	5.88	1	*3-100	10	0.7
1995	Mon-N	103	314	38	100	22	1	14	55	25	53	3	8	.318	.372	.529	.901	130	10	58	6.73	7	3-83/1-3	12	1.7
1996	Hou-N	132	431	55	121	38	1	17	95	23	58	12	6	.281	.330	.492	.822	123	12	67	5.39	-6	*3-110	19	0.7
1997	*Hou-N	96	301	37	77	24	1	8	43	25	53	1	5	.256	.323	.422	.745	97	-4	39	4.27	-2	3-85/D-3	5	-0.5
1998	*Hou-N	102	299	48	94	17	1	13	52	31	50	3	1	.314	.392	.508	.900	138	17	59	7.33	-1	3-87/D-1	12	1.7
1999	Mil-N	106	259	26	59	11	1	2	23	17	50	0	0	.228	.283	.301	.584	49	-21	22	2.95	-3	1-64	1	-2.7
2000	Mil-N	32	46	1	7	2	0	1	2	4	13	0	1	.152	.220	.261	.481	21	-6	2	1.55	-4	/3-9	0	-0.9
	Bos-A	1	4	0	0	0	0	0	0	0	2	0	0	.000	.000	.000	.000	-97	-1	0	.00	-1	/3-1	0	-0.2
Total	**11**	**860**	**2413**	**310**	**657**	**153**	**10**	**81**	**369**	**206**	**438**	**47**	**24**	**.272**	**.338**	**.445**	**.782**	**105**	**11**	**365**	**5.27**	**-4**	**3-629/1-67,D-4**	**74**	**1.2**

• BERRY, Tom Thomas Haney Berry b: 12/31/1842, Chester, PA d: 6/6/1915, Chester, PA, 5'6", 140 lbs. Deb: 9/2/1871

YEAR	TM-L	G	AB	R	H	2B	3B	HR	RBI	BB	SO	SB	CS	AVG	OBP	SLG	OPS	OPS+	BR/A	RC	RC/G	FR	G/POS	WS	TPW
1871	Ath-n	1	4	0	1	0	0	0	0	0	0	0	0	.250	.250	.250	.500	45	-0	0	2.69	0	/O-1	....	0.0

YEAR TM-L	G	AB	R	H	2B	3B	HR	RBI	BB	SO	SB	CS	AVG	OBP	SLG	OPS	OPS+	BR/A	RC	RC/G	FR	G/POS	WS	TPW
• BERRYHILL, Damon	Damon Scott Berryhill b: 12/3/1963, South Laguna, CA BB/TR, 6', 205 lbs. Deb: 9/5/1987																							
1987 Chi-N	12	28	2	5	1	0	0	1	3	5	0	1	.179	.258	.214	.472	26	-3	1	1.42	-1	C-11	0	-0.5
1988 Chi-N	95	309	19	80	19	1	7	38	17	56	1	0	.259	.298	.395	.692	93	-4	33	3.66	-1	C-90	7	0.1
1989 Chi-N	91	334	37	86	13	0	5	41	16	54	1	0	.257	.295	.341	.637	76	-11	31	3.10	1	C-89	12	-0.5
1990 Chi-N	17	53	6	10	4	0	1	9	5	14	0	0	.189	.259	.321	.579	54	-3	4	2.17	-2	C-15	0	-0.5
1991 Chi-N	62	159	13	30	7	0	5	14	11	41	1	2	.189	.246	.327	.573	57	-10	12	2.49	-1	C-48	1	-1.0
Atl-N	1	1	0	0	0	0	0	0	0	1	0	0	.000	.000	.000	.000	-94	-0	0	.00	0	/C-1	0	0.0
Yr.	63	160	13	30	7	0	5	14	11	42	1	2	.188	.244	.325	.569	56	-11	12	2.47	-1	C-49	1	-1.0
1992*Atl-N	101	307	21	70	16	1	10	43	17	67	0	2	.228	.271	.384	.655	79	-11	31	3.38	-4	C-84	10	-1.1
1993*Atl-N	115	335	24	82	18	2	8	43	21	64	0	0	.245	.293	.382	.675	78	-11	37	3.75	-2	*C-105	8	-0.7
1994 Bos-A	82	255	30	67	17	2	6	34	19	59	0	1	.263	.314	.416	.730	82	-8	32	4.39	0	C-67/D-6	5	-0.4
1995 Cin-N	34	82	6	15	3	0	2	11	10	19	0	0	.183	.272	.293	.564	49	-6	7	2.34	-1	C-29/1-1	1	-0.5
1997*SF-N	73	167	17	43	8	0	3	23	20	29	0	0	.257	.337	.359	.696	85	-3	21	4.34	-1	C-51/1-1	5	-0.1
Total 10	**683**	**2030**	**175**	**488**	**106**	**6**	**47**	**257**	**139**	**409**	**3**	**6**	**.240**	**.291**	**.368**	**.659**	**77**	**-72**	**208**	**3.44**	**-13**	**C-590/D-6,1-2**	**49**	**-5.1**
• BERTE, Harry	Harry Thomas Berte b: 5/10/1872, Covington, KY d: 5/6/1952, Los Angeles, CA TR, 5'10" Deb: 9/17/1903																							
1903 StL-N	4	15	1	5	0	0	0	1	1	....	0	....	.333	.375	.333	.708	106	0	2	5.09	-1	/2-3,S-1	0	-0.1
• BERTELL, Dick	Richard George Bertell b: 11/21/1935, Oak Park, IL d: 12/20/1999, Mission Viejo, CA BR/TR, 6'.5", 200 lbs. Deb: 9/22/1960																							
1960 Chi-N	5	15	0	2	0	0	0	2	3	1	0	0	.133	.278	.133	.411	17	-2	1	1.67	1	/C-5	0	0.0
1961 Chi-N	92	267	20	73	7	1	2	33	15	33	0	0	.273	.312	.330	.642	70	-12	26	3.47	1	C-90	5	-0.7
1962 Chi-N	77	215	19	65	6	2	2	18	13	30	0	1	.302	.345	.377	.722	90	-3	27	4.57	-1	C-76	5	-0.1
1963 Chi-N	100	322	15	75	7	2	2	14	24	41	0	2	.233	.286	.286	.572	62	-16	25	2.60	6	C-99	8	-0.5
1964 Chi-N	112	353	29	84	11	3	4	35	33	67	2	1	.238	.307	.320	.627	74	-11	34	3.17	-7	*C-110	5	-1.3
1965 Chi-N	34	84	6	18	2	0	0	7	11	10	0	0	.214	.305	.238	.543	54	-5	7	2.63	3	C-34	2	0.0
SF-N	22	48	1	9	1	0	0	3	7	5	0	0	.188	.291	.208	.499	42	-3	3	2.04	-1	C-22	1	-0.3
Yr.	56	132	7	27	3	0	0	10	18	15	0	0	.205	.300	.227	.527	50	-8	10	2.41	2	C-56	3	-0.4
1967 Chi-N	2	6	1	1	0	1	0	0	0	1	0	0	.167	.167	.500	.667	80	-0	1	2.26	-0	/C-2	0	0.0
Total 7	**444**	**1310**	**91**	**327**	**34**	**9**	**10**	**112**	**106**	**188**	**2**	**4**	**.250**	**.307**	**.312**	**.619**	**69**	**-52**	**124**	**3.19**	**3**	**C-438**	**26**	**-3.0**
• BERTHRONG, Harry	Henry W. Berthrong b: 12/31/1843, Munford, NY d: 4/24/1928, Chelsea, MA TR, 5'6.5", 140 lbs. Deb: 5/5/1871 U																							
1871 Oly-n	17	73	17	17	1	1	0	8	4	2	3	1	.233	.273	.274	.547	61	-3	6	3.55	-3	0-12(11-1-0)/2-5,C-1	....	-0.4
• BERTOIA, Reno	Reno Peter Bertoia b: 1/8/1935, St. Vito Udine, Italy BR/TR, 5'11.5", 185 lbs. Deb: 9/22/1953																							
1953 Det-A	1	1	0	0	0	0	0	0	0	1	0	0	.000	.000	.000	.000	-101	-0	0	.00	-1	/2-1	0	-0.1
1954 Det-A	54	37	13	6	2	0	1	2	5	9	1	0	.162	.262	.297	.559	54	-2	3	2.92	-4	2-15/3-8,S-3	1	-0.5
1955 Det-A	38	68	13	14	2	1	1	10	5	11	0	0	.206	.260	.309	.569	54	-5	6	2.60	2	3-14/2-6,S-5	1	-0.3
1956 Det-A	22	66	7	12	2	0	1	5	6	12	0	0	.182	.260	.258	.518	37	-6	4	1.80	6	2-18/3-2	1	0.1
1957 Det-A	97	295	28	81	16	2	4	28	19	43	2	3	.275	.327	.383	.710	91	-5	36	4.18	-5	3-83/S-7,2-2	6	-1.0
1958 Det-A	86	240	28	56	6	0	6	27	20	35	5	2	.233	.298	.333	.631	68	-10	25	3.31	1	3-68/S-5,0-1	4	-0.9
1959 Was-A	90	308	33	73	10	0	8	29	29	48	2	5	.237	.305	.347	.652	79	-11	30	3.21	-8	2-71/3-5,S-1	5	-1.3
1960 Was-A	121	460	44	122	17	7	4	45	26	58	3	5	.265	.316	.359	.674	81	-14	50	3.66	-3	*3-112,2-21	9	-1.7
1961 Min-A	35	104	17	22	2	0	1	8	20	12	0	0	.212	.339	.260	.598	59	-5	10	3.14	-2	3-32	1	-0.7
KC-A	39	120	12	29	2	0	0	13	9	15	1	0	.242	.295	.258	.553	49	-8	9	2.28	4	3-29/2-6	1	-0.4
Det-A	24	46	6	10	1	0	1	4	3	8	2	0	.217	.265	.304	.570	50	-3	4	3.05	-1	3-13/2-7,S-1	1	-0.4
Yr.	98	270	35	61	5	0	2	25	32	35	3	0	.226	.308	.267	.575	53	-17	24	2.74	1	3-74,2-13/S-1	3	-1.5
1962 Det-A	5	0	3	0	0	0	0	0	0	0	0	0	....	....	....	....	-97	0	0	....	-1	/2-1,3-1,S-1	0	0.0
Total 10	**612**	**1745**	**204**	**425**	**60**	**10**	**27**	**171**	**142**	**252**	**16**	**15**	**.244**	**.306**	**.336**	**.642**	**73**	**-69**	**177**	**3.33**	**-11**	**3-367,2-148/S-23,0-1**	**30**	**-7.2**
• BESCHER, Bob	Robert Henry Bescher b: 2/25/1884, London, OH d: 11/29/1942, London, OH BB/TL, 6'1", 200 lbs. Deb: 9/5/1908 Career OF: 1052-120-18																							
1908 Cin-N	32	114	16	31	5	5	0	17	9	....	10	....	.272	.336	.404	.740	140	5	18	5.63	2	0-32(32-0-0)	6	0.6
1909 Cin-N	124	446	73	107	17	6	1	34	56	....	**54**	....	.240	.335	.312	.647	102	3	63	4.81	-4	*0-117(115-0-2)	16	-0.8
1910 Cin-N	150	589	95	147	20	10	4	48	81	75	**70**	....	.250	.344	.338	.682	104	5	91	5.26	-1	*0-150(150-0-0)	18	-0.5
1911 Cin-N	153	599	106	165	32	10	1	45	102	78	**81**	....	.275	.385	.367	.753	115	17	115	6.72	-12	*0-153(153-0-0)	20	-0.1
1912 Cin-N	145	548	**120**	154	29	11	4	38	83	61	**67**	....	.281	.381	.396	.777	116	15	107	6.77	-4	*0-143(143-0-0)	23	0.5
1913 Cin-N	141	511	86	132	22	11	1	37	**94**	68	38	....	.258	.377	.350	.727	109	11	77	5.11	3	*0-138(138-0-0)	17	0.8
1914 NY-N	135	512	82	138	23	4	6	35	45	48	36	....	.270	.336	.365	.701	112	7	70	4.78	1	*0-126(15-111-0)	18	0.1
1915 StL-N	130	486	71	128	15	7	4	34	52	53	27	19	.263	.342	.348	.690	109	4	61	4.13	-3	*0-129(128-0-1)	15	-0.5
1916 StL-N	151	561	78	132	24	8	6	43	60	50	39	12	.235	.316	.339	.654	101	5	67	3.90	2	*0-151(151-2-1)	16	0.1
1917 StL-N	42	110	10	17	1	1	1	8	20	13	3	....	.155	.290	.209	.499	56	-5	8	2.03	-2	0-32(27-4-0)	1	-0.9
1918 Cle-A	25	60	12	20	2	1	0	6	17	5	3	....	.333	.487	.400	.887	153	6	13	7.99	0	0-17(0-3-14)	4	0.6
Total 11	**1228**	**4536**	**749**	**1171**	**190**	**74**	**28**	**345**	**619**	**451**	**428**	**31**	**.258**	**.353**	**.351**	**.704**	**109**	**74**	**691**	**5.15**	**-17**	***0-1188**	**154**	**-0.2**
• BESTICK, William	William Bestick b: New York, NY Deb: 6/20/1872																							
1872 Eck-n	4	14	0	4	0	0	0	1	0	0	0	0	.286	.286	.286	.571	90	0	1	3.63	-1	/C-4	....	0.0
• BESWICK, Jim	James William Beswick b: 2/12/1958, Wilkinsburg, PA BB/TR, 6'1", 180 lbs. Deb: 8/9/1978																							
1978 SD-N	17	20	2	1	0	0	0	0	1	7	0	0	.050	.095	.050	.145	-63	-4	0	.00	0	/0-6(0-2-4)	0	-0.5
• BETCHER, Frank	Franklin Lyle Betcher b: 2/15/1888, Philadelphia, PA d: 11/27/1981, Wynnewood, PA BB/TR, 5'11", 173 lbs. Deb: 5/21/1910																							
1910 StL-N	35	89	7	18	2	0	0	6	7	14	1	....	.202	.276	.225	.500	48	-6	6	2.09	-1	S-12/3-7,2-6,0-2(1-1-0)	1	-0.7
• BETEMIT, Wilson	Wilson Betemit b: 11/2/1981, Santo Domingo, Dominican Republic BB/TR, 6'2", 155 lbs. Deb: 9/18/2001																							
2001 Atl-N	8	3	1	0	0	0	0	0	2	3	1	0	.000	.400	.000	.400	16	-0	0	3.74	0	/S-1	0	0.0
• BETHEA, Bill	William Lamar "Spot" Bethea b: 1/1/1942, Houston, TX BR/TR, 6', 175 lbs. Deb: 9/13/1964																							
1964 Min-A	10	30	4	5	1	0	0	2	4	4	0	0	.167	.265	.200	.465	31	-3	2	2.02	-1	/2-7,S-3	0	-0.3
• BETTENCOURT, Larry	Lawrence Joseph Bettencourt b: 9/22/1905, Newark, CA d: 9/15/1978, New Orleans, LA BR/TR, 5'11", 195 lbs. Deb: 6/2/1928 Career OF: 4-0-61																							
1928 StL-A	67	159	30	45	9	4	4	24	22	19	2	1	.283	.377	.465	.842	117	4	29	6.43	-2	3-41/0-2(0-0-2),C-1	6	0.4
1931 StL-A	74	206	27	53	9	2	3	26	31	35	4	3	.257	.357	.364	.721	87	-3	28	4.78	-1	0-58(2-0-56)	4	-0.6
1932 StL-A	27	30	4	4	1	0	1	3	7	6	1	0	.133	.297	.267	.564	45	-2	3	3.01	0	/0-4(2-0-3),3-2	0	-0.2
Total 3	**168**	**395**	**61**	**102**	**19**	**6**	**8**	**53**	**60**	**60**	**7**	**4**	**.258**	**.360**	**.397**	**.758**	**96**	**-0**	**60**	**5.28**	**-3**	**/0-64,3-43,C-1**	**10**	**-0.4**
• BETZEL, Bruno	Christian Frederick Albert John Henry David Betzel b: 12/6/1894, Chattanooga, TN d: 2/7/1965, West Hollywood, FL BR/TR, 5'9", 158 lbs. Deb: 9/3/1914 Career OF: 14-10-28																							
1914 StL-N	7	9	2	0	0	0	0	0	1	1	0	....	.000	.100	.000	.100	-70	-2	0	.00	0	/2-4,3-1	0	-0.2
1915 StL-N	117	367	42	92	12	4	0	27	18	48	10	13	.251	.291	.305	.596	80	-13	33	2.89	3	*3-105/2-3,S-2	7	-0.8
1916 StL-N	142	510	49	119	15	11	1	37	39	77	22	16	.233	.288	.312	.600	84	-12	47	2.95	11	*2-113,3-33/0-7(1-2-4)	12	0.1
1917 StL-N	106	328	24	71	4	3	1	17	20	47	9	....	.216	.266	.256	.522	62	-15	24	2.33	6	2-75,0-23(12-1-9)/3-4	5	-1.0
1918 StL-N	76	230	18	51	6	7	0	13	12	16	8	....	.222	.260	.309	.569	76	-7	20	2.74	-6	3-34,0-21(1-7-15),2-10	3	-1.4
Total 5	**448**	**1444**	**135**	**333**	**37**	**25**	**2**	**94**	**90**	**189**	**49**	**29**	**.231**	**.278**	**.295**	**.573**	**76**	**-49**	**124**	**2.74**	**14**	**2-205,3-177/0-51,S-2**	**27**	**-3.2**
• BEVACQUA, Kurt	Kurt Anthony Bevacqua b: 1/23/1947, Miami Beach, FL BR/TR, 6', 185 lbs. Deb: 6/22/1971 Career OF: 47-0-25																							
1971 Cle-A	55	137	9	28	3	1	3	13	4	28	0	0	.204	.227	.307	.534	46	-10	9	2.00	-4	2-36/0-5(2-0-3),3-3,S-2	1	-1.3
1972 Cle-A	19	35	2	4	0	0	1	1	3	10	0	0	.114	.184	.200	.384	14	-4	1	1.00	1	0-11(8-0-3)/3-1	0	-0.3
1973 KC-A	99	276	39	71	8	3	2	40	25	42	2	3	.257	.321	.330	.651	78	-8	29	3.50	-6	3-40,2-16,D-16,0-10(5-0-5)/1	5	-1.5
1974 Pit-N	18	35	1	4	1	0	0	0	2	10	0	0	.114	.162	.143	.305	-15	-5	0	.34	-1	/3-8,0-1	0	-0.6
KC-A	39	90	10	19	0	0	0	3	9	20	1	1	.211	.290	.211	.501	43	-6	6	1.99	-2	1-14,3-13/2-7,D-3,S-2	0	-1.0
1975 Mil-A	104	258	30	59	14	0	2	24	26	45	3	4	.229	.302	.306	.608	72	-10	24	2.95	-7	3-60,2-32/S-5,1-3,D-1	4	-1.5
1976 Mil-A	12	7	3	1	0	0	0	0	0	0	0	0	.143	.143	.143	.286	-17	-1	0	.64	0	/D-3,2-2	0	-0.1

YEAR TM-L	G	AB	R	H	2B	3B	HR	RBI	BB	SO	SB	CS	AVG	OBP	SLG	OPS	OPS+	BR/A	RC	RC/G	FR	G/POS	WS	TPW
1977 Tex-A	39	96	13	32	7	2	5	28	6	13	0	1	.333	.373	.604	.977	159	7	18	6.65	0	O-14(6-0-8),3-11/1-5,2-5,D	4	0.7
1978 Tex-A	90	248	21	55	12	0	6	30	18	31	1	2	.222	.274	.343	.617	72	-10	22	2.80	-14	3-49,D-16,2-13/1-1	2	-2.5
1979 SD-N	114	297	23	75	12	4	1	34	38	25	2	5	.253	.337	.330	.667	88	-6	31	3.37	0	3-64,2-16/1-8,O-8(8-0-0)	6	-0.6
1980 SD-N	62	71	4	19	6	1	0	12	6	1	1	1	.268	.325	.380	.705	102	-0	9	4.23	0	3-13/O-4(4-0-0),2-2,1-1	2	-0.1
Pit-N	22	43	1	7	1	0	0	4	6	7	0	0	.163	.280	.186	.466	32	-4	2	1.67	-1	/3-9,1-2	0	-0.5
Yr.	84	114	5	26	7	1	0	16	12	8	1	1	.228	.307	.307	.614	75	-4	11	3.20	-1	3-22/O-4(4-0-0),1-3,2-2	2	-0.6
1981 Pit-N	29	27	2	7	1	0	1	4	4	6	0	0	.259	.355	.407	.762	112	1	4	4.50	0	/2-4,3-2	1	0.0
1982 SD-N	64	123	15	31	9	0	0	24	17	22	2	0	.252	.343	.325	.668	93	-0	14	3.69	0	1-30/O-3(2-0-1),3-1	3	-0.2
1983 SD-N	74	156	17	38	7	0	2	24	18	33	0	3	.244	.322	.327	.649	83	-5	16	3.42	2	1-27,3-12,O-12(9-0-3)	3	-0.5
1984*SD-N	59	80	7	16	3	0	1	9	14	19	0	0	.200	.326	.275	.601	71	-3	7	2.60	1	1-20,3-10/O-3(1-0-2)	1	-0.2
1985 SD-N	71	138	17	33	6	0	3	25	25	17	0	0	.239	.356	.348	.704	99	1	18	4.39	1	3-33/1-9,O-1	4	0.1
Total 15	**970**	**2117**	**214**	**499**	**90**	**11**	**27**	**275**	**221**	**329**	**12**	**20**	**.236**	**.309**	**.327**	**.636**	**78**	**-64**	**210**	**3.21**	**-29**	**3-329,2-133,1-129/O-72,D-42,S**	**36**	**-10.2**

• BEVAN, Hal Harold Joseph Bevan b: 11/15/1930, New Orleans, LA d: 10/5/1968, New Orleans, LA BR/TR, 6'2", 198 lbs. Deb: 4/24/1952

YEAR TM-L	G	AB	R	H	2B	3B	HR	RBI	BB	SO	SB	CS	AVG	OBP	SLG	OPS	OPS+	BR/A	RC	RC/G	FR	G/POS	WS	TPW
1952 Bos-A	1	1	0	0	0	0	0	0	0	0	0	0	.000	.000	.000	.000	-93	-0	0	.00	0	/3-1	0	-0.1
Phi-A	8	17	1	6	0	0	0	4	0	1	2	0	.353	.353	.353	.706	91	0	2	4.76	0	/3-6	1	0.0
Yr.	9	18	1	6	0	0	0	4	0	1	2	0	.333	.333	.333	.667	81	-0	2	4.39	0	/3-7	1	0.0
1955 KC-A	3	3	0	0	0	0	0	0	0	0	0	0	.000	.000	.000	.000	-99	-1	0	.00	0	/3-1	0	-0.1
1961 Cin-N	3	3	1	1	0	0	1	1	0	2	0	0	.333	.333	1.333	1.667	311	1	1	18.00	0	....	0	0.1
Total 3	**15**	**24**	**2**	**7**	**0**	**0**	**1**	**5**	**0**	**3**	**2**	**0**	**.292**	**.292**	**.417**	**.708**	**87**	**-0**	**3**	**5.17**	**-1**	**/3-8**	**1**	**-0.1**

• BEVILLE, Monte Henry Monte Beville b: 2/24/1875, Dublin, IN d: 1/24/1955, Grand Rapids, MI BL/TR, 5'11", 180 lbs. Deb: 4/24/1903 U

YEAR TM-L	G	AB	R	H	2B	3B	HR	RBI	BB	SO	SB	CS	AVG	OBP	SLG	OPS	OPS+	BR/A	RC	RC/G	FR	G/POS	WS	TPW
1903 NY-A	82	258	23	50	14	1	0	29	16	....	4	....	.194	.252	.256	.508	49	-16	19	2.32	-7	C-75/1-3	3	-1.7
1904 NY-A	9	22	2	6	2	0	0	2	2	....	0	....	.273	.333	.364	.697	115	0	3	4.53	-1	/1-4,C-3	1	-0.1
Det-A	54	174	14	36	5	1	0	13	8	....	2	....	.207	.250	.247	.497	59	-8	12	2.26	-4	C-30,1-24	2	-1.1
Yr.	63	196	16	42	7	1	0	15	10	....	2	....	.214	.260	.260	.520	65	-8	15	2.49	-6	C-33,1-28	3	-1.2
Total 2	**145**	**454**	**39**	**92**	**21**	**2**	**0**	**44**	**26**	**....**	**6**	**....**	**.203**	**.255**	**.258**	**.513**	**56**	**-23**	**34**	**2.39**	**-13**	**C-108/1-31**	**6**	**-2.9**

• BIANCALANA, Buddy Roland Americo Biancalana b: 2/2/1960, Greenbrae, CA BB/TR, 5'11", 160 lbs. Deb: 9/12/1982

YEAR TM-L	G	AB	R	H	2B	3B	HR	RBI	BB	SO	SB	CS	AVG	OBP	SLG	OPS	OPS+	BR/A	RC	RC/G	FR	G/POS	WS	TPW
1982 KC-A	3	2	0	1	0	1	0	0	1	0	0	0	.500	.667	1.500	2.167	474	1	1	14.67	1	/S-3	0	0.2
1983 KC-A	6	15	2	3	0	0	0	0	0	7	1	0	.200	.200	.200	.400	10	-2	1	1.58	0	/S-6	0	-0.1
1984*KC-A	66	134	18	26	6	1	2	9	6	44	1	2	.194	.229	.299	.527	44	-11	9	1.99	2	S-33,2-29/D-1	2	-0.6
1985*KC-A	81	138	21	26	5	1	1	6	17	34	1	4	.188	.277	.261	.538	48	-11	10	2.29	-4	S-74/2-4,D-2	3	-1.0
1986 KC-A	100	190	24	46	4	4	2	8	15	50	5	1	.242	.298	.337	.634	71	-7	20	3.52	-9	S-89,2-12	4	-0.8
1987 KC-A	37	47	4	10	1	0	1	7	1	10	0	0	.213	.229	.298	.527	37	-4	3	2.09	-1	S-22,2-12/D-1	1	-0.4
Hou-N	18	24	1	1	0	0	0	0	1	12	0	0	.042	.080	.042	.122	-69	-6	0	.12	-2	S-16/2-3	0	-0.7
Total 6	**311**	**550**	**70**	**113**	**16**	**7**	**6**	**30**	**41**	**157**	**8**	**7**	**.205**	**.261**	**.293**	**.553**	**51**	**-40**	**44**	**2.52**	**-14**	**S-243/2-60,D-4**	**10**	**-3.4**

• BIANCO, Tommy Thomas Anthony Bianco b: 12/16/1952, Rockville Centre, NY BB/TR, 5'11", 190 lbs. Deb: 5/28/1975

YEAR TM-L	G	AB	R	H	2B	3B	HR	RBI	BB	SO	SB	CS	AVG	OBP	SLG	OPS	OPS+	BR/A	RC	RC/G	FR	G/POS	WS	TPW
1975 Mil-A	18	34	6	6	1	0	0	0	3	7	0	0	.176	.263	.206	.469	34	-3	2	1.77	-1	/3-7,1-5,D-2	0	-0.4

• BIASETTI, Hank Henry Arcado Biasetti b: 1/14/1922, Beano, Italy d: 4/20/1996, Dearborn, MI BL/TL, 5'11", 175 lbs. Deb: 4/23/1949

YEAR TM-L	G	AB	R	H	2B	3B	HR	RBI	BB	SO	SB	CS	AVG	OBP	SLG	OPS	OPS+	BR/A	RC	RC/G	FR	G/POS	WS	TPW
1949 Phi-A	21	24	6	2	2	0	0	2	8	5	0	0	.083	.313	.167	.479	30	-2	2	2.38	-1	/1-8	0	-0.3

• BICHETTE, Dante Alphonse Dante Bichette b: 11/18/1963, West Palm Beach, FL BR/TR, 6'3", 225 lbs. Deb: 9/5/1988 Career OF: 649-56-907

YEAR TM-L	G	AB	R	H	2B	3B	HR	RBI	BB	SO	SB	CS	AVG	OBP	SLG	OPS	OPS+	BR/A	RC	RC/G	FR	G/POS	WS	TPW
1988 Cal-A	21	46	1	12	2	0	0	8	0	7	0	0	.261	.261	.304	.565	59	-3	4	2.74	1	O-21(3-17-5)	1	-0.2
1989 Cal-A	48	138	13	29	7	0	3	15	6	24	3	0	.210	.243	.326	.569	60	-7	11	2.55	6	O-40(12-6-23)/D-1	2	-0.3
1990 Cal-A	109	349	40	89	15	1	15	53	16	79	5	2	.255	.293	.433	.726	103	-0	42	4.12	2	*O-105(51-16-53)	7	-0.2
1991 Mil-A	134	445	53	106	18	3	15	59	22	107	14	8	.238	.276	.393	.669	85	-12	45	3.35	3	*O-127(1-7-120)/3-1	7	-1.2
1992 Mil-A	112	387	37	111	27	2	5	41	16	74	18	7	.287	.320	.406	.726	104	1	46	4.16	-3	*O-101(0-1-101)/D-4	8	-0.4
1993 Col-N	141	538	93	167	43	5	21	89	28	99	14	8	.310	.353	.526	.879	113	8	98	6.68	5	*O-137(0-9-134)	19	0.6
1994 Col-N★	116	484	74	147	33	2	27	95	19	70	21	8	.304	.335	.548	.883	107	4	80	5.96	-3	*O-116(0-0-116)	13	-0.5
1995*Col-N★	139	579	102	**197**	38	2	**40**	**128**	22	96	13	9	.340	.369	**.620**	.989	120	15	121	7.91	-5	*O-136(120-0-35)	23	0.3
1996 Col-N★	159	633	114	198	39	3	31	141	45	105	31	12	.313	.364	.531	.895	107	7	117	6.63	-8	*O-156(19-0-138)	20	-0.9
1997 Col-N	151	561	81	173	31	2	26	118	30	90	6	5	.308	.347	.510	.857	98	-3	94	6.16	-5	*O-139(128-0-16)/D-5	15	-1.4
1998 Col-N★	161	662	97	**219**	48	2	22	122	28	76	14	4	.331	.359	.509	.868	103	3	113	6.44	7	*O-156(134-0-29)/D-1	17	0.3
1999 Col-N	151	593	104	177	38	2	34	133	54	84	6	6	.298	.359	.541	.900	97	-5	110	6.67	2	*O-144(144-0-0)/D-2	15	-0.8
2000 Cin-N	125	461	67	136	27	2	16	76	41	69	5	2	.295	.358	.466	.824	104	2	73	5.57	1	*O-121(0-0-121)	12	-0.3
Bos-A	30	114	13	33	5	0	7	14	8	22	0	0	.289	.336	.518	.854	109	1	19	6.12	0	D-30	2	-0.1
2001 Bos-A	107	391	45	112	30	1	12	49	20	76	2	2	.286	.326	.460	.786	103	-0	54	4.96	-2	O-53(37-0-16),D-45	7	-0.7
Total 14	**1704**	**6381**	**934**	**1906**	**401**	**27**	**274**	**1141**	**355**	**1078**	**152**	**73**	**.299**	**.340**	**.499**	**.839**	**103**	**12**	**1027**	**5.77**	**1**	***O-1552/D-88,3-1**	**168**	**-5.8**

• BIECHER, Ed Edward "Scrap Iron" Biecher b: 5/1876, IN d: 7/15/1939, St. Louis, MO Deb: 9/26/1897 Career OF: 3-8-0

YEAR TM-L	G	AB	R	H	2B	3B	HR	RBI	BB	SO	SB	CS	AVG	OBP	SLG	OPS	OPS+	BR/A	RC	RC/G	FR	G/POS	WS	TPW
1897 StL-N	3	12	1	4	0	0	0	1	0	....	1	....	.333	.333	.333	.667	78	-0	2	5.66	0	/O-3(3-0-0)	0	-0.1
1898 Cle-N	8	25	1	5	2	0	0	0	0	....	0	....	.200	.200	.280	.480	38	-2	2	1.92	0	/O-8(0-8-0)	0	-0.3
Total 2	**11**	**37**	**2**	**9**	**2**	**0**	**0**	**1**	**0**	**....**	**1**	**....**	**.243**	**.243**	**.297**	**.541**	**50**	**-3**	**3**	**2.95**	**0**	**/O-11**	**0**	**-0.3**

• BIELASKI, Oscar Oscar Bielaski b: 3/21/1847, Washington, DC d: 11/8/1911, Washington, DC BR/TR, 5'10.5", 170 lbs. Deb: 4/24/1872 U NA OF: 6-1-137

YEAR TM-L	G	AB	R	H	2B	3B	HR	RBI	BB	SO	SB	CS	AVG	OBP	SLG	OPS	OPS+	BR/A	RC	RC/G	FR	G/POS	WS	TPW
1872 Nat-n	10	46	13	9	0	0	0	3	0	0	0	0	.196	.196	.196	.391	18	-5	2	1.51	-1	O-10(0-0-10)	....	-0.4
1873 Was-n	38	173	35	49	3	2	0	23	4	5	0	1	.283	.299	.324	.623	88	-2	17	4.19	2	*O-38(2-0-36)	....	0.2
1874 Bal-n	43	187	24	45	0	0	0	8	2	4	3	1	.241	.249	.241	.489	58	-8	12	2.57	6	*O-43(0-1-43)/1-1	....	0.0
1875 Chi-n	51	201	21	48	1	0	0	11	2	5	5	5	.239	.246	.244	.490	70	-7	14	2.55	1	*O-51(4-0-48)	....	-0.3
1876 Chi-N	32	141	24	29	3	0	0	10	2	3	....	....	.206	.220	.230	.450	45	-9	7	1.84	-3	O-32(0-0-32)	0	-1.0
Total 4 n	**142**	**607**	**93**	**151**	**4**	**2**	**0**	**45**	**8**	**14**	**8**	**7**	**.249**	**.259**	**.262**	**.520**	**68**	**-23**	**45**	**2.91**	**7**	**O-142/1-1**	**....**	**-0.5**

• BIERBAUER, Lou Louis W. Bierbauer b: 9/23/1865, Erie, PA d: 1/31/1926, Erie, PA BL/TR, 5'8", 140 lbs. Deb: 4/17/1886

YEAR TM-L	G	AB	R	H	2B	3B	HR	RBI	BB	SO	SB	CS	AVG	OBP	SLG	OPS	OPS+	BR/A	RC	RC/G	FR	G/POS	WS	TPW
1886 Phi-a	137	522	56	118	17	5	2	47	21	....	19	....	.226	.256	.289	.545	70	-20	45	2.98	-6	*2-133/C-4,P-2,S-2	10	-1.8
1887 Phi-a	126	543	74	157	19	7	1	82	13	....	40	....	.289	.289	.340	.629	75	-20	65	4.56	5	*2-126/P-1	10	-0.8
1888 Phi-a	134	535	83	143	20	9	0	80	25	....	34	....	.267	.301	.338	.640	105	2	66	4.57	25	*2-121,3-13/P-1	19	3.0
1889 Phi-a	130	549	80	167	27	7	7	105	29	30	17	....	.304	.344	.417	.761	117	10	87	6.01	35	*2-130/C-1	18	4.2
1890 Bro-P	133	589	128	180	31	11	7	99	40	15	16	....	.306	.350	.431	.781	102	-3	97	6.39	24	*2-133	20	2.0
1891 Pit-N	121	500	60	103	13	6	1	47	28	19	12	....	.206	.252	.262	.514	51	-32	37	2.52	3	*2-121	4	-2.2
1892 Pit-N	152	649	81	153	20	9	8	65	25	29	11	....	.236	.264	.331	.595	79	-21	61	3.33	23	*2-152	17	0.9
1893 Pit-N	128	528	84	150	19	11	4	94	36	12	11	....	.284	.335	.384	.719	93	-8	73	5.14	14	*2-128	13	1.0
1894 Pit-N	131	528	87	160	20	13	3	109	26	10	19	....	.303	.337	.407	.744	80	-20	81	5.71	4	*2-130	12	-0.7
1895 Pit-N	118	470	54	122	13	11	1	69	19	8	18	....	.260	.291	.340	.632	64	-26	54	4.01	9	*2-117	8	-0.9
1896 Pit-N	59	258	33	74	10	6	0	39	5	7	7	....	.287	.300	.372	.672	80	-9	32	4.55	11	2-59	6	0.5
1897 StL-N	12	46	1	10	0	0	0	1	0	....	2	....	.217	.217	.217	.435	15	-6	3	2.02	-2	2-12	0	-0.6
1898 StL-N	4	9	0	0	0	0	0	0	1	....	0	....	.000	.100	.000	.100	-69	-2	0	.00	-1	/2-2,3-1,S-1	0	-0.2
Total 13	**1385**	**5726**	**821**	**1537**	**209**	**95**	**34**	**837**	**268**	**130**	**206**	**....**	**.268**	**.301**	**.354**	**.656**	**83**	**-153**	**701**	**4.45**	**144**	***2-1364/3-14,C-5,P-4,S-3**	**137**	**4.1**

• BIERMAN, Charlie Charles S. Bierman b: 1845, Hoboken, NJ d: 8/4/1879, Hoboken, NJ, 6', 180 lbs. Deb: 6/21/1871

YEAR TM-L	G	AB	R	H	2B	3B	HR	RBI	BB	SO	SB	CS	AVG	OBP	SLG	OPS	OPS+	BR/A	RC	RC/G	FR	G/POS	WS	TPW
1871 Kek-n	1	2	0	0	0	0	0	0	1	0	0	0	.000	.333	.000	.333	6	-0	0	.00	0	/1-1	....	0.0

• BIESER, Steve Steven Ray Bieser b: 8/4/1967, Perryville, MO BL/TR, 5'10", 170 lbs. Deb: 4/1/1997 Career OF: 10-13-1

YEAR TM-L	G	AB	R	H	2B	3B	HR	RBI	BB	SO	SB	CS	AVG	OBP	SLG	OPS	OPS+	BR/A	RC	RC/G	FR	G/POS	WS	TPW
1997 NY-N	47	69	16	17	3	0	0	4	7	20	2	3	.246	.350	.290	.640	72	-3	7	3.60	0	O-21(9-13-1)/C-2	1	-0.3
1998 Pit-N	13	11	2	3	1	0	0	1	2	2	0	0	.273	.385	.364	.748	97	0	1	4.17	0	/O-1	0	0.0
Total 2	**60**	**80**	**18**	**20**	**4**	**0**	**0**	**5**	**9**	**22**	**2**	**3**	**.250**	**.355**	**.300**	**.655**	**76**	**-3**	**9**	**3.68**	**0**	**/O-22,C-2**	**1**	**-0.3**

• BIGBEE, Carson Carson Lee "Skeeter" Bigbee b: 3/31/1895, Waterloo, OR d: 10/17/1964, Portland, OR BL/TR, 5'9", 157 lbs. Deb: 8/25/1916 Career OF: 892-109-32

YEAR TM-L	G	AB	R	H	2B	3B	HR	RBI	BB	SO	SB	CS	AVG	OBP	SLG	OPS	OPS+	BR/A	RC	RC/G	FR	G/POS	WS	TPW
1916 Pit-N	43	164	17	41	3	6	0	3	7	14	8	....	.250	.285	.341	.626	91	-2	19	3.77	-2	2-23,O-19(19-0-0)/3-1	3	-0.6

YEAR TM-L	G	AB	R	H	2B	3B	HR	RBI	BB	SO	SB	CS	AVG	OBP	SLG	OPS	OPS+	BR/A	RC	RC/G	FR	G/POS	WS	TPW
1917 Pit-N	133	469	46	112	11	6	0	21	37	16	19	....	.239	.301	.288	.589	78	-11	46	3.16	-7	*O-107(85-5-17),2-16/S-2	7	-2.5
1918 Pit-N	92	310	47	79	11	3	1	19	42	10	19	....	.255	.344	.319	.663	99	1	40	4.23	0	O-92(87-0-5)	10	-0.3
1919 Pit-N	125	478	61	132	11	4	2	27	37	26	31	....	.276	.332	.328	.660	95	-2	59	4.31	6	*O-124(50-75-0)	18	-0.3
1920 Pit-N	137	550	78	154	19	15	4	32	45	28	31	15	.280	.341	.391	.732	107	7	74	4.72	-1	*O-133(128-6-0)	18	0.1
1921 Pit-N	147	632	100	204	23	17	3	42	41	19	21	20	.323	.364	.427	.791	106	4	94	5.41	8	*O-146(133-13-0)	21	0.1
1922 Pit-N	150	614	113	215	29	15	5	99	56	13	24	15	.350	.405	.471	.876	124	23	116	7.11	7	*O-150(146-4-0)	23	1.8
1923 Pit-N	123	499	79	149	18	7	0	54	43	15	10	9	.299	.355	.363	.718	88	-8	65	4.63	6	*O-122(122-0-0)	13	-1.1
1924 Pit-N	89	282	42	74	4	1	0	15	26	12	15	7	.262	.331	.284	.615	65	-12	29	3.41	2	O-75(75-0-0)	5	-1.5
1925*Pit-N	66	126	31	30	7	0	0	8	7	8	2	2	.238	.278	.294	.572	43	-11	10	2.67	-1	O-42(30-2-10)	1	-1.3
1926 Pit-N	42	68	15	15	3	1	2	4	3	0	2	....	.221	.264	.382	.646	68	-3	7	3.26	0	O-21(17-4-0)	1	-0.4
Total 11	1147	4192	629	1205	139	75	17	324	344	161	182	68	.287	.345	.369	.713	96	-14	558	4.65	18	*O-1031/2-39,S-2,3-1	120	-6.2

• BIGBEE, Lyle Lyle Randolph "Al" Bigbee b: 8/22/1893, Sweet Home, OR d: 8/5/1942, Portland, OR BL/TR, 6', 180 lbs. Deb: 4/15/1920 ♦

YEAR TM-L	G	AB	R	H	2B	3B	HR	RBI	BB	SO	SB	CS	AVG	OBP	SLG	OPS	OPS+	BR/A	RC	RC/G	FR	G/POS	WS	TPW
1920 Phi-A	38	75	5	14	2	0	1	8	9	12	1	0	.187	.282	.253	.536	42	-4	6	2.59	-2	O-13(11-0-1),P-12	0	-2.5
1921 Pit-N	5	2	0	0	0	0	0	0	0	1	0	0	.000	.000	.000	.000	-98	-0	0	.00	0	/P-5	1	0.2
Total 2	43	77	5	14	2	0	1	8	9	13	1	0	.182	.276	.247	.523	39	-4	6	2.51	-2	/P-17,O-13	1	-2.3

• BIGBIE, Larry Larry Robert Bigbie b: 11/4/1977, Hobart, IN BL/TR, 6'4", 190 lbs. Deb: 6/23/2001 Career OF: 87-22-28

YEAR TM-L	G	AB	R	H	2B	3B	HR	RBI	BB	SO	SB	CS	AVG	OBP	SLG	OPS	OPS+	BR/A	RC	RC/G	FR	G/POS	WS	TPW
2001 Bal-A	47	131	15	30	6	0	2	11	17	42	4	1	.229	.318	.321	.638	73	-4	14	3.70	-2	O-40(5-19-17)	2	-0.7
2002 Bal-A	16	34	1	6	1	0	0	3	1	11	1	0	.176	.200	.206	.406	9	-4	1	1.25	0	O-12(6-1-6)	0	-0.4
2003 Bal-A	83	287	43	87	15	1	9	31	29	60	7	1	.303	.367	.456	.824	120	9	51	6.64	1	O-80(76-2-5)	9	0.7
Total 3	146	452	59	123	22	1	11	45	47	113	12	2	.272	.341	.398	.739	98	1	66	5.26	-1	O-132	11	-0.4

• BIGELOW, Elliot Elliott Allardice "Babe,Gilly" Bigelow b: 10/13/1897, Tarpon Springs, FL d: 8/10/1933, Tampa, FL BL/TL, 5'11", 185 lbs. Deb: 4/18/1929

YEAR TM-L	G	AB	R	H	2B	3B	HR	RBI	BB	SO	SB	CS	AVG	OBP	SLG	OPS	OPS+	BR/A	RC	RC/G	FR	G/POS	WS	TPW
1929 Bos-A	100	211	23	60	16	0	1	26	23	18	1	4	.284	.357	.374	.732	91	-4	28	4.68	1	O-59(2-2-55)	4	-0.5

• BIGGIO, Craig Craig Alan Biggio b: 12/14/1965, Smithtown, NY BR/TR, 5'11", 180 lbs. Deb: 6/26/1988 Career OF: 26-189-2

YEAR TM-L	G	AB	R	H	2B	3B	HR	RBI	BB	SO	SB	CS	AVG	OBP	SLG	OPS	OPS+	BR/A	RC	RC/G	FR	G/POS	WS	TPW
1988 Hou-N	50	123	14	26	6	1	3	5	7	29	6	1	.211	.254	.350	.603	74	-4	11	3.06	1	C-50	1	0.0
1989 Hou-N	134	443	64	114	21	2	13	60	49	64	21	3	.257	.339	.402	.741	115	12	65	4.98	-6	*C-125/O-5(1-4-0)	18	1.6
1990 Hou-N	150	555	53	153	24	2	4	42	53	79	25	11	.276	.342	.348	.690	93	-4	68	4.22	1	*C-113,O-50(17-34-2)	18	0.3
1991 Hou-N★	149	546	79	161	23	4	4	46	53	71	19	6	.295	.359	.374	.733	113	12	79	5.33	1	*C-139/2-3,O-2(1-1-0)	20	2.2
1992 Hou-N★	162	613	96	170	32	3	6	39	94	95	38	15	.277	.380	.369	.748	118	21	95	5.47	-7	*2-161	32	1.9
1993 Hou-N	155	610	98	175	41	5	21	64	77	93	15	17	.287	.376	.474	.850	130	23	107	6.15	5	*2-155	26	3.5
1994 Hou-N★	114	437	88	139	**44**	5	6	56	62	58	**39**	4	.318	.412	.483	.895	140	35	98	8.54	-5	*2-113	26	3.5
1995 Hou-N★	141	553	**123**	167	30	2	22	77	80	85	33	8	.302	.411	.483	.894	145	43	121	7.83	-15	*2-141	29	3.4
1996 Hou-N★	162	605	113	174	24	4	15	75	75	72	25	7	.288	.390	.415	.805	122	26	107	6.23	-8	*2-162	32	2.5
1997*Hou-N★	162	619	**146**	191	37	8	22	81	84	107	47	10	.309	.419	.501	.920	145	52	148	8.95	13	*2-160/D-1	38	7.2
1998*Hou-N★	160	646	123	210	**51**	2	20	88	64	113	50	8	.325	.405	.503	.908	141	48	142	8.33	-13	*2-159/D-1	35	4.2
1999*Hou-N	160	639	123	188	**56**	0	16	73	88	107	28	14	.294	.389	.457	.846	115	17	120	6.74	8	*2-155/O-6(6-0-0),D-2	31	3.0
2000 Hou-N	101	377	67	101	13	5	8	35	61	73	12	2	.268	.392	.393	.785	94	1	64	5.76	4	*2-100	11	1.0
2001*Hou-N	155	617	118	180	35	3	20	70	66	100	7	4	.292	.385	.455	.841	110	12	112	6.63	-17	*2-154/D-1	25	0.3
2002 Hou-N	145	577	96	146	36	3	15	58	50	111	16	2	.253	.331	.404	.735	88	-7	79	4.65	-10	*2-142/O-1	15	-1.0
2003 Hou-N	153	628	102	166	44	2	15	62	57	116	8	4	.264	.351	.412	.764	94	-4	97	5.50	-2	*O-150(0-150-0)	20	-0.5
Total 16	2253	8588	1503	2461	517	51	210	931	1020	1373	389	116	.287	.378	.432	.810	118	283	1513	6.29	-50	*2-1605,C-427,O-214/D-5	377	33.0

• BIGLER, Pete Ivan Edward Bigler b: 12/13/1892, Bradford, OH d: 4/1/1975, Coldwater, MI BR/TR, 5'9", 150 lbs. Deb: 5/6/1917

YEAR TM-L	G	AB	R	H	2B	3B	HR	RBI	BB	SO	SB	CS	AVG	OBP	SLG	OPS	OPS+	BR/A	RC	RC/G	FR	G/POS	WS	TPW
1917 StL-A	1	0	0	0	0	0	0	0	0	0	0	....	....	....	....	....	-104	0	0	....	0	....	0	0.0

• BIGNELL, George George William Bignell b: 7/18/1858, Taunton, MA d: 1/16/1925, Providence, RI, 5'9", 160 lbs. Deb: 9/27/1884

YEAR TM-L	G	AB	R	H	2B	3B	HR	RBI	BB	SO	SB	CS	AVG	OBP	SLG	OPS	OPS+	BR/A	RC	RC/G	FR	G/POS	WS	TPW
1884 Mil-U	4	9	4	2	0	0	0	....	1	....	....	....	.222	.300	.222	.522	79	-0	1	2.46	1	/C-4	0	0.1

• BIITTNER, Larry Lawrence David Biittner b: 7/27/1945, Pocahontas, IA BL/TL, 6'2", 205 lbs. Deb: 7/17/1970 Career OF: 268-15-219

YEAR TM-L	G	AB	R	H	2B	3B	HR	RBI	BB	SO	SB	CS	AVG	OBP	SLG	OPS	OPS+	BR/A	RC	RC/G	FR	G/POS	WS	TPW
1970 Was-A	2	2	0	0	0	0	0	0	0	0	0	0	.000	.000	.000	.000	-105	-1	0	.00	0	....	0	-0.1
1971 Was-A	66	171	12	44	4	1	0	16	16	20	1	0	.257	.324	.292	.617	80	-4	16	3.12	1	O-41(7-0-38)/1-3	3	-0.6
1972 Tex-A	137	382	34	99	18	1	3	31	29	37	1	3	.259	.315	.335	.650	98	-3	40	3.56	3	1-65,O-65(28-8-32)	10	-0.6
1973 Tex-A	83	258	19	65	8	2	1	12	20	21	1	0	.252	.308	.310	.618	78	-7	24	3.21	3	O-57(19-2-38),1-20/D-3	3	-0.8
1974 Mon-N	18	26	2	7	1	0	0	3	0	2	0	0	.269	.269	.308	.577	58	-2	2	2.98	1	/O-4(4-0-0)	0	-0.1
1975 Mon-N	121	346	34	109	13	5	3	28	34	33	2	1	.315	.376	.408	.784	112	6	51	5.43	1	O-93(35-4-55)	11	0.3
1976 Mon-N	11	32	2	6	1	0	0	1	0	3	0	0	.188	.188	.219	.406	14	-4	1	.84	1	/O-7(3-0-4)	0	-0.3
Chi-N	78	192	21	47	13	1	0	17	10	6	0	2	.245	.286	.323	.609	66	-10	17	2.91	6	1-33,O-24(22-0-3)	2	-0.7
Yr.	89	224	23	53	14	1	0	18	10	9	0	2	.237	.272	.308	.580	59	-13	17	2.59	7	1-33,O-31(25-0-7)	2	-1.0
1977 Chi-N	138	493	74	147	28	1	12	62	35	36	2	1	.298	.346	.432	.778	96	-2	70	5.12	4	1-80,O-52(52-0-0)/P-1	11	-1.0
1978 Chi-N	120	343	32	88	15	1	4	50	23	37	0	1	.257	.305	.341	.646	72	-14	35	3.45	5	1-62,O-29(29-0-0)	5	-1.4
1979 Chi-N	111	272	35	79	13	3	3	50	21	23	1	1	.290	.341	.393	.735	91	-3	34	4.50	-1	O-44(23-1-21),1-32	5	-0.7
1980 Chi-N	127	273	21	68	12	2	1	34	18	33	1	3	.249	.300	.319	.619	68	-13	25	3.09	3	1-41,O-38(20-0-17)	3	-1.4
1981 Cin-N	42	61	1	13	4	0	0	8	4	4	0	0	.213	.262	.279	.540	52	-4	4	2.02	1	/1-8,O-3(0-0-3)	0	-0.3
1982 Cin-N	97	184	18	57	9	2	2	24	17	16	1	0	.310	.374	.413	.787	118	5	27	5.15	0	O-31(26-0-6),1-15	5	0.3
1983 Tex-A	66	116	5	32	5	1	0	18	9	16	0	0	.276	.328	.336	.664	85	-2	13	4.16	1	1-22/D-9,O-2(0-0-2)	2	-0.2
Total 14	1217	3151	310	861	144	20	29	354	236	287	10	12	.273	.326	.359	.685	87	-55	358	3.96	31	O-490,1-381/D-12,P-1	60	-7.5

• BILARDELLO, Dann Dann James Bilardello b: 5/26/1959, Santa Cruz, CA BR/TR, 6', 190 lbs. Deb: 4/11/1983

YEAR TM-L	G	AB	R	H	2B	3B	HR	RBI	BB	SO	SB	CS	AVG	OBP	SLG	OPS	OPS+	BR/A	RC	RC/G	FR	G/POS	WS	TPW
1983 Cin-N	109	298	27	71	18	0	9	38	15	49	2	1	.238	.277	.389	.666	80	-10	30	3.30	7	*C-105	9	0.1
1984 Cin-N	68	182	16	38	7	0	2	10	19	34	0	1	.209	.287	.280	.567	57	-11	14	2.48	3	C-68	3	-0.5
1985 Cin-N	42	102	6	17	0	0	1	9	4	15	0	0	.167	.206	.196	.402	12	-12	3	1.01	0	C-42	2	-1.0
1986 Mon-N	79	191	12	37	5	0	4	17	14	32	1	0	.194	.249	.283	.532	47	-14	13	2.15	-1	C-77	2	-1.2
1989 Pit-N	33	80	11	18	6	0	2	8	2	18	1	2	.225	.244	.375	.619	77	-4	6	2.64	-2	C-33	2	-0.4
1990 Pit-N	19	37	1	2	0	0	0	3	4	10	0	0	.054	.146	.054	.200	-44	-7	1	.39	1	C-19	1	-0.6
1991 SD-N	15	26	4	7	2	1	0	5	3	4	0	0	.269	.345	.423	.768	111	0	4	5.77	0	C-13	2	0.2
1992 SD-N	17	33	2	4	1	0	0	1	4	8	0	0	.121	.216	.152	.368	6	-4	1	1.05	1	C-14	1	-0.2
Total 8	382	949	79	194	39	1	18	91	65	170	4	4	.204	.258	.305	.562	54	-61	73	2.43	10	C-371	22	-3.7

• BILKO, Steve Stephen Thomas Bilko b: 11/13/1928, Nanticoke, PA d: 3/7/1978, Wilkes-Barre, PA BR/TR, 6'1", 230 lbs. Deb: 9/22/1949

YEAR TM-L	G	AB	R	H	2B	3B	HR	RBI	BB	SO	SB	CS	AVG	OBP	SLG	OPS	OPS+	BR/A	RC	RC/G	FR	G/POS	WS	TPW
1949 StL-N	6	17	3	5	2	0	0	2	5	6	0	....	.294	.455	.412	.866	128	1	4	8.49	0	/1-5	1	0.1
1950 StL-N	10	33	1	6	1	0	0	2	4	10	0	....	.182	.270	.212	.482	27	-3	2	1.89	0	/1-9	0	-0.3
1951 StL-N	21	72	5	16	4	0	2	12	9	10	0	0	.222	.309	.361	.670	79	-2	9	4.02	0	1-19	1	-0.3
1952 StL-N	20	72	7	19	6	1	1	6	4	15	0	0	.264	.303	.417	.719	97	-1	9	4.19	3	1-20	1	0.2
1953 StL-N	154	570	72	143	23	3	21	84	70	125	0	1	.251	.334	.412	.746	93	-6	79	4.81	4	*1-154	12	-1.0
1954 StL-N	8	14	1	2	0	0	0	1	3	1	0	0	.143	.294	.143	.437	18	-2	0	.95	2	/1-6	0	0.0
Chi-N	47	92	11	22	8	1	4	12	11	24	0	0	.239	.320	.478	.799	104	0	12	4.36	5	1-22	2	0.4
Yr.	55	106	12	24	8	1	4	13	14	25	0	0	.226	.317	.434	.751	91	-1	13	3.83	7	1-28	2	0.4
1958 Cin-N	31	87	12	23	4	2	4	17	10	20	0	0	.264	.340	.494	.834	111	1	13	4.95	-1	1-21	2	-0.1
LA-N	47	101	13	21	1	2	7	18	8	37	0	0	.208	.266	.465	.731	86	-3	11	3.58	0	1-25	2	-0.4
Yr.	78	188	25	44	5	4	11	35	18	57	0	0	.234	.301	.479	.780	98	-1	24	4.21	-1	1-46	4	-0.5
1960 Det-A	78	222	20	46	11	2	9	25	27	31	0	1	.207	.293	.396	.690	80	-7	25	3.70	1	1-62	3	-1.0
1961 LA-A	114	294	49	82	16	1	20	59	58	81	1	1	.279	.398	.544	.942	134	15	65	7.80	3	1-86/O-3(0-0-3)	10	1.4
1962 LA-A	64	164	26	47	9	1	8	38	25	35	1	1	.287	.387	.500	.887	141	10	32	6.65	0	1-50	8	0.7
Total 10	600	1738	220	432	85	13	76	276	234	395	2	4	.249	.339	.444	.782	103	4	262	5.10	17	1-479/O-3	42	-0.3

• BILLINGS, Dick Richard Arlin Billings b: 12/4/1942, Detroit, MI BR/TR, 6'1", 195 lbs. Deb: 9/11/1968 Career OF: 78-1-15

YEAR TM-L	G	AB	R	H	2B	3B	HR	RBI	BB	SO	SB	CS	AVG	OBP	SLG	OPS	OPS+	BR/A	RC	RC/G	FR	G/POS	WS	TPW
1968 Was-A	12	33	3	6	1	0	1	3	5	13	0	0	.182	.289	.303	.593	82	-1	3	2.78	0	/O-8(8-0-0),3-4	1	-0.1
1969 Was-A	27	37	3	5	0	0	0	0	6	8	0	1	.135	.256	.135	.391	13	-5	1	.80	1	/O-6(5-1-0),3-1	0	-0.5

YEAR	TM-L	G	AB	R	H	2B	3B	HR	RBI	BB	SO	SB	CS	AVG	OBP	SLG	OPS	OPS+	BR/A	RC	RC/G	FR	G/POS	WS	TPW
1970	Was-A	11	24	3	6	2	0	1	1	2	3	0	0	.250	.308	.458	.766	114	0	3	4.41	0	/C-8	1	0.0
1971	Was-A	116	349	32	86	14	0	6	48	21	54	2	5	.246	.299	.338	.637	85	-9	34	3.34	3	C-62,0-32(22-0-12)/3-2	8	-0.5
1972	Tex-A	133	469	41	119	15	1	5	58	29	77	1	5	.254	.300	.322	.622	89	-9	42	3.03	3	C-92,0-41(39-0-2)/3-5,1-1	12	-0.5
1973	Tex-A	81	280	17	50	11	0	3	32	20	43	1	1	.179	.238	.250	.488	39	-23	15	1.64	-2	C-72/0-4(3-0-1),1-3,D-2	2	-2.3
1974	Tex-A	16	31	2	7	1	0	0	0	4	6	2	0	.226	.314	.258	.572	68	-1	3	3.11	0	C-13/D-1,0-1	1	0.0
	StL-N	1	5	0	1	0	0	0	0	0	1	0	0	.200	.200	.200	.400	12	-1	0	1.35	0	/C-1	0	0.0
1975	StL-N	3	3	0	0	0	0	0	0	0	2	0	0	.000	.000	.000	.000	-97	-1	0	.00	0	....	0	-0.1
Total	8	400	1231	101	280	44	1	16	142	87	207	6	12	.227	.283	.304	.587	73	-48	102	2.70	4	C-248/0-92,3-12,1-4,D-3	25	-4.0

• BILLINGS, Josh John Augustus Billings b: 11/30/1891, Grantville, KS d: 12/30/1981, Santa Monica, CA BR/TR, 5'11", 165 lbs. Deb: 9/9/1913

YEAR	TM-L	G	AB	R	H	2B	3B	HR	RBI	BB	SO	SB	CS	AVG	OBP	SLG	OPS	OPS+	BR/A	RC	RC/G	FR	G/POS	WS	TPW
1913	Cle-A	1	3	0	0	0	0	0	0	0	3	0	....	.000	.000	.000	.000	-97	-1	0	.00	0	/C-1	0	-0.1
1914	Cle-A	11	8	3	2	1	0	0	0	1	1	1	....	.250	.333	.375	.708	109	0	1	5.67	-1	/C-3	0	-0.1
1915	Cle-A	8	21	2	4	1	0	0	0	0	6	1	....	.190	.190	.238	.429	28	-2	1	1.86	0	/C-7,0-1	0	-0.1
1916	Cle-A	22	31	2	5	0	0	0	1	2	11	0	....	.161	.212	.161	.373	12	-3	1	1.24	0	C-12	0	-0.3
1917	Cle-A	66	129	8	23	3	2	0	9	8	21	2	....	.178	.243	.233	.475	42	-9	8	1.85	0	C-48	2	-0.6
1918	Cle-A	2	3	0	1	0	0	0	0	0	0	0	....	.333	.333	.333	.667	92	-0	0	4.00	0	/C-1	0	0.0
1919	StL-A	38	76	9	15	1	1	0	3	1	12	0	....	.197	.218	.237	.455	27	-8	4	1.62	2	C-26/1-1	1	-0.4
1920	StL-A	66	155	19	43	5	2	0	11	11	10	1	0	.277	.353	.335	.688	80	-3	20	4.45	-2	C-40	3	-0.2
1921	StL-A	20	46	2	10	0	0	0	4	0	7	0	0	.217	.217	.217	.435	11	-6	2	1.54	0	C-12	1	-0.5
1922	StL-A	5	7	0	3	1	0	0	1	0	0	0	0	.429	.429	.571	1.000	153	1	2	10.90	0	/C-3	0	0.1
1923	StL-A	4	9	0	0	0	0	0	0	0	2	0	0	.000	.000	.000	.000	-95	-3	0	.00	0	/C-4	0	-0.2
Total	11	243	488	45	106	12	5	0	29	23	73	5	0	.217	.268	.262	.530	47	-34	40	2.60	0	C-157/1-1,0-1	7	-2.5

• BINKS, George George Alvin "Bingo" Binks b: 7/11/1916, Chicago, IL BL/TL, 6', 175 lbs. Deb: 9/23/1944 Career OF: 71-88-100

YEAR	TM-L	G	AB	R	H	2B	3B	HR	RBI	BB	SO	SB	CS	AVG	OBP	SLG	OPS	OPS+	BR/A	RC	RC/G	FR	G/POS	WS	TPW
1944	Was-A	5	12	0	3	0	0	0	0	0	1	0	0	.250	.250	.250	.500	45	-1	1	2.31	-0	/0-3(0-0-3)	0	-0.1
1945	Was-A	145	550	62	153	32	6	6	81	34	52	11	7	.278	.324	.391	.715	117	9	69	4.43	4	*0-128(27-79-26),1-20	20	0.8
1946	Was-A	65	134	13	26	3	0	0	12	6	16	1	0	.194	.229	.216	.445	26	-13	7	1.60	-1	0-28(15-9-5)	1	-1.6
1947	Phi-A	104	333	33	86	19	4	2	34	23	36	8	2	.258	.308	.357	.665	83	-7	38	3.94	1	0-75(25-0-51),1-13	7	-1.0
1948	Phi-A	17	41	2	4	1	0	0	2	2	2	1	0	.098	.140	.122	.261	-30	-8	1	.53	0	0-14(2-0-12)	0	-0.8
	StL-A	15	23	2	5	0	0	0	1	2	1	0	0	.217	.280	.217	.497	32	-2	2	2.34	-1	/0-5(2-0-3),1-4	0	-0.3
	Yr.	32	64	4	9	1	0	0	3	4	3	1	0	.141	.191	.156	.347	-6	-10	2	1.14	0	0-19(4-0-15)/1-4	0	-1.0
Total	5	351	1093	112	277	55	10	8	130	67	108	21	9	.253	.299	.344	.643	87	-22	117	3.67	4	0-253/1-37	28	-3.0

• BIRAS, Steve Stephen Alexander Biras b: 2/26/1922, East St. Louis, IL d: 4/21/1965, St. Louis, MO BR/TR, 5'11", 185 lbs. Deb: 9/15/1944

YEAR	TM-L	G	AB	R	H	2B	3B	HR	RBI	BB	SO	SB	CS	AVG	OBP	SLG	OPS	OPS+	BR/A	RC	RC/G	FR	G/POS	WS	TPW
1944	Cle-A	2	2	0	2	0	0	0	2	0	0	0	0	1.000	1.000	1.000	2.000	491	1	2	∞	-1	/2-1	0	0.0

• BIRCHALL, Jud Adoniram Judson Birchall b: 9/12/1855, Philadelphia, PA d: 12/22/1887, Philadelphia, PA Deb: 5/2/1882 Career OF: 221-0-1

YEAR	TM-L	G	AB	R	H	2B	3B	HR	RBI	BB	SO	SB	CS	AVG	OBP	SLG	OPS	OPS+	BR/A	RC	RC/G	FR	G/POS	WS	TPW
1882	Phi-a	75	338	65	89	12	1	0	27	8	....	....	....	.263	.280	.305	.585	87	-6	30	3.33	2	*0-74(74-0-0)/2-1	10	-0.7
1883	Phi-a	96	448	95	108	10	1	1	24	20	....	....	....	.241	.274	.275	.548	71	-15	34	2.84	5	*0-96(96-0-0)	11	-1.2
1884	Phi-a	54	221	36	57	2	2	0	0	4	....	....	....	.258	.287	.285	.572	82	-5	19	3.11	4	0-52(51-0-1)/3-2	4	-0.2
Total	3	225	1007	196	254	24	4	1	51	32	....	....	....	.252	.279	.287	.566	79	-27	83	3.06	11	0-222/3-2,2-1	25	-2.1

• BIRD, Frank Frank Zepherin "Dodo" Bird b: 3/10/1869, Spencer, MA d: 5/20/1958, Worcester, MA BR/TR, 5'10", 195 lbs. Deb: 4/16/1892

YEAR	TM-L	G	AB	R	H	2B	3B	HR	RBI	BB	SO	SB	CS	AVG	OBP	SLG	OPS	OPS+	BR/A	RC	RC/G	FR	G/POS	WS	TPW
1892	StL-N	17	50	9	10	3	1	1	1	6	11	2	....	.200	.286	.360	.646	100	-0	6	3.95	0	C-17	1	0.1

• BIRD, George George Raymond Bird b: 6/23/1850, Stillman Valley, IL d: 11/9/1940, Rockford, IL BR/TR, 5'9", 150 lbs. Deb: 5/6/1871

YEAR	TM-L	G	AB	R	H	2B	3B	HR	RBI	BB	SO	SB	CS	AVG	OBP	SLG	OPS	OPS+	BR/A	RC	RC/G	FR	G/POS	WS	TPW
1871	Rok-n	25	106	19	28	2	5	0	13	3	2	1	0	.264	.284	.377	.662	92	-1	12	4.83	-4	*0-25(1-25-0)	....	-0.3

• BIRDSALL, Dave David Solomon Birdsall b: 7/16/1838, New York, NY d: 12/30/1896, Boston, MA BR/TR, 5'9", 126 lbs. Deb: 5/5/1871 U NA OF: 4-0-34

YEAR	TM-L	G	AB	R	H	2B	3B	HR	RBI	BB	SO	SB	CS	AVG	OBP	SLG	OPS	OPS+	BR/A	RC	RC/G	FR	G/POS	WS	TPW
1871	Bos-n	29	152	51	46	3	3	0	24	4	4	6	0	.303	.321	.362	.682	93	-1	20	5.96	1	*0-27(0-0-27)/C-7	....	0.1
1872	Bos-n	16	76	11	16	3	0	0	15	1	0	0	2	.211	.221	.250	.471	42	-6	4	2.15	1	C-12/0-8(4-0-4)	....	-0.4
1873	Bos-n	3	12	4	1	0	0	0	1	0	0	0	0	.083	.083	.083	.167	-46	-2	0	.24	-1	/0-3(0-0-3)	....	-0.2
Total	3 n	48	240	66	63	6	3	0	40	5	4	6	2	.263	.278	.313	.590	70	-10	24	4.29	1	/0-38,C-19	....	-0.5

• BIRMINGHAM, Joe Joseph Leo "Dode" Birmingham
b: 8/6/1884, Elmira, NY d: 4/24/1946, Tampico, Mexico BR/TR, 5'10", 185 lbs. Deb: 9/12/1906 M Career OF: 38-647-28

YEAR	TM-L	G	AB	R	H	2B	3B	HR	RBI	BB	SO	SB	CS	AVG	OBP	SLG	OPS	OPS+	BR/A	RC	RC/G	FR	G/POS	WS	TPW
1906	Cle-A	10	40	5	11	2	1	0	6	1	....	2	....	.275	.293	.375	.668	110	0	5	4.66	1	/0-9(9-0-0),3-1	1	0.1
1907	Cle-A	137	476	55	112	10	9	1	33	16	....	23	....	.235	.265	.300	.565	79	-13	46	3.27	11	*0-133(17-101-16)/S-3	13	-0.9
1908	Cle-A	122	413	32	88	10	1	2	38	19	....	15	....	.213	.253	.257	.510	65	-16	30	2.33	3	*0-121(1-119-1)/S-1	10	-2.1
1909	Cle-A	100	343	29	99	10	5	1	38	19	....	12	....	.289	.333	.356	.689	113	5	44	4.58	0	0-98(0-98-0)	13	0.0
1910	Cle-A	104	367	41	84	11	2	0	35	23	....	18	....	.229	.284	.270	.553	72	-12	33	2.92	11	*0-103(1-102-0)/3-1	8	-0.6
1911	Cle-A	125	447	55	136	18	5	2	51	15	....	16	....	.304	.334	.380	.714	98	-3	61	4.92	6	*0-102(3-96-3),3-16	14	-0.3
1912	Cle-A	107	369	49	94	19	3	1	45	26	....	15	....	.255	.311	.331	.641	81	-10	43	3.83	-3	0-96(3-93-0)/1-9	7	-1.9
1913	Cle-A	47	131	16	37	9	1	0	15	8	22	7	....	.282	.324	.366	.690	99	-1	18	4.37	-3	0-36(4-32-0)	3	-0.6
1914	Cle-A	19	47	2	6	0	0	0	4	2	5	0	1	.128	.163	.128	.291	-12	-7	1	.59	-0	0-14(0-6-8)	0	-0.8
Total	9	771	2633	284	667	89	27	7	265	129	27	108	1	.253	.294	.316	.610	84	-57	281	3.59	27	0-712/3-18,1-9,S-4	69	-7.2

• BISCHOFF, John John George "Smiley" Bischoff b: 10/28/1894, Edwardsville, IL d: 12/28/1981, Granite City, IL BR/TR, 5'7", 165 lbs. Deb: 4/18/1925

YEAR	TM-L	G	AB	R	H	2B	3B	HR	RBI	BB	SO	SB	CS	AVG	OBP	SLG	OPS	OPS+	BR/A	RC	RC/G	FR	G/POS	WS	TPW
1925	Chi-A	7	11	1	1	0	0	0	0	1	5	0	0	.091	.167	.091	.258	-35	-2	0	.53	0	/C-4	0	-0.2
	Bos-A	41	133	13	37	9	1	1	16	6	11	1	2	.278	.309	.383	.693	75	-6	15	3.97	0	C-40	2	-0.3
	Yr.	48	144	14	38	9	1	1	16	7	16	1	2	.264	.298	.361	.659	66	-8	15	3.66	1	C-44	2	-0.5
1926	Bos-A	59	127	6	33	11	2	0	19	15	16	1	3	.260	.343	.378	.721	91	-3	16	4.41	0	C-46	2	0.0
Total	2	107	271	20	71	20	3	1	35	22	32	2	5	.262	.320	.369	.689	78	-11	32	4.01	0	/C-90	4	-0.5

• BISHOP, Frank Frank H. Bishop b: 9/21/1860, Belvidere, IL d: 6/18/1929, Chicago, IL Deb: 5/27/1884

YEAR	TM-L	G	AB	R	H	2B	3B	HR	RBI	BB	SO	SB	CS	AVG	OBP	SLG	OPS	OPS+	BR/A	RC	RC/G	FR	G/POS	WS	TPW
1884	CP-U	4	16	1	3	1	0	0	....	0	....	....	....	.188	.188	.250	.438	50	-1	1	1.66	-1	/3-3,S-1	0	-0.2

• BISHOP, Max Max Frederick "Tilly,Camera Eye" Bishop b: 9/5/1899, Waynesboro, PA d: 2/24/1962, Waynesboro, PA BL/TR, 5'8.5", 165 lbs. Deb: 4/15/1924

YEAR	TM-L	G	AB	R	H	2B	3B	HR	RBI	BB	SO	SB	CS	AVG	OBP	SLG	OPS	OPS+	BR/A	RC	RC/G	FR	G/POS	WS	TPW
1924	Phi-A	91	294	52	75	13	2	2	21	54	30	4	3	.255	.380	.333	.713	84	-4	41	4.84	10	2-80	10	0.8
1925	Phi-A	105	368	66	103	18	4	4	27	87	37	5	9	.280	.420	.383	.803	98	2	65	6.05	9	*2-104	14	1.3
1926	Phi-A	122	400	77	106	20	2	0	33	116	41	4	5	.265	.431	.325	.756	94	5	67	5.68	10	*2-119	16	1.7
1927	Phi-A	117	372	80	103	15	1	0	22	105	28	8	6	.277	.442	.323	.764	95	6	63	5.97	1	*2-106	15	0.9
1928	Phi-A	126	472	104	149	27	5	6	50	97	36	9	9	.316	.435	.432	.868	125	23	95	7.28	4	*2-125	24	2.9
1929*	Phi-A	129	475	102	110	19	6	3	36	**128**	44	1	4	.232	.398	.316	.713	83	-5	70	4.90	4	*2-129	15	0.2
1930*	Phi-A	130	441	117	111	27	6	10	38	128	60	3	2	.252	.426	.408	.834	108	14	88	6.80	11	*2-127	21	2.5
1931*	Phi-A	130	497	115	146	30	4	5	37	112	51	3	1	.294	.426	.400	.826	111	18	94	7.01	19	*2-130	25	4.3
1932	Phi-A	114	409	89	104	24	2	5	37	110	43	2	2	.254	.412	.359	.772	98	6	69	5.94	7	*2-106	15	1.8
1933	Phi-A	117	391	80	115	27	1	4	42	106	46	1	5	.294	.446	.399	.845	124	21	78	7.14	-6	*2-113	17	2.0
1934	Bos-A	97	253	65	66	13	1	1	22	82	22	3	2	.261	.445	.332	.777	96	5	46	6.26	3	2-57,1-15	10	1.0
1935	Bos-A	60	122	19	28	3	1	1	14	28	14	0	2	.230	.377	.295	.673	71	-5	16	3.98	-3	2-34,1-11/S-2	2	-0.6
Total	12	1338	4494	966	1216	236	35	41	379	1153	452	43	50	.271	.423	.366	.789	102	86	792	6.13	68	*2-1230/1-26,S-2	184	18.8

• BISHOP, Mike Michael David Bishop b: 11/5/1958, Santa Maria, CA BR/TR, 6'2", 188 lbs. Deb: 4/16/1983

YEAR	TM-L	G	AB	R	H	2B	3B	HR	RBI	BB	SO	SB	CS	AVG	OBP	SLG	OPS	OPS+	BR/A	RC	RC/G	FR	G/POS	WS	TPW
1983	NY-N	3	8	2	1	1	0	0	0	3	4	0	0	.125	.364	.250	.614	74	-0	1	3.90	0	/C-3	0	0.0

• BISLAND, Rivington Rivington Martin Bisland b: 2/17/1890, New York, NY d: 1/11/1973, Salzburg, Austria BR/TR, 5'9", 155 lbs. Deb: 9/13/1912

YEAR	TM-L	G	AB	R	H	2B	3B	HR	RBI	BB	SO	SB	CS	AVG	OBP	SLG	OPS	OPS+	BR/A	RC	RC/G	FR	G/POS	WS	TPW
1912	Pit-N	1	1	0	0	0	0	0	0	0	0	0	....	.000	.000	.000	.000	-102	-0	0	.00	0	....	0	0.0
1913	StL-A	12	44	3	6	0	0	0	3	2	5	0	....	.136	.191	.136	.328	-4	-6	1	.70	0	S-12	0	-0.6
1914	Cle-A	18	57	9	6	1	0	0	2	6	2	2	5	.105	.190	.123	.313	-5	-9	1	.49	-1	S-15/3-1	0	-1.0
Total	3	31	102	12	12	1	0	0	5	8	7	2	5	.118	.189	.127	.317	-6	-15	2	.56	-1	/S-27,3-1	0	-1.6

YEAR TM-L	G	AB	R	H	2B	3B	HR	RBI	BB	SO	SB	CS	AVG	OBP	SLG	OPS	OPS+	BR/A	RC	RC/G	FR	G/POS	WS	TPW
• BISSONETTE, Del	Delphia Louis Bissonette b: 9/6/1899, Winthrop, ME d: 6/9/1972, Augusta, ME BL/TL, 5'11", 180 lbs. Deb: 4/11/1928 M/C																							
1928 Bro-N	155	587	90	188	30	13	25	106	70	75	5	....	.320	.396	.543	.940	145	38	125	7.96	-4	*1-155	25	2.3
1929 Bro-N	116	431	68	121	28	10	12	75	46	58	2	....	.281	.351	.476	.827	105	2	71	5.84	-5	*1-113	11	-1.0
1930 Bro-N	146	572	102	192	33	13	16	113	56	66	4	....	.336	.396	.523	.919	121	20	115	7.61	-5	*1-146	17	0.5
1931 Bro-N	152	587	90	170	19	14	12	87	59	53	4	....	.290	.354	.431	.785	111	9	93	5.73	-8	*1-152	19	-1.4
1933 Bro-N	35	114	9	28	7	0	1	10	2	17	2	....	.246	.259	.333	.592	71	-5	9	2.48	0	1-32	1	-0.8
Total 5	**604**	**2291**	**359**	**699**	**117**	**50**	**66**	**391**	**233**	**269**	**17**	**....**	**.305**	**.371**	**.486**	**.857**	**119**	**64**	**412**	**6.57**	**-23**	**1-598**	**73**	**-0.4**
• BITTMANN, Red	Henry Peter Bittmann b: 7/22/1862, Cincinnati, OH d: 11/8/1929, Cincinnati, OH Deb: 10/10/1889 U																							
1889 KC-a	4	14	2	4	0	0	0	2	1	1	1	....	.286	.333	.286	.619	73	-1	2	4.53	0	/2-4	0	0.0
• BJORKMAN, George	George Anton Bjorkman b: 8/26/1956, Ontario, CA BR/TR, 6'2", 190 lbs. Deb: 7/10/1983																							
1983 Hou-N	29	75	8	17	4	0	2	14	16	29	0	0	.227	.370	.360	.730	110	2	11	4.93	-1	C-29	3	0.3
• BLACK, Bill	John William "Jigger" Black b: 8/12/1899, Philadelphia, PA d: 1/14/1968, Philadelphia, PA BL/TR, 5'11", 168 lbs. Deb: 5/4/1924																							
1924 Chi-A	6	5	0	1	0	0	0	0	0	0	0	0	.200	.200	.200	.400	3	-1	0	1.27	-1	/2-1	0	-0.1
• BLACK, Bob	Robert Benjamin Black b: 12/10/1862, Cincinnati, OH d: 3/21/1933, Sioux City, IA, 5'5.5", 155 lbs. Deb: 8/19/1884 ♦																							
1884 KC-U	38	146	25	36	14	2	1	....	10	....	....	....	.247	.295	.390	.685	149	10	17	4.39	-2	O-19(5-7-7),P-16/2-6,S-1	7	0.1
• BLACK, John	John Falcnor "Jack" Black b: 2/23/1890, Covington, KY d: 3/20/1962, Rutherford, NJ BR/TR, 6'1", 185 lbs. Deb: 6/20/1911																							
1911 StL-A	54	186	13	28	4	0	0	7	10	....	4	....	.151	.202	.172	.374	5	-24	7	1.14	-1	1-54	0	-2.5
• BLACKABY, Ethan	Ethan Allen Blackaby b: 7/24/1940, Cincinnati, OH BL/TL, 5'11", 190 lbs. Deb: 9/6/1962 Career OF: 4-1-3																							
1962 Mil-N	6	13	0	2	1	0	0	0	1	8	0	0	.154	.214	.231	.445	20	-1	1	1.71	-0	/O-3(2-1-0)	0	-0.2
1964 Mil-N	9	12	0	1	0	0	0	1	1	2	0	0	.083	.154	.083	.237	-31	-2	0	.48	-1	/O-5(2-0-3)	0	-0.3
Total 2	**15**	**25**	**0**	**3**	**1**	**0**	**0**	**1**	**2**	**10**	**0**	**0**	**.120**	**.185**	**.160**	**.345**	**-5**	**-4**	**1**	**1.10**	**-1**	**/O-8**	**0**	**-0.5**
• BLACKBURN, Earl	Earl Stuart Blackburn b: 11/1/1892, Leesville, OH d: 8/3/1966, Mansfield, OH BR/TR, 5'11", 180 lbs. Deb: 9/17/1912																							
1912 Pit-N	1	0	0	0	0	0	0	0	0	0	0	....	....	....	....	....	-102	0	0	....	0	/C-1	0	0.0
Cin-N	1	0	0	0	0	0	0	0	1	0	0	....	....	1.000	....	1.000	191	0	0	....	0	/C-1	0	0.0
Yr.	2	0	0	0	0	0	0	0	1	0	0	....	....	1.000	....	1.000	191	0	0	....	0	/C-2	0	0.0
1913 Cin-N	17	27	1	7	0	0	0	3	2	5	2	....	.259	.310	.259	.570	64	-1	3	3.24	-3	C-12	0	-0.3
1915 Bos-N	3	6	0	1	0	0	0	0	2	1	0	....	.167	.375	.167	.542	68	-0	0	1.99	0	/C-3	1	0.1
1916 Bos-N	47	110	12	30	4	4	0	7	9	21	2	....	.273	.328	.382	.710	124	3	15	4.62	-2	C-44	6	0.5
1917 Chi-N	2	2	0	0	0	0	0	0	0	0	0	....	.000	.000	.000	.000	-93	-0	0	.00	0	....	0	0.0
Total 5	**71**	**145**	**13**	**38**	**4**	**4**	**0**	**10**	**14**	**27**	**4**	**....**	**.262**	**.327**	**.345**	**.672**	**108**	**2**	**18**	**4.17**	**-4**	**/C-61**	**7**	**0.2**
• BLACKBURNE, Lena	Russell Aubrey "Slats" Blackburne b: 10/23/1886, Clifton Heights, PA d: 2/29/1968, Riverside, NJ BR/TR, 5'11", 160 lbs. Deb: 4/14/1910 M/C																							
1910 Chi-A	75	242	16	42	3	1	0	10	19	....	4	....	.174	.245	.194	.439	40	-16	13	1.62	13	S-74	4	-0.1
1912 Chi-A	5	1	0	0	0	0	0	0	1	....	1	....	.000	.500	.000	.500	48	0	1	13.06	-1	/S-4,3-1	0	-0.1
1914 Chi-A	144	474	52	105	10	5	1	35	66	58	25	15	.222	.324	.270	.594	80	-10	49	3.15	-9	*2-143	12	-1.8
1915 Chi-A	96	283	33	61	5	1	0	25	35	34	13	11	.216	.304	.240	.544	61	-15	25	2.57	-12	3-83/S-9	5	-2.5
1918 Cin-N	125	435	34	99	8	10	1	45	25	30	6	....	.228	.271	.299	.570	75	-14	36	2.67	10	*S-125	10	0.6
1919 Bos-N	31	80	5	21	3	1	0	4	6	7	3	....	.263	.322	.325	.647	99	-0	9	3.82	-3	3-24/1-1,2-1,S-1	2	-0.2
Phi-N	72	291	32	58	10	5	2	19	10	22	2	....	.199	.228	.289	.517	51	-18	20	2.08	3	3-72/1-1	2	-1.4
Yr.	103	371	37	79	13	6	2	23	16	29	5	....	.213	.249	.296	.546	62	-18	30	2.43	0	3-96/1-2,2-1,S-1	4	-1.7
1927 Chi-A	1	1	1	1	0	0	0	1	0	0	0	0	1.000	1.000	1.000	2.000	431	0	1	∞	0	....	0	0.0
1929 Chi-A	1	0	0	0	0	0	0	0	0	0	0	0	....	....	....	....	-101	0	0	....	-0	/P-1	0	0.0
Total 8	**550**	**1807**	**173**	**387**	**39**	**23**	**4**	**139**	**162**	**151**	**54**	**26**	**.214**	**.284**	**.268**	**.552**	**67**	**-73**	**154**	**2.59**	**1**	**S-213,3-180,2-144/1-2,P-1**	**35**	**-5.6**
• BLACKERBY, George	George Franklin Blackerby b: 11/18/1903, Luther, OK d: 3/30/1987, Wichita Falls, TX BR/TR, 6'1", 176 lbs. Deb: 8/10/1928																							
1928 Chi-A	30	83	8	21	0	0	0	12	4	10	2	1	.253	.287	.253	.540	44	-7	6	2.51	-1	O-20(20-0-0)	0	-0.9
• BLACKWELL, Fred	Frederick William Blackwell b: 9/7/1891, Bowling Green, KY d: 12/8/1975, Morgantown, KY BL/TR, 5'10.5", 160 lbs. Deb: 9/25/1917																							
1917 Pit-N	3	10	1	2	0	0	0	2	0	3	0	....	.200	.200	.200	.400	22	-1	0	1.17	0	/C-3	0	-0.1
1918 Pit-N	8	13	1	2	0	0	0	4	3	4	0	....	.154	.313	.154	.466	42	-1	1	1.72	0	/C-8	0	-0.1
1919 Pit-N	24	65	3	14	3	0	0	4	3	9	0	....	.215	.261	.262	.522	55	-4	5	2.18	-4	C-22	1	-0.6
Total 3	**35**	**88**	**5**	**18**	**3**	**0**	**0**	**10**	**6**	**16**	**0**	**....**	**.205**	**.263**	**.239**	**.502**	**50**	**-5**	**6**	**2.00**	**-4**	**/C-33**	**1**	**-0.8**
• BLACKWELL, Tim	Timothy P. Blackwell b: 8/19/1952, San Diego, CA BB/TR, 5'11", 180 lbs. Deb: 7/3/1974																							
1974 Bos-A	44	122	9	30	1	1	0	8	10	21	1	1	.246	.308	.270	.579	63	-6	10	2.81	-1	C-44	2	-0.4
1975 Bos-A	59	132	15	26	3	2	0	6	19	13	0	0	.197	.303	.250	.553	53	-8	11	2.65	-1	C-57/D-2	3	-0.6
1976 Phi-N	4	8	0	2	0	0	0	1	0	1	0	0	.250	.250	.250	.500	41	-1	1	2.25	0	/C-4	0	-0.1
1977 Phi-N	1	0	1	0	0	0	0	0	0	0	0	0	....	....	....	....	-96	0	0	....	0	/C-1	0	0.0
Mon-N	16	22	3	2	1	0	0	0	2	7	0	0	.091	.167	.136	.303	-18	-4	0	.56	-1	C-14	0	-0.5
Yr.	17	22	4	2	1	0	0	0	2	7	0	0	.091	.167	.136	.303	-18	-4	0	.56	-1	C-15	0	-0.5
1978 Chi-N	49	103	8	23	3	0	0	7	23	17	0	0	.223	.370	.252	.623	68	-3	11	3.42	0	C-49	3	-0.1
1979 Chi-N	63	122	8	20	3	1	0	12	32	25	0	0	.164	.342	.205	.547	48	-7	11	2.76	-1	C-63	2	-0.6
1980 Chi-N	103	320	24	87	16	4	5	30	41	62	0	1	.272	.355	.394	.748	101	1	46	5.08	13	*C-103	14	2.0
1981 Chi-N	58	158	21	37	10	2	1	11	23	23	2	1	.234	.331	.342	.673	87	-2	19	4.09	1	C-56	5	0.2
1982 Mon-N	23	42	2	8	2	1	0	3	3	11	0	0	.190	.244	.286	.530	47	-3	3	2.19	1	C-18	1	-0.2
1983 Mon-N	6	15	0	3	1	0	0	2	1	3	0	0	.200	.250	.267	.517	43	-1	1	1.66	-1	/C-5	0	-0.2
Total 10	**426**	**1044**	**91**	**238**	**40**	**11**	**6**	**80**	**154**	**183**	**3**	**3**	**.228**	**.329**	**.305**	**.634**	**73**	**-33**	**113**	**3.57**	**10**	**C-414/D-2**	**30**	**-0.6**
• BLADES, Ray	Francis Raymond Blades b: 8/6/1896, Mount Vernon, IL d: 5/18/1979, Lincoln, IL BR/TR, 5'7.5", 163 lbs. Deb: 8/19/1922 M/C Career OF: 500-4-124																							
1922 StL-N	37	130	27	39	2	4	3	21	25	21	3	3	.300	.428	.446	.874	132	8	26	7.15	-1	O-29(28-0-1)/S-4,3-1	5	0.5
1923 StL-N	98	317	48	78	21	5	5	44	37	46	4	2	.246	.342	.391	.733	95	-1	45	4.85	4	O-83(81-1-3)/3-4	8	-0.3
1924 StL-N	131	456	86	142	21	13	11	68	35	38	7	9	.311	.373	.487	.860	131	19	81	6.40	-4	*O-109(106-3-1)/2-7,3-7	15	0.6
1925 StL-N	122	462	112	158	37	8	12	57	59	47	6	8	.342	.423	.535	.958	140	28	105	8.74	6	*O-114(114-0-0)/3-1	20	2.4
1926 StL-N	107	416	81	127	17	12	8	43	62	57	6	....	.305	.409	.462	.871	129	20	80	7.01	-1	*O-105(105-0-0)	19	1.1
1927 StL-N	61	180	33	57	8	5	2	29	28	22	3	....	.317	.414	.450	.864	127	8	34	6.91	-6	O-50(29-0-21)	8	-0.1
1928*StL-N	51	85	9	20	7	1	1	19	20	26	0	....	.235	.393	.376	.769	100	1	14	5.25	-1	O-19(4-0-15)	3	-0.1
1930*StL-N	45	101	26	40	6	2	4	25	21	15	1	....	.396	.504	.614	1.118	163	12	32	12.63	-3	O-32(13-0-21)	6	0.6
1931*StL-N	35	67	10	19	4	0	1	5	10	7	1	....	.284	.392	.388	.780	106	1	11	5.82	-2	O-20(7-0-13)	2	-0.1
1932 StL-N	80	201	35	46	10	1	3	29	34	31	2	....	.229	.340	.333	.674	80	-5	25	4.16	-2	O-62(13-0-49)/3-1	4	-1.0
Total 10	**767**	**2415**	**467**	**726**	**133**	**51**	**50**	**340**	**331**	**310**	**33**	**22**	**.301**	**.395**	**.460**	**.855**	**123**	**92**	**453**	**6.75**	**-10**	**O-623/3-14,2-7,S-4**	**90**	**3.6**
• BLADT, Rick	Richard Alan Bladt b: 12/9/1946, Santa Cruz, CA BR/TR, 6'1", 160 lbs. Deb: 6/15/1969 Career OF: 2-56-1																							
1969 Chi-N	10	13	1	2	0	0	0	1	0	5	0	0	.154	.154	.154	.308	-12	-2	0	.76	0	/O-7(2-5-1)	0	-0.2
1975 NY-A	52	117	13	26	3	1	1	11	11	8	6	2	.222	.295	.291	.585	68	-4	11	3.07	1	O-51(0-51-0)	2	-0.4
Total 2	**62**	**130**	**14**	**28**	**3**	**1**	**1**	**12**	**11**	**13**	**6**	**2**	**.215**	**.282**	**.277**	**.559**	**61**	**-6**	**11**	**2.83**	**2**	**/O-58**	**2**	**-0.6**
• BLAEMIRE, Rae	Rae Bertrum Blaemire b: 2/8/1911, Gary, IN d: 12/23/1975, Champaign, IL BR/TR, 6', 178 lbs. Deb: 9/13/1941																							
1941 NY-N	2	5	0	2	0	0	0	0	0	0	0	....	.400	.400	.400	.800	123	0	1	7.20	0	/C-2	0	0.0
• BLAIR, Buddy	Louis Nathan Blair b: 9/10/1910, Columbia, MS d: 6/7/1996, Monroe, LA BL/TR, 6', 186 lbs. Deb: 4/14/1942																							
1942 Phi-A	137	484	48	135	26	8	5	66	30	30	1	6	.279	.325	.397	.722	103	-2	59	4.26	-3	*3-126	15	-0.1
• BLAIR, Footsie	Clarence Vick Blair b: 7/13/1900, Enterprise, OK d: 7/1/1982, Texarkana, TX BL/TR, 6'1", 180 lbs. Deb: 4/28/1929																							
1929*Chi-N	26	72	10	23	5	0	1	8	3	4	1	....	.319	.347	.431	.777	91	-1	10	5.24	0	/3-8,1-7,2-2	2	-0.1
1930 Chi-N	134	578	97	158	24	12	6	59	20	58	9	....	.273	.306	.388	.693	66	-34	66	4.03	10	*2-115,3-13	9	-1.8

YEAR TM-L	G	AB	R	H	2B	3B	HR	RBI	BB	SO	SB	CS	AVG	OBP	SLG	OPS	OPS+	BR/A	RC	RC/G	FR	G/POS	WS	TPW
1931 Chi-N	86	240	31	62	19	4	3	29	14	26	1	....	.258	.302	.408	.710	88	-5	30	4.31	-11	2-44,1-23/3-1	5	-1.4
Total 3	246	890	138	243	48	16	10	96	37	88	11	....	.273	.308	.397	.705	74	-40	106	4.20	-1	2-161/1-30,3-22	16	-3.3

• BLAIR, Paul Paul L D "Motormouth" Blair b: 2/1/1944, Cushing, OK BR/TR, 6', 171 lbs. Deb: 9/9/1964 Career OF: 31-1801-58

YEAR TM-L	G	AB	R	H	2B	3B	HR	RBI	BB	SO	SB	CS	AVG	OBP	SLG	OPS	OPS+	BR/A	RC	RC/G	FR	G/POS	WS	TPW
1964 Bal-A	8	1	0	0	0	0	0	0	0	1	0	1	.000	.000	.000	.000	-100	-1	0	.00	-1	/0-6(0-6-0)	0	-0.2
1965 Bal-A	119	364	49	85	19	2	5	25	32	52	8	5	.234	.303	.338	.640	80	-10	38	3.41	-1	*0-116(0-116-0)	10	-1.5
1966*Bal-A	133	303	35	84	20	2	6	33	15	36	5	6	.277	.311	.416	.727	109	1	37	4.27	-7	*0-127(2-125-0)	9	-1.0
1967 Bal-A	151	552	72	162	27	**12**	11	64	50	68	8	6	.293	.357	.446	.803	137	25	87	5.62	13	*0-146(0-146-0)	24	3.6
1968 Bal-A	141	421	48	89	22	1	7	38	37	60	4	2	.211	.278	.318	.597	80	-10	39	3.04	5	*0-132(0-132-0)/3-1	11	-1.0
1969*Bal-A★	150	625	102	178	32	5	26	76	40	72	20	6	.285	.330	.477	.807	122	17	97	5.46	15	*0-150(0-150-0)	28	2.9
1970*Bal-A	133	480	79	128	24	2	18	65	56	93	24	11	.267	.347	.438	.784	114	10	74	5.23	9	*0-128(0-128-0)/3-1	22	1.5
1971*Bal-A	141	516	75	135	24	8	10	44	32	94	14	11	.262	.306	.397	.703	99	-4	60	3.99	-4	*0-138(0-138-0)	15	-1.3
1972 Bal-A	142	477	47	111	20	8	8	49	25	78	7	8	.233	.271	.358	.629	84	-13	41	2.74	8	*0-139(0-139-0)	11	-1.0
1973*Bal-A★	146	500	73	140	25	3	10	64	43	72	18	8	.280	.337	.402	.739	108	6	67	4.68	12	*0-144(0-144-0)/D-1	18	1.4
1974*Bal-A	151	552	77	144	27	4	17	62	43	59	27	9	.261	.317	.417	.733	113	10	73	4.41	8	*0-151(0-151-0)	21	1.4
1975 Bal-A	140	440	51	96	13	4	5	31	25	82	17	11	.218	.260	.300	.560	62	-24	34	2.36	6	*0-138(0-138-0)/1-1,D-1	6	-2.2
1976 Bal-A	145	375	29	74	16	0	3	16	22	49	15	6	.197	.246	.264	.510	52	-22	23	1.82	-1	*0-139(0-139-0)/D-1	3	-2.7
1977*NY-A	83	164	20	43	4	3	4	25	9	16	3	2	.262	.309	.396	.705	92	-2	18	3.53	-3	0-79(6-42-33)/D-1	3	-0.7
1978*NY-A	75	125	10	22	5	0	2	13	9	17	1	1	.176	.231	.264	.495	40	-10	7	1.73	-3	0-64(1-49-16)/2-5,S-4,3-3	1	-1.4
1979 NY-A	2	5	0	1	0	0	0	0	0	1	0	0	.200	.200	.200	.400	8	-1	0	1.35	0	/0-2(0-1-1)	0	-0.1
Cin-N	75	140	7	21	4	1	2	15	11	27	0	0	.150	.212	.236	.448	22	-15	7	1.43	0	0-67(16-56-2)	1	-1.7
1980 NY-A	12	2	2	0	0	0	0	0	0	0	0	0	.000	.000	.000	.000	-102	-1	0	.00	0	0-12(6-1-6)	0	-0.1
Total 17	1947	6042	776	1513	282	55	134	620	449	877	171	93	.250	.305	.382	.687	96	-46	702	3.86	56	*0-1878/2-5,3-5,D-4,S-4,1-1	183	-3.8

• BLAIR, Walter Walter Allen "Heavy" Blair b: 10/13/1883, Landrus, PA d: 8/20/1948, Lewisburg, PA BR/TR, 6', 185 lbs. Deb: 9/17/1907 M

YEAR TM-L	G	AB	R	H	2B	3B	HR	RBI	BB	SO	SB	CS	AVG	OBP	SLG	OPS	OPS+	BR/A	RC	RC/G	FR	G/POS	WS	TPW
1907 NY-A	7	22	1	4	0	0	0	1	2	....	0	....	.182	.250	.182	.432	35	-2	1	1.51	1	/C-7	0	0.0
1908 NY-A	76	211	9	40	5	1	1	13	11	....	4	....	.190	.237	.237	.474	53	-11	13	1.86	-5	C-60/0-9(2-0-7),1-3	1	-1.3
1909 NY-A	42	110	5	23	2	2	0	11	7	....	2	....	.209	.269	.264	.533	68	-4	8	2.39	-1	C-42	2	-0.3
1910 NY-A	6	22	2	5	0	1	0	2	0	....	0	....	.227	.227	.318	.545	67	-1	2	2.27	1	/C-6	0	0.0
1911 NY-A	85	222	18	43	9	2	0	26	16	....	2	....	.194	.257	.252	.510	40	-19	16	2.12	1	C-84/1-1	4	-1.2
1914 Buf-F	128	378	22	92	11	2	0	33	32	64	6	....	.243	.304	.283	.587	65	-17	33	2.88	9	*C-128	13	0.2
1915 Buf-F	98	290	23	65	15	3	2	20	18	32	4	....	.224	.274	.317	.591	74	-11	25	2.82	11	C-97	8	0.8
Total 7	442	1255	80	272	42	11	3	106	86	96	18	....	.217	.272	.275	.547	60	-64	97	2.47	17	C-424/0-9,1-4	28	-1.8

• BLAKE, Casey William Casey Blake b: 8/23/1973, Des Moines, IA BR/TR, 6'2", 200 lbs. Deb: 8/14/1999

YEAR TM-L	G	AB	R	H	2B	3B	HR	RBI	BB	SO	SB	CS	AVG	OBP	SLG	OPS	OPS+	BR/A	RC	RC/G	FR	G/POS	WS	TPW
1999 Tor-A	14	39	6	10	2	0	1	1	2	7	0	0	.256	.293	.385	.677	70	-2	4	3.75	0	3-14	1	-0.2
2000 Min-A	7	16	1	3	2	0	0	1	3	7	0	0	.188	.350	.313	.663	67	-1	2	3.37	-1	/3-5,1-1,D-1	0	-0.1
2001 Min-A	13	22	1	7	1	0	0	2	3	8	1	0	.318	.400	.364	.764	101	0	4	6.51	0	/3-5,D-4,1-3	1	0.0
Bal-A	6	15	2	2	0	0	1	2	1	4	2	0	.133	.188	.333	.521	35	-1	1	2.45	-1	/1-5,D-1	0	-0.3
Yr.	19	37	3	9	1	0	1	4	4	12	3	0	.243	.317	.351	.668	75	-1	5	4.63	-1	/1-8,3-5,D-5	1	-0.3
2002 Min-A	9	20	2	4	1	0	0	1	2	7	0	0	.200	.273	.250	.523	40	-2	2	2.54	-1	/3-5,1-3,D-1	0	-0.3
2003 Cle-A	152	557	80	143	35	0	17	67	38	109	7	9	.257	.316	.411	.727	93	-9	70	4.18	8	*3-140,1-31	11	0.0
Total 5	201	669	92	169	41	0	19	74	49	142	10	9	.253	.314	.399	.713	88	-14	82	4.11	5	3-169/1-43,D-7	13	-0.9

• BLAKE, Harry Harry Cooper Blake b: 6/16/1874, Portsmouth, OH d: 10/14/1919, Chicago, IL BR/TR, 5'7", 165 lbs. Deb: 7/7/1894 Career OF: 12-132-372

YEAR TM-L	G	AB	R	H	2B	3B	HR	RBI	BB	SO	SB	CS	AVG	OBP	SLG	OPS	OPS+	BR/A	RC	RC/G	FR	G/POS	WS	TPW
1894 Cle-N	73	296	51	78	15	4	1	51	30	22	1	....	.264	.335	.351	.687	63	-19	36	4.30	3	0-73(0-4-69)	4	-1.5
1895*Cle-N	85	318	50	88	10	1	3	45	30	33	11	....	.277	.341	.343	.684	72	-14	44	4.85	-2	0-83(0-0-83)	7	-1.6
1896*Cle-N	104	383	66	92	12	5	1	43	46	30	10	....	.240	.322	.305	.627	62	-21	43	3.81	4	*0-103(0-12-92)/S-1	6	-1.9
1897 Cle-N	32	117	17	30	3	1	1	15	12	....	5	....	.256	.331	.325	.656	70	-5	15	4.42	3	0-32(2-25-5)	3	-0.4
1898 Cle-N	136	474	65	116	18	7	0	58	69	....	12	....	.245	.342	.312	.654	89	-4	59	4.14	7	*0-136(1-22-114)/1-2	12	-0.5
1899 StL-N	97	292	50	70	9	4	2	41	43	....	16	....	.240	.341	.318	.660	79	-7	39	4.52	3	0-87(9-69-9)/2-4,1-1,C-1,S	7	-0.8
Total 6	527	1880	299	474	67	22	8	253	230	85	55	....	.252	.336	.324	.660	74	-70	236	4.29	17	0-514/2-4,1-3,S-2,C-1	39	-6.8

• BLAKELY, Linc Lincoln Howard Blakely b: 2/12/1912, Oakland, CA d: 9/28/1976, Oakland, CA BR/TR, 6', 180 lbs. Deb: 4/29/1934

YEAR TM-L	G	AB	R	H	2B	3B	HR	RBI	BB	SO	SB	CS	AVG	OBP	SLG	OPS	OPS+	BR/A	RC	RC/G	FR	G/POS	WS	TPW
1934 Cin-N	34	102	11	23	1	1	0	10	5	14	1	....	.225	.269	.255	.523	42	-8	6	1.90	2	0-28(6-22-0)	1	-0.6

• BLAKISTON, Bob Robert J. Blakiston b: 10/2/1855, San Francisco, CA d: 12/25/1918, San Francisco, CA, 5'8.5", 180 lbs. Deb: 5/2/1882 U Career OF: 2-66-37

YEAR TM-L	G	AB	R	H	2B	3B	HR	RBI	BB	SO	SB	CS	AVG	OBP	SLG	OPS	OPS+	BR/A	RC	RC/G	FR	G/POS	WS	TPW
1882 Phi-a	72	281	40	64	4	1	0	20	9	....	....	....	.228	.252	.249	.501	62	-12	18	2.33	-1	0-38(0-4-34),3-34/2-1	5	-1.2
1883 Phi-a	44	167	26	41	3	3	0	26	9	....	....	....	.246	.284	.299	.583	81	-4	15	3.24	1	0-37(2-35-0)/1-6,3-5	5	-0.4
1884 Phi-a	32	128	21	33	6	0	0	0	11	....	....	....	.258	.336	.305	.640	104	1	13	3.88	2	0-28(0-27-1)/3-2,1-1,2-1,S	4	0.1
Ind-a	6	18	0	4	1	0	0	0	1	....	....	....	.222	.263	.278	.541	79	-0	1	2.65	0	/1-5,0-1	0	-0.1
Yr.	38	146	21	37	7	0	0	0	12	....	....	....	.253	.327	.301	.629	101	1	15	3.73	1	0-29(0-27-3)/1-6,3-2,2-1,S	4	0.0
Total 3	154	594	87	142	14	4	0	46	30	....	....	....	.239	.280	.276	.556	77	-16	47	2.92	1	0-104/3-41,1-12,2-2,S-1	14	-1.5

• BLALOCK, Hank Hank Joe Blalock b: 11/21/1980, San Diego, CA BL/TR, 6'1", 192 lbs. Deb: 4/1/2002

YEAR TM-L	G	AB	R	H	2B	3B	HR	RBI	BB	SO	SB	CS	AVG	OBP	SLG	OPS	OPS+	BR/A	RC	RC/G	FR	G/POS	WS	TPW
2002 Tex-A	49	147	16	31	8	0	3	17	20	43	0	0	.211	.310	.327	.636	66	-7	16	3.56	-6	3-46	1	-1.2
2003 Tex-A★	143	567	89	170	33	3	29	90	44	97	2	3	.300	.351	.522	.873	116	11	99	6.37	-6	*3-141/2-4	17	0.7
Total 2	192	714	105	201	41	3	32	107	64	140	2	3	.282	.342	.482	.824	105	4	115	5.73	-13	3-187/2-4	18	-0.6

• BLANCHARD, Johnny John Edwin Blanchard b: 2/26/1933, Minneapolis, MN BL/TR, 6'1", 198 lbs. Deb: 9/25/1955 Career OF: 54-0-115

YEAR TM-L	G	AB	R	H	2B	3B	HR	RBI	BB	SO	SB	CS	AVG	OBP	SLG	OPS	OPS+	BR/A	RC	RC/G	FR	G/POS	WS	TPW
1955 NY-A	1	3	0	0	0	0	0	0	1	0	0	0	.000	.250	.000	.250	-29	-1	0	.59	0	/C-1	0	0.0
1959 NY-A	49	59	6	10	1	0	2	4	7	12	0	0	.169	.258	.288	.546	51	-4	4	2.26	-1	C-12/0-8(1-0-7),1-1	0	-0.5
1960*NY-A	53	99	8	24	3	1	4	14	6	17	0	0	.242	.292	.414	.707	94	-1	12	4.04	-1	C-28	3	-0.1
1961*NY-A	93	243	38	74	10	1	21	54	27	28	1	0	.305	.383	.613	.996	170	24	56	8.60	-0	C-48,0-15(8-0-7)	17	2.5
1962*NY-A	93	246	33	57	7	0	13	39	28	32	0	0	.232	.313	.419	.731	98	-1	33	4.63	-2	0-47(15-0-32),C-15/1-2	7	-0.5
1963*NY-A	76	218	22	49	4	0	16	45	26	30	0	0	.225	.307	.463	.771	113	3	31	4.69	-1	0-64(22-0-42)	8	0.0
1964*NY-A	77	161	18	41	8	0	7	28	24	24	1	0	.255	.351	.435	.786	115	4	24	5.04	-3	C-25,0-14(6-0-8)/1-3	7	0.2
1965 NY-A	12	34	1	5	1	0	1	3	7	3	0	0	.147	.293	.265	.557	60	-2	3	2.47	-1	C-12	1	-0.2
KC-A	52	120	10	24	2	0	2	11	8	16	0	0	.200	.256	.267	.522	49	-8	8	2.14	-1	0-20(1-0-19),C-14	1	-0.9
Yr.	64	154	11	29	3	0	3	14	15	19	0	0	.188	.265	.266	.531	52	-10	11	2.22	-1	C-26,0-20(1-0-19)	2	-1.1
Mil-N	10	10	1	1	0	0	1	2	2	1	0	0	.100	.250	.400	.650	79	-0	1	3.39	0	/0-1	0	0.0
Total 8	516	1193	137	285	36	2	67	200	136	163	2	0	.239	.320	.441	.761	109	14	173	4.90	-9	0-169,C-155/1-6	44	0.2

• BLANCO, Damaso Damaso (Caripe) Blanco b: 11/12/1941, Curiepe, Venezuela BR/TR, 5'10", 165 lbs. Deb: 5/26/1972

YEAR TM-L	G	AB	R	H	2B	3B	HR	RBI	BB	SO	SB	CS	AVG	OBP	SLG	OPS	OPS+	BR/A	RC	RC/G	FR	G/POS	WS	TPW
1972 SF-N	39	20	5	7	1	0	0	2	4	3	2	1	.350	.458	.400	.858	144	1	4	6.44	-4	3-19/S-8,2-3	1	-0.2
1973 SF-N	28	12	4	0	0	0	0	0	1	2	0	0	.000	.077	.000	.077	-74	-3	0	.05	-4	/3-7,S-5,2-3	0	-0.7
1974 SF-N	5	1	0	0	0	0	0	0	0	1	1	0	.000	.000	.000	.000	-95	-0	0	.00	0	....	0	0.0
Total 3	72	33	9	7	1	0	0	2	5	6	3	1	.212	.316	.242	.558	65	-1	4	3.57	-8	/3-26,S-13,2-6	1	-0.9

• BLANCO, Henry Henry Ramon Blanco b: 8/29/1971, Caracas, Venezuela BR/TR, 5'11", 170 lbs. Deb: 7/25/1997

YEAR TM-L	G	AB	R	H	2B	3B	HR	RBI	BB	SO	SB	CS	AVG	OBP	SLG	OPS	OPS+	BR/A	RC	RC/G	FR	G/POS	WS	TPW
1997 LA-N	3	5	1	2	0	0	1	1	0	1	0	0	.400	.400	1.000	1.400	273	1	2	18.00	0	/1-1,3-1	0	0.1
1999 Col-N	88	263	30	61	12	3	6	28	34	38	1	1	.232	.322	.369	.691	58	-17	33	4.17	6	C-86/0-1	6	-0.5
2000 Mil-N	93	284	29	67	24	0	7	31	36	60	0	3	.236	.322	.394	.716	81	-10	34	3.97	9	C-88	9	0.5
2001 Mil-N	104	314	33	66	18	3	6	31	34	72	3	1	.210	.291	.344	.635	65	-16	31	3.13	10	*C-102	6	0.0
2002*Atl-N	81	221	17	45	9	1	6	22	20	51	0	2	.204	.273	.335	.608	58	-15	19	2.75	-5	C-79	4	-1.5
2003 Atl-N	55	151	11	30	8	0	1	13	10	21	0	0	.199	.253	.272	.525	37	-14	10	2.19	-1	C-52	2	-1.2
Total 6	424	1238	121	271	71	7	27	126	134	243	4	7	.219	.298	.353	.651	64	-72	130	3.39	19	C-407/1-1,3-1,0-1	27	-2.5

• BLANCO, Ossie Oswaldo Carlos (Diaz) Blanco b: 9/8/1945, Caracas, Venezuela BR/TR, 6', 185 lbs. Deb: 5/26/1970

YEAR TM-L	G	AB	R	H	2B	3B	HR	RBI	BB	SO	SB	CS	AVG	OBP	SLG	OPS	OPS+	BR/A	RC	RC/G	FR	G/POS	WS	TPW
1970 Chi-A	34	66	4	13	0	0	0	8	3	14	0	1	.197	.232	.197	.429	19	-8	3	1.38	-1	1-22/0-1	0	-1.1

YEAR TM-L	G	AB	R	H	2B	3B	HR	RBI	BB	SO	SB	CS	AVG	OBP	SLG	OPS	OPS+	BR/A	RC	RC/G	FR	G/POS	WS	TPW
1974 Cle-A	18	36	1	7	0	0	0	2	7	4	0	3	.194	.326	.194	.520	53	-3	2	1.68	-1	1-16/D-1	0	-0.5
Total 2	**52**	**102**	**5**	**20**	**0**	**0**	**0**	**10**	**10**	**18**	**0**	**4**	**.196**	**.268**	**.196**	**.464**	**32**	**-11**	**5**	**1.49**	**-2**	**/1-38,D-1,0-1**	**0**	**-1.6**
• BLANK, Coonie	Frank Ignatz Blank b: 10/18/1892, St. Louis, MO d: 12/8/1961, St. Louis, MO BR/TR, 5'11", 165 lbs. Deb: 8/15/1909																							
1909 StL-N	1	2	0	0	0	0	0	0	0	....	0	....	.000	.000	.000	.000	-107	-0	0	.00	0	/C-1	0	-0.1
• BLANKENSHIP, Cliff	Clifford Douglas Blankenship b: 4/10/1880, Columbus, GA d: 4/26/1956, Oakland, CA BR/TR, 5'10.5", 165 lbs. Deb: 4/17/1905 U																							
1905 Cin-N	19	56	8	11	1	1	0	7	4	....	1	....	.196	.250	.250	.500	44	-4	4	2.24	-4	1-15	0	-0.8
1907 Was-A	37	102	4	23	2	0	0	6	3	....	3	....	.225	.248	.245	.493	62	-5	7	2.40	1	C-22/1-9	1	-0.2
1909 Was-A	39	60	4	15	1	0	0	9	0	....	2	....	.250	.250	.267	.517	66	-3	4	2.46	-2	C-17/O-4(1-1-2)	1	-0.4
Total 3	**95**	**218**	**16**	**49**	**4**	**1**	**0**	**22**	**7**	**....**	**6**	**....**	**.225**	**.249**	**.252**	**.501**	**58**	**-11**	**16**	**2.37**	**-5**	**/C-39,1-24,O-4**	**2**	**-1.5**
• BLANKENSHIP, Lance	Lance Robert Blankenship b: 12/6/1963, Portland, OR BR/TR, 6', 185 lbs. Deb: 9/4/1988 Career OF: 71-66-71																							
1988 Oak-A	10	3	1	0	0	0	0	0	0	1	0	1	.000	.000	.000	.000	-104	-1	0	.00	-2	/2-4,D-4	0	-0.3
1989*Oak-A	58	125	22	29	5	1	1	4	8	31	5	1	.232	.278	.312	.590	68	-5	12	3.21	4	O-25(4-0-21),2-24,D-10	2	-0.1
1990*Oak-A	86	136	18	26	3	0	0	10	20	23	3	1	.191	.295	.213	.508	46	-9	9	2.05	1	3-28,O-28(10-1-17),2-20/D-6,1	2	-0.8
1991 Oak-A	90	185	33	46	8	0	3	21	23	42	12	3	.249	.341	.341	.682	95	1	24	4.42	6	2-45,O-28(18-0-11),3-14/D-6	7	0.7
1992*Oak-A	123	349	59	84	24	1	3	34	82	57	21	7	.241	.394	.341	.735	113	14	55	5.06	17	2-78,O-51(22-16-20)/1-7,D	15	3.2
1993 Oak-A	94	252	43	48	8	1	2	23	67	64	13	5	.190	.364	.254	.618	74	-4	29	3.48	0	O-66(17-49-2),2-19/1-6,D-5,S	7	-0.4
Total 6	**461**	**1050**	**176**	**233**	**48**	**3**	**9**	**92**	**200**	**218**	**54**	**18**	**.222**	**.352**	**.299**	**.651**	**87**	**-4**	**129**	**3.91**	**26**	**O-198,2-190/3-42,D-34,1-14,S**	**33**	**2.2**
• BLANKS, Larvell	Larvell "Sugar Bear" Blanks b: 1/28/1950, Del Rio, TX BR/TR, 5'8", 167 lbs. Deb: 7/19/1972																							
1972 Atl-N	33	85	10	28	5	0	1	7	7	12	0	0	.329	.380	.424	.804	117	2	13	5.76	2	2-18/S-4,3-2	4	0.7
1973 Atl-N	17	18	1	4	0	0	0	0	1	3	0	0	.222	.263	.222	.485	33	-2	1	1.61	-2	/3-3,2-2,S-2	0	-0.4
1974 Atl-N	3	8	0	2	0	0	0	1	0	0	0	0	.250	.250	.250	.500	38	-1	1	2.25	0	/S-2	0	-0.1
1975 Atl-N	141	471	49	110	13	3	3	38	38	43	4	3	.234	.294	.293	.587	61	-26	40	2.86	-18	*S-129,2-12	7	-3.0
1976 Cle-A	104	328	45	92	8	7	5	41	30	31	1	2	.280	.341	.393	.734	116	6	41	4.14	-1	S-56,2-46/D-3,3-2	12	1.2
1977 Cle-A	105	322	43	92	10	4	6	38	19	37	3	0	.286	.327	.398	.725	100	0	42	4.57	-4	S-66,3-18,2-12/D-6	9	0.1
1978 Cle-A	70	193	19	49	10	0	2	20	10	16	0	0	.254	.291	.337	.627	77	-6	18	2.99	-8	S-43,2-17/3-3,D-1	3	-1.0
1979 Tex-A	68	120	13	24	5	0	1	15	11	9	0	0	.200	.267	.267	.534	45	-9	9	2.46	-4	S-49,2-16/D-1	1	-1.0
1980 Atl-N	88	221	23	45	6	0	2	12	16	27	1	2	.204	.257	.258	.515	43	-18	14	2.00	3	S-56,3-43/2-1	3	-1.3
Total 9	**629**	**1766**	**203**	**446**	**57**	**14**	**20**	**172**	**132**	**178**	**9**	**7**	**.253**	**.306**	**.335**	**.640**	**79**	**-53**	**179**	**3.37**	**-32**	**S-407,2-124/3-71,D-11**	**39**	**-4.6**
• BLASINGAME, Don	Don Lee "Blazer" Blasingame b: 3/16/1932, Corinth, MS BL/TR, 5'10", 165 lbs. Deb: 9/20/1955																							
1955 StL-N	5	16	4	6	1	0	0	0	6	0	1	1	.375	.545	.438	.983	165	2	4	10.05	1	/2-3,S-2	1	0.4
1956 StL-N	150	587	94	153	22	7	0	27	72	52	8	8	.261	.344	.322	.666	81	-15	70	4.21	9	2-98,S-49/3-2	17	0.6
1957 StL-N	154	650	108	176	25	7	8	58	71	49	21	9	.271	.343	.368	.711	89	-7	87	4.79	21	*2-154	24	2.6
1958 StL-N★	143	547	71	150	19	10	2	36	57	47	20	5	.274	.344	.356	.700	82	-10	69	4.44	-4	*2-137	13	-0.4
1959 StL-N	150	615	90	178	26	7	1	24	67	42	15	15	.289	.361	.359	.720	87	-12	83	4.84	10	*2-150	18	0.9
1960 SF-N	136	523	72	123	12	8	2	31	49	53	14	2	.235	.303	.300	.603	70	-18	52	3.41	-7	*2-133	13	-1.6
1961 SF-N	3	1	1	0	0	0	0	0	2	1	0	0	.000	.667	.000	.667	100	0	0	9.36	0	....	0	0.0
*Cin-N	123	450	59	100	18	4	1	21	39	38	4	3	.222	.287	.287	.574	52	-31	38	2.80	-2	*2-116	6	-2.3
Yr.	126	451	60	100	18	4	1	21	41	39	4	3	.222	.289	.286	.576	52	-30	39	2.82	-2	*2-116	6	-2.3
1962 Cin-N	141	494	77	139	9	7	2	35	63	44	4	3	.281	.365	.340	.705	88	-6	66	4.81	3	*2-137	17	0.8
1963 Cin-N	18	31	4	5	2	0	0	0	7	5	0	1	.161	.316	.226	.542	57	-2	3	2.55	-1	2-11/3-2	1	-0.2
Was-A	69	254	29	65	10	2	2	12	24	18	3	2	.256	.320	.335	.655	84	-5	29	4.03	4	2-64	7	0.4
1964 Was-A	143	506	56	135	17	2	1	34	40	44	8	5	.267	.321	.314	.635	78	-15	54	3.79	-7	*2-135	12	-1.2
1965 Was-A	129	403	47	90	8	8	1	18	35	45	5	4	.223	.289	.290	.579	66	-18	36	2.96	-1	*2-110	7	-1.2
1966 Was-A	68	200	18	43	9	0	1	11	18	21	2	1	.215	.280	.275	.555	61	-10	17	2.83	-1	2-58/S-1	4	-0.7
KC-A	12	19	1	3	0	0	0	1	2	3	0	1	.158	.238	.158	.396	17	-2	1	1.06	1	/2-4	0	-0.2
Yr.	80	219	19	46	9	0	1	12	20	24	2	2	.210	.276	.265	.541	57	-12	18	2.66	0	2-62/S-1	4	-0.8
Total 12	**1444**	**5296**	**731**	**1366**	**178**	**62**	**21**	**308**	**552**	**462**	**105**	**60**	**.258**	**.330**	**.327**	**.657**	**78**	**-150**	**610**	**4.01**	**26**	***2-1310/S-52,3-4**	**140**	**-1.8**
• BLATNIK, Johnny	John Louis Blatnik b: 3/10/1921, Bridgeport, OH BR/TR, 6', 195 lbs. Deb: 4/21/1948 Career OF: 108-0-9																							
1948 Phi-N	121	415	56	108	27	8	6	45	31	77	3	....	.260	.315	.407	.722	96	-4	51	4.28	-3	*O-105(105-0-0)	9	-1.5
1949 Phi-N	6	8	3	1	0	0	0	0	4	1	0	....	.125	.417	.125	.542	53	-0	1	3.28	0	/O-2(0-0-2)	0	0.0
1950 Phi-N	4	4	0	1	0	0	0	0	2	3	0	....	.250	.500	.250	.750	106	0	1	6.84	-0	/O-1	0	0.0
StL-N	7	20	0	3	0	0	0	1	3	2	0	....	.150	.261	.150	.411	11	-3	1	1.23	0	/O-7(2-0-7)	0	-0.3
Yr.	11	24	0	4	0	0	0	1	5	5	0	....	.167	.310	.167	.477	30	-2	2	2.03	-0	/O-8(3-0-7)	0	-0.2
Total 3	**138**	**447**	**59**	**113**	**27**	**8**	**6**	**46**	**40**	**83**	**3**	**....**	**.253**	**.317**	**.389**	**.706**	**91**	**-6**	**54**	**4.12**	**-3**	**O-115**	**9**	**-1.8**
• BLATTNER, Buddy	Robert Garnett Blattner b: 2/8/1920, St. Louis, MO BR/TR, 6'.5", 180 lbs. Deb: 4/18/1942																							
1942 StL-N	19	23	3	1	0	0	0	1	3	6	0	....	.043	.185	.043	.229	-29	-4	0	.35	-1	S-13/2-3	0	-0.4
1946 NY-N	126	420	63	107	18	6	11	49	56	52	12	....	.255	.351	.405	.755	113	8	63	5.25	-2	*2-114/1-1	13	1.3
1947 NY-N	55	153	28	40	9	2	0	13	21	19	4	....	.261	.351	.346	.697	85	-3	20	4.75	-1	2-34,3-11	4	-0.2
1948 NY-N	8	20	3	4	1	0	0	0	3	2	2	....	.200	.304	.250	.554	51	-1	2	2.92	2	/2-7	0	0.1
1949 Phi-N	64	97	15	24	6	0	5	21	19	17	0	....	.247	.371	.464	.835	126	4	18	6.21	-3	2-15,3-12/S-1	4	0.1
Total 5	**272**	**713**	**112**	**176**	**34**	**8**	**16**	**84**	**102**	**96**	**18**	**....**	**.247**	**.347**	**.384**	**.731**	**103**	**4**	**103**	**5.01**	**-5**	**2-173/3-23,S-14,1-1**	**21**	**0.9**
• BLAUSER, Jeff	Jeffrey Michael Blauser b: 11/8/1965, Los Gatos, CA BR/TR, 6', 170 lbs. Deb: 7/5/1987 Career OF: 1-3-0																							
1987 Atl-N	51	165	11	40	6	3	2	15	18	34	7	3	.242	.328	.352	.679	76	-5	19	3.95	2	S-50	4	0.1
1988 Atl-N	18	67	7	16	3	1	2	7	2	11	0	1	.239	.271	.403	.674	87	-2	7	3.25	1	/2-9,S-8	1	0.0
1989 Atl-N	142	456	63	123	24	2	12	46	38	101	5	2	.270	.327	.410	.737	107	3	62	4.73	-9	3-78,2-39,S-30/O-2(0-2-0)	12	-0.3
1990 Atl-N	115	386	46	104	24	3	8	39	35	70	3	5	.269	.338	.409	.747	99	-2	54	4.95	-11	S-93,2-14/3-9,O-1	10	-0.6
1991*Atl-N	129	352	49	91	14	3	11	54	54	59	5	6	.259	.360	.409	.769	109	4	54	5.25	-4	S-85,2-32,3-18	13	0.5
1992*Atl-N	123	343	61	90	19	3	14	46	46	82	5	5	.262	.356	.458	.814	122	9	59	5.85	-3	*S-106,2-21/3-1	18	1.2
1993*Atl-N★	161	597	110	182	29	2	15	73	85	109	16	6	.305	.405	.436	.841	124	26	112	6.77	-5	*S-161	29	3.3
1994 Atl-N	96	380	56	98	21	4	6	45	38	64	1	3	.258	.333	.382	.715	84	-10	48	4.18	-2	S-96	10	-0.3
1995*Atl-N	115	431	60	91	16	2	12	31	57	107	8	5	.211	.320	.341	.661	72	-17	50	3.84	-3	*S-115	10	-1.1
1996*Atl-N	83	265	48	65	14	1	10	35	40	54	6	0	.245	.357	.419	.776	98	1	42	5.44	-14	S-79	9	-0.7
1997*Atl-N★	151	519	90	160	31	4	17	70	70	101	5	1	.308	.411	.482	.892	130	27	107	7.45	-6	*S-149/D-1	27	3.2
1998*Chi-N	119	361	49	79	11	3	4	26	60	93	2	2	.219	.343	.299	.642	68	-15	42	3.82	-15	*S-106	6	-2.1
1999 Chi-N	104	200	41	48	5	2	9	26	26	52	2	2	.240	.350	.420	.770	95	-2	32	5.51	-4	2-25,S-22,3-18/O-1	5	-0.3
Total 13	**1407**	**4522**	**691**	**1187**	**217**	**33**	**122**	**513**	**569**	**937**	**65**	**41**	**.262**	**.356**	**.406**	**.762**	**102**	**18**	**687**	**5.24**	**-74**	***S-1100,2-140,3-124/O-4,D-1**	**154**	**2.9**
• BLAYLOCK, Marv	Marvin Edward Blaylock b: 9/30/1929, Fort Smith, AR d: 10/23/1993, Conway, AR BL/TL, 6'1.5", 175 lbs. Deb: 9/26/1950 Career OF: 4-0-5																							
1950 NY-N	1	1	0	0	0	0	0	0	0	0	0	....	.000	.000	.000	.000	-99	-0	0	.00	0	....	0	0.0
1955 Phi-N	113	259	30	54	7	7	3	24	31	43	6	1	.208	.296	.324	.620	65	-12	27	3.34	7	1-77/O-6(4-0-2)	4	-0.9
1956 Phi-N	136	460	61	117	14	8	10	50	50	86	5	1	.254	.330	.385	.715	93	-3	60	4.44	1	*1-124/O-1	13	-0.9
1957 Phi-N	37	26	5	4	0	0	2	4	3	8	0	0	.154	.313	.385	.697	89	-0	4	4.43	-1	1-12/O-1	1	-0.1
Total 4	**287**	**746**	**96**	**175**	**21**	**15**	**15**	**78**	**84**	**137**	**11**	**2**	**.235**	**.317**	**.363**	**.680**	**83**	**-15**	**90**	**4.04**	**7**	**1-213/O-8**	**18**	**-1.9**
• BLEFARY, Curt	Curtis Le Roy Blefary b: 7/5/1943, Brooklyn, NY d: 1/28/2001, Pompano Beach, FL BL/TR, 6'2", 195 lbs. Deb: 4/14/1965 Career OF: 323-0-232																							
1965 Bal-A	144	462	72	120	23	4	22	70	88	73	4	2	.260	.382	.470	.851	138	26	87	6.50	6	*O-136(63-0-73)	26	2.7
1966*Bal-A	131	419	73	107	14	3	23	64	73	56	1	4	.255	.373	.468	.841	142	24	77	6.24	3	*O-109(109-0-0),1-20	20	2.4
1967 Bal-A	155	554	69	134	19	5	22	81	73	94	4	4	.242	.339	.413	.752	122	16	81	5.00	7	*O-103(86-0-19),1-52	19	1.5
1968 Bal-A	137	451	50	90	8	1	15	39	65	66	6	3	.200	.306	.322	.627	90	-4	49	3.42	-2	O-92(55-0-46),C-40,1-12	13	-1.2
1969 Hou-N	155	542	66	137	26	7	12	67	77	79	8	7	.253	.350	.393	.743	110	8	77	4.86	-1	*1-152/O-1	17	-0.5
1970 NY-A	99	269	34	57	6	0	9	37	43	37	1	3	.212	.327	.335	.662	87	-4	31	3.68	-4	O-79(0-0-79)/1-6	6	-1.3
1971 NY-A	21	36	4	7	1	0	1	2	3	5	0	0	.194	.256	.306	.562	62	-2	3	2.45	0	/O-6(0-0-6),1-4	1	-0.3

YEAR TM-L	G	AB	R	H	2B	3B	HR	RBI	BB	SO	SB	CS	AVG	OBP	SLG	OPS	OPS+	BR/A	RC	RC/G	FR	G/POS	WS	TPW
• BOCCABELLA, John	John Dominic Boccabella b: 6/29/1941, San Francisco, CA BR/TR, 6'1", 200 lbs. Deb: 9/2/1963 Career OF: 41-0-5																							
1963 Chi-N	24	74	7	14	4	1	1	5	6	21	0	1	.189	.250	.311	.561	57	-4	5	2.22	-1	1-24	1	-0.7
1964 Chi-N	9	23	4	9	2	1	0	6	0	3	0	0	.391	.391	.565	.957	159	2	5	8.14	0	/1-5,0-2(2-0-0)	1	0.1
1965 Chi-N	6	12	2	4	0	0	2	4	1	2	0	0	.333	.385	.833	1.218	227	2	4	13.32	0	/1-2,0-1	1	0.2
1966 Chi-N	75	206	22	47	9	0	6	25	14	39	0	1	.228	.277	.359	.636	74	-8	19	2.91	1	0-33(33-0-0),1-30/C-5	2	-1.0
1967 Chi-N	25	35	0	6	1	1	0	8	3	7	0	0	.171	.256	.257	.514	45	-2	2	2.02	-1	/0-9(4-0-5),1-3,C-1	0	-0.4
1968 Chi-N	7	14	0	1	0	0	0	1	2	2	0	0	.071	.188	.071	.259	-19	-2	0	.69	-1	/C-4,0-1	0	-0.3
1969 Mon-N	40	86	4	9	2	0	1	6	6	30	1	0	.105	.172	.163	.335	-6	-12	2	.83	2	C-32	1	-0.9
1970 Mon-N	61	145	18	39	3	1	5	17	11	24	0	1	.269	.321	.407	.727	94	-2	18	4.44	7	1-33,C-24/3-1	4	0.3
1971 Mon-N	74	177	15	39	11	0	3	15	14	26	0	1	.220	.281	.333	.615	73	-7	15	2.81	1	1-37,C-37/3-2	3	-0.7
1972 Mon-N	83	207	14	47	8	1	1	10	9	29	1	2	.227	.263	.290	.553	56	-13	15	2.36	2	C-73/1-7,3-1	4	-0.9
1973 Mon-N	118	403	25	94	13	0	7	46	26	57	1	1	.233	.281	.318	.599	63	-21	33	2.67	3	*C-117/1-1	6	-1.3
1974 SF-N	29	80	6	11	3	0	0	5	4	6	0	0	.138	.179	.175	.354	-1	-11	2	.86	-1	C-26	1	-1.2
Total 12	551	1462	117	320	56	5	26	148	96	246	3	7	.219	.269	.317	.587	62	-79	122	2.68	13	C-319,1-142/0-46,3-4	24	-6.7
• BOCEK, Milt	Milton Frank Bocek b: 7/16/1912, Chicago, IL BR/TR, 6'1", 185 lbs. Deb: 9/3/1933 Career OF: 12-2-2																							
1933 Chi-A	11	22	3	8	1	0	1	3	4	6	0	0	.364	.462	.545	1.007	173	3	6	10.94	0	/0-6(3-1-2)	1	0.2
1934 Chi-A	19	38	3	8	1	0	0	3	5	5	0	0	.211	.302	.237	.539	39	-3	3	2.64	2	0-10(9-1-0)	0	-0.2
Total 2	30	60	6	16	2	0	1	6	9	11	0	0	.267	.362	.350	.712	90	-1	9	5.28	2	/0-16	1	0.0
• BOCHTE, Bruce	Bruce Anton Bochte b: 11/12/1950, Pasadena, CA BL/TL, 6'3", 200 lbs. Deb: 7/19/1974 Career OF: 372-52-22																							
1974 Cal-A	57	196	24	53	4	1	5	26	18	23	6	3	.270	.335	.378	.712	111	3	24	4.15	-2	0-39(32-5-3),1-24	5	-0.3
1975 Cal-A	107	375	41	107	19	3	3	48	45	43	3	4	.285	.365	.376	.741	118	9	53	5.01	-6	*1-105/D-1	13	-0.5
1976 Cal-A	146	466	53	120	17	1	2	49	64	53	4	5	.258	.350	.311	.661	101	2	52	3.75	1	0-86(71-0-18),1-59/D-1	15	-0.6
1977 Cal-A	25	100	12	29	4	0	2	8	7	4	3	2	.290	.336	.390	.726	101	-0	12	4.32	1	0-24(0-24-0)/D-1	3	0.1
Cle-A	112	392	52	119	19	1	5	43	40	38	3	2	.304	.368	.395	.763	112	7	54	4.83	1	0-76(74-3-1),1-36/D-1	11	0.2
Yr.	137	492	64	148	23	1	7	51	47	42	6	4	.301	.362	.394	.756	110	7	67	4.73	2	*0-100(74-27-1),1-36/D-2	14	0.3
1978 Sea-A	140	486	58	128	25	3	11	51	60	47	3	4	.263	.346	.395	.741	108	6	67	4.64	0	0-91(82-19-0),D-43/1-1	12	0.1
1979 Sea-A★	150	554	81	175	38	6	16	100	67	64	2	2	.316	.392	.493	.884	135	28	100	6.43	1	*1-147	19	2.0
1980 Sea-A	148	520	62	156	34	4	13	78	72	81	2	3	.300	.385	.456	.841	128	22	90	6.15	7	*1-133,D-11	19	2.0
1981 Sea-A	99	335	39	87	16	0	6	30	47	53	1	3	.260	.354	.361	.715	102	2	44	4.66	-2	1-82,0-14(14-0-0)/D-1	9	-0.6
1982 Sea-A	144	509	58	151	21	0	12	70	67	71	8	5	.297	.382	.409	.790	114	12	79	5.51	3	0-99(99-1-0),1-34,D-12	15	0.9
1984 Oak-A	148	469	58	124	23	0	5	52	52	59	2	5	.264	.338	.345	.683	96	-3	54	3.92	-7	*1-144/D-2	10	-1.8
1985 Oak-A	137	424	48	125	17	1	14	60	49	58	3	1	.295	.368	.439	.807	129	18	67	5.73	0	*1-128	17	1.1
1986 Oak-A	125	407	57	104	13	1	6	43	65	68	3	2	.256	.358	.337	.695	98	1	52	4.44	3	*1-115/D-1	11	-0.2
Total 12	1538	5233	643	1478	250	21	100	658	653	662	43	41	.282	.363	.396	.759	113	107	749	4.99	1	*1-1008,0-429/D-74	159	2.5
• BOCHY, Bruce	Bruce Douglas Bochy b: 4/16/1955, Landes De Bussac, France BR/TR, 6'3", 210 lbs. Deb: 7/19/1978 M/C																							
1978 Hou-N	54	154	8	41	8	0	3	15	11	35	0	0	.266	.315	.377	.692	100	-1	16	3.52	1	C-53	4	0.2
1979 Hou-N	56	129	11	28	4	0	1	6	13	25	0	0	.217	.294	.271	.565	58	-7	10	2.48	-1	C-55	2	-0.7
1980*Hou-N	22	22	0	4	1	0	0	0	5	7	0	0	.182	.357	.227	.584	72	-0	2	3.38	-1	C-10/1-1	0	-0.1
1982 NY-N	17	49	4	15	4	0	2	8	4	6	0	0	.306	.358	.510	.869	141	3	9	6.82	0	C-16/1-1	3	0.4
1983 SD-N	23	42	2	9	1	1	0	3	0	9	0	0	.214	.214	.286	.500	39	-4	2	1.51	0	C-11	0	-0.3
1984*SD-N	37	92	10	21	5	1	4	15	3	21	0	1	.228	.253	.435	.687	90	-2	9	3.22	0	C-36	3	-0.2
1985 SD-N	48	112	16	30	2	0	6	13	6	30	0	0	.268	.305	.446	.752	109	1	15	4.85	-1	C-46	4	0.2
1986 SD-N	63	127	16	32	9	0	8	22	14	23	1	0	.252	.326	.512	.838	130	5	21	5.69	1	C-48	6	0.8
1987 SD-N	38	75	8	12	3	0	2	11	11	21	0	1	.160	.267	.280	.547	47	-6	5	2.09	-1	C-23	0	-0.7
Total 9	358	802	75	192	37	2	26	93	67	177	1	2	.239	.300	.388	.687	92	-13	89	3.73	-2	C-298/1-2	22	-0.3
• BOCKMAN, Eddie	Joseph Edward Bockman b: 7/26/1920, Santa Ana, CA BR/TR, 5'9", 175 lbs. Deb: 9/11/1946																							
1946 NY-A	4	12	2	1	1	0	0	0	1	4	0	0	.083	.154	.167	.321	-10	-2	0	.87	0	/3-4	0	-0.2
1947 Cle-A	46	66	8	17	2	2	1	14	5	17	0	0	.258	.310	.394	.704	97	-0	9	4.77	2	3-12/2-4,0-1,S-1	2	0.2
1948 Pit-N	70	176	23	42	7	1	4	23	17	35	2	....	.239	.309	.358	.667	78	-6	19	3.51	4	3-51/2-1	4	-0.1
1949 Pit-N	79	220	21	49	6	1	6	19	23	31	3	....	.223	.296	.341	.637	69	-10	23	3.54	0	3-68/2-5	4	-1.0
Total 4	199	474	54	109	16	4	11	56	46	87	5	0	.230	.299	.350	.650	74	-18	51	3.61	7	3-135/2-10,0-1,S-1	10	-1.1
• BODIE, Ping	Frank Stephen Bodie b: 10/8/1887, San Francisco, CA d: 12/17/1961, San Francisco, CA BR/TR, 5'8", 195 lbs. Deb: 4/22/1911 Career OF: 293-625-77																							
1911 Chi-A	145	551	75	159	27	13	4	97	49	....	14	....	.289	.348	.407	.754	113	8	82	5.23	3	*0-128(0-107-21),2-16	20	0.3
1912 Chi-A	138	472	58	139	24	7	5	72	43	....	12	....	.294	.358	.407	.765	122	13	73	5.42	-8	*0-130(8-72-50)	17	-0.1
1913 Chi-A	127	406	39	107	14	8	8	48	35	57	5	....	.264	.325	.397	.722	112	4	54	4.27	-4	*0-119(43-76-0)	16	-0.7
1914 Chi-A	107	327	21	75	9	5	3	29	21	35	12	11	.229	.278	.315	.593	79	-12	32	2.85	3	0-95(2-92-1)	6	-1.7
1917 Phi-A	148	557	51	162	28	11	7	74	53	40	13	....	.291	.356	.418	.774	138	24	86	5.34	10	*0-145(145-0-0)/1-1	22	3.1
1918 NY-A	91	324	36	83	12	6	3	46	27	24	6	....	.256	.319	.358	.677	102	-0	39	3.85	5	0-90(90-0-0)	9	0.1
1919 NY-A	134	475	45	132	27	8	6	59	36	46	15	....	.278	.334	.406	.740	106	3	67	4.86	-3	*0-134(0-129-5)	18	-0.9
1920 NY-A	129	471	63	139	26	12	7	79	40	30	6	14	.295	.350	.446	.796	106	-1	70	5.15	-10	*0-129(0-129-0)	16	-1.8
1921 NY-A	31	87	5	15	2	2	0	12	8	8	0	1	.172	.242	.241	.483	23	-11	5	1.85	-2	0-25(5-20-0)	0	-1.3
Total 9	1050	3670	393	1011	169	72	43	516	312	240	83	26	.275	.335	.396	.731	110	28	508	4.64	-7	0-995/2-16,1-1	124	-2.9
• BOECKEL, Tony	Norman Doxie Boeckel b: 8/25/1892, Los Angeles, CA d: 2/16/1924, La Jolla, CA BR/TR, 5'10.5", 175 lbs. Deb: 7/23/1917																							
1917 Pit-N	64	219	16	58	11	1	0	23	8	31	6	....	.265	.297	.324	.621	87	-4	22	3.42	2	3-62	4	0.0
1919 Pit-N	45	152	18	38	9	2	0	16	18	20	11	....	.250	.333	.336	.669	97	0	20	4.32	-2	3-45	5	0.0
Bos-N	95	365	42	91	11	5	1	26	35	13	10	....	.249	.317	.315	.632	94	-2	38	3.51	-3	3-93	9	-0.3
Yr.	140	517	60	129	20	7	1	42	53	33	21	....	.250	.322	.321	.643	95	-2	58	3.75	-5	*3-138	14	-0.3
1920 Bos-N	153	582	70	156	28	5	3	62	38	50	18	15	.268	.314	.349	.663	94	-5	62	3.67	-12	*3-149/S-3,2-1	13	-1.4
1921 Bos-N	153	592	93	185	20	13	10	84	52	41	20	15	.313	.370	.441	.811	120	18	95	5.75	-8	*3-153	23	2.0
1922 Bos-N	119	402	61	116	19	6	6	47	35	32	14	8	.289	.349	.410	.759	99	0	58	5.04	-8	*3-106	11	-0.1
1923 Bos-N	148	568	72	169	32	4	7	79	51	31	11	8	.298	.357	.405	.762	105	5	83	5.24	-12	*3-147/S-1	15	0.3
Total 6	777	2880	372	813	130	36	27	337	237	218	90	46	.282	.339	.381	.720	102	12	378	4.58	-42	3-755/S-4,2-1	80	0.5
• BOEHMER, Len	Leonard Joseph Stephen Boehmer b: 6/28/1941, Flinthill, MO BR/TR, 6'1", 192 lbs. Deb: 6/18/1967																							
1967 Cin-N	2	3	0	0	0	0	0	0	0	0	0	0	.000	.000	.000	.000	-90	-1	0	.00	0	/2-1	0	-0.1
1969 NY-A	45	108	5	19	4	0	0	7	8	10	0	1	.176	.233	.213	.446	26	-11	5	1.41	0	1-21/3-8,2-1,S-1	1	-1.4
1971 NY-A	3	5	0	0	0	0	0	0	0	0	0	0	.000	.000	.000	.000	-107	-1	0	.00	0	/3-1	0	-0.2
Total 3	50	116	5	19	4	0	0	7	8	10	0	1	.164	.218	.198	.416	18	-13	5	1.30	-1	/1-21,3-9,2-2,S-1	1	-1.6
• BOGAR, Tim	Timothy Paul Bogar b: 10/28/1966, Indianapolis, IN BR/TR, 6'2", 198 lbs. Deb: 4/21/1993 Career OF: 2-0-0																							
1993 NY-N	78	205	19	50	13	0	3	25	14	29	0	1	.244	.302	.351	.653	75	-8	22	3.71	5	S-66/3-7,2-6	6	0.2
1994 NY-N	50	52	5	8	0	0	2	5	4	11	1	0	.154	.214	.269	.484	25	-6	3	1.77	0	3-22,1-14/S-7,2-1,0-1	1	-0.6
1995 NY-N	78	145	17	42	7	0	1	21	9	25	1	0	.290	.331	.359	.690	85	-3	18	4.40	2	S-27,3-25,1-10/2-7,0-1	4	0.0
1996 NY-N	91	89	17	19	4	0	0	6	8	20	1	3	.213	.293	.258	.551	49	-8	7	2.49	1	1-32,3-25,S-19/2-8	1	-0.6
1997 Hou-N	97	241	30	60	14	4	4	30	24	42	4	1	.249	.325	.390	.715	90	-3	32	4.44	2	S-80,3-14/1-1	7	0.4
1998 Hou-N	79	156	12	24	4	1	1	8	9	36	2	1	.154	.210	.212	.421	11	-20	6	1.24	5	S-55,2-11,3-11/D-1	3	-1.2
1999*Hou-N	107	309	44	74	16	2	4	31	38	52	3	5	.239	.330	.343	.674	72	-15	34	3.62	5	S-90,3-12/2-1	7	-0.3
2000 Hou-N	110	304	32	63	9	2	7	33	35	56	1	5	.207	.295	.319	.614	52	-23	27	2.71	4	S-95/2-2,P-2,3-1	5	-1.1
2001 LA-N	12	15	4	5	2	0	2	2	2	1	0	0	.333	.412	.867	1.278	235	3	6	15.03	-1	/1-3,S-2,3-1	0	0.1
Total 9	702	1516	180	345	69	9	24	161	143	272	13	12	.228	.301	.332	.634	65	-83	154	3.32	22	S-441,3-118/1-60,2-36,0-2,P,D	34	-3.0
• BOGENER, Terry	Terry Wayne Bogener b: 9/28/1955, Hannibal, MO BL/TL, 6', 193 lbs. Deb: 6/14/1982																							
1982 Tex-A	24	60	6	13	2	1	1	4	4	8	2	0	.217	.288	.333	.621	74	-2	6	2.92	0	0-16(4-10-2)/D-4	0	-0.2

YEAR TM-L	G	AB	R	H	2B	3B	HR	RBI	BB	SO	SB	CS	AVG	OBP	SLG	OPS	OPS+	BR/A	RC	RC/G	FR	G/POS	WS	TPW
• BOGGS, Wade	Wade Anthony Boggs b: 6/15/1958, Omaha, NE BL/TR, 6'2", 197 lbs. Deb: 4/10/1982 C																							
1982 Bos-A	104	338	51	118	14	1	5	44	35	21	1	0	.349	.410	.441	.851	126	14	61	6.96	12	1-49,3-44/D-3,0-1	15	2.3
1983 Bos-A	153	582	100	210	44	7	5	74	92	36	3	3	**.361**	**.449**	.486	.935	147	43	130	**8.80**	13	*3-153	34	5.4
1984 Bos-A	158	625	109	203	31	4	6	55	89	44	3	2	.325	.409	.416	.825	123	25	110	6.64	16	*3-156/D-2	28	3.9
1985 Bos-A★	161	653	107	**240**	42	3	8	78	96	61	2	1	**.368**	**.452**	.478	.929	149	51	143	8.81	-1	*3-161	31	4.7
1986*Bos-A★	149	580	107	207	47	2	8	71	**105**	44	0	4	**.357**	**.455**	.486	.942	156	51	133	**9.05**	-2	*3-149	**37**	4.5
1987 Bos-A★	147	551	108	200	40	6	24	89	105	48	1	3	**.363**	**.467**	.588	**1.055**	**173**	**63**	154	**11.03**	-5	*3-145/1-1,D-1	32	5.3
1988*Bos-A★	155	584	**128**	214	**45**	6	5	58	**125**	34	2	3	**.366**	**.480**	.490	**.970**	165	61	140	**9.40**	-4	*3-151/D-3	31	5.9
1989 Bos-A★	156	621	**113**	205	**51**	7	3	54	107	51	2	6	.330	**.434**	.449	.883	141	39	122	7.36	-3	*3-152/D-3	29	3.7
1990*Bos-A★	155	619	89	187	44	5	6	63	87	68	0	0	.302	.389	.418	.807	120	20	103	6.12	-26	*3-152/D-3	24	-0.5
1991 Bos-A★	144	546	93	181	42	2	8	51	89	32	1	2	.332	.425	.460	.885	138	33	107	7.40	4	*3-140	25	3.7
1992 Bos-A★	143	514	62	133	22	4	7	50	74	31	1	3	.259	.356	.358	.714	94	-2	67	4.54	-4	*3-117,D-21	15	-0.6
1993 NY-A★	143	560	83	169	26	1	2	59	74	49	0	1	.302	.383	.363	.746	105	7	82	5.34	16	*3-134/D-8	20	2.4
1994 NY-A★	97	366	61	125	19	1	11	55	61	29	2	1	.342	.437	.489	.926	144	27	80	8.42	8	3-93/1-4	18	3.4
1995*NY-A★	126	460	76	149	22	4	5	63	74	50	1	1	.324	.418	.422	.839	120	17	83	6.79	4	*3-117/1-9	18	2.1
1996*NY-A★	132	501	80	156	29	2	2	41	67	32	1	2	.311	.393	.389	.782	99	1	79	5.86	1	*3-123/D-4	15	0.3
1997*NY-A	104	353	55	103	23	1	4	28	48	38	0	1	.292	.377	.397	.773	103	3	56	5.81	4	3-76,D-19/P-1	10	0.7
1998 TB-A	123	435	51	122	23	4	7	52	46	54	3	2	.280	.349	.400	.749	93	-5	59	4.85	4	3-78,D-33	6	-0.2
1999 TB-A	90	292	40	88	14	1	2	29	38	23	1	0	.301	.382	.377	.759	93	-1	41	4.97	-4	3-74/D-8,1-4,P-1	6	-0.5
Total 18	2440	9180	1513	3010	578	61	118	1014	1412	745	24	35	.328	.419	.443	.861	130	447	1751	7.20	31	*3-2215,D-108/1-67,P-2,0-1	394	46.5
• BOHN, Charlie	Charles Bohn b: 1857, Cleveland, OH d: 8/1/1903, Cleveland, OH BR/TR, 5'9", 165 lbs. Deb: 6/20/1882 ♦																							
1882 Lou-a	4	13	0	2	0	0	0	....	0	....	....	....	.154	.154	.154	.308	4	-1	0	.80	0	/0-2(0-2-0),P-2	1	-0.2
• BOHNE, Sam	Samuel Arthur Bohne b: 10/22/1896, San Francisco, CA d: 5/23/1977, Palo Alto, CA BR/TR, 5'8.5", 175 lbs. Deb: 9/9/1916																							
1916 StL-N	14	38	3	9	0	0	0	0	4	6	3	....	.237	.310	.237	.546	69	-1	4	3.21	-3	S-14	1	-0.3
1921 Cin-N	153	613	98	175	28	16	3	44	54	38	26	22	.285	.347	.398	.745	101	0	83	4.57	18	*2-102,3-53	20	2.4
1922 Cin-N	112	383	53	105	14	5	3	51	39	18	13	8	.274	.344	.360	.705	83	-8	49	4.37	12	2-85,S-20	12	0.8
1923 Cin-N	139	539	77	136	18	10	3	47	48	37	16	19	.252	.316	.340	.655	74	-23	56	3.39	6	2-96,3-35/S-9,1-1	12	-1.1
1924 Cin-N	100	349	42	89	15	9	4	46	18	24	9	6	.255	.293	.384	.677	81	-10	39	3.70	-11	2-48,S-40,3-12	7	-1.5
1925 Cin-N	73	214	24	55	9	1	2	24	14	14	6	4	.257	.303	.336	.639	65	-12	22	3.41	-2	S-49,2-10/0-4(1-0-4),1-2,3	4	-0.9
1926 Cin-N	25	54	8	11	0	2	0	5	4	8	1	....	.204	.259	.278	.536	46	-4	4	2.23	-2	S-20	0	-0.5
Bro-N	47	125	4	25	3	2	1	11	12	9	1	....	.200	.270	.280	.550	49	-9	10	2.43	2	2-31,3-15	2	-0.5
Yr.	72	179	12	36	3	4	1	16	16	17	2	....	.201	.267	.279	.546	48	-13	14	2.36	0	2-31,S-20,3-15	2	-1.0
Total 7	663	2315	309	605	87	45	16	228	193	154	75	59	.261	.321	.359	.679	81	-67	266	3.82	21	2-372,S-152,3-117/0-4,1-3	58	-1.6
• BOISCLAIR, Bruce	Bruce Armand Boisclair b: 12/9/1952, Putnam, CT BL/TL, 6'2", 190 lbs. Deb: 9/11/1974 Career OF: 87-53-150																							
1974 NY-N	7	12	0	3	1	0	0	1	1	4	0	0	.250	.308	.333	.641	81	-0	1	2.65	1	/0-5(2-3-0)	0	0.0
1976 NY-N	110	286	42	82	13	3	2	13	28	55	9	5	.287	.350	.374	.724	112	4	38	4.77	-2	0-87(35-39-20)	10	-0.1
1977 NY-N	127	307	41	90	21	1	4	44	31	57	6	4	.293	.360	.407	.767	110	5	46	5.28	-5	0-91(30-9-55)/1-9	8	-0.4
1978 NY-N	107	214	24	48	7	1	4	15	23	43	3	3	.224	.300	.322	.622	77	-7	21	3.12	1	0-69(12-2-58)/1-1	3	-1.0
1979 NY-N	59	98	7	18	5	1	0	4	3	24	0	2	.184	.216	.255	.471	29	-11	5	1.47	1	0-24(8-0-17)/1-1	0	-1.1
Total 5	410	917	114	241	47	6	10	77	86	183	18	14	.263	.327	.360	.687	94	-10	111	4.10	-5	0-276/1-11	21	-2.6
• BOKEN, Bob	Robert Anthony Boken b: 2/23/1908, Maryville, IL d: 10/8/1988, Las Vegas, NV BR/TR, 6'2", 165 lbs. Deb: 4/25/1933																							
1933 Was-A	55	133	19	37	5	2	3	26	9	16	0	0	.278	.324	.414	.737	95	-1	18	4.84	0	2-31,3-19,S-10	4	0.0
1934 Was-A	11	27	5	6	1	1	0	6	3	1	2	0	.222	.300	.333	.633	66	-1	3	3.93	0	/3-6,2-1	0	-0.1
Chi-A	81	297	30	70	9	1	3	40	15	32	2	1	.236	.275	.303	.578	47	-24	25	2.85	-17	2-57,S-22	1	-3.3
Yr.	92	324	35	76	10	2	3	46	18	33	4	1	.235	.277	.306	.583	49	-25	28	2.94	-17	2-58,S-22/3-6	1	-3.4
Total 2	147	457	54	113	15	4	6	72	27	49	4	1	.247	.291	.337	.628	63	-26	46	3.47	-17	/2-89,S-32,3-25	5	-3.4
• BOLAND,	Boland Deb: 9/4/1875																							
1875 Atl-n	1	4	0	0	0	0	0	0	0	0	0	0	.000	.000	.000	.000	-115	-1	0	.00	0	/3-1	....	-0.1
• BOLAND, Ed	Edward John Boland b: 4/18/1908, Long Island City, NY d: 2/5/1993, Clearwater, FL BL/TL, 5'10", 165 lbs. Deb: 9/18/1934 Career OF: 2-2-27																							
1934 Phi-N	8	30	2	9	1	1	0	5	0	2	1	....	.300	.300	.400	.700	76	-1	4	4.74	0	/0-7(0-0-7)	0	-0.2
1935 Phi-N	30	47	5	10	0	0	0	4	4	6	1	....	.213	.275	.213	.487	30	-5	3	2.26	-2	0-10(2-2-6)	0	-0.7
1944 Was-A	19	59	4	16	4	0	0	14	0	6	0	0	.271	.271	.339	.610	77	-2	5	3.20	0	0-14(0-0-14)	1	-0.3
Total 3	57	136	11	35	5	1	0	23	4	14	2	0	.257	.279	.309	.587	60	-8	12	3.18	-3	/0-31	1	-1.2
• BOLD, Charlie	Charles Dickens "Dutch" Bold b: 10/27/1894, Karlskrona, Sweden d: 7/29/1978, Chelsea, MA BR/TR, 6'2", 185 lbs. Deb: 8/24/1914																							
1914 StL-A	2	1	0	0	0	0	0	0	0	1	0	....	.000	.000	.000	.000	-104	-0	0	.00	0	/1-1	0	-0.1
• BOLES, Carl	Carl Theodore Boles b: 10/31/1934, Center Point, AR BR/TR, 5'11", 185 lbs. Deb: 8/2/1962																							
1962 SF-N	19	24	4	9	0	0	0	1	0	6	0	0	.375	.375	.375	.750	104	0	3	4.00	-1	/0-7(7-0-0)	1	-0.1
• BOLEY, Joe	John Peter Boley b: 7/19/1896, Mahanoy City, PA d: 12/30/1962, Mahanoy City, PA BR/TR, 5'11", 170 lbs. Deb: 4/12/1927																							
1927 Phi-A	118	370	49	115	18	8	1	52	26	14	8	5	.311	.361	.411	.772	95	-3	55	5.30	1	*S-114	12	0.8
1928 Phi-A	132	425	49	112	20	3	0	49	32	11	5	1	.264	.317	.325	.641	67	-19	46	3.65	-8	*S-132	10	-1.2
1929*Phi-A	91	303	36	76	17	6	2	47	24	16	1	0	.251	.310	.366	.676	71	-13	36	4.02	3	S-88/3-1	8	-0.1
1930*Phi-A	121	420	41	116	22	2	4	55	32	26	0	0	.276	.335	.367	.701	74	-16	53	4.50	2	*S-120	12	-0.2
1931*Phi-A	67	224	26	51	9	3	0	20	15	13	1	1	.228	.282	.295	.577	49	-16	19	2.86	0	S-62/2-1	3	-1.1
1932 Phi-A	10	34	2	7	2	0	0	4	1	4	0	1	.206	.229	.265	.493	26	-4	2	1.67	-3	S-10	0	-0.6
Cle-A	1	4	0	1	0	0	0	0	0	0	0	0	.250	.250	.250	.500	28	-0	0	2.12	-1	/S-1	0	-0.1
Yr.	11	38	2	8	2	0	0	4	1	4	0	1	.211	.231	.263	.494	27	-5	2	1.71	-3	S-11	0	-0.7
Total 6	540	1780	203	478	88	22	7	227	130	84	15	8	.269	.323	.354	.677	72	-72	211	4.09	-5	S-527/2-1,3-1	45	-2.5
• BOLGER, Jim	James Cyril "Dutch" Bolger b: 2/23/1932, Cincinnati, OH BR/TR, 6'2", 180 lbs. Deb: 6/24/1950 Career OF: 64-86-23																							
1950 Cin-N	2	1	0	0	0	0	0	0	0	0	0	....	.000	.000	.000	.000	-100	-0	0	.00	0	/0-2(2-0-0)	0	-0.1
1951 Cin-N	2	0	1	0	0	0	0	0	0	0	1	0	....	....	....	....	-98	0	0	....	0	....	0	0.0
1954 Cin-N	5	3	1	1	0	0	0	0	0	1	0	0	.333	.333	.333	.667	72	-0	0	4.50	0	/0-2(0-2-0)	0	-0.1
1955 Chi-N	64	160	19	33	5	4	0	7	9	17	2	2	.206	.257	.288	.545	44	-13	11	2.30	-4	0-51(3-49-0)	2	-2.0
1957 Chi-N	112	273	28	75	4	1	5	29	10	36	0	1	.275	.308	.352	.659	78	-9	27	3.34	-2	0-63(24-28-17)/3-3	4	-1.5
1958 Chi-N	84	120	15	27	4	1	1	11	9	20	0	1	.225	.285	.300	.585	56	-8	10	2.83	-1	0-37(28-6-5)	1	-1.1
1959 Cle-A	8	7	0	0	0	0	0	0	1	1	0	0	.000	.125	.000	.125	-65	-2	0	.13	0	....	0	-0.2
Phi-N	35	48	1	4	1	0	0	1	3	8	0	0	.083	.137	.104	.241	-34	-9	0	.19	-1	/0-9(7-1-1)	0	-1.0
Total 7	312	612	65	140	14	6	6	48	32	83	3	4	.229	.274	.301	.575	54	-41	49	2.61	-9	0-164/3-3	7	-5.8
• BOLICK, Frank	Frank Charles Bolick b: 6/28/1966, Ashland, PA BB/TR, 5'10", 180 lbs. Deb: 4/5/1993																							
1993 Mon-N	95	213	25	45	13	0	4	24	23	37	1	0	.211	.300	.329	.629	65	-10	22	3.40	4	1-51,3-24	3	-0.9
1998 Ana-A	21	45	3	7	2	0	1	2	11	8	0	0	.156	.321	.267	.588	55	-3	5	3.12	0	/D-9,3-7,1-1,0-1	0	-0.3
Total 2	116	258	28	52	15	0	5	26	34	45	1	0	.202	.304	.318	.622	63	-13	26	3.35	4	/1-52,3-31,D-9,0-1	3	-1.2
• BOLLING, Frank	Frank Elmore Bolling b: 11/16/1931, Mobile, AL BR/TR, 6'1", 175 lbs. Deb: 4/13/1954																							
1954 Det-A	117	368	46	87	15	2	6	38	36	51	3	5	.236	.304	.337	.641	77	-13	38	3.44	-14	*2-113	6	-2.1
1956 Det-A	102	366	53	103	21	7	7	45	42	51	6	2	.281	.359	.434	.793	108	5	60	5.76	-1	*2-102	13	1.1
1957 Det-A	146	576	72	149	27	6	15	40	57	64	4	9	.259	.328	.405	.732	96	-6	73	4.26	23	*2-146	17	3.0
1958 Det-A	154	610	91	164	25	4	14	75	54	54	6	4	.269	.332	.392	.724	92	-6	81	4.63	15	*2-154	21	2.1
1959 Det-A	127	459	56	122	18	3	13	55	45	37	2	2	.266	.341	.403	.744	98	-1	65	4.96	10	*2-126	15	1.9
1960 Det-A	139	536	64	136	20	4	9	59	40	48	7	4	.254	.308	.356	.664	74	-20	58	3.76	6	*2-138	12	-0.3
1961 Mil-N★	148	585	86	153	16	4	15	56	57	62	7	3	.262	.330	.379	.710	93	-5	70	3.98	5	*2-148	17	1.3

YEAR TM-L	G	AB	R	H	2B	3B	HR	RBI	BB	SO	SB	CS	AVG	OBP	SLG	OPS	OPS+	BR/A	RC	RC/G	FR	G/POS	WS	TPW
1962 Mil-N★	122	406	45	110	17	4	9	43	35	45	2	2	.271	.335	.399	.734	99	-1	55	4.72	-4	*2-119	14	0.4
1963 Mil-N	142	542	73	132	18	2	5	43	41	47	2	1	.244	.300	.312	.612	77	-15	52	3.16	-1	*2-141	12	-0.3
1964 Mil-N	120	352	35	70	11	1	5	34	21	44	0	1	.199	.248	.278	.526	48	-25	24	2.12	-4	*2-117	2	-2.2
1965 Mil-N	148	535	55	141	26	3	7	50	24	41	0	4	.264	.295	.363	.658	84	-14	54	3.42	-6	*2-147	11	-0.9
1966 Atl-N	75	227	16	48	7	0	1	18	10	14	1	1	.211	.248	.256	.503	40	-18	14	2.05	1	2-67	1	-1.4
Total 12	1540	5562	692	1415	221	40	106	556	462	558	40	38	.254	.315	.366	.681	85	-121	643	3.92	29	*2-1518	141	2.7

• BOLLING, Jack John Edward Bolling b: 2/20/1917, Mobile, AL d: 4/13/1998, Panama City, FL BL/TL, 5'11", 168 lbs. Deb: 6/10/1939

YEAR TM-L	G	AB	R	H	2B	3B	HR	RBI	BB	SO	SB	CS	AVG	OBP	SLG	OPS	OPS+	BR/A	RC	RC/G	FR	G/POS	WS	TPW
1939 Phi-N	69	211	27	61	11	0	3	13	11	10	6	....	.289	.324	.384	.708	94	-3	25	4.41	2	1-48	4	-0.5
1944 Bro-N	56	131	21	46	14	1	1	25	14	4	0	....	.351	.418	.496	.914	159	11	27	8.08	2	1-27	7	1.2
Total 2	125	342	48	107	25	1	4	38	25	14	6	....	.313	.361	.427	.788	120	8	52	5.76	5	/1-75	11	0.7

• BOLLING, Milt Milton Joseph Bolling b: 8/9/1930, Mississippi City, MS BR/TR, 6'1", 180 lbs. Deb: 9/10/1952

YEAR TM-L	G	AB	R	H	2B	3B	HR	RBI	BB	SO	SB	CS	AVG	OBP	SLG	OPS	OPS+	BR/A	RC	RC/G	FR	G/POS	WS	TPW
1952 Bos-A	11	36	4	8	1	0	1	3	3	5	0	1	.222	.282	.333	.615	66	-2	3	3.12	2	S-11	1	0.1
1953 Bos-A	109	323	30	85	12	1	5	28	23	41	1	4	.263	.318	.353	.671	77	-12	37	3.88	6	*S-109	9	0.2
1954 Bos-A	113	370	42	92	20	3	6	36	47	55	2	4	.249	.340	.368	.707	84	-8	49	4.43	-2	*S-107/3-5	10	-0.1
1955 Bos-A	6	5	0	1	0	0	0	0	0	1	0	0	.200	.200	.200	.400	7	-1	0	1.31	0	/S-2	0	-0.1
1956 Bos-A	45	118	19	25	3	2	3	8	18	20	0	1	.212	.321	.347	.669	68	-6	14	3.62	-5	S-26,3-11/2-1	2	-0.9
1957 Bos-A	1	1	0	0	0	0	0	0	0	0	0	0	.000	.000	.000	.000	-95	-0	0	.00	0	....	0	0.0
Was-A	91	277	29	63	12	1	4	19	18	59	2	2	.227	.279	.321	.601	64	-14	22	2.58	1	2-53,S-37/3-1	3	-0.7
Yr.	92	278	29	63	12	1	4	19	18	59	2	2	.227	.279	.320	.599	64	-15	22	2.56	1	2-53,S-37/3-1	3	-0.8
1958 Det-A	24	31	3	6	2	0	0	0	5	7	0	0	.194	.306	.258	.564	53	-2	3	3.03	-1	S-13/2-1,3-1	0	-0.2
Total 7	400	1161	127	280	50	7	19	94	114	188	5	12	.241	.314	.345	.660	74	-45	129	3.64	1	S-305/2-55,3-18	25	-1.8

• BOLLWEG, Don Donald Raymond Bollweg b: 2/12/1921, Wheaton, IL d: 5/26/1996, Wheaton, IL BL/TL, 6'1", 190 lbs. Deb: 9/28/1950

YEAR TM-L	G	AB	R	H	2B	3B	HR	RBI	BB	SO	SB	CS	AVG	OBP	SLG	OPS	OPS+	BR/A	RC	RC/G	FR	G/POS	WS	TPW
1950 StL-N	4	11	1	2	0	0	0	1	1	1	0	....	.182	.250	.182	.432	15	-1	0	1.02	-1	/1-4	0	-0.2
1951 StL-N	6	9	1	1	1	0	0	2	0	1	0	0	.111	.111	.222	.333	-13	-1	0	.77	-1	/1-2	0	-0.2
1953*NY-A	70	155	24	46	6	4	6	24	21	31	1	0	.297	.384	.503	.887	143	10	33	8.13	-5	1-43	8	0.3
1954 Phi-A	103	268	35	60	15	3	5	24	35	33	1	0	.224	.320	.358	.678	85	-5	33	4.15	-1	1-71	6	-1.0
1955 KC-A	12	9	1	1	0	0	0	2	3	2	0	0	.111	.333	.111	.444	23	-1	0	1.42	0	/1-3	0	-0.1
Total 5	195	452	62	110	22	7	11	53	60	68	2	0	.243	.337	.396	.733	100	1	67	5.17	-7	1-123	14	-1.3

• BOLTON, Cecil Cecil Glenford "Glenn" Bolton b: 2/13/1904, Booneville, MS d: 8/25/1993, Jackson, MS BL/TR, 6'4", 195 lbs. Deb: 9/21/1928

YEAR TM-L	G	AB	R	H	2B	3B	HR	RBI	BB	SO	SB	CS	AVG	OBP	SLG	OPS	OPS+	BR/A	RC	RC/G	FR	G/POS	WS	TPW
1928 Cle-A	4	13	1	2	0	2	0	0	2	2	0	0	.154	.267	.462	.728	87	-0	2	4.02	-1	/1-4	0	-0.2

• BOLTON, Cliff William Clifton Bolton b: 4/10/1907, High Point, NC d: 4/21/1979, Lexington, NC BL/TR, 5'9", 160 lbs. Deb: 4/20/1931

YEAR TM-L	G	AB	R	H	2B	3B	HR	RBI	BB	SO	SB	CS	AVG	OBP	SLG	OPS	OPS+	BR/A	RC	RC/G	FR	G/POS	WS	TPW
1931 Was-A	23	43	3	11	1	1	0	6	1	5	0	0	.256	.273	.326	.598	56	-3	4	3.09	-1	C-13	0	-0.3
1933*Was-A	33	39	4	16	1	1	0	6	6	3	0	0	.410	.500	.487	.987	164	4	10	11.51	-1	/C-9,0-1	3	0.3
1934 Was-A	42	148	12	40	9	1	1	17	11	9	2	0	.270	.321	.365	.686	80	-4	18	4.35	-2	C-39	3	-0.4
1935 Was-A	110	375	47	114	18	11	2	55	58	13	0	1	.304	.399	.427	.825	117	12	67	6.71	-8	*C-106	13	0.9
1936 Was-A	86	289	41	84	18	4	2	51	25	12	1	2	.291	.349	.401	.751	90	-6	41	5.19	-1	C-83	9	-0.2
1937 Det-A	27	57	6	15	2	0	1	7	8	6	0	0	.263	.354	.351	.705	76	-2	8	4.73	0	C-13	2	-0.1
1941 Was-A	14	11	0	0	0	0	0	1	1	2	0	0	.000	.083	.000	.083	-80	-3	0	.05	-1	/C-3	0	-0.3
Total 7	335	962	113	280	49	18	6	143	110	50	3	3	.291	.366	.398	.764	99	-1	147	5.64	-14	C-266/0-1	30	0.0

• BOND, Tommy Thomas Henry Bond b: 4/2/1856, Granard, Ireland d: 1/24/1941, Boston, MA BR/TR, 5'7.5", 160 lbs. Deb: 5/5/1874 M/U Career OF: 0-3-60 ♦

YEAR TM-L	G	AB	R	H	2B	3B	HR	RBI	BB	SO	SB	CS	AVG	OBP	SLG	OPS	OPS+	BR/A	RC	RC/G	FR	G/POS	WS	TPW
1874 Atl-n	55	245	25	54	10	1	0	20	1	5	0	0	.220	.224	.269	.493	65	2	15	2.38	9	*P-55	....	-1.5
1875 Har-n	72	289	32	77	11	3	0	33	0	5	5	1	.266	.266	.325	.592	99	3	27	3.74	7	P-40,0-29(0-0-29)/1-4,2-3	....	3.2
1876 Har-N	45	182	18	50	8	0	0	21	0	4	....	....	.275	.275	.319	.593	90	-0	16	3.46	6	*P-45	47	1.0
1877 Bos-N	61	259	32	59	4	3	0	30	1	15	....	....	.228	.231	.266	.497	54	-5	16	2.24	4	*P-58/0-3(0-0-3)	47	3.4
1878 Bos-N	59	236	22	50	4	1	0	23	0	9	....	....	.212	.212	.237	.449	44	-5	12	1.80	2	*P-59/0-2(0-0-2)	**60**	0.3
1879 Bos-N	65	257	35	62	3	1	0	21	6	8	....	....	.241	.259	.261	.519	70	0	18	2.55	7	*P-64/0-5(0-1-4),1-1	50	1.0
1880 Bos-N	76	282	27	62	4	1	0	24	8	14	....	....	.220	.241	.241	.483	66	-5	17	2.10	12	*P-63,0-26(0-0-26)/1-1,3-1	21	-1.0
1881 Bos-N	3	10	0	2	0	0	0	0	0	0	....	....	.200	.200	.200	.400	27	-0	0	1.38	0	/P-3	1	-0.4
1882 Wor-N	8	30	1	4	0	0	0	2	2	3	....	....	.133	.188	.133	.321	5	-3	1	.81	-2	/0-8(0-1-7),P-2	0	-0.6
1884 Bos-U	37	162	21	48	8	0	0	....	4	....	....	....	.296	.313	.346	.659	124	6	18	4.42	2	P-23,0-17(0-0-17)/3-1	17	0.2
Ind-a	7	23	0	3	1	1	0	0	0	....	....	....	.130	.130	.261	.391	25	-1	1	1.10	-2	/P-5,0-2(0-1-1)	0	-1.0
Total 2 n	127	534	57	131	21	4	0	53	1	10	5	1	.245	.247	.300	.546	83	5	42	3.10	16	/P-95,0-29,1-4,2-3	....	1.7
Total 8	361	1441	156	340	32	7	0	121	21	53	....	....	.236	.247	.268	.515	68	-14	99	2.51	29	P-322/0-63,1-2,3-2	243	2.9

• BOND, Walt Walter Franklin Bond b: 10/19/1937, Denmark, TN d: 9/14/1967, Houston, TX BL/TR, 6'7", 228 lbs. Deb: 4/19/1960 Career OF: 57-13-104

YEAR TM-L	G	AB	R	H	2B	3B	HR	RBI	BB	SO	SB	CS	AVG	OBP	SLG	OPS	OPS+	BR/A	RC	RC/G	FR	G/POS	WS	TPW
1960 Cle-A	40	131	19	29	2	1	5	18	13	14	4	1	.221	.306	.366	.673	84	-3	15	3.89	1	0-36(5-11-20)	3	-0.3
1961 Cle-A	38	52	7	9	1	1	2	7	6	10	1	0	.173	.271	.346	.617	65	-2	5	3.13	0	0-12(0-1-11)	1	-0.3
1962 Cle-A	12	50	10	19	3	0	6	17	4	9	1	0	.380	.426	.800	1.226	228	9	17	14.20	0	0-12(3-0-10)	5	0.8
1964 Hou-N	148	543	63	138	16	7	20	85	38	90	2	2	.254	.312	.420	.732	110	6	70	4.41	-6	1-76,0-71(28-1-42)	16	-0.8
1965 Hou-N	117	407	46	107	17	2	7	47	42	51	2	1	.263	.339	.366	.705	106	4	52	4.52	-3	1-74,0-38(18-0-21)	12	-0.5
1967 Min-A	10	16	4	5	1	0	1	5	3	1	0	0	.313	.421	.563	.984	174	2	4	9.27	0	/0-3(3-0-0)	1	0.1
Total 6	365	1199	149	307	40	11	41	179	106	175	10	4	.256	.325	.410	.736	110	16	163	4.73	-7	0-172,1-150	38	-1.0

• BONDS, Barry Barry Lamar Bonds b: 7/24/1964, Riverside, CA BL/TL, 6'1", 228 lbs. Deb: 5/30/1986 Career OF: 2343-171-1

YEAR TM-L	G	AB	R	H	2B	3B	HR	RBI	BB	SO	SB	CS	AVG	OBP	SLG	OPS	OPS+	BR/A	RC	RC/G	FR	G/POS	WS	TPW
1986 Pit-N	113	413	72	92	26	3	16	48	65	102	36	7	.223	.331	.416	.748	103	6	64	5.15	8	*0-110(0-110-0)	15	1.3
1987 Pit-N	150	551	99	144	34	9	25	59	54	88	32	10	.261	.331	.492	.822	114	11	93	5.91	12	*0-145(101-46-1)	22	1.7
1988 Pit-N	144	538	97	152	30	5	24	58	72	82	17	11	.283	.369	.491	.860	147	32	100	6.71	2	*0-136(135-3-0)	26	3.0
1989 Pit-N	159	580	96	144	34	6	19	58	93	93	32	10	.248	.353	.426	.779	126	24	92	5.39	8	*0-156(156-0-0)	23	2.8
1990*Pit-N★	151	519	104	156	32	3	33	114	93	83	52	13	.301	.410	**.565**	**.974**	**172**	**59**	128	**8.86**	8	*0-150(149-2-0)	**37**	**6.4**
1991*Pit-N	153	510	95	149	28	5	25	116	107	73	43	13	.292	**.419**	.514	**.932**	**163**	**52**	118	**8.08**	6	*0-150(150-4-0)	**37**	5.5
1992*Pit-N★	140	473	**109**	147	36	5	34	103	**127**	69	39	8	.311	**.461**	**.624**	**1.085**	**207**	**80**	148	**11.39**	3	*0-139(139-0-0)	**41**	**8.3**
1993 SF-N★	159	539	129	181	38	4	**46**	**123**	126	79	29	12	.336	**.463**	**.677**	**1.140**	**207**	**89**	172	**11.98**	-2	*0-157(157-0-0)	**47**	**8.1**
1994 SF-N★	112	391	89	122	18	1	37	81	**74**	43	29	9	.312	.429	.647	1.076	184	53	115	10.89	2	*0-112(112-0-0)	25	4.9
1995 SF-N★	144	506	109	149	30	7	33	104	**120**	83	31	10	.294	**.434**	.577	**1.011**	169	**59**	134	9.43	2	*0-143(143-0-0)	**36**	**5.4**
1996 SF-N★	158	517	122	159	27	3	42	129	**151**	76	40	7	.308	.465	.615	1.080	190	**83**	162	**11.46**	1	*0-152(149-6-0)	39	**7.5**
1997*SF-N★	159	532	123	155	26	5	40	101	**145**	87	37	8	.291	.450	.585	1.034	174	71	151	10.14	0	*0-159(159-0-0)	36	6.3
1998 SF-N★	156	552	120	167	44	7	37	122	130	92	28	12	.303	.442	.609	1.051	184	75	153	9.83	1	*0-155(155-0-0)	34	6.8
1999 SF-N	102	355	91	93	20	2	34	83	73	62	15	2	.262	.392	.617	1.009	162	36	91	9.02	1	0-96(96-0-0)/D-4	19	3.1
2000*SF-N★	143	480	129	147	28	4	49	106	**117**	77	11	3	.306	.445	.688	1.133	**195**	**75**	155	12.00	5	*0-141(141-0-0)	32	**7.1**
2001 SF-N★	153	476	129	156	32	2	**73**	137	**177**	93	13	3	.328	**.517**	**.863**	**1.380**	**267**	**135**	230	**18.85**	-4	*0-143(143-0-0)/D-6	**54**	**12.2**
2002*SF-N★	143	403	117	149	31	2	46	110	**198**	47	9	2	**.370**	**.584**	**.799**	**1.383**	**272**	**128**	208	**21.44**	-5	*0-135(135-0-0)/D-5	**49**	**11.7**
2003*SF-N★	130	390	111	133	22	1	45	90	**148**	58	7	0	.341	**.531**	**.749**	**1.280**	**236**	**94**	166	**16.87**	2	*0-123(123-0-0)/D-6	39	**8.9**
Total 18	2569	8725	1941	2595	536	74	658	1742	2070	1387	500	140	.297	.437	.602	1.039	183	1163	2480	10.31	50	*0-2502/D-21	611	111.1

• BONDS, Bobby Bobby Lee Bonds b: 3/15/1946, Riverside, CA d: 8/23/2003, San Carlos, CA BR/TR, 6'1", 190 lbs. Deb: 6/25/1968 C Career OF: 65-285-1472

YEAR TM-L	G	AB	R	H	2B	3B	HR	RBI	BB	SO	SB	CS	AVG	OBP	SLG	OPS	OPS+	BR/A	RC	RC/G	FR	G/POS	WS	TPW
1968 SF-N	81	307	55	78	10	5	9	35	38	84	16	7	.254	.338	.407	.745	123	10	46	5.16	-2	0-80(0-35-62)	15	0.3
1969 SF-N	158	622	**120**	161	25	6	32	90	81	187	45	4	.259	.353	.473	.826	132	36	114	6.41	2	*0-155(0-77-99)	31	3.2
1970 SF-N	157	663	134	200	36	10	26	78	77	189	48	10	.302	.376	.504	.880	135	39	134	7.50	3	*0-157(1-32-141)	32	3.4
1971*SF-N★	155	619	110	178	32	4	33	102	62	137	26	8	.288	.357	.512	.869	146	38	115	6.67	1	*0-154(0-33-133)	32	3.4
1972 SF-N	153	626	118	162	29	5	26	80	60	137	44	6	.259	.329	.446	.774	116	19	96	5.29	2	*0-153(0-12-143)	23	1.5
1973 SF-N★	160	643	**131**	182	34	4	39	96	87	148	43	17	.283	.372	.530	.902	141	38	130	7.16	4	*0-158(0-2-158)	31	3.5
1974 SF-N	150	567	97	145	22	8	21	71	95	134	41	11	.256	.366	.434	.800	118	19	100	6.13	2	*0-148(0-8-141)	23	1.5
1975 NY-A★	145	529	93	143	26	3	32	85	89	137	30	17	.270	.378	.512	.891	154	39	103	6.68	4	*0-129(1-44-90),D-12	24	3.7
1976 Cal-A	99	378	48	100	10	3	10	54	41	90	30	15	.265	.341	.386	.727	120	10	50	4.40	5	0-98(0-0-98)/D-1	16	1.0

YEAR	TM-L	G	AB	R	H	2B	3B	HR	RBI	BB	SO	SB	CS	AVG	OBP	SLG	OPS	OPS+	BR/A	RC	RC/G	FR	G/POS	WS	TPW
1977	Cal-A	158	592	103	156	23	9	37	115	74	141	41	18	.264	.347	.520	.868	138	32	107	6.08	0	*O-140(0-0-140),D-18	24	2.4
1978	Chi-A	26	90	8	25	4	0	2	8	10	10	6	2	.278	.350	.389	.739	107	1	13	4.80	0	O-22(0-0-22)/D-3	3	0.0
	Tex-A	130	475	85	126	15	4	29	82	69	110	37	20	.265	.361	.497	.858	139	24	82	5.70	5	*O-111(0-0-111),D-18	20	2.4
	Yr.	156	565	93	151	19	4	31	90	79	120	43	22	.267	.359	.480	.839	134	26	95	5.56	5	*O-133(0-0-133),D-21	23	2.4
1979	Cle-A	146	538	93	148	24	1	25	85	74	135	34	23	.275	.371	.463	.834	123	16	92	5.73	2	*O-116(0-0-116),D-29	21	1.1
1980	StL-N	86	231	37	47	5	3	5	24	33	74	15	5	.203	.308	.316	.624	72	-7	25	3.38	0	O-70(63-0-15)	4	-1.1
1981	Chi-N	45	163	26	35	7	1	6	19	24	44	5	6	.215	.323	.380	.703	95	-2	19	3.68	-3	O-45(0-42-3)	3	-0.6
Total 14		**1849**	**7043**	**1258**	**1886**	**302**	**66**	**332**	**1024**	**914**	**1757**	**461**	**169**	**.268**	**.356**	**.471**	**.827**	**130**	**312**	**1224**	**6.00**	**24**	***O-1736/D-81**	**302**	**25.7**

• BONE, George George Drummond Bone b: 8/28/1876, New Haven, CT d: 5/26/1918, West Haven, CT BB/TR, 5'7", 152 lbs. Deb: 9/18/1901

YEAR	TM-L	G	AB	R	H	2B	3B	HR	RBI	BB	SO	SB	CS	AVG	OBP	SLG	OPS	OPS+	BR/A	RC	RC/G	FR	G/POS	WS	TPW
1901	Mil-A	12	43	6	13	2	0	0	6	4	....	0	....	.302	.362	.349	.711	103	0	6	4.91	-1	S-12	1	0.0

• BONGIOVANNI, Nino Anthony Thomas Bongiovanni b: 12/21/1911, New Orleans, LA BL/TL, 5'10", 175 lbs. Deb: 4/23/1938 Career OF: 8-1-32

YEAR	TM-L	G	AB	R	H	2B	3B	HR	RBI	BB	SO	SB	CS	AVG	OBP	SLG	OPS	OPS+	BR/A	RC	RC/G	FR	G/POS	WS	TPW
1938	Cin-N	2	7	0	2	1	0	0	0	0	0	0	....	.286	.286	.429	.714	97	-0	1	4.04	0	/O-2(2-0-0)	0	0.0
1939*	Cin-N	66	159	17	41	6	0	0	16	9	8	0	....	.258	.298	.296	.593	59	-9	15	3.23	1	O-39(6-1-32)	3	-1.0
Total 2		**68**	**166**	**17**	**43**	**7**	**0**	**0**	**16**	**9**	**8**	**0**	**....**	**.259**	**.297**	**.301**	**.598**	**61**	**-9**	**15**	**3.27**	**2**	**/O-41**	**3**	**-1.0**

• BONILLA, Bobby Roberto Martin Antonio Bonilla b: 2/23/1963, Bronx, NY BB/TR, 6'3", 240 lbs. Deb: 4/9/1986 Career OF: 206-10-698

YEAR	TM-L	G	AB	R	H	2B	3B	HR	RBI	BB	SO	SB	CS	AVG	OBP	SLG	OPS	OPS+	BR/A	RC	RC/G	FR	G/POS	WS	TPW
1986	Chi-A	75	234	27	63	10	2	2	26	33	49	4	1	.269	.362	.355	.717	93	-0	32	4.86	0	O-43(39-4-4),1-30	7	-0.4
	Pit-N	63	192	28	46	6	2	1	17	29	39	4	4	.240	.342	.307	.650	79	-5	21	3.57	1	O-51(37-6-24)/1-4,3-4	3	-0.6
1987	Pit-N	141	466	58	140	33	3	15	77	39	64	3	5	.300	.357	.481	.838	119	10	78	6.08	-12	3-89,O-46(17-0-34)/1-6	16	-0.5
1988	Pit-N★	159	584	87	160	32	7	24	100	85	82	3	5	.274	.370	.476	.846	143	32	106	6.51	2	*3-159	31	3.8
1989	Pit-N★	163	616	96	173	37	10	24	86	76	93	8	8	.281	.361	.490	.851	146	35	108	6.23	12	*3-156/1-8,O-1	29	5.1
1990*	Pit-N★	160	625	112	175	39	7	32	120	45	103	4	3	.280	.329	.518	.848	135	24	104	5.84	-5	*O-149(0-0-149),3-14/1-3	23	1.6
1991*	Pit-N★	157	577	102	174	**44**	6	18	100	90	67	2	4	.302	.398	.492	.890	151	41	114	7.13	4	*O-104(0-0-104),3-67/1-4	31	4.3
1992	NY-N	128	438	62	109	23	0	19	70	66	73	4	3	.249	.349	.432	.780	121	13	66	5.19	5	*O-121(0-0-121)/1-6	18	1.6
1993	NY-N★	139	502	81	133	21	3	34	87	72	96	3	3	.265	.357	.522	.879	134	23	93	6.38	2	O-85(0-0-85),3-52/1-6	16	2.0
1994	NY-N	108	403	60	117	24	1	20	67	55	101	1	3	.290	.376	.504	.879	128	16	75	6.71	8	*3-107	19	2.5
1995	NY-N★	80	317	49	103	25	4	18	53	31	48	0	3	.325	.387	.599	.986	160	25	68	7.96	-3	3-46,O-31(31-0-0),1-10	13	2.0
	Bal-A	61	237	47	79	12	4	10	46	23	31	0	2	.333	.395	.544	.939	139	12	47	7.28	2	O-39(1-0-38),3-24	9	1.2
1996*	Bal-A	159	595	107	171	27	5	28	116	75	85	1	3	.287	.372	.491	.863	116	14	109	6.43	1	*O-108(0-0-108),D-44/1-9,3	19	0.6
1997*	Fla-N	153	562	77	167	39	3	17	96	73	94	6	6	.297	.383	.468	.851	127	22	98	6.22	-12	*3-149/D-3,1-2	21	1.2
1998	Fla-N	28	97	11	27	5	0	4	15	12	22	0	1	.278	.358	.454	.811	116	2	14	4.77	-2	3-26	2	0.1
	LA-N	72	236	28	56	6	1	7	30	29	37	1	1	.237	.321	.360	.681	84	-6	26	3.58	-8	3-59,O-12(12-0-0)	3	-1.3
	Yr.	100	333	39	83	11	1	11	45	41	59	1	2	.249	.332	.387	.719	93	-4	40	3.92	-10	3-85,O-12(12-0-0)	5	-1.3
1999*	NY-N	60	119	12	19	5	0	4	18	19	16	0	1	.160	.281	.303	.583	49	-10	10	2.55	1	O-25(2-0-23)/1-4,D-3	0	-1.0
2000*	Atl-N	114	239	23	61	13	3	5	28	37	51	0	0	.255	.357	.397	.755	90	-3	36	5.37	-9	O-64(63-0-1)/3-1,D-1	6	-1.3
2001	StL-N	93	174	17	37	7	0	5	21	23	53	1	1	.213	.308	.339	.647	68	-8	18	3.49	-2	1-33,O-10(4-0-6)/D-2,P-1	1	-1.4
Total 16		**2113**	**7213**	**1084**	**2010**	**408**	**61**	**287**	**1173**	**912**	**1204**	**45**	**57**	**.279**	**.362**	**.472**	**.833**	**125**	**234**	**1222**	**5.97**	**-14**	**3-957,O-889,1-125/D-53,P-1**	**267**	**19.4**

• BONILLA, Juan Juan Guillermo Bonilla b: 1/12/1956, Santurce, Puerto Rico BR/TR, 5'9", 170 lbs. Deb: 4/9/1981

YEAR	TM-L	G	AB	R	H	2B	3B	HR	RBI	BB	SO	SB	CS	AVG	OBP	SLG	OPS	OPS+	BR/A	RC	RC/G	FR	G/POS	WS	TPW
1981	SD-N	99	369	30	107	13	2	1	25	25	23	4	9	.290	.338	.344	.683	101	-3	41	3.81	-16	2-97	8	-1.5
1982	SD-N	45	182	21	51	6	2	0	8	11	15	0	1	.280	.325	.335	.660	90	-3	20	3.94	-1	2-45	5	-0.1
1983	SD-N	152	556	55	132	17	4	4	45	50	40	3	0	.237	.304	.304	.608	71	-21	50	2.99	2	*2-149	12	-1.1
1985	NY-A	8	16	0	2	1	0	0	2	0	3	0	0	.125	.125	.188	.313	-16	-3	0	.72	1	/2-7	0	-0.2
1986	Bal-A	102	284	33	69	10	1	1	18	25	21	0	0	.243	.311	.296	.607	67	-12	25	2.84	-3	2-70,3-33/D-2	3	-1.3
1987	NY-A	23	55	6	14	3	0	1	3	5	6	0	0	.255	.317	.364	.680	81	-2	6	3.62	-1	2-22/3-1,D-1	1	-0.1
Total 6		**429**	**1462**	**145**	**375**	**50**	**9**	**7**	**101**	**116**	**108**	**7**	**10**	**.256**	**.315**	**.317**	**.632**	**80**	**-43**	**142**	**3.27**	**-18**	**2-390/3-34,D-3**	**29**	**-4.3**

• BONIN, Luther Ernest Luther "Bonnie" Bonin b: 1/13/1888, Greenhill, IN d: 1/3/1966, Sycamore, OH BL/TR, 5'9.5", 178 lbs. Deb: 4/13/1913

YEAR	TM-L	G	AB	R	H	2B	3B	HR	RBI	BB	SO	SB	CS	AVG	OBP	SLG	OPS	OPS+	BR/A	RC	RC/G	FR	G/POS	WS	TPW
1913	StL-A	1	1	0	0	0	0	0	0	0	0	0	....	.000	.000	.000	.000	-103	-0	0	.00	0	....	0	0.0
1914	Buf-F	20	76	6	14	4	1	0	4	7	11	3	....	.184	.253	.263	.516	45	-6	6	2.21	1	O-20(0-0-20)	1	-0.6
Total 2		**21**	**77**	**6**	**14**	**4**	**1**	**0**	**4**	**7**	**11**	**3**	**....**	**.182**	**.250**	**.260**	**.510**	**43**	**-6**	**6**	**2.18**	**1**	**/O-20**	**1**	**-0.6**

• BONNELL, Barry Robert Barry "Preacher" Bonnell b: 10/27/1953, Clermont County, OH BR/TR, 6'3", 200 lbs. Deb: 5/4/1977 Career OF: 395-344-214

YEAR	TM-L	G	AB	R	H	2B	3B	HR	RBI	BB	SO	SB	CS	AVG	OBP	SLG	OPS	OPS+	BR/A	RC	RC/G	FR	G/POS	WS	TPW
1977	Atl-N	100	360	41	108	11	0	1	45	37	32	7	5	.300	.368	.339	.707	81	-8	45	4.58	-2	O-75(2-63-10),3-32	9	-1.2
1978	Atl-N	117	304	36	73	11	3	1	16	20	30	12	6	.240	.287	.306	.593	59	-17	23	2.47	-1	*O-105(53-55-11),3-15	3	-2.2
1979	Atl-N	127	375	47	97	20	3	12	45	26	55	8	7	.259	.312	.424	.736	92	-6	46	4.11	-5	*O-124(77-74-0)/3-1	8	-1.5
1980	Tor-A	130	463	55	124	22	4	13	56	37	59	3	4	.268	.325	.417	.742	97	-3	59	4.39	4	*O-122(5-57-61)/D-3	12	-0.3
1981	Tor-A	66	227	21	50	7	4	4	28	12	25	4	3	.220	.263	.339	.602	68	-10	18	2.54	-1	O-66(9-18-41)	2	-1.5
1982	Tor-A	140	437	59	128	26	3	6	49	32	51	14	2	.293	.345	.407	.753	97	1	63	5.22	-7	*O-125(99-39-7)/3-9,D-6	14	-1.0
1983	Tor-A	121	377	49	120	21	3	10	54	33	52	10	7	.318	.373	.469	.843	123	11	64	6.18	1	*O-117(62-22-51)/3-4,D-1	14	0.8
1984	Sea-A	110	363	42	96	15	4	8	48	25	51	5	2	.264	.315	.394	.709	96	-2	43	4.13	-1	O-94(70-16-20),3-10/D-8,1	7	-0.6
1985	Sea-A	48	111	9	27	8	0	1	10	6	19	1	2	.243	.282	.342	.624	70	-6	10	3.17	0	O-22(9-0-13)/1-5,D-2	1	-0.7
1986	Sea-A	17	51	4	10	2	0	0	4	1	13	0	1	.196	.212	.235	.447	21	-6	2	1.16	-0	/O-9(9-0-0),1-8,D-2	0	-0.7
Total 10		**976**	**3068**	**363**	**833**	**143**	**24**	**56**	**355**	**229**	**387**	**64**	**39**	**.272**	**.325**	**.389**	**.713**	**90**	**-47**	**374**	**4.21**	**-12**	**O-859/3-71,D-22,1-18**	**70**	**-9.0**

• BONNER, Bobby Robert Averill Bonner b: 8/12/1956, Uvalde, TX BR/TR, 6', 185 lbs. Deb: 9/12/1980

YEAR	TM-L	G	AB	R	H	2B	3B	HR	RBI	BB	SO	SB	CS	AVG	OBP	SLG	OPS	OPS+	BR/A	RC	RC/G	FR	G/POS	WS	TPW
1980	Bal-A	4	4	1	0	0	0	0	1	0	0	0	0	.000	.000	.000	.000	-101	-1	0	.00	0	/S-3	0	-0.1
1981	Bal-A	10	27	6	8	2	0	0	2	1	4	1	0	.296	.321	.370	.692	99	0	4	4.73	1	/S-9	1	0.2
1982	Bal-A	41	77	8	13	3	1	0	5	3	12	0	0	.169	.200	.234	.434	19	-9	3	1.23	-2	S-38/2-3	1	-0.8
1983	Bal-A	6	0	0	0	0	0	0	0	0	0	0	0	....	....	....	....	-102	0	0	....	-3	/2-5,D-1	0	-0.3
Total 4		**61**	**108**	**15**	**21**	**5**	**1**	**0**	**8**	**4**	**16**	**1**	**0**	**.194**	**.223**	**.259**	**.482**	**35**	**-10**	**7**	**1.91**	**-4**	**/S-50,2-8,D-1**	**2**	**-1.0**

• BONNER, Frank Frank J. Bonner b: 8/20/1869, Lowell, MA d: 12/31/1905, Kansas City, MO BR/TR, 5'7.5", 169 lbs. Deb: 4/26/1894 U Career OF: 2-1-6

YEAR	TM-L	G	AB	R	H	2B	3B	HR	RBI	BB	SO	SB	CS	AVG	OBP	SLG	OPS	OPS+	BR/A	RC	RC/G	FR	G/POS	WS	TPW
1894*	Bal-N	33	118	27	38	10	2	0	24	17	5	12	....	.322	.412	.441	.852	101	1	27	8.78	-4	2-27/O-4(2-1-1),3-2,S-1	4	-0.2
1895	Bal-N	11	42	9	14	1	1	0	7	5	1	4	....	.333	.404	.405	.809	106	1	9	8.04	-2	3-11	1	-0.1
	StL-N	15	59	3	8	0	1	1	8	1	8	2	....	.136	.164	.220	.384	-2	-9	3	1.33	-5	3-10/O-5(0-0-5),C-1	0	-1.1
	Yr.	26	101	12	22	1	2	1	15	6	9	6	....	.218	.269	.297	.566	46	-9	11	3.82	-6	3-21/O-5(0-0-5),C-1	1	-1.2
1896	Bro-N	9	34	8	6	2	0	0	5	2	8	1	....	.176	.263	.235	.498	34	-3	2	2.30	1	/2-9	0	-0.2
1899	Was-N	85	347	41	95	20	4	2	44	18	....	6	....	.274	.313	.372	.685	88	-7	44	4.54	-1	2-85	7	-0.4
1902	Cle-A	34	132	14	37	6	0	0	14	5	....	1	....	.280	.312	.326	.637	80	-4	14	3.91	-9	2-34	2	-1.2
	Phi-A	11	44	2	8	0	0	0	3	0	....	0	....	.182	.200	.182	.382	6	-6	2	1.21	0	2-11	0	-0.5
	Yr.	45	176	16	45	6	0	0	17	5	....	1	....	.256	.284	.290	.574	62	-9	16	3.18	-9	2-45	2	-1.7
1903	Bos-N	48	173	11	38	5	0	1	10	7	....	2	....	.220	.262	.266	.528	53	-11	13	2.55	2	2-24,S-22	1	-0.8
Total 6		**246**	**949**	**115**	**244**	**44**	**8**	**4**	**115**	**55**	**22**	**28**	**....**	**.257**	**.305**	**.333**	**.638**	**72**	**-38**	**114**	**4.21**	**-18**	**2-190/3-23,S-23,O-9,C-1**	**15**	**-4.5**

• BONURA, Zeke Henry John Bonura b: 9/20/1908, New Orleans, LA d: 3/9/1987, New Orleans, LA BR/TR, 6', 210 lbs. Deb: 4/17/1934

YEAR	TM-L	G	AB	R	H	2B	3B	HR	RBI	BB	SO	SB	CS	AVG	OBP	SLG	OPS	OPS+	BR/A	RC	RC/G	FR	G/POS	WS	TPW
1934	Chi-A	127	510	86	154	35	4	27	110	64	31	0	2	.302	.380	.545	.925	132	22	106	7.86	8	*1-127	20	1.6
1935	Chi-A	138	550	107	162	34	4	21	92	57	28	4	0	.295	.364	.485	.849	115	12	99	6.78	9	*1-138	17	0.8
1936	Chi-A	148	587	120	194	39	7	12	138	94	29	4	2	.330	.426	.482	.908	120	22	126	8.43	10	*1-146	24	1.6
1937	Chi-A	116	447	79	154	41	2	19	100	49	24	5	1	.345	.412	.573	.984	146	31	107	9.50	-2	*1-115	21	1.8
1938	Was-A	137	540	72	156	27	3	22	114	44	29	2	2	.289	.346	.472	.818	111	6	88	6.03	3	*1-129	16	-0.3
1939	NY-N	123	455	75	146	26	6	11	85	46	22	1	....	.321	.388	.477	.865	130	20	80	6.26	4	*1-122	19	1.3
1940	Was-A	79	311	41	85	16	3	3	45	40	13	2	0	.273	.358	.373	.731	96	0	45	5.18	-6	1-79	8	-1.3
	Chi-N	49	182	20	48	14	0	4	20	10	4	1	....	.264	.302	.407	.709	96	-2	18	3.38	5	1-44	2	-0.1
Total 7		**917**	**3582**	**600**	**1099**	**232**	**29**	**119**	**704**	**404**	**180**	**19**	**7**	**.307**	**.380**	**.487**	**.867**	**121**	**111**	**670**	**6.98**	**31**	**1-900**	**127**	**5.3**

• BOOE, Everett Everitt Little Booe b: 9/28/1891, Mocksville, NC d: 3/21/1969, Kenedy, TX BL/TR, 5'8.5", 165 lbs. Deb: 4/13/1913 Career OF: 28-22-35

YEAR	TM-L	G	AB	R	H	2B	3B	HR	RBI	BB	SO	SB	CS	AVG	OBP	SLG	OPS	OPS+	BR/A	RC	RC/G	FR	G/POS	WS	TPW
1913	Pit-N	29	80	9	16	0	2	0	2	6	9	2	....	.200	.256	.250	.506	47	-6	5	2.10	0	O-22(1-21-0)	1	-0.6

YEAR TM-L	G	AB	R	H	2B	3B	HR	RBI	BB	SO	SB	CS	AVG	OBP	SLG	OPS	OPS+	BR/A	RC	RC/G	FR	G/POS	WS	TPW
1914 Ind-F	20	31	5	7	1	0	0	6	7	6	4	....	.226	.368	.258	.626	72	-1	4	4.29	-1	/O-5(4-1-0),S-3	1	-0.2
Buf-F	76	241	29	54	9	2	0	14	21	50	8	....	.224	.289	.278	.567	59	-13	21	2.77	-2	O-58(23-0-35)/S-8,3-2,2-1	4	-1.8
Yr.	96	272	34	61	10	2	0	20	28	56	12	....	.224	.299	.276	.575	61	-14	25	2.94	-4	O-63(27-1-35),S-11/3-2,2-1	5	-2.0
Total 2	125	352	43	77	10	4	0	22	34	65	14	....	.219	.289	.270	.559	58	-19	31	2.75	-3	/O-85,S-11,3-2,2-1	6	-2.7
• BOOKER, Buddy	Richard Lee Booker b: 5/28/1942, Lynchburg, VA BL/TR, 5'10", 170 lbs. Deb: 6/4/1966																							
1966 Cle-A	18	28	6	6	1	0	2	5	2	6	0	0	.214	.267	.464	.731	105	0	3	3.04	-1	C-12	0	-0.1
1968 Chi-A	5	5	0	0	0	0	0	0	1	2	0	0	.000	.167	.000	.167	-46	-1	0	.23	-1	/C-3	0	-0.2
Total 2	23	33	6	6	1	0	2	5	3	8	0	0	.182	.250	.394	.644	80	-1	3	2.56	-2	/C-15	0	-0.3
• BOOKER, Rod	Roderick Stewart Booker b: 9/4/1958, Los Angeles, CA BL/TR, 6', 175 lbs. Deb: 4/29/1987																							
1987 StL-N	44	47	9	13	1	1	0	8	7	7	2	0	.277	.370	.340	.711	88	-0	7	5.26	-3	2-18/3-4,S-1	2	-0.2
1988 StL-N	18	35	6	12	3	0	0	3	4	3	2	2	.343	.410	.429	.839	140	1	6	6.62	-1	3-13/2-1	1	0.1
1989 StL-N	10	8	1	2	0	0	0	0	0	1	0	0	.250	.250	.250	.500	42	-1	1	2.25	-1	/2-5,3-1	0	-0.1
1990 Phi-N	73	131	19	29	5	2	0	10	15	26	3	1	.221	.301	.290	.591	64	-6	10	2.50	-2	S-27,2-23,3-10	1	-0.6
1991 Phi-N	28	53	3	12	1	0	0	7	1	7	0	0	.226	.241	.245	.486	37	-4	3	1.85	1	S-20/3-3	1	-0.3
Total 5	173	274	38	68	10	3	0	28	27	44	7	3	.248	.316	.307	.622	72	-10	27	3.27	-5	/S-48,2-47,3-31	5	-1.2
• BOOL, Al	Albert J. Bool b: 8/24/1897, Lincoln, NE d: 9/27/1981, Lincoln, NE BR/TR, 5'11", 180 lbs. Deb: 9/29/1928																							
1928 Was-A	2	7	0	1	0	0	0	1	0	0	0	0	.143	.143	.143	.286	-25	-1	0	.69	0	/C-2	0	-0.1
1930 Pit-N	78	216	30	56	12	4	7	46	25	29	0	....	.259	.336	.449	.785	87	-5	32	5.16	4	C-65	7	0.3
1931 Bos-N	49	85	5	16	1	0	0	6	9	13	0	....	.188	.266	.200	.466	28	-8	5	1.88	2	C-37	1	-0.5
Total 3	129	308	35	73	13	4	7	53	34	42	0	0	.237	.313	.373	.686	68	-15	38	4.07	6	C-104	8	-0.4
• BOONE, Aaron	Aaron John Boone b: 3/9/1973, La Mesa, CA BR/TR, 6'2", 190 lbs. Deb: 6/20/1997																							
1997 Cin-N	16	49	5	12	1	0	0	5	2	5	1	0	.245	.275	.265	.540	41	-4	4	2.52	-1	3-13/2-1	0	-0.5
1998 Cin-N	58	181	24	51	13	2	2	28	15	36	6	1	.282	.353	.409	.762	99	1	28	5.35	1	3-52/2-1,S-1	6	0.3
1999 Cin-N	139	472	56	132	26	5	14	72	30	79	17	6	.280	.333	.445	.778	92	-6	71	5.29	11	*3-136/S-6	15	0.6
2000 Cin-N	84	291	44	83	18	0	12	43	24	52	6	1	.285	.360	.471	.831	105	3	51	6.25	6	3-84/S-2	10	0.9
2001 Cin-N	103	381	54	112	26	2	14	62	29	71	6	3	.294	.356	.483	.839	109	5	65	6.01	2	*3-103	13	0.9
2002 Cin-N	162	606	83	146	38	2	26	87	56	111	32	8	.241	.315	.439	.754	94	-4	87	4.79	9	*3-154,S-16	19	0.9
2003 Cin-N★	106	403	61	110	19	3	18	65	35	74	15	3	.273	.339	.469	.808	110	7	66	5.83	13	3-83,2-19/S-5	17	2.2
*NY-A	54	189	31	48	13	0	6	31	11	30	8	0	.254	.305	.418	.723	90	-1	24	4.17	6	3-54	6	0.5
Total 7	722	2572	358	694	154	14	92	393	202	458	91	22	.270	.335	.448	.783	99	-0	394	5.32	47	3-679/S-30,2-21	86	5.8
• BOONE, Bob	Robert Raymond Boone b: 11/19/1947, San Diego, CA BR/TR, 6'2.5", 202 lbs. Deb: 9/10/1972 M/C																							
1972 Phi-N	16	51	4	14	1	0	1	4	5	7	1	0	.275	.339	.353	.692	94	-0	6	3.99	-1	C-14	1	-0.1
1973 Phi-N	145	521	42	136	20	2	10	61	41	36	3	4	.261	.315	.365	.680	85	-12	60	3.94	9	*C-145	16	0.5
1974 Phi-N	146	488	41	118	24	3	3	52	35	29	3	1	.242	.298	.322	.620	70	-20	45	3.03	-4	*C-146	8	-1.8
1975 Phi-N	97	289	28	71	14	2	2	20	32	14	1	3	.246	.323	.329	.652	78	-9	30	3.43	3	C-92/3-3	7	-0.3
1976*Phi-N★	121	361	40	98	18	2	4	54	45	44	2	5	.271	.354	.366	.719	101	0	45	4.24	-6	*C-108/1-4	14	-0.2
1977*Phi-N	132	440	55	125	26	4	11	66	42	54	5	5	.284	.349	.436	.786	105	2	66	5.28	2	*C-131/3-2	18	1.0
1978*Phi-N★	132	435	48	123	18	4	12	62	46	37	2	5	.283	.353	.425	.778	115	7	62	4.89	-6	*C-129/1-3,O-1	17	0.7
1979 Phi-N★	119	398	38	114	21	3	9	58	49	33	1	4	.286	.367	.422	.790	111	6	61	5.45	-3	*C-117/3-2	16	0.9
1980*Phi-N	141	480	34	110	23	1	9	55	48	41	3	4	.229	.301	.338	.638	74	-18	48	3.34	-3	*C-138	11	-1.5
1981*Phi-N	76	227	19	48	7	0	4	24	22	16	2	2	.211	.281	.295	.576	61	-12	18	2.61	-3	C-75	3	-1.2
1982*Cal-A	143	472	42	121	17	0	7	58	39	34	0	2	.256	.313	.337	.650	79	-14	51	3.51	9	*C-143	13	0.1
1983 Cal-A★	142	468	46	120	18	0	9	52	24	42	4	3	.256	.293	.353	.645	77	-16	44	3.04	7	*C-142	9	-0.2
1984 Cal-A	139	450	33	91	16	1	3	32	25	45	3	3	.202	.244	.262	.506	40	-37	28	1.94	1	*C-137	7	-2.9
1985 Cal-A	150	460	37	114	17	0	5	55	37	35	1	2	.248	.308	.317	.625	72	-18	45	3.19	4	*C-147	12	-0.7
1986*Cal-A	144	442	48	98	12	2	7	49	43	30	1	0	.222	.291	.305	.596	63	-22	39	2.80	6	*C-144	10	-0.9
1987 Cal-A	128	389	42	94	18	0	3	33	35	36	0	2	.242	.306	.311	.617	66	-19	37	3.10	1	*C-127/D-1	10	-1.2
1988 Cal-A	122	352	38	104	17	0	5	39	29	26	2	2	.295	.352	.386	.739	110	4	47	4.76	6	*C-121	17	1.7
1989 KC-A	131	405	33	111	13	2	1	43	49	37	3	2	.274	.355	.323	.679	93	-2	47	3.87	3	*C-129	20	1.0
1990 KC-A	40	117	11	28	3	0	0	9	17	12	1	1	.239	.336	.265	.601	71	-4	11	3.28	-3	C-40	1	-0.4
Total 19	2264	7245	679	1838	303	26	105	826	663	608	38	50	.254	.318	.346	.664	82	-184	790	3.64	22	*C-2225/1-7,3-7,D-1,O-1	210	-5.6
• BOONE, Bret	Bret Robert Boone b: 4/6/1969, El Cajon, CA BR/TR, 5'10", 180 lbs. Deb: 8/19/1992																							
1992 Sea-A	33	129	15	25	4	0	4	15	4	34	1	1	.194	.224	.318	.542	50	-9	8	1.97	-2	2-32/3-6	1	-1.1
1993 Sea-A	76	271	31	68	12	2	12	38	17	52	2	3	.251	.305	.443	.748	97	-3	35	4.23	-3	2-74/D-1	8	-0.3
1994 Cin-N	108	381	59	122	25	2	12	68	24	74	3	4	.320	.373	.491	.864	124	12	67	6.35	-14	*2-106/3-2	15	0.2
1995*Cin-N	138	513	63	137	34	2	15	68	41	84	5	1	.267	.329	.429	.757	98	-2	71	4.79	-2	*2-138	15	0.2
1996 Cin-N	142	520	56	121	21	3	12	69	31	100	3	2	.233	.280	.354	.634	66	-28	51	3.26	2	*2-141	10	-1.8
1997 Cin-N	139	443	40	99	25	1	7	46	45	101	5	5	.223	.301	.332	.633	64	-25	44	3.20	6	*2-136	8	-1.2
1998 Cin-N★	157	583	76	155	38	1	24	95	48	104	6	4	.266	.326	.458	.784	102	-0	80	4.64	12	*2-156	18	1.9
1999*Atl-N	152	608	102	153	38	1	20	63	47	112	14	9	.252	.311	.416	.727	82	-20	77	4.28	-3	*2-151	17	-1.5
2000 SD-N	127	463	61	116	18	2	19	74	50	97	8	4	.251	.330	.421	.751	95	-5	64	4.68	3	*2-126	15	0.4
2001*Sea-A★	158	623	118	206	37	3	37	**141**	40	110	5	5	.331	.379	.578	.957	156	47	133	7.95	11	*2-156/D-2	32	6.3
2002 Sea-A	155	608	88	169	34	3	24	107	53	102	12	5	.278	.342	.462	.804	115	13	96	5.60	-8	*2-153/D-1	25	1.2
2003 Sea-A★	159	622	111	183	35	5	35	117	68	125	16	3	.294	.370	.535	.906	139	37	123	7.11	16	*2-158	30	**5.8**
Total 12	1544	5764	820	1554	321	25	221	901	468	1095	80	46	.270	.331	.449	.780	104	16	849	5.08	19	*2-1527/3-8,D-4	194	10.2
• BOONE, Ike	Isaac Morgan Boone b: 2/17/1897, Samantha, AL d: 8/1/1958, Northport, AL BL/TR, 6', 195 lbs. Deb: 4/22/1922 Career OF: 30-4-258																							
1922 NY-N	2	2	0	1	0	0	0	0	0	1	0	0	.500	.500	.500	1.000	157	0	0	12.72	0	....	0	0.0
1923 Bos-A	5	15	1	4	0	1	0	2	1	0	0	1	.267	.313	.400	.713	86	-1	2	3.32	0	/O-4(0-4-0)	0	-0.1
1924 Bos-A	128	487	72	164	31	4	13	98	54	32	2	2	.337	.404	.497	.901	131	23	99	7.99	-8	*O-124(0-0-124)	18	0.5
1925 Bos-A	133	476	79	157	34	5	9	68	60	19	1	4	.330	.406	.479	.885	124	18	94	7.50	-9	*O-118(0-0-118)	15	0.0
1927 Chi-A	29	53	10	12	4	0	1	11	3	4	0	0	.226	.268	.358	.626	63	-3	5	3.23	0	O-11(1-0-10)	1	-0.4
1930 Bro-N	40	101	13	30	9	1	3	13	14	8	0	....	.297	.383	.495	.878	111	2	19	6.89	1	O-27(27-0-0)	3	0.1
1931 Bro-N	6	5	0	1	0	0	0	0	1	1	0	....	.200	.333	.200	.533	47	-0	0	2.64	0	....	0	0.0
1932 Bro-N	13	21	2	3	1	0	0	2	5	2	0	....	.143	.308	.190	.498	38	-2	2	2.28	1	/O-8(2-0-6)	0	-0.1
Total 8	356	1160	177	372	79	11	26	194	138	67	3	7	.321	.394	.475	.869	121	37	221	7.23	-16	O-292	37	0.0
• BOONE, Lute	Lute Joseph "Danny" Boone b: 5/6/1890, Pittsburgh, PA d: 7/29/1982, Pittsburgh, PA BR/TR, 5'9", 160 lbs. Deb: 9/9/1913																							
1913 NY-A	6	12	3	4	0	0	0	1	3	1	0	....	.333	.467	.333	.800	134	1	2	5.75	-1	/S-4	1	0.0
1914 NY-A	106	370	34	82	8	2	0	21	31	41	10	18	.222	.285	.254	.539	63	-23	26	2.19	22	2-90/3-9,O-1	6	0.1
1915 NY-A	130	431	44	88	12	2	5	43	41	53	14	17	.204	.285	.276	.562	68	-22	35	2.46	19	*2-115,S-11/3-4	8	0.0
1916 NY-A	46	124	14	23	4	0	1	8	8	10	7	....	.185	.252	.242	.494	47	-8	10	2.42	0	3-25,S-12/2-8	2	-0.8
1918 Pit-N	27	91	7	18	3	0	0	3	8	6	1	....	.198	.263	.231	.493	49	-5	6	2.04	-4	S-26/2-1	1	-0.8
Total 5	315	1028	102	215	27	4	6	76	91	111	32	35	.209	.282	.261	.543	63	-57	79	2.35	35	2-214/S-53,3-38,O-1	18	-1.5
• BOONE, Ray	Raymond Otis "Ike" Boone b: 7/27/1923, San Diego, CA BR/TR, 6', 188 lbs. Deb: 9/3/1948																							
1948*Cle-A	6	5	0	2	1	0	0	1	0	1	0	0	.400	.400	.600	1.000	168	0	1	11.07	-1	/S-4	0	0.0
1949 Cle-A	86	258	39	65	4	4	4	26	38	17	0	2	.252	.352	.345	.697	87	-5	32	4.00	-4	S-76	8	-0.4
1950 Cle-A	109	365	53	110	14	6	7	58	56	27	4	3	.301	.397	.430	.827	116	10	65	6.53	-1	*S-102	16	1.4
1951 Cle-A	151	544	65	127	14	1	12	51	48	36	5	3	.233	.302	.329	.631	75	-20	55	3.40	5	*S-151	14	-0.5
1952 Cle-A	103	316	57	83	8	2	7	45	53	33	0	1	.263	.372	.367	.739	114	8	45	4.93	4	S-96/3-2,2-1	13	1.8
1953 Cle-A	34	112	21	27	1	2	4	21	24	21	1	2	.241	.375	.393	.768	110	2	18	5.13	-1	S-31	5	0.4
Det-A	101	385	73	120	16	6	22	93	48	47	2	1	.312	.395	.556	.951	156	30	89	8.65	1	3-97/S-3	22	3.2
Yr.	135	497	94	147	17	8	26	114	72	68	3	3	.296	.390	.519	.909	145	32	106	7.76	1	3-97,S-34	27	3.6

YEAR TM-L	G	AB	R	H	2B	3B	HR	RBI	BB	SO	SB	CS	AVG	OBP	SLG	OPS	OPS+	BR/A	RC	RC/G	FR	G/POS	WS	TPW
1954 Det-A★	148	543	76	160	19	7	20	85	71	53	4	2	.295	.378	.466	.844	133	25	95	6.27	5	*3-148/S-1	22	3.1
1955 Det-A	135	500	61	142	22	7	20	**116**	50	49	1	1	.284	.350	.476	.826	123	14	80	5.66	5	*3-126	19	1.9
1956 Det-A★	131	481	77	148	14	6	25	81	77	46	0	0	.308	.406	.518	.924	142	31	103	7.86	2	*3-130	22	3.2
1957 Det-A	129	462	48	126	25	3	12	65	57	47	1	1	.273	.356	.418	.774	108	6	68	5.04	-6	*1-117/3-4	12	-0.6
1958 Det-A	39	114	16	27	4	1	6	20	14	13	0	2	.237	.326	.447	.773	103	-0	16	4.48	-2	1-32	3	-0.4
Chi-A	77	246	25	60	12	1	7	41	18	33	1	1	.244	.298	.386	.684	89	-5	27	3.75	-1	1-63	4	-0.9
Yr.	116	360	41	87	16	2	13	61	32	46	1	3	.242	.307	.406	.713	93	-5	43	3.99	-3	1-95	7	-1.3
1959 Chi-A	9	21	3	5	0	0	1	5	7	5	1	0	.238	.429	.381	.810	126	2	5	6.83	0	/1-6	1	0.2
KC-A	61	132	19	36	6	0	2	12	27	17	1	0	.273	.396	.364	.760	108	3	21	5.44	0	1-38/3-3	4	0.2
Yr.	70	153	22	41	6	0	3	17	34	22	2	0	.268	.401	.366	.767	111	5	25	5.65	1	1-44/3-3	5	0.4
Mil-N	13	15	3	3	0	0	1	2	4	2	0	0	.200	.368	.400	.768	114	0	2	4.37	0	/1-3	0	0.0
1960 Mil-N	7	12	3	3	1	0	0	4	5	1	0	0	.250	.471	.333	.804	134	1	2	7.48	0	/1-4	1	0.1
Bos-A	34	78	6	16	1	0	1	11	11	15	0	0	.205	.303	.256	.560	51	-5	6	2.70	-1	1-22	0	-0.7
Total 13	1373	4589	645	1260	162	46	151	737	608	463	21	19	.275	.363	.429	.791	114	99	731	5.55	9	3-510,S-464,1-285/2-1	166	11.9

• BOOTH, Booth Deb: 5/1/1875

YEAR TM-L	G	AB	R	H	2B	3B	HR	RBI	BB	SO	SB	CS	AVG	OBP	SLG	OPS	OPS+	BR/A	RC	RC/G	FR	G/POS	WS	TPW
1875 NH-n	1	2	0	0	0	0	0	0	0	1	0	0	.000	.000	.000	.000	-115	-0	0	.00	0	/S-1	....	-0.1

• BOOTH, Amos Amos Smith "Darling" Booth b: 9/4/1852, Cincinnati, OH d: 7/1/1921, Miamisburg, OH BR/TR, 5'9", 159 lbs. Deb: 4/25/1876 U Career OF: 1-0-3 ♦

YEAR TM-L	G	AB	R	H	2B	3B	HR	RBI	BB	SO	SB	CS	AVG	OBP	SLG	OPS	OPS+	BR/A	RC	RC/G	FR	G/POS	WS	TPW
1876 Cin-N	63	281	31	71	3	0	0	14	9	11	....	....	.253	.285	.272	.557	101	3	22	3.01	-11	3-24,C-24,S-22/O-3(0-0-3),P	4	-1.1
1877 Cin-N	44	157	16	27	2	1	0	13	12	10	....	....	.172	.231	.197	.428	40	-7	7	1.55	-7	S-13,C-12,P-12,2-10/3-3,O	2	-1.4
1880 Cin-N	1	2	0	0	0	0	0	0	0	0	....	....	.000	.000	.000	.000	-101	-0	0	.00	0	/3-1	0	-0.1
1882 Bal-a	1	3	0	0	0	0	0	....	0	....	....	....	.000	.000	.000	.000	-108	-1	0	.00	0	/3-1	0	0.0
Lou-a	1	4	0	0	0	0	0	....	0	....	....	....	.000	.000	.000	.000	-106	-1	0	.00	0	/2-1	0	0.0
Yr.	2	7	0	0	0	0	0	....	0	....	....	....	.000	.000	.000	.000	-107	-1	0	.00	0	/2-1,3-1	0	-0.1
Total 4	110	447	47	98	5	1	0	27	21	21	....	....	.219	.259	.240	.499	74	-6	29	2.37	-18	/C-36,S-35,3-29,P-15,2-11,O	6	-2.7

• BOOTH, Eddie Edward H. Booth b: Brooklyn, NY Deb: 4/26/1872 NA OF: 68-8-83

YEAR TM-L	G	AB	R	H	2B	3B	HR	RBI	BB	SO	SB	CS	AVG	OBP	SLG	OPS	OPS+	BR/A	RC	RC/G	FR	G/POS	WS	TPW
1872 Man-n	24	117	25	38	4	2	0	12	0	1	0	0	.325	.325	.393	.718	127	4	15	6.01	-3	2-20/O-4(0-3-1)	....	0.0
Atl-n	15	62	11	19	4	0	0	8	0	0	0	2	.306	.306	.371	.677	92	-2	7	4.98	1	O-14(6-0-8)/2-1	....	-0.1
Yr.	39	179	36	57	8	2	0	20	0	1	0	2	.318	.318	.385	.704	115	2	23	5.63	-2	2-21,O-18(6-3-9)	....	-0.1
1873 Res-n	18	72	11	21	3	2	0	4	0	2	0	0	.292	.292	.389	.681	109	1	8	5.01	-3	O-17(15-0-2)/2-1	....	-0.1
Atl-n	16	69	8	14	3	1	0	8	3	0	0	1	.203	.236	.275	.511	58	-3	5	2.50	1	O-16(0-4-12)	....	-0.1
Yr.	34	141	19	35	6	3	0	12	3	2	0	1	.248	.264	.333	.597	83	-2	13	3.70	-2	O-33(15-4-14)/2-1	....	-0.2
1874 Atl-n	44	185	24	47	4	3	1	16	3	3	0	0	.254	.266	.324	.590	100	2	16	3.56	-5	*O-44(44-0-0)/2-1	....	-0.2
1875 Mut-n	68	281	33	56	3	4	0	18	0	2	4	3	.199	.199	.238	.438	49	-15	15	1.88	1	*O-63(3-1-60)/2-8	....	-0.9
1876 NY-N	57	230	17	49	2	1	0	7	2	4	....	....	.213	.222	.232	.454	59	-7	12	1.88	-8	*O-53(0-2-51)/2-5,P-1	2	-1.7
Total 4 n	185	786	112	195	21	12	1	66	6	8	4	6	.248	.254	.309	.563	82	-13	66	3.37	-8	O-158/2-31	....	-1.4

• BOOTY, Josh Joshua Gibson Booty b: 4/29/1975, Starkville, MS BR/TR, 6'3", 210 lbs. Deb: 9/24/1996

YEAR TM-L	G	AB	R	H	2B	3B	HR	RBI	BB	SO	SB	CS	AVG	OBP	SLG	OPS	OPS+	BR/A	RC	RC/G	FR	G/POS	WS	TPW
1996 Fla-N	2	2	1	1	0	0	0	0	0	0	0	0	.500	.500	.500	1.000	170	0	0	.00	0	/3-1	0	0.0
1997 Fla-N	4	5	2	3	0	0	0	1	1	1	0	0	.600	.667	.600	1.267	246	1	2	29.34	0	/3-4	1	0.1
1998 Fla-N	7	19	0	3	1	0	0	3	3	8	0	0	.158	.273	.211	.483	31	-2	1	2.20	-1	/3-7	0	-0.3
Total 3	13	26	3	7	1	0	0	4	4	9	0	0	.269	.367	.308	.674	83	-0	3	4.69	-2	/3-12	1	-0.2

• BORCHARD, Joe Joseph Edward Borchard b: 11/25/1978, Panorama City, CA BB/TR, 6'5", 220 lbs. Deb: 9/2/2002 Career OF: 10-21-3

YEAR TM-L	G	AB	R	H	2B	3B	HR	RBI	BB	SO	SB	CS	AVG	OBP	SLG	OPS	OPS+	BR/A	RC	RC/G	FR	G/POS	WS	TPW
2002 Chi-A	16	36	5	8	0	0	2	5	1	14	0	0	.222	.243	.389	.632	63	-2	3	3.34	-1	O-15(10-5-3)	1	-0.3
2003 Chi-A	16	49	5	9	1	0	1	5	5	18	0	1	.184	.259	.265	.525	39	-5	4	2.22	-2	O-16(0-16-0)	0	-0.6
Total 2	32	85	10	17	1	0	3	10	6	32	0	1	.200	.253	.318	.570	48	-7	7	2.66	-3	/O-31	1	-0.9

• BORDAGARAY, Frenchy Stanley George Bordagaray b: 1/3/1910, Coalinga, CA d: 4/13/2000, Ventura, CA BR/TR, 5'7.5", 175 lbs. Deb: 4/17/1934 Career OF: 111-170-171

YEAR TM-L	G	AB	R	H	2B	3B	HR	RBI	BB	SO	SB	CS	AVG	OBP	SLG	OPS	OPS+	BR/A	RC	RC/G	FR	G/POS	WS	TPW
1934 Chi-A	29	87	12	28	3	1	0	2	3	8	1	2	.322	.344	.379	.724	84	-3	11	4.55	0	O-17(2-1-14)	1	-0.4
1935 Bro-N	120	422	69	119	19	6	1	39	17	29	18	....	.282	.319	.363	.682	85	-9	51	4.36	4	*O-105(17-61-27)	9	-0.9
1936 Bro-N	125	372	63	117	21	3	4	31	17	42	12	....	.315	.346	.419	.766	104	1	54	5.31	-1	O-92(14-46-33),2-11/3-6	11	-0.3
1937 StL-N	96	300	43	88	11	4	1	37	15	25	11	....	.293	.331	.367	.698	87	-5	37	4.54	-2	3-50,O-28(3-7-15)	8	-0.7
1938 StL-N	81	156	19	44	5	1	0	21	8	9	2	....	.282	.325	.327	.652	75	-5	17	3.90	-2	O-29(6-14-9)/3-4	2	-0.8
1939*Cin-N	63	122	19	24	5	1	0	12	9	10	3	....	.197	.252	.254	.506	36	-11	8	2.20	0	O-43(21-3-19)/2-2	1	-1.3
1941*NY-A	36	73	10	19	1	0	0	4	6	8	1	0	.260	.325	.274	.599	61	-4	7	3.68	0	O-19(6-0-13)	1	-0.4
1942 Bro-N	48	58	11	14	2	0	0	5	3	3	2	....	.241	.279	.276	.555	62	-3	4	2.62	-1	O-17(0-10-7)	1	-0.4
1943 Bro-N	89	268	47	81	18	2	0	19	30	15	6	....	.302	.379	.384	.763	120	8	42	5.91	-6	O-53(28-6-20),3-25	11	0.0
1944 Bro-N	130	501	85	141	26	4	6	51	36	22	3	....	.281	.331	.385	.716	103	1	64	4.53	-11	3-98,O-25(5-15-8)	14	-1.0
1945 Bro-N	113	273	32	70	9	6	2	49	29	15	7	....	.256	.328	.355	.683	91	-4	33	4.31	-7	3-57,O-22(9-7-6)	7	-1.1
Total 11	930	2632	410	745	120	28	14	270	173	186	66	2	.283	.331	.366	.697	91	-34	329	4.49	-26	O-450,3-240/2-13	66	-7.3

• BORDERS, Pat Patrick Lance Borders b: 5/14/1963, Columbus, OH BR/TR, 6'2", 200 lbs. Deb: 4/6/1988

YEAR TM-L	G	AB	R	H	2B	3B	HR	RBI	BB	SO	SB	CS	AVG	OBP	SLG	OPS	OPS+	BR/A	RC	RC/G	FR	G/POS	WS	TPW
1988 Tor-A	56	154	15	42	6	3	5	21	3	24	0	0	.273	.287	.448	.735	102	-1	18	4.01	-3	C-43/D-7,2-1,3-1	3	-0.1
1989*Tor-A	94	241	22	62	11	1	3	29	11	45	2	1	.257	.292	.349	.641	85	-6	23	3.27	0	C-68,D-18	5	-0.3
1990 Tor-A	125	346	36	99	24	2	15	49	18	57	0	1	.286	.321	.497	.819	119	6	48	4.81	2	*C-115/D-1	12	1.5
1991*Tor-A	105	291	22	71	17	0	5	36	11	45	0	0	.244	.274	.354	.628	70	-13	27	3.03	1	*C-102	5	-0.7
1992*Tor-A	138	480	47	116	26	2	13	53	33	75	1	1	.242	.293	.385	.679	85	-11	53	3.71	3	*C-137	12	0.0
1993*Tor-A	138	488	38	124	30	0	9	55	20	66	2	2	.254	.286	.371	.657	75	-19	47	3.20	-1	*C-138	8	-1.0
1994 Tor-A	85	295	24	73	13	1	3	26	15	50	1	1	.247	.284	.329	.613	57	-20	26	3.06	3	C-85	4	-1.0
1995 KC-A	52	143	14	33	8	1	4	13	7	22	0	0	.231	.267	.385	.651	66	-8	15	3.58	1	C-45/D-3	2	-0.4
Hou-N	11	35	1	4	0	0	0	0	2	7	0	0	.114	.162	.114	.276	-27	-6	0	.38	-0	C-11	0	-0.6
1996 StL-N	26	69	3	22	3	0	0	4	1	14	0	1	.319	.329	.362	.691	83	-2	8	4.12	0	C-17/1-1	2	-0.1
Cal-A	19	57	6	13	3	0	2	8	3	11	0	1	.228	.267	.386	.653	64	-4	5	3.07	2	C-19	1	-0.1
Chi-A	31	94	6	26	1	0	3	6	5	18	0	1	.277	.313	.383	.696	79	-3	11	4.09	1	C-30/D-1	1	-0.1
Yr.	50	151	12	39	4	0	5	14	8	29	0	1	.258	.296	.384	.680	73	-7	16	3.69	2	C-49/D-1	2	-0.2
1997 Cle-A	55	159	17	47	7	1	4	15	9	27	0	2	.296	.341	.428	.769	96	-2	21	4.82	-1	C-53	3	0.1
1998 Cle-A	54	160	12	38	6	0	0	6	10	40	0	2	.238	.291	.275	.566	47	-13	13	2.60	-2	C-53/3-1	1	-1.1
1999 Cle-A	6	20	2	6	0	1	0	3	0	3	0	1	.300	.300	.400	.700	73	-1	2	3.60	-1	/C-5,3-1	0	-0.2
Tor-A	6	14	1	3	0	0	1	3	1	2	0	0	.214	.267	.429	.695	72	-1	2	4.10	0	/C-3,D-3	1	0.0
Yr.	12	34	3	9	0	1	1	6	1	5	0	1	.265	.286	.412	.697	73	-2	4	3.81	-1	/C-8,D-3,3-1	1	-0.3
2001 Sea-A	5	6	1	3	0	0	0	0	0	1	0	0	.500	.500	.500	1.000	175	1	2	10.18	-1	/C-5	0	0.0
2002 Sea-A	4	4	0	2	1	0	0	1	0	1	0	0	.500	.500	.750	1.250	234	1	2	20.25	0	/C-2,D-2	0	0.0
2003 Sea-A	12	14	1	2	1	0	0	1	1	5	0	0	.143	.200	.214	.414	10	-2	1	1.47	0	/C-7,3-2,D-1	0	-0.1
Total 15	1022	3070	268	786	157	12	67	329	150	513	6	13	.256	.293	.380	.673	80	-105	321	3.57	5	C-938/D-36,3-5,1-1,2-1	60	-4.2

• BORDICK, Mike Michael Todd Bordick b: 7/21/1965, Marquette, MI BR/TR, 5'11", 175 lbs. Deb: 4/11/1990

YEAR TM-L	G	AB	R	H	2B	3B	HR	RBI	BB	SO	SB	CS	AVG	OBP	SLG	OPS	OPS+	BR/A	RC	RC/G	FR	G/POS	WS	TPW
1990*Oak-A	25	14	0	1	0	0	0	0	1	4	0	0	.071	.133	.071	.205	-43	-3	0	.35	-6	3-10/S-9,2-7	0	-0.9
1991 Oak-A	90	235	21	56	5	1	0	21	14	37	3	4	.238	.290	.268	.558	59	-14	19	2.56	-7	S-84/2-5,3-1	6	-1.4
1992*Oak-A	154	504	62	151	19	4	3	48	40	59	12	6	.300	.362	.371	.733	111	8	69	4.82	21	2-95,S-70	22	3.8
1993 Oak-A	159	546	60	136	21	2	3	48	60	58	10	10	.249	.335	.311	.647	80	-15	60	3.63	-3	*S-159/2-1	14	-0.5
1994 Oak-A	114	391	38	99	18	4	2	37	38	44	7	2	.253	.324	.335	.659	77	-12	44	3.80	8	*S-112/2-4	8	0.5
1995 Oak-A	126	428	46	113	13	0	8	44	35	48	11	3	.264	.327	.350	.677	81	-11	51	4.08	2	*S-126/D-1	10	0.2
1996 Oak-A	155	525	46	126	18	4	5	54	52	59	5	6	.240	.310	.318	.628	61	-33	53	3.38	4	*S-155	10	-1.5
1997*Bal-A	153	509	55	120	19	1	7	46	33	66	0	2	.236	.285	.318	.603	59	-32	42	2.61	-2	*S-153	7	-2.1
1998 Bal-A	151	465	59	121	29	1	13	51	39	65	6	7	.260	.331	.411	.741	93	-7	61	4.30	2	*S-150	13	0.6
1999 Bal-A	160	631	93	175	35	7	10	77	54	102	14	4	.277	.339	.403	.742	92	-7	83	4.44	24	*S-159	17	2.7
2000 Bal-A★	100	391	70	116	22	1	16	59	34	71	6	5	.297	.354	.481	.835	114	7	63	5.70	-10	*S-100	13	0.4

YEAR TM-L	G	AB	R	H	2B	3B	HR	RBI	BB	SO	SB	CS	AVG	OBP	SLG	OPS	OPS+	BR/A	RC	RC/G	FR	G/POS	WS	TPW
*NY-N	56	192	18	50	8	0	4	21	15	28	3	1	.260	.321	.365	.685	76	-7	23	4.10	-3	S-56	3	-0.5
2001 Bal-A	58	229	32	57	13	0	7	30	17	36	9	3	.249	.317	.397	.715	92	-2	30	4.35	-3	S-58	6	-0.1
2002 Bal-A	117	367	37	85	19	3	8	36	35	63	7	4	.232	.304	.365	.669	81	-11	40	3.60	20	*S-117	12	1.8
2003 Tor-A	102	343	39	94	18	2	5	54	33	60	3	1	.274	.341	.382	.723	89	-5	45	4.69	2	S-69,3-22,2-13/D-1	10	0.3
Total 14	1720	5770	676	1500	257	30	91	626	500	800	96	58	.260	.326	.362	.688	83	-144	682	3.98	48	*S-1577,2-125/3-33,D-2	151	3.3
• BORGMANN, Glenn	Glenn Dennis Borgmann b: 5/25/1950, Paterson, NJ BR/TR, 6'4", 210 lbs. Deb: 7/1/1972																							
1972 Min-A	56	175	11	41	4	0	3	14	25	25	0	0	.234	.330	.309	.639	86	-2	18	3.51	-2	C-56	5	-0.1
1973 Min-A	12	34	7	9	2	0	0	9	6	10	0	0	.265	.375	.324	.699	95	0	5	4.97	-1	C-12	1	0.0
1974 Min-A	128	345	33	87	8	1	3	45	39	44	2	1	.252	.330	.307	.637	81	-7	36	3.52	2	*C-128	12	0.0
1975 Min-A	125	352	34	73	15	2	2	33	47	59	0	1	.207	.304	.278	.583	64	-16	31	2.80	6	*C-125	8	-0.5
1976 Min-A	24	65	10	16	3	0	1	6	19	7	1	1	.246	.417	.338	.755	120	3	11	5.37	-1	C-24	3	0.4
1977 Min-A	17	43	12	11	1	0	2	7	11	9	0	0	.256	.407	.419	.826	128	2	8	6.64	0	C-17	2	0.3
1978 Min-A	49	123	16	26	4	1	3	15	18	17	0	0	.211	.312	.333	.645	80	-3	15	3.83	1	C-46/D-1	4	0.0
1979 Min-A	31	70	4	14	3	0	0	8	12	11	1	0	.200	.317	.243	.560	52	-4	6	2.63	-1	C-31	2	-0.3
1980 Chi-A	32	87	10	19	2	0	2	14	14	9	0	0	.218	.327	.310	.637	76	-2	10	3.74	2	C-32	3	0.1
Total 9	474	1294	137	296	42	4	16	151	191	191	4	3	.229	.329	.304	.634	79	-28	140	3.53	6	C-471/D-1	40	-0.2
• BORKOWSKI, Bob	Robert Vilarian Borkowski b: 1/27/1926, Dayton, OH BR/TR, 6', 182 lbs. Deb: 4/22/1950 Career OF: 59-107-153																							
1950 Chi-N	85	256	27	70	7	4	4	29	16	30	1	....	.273	.319	.379	.698	84	-7	29	3.98	2	O-65(7-29-30)/1-1	5	-0.6
1951 Chi-N	58	89	9	14	1	0	0	10	3	16	0	0	.157	.185	.169	.353	-4	-13	2	.72	-1	O-25(7-9-9)	0	-1.5
1952 Cin-N	126	377	42	95	11	4	4	24	26	53	1	3	.252	.300	.334	.634	76	-14	39	3.64	-7	*O-103(15-64-26)/1-5	7	-2.5
1953 Cin-N	94	249	32	67	11	1	7	29	21	41	0	1	.269	.328	.406	.734	89	-4	34	4.76	-2	O-67(3-3-61)/1-2	5	-0.8
1954 Cin-N	73	162	13	43	12	1	1	19	8	18	0	2	.265	.304	.370	.674	73	-8	15	3.04	0	O-36(13-0-23)/1-3	1	-0.9
1955 Cin-N	25	18	1	3	1	0	0	1	1	2	0	0	.167	.211	.222	.433	14	-2	1	1.14	-1	O-11(11-0-0)/1-1	0	-0.3
Bro-N	9	19	2	2	0	0	0	0	1	6	0	0	.105	.150	.105	.255	-30	-4	0	.54	0	/O-9(3-2-4)	0	-0.4
Yr.	34	37	3	5	1	0	0	1	2	8	0	0	.135	.179	.162	.342	-8	-6	1	.84	-1	O-20(14-2-4)/1-1	0	-0.7
Total 6	470	1170	126	294	43	10	16	112	76	166	2	6	.251	.299	.346	.645	71	-51	120	3.50	-9	O-316/1-12	18	-7.1
• BOROM, Red	Edward Jones Borom b: 10/30/1915, Spartanburg, SC BL/TR, 5'11", 175 lbs. Deb: 4/23/1944																							
1944 Det-A	7	14	1	1	0	0	0	1	2	2	0	0	.071	.188	.071	.259	-23	-2	0	.44	0	/2-4,S-1	0	-0.2
1945*Det-A	55	130	19	35	4	0	0	9	7	8	4	2	.269	.307	.300	.607	72	-5	13	3.19	2	2-28/3-4,S-2	3	-0.1
Total 2	62	144	20	36	4	0	0	10	9	10	4	2	.250	.294	.278	.572	62	-7	13	2.85	2	/2-32,3-4,S-3	3	-0.4
• BOROS, Steve	Stephen Boros b: 9/3/1936, Flint, MI BR/TR, 6', 185 lbs. Deb: 6/19/1957 M/C																							
1957 Det-A	24	41	4	6	1	0	0	2	1	8	0	0	.146	.167	.171	.337	-7	-6	1	.63	0	/3-9,S-5	0	-0.6
1958 Det-A	6	2	0	0	0	0	0	0	0	0	0	0	.000	.000	.000	.000	-93	-1	0	.00	0	/2-1	0	-0.1
1961 Det-A	116	396	51	107	18	2	5	62	68	42	4	2	.270	.388	.364	.751	98	3	61	5.31	-8	*3-116	13	-0.5
1962 Det-A	116	356	46	81	14	1	16	47	53	62	3	1	.228	.333	.407	.740	94	-2	50	4.73	-1	*3-105/2-6	9	-0.2
1963 Chi-N	41	90	9	19	5	1	3	7	12	19	0	2	.211	.304	.389	.693	93	-1	11	3.75	-1	1-14,O-11(0-0-11)	2	-0.4
1964 Cin-N	117	370	31	95	12	3	2	31	47	43	4	1	.257	.344	.322	.665	86	-4	41	3.79	3	*3-114	10	-0.2
1965 Cin-N	2	0	0	0	0	0	0	0	0	0	0	0	....	....	....	....	-94	0	0		0	/3-2	0	0.0
Total 7	422	1255	141	308	50	7	26	149	181	174	11	6	.245	.346	.359	.705	90	-11	164	4.40	-6	3-346/1-14,O-11,2-7,S-5	34	-1.9
• BORTON, Babe	William Baker Borton b: 8/14/1888, Marion, IL d: 7/29/1954, Berkeley, CA BL/TL, 6', 178 lbs. Deb: 9/2/1912																							
1912 Chi-A	31	105	15	39	3	1	0	17	8	....	1	....	.371	.416	.419	.835	143	6	19	6.95	1	1-30	5	0.7
1913 Chi-A	28	80	9	22	5	0	0	13	23	5	1	....	.275	.442	.338	.780	130	5	12	5.26	-2	1-26	4	0.3
NY-A	33	108	8	14	2	0	0	11	18	19	1	....	.130	.260	.148	.408	20	-10	5	1.24	3	1-33	1	-0.8
Yr.	61	188	17	36	7	0	0	24	41	24	2	....	.191	.342	.229	.571	69	-5	17	2.77	2	1-59	5	-0.5
1915 StL-F	159	549	**97**	157	20	14	3	83	**92**	64	17	....	.286	.395	.390	.785	125	22	90	5.68	-15	*1-159	20	0.5
1916 StL-A	66	98	10	22	1	2	1	12	19	13	1	....	.224	.350	.306	.657	102	1	11	3.74	-2	1-22	3	-0.1
Total 4	317	940	139	254	31	17	4	136	160	101	21	....	.270	.381	.352	.734	113	24	137	4.96	-14	1-270	33	0.6
• BOSCH, Don	Donald John Bosch b: 7/15/1942, San Francisco, CA BB/TR, 5'10", 160 lbs. Deb: 9/19/1966 Career OF: 6-99-1																							
1966 Pit-N	3	2	0	0	0	0	0	0	0	0	0	0	.000	.000	.000	.000	-100	-1	0	.00	0	/O-1	0	-0.1
1967 NY-N	44	93	7	13	0	1	0	2	5	24	3	1	.140	.184	.161	.345	-1	-12	3	.84	0	O-39(0-39-0)	1	-1.4
1968 NY-N	50	111	14	19	1	0	3	7	9	33	0	2	.171	.233	.261	.495	48	-8	6	1.74	1	O-33(4-30-0)	1	-1.0
1969 Mon-N	49	112	13	20	5	0	1	4	8	20	1	0	.179	.233	.250	.483	35	-10	7	1.99	-1	O-32(2-29-1)	0	-1.2
Total 4	146	318	34	52	6	1	4	13	22	77	4	3	.164	.218	.226	.444	29	-30	16	1.53	-1	O-105	2	-3.6
• BOSETTI, Rick	Richard Alan Bosetti b: 8/5/1953, Redding, CA BR/TR, 5'11", 185 lbs. Deb: 9/9/1976 Career OF: 33-382-7																							
1976 Phi-N	13	18	6	5	1	0	0	0	1	3	3	0	.278	.316	.333	.649	82	0	2	3.75	0	/O-6(1-4-1)	0	0.0
1977 StL-N	41	69	12	16	0	0	0	3	6	11	4	4	.232	.303	.232	.535	46	-6	5	2.36	2	O-35(27-7-3)	1	-0.5
1978 Tor-A	136	568	61	147	25	5	5	42	30	65	6	10	.259	.300	.347	.646	80	-19	58	3.51	13	*O-135(0-135-0)	12	-0.8
1979 Tor-A	162	619	59	161	35	2	8	65	22	70	13	12	.260	.289	.362	.651	73	-27	58	3.15	9	*O-162(0-162-0)	9	-1.9
1980 Tor-A	53	188	24	40	7	1	4	18	15	29	4	6	.213	.278	.324	.603	62	-12	16	2.76	-1	O-51(0-51-0)	2	-1.4
1981 Tor-A	25	47	5	11	2	0	0	4	2	6	0	2	.234	.265	.277	.542	53	-4	3	1.66	-1	O-19(5-13-2)/D-1	1	-0.5
*Oak-A	9	19	4	2	0	0	0	1	3	3	0	0	.105	.227	.105	.333	-2	-2	1	1.00	0	/O-5(0-4-1),D-2	0	-0.3
Yr.	34	66	9	13	2	0	0	5	5	9	0	2	.197	.254	.227	.481	36	-6	3	1.47	-1	O-24(5-17-3)/D-3	1	-0.8
1982 Oak-A	6	15	1	3	0	0	0	0	0	1	0	0	.200	.200	.200	.400	11	-2	0	.85	1	/O-6(0-6-0)	0	-0.1
Total 7	445	1543	172	385	70	8	17	133	79	188	30	34	.250	.290	.338	.628	71	-71	143	3.10	23	O-419/D-3	25	-5.5
• BOSLEY, Thad	Thaddis Bosley b: 9/17/1956, Oceanside, CA BL/TL, 6'3", 175 lbs. Deb: 6/29/1977 C Career OF: 267-122-108																							
1977 Cal-A	58	212	19	63	10	2	0	19	16	32	5	4	.297	.349	.363	.713	98	-1	27	4.42	-3	O-55(20-35-1)	5	-0.6
1978 Chi-A	66	219	25	59	5	1	2	13	13	32	12	11	.269	.310	.329	.639	79	-8	20	3.04	-2	O-64(15-39-14)	4	-1.3
1979 Chi-A	36	77	13	24	1	1	1	8	9	14	4	1	.312	.384	.390	.773	109	2	12	6.09	1	O-28(22-1-5)/D-1	3	0.1
1980 Chi-A	70	147	12	33	2	0	2	14	10	27	3	2	.224	.274	.279	.553	52	-10	10	2.24	-2	O-52(32-18-4)	1	-1.3
1981*Mil-A	42	105	11	24	2	0	0	3	6	13	2	1	.229	.270	.248	.518	53	-6	7	2.02	-1	O-37(7-8-22)/D-1	0	-0.9
1982 Sea-A	22	46	3	8	1	0	0	2	4	8	3	1	.174	.240	.196	.436	21	-5	2	1.57	0	O-19(15-3-2)	0	-0.5
1983 Chi-N	43	72	12	21	4	1	2	12	10	12	1	1	.292	.378	.458	.836	125	2	13	6.70	0	O-20(16-1-3)	3	0.2
1984*Chi-N	55	98	17	29	2	2	2	14	13	22	5	1	.296	.378	.418	.797	113	3	17	6.29	0	O-33(11-2-21)	4	0.1
1985 Chi-N	108	180	25	59	6	3	7	27	20	29	5	1	.328	.395	.511	.906	137	10	37	7.94	-2	O-55(46-7-8)	8	0.6
1986 Chi-N	87	120	15	33	4	1	1	9	18	24	3	0	.275	.370	.350	.720	92	0	17	4.92	-1	O-41(32-2-8)	3	-0.2
1987 KC-A	80	140	13	39	6	1	1	16	9	26	0	0	.279	.322	.357	.679	78	-4	16	4.11	-1	O-28(13-1-14),D-13	2	-0.7
1988 KC-A	15	21	1	4	0	0	0	2	2	6	0	0	.190	.261	.190	.451	28	-2	1	1.79	0	/O-6(1-4-1),D-4	0	-0.3
Cal-A	35	75	9	21	5	0	0	7	6	12	1	1	.280	.333	.347	.680	93	-1	9	3.77	-1	O-26(24-0-2)/D-2	1	-0.2
Yr.	50	96	10	25	5	0	0	9	8	18	1	1	.260	.317	.313	.630	79	-3	10	3.32	-1	O-32(25-4-3)/D-6	1	-0.5
1989 Tex-A	37	40	5	9	2	0	1	9	3	11	2	0	.225	.279	.350	.629	75	-1	4	2.95	1	/O-8(6-0-2),D-5	1	-0.1
1990 Tex-A	30	29	3	4	0	0	1	3	4	7	1	0	.138	.242	.241	.484	36	-2	2	1.83	-1	/O-9(7-1-1),D-4	0	-0.3
Total 14	784	1581	183	430	50	12	20	158	143	275	47	24	.272	.333	.357	.689	88	-24	194	4.22	-13	O-481/D-30	35	-5.1
• BOSS, Harley	Elmer Harley "Lefty" Boss b: 11/19/1908, Hodge, LA d: 5/15/1964, Nashville, TN BL/TL, 5'11.5", 185 lbs. Deb: 7/19/1928																							
1928 Was-A	12	12	1	3	0	0	0	2	3	1	0	0	.250	.400	.250	.650	75	-0	1	4.27	-1	/1-5	0	-0.1
1929 Was-A	28	66	9	18	2	1	0	6	2	6	0	0	.273	.294	.333	.627	61	-4	6	3.51	-0	1-18	1	-0.4
1930 Was-A	3	3	0	0	0	0	0	0	0	0	0	0	.000	.000	.000	.000	-100	-1	0	.00	0	/1-1	0	-0.1
1933 Cle-A	112	438	54	118	17	7	1	53	25	27	2	5	.269	.310	.347	.657	71	-20	46	3.70	5	*1-110	6	-2.4
Total 4	155	519	64	139	19	8	1	61	30	34	2	5	.268	.309	.341	.650	69	-25	54	3.66	4	1-134	7	-3.1
• BOSTICK, Henry	Henry Landers Bostick b: 1/12/1895, Boston, MA d: 9/16/1968, Denver, CO BR/TR Deb: 5/18/1915																							
1915 Phi-A	2	7	0	0	0	0	0	2	1	1	0	....	.000	.125	.000	.125	-65	-1	0	.00	0	/3-2	0	-0.1

• BOSTOCK, Lyman — Lyman Wesley Bostock b: 11/22/1950, Birmingham, AL d: 9/23/1978, Gary, IN BL/TR, 6'1", 180 lbs. Deb: 4/8/1975 Career OF: 72-297-151

YEAR TM-L	G	AB	R	H	2B	3B	HR	RBI	BB	SO	SB	CS	AVG	OBP	SLG	OPS	OPS+	BR/A	RC	RC/G	FR	G/POS	WS	TPW
1975 Min-A	98	369	52	104	21	5	0	29	28	42	2	3	.282	.332	.366	.698	95	-3	44	4.28	-5	0-92(12-28-55)/D-1	8	-1.2
1976 Min-A	128	474	75	153	21	9	4	60	33	37	12	6	.323	.368	.430	.798	130	17	71	5.49	-4	*0-124(0-121-3)	19	1.0
1977 Min-A	153	593	104	199	36	12	14	90	51	59	16	7	.336	.394	.508	.901	146	39	116	7.32	0	*0-149(60-90-3)	27	3.4
1978 Cal-A	147	568	74	168	24	4	5	71	59	36	15	12	.296	.364	.379	.743	113	10	72	4.37	-2	*0-146(0-58-90)/D-1	19	0.2
Total 4	526	2004	305	624	102	30	23	250	171	174	45	28	.311	.368	.427	.795	124	62	303	5.45	-11	0-511/D-2	73	3.4

• BOSTON, Daryl — Daryl Lamont Boston b: 1/4/1963, Cincinnati, OH BL/TL, 6'3", 203 lbs. Deb: 5/13/1984 Career OF: 276-499-94

YEAR TM-L	G	AB	R	H	2B	3B	HR	RBI	BB	SO	SB	CS	AVG	OBP	SLG	OPS	OPS+	BR/A	RC	RC/G	FR	G/POS	WS	TPW
1984 Chi-A	35	83	8	14	3	1	0	3	4	20	6	0	.169	.207	.229	.436	20	-8	5	1.88	-1	0-34(0-30-5)/D-1	1	-1.0
1985 Chi-A	95	232	20	53	13	1	3	15	14	44	8	6	.228	.272	.332	.604	62	-13	20	2.84	-3	0-93(0-90-4)/D-2	4	-1.8
1986 Chi-A	56	199	29	53	11	3	5	22	21	33	9	5	.266	.336	.427	.764	103	1	28	4.75	1	0-53(0-53-0)/D-1	7	0.0
1987 Chi-A	103	337	51	87	21	2	10	29	25	68	12	6	.258	.309	.421	.731	89	-6	43	4.35	2	0-92(51-45-0)/D-5	8	-0.6
1988 Chi-A	105	281	37	61	12	2	15	31	21	44	9	3	.217	.272	.434	.706	95	-3	32	3.75	-2	0-85(44-43-1)/D-5	7	-0.7
1989 Chi-A	101	218	34	55	3	4	5	23	24	31	7	2	.252	.326	.372	.698	99	0	29	4.50	-1	0-75(57-2-21)/D-9	6	-0.3
1990 Chi-A	5	1	0	0	0	0	0	0	0	0	1	0	.000	.000	.000	.000	-102	-0	0	.00	0	/D-3,0-1	0	0.0
NY-N	115	366	65	100	21	2	12	45	28	50	18	7	.273	.328	.440	.768	110	4	52	5.02	0	*0-109(1-108-0)	12	0.3
1991 NY-N	137	255	40	70	16	4	4	21	30	42	15	8	.275	.351	.416	.767	116	5	38	5.29	-2	*0-115(9-74-37)	9	0.2
1992 NY-N	130	289	37	72	14	2	11	35	38	60	12	6	.249	.342	.426	.768	118	7	43	4.99	1	0-95(66-16-14)	12	0.6
1993 Col-N	124	291	46	76	15	1	14	40	26	57	1	6	.261	.326	.464	.790	93	-6	42	4.95	-0	0-79(41-31-9)	4	-0.7
1994 NY-A	52	77	11	14	2	0	4	14	6	20	0	1	.182	.250	.364	.614	58	-6	7	3.00	1	0-16(7-7-2)/D-9	1	-0.5
Total 11	1058	2629	378	655	131	22	83	278	237	469	98	50	.249	.313	.410	.724	95	-24	339	4.38	-6	0-847/D-35	71	-4.6

• BOSWELL, Ken — Kenneth George Boswell b: 2/23/1946, Austin, TX BL/TR, 6', 172 lbs. Deb: 9/18/1967 Career OF: 3-0-5

YEAR TM-L	G	AB	R	H	2B	3B	HR	RBI	BB	SO	SB	CS	AVG	OBP	SLG	OPS	OPS+	BR/A	RC	RC/G	FR	G/POS	WS	TPW
1967 NY-N	11	40	2	9	3	0	1	4	1	5	0	0	.225	.244	.375	.619	76	-1	3	1.99	2	/2-6,3-4	1	0.2
1968 NY-N	75	284	37	74	7	2	4	11	16	27	7	2	.261	.302	.342	.644	92	-2	29	3.54	4	2-69	7	0.9
1969*NY-N	102	362	48	101	14	7	3	32	36	47	7	3	.279	.348	.381	.729	102	2	47	4.46	3	2-96	13	1.1
1970 NY-N	105	351	32	89	13	2	5	44	41	32	5	4	.254	.335	.345	.680	82	-9	39	3.68	6	*2-101	9	0.4
1971 NY-N	116	392	46	107	20	1	5	40	36	31	5	2	.273	.337	.367	.705	101	1	48	4.26	-7	*2-109	11	0.1
1972 NY-N	100	355	35	75	9	1	9	33	32	35	2	2	.211	.276	.318	.595	70	-15	29	2.53	-16	2-94	5	-2.7
1973*NY-N	76	110	12	25	2	1	2	14	12	11	0	0	.227	.303	.318	.621	74	-4	11	3.46	1	3-17/2-3	2	-0.3
1974 NY-N	96	222	19	48	6	1	2	15	18	19	0	1	.216	.278	.279	.557	57	-13	16	2.35	1	2-28,3-20/0-7(2-0-5)	2	-1.1
1975 Hou-N	86	178	16	43	8	2	0	21	30	12	0	3	.242	.354	.309	.663	92	-2	19	3.46	-1	2-31,3-23	3	-0.2
1976 Hou-N	91	126	12	33	8	1	0	18	8	8	1	0	.262	.306	.341	.647	92	-2	11	2.92	-2	3-16/2-3,0-1	2	-0.4
1977 Hou-N	72	97	7	21	1	1	0	12	10	12	0	0	.216	.290	.247	.537	50	-7	6	2.13	0	2-26/3-2	1	-0.6
Total 11	930	2517	266	625	91	19	31	244	240	239	27	17	.248	.316	.337	.652	85	-51	259	3.41	-8	2-566/3-82,0-8	56	-2.6

• BOTTARINI, John — John Charles Bottarini b: 9/14/1908, Crockett, CA d: 10/8/1976, Jemez Springs, NM BR/TR, 6', 190 lbs. Deb: 4/22/1937

YEAR TM-L	G	AB	R	H	2B	3B	HR	RBI	BB	SO	SB	CS	AVG	OBP	SLG	OPS	OPS+	BR/A	RC	RC/G	FR	G/POS	WS	TPW
1937 Chi-N	26	40	3	11	3	0	1	7	5	10	0	....	.275	.370	.425	.795	111	1	7	6.53	0	C-18/0-1	2	0.1

• BOTTOMLEY, Jim — James Leroy "Sunny Jim" Bottomley b: 4/23/1900, Oglesby, IL d: 12/11/1959, St. Louis, MO BL/TL, 6', 180 lbs. Deb: 8/18/1922 M/C HOF: 1974

YEAR TM-L	G	AB	R	H	2B	3B	HR	RBI	BB	SO	SB	CS	AVG	OBP	SLG	OPS	OPS+	BR/A	RC	RC/G	FR	G/POS	WS	TPW
1922 StL-N	37	151	29	49	8	5	5	35	6	13	3	1	.325	.358	.543	.902	136	8	29	7.30	-4	1-34	6	0.2
1923 StL-N	134	523	79	194	34	14	8	94	45	44	4	6	.371	.425	.535	.960	155	41	117	8.88	-7	*1-130	24	2.4
1924 StL-N	137	528	87	167	31	12	14	111	35	35	5	4	.316	.362	.500	.862	131	22	94	6.55	-9	*1-133/2-1	16	0.5
1925 StL-N	153	619	92	**227**	**44**	12	21	128	47	36	3	4	.367	.413	.578	.992	147	43	145	9.41	3	*1-153	27	3.3
1926*StL-N	154	603	98	180	**40**	14	19	**120**	58	52	4	....	.299	.364	.506	.870	127	21	109	6.38	-2	*1-154	23	0.9
1927 StL-N	152	574	95	174	31	15	19	124	74	49	8	....	.303	.387	.509	.896	134	28	112	6.86	-3	*1-152	26	1.5
1928*StL-N	149	576	123	187	42	**20**	**31**	**136**	71	54	10	....	.325	.402	.628	1.030	162	51	142	9.07	-8	*1-148	30	3.1
1929 StL-N	146	560	108	176	31	12	29	137	70	54	3	....	.314	.391	.568	.959	133	28	122	7.91	-4	*1-145	21	1.2
1930*StL-N	131	487	92	148	33	7	15	97	44	36	5	....	.304	.368	.493	.860	102	1	86	6.18	-10	*1-124	13	-1.5
1931*StL-N	108	382	73	133	34	5	9	75	34	24	3	....	.348	.403	.534	.937	144	24	84	8.65	-4	1-93	19	1.1
1932 StL-N	91	311	45	92	16	3	11	48	25	32	2	....	.296	.350	.473	.823	115	6	52	6.17	-4	1-74	9	-0.5
1933 Cin-N	145	549	57	137	23	9	13	83	42	28	3	....	.250	.311	.395	.706	102	1	68	4.24	3	*1-145	15	-1.0
1934 Cin-N	142	556	72	158	31	11	11	78	33	40	1	....	.284	.324	.439	.763	105	2	80	5.27	-4	*1-139	13	-1.5
1935 Cin-N	107	399	44	103	21	1	1	49	18	24	3	....	.258	.294	.323	.617	68	-18	37	3.21	0	1-97	4	-2.7
1936 StL-A	140	544	72	162	39	11	12	95	44	55	0	0	.298	.354	.476	.830	100	-2	92	6.31	-11	*1-140	11	-2.3
1937 StL-A	65	109	11	26	7	0	1	12	18	15	1	0	.239	.346	.330	.677	71	-4	14	4.38	0	1-24	1	-0.5
Total 16	1991	7471	1177	2313	465	151	219	1422	664	591	58	15	.310	.369	.500	.869	124	251	1384	6.76	-65	*1-1885/2-1	258	4.1

• BOUCHEE, Ed — Edward Francis Bouchee b: 3/7/1933, Livingston, MT BL/TL, 6', 205 lbs. Deb: 9/19/1956

YEAR TM-L	G	AB	R	H	2B	3B	HR	RBI	BB	SO	SB	CS	AVG	OBP	SLG	OPS	OPS+	BR/A	RC	RC/G	FR	G/POS	WS	TPW
1956 Phi-N	9	22	0	6	2	0	0	1	5	6	0	0	.273	.407	.364	.771	112	1	4	6.39	0	/1-6	1	0.0
1957 Phi-N	154	574	78	168	35	8	17	76	84	91	1	0	.293	.396	.470	.866	136	33	110	7.01	7	*1-154	27	3.2
1958 Phi-N	89	334	55	86	19	5	9	39	51	74	1	0	.257	.356	.425	.781	107	5	51	5.28	3	1-89	9	0.3
1959 Phi-N	136	499	75	142	29	4	15	74	70	74	0	4	.285	.378	.449	.827	117	13	85	6.00	3	*1-134	17	0.8
1960 Phi-N	22	65	1	17	4	0	0	8	9	11	0	0	.262	.360	.323	.683	88	-1	8	4.36	0	1-22	1	-0.1
Chi-N	98	299	33	71	11	1	5	44	45	51	2	0	.237	.341	.331	.672	86	-4	37	4.20	0	1-80	7	-0.8
Yr.	120	364	34	88	15	1	5	52	54	62	2	0	.242	.344	.330	.674	86	-4	45	4.23	1	*1-102	8	-0.9
1961 Chi-N	112	319	49	79	12	3	12	38	58	77	1	4	.248	.372	.417	.789	107	4	53	5.70	1	*1-107	9	0.0
1962 NY-N	50	87	7	14	2	0	3	10	18	17	0	0	.161	.305	.287	.592	59	-5	8	2.98	3	1-19	0	-0.2
Total 7	670	2199	298	583	114	21	61	290	340	401	5	8	.265	.370	.419	.790	111	47	356	5.66	18	1-611	71	3.1

• BOUCHER, Al — Alexander Francis "Bo" Boucher b: 11/13/1881, Franklin, MA d: 6/23/1974, Torrance, CA BR/TR, 5'8.5", 156 lbs. Deb: 4/16/1914

YEAR TM-L	G	AB	R	H	2B	3B	HR	RBI	BB	SO	SB	CS	AVG	OBP	SLG	OPS	OPS+	BR/A	RC	RC/G	FR	G/POS	WS	TPW
1914 StL-F	147	516	62	119	26	4	2	49	52	88	13	....	.231	.304	.308	.612	70	-20	52	3.16	-5	*3-147	9	-2.2

• BOUCHER, Medric — Medric Charles Francis Boucher b: 3/12/1886, St. Louis, MO d: 3/12/1974, Martinez, CA BR/TR, 5'10", 165 lbs. Deb: 5/20/1914

YEAR TM-L	G	AB	R	H	2B	3B	HR	RBI	BB	SO	SB	CS	AVG	OBP	SLG	OPS	OPS+	BR/A	RC	RC/G	FR	G/POS	WS	TPW
1914 Bal-F	16	16	2	5	1	1	0	2	1	1	0	....	.313	.353	.500	.853	142	1	3	6.20	-1	/C-7,1-1,0-1	1	0.0
Pit-F	1	1	0	0	0	0	0	0	0	0	0	....	.000	.000	.000	.000	-106	-0	0	.00	0	....	0	0.0
Yr.	17	17	2	5	1	1	0	2	1	1	0	....	.294	.333	.471	.804	129	1	3	5.68	-1	/C-7,1-1,0-1	1	0.0

• BOUDREAU, Lou — Louis Boudreau b: 7/17/1917, Harvey, IL d: 8/10/2001, Olympia Fields, IL BR/TR, 5'11", 185 lbs. Deb: 9/9/1938 M HOF: 1970

YEAR TM-L	G	AB	R	H	2B	3B	HR	RBI	BB	SO	SB	CS	AVG	OBP	SLG	OPS	OPS+	BR/A	RC	RC/G	FR	G/POS	WS	TPW
1938 Cle-A	1	1	0	0	0	0	0	0	1	0	0	0	.000	.500	.000	.500	36	0	0	3.31	0	/3-1	0	0.0
1939 Cle-A	53	225	42	58	15	4	0	19	28	24	2	1	.258	.340	.360	.700	82	-6	28	4.36	8	S-53	7	0.6
1940 Cle-A★	155	627	97	185	46	10	9	101	73	39	6	3	.295	.370	.443	.814	113	13	103	5.87	25	*S-155	30	4.7
1941 Cle-A★	148	579	95	149	**45**	8	10	56	85	57	9	4	.257	.355	.415	.770	108	9	92	5.39	13	*S-147	22	3.1
1942 Cle-A★	147	506	57	143	18	10	2	58	75	39	7	16	.283	.379	.370	.749	118	10	73	4.77	6	*S-146	23	2.7
1943 Cle-A★	152	539	69	154	32	7	3	67	90	31	4	7	.286	.388	.388	.776	135	26	87	5.52	26	*S-152/C-1	32	**7.0**
1944 Cle-A★	150	584	91	191	**45**	5	3	67	73	39	11	3	**.327**	.406	.437	.843	146	39	112	7.10	16	*S-149/C-1	28	7.1
1945 Cle-A★	97	345	50	106	24	1	3	48	35	20	0	4	.307	.374	.409	.783	133	13	53	5.28	13	S-97	17	3.7
1946 Cle-A	140	515	51	151	30	6	6	62	40	14	6	7	.293	.345	.410	.755	118	9	72	4.93	23	*S-139	24	4.4
1947 Cle-A★	150	538	79	165	**45**	3	4	67	67	10	1	0	.307	.388	.424	.811	129	23	95	6.46	20	*S-148	28	5.4
1948*Cle-A★	152	560	116	199	34	6	18	106	98	9	3	2	.355	.453	.534	.987	166	57	143	9.79	10	*S-151/C-1	34	**7.5**
1949 Cle-A	134	475	53	135	20	3	4	60	70	10	0	1	.284	.381	.364	.745	99	2	68	4.96	8	S-88,3-38/1-6,2-1	17	1.5
1950 Cle-A	81	260	23	70	13	2	1	29	31	5	1	2	.269	.349	.346	.695	81	-7	32	4.19	6	S-61/1-8,2-2,3-2	7	0.2
1951 Bos-A	82	273	37	73	18	1	5	47	30	12	1	0	.267	.353	.396	.748	93	-2	39	4.89	3	S-52,3-15/1-2	8	0.4
1952 Bos-A	4	2	1	0	0	0	0	2	0	0	0	0	.000	.000	.000	.000	-93	-1	0	.00	-1	/3-1,S-1	0	-0.1
Total 15	1646	6029	861	1779	385	66	68	789	796	309	51	50	.295	.380	.415	.795	122	187	996	5.82	176	*S-1539/3-57,1-16,2-3,C-3	277	48.1

• BOURJOS, Chris — Christopher Bourjos b: 10/16/1954, Chicago, IL BR/TR, 6', 185 lbs. Deb: 8/31/1980

YEAR TM-L	G	AB	R	H	2B	3B	HR	RBI	BB	SO	SB	CS	AVG	OBP	SLG	OPS	OPS+	BR/A	RC	RC/G	FR	G/POS	WS	TPW
1980 SF-N	13	22	4	5	1	0	1	2	2	7	0	0	.227	.292	.409	.701	96	-0	2	3.57	0	/0-6(2-0-4)	0	-0.1

• BOURNIGAL, Rafael — Rafael Antonio (Pelletier) Bournigal b: 5/12/1966, Azua, Dominican Republic BR/TR, 5'11", 165 lbs. Deb: 9/1/1992

YEAR TM-L	G	AB	R	H	2B	3B	HR	RBI	BB	SO	SB	CS	AVG	OBP	SLG	OPS	OPS+	BR/A	RC	RC/G	FR	G/POS	WS	TPW
1992 LA-N	10	20	1	3	1	0	0	0	1	2	0	0	.150	.227	.200	.427	22	-2	1	1.63	-1	/S-9	0	-0.3

YEAR TM-L	G	AB	R	H	2B	3B	HR	RBI	BB	SO	SB	CS	AVG	OBP	SLG	OPS	OPS+	BR/A	RC	RC/G	FR	G/POS	WS	TPW
1993 LA-N	8	18	0	9	1	0	0	3	0	2	0	0	.500	.500	.556	1.056	193	2	5	15.00	-2	/2-4,S-4	1	0.1
1994 LA-N	40	116	2	26	3	1	0	11	9	5	0	0	.224	.291	.267	.559	50	-8	9	2.47	0	S-40	2	-0.5
1996 Oak-A	88	252	33	61	14	2	0	18	16	19	4	3	.242	.290	.313	.603	54	-19	22	2.90	4	2-64,S-23	3	-1.1
1997 Oak-A	79	222	29	62	9	0	1	20	16	19	2	1	.279	.339	.333	.672	78	-7	24	3.55	-3	S-74/2-7	4	-0.5
1998 Oak-A	85	209	23	47	11	0	1	19	10	11	6	1	.225	.267	.292	.559	46	-16	16	2.46	3	2-48,S-38/D-1	2	-0.9
1999 Sea-A	55	95	16	26	5	0	2	14	7	6	0	0	.274	.324	.389	.713	79	-3	11	3.85	-1	S-28,2-17/3-8,D-1,O-1	3	-0.2
Total 7	**365**	**932**	**104**	**234**	**44**	**3**	**4**	**85**	**59**	**64**	**12**	**5**	**.251**	**.303**	**.318**	**.620**	**62**	**-52**	**88**	**3.11**	**-0**	**S-216,2-140/3-8,D-2,O-1**	**15**	**-3.3**

• BOURQUE, Pat
Patrick Daniel Bourque b: 3/23/1947, Worcester, MA BL/TL, 6', 210 lbs. Deb: 9/6/1971

YEAR TM-L	G	AB	R	H	2B	3B	HR	RBI	BB	SO	SB	CS	AVG	OBP	SLG	OPS	OPS+	BR/A	RC	RC/G	FR	G/POS	WS	TPW
1971 Chi-N	14	37	3	7	0	1	1	3	3	9	0	0	.189	.250	.324	.574	54	-2	3	2.46	2	1-11	0	-0.1
1972 Chi-N	11	27	3	7	1	0	0	5	2	2	0	0	.259	.310	.296	.607	66	-1	3	3.57	1	/1-7	1	-0.1
1973 Chi-N	57	139	11	29	6	0	7	20	16	21	1	1	.209	.299	.403	.702	86	-3	18	4.31	4	1-38	3	-0.2
*Oak-A	23	42	8	8	4	1	2	9	15	10	0	0	.190	.404	.476	.880	155	4	9	6.64	0	D-15/1-5	2	0.3
1974 Oak-A	73	96	6	22	4	0	1	16	15	20	0	2	.229	.333	.302	.635	90	-2	10	3.46	-1	1-39/D-8	2	-0.4
Min-A	23	64	5	14	2	0	1	8	7	11	0	0	.219	.296	.297	.593	68	-2	6	2.89	2	1-21	1	-0.1
Yr.	96	160	11	36	6	0	2	24	22	31	0	2	.225	.319	.300	.619	81	-4	16	3.24	1	1-60/D-8	3	-0.6
Total 4	**201**	**405**	**36**	**87**	**17**	**2**	**12**	**61**	**58**	**73**	**1**	**3**	**.215**	**.316**	**.356**	**.672**	**89**	**-6**	**48**	**3.93**	**8**	**1-121/D-23**	**9**	**-0.6**

• BOWA, Larry
Lawrence Robert Bowa b: 12/6/1945, Sacramento, CA BB/TR, 5'10", 155 lbs. Deb: 4/7/1970 M/C

YEAR TM-L	G	AB	R	H	2B	3B	HR	RBI	BB	SO	SB	CS	AVG	OBP	SLG	OPS	OPS+	BR/A	RC	RC/G	FR	G/POS	WS	TPW
1970 Phi-N	145	547	50	137	17	6	0	34	21	48	24	13	.250	.278	.303	.582	57	-35	45	2.74	-6	*S-143/2-1	10	-2.4
1971 Phi-N	159	650	74	162	18	5	0	25	36	61	28	11	.249	.294	.292	.586	66	-27	59	3.12	0	*S-157	12	-0.9
1972 Phi-N	152	579	67	145	11	**13**	1	31	32	51	17	9	.250	.292	.320	.612	72	-22	54	3.12	0	*S-150	12	-0.4
1973 Phi-N	122	446	42	94	11	3	0	23	24	31	10	6	.211	.253	.249	.502	38	-38	28	2.05	0	*S-122	5	-2.5
1974 Phi-N★	162	669	97	184	19	10	1	36	23	52	39	11	.275	.300	.338	.638	75	-21	69	3.50	-18	*S-162	15	-2.1
1975 Phi-N★	136	583	79	178	18	9	2	38	24	32	24	6	.305	.335	.377	.712	94	-4	75	4.61	-12	*S-135	15	0.1
1976*Phi-N★	156	624	71	155	15	9	0	49	32	31	30	8	.248	.285	.301	.586	64	-27	55	2.94	2	*S-156	14	-0.7
1977*Phi-N	154	624	93	175	19	3	4	41	32	32	32	3	.280	.316	.340	.655	73	-19	70	3.95	-5	*S-154	16	-0.7
1978*Phi-N★	156	654	78	192	31	5	3	43	24	40	27	5	.294	.320	.370	.690	91	-6	80	4.45	7	*S-156	22	1.8
1979 Phi-N★	147	539	74	130	17	11	0	31	61	32	20	9	.241	.319	.314	.633	71	-20	57	3.42	-7	*S-146	12	-1.1
1980*Phi-N	147	540	57	144	16	4	2	39	24	28	21	6	.267	.302	.322	.624	70	-20	53	3.39	-19	*S-147	9	-2.5
1981*Phi-N	103	360	34	102	14	3	0	31	26	17	16	7	.283	.332	.339	.670	87	-6	40	3.91	-18	*S-102	9	-1.4
1982 Chi-N	142	499	50	123	15	7	0	29	39	38	8	3	.246	.302	.305	.607	68	-21	47	3.15	-33	*S-140	5	-4.0
1983 Chi-N	147	499	73	133	20	5	2	43	35	30	7	3	.267	.315	.339	.653	77	-15	56	3.93	-3	*S-145	13	-0.4
1984*Chi-N	133	391	33	87	14	2	0	17	28	24	10	4	.223	.274	.269	.543	49	-26	30	2.56	-4	*S-132	6	-1.8
1985 Chi-N	72	195	13	48	6	4	0	13	11	20	5	1	.246	.286	.318	.604	62	-10	18	3.13	6	S-66	4	0.3
NY-N	14	19	2	2	1	0	0	2	2	2	0	0	.105	.190	.158	.348	-2	-3	1	1.10	-1	/S-9,2-4	0	-0.3
Yr.	86	214	15	50	7	4	0	15	13	22	5	1	.234	.278	.304	.581	56	-12	19	2.92	5	S-75/2-4	4	-0.1
Total 16	**2247**	**8418**	**987**	**2191**	**262**	**99**	**15**	**525**	**474**	**569**	**318**	**105**	**.260**	**.301**	**.320**	**.621**	**71**	**-319**	**836**	**3.39**	**-110**	***S-2222/2-5**	**179**	**-19.2**

• BOWCOCK, Benny
Benjamin James Bowcock b: 10/28/1879, Fall River, MA d: 6/16/1961, Taunton, MA BR/TR, 5'7", 150 lbs. Deb: 9/18/1903

YEAR TM-L	G	AB	R	H	2B	3B	HR	RBI	BB	SO	SB	CS	AVG	OBP	SLG	OPS	OPS+	BR/A	RC	RC/G	FR	G/POS	WS	TPW
1903 StL-A	14	50	7	16	3	1	1	10	3	....	1	....	.320	.358	.480	.838	154	3	9	6.90	-5	2-14	2	-0.2

• BOWDEN, Tim
David Timon Bowden b: 8/15/1891, McDonough, GA d: 10/25/1949, Emory, GA BL/TR, 5'10", 175 lbs. Deb: 9/17/1914

YEAR TM-L	G	AB	R	H	2B	3B	HR	RBI	BB	SO	SB	CS	AVG	OBP	SLG	OPS	OPS+	BR/A	RC	RC/G	FR	G/POS	WS	TPW
1914 StL-A	7	9	0	2	0	0	0	0	1	6	0	....	.222	.300	.222	.522	59	-0	1	2.27	0	/O-4(0-1-3)	0	-0.1

• BOWEN, Chick
Emmons Joseph Bowen b: 7/26/1897, New Haven, CT d: 8/9/1948, New Haven, CT BR/TR, 5'7", 165 lbs. Deb: 9/15/1919

YEAR TM-L	G	AB	R	H	2B	3B	HR	RBI	BB	SO	SB	CS	AVG	OBP	SLG	OPS	OPS+	BR/A	RC	RC/G	FR	G/POS	WS	TPW
1919 NY-N	3	5	0	1	0	0	0	1	1	2	0	....	.200	.333	.200	.533	63	-0	0	2.06	0	/O-2(0-1-1)	0	0.0

• BOWEN, Rob
Robert McClure Bowen b: 2/24/1981, Bedford, TX BB/TR, 6'2", 225 lbs. Deb: 9/1/2003

YEAR TM-L	G	AB	R	H	2B	3B	HR	RBI	BB	SO	SB	CS	AVG	OBP	SLG	OPS	OPS+	BR/A	RC	RC/G	FR	G/POS	WS	TPW
2003 Min-A	7	10	0	1	0	0	0	1	0	4	0	0	.100	.100	.100	.200	-47	-2	0	.00	0	/C-7	0	-0.2

• BOWEN, Sam
Samuel Thomas Bowen b: 9/18/1952, Brunswick, GA BR/TR, 5'9", 170 lbs. Deb: 8/25/1977 Career OF: 4-8-1

YEAR TM-L	G	AB	R	H	2B	3B	HR	RBI	BB	SO	SB	CS	AVG	OBP	SLG	OPS	OPS+	BR/A	RC	RC/G	FR	G/POS	WS	TPW
1977 Bos-A	3	2	0	0	0	0	0	0	0	2	0	0	.000	.000	.000	.000	-89	-1	0	.00	0	/O-3(2-1-0)	0	-0.1
1978 Bos-A	6	7	3	1	0	0	1	1	1	2	0	0	.143	.250	.571	.821	113	0	1	4.79	0	/O-4(1-3-0)	0	0.0
1980 Bos-A	7	13	0	2	0	0	0	0	2	3	1	0	.154	.267	.154	.421	17	-1	1	1.99	1	/O-6(1-4-1)	0	0.0
Total 3	**16**	**22**	**3**	**3**	**0**	**0**	**1**	**1**	**3**	**7**	**1**	**0**	**.136**	**.240**	**.273**	**.513**	**39**	**-2**	**2**	**2.67**	**0**	**/O-13**	**0**	**-0.2**

• BOWENS, Sam
Samuel Edward Bowens b: 3/23/1939, Wilmington, NC d: 3/28/2003, Wilmington, NC BR/TR, 6'1.5", 195 lbs. Deb: 9/7/1963 Career OF: 108-10-284

YEAR TM-L	G	AB	R	H	2B	3B	HR	RBI	BB	SO	SB	CS	AVG	OBP	SLG	OPS	OPS+	BR/A	RC	RC/G	FR	G/POS	WS	TPW
1963 Bal-A	15	48	8	16	3	1	1	9	4	5	1	1	.333	.385	.500	.885	149	3	9	7.56	-1	O-13(0-0-13)	3	0.2
1964 Bal-A	139	501	58	132	25	2	22	71	42	99	4	3	.263	.325	.453	.779	114	8	71	4.89	-0	*O-135(32-0-120)	18	-0.2
1965 Bal-A	84	203	16	33	4	1	7	20	10	41	7	1	.163	.202	.296	.497	39	-16	10	1.45	2	O-68(11-0-58)	2	-2.0
1966 Bal-A	89	243	26	51	9	1	6	20	17	52	9	3	.210	.275	.329	.605	74	-8	21	2.76	2	O-68(32-4-41)	3	-1.1
1967 Bal-A	62	120	13	22	2	1	5	12	11	43	3	4	.183	.258	.342	.599	76	-5	10	2.75	0	O-32(16-0-16)	1	-0.7
1968 Was-A	57	115	14	22	4	0	4	7	11	39	0	0	.191	.262	.330	.592	81	-3	11	3.09	-1	O-27(11-3-14)	2	-0.6
1969 Was-A	33	57	6	11	1	0	0	4	5	14	1	1	.193	.258	.211	.469	34	-5	3	1.76	-1	O-30(6-3-22)	0	-0.7
Total 7	**479**	**1287**	**141**	**287**	**48**	**6**	**45**	**143**	**100**	**293**	**25**	**13**	**.223**	**.284**	**.375**	**.659**	**86**	**-25**	**136**	**3.44**	**1**	**O-373**	**29**	**-5.1**

• BOWERMAN, Frank
Frank Eugene "Mike" Bowerman b: 12/5/1868, Romeo, MI d: 11/30/1948, Romeo, MI BR/TR, 6'2", 190 lbs. Deb: 8/24/1895 M

YEAR TM-L	G	AB	R	H	2B	3B	HR	RBI	BB	SO	SB	CS	AVG	OBP	SLG	OPS	OPS+	BR/A	RC	RC/G	FR	G/POS	WS	TPW
1895 Bal-N	1	1	0	0	0	0	0	0	0	0	0	....	.000	.000	.000	.000	-97	-0	0	.00	0	/C-1	0	0.0
1896 Bal-N	4	16	0	2	0	0	0	4	1	0	0	....	.125	.176	.125	.301	-20	-3	0	.68	0	/C-3,1-1	0	-0.2
1897*Bal-N	38	130	16	41	5	0	1	21	1	....	3	....	.315	.331	.377	.708	87	-3	18	5.23	-5	C-36	3	-0.4
1898 Bal-N	5	16	5	7	1	0	0	1	2	....	1	....	.438	.526	.500	1.026	191	2	5	14.30	1	/C-4	1	0.3
Pit-N	69	241	17	66	6	3	0	29	7	....	4	....	.274	.297	.324	.621	79	-7	25	3.77	3	C-59/1-9	6	0.2
Yr.	74	257	22	73	7	3	0	30	9	....	5	....	.284	.313	.335	.648	87	-5	30	4.28	4	C-63/1-9	7	0.5
1899 Pit-N	110	427	51	111	16	10	3	53	12	....	10	....	.260	.288	.365	.654	79	-15	50	4.06	9	C-79,1-28	9	0.2
1900 NY-N	80	270	25	65	5	3	1	42	6	....	10	....	.241	.268	.293	.560	57	-16	25	3.16	8	C-75/S-2	4	-0.1
1901 NY-N	59	191	20	38	5	3	0	14	7	....	3	....	.199	.235	.257	.492	44	-14	13	2.18	5	C-46/2-3,3-3,S-3,1-1	2	-0.3
1902 NY-N	109	373	38	93	14	6	0	27	13	....	12	....	.249	.275	.319	.594	84	-9	37	3.48	3	C-98/1-3	7	0.4
1903 NY-N	64	210	22	58	6	2	1	31	6	....	5	....	.276	.306	.338	.644	80	-6	24	4.13	-3	C-55/1-4,O-1	7	-0.3
1904 NY-N	93	289	38	67	11	4	2	27	16	....	7	....	.232	.288	.318	.607	84	-6	30	3.42	-6	C-79/1-9,2-2,P-1	9	-0.5
1905 NY-N	98	297	37	80	8	1	3	41	12	....	6	....	.269	.322	.333	.655	93	-3	36	4.13	-9	C-72,1-17/2-1	9	-0.5
1906 NY-N	103	285	23	65	7	3	1	42	15	....	5	....	.228	.274	.284	.558	72	-10	25	2.86	1	C-67,1-20	7	-0.4
1907 NY-N	96	311	31	81	8	2	0	32	17	....	11	....	.260	.309	.299	.608	88	-5	35	3.70	-6	C-62,1-29	8	-0.6
1908 Bos-N	86	254	16	58	8	1	1	25	13	....	4	....	.228	.274	.280	.554	78	-7	20	2.61	2	C-63,1-11	5	0.1
1909 Bos-N	33	99	6	21	2	0	0	4	2	....	0	....	.212	.228	.232	.460	41	-7	5	1.65	0	C-27	1	-0.5
Total 15	**1048**	**3410**	**345**	**853**	**102**	**38**	**13**	**393**	**130**	**0**	**81**	**....**	**.250**	**.287**	**.314**	**.601**	**77**	**-108**	**348**	**3.49**	**3**	**C-826,1-132/2-6,S-5,3-3,O-1,P**	**78**	**-2.8**

• BOWERS, Billy
Grover Bill Bowers b: 3/25/1922, Parkin, AR d: 9/17/1996, Wynne, AR BL/TR, 5'9.5", 176 lbs. Deb: 4/24/1949

YEAR TM-L	G	AB	R	H	2B	3B	HR	RBI	BB	SO	SB	CS	AVG	OBP	SLG	OPS	OPS+	BR/A	RC	RC/G	FR	G/POS	WS	TPW
1949 Chi-A	26	78	5	15	2	1	0	6	4	5	1	1	.192	.232	.244	.475	27	-9	4	1.42	0	O-20(3-10-8)	1	-0.9

• BOWERS, Brent
Brent Raymond Bowers b: 5/2/1971, Bridgeview, IL BL/TR, 6'3", 200 lbs. Deb: 8/16/1996

YEAR TM-L	G	AB	R	H	2B	3B	HR	RBI	BB	SO	SB	CS	AVG	OBP	SLG	OPS	OPS+	BR/A	RC	RC/G	FR	G/POS	WS	TPW
1996 Bal-A	21	39	6	12	2	0	0	3	0	7	0	0	.308	.308	.359	.667	68	-2	4	3.81	1	O-21(21-0-0)	0	-0.2

• BOWES, Frank
Frank M. Bowes b: 1865, Bath, NY d: 1/21/1895, Brooklyn, NY TR, 5'9", 160 lbs. Deb: 4/17/1890

YEAR TM-L	G	AB	R	H	2B	3B	HR	RBI	BB	SO	SB	CS	AVG	OBP	SLG	OPS	OPS+	BR/A	RC	RC/G	FR	G/POS	WS	TPW
1890 Bro-a	61	232	28	51	5	2	0	24	7	....	11	....	.220	.246	.259	.504	50	-15	18	2.62	-5	C-25,O-19(4-2-13),3-13/1-3,S	2	-1.6

• BOWIE, Jim
James R. Bowie b: 2/17/1965, Tokyo, Japan BL/TL, 6', 205 lbs. Deb: 8/3/1994

YEAR TM-L	G	AB	R	H	2B	3B	HR	RBI	BB	SO	SB	CS	AVG	OBP	SLG	OPS	OPS+	BR/A	RC	RC/G	FR	G/POS	WS	TPW
1994 Oak-A	6	14	0	3	0	0	0	0	0	2	0	0	.214	.214	.214	.429	12	-2	0	.97	0	/1-6	0	-0.2

• BOWLIN, Weldon
Lois Weldon "Hoss" Bowlin b: 12/10/1940, Paragould, AR BR/TR, 5'9", 155 lbs. Deb: 9/16/1967

YEAR TM-L	G	AB	R	H	2B	3B	HR	RBI	BB	SO	SB	CS	AVG	OBP	SLG	OPS	OPS+	BR/A	RC	RC/G	FR	G/POS	WS	TPW
1967 KC-A	2	5	0	1	0	0	0	0	0	0	0	0	.200	.200	.200	.400	19	-1	0	1.35	0	/3-2	0	0.0

YEAR TM-L	G	AB	R	H	2B	3B	HR	RBI	BB	SO	SB	CS	AVG	OBP	SLG	OPS	OPS+	BR/A	RC	RC/G	FR	G/POS	WS	TPW
• BOWLING, Steve	Stephen Shaddon Bowling b: 6/26/1952, Tulsa, OK BR/TR, 6', 185 lbs. Deb: 9/7/1976 Career OF: 20-37-47																							
1976 Mil-A	14	42	4	7	2	0	0	2	2	5	0	0	.167	.205	.214	.419	23	-4	2	1.50	-0	O-13(0-13-0)/D-1	1	-0.5
1977 Tor-A	89	194	19	40	8	1	1	13	37	42	2	3	.206	.333	.273	.607	67	-8	18	2.93	5	O-87(20-24-47)	2	-0.6
Total 2	**103**	**236**	**23**	**47**	**10**	**1**	**1**	**15**	**39**	**47**	**2**	**3**	**.199**	**.313**	**.263**	**.575**	**60**	**-12**	**20**	**2.69**	**5**	**O-100/D-1**	**3**	**-1.1**
• BOWMAN, Bill	William George Bowman b: 1869, Chicago, IL d: 4/6/1918, Arlington Heights, IL, 5'11", 180 lbs. Deb: 6/18/1891																							
1891 Chi-N	15	45	2	4	1	0	0	5	5	9	0	....	.089	.196	.111	.307	-10	-6	1	.66	0	C-15	1	-0.5
• BOWMAN, Bob	Robert Leroy Bowman b: 5/10/1931, Laytonville, CA BR/TR, 6'1", 195 lbs. Deb: 4/16/1955 Career OF: 35-4-128																							
1955 Phi-N	3	3	0	0	0	0	0	0	0	0	0	0	.000	.000	.000	.000	-102	-1	0	.00	0	/O-2(1-0-1)	0	-0.1
1956 Phi-N	6	16	2	3	0	1	1	2	0	6	0	0	.188	.188	.500	.688	78	-1	2	3.12	-1	/O-5(0-1-4)	0	-0.1
1957 Phi-N	99	237	31	63	8	2	6	23	27	50	0	0	.266	.356	.392	.748	104	2	35	5.07	-3	O-81(3-0-79)	7	-0.3
1958 Phi-N	91	184	31	53	11	2	8	24	16	30	0	1	.288	.345	.500	.845	122	5	31	5.99	-6	O-57(20-1-37)	5	-0.3
1959 Phi-N	57	79	7	10	0	0	2	5	5	23	0	0	.127	.179	.203	.381	1	-11	3	.93	1	O-20(11-2-7)/P-5	0	-1.2
Total 5	**256**	**519**	**71**	**129**	**19**	**5**	**17**	**54**	**48**	**109**	**0**	**1**	**.249**	**.319**	**.403**	**.722**	**93**	**-5**	**70**	**4.55**	**-9**	**O-165/P-5**	**12**	**-2.1**
• BOWMAN, Elmer	Elmari Wilhelm "Big Bow" Bowman b: 3/19/1897, Proctor, VT d: 12/17/1985, Los Angeles, CA BR/TR, 6'.5", 193 lbs. Deb: 8/3/1920																							
1920 Was-A	2	1	1	0	0	0	0	0	1	0	0	0	.000	.500	.000	.500	42	0	0	3.31	0	....	0	0.0
• BOWMAN, Ernie	Ernest Ferrell Bowman b: 7/28/1935, Johnson City, TN BR/TR, 5'10", 160 lbs. Deb: 4/12/1961																							
1961 SF-N	38	38	10	8	0	2	0	2	1	8	2	0	.211	.231	.316	.547	45	-3	3	2.33	-2	2-13,S-12/3-7	0	-0.4
1962*SF-N	46	42	9	8	1	0	1	4	1	10	0	1	.190	.227	.286	.513	37	-4	2	1.68	-2	2-17,3-11,S-10	1	-0.5
1963 SF-N	81	125	10	23	3	0	0	4	0	15	1	2	.184	.184	.208	.392	13	-15	4	1.04	-2	S-40,2-26,3-12	1	-1.4
Total 3	**165**	**205**	**29**	**39**	**4**	**2**	**1**	**10**	**2**	**33**	**3**	**3**	**.190**	**.202**	**.244**	**.446**	**24**	**-22**	**9**	**1.40**	**-6**	**/S-62,2-56,3-30**	**2**	**-2.4**
• BOWSER, Red	James Harvey Bowser b: 9/20/1881, Freeport, PA d: 5/22/1943, Moundsville, WV Deb: 9/13/1910																							
1910 Chi-A	1	2	0	0	0	0	0	0	0	....	0	....	.000	.000	.000	.000	-105	-0	0	.00	0	/O-1	0	-0.1
• BOYD, Bill	William J. Boyd b: 12/22/1852, New York, NY d: 9/30/1912, Jamaica, NY Deb: 4/22/1872 M/U NA OF: 0-0-57																							
1872 Mut-n	35	165	26	44	6	1	1	32	6	7	4	2	.267	.292	.333	.626	98	1	18	4.46	-6	*3-34/O-1	....	-0.4
1873 Atl-n	50	228	31	63	5	4	1	31	2	2	1	1	.276	.283	.346	.629	96	1	23	4.26	3	*O-43(0-0-43)/3-8	....	0.5
1874 Har-n	26	117	22	41	8	4	0	20	1	2	1	0	.350	.356	.487	.843	159	7	21	8.35	-9	3-25/O-1	....	-0.2
1875 Atl-n	36	151	14	44	11	0	1	10	1	0	0	0	.291	.296	.384	.680	154	9	18	4.85	-10	2-15,O-12(0-0-12)/3-9,1-2,P,S	....	0.0
Total 4 n	**147**	**661**	**93**	**192**	**30**	**9**	**3**	**93**	**10**	**11**	**6**	**3**	**.290**	**.301**	**.377**	**.678**	**121**	**19**	**80**	**5.10**	**-22**	**/3-76,O-57,2-15,1-2,P-1,S-1**	**....**	**-0.1**
• BOYD, Bob	Robert Richard "Rope" Boyd b: 10/1/1925, Potts Camp, MS BL/TL, 5'10", 170 lbs. Deb: 9/8/1951 Career OF: 32-0-6																							
1951 Chi-A	12	18	3	3	0	1	0	4	3	3	0	0	.167	.286	.278	.563	54	-1	2	3.04	-1	/1-6	0	-0.2
1953 Chi-A	55	165	20	49	6	2	3	23	13	11	1	4	.297	.352	.412	.764	102	-1	23	4.97	-1	1-29,O-16(15-0-1)	5	-0.5
1954 Chi-A	29	56	10	10	3	0	0	5	4	3	2	0	.179	.233	.232	.465	27	-5	3	1.52	0	O-13(13-0-0),1-12	0	-0.7
1956 Bal-A	70	225	28	70	8	3	2	11	30	14	0	5	.311	.395	.400	.795	119	5	35	5.43	-3	1-60/O-8(3-0-5)	8	-0.1
1957 Bal-A	141	485	73	154	16	8	4	34	55	31	2	4	.318	.389	.408	.798	126	18	80	6.21	-3	*1-132/O-1	19	0.8
1958 Bal-A	125	401	58	124	21	5	7	36	25	24	1	1	.309	.353	.439	.792	123	12	62	5.85	4	1-99	15	1.0
1959 Bal-A	128	415	42	110	20	2	3	41	29	14	3	1	.265	.315	.345	.659	83	-10	44	3.57	-6	*1-109	6	-2.2
1960 Bal-A	71	82	9	26	5	2	0	9	6	5	0	0	.317	.364	.427	.790	114	2	12	5.20	0	1-17	3	0.1
1961 KC-A	26	48	7	11	2	0	0	9	1	2	0	2	.229	.245	.271	.516	37	-5	2	1.63	-1	/1-8	0	-0.6
Mil-N	36	41	3	10	0	0	0	3	1	7	0	0	.244	.262	.244	.506	38	-4	3	2.05	1	/1-3	0	-0.2
Total 9	**693**	**1936**	**253**	**567**	**81**	**23**	**19**	**175**	**167**	**114**	**9**	**17**	**.293**	**.351**	**.388**	**.739**	**105**	**10**	**266**	**4.89**	**-11**	**1-475/O-38**	**56**	**-2.6**
• BOYD, Frank	Frank Jay Boyd b: 4/2/1868, West Middletown, PA d: 12/16/1937, Oil City, PA BR/TR Deb: 5/18/1893																							
1893 Cle-N	2	5	3	1	1	0	0	3	1	0	0	....	.200	.333	.400	.733	89	-0	1	4.53	1	/C-2	0	0.0
• BOYD, Jake	Jacob Henry Boyd b: 1/19/1874, Martinsburg, WV d: 8/12/1932, Gettysburg, PA TL, 160 lbs. Deb: 9/20/1894 Career OF: 4-0-20 ♦																							
1894 Was-N	6	21	1	3	0	0	0	1	1	4	2	....	.143	.182	.143	.325	-21	-3	1	1.35	1	/O-3(1-0-2),P-3	0	-0.7
1895 Was-N	52	159	29	43	5	1	1	16	20	28	2	....	.270	.376	.333	.710	85	0	21	4.94	-8	O-21(3-0-18),P-14,2-10/S-8,3	3	-2.0
1896 Was-N	4	13	1	1	0	0	0	1	1	1	0	....	.077	.200	.077	.277	-25	-1	0	.45	-0	/P-4	0	-0.8
Total 3	**62**	**193**	**31**	**47**	**5**	**1**	**1**	**18**	**22**	**33**	**4**	**....**	**.244**	**.345**	**.295**	**.641**	**67**	**-4**	**22**	**4.13**	**-7**	**/O-24,P-21,2-10,S-8,3-1**	**3**	**-3.4**
• BOYER, Clete	Cletis Leroy Boyer b: 2/9/1937, Cassville, MO BR/TR, 6', 182 lbs. Deb: 6/5/1955 C																							
1955 KC-A	47	79	3	19	1	0	0	6	3	17	0	0	.241	.268	.253	.521	40	-7	5	2.06	-2	S-12,3-11,2-10	1	-0.8
1956 KC-A	67	129	15	28	3	1	1	4	11	24	1	1	.217	.284	.279	.563	49	-10	10	2.66	2	2-51/3-7	1	-0.4
1957 KC-A	10	0	0	0	0	0	0	0	0	0	0	0	....	....	....	....	-98	0	0	....	-1	/2-1,3-1	0	-0.1
1959 NY-A	47	114	4	20	2	0	0	3	6	23	1	0	.175	.217	.193	.410	14	-13	5	1.34	1	S-26,3-16	1	-1.1
1960*NY-A	124	393	54	95	20	1	14	46	23	85	2	3	.242	.289	.405	.693	90	-8	44	3.75	15	3-99,S-33	11	0.9
1961*NY-A	148	504	61	113	19	5	11	55	63	83	1	3	.224	.313	.347	.660	80	-15	55	3.57	33	*3-141,S-12/O-1	15	1.9
1962*NY-A	158	566	85	154	24	1	18	68	51	106	3	2	.272	.335	.413	.749	103	2	76	4.62	39	*3-157	21	4.1
1963*NY-A	152	557	59	140	20	3	12	54	33	91	4	2	.251	.296	.363	.658	84	-13	60	3.78	21	*3-141/S-9,2-1	17	0.9
1964*NY-A	147	510	43	111	10	5	8	52	36	93	6	1	.218	.271	.304	.574	59	-28	41	2.65	15	*3-123,S-21	8	-1.2
1965 NY-A	148	514	69	129	23	6	18	58	39	79	4	1	.251	.306	.424	.730	106	3	63	4.17	17	*3-147/S-2	18	2.1
1966 NY-A	144	500	59	120	22	4	14	57	46	48	6	0	.240	.307	.384	.691	101	2	60	4.08	3	3-85,S-59	16	1.0
1967 Atl-N	154	572	63	140	18	3	26	96	39	81	6	3	.245	.295	.423	.718	105	2	68	4.06	8	*3-150/S-6	17	1.1
1968 Atl-N	71	273	19	62	7	2	4	17	16	32	2	0	.227	.275	.311	.586	75	-8	22	2.74	4	3-69	5	-0.5
1969*Atl-N	144	496	57	124	16	1	14	57	55	87	3	7	.250	.333	.371	.701	96	-4	58	3.88	13	*3-141	15	0.9
1970 Atl-N	134	475	44	117	14	1	16	62	41	71	2	5	.246	.308	.381	.689	79	-17	53	3.75	12	*3-126/S-5	11	-0.5
1971 Atl-N	30	98	10	24	1	0	6	19	8	11	0	0	.245	.302	.439	.741	101	-0	13	4.59	4	3-25/S-1	3	0.4
Total 16	**1725**	**5780**	**645**	**1396**	**200**	**33**	**162**	**654**	**470**	**931**	**41**	**28**	**.242**	**.301**	**.372**	**.673**	**87**	**-115**	**635**	**3.69**	**183**	***3-1439,S-186/2-63,O-1**	**160**	**8.6**
• BOYER, Ken	Kenton Lloyd Boyer b: 5/20/1931, Liberty, MO d: 9/7/1982, St. Louis, MO BR/TR, 6'1.5", 200 lbs. Deb: 4/12/1955 M/C Career OF: 0-111-0																							
1955 StL-N	147	530	78	140	27	2	18	62	37	67	22	17	.264	.313	.425	.738	93	-9	67	4.32	6	*3-139,S-18	14	-0.2
1956 StL-N★	150	595	91	182	30	2	26	98	38	65	8	3	.306	.349	.494	.843	123	18	97	5.95	5	*3-149	23	2.3
1957 StL-N	142	544	79	144	18	3	19	62	44	77	12	8	.265	.321	.414	.734	94	-6	70	4.40	1	*O-105(0-105-0),3-41	16	-1.1
1958 StL-N	150	570	101	175	21	9	23	90	49	53	11	6	.307	.365	.496	.861	120	16	100	6.32	20	*3-144/O-6(0-6-0),S-1	24	3.6
1959 StL-N★	149	563	86	174	18	5	28	94	67	77	12	6	.309	.384	.508	.892	127	23	112	7.52	5	*3-143,S-12	24	2.8
1960 StL-N★	151	552	95	168	26	10	32	97	56	77	8	7	.304	.373	.562	.934	139	29	111	7.36	14	*3-146	31	4.3
1961 StL-N★	153	589	109	194	26	11	24	95	68	91	6	3	.329	.400	.533	.933	132	29	126	8.21	9	*3-153	27	3.7
1962 StL-N★	160	611	92	178	27	5	24	98	75	104	12	7	.291	.370	.470	.839	113	12	105	6.19	4	*3-160	22	1.6
1963 StL-N★	159	617	86	176	28	2	24	111	70	90	1	0	.285	.360	.454	.814	121	20	98	5.71	0	*3-159	23	2.1
1964*StL-N★	162	628	100	185	30	10	24	**119**	70	85	3	5	.295	.367	.489	.856	128	23	107	6.07	6	*3-162	28	3.1
1965 StL-N	144	535	71	139	18	2	13	75	57	73	2	7	.260	.332	.374	.706	90	-8	64	4.00	-6	*3-143	13	-1.5
1966 NY-N	136	496	62	132	28	2	14	61	30	64	4	3	.266	.308	.415	.723	101	-1	59	4.08	1	*3-130/1-2	17	0.1
1967 NY-N	56	166	17	39	7	2	3	13	26	22	2	1	.235	.339	.355	.694	100	1	20	3.98	2	3-44/1-8	5	0.3
Chi-A	57	180	17	47	5	1	4	21	7	25	0	2	.261	.289	.367	.655	96	-2	18	3.33	1	3-33,1-18	4	-0.2
1968 Chi-A	10	24	0	3	0	0	0	0	1	6	0	0	.125	.160	.125	.285	-13	-3	0	.31	-0	/3-5,1-1	0	-0.4
LA-N	83	221	20	60	7	2	6	41	16	34	2	2	.271	.324	.403	.726	127	6	29	4.59	-6	3-34,1-32	8	-0.1
1969 LA-N	25	34	0	7	2	0	0	4	2	7	0	0	.206	.250	.265	.515	48	-2	2	1.72	0	/1-4	0	-0.3
Total 15	**2034**	**7455**	**1104**	**2143**	**318**	**68**	**282**	**1141**	**713**	**1017**	**105**	**77**	**.287**	**.351**	**.462**	**.813**	**115**	**145**	**1184**	**5.65**	**62**	***3-1785,O-111/1-65,S-31**	**279**	**20.1**
• BOYLAND, Doe	Dorian Scott Boyland b: 1/6/1955, Chicago, IL BL/TL, 6'4", 200 lbs. Deb: 9/4/1978																							
1978 Pit-N	6	8	1	2	0	0	0	1	0	1	0	0	.250	.250	.250	.500	38	-1	1	2.25	0	/1-1	0	-0.1
1979 Pit-N	4	3	0	0	0	0	0	0	0	2	0	0	.000	.000	.000	.000	-96	-1	0	.00	0	....	0	-0.1

YEAR	TM-L	G	AB	R	H	2B	3B	HR	RBI	BB	SO	SB	CS	AVG	OBP	SLG	OPS	OPS+	BR/A	RC	RC/G	FR	G/POS	WS	TPW
1981	Pit-N	11	8	0	0	0	0	0	0	1	3	0	0	.000	.111	.000	.111	-64	-2	0	.10	0	....	0	-0.2
Total	3	21	19	1	2	0	0	0	1	1	6	0	0	.105	.150	.105	.255	-28	-3	1	.84	0	/1-1	0	-0.4
• BOYLE, Buzz	Ralph Francis Boyle b: 2/9/1908, Cincinnati, OH d: 11/12/1978, Cincinnati, OH BL/TL, 5'11.5", 170 lbs. Deb: 9/11/1929 Career OF: 80-71-203																								
1929	Bos-N	17	57	8	15	2	1	1	2	6	11	2	....	.263	.333	.386	.719	81	-2	7	4.26	1	0-17(17-0-0)	1	-0.2
1930	Bos-N	1	1	0	0	0	0	0	0	0	1	0	....	.000	.000	.000	.000	-103	-0	0	.00	0	/0-1	0	0.0
1933	Bro-N	93	338	38	101	13	4	0	31	16	24	7	....	.299	.331	.361	.691	102	0	42	4.71	-7	0-90(45-34-10)	9	-1.1
1934	Bro-N	128	472	88	144	26	10	7	48	51	44	8	....	.305	.376	.447	.823	126	18	84	6.69	9	*0-121(18-19-86)	17	2.0
1935	Bro-N	127	475	51	129	17	9	4	44	43	45	7	....	.272	.332	.371	.703	90	-6	62	4.75	7	*0-124(0-17-107)	12	-0.5
Total	5	366	1343	185	389	58	24	12	125	116	125	24	....	.290	.347	.395	.743	105	10	196	5.38	10	0-353	39	0.2
• BOYLE, Eddie	Edward J. Boyle b: 5/8/1874, Cincinnati, OH d: 2/9/1941, Cincinnati, OH BR/TR, 6'3", 200 lbs. Deb: 4/17/1896																								
1896	Lou-N	3	9	0	0	0	0	0	0	2	2	0	....	.000	.182	.000	.182	-52	-2	0	.00	-0	/C-3	0	-0.1
	Pit-N	2	5	0	0	0	0	0	0	0	1	0	....	.000	.000	.000	.000	-104	-1	0	.00	0	/C-2	0	-0.1
	Yr.	5	14	0	0	0	0	0	0	2	3	0	....	.000	.125	.000	.125	-68	-3	0	.00	0	/C-5	0	-0.3
• BOYLE, Henry	Henry J. "Handsome Henry" Boyle b: 9/20/1860, Philadelphia, PA d: 5/25/1932, Philadelphia, PA BR/TR, 6'1" Deb: 7/9/1884 U Career OF: 54-18-13 ♦																								
1884	StL-U	65	262	41	68	10	3	4	....	9	....	....	....	.260	.284	.366	.651	114	4	28	4.04	4	0-43(40-2-2),P-19/3-4,1-1,2,S	25	1.9
1885	StL-N	72	258	24	52	9	1	1	21	13	38	....	....	.202	.240	.256	.496	64	-3	16	2.13	-4	P-42,0-31(12-10-9)/2-2	24	-1.5
1886	StL-N	30	108	8	27	2	2	1	13	5	19	0	....	.250	.283	.333	.617	93	4	10	3.48	-1	P-25/0-6(0-5-1)	15	3.0
1887	Ind-N	41	150	17	36	9	1	2	13	9	18	2	....	.240	.250	.312	.562	57	-0	12	2.74	-5	P-38/0-4(2-1-1)	15	1.1
1888	Ind-N	37	125	13	18	2	0	1	6	6	31	1	....	.144	.189	.184	.373	19	-3	5	1.18	2	P-37/1-1	13	-0.8
1889	Ind-N	46	155	17	38	10	0	1	17	9	23	4	....	.245	.291	.329	.620	72	6	16	3.71	-5	P-46/3-1	28	1.0
Total	6	291	1058	120	239	42	7	10	70	51	129	7	....	.226	.258	.301	.559	74	9	87	2.90	-9	P-207/0-84,3-5,2-3,1-2,S-1	120	4.7
• BOYLE, Jack	John Anthony "Honest Jack" Boyle b: 3/22/1866, Cincinnati, OH d: 1/7/1913, Cincinnati, OH BR/TR, 6'4", 190 lbs. Deb: 10/8/1886 U Career OF: 6-2-7																								
1886	Cin-a	1	5	0	1	0	0	0	0	0	....	0	....	.200	.200	.200	.400	25	-0	0	1.38	0	/C-1	0	-0.1
1887*	StL-a	88	370	48	86	3	1	2	41	20	....	7	....	.232	.237	.220	.457	25	-38	20	1.94	-10	*C-86/1-2,0-2(0-0-2),3-1	3	-3.3
1888*	StL-a	71	257	33	62	8	1	1	23	13	....	11	....	.241	.286	.292	.578	77	-8	25	3.49	3	C-70/0-1	9	0.2
1889	StL-a	99	347	54	85	11	5	3	42	21	42	5	....	.245	.301	.331	.633	71	-16	37	3.75	3	C-80,3-12/0-5(3-0-2),1-4,2	9	-0.6
1890	Chi-P	100	369	56	96	9	5	1	49	44	29	11	....	.260	.347	.320	.667	75	-13	46	4.54	-8	C-50,3-30,S-16/1-7,0-2(0-0-2)	9	-1.3
1891	StL-a	121	434	76	122	18	8	5	79	44	35	18	....	.281	.363	.394	.757	101	-2	71	6.01	-7	C-91,S-26/3-8,1-3,2-3,0-3(1-1-1)	15	-0.1
1892	NY-N	120	436	52	80	8	8	0	32	36	41	10	....	.183	.252	.239	.491	49	-27	29	2.23	8	C-79,1-40/0-2(2-0-0),S-2	4	-1.2
1893	Phi-N	116	504	105	144	29	9	4	81	41	30	22	....	.286	.351	.403	.754	100	-1	81	5.96	-2	*1-112/C-6,2-2	11	-0.3
1894	Phi-N	117	510	103	152	23	10	4	89	46	27	21	....	.298	.360	.406	.765	87	-11	84	6.10	-3	*1-114/2-1,3-1	9	-1.1
1895	Phi-N	133	565	90	143	17	4	0	67	35	23	13	....	.253	.302	.297	.600	55	-39	59	3.59	-10	*1-133	3	-4.0
1896	Phi-N	40	145	17	43	4	1	1	28	6	7	3	....	.297	.346	.359	.705	87	-3	20	5.04	-5	C-28,1-12	3	-0.4
1897	Phi-N	75	288	37	73	9	1	2	36	19	....	3	....	.253	.306	.313	.619	65	-14	30	3.60	-1	C-50,1-24	4	-0.9
1898	Phi-N	6	22	0	2	0	1	0	3	1	....	0	....	.091	.130	.182	.312	-11	-3	1	.77	-1	/1-4,C-3	0	-0.4
Total	13	1087	4252	671	1089	139	54	23	570	326	234	124	....	.256	.315	.327	.642	72	-176	503	4.19	-34	C-544,1-455/3-52,S-44,0-15,2	79	-13.6
• BOYLE, Jack	John Bellew Boyle b: 7/9/1889, Morris, IL d: 4/3/1971, Fort Lauderdale, FL BL/TR, 5'11.5", 165 lbs. Deb: 6/28/1912																								
1912	Phi-N	15	25	4	7	1	0	0	2	1	5	0	....	.280	.308	.320	.628	67	-1	2	3.35	1	/3-6,S-2	0	0.0
• BOYLE, Jim	James John Boyle b: 1/19/1904, Cincinnati, OH d: 12/24/1958, Cincinnati, OH BR/TR, 6', 180 lbs. Deb: 6/20/1926																								
1926	NY-N	1	0	0	0	0	0	0	0	0	0	0	....	....	....	....	....	-101	0	0	....	0	/C-1	0	0.0
• BRACK, Gibby	Gilbert Herman Brack b: 3/29/1908, Chicago, IL d: 1/20/1960, Greenville, TX BR/TR, 5'9", 170 lbs. Deb: 4/23/1937 Career OF: 58-88-91																								
1937	Bro-N	112	372	60	102	27	9	5	38	44	93	9	....	.274	.351	.435	.786	111	6	60	5.79	1	*0-101(37-44-21)	11	0.2
1938	Bro-N	40	56	10	12	2	1	1	6	4	14	1	....	.214	.267	.339	.606	64	-3	5	3.36	2	0-13(7-0-6)	1	-0.2
	Phi-N	72	282	40	81	20	4	4	28	18	30	2	....	.287	.332	.429	.761	108	2	41	5.31	-2	0-68(12-38-24)	8	-0.2
	Yr.	112	338	50	93	22	5	5	34	22	44	3	....	.275	.321	.414	.736	100	-1	46	4.97	0	0-81(19-38-30)	9	-0.5
1939	Phi-N	91	270	40	78	21	4	6	41	26	49	1	....	.289	.351	.463	.814	123	8	45	6.02	-5	0-48(2-6-40),1-19	8	-0.2
Total	3	315	980	150	273	70	18	16	113	92	186	13	....	.279	.341	.436	.777	110	13	151	5.57	-5	0-230/1-19	28	-0.4
• BRADFORD, Buddy	Charles William Bradford b: 7/25/1944, Mobile, AL BR/TR, 5'11", 191 lbs. Deb: 9/9/1966 Career OF: 107-267-259																								
1966	Chi-A	14	28	3	4	0	0	0	0	2	6	0	0	.143	.200	.143	.343		-4	1	1.02	-1	/0-9(5-0-4)	0	-0.5
1967	Chi-A	24	20	6	2	1	0	0	1	1	7	1	0	.100	.143	.150	.293	-14	-3	1	.75	-1	0-14(6-1-8)	0	-0.4
1968	Chi-A	103	281	32	61	11	0	5	24	23	67	8	4	.217	.281	.310	.591	78	-7	24	2.69	-2	0-99(35-25-58)	4	-1.7
1969	Chi-A	93	273	36	70	8	2	11	27	34	75	5	2	.256	.347	.421	.769	109	4	42	5.32	0	0-88(0-48-59)	8	0.1
1970	Chi-A	32	91	8	17	3	0	2	8	10	30	1	2	.187	.267	.286	.553	51	-7	6	1.91	0	0-27(2-20-9)	0	-0.8
	Cle-A	75	163	25	32	6	1	7	23	21	43	0	1	.196	.292	.374	.666	78	-5	16	3.10	-5	0-64(1-58-5)/3-1	2	-1.3
	Yr.	107	254	33	49	9	1	9	31	31	73	1	3	.193	.283	.343	.626	69	-12	22	2.66	-5	0-91(3-78-14)/3-1	2	-2.1
1971	Cle-A	20	38	4	6	2	1	0	3	6	10	0	0	.158	.273	.263	.536	48	-3	3	2.04	-2	0-18(0-18-0)	0	-0.5
	Cin-N	79	100	17	20	3	0	2	12	14	23	4	2	.200	.316	.290	.606	77	-2	10	3.11	1	0-66(36-26-5)	2	-0.4
1972	Chi-A	35	48	13	13	2	0	2	8	4	13	3	2	.271	.340	.438	.777	127	1	6	3.87	-1	0-28(3-22-3)	2	0.0
1973	Chi-A	53	168	24	40	3	1	8	15	17	43	4	5	.238	.316	.411	.726	100	-2	20	3.99	4	0-51(1-48-2)	5	0.1
1974	Chi-A	39	96	16	32	2	0	5	10	13	11	1	2	.333	.418	.510	.929	162	8	20	7.55	-1	0-32(10-0-24)/D-1	5	0.6
1975	Chi-A	25	58	8	9	3	1	2	15	8	22	3	2	.155	.290	.345	.635	78	-2	6	2.94	0	0-18(3-0-15)/D-4	1	-0.3
	StL-N	50	81	12	22	1	0	4	15	12	24	0	2	.272	.366	.432	.798	116	1	12	5.01	-1	0-25(3-1-21)	2	-0.1
1976	Chi-A	55	160	20	35	5	2	4	14	19	37	6	0	.219	.309	.350	.659	92	-0	20	4.24	-3	0-48(2-0-46)/D-3	4	-0.6
Total	11	697	1605	224	363	50	8	52	175	184	411	36	24	.226	.313	.364	.678	91	-20	185	3.75	-11	0-587/D-8,3-1	35	-5.7
• BRADFORD, Vic	Henry Victor Bradford b: 3/5/1915, Brownsville, TN d: 6/10/1994, Paris, KY BR/TR, 6'2", 190 lbs. Deb: 5/1/1943																								
1943	NY-N	6	5	1	1	0	0	0	1	1	1	0	....	.200	.333	.200	.533	55	-0	0	2.84	0	/0-1	0	0.0
• BRADLEY, Al	Albert Joseph Bradley b: 5/23/1856, Brady's Bend, PA d: 2/5/1937, Altoona, PA, 5'10", 185 lbs. Deb: 5/21/1884																								
1884	Was-U	1	3	0	0	0	0	0	....	2	....	....	....	.000	.400	.000	.400	47	0	0	.00	0	/0-1	0	0.0
• BRADLEY, Bill	William Joseph Bradley b: 2/13/1878, Cleveland, OH d: 3/11/1954, Cleveland, OH BR/TR, 6', 185 lbs. Deb: 8/26/1899 M																								
1899	Chi-N	35	129	26	40	6	1	2	18	12	....	4	....	.310	.378	.419	.796	122	4	23	6.65	-5	3-30/S-5	5	0.0
1900	Chi-N	122	444	63	125	21	8	5	49	27	....	14	....	.282	.330	.399	.728	104	1	65	5.31	12	*3-106,1-15	16	1.4
1901	Cle-A	133	516	95	151	28	13	1	55	26	....	15	....	.293	.336	.403	.739	109	5	77	5.57	10	*3-133/P-1	19	1.8
1902	Cle-A	137	550	104	187	39	12	11	77	27	....	11	....	.340	.375	.515	.890	151	35	114	8.00	10	*3-137	26	**4.7**
1903	Cle-A	136	536	101	168	36	22	6	68	25	....	21	....	.313	.348	.496	.844	153	32	104	7.05	9	*3-136	29	4.7
1904	Cle-A	154	609	94	183	32	8	5	83	26	....	23	....	.300	.334	.404	.738	134	21	95	5.56	9	*3-154	28	3.9
1905	Cle-A	146	541	63	145	34	6	0	51	27	....	22	....	.268	.321	.353	.674	112	7	72	4.61	15	*3-146	22	2.8
1906	Cle-A	82	302	32	83	16	2	2	25	18	....	13	....	.275	.324	.361	.685	116	5	42	4.77	8	3-82	11	1.7
1907	Cle-A	139	498	48	111	20	1	0	34	35	....	20	....	.223	.286	.267	.553	76	-13	50	3.09	2	*3-139	12	-0.8
1908	Cle-A	148	548	70	133	24	7	1	46	29	....	18	....	.243	.297	.318	.614	99	-1	61	3.34	-21	*3-118,S-30	15	-2.0
1909	Cle-A	95	334	30	62	6	3	0	22	19	....	8	....	.186	.236	.222	.458	43	-22	20	1.81	-7	3-87/1-3,2-3	3	-3.1
1910	Cle-A	61	214	12	42	3	0	0	12	10	....	6	....	.196	.236	.210	.446	39	-15	12	1.76	-3	3-61	2	-1.8
1914	Bro-F	7	6	1	3	1	0	0	3	0	0	0	....	.500	.500	.667	1.167	229	1	2	16.32	0	....	1	0.1
1915	KC-F	66	203	15	38	9	1	0	9	9	18	6	....	.187	.225	.241	.467	38	-16	12	1.81	-6	3-61	2	-2.3
Total	14	1461	5430	754	1471	275	84	33	552	290	18	181	....	.271	.317	.371	.687	107	45	751	4.71	34	*3-1390/S-35,1-18,2-3,P-1	191	11.3
• BRADLEY, George	George Washington "Grin" Bradley b: 7/13/1852, Reading, PA d: 10/2/1931, Philadelphia, PA BR/TR, 5'10.5", 175 lbs. Deb: 5/4/1875 U Career OF: 11-19-16 ♦																								
1875	StL-n	60	254	28	62	7	3	0	24	1	19	3	3	.244	.247	.295	.542	96	6	20	2.99	2	*P-60/S-2,2-1,0-1	....	0.5
1876	StL-N	64	268	29	66	7	6	0	28	3	12	....	....	.246	.257	.321	.578	97	4	22	3.16	3	*P-64	**57**	2.3

YEAR TM-L	G	AB	R	H	2B	3B	HR	RBI	BB	SO	SB	CS	AVG	OBP	SLG	OPS	OPS+	BR/A	RC	RC/G	FR	G/POS	WS	TPW
1877 Chi-N	55	214	31	52	7	3	0	12	6	19	....	....	.243	.264	.304	.567	70	-2	18	2.98	-2	*P-50,3-16/1-3,0-1	19	-1.4
1879 Tro-N	63	251	36	62	9	5	0	23	1	20	....	....	.247	.250	.323	.573	93	6	21	3.08	5	P-54/3-5,1-3,0-1,S-1	14	0.4
1880 Pro-N	82	309	32	70	7	6	0	23	5	38	....	....	.227	.239	.288	.527	80	-4	22	2.51	17	*3-57,P-28/0-7(1-0-6),1-2	24	2.6
1881 Det-N	1	4	0	0	0	0	0	0	0	0	....	....	.000	.000	.000	.000	-96	-1	0	.00	0	/S-1	0	-0.1
Cle-N	60	241	21	60	10	1	2	18	4	25	....	....	.249	.261	.324	.585	87	-3	21	3.12	-5	3-48/P-6,S-6,0-1	5	-1.2
Yr.	61	245	21	60	10	1	2	18	4	25	....	....	.245	.257	.318	.575	84	-4	21	3.05	-5	3-48/S-7,P-6,0-1	5	-1.3
1882 Cle-N	30	115	16	21	5	0	0	6	4	16	....	....	.183	.210	.226	.436	41	-6	6	1.64	3	P-18/0-9(5-4-0),1-6	5	-2.5
1883 Cle-N	4	16	0	5	0	1	0	1	0	1	....	....	.313	.313	.438	.750	126	0	2	5.61	0	/S-4	1	0.0
Phi-a	76	312	47	73	8	5	1	36	8	....	....	....	.234	.253	.301	.554	72	-8	24	2.86	0	3-44,P-26,0-11(0-11-0)/1-2	22	0.8
1884 Cin-U	58	226	31	43	4	7	0	....	7	....	....	....	.190	.215	.270	.485	58	-8	13	2.05	0	P-41,0-16(4-4-8)/S-5,1-2	28	0.8
1886 Phi-a	13	48	1	4	0	1	0	1	1	....	2	....	.083	.102	.125	.227	-29	-7	1	.51	1	S-13	1	-0.5
1888 Bal-a	1	3	0	0	0	0	0	0	0	....	0	....	.000	.000	.000	.000	-103	-1	0	.00	-1	/S-1	0	-0.1
Total 10	**507**	**2007**	**244**	**456**	**57**	**35**	**3**	**148**	**39**	**131**	**2**	**....**	**.227**	**.242**	**.295**	**.538**	**75**	**-29**	**150**	**2.68**	**20**	**P-287,3-170/0-46,S-31,1-18**	**176**	**1.1**

• BRADLEY, George George Washington Bradley b: 4/1/1914, Greenwood, AR d: 10/19/1982, Lawrenceburg, TN BR/TR, 6'1.5", 185 lbs. Deb: 4/28/1946

YEAR TM-L	G	AB	R	H	2B	3B	HR	RBI	BB	SO	SB	CS	AVG	OBP	SLG	OPS	OPS+	BR/A	RC	RC/G	FR	G/POS	WS	TPW
1946 StL-A	4	12	2	2	1	0	0	3	0	1	0	0	.167	.167	.250	.417	15	-1	0	.00	0	/0-3(0-3-0)	0	-0.2

• BRADLEY, Hugh Hugh Frederick "Corns" Bradley b: 5/23/1885, Grafton, MA d: 1/26/1949, Worcester, MA BR/TR, 5'10", 175 lbs. Deb: 4/25/1910 Career OF: 0-0-23

YEAR TM-L	G	AB	R	H	2B	3B	HR	RBI	BB	SO	SB	CS	AVG	OBP	SLG	OPS	OPS+	BR/A	RC	RC/G	FR	G/POS	WS	TPW
1910 Bos-A	32	83	8	14	6	2	0	7	5	....	2	....	.169	.216	.289	.505	57	-5	6	1.99	-1	1-21/C-3,0-1	0	-0.6
1911 Bos-A	12	41	9	13	2	0	1	4	2	....	1	....	.317	.364	.439	.803	125	1	7	6.12	1	1-12	1	0.1
1912 Bos-A	40	137	16	26	11	1	1	19	15	....	3	....	.190	.275	.307	.581	63	-7	13	2.78	2	1-40	1	-0.6
1914 Pit-F	118	427	41	131	20	6	0	61	27	27	7	....	.307	.359	.382	.741	117	10	60	4.91	2	*1-118	12	1.0
1915 Pit-F	26	66	3	18	4	1	0	6	4	5	2	....	.273	.314	.364	.678	95	-1	8	4.11	-1	0-15(0-0-15)	1	-0.2
Bro-F	37	126	7	31	3	2	0	18	4	9	6	....	.246	.269	.302	.571	69	-5	12	2.96	2	1-26/0-7(0-0-7),C-1	1	-0.5
New-F	12	33	0	5	0	0	0	2	2	3	2	....	.152	.243	.152	.395	18	-3	2	1.49	-1	/1-8	0	-0.5
Yr.	75	225	10	54	7	3	0	26	10	17	10	....	.240	.278	.298	.576	69	-9	21	3.03	0	1-34,0-22(0-0-22)/C-1	2	-1.2
Total 5	**277**	**913**	**84**	**238**	**46**	**12**	**2**	**117**	**59**	**44**	**23**	**....**	**.261**	**.314**	**.344**	**.658**	**92**	**-10**	**106**	**3.83**	**3**	**1-225/0-23,C-4**	**16**	**-1.3**

• BRADLEY, Jack John Thomas Bradley b: 9/20/1893, Denver, CO d: 3/18/1969, Tulsa, OK BR/TR, 5'11", 175 lbs. Deb: 6/18/1916

YEAR TM-L	G	AB	R	H	2B	3B	HR	RBI	BB	SO	SB	CS	AVG	OBP	SLG	OPS	OPS+	BR/A	RC	RC/G	FR	G/POS	WS	TPW
1916 Cle-A	2	3	0	0	0	0	0	0	0	1	0	....	.000	.000	.000	.000	-94	-1	0	.00	0	/C-1	0	-0.1

• BRADLEY, Mark Mark Allen Bradley b: 12/3/1956, Elizabethtown, KY BR/TR, 6'1", 180 lbs. Deb: 9/3/1981 Career OF: 16-7-23

YEAR TM-L	G	AB	R	H	2B	3B	HR	RBI	BB	SO	SB	CS	AVG	OBP	SLG	OPS	OPS+	BR/A	RC	RC/G	FR	G/POS	WS	TPW
1981 LA-N	9	6	2	1	1	0	0	0	0	1	0	0	.167	.167	.333	.500	40	-1	0	1.80	0	/0-6(1-0-5)	0	0.0
1982 LA-N	8	3	1	1	0	0	0	0	0	0	0	0	.333	.333	.333	.667	89	-0	0	4.50	0	/0-3(1-0-2)	0	0.0
1983 NY-N	73	104	10	21	4	0	3	5	11	35	4	2	.202	.278	.327	.605	68	-5	9	2.92	0	0-35(14-7-16)	1	-0.6
Total 3	**90**	**113**	**13**	**23**	**5**	**0**	**3**	**5**	**11**	**36**	**4**	**2**	**.204**	**.274**	**.327**	**.602**	**67**	**-5**	**10**	**2.90**	**0**	**/0-44**	**1**	**-0.6**

• BRADLEY, Milton Milton Obelle Bradley b: 4/15/1978, Harbor City, CA BB/TR, 6', 180 lbs. Deb: 7/19/2000 Career OF: 13-287-3

YEAR TM-L	G	AB	R	H	2B	3B	HR	RBI	BB	SO	SB	CS	AVG	OBP	SLG	OPS	OPS+	BR/A	RC	RC/G	FR	G/POS	WS	TPW
2000 Mon-N	42	154	20	34	8	1	2	15	14	32	2	1	.221	.290	.325	.615	53	-11	15	3.16	1	0-41(0-40-0)	3	-0.9
2001 Mon-N	67	220	19	49	16	3	1	19	19	62	7	4	.223	.288	.336	.624	59	-14	20	3.02	3	0-65(13-52-2)	3	-1.1
Cle-A	10	18	3	4	1	0	0	0	2	3	1	1	.222	.300	.278	.578	53	-1	1	2.04	0	/0-9(0-8-1),D-1	0	-0.1
2002 Cle-A	98	325	48	81	18	3	9	38	32	58	6	3	.249	.317	.406	.723	92	-4	39	4.08	4	0-94(0-94-0)/D-1	6	0.0
2003 Cle-A	101	377	61	121	34	2	10	56	64	73	17	7	.321	.426	.501	.927	148	30	83	8.06	3	0-93(0-93-0)/D-8	18	3.2
Total 4	**318**	**1094**	**151**	**289**	**77**	**9**	**22**	**128**	**131**	**228**	**33**	**16**	**.264**	**.347**	**.411**	**.758**	**100**	**-0**	**159**	**4.96**	**11**	**0-302/D-10**	**30**	**1.1**

• BRADLEY, Phil Philip Poole Bradley b: 3/11/1959, Bloomington, IN BR/TR, 6', 185 lbs. Deb: 9/2/1983 Career OF: 856-145-31

YEAR TM-L	G	AB	R	H	2B	3B	HR	RBI	BB	SO	SB	CS	AVG	OBP	SLG	OPS	OPS+	BR/A	RC	RC/G	FR	G/POS	WS	TPW
1983 Sea-A	23	67	8	18	2	0	0	5	8	5	3	1	.269	.347	.299	.645	77	-2	8	4.16	-1	0-21(0-27-0)/D-1	1	-0.2
1984 Sea-A	124	322	49	97	12	4	0	24	34	61	21	8	.301	.373	.363	.737	106	5	46	5.00	-3	*0-117(48-68-14)/D-3	9	-0.1
1985 Sea-A★	159	641	100	192	33	8	26	88	55	129	22	9	.300	.366	.498	.863	133	30	116	6.53	2	*0-159(126-28-10)	26	2.4
1986 Sea-A	143	526	88	163	27	4	12	50	77	134	21	12	.310	.406	.445	.851	130	25	99	6.92	-1	*0-140(138-5-0)	19	1.7
1987 Sea-A	158	603	101	179	38	10	14	67	84	119	40	10	.297	.390	.463	.853	119	23	113	6.67	-3	*0-158(158-0-0)	21	1.2
1988 Phi-N	154	569	77	150	30	5	11	56	54	106	11	9	.264	.344	.392	.736	109	5	78	4.68	-1	*0-153(153-3-1)	17	-0.1
1989 Bal-A	144	545	83	151	23	10	11	55	70	103	20	6	.277	.367	.417	.783	124	21	87	5.58	-4	*0-140(140-0-0)/D-2	20	1.2
1990 Bal-A	72	289	39	78	9	1	4	26	30	35	10	4	.270	.353	.349	.702	100	2	36	4.26	1	0-70(70-0-0)/D-2	9	0.1
Chi-A	45	133	20	30	5	1	0	5	20	26	7	3	.226	.344	.278	.622	78	-3	15	3.52	0	0-38(23-14-6)/D-7	2	-0.4
Yr.	117	422	59	108	14	2	4	31	50	61	17	7	.256	.350	.327	.677	93	-1	51	4.02	1	*0-108(93-14-6)/D-9	11	-0.3
Total 8	**1022**	**3695**	**565**	**1058**	**179**	**43**	**78**	**376**	**432**	**718**	**155**	**62**	**.286**	**.371**	**.421**	**.792**	**117**	**108**	**598**	**5.69**	**-11**	**0-996/D-15**	**124**	**5.7**

• BRADLEY, Scott Scott William Bradley b: 3/22/1960, Glen Ridge, NJ BL/TR, 5'11", 185 lbs. Deb: 9/9/1984 Career OF: 7-0-6

YEAR TM-L	G	AB	R	H	2B	3B	HR	RBI	BB	SO	SB	CS	AVG	OBP	SLG	OPS	OPS+	BR/A	RC	RC/G	FR	G/POS	WS	TPW
1984 NY-A	9	21	3	6	1	0	0	2	1	1	0	0	.286	.318	.333	.652	84	-0	2	4.16	-1	/0-5(5-0-0),C-3	0	-0.2
1985 NY-A	19	49	4	8	2	1	0	1	1	5	0	0	.163	.196	.245	.441	20	-5	2	1.23	-1	/D-9,C-3	0	-0.6
1986 Chi-A	9	21	3	6	0	0	0	0	1	0	0	2	.286	.375	.286	.661	80	-1	2	2.54	0	/D-6,0-1	0	-0.2
Sea-A	68	199	17	60	8	3	5	28	12	7	1	0	.302	.347	.447	.795	113	4	27	4.69	0	C-59/D-3	6	0.6
Yr.	77	220	20	66	8	3	5	28	13	7	1	2	.300	.350	.432	.782	110	2	29	4.47	0	C-59/D-9,0-1	6	0.4
1987 Sea-A	102	342	34	95	15	1	5	43	15	18	0	1	.278	.314	.371	.685	77	-12	36	3.68	-2	C-82/3-8,D-6,0-2(0-0-2)	6	-1.1
1988 Sea-A	103	335	45	86	17	1	4	33	17	16	1	1	.257	.297	.349	.646	77	-11	32	3.28	3	C-85/D-4,0-4(0-0-4),3-3,1	7	-0.3
1989 Sea-A	103	270	21	74	16	0	3	37	21	23	1	1	.274	.329	.367	.695	93	-3	32	4.19	0	C-70/D-6,1-2,0-1	8	0.1
1990 Sea-A	101	233	11	52	9	0	1	28	15	20	0	1	.223	.270	.275	.545	52	-15	17	2.31	-1	C-63/D-6,3-5,1-1	4	-1.3
1991 Sea-A	83	172	10	35	7	0	0	11	19	19	0	1	.203	.283	.244	.527	47	-12	13	2.43	-2	C-65/3-4,D-2,1-1	2	-1.2
1992 Sea-A	2	1	0	0	0	0	0	0	1	1	0	0	.000	.500	.000	.500	51	0	0	3.51	0	/C-1	0	0.0
Cin-N	5	5	1	2	0	0	0	1	1	0	0	0	.400	.500	.400	.900	154	0	1	10.17	-1	/C-2	0	0.0
Total 9	**604**	**1648**	**149**	**424**	**75**	**6**	**18**	**184**	**104**	**110**	**3**	**6**	**.257**	**.306**	**.343**	**.649**	**76**	**-57**	**165**	**3.38**	**-4**	**C-433/D-42,3-20,0-13,1-6**	**33**	**-4.0**

• BRADSHAW, Dallas Dallas Carl "Windy" Bradshaw b: 11/23/1895, Wolf Creek, IL d: 12/11/1939, Herrin, IL BL/TR, 5'7", 145 lbs. Deb: 6/5/1917

YEAR TM-L	G	AB	R	H	2B	3B	HR	RBI	BB	SO	SB	CS	AVG	OBP	SLG	OPS	OPS+	BR/A	RC	RC/G	FR	G/POS	WS	TPW
1917 Phi-A	2	4	0	0	0	0	0	0	0	1	0	....	.000	.000	.000	.000	-101	-1	0	.00	0	/2-1	0	-0.1

• BRADSHAW, George George Thomas Bradshaw b: 9/12/1924, Salisbury, NC d: 11/4/1994, Hendersonville, NC BR/TR, 6'2", 185 lbs. Deb: 8/10/1952

YEAR TM-L	G	AB	R	H	2B	3B	HR	RBI	BB	SO	SB	CS	AVG	OBP	SLG	OPS	OPS+	BR/A	RC	RC/G	FR	G/POS	WS	TPW
1952 Was-A	10	23	3	5	2	0	0	6	1	2	0	0	.217	.280	.304	.584	65	-1	2	2.08	-1	/C-9	0	-0.2

• BRADSHAW, Terry Terry Leon Bradshaw b: 2/3/1969, Franklin, VA BL/TR, 6', 180 lbs. Deb: 5/4/1995 Career OF: 10-6-2

YEAR TM-L	G	AB	R	H	2B	3B	HR	RBI	BB	SO	SB	CS	AVG	OBP	SLG	OPS	OPS+	BR/A	RC	RC/G	FR	G/POS	WS	TPW
1995 StL-N	19	44	6	10	1	1	0	2	2	10	1	2	.227	.261	.295	.556	46	-4	3	2.29	0	0-10(6-3-1)	0	-0.4
1996 StL-N	15	21	4	7	1	0	0	3	3	2	0	1	.333	.417	.381	.798	113	0	3	5.65	-1	/0-7(4-3-1)	1	0.0
Total 2	**34**	**65**	**10**	**17**	**2**	**1**	**0**	**5**	**5**	**12**	**1**	**3**	**.262**	**.314**	**.323**	**.637**	**70**	**-4**	**6**	**3.32**	**0**	**/0-17**	**1**	**-0.5**

• BRADY, Brady Deb: 9/25/1875

YEAR TM-L	G	AB	R	H	2B	3B	HR	RBI	BB	SO	SB	CS	AVG	OBP	SLG	OPS	OPS+	BR/A	RC	RC/G	FR	G/POS	WS	TPW
1875 Chi-n	1	4	1	1	0	1	0	0	0	0	0	0	.250	.250	.750	1.000	231	1	1	7.56	1	/0-1	....	0.1

• BRADY, Bob Robert Jay Brady b: 11/8/1922, Lewiston, PA d: 4/22/1996, Manchester, CT BL/TR, 6'1", 175 lbs. Deb: 8/24/1946

YEAR TM-L	G	AB	R	H	2B	3B	HR	RBI	BB	SO	SB	CS	AVG	OBP	SLG	OPS	OPS+	BR/A	RC	RC/G	FR	G/POS	WS	TPW
1946 Bos-N	3	5	0	1	0	0	0	0	1	1	0	....	.200	.333	.200	.533	52	-0	0	2.84	0	/C-1	0	0.0
1947 Bos-N	1	1	0	0	0	0	0	0	0	0	0	....	.000	.000	.000	.000	-102	-0	0	.00	0	....	0	0.0
Total 2	**4**	**6**	**0**	**1**	**0**	**0**	**0**	**0**	**1**	**1**	**0**	**....**	**.167**	**.286**	**.167**	**.452**	**30**	**-1**	**0**	**2.27**	**0**	**/C-1**	**0**	**0.0**

• BRADY, Brian Brian Phelan Brady b: 7/11/1962, Elmhurst, NY BL/TL, 5'11", 185 lbs. Deb: 4/16/1989

YEAR TM-L	G	AB	R	H	2B	3B	HR	RBI	BB	SO	SB	CS	AVG	OBP	SLG	OPS	OPS+	BR/A	RC	RC/G	FR	G/POS	WS	TPW
1989 Cal-A	2	2	0	1	1	0	0	1	0	1	0	0	.500	.500	1.000	1.500	318	1	1	27.00	0	/0-1	0	0.0

• BRADY, Cliff Clifford Francis Brady b: 3/6/1897, St. Louis, MO d: 9/25/1974, Belleville, IL BR/TR, 5'5.5", 140 lbs. Deb: 8/8/1920

YEAR TM-L	G	AB	R	H	2B	3B	HR	RBI	BB	SO	SB	CS	AVG	OBP	SLG	OPS	OPS+	BR/A	RC	RC/G	FR	G/POS	WS	TPW
1920 Bos-A	53	180	16	41	5	1	0	12	13	12	0	1	.228	.284	.267	.550	48	-13	14	2.57	6	2-53	2	-0.6

• BRADY, Doug Stephen Douglas Brady b: 11/23/1969, Jacksonville, IL BB/TR, 5'11", 165 lbs. Deb: 9/5/1995

YEAR TM-L	G	AB	R	H	2B	3B	HR	RBI	BB	SO	SB	CS	AVG	OBP	SLG	OPS	OPS+	BR/A	RC	RC/G	FR	G/POS	WS	TPW
1995 Chi-A	12	21	4	4	1	0	0	3	2	4	0	1	.190	.261	.238	.499	32	-3	1	1.36	2	/2-6,D-3	0	0.0

YEAR	TM-L	G	AB	R	H	2B	3B	HR	RBI	BB	SO	SB	CS	AVG	OBP	SLG	OPS	OPS+	BR/A	RC	RC/G	FR	G/POS	WS	TPW
• BRADY, Steve	Stephen A. Brady b: 7/14/1851, Worcester, MA d: 11/1/1917, Hartford, CT, 5'9.5", 165 lbs. Deb: 7/23/1874 NA OF: 1-6-7 Career OF: 0-0-354																								
1874	Har-n	27	118	19	37	5	1	0	14	2	10	1	2	.314	.325	.373	.698	117	1	15	5.42	-10	3-16,0-11(0-5-6)/S-1	....	-0.6
1875	Har-n	1	4	0	0	0	0	0	0	0	1	0	0	.000	.000	.000	.000	-95	-1	0	.00	1	/0-1	....	0.0
	Was-n	21	91	7	13	0	0	0	3	0	4	5	0	.143	.143	.143	.286		-7	3	1.00	-7	2-18/0-2(1-0-1),1-1,C-1	....	-1.3
	Yr.	22	95	7	13	0	0	0	3	0	5	5	0	.137	.137	.137	.274	-4	-8	3	.95	-6	2-18/0-3(1-1-1),1-1,C-1	....	-1.3
1883	NY-a	97	432	69	117	12	6	0	0	11	....	....	....	.271	.289	.326	.615	93	-4	42	3.71	9	*1-81,0-16(0-0-16)	9	-0.2
1884*	NY-a	112	485	102	122	11	3	1	0	21	....	....	....	.252	.283	.293	.575	90	-5	41	3.12	4	*0-110(0-0-110)/1-5,2-1	13	-0.3
1885	NY-a	108	434	60	128	14	5	3	58	25	....	....	....	.295	.342	.371	.713	136	19	56	4.98	-7	*0-105(0-0-105)/1-4,2-2,3	18	1.0
1886	NY-a	124	466	56	112	8	5	0	39	35	....	16	....	.240	.298	.279	.577	85	-7	45	3.40	-4	*0-123(0-0-123)/1-1	8	-1.1
Total	2 n	49	213	26	50	5	1	0	17	2	15	6	2	.235	.242	.268	.509	63	-7	18	3.20	-16	/2-18,3-16,0-14,1-1,C-1,S-1	....	-1.9
Total	4	441	1817	287	479	45	19	4	97	92	....	16	....	.264	.302	.316	.618	100	3	184	3.76	2	0-354/1-91,2-3,3-1	48	-0.7
• BRAGAN, Bobby	Robert Randall "Nig" Bragan b: 10/30/1917, Birmingham, AL BR/TR, 5'10.5", 175 lbs. Deb: 4/16/1940 M/C																								
1940	Phi-N	132	474	36	105	14	1	7	44	28	34	2	....	.222	.265	.300	.565	58	-28	37	2.60	-2	*S-132/3-2	4	-2.1
1941	Phi-N	154	557	37	140	19	3	4	69	26	29	7	....	.251	.285	.318	.603	72	-22	48	2.87	-15	*S-154/2-2,3-1	6	-2.7
1942	Phi-N	109	335	17	73	12	2	2	15	20	21	0	....	.218	.264	.284	.548	63	-16	24	2.33	1	S-78,C-22/2-4,3-3	3	-0.9
1943	Bro-N	74	220	17	58	7	2	2	24	15	16	0	....	.264	.311	.341	.652	88	-4	23	3.45	-2	C-57,3-12	6	-0.2
1944	Bro-N	94	266	26	71	8	4	0	17	13	14	2	....	.267	.304	.327	.631	79	-8	25	3.13	1	S-51,C-35/3-6,2-1	5	-0.2
1947*	Bro-N	25	36	3	7	2	0	0	3	7	3	1	....	.194	.326	.250	.576	53	-2	4	3.28	1	C-21	1	-0.1
1948	Bro-N	9	12	0	2	0	0	0	0	1	0	0	....	.167	.231	.167	.397	9	-2	1	1.46	0	/C-5	0	-0.1
Total	7	597	1900	136	456	62	12	15	172	110	117	12	....	.240	.282	.309	.591	69	-82	160	2.81	-16	S-415,C-140/3-24,2-7	25	-6.3
• BRAGG, Darren	Darren William Bragg b: 9/7/1969, Waterbury, CT BL/TR, 5'9", 180 lbs. Deb: 4/12/1994 Career OF: 203-266-341																								
1994	Sea-A	8	19	4	3	1	0	0	2	2	5	0	0	.158	.238	.211	.449	17	-2	1	1.71	0	/D-3,0-3(3-0-0)	0	-0.3
1995	Sea-A	52	145	20	34	5	1	3	12	18	37	9	0	.234	.335	.345	.680	77	-3	20	4.56	3	0-47(32-0-17)/D-2	2	-0.2
1996	Sea-A	69	195	36	53	12	1	7	25	33	35	8	5	.272	.383	.451	.834	110	3	35	6.21	3	0-63(48-5-16)	5	0.3
	Bos-A	58	222	38	56	14	1	3	22	36	39	6	4	.252	.362	.365	.726	83	-5	31	4.80	0	0-58(7-47-29)	5	-0.6
	Yr.	127	417	74	109	26	2	10	47	69	74	14	9	.261	.371	.405	.777	96	-2	67	5.46	2	*0-121(55-52-45)	10	-0.3
1997	Bos-A	153	513	65	132	35	2	9	57	61	102	10	6	.257	.340	.386	.726	87	-9	66	4.34	0	*0-150(1-118-41)/3-1	11	-1.0
1998*	Bos-A	129	409	51	114	29	3	8	57	42	99	5	3	.279	.354	.423	.777	99	-0	59	4.96	-2	*0-124(7-12-112)/D-4	11	-0.8
1999	StL-N	93	273	38	71	12	1	6	26	44	67	3	0	.260	.369	.377	.746	89	-3	41	5.27	0	0-88(22-43-33)	7	-0.4
2000	Col-N	71	149	16	33	7	1	3	21	17	41	4	1	.221	.301	.342	.643	50	-12	16	3.51	-3	0-43(34-0-9)	2	-1.5
2001	NY-N	18	57	4	15	6	0	0	5	4	23	3	2	.263	.323	.368	.691	82	-2	7	4.18	-1	0-16(8-2-10)	2	-0.3
	NY-A	5	4	1	1	1	0	0	0	0	1	0	0	.250	.250	.500	.750	90	-0	1	4.50	0	/0-3(0-0-3)	0	0.0
2002*	Atl-N	109	212	34	57	15	2	3	15	24	52	5	2	.269	.349	.401	.750	96	-1	31	5.07	2	0-63(12-18-36)/D-3	6	-0.1
2003*	Atl-N	104	162	21	39	5	1	0	9	13	38	2	1	.241	.305	.284	.589	55	-11	15	3.17	-2	0-78(29-21-35)	1	-1.4
Total	10	869	2360	328	608	142	13	42	251	294	539	55	24	.258	.346	.382	.728	86	-44	324	4.67	-1	0-736/D-12,3-1	52	-6.2
• BRAGGS, Glenn	Glenn Erick Braggs b: 10/17/1962, San Bernardino, CA BR/TR, 6'3", 210 lbs. Deb: 7/18/1986 Career OF: 328-3-302																								
1986	Mil-A	58	215	19	51	8	2	4	18	11	47	1	1	.237	.278	.349	.626	67	-11	20	3.01	-3	0-56(51-3-5)/D-2	2	-1.6
1987	Mil-A	132	505	67	136	28	7	13	77	47	96	12	5	.269	.336	.430	.766	98	-1	69	4.60	6	*0-123(0-0-123)/D-8	12	-0.1
1988	Mil-A	72	272	30	71	14	0	10	42	14	60	6	4	.261	.309	.423	.732	102	-1	34	4.28	1	0-54(0-0-54),D-18	9	-0.2
1989	Mil-A	144	514	77	127	12	3	15	66	42	111	17	5	.247	.309	.370	.679	91	-5	58	3.80	-2	*0-132(127-0-9),D-13	10	-1.3
1990	Mil-A	37	113	17	28	5	0	3	13	12	21	5	3	.248	.336	.372	.708	98	-0	15	4.33	-1	0-32(13-0-20)/D-2	2	-0.2
	*Cin-N	72	201	22	60	9	1	6	28	26	43	3	4	.299	.387	.443	.830	123	6	35	6.33	6	0-60(26-0-35)	9	1.0
1991	Cin-N	85	250	36	65	10	0	11	39	23	46	11	3	.260	.327	.432	.759	108	3	36	4.98	-2	0-74(55-0-27)	7	-0.2
1992	Cin-N	92	266	40	63	16	3	8	38	36	48	3	1	.237	.332	.410	.742	106	3	35	4.40	-2	0-79(56-0-29)	7	-0.1
Total	7	692	2336	308	601	102	16	70	321	211	472	58	26	.257	.325	.405	.730	99	-6	302	4.38	3	0-610/D-43	58	-2.7
• BRAIN, Dave	David Leonard Brain b: 1/24/1879, Hereford, England d: 5/25/1959, Los Angeles, CA BR/TR, 5'10", 170 lbs. Deb: 4/24/1901 Career OF: 26-15-5																								
1901	Chi-A	5	20	2	7	1	0	0	5	1	....	0	....	.350	.381	.400	.781	120	1	3	6.37	0	/2-5	1	0.1
1903	StL-N	119	464	44	107	8	15	1	60	25	....	21	....	.231	.270	.319	.589	70	-20	47	3.46	-3	S-72,3-46	7	-1.8
1904	StL-N	127	488	57	130	24	12	7	72	17	....	18	....	.266	.291	.408	.699	120	8	66	4.64	3	S-59,3-30,0-19(7-11-1),2-13/1	18	1.4
1905	StL-N	44	158	11	36	4	5	1	17	8	....	4	....	.228	.269	.335	.605	82	-4	16	3.35	-5	S-29/3-6,0-6(0-4-2)	3	-0.8
	Pit-N	85	307	31	79	17	6	3	46	15	....	8	....	.257	.296	.381	.677	99	-2	39	4.26	5	3-78/S-4	11	0.5
	Yr.	129	465	42	115	21	11	4	63	23	....	12	....	.247	.287	.366	.653	93	-6	55	3.95	0	3-84,S-33/0-6(0-4-2)	14	-0.3
1906	Bos-N	139	525	43	131	19	5	5	45	29	....	11	....	.250	.293	.333	.626	98	-4	58	3.65	13	*3-139	12	1.4
1907	Bos-N	133	509	60	142	24	9	**10**	56	29	....	10	....	.279	.324	.420	.745	134	16	75	5.21	16	*3-130/0-3(3-0-0)	22	4.1
1908	Cin-N	16	55	4	6	0	0	0	1	8	....	0	....	.109	.222	.109	.331	7	-5	1	.72	-2	0-16(16-0-0)	0	-0.9
	NY-N	11	17	2	3	0	0	0	1	2	....	1	....	.176	.263	.176	.440	39	-1	1	1.87	-3	/2-3,0-3(0-0-2),3-2,S-1	0	-0.5
	Yr.	27	72	6	9	0	0	0	2	10	....	1	....	.125	.232	.125	.357	14	-6	2	.97	-4	0-19(16-0-2)/2-3,3-2,S-1	0	-1.4
Total	7	679	2543	254	641	97	52	27	303	134	....	73	....	.252	.292	.363	.655	101	-11	307	4.09	25	3-431,S-165/0-47,2-21,1-4	74	3.5
• BRAINERD, Fred	Frederick F. Brainerd b: 2/17/1892, Champaign, IL d: 4/17/1959, Galveston, TX BR/TR, 6', 176 lbs. Deb: 10/6/1914																								
1914	NY-N	2	5	1	1	0	0	0	0	1	0	0	....	.200	.333	.200	.533	62	-0	1	2.61	0	/2-2	0	0.0
1915	NY-N	91	249	31	50	7	2	1	21	21	44	6	7	.201	.266	.257	.523	62	-13	17	2.16	4	1-43,3-15/S-9,2-1,0-1	3	-1.0
1916	NY-N	2	7	0	0	0	0	0	0	0	0	0	....	.000	.000	.000	.000	-106	-2	0	.00	-1	/3-2	0	-0.3
Total	3	95	261	32	51	7	2	1	21	22	44	6	7	.195	.261	.249	.510	58	-15	17	2.10	3	/1-43,3-17,S-9,2-3,0-1	3	-1.3
• BRAMHALL, Art	Arthur Washington Bramhall b: 2/22/1909, Oak Park, IL d: 9/4/1985, Madison, WI BR/TR, 5'11", 170 lbs. Deb: 4/18/1935																								
1935	Phi-N	2	1	0	0	0	0	0	0	0	0	0	....	.000	.000	.000	.000	-91	-0	0	.00	0	/3-1,S-1	0	-0.1
• BRANCATO, Al	Albert "Bronk" Brancato b: 5/29/1919, Philadelphia, PA BR/TR, 5'9.5", 188 lbs. Deb: 9/7/1939																								
1939	Phi-A	21	68	12	14	5	0	1	8	8	4	1	0	.206	.299	.324	.622	60	-4	7	3.00	-1	3-20/S-1	1	-0.4
1940	Phi-A	107	298	42	57	11	2	1	23	28	36	3	1	.191	.265	.252	.517	35	-28	20	2.14	-5	S-80,3-25	2	-2.6
1941	Phi-A	144	530	60	124	20	9	2	49	59	49	1	5	.234	.311	.317	.628	68	-26	54	3.39	-11	*S-139/3-7	8	-2.6
1945	Phi-A	10	34	3	4	1	0	0	0	1	3	0	0	.118	.143	.147	.290	-16	-5	1	.69	-1	S-10	0	-0.6
Total	4	282	930	117	199	37	11	4	80	96	92	5	6	.214	.290	.290	.580	54	-63	81	2.84	-19	S-230/3-52	11	-6.2
• BRAND, Ron	Ronald George Brand b: 1/13/1940, Los Angeles, CA BR/TR, 5'7.5", 170 lbs. Deb: 5/26/1963 Career OF: 14-5-2																								
1963	Pit-N	46	66	8	19	2	0	1	7	10	11	0	0	.288	.390	.364	.753	117	2	10	5.69	-3	C-33/2-2,3-2	3	0.1
1965	Hou-N	117	391	27	92	6	3	2	37	19	34	10	5	.235	.281	.281	.563	63	-19	28	2.32	0	*C-102/3-6,0-5(5-0-0)	4	-1.5
1966	Hou-N	56	123	12	30	2	0	0	10	9	13	0	2	.244	.306	.260	.566	64	-7	9	2.22	-1	C-25/2-9,0-3(3-0-0),3-1	1	-0.7
1967	Hou-N	84	215	22	52	8	1	0	18	23	17	4	0	.242	.321	.288	.609	78	-4	21	3.22	2	C-67/2-1,0-1	6	0.1
1968	Hou-N	43	81	7	13	2	0	0	4	9	11	1	1	.160	.261	.185	.446	36	-6	5	1.70	1	C-29/3-1,0-1	1	-0.4
1969	Mon-N	103	287	19	74	12	0	0	20	30	19	2	3	.258	.330	.300	.630	77	-8	27	3.16	2	C-84/0-2(1-1-0)	4	-0.3
1970	Mon-N	72	126	10	30	2	3	0	9	9	16	2	1	.238	.289	.302	.590	59	-8	12	3.16	-4	S-19,3-12/C-9,0-5(1-3-1),2	2	-1.0
1971	Mon-N	47	56	3	12	0	0	0	1	3	5	1	1	.214	.254	.214	.469	34	-5	3	1.89	-2	S-22/3-4,0-4(3-1-0),2-1,C	0	-0.6
Total	8	568	1345	108	322	34	7	3	106	112	126	20	13	.239	.305	.282	.586	68	-54	114	2.79	-5	C-350/S-41,3-26,0-21,2-16	21	-4.2
• BRANDT, Jackie	John George Brandt b: 4/28/1934, Omaha, NE BR/TR, 5'11", 170 lbs. Deb: 4/21/1956 Career OF: 354-651-237																								
1956	StL-N	27	42	9	12	3	0	1	3	4	5	0	1	.286	.362	.429	.790	111	0	6	5.07	0	0-26(3-3-20)	1	0.0
	NY-N	98	351	45	105	16	8	11	47	17	31	3	4	.299	.332	.484	.816	116	6	55	5.75	0	0-96(86-3-26)	11	0.1
	Yr.	125	393	54	117	19	8	12	50	21	36	3	5	.298	.335	.478	.813	116	6	61	5.67	1	*0-122(89-6-46)	12	0.1
1958	SF-N	18	52	7	13	1	0	0	3	6	5	1	0	.250	.328	.269	.597	62	-2	5	3.61	0	0-14(11-1-3)	1	-0.3
1959	SF-N	137	429	63	116	16	5	12	57	35	69	11	4	.270	.325	.415	.740	98	-1	58	4.70	0	*0-116(111-4-6),3-18/1-3,2	12	-0.7
1960	Bal-A	145	511	73	130	24	6	15	65	47	69	5	3	.254	.321	.413	.734	98	-3	69	4.64	0	*0-142(17-102-51)/3-2,1-1	17	-0.9
1961	Bal-A★	139	516	93	153	18	5	16	72	62	51	10	2	.297	.373	.444	.817	120	17	85	5.96	-5	*0-136(21-120-34)/3-1	21	0.5
1962	Bal-A	143	505	76	129	29	5	19	75	55	64	9	3	.255	.333	.446	.779	113	9	76	5.15	1	*0-138(0-109-30)/3-2	18	0.4
1963	Bal-A	142	451	49	112	15	5	15	61	34	85	4	5	.248	.301	.404	.705	97	-4	51	3.81	-5	*0-134(30-92-39)/3-1	12	-1.5

YEAR TM-L	G	AB	R	H	2B	3B	HR	RBI	BB	SO	SB	CS	AVG	OBP	SLG	OPS	OPS+	BR/A	RC	RC/G	FR	G/POS	WS	TPW
1964 Bal-A	137	523	66	127	25	1	13	47	45	104	1	4	.243	.306	.369	.676	87	-11	59	3.86	8	*0-134(10-131-0)	16	-0.8
1965 Bal-A	96	243	35	59	17	0	8	24	21	40	1	2	.243	.303	.412	.715	99	-2	30	4.15	1	0-84(39-37-22)	8	-0.4
1966 Phi-N	82	164	16	41	6	1	1	15	17	36	0	2	.250	.320	.317	.638	78	-5	16	3.28	-1	0-71(17-49-6)	3	-0.8
1967 Phi-N	16	19	1	2	1	0	0	1	0	6	0	0	.105	.105	.158	.263	-25	-3	0	.50	0	/0-3(3-0-0)	0	-0.4
Hou-N	41	89	7	21	4	1	1	15	8	9	0	0	.236	.299	.337	.636	84	-2	9	3.56	-1	1-14/0-6(6-0-0),3-1	2	-0.3
Yr.	57	108	8	23	5	1	1	16	8	15	0	0	.213	.267	.306	.573	67	-5	10	2.97	-1	1-14/0-9(9-0-0),3-1	2	-0.7
Total 11	1221	3895	540	1020	175	37	112	485	351	574	45	30	.262	.325	.412	.737	101	-1	520	4.62	-1	*0-1100/3-25,1-18,2-1	122	-5.2

• BRANNAN, Otis Otis Owen Brannan b: 3/13/1899, Greenbrier, AR d: 6/6/1967, Little Rock, AR BL/TR, 5'9", 160 lbs. Deb: 4/11/1928

YEAR TM-L	G	AB	R	H	2B	3B	HR	RBI	BB	SO	SB	CS	AVG	OBP	SLG	OPS	OPS+	BR/A	RC	RC/G	FR	G/POS	WS	TPW
1928 StL-A	135	483	68	118	18	3	10	66	60	19	3	9	.244	.333	.356	.689	79	-17	59	3.93	9	*2-135	12	-0.4
1929 StL-A	23	51	4	15	1	0	1	8	4	4	0	0	.294	.345	.373	.718	82	-1	7	4.61	2	2-19	1	0.1
Total 2	158	534	72	133	19	3	11	74	64	23	3	9	.249	.334	.358	.692	79	-18	66	3.99	11	2-154	13	-0.4

• BRANNOCK, Mike Michael J. Brannock b: 1853, Guelph, Canada, 5'8", 162 lbs. Deb: 10/21/1871

YEAR TM-L	G	AB	R	H	2B	3B	HR	RBI	BB	SO	SB	CS	AVG	OBP	SLG	OPS	OPS+	BR/A	RC	RC/G	FR	G/POS	WS	TPW
1871 Chi-n	3	14	2	1	0	0	0	0	0	0	0	0	.071	.071	.071	.143	-53	-3	0	.18	-1	/3-3	....	-0.3
1875 Chi-n	2	9	2	1	0	0	0	0	0	0	2	0	.111	.111	.111	.222	-22	-1	0	1.26	-1	/3-2	....	-0.2
Total 2 n	5	23	4	2	0	0	0	0	0	0	2	0	.087	.087	.087	.174	-41	-4	0	.59	-2	/3-5	....	-0.4

• BRANOM, Dud Edgar Dudley Branom b: 11/30/1897, Sulpher Springs, TX d: 2/4/1980, Sun City, AZ BL/TL, 6'1", 190 lbs. Deb: 4/12/1927

YEAR TM-L	G	AB	R	H	2B	3B	HR	RBI	BB	SO	SB	CS	AVG	OBP	SLG	OPS	OPS+	BR/A	RC	RC/G	FR	G/POS	WS	TPW
1927 Phi-A	30	94	8	22	1	0	0	13	2	5	2	1	.234	.250	.245	.495	27	-10	6	2.00	1	1-26	0	-1.1

• BRANSFIELD, Kitty William Edward Bransfield b: 1/7/1875, Worcester, MA d: 5/1/1947, Worcester, MA BR/TR, 5'11", 207 lbs. Deb: 8/22/1898 U

YEAR TM-L	G	AB	R	H	2B	3B	HR	RBI	BB	SO	SB	CS	AVG	OBP	SLG	OPS	OPS+	BR/A	RC	RC/G	FR	G/POS	WS	TPW
1898 Bos-N	5	9	2	2	0	1	0	1	0	....	0	....	.222	.222	.444	.667	85	-0	1	3.45	-1	/C-4,1-1	0	-0.1
1901 Pit-N	139	566	92	167	26	16	0	91	29	....	23	....	.295	.335	.398	.733	109	5	86	5.59	-6	*1-139	17	-0.4
1902 Pit-N	102	413	49	126	21	8	0	69	17	....	23	....	.305	.336	.395	.730	121	8	65	5.80	-4	*1-101	15	0.3
1903*Pit-N	127	505	69	134	23	7	2	57	33	....	13	....	.265	.314	.350	.665	87	-10	63	4.33	3	*1-127	10	-0.9
1904 Pit-N	139	520	47	116	17	9	0	60	22	....	11	....	.223	.259	.290	.549	68	-21	45	2.77	0	*1-139	6	-2.5
1905 Phi-N	151	580	55	150	23	9	3	76	27	....	27	....	.259	.294	.345	.639	93	-7	70	4.08	-3	*1-151	13	-1.3
1906 Phi-N	140	524	47	144	28	5	1	60	16	....	12	....	.275	.300	.353	.653	104	-1	62	4.11	-1	*1-139	14	-0.5
1907 Phi-N	94	348	25	81	15	2	0	38	14	....	8	....	.233	.262	.287	.550	73	-12	30	2.83	-6	1-92	4	-2.3
1908 Phi-N	144	527	53	160	25	7	3	71	23	....	30	....	.304	.335	.395	.730	129	15	79	5.34	-3	*1-143	20	1.0
1909 Phi-N	140	527	47	154	27	6	1	59	18	....	17	....	.292	.319	.372	.691	114	5	68	4.46	0	*1-138	14	0.3
1910 Phi-N	123	427	39	102	17	4	3	52	20	34	10	....	.239	.275	.319	.593	71	-18	40	3.04	-6	*1-110	6	-2.8
1911 Phi-N	23	43	4	11	1	1	0	3	0	5	1	....	.256	.256	.326	.581	61	-3	4	2.93	0	/1-8	0	-0.3
Chi-N	3	10	0	4	2	0	0	0	2	2	0	....	.400	.500	.600	1.100	207	2	3	12.88	0	/1-3	1	0.1
Yr.	26	53	4	15	3	1	0	3	2	7	1	....	.283	.309	.377	.686	93	-1	7	4.46	0	1-11	1	-0.1
Total 12	1330	4999	529	1351	225	75	13	637	221	41	175	....	.270	.304	.353	.657	98	-39	615	4.25	-27	*1-1291/C-4	120	-9.4

• BRANSON, Jeff Jeffery Glenn Branson b: 1/26/1967, Waynesboro, MS BL/TR, 6', 180 lbs. Deb: 4/12/1992

YEAR TM-L	G	AB	R	H	2B	3B	HR	RBI	BB	SO	SB	CS	AVG	OBP	SLG	OPS	OPS+	BR/A	RC	RC/G	FR	G/POS	WS	TPW
1992 Cin-N	72	115	12	34	7	1	0	15	5	16	0	1	.296	.325	.374	.699	95	-1	13	3.80	-5	2-33/3-8,S-1	3	-0.6
1993 Cin-N	125	381	40	92	15	1	3	22	19	73	4	1	.241	.278	.310	.587	57	-24	34	2.97	2	S-59,2-45,3-14/1-1	4	-1.5
1994 Cin-N	58	109	18	31	4	1	6	16	5	16	0	0	.284	.316	.505	.820	110	1	16	5.04	-2	2-19,3-18/S-8,1-2	4	0.0
1995*Cin-N	122	331	43	86	18	2	12	45	44	69	2	1	.260	.350	.435	.785	106	3	50	5.14	14	3-98,S-32/2-6,1-1	12	1.9
1996 Cin-N	129	311	34	76	16	4	9	37	31	67	2	0	.244	.315	.408	.723	90	-5	39	4.19	7	3-64,S-38,2-31	7	0.5
1997 Cin-N	65	98	9	15	3	1	1	5	7	23	1	0	.153	.210	.235	.444	16	-12	5	1.42	1	3-27,2-14,S-11	1	-1.1
*Cle-A	29	72	5	19	4	0	2	7	7	17	0	2	.264	.338	.403	.740	89	-2	9	4.38	2	2-19/3-6,S-2,D-1	1	0.1
1998*Cle-A	63	100	6	20	4	1	1	9	3	21	0	0	.200	.223	.290	.513	31	-10	6	2.10	-3	2-31,3-20/1-3,S-2	1	-1.2
2000 LA-N	18	17	3	4	1	0	0	0	1	6	0	0	.235	.278	.294	.572	47	-1	1	2.25	-1	/S-7,2-3,3-3	0	-0.2
2001 LA-N	13	21	3	6	0	0	0	1	0	4	0	0	.286	.286	.286	.571	52	-2	2	3.09	-1	/2-6,S-2,3-1	0	-0.2
Total 9	694	1555	173	383	72	11	34	156	122	312	9	5	.246	.303	.372	.675	78	-54	174	3.76	15	3-259,2-207,S-162/1-7,D-1	33	-2.2

• BRANT, Marshall Marshall Lee Brant b: 9/17/1955, Garberville, CA BR/TR, 6'5", 185 lbs. Deb: 10/1/1980

YEAR TM-L	G	AB	R	H	2B	3B	HR	RBI	BB	SO	SB	CS	AVG	OBP	SLG	OPS	OPS+	BR/A	RC	RC/G	FR	G/POS	WS	TPW
1980 NY-A	3	6	0	0	0	0	0	0	0	3	0	0	.000	.000	.000	.000	-102	-2	0	.00	0	/1-2,D-1	0	-0.2
1983 Oak-A	5	14	2	2	0	0	0	2	0	3	0	0	.143	.143	.143	.286	-22	-2	0	.64	-1	/1-3,D-1	0	-0.3
Total 2	8	20	2	2	0	0	0	2	0	6	0	0	.100	.100	.100	.200	-46	-4	0	.43	-1	/1-5,D-2	0	-0.5

• BRANTLEY, Mickey Michael Charles Brantley b: 6/17/1961, Catskill, NY BR/TR, 5'10", 180 lbs. Deb: 8/9/1986 C Career OF: 137-125-50

YEAR TM-L	G	AB	R	H	2B	3B	HR	RBI	BB	SO	SB	CS	AVG	OBP	SLG	OPS	OPS+	BR/A	RC	RC/G	FR	G/POS	WS	TPW
1986 Sea-A	27	102	12	20	3	2	3	7	10	21	1	1	.196	.268	.353	.621	67	-5	9	2.83	1	0-25(1-25-0)	1	-0.4
1987 Sea-A	92	351	52	106	23	2	14	54	24	44	13	4	.302	.347	.499	.845	115	7	62	6.61	0	0-82(6-51-35)/D-8	11	0.4
1988 Sea-A	149	577	76	152	25	4	15	56	26	64	18	7	.263	.298	.399	.696	89	-10	66	3.93	-5	*0-147(118-49-4)/D-2	10	-2.0
1989 Sea-A	34	108	14	17	5	0	0	8	7	7	2	2	.157	.209	.204	.412	16	-13	5	1.31	0	0-23(12-0-11)/D-7	1	-1.4
Total 4	302	1138	154	295	56	8	32	125	67	136	34	14	.259	.302	.407	.708	88	-20	142	4.30	-4	0-277/D-17	23	-3.3

• BRANYAN, Russ Russell Oles Branyan b: 12/19/1975, Warner Robins, GA BL/TR, 6'3", 195 lbs. Deb: 9/26/1998 Career OF: 133-0-17

YEAR TM-L	G	AB	R	H	2B	3B	HR	RBI	BB	SO	SB	CS	AVG	OBP	SLG	OPS	OPS+	BR/A	RC	RC/G	FR	G/POS	WS	TPW
1998 Cle-A	1	4	0	0	0	0	0	0	0	2	0	0	.000	.000	.000	.000	-97	-1	0	.00	0	/3-1	0	-0.1
1999 Cle-A	11	38	4	8	2	0	1	6	3	19	0	0	.211	.286	.342	.628	57	-3	4	3.61	1	/3-8,D-3	1	-0.2
2000 Cle-A	67	193	32	46	7	2	16	38	22	76	0	0	.238	.329	.544	.873	113	3	36	6.42	2	0-33(18-0-15),D-23/3-1	5	0.2
2001*Cle-A	113	315	48	73	16	2	20	54	38	132	1	1	.232	.320	.486	.806	107	2	51	5.53	-4	3-72,0-33(31-0-2)/D-7	10	-0.2
2002 Cle-A	50	161	16	33	4	0	8	17	17	65	1	2	.205	.281	.379	.660	74	-7	17	3.35	-2	0-43(42-0-0)/3-8,D-1	1	-1.0
Cin-N	84	217	34	53	9	1	16	39	34	86	3	1	.244	.352	.516	.868	122	7	42	6.64	0	0-25(25-0-0),1-18,3-16/D-4	7	0.4
2003 Cin-N	74	176	22	38	12	0	9	26	27	69	0	0	.216	.324	.438	.761	98	-1	27	5.19	7	3-20,0-17(17-0-0),1-14/D-1	5	0.4
Total 6	400	1104	156	251	50	5	70	180	141	449	5	4	.227	.321	.472	.793	103	1	176	5.41	4	0-151,3-126/D-39,1-32	29	-0.4

• BRASHEAR, Roy Roy Parks Brashear b: 1/3/1874, Ashtabula, OH d: 4/20/1951, Los Angeles, CA BR/TR, 5'11", 190 lbs. Deb: 4/25/1902

YEAR TM-L	G	AB	R	H	2B	3B	HR	RBI	BB	SO	SB	CS	AVG	OBP	SLG	OPS	OPS+	BR/A	RC	RC/G	FR	G/POS	WS	TPW
1902 StL-N	110	388	36	107	8	2	1	40	32	....	9	....	.276	.333	.314	.647	104	2	46	4.19	-4	1-67,2-21,0-16(1-7-8)/S-3	11	-0.4
1903 Phi-N	20	75	9	17	3	0	0	4	6	....	2	....	.227	.284	.267	.551	59	-4	7	2.94	-2	2-18/1-2	1	-0.6
Total 2	130	463	45	124	11	2	1	44	38	....	11	....	.268	.325	.307	.631	97	-2	53	3.98	-6	/1-69,2-39,0-16,S-3	12	-0.9

• BRATCHER, Joe Joseph Warlick "Goobers" Bratcher b: 7/22/1898, Grand Saline, TX d: 10/13/1977, Fort Worth, TX BL/TR, 5'8.5", 140 lbs. Deb: 8/26/1924

YEAR TM-L	G	AB	R	H	2B	3B	HR	RBI	BB	SO	SB	CS	AVG	OBP	SLG	OPS	OPS+	BR/A	RC	RC/G	FR	G/POS	WS	TPW
1924 StL-N	4	1	1	0	0	0	0	0	0	0	0	0	.000	.000	.000	.000	-102	-0	0	.00	0	/0-1	0	-0.1

• BRATSCHI, Fred Frederick Oscar "Fritz" Bratschi b: 1/16/1892, Alliance, OH d: 1/10/1962, Massillon, OH BR/TR, 5'10", 170 lbs. Deb: 7/24/1921 Career OF: 30-0-12

YEAR TM-L	G	AB	R	H	2B	3B	HR	RBI	BB	SO	SB	CS	AVG	OBP	SLG	OPS	OPS+	BR/A	RC	RC/G	FR	G/POS	WS	TPW
1921 Chi-A	16	28	0	8	1	0	0	3	0	2	0	0	.286	.286	.321	.607	55	-2	2	3.27	1	/0-5(1-0-4)	0	-0.1
1926 Bos-A	72	167	12	46	10	1	0	19	14	15	0	1	.275	.335	.347	.682	81	-5	20	4.23	-4	0-37(29-0-8)	2	-1.1
1927 Bos-A	1	1	0	0	0	0	0	0	0	0	0	0	.000	.000	.000	.000	-102	-0	0	.00	0	....	0	0.0
Total 3	89	196	12	54	11	1	0	22	14	17	0	1	.276	.327	.342	.669	77	-7	22	4.07	-3	/0-42	2	-1.3

• BRAUN, Steve Stephen Russell Braun b: 5/8/1948, Trenton, NJ BL/TR, 5'10", 180 lbs. Deb: 4/6/1971 C Career OF: 465-0-35

YEAR TM-L	G	AB	R	H	2B	3B	HR	RBI	BB	SO	SB	CS	AVG	OBP	SLG	OPS	OPS+	BR/A	RC	RC/G	FR	G/POS	WS	TPW
1971 Min-A	128	343	51	87	12	2	5	35	48	50	8	3	.254	.354	.344	.698	95	0	44	4.38	-10	3-73,2-28,S-10/0-2(2-0-0)	10	-0.8
1972 Min-A	121	402	40	116	21	0	2	50	45	38	4	5	.289	.363	.356	.719	109	5	51	4.40	-4	3-74,2-20,S-11/0-9(8-0-1)	14	0.3
1973 Min-A	115	361	46	102	28	5	6	42	74	48	4	3	.283	.409	.438	.846	133	20	68	6.72	-5	*3-102/0-6(6-0-0)	16	1.5
1974 Min-A	129	453	53	127	12	1	8	40	56	51	4	4	.280	.362	.364	.726	105	5	62	4.93	1	*0-108(108-0-0),3-17	13	0.0
1975 Min-A	136	453	70	137	18	3	11	45	66	55	0	2	.302	.392	.428	.821	129	19	79	6.40	0	*0-106(106-0-0)/1-9,D-9,3,2	17	1.3
1976 Min-A	122	417	73	120	12	3	3	61	67	43	12	4	.288	.388	.353	.740	115	12	63	5.47	1	D-71,0-32(30-0-3),3-16	16	1.1
1977 Sea-A	139	451	51	106	19	1	5	31	80	59	8	3	.235	.353	.315	.668	84	-5	54	3.93	3	0-100(100-0-0),D-32/3-1	10	-0.8
1978 Sea-A	32	74	11	17	4	0	3	15	9	5	1	0	.230	.313	.405	.719	101	0	9	3.78	-0	D-14/0-4(2-0-2)	1	0.0
*KC-A	64	137	16	36	10	1	0	14	28	16	3	2	.263	.388	.350	.738	106	3	21	5.36	-1	0-33(33-0-0),3-11	5	0.1
Yr.	96	211	27	53	14	1	3	29	37	21	4	2	.251	.363	.370	.733	105	3	30	4.78	-1	0-37(35-0-2),D-14,3-11	6	0.1
1979 KC-A	58	116	15	31	2	0	4	10	22	11	0	0	.267	.384	.388	.772	107	2	19	5.71	2	0-18(18-0-0),D-11/3-2	4	0.4
1980 KC-A	14	23	0	1	0	0	0	1	2	2	0	0	.043	.120	.043	.163	-53	-5	0	.22	-1	/0-5(3-0-2),D-1	0	-0.5
Tor-A	37	55	4	15	2	0	1	9	8	5	0	0	.273	.365	.364	.729	96	0	7	4.68	0	D-13/3-1	1	0.0

YEAR TM-L	G	AB	R	H	2B	3B	HR	RBI	BB	SO	SB	CS	AVG	OBP	SLG	OPS	OPS+	BR/A	RC	RC/G	FR	G/POS	WS	TPW
Yr.	51	78	4	16	2	0	1	10	10	7	0	0	.205	.295	.269	.565	54	-5	7	3.15	-1	D-14/0-5(3-0-2),3-1	1	-0.6
1981 StL-N	44	46	9	9	2	1	0	2	15	7	1	0	.196	.393	.283	.676	92	1	7	4.61	1	0-12(6-0-6)/3-1	2	0.1
1982*StL-N	58	62	6	17	4	0	0	4	11	10	0	0	.274	.384	.339	.722	102	1	8	4.88	-1	/0-8(6-0-2),3-5	2	0.0
1983 StL-N	78	92	8	25	2	1	3	7	21	7	0	1	.272	.407	.413	.820	128	4	17	6.55	0	0-22(18-0-5)/3-4	4	0.4
1984 StL-N	86	98	6	27	3	1	0	16	17	17	0	0	.276	.383	.327	.709	104	1	14	5.30	0	0-19(12-0-7)/3-1	4	0.1
1985*StL-N	64	67	7	16	4	0	1	6	10	9	0	0	.239	.346	.343	.689	94	-0	9	4.64	0	0-14(7-0-7)	2	0.0
Total 15	1425	3650	466	989	155	19	52	388	579	433	45	27	.271	.373	.367	.740	108	65	532	5.11	-13	0-498,3-310,D-151/2-49,S-21,1	121	2.9

• BRAVO, Angel Angel Alfonso (Urdaneta) Bravo b: 8/4/1942, Maracaibo, Venezuela BL/TL, 5'8", 150 lbs. Deb: 6/6/1969 Career OF: 12-39-9

YEAR TM-L	G	AB	R	H	2B	3B	HR	RBI	BB	SO	SB	CS	AVG	OBP	SLG	OPS	OPS+	BR/A	RC	RC/G	FR	G/POS	WS	TPW
1969 Chi-A	27	90	10	26	4	2	1	3	3	5	2	0	.289	.319	.411	.730	98	-0	12	4.95	-1	0-25(2-24-3)	2	-0.2
1970*Cin-N	65	65	10	18	1	1	0	3	9	13	0	1	.277	.365	.323	.688	82	-2	8	4.40	0	0-22(5-12-5)	1	-0.2
1971 Cin-N	5	5	0	1	0	0	0	0	0	1	0	0	.200	.200	.200	.400	14	-1	0	1.35	0	....	0	-0.1
SD-N	52	58	6	9	2	0	0	6	8	12	0	1	.155	.269	.190	.458	34	-5	3	1.80	-1	/0-9(5-3-1)	0	-0.7
Yr.	57	63	6	10	2	0	0	6	8	13	0	1	.159	.264	.190	.454	33	-6	4	1.77	-1	/0-9(5-3-1)	0	-0.7
Total 3	149	218	26	54	7	3	1	12	20	31	2	2	.248	.317	.321	.638	74	-8	24	3.77	-2	/0-56	3	-1.1

• BRAY, Buster Clarence Wilbur Bray b: 4/1/1913, Birmingham, AL d: 9/4/1982, Evansville, IN BL/TL, 6', 170 lbs. Deb: 4/18/1941

YEAR TM-L	G	AB	R	H	2B	3B	HR	RBI	BB	SO	SB	CS	AVG	OBP	SLG	OPS	OPS+	BR/A	RC	RC/G	FR	G/POS	WS	TPW
1941 Bos-N	4	11	2	1	1	0	0	1	1	2	0	....	.091	.167	.182	.348	-2	-2	0	1.02	-0	/0-3(0-3-0)	0	-0.2

• BRAZILL, Frank Frank Leo Brazill b: 8/11/1899, Spangler, PA d: 11/3/1976, Oakland, CA BL/TR, 5'11.5", 175 lbs. Deb: 4/13/1921

YEAR TM-L	G	AB	R	H	2B	3B	HR	RBI	BB	SO	SB	CS	AVG	OBP	SLG	OPS	OPS+	BR/A	RC	RC/G	FR	G/POS	WS	TPW
1921 Phi-A	66	177	17	48	3	1	0	19	23	21	2	4	.271	.361	.299	.661	70	-8	20	3.89	-0	1-36/3-9	2	-0.9
1922 Phi-A	6	13	0	1	0	0	0	1	0	1	0	0	.077	.077	.077	.154	-58	-3	0	.16	0	/3-2	0	-0.3
Total 2	72	190	17	49	3	1	0	20	23	22	2	4	.258	.344	.284	.628	62	-11	20	3.59	-1	/1-36,3-11	2	-1.2

• BREAM, Sid Sidney Eugene Bream b: 8/3/1960, Carlisle, PA BL/TL, 6'4", 220 lbs. Deb: 9/1/1983

YEAR TM-L	G	AB	R	H	2B	3B	HR	RBI	BB	SO	SB	CS	AVG	OBP	SLG	OPS	OPS+	BR/A	RC	RC/G	FR	G/POS	WS	TPW
1983 LA-N	15	11	0	2	0	0	0	2	2	2	0	0	.182	.308	.182	.490	39	-1	1	1.57	0	/1-4	0	-0.1
1984 LA-N	27	49	2	9	3	0	0	6	6	9	1	0	.184	.273	.245	.518	47	-3	4	2.24	1	1-14	0	-0.3
1985 LA-N	24	53	4	7	0	0	3	6	7	10	0	0	.132	.233	.302	.535	50	-4	4	2.28	1	1-16	0	-0.4
Pit-N	26	95	14	27	7	0	3	15	11	14	0	2	.284	.358	.453	.811	127	2	14	4.88	1	1-25	2	0.2
Yr.	50	148	18	34	7	0	6	21	18	24	0	2	.230	.313	.399	.712	98	-1	18	3.86	2	1-41	2	-0.2
1986 Pit-N	154	522	73	140	37	5	16	77	60	73	13	7	.268	.345	.450	.795	115	10	79	5.21	17	*1-153/0-2(2-0-0)	15	1.8
1987 Pit-N	149	516	64	142	25	3	13	65	49	69	9	8	.275	.338	.411	.749	97	-5	66	4.37	10	*1-144	10	-0.4
1988 Pit-N	148	462	50	122	37	0	10	65	47	64	9	9	.264	.333	.409	.742	114	5	61	4.40	18	*1-138	16	1.6
1989 Pit-N	19	36	3	8	3	0	0	4	12	10	0	4	.222	.417	.306	.722	114	-0	5	3.85	0	1-13	1	-0.1
1990*Pit-N	147	389	39	105	23	2	15	67	48	65	8	4	.270	.353	.455	.808	125	13	64	5.70	6	*1-142	15	1.1
1991*Atl-N	91	265	32	67	12	0	11	45	25	31	0	3	.253	.317	.423	.740	100	-2	33	4.10	0	1-85	6	-0.7
1992*Atl-N	125	372	30	97	25	1	10	61	46	51	6	0	.261	.344	.414	.758	107	5	57	5.41	-3	*1-120	15	-0.5
1993*Atl-N	117	277	33	72	14	1	9	35	31	43	4	2	.260	.334	.415	.750	98	-1	38	4.81	3	1-90	8	-0.4
1994 Hou-N	46	61	7	21	5	0	0	7	9	9	0	1	.344	.429	.426	.855	131	3	11	6.80	2	1-10	2	0.4
Total 12	1088	3108	351	819	191	12	90	455	353	450	50	40	.264	.340	.420	.759	108	24	436	4.77	55	1-954/0-2	90	2.2

• BREAZEALE, Jim James Leo Breazeale b: 10/3/1949, Houston, TX BL/TR, 6'2", 210 lbs. Deb: 9/13/1969

YEAR TM-L	G	AB	R	H	2B	3B	HR	RBI	BB	SO	SB	CS	AVG	OBP	SLG	OPS	OPS+	BR/A	RC	RC/G	FR	G/POS	WS	TPW
1969 Atl-N	2	1	1	0	0	0	0	0	2	0	0	0	.000	.667	.000	.667	101	0	0	9.36	0	/1-1	0	0.0
1971 Atl-N	10	21	1	4	0	0	1	3	0	3	0	0	.190	.190	.333	.524	43	-2	1	2.05	0	/1-4	0	-0.2
1972 Atl-N	52	85	10	21	2	0	5	17	6	12	0	1	.247	.297	.447	.744	100	-1	10	4.18	-2	1-16/3-1	2	-0.4
1978 Chi-A	25	72	8	15	3	0	3	13	8	10	0	0	.208	.288	.375	.663	84	-2	8	3.45	-2	1-19/D-4	1	-0.4
Total 4	89	179	20	40	5	0	9	33	16	25	0	1	.223	.287	.402	.689	87	-4	20	3.65	-4	/1-40,D-4,3-1	3	-1.0

• BREDE, Brent Brent David Brede b: 9/13/1971, Belleville, IL BL/TL, 6'4", 190 lbs. Deb: 9/8/1996 Career OF: 29-0-86

YEAR TM-L	G	AB	R	H	2B	3B	HR	RBI	BB	SO	SB	CS	AVG	OBP	SLG	OPS	OPS+	BR/A	RC	RC/G	FR	G/POS	WS	TPW
1996 Min-A	10	20	2	6	0	1	0	2	1	5	0	0	.300	.333	.400	.733	83	-1	2	4.25	1	/0-7(0-0-7)	0	0.0
1997 Min-A	61	190	25	52	11	1	3	21	21	38	7	2	.274	.349	.389	.739	91	-1	28	5.29	-3	0-42(3-0-40),1-15/D-1	3	-0.7
1998 Ari-N	98	212	23	48	9	3	2	17	24	43	1	0	.226	.311	.325	.636	68	-9	22	3.44	-1	0-58(26-0-39),1-12/D-1	3	-1.3
Total 3	169	422	50	106	20	5	5	40	46	86	8	2	.251	.329	.358	.687	79	-12	52	4.28	-3	0-107/1-27,D-2	6	-2.0

• BREEDEN, Danny Danny Richard Breeden b: 6/27/1942, Albany, GA BR/TR, 5'11.5", 185 lbs. Deb: 7/24/1969

YEAR TM-L	G	AB	R	H	2B	3B	HR	RBI	BB	SO	SB	CS	AVG	OBP	SLG	OPS	OPS+	BR/A	RC	RC/G	FR	G/POS	WS	TPW
1969 Cin-N	3	8	0	1	0	0	0	1	0	3	0	0	.125	.125	.125	.250	-28	-1	0	.63	0	/C-3	0	-0.1
1971 Chi-N	25	65	3	10	1	0	0	4	9	18	0	0	.154	.267	.169	.436	22	-6	4	1.58	-2	C-25	1	-0.7
Total 2	28	73	3	11	1	0	0	5	9	21	0	0	.151	.253	.164	.417	16	-8	4	1.45	-1	/C-28	1	-0.8

• BREEDEN, Hal Harold Noel Breeden b: 6/28/1944, Albany, GA BR/TL, 6'2", 200 lbs. Deb: 4/7/1971

YEAR TM-L	G	AB	R	H	2B	3B	HR	RBI	BB	SO	SB	CS	AVG	OBP	SLG	OPS	OPS+	BR/A	RC	RC/G	FR	G/POS	WS	TPW
1971 Chi-N	23	36	1	5	1	0	1	2	2	7	0	0	.139	.184	.250	.434	19	-4	2	1.52	1	/1-8	0	-0.3
1972 Mon-N	42	87	6	20	2	0	3	10	7	15	0	0	.230	.287	.356	.644	80	-2	9	3.51	0	1-26/0-1	2	-0.4
1973 Mon-N	105	258	36	71	10	6	15	43	29	45	0	1	.275	.353	.535	.888	138	12	47	6.51	4	1-66	11	1.2
1974 Mon-N	79	190	14	47	13	0	2	20	24	35	0	1	.247	.332	.347	.679	85	-4	21	3.79	2	1-56	3	-0.6
1975 Mon-N	24	37	4	5	2	0	0	1	7	5	0	0	.135	.273	.189	.462	29	-3	2	1.64	-1	1-12	0	-0.5
Total 5	273	608	61	148	28	6	21	76	69	107	0	2	.243	.323	.413	.735	99	-1	81	4.56	6	1-168/0-1	16	-0.6

• BREEDING, Marv Marvin Eugene Breeding b: 3/8/1934, Decatur, AL BR/TR, 6', 175 lbs. Deb: 4/19/1960

YEAR TM-L	G	AB	R	H	2B	3B	HR	RBI	BB	SO	SB	CS	AVG	OBP	SLG	OPS	OPS+	BR/A	RC	RC/G	FR	G/POS	WS	TPW
1960 Bal-A	152	551	69	147	25	2	3	43	35	80	10	4	.267	.314	.336	.650	77	-18	59	3.78	12	*2-152	16	0.5
1961 Bal-A	90	244	32	51	8	0	1	16	14	33	5	2	.209	.252	.254	.506	36	-22	16	2.19	3	2-80	4	-1.3
1962 Bal-A	95	240	27	59	10	1	2	18	8	41	2	2	.246	.273	.321	.594	62	-14	21	3.05	2	2-73/3-1,S-1	5	-0.6
1963 Was-A	58	197	20	54	7	2	1	14	7	21	1	1	.274	.299	.345	.644	80	-6	20	3.77	-5	3-29,2-22/S-2	4	-1.0
LA-N	20	36	6	6	0	0	0	1	2	5	1	0	.167	.211	.167	.377	11	-4	2	1.36	-1	2-17/3-1,S-1	0	-0.5
Total 4	415	1268	154	317	50	5	7	92	66	180	19	9	.250	.289	.314	.603	65	-64	118	3.24	10	2-344/3-31,S-4	29	-2.9

• BREMER, Herb Herbert Frederick Bremer b: 10/25/1913, Chicago, IL d: 11/28/1979, Columbus, GA BR/TR, 6', 195 lbs. Deb: 9/16/1937

YEAR TM-L	G	AB	R	H	2B	3B	HR	RBI	BB	SO	SB	CS	AVG	OBP	SLG	OPS	OPS+	BR/A	RC	RC/G	FR	G/POS	WS	TPW
1937 StL-N	11	33	2	7	1	0	0	3	2	4	0	....	.212	.257	.242	.500	36	-3	2	1.98	0	C-10	1	-0.2
1938 StL-N	50	151	14	33	5	1	2	14	9	36	1	....	.219	.263	.305	.567	53	-10	13	2.84	0	C-50	2	-0.7
1939 StL-N	9	9	0	1	0	0	0	1	0	2	0	....	.111	.111	.111	.222	-38	-2	0	.38	-1	/C-8	0	-0.2
Total 3	70	193	16	41	6	1	2	18	11	42	1	....	.212	.255	.285	.540	46	-15	15	2.56	0	/C-68	3	-1.1

• BRENEGAN, Sam Olaf Selmar Brenegan b: 9/1/1890, Galesville, WI d: 4/20/1956, Galesville, WI BL/TR, 6'2", 185 lbs. Deb: 4/24/1914

YEAR TM-L	G	AB	R	H	2B	3B	HR	RBI	BB	SO	SB	CS	AVG	OBP	SLG	OPS	OPS+	BR/A	RC	RC/G	FR	G/POS	WS	TPW
1914 Pit-N	1	0	0	0	0	0	0	0	0	0	0	....	....	....	....	....	-105	0	0	....	-1	/C-1	0	-0.1

• BRENLY, Bob Robert Earl Brenly b: 2/25/1954, Coshocton, OH BR/TR, 6'2", 210 lbs. Deb: 8/14/1981 M/C Career OF: 3-0-3

YEAR TM-L	G	AB	R	H	2B	3B	HR	RBI	BB	SO	SB	CS	AVG	OBP	SLG	OPS	OPS+	BR/A	RC	RC/G	FR	G/POS	WS	TPW
1981 SF-N	19	45	5	15	2	1	1	4	6	4	0	1	.333	.423	.489	.912	161	3	9	7.73	-2	C-14/3-3,0-1	3	0.2
1982 SF-N	65	180	26	51	4	1	4	15	18	26	6	2	.283	.352	.383	.735	106	2	25	5.03	-2	C-61/3-1	8	0.3
1983 SF-N	104	281	36	63	12	2	7	34	37	48	10	7	.224	.319	.356	.675	89	-5	30	3.33	6	C-90,1-10/0-2(1-0-1)	8	0.5
1984 SF-N★	145	506	74	147	28	0	20	80	48	52	6	9	.291	.355	.464	.820	133	18	79	5.44	-2	*C-127,1-22/0-3(1-0-2)	20	2.2
1985 SF-N	133	440	41	97	16	1	19	56	57	62	1	4	.220	.313	.391	.704	101	-2	55	4.12	-2	*C-110,3-17,1-10	12	0.1
1986 SF-N	149	472	60	116	26	0	16	62	74	97	10	6	.246	.352	.403	.754	113	9	71	5.14	-7	*C-101,3-45,1-19	20	0.5
1987*SF-N	123	375	55	100	19	1	18	51	47	85	10	7	.267	.353	.467	.820	121	10	63	5.72	6	*C-108/1-6,3-2	18	2.0
1988 SF-N	73	206	13	39	7	0	5	22	20	40	1	2	.189	.268	.296	.564	64	-10	17	2.54	-5	C-69	3	-1.2
1989 Tor-A	48	88	9	15	3	1	1	6	10	17	1	0	.170	.255	.261	.516	49	-6	6	2.20	0	D-28,C-13/1-5	0	-0.6
SF-N	12	22	2	4	2	0	0	3	1	7	0	0	.182	.217	.273	.490	40	-2	1	1.47	0	C-12	1	-0.1
Total 9	871	2615	321	647	119	7	91	333	318	438	45	38	.247	.333	.403	.736	107	18	356	4.57	-7	C-705/1-72,3-68,D-28,0-6	93	3.9

• BRENNAN, Jim Jack Brennan b: 1862, St. Louis, MO d: 10/18/1904, Philadelphia, PA Deb: 4/20/1884 U Career OF: 13-9-15

YEAR TM-L	G	AB	R	H	2B	3B	HR	RBI	BB	SO	SB	CS	AVG	OBP	SLG	OPS	OPS+	BR/A	RC	RC/G	FR	G/POS	WS	TPW
1884 StL-U	56	231	38	50	6	1	0	....	12	....	....	....	.216	.255	.251	.506	69	-7	15	2.35	8	C-33,0-16(7-4-6)/3-7,S-1	5	0.2
1885 StL-N	3	10	0	1	0	0	0	1	1	1	....	....	.100	.182	.100	.282	-7	-1	0	.56	-1	/0-2(2-0-0),3-1	0	-0.2
1888 KC-a	34	118	5	20	2	0	0	6	3	....	3	....	.169	.203	.186	.390	24	-10	5	1.43	1	C-25/3-5,0-5(2-1-2)	1	-0.7

YEAR TM-L	G	AB	R	H	2B	3B	HR	RBI	BB	SO	SB	CS	AVG	OBP	SLG	OPS	OPS+	BR/A	RC	RC/G	FR	G/POS	WS	TPW
1889 Phi-a	31	113	12	25	4	0	0	15	10	15	1	....	.221	.285	.257	.541	55	-7	9	2.63	3	C-13/2-7,0-7(0-4-3),3-4	1	-0.3
1890 Cle-P	59	233	32	59	3	7	0	26	13	29	8	....	.253	.304	.326	.630	74	-8	26	4.06	0	C-42,3-14/0-6(2-0-4)	3	-0.4
Total 5	183	705	87	155	15	8	0	48	39	45	12	....	.220	.267	.264	.530	60	-34	55	2.74	10	C-113/0-36,3-31,2-7,S-1	10	-1.3

• BRENZEL, Bill William Richard Brenzel b: 3/3/1910, Oakland, CA d: 6/12/1979, Oakland, CA BR/TR, 5'10", 173 lbs. Deb: 4/13/1932

YEAR TM-L	G	AB	R	H	2B	3B	HR	RBI	BB	SO	SB	CS	AVG	OBP	SLG	OPS	OPS+	BR/A	RC	RC/G	FR	G/POS	WS	TPW
1932 Pit-N	9	24	0	1	1	0	0	2	0	4	0	....	.042	.042	.083	.125	-69	-6	0	.09	-1	/C-9	0	-0.6
1934 Cle-A	15	51	4	11	3	0	0	3	2	1	0	0	.216	.245	.275	.520	33	-5	4	2.23	0	C-15	1	-0.4
1935 Cle-A	52	142	12	31	5	1	0	14	6	10	2	2	.218	.250	.268	.518	33	-15	10	2.12	-5	C-51	1	-1.6
Total 3	76	217	16	43	9	1	0	19	8	15	2	2	.198	.227	.249	.476	23	-26	13	1.89	-5	/C-75	2	-2.5

• BRESNAHAN, Roger Roger Philip "The Duke Of Tralee" Bresnahan
b: 6/11/1879, Toledo, OH d: 12/4/1944, Toledo, OH BR/TR, 5'9", 200 lbs. Deb: 8/27/1897 M/C HOF: 1945 Career OF: 19-221-41 ◆

YEAR TM-L	G	AB	R	H	2B	3B	HR	RBI	BB	SO	SB	CS	AVG	OBP	SLG	OPS	OPS+	BR/A	RC	RC/G	FR	G/POS	WS	TPW
1897 Was-N	6	16	1	6	0	0	0	3	1	....	0	....	.375	.412	.375	.787	109	1	3	6.71	-1	/P-6,0-1	3	0.2
1900 Chi-N	2	2	0	0	0	0	0	0	0	....	0	....	.000	.000	.000	.000	-104	-1	0	.00	-1	/C-1	0	-0.1
1901 Bal-A	86	295	40	79	9	9	1	32	23	....	10	....	.268	.323	.369	.692	88	-5	40	4.80	-11	C-69/0-8(7-0-1),3-4,2-2,P	6	-1.0
1902 Bal-A	65	235	30	64	8	6	4	34	21	....	12	....	.272	.337	.409	.746	102	0	38	5.72	-9	3-30,C-22,0-15(0-15-0)	6	-0.6
NY-N	51	178	16	51	9	3	1	22	16	....	6	....	.287	.352	.388	.740	129	6	28	5.54	-1	0-27(0-0-27),C-16/1-4,S-4,3	6	0.6
1903 NY-N	113	406	87	142	30	8	4	55	61	....	34	....	.350	.443	.493	.936	160	35	108	10.32	2	0-84(4-79-1),1-13,C-11/3-4	27	3.3
1904 NY-N	109	402	81	114	22	7	5	33	58	....	13	....	.284	.381	.410	.791	138	20	70	6.24	8	0-93(7-81-5),1-10/S-4,2-1,3	23	2.5
1905*NY-N	104	331	58	100	18	3	0	46	50	....	11	....	.302	.411	.375	.785	132	17	58	6.33	-9	C-87/0-8(0-2-4)	19	1.7
1906 NY-N	124	405	69	114	22	4	0	43	81	....	25	....	.281	**.419**	.356	.775	139	26	73	6.45	2	C-82,0-40(0-39-3)	29	3.7
1907 NY-N	110	328	57	83	9	7	4	38	61	....	15	....	.253	.380	.360	.740	128	14	53	5.46	-8	C-95/1-6,0-2(0-2-0),3-1	18	1.7
1908 NY-N	140	449	70	127	25	3	1	54	**83**	....	14	....	.283	.401	.359	.760	136	25	73	5.46	-12	*C-139	27	3.0
1909 StL-N	72	234	27	57	4	1	0	23	46	....	11	....	.244	.370	.269	.639	105	5	28	3.95	4	C-59/2-9,3-1	8	1.6
1910 StL-N	88	234	35	65	15	3	0	27	55	17	13	....	.278	.419	.368	.787	135	15	42	6.19	-4	C-77/0-2(1-1-0),P-1	13	2.0
1911 StL-N	81	227	22	63	17	8	3	41	45	19	4	....	.278	.404	.463	.866	146	16	44	6.73	0	C-77/2-2	14	2.1
1912 StL-N	48	108	8	36	7	2	1	15	14	9	4	....	.333	.419	.463	.882	145	7	22	7.88	7	C-28	6	1.6
1913 Chi-N	69	162	20	37	5	2	1	21	21	11	7	....	.228	.324	.302	.627	79	-4	18	3.46	-2	C-58	5	-0.2
1914 Chi-N	101	248	42	69	10	4	0	24	49	20	14	....	.278	.401	.351	.752	125	11	40	5.49	1	C-85,2-14/0-1	14	1.9
1915 Chi-N	77	221	19	45	8	1	1	19	29	23	19	3	.204	.296	.262	.558	69	-4	22	3.14	1	C-68	7	0.3
Total 17	1446	4481	682	1252	218	71	26	530	714	99	212	3	.279	.386	.377	.764	126	184	758	5.92	-33	C-974,0-281/3-42,1-33,2,P,S	231	24.3

• BRESSLER, Rube Raymond Bloom Bressler b: 10/23/1894, Coder, PA d: 11/7/1966, Mount Washington, OH BR/TL, 6', 187 lbs. Deb: 4/24/1914 Career OF: 732-8-99 ◆

YEAR TM-L	G	AB	R	H	2B	3B	HR	RBI	BB	SO	SB	CS	AVG	OBP	SLG	OPS	OPS+	BR/A	RC	RC/G	FR	G/POS	WS	TPW
1914 Phi-A	29	51	6	11	1	1	0	4	6	7	0	....	.216	.310	.275	.585	79	4	5	2.97	-2	P-29	14	1.9
1915 Phi-A	33	55	9	8	0	1	1	4	9	13	0	....	.145	.277	.236	.513	56	2	4	2.18	0	P-32	1	-4.5
1916 Phi-A	4	5	1	1	0	1	0	1	0	0	0	....	.200	.200	.600	.800	147	1	1	3.34	-1	/P-4	0	-0.6
1917 Cin-N	3	5	0	1	0	0	0	0	0	2	0	....	.200	.200	.200	.400	24	-0	0	1.17	0	/P-2	0	-0.4
1918 Cin-N	23	62	10	17	5	0	0	6	5	4	0	....	.274	.328	.355	.683	110	4	7	3.94	2	P-17/0-3(3-0-1)	9	0.6
1919 Cin-N	61	165	22	34	3	4	2	17	23	15	2	....	.206	.311	.309	.620	89	-0	17	3.12	0	0-48(41-0-7),P-13	6	-0.8
1920 Cin-N	21	30	4	8	1	0	0	3	1	4	1	0	.267	.290	.300	.590	71	-0	3	3.20	-1	P-10/0-3(0-1-2),1-2	2	0.2
1921 Cin-N	109	323	41	99	18	6	1	54	39	20	5	5	.307	.385	.409	.793	115	9	52	5.64	-7	0-85(9-0-76)/1-6	10	-0.4
1922 Cin-N	52	53	7	14	0	2	0	8	4	4	1	0	.264	.316	.340	.655	70	-2	6	3.96	-1	/1-3,0-2(1-0-1)	1	-0.3
1923 Cin-N	54	119	25	33	3	1	0	18	20	4	3	1	.277	.399	.319	.718	93	1	17	5.17	-2	1-22/0-6(3-0-3)	4	-0.2
1924 Cin-N	115	383	41	133	14	13	4	49	22	20	9	10	.347	.389	.483	.872	134	17	69	6.85	5	1-50,0-49(45-0-4)	15	1.4
1925 Cin-N	97	319	43	111	17	6	4	61	40	16	9	5	.348	.424	.476	.900	133	18	66	7.96	-3	1-52,0-38(36-0-2)	14	0.8
1926 Cin-N	86	297	58	106	15	9	1	51	37	20	3	....	.357	.433	.478	.911	149	22	61	7.83	-1	0-80(80-0-0)/1-4	15	1.5
1927 Cin-N	124	467	43	136	14	8	3	77	32	22	4	....	.291	.338	.375	.713	93	-5	58	4.28	8	*0-120(120-0-0)	12	-0.6
1928 Bro-N	145	501	78	148	29	13	4	70	80	33	2	....	.295	.398	.429	.827	118	16	88	6.09	-6	*0-137(137-0-0)	18	0.0
1929 Bro-N	136	456	72	145	22	8	9	77	67	27	4	....	.318	.406	.461	.867	117	14	86	6.88	-1	*0-122(122-0-0)	14	0.3
1930 Bro-N	109	335	53	100	12	8	3	52	51	19	4	....	.299	.394	.409	.803	96	0	56	5.87	8	0-90(90-0-0)/1-7	10	0.0
1931 Bro-N	67	153	22	43	4	5	0	26	11	10	0	....	.281	.329	.373	.702	89	-2	19	4.44	0	0-35(23-7-3)/1-1	3	-0.3
1932 Phi-N	27	83	9	19	6	1	0	6	2	5	0	....	.229	.247	.325	.572	47	-6	7	2.66	3	0-18(18-0-0)	1	-0.4
StL-N	10	19	0	3	0	0	0	2	0	1	0	....	.158	.158	.158	.316	-14	-3	1	.81	0	/0-4(4-0-0)	0	-0.3
Yr.	37	102	9	22	6	1	0	8	2	6	0	....	.216	.231	.294	.525	35	-9	7	2.26	3	0-22(22-0-0)	1	-0.8
Total 19	1305	3881	544	1170	164	87	32	586	449	246	47	21	.301	.378	.413	.791	110	88	623	5.68	1	0-840,1-147,P-107	149	-2.2

• BRESSOUD, Eddie Edward Francis Bressoud b: 5/2/1932, Los Angeles, CA BR/TR, 6'1", 175 lbs. Deb: 6/14/1956

YEAR TM-L	G	AB	R	H	2B	3B	HR	RBI	BB	SO	SB	CS	AVG	OBP	SLG	OPS	OPS+	BR/A	RC	RC/G	FR	G/POS	WS	TPW
1956 NY-N	49	163	15	37	4	2	0	9	12	20	1	0	.227	.284	.276	.560	52	-11	13	2.61	-5	S-48	1	-1.2
1957 NY-N	49	127	11	34	2	2	5	10	4	19	0	1	.268	.301	.433	.734	94	-2	16	4.29	-5	S-33,3-12	3	-0.4
1958 SF-N	66	137	19	36	5	3	0	8	14	22	0	1	.263	.331	.343	.674	81	-4	16	4.00	-7	2-57/3-6,S-4	3	-0.8
1959 SF-N	104	315	36	79	17	2	9	26	28	55	0	0	.251	.312	.403	.715	91	-5	40	4.39	-2	S-92/1-1,2-1,3-1	8	0.1
1960 SF-N	116	386	37	87	19	6	9	43	35	72	1	2	.225	.293	.376	.669	87	-8	41	3.44	1	*S-115	11	0.2
1961 SF-N	59	114	14	24	6	0	3	11	11	23	1	1	.211	.280	.342	.622	66	-6	9	2.53	-1	S-34/3-3,2-1	1	-0.5
1962 Bos-A	153	599	79	166	40	9	14	68	46	118	2	3	.277	.331	.444	.775	103	0	85	4.99	14	*S-153	21	2.8
1963 Bos-A	140	497	61	129	23	6	20	60	52	93	1	1	.260	.332	.451	.783	113	8	75	5.24	-8	*S-137	17	1.3
1964 Bos-A★	158	566	86	166	41	3	15	55	72	99	1	1	.293	.374	.456	.830	123	20	99	6.46	-18	*S-158	25	1.6
1965 Bos-A	107	296	29	67	11	1	8	25	29	77	0	1	.226	.298	.351	.649	79	-9	32	3.65	-1	S-86/3-2,0-1	6	-0.3
1966 NY-N	133	405	48	91	15	5	10	49	47	107	2	2	.225	.307	.360	.667	87	-7	45	3.56	-5	S-94,3-32/1-9,2-7	11	-0.6
1967*StL-N	52	67	8	9	1	1	1	1	9	18	0	0	.134	.237	.224	.461	33	-6	4	1.88	-1	S-48/3-1	1	-0.5
Total 12	1186	3672	443	925	184	40	94	365	359	723	9	13	.252	.321	.401	.721	95	-28	474	4.42	-38	*S-1002/2-66,3-57,1-10,0-1	108	1.7

• BRETON, Jim John Frederick Breton b: 7/15/1891, Chicago, IL d: 5/30/1973, Beloit, WI BR/TR, 5'10.5", 178 lbs. Deb: 8/25/1913

YEAR TM-L	G	AB	R	H	2B	3B	HR	RBI	BB	SO	SB	CS	AVG	OBP	SLG	OPS	OPS+	BR/A	RC	RC/G	FR	G/POS	WS	TPW
1913 Chi-A	12	30	1	5	1	1	0	2	1	5	0	....	.167	.194	.267	.460	35	-3	1	1.46	2	/S-7,3-3	1	0.0
1914 Chi-A	81	231	21	49	7	2	0	24	24	42	9	6	.212	.292	.260	.552	67	-10	20	2.65	-9	3-79	3	-1.8
1915 Chi-A	16	36	3	5	1	0	0	1	5	9	2	1	.139	.262	.167	.429	27	-3	3	1.82	-3	3-14/2-1,S-1	0	-0.6
Total 3	109	297	25	59	9	3	0	27	30	56	11	7	.199	.279	.249	.528	59	-16	24	2.41	-10	/3-96,S-8,2-1	4	-2.4

• BRETT, George George Howard Brett b: 5/15/1953, Glen Dale, WV BL/TR, 6', 200 lbs. Deb: 8/2/1973 HOF: 1999 Career OF: 22-0-14

YEAR TM-L	G	AB	R	H	2B	3B	HR	RBI	BB	SO	SB	CS	AVG	OBP	SLG	OPS	OPS+	BR/A	RC	RC/G	FR	G/POS	WS	TPW
1973 KC-A	13	40	2	5	2	0	0	0	0	5	0	0	.125	.125	.175	.300	-15	-6	1	.69	-1	3-13	0	-0.8
1974 KC-A	133	457	49	129	21	5	2	47	21	38	8	5	.282	.314	.363	.677	89	-7	50	3.86	-9	*3-132/S-1	9	-1.7
1975 KC-A	159	634	84	**195**	35	**13**	11	89	46	49	13	10	.308	.356	.456	.812	125	18	102	5.81	-7	*3-159/S-1	25	1.0
1976*KC-A★	159	645	94	**215**	34	**14**	7	67	49	36	21	11	**.333**	.381	.462	.843	145	35	114	6.69	5	*3-157/S-4	**33**	4.3
1977*KC-A★	139	564	105	176	32	13	22	88	55	24	14	12	.312	.375	.532	.907	143	31	108	6.95	23	*3-135/D-3,S-1	29	5.2
1978*KC-A★	128	510	79	150	**45**	8	9	62	39	35	23	7	.294	.345	.467	.812	123	17	83	5.91	21	*3-128/S-1	23	3.8
1979 KC-A★	154	645	119	**212**	42	**20**	23	107	51	36	17	10	.329	.378	.563	.941	147	40	134	7.95	28	*3-149/1-8,D-1	33	**6.4**
1980*KC-A★	117	449	87	175	33	9	24	118	58	22	15	6	**.390**	**.461**	**.664**	**1.124**	**202**	**65**	135	**12.24**	10	*3-112/1-1	**36**	**7.4**
1981*KC-A★	89	347	42	109	27	7	6	43	27	23	14	6	.314	.365	.484	.849	144	19	60	6.33	-1	3-88	14	1.8
1982 KC-A★	144	552	101	166	32	9	21	82	71	51	6	1	.301	.381	.505	.887	141	33	107	7.17	7	*3-134,0-12(12-0-0)	27	3.8
1983 KC-A★	123	464	90	144	38	2	25	93	57	39	0	1	.310	.387	**.563**	**.949**	157	36	100	8.13	-11	*3-102,1-14,0-13(6-0-7)/D-1	24	2.3
1984*KC-A★	104	377	42	107	21	3	13	69	38	37	0	2	.284	.349	.459	.808	121	10	58	5.39	4	*3-101	14	1.3
1985*KC-A★	155	550	108	184	38	5	30	112	103	49	9	1	.335	.442	**.585**	**1.028**	**178**	**66**	146	**10.17**	1	*3-152/D-1	37	6.4
1986 KC-A★	124	441	70	128	28	4	16	73	80	45	1	2	.290	.404	.481	.885	137	26	89	7.42	-1	*3-115/D-7,S-2	19	2.3
1987 KC-A	115	427	71	124	18	2	22	78	72	47	6	3	.290	.394	.496	.890	131	21	85	7.08	-4	1-83,D-21,3-11	15	1.1
1988 KC-A★	157	589	90	180	42	3	24	103	82	51	14	3	.306	.393	.509	.903	149	42	119	7.43	-6	*1-124,D-33/S-1	26	2.6
1989 KC-A	124	457	67	129	26	3	12	80	59	47	14	4	.282	.368	.431	.799	125	18	71	5.33	6	*1-104,D-17/0-2(2-0-0)	17	1.6
1990 KC-A	142	544	82	179	**45**	7	14	87	56	63	9	2	**.329**	.392	.515	.906	154	40	106	7.30	0	*1-102,D-32/0-9(2-0-7),3-1	26	3.2
1991 KC-A	131	505	77	129	40	2	10	61	58	75	2	0	.255	.332	.402	.734	102	2	65	4.31	-1	*D-118,1-10	8	-0.4
1992 KC-A	152	592	55	169	35	5	7	61	35	69	8	6	.285	.332	.397	.729	101	-1	74	4.48	0	*D-132,1-15/3-3	11	-0.8
1993 KC-A	145	560	69	149	31	3	19	75	39	67	7	5	.266	.317	.434	.751	94	-7	71	4.28	0	*D-140	6	-1.6
Total 21	2707	10349	1583	3154	665	137	317	1595	1096	908	201	97	.305	.373	.487	.861	135	496	1878	6.61	65	*3-1692,D-506,1-461/0-36,S	432	49.1

YEAR TM-L	G	AB	R	H	2B	3B	HR	RBI	BB	SO	SB	CS	AVG	OBP	SLG	OPS	OPS+	BR/A	RC	RC/G	FR	G/POS	WS	TPW
• BREWER, Mike	Michael Quinn Brewer b: 10/24/1959, Shreveport, LA BR/TR, 6'5", 190 lbs. Deb: 6/11/1986																							
1986 KC-A	12	18	0	3	1	0	0	0	2	6	0	1	.167	.250	.222	.472	29	-2	1	1.53	0	/0-9(0-0-9),D-1	0	-0.3
• BREWER, Rod	Rodney Lee Brewer b: 2/24/1966, Eustis, FL BL/TL, 6'3", 210 lbs. Deb: 9/5/1990 Career OF: 19-0-22																							
1990 StL-N	14	25	4	6	1	0	0	2	0	4	0	0	.240	.240	.280	.520	42	-2	1	1.89	1	/1-9	0	-0.2
1991 StL-N	19	13	0	1	0	0	0	1	0	5	0	0	.077	.077	.077	.154	-56	-3	0	.17	-1	1-15/0-3(0-0-3)	0	-0.4
1992 StL-N	29	103	11	31	6	0	0	10	8	12	0	1	.301	.357	.359	.716	107	1	13	4.83	2	1-27/0-4(4-0-0)	3	0.1
1993 StL-N	110	147	15	42	8	0	2	20	17	26	1	0	.286	.364	.381	.745	102	1	20	4.78	-2	0-33(15-0-19),1-32/P-1	4	-0.8
Total 4	**172**	**288**	**30**	**80**	**15**	**0**	**2**	**33**	**25**	**47**	**1**	**1**	**.278**	**.340**	**.351**	**.690**	**92**	**-3**	**35**	**4.28**	**0**	**/1-83,0-40,P-1**	**7**	**-1.3**
• BREWER, Tony	Anthony Bruce Brewer b: 11/25/1957, Coushatta, LA BR/TR, 5'11", 190 lbs. Deb: 8/1/1984																							
1984 LA-N	24	37	3	4	1	0	1	4	4	9	1	0	.108	.195	.216	.411	16	-4	2	1.26	-0	0-10(8-0-2)	0	-0.5
• BREWSTER, Charlie	Charles Lawrence Brewster b: 12/27/1916, Marthaville, LA d: 10/1/2000, Alma, GA BR/TR, 5'8.5", 175 lbs. Deb: 5/2/1943																							
1943 Cin-N	7	8	0	1	0	0	0	0	0	1	0	....	.125	.125	.125	.250	-28	-1	0	.57	0	/2-2	0	-0.1
Phi-N	49	159	13	35	2	0	0	12	10	19	1	....	.220	.275	.233	.508	49	-10	11	2.25	-14	S-46	0	-2.2
Yr.	56	167	13	36	2	0	0	12	10	20	1	....	.216	.268	.228	.496	45	-12	11	2.16	-14	S-46/2-2	0	-2.3
1944 Chi-N	10	44	4	11	2	0	0	2	5	7	0	....	.250	.327	.295	.622	76	-1	4	3.48	-1	S-10	1	-0.2
1946 Cle-A	3	2	0	0	0	0	0	0	1	1	0	0	.000	.333	.000	.333	-1	-0	0	1.17	0	/S-1	0	0.0
Total 3	**69**	**213**	**17**	**47**	**4**	**0**	**0**	**14**	**16**	**28**	**1**	**0**	**.221**	**.281**	**.239**	**.521**	**51**	**-13**	**15**	**2.40**	**-15**	**/S-57,2-2**	**1**	**-2.5**
• BRICKELL, Fred	George Frederick Brickell b: 11/9/1906, Saffordville, KS d: 4/8/1961, Wichita, KS BL/TR, 5'7", 160 lbs. Deb: 8/19/1926 Career OF: 89-236-23																							
1926 Pit-N	24	55	11	19	3	1	0	4	3	6	0	....	.345	.400	.436	.836	119	2	9	6.80	1	0-14(14-0-0)	2	0.1
1927*Pit-N	32	21	6	6	1	0	1	4	1	0	0	....	.286	.318	.476	.794	103	-0	3	4.93	0	/0-3(1-0-2)	0	0.0
1928 Pit-N	81	202	34	65	4	4	3	41	20	18	5	....	.322	.383	.426	.809	107	2	33	6.04	1	0-50(44-0-8)	7	0.0
1929 Pit-N	60	118	13	37	4	2	0	17	7	12	3	....	.314	.352	.381	.733	80	-4	15	4.82	1	0-27(14-0-13)	3	-0.5
1930 Pit-N	68	219	36	65	9	3	1	14	15	20	3	....	.297	.342	.379	.721	74	-9	28	4.52	-2	0-61(11-50-0)	4	-1.2
Phi-N	53	240	33	59	12	6	0	17	13	21	1	....	.246	.290	.346	.636	49	-21	24	3.34	1	0-53(0-53-0)	1	-1.9
Yr.	121	459	69	124	21	9	1	31	28	41	4	....	.270	.315	.362	.677	61	-30	51	3.89	-1	*0-114(11-103-0)	5	-3.1
1931 Phi-N	130	514	77	130	14	5	1	31	42	39	5	....	.253	.316	.305	.621	63	-26	52	3.50	-2	*0-122(0-122-0)	7	-3.1
1932 Phi-N	45	66	9	22	6	1	0	2	4	5	2	....	.333	.389	.455	.843	112	1	12	7.05	-0	0-12(1-11-0)	2	0.1
1933 Phi-N	8	13	2	4	1	1	0	1	1	0	0	....	.308	.357	.538	.896	136	1	3	7.97	1	/0-4(4-0-0)	0	0.1
Total 8	**501**	**1448**	**221**	**407**	**54**	**23**	**6**	**131**	**106**	**121**	**19**	**....**	**.281**	**.335**	**.363**	**.697**	**75**	**-54**	**178**	**4.39**	**0**	**0-346**	**26**	**-6.4**
• BRICKELL, Fritz	Fritz Darrell Brickell b: 3/19/1935, Wichita, KS d: 10/15/1965, Wichita, KS BR/TR, 5'5.5", 157 lbs. Deb: 4/30/1958																							
1958 NY-A	2	0	0	0	0	0	0	0	0	0	0	0	....	....	....	....	-104	0	0	....	-1	/2-2	0	-0.1
1959 NY-A	18	39	4	10	1	0	1	4	1	10	0	0	.256	.275	.359	.634	75	-1	4	3.14	-3	S-15/2-3	1	-0.4
1961 LA-A	21	49	3	6	0	0	0	3	6	9	0	0	.122	.218	.122	.341	-6	-7	1	.63	-3	S-17	0	-0.9
Total 3	**41**	**88**	**7**	**16**	**1**	**0**	**1**	**7**	**7**	**19**	**0**	**0**	**.182**	**.242**	**.227**	**.469**	**29**	**-9**	**5**	**1.63**	**-7**	**/S-32,2-5**	**1**	**-1.4**
• BRICKLEY, George	George Vincent Brickley b: 7/19/1894, Everett, MA d: 2/23/1947, Everett, MA BR/TR, 5'9", 180 lbs. Deb: 9/26/1913																							
1913 Phi-A	5	12	0	2	0	1	0	0	0	4	0	....	.167	.231	.333	.564	66	-1	1	2.17	0	/0-4(0-0-4)	0	-0.1
• BRIDEWESER, Jim	James Ehrenfeld Brideweser b: 2/13/1927, Lancaster, OH d: 8/25/1989, El Toro, CA BR/TR, 6', 165 lbs. Deb: 9/29/1951																							
1951 NY-A	2	8	1	3	0	0	0	0	0	1	0	0	.375	.375	.375	.750	107	0	1	6.23	0	/S-2	0	0.0
1952 NY-A	42	38	12	10	0	0	0	2	3	5	0	0	.263	.317	.263	.580	67	-2	3	2.66	-4	S-22/2-4,3-1	1	-0.5
1953 NY-A	7	3	3	3	0	1	0	3	1	0	0	0	1.000	1.000	1.667	2.667	631	2	5	∞	-1	/S-3	1	0.1
1954 Bal-A	73	204	18	54	7	2	0	12	15	27	1	1	.265	.318	.319	.637	81	-6	20	3.48	-3	S-48,2-19	4	-0.4
1955 Chi-A	34	58	6	12	3	2	0	4	3	7	0	0	.207	.246	.328	.573	52	-4	4	2.10	-1	S-26/3-3,2-2	1	-0.4
1956 Chi-A	10	11	0	2	1	0	0	1	0	3	0	0	.182	.250	.273	.523	37	-1	1	2.45	0	S-10	0	-0.1
Det-A	70	156	23	34	4	0	0	10	20	19	3	1	.218	.307	.244	.550	47	-11	13	2.60	2	S-32,2-31/3-4	2	-0.5
Yr.	80	167	23	36	5	0	0	11	20	22	3	1	.216	.303	.246	.549	46	-12	13	2.59	2	S-42,2-31/3-4	2	-0.6
1957 Bal-A	91	142	16	38	7	1	1	18	21	15	2	0	.268	.362	.352	.714	102	2	19	4.49	-1	S-74/3-3,2-1	6	0.5
Total 7	**329**	**620**	**79**	**156**	**22**	**6**	**1**	**50**	**63**	**77**	**6**	**2**	**.252**	**.323**	**.311**	**.634**	**76**	**-19**	**66**	**3.30**	**-9**	**S-217/2-57,3-11**	**15**	**-1.4**
• BRIDGES, Rocky	Everett Lamar Bridges b: 8/7/1927, Refugio, TX BR/TR, 5'8", 175 lbs. Deb: 4/17/1951 C																							
1951 Bro-N	63	134	13	34	7	0	1	15	10	10	0	0	.254	.306	.328	.634	69	-6	12	2.83	-4	3-40,2-10/S-9	1	-0.9
1952 Bro-N	51	56	9	11	3	0	0	2	7	9	0	1	.196	.286	.250	.536	49	-4	4	2.13	0	2-24,S-13/3-6	1	-0.3
1953 Cin-N	122	432	52	98	13	2	1	21	37	42	6	3	.227	.288	.273	.561	47	-33	35	2.68	11	*2-115/S-6,3-3	5	-1.3
1954 Cin-N	53	52	4	12	1	0	0	2	7	7	0	1	.231	.322	.250	.572	50	-4	4	2.71	-2	S-20,2-19,3-13	1	-0.5
1955 Cin-N	95	168	20	48	4	0	1	18	15	19	1	1	.286	.344	.327	.672	75	-6	19	3.91	-2	3-59,S-26/2-9	3	-0.7
1956 Cin-N	71	19	9	4	0	0	0	1	4	3	1	2	.211	.348	.211	.558	52	-2	1	2.30	-12	3-51/2-8,S-7,0-1	0	-1.4
1957 Cin-N	5	1	1	0	0	0	0	0	1	1	0	0	.000	.500	.000	.500	46	0	0	3.51	-2	/2-2,3-1,S-1	0	-0.1
Was-A	120	391	40	89	17	2	3	47	40	32	0	2	.228	.303	.304	.607	67	-18	34	2.75	8	*S-108,2-14/3-1	7	0.0
1958 Was-A★	116	377	38	99	14	3	5	28	27	32	0	3	.263	.317	.355	.672	86	-8	38	3.45	6	*S-112/2-3,3-3	11	0.6
1959 Det-A	116	381	38	102	16	3	3	35	30	35	1	2	.268	.323	.349	.672	80	-11	40	3.60	10	*S-110/2-5	9	0.8
1960 Det-A	10	5	0	1	0	0	0	0	0	0	0	0	.200	.200	.200	.400	8	-1	0	.00	0	/3-7,S-3	0	0.0
Cle-A	10	27	1	9	0	0	0	3	1	2	0	0	.333	.357	.333	.690	91	-0	3	3.99	-0	/S-7,3-3	1	0.0
Yr.	20	32	1	10	0	0	0	3	1	2	0	0	.313	.333	.313	.646	79	-1	3	3.19	0	3-10,S-10	1	0.0
StL-N	3	0	0	0	0	0	0	0	0	0	0	0	....	....	....	....	-92	0	0	....	0	/2-3	0	0.0
1961 LA-A	84	229	20	55	5	1	2	15	26	37	1	0	.240	.320	.297	.617	59	-13	23	3.45	-1	2-58,S-25/3-4	4	-0.7
Total 11	**919**	**2272**	**245**	**562**	**80**	**11**	**16**	**187**	**205**	**229**	**10**	**15**	**.247**	**.312**	**.313**	**.625**	**68**	**-105**	**215**	**3.13**	**10**	**S-447,2-270,3-191/0-1**	**43**	**-4.7**
• BRIDWELL, Al	Albert Henry Bridwell b: 1/4/1884, Friendship, OH d: 1/23/1969, Portsmouth, OH BL/TR, 5'9", 170 lbs. Deb: 4/16/1905 Career OF: 3-2-14																							
1905 Cin-N	82	254	17	64	3	1	0	17	19	....	8	....	.252	.309	.272	.581	66	-10	26	3.35	0	3-43,0-18(3-2-13)/2-7,S-5,1	4	-1.0
1906 Bos-N	120	459	41	104	9	1	0	22	44	....	6	....	.227	.297	.251	.548	73	-13	39	2.74	1	*S-119/0-1	7	-1.0
1907 Bos-N	140	509	49	111	8	2	0	26	61	....	17	....	.218	.309	.242	.551	73	-13	46	2.92	-9	*S-140	11	-2.0
1908 NY-N	147	467	53	133	14	1	0	46	52	....	20	....	.285	.364	.319	.683	113	10	63	4.61	1	*S-147	24	1.8
1909 NY-N	145	476	59	140	11	5	0	55	67	....	32	....	.294	.386	.338	.724	123	17	75	5.53	-4	*S-145	24	1.9
1910 NY-N	142	492	74	136	15	7	0	48	73	23	14	....	.276	.374	.335	.710	107	8	68	4.73	3	*S-141	22	1.6
1911 NY-N	76	263	28	71	10	1	0	31	33	10	8	....	.270	.358	.316	.673	87	-3	33	4.27	1	S-76	10	0.3
Bos-N	51	182	29	53	5	0	0	10	33	8	2	....	.291	.403	.319	.721	95	1	25	4.76	-7	S-51	5	-0.3
Yr.	127	445	57	124	15	1	0	41	66	18	10	....	.279	.377	.317	.694	90	-2	59	4.47	-7	*S-127	15	0.0
1912 Bos-N	31	106	6	25	5	1	0	14	5	5	2	....	.236	.270	.302	.572	55	-7	9	2.75	-7	S-31	1	-1.1
1913 Chi-N	136	405	35	97	6	6	1	37	74	28	12	....	.240	.358	.291	.650	86	-3	47	3.68	-1	*S-136	15	0.5
1914 StL-F	117	381	46	90	6	5	1	33	71	18	9	....	.236	.359	.286	.645	80	-6	45	3.61	-1	*S-103,2-11	11	0.0
1915 StL-F	65	175	20	40	3	2	0	9	25	6	6	....	.229	.328	.269	.597	73	-5	18	3.21	1	2-42,3-15/1-1	4	-0.3
Total 11	**1252**	**4169**	**457**	**1064**	**95**	**32**	**2**	**348**	**557**	**98**	**136**	**....**	**.255**	**.347**	**.295**	**.642**	**90**	**-26**	**495**	**3.91**	**-23**	***S-1094/2-60,3-58,0-19,1-2**	**138**	**0.5**
• BRIEF, Bunny	Anthony Vincent Brief b: 7/3/1892, Remus, MI d: 2/10/1963, Milwaukee, WI BR/TR, 6', 185 lbs. Deb: 9/22/1912 Career OF: 17-0-0																							
1912 StL-A	15	42	9	13	3	0	0	5	6	....	2	....	.310	.408	.381	.789	131	2	8	6.11	-2	/0-9(9-0-0),1-4	1	0.0
1913 StL-A	85	258	24	56	11	6	1	26	21	46	3	....	.217	.284	.318	.602	78	-8	24	2.87	-2	1-62/0-8(8-0-0)	3	-1.2
1915 Chi-A	48	154	13	33	6	2	2	17	16	28	8	6	.214	.305	.318	.623	84	-4	16	3.17	0	1-46	3	-0.5
1917 Pit-N	36	115	15	25	5	1	2	11	15	21	4	....	.217	.318	.330	.649	96	-0	14	3.63	2	1-34	2	0.1
Total 4	**184**	**569**	**61**	**127**	**25**	**9**	**5**	**59**	**58**	**95**	**17**	**6**	**.223**	**.306**	**.325**	**.631**	**88**	**-10**	**62**	**3.33**	**-2**	**1-146/0-17**	**9**	**-1.6**
• BRIGGS, Charlie	Charles R. Briggs b: 9/1860, Batavia, IL d: 3/10/1920, Seattle, WA, 5'7", 170 lbs. Deb: 5/2/1884																							
1884 CP-U	49	182	29	31	8	2	1	....	11	....	....	....	.170	.218	.253	.470	62	-6	10	1.90	-8	0-37(3-28-6),2-12/S-2	1	-1.3
• BRIGGS, Dan	Dan Lee Briggs b: 11/18/1952, Scotia, CA BL/TL, 6', 180 lbs. Deb: 9/10/1975 Career OF: 41-63-30																							
1975 Cal-A	13	31	3	7	1	0	1	3	2	6	0	2	.226	.273	.355	.628	82	-2	2	2.48	-1	/1-6,0-5(5-0-0),D-2	0	-0.4

YEAR	TM-L	G	AB	R	H	2B	3B	HR	RBI	BB	SO	SB	CS	AVG	OBP	SLG	OPS	OPS+	BR/A	RC	RC/G	FR	G/POS	WS	TPW
1976	Cal-A	77	248	19	53	13	2	1	14	13	47	0	3	.214	.256	.294	.550	65	-13	17	2.16	-1	1-44,0-40(2-32-9)/D-1	2	-1.9
1977	Cal-A	59	74	6	12	2	0	1	4	8	14	0	0	.162	.244	.230	.474	31	-7	4	1.62	0	1-45,0-13(0-12-1)	0	-0.8
1978	Cle-A	15	49	4	8	0	1	1	1	4	9	0	0	.163	.226	.265	.492	38	-4	3	1.66	1	0-15(0-0-15)	0	-0.4
1979	SD-N	104	227	34	47	4	3	8	30	18	45	2	1	.207	.280	.357	.637	77	-8	23	3.31	0	1-50,0-44(25-16-3)	3	-1.2
1981	Mon-N	9	11	0	1	0	0	0	0	0	3	0	1	.091	.091	.091	.182	-48	-3	0	.00	0	/1-3,0-3(1-2-1)	0	-0.3
1982	Chi-N	48	48	1	6	0	0	0	1	0	9	0	0	.125	.143	.125	.268	-24	-8	1	.50	0	0-10(8-1-1)/1-4	0	-0.8
Total	7	325	688	67	134	20	6	12	53	45	133	2	7	.195	.251	.294	.545	57	-44	50	2.28	0	1-152,0-130/D-3	5	-5.7

• BRIGGS, Grant Grant Briggs b: 3/16/1865, Pittsburgh, PA d: 5/31/1928, Pittsburgh, PA, 5'11", 170 lbs. Deb: 4/17/1890 Career OF: 6-26-9

YEAR	TM-L	G	AB	R	H	2B	3B	HR	RBI	BB	SO	SB	CS	AVG	OBP	SLG	OPS	OPS+	BR/A	RC	RC/G	FR	G/POS	WS	TPW
1890	Syr-a	86	316	44	57	6	5	0	21	16	....	7	....	.180	.222	.231	.453	37	-24	18	1.86	1	C-46,0-33(4-25-4)/3-5,S-4	2	-1.8
1891	Lou-a	1	4	0	1	0	0	0	0	0	0	0	....	.250	.250	.250	.500	44	-0	0	2.26	0	/C-1	0	0.0
1892	StL-N	22	55	2	4	1	0	0	1	5	16	2	....	.073	.164	.091	.255	-24	-8	1	.62	-2	C-15/0-8(2-1-5)	0	-0.9
1895	Lou-N	1	3	0	0	0	0	0	0	0	1	0	....	.000	.000	.000	.000	-107	-1	0	.00	0	/C-1	0	-0.1
Total	4	110	378	46	62	7	5	0	22	21	17	9	....	.164	.212	.209	.421	27	-33	20	1.64	-1	/C-63,0-41,3-5,S-4	2	-2.8

• BRIGGS, Johnny John Edward Briggs b: 3/10/1944, Paterson, NJ BL/TL, 6'1", 195 lbs. Deb: 4/17/1964 Career OF: 698-294-78

YEAR	TM-L	G	AB	R	H	2B	3B	HR	RBI	BB	SO	SB	CS	AVG	OBP	SLG	OPS	OPS+	BR/A	RC	RC/G	FR	G/POS	WS	TPW
1964	Phi-N	61	66	16	17	2	0	1	6	9	12	1	1	.258	.347	.333	.680	94	-0	8	3.91	-1	0-19(9-9-1)/1-1	2	-0.2
1965	Phi-N	93	229	47	54	9	4	4	23	42	44	3	2	.236	.354	.362	.717	104	3	33	4.92	-3	0-66(4-62-0)	8	-0.3
1966	Phi-N	81	255	43	72	13	5	10	23	41	55	3	2	.282	.382	.490	.872	140	15	50	7.22	-4	0-69(2-68-0)	13	0.9
1967	Phi-N	106	332	47	77	12	4	9	30	41	72	3	5	.232	.316	.373	.690	96	-3	40	4.02	-2	0-94(31-65-1)	9	-0.9
1968	Phi-N	110	338	36	86	13	1	7	31	58	72	8	5	.254	.365	.361	.726	118	10	49	5.01	-4	0-65(10-34-21),1-36	16	0.2
1969	Phi-N	124	361	51	86	20	3	12	46	64	78	9	6	.238	.353	.410	.763	116	9	56	5.34	-3	*0-108(76-32-12)/1-2	13	0.1
1970	Phi-N	110	341	43	92	15	7	9	47	39	65	5	4	.270	.345	.434	.779	110	4	48	4.69	-1	0-95(79-11-15)	9	-0.3
1971	Phi-N	10	22	3	4	1	0	0	3	6	2	0	0	.182	.357	.227	.584	69	-1	2	3.38	0	/0-8(8-0-0)	0	-0.1
	Mil-A	125	375	51	99	11	1	21	59	71	79	1	2	.264	.383	.467	.849	141	22	71	6.66	2	0-65(55-0-11),1-60	18	1.7
1972	Mil-A	135	418	58	111	14	1	21	65	54	67	1	2	.266	.351	.455	.805	141	21	67	5.60	0	*0-106(98-12-0),1-28	20	1.6
1973	Mil-A	142	488	78	120	20	7	18	57	87	83	15	9	.246	.362	.426	.788	124	18	80	5.59	-1	*0-137(137-0-0)/D-1	18	0.8
1974	Mil-A	154	554	72	140	30	8	17	73	71	102	9	7	.253	.338	.428	.765	120	14	82	5.09	-1	*0-149(148-1-0)/D-2	20	0.4
1975	Mil-A	28	74	12	22	1	0	3	5	20	13	0	2	.297	.447	.432	.879	149	6	15	7.58	1	0-21(21-0-0)/D-1	4	0.6
	Min-A	87	264	44	61	9	2	7	39	60	41	6	2	.231	.373	.360	.733	106	6	41	5.25	8	1-49,0-35(20-0-17)/D-2	9	0.8
	Yr.	115	338	56	83	10	2	10	44	80	54	6	4	.246	.390	.376	.766	115	11	56	5.74	9	0-56(41-0-17),1-49/D-3	13	1.4
Total	12	1366	4117	601	1041	170	43	139	507	663	785	64	49	.253	.357	.416	.773	121	123	643	5.37	-10	*0-1037,1-176/D-6	159	5.4

• BRIGHT, Harry Harry James Bright b: 9/22/1929, Kansas City, MO d: 3/13/2000, Sacramento, CA BR/TR, 6', 190 lbs. Deb: 8/7/1958

YEAR	TM-L	G	AB	R	H	2B	3B	HR	RBI	BB	SO	SB	CS	AVG	OBP	SLG	OPS	OPS+	BR/A	RC	RC/G	FR	G/POS	WS	TPW
1958	Pit-N	15	24	4	6	1	0	1	3	1	6	0	0	.250	.280	.417	.697	83	-1	3	4.12	-1	/3-7	1	-0.1
1959	Pit-N	40	48	4	12	1	0	3	8	5	10	0	0	.250	.321	.458	.779	105	0	7	5.47	0	/0-4(3-0-1),3-3,2-1	1	0.0
1960	Pit-N	4	4	0	0	0	0	0	0	0	2	0	0	.000	.000	.000	.000	-99	-1	0	.00	0	....	0	-0.1
1961	Was-A	72	183	20	44	6	0	4	21	19	23	0	2	.240	.312	.339	.651	78	-7	18	3.31	2	3-40/C-8,2-1	3	-0.4
1962	Was-A	113	392	55	107	15	4	17	67	26	51	2	1	.273	.321	.462	.783	109	3	54	4.80	1	1-99/C-3,3-1	8	-0.1
1963	Cin-N	1	1	0	0	0	0	0	0	0	1	0	0	.000	.000	.000	.000	-97	-0	0	.00	0	/1-1	0	0.0
	*NY-A	60	157	15	37	7	0	7	23	13	31	0	0	.236	.298	.414	.712	98	-1	19	4.04	-6	1-35,3-12	4	-0.9
1964	NY-A	4	5	0	1	0	0	0	0	1	1	0	0	.200	.333	.200	.533	52	-0	0	2.84	0	/1-2	0	-0.1
1965	Chi-N	27	25	1	7	1	0	0	4	0	8	0	0	.280	.280	.320	.600	67	-1	2	3.26	0	....	0	-0.1
Total	8	336	839	99	214	31	4	32	126	65	133	2	3	.255	.311	.416	.727	96	-7	104	4.25	-4	1-137/3-63,C-11,0-4,2-2	17	-1.9

• BRILEY, Greg Gregory "Pee Wee" Briley b: 5/24/1965, Greenville, NC BL/TR, 5'9", 165 lbs. Deb: 6/27/1988 Career OF: 303-18-163

YEAR	TM-L	G	AB	R	H	2B	3B	HR	RBI	BB	SO	SB	CS	AVG	OBP	SLG	OPS	OPS+	BR/A	RC	RC/G	FR	G/POS	WS	TPW
1988	Sea-A	13	36	6	9	2	0	1	4	5	6	0	1	.250	.341	.389	.730	100	-0	5	4.48	-1	0-11(11-0-0)	0	-0.1
1989	Sea-A	115	394	52	105	22	4	13	52	39	82	11	5	.266	.340	.442	.782	115	8	59	5.15	1	*0-105(96-0-10),2-10/D-2	11	0.6
1990	Sea-A	125	337	40	83	18	2	5	29	37	48	16	4	.246	.323	.356	.679	89	-3	41	4.13	-2	*0-107(43-0-67)/D-4	8	-0.9
1991	Sea-A	139	381	39	99	17	3	2	26	27	51	23	11	.260	.309	.336	.645	78	-11	39	3.47	-1	*0-125(94-4-46)/D-2,2-1,3	6	-1.5
1992	Sea-A	86	200	18	55	10	0	5	12	4	31	9	2	.275	.293	.400	.693	92	-2	23	4.01	-2	0-42(27-13-4),D-12/2-4,3-4	2	-0.5
1993	Fla-N	120	170	17	33	6	0	3	12	12	42	6	2	.194	.251	.282	.534	40	-14	12	2.17	-1	0-67(32-1-36)	1	-1.7
Total	6	598	1518	172	384	75	9	29	135	124	260	65	25	.253	.313	.372	.684	88	-24	178	3.98	-5	0-457/D-20,2-15,3-5	28	-4.1

• BRINKER, Bill William Hutchinson "Dode" Brinker b: 8/30/1883, Warrensburg, MO d: 2/5/1965, Arcadia, CA BB/TR, 6'1", 190 lbs. Deb: 4/24/1912

YEAR	TM-L	G	AB	R	H	2B	3B	HR	RBI	BB	SO	SB	CS	AVG	OBP	SLG	OPS	OPS+	BR/A	RC	RC/G	FR	G/POS	WS	TPW
1912	Phi-N	9	18	1	4	1	0	0	2	2	3	0	....	.222	.300	.278	.578	55	-1	1	2.63	0	/3-2,0-2(1-1-0)	0	-0.1

• BRINKMAN, Chuck Charles Ernest Brinkman b: 9/16/1944, Cincinnati, OH BR/TR, 6'1", 185 lbs. Deb: 7/10/1969

YEAR	TM-L	G	AB	R	H	2B	3B	HR	RBI	BB	SO	SB	CS	AVG	OBP	SLG	OPS	OPS+	BR/A	RC	RC/G	FR	G/POS	WS	TPW
1969	Chi-A	14	15	2	1	0	0	0	0	1	5	0	0	.067	.125	.067	.192	-43	-3	0	.43	0	C-14	0	-0.3
1970	Chi-A	9	20	4	5	1	0	0	0	3	3	0	0	.250	.348	.300	.648	77	-0	2	4.24	0	/C-9	1	0.0
1971	Chi-A	15	20	0	4	0	0	0	1	3	5	0	0	.200	.304	.200	.504	44	-1	1	2.33	0	C-14	0	-0.1
1972	Chi-A	35	52	1	7	0	0	0	0	4	7	0	0	.135	.196	.135	.331		-6	1	.65	1	C-33	1	-0.5
1973	Chi-A	63	139	13	26	6	0	1	10	11	37	0	0	.187	.252	.252	.503	41	-11	9	2.01	5	C-63	3	-0.3
1974	Chi-A	8	14	1	2	0	0	0	0	1	3	0	0	.143	.200	.143	.343		-2	0	.63	0	/C-8	0	-0.2
	Pit-N	4	7	1	1	0	0	0	1	0	0	0	0	.143	.143	.143	.286	-21	-1	0	.73	0	/C-4	0	-0.1
Total	6	148	267	22	46	7	0	1	12	23	60	0	0	.172	.241	.210	.450	28	-25	15	1.69	7	C-145	5	-1.5

• BRINKMAN, Ed Edwin Albert Brinkman b: 12/8/1941, Cincinnati, OH BR/TR, 6', 170 lbs. Deb: 9/6/1961 C

YEAR	TM-L	G	AB	R	H	2B	3B	HR	RBI	BB	SO	SB	CS	AVG	OBP	SLG	OPS	OPS+	BR/A	RC	RC/G	FR	G/POS	WS	TPW
1961	Was-A	4	11	0	1	0	0	0	0	1	1	0	0	.091	.167	.091	.258	-31	-2	0	.57	0	/3-3	0	-0.2
1962	Was-A	54	133	8	22	7	1	0	4	11	28	1	0	.165	.229	.233	.462	25	-14	6	1.49	-6	S-38,3-10	1	-1.7
1963	Was-A	145	514	44	117	20	3	7	45	31	86	5	3	.228	.277	.319	.596	67	-24	46	3.00	1	*S-143	9	-1.1
1964	Was-A	132	447	54	100	20	3	8	34	26	99	2	2	.224	.273	.336	.608	68	-20	41	3.06	3	*S-125	9	-0.7
1965	Was-A	154	444	35	82	13	2	5	35	38	82	1	2	.185	.252	.257	.509	46	-32	28	1.99	-1	*S-150	6	-2.3
1966	Was-A	158	582	42	133	18	9	7	48	29	105	7	9	.229	.265	.326	.592	70	-26	45	2.49	16	*S-158	11	0.3
1967	Was-A	109	320	21	60	9	2	1	18	24	58	1	3	.188	.253	.238	.490	47	-22	20	1.96	8	*S-109	6	-0.6
1968	Was-A	77	193	12	36	3	0	0	6	19	31	0	0	.187	.259	.202	.462	43	-13	10	1.64	-4	S-74/2-2,0-1	2	-1.3
1969	Was-A	151	576	71	153	18	5	2	43	50	42	2	2	.266	.330	.325	.654	88	-9	59	3.49	9	*S-150	16	1.8
1970	Was-A	158	625	63	164	17	2	1	40	60	41	8	9	.262	.332	.301	.633	79	-18	62	3.44	18	*S-157	16	2.0
1971	Det-A	159	527	40	120	18	2	1	37	44	54	1	4	.228	.296	.275	.571	60	-28	42	2.62	11	*S-159	11	0.2
1972	*Det-A	156	516	42	105	19	1	6	49	38	51	0	0	.203	.262	.279	.541	59	-26	37	2.27	6	*S-156	10	-0.2
1973	Det-A★	162	515	55	122	16	4	7	40	34	79	0	1	.237	.285	.324	.610	67	-23	44	2.72	-9	*S-162	7	-1.4
1974	Det-A	153	502	55	111	15	3	14	54	29	71	2	0	.221	.268	.347	.614	73	-18	45	2.96	2	*S-151/3-2	11	0.2
1975	StL-N	28	75	6	18	4	0	1	6	7	10	0	0	.240	.313	.333	.647	77	-2	7	3.25	0	S-24	2	0.1
	Tex-A	1	2	0	0	0	0	0	0	0	1	0	0	.000	.000	.000	.000	-101	-1	0	.00	0	/3-1	0	-0.1
	NY-A	44	63	2	11	4	1	0	2	3	6	0	0	.175	.224	.270	.494	40	-5	3	1.58	-1	S-39/2-3,3-3	1	-0.4
	Yr.	45	65	2	11	4	1	0	2	3	7	0	0	.169	.217	.262	.479	36	-6	3	1.52	-1	S-39/3-4,2-3	1	-0.5
Total	15	1845	6045	550	1355	201	38	60	461	444	845	30	35	.224	.282	.300	.581	65	-283	497	2.68	51	*S-1795/3-19,2-5,0-1	118	-5.5

• BRINKOPF, Leon Leon Clarence Brinkopf b: 10/20/1926, Cape Girardeau, MO d: 7/2/1998, Cape Girardeau, MO BR/TR, 5'11.5", 185 lbs. Deb: 4/18/1952

YEAR	TM-L	G	AB	R	H	2B	3B	HR	RBI	BB	SO	SB	CS	AVG	OBP	SLG	OPS	OPS+	BR/A	RC	RC/G	FR	G/POS	WS	TPW
1952	Chi-N	9	22	1	4	0	0	0	2	4	5	0	0	.182	.308	.182	.490	38	-2	2	2.37	0	/S-6	0	-0.1

• BRIODY, Fatty Charles F. "Alderman" Briody b: 8/13/1858, Lansingburg, NY d: 6/22/1903, Chicago, IL TR, 5'8.5", 190 lbs. Deb: 6/16/1880 U Career OF: 0-2-2

YEAR	TM-L	G	AB	R	H	2B	3B	HR	RBI	BB	SO	SB	CS	AVG	OBP	SLG	OPS	OPS+	BR/A	RC	RC/G	FR	G/POS	WS	TPW
1880	Tro-N	1	4	0	0	0	0	0	0	0	0	....	....	.000	.000	.000	.000	-95	-1	0	.00	-1	/C-1	0	-0.1
1882	Cle-N	53	194	30	50	13	0	0	13	9	13	....	....	.258	.291	.325	.615	100	0	19	3.58	1	C-53	6	0.6
1883	Cle-N	40	145	23	34	5	1	0	10	3	13	....	....	.234	.250	.283	.533	62	-6	11	2.60	1	C-33/2-4,1-2,3-1	3	-0.2
1884	Cle-N	43	148	17	25	6	0	1	12	6	19	....	....	.169	.201	.230	.431	34	-11	7	1.57	8	C-42/0-1	2	0.1
	Cin-U	22	89	11	30	2	2	0	....	1	....	....	....	.337	.344	.404	.749	141	3	13	6.03	2	C-22	5	0.6
1885	StL-N	62	215	14	42	9	0	1	17	12	23	....	....	.195	.238	.251	.489	62	-8	13	2.05	2	C-60/2-1,3-1,0-1	2	-0.1
1886	KC-N	56	215	14	51	10	3	0	29	3	35	0	....	.237	.248	.312	.559	65	-10	17	2.80	7	C-54/0-2(0-1-1),1-1	2	0.1
1887	Det-N	33	137	24	38	6	1	1	26	9	10	6	....	.277	.283	.313	.595	63	-7	13	3.57	5	C-33	4	0.1

YEAR TM-L	G	AB	R	H	2B	3B	HR	RBI	BB	SO	SB	CS	AVG	OBP	SLG	OPS	OPS+	BR/A	RC	RC/G	FR	G/POS	WS	TPW
1888 KC-a	13	48	1	10	1	0	0	8	1	....	0	....	.208	.224	.229	.454	43	-3	3	1.80	-2	C-13	0	-0.4
Total 8	323	1195	134	280	52	7	3	115	44	113	6	....	.234	.257	.292	.548	70	-43	95	2.83	25	C-311/2-5,0-4,1-3,3-2	24	0.7
• BRISTOW, George	George T. Bristow b: 5/1870, Paw Paw, IL TR, 5'10" Deb: 4/15/1899																							
1899 Cle-N	3	8	0	1	1	0	0	0	0	....	0	....	.125	.222	.250	.472	32	-1	0	1.72	0	/0-3(1-0-2)	0	0.0
• BRITO, Bernardo	Bernardo Brito b: 12/4/1963, San Cristobal, Dominican Republic BR/TR, 6'1", 190 lbs. Deb: 9/15/1992 Career OF: 13-0-0																							
1992 Min-A	8	14	1	2	1	0	0	2	0	4	0	1	.143	.143	.214	.357	-1	-2	0	.45	0	/0-3(3-0-0),D-1	0	-0.3
1993 Min-A	27	54	8	13	2	0	4	9	1	20	0	0	.241	.255	.500	.755	97	-1	6	4.14	0	0-10(10-0-0)/D-7	1	-0.1
1995 Min-A	5	5	1	1	0	0	1	1	0	3	0	0	.200	.333	.800	1.133	183	1	1	3.83	0	/D-3	0	0.0
Total 3	40	73	10	16	3	0	5	12	1	27	0	1	.219	.240	.466	.706	85	-3	7	3.27	0	/0-13,D-11	1	-0.3
• BRITO, Jorge	Jorge Manuel (Uceta) Brito b: 6/22/1966, Moncion, Dominican Republic BR/TR, 6'1", 190 lbs. Deb: 4/30/1995																							
1995 Col-N	18	51	5	11	3	0	0	7	2	17	1	0	.216	.259	.275	.534	32	-5	4	2.40	-1	C-18	1	-0.5
1996 Col-N	8	14	1	1	0	0	0	0	1	8	0	0	.071	.235	.071	.307	-12	-2	1	.99	1	/C-8	0	-0.1
Total 2	26	65	6	12	3	0	0	7	3	25	1	0	.185	.254	.231	.484	21	-7	4	2.05	0	/C-26	1	-0.6
• BRITO, Juan	Juan Ramon Brito b: 11/7/1979, Santiago, Dominican Republic BR/TR, 5'11", 205 lbs. Deb: 5/3/2002																							
2002 KC-A	9	23	1	7	2	0	0	1	0	3	0	0	.304	.304	.391	.696	74	-1	2	2.93	-0	/C-9	0	0.0
• BRITO, Tilson	Tilson Manuel (Jiminez) Brito b: 5/28/1972, Santo Domingo, Dominican Republic BR/TR, 6', 175 lbs. Deb: 4/1/1996																							
1996 Tor-A	26	80	10	19	7	0	1	7	10	18	1	1	.238	.344	.363	.707	79	-3	11	4.67	1	2-18/S-5,D-2	2	-0.1
1997 Tor-A	49	126	9	28	3	0	0	8	9	28	1	0	.222	.285	.246	.531	40	-11	9	2.50	2	2-25,3-17/S-8	2	-0.6
Oak-A	17	46	8	13	2	1	2	6	1	10	0	0	.283	.298	.500	.798	106	0	7	5.36	1	3-10/S-6,2-2	2	0.1
Yr.	66	172	17	41	5	1	2	14	10	38	1	0	.238	.288	.314	.602	57	-11	16	3.23	3	2-27,3-27,S-14	4	-0.5
Total 2	92	252	27	60	12	1	3	21	20	56	2	1	.238	.307	.329	.636	65	-13	27	3.69	4	/2-45,3-27,S-19,D-2	6	-0.6
• BRITTAIN, Gus	August Schuster Brittain b: 11/29/1909, Wilmington, NC d: 2/16/1974, Wilmington, NC BR/TR, 5'10", 192 lbs. Deb: 7/22/1937																							
1937 Cin-N	3	6	0	1	0	0	0	0	0	3	0	....	.167	.167	.167	.333	-10	-1	0	.92	0	/C-1	0	-0.1
• BRITTON, Gil	Stephen Gilbert Britton b: 9/21/1891, Parsons, KS d: 6/20/1983, Parsons, KS BR/TR, 5'10", 160 lbs. Deb: 9/20/1913																							
1913 Pit-N	3	12	0	0	0	0	0	0	0	2	0	....	.000	.000	.000	.000	-105	-3	0	.00	0	/S-3	0	-0.3
• BROCK, Greg	Gregory Allen Brock b: 6/14/1957, McMinnville, OR BL/TR, 6'3", 205 lbs. Deb: 9/1/1982																							
1982 LA-N	18	17	1	2	1	0	0	1	1	5	0	0	.118	.167	.176	.343	-4	-2	1	.90	0	/1-3	0	-0.3
1983*LA-N	146	455	64	102	14	2	20	66	83	81	5	1	.224	.345	.396	.741	105	6	64	4.69	3	*1-140	15	0.1
1984 LA-N	88	271	33	61	6	0	14	34	39	37	8	0	.225	.323	.402	.725	104	3	37	4.59	2	1-83	8	0.1
1985*LA-N	129	438	64	110	19	0	21	66	54	72	4	2	.251	.333	.438	.772	118	10	65	5.08	1	*1-122	15	0.3
1986 LA-N	115	325	33	76	13	0	16	52	37	60	2	5	.234	.312	.422	.734	108	1	42	4.28	5	1-99	9	0.1
1987 Mil-A	141	532	81	159	29	3	13	85	57	63	5	4	.299	.373	.438	.811	111	9	88	6.07	-1	*1-141	17	-0.1
1988 Mil-A	115	364	53	77	16	1	6	50	63	48	6	2	.212	.333	.310	.643	81	-7	39	3.47	7	*1-114/D-1	7	-0.8
1989 Mil-A	107	373	40	99	16	0	12	52	43	49	6	1	.265	.346	.405	.751	112	7	53	4.93	-3	*1-100/D-7	10	-0.3
1990 Mil-A	123	367	42	91	23	0	7	50	43	45	4	2	.248	.330	.368	.698	96	-2	46	4.22	-5	*1-115	9	-1.5
1991 Mil-A	31	60	9	17	4	0	1	6	14	9	1	1	.283	.419	.400	.819	131	3	11	6.45	-1	1-25	3	0.2
Total 10	1013	3202	420	794	141	6	110	462	434	469	41	18	.248	.340	.399	.739	105	28	446	4.74	8	1-942/D-8	93	-2.2
• BROCK, John	John Roy Brock b: 10/16/1896, Hamilton, IL d: 10/27/1951, Clayton, MO BR/TR, 5'6.5", 165 lbs. Deb: 8/10/1917																							
1917 StL-N	7	15	4	6	1	0	0	2	0	2	2	....	.400	.400	.467	.867	170	1	3	9.55	0	/C-4	1	0.1
1918 StL-N	27	52	9	11	2	0	0	4	3	10	5	....	.212	.255	.250	.505	56	-3	4	2.61	0	C-18/0-1	0	-0.2
Total 2	34	67	13	17	3	0	0	6	3	12	7	....	.254	.286	.299	.584	80	-2	8	3.81	0	/C-22,0-1	1	-0.1
• BROCK, Lou	Louis Clark Brock b: 6/18/1939, El Dorado, AR BL/TL, 5'11.5", 170 lbs. Deb: 9/10/1961 HOF: 1985 Career OF: 2164-115-240																							
1961 Chi-N	4	11	1	1	0	0	0	0	1	3	0	0	.091	.167	.091	.258	-29	-2	0	.57	-1	/0-3(0-3-0)	0	-0.3
1962 Chi-N	123	434	73	114	24	7	9	35	35	96	16	7	.263	.322	.412	.734	92	-5	58	4.67	-1	*0-106(0-106-0)	9	-0.9
1963 Chi-N	148	547	79	141	19	11	9	37	31	122	24	12	.258	.302	.382	.684	91	-7	64	4.07	15	*0-140(0-0-140)	15	-0.2
1964 Chi-N	52	215	30	54	9	2	5	14	13	40	10	3	.251	.300	.340	.640	77	-6	23	3.62	4	0-52(0-2-51)	4	-0.6
*StL-N	103	419	81	146	21	9	12	44	27	87	33	15	.348	.391	.527	.918	143	25	86	7.63	-1	*0-102(99-2-4)	22	1.8
Yr.	155	634	111	200	30	11	14	58	40	127	43	18	.315	.360	.464	.824	121	19	109	6.21	2	*0-154(99-4-55)	26	1.2
1965 StL-N	155	631	107	182	35	8	16	69	45	116	63	27	.288	.345	.445	.791	110	11	99	5.47	-1	*0-153(150-2-7)	22	0.1
1966 StL-N	156	643	94	183	24	12	15	46	31	134	**74**	18	.285	.321	.429	.750	106	13	91	5.07	-3	*0-154(122-0-34)	21	0.0
1967*StL-N★	159	689	**113**	206	32	12	21	76	24	109	**52**	18	.299	.328	.472	.800	128	26	106	5.57	1	*0-157(157-0-0)	30	1.9
1968*StL-N	159	660	92	184	**46**	**14**	6	51	46	124	**62**	12	.279	.329	.418	.747	125	27	98	5.33	-4	*0-156(156-0-0)	31	1.6
1969 StL-N	157	655	97	195	33	10	12	47	50	115	**53**	14	.298	.349	.434	.783	118	20	105	5.92	-6	*0-157(157-0-0)	23	0.5
1970 StL-N	155	664	114	202	29	5	13	57	60	99	51	15	.304	.363	.422	.784	107	11	105	5.77	-4	*0-152(149-0-3)	20	-0.1
1971 StL-N★	157	640	**126**	200	37	7	7	61	76	107	**64**	19	.313	.386	.425	.811	125	29	114	6.61	-11	*0-157(156-0-1)	30	0.9
1972 StL-N★	153	621	81	193	26	8	3	42	47	93	**63**	18	.311	.360	.393	.753	115	19	93	5.48	-8	*0-149(149-0-0)	21	0.2
1973 StL-N	160	650	110	193	29	8	7	63	71	112	**70**	20	.297	.366	.398	.765	112	19	101	5.55	-11	*0-159(159-0-0)	26	-0.1
1974 StL-N★	153	635	105	194	25	7	3	48	61	88	**118**	33	.306	.368	.381	.749	111	21	98	5.44	-1	*0-152(152-0-0)	22	1.3
1975 StL-N★	136	528	78	163	27	6	3	47	38	64	56	16	.309	.359	.400	.758	106	9	79	5.48	-4	*0-128(128-0-0)	18	-0.2
1976 StL-N	133	498	73	150	24	5	4	67	35	75	56	19	.301	.348	.394	.742	109	9	65	4.41	0	*0-123(123-0-0)	13	0.3
1977 StL-N	141	489	69	133	22	6	2	46	30	74	35	24	.272	.317	.354	.670	81	-16	52	3.61	0	*0-130(130-0-0)	9	-2.0
1978 StL-N	92	298	31	66	9	0	0	12	17	29	17	5	.221	.263	.252	.515	45	-21	21	2.30	-3	0-79(79-0-0)	2	-2.8
1979 StL-N★	120	405	56	123	15	4	5	38	23	43	21	12	.304	.346	.398	.743	101	-0	54	4.76	0	0-98(98-0-0)	10	-0.5
Total 19	2616	10332	1610	3023	486	141	149	900	761	1730	938	307	.293	.344	.410	.754	109	181	1512	5.22	-38	*0-2507	348	0.7
• BROCK, Tarrik	Tarrik Jumaan Brock b: 12/25/1973, Goleta, CA BL/TL, 6'3", 185 lbs. Deb: 3/29/2000																							
2000 Chi-N	13	12	1	2	0	0	0	0	4	4	1	1	.167	.375	.167	.542	44	-1	1	2.73	0	0-10(9-2-0)	0	-0.1
• BRODERICK, Matt	Matthew Thomas Broderick b: 12/1/1877, Lattimer, PA d: 2/26/1940, Freeland, PA BR/TR, 5'6.5", 135 lbs. Deb: 5/1/1903																							
1903 Bro-N	2	2	0	0	0	0	0	0	0	....	0	....	.000	.000	.000	.000	-103	-1	0	.00	0	/2-1	0	-0.1
• BRODIE, Steve	Walter Scott Brodie b: 9/11/1868, Warrenton, VA d: 10/30/1935, Baltimore, MD BL/TR, 5'11", 180 lbs. Deb: 4/21/1890 Career OF: 17-1242-168																							
1890 Bos-N	132	514	77	152	19	9	0	67	66	20	29	....	.296	.387	.368	.755	111	9	87	6.34	1	*0-132(2-19-114)	17	0.7
1891 Bos-N	133	523	84	136	13	6	2	78	63	39	25	....	.260	.351	.319	.670	85	-9	69	4.81	3	*0-133(1-102-31)	16	-1.0
1892 StL-N	154	602	85	153	10	9	4	60	52	31	28	....	.254	.318	.321	.638	98	-1	72	4.33	-4	*0-137(1-121-17),2-16/3-2	12	-1.2
1893 StL-N	107	469	71	149	16	8	2	79	33	16	41	....	.318	.376	.399	.775	106	4	88	7.28	3	*0-107(0-102-5)	15	0.0
Bal-N	25	97	18	35	7	2	0	19	12	2	8	....	.361	.446	.474	.921	142	7	25	10.56	0	0-25(2-24-0)	4	0.4
Yr.	132	566	89	184	23	10	2	98	45	18	49	....	.325	.389	.412	.800	112	10	113	7.81	3	*0-132(2-126-5)	19	0.4
1894*Bal-N	129	573	134	210	25	11	3	113	18	8	42	....	.366	.399	.464	.863	103	1	126	9.02	-5	*0-129(0-129-0)	19	-0.9
1895*Bal-N	131	528	85	184	27	10	2	134	26	15	35	....	.348	.394	.449	.843	114	10	111	8.48	4	*0-131(0-131-0)	20	0.4
1896*Bal-N	132	516	98	153	19	11	2	87	36	17	25	....	.297	.363	.388	.751	96	-3	84	6.09	5	*0-132(0-132-0)	16	-0.6
1897 Pit-N	100	370	47	108	7	12	2	53	25	....	11	....	.292	.348	.392	.740	99	-1	57	5.56	-4	*0-100(0-100-0)	10	-0.9
1898 Pit-N	42	156	15	41	5	0	0	21	6	....	3	....	.263	.303	.295	.598	73	-6	16	3.50	1	0-42(0-42-0)	3	-0.7
Bal-N	23	98	12	30	3	2	0	19	5	....	3	....	.306	.346	.378	.724	105	0	14	5.53	1	0-23(0-23-0)	3	0.0
Yr.	65	254	27	71	8	2	0	40	11	....	6	....	.280	.320	.327	.646	85	-5	30	4.23	2	0-65(0-65-0)	6	-0.7
1899 Bal-N	137	531	82	164	26	1	3	87	31	....	19	....	.309	.373	.379	.751	101	1	86	5.95	-7	*0-137(0-136-1)	15	-1.3
1901 Bal-A	83	306	41	95	6	6	2	41	25	....	9	....	.310	.378	.389	.766	108	4	51	6.09	-10	0-83(11-72-0)	9	-0.9
1902 NY-N	110	420	37	118	8	2	3	42	22	....	11	....	.281	.326	.331	.657	104	1	51	4.37	6	*0-109(0-109-0)	11	0.2
Total 12	1438	5703	886	1728	191	89	25	900	420	148	289	....	.303	.365	.381	.745	102	18	937	6.16	-5	*0-1420/2-16,3-2	170	-5.8
• BROGNA, Rico	Rico Joseph Brogna b: 4/18/1970, Turners Falls, MA BL/TL, 6'2", 200 lbs. Deb: 8/8/1992																							
1992 Det-A	9	26	3	5	1	0	1	3	3	5	0	0	.192	.276	.346	.622	73	-1	3	3.47	1	/1-8,D-2	0	-0.1

YEAR TM-L	G	AB	R	H	2B	3B	HR	RBI	BB	SO	SB	CS	AVG	OBP	SLG	OPS	OPS+	BR/A	RC	RC/G	FR	G/POS	WS	TPW
1994 NY-N	39	131	16	46	11	2	7	20	6	29	1	0	.351	.380	.626	1.006	158	10	31	9.40	2	1-35	7	0.9
1995 NY-N	134	495	72	143	27	2	22	76	39	111	0	0	.289	.343	.485	.828	119	12	81	5.96	3	*1-131	15	0.4
1996 NY-N	55	188	18	48	10	1	7	30	19	50	0	0	.255	.324	.431	.755	101	-0	26	4.78	-2	1-52	4	-0.7
1997 Phi-N	148	543	68	137	36	1	20	81	33	116	12	3	.252	.295	.433	.728	88	-11	67	4.26	7	*1-145	11	-1.7
1998 Phi-N	153	565	77	150	36	3	20	104	49	125	7	7	.265	.324	.446	.770	98	-4	78	4.76	10	*1-151	15	-0.8
1999 Phi-N	157	619	90	172	29	4	24	102	54	132	8	5	.278	.338	.454	.792	95	-7	91	5.16	6	*1-157	13	-1.4
2000 Phi-N	38	129	12	32	14	0	1	13	7	28	1	0	.248	.297	.380	.677	69	-6	14	3.67	-1	1-34	1	-0.9
Bos-A	43	56	8	11	3	0	1	8	3	13	0	0	.196	.237	.304	.541	35	-6	4	2.28	-2	1-37/D-2	1	-0.8
2001 Atl-N	72	206	15	51	9	0	3	21	14	46	3	1	.248	.299	.335	.634	62	-11	19	3.05	2	1-67	2	-1.4
Total 9	**848**	**2958**	**379**	**795**	**176**	**13**	**106**	**458**	**227**	**655**	**32**	**16**	**.269**	**.322**	**.445**	**.767**	**97**	**-26**	**413**	**4.89**	**26**	**1-817/D-4**	**69**	**-6.5**

• BROHAMER, Jack John Anthony Brohamer b: 2/26/1950, Maywood, CA BL/TR, 5'10", 165 lbs. Deb: 4/18/1972

YEAR TM-L	G	AB	R	H	2B	3B	HR	RBI	BB	SO	SB	CS	AVG	OBP	SLG	OPS	OPS+	BR/A	RC	RC/G	FR	G/POS	WS	TPW
1972 Cle-A	136	527	49	123	13	2	5	35	27	46	3	2	.233	.272	.294	.566	66	-23	42	2.68	7	*2-132/3-1	10	-0.7
1973 Cle-A	102	300	29	66	12	1	4	29	32	23	0	2	.220	.295	.307	.602	69	-13	28	3.01	2	2-97	6	-0.5
1974 Cle-A	101	315	33	85	11	1	2	30	26	22	2	1	.270	.331	.330	.662	92	-3	36	4.04	11	2-99	11	1.4
1975 Cle-A	69	217	15	53	5	0	6	16	14	14	2	2	.244	.290	.350	.640	80	-7	21	3.27	-3	2-66	4	-0.6
1976 Chi-A	119	354	33	89	12	2	7	40	44	28	1	3	.251	.339	.356	.695	103	1	43	3.98	5	*2-117/3-1	11	1.4
1977 Chi-A	59	152	26	39	10	3	2	20	21	8	0	0	.257	.351	.401	.752	105	2	23	5.19	-1	3-38,2-18/D-1	6	0.1
1978 Bos-A	81	244	34	57	14	1	1	25	25	13	1	3	.234	.305	.311	.616	67	-11	23	3.03	0	3-30,D-25,2-23	3	-1.1
1979 Bos-A	64	192	25	51	7	1	1	11	15	15	0	3	.266	.319	.328	.647	71	-9	18	3.11	-1	2-36,3-22	2	-0.9
1980 Bos-A	21	57	5	18	2	0	1	6	4	3	0	0	.316	.361	.404	.764	104	0	8	5.09	-1	3-13/2-4,D-3	1	-0.1
Cle-A	53	142	13	32	5	1	1	15	14	6	0	1	.225	.295	.296	.591	62	-8	12	2.62	-3	2-47/D-1	1	-0.9
Yr.	74	199	18	50	7	1	2	21	18	9	0	1	.251	.313	.327	.640	74	-7	20	3.25	-4	2-51,3-13/D-4	2	-1.0
Total 9	**805**	**2500**	**262**	**613**	**91**	**12**	**30**	**227**	**222**	**178**	**9**	**17**	**.245**	**.309**	**.327**	**.636**	**80**	**-69**	**253**	**3.38**	**15**	**2-639,3-105/D-30**	**55**	**-1.8**

• BRONKIE, Herman Herman Charles "Dutch" Bronkie b: 3/30/1885, South Manchester, CT d: 5/27/1968, Somers, CT BR/TR, 5'9", 165 lbs. Deb: 9/20/1910

YEAR TM-L	G	AB	R	H	2B	3B	HR	RBI	BB	SO	SB	CS	AVG	OBP	SLG	OPS	OPS+	BR/A	RC	RC/G	FR	G/POS	WS	TPW
1910 Cle-A	5	10	1	2	0	0	0	0	1	....	1	....	.200	.273	.200	.473	48	-1	1	2.54	-3	/3-3,S-1	0	-0.4
1911 Cle-A	2	6	0	1	0	0	0	0	0	....	0	....	.167	.167	.167	.333	-7	-1	0	.78	-1	/3-2	0	-0.1
1912 Cle-A	6	16	1	0	0	0	0	0	1	....	0	....	.000	.059	.000	.059	-80	-4	0	.08	1	/3-6	0	-0.3
1914 Chi-N	1	1	1	1	1	0	0	1	0	0	0	....	1.000	1.000	2.000	3.000	787	1	2	∞	-1	/3-1	0	0.0
1918 StL-N	18	68	7	15	3	0	1	7	2	4	0	....	.221	.243	.309	.552	70	-3	5	2.35	0	3-18	1	-0.3
1919 StL-A	67	196	23	50	6	4	0	14	23	23	2	....	.255	.336	.327	.663	84	-4	22	3.76	3	3-34,2-16/1-2	5	0.1
1922 StL-A	23	64	7	18	4	1	0	2	6	7	0	2	.281	.343	.375	.718	84	-2	8	4.01	0	3-18	1	-0.1
Total 7	**122**	**361**	**40**	**87**	**14**	**5**	**1**	**24**	**33**	**34**	**3**	**2**	**.241**	**.306**	**.316**	**.622**	**74**	**-13**	**38**	**3.22**	**0**	**/3-82,2-16,1-2,S-1**	**7**	**-1.1**

• BROOKENS, Tom Thomas Dale Brookens b: 8/10/1953, Chambersburg, PA BR/TR, 5'10", 170 lbs. Deb: 7/10/1979 Career OF: 0-2-6

YEAR TM-L	G	AB	R	H	2B	3B	HR	RBI	BB	SO	SB	CS	AVG	OBP	SLG	OPS	OPS+	BR/A	RC	RC/G	FR	G/POS	WS	TPW
1979 Det-A	60	190	23	50	5	2	4	21	11	40	10	3	.263	.310	.374	.684	81	-4	23	4.03	4	3-42,2-19/D-1	6	0.0
1980 Det-A	151	509	64	140	25	9	10	66	32	71	13	11	.275	.319	.418	.738	98	-5	64	4.34	4	*3-138/2-9,D-1,S-1	14	-0.2
1981 Det-A	71	239	19	58	10	1	4	25	14	43	5	3	.243	.290	.343	.633	79	-7	23	3.18	0	3-71	5	-0.9
1982 Det-A	140	398	40	92	15	3	9	58	27	63	5	9	.231	.280	.352	.632	72	-19	36	2.92	-1	*3-113,2-26/S-9,0-1	5	-2.0
1983 Det-A	138	332	50	71	13	3	6	32	29	46	10	4	.214	.281	.325	.606	68	-14	32	3.11	0	*3-103,S-30,2-10/D-1	6	-1.3
1984*Det-A	113	224	32	55	11	4	5	26	19	33	6	6	.246	.307	.397	.705	94	-3	27	3.92	0	3-68,S-28,2-26/D-1	7	-0.1
1985 Det-A	156	485	54	115	34	6	7	47	27	78	14	5	.237	.277	.375	.653	77	-16	50	3.42	8	*3-151/S-8,2-3,C-1,D-1	9	-0.9
1986 Det-A	98	281	42	76	11	2	3	25	20	42	11	8	.270	.321	.356	.677	84	-7	32	3.80	-2	3-35,2-31,D-14,S-14/0-3(0-1-3)	6	-0.7
1987*Det-A	143	444	59	107	15	3	13	59	33	63	7	4	.241	.296	.376	.673	80	-14	49	3.67	7	*3-122,S-16,2-11	9	-0.6
1988 Det-A	136	441	62	107	23	5	5	38	44	74	4	4	.243	.316	.351	.667	90	-7	49	3.73	0	*3-136/S-3,2-1	11	-0.6
1989 NY-A	66	168	14	38	6	0	4	14	11	27	1	3	.226	.274	.333	.607	71	-8	14	2.77	-3	3-51/S-7,2-5,D-3,0-3(0-0-3)	1	-1.1
1990 Cle-A	64	154	18	41	7	2	1	20	14	25	0	0	.266	.327	.357	.685	92	-2	18	4.11	-1	3-35,2-21/S-3,1-2,D-1	5	-0.2
Total 12	**1336**	**3865**	**477**	**950**	**175**	**40**	**71**	**431**	**281**	**605**	**86**	**60**	**.246**	**.299**	**.367**	**.666**	**83**	**-106**	**417**	**3.59**	**14**	***3-1065,2-162,S-119/D,0,1,C**	**84**	**-8.6**

• BROOKS, Bobby Robert Brooks b: 11/1/1945, Los Angeles, CA d: 10/11/1994, Harbor City, CA BR/TR, 5'8.5", 165 lbs. Deb: 9/1/1969 Career OF: 21-11-7

YEAR TM-L	G	AB	R	H	2B	3B	HR	RBI	BB	SO	SB	CS	AVG	OBP	SLG	OPS	OPS+	BR/A	RC	RC/G	FR	G/POS	WS	TPW
1969 Oak-A	29	79	13	19	5	0	3	10	20	24	0	2	.241	.400	.418	.818	135	4	15	6.24	1	0-21(16-0-5)	4	0.4
1970 Oak-A	7	18	2	6	1	0	2	5	1	7	0	1	.333	.368	.722	1.091	201	2	4	8.70	0	/0-5(4-0-2)	1	0.2
1972 Oak-A	15	39	4	7	0	0	0	5	8	8	0	1	.179	.319	.179	.499	54	-2	2	1.74	1	0-11(0-11-0)	1	-0.1
1973 Cal-A	4	7	0	1	0	0	0	0	0	3	0	0	.143	.143	.143	.286	-21	-1	0	.64	0	/0-1	0	-0.1
Total 4	**55**	**143**	**19**	**33**	**6**	**0**	**5**	**20**	**29**	**42**	**0**	**4**	**.231**	**.364**	**.378**	**.742**	**114**	**2**	**21**	**4.88**	**2**	**/0-38**	**6**	**0.3**

• BROOKS, Harry Henry Frank Brooks b: 11/30/1865, Philadelphia, PA d: 12/5/1945, Philadelphia, PA Deb: 7/24/1886

YEAR TM-L	G	AB	R	H	2B	3B	HR	RBI	BB	SO	SB	CS	AVG	OBP	SLG	OPS	OPS+	BR/A	RC	RC/G	FR	G/POS	WS	TPW
1886 NY-a	1	1	0	0	0	0	0	0	0	....	0	....	.000	.000	.000	.000	-105	-0	0	.00	-1	/0-1,P-1	0	-0.7

• BROOKS, Hubie Hubert Brooks b: 9/24/1956, Los Angeles, CA BR/TR, 6', 200 lbs. Deb: 9/4/1980 Career OF: 7-0-576

YEAR TM-L	G	AB	R	H	2B	3B	HR	RBI	BB	SO	SB	CS	AVG	OBP	SLG	OPS	OPS+	BR/A	RC	RC/G	FR	G/POS	WS	TPW
1980 NY-N	24	81	8	25	2	1	1	10	5	9	1	1	.309	.364	.395	.759	115	1	12	5.38	2	3-23	3	0.3
1981 NY-N	98	358	34	110	21	2	4	38	23	65	9	5	.307	.351	.411	.761	117	7	50	4.99	-1	3-93/0-3(1-0-2),S-1	11	0.5
1982 NY-N	126	457	40	114	21	2	2	40	28	76	6	3	.249	.300	.317	.617	73	-17	43	3.15	-11	*3-126	6	-3.0
1983 NY-N	150	586	53	147	18	4	5	58	24	96	6	4	.251	.285	.321	.606	68	-27	51	2.95	5	*3-145/2-7	10	-2.5
1984 NY-N	153	561	61	159	23	2	16	73	48	79	6	5	.283	.342	.417	.759	114	8	75	4.78	-13	*3-129,S-26	21	-0.3
1985 Mon-N	156	605	67	163	34	7	13	100	34	79	6	9	.269	.314	.413	.727	108	0	71	3.98	-35	*S-155	15	-1.9
1986 Mon-N★	80	306	50	104	18	5	14	58	25	60	4	2	.340	.393	.569	.962	164	25	65	7.92	-14	S-80	15	2.1
1987 Mon-N★	112	430	57	113	22	3	14	72	24	72	4	3	.263	.303	.426	.729	88	-10	54	4.39	-9	*S-109	11	-0.9
1988 Mon-N	151	588	61	164	35	2	20	90	35	108	7	3	.279	.321	.447	.768	113	7	78	4.64	2	*0-149(0-0-149)	19	0.6
1989 Mon-N	148	542	56	145	30	1	14	70	39	108	6	11	.268	.321	.404	.725	105	-2	65	4.05	4	*0-140(0-0-140)	13	-0.2
1990 LA-N	153	568	74	151	28	1	20	91	33	108	2	5	.266	.313	.424	.737	104	-2	71	4.30	-8	*0-150(0-0-151)	14	-1.4
1991 NY-N	103	357	48	85	11	1	16	50	44	62	3	1	.238	.327	.409	.736	106	3	49	4.63	2	*0-100(0-0-100)	7	0.3
1992 Cal-A	82	306	28	66	13	0	8	36	12	46	3	3	.216	.248	.337	.584	62	-18	22	2.36	0	D-70/1-6	1	-2.2
1993 KC-A	75	168	14	48	12	0	1	24	11	27	0	1	.286	.333	.375	.708	85	-4	20	4.21	1	0-40(6-34)/D-9,1-3	3	-0.5
1994 KC-A	34	61	5	14	2	0	1	14	2	10	1	0	.230	.254	.311	.565	43	-5	5	2.35	0	D-19/1-4	0	-0.6
Total 15	**1645**	**5974**	**656**	**1608**	**290**	**31**	**149**	**824**	**387**	**1005**	**64**	**56**	**.269**	**.318**	**.403**	**.721**	**100**	**-31**	**728**	**4.22**	**-76**	**0-582,3-516,S-371/D-98,1-13,2**	**149**	**-9.6**

• BROOKS, Jerry Jerome Edward Brooks b: 3/23/1967, Syracuse, NY BR/TR, 6', 195 lbs. Deb: 9/6/1993 Career OF: 0-0-4

YEAR TM-L	G	AB	R	H	2B	3B	HR	RBI	BB	SO	SB	CS	AVG	OBP	SLG	OPS	OPS+	BR/A	RC	RC/G	FR	G/POS	WS	TPW
1993 LA-N	9	9	2	2	1	0	1	1	0	2	0	0	.222	.222	.667	.889	135	0	1	5.14	0	/0-2(0-0-2)	0	0.0
1996 Fla-N	8	5	2	2	0	1	0	3	1	1	0	0	.400	.571	.800	1.371	265	1	3	23.25	0	/0-2(0-0-2),1-1	1	0.1
Total 2	**17**	**14**	**4**	**4**	**1**	**1**	**1**	**4**	**1**	**3**	**0**	**0**	**.286**	**.375**	**.714**	**1.089**	**192**	**2**	**4**	**10.57**	**-1**	**/0-4,1-1**	**1**	**0.1**

• BROOKS, Mandy Jonathan Joseph Brooks b: 8/18/1897, Milwaukee, WI d: 6/17/1962, Kirkwood, MO BR/TR, 5'9", 165 lbs. Deb: 5/30/1925 Career OF: 4-94-9

YEAR TM-L	G	AB	R	H	2B	3B	HR	RBI	BB	SO	SB	CS	AVG	OBP	SLG	OPS	OPS+	BR/A	RC	RC/G	FR	G/POS	WS	TPW
1925 Chi-N	90	349	55	98	25	7	14	72	19	28	10	3	.281	.322	.513	.835	108	3	57	5.79	6	0-89(0-89-0)	12	0.5
1926 Chi-N	26	48	7	9	1	0	1	6	5	5	0	....	.188	.278	.271	.549	48	-4	4	2.41	2	0-18(4-5-9)	0	-0.3
Total 2	**116**	**397**	**62**	**107**	**26**	**7**	**15**	**78**	**24**	**33**	**10**	**3**	**.270**	**.316**	**.484**	**.800**	**100**	**-0**	**61**	**5.32**	**7**	**0-107**	**12**	**0.2**

• BROSIUS, Scott Scott David Brosius b: 8/15/1966, Hillsboro, OR BR/TR, 6'1", 185 lbs. Deb: 8/7/1991 Career OF: 37-68-74

YEAR TM-L	G	AB	R	H	2B	3B	HR	RBI	BB	SO	SB	CS	AVG	OBP	SLG	OPS	OPS+	BR/A	RC	RC/G	FR	G/POS	WS	TPW
1991 Oak-A	36	68	9	16	5	0	2	4	3	11	3	1	.235	.268	.397	.665	86	-1	7	3.20	-6	2-18,0-13(5-0-10)/3-7,D-1	1	-0.8
1992 Oak-A	38	87	13	19	2	0	4	13	3	13	3	0	.218	.261	.379	.640	82	-2	9	3.65	-2	0-20(4-0-19),3-12/1-3,D-1,S	2	-0.4
1993 Oak-A	70	213	26	53	10	1	6	25	14	37	6	0	.249	.298	.390	.688	89	-3	25	3.89	-1	0-46(8-34-6),1-11,3-10/S-6,D	5	-0.5
1994 Oak-A	96	324	31	77	14	1	14	49	24	57	2	6	.238	.294	.417	.711	88	-9	37	3.70	2	3-93/0-7(2-2-4),1-1	6	-0.6
1995 Oak-A	123	389	69	102	19	2	17	46	41	67	4	2	.262	.345	.452	.797	112	6	63	5.68	-4	3-60,0-49(8-22-22),1-18/2-3,S,D	10	0.1
1996 Oak-A	114	428	73	130	25	0	22	71	59	85	7	2	.304	.397	.516	.913	132	23	89	7.60	13	*3-109,1-10/0-4(3-2-0)	19	3.4
1997 Oak-A	129	479	59	97	20	1	11	41	34	102	9	4	.203	.261	.317	.578	51	-35	40	2.65	6	*3-107,S-30,0-22(6-6-11)	5	-2.6
1998*NY-A★	152	530	86	159	34	0	19	98	52	97	11	8	.300	.373	.472	.845	122	17	96	6.59	16	*3-150/1-3,0-1	27	3.3
1999*NY-A	133	473	64	117	26	1	17	71	39	74	9	3	.247	.313	.414	.727	84	-12	60	4.23	7	*3-132/D-1	13	-0.3
2000*NY-A	135	470	57	108	20	0	16	64	45	73	0	3	.230	.300	.374	.674	70	-24	49	3.46	7	*3-134/1-2,0-2(1-0-1),D-1	8	-1.4

YEAR TM-L	G	AB	R	H	2B	3B	HR	RBI	BB	SO	SB	CS	AVG	OBP	SLG	OPS	OPS+	BR/A	RC	RC/G	FR	G/POS	WS	TPW
2001*NY-A	120	428	57	123	25	2	13	49	34	83	3	1	.287	.347	.446	.793	106	3	66	5.42	6	*3-120/0-2(0-2-0)	15	1.1
Total 11	1146	3889	544	1001	200	8	141	531	348	699	57	30	.257	.326	.422	.748	95	-38	540	4.75	44	3-934,0-166/1-48,S-40,2-21,D	111	1.3

• BROSKIE, Sig Sigmund Theodore "Chops" Broskie b: 3/23/1911, Iselin, PA d: 5/17/1975, Canton, OH BR/TR, 5'11.5", 200 lbs. Deb: 9/11/1940

YEAR TM-L	G	AB	R	H	2B	3B	HR	RBI	BB	SO	SB	CS	AVG	OBP	SLG	OPS	OPS+	BR/A	RC	RC/G	FR	G/POS	WS	TPW
1940 Bos-N	11	22	1	6	1	0	0	4	1	2	0	....	.273	.304	.318	.623	76	-1	2	3.73	0	C-11	1	0.0

• BROTTEM, Tony Anton Christian Brottem b: 4/30/1892, Halstad, MN d: 8/5/1929, Chicago, IL BR/TR, 6'.5", 176 lbs. Deb: 4/17/1916

YEAR TM-L	G	AB	R	H	2B	3B	HR	RBI	BB	SO	SB	CS	AVG	OBP	SLG	OPS	OPS+	BR/A	RC	RC/G	FR	G/POS	WS	TPW
1916 StL-N	26	33	3	6	1	0	0	4	3	10	1	....	.182	.250	.212	.462	43	-2	2	1.89	1	C-15/0-2(0-1-1)	0	-0.1
1918 StL-N	2	4	0	0	0	0	0	0	1	0	0	....	.000	.200	.000	.200	-39	-1	0	.00	1	/1-2	0	0.0
1921 Was-A	4	7	1	1	0	0	0	0	2	1	0	0	.143	.333	.143	.476	26	-1	0	2.15	0	/C-4	0	0.0
Pit-N	30	91	6	22	2	0	0	9	3	11	0	1	.242	.266	.264	.530	40	-8	6	2.29	-1	C-29	1	-0.7
Total 3	62	135	10	29	3	0	0	13	9	22	1	1	.215	.264	.237	.501	37	-11	9	2.10	1	/C-48,1-2,0-2	1	-0.8

• BROUGHTON, Cal Cecil Calvert Broughton b: 12/28/1860, Magnolia, WI d: 3/15/1939, Evansville, WI BR/TR, 5'10" Deb: 5/2/1883 Career OF: 1-4-1

YEAR TM-L	G	AB	R	H	2B	3B	HR	RBI	BB	SO	SB	CS	AVG	OBP	SLG	OPS	OPS+	BR/A	RC	RC/G	FR	G/POS	WS	TPW
1883 Cle-N	4	10	2	2	0	0	0	1	2	2	....	....	.200	.333	.200	.533	68	-0	1	2.35	0	/C-4	0	0.0
Bal-a	9	32	1	6	0	0	0	0	1	....	....	....	.188	.212	.188	.400	29	-3	1	1.40	-2	/C-8,0-1	0	-0.3
1884 Mil-U	11	39	5	12	5	0	0	....	0	....	....	....	.308	.308	.436	.744	149	2	5	5.56	2	/C-7,0-5(1-4-0)	2	0.4
1885 StL-a	4	17	1	1	0	0	0	1	0	....	....	....	.059	.059	.059	.118	-60	-3	0	.10	-1	/C-4	0	-0.3
NY-a	11	41	1	6	1	0	0	1	1	....	....	....	.146	.167	.171	.337	7	-4	1	.92	-1	C-11	0	-0.3
Yr.	15	58	2	7	1	0	0	2	1	....	....	....	.121	.136	.138	.274	-12	-7	1	.67	-1	C-15	0	-0.7
1888 Det-N	1	4	0	0	0	0	0	0	0	0	0	....	.000	.000	.000	.000	-100	-1	0	.00	1	/C-1	0	0.0
Total 4	40	143	10	27	6	0	0	3	4	2	0	....	.189	.211	.231	.442	44	-9	9	2.06	0	/C-35,0-6	2	-0.6

• BROUHARD, Mark Mark Steven Brouhard b: 5/22/1956, Burbank, CA BR/TR, 6'1", 210 lbs. Deb: 4/12/1980 Career OF: 114-0-110

YEAR TM-L	G	AB	R	H	2B	3B	HR	RBI	BB	SO	SB	CS	AVG	OBP	SLG	OPS	OPS+	BR/A	RC	RC/G	FR	G/POS	WS	TPW
1980 Mil-A	45	125	17	29	6	0	5	16	7	24	1	0	.232	.278	.400	.678	86	-3	13	3.67	0	D-21,0-12(4-0-8),1-10	2	-0.4
1981 Mil-A	60	186	19	51	6	3	2	20	7	41	1	1	.274	.308	.371	.679	100	-1	19	3.54	4	0-51(7-0-46)/D-7	5	0.1
1982*Mil-A	40	108	16	29	4	1	4	10	9	17	0	3	.269	.336	.435	.771	117	1	14	4.40	0	0-30(7-0-23)/D-7	3	0.0
1983 Mil-A	56	185	25	51	10	1	7	23	9	39	0	4	.276	.316	.454	.770	118	2	23	4.16	-2	0-42(38-0-8),D-11	5	-0.2
1984 Mil-A	66	197	20	47	7	0	6	22	16	36	0	3	.239	.302	.365	.668	87	-5	21	3.56	3	0-52(48-0-4)/D-8	3	-0.4
1985 Mil-A	37	108	11	28	7	2	1	13	5	26	0	0	.259	.298	.389	.687	87	-2	12	3.97	-1	0-29(10-0-21)/D-1	2	-0.5
Total 6	304	909	108	235	40	7	25	104	53	183	2	11	.259	.307	.400	.707	100	-8	103	3.84	4	0-216/D-55,1-10	20	-1.5

• BROUSSARD, Ben Benjamin Isaac Broussard b: 9/24/1976, Beaumont, TX BL/TL, 6'2", 220 lbs. Deb: 6/22/2002

YEAR TM-L	G	AB	R	H	2B	3B	HR	RBI	BB	SO	SB	CS	AVG	OBP	SLG	OPS	OPS+	BR/A	RC	RC/G	FR	G/POS	WS	TPW
2002 Cle-A	39	112	10	27	4	0	4	9	7	25	0	0	.241	.292	.384	.676	79	-4	12	3.67	-2	0-32(32-0-0)/1-4,D-3	0	-0.7
2003 Cle-A	116	386	53	96	21	3	16	55	32	75	5	2	.249	.314	.443	.757	100	-1	54	4.81	-4	*1-114	9	-1.4
Total 2	155	498	63	123	25	3	20	64	39	100	5	2	.247	.309	.430	.739	95	-4	66	4.55	-6	1-118/0-32,D-3	9	-2.0

• BROUTHERS, Art Arthur H. Brouthers b: 11/25/1882, Montgomery, AL d: 9/28/1959, Charleston, SC TR, 6'1" Deb: 4/14/1906

YEAR TM-L	G	AB	R	H	2B	3B	HR	RBI	BB	SO	SB	CS	AVG	OBP	SLG	OPS	OPS+	BR/A	RC	RC/G	FR	G/POS	WS	TPW
1906 Phi-A	37	144	18	30	5	1	0	14	5	....	4	....	.208	.240	.257	.497	54	-8	11	2.38	-2	3-35/2-1	1	-1.0

• BROUTHERS, Dan Dennis Joseph "Big Dan" Brouthers b: 5/8/1858, Sylvan Lake, NY d: 8/2/1932, East Orange, NJ BL/TL, 6'2", 207 lbs. Deb: 6/23/1879 HOF: 1945

YEAR TM-L	G	AB	R	H	2B	3B	HR	RBI	BB	SO	SB	CS	AVG	OBP	SLG	OPS	OPS+	BR/A	RC	RC/G	FR	G/POS	WS	TPW
1879 Tro-N	39	168	17	46	12	1	4	17	1	18	....	....	.274	.278	.429	.707	138	7	21	4.71	-7	1-37/P-3	5	-0.7
1880 Tro-N	3	12	0	2	0	0	0	1	1	0	....	....	.167	.231	.167	.397	35	-1	0	1.30	-1	/1-3	0	-0.2
1881 Buf-N	65	270	60	86	18	9	**8**	45	18	22	....	....	.319	.361	**.541**	.902	182	25	54	7.93	-5	0-35(33-0-2),1-30	15	1.6
1882 Buf-N	84	351	71	**129**	23	11	6	63	21	7	....	....	**.368**	**.403**	**.547**	**.950**	**198**	**38**	79	**9.83**	6	*1-84	20	3.4
1883 Buf-N	98	425	85	**159**	41	**17**	3	**97**	16	17	....	....	**.374**	**.397**	**.572**	**.969**	**186**	**42**	99	**10.22**	7	*1-97/3-1,P-1	24	3.0
1884 Buf-N	94	398	82	130	22	15	14	79	33	20	....	....	.327	.378	**.563**	**.941**	**185**	38	87	8.91	4	*1-93/3-1	22	3.0
1885 Buf-N	98	407	87	146	32	11	7	59	34	10	....	....	.359	.408	**.543**	**.951**	199	44	92	**9.56**	-3	*1-98	26	3.1
1886 Det-N	121	489	139	181	**40**	15	**11**	72	66	16	21	....	.370	.445	**.581**	**1.026**	**204**	**63**	139	12.20	0	*1-121	31	4.7
1887*Det-N	123	571	**153**	**240**	**36**	20	12	101	71	9	34	....	.420	**.426**	.562	**.988**	**167**	**47**	138	**11.02**	-12	*1-123	26	2.1
1888 Det-N	129	522	**118**	160	**33**	11	9	66	68	13	34	....	.307	.399	.464	.862	174	**48**	113	8.41	1	*1-129	27	3.6
1889 Bos-N	126	485	105	181	26	9	7	118	66	6	22	....	**.373**	**.462**	.507	**.969**	161	43	127	**11.06**	3	*1-126	**28**	3.1
1890 Bos-P	123	460	117	152	36	9	1	97	99	17	28	....	.330	**.466**	.454	.921	137	32	113	9.93	-7	*1-123	19	1.1
1891 Bos-a	130	486	117	170	26	19	5	109	87	20	31	....	**.350**	**.471**	**.512**	**.983**	**184**	**60**	135	**11.33**	-11	*1-130	29	3.3
1892 Bro-N	152	588	121	**197**	30	20	5	**124**	84	30	31	....	**.335**	.432	.480	**.911**	**182**	**63**	138	**9.56**	14	*1-152	**34**	**7.0**
1893 Bro-N	77	282	57	95	21	11	2	59	52	10	9	....	.337	.450	.511	.961	162	28	71	10.00	7	1-77	16	2.8
1894*Bal-N	123	525	137	182	39	23	9	128	67	9	38	....	.347	.425	.560	.985	130	25	145	10.97	-5	*1-123	21	1.5
1895 Bal-N	5	23	2	6	2	0	0	5	1	1	0	....	.261	.292	.348	.639	63	-1	3	3.76	0	/1-5	0	-0.1
Lou-N	24	97	13	30	10	1	2	15	11	2	1	....	.309	.380	.495	.874	133	5	19	7.68	-2	1-24	3	0.2
Yr.	29	120	15	36	12	1	2	20	12	3	1	....	.300	.364	.467	.830	119	3	22	6.85	-2	1-29	3	0.1
1896 Phi-N	57	218	42	75	13	3	1	41	44	11	7	....	.344	.462	.445	.907	141	17	49	9.10	-3	1-57	9	1.2
1904 NY-N	2	5	0	0	0	0	0	0	0	....	0	....	.000	.000	.000	.000	-96	-1	0	.00	0	/1-1	0	-0.1
Total 19	1673	6782	1523	2367	460	205	106	1296	840	238	256	....	.349	.423	.519	.942	170	621	1622	9.86	-15	*1-1633/0-35,P-4,3-2	355	43.5

• BROVIA, Joe Joseph John "Ox" Brovia b: 2/18/1922, Davenport, CA d: 8/15/1994, Santa Cruz, CA BL/TR, 6'3", 195 lbs. Deb: 7/3/1955

YEAR TM-L	G	AB	R	H	2B	3B	HR	RBI	BB	SO	SB	CS	AVG	OBP	SLG	OPS	OPS+	BR/A	RC	RC/G	FR	G/POS	WS	TPW
1955 Cin-N	21	18	0	2	0	0	0	4	1	6	0	0	.111	.158	.111	.269	-26	-3	0	.66	0	....	0	-0.3

• BROWER, Bob Robert Richard Brower b: 1/10/1960, Jamaica, NY BR/TR, 5'11", 185 lbs. Deb: 9/3/1986 Career OF: 88-110-26

YEAR TM-L	G	AB	R	H	2B	3B	HR	RBI	BB	SO	SB	CS	AVG	OBP	SLG	OPS	OPS+	BR/A	RC	RC/G	FR	G/POS	WS	TPW
1986 Tex-A	21	9	3	1	1	0	0	0	0	3	1	2	.111	.111	.222	.333	-12	-2	0	.00	-1	0-17(16-1-1)/D-1	0	-0.3
1987 Tex-A	127	303	63	79	10	3	14	46	36	66	15	9	.261	.339	.452	.791	107	2	47	5.23	-3	*0-106(45-67-6)/D-7	10	-0.3
1988 Tex-A	82	201	29	45	7	0	1	11	27	38	10	5	.224	.316	.274	.589	65	-9	18	2.86	0	0-59(26-33-4),D-13	1	-1.0
1989 NY-A	26	69	9	16	3	0	2	3	6	11	3	1	.232	.293	.362	.656	85	-1	7	3.68	0	0-25(1-9-15)/D-1	0	-0.2
Total 4	256	582	104	141	21	3	17	60	69	118	29	17	.242	.323	.376	.699	88	-10	73	4.10	-3	0-207/D-22	11	-1.8

• BROWER, Frank Frank Willard "Turkeyfoot" Brower
b: 3/26/1893, Gainesville, VA d: 11/20/1960, Baltimore, MD BL/TR, 6'2", 180 lbs. Deb: 8/14/1920 Career OF: 4-0-190

YEAR TM-L	G	AB	R	H	2B	3B	HR	RBI	BB	SO	SB	CS	AVG	OBP	SLG	OPS	OPS+	BR/A	RC	RC/G	FR	G/POS	WS	TPW
1920 Was-A	36	119	21	37	7	2	1	13	9	11	1	1	.311	.374	.429	.803	115	3	19	5.95	-1	0-20(1-0-19)/1-9,3-1	4	0.1
1921 Was-A	83	203	31	53	12	3	1	35	18	7	1	1	.261	.330	.365	.695	81	-6	25	4.27	3	0-46(0-0-46)/1-4	4	-0.6
1922 Was-A	139	471	61	138	20	6	9	71	52	25	8	6	.293	.375	.418	.793	112	10	76	5.75	-3	*0-121(0-0-121)/1-7	16	-0.3
1923 Cle-A	126	397	77	113	25	8	16	66	62	32	6	5	.285	.392	.509	.901	136	21	82	7.27	-7	*1-112/0-4(1-0-3)	15	0.7
1924 Cle-A	66	107	16	30	10	1	3	20	27	9	1	1	.280	.434	.477	.910	133	7	24	8.21	0	1-26/P-4,0-3(2-0-1)	5	1.0
Total 5	450	1297	206	371	74	20	30	205	168	84	17	14	.286	.379	.443	.822	117	36	227	6.19	-7	0-194,1-158/P-4,3-1	44	0.9

• BROWER, Louis Louis Lester Brower b: 7/1/1900, Cleveland, OH d: 3/4/1994, Tyler, TX BR/TR, 5'10", 155 lbs. Deb: 6/13/1931

YEAR TM-L	G	AB	R	H	2B	3B	HR	RBI	BB	SO	SB	CS	AVG	OBP	SLG	OPS	OPS+	BR/A	RC	RC/G	FR	G/POS	WS	TPW
1931 Det-A	21	62	3	10	1	0	0	6	8	5	1	0	.161	.278	.177	.455	21	-6	4	1.93	-7	S-20/2-2	0	-1.1

• BROWN, Adrian Adrian Demond Brown b: 2/7/1974, McComb, MS BR/TR, 6', 175 lbs. Deb: 5/16/1997 Career OF: 17-246-94

YEAR TM-L	G	AB	R	H	2B	3B	HR	RBI	BB	SO	SB	CS	AVG	OBP	SLG	OPS	OPS+	BR/A	RC	RC/G	FR	G/POS	WS	TPW
1997 Pit-N	48	147	17	28	6	0	1	10	13	18	8	4	.190	.274	.252	.526	38	-13	11	2.25	-0	0-38(0-35-3)	1	-1.3
1998 Pit-N	41	152	20	43	4	1	0	5	9	18	4	0	.283	.323	.322	.645	70	-6	16	3.84	1	0-38(3-34-1)	2	-0.5
1999 Pit-N	116	226	34	61	5	2	4	17	33	39	5	3	.270	.365	.363	.728	85	-4	31	4.72	0	0-96(4-29-66)	3	-0.6
2000 Pit-N	104	308	64	97	18	3	4	28	29	34	13	1	.315	.374	.432	.806	104	4	54	6.77	2	0-92(7-71-15)	9	0.6
2001 Pit-N	8	31	3	6	0	0	1	2	3	3	2	1	.194	.265	.290	.555	43	-3	2	2.23	0	/0-7(0-7-0)	0	-0.3
2002 Pit-N	91	208	20	45	10	2	1	21	19	34	10	6	.216	.285	.298	.583	53	-15	17	2.63	-2	0-71(0-64-9)	2	-1.7
2003*Bos-A	9	15	2	3	0	0	0	1	1	4	2	0	.200	.250	.200	.450	20	-1	1	2.42	0	/0-9(3-6-0)	0	-0.2
Total 7	417	1087	160	283	43	8	11	84	107	150	44	15	.260	.330	.345	.675	74	-38	134	4.20	0	0-351	17	-3.9

• BROWN, Bill William Verna "Verna" Brown b: 7/8/1893, Coleman, TX d: 5/13/1965, Lubbock, TX BL/TL, 5'8", 185 lbs. Deb: 8/15/1912

YEAR TM-L	G	AB	R	H	2B	3B	HR	RBI	BB	SO	SB	CS	AVG	OBP	SLG	OPS	OPS+	BR/A	RC	RC/G	FR	G/POS	WS	TPW
1912 StL-A	9	20	0	4	0	0	0	1	0	....	0	....	.200	.200	.200	.400	15	-2	1	1.27	-1	/0-7(6-1-0)	0	-0.3

• BROWN, Bobby Rogers Lee Brown b: 5/25/1954, Norfolk, VA BB/TR, 6'2", 205 lbs. Deb: 4/5/1979 Career OF: 182-148-77

YEAR TM-L	G	AB	R	H	2B	3B	HR	RBI	BB	SO	SB	CS	AVG	OBP	SLG	OPS	OPS+	BR/A	RC	RC/G	FR	G/POS	WS	TPW
1979 Tor-A	4	10	1	0	0	0	0	0	2	1	0	0	.000	.167	.000	.167	-50	-2	0	.23	0	/0-4(2-0-2)	0	-0.2

YEAR TM-L	G	AB	R	H	2B	3B	HR	RBI	BB	SO	SB	CS	AVG	OBP	SLG	OPS	OPS+	BR/A	RC	RC/G	FR	G/POS	WS	TPW
NY-A	30	68	7	17	3	1	0	3	2	17	2	1	.250	.271	.324	.595	61	-4	6	3.11	-1	O-27(7-20-0)/D-1	1	-0.6
Yr.	34	78	8	17	3	1	0	3	4	18	2	1	.218	.256	.282	.538	45	-6	6	2.65	-1	O-31(9-20-2)/D-1	1	-0.8
1980*NY-A	137	412	65	107	12	5	14	47	29	82	27	8	.260	.308	.415	.723	98	0	52	4.33	-4	*O-131(28-81-25)/D-1	11	-0.8
1981*NY-A	31	62	5	14	1	0	0	6	5	15	4	2	.226	.284	.242	.526	53	-4	5	2.29	0	O-29(6-11-14)/D-2	1	-0.5
1982 Sea-A	79	245	29	59	7	1	4	17	17	32	28	6	.241	.290	.327	.617	67	-8	25	3.42	1	O-68(51-14-4)/D-3	4	-1.0
1983 SD-N	57	225	40	60	5	3	5	22	23	38	27	9	.267	.335	.382	.717	102	2	31	4.77	-2	O-54(52-0-4)	8	-0.2
1984*SD-N	85	171	28	43	7	2	3	29	11	33	16	4	.251	.297	.368	.665	86	-2	18	3.41	-1	O-53(27-13-16)	5	-0.5
1985 SD-N	79	84	8	13	3	0	0	6	5	20	6	4	.155	.202	.190	.393	11	-11	3	.97	1	O-28(9-9-12)	0	-1.1
Total 7	502	1277	183	313	38	12	26	130	94	238	110	34	.245	.297	.355	.652	80	-27	140	3.64	-7	O-394/D-7	30	-4.9
• BROWN, Bobby	Robert William "Doc" Brown b: 10/25/1924, Seattle, WA BL/TR, 6'1", 180 lbs. Deb: 9/22/1946 Career OF: 4-2-4																							
1946 NY-A	7	24	1	8	1	0	0	1	4	0	0	0	.333	.429	.375	.804	124	1	4	5.28	0	/S-5,3-2	1	0.2
1947*NY-A	69	150	21	45	6	1	1	18	21	9	0	2	.300	.390	.373	.763	114	3	23	5.34	-2	3-27,S-11/O-3(0-2-1)	5	0.2
1948 NY-A	113	363	62	109	19	5	3	48	48	16	0	1	.300	.383	.405	.788	111	6	60	6.06	2	3-41,S-26,2-17/O-4(3-0-1)	14	1.0
1949*NY-A	104	343	61	97	14	4	6	61	38	18	4	3	.283	.359	.399	.759	101	-0	50	5.26	1	3-86/O-3(1-0-2)	12	0.0
1950*NY-A	95	277	33	74	4	2	4	37	39	18	3	1	.267	.360	.339	.699	82	-6	35	4.28	2	3-82	7	-0.4
1951*NY-A	103	313	44	84	15	2	6	51	47	18	1	1	.268	.369	.387	.756	108	5	49	5.53	-4	3-90	13	0.0
1952 NY-A	29	89	6	22	2	0	1	14	9	6	1	1	.247	.323	.303	.627	80	-2	9	3.45	1	3-24	2	-0.2
1954 NY-A	28	60	5	13	1	0	1	7	8	3	0	1	.217	.309	.283	.592	65	-3	5	2.51	2	3-17	1	-0.2
Total 8	548	1619	233	452	62	14	22	237	214	88	9	10	.279	.367	.376	.742	100	4	234	5.10	1	3-369/S-42,2-17,O-10	55	0.7
• BROWN, Brant	Brant Michael Brown b: 6/22/1971, Porterville, CA BL/TL, 6'3", 220 lbs. Deb: 6/15/1996 Career OF: 101-101-67																							
1996 Chi-N	29	69	11	21	1	0	5	9	2	17	3	3	.304	.333	.536	.870	121	1	11	5.53	3	1-18	1	0.3
1997 Chi-N	46	137	15	32	7	1	5	15	7	28	2	1	.234	.286	.409	.694	77	-5	16	3.93	0	O-27(27-0-0),1-12	2	-0.7
1998*Chi-N	124	347	56	101	17	7	14	48	30	95	4	5	.291	.349	.501	.851	116	6	61	6.51	-6	*O-102(48-69-0)/1-7	13	0.0
1999 Pit-N	130	341	49	79	20	3	16	58	22	114	3	4	.232	.286	.449	.735	82	-13	43	4.19	1	O-82(0-23-59)/1-7,D-6	7	-1.5
2000 Fla-N	41	73	4	14	6	0	2	6	3	33	1	0	.192	.224	.356	.580	45	-6	6	2.59	-1	O-13(8-0-5)/1-5	0	-0.7
Chi-N	54	89	7	14	1	0	3	10	10	29	2	1	.157	.250	.270	.520	32	-10	6	2.11	0	O-28(18-9-3)/1-7	1	-1.0
Yr.	95	162	11	28	7	0	5	16	13	62	3	1	.173	.239	.309	.547	38	-16	12	2.31	-1	O-41(26-9-8),1-12	1	-1.7
Total 5	424	1056	142	261	52	11	45	146	74	316	15	14	.247	.303	.445	.748	88	-27	142	4.63	-3	O-252/1-56,D-6	24	-3.6
• BROWN, Chris	John Christopher Brown b: 8/15/1961, Jackson, MS BR/TR, 6', 210 lbs. Deb: 9/3/1984																							
1984 SF-N	23	84	6	24	7	0	1	11	9	19	2	1	.286	.362	.405	.766	119	2	12	4.77	-3	3-23	2	-0.2
1985 SF-N	131	432	50	117	20	3	16	61	38	78	2	3	.271	.345	.442	.787	125	13	61	4.87	5	*3-120	16	1.7
1986 SF-N★	116	416	57	132	16	3	7	49	33	43	13	9	.317	.380	.421	.801	127	14	65	5.76	-9	*3-111/S-2	16	0.4
1987 SF-N	38	132	17	32	6	0	6	17	9	16	1	3	.242	.306	.424	.730	95	-3	14	3.44	-6	3-37/S-1	2	-0.9
SD-N	44	155	17	36	3	0	6	23	11	30	3	1	.232	.296	.368	.664	77	-5	16	3.22	1	3-43	2	-0.5
Yr.	82	287	34	68	9	0	12	40	20	46	4	4	.237	.300	.394	.694	86	-8	30	3.32	-5	3-80/S-1	4	-1.4
1988 SD-N	80	247	14	58	6	0	2	19	19	49	0	0	.235	.297	.283	.581	69	-10	20	2.67	-2	3-72	3	-1.2
1989 Det-A	17	57	3	11	3	0	0	4	1	17	0	0	.193	.207	.246	.453	28	-6	2	1.22	-1	3-17	0	-0.7
Total 6	449	1523	164	410	61	6	38	184	120	252	21	17	.269	.335	.392	.727	105	5	190	4.26	-16	3-423/S-3	41	-1.4
• BROWN, Curtis	Curtis Brown b: 9/14/1945, Sacramento, CA BR/TR, 5'11", 180 lbs. Deb: 5/27/1973																							
1973 Mon-N	1	4	0	0	0	0	0	0	0	0	0	0	.000	.000	.000	.000	-97	-1	0	.00	0	/O-1	0	-0.1
• BROWN, Darrell	Darrell Wayne Brown b: 10/29/1955, Oklahoma City, OK BB/TR, 6', 184 lbs. Deb: 4/11/1981 Career OF: 26-113-9																							
1981 Det-A	16	4	4	1	0	0	0	0	0	1	1	0	.250	.250	.250	.500	43	-0	0	3.42	-1	/O-6(1-2-3),D-4	0	-0.1
1982 Oak-A	8	18	2	6	0	1	0	3	1	2	1	0	.333	.368	.444	.813	128	1	3	6.76	0	/O-7(1-0-6),D-1	1	0.1
1983 Min-A	91	309	40	84	6	2	0	22	10	28	3	3	.272	.297	.304	.601	64	-16	26	2.89	-5	O-81(5-76-0)/D-3	3	-2.2
1984 Min-A	95	260	36	71	9	3	1	19	14	16	4	1	.273	.310	.342	.653	77	-8	27	3.71	2	O-55(19-35-0),D-13	5	-0.7
Total 4	210	591	82	162	15	6	1	44	25	47	9	4	.274	.305	.325	.630	71	-23	57	3.36	-3	O-149/D-21	9	-3.0
• BROWN, Dee	Dermal Bram Brown b: 3/27/1978, Bronx, NY BL/TR, 5'11", 215 lbs. Deb: 9/14/1998 Career OF: 110-4-22																							
1998 KC-A	5	3	2	0	0	0	0	0	0	1	0	0	.000	.000	.000	.000	-97	-1	0	.00	0	/D-3,O-2(0-0-2)	0	-0.1
1999 KC-A	12	25	1	2	0	0	0	0	2	7	0	0	.080	.148	.080	.228	-39	-5	0	.44	2	/O-3(3-0-0),D-2	0	-0.4
2000 KC-A	15	25	4	4	1	0	0	4	3	9	0	0	.160	.250	.200	.450	15	-3	1	1.86	1	/O-5(5-0-0)	0	-0.2
2001 KC-A	106	380	39	93	19	0	7	40	22	81	5	3	.245	.288	.350	.638	62	-22	35	3.13	-1	O-83(77-4-3),D-20	4	-2.7
2002 KC-A	16	51	5	12	3	1	1	7	4	20	0	0	.235	.291	.392	.683	71	-2	6	4.24	-1	/O-8(8-0-0),D-5	0	-0.4
2003 KC-A	50	132	16	30	7	0	2	14	8	37	1	1	.227	.282	.326	.607	53	-9	13	3.28	3	O-33(17-0-17),D-10	2	-0.8
Total 6	204	616	67	141	30	1	10	65	39	155	6	4	.229	.278	.330	.608	54	-43	56	3.05	2	O-134/D-40	6	-4.6
• BROWN, Delos	Delos Hight Brown b: 10/4/1892, Anna, IL d: 12/21/1964, Carbondale, IL BR/TR, 5'9", 160 lbs. Deb: 6/12/1914																							
1914 Chi-A	1	1	0	0	0	0	0	0	0	1	0	....	.000	.000	.000	.000	-101	-0	0	.00	0	....	0	0.0
• BROWN, Dick	Richard Ernest Brown b: 1/17/1935, Shinnston, WV d: 4/12/1970, Baltimore, MD BR/TR, 6'2", 190 lbs. Deb: 6/20/1957																							
1957 Cle-A	34	114	10	30	4	0	4	22	4	23	1	1	.263	.288	.404	.692	88	-3	13	3.92	0	C-33	3	-0.1
1958 Cle-A	68	173	20	41	5	0	7	20	14	27	1	0	.237	.305	.387	.693	91	-2	21	4.08	-1	C-62	5	-0.1
1959 Cle-A	48	141	15	31	7	0	5	16	11	39	0	0	.220	.290	.376	.666	85	-3	16	3.85	0	C-48	5	-0.1
1960 Chi-A	16	43	4	7	0	0	3	5	3	11	0	0	.163	.217	.372	.589	57	-3	3	2.35	0	C-14	1	-0.2
1961 Det-A	93	308	32	82	12	2	16	45	22	57	0	2	.266	.315	.474	.789	104	-1	42	4.68	-1	C-91	11	0.3
1962 Det-A	134	431	40	104	12	0	12	40	21	66	0	1	.241	.280	.353	.632	67	-22	40	3.11	3	*C-132	10	-1.3
1963 Bal-A	59	171	13	42	7	0	2	13	15	35	1	0	.246	.310	.322	.632	79	-4	18	3.54	0	C-58	5	-0.1
1964 Bal-A	88	230	24	59	6	0	8	32	12	45	2	0	.257	.296	.387	.683	89	-4	24	3.56	-1	C-84	6	-0.1
1965 Bal-A	96	255	17	59	9	1	5	30	17	53	2	2	.231	.282	.333	.615	73	-10	22	2.80	-3	C-92	5	-0.9
Total 9	636	1866	175	455	62	3	62	223	119	356	7	6	.244	.293	.380	.673	82	-51	199	3.59	-2	C-614	51	-2.6
• BROWN, Drummond	Drummond Nicol Brown b: 1/31/1885, Los Angeles, CA d: 1/27/1927, Platte County, MO BR/TR, 6', 180 lbs. Deb: 4/25/1913																							
1913 Bos-N	15	34	3	11	1	0	1	2	2	9	0	....	.324	.361	.441	.802	126	1	5	5.61	-2	C-12	2	0.0
1914 KC-F	31	58	4	11	3	0	0	5	7	6	1	....	.190	.277	.241	.518	51	-4	4	2.23	-1	C-23/1-2	0	-0.3
1915 KC-F	77	227	13	55	10	1	1	26	12	23	3	....	.242	.289	.308	.598	78	-7	21	3.00	1	C-65/1-1	7	-0.1
Total 3	123	319	20	77	14	1	2	33	21	38	4	....	.241	.294	.310	.605	78	-9	31	3.09	-2	C-100/1-3	9	-0.4
• BROWN, Ed	Edward P. Brown b: Chicago, IL TR, 178 lbs. Deb: 8/19/1882 Career OF: 4-0-13																							
1882 StL-a	17	60	4	11	0	0	0	....	4	....	....	....	.183	.234	.183	.418	41	-4	3	1.51	-2	O-15(2-0-13)/2-2,P-1	0	-0.4
1884 Tol-a	42	153	13	27	3	0	0	0	2	....	....	....	.176	.187	.196	.383	24	-13	6	1.26	-11	3-40/O-2(2-0-0),C-1,P-1	0	-2.5
Total 2	59	213	17	38	3	0	0	0	6	....	....	....	.178	.201	.192	.393	29	-16	8	1.33	-13	/3-40,O-17,2-2,P-2,C-1	0	-3.0
• BROWN, Eddie	Edward William "Glass Arm Eddie" Brown b: 7/17/1891, Milligan, NE d: 9/10/1956, Vallejo, CA BR/TR, 6'3", 190 lbs. Deb: 9/26/1920 Career OF: 305-425-3																							
1920 NY-N	3	8	1	1	1	0	0	0	0	3	0	0	.125	.125	.250	.375	6	-1	0	.91	0	/O-2(0-2-0)	0	-0.1
1921 NY-N	70	128	16	36	6	2	0	12	4	11	1	0	.281	.324	.359	.683	80	-3	15	4.25	-2	O-30(2-26-2)	3	-0.6
1924 Bro-N	114	455	56	140	30	4	5	78	26	15	3	5	.308	.345	.424	.769	109	4	65	5.24	-5	*O-114(0-114-0)	16	-0.6
1925 Bro-N	153	618	88	189	39	11	5	99	22	18	3	4	.306	.332	.429	.761	95	-6	86	4.98	0	*O-153(0-153-0)	15	-1.1
1926 Bos-N	153	612	71	**201**	31	8	2	84	23	20	5	....	.328	.355	.415	.770	117	12	86	5.28	0	*O-153(73-80-0)	19	0.3
1927 Bos-N	155	558	64	171	35	6	2	75	28	20	11	....	.306	.340	.401	.741	106	3	73	4.70	1	*O-150(150-0-0)/1-1	14	-0.7
1928 Bos-N	142	523	45	140	28	2	2	59	24	22	6	....	.268	.305	.340	.645	72	-22	53	3.45	-5	*O-129(80-50-1)/1-1	6	-3.4
Total 7	790	2902	341	878	170	33	16	407	127	109	29	9	.303	.334	.400	.735	99	-13	379	4.69	-11	O-731/1-2	73	-6.2
• BROWN, Emil	Emil Quincy Brown b: 12/29/1974, Chicago, IL BR/TR, 6'2", 195 lbs. Deb: 4/3/1997 Career OF: 65-78-27																							
1997 Pit-N	66	95	16	17	2	1	2	6	10	32	5	1	.179	.304	.284	.588	54	-6	10	3.26	-2	O-42(30-8-4)	1	-0.9
1998 Pit-N	13	39	2	10	1	0	0	3	1	11	0	0	.256	.293	.282	.575	51	-3	3	3.14	1	O-10(9-1-1)	0	-0.2

YEAR TM-L	G	AB	R	H	2B	3B	HR	RBI	BB	SO	SB	CS	AVG	OBP	SLG	OPS	OPS+	BR/A	RC	RC/G	FR	G/POS	WS	TPW
1999 Pit-N	6	14	0	2	1	0	0	0	0	3	0	0	.143	.143	.214	.357	-11	-2	0	.96	0	/0-6(6-0-0)	0	-0.3
2000 Pit-N	50	119	13	26	5	0	3	16	11	34	3	1	.218	.301	.336	.637	61	-7	12	3.36	1	0-38(14-12-18)	1	-0.6
2001 Pit-N	61	123	18	25	4	1	3	13	15	42	10	4	.203	.300	.325	.625	60	-7	13	3.30	2	0-54(2-51-2)	2	-0.5
SD-N	13	14	3	1	0	0	0	0	1	7	2	0	.071	.133	.071	.205	-49	-3	0	.64	-1	0-11(4-6-2)	0	-0.3
Yr.	74	137	21	26	4	1	3	13	16	49	12	4	.190	.284	.299	.583	50	-9	13	3.00	1	0-65(6-57-4)	2	-0.8
Total 5	209	404	52	81	13	2	8	38	38	129	20	6	.200	.290	.302	.592	52	-27	39	3.11	1	0-161	4	-2.8

• BROWN, Fred Fred Herbert Brown b: 4/12/1879, Ossipee, NH d: 2/3/1955, Somersworth, NH BR/TR, 5'10.5", 190 lbs. Deb: 5/4/1901 Career OF: 3-0-4

YEAR TM-L	G	AB	R	H	2B	3B	HR	RBI	BB	SO	SB	CS	AVG	OBP	SLG	OPS	OPS+	BR/A	RC	RC/G	FR	G/POS	WS	TPW
1901 Bos-N	7	14	1	2	0	0	0	2	0	....	0	....	.143	.143	.143	.286	-16	-2	0	.65	0	/0-5(3-0-2)	0	-0.2
1902 Bos-N	2	6	1	2	1	0	0	0	0	....	0	....	.333	.333	.500	.833	155	0	1	6.79	1	/0-2(0-0-2)	0	0.1
Total 2	9	20	2	4	1	0	0	2	0	....	0	....	.200	.200	.250	.450	36	-2	1	2.18	1	/0-7	0	-0.1

• BROWN, Gates William James Brown b: 5/2/1939, Crestline, OH BL/TR, 5'11", 220 lbs. Deb: 6/19/1963 C Career OF: 421-0-7

YEAR TM-L	G	AB	R	H	2B	3B	HR	RBI	BB	SO	SB	CS	AVG	OBP	SLG	OPS	OPS+	BR/A	RC	RC/G	FR	G/POS	WS	TPW
1963 Det-A	55	82	16	22	3	1	2	14	8	13	2	1	.268	.341	.402	.743	104	1	11	4.44	2	0-16(16-0-0)	2	0.2
1964 Det-A	123	426	65	116	22	6	15	54	31	53	11	4	.272	.328	.458	.785	114	8	64	5.35	2	*0-106(106-0-0)	15	0.3
1965 Det-A	96	227	33	58	14	2	10	43	17	33	6	0	.256	.307	.467	.774	115	5	34	5.11	-2	0-56(49-0-7)	8	0.0
1966 Det-A	88	169	27	45	5	1	7	27	18	19	3	0	.266	.344	.432	.776	119	5	26	5.38	0	0-43(43-0-0)	7	0.3
1967 Det-A	51	91	17	17	1	1	2	9	13	15	0	0	.187	.288	.286	.574	68	-3	8	2.66	1	0-20(20-0-0)	1	-0.3
1968*Det-A	67	92	15	34	7	2	6	15	12	4	0	0	.370	.442	.685	1.127	231	14	28	12.54	0	0-17(17-0-0)/1-1	8	1.6
1969 Det-A	60	93	13	19	1	2	1	6	5	17	0	0	.204	.253	.290	.543	49	-7	7	2.35	0	0-14(14-0-0)	0	-0.8
1970 Det-A	81	124	18	28	3	0	3	24	20	14	0	0	.226	.338	.323	.661	82	-2	15	3.87	-1	0-26(26-0-0)	2	-0.4
1971 Det-A	82	195	37	66	2	3	11	29	21	17	4	2	.338	.408	.549	.957	162	16	44	8.72	-1	0-56(56-0-0)	12	1.4
1972*Det-A	103	252	33	58	5	0	10	31	26	28	3	0	.230	.307	.369	.676	97	-0	29	3.79	4	0-72(72-0-0)	7	0.0
1973 Det-A	125	377	48	89	11	1	12	50	52	41	1	1	.236	.330	.366	.696	90	-4	44	3.90	0	*D-119/0-2(2-0-0)	6	-0.8
1974 Det-A	73	99	7	24	2	0	4	17	10	15	0	0	.242	.312	.384	.696	96	-1	12	4.31	0	D-13	2	-0.1
1975 Det-A	47	35	1	6	2	0	1	3	9	6	0	0	.171	.356	.314	.670	87	-0	4	3.61	0	....	0	0.0
Total 13	1051	2262	330	582	78	19	84	322	242	275	30	8	.257	.333	.420	.753	110	32	324	4.96	4	0-428,D-132/1-1	70	1.4

• BROWN, Ike Isaac Brown b: 4/13/1942, Memphis, TN d: 5/17/2001, Memphis, TN BR/TR, 6', 205 lbs. Deb: 6/17/1969 Career OF: 44-0-7

YEAR TM-L	G	AB	R	H	2B	3B	HR	RBI	BB	SO	SB	CS	AVG	OBP	SLG	OPS	OPS+	BR/A	RC	RC/G	FR	G/POS	WS	TPW
1969 Det-A	70	170	24	39	4	3	5	12	26	43	2	3	.229	.338	.376	.715	96	-1	21	3.80	0	2-45,3-12/0-3(1-0-2),S-1	5	0.2
1970 Det-A	56	94	17	27	5	0	4	15	13	26	0	0	.287	.380	.468	.848	131	4	17	6.33	-5	2-23/0-4(3-0-1),3-1	4	0.0
1971 Det-A	59	110	20	28	1	0	8	19	19	25	0	1	.255	.364	.482	.846	133	5	19	5.65	-2	1-17/0-9(8-0-1),2-8,3-4,S	5	0.2
1972*Det-A	51	84	12	21	3	0	2	10	17	23	1	2	.250	.376	.357	.733	115	2	11	4.11	-1	0-22(20-0-3),1-13/2-3,3-1,S	3	0.0
1973 Det-A	42	76	12	22	2	1	1	9	15	13	0	1	.289	.407	.382	.788	115	2	12	5.78	1	1-21,0-12(12-0-0)/3-2,D-2	3	0.1
1974 Det-A	2	2	0	0	0	0	0	0	0	0	0	0	.000	.000	.000	.000	-97	-1	0	.00	0	/3-2	0	-0.1
Total 6	280	536	85	137	15	4	20	65	90	130	3	7	.256	.366	.410	.776	115	11	80	4.89	-6	/2-79,1-51,0-50,3-22,S-3,D-2	20	0.4

• BROWN, Jake Jerald Ray Brown b: 3/3/1948, Sumrall, MS d: 12/18/1981, Houston, TX BR/TR, 6'2", 200 lbs. Deb: 5/17/1975

YEAR TM-L	G	AB	R	H	2B	3B	HR	RBI	BB	SO	SB	CS	AVG	OBP	SLG	OPS	OPS+	BR/A	RC	RC/G	FR	G/POS	WS	TPW
1975 SF-N	41	43	6	9	3	0	0	4	5	13	0	0	.209	.292	.279	.571	57	-2	4	3.08	-1	0-14(9-1-4)	0	-0.4

• BROWN, Jarvis Jarvis Ardel Brown b: 3/26/1967, Waukegan, IL BR/TR, 5'7", 170 lbs. Deb: 7/2/1991 Career OF: 15-77-44

YEAR TM-L	G	AB	R	H	2B	3B	HR	RBI	BB	SO	SB	CS	AVG	OBP	SLG	OPS	OPS+	BR/A	RC	RC/G	FR	G/POS	WS	TPW
1991*Min-A	38	37	10	8	0	0	0	0	2	8	7	1	.216	.256	.216	.473	31	-2	3	2.48	-2	0-32(3-11-19)/D-4	0	-0.4
1992 Min-A	35	15	8	1	0	0	0	0	2	4	2	2	.067	.222	.067	.289	-15	-3	0	.53	-1	0-31(4-9-18)/D-2	0	-0.4
1993 SD-N	47	133	21	31	9	2	0	8	15	26	3	3	.233	.338	.331	.668	78	-4	15	3.63	0	0-43(5-40-0)	2	-0.4
1994 Atl-N	17	15	3	2	1	0	1	1	0	2	0	0	.133	.133	.400	.533	31	-2	0	.73	0	/0-9(3-4-2)	0	-0.2
1995 Bal-A	18	27	2	4	1	0	0	1	7	9	1	1	.148	.324	.185	.509	36	-3	2	2.41	0	0-17(0-13-5)	0	-0.3
Total 5	155	227	44	46	11	2	1	10	26	49	13	7	.203	.304	.282	.586	56	-14	21	2.83	-4	0-132/D-6	2	-1.8

• BROWN, Jim James W. H. Brown b: 12/12/1860, Clinton County, PA d: 4/6/1908, Williamsport, PA Deb: 4/17/1884 ♦

YEAR TM-L	G	AB	R	H	2B	3B	HR	RBI	BB	SO	SB	CS	AVG	OBP	SLG	OPS	OPS+	BR/A	RC	RC/G	FR	G/POS	WS	TPW
1884 Alt-U	21	88	12	22	2	2	1	....	1	....	....	....	.250	.258	.352	.611	103	1	8	3.48	-5	0-14(2-4-8),P-11	2	-1.3
NY-N	1	3	0	0	0	0	0	0	0	1	....	....	.000	.000	.000	.000	-98	-1	0	.00	0	/P-1	0	-0.2
StP-U	6	16	5	5	4	0	0	....	1	....	....	....	.313	.353	.563	.915	205	2	3	8.29	0	/P-6,1-1,0-1	2	-0.3
Yr.	27	104	17	27	6	2	1	....	2	....	....	....	.260	.274	.385	.658	120	3	11	4.17	-5	P-17,0-15(2-4-9)/1-1	4	-1.5
1886 Phi-a	1	3	0	0	0	0	0	0	0	....	0	....	.000	.000	.000	.000	-99	-1	0	.00	0	/P-1	0	0.0
Total 2	29	110	17	27	6	2	1	0	2	1	0	....	.245	.259	.364	.623	108	1	11	3.87	-5	/P-19,0-15,1-1	4	-1.8

• BROWN, Jim James Donaldson "Don,Moose" Brown b: 3/31/1897, Laurel, MD BR/TR, 6', 178 lbs. Deb: 9/13/1915 Career OF: 0-7-6

YEAR TM-L	G	AB	R	H	2B	3B	HR	RBI	BB	SO	SB	CS	AVG	OBP	SLG	OPS	OPS+	BR/A	RC	RC/G	FR	G/POS	WS	TPW
1915 StL-N	1	2	0	1	0	0	0	0	2	1	0	....	.500	.750	.500	1.250	281	1	1	19.88	-0	/0-1	0	0.1
1916 Phi-A	14	42	6	10	2	1	1	5	4	9	0	....	.238	.304	.405	.709	118	1	6	4.15	-0	0-12(0-6-6)	1	0.0
Total 2	15	44	6	11	2	1	1	5	6	10	0	....	.250	.340	.409	.749	131	2	6	4.59	0	/0-13	1	0.1

• BROWN, Jimmy James Roberson Brown b: 4/25/1910, Jamesville, NC d: 12/29/1977, Bath, NC BB/TR, 5'8.5", 165 lbs. Deb: 4/23/1937

YEAR TM-L	G	AB	R	H	2B	3B	HR	RBI	BB	SO	SB	CS	AVG	OBP	SLG	OPS	OPS+	BR/A	RC	RC/G	FR	G/POS	WS	TPW
1937 StL-N	138	525	86	145	20	9	2	53	27	29	10	....	.276	.313	.360	.673	81	-15	58	3.72	3	*2-112,S-25/3-1	11	-0.4
1938 StL-N	108	382	50	115	12	6	0	38	27	9	7	....	.301	.350	.364	.714	91	-4	50	4.96	0	2-49,S-30,3-24	10	0.2
1939 StL-N	147	645	88	192	31	8	3	51	32	18	4	....	.298	.335	.384	.719	87	-12	83	4.70	14	*S-104,2-50	18	1.2
1940 StL-N	107	454	56	127	17	4	0	30	24	15	9	....	.280	.317	.335	.652	76	-15	48	3.84	-3	2-48,3-41,S-28	9	-1.3
1941 StL-N	132	549	81	168	28	9	3	56	45	22	2	....	.306	.363	.406	.769	109	7	83	5.58	9	*3-123,2-11	21	2.1
1942*StL-N★	145	606	75	155	28	4	1	71	52	11	4	....	.256	.315	.320	.635	80	-15	63	3.62	4	2-82,3-66,S-12	16	-0.4
1943 StL-N	34	110	6	20	4	2	0	8	6	1	0	....	.182	.224	.255	.479	36	-9	7	1.97	3	2-19/3-9,S-6	2	-0.5
1946 Pit-N	79	241	23	58	6	0	0	12	18	5	3	....	.241	.293	.266	.559	58	-13	18	2.53	-2	S-30,2-21/3-9	2	-1.4
Total 8	890	3512	465	980	146	42	9	319	231	110	39	....	.279	.326	.352	.678	84	-78	411	4.15	26	2-392,3-273,S-235	89	-0.4

• BROWN, Joe Joseph E. Brown b: 4/4/1859, Warren, PA d: 6/28/1888, Warren, PA, 5'10", 162 lbs. Deb: 8/16/1884 ♦

YEAR TM-L	G	AB	R	H	2B	3B	HR	RBI	BB	SO	SB	CS	AVG	OBP	SLG	OPS	OPS+	BR/A	RC	RC/G	FR	G/POS	WS	TPW
1884 Chi-N	15	61	6	13	1	0	0	3	0	15	....	....	.213	.213	.230	.443	36	-3	3	1.75	0	/0-9(0-1-9),P-7,1-1,C-1	2	-1.3
1885 Bal-a	5	19	2	3	0	0	0	0	0	....	....	....	.158	.158	.158	.316		-1	0	.82	0	/P-4,2-1	0	-0.9
Total 2	20	80	8	16	1	0	0	3	0	15	....	....	.200	.200	.213	.413	28	-5	4	1.52	-1	/P-11,0-9,1-2,1-2,C-1	2	-2.2

• BROWN, Kevin Kevin Lee Brown b: 4/21/1973, Valparaiso, IN BR/TR, 6'2", 200 lbs. Deb: 9/12/1996

YEAR TM-L	G	AB	R	H	2B	3B	HR	RBI	BB	SO	SB	CS	AVG	OBP	SLG	OPS	OPS+	BR/A	RC	RC/G	FR	G/POS	WS	TPW
1996 Tex-A	3	4	1	0	0	0	0	1	2	2	0	0	.000	.429	.000	.429	20	-0	0	2.63	0	/C-2,D-1	0	0.0
1997 Tex-A	4	5	1	2	0	0	1	1	0	0	0	0	.400	.400	1.000	1.400	237	1	2	18.00	-1	/C-4	0	0.0
1998 Tor-A	52	110	17	29	7	1	2	15	9	31	0	0	.264	.331	.400	.731	89	-2	15	4.67	1	C-52	3	0.1
1999 Tor-A	2	9	1	4	2	0	0	1	0	3	0	0	.444	.444	.667	1.111	176	1	3	14.40	-0	/C-2	1	0.1
2000 Mil-N	5	17	3	4	3	0	0	1	1	5	0	0	.235	.278	.412	.690	72	-1	2	4.19	-2	/C-5	0	-0.2
2001 Mil-N	17	43	7	9	0	1	4	12	2	18	0	0	.209	.261	.535	.796	100	-0	6	4.39	-1	C-16	1	-0.1
2002 Bos-A	2	1	0	0	0	0	0	0	0	0	0	0	.000	.000	.000	.000	-98	-0	0	.00	0	/C-2	0	-0.1
Total 7	85	189	30	48	12	2	7	31	14	59	0	0	.254	.319	.450	.769	93	-2	28	5.05	-3	/C-83,D-1	5	0.0

• BROWN, Larry Larry Leslie Brown b: 3/1/1940, Shinnston, WV BR/TR, 5'10", 165 lbs. Deb: 7/6/1963

YEAR TM-L	G	AB	R	H	2B	3B	HR	RBI	BB	SO	SB	CS	AVG	OBP	SLG	OPS	OPS+	BR/A	RC	RC/G	FR	G/POS	WS	TPW
1963 Cle-A	74	247	28	63	6	0	5	18	22	27	4	3	.255	.319	.340	.659	85	-5	27	3.67	-4	S-46,2-27	6	-0.3
1964 Cle-A	115	335	33	77	12	1	12	40	24	55	1	2	.230	.285	.379	.664	84	-9	34	3.31	6	*2-103/S-4	8	0.6
1965 Cle-A	124	438	52	111	22	2	8	40	38	62	5	7	.253	.316	.368	.683	93	-6	51	3.89	8	S-95,2-26	14	1.2
1966 Cle-A	105	340	29	78	12	0	3	17	36	58	0	1	.229	.309	.291	.600	74	-11	30	2.94	1	S-90,2-10	8	-0.4
1967 Cle-A	152	485	38	110	16	2	7	37	53	62	4	4	.227	.311	.311	.622	83	-9	48	3.17	5	*S-150	14	1.0
1968 Cle-A	154	495	43	116	18	3	6	35	43	46	1	1	.234	.302	.319	.621	90	-6	47	3.18	12	*S-154	17	2.2
1969 Cle-A	132	469	48	112	10	2	4	24	44	43	5	3	.239	.305	.294	.600	66	-21	43	3.08	3	*S-101,3-29/2-5	10	-0.7
1970 Cle-A	72	155	17	40	5	2	0	15	20	14	1	0	.258	.343	.316	.659	79	-3	17	3.67	-2	S-27,3-17,2-16	3	-0.2
1971 Cle-A	13	50	4	11	1	0	0	5	3	3	1	0	.220	.278	.240	.518	44	-4	3	2.07	-3	S-13	0	-0.5
Oak-A	70	189	14	37	2	1	1	9	7	19	1	2	.196	.228	.233	.461	31	-18	9	1.43	8	S-31,2-23,3-10	3	-0.6
Yr.	83	239	18	48	3	1	1	14	10	22	1	2	.201	.239	.234	.473	34	-21	12	1.56	5	S-44,2-23,3-10	3	-1.2
1972 Oak-A	47	142	11	26	2	0	0	4	13	8	0	0	.183	.252	.197	.449	37	-11	6	1.31	2	2-46/3-1	2	-0.7

YEAR TM-L	G	AB	R	H	2B	3B	HR	RBI	BB	SO	SB	CS	AVG	OBP	SLG	OPS	OPS+	BR/A	RC	RC/G	FR	G/POS	WS	TPW
1973*Bal-A	17	28	4	7	0	0	1	5	5	4	0	0	.250	.364	.357	.721	104	0	4	4.36	-1	3-15/2-1	1	-0.1
1974 Tex-A	54	76	10	15	2	0	0	5	9	13	0	0	.197	.282	.224	.506	48	-5	4	1.77	0	3-47/2-8,S-1	1	-0.5
Total 12	1129	3449	331	803	108	13	47	254	317	414	22	23	.233	.301	.313	.614	76	-107	324	3.07	32	S-712,2-265,3-119	87	0.9
• BROWN, Leon — Leon Brown b: 11/16/1949, Sacramento, CA BR/TR, 6', 185 lbs. Deb: 5/19/1976																								
1976 NY-N	64	70	11	15	3	0	0	2	4	4	2	4	.214	.257	.257	.514	49	-6	3	1.42	0	0-43(39-28-6)	1	-0.8
• BROWN, Lew — Lewis J. "Blower" Brown b: 2/1/1858, Leominster, MA d: 1/15/1889, Boston, MA BR/TR, 5'10.5", 185 lbs. Deb: 6/17/1876 Career OF: 0-1-23																								
1876 Bos-N	45	198	23	41	6	6	2	21	3	22	....	....	.207	.222	.333	.556	81	-4	15	2.69	1	*C-45/0-1	5	-0.2
1877 Bos-N	58	221	27	56	12	8	1	31	6	33	....	....	.253	.273	.394	.667	104	0	24	4.06	9	*C-55/1-4	9	1.0
1878 Pro-N	58	243	44	74	21	6	1	43	7	37	....	....	.305	.324	.453	.777	153	13	37	5.94	2	*C-45,1-15/0-1,P-1	12	1.3
1879 Pro-N	53	229	23	59	13	4	2	38	4	24	....	....	.258	.270	.376	.646	112	3	24	3.93	-6	C-48/0-6(0-0-6)	8	-0.2
Chi-N	6	21	2	6	1	0	0	3	1	4	....	....	.286	.318	.333	.652	109	0	2	4.26	1	/1-6	1	0.1
Yr.	59	250	25	65	14	4	2	41	5	28	....	....	.260	.275	.372	.647	112	3	26	3.95	-5	C-48/1-6,0-6(0-0-6)	9	-0.1
1881 Det-N	27	108	16	26	3	1	3	14	3	16	....	....	.241	.261	.370	.632	92	-1	11	3.53	-1	1-27	2	-0.4
Pro-N	18	75	9	18	3	1	0	10	4	13	....	....	.240	.278	.307	.585	85	-1	7	3.11	-1	0-13(0-0-13)/1-5	2	-0.3
Yr.	45	183	25	44	6	2	3	24	7	29	....	....	.240	.268	.344	.613	89	-2	17	3.36	-3	1-32,0-13(0-0-13)	4	-0.6
1883 Bos-N	14	54	5	13	4	1	0	9	3	6	....	....	.241	.281	.352	.633	89	-1	5	3.67	-1	1-14	1	-0.2
Lou-a	14	60	6	11	2	1	0	0	1	....	....	....	.183	.197	.250	.447	46	-3	3	1.73	-2	1-14/C-1	0	-0.6
1884 Bos-U	85	325	50	75	18	3	1	....	13	....	....	....	.231	.260	.314	.574	95	-1	27	3.05	7	C-54,1-33/0-2(0-0-2),P-1	10	0.3
Total 7	378	1534	205	379	83	31	10	169	45	155	....	....	.247	.269	.362	.631	104	5	155	3.72	8	C-248,1-118/0-23,P-2	50	0.9
• BROWN, Lindsay — John Lindsay "Red" Brown b: 7/22/1911, Mason, TX d: 1/1/1967, San Antonio, TX BR/TR, 5'10", 160 lbs. Deb: 7/13/1937																								
1937 Bro-N	48	115	16	31	3	1	0	6	3	17	1	....	.270	.288	.313	.601	62	-6	10	2.89	-3	S-45	1	-0.7
• BROWN, Marty — Marty Leo Brown b: 1/23/1963, Lawton, OK BR/TR, 6'1", 190 lbs. Deb: 9/4/1988																								
1988 Cin-N	10	16	0	3	1	0	0	2	1	2	0	1	.188	.235	.250	.485	38	-2	1	1.45	1	/3-8	0	-0.1
1989 Cin-N	16	30	2	5	1	0	0	4	4	9	0	0	.167	.265	.200	.465	34	-3	2	2.02	0	3-11	0	-0.2
1990 Bal-A	9	15	1	3	0	0	0	0	1	7	0	0	.200	.250	.200	.450	28	-1	1	1.27	-1	/D-4,2-3,3-2	0	-0.2
Total 3	35	61	3	11	2	0	0	6	6	18	0	1	.180	.254	.213	.467	33	-6	3	1.68	0	/3-21,D-4,2-3	0	-0.6
• BROWN, Mike — Michael Charles Brown b: 12/29/1959, San Francisco, CA BR/TR, 6'2", 195 lbs. Deb: 7/21/1983 Career OF: 39-4-229																								
1983 Cal-A	31	104	12	24	5	1	3	9	7	20	1	0	.231	.279	.385	.664	81	-3	11	3.47	1	0-31(18-3-11)	1	-0.3
1984 Cal-A	62	148	19	42	8	3	7	22	13	23	0	2	.284	.342	.520	.862	136	6	22	5.13	0	0-44(2-0-43)/D-3	5	0.5
1985 Cal-A	60	153	23	41	9	1	4	20	7	21	0	1	.268	.304	.418	.723	96	-2	16	3.47	1	0-48(1-1-46)/D-7	3	-0.2
Pit-N	57	205	29	68	18	2	5	33	22	27	2	2	.332	.396	.512	.909	154	14	40	7.03	-4	0-56(0-0-56)	8	0.8
1986 Pit-N	87	243	18	53	7	0	4	26	27	32	2	3	.218	.296	.296	.593	62	-13	20	2.65	1	0-71(0-0-71)	2	-1.6
1988 Cal-A	18	50	4	11	2	0	0	3	1	12	0	0	.220	.235	.260	.495	40	-4	3	1.70	1	0-18(18-0-2)	0	-0.4
Total 5	315	903	105	239	49	7	23	113	77	135	5	8	.265	.323	.411	.734	102	-2	112	4.15	0	0-268/D-10	19	-1.3
• BROWN, Oliver — Oliver S. Brown b: 5/3/1849, Brooklyn, NY d: 9/23/1932, Brooklyn, NY BR, 6' Deb: 8/1/1872 NA OF: 0-1-5																								
1872 Atl-n	4	15	0	2	0	0	0	0	0	1	0	0	.133	.133	.133	.267	-15	-2	0	.65	0	/0-4(0-0-4)	....	-0.1
1875 Atl-n	3	10	0	0	0	0	0	0	0	0	0	0	.000	.000	.000	.000	-115	-2	0	.00	-1	/1-2,0-2(0-1-1)	....	-0.2
Total 2 n	7	25	0	2	0	0	0	0	0	1	0	0	.080	.080	.080	.160	-55	-4	0	.37	0	/0-6,1-2	....	-0.3
• BROWN, Ollie — Ollie Lee "Downtown" Brown b: 2/11/1944, Tuscaloosa, AL BR/TR, 6'2", 200 lbs. Deb: 9/10/1965 Career OF: 75-39-910																								
1965 SF-N	6	10	0	2	1	0	0	0	0	2	0	0	.200	.200	.300	.500	38	-1	1	2.03	0	/0-4(0-0-4)	0	-0.1
1966 SF-N	115	348	32	81	7	1	7	33	33	66	2	5	.233	.303	.319	.622	71	-14	30	2.84	-4	*0-114(1-16-107)	6	-2.7
1967 SF-N	120	412	44	110	12	1	13	53	25	65	0	2	.267	.315	.396	.711	103	0	47	3.91	-2	*0-115(0-10-111)	11	-1.0
1968 SF-N	40	95	7	22	4	0	0	11	3	23	1	0	.232	.270	.274	.544	64	-4	7	2.64	-1	0-35(3-3-30)	1	-0.7
1969 SD-N	151	568	76	150	18	3	20	61	44	97	10	6	.264	.320	.412	.732	108	4	73	4.47	1	*0-148(0-0-148)	16	-0.3
1970 SD-N	139	534	79	156	34	1	23	89	34	78	5	3	.292	.335	.489	.823	122	13	82	5.51	-1	*0-137(0-0-137)	16	0.5
1971 SD-N	145	484	36	132	16	0	9	55	52	74	3	3	.273	.347	.362	.709	108	5	61	4.50	1	*0-134(0-1-134)	13	-0.1
1972 SD-N	23	70	3	12	2	0	0	3	5	9	0	0	.171	.227	.200	.427	24	-7	3	1.45	-0	0-17(0-0-17)	0	-0.8
Oak-A	20	54	5	13	1	0	1	4	6	14	1	1	.241	.317	.315	.631	93	-1	6	3.63	0	0-16(0-9-9)	2	-0.2
Mil-A	66	179	21	50	8	0	3	25	17	24	0	2	.279	.345	.374	.719	116	3	20	3.80	4	0-56(0-0-56)/3-1	6	0.5
Yr.	86	233	26	63	9	0	4	29	23	38	1	3	.270	.339	.361	.699	111	2	26	3.76	4	0-72(0-9-65)/3-1	8	0.3
1973 Mil-A	97	296	28	83	10	1	7	32	33	53	4	1	.280	.356	.392	.748	113	6	42	5.05	0	D-82/0-4(0-0-4)	7	0.4
1974 Hou-N	27	69	8	15	1	0	3	6	4	15	0	0	.217	.260	.362	.623	76	-3	6	2.92	-1	0-20(0-0-20)	1	-0.5
Phi-N	43	99	11	24	5	2	4	13	6	20	0	1	.242	.286	.455	.740	100	-1	11	3.53	-1	0-33(24-0-9)	2	-0.3
Yr.	70	168	19	39	6	2	7	19	10	35	0	1	.232	.275	.417	.692	90	-4	17	3.28	-2	0-53(24-0-29)	3	-0.8
1975 Phi-N	84	145	19	44	12	0	6	26	15	29	1	1	.303	.369	.510	.879	137	7	28	7.23	-1	0-63(23-0-48)	6	0.4
1976*Phi-N	92	209	30	53	10	1	5	30	33	33	2	1	.254	.355	.383	.738	106	3	31	5.12	2	0-75(9-0-69)	7	0.2
1977*Phi-N	53	70	5	17	3	1	1	13	4	14	1	1	.243	.284	.357	.641	68	-4	6	2.83	0	0-21(15-0-7)	1	-0.4
Total 13	1221	3642	404	964	144	11	102	454	314	616	30	27	.265	.326	.394	.720	103	8	455	4.32	-3	0-992/D-82,3-1	95	-5.0
• BROWN, Oscar — Oscar Lee Brown b: 2/8/1946, Long Beach, CA BR/TR, 6', 175 lbs. Deb: 9/3/1969 Career OF: 47-27-42																								
1969 Atl-N	7	4	2	1	0	0	0	0	0	1	0	0	.250	.250	.250	.500	40	-0	0	2.25	0	/0-3(0-2-1)	0	-0.1
1970 Atl-N	28	47	6	18	2	1	1	7	7	7	0	2	.383	.473	.532	1.005	159	4	11	9.01	-1	0-25(8-12-5)	3	0.2
1971 Atl-N	27	43	4	9	4	0	0	5	3	8	0	0	.209	.261	.302	.563	55	-3	4	2.85	0	0-15(6-7-3)	0	-0.3
1972 Atl-N	76	164	19	37	5	1	3	16	4	29	0	2	.226	.244	.323	.567	55	-11	11	2.29	1	0-59(28-3-28)	1	-1.3
1973 Atl-N	22	58	3	12	3	0	0	0	3	10	0	0	.207	.246	.259	.505	37	-5	4	2.07	1	0-13(5-3-5)	0	-0.5
Total 5	160	316	34	77	14	2	4	28	17	55	0	4	.244	.284	.339	.623	69	-15	30	3.23	1	0-115	4	-2.0
• BROWN, Randy — Edwin Randolph Brown b: 8/29/1944, Leesburg, FL BL/TR, 5'7", 170 lbs. Deb: 9/11/1969																								
1969 Cal-A	13	25	3	4	1	0	0	0	6	1	0	0	.160	.323	.200	.523	51	-1	2	2.72	1	C-10/0-1	1	0.0
1970 Cal-A	5	4	0	0	0	0	0	0	0	0	0	0	.000	.000	.000	.000	-104	-1	0	.00	-1	/C-5	0	-0.2
Total 2	18	29	3	4	1	0	0	0	6	1	0	0	.138	.286	.172	.458	34	-2	2	2.29	0	/C-15,0-1	1	-0.2
• BROWN, Robert — Robert Brown Deb: 7/29/1874																								
1874 Bal-n	2	9	0	0	0	0	0	0	0	0	0	0	.000	.000	.000	.000	-101	-2	0	.00	-1	/S-2	....	-0.2
• BROWN, Roosevelt — Roosevelt Lawayne Brown b: 8/3/1975, Vicksburg, MS BL/TR, 5'11", 200 lbs. Deb: 5/18/1999 Career OF: 106-20-13																								
1999 Chi-N	33	64	6	14	6	1	1	10	2	14	1	0	.219	.242	.391	.633	57	-4	6	2.71	0	0-18(13-5-1)	0	-0.5
2000 Chi-N	45	91	11	32	8	0	3	14	4	22	0	1	.352	.385	.538	.924	133	4	19	8.21	0	0-28(24-1-5)	3	0.3
2001 Chi-N	39	83	13	22	6	1	4	22	7	12	0	0	.265	.330	.506	.836	117	2	13	5.44	-2	0-22(21-1-3)/D-3	4	-0.1
2002 Chi-N	111	204	14	43	12	0	3	23	23	50	2	2	.211	.300	.314	.614	63	-11	20	3.17	-2	0-64(48-13-4)/D-1	2	-1.4
Total 4	228	442	44	111	32	2	11	69	36	98	3	3	.251	.315	.407	.722	86	-10	57	4.41	-3	0-132/D-4	9	-1.7
• BROWN, Sam — Samuel Wakefield Brown b: 5/21/1878, Webster, PA d: 11/8/1931, Mount Pleasant, PA BR/TR Deb: 4/21/1906 U																								
1906 Bos-N	71	231	12	48	6	1	0	20	13	....	4	....	.208	.262	.242	.505	59	-11	17	2.33	3	C-35,0-13(6-4-1),3-12/1-3,2	2	-0.5
1907 Bos-N	70	208	17	40	6	0	0	14	12	....	0	....	.192	.250	.221	.471	48	-13	13	1.89	4	C-63/1-2	2	-0.2
Total 2	141	439	29	88	12	1	0	34	25	....	4	....	.200	.256	.232	.489	54	-24	30	2.12	8	/C-98,0-13,3-12,1-5,2-2	4	-0.7
• BROWN, Tom — Thomas William Brown b: 12/12/1940, Laureldale, PA BB/TL, 6'1", 190 lbs. Deb: 4/8/1963																								
1963 Was-A	61	116	8	17	4	0	1	4	11	45	2	1	.147	.227	.207	.433	23	-12	6	1.66	0	0-16(10-5-1),1-14	0	-1.4
• BROWN, Tom — Thomas Tarlton Brown b: 9/21/1860, Liverpool, England d: 10/25/1927, Washington, DC BL/TR, 5'10", 168 lbs. Deb: 7/6/1882 M/U Career OF: 96-1096-593 ♦																								
1882 Bal-a	45	181	30	55	5	2	1	23	6	....	....	....	.304	.326	.370	.696	145	9	22	4.98	-1	0-45(0-0-45)/P-2	8	0.9
1883 Col-a	97	420	69	115	12	7	5	32	20	....	....	....	.274	.307	.371	.678	127	14	49	4.50	-1	*0-96(0-0-96)/P-3	12	0.7

YEAR TM-L	G	AB	R	H	2B	3B	HR	RBI	BB	SO	SB	CS	AVG	OBP	SLG	OPS	OPS+	BR/A	RC	RC/G	FR	G/POS	WS	TPW
1884 Col-a	107	451	93	123	9	11	5	32	24	....	....	....	.273	.315	.375	.690	135	19	55	4.58	-3	*O-107(0-0-107)/P-4	18	0.6
1885 Pit-a	108	437	81	134	16	12	4	68	34	....	....	....	.307	.366	.426	.792	152	27	70	6.22	-3	*O-108(0-0-108)/P-2	20	2.0
1886 Pit-a	115	460	106	131	11	11	1	51	56	....	30	....	.285	.365	.363	.728	129	18	74	6.05	3	*O-115(1-1-115)/P-1	19	1.5
1887 Pit-N	47	203	30	58	3	4	0	6	11	40	12	....	.286	.289	.302	.591	68	-8	21	3.79	2	O-47(0-47-0)	3	-0.6
Ind-N	36	148	20	33	3	0	2	9	8	25	13	....	.223	.228	.243	.471	32	-13	11	2.53	-2	O-36(0-17-19)	0	-1.3
Yr.	83	351	50	91	6	4	2	15	19	65	25	....	.259	.263	.277	.541	53	-20	32	3.24	0	O-83(0-64-19)	3	-1.9
1888 Bos-N	107	420	62	104	10	7	9	49	30	68	46	....	.248	.299	.369	.668	108	3	62	5.27	-1	*O-107(6-2-99)	13	0.0
1889 Bos-N	90	362	93	84	10	5	2	24	59	56	63	....	.232	.341	.304	.645	76	-10	61	5.77	3	O-90(88-0-2)	12	-0.9
1890 Bos-P	128	543	146	149	23	14	4	61	86	84	79	....	.274	.377	.390	.767	98	-1	112	7.70	2	*O-128(0-128-0)	18	-0.3
1891 Bos-a	137	589	**177**	**189**	30	**21**	5	72	70	96	**106**	....	.321	.397	.469	.865	150	37	155	10.29	-6	*O-137(0-137-0)	**31**	2.2
1892 Lou-N	153	660	105	150	16	8	2	45	47	94	78	....	.227	.284	.285	.569	78	-17	77	4.10	16	*O-153(0-153-0)	16	-1.0
1893 Lou-N	122	529	104	127	15	7	5	54	56	63	**66**	....	.240	.319	.323	.642	77	-16	77	5.10	21	*O-122(0-122-0)	11	-0.3
1894 Lou-N	130	541	123	137	22	14	9	57	60	74	66	....	.253	.331	.396	.727	80	-17	95	6.12	0	*O-129(0-129-0)	9	-1.9
1895 StL-N	84	355	73	78	11	4	1	31	48	44	34	....	.220	.316	.282	.598	56	-22	44	4.23	-1	O-83(1-82-0)	3	-2.3
Was-N	34	134	25	32	8	3	2	16	18	16	8	....	.239	.329	.388	.717	86	-3	20	5.33	-3	O-34(0-34-0)	2	-0.7
Yr.	118	489	98	110	19	7	3	47	66	60	42	....	.225	.320	.311	.630	64	-26	64	4.52	-4	*O-117(1-116-0)	5	-3.0
1896 Was-N	116	435	87	128	17	6	2	59	58	49	28	....	.294	.385	.375	.759	101	3	77	6.37	-6	*O-116(0-114-2)	12	-0.9
1897 Was-N	116	469	91	137	17	2	5	45	52	....	25	....	.292	.364	.369	.733	94	-3	75	5.84	-2	*O-115(0-115-0)	11	-1.1
1898 Was-N	16	55	8	9	1	0	0	2	5	....	3	....	.164	.233	.182	.415	19	-6	3	1.79	-1	O-15(0-15-0)	0	-0.8
Total 17	1788	7392	1523	1973	239	138	64	736	748	709	657	....	.267	.336	.361	.697	102	14	1160	5.71	17	*O-1783/P-12	218	-4.2

• BROWN, Tommy Thomas Michael "Buckshot" Brown b: 12/6/1927, Brooklyn, NY BR/TR, 6'1", 170 lbs. Deb: 8/3/1944 Career OF: 87-0-6

YEAR TM-L	G	AB	R	H	2B	3B	HR	RBI	BB	SO	SB	CS	AVG	OBP	SLG	OPS	OPS+	BR/A	RC	RC/G	FR	G/POS	WS	TPW
1944 Bro-N	46	146	17	24	4	0	0	8	8	17	0	....	.164	.208	.192	.400	13	-17	6	1.24	-7	S-46	1	-2.1
1945 Bro-N	57	196	13	48	3	4	2	19	6	16	3	....	.245	.267	.332	.599	66	-10	17	2.98	-2	S-55/O-1	4	-0.8
1947 Bro-N	15	34	3	8	1	0	0	2	1	6	0	....	.235	.257	.265	.522	37	-3	2	2.12	2	/3-6,O-3(3-0-0),S-1	0	-0.2
1948 Bro-N	54	145	18	35	4	0	2	20	7	17	1	....	.241	.281	.310	.591	58	-9	12	2.71	-3	3-43/1-1	1	-1.2
1949*Bro-N	41	89	14	27	2	0	3	18	6	8	0	....	.303	.347	.427	.774	102	0	13	5.71	-3	O-27(27-0-0)	3	-0.5
1950 Bro-N	48	86	15	25	2	1	8	20	11	9	0	....	.291	.378	.616	.994	153	6	19	7.85	1	O-16(16-0-0)	4	0.6
1951 Bro-N	11	25	2	4	2	0	0	1	2	4	0	0	.160	.222	.240	.462	24	-3	1	1.91	0	/O-5(5-0-0)	0	-0.3
Phi-N	78	196	24	43	2	1	10	32	15	21	1	2	.219	.278	.393	.671	80	-7	19	3.19	-5	O-32(32-0-0),2-14,1-12/3-1	2	-1.3
Yr.	89	221	26	47	4	1	10	33	17	25	1	2	.213	.272	.376	.648	73	-10	21	3.04	-5	O-37(37-0-0),2-14,1-12/3-1	2	-1.7
1952 Phi-N	18	25	2	4	1	0	1	2	4	3	0	0	.160	.276	.320	.596	65	-1	3	3.28	0	/1-3,O-3(3-0-0)	0	-0.1
Chi-N	61	200	24	64	11	0	3	24	12	24	1	2	.320	.358	.420	.778	114	3	29	5.48	-11	S-39,2-10/1-5	6	-0.6
Yr.	79	225	26	68	12	0	4	26	16	27	1	2	.302	.349	.409	.757	108	2	32	5.20	-11	S-39,2-10/1-8,O-3(3-0-0)	6	-0.7
1953 Chi-N	65	138	19	27	7	1	2	13	13	17	1	0	.196	.279	.304	.584	51	-10	11	2.37	-3	S-25/O-6(1-0-5)	1	-1.0
Total 9	494	1280	151	309	39	7	31	159	85	142	7	4	.241	.292	.355	.647	74	-50	132	3.48	-31	S-166/O-93,3-50,2-24,1-21	22	-7.5

• BROWN, Willard Willard Jessie Brown b: 6/26/1915, Shreveport, LA d: 8/8/1996, Houston, TX BR/TR, 5'11.5", 200 lbs. Deb: 7/19/1947

YEAR TM-L	G	AB	R	H	2B	3B	HR	RBI	BB	SO	SB	CS	AVG	OBP	SLG	OPS	OPS+	BR/A	RC	RC/G	FR	G/POS	WS	TPW
1947 StL-A	21	67	4	12	3	0	1	6	0	7	2	2	.179	.179	.269	.448	23	-8	2	1.06	-1	O-18(0-1-17)	0	-0.9

• BROWN, Willard Willard "Big Bill,California" Brown
b: 1866, San Francisco, CA d: 12/20/1897, San Francisco, CA BR/TR, 6'2", 190 lbs. Deb: 5/10/1887 U Career OF: 2-5-13

YEAR TM-L	G	AB	R	H	2B	3B	HR	RBI	BB	SO	SB	CS	AVG	OBP	SLG	OPS	OPS+	BR/A	RC	RC/G	FR	G/POS	WS	TPW
1887 NY-N	49	180	17	47	3	2	0	25	10	15	10	....	.261	.273	.259	.532	51	-11	15	3.01	-4	C-46/3-3,O-2(0-0-2)	2	-0.9
1888*NY-N	20	59	4	16	1	0	0	6	1	8	1	....	.271	.283	.288	.571	83	-1	5	3.28	-5	C-20	2	-0.5
1889*NY-N	40	139	16	36	10	0	1	29	9	9	6	....	.259	.318	.353	.670	87	-3	18	4.61	-3	C-37/O-3(0-3-0)	4	-0.3
1890 NY-P	60	230	47	64	8	4	4	43	13	13	5	....	.278	.320	.400	.720	84	-8	32	5.17	-1	C-34,O-13(2-0-11)/1-9,3-3,2	5	-0.5
1891 Phi-N	115	441	62	107	20	4	0	50	34	35	7	....	.243	.303	.306	.609	75	-15	44	3.56	3	*1-97,C-19/O-2(0-2-0)	8	-1.7
1893 Bal-N	7	32	5	4	3	0	0	5	1	3	0	....	.125	.152	.219	.370	-2	-5	1	1.03	0	/1-7	0	-0.4
Lou-N	111	461	80	140	23	7	1	85	50	32	9	....	.304	.373	.390	.764	112	9	72	5.97	0	*1-111/C-1	13	0.7
Yr.	118	493	85	144	26	7	1	90	51	35	9	....	.292	.360	.379	.739	105	4	73	5.57	0	*1-118/C-1	13	0.3
1894 Lou-N	13	48	5	10	2	0	0	9	5	7	1	....	.208	.283	.250	.533	32	-5	4	2.58	3	1-13	0	-0.1
StL-N	3	9	0	1	0	0	0	0	0	2	0	....	.111	.111	.111	.222	-46	-2	0	.37	0	/1-3	0	-0.1
Yr.	16	57	5	11	2	0	0	9	5	9	1	....	.193	.258	.228	.486	20	-7	4	2.20	4	1-16	0	-0.3
Total 7	418	1599	236	425	70	17	6	252	123	124	39	....	.266	.319	.338	.657	83	-40	191	4.35	-6	1-240,C-157/O-20,3-6,2-2	34	-3.8

• BROWNE, Byron Byron Ellis Browne b: 12/27/1942, St. Joseph, MO BR/TR, 6'2", 200 lbs. Deb: 9/9/1965 Career OF: 99-79-103

YEAR TM-L	G	AB	R	H	2B	3B	HR	RBI	BB	SO	SB	CS	AVG	OBP	SLG	OPS	OPS+	BR/A	RC	RC/G	FR	G/POS	WS	TPW
1965 Chi-N	4	6	0	0	0	0	0	0	0	2	0	0	.000	.000	.000	.000	-98	-2	0	.00	0	/O-4(4-0-0)	0	-0.2
1966 Chi-N	120	419	46	102	15	7	16	51	40	143	3	3	.243	.317	.427	.744	103	1	57	4.66	-5	*O-114(67-42-10)	10	-0.9
1967 Chi-N	10	19	3	3	2	0	0	2	4	5	1	1	.158	.304	.263	.568	61	-1	2	2.56	0	/O-8(0-2-6)	0	-0.2
1968 Hou-N	10	13	0	3	0	0	0	1	4	6	0	0	.231	.412	.231	.643	99	0	1	3.50	2	/O-2(0-0-2)	1	0.2
1969 StL-N	22	53	9	12	0	1	1	7	11	14	0	0	.226	.359	.321	.680	91	-0	6	4.04	2	O-16(5-5-8)	2	0.1
1970 Phi-N	104	270	29	67	17	2	10	36	33	72	1	2	.248	.330	.437	.767	107	1	36	4.38	-2	O-88(6-23-61)	7	-0.4
1971 Phi-N	58	68	5	14	3	0	3	5	8	23	0	0	.206	.289	.382	.672	89	-1	8	4.06	0	O-30(17-4-10)	2	-0.2
1972 Phi-N	21	21	2	4	0	0	0	0	1	8	0	0	.190	.227	.190	.418	19	-2	1	1.16	-1	/O-9(0-3-6)	0	-0.4
Total 8	349	869	94	205	37	10	30	102	101	273	5	6	.236	.319	.405	.724	98	-3	111	4.28	-5	O-271	22	-2.0

• BROWNE, Earl Earl James "Snitz" Browne b: 3/5/1911, Louisville, KY d: 1/12/1993, Whittier, CA BL/TL, 6', 175 lbs. Deb: 9/12/1935 Career OF: 14-5-43

YEAR TM-L	G	AB	R	H	2B	3B	HR	RBI	BB	SO	SB	CS	AVG	OBP	SLG	OPS	OPS+	BR/A	RC	RC/G	FR	G/POS	WS	TPW
1935 Pit-N	9	32	6	8	2	0	0	6	2	8	0	....	.250	.294	.313	.607	61	-2	3	2.53	0	/1-9	0	-0.2
1936 Pit-N	8	23	7	7	1	2	0	3	1	4	0	....	.304	.333	.522	.855	124	1	4	7.07	0	/O-4(4-0-0),1-1	1	0.1
1937 Phi-N	105	332	42	97	19	3	6	52	21	41	4	....	.292	.342	.422	.763	98	-1	48	5.20	2	O-54(8-5-43),1-23	7	-0.4
1938 Phi-N	21	74	4	19	4	0	0	8	5	11	0	....	.257	.304	.311	.615	69	-3	7	3.25	0	1-16/O-2(2-0-0)	1	-0.5
Total 4	143	461	59	131	26	5	6	69	29	64	4	....	.284	.332	.401	.733	92	-5	61	4.75	3	/O-60,1-49	9	-1.0

• BROWNE, George George Edward Browne b: 1/12/1876, Richmond, VA d: 12/9/1920, Hyde Park, NY BL/TR, 5'10.5", 160 lbs. Deb: 9/27/1901 Career OF: 208-53-816

YEAR TM-L	G	AB	R	H	2B	3B	HR	RBI	BB	SO	SB	CS	AVG	OBP	SLG	OPS	OPS+	BR/A	RC	RC/G	FR	G/POS	WS	TPW
1901 Phi-N	8	26	2	5	1	0	0	4	1	....	2	....	.192	.250	.231	.481	39	-2	2	2.59	0	/O-8(6-1-1)	0	-0.2
1902 Phi-N	70	281	41	73	7	1	0	26	16	....	11	....	.260	.304	.292	.596	84	-5	30	3.69	5	O-70(70-0-0)	6	-0.4
NY-N	53	216	30	69	9	5	0	14	9	....	13	....	.319	.355	.407	.763	136	8	37	6.48	-1	O-53(51-0-2)	7	0.5
Yr.	123	497	71	142	16	6	0	40	25	....	24	....	.286	.326	.342	.668	107	3	67	4.85	5	*O-123(121-0-2)	13	0.0
1903 NY-N	141	591	105	185	20	3	3	45	43	....	27	....	.313	.364	.372	.736	106	4	94	5.92	-4	*O-141(1-0-140)	19	-0.6
1904 NY-N	150	596	**99**	169	16	5	4	39	39	....	24	....	.284	.332	.347	.679	105	3	81	4.70	2	*O-149(0-0-149)	20	-0.1
1905*NY-N	127	536	95	157	16	14	4	43	20	....	26	....	.293	.321	.397	.718	111	4	80	5.31	-5	*O-127(0-0-127)	16	-0.6
1906 NY-N	122	477	61	126	10	4	0	38	27	....	32	....	.264	.304	.302	.605	87	-8	58	3.98	1	*O-121(0-0-121)	10	-1.4
1907 NY-N	127	458	54	119	11	10	5	37	31	....	15	....	.260	.308	.360	.668	106	1	59	4.26	-8	*O-121(0-0-121)	11	-1.3
1908 Bos-N	138	536	61	122	10	6	1	34	36	....	17	....	.228	.276	.274	.550	77	-14	45	2.73	7	*O-138(12-17-109)	8	-1.6
1909 Chi-N	12	39	7	8	0	1	0	1	5	....	3	....	.205	.295	.256	.552	70	-1	4	3.11	0	O-12(0-11-1)	1	-0.2
Was-A	103	393	40	107	15	5	1	16	17	....	13	....	.272	.308	.344	.651	111	3	45	3.95	-2	*O-101(63-4-34)	10	-0.5
1910 Was-A	7	22	1	4	0	0	0	0	1	....	0	....	.182	.217	.182	.399	26	-2	1	1.17	-1	/O-5(5-0-0)	0	-0.3
Chi-A	30	112	17	27	4	1	0	4	12	....	5	....	.241	.315	.295	.609	96	-0	12	3.52	-1	O-29(0-20-9)	3	-0.3
Yr.	37	134	18	31	4	1	0	4	13	....	5	....	.231	.299	.276	.575	85	-2	13	3.12	-2	O-34(5-20-9)	3	-0.6
1911 Bro-N	8	12	1	4	0	0	0	2	1	1	2	....	.333	.385	.333	.718	106	0	2	7.32	0	/O-2(0-2-0)	0	0.0
1912 Phi-N	6	5	0	1	0	0	0	0	1	0	0	....	.200	.333	.200	.533	45	-0	0	2.07	0	....	0	0.0
Total 12	1102	4300	614	1176	119	55	18	303	259	1	190	....	.273	.318	.339	.657	100	-9	550	4.41	-7	*O-1077	111	-7.4

• BROWNE, Jerry Jerome Austin Browne b: 2/13/1966, Christiansted, V.I. BB/TR, 5'10", 170 lbs. Deb: 9/6/1986 Career OF: 98-67-25

YEAR TM-L	G	AB	R	H	2B	3B	HR	RBI	BB	SO	SB	CS	AVG	OBP	SLG	OPS	OPS+	BR/A	RC	RC/G	FR	G/POS	WS	TPW
1986 Tex-A	12	24	6	10	2	0	0	3	1	4	0	2	.417	.440	.500	.940	151	1	4	7.45	-1	/2-8	1	0.0
1987 Tex-A	132	454	63	123	16	6	1	38	61	50	27	17	.271	.360	.339	.699	87	-8	59	4.36	-8	*2-130/D-1	13	-0.9
1988 Tex-A	73	214	26	49	9	2	1	17	25	32	7	5	.229	.310	.304	.613	71	-9	20	3.07	-12	2-70/D-1	2	-1.9
1989 Cle-A	153	598	83	179	31	4	5	45	68	64	14	6	.299	.372	.390	.761	113	13	90	5.38	-36	*2-151/D-2	17	-1.9
1990 Cle-A	140	513	92	137	26	5	6	50	72	46	12	7	.267	.359	.372	.732	105	6	72	4.64	-8	*2-139	17	0.1
1991 Cle-A	107	290	28	66	5	2	1	29	27	29	2	4	.228	.296	.269	.565	57	-18	24	2.61	-5	2-47,O-17(17-0-0),3-15/D-7	3	-2.2

YEAR TM-L	G	AB	R	H	2B	3B	HR	RBI	BB	SO	SB	CS	AVG	OBP	SLG	OPS	OPS+	BR/A	RC	RC/G	FR	G/POS	WS	TPW
1992*Oak-A	111	324	43	93	12	2	3	40	40	40	3	3	.287	.372	.364	.736	113	7	46	4.76	-5	3-58,0-43(17-23-6),2-19/D-1,S	13	0.1
1993 Oak-A	76	260	27	65	13	0	2	19	22	17	4	0	.250	.309	.323	.632	74	-8	26	3.32	-2	0-56(30-26-4),3-13/2-3,1-2	2	-1.1
1994 Fla-N	101	329	42	97	17	4	3	30	52	23	3	0	.295	.394	.398	.792	104	5	56	6.23	-4	3-62,0-30(23-7-4),2-15	10	0.2
1995 Fla-N	77	184	21	47	4	0	1	17	25	20	1	1	.255	.348	.293	.641	71	-7	20	3.42	4	0-29(11-11-11),2-27/3-7	2	-0.3
Total 10	982	3190	431	866	135	25	23	288	393	325	73	45	.271	.354	.351	.705	94	-19	417	4.42	-76	2-609,0-175,3-155/D-12,1-2,S	80	-7.8

• BROWNE, Pidge Prentice Almont Browne b: 3/21/1929, Peekskill, NY d: 6/3/1997, Houston, TX BL/TL, 6'1", 190 lbs. Deb: 4/13/1962

YEAR TM-L	G	AB	R	H	2B	3B	HR	RBI	BB	SO	SB	CS	AVG	OBP	SLG	OPS	OPS+	BR/A	RC	RC/G	FR	G/POS	WS	TPW
1962 Hou-N	65	100	8	21	4	2	1	10	13	9	0	0	.210	.301	.320	.621	72	-4	8	2.51	1	1-26	1	-0.4

• BROWNING, Pete Louis Rogers "Gladiator" Browning b: 6/17/1861, Louisville, KY d: 9/10/1905, Louisville, KY BR/TR, 6', 180 lbs. Deb: 5/2/1882 Career OF: 477-490-35

YEAR TM-L	G	AB	R	H	2B	3B	HR	RBI	BB	SO	SB	CS	AVG	OBP	SLG	OPS	OPS+	BR/A	RC	RC/G	FR	G/POS	WS	TPW
1882 Lou-a	69	288	67	109	17	3	5	....	26	....	....	....	**.378**	**.430**	**.510**	**.940**	**228**	**40**	65	**10.13**	7	2-42,S-18,3-13	20	**4.5**
1883 Lou-a	84	358	95	121	15	9	4	0	23	....	....	....	.338	.378	.464	.842	183	34	64	7.60	-6	0-48(34-11-3),S-26,3-10/2-3,1	20	2.4
1884 Lou-a	103	447	101	150	33	8	4	47	13	....	....	....	.336	.357	.472	.829	176	36	77	7.15	-9	3-52,0-24(1-23-0),1-23/2-4,P	23	2.1
1885 Lou-a	112	481	98	**174**	34	10	9	73	25	....	....	....	**.362**	**.393**	.530	**.923**	190	**47**	103	**9.04**	4	*0-112(0-112-0)	**28**	**4.3**
1886 Lou-a	112	467	86	159	29	6	2	68	30	....	26	....	.340	.389	.441	.830	151	26	92	8.11	-8	*0-112(31-82-0)	17	1.3
1887 Lou-a	134	602	137	**275**	35	16	4	118	55	....	103	....	.457	.464	.547	1.011	178	58	191	15.78	-1	*0-134(0-134-0)	30	4.2
1888 Lou-a	99	383	58	120	22	8	3	72	37	....	36	....	.313	.380	.436	.816	164	28	79	8.11	-7	*0-99(20-79-0)	17	1.6
1889 Lou-a	83	324	39	83	19	5	2	32	34	30	21	....	.256	.327	.364	.691	98	-1	47	5.12	-2	0-83(83-0-0)	4	-0.5
1890 Cle-P	118	493	112	184	**40**	8	5	93	75	36	35	....	**.373**	.459	.517	.976	**175**	**57**	136	**11.92**	4	*0-118(118-0-0)	23	**4.5**
1891 Pit-N	50	203	35	59	14	1	4	28	27	31	4	....	.291	.377	.429	.805	138	10	35	6.59	5	0-50(48-0-2)	8	1.2
Cin-N	55	216	29	74	10	3	0	33	24	23	12	....	.343	.413	.417	.830	141	12	43	8.21	1	0-55(54-1-0)	9	1.0
Yr.	105	419	64	133	24	4	4	61	51	54	16	....	.317	.395	.422	.818	139	22	78	7.39	6	*0-105(102-1-2)	17	2.2
1892 Cin-N	83	307	47	93	12	5	3	52	40	26	8	....	.303	.383	.404	.787	140	16	52	6.54	-1	0-82(23-46-16)/1-2	13	0.8
Lou-N	21	77	10	19	4	0	0	4	12	7	5	....	.247	.348	.299	.647	104	1	10	4.65	-1	0-21(21-0-0)	2	-0.2
Yr.	104	384	57	112	16	5	3	56	52	33	13	....	.292	.376	.383	.759	133	17	62	6.14	-2	*0-103(44-46-16)/1-2	15	0.6
1893 Lou-N	57	220	38	78	11	3	1	37	44	15	8	....	.355	.466	.445	.912	155	21	51	9.45	-5	0-57(44-0-13)	11	1.0
1894 StL-N	2	7	1	1	0	0	0	0	0	0	0	....	.143	.143	.143	.286	-31	-2	0	.63	0	/0-2(0-2-0)	0	-0.1
Bro-N	1	2	1	2	0	0	0	2	1	0	0	....	1.000	1.000	1.000	2.000	413	1	2	∞	0	/0-1	0	0.1
Yr.	3	9	2	3	0	0	0	2	1	0	0	....	.333	.400	.333	.733	102	-0	2	.63	0	/0-3(0-2-1)	0	0.0
Total 13	1183	4875	954	1701	295	85	46	659	466	168	258	....	.349	.403	.467	.869	164	386	1048	8.93	-19	0-998/3-75,2-49,S-44,1-26,P	225	28.2

• BRUBAKER, Bill Wilber Lee Brubaker b: 11/7/1910, Cleveland, OH d: 4/2/1978, Laguna Hills, CA BR/TR, 6'2", 185 lbs. Deb: 9/8/1932

YEAR TM-L	G	AB	R	H	2B	3B	HR	RBI	BB	SO	SB	CS	AVG	OBP	SLG	OPS	OPS+	BR/A	RC	RC/G	FR	G/POS	WS	TPW
1932 Pit-N	7	24	3	10	3	0	0	4	3	4	1	....	.417	.481	.542	1.023	178	3	6	11.98	1	/3-7	2	0.4
1933 Pit-N	2	2	0	0	0	0	0	0	0	0	0	....	.000	.000	.000	.000	-100	-1	0	.00	0	/3-1	0	0.0
1934 Pit-N	3	6	0	2	1	0	0	1	1	0	0	....	.333	.429	.500	.929	144	0	1	9.65	1	/3-3	0	0.1
1935 Pit-N	6	11	1	0	0	0	0	0	2	5	0	....	.000	.154	.000	.154	-53	-2	0	.20	-1	/3-5	0	-0.3
1936 Pit-N	145	554	77	160	27	4	6	102	50	96	5	....	.289	.352	.384	.736	96	-2	76	4.84	-6	*3-145	15	-0.3
1937 Pit-N	120	413	57	105	20	4	6	48	47	51	2	....	.254	.335	.366	.700	90	-5	52	4.24	5	*3-115/S-3,1-1	12	0.4
1938 Pit-N	45	112	18	33	5	0	3	19	9	14	2	....	.295	.347	.420	.767	109	1	16	5.25	-5	3-18/1-9,S-3,0-1	3	-0.4
1939 Pit-N	100	345	41	80	23	1	7	43	29	51	3	....	.232	.297	.365	.662	78	-11	36	3.54	-4	2-65,3-32/S-1	6	-1.0
1940 Pit-N	38	78	8	15	3	1	0	7	8	16	0	....	.192	.267	.256	.524	45	-6	6	2.49	-2	3-19/S-8,1-4	1	-0.7
1943 Bos-N	13	19	3	8	3	0	0	1	2	2	0	....	.421	.476	.579	1.055	207	3	5	13.46	-1	/3-5,1-3	2	0.2
Total 10	479	1564	208	413	85	10	22	225	151	239	13	....	.264	.333	.373	.706	90	-20	200	4.41	-12	3-350/2-65,1-17,S-15,0-1	41	-1.6

• BRUCE, Lou Louis R. Bruce b: 1/16/1877, St. Regis, NY d: 2/9/1968, Ilion, NY BL/TR, 5'5", 145 lbs. Deb: 6/22/1904

YEAR TM-L	G	AB	R	H	2B	3B	HR	RBI	BB	SO	SB	CS	AVG	OBP	SLG	OPS	OPS+	BR/A	RC	RC/G	FR	G/POS	WS	TPW
1904 Phi-A	30	101	9	27	3	0	0	8	5	....	2	....	.267	.302	.297	.599	85	-1	11	3.53	1	0-25(11-10-5)/P-2,2-1,3-1	2	-0.5

• BRUCKER, Earle Earle Francis Brucker, Sr. b: 5/6/1901, Albany, NY d: 5/8/1981, San Diego, CA BR/TR, 5'11", 175 lbs. Deb: 4/19/1937 M/C

YEAR TM-L	G	AB	R	H	2B	3B	HR	RBI	BB	SO	SB	CS	AVG	OBP	SLG	OPS	OPS+	BR/A	RC	RC/G	FR	G/POS	WS	TPW
1937 Phi-A	102	317	40	82	16	5	6	37	48	30	1	2	.259	.356	.397	.754	91	-4	47	5.18	-3	C-92	7	-0.2
1938 Phi-A	53	171	26	64	21	1	3	35	19	16	1	1	.374	.437	.561	.998	152	14	42	10.22	-1	C-44/1-1	7	1.4
1939 Phi-A	62	172	18	50	15	1	3	31	24	16	0	1	.291	.381	.442	.823	112	3	28	5.75	1	C-47	6	0.7
1940 Phi-A	23	46	3	9	1	1	0	2	6	3	0	0	.196	.288	.261	.549	44	-4	3	1.93	1	C-13	0	-0.2
1943 Phi-A	1	1	0	0	0	0	0	0	0	0	0	0	.000	.000	.000	.000	-101	-0	0	.00	0	....	0	0.0
Total 5	241	707	87	205	53	8	12	105	97	65	2	4	.290	.376	.438	.815	107	9	120	6.11	-2	C-196/1-1	20	1.6

• BRUCKER, Earle Earle Francis Brucker, Jr. b: 8/25/1925, Los Angeles, CA BL/TR, 6'2", 210 lbs. Deb: 10/2/1948

YEAR TM-L	G	AB	R	H	2B	3B	HR	RBI	BB	SO	SB	CS	AVG	OBP	SLG	OPS	OPS+	BR/A	RC	RC/G	FR	G/POS	WS	TPW
1948 Phi-A	2	6	0	1	1	0	0	0	1	1	0	0	.167	.286	.333	.619	64	-0	1	3.56	-0	/C-2	0	0.0

• BRUETT, J.T. Joseph Timothy Bruett b: 10/8/1967, Milwaukee, WI BL/TL, 5'11", 175 lbs. Deb: 6/3/1992 Career OF: 7-24-30

YEAR TM-L	G	AB	R	H	2B	3B	HR	RBI	BB	SO	SB	CS	AVG	OBP	SLG	OPS	OPS+	BR/A	RC	RC/G	FR	G/POS	WS	TPW
1992 Min-A	56	76	7	19	4	0	0	2	6	12	6	3	.250	.313	.303	.616	71	-3	8	3.42	0	0-45(5-20-22)/D-3	1	-0.4
1993 Min-A	17	20	2	5	2	0	0	1	1	4	0	0	.250	.318	.350	.668	79	-1	2	3.46	-1	0-13(2-4-8)	0	-0.2
Total 2	73	96	9	24	6	0	0	3	7	16	6	3	.250	.314	.313	.627	73	-3	10	3.43	-1	/0-58,D-3	1	-0.5

• BRUGGY, Frank Frank Leo Bruggy b: 5/4/1891, Elizabeth, NJ d: 4/5/1959, Elizabeth, NJ BR/TR, 5'11", 195 lbs. Deb: 4/13/1921

YEAR TM-L	G	AB	R	H	2B	3B	HR	RBI	BB	SO	SB	CS	AVG	OBP	SLG	OPS	OPS+	BR/A	RC	RC/G	FR	G/POS	WS	TPW
1921 Phi-N	96	277	28	86	11	2	5	28	23	37	6	2	.310	.370	.419	.788	100	2	44	5.89	-5	C-86/1-2	8	0.2
1922 Phi-A	53	111	10	31	7	0	0	9	6	11	1	2	.279	.322	.342	.664	71	-5	12	3.79	-1	C-31	2	-0.5
1923 Phi-A	54	105	4	22	3	0	1	6	4	9	1	1	.210	.245	.267	.512	34	-10	7	2.13	-1	C-34/1-5	1	-1.0
1924 Phi-A	50	113	9	30	6	0	0	8	8	15	4	0	.265	.314	.319	.633	63	-5	12	3.78	-4	C-44	2	-0.7
1925 Cin-N	6	14	2	3	0	0	0	1	2	0	0	0	.214	.313	.214	.527	38	-1	1	2.54	-2	/C-6	0	-0.2
Total 5	259	620	53	172	27	2	6	52	43	72	12	5	.277	.329	.356	.686	76	-20	76	4.35	-13	C-201/1-7	13	-2.2

• BRUMBAUGH, Cliff Clifford Michael Brumbaugh b: 4/21/1974, Wilmington, DE BR/TR, 6'2", 205 lbs. Deb: 5/30/2001

YEAR TM-L	G	AB	R	H	2B	3B	HR	RBI	BB	SO	SB	CS	AVG	OBP	SLG	OPS	OPS+	BR/A	RC	RC/G	FR	G/POS	WS	TPW
2001 Tex-A	7	10	1	0	0	0	0	0	1	5	0	0	.000	.091	.000	.091	-71	-3	0	.06	-1	/0-6(2-0-4)	0	-0.3
Col-N	14	36	5	10	2	0	1	4	2	9	0	1	.278	.316	.417	.732	71	-2	3	2.94	-1	0-11(4-0-8)	0	-0.3

• BRUMFIELD, Jacob Jacob Donnell Brumfield b: 5/27/1965, Bogalusa, LA BR/TR, 6', 185 lbs. Deb: 4/6/1992 Career OF: 94-329-67

YEAR TM-L	G	AB	R	H	2B	3B	HR	RBI	BB	SO	SB	CS	AVG	OBP	SLG	OPS	OPS+	BR/A	RC	RC/G	FR	G/POS	WS	TPW
1992 Cin-N	24	30	6	4	0	0	0	2	2	4	6	0	.133	.212	.133	.345		-3	2	1.68	0	0-16(7-8-1)	0	-0.3
1993 Cin-N	103	272	40	73	17	3	6	23	21	47	20	8	.268	.323	.419	.742	97	-1	38	4.80	-3	0-96(24-68-5)/2-4	8	-0.5
1994 Cin-N	68	122	36	38	10	2	4	11	15	18	6	3	.311	.387	.525	.911	136	7	24	7.00	-1	0-43(14-24-6)	5	0.5
1995 Pit-N	116	402	64	109	23	2	4	26	37	71	22	12	.271	.340	.368	.708	85	-9	52	4.56	2	*0-104(0-104-0)	9	-0.6
1996 Pit-N	29	80	11	20	9	0	2	8	5	17	3	1	.250	.294	.438	.732	87	-2	9	3.63	0	0-22(0-22-0)	1	-0.2
Tor-A	90	308	52	79	19	2	12	52	24	58	12	3	.256	.318	.448	.767	91	-4	42	4.65	1	0-83(18-39-37)/D-5	8	-0.5
1997 Tor-A	58	174	22	36	5	1	2	20	14	31	4	4	.207	.270	.282	.551	44	-15	13	2.30	4	0-47(14-24-10)/D-4	2	-1.2
1999 LA-N	18	17	4	5	0	1	0	1	0	5	0	0	.294	.294	.412	.706	81	-1	2	4.63	0	0-11(7-4-0)	1	-0.1
Tor-A	62	170	25	40	8	3	2	19	19	39	1	2	.235	.312	.353	.665	68	-9	19	3.73	1	0-53(10-36-8)/D-6	3	-0.8
Total 7	568	1575	260	404	91	14	32	162	137	290	74	33	.257	.321	.393	.714	84	-37	201	4.34	3	0-475/D-15,2-4	37	-3.6

• BRUMLEY, Mike Anthony Michael Brumley b: 4/9/1963, Oklahoma City, OK BB/TR, 5'10", 165 lbs. Deb: 6/16/1987 Career OF: 9-6-3

YEAR TM-L	G	AB	R	H	2B	3B	HR	RBI	BB	SO	SB	CS	AVG	OBP	SLG	OPS	OPS+	BR/A	RC	RC/G	FR	G/POS	WS	TPW
1987 Chi-N	39	104	8	21	2	2	1	9	10	30	7	1	.202	.278	.288	.567	49	-7	9	2.84	-0	S-34/2-1	1	-0.4
1989 Det-A	92	212	33	42	5	2	1	11	14	45	8	4	.198	.251	.255	.506	44	-16	14	2.02	-5	S-42,2-24,3-11/D-8,0-4(1-1-2)	2	-1.8
1990 Sea-A	62	147	19	33	5	4	0	7	10	22	2	0	.224	.274	.313	.587	63	-7	12	2.67	-1	S-47/2-6,3-3,0-2(1-1-0),D	2	-0.5
1991 Bos-A	63	118	16	25	5	0	0	5	10	22	2	0	.212	.273	.254	.528	45	-8	9	2.64	1	S-31,3-17/2-7,0-4(0-4-0),D	2	-0.6
1992 Bos-A	2	1	0	0	0	0	0	0	0	0	0	0	.000	.000	.000	.000	-94	-0	0	.00	0	....	0	0.0
1993 Hou-N	8	10	1	3	0	0	0	2	1	3	0	1	.300	.364	.300	.664	83	-1	1	3.00	-1	/3-1,0-1,S-1	0	-0.1
1994 Oak-A	11	25	0	6	0	0	0	2	1	8	0	0	.240	.269	.240	.509	36	-2	2	2.40	-1	/2-4,3-4,0-3(3-0-0),S-1	0	-0.3
1995 Hou-N	18	18	1	1	0	0	1	2	0	6	1	0	.056	.056	.222	.278	-33	-3	0	.40	-2	/0-3(3-0-0),S-3,1-1,3-1	0	-0.5
Total 8	295	635	78	131	17	8	3	38	46	136	20	6	.206	.262	.272	.535	47	-45	47	2.39	-9	S-159/2-42,3-37,0-17,D-11,1	7	-4.3

• BRUMLEY, Mike Tony Mike Brumley b: 7/10/1938, Granite, OK BL/TR, 5'10", 195 lbs. Deb: 4/18/1964

YEAR TM-L	G	AB	R	H	2B	3B	HR	RBI	BB	SO	SB	CS	AVG	OBP	SLG	OPS	OPS+	BR/A	RC	RC/G	FR	G/POS	WS	TPW
1964 Was-A	136	426	36	104	19	2	2	35	40	54	1	1	.244	.310	.312	.623	74	-14	40	3.16	-1	*C-132	8	-1.0
1965 Was-A	79	216	15	45	4	0	3	15	20	33	1	1	.208	.282	.269	.550	58	-12	16	2.44	0	C-66	2	-0.9

YEAR TM-L	G	AB	R	H	2B	3B	HR	RBI	BB	SO	SB	CS	AVG	OBP	SLG	OPS	OPS+	BR/A	RC	RC/G	FR	G/POS	WS	TPW
1966 Was-A	9	18	1	2	1	0	0	0	0	2	0	0	.111	.111	.167	.278	-22	-3	0	.56	0	/C-7	0	-0.3
Total 3	224	660	52	151	24	2	5	50	60	89	2	2	.229	.296	.294	.590	66	-29	57	2.84	-1	C-205	10	-2.1

• BRUMMER, Glenn Glenn Edward Brummer b: 11/23/1954, Olney, IL BR/TR, 6', 200 lbs. Deb: 5/25/1981

YEAR TM-L	G	AB	R	H	2B	3B	HR	RBI	BB	SO	SB	CS	AVG	OBP	SLG	OPS	OPS+	BR/A	RC	RC/G	FR	G/POS	WS	TPW
1981 StL-N	21	30	2	6	1	0	0	2	1	2	0	0	.200	.226	.233	.459	30	-3	2	1.51	0	C-19	0	-0.3
1982*StL-N	35	64	4	15	4	0	0	8	0	12	2	0	.234	.234	.297	.531	47	-4	5	2.59	-2	C-32	1	-0.5
1983 StL-N	45	87	7	24	7	0	0	9	10	11	1	3	.276	.351	.356	.707	96	-1	10	3.57	-2	C-41	2	-0.2
1984 StL-N	28	58	3	12	0	0	1	3	3	7	0	0	.207	.246	.259	.505	43	-5	3	1.37	-1	C-26	1	-0.5
1985 Tex-A	49	108	7	30	4	0	0	5	11	22	1	5	.278	.355	.315	.670	84	-4	11	3.56	-3	C-47/D-1,0-1	2	-0.5
Total 5	178	347	23	87	16	0	1	27	25	54	4	8	.251	.305	.305	.610	70	-17	30	2.81	-8	C-165/D-1,0-1	6	-2.0

• BRUNANSKY, Tom Thomas Andrew Brunansky b: 8/20/1960, Covina, CA BR/TR, 6'4", 211 lbs. Deb: 4/9/1981 Career OF: 88-81-1569

YEAR TM-L	G	AB	R	H	2B	3B	HR	RBI	BB	SO	SB	CS	AVG	OBP	SLG	OPS	OPS+	BR/A	RC	RC/G	FR	G/POS	WS	TPW
1981 Cal-A	11	33	7	5	0	0	3	6	8	10	1	0	.152	.317	.424	.741	112	1	5	5.08	2	0-11(11-0-0)	1	0.3
1982 Min-A	127	463	77	126	30	1	20	46	71	101	1	2	.272	.378	.471	.849	128	20	84	6.43	1	*0-127(3-38-97)	18	1.6
1983 Min-A	151	542	70	123	24	5	28	82	61	95	2	5	.227	.310	.445	.754	101	-2	72	4.43	8	*0-146(0-38-119)/D-4	15	-0.1
1984 Min-A	155	567	75	144	21	0	32	85	57	94	4	5	.254	.322	.460	.782	109	5	81	4.87	-2	*0-153(0-0-153)/D-1	17	-0.5
1985 Min-A★	157	567	71	137	28	4	27	90	71	86	5	3	.242	.326	.448	.774	103	2	83	4.89	-1	*0-155(0-1-155)	16	-0.6
1986 Min-A	157	593	69	152	28	1	23	75	53	98	12	4	.256	.318	.423	.742	97	-2	78	4.52	0	*0-152(0-1-152)/D-2	12	-0.9
1987*Min-A	155	532	83	138	22	2	32	85	74	104	11	11	.259	.354	.489	.843	116	10	90	5.78	1	*0-138(58-0-107),D-17	20	0.4
1988 Min-A	14	49	5	9	1	0	1	6	7	11	1	2	.184	.286	.265	.551	54	-4	4	2.47	-2	0-13(1-0-12)/D-1	0	-0.5
StL-N	143	523	69	128	22	4	22	79	79	82	16	6	.245	.348	.428	.776	120	16	79	4.99	2	*0-143(1-0-143)	16	1.5
1989 StL-N	158	556	67	133	29	3	20	85	59	107	5	9	.239	.314	.410	.724	102	-2	70	4.22	1	*0-155(0-1-155)/1-1	16	-0.6
1990 StL-N	19	57	5	9	3	0	1	2	12	10	0	0	.158	.314	.263	.577	60	-3	6	3.02	0	0-17(0-0-17)	0	-0.4
*Bos-A	129	461	61	123	24	5	15	71	54	105	5	10	.267	.347	.438	.786	113	5	67	4.89	3	*0-121(0-1-121)/D-7	12	0.5
1991 Bos-A	142	459	54	105	24	1	16	70	49	72	1	2	.229	.307	.390	.697	87	-9	56	4.04	3	*0-137(0-1-136)/D-1	11	-1.0
1992 Bos-A	138	458	47	122	31	3	15	74	66	96	2	5	.266	.359	.445	.804	116	9	73	5.46	4	0-92(0-0-92),1-28,D-17	15	0.8
1993 Mil-A	80	224	20	41	7	3	6	29	25	59	3	4	.183	.265	.321	.586	58	-15	18	2.56	-1	0-71(0-0-71)/D-6	1	-1.9
1994 Mil-A	16	28	2	6	2	0	0	0	1	9	0	0	.214	.241	.286	.527	34	-3	2	2.01	-1	/0-6(0-0-6),1-2,D-2	0	-0.4
Bos-A	48	177	22	42	10	1	10	34	23	48	0	2	.237	.325	.475	.800	98	-2	27	5.18	-2	0-42(14-0-33)/1-5,D-3	5	-0.6
Yr.	64	205	24	48	12	1	10	34	24	57	0	2	.234	.314	.449	.763	90	-5	29	4.74	-3	0-48(14-0-39)/1-7,D-5	5	-1.0
Total 14	1800	6289	804	1543	306	33	271	919	770	1187	69	70	.245	.331	.434	.764	105	27	895	4.79	17	*0-1679/D-61,1-36	175	-2.5

• BRUNSBERG, Arlo Arlo Adolph Brunsberg b: 8/15/1940, Fertile, MN BL/TR, 6', 195 lbs. Deb: 9/23/1966

YEAR TM-L	G	AB	R	H	2B	3B	HR	RBI	BB	SO	SB	CS	AVG	OBP	SLG	OPS	OPS+	BR/A	RC	RC/G	FR	G/POS	WS	TPW
1966 Det-A	2	3	1	1	1	0	0	0	0	0	0	0	.333	.500	.667	1.167	227	1	1	15.26	0	/C-2	0	0.0

• BRUNTLETT, Eric Eric Kevin Bruntlett b: 3/29/1978, Lafayette, IN BR/TR, 6', 200 lbs. Deb: 6/27/2003

YEAR TM-L	G	AB	R	H	2B	3B	HR	RBI	BB	SO	SB	CS	AVG	OBP	SLG	OPS	OPS+	BR/A	RC	RC/G	FR	G/POS	WS	TPW
2003 Hou-N	31	54	3	14	3	0	1	4	0	10	0	0	.259	.259	.370	.630	59	-3	5	3.07	-2	S-10/2-9,0-2(1-1-0),3-1	1	-0.4

• BRUSH, Bob Robert Brush b: 3/8/1875, Osage, IA d: 4/2/1944, San Bernardino, CA Deb: 4/20/1907

YEAR TM-L	G	AB	R	H	2B	3B	HR	RBI	BB	SO	SB	CS	AVG	OBP	SLG	OPS	OPS+	BR/A	RC	RC/G	FR	G/POS	WS	TPW
1907 Bos-N	2	2	0	0	0	0	0	0	0	....	0	....	.000	.000	.000	.000	-100	-0	0	.00	0	/1-1	0	-0.1

• BRUTON, Bill William Haron Bruton b: 11/9/1925, Panola, AL d: 12/5/1995, Marshallton, DE BL/TR, 6'.5", 169 lbs. Deb: 4/13/1953 Career OF: 10-1550-1

YEAR TM-L	G	AB	R	H	2B	3B	HR	RBI	BB	SO	SB	CS	AVG	OBP	SLG	OPS	OPS+	BR/A	RC	RC/G	FR	G/POS	WS	TPW
1953 Mil-N	151	613	82	153	18	14	1	41	44	100	**26**	11	.250	.306	.330	.636	70	-26	65	3.60	4	*0-150(0-150-0)	14	-2.8
1954 Mil-N	142	567	89	161	20	7	4	30	40	78	**34**	13	.284	.336	.365	.701	88	-8	73	4.61	3	*0-141(0-141-0)	17	-1.1
1955 Mil-N	149	636	106	175	30	12	9	47	43	72	**25**	11	.275	.325	.403	.728	96	-3	86	4.86	13	*0-149(0-149-0)	22	0.3
1956 Mil-N	147	525	73	143	23	**15**	8	56	26	63	8	6	.272	.308	.419	.727	99	-4	66	4.21	1	*0-145(0-145-0)	17	-1.0
1957 Mil-N	79	306	41	85	16	9	5	30	19	35	11	4	.278	.322	.438	.760	109	4	44	5.08	0	0-79(0-79-0)	11	0.0
1958*Mil-N	100	325	47	91	11	3	3	28	27	37	4	1	.280	.339	.360	.699	93	-3	41	4.46	-3	0-96(0-96-0)	10	-1.0
1959 Mil-N	133	478	72	138	22	6	6	41	35	54	13	5	.289	.339	.397	.736	104	3	64	4.80	0	*0-133(0-133-0)	14	-0.3
1960 Mil-N	151	629	**112**	180	27	**13**	12	54	41	97	22	13	.286	.332	.428	.760	114	10	89	5.13	-6	*0-149(0-149-0)	24	-0.4
1961 Det-A	160	596	99	153	15	5	17	63	61	66	22	6	.257	.329	.384	.713	87	-9	79	4.58	2	*0-155(0-155-0)	17	-1.1
1962 Det-A	147	561	90	156	27	5	16	74	55	67	14	7	.278	.348	.430	.777	104	3	84	5.24	-1	*0-145(0-145-0)	19	-0.2
1963 Det-A	145	524	84	134	21	8	8	48	59	70	14	7	.256	.331	.372	.703	93	-4	67	4.40	2	*0-138(0-138-0)	15	-0.6
1964 Det-A	106	296	42	82	11	5	5	33	32	54	14	5	.277	.348	.399	.746	105	3	42	4.97	-2	0-81(10-70-1)	10	-0.1
Total 12	1610	6056	937	1651	241	102	94	545	482	793	207	89	.273	.329	.393	.722	96	-32	801	4.63	14	*0-1561	190	-8.4

• BRUYETTE, Ed Edward T. Bruyette b: 8/31/1874, Manawa, WI d: 8/5/1940, Peshastin, WA BL/TR, 5'10", 170 lbs. Deb: 8/6/1901

YEAR TM-L	G	AB	R	H	2B	3B	HR	RBI	BB	SO	SB	CS	AVG	OBP	SLG	OPS	OPS+	BR/A	RC	RC/G	FR	G/POS	WS	TPW
1901 Mil-A	26	82	7	15	3	0	0	4	12	....	1	....	.183	.295	.220	.514	46	-5	6	2.30	-5	0-21(0-21-0)/2-3,3-1,S-1	0	-1.0

• BRYAN, Billy William Ronald Bryan b: 12/4/1938, Morgan, GA BL/TR, 6'4", 200 lbs. Deb: 9/12/1961

YEAR TM-L	G	AB	R	H	2B	3B	HR	RBI	BB	SO	SB	CS	AVG	OBP	SLG	OPS	OPS+	BR/A	RC	RC/G	FR	G/POS	WS	TPW
1961 KC-A	9	19	2	3	0	0	1	2	2	7	0	0	.158	.238	.316	.554	46	-2	1	1.97	-0	/C-4	0	-0.1
1962 KC-A	25	74	5	11	2	1	2	7	5	32	0	0	.149	.203	.284	.486	28	-8	5	1.94	-2	C-22	0	-0.8
1963 KC-A	24	65	11	11	1	1	3	7	9	22	0	0	.169	.270	.354	.624	70	-3	6	3.03	-2	C-24	1	-0.4
1964 KC-A	93	220	19	53	9	2	13	36	16	69	0	0	.241	.292	.477	.770	107	1	29	4.44	1	C-65	6	0.5
1965 KC-A	108	325	36	82	11	5	14	51	29	87	0	0	.252	.317	.446	.764	116	6	47	5.16	1	C-95	12	1.2
1966 KC-A	32	76	0	10	4	0	0	7	6	17	0	0	.132	.195	.184	.379	10	-9	3	1.06	-0	C-21/1-3	1	-0.9
NY-A	27	69	5	15	2	0	4	5	5	19	0	0	.217	.270	.420	.691	99	-0	8	3.82	1	C-14/1-3	2	0.1
Yr.	59	145	5	25	6	0	4	12	11	36	0	0	.172	.231	.297	.527	52	-9	10	2.28	1	C-35/1-6	3	-0.7
1967 NY-A	16	12	1	2	0	0	1	2	5	3	0	0	.167	.412	.417	.828	151	1	3	7.00	0	/C-1	1	0.2
1968 Was-A	40	108	7	22	3	0	3	8	14	27	0	1	.204	.301	.315	.616	90	-1	11	3.26	-1	C-28	3	-0.1
Total 8	374	968	86	209	32	9	41	125	91	283	0	1	.216	.285	.395	.680	91	-15	112	3.87	-1	C-274/1-6	26	-0.2

• BRYANT, Derek Derek Roszell Bryant b: 10/9/1951, Lexington, KY BR/TR, 5'11", 185 lbs. Deb: 4/24/1979

YEAR TM-L	G	AB	R	H	2B	3B	HR	RBI	BB	SO	SB	CS	AVG	OBP	SLG	OPS	OPS+	BR/A	RC	RC/G	FR	G/POS	WS	TPW
1979 Oak-A	39	106	8	19	2	1	0	13	10	10	0	0	.179	.250	.217	.467	29	-10	6	1.62	0	0-33(25-0-10)/D-2	0	-1.2

• BRYANT, Don Donald Ray Bryant b: 7/13/1941, Jasper, FL BR/TR, 6'5", 200 lbs. Deb: 7/17/1966 C

YEAR TM-L	G	AB	R	H	2B	3B	HR	RBI	BB	SO	SB	CS	AVG	OBP	SLG	OPS	OPS+	BR/A	RC	RC/G	FR	G/POS	WS	TPW
1966 Chi-N	13	26	2	8	2	0	0	4	1	4	1	0	.308	.357	.385	.742	105	0	4	5.04	0	C-10	1	0.1
1969 Hou-N	31	59	2	11	1	0	1	6	4	13	0	0	.186	.250	.254	.504	42	-5	4	2.06	0	C-28	1	-0.4
1970 Hou-N	15	24	2	5	0	0	0	3	1	8	0	0	.208	.240	.208	.448	22	-3	1	1.80	-1	C-13	0	-0.3
Total 3	59	109	6	24	3	0	1	13	6	25	1	0	.220	.274	.275	.549	53	-7	9	2.64	-1	/C-51	2	-0.6

• BRYANT, George George F. Bryant b: 2/10/1857, Bridgeport, CT d: 6/12/1907, Boston, MA Deb: 8/6/1885

YEAR TM-L	G	AB	R	H	2B	3B	HR	RBI	BB	SO	SB	CS	AVG	OBP	SLG	OPS	OPS+	BR/A	RC	RC/G	FR	G/POS	WS	TPW
1885 Det-N	1	4	0	0	0	0	0	1	0	2	....	....	.000	.000	.000	.000	-100	-1	0	.00	0	/2-1	0	-0.1

• BRYANT, Ralph Ralph Wendell Bryant b: 5/20/1961, Fort Gaines, GA BL/TR, 6'2", 200 lbs. Deb: 9/8/1985 Career OF: 10-0-39

YEAR TM-L	G	AB	R	H	2B	3B	HR	RBI	BB	SO	SB	CS	AVG	OBP	SLG	OPS	OPS+	BR/A	RC	RC/G	FR	G/POS	WS	TPW
1985 LA-N	6	6	0	2	0	0	0	1	0	2	0	0	.333	.333	.333	.667	90	-0	1	4.50	0	/0-3(2-0-1)	0	-0.1
1986 LA-N	27	75	15	19	4	2	6	13	5	25	0	1	.253	.309	.600	.909	156	4	13	6.04	0	0-26(0-0-26)	3	0.3
1987 LA-N	46	69	7	17	2	1	2	10	10	24	2	1	.246	.350	.391	.741	99	0	10	5.15	-2	0-19(8-0-12)	2	-0.2
Total 3	79	150	22	38	6	3	8	24	15	51	2	2	.253	.329	.493	.823	126	4	24	5.58	-2	/0-48	5	0.0

• BRYE, Steve Stephen Robert Brye b: 2/4/1949, Alameda, CA BR/TR, 6', 190 lbs. Deb: 9/3/1970 Career OF: 204-339-102

YEAR TM-L	G	AB	R	H	2B	3B	HR	RBI	BB	SO	SB	CS	AVG	OBP	SLG	OPS	OPS+	BR/A	RC	RC/G	FR	G/POS	WS	TPW
1970 Min-A	9	11	1	2	1	0	0	2	2	4	0	0	.182	.308	.273	.580	60	-1	1	3.25	0	/0-6(6-0-1)	0	-0.1
1971 Min-A	28	107	10	24	1	0	3	11	7	15	3	1	.224	.272	.318	.590	64	-5	9	2.60	0	0-28(25-7-0)	1	-0.7
1972 Min-A	100	253	18	61	9	3	0	12	17	38	3	1	.241	.292	.300	.592	73	-8	22	3.00	6	0-93(74-20-2)	6	-0.7
1973 Min-A	92	278	39	73	9	5	6	33	35	43	3	5	.263	.345	.396	.741	104	1	38	4.72	-2	0-87(12-72-4)/D-1	8	-0.4
1974 Min-A	135	488	52	138	32	1	2	41	22	59	1	3	.283	.320	.365	.685	93	-6	54	3.95	-2	*0-129(0-128-1)	11	-1.2
1975 Min-A	86	246	41	62	13	1	9	34	21	37	2	1	.252	.316	.423	.739	105	1	32	4.47	0	0-72(19-5-48)/D-6	6	-0.2
1976 Min-A	87	258	33	68	11	0	2	23	13	31	1	2	.264	.299	.329	.628	82	-7	24	3.13	-4	0-78(11-57-17)/D-3	4	-1.4
1977 Mil-A	94	241	27	60	14	3	7	28	16	39	1	0	.249	.298	.419	.718	93	-3	30	4.18	4	0-83(29-43-17)/D-6	6	-0.1
1978 Pit-N	66	115	16	27	7	0	1	9	11	10	2	1	.235	.307	.322	.629	73	-4	12	3.38	0	0-47(28-7-12)	2	-0.6
Total 9	697	1997	237	515	97	13	30	193	144	276	16	14	.258	.311	.365	.676	89	-31	222	3.81	4	0-623/D-16	44	-5.2

YEAR TM-L	G	AB	R	H	2B	3B	HR	RBI	BB	SO	SB	CS	AVG	OBP	SLG	OPS	OPS+	BR/A	RC	RC/G	FR	G/POS	WS	TPW
• BUBSER, Hal	Harold Fred Bubser b: 9/28/1895, Chicago, IL d: 6/22/1959, Melrose Park, IL BR/TR, 5'11", 170 lbs. Deb: 4/15/1922																							
1922 Chi-A	3	3	0	0	0	0	0	0	0	2	0	0	.000	.000	.000	.000	-101	-1	0	.00	0	....	0	-0.1
• BUCHA, Johnny	John George Bucha b: 1/22/1925, Allentown, PA d: 4/28/1996, Bethlehem, PA BR/TR, 5'11", 190 lbs. Deb: 5/2/1948																							
1948 StL-N	2	1	0	0	0	0	0	0	1	0	0	....	.000	.500	.000	.500	43	0	0	3.51	0	/C-1	0	0.0
1950 StL-N	22	36	1	5	1	0	0	1	4	7	0	....	.139	.225	.167	.392	5	-5	1	1.01	-1	C-17	0	-0.5
1953 Det-A	60	158	17	35	9	0	1	14	20	14	1	1	.222	.309	.297	.606	65	-7	16	3.26	0	C-56	3	-0.5
Total 3	**84**	**195**	**18**	**40**	**10**	**0**	**1**	**15**	**25**	**21**	**1**	**1**	**.205**	**.295**	**.272**	**.567**	**54**	**-12**	**17**	**2.80**	**-1**	**/C-74**	**3**	**-1.1**
• BUCHANAN, Brian	Brian James Buchanan b: 7/21/1973, Miami, FL BR/TR, 6'4", 230 lbs. Deb: 5/19/2000 Career OF: 24-0-130																							
2000 Min-A	30	82	10	19	3	0	1	8	8	22	0	2	.232	.308	.305	.613	54	-7	7	2.71	-3	O-25(2-0-24)/D-2	0	-1.0
2001 Min-A	69	197	28	54	12	0	10	32	19	58	1	1	.274	.344	.487	.831	113	3	34	6.19	-2	O-46(7-0-39),D-19	5	-0.1
2002 Min-A	44	135	19	34	5	1	5	15	6	33	2	1	.252	.294	.415	.709	85	-3	15	3.90	0	O-24(0-0-24),D-17	1	-0.5
SD-N	48	92	12	27	5	0	6	13	9	26	0	1	.293	.363	.543	.906	148	5	18	6.96	-1	1-15,O-14(0-0-14)	4	0.3
2003 SD-N	115	198	29	52	10	2	8	29	24	51	6	2	.263	.351	.455	.806	119	6	31	5.21	1	O-43(15-0-29),1-24/D-4	5	0.4
Total 4	**306**	**704**	**98**	**186**	**35**	**3**	**30**	**97**	**66**	**190**	**9**	**7**	**.264**	**.335**	**.450**	**.785**	**107**	**5**	**104**	**5.12**	**-5**	**O-152/D-42,1-39**	**15**	**-1.0**
• BUCHEK, Jerry	Gerald Peter Buchek b: 5/9/1942, St. Louis, MO BR/TR, 5'11", 185 lbs. Deb: 6/30/1961																							
1961 StL-N	31	90	6	12	2	0	0	9	0	28	0	0	.133	.152	.156	.308	-16	-15	1	.41	-2	S-31	0	-1.6
1963 StL-N	3	4	0	1	0	0	0	0	0	2	0	0	.250	.250	.250	.500	41	-0	0	2.25	0	/S-1	0	0.0
1964*StL-N	35	30	7	6	0	2	0	1	3	11	0	0	.200	.273	.333	.606	64	-1	3	3.31	-4	S-20/2-9,3-1	1	-0.4
1965 StL-N	55	166	17	41	8	3	3	21	13	46	1	0	.247	.302	.386	.687	84	-3	19	3.90	7	2-33,S-18/3-1	5	0.8
1966 StL-N	100	284	23	67	10	4	4	25	23	71	0	5	.236	.293	.342	.635	76	-11	26	2.91	2	2-49,S-48/3-4	6	-0.4
1967 NY-N	124	411	35	97	11	2	14	41	26	101	3	5	.236	.285	.375	.659	89	-8	41	3.29	-1	2-95,3-17/S-9	9	-0.2
1968 NY-N	73	192	8	35	4	0	1	11	10	53	1	1	.182	.234	.219	.453	36	-15	9	1.38	-1	3-37,2-12/O-9(9-0-0)	2	-1.8
Total 7	**421**	**1177**	**96**	**259**	**35**	**11**	**22**	**108**	**75**	**312**	**5**	**11**	**.220**	**.271**	**.325**	**.595**	**68**	**-55**	**98**	**2.70**	**0**	**2-198,S-127/3-60,O-9**	**23**	**-3.4**
• BUCHER, Jim	James Quinter Bucher b: 3/11/1911, Manassas, VA BL/TR, 5'11", 170 lbs. Deb: 4/18/1934 Career OF: 32-1-40																							
1934 Bro-N	47	84	12	19	5	2	0	8	4	7	1	....	.226	.261	.333	.595	61	-5	7	3.01	-3	2-20/3-6	1	-0.7
1935 Bro-N	123	473	72	143	22	1	7	58	10	33	4	....	.302	.317	.397	.714	93	-6	58	4.59	-1	2-41,3-39,O-37(21-0-16)	12	-0.5
1936 Bro-N	110	370	49	93	12	8	2	41	29	27	5	....	.251	.306	.343	.649	74	-14	40	3.79	-1	3-39,2-32,O-30(7-0-23)	6	-1.4
1937 Bro-N	125	380	44	96	11	2	4	37	20	18	5	....	.253	.295	.324	.619	67	-18	37	3.39	-7	2-49,3-43/O-6(4-1-1)	5	-2.0
1938 StL-N	17	57	7	13	3	1	0	7	2	2	0	....	.228	.254	.316	.570	53	-4	4	2.40	-1	2-14/3-1	0	-0.5
1944 Bos-A	80	277	39	76	9	2	4	31	19	13	3	3	.274	.326	.365	.690	98	-2	33	4.14	-4	3-44,2-21	7	-0.4
1945 Bos-A	52	151	19	34	4	3	0	11	7	13	1	3	.225	.264	.291	.556	60	-9	11	2.44	0	3-32/2-2	1	-0.9
Total 7	**554**	**1792**	**242**	**474**	**66**	**19**	**17**	**193**	**91**	**113**	**19**	**6**	**.265**	**.302**	**.351**	**.653**	**78**	**-58**	**192**	**3.75**	**-18**	**3-204,2-179/O-73**	**32**	**-6.5**
• BUCKLEY, Dick	Richard D. Buckley b: 9/21/1858, Troy, NY d: 12/12/1929, Pittsburgh, PA BR/TR, 5'10", 195 lbs. Deb: 4/20/1888 Career OF: 1-0-1																							
1888 Ind-N	71	260	28	71	9	3	5	22	6	24	4	....	.273	.289	.388	.678	112	2	31	4.45	-11	C-51,3-22/1-1,O-1	8	-0.4
1889 Ind-N	68	260	35	67	11	0	8	41	15	32	5	....	.258	.301	.392	.693	91	-5	33	4.53	-3	C-55,3-12/1-1,O-1	4	-0.3
1890 NY-N	70	266	39	68	11	0	2	26	23	35	3	....	.256	.324	.320	.644	88	-4	29	3.91	4	C-62/3-8	7	0.5
1891 NY-N	75	253	23	55	9	1	4	31	11	30	3	....	.217	.258	.308	.567	67	-11	21	2.93	3	C-74/3-1	6	-0.2
1892 StL-N	121	410	43	93	17	4	5	52	22	34	7	....	.227	.275	.324	.599	85	-9	39	3.36	-4	*C-119/1-2	8	-0.1
1893 StL-N	9	23	2	4	1	0	0	1	0	0	0	....	.174	.174	.217	.391	4	-3	1	1.24	-1	/C-9	0	-0.3
1894 StL-N	29	89	5	16	1	2	1	3	6	3	1	....	.180	.240	.270	.509	23	-12	6	2.19	2	C-27/1-1	2	-0.6
Phi-N	43	160	18	47	7	3	1	26	6	13	0	....	.294	.327	.394	.721	75	-7	21	4.86	0	C-42/1-1	3	-0.2
Yr.	72	249	23	63	8	5	2	29	12	16	1	....	.253	.295	.349	.645	56	-19	27	3.81	2	C-69/1-2	5	-0.8
1895 Phi-N	38	112	20	28	6	1	0	14	9	17	2	....	.250	.333	.321	.655	69	-5	14	4.16	-5	C-38	2	-0.5
Total 8	**524**	**1833**	**213**	**449**	**72**	**14**	**26**	**216**	**98**	**188**	**25**	**....**	**.245**	**.291**	**.342**	**.633**	**82**	**-54**	**196**	**3.77**	**-14**	**C-477/3-43,1-6,O-2**	**40**	**-2.2**
• BUCKLEY, Kevin	Kevin John Buckley b: 1/16/1959, Quincy, MA BR/TR, 6'1", 200 lbs. Deb: 9/4/1984																							
1984 Tex-A	5	7	1	2	1	0	0	0	2	4	0	0	.286	.444	.429	.873	138	1	2	8.45	0	/D-3	0	0.0
• BUCKNER, Bill	William Joseph "Billy Buck" Buckner b: 12/14/1949, Vallejo, CA BL/TL, 6', 185 lbs. Deb: 9/21/1969 C Career OF: 493-0-168																							
1969 LA-N	1	1	0	0	0	0	0	0	0	0	0	0	.000	.000	.000	.000	-108	-0	0	.00	0	....	0	0.0
1970 LA-N	28	68	6	13	3	1	0	4	3	7	0	1	.191	.225	.265	.490	32	-7	4	1.89	0	O-20(19-0-1)/1-1	1	-0.8
1971 LA-N	108	358	37	99	15	1	5	41	11	18	4	1	.277	.307	.366	.673	96	-3	40	3.90	0	O-86(6-0-81),1-11	9	-0.8
1972 LA-N	105	383	47	122	14	3	5	37	17	13	10	3	.319	.349	.410	.759	118	9	52	4.96	0	O-61(19-0-52),1-35	13	0.2
1973 LA-N	140	575	68	158	20	0	8	46	17	34	12	2	.275	.299	.351	.650	83	-13	58	3.51	2	1-93,O-48(35-0-13)	11	-2.3
1974*LA-N	145	580	83	182	30	3	7	58	30	24	31	13	.314	.352	.412	.764	118	13	81	5.09	-10	*O-137(134-0-4)/1-6	21	-0.6
1975 LA-N	92	288	30	70	11	2	6	31	17	15	8	3	.243	.290	.358	.648	82	-8	27	3.07	0	O-72(72-0-0)	5	-1.2
1976 LA-N	154	642	76	193	28	4	7	60	26	26	28	9	.301	.329	.389	.718	105	4	82	4.66	-2	*O-153(149-0-5)/1-1	20	-0.7
1977 Chi-N	122	426	40	121	27	0	11	60	21	23	7	5	.284	.319	.425	.744	88	-9	52	4.19	-4	1-99	7	-1.9
1978 Chi-N	117	446	47	144	26	1	5	74	18	17	7	5	.323	.349	.419	.768	102	-0	59	4.85	5	*1-105	12	-0.2
1979 Chi-N	149	591	72	168	34	7	14	66	30	28	9	4	.284	.321	.437	.758	96	-5	78	4.70	6	*1-140	14	-0.7
1980 Chi-N	145	578	69	187	41	3	10	68	30	18	1	2	**.324**	.357	.457	.814	117	11	90	5.88	7	1-94,O-50(42-0-12)	17	1.1
1981 Chi-N★	106	421	45	131	**35**	3	10	75	26	16	5	2	.311	.353	.480	.832	129	14	65	5.59	-3	*1-105	13	0.5
1982 Chi-N	161	657	93	201	34	5	15	105	36	26	15	5	.306	.347	.441	.788	116	13	98	5.46	16	*1-161	21	2.1
1983 Chi-N	153	626	79	175	**38**	6	16	66	25	30	12	4	.280	.313	.436	.749	101	-2	83	4.75	18	*1-144,O-15(15-0-0)	16	0.7
1984 Chi-N	21	43	3	9	0	0	0	2	1	1	0	0	.209	.244	.209	.454	26	-4	2	1.59	1	/1-7,O-2(2-0-0)	0	-0.4
Bos-A	114	439	51	122	21	2	11	67	24	38	2	2	.278	.323	.410	.733	97	-3	55	4.49	3	*1-113	9	-0.6
1985 Bos-A	162	673	89	201	46	3	16	110	30	36	18	4	.299	.330	.447	.778	106	6	96	5.14	9	*1-162	16	0.5
1986*Bos-A	153	629	73	168	39	2	18	102	40	25	6	4	.267	.315	.421	.736	98	-4	76	4.10	14	*1-138,D-15	13	0.1
1987 Bos-A	75	286	23	78	6	1	2	42	13	19	1	3	.273	.304	.322	.626	65	-16	25	3.01	-1	1-74	1	-2.1
Cal-A	57	183	16	56	12	1	3	32	9	7	1	0	.306	.339	.432	.770	106	1	26	5.40	0	D-39/1-5	4	0.0
Yr.	132	469	39	134	18	2	5	74	22	26	2	3	.286	.318	.365	.682	81	-15	52	3.89	-1	1-79,D-39	5	-2.1
1988 Cal-A	19	43	1	9	0	0	0	9	4	0	2	0	.209	.277	.209	.486	39	-3	3	1.94	0	D-11/1-1	0	-0.3
KC-A	89	242	18	62	14	0	3	34	13	19	3	1	.256	.294	.351	.645	79	-7	24	3.32	0	D-42,1-21	3	-1.0
Yr.	108	285	19	71	14	0	3	43	17	19	5	1	.249	.291	.330	.621	73	-10	27	3.10	0	D-53,1-22	3	-1.3
1989 KC-A	79	176	7	38	4	1	1	16	6	11	1	0	.216	.242	.267	.509	43	-13	11	2.03	-1	1-24,D-19	0	-1.6
1990 Bos-A	22	43	4	8	0	0	1	3	3	2	0	0	.186	.239	.256	.495	37	-4	3	1.82	0	1-15	0	-0.5
Total 22	**2517**	**9397**	**1077**	**2715**	**498**	**49**	**174**	**1208**	**450**	**453**	**183**	**73**	**.289**	**.324**	**.408**	**.732**	**99**	**-29**	**1190**	**4.50**	**62**	***1-1555,O-644,D-126**	**226**	**-10.4**
• BUDASKA, Mark	Mark David Budaska b: 12/27/1952, Sharon, PA BB/TL, 6', 180 lbs. Deb: 6/6/1978																							
1978 Oak-A	4	4	0	1	1	0	0	0	1	2	0	0	.250	.400	.500	.900	160	0	1	8.14	-1	/O-2(1-0-1)	0	0.0
1981 Oak-A	9	32	3	5	1	0	0	2	4	10	0	1	.156	.250	.188	.438	29	-3	2	1.51	0	/D-9	0	-0.4
Total 2	**13**	**36**	**3**	**6**	**2**	**0**	**0**	**2**	**5**	**12**	**0**	**1**	**.167**	**.268**	**.222**	**.491**	**45**	**-3**	**2**	**2.15**	**-1**	**/D-9,O-2**	**0**	**-0.4**
• BUDD,	Budd b: Cleveland, OH Deb: 9/10/1890																							
1890 Cle-P	1	4	0	0	0	0	0	0	0	3	0	....	.000	.000	.000	.000	-109	-1	0	.00	0	/O-1	0	-0.1
• BUDDIN, Don	Donald Thomas Buddin b: 5/5/1934, Turbeville, SC BR/TR, 5'11", 178 lbs. Deb: 4/17/1956																							
1956 Bos-A	114	377	49	90	24	0	5	37	65	62	2	0	.239	.357	.342	.699	76	-11	49	4.24	4	*S-113	9	0.3
1958 Bos-A	136	497	74	118	25	2	12	43	82	106	0	4	.237	.350	.368	.718	92	-4	66	4.40	-2	*S-136	14	0.5
1959 Bos-A	151	485	75	117	24	1	10	53	92	99	6	1	.241	.368	.357	.724	95	2	72	5.05	-10	*S-150	16	0.3
1960 Bos-A	124	428	62	105	21	5	6	36	62	59	4	2	.245	.342	.360	.702	87	-6	53	4.15	-18	*S-124	9	-1.4
1961 Bos-A	115	339	58	89	22	3	6	42	72	45	2	1	.263	.395	.398	.793	110	8	58	5.91	-8	*S-109	15	1.0
1962 Hou-N	40	80	10	13	4	1	2	10	17	17	0	0	.163	.316	.313	.629	75	-2	8	3.02	-2	S-27/3-9	2	-0.2
Det-A	31	83	14	19	3	0	0	4	20	16	1	0	.229	.385	.265	.650	76	-1	11	4.48	1	S-19/2-5,3-2	3	0.2
Total 6	**711**	**2289**	**342**	**551**	**123**	**12**	**41**	**225**	**410**	**404**	**15**	**8**	**.241**	**.360**	**.359**	**.719**	**91**	**-14**	**317**	**4.63**	**-34**	**S-678/3-11,2-5**	**68**	**0.7**

YEAR TM-L	G	AB	R	H	2B	3B	HR	RBI	BB	SO	SB	CS	AVG	OBP	SLG	OPS	OPS+	BR/A	RC	RC/G	FR	G/POS	WS	TPW
• BUDZINSKI, Mark	Mark Joseph Budzinski b: 8/26/1973, Baltimore, MD BL/TL, 6'2", 180 lbs. Deb: 8/3/2003																							
2003 Cin-N	4	7	0	0	0	0	0	0	0	4	0	0	.000	.000	.000	.000	-102	-2	0	.00	0	/0-1	0	-0.2
• BUECHELE, Steve	Steven Bernard Buechele b: 9/26/1961, Lancaster, CA BR/TR, 6'2", 190 lbs. Deb: 7/19/1985 Career OF: 3-0-0																							
1985 Tex-A	69	219	22	48	6	3	6	21	14	38	3	2	.219	.272	.356	.629	70	-10	18	2.64	8	3-69/2-1	3	-0.3
1986 Tex-A	153	461	54	112	19	2	18	54	35	98	5	8	.243	.303	.410	.713	90	-10	54	3.87	6	*3-137,2-33/0-2(1-0-0)	12	-0.4
1987 Tex-A	136	363	45	86	20	0	13	50	28	66	2	2	.237	.293	.399	.693	81	-11	42	3.82	-7	*3-123,2-18/0-2(2-0-0)	7	-1.8
1988 Tex-A	155	503	68	126	21	4	16	58	65	79	2	4	.250	.342	.404	.746	105	3	71	4.86	6	*3-153/2-2	15	1.1
1989 Tex-A	155	486	60	114	22	2	16	59	36	107	1	3	.235	.294	.387	.681	89	-10	50	3.36	15	*3-145,2-18/D-1,S-1	11	0.7
1990 Tex-A	91	251	30	54	10	0	7	30	27	63	1	0	.215	.296	.339	.635	77	-7	26	3.37	5	3-88/2-4	7	-0.2
1991 Tex-A	121	416	58	111	17	2	18	66	39	69	0	4	.267	.337	.447	.784	117	7	60	4.89	8	*3-111,2-13/S-4	18	1.6
*Pit-N	31	114	16	28	5	1	4	19	10	28	0	1	.246	.317	.412	.730	105	0	14	4.22	2	3-31	4	0.2
1992 Pit-N	80	285	27	71	14	1	8	43	34	61	0	2	.249	.333	.389	.723	105	1	37	4.48	3	3-80	10	0.6
Chi-N	65	239	25	66	9	3	1	21	18	44	1	1	.276	.340	.351	.691	94	-2	29	4.25	-4	3-63/2-2	5	-0.6
Yr.	145	524	52	137	23	4	9	64	52	105	1	3	.261	.336	.372	.708	100	-0	66	4.38	-1	*3-143/2-2	15	-0.1
1993 Chi-N	133	460	53	125	27	2	15	65	48	87	1	1	.272	.347	.437	.784	110	6	69	5.25	-6	*3-129/1-6	14	0.2
1994 Chi-N	104	339	33	82	11	1	14	52	39	80	1	0	.242	.327	.404	.731	91	-5	46	4.56	-7	3-99/1-6,2-1	9	-1.0
1995 Chi-N	32	106	10	20	2	0	1	9	11	19	0	0	.189	.265	.236	.501	34	-10	7	2.21	-4	3-32	1	-1.3
Tex-A	9	24	0	3	0	0	0	0	4	3	0	0	.125	.250	.125	.375	1	-3	1	1.22	0	/3-9	0	-0.3
Total 11	1334	4266	501	1046	183	21	137	547	408	842	17	28	.245	.317	.394	.712	94	-50	524	4.13	25	*3-1269/2-92,1-12,S-5,0-4,D	116	-1.6
• BUELOW, Charlie	Charles John Buelow b: 1/12/1877, Dubuque, IA d: 5/4/1951, Dubuque, IA BR/TR Deb: 6/1/1901 U																							
1901 NY-N	22	72	3	8	4	0	0	4	2	....	0	....	.111	.147	.167	.313	-10	-10	2	.75	0	3-17/2-2	1	-0.9
• BUELOW, Fritz	Frederick William Alexander Buelow b: 2/13/1876, Berlin, Germany d: 12/27/1933, Detroit, MI BR/TR, 5'10.5", 170 lbs. Deb: 9/28/1899 U Career OF: 3-0-8																							
1899 StL-N	7	15	4	7	0	2	0	2	2	....	0	....	.467	.556	.733	1.289	246	3	6	20.75	-1	/C-4,0-2(2-0-0)	1	0.2
1900 StL-N	6	17	2	4	0	0	0	3	0	....	0	....	.235	.235	.235	.471	30	-2	1	1.97	-1	/C-4,0-1	0	-0.2
1901 Det-A	70	231	28	52	5	5	2	29	11	....	2	....	.225	.269	.316	.585	59	-14	22	3.06	0	C-69	3	-0.7
1902 Det-A	66	224	23	50	5	2	2	29	9	....	3	....	.223	.256	.290	.547	50	-16	18	2.73	-1	C-63/1-2	2	-1.0
1903 Det-A	63	192	24	41	3	6	1	13	6	....	4	....	.214	.249	.307	.556	68	-8	17	2.81	-2	C-60/1-2	3	-0.4
1904 Det-A	42	136	6	15	1	1	0	5	8	....	2	....	.110	.160	.132	.292	-7	-16	4	.80	1	C-42	2	-1.2
Cle-A	42	119	11	21	4	1	0	5	11	....	2	....	.176	.252	.227	.479	52	-6	8	2.10	-2	C-42	1	-0.5
Yr.	84	255	17	36	5	2	0	10	19	....	4	....	.141	.204	.176	.380	21	-22	12	1.39	-1	C-84	3	-1.7
1905 Cle-A	75	239	11	41	4	1	1	18	6	....	7	....	.172	.198	.209	.408	29	-20	12	1.59	-4	C-60/0-8(0-0-8),1-3,3-2	2	-1.9
1906 Cle-A	34	86	7	14	2	0	0	7	9	....	0	....	.163	.250	.186	.436	38	-6	5	1.65	-3	C-33/1-1	1	-0.6
1907 StL-A	26	75	9	11	1	0	0	1	7	....	0	....	.147	.220	.160	.380	21	-6	3	1.22	2	C-25	1	-0.2
Total 9	431	1334	125	256	25	18	6	112	69	....	20	....	.192	.238	.251	.489	45	-90	97	2.27	-10	C-402/0-11,1-8,3-2	16	-6.5
• BUES, Art	Arthur Frederick Bues b: 3/3/1888, Milwaukee, WI d: 11/7/1954, Whitefish Bay, WI BR/TR, 5'11", 184 lbs. Deb: 4/17/1913																							
1913 Bos-N	2	1	0	0	0	0	0	0	0	1	0	....	.000	.000	.000	.000	-98	-0	0	.00	-1	/2-1,3-1	0	-0.1
1914 Chi-N	14	45	3	10	1	1	0	4	5	6	1	....	.222	.300	.289	.589	76	-1	4	2.90	0	3-12	1	-0.1
Total 2	16	46	3	10	1	1	0	4	5	7	1	....	.217	.294	.283	.577	72	-2	4	2.82	-1	/3-13,2-1	1	-0.3
• BUFFINTON, Charlie	Charles G. Buffinton b: 6/14/1861, Fall River, MA d: 9/23/1907, Fall River, MA BR/TR, 6'1" Deb: 5/17/1882 M/U Career OF: 16-47-78 ♦																							
1882 Bos-N	15	50	5	13	1	0	0	4	2	3	....	....	.260	.288	.280	.568	83	-1	4	3.08	-1	/0-7(0-0-7),P-5,1-4	2	-0.7
1883 Bos-N	86	341	28	81	8	3	1	26	6	24	....	....	.238	.251	.287	.538	62	-10	25	2.66	-8	0-51(0-13-40),P-43/1-2	28	-1.0
1884 Bos-N	87	352	48	94	18	3	1	39	16	12	....	....	.267	.299	.344	.643	102	11	37	3.95	0	P-67,0-13(0-13-1),1-11	62	4.2
1885 Bos-N	82	338	26	81	12	3	1	33	3	26	....	....	.240	.246	.302	.548	79	1	26	2.71	0	P-51,0-18(1-11-6),1-15	28	0.3
1886 Bos-N	44	176	27	51	4	1	1	30	6	12	3	....	.290	.313	.341	.654	102	4	20	4.37	-6	1-19,P-18/0-9(0-1-8)	8	-2.0
1887 Phi-N	66	280	34	83	12	1	1	46	11	3	8	....	.296	.299	.331	.630	71	-3	30	4.00	3	P-40,0-22(7-7-8),1-10	23	1.8
1888 Phi-N	46	160	14	29	4	1	0	12	7	5	1	....	.181	.216	.219	.434	37	-1	8	1.64	9	P-46/0-1	44	5.2
1889 Phi-N	47	154	16	32	2	0	0	21	9	5	0	....	.208	.256	.221	.477	31	-2	9	1.94	1	P-47/0-1	33	5.2
1890 Phi-P	42	150	24	41	3	2	1	24	9	3	1	....	.273	.319	.340	.659	74	3	17	4.21	1	P-36/0-5(1-2-2),1-3	21	1.5
1891 Bos-a	58	181	16	34	2	1	1	16	19	15	0	....	.188	.269	.227	.495	42	-3	11	2.04	6	P-48,0-10(5-0-6)/1-4	31	2.3
1892 Bal-N	13	43	7	15	1	1	0	4	3	6	1	....	.349	.391	.419	.810	141	4	8	7.35	1	P-13	3	-0.7
Total 11	586	2225	245	554	67	16	7	255	91	114	14	....	.249	.276	.299	.576	72	3	195	3.15	5	P-414,0-137/1-68	283	16.0
• BUFORD, Damon	Damon Jackson Buford b: 6/12/1970, Baltimore, MD BR/TR, 5'10", 170 lbs. Deb: 5/4/1993 Career OF: 52-519-62																							
1993 Bal-A	53	79	18	18	5	0	2	9	9	19	2	2	.228	.315	.367	.682	79	-3	9	3.83	0	0-30(5-24-1),D-17	2	-0.3
1994 Bal-A	4	2	2	1	0	0	0	0	0	1	0	0	.500	.500	.500	1.000	151	0	1	13.50	0	/D-1,0-1	0	0.0
1995 Bal-A	24	32	6	2	0	0	0	2	6	7	3	1	.063	.211	.063	.273	-24	-6	1	.93	0	0-24(0-15-9)	1	-0.6
NY-N	44	136	24	32	5	0	4	12	19	28	7	7	.235	.350	.360	.710	91	-3	17	3.96	0	0-39(25-16-0)	3	-0.4
1996*Tex-A	90	145	30	41	9	0	6	20	15	34	8	5	.283	.350	.469	.819	99	-1	23	5.41	0	0-80(14-25-44)	4	-0.2
1997 Tex-A	122	366	49	82	18	0	8	39	30	83	18	7	.224	.288	.339	.627	60	-22	36	3.18	5	*0-117(0-117-0)/D-3	4	-1.5
1998*Bos-A	86	216	37	61	14	4	10	42	22	43	5	5	.282	.351	.523	.875	121	5	38	6.07	2	0-67(0-67-0),D-15/2-1,3-1	9	0.6
1999*Bos-A	91	297	39	72	15	2	6	38	21	74	9	2	.242	.297	.367	.664	66	-15	33	3.78	1	0-84(5-82-0)/D-5	6	-1.3
2000 Chi-N	150	495	64	124	18	3	15	48	47	118	4	6	.251	.325	.390	.715	81	-17	62	4.30	-6	*0-148(2-140-7)	9	-2.1
2001 Chi-N	35	85	11	15	2	0	3	8	4	23	0	0	.176	.213	.306	.519	34	-9	5	1.80	-2	0-34(0-33-1)	1	-1.0
Total 9	699	1853	280	448	86	9	54	218	173	430	56	35	.242	.313	.385	.699	77	-69	224	4.03	-1	0-624/D-41,2-1,3-1	39	-6.8
• BUFORD, Don	Donald Alvin Buford b: 2/2/1937, Linden, TX BB/TR, 5'7", 165 lbs. Deb: 9/14/1963 C Career OF: 512-41-7																							
1963 Chi-A	12	42	9	12	1	2	0	5	5	7	1	0	.286	.362	.405	.766	116	1	6	5.44	-3	/3-9,2-2	1	-0.2
1964 Chi-A	135	442	62	116	14	6	4	30	46	62	12	7	.262	.339	.348	.687	94	-3	54	4.17	1	2-92,3-37	15	0.5
1965 Chi-A	155	586	93	166	22	5	10	47	67	76	17	7	.283	.361	.389	.750	120	18	87	5.30	13	*2-139,3-41	30	**4.4**
1966 Chi-A	163	607	85	148	26	7	8	52	69	71	51	22	.244	.324	.349	.673	100	3	74	3.99	-4	*3-133,2-37,0-11(8-0-3)	21	0.1
1967 Chi-A	156	535	61	129	10	9	4	32	65	51	34	21	.241	.324	.316	.640	93	-4	58	3.59	-7	*3-121,2-51/0-1	17	-0.8
1968 Bal-A	130	426	65	120	13	4	15	46	57	46	27	12	.282	.372	.437	.808	144	25	74	6.15	-1	0-65(27-41-2),2-58/3-2	25	2.9
1969*Bal-A	144	554	99	161	31	3	11	64	96	62	19	18	.291	.400	.417	.817	128	22	97	6.19	-5	*0-128(128-0-0),2-10/3-6	24	1.0
1970*Bal-A	144	504	99	137	15	2	17	66	109	55	16	8	.272	.409	.411	.820	125	25	97	6.79	5	*0-130(130-0-0)/2-3,3-3	26	2.3
1971*Bal-A★	122	449	**99**	130	19	4	19	54	89	62	15	7	.290	.415	.477	.891	153	37	97	7.87	-1	*0-115(114-0-1)	26	3.2
1972 Bal-A	125	408	46	84	6	2	5	22	69	83	8	3	.206	.326	.267	.594	76	-8	40	3.25	-4	*0-105(104-0-1)	9	-2.0
Total 10	1286	4553	718	1203	157	44	93	418	672	575	200	105	.264	.364	.379	.743	115	115	686	5.19	-6	0-555,2-392,3-352	194	11.4
• BUHNER, Jay	Jay Campbell "Bone" Buhner b: 8/13/1964, Louisville, KY BR/TR, 6'3", 205 lbs. Deb: 9/11/1987 Career OF: 17-30-1356																							
1987 NY-A	7	22	0	5	2	0	0	1	1	6	0	0	.227	.261	.318	.579	53	-2	2	2.37	1	/0-7(2-3-2)	0	-0.1
1988 NY-A	25	69	8	13	0	0	3	13	3	25	0	0	.188	.253	.319	.572	60	-4	6	2.65	0	0-22(3-16-3)	1	-0.5
Sea-A	60	192	28	43	13	1	10	25	25	68	1	1	.224	.323	.458	.781	111	2	29	4.94	5	0-59(1-2-55)	6	0.6
Yr.	85	261	36	56	13	1	13	38	28	93	1	1	.215	.305	.421	.727	98	-1	34	4.33	5	0-81(4-18-58)	7	0.2
1989 Sea-A	58	204	27	56	15	1	9	33	19	55	1	4	.275	.342	.490	.832	128	5	34	6.07	1	0-57(0-2-56)	8	0.5
1990 Sea-A	51	163	16	45	12	0	7	33	17	50	2	2	.276	.359	.479	.837	131	6	27	5.65	-1	0-40(0-1-39),D-10	6	0.4
1991 Sea-A	137	406	64	99	14	4	27	77	53	117	0	1	.244	.340	.498	.837	128	15	68	5.70	6	*0-131(1-3-131)	13	1.7
1992 Sea-A	152	543	69	132	16	3	25	79	71	146	0	6	.243	.337	.422	.759	111	6	77	4.74	4	*0-150(0-2-150)	16	0.5
1993 Sea-A	158	563	91	153	28	3	27	98	100	144	2	5	.272	.383	.476	.859	128	23	105	6.49	-4	*0-148(0-0-148),D-10	22	1.1
1994 Sea-A	101	358	74	100	23	4	21	68	66	63	0	1	.279	.399	.542	.941	137	21	80	7.96	4	0-96(0-1-95)/D-4	13	1.8
1995*Sea-A	126	470	86	123	23	0	40	121	60	120	0	1	.262	.347	.566	.912	131	19	89	6.45	-9	*0-120(0-0-120)/D-4	16	0.4
1996 Sea-A★	150	564	107	153	29	0	44	138	84	159	0	1	.271	.374	.557	.931	131	26	120	7.48	-9	*0-142(0-0-142)/D-8	22	0.8
1997*Sea-A	157	540	104	131	18	2	40	109	119	175	0	0	.243	.384	.506	.890	131	28	106	6.63	-3	*0-154(0-0-154)/D-2	19	1.6
1998 Sea-A	72	244	33	59	7	1	15	45	38	71	0	0	.242	.346	.463	.809	108	3	42	5.95	1	0-70(0-0-70)/D-1	8	0.0
1999 Sea-A	87	266	37	59	11	0	14	38	69	100	0	0	.222	.391	.421	.812	105	5	49	6.15	1	0-85(0-0-85)/1-1	8	0.2

YEAR TM-L	G	AB	R	H	2B	3B	HR	RBI	BB	SO	SB	CS	AVG	OBP	SLG	OPS	OPS+	BR/A	RC	RC/G	FR	G/POS	WS	TPW
2000*Sea-A	112	364	50	92	20	0	26	82	59	98	0	2	.253	.363	.522	.885	128	15	69	6.48	-4	*O-104(0-0-104)/D-1	16	0.5
2001*Sea-A	19	45	4	10	2	0	2	5	8	9	0	0	.222	.340	.400	.740	100	0	6	4.04	-1	O-12(10-0-2)/D-4	0	-0.1
Total 15	1472	5013	798	1273	233	19	310	965	792	1406	6	24	.254	.362	.494	.855	124	169	908	6.20	-9	*O-1397/D-44,1-1	174	9.3
• BUKER, Harry	Henry L. "Happy" Buker b: 1859, Chicago, IL d: 8/10/1899, Chicago, IL, 140 lbs. Deb: 6/11/1884																							
1884 Det-N	30	111	5	15	1	0	0	3	4	15	....	....	.135	.165	.144	.309	-2	-12	3	.78	0	S-19,O-11(0-0-11)	1	-1.1
• BULLARD, George	George Donald "Curly" Bullard b: 10/24/1928, Lynn, MA d: 12/23/2002, Lynn, MA BR/TR, 5'9.5", 165 lbs. Deb: 9/17/1954																							
1954 Det-A	4	1	0	0	0	0	0	0	0	0	0	0	.000	.000	.000	.000	-102	-0	0	.00	-1	/S-1	0	-0.1
• BULLAS, Sim	Simeon Edward Bullas b: 4/10/1861, Cleveland, OH d: 1/14/1908, Cleveland, OH BR, 5'7.5", 150 lbs. Deb: 5/2/1884																							
1884 Tol-a	13	45	4	4	0	1	0	0	1	....	....	....	.089	.109	.133	.242	-21	-6	1	.45	-1	C-12/O-2(2-0-0)	0	-0.6
• BULLETT, Scott	Scott Douglas Bullett b: 12/25/1968, Martinsburg, WV BB/TL, 6'2", 200 lbs. Deb: 9/3/1991 Career OF: 83-42-24																							
1991 Pit-N	11	4	2	0	0	0	0	0	0	3	1	1	.000	.200	.000	.200	-40	-1	0	.00	0	/O-3(1-1-1)	0	-0.1
1993 Pit-N	23	55	2	11	0	2	0	4	3	15	3	2	.200	.241	.273	.514	37	-5	3	1.87	0	O-19(0-18-1)	0	-0.6
1995 Chi-N	104	150	19	41	5	7	3	22	12	30	8	3	.273	.331	.460	.791	108	2	22	5.06	-1	O-64(54-12-0)	4	0.0
1996 Chi-N	109	165	26	35	5	0	3	16	10	54	7	3	.212	.257	.297	.554	44	-14	13	2.51	1	O-58(28-11-22)	1	-1.4
Total 4	247	374	49	87	10	9	6	42	25	102	19	9	.233	.284	.356	.640	68	-18	38	3.34	-1	O-144	5	-2.1
• BULLING, Bud	Terry Charles Bulling b: 12/15/1952, Lynwood, CA BR/TR, 6'1", 200 lbs. Deb: 7/3/1977																							
1977 Min-A	15	32	2	5	1	0	0	5	5	5	0	0	.156	.270	.188	.458	28	-3	2	1.68	-1	C-10/D-3	0	-0.4
1981 Sea-A	62	154	15	38	3	0	2	15	21	20	0	0	.247	.341	.305	.646	84	-2	18	3.91	-3	C-62	4	-0.3
1982 Sea-A	56	154	17	34	7	0	1	8	19	16	2	1	.221	.306	.286	.592	62	-7	13	2.80	0	C-56	3	-0.5
1983 Sea-A	5	5	0	0	0	0	0	0	0	0	0	0	.000	.000	.000	.000	-96	-1	0	.00	0	/C-5	0	-0.1
Total 4	138	345	34	77	11	0	3	28	45	41	2	1	.223	.315	.281	.596	67	-14	33	3.11	-4	C-133/D-3	7	-1.3
• BULLOCK, Eric	Eric Gerald Bullock b: 2/16/1960, Los Angeles, CA BL/TL, 5'11", 185 lbs. Deb: 8/26/1985 Career OF: 19-1-10																							
1985 Hou-N	18	25	3	7	2	0	0	2	1	3	0	1	.280	.308	.360	.668	89	-1	2	3.54	-1	/O-7(4-0-3)	1	-0.2
1986 Hou-N	6	21	0	1	0	0	0	1	0	3	2	0	.048	.048	.048	.095	-76	-5	0	.13	0	/O-6(6-0-0)	0	-0.5
1988 Min-A	16	17	3	5	0	0	0	3	3	1	1	0	.294	.400	.294	.694	95	0	3	5.67	-1	/O-4(3-0-2),D-2	0	0.0
1989 Phi-N	6	4	1	0	0	0	0	0	0	2	0	0	.000	.000	.000	.000	-100	-1	0	.00	0	/O-3(0-1-2)	0	-0.1
1990 Mon-N	4	2	0	1	0	0	0	0	0	0	0	0	.500	.500	.500	1.000	183	0	1	13.50	0	....	0	0.0
1991 Mon-N	73	72	6	16	4	0	1	6	9	13	6	1	.222	.309	.319	.628	78	-1	7	3.29	1	/O-9(6-0-3),1-3	1	-0.1
1992 Mon-N	8	5	0	0	0	0	0	0	0	1	0	0	.000	.000	.000	.000	-101	-1	0	.00	0	....	0	-0.1
Total 7	131	146	13	30	6	0	1	12	13	23	9	2	.205	.270	.267	.538	53	-8	13	2.88	-1	/O-29,1-3,D-2	2	-1.1
• BUMBRY, Al	Alonza Benjamin Bumbry b: 4/21/1947, Fredericksburg, VA BL/TR, 5'8", 175 lbs. Deb: 9/5/1972 C Career OF: 382-928-31																							
1972 Bal-A	9	11	5	4	0	1	0	0	0	0	1	1	.364	.364	.545	.909	164	1	2	6.00	0	/O-2(2-0-0)	1	0.0
1973*Bal-A	110	356	73	120	15	**11**	7	34	34	49	23	10	.337	.399	.500	.899	153	26	72	7.70	-1	O-86(62-1-29)/D-7	17	2.2
1974*Bal-A	94	270	35	63	10	3	1	19	21	46	12	4	.233	.291	.304	.595	74	-8	25	3.10	-2	O-67(67-0-0)/D-7	4	-1.5
1975 Bal-A	114	349	47	94	19	4	2	32	32	81	16	3	.269	.338	.364	.702	105	5	47	4.78	0	D-48,O-39(35-3-1)/3-1	10	0.2
1976 Bal-A	133	450	71	113	15	7	9	36	43	76	42	10	.251	.318	.376	.693	109	10	57	4.31	2	*O-116(82-57-0),D-10	16	0.7
1977 Bal-A	133	518	74	164	31	3	4	41	45	88	19	8	.317	.373	.411	.785	121	17	83	6.00	-4	*O-130(52-112-0)	24	1.0
1978 Bal-A	33	114	21	27	5	2	2	6	17	15	5	3	.237	.346	.368	.714	108	2	15	4.14	0	O-28(16-17-0)	3	0.1
1979*Bal-A	148	569	80	162	29	1	7	49	43	74	37	12	.285	.338	.376	.714	96	-0	76	4.74	-4	*O-146(5-146-0)	19	-0.6
1980 Bal-A★	160	645	118	205	29	9	9	53	78	75	44	11	.318	.394	.433	.826	127	32	118	6.74	8	*O-160(1-160-0)	33	3.8
1981 Bal-A	101	392	61	107	18	2	1	27	51	51	22	15	.273	.360	.337	.696	102	2	49	4.26	2	*O-100(0-100-0)	13	0.2
1982 Bal-A	150	562	77	147	20	4	5	40	44	77	10	5	.262	.315	.338	.653	80	-15	60	3.63	1	*O-147(3-146-0)/D-1	12	-1.7
1983*Bal-A	124	378	63	104	14	4	3	31	31	33	12	5	.275	.330	.357	.687	91	-4	47	4.45	-5	*O-104(17-99-0),D-11	10	-1.1
1984 Bal-A	119	344	47	93	12	1	3	24	25	35	9	5	.270	.320	.337	.657	84	-8	35	3.51	2	O-99(28-82-0)/D-9	7	-0.8
1985 SD-N	68	95	6	19	3	0	1	10	7	9	2	0	.200	.255	.263	.518	46	-7	6	2.02	-1	O-17(12-5-1)	0	-0.9
Total 14	1496	5053	778	1422	220	52	54	402	471	709	254	92	.281	.345	.378	.723	104	52	692	4.83	-2	*O-1241/D-93,3-1	169	1.5
• BUNCE, Josh	Joshua Bunce b: 5/10/1847, Brooklyn, NY d: 4/28/1912, Brooklyn, NY Deb: 8/27/1877 U																							
1877 Har-N	1	4	0	0	0	0	0	0	0	0	....	....	.000	.000	.000	.000	-112	-1	0	.00	0	/O-1	0	-0.1
• BURBRINK, Nelson	Nelson Edward Burbrink b: 12/28/1921, Cincinnati, OH d: 4/12/2001, Largo, FL BR/TR, 5'10", 195 lbs. Deb: 6/5/1955																							
1955 StL-N	58	170	11	47	8	1	0	15	14	13	1	1	.276	.335	.335	.670	79	-5	19	3.84	-2	C-55	3	-0.5
• BURCH, Al	Albert William Burch b: 10/7/1883, Albany, NY d: 10/5/1926, Brooklyn, NY BL/TR, 5'8.5", 160 lbs. Deb: 6/19/1906 Career OF: 115-324-123																							
1906 StL-N	91	335	40	89	5	1	0	11	37	....	15	....	.266	.339	.287	.625	99	1	40	4.06	2	O-91(0-58-33)	8	-0.1
1907 StL-N	48	154	18	35	3	1	0	5	17	....	7	....	.227	.304	.260	.564	79	-3	15	3.20	1	O-48(0-48-0)	4	-0.5
Bro-N	40	120	12	35	2	2	0	12	11	....	5	....	.292	.351	.342	.693	127	4	17	5.06	1	O-36(27-5-5)/2-1	5	0.3
Yr.	88	274	30	70	5	3	0	17	28	....	12	....	.255	.325	.296	.620	100	1	31	3.98	1	O-84(27-53-5)/2-1	9	-0.3
1908 Bro-N	123	456	45	111	8	4	2	18	33	....	15	....	.243	.294	.292	.586	91	-5	43	3.15	12	*O-116(47-44-28)	11	0.1
1909 Bro-N	152	601	80	163	20	6	1	30	51	....	38	....	.271	.329	.329	.659	108	5	76	4.44	0	*O-151(41-102-9)/1-1	17	-0.3
1910 Bro-N	103	352	41	83	8	3	1	20	22	30	13	....	.236	.281	.284	.565	67	-16	31	2.93	-1	O-70(0-26-45),1-13	4	-2.2
1911 Bro-N	54	167	18	38	2	3	0	7	15	22	3	....	.228	.291	.275	.567	61	-9	14	2.77	0	O-43(0-41-3)/2-3	2	-1.2
Total 6	611	2185	254	554	48	20	4	103	186	52	96	....	.254	.312	.299	.612	92	-23	236	3.67	14	O-555/1-14,2-4	51	-4.0
• BURCH, Ernie	Earnest W. Burch b: 9/9/1856, DeKalb County, IL d: 10/12/1892, Guthrie, OK BL, 5'10", 190 lbs. Deb: 8/15/1884 Career OF: 185-0-9																							
1884 Cle-N	32	124	9	26	4	0	0	7	5	24	....	....	.210	.240	.242	.482	50	-7	7	2.07	4	O-32(23-0-9)	1	-0.3
1886 Bro-a	113	456	78	119	22	6	2	72	39	....	16	....	.261	.321	.349	.669	109	4	58	4.61	-11	*O-113(113-0-0)	14	-0.9
1887 Bro-a	49	217	47	84	4	4	2	26	29	....	15	....	.387	.395	.388	.784	118	6	36	7.24	1	O-49(49-0-0)	6	0.4
Total 3	194	797	134	229	30	10	4	105	73	24	31	....	.287	.328	.341	.669	102	3	101	4.79	-5	O-194	21	-0.8
• BURDA, Bob	Edward Robert Burda b: 7/16/1938, St. Louis, MO BL/TL, 5'11", 180 lbs. Deb: 8/25/1962 Career OF: 12-0-86																							
1962 StL-N	7	14	0	1	0	0	0	0	3	1	1	0	.071	.235	.071	.307	-12	-2	1	1.12	0	/O-6(1-0-5)	0	-0.3
1965 SF-N	31	27	0	3	0	0	0	5	5	6	0	0	.111	.250	.111	.361	6	-3	1	.91	-1	1-11/O-1	0	-0.4
1966 SF-N	37	43	3	7	3	0	0	2	2	5	0	0	.163	.200	.233	.433	19	-5	2	1.36	-0	/1-7,O-4(3-0-1)	0	-0.5
1969 SF-N	97	161	20	37	8	0	6	27	21	12	0	1	.230	.319	.391	.710	100	-0	21	4.30	0	1-45,O-19(5-0-15)	4	-0.3
1970 SF-N	28	23	1	6	0	0	0	3	5	2	0	0	.261	.414	.261	.675	86	0	3	4.63	-1	/1-8,O-1	0	-0.1
Mil-A	78	222	19	55	9	0	4	20	16	17	1	0	.248	.307	.342	.649	78	-6	24	3.59	-1	O-64(0-0-64)/1-7	4	-1.0
1971 StL-N	65	71	6	21	0	0	1	12	10	11	0	0	.296	.390	.338	.728	104	1	10	4.95	0	1-13/O-1	2	0.1
1972 Bos-A	45	73	4	12	1	0	2	9	8	11	0	0	.164	.247	.260	.507	48	-5	4	1.78	-1	1-15/O-1	0	-0.8
Total 7	388	634	53	142	21	0	13	78	70	65	2	1	.224	.306	.319	.625	74	-20	64	3.34	-4	1-106/O-97	10	-3.4
• BURDOCK, Jack	John Joseph "Black Jack" Burdock b: 4/1852, Brooklyn, NY d: 11/27/1931, Brooklyn, NY BR/TR, 5'9.5", 158 lbs. Deb: 5/2/1872 M/U																							
1872 Atl-n	37	174	26	46	3	0	0	15	1	1	0	1	.264	.269	.282	.550	59	-11	13	3.24	-14	*S-36/C-4,2-2	....	-1.8
1873 Atl-n	55	245	56	62	7	1	2	36	7	4	3	1	.253	.274	.314	.588	83	-1	22	3.72	-8	*2-55/C-2	....	-0.9
1874 Mut-n	61	273	45	75	11	4	1	27	1	5	4	0	.275	.277	.355	.633	98	-1	29	4.35	16	*3-60/O-3(2-1-0)	....	1.2
1875 Har-n	74	350	72	103	12	5	0	35	3	13	20	11	.294	.300	.357	.657	121	6	45	5.10	7	*2-73/3-2,C-1	....	0.7
1876 Har-N	69	322	66	80	9	1	0	23	13	16	....	....	.248	.289	.294	.583	87	-5	27	3.29	5	*2-69/3-1	8	0.3
1877 Har-N	58	277	35	72	6	0	0	9	2	16	....	....	.260	.265	.282	.547	81	-5	21	2.84	9	*2-55/3-3	6	0.6
1878 Bos-N	60	246	37	64	12	6	0	25	3	17	....	....	.260	.269	.358	.627	97	-2	24	3.67	21	*2-60	11	2.0
1879 Bos-N	84	359	64	86	10	3	0	36	9	28	....	....	.240	.258	.284	.542	77	-9	27	2.77	13	*2-84	8	0.8
1880 Bos-N	86	356	58	90	17	4	2	35	8	26	....	....	.253	.269	.340	.609	108	3	33	3.45	6	*2-86	11	1.2
1881 Bos-N	73	282	36	67	12	4	1	24	7	18	....	....	.238	.256	.319	.575	83	-5	24	2.97	-8	*2-72/S-1	6	-0.9
1882 Bos-N	83	319	36	76	6	7	0	27	9	24	....	....	.238	.259	.301	.560	79	-8	26	2.89	11	*2-83	7	0.6
1883 Bos-N	96	400	80	132	27	8	5	88	14	35	....	....	.330	.353	.475	.828	145	21	69	7.05	0	*2-96	19	2.1

YEAR TM-L	G	AB	R	H	2B	3B	HR	RBI	BB	SO	SB	CS	AVG	OBP	SLG	OPS	OPS+	BR/A	RC	RC/G	FR	G/POS	WS	TPW
1884 Bos-N	87	361	65	97	14	4	6	49	15	52	....	....	.269	.298	.380	.677	112	4	42	4.36	4	*2-87/3-1	13	1.0
1885 Bos-N	45	169	18	24	5	0	0	7	8	18	....	....	.142	.181	.172	.352	15	-15	5	1.00	-9	2-45	1	-2.2
1886 Bos-N	59	221	26	48	6	1	0	25	11	27	3	....	.217	.254	.253	.508	57	-11	15	2.40	-3	2-59	2	-1.1
1887 Bos-N	65	255	36	79	6	0	0	29	18	22	19	....	.310	.320	.283	.603	71	-8	28	4.25	-24	2-65	3	-2.5
1888 Bos-N	22	79	5	16	0	0	0	4	2	5	1	....	.203	.232	.203	.434	38	-6	4	1.73	-3	2-22	0	-0.8
Bro-a	70	246	15	30	1	2	1	8	8	....	9	....	.122	.166	.154	.320	3	-27	8	1.00	7	2-70	3	-1.6
1891 Bro-N	3	12	1	1	0	0	0	1	1	1	0	....	.083	.154	.083	.237	-31	-2	0	.39	0	/2-3	0	-0.1
Total 4 n	227	1042	199	286	33	10	3	113	12	23	27	13	.274	.283	.334	.617	96	-8	109	4.27	1	2-130/3-62,S-36,C-7,O-3	....	-0.9
Total 14	960	3904	578	962	131	40	15	390	128	305	32	....	.246	.270	.310	.580	83	-73	354	3.31	29	2-956/3-5,S-1	98	-0.6

• BURG, Joe Joseph Peter Burg b: 6/4/1882, Chicago, IL d: 4/28/1969, Joliet, IL BR/TR, 5'10", 143 lbs. Deb: 9/26/1910

YEAR TM-L	G	AB	R	H	2B	3B	HR	RBI	BB	SO	SB	CS	AVG	OBP	SLG	OPS	OPS+	BR/A	RC	RC/G	FR	G/POS	WS	TPW
1910 Bos-N	13	46	7	15	0	1	0	10	7	12	5	....	.326	.415	.370	.785	124	2	9	7.39	1	3-12/S-1	1	0.3

• BURGESS, Smoky Forrest Harrill Burgess b: 2/6/1927, Caroleen, NC d: 9/15/1991, Asheville, NC BL/TR, 5'8.5", 187 lbs. Deb: 4/19/1949

YEAR TM-L	G	AB	R	H	2B	3B	HR	RBI	BB	SO	SB	CS	AVG	OBP	SLG	OPS	OPS+	BR/A	RC	RC/G	FR	G/POS	WS	TPW
1949 Chi-N	46	56	4	15	0	0	1	12	4	4	0	....	.268	.317	.321	.638	73	-2	6	3.67	1	/C-8	1	-0.1
1951 Chi-N	94	219	21	55	4	2	2	20	21	12	2	0	.251	.317	.315	.632	69	-9	21	3.30	2	C-64	4	-0.4
1952 Phi-N	110	371	49	110	27	2	6	56	49	21	3	1	.296	.380	.429	.809	125	14	65	6.57	-8	*C-104	17	1.3
1953 Phi-N	102	312	31	91	17	5	4	36	37	17	3	2	.292	.370	.417	.787	105	3	48	5.58	-5	C-95	12	0.3
1954 Phi-N★	108	345	41	127	27	5	4	46	42	11	1	5	.368	.437	.510	.947	146	23	75	8.47	-3	C-91	15	2.4
1955 Phi-N	7	21	4	4	2	0	1	1	3	1	0	0	.190	.292	.429	.720	90	-0	2	2.14	0	/C-6	0	0.0
Cin-N★	116	421	67	129	15	3	20	77	47	35	1	1	.306	.377	.499	.876	123	14	78	6.77	-6	*C-107	16	1.4
Yr.	123	442	71	133	17	3	21	78	50	36	1	1	.301	.373	.495	.869	121	14	80	6.49	-6	*C-113	16	1.4
1956 Cin-N	90	229	28	63	10	0	12	39	26	18	0	1	.275	.349	.476	.825	112	4	37	5.77	0	C-55	10	0.6
1957 Cin-N	90	205	29	58	14	1	14	39	24	16	0	0	.283	.358	.566	.924	134	10	41	7.22	-3	C-45	9	0.9
1958 Cin-N	99	251	28	71	12	1	6	31	22	20	0	0	.283	.343	.410	.753	93	-2	34	4.88	-2	C-58	7	-0.1
1959 Pit-N★	114	377	41	112	28	5	11	59	31	16	0	0	.297	.354	.485	.839	122	11	62	5.96	-4	*C-101	16	1.2
1960*Pit-N★	110	337	33	99	15	2	7	39	35	13	0	1	.294	.360	.412	.773	110	5	50	5.39	-2	C-89	15	0.8
1961 Pit-N★	100	323	37	98	17	3	12	52	30	16	1	0	.303	.366	.486	.852	123	11	57	6.58	-6	C-92	13	0.9
1962 Pit-N	103	360	38	118	19	2	13	61	31	19	0	1	.328	.381	.500	.881	134	17	68	7.10	-5	*C-101	19	1.6
1963 Pit-N	91	264	20	74	10	1	6	37	24	14	0	1	.280	.343	.394	.737	111	4	32	4.23	-1	C-72	8	0.7
1964 Pit-N★	68	171	9	42	3	1	2	17	13	14	2	1	.246	.303	.310	.613	73	-6	14	2.73	-2	C-44	2	-0.6
Chi-A	7	5	1	1	0	0	1	1	2	0	0	0	.200	.429	.800	1.229	239	1	2	11.57	0	....	1	0.1
1965 Chi-A	80	77	2	22	4	0	2	24	11	7	0	0	.286	.375	.416	.791	132	4	12	5.57	0	/C-5	3	0.4
1966 Chi-A	79	67	0	21	5	0	0	15	11	8	0	0	.313	.418	.388	.806	143	4	12	6.90	0	/C-2	3	0.5
1967 Chi-A	77	60	2	8	1	0	2	11	14	8	0	0	.133	.307	.250	.557	69	-1	5	2.42	0	....	1	-0.1
Total 18	1691	4471	485	1318	230	33	126	673	477	270	13	14	.295	.364	.446	.810	116	105	722	5.83	-44	*C-1139	172	11.6

• BURGESS, Tom Thomas Roland "Tim" Burgess b: 9/1/1927, London, Canada BL/TL, 6', 180 lbs. Deb: 4/17/1954 C Career OF: 2-0-4

YEAR TM-L	G	AB	R	H	2B	3B	HR	RBI	BB	SO	SB	CS	AVG	OBP	SLG	OPS	OPS+	BR/A	RC	RC/G	FR	G/POS	WS	TPW
1954 StL-N	17	21	2	1	1	0	0	1	3	9	0	0	.048	.167	.095	.262	-30	-4	0	.63	0	/O-4(0-0-4)	0	-0.5
1962 LA-A	87	143	17	28	7	1	2	13	36	20	2	0	.196	.358	.301	.658	82	-1	18	4.14	-3	1-35/O-2(2-0-0)	3	-0.6
Total 2	104	164	19	29	8	1	2	14	39	29	2	0	.177	.335	.274	.609	69	-5	19	3.63	-3	/1-35,O-6	3	-1.1

• BURGO, Bill William Ross Burgo b: 11/5/1919, Johnstown, PA d: 10/19/1988, Morgan City, LA BR/TR, 5'8", 185 lbs. Deb: 9/22/1943 Career OF: 31-0-8

YEAR TM-L	G	AB	R	H	2B	3B	HR	RBI	BB	SO	SB	CS	AVG	OBP	SLG	OPS	OPS+	BR/A	RC	RC/G	FR	G/POS	WS	TPW
1943 Phi-A	17	70	12	26	4	2	1	9	4	1	0	2	.371	.421	.529	.950	178	6	16	9.15	2	O-17(17-0-0)	5	0.7
1944 Phi-A	27	88	6	21	2	0	1	3	7	3	1	3	.239	.316	.295	.612	76	-4	8	2.96	2	O-22(14-0-8)	1	-0.4
Total 2	44	158	18	47	6	2	2	12	11	4	1	5	.297	.362	.399	.761	121	2	23	5.37	3	/O-39	6	0.3

• BURICH, Bill William Max Burich b: 5/29/1918, Calumet, MI BR/TR, 6', 180 lbs. Deb: 4/15/1942

YEAR TM-L	G	AB	R	H	2B	3B	HR	RBI	BB	SO	SB	CS	AVG	OBP	SLG	OPS	OPS+	BR/A	RC	RC/G	FR	G/POS	WS	TPW
1942 Phi-N	25	80	3	23	1	0	0	7	6	13	2	....	.288	.337	.300	.637	92	-1	8	3.84	-4	S-19/3-3	1	-0.3
1946 Phi-N	2	1	1	0	0	0	0	0	0	0	0	....	.000	.000	.000	.000	-103	-0	0	.00	0	/3-1	0	-0.1
Total 2	27	81	4	23	1	0	0	7	6	13	2	....	.284	.333	.296	.630	90	-1	8	3.78	-4	/S-19,3-4	1	-0.4

• BURK, Mack Mack Edwin Burk b: 4/21/1935, Nacogdoches, TX BR/TR, 6'4", 180 lbs. Deb: 5/25/1956

YEAR TM-L	G	AB	R	H	2B	3B	HR	RBI	BB	SO	SB	CS	AVG	OBP	SLG	OPS	OPS+	BR/A	RC	RC/G	FR	G/POS	WS	TPW
1956 Phi-N	15	1	3	1	0	0	0	0	0	0	0	0	1.000	1.000	1.000	2.000	448	0	1	∞	0	/C-1	0	0.0
1958 Phi-N	1	1	0	0	0	0	0	0	0	1	0	0	.000	.000	.000	.000	-101	-0	0	.00	0	....	0	0.0
Total 2	16	2	3	1	0	0	0	0	0	1	0	0	.500	.500	.500	1.000	173	0	1	.00	0	/C-1	0	0.0

• BURKAM, Chris Chauncey De Pew Burkam b: 10/13/1892, Benton Harbor, MI d: 5/9/1964, Kalamazoo, MI BL/TR, 5'11", 175 lbs. Deb: 6/24/1915

YEAR TM-L	G	AB	R	H	2B	3B	HR	RBI	BB	SO	SB	CS	AVG	OBP	SLG	OPS	OPS+	BR/A	RC	RC/G	FR	G/POS	WS	TPW
1915 StL-A	1	1	0	0	0	0	0	0	0	1	0	....	.000	.000	.000	.000	-104	-0	0	.00	0	....	0	0.0

• BURKE, Dan Daniel L. Burke b: 10/25/1868, Abington, MA d: 3/20/1933, Taunton, MA BR/TR, 5'10", 190 lbs. Deb: 4/18/1890

YEAR TM-L	G	AB	R	H	2B	3B	HR	RBI	BB	SO	SB	CS	AVG	OBP	SLG	OPS	OPS+	BR/A	RC	RC/G	FR	G/POS	WS	TPW
1890 Roc-a	32	102	14	22	1	0	0	9	17	....	2	....	.216	.333	.225	.559	70	-2	9	2.83	0	O-29(0-19-10)/C-4,1-2	2	-0.2
Syr-a	9	20	1	0	0	0	0	0	5	....	0	....	.000	.231	.000	.231	-35	-3	0	.00	-2	/C-9	0	-0.4
Yr.	41	122	15	22	1	0	0	9	22	....	2	....	.180	.315	.189	.504	51	-5	9	2.26	-2	O-29(0-19-10),C-13/1-2	2	-0.6
1892 Bos-N	1	4	0	0	0	0	0	0	0	2	0	....	.000	.000	.000	.000	-92	-1	0	.00	-1	/C-1	0	-0.1
Total 2	42	126	15	22	1	0	0	9	22	2	2	....	.175	.307	.183	.489	47	-6	9	2.18	-3	/O-29,C-14,1-2	2	-0.7

• BURKE, Eddie Edward D. Burke b: 10/6/1866, Northumberland, PA d: 11/26/1907, Utica, NY BL/TR, 5'6", 161 lbs. Deb: 4/19/1890 Career OF: 609-172-9

YEAR TM-L	G	AB	R	H	2B	3B	HR	RBI	BB	SO	SB	CS	AVG	OBP	SLG	OPS	OPS+	BR/A	RC	RC/G	FR	G/POS	WS	TPW
1890 Phi-N	100	430	85	113	16	11	4	50	49	40	38	....	.263	.349	.379	.728	109	5	72	6.01	0	*O-96(0-96-0)/2-4	14	0.2
Pit-N	31	124	17	26	5	2	1	7	14	9	6	....	.210	.295	.306	.601	85	-2	13	3.60	-2	O-31(0-31-0)	1	-0.4
Yr.	131	554	102	139	21	13	5	57	63	49	44	....	.251	.337	.363	.700	104	3	85	5.44	-1	*O-127(0-127-0)/2-4	15	-0.2
1891 Mil-a	35	144	31	34	9	0	2	21	12	19	7	....	.236	.337	.340	.678	78	-5	19	4.66	2	O-35(0-35-0)	4	-0.4
1892 Cin-N	15	41	6	6	1	0	0	4	9	4	2	....	.146	.300	.171	.471	44	-2	3	2.13	0	O-14(3-5-6)/3-1	0	-0.2
NY-N	89	363	81	94	10	5	6	41	46	37	42	....	.259	.350	.364	.714	118	9	62	6.27	-6	2-59,O-30(30-0-0)	14	0.2
Yr.	104	404	87	100	11	5	6	45	55	41	44	....	.248	.345	.344	.689	110	7	65	5.79	-6	2-59,O-44(33-5-6)/3-1	14	0.0
1893 NY-N	135	537	122	150	23	10	9	80	51	32	54	....	.279	.369	.410	.778	106	5	104	7.09	7	*O-135(135-0-0)	15	-0.1
1894*NY-N	138	574	124	176	23	11	4	77	39	35	34	....	.307	.361	.406	.767	85	-14	99	6.46	0	*O-136(136-0-0)	15	-2.1
1895 NY-N	39	167	38	43	6	2	1	12	7	9	14	....	.257	.299	.335	.635	65	-9	22	4.65	2	O-39(39-0-0)	3	-0.8
Cin-N	56	228	52	61	8	6	1	25	22	14	19	....	.268	.343	.368	.711	80	-7	36	5.81	0	O-56(56-0-1)	5	-1.0
Yr.	95	395	90	104	14	8	2	37	29	23	33	....	.263	.325	.354	.679	74	-16	58	5.32	2	*O-95(95-0-1)	8	-1.9
1896 Cin-N	122	521	120	177	24	9	1	52	41	29	53	....	.340	.392	.426	.818	108	6	111	8.37	0	*O-122(116-5-1)	20	-0.4
1897 Cin-N	95	387	71	103	17	1	1	41	29	....	22	....	.266	.327	.323	.650	67	-19	50	4.58	-1	*O-95(94-0-1)	7	-2.4
Total 8	855	3516	747	983	142	57	30	410	319	228	291	....	.280	.352	.378	.730	94	-34	591	6.15	3	O-789/2-63,3-1	98	-7.5

• BURKE, Frank Frank Aloysius Burke b: 2/16/1880, Carbon County, PA d: 9/17/1946, Los Angeles, CA TR Deb: 9/14/1906 Career OF: 32-7-2

YEAR TM-L	G	AB	R	H	2B	3B	HR	RBI	BB	SO	SB	CS	AVG	OBP	SLG	OPS	OPS+	BR/A	RC	RC/G	FR	G/POS	WS	TPW
1906 NY-N	8	9	2	3	1	1	0	1	1	....	1	....	.333	.400	.667	1.067	227	1	3	12.44	-1	/O-4(0-3-1)	1	0.1
1907 Bos-N	43	129	6	23	0	1	0	8	11	....	3	....	.178	.243	.194	.437	37	-9	8	1.78	-3	O-36(32-4-1)	0	-1.7
Total 2	51	138	8	26	1	2	0	9	12	....	4	....	.188	.253	.225	.478	49	-8	10	2.33	-4	/O-40	1	-1.6

• BURKE, Glenn Glenn Lawrence Burke b: 11/16/1952, Oakland, CA d: 5/30/1995, San Leandro, CA BR/TR, 6', 195 lbs. Deb: 4/9/1976 Career OF: 49-135-22

YEAR TM-L	G	AB	R	H	2B	3B	HR	RBI	BB	SO	SB	CS	AVG	OBP	SLG	OPS	OPS+	BR/A	RC	RC/G	FR	G/POS	WS	TPW
1976 LA-N	25	46	9	11	2	0	0	5	3	8	3	2	.239	.300	.283	.583	67	-2	4	2.63	-1	O-20(5-15-0)	1	-0.4
1977*LA-N	83	169	16	43	8	0	1	13	5	22	13	5	.254	.280	.320	.600	61	-9	15	2.93	-5	O-74(5-64-6)	2	-1.6
1978 LA-N	16	19	2	4	0	0	0	2	0	4	1	0	.211	.211	.211	.421	18	-2	1	1.71	-1	O-15(4-11-0)	0	-0.3
Oak-A	78	200	19	47	6	1	1	14	10	26	15	8	.235	.271	.290	.561	61	-11	14	2.14	-4	O-67(13-45-14)/D-2,1-1	2	-1.7
1979 Oak-A	23	89	4	19	2	1	0	4	4	10	3	1	.213	.247	.258	.506	39	-7	5	1.88	0	O-23(22-0-2)	0	-0.8
Total 4	225	523	50	124	18	2	2	38	22	70	35	16	.237	.271	.291	.561	56	-31	38	2.37	-12	O-199/D-2,1-1	5	-4.8

• BURKE, Jamie Jamie Burke b: 9/24/1971, Roseburg, OR BR/TR, 6', 195 lbs. Deb: 5/9/2001

YEAR TM-L	G	AB	R	H	2B	3B	HR	RBI	BB	SO	SB	CS	AVG	OBP	SLG	OPS	OPS+	BR/A	RC	RC/G	FR	G/POS	WS	TPW
2001 Ana-A	9	5	1	1	0	0	0	0	0	2	0	0	.200	.200	.200	.400	6	-1	0	1.35	1	/C-8,1-1	0	0.0

YEAR TM-L	G	AB	R	H	2B	3B	HR	RBI	BB	SO	SB	CS	AVG	OBP	SLG	OPS	OPS+	BR/A	RC	RC/G	FR	G/POS	WS	TPW
2003 Chi-A	6	8	0	3	0	0	0	2	0	0	0	0	.375	.375	.375	.750	99	-0	1	6.08	-1	/C-4,1-1,D-1	1	-0.1
Total 2	15	13	1	4	0	0	0	2	0	2	0	0	.308	.308	.308	.615	63	-1	1	3.98	0	/C-12,1-2,D-1	1	-0.1

• BURKE, Jimmy James Timothy "Sunset Jimmy" Burke
b: 10/12/1874, St. Louis, MO d: 3/26/1942, St. Louis, MO BR/TR, 5'7", 160 lbs. Deb: 10/6/1898 M/C Career OF: 11-0-12

YEAR TM-L	G	AB	R	H	2B	3B	HR	RBI	BB	SO	SB	CS	AVG	OBP	SLG	OPS	OPS+	BR/A	RC	RC/G	FR	G/POS	WS	TPW
1898 Cle-N	13	38	1	4	1	0	0	1	2	....	1	....	.105	.150	.132	.282	-19	-6	1	.80	0	3-13	0	-0.6
1899 StL-N	2	6	1	2	0	0	0	0	1	....	0	....	.333	.429	.333	.762	108	0	1	5.82	0	/2-2	0	0.0
1901 Mil-A	64	233	24	48	8	0	0	26	17	....	6	....	.206	.266	.240	.506	43	-17	18	2.45	-9	3-64	1	-2.2
Chi-A	42	148	20	39	5	0	0	21	12	....	11	....	.264	.327	.297	.624	76	-4	19	4.40	-1	S-31,3-11	4	-0.3
Yr.	106	381	44	87	13	0	0	47	29	....	17	....	.228	.290	.262	.552	56	-21	37	3.19	-10	3-75,S-31	5	-2.5
Pit-N	14	51	4	10	0	0	0	4	4	....	0	....	.196	.268	.196	.464	35	-4	3	1.87	3	3-14	1	-0.1
1902 Pit-N	60	203	24	60	12	2	0	26	17	....	9	....	.296	.359	.374	.733	122	5	32	5.73	0	2-27,0-18(7-0-11)/3-9,S-4	9	0.6
1903 StL-N	115	431	55	123	13	3	0	42	23	....	28	....	.285	.326	.329	.656	90	-6	58	4.85	5	3-93,2-15/0-5(4-0-1)	11	0.1
1904 StL-N	118	406	37	92	10	3	0	37	15	....	17	....	.227	.271	.266	.537	69	-15	37	2.89	-8	*3-118	6	-2.0
1905 StL-N	122	431	34	97	9	5	1	30	21	....	15	....	.225	.275	.276	.552	66	-18	39	2.95	4	*3-122	8	-1.1
Total 7	550	1947	200	475	58	13	1	187	112	....	87	....	.244	.295	.289	.584	73	-65	207	3.57	-7	3-444/2-44,S-35,0-23	40	-5.6

• BURKE, Joe Joseph A. Burke b: 12/7/1867, Nashville, TN d: 11/3/1940, Cincinnati, OH, 5'7", 160 lbs. Deb: 9/26/1890

YEAR TM-L	G	AB	R	H	2B	3B	HR	RBI	BB	SO	SB	CS	AVG	OBP	SLG	OPS	OPS+	BR/A	RC	RC/G	FR	G/POS	WS	TPW
1890 StL-a	2	6	3	4	0	0	0	2	1	....	0	....	.667	.750	.667	1.417	278	2	3	40.74	-0	/3-2	1	0.2
1891 Cin-a	1	4	0	1	0	0	0	1	0	2	0	....	.250	.250	.250	.500	40	-0	0	2.26	1	/2-1	0	0.1
Total 2	3	10	3	5	0	0	0	3	1	2	0	....	.500	.583	.500	1.083	199	1	3	17.66	1	/3-2,2-1	1	0.2

• BURKE, John John Patrick Burke b: 1/27/1877, Hazleton, PA d: 8/4/1950, Jersey City, NJ BR/TR Deb: 6/27/1902 ♦

YEAR TM-L	G	AB	R	H	2B	3B	HR	RBI	BB	SO	SB	CS	AVG	OBP	SLG	OPS	OPS+	BR/A	RC	RC/G	FR	G/POS	WS	TPW
1902 NY-N	4	13	0	2	0	0	0	0	0	....	0	....	.154	.154	.154	.308	-5	-1	0	.76	0	/0-2(0-0-2),P-2	0	-0.6

• BURKE, Leo Leo Patrick Burke b: 5/6/1934, Hagerstown, MD BR/TR, 5'11", 190 lbs. Deb: 9/7/1958 Career OF: 7-1-37

YEAR TM-L	G	AB	R	H	2B	3B	HR	RBI	BB	SO	SB	CS	AVG	OBP	SLG	OPS	OPS+	BR/A	RC	RC/G	FR	G/POS	WS	TPW
1958 Bal-A	7	11	4	5	1	0	1	4	1	2	0	0	.455	.500	.818	1.318	270	2	5	20.84	-1	/0-3(1-1-1),3-1	1	0.2
1959 Bal-A	5	10	0	2	0	0	0	1	0	5	0	0	.200	.273	.200	.473	33	-1	0	1.23	0	/2-2,3-2	0	-0.1
1961 LA-A	6	5	0	0	0	0	0	0	0	1	0	0	.000	.000	.000	.000	-90	-1	0	.00	0	....	0	-0.1
1962 LA-A	19	64	8	17	1	0	4	14	5	11	0	0	.266	.329	.469	.797	115	1	10	5.53	-2	0-12(4-0-8)/3-4,S-1	2	-0.1
1963 StL-N	30	49	6	10	2	1	1	5	4	12	0	0	.204	.264	.347	.611	68	-2	4	2.99	-1	0-11(2-0-9)/3-5	1	-0.4
Chi-N	27	49	4	9	0	0	2	7	4	13	0	1	.184	.245	.306	.551	55	-3	3	2.08	-1	2-10/1-4	1	-0.4
Yr.	57	98	10	19	2	1	3	12	8	25	0	1	.194	.255	.327	.581	61	-5	8	2.52	-3	0-11(2-0-9),2-10/3-5,1-4	2	-0.8
1964 Chi-N	59	103	11	27	3	1	1	14	7	31	0	0	.262	.315	.340	.655	81	-2	11	3.79	-1	0-18(0-0-18)/2-5,3-4,1-2,C	2	-0.4
1965 Chi-N	12	10	0	2	0	0	0	0	0	4	0	0	.200	.200	.200	.400	13	-1	0	.60	-1	/C-2,0-1	0	-0.2
Total 7	165	301	33	72	7	2	9	45	21	79	0	1	.239	.295	.365	.661	83	-7	34	3.83	-7	/0-45,2-17,3-16,1-6,C-3,S-1	7	-1.6

• BURKE, Les Leslie Kingston "Buck" Burke b: 12/18/1902, Lynn, MA d: 5/6/1975, Danvers, MA BL/TR, 5'9", 168 lbs. Deb: 5/2/1923

YEAR TM-L	G	AB	R	H	2B	3B	HR	RBI	BB	SO	SB	CS	AVG	OBP	SLG	OPS	OPS+	BR/A	RC	RC/G	FR	G/POS	WS	TPW
1923 Det-A	7	10	2	1	0	0	0	2	0	1	0	0	.100	.100	.100	.200	-48	-2	0	.28	-1	/3-2,2-1	0	-0.3
1924 Det-A	72	241	30	61	10	4	0	17	22	20	2	4	.253	.321	.328	.649	69	-12	26	3.55	-3	2-58/S-6	4	-1.3
1925 Det-A	77	180	32	52	6	3	0	24	17	8	4	1	.289	.357	.356	.712	82	-4	25	4.57	5	2-52	4	0.2
1926 Det-A	38	75	9	17	1	0	0	4	7	3	1	2	.227	.301	.240	.541	42	-7	6	2.40	-1	2-15/3-7,S-1	1	-0.7
Total 4	194	506	73	131	17	7	0	47	46	32	7	7	.259	.327	.320	.647	68	-25	56	3.66	-1	2-126/3-9,S-7	9	-2.1

• BURKE, Mike Michael E. Burke b: 1855, Cincinnati, OH d: 6/9/1889, Albany, NY BR/TR, 6', 190 lbs. Deb: 5/1/1879

YEAR TM-L	G	AB	R	H	2B	3B	HR	RBI	BB	SO	SB	CS	AVG	OBP	SLG	OPS	OPS+	BR/A	RC	RC/G	FR	G/POS	WS	TPW
1879 Cin-N	28	117	13	26	3	0	0	8	2	5	....	....	.222	.235	.248	.483	63	-4	7	2.15	-6	S-19/3-5,0-5(0-1-4)	1	-0.8

• BURKE, Pat Patrick Edward Burke b: 5/13/1901, St. Louis, MO d: 7/7/1965, St. Louis, MO BR/TR, 5'10.5", 170 lbs. Deb: 9/23/1924

YEAR TM-L	G	AB	R	H	2B	3B	HR	RBI	BB	SO	SB	CS	AVG	OBP	SLG	OPS	OPS+	BR/A	RC	RC/G	FR	G/POS	WS	TPW
1924 StL-A	1	3	0	0	0	0	0	1	0	0	0	0	.000	.000	.000	.000	-94	-1	0	.00	0	/3-1	0	-0.1

• BURKETT, Jesse Jesse Cail "Crab" Burkett
b: 12/4/1868, Wheeling, WV d: 5/27/1953, Worcester, MA BL/TL, 5'8", 155 lbs. Deb: 4/22/1890 C HOF: 1946 Career OF: 1935-7-115 ♦

YEAR TM-L	G	AB	R	H	2B	3B	HR	RBI	BB	SO	SB	CS	AVG	OBP	SLG	OPS	OPS+	BR/A	RC	RC/G	FR	G/POS	WS	TPW
1890 NY-N	101	401	67	124	23	13	4	60	33	52	14	....	.309	.366	.461	.827	141	21	75	7.14	5	0-90(11-2-77),P-21	14	-0.4
1891 Cle-N	40	167	29	45	7	4	0	13	23	19	1	....	.269	.358	.359	.717	105	1	22	4.95	-2	0-40(6-2-35)	4	-0.1
1892*Cle-N	145	608	119	167	15	14	6	66	67	59	36	....	.275	.348	.375	.723	114	10	94	5.76	-2	*0-145(145-0-0)	23	-0.6
1893 Cle-N	125	511	145	178	25	15	6	82	98	23	39	....	.348	.459	.491	.951	144	37	137	10.87	-7	*0-125(125-0-0)	24	1.5
1894 Cle-N	125	523	138	187	27	14	8	94	84	27	28	....	.358	.447	.509	.956	125	25	135	10.43	-5	*0-125(125-0-0)/P-1	21	0.7
1895*Cle-N	132	555	153	**225**	22	13	5	83	74	32	41	....	**.405**	.482	.519	1.001	149	46	163	13.08	-2	*0-131(130-0-1)	35	2.6
1896*Cle-N	133	586	**160**	**240**	27	16	6	72	49	19	34	....	**.410**	.461	.541	1.002	155	47	166	12.56	1	*0-133(133-0-0)	**35**	3.0
1897 Cle-N	127	517	129	198	28	7	2	60	76	....	28	....	.383	.468	.476	.944	142	37	133	10.70	1	*0-127(127-1-0)	23	2.2
1898 Cle-N	150	624	114	213	18	9	0	42	69	....	19	....	.341	.415	.399	.814	135	32	114	7.31	-8	*0-150(148-1-1)	29	1.0
1899 StL-N	141	558	116	221	21	8	7	71	67	....	25	....	.396	.463	.500	.963	160	49	145	11.14	2	*0-140(139-0-1)/2-1	30	3.5
1900 StL-N	141	559	88	203	11	15	7	68	62	....	32	....	.363	.429	.474	.904	150	40	133	9.39	1	*0-141(140-1-0)	25	2.6
1901 StL-N	142	601	**142**	**226**	20	15	10	75	59	....	27	....	**.376**	**.440**	.509	.949	**184**	**66**	151	**10.56**	2	*0-142(142-0-0)	**38**	**5.8**
1902 StL-A	138	553	97	169	29	9	5	52	71	....	23	....	.306	.390	.418	.807	126	22	102	6.93	7	*0-137(137-0-0)/3-1,P-1,S	25	1.9
1903 StL-A	132	515	73	151	20	7	3	40	52	....	17	....	.293	.361	.377	.738	125	18	79	5.67	-3	*0-132(132-0-0)	22	0.7
1904 StL-A	147	575	72	156	15	10	2	27	78	....	12	....	.271	.363	.343	.706	132	25	78	4.92	8	*0-147(147-0-0)	25	2.8
1905 Bos-A	148	573	78	147	12	13	4	47	67	....	13	....	.257	.339	.344	.682	115	12	74	4.51	-3	*0-148(148-0-0)	22	0.0
Total 16	2067	8426	1720	2850	320	182	75	952	1029	231	389	....	.338	.415	.446	.861	139	488	1801	8.45	-4	*0-2053/P-23,2-1,3-1,S-1	389	27.5

• BURKHART, Morgan Morgan Burkhart b: 1/29/1972, St. Louis, MO BB/TL, 5'11", 225 lbs. Deb: 6/27/2000

YEAR TM-L	G	AB	R	H	2B	3B	HR	RBI	BB	SO	SB	CS	AVG	OBP	SLG	OPS	OPS+	BR/A	RC	RC/G	FR	G/POS	WS	TPW
2000 Bos-A	25	73	16	21	3	0	4	18	17	25	0	0	.288	.447	.493	.940	134	5	18	9.00	-1	D-19/1-5,0-1	2	0.3
2001 Bos-A	11	33	3	6	1	0	1	4	1	11	0	0	.182	.206	.303	.509	31	-3	2	1.75	0	/D-6,1-5	0	-0.4
2003 KC-A	6	15	1	3	0	0	0	1	1	2	0	0	.200	.250	.200	.450	18	-2	1	1.83	0	/1-2,D-2	0	-0.2
Total 3	42	121	20	30	4	0	5	23	19	38	0	0	.248	.368	.405	.773	97	-0	21	5.93	-1	/D-27,1-12,0-1	2	-0.4

• BURKS, Ellis Ellis Rena Burks b: 9/11/1964, Vicksburg, MS BR/TR, 6'2", 205 lbs. Deb: 4/30/1987 Career OF: 290-1062-360

YEAR TM-L	G	AB	R	H	2B	3B	HR	RBI	BB	SO	SB	CS	AVG	OBP	SLG	OPS	OPS+	BR/A	RC	RC/G	FR	G/POS	WS	TPW
1987 Bos-A	133	558	94	152	30	2	20	59	41	98	27	6	.272	.324	.441	.765	98	-0	85	5.49	4	*0-132(0-132-0)/D-1	15	0.2
1988*Bos-A	144	540	93	159	37	5	18	92	62	89	25	9	.294	.370	.481	.852	131	24	99	6.57	-2	*0-142(0-142-0)/D-2	24	2.0
1989 Bos-A	97	399	73	121	19	6	12	61	36	52	21	5	.303	.368	.471	.839	127	17	71	6.44	1	0-95(0-96-0)/D-1	16	1.7
1990*Bos-A★	152	588	89	174	33	8	21	89	48	82	9	11	.296	.350	.486	.836	126	16	92	5.57	-8	*0-143(0-143-0)/D-6	21	0.6
1991 Bos-A	130	474	56	119	33	3	14	56	39	81	6	11	.251	.316	.422	.738	97	-6	60	4.32	-6	*0-126(0-126-0)/D-2	10	-1.4
1992 Bos-A	66	235	35	60	8	3	8	30	25	48	5	2	.255	.330	.417	.747	101	0	32	4.76	-3	0-63(0-63-0)/D-1	5	-0.3
1993*Chi-A	146	499	75	137	24	4	17	74	60	97	6	9	.275	.357	.441	.798	116	9	77	5.31	-2	*0-146(0-21-132)	14	0.0
1994 Col-N	42	149	33	48	8	3	13	24	16	39	3	1	.322	.388	.678	1.066	147	10	39	9.91	-4	0-39(0-39-0)	5	0.6
1995*Col-N	103	278	41	74	10	6	14	49	39	72	7	3	.266	.361	.496	.857	96	-1	50	6.27	-4	0-80(23-65-1)	8	-0.6
1996 Col-N★	156	613	**142**	211	45	8	40	128	61	114	32	6	.344	.409	**.639**	1.048	138	38	158	9.88	-0	*0-152(129-32-0)	28	3.2
1997 Col-N	119	424	91	123	19	2	32	82	47	75	7	2	.290	.365	.571	.936	114	9	84	7.02	-3	*0-112(67-89-0)	15	0.5
1998 Col-N	100	357	54	102	22	5	16	54	39	80	3	7	.286	.359	.510	.869	103	-1	62	5.96	-3	0-98(45-78-0)	8	-0.4
SF-N	42	147	22	45	6	1	5	22	19	31	8	1	.306	.396	.463	.859	133	9	30	7.07	-3	0-41(0-36-10)	6	0.6
Yr.	142	504	76	147	28	6	21	76	58	111	11	8	.292	.370	.496	.866	112	9	91	6.28	-5	*0-139(45-114-10)	14	0.2
1999 SF-N	120	390	73	110	19	0	31	96	69	86	7	5	.282	.398	.569	.967	152	31	89	8.00	0	*0-107(0-0-107)/D-3	24	2.4
2000*SF-N	122	393	74	135	21	5	24	96	56	49	5	1	.344	.427	.606	1.032	170	43	102	9.95	0	*0-108(0-0-108)/D-2	21	3.6
2001*Cle-A	124	439	83	123	29	1	28	74	62	85	5	1	.280	.375	.542	.918	136	24	88	6.95	0	*D-102,0-20(18-0-2)	14	1.6
2002 Cle-A	138	518	92	156	28	0	32	91	44	108	2	3	.301	.363	.541	.903	138	26	98	6.97	-1	*D-127/0-6(6-0-0)	21	1.6
2003 Cle-A	55	198	27	52	11	1	6	28	27	46	1	1	.263	.360	.419	.779	108	3	31	5.48	0	D-51/0-2(2-0-0)	5	0.0
Total 17	1989	7199	1247	2101	402	63	351	1205	790	1332	179	84	.292	.367	.511	.878	124	251	1347	6.68	-33	*0-1612,D-298	260	15.8

• BURLESON, Rick Richard Paul "Rooster" Burleson b: 4/29/1951, Lynwood, CA BR/TR, 5'10", 165 lbs. Deb: 5/4/1974 C

YEAR TM-L	G	AB	R	H	2B	3B	HR	RBI	BB	SO	SB	CS	AVG	OBP	SLG	OPS	OPS+	BR/A	RC	RC/G	FR	G/POS	WS	TPW
1974 Bos-A	114	384	36	109	22	0	4	44	21	34	3	3	.284	.324	.372	.697	93	-4	43	3.90	0	S-88,2-31/3-2	11	0.9
1975*Bos-A	158	580	66	146	25	1	6	62	45	44	8	5	.252	.309	.329	.638	74	-20	58	3.23	12	*S-158	14	1.2

YEAR TM-L	G	AB	R	H	2B	3B	HR	RBI	BB	SO	SB	CS	AVG	OBP	SLG	OPS	OPS+	BR/A	RC	RC/G	FR	G/POS	WS	TPW
1976 Bos-A	152	540	75	157	27	1	7	42	60	37	14	9	.291	.367	.383	.750	107	6	76	4.91	7	*S-152	21	3.3
1977 Bos-A★	154	663	80	194	36	7	3	52	47	69	13	12	.293	.341	.382	.723	87	-13	83	4.44	13	*S-154	21	1.6
1978 Bos-A★	145	626	75	155	32	5	5	49	40	71	8	8	.248	.297	.339	.636	71	-26	60	3.18	21	*S-144	16	1.1
1979 Bos-A★	153	627	93	174	32	5	5	60	35	54	9	5	.278	.319	.368	.687	80	-18	72	4.00	22	*S-153	19	1.9
1980 Bos-A	155	644	89	179	29	2	8	51	62	51	12	13	.278	.343	.366	.710	90	-11	76	4.00	18	*S-155	18	2.3
1981 Cal-A★	109	430	53	126	17	1	5	33	42	38	4	6	.293	.360	.372	.732	111	6	58	4.70	22	*S-109	17	4.2
1982 Cal-A	11	45	4	7	1	0	0	2	6	3	0	0	.156	.255	.178	.433	21	-5	2	1.34	6	S-11	1	0.3
1983 Cal-A	33	119	22	34	7	0	0	11	12	12	0	2	.286	.351	.345	.696	93	-2	13	3.78	-1	S-31	3	0.1
1984 Cal-A	7	4	2	0	0	0	0	0	0	2	0	0	.000	.000	.000	.000	-101	-1	0	.00	0	....	0	-0.1
1986*Cal-A	93	271	35	77	14	0	5	29	33	32	1	3	.284	.364	.391	.755	107	2	40	5.29	0	D-38,S-37/2-6,3-4	9	0.4
1987 Bal-A	62	206	26	43	14	1	2	14	17	30	0	2	.209	.279	.316	.594	59	-13	17	2.59	-4	2-55/D-7	2	-1.4
Total 13	1346	5139	656	1401	256	23	50	449	420	477	72	68	.273	.331	.361	.692	87	-97	599	3.97	117	*S-1192/2-92,D-45,3-6	152	15.8

• BURNETT, Hercules Hercules H. Burnett b: 8/13/1869, Louisville, KY d: 10/4/1936, Louisville, KY BR, 5'11", 177 lbs. Deb: 6/26/1888 Career OF: 0-4-1

YEAR TM-L	G	AB	R	H	2B	3B	HR	RBI	BB	SO	SB	CS	AVG	OBP	SLG	OPS	OPS+	BR/A	RC	RC/G	FR	G/POS	WS	TPW
1888 Lou-a	1	4	1	0	0	0	0	0	1	....	1	....	.000	.200	.000	.200	-35	-1	0	1.38	0	/O-1	0	-0.1
1895 Lou-N	5	17	6	7	0	1	2	3	2	2	2	....	.412	.474	.882	1.356	261	4	8	20.08	-1	/O-4(0-4-0),1-1	1	0.2
Total 2	6	21	7	7	0	1	2	3	3	2	3	....	.333	.417	.714	1.131	202	3	8	15.09	-1	/O-5,1-1	1	0.2

• BURNETT, Jack John P. Burnett b: 12/2/1889, MO d: 9/8/1929, Taft, CA Deb: 7/2/1907

YEAR TM-L	G	AB	R	H	2B	3B	HR	RBI	BB	SO	SB	CS	AVG	OBP	SLG	OPS	OPS+	BR/A	RC	RC/G	FR	G/POS	WS	TPW
1907 StL-N	59	206	18	49	8	4	0	12	15	....	5	....	.238	.296	.316	.611	95	-2	22	3.50	-2	O-59(0-59-0)	5	-0.7

• BURNETT, Johnny John Henderson Burnett b: 11/1/1904, Bartow, FL d: 8/12/1959, Tampa, FL BL/TR, 5'11", 175 lbs. Deb: 5/7/1927 Career OF: 1-0-2

YEAR TM-L	G	AB	R	H	2B	3B	HR	RBI	BB	SO	SB	CS	AVG	OBP	SLG	OPS	OPS+	BR/A	RC	RC/G	FR	G/POS	WS	TPW
1927 Cle-A	17	8	5	0	0	0	0	0	0	3	1	0	.000	.000	.000	.000	-99	-2	0	.00	0	/2-2	0	-0.2
1928 Cle-A	3	10	3	5	0	0	0	1	0	1	0	0	.500	.500	.500	1.000	162	1	2	12.72	0	/S-2	1	0.2
1929 Cle-A	19	33	2	5	1	0	0	2	1	2	0	0	.152	.200	.182	.382	-1	-5	1	1.18	-2	S-10/2-8	1	-0.6
1930 Cle-A	54	170	28	53	13	0	0	20	17	8	2	2	.312	.378	.388	.766	91	-2	26	5.41	0	3-27,S-19	5	0.1
1931 Cle-A	111	427	85	128	25	5	1	52	39	25	5	2	.300	.360	.389	.749	92	-3	61	5.34	-4	S-63,2-35,3-21/O-1	12	0.0
1932 Cle-A	129	512	81	152	23	5	4	53	46	27	2	5	.297	.359	.385	.744	87	-10	72	5.04	-16	*S-103,2-26	12	-1.6
1933 Cle-A	83	261	39	71	11	2	1	29	23	14	3	2	.272	.333	.341	.674	76	-9	31	4.09	-4	S-41,2-17,3-12	6	-0.8
1934 Cle-A	72	208	28	61	11	2	3	30	18	11	1	1	.293	.352	.409	.761	94	-2	30	5.35	-5	3-42/S-9,2-3,O-2(1-0-1)	6	-0.4
1935 StL-A	70	206	17	46	10	1	0	26	19	16	1	0	.223	.289	.282	.570	46	-16	18	2.87	-1	3-31,S-18,2-12	2	-1.4
Total 9	558	1835	288	521	94	15	9	213	163	107	15	12	.284	.345	.366	.712	81	-48	241	4.69	-32	S-265,3-133,2-103/O-3	45	-4.9

• BURNITZ, Jeromy Jeromy Neal Burnitz b: 4/15/1969, Westminster, CA BL/TR, 6', 190 lbs. Deb: 6/21/1993 Career OF: 84-94-1045

YEAR TM-L	G	AB	R	H	2B	3B	HR	RBI	BB	SO	SB	CS	AVG	OBP	SLG	OPS	OPS+	BR/A	RC	RC/G	FR	G/POS	WS	TPW
1993 NY-N	86	263	49	64	10	6	13	38	38	66	3	6	.243	.341	.475	.816	117	4	43	5.47	0	O-79(0-20-61)	8	0.1
1994 NY-N	45	143	26	34	4	0	3	15	23	45	1	1	.238	.347	.329	.676	78	-4	18	4.25	-4	O-42(0-0-42)	2	-1.0
1995 Cle-A	9	7	4	4	1	0	0	0	0	0	0	0	.571	.571	.714	1.286	229	1	3	25.71	0	/O-6(5-1-0),D-2	1	0.1
1996 Cle-A	71	128	30	36	10	0	7	26	25	31	2	1	.281	.406	.523	.930	134	7	28	8.01	0	O-30(10-5-15),D-15	5	0.5
Mil-A	23	72	8	17	4	0	2	14	8	16	2	0	.236	.329	.375	.704	75	-2	10	4.53	0	O-22(0-8-14)	1	-0.3
Yr.	94	200	38	53	14	0	9	40	33	47	4	1	.265	.380	.470	.850	113	5	38	6.70	0	O-52(10-13-29),D-15	6	0.3
1997 Mil-A	153	494	85	139	37	8	27	85	75	111	20	13	.281	.382	.553	.934	139	27	104	7.42	1	*O-149(5-26-124)	20	2.2
1998 Mil-N	161	609	92	160	28	1	38	125	70	158	7	4	.263	.343	.499	.842	118	14	105	6.05	-3	*O-161(0-1-161)	19	0.2
1999 Mil-N★	130	467	87	126	33	2	33	103	91	124	7	3	.270	.406	.561	.967	143	34	111	8.32	-3	*O-127(0-0-127)/D-3	19	2.2
2000 Mil-N	161	564	91	131	29	2	31	98	99	121	6	4	.232	.360	.456	.816	106	7	97	5.71	-3	*O-158(0-0-158)/D-1	16	-0.5
2001 Mil-N	154	562	104	141	32	4	34	100	80	150	0	4	.251	.349	.504	.853	120	15	100	6.19	3	*O-154(0-0-153)	18	0.9
2002 NY-N	154	479	65	103	15	0	19	54	58	135	10	7	.215	.313	.365	.678	81	-14	55	3.75	-5	*O-140(0-0-140)/D-1	7	-2.6
2003 NY-N	65	234	38	64	18	0	18	45	21	55	1	4	.274	.344	.581	.925	140	11	44	6.71	-3	O-65(10-21-48)	10	0.5
LA-N	61	230	25	47	4	0	13	32	14	57	4	0	.204	.253	.391	.644	69	-11	24	3.46	-2	O-60(54-12-2)	2	-1.5
Yr.	126	464	63	111	22	0	31	77	35	112	5	4	.239	.300	.487	.787	105	-0	68	5.06	-5	*O-125(64-33-50)	12	-0.9
Total 11	1273	4252	704	1066	225	23	238	735	602	1069	63	47	.251	.352	.482	.835	115	88	743	5.99	-18	*O-1193/D-22	128	1.0

• BURNS, C.B. Charles Birmingham Burns b: 5/15/1879, Bayview, MD d: 6/6/1968, Havre de Grace, MD BR/TR, 6', 175 lbs. Deb: 8/19/1902

YEAR TM-L	G	AB	R	H	2B	3B	HR	RBI	BB	SO	SB	CS	AVG	OBP	SLG	OPS	OPS+	BR/A	RC	RC/G	FR	G/POS	WS	TPW
1902 Bal-A	1	1	0	1	0	0	0	0	0	....	0	....	1.000	1.000	1.000	2.000	436	0	1	∞	0	....	0	0.0

• BURNS, Dick Richard Simon Burns b: 12/26/1863, Holyoke, MA d: 11/16/1937, Holyoke, MA BL/TL, 5'7", 140 lbs. Deb: 5/3/1883 Career OF: 7-48-30 ♦

YEAR TM-L	G	AB	R	H	2B	3B	HR	RBI	BB	SO	SB	CS	AVG	OBP	SLG	OPS	OPS+	BR/A	RC	RC/G	FR	G/POS	WS	TPW
1883 Det-N	37	140	11	26	7	1	0	5	2	22	....	....	.186	.197	.250	.447	36	-7	7	1.71	-4	O-24(1-1-23),P-17	2	-2.5
1884 Cin-U	79	350	84	107	17	**12**	4	....	5	....	....	....	.306	.315	.457	.773	147	17	52	5.96	-3	O-44(6-33-7),P-40/S-2	**41**	3.5
1885 StL-N	14	54	2	12	2	1	0	4	3	8	....	....	.222	.263	.296	.559	86	-1	4	2.77	-2	O-14(0-14-0)/P-1	1	-0.5
Total 3	130	544	97	145	26	14	4	9	10	30	....	....	.267	.280	.388	.668	112	9	63	4.41	-9	/O-82,P-58,S-2	44	0.5

• BURNS, Ed Edward James Burns b: 10/31/1888, San Francisco, CA d: 5/30/1942, Monterey, CA BR/TR, 5'6", 165 lbs. Deb: 6/25/1912

YEAR TM-L	G	AB	R	H	2B	3B	HR	RBI	BB	SO	SB	CS	AVG	OBP	SLG	OPS	OPS+	BR/A	RC	RC/G	FR	G/POS	WS	TPW
1912 StL-N	1	1	0	0	0	0	0	1	0	0	0	....	.000	.000	.000	.000	-102	-0	0	.00	0	/C-1	0	-0.1
1913 Phi-N	17	30	3	6	3	0	0	3	6	3	2	....	.200	.351	.300	.651	83	-0	4	3.81	0	C-15	1	0.1
1914 Phi-N	70	139	8	36	3	4	0	16	20	12	5	....	.259	.352	.338	.690	99	1	18	4.34	2	C-55	6	0.6
1915*Phi-N	67	174	11	42	5	0	0	16	20	12	1	....	.241	.327	.270	.597	80	-3	16	3.14	1	C-62	6	0.2
1916 Phi-N	78	219	14	51	8	1	0	14	16	18	3	....	.233	.294	.279	.573	74	-6	20	2.94	-5	C-75/O-1,S-1	6	-0.7
1917 Phi-N	20	49	2	10	1	0	0	6	1	5	2	....	.204	.220	.224	.444	35	-4	3	1.73	1	C-15	1	-0.3
1918 Phi-N	68	184	10	38	1	1	0	9	20	9	1	....	.207	.288	.223	.511	53	-10	12	2.11	1	C-68	3	-0.4
Total 7	321	796	48	183	21	6	0	65	83	59	14	....	.230	.308	.271	.579	73	-23	72	2.97	0	C-291/O-1,S-1	23	-0.6

• BURNS, George George Henry "Tioga George" Burns b: 1/31/1893, Niles, OH d: 1/7/1978, Kirkland, WA BR/TR, 6'1.5", 180 lbs. Deb: 4/14/1914 Career OF: 1-0-49

YEAR TM-L	G	AB	R	H	2B	3B	HR	RBI	BB	SO	SB	CS	AVG	OBP	SLG	OPS	OPS+	BR/A	RC	RC/G	FR	G/POS	WS	TPW
1914 Det-A	137	478	55	139	22	5	5	57	32	56	23	13	.291	.351	.389	.740	119	9	70	4.97	2	*1-137	17	0.9
1915 Det-A	105	392	49	99	18	3	5	50	22	51	9	3	.253	.301	.352	.653	91	-6	45	3.82	3	*1-104	10	-0.5
1916 Det-A	135	479	60	137	22	6	4	73	22	30	12	....	.286	.327	.382	.709	109	3	66	4.75	-2	*1-124	15	-0.2
1917 Det-A	119	407	42	92	14	10	1	40	15	33	3	....	.226	.264	.317	.581	77	-13	34	2.69	1	*1-104	5	-1.6
1918 Phi-A	130	505	61	**178**	22	9	6	70	23	25	8	....	.352	.390	.467	**.857**	157	**32**	91	6.95	4	*1-128/O-2(1-0-1)	24	3.6
1919 Phi-A	126	470	63	139	29	9	8	57	19	18	15	....	.296	.339	.447	.786	118	9	72	5.57	1	1-86,O-34(0-0-34)	11	0.7
1920 Phi-A	22	60	1	14	3	0	1	7	6	7	4	0	.233	.313	.333	.647	71	-1	7	4.07	0	O-13(0-0-13)	1	-0.2
*Cle-A	44	56	7	15	4	1	0	13	4	3	1	0	.268	.339	.375	.714	86	-1	8	4.68	1	1-12/O-1	1	0.0
Yr.	66	116	8	29	7	1	1	20	10	10	5	0	.250	.326	.353	.679	78	-2	15	4.36	1	O-14(0-0-14),1-12	2	-0.2
1921 Cle-A	84	244	52	88	21	4	0	49	13	19	3	1	.361	.398	.480	.877	121	8	46	7.54	3	1-73	9	0.7
1922 Bos-A	147	558	71	171	32	5	12	73	20	28	8	2	.306	.341	.446	.787	104	3	85	5.56	3	*1-140	15	-0.3
1923 Bos-A	146	551	91	181	47	5	7	82	45	33	9	7	.328	.386	.470	.856	124	19	100	6.81	7	*1-146	21	1.5
1924 Cle-A	129	462	64	143	37	5	4	68	29	27	14	5	.310	.370	.437	.807	106	5	77	5.86	4	*1-127	12	0.1
1925 Cle-A	127	488	69	164	41	4	6	79	24	24	16	11	.336	.371	.473	.844	112	7	83	6.39	-2	*1-126	14	-0.3
1926 Cle-A	151	603	97	**216**	**64**	3	4	114	28	33	13	7	.358	.394	.494	.889	129	25	116	7.44	0	*1-151	24	1.4
1927 Cle-A	140	549	84	175	51	2	3	78	42	27	13	11	.319	.375	.435	.810	109	5	89	5.96	1	*1-139	17	-0.3
1928 Cle-A	82	209	29	52	12	1	5	30	17	11	2	3	.249	.323	.388	.711	85	-5	26	4.22	0	1-53	3	-0.8
NY-A	4	4	1	2	0	0	0	0	0	1	0	0	.500	.500	.500	1.000	169	0	1	12.72	0	/1-2	0	0.0
Yr.	86	213	30	54	12	1	5	30	17	12	2	3	.254	.326	.390	.716	86	-5	27	4.32	0	1-55	3	-0.8
1929 NY-A	9	9	0	0	0	0	0	0	0	4	0	0	.000	.000	.000	.000	-107	-3	0	.00	0	....	0	-0.2
*Phi-A	29	49	5	13	5	0	1	11	2	3	1	0	.265	.294	.429	.723	81	-1	6	4.47	0	1-19	1	-0.2
Yr.	38	58	5	13	5	0	1	11	2	7	1	0	.224	.250	.362	.612	53	-4	6	3.60	0	1-19	1	-0.5
Total 16	1866	6573	901	2018	444	72	72	951	363	433	154	63	.307	.354	.429	.783	112	93	1022	5.60	24	*1-1671/O-50	200	4.1

• BURNS, George George Joseph Burns b: 11/24/1889, Utica, NY d: 8/15/1966, Gloversville, NY BR/TR, 5'7", 160 lbs. Deb: 10/3/1911 C Career OF: 1262-186-406

YEAR TM-L	G	AB	R	H	2B	3B	HR	RBI	BB	SO	SB	CS	AVG	OBP	SLG	OPS	OPS+	BR/A	RC	RC/G	FR	G/POS	WS	TPW
1911 NY-N	6	17	2	1	0	0	0	0	1	0	0	....	.059	.111	.059	.170	-51	-3	0	.24	0	/O-6(1-4-1)	0	-0.4
1912 NY-N	29	51	11	15	4	0	0	3	8	8	7	....	.294	.400	.373	.773	108	1	10	7.23	1	O-23(13-5-5)	2	0.2
1913*NY-N	150	605	81	173	37	4	2	54	58	74	40	....	.286	.352	.370	.723	106	5	88	5.06	3	*O-150(119-0-32)	22	0.2
1914 NY-N	154	561	**100**	170	35	10	3	60	89	53	**62**	....	.303	.403	.417	.820	149	**38**	113	7.24	4	*O-154(102-0-54)	**31**	3.7
1915 NY-N	155	622	83	169	27	14	3	51	56	57	27	20	.272	.333	.375	.707	121	12	79	4.34	-8	*O-155(140-0-15)	24	-0.3

YEAR TM-L	G	AB	R	H	2B	3B	HR	RBI	BB	SO	SB	CS	AVG	OBP	SLG	OPS	OPS+	BR/A	RC	RC/G	FR	G/POS	WS	TPW
1916 NY-N	155	623	**105**	174	24	8	5	41	63	47	37	26	.279	.346	.368	.714	126	16	82	4.39	2	*O-155(155-0-0)	25	1.4
1917*NY-N	152	597	**103**	180	25	13	5	45	**75**	55	40	....	.302	.380	.412	.792	148	36	102	6.30	5	*O-152(152-0-0)	34	3.9
1918 NY-N	119	465	80	135	22	6	4	51	43	37	40	....	.290	.354	.389	.743	129	16	74	5.63	8	*O-119(119-0-0)	23	2.2
1919 NY-N	139	534	**86**	162	30	9	2	46	**82**	37	**40**	....	.303	**.396**	.404	.801	142	32	96	**6.57**	6	*O-139(139-0-0)	32	3.6
1920 NY-N	154	631	**115**	181	35	9	6	46	**76**	48	22	22	.287	.365	.399	.765	121	17	91	5.06	18	*O-154(154-1-0)	24	3.1
1921*NY-N	149	605	111	181	28	9	4	61	**80**	24	19	20	.299	.386	.395	.781	107	8	93	5.48	1	*O-149(90-59-0)/3-1	22	0.0
1922 Cin-N	156	631	104	180	20	10	1	53	78	38	30	23	.285	.366	.353	.719	88	-10	83	4.55	1	*O-156(0-109-47)	19	-1.6
1923 Cin-N	154	614	99	168	27	13	3	45	**101**	46	12	14	.274	.376	.375	.751	101	3	90	5.10	-1	*O-154(0-3-151)	20	-1.0
1924 Cin-N	93	336	43	86	19	2	2	33	29	21	3	6	.256	.315	.342	.657	77	-12	36	3.63	5	O-90(12-1-79)	6	-1.3
1925 Phi-N	88	349	65	102	29	1	1	22	33	20	4	8	.292	.353	.390	.743	82	-11	47	4.76	-2	O-88(66-4-22)	6	-1.8
Total 15	**1853**	**7241**	**1188**	**2077**	**362**	**108**	**41**	**611**	**872**	**565**	**383**	**139**	**.287**	**.366**	**.384**	**.749**	**117**	**149**	**1085**	**5.25**	**44**	***O-1844/3-1**	**290**	**11.8**

• BURNS, Jack John Joseph Burns b: 5/13/1880, Avoca, PA d: 6/24/1957, Waterford, CT BR/TR, 5'10", 160 lbs. Deb: 9/11/1903

YEAR TM-L	G	AB	R	H	2B	3B	HR	RBI	BB	SO	SB	CS	AVG	OBP	SLG	OPS	OPS+	BR/A	RC	RC/G	FR	G/POS	WS	TPW
1903 Det-A	11	37	2	10	0	0	0	3	1	....	0	....	.270	.325	.270	.595	82	-1	4	3.32	2	2-11	1	0.2
1904 Det-A	4	16	3	2	0	0	0	1	1	....	1	....	.125	.176	.125	.301	-4	-2	1	1.03	-1	/2-4	0	-0.3
Total 2	**15**	**53**	**5**	**12**	**0**	**0**	**0**	**4**	**2**	**....**	**1**	**....**	**.226**	**.281**	**.226**	**.507**	**58**	**-2**	**4**	**2.58**	**2**	**/2-15**	**1**	**-0.1**

• BURNS, Jack John Irving "Slug" Burns b: 8/31/1907, Cambridge, MA d: 4/18/1975, Brighton, MA BL/TL, 5'10.5", 175 lbs. Deb: 9/17/1930 C

YEAR TM-L	G	AB	R	H	2B	3B	HR	RBI	BB	SO	SB	CS	AVG	OBP	SLG	OPS	OPS+	BR/A	RC	RC/G	FR	G/POS	WS	TPW
1930 StL-A	8	30	5	9	3	0	0	2	5	5	0	0	.300	.400	.400	.800	100	0	5	6.21	1	/1-8	1	0.1
1931 StL-A	144	570	75	148	27	7	4	70	42	58	19	12	.260	.312	.353	.664	72	-23	63	3.75	11	*1-143	7	-2.3
1932 StL-A	150	617	111	188	33	8	11	70	61	43	17	11	.305	.368	.438	.806	102	1	100	5.76	0	*1-150	15	-1.2
1933 StL-A	144	556	89	160	43	4	7	71	56	51	11	11	.288	.353	.417	.770	97	-4	81	5.22	-5	*1-143	10	-2.1
1934 StL-A	154	612	86	157	28	8	13	73	62	47	9	3	.257	.327	.392	.719	78	-21	81	4.59	-3	*1-154	9	-3.6
1935 StL-A	143	549	77	157	28	1	5	67	68	49	3	2	.286	.366	.368	.734	86	-9	78	5.00	-14	*1-141	9	-3.4
1936 StL-A	9	14	2	3	1	0	0	1	3	1	0	0	.214	.353	.286	.639	58	-1	2	3.90	-0	/1-2	0	-0.1
Det-A	138	558	96	158	36	3	4	63	79	45	4	8	.283	.375	.380	.755	87	-12	82	5.25	0	*1-138	12	-2.2
Yr.	147	572	98	161	37	3	4	64	82	46	4	8	.281	.374	.378	.752	86	-13	84	5.21	0	*1-140	12	-2.3
Total 7	**890**	**3506**	**541**	**980**	**199**	**31**	**44**	**417**	**376**	**299**	**63**	**47**	**.280**	**.351**	**.392**	**.742**	**87**	**-69**	**493**	**4.93**	**-11**	**1-879**	**63**	**-14.9**

• BURNS, Jim James M. Burns b: St. Louis, MO d: 2/17/1909, Chicago, IL, 5'7", 168 lbs. Deb: 9/25/1888 Career OF: 15-139-16

YEAR TM-L	G	AB	R	H	2B	3B	HR	RBI	BB	SO	SB	CS	AVG	OBP	SLG	OPS	OPS+	BR/A	RC	RC/G	FR	G/POS	WS	TPW
1888 KC-a	15	66	13	20	0	0	0	4	1	....	6	....	.303	.343	.303	.646	101	0	9	5.36	2	O-15(15-0-0)	2	0.1
1889 KC-a	134	579	103	176	23	11	5	97	20	68	56	....	.304	.335	.408	.743	105	-1	100	6.59	-8	*O-134(0-134-0)/3-1	17	-1.1
1891 Was-a	20	82	15	26	6	0	0	10	6	10	2	....	.317	.378	.390	.768	125	3	13	6.23	-4	O-20(0-5-16)/S-1	2	-0.1
Total 3	**169**	**727**	**131**	**222**	**29**	**11**	**5**	**111**	**27**	**78**	**64**	**....**	**.305**	**.341**	**.396**	**.737**	**107**	**2**	**123**	**6.44**	**-10**	**O-169/3-1,S-1**	**21**	**-1.1**

• BURNS, Joe Joseph James Burns b: 6/17/1916, Bryn Mawr, PA d: 6/24/1974, Bryn Mawr, PA BR/TR, 5'10.5", 175 lbs. Deb: 4/24/1943 Career OF: 1-1-21

YEAR TM-L	G	AB	R	H	2B	3B	HR	RBI	BB	SO	SB	CS	AVG	OBP	SLG	OPS	OPS+	BR/A	RC	RC/G	FR	G/POS	WS	TPW
1943 Bos-N	52	135	12	28	3	0	1	5	8	25	2	....	.207	.262	.252	.514	50	-9	8	1.92	-1	3-34/O-4(1-1-2)	1	-1.0
1944 Phi-A	28	75	5	18	2	0	1	8	4	8	0	1	.240	.278	.307	.585	68	-4	7	2.99	-3	3-17/2-9	1	-0.6
1945 Phi-A	31	90	7	23	1	1	0	3	4	17	0	1	.256	.287	.289	.576	68	-4	7	2.69	-3	O-19(0-0-19)/3-5,1-1	0	-0.9
Total 3	**111**	**300**	**24**	**69**	**6**	**1**	**2**	**16**	**16**	**50**	**2**	**2**	**.230**	**.274**	**.277**	**.550**	**59**	**-17**	**22**	**2.40**	**-6**	**/3-56,O-23,2-9,1-1**	**2**	**-2.5**

• BURNS, Joe Joseph Francis Burns b: 2/25/1900, Trenton, NJ d: 1/7/1986, Trenton, NJ BR/TR, 6', 175 lbs. Deb: 4/18/1924

YEAR TM-L	G	AB	R	H	2B	3B	HR	RBI	BB	SO	SB	CS	AVG	OBP	SLG	OPS	OPS+	BR/A	RC	RC/G	FR	G/POS	WS	TPW
1924 Chi-A	8	19	1	2	0	0	0	0	0	2	0	0	.105	.105	.105	.211	-47	-4	0	.35	0	/C-6	0	-0.4

• BURNS, Joe Joseph Francis Burns b: 3/26/1889, Ipswich, MA d: 7/12/1987, Beverly, MA BL/TL, 5'11", 170 lbs. Deb: 6/19/1910

YEAR TM-L	G	AB	R	H	2B	3B	HR	RBI	BB	SO	SB	CS	AVG	OBP	SLG	OPS	OPS+	BR/A	RC	RC/G	FR	G/POS	WS	TPW
1910 Cin-N	1	1	0	1	0	0	0	0	0	0	1	....	1.000	1.000	1.000	2.000	506	0	2	∞	0	....	0	0.1
1913 Det-A	4	13	0	5	0	0	0	1	2	4	0	....	.385	.500	.385	.885	162	1	2	7.71	0	/O-4(4-0-0)	1	0.1
Total 2	**5**	**14**	**0**	**6**	**0**	**0**	**0**	**1**	**2**	**4**	**1**	**....**	**.429**	**.529**	**.429**	**.958**	**182**	**2**	**4**	**7.71**	**0**	**/O-4**	**1**	**0.2**

• BURNS, Oyster Thomas P. Burns b: 9/6/1864, Philadelphia, PA d: 11/11/1928, Brooklyn, NY BR/TR, 5'8", 183 lbs. Deb: 8/18/1884 U Career OF: 100-15-780 ♦

YEAR TM-L	G	AB	R	H	2B	3B	HR	RBI	BB	SO	SB	CS	AVG	OBP	SLG	OPS	OPS+	BR/A	RC	RC/G	FR	G/POS	WS	TPW
1884 Wil-U	2	7	0	1	0	1	0	....	1	....	....	....	.143	.250	.429	.679	122	0	1	3.59	0	/S-2	0	0.0
Bal-a	35	131	34	39	2	6	6	23	7	....	....	....	.298	.348	.542	.890	179	11	25	7.56	-4	O-24(0-0-24),2-10/P-2,3-1	9	0.8
1885 Bal-a	78	321	47	74	11	6	5	37	16	....	....	....	.231	.280	.349	.629	99	2	32	3.51	-1	O-45(1-0-44),P-15,S-10/2-6,3,1	13	0.1
1887 Bal-a	140	614	122	251	33	**19**	9	99	63	....	58	....	.409	.414	.519	.933	169	53	146	10.85	-14	*S-98,3-42/P-3,2-1	28	2.9
1888 Bal-a	79	325	54	97	18	9	4	42	24	....	23	....	.298	.349	.446	.795	158	21	60	7.11	-6	O-56(46-0-10),S-23/P-5,3-2,2	15	1.1
Bro-a	52	204	40	58	9	6	2	25	14	....	21	....	.284	.339	.417	.756	142	9	37	6.82	-7	S-36,O-14(0-14-0)/2-3	9	0.3
Yr.	131	529	94	155	27	15	6	67	38	....	44	....	.293	.345	.435	.780	152	30	97	7.00	-13	O-70(46-14-10),S-59/P-5,2,3	24	1.4
1889*Bro-a	131	504	105	153	19	13	5	100	68	26	32	....	.304	.391	.423	.813	131	22	98	7.41	-4	*O-113(0-0-113),S-19	25	1.4
1890*Bro-N	119	472	102	134	22	12	**13**	**128**	51	42	21	....	.284	.359	.464	.823	139	21	88	6.92	-3	*O-116(0-0-116)/3-3	21	1.4
1891 Bro-N	123	470	75	134	24	13	4	83	53	30	21	....	.285	.358	.417	.775	126	15	80	6.39	-3	*O-113(0-0-113)/S-6,3-5	15	1.0
1892 Bro-N	141	542	88	171	27	18	4	96	65	42	33	....	.315	.395	.454	.849	162	42	113	8.22	-9	*O-129(2-0-127)/3-7,S-5	26	2.4
1893 Bro-N	109	415	68	112	22	8	7	60	36	16	14	....	.270	.334	.412	.746	102	-0	63	5.54	-1	*O-108(0-1-108)/S-1	12	-0.6
1894 Bro-N	126	509	106	180	32	14	5	107	44	18	30	....	.354	.408	.501	.909	127	23	119	9.43	-8	*O-125(0-0-125)	18	0.7
1895 Bro-N	20	76	7	14	0	1	0	7	8	2	0	....	.184	.271	.211	.481	27	-8	4	1.93	1	O-19(19-0-0)	1	-0.7
NY-N	33	114	21	35	5	3	1	25	14	6	10	....	.307	.388	.430	.817	113	3	24	7.95	-1	O-32(32-0-0)/1-1	4	-0.1
Yr.	53	190	28	49	5	4	1	32	22	8	10	....	.258	.341	.342	.683	79	-5	28	5.32	0	O-51(51-0-0)/1-1	5	-0.8
Total 11	**1188**	**4704**	**869**	**1453**	**224**	**129**	**65**	**832**	**464**	**182**	**263**	**....**	**.309**	**.368**	**.445**	**.814**	**136**	**214**	**890**	**7.32**	**-61**	**O-894,S-200/3-66,P-25,2-21,1**	**196**	**10.7**

• BURNS, Pat Patrick Burns Deb: 8/11/1884

YEAR TM-L	G	AB	R	H	2B	3B	HR	RBI	BB	SO	SB	CS	AVG	OBP	SLG	OPS	OPS+	BR/A	RC	RC/G	FR	G/POS	WS	TPW
1884 Bal-a	6	25	3	5	2	1	0	0	3	....	....	....	.200	.286	.360	.646	105	0	3	3.62	-1	/1-6	1	-0.1
Bal-U	1	4	0	2	0	0	0	....	0	....	....	....	.500	.500	.500	1.000	217	0	1	14.35	0	/1-1	0	0.0

• BURNS, Tom Thomas Everett Burns b: 3/30/1857, Honesdale, PA d: 3/19/1902, Jersey City, NJ BR/TR, 5'7", 152 lbs. Deb: 5/1/1880 M/U Career OF: 10-2-2

YEAR TM-L	G	AB	R	H	2B	3B	HR	RBI	BB	SO	SB	CS	AVG	OBP	SLG	OPS	OPS+	BR/A	RC	RC/G	FR	G/POS	WS	TPW
1880 Chi-N	85	333	47	103	17	3	0	43	12	23	....	....	.309	.333	.378	.712	132	11	43	5.15	-24	*S-79/3-9,C-2,P-1	15	-0.9
1881 Chi-N	84	342	41	95	20	3	4	42	14	22	....	....	.278	.306	.389	.695	109	3	42	4.56	-8	*S-80/2-3,3-3	12	-0.1
1882 Chi-N	84	355	55	88	23	6	0	48	15	28	....	....	.248	.278	.346	.625	98	-1	35	3.61	4	2-43,S-41	10	0.5
1883 Chi-N	97	405	69	119	37	7	2	67	13	31	....	....	.294	.316	.435	.750	116	6	57	5.48	-5	*S-79,2-19/O-1	16	0.3
1884 Chi-N	83	343	54	84	14	2	7	44	13	50	....	....	.245	.272	.359	.631	89	-6	34	3.65	-14	*S-80/3-3	7	-1.5
1885*Chi-N	111	445	82	121	23	9	7	71	16	48	....	....	.272	.297	.411	.708	111	2	56	4.65	-10	*S-111/2-1	18	-0.4
1886*Chi-N	112	445	64	123	18	10	3	65	14	40	15	....	.276	.298	.382	.680	92	-8	57	4.75	8	*3-112	14	0.2
1887 Chi-N	115	458	57	146	20	10	3	60	34	32	32	....	.319	.320	.380	.700	83	-12	63	5.38	12	*3-107/O-8(6-2-0)	13	0.2
1888 Chi-N	134	483	60	115	12	6	3	70	26	49	34	....	.238	.281	.306	.588	81	-11	52	3.85	10	*3-134	13	0.2
1889 Chi-N	136	525	64	127	27	6	4	66	32	57	18	....	.242	.288	.339	.627	71	-23	58	3.85	2	*3-136	11	-1.5
1890 Chi-N	139	538	86	149	17	6	5	86	57	45	44	....	.277	.348	.359	.707	102	1	85	5.77	6	*3-139	20	0.9
1891 Chi-N	59	243	36	55	8	1	1	17	21	21	18	....	.226	.288	.280	.568	66	-11	25	3.64	-3	3-53/S-4,O-2(2-0-0)	5	-1.1
1892 Pit-N	12	39	7	8	0	0	0	4	3	8	1	....	.205	.262	.205	.467	41	-3	2	2.10	-4	/3-8,O-3(1-0-2)	0	-0.6
Total 13	**1251**	**4954**	**722**	**1333**	**236**	**69**	**39**	**683**	**270**	**454**	**162**	**....**	**.269**	**.303**	**.364**	**.667**	**95**	**-52**	**610**	**4.54**	**-25**	**3-704,S-474/2-66,O-14,C-2,P**	**154**	**-3.8**

• BURR, Alex Alexander Thomson Burr b: 11/1/1893, Chicago, IL d: 10/12/1918, Cazaux, France BR/TR, 6'3.5", 190 lbs. Deb: 4/21/1914

YEAR TM-L	G	AB	R	H	2B	3B	HR	RBI	BB	SO	SB	CS	AVG	OBP	SLG	OPS	OPS+	BR/A	RC	RC/G	FR	G/POS	WS	TPW
1914 NY-A	1	0	0	0	0	0	0	0	0	0	0	....	....	....	....	....	-100	0	0	....	0	/O-1	0	0.0

• BURRELL, Buster Frank Andrew Burrell b: 12/22/1866, Weymouth, MA d: 5/8/1962, Weymouth, MA BR/TR, 5'10", 165 lbs. Deb: 8/1/1891

YEAR TM-L	G	AB	R	H	2B	3B	HR	RBI	BB	SO	SB	CS	AVG	OBP	SLG	OPS	OPS+	BR/A	RC	RC/G	FR	G/POS	WS	TPW
1891 NY-N	15	53	1	5	0	0	0	1	3	12	2	....	.094	.158	.094	.252	-27	-8	1	.64	-2	C-15/O-1	0	-0.9
1895 Bro-N	12	28	7	4	0	0	1	5	4	3	0	....	.143	.250	.250	.500	32	-3	2	2.02	-1	C-12	0	-0.3
1896 Bro-N	62	206	19	62	11	3	0	23	15	13	1	....	.301	.348	.383	.732	98	-1	29	5.21	-4	C-60	6	0.0
1897 Bro-N	33	103	15	25	2	0	2	18	10	....	1	....	.243	.310	.320	.630	70	-4	11	3.66	-1	C-27/1-4	2	-0.3
Total 4	**122**	**390**	**42**	**96**	**13**	**3**	**3**	**47**	**32**	**28**	**4**	**....**	**.246**	**.305**	**.318**	**.623**	**69**	**-16**	**43**	**3.81**	**-9**	**C-114/1-4,O-1**	**8**	**-1.4**

• BURRELL, Pat Patrick Brian "Pat the Bat" Burrell b: 10/10/1976, Eureka Springs, AR BR/TR, 6'4", 225 lbs. Deb: 5/24/2000 Career OF: 491-0-0

YEAR TM-L	G	AB	R	H	2B	3B	HR	RBI	BB	SO	SB	CS	AVG	OBP	SLG	OPS	OPS+	BR/A	RC	RC/G	FR	G/POS	WS	TPW
2000 Phi-N	111	408	57	106	27	1	18	79	63	139	0	0	.260	.360	.463	.823	105	4	72	6.27	-6	1-58,O-48(48-0-0)/D-4	12	-1.0
2001 Phi-N	155	539	70	139	29	2	27	89	70	162	2	1	.258	.349	.469	.818	112	10	89	5.77	-2	*O-146(146-0-0)/D-5	17	0.1

YEAR TM-L	G	AB	R	H	2B	3B	HR	RBI	BB	SO	SB	CS	AVG	OBP	SLG	OPS	OPS+	BR/A	RC	RC/G	FR	G/POS	WS	TPW
2002 Phi-N	157	586	96	165	39	2	37	116	89	153	1	0	.282	.379	.544	.923	146	40	121	7.39	-4	*O-157(157-0-0)	25	2.9
2003 Phi-N	146	522	57	109	31	4	21	64	72	142	0	0	.209	.309	.404	.714	90	-9	64	4.02	-4	*O-140(140-0-0)/D-2	9	-1.8
Total 4	**569**	**2055**	**280**	**519**	**126**	**9**	**103**	**348**	**294**	**596**	**3**	**1**	**.253**	**.350**	**.473**	**.823**	**115**	**44**	**346**	**5.84**	**-15**	**O-491/1-58,D-11**	**63**	**0.3**
• BURRIGHT, Larry	Larry Allen "Possum" Burright b: 7/10/1937, Roseville, IL BR/TR, 5'11", 170 lbs. Deb: 4/12/1962																							
1962 LA-N	115	249	35	51	6	5	4	30	21	67	4	3	.205	.267	.317	.584	60	-15	20	2.61	-4	*2-109/S-1	4	-1.3
1963 NY-N	41	100	9	22	2	1	0	3	8	25	1	0	.220	.291	.260	.551	59	-5	8	2.91	2	S-19,2-15/3-1	2	0.0
1964 NY-N	3	7	0	0	0	0	0	0	0	0	0	0	.000	.000	.000	.000	-102	-2	0	.00	2	/2-3	0	0.0
Total 3	**159**	**356**	**44**	**73**	**8**	**6**	**4**	**33**	**29**	**92**	**5**	**3**	**.205**	**.269**	**.295**	**.564**	**57**	**-22**	**29**	**2.63**	**-1**	**2-127/S-20,3-1**	**6**	**-1.3**
• BURRIS, Paul	Paul Robert Burris b: 7/21/1923, Hickory, NC d: 10/3/1999, Charlotte, NC BR/TR, 6', 190 lbs. Deb: 10/2/1948																							
1948 Bos-N	2	4	0	2	0	0	0	0	0	0	0	....	.500	.500	.500	1.000	174	0	1	13.50	0	/C-2	0	0.1
1950 Bos-N	10	23	1	4	1	0	0	3	1	2	0	....	.174	.208	.217	.426	13	-3	1	.85	0	/C-8	0	-0.3
1952 Bos-N	55	168	14	37	4	0	2	21	7	19	0	0	.220	.256	.280	.535	50	-11	10	1.97	-1	C-50	2	-1.0
1953 Mil-N	2	1	0	0	0	0	0	0	0	0	0	0	.000	.000	.000	.000	-107	-0	0	.00	-1	/C-2	0	-0.1
Total 4	**69**	**196**	**15**	**43**	**5**	**0**	**2**	**24**	**8**	**21**	**0**	**0**	**.219**	**.254**	**.276**	**.529**	**47**	**-14**	**12**	**1.95**	**-2**	**/C-62**	**2**	**-1.4**
• BURROUGHS, Henry	Henry S. Burroughs b: 1845, NJ d: 3/31/1878, Newark, NJ, 5'8", 147 lbs. Deb: 5/5/1871 NA OF: 4-2-4																							
1871 Oly-n	12	63	11	15	2	3	1	14	1	1	0	0	.238	.250	.413	.663	91	-1	7	4.37	-1	/O-8(4-0-4),3-5,2-1	....	-0.1
1872 Oly-n	2	7	1	1	0	0	0	0	1	0	0	0	.143	.250	.143	.393	25	-0	0	1.32	0	/O-2(0-2-0)	....	0.0
Total 2 n	**14**	**70**	**12**	**16**	**2**	**3**	**1**	**14**	**2**	**1**	**0**	**0**	**.229**	**.250**	**.386**	**.636**	**84**	**-1**	**7**	**4.03**	**-1**	**/O-10,3-5,2-1**	**....**	**-0.1**
• BURROUGHS, Jeff	Jeffrey Alan Burroughs b: 3/7/1951, Long Beach, CA BR/TR, 6'1", 200 lbs. Deb: 7/20/1970 Career OF: 445-0-845																							
1970 Was-A	6	12	1	2	0	0	0	1	2	5	0	0	.167	.286	.167	.452	29	-1	1	1.94	0	/O-3(0-0-3)	0	-0.1
1971 Was-A	59	181	20	42	9	0	5	25	22	55	1	0	.232	.319	.365	.683	99	0	22	4.09	-1	O-50(34-0-23)	5	-0.3
1972 Tex-A	22	65	4	12	1	0	1	3	5	22	0	2	.185	.243	.246	.489	48	-5	3	1.52	-1	O-19(17-0-2)/1-1	0	-0.8
1973 Tex-A	151	526	71	147	17	1	30	85	67	88	0	0	.279	.362	.487	.849	143	30	95	6.47	1	*O-148(43-0-106)/1-3,D-1	23	2.4
1974 Tex-A★	152	554	84	167	33	2	25	**118**	91	104	2	3	.301	.405	.504	.908	164	49	113	7.29	-9	*O-150(0-0-150)/1-2,D-1	**33**	3.4
1975 Tex-A	152	585	81	132	20	0	29	94	79	155	4	4	.226	.319	.409	.727	105	3	76	4.31	-9	*O-148(0-0-148)/D-3	15	-1.4
1976 Tex-A	158	604	71	143	22	2	18	86	69	93	0	0	.237	.317	.369	.686	98	-1	69	3.79	0	*O-155(0-0-155)/D-3	14	-0.9
1977 Atl-N	154	579	91	157	19	1	41	114	86	126	4	1	.271	.365	.520	.885	120	18	114	7.07	-11	*O-154(0-0-154)	22	0.0
1978 Atl-N★	153	488	72	147	30	6	23	77	**117**	92	1	2	.301	**.436**	.529	.965	151	40	116	8.61	2	*O-146(146-0-0)	27	3.8
1979 Atl-N	116	397	49	89	14	1	11	47	73	75	2	2	.224	.349	.348	.696	84	-6	50	4.11	0	*O-110(110-0-0)	8	-1.1
1980 Atl-N	99	278	35	73	14	0	13	51	35	57	1	1	.263	.349	.453	.802	118	7	45	5.70	-4	O-73(73-0-0)	11	0.0
1981 Sea-A	89	319	32	81	13	1	10	41	41	64	0	1	.254	.339	.395	.734	107	3	43	4.72	-3	O-87(1-0-86)/D-1	8	-0.4
1982 Oak-A	113	285	42	79	13	2	16	48	45	61	1	3	.277	.376	.505	.881	146	18	54	6.54	-1	D-48,O-34(17-0-18)	14	1.4
1983 Oak-A	121	401	43	108	15	1	10	56	47	79	0	2	.269	.346	.387	.733	108	4	51	4.34	0	*D-114	9	0.0
1984 Oak-A	58	71	5	15	1	0	2	8	18	23	0	0	.211	.371	.310	.681	97	1	9	4.29	-1	D-23/O-4(4-0-0)	2	0.0
1985*Tor-A	86	191	19	49	9	3	6	28	34	36	0	1	.257	.369	.429	.798	115	5	30	5.38	0	D-75	5	0.3
Total 16	**1689**	**5536**	**720**	**1443**	**230**	**20**	**240**	**882**	**831**	**1135**	**16**	**22**	**.261**	**.359**	**.439**	**.798**	**121**	**164**	**892**	**5.56**	**-35**	***O-1281,D-269/1-6**	**196**	**6.4**
• BURROUGHS, Sean	Sean Patrick Burroughs b: 9/12/1980, Atlanta, GA BL/TR, 6'2", 200 lbs. Deb: 4/2/2002																							
2002 SD-N	63	192	18	52	5	1	1	11	12	30	2	0	.271	.317	.323	.640	76	-6	19	3.51	-3	3-48,2-13	2	-0.8
2003 SD-N	146	517	62	148	27	6	7	58	44	75	7	2	.286	.355	.402	.757	107	6	74	5.13	0	*3-137	16	0.8
Total 2	**209**	**709**	**80**	**200**	**32**	**7**	**8**	**69**	**56**	**105**	**9**	**2**	**.282**	**.345**	**.381**	**.726**	**99**	**-0**	**93**	**4.69**	**-3**	**3-185/2-13**	**18**	**0.0**
• BURRUS, Dick	Maurice Lennon Burrus b: 1/29/1898, Hatteras, NC d: 2/2/1972, Elizabeth City, NC BL/TL, 5'11", 175 lbs. Deb: 6/23/1919 Career OF: 0-2-10																							
1919 Phi-A	70	194	17	50	3	4	0	8	9	25	2	....	.258	.294	.314	.609	70	-8	18	3.12	-3	1-38,O-10(0-2-8)	2	-1.3
1920 Phi-A	71	135	11	25	8	0	0	10	5	7	0	3	.185	.225	.244	.470	24	-16	7	1.60	-1	1-31/O-2(0-0-2)	0	-1.7
1925 Bos-N	152	588	82	200	41	4	5	87	51	29	8	9	.340	.396	.449	.845	126	23	104	6.75	-4	*1-151	21	0.8
1926 Bos-N	131	486	59	131	21	1	3	61	37	16	4	....	.270	.324	.335	.659	85	-10	53	3.70	5	*1-128	10	-1.3
1927 Bos-N	72	220	22	70	8	3	0	32	17	10	3	....	.318	.370	.382	.752	110	3	31	5.00	-1	1-61	6	-0.1
1928 Bos-N	64	137	15	37	6	0	3	13	19	8	1	....	.270	.367	.380	.747	101	1	20	5.06	-1	1-32	3	-0.3
Total 6	**560**	**1760**	**206**	**513**	**87**	**12**	**11**	**211**	**138**	**95**	**18**	**12**	**.291**	**.347**	**.373**	**.720**	**97**	**-7**	**231**	**4.67**	**-5**	**1-441/O-12**	**42**	**-3.8**
• BURT, Frank	Frank J. Burt b: Camden, NJ Deb: 5/2/1882																							
1882 Bal-a	10	36	2	4	2	1	0	....	1	....	....	....	.111	.135	.222	.357	20	-3	1	.97	-1	O-10(10-0-0)	0	-0.3
• BURTON, Ellis	Ellis Narrington Burton b: 8/12/1936, Los Angeles, CA BB/TR, 5'11", 165 lbs. Deb: 9/18/1958 Career OF: 32-112-45																							
1958 StL-N	8	30	5	7	0	1	2	4	3	8	0	1	.233	.324	.500	.824	110	-0	4	4.59	-1	/O-7(5-0-2)	1	-0.1
1960 StL-N	29	28	5	6	1	0	0	2	4	14	0	2	.214	.313	.250	.563	52	-3	2	2.22	-2	O-23(14-5-4)	0	-0.5
1963 Cle-A	26	31	6	6	3	0	1	1	4	4	0	0	.194	.286	.387	.673	87	-1	3	3.48	0	O-16(9-0-7)	0	-0.1
Chi-N	93	322	45	74	16	1	12	41	36	59	6	3	.230	.315	.398	.712	98	0	41	4.17	-2	O-90(1-76-21)	9	-0.5
1964 Chi-N	42	105	12	20	3	2	2	7	17	22	4	0	.190	.303	.314	.618	71	-3	11	3.31	0	O-29(1-21-11)	1	-0.4
1965 Chi-N	17	40	6	7	1	0	0	4	1	10	1	0	.175	.195	.200	.395	11	-4	2	1.41	1	O-12(2-10-0)	0	-0.5
Total 5	**215**	**556**	**79**	**120**	**24**	**4**	**17**	**59**	**65**	**117**	**11**	**6**	**.216**	**.304**	**.365**	**.669**	**85**	**-10**	**64**	**3.67**	**-3**	**O-177**	**11**	**-2.0**
• BUSBY, Jim	James Franklin Busby b: 1/8/1927, Kenedy, TX d: 7/8/1996, Augusta, GA BR/TR, 6'1", 175 lbs. Deb: 4/23/1950 C Career OF: 12-1267-3																							
1950 Chi-A	18	48	5	10	0	0	0	4	1	5	0	2	.208	.224	.208	.433	12	-7	2	1.13	1	O-12(0-12-1)	0	-0.6
1951 Chi-A★	143	477	59	135	15	2	5	68	40	46	26	11	.283	.344	.354	.698	91	-5	58	4.24	6	*O-139(0-139-0)	12	-0.2
1952 Chi-A	16	39	5	5	0	0	0	0	2	7	0	2	.128	.171	.128	.299	-16	-7	1	.43	-1	O-16(0-16-0)	1	-0.9
Was-A	129	512	58	125	24	4	2	47	22	48	5	6	.244	.281	.318	.599	69	-24	44	2.90	-3	*O-128(0-128-0)	10	-3.2
Yr.	145	551	63	130	24	4	2	47	24	55	5	8	.236	.273	.305	.578	63	-31	45	2.69	-4	*O-144(0-144-0)	11	-4.1
1953 Was-A	150	586	68	183	28	7	6	82	38	45	13	6	.312	.358	.415	.773	111	9	90	5.72	10	*O-150(0-150-0)	25	1.1
1954 Was-A	155	628	83	187	22	7	7	80	43	56	17	2	.298	.346	.389	.734	107	8	88	5.14	3	*O-155(0-155-0)	22	0.4
1955 Was-A	47	191	23	44	6	2	6	14	13	22	5	0	.230	.279	.377	.656	79	-5	20	3.54	-1	O-47(0-47-0)	3	-0.9
Chi-A	99	337	38	82	13	4	1	27	25	37	7	3	.243	.296	.315	.610	62	-18	32	3.16	4	O-99(0-99-0)	6	-1.9
Yr.	146	528	61	126	19	6	7	41	38	59	12	3	.239	.290	.337	.627	68	-24	52	3.30	2	*O-146(0-146-0)	9	-2.8
1956 Cle-A	135	494	72	116	17	3	12	50	43	47	8	3	.235	.301	.354	.656	71	-21	52	3.52	-2	*O-133(0-133-0)	12	-2.9
1957 Cle-A	30	74	9	14	2	1	2	4	1	8	0	1	.189	.200	.324	.524	41	-7	4	1.47	-1	O-26(2-25-0)	0	-0.9
Bal-A	86	288	31	72	10	1	3	19	23	36	6	3	.250	.305	.323	.628	76	-9	30	3.48	4	O-85(0-85-0)	7	-1.0
Yr.	116	362	40	86	12	2	5	23	24	44	6	4	.238	.285	.323	.608	70	-16	33	3.03	3	*O-111(2-110-0)	7	-1.9
1958 Bal-A	113	215	32	51	7	2	3	19	24	37	6	4	.237	.322	.330	.653	84	-4	24	3.79	-4	*O-103(0-103-0)/3-1	6	-1.2
1959 Bos-A	61	102	16	23	8	0	1	5	5	18	0	1	.225	.269	.333	.602	61	-6	8	2.64	-2	O-34(8-25-1)	1	-0.9
1960 Bos-A	1	0	0	0	0	0	0	0	0	0	0	0	....	....	....	....	-97	0	0	....	0	/O-1	0	0.0
Bal-A	79	159	25	41	7	1	0	12	20	14	2	3	.258	.341	.314	.655	79	-5	17	3.59	0	O-71(0-71-0)	4	-0.8
Yr.	80	159	25	41	7	1	0	12	20	14	2	3	.258	.341	.314	.655	79	-5	17	3.59	0	O-72(1-71-0)	4	-0.8
1961 Bal-A	75	89	15	23	3	1	0	6	8	10	2	0	.258	.320	.315	.634	72	-3	10	3.81	-1	O-71(0-71-0)	3	-0.5
1962 Hou-N	15	11	2	2	0	0	0	1	2	3	0	1	.182	.308	.182	.490	38	-1	1	1.57	-1	O-10(1-8-1)/C-1	0	-0.3
Total 13	**1352**	**4250**	**541**	**1113**	**162**	**35**	**48**	**438**	**310**	**439**	**97**	**48**	**.262**	**.316**	**.350**	**.666**	**82**	**-108**	**481**	**3.89**	**11**	***O-1280/3-1,C-1**	**112**	**-14.8**
• BUSBY, Paul	Paul Miller "Red" Busby b: 8/25/1918, Waynesboro, MS BL/TR, 6'1", 175 lbs. Deb: 9/14/1941 Career OF: 2-2-9																							
1941 Phi-N	10	16	3	5	0	0	0	2	0	1	0	....	.313	.313	.313	.625	79	-0	2	3.84	0	/O-3(0-2-1)	0	-0.1
1943 Phi-N	26	40	13	10	1	0	0	5	2	1	2	....	.250	.286	.275	.561	65	-2	3	2.17	0	O-10(2-0-8)	0	-0.3
Total 2	**36**	**56**	**16**	**15**	**1**	**0**	**0**	**7**	**2**	**2**	**2**	**....**	**.268**	**.293**	**.286**	**.579**	**69**	**-2**	**5**	**2.54**	**-1**	**/O-13**	**0**	**-0.4**
• BUSCH, Ed	Edgar John Busch b: 11/16/1917, Lebanon, IL d: 1/17/1987, St. Clair County, IL BR/TR, 5'10", 175 lbs. Deb: 9/30/1943																							
1943 Phi-A	4	17	2	5	0	0	0	0	1	2	0	1	.294	.368	.294	.663	95	-0	2	3.70	-1	/S-4	0	-0.2
1944 Phi-A	140	484	41	131	11	3	0	40	29	17	5	3	.271	.313	.306	.619	78	-14	44	3.09	-12	*S-111,2-27/3-4	8	-1.6

YEAR TM-L	G	AB	R	H	2B	3B	HR	RBI	BB	SO	SB	CS	AVG	OBP	SLG	OPS	OPS+	BR/A	RC	RC/G	FR	G/POS	WS	TPW
1945 Phi-A	126	416	37	104	10	3	0	35	32	9	2	3	.250	.305	.288	.594	73	-15	37	2.94	-7	*S-116/2-2,3-2,1-1	7	-1.3
Total 3	270	917	80	240	21	6	0	75	62	28	7	7	.262	.311	.298	.608	76	-29	82	3.03	-20	S-231/2-29,3-6,1-1	15	-3.1

• BUSCH, Mike Michael Anthony Busch b: 7/7/1968, Davenport, IA BR/TR, 6'5", 249 lbs. Deb: 8/30/1995

YEAR TM-L	G	AB	R	H	2B	3B	HR	RBI	BB	SO	SB	CS	AVG	OBP	SLG	OPS	OPS+	BR/A	RC	RC/G	FR	G/POS	WS	TPW
1995 LA-N	13	17	3	4	0	0	3	6	0	7	0	0	.235	.235	.765	1.000	165	1	3	6.35	-1	3-10/1-2	1	0.1
1996 LA-N	38	83	8	18	4	0	4	17	5	33	0	0	.217	.261	.410	.671	80	-3	8	3.39	-4	3-23/1-1	1	-0.7
Total 2	51	100	11	22	4	0	7	23	5	40	0	0	.220	.257	.470	.727	94	-2	11	3.88	-5	/3-33,1-3	2	-0.6

• BUSH, Donie Owen Joseph Bush b: 10/8/1887, Indianapolis, IN d: 3/28/1972, Indianapolis, IN BB/TR, 5'6", 140 lbs. Deb: 9/18/1908 M

YEAR TM-L	G	AB	R	H	2B	3B	HR	RBI	BB	SO	SB	CS	AVG	OBP	SLG	OPS	OPS+	BR/A	RC	RC/G	FR	G/POS	WS	TPW
1908 Det-A	20	68	13	20	1	1	0	4	7	....	2	....	.294	.360	.338	.698	122	2	9	4.65	-2	S-20	3	0.1
1909*Det-A	157	532	114	145	18	2	0	33	**88**	....	53	....	.273	.380	.314	.694	114	15	89	5.25	7	*S-157	27	3.1
1910 Det-A	142	496	90	130	13	4	3	34	**78**	....	49	....	.262	.365	.323	.687	108	9	78	5.13	14	*S-141/3-1	24	3.0
1911 Det-A	150	561	126	130	18	5	1	36	**98**	....	40	....	.232	.349	.287	.636	74	-15	73	4.09	20	*S-150	18	1.6
1912 Det-A	144	511	107	118	14	8	2	38	**117**	....	35	....	.231	.377	.301	.679	98	7	72	4.61	12	*S-144	19	2.9
1913 Det-A	153	597	98	150	19	10	1	40	80	32	44	....	.251	.344	.322	.665	96	-0	77	4.26	-6	*S-153	18	0.5
1914 Det-A	157	596	97	150	18	4	0	32	**112**	54	35	26	.252	.373	.295	.668	98	2	71	3.90	19	*S-157	22	3.5
1915 Det-A	155	561	99	128	12	8	1	44	118	44	35	27	.228	.364	.283	.648	89	-5	65	3.59	4	*S-155	20	1.1
1916 Det-A	145	550	73	124	5	9	0	34	75	42	19	....	.225	.319	.267	.587	74	-15	57	3.27	-9	*S-144	12	-1.6
1917 Det-A	147	581	**112**	163	18	3	0	24	80	40	34	....	.281	.370	.322	.691	111	12	78	4.73	-10	*S-147	21	1.4
1918 Det-A	128	500	74	117	10	3	0	22	79	31	9	....	.234	.340	.266	.606	86	-4	48	3.08	-16	*S-128	13	-1.3
1919 Det-A	129	509	82	124	11	6	0	26	75	36	22	....	.244	.343	.289	.632	80	-10	57	3.68	-1	*S-129	15	-0.1
1920 Det-A	141	506	85	133	18	5	1	33	73	32	15	7	.263	.357	.324	.681	83	-7	66	4.08	-23	*S-140	9	-1.9
1921 Det-A	104	402	72	113	6	5	0	27	45	23	8	11	.281	.355	.321	.676	74	-16	48	3.75	-2	S-81,2-23	6	-0.8
Was-A	23	84	15	18	1	0	0	2	12	4	2	2	.214	.313	.226	.539	41	-7	7	2.52	-1	S-21	1	-0.6
Yr.	127	486	87	131	7	5	0	29	57	27	10	13	.270	.347	.305	.652	69	-23	55	3.55	-3	*S-102,2-23	7	-1.4
1922 Was-A	41	134	17	32	4	1	0	7	21	7	1	1	.239	.342	.284	.626	68	-5	14	3.58	5	3-37/2-1	3	0.2
1923 Was-A	10	22	6	9	0	0	0	0	0	1	1	1	.409	.409	.409	.818	122	0	3	4.78	-1	/3-5,2-2	1	0.0
Total 16	1946	7210	1280	1804	186	74	9	436	1158	346	404	75	.250	.356	.300	.656	91	-41	912	4.09	12	*S-1867/3-43,2-26	232	11.0

• BUSH, Homer Homer Giles Bush b: 11/12/1972, East St. Louis, IL BR/TR, 5'10", 180 lbs. Deb: 8/16/1997

YEAR TM-L	G	AB	R	H	2B	3B	HR	RBI	BB	SO	SB	CS	AVG	OBP	SLG	OPS	OPS+	BR/A	RC	RC/G	FR	G/POS	WS	TPW
1997 NY-A	10	11	2	4	0	0	0	3	0	0	0	0	.364	.364	.364	.727	91	-0	1	5.61	-1	/2-8,D-1	1	-0.1
1998*NY-A	45	71	17	27	3	0	1	5	5	19	6	3	.380	.421	.465	.886	135	4	14	7.46	-2	2-24,D-12/3-3,S-2	3	0.2
1999 Tor-A	128	485	69	155	26	4	5	55	21	82	32	8	.320	.355	.421	.776	96	-0	74	5.55	4	*2-109,S-18	15	1.0
2000 Tor-A	76	297	38	64	8	0	1	18	18	60	9	4	.215	.272	.253	.524	33	-30	20	2.12	15	2-75	4	-1.1
2001 Tor-A	78	271	32	83	11	1	3	27	8	50	13	4	.306	.340	.387	.728	89	-3	37	4.99	12	2-78	9	1.1
2002 Tor-A	23	78	9	18	2	0	1	2	2	12	2	0	.231	.268	.295	.563	48	-5	6	2.64	-1	2-22	1	-0.5
Fla-N	40	54	7	12	0	0	0	5	3	13	2	1	.222	.263	.222	.485	31	-5	3	2.12	-7	2-12/S-4	0	-1.2
Total 6	400	1267	174	363	50	5	11	115	57	236	64	20	.287	.327	.360	.687	76	-42	155	4.31	20	2-328/S-24,D-13,3-3	33	-0.5

• BUSH, Randy Robert Randall Bush b: 10/5/1958, Dover, DE BL/TL, 6'1", 186 lbs. Deb: 5/1/1982 Career OF: 184-1-371

YEAR TM-L	G	AB	R	H	2B	3B	HR	RBI	BB	SO	SB	CS	AVG	OBP	SLG	OPS	OPS+	BR/A	RC	RC/G	FR	G/POS	WS	TPW
1982 Min-A	55	119	13	29	6	1	4	13	8	28	0	0	.244	.308	.412	.719	93	-1	16	4.58	0	D-26/O-6(6-0-0)	2	-0.2
1983 Min-A	124	373	43	93	24	3	11	56	34	51	0	1	.249	.324	.418	.742	99	-1	50	4.68	1	*D-103/1-3	8	-0.4
1984 Min-A	113	311	46	69	17	1	11	43	31	60	1	2	.222	.301	.389	.690	85	-7	38	4.03	0	D-89/1-2	5	-1.0
1985 Min-A	97	234	26	56	13	3	10	35	24	30	3	0	.239	.323	.449	.772	103	1	36	5.24	-2	O-41(39-0-4),D-28/1-1	6	-0.2
1986 Min-A	130	357	50	96	19	7	7	45	39	63	5	3	.269	.348	.420	.768	105	3	53	5.21	-4	*O-102(90-0-13)/D-6,1-3	9	-0.6
1987*Min-A	122	293	46	74	10	2	11	46	43	49	10	3	.253	.354	.413	.767	99	1	45	5.13	-3	O-75(2-0-72)/1-9,D-9	9	-0.4
1988 Min-A	136	394	51	103	20	3	14	51	58	49	8	6	.261	.369	.434	.803	120	12	64	5.58	-2	*O-109(1-0-108)/D-7,1-6	14	0.7
1989 Min-A	141	391	60	103	17	4	14	54	48	73	5	8	.263	.348	.435	.783	112	4	54	4.67	-1	*O-109(34-1-88),1-25/D-5	13	-0.1
1990 Min-A	73	181	17	44	8	0	6	18	21	27	0	3	.243	.341	.387	.728	97	-1	24	4.57	0	O-32(2-0-32),D-29/1-6	3	-0.3
1991*Min-A	93	165	21	50	10	1	6	23	24	25	0	2	.303	.401	.485	.886	137	9	31	6.96	1	O-38(7-0-32),1-12,D-10	6	0.8
1992 Min-A	100	182	14	39	8	1	2	22	11	37	1	1	.214	.267	.302	.569	57	-11	14	2.46	-1	D-24,O-24(3-0-21)/1-8	1	-1.3
1993 Min-A	35	45	1	7	2	0	0	3	7	13	0	0	.156	.269	.200	.469	28	-4	2	1.47	-1	/D-5,1-4,O-1	0	-0.5
Total 12	1219	3045	388	763	154	26	96	409	348	505	33	29	.251	.337	.413	.750	101	4	428	4.78	-13	O-537,D-341/1-79	76	-3.6

• BUSHONG, Doc Albert John Bushong b: 9/15/1856, Philadelphia, PA d: 8/19/1908, Brooklyn, NY BR/TR, 5'11", 165 lbs. Deb: 7/19/1875 U Career OF: 0-3-3

YEAR TM-L	G	AB	R	H	2B	3B	HR	RBI	BB	SO	SB	CS	AVG	OBP	SLG	OPS	OPS+	BR/A	RC	RC/G	FR	G/POS	WS	TPW
1875 Atl-n	1	5	0	3	0	1	0	0	0	0	0	0	.600	.600	1.000	1.600	511	2	3	45.36	0	/C-1	....	0.1
1876 Phi-N	5	21	4	1	0	0	0	1	0	0	....	....	.048	.048	.048	.095	-69	-4	0	.07	0	/C-5	0	-0.3
1880 Wor-N	41	146	13	25	3	0	0	19	1	16	....	....	.171	.177	.192	.369	23	-12	5	1.15	12	C-40/3-1,O-1	3	0.1
1881 Wor-N	76	275	35	64	7	4	0	21	21	23	....	....	.233	.287	.287	.574	76	-7	23	2.98	14	*C-76	8	0.8
1882 Wor-N	69	253	20	40	4	1	1	15	5	17	....	....	.158	.174	.194	.368	17	-23	9	1.13	1	*C-69	1	-1.4
1883 Cle-N	63	215	15	37	5	0	0	9	7	19	....	....	.172	.198	.195	.394	20	-20	9	1.32	2	C-63	4	-1.1
1884 Cle-N	62	203	24	48	6	1	0	10	17	11	....	....	.236	.295	.276	.571	78	-5	17	3.01	-1	C-62/O-1	4	-0.1
1885*StL-a	85	300	42	80	13	5	0	21	11	....	....	....	.267	.297	.343	.640	97	-2	31	3.85	2	*C-85/3-1	15	0.7
1886*StL-a	107	386	56	86	8	0	1	31	31	....	12	....	.223	.281	.251	.532	64	-17	31	2.82	-8	*C-106/1-1	11	-1.3
1887*StL-a	53	212	35	62	4	0	0	26	11	....	14	....	.292	.299	.274	.573	54	-13	21	3.81	3	C-52/3-2,O-2(0-0-2)	4	-0.5
1888 Bro-a	69	253	23	53	5	1	0	16	5	....	9	....	.209	.231	.237	.468	50	-15	16	2.20	-3	C-69	4	-1.1
1889*Bro-a	25	84	15	13	1	0	0	8	9	7	2	....	.155	.237	.167	.403	15	-9	4	1.45	1	C-25	1	-0.5
1890*Bro-N	16	55	5	13	2	0	0	7	6	4	2	....	.236	.311	.273	.584	70	-2	5	3.42	-3	C-15/O-2(0-2-0)	1	-0.4
Total 12	671	2403	287	522	58	12	2	184	124	97	39	....	.217	.254	.250	.505	55	-128	172	2.48	19	C-667/O-6,3-4,1-1	56	-5.1

• BUSKEY, Joe Joseph Henry "Jazzbow" Buskey b: 12/18/1902, Cumberland, MD d: 4/11/1949, Cumberland, MD BR/TR, 5'10", 175 lbs. Deb: 4/19/1926

YEAR TM-L	G	AB	R	H	2B	3B	HR	RBI	BB	SO	SB	CS	AVG	OBP	SLG	OPS	OPS+	BR/A	RC	RC/G	FR	G/POS	WS	TPW
1926 Phi-N	5	8	1	0	0	0	0	0	1	1	0	....	.000	.111	.000	.111	-65	-2	0	.26	-2	/S-5	0	-0.4

• BUSKEY, Mike Michael Thomas Buskey b: 1/13/1949, San Francisco, CA BR/TR, 5'11", 160 lbs. Deb: 9/2/1977

YEAR TM-L	G	AB	R	H	2B	3B	HR	RBI	BB	SO	SB	CS	AVG	OBP	SLG	OPS	OPS+	BR/A	RC	RC/G	FR	G/POS	WS	TPW
1977 Phi-N	6	7	1	2	0	1	0	1	0	1	0	0	.286	.375	.571	.946	143	0	2	8.63	-1	/S-6	0	-0.1

• BUSSE, Ray Raymond Edward Busse b: 9/25/1948, Daytona Beach, FL BR/TR, 6'4", 175 lbs. Deb: 7/24/1971

YEAR TM-L	G	AB	R	H	2B	3B	HR	RBI	BB	SO	SB	CS	AVG	OBP	SLG	OPS	OPS+	BR/A	RC	RC/G	FR	G/POS	WS	TPW
1971 Hou-N	10	34	2	5	3	0	0	4	2	9	0	0	.147	.194	.235	.430	22	-4	2	1.54	0	/S-5,3-3	0	-0.4
1973 StL-N	24	70	6	10	4	2	2	5	5	21	0	1	.143	.200	.343	.543	48	-6	3	1.36	-2	S-23	1	-0.5
Hou-N	15	17	1	1	0	0	0	0	1	12	0	0	.059	.111	.059	.170	-52	-3	0	.24	1	/S-5,3-3	0	-0.3
Yr.	39	87	7	11	4	2	2	5	6	33	0	1	.126	.183	.287	.470	29	-9	3	1.14	-1	S-28/3-3	1	-0.8
1974 Hou-N	19	34	3	7	1	0	0	0	3	12	0	0	.206	.270	.235	.506	44	-3	2	1.77	0	/3-8	0	-0.3
Total 3	68	155	12	23	8	2	2	9	11	54	0	1	.148	.205	.265	.469	31	-15	7	1.36	-2	/S-33,3-14	1	-1.5

• BUTCHER, Hank Henry Joseph Butcher b: 7/12/1886, Chicago, IL d: 12/28/1979, Hazel Crest, IL BR/TR, 5'10", 180 lbs. Deb: 7/8/1911 Career OF: 44-4-6

YEAR TM-L	G	AB	R	H	2B	3B	HR	RBI	BB	SO	SB	CS	AVG	OBP	SLG	OPS	OPS+	BR/A	RC	RC/G	FR	G/POS	WS	TPW
1911 Cle-A	38	133	21	32	7	3	1	11	11	....	9	....	.241	.303	.361	.664	84	-3	17	4.25	2	O-34(24-4-6)	3	-0.2
1912 Cle-A	26	82	9	16	4	1	1	10	6	....	1	....	.195	.250	.305	.555	57	-5	6	2.44	0	O-21(20-0-0)	1	-0.6
Total 2	64	215	30	48	11	4	2	21	17	....	10	....	.223	.283	.340	.623	73	-8	23	3.52	2	/O-55	4	-0.9

• BUTERA, Sal Salvatore Philip Butera b: 9/25/1952, Richmond Hill, NY BR/TR, 6', 190 lbs. Deb: 4/10/1980 C

YEAR TM-L	G	AB	R	H	2B	3B	HR	RBI	BB	SO	SB	CS	AVG	OBP	SLG	OPS	OPS+	BR/A	RC	RC/G	FR	G/POS	WS	TPW
1980 Min-A	34	85	4	23	1	0	0	2	3	6	0	0	.271	.303	.282	.586	57	-5	7	2.62	-3	C-32/D-2	0	-0.7
1981 Min-A	62	167	13	40	7	1	0	18	22	14	0	0	.240	.328	.293	.621	75	-4	16	3.08	1	C-59/1-1,D-1	4	-0.1
1982 Min-A	54	126	9	32	2	0	0	8	17	12	0	0	.254	.347	.270	.617	70	-4	12	3.17	1	C-53	2	-0.1
1983 Det-A	4	5	1	1	0	0	0	0	0	0	0	0	.200	.200	.200	.400	11	-1	0	1.35	0	/C-4	0	-0.1
1984 Mon-N	3	3	0	0	0	0	0	0	1	0	0	0	.000	.250	.000	.250	-26	-0	0	.59	0	/C-2	0	-0.1
1985 Mon-N	67	120	11	24	1	0	3	12	13	12	0	0	.200	.284	.283	.567	63	-6	11	2.83	-1	C-66/P-1	3	-0.5
1986 Cin-N	56	113	14	27	6	1	2	16	21	10	0	0	.239	.358	.363	.721	95	0	15	4.26	-2	C-53/P-1	4	0.0
1987 Cin-N	5	11	1	2	0	0	1	2	1	6	0	0	.182	.250	.455	.705	78	-0	1	3.95	0	/C-5	0	-0.1
*Min-A	51	111	7	19	5	0	1	12	7	16	0	0	.171	.220	.243	.464	22	-13	5	1.26	-1	C-51	1	-1.1

YEAR TM-L	G	AB	R	H	2B	3B	HR	RBI	BB	SO	SB	CS	AVG	OBP	SLG	OPS	OPS+	BR/A	RC	RC/G	FR	G/POS	WS	TPW
1988 Tor-A	23	60	3	14	2	1	1	6	1	9	0	0	.233	.246	.350	.596	65	-3	5	2.77	0	C-23	1	-0.2
Total 9	359	801	63	182	24	3	8	76	86	85	0	0	.227	.304	.295	.599	65	-37	71	2.86	-5	C-348/D-3,P-2,1-1	15	-2.7
• BUTKA, Ed	Edward Luke "Babe" Butka b: 1/7/1916, Canonsburg, PA BR/TR, 6'3", 193 lbs. Deb: 9/26/1943																							
1943 Was-A	3	9	0	3	1	0	0	1	0	3	0	0	.333	.333	.444	.778	132	0	1	6.15	1	/1-3	0	0.1
1944 Was-A	15	41	1	8	1	0	0	1	2	11	0	0	.195	.233	.220	.452	31	-4	2	1.85	0	1-14	0	-0.5
Total 2	18	50	1	11	2	0	0	2	2	14	0	0	.220	.250	.260	.510	48	-3	4	2.52	1	/1-17	0	-0.4
• BUTLER, Art	Arthur Edward Butler b: 12/19/1887, Fall River, MA d: 10/7/1984, Fall River, MA BR/TR, 5'9", 160 lbs. Deb: 4/14/1911 Career OF: 2-10-6																							
1911 Bos-N	27	68	11	12	2	0	0	2	6	6	0	....	.176	.263	.206	.469	30	-6	4	1.63	-4	3-14/2-4,S-1	0	-1.0
1912 Pit-N	43	154	19	42	4	2	1	17	15	13	2	....	.273	.337	.344	.681	88	-2	19	4.07	-13	2-43	4	-1.4
1913 Pit-N	82	214	40	60	9	3	0	20	32	14	9	....	.280	.379	.350	.729	114	6	31	4.94	-7	2-28,S-26/3-2,0-2(0-0-2)	8	0.1
1914 StL-N	86	274	29	55	12	3	1	24	39	23	14	....	.201	.311	.277	.589	76	-7	28	3.12	-15	S-83/0-1	6	-1.7
1915 StL-N	130	469	73	119	12	5	1	31	47	34	26	14	.254	.323	.307	.630	91	-5	52	3.60	-36	*S-125/2-2	10	-3.6
1916 StL-N	86	110	9	23	5	0	0	7	7	12	3	....	.209	.256	.255	.511	57	-6	8	2.38	-2	0-15(2-9-4)/2-8,3-1,S-1	1	-0.9
Total 6	454	1289	181	311	44	13	3	101	146	102	54	14	.241	.323	.303	.626	85	-20	141	3.54	-77	S-236/2-85,0-18,3-17	29	-8.5
• BUTLER, Bill	William J. Butler b: 1861, New Orleans, LA Deb: 6/29/1884																							
1884 Ind-a	9	31	7	7	3	2	0	0	1	....	....	....	.226	.250	.452	.702	128	1	4	4.11	-1	/0-9(1-1-7)	1	0.0
• BUTLER, Brent	Justin Brent Butler b: 2/11/1978, Laurinburg, NC BR/TR, 6', 180 lbs. Deb: 7/4/2001																							
2001 Col-N	53	119	17	29	7	1	1	14	7	7	1	1	.244	.291	.345	.636	52	-9	11	3.04	-4	2-23,S-10/3-9	1	-1.1
2002 Col-N	113	344	55	89	18	4	9	42	10	40	2	6	.259	.290	.413	.702	71	-17	38	3.70	-10	2-72,3-33,S-13	6	-2.3
2003 Col-N	37	90	13	19	3	1	1	4	7	13	1	0	.211	.276	.300	.576	44	-7	7	2.73	-5	2-20/3-8,S-4	1	-1.1
Total 3	203	553	85	137	28	6	11	60	24	60	4	7	.248	.288	.380	.667	62	-34	56	3.39	-19	2-115/3-50,S-27	8	-4.5
• BUTLER, Brett	Brett Morgan Butler b: 6/15/1957, Los Angeles, CA BL/TL, 5'10", 160 lbs. Deb: 8/20/1981 Career OF: 181-1986-10																							
1981 Atl-N	40	126	17	32	2	3	0	4	19	17	9	1	.254	.352	.317	.669	89	0	17	4.86	0	0-37(25-11-5)	4	-0.1
1982*Atl-N	89	240	35	52	2	0	0	7	25	35	21	8	.217	.291	.225	.516	44	-16	19	2.50	-1	0-77(0-77-0)	2	-1.9
1983 Atl-N	151	549	84	154	21	**13**	5	37	54	56	39	23	.281	.347	.393	.741	97	-3	75	4.73	6	*0-143(109-38-4)	16	-0.3
1984 Cle-A	159	602	108	162	25	9	3	49	86	62	52	22	.269	.364	.355	.720	98	4	86	4.80	2	*0-156(0-155-1)	19	0.4
1985 Cle-A	152	591	106	184	28	14	5	50	63	42	47	20	.311	.379	.431	.810	122	21	100	6.02	11	*0-150(0-150-0)/D-1	23	3.0
1986 Cle-A	161	587	92	163	17	**14**	4	51	70	65	32	15	.278	.359	.375	.733	102	4	84	4.82	-2	*0-159(0-159-0)	20	-0.1
1987 Cle-A	137	522	91	154	25	8	9	41	91	55	33	16	.295	.401	.425	.826	118	18	97	6.73	0	*0-136(0-136-0)	20	1.6
1988 SF-N	157	568	**109**	163	27	9	6	43	97	64	43	20	.287	.395	.398	.793	134	30	99	6.14	0	*0-155(0-156-0)	27	3.0
1989*SF-N	154	594	100	168	22	4	4	36	59	69	31	16	.283	.351	.354	.704	105	4	78	4.57	4	*0-152(0-152-0)	20	0.7
1990 SF-N	160	622	108	**192**	20	9	3	44	90	62	51	19	.309	.401	.384	.785	122	26	108	6.26	-1	*0-159(0-159-0)	27	2.3
1991 LA-N★	161	615	**112**	182	13	5	2	38	**108**	79	38	28	.296	.402	.343	.745	114	14	93	5.34	5	*0-161(0-161-0)	26	1.8
1992 LA-N	157	553	86	171	14	11	3	39	95	67	41	21	.309	.413	.391	.804	131	28	99	6.21	-1	*0-155(0-155-0)	24	2.7
1993 LA-N	156	607	80	181	21	10	1	42	86	69	39	19	.298	.390	.371	.760	111	14	96	5.52	-3	*0-155(0-155-0)	23	1.3
1994 LA-N	111	417	79	131	13	**9**	8	33	68	52	27	8	.314	.413	.446	.859	133	26	86	7.60	5	*0-111(0-111-0)	19	3.1
1995 NY-N	90	367	54	114	13	7	1	25	43	42	21	7	.311	.383	.392	.775	108	7	59	5.89	5	0-90(0-90-0)	12	1.2
*LA-N	39	146	24	40	5	2	0	13	24	9	11	1	.274	.376	.336	.712	98	3	23	5.28	-4	0-38(0-38-0)	4	-0.1
Yr.	129	513	78	154	18	**9**	1	38	67	51	32	8	.300	.381	.376	.757	105	10	82	5.70	0	*0-128(0-128-0)	16	1.1
1996 LA-N	34	131	22	35	1	1	0	8	9	22	8	3	.267	.319	.290	.609	67	-6	13	3.44	-1	0-34(0-34-0)	2	-0.6
1997 LA-N	105	343	52	97	8	3	0	18	42	40	15	10	.283	.363	.324	.686	88	-5	44	4.40	3	0-91(47-49-0)/D-1	7	-0.4
Total 17	2213	8180	1359	2375	277	131	54	578	1129	907	558	257	.290	.379	.376	.755	110	170	1277	5.45	28	*0-2159/D-2	295	17.5
• BUTLER, Dick	Richard H. Butler b: Brooklyn, NY Deb: 6/16/1897 U																							
1897 Lou-N	10	38	3	7	0	0	0	2	0	....	1	....	.184	.184	.184	.368	-3	-6	2	1.33	-1	C-10	0	-0.5
1899 Was-N	12	36	4	10	0	1	0	1	2	....	1	....	.278	.316	.333	.649	79	-1	4	4.29	1	C-11	1	0.1
Total 2	22	74	7	17	0	1	0	3	2	....	2	....	.230	.250	.257	.507	38	-7	6	2.66	0	/C-21	1	-0.4
• BUTLER, Frank	Frank Dean "Stuffy,Goldbrick" Butler b: 7/18/1860, Savannah, GA d: 7/18/1945, Jacksonville, FL BL/TL, 5'7" Deb: 7/30/1895																							
1895 NY-N	5	22	5	6	1	0	0	2	1	1	0	....	.273	.304	.318	.623	62	-1	2	3.68	0	/0-5(4-0-1)	0	-0.1
• BUTLER, John	John Albert Butler b: 7/26/1879, Boston, MA d: 2/2/1950, Boston, MA BR/TR, 5'7", 170 lbs. Deb: 9/28/1901																							
1901 Mil-A	1	3	0	0	0	0	0	0	1	....	0	....	.000	.250	.000	.250	-28	-0	0	.00	-0	/C-1	0	0.0
1904 StL-N	12	37	0	6	1	0	0	1	4	....	0	....	.162	.262	.189	.451	42	-2	2	1.58	-2	C-12	0	-0.3
1906 Bro-N	1	0	0	0	0	0	0	0	0	....	0	....	....	....	....	....	-108	0	0	....	0	/C-1	0	0.0
1907 Bro-N	30	79	6	10	1	0	0	2	9	....	0	....	.127	.216	.139	.355	12	-8	3	1.11	-1	C-28/0-1	1	-0.7
Total 4	44	119	6	16	2	0	0	3	14	....	0	....	.134	.231	.151	.383	20	-10	5	1.21	-3	/C-42,0-1	1	-1.1
• BUTLER, Johnny	John Stephen "Trolley Line" Butler b: 3/20/1893, Fall River, KS d: 4/29/1967, Seal Beach, CA BR/TR, 6', 175 lbs. Deb: 4/18/1926 C																							
1926 Bro-N	147	501	54	135	27	5	1	68	54	44	6	....	.269	.346	.349	.696	89	-6	62	4.21	-1	*S-102,3-42/2-8	15	0.6
1927 Bro-N	149	521	39	124	13	6	2	57	34	33	9	....	.238	.292	.298	.590	58	-31	46	2.87	-1	S-90,3-60	8	-1.8
1928 Chi-N	62	174	17	47	7	0	0	16	19	7	2	....	.270	.352	.310	.662	75	-5	20	3.88	-3	3-59/S-2	5	-0.4
1929 StL-N	17	55	5	9	1	1	0	5	4	5	0	....	.164	.220	.218	.439	9	-8	3	1.51	0	/3-9,S-8	1	-0.6
Total 4	375	1251	115	315	48	12	3	146	111	89	17	....	.252	.320	.317	.636	71	-51	130	3.47	-4	S-202,3-170/2-8	29	-2.2
• BUTLER, Kid	Frank Edward Butler b: 5/1861, Boston, MA d: 4/9/1921, South Boston, MA, 5'6", 140 lbs. Deb: 5/20/1884																							
1884 Bos-U	71	255	36	43	15	0	0	....	12	....	....	....	.169	.206	.227	.433	47	-13	12	1.62	-3	0-53(37-7-9),2-12/S-6,3-2	3	-1.5
• BUTLER, Kid	Willis Everett Butler b: 8/9/1887, Franklin, PA d: 2/22/1964, Richmond, CA BR/TR, 5'11", 155 lbs. Deb: 4/30/1907																							
1907 StL-A	20	59	4	13	2	0	0	6	2	....	1	....	.220	.246	.254	.500	60	-3	4	2.35	2	2-11/3-5,S-1	1	-0.1
• BUTLER, Rich	Richard Dwight Butler b: 5/1/1973, Toronto, Canada BL/TR, 6'1", 180 lbs. Deb: 9/6/1997 Career OF: 44-0-26																							
1997 Tor-A	7	14	3	4	1	0	0	2	2	3	0	1	.286	.375	.357	.732	92	-1	2	4.23	0	/0-3(3-0-0),D-1	1	0.0
1998 TB-A	72	217	25	49	3	3	7	20	15	37	4	2	.226	.282	.364	.646	65	-12	22	3.36	3	0-61(39-0-22)	2	-1.1
1999 TB-A	7	20	2	3	1	0	0	0	2	4	0	0	.150	.227	.200	.427	10	-3	1	1.63	0	/0-6(2-0-4)	0	-0.3
Total 3	86	251	30	56	5	3	7	22	19	44	4	3	.223	.283	.351	.634	62	-15	25	3.27	3	/0-70,D-1	3	-1.4
• BUTLER, Rob	Robert Frank John Butler b: 4/10/1970, East York, Canada BL/TL, 5'11", 185 lbs. Deb: 6/12/1993 Career OF: 38-28-10																							
1993*Tor-A	17	48	8	13	4	0	0	2	7	12	2	2	.271	.375	.354	.729	97	-0	7	4.98	-1	0-16(15-1-0)	1	-0.2
1994 Tor-A	41	74	13	13	0	1	0	5	7	8	0	1	.176	.256	.203	.459	20	-9	4	1.48	-2	0-31(17-13-2)/D-1	0	-1.0
1997 Phi-N	43	89	10	26	9	1	0	13	5	8	1	0	.292	.330	.416	.746	94	-1	12	4.91	2	0-25(4-14-8)	3	0.1
1999 Tor-A	8	7	1	1	0	0	0	1	0	0	0	0	.143	.250	.143	.393	4	-1	0	1.42	0	/D-3,0-2(2-0-0)	0	-0.1
Total 4	109	218	32	53	13	2	0	21	19	28	3	3	.243	.313	.321	.634	65	-11	23	3.46	-1	/0-74,D-4	4	-1.3
• BUTTERY, Frank	Frank Buttery b: 5/13/1851, Silvermine, CT d: 12/16/1902, Silvermine, CT Deb: 4/26/1872 ♦																							
1872 Man-n	18	93	19	24	0	0	0	8	0	2	0	0	.258	.258	.258	.516	63	-3	6	2.85	-3	/0-8(0-0-8),P-7,3-5	....	-0.1
• BUZAS, Joe	Joseph John Buzas b: 10/2/1919, Alpha, NJ d: 3/19/2003, Salt Lake City, UT BR/TR, 6'1", 180 lbs. Deb: 4/17/1945																							
1945 NY-A	30	65	8	17	2	1	0	6	2	5	2	0	.262	.284	.323	.607	73	-2	6	3.16	-1	S-12	1	-0.2
• BYERS, Bill	James William Byers b: 10/3/1877, Bridgeton, IN d: 9/8/1948, Baltimore, MD BL/TR, 5'7" Deb: 4/15/1904																							
1904 StL-N	19	60	3	13	0	0	0	4	1	....	0	....	.217	.230	.217	.446	40	-4	3	1.72	-2	C-16/1-1	0	-0.5
• BYERS, Burley	Burley Byers b: 12/19/1875, Louisville, KY d: 5/30/1933, Louisville, KY, 175 lbs. Deb: 6/17/1899																							
1899 Lou-N	1	3	0	0	0	0	0	0	0	....	0	....	.000	.000	.000	.000	-100	-1	0	.00	-1	/S-1	0	-0.2

YEAR TM-L	G	AB	R	H	2B	3B	HR	RBI	BB	SO	SB	CS	AVG	OBP	SLG	OPS	OPS+	BR/A	RC	RC/G	FR	G/POS	WS	TPW
• BYERS, Randy	Randell Parker Byers b: 10/2/1964, Bridgeton, NJ BL/TR, 6'2", 180 lbs. Deb: 9/7/1987 Career OF: 6-0-1																							
1987 SD-N	10	16	1	5	1	0	0	1	1	5	1	0	.313	.353	.375	.728	96	0	2	5.87	1	/O-5(5-0-0)	0	0.1
1988 SD-N	11	10	0	2	1	0	0	0	0	5	0	0	.200	.200	.300	.500	42	-1	1	2.03	0	/O-2(1-0-1)	0	-0.1
Total 2	21	26	1	7	2	0	0	1	1	10	1	0	.269	.296	.346	.642	76	-1	3	4.25	0	/O-7	0	-0.1
• BYRD, Jim	James Edward Byrd b: 10/3/1968, Wewahitchka, FL BR/TR, 6'1", 185 lbs. Deb: 5/31/1993																							
1993 Bos-A	2	0	0	0	0	0	0	0	0	0	0	0	....	....	....	....	-94	0	0	....	0	....	0	0.0
• BYRD, Marlon	Marlon Jerrard Byrd b: 8/30/1977, Boynton Beach, FL BR/TR, 6', 225 lbs. Deb: 9/8/2002 Career OF: 0-139-2																							
2002 Phi-N	10	35	2	8	2	0	1	1	1	8	0	2	.229	.250	.371	.621	64	-3	3	2.40	-1	O-10(0-8-2)	0	-0.4
2003 Phi-N	135	495	86	150	28	4	7	45	44	94	11	1	.303	.368	.418	.786	112	11	79	5.94	-4	*O-131(0-131-0)	16	0.8
Total 2	145	530	88	158	30	4	8	46	45	102	11	3	.298	.361	.415	.776	109	8	82	5.68	-5	O-141	16	0.4
• BYRD, Sammy	Samuel Dewey "Babe Ruth's Legs" Byrd b: 10/15/1907, Bremen, GA d: 5/11/1981, Mesa, AZ BR/TR, 5'10.5", 175 lbs. Deb: 5/11/1929 Career OF: 201-258-197																							
1929 NY-A	62	170	32	53	12	0	5	28	28	18	1	4	.312	.409	.471	.880	135	9	33	6.97	1	O-54(6-16-32)	7	0.6
1930 NY-A	92	218	46	62	12	2	6	31	30	18	5	1	.284	.371	.440	.811	110	5	38	6.12	-1	O-85(47-12-26)	6	0.0
1931 NY-A	115	248	51	67	18	2	3	32	29	26	5	0	.270	.349	.395	.744	101	3	36	5.25	-4	O-88(26-34-34)	6	-0.4
1932*NY-A	105	209	49	62	12	1	8	30	30	20	1	2	.297	.385	.478	.863	129	9	39	6.80	-4	O-91(11-70-11)	8	0.3
1933 NY-A	85	107	26	30	6	1	2	11	15	12	0	1	.280	.369	.411	.780	113	2	17	5.63	-3	O-71(23-15-35)	3	-0.2
1934 NY-A	106	191	32	47	8	0	3	23	18	22	1	2	.246	.318	.335	.653	73	-8	21	3.64	0	*O-104(34-13-59)	4	-1.1
1935 Cin-N	121	416	51	109	25	4	9	52	37	51	4	....	.262	.322	.406	.729	97	-2	56	4.74	-1	*O-115(39-76-0)	11	-0.7
1936 Cin-N	59	141	17	35	8	0	2	13	11	11	0	....	.248	.303	.348	.650	80	-4	15	3.58	-1	O-37(15-22-0)	2	-0.6
Total 8	745	1700	304	465	101	10	38	220	198	178	17	10	.274	.350	.412	.762	104	13	255	5.27	-13	O-645	47	-2.2
• BYRNE, Bobby	Robert Matthew Byrne b: 12/31/1884, St. Louis, MO d: 12/31/1964, Wayne, PA BR/TR, 5'7.5", 145 lbs. Deb: 4/11/1907																							
1907 StL-N	149	559	55	143	11	5	0	29	35	....	21	....	.256	.307	.293	.600	91	-6	61	3.62	11	*3-148/S-1	15	1.1
1908 StL-N	127	439	27	84	7	1	0	14	23	....	16	....	.191	.238	.212	.450	46	-27	27	1.86	2	*3-122/S-4	4	-2.4
1909 StL-N	105	421	61	90	13	6	1	33	46	....	21	....	.214	.302	.280	.582	86	-6	42	3.18	15	*3-105	9	1.4
*Pit-N	46	168	31	43	6	2	0	7	32	....	8	....	.256	.387	.315	.703	113	5	24	4.81	7	3-46	9	1.5
Yr.	151	589	92	133	19	8	1	40	78	....	29	....	.226	.327	.290	.618	94	-1	65	3.62	22	*3-151	18	2.9
1910 Pit-N	148	602	101	**178**	**43**	12	2	52	66	27	36	....	.296	.366	.417	.783	121	15	104	6.20	1	*3-148	27	2.1
1911 Pit-N	153	598	96	155	24	17	2	52	67	41	23	....	.259	.342	.366	.708	95	-4	82	4.68	7	*3-152	20	0.7
1912 Pit-N	130	528	99	152	31	11	3	35	54	40	20	....	.288	.358	.405	.764	110	7	83	5.45	-15	*3-130	18	-0.3
1913 Pit-N	113	448	54	121	22	0	1	47	29	28	10	....	.270	.322	.326	.647	89	-6	49	3.66	-3	*3-110	12	-0.7
Phi-N	19	58	9	13	1	0	1	4	5	3	2	....	.224	.308	.293	.601	69	-2	6	3.09	2	3-15	1	0.0
Yr.	132	506	63	134	23	0	2	51	34	31	12	....	.265	.320	.322	.642	87	-9	54	3.59	-2	*3-125	13	-0.7
1914 Phi-N	126	467	61	127	12	1	0	26	45	44	9	....	.272	.339	.302	.640	85	-7	49	3.67	-8	*2-101,3-22	11	-1.4
1915*Phi-N	105	387	50	81	6	4	0	21	39	28	4	12	.209	.290	.245	.536	62	-21	28	2.24	-5	*3-105	6	-2.6
1916 Phi-N	48	141	22	33	10	1	0	9	14	7	6	....	.234	.308	.319	.627	89	-1	17	3.73	-1	3-40	5	-0.1
1917 Phi-N	13	14	1	5	0	0	0	0	1	2	0	....	.357	.400	.357	.757	128	1	2	5.33	-1	/3-4	0	0.0
Chi-A	1	1	0	0	0	0	0	0	0	0	0	....	.000	.000	.000	.000	-98	-0	0	.00	-1	/2-1	0	-0.1
Total 11	1283	4831	667	1225	186	60	10	329	456	220	176	12	.254	.324	.323	.647	90	-53	573	3.94	11	*3-1147,2-102/S-5	137	-0.9
• BYRNES, Eric	Eric James Byrnes b: 2/16/1976, Redwood City, CA BR/TR, 6'2", 205 lbs. Deb: 8/22/2000 Career OF: 105-94-32																							
2000 Oak-A	10	10	5	3	0	0	0	0	0	1	2	1	.300	.364	.300	.664	72	-0	1	3.96	0	/O-4(1-0-3),D-2	0	0.0
2001*Oak-A	19	38	9	9	1	0	3	5	4	6	1	0	.237	.326	.500	.826	113	1	7	6.31	-1	O-12(8-2-5)/D-3	1	-0.1
2002*Oak-A	90	94	24	23	4	2	3	11	4	17	3	0	.245	.297	.426	.723	89	-1	12	4.09	-1	O-79(52-10-22)/D-5	2	-0.3
2003*Oak-A	121	414	64	109	27	9	12	51	42	71	10	2	.263	.334	.459	.793	105	4	66	5.75	-5	*O-117(44-82-2)/D-1	16	-0.2
Total 4	240	556	102	144	32	11	18	67	50	95	16	3	.259	.328	.453	.781	102	3	86	5.46	-7	O-212/D-11	19	-0.6
• BYRNES, Jim	James Joseph Byrnes b: 1/5/1880, San Francisco, CA d: 7/31/1941, San Francisco, CA BR/TR, 5'9", 150 lbs. Deb: 4/19/1906																							
1906 Phi-A	10	23	2	4	0	1	0	0	0	....	0	....	.174	.174	.261	.435	34	-2	1	1.49	-1	/C-9	0	-0.2
• BYRNES, Milt	Milton John "Skippy" Byrnes b: 11/15/1916, St. Louis, MO d: 2/1/1979, St. Louis, MO BL/TL, 5'10.5", 170 lbs. Deb: 4/21/1943 Career OF: 95-174-109																							
1943 StL-A	129	429	58	120	28	7	4	50	53	49	1	4	.280	.362	.406	.767	122	11	65	5.32	3	*O-114(23-66-26)	15	1.0
1944*StL-A	128	407	63	120	20	4	4	45	68	50	1	7	.295	.396	.393	.789	119	11	67	5.76	-2	*O-122(41-52-36)	19	0.3
1945 StL-A	133	442	53	110	29	4	8	59	78	84	1	3	.249	.363	.387	.750	112	9	69	5.16	2	*O-125(31-56-47)/1-2	18	0.5
Total 3	390	1278	174	350	77	15	16	154	199	183	3	14	.274	.373	.395	.768	117	31	201	5.40	3	O-361/1-2	52	1.9
• CABALLERO, Putsy	Ralph Joseph Caballero b: 11/5/1927, New Orleans, LA BR/TR, 5'10", 175 lbs. Deb: 9/14/1944																							
1944 Phi-N	4	4	0	0	0	0	0	0	0	1	0	....	.000	.000	.000	.000	-103	-1	0	.00	-0	/3-2	0	-0.1
1945 Phi-N	9	1	1	0	0	0	0	1	0	0	0	....	.000	.000	.000	.000	-103	-0	0	.00	-1	/3-5	0	-0.1
1947 Phi-N	2	7	2	1	0	0	0	0	1	0	0	....	.143	.250	.143	.393	7	-1	0	1.42	0	/2-2,3-1	0	0.0
1948 Phi-N	113	351	33	86	12	1	0	19	24	18	7	....	.245	.293	.285	.578	58	-21	29	2.80	7	3-79,2-23	4	-1.3
1949 Phi-N	29	68	8	19	3	0	0	3	0	3	0	....	.279	.279	.324	.603	63	-4	6	2.88	0	2-21/S-1	1	-0.3
1950*Phi-N	46	24	12	4	0	0	0	0	2	2	1	....	.167	.231	.167	.397	7	-3	1	1.41	-3	/2-5,3-4,S-2	0	-0.6
1951 Phi-N	84	161	15	30	3	2	1	11	12	7	1	2	.186	.243	.248	.491	33	-16	9	1.70	-6	2-54/3-3,S-1	2	-1.9
1952 Phi-N	35	42	10	10	3	0	0	6	2	3	1	0	.238	.273	.310	.582	62	-2	2	1.65	-2	/S-8,2-7,3-7	0	-0.3
Total 8	322	658	81	150	21	3	1	40	41	34	10	2	.228	.273	.274	.547	49	-48	47	2.35	-3	2-112,3-101/S-12	7	-4.6
• CABELL, Enos	Enos Milton Cabell b: 10/8/1949, Fort Riley, KS BR/TR, 6'4", 185 lbs. Deb: 9/17/1972 Career OF: 42-1-72																							
1972 Bal-A	3	5	0	0	0	0	0	1	0	0	0	0	.000	.000	.000	.000	-97	-1	0	.00	0	/1-1	0	-0.2
1973 Bal-A	32	47	12	10	2	0	1	3	3	7	1	3	.213	.260	.319	.579	63	-4	3	1.86	-2	1-23/3-1	0	-0.7
1974*Bal-A	80	174	24	42	4	2	3	17	7	20	5	3	.241	.271	.339	.610	77	-6	14	2.65	-1	1-28,O-22(1-0-22),3-19/2-1,D	2	-1.0
1975 Hou-N	117	348	43	92	17	6	2	43	18	53	12	3	.264	.306	.365	.671	92	-4	38	3.77	4	O-67(37-0-32),1-25,3-22	7	-0.4
1976 Hou-N	144	586	85	160	13	7	2	43	29	79	35	8	.273	.310	.329	.639	89	-5	61	3.62	-10	*3-143/1-3	16	-1.7
1977 Hou-N	150	625	101	176	36	7	16	68	27	55	42	22	.282	.315	.438	.753	109	4	82	4.55	-4	*3-144/1-8,S-1	17	-0.1
1978 Hou-N	162	660	92	195	31	8	7	71	22	80	33	15	.295	.323	.398	.722	109	5	81	4.35	-6	*3-153,1-14/S-1	20	-0.4
1979 Hou-N	155	603	60	164	30	5	6	67	21	68	37	18	.272	.300	.368	.668	86	-14	60	3.37	-8	*3-132,1-51	12	-2.6
1980*Hou-N	152	604	69	167	23	8	2	55	26	84	21	13	.276	.307	.351	.658	90	-11	61	3.51	-15	*3-150/1-1	11	-2.9
1981 SF-N	96	396	41	101	20	1	2	36	10	47	6	7	.255	.275	.326	.601	71	-18	33	2.85	1	1-69,3-22	4	-2.4
1982 Det-A	125	464	45	121	17	3	2	37	15	48	15	6	.261	.285	.323	.609	67	-21	41	3.04	1	1-83,3-59/O-3(1-0-2)	4	-2.4
1983 Det-A	121	392	62	122	23	5	5	46	16	41	4	8	.311	.340	.434	.774	114	4	51	4.51	9	*1-106/D-8,3-4,S-1	10	0.7
1984 Hou-N	127	436	52	135	17	3	8	44	21	47	8	11	.310	.343	.417	.760	121	7	56	4.58	-2	*1-112	12	-0.2
1985 Hou-N	60	143	20	35	8	1	2	14	16	15	3	1	.245	.321	.357	.677	92	-1	16	3.80	-1	1-49	3	-0.5
*LA-N	57	192	20	56	11	0	0	22	14	21	6	2	.292	.340	.349	.689	96	-1	24	4.70	1	3-32,1-21/O-4(1-0-3)	7	-0.1
Yr.	117	335	40	91	19	1	2	36	30	36	9	3	.272	.332	.352	.684	94	-2	40	4.30	0	1-70,3-32/O-4(1-0-3)	10	-0.6
1986 LA-N	107	277	27	71	11	0	2	29	14	26	10	4	.256	.297	.318	.615	75	-10	26	3.19	-2	1-61,O-16(2-1-13)/3-7	4	-1.5
Total 15	1688	5952	753	1647	263	56	60	596	259	691	238	124	.277	.309	.370	.679	93	-77	646	3.76	-34	3-888,1-655,O-112/D-9,S-3,2	129	-16.3
• CABRERA, Al	Alfredo A. Cabrera b: 5/11/1881, Canary Islands, Spain d: 1964, Batabano, Cuba TR Deb: 5/16/1913																							
1913 StL-N	1	2	0	0	0	0	0	0	0	0	0	0	.000	.000	.000	.000	-101	-1	0	.00	-1	/S-1	0	-0.1
• CABRERA, Alex	Alexander Alberto Cabrera b: 12/24/1971, Caripito, Venezuela BR/TR, 6'2", 217 lbs. Deb: 6/26/2000																							
2000 Ari-N	31	80	10	21	2	1	5	14	4	21	0	0	.263	.306	.500	.806	96	-1	11	4.72	1	1-15,O-12(1-0-11)	1	-0.1
• CABRERA, Francisco	Francisco (Paulino) Cabrera b: 10/10/1966, Santo Domingo, Dominican Republic BR/TR, 6'4", 193 lbs. Deb: 7/24/1989																							
1989 Tor-A	3	12	1	2	1	0	0	0	1	3	0	0	.167	.231	.250	.481	38	-1	1	2.03	0	/D-3	0	-0.1
Atl-N	4	14	0	3	2	0	0	0	0	3	0	0	.214	.214	.357	.571	59	-1	1	2.63	-1	/1-2,C-1	0	-0.2
1990 Atl-N	63	137	14	38	5	1	7	25	5	21	1	0	.277	.303	.482	.785	106	0	19	4.84	-4	1-48/C-3	4	-0.6

YEAR TM-L	G	AB	R	H	2B	3B	HR	RBI	BB	SO	SB	CS	AVG	OBP	SLG	OPS	OPS+	BR/A	RC	RC/G	FR	G/POS	WS	TPW
1991*Atl-N	44	95	7	23	6	0	4	23	6	20	1	1	.242	.287	.432	.719	94	-1	10	3.36	-1	C-17,1-14	2	-0.2
1992*Atl-N	12	10	2	3	0	0	2	3	1	1	0	0	.300	.364	.900	1.264	233	2	3	12.99	0	/C-1	1	0.1
1993*Atl-N	70	83	8	20	3	0	4	11	8	21	0	0	.241	.308	.422	.729	92	-1	11	4.37	2	1-12/C-2	1	0.0
Total 5	**196**	**351**	**32**	**89**	**17**	**1**	**17**	**62**	**21**	**69**	**2**	**1**	**.254**	**.296**	**.453**	**.749**	**99**	**-2**	**44**	**4.32**	**-4**	**/1-76,C-24,D-3**	**8**	**-0.9**

• CABRERA, Jolbert Jolbert Alexis Cabrera b: 12/8/1972, Cartagena, Colombia BR/TR, 6', 177 lbs. Deb: 4/12/1998 Career OF: 103-127-65

YEAR TM-L	G	AB	R	H	2B	3B	HR	RBI	BB	SO	SB	CS	AVG	OBP	SLG	OPS	OPS+	BR/A	RC	RC/G	FR	G/POS	WS	TPW
1998 Cle-A	1	2	0	0	0	0	0	0	0	1	0	0	.000	.000	.000	.000	-97	-1	0	.00	0	/S-1	0	-0.1
1999 Cle-A	30	37	6	7	1	0	0	0	1	8	3	0	.189	.231	.216	.447	14	-4	2	1.80	-2	O-16(4-12-0)/2-6	0	-0.5
2000 Cle-A	100	175	27	44	3	1	2	15	8	15	6	4	.251	.292	.314	.606	53	-13	16	3.17	2	O-74(24-26-29),2-19/S-8,D	2	-1.0
2001*Cle-A	141	287	50	75	16	3	1	38	16	41	10	4	.261	.314	.348	.662	73	-11	32	3.88	-3	O-83(36-35-18),2-28,3-27,S	6	-1.2
2002 Cle-A	38	72	5	8	1	0	0	7	5	13	1	1	.111	.179	.125	.304	-17	-12	1	.57	-1	O-34(5-16-13)/2-3,D-1	0	-1.3
LA-N	10	12	3	4	1	0	0	1	2	2	0	0	.333	.429	.417	.845	133	1	2	7.25	1	/O-4(3-0-1),3-3,2-1	1	0.1
2003 LA-N	128	347	43	98	32	2	6	37	17	62	6	4	.282	.334	.438	.772	105	1	48	4.82	-8	O-63(31-38-4),2-59/S-9,1-8,3	9	-0.5
Total 6	**448**	**932**	**134**	**236**	**54**	**6**	**9**	**98**	**49**	**142**	**26**	**13**	**.253**	**.305**	**.353**	**.658**	**73**	**-39**	**102**	**3.73**	**-11**	**O-274,2-116/3-35,S-32,1-8,D**	**18**	**-4.5**

• CABRERA, Miguel Jose Miguel Torres Cabrera b: 4/18/1983, Maracay, Venezuela BR/TR, 6'2", 185 lbs. Deb: 6/20/2003

YEAR TM-L	G	AB	R	H	2B	3B	HR	RBI	BB	SO	SB	CS	AVG	OBP	SLG	OPS	OPS+	BR/A	RC	RC/G	FR	G/POS	WS	TPW
2003*Fla-N	87	314	39	84	21	3	12	62	25	84	0	2	.268	.326	.468	.794	108	2	44	4.74	-3	O-55(55-0-0),3-34	12	-0.3

• CABRERA, Orlando Orlando Luis Cabrera b: 11/2/1974, Cartagena, Colombia BR/TR, 5'11", 165 lbs. Deb: 9/3/1997

YEAR TM-L	G	AB	R	H	2B	3B	HR	RBI	BB	SO	SB	CS	AVG	OBP	SLG	OPS	OPS+	BR/A	RC	RC/G	FR	G/POS	WS	TPW
1997 Mon-N	16	18	4	4	0	0	0	2	1	3	1	2	.222	.263	.222	.485	29	-3	1	.80	-1	/S-6,2-4	0	-0.3
1998 Mon-N	79	261	44	73	16	5	3	22	18	27	6	2	.280	.326	.414	.740	94	-2	35	4.62	-7	S-52,2-28	6	-0.5
1999 Mon-N	104	382	48	97	23	5	8	39	18	38	2	2	.254	.293	.403	.696	76	-17	42	3.82	4	*S-102	8	-0.4
2000 Mon-N	125	422	47	100	25	1	13	55	25	28	4	4	.237	.281	.393	.675	66	-25	43	3.37	-3	*S-124/2-1	9	-1.8
2001 Mon-N	162	626	64	173	41	6	14	96	43	54	19	7	.276	.327	.428	.755	91	-8	85	4.74	24	*S-162	26	2.8
2002 Mon-N	153	563	64	148	43	1	7	56	48	53	25	7	.263	.323	.380	.703	82	-13	69	4.11	6	*S-153	14	0.6
2003 Mon-N	162	626	95	186	47	2	17	80	52	64	24	2	.297	.352	.460	.812	93	-2	101	5.80	0	*S-162	18	1.1
Total 7	**801**	**2898**	**366**	**781**	**195**	**20**	**62**	**350**	**205**	**267**	**81**	**26**	**.269**	**.320**	**.415**	**.735**	**84**	**-70**	**376**	**4.46**	**22**	**S-761/2-33**	**81**	**1.5**

• CACEK, Craig Craig Thomas Cacek b: 9/10/1954, Hollywood, CA BR/TR, 6'1", 200 lbs. Deb: 6/18/1977

YEAR TM-L	G	AB	R	H	2B	3B	HR	RBI	BB	SO	SB	CS	AVG	OBP	SLG	OPS	OPS+	BR/A	RC	RC/G	FR	G/POS	WS	TPW
1977 Hou-N	7	20	0	1	0	0	0	1	1	3	0	0	.050	.095	.050	.145	-66	-5	0	.00	-1	/1-6	0	-0.6

• CACERES, Edgar Edgar F. Caceres b: 6/6/1964, Barquisimeto, Venezuela BB/TR, 6'1", 170 lbs. Deb: 6/8/1995

YEAR TM-L	G	AB	R	H	2B	3B	HR	RBI	BB	SO	SB	CS	AVG	OBP	SLG	OPS	OPS+	BR/A	RC	RC/G	FR	G/POS	WS	TPW
1995 KC-A	55	117	13	28	6	2	1	17	8	15	2	2	.239	.294	.350	.644	66	-7	11	3.15	-1	2-36/S-8,1-6,3-3,D-3	2	-0.6

• CADY, Charlie Charles B. Cady b: 12/1865, Chicago, IL d: 6/7/1909, Kankakee, IL, 5'11", 180 lbs. Deb: 9/5/1883 Career OF: 0-2-2 ♦

YEAR TM-L	G	AB	R	H	2B	3B	HR	RBI	BB	SO	SB	CS	AVG	OBP	SLG	OPS	OPS+	BR/A	RC	RC/G	FR	G/POS	WS	TPW
1883 Cle-N	3	11	0	0	0	0	0	0	1	5	....	....	.000	.083	.000	.083	-73	-2	0	.00	0	/O-2(0-0-2),P-1	0	-0.6
1884 CP-U	6	20	4	2	1	1	0	....	1	....	....	....	.100	.143	.250	.393	32	-1	1	1.14	0	/P-4,O-2(0-2-0)	2	-0.1
KC-U	2	3	0	0	0	0	0	....	0	....	....	....	.000	.000	.000	.000	-115	-1	0	.00	-2	/2-1,C-1	0	-0.2
Yr.	8	23	4	2	1	1	0	....	1	....	....	....	.087	.125	.217	.342	14	-2	1	.98	-2	/P-4,O-2(0-2-0),2-1,C-1	2	-0.3
Total 2	**11**	**34**	**4**	**2**	**1**	**1**	**0**	**0**	**2**	**5**	**....**	**....**	**.059**	**.111**	**.147**	**.258**	**-15**	**-3**	**1**	**.64**	**-2**	**/P-5,O-4,2-1,C-1**	**2**	**-0.8**

• CADY, Hick Forrest Leroy Cady b: 1/26/1886, Bishop Hill, IL d: 3/3/1946, Cedar Rapids, IA BR/TR, 6'2", 179 lbs. Deb: 4/26/1912

YEAR TM-L	G	AB	R	H	2B	3B	HR	RBI	BB	SO	SB	CS	AVG	OBP	SLG	OPS	OPS+	BR/A	RC	RC/G	FR	G/POS	WS	TPW
1912*Bos-A	47	135	19	35	13	2	0	9	10	....	0	....	.259	.324	.385	.710	98	-1	17	4.16	-2	C-43/1-4	6	0.1
1913 Bos-A	40	96	10	24	5	2	0	6	5	14	1	....	.250	.294	.344	.638	84	-2	10	3.31	0	C-39	3	0.0
1914 Bos-A	61	159	14	41	6	1	0	8	12	22	2	1	.258	.310	.308	.618	86	-3	16	3.46	2	C-58	6	0.3
1915*Bos-A	78	205	25	57	10	2	0	17	19	25	0	2	.278	.342	.346	.689	109	1	25	4.20	3	C-77	11	1.0
1916*Bos-A	78	162	5	31	6	3	0	13	15	16	0	....	.191	.264	.265	.529	59	-8	12	2.33	-4	C-63/1-3	3	-1.0
1917 Bos-A	17	46	4	7	1	1	0	2	1	6	0	....	.152	.170	.217	.388	18	-5	2	1.04	-1	C-14	1	-0.5
1919 Phi-N	34	98	6	21	6	0	1	19	4	8	1	....	.214	.252	.306	.559	63	-5	8	2.46	1	C-29	1	-0.2
Total 7	**355**	**901**	**83**	**216**	**47**	**11**	**1**	**74**	**66**	**91**	**4**	**3**	**.240**	**.297**	**.320**	**.616**	**82**	**-23**	**89**	**3.25**	**-2**	**C-323/1-7**	**31**	**-0.4**

• CAFEGO, Tom Thomas Cafego b: 8/21/1911, Whipple, WV d: 10/29/1961, Detroit, MI BL/TR, 5'10", 160 lbs. Deb: 9/3/1937

YEAR TM-L	G	AB	R	H	2B	3B	HR	RBI	BB	SO	SB	CS	AVG	OBP	SLG	OPS	OPS+	BR/A	RC	RC/G	FR	G/POS	WS	TPW
1937 StL-A	4	4	1	0	0	0	0	0	0	1	0	0	.000	.000	.000	.000	-99	-1	0	.00	0	/O-1	0	-0.2

• CAFFIE, Joe Joseph Clifford "Rabbit" Caffie b: 2/14/1931, Ramer, AL BL/TR, 5'10.5", 180 lbs. Deb: 9/13/1956 Career OF: 13-0-18

YEAR TM-L	G	AB	R	H	2B	3B	HR	RBI	BB	SO	SB	CS	AVG	OBP	SLG	OPS	OPS+	BR/A	RC	RC/G	FR	G/POS	WS	TPW
1956 Cle-A	12	38	7	13	0	0	0	1	4	8	3	2	.342	.432	.342	.774	104	1	6	6.23	0	O-10(10-0-0)	2	0.0
1957 Cle-A	32	89	14	24	2	1	3	10	4	11	0	1	.270	.301	.416	.717	95	-1	11	4.13	0	O-19(3-0-18)	2	-0.2
Total 2	**44**	**127**	**21**	**37**	**2**	**1**	**3**	**11**	**8**	**19**	**3**	**3**	**.291**	**.343**	**.394**	**.737**	**98**	**-1**	**17**	**4.72**	**0**	**/O-29**	**4**	**-0.2**

• CAFFYN, Ben Benjamin Thomas Caffyn b: 2/10/1880, Peoria, IL d: 11/22/1942, Peoria, IL BL/TL, 5'10", 175 lbs. Deb: 8/21/1906

YEAR TM-L	G	AB	R	H	2B	3B	HR	RBI	BB	SO	SB	CS	AVG	OBP	SLG	OPS	OPS+	BR/A	RC	RC/G	FR	G/POS	WS	TPW
1906 Cle-A	30	103	16	20	4	0	0	3	12	....	2	....	.194	.291	.233	.524	65	-3	8	2.49	-2	O-29(28-1-0)	1	-0.8

• CAGE, Wayne Wayne Levell Cage b: 11/23/1951, Monroe, LA BL/TL, 6'4", 205 lbs. Deb: 4/22/1978

YEAR TM-L	G	AB	R	H	2B	3B	HR	RBI	BB	SO	SB	CS	AVG	OBP	SLG	OPS	OPS+	BR/A	RC	RC/G	FR	G/POS	WS	TPW
1978 Cle-A	36	98	11	24	6	1	4	13	9	28	1	2	.245	.308	.449	.757	112	1	13	4.35	1	D-20,1-11	3	0.0
1979 Cle-A	29	56	6	13	2	0	1	6	5	16	0	2	.232	.295	.321	.617	66	-4	5	2.79	1	/D-9,1-7	0	-0.3
Total 2	**65**	**154**	**17**	**37**	**8**	**1**	**5**	**19**	**14**	**44**	**1**	**4**	**.240**	**.304**	**.403**	**.706**	**95**	**-3**	**17**	**3.77**	**1**	**/D-29,1-18**	**3**	**-0.3**

• CAHILL, John John Patrick Parnell "Patsy" Cahill
b: 4/30/1865, San Francisco, CA d: 10/31/1901, Pleasanton, CA BR/TR, 5'7.5", 168 lbs. Deb: 5/31/1884 Career OF: 56-4-176 ♦

YEAR TM-L	G	AB	R	H	2B	3B	HR	RBI	BB	SO	SB	CS	AVG	OBP	SLG	OPS	OPS+	BR/A	RC	RC/G	FR	G/POS	WS	TPW
1884 Col-a	59	210	28	46	3	3	0	0	6	....	....	....	.219	.248	.262	.510	72	-5	14	2.34	1	O-56(56-0-0)/S-5,P-2	3	-0.9
1886 StL-N	125	463	43	92	17	6	1	32	9	79	16	....	.199	.214	.268	.482	49	-27	31	2.23	2	*O-124(0-1-123)/P-2,3-1,S	3	-2.5
1887 Ind-N	68	272	22	63	4	3	0	26	9	5	34	....	.232	.234	.243	.478	34	-22	24	2.99	-5	O-56(0-3-53)/3-9,P-6,S-1	1	-4.4
Total 3	**252**	**945**	**93**	**201**	**24**	**12**	**1**	**58**	**24**	**84**	**50**	**....**	**.213**	**.227**	**.260**	**.487**	**50**	**-55**	**68**	**2.47**	**-2**	**O-236/3-10,P-10,S-7**	**7**	**-7.8**

• CAHILL, Tom Thomas H. Cahill b: 10/1868, Fall River, MA d: 12/25/1894, Scranton, PA, 5'7" Deb: 4/9/1891

YEAR TM-L	G	AB	R	H	2B	3B	HR	RBI	BB	SO	SB	CS	AVG	OBP	SLG	OPS	OPS+	BR/A	RC	RC/G	FR	G/POS	WS	TPW
1891 Lou-a	119	430	68	109	17	7	3	44	41	51	38	....	.253	.327	.347	.674	94	-4	63	5.18	3	C-56,S-49,O-12(9-2-1)/2-6,3	13	0.4

• CAIRO, Miguel Miguel Jesus Cairo b: 5/4/1974, Anaco, Venezuela BR/TR, 6', 160 lbs. Deb: 4/17/1996 Career OF: 47-0-11

YEAR TM-L	G	AB	R	H	2B	3B	HR	RBI	BB	SO	SB	CS	AVG	OBP	SLG	OPS	OPS+	BR/A	RC	RC/G	FR	G/POS	WS	TPW
1996 Tor-A	9	27	5	6	2	0	0	1	2	9	0	0	.222	.300	.296	.596	52	-2	2	2.87	0	/2-9	0	-0.2
1997 Chi-N	16	29	7	7	1	0	0	1	2	3	0	0	.241	.313	.276	.588	54	-2	3	3.37	-0	/2-9,S-2	0	-0.1
1998 TB-A	150	515	49	138	26	5	5	46	24	44	19	8	.268	.308	.367	.675	73	-21	58	3.83	15	*2-148/D-2	10	0.1
1999 TB-A	120	465	61	137	15	5	3	36	24	46	22	7	.295	.339	.368	.706	79	-13	57	4.30	13	*2-117/D-2	10	0.5
2000 TB-A	119	375	49	98	18	2	1	34	29	34	28	7	.261	.318	.328	.646	65	-17	42	3.73	-2	*2-108/D-2	10	-1.3
2001 Chi-N	66	123	20	35	3	1	2	9	16	21	2	1	.285	.367	.374	.741	97	-0	18	4.76	-5	3-40,2-11/S-1	2	-0.4
*StL-N	27	33	5	11	5	0	1	7	2	2	0	0	.333	.371	.576	.947	141	2	7	7.86	0	/O-6(6-0-0),2-5,3-3,1-1,S-1	2	0.1
Yr.	93	156	25	46	8	1	3	16	18	23	2	1	.295	.368	.417	.784	106	2	24	5.34	-5	3-43,2-16/O-6(6-0-0),S-2,1	4	-0.2
2002*StL-N	108	184	28	46	9	2	2	23	13	36	1	1	.250	.310	.353	.663	76	-7	20	3.51	-1	O-24(19-0-5),2-18/3-7,S-6,1,D	3	-0.7
2003 StL-N	92	261	41	64	15	2	5	32	13	30	4	1	.245	.296	.375	.672	77	-9	29	3.64	-8	2-40,O-27(22-0-6),3-12/S-7,1	3	-1.6
Total 8	**707**	**2012**	**265**	**542**	**94**	**17**	**19**	**189**	**125**	**225**	**76**	**25**	**.269**	**.320**	**.361**	**.682**	**76**	**-69**	**235**	**3.96**	**11**	**2-465/3-62,O-57,S-17,D-9,1**	**40**	**-3.7**

• CAITHAMER, George George Theodore "Sidee" Caithamer b: 7/22/1910, Chicago, IL d: 6/1/1954, Chicago, IL BR/TR, 5'7.5", 168 lbs. Deb: 9/17/1934

YEAR TM-L	G	AB	R	H	2B	3B	HR	RBI	BB	SO	SB	CS	AVG	OBP	SLG	OPS	OPS+	BR/A	RC	RC/G	FR	G/POS	WS	TPW
1934 Chi-A	5	19	1	6	1	0	0	3	1	5	0	0	.316	.350	.368	.718	83	-0	2	4.71	0	/C-5	1	0.0

• CALDERON, Ivan Ivan (Perez) Calderon
b: 3/19/1962, Fajardo, Puerto Rico d: 12/27/2003, Loiza, Puerto Rico BR/TR, 6'1", 220 lbs. Deb: 8/10/1984 Career OF: 378-11-383

YEAR TM-L	G	AB	R	H	2B	3B	HR	RBI	BB	SO	SB	CS	AVG	OBP	SLG	OPS	OPS+	BR/A	RC	RC/G	FR	G/POS	WS	TPW
1984 Sea-A	11	24	2	5	1	0	1	1	2	5	1	0	.208	.269	.375	.644	77	-1	2	1.90	0	O-11(4-6-1)	0	-0.1
1985 Sea-A	67	210	37	60	16	4	8	28	19	45	4	2	.286	.351	.514	.865	132	9	34	5.67	2	O-53(33-1-22)/D-3,1-2	7	0.9
1986 Sea-A	37	131	13	31	5	0	2	13	6	33	3	1	.237	.275	.321	.596	61	-7	12	3.13	-1	O-32(2-2-31)	1	-0.9
Chi-A	13	33	3	10	2	1	0	2	3	6	0	0	.303	.361	.424	.785	109	0	5	6.16	0	/D-6,O-5(5-0-0)	1	0.0
Yr.	50	164	16	41	7	1	2	15	9	39	3	1	.250	.293	.341	.635	71	-7	17	3.69	-1	O-37(7-2-31)/D-6	2	-1.0
1987 Chi-A	144	542	93	159	38	2	28	83	60	109	10	5	.293	.365	.526	.891	129	22	102	6.80	0	*O-139(6-0-135)/D-3	20	1.5
1988 Chi-A	73	264	40	56	14	0	14	35	34	66	4	4	.212	.302	.424	.726	101	-1	33	4.03	1	O-67(4-0-63)/D-3	7	-0.2

YEAR TM-L	G	AB	R	H	2B	3B	HR	RBI	BB	SO	SB	CS	AVG	OBP	SLG	OPS	OPS+	BR/A	RC	RC/G	FR	G/POS	WS	TPW
1989 Chi-A	157	622	83	178	34	9	14	87	43	94	7	1	.286	.335	.437	.773	119	15	87	4.97	0	*0-103(17-0-89),D-36,1-26	18	0.9
1990 Chi-A	158	607	85	166	44	2	14	74	51	79	32	16	.273	.331	.422	.753	112	8	76	4.19	2	*0-130(130-0-3),D-27/1-2	22	0.4
1991 Mon-N★	134	470	69	141	22	3	19	75	53	64	31	16	.300	.375	.481	.855	141	25	85	6.30	2	*0-122(122-0-0)/1-4	21	2.4
1992 Mon-N	48	170	19	45	14	2	3	24	14	22	1	2	.265	.324	.424	.748	111	1	22	4.55	0	0-46(46-0-0)	5	0.0
1993 Bos-A	73	213	25	47	8	2	1	19	21	28	4	2	.221	.294	.291	.585	54	-14	17	2.53	0	0-47(9-2-39),D-19	2	-1.6
Chi-A	9	26	1	3	2	0	0	3	0	5	0	0	.115	.115	.192	.308	-19	-4	0	.21	0	/D-6	0	-0.5
Yr.	82	239	26	50	10	2	1	22	21	33	4	2	.209	.276	.280	.556	47	-18	17	2.25	0	0-47(9-2-39),D-25	2	-2.0
Total 10	**924**	**3312**	**470**	**901**	**200**	**25**	**104**	**444**	**306**	**556**	**97**	**49**	**.272**	**.336**	**.442**	**.778**	**114**	**54**	**475**	**4.93**	**7**	**0-755,D-103/1-34**	**104**	**2.8**
• CALDERONE, Sam	Samuel Francis Calderone b: 2/6/1926, Beverly, NJ BR/TR, 5'10.5", 185 lbs. Deb: 4/19/1950																							
1950 NY-N	34	67	9	20	1	0	1	12	2	5	0	....	.299	.319	.358	.677	77	-2	7	3.86	-1	C-33	1	-0.2
1953 NY-N	35	45	4	10	2	0	0	8	1	4	0	0	.222	.239	.267	.506	31	-5	3	2.32	0	C-31	1	-0.4
1954 Mil-N	22	29	3	11	2	0	0	5	4	4	0	0	.379	.455	.448	.903	146	2	6	8.09	1	C-16	2	0.3
Total 3	**91**	**141**	**16**	**41**	**5**	**0**	**1**	**25**	**7**	**13**	**0**	**0**	**.291**	**.324**	**.348**	**.672**	**79**	**-5**	**16**	**4.15**	**0**	**/C-80**	**4**	**-0.3**
• CALDWELL, Bruce	Bruce Caldwell b: 2/8/1906, Ashton, RI d: 2/15/1959, West Haven, CT BR/TR, 6', 195 lbs. Deb: 6/30/1928																							
1928 Cle-A	18	27	2	6	1	1	0	3	2	2	1	0	.222	.300	.333	.633	65	-1	3	3.63	0	0-10(0-0-10)/1-1	0	-0.2
1932 Bro-N	7	11	2	1	0	0	0	2	2	2	0	....	.091	.231	.091	.322	-10	-2	0	.88	-1	/1-6	0	-0.3
Total 2	**25**	**38**	**4**	**7**	**1**	**1**	**0**	**5**	**4**	**4**	**1**	**0**	**.184**	**.279**	**.263**	**.542**	**43**	**-3**	**3**	**2.77**	**-1**	**/0-10,1-7**	**0**	**-0.4**
• CALHOUN, Bill	William Davitte "Mary" Calhoun b: 6/23/1890, Rockmart, GA d: 1/28/1955, Sandersville, GA BL/TL, 6', 180 lbs. Deb: 4/24/1913																							
1913 Bos-N	6	13	0	1	0	0	0	0	0	3	0	....	.077	.077	.077	.154	-55	-3	0	.12	0	/1-3	0	-0.3
• CALHOUN, Jack	John Charles "Red" Calhoun b: 12/14/1879, Pittsburgh, PA d: 2/27/1947, Cincinnati, OH BR/TR, 6', 185 lbs. Deb: 6/27/1902																							
1902 StL-N	20	64	3	10	2	1	0	8	8	....	1	....	.156	.260	.219	.479	50	-3	4	1.96	-1	3-12/1-5,0-1	1	-0.5
• CALLAGHAN, Marty	Martin Francis Callaghan b: 6/9/1900, Norwood, MA d: 6/23/1975, Norfolk, MA BL/TL, 5'10", 157 lbs. Deb: 4/13/1922 Career OF: 95-70-51																							
1922 Chi-N	74	175	31	45	7	4	0	20	17	17	2	3	.257	.326	.343	.669	71	-8	20	3.87	-4	0-53(12-10-31)	3	-1.4
1923 Chi-N	61	129	18	29	1	3	0	14	8	18	2	5	.225	.275	.279	.554	47	-11	9	2.28	-0	0-38(19-0-19)	1	-1.3
1928 Cin-N	81	238	29	69	11	4	0	24	27	10	5	....	.290	.362	.370	.732	93	-2	33	4.51	1	0-69(48-22-1)	7	-0.5
1930 Cin-N	79	225	28	62	9	2	0	16	19	25	1	....	.276	.335	.333	.668	66	-12	25	3.78	0	0-54(16-38-0)	3	-1.3
Total 4	**295**	**767**	**106**	**205**	**28**	**13**	**0**	**74**	**71**	**70**	**10**	**8**	**.267**	**.332**	**.338**	**.669**	**73**	**-33**	**87**	**3.77**	**-4**	**0-214**	**14**	**-4.6**
• CALLAGHAN, Pat	Patrick J. Callaghan b: New York, NY d: 2/4/1940, Louisville, KY Deb: 5/1/1884																							
1884 Ind-a	61	258	38	67	8	5	2	0	8	....	....	....	.260	.282	.353	.635	109	2	26	3.79	-11	3-61	5	-0.7
• CALLAHAN, Dave	David Joseph Callahan b: 7/20/1888, Ottawa, IL d: 10/28/1969, Ottawa, IL BL/TR, 5'10", 165 lbs. Deb: 9/14/1910 Career OF: 12-4-0																							
1910 Cle-A	13	44	6	8	1	0	0	2	4	....	5	....	.182	.265	.205	.470	47	-3	4	2.58	0	0-12(12-0-0)	0	-0.3
1911 Cle-A	6	16	1	4	0	1	0	0	1	....	0	....	.250	.294	.375	.669	85	-0	2	3.67	0	/0-4(0-4-0)	0	0.0
Total 2	**19**	**60**	**7**	**12**	**1**	**1**	**0**	**2**	**5**	**....**	**5**	**....**	**.200**	**.273**	**.250**	**.523**	**56**	**-3**	**5**	**2.84**	**1**	**/0-16**	**0**	**-0.4**
• CALLAHAN, Ed	Edward Joseph Callahan b: 12/11/1857, Boston, MA d: 2/5/1947, New York, NY Deb: 7/19/1884 U																							
1884 StL-U	1	3	0	0	0	0	0	....	0	....	....	....	.000	.000	.000	.000	-96	-1	0	.00	1	/0-1	0	0.0
KC-U	3	11	0	4	0	0	0	....	0	....	....	....	.364	.364	.364	.727	169	1	1	5.96	-0	/S-3	1	0.1
Bos-U	4	13	2	5	0	0	0	....	1	....	....	....	.385	.429	.385	.813	179	1	2	7.69	0	/0-4(1-0-3)	1	0.1
Yr.	8	27	2	9	0	0	0	....	1	....	....	....	.333	.357	.333	.690	146	1	4	5.74	0	/0-5(2-0-3),S-3	2	0.1
• CALLAHAN, Jim	James Timothy "Red" Callahan b: 1/12/1879, Allegheny County, PA d: 3/9/1968, Carnegie, PA BR/TR, 5'9", 145 lbs. Deb: 5/25/1902																							
1902 NY-N	1	4	0	0	0	0	0	0	1	....	0	....	.000	.200	.000	.200	-38	-1	0	.00	0	/0-1	0	-0.1
• CALLAHAN, Leo	Leo David Callahan b: 8/9/1890, Jamaica Plain, MA d: 5/2/1982, Erie, PA BL/TL, 5'8", 142 lbs. Deb: 4/9/1913 Career OF: 14-13-40																							
1913 Bro-N	33	41	6	7	3	1	0	3	4	5	0	....	.171	.244	.293	.537	52	-3	3	2.04	-1	/0-8(2-4-2)	0	-0.5
1919 Phi-N	81	235	26	54	14	4	1	9	29	19	5	....	.230	.317	.336	.653	90	-2	26	3.59	1	0-58(12-9-38)	5	-0.4
Total 2	**114**	**276**	**32**	**61**	**17**	**5**	**1**	**12**	**33**	**24**	**5**	**....**	**.221**	**.306**	**.330**	**.636**	**84**	**-5**	**29**	**3.35**	**0**	**/0-66**	**5**	**-0.9**
• CALLAHAN, Nixey	James Joseph Callahan b: 3/18/1874, Fitchburg, MA d: 10/4/1934, Boston, MA BR/TR, 5'10.5", 180 lbs. Deb: 5/12/1894 M/U Career OF: 401-30-59 ♦																							
1894 Phi-N	9	21	4	5	0	0	0	0	0	7	0	....	.238	.238	.238	.476	16	-1	1	1.98	0	/P-9	0	-1.4
1897 Chi-N	94	360	60	105	18	6	3	47	10	....	12	....	.292	.320	.400	.720	86	-4	52	5.24	-1	2-30,P-23,0-21(12-9-0),S-18/3	19	0.5
1898 Chi-N	43	164	27	43	7	5	0	22	4	....	3	....	.262	.280	.366	.646	85	3	18	3.91	-1	P-31/0-9(1-0-8),1-1,2-1,S	23	3.2
1899 Chi-N	47	150	21	39	4	3	0	18	8	....	9	....	.260	.306	.327	.633	76	3	19	4.29	4	P-35/0-9(0-7-2),S-2,2-1	23	2.3
1900 Chi-N	32	115	16	27	3	2	0	9	6	....	5	....	.235	.273	.296	.568	59	2	11	3.26	5	P-32	14	0.1
1901 Chi-A	45	118	15	39	7	3	1	19	10	....	10	....	.331	.383	.466	.849	138	12	26	8.25	4	P-27/3-6,2-2	23	3.2
1902 Chi-A	70	218	27	51	7	2	0	13	6	....	4	....	.234	.261	.284	.545	53	-2	19	2.81	5	P-35,0-23(6-3-15)/S-1	16	-1.4
1903 Chi-A	118	439	47	128	26	5	2	56	20	....	24	....	.292	.324	.387	.711	118	9	66	5.39	-5	*3-102/0-8(6-0-2),P-3	16	0.2
1904 Chi-A	132	482	66	126	23	2	0	54	39	....	29	....	.261	.318	.317	.635	105	4	63	4.31	-11	*0-104(104-0-0),2-28	17	-1.5
1905 Chi-A	96	345	50	94	18	6	1	43	29	....	26	....	.272	.336	.368	.704	128	11	54	5.46	-2	0-93(71-1-21)	16	0.4
1911 Chi-A	120	466	64	131	13	5	3	60	15	....	45	....	.281	.306	.350	.656	85	-12	63	4.60	-7	*0-114(93-10-11)	11	-2.4
1912 Chi-A	111	408	45	111	9	7	1	52	12	....	19	....	.272	.298	.336	.634	84	-11	47	3.81	-16	*0-107(107-0-0)	7	-3.1
1913 Chi-A	6	9	0	2	0	0	0	1	0	2	0	....	.222	.222	.222	.444	30	-1	0	1.47	-0	/0-1	0	-0.1
Total 13	**923**	**3295**	**442**	**901**	**135**	**46**	**11**	**394**	**159**	**9**	**186**	**....**	**.273**	**.311**	**.352**	**.663**	**95**	**14**	**439**	**4.58**	**-24**	**0-489,P-195,3-110/2-62,S-22,1**	**185**	**0.0**
• CALLAHAN, Wesley	Wesley Leroy Callahan b: 7/3/1888, Lyons, IN d: 9/13/1953, Dayton, OH BR/TR, 5'7.5", 155 lbs. Deb: 9/7/1913																							
1913 StL-N	7	14	0	4	0	0	0	1	2	2	1	....	.286	.375	.286	.661	91	-0	2	4.45	-1	/S-6	1	-0.1
• CALLAWAY, Frank	Frank Burnett Callaway b: 2/26/1898, Knoxville, TN d: 8/21/1987, Knoxville, TN BR/TR, 6', 170 lbs. Deb: 9/17/1921																							
1921 Phi-A	14	50	7	12	1	1	0	4	2	11	1	0	.240	.283	.300	.583	48	-4	5	3.00	-4	S-14	0	-0.6
1922 Phi-A	29	48	5	13	0	2	0	4	0	13	0	0	.271	.271	.354	.625	60	-3	4	3.22	-1	2-11/3-5,S-4	0	-0.4
Total 2	**43**	**98**	**12**	**25**	**1**	**3**	**0**	**8**	**2**	**24**	**1**	**0**	**.255**	**.277**	**.327**	**.604**	**54**	**-7**	**9**	**3.11**	**-5**	**/S-18,2-11,3-5**	**0**	**-0.9**
• CALLISON, Johnny	John Wesley Callison b: 3/12/1939, Qualls, OK BL/TR, 5'10", 175 lbs. Deb: 9/9/1958 Career OF: 189-26-1586																							
1958 Chi-A	18	64	10	19	4	2	1	12	6	14	1	0	.297	.357	.469	.826	128	3	11	6.33	1	0-18(18-0-0)	3	0.3
1959 Chi-A	49	104	12	18	3	0	3	12	13	20	0	1	.173	.271	.288	.560	54	-7	7	2.18	-1	0-41(41-0-0)	1	-1.0
1960 Phi-N	99	288	36	75	11	5	9	30	45	70	0	4	.260	.360	.427	.787	114	5	46	5.70	3	0-86(32-16-47)	10	0.5
1961 Phi-N	138	455	74	121	20	11	9	47	69	76	10	4	.266	.366	.418	.784	109	9	74	5.60	3	*0-124(90-1-35)	13	0.4
1962 Phi-N★	157	603	107	181	26	**10**	23	83	54	96	10	3	.300	.363	.491	.854	131	26	110	6.72	17	*0-152(3-5-151)	27	3.3
1963 Phi-N	157	626	96	178	36	11	26	78	50	111	8	3	.284	.339	.502	.841	140	32	107	6.10	24	*0-157(2-1-156)	32	4.9
1964 Phi-N★	162	654	101	179	30	10	31	104	36	95	6	3	.274	.318	.492	.810	126	20	103	5.64	11	*0-162(2-0-162)	29	2.0
1965 Phi-N★	160	619	93	162	25	**16**	32	101	57	117	6	5	.262	.330	.509	.839	135	26	105	5.98	15	*0-159(0-0-159)	28	3.1
1966 Phi-N	155	612	93	169	**40**	7	11	55	56	83	8	8	.276	.340	.418	.758	109	7	86	4.94	2	*0-154(0-0-154)	20	-0.3
1967 Phi-N	149	556	62	145	30	5	14	64	55	63	6	12	.261	.331	.408	.739	109	3	72	4.48	4	*0-147(0-0-147)	17	-0.4
1968 Phi-N	121	398	46	97	18	4	14	40	42	70	4	3	.244	.321	.415	.735	119	9	54	4.59	1	*0-109(0-0-109)	16	0.3
1969 Phi-N	134	495	66	131	29	5	16	64	49	73	2	1	.265	.335	.440	.775	119	12	74	5.32	7	*0-129(0-0-129)	17	1.3
1970 Chi-N	147	477	65	126	23	2	19	68	60	63	7	2	.264	.350	.440	.790	98	-0	75	5.50	2	*0-144(0-3-143)	14	-0.5
1971 Chi-N	103	290	27	61	12	1	8	38	36	55	2	1	.210	.302	.341	.643	71	-10	31	3.42	-3	0-89(1-0-88)	5	-1.9
1972 NY-A	92	275	28	71	10	0	9	34	18	34	3	0	.258	.304	.393	.696	110	3	33	4.05	-2	0-74(0-0-74)	8	-0.3
1973 NY-A	45	136	10	24	4	0	1	10	4	24	1	1	.176	.200	.228	.428	21	-15	5	1.11	-1	0-32(0-0-32),D-10	1	-1.7
Total 16	**1886**	**6652**	**926**	**1757**	**321**	**89**	**226**	**840**	**650**	**1064**	**74**	**51**	**.264**	**.333**	**.441**	**.774**	**115**	**122**	**992**	**5.21**	**83**	***0-1777/D-10**	**241**	**9.9**
• CALLOWAY, Ron	Ronald Isiah Calloway b: 9/4/1976, San Jose, CA BL/TL, 6'1", 210 lbs. Deb: 3/31/2003																							
2003 Mon-N	126	340	36	81	17	1	9	52	20	80	9	2	.238	.285	.374	.658	59	-20	34	3.23	1	0-97(50-2-47)	5	-2.3

YEAR TM-L	G	AB	R	H	2B	3B	HR	RBI	BB	SO	SB	CS	AVG	OBP	SLG	OPS	OPS+	BR/A	RC	RC/G	FR	G/POS	WS	TPW
• CALVO, Jack	Jacinto (Gonzalez) Calvo b: 6/11/1894, Havana, Cuba d: 6/15/1965, Miami, FL BL/TL, 5'10", 156 lbs. Deb: 5/9/1913 Career OF: 11-1-10																							
1913 Was-A	17	33	5	8	0	0	1	2	1	4	0	....	.242	.265	.333	.598	73	-1	3	2.78	0	0-13(5-0-7)	1	-0.2
1920 Was-A	17	23	5	1	0	1	0	2	2	2	0	0	.043	.120	.130	.250	-35	-4	0	.51	-1	0-10(6-1-3)	0	-0.5
Total 2	34	56	10	9	0	1	1	4	3	6	0	0	.161	.203	.250	.453	29	-6	4	1.76	-1	/0-23	1	-0.7
• CAMELLI, Hank	Henry Richard Camelli b: 12/12/1914, Gloucester, MA d: 7/14/1996, Wellesley, MA BR/TR, 5'11", 190 lbs. Deb: 10/3/1943																							
1943 Pit-N	1	3	1	0	0	0	0	0	1	0	0	....	.000	.250	.000	.250	-24	-0	0	.59	0	/C-1	0	0.0
1944 Pit-N	63	125	14	37	5	1	1	10	18	12	0	....	.296	.385	.376	.761	110	2	18	4.97	-2	C-61	5	0.3
1945 Pit-N	1	2	0	0	0	0	0	0	1	0	0	....	.000	.333	.000	.333	-3	-0	0	1.17	0	/C-1	0	0.0
1946 Pit-N	42	96	8	20	2	2	0	5	8	9	0	....	.208	.269	.271	.540	52	-6	7	2.55	0	C-39	1	-0.4
1947 Bos-N	52	150	10	29	8	1	1	11	18	18	0	....	.193	.280	.280	.560	50	-11	11	2.26	-2	C-51	3	-1.0
Total 5	159	376	33	86	15	4	2	26	46	39	0	....	.229	.313	.306	.619	70	-15	36	3.15	-4	C-153	9	-1.1
• CAMERON, Jack	John Stanley "Happy Jack" Cameron b: 9/22/1884, Cape Breton, Canada d: 7/12/1963, Charlotte, NC TR, 5'10", 170 lbs. Deb: 9/13/1906																							
1906 Bos-N	18	61	3	11	0	0	0	4	2	....	0	....	.180	.206	.180	.387	21	-5	2	1.21	0	0-16(15-0-1)/P-2	0	-0.5
• CAMERON, Mike	Michael Terrance Cameron b: 1/8/1973, La Grange, GA BR/TR, 6'1", 170 lbs. Deb: 8/27/1995 Career OF: 3-997-71																							
1995 Chi-A	28	38	4	7	2	0	1	2	3	15	0	0	.184	.244	.316	.560	46	-3	3	2.59	0	0-28(0-3-26)	0	-0.3
1996 Chi-A	11	11	1	1	0	0	0	0	1	3	0	1	.091	.167	.091	.258	-34	-3	0	.26	-1	/0-8(2-4-5),D-2	0	-0.4
1997 Chi-A	116	379	63	98	18	3	14	55	55	105	23	2	.259	.360	.433	.793	110	11	65	5.86	1	*0-112(0-102-37)/D-4	17	1.1
1998 Chi-A	141	396	53	83	16	5	8	43	37	101	27	11	.210	.287	.336	.623	63	-21	39	3.19	-1	*0-138(0-136-2)	6	-2.0
1999 Cin-N	146	542	93	139	34	9	21	66	80	145	38	12	.256	.358	.469	.827	104	6	99	6.23	-2	*0-146(0-146-0)	19	0.5
2000*Sea-A	155	543	96	145	28	4	19	78	78	133	24	7	.267	.368	.438	.807	109	12	94	5.90	2	*0-155(1-155-1)	19	1.4
2001*Sea-A★	150	540	99	144	30	5	25	110	69	155	34	5	.267	.360	.480	.840	126	26	98	6.21	5	*0-149(0-149-0)/D-1	29	3.1
2002 Sea-A	158	545	84	130	26	5	25	80	79	176	31	8	.239	.342	.442	.785	110	13	89	5.43	0	*0-155(0-155-0)	19	1.3
2003 Sea-A	147	534	74	135	31	5	18	76	70	137	17	7	.253	.345	.431	.776	106	6	81	5.16	11	*0-147(0-147-0)	21	1.8
Total 9	1052	3528	567	882	185	36	131	510	472	970	194	53	.250	.346	.434	.781	105	47	567	5.43	15	*0-1038/D-7	130	6.5
• CAMILLI, Dolph	Adolph Louis Camilli b: 4/23/1907, San Francisco, CA d: 10/21/1997, San Mateo, CA BL/TL, 5'10", 185 lbs. Deb: 9/9/1933																							
1933 Chi-N	16	58	8	13	2	1	2	7	4	11	3	....	.224	.274	.397	.671	90	-1	6	3.37	1	1-16	1	-0.2
1934 Chi-N	32	120	17	33	8	0	4	19	5	25	1	....	.275	.315	.442	.757	102	-0	18	5.43	3	1-32	3	0.0
Phi-N	102	378	52	100	20	3	12	68	48	69	3	....	.265	.350	.429	.779	95	-2	59	5.53	-2	*1-102	7	-1.3
Yr.	134	498	69	133	28	3	16	87	53	94	4	....	.267	.342	.432	.774	97	-2	77	5.51	1	*1-134	10	-1.3
1935 Phi-N	156	602	88	157	23	5	25	83	65	113	9	....	.261	.336	.440	.776	97	-3	93	5.53	-2	*1-156	14	-1.9
1936 Phi-N	151	530	106	167	29	13	28	102	116	84	5	....	.315	.441	.577	1.018	156	48	148	10.75	-6	*1-150	22	2.7
1937 Phi-N	131	475	101	161	23	7	27	80	90	82	6	....	.339	**.446**	.587	1.034	165	47	137	**11.53**	0	*1-131	25	3.5
1938 Bro-N	146	509	106	128	25	11	24	100	**119**	101	6	....	.251	.393	.485	.879	137	31	110	7.64	2	*1-145	25	1.9
1939 Bro-N★	157	565	105	164	30	12	26	104	**110**	107	1	....	.290	.409	.524	.933	144	39	128	8.25	15	*1-157	28	3.9
1940 Bro-N	142	512	92	147	29	13	23	96	89	83	9	....	.287	.397	.529	.926	144	33	114	8.29	2	*1-140	25	2.3
1941*Bro-N★	149	529	92	151	29	6	**34**	**120**	104	115	3	....	.285	.407	.556	.962	162	**46**	128	8.96	7	*1-148	29	4.1
1942 Bro-N	150	524	89	132	23	7	26	109	97	85	10	....	.252	.372	.471	.843	144	31	97	6.51	3	*1-150	28	2.2
1943 Bro-N	95	353	56	87	15	6	6	43	65	48	2	....	.246	.365	.374	.739	113	9	52	5.13	3	1-95	13	0.7
1945 Bos-A	63	198	24	42	5	2	2	19	35	38	2	0	.212	.330	.288	.618	78	-3	21	3.54	1	1-54	4	-0.6
Total 12	1490	5353	936	1482	261	86	239	950	947	961	60	0	.277	.388	.492	.880	134	274	1111	7.55	26	*1-1476	224	17.2
• CAMILLI, Doug	Douglas Joseph Camilli b: 9/22/1936, Philadelphia, PA BR/TR, 5'11", 195 lbs. Deb: 9/25/1960 C																							
1960 LA-N	6	24	4	8	2	0	1	3	1	4	0	0	.333	.385	.542	.926	141	1	5	8.78	0	/C-6	1	0.1
1961 LA-N	13	30	3	4	0	0	3	4	1	9	0	0	.133	.161	.433	.595	47	-3	2	1.71	0	C-12	1	-0.2
1962 LA-N	45	88	16	25	5	2	4	22	12	21	0	0	.284	.370	.523	.893	145	6	16	6.32	-1	C-39	5	0.6
1963 LA-N	49	117	9	19	1	1	3	10	11	22	0	0	.162	.234	.265	.499	47	-8	7	1.73	-4	C-47	2	-1.0
1964 LA-N	50	123	1	22	3	0	0	10	8	19	0	0	.179	.229	.203	.432	25	-12	6	1.38	0	C-46	2	-1.1
1965 Was-A	75	193	13	37	6	1	3	18	16	34	0	0	.192	.257	.280	.537	53	-12	14	2.39	-1	C-59	2	-1.1
1966 Was-A	44	107	5	22	4	0	2	8	3	19	0	0	.206	.234	.299	.533	53	-7	7	1.97	1	C-39	1	-0.5
1967 Was-A	30	82	5	15	1	0	2	5	4	16	0	0	.183	.221	.268	.489	46	-6	5	1.91	-1	C-24	1	-0.6
1969 Was-A	1	3	0	1	0	0	0	0	0	2	0	0	.333	.333	.333	.667	92	-0	0	4.50	0	/C-1	0	0.0
Total 9	313	767	56	153	22	4	18	80	56	146	0	0	.199	.257	.309	.566	61	-40	61	2.56	-5	C-273	15	-3.7
• CAMILLI, Lou	Louis Steven Camilli b: 9/24/1946, El Paso, TX BB/TR, 5'10", 170 lbs. Deb: 8/9/1969																							
1969 Cle-A	13	14	0	0	0	0	0	0	0	3	0	0	.000	.000	.000	.000	-97	-4	0	.00	-1	3-13	0	-0.5
1970 Cle-A	16	15	0	0	0	0	0	0	2	2	0	0	.000	.118	.000	.118	-62	-3	0	.05	-1	/S-3,2-2,3-1	0	-0.4
1971 Cle-A	39	81	5	16	2	0	0	0	8	10	0	0	.198	.270	.222	.492	37	-6	5	1.86	-2	S-23,2-16	1	-0.6
1972 Cle-A	39	41	2	6	2	0	0	3	3	8	0	0	.146	.205	.195	.400	19	-4	2	1.40	0	/S-8,2-2	0	-0.5
Total 4	107	151	7	22	4	0	0	3	13	23	0	0	.146	.213	.172	.386	10	-18	7	1.30	-4	/S-34,2-20,3-14	1	-2.0
• CAMINITI, Ken	Kenneth Gene Caminiti b: 4/21/1963, Hanford, CA BB/TR, 6', 200 lbs. Deb: 7/16/1987																							
1987 Hou-N	63	203	10	50	7	1	3	23	12	44	0	0	.246	.288	.335	.623	67	-10	19	3.10	3	3-61	3	-0.8
1988 Hou-N	30	83	5	15	2	0	1	7	5	18	0	0	.181	.227	.241	.468	36	-7	4	1.56	0	3-28	1	-0.7
1989 Hou-N	161	585	71	149	31	3	10	72	51	93	4	1	.255	.318	.369	.687	99	-1	70	4.19	19	*3-160	25	2.1
1990 Hou-N	153	541	52	131	20	2	4	51	48	97	9	4	.242	.304	.309	.613	71	-22	50	3.09	-1	*3-149	11	-2.2
1991 Hou-N	152	574	65	145	30	3	13	80	46	85	4	5	.253	.314	.383	.697	101	-2	65	3.82	14	*3-152	17	1.3
1992 Hou-N	135	506	68	149	31	2	13	62	44	68	10	4	.294	.352	.441	.793	129	19	76	5.37	-2	*3-129	21	1.8
1993 Hou-N	143	543	75	142	31	0	13	75	49	88	8	5	.262	.323	.390	.713	93	-7	66	4.16	8	*3-143	14	0.4
1994 Hou-N★	111	406	63	115	28	2	18	75	43	71	4	3	.283	.355	.495	.850	125	14	70	6.19	0	*3-108	16	1.5
1995 SD-N	143	526	74	159	33	0	26	94	69	94	12	5	.302	.384	.513	.898	140	31	105	7.26	8	*3-143	24	4.0
1996*SD-N★	146	546	109	178	37	2	40	130	78	99	11	5	.326	.414	.621	1.035	179	62	138	9.37	12	*3-145	38	7.5
1997 SD-N★	137	486	92	141	28	0	26	90	80	118	11	2	.290	.394	.508	.902	147	36	100	7.41	13	*3-133	26	5.0
1998*SD-N	131	452	87	114	29	0	29	82	71	108	6	2	.252	.359	.509	.867	134	23	87	6.60	-10	*3-126	20	1.5
1999*Hou-N	78	273	45	78	11	1	13	56	46	58	6	2	.286	.394	.476	.871	121	10	53	6.83	1	3-75	10	1.2
2000 Hou-N	59	208	42	63	13	0	15	45	42	37	3	0	.303	.422	.582	1.004	142	16	52	9.10	-8	3-58	9	0.7
2001 Tex-A	54	185	24	43	8	1	9	25	22	41	0	0	.232	.321	.432	.753	93	-2	25	4.62	1	3-53	4	-0.1
*Atl-N	64	171	12	38	9	0	6	16	21	44	0	1	.222	.307	.380	.687	75	-7	21	4.04	-3	1-33,3-13/D-1	3	-1.2
Total 15	1760	6288	894	1710	348	17	239	983	727	1163	88	39	.272	.350	.447	.797	117	153	1000	5.57	55	*3-1676/1-33,D-1	242	22.1
• CAMP, Howie	Howard Lee "Red" Camp b: 7/1/1893, Mumford, AL d: 5/8/1960, Eastaboga, AL BL/TR, 5'9", 169 lbs. Deb: 9/19/1917																							
1917 NY-A	5	21	3	6	1	0	0	0	1	2	0	....	.286	.318	.333	.652	98	-0	2	3.63	0	/0-5(0-4-1)	0	0.0
• CAMP, Lew	Robert Plantagenet Llewellan Camp b: 2/23/1868, Columbus, OH d: 10/1/1948, Omaha, NE BL/TR, 6', 175 lbs. Deb: 8/26/1892 Career OF: 0-13-1																							
1892 StL-N	42	145	19	30	3	1	2	13	17	27	12	....	.207	.294	.283	.577	79	-3	16	3.76	-14	3-39/0-3(0-2-1)	3	-1.6
1893 Chi-N	38	156	37	41	7	7	2	17	19	19	30	....	.263	.347	.436	.782	109	1	35	8.02	-4	3-16,0-11(0-11-0)/2-9,S-3	5	-0.2
1894 Chi-N	8	33	1	6	2	0	0	1	1	6	0	....	.182	.206	.242	.448	7	-5	2	1.63	-4	/2-8	0	-0.7
Total 3	88	334	57	77	12	8	4	31	37	52	42	....	.231	.311	.350	.661	86	-7	53	5.44	-22	/3-55,2-17,0-14,S-3	8	-2.4
• CAMPANELLA, Roy	Roy Campanella b: 11/19/1921, Philadelphia, PA d: 6/26/1993, Woodland Hills, CA BR/TR, 5'9.5", 200 lbs. Deb: 4/20/1948 HOF: 1969																							
1948 Bro-N	83	279	32	72	11	3	9	45	36	45	3	....	.258	.345	.416	.761	101	1	42	5.32	5	C-78	12	1.0
1949*Bro-N★	130	436	65	125	22	2	22	82	67	36	3	....	.287	.385	.498	.883	130	20	86	7.15	-3	*C-127	24	2.3
1950 Bro-N★	126	437	70	123	19	3	31	89	55	51	1	....	.281	.364	.551	.916	134	21	84	6.89	-4	*C-123	22	2.3
1951 Bro-N★	143	505	90	164	33	1	33	108	53	51	1	2	.325	.393	.590	.983	158	39	114	8.51	1	*C-140	33	4.8
1952*Bro-N★	128	468	73	126	18	1	22	97	57	59	8	4	.269	.352	.453	.805	120	13	72	5.21	-2	*C-122	22	1.8
1953*Bro-N★	144	519	103	162	26	3	41	**142**	67	58	4	2	.312	.395	.611	1.006	154	41	128	9.26	0	*C-140	33	4.6
1954 Bro-N★	111	397	43	82	14	3	19	51	42	49	1	4	.207	.286	.401	.686	74	-18	42	3.40	1	*C-111	10	-1.2

YEAR TM-L	G	AB	R	H	2B	3B	HR	RBI	BB	SO	SB	CS	AVG	OBP	SLG	OPS	OPS+	BR/A	RC	RC/G	FR	G/POS	WS	TPW
1955*Bro-N★	123	446	81	142	20	1	32	107	56	41	2	3	.318	.402	.583	.985	153	34	101	8.15	-3	*C-121	28	3.7
1956*Bro-N★	124	388	39	85	6	1	20	73	66	61	1	0	.219	.334	.394	.728	88	-5	49	4.00	-5	*C-121	12	-0.4
1957 Bro-N	103	330	31	80	9	0	13	62	34	50	1	0	.242	.321	.388	.709	81	-8	40	3.98	2	*C-100	11	-0.1
Total 10	1215	4205	627	1161	178	18	242	856	533	501	25	15	.276	.362	.500	.861	123	138	759	6.30	-9	*C-1183	207	18.9

• CAMPANERIS, Bert Dagoberto (Blanco) "Campy" Campaneris b: 3/9/1942, Pueblo Nuevo, Cuba BR/TR, 5'10", 160 lbs. Deb: 7/23/1964 Career OF: 68-2-1

YEAR TM-L	G	AB	R	H	2B	3B	HR	RBI	BB	SO	SB	CS	AVG	OBP	SLG	OPS	OPS+	BR/A	RC	RC/G	FR	G/POS	WS	TPW
1964 KC-A	67	269	27	69	14	3	4	22	15	41	10	2	.257	.306	.375	.681	86	-4	32	4.19	-2	S-38,0-27(27-0-0)/3-6	6	-0.5
1965 KC-A	144	578	67	156	23	**12**	6	42	41	71	**51**	19	.270	.328	.382	.710	103	4	76	4.52	-10	*S-109,0-39(38-2-1)/1-1,2,3,C,P	18	0.1
1966 KC-A	142	573	82	153	29	10	5	42	25	72	**52**	10	.267	.303	.379	.682	98	4	70	4.29	-6	*S-138	22	1.0
1967 KC-A	147	601	85	149	29	6	3	32	36	82	**55**	16	.248	.298	.331	.629	88	-4	64	3.64	-4	*S-145	16	0.5
1968 Oak-A★	159	642	87	**177**	25	9	4	38	50	69	**62**	22	.276	.332	.361	.693	116	16	82	4.39	10	*S-155/0-3(3-0-0)	29	4.4
1969 Oak-A	135	547	71	142	15	2	2	25	30	62	62	8	.260	.303	.305	.608	74	-9	59	3.70	2	*S-125	16	0.8
1970 Oak-A	147	603	97	168	28	4	22	64	36	73	**42**	10	.279	.323	.448	.771	115	14	91	5.36	11	*S-143	26	4.4
1971*Oak-A	134	569	80	143	18	4	5	47	29	64	34	7	.251	.290	.323	.613	75	-15	56	3.38	14	*S-133	15	1.6
1972*Oak-A★	149	625	85	150	25	2	8	32	32	88	**52**	14	.240	.279	.325	.604	84	-9	59	3.07	20	*S-148	21	3.4
1973*Oak-A★	151	601	89	150	17	6	4	46	50	79	34	10	.250	.311	.318	.629	82	-11	63	3.51	26	*S-149	20	3.4
1974*Oak-A★	134	527	77	153	18	8	2	41	47	81	34	15	.290	.348	.366	.715	113	10	70	4.62	9	*S-133/D-1	22	3.7
1975*Oak-A★	137	509	69	135	15	3	4	46	50	71	24	12	.265	.339	.330	.669	92	-4	60	3.88	1	*S-137	17	1.3
1976 Oak-A	149	536	67	137	14	1	1	52	63	80	54	12	.256	.337	.291	.628	89	2	64	3.90	3	*S-149	19	2.4
1977 Tex-A★	150	552	77	140	19	7	5	46	47	86	27	20	.254	.317	.341	.657	78	-18	60	3.37	23	*S-149	15	2.0
1978 Tex-A	98	269	30	50	5	3	1	17	20	36	22	4	.186	.247	.238	.485	37	-19	19	1.95	-5	S-89/D-4	3	-1.6
1979 Tex-A	8	9	2	1	0	0	0	0	1	3	1	0	.111	.200	.111	.311	-14	-1	0	1.20	-1	/S-8	0	-0.2
*Cal-A	85	239	27	56	4	4	0	15	19	32	12	4	.234	.296	.285	.581	59	-12	21	2.67	14	S-82/D-1	5	0.9
Yr.	93	248	29	57	4	4	0	15	20	35	13	4	.230	.293	.278	.571	57	-13	21	2.62	12	S-90/D-1	5	0.7
1980 Cal-A	77	210	32	53	8	1	2	18	14	33	10	5	.252	.302	.329	.631	75	-7	21	3.22	-3	S-64/D-2,2-1	4	-0.4
1981 Cal-A	55	82	11	21	2	1	1	10	5	10	5	2	.256	.299	.341	.640	84	-2	9	3.61	-2	3-45/S-3,2-2	2	-0.4
1983 NY-A	60	143	19	46	5	0	0	11	8	9	6	7	.322	.358	.357	.714	101	-2	16	3.90	1	2-32,3-24	4	0.1
Total 19	2328	8684	1181	2249	313	86	79	646	618	1142	649	199	.259	.313	.342	.655	89	-67	992	3.83	101	*S-2097/3-76,0-69,2,D,1,C,P	280	26.9

• CAMPANIS, Al Alexander Sebastian Campanis b: 11/2/1916, Kos, Greece d: 6/21/1998, Fullerton, CA BB/TR, 6', 185 lbs. Deb: 9/23/1943

YEAR TM-L	G	AB	R	H	2B	3B	HR	RBI	BB	SO	SB	CS	AVG	OBP	SLG	OPS	OPS+	BR/A	RC	RC/G	FR	G/POS	WS	TPW
1943 Bro-N	7	20	3	2	0	0	0	0	4	5	0	....	.100	.250	.100	.350	3	-2	1	1.14	2	/2-7	0	0.0

• CAMPANIS, Jim James Alexander Campanis b: 2/9/1944, New York, NY BR/TR, 6', 195 lbs. Deb: 9/20/1966

YEAR TM-L	G	AB	R	H	2B	3B	HR	RBI	BB	SO	SB	CS	AVG	OBP	SLG	OPS	OPS+	BR/A	RC	RC/G	FR	G/POS	WS	TPW
1966 LA-N	1	1	0	0	0	0	0	0	0	0	0	0	.000	.000	.000	.000	-109	-0	0	.00	0	/C-1	0	0.0
1967 LA-N	41	62	3	10	1	0	2	2	9	14	0	0	.161	.268	.274	.542	60	-3	5	2.28	0	C-23	1	-0.3
1968 LA-N	4	11	0	1	0	0	0	0	1	2	0	0	.091	.167	.091	.258	-23	-2	0	.26	1	/C-4	0	-0.1
1969 KC-A	30	83	4	13	5	0	0	5	5	19	0	0	.157	.205	.217	.421	18	-9	3	1.11	-2	C-26	1	-1.0
1970 KC-A	31	54	6	7	0	0	2	2	4	14	0	0	.130	.203	.241	.444	22	-6	3	1.47	0	C-13/0-1	0	-0.5
1973 Pit-N	6	6	0	1	0	0	0	0	0	0	0	0	.167	.167	.167	.333	-8	-1	0	.90	0	....	0	-0.1
Total 6	113	217	13	32	6	0	4	9	19	49	0	0	.147	.219	.230	.450	28	-21	11	1.47	-1	/C-67,0-1	2	-2.0

• CAMPAU, Count Charles Columbus Campau b: 10/17/1863, Detroit, MI d: 4/3/1938, New Orleans, LA BL/TR, 5'11", 160 lbs. Deb: 7/7/1888 M Career OF: 41-2-103

YEAR TM-L	G	AB	R	H	2B	3B	HR	RBI	BB	SO	SB	CS	AVG	OBP	SLG	OPS	OPS+	BR/A	RC	RC/G	FR	G/POS	WS	TPW
1888 Det-N	70	251	28	51	5	3	1	18	19	36	27	....	.203	.259	.259	.518	66	-9	24	3.30	-5	0-70(0-0-70)	4	-1.5
1890 StL-a	75	314	68	101	9	12	**9**	75	26	....	36	....	.322	.374	.513	.886	141	12	75	9.38	3	0-74(39-2-33)/1-1,3-1	12	1.2
1894 Was-N	2	7	1	1	0	0	0	0	1	4	0	....	.143	.250	.143	.393	-3	-1	0	1.11	0	/0-2(2-0-0)	0	-0.1
Total 3	147	572	97	153	14	15	10	93	46	40	63	....	.267	.322	.397	.719	106	2	100	6.36	-2	0-146/1-1,3-1	16	-0.4

• CAMPBELL, Bruce Bruce Douglas Campbell b: 10/20/1909, Chicago, IL d: 6/17/1995, Fort Myers Beach, FL BL/TR, 6'1", 185 lbs. Deb: 9/12/1930 Career OF: 31-0-1164

YEAR TM-L	G	AB	R	H	2B	3B	HR	RBI	BB	SO	SB	CS	AVG	OBP	SLG	OPS	OPS+	BR/A	RC	RC/G	FR	G/POS	WS	TPW
1930 Chi-A	5	10	4	5	1	1	0	5	1	2	0	0	.500	.545	.800	1.345	245	2	4	22.92	0	/0-4(4-0-0)	1	0.2
1931 Chi-A	4	17	4	7	2	0	2	5	0	4	0	0	.412	.444	.882	1.327	256	4	7	17.25	0	/0-4(4-0-0)	1	0.3
1932 Chi-A	7	18	3	4	1	0	0	2	0	2	0	1	.222	.222	.278	.500	31	-2	1	1.41	0	/0-4(3-0-1)	0	-0.2
StL-A	139	593	83	169	35	11	14	85	40	102	7	5	.285	.336	.452	.788	97	-5	90	5.49	3	*0-139(0-0-139)	13	-1.0
Yr.	146	611	86	173	36	11	14	87	40	104	7	6	.283	.333	.447	.780	95	-7	90	5.36	3	*0-143(3-0-140)	13	-1.2
1933 StL-A	148	567	87	157	38	8	16	106	69	77	10	4	.277	.357	.457	.814	108	7	95	6.07	-5	*0-144(0-0-144)	13	-0.7
1934 StL-A	138	481	62	134	25	6	9	74	51	64	5	4	.279	.350	.412	.762	88	-9	71	5.32	-2	*0-123(0-0-123)	10	-1.8
1935 Cle-A	80	308	56	100	26	3	7	54	31	33	2	1	.325	.390	.497	.887	126	12	60	7.59	-4	0-75(0-0-75)	12	0.3
1936 Cle-A	76	172	35	64	15	2	6	30	19	17	2	1	.372	.440	.587	1.028	150	14	45	10.82	1	0-47(0-0-47)	7	1.1
1937 Cle-A	134	448	82	135	42	11	4	61	67	49	4	5	.301	.392	.471	.863	116	11	85	6.97	3	*0-123(0-0-123)	16	0.6
1938 Cle-A	133	511	90	148	27	12	12	72	53	57	11	7	.290	.360	.460	.820	106	3	85	5.98	1	*0-122(0-0-122)	15	-0.3
1939 Cle-A	130	450	84	129	23	13	8	72	67	48	7	6	.287	.383	.449	.832	116	11	81	6.41	-5	*0-115(0-0-115)	16	-0.1
1940*Det-A	103	297	56	84	15	5	8	44	45	28	2	7	.283	.381	.448	.829	104	0	51	5.88	0	0-74(0-0-74)	8	-0.3
1941 Det-A	141	512	72	141	28	10	15	93	68	67	3	3	.275	.364	.457	.821	105	4	90	6.37	-6	*0-133(0-0-133)	15	-1.0
1942 Was-A	122	378	41	105	17	5	5	63	37	34	0	6	.278	.344	.389	.733	107	1	51	4.90	-4	0-87(20-0-68)	11	-0.9
Total 13	1360	4762	759	1382	295	87	106	766	548	584	53	50	.290	.367	.455	.822	109	51	815	6.23	-19	*0-1194	138	-3.9

• CAMPBELL, Dave David Wilson Campbell b: 1/14/1942, Manistee, MI BR/TR, 6'1", 185 lbs. Deb: 9/17/1967 Career OF: 4-0-0

YEAR TM-L	G	AB	R	H	2B	3B	HR	RBI	BB	SO	SB	CS	AVG	OBP	SLG	OPS	OPS+	BR/A	RC	RC/G	FR	G/POS	WS	TPW
1967 Det-A	2	2	0	0	0	0	0	0	0	1	0	0	.000	.000	.000	.000	-97	-0	0	.00	0	/1-1	0	-0.1
1968 Det-A	9	8	1	1	0	0	1	2	1	3	0	0	.125	.222	.500	.722	110	0	1	3.65	0	/2-5	0	0.0
1969 Det-A	32	39	4	4	1	0	0	2	4	15	0	1	.103	.205	.128	.333	-5	-6	1	.86	-2	1-13/2-5,3-1	0	-0.8
1970 SD-N	154	581	71	127	28	2	12	40	40	115	18	6	.219	.270	.336	.606	64	-30	54	3.04	14	*2-153	10	-0.7
1971 SD-N	108	365	38	83	14	2	7	29	37	75	9	6	.227	.299	.334	.633	85	-8	38	3.32	-3	2-69,3-40/S-4,1-2,0-2(2-0-0)	7	-0.7
1972 SD-N	33	100	6	24	5	0	0	3	11	12	0	4	.240	.315	.290	.605	78	-4	8	2.67	1	3-31/2-1	2	-0.4
1973 SD-N	33	98	2	22	3	0	0	8	7	15	1	1	.224	.276	.255	.531	52	-7	6	2.05	-2	2-27/1-3,3-2	1	-0.7
StL-N	13	21	1	0	0	0	0	1	1	6	0	0	.000	.045	.000	.045	-87	-5	0	.06	0	/2-6	0	-0.5
Hou-N	9	15	1	4	2	0	0	2	0	4	0	0	.267	.267	.400	.667	83	-0	2	3.93	1	/3-5,1-2,0-1	1	0.0
Yr.	55	134	4	26	5	0	0	11	8	25	1	1	.194	.239	.231	.471	33	-12	8	1.83	-1	2-33/3-7,1-5,0-1	2	-1.2
1974 Hou-N	35	23	4	2	1	0	0	2	1	8	1	0	.087	.125	.130	.255	-30	-4	1	.63	0	/2-9,1-6,3-2,0-1	0	-0.4
Total 8	428	1252	128	267	54	4	20	89	102	254	29	18	.213	.274	.311	.584	64	-66	110	2.83	8	2-275/3-81,1-27,0-4,S-4	21	-4.4

• CAMPBELL, Gilly William Gilthorpe Campbell b: 2/13/1908, Kansas City, KS d: 2/21/1973, Los Angeles, CA BL/TR, 5'7.5", 182 lbs. Deb: 4/25/1933

YEAR TM-L	G	AB	R	H	2B	3B	HR	RBI	BB	SO	SB	CS	AVG	OBP	SLG	OPS	OPS+	BR/A	RC	RC/G	FR	G/POS	WS	TPW
1933 Chi-N	46	89	11	25	3	1	1	10	7	4	0	....	.281	.347	.371	.718	105	1	12	5.00	-1	C-20	3	0.1
1935 Cin-N	88	218	26	56	7	0	3	30	42	7	3	....	.257	.379	.330	.710	95	1	30	4.87	-1	C-66/1-5,0-1	8	0.4
1936 Cin-N	89	235	28	63	13	1	1	40	43	14	2	....	.268	.384	.345	.728	104	4	35	5.27	2	C-71/1-1	9	1.0
1937 Cin-N	18	40	3	11	2	0	0	2	5	1	0	....	.275	.356	.325	.681	90	-0	5	4.84	-1	C-17	1	-0.1
1938 Bro-N	54	126	10	31	5	0	0	11	19	9	0	....	.246	.354	.286	.639	76	-3	13	3.54	-1	C-44	3	-0.1
Total 5	295	708	78	186	30	2	5	93	116	35	5	....	.263	.371	.332	.703	96	3	95	4.77	-1	C-218/1-6,0-1	24	1.3

• CAMPBELL, Hutch Marc Thaddeus Campbell b: 11/29/1884, Punxsutawney, PA d: 2/13/1946, New Bethlehem, PA BL/TR, 5'10", 155 lbs. Deb: 9/30/1907

YEAR TM-L	G	AB	R	H	2B	3B	HR	RBI	BB	SO	SB	CS	AVG	OBP	SLG	OPS	OPS+	BR/A	RC	RC/G	FR	G/POS	WS	TPW
1907 Pit-N	2	4	0	1	0	0	0	1	1	....	0	....	.250	.400	.250	.650	102	0	0	3.55	0	/S-2	0	0.0

• CAMPBELL, Jim James Robert Campbell b: 6/24/1937, Palo Alto, CA BR/TR, 6', 190 lbs. Deb: 7/17/1962

YEAR TM-L	G	AB	R	H	2B	3B	HR	RBI	BB	SO	SB	CS	AVG	OBP	SLG	OPS	OPS+	BR/A	RC	RC/G	FR	G/POS	WS	TPW
1962 Hou-N	27	86	6	19	4	0	3	6	6	23	0	0	.221	.272	.372	.644	77	-3	8	3.10	1	C-25	2	-0.1
1963 Hou-N	55	158	9	35	3	0	4	19	10	40	0	0	.222	.268	.316	.584	72	-6	12	2.40	2	C-42	2	-0.2
Total 2	82	244	15	54	7	0	7	25	16	63	0	0	.221	.269	.336	.605	74	-9	20	2.64	2	/C-67	4	-0.3

• CAMPBELL, Jim James Robert Campbell b: 1/10/1943, Hartsville, SC BL/TR, 6', 205 lbs. Deb: 4/11/1970

YEAR TM-L	G	AB	R	H	2B	3B	HR	RBI	BB	SO	SB	CS	AVG	OBP	SLG	OPS	OPS+	BR/A	RC	RC/G	FR	G/POS	WS	TPW
1970 StL-N	13	13	0	3	0	0	0	1	0	3	0	0	.231	.231	.231	.462	24	-1	1	1.87	0	....	0	-0.1

• CAMPBELL, Joe Joseph Earl Campbell b: 3/10/1944, Louisville, KY BR/TR, 6'1", 175 lbs. Deb: 5/3/1967

YEAR TM-L	G	AB	R	H	2B	3B	HR	RBI	BB	SO	SB	CS	AVG	OBP	SLG	OPS	OPS+	BR/A	RC	RC/G	FR	G/POS	WS	TPW
1967 Chi-N	1	3	0	0	0	0	0	0	0	3	0	0	.000	.000	.000	.000	-96	-1	0	.00	0	/0-1	0	-0.1

YEAR TM-L	G	AB	R	H	2B	3B	HR	RBI	BB	SO	SB	CS	AVG	OBP	SLG	OPS	OPS+	BR/A	RC	RC/G	FR	G/POS	WS	TPW
• CAMPBELL, Mike	Mathew Campbell b: 8/1/1850, Ireland d: 1/12/1926, Scotch Plains, NJ Deb: 4/28/1873																							
1873 Res-n	21	83	9	12	0	0	0	3	3	6	1	0	.145	.174	.145	.319	-5	-9	2	1.00	2	1-18/S-3,O-1	....	-0.5
• CAMPBELL, Paul	Paul McLaughlin Campbell b: 9/1/1917, Paw Creek, NC BL/TL, 5'10", 185 lbs. Deb: 4/15/1941																							
1941 Bos-A	1	0	0	0	0	0	0	0	0	0	0	0	....	....	....	....	-98	0	0	....	0	....	0	0.0
1942 Bos-A	26	15	4	1	0	0	0	0	1	5	1	0	.067	.125	.067	.192	-44	-3	0	.44	-1	/O-4(0-4-0)	0	-0.3
1946*Bos-A	28	26	3	3	1	0	0	0	2	7	0	0	.115	.179	.154	.332	-6	-4	1	.97	-1	/1-5	0	-0.5
1948 Det-A	59	83	15	22	1	1	1	11	1	10	0	0	.265	.274	.337	.611	60	-5	8	3.47	1	1-27	1	-0.4
1949 Det-A	87	255	38	71	15	4	3	30	24	32	3	3	.278	.343	.404	.747	97	-3	38	5.21	-1	1-74	7	-0.5
1950 Det-A	3	1	1	0	0	0	0	0	0	0	0	0	.000	.000	.000	.000	-97	-0	0	.00	0	....	0	0.0
Total 6	**204**	**380**	**61**	**97**	**17**	**5**	**4**	**41**	**28**	**54**	**4**	**3**	**.255**	**.308**	**.358**	**.666**	**77**	**-14**	**47**	**4.25**	**-1**	**1-106/O-4**	**8**	**-1.8**
• CAMPBELL, Ron	Ronald Thomas Campbell b: 4/5/1940, Chattanooga, TN BR/TR, 6'1", 180 lbs. Deb: 9/1/1964																							
1964 Chi-N	26	92	7	25	6	1	1	10	1	21	0	1	.272	.280	.391	.671	83	-3	10	3.79	1	2-26	2	0.1
1965 Chi-N	2	2	0	0	0	0	0	0	0	0	0	0	.000	.000	.000	.000	-98	-0	0	.00	0	....	0	-0.1
1966 Chi-N	24	60	4	13	1	0	0	4	6	5	1	1	.217	.288	.233	.521	46	-4	4	1.87	2	S-11/3-7	0	-0.2
Total 3	**52**	**154**	**11**	**38**	**7**	**1**	**1**	**14**	**7**	**26**	**1**	**2**	**.247**	**.280**	**.325**	**.604**	**66**	**-8**	**13**	**2.92**	**3**	**/2-26,S-11,3-7**	**2**	**-0.2**
• CAMPBELL, Sam	Samuel Campbell b: Philadelphia, PA Deb: 10/11/1890																							
1890 Phi-a	2	5	0	0	0	0	0	0	1	....	0	....	.000	.167	.000	.167	-52	-1	0	.00	-1	/2-2	0	-0.2
• CAMPBELL, Soup	Clarence Campbell b: 3/7/1915, Sparta, VA d: 2/16/2000, Sparta, VA BL/TR, 6'1", 188 lbs. Deb: 4/21/1940 Career OF: 28-64-4																							
1940 Cle-A	35	62	8	14	1	0	0	2	7	12	0	0	.226	.304	.242	.546	45	-5	5	2.75	0	O-16(8-5-4)	1	-0.5
1941 Cle-A	104	328	36	82	10	4	3	35	31	21	1	9	.250	.317	.332	.649	75	-15	32	3.27	0	O-78(20-59-0)	4	-1.7
Total 2	**139**	**390**	**44**	**96**	**11**	**4**	**3**	**37**	**38**	**33**	**1**	**9**	**.246**	**.315**	**.318**	**.633**	**71**	**-20**	**37**	**3.19**	**0**	**/O-94**	**5**	**-2.3**
• CAMPBELL, Vin	Arthur Vincent Campbell b: 1/30/1888, St. Louis, MO d: 11/16/1969, Towson, MD BL/TR, 6', 185 lbs. Deb: 6/6/1908 Career OF: 48-268-181																							
1908 Chi-N	1	1	0	0	0	0	0	0	0	....	0	....	.000	.000	.000	.000	-96	-0	0	.00	0	....	0	0.0
1910 Pit-N	97	282	42	92	9	5	4	21	26	23	17	....	.326	.391	.436	.827	133	12	55	7.05	-4	O-74(38-17-18)	12	0.4
1911 Pit-N	42	93	12	29	3	1	0	10	8	7	6	....	.312	.366	.366	.732	101	0	14	5.71	-2	O-21(9-1-11)	3	-0.2
1912 Bos-N	145	624	102	185	32	9	3	48	32	44	19	....	.296	.334	.391	.725	96	-6	87	4.82	-8	*O-144(0-144-0)	11	-2.3
1914 Ind-F	134	544	92	173	23	11	7	44	37	47	26	....	.318	.368	.439	.807	116	11	93	6.20	-4	*O-132(1-94-37)	20	0.0
1915 New-F	127	525	78	163	18	10	1	44	29	35	24	....	.310	.352	.389	.741	125	15	76	5.35	-6	*O-126(0-12-115)	19	0.2
Total 6	**546**	**2069**	**326**	**642**	**85**	**36**	**15**	**167**	**132**	**156**	**92**	**....**	**.310**	**.357**	**.408**	**.765**	**114**	**32**	**325**	**5.65**	**-24**	**O-497**	**65**	**-1.9**
• CAMPOS, Frank	Francisco Jose (Lopez) Campos b: 5/11/1924, Havana, Cuba BL/TL, 5'11", 180 lbs. Deb: 9/11/1951 Career OF: 13-1-17																							
1951 Was-A	8	26	4	11	3	1	0	3	0	1	0	0	.423	.423	.615	1.038	182	3	7	12.49	0	/O-7(0-0-7)	1	0.2
1952 Was-A	53	112	9	29	6	1	0	8	1	13	0	0	.259	.278	.330	.609	71	-5	11	3.31	-2	O-23(13-1-10)	2	-0.8
1953 Was-A	10	9	0	1	0	0	0	2	1	0	0	0	.111	.200	.111	.311	-15	-1	0	.39	0	....	0	-0.1
Total 3	**71**	**147**	**13**	**41**	**9**	**2**	**0**	**13**	**2**	**14**	**0**	**0**	**.279**	**.298**	**.367**	**.665**	**84**	**-3**	**18**	**4.32**	**-2**	**/O-30**	**3**	**-0.7**
• CAMPUSANO, Sil	Silvestre (Diaz) Campusano b: 12/31/1965, Santo Domingo, Dominican Republic BR/TR, 6', 175 lbs. Deb: 4/4/1988 Career OF: 32-75-26																							
1988 Tor-A	73	142	14	31	10	2	2	12	9	33	0	0	.218	.284	.359	.643	79	-4	16	3.69	-3	O-69(15-35-19)/D-2	3	-0.9
1990 Phi-N	66	85	10	18	1	1	2	9	6	16	1	0	.212	.272	.318	.589	62	-4	8	3.02	0	O-47(16-25-7)	0	-0.5
1991 Phi-N	15	35	2	4	0	0	1	2	1	10	0	0	.114	.139	.200	.339	-6	-5	1	.89	0	O-15(1-15-0)	0	-0.5
Total 3	**154**	**262**	**26**	**53**	**11**	**3**	**5**	**23**	**16**	**59**	**1**	**0**	**.202**	**.261**	**.324**	**.586**	**62**	**-14**	**24**	**3.06**	**-3**	**O-131/D-2**	**3**	**-2.0**
• CANALE, George	George Anthony Canale b: 8/11/1965, Memphis, TN BL/TR, 6'1", 190 lbs. Deb: 9/3/1989																							
1989 Mil-A	13	26	5	5	1	0	1	3	2	3	0	1	.192	.250	.346	.596	67	-2	2	2.44	-1	1-11	1	-0.4
1990 Mil-A	10	13	4	1	1	0	0	0	2	6	0	1	.077	.200	.154	.354		-2	0	.70	0	/1-6,D-3	0	-0.2
1991 Mil-A	21	34	6	6	2	0	3	10	8	6	0	0	.176	.333	.500	.833	130	1	4	3.17	2	1-19	1	0.3
Total 3	**44**	**73**	**15**	**12**	**4**	**0**	**4**	**13**	**12**	**15**	**0**	**2**	**.164**	**.282**	**.384**	**.666**	**87**	**-2**	**7**	**2.48**	**2**	**/1-36,D-3**	**2**	**-0.3**
• CANATE, Willie	Emisael William (Librada) Canate b: 12/11/1971, Maracaibo, Venezuela BR/TR, 6', 170 lbs. Deb: 4/16/1993																							
1993*Tor-A	38	47	12	10	0	0	1	3	6	15	1	1	.213	.315	.277	.591	60	-3	4	2.61	0	O-31(17-6-9)/D-1	0	-0.3
• CANAVAN, Jim	James Edward Canavan b: 11/26/1866, New Bedford, MA d: 5/27/1949, New Bedford, MA BR/TR, 5'8", 160 lbs. Deb: 4/8/1891 Career OF: 105-10-104																							
1891 Cin-a	101	426	74	97	13	14	7	66	27	44	21	....	.228	.282	.373	.655	80	-16	52	4.19	-12	*S-101	7	-2.2
Mil-a	35	142	33	38	2	4	3	21	16	10	7	....	.268	.342	.401	.743	94	-3	22	5.71	-1	2-24,S-11	4	-0.2
Yr.	136	568	107	135	15	18	10	87	43	54	28	....	.238	.297	.380	.677	84	-19	74	4.55	-13	*S-112,2-24	11	-2.4
1892 Chi-N	118	439	48	73	10	11	0	32	48	48	33	....	.166	.248	.239	.488	47	-29	35	2.59	-4	*2-112/O-4(1-3-0),S-2	5	-2.6
1893 Cin-N	121	461	65	104	13	7	5	64	51	20	31	....	.226	.305	.317	.622	64	-26	55	4.11	0	*O-117(96-6-16)/2-5,3-1	8	-2.9
1894 Cin-N	103	364	81	100	16	10	13	74	64	25	13	....	.275	.383	.481	.864	103	1	74	7.27	-1	*O-95(8-1-88)/S-3,3-2,1-1,2	10	-0.4
1897 Bro-N	63	240	25	52	9	3	2	34	26	....	9	....	.217	.299	.304	.603	63	-12	25	3.54	-16	2-63	3	-2.2
Total 5	**541**	**2072**	**326**	**464**	**63**	**49**	**30**	**291**	**232**	**147**	**114**	**....**	**.224**	**.305**	**.345**	**.650**	**73**	**-85**	**264**	**4.34**	**-34**	**O-216,2-205,S-117/3-3,1-1**	**37**	**-10.4**
• CANCEL, Robinson	Robinson Castro Cancel b: 5/4/1976, Lajas, Puerto Rico BR/TR, 6', 195 lbs. Deb: 9/3/1999																							
1999 Mil-N	15	44	5	8	2	0	0	5	2	12	0	0	.182	.234	.227	.461	18	-6	3	1.89	1	C-15	0	-0.3
• CANDAELE, Casey	Casey Todd Candaele b: 1/12/1961, Lompoc, CA BB/TR, 5'9", 165 lbs. Deb: 6/5/1986 Career OF: 86-78-38																							
1986 Mon-N	30	104	9	24	4	1	0	6	5	15	3	5	.231	.266	.288	.555	53	-8	6	1.93	2	2-24/3-4	1	-0.5
1987 Mon-N	138	449	62	122	23	4	1	23	38	28	7	10	.272	.331	.347	.679	78	-17	51	3.97	-3	2-68,O-67(8-45-16),S-25/1-1	12	-1.7
1988 Mon-N	36	116	9	20	5	1	0	4	10	11	1	0	.172	.238	.233	.471	34	-10	6	1.43	4	2-35	2	-0.5
Hou-N	21	31	2	5	3	0	0	1	1	6	0	1	.161	.188	.258	.446	28	-3	1	1.28	0	2-10/O-5(0-3-2),3-1	0	-0.4
Yr.	57	147	11	25	8	1	0	5	11	17	1	1	.170	.228	.238	.466	33	-13	7	1.40	4	2-45/O-5(0-3-2),3-1	2	-0.9
1990 Hou-N	130	262	30	75	8	6	3	22	31	42	7	5	.286	.364	.397	.761	112	4	38	5.18	-1	O-58(36-12-13),2-49,S-13/3	11	0.4
1991 Hou-N	151	461	44	121	20	7	4	50	40	49	9	3	.262	.321	.362	.684	97	-1	55	4.24	6	*2-109,O-26(18-5-4),3-11	14	0.7
1992 Hou-N	135	320	19	68	12	1	1	18	24	36	7	1	.213	.274	.266	.539	56	-17	25	2.50	-1	S-65,3-29,O-21(20-1-1)/2-9	4	-1.5
1993 Hou-N	75	121	18	29	8	0	1	7	10	14	2	3	.240	.298	.331	.628	70	-6	12	3.41	-3	2-19,O-17(4-12-2),S-14/3-4	2	-0.8
1996*Cle-A	24	44	8	11	2	0	1	4	1	9	0	0	.250	.267	.364	.630	58	-3	4	3.55	1	2-11/3-3,S-1	1	-0.1
1997 Cle-A	14	26	5	8	1	0	0	4	1	1	1	0	.308	.333	.346	.679	75	-1	3	4.89	1	/2-9,3-1,D-1	1	0.1
Total 9	**754**	**1934**	**206**	**483**	**86**	**20**	**11**	**139**	**161**	**211**	**37**	**28**	**.250**	**.309**	**.332**	**.641**	**78**	**-63**	**203**	**3.56**	**8**	**2-343,O-194,S-118/3-54,1-1,D**	**48**	**-4.3**
• CANGELOSI, John	John Anthony Cangelosi b: 3/10/1963, Brooklyn, NY BB/TL, 5'8", 160 lbs. Deb: 6/30/1985 Career OF: 265-317-70																							
1985 Chi-A	5	2	2	0	0	0	0	0	0	1	0	0	.000	.333	.000	.333	1	-0	0	1.76	-1	/O-3(0-4-0),D-2	0	-0.1
1986 Chi-A	137	438	65	103	16	3	2	32	71	61	50	17	.235	.351	.299	.650	77	-8	55	4.07	-4	*O-129(29-98-5)/D-3	11	-1.4
1987 Pit-N	104	182	44	50	8	3	4	18	46	33	21	6	.275	.429	.418	.846	125	11	39	7.33	1	O-47(27-16-8)	8	1.1
1988 Pit-N	75	118	18	30	4	1	0	8	17	16	9	4	.254	.353	.305	.658	92	-0	15	4.22	-1	O-24(11-12-3)/P-1	4	-0.1
1989 Pit-N	112	160	18	35	4	2	0	9	35	20	11	8	.219	.369	.269	.637	88	-1	19	3.74	-1	O-46(12-24-10)	4	-0.3
1990 Pit-N	58	76	13	15	2	0	0	1	11	12	7	2	.197	.307	.224	.531	50	-4	6	2.55	0	O-12(3-9-0)	1	-0.5
1992 Tex-A	73	85	12	16	2	0	1	6	18	16	6	5	.188	.330	.247	.577	66	-4	8	2.91	1	O-65(36-24-10)/D-6	1	-0.4
1994 NY-N	62	111	14	28	4	0	0	4	19	20	5	1	.252	.371	.288	.660	76	-2	14	4.42	2	O-50(24-13-19)	3	-0.1
1995 Hou-N	90	201	46	64	5	2	2	18	48	42	21	5	.318	.458	.393	.852	137	18	44	8.04	-1	O-59(26-32-1)/P-1	10	1.6
1996 Hou-N	108	262	49	69	11	4	1	16	44	41	17	9	.263	.379	.347	.727	101	3	38	4.95	2	O-78(53-29-0)	7	0.3
1997*Fla-N	103	192	28	47	8	0	1	12	19	33	5	1	.245	.322	.302	.625	68	-8	20	3.61	-2	O-58(34-23-6)/P-1	3	-1.0
1998 Fla-N	104	171	19	43	8	0	1	10	30	23	2	3	.251	.366	.316	.682	85	-3	21	4.00	0	O-45(9-33-8)/D-1	2	-0.4
1999 Col-N	7	6	0	1	1	0	0	0	0	4	0	0	.167	.167	.333	.500	18	-1	0	1.80	-0	/O-1	0	-0.1
Total 13	**1038**	**2004**	**328**	**501**	**73**	**15**	**12**	**134**	**358**	**322**	**154**	**61**	**.250**	**.372**	**.319**	**.691**	**91**	**1**	**281**	**4.65**	**-3**	**O-617/D-12,P-3**	**54**	**-1.3**
• CANIZARO, Jay	Jason Kyle Canizaro b: 7/4/1973, Beaumont, TX BR/TR, 5'9", 170 lbs. Deb: 4/28/1996																							
1996 SF-N	43	120	11	24	4	1	2	8	9	38	0	2	.200	.262	.300	.562	50	-10	8	2.08	0	2-35/S-7	1	-0.8

YEAR TM-L	G	AB	R	H	2B	3B	HR	RBI	BB	SO	SB	CS	AVG	OBP	SLG	OPS	OPS+	BR/A	RC	RC/G	FR	G/POS	WS	TPW
1999 SF-N	12	18	5	8	2	0	1	9	1	2	1	0	.444	.474	.722	1.196	212	3	7	17.62	0	/2-4	2	0.3
2000 Min-A	102	346	43	93	21	1	7	40	24	57	4	2	.269	.318	.396	.714	76	-13	42	4.35	-24	2-90/D-2	7	-3.0
2002 Min-A	38	112	14	24	8	1	0	11	10	22	0	1	.214	.285	.304	.588	56	-8	10	2.92	1	2-30/3-8	2	-0.5
Total 4	195	596	73	149	35	3	10	68	44	119	5	5	.250	.305	.369	.674	71	-28	67	3.85	-22	2-159/3-8,S-7,D-2	12	-4.0
• CANNELL, Rip	Virgin Wirt Cannell b: 1/23/1880, South Bridgton, ME d: 8/26/1948, Bridgton, ME BL/TR, 5'10.5", 180 lbs. Deb: 4/14/1904 Career OF: 18-159-72																							
1904 Bos-N	100	346	32	81	5	1	0	18	23	....	10	....	.234	.286	.254	.540	70	-12	30	2.83	-12	0-93(15-10-69)	3	-3.0
1905 Bos-N	154	567	52	140	14	4	0	36	51	....	17	....	.247	.311	.286	.597	80	-13	59	3.48	-8	*0-154(3-149-3)	10	-2.9
Total 2	254	913	84	221	19	5	0	54	74	....	27	....	.242	.302	.274	.576	76	-25	88	3.23	-20	0-247	13	-5.9
• CANNIZZARO, Chris	Christopher John Cannizzaro b: 5/3/1938, Oakland, CA BR/TR, 6', 190 lbs. Deb: 4/17/1960 C																							
1960 StL-N	7	9	0	2	0	0	0	1	1	3	0	0	.222	.300	.222	.522	42	-1	1	2.56	1	/C-6	1	0.0
1961 StL-N	6	2	0	1	0	0	0	0	0	0	0	0	.500	.500	.500	1.000	151	0	1	13.50	-1	/C-5	0	-0.1
1962 NY-N	59	133	9	32	2	1	0	9	19	26	1	1	.241	.340	.271	.611	65	-6	13	3.11	1	C-56/0-1	2	-0.3
1963 NY-N	16	33	4	8	1	0	0	4	1	8	0	0	.242	.265	.273	.537	54	-2	3	2.61	1	C-15	0	-0.1
1964 NY-N	60	164	11	51	10	0	0	10	14	28	0	5	.311	.369	.372	.741	112	1	21	4.58	4	C-53	6	0.8
1965 NY-N	114	251	17	46	8	2	0	7	28	60	0	2	.183	.270	.231	.502	44	-19	16	2.02	5	*C-112	3	-0.9
1968 Pit-N	25	58	5	14	2	2	1	7	9	13	0	0	.241	.343	.397	.740	123	2	8	4.27	-1	C-25	2	0.2
1969 SD-N★	134	418	23	92	14	3	4	33	42	81	0	1	.220	.291	.297	.588	68	-18	34	2.63	1	*C-132	6	-1.1
1970 SD-N	111	341	27	95	13	3	5	42	48	49	2	7	.279	.369	.378	.748	105	1	47	4.67	-2	*C-110	10	0.4
1971 SD-N	21	63	2	12	1	0	1	8	11	10	0	0	.190	.320	.254	.574	69	-2	4	2.02	1	C-19	1	-0.1
Chi-N	71	197	18	42	8	1	5	23	28	24	0	0	.213	.314	.340	.654	74	-6	19	2.97	-1	C-70	4	-0.4
Yr.	92	260	20	54	9	1	6	31	39	34	0	0	.208	.316	.319	.635	73	-8	24	2.74	0	C-89	5	-0.5
1972 LA-N	73	200	14	48	6	0	2	18	31	38	0	1	.240	.342	.300	.642	86	-3	22	3.66	-3	C-72	6	-0.4
1973 LA-N	17	21	0	4	0	0	0	3	3	3	0	0	.190	.292	.190	.482	38	-2	1	2.12	-1	C-13	0	-0.2
1974 SD-N	26	60	2	11	1	0	0	4	6	11	0	0	.183	.258	.200	.458	31	-5	3	1.50	0	C-26	1	-0.5
Total 13	740	1950	132	458	66	12	18	169	241	354	3	17	.235	.321	.309	.630	77	-59	192	3.20	4	C-714/0-1	42	-2.6
• CANNON, Joe	Joseph Jerome Cannon b: 7/13/1953, Camp LeJeune, NC BL/TR, 6'3", 193 lbs. Deb: 9/22/1977 Career OF: 41-18-40																							
1977 Hou-N	9	17	3	2	2	0	0	1	0	5	1	1	.118	.118	.235	.353	-9	-3	0	.45	0	/0-3(3-0-0)	0	-0.3
1978 Hou-N	8	18	1	4	0	0	0	1	0	1	0	1	.222	.222	.222	.444	26	-2	1	1.20	-1	/0-5(3-2-0)	0	-0.4
1979 Tor-A	61	142	14	30	1	1	1	5	1	34	12	2	.211	.217	.254	.470	26	-13	8	1.85	1	0-50(17-0-40)	1	-1.3
1980 Tor-A	70	50	16	4	0	0	0	4	0	14	2	2	.080	.098	.080	.178	-48	-11	0	.18	0	0-33(18-16-0)/D-1	0	-1.1
Total 4	148	227	34	40	3	1	1	11	1	54	15	6	.176	.183	.211	.395	7	-29	9	1.28	0	/0-91,D-1	1	-3.1
• CANSECO, Jose	Jose (Capas) Canseco b: 7/2/1964, Havana, Cuba BR/TR, 6'3", 240 lbs. Deb: 9/2/1985 Career OF: 356-1-679																							
1985 Oak-A	29	96	16	29	3	0	5	13	4	31	1	1	.302	.330	.490	.820	130	3	15	5.89	-1	0-26(13-1-16)	4	0.1
1986 Oak-A★	157	600	85	144	29	1	33	117	65	175	15	7	.240	.322	.457	.779	118	14	89	4.94	-9	*0-155(124-0-46)/D-1	21	-0.2
1987 Oak-A	159	630	81	162	35	3	31	113	50	157	15	3	.257	.314	.470	.784	111	10	91	4.94	6	*0-130(130-0-0),D-30	17	0.8
1988*Oak-A★	158	610	120	187	34	0	**42**	**124**	78	128	40	16	.307	.394	**.569**	.963	**172**	**61**	136	7.94	3	*0-144(0-0-144),D-13	**39**	**6.0**
1989*Oak-A★	65	227	40	61	9	1	17	57	23	69	6	3	.269	.341	.542	.883	151	14	41	6.22	1	0-56(0-0-56)/D-5	14	1.3
1990*Oak-A★	131	481	83	132	14	2	37	101	72	158	19	10	.274	.375	.543	.917	160	39	98	7.12	2	0-88(0-0-88),D-43	26	3.7
1991 Oak-A	154	572	115	152	32	1	**44**	122	78	152	26	6	.266	.363	.556	.919	159	49	116	6.99	-10	*0-131(0-0-131),D-24	31	3.4
1992 Oak-A★	97	366	66	90	11	0	22	72	48	104	5	7	.246	.338	.456	.794	127	11	52	4.67	-2	0-77(0-0-77),D-20	12	0.6
Tex-A	22	73	8	17	4	0	4	15	15	24	1	0	.233	.385	.452	.837	138	5	14	6.71	0	0-13(0-0-13)/D-8	4	0.4
Yr.	119	439	74	107	15	0	26	87	63	128	6	7	.244	.346	.456	.802	129	16	66	4.99	-2	0-90(0-0-90),D-28	16	1.1
1993 Tex-A	60	231	30	59	14	1	10	46	16	62	6	6	.255	.312	.455	.767	107	0	30	4.30	1	0-49(0-0-49)/P-1	8	-0.4
1994 Tex-A	111	429	88	121	19	2	31	90	69	114	15	8	.282	.388	.552	.940	139	26	87	6.95	0	*D-111	16	1.6
1995*Bos-A	102	396	64	121	25	1	24	81	42	93	4	0	.306	.382	.556	.938	136	21	85	7.90	0	*D-101/0-1	15	1.3
1996 Bos-A	96	360	68	104	22	1	28	82	63	82	3	1	.289	.403	.589	.992	144	25	89	8.97	0	D-84,0-11(10-0-2)	13	1.8
1997 Oak-A	108	388	56	91	19	0	23	74	51	122	8	2	.235	.328	.461	.789	105	3	57	4.85	-4	D-56,0-44(19-0-27)	8	-0.6
1998 Tor-A	151	583	98	138	26	0	46	107	65	159	29	17	.237	.320	.518	.838	113	7	95	5.40	-1	D-78,0-73(50-0-26)	15	-0.2
1999 TB-A★	113	430	75	120	18	1	34	95	58	135	3	0	.279	.374	.563	.937	133	22	90	7.32	1	*D-109/0-6(6-0-0)	13	1.3
2000 TB-A	61	218	31	56	15	0	9	30	41	65	2	0	.257	.384	.450	.834	111	6	40	6.49	0	D-60	5	0.2
*NY-A	37	111	16	27	3	0	6	19	23	37	0	0	.243	.373	.432	.806	104	1	19	5.88	0	D-26/0-5(4-0-1)	3	-0.1
Yr.	98	329	47	83	18	0	15	49	64	102	2	0	.252	.380	.444	.824	109	7	60	6.28	0	D-86/0-5(4-0-1)	8	0.1
2001 Chi-A	76	256	46	66	8	0	16	49	45	75	2	1	.258	.371	.477	.847	117	7	48	6.49	0	D-68/0-2(0-0-2)	8	0.2
Total 17	1887	7057	1186	1877	340	14	462	1407	906	1942	200	88	.266	.356	.515	.871	133	324	1291	6.30	-13	*0-1011,D-837/P-1	272	21.5
• CANSECO, Ozzie	Osvaldo (Capas) Canseco b: 7/2/1964, Havana, Cuba BR/TR, 6'2", 220 lbs. Deb: 7/18/1990 Career OF: 13-0-2																							
1990 Oak-A	9	19	1	2	1	0	0	1	1	10	0	0	.105	.150	.158	.308	-14	-3	0	.78	-0	/D-4,0-2(1-0-1)	0	-0.3
1992 StL-N	9	29	7	8	5	0	0	3	7	4	0	0	.276	.417	.448	.865	150	2	6	7.07	-1	/0-8(7-0-1)	1	0.2
1993 StL-N	6	17	0	3	0	0	0	0	1	3	0	0	.176	.222	.176	.399	8	-2	1	1.40	-1	/0-5(5-0-0)	0	-0.3
Total 3	24	65	8	13	6	0	0	4	9	17	0	0	.200	.297	.292	.590	71	-3	7	3.55	-1	/0-15,D-4	1	-0.4
• CANTZ, Bart	Bartholomew L. Cantz b: 1/29/1860, Philadelphia, PA d: 2/12/1943, Philadelphia, PA Deb: 7/25/1888 Career OF: 1-0-5																							
1888 Bal-a	37	126	7	21	2	1	0	9	2	....	0	....	.167	.180	.198	.378	22	-11	5	1.18	-2	C-33/0-4(1-0-3)	1	-1.0
1889 Bal-a	20	69	6	12	2	0	0	8	4	14	2	....	.174	.219	.203	.422	21	-7	4	1.67	-5	C-18/0-2(0-0-2)	1	-1.0
1890 Phi-a	5	22	1	1	0	0	0	1	0	....	0	....	.045	.045	.045	.091	-75	-5	0	.06	1	/C-5	0	-0.3
Total 3	62	217	14	34	4	1	0	18	6	14	2	....	.157	.179	.184	.364	12	-23	8	1.21	-7	/C-56,0-6	2	-2.3
• CAPRA, Nick	Nick Lee Capra b: 3/8/1958, Denver, CO BR/TR, 5'8", 165 lbs. Deb: 9/6/1982 Career OF: 9-13-12																							
1982 Tex-A	13	15	2	4	0	0	1	1	3	4	2	1	.267	.421	.467	.888	151	1	3	5.96	1	/0-9(4-1-4)	1	0.2
1983 Tex-A	8	2	2	0	0	0	0	0	0	0	0	0	.000	.000	.000	.000	-102	-1	0	.00	-1	/0-4(1-1-2)	0	-0.1
1985 Tex-A	8	8	1	1	0	0	0	0	0	0	0	0	.125	.125	.125	.250	-31	-1	0	.48	0	/0-8(1-3-4)	0	-0.2
1988 KC-A	14	29	3	4	1	0	0	0	2	3	1	0	.138	.194	.172	.366	3	-4	1	.56	0	0-11(2-7-2)/D-1	0	-0.4
1991 Tex-A	2	0	1	0	0	0	0	0	1	0	0	0	....	1.000	....	1.000	205	0	0	∞	-0	/0-2(1-1-0)	0	0.0
Total 5	45	54	9	9	1	0	1	1	6	7	3	1	.167	.262	.241	.503	45	-4	4	1.93	0	/0-34,D-1	1	-0.5
• CAPRI, Pat	Patrick Nicholas Capri b: 11/27/1918, New York, NY d: 6/14/1989, New York, NY BR/TR, 6'.5", 170 lbs. Deb: 7/16/1944																							
1944 Bos-N	7	1	1	0	0	0	0	0	0	1	0	....	.000	.000	.000	.000	-96	-0	0	.00	0	/2-1	0	0.0
• CAPRON, Ralph	Ralph Earl Capron b: 6/16/1889, Minneapolis, MN d: 9/19/1980, Los Angeles, CA BL/TR, 5'11.5", 165 lbs. Deb: 4/25/1912																							
1912 Pit-N	1	0	0	0	0	0	0	0	0	0	0	....	....	....	....	....	-102	0	0	....	0	....	0	0.0
1913 Phi-N	2	1	1	0	0	0	0	0	0	0	0	....	.000	.000	.000	.000	-96	-0	0	.00	0	/0-1	0	0.0
Total 2	3	1	1	0	0	0	0	0	0	0	0	....	.000	.000	.000	.000	-96	-0	0	.00	0	/0-1	0	0.0
• CARABALLO, Ramon	Ramon (Sanchez) Caraballo b: 5/23/1969, Rio San Juan, Dominican Republic BB/TR, 5'7", 150 lbs. Deb: 9/9/1993																							
1993 Atl-N	6	0	0	0	0	0	0	0	0	0	0	0	....	....	....	....	-99	0	0	....	-1	/2-5	0	-0.1
1995 StL-N	34	99	10	20	4	1	2	3	6	33	3	2	.202	.269	.323	.592	55	-7	9	2.81	-1	2-24	1	-0.7
Total 2	40	99	10	20	4	1	2	3	6	33	3	2	.202	.269	.323	.592	55	-7	9	2.81	-2	/2-29	1	-0.7
• CARBINE, John	John C. Carbine b: 10/12/1855, Syracuse, NY d: 9/11/1915, Forest Park, IL, 6', 187 lbs. Deb: 5/8/1875																							
1875 Wes-n	10	36	0	3	0	0	0	2	0	1	0	0	.083	.083	.083	.167	-40	-5	0	.23	2	1-10	....	-0.3
1876 Lou-N	7	25	3	4	0	0	0	1	0	0	....	....	.160	.160	.160	.320	6	-3	1	.87	1	/1-6,0-1	0	-0.2
• CARBO, Bernie	Bernardo Carbo b: 8/5/1947, Detroit, MI BL/TR, 5'11", 175 lbs. Deb: 9/2/1969 Career OF: 299-0-406																							
1969 Cin-N	4	3	0	0	0	0	0	0	0	2	0	0	.000	.000	.000	.000	-95	-1	0	.00	0	....	0	-0.1
1970*Cin-N	125	365	54	113	19	3	21	63	94	77	10	4	.310	.456	.551	1.006	162	38	100	10.11	-0	*0-119(118-0-1)	25	3.2
1971 Cin-N	106	310	33	68	20	1	5	20	54	56	2	1	.219	.339	.339	.678	97	1	38	4.11	4	0-90(90-0-0)	9	0.0
1972 Cin-N	19	21	2	3	0	0	0	0	6	3	0	0	.143	.357	.143	.500	50	-1	2	2.44	0	/0-4(0-0-4)	0	-0.1

YEAR TM-L	G	AB	R	H	2B	3B	HR	RBI	BB	SO	SB	CS	AVG	OBP	SLG	OPS	OPS+	BR/A	RC	RC/G	FR	G/POS	WS	TPW
StL-N	99	302	42	78	13	1	7	34	57	56	0	1	.258	.385	.377	.762	119	10	47	5.33	7	0-92(0-0-92)/3-1	12	1.4
Yr.	118	323	44	81	13	1	7	34	63	59	0	1	.251	.383	.362	.745	114	10	48	5.12	7	0-96(0-0-96)/3-1	12	1.3
1973 StL-N	111	308	42	88	18	0	8	40	58	52	2	0	.286	.401	.422	.823	129	15	56	6.54	0	0-94(2-0-93)	16	1.1
1974 Bos-A	117	338	40	84	20	0	12	61	58	90	4	3	.249	.365	.414	.779	116	9	52	5.29	1	0-87(33-0-56),D-15	12	0.6
1975*Bos-A	107	319	64	82	21	3	15	50	83	69	2	4	.257	.412	.483	.895	140	20	68	7.33	2	0-85(38-0-47),D-13	17	1.8
1976 Bos-A	17	55	5	13	4	0	2	6	8	17	1	0	.236	.333	.418	.752	106	1	8	5.43	-0	D-15/O-1	2	0.0
Mil-A	69	183	20	43	7	0	3	15	33	55	1	2	.235	.352	.322	.674	100	1	22	3.91	3	0-33(4-0-29),D-24	5	0.2
Yr.	86	238	25	56	11	0	5	21	41	72	2	2	.235	.348	.345	.692	102	2	30	4.24	3	D-39,0-34(5-0-29)	7	0.2
1977 Bos-A	86	228	36	66	6	1	15	34	47	72	1	2	.289	.411	.522	.933	136	13	51	8.14	-1	0-67(8-0-59)/D-7	11	0.8
1978 Bos-A	17	46	7	12	3	0	1	6	8	8	1	1	.261	.370	.391	.762	103	0	6	4.34	1	/0-9(1-0-8),D-8	1	0.0
Cle-A	60	174	21	50	8	0	4	16	20	31	1	0	.287	.364	.402	.766	117	5	25	5.18	0	D-49/0-4(0-0-4)	5	0.3
Yr.	77	220	28	62	11	0	5	22	28	39	2	1	.282	.365	.400	.765	114	5	31	4.99	0	D-57,0-13(1-0-12)	6	0.3
1979 StL-N	52	64	6	18	1	0	3	12	10	22	1	0	.281	.378	.438	.816	121	2	12	6.66	-1	0-17(4-0-13)	2	0.1
1980 StL-N	14	11	0	2	0	0	0	0	1	0	0	0	.182	.250	.182	.432	22	-1	1	1.73	0	....	0	-0.1
Pit-N	7	6	0	2	0	0	0	1	1	1	0	0	.333	.429	.333	.762	113	0	1	6.54	0	....	0	0.0
Yr.	21	17	0	4	0	0	0	1	2	1	0	0	.235	.316	.235	.551	54	-1	2	3.11	0	....	0	-0.1
Total 12	**1010**	**2733**	**372**	**722**	**140**	**9**	**96**	**358**	**538**	**611**	**26**	**18**	**.264**	**.389**	**.427**	**.816**	**124**	**114**	**489**	**6.23**	**15**	**0-702,D-131/3-1**	**117**	**9.3**

• CARDENAL, Jose Jose Rosario Domec Cardenal b: 10/7/1943, Matanzas, Cuba BR/TR, 5'10", 150 lbs. Deb: 4/14/1963 C Career OF: 427-847-549

YEAR TM-L	G	AB	R	H	2B	3B	HR	RBI	BB	SO	SB	CS	AVG	OBP	SLG	OPS	OPS+	BR/A	RC	RC/G	FR	G/POS	WS	TPW
1963 SF-N	9	5	1	1	0	0	0	2	1	1	0	1	.200	.333	.200	.533	58	-1	0	1.13	0	/0-2(0-1-1)	0	-0.1
1964 SF-N	20	15	3	0	0	0	0	0	2	3	2	0	.000	.118	.000	.118	-62	-3	0	.33	1	0-16(8-2-6)	0	-0.3
1965 Cal-A	134	512	58	128	23	2	11	57	27	72	37	17	.250	.290	.367	.657	87	-9	54	3.50	7	*0-129(0-129-0)/3-2,2-1	14	-0.7
1966 Cal-A	154	561	67	155	15	3	16	48	34	69	24	11	.276	.322	.399	.721	109	6	72	4.54	7	*0-146(7-140-0)	20	0.9
1967 Cal-A	108	381	40	90	13	5	6	27	15	63	10	5	.236	.269	.344	.613	83	-9	35	3.07	4	*0-101(27-70-17)	8	-1.0
1968 Cle-A	157	583	78	150	21	7	7	44	39	74	40	18	.257	.306	.353	.659	101	0	65	3.80	3	*0-153(0-153-0)	21	-0.2
1969 Cle-A	146	557	75	143	26	3	11	45	49	58	36	6	.257	.317	.373	.690	89	-4	67	4.01	1	*0-142(1-141-0)/3-5	14	-0.7
1970 StL-N	148	552	73	162	32	6	10	74	45	70	26	9	.293	.348	.428	.775	104	4	81	5.28	-8	*0-134(0-133-1)	16	-0.7
1971 StL-N	89	301	37	73	12	4	7	48	29	35	12	3	.243	.309	.379	.688	90	-3	35	3.86	2	0-83(0-8-78)	8	-0.6
Mil-A	53	198	20	51	10	0	3	32	13	20	9	5	.258	.307	.354	.660	87	-4	21	3.47	2	0-52(0-45-7)	5	-0.4
1972 Chi-N	143	533	96	155	24	6	17	70	55	58	25	14	.291	.358	.454	.812	117	12	83	5.46	-2	*0-137(8-16-125)	18	0.3
1973 Chi-N	145	522	80	158	33	2	11	68	58	62	19	7	.303	.378	.437	.815	116	14	86	5.84	-3	*0-142(1-2-142)	18	0.4
1974 Chi-N	143	542	75	159	35	3	13	72	56	67	23	9	.293	.361	.441	.802	118	14	84	5.45	5	*0-137(32-1-108)	17	1.2
1975 Chi-N	154	574	85	182	30	2	9	68	77	50	34	12	.317	.402	.423	.825	123	23	103	6.54	6	*0-151(137-0-18)	26	2.1
1976 Chi-N	136	521	64	156	25	2	8	47	32	39	23	14	.299	.341	.401	.742	101	-1	71	4.89	3	*0-128(127-0-2)	16	-0.6
1977 Chi-N	100	226	33	54	12	1	3	18	28	30	5	4	.239	.325	.341	.666	71	-9	24	3.44	-2	0-62(54-6-2)/2-1,S-1	3	-1.4
1978*Phi-N	87	201	27	50	12	0	4	33	23	16	2	3	.249	.326	.368	.694	93	-3	23	3.93	-5	1-50,0-13(10-0-4)	4	-1.1
1979 Phi-N	29	48	4	10	3	0	0	9	8	8	1	0	.208	.321	.271	.592	61	-2	4	2.71	0	0-12(9-0-6)/1-1	0	-0.3
NY-N	11	37	8	11	4	0	2	4	6	3	1	0	.297	.409	.568	.977	170	4	10	9.92	-1	/0-9(0-0-9),1-2	2	0.3
Yr.	40	85	12	21	7	0	2	13	14	11	2	0	.247	.360	.400	.760	109	2	14	5.50	-1	0-21(9-0-15)/1-3	2	0.0
1980 NY-N	26	42	4	7	1	0	0	4	6	4	0	1	.167	.271	.190	.461	32	-4	2	1.25	0	/0-6(2-0-4),1-5	0	-0.5
*KC-A	25	53	8	18	2	0	0	5	5	5	0	0	.340	.397	.377	.774	112	1	9	6.12	0	0-23(4-0-19)	2	0.0
Total 18	**2017**	**6964**	**936**	**1913**	**333**	**46**	**138**	**775**	**608**	**807**	**329**	**139**	**.275**	**.335**	**.395**	**.730**	**102**	**28**	**928**	**4.61**	**16**	***0-1778/1-58,3-7,2-2,S-1**	**212**	**-3.4**

• CARDENAS, Leo Leonardo Lazaro (Alfonso) "Chico,Mr. Automatic" Cardenas b: 12/17/1938, Matanzas, Cuba BR/TR, 5'11", 163 lbs. Deb: 7/25/1960

YEAR TM-L	G	AB	R	H	2B	3B	HR	RBI	BB	SO	SB	CS	AVG	OBP	SLG	OPS	OPS+	BR/A	RC	RC/G	FR	G/POS	WS	TPW
1960 Cin-N	48	142	13	33	2	4	1	12	6	32	0	0	.232	.264	.324	.587	59	-8	12	2.92	-1	S-47	2	-0.6
1961*Cin-N	74	198	23	61	18	1	5	24	15	39	1	0	.308	.357	.485	.842	119	5	33	6.23	-1	S-63	8	0.9
1962 Cin-N	153	589	77	173	31	4	10	60	39	99	2	5	.294	.343	.411	.754	98	-4	79	4.69	4	*S-149	21	1.3
1963 Cin-N	158	565	42	133	22	4	7	48	23	101	3	5	.235	.270	.326	.596	69	-25	46	2.72	9	*S-157	12	-0.2
1964 Cin-N★	163	597	61	150	32	2	9	69	41	110	4	4	.251	.302	.357	.658	82	-15	63	3.60	7	*S-163	17	0.6
1965 Cin-N★	156	557	65	160	25	11	11	57	60	100	1	4	.287	.358	.431	.788	113	10	81	5.14	16	*S-155	22	4.2
1966 Cin-N★	160	568	59	145	25	4	20	81	45	87	9	4	.255	.311	.419	.730	92	-5	69	4.07	7	*S-160	19	1.6
1967 Cin-N	108	379	30	97	14	3	2	21	34	77	4	5	.256	.320	.325	.645	76	-12	38	3.43	5	*S-108	11	0.3
1968 Cin-N★	137	452	45	106	13	2	7	41	36	83	2	1	.235	.294	.319	.612	79	-11	39	2.86	-22	*S-136	5	-2.4
1969*Min-A	160	578	67	162	24	4	10	70	66	96	5	6	.280	.358	.388	.746	106	5	78	4.60	30	*S-160	23	5.7
1970*Min-A	160	588	67	145	34	4	11	65	42	101	2	5	.247	.301	.374	.675	84	-16	65	3.69	17	*S-160	19	2.1
1971 Min-A★	153	554	59	146	25	4	18	75	51	69	3	3	.264	.327	.421	.747	107	4	73	4.46	7	*S-153	22	3.0
1972 Cal-A	150	551	25	123	11	2	6	42	35	73	1	2	.223	.272	.283	.555	69	-22	41	2.41	2	*S-150	11	-0.2
1973 Cle-A	72	195	9	42	4	0	0	12	13	42	1	4	.215	.264	.236	.500	41	-17	11	1.83	-7	S-67/3-5	2	-1.8
1974 Tex-A	34	92	5	25	3	0	0	7	2	14	1	0	.272	.287	.304	.592	72	-3	8	2.97	-1	3-21,S-10/D-4	2	-0.3
1975 Tex-A	55	102	15	24	2	0	1	5	14	12	0	0	.235	.328	.284	.612	75	-3	11	3.64	-2	3-43/S-5,2-3	3	-0.5
Total 16	**1941**	**6707**	**662**	**1725**	**285**	**49**	**118**	**689**	**522**	**1135**	**39**	**48**	**.257**	**.313**	**.367**	**.681**	**88**	**-116**	**748**	**3.78**	**70**	***S-1843/3-69,D-4,2-3**	**199**	**13.7**

• CARDONA, Javier Javier Peterson Cardona b: 9/15/1975, Santurce, Puerto Rico BR/TR, 6'1", 185 lbs. Deb: 5/31/2000

YEAR TM-L	G	AB	R	H	2B	3B	HR	RBI	BB	SO	SB	CS	AVG	OBP	SLG	OPS	OPS+	BR/A	RC	RC/G	FR	G/POS	WS	TPW
2000 Det-A	26	40	1	7	1	0	1	2	0	9	0	0	.175	.195	.275	.470	18	-5	2	1.51	-3	C-26	1	-0.7
2001 Det-A	46	96	10	25	8	0	1	10	2	12	0	1	.260	.283	.375	.658	75	-4	9	3.30	-8	C-44/D-1	1	-1.0
2002 SD-N	15	39	2	4	1	0	0	2	2	10	0	0	.103	.146	.128	.275	-30	-7	1	.52	-1	C-14	1	-0.8
Total 3	**87**	**175**	**13**	**36**	**10**	**0**	**2**	**14**	**4**	**31**	**0**	**1**	**.206**	**.232**	**.297**	**.529**	**38**	**-17**	**12**	**2.19**	**-13**	**/C-84,D-1**	**3**	**-2.5**

• CAREW, Rod Rodney Cline Carew b: 10/1/1945, Gatun, Panama BL/TR, 6', 182 lbs. Deb: 4/11/1967 C HOF: 1991

YEAR TM-L	G	AB	R	H	2B	3B	HR	RBI	BB	SO	SB	CS	AVG	OBP	SLG	OPS	OPS+	BR/A	RC	RC/G	FR	G/POS	WS	TPW
1967 Min-A★	137	514	66	150	22	7	8	51	37	91	5	9	.292	.342	.409	.750	112	5	68	4.65	-5	*2-134	19	1.3
1968 Min-A★	127	461	46	126	27	2	1	42	26	71	12	4	.273	.314	.347	.661	95	-2	49	3.75	-9	*2-117/S-4	13	-0.1
1969*Min-A★	123	458	79	152	30	4	8	56	37	72	19	8	**.332**	.386	.467	.853	135	21	83	6.88	4	*2-118	21	3.4
1970*Min-A★	51	191	27	70	12	3	4	28	11	28	4	6	.366	.407	.524	.930	152	12	39	8.29	1	2-45/1-1	11	1.6
1971 Min-A★	147	577	88	177	16	10	2	48	45	81	6	7	.307	.358	.380	.737	106	3	73	4.48	-17	*2-142/3-2	17	-0.5
1972 Min-A★	142	535	61	170	21	6	0	51	43	60	12	6	**.318**	.371	.379	.750	118	13	75	5.16	6	*2-139	22	3.2
1973 Min-A★	149	580	98	**203**	30	**11**	6	62	62	55	41	16	**.350**	.415	.471	.885	143	37	113	7.22	13	*2-147	28	6.1
1974 Min-A★	153	599	86	**218**	30	5	3	55	74	49	38	16	**.364**	**.435**	.446	.880	148	43	118	7.39	7	*2-148	**32**	**6.2**
1975 Min-A★	143	535	89	192	24	4	14	80	64	40	35	9	**.359**	**.428**	.497	.926	158	47	118	8.39	0	*2-123,1-14/D-2	30	5.5
1976 Min-A★	156	605	97	200	29	12	9	90	67	52	49	22	.331	.398	.463	.861	147	**38**	111	6.63	-3	*1-152/2-7	30	2.5
1977 Min-A★	155	616	**128**	**239**	38	**16**	14	100	69	55	23	13	**.388**	**.452**	.570	**1.022**	**179**	**69**	160	**10.76**	4	*1-151/2-4,D-1	**37**	**6.3**
1978 Min-A★	152	564	85	188	26	10	5	70	78	62	27	7	**.333**	**.415**	.441	.857	138	36	105	6.94	-6	*1-148/2-4,0-1	22	2.2
1979*Cal-A★	110	409	78	130	15	3	3	44	73	46	18	8	.318	.421	.391	.812	125	20	73	6.38	-6	*1-103/D-6	16	0.7
1980 Cal-A★	144	540	74	179	34	7	3	59	59	38	23	15	.331	.398	.437	.835	132	24	92	6.13	0	*1-103,D-32	20	1.6
1981 Cal-A★	93	364	57	111	17	1	2	21	45	45	16	9	.305	.381	.374	.755	118	10	53	5.07	1	1-90/D-2	12	0.5
1982*Cal-A★	138	523	88	167	25	5	3	44	67	49	10	17	.319	.399	.403	.802	121	13	83	5.61	3	*1-134	17	0.8
1983 Cal-A★	129	472	66	160	24	2	2	44	57	48	6	7	.339	.411	.411	.822	128	19	78	6.18	-11	1-89,D-24/2-2	16	0.2
1984 Cal-A★	93	329	42	97	8	1	3	31	40	39	4	3	.295	.371	.353	.724	102	2	44	4.75	-2	1-83/D-1	9	-0.4
1985 Cal-A	127	443	69	124	17	3	2	39	64	47	5	5	.280	.372	.345	.717	98	1	60	4.70	-10	*1-116	12	-1.5
Total 19	**2469**	**9315**	**1424**	**3053**	**445**	**112**	**92**	**1015**	**1018**	**1028**	**353**	**187**	**.328**	**.395**	**.429**	**.825**	**131**	**413**	**1595**	**6.28**	**-31**	***1-1184,2-1130/D-68,S-4,3-2,0**	**384**	**39.6**

• CAREY, Andy Andrew Arthur Carey b: 10/18/1931, Oakland, CA BR/TR, 6'1.5", 195 lbs. Deb: 5/2/1952

YEAR TM-L	G	AB	R	H	2B	3B	HR	RBI	BB	SO	SB	CS	AVG	OBP	SLG	OPS	OPS+	BR/A	RC	RC/G	FR	G/POS	WS	TPW
1952 NY-A	16	40	6	6	0	0	0	1	3	10	0	0	.150	.209	.150	.359	1	-5	1	.88	-1	3-14/S-1	0	-0.7
1953 NY-A	51	81	14	26	5	0	4	8	9	12	2	1	.321	.389	.531	.920	151	6	17	8.10	2	3-40/S-2,2-1	5	0.8
1954 NY-A	122	411	60	124	14	6	8	65	43	38	5	5	.302	.377	.423	.801	123	13	64	5.42	8	*3-120	18	2.1
1955*NY-A	135	510	73	131	19	**11**	7	47	44	51	3	3	.257	.317	.378	.696	88	-11	60	4.00	17	*3-135	14	0.6
1956*NY-A	132	422	54	100	18	2	7	50	45	53	9	6	.237	.313	.339	.652	75	-16	45	3.51	0	*3-131	8	-1.6
1957*NY-A	85	247	30	63	6	5	6	33	15	42	2	2	.255	.311	.393	.704	92	-3	29	3.88	0	3-81	7	-0.4
1958*NY-A	102	315	39	90	19	4	12	45	34	43	1	2	.286	.366	.486	.852	137	16	57	6.32	10	3-99	15	2.6
1959 NY-A	41	101	11	26	1	0	3	9	7	17	1	1	.257	.306	.356	.662	84	-3	10	3.33	-2	3-34	2	-0.5
1960 NY-A	4	3	1	1	0	0	0	1	0	1	0	0	.333	.333	.333	.667	86	-0	0	4.50	0	/3-2,0-1	0	-0.1

YEAR TM-L	G	AB	R	H	2B	3B	HR	RBI	BB	SO	SB	CS	AVG	OBP	SLG	OPS	OPS+	BR/A	RC	RC/G	FR	G/POS	WS	TPW
KC-A	102	343	30	80	14	4	12	53	26	52	0	0	.233	.289	.402	.692	84	-9	36	3.40	4	3-91	7	-0.6
Yr.	106	346	31	81	14	4	12	54	26	53	0	0	.234	.290	.402	.691	84	-9	36	3.40	3	3-93/0-1	7	-0.6
1961 KC-A	39	123	20	30	6	2	3	11	15	23	0	0	.244	.336	.398	.734	95	-1	17	4.65	4	3-39	4	0.3
Chi-A	56	143	21	38	12	3	0	14	11	24	0	1	.266	.327	.392	.719	92	-2	19	4.52	-2	3-54	4	-0.4
Yr.	95	266	41	68	18	5	3	25	26	47	0	1	.256	.331	.395	.726	94	-3	36	4.58	1	3-93	8	-0.2
1962 LA-N	53	111	12	26	5	1	2	13	16	23	0	0	.234	.336	.351	.687	90	-1	14	4.38	0	3-42	3	-0.1
Total 11	938	2850	371	741	119	38	64	350	268	389	23	21	.260	.329	.396	.725	98	-17	369	4.38	38	3-882/S-3,2-1,0-1	87	2.0

• CAREY, Max Max George "Scoops" Carey b: 1/11/1890, Terre Haute, IN d: 5/30/1976, Miami, FL BB/TR, 5'11.5", 170 lbs. Deb: 10/3/1910 M/C HOF: 1961 Career OF: 655-1646-145

YEAR TM-L	G	AB	R	H	2B	3B	HR	RBI	BB	SO	SB	CS	AVG	OBP	SLG	OPS	OPS+	BR/A	RC	RC/G	FR	G/POS	WS	TPW
1910 Pit-N	2	6	2	3	0	1	0	2	2	1	0	....	.500	.625	.833	1.458	306	2	3	27.09	2	/0-2(2-0-0)	1	0.4
1911 Pit-N	129	427	77	110	15	10	5	43	44	75	27	....	.258	.337	.375	.712	95	-3	64	4.85	0	*0-122(46-76-0)	14	-1.0
1912 Pit-N	150	587	114	177	23	8	5	66	61	79	45	....	.302	.372	.394	.766	111	10	104	5.94	5	*0-150(145-6-0)	22	0.9
1913 Pit-N	154	620	**99**	172	23	10	5	49	55	67	**61**	....	.277	.339	.371	.710	107	6	92	5.10	6	*0-154(144-11-0)	20	0.5
1914 Pit-N	156	593	76	144	25	**17**	1	31	59	56	38	....	.243	.313	.347	.661	101	-0	72	4.07	4	*0-154(154-0-0)	17	-0.2
1915 Pit-N	140	564	76	143	26	5	3	27	57	58	**36**	17	.254	.326	.333	.660	101	2	66	3.96	8	*0-139(139-0-0)	16	0.4
1916 Pit-N	154	599	90	158	23	11	7	42	59	58	**63**	19	.264	.337	.374	.711	117	18	87	4.79	17	*0-154(21-134-0)	25	3.0
1917 Pit-N	155	588	82	174	21	12	1	51	58	38	**46**	....	.296	.369	.378	.746	125	20	94	5.71	14	*0-153(0-153-0)	23	2.7
1918 Pit-N	126	468	70	128	14	6	3	48	**62**	25	**58**	....	.274	.363	.348	.712	113	10	76	5.54	15	*0-126(0-126-0)	22	1.9
1919 Pit-N	66	244	41	75	10	2	0	9	25	24	18	....	.307	.376	.365	.741	119	7	38	5.72	-4	0-63(0-63-0)	11	-0.2
1920 Pit-N	130	485	74	140	18	4	1	35	59	31	**52**	10	.289	.369	.348	.718	104	14	72	5.10	-13	*0-129(0-129-0)	20	-0.7
1921 Pit-N	140	521	85	161	34	4	7	56	70	30	37	12	.309	.395	.430	.825	115	19	95	6.26	1	*0-139(0-139-0)	24	1.4
1922 Pit-N	155	629	140	207	28	12	10	70	**80**	26	**51**	2	.329	.408	.459	.868	122	36	131	7.86	1	*0-155(3-152-0)	29	2.8
1923 Pit-N	153	610	120	188	32	**19**	6	63	73	28	**51**	8	.308	.388	.452	.841	119	27	117	7.06	11	*0-153(0-153-0)	29	3.0
1924 Pit-N	149	599	113	178	30	9	8	55	58	17	**49**	13	.297	.366	.417	.783	108	15	97	5.70	6	*0-149(0-149-0)	25	1.4
1925*Pit-N	133	542	109	186	39	13	5	44	66	19	**46**	11	.343	.418	.491	.909	123	27	118	8.36	2	*0-130(0-130-0)	26	2.2
1926 Pit-N	86	324	46	72	14	5	0	28	30	14	10	....	.222	.288	.296	.584	55	-21	28	2.76	0	0-82(0-82-0)	5	-2.4
Bro-N	27	100	18	26	3	1	0	7	8	5	0	....	.260	.315	.310	.625	70	-4	10	3.26	-3	0-27(0-27-0)	2	-0.8
Yr.	113	424	64	98	17	6	0	35	38	19	10	....	.231	.294	.300	.594	58	-25	38	2.88	-3	*0-109(0-109-0)	7	-3.2
1927 Bro-N	144	538	70	143	30	10	1	54	64	18	32	....	.266	.345	.364	.709	90	-6	69	4.32	3	*0-141(0-39-108)	13	-1.3
1928 Bro-N	108	296	41	73	11	0	2	19	47	24	18	....	.247	.354	.304	.658	74	-9	34	3.85	-2	0-95(1-75-35)	7	-1.5
1929 Bro-N	19	23	2	7	0	0	0	1	3	2	0	....	.304	.407	.304	.712	81	-0	3	4.95	0	/0-4(0-2-2)	0	-0.1
Total 20	2476	9363	1545	2665	419	159	70	800	1040	695	738	92	.285	.361	.386	.747	107	169	1472	5.44	71	*0-2421	351	12.5

• CAREY, Paul Paul Stephen Carey b: 1/8/1968, Boston, MA BL/TR, 6'4", 215 lbs. Deb: 5/25/1993

YEAR TM-L	G	AB	R	H	2B	3B	HR	RBI	BB	SO	SB	CS	AVG	OBP	SLG	OPS	OPS+	BR/A	RC	RC/G	FR	G/POS	WS	TPW
1993 Bal-A	18	47	1	10	1	0	0	3	5	14	0	0	.213	.288	.234	.523	41	-4	3	1.71	-2	/1-9,D-5	0	-0.6

• CAREY, Roger Roger J. Carey b: 1865, NY d: 2/8/1895, New York, NY Deb: 7/9/1887

YEAR TM-L	G	AB	R	H	2B	3B	HR	RBI	BB	SO	SB	CS	AVG	OBP	SLG	OPS	OPS+	BR/A	RC	RC/G	FR	G/POS	WS	TPW
1887 NY-N	1	4	0	0	0	0	0	2	0	1	0	....	.000	.000	.000	.000	-105	-1	0	.00	1	/2-1	0	0.0

• CAREY, Scoops George C. Carey b: 12/4/1870, Pittsburgh, PA d: 12/17/1916, East Liverpool, OH BR/TR, 5'11", 175 lbs. Deb: 4/26/1895

YEAR TM-L	G	AB	R	H	2B	3B	HR	RBI	BB	SO	SB	CS	AVG	OBP	SLG	OPS	OPS+	BR/A	RC	RC/G	FR	G/POS	WS	TPW
1895*Bal-N	123	490	59	128	21	6	1	75	27	32	2	....	.261	.305	.335	.640	63	-29	53	3.86	-8	*1-123/3-1,0-1,S-1	4	-3.0
1898 Lou-N	8	32	1	6	1	1	0	1	1	....	0	....	.188	.212	.281	.493	42	-3	2	1.99	0	/1-8	0	-0.2
1902 Was-A	120	452	46	142	35	11	0	60	20	....	3	....	.314	.350	.440	.790	117	9	73	6.14	-0	*1-120	13	0.6
1903 Was-A	48	183	8	37	3	2	0	23	4	....	0	....	.202	.223	.240	.464	38	-14	10	1.84	-4	1-47	0	-1.9
Total 4	299	1157	114	313	60	20	1	159	52	32	5	....	.271	.308	.360	.667	80	-37	139	4.29	-11	1-298/3-1,0-1,S-1	17	-4.5

• CAREY, Tom Thomas Francis Aloysius "Scoops" Carey b: 10/11/1906, Hoboken, NJ d: 2/21/1970, Rochester, NY BR/TR, 5'8.5", 170 lbs. Deb: 7/19/1935 C

YEAR TM-L	G	AB	R	H	2B	3B	HR	RBI	BB	SO	SB	CS	AVG	OBP	SLG	OPS	OPS+	BR/A	RC	RC/G	FR	G/POS	WS	TPW
1935 StL-A	76	296	29	86	18	4	0	42	13	11	0	2	.291	.320	.378	.699	77	-12	35	4.32	-6	2-76	4	-1.2
1936 StL-A	134	488	58	133	27	6	1	57	27	25	2	1	.273	.315	.359	.673	64	-29	55	4.09	-11	*2-128/S-1	5	-2.8
1937 StL-A	130	487	54	134	24	1	1	40	21	26	1	2	.275	.306	.335	.641	61	-30	49	3.64	-22	2-87,S-44/3-1	4	-4.1
1939 Bos-A	54	161	17	39	6	2	0	20	3	9	0	0	.242	.265	.304	.569	44	-14	12	2.56	3	2-35,S-10	2	-0.8
1940 Bos-A	43	62	4	20	4	0	0	7	2	1	0	0	.323	.344	.387	.731	86	-1	8	4.65	0	S-20/2-4,3-4	2	-0.1
1941 Bos-A	25	21	7	4	0	0	0	2	0	0	0	0	.190	.190	.190	.381	1	-3	1	.88	-2	/2-9,S-8,3-1	0	-0.4
1942 Bos-A	1	1	0	1	0	0	0	1	0	0	0	0	1.000	1.000	1.000	2.000	448	0	1	∞	0	/2-1	0	0.0
1946 Bos-A	3	5	0	1	0	0	0	0	0	1	0	0	.200	.200	.200	.400	11	-1	0	.00	0	/2-3	0	0.0
Total 8	466	1521	169	418	79	13	2	169	66	73	3	5	.275	.308	.348	.655	63	-90	161	3.77	-39	2-343/S-83,3-6	17	-9.4

• CAREY, Tom Thomas John Carey b: 1849, Brooklyn, NY d: 2/13/1899, Los Angeles, CA BR/TR, 5'8", 145 lbs. Deb: 5/4/1871 M/U

YEAR TM-L	G	AB	R	H	2B	3B	HR	RBI	BB	SO	SB	CS	AVG	OBP	SLG	OPS	OPS+	BR/A	RC	RC/G	FR	G/POS	WS	TPW
1871 Kek-n	19	87	16	20	2	0	0	10	2	1	5	0	.230	.247	.253	.500	43	-6	7	3.22	4	2-19	....	-0.2
1872 Bal-n	42	198	42	57	7	0	2	27	0	2	4	1	.288	.288	.354	.641	92	-3	22	4.77	-5	2-29/S-9,3-3,0-3(0-0-3),1	....	-0.6
1873 Bal-n	56	290	76	97	19	3	1	55	1	2	1	3	.334	.337	.431	.768	127	8	43	6.77	1	*2-54/3-4,S-3	....	0.4
1874 Mut-n	64	286	56	82	10	3	1	39	2	4	3	0	.287	.292	.353	.645	102	0	31	4.57	-8	*S-51,2-13	....	-0.7
1875 Har-n	86	382	63	101	6	2	0	38	1	3	13	3	.264	.266	.291	.557	89	-4	34	3.52	-3	*S-86/2-1	....	-0.7
1876 Har-N	68	292	51	78	7	0	0	26	3	4	....	....	.267	.277	.294	.572	83	-6	24	3.21	3	*S-68	8	0.0
1877 Har-N	60	274	38	70	3	2	1	20	0	9	....	....	.255	.255	.292	.547	80	-5	21	2.82	-6	*S-60	6	-0.7
1878 Pro-N	61	253	33	60	10	3	0	24	0	14	....	....	.237	.237	.300	.538	76	-7	18	2.63	-6	*S-61	5	-1.0
1879 Cle-N	80	335	30	80	14	1	0	32	5	20	....	....	.239	.250	.287	.537	77	-8	25	2.70	-2	*S-80	7	-0.5
Total 5 n	267	1243	253	357	44	8	4	169	6	12	26	7	.287	.291	.345	.636	98	-4	137	4.65	-10	S-149,2-116/3-7,0-3,1-1	....	-1.9
Total 4	269	1154	152	288	34	6	1	102	8	47	....	....	.250	.255	.293	.548	79	-26	88	2.84	-11	S-269	26	-2.2

• CARFREY, Ed Ed Carfrey Deb: 4/19/1890

YEAR TM-L	G	AB	R	H	2B	3B	HR	RBI	BB	SO	SB	CS	AVG	OBP	SLG	OPS	OPS+	BR/A	RC	RC/G	FR	G/POS	WS	TPW
1890 Phi-a	1	4	0	1	0	0	0	....	0	....	0	....	.250	.250	.250	.500	48	-0	0	2.26	0	/S-1	0	-0.1

• CARGO, Bobby Robert J. Cargo b: 10/1868, Pittsburgh, PA d: 4/27/1904, Atlanta, GA BR/TR Deb: 10/6/1892

YEAR TM-L	G	AB	R	H	2B	3B	HR	RBI	BB	SO	SB	CS	AVG	OBP	SLG	OPS	OPS+	BR/A	RC	RC/G	FR	G/POS	WS	TPW
1892 Pit-N	2	4	0	1	0	0	0	0	0	0	0	....	.250	.250	.250	.500	51	-0	0	2.31	-1	/S-2	0	-0.1

• CARISCH, Fred Frederick Behlmer Carisch b: 11/14/1881, Fountain City, WI d: 4/19/1977, San Gabriel, CA BR/TR, 5'10.5", 174 lbs. Deb: 8/31/1903 C

YEAR TM-L	G	AB	R	H	2B	3B	HR	RBI	BB	SO	SB	CS	AVG	OBP	SLG	OPS	OPS+	BR/A	RC	RC/G	FR	G/POS	WS	TPW
1903 Pit-N	5	18	4	6	4	0	1	5	0	....	0	....	.333	.333	.722	1.056	192	2	4	9.81	1	/C-4	1	0.3
1904 Pit-N	37	125	9	31	3	1	0	8	9	....	3	....	.248	.299	.288	.587	79	-3	12	3.30	2	C-22,1-14	3	0.1
1905 Pit-N	32	107	7	22	0	3	0	8	2	....	1	....	.206	.227	.262	.489	44	-8	7	2.10	0	C-30	2	-0.4
1906 Pit-N	4	12	0	1	0	0	0	0	1	....	1	....	.083	.154	.083	.237	-25	-2	0	.75	-1	/C-4	0	-0.2
1912 Cle-A	24	69	4	19	3	1	0	5	1	....	3	....	.275	.286	.348	.634	78	-2	8	3.77	3	C-23	2	0.2
1913 Cle-A	82	222	11	48	4	2	0	26	21	19	6	....	.216	.287	.252	.539	56	-12	17	2.42	3	C-79	6	-0.4
1914 Cle-A	40	102	8	22	3	2	0	5	12	18	2	2	.216	.298	.284	.583	72	-4	9	2.84	0	C-38	2	-0.2
1923 Det-A	2	0	0	0	0	0	0	0	0	0	0	0	....	....	....	....	-102	0	0	....	-1	/C-2	0	0.0
Total 8	226	655	43	149	17	9	1	57	46	37	16	2	.227	.280	.285	.566	65	-29	57	2.87	7	C-202/1-14	16	-0.6

• CARL, Fred Frederick E. Carl b: 9/8/1858, Baltimore, MD d: 5/4/1919, Washington, DC BL/TL, 5'6", 158 lbs. Deb: 7/25/1889

YEAR TM-L	G	AB	R	H	2B	3B	HR	RBI	BB	SO	SB	CS	AVG	OBP	SLG	OPS	OPS+	BR/A	RC	RC/G	FR	G/POS	WS	TPW
1889 Lou-a	25	99	13	20	2	2	0	13	16	22	0	....	.202	.313	.263	.576	66	-4	8	2.80	0	0-18(2-4-12)/2-6,3-1	1	-0.4

• CARL, Lew Lewis Adolph Carl b: 1836, Baltimore, MD d: 5/19/1885, Newark, NJ Deb: 9/9/1874

YEAR TM-L	G	AB	R	H	2B	3B	HR	RBI	BB	SO	SB	CS	AVG	OBP	SLG	OPS	OPS+	BR/A	RC	RC/G	FR	G/POS	WS	TPW
1874 Bal-n	1	3	0	0	0	0	0	0	0	0	0	0	.000	.000	.000	.000	-101	-1	0	.00	-1	/C-1	....	-0.1

• CARLETON, Jim James Leslie Carleton b: 8/20/1848, Clinton, CT d: 4/25/1910, Detroit, MI, 5'8", 155 lbs. Deb: 5/4/1871

YEAR TM-L	G	AB	R	H	2B	3B	HR	RBI	BB	SO	SB	CS	AVG	OBP	SLG	OPS	OPS+	BR/A	RC	RC/G	FR	G/POS	WS	TPW
1871 Cle-n	29	127	31	32	8	1	0	18	8	3	2	1	.252	.296	.331	.627	84	-2	13	4.38	1	*1-29	....	0.0
1872 Cle-n	7	38	8	12	1	0	0	4	1	0	1	0	.316	.333	.342	.675	114	1	5	5.70	1	/1-7	....	0.2
Total 2 n	36	165	39	44	9	1	0	22	9	3	3	1	.267	.305	.333	.638	91	-1	18	4.67	2	/1-36	....	0.1

• CARLIN, Jim James Arthur Carlin b: 2/23/1918, Wylam, AL BR/TR, 5'11", 165 lbs. Deb: 7/26/1941

YEAR TM-L	G	AB	R	H	2B	3B	HR	RBI	BB	SO	SB	CS	AVG	OBP	SLG	OPS	OPS+	BR/A	RC	RC/G	FR	G/POS	WS	TPW
1941 Phi-N	16	21	2	3	1	0	1	2	3	4	0	....	.143	.250	.333	.583	66	-1	2	2.30	-1	/0-9(0-4-5),3-2	0	-0.2

YEAR TM-L	G	AB	R	H	2B	3B	HR	RBI	BB	SO	SB	CS	AVG	OBP	SLG	OPS	OPS+	BR/A	RC	RC/G	FR	G/POS	WS	TPW
• CARLISLE, Walter	Walter G. "Rosy" Carlisle b: 7/6/1883, Yorkshire, England d: 5/27/1945, Los Angeles, CA BB/TR, 5'9", 154 lbs. Deb: 5/8/1908																							
1908 Bos-A	3	10	0	1	0	0	0	0	1	....	1	....	.100	.182	.100	.282	-8	-1	0	.97	1	/O-3(3-0-0)	0	-0.1
• CARLSTROM, Swede	Albin Oscar Carlstrom b: 10/26/1886, Elizabeth, NJ d: 4/23/1935, Elizabeth, NJ BR/TR, 6', 167 lbs. Deb: 9/12/1911																							
1911 Bos-A	2	6	0	1	0	0	0	0	0	....	0	....	.167	.167	.167	.333	-7	-1	0	.97	0	/S-2	0	0.0
• CARLYLE, Cleo	Hiram Cleo Carlyle b: 9/7/1902, Fairburn, GA d: 11/12/1967, Los Angeles, CA BL/TR, 6', 170 lbs. Deb: 5/16/1927																							
1927 Bos-A	95	278	31	65	12	8	1	28	36	40	4	4	.234	.324	.345	.669	75	-11	33	3.82	-1	O-83(30-3-50)	4	-1.6
• CARLYLE, Roy	Roy Edward "Dizzy" Carlyle b: 12/10/1900, Buford, GA d: 11/22/1956, Norcross, GA BL/TR, 6'2.5", 195 lbs. Deb: 4/16/1925 Career OF: 43-0-77																							
1925 Was-A	1	1	0	0	0	0	0	0	0	1	0	0	.000	.000	.000	.000	-102	-0	0	.00	0	....	0	0.0
Bos-A	93	276	36	90	20	3	7	49	16	28	1	1	.326	.365	.496	.862	117	6	49	6.74	-6	O-67(43-0-24)	7	-0.5
Yr.	94	277	36	90	20	3	7	49	16	29	1	1	.325	.364	.495	.859	116	6	49	6.71	-6	O-67(43-0-24)	7	-0.5
1926 Bos-A	45	165	22	47	6	2	2	16	4	18	0	0	.285	.310	.382	.692	82	-5	19	4.31	-3	O-38(0-0-38)	2	-1.0
NY-A	35	62	3	20	5	1	0	11	4	9	0	0	.323	.373	.435	.809	112	1	10	6.40	0	O-15(0-0-15)	3	0.0
Yr.	80	227	25	67	11	3	2	27	8	27	0	0	.295	.328	.396	.724	91	-4	29	4.86	-3	O-53(0-0-53)	5	-1.0
Total 2	**174**	**504**	**61**	**157**	**31**	**6**	**9**	**76**	**24**	**56**	**1**	**1**	**.312**	**.348**	**.450**	**.798**	**105**	**2**	**79**	**5.87**	**-9**	**O-120**	**12**	**-1.5**
• CARMAN, George	George Wartman Carman b: 3/29/1866, Philadelphia, PA d: 6/16/1929, Lancaster, PA Deb: 9/4/1890																							
1890 Phi-a	27	93	9	16	2	0	0	7	8	....	5	....	.172	.245	.194	.439	30	-8	6	1.99	-9	S-14,O-10(0-0-10)/2-2,3-1	0	-1.5
• CARMEL, Duke	Leon James Carmel b: 4/23/1937, New York, NY BL/TL, 6'3", 202 lbs. Deb: 9/10/1959 Career OF: 28-35-12																							
1959 StL-N	10	23	2	3	1	0	0	3	1	6	0	1	.130	.167	.174	.341	-9	-4	1	.68	-1	O-10(2-8-3)	0	-0.5
1960 StL-N	4	3	0	0	0	0	0	0	1	1	1	1	.000	.250	.000	.250	-23	-1	0	.00	0	/1-2,O-1	0	-0.1
1963 StL-N	57	44	9	10	1	0	1	2	9	11	0	0	.227	.358	.318	.677	88	-0	6	4.65	-1	O-38(26-6-8)/1-1	2	-0.3
NY-N	47	149	11	35	5	3	3	18	16	37	2	2	.235	.309	.369	.678	93	-2	18	4.08	-3	O-21(0-21-0),1-18	4	-0.7
Yr.	104	193	20	45	6	3	4	20	25	48	2	2	.233	.321	.358	.679	92	-2	24	4.21	-4	O-59(26-27-8),1-19	6	-0.9
1965 NY-A	6	8	0	0	0	0	0	0	0	5	0	0	.000	.000	.000	.000	-101	-2	0	.00	0	/1-2	0	-0.2
Total 4	**124**	**227**	**22**	**48**	**7**	**3**	**4**	**23**	**27**	**60**	**3**	**4**	**.211**	**.295**	**.322**	**.617**	**75**	**-9**	**24**	**3.53**	**-5**	**/O-70,1-23**	**6**	**-1.7**
• CARNETT, Eddie	Edwin Elliott "Lefty" Carnett b: 10/21/1916, Springfield, MO BL/TL, 6', 185 lbs. Deb: 4/19/1941 Career OF: 70-26-13 ♦																							
1941 Bos-N	2	0	0	0	0	0	0	0	0	0	0	0	....	....	....	....	-104	0	0	....	0	/P-2	0	-0.3
1944 Chi-A	126	457	51	126	18	8	1	60	26	35	5	2	.276	.322	.357	.678	95	-3	55	4.33	-7	O-88(62-25-6),1-25/P-2	13	-1.8
1945 Cle-A	30	73	5	16	7	0	0	7	2	9	0	1	.219	.250	.315	.565	66	-4	5	2.49	-1	O-16(8-1-7)/P-2	1	-0.5
Total 3	**158**	**530**	**56**	**142**	**25**	**8**	**1**	**67**	**28**	**44**	**5**	**3**	**.268**	**.312**	**.351**	**.663**	**91**	**-7**	**60**	**4.06**	**-7**	**O-104/1-25,P-6**	**14**	**-2.6**
• CARNEY, Bill	William John Carney b: 3/25/1874, St. Paul, MN d: 7/31/1938, Hopkins, MN BB/TR, 5'10" Deb: 8/22/1904																							
1904 Chi-N	2	7	0	0	0	0	0	0	1	....	0	....	.000	.125	.000	.125	-60	-1	0	.00	1	/O-2(0-0-2)	0	-0.1
• CARNEY, John	John Joseph "Handsome Jack" Carney b: 11/10/1866, Salem, MA d: 10/19/1925, Litchfield, NH BR/TR, 5'10.5", 175 lbs. Deb: 4/24/1889 U Career OF: 2-0-37																							
1889 Was-N	69	273	25	63	7	0	1	29	14	14	12	....	.231	.271	.267	.538	54	-17	24	2.98	-8	1-53,O-16(1-0-15)	1	-2.5
1890 Buf-P	28	107	11	29	3	0	0	13	7	14	2	....	.271	.333	.299	.632	76	-3	12	4.02	-2	1-24/O-4(1-0-3)	1	-0.5
Cle-P	25	89	15	31	5	3	0	21	14	5	6	....	.348	.442	.472	.914	157	8	22	10.13	-2	O-19(0-0-19)/1-6	4	0.4
Yr.	53	196	26	60	8	3	0	34	21	19	8	....	.306	.385	.378	.762	114	5	33	6.63	-4	1-30,O-23(1-0-22)	5	-0.1
1891 Cin-a	99	367	47	102	10	8	3	43	35	18	15	....	.278	.346	.373	.719	97	-3	54	5.39	2	*1-99	8	-0.8
Mil-a	31	110	22	33	5	2	3	23	13	8	5	....	.300	.389	.464	.853	119	2	22	7.68	5	1-31	5	0.3
Yr.	130	477	69	135	15	10	6	66	48	26	20	....	.283	.356	.394	.750	102	-1	76	5.90	7	*1-130	13	-0.5
Total 3	**252**	**946**	**120**	**258**	**30**	**13**	**7**	**129**	**83**	**59**	**40**	**....**	**.273**	**.338**	**.354**	**.693**	**91**	**-13**	**133**	**5.15**	**-5**	**1-213/O-39**	**19**	**-3.1**
• CARNEY, Pat	Patrick Joseph "Doc" Carney b: 8/7/1876, Holyoke, MA d: 1/9/1953, Worcester, MA BL/TL, 6', 200 lbs. Deb: 9/20/1901 Career OF: 8-9-298 ♦																							
1901 Bos-N	13	55	6	16	2	1	0	6	3	....	0	....	.291	.339	.364	.703	95	-0	7	4.72	-2	O-13(0-0-13)	1	-0.3
1902 Bos-N	137	522	75	141	17	4	2	65	42	....	27	....	.270	.339	.330	.668	105	5	70	4.79	-8	*O-137(3-0-135)/P-2	17	-1.3
1903 Bos-N	110	392	37	94	12	4	1	49	28	....	10	....	.240	.297	.298	.596	73	-11	39	3.44	-2	O-92(3-0-90),P-10/1-1	8	-2.4
1904 Bos-N	78	279	24	57	5	2	0	11	12	....	6	....	.204	.240	.237	.476	49	-16	19	2.10	0	O-71(2-9-60)/P-4,1-1	1	-2.8
Total 4	**338**	**1248**	**142**	**308**	**36**	**11**	**3**	**131**	**85**	**....**	**43**	**....**	**.247**	**.304**	**.300**	**.605**	**82**	**-23**	**134**	**3.71**	**-12**	**O-313/P-16,1-2**	**27**	**-6.9**
• CARPENTER, Bubba	Charles Sydney Carpenter b: 7/23/1968, Dallas, TX BL/TL, 6'1", 185 lbs. Deb: 5/13/2000																							
2000 Col-N	15	27	4	6	0	0	3	5	4	13	0	0	.222	.323	.556	.878	93	-0	5	6.65	-1	/O-6(5-0-1),D-2	1	-0.2
• CARPENTER, Hick	Warren William Carpenter b: 8/16/1855, Grafton, MA d: 4/18/1937, San Diego, CA BR/TL, 5'11", 186 lbs. Deb: 5/1/1879 Career OF: 0-0-12																							
1879 Syr-N	65	261	30	53	6	0	0	20	2	15	....	....	.203	.209	.226	.435	49	-12	13	1.70	-4	1-34,3-18,O-11(0-0-11)/2-3	2	-1.6
1880 Cin-N	77	300	32	72	6	4	0	23	2	15	....	....	.240	.245	.287	.532	80	-6	22	2.61	2	*3-67/1-9,S-1	5	-0.2
1881 Wor-N	83	347	40	75	12	2	2	31	3	19	....	....	.216	.223	.280	.502	54	-19	22	2.20	-1	*3-83	4	-1.7
1882 Cin-a	80	351	78	**120**	15	5	1	**67**	10	....	....	....	.342	.360	.422	.782	154	18	55	6.62	6	*3-80	18	2.4
1883 Cin-a	95	435	99	130	18	4	3	40	19	....	....	....	.299	.328	.379	.708	120	9	56	5.10	8	*3-95	16	1.6
1884 Cin-a	108	474	80	121	16	2	4	60	6	....	....	....	.255	.271	.323	.593	88	-8	42	3.31	0	*3-108/O-1	12	-0.5
1885 Cin-a	112	473	89	131	12	8	2	61	9	....	....	....	.277	.295	.349	.644	101	-1	50	3.94	0	*3-112	13	0.1
1886 Cin-a	111	458	67	101	8	5	2	61	18	....	8	....	.221	.262	.273	.535	66	-20	36	2.71	-8	*3-111	7	-2.2
1887 Cin-a	127	517	70	143	12	6	1	50	19	....	44	....	.277	.282	.303	.585	62	-27	56	4.07	-6	*3-127	7	-2.5
1888 Cin-a	136	551	68	147	14	5	3	67	5	....	59	....	.267	.280	.327	.607	89	-10	69	4.58	-8	*3-136	14	-1.4
1889 Cin-a	123	486	67	127	23	6	0	63	18	41	47	....	.261	.293	.333	.627	76	-18	63	4.64	-21	*3-121/1-2	7	-3.1
1892 StL-N	1	3	0	1	0	0	0	0	1	1	0	....	.333	.500	.333	.833	161	0	1	6.92	0	/3-1	0	0.0
Total 12	**1118**	**4656**	**720**	**1221**	**142**	**47**	**18**	**543**	**112**	**91**	**158**	**....**	**.262**	**.281**	**.322**	**.603**	**86**	**-95**	**483**	**3.83**	**-33**	***3-1059/1-45,O-12,2-3,S-1**	**105**	**-9.1**
• CARR, Charlie	Charles Carbitt Carr b: 12/27/1876, Coatesville, PA d: 11/25/1932, Memphis, TN BR/TR, 6'2", 195 lbs. Deb: 9/15/1898																							
1898 Was-N	20	73	6	14	2	0	0	4	2	....	2	....	.192	.213	.219	.433	24	-7	4	1.79	-3	1-20	0	-1.0
1901 Phi-A	2	8	0	1	0	0	0	0	0	....	0	....	.125	.125	.125	.250	-29	-1	0	.49	0	/1-2	0	-0.1
1903 Det-A	135	548	59	154	23	11	2	79	10	....	10	....	.281	.296	.374	.671	103	0	67	4.34	8	*1-135	13	0.6
1904 Det-A	92	360	29	77	13	3	0	40	14	....	6	....	.214	.245	.267	.512	64	-15	28	2.43	11	1-92	2	-0.7
Cle-A	32	120	9	27	5	1	0	7	4	....	0	....	.225	.250	.283	.533	69	-4	9	2.50	-1	1-32	1	-0.7
Yr.	124	480	38	104	18	4	0	47	18	....	6	....	.217	.246	.271	.517	65	-20	37	2.45	10	*1-124	3	-1.4
1905 Cle-A	89	306	29	72	12	4	1	31	13	....	12	....	.235	.266	.310	.577	82	-7	31	3.28	5	1-87	5	-0.4
1906 Cin-N	22	94	9	18	2	3	0	10	2	....	0	....	.191	.216	.277	.493	51	-6	6	1.98	0	1-22	0	-0.7
1914 Ind-F	115	441	44	129	11	10	3	69	26	47	19	....	.293	.333	.383	.717	93	-5	60	4.70	-5	*1-115	10	-1.2
Total 7	**507**	**1950**	**185**	**492**	**68**	**32**	**6**	**240**	**71**	**47**	**49**	**....**	**.252**	**.280**	**.329**	**.610**	**82**	**-47**	**205**	**3.51**	**16**	**1-505**	**31**	**-4.1**
• CARR, Chuck	Charles Lee Glenn Carr b: 8/10/1967, San Bernardino, CA BB/TR, 5'10", 165 lbs. Deb: 4/28/1990 Career OF: 7-473-6																							
1990 NY-N	4	2	0	0	0	0	0	0	0	2	1	0	.000	.000	.000	.000	-100	-0	0	.00	0	/O-1	0	-0.1
1991 NY-N	12	11	1	2	0	0	0	1	0	2	1	0	.182	.182	.182	.364	3	-1	0	1.37	0	/O-9(0-9-0)	0	-0.2
1992 StL-N	22	64	8	14	3	0	0	3	9	6	10	2	.219	.315	.266	.581	68	-1	7	3.54	0	O-19(5-9-6)	1	-0.2
1993 Fla-N	142	551	75	147	19	2	4	41	49	74	**58**	22	.267	.329	.330	.659	73	-18	64	3.91	2	*O-139(0-139-0)	12	-1.4
1994 Fla-N	106	433	61	114	19	2	2	30	22	71	32	8	.263	.307	.330	.637	64	-20	47	3.70	4	*O-104(0-104-0)	8	-1.5
1995 Fla-N	105	308	54	70	20	0	2	20	46	49	25	11	.227	.331	.312	.643	71	-12	36	3.76	-1	*O-103(0-103-0)	6	-1.2
1996 Mil-A	27	106	18	29	6	1	1	11	6	21	5	4	.274	.313	.377	.690	71	-6	12	3.86	2	O-27(0-27-0)	4	-0.3
1997 Mil-A	26	46	3	6	3	0	0	0	2	11	1	0	.130	.184	.196	.379	-1	-7	2	1.28	0	O-23(0-23-0)/D-1	0	-0.6
*Hou-N	63	192	34	53	11	2	4	17	15	37	11	5	.276	.335	.417	.752	99	-0	28	5.02	0	O-60(1-59-0)	5	0.0
Total 8	**507**	**1713**	**254**	**435**	**81**	**7**	**13**	**123**	**149**	**273**	**144**	**52**	**.254**	**.318**	**.332**	**.650**	**70**	**-64**	**197**	**3.83**	**7**	**O-485/D-1**	**36**	**-5.3**
• CARR, Lew	Lewis Smith Carr b: 8/15/1872, Union Springs, NY d: 6/15/1954, Moravia, NY BR/TR, 6'2", 200 lbs. Deb: 7/4/1901																							
1901 Pit-N	9	28	2	7	1	1	0	4	2	....	0	....	.250	.344	.357	.701	100	0	4	4.45	-2	/S-9,3-1	1	-0.1

YEAR TM-L	G	AB	R	H	2B	3B	HR	RBI	BB	SO	SB	CS	AVG	OBP	SLG	OPS	OPS+	BR/A	RC	RC/G	FR	G/POS	WS	TPW
• CARRASQUEL, Chico	Alfonso (Colon) Carrasquel b: 1/23/1926, Caracas, Venezuela BR/TR, 6', 170 lbs. Deb: 4/18/1950																							
1950 Chi-A	141	524	72	148	21	5	4	46	66	46	0	2	.282	.368	.365	.733	91	-6	73	4.89	9	*S-141	14	1.1
1951 Chi-A★	147	538	41	142	22	4	2	58	46	39	14	4	.264	.325	.331	.656	79	-14	60	3.88	24	*S-147	17	2.0
1952 Chi-A	100	359	36	89	7	4	1	42	33	27	2	2	.248	.315	.298	.613	71	-14	36	3.45	-3	S-99	8	-1.1
1953 Chi-A★	149	552	72	154	30	4	2	47	38	47	5	3	.279	.330	.359	.689	83	-13	65	4.14	4	*S-149	16	0.3
1954 Chi-A★	155	620	106	158	28	3	12	62	85	67	7	6	.255	.349	.368	.717	93	-4	84	4.68	19	*S-155	24	2.8
1955 Chi-A★	145	523	83	134	11	2	11	52	61	59	1	1	.256	.338	.348	.686	82	-12	64	4.24	0	*S-144	15	-0.1
1956 Cle-A	141	474	60	115	15	1	7	48	52	61	0	4	.243	.325	.323	.648	70	-21	51	3.60	-2	*S-141/3-1	12	-1.2
1957 Cle-A	125	392	37	108	14	1	8	57	41	53	0	2	.276	.356	.378	.734	101	1	51	4.43	-3	*S-122	14	0.9
1958 Cle-A	49	156	14	40	6	0	2	21	14	12	0	0	.256	.318	.333	.651	81	-4	16	3.61	-3	S-32,3-14	3	-0.5
KC-A	59	160	19	34	5	1	2	13	21	15	0	1	.213	.304	.294	.598	64	-8	15	3.06	-3	3-32,S-22	3	-1.0
Yr.	108	316	33	74	11	1	4	34	35	27	0	1	.234	.311	.313	.624	72	-11	31	3.33	-7	S-54,3-46	6	-1.5
1959 Bal-A	114	346	28	77	13	0	4	28	34	41	2	3	.223	.294	.295	.589	64	-18	30	2.74	3	S-89,2-22/3-2,1-1	6	-0.8
Total 10	1325	4644	568	1199	172	25	55	474	491	467	31	28	.258	.334	.342	.676	82	-112	546	4.02	45	*S-1241/3-49,2-22,1-1	132	2.3
• CARREON, Cam	Camilo Carreon b: 8/6/1937, Colton, CA d: 9/2/1987, Tucson, AZ BR/TR, 6'1.5", 198 lbs. Deb: 9/27/1959																							
1959 Chi-A	1	1	0	0	0	0	0	0	0	0	0	0	.000	.000	.000	.000	-101	-0	0	.00	-0	/C-1	0	0.0
1960 Chi-A	8	17	2	4	0	0	0	2	1	3	0	0	.235	.278	.235	.513	41	-1	1	2.46	0	/C-7	0	-0.1
1961 Chi-A	78	229	32	62	5	1	4	27	21	24	0	1	.271	.332	.354	.686	85	-5	26	3.93	-1	C-71	8	-0.3
1962 Chi-A	106	313	31	80	19	1	4	37	33	37	1	1	.256	.329	.361	.690	86	-6	36	3.96	-3	C-93	10	-0.4
1963 Chi-A	101	270	28	74	10	1	2	35	23	32	1	1	.274	.333	.341	.674	91	-3	30	3.80	1	C-92	8	0.2
1964 Chi-A	37	95	12	26	5	0	0	4	7	13	0	0	.274	.330	.326	.656	86	-2	9	3.29	1	C-34	3	0.0
1965 Cle-A	19	52	6	12	2	1	1	7	9	6	1	1	.231	.344	.365	.710	101	0	6	3.85	0	C-19	2	0.2
1966 Bal-A	4	9	2	2	2	0	0	2	3	2	0	0	.222	.417	.444	.861	150	1	2	7.68	0	/C-3	1	0.1
Total 8	354	986	113	260	43	4	11	114	97	117	3	4	.264	.331	.349	.680	88	-17	111	3.84	-1	C-320	32	-0.3
• CARREON, Mark	Mark Steven Carreon b: 7/19/1963, Chicago, IL BR/TL, 6', 195 lbs. Deb: 9/8/1987 Career OF: 175-68-151																							
1987 NY-N	9	12	0	3	0	0	0	1	1	1	0	1	.250	.308	.250	.558	53	-1	1	2.03	0	/0-5(5-0-0)	0	-0.2
1988 NY-N	7	9	5	5	2	0	1	1	2	1	0	0	.556	.636	1.111	1.747	413	4	7	45.19	0	/0-4(4-0-0)	2	0.4
1989 NY-N	68	133	20	41	6	0	6	16	12	17	2	3	.308	.370	.489	.859	151	7	24	6.69	-1	0-39(18-0-21)	5	0.6
1990 NY-N	82	188	30	47	12	0	10	26	15	29	1	0	.250	.312	.473	.786	113	3	29	5.49	-1	0-60(16-36-13)	7	0.1
1991 NY-N	106	254	18	66	6	0	4	21	12	26	2	1	.260	.299	.331	.629	77	-8	22	2.89	0	0-77(43-22-22)	1	-1.1
1992 Det-A	101	336	34	78	11	1	10	41	22	57	3	1	.232	.281	.360	.641	78	-11	32	3.09	0	0-83(64-1-19),D-13	3	-1.5
1993 SF-N	78	150	22	49	9	1	7	33	13	16	1	0	.327	.384	.540	.924	149	10	28	6.72	-1	0-41(9-5-30)/1-3	8	0.8
1994 SF-N	51	100	8	27	4	0	3	20	7	20	0	0	.270	.330	.400	.730	94	-1	14	4.86	-1	0-33(10-0-24)	4	-0.3
1995 SF-N	117	396	53	119	24	0	17	65	23	37	0	1	.301	.345	.490	.835	121	10	66	6.14	-2	1-81,0-22(3-0-19)	15	-0.1
1996 SF-N	81	292	40	76	22	3	9	51	22	33	2	3	.260	.319	.449	.767	104	-1	40	4.77	-4	1-73/0-5(3-0-2)	7	-1.0
Cle-A	38	142	16	46	12	0	2	14	11	9	1	1	.324	.385	.451	.835	111	2	24	6.42	-1	1-34/0-5(0-4-1),D-2	4	-0.2
Total 10	738	2012	246	557	108	5	69	289	140	246	12	11	.277	.330	.438	.768	108	14	285	5.01	-12	0-374,1-191/D-15	56	-2.3
• CARRIGAN, Bill	William Francis "Rough" Carrigan b: 10/22/1883, Lewiston, ME d: 7/8/1969, Lewiston, ME BR/TR, 5'9", 175 lbs. Deb: 7/7/1906 M																							
1906 Bos-A	37	109	5	23	0	0	0	10	5	....	3	....	.211	.252	.211	.463	45	-7	7	2.11	0	C-35	1	-0.3
1908 Bos-A	57	149	13	35	5	2	0	14	3	....	1	....	.235	.255	.295	.550	76	-4	12	2.49	5	C-47/1-3	4	0.5
1909 Bos-A	94	280	25	83	13	2	1	36	17	....	2	....	.296	.341	.368	.709	121	6	36	4.49	1	C-77/1-8	12	1.7
1910 Bos-A	114	342	36	85	11	1	3	53	23	....	10	....	.249	.307	.313	.620	92	-3	37	3.48	-15	*C-110	8	-0.9
1911 Bos-A	72	232	29	67	6	1	1	30	26	....	5	....	.289	.373	.336	.709	99	1	31	4.74	0	C-62/1-6	8	0.5
1912*Bos-A	87	266	34	70	7	1	0	24	38	....	7	....	.263	.359	.297	.656	84	-4	31	4.00	-7	C-87	10	-0.5
1913 Bos-A	87	256	17	62	15	5	0	28	27	26	6	....	.242	.319	.340	.659	91	-3	29	3.66	5	C-82	9	0.8
1914 Bos-A	82	178	18	45	5	1	1	22	40	18	1	2	.253	.395	.309	.704	112	5	24	4.35	0	C-78	11	1.2
1915*Bos-A	46	95	10	19	3	0	0	7	16	12	0	....	.200	.321	.232	.553	68	-3	8	2.70	2	C-44	4	0.2
1916*Bos-A	33	63	7	17	2	1	0	11	11	3	2	....	.270	.378	.333	.712	113	2	9	4.87	-2	C-27	4	0.2
Total 10	709	1970	194	506	67	14	6	235	206	59	37	2	.257	.334	.314	.648	94	-11	224	3.77	-12	C-649/1-17	71	3.3
• CARRILLO, Matias	Matias (Garcia) Carrillo b: 2/24/1963, Los Mochis, Mexico BL/TL, 5'11", 190 lbs. Deb: 5/23/1991 Career OF: 27-13-34																							
1991 Mil-A	3	0	0	0	0	0	0	0	0	0	0	0	....	....	....	....	-103	0	0	....	0	/0-3(3-0-0)	0	-0.1
1993 Fla-N	24	55	4	14	6	0	0	3	1	7	0	0	.255	.281	.364	.644	67	-3	4	2.29	0	0-16(4-5-9)	0	-0.3
1994 Fla-N	80	136	13	34	7	0	0	9	9	31	3	3	.250	.297	.301	.598	55	-10	11	2.65	2	0-49(20-8-25)	1	-0.9
Total 3	107	191	17	48	13	0	0	12	10	38	3	3	.251	.292	.319	.611	58	-12	15	2.54	1	/0-68	1	-1.3
• CARROLL, Chick	Edward Carroll b: 1868, AR d: 7/13/1908, Chicago, IL Deb: 4/17/1884																							
1884 Was-U	4	16	1	4	0	0	0	....	0	....	....	....	.250	.250	.250	.500	72	-0	1	2.39	-1	/0-4(4-0-0)	0	-0.1
• CARROLL, Cliff	Samuel Clifford Carroll b: 10/18/1859, Clay Grove, IA d: 6/12/1923, Portland, OR BB/TR, 5'8", 163 lbs. Deb: 8/3/1882 Career OF: 731-4-260																							
1882 Pro-N	10	41	4	5	0	0	0	2	0	4	....	....	.122	.122	.122	.244	-22	-5	1	.48	2	0-10(2-0-8)	1	-0.3
1883 Pro-N	58	238	37	63	12	3	1	20	4	28	....	....	.265	.277	.353	.630	87	-4	24	3.75	6	0-58(56-1-1)	7	0.0
1884*Pro-N	113	452	90	118	16	4	3	54	29	39	....	....	.261	.306	.334	.640	103	3	47	3.89	2	*0-113(113-0-0)	17	0.0
1885 Pro-N	104	426	62	99	12	3	1	40	29	29	....	....	.232	.281	.282	.563	86	-5	35	2.86	3	*0-104(104-0-0)	12	-0.6
1886 Was-N	111	433	73	99	11	6	2	22	44	26	31	....	.229	.300	.296	.595	86	-4	49	3.95	-2	*0-111(109-1-1)	6	-0.9
1887 Was-N	103	437	79	121	17	4	4	37	17	30	40	....	.277	.291	.336	.627	78	-12	54	4.53	0	*0-103(102-1-0)	6	-1.3
1888 Pit-N	5	20	1	0	0	0	0	0	0	8	2	....	.000	.000	.000	.000	-108	-4	0	.00	-1	/0-5(1-0-4)	0	-0.5
1890 Chi-N	136	582	134	166	16	6	7	65	53	34	34	....	.285	.352	.369	.721	106	4	90	5.72	14	*0-136(112-0-24)	20	1.1
1891 Chi-N	130	515	87	132	20	8	7	80	50	42	31	....	.256	.340	.367	.707	106	4	77	5.40	-2	*0-130(0-1-130)	16	0.0
1892 StL-N	101	407	82	111	14	8	4	49	47	22	30	....	.273	.363	.376	.739	130	17	68	6.22	2	*0-101(99-0-3)	13	0.9
1893 Bos-N	120	438	80	98	7	5	2	54	88	28	29	....	.224	.360	.276	.636	65	-20	55	4.31	0	*0-120(33-0-89)	11	-2.3
Total 11	991	3989	729	1012	125	47	31	423	361	290	197	....	.254	.320	.329	.649	93	-29	499	4.51	22	0-991	109	-3.9
• CARROLL, Dixie	Dorsey Lee Carroll b: 5/9/1891, Paducah, KY d: 10/13/1984, Jacksonville, FL BL/TR, 5'11", 165 lbs. Deb: 9/12/1919																							
1919 Bos-N	15	49	10	13	3	1	0	7	7	1	5	....	.265	.379	.367	.747	130	2	8	5.78	2	0-13(6-8-1)	2	0.3
• CARROLL, Doc	Ralph Arthur "Red" Carroll b: 12/28/1891, Worcester, MA d: 6/27/1983, Worcester, MA BR/TR, 6', 170 lbs. Deb: 6/27/1916																							
1916 Phi-A	10	22	1	2	0	0	0	0	1	8	0	....	.091	.167	.091	.258	-24	-3	1	.67	0	C-10	0	-0.3
• CARROLL, Fred	Frederick Herbert Carroll b: 7/2/1864, Sacramento, CA d: 11/7/1904, San Rafael, CA BR/TR, 5'11", 185 lbs. Deb: 5/1/1884 U Career OF: 144-67-108																							
1884 Col-a	69	252	46	70	13	5	6	0	13	....	....	....	.278	.326	.440	.766	160	17	37	5.60	5	C-54,0-15(12-2-1)	14	2.4
1885 Pit-a	71	280	45	75	13	8	0	30	7	....	....	....	.268	.298	.371	.669	112	3	32	4.18	4	C-60,0-12(10-2-0)	9	1.1
1886 Pit-a	122	486	92	140	28	11	5	64	52	....	20	....	.288	.362	.422	.783	146	26	83	6.51	-12	C-70,0-27(15-10-2),1-25/S-1	22	1.5
1887 Pit-N	102	457	71	174	24	15	6	54	36	21	23	....	.381	.383	.499	.882	152	30	92	8.58	-15	0-46(8-33-5),C-40,1-17/S-1	18	1.4
1888 Pit-N	97	366	62	91	14	5	2	48	32	31	18	....	.249	.326	.331	.657	119	10	46	4.56	-16	C-54,0-38(31-2-5)/1-5,3-1	13	-0.3
1889 Pit-N	91	318	80	105	21	11	2	51	85	26	19	....	.330	.486	.484	.970	190	49	86	10.71	-3	C-43,0-41(24-12-5)/1-7,3-1	23	4.1
1890 Pit-P	111	416	95	124	20	7	2	71	75	22	35	....	.298	.418	.394	.813	128	24	85	7.89	-11	C-56,0-49(42-6-1)/1-7	16	1.2
1891 Pit-N	91	353	55	77	13	4	4	48	48	36	22	....	.218	.315	.312	.627	85	-6	43	4.17	4	0-91(2-0-89)	8	-0.3
Total 8	754	2928	546	856	146	66	27	366	348	136	137	....	.292	.370	.408	.778	137	154	504	6.54	-43	C-377,0-319/1-61,3-2,S-2	123	11.2
• CARROLL, Jamey	Jamey Blake Carroll b: 2/18/1974, Evansville, IN BR/TR, 5'10", 175 lbs. Deb: 9/11/2002																							
2002 Mon-N	16	71	16	22	5	3	1	6	4	12	1	0	.310	.347	.507	.854	117	2	13	6.27	-3	3-13/S-3,2-1	3	0.0
2003 Mon-N	105	227	31	59	10	1	1	10	19	39	5	2	.260	.325	.326	.651	60	-13	23	3.30	8	3-67,S-14,2-11	3	-0.4
Total 2	121	298	47	81	15	4	2	16	23	51	6	2	.272	.330	.369	.699	73	-11	36	3.96	5	/3-80,S-17,2-12	6	-0.4
• CARROLL, Pat	Patrick Carroll b: 3/1853, Philadelphia, PA d: 2/14/1916, Philadelphia, PA Deb: 5/10/1884 U																							
1884 Alt-U	11	49	4	13	1	0	0	....	1	....	....	....	.265	.280	.286	.566	91	-1	4	3.13	-1	/C-8,0-3(0-0-3)	0	-0.1
Phi-U	5	19	1	3	1	0	0	....	0	....	....	....	.158	.158	.211	.368	25	-1	1	1.13	4	/C-5	0	0.3

YEAR TM-L	G	AB	R	H	2B	3B	HR	RBI	BB	SO	SB	CS	AVG	OBP	SLG	OPS	OPS+	BR/A	RC	RC/G	FR	G/POS	WS	TPW
Yr.	16	68	5	16	2	0	0	....	1	....	....	....	.235	.246	.265	.511	73	-2	5	2.51	3	C-13/0-3(0-0-3)	0	0.2

• CARROLL, Scrappy John E. Carroll b: 8/27/1860, Buffalo, NY d: 11/14/1942, Buffalo, NY BR, 5'7.5" Deb: 9/27/1884 Career OF: 21-6-48

YEAR TM-L	G	AB	R	H	2B	3B	HR	RBI	BB	SO	SB	CS	AVG	OBP	SLG	OPS	OPS+	BR/A	RC	RC/G	FR	G/POS	WS	TPW
1884 StP-U	9	31	3	3	1	0	0	....	2	....	....	....	.097	.152	.129	.281	-4	-3	1	.62	3	/0-8(0-0-8),3-2	0	-0.1
1885 Buf-N	13	40	1	3	0	0	0	1	2	8	....	....	.075	.119	.075	.194	-35	-6	0	.27	1	0-13(7-6-0)	0	-0.5
1887 Cle-a	57	231	30	58	5	1	0	19	15	....	19	....	.251	.264	.231	.495	40	-17	19	2.91	-5	0-54(14-0-40)/3-3,2-1	0	-1.9
Total 3	79	302	34	64	6	1	0	20	19	8	19	....	.212	.232	.199	.431	25	-26	20	2.23	-2	/0-75,3-5,2-1	0	-2.5

• CARROLL, Tom Thomas Edward Carroll b: 9/17/1936, Jamaica, NY BR/TR, 6'3", 186 lbs. Deb: 5/7/1955

YEAR TM-L	G	AB	R	H	2B	3B	HR	RBI	BB	SO	SB	CS	AVG	OBP	SLG	OPS	OPS+	BR/A	RC	RC/G	FR	G/POS	WS	TPW
1955*NY-A	14	6	3	2	0	0	0	0	0	2	0	0	.333	.333	.333	.667	81	-0	1	4.50	0	/S-4	0	-0.1
1956 NY-A	36	17	11	6	0	0	0	0	1	3	1	0	.353	.389	.353	.742	100	0	3	6.47	0	3-11/S-1	1	0.1
1959 KC-A	14	7	1	1	0	0	0	1	0	1	0	0	.143	.143	.143	.286	-21	-1	0	.64	-1	/S-9,3-3	0	-0.2
Total 3	64	30	15	9	0	0	0	1	1	6	1	0	.300	.323	.300	.623	69	-1	3	4.43	-1	/3-14,S-14	1	-0.2

• CARSON, Kit Walter Lloyd Carson b: 11/15/1912, Colton, CA d: 6/21/1983, Long Beach, CA BL/TL, 6', 180 lbs. Deb: 7/21/1934 Career OF: 0-0-8

YEAR TM-L	G	AB	R	H	2B	3B	HR	RBI	BB	SO	SB	CS	AVG	OBP	SLG	OPS	OPS+	BR/A	RC	RC/G	FR	G/POS	WS	TPW
1934 Cle-A	5	18	4	5	2	1	0	1	2	3	0	0	.278	.350	.500	.850	115	0	3	6.52	0	/0-4(0-0-4)	1	0.0
1935 Cle-A	16	22	1	5	2	0	0	1	2	6	0	1	.227	.292	.318	.610	57	-2	2	2.66	0	/0-4(0-0-4)	0	-0.2
Total 2	21	40	5	10	4	1	0	2	4	9	0	1	.250	.318	.400	.718	83	-2	5	4.28	0	/0-8	1	-0.2

• CARSWELL, Frank Frank Willis Carswell b: 11/6/1919, Palestine, TX d: 10/16/1998, Houston, TX BR/TR, 6', 195 lbs. Deb: 4/17/1953

YEAR TM-L	G	AB	R	H	2B	3B	HR	RBI	BB	SO	SB	CS	AVG	OBP	SLG	OPS	OPS+	BR/A	RC	RC/G	FR	G/POS	WS	TPW
1953 Det-A	16	15	2	4	0	0	0	2	3	1	0	0	.267	.389	.267	.656	81	-0	2	4.66	0	/0-3(3-0-0)	0	-0.1

• CARTER, Blackie Otis Leonard Carter b: 9/30/1902, Langley, SC d: 9/10/1976, Greenville, SC BR/TR, 5'10", 175 lbs. Deb: 10/3/1925 Career OF: 4-0-1

YEAR TM-L	G	AB	R	H	2B	3B	HR	RBI	BB	SO	SB	CS	AVG	OBP	SLG	OPS	OPS+	BR/A	RC	RC/G	FR	G/POS	WS	TPW
1925 NY-N	1	4	0	0	0	0	0	0	0	1	0	0	.000	.000	.000	.000	-104	-1	0	.00	1	/0-1	0	-0.1
1926 NY-N	5	17	4	4	1	0	1	1	1	0	0	....	.235	.278	.471	.748	100	-0	2	4.27	0	/0-4(3-0-1)	0	0.0
Total 2	6	21	4	4	1	0	1	1	1	1	0	0	.190	.227	.381	.608	62	-1	2	3.26	1	/0-5	0	-0.1

• CARTER, Gary Gary Edmund "Kid" Carter b: 4/8/1954, Culver City, CA BR/TR, 6'2", 215 lbs. Deb: 9/16/1974 HOF: 2003 Career OF: 5-0-132

YEAR TM-L	G	AB	R	H	2B	3B	HR	RBI	BB	SO	SB	CS	AVG	OBP	SLG	OPS	OPS+	BR/A	RC	RC/G	FR	G/POS	WS	TPW
1974 Mon-N	9	27	5	11	0	1	1	6	1	2	2	0	.407	.429	.593	1.021	174	3	7	11.71	1	/C-6,0-2(0-0-2)	2	0.4
1975 Mon-N★	144	503	58	136	20	1	17	68	72	83	5	2	.270	.363	.416	.778	111	9	80	5.53	-1	0-92(0-0-92),C-66/3-1	18	0.7
1976 Mon-N	91	311	31	68	8	1	6	38	30	43	0	2	.219	.289	.309	.598	67	-14	28	2.89	8	C-60,0-36(2-0-34)	6	-0.5
1977 Mon-N	154	522	86	148	29	2	31	84	58	103	5	5	.284	.361	.525	.886	138	26	98	6.67	7	*C-146/0-1	25	4.1
1978 Mon-N	157	533	76	136	27	1	20	72	62	70	10	6	.255	.338	.422	.760	113	8	77	4.92	9	*C-152/1-1	22	2.6
1979 Mon-N★	141	505	74	143	26	5	22	75	40	62	3	2	.283	.342	.485	.827	124	15	82	5.77	10	*C-138	27	3.3
1980 Mon-N★	154	549	76	145	25	5	29	101	58	78	3	2	.264	.336	.486	.822	127	17	89	5.69	11	*C-149	30	3.8
1981*Mon-N★	100	374	48	94	20	2	16	68	35	35	1	5	.251	.317	.444	.761	113	3	51	4.59	5	*C-100/1-1	17	1.4
1982 Mon-N★	154	557	91	163	32	1	29	97	78	64	2	5	.293	.385	.510	.895	146	34	107	6.79	9	*C-153	31	5.3
1983 Mon-N★	145	541	63	146	37	3	17	79	51	57	1	1	.270	.341	.444	.784	116	11	80	5.17	15	*C-144/1-1	24	3.4
1984 Mon-N★	159	596	75	175	32	1	27	**106**	64	57	2	2	.294	.368	.487	.854	145	34	108	6.74	-0	*C-143,1-25	30	4.1
1985 NY-N★	149	555	83	156	17	1	32	100	69	46	1	1	.281	.367	.488	.855	141	30	97	6.19	2	*C-143/1-6,0-1	33	4.1
1986*NY-N★	132	490	81	125	14	2	24	105	62	63	1	0	.255	.346	.439	.785	118	13	72	4.82	2	*C-122/1-9,0-4(2-0-2),3-1	23	2.1
1987 NY-N★	139	523	55	123	18	2	20	83	42	73	0	0	.235	.293	.392	.685	84	-14	58	3.74	2	*C-135/1-4,0-1	13	-0.6
1988*NY-N★	130	455	39	110	16	2	11	46	34	52	0	2	.242	.304	.358	.663	94	-5	50	3.70	-1	*C-119,1-10/3-1	12	0.0
1989 NY-N	50	153	14	28	8	0	2	15	12	15	0	0	.183	.242	.275	.517	50	-10	10	1.98	2	C-47/1-1	2	-0.7
1990 SF-N	92	244	24	62	10	0	9	27	25	31	1	1	.254	.326	.406	.732	104	1	33	4.81	-3	C-80/1-3	8	0.2
1991 LA-N	101	248	22	61	14	0	6	26	22	26	2	2	.246	.325	.375	.700	98	-1	28	3.76	4	C-68,1-10	7	0.6
1992 Mon-N	95	285	24	62	18	1	5	29	33	37	0	4	.218	.303	.340	.643	83	-8	29	3.37	2	C-85/1-5	7	-0.2
Total 19	2296	7971	1025	2092	371	31	324	1225	848	997	39	42	.262	.338	.439	.777	116	149	1185	5.13	83	*C-2056,0-137/1-76,3-3	337	34.2

• CARTER, Howie John Howard Carter b: 10/13/1904, New York, NY d: 7/24/1991, New York, NY BR/TR, 5'10", 154 lbs. Deb: 6/21/1926

YEAR TM-L	G	AB	R	H	2B	3B	HR	RBI	BB	SO	SB	CS	AVG	OBP	SLG	OPS	OPS+	BR/A	RC	RC/G	FR	G/POS	WS	TPW
1926 Cin-N	5	1	0	0	0	0	0	0	0	0	0	....	.000	.000	.000	.000	-103	-0	0	.00	-1	/2-3,S-1	0	-0.2

• CARTER, Joe Joseph Chris Carter b: 3/7/1960, Oklahoma City, OK BR/TR, 6'3", 215 lbs. Deb: 7/30/1983 Career OF: 775-432-624

YEAR TM-L	G	AB	R	H	2B	3B	HR	RBI	BB	SO	SB	CS	AVG	OBP	SLG	OPS	OPS+	BR/A	RC	RC/G	FR	G/POS	WS	TPW
1983 Chi-N	23	51	6	9	1	1	0	1	0	21	1	0	.176	.176	.235	.412	13	-6	2	1.23	-1	0-16(14-2-1)	0	-0.7
1984 Cle-A	66	244	32	67	6	1	13	41	11	48	2	4	.275	.309	.467	.776	109	1	34	4.95	1	0-59(48-14-0)/1-7	7	0.0
1985 Cle-A	143	489	64	128	27	0	15	59	25	74	24	6	.262	.300	.409	.709	93	-4	60	4.20	-1	*0-135(122-4-30),1-11/D-7,2,3	11	-1.1
1986 Cle-A	162	663	108	200	36	9	29	**121**	32	95	29	7	.302	.339	.514	.853	130	28	116	6.42	0	*0-104(45-9-78),1-70	28	1.9
1987 Cle-A	149	588	83	155	27	2	32	106	27	105	31	6	.264	.306	.480	.786	103	4	87	5.19	-7	1-84,0-62(42-13-14)/D-5	14	-1.0
1988 Cle-A	157	621	85	168	36	6	27	98	35	82	27	5	.271	.317	.478	.795	116	14	96	5.52	1	*0-156(0-155-0)	26	1.3
1989 Cle-A	162	651	84	158	32	4	35	105	39	112	13	5	.243	.294	.465	.759	109	4	89	4.70	1	*0-146(56-103-1),1-11/D-8	20	0.1
1990 SD-N	162	634	79	147	27	1	24	115	48	93	22	6	.232	.293	.391	.684	86	-13	72	3.80	-2	*0-150(51-112-0),1-14	16	-2.0
1991*Tor-A★	162	638	89	174	42	3	33	108	49	112	20	9	.273	.334	.503	.837	124	19	108	5.95	-5	*0-151(57-0-100),D-11	23	0.9
1992*Tor-A★	158	622	97	164	30	7	34	119	36	109	12	5	.264	.315	.498	.814	119	13	94	5.17	-1	*0-129(6-0-123),D-24/1-4	24	0.7
1993*Tor-A★	155	603	92	153	33	5	33	121	47	113	8	3	.254	.317	.489	.806	113	9	93	5.31	-12	*0-151(55-0-96)/D-3	17	-1.1
1994 Tor-A★	111	435	70	118	25	2	27	103	33	64	11	0	.271	.326	.524	.850	114	9	75	6.07	-4	*0-110(0-0-110)/D-1	14	-0.1
1995 Tor-A	139	558	70	141	23	0	25	76	37	87	12	1	.253	.303	.428	.731	88	-10	72	4.48	-4	*0-128(116-20-0)/1-7,D-5	8	-1.8
1996 Tor-A★	157	625	84	158	35	7	30	107	44	106	7	6	.253	.309	.475	.784	95	-10	89	4.87	-7	*0-115(115-0-0),1-41,D-15	13	-2.3
1997 Tor-A	157	612	76	143	30	4	21	102	40	105	8	2	.234	.288	.399	.687	77	-22	69	3.81	1	D-65,0-51(41-0-10),1-42	10	-3.0
1998 Bal-A	85	283	36	70	15	1	11	34	18	48	3	1	.247	.297	.424	.721	86	-7	34	4.16	1	0-50(3-0-47),D-32/1-1	3	-0.9
SF-N	41	105	15	31	7	0	7	29	6	13	1	0	.295	.333	.562	.895	138	5	19	6.49	0	0-17(4-0-14),1-16	6	0.4
Total 16	2189	8422	1170	2184	432	53	396	1445	527	1387	231	66	.259	.310	.464	.774	105	34	1209	4.98	-37	*0-1730,1-308,D-176/2-1,3-1	240	-8.8

• CARTER, Steve Steven Jerome Carter b: 12/3/1964, Charlottesville, VA BL/TR, 6'4", 201 lbs. Deb: 4/16/1989 Career OF: 1-2-6

YEAR TM-L	G	AB	R	H	2B	3B	HR	RBI	BB	SO	SB	CS	AVG	OBP	SLG	OPS	OPS+	BR/A	RC	RC/G	FR	G/POS	WS	TPW
1989 Pit-N	9	16	2	2	1	0	1	3	2	5	0	0	.125	.222	.375	.597	70	-1	1	2.68	0	/0-5(0-0-5)	0	-0.1
1990 Pit-N	5	5	0	1	0	0	0	0	0	1	0	0	.200	.200	.200	.400	11	-1	0	1.35	-0	/0-3(1-2-1)	0	-0.1
Total 2	14	21	2	3	1	0	1	3	2	6	0	0	.143	.217	.333	.551	57	-1	2	2.39	0	/0-8	0	-0.2

• CARTWRIGHT, Ed Edward Charles "Jumbo" Cartwright b: 10/6/1859, Johnstown, PA d: 9/3/1933, St. Petersburg, FL BR/TR, 5'10", 220 lbs. Deb: 7/10/1890

YEAR TM-L	G	AB	R	H	2B	3B	HR	RBI	BB	SO	SB	CS	AVG	OBP	SLG	OPS	OPS+	BR/A	RC	RC/G	FR	G/POS	WS	TPW
1890 StL-a	75	300	70	90	12	4	8	60	29	....	26	....	.300	.367	.447	.814	122	6	60	7.60	0	1-75	9	0.0
1894 Was-N	132	507	88	149	35	13	12	106	57	43	31	....	.294	.374	.485	.859	109	7	106	7.71	0	*1-132	11	0.4
1895 Was-N	122	472	95	156	34	17	3	90	54	41	50	....	.331	.400	.494	.894	131	22	116	9.83	9	*1-122	14	2.4
1896 Was-N	133	499	76	138	15	10	1	62	54	44	28	....	.277	.350	.353	.702	85	-10	74	5.33	-7	*1-133	10	-1.5
1897 Was-N	33	124	19	29	4	0	0	15	8	....	9	....	.234	.286	.266	.552	46	-10	12	3.43	-1	1-33	0	-0.9
Total 5	495	1902	348	562	100	44	24	333	202	128	144	....	.295	.368	.432	.800	107	15	369	7.25	1	1-495	44	0.5

• CARTY, Rico Ricardo Adolfo Jacobo "Beeg Mon" Carty
b: 9/1/1939, San Pedro de Macoris, Dominican Republic BR/TR, 6'3", 200 lbs. Deb: 9/15/1963 Career OF: 789-1-18

YEAR TM-L	G	AB	R	H	2B	3B	HR	RBI	BB	SO	SB	CS	AVG	OBP	SLG	OPS	OPS+	BR/A	RC	RC/G	FR	G/POS	WS	TPW
1963 Mil-N	2	2	0	0	0	0	0	0	0	2	0	0	.000	.000	.000	.000	-101	-0	0	.00	0	....	0	-0.1
1964 Mil-N	133	455	72	150	28	4	22	88	43	78	1	2	.330	.391	.554	.945	162	37	94	7.73	1	*0-121(118-1-2)	27	3.4
1965 Mil-N	83	271	37	84	18	1	10	35	17	44	1	4	.310	.357	.494	.852	136	11	44	5.94	0	0-73(73-0-0)	10	0.7
1966 Atl-N	151	521	73	170	25	2	15	76	60	74	4	6	.326	.396	.468	.864	137	27	94	6.67	0	*0-126(126-0-1),C-17/1-2,3	21	2.1
1967 Atl-N	134	444	41	113	16	2	15	64	49	70	4	3	.255	.330	.401	.731	110	6	55	4.22	-1	*0-112(97-0-15)/1-9	12	-0.2
1969*Atl-N	104	304	47	104	15	0	16	58	32	28	0	2	.342	.405	.549	.954	164	25	61	7.39	-2	0-79(79-0-0)	17	2.1
1970 Atl-N★	136	478	84	175	23	3	25	101	77	46	1	2	**.366**	**.456**	.584	1.040	167	48	125	**10.31**	1	*0-133(133-0-0)	27	4.2
1972 Atl-N	86	271	31	75	12	2	6	29	44	33	0	0	.277	.378	.402	.780	111	6	42	5.57	5	0-78(78-0-0)	10	0.9
1973 Tex-A	86	306	24	71	12	0	3	33	36	39	2	0	.232	.315	.301	.616	77	-8	30	3.24	0	0-53(53-0-0),D-31	4	-1.1
Chi-N	22	70	4	15	0	0	1	8	6	10	0	0	.214	.276	.257	.533	45	-5	4	1.70	0	0-19(19-0-0)	0	-0.7
Oak-A	7	8	1	2	1	0	1	1	2	1	0	0	.250	.400	.750	1.150	230	1	3	11.74	0	/D-2	1	0.1
Yr.	93	314	25	73	13	0	4	34	38	40	2	0	.232	.317	.312	.629	82	-6	32	3.44	0	0-53(53-0-0),D-33	5	-1.0
1974 Cle-A	33	91	6	33	5	0	1	16	5	9	0	0	.363	.396	.451	.846	144	5	15	6.52	-1	D-14/1-8	4	0.3
1975 Cle-A	118	383	57	118	19	1	18	64	45	31	2	2	.308	.384	.504	.888	149	25	70	6.57	-1	D-72,1-26,0-12(12-0-0)	16	2.0

YEAR TM-L	G	AB	R	H	2B	3B	HR	RBI	BB	SO	SB	CS	AVG	OBP	SLG	OPS	OPS+	BR/A	RC	RC/G	FR	G/POS	WS	TPW
1976 Cle-A	152	552	67	171	34	0	13	83	67	45	1	1	.310	.384	.442	.827	143	31	92	6.08	-1	*D-137,1-12/O-1	24	2.6
1977 Cle-A	127	461	50	129	23	1	15	80	56	51	1	2	.280	.358	.432	.790	118	12	68	5.20	1	*D-123/1-2	12	0.8
1978 Tor-A	104	387	51	110	16	0	20	68	36	41	1	1	.284	.345	.481	.826	127	13	64	5.88	0	*D-101	13	1.0
Oak-A	41	141	19	39	5	1	11	31	21	16	0	0	.277	.370	.560	.931	167	12	27	6.55	0	D-41	6	1.1
Yr.	145	528	70	149	21	1	31	99	57	57	1	1	.282	.352	.502	.854	138	26	91	6.07	0	*D-142	19	2.1
1979 Tor-A	132	461	48	118	26	0	12	55	46	45	3	1	.256	.325	.390	.715	91	-5	54	3.98	0	*D-129	5	-1.0
Total 15	1651	5606	712	1677	278	17	204	890	642	663	21	26	.299	.372	.464	.836	132	241	941	6.03	2	O-807,D-650/1-59,C-17,3-1	209	18.5
• CARUSO, Mike	Michael John Caruso b: 5/27/1977, Queens, NY BL/TR, 6'1", 172 lbs. Deb: 3/31/1998																							
1998 Chi-A	133	523	81	160	17	6	5	55	14	38	22	6	.306	.333	.390	.723	90	-7	68	4.75	-7	*S-131	13	-0.3
1999 Chi-A	136	529	60	132	11	4	2	35	20	36	12	14	.250	.281	.297	.578	47	-46	42	2.64	-8	*S-132/D-2	5	-4.0
2002 KC-A	12	20	3	2	0	0	0	0	1	2	0	0	.100	.143	.100	.243	-30	-4	0	.48	-1	/S-5,2-4,3-2	0	-0.4
Total 3	281	1072	144	294	28	10	7	90	35	76	34	20	.274	.303	.339	.642	67	-57	111	3.57	-16	S-268/2-4,3-2,D-2	18	-4.8
• CARUTHERS, Bob	Robert Lee "Parisian Bob" Caruthers b: 1/5/1864, Memphis, TN d: 8/5/1911, Peoria, IL BL/TR, 5'7", 138 lbs. Deb: 9/7/1884 M/U Career OF: 58-30-280 ♦																							
1884 StL-a	23	82	15	22	2	0	2	0	4	....	....	....	.268	.302	.366	.668	113	2	9	4.26	-4	O-16(0-0-16),P-13	10	0.3
1885*StL-a	60	222	37	50	10	2	1	12	20	....	....	....	.225	.289	.302	.591	83	5	20	3.12	0	P-53/O-7(6-0-1)	51	5.1
1886*StL-a	87	317	91	106	21	14	4	61	64	....	26	....	.334	.448	.527	.974	196	43	89	11.33	-4	P-44,O-43(1-0-42)/2-2	57	7.7
1887*StL-a	98	430	102	196	23	11	8	73	66	....	49	....	.456	.463	.547	1.010	164	40	118	13.59	10	O-54(3-2-50),P-39/1-7	**54**	**6.5**
1888 Bro-a	94	335	58	77	10	5	5	53	45	....	23	....	.230	.328	.334	.662	113	13	45	4.75	-1	O-51(4-16-31),P-44	46	3.3
1889*Bro-a	59	172	45	43	8	3	2	31	44	17	9	....	.250	.408	.366	.775	121	17	30	6.19	1	P-56/O-3(0-1-2),1-2	46	3.9
1890*Bro-N	71	238	46	63	7	4	1	29	47	18	13	....	.265	.397	.340	.737	115	14	38	5.79	-3	O-39(37-1-1),P-37	30	1.6
1891 Bro-N	56	171	24	48	5	3	2	23	25	13	4	....	.281	.372	.380	.753	120	13	26	5.78	-2	P-38,O-17(1-2-14)/2-1	22	2.2
1892 StL-N	143	513	76	142	16	8	3	69	86	29	24	....	.277	.386	.357	.742	131	27	82	5.96	-14	*O-122(6-7-110),P-16/2-6,1	19	-1.7
1893 Chi-N	1	3	0	0	0	0	0	0	0	1	0	....	.000	.000	.000	.000	-102	-1	0	.00	-0	/O-1	0	-0.1
Cin-N	13	48	14	14	2	0	1	8	16	1	4	....	.292	.477	.396	.873	130	4	11	8.76	-1	O-13(O-0-13)	2	0.2
Yr.	14	51	14	14	2	0	1	8	16	2	4	....	.275	.456	.373	.828	120	3	11	8.05	-1	O-14(O-1-13)	2	0.1
Total 10	705	2531	508	761	104	50	29	359	417	79	152	....	.301	.391	.400	.791	134	178	469	7.13	-17	O-366,P-340/1-13,2-9	337	28.8
• CASANOVA, Paul	Paulino (Ortiz) Casanova b: 12/21/1941, Colon, Cuba BR/TR, 6'4", 200 lbs. Deb: 9/18/1965																							
1965 Was-A	5	13	2	4	1	0	0	1	1	3	0	0	.308	.357	.385	.742	112	0	0	.78	-1	/C-4	0	0.0
1966 Was-A	122	429	45	109	16	5	13	44	14	78	1	2	.254	.279	.406	.685	95	-5	46	3.69	-3	*C-119	12	-0.2
1967 Was-A★	141	528	47	131	19	1	9	53	17	65	1	1	.248	.274	.339	.613	83	-13	44	2.80	1	*C-137	12	-0.5
1968 Was-A	96	322	19	63	6	0	4	25	7	52	0	1	.196	.213	.252	.464	42	-24	16	1.54	0	C-92	2	-2.2
1969 Was-A	124	379	26	82	9	2	4	37	18	52	0	0	.216	.258	.282	.540	54	-24	26	2.18	0	*C-122	6	-2.0
1970 Was-A	104	328	25	75	17	3	6	30	10	47	0	0	.229	.254	.354	.607	69	-15	28	2.93	0	*C-100	5	-1.2
1971 Was-A	94	311	19	63	9	1	5	26	14	52	0	3	.203	.239	.286	.525	51	-22	19	1.98	-2	C-83	3	-2.2
1972 Atl-N	49	136	8	28	3	0	2	10	4	28	0	1	.206	.229	.272	.501	38	-12	6	1.50	-1	C-43	1	-1.2
1973 Atl-N	82	236	18	51	7	0	7	18	11	36	0	2	.216	.254	.335	.589	58	-15	18	2.58	3	C-78	3	-0.9
1974 Atl-N	42	104	5	21	0	0	0	8	5	17	0	0	.202	.239	.202	.440	23	-11	5	1.54	1	C-33	2	-0.9
Total 10	859	2786	214	627	87	12	50	252	101	430	2	10	.225	.254	.319	.573	64	-141	209	2.47	-2	C-811	46	-11.3
• CASANOVA, Raul	Raul Casanova b: 8/23/1972, Humacao, Puerto Rico BB/TR, 6', 192 lbs. Deb: 5/24/1996																							
1996 Det-A	25	85	6	16	1	0	4	9	6	18	0	0	.188	.242	.341	.583	45	-8	5	1.93	0	C-22/D-3	0	-0.6
1997 Det-A	101	304	27	74	10	1	5	24	26	48	1	1	.243	.309	.332	.642	68	-14	30	3.36	-2	C-92/D-1	2	-1.0
1998 Det-A	16	42	4	6	2	0	1	3	5	10	0	0	.143	.250	.262	.512	33	-4	3	2.36	-1	C-14	0	-0.4
2000 Mil-N	86	231	20	57	13	3	6	36	26	48	1	2	.247	.333	.407	.740	87	-5	31	4.59	0	C-72/D-3	8	-0.1
2001 Mil-N	71	192	21	50	10	0	11	33	12	29	0	0	.260	.307	.484	.792	103	-0	28	5.13	-2	C-56/D-1	6	0.1
2002 Mil-N	31	87	3	16	1	0	1	8	10	18	0	0	.184	.276	.230	.505	35	-8	5	1.95	0	C-28	1	-0.6
Bal-A	2	1	0	0	0	0	0	0	0	1	0	0	.000	.000	.000	.000	-105	-0	0	.00	0	/C-2	0	0.0
Total 6	332	942	81	219	37	4	28	113	85	172	2	3	.232	.303	.369	.672	73	-40	104	3.67	-5	C-286/D-8	17	-2.6
• CASE, George	George Washington Case b: 11/11/1915, Trenton, NJ d: 1/23/1989, Trenton, NJ BR/TR, 6', 183 lbs. Deb: 9/8/1937 C Career OF: 534-243-422																							
1937 Was-A	22	90	14	26	6	2	0	11	3	5	2	1	.289	.312	.400	.712	82	-3	11	4.46	-1	O-22(8-1-14)	2	-0.5
1938 Was-A	107	433	69	132	27	3	2	40	39	28	11	6	.305	.362	.395	.757	96	-2	63	5.32	-3	*O-101(0-19-82)	10	-1.0
1939 Was-A★	128	530	103	160	20	7	2	35	56	36	**51**	17	.302	.369	.377	.746	98	5	80	5.38	0	*O-123(7-79-38)	15	0.0
1940 Was-A	154	656	109	192	29	5	5	56	52	39	**35**	10	.293	.349	.375	.724	94	-1	94	5.21	-1	*O-154(0-118-36)	17	-0.7
1941 Was-A	153	649	95	176	32	8	2	53	51	37	**33**	9	.271	.325	.354	.680	83	-12	82	4.46	11	*O-151(115-0-36)	15	-1.0
1942 Was-A	125	513	101	164	26	2	5	43	44	30	**44**	6	.320	.377	.407	.784	122	22	88	6.48	-6	*O-120(86-0-34)	22	0.9
1943 Was-A★	141	613	**102**	180	36	5	1	52	41	27	**61**	14	.294	.341	.374	.715	113	17	88	5.22	2	*O-140(18-0-122)	25	1.0
1944 Was-A★	119	464	63	116	14	2	2	32	49	22	49	18	.250	.326	.302	.627	84	-5	50	3.59	1	*O-114(83-7-28)	10	-1.3
1945 Was-A★	123	504	72	148	19	5	1	31	49	27	30	16	.294	.360	.357	.717	118	12	68	4.80	9	*O-123(87-15-27)	21	1.4
1946 Cle-A	118	484	46	109	23	4	1	22	34	38	**28**	11	.225	.280	.295	.576	65	-21	43	2.88	-4	*O-118(118-0-0)	5	-3.5
1947 Was-A	36	80	11	12	1	0	0	2	8	8	5	1	.150	.227	.163	.390	10	-9	4	1.53	-1	O-21(12-4-5)	0	-1.1
Total 11	1226	5016	785	1415	233	43	21	377	426	297	349	109	.282	.341	.358	.699	96	2	670	4.74	5	*O-1187	142	-5.8
• CASEY, Bob	Orrin Robinson Casey b: 1/26/1859, Adolphustown, Canada d: 11/28/1936, Syracuse, NY, 5'11", 190 lbs. Deb: 7/17/1882																							
1882 Det-N	9	39	5	9	2	1	1	7	0	15	....	....	.231	.231	.410	.641	101	-0	4	3.47	-4	/3-8,2-1	1	-0.4
• CASEY, Dennis	Dennis Patrick Casey b: 3/30/1858, Binghamton, NY d: 1/19/1909, Binghamton, NY BL/TR, 5'9", 164 lbs. Deb: 8/18/1884 Career OF: 0-102-0																							
1884 Wil-U	2	8	1	2	1	0	0	....	0	....	....	....	.250	.250	.375	.625	106	0	1	3.59	0	/O-2(0-2-0)	0	0.0
Bal-a	37	149	20	37	7	4	3	0	5	....	....	....	.248	.273	.409	.682	115	2	17	4.19	-1	O-37(0-37-0)	5	-0.1
1885 Bal-a	63	264	50	76	10	5	3	29	21	....	....	....	.288	.347	.398	.745	137	12	37	5.37	-7	O-63(0-63-0)	9	0.2
Total 2	102	421	71	115	18	9	6	29	26	....	....	....	.273	.320	.401	.721	129	13	55	4.90	-8	O-102	14	0.1
• CASEY, Doc	James Patrick Casey b: 3/15/1870, Lawrence, MA d: 12/31/1936, Detroit, MI BB/TR, 5'6", 157 lbs. Deb: 9/14/1898																							
1898 Was-N	28	112	13	31	2	0	0	15	3	....	15	....	.277	.302	.295	.596	71	-4	15	4.83	-2	3-22/S-4,C-3	2	-0.5
1899 Was-N	9	34	3	4	2	0	0	2	2	....	1	....	.118	.167	.176	.343	-6	-5	1	1.10	-2	/3-9	0	-0.6
Bro-N	134	525	75	141	14	8	1	43	25	....	27	....	.269	.313	.331	.644	75	-19	65	4.43	-17	*3-134	11	-3.1
Yr.	143	559	78	145	16	8	1	45	27	....	28	....	.259	.304	.322	.626	70	-24	66	4.19	-19	*3-143	11	-3.7
1900 Bro-N	1	3	0	1	0	0	0	1	0	....	0	....	.333	.500	.333	.833	125	0	1	6.79	0	/3-1	0	0.0
1901 Det-A	128	540	105	153	16	9	2	46	32	....	34	....	.283	.335	.357	.692	88	-9	79	5.27	-4	*3-127	15	-0.8
1902 Det-A	132	520	69	142	18	7	3	55	44	....	22	....	.273	.338	.352	.690	90	-7	72	4.94	0	*3-132	14	-0.2
1903 Chi-N	112	435	56	126	8	3	1	40	19	....	11	....	.290	.324	.329	.653	89	-7	54	4.32	-10	*3-112	9	-1.3
1904 Chi-N	136	548	71	147	20	4	1	43	18	....	21	....	.268	.300	.325	.625	93	-6	64	3.92	-4	*3-134/C-2	16	-0.7
1905 Chi-N	144	526	66	122	21	10	1	56	41	....	22	....	.232	.295	.316	.611	79	-14	59	3.63	-1	*3-142/S-1	13	-1.2
1906 Bro-N	149	571	71	133	17	8	0	34	52	....	22	....	.233	.306	.291	.597	93	-4	61	3.50	-12	*3-149	16	-1.3
1907 Bro-N	141	527	55	122	19	3	0	19	34	....	16	....	.231	.282	.279	.561	82	-12	51	3.03	-6	*3-138	12	-1.6
Total 10	1114	4341	584	1122	137	52	9	354	270	....	191	....	.258	.310	.320	.630	85	-87	522	4.08	-58	*3-1100/C-5,S-5	108	-11.3
• CASEY, Joe	Joseph Felix Casey b: 8/15/1887, Boston, MA d: 6/2/1966, Melrose, MA BR/TR, 5'9", 180 lbs. Deb: 10/1/1909																							
1909 Det-A	3	5	1	0	0	0	0	0	1	....	0	....	.000	.167	.000	.167	-45	-1	0	.00	1	/C-3	0	0.0
1910 Det-A	23	62	3	12	3	0	0	2	2	....	1	....	.194	.231	.242	.473	45	-4	4	1.82	-0	C-22	1	-0.2
1911 Det-A	15	33	2	5	0	0	0	3	3	....	0	....	.152	.222	.152	.374	5	-4	1	.97	-1	C-12/O-3(0-3-0)	0	-0.5
1918 Was-A	9	17	3	4	0	0	0	2	2	2	0	....	.235	.316	.235	.551	67	-1	1	2.34	0	/C-8	0	0.0
Total 4	50	117	9	21	3	0	0	7	8	2	1	....	.179	.238	.205	.443	33	-10	6	1.55	-1	/C-45,O-3	1	-0.7
• CASEY, Sean	Sean Thomas "The Mayor" Casey b: 7/2/1974, Willingboro, NJ BL/TR, 6'4", 215 lbs. Deb: 9/12/1997																							
1997 Cle-A	6	10	1	2	0	0	0	1	1	2	0	0	.200	.333	.200	.533	42	-1	1	2.84	0	/D-3,1-1	0	-0.1

YEAR TM-L	G	AB	R	H	2B	3B	HR	RBI	BB	SO	SB	CS	AVG	OBP	SLG	OPS	OPS+	BR/A	RC	RC/G	FR	G/POS	WS	TPW
1998 Cin-N	96	302	44	82	21	1	7	52	43	45	1	1	.272	.368	.417	.785	105	3	46	5.29	-5	1-86	10	-0.9
1999 Cin-N★	151	594	103	197	42	3	25	99	61	88	0	2	.332	.402	.539	.941	132	28	126	8.13	-8	*1-148/D-1	23	0.6
2000 Cin-N	133	480	69	151	33	2	20	85	52	80	1	0	.315	.390	.517	.906	124	18	95	7.28	-5	*1-129	17	0.2
2001 Cin-N★	145	533	69	165	40	0	13	89	43	63	3	1	.310	.371	.458	.829	108	7	88	6.12	-4	*1-136/D-3	18	-0.9
2002 Cin-N	120	425	56	111	25	0	6	42	43	47	2	1	.261	.336	.362	.699	82	-11	52	4.25	0	*1-108/D-1	6	-2.1
2003 Cin-N	147	573	71	167	19	3	14	80	51	58	4	0	.291	.351	.408	.760	99	0	80	5.05	-8	*1-144	16	-2.0
Total 7	798	2917	413	875	180	9	85	448	294	383	11	5	.300	.371	.455	.826	109	45	487	6.10	-31	1-752/D-8	90	-5.1
• CASH, Dave	David Cash b: 6/11/1948, Utica, NY BR/TR, 5'11", 175 lbs. Deb: 9/13/1969 C																							
1969 Pit-N	18	61	8	17	3	1	0	4	9	9	2	0	.279	.371	.361	.732	108	2	9	4.81	4	2-17	3	0.7
1970*Pit-N	64	210	30	66	7	6	1	28	17	25	5	2	.314	.368	.419	.787	114	4	30	5.21	-1	2-55	8	0.7
1971*Pit-N	123	478	79	138	17	4	2	34	46	33	13	5	.289	.351	.354	.705	99	1	61	4.53	7	*2-105,3-24/S-3	16	1.5
1972*Pit-N	99	425	58	120	22	4	3	30	22	31	9	9	.282	.318	.374	.692	98	-4	48	3.97	31	2-97	15	3.6
1973 Pit-N	116	436	59	118	21	2	2	31	38	36	2	5	.271	.329	.342	.671	88	-8	49	3.90	4	2-92,3-17	12	0.1
1974 Phi-N★	162	687	89	206	26	11	2	58	46	33	20	8	.300	.352	.378	.730	100	1	93	4.97	27	*2-162	26	4.1
1975 Phi-N★	162	699	111	**213**	40	3	4	57	56	34	13	6	.305	.360	.388	.747	103	4	100	5.32	13	*2-162	24	2.8
1976*Phi-N★	160	666	92	189	14	**12**	1	56	54	13	10	12	.284	.339	.345	.685	92	-10	75	3.98	13	*2-158	21	1.5
1977 Mon-N	153	650	91	188	42	7	0	43	52	33	21	12	.289	.344	.375	.719	96	-4	82	4.48	0	*2-153	17	0.4
1978 Mon-N	159	658	66	166	26	3	3	43	37	29	12	6	.252	.292	.315	.607	70	-27	58	3.02	12	*2-159	11	-0.8
1979 Mon-N	76	187	24	60	11	1	2	19	12	12	7	4	.321	.362	.422	.784	114	3	27	5.14	0	2-47	7	0.5
1980 SD-N	130	397	25	90	14	2	1	23	35	21	6	5	.227	.289	.280	.569	63	-21	30	2.40	-7	*2-123	5	-2.3
Total 12	1422	5554	732	1571	243	56	21	426	424	309	120	74	.283	.336	.358	.694	93	-60	661	4.21	101	*2-1330/3-41,S-3	165	12.8
• CASH, Kevin	Kevin Forrest Cash b: 12/6/1977, Tampa, FL BR/TR, 6', 185 lbs. Deb: 9/6/2002																							
2002 Tor-A	7	14	1	2	0	0	0	0	1	4	0	0	.143	.200	.143	.343	-6	-2	0	.63	0	/C-7	0	-0.1
2003 Tor-A	34	106	10	15	3	0	1	8	4	22	0	0	.142	.180	.198	.378		-16	3	.80	-4	C-34	1	-1.7
Total 2	41	120	11	17	3	0	1	8	5	26	0	0	.142	.183	.192	.374	-1	-18	3	.78	-4	/C-41	1	-1.8
• CASH, Norm	Norman Dalton Cash b: 11/10/1934, Justiceburg, TX d: 10/12/1986, Beaver Island, MI BL/TL, 6', 190 lbs. Deb: 6/18/1958 Career OF: 4-0-7																							
1958 Chi-A	13	8	2	2	0	0	0	0	0	1	0	0	.250	.250	.250	.500	39	-1	1	2.25	0	/O-4(1-0-3)	0	-0.1
1959*Chi-A	58	104	16	25	0	1	4	16	18	9	1	1	.240	.378	.375	.753	109	2	17	5.44	-2	1-31	4	-0.1
1960 Det-A	121	353	64	101	16	3	18	63	65	58	4	2	.286	.406	.501	.907	135	20	79	8.29	3	1-99/O-4(3-0-1)	16	1.8
1961 Det-A★	159	535	119	**193**	22	8	41	132	124	85	11	5	**.361**	**.488**	.662	**1.150**	197	83	178	**13.07**	10	*1-157	42	**8.3**
1962 Det-A	148	507	94	123	16	2	39	89	104	82	6	3	.243	.385	.513	.897	134	28	104	6.96	8	*1-146/O-3(0-0-3)	23	2.8
1963 Det-A	147	493	67	133	19	1	26	79	89	76	2	3	.270	.388	.471	.858	135	26	94	6.74	0	*1-142	23	1.9
1964 Det-A	144	479	63	123	15	5	23	83	70	66	2	1	.257	.355	.453	.808	121	15	78	5.63	8	*1-137	18	1.6
1965 Det-A	142	467	79	124	23	1	30	82	77	62	6	6	.266	.374	.512	.886	147	29	91	6.76	7	*1-139	24	3.0
1966 Det-A★	160	603	98	168	18	3	32	93	66	91	2	1	.279	.354	.478	.831	133	27	101	5.98	2	*1-158	27	2.0
1967 Det-A	152	488	64	118	16	5	22	72	81	100	3	2	.242	.354	.430	.785	127	19	78	5.53	5	*1-146	21	1.8
1968*Det-A	127	411	50	108	15	1	25	63	39	70	1	1	.263	.331	.487	.818	141	19	63	5.34	11	*1-117	18	2.7
1969 Det-A	142	483	81	135	15	4	22	74	63	80	2	1	.280	.370	.464	.833	126	18	85	6.34	3	*1-134	21	1.1
1970 Det-A	130	370	58	96	18	2	15	53	72	58	0	1	.259	.387	.441	.828	127	16	64	5.79	0	*1-114	16	0.9
1971 Det-A★	135	452	72	128	10	3	32	91	59	86	1	0	.283	.375	.531	.905	148	29	93	7.55	-5	*1-131	24	1.6
1972*Det-A★	137	440	51	114	16	0	22	61	50	64	0	2	.259	.340	.445	.786	128	15	66	5.17	-3	*1-134	18	0.2
1973 Det-A	121	363	51	95	19	0	19	40	47	73	1	0	.262	.359	.471	.830	124	13	63	6.21	1	*1-114/D-3	15	0.6
1974 Det-A	53	149	17	34	3	2	7	12	19	30	1	1	.228	.327	.416	.744	109	2	21	4.90	-1	1-44	5	-0.2
Total 17	2089	6705	1046	1820	241	41	377	1103	1043	1091	43	30	.271	.377	.488	.865	137	361	1278	6.73	48	*1-1943/O-11,D-3	315	29.7
• CASH, Ron	Ronald Forrest Cash b: 11/20/1949, Atlanta, GA BR/TR, 6', 180 lbs. Deb: 9/4/1973																							
1973 Det-A	14	39	8	16	1	1	0	6	5	5	0	0	.410	.477	.487	.964	161	4	9	9.64	0	/O-7(7-0-0),3-6	2	0.4
1974 Det-A	20	62	6	14	2	0	0	5	0	11	0	1	.226	.226	.258	.484	38	-6	3	1.50	-2	1-15/3-4	0	-0.9
Total 2	34	101	14	30	3	1	0	11	5	16	0	1	.297	.330	.347	.677	90	-2	12	4.21	-2	/1-15,3-10,O-7	2	-0.5
• CASIMIRO, Carlos	Carlos Rafael Casimiro b: 11/8/1976, San Pedro de Macoris, Dominican Republic BR/TR, 5'11", 175 lbs. Deb: 7/31/2000																							
2000 Bal-A	2	8	0	1	1	0	0	3	0	2	0	0	.125	.125	.250	.375	-9	-1	0	.96	0	/D-2	0	-0.1
• CASKIN, Ed	Edward James Caskin b: 12/30/1851, Danvers, MA d: 10/9/1924, Danvers, MA BR/TR, 5'9.5", 165 lbs. Deb: 5/1/1879 U																							
1879 Tro-N	70	304	32	78	13	2	0	21	2	14	....	....	.257	.261	.313	.574	94	-1	25	3.15	0	S-42,C-22/2-6	6	0.2
1880 Tro-N	82	333	36	75	5	4	0	28	7	24	....	....	.225	.241	.264	.505	68	-12	22	2.32	10	*S-82/C-2	7	0.2
1881 Tro-N	63	234	33	53	7	1	0	21	13	29	....	....	.226	.267	.265	.532	64	-10	17	2.53	1	*S-63	5	-0.5
1883 NY-N	95	383	47	91	11	2	1	40	14	25	....	....	.238	.264	.285	.549	68	-14	30	2.78	2	*S-81,2-13/C-1	7	-0.8
1884 NY-N	100	351	49	81	11	1	1	40	34	55	....	....	.231	.299	.276	.575	80	-7	30	3.02	3	*S-96/C-6	10	-0.1
1885 StL-N	71	262	31	47	3	0	0	12	12	22	....	....	.179	.215	.191	.406	34	-18	11	1.39	-2	3-69/C-2,S-1	2	-1.7
1886 NY-N	1	4	1	2	0	0	0	1	0	1	0	....	.500	.500	.500	1.000	203	0	1	13.84	0	/S-1	0	0.0
Total 7	482	1871	229	427	50	10	2	163	82	170	0	....	.228	.261	.269	.529	69	-61	136	2.58	15	S-366/3-69,C-33,2-19	37	-2.6
• CASSADY, Harry	Harry Delbert Cassady b: 7/20/1880, Bellflower, IL d: 4/19/1969, Fresno, CA BL/TL, 5'8", 145 lbs. Deb: 8/8/1904 Career OF: 0-0-21																							
1904 Pit-N	12	44	8	9	0	0	0	3	2	....	2	....	.205	.239	.205	.444	36	-3	3	2.00	0	O-12(0-0-12)	0	-0.4
1905 Was-A	10	30	1	4	0	0	0	1	0	....	0	....	.133	.133	.133	.267	-16	-4	1	.61	0	/O-9(0-0-9)	0	-0.4
Total 2	22	74	9	13	0	0	0	4	2	....	2	....	.176	.197	.176	.373	15	-7	3	1.40	1	/O-21	0	-0.8
• CASSIDY, Joe	Joseph Phillip Cassidy b: 2/8/1883, Chester, PA d: 3/25/1906, Chester, PA BR/TR Deb: 4/18/1904																							
1904 Was-A	152	581	63	140	12	**19**	1	33	15	....	17	....	.241	.265	.332	.597	90	-9	59	3.40	-10	S-99,O-32(1-20-11),3-23	11	-1.9
1905 Was-A	151	576	67	124	16	4	1	43	25	....	23	....	.215	.250	.262	.513	65	-24	47	2.63	29	*S-151	10	1.2
Total 2	303	1157	130	264	28	23	2	76	40	....	40	....	.228	.258	.297	.555	77	-33	106	3.01	19	S-250/O-32,3-23	21	-0.7
• CASSIDY, John	John P. Cassidy b: 1855, Brooklyn, NY d: 7/3/1891, Brooklyn, NY BR/TL, 5'8", 168 lbs. Deb: 4/24/1875 U Career OF: 1-147-411 ♦																							
1875 Atl-n	41	166	14	29	3	2	1	6	0	4	0	0	.175	.175	.235	.410	47	-4	7	1.50	-2	P-30,O-12(1-0-11),1-10/2-2	....	-2.5
NH-n	6	22	3	3	1	0	0	1	0	1	0	1	.136	.136	.182	.318	11	-2	1	.82	1	/1-6	....	-0.1
Yr.	47	188	17	32	4	2	1	7	0	5	0	1	.170	.170	.229	.399	43	-6	8	1.42	-1	P-30,1-16,O-12(1-0-11)/2-2	....	-2.6
1876 Har-N	12	48	6	13	2	0	0	8	1	0	....	....	.271	.292	.319	.611	95	-0	4	3.69	2	/O-8(0-8-0),1-4	1	0.1
1877 Har-N	60	251	43	95	10	5	0	27	3	3	....	....	.378	.386	.458	.844	184	24	45	8.02	-4	*O-58(0-1-57)/P-2	13	1.3
1878 Chi-N	60	256	33	68	7	1	0	29	9	11	....	....	.266	.291	.301	.591	89	-3	23	3.35	9	*O-60(0-0-60)/C-1	5	0.5
1879 Tro-N	9	37	4	7	1	0	0	1	2	4	....	....	.189	.231	.216	.447	52	-2	2	1.77	-1	/O-8(0-3-5),1-2	0	-0.3
1880 Tro-N	83	352	40	89	14	8	0	29	12	34	....	....	.253	.277	.338	.616	102	0	34	3.54	-6	*O-82(0-47-35)/2-1	8	-0.8
1881 Tro-N	85	370	57	82	13	3	1	11	18	21	....	....	.222	.258	.281	.539	66	-15	27	2.58	-11	*O-84(0-84-0)/S-1	5	-2.8
1882 Tro-N	29	121	14	21	3	1	0	9	3	16	....	....	.174	.194	.215	.408	32	-9	5	1.42	-8	O-16(0-12-4),3-13	0	-1.5
1883 Pro-N	89	366	46	87	16	5	0	42	9	38	....	....	.238	.256	.309	.565	69	-14	30	2.92	5	*O-88(1-0-87)/1-1,2-1	7	-1.0
1884 Bro-a	106	433	57	109	11	6	2	0	19		....	....	.252	.286	.319	.605	96	-2	41	3.44	-12	*O-101(0-0-101)/3-4,S-1	10	-1.4
1885 Bro-a	54	221	36	47	6	2	1	28	8		....	....	.213	.250	.271	.521	64	-9	15	2.39	-5	O-54(0-0-54)	2	-1.3
Total 10	587	2455	336	618	83	31	4	184	84	127	....	....	.252	.278	.316	.594	90	-30	227	3.39	-32	O-559/3-17,1-7,2-2,P-2,S-2,C	51	-7.3
• CASSIDY, Pete	Peter Francis Cassidy b: 4/8/1873, Wilmington, DE d: 7/9/1929, Wilmington, DE BR/TR, 5'10", 165 lbs. Deb: 4/18/1896																							
1896 Lou-N	49	184	16	39	1	1	0	12	7	7	5	....	.212	.256	.228	.485	29	-19	13	2.28	-7	1-38,S-11	1	-2.1
1899 Bro-N	6	20	2	3	1	0	0	4	1	....	1	....	.150	.261	.200	.461	26	-2	1	2.08	-1	/3-3,S-2	0	-0.3
Was-N	46	178	21	56	13	0	3	32	9	....	5	....	.315	.365	.438	.803	121	5	31	6.74	-2	1-37/3-6,S-3	6	0.3
Yr.	52	198	23	59	14	0	3	36	10	....	6	....	.298	.353	.414	.768	111	3	32	6.17	-3	1-37/3-9,S-5	6	0.0
Total 2	101	382	39	98	15	1	3	48	17	7	11	....	.257	.307	.325	.632	72	-16	45	4.16	-10	/1-75,S-16,3-9	7	-2.1

YEAR TM-L	G	AB	R	H	2B	3B	HR	RBI	BB	SO	SB	CS	AVG	OBP	SLG	OPS	OPS+	BR/A	RC	RC/G	FR	G/POS	WS	TPW
• CASSINI, Jack	Jack Dempsey "Gabby,Scat" Cassini b: 10/26/1919, Dearborn, MI BR/TR, 5'10", 175 lbs. Deb: 4/19/1949																							
1949 Pit-N	8	0	3	0	0	0	0	0	0	0	0	....	....	....	....	....	-97	0	0	....	0	....	0	0.0
• CASTELLANO, Pedro	Pedro Orlando (Arrieta) Castellano b: 3/11/1970, Barquisimeto, Venezuela BR/TR, 6'1", 175 lbs. Deb: 5/30/1993																							
1993 Col-N	34	71	12	13	2	0	3	7	8	16	1	1	.183	.266	.338	.604	52	-5	6	2.88	-1	3-13,1-10/S-5,2-4	0	-0.6
1995 Col-N	4	5	0	0	0	0	0	0	2	3	0	0	.000	.286	.000	.286	-13	-1	0	.80	-1	/3-3	0	-0.2
1996 Col-N	13	17	1	2	0	0	0	2	3	6	0	0	.118	.286	.118	.403	9	-2	1	1.43	1	/2-3,3-1,0-1	0	-0.1
Total 3	51	93	13	15	2	0	3	9	13	25	1	1	.161	.271	.280	.551	39	-8	7	2.48	-1	/3-17,1-10,2-7,S-5,0-1	0	-0.9
• CASTIGLIA, Jim	James Vincent Castiglia b: 9/30/1918, Passaic, NJ BL/TR, 5'11", 200 lbs. Deb: 4/14/1942																							
1942 Phi-A	16	18	2	7	0	0	0	2	1	3	0	0	.389	.421	.389	.810	129	1	3	7.68	0	/C-3	1	0.0
• CASTIGLIONE, Pete	Peter Paul Castiglione b: 2/13/1921, Greenwich, CT BR/TR, 5'11", 175 lbs. Deb: 9/10/1947 Career OF: 1-0-2																							
1947 Pit-N	13	50	6	14	0	0	0	1	2	5	0	....	.280	.308	.280	.588	55	-3	4	3.35	-1	S-13	1	-0.3
1948 Pit-N	4	2	0	0	0	0	0	0	0	0	1	....	.000	.000	.000	.000	-98	-1	0	.00	0	/S-1	0	-0.1
1949 Pit-N	118	448	57	120	20	2	6	43	20	43	2	....	.268	.299	.362	.661	74	-18	49	3.88	4	3-98,S-17/0-2(0-0-2)	9	-1.3
1950 Pit-N	94	263	29	67	10	3	3	22	23	23	1	....	.255	.317	.350	.667	73	-11	29	3.74	-9	3-35,S-29/2-9,1-3	3	-1.7
1951 Pit-N	132	482	62	126	19	4	7	42	34	28	2	2	.261	.311	.361	.672	78	-16	55	3.90	4	3-99,S-28	9	-1.1
1952 Pit-N	67	214	27	57	9	1	4	18	17	8	3	3	.266	.323	.374	.697	90	-3	27	4.38	2	3-57/1-1,0-1	4	-0.2
1953 Pit-N	45	159	14	33	2	1	4	21	5	14	1	1	.208	.236	.308	.545	41	-14	11	2.16	2	3-43	1	-1.2
StL-N	67	52	9	9	2	0	0	3	2	5	0	0	.173	.204	.212	.415	8	-7	2	1.03	-8	3-51/2-9,S-3	1	-1.4
Yr.	112	211	23	42	4	1	4	24	7	19	1	1	.199	.228	.284	.513	33	-21	13	1.88	-6	3-94/2-9,S-3	2	-2.6
1954 StL-N	5	0	1	0	0	0	0	0	0	0	0	0	....	....	....	....	-99	0	0	....	-1	/3-5	0	-0.1
Total 8	545	1670	205	426	62	11	24	150	103	126	10	6	.255	.300	.349	.648	71	-73	178	3.63	-7	3-388/S-91,2-18,1-4,0-3	28	-7.4
• CASTILLA, Vinny	Vinicio (Soria) Castilla b: 7/4/1967, Oaxaca, Mexico BR/TR, 6'1", 185 lbs. Deb: 9/1/1991																							
1991 Atl-N	12	5	1	1	0	0	0	0	0	2	0	0	.200	.200	.200	.400	12	-1	0	1.37	-3	S-12	0	-0.3
1992 Atl-N	9	16	1	4	1	0	0	1	1	4	0	0	.250	.333	.313	.646	79	-0	2	3.95	1	/3-4,S-4	1	0.0
1993 Col-N	105	337	36	86	9	7	9	30	13	45	2	5	.255	.287	.404	.690	71	-17	34	3.42	-8	*S-104	3	-1.6
1994 Col-N	52	130	16	43	11	1	3	18	7	23	2	1	.331	.365	.500	.865	105	1	23	6.46	-1	S-18,2-14/3-9,1-2	5	0.1
1995*Col-N★	139	527	82	163	34	2	32	90	30	87	2	8	.309	.351	.564	.915	106	1	95	6.46	-16	*3-137/S-5	13	-1.3
1996 Col-N	160	629	97	191	34	0	40	113	35	88	7	2	.304	.345	.548	.894	106	4	112	6.49	15	*3-160	23	2.1
1997 Col-N	159	612	94	186	25	2	40	113	44	108	2	4	.304	.358	.547	.906	108	5	113	6.79	-10	*3-157	21	-0.2
1998 Col-N★	162	645	108	206	28	4	46	144	40	89	5	9	.319	.365	.589	.954	120	15	124	7.03	-9	*3-162/S-1	21	0.8
1999 Col-N	158	615	83	169	24	1	33	102	53	75	2	3	.275	.333	.478	.811	80	-21	94	5.43	-14	*3-157	11	-3.1
2000 TB-A	85	331	22	73	9	1	6	42	14	41	1	2	.221	259	.308	.567	43	-30	24	2.39	6	3-83	3	-2.1
2001 TB-A	24	93	7	20	6	0	2	9	3	22	0	0	.215	.247	.344	.592	54	-6	7	2.54	3	3-24	1	-0.3
*Hou-N	122	445	62	120	28	1	23	82	32	86	1	4	.270	.323	.492	.815	101	-2	63	4.81	4	*3-121/S-3	12	0.4
2002*Atl-N	143	543	56	126	23	2	12	61	22	69	4	1	.232	.271	.348	.619	61	-32	46	2.77	-13	*3-139	2	-4.3
2003*Atl-N	147	542	65	150	28	3	22	76	26	86	1	2	.277	.313	.461	.775	99	-4	70	4.47	-2	*3-147	14	-0.4
Total 13	1477	5470	730	1538	260	24	268	881	320	825	29	41	.281	.326	.484	.810	92	-88	808	5.18	-46	*3-1300,S-147/2-14,1-2	130	-10.2
• CASTILLO, Alberto	Alberto Terrero Castillo b: 2/10/1970, San Juan de la Maguana, Dominican Republic BR/TR, 6', 185 lbs. Deb: 5/28/1995																							
1995 NY-N	13	29	2	3	0	0	0	0	3	9	1	0	.103	.212	.103	.316	-14	-5	1	1.00	0	C-12	0	-0.4
1996 NY-N	6	11	1	4	0	0	0	0	0	4	0	0	.364	.364	.364	.727	97	-0	1	5.61	0	/C-6	1	0.0
1997 NY-N	35	59	3	12	1	0	0	7	9	16	0	1	.203	.309	.220	.529	43	-5	4	2.02	-2	C-34	1	-0.5
1998 NY-N	38	83	13	17	4	0	2	7	9	17	0	2	.205	.290	.325	.616	63	-5	8	2.86	1	C-35/D-1	3	-0.2
1999 StL-N	93	255	21	67	8	0	4	31	24	48	0	0	.263	.331	.341	.672	70	-12	29	3.92	3	C-91	7	-0.3
2000 Tor-A	66	185	14	39	7	0	1	16	21	36	0	0	.211	.291	.265	.556	41	-17	15	2.70	6	C-66	4	-0.6
2001 Tor-A	66	131	9	26	4	0	1	4	7	30	1	1	.198	.255	.252	.507	34	-13	9	2.09	6	C-66	3	-0.4
2002 NY-A	15	37	3	5	1	1	0	4	1	12	0	0	.135	.158	.216	.374	-2	-5	1	.70	3	C-14	0	-0.2
2003 SF-N	11	15	2	3	1	0	1	4	0	5	0	0	.200	.200	.467	.667	69	-1	1	3.15	2	C-10	1	0.1
Total 9	343	805	68	176	26	1	9	73	74	177	2	4	.219	.290	.287	.577	49	-63	70	2.79	18	C-334/D-1	20	-2.5
• CASTILLO, Braulio	Braulio Robinson Medrano Castillo b: 5/13/1968, Elias Pina, Dominican Republic BR/TR, 6', 160 lbs. Deb: 8/18/1991 Career OF: 2-30-18																							
1991 Phi-N	28	52	3	9	3	0	0	2	1	15	1	1	.173	.189	.231	.419	18	-6	2	1.16	1	0-26(0-24-2)	1	-0.6
1992 Phi-N	28	76	12	15	3	1	2	7	4	15	1	0	.197	.238	.342	.580	62	-4	6	2.67	-2	0-24(2-6-16)	0	-0.7
Total 2	56	128	15	24	6	1	2	9	5	30	2	1	.188	.218	.297	.515	45	-10	8	2.04	-1	/0-50	1	-1.3
• CASTILLO, Carmen	Monte Carmelo Castillo b: 6/8/1958, San Pedro de Macoris, Dominican Republic BR/TR, 6'1", 190 lbs. Deb: 7/17/1982 Career OF: 60-8-320																							
1982 Cle-A	47	120	11	25	4	0	2	11	6	17	0	0	.208	.258	.292	.549	51	-8	9	2.45	-2	0-43(19-8-20)/D-2	1	-1.1
1983 Cle-A	23	36	9	10	2	1	1	3	4	6	1	1	.278	.366	.472	.838	124	1	6	6.43	1	0-19(0-0-19)/D-1	1	0.2
1984 Cle-A	87	211	36	55	9	2	10	36	21	32	1	3	.261	.333	.464	.798	116	3	30	4.86	0	0-70(0-0-70)/D-2	6	0.1
1985 Cle-A	67	184	27	45	5	1	11	25	11	40	3	0	.245	.298	.462	.760	105	1	24	4.50	-2	0-51(0-0-51)/D-9	4	-0.4
1986 Cle-A	85	205	34	57	9	0	8	32	9	48	2	1	.278	.312	.439	.751	103	0	25	4.20	1	0-37(0-0-37),D-35	4	-0.1
1987 Cle-A	89	220	27	55	17	0	11	31	16	52	1	1	.250	.301	.477	.778	101	-1	33	5.15	1	D-43,0-23(1-0-22)	5	-0.1
1988 Cle-A	66	176	12	48	8	0	4	14	5	31	6	2	.273	.297	.386	.683	87	-3	19	3.85	-3	0-45(30-0-16)/D-9	3	-0.7
1989 Min-A	94	218	23	56	13	3	8	33	15	40	1	2	.257	.308	.454	.762	105	-0	29	4.45	-1	0-67(7-0-61),D-16	5	-0.4
1990 Min-A	64	137	11	30	4	0	0	12	3	23	0	1	.219	.241	.248	.489	35	-13	8	1.95	-1	D-35,0-21(2-0-21)	0	-1.5
1991 Min-A	9	12	0	2	0	1	0	0	0	2	0	0	.167	.231	.333	.564	52	-1	1	2.65	0	/0-4(1-0-3),D-2	0	-0.1
Total 10	631	1519	190	383	71	8	55	197	90	291	15	11	.252	.300	.418	.718	94	-20	184	4.15	-6	0-380,D-154	29	-4.2
• CASTILLO, Juan	Juan (Bryas) Castillo b: 1/25/1962, San Pedro de Macoris, Dominican Republic BB/TR, 5'11", 162 lbs. Deb: 4/12/1986 Career OF: 1-0-1																							
1986 Mil-A	26	54	6	9	0	1	0	5	5	12	1	1	.167	.250	.204	.454	24	-6	3	1.48	0	2-17/S-4,3-2,D-2,0-1	1	-0.4
1987 Mil-A	116	321	44	72	11	4	3	28	33	76	15	7	.224	.303	.312	.614	62	-17	33	3.29	-4	2-97,S-13/3-7	6	-1.5
1988 Mil-A	54	90	10	20	0	0	0	2	3	14	2	0	.222	.247	.222	.470	32	-8	5	1.96	1	2-18,3-17,S-13/D-3,0-1	1	-0.6
1989 Mil-A	3	4	0	0	0	0	0	3	0	2	0	0	.000	.000	.000	.000	-101	-1	0	.00	0	/2-3	0	-0.1
Total 4	199	469	60	101	11	5	3	38	41	104	18	8	.215	.284	.279	.563	50	-32	41	2.78	-3	2-135/S-30,3-26,D-5,0-2	8	-2.7
• CASTILLO, Luis	Luis Antonio (Donato) Castillo b: 9/12/1975, San Pedro de Macoris, Dominican Republic BB/TR, 5'11", 145 lbs. Deb: 8/8/1996																							
1996 Fla-N	41	164	26	43	2	1	1	8	14	46	17	4	.262	.320	.305	.625	68	-5	19	3.98	6	2-41	3	0.2
1997 Fla-N	75	263	27	63	8	0	0	8	27	53	16	10	.240	.310	.270	.580	56	-17	22	2.75	6	2-70	3	-0.8
1998 Fla-N	44	153	21	31	3	2	1	10	22	33	3	0	.203	.307	.268	.575	55	-9	15	3.20	-4	2-44	3	-1.1
1999 Fla-N	128	487	76	147	23	4	0	28	67	85	50	17	.302	.386	.366	.752	97	4	78	5.70	-6	*2-126	14	0.3
2000 Fla-N	136	539	101	180	17	3	2	17	78	86	**62**	22	.334	.418	.388	.806	110	17	96	6.44	-12	*2-136	18	1.1
2001 Fla-N	134	537	76	141	16	10	2	45	67	90	33	16	.263	.345	.341	.686	81	-13	68	4.30	10	*2-133	14	0.3
2002 Fla-N★	146	606	86	185	18	5	2	39	55	76	**48**	15	.305	.365	.361	.726	96	2	86	5.17	-5	*2-144	19	0.4
2003*Fla-N★	152	595	99	187	19	6	6	39	63	60	21	19	.314	.382	.397	.778	108	5	91	5.46	7	*2-152	22	1.9
Total 8	856	3344	512	977	106	31	14	194	393	529	250	103	.292	.368	.355	.723	92	-17	473	4.99	1	2-846	96	2.4
• CASTILLO, Manny	Esteban Manuel Antonio (Cabrera) Castillo b: 4/1/1957, Santo Domingo, Dominican Republic BB/TR, 5'9", 160 lbs. Deb: 9/1/1980																							
1980 KC-A	7	10	1	2	0	0	0	0	0	0	0	0	.200	.200	.200	.400	10	-1	0	1.35	1	/3-3,D-2,2-1	0	-0.1
1982 Sea-A	138	506	49	130	29	1	3	49	22	35	2	8	.257	.291	.336	.627	70	-25	46	3.03	-17	*3-130/2-9	4	-4.3
1983 Sea-A	91	203	13	42	6	3	0	24	7	20	1	1	.207	.237	.266	.503	37	-18	12	1.93	-6	3-55,1-11/D-6,2-5,P-1	1	-3.0
Total 3	236	719	63	174	35	4	3	73	29	55	3	9	.242	.274	.314	.589	60	-44	58	2.68	-22	3-188/2-15,1-11,D-8,P-1	5	-7.3
• CASTILLO, Marty	Martin Horace Castillo b: 1/16/1957, Long Beach, CA BR/TR, 6'1", 190 lbs. Deb: 8/19/1981																							
1981 Det-A	6	8	1	1	0	0	0	0	0	2	0	0	.125	.125	.125	.250	-27	-1	0	.48	1	/3-4,C-1,0-1	0	-0.1
1982 Det-A	1	0	0	0	0	0	0	0	0	0	0	0	....	....	....	....	-100	0	0	....	0	/C-1	0	0.0
1983 Det-A	67	119	10	23	4	0	2	10	7	22	2	0	.193	.238	.277	.515	42	-9	8	1.96	0	3-58,C-10	2	-0.9

YEAR TM-L	G	AB	R	H	2B	3B	HR	RBI	BB	SO	SB	CS	AVG	OBP	SLG	OPS	OPS+	BR/A	RC	RC/G	FR	G/POS	WS	TPW
1984*Det-A	70	141	16	33	5	2	4	17	10	33	1	0	.234	.285	.383	.668	83	-3	15	3.47	-4	C-36,3-33/D-1	3	-0.6
1985 Det-A	57	84	4	10	2	0	2	5	2	19	0	2	.119	.140	.214	.354	-5	-13	2	.68	1	C-32,3-25	2	-1.1
Total 5	**201**	**352**	**31**	**67**	**11**	**2**	**8**	**32**	**19**	**76**	**3**	**2**	**.190**	**.232**	**.301**	**.533**	**47**	**-27**	**25**	**2.17**	**-2**	**3-120/C-80,D-1,0-1**	**7**	**-2.7**
• CASTILLO, Tony	Anthony Castillo b: 6/14/1957, San Jose, CA BR/TR, 6'4", 190 lbs. Deb: 9/22/1978																							
1978 SD-N	5	8	0	1	0	0	0	1	0	2	0	0	.125	.125	.125	.250	-33	-1	0	.57	0	/C-5	0	-0.2
• CASTINO, John	John Anthony Castino b: 10/23/1954, Evanston, IL BR/TR, 5'11", 175 lbs. Deb: 4/6/1979																							
1979 Min-A	148	393	49	112	13	8	5	52	27	72	5	2	.285	.333	.397	.729	92	-4	52	4.42	-5	*3-143/S-5	9	-1.0
1980 Min-A	150	546	67	165	17	7	13	64	29	67	7	5	.302	.337	.430	.768	101	-0	75	4.77	13	*3-138,S-18	18	1.2
1981 Min-A	101	381	41	102	13	**9**	6	36	18	52	4	5	.268	.303	.396	.699	94	-5	45	4.08	7	3-98/2-4	12	0.1
1982 Min-A	117	410	48	99	12	6	6	37	36	51	2	5	.241	.306	.344	.650	76	-15	41	3.35	6	2-96,3-21/0-6(5-1-0),D-1	8	-0.4
1983 Min-A	142	563	83	156	30	4	11	57	62	54	4	2	.277	.350	.403	.753	103	3	81	5.06	10	*2-132/3-8,D-1	21	2.0
1984 Min-A	8	27	5	12	1	0	0	3	5	2	0	0	.444	.531	.481	1.013	174	3	6	10.26	1	/3-8	2	0.4
Total 6	**666**	**2320**	**293**	**646**	**86**	**34**	**41**	**249**	**177**	**298**	**22**	**19**	**.278**	**.331**	**.398**	**.729**	**95**	**-18**	**300**	**4.46**	**32**	**3-416,2-232/S-23,0-6,D-2**	**70**	**2.3**
• CASTINO, Vince	Vincent Charles Castino b: 10/11/1917, Willisville, IL d: 3/6/1967, Sacramento, CA BR/TR, 5'9", 175 lbs. Deb: 6/24/1943																							
1943 Chi-A	33	101	14	23	1	0	2	16	12	11	0	0	.228	.310	.297	.607	78	-3	10	3.20	-2	C-30	2	-0.3
1944 Chi-A	29	78	8	18	5	0	0	3	10	13	0	1	.231	.326	.295	.621	79	-2	8	3.47	2	C-26	2	0.1
1945 Chi-A	26	36	2	8	1	0	0	4	3	7	0	0	.222	.282	.250	.532	56	-2	2	2.08	0	C-25	0	-0.2
Total 3	**88**	**215**	**24**	**49**	**7**	**0**	**2**	**23**	**25**	**31**	**0**	**1**	**.228**	**.311**	**.288**	**.600**	**75**	**-7**	**20**	**3.10**	**-1**	**/C-81**	**4**	**-0.4**
• CASTLE, Don	Donald Hardy Castle b: 2/1/1950, Kokomo, IN BL/TL, 6'1", 205 lbs. Deb: 9/11/1973																							
1973 Tex-A	4	13	0	4	1	0	0	2	1	3	0	0	.308	.357	.385	.742	114	0	1	2.77	0	/D-3	0	0.0
• CASTLE, John	John Francis Castle b: 6/1/1883, Honey Brook, PA d: 4/13/1929, Philadelphia, PA, 5'10.5" Deb: 4/25/1910																							
1910 Phi-N	3	4	1	1	0	0	0	0	0	0	1	....	.250	.250	.250	.500	44	-0	0	4.09	0	/0-2(1-1-0)	0	-0.1
• CASTLEMAN, Foster	Foster Ephraim Castleman b: 1/1/1931, Nashville, TN BR/TR, 6', 175 lbs. Deb: 8/4/1954																							
1954 NY-N	13	12	0	3	0	0	0	1	0	3	0	0	.250	.308	.250	.558	47	-1	1	1.99	-1	/3-2	0	-0.2
1955 NY-N	15	28	3	6	1	0	2	4	2	4	0	0	.214	.267	.464	.731	89	-1	4	4.25	-1	/2-6,3-1	1	-0.1
1956 NY-N	124	385	33	87	16	3	14	45	15	50	2	1	.226	.259	.392	.651	72	-16	37	3.14	4	*3-107/S-2,2-1	6	-1.3
1957 NY-N	18	37	7	6	2	0	1	1	2	8	0	0	.162	.205	.297	.502	33	-4	2	2.06	-1	/3-7,2-1,S-1	0	-0.4
1958 Bal-A	98	200	15	34	5	0	3	14	16	34	2	0	.170	.242	.240	.482	35	-17	12	1.80	-2	S-91/2-4,3-4,0-1	3	-1.4
Total 5	**268**	**662**	**58**	**136**	**24**	**3**	**20**	**65**	**35**	**99**	**4**	**1**	**.205**	**.252**	**.341**	**.593**	**59**	**-39**	**55**	**2.68**	**0**	**3-121/S-94,2-12,0-1**	**10**	**-3.4**
• CASTRO, Juan	Juan Gabriel Castro b: 6/20/1972, Los Mochis, Mexico BR/TR, 5'10", 165 lbs. Deb: 9/2/1995																							
1995 LA-N	11	4	0	1	0	0	0	0	1	1	0	0	.250	.400	.250	.650	84	-0	1	4.54	0	/3-7,S-4	0	0.0
1996*LA-N	70	132	16	26	5	3	0	5	10	27	1	0	.197	.254	.280	.534	44	-11	10	2.28	-4	S-30,3-23/2-9,0-1	2	-1.2
1997 LA-N	40	75	3	11	3	1	0	4	7	20	0	0	.147	.220	.213	.433	15	-9	4	1.41	-1	S-22,2-14/3-3	1	-0.9
1998 LA-N	89	220	25	43	7	0	2	14	15	37	0	0	.195	.247	.255	.501	34	-21	14	1.98	2	S-47,2-38,3-12	3	-1.5
1999 LA-N	2	1	0	0	0	0	0	0	0	1	0	0	.000	.000	.000	.000	-106	-0	0	.00	0	/2-1,S-1	0	0.0
2000 Cin-N	82	224	20	54	12	2	4	23	14	33	0	2	.241	.286	.366	.652	62	-15	21	2.99	-2	S-57,2-21/3-7	3	-1.2
2001 Cin-N	96	242	27	54	10	0	3	13	13	50	0	0	.223	.263	.302	.564	43	-21	18	2.33	-15	S-46,2-37,3-19/1-1	1	-3.1
2002 Cin-N	54	82	5	18	3	0	2	11	7	18	0	0	.220	.281	.329	.610	58	-5	8	3.36	0	S-25,2-17/1-1,3-1	2	-0.4
2003 Cin-N	113	320	28	81	14	1	9	33	18	58	2	3	.253	.293	.388	.680	77	-13	34	3.59	3	2-56,3-30,S-24/1-1	7	-0.6
Total 9	**557**	**1300**	**124**	**288**	**54**	**7**	**20**	**103**	**85**	**245**	**3**	**5**	**.222**	**.269**	**.320**	**.589**	**53**	**-95**	**109**	**2.68**	**-18**	**S-256,2-193,3-102/1-3,0-1**	**19**	**-8.9**
• CASTRO, Luis	Luis Manuel "Jud" Castro b: 1876, Medellin, Colombia d: 9/24/1941, New York, NY BR/TR, 5'7" Deb: 4/23/1902																							
1902 Phi-A	42	143	18	35	8	1	1	15	4	....	2	....	.245	.265	.336	.601	63	-8	14	3.32	-13	2-36/0-3(0-2-1),S-1	1	-2.0
• CASTRO, Ramon	Ramon Abraham Castro b: 3/1/1976, Vega Baja, Puerto Rico BR/TR, 6'3", 225 lbs. Deb: 8/27/1999																							
1999 Fla-N	24	67	4	12	4	0	2	4	10	14	0	0	.179	.286	.328	.614	58	-4	7	3.10	2	C-24	1	-0.1
2000 Fla-N	50	138	10	33	4	0	2	14	16	36	0	0	.239	.323	.312	.634	64	-7	15	3.64	0	C-50	3	-0.5
2001 Fla-N	7	11	0	2	0	0	0	1	1	1	0	0	.182	.250	.182	.432	15	-1	1	1.70	0	/C-3	0	-0.2
2002 Fla-N	54	101	11	24	4	0	6	18	14	24	0	0	.238	.330	.455	.786	109	1	15	4.62	-2	C-37/D-1	4	0.1
2003 Fla-N	40	53	6	15	2	0	5	8	4	11	0	0	.283	.333	.604	.937	143	3	11	7.83	-1	C-18/D-1	2	0.3
Total 5	**175**	**370**	**31**	**86**	**14**	**0**	**15**	**45**	**45**	**86**	**0**	**0**	**.232**	**.317**	**.392**	**.709**	**85**	**-9**	**47**	**4.29**	**-2**	**C-132/D-2**	**10**	**-0.4**
• CATALANOTTO, Frank	Frank John Catalanotto b: 4/27/1974, Smithtown, NY BL/TR, 6', 170 lbs. Deb: 9/3/1997 Career OF: 165-0-59																							
1997 Det-A	13	26	2	8	2	0	0	3	3	7	0	0	.308	.379	.385	.764	101	0	4	6.13	0	/2-6,D-3	1	0.0
1998 Det-A	89	213	23	60	13	2	6	25	12	39	3	2	.282	.332	.446	.778	99	-1	31	5.08	-1	2-31,D-23,1-18/3-3	4	-0.3
1999 Det-A	100	286	41	79	19	0	11	35	15	49	3	4	.276	.332	.458	.790	98	-3	42	5.15	0	1-32,2-32,3-21/D-9	5	-0.4
2000 Tex-A	103	282	55	82	13	2	10	42	33	36	6	2	.291	.377	.457	.834	108	5	51	6.45	-5	2-50,D-20,1-17/0-1	8	0.0
2001 Tex-A	133	463	77	153	31	5	11	54	39	55	15	5	.330	.392	.490	.882	126	19	92	7.69	-3	0-92(78-0-15),2-13,3-11/1-5,D	17	1.2
2002 Tex-A	68	212	42	57	16	6	3	23	25	27	9	5	.269	.367	.443	.811	109	3	36	5.79	-5	0-26(26-0-0),2-23,1-15/D-8	7	-0.3
2003 Tor-A	133	489	83	146	34	6	13	59	35	62	2	2	.299	.353	.472	.825	113	8	81	6.06	-7	*0-100(61-0-43),D-20/1-5	15	-0.4
Total 7	**639**	**1971**	**323**	**585**	**128**	**21**	**54**	**241**	**162**	**275**	**38**	**20**	**.297**	**.362**	**.465**	**.828**	**111**	**32**	**336**	**6.20**	**-22**	**0-219,2-155/1-92,D-87,3-35**	**57**	**-0.4**
• CATER, Danny	Danny Anderson Cater b: 2/25/1940, Austin, TX BR/TR, 6', 180 lbs. Deb: 4/14/1964 Career OF: 293-2-16																							
1964 Phi-N	60	152	13	45	9	1	1	13	7	15	1	0	.296	.327	.388	.715	102	0	18	4.19	1	0-39(36-1-2)/1-7,3-1	4	-0.1
1965 Chi-A	142	514	74	139	18	4	14	55	33	65	3	3	.270	.318	.403	.721	110	4	61	4.12	-4	*0-127(127-1-0),3-11/1-3	16	-0.7
1966 Chi-A	21	60	3	11	1	1	0	4	0	10	3	1	.183	.197	.233	.430	25	-6	3	1.35	-1	0-18(16-0-3)	0	-0.8
KC-A	116	425	47	124	16	3	7	52	28	37	1	4	.292	.337	.393	.730	113	5	53	4.48	-2	1-53,3-42,0-22(21-0-1)	15	-0.1
Yr.	137	485	50	135	17	4	7	56	28	47	4	5	.278	.320	.373	.694	102	-1	56	4.02	-3	1-53,3-42,0-40(37-0-4)	15	-0.9
1967 KC-A	142	529	55	143	17	4	4	46	34	56	4	5	.270	.319	.340	.659	98	-3	54	3.58	-1	3-56,0-55(55-0-0),1-44	11	-0.9
1968 Oak-A	147	504	53	146	28	3	6	62	35	43	8	7	.290	.338	.393	.731	127	14	61	4.15	3	*1-121,0-20(19-0-2)/2-1	17	1.1
1969 Oak-A	152	584	64	153	24	2	10	76	28	40	1	4	.262	.298	.361	.659	87	-14	55	3.19	9	*1-132,0-20(19-0-1)/2-4	10	-1.6
1970 NY-A	155	582	64	175	26	5	6	76	34	44	4	2	.301	.341	.393	.735	108	5	74	4.61	2	*1-131,3-42/0-7(0-0-7)	19	-0.2
1971 NY-A	121	428	39	118	16	5	4	50	19	25	0	3	.276	.310	.364	.674	96	-5	42	3.39	6	1-78,3-52	8	-0.4
1972 Bos-A	92	317	32	75	17	1	8	39	15	33	0	1	.237	.275	.372	.648	87	-7	28	2.80	4	1-90	4	-1.0
1973 Bos-A	63	195	30	61	12	0	1	24	10	22	0	0	.313	.350	.390	.739	102	1	25	4.80	0	1-37,3-21/D-3	5	-0.2
1974 Bos-A	56	126	14	31	5	0	5	20	10	13	1	0	.246	.312	.405	.716	98	-0	15	3.98	1	1-23,D-14	2	0.0
1975 StL-N	22	35	3	8	2	0	0	2	1	3	0	0	.229	.250	.286	.536	47	-3	3	2.50	0	1-12	0	-0.3
Total 12	**1289**	**4451**	**491**	**1229**	**191**	**29**	**66**	**519**	**254**	**406**	**26**	**30**	**.276**	**.318**	**.377**	**.695**	**102**	**-8**	**492**	**3.83**	**20**	**1-731,0-308,3-225/D-17,2-5**	**111**	**-5.3**
• CATHER, Ted	Theodore Physick Cather b: 5/20/1889, Chester, PA d: 4/9/1945, Elkton, MD BR/TR, 5'10.5", 178 lbs. Deb: 9/23/1912 Career OF: 91-17-65																							
1912 StL-N	5	19	4	8	1	1	0	2	0	4	1	....	.421	.421	.579	1.000	176	2	5	11.44	2	/0-5(0-4-1)	1	0.3
1913 StL-N	67	183	16	39	8	4	0	12	9	24	7	....	.213	.250	.301	.551	58	-11	15	2.51	-0	0-57(14-1-42)/1-1,P-1	1	-1.5
1914 StL-N	39	99	11	27	7	0	0	13	3	15	4	....	.273	.294	.343	.638	90	-2	11	3.70	0	0-28(23-5-0)	2	-0.3
*Bos-N	50	145	19	43	11	2	0	27	7	28	7	....	.297	.338	.400	.738	120	3	21	5.08	-2	0-48(23-7-20)	5	-0.1
Yr.	89	244	30	70	18	2	0	40	10	43	11	....	.287	.320	.377	.697	108	1	32	4.52	-2	0-76(46-12-20)	7	-0.4
1915 Bos-N	40	102	10	21	3	1	2	18	15	19	2	4	.206	.319	.314	.633	94	-2	11	3.08	-2	0-32(31-0-2)	2	-0.5
Total 4	**201**	**548**	**60**	**138**	**30**	**8**	**2**	**72**	**34**	**90**	**21**	**4**	**.252**	**.300**	**.347**	**.647**	**91**	**-9**	**62**	**3.71**	**-2**	**0-170/1-1,P-1**	**11**	**-2.1**
• CATON, Howdy	James Howard "Buster" Caton b: 7/16/1896, Zanesville, OH d: 1/8/1948, Zanesville, OH BR/TR, 5'6", 165 lbs. Deb: 9/17/1917																							
1917 Pit-N	14	57	6	12	1	2	0	4	6	7	0	....	.211	.286	.298	.584	77	-2	5	2.63	-1	S-14	1	-0.2
1918 Pit-N	80	303	37	71	5	7	0	17	32	16	12	....	.234	.312	.297	.609	83	-5	31	3.32	-3	S-79	8	-0.3
1919 Pit-N	39	102	13	18	1	2	0	5	12	10	2	....	.176	.263	.225	.489	46	-6	7	2.01	-4	S-17,3-14/0-1	1	-1.0
1920 Pit-N	98	352	29	83	11	5	0	27	33	19	4	9	.236	.305	.295	.600	71	-14	32	2.93	-9	S-96	7	-1.7
Total 4	**231**	**814**	**85**	**184**	**18**	**16**	**0**	**53**	**83**	**52**	**18**	**9**	**.226**	**.301**	**.287**	**.588**	**72**	**-27**	**74**	**2.93**	**-17**	**S-206/3-14,0-1**	**17**	**-3.1**

YEAR TM-L	G	AB	R	H	2B	3B	HR	RBI	BB	SO	SB	CS	AVG	OBP	SLG	OPS	OPS+	BR/A	RC	RC/G	FR	G/POS	WS	TPW
• CATTERSON, Tom	Thomas Henry Catterson b: 8/25/1884, Warwick, RI d: 2/5/1920, Portland, ME BL/TL, 5'10", 170 lbs. Deb: 9/19/1908 Career OF: 18-6-0																							
1908 Bro-N	19	68	5	13	1	1	1	2	5	....	0	....	.191	.257	.279	.536	74	-2	5	2.22	0	0-18(18-0-0)	1	-0.3
1909 Bro-N	9	18	0	4	0	0	0	1	3	....	0	....	.222	.333	.222	.556	75	-0	1	2.54	-1	/0-6(0-6-0)	0	-0.1
Total 2	28	86	5	17	1	1	1	3	8	....	0	....	.198	.274	.267	.541	74	-2	6	2.29	0	/0-24	1	-0.5
• CAULFIELD, Jake	John Joseph Caulfield b: 11/23/1917, Los Angeles, CA d: 12/16/1986, San Francisco, CA BR/TR, 5'11", 170 lbs. Deb: 4/24/1946																							
1946 Phi-A	44	94	13	26	8	0	0	10	4	11	0	0	.277	.306	.362	.668	87	-2	10	3.96	-4	S-31/3-1	1	-0.5
• CAUSEY, Wayne	James Wayne Causey b: 12/26/1936, Ruston, LA BL/TR, 5'10.5", 175 lbs. Deb: 6/5/1955																							
1955 Bal-A	68	175	14	34	2	1	1	9	17	25	0	1	.194	.269	.234	.504	39	-15	12	2.22	-5	3-55/2-7,S-1	1	-2.0
1956 Bal-A	53	88	7	15	0	1	1	4	8	23	0	0	.170	.240	.227	.467	26	-9	5	1.74	-1	3-30/2-7	1	-1.0
1957 Bal-A	14	10	2	2	0	0	0	1	5	2	0	0	.200	.500	.200	.700	105	1	2	5.03	-1	/2-6,3-5	1	0.0
1961 KC-A	104	312	37	86	14	1	8	49	37	28	0	0	.276	.352	.404	.756	101	1	46	5.15	6	3-88,S-11/2-9	11	0.8
1962 KC-A	117	305	40	77	14	1	4	38	41	30	2	0	.252	.345	.344	.689	83	-5	38	4.20	-7	S-51,3-26/2-9	7	-0.7
1963 KC-A	139	554	72	155	32	4	8	44	56	54	4	2	.280	.346	.395	.741	103	3	77	4.99	3	*S-135/3-2	20	1.8
1964 KC-A	157	604	82	170	31	4	8	49	88	65	0	1	.281	.379	.386	.765	110	12	90	5.30	-6	*S-131,2-17/3-9	20	2.1
1965 KC-A	144	513	48	134	17	8	3	34	61	48	1	3	.261	.342	.343	.685	97	-2	63	4.25	-2	S-62,2-45,3-35	15	0.5
1966 KC-A	28	79	1	18	0	0	0	5	7	6	1	0	.228	.291	.228	.519	53	-4	5	2.16	-3	3-15,S-10	1	-0.7
Chi-A	78	164	23	40	8	2	0	13	24	13	2	0	.244	.340	.317	.657	97	1	20	4.04	-3	2-60/3-1,S-1	6	0.1
Yr.	106	243	24	58	8	2	0	18	31	19	3	0	.239	.325	.288	.613	83	-4	25	3.42	-6	2-60,3-16,S-11	7	-0.6
1967 Chi-A	124	292	21	66	10	3	1	28	32	35	2	5	.226	.305	.291	.596	80	-8	27	3.03	-3	2-96/S-2	8	-0.6
1968 Chi-A	59	100	8	18	2	0	0	7	14	7	0	0	.180	.287	.200	.487	49	-5	7	2.22	-6	2-41	1	-1.1
Cal-A	4	11	0	0	0	0	0	0	0	1	0	0	.000	.000	.000	.000	-104	-3	0	.00	1	/2-4	0	-0.1
Yr.	63	111	8	18	2	0	0	7	14	8	0	0	.162	.262	.180	.442	36	-8	7	1.94	-4	2-45	1	-1.2
Atl-N	16	37	2	4	0	1	1	4	0	4	0	0	.108	.108	.243	.351	3	-4	1	.79	-1	/2-6,3-2,S-2	0	-0.6
Total 11	1105	3244	357	819	130	26	35	285	390	341	12	12	.252	.335	.341	.676	89	-39	394	4.14	-28	S-406,2-307,3-268	92	-1.5
• CAVANAUGH, John	John J. Cavanaugh b: 6/5/1900, Reading, PA d: 1/14/1961, New Brunswick, NJ BR/TR, 5'9", 158 lbs. Deb: 7/7/1919																							
1919 Phi-N	1	1	0	0	0	0	0	0	0	1	0	....	.000	.000	.000	.000	-93	-0	0	.00	0	/3-1	0	-0.1
• CAVARRETTA, Phil	Philip Joseph Cavarretta b: 7/19/1916, Chicago, IL BL/TL, 5'11.5", 175 lbs. Deb: 9/16/1934 M/C Career OF: 148-234-172																							
1934 Chi-N	7	21	5	8	0	1	1	6	2	3	1	....	.381	.435	.619	1.054	182	2	6	12.50	1	/1-5	1	0.3
1935*Chi-N	146	589	85	162	28	12	8	82	39	61	4	....	.275	.322	.404	.726	93	-6	79	4.80	-6	*1-145	14	-2.5
1936 Chi-N	124	458	55	125	18	1	9	56	17	36	8	....	.273	.306	.376	.682	81	-14	53	4.12	-5	*1-115	7	-2.9
1937 Chi-N	106	329	43	94	18	7	5	56	32	35	7	....	.286	.349	.429	.778	106	3	50	5.46	2	0-55(7-47-1),1-43	11	0.0
1938*Chi-N	92	268	29	64	11	4	1	28	14	27	4	....	.239	.287	.321	.608	65	-13	25	3.14	-2	0-52(7-8-37),1-28	3	-2.0
1939 Chi-N	22	55	4	15	3	1	0	0	4	3	2	....	.273	.322	.364	.686	82	-1	6	4.23	-1	1-13/0-1	1	-0.3
1940 Chi-N	65	193	34	54	11	4	2	22	31	18	3	....	.280	.388	.409	.797	122	7	33	6.23	-2	1-52	7	0.0
1941 Chi-N	107	346	46	99	18	4	6	40	53	28	2	....	.286	.384	.413	.797	129	15	58	6.08	-3	0-66(8-53-6),1-33	14	0.8
1942 Chi-N	136	482	59	130	28	4	3	54	71	42	7	....	.270	.365	.363	.728	118	13	71	5.21	1	0-70(4-67-0),1-61	16	0.7
1943 Chi-N	143	530	93	154	27	9	8	73	75	42	3	....	.291	.382	.421	.802	134	25	89	6.06	-10	*1-134/0-7(0-7-0)	18	0.8
1944 Chi-N★	152	614	106	**197**	35	15	5	82	67	42	4	....	.321	.390	.451	.841	137	31	111	6.90	-9	*1-139,0-13(0-13-0)	25	1.5
1945*Chi-N★	132	498	94	177	34	10	6	97	81	34	5	....	**.355**	**.449**	.500	.949	167	49	119	9.75	-1	*1-120,0-11(11-0-0)	30	4.1
1946 Chi-N★	139	510	89	150	28	10	8	78	88	54	2	....	.294	.401	.435	.836	140	30	92	6.59	4	0-86(7-13-78),1-51	25	3.2
1947 Chi-N★	127	459	56	144	22	5	2	63	58	35	2	....	.314	.391	.397	.787	114	11	76	6.31	1	*0-100(69-26-8),1-24	16	0.6
1948 Chi-N	111	334	41	93	16	5	3	40	35	29	4	....	.278	.349	.383	.732	102	1	48	5.25	1	1-41,0-40(30-0-10)	9	-0.1
1949 Chi-N	105	360	46	106	22	4	8	49	45	31	2	....	.294	.374	.444	.819	122	12	62	6.26	5	1-70,0-25(3-0-21)	14	1.3
1950 Chi-N	82	256	49	70	11	1	10	31	40	31	1	....	.273	.376	.441	.817	115	7	45	6.24	-1	1-67/0-3(0-0-3)	8	0.4
1951 Chi-N	89	206	24	64	7	1	6	28	27	28	0	0	.311	.393	.442	.835	122	7	39	7.12	2	1-53	8	0.8
1952 Chi-N	41	63	7	15	1	1	1	8	9	3	0	0	.238	.333	.333	.667	84	-1	8	4.47	1	1-13	2	0.0
1953 Chi-N	27	21	3	6	3	0	0	3	6	3	0	0	.286	.444	.429	.873	126	1	5	8.63	0	....	1	0.1
1954 Chi-A	71	158	21	50	6	0	3	24	26	12	4	0	.316	.419	.411	.831	124	8	31	7.51	0	1-44/0-9(2-0-7)	7	0.6
1955 Chi-A	6	4	1	0	0	0	0	0	0	1	0	0	.000	.000	.000	.000	-97	-1	0	.00	0	/1-3	0	-0.1
Total 22	2030	6754	990	1977	347	99	95	920	820	598	65	0	.293	.372	.416	.788	119	187	1106	6.01	-21	*1-1254,0-538	237	7.2
• CAVENEY, Ike	James Christopher Caveney b: 12/10/1894, San Francisco, CA d: 7/6/1949, San Francisco, CA BR/TR, 5'9", 168 lbs. Deb: 4/12/1922																							
1922 Cin-N	118	394	41	94	12	9	3	54	29	33	6	6	.239	.301	.338	.638	66	-21	41	3.29	-6	*S-118	8	-1.3
1923 Cin-N	138	488	58	135	21	9	4	63	26	41	5	4	.277	.315	.381	.696	84	-12	58	4.09	-3	*S-138	13	0.0
1924 Cin-N	95	337	36	92	19	1	4	32	14	21	2	3	.273	.310	.371	.681	83	-9	38	3.97	-10	S-90/2-5	7	-0.9
1925 Cin-N	115	358	38	89	9	5	2	47	28	31	2	0	.249	.303	.318	.622	60	-20	36	3.40	1	*S-111	8	-0.7
Total 4	466	1577	173	410	61	24	13	196	97	126	15	13	.260	.307	.354	.661	74	-61	174	3.70	-19	S-457/2-5	36	-2.9
• CEDENO, Andujar	Andujar (Donastorg) Cedeno b: 8/21/1969, La Romana, Dominican Republic d: 10/28/2000, Santo Domingo, Dominican Republic BR/TR, 6'1", 168 lbs. Deb: 9/2/1990																							
1990 Hou-N	7	8	0	0	0	0	0	0	0	5	0	0	.000	.000	.000	.000	-103	-2	0	.00	-1	/S-3	0	-0.3
1991 Hou-N	67	251	27	61	13	2	9	36	9	74	4	3	.243	.272	.418	.690	97	-3	27	3.71	-9	S-66	5	-0.7
1992 Hou-N	71	220	15	38	13	2	2	13	14	71	2	0	.173	.232	.277	.509	46	-16	15	2.22	1	S-70	3	-1.1
1993 Hou-N	149	505	69	143	24	4	11	56	48	97	9	7	.283	.349	.412	.761	107	4	69	4.69	-12	*S-149/3-1	13	0.2
1994 Hou-N	98	342	38	90	26	0	9	49	29	79	1	1	.263	.335	.418	.753	100	-1	48	4.97	-6	S-95	12	0.2
1995 SD-N	120	390	42	82	16	2	6	31	28	92	5	3	.210	.272	.308	.580	55	-27	31	2.55	-6	*S-116/3-1	5	-2.3
1996 SD-N	49	154	10	36	2	1	3	18	9	32	3	2	.234	.280	.318	.599	61	-9	12	2.51	-1	S-47/3-2	3	-0.7
Det-A	52	179	19	35	4	2	7	20	4	37	2	1	.196	.213	.358	.571	41	-17	11	1.89	-7	S-51/3-1	1	-1.9
Hou-N	3	2	1	0	0	0	0	0	2	1	0	0	.000	.500	.000	.500	50	0	0	3.51	0	/S-2,3-1	0	0.1
Yr.	52	156	11	36	2	1	3	18	11	33	3	2	.231	.286	.314	.600	61	-9	12	2.53	-1	S-49/3-3	3	-0.6
Total 7	616	2051	221	485	98	13	47	223	143	488	26	17	.236	.293	.366	.659	78	-72	212	3.47	-40	S-599/3-6	42	-6.5
• CEDENO, Cesar	Cesar (Encarnacion) Cedeno b: 2/25/1951, Santo Domingo, Dominican Republic BR/TR, 6'2", 195 lbs. Deb: 6/20/1970 Career OF: 138-1457-144																							
1970 Hou-N	90	355	46	110	21	4	7	42	15	57	17	4	.310	.341	.451	.792	115	8	53	5.51	-3	0-90(0-75-17)	12	0.1
1971 Hou-N	161	611	85	161	**40**	6	10	81	25	102	20	9	.264	.296	.398	.693	97	-5	70	3.94	-6	*0-157(11-125-30)/1-2	17	-1.7
1972 Hou-N★	139	559	103	179	**39**	8	22	82	56	62	55	21	.320	.387	.537	.924	163	48	115	7.45	4	*0-137(0-137-0)	33	5.2
1973 Hou-N★	139	525	86	168	35	2	25	70	41	79	56	15	.320	.377	.537	.914	151	40	102	7.00	4	*0-136(0-136-0)	30	4.3
1974 Hou-N★	160	610	95	164	29	5	26	102	64	103	57	17	.269	.342	.461	.803	129	26	99	5.57	9	*0-157(0-157-0)	27	3.2
1975 Hou-N	131	500	93	144	31	3	13	63	62	52	50	17	.288	.374	.440	.814	135	28	85	5.84	0	*0-131(0-131-0)	20	2.5
1976 Hou-N★	150	575	89	171	26	5	18	83	55	51	58	15	.297	.360	.454	.814	143	37	94	5.80	1	*0-146(0-146-0)	30	3.6
1977 Hou-N	141	530	92	148	36	8	14	71	47	50	61	14	.279	.350	.457	.807	126	27	89	5.77	6	*0-137(0-137-0)	23	3.1
1978 Hou-N	50	192	31	54	8	2	7	23	15	24	23	2	.281	.333	.453	.786	127	10	31	5.78	1	0-50(0-50-0)	9	1.2
1979 Hou-N	132	470	57	123	27	4	6	54	64	52	30	13	.262	.354	.374	.728	105	6	63	4.39	-3	1-91,0-40(0-40-0)	17	-0.3
1980*Hou-N	137	499	71	154	32	8	10	73	66	72	48	15	.309	.390	.465	.855	149	38	93	6.65	-2	*0-136(0-136-0)	26	3.6
1981*Hou-N	82	306	42	83	19	0	5	34	24	31	12	7	.271	.326	.382	.709	106	1	37	4.15	-1	1-46,0-34(0-34-0)	9	-0.4
1982 Cin-N	138	492	52	142	35	1	8	57	41	41	16	11	.289	.348	.413	.761	110	5	67	4.73	-6	*0-131(0-131-0)/1-1	13	-0.3
1983 Cin-N	98	332	40	77	16	0	9	39	33	53	13	9	.232	.307	.361	.669	82	-10	38	3.75	1	0-73(0-1-73),1-17	7	-1.4
1984 Cin-N	110	380	59	105	24	2	10	47	25	54	19	3	.276	.323	.429	.752	105	4	52	4.72	-2	0-77(52-14-19),1-44	11	-0.3
1985 Cin-N	83	220	24	53	12	0	3	30	19	35	9	5	.241	.310	.336	.646	77	-7	23	3.41	-1	0-53(46-4-4),1-34	4	-1.2
*StL-N	28	76	14	33	4	1	6	19	5	7	5	1	.434	.469	.750	1.219	238	14	26	14.93	-2	1-23/0-2(1-0-1)	7	1.1
Yr.	111	296	38	86	16	1	9	49	24	42	14	6	.291	.350	.443	.792	117	7	49	5.80	-4	1-57,0-55(47-4-5)	11	-0.1
1986 LA-N	37	78	5	18	2	1	0	6	7	13	1	1	.231	.294	.282	.576	64	-4	7	3.00	-1	0-31(28-3-0)	1	-0.6
Total 17	2006	7310	1084	2087	436	60	199	976	664	938	550	179	.285	.350	.443	.793	124	267	1144	5.45	-2	*0-1718,1-258	296	21.8
• CEDENO, Domingo	Domingo Antonio (Donastorg) Cedeno b: 11/4/1968, La Romana, Dominican Republic BB/TR, 6'1", 170 lbs. Deb: 5/19/1993																							
1993 Tor-A	15	46	5	8	0	0	0	7	1	10	1	0	.174	.191	.174	.365	-1	-6	1	.91	2	S-10/2-5	1	-0.3

YEAR TM-L	G	AB	R	H	2B	3B	HR	RBI	BB	SO	SB	CS	AVG	OBP	SLG	OPS	OPS+	BR/A	RC	RC/G	FR	G/POS	WS	TPW
1994 Tor-A	47	97	14	19	2	3	0	10	10	31	1	2	.196	.271	.278	.549	42	-9	8	2.36	-3	2-28/S-8,3-6,0-1	1	-1.0
1995 Tor-A	51	161	18	38	6	1	4	14	10	35	0	1	.236	.289	.360	.649	68	-9	16	3.44	4	S-30,2-20/3-1	2	-0.1
1996 Tor-A	77	282	44	79	10	2	2	17	15	60	5	3	.280	.321	.351	.672	70	-13	31	3.83	9	2-62/3-6,S-5	4	-0.1
Chi-A	12	19	2	3	2	0	0	3	0	4	1	0	.158	.158	.263	.421	4	-3	1	.87	-1	/2-2,S-2,D-1	0	-0.3
Yr.	89	301	46	82	12	2	2	20	15	64	6	3	.272	.311	.346	.657	66	-16	32	3.59	8	2-64/S-7,3-6,D-1	4	-0.4
1997 Tex-A	113	365	49	103	19	6	4	36	27	77	3	3	.282	.335	.400	.735	86	-8	49	4.84	-3	2-65,S-43/3-3,D-2	9	-0.6
1998 Tex-A	61	141	19	37	9	1	2	21	10	32	2	1	.262	.311	.383	.694	76	-5	16	3.92	-3	S-35,D-14/2-7	2	-0.6
1999 Sea-A	21	42	4	9	2	0	2	8	5	9	1	1	.214	.313	.405	.717	79	-2	5	3.99	0	S-20/2-1,3-1	2	0.0
Phi-N	32	66	5	10	4	0	1	5	5	22	0	1	.152	.211	.258	.469	17	-9	3	1.41	-1	S-19/2-1	1	-0.9
Total 7	**429**	**1219**	**160**	**306**	**54**	**13**	**15**	**121**	**83**	**280**	**14**	**12**	**.251**	**.303**	**.354**	**.656**	**67**	**-64**	**131**	**3.61**	**3**	**2-191,S-172/3-17,D-17,0-1**	**22**	**-4.1**

• CEDENO, Roger Roger Leandro Cedeno b: 8/16/1974, Valencia, Venezuela BB/TR, 6'1", 165 lbs. Deb: 6/20/1995 Career OF: 265-281-333

YEAR TM-L	G	AB	R	H	2B	3B	HR	RBI	BB	SO	SB	CS	AVG	OBP	SLG	OPS	OPS+	BR/A	RC	RC/G	FR	G/POS	WS	TPW
1995 LA-N	40	42	4	10	2	0	0	3	3	10	1	0	.238	.289	.286	.575	57	-2	4	2.86	-1	0-36(19-13-5)	1	-0.4
1996 LA-N	86	211	26	52	11	1	2	18	24	47	5	1	.246	.326	.336	.663	82	-5	26	4.32	-2	0-71(20-50-4)	7	-0.7
1997 LA-N	80	194	31	53	10	2	3	17	25	44	9	1	.273	.365	.392	.757	106	4	31	5.72	-1	0-71(13-55-4)	9	0.3
1998 LA-N	105	240	33	58	11	1	2	17	27	57	8	2	.242	.318	.321	.639	73	-8	27	3.88	1	0-77(45-29-10)	3	-0.8
1999*NY-N	155	453	90	142	23	4	4	36	60	100	66	17	.313	.397	.408	.806	108	15	84	6.59	3	*0-149(13-21-127)/2-1	17	1.2
2000 Hou-N	74	259	54	73	2	5	6	26	43	47	25	11	.282	.384	.398	.782	93	-1	42	5.48	-5	0-67(23-29-17)	5	-0.7
2001 Det-A	131	523	79	153	14	11	6	48	36	83	55	15	.293	.340	.396	.736	98	3	75	5.05	-12	*0-121(0-67-55)/D-7	14	-1.1
2002 NY-N	149	511	65	133	19	2	7	41	42	92	25	4	.260	.319	.346	.665	78	-13	59	4.02	-6	*0-132(132-0-0)	10	-2.4
2003 NY-N	148	484	70	129	25	4	7	37	38	86	14	9	.267	.321	.378	.699	84	-13	58	4.15	-4	*0-128(0-17-111)	8	-2.1
Total 9	**968**	**2917**	**452**	**803**	**117**	**30**	**37**	**243**	**298**	**566**	**208**	**60**	**.275**	**.345**	**.374**	**.719**	**90**	**-19**	**406**	**4.85**	**-26**	**0-852/D-7,2-1**	**74**	**-6.7**

• CEPEDA, Orlando Orlando Manuel (Penne) "Cha Cha,Baby Bull" Cepeda
b: 9/17/1937, Ponce, Puerto Rico BR/TR, 6'2", 210 lbs. Deb: 4/15/1958 C HOF: 1999 Career OF: 214-0-18

YEAR TM-L	G	AB	R	H	2B	3B	HR	RBI	BB	SO	SB	CS	AVG	OBP	SLG	OPS	OPS+	BR/A	RC	RC/G	FR	G/POS	WS	TPW
1958 SF-N	148	603	88	188	**38**	4	25	96	29	84	15	11	.312	.346	.512	.859	126	19	97	5.80	1	*1-147	20	1.1
1959 SF-N★	151	605	92	192	35	4	27	105	33	100	23	9	.317	.358	.522	.880	134	28	110	6.81	-2	*1-122,0-44(44-0-0)/3-4	23	1.8
1960 SF-N★	151	569	81	169	36	3	24	96	34	91	15	6	.297	.345	.497	.843	136	26	95	6.10	-2	0-91(91-0-0),1-63	26	1.6
1961 SF-N★	152	585	105	182	28	4	**46**	**142**	39	91	12	8	.311	.363	.609	.972	158	44	118	7.33	1	1-81,0-80(64-0-17)	29	3.6
1962*SF-N★	162	625	105	191	26	1	35	114	37	97	10	4	.306	.350	.518	.869	132	26	108	6.34	3	*1-160/0-2(1-0-1)	26	1.9
1963 SF-N★	156	579	100	183	33	4	34	97	37	70	8	3	.316	.367	.563	.930	166	48	113	7.29	0	*1-150/0-3(3-0-0)	30	4.2
1964 SF-N★	142	529	75	161	27	2	31	97	43	83	9	4	.304	.366	.539	.904	148	33	101	6.97	-9	*1-139/0-1	23	1.7
1965 SF-N	33	34	1	6	1	0	1	5	3	9	0	0	.176	.243	.294	.537	49	-2	2	2.04	0	/1-4,0-2(2-0-0)	0	-0.3
1966 SF-N	19	49	5	14	2	0	3	15	4	11	0	1	.286	.352	.510	.862	132	2	9	6.45	-2	/0-8(8-0-0),1-6	2	-0.1
StL-N	123	452	65	137	24	0	17	58	34	68	9	8	.303	.369	.469	.838	131	18	75	5.84	-7	*1-120	17	0.4
Yr.	142	501	70	151	26	0	20	73	38	79	9	9	.301	.367	.473	.840	131	20	83	5.89	-8	*1-126/0-8(8-0-0)	19	0.4
1967*StL-N★	151	563	91	183	37	0	25	**111**	62	75	11	2	.325	.403	.524	.927	166	52	118	7.86	1	*1-151	34	4.8
1968*StL-N	157	600	71	149	26	2	16	73	43	96	8	6	.248	.308	.378	.687	107	4	68	3.85	-4	*1-154	17	-1.1
1969*Atl-N	154	573	74	147	28	2	22	88	55	76	12	5	.257	.327	.428	.755	109	7	79	4.81	10	*1-153	19	0.6
1970 Atl-N	148	567	87	173	33	0	34	111	47	75	6	5	.305	.368	.543	.911	133	24	108	7.00	7	*1-148	21	1.9
1971 Atl-N	71	250	31	69	10	1	14	44	22	29	3	6	.276	.335	.492	.827	124	5	35	4.59	2	1-63	7	0.2
1972 Atl-N	28	84	6	25	3	0	4	9	7	17	0	0	.298	.352	.476	.828	122	2	14	6.37	1	1-22	3	0.2
Oak-A	3	3	0	0	0	0	0	0	0	0	0	0	.000	.000	.000	.000	-105	-1	0	.00	0	....	0	-0.1
1973 Bos-A	142	550	51	159	25	0	20	86	50	81	0	2	.289	.352	.444	.795	116	11	79	5.03	0	*D-142	13	0.6
1974 KC-A	33	107	3	23	5	0	1	18	9	16	1	0	.215	.282	.290	.572	61	-5	8	2.48	0	D-26	0	-0.6
Total 17	**2124**	**7927**	**1131**	**2351**	**417**	**27**	**379**	**1365**	**588**	**1169**	**142**	**80**	**.297**	**.353**	**.499**	**.852**	**133**	**340**	**1338**	**6.07**	**3**	***1-1683,0-231,D-168/3-4**	**310**	**22.5**

• CEPICKY, Matt Matthew William Cepicky b: 11/10/1977, St. Louis, MO BL/TR, 6'2", 215 lbs. Deb: 7/31/2002 Career OF: 19-0-2

YEAR TM-L	G	AB	R	H	2B	3B	HR	RBI	BB	SO	SB	CS	AVG	OBP	SLG	OPS	OPS+	BR/A	RC	RC/G	FR	G/POS	WS	TPW
2002 Mon-N	32	74	7	16	3	0	3	15	4	21	0	0	.216	.256	.378	.635	62	-4	7	3.44	-1	0-17(16-0-1)	1	-0.6
2003 Mon-N	5	8	0	2	1	0	0	0	0	2	0	0	.250	.250	.375	.625	51	-1	1	3.38	-1	/0-4(3-0-1)	0	-0.1
Total 2	**37**	**82**	**7**	**18**	**4**	**0**	**3**	**15**	**4**	**23**	**0**	**0**	**.220**	**.256**	**.378**	**.634**	**61**	**-5**	**8**	**3.43**	**-2**	**/0-21**	**1**	**-0.8**

• CERMAK, Ed Edward Hugo Cermak b: 3/10/1882, Cleveland, OH d: 11/22/1911, Cleveland, OH BR/TR, 5'11", 170 lbs. Deb: 9/9/1901

YEAR TM-L	G	AB	R	H	2B	3B	HR	RBI	BB	SO	SB	CS	AVG	OBP	SLG	OPS	OPS+	BR/A	RC	RC/G	FR	G/POS	WS	TPW
1901 Cle-A	1	4	0	0	0	0	0	0	0	....	0	....	.000	.000	.000	.000	-104	-1	0	.00	2	/0-1	0	0.0

• CERONE, Rick Richard Aldo Cerone b: 5/19/1954, Newark, NJ BR/TR, 5'11", 192 lbs. Deb: 8/17/1975

YEAR TM-L	G	AB	R	H	2B	3B	HR	RBI	BB	SO	SB	CS	AVG	OBP	SLG	OPS	OPS+	BR/A	RC	RC/G	FR	G/POS	WS	TPW
1975 Cle-A	7	12	1	3	1	0	0	0	1	0	0	0	.250	.308	.333	.641	81	-0	1	3.69	0	/C-7	0	-0.1
1976 Cle-A	7	16	1	2	0	0	0	1	0	2	0	0	.125	.125	.125	.250	-27	-3	0	.48	0	/C-6,D-1	0	-0.3
1977 Tor-A	31	100	7	20	4	0	1	10	6	12	0	0	.200	.245	.270	.515	40	-8	6	2.01	0	C-31	1	-0.7
1978 Tor-A	88	282	25	63	8	2	3	20	23	32	0	3	.223	.284	.298	.582	63	-15	23	2.66	1	C-84/D-2	4	-1.1
1979 Tor-A	136	469	47	112	27	4	7	61	37	40	1	4	.239	.296	.358	.654	75	-19	50	3.61	-1	*C-136	8	-1.2
1980*NY-A	147	519	70	144	30	4	14	85	32	56	1	3	.277	.327	.432	.758	108	3	70	4.60	1	*C-147	21	1.2
1981*NY-A	71	234	23	57	13	2	2	21	12	24	0	2	.244	.280	.342	.622	80	-8	20	2.68	-5	C-69	4	-1.0
1982 NY-A	89	300	29	68	10	0	5	28	19	27	0	2	.227	.275	.310	.585	61	-17	23	2.44	-8	C-89	2	-2.1
1983 NY-A	80	246	18	54	7	0	2	22	15	29	0	0	.220	.267	.272	.540	51	-17	18	2.40	-7	C-78/3-1	2	-2.0
1984 NY-A	38	120	8	25	3	0	2	13	9	15	1	0	.208	.269	.283	.553	55	-7	9	2.30	-2	C-38	2	-0.7
1985 Atl-N	96	282	15	61	9	0	3	25	29	25	0	3	.216	.292	.280	.572	57	-17	20	2.27	1	C-91	3	-1.3
1986 Mil-A	68	216	22	56	14	0	4	18	15	28	1	1	.259	.310	.380	.690	84	-5	25	3.84	4	C-68	7	0.2
1987 NY-A	113	284	28	69	12	1	4	23	30	46	0	1	.243	.324	.335	.658	76	-10	31	3.61	0	*C-111/1-2,P-2	9	-0.4
1988 Bos-A	84	264	31	71	13	1	3	27	20	32	0	0	.269	.328	.360	.687	89	-4	31	4.17	-1	C-83/D-1	7	0.0
1989 Bos-A	102	296	28	72	16	1	4	48	34	40	0	0	.243	.325	.345	.670	84	-6	33	3.70	-1	C-97/D-1,0-1	8	-0.1
1990 NY-A	49	139	12	42	6	0	2	11	5	13	0	0	.302	.326	.388	.715	99	-1	17	4.35	-1	C-35/D-6,2-1	4	0.0
1991 NY-N	90	227	18	62	13	0	2	16	30	24	1	1	.273	.360	.357	.717	103	2	29	4.42	-1	C-81	7	0.5
1992 Mon-N	33	63	10	17	4	0	1	7	3	5	1	2	.270	.313	.381	.694	97	-1	7	4.02	0	C-28	2	0.0
Total 18	**1329**	**4069**	**393**	**998**	**190**	**15**	**59**	**436**	**320**	**450**	**6**	**22**	**.245**	**.304**	**.343**	**.647**	**78**	**-132**	**413**	**3.38**	**-20**	***C-1279/D-11,1-2,P-2,2-1,3,0**	**91**	**-9.0**

• CERV, Bob Robert Henry Cerv b: 5/5/1926, Weston, NE BR/TR, 6' Deb: 8/1/1951 Career OF: 497-72-36

YEAR TM-L	G	AB	R	H	2B	3B	HR	RBI	BB	SO	SB	CS	AVG	OBP	SLG	OPS	OPS+	BR/A	RC	RC/G	FR	G/POS	WS	TPW
1951 NY-A	12	28	4	6	1	0	0	2	4	6	0	0	.214	.313	.250	.563	55	-2	2	2.71	-1	/0-9(0-0-9)	0	-0.3
1952 NY-A	36	87	11	21	3	2	1	8	9	22	0	1	.241	.313	.356	.669	91	-2	10	4.15	-1	0-27(15-12-0)	2	-0.4
1953 NY-A	8	6	0	0	0	0	0	0	1	1	0	0	.000	.143	.000	.143	-61	-1	0	.17	0	....	0	-0.1
1954 NY-A	56	100	14	26	6	0	5	13	11	17	0	2	.260	.333	.470	.803	122	2	14	4.86	-1	0-24(24-0-0)	3	0.0
1955*NY-A	55	85	17	29	4	2	3	22	7	16	4	0	.341	.411	.541	.952	156	8	20	9.43	0	0-20(13-7-1)	5	0.7
1956*NY-A	54	115	16	35	5	6	3	25	18	13	0	1	.304	.398	.530	.929	148	8	24	7.60	2	0-44(29-15-1)	6	0.8
1957 KC-A	124	345	35	94	14	2	11	44	20	57	1	1	.272	.314	.420	.734	97	-2	42	4.17	0	0-89(40-35-22)	7	-0.7
1958 KC-A★	141	515	93	157	20	7	38	104	50	82	3	3	.305	.372	.592	.964	158	39	106	7.50	17	*0-136(136-0-0)	29	5.0
1959 KC-A	125	463	61	132	22	4	20	87	35	87	3	2	.285	.339	.479	.819	120	11	72	5.43	-2	*0-119(119-0-0)	15	0.1
1960 KC-A	23	78	14	20	1	1	6	12	10	17	0	0	.256	.341	.526	.867	130	3	14	6.11	2	0-21(21-0-0)	3	0.4
*NY-A	87	216	32	54	11	1	8	28	30	36	0	0	.250	.349	.421	.771	114	5	32	5.18	3	0-51(50-1-1)/1-3	8	0.4
Yr.	110	294	46	74	12	2	14	40	40	53	0	0	.252	.347	.449	.796	118	8	46	5.43	5	0-72(71-1-1)/1-3	11	0.8
1961 LA-A	18	57	3	9	3	0	2	6	1	8	0	0	.158	.172	.316	.488	25	-7	2	.97	-1	0-15(15-0-0)	0	-0.8
NY-A	57	118	17	32	5	1	6	20	12	17	1	0	.271	.344	.483	.827	125	4	18	5.32	1	0-30(28-2-0)/1-3	4	0.3
Yr.	75	175	20	41	8	1	8	26	13	25	1	0	.234	.291	.429	.720	93	-2	20	3.71	0	0-45(43-2-0)/1-3	4	-0.4
1962 NY-A	14	17	1	2	1	0	0	0	2	3	0	0	.118	.250	.176	.426	18	-2	1	1.70	0	/0-3(1-0-2)	0	-0.2
Hou-N	19	31	2	7	0	0	2	3	2	10	0	0	.226	.273	.419	.692	89	-1	3	2.98	0	/0-6(6-0-0)	0	-0.1
Total 12	**829**	**2261**	**320**	**624**	**96**	**26**	**105**	**374**	**212**	**392**	**12**	**10**	**.276**	**.343**	**.481**	**.823**	**122**	**62**	**361**	**5.59**	**20**	**0-594/1-6**	**82**	**5.3**

• CEY, Ron Ronald Charles "Penguin" Cey b: 2/15/1948, Tacoma, WA BR/TR, 5'10" Deb: 9/3/1971

YEAR TM-L	G	AB	R	H	2B	3B	HR	RBI	BB	SO	SB	CS	AVG	OBP	SLG	OPS	OPS+	BR/A	RC	RC/G	FR	G/POS	WS	TPW
1971 LA-N	2	2	0	0	0	0	0	0	0	2	0	0	.000	.000	.000	.000	-106	-1	0	.00	0	....	0	-0.1
1972 LA-N	11	37	3	10	1	0	1	3	7	10	0	0	.270	.400	.378	.778	125	2	6	6.43	0	3-11	2	0.2
1973 LA-N	152	507	60	124	18	4	15	80	74	77	1	1	.245	.343	.385	.728	106	6	66	4.32	20	*3-146	17	2.6

YEAR TM-L	G	AB	R	H	2B	3B	HR	RBI	BB	SO	SB	CS	AVG	OBP	SLG	OPS	OPS+	BR/A	RC	RC/G	FR	G/POS	WS	TPW
1974*LA-N★	159	577	88	151	20	2	18	97	76	68	1	1	.262	.355	.397	.751	115	12	82	4.83	22	*3-158	23	3.5
1975 LA-N★	158	566	72	160	29	2	25	101	78	74	5	2	.283	.376	.473	.850	141	32	101	6.31	14	*3-158	27	4.7
1976 LA-N★	145	502	69	139	18	3	23	80	89	74	0	4	.277	.389	.462	.851	143	30	92	6.47	18	*3-144	27	5.1
1977*LA-N★	153	564	77	136	22	3	30	110	93	106	3	4	.241	.351	.450	.801	114	11	92	5.46	15	*3-153	21	2.4
1978*LA-N★	159	555	84	150	32	0	23	84	96	96	2	5	.270	.384	.452	.837	134	27	99	6.19	7	*3-158	25	3.4
1979 LA-N★	150	487	77	137	20	1	28	81	86	85	3	3	.281	.391	.499	.890	143	31	97	7.15	13	*3-150	25	4.4
1980 LA-N	157	551	81	140	25	0	28	77	69	92	2	2	.254	.342	.452	.794	122	16	84	5.24	14	*3-157	23	2.9
1981*LA-N	85	312	42	90	15	2	13	50	40	55	0	2	.288	.375	.474	.849	145	18	55	6.37	8	3-84	16	2.7
1982 LA-N	150	556	62	141	23	1	24	79	57	99	3	2	.254	.327	.428	.755	113	8	76	4.63	12	*3-149	17	1.9
1983 Chi-N	159	581	73	160	33	1	24	90	62	85	0	0	.275	.350	.460	.810	117	13	90	5.40	-31	*3-157	16	-2.1
1984*Chi-N	146	505	71	121	27	0	25	97	61	108	3	2	.240	.329	.442	.770	105	3	74	4.94	-26	*3-144	17	-2.6
1985 Chi-N	145	500	64	116	18	2	22	63	58	106	1	1	.232	.317	.408	.725	91	-6	65	4.42	-16	*3-140	10	-2.5
1986 Chi-N	97	256	42	70	21	0	13	36	44	66	0	0	.273	.386	.508	.894	134	13	53	7.31	-4	3-77	11	0.8
1987 Oak-A	45	104	12	23	6	0	4	11	22	32	0	0	.221	.362	.394	.756	108	2	16	4.87	-1	D-30/1-7,3-3	3	0.0
Total 17	2073	7162	977	1868	328	21	316	1139	1012	1235	24	29	.261	.357	.445	.802	122	215	1149	5.52	65	*3-1989/D-30,1-7	280	27.4

• CHACON, Elio Elio (Rodriguez) Chacon b: 10/26/1936, Caracas, Venezuela d: 4/24/1992, Caracas, Venezuela BR/TR, 5'9" Deb: 4/20/1960 Career OF: 3-0-7

YEAR TM-L	G	AB	R	H	2B	3B	HR	RBI	BB	SO	SB	CS	AVG	OBP	SLG	OPS	OPS+	BR/A	RC	RC/G	FR	G/POS	WS	TPW
1960 Cin-N	49	116	14	21	1	0	0	7	14	23	7	1	.181	.275	.190	.464	29	-10	8	2.20	-1	2-43/0-2(0-0-2)	1	-0.9
1961*Cin-N	61	132	26	35	4	2	2	5	21	22	1	4	.265	.374	.371	.745	97	-1	20	5.06	2	2-42/0-7(3-0-5)	5	0.4
1962 NY-N	118	368	49	87	10	3	2	27	76	64	12	7	.236	.369	.296	.665	80	-7	44	3.88	-18	*S-110/2-2,3-1	5	-1.6
Total 3	228	616	89	143	15	5	4	39	111	109	20	12	.232	.353	.292	.645	74	-18	71	3.79	-17	S-110/2-87,0-9,3-1	11	-2.0

• CHADBOURNE, Chet Chester James Chadbourne b: 10/28/1884, Parkman, ME d: 6/21/1943, Los Angeles, CA BL/TR, 5'9" Deb: 9/17/1906 Career OF: 161-174-0

YEAR TM-L	G	AB	R	H	2B	3B	HR	RBI	BB	SO	SB	CS	AVG	OBP	SLG	OPS	OPS+	BR/A	RC	RC/G	FR	G/POS	WS	TPW
1906 Bos-A	11	43	7	13	1	0	0	3	3	....	1	....	.302	.348	.326	.673	111	1	5	4.69	3	2-11/S-1	1	0.4
1907 Bos-A	10	38	0	11	0	0	0	1	7	....	1	....	.289	.400	.289	.689	122	2	5	4.83	0	0-10(10-0-0)	2	0.1
1914 KC-F	147	581	92	161	22	8	1	37	69	49	42	....	.277	.359	.348	.706	107	7	83	4.91	14	*0-146(146-0-0)	19	1.6
1915 KC-F	152	587	75	133	16	9	1	35	62	29	29	....	.227	.307	.290	.596	78	-15	59	3.26	5	*0-152(5-147-0)	18	-2.1
1918 Bos-N	27	104	9	27	2	1	0	6	5	5	5	....	.260	.300	.298	.598	86	-2	11	3.37	-2	0-27(0-27-0)	2	-0.6
Total 5	347	1353	183	345	41	18	2	82	146	83	78	....	.255	.333	.316	.649	93	-7	164	4.02	19	0-335/2-11,S-1	42	-0.7

• CHALK, Dave David Lee Chalk b: 8/30/1950, Del Rio, TX BR/TR, 5'10" Deb: 9/4/1973

YEAR TM-L	G	AB	R	H	2B	3B	HR	RBI	BB	SO	SB	CS	AVG	OBP	SLG	OPS	OPS+	BR/A	RC	RC/G	FR	G/POS	WS	TPW
1973 Cal-A	24	69	14	16	2	0	0	6	9	13	0	0	.232	.329	.261	.590	74	-2	6	3.07	1	S-22	2	0.2
1974 Cal-A★	133	465	44	117	9	3	5	31	30	57	10	10	.252	.307	.316	.623	84	-11	41	2.86	-6	S-99,3-38	7	-0.7
1975 Cal-A★	149	513	59	140	24	2	3	56	66	49	6	9	.273	.358	.345	.703	107	5	64	4.17	9	*3-149	18	1.3
1976 Cal-A	142	438	39	95	14	1	0	33	49	62	0	0	.217	.310	.253	.563	71	-14	36	2.59	-6	*S-102,3-49	8	-1.0
1977 Cal-A	149	519	58	144	27	2	3	45	52	69	12	8	.277	.349	.355	.703	96	-2	65	4.25	-1	*3-141/2-7,S-4	14	-0.4
1978 Cal-A	135	470	42	119	12	0	1	34	38	34	5	8	.253	.318	.285	.604	74	-17	43	3.06	2	S-97,2-29,3-22/D-1	10	-0.5
1979 Tex-A	9	8	0	2	0	0	0	0	0	0	0	0	.250	.250	.250	.500	36	-1	0	.95	-1	/S-3,D-2,2-1	0	-0.2
Oak-A	66	212	15	47	6	0	2	13	29	14	2	1	.222	.318	.278	.596	66	-9	20	3.02	-8	2-37,3-16,S-16	3	-1.3
Yr.	75	220	15	49	6	0	2	13	29	14	2	1	.223	.316	.277	.593	65	-10	20	2.94	-9	2-38,S-19,3-16/D-2	3	-1.5
1980*KC-A	69	167	19	42	10	1	1	20	18	27	1	1	.251	.332	.341	.673	84	-3	19	3.82	0	3-33,2-17/D-6,S-1	4	-0.3
1981 KC-A	27	49	2	11	3	0	0	5	4	2	0	1	.224	.283	.286	.569	65	-3	4	2.42	0	3-14,2-10/S-1	0	-0.3
Total 9	903	2910	292	733	107	9	15	243	295	327	36	38	.252	.328	.310	.638	85	-57	299	3.37	-11	3-462,S-345,2-101/D-9	66	-3.1

• CHAMBERLAIN, Joe Joseph Jeremiah Chamberlain b: 5/10/1910, San Francisco, CA d: 1/28/1983, San Francisco, CA BR/TR, 6'1", 175 lbs. Deb: 4/17/1934

YEAR TM-L	G	AB	R	H	2B	3B	HR	RBI	BB	SO	SB	CS	AVG	OBP	SLG	OPS	OPS+	BR/A	RC	RC/G	FR	G/POS	WS	TPW
1934 Chi-A	43	141	13	34	5	1	2	17	6	38	1	1	.241	.272	.333	.605	54	-11	13	3.07	-5	S-26,3-14/2-1	1	-1.3

• CHAMBERLAIN, Wes Wesley Polk Chamberlain b: 4/13/1966, Chicago, IL BR/TR, 6'2", 210 lbs. Deb: 8/31/1990 Career OF: 133-0-193

YEAR TM-L	G	AB	R	H	2B	3B	HR	RBI	BB	SO	SB	CS	AVG	OBP	SLG	OPS	OPS+	BR/A	RC	RC/G	FR	G/POS	WS	TPW
1990 Phi-N	18	46	9	13	3	0	2	4	1	9	4	0	.283	.298	.478	.776	110	1	7	5.93	-1	0-10(10-0-2)	2	-0.1
1991 Phi-N	101	383	51	92	16	3	13	50	31	73	9	4	.240	.300	.399	.700	96	-3	45	4.01	-6	0-98(95-0-3)	12	-1.3
1992 Phi-N	76	275	26	71	18	0	9	41	10	55	4	0	.258	.287	.422	.709	99	-1	32	3.99	-4	0-73(28-0-48)	5	-0.8
1993*Phi-N	96	284	34	80	20	2	12	45	17	51	2	1	.282	.325	.493	.817	117	5	43	5.32	5	0-76(0-0-76)	9	0.7
1994 Phi-N	24	69	7	19	5	0	2	6	3	12	0	0	.275	.306	.435	.740	88	-1	8	4.14	1	0-18(0-0-18)	1	-0.1
Bos-A	51	164	13	42	9	1	4	20	12	38	0	2	.256	.307	.396	.703	76	-7	18	3.67	2	0-34(0-0-34),D-12	1	-0.7
1995 Bos-A	19	42	4	5	1	0	1	1	3	11	1	0	.119	.178	.214	.392	1	-6	1	.95	0	0-12(0-0-12)/D-5	0	-0.6
Total 6	385	1263	144	322	72	6	43	167	77	249	20	7	.255	.300	.424	.723	96	-13	154	4.20	-2	0-321/D-17	30	-2.9

• CHAMBERS, Al Albert Eugene Chambers b: 3/24/1961, Harrisburg, PA BL/TL, 6'4" Deb: 7/23/1983 Career OF: 16-0-0

YEAR TM-L	G	AB	R	H	2B	3B	HR	RBI	BB	SO	SB	CS	AVG	OBP	SLG	OPS	OPS+	BR/A	RC	RC/G	FR	G/POS	WS	TPW
1983 Sea-A	31	67	11	14	3	0	1	7	18	20	0	1	.209	.376	.299	.675	85	-1	9	4.23	-0	D-22/0-3(3-0-0)	1	-0.1
1984 Sea-A	22	49	4	11	1	0	1	4	3	12	2	1	.224	.269	.306	.575	60	-3	4	2.91	-1	0-13(13-0-0)/D-1	0	-0.4
1985 Sea-A	4	4	0	0	0	0	0	0	0	2	0	0	.000	.000	.000	.000	-99	-1	0	.00	0	....	0	-0.1
Total 3	57	120	15	25	4	0	2	11	21	34	2	2	.208	.326	.292	.618	71	-5	13	3.53	-1	/D-23,0-16	1	-0.6

• CHAMBLEE, Jim James Nathaniel Chamblee b: 5/6/1975, Denton, TX BR/TR, 6'4", 186 lbs. Deb: 8/24/2003

YEAR TM-L	G	AB	R	H	2B	3B	HR	RBI	BB	SO	SB	CS	AVG	OBP	SLG	OPS	OPS+	BR/A	RC	RC/G	FR	G/POS	WS	TPW
2003 Cin-N	2	2	0	0	0	0	0	0	0	2	0	0	.000	.000	.000	.000	-102	-1	0	.00	0	/3-1	0	-0.1

• CHAMBLISS, Chris Carroll Christopher Chambliss b: 12/26/1948, Dayton, OH BL/TR, 6'1" Deb: 5/28/1971 C

YEAR TM-L	G	AB	R	H	2B	3B	HR	RBI	BB	SO	SB	CS	AVG	OBP	SLG	OPS	OPS+	BR/A	RC	RC/G	FR	G/POS	WS	TPW
1971 Cle-A	111	415	49	114	20	4	9	48	40	83	2	0	.275	.341	.407	.749	102	2	58	5.04	-8	*1-108	11	-1.6
1972 Cle-A	121	466	51	136	27	2	6	44	26	63	3	4	.292	.329	.397	.726	112	5	59	4.57	-2	*1-119	13	-0.8
1973 Cle-A	155	572	70	156	30	2	11	53	58	76	4	8	.273	.343	.390	.733	104	1	74	4.51	3	*1-154	16	-0.8
1974 Cle-A	17	67	8	22	4	0	0	7	5	5	0	1	.328	.375	.388	.763	121	1	9	5.39	-1	1-17	2	-0.1
NY-A	110	400	38	97	16	3	6	43	23	43	0	0	.243	.284	.343	.626	82	-10	38	3.22	3	*1-106	7	-1.6
Yr.	127	467	46	119	20	3	6	50	28	48	0	1	.255	.297	.349	.646	87	-9	47	3.50	2	*1-123	9	-1.7
1975 NY-A	150	562	66	171	38	4	9	72	29	50	0	1	.304	.340	.434	.774	121	13	77	4.91	0	*1-147	15	0.1
1976*NY-A★	156	641	79	188	32	6	17	96	27	80	1	0	.293	.325	.441	.766	124	16	90	5.19	-3	*1-155/D-1	21	0.0
1977*NY-A	157	600	90	172	32	6	17	90	45	73	4	0	.287	.338	.445	.783	113	11	85	5.07	-3	*1-157	17	-0.1
1978*NY-A	162	625	81	171	26	3	12	90	41	60	2	1	.274	.323	.382	.706	100	-0	79	4.56	4	*1-155/D-7	19	-0.7
1979 NY-A	149	554	61	155	27	3	18	63	34	53	3	2	.280	.327	.437	.764	106	3	78	5.07	-6	*1-134,D-16	16	-1.2
1980 Atl-N	158	602	83	170	37	2	18	72	49	73	7	3	.282	.340	.440	.781	113	9	90	5.36	4	*1-158	21	0.4
1981 Atl-N	107	404	44	110	25	2	8	51	44	41	4	1	.272	.345	.403	.749	109	5	56	4.83	11	*1-107	12	1.1
1982*Atl-N	157	534	57	144	25	2	20	86	57	57	7	3	.270	.340	.436	.776	111	8	79	5.18	11	*1-151	19	1.0
1983 Atl-N	131	447	59	125	24	3	20	78	63	68	2	7	.280	.369	.481	.850	124	13	78	6.16	-1	*1-126	16	0.5
1984 Atl-N	135	389	47	100	14	0	9	44	58	54	1	2	.257	.355	.362	.717	95	-1	51	4.47	6	*1-109	10	-0.2
1985 Atl-N	101	170	16	40	7	0	3	21	18	22	0	0	.235	.309	.329	.638	74	-6	17	3.35	2	1-39	2	-0.6
1986 Atl-N	97	122	13	38	8	0	2	14	15	24	0	2	.311	.387	.426	.813	117	3	20	5.97	-2	1-20	4	0.0
1988 NY-A	1	1	0	0	0	0	0	0	0	1	0	0	.000	.000	.000	.000	-101	-0	0	.00	0	....	0	0.0
Total 17	2175	7571	912	2109	392	42	185	972	632	926	40	35	.279	.336	.415	.751	108	73	1036	4.87	18	*1-1962/D-24	221	-4.5

• CHAMPION, Mike Robert Michael Champion b: 2/10/1955, Montgomery, AL BR/TR, 6', 185 lbs. Deb: 9/14/1976

YEAR TM-L	G	AB	R	H	2B	3B	HR	RBI	BB	SO	SB	CS	AVG	OBP	SLG	OPS	OPS+	BR/A	RC	RC/G	FR	G/POS	WS	TPW
1976 SD-N	11	38	4	9	2	0	1	2	1	3	0	0	.237	.256	.368	.625	82	-1	3	2.90	-3	2-11	0	-0.4
1977 SD-N	150	507	35	116	14	6	1	43	27	85	3	3	.229	.271	.286	.557	55	-33	39	2.55	-32	*2-149	2	-5.8
1978 SD-N	32	53	3	12	0	2	0	4	5	13	0	0	.226	.293	.302	.595	72	-2	5	3.03	-1	2-20/3-4	1	-0.3
Total 3	193	598	42	137	16	8	2	49	33	101	3	3	.229	.272	.293	.564	58	-37	47	2.61	-37	2-180/3-4	3	-6.5

• CHANCE, Bob Robert Chance b: 9/10/1940, Statesboro, GA BL/TR, 6'2", 219 lbs. Deb: 9/4/1963 Career OF: 1-0-47

YEAR TM-L	G	AB	R	H	2B	3B	HR	RBI	BB	SO	SB	CS	AVG	OBP	SLG	OPS	OPS+	BR/A	RC	RC/G	FR	G/POS	WS	TPW
1963 Cle-A	16	52	5	15	4	0	2	7	1	10	0	1	.288	.302	.481	.783	116	0	7	4.51	-2	0-14(0-0-14)	2	-0.2
1964 Cle-A	120	390	45	109	16	1	14	75	40	101	3	3	.279	.351	.433	.784	118	9	58	5.26	-9	1-81,0-31(1-0-30)	13	-0.6
1965 Was-A	72	199	20	51	9	0	4	14	18	44	0	1	.256	.318	.362	.680	94	-2	24	4.31	-2	1-48/0-3(0-0-3)	5	-0.8
1966 Was-A	37	57	1	10	3	0	1	8	2	23	0	0	.175	.203	.281	.484	38	-5	3	1.53	-1	1-13	0	-0.7
1967 Was-A	27	42	5	9	2	0	3	7	7	13	0	0	.214	.340	.476	.816	144	3	8	6.14	0	1-10	2	0.2

YEAR TM-L	G	AB	R	H	2B	3B	HR	RBI	BB	SO	SB	CS	AVG	OBP	SLG	OPS	OPS+	BR/A	RC	RC/G	FR	G/POS	WS	TPW
1969 Cal-A	5	7	0	1	0	0	0	1	0	4	0	0	.143	.143	.143	.286	-21	-1	0	.64	0	/1-1	0	-0.2
Total 6	277	747	76	195	34	1	24	112	68	195	3	5	.261	.326	.406	.732	106	4	99	4.64	-15	1-153/0-48	22	-2.3

• CHANCE, Frank
Frank Leroy "Husk,The Peerless Leader" Chance
b: 9/9/1877, Fresno, CA d: 9/15/1924, Los Angeles, CA BR/TR, 6', 190 lbs. Deb: 4/29/1898 M/U HOF: 1946 Career OF: 6-2-65

YEAR TM-L	G	AB	R	H	2B	3B	HR	RBI	BB	SO	SB	CS	AVG	OBP	SLG	OPS	OPS+	BR/A	RC	RC/G	FR	G/POS	WS	TPW
1898 Chi-N	53	147	32	41	4	3	1	14	7	....	7	....	.279	.338	.367	.705	102	0	21	5.24	-3	C-33,0-17(1-1-15)/1-3	4	-0.2
1899 Chi-N	64	192	37	55	6	2	1	22	15	....	10	....	.286	.351	.354	.705	96	-1	28	5.39	0	C-57/1-1,0-1	7	0.3
1900 Chi-N	56	149	26	44	9	3	0	13	15	....	8	....	.295	.413	.396	.809	129	8	30	6.93	-2	C-51/1-1	7	0.9
1901 Chi-N	69	241	38	67	12	4	0	36	29	....	27	....	.278	.376	.361	.737	119	8	44	6.62	-1	0-51(4-1-46),C-13/1-6	9	0.5
1902 Chi-N	76	242	40	70	9	4	1	31	37	....	29	....	.289	.401	.372	.773	143	15	48	7.36	-4	1-38,C-29/0-4(0-0-4)	13	1.3
1903 Chi-N	125	441	83	144	24	10	2	81	78	....	**67**	....	.327	.439	.440	.878	155	38	118	**10.42**	4	*1-121/C-2	31	3.8
1904 Chi-N	124	451	89	140	16	10	6	49	36	....	42	....	.310	.382	.430	.812	150	27	93	7.54	7	*1-123/C-1	29	3.4
1905 Chi-N	118	392	92	124	16	12	2	70	78	....	38	....	.316	**.450**	.434	.883	157	35	98	9.00	2	*1-115	25	3.6
1906*Chi-N	136	474	**103**	151	24	10	3	71	70	....	**57**	....	.319	.419	.430	.849	156	35	114	8.70	4	*1-136	35	4.1
1907*Chi-N	111	382	58	112	19	2	1	49	51	....	35	....	.293	.395	.361	.756	129	16	71	6.68	9	*1-109	23	2.6
1908*Chi-N	129	452	65	123	27	4	2	55	37	....	27	....	.272	.338	.363	.701	119	10	64	4.85	6	*1-126	20	1.5
1909 Chi-N	93	324	53	88	16	4	0	46	30	....	29	....	.272	.341	.346	.686	110	4	48	5.03	-1	1-92	14	0.2
1910*Chi-N	88	295	54	88	12	8	0	36	37	15	16	....	.298	.395	.393	.788	131	13	52	6.33	2	1-87	14	1.5
1911 Chi-N	31	88	23	21	6	3	1	17	25	13	9	....	.239	.432	.409	.841	136	6	20	7.16	-2	1-29	5	0.4
1912 Chi-N	2	5	2	1	0	0	0	0	3	0	1	....	.200	.500	.200	.700	95	0	1	6.19	0	/1-2	0	0.0
1913 NY-A	12	24	3	5	0	0	0	6	8	1	1	....	.208	.406	.208	.615	81	0	3	3.24	0	/1-7	1	0.0
1914 NY-A	1	0	0	0	0	0	0	0	0	0	0	....	....	....	....	....	-100	0	0	....	0	/1-1	0	0.0
Total 17	1288	4299	798	1274	200	79	20	596	556	29	403	....	.296	.394	.394	.788	135	217	854	7.12	19	1-997,C-186/0-73	237	24.0

• CHANEY, Darrel
Darrel Lee Chaney b: 3/9/1948, Hammond, IN BB/TR, 6'2", 190 lbs. Deb: 4/11/1969

YEAR TM-L	G	AB	R	H	2B	3B	HR	RBI	BB	SO	SB	CS	AVG	OBP	SLG	OPS	OPS+	BR/A	RC	RC/G	FR	G/POS	WS	TPW
1969 Cin-N	93	209	21	40	5	2	0	15	24	75	1	0	.191	.278	.234	.512	43	-15	15	2.38	-4	S-91	2	-1.2
1970*Cin-N	57	95	7	22	3	0	1	4	3	26	1	1	.232	.263	.295	.557	47	-8	8	2.67	-3	S-30,2-18/3-3	1	-0.8
1971 Cin-N	10	24	2	3	0	0	0	1	1	3	0	1	.125	.160	.125	.285	-19	-4	0	.48	-1	/S-7,2-1,3-1	0	-0.5
1972*Cin-N	83	196	29	49	7	2	2	19	29	28	1	3	.250	.347	.337	.683	101	0	24	4.17	2	S-64,2-12,3-10	8	0.8
1973*Cin-N	105	227	27	41	7	1	0	14	26	50	4	3	.181	.268	.220	.488	39	-19	15	2.02	8	S-75,2-14,3-12	4	-0.3
1974 Cin-N	117	135	27	27	6	1	2	16	26	33	1	2	.200	.329	.304	.633	79	-4	14	3.39	-5	3-81,2-38,S-12	4	-0.7
1975*Cin-N	71	160	18	35	6	0	2	26	14	38	3	0	.219	.282	.294	.575	59	-8	14	2.87	9	S-34,2-23,3-13	4	0.5
1976 Atl-N	153	496	42	125	20	8	1	50	54	92	5	7	.252	.327	.331	.657	82	-13	54	3.65	-11	*S-151/2-1,3-1	12	-0.7
1977 Atl-N	74	209	22	42	7	2	3	15	17	44	0	0	.201	.261	.297	.558	44	-17	15	2.21	0	S-41,2-24	2	-1.2
1978 Atl-N	89	245	27	55	9	1	3	20	25	48	1	0	.224	.296	.306	.602	62	-12	24	3.28	-6	S-77/3-8,2-1	4	-1.2
1979 Atl-N	63	117	15	19	5	0	0	10	19	34	2	1	.162	.279	.205	.485	32	-11	8	2.03	-3	S-39/2-5,3-4,C-1	1	-1.1
Total 11	915	2113	237	458	75	17	14	190	238	471	19	18	.217	.297	.288	.585	62	-110	191	2.94	-15	S-621,2-137,3-133/C-1	42	-6.3

• CHANNELL, Les
Lester Clark "Goat,Gint" Channell b: 3/3/1886, Crestline, OH d: 5/7/1954, Denver, CO BL/TL, 6', 180 lbs. Deb: 5/11/1910

YEAR TM-L	G	AB	R	H	2B	3B	HR	RBI	BB	SO	SB	CS	AVG	OBP	SLG	OPS	OPS+	BR/A	RC	RC/G	FR	G/POS	WS	TPW
1910 NY-A	6	19	3	6	0	0	0	3	2	....	2	....	.316	.381	.316	.697	112	0	3	5.95	-1	/0-6(6-0-0)	1	-0.1
1914 NY-A	1	1	0	1	1	0	0	0	0	0	0	....	1.000	1.000	2.000	3.000	803	1	2	∞	0	....	0	0.1
Total 2	7	20	3	7	1	0	0	3	2	0	2	....	.350	.409	.400	.809	143	1	5	5.95	-1	/0-6	1	0.0

• CHANT, Charlie
Charles Joseph Chant b: 8/7/1951, Bell, CA BR/TR, 6', 190 lbs. Deb: 9/12/1975 Career OF: 10-2-7

YEAR TM-L	G	AB	R	H	2B	3B	HR	RBI	BB	SO	SB	CS	AVG	OBP	SLG	OPS	OPS+	BR/A	RC	RC/G	FR	G/POS	WS	TPW
1975 Oak-A	5	5	1	0	0	0	0	0	0	0	0	0	.000	.000	.000	.000	-102	-1	0	.00	-1	/0-5(3-0-2),D-1	0	-0.2
1976 StL-N	15	14	0	2	0	0	0	0	0	4	0	0	.143	.143	.143	.286	-19	-2	0	.64	1	0-14(7-2-5)	0	-0.2
Total 2	20	19	1	2	0	0	0	0	0	4	0	0	.105	.105	.105	.211	-41	-3	0	.45	0	/0-19,D-1	0	-0.4

• CHAPLIN, Ed
Bert Edgar Chaplin b: 9/25/1893, Pelzer, SC d: 8/15/1978, Sanford, FL BL/TR, 5'7", 158 lbs. Deb: 9/4/1920

YEAR TM-L	G	AB	R	H	2B	3B	HR	RBI	BB	SO	SB	CS	AVG	OBP	SLG	OPS	OPS+	BR/A	RC	RC/G	FR	G/POS	WS	TPW
1920 Bos-A	4	5	2	1	1	0	0	1	4	1	0	0	.200	.556	.400	.956	163	1	2	10.74	0	/C-2	1	0.1
1921 Bos-A	3	2	0	0	0	0	0	0	0	1	0	0	.000	.000	.000	.000	-103	-1	0	.00	0	/C-1	0	-0.1
1922 Bos-A	28	69	8	13	1	1	0	6	9	9	2	1	.188	.282	.232	.514	35	-6	5	2.31	0	C-21	1	-0.5
Total 3	35	76	10	14	2	1	0	7	13	11	2	1	.184	.303	.237	.540	45	-6	7	2.75	0	/C-24	2	-0.4

• CHAPMAN, Ben
William Benjamin Chapman b: 12/25/1908, Nashville, TN d: 7/7/1993, Hoover, AL BR/TR, 6', 190 lbs. Deb: 4/15/1930 M/C Career OF: 404-583-541

YEAR TM-L	G	AB	R	H	2B	3B	HR	RBI	BB	SO	SB	CS	AVG	OBP	SLG	OPS	OPS+	BR/A	RC	RC/G	FR	G/POS	WS	TPW
1930 NY-A	138	513	74	162	31	10	10	81	43	58	14	6	.316	.371	.474	.845	118	15	91	6.62	-3	3-91,2-45	17	1.7
1931 NY-A	149	600	120	189	28	11	17	122	75	77	**61**	23	.315	.396	.483	.879	138	41	119	7.17	4	*0-137(90-0-50),2-11	22	3.4
1932*NY-A	151	581	101	174	41	15	10	107	71	55	**38**	18	.299	.381	.473	.854	126	25	107	6.58	0	*0-150(81-0-86)	22	1.4
1933 NY-A★	147	565	112	176	36	4	9	98	72	45	**27**	18	.312	.393	.437	.830	127	23	99	6.27	8	*0-147(76-0-77)	21	2.2
1934 NY-A★	149	588	82	181	21	**13**	5	86	67	68	26	16	.308	.381	.413	.795	113	11	94	5.81	-1	*0-149(41-87-23)	19	0.4
1935 NY-A★	140	553	118	160	38	8	8	74	61	39	17	10	.289	.361	.430	.791	110	8	87	5.56	11	*0-138(0-138-0)	21	1.4
1936 NY-A	36	139	19	37	14	3	1	21	15	20	1	2	.266	.338	.432	.769	92	-3	20	5.04	0	0-36(0-36-0)	4	-0.3
Was-A★	97	401	91	133	36	7	4	60	69	18	19	7	.332	.431	.486	.917	133	26	89	8.56	0	0-97(0-97-0)	19	2.1
Yr.	133	540	110	170	50	10	5	81	84	38	20	9	.315	.408	.472	.880	123	23	109	7.58	0	*0-133(0-133-0)	23	1.7
1937 Was-A	35	130	23	34	7	1	0	12	26	7	8	0	.262	.385	.331	.715	86	0	20	5.50	-2	0-32(0-32-0)	4	-0.2
Bos-A	113	423	76	130	23	11	7	57	57	35	27	12	.307	.391	.463	.854	110	8	79	6.75	3	*0-112(2-10-100)/S-1	15	0.4
Yr.	148	553	99	164	30	12	7	69	83	42	**35**	12	.297	.389	.432	.822	104	9	99	6.45	1	*0-144(2-42-100)/S-1	19	0.3
1938 Bos-A	127	480	92	163	40	8	6	80	65	33	13	6	.340	.418	.494	.912	122	18	102	8.17	8	*0-126(1-0-125)/3-1	19	1.7
1939 Cle-A	149	545	101	158	31	9	6	82	87	30	18	6	.290	.390	.413	.802	109	12	91	5.68	-7	*0-146(2-137-9)	19	0.1
1940 Cle-A	143	548	82	157	40	6	4	50	78	45	13	7	.286	.377	.403	.781	105	7	85	5.50	0	*0-140(62-18-62)	18	0.0
1941 Was-A	28	110	9	28	6	0	1	10	10	6	2	2	.255	.317	.336	.653	76	-4	10	2.96	1	0-26(26-0-0)	1	-0.4
Chi-A	57	190	26	43	9	1	2	19	19	14	2	2	.226	.297	.316	.612	63	-11	19	3.34	1	0-49(21-22-7)	4	-1.2
Yr.	85	300	35	71	15	1	3	29	29	20	4	4	.237	.304	.323	.627	68	-15	29	3.19	2	0-75(47-22-7)	5	-1.6
1944 Bro-N	20	38	11	14	4	0	0	11	5	4	1	....	.368	.442	.474	.916	161	6	9	9.24	-2	P-11	6	1.1
1945 Bro-N	13	22	2	3	0	0	0	3	2	1	0	....	.136	.208	.136	.345	-3	-0	1	.79	0	P-10	1	-1.1
Phi-N	24	51	4	16	2	0	0	4	2	1	0	....	.314	.340	.353	.693	95	-0	5	3.39	-1	0-10(2-6-2)/3-4,P-3	1	-0.4
Yr.	37	73	6	19	2	0	0	7	4	2	0	....	.260	.299	.288	.586	65	-1	5	2.51	0	P-13,0-10(2-6-2)/3-4	2	-1.5
1946 Phi-N	1	1	1	0	0	0	0	0	0	0	0	....	.000	.000	.000	.000	-103	-0	0	.00	-0	/P-1	0	0.0
Total 15	1717	6478	1144	1958	407	107	90	977	824	556	287	135	.302	.383	.440	.823	115	182	1127	6.24	21	*0-1495/3-96,2-56,P-25,S-1	233	12.3

• CHAPMAN, Calvin
Calvin Louis Chapman b: 12/20/1910, Courtland, MS d: 4/1/1983, Batesville, MS BL/TR, 5'9", 160 lbs. Deb: 9/10/1935

YEAR TM-L	G	AB	R	H	2B	3B	HR	RBI	BB	SO	SB	CS	AVG	OBP	SLG	OPS	OPS+	BR/A	RC	RC/G	FR	G/POS	WS	TPW
1935 Cin-N	15	53	6	18	1	0	0	3	4	5	2	....	.340	.386	.358	.744	105	1	8	6.11	-2	S-12/2-4	2	0.0
1936 Cin-N	96	219	35	54	7	3	1	22	16	19	5	....	.247	.301	.320	.620	72	-9	22	3.50	-1	0-31(21-1-9),2-23/3-1	3	-1.0
Total 2	111	272	41	72	8	3	1	25	20	24	7	....	.265	.317	.327	.645	78	-8	30	3.95	-3	/0-31,2-27,S-12,3-1	5	-1.0

• CHAPMAN, Fred
William Fred "Chappie" Chapman b: 7/17/1916, Liberty, SC d: 3/27/1997, Kannapolis, NC BR/TR, 6'1", 185 lbs. Deb: 9/15/1939

YEAR TM-L	G	AB	R	H	2B	3B	HR	RBI	BB	SO	SB	CS	AVG	OBP	SLG	OPS	OPS+	BR/A	RC	RC/G	FR	G/POS	WS	TPW
1939 Phi-A	15	49	5	14	1	1	0	1	1	3	1	0	.286	.300	.347	.647	66	-2	5	4.04	-2	S-15	1	-0.3
1940 Phi-A	26	69	6	11	1	0	0	4	6	10	1	1	.159	.227	.174	.401	6	-10	3	1.21	-6	S-25	0	-1.3
1941 Phi-A	35	69	1	11	1	0	0	4	4	15	1	2	.159	.205	.174	.379	1	-10	2	1.01	-1	S-28/3-2,2-1	1	-1.0
Total 3	76	187	12	36	3	1	0	9	11	28	3	3	.193	.237	.219	.457	19	-23	11	1.76	-9	/S-68,3-2,2-1	2	-2.7

• CHAPMAN, Glenn
Glenn Justice "Pete" Chapman b: 1/21/1906, Cambridge City, IN d: 11/5/1988, Richmond, IN BR/TR, 5'11.5", 170 lbs. Deb: 4/18/1934

YEAR TM-L	G	AB	R	H	2B	3B	HR	RBI	BB	SO	SB	CS	AVG	OBP	SLG	OPS	OPS+	BR/A	RC	RC/G	FR	G/POS	WS	TPW
1934 Bro-N	67	93	19	26	5	1	1	10	7	19	1	....	.280	.330	.387	.717	96	-1	12	4.86	-2	0-40(27-0-14),2-14	2	-0.3

• CHAPMAN, Harry
Harry E. Chapman b: 10/26/1887, Severance, KS d: 10/21/1918, Nevada, MO BR/TR, 5'11", 160 lbs. Deb: 10/6/1912

YEAR TM-L	G	AB	R	H	2B	3B	HR	RBI	BB	SO	SB	CS	AVG	OBP	SLG	OPS	OPS+	BR/A	RC	RC/G	FR	G/POS	WS	TPW
1912 Chi-N	1	4	1	1	0	1	0	1	0	0	1	....	.250	.250	.750	1.000	168	0	1	8.02	1	/C-1	0	0.1
1913 Cin-N	2	2	0	1	0	0	0	0	0	1	0	....	.500	.500	.500	1.000	187	0	0	12.24	0	....	0	0.0
1914 StL-F	64	181	16	38	2	1	0	14	13	27	2	....	.210	.270	.232	.502	41	-14	12	2.02	0	C-51/1-1,2-1,0-1	2	-1.0
1915 StL-F	62	186	19	37	6	3	1	29	22	24	4	....	.199	.284	.280	.563	63	-9	16	2.64	0	C-53	3	-0.5

YEAR TM-L	G	AB	R	H	2B	3B	HR	RBI	BB	SO	SB	CS	AVG	OBP	SLG	OPS	OPS+	BR/A	RC	RC/G	FR	G/POS	WS	TPW
1916 StL-A	18	31	2	3	0	0	0	0	2	5	0	....	.097	.152	.097	.248	-27	-5	1	.58	0	C-14	0	-0.4
Total 5	**147**	**404**	**38**	**80**	**8**	**5**	**1**	**44**	**37**	**57**	**7**	**....**	**.198**	**.269**	**.250**	**.519**	**48**	**-27**	**30**	**2.27**	**1**	**C-119/1-1,2-1,O-1**	**5**	**-1.8**
• CHAPMAN, Jack	John Curtis "Death To Flying Things" Chapman b: 5/8/1843, Brooklyn, NY d: 6/10/1916, Brooklyn, NY TR, 5'11", 170 lbs. Deb: 5/5/1874 M/U NA OF: 0-1-95																							
1874 Atl-n	53	242	32	64	10	2	0	25	4	11	2	1	.264	.276	.322	.599	103	3	23	3.80	4	*O-53(0-1-52)/1-1	....	0.8
1875 StL-n	43	195	28	44	5	3	0	30	1	7	4	1	.226	.230	.282	.512	84	-1	14	2.69	-3	O-43(0-0-43)/1-1	....	-0.1
1876 Lou-N	17	68	4	16	1	0	0	5	1	3	....	....	.235	.250	.254	.504	58	-3	4	2.39	-3	O-17(5-1-11)/3-1	0	-0.6
Total 2 n	**96**	**437**	**60**	**108**	**15**	**5**	**0**	**55**	**5**	**18**	**6**	**2**	**.247**	**.256**	**.304**	**.560**	**95**	**2**	**37**	**3.29**	**1**	**/O-96,1-2**	**....**	**0.7**
• CHAPMAN, John	John Joseph Chapman b: 10/15/1899, Centralia, PA d: 11/3/1953, Philadelphia, PA BR/TR, 5'10.5", 175 lbs. Deb: 6/28/1924																							
1924 Phi-A	19	71	7	20	4	1	0	7	4	8	0	0	.282	.329	.366	.695	78	-2	9	4.24	-5	S-19	2	-0.5
• CHAPMAN, Kelvin	Kelvin Keith Chapman b: 6/2/1956, Willits, CA BR/TR, 5'11", 173 lbs. Deb: 4/5/1979																							
1979 NY-N	35	80	7	12	1	2	0	4	5	15	0	0	.150	.200	.213	.413	13	-10	4	1.35	0	2-22/3-1	1	-0.9
1984 NY-N	75	197	27	57	13	0	3	23	19	30	8	7	.289	.358	.401	.759	115	3	26	4.45	-1	2-57/3-3	8	0.5
1985 NY-N	62	144	16	25	3	0	0	7	9	15	5	4	.174	.232	.194	.427	21	-16	7	1.40	-2	2-48/3-1	2	-1.7
Total 3	**172**	**421**	**50**	**94**	**17**	**2**	**3**	**34**	**33**	**60**	**13**	**11**	**.223**	**.286**	**.295**	**.581**	**64**	**-23**	**36**	**2.74**	**-3**	**2-127/3-5**	**11**	**-2.1**
• CHAPMAN, Ray	Raymond Johnson Chapman b: 1/15/1891, Beaver Dam, KY d: 8/17/1920, New York, NY BR/TR, 5'10", 170 lbs. Deb: 8/30/1912 Career OF: 0-1-0																							
1912 Cle-A	31	109	29	34	6	3	0	19	10	....	10	....	.312	.375	.422	.797	124	3	22	6.44	-5	S-31	4	0.1
1913 Cle-A	141	508	78	131	19	7	3	39	46	51	29	....	.258	.322	.341	.662	91	-6	66	4.00	-7	*S-138/O-1	15	-0.3
1914 Cle-A	106	375	59	103	16	10	2	42	48	48	24	9	.275	.358	.387	.745	119	10	58	5.18	-20	S-72,2-33	13	-0.4
1915 Cle-A	154	570	101	154	14	17	3	67	70	82	36	15	.270	.353	.370	.723	114	11	84	4.85	1	*S-154	17	2.5
1916 Cle-A	109	346	50	80	10	5	0	27	50	46	21	14	.231	.330	.289	.619	81	-8	41	3.30	3	S-52,3-36,2-16	10	0.0
1917 Cle-A	156	563	98	170	28	13	2	36	61	65	52	....	.302	.370	.409	.779	128	19	105	5.95	18	*S-156	30	5.4
1918 Cle-A	128	446	**84**	119	19	8	1	32	**84**	46	30	....	.267	.390	.352	.742	113	12	74	5.24	1	*S-128/O-1	21	2.5
1919 Cle-A	115	433	75	130	23	10	3	53	31	38	18	....	.300	.351	.420	.772	109	5	72	5.31	0	*S-115	18	1.3
1920 Cle-A	111	435	97	132	27	8	3	49	52	38	13	9	.303	.380	.423	.803	109	7	72	5.43	18	*S-111	20	3.2
Total 9	**1051**	**3785**	**671**	**1053**	**162**	**81**	**17**	**364**	**452**	**414**	**233**	**47**	**.278**	**.358**	**.377**	**.735**	**110**	**53**	**595**	**4.98**	**9**	**S-957/2-49,3-36,O-2**	**148**	**14.2**
• CHAPMAN, Sam	Samuel Blake Chapman b: 4/11/1916, Tiburon, CA BR/TR, 6', 190 lbs. Deb: 5/16/1938 Career OF: 242-1068-8																							
1938 Phi-A	114	406	60	105	17	7	17	63	55	94	3	4	.259	.353	.461	.813	105	1	67	5.84	-4	*O-110(103-8-0)	9	-0.8
1939 Phi-A	140	498	74	134	24	6	15	64	51	62	11	4	.269	.338	.432	.770	98	-2	73	5.14	-7	*O-117(0-117-0),1-19	12	-1.3
1940 Phi-A	134	508	88	140	26	3	23	75	46	96	2	6	.276	.337	.474	.811	110	4	78	5.36	-1	*O-129(0-129-0)	14	0.0
1941 Phi-A	143	552	97	178	29	9	25	106	47	49	6	9	.322	.378	.543	.921	145	30	110	7.50	8	*O-141(0-140-1)	25	3.4
1945 Phi-A	9	30	3	6	2	0	0	1	2	4	0	0	.200	.250	.267	.517	50	-2	2	2.45	0	/O-8(0-8-0)	0	-0.3
1946 Phi-A★	146	545	77	142	22	5	20	67	54	66	1	3	.261	.327	.429	.757	111	6	73	4.56	0	*O-145(89-59-0)	12	-0.2
1947 Phi-A	149	551	84	139	18	5	14	83	65	70	3	4	.252	.331	.379	.710	95	-4	71	4.35	7	*O-146(12-134-0)	17	-0.2
1948 Phi-A	123	445	58	115	18	6	13	70	55	50	6	1	.258	.341	.413	.755	100	0	63	4.79	-1	*O-118(0-118-0)	14	-0.4
1949 Phi-A	154	589	89	164	24	4	24	108	80	68	3	4	.278	.367	.455	.822	121	15	97	5.77	3	*O-154(0-154-0)	24	1.4
1950 Phi-A	144	553	93	139	20	6	23	95	68	79	3	3	.251	.338	.434	.772	98	-4	83	5.16	3	*O-140(0-140-0)	13	-0.4
1951 Phi-A	18	65	7	11	1	0	0	5	12	12	0	0	.169	.299	.185	.483	32	-6	4	2.03	-1	O-17(0-17-0)	0	-0.8
Cle-A	94	246	24	56	9	1	6	36	27	32	3	0	.228	.304	.346	.650	80	-6	27	3.71	-3	O-84(38-44-7)/1-1	5	-1.2
Yr.	112	311	31	67	10	1	6	41	39	44	3	0	.215	.303	.312	.615	69	-12	31	3.33	-4	*O-101(38-61-7)/1-1	5	-1.9
Total 11	**1368**	**4988**	**754**	**1329**	**210**	**52**	**180**	**773**	**562**	**682**	**41**	**38**	**.266**	**.342**	**.438**	**.780**	**107**	**31**	**748**	**5.21**	**3**	***O-1309/1-20**	**145**	**-0.8**
• CHAPMAN, Travis	Travis A. Chapman b: 6/5/1978, Jacksonville, FL BR/TR, 6'2", 185 lbs. Deb: 9/9/2003																							
2003 Phi-N	1	1	0	0	0	0	0	0	0	0	0	0	.000	.000	.000	.000	-107	-0	0	.00	0	/3-1	0	-0.1
• CHAPPAS, Harry	Harry Perry Chappas b: 10/26/1957, Mount Rainier, MD BB/TR, 5'3", 150 lbs. Deb: 9/7/1978																							
1978 Chi-A	20	75	11	20	1	0	0	6	6	11	1	2	.267	.329	.280	.609	72	-3	8	3.22	1	S-20	2	0.0
1979 Chi-A	26	59	9	17	1	0	1	4	5	5	1	1	.288	.354	.356	.710	92	-1	7	4.26	-2	S-23	1	0.0
1980 Chi-A	26	50	6	8	2	0	0	2	4	10	0	2	.160	.236	.200	.436	21	-6	2	1.39	1	S-19/D-2,2-1	1	-0.4
Total 3	**72**	**184**	**26**	**45**	**4**	**0**	**1**	**12**	**15**	**26**	**2**	**5**	**.245**	**.312**	**.283**	**.594**	**65**	**-10**	**17**	**2.99**	**0**	**/S-62,D-2,2-1**	**4**	**-0.4**
• CHAPPELL, Larry	La Verne Ashford Chappell b: 2/19/1890, McClusky, IL d: 11/8/1918, San Francisco, CA BL/TR, 6', 186 lbs. Deb: 7/18/1913 Career OF: 71-8-4																							
1913 Chi-A	60	208	20	48	8	1	0	15	18	22	7	....	.231	.295	.279	.574	69	-8	18	2.85	-1	O-59(52-7-0)	4	-1.3
1914 Chi-A	21	39	3	9	0	0	0	1	4	11	0	....	.231	.302	.231	.533	61	-2	3	2.40	-1	/O-9(7-0-2)	0	-0.4
1915 Chi-A	1	1	0	0	0	0	0	0	0	0	0	....	.000	.000	.000	.000	-97	-0	0	.00	0	....	0	0.0
1916 Cle-A	3	2	0	0	0	0	0	0	1	0	1	....	.000	.333	.000	.333	1	-0	0	3.68	0	....	0	0.0
Bos-N	20	53	4	12	1	1	0	9	2	8	1	....	.226	.268	.283	.551	73	-2	4	2.69	-2	O-14(12-0-2)	1	-0.5
1917 Bos-N	4	2	0	0	0	0	0	1	0	1	0	....	.000	.000	.000	.000	-106	-0	0	.00	0	/O-1	0	-0.1
Total 5	**109**	**305**	**27**	**69**	**9**	**2**	**0**	**26**	**25**	**42**	**9**	**....**	**.226**	**.289**	**.269**	**.558**	**66**	**-13**	**26**	**2.74**	**-4**	**/O-83**	**5**	**-2.2**
• CHARBONEAU, Joe	Joseph Charboneau b: 6/17/1955, Belvidere, IL BR/TR, 6'2", 205 lbs. Deb: 4/11/1980 Career OF: 100-0-14																							
1980 Cle-A	131	453	76	131	17	2	23	87	49	70	2	4	.289	.362	.488	.850	130	17	72	5.48	-2	O-67(67-0-1),D-57	15	1.1
1981 Cle-A	48	138	14	29	7	1	4	18	7	22	1	0	.210	.248	.362	.611	75	-5	11	2.62	-1	O-27(24-0-5),D-14	1	-0.7
1982 Cle-A	22	56	7	12	2	1	2	9	5	7	0	0	.214	.290	.393	.683	86	-1	6	3.51	-1	O-18(9-0-8)/D-1	1	-0.2
Total 3	**201**	**647**	**97**	**172**	**26**	**4**	**29**	**114**	**61**	**99**	**3**	**4**	**.266**	**.333**	**.453**	**.786**	**115**	**12**	**90**	**4.66**	**-3**	**O-112/D-72**	**17**	**0.1**
• CHARLES, Chappy	Raymond Charles b: 3/25/1881, Phillipsburg, NJ d: 8/4/1959, Bethlehem, PA BR/TR, 5'11", 175 lbs. Deb: 4/15/1908																							
1908 StL-N	121	454	39	93	14	3	1	17	19	....	15	....	.205	.238	.256	.494	61	-21	31	2.14	-16	2-65,S-31,3-23	2	-4.1
1909 StL-N	99	339	33	80	7	3	0	29	31	....	7	....	.236	.309	.274	.584	87	-5	31	3.01	-8	2-71,S-26/3-2	6	-1.3
Cin-N	13	43	3	11	2	0	0	5	4	....	2	....	.256	.319	.302	.621	94	-0	5	3.74	-1	2-10/S-3	1	-0.2
Yr.	112	382	36	91	9	3	0	34	35	....	9	....	.238	.310	.277	.588	87	-5	36	3.09	-10	2-81,S-29/3-2	7	-1.4
1910 Cin-N	4	15	1	2	0	1	0	0	0	1	0	....	.133	.133	.267	.400	17	-2	0	.93	-1	/S-4	0	-0.3
Total 3	**237**	**851**	**76**	**186**	**23**	**7**	**1**	**51**	**54**	**1**	**24**	**....**	**.219**	**.270**	**.266**	**.536**	**72**	**-28**	**68**	**2.53**	**-27**	**2-146/S-64,3-25**	**9**	**-5.8**
• CHARLES, Ed	Edwin Douglas "Ez,The Poet" Charles b: 4/29/1933, Daytona Beach, FL BR/TR, 5'10", 170 lbs. Deb: 4/11/1962																							
1962 KC-A	147	535	81	154	24	7	17	74	54	70	20	4	.288	.358	.454	.812	113	13	89	5.93	3	*3-140/2-2	21	1.6
1963 KC-A	158	603	82	161	28	2	15	79	58	79	15	8	.267	.336	.395	.731	100	0	77	4.28	-9	*3-158	16	-0.9
1964 KC-A	150	557	69	134	25	2	16	63	64	92	12	7	.241	.323	.379	.702	92	-6	66	3.88	-14	*3-147	10	-2.1
1965 KC-A	134	480	55	129	19	7	8	56	44	72	13	4	.269	.335	.388	.723	106	5	64	4.62	3	*3-128/2-1,S-1	16	0.9
1966 KC-A	118	385	52	110	18	8	9	42	30	53	12	5	.286	.337	.444	.782	126	13	56	5.16	-1	*3-104/1-1,O-1	18	1.3
1967 KC-A	19	61	5	15	1	0	0	5	12	13	1	0	.246	.378	.262	.641	95	1	7	3.88	1	3-18	2	0.2
NY-N	101	323	32	77	13	2	3	31	24	58	4	1	.238	.305	.319	.624	80	-7	33	3.40	5	3-89	8	-0.3
1968 NY-N	117	369	41	102	11	1	15	53	28	57	5	4	.276	.331	.434	.764	127	11	52	4.84	2	*3-106/1-2	14	1.5
1969*NY-N	61	169	21	35	8	1	3	18	18	31	4	2	.207	.287	.320	.607	68	-7	15	2.79	-0	3-52	3	-0.8
Total 8	**1005**	**3482**	**438**	**917**	**147**	**30**	**86**	**421**	**332**	**525**	**86**	**35**	**.263**	**.332**	**.397**	**.729**	**104**	**23**	**458**	**4.49**	**-9**	**3-942/1-3,2-3,O-1,S-1**	**108**	**1.5**
• CHARLES, Frank	Franklin Scott Charles b: 2/23/1969, Fontana, CA BR/TR, 6'4", 210 lbs. Deb: 9/5/2000																							
2000 Hou-N	4	7	1	3	1	0	0	2	0	2	0	0	.429	.429	.571	1.000	142	0	2	11.57	1	/C-1	1	0.1
• CHARTAK, Mike	Michael George "Shotgun" Chartak b: 4/28/1916, Brooklyn, NY d: 7/25/1967, Cedar Rapids, IA BL/TL, 6'2", 180 lbs. Deb: 9/13/1940 Career OF: 4-0-171																							
1940 NY-A	11	15	2	2	1	0	0	3	5	5	0	0	.133	.350	.200	.550	49	-1	2	3.18	0	/O-3(0-0-3)	0	-0.1
1942 NY-A	5	5	0	0	0	0	0	0	0	0	0	0	.000	.000	.000	.000	-102	-1	0	.00	0	....	0	-0.1
Was-A	24	92	11	20	4	2	1	8	14	16	0	1	.217	.321	.337	.658	86	-2	10	3.73	-1	O-24(0-0-24)	2	-0.5
StL-A	73	237	37	59	11	2	9	43	40	27	3	3	.249	.362	.426	.788	119	6	39	5.59	7	O-64(0-0-64)	9	1.0
Yr.	102	334	48	79	15	4	10	51	54	43	3	4	.237	.346	.395	.741	107	3	49	4.96	6	O-88(0-0-88)	11	0.4
1943 StL-A	108	344	38	88	16	2	10	37	39	55	1	3	.256	.333	.401	.734	112	4	47	4.65	-2	O-77(0-0-77),1-18	10	-0.4

YEAR TM-L	G	AB	R	H	2B	3B	HR	RBI	BB	SO	SB	CS	AVG	OBP	SLG	OPS	OPS+	BR/A	RC	RC/G	FR	G/POS	WS	TPW
1944*StL-A	35	72	8	17	2	1	1	7	6	9	0	0	.236	.304	.333	.637	77	-2	8	3.67	0	1-12/0-7(4-0-3)	2	-0.3
Total 4	**256**	**765**	**96**	**186**	**34**	**7**	**21**	**98**	**104**	**112**	**4**	**7**	**.243**	**.337**	**.388**	**.725**	**105**	**5**	**105**	**4.66**	**4**	**0-175/1-30**	**23**	**-0.4**

• CHASE, Hal

Harold Homer "Prince Hal" Chase b: 2/13/1883, Los Gatos, CA d: 5/18/1947, Colusa, CA BR/TL, 6', 175 lbs. Deb: 4/14/1905 M Career OF: 23-26-1

YEAR TM-L	G	AB	R	H	2B	3B	HR	RBI	BB	SO	SB	CS	AVG	OBP	SLG	OPS	OPS+	BR/A	RC	RC/G	FR	G/POS	WS	TPW
1905 NY-A	128	465	60	116	16	6	3	49	15	....	22	....	.249	.277	.329	.606	83	-11	52	3.72	-7	*1-124/S-2,2-1	9	-2.2
1906 NY-A	151	597	84	193	23	10	0	76	13	....	28	....	.323	.341	.395	.736	118	10	95	5.86	-1	*1-150/2-1	20	0.7
1907 NY-A	125	498	72	143	23	3	2	68	19	....	32	....	.287	.315	.357	.672	106	1	69	4.99	-5	*1-121/0-4(4-0-0)	17	-0.6
1908 NY-A	106	405	50	104	11	3	1	36	15	....	27	....	.257	.285	.306	.591	91	-5	42	3.53	-1	1-98/2-3,0-3(3-0-0),3-1,P	10	-0.9
1909 NY-A	118	474	60	134	17	3	4	63	20	....	25	....	.283	.317	.357	.674	112	5	61	4.45	0	*1-118/S-1	17	0.3
1910 NY-A	130	524	67	152	20	5	3	73	16	....	40	....	.290	.312	.365	.677	106	1	71	4.73	2	*1-130	17	0.0
1911 NY-A	133	527	82	166	32	7	3	62	21	....	36	....	.315	.342	.419	.762	105	1	87	5.91	5	*1-124/0-7(0-7-0),2-2	14	0.3
1912 NY-A	131	522	61	143	21	9	4	58	17	....	33	....	.274	.299	.372	.671	86	-13	67	4.33	3	*1-122/2-7	9	-1.2
1913 NY-A	39	146	15	31	2	4	0	9	11	13	5	....	.212	.268	.281	.548	60	-8	12	2.52	-5	1-29/2-5,0-5(0-5-0)	1	-1.4
Chi-A	102	384	49	110	11	10	2	39	16	41	9	....	.286	.320	.383	.703	107	1	48	4.30	1	*1-102	11	0.0
Yr.	141	530	64	141	13	14	2	48	27	54	14	....	.266	.305	.355	.660	94	-7	60	3.78	-4	*1-131/2-5,0-5(0-5-0)	12	-1.4
1914 Chi-A	58	206	27	55	10	5	0	20	23	19	9	4	.267	.343	.364	.708	114	4	28	4.59	3	1-58	7	0.7
Buf-F	75	291	43	101	19	9	3	48	6	31	10	....	.347	.365	.505	.870	140	13	54	7.09	0	1-73	14	1.2
1915 Buf-F	145	567	85	165	31	10	**17**	89	20	50	23	....	.291	.316	.471	.787	130	16	86	5.45	-1	*1-143/0-1	23	1.3
1916 Cin-N	142	542	66	**184**	29	12	4	82	19	48	22	11	**.339**	.363	.459	.822	**155**	32	93	6.40	-9	1-98,0-25(14-14-0),2-16	22	2.4
1917 Cin-N	152	602	71	167	28	15	4	86	15	49	21	....	.277	.296	.394	.690	115	7	72	4.19	-8	*1-151	17	-0.4
1918 Cin-N	74	259	30	78	12	6	2	38	13	15	5	....	.301	.339	.417	.756	132	9	37	5.11	-6	1-67/0-2(2-0-0)	9	0.2
1919 NY-N	110	408	58	116	17	7	5	45	17	40	16	....	.284	.318	.397	.715	115	6	54	4.60	-4	*1-107	14	0.0
Total 15	**1919**	**7417**	**980**	**2158**	**322**	**124**	**57**	**941**	**276**	**306**	**363**	**15**	**.291**	**.319**	**.391**	**.710**	**112**	**68**	**1027**	**4.88**	**-33**	***1-1815/0-47,2-35,S-3,3-1,P**	**231**	**0.1**

• CHATHAM, Buster

Charles L. Chatham b: 12/25/1901, West, TX d: 12/15/1975, Waco, TX BR/TR, 5'5", 150 lbs. Deb: 6/1/1930

YEAR TM-L	G	AB	R	H	2B	3B	HR	RBI	BB	SO	SB	CS	AVG	OBP	SLG	OPS	OPS+	BR/A	RC	RC/G	FR	G/POS	WS	TPW
1930 Bos-N	112	404	48	108	20	11	5	56	37	41	8	....	.267	.332	.408	.740	80	-13	54	4.48	-2	3-92,S-17	10	-0.7
1931 Bos-N	17	44	4	10	1	0	1	3	6	6	0	....	.227	.320	.318	.638	75	-1	5	3.70	-2	/3-6,S-6	1	-0.3
Total 2	**129**	**448**	**52**	**118**	**21**	**11**	**6**	**59**	**43**	**47**	**8**	**....**	**.263**	**.331**	**.400**	**.730**	**80**	**-15**	**59**	**4.40**	**-4**	**/3-98,S-23**	**11**	**-1.0**

• CHATTERTON, Jim

James M. Chatterton b: 10/14/1864, Brooklyn, NY d: 12/15/1944, Tewksbury, MA Deb: 6/7/1884

YEAR TM-L	G	AB	R	H	2B	3B	HR	RBI	BB	SO	SB	CS	AVG	OBP	SLG	OPS	OPS+	BR/A	RC	RC/G	FR	G/POS	WS	TPW
1884 KC-U	4	15	4	2	1	0	0	....	2	....	....	....	.133	.235	.200	.435	56	-0	1	1.56	1	/1-2,0-2(0-0-2),P-1	0	0.0

• CHAVARRIA, Ossie

Osvaldo (Quijano) Chavarria b: 8/5/1940, Colon, Panama BR/TR, 5'11", 155 lbs. Deb: 4/14/1966 Career OF: 21-0-8

YEAR TM-L	G	AB	R	H	2B	3B	HR	RBI	BB	SO	SB	CS	AVG	OBP	SLG	OPS	OPS+	BR/A	RC	RC/G	FR	G/POS	WS	TPW
1966 KC-A	86	191	26	46	10	0	2	10	18	43	3	2	.241	.306	.325	.631	84	-4	19	3.26	1	0-26(19-0-7),S-23,2-14/1-8,3	4	-0.2
1967 KC-A	38	59	2	6	2	0	0	4	7	16	1	0	.102	.209	.136	.345	4	-7	2	1.13	0	2-17/3-7,0-3(2-0-1),S-2	1	-0.6
Total 2	**124**	**250**	**28**	**52**	**12**	**0**	**2**	**14**	**25**	**59**	**4**	**2**	**.208**	**.283**	**.280**	**.563**	**65**	**-11**	**21**	**2.71**	**1**	**/2-31,0-29,S-25,3-12,1-8**	**5**	**-0.8**

• CHAVEZ, Endy

Endy DeJesus Chavez b: 2/7/1978, Valencia, Venezuela BL/TL, 6', 165 lbs. Deb: 5/29/2001 Career OF: 22-175-2

YEAR TM-L	G	AB	R	H	2B	3B	HR	RBI	BB	SO	SB	CS	AVG	OBP	SLG	OPS	OPS+	BR/A	RC	RC/G	FR	G/POS	WS	TPW
2001 KC-A	29	77	4	16	2	0	0	5	3	8	0	2	.208	.238	.234	.471	23	-10	3	1.34	1	0-28(22-5-2)	0	-0.9
2002 Mon-N	36	125	20	37	8	5	1	9	5	16	3	5	.296	.323	.464	.787	101	-2	17	4.66	7	0-35(0-35-0)	3	0.5
2003 Mon-N	141	483	66	121	25	5	5	47	31	59	18	7	.251	.296	.354	.650	58	-30	51	3.54	1	*0-135(0-135-0)	9	-2.7
Total 3	**206**	**685**	**90**	**174**	**35**	**10**	**6**	**61**	**39**	**83**	**21**	**14**	**.254**	**.294**	**.361**	**.655**	**62**	**-41**	**72**	**3.48**	**9**	**0-198**	**12**	**-3.1**

• CHAVEZ, Eric

Eric Cesar Chavez b: 12/7/1977, Los Angeles, CA BL/TR, 6'1", 204 lbs. Deb: 9/8/1998

YEAR TM-L	G	AB	R	H	2B	3B	HR	RBI	BB	SO	SB	CS	AVG	OBP	SLG	OPS	OPS+	BR/A	RC	RC/G	FR	G/POS	WS	TPW
1998 Oak-A	16	45	6	14	4	1	0	6	3	5	1	1	.311	.354	.444	.799	109	0	7	5.38	1	3-13	2	0.1
1999 Oak-A	115	356	47	88	21	2	13	50	46	56	1	1	.247	.333	.427	.760	96	-3	51	5.01	-8	*3-105/D-3,S-2	9	-0.8
2000*Oak-A	153	501	89	139	23	4	26	86	62	94	2	2	.277	.358	.495	.853	116	11	89	6.38	-9	*3-146/S-2,D-1	16	0.4
2001*Oak-A	151	552	91	159	43	0	32	114	41	99	8	2	.288	.342	.540	.882	127	20	102	6.72	13	*3-149/1-1,D-1,S-1	26	3.3
2002*Oak-A	153	585	87	161	31	3	34	109	65	119	8	3	.275	.349	.513	.862	125	20	106	6.52	8	*3-143/D-9,0-1	25	2.8
2003*Oak-A	156	588	94	166	39	5	29	101	62	89	8	3	.282	.352	.514	.865	123	19	104	6.37	23	*3-154	25	4.3
Total 6	**744**	**2627**	**414**	**727**	**161**	**15**	**134**	**466**	**279**	**462**	**28**	**12**	**.277**	**.348**	**.502**	**.850**	**119**	**68**	**459**	**6.27**	**28**	**3-710/D-14,S-5,1-1,0-1**	**103**	**10.1**

• CHAVEZ, Raul

Raul Alexander Chavez b: 3/18/1973, Valencia, Venezuela BR/TR, 5'11", 175 lbs. Deb: 8/30/1996

YEAR TM-L	G	AB	R	H	2B	3B	HR	RBI	BB	SO	SB	CS	AVG	OBP	SLG	OPS	OPS+	BR/A	RC	RC/G	FR	G/POS	WS	TPW
1996 Mon-N	4	5	1	1	0	0	0	0	1	1	1	0	.200	.333	.200	.533	44	-0	0	1.60	0	/C-3	0	0.0
1997 Mon-N	13	26	0	7	0	0	0	2	0	5	1	0	.269	.269	.269	.538	42	-2	2	2.81	1	C-13	0	-0.1
1998 Sea-A	1	1	0	0	0	0	0	0	0	0	0	0	.000	.000	.000	.000	-100	-0	0	.00	-0	/C-1	0	0.0
2000 Hou-N	14	43	3	11	2	0	1	5	3	6	0	0	.256	.304	.372	.676	66	-2	3	2.28	-3	C-14	0	-0.5
2002 Hou-N	2	4	1	1	1	0	0	0	1	0	0	0	.250	.500	.500	1.000	157	1	1	11.34	-1	/C-2	0	0.0
2003 Hou-N	19	37	5	10	1	1	1	4	1	6	0	0	.270	.289	.432	.722	81	-1	3	3.08	-2	C-16	1	-0.2
Total 6	**53**	**116**	**10**	**30**	**4**	**1**	**2**	**11**	**6**	**18**	**2**	**0**	**.259**	**.301**	**.362**	**.663**	**67**	**-5**	**10**	**2.86**	**-5**	**/C-49**	**1**	**-0.8**

• CHEEK, Harry

Harry G. Cheek b: 3/1/1879, Sedalia, MO d: 6/25/1956, Paramus, NJ TR Deb: 4/30/1910

YEAR TM-L	G	AB	R	H	2B	3B	HR	RBI	BB	SO	SB	CS	AVG	OBP	SLG	OPS	OPS+	BR/A	RC	RC/G	FR	G/POS	WS	TPW
1910 Phi-N	2	4	1	2	1	0	0	0	0	0	0	....	.500	.500	.750	1.250	255	1	1	19.19	-1	/C-2	0	0.0

• CHEN, Chin-Feng

Chin-Feng Chen b: 10/28/1977, Tainan City, Taiwan BR/TR, 6'1", 189 lbs. Deb: 9/14/2002

YEAR TM-L	G	AB	R	H	2B	3B	HR	RBI	BB	SO	SB	CS	AVG	OBP	SLG	OPS	OPS+	BR/A	RC	RC/G	FR	G/POS	WS	TPW
2002 LA-N	3	5	1	0	0	0	0	0	1	3	0	0	.000	.167	.000	.167	-55	-1	0	.23	0	/0-1	0	-0.1
2003 LA-N	1	1	0	0	0	0	0	0	0	0	0	0	.000	.000	.000	.000	-106	-0	0	.00	0	....	0	0.0
Total 2	**4**	**6**	**1**	**0**	**0**	**0**	**0**	**0**	**1**	**3**	**0**	**0**	**.000**	**.143**	**.000**	**.143**	**-62**	**-1**	**0**	**.20**	**0**	**/0-1**	**0**	**-0.1**

• CHERVINKO, Paul

Paul Chervinko b: 7/28/1910, Trauger, PA d: 6/3/1976, Danville, IL BR/TR, 5'8", 185 lbs. Deb: 5/30/1937

YEAR TM-L	G	AB	R	H	2B	3B	HR	RBI	BB	SO	SB	CS	AVG	OBP	SLG	OPS	OPS+	BR/A	RC	RC/G	FR	G/POS	WS	TPW
1937 Bro-N	30	48	1	7	0	1	0	2	3	16	0	....	.146	.196	.188	.384	5	-6	2	1.14	1	C-26	0	-0.5
1938 Bro-N	12	27	0	4	0	0	0	3	2	0	0	....	.148	.207	.148	.355	-1	-4	1	.71	0	C-12	0	-0.3
Total 2	**42**	**75**	**1**	**11**	**0**	**1**	**0**	**5**	**5**	**16**	**0**	**....**	**.147**	**.200**	**.173**	**.373**	**2**	**-10**	**2**	**.97**	**0**	**/C-38**	**0**	**-0.8**

• CHILDS, Cupid

Clarence Algernon Childs b: 8/8/1867, Calvert County, MD d: 11/8/1912, Baltimore, MD BL/TR, 5'8", 185 lbs. Deb: 4/23/1888

YEAR TM-L	G	AB	R	H	2B	3B	HR	RBI	BB	SO	SB	CS	AVG	OBP	SLG	OPS	OPS+	BR/A	RC	RC/G	FR	G/POS	WS	TPW
1888 Phi-N	2	4	0	0	0	0	0	0	0	0	0	....	.000	.000	.000	.000	-95	-1	0	.00	0	/2-2	0	-0.1
1890 Syr-a	126	493	109	170	**33**	14	2	89	72	....	56	....	.345	.434	**.481**	**.915**	**189**	**59**	130	10.70	14	*2-125/S-1	**31**	**6.8**
1891 Cle-N	141	551	120	155	21	12	2	83	97	32	39	....	.281	.395	.374	.769	119	18	99	6.77	-18	*2-141	21	0.4
1892*Cle-N	145	558	**136**	177	14	11	3	53	117	20	26	....	.317	**.443**	.398	.841	149	42	113	7.98	10	*2-145	32	5.5
1893 Cle-N	124	485	145	158	19	10	3	65	120	12	23	....	.326	.463	.425	.888	129	29	109	8.81	3	*2-123	23	3.0
1894 Cle-N	118	479	143	169	21	12	2	52	107	11	17	....	.353	.475	.459	.935	122	25	116	9.69	6	*2-118	20	2.8
1895*Cle-N	120	466	96	134	15	4	4	90	74	24	20	....	.288	.392	.363	.755	89	-5	76	6.06	14	*2-119	18	1.2
1896*Cle-N	132	498	106	177	24	9	1	106	100	18	25	....	.355	.467	.446	.913	134	32	120	9.53	33	*2-132	27	6.0
1897 Cle-N	114	444	105	150	15	9	1	61	74	....	25	....	.338	.435	.419	.854	119	17	96	8.21	35	*2-114	18	4.8
1898 Cle-N	110	413	90	119	9	4	1	31	69	....	9	....	.288	.395	.337	.732	112	11	62	5.36	9	*2-110	18	2.3
1899 StL-N	125	464	73	123	11	11	1	48	74	....	11	....	.265	.369	.343	.711	93	-1	66	4.96	-21	*2-125	12	-1.5
1900 Chi-N	137	531	67	128	14	5	0	44	57	....	15	....	.241	.323	.286	.609	71	-18	58	3.64	11	*2-137	12	-0.1
1901 Chi-N	63	236	24	61	9	0	0	21	30	....	3	....	.258	.359	.297	.656	95	1	27	4.07	5	2-63	6	0.6
Total 13	**1457**	**5622**	**1214**	**1721**	**205**	**101**	**20**	**743**	**991**	**117**	**269**	**....**	**.306**	**.416**	**.389**	**.805**	**120**	**208**	**1073**	**7.15**	**101**	***2-1454/S-1**	**238**	**31.7**

• CHILDS, Pete

Peter Pierre Childs b: 11/15/1871, Philadelphia, PA d: 2/15/1922, Philadelphia, PA TR Deb: 4/24/1901

YEAR TM-L	G	AB	R	H	2B	3B	HR	RBI	BB	SO	SB	CS	AVG	OBP	SLG	OPS	OPS+	BR/A	RC	RC/G	FR	G/POS	WS	TPW
1901 StL-N	29	79	12	21	1	0	0	8	14	....	0	....	.266	.389	.278	.668	100	1	9	4.01	-3	2-19/0-2(1-1-0),S-1	2	-0.2
Chi-N	60	210	23	48	5	1	0	14	26	....	4	....	.229	.319	.262	.581	72	-6	20	3.18	8	2-60	4	0.3
Yr.	89	289	35	69	6	1	0	22	40	....	4	....	.239	.339	.266	.606	80	-4	29	3.39	5	2-79/0-2(1-1-0),S-1	6	0.1
1902 Phi-N	123	403	25	78	5	0	0	25	34	....	6	....	.194	.256	.206	.462	43	-26	25	1.96	-18	*2-123	3	-4.5
Total 2	**212**	**692**	**60**	**147**	**11**	**1**	**0**	**47**	**74**	**....**	**10**	**....**	**.212**	**.292**	**.231**	**.523**	**59**	**-31**	**53**	**2.53**	**-13**	**2-202/0-2,S-1**	**9**	**-4.4**

• CHILDS, Sam

Samuel Beresford Childs b: 11/6/1861, East Hartford, CT d: 5/21/1938, Denver, CO Deb: 5/31/1883

YEAR TM-L	G	AB	R	H	2B	3B	HR	RBI	BB	SO	SB	CS	AVG	OBP	SLG	OPS	OPS+	BR/A	RC	RC/G	FR	G/POS	WS	TPW
1883 Col-a	1	3	0	0	0	0	0	0	0	....	....	....	.000	.000	.000	.000	-109	-1	0	.00	-0	/1-1	0	-0.1

YEAR TM-L	G	AB	R	H	2B	3B	HR	RBI	BB	SO	SB	CS	AVG	OBP	SLG	OPS	OPS+	BR/A	RC	RC/G	FR	G/POS	WS	TPW
• CHILES, Pearce	Pearce Nuget "What's The Use" Chiles b: 5/28/1867, Deepwater, MO BR/TR, 5'11", 185 lbs. Deb: 4/18/1899 Career OF: 13-2-34																							
1899 Phi-N	97	338	57	108	28	7	2	76	16	....	6	....	.320	.352	.462	.814	127	10	59	6.72	-9	0-46(13-2-31),1-25,2-16	12	-0.1
1900 Phi-N	33	111	13	24	6	2	1	23	6	....	4	....	.216	.256	.333	.590	63	-6	11	3.26	-1	1-16,2-12/0-3(0-0-3)	1	-0.6
Total 2	**130**	**449**	**70**	**132**	**34**	**9**	**3**	**99**	**22**	**....**	**10**	**....**	**.294**	**.328**	**.430**	**.758**	**111**	**4**	**70**	**5.75**	**-10**	**/0-49,1-41,2-28**	**13**	**-0.7**
• CHILES, Rich	Richard Francis Chiles b: 11/22/1949, Sacramento, CA BL/TL, 5'11", 170 lbs. Deb: 4/20/1971 Career OF: 87-8-26																							
1971 Hou-N	67	119	12	27	5	1	2	15	6	20	0	1	.227	.270	.336	.606	72	-5	10	2.89	-1	0-27(25-0-2)	1	-0.7
1972 Hou-N	9	11	0	3	1	0	0	2	1	1	0	0	.273	.333	.364	.697	100	0	1	4.79	-0	/0-2(2-0-0)	0	0.0
1973 NY-N	8	25	2	3	2	0	0	1	0	2	0	0	.120	.120	.200	.320	-13	-4	0	.23	1	/0-8(0-8-0)	0	-0.3
1976 Hou-N	5	4	1	2	1	0	0	0	0	0	0	0	.500	.500	.750	1.250	276	1	2	20.25	-0	/0-1	0	0.1
1977 Min-A	108	261	31	69	16	1	3	36	23	17	0	1	.264	.329	.368	.696	91	-3	32	4.15	-1	D-61,0-22(1-0-21)	4	-0.7
1978 Min-A	87	198	22	53	12	0	1	22	20	25	1	2	.268	.341	.343	.684	91	-2	22	3.64	2	0-61(58-0-3)/D-8	3	-0.3
Total 6	**284**	**618**	**68**	**157**	**37**	**2**	**6**	**76**	**50**	**65**	**1**	**4**	**.254**	**.315**	**.350**	**.665**	**85**	**-14**	**67**	**3.63**	**1**	**0-121/D-69**	**8**	**-1.9**
• CHIOZZA, Dino	Dino Joseph Chiozza b: 6/30/1912, Memphis, TN d: 4/23/1972, Memphis, TN BL/TR, 6', 170 lbs. Deb: 7/14/1935																							
1935 Phi-N	2	0	1	0	0	0	0	0	0	0	0	....	....	....	....	....	-91	0	0	....	-1	/S-2	0	-0.1
• CHIOZZA, Lou	Louis Peo Chiozza b: 5/17/1910, Tallulah, LA d: 2/28/1971, Memphis, TN BL/TR, 6', 172 lbs. Deb: 4/17/1934 Career OF: 22-107-5																							
1934 Phi-N	134	484	66	147	28	5	0	44	34	35	9	....	.304	.357	.382	.739	86	-8	68	5.17	-13	2-85,3-26,0-17(13-0-4)	9	-1.5
1935 Phi-N	124	472	71	134	26	6	3	47	33	44	5	....	.284	.333	.383	.717	84	-11	64	4.93	2	*2-120/3-2	11	-0.1
1936 Phi-N	144	572	83	170	32	6	1	48	37	39	17	....	.297	.346	.379	.726	87	-10	80	5.27	-6	0-90(4-85-1),2-33,3-26	11	-1.6
1937*NY-N	117	439	49	102	11	2	4	29	20	30	6	....	.232	.266	.294	.560	51	-31	36	2.83	-8	3-93,0-12(0-12-0)/2-2	4	-3.5
1938 NY-N	57	179	15	42	7	2	3	17	12	7	5	....	.235	.283	.346	.629	72	-7	18	3.48	-2	2-34,0-16(5-10-0)/3-1	3	-0.8
1939 NY-N	40	142	19	38	3	1	3	12	9	10	3	....	.268	.311	.366	.677	81	-4	17	4.20	-4	3-30/S-8	3	-0.6
Total 6	**616**	**2288**	**303**	**633**	**107**	**22**	**14**	**197**	**145**	**165**	**45**	**....**	**.277**	**.324**	**.361**	**.685**	**78**	**-71**	**283**	**4.47**	**-30**	**2-274,3-178,0-135/S-8**	**41**	**-8.1**
• CHIPPLE, Walt	Walter John Chipple b: 9/26/1918, Utica, NY d: 6/8/1988, Tonawanda, NY BR/TR, 6'.5", 168 lbs. Deb: 4/17/1945																							
1945 Was-A	18	44	4	6	0	0	0	5	5	6	0	1	.136	.224	.136	.361	6	-5	1	.94	2	0-13(1-11-1)	1	-0.4
• CHISM, Tom	Thomas Raymond Chism b: 5/9/1954, Chester, PA BL/TL, 6'1", 195 lbs. Deb: 9/13/1979																							
1979 Bal-A	6	3	0	0	0	0	0	0	0	0	0	0	.000	.000	.000	.000	-104	-1	0	.00	0	/1-4	0	-0.1
• CHITI, Harry	Harry Chiti b: 11/16/1932, Kincaid, IL d: 1/31/2002, Haines City, FL BR/TR, 6'2.5", 225 lbs. Deb: 9/27/1950																							
1950 Chi-N	3	6	0	2	0	0	0	0	0	0	0	....	.333	.333	.333	.667	77	-0	1	4.50	0	/C-1	0	0.0
1951 Chi-N	9	31	1	11	2	0	0	5	2	2	0	0	.355	.394	.419	.813	117	1	4	4.75	1	/C-8	1	0.2
1952 Chi-N	32	113	14	31	5	0	5	13	5	8	0	1	.274	.305	.451	.756	106	-0	15	4.56	1	C-32	3	0.2
1955 Chi-N	113	338	24	78	6	1	11	41	25	68	0	0	.231	.286	.352	.638	68	-16	33	3.23	3	*C-113	7	-0.8
1956 Chi-N	72	203	17	43	6	4	4	18	19	35	0	0	.212	.283	.340	.622	68	-9	18	2.80	1	C-67	3	-0.5
1958 KC-A	103	295	32	79	11	3	9	44	18	48	3	2	.268	.316	.417	.733	98	-1	37	4.29	0	C-83	10	0.3
1959 KC-A	55	162	20	44	11	1	5	25	17	26	0	1	.272	.344	.444	.789	113	2	22	4.66	1	C-47	5	0.5
1960 KC-A	58	190	16	42	7	0	5	28	17	33	1	0	.221	.288	.337	.625	68	-9	18	2.94	0	C-52	2	-0.6
Det-A	37	104	9	17	0	0	2	5	10	12	0	3	.163	.237	.221	.458	23	-13	4	1.13	-1	C-36	1	-1.2
Yr.	95	294	25	59	7	0	7	33	27	45	1	3	.201	.270	.296	.566	52	-21	22	2.25	0	C-88	3	-1.7
1961 Det-A	5	12	0	1	0	0	0	0	1	2	0	0	.083	.154	.083	.237	-34	-2	0	.22	0	/C-5	0	-0.2
1962 NY-N	15	41	2	8	1	0	0	0	1	8	0	0	.195	.233	.220	.452	22	-5	2	1.37	-1	C-14	0	-0.5
Total 10	**502**	**1495**	**135**	**356**	**49**	**9**	**41**	**179**	**115**	**242**	**4**	**7**	**.238**	**.296**	**.365**	**.661**	**77**	**-52**	**153**	**3.36**	**5**	**C-458**	**32**	**-2.5**
• CHOI, Hee Seop	Hee Seop Choi b: 3/16/1979, Chun-Nam, South Korea BL/TL, 6'5", 235 lbs. Deb: 9/3/2002																							
2002 Chi-N	24	50	6	9	1	0	2	4	7	15	0	0	.180	.281	.320	.601	59	-3	4	2.75	0	1-22	0	-0.5
2003 Chi-N	80	202	31	44	17	0	8	28	37	71	1	1	.218	.350	.421	.771	101	1	32	5.38	1	1-69	5	-0.3
Total 2	**104**	**252**	**37**	**53**	**18**	**0**	**10**	**32**	**44**	**86**	**1**	**1**	**.210**	**.337**	**.401**	**.737**	**93**	**-2**	**37**	**4.83**	**0**	**/1-91**	**5**	**-0.8**
• CHOUINARD, Felix	Felix George Chouinard b: 10/5/1887, Chicago, IL d: 4/28/1955, Hines, IL BR/TR, 5'7", 150 lbs. Deb: 9/11/1910 Career OF: 9-43-3																							
1910 Chi-A	24	82	6	16	3	2	0	9	8	....	4	....	.195	.275	.280	.555	78	-2	7	2.80	5	0-23(0-23-0)/2-1	3	0.2
1911 Chi-A	14	17	3	3	0	0	0	0	0	....	0	....	.176	.176	.176	.353	-2	-2	1	1.04	0	/2-4,0-4(0-3-1)	0	-0.3
1914 Pit-F	9	30	2	9	1	0	1	3	0	4	1	....	.300	.300	.433	.733	114	0	4	4.71	0	/2-4,0-3(2-1-0),S-1	1	0.0
Bro-F	32	79	7	20	1	2	0	8	4	13	3	....	.253	.289	.316	.606	72	-3	8	3.23	0	0-20(5-14-2)	1	-0.5
Bal-F	5	9	3	4	0	0	0	1	0	1	0	....	.444	.444	.444	.889	154	1	2	8.66	0	/0-2(1-1-0)	1	0.0
Yr.	46	118	12	33	2	2	1	12	4	18	4	....	.280	.303	.356	.659	88	-2	13	3.90	0	0-25(8-16-2)/2-4,S-1	3	-0.4
1915 Bro-F	4	4	1	2	0	0	0	2	0	0	0	....	.500	.500	.500	1.000	199	0	1	9.48	0	/0-2(1-1-0)	0	0.0
Total 4	**88**	**221**	**22**	**54**	**5**	**4**	**1**	**23**	**12**	**18**	**8**	**....**	**.244**	**.286**	**.317**	**.603**	**79**	**-6**	**22**	**3.30**	**4**	**/0-54,2-9,S-1**	**6**	**-0.5**
• CHOZEN, Harry	Harry Chozen b: 9/27/1915, Winnebago, MN d: 9/16/1994, Houston, TX BR/TR, 5'9", 190 lbs. Deb: 9/21/1937																							
1937 Cin-N	1	4	0	1	0	0	0	0	0	0	0	....	.250	.250	.250	.500	38	-0	0	2.31	0	/C-1	0	-0.1
• CHRISLEY, Neil	Barbra O'Neil Chrisley b: 12/16/1931, Calhoun Falls, SC BL/TR, 6'3", 187 lbs. Deb: 4/15/1957 Career OF: 76-12-61																							
1957 Was-A	26	51	6	8	2	1	0	3	7	7	0	0	.157	.259	.235	.494	36	-4	4	2.24	-1	0-11(4-0-7)	0	-0.6
1958 Was-A	105	233	19	50	7	4	5	26	16	18	1	3	.215	.265	.343	.608	67	-12	19	2.69	-0	0-69(38-7-25)/3-1	2	-1.6
1959 Det-A	65	106	7	14	3	0	6	11	12	10	0	0	.132	.227	.330	.557	48	-8	8	2.42	-1	0-21(3-1-17)	0	-0.9
1960 Det-A	96	220	27	56	10	3	5	24	19	26	2	0	.255	.317	.395	.712	86	-4	28	4.29	-2	0-47(31-4-12)/1-2	4	-0.9
1961 Mil-N	10	9	1	2	0	0	0	0	1	1	0	0	.222	.300	.222	.522	44	-1	1	2.62	0	....	0	-0.1
Total 5	**302**	**619**	**60**	**130**	**22**	**8**	**16**	**64**	**55**	**62**	**3**	**3**	**.210**	**.277**	**.349**	**.626**	**68**	**-29**	**60**	**3.15**	**-4**	**0-148/1-2,3-1**	**6**	**-4.1**
• CHRISTENBURY, Lloyd	Lloyd Reid "Low" Christenbury b: 10/19/1893, Mecklenburg County, NC d: 12/13/1944, Birmingham, AL BL/TR, 5'7", 165 lbs. Deb: 9/20/1919 Career OF: 37-7-9																							
1919 Bos-N	7	31	5	9	1	0	0	4	2	2	0	....	.290	.333	.323	.656	102	0	3	3.74	1	/0-7(7-0-0)	1	0.1
1920 Bos-N	65	106	17	22	2	2	0	14	13	12	0	1	.208	.300	.264	.564	66	-4	9	2.71	-2	0-14(0-7-7)/S-7,2-6,3-2	1	-0.7
1921 Bos-N	62	125	34	44	6	2	3	16	21	7	3	4	.352	.449	.504	.953	161	12	28	8.48	-6	2-32/3-2,S-2	7	0.7
1922 Bos-N	71	152	22	38	5	2	1	13	18	11	2	4	.250	.337	.329	.666	76	-6	17	3.71	1	0-32(30-0-2)/2-5,3-2	2	-0.7
Total 4	**205**	**414**	**78**	**113**	**14**	**6**	**4**	**47**	**54**	**32**	**5**	**9**	**.273**	**.362**	**.365**	**.727**	**101**	**2**	**58**	**4.74**	**-7**	**/0-53,2-43,S-9,3-6**	**11**	**-0.6**
• CHRISTENSEN, Bruce	Bruce Ray Christensen b: 2/22/1948, Madison, WI BL/TR, 5'11", 160 lbs. Deb: 7/17/1971																							
1971 Cal-A	29	63	4	17	1	0	0	3	6	5	0	1	.270	.333	.286	.619	83	-2	6	3.03	0	S-24	1	0.1
• CHRISTENSEN, Cuckoo	Walter Niels "Seacap" Christensen b: 10/24/1899, San Francisco, CA d: 12/20/1984, Menlo Park, CA BL/TL, 5'6.5", 156 lbs. Deb: 4/13/1926 Career OF: 83-54-13																							
1926 Cin-N	114	329	41	115	15	7	0	41	40	18	8	....	.350	.426	.438	.864	136	19	62	7.11	0	0-93(72-19-9)	16	1.3
1927 Cin-N	57	185	25	47	6	0	0	16	20	16	4	....	.254	.330	.286	.617	68	-7	18	3.32	-1	0-50(11-35-4)	3	-1.0
Total 2	**171**	**514**	**66**	**162**	**21**	**7**	**0**	**57**	**60**	**34**	**12**	**....**	**.315**	**.392**	**.383**	**.775**	**112**	**12**	**80**	**5.65**	**-1**	**0-143**	**19**	**0.3**
• CHRISTENSEN, John	John Lawrence Christensen b: 9/15/1960, Downey, CA BR/TR, 6'3", 205 lbs. Deb: 9/13/1984 Career OF: 11-2-91																							
1984 NY-N	5	11	2	3	2	0	0	3	1	2	0	1	.273	.333	.455	.788	121	-0	1	3.60	-1	/0-5(3-0-2)	0	-0.1
1985 NY-N	51	113	10	21	4	1	3	13	19	23	1	2	.186	.303	.319	.622	76	-4	11	3.02	-2	0-38(6-2-31)	2	-0.8
1987 Sea-A	53	132	19	32	6	1	2	12	12	28	2	0	.242	.306	.348	.654	69	-5	14	3.70	2	0-43(2-0-41)/D-8	2	-0.5
1988 Min-A	23	38	5	10	4	0	0	5	3	5	0	0	.263	.349	.368	.717	98	0	5	4.56	0	0-17(0-0-17)/D-1	2	-0.1
Total 4	**132**	**294**	**36**	**66**	**16**	**2**	**5**	**33**	**35**	**58**	**3**	**3**	**.224**	**.311**	**.344**	**.655**	**78**	**-10**	**32**	**3.52**	**-1**	**0-103/D-9**	**6**	**-1.4**
• CHRISTENSEN, McKay	McKay Andrew Christensen b: 8/14/1975, Upland, CA BL/TL, 5'11", 180 lbs. Deb: 4/6/1999 Career OF: 5-74-0																							
1999 Chi-A	28	53	10	12	1	0	1	6	4	7	2	1	.226	.281	.302	.583	49	-4	5	2.69	-1	0-27(0-27-0)	1	-0.5
2000*Chi-A	32	19	4	2	0	0	0	1	2	6	1	1	.105	.227	.105	.333	-12	-3	1	.90	0	0-29(0-29-0)	0	-0.3
2001 Chi-A	7	4	0	1	0	0	0	0	0	2	0	0	.250	.400	.250	.650	74	-0	1	4.54	-1	/0-6(0-6-0)	0	-0.1

YEAR TM-L	G	AB	R	H	2B	3B	HR	RBI	BB	SO	SB	CS	AVG	OBP	SLG	OPS	OPS+	BR/A	RC	RC/G	FR	G/POS	WS	TPW
LA-N	28	49	7	16	2	0	1	7	3	10	3	2	.327	.400	.429	.829	124	2	9	6.77	-2	0-14(3-11-0)	2	0.0
2002 NY-N	4	3	1	1	0	0	0	0	1	1	0	0	.333	.500	.333	.833	130	0	1	8.51	0	/0-3(2-1-0)	0	0.0
Total 4	99	128	22	32	3	0	2	14	10	26	6	4	.250	.329	.320	.649	71	-6	15	3.92	-3	/0-79	3	-0.8
• CHRISTENSON, Ryan	Ryan Alan Christenson b: 3/28/1974, Redlands, CA BR/TR, 5'11", 191 lbs. Deb: 4/20/1998 Career OF: 88-321-21																							
1998 Oak-A	117	370	56	95	22	2	5	40	36	106	5	6	.257	.324	.368	.692	81	-12	46	4.21	0	*O-116(1-113-4)	9	-1.0
1999 Oak-A	106	268	41	56	12	1	4	24	38	58	7	5	.209	.309	.306	.615	60	-16	27	3.09	-2	*O-104(0-104-0)/D-1	3	-1.6
2000*Oak-A	121	129	31	32	2	2	4	18	19	33	1	2	.248	.349	.388	.737	88	-3	19	4.81	-2	*O-114(76-27-14)	3	-0.5
2001 Oak-A	7	4	1	0	0	0	0	0	0	1	0	0	.000	.000	.000	.000	-100	-1	0	.00	0	/O-4(1-1-3),D-1	0	-0.1
Ari-N	19	4	3	1	1	0	0	1	1	1	1	0	.250	.400	.500	.900	123	0	1	10.01	0	/O-5(4-1-0)	0	0.0
2002 Mil-N	22	58	5	9	4	0	1	3	5	13	0	0	.155	.222	.276	.498	31	-6	4	1.89	-1	O-21(6-16-0)	0	-0.7
2003 Tex-A	60	165	22	29	7	0	2	16	15	44	2	2	.176	.257	.255	.511	33	-17	11	2.09	0	O-59(0-59-0)	1	-1.5
Total 6	452	998	159	222	48	5	16	102	114	256	16	15	.222	.306	.329	.635	65	-54	108	3.46	-5	O-423/D-2	16	-5.5
• CHRISTIAN, Bob	Robert Charles Christian b: 10/17/1945, Chicago, IL d: 2/20/1974, San Diego, CA BR/TR, 5'10", 180 lbs. Deb: 9/2/1968 Career OF: 41-0-2																							
1968 Det-A	3	3	0	1	1	0	0	0	0	0	0	0	.333	.333	.667	1.000	191	0	1	9.00	0	/1-1,O-1	0	0.0
1969 Chi-A	39	129	11	28	4	0	3	16	10	19	3	0	.217	.279	.318	.596	63	-6	12	2.97	-1	O-38(37-0-1)	1	-1.0
1970 Chi-A	12	15	3	4	0	0	1	3	1	4	0	0	.267	.313	.467	.779	108	0	2	5.57	0	/O-4(4-0-0)	0	0.0
Total 3	54	147	14	33	5	0	4	19	11	23	3	0	.224	.283	.340	.623	70	-6	15	3.31	-1	/O-43,1-1	1	-1.0
• CHRISTMAN, Mark	Marquette Joseph Christman b: 10/21/1913, Maplewood, MO d: 10/9/1976, St. Louis, MO BR/TR, 5'11", 180 lbs. Deb: 4/20/1938																							
1938 Det-A	95	318	35	79	6	4	1	44	27	21	5	2	.248	.307	.302	.609	50	-25	31	3.35	6	3-69,S-21	5	-1.3
1939 Det-A	6	16	0	4	2	0	0	0	0	2	0	0	.250	.250	.375	.625	54	-1	1	1.45	0	/3-5	0	-0.1
StL-A	79	222	27	48	6	3	0	20	20	10	2	1	.216	.281	.270	.551	41	-20	16	2.31	-2	S-64/2-1	2	-1.6
Yr.	85	238	27	52	8	3	0	20	20	12	2	1	.218	.279	.277	.556	41	-21	17	2.25	-3	S-64/3-5,2-1	2	-1.8
1943 StL-A	98	336	31	91	11	5	2	35	19	19	0	3	.271	.318	.351	.669	93	-4	38	3.95	0	3-37,S-24,1-20,2-14	9	-0.3
1944*StL-A	148	547	56	148	25	1	6	83	47	37	5	2	.271	.332	.353	.684	90	-6	64	4.03	7	*3-145/1-3	21	0.2
1945 StL-A	78	289	32	80	7	4	4	34	19	19	1	0	.277	.328	.370	.698	98	-1	36	4.49	6	3-77	9	0.6
1946 StL-A	128	458	40	118	22	2	1	41	22	29	0	2	.258	.295	.321	.616	68	-20	41	3.06	8	3-77,S-47	8	-1.1
1947 Was-A	110	374	27	83	15	2	1	33	32	16	4	4	.222	.287	.281	.568	60	-21	30	2.64	-5	*S-106/2-1	6	-2.0
1948 Was-A	120	409	38	106	17	2	1	40	25	19	0	3	.259	.303	.318	.621	67	-21	37	3.10	-14	*S-102/3-9,2-3	4	-2.8
1949 Was-A	49	112	8	24	2	0	3	18	8	7	0	0	.214	.273	.313	.585	56	-8	9	2.55	1	3-23/1-6,S-4,2-1	1	-0.6
Total 9	911	3081	294	781	113	23	19	348	219	179	17	17	.253	.306	.324	.630	72	-128	302	3.34	5	3-442,S-368/1-29,2-20	65	-9.1
• CHRISTMAS, Steve	Stephen Randall Christmas b: 12/9/1957, Orlando, FL BL/TR, 6', 190 lbs. Deb: 9/1/1983																							
1983 Cin-N	9	17	0	1	0	0	0	1	1	3	0	0	.059	.111	.059	.170	-50	-3	0	.14	0	/C-7	0	-0.3
1984 Chi-A	12	11	1	4	1	0	1	4	0	2	0	0	.364	.364	.727	1.091	185	1	3	11.22	-0	/C-1	1	0.1
1986 Chi-N	3	9	0	1	1	0	0	2	0	1	0	0	.111	.111	.222	.333	-10	-1	0	.75	1	/1-1,C-1	0	-0.1
Total 3	24	37	1	6	2	0	1	7	1	6	0	0	.162	.184	.297	.482	26	-4	3	2.64	1	/C-9,1-1	1	-0.3
• CHRISTOPHER, Joe	Joseph O'Neal Christopher b: 12/13/1935, Frederiksted, V.I. BR/TR, 5'10", 176 lbs. Deb: 5/26/1959 Career OF: 152-54-277																							
1959 Pit-N	15	12	6	0	0	0	0	0	1	4	0	0	.000	.077	.000	.077	-78	-3	0	.12	0	/O-9(0-0-9)	0	-0.4
1960*Pit-N	50	56	21	13	2	0	1	3	5	8	1	0	.232	.295	.321	.617	68	-2	6	3.67	0	O-17(11-5-1)	1	-0.3
1961 Pit-N	76	186	25	49	7	3	0	14	18	24	6	4	.263	.328	.333	.662	76	-6	19	3.47	0	O-55(45-5-5)	3	-0.9
1962 NY-N	119	271	36	66	10	2	6	32	35	42	11	3	.244	.339	.362	.700	87	-3	36	4.52	1	O-94(19-34-42)	4	-0.6
1963 NY-N	64	149	19	33	5	1	1	8	13	21	1	3	.221	.297	.289	.586	68	-7	13	2.81	-2	O-45(6-0-40)	2	-1.2
1964 NY-N	154	543	78	163	26	8	16	76	48	92	6	5	.300	.363	.466	.829	135	25	88	5.76	-3	*O-145(7-10-129)	21	1.3
1965 NY-N	148	437	38	109	18	3	5	40	35	82	4	4	.249	.314	.339	.652	87	-8	46	3.54	1	*O-112(62-0-51)	8	-1.4
1966 Bos-A	12	13	1	1	0	0	0	0	2	4	0	0	.077	.200	.077	.277	-15	-2	0	.68	0	/O-2(2-0-0)	0	-0.2
Total 8	638	1667	224	434	68	17	29	173	157	277	29	19	.260	.331	.374	.705	97	-7	208	4.26	-5	O-479	39	-3.8
• CHRISTOPHER, Loyd	Lloyd Eugene Christopher b: 12/31/1919, Richmond, CA d: 9/5/1991, Richmond, CA BR/TR, 6'2", 190 lbs. Deb: 4/20/1945 Career OF: 8-3-0																							
1945 Bos-A	8	14	4	4	0	0	0	4	3	2	0	0	.286	.412	.286	.697	101	0	2	5.43	-0	/O-3(0-3-0)	0	0.0
Chi-N	1	0	0	0	0	0	0	0	0	0	0	....	....	....	....	....	-102	0	0	....	0	/O-1	0	0.0
1947 Chi-A	7	23	1	5	0	1	0	0	2	4	0	1	.217	.280	.304	.584	65	-2	1	1.58	1	/O-7(7-0-0)	0	-0.1
Total 2	16	37	5	9	0	1	0	4	5	6	0	1	.243	.333	.297	.631	80	-1	3	2.82	1	/O-11	0	-0.1
• CHURCH, Hi	Hiram Lincoln Church b: 11/23/1863, Central Square, NY d: 2/23/1926, Jacksonville, FL Deb: 8/23/1890																							
1890 Bro-a	3	9	1	1	0	0	0	0	0	....	0	....	.111	.111	.111	.222	-36	-2	0	.38	0	/O-3(3-0-0)	0	-0.2
• CHURRY, John	John Churry b: 11/26/1900, Johnstown, PA d: 2/8/1970, Zanesville, OH BR/TR, 5'9", 172 lbs. Deb: 5/24/1924																							
1924 Chi-N	6	7	0	1	1	0	0	0	2	0	0	0	.143	.333	.286	.619	67	-0	1	3.56	0	/C-3	0	0.0
1925 Chi-N	3	6	1	3	0	0	0	1	0	0	0	0	.500	.500	.500	1.000	154	0	1	12.72	0	/C-3	0	0.1
1926 Chi-N	2	4	0	0	0	0	0	0	1	2	0	....	.000	.200	.000	.200	-42	-1	0	.31	0	/C-1	0	-0.1
1927 Chi-N	1	1	0	1	0	0	0	0	0	0	0	....	1.000	1.000	1.000	2.000	436	0	1	∞	-0	/C-1	0	0.0
Total 4	12	18	1	5	1	0	0	1	3	2	0	0	.278	.381	.333	.714	83	-0	3	4.68	-0	/C-8	0	0.0
• CIAFFONE, Larry	Lawrence Thomas "Symphony Larry" Ciaffone b: 8/17/1924, Brooklyn, NY d: 12/14/1991, Brooklyn, NY BR/TR, 5'9.5", 185 lbs. Deb: 4/17/1951																							
1951 StL-N	5	5	0	0	0	0	0	0	1	2	0	0	.000	.167	.000	.167	-51	-1	0	.23	0	/O-1	0	-0.1
• CIANFROCCO, Archi	Angelo Dominic Cianfrocco b: 10/6/1966, Rome, NY BR/TR, 6'5", 215 lbs. Deb: 4/8/1992 Career OF: 8-0-17																							
1992 Mon-N	86	232	25	56	5	2	6	30	11	66	3	0	.241	.279	.358	.636	80	-6	24	3.56	3	1-56,3-19/O-5(5-0-0)	4	-0.7
1993 Mon-N	12	17	3	4	1	0	1	1	0	5	0	0	.235	.235	.471	.706	80	-1	2	3.91	0	1-11	0	-0.1
SD-N	84	279	27	68	10	2	11	47	17	64	2	0	.244	.294	.412	.707	85	-7	32	3.83	-4	3-64,1-31	6	-1.1
Yr.	96	296	30	72	11	2	12	48	17	69	2	0	.243	.291	.416	.707	85	-7	34	3.83	-4	3-64,1-42	6	-1.2
1994 SD-N	59	146	9	32	8	0	4	13	3	39	2	0	.219	.255	.356	.611	59	-9	13	3.04	-1	3-37,1-16/S-1	1	-1.0
1995 SD-N	51	118	22	31	7	0	5	31	11	28	0	2	.263	.336	.449	.785	109	0	17	4.86	-1	1-30,S-15/O-7(2-0-5),2-3,3	5	-0.1
1996*SD-N	79	192	21	54	13	3	2	32	8	56	1	0	.281	.317	.411	.728	96	-2	24	4.61	-2	1-33,3-11,S-10/O-8(1-0-7),2,C	5	-0.4
1997 SD-N	89	220	25	54	12	0	4	26	25	80	7	1	.245	.331	.355	.685	87	-3	25	3.75	2	1-39,3-38,2-12/S-5,O-2(0-0-2)	5	-0.2
1998 SD-N	40	72	4	9	3	0	1	5	5	22	1	0	.125	.192	.208	.401	6	-10	3	1.08	-1	1-19,3-13/2-3,O-3(0-0-3)	0	-1.2
Total 7	500	1276	136	308	59	7	34	185	80	360	16	3	.241	.294	.379	.673	81	-36	140	3.70	-4	1-235,3-185/S-31,O-25,2-24,C	26	-4.8
• CIAS, Darryl	Darryl Richard Cias b: 4/23/1957, New York, NY BR/TR, 5'11", 190 lbs. Deb: 4/27/1983																							
1983 Oak-A	19	18	1	6	1	0	0	1	2	4	1	0	.333	.400	.389	.789	126	1	3	7.24	-1	C-19	1	0.0
• CICERO, Joe	Joseph Francis "Dody" Cicero b: 11/18/1910, Atlantic City, NJ d: 3/30/1983, Clearwater, FL BR/TR, 5'8", 167 lbs. Deb: 9/20/1929 Career OF: 3-6-10																							
1929 Bos-A	10	32	6	10	2	2	0	4	0	2	0	0	.313	.313	.500	.813	108	0	5	5.78	0	/O-7(1-6-0)	1	0.0
1930 Bos-A	18	30	5	5	1	2	0	4	1	5	0	0	.167	.194	.333	.527	32	-3	2	1.98	-1	/O-5(1-0-4),3-2	0	-0.4
1945 Phi-A	12	19	3	3	0	0	0	0	1	6	0	0	.158	.238	.158	.396	16	-2	1	1.49	0	/O-7(1-0-6)	0	-0.3
Total 3	40	81	14	18	3	4	0	8	2	13	0	0	.222	.250	.358	.608	56	-5	8	3.14	-1	/O-19,3-2	1	-0.6
• CIESLAK, Ted	Thaddeus Walter Cieslak b: 11/22/1912, Milwaukee, WI d: 5/9/1993, Milwaukee, WI BR/TR, 5'10", 175 lbs. Deb: 4/18/1944																							
1944 Phi-N	85	220	18	54	10	0	2	11	21	17	1	....	.245	.314	.318	.632	81	-5	22	3.42	-9	3-48/O-5(5-0-0)	3	-1.4
• CIHOCKI, Al	Albert Joseph Cihocki b: 5/7/1924, Nanticoke, PA BR/TR, 5'11", 185 lbs. Deb: 4/17/1945																							
1945 Cle-A	92	283	21	60	9	3	0	24	11	48	2	1	.212	.241	.265	.507	49	-19	19	2.07	0	S-41,3-29,2-23	4	-1.6
• CIHOCKI, Ed	Edward Joseph "Cy" Cihocki b: 5/9/1907, Wilmington, DE d: 11/9/1987, Newark, DE BR/TR, 5'8", 163 lbs. Deb: 5/29/1932																							
1932 Phi-A	1	1	0	0	0	0	0	0	0	0	0	0	.000	.000	.000	.000	-97	-0	0	.00	0	....	0	0.0
1933 Phi-A	33	97	6	14	2	3	0	9	7	16	0	0	.144	.202	.227	.429	13	-12	5	1.47	-1	S-28/2-1,3-1	1	-1.1
Total 2	34	98	6	14	2	3	0	9	7	16	0	0	.143	.200	.224	.424	12	-13	5	1.46	-1	/S-28,2-1,3-1	1	-1.1

YEAR TM-L	G	AB	R	H	2B	3B	HR	RBI	BB	SO	SB	CS	AVG	OBP	SLG	OPS	OPS+	BR/A	RC	RC/G	FR	G/POS	WS	TPW
• CIMOLI, Gino	Gino Nicholas Cimoli b: 12/18/1929, San Francisco, CA BR/TR, 6'1", 200 lbs. Deb: 4/19/1956 Career OF: 270-263-434																							
1956*Bro-N	73	36	3	4	1	0	0	4	1	8	1	0	.111	.135	.139	.274	-24	-6	1	.50	-2	0-62(52-8-3)	0	-1.0
1957 Bro-N★	142	532	88	156	22	5	10	57	39	86	3	1	.293	.346	.410	.756	93	-4	76	5.06	0	*0-138(81-24-51)	15	-1.2
1958 LA-N	109	325	35	80	6	3	9	27	18	49	3	3	.246	.292	.366	.658	70	-15	30	3.01	-2	*0-104(34-68-12)	4	-2.1
1959 StL-N	143	519	61	145	40	7	8	72	37	83	7	0	.279	.330	.430	.759	94	-3	70	4.69	4	*0-141(43-45-55)	11	-0.5
1960*Pit-N	101	307	36	82	14	4	0	28	32	43	1	0	.267	.338	.339	.677	85	-5	35	3.99	-1	0-91(27-58-17)	7	-1.1
1961 Pit-N	21	67	4	20	3	1	0	6	2	13	0	0	.299	.319	.373	.692	83	-2	7	3.52	0	0-19(14-5-0)	1	-0.3
Mil-N	37	117	12	23	5	0	3	4	11	15	1	0	.197	.266	.316	.582	57	-7	10	2.68	-4	0-31(0-30-1)	1	-1.2
Yr.	58	184	16	43	8	1	3	10	13	28	1	0	.234	.284	.337	.621	66	-9	17	2.97	-5	0-50(14-35-1)	2	-1.5
1962 KC-A	152	550	67	151	20	**15**	10	71	40	89	2	1	.275	.326	.420	.746	96	-4	74	4.70	-7	*0-147(5-10-138)	13	-2.0
1963 KC-A	145	529	56	139	19	11	4	48	39	72	3	1	.263	.316	.363	.679	86	-10	60	3.92	3	*0-136(2-13-130)	11	-1.7
1964 KC-A	4	9	1	0	0	0	0	0	0	1	0	0	.000	.000	.000	.000	-97	-2	0	.00	0	/0-4(1-0-3)	0	-0.3
Bal-A	38	58	6	8	3	2	0	3	2	13	0	0	.138	.167	.259	.425	16	-7	2	1.21	-1	0-35(11-2-23)	0	-1.0
Yr.	42	67	7	8	3	2	0	3	2	14	0	0	.119	.145	.224	.369	2	-9	2	1.01	-2	0-39(12-2-26)	0	-1.2
1965 Cal-A	4	5	1	0	0	0	0	1	0	2	0	0	.000	.000	.000	.000	-102	-1	0	.00	0	/0-1	0	-0.1
Total 10	**969**	**3054**	**370**	**808**	**133**	**48**	**44**	**321**	**221**	**474**	**21**	**6**	**.265**	**.317**	**.383**	**.700**	**84**	**-66**	**365**	**4.09**	**-11**	**0-909**	**63**	**-12.5**
• CINTRON, Alex	Alexander Cintron b: 12/17/1978, Humacao, Puerto Rico BB/TR, 6'1", 170 lbs. Deb: 7/24/2001																							
2001 Ari-N	8	7	0	2	0	1	0	0	0	0	0	0	.286	.286	.571	.857	107	0	1	6.17	0	/S-7	0	0.0
2002*Ari-N	38	75	11	16	6	0	0	4	12	13	0	0	.213	.322	.293	.615	58	-4	8	3.19	1	2-18/3-9,S-8	1	-0.2
2003 Ari-N	117	448	70	142	26	6	13	51	29	33	2	3	.317	.361	.489	.850	108	4	78	6.48	-9	S-93,3-16/2-9	14	0.3
Total 3	**163**	**530**	**81**	**160**	**32**	**7**	**13**	**55**	**41**	**46**	**2**	**3**	**.302**	**.354**	**.462**	**.817**	**101**	**-0**	**86**	**5.94**	**-8**	**S-108/2-27,3-25**	**15**	**0.1**
• CIPRIANI, Frank	Frank Dominick Cipriani b: 4/14/1941, Buffalo, NY BR/TR, 6', 180 lbs. Deb: 9/8/1961																							
1961 KC-A	13	36	2	9	0	0	0	2	2	4	0	0	.250	.289	.250	.539	45	-3	3	2.42	-1	0-11(0-0-11)	0	-0.4
• CIRILLO, Jeff	Jeffrey Howard Cirillo b: 9/23/1969, Pasadena, CA BR/TR, 6'2", 190 lbs. Deb: 5/11/1994																							
1994 Mil-A	39	126	17	30	9	0	3	12	11	16	0	1	.238	.309	.381	.690	73	-6	14	3.75	-3	3-37/2-1	2	-0.8
1995 Mil-A	125	328	57	91	19	4	9	39	47	42	7	2	.277	.375	.442	.817	106	4	57	6.06	2	*3-108,2-25/1-3,S-2	10	0.8
1996 Mil-A	158	566	101	184	46	5	15	83	58	69	4	9	.325	.395	.504	.898	120	15	109	7.06	-5	*3-154/D-3,1-2,2-1	20	1.1
1997 Mil-A★	154	580	74	167	46	2	10	82	60	74	4	3	.288	.369	.426	.794	106	6	93	5.73	22	*3-150/D-2	24	2.8
1998 Mil-N	156	604	97	194	31	1	14	68	79	88	10	4	.321	.403	.445	.849	123	24	106	6.42	22	*3-149/1-6	26	4.7
1999 Mil-N	157	607	98	198	35	1	15	88	75	83	7	4	.326	.405	.461	.866	120	20	115	7.07	12	*3-155	22	3.3
2000 Col-N★	157	598	111	195	53	2	11	115	67	72	3	4	.326	.399	.477	.876	96	-2	111	6.86	1	*3-155	19	0.1
2001 Col-N	138	528	72	165	26	4	17	83	43	63	12	2	.313	.370	.473	.843	95	-1	91	6.31	21	*3-137	14	2.1
2002 Sea-A	146	485	51	121	20	0	6	54	31	67	8	4	.249	.307	.328	.635	71	-20	49	3.29	8	*3-141,1-11	9	-1.0
2003 Sea-A	87	258	24	53	11	0	2	23	24	32	1	1	.205	.286	.271	.557	50	-19	21	2.57	-3	3-85/1-1	3	-2.0
Total 10	**1317**	**4680**	**702**	**1398**	**296**	**19**	**102**	**647**	**495**	**606**	**56**	**34**	**.299**	**.373**	**.435**	**.809**	**102**	**23**	**766**	**5.84**	**78**	***3-1271/2-27,1-23,D-5,S-2**	**149**	**11.3**
• CISAR, George	George Joseph Cisar b: 8/25/1912, Chicago, IL BR/TR, 6', 175 lbs. Deb: 9/9/1937																							
1937 Bro-N	20	29	8	6	0	0	0	4	2	6	3	....	.207	.258	.207	.465	27	-3	1	1.39	0	0-13(9-0-4)	0	-0.4
• CISSELL, Bill	Chalmer William Cissell b: 1/3/1904, Perryville, MO d: 3/15/1949, Chicago, IL BR/TR, 5'11", 170 lbs. Deb: 4/11/1928																							
1928 Chi-A	125	443	66	115	22	3	1	60	29	41	18	6	.260	.307	.330	.636	68	-19	46	3.57	4	*S-123	11	-0.2
1929 Chi-A	152	618	83	173	27	12	5	62	28	53	25	17	.280	.312	.387	.699	80	-22	72	3.95	-2	*S-152	12	-0.6
1930 Chi-A	141	562	82	152	28	9	2	48	28	32	16	9	.270	.307	.363	.670	72	-25	62	3.82	-19	*2-107,3-24,S-10	8	-3.4
1931 Chi-A	109	409	42	90	13	5	1	46	16	26	18	6	.220	.256	.284	.540	44	-30	31	2.46	-2	S-83,2-23/3-1	3	-2.3
1932 Chi-A	12	43	7	11	1	1	1	5	1	0	0	0	.256	.273	.395	.668	76	-2	5	3.74	-2	S-12	1	-0.3
Cle-A	131	541	78	173	35	6	6	93	28	25	18	15	.320	.354	.440	.794	98	-5	80	5.48	10	*2-129/S-6	15	1.3
Yr.	143	584	85	184	36	7	7	98	29	25	18	15	.315	.349	.437	.785	97	-7	85	5.35	8	*2-129,S-18	16	1.0
1933 Cle-A	112	409	53	94	21	3	6	33	31	29	6	6	.230	.284	.340	.624	62	-25	39	3.16	-8	2-62,S-46/3-1	6	-2.4
1934 Bos-A	102	416	71	111	13	4	4	44	28	23	11	4	.267	.315	.346	.661	66	-22	46	3.90	-7	2-96/S-7,3-2	7	-2.1
1937 Phi-A	34	117	15	31	7	0	1	14	17	10	0	0	.265	.358	.350	.709	81	-3	16	4.78	3	2-33	2	0.2
1938 NY-N	38	149	19	40	6	0	2	18	6	11	1	....	.268	.297	.349	.646	76	-5	14	3.32	5	2-33/3-6	3	0.2
Total 9	**956**	**3707**	**516**	**990**	**173**	**43**	**29**	**423**	**212**	**250**	**113**	**63**	**.267**	**.308**	**.360**	**.669**	**72**	**-156**	**412**	**3.82**	**-18**	**2-483,S-439/3-34**	**68**	**-9.7**
• CLABAUGH, Moose	John William Clabaugh b: 11/13/1901, Albany, MO d: 7/11/1984, Tucson, AZ BL/TR, 6', 185 lbs. Deb: 8/30/1926																							
1926 Bro-N	11	14	2	1	1	0	0	1	0	1	0	....	.071	.133	.143	.276	-26	-3	0	.56	-1	/0-2(2-0-0)	0	-0.3
• CLACK, Bobby	Robert S. "Gentlemanly Bob" Clack b: 6/1850, England d: 10/22/1933, Danvers, MA BR/TR, 5'9", 153 lbs. Deb: 5/13/1874 U NA OF: 1-46-1																							
1874 Atl-n	33	135	22	23	1	0	0	13	4	2	0	0	.170	.194	.178	.372	23	-9	5	1.28	1	0-31(1-30-0)/1-2	....	-0.6
1875 Atl-n	17	59	1	6	0	0	0	1	0	3	0	0	.102	.102	.102	.203	-33	-7	1	.35	2	0-17(0-16-1)/1-1	....	-0.4
1876 Cin-N	32	123	10	19	0	1	0	5	5	12	....	....	.154	.195	.178	.373	29	-7	4	1.19	-3	0-17(0-3-14)/2-8,1-5,3-3,P	0	-0.9
Total 2 n	**50**	**194**	**23**	**29**	**1**	**0**	**0**	**14**	**4**	**5**	**0**	**0**	**.149**	**.167**	**.155**	**.321**	**6**	**-16**	**5**	**.98**	**3**	**/0-48,1-3**	**....**	**-1.1**
• CLAIRE, Danny	David Matthew Claire b: 11/17/1897, Ludington, MI d: 1/7/1956, Las Vegas, NV BR/TR, 5'8", 164 lbs. Deb: 9/17/1920																							
1920 Det-A	3	7	1	1	0	0	0	0	0	0	0	0	.143	.143	.143	.286	-25	-1	0	.61	-1	/S-3	0	-0.2
• CLANCY, Al	Albert Harrison Clancy b: 8/14/1888, Santa Fe, NM d: 10/17/1951, Las Cruces, NM BR/TR, 5'10.5", 175 lbs. Deb: 6/20/1911																							
1911 StL-A	3	5	0	0	0	0	0	0	0	....	0	....	.000	.167	.000	.167	-54	-1	0	.00	0	/3-2	0	-0.1
• CLANCY, Bill	William Edward Clancy b: 4/12/1879, Redfield, NY d: 2/10/1948, Oriskany, NY BR/TR, 6'2", 180 lbs. Deb: 4/14/1905																							
1905 Pit-N	56	227	23	52	11	3	2	34	4	....	3	....	.229	.246	.330	.576	69	-10	20	2.90	-2	1-52/0-4(0-0-4)	2	-1.4
• CLANCY, Bud	John William Clancy b: 9/15/1900, Odell, IL d: 9/26/1968, Ottumwa, IA BL/TL, 6', 170 lbs. Deb: 8/29/1924																							
1924 Chi-A	13	35	5	9	1	0	0	6	3	2	3	2	.257	.316	.286	.602	58	-2	3	2.77	-1	/1-8	0	-0.4
1925 Chi-A	4	3	0	0	0	0	0	0	1	0	0	0	.000	.250	.000	.250	-34	-1	0	.55	0	....	0	0.0
1926 Chi-A	12	38	3	13	2	2	0	7	1	1	0	0	.342	.375	.500	.875	132	2	7	6.45	0	1-10	1	0.1
1927 Chi-A	130	464	46	139	21	2	3	53	24	24	4	3	.300	.337	.373	.710	86	-10	59	4.42	2	*1-123	8	-1.5
1928 Chi-A	130	487	64	132	19	11	2	37	42	25	6	9	.271	.331	.368	.699	85	-13	60	4.02	3	*1-128	9	-1.8
1929 Chi-A	92	290	36	82	14	6	3	45	16	19	3	1	.283	.320	.403	.724	86	-6	38	4.52	-0	1-74	5	-1.0
1930 Chi-A	68	234	28	57	8	3	3	27	12	18	3	1	.244	.286	.342	.628	61	-14	23	3.36	-2	1-60	2	-1.8
1932 Bro-N	53	196	14	60	4	2	0	16	6	13	0	....	.306	.327	.347	.674	83	-5	22	4.19	0	1-53	4	-1.0
1934 Phi-N	20	49	8	12	0	0	1	7	6	4	0	....	.245	.339	.306	.645	65	-2	6	4.26	-1	1-10	1	-0.4
Total 9	**522**	**1796**	**204**	**504**	**69**	**26**	**12**	**198**	**111**	**106**	**19**	**16**	**.281**	**.325**	**.368**	**.693**	**82**	**-52**	**218**	**4.15**	**1**	**1-466**	**30**	**-7.9**
• CLANTON, Uke	Eucal "Cat" Clanton b: 2/19/1898, Powell, MO d: 2/24/1960, Antlers, OK BL/TL, 5'8", 165 lbs. Deb: 9/21/1922																							
1922 Cle-A	1	1	0	0	0	0	0	0	0	1	0	0	.000	.000	.000	.000	-99	-0	0	.00	0	/1-1	0	-0.1
• CLAPINSKI, Chris	Christopher Alan Clapinski b: 8/20/1971, Buffalo, NY BB/TR, 6', 175 lbs. Deb: 7/17/1999 Career OF: 6-0-0																							
1999 Fla-N	36	56	6	13	1	2	0	2	9	12	1	0	.232	.348	.321	.670	75	-2	7	4.32	-2	/3-9,S-6,0-3(3-0-0),2-2,D-1	1	-0.3
2000 Fla-N	34	49	12	15	4	1	1	7	5	7	0	0	.306	.370	.490	.860	120	1	9	6.69	-2	2-14/3-3,0-3(3-0-0),S-1	2	0.0
Total 2	**70**	**105**	**18**	**28**	**5**	**3**	**1**	**9**	**14**	**19**	**1**	**0**	**.267**	**.358**	**.400**	**.758**	**96**	**-0**	**16**	**5.39**	**-4**	**/2-16,3-12,S-7,0-6,D-1**	**3**	**-0.3**
• CLAPP, Aaron	Aaron Bronson Clapp b: 7/1856, Ithaca, NY d: 1/13/1914, Sayre, PA TR, 5'8", 175 lbs. Deb: 5/1/1879																							
1879 Tro-N	36	146	24	39	9	3	0	18	6	10	....	....	.267	.296	.370	.666	126	5	16	4.29	-5	1-25,0-11(7-1-3)	4	-0.2
• CLAPP, John	John Edgar Clapp b: 7/17/1851, Ithaca, NY d: 12/18/1904, Ithaca, NY BR/TR, 5'7", 194 lbs. Deb: 4/26/1872 M/U NA OF: 0-3-14 Career OF: 62-19-21																							
1872 Man-n	19	97	28	28	6	1	1	10	1	0	2	1	.289	.296	.402	.698	120	3	12	5.51	5	C-19/S-2,0-1	....	0.6
1873 Ath-n	45	204	36	62	10	2	1	28	2	2	4	5	.304	.311	.387	.698	99	-3	26	5.48	0	*C-43/S-6,2-1,0-1	....	-0.2
1874 Ath-n	39	165	46	48	7	4	3	20	1	1	2	0	.291	.295	.436	.732	121	3	22	5.74	0	C-27,0-15(0-1-14)/S-1	....	0.3

YEAR TM-L	G	AB	R	H	2B	3B	HR	RBI	BB	SO	SB	CS	AVG	OBP	SLG	OPS	OPS+	BR/A	RC	RC/G	FR	G/POS	WS	TPW
1875 Ath-n	60	292	65	77	8	7	0	39	7	1	9	5	.264	.281	.339	.620	103	-1	31	4.17	4	*C-60	....	0.3
1876 StL-N	64	306	60	91	4	2	0	29	8	2	....	....	.297	.324	.332	.656	125	9	33	4.44	3	*C-61/O-4(0-1-3),2-1	14	1.2
1877 StL-N	60	255	47	81	6	6	0	34	8	6	....	....	.318	.338	.388	.727	135	11	34	5.43	-5	*C-53,O-10(2-0-9)/1-1	10	0.6
1878 Ind-N	63	263	42	80	10	2	0	29	13	8	....	....	.304	.337	.357	.694	148	15	32	4.88	-4	*O-44(44-0-0),1-12/C-9,S-3,2	10	0.8
1879 Buf-N	70	292	47	77	12	5	1	36	11	11	....	....	.264	.290	.349	.640	107	2	30	3.95	-9	*C-63/O-7(0-0-7)	9	-0.5
1880 Cin-N	80	323	33	91	16	4	1	20	21	10	....	....	.282	.326	.365	.691	135	12	39	4.67	16	*C-73,O-10(1-9-0)	12	2.9
1881 Cle-N	68	261	47	66	12	2	0	25	**35**	6	....	....	.253	.341	.314	.655	113	7	29	3.97	-2	C-48,O-21(15-6-0)	8	0.5
1883 NY-N	20	73	6	13	0	0	0	5	5	4	....	....	.178	.231	.178	.409	27	-6	3	1.41	2	C-16/O-5(0-3-2)	1	-0.3
Total 4 n	163	758	175	215	31	14	5	97	11	4	17	11	.284	.294	.381	.675	108	1	92	5.02	9	C-149/O-17,S-9,2-1	....	1.1
Total 7	425	1773	282	499	60	21	2	178	101	47	....	....	.281	.322	.344	.665	123	50	201	4.38	1	C-323,O-101/1-13,S-3,2-2	64	5.3

• CLAPP, Stubby

Richard Keith Clapp b: 2/24/1973, Windsor, Canada BB/TR, 5'8", 175 lbs. Deb: 6/18/2001

2001 StL-N	23	25	0	5	2	0	0	1	1	7	0	0	.200	.231	.280	.511	31	-3	2	2.26	1	/2-4,O-4(4-0-0)	0	-0.2

• CLARE, Denny

Dennis J. Clare b: 1/1853, Brooklyn, NY d: 11/26/1928, Brooklyn, NY Deb: 9/14/1872

1872 Atl-n	2	7	1	1	0	0	0	0	0	0	0	0	.143	.143	.143	.286	-10	-1	0	.76	-2	/2-2,S-1	....	-0.2

• CLAREY, Doug

Douglas William Clarey b: 4/20/1954, Los Angeles, CA BR/TR, 6', 180 lbs. Deb: 4/20/1976

1976 StL-N	9	4	2	1	0	0	1	2	0	1	0	0	.250	.250	1.000	1.250	240	1	1	9.00	-3	/2-7	0	-0.3

• CLARK, Allie

Alfred Aloysius Clark b: 6/16/1923, South Amboy, NJ BR/TR, 6', 185 lbs. Deb: 8/5/1947 Career OF: 62-3-178

1947*NY-A	24	67	9	25	5	0	1	14	5	2	0	0	.373	.417	.493	.909	154	5	12	6.87	0	O-16(6-0-10)	3	0.4
1948*Cle-A	81	271	43	84	5	2	9	38	23	13	0	2	.310	.364	.443	.807	117	5	41	5.39	1	O-65(21-0-44)/3-5,1-1	8	0.3
1949 Cle-A	35	74	8	13	4	0	1	9	4	7	0	0	.176	.218	.270	.488	29	-8	4	1.78	0	O-17(1-0-16)/1-1	0	-0.8
1950 Cle-A	59	163	19	35	6	1	6	21	11	10	0	1	.215	.264	.374	.639	64	-10	12	2.36	-1	O-41(25-0-17)	1	-1.3
1951 Cle-A	3	10	3	3	2	0	1	3	1	2	0	0	.300	.364	.800	1.164	221	1	3	11.87	-0	/O-3(0-0-3)	1	0.1
Phi-A	56	161	20	40	10	1	4	22	15	7	2	0	.248	.320	.398	.718	91	-2	20	4.30	1	O-32(1-1-30),3-10	3	-0.1
Yr.	59	171	23	43	12	1	5	25	16	9	2	0	.251	.323	.421	.744	99	-0	23	4.69	1	O-35(1-1-33),3-10	4	0.0
1952 Phi-A	71	186	23	51	12	0	7	29	10	19	0	2	.274	.315	.452	.766	105	-1	24	4.41	-1	O-48(7-2-39)/1-2	5	-0.3
1953 Phi-A	20	74	6	15	4	0	3	13	3	5	0	0	.203	.234	.378	.612	61	-5	6	2.68	0	O-19(0-0-19)	0	-0.5
Chi-A	9	15	0	1	0	0	0	0	0	5	0	0	.067	.067	.067	.133	-62	-3	0	.00	0	/1-1,O-1	0	-0.4
Yr.	29	89	6	16	4	0	3	13	3	10	0	0	.180	.207	.326	.532	41	-8	6	2.10	0	O-20(1-0-19)/1-1	0	-0.8
Total 7	358	1021	131	267	48	4	32	149	72	70	2	5	.262	.312	.410	.722	93	-18	123	4.06	0	O-242/3-15,1-5	21	-2.5

• CLARK, Bob

Robert H. Clark b: 5/18/1863, Covington, KY d: 8/21/1919, Covington, KY BR/TR, 5'10", 175 lbs. Deb: 4/17/1886 Career OF: 7-2-22

1886 Bro-a	71	269	37	58	8	2	0	26	17	....	14	....	.216	.262	.260	.522	63	-12	23	2.89	-7	C-44,O-17(6-1-11),S-12	5	-1.3
1887 Bro-a	48	184	24	54	3	1	0	18	7	....	15	....	.293	.297	.294	.591	64	-9	20	4.24	-6	C-45/O-3(0-0-3)	3	-0.9
1888 Bro-a	45	150	23	36	5	3	1	20	9	....	11	....	.240	.292	.333	.625	100	-0	18	4.32	-3	C-36/O-8(1-1-6),1-1	5	0.0
1889*Bro-a	53	182	32	50	5	2	0	22	26	7	18	....	.275	.368	.324	.693	97	1	29	5.84	-4	C-53	9	0.1
1890*Bro-N	43	151	24	33	3	3	0	15	15	8	10	....	.219	.306	.278	.584	70	-5	16	3.66	-10	C-42/O-1	4	-1.0
1891 Cin-N	16	54	2	6	0	0	0	3	6	9	3	....	.111	.213	.111	.324	-5	-7	2	1.11	-1	C-16	0	-0.6
1893 Lou-N	12	28	3	3	1	0	0	3	5	5	0	....	.107	.242	.143	.385	4	-4	1	1.05	2	C-10/O-1,S-1	0	-0.1
Total 7	288	1018	145	240	25	11	1	107	85	29	71	....	.236	.296	.280	.576	71	-36	110	3.77	-28	C-246/O-30,S-13,1-1	26	-3.8

• CLARK, Bobby

Robert Cale Clark b: 6/13/1955, Sacramento, CA BR/TR, 6', 190 lbs. Deb: 8/21/1979 Career OF: 147-144-116

1979*Cal-A	19	54	8	16	2	2	1	5	5	11	1	1	.296	.356	.463	.819	123	1	8	4.86	1	O-19(16-3-2)	2	0.2
1980 Cal-A	78	261	26	60	10	1	5	23	11	42	0	1	.230	.266	.333	.600	65	-14	21	2.76	-1	O-77(33-46-0)	2	-1.7
1981 Cal-A	34	88	12	22	2	1	4	19	7	18	0	0	.250	.305	.432	.737	110	1	11	4.49	1	O-34(27-8-1)	3	0.1
1982*Cal-A	102	90	11	19	1	0	2	8	0	29	1	0	.211	.211	.289	.500	36	-8	5	1.96	-2	*O-102(24-24-57)	1	-1.2
1983 Cal-A	76	212	17	49	9	1	5	21	9	45	0	0	.231	.262	.354	.616	68	-10	18	2.79	-2	O-72(43-4-28)/D-2,3-1	2	-1.4
1984 Mil-A	58	169	17	44	7	2	2	16	16	35	1	5	.260	.328	.361	.689	94	-3	17	3.19	-4	O-56(3-42-16)	2	-0.9
1985 Mil-A	29	93	6	21	3	0	0	8	7	19	1	1	.226	.280	.258	.538	49	-7	6	2.24	-2	O-27(1-17-12)	1	-0.9
Total 7	396	967	97	231	34	7	19	100	55	199	4	8	.239	.282	.347	.629	74	-39	87	2.98	-9	O-387/D-2,3-1	13	-5.9

• CLARK, Brady

Brady William Clark b: 4/18/1973, Portland, OR BR/TR, 6'2", 195 lbs. Deb: 9/3/2000 Career OF: 69-18-108

2000 Cin-N	11	11	1	3	1	0	0	2	0	2	0	0	.273	.273	.364	.636	58	-1	1	3.68	1	/O-5(2-0-3)	0	0.0
2001 Cin-N	89	129	22	34	3	0	6	18	22	16	4	1	.264	.375	.426	.801	102	2	21	5.26	-1	O-43(26-7-14)/D-1	4	-0.1
2002 Cin-N	51	66	6	10	3	0	0	9	6	9	1	2	.152	.233	.197	.430	14	-9	3	1.19	-1	O-22(15-3-6)	0	-1.1
NY-N	10	12	3	5	1	0	0	1	1	2	0	0	.417	.462	.500	.962	160	1	3	11.14	0	/O-6(1-2-3)	1	0.1
Yr.	61	78	9	15	4	0	0	10	7	11	1	2	.192	.267	.244	.511	36	-8	6	2.22	-2	O-28(16-5-9)	1	-1.0
2003 Mil-N	128	315	33	86	21	1	6	40	21	40	13	2	.273	.336	.403	.739	94	-1	42	4.51	1	*O-105(25-6-82)	7	-0.3
Total 4	289	533	65	138	29	1	12	70	50	69	18	5	.259	.335	.385	.720	87	-8	70	4.32	-1	O-181/D-1	12	-1.4

• CLARK, Cap

John Carrol Clark b: 9/19/1906, Snow Camp, NC d: 2/16/1957, Fayetteville, NC BL/TR, 5'11", 180 lbs. Deb: 4/23/1938

1938 Phi-N	52	74	11	19	1	1	0	4	9	10	0	....	.257	.337	.297	.635	75	-2	8	4.08	-1	C-29	1	-0.2

• CLARK, Dad

Alfred Robert "Fred" Clark b: 7/16/1873, San Francisco, CA d: 7/26/1956, Ogden, UT BL/TL, 5'11", 170 lbs. Deb: 7/3/1902

1902 Chi-N	12	43	1	8	1	0	0	2	4	....	1	....	.186	.255	.209	.465	45	-3	3	2.02	-2	1-12	0	-0.5

• CLARK, Danny

Daniel Curren Clark b: 1/18/1894, Meridian, MS d: 5/23/1937, Meridian, MS BL/TR, 5'9", 167 lbs. Deb: 4/12/1922 Career OF: 0-0-14

1922 Det-A	83	185	31	54	11	3	3	26	15	11	1	0	.292	.345	.432	.777	105	1	28	5.48	-2	2-38/O-5(0-0-5),3-1	5	0.0
1924 Bos-A	104	325	36	90	23	3	2	54	51	19	4	7	.277	.378	.385	.763	97	-1	49	5.10	-1	3-94	10	0.2
1927 StL-N	58	72	8	17	2	2	0	13	8	7	0	....	.236	.313	.319	.632	67	-3	7	3.45	1	/O-9(0-0-9)	1	-0.3
Total 3	245	582	75	161	36	8	5	93	74	37	5	7	.277	.360	.392	.752	96	-3	85	5.01	-2	/3-95,2-38,O-14	16	-0.1

• CLARK, Dave

David Earl Clark b: 9/3/1962, Tupelo, MS BL/TR, 6'2", 210 lbs. Deb: 9/3/1986 C Career OF: 215-1-228

1986 Cle-A	18	58	10	16	1	0	3	9	7	11	1	0	.276	.354	.448	.802	119	2	10	5.68	0	O-10(0-0-10)/D-7	2	0.1
1987 Cle-A	29	87	11	18	5	0	3	12	2	24	1	0	.207	.225	.368	.593	53	-6	6	2.20	0	O-13(1-0-12),D-12	0	-0.7
1988 Cle-A	63	156	11	41	4	1	3	18	17	28	0	2	.263	.335	.359	.694	92	-2	17	3.57	-1	D-27,O-23(10-1-15)	2	-0.5
1989 Cle-A	102	253	21	60	12	0	8	29	30	63	0	2	.237	.318	.379	.697	94	-3	29	3.89	-1	D-55,O-21(12-0-11)	3	-0.5
1990 Chi-N	84	171	22	47	4	2	5	20	8	40	7	1	.275	.307	.409	.717	89	-2	21	4.36	1	O-39(39-0-0)	3	-0.2
1991 KC-A	11	10	1	2	0	0	0	1	1	1	0	0	.200	.273	.200	.473	33	-1	1	2.08	0	/D-1,O-1	0	-0.1
1992 Pit-N	23	33	3	7	0	0	2	7	6	8	0	0	.212	.333	.394	.727	106	0	5	4.90	0	/O-8(1-0-7)	1	0.0
1993 Pit-N	110	277	43	75	11	2	11	46	38	58	1	0	.271	.361	.444	.805	114	6	44	5.50	-1	O-91(40-0-53)	9	0.2
1994 Pit-N	86	223	37	66	11	1	10	46	22	48	2	2	.296	.359	.489	.848	117	5	38	6.16	1	O-57(10-0-48)	9	0.2
1995 Pit-N	77	196	30	55	6	0	4	24	24	38	3	3	.281	.362	.372	.734	92	-2	25	4.35	-2	O-61(34-0-29)	3	-0.7
1996 Pit-N	92	211	28	58	12	2	8	35	31	51	2	1	.275	.368	.464	.832	115	5	36	6.05	0	O-61(34-0-28)	7	0.2
*LA-N	15	15	0	3	0	0	0	1	3	2	0	0	.200	.333	.200	.533	49	-1	1	2.84	0	/O-1	1	-0.1
Yr.	107	226	28	61	12	2	8	36	34	53	2	1	.270	.365	.447	.812	110	4	37	5.82	0	O-62(35-0-28)	8	0.1
1997 Chi-N	102	143	19	43	8	0	5	32	19	34	1	0	.301	.390	.462	.852	119	5	27	7.00	0	O-25(24-0-1)/D-4	5	0.4
1998*Hou-N	93	131	12	27	7	0	0	4	14	45	1	1	.206	.288	.260	.547	47	-10	10	2.57	-1	O-22(9-0-13)/D-4	0	-1.2
Total 13	905	1964	248	518	81	8	62	284	222	451	19	12	.264	.340	.408	.748	98	-5	270	4.74	-5	O-433,D-110	45	-2.8

• CLARK, Earl

Bailey Earl Clark b: 11/6/1907, Washington, DC d: 1/16/1938, Washington, DC BR/TR, 5'10", 160 lbs. Deb: 8/17/1927 Career OF: 40-146-36

1927 Bos-N	13	44	6	12	1	0	0	3	2	4	0	....	.273	.304	.295	.600	66	-2	4	2.94	0	O-13(10-3-0)	0	-0.3
1928 Bos-N	28	112	18	34	9	1	0	10	4	8	0	....	.304	.339	.402	.741	98	-1	15	4.73	-2	O-27(0-27-0)	2	-0.4
1929 Bos-N	84	279	43	88	13	3	1	30	12	30	6	....	.315	.346	.394	.740	86	-6	37	4.73	3	O-74(4-70-1)	7	-0.6
1930 Bos-N	82	233	29	69	11	3	3	28	7	22	3	....	.296	.320	.408	.727	77	-9	29	4.47	0	O-63(1-40-22)	5	-1.1
1931 Bos-N	16	50	8	11	2	0	0	4	7	4	1	....	.220	.316	.260	.576	58	-3	5	2.97	1	O-14(14-0-0)	1	-0.3
1932 Bos-N	50	44	11	11	2	0	0	4	2	7	1	....	.250	.283	.295	.578	58	-3	4	2.89	0	O-16(6-3-6)	1	-0.3
1933 Bos-N	7	23	3	8	1	0	0	1	2	1	0	....	.348	.400	.391	.791	138	1	4	5.64	0	/O-6(3-3-0)	1	0.1

YEAR TM-L	G	AB	R	H	2B	3B	HR	RBI	BB	SO	SB	CS	AVG	OBP	SLG	OPS	OPS+	BR/A	RC	RC/G	FR	G/POS	WS	TPW
1934 StL-A	13	41	4	7	2	0	0	1	1	3	0	0	.171	.190	.220	.410	5	-6	2	1.32	0	/0-9(2-0-7)	0	-0.6
Total 8	293	826	122	240	41	7	4	81	37	79	11	0	.291	.324	.372	.696	78	-28	98	4.17	0	0-222	17	-3.6
• CLARK, Glen	Glen Ester Clark b: 3/7/1941, Austin, TX BB/TR, 6'1", 190 lbs. Deb: 6/3/1967																							
1967 Atl-N	4	4	0	0	0	0	0	0	0	1	0	0	.000	.000	.000	.000	-101	-1	0	.00	0	....	0	-0.1
• CLARK, Howie	Howard Roddy Clark b: 2/13/1974, San Diego, CA BL/TR, 5'10", 191 lbs. Deb: 7/16/2002 Career OF: 8-0-1																							
2002 Bal-A	14	53	3	16	5	0	0	4	3	6	0	0	.302	.362	.396	.758	107	1	6	3.95	0	/D-8,0-4(4-0-0),1-1	0	0.0
2003 Tor-A	38	70	9	25	3	1	0	7	3	6	0	1	.357	.400	.429	.829	117	1	11	5.78	0	3-13/D-6,0-5(4-0-1),2-3,1,S	2	0.2
Total 2	52	123	12	41	8	1	0	11	6	12	0	1	.333	.383	.415	.798	113	2	17	4.96	0	/D-14,3-13,0-9,1-3,2-3,S-1	2	0.1
• CLARK, Jack	Jack Anthony "Jack the Ripper" Clark b: 11/10/1955, New Brighton, PA BR/TR, 6'2", 205 lbs. Deb: 9/12/1975 C Career OF: 11-23-1014																							
1975 SF-N	8	17	3	4	0	0	0	2	1	2	1	0	.235	.278	.235	.513	42	-1	1	2.69	0	/0-3(1-2-1),3-2	0	-0.2
1976 SF-N	26	102	14	23	6	2	2	10	8	18	6	2	.225	.282	.382	.664	85	-2	12	3.71	1	0-26(5-20-8)	3	-0.3
1977 SF-N	136	413	64	104	17	4	13	51	49	73	12	4	.252	.334	.407	.741	98	0	58	4.85	1	*0-114(0-1-113)	11	-0.5
1978 SF-N★	156	592	90	181	46	8	25	98	50	72	15	11	.306	.363	.537	.900	155	38	109	6.54	6	*0-152(0-0-152)	30	3.8
1979 SF-N★	143	527	84	144	25	2	26	86	63	95	11	8	.273	.352	.476	.828	133	22	88	5.84	1	*0-140(0-0-140)/3-2	23	1.7
1980 SF-N	127	437	77	124	20	8	22	82	74	52	2	5	.284	.390	.517	.907	155	32	87	6.89	-6	*0-120(0-0-120)	24	2.0
1981 SF-N	99	385	60	103	19	2	17	53	45	45	1	1	.268	.346	.460	.805	129	14	59	5.33	7	0-98(0-0-98)	15	1.8
1982 SF-N	157	563	90	154	30	3	27	103	90	91	6	9	.274	.375	.481	.856	138	28	98	5.96	-2	*0-155(0-0-155)	26	1.8
1983 SF-N	135	492	82	132	25	0	20	66	74	79	5	3	.268	.365	.441	.806	126	19	80	5.61	8	*0-133(0-0-133)/1-2	20	2.0
1984 SF-N	57	203	33	65	9	1	11	44	43	29	1	1	.320	.439	.537	.976	179	23	47	8.48	1	0-54(0-0-55)/1-4	12	2.3
1985*StL-N★	126	442	71	124	26	3	22	87	83	88	1	4	.281	.397	.502	.899	151	31	89	7.15	-6	*1-121,0-12(0-0-12)	22	1.9
1986 StL-N	65	232	34	55	12	2	9	23	45	61	1	1	.237	.363	.422	.786	117	6	38	5.58	-4	1-64	9	-0.1
1987*StL-N★	131	419	93	120	23	1	35	106	**136**	139	1	2	.286	**.461**	**.597**	**1.058**	**174**	53	127	**11.08**	-10	*1-126/0-1	33	3.5
1988 NY-A	150	496	81	120	14	0	27	93	113	141	3	2	.242	.385	.433	.818	130	25	88	5.98	-2	*D-112,0-19(5-0-14),1-10	21	1.8
1989 SD-N	142	455	76	110	19	1	26	94	**132**	145	6	2	.242	.413	.459	.873	149	38	95	7.11	-3	*1-131,0-12(0-0-12)	31	2.7
1990 SD-N	115	334	59	89	12	1	25	62	**104**	91	4	3	.266	.443	.533	.976	166	36	84	8.64	-2	*1-110	17	2.8
1991 Bos-A	140	481	75	120	18	1	28	87	96	133	0	2	.249	.378	.466	.843	126	19	86	6.03	0	*D-135	15	1.4
1992 Bos-A	81	257	32	54	11	0	5	33	56	87	1	1	.210	.356	.311	.667	83	-3	33	4.13	-1	D-64,1-13	4	-0.7
Total 18	1994	6847	1118	1826	332	39	340	1180	1262	1441	77	61	.267	.383	.476	.858	138	377	1279	6.46	-11	*0-1039,1-581,D-311/3-4	316	27.8
• CLARK, Jerald	Jerald Dwayne Clark b: 8/10/1963, Crockett, TX BR/TR, 6'4", 202 lbs. Deb: 9/19/1988 Career OF: 311-11-70																							
1988 SD-N	6	15	0	3	1	0	0	3	0	4	0	0	.200	.200	.267	.467	33	-1	1	1.80	1	/0-4(4-0-0)	1	-0.1
1989 SD-N	17	41	5	8	2	0	1	7	3	9	0	1	.195	.250	.317	.567	61	-3	3	2.49	1	0-14(10-0-4)	0	-0.2
1990 SD-N	53	101	12	27	4	1	5	11	5	24	0	0	.267	.302	.475	.777	109	1	14	4.67	-1	1-15,0-13(5-0-9)	1	-0.1
1991 SD-N	118	369	26	84	16	0	10	47	31	90	2	1	.228	.298	.352	.650	80	-10	38	3.43	1	0-96(85-0-13),1-16	7	-1.4
1992 SD-N	146	496	45	120	22	6	12	58	22	97	3	0	.242	.280	.383	.663	84	-12	53	3.68	4	*0-134(115-1-22),1-11	11	-1.4
1993 Col-N	140	478	65	135	26	6	13	67	20	60	9	6	.282	.325	.444	.768	89	-9	65	4.80	-5	0-96(80-0-17),1-37	11	-2.2
1995 Min-A	36	109	17	37	8	3	3	15	2	11	3	0	.339	.357	.550	.908	132	5	19	6.74	0	0-23(12-10-5),1-11/D-3	2	0.4
Total 7	516	1609	170	414	79	16	44	208	83	295	17	8	.257	.302	.408	.711	88	-30	193	4.15	1	0-380/1-90,D-3	33	-4.9
• CLARK, Jermaine	Jermaine Marcel Clark b: 9/29/1976, Berkeley, CA BL/TR, 5'10", 175 lbs. Deb: 4/3/2001																							
2001 Det-A	3	0	1	0	0	0	0	0	0	0	0	0	....	....	....	....	-105	0	0	....	0	/D-1	0	0.0
2003 Tex-A	10	9	0	0	0	0	0	0	3	0	0	0	.000	.250	.000	.250	-24	-2	0	.59	-1	/0-6(5-1-0),2-2	0	-0.3
SD-N	1	2	0	0	0	0	0	1	0	1	0	1	.000	.000	.000	.000	-110	-1	0	.00	-0	/0-1	0	-0.1
Tex-A	14	37	2	8	2	0	0	6	3	4	2	1	.216	.275	.270	.545	41	-3	3	2.25	2	0-11(11-0-0)/2-5	1	-0.1
Yr.	24	46	2	8	2	0	0	6	6	4	2	1	.174	.269	.217	.487	27	-5	3	1.90	1	0-17(16-1-0)/2-7	1	-0.4
Total 2	28	48	3	8	2	0	0	7	6	5	2	2	.167	.259	.208	.468	20	-6	3	1.73	1	/0-18,2-7,D-1	1	-0.5
• CLARK, Jim	James Clark b: 9/21/1927, Baggaley, PA d: 10/24/1990, Santa Monica, CA BR/TR, 5'9", 150 lbs. Deb: 8/17/1948																							
1948 Was-A	9	12	1	3	0	0	0	0	0	2	0	0	.250	.250	.250	.500	34	-1	1	2.31	0	/3-1,S-1	0	-0.1
• CLARK, Jim	James Francis Clark b: 12/26/1887, Brooklyn, NY d: 3/20/1969, Beaumont, TX BR/TR, 5'11", 175 lbs. Deb: 9/2/1911																							
1911 StL-N	14	18	2	3	0	1	0	3	3	4	2	....	.167	.286	.278	.563	59	-1	2	3.34	0	/0-8(1-6-1)	0	-0.2
1912 StL-N	2	1	0	0	0	0	0	0	0	1	0	....	.000	.000	.000	.000	-102	-0	0	.00	0	....	0	0.0
Total 2	16	19	2	3	0	1	0	3	3	5	2	....	.158	.273	.263	.536	52	-1	2	3.13	0	/0-8	0	-0.2
• CLARK, Jim	James Edward Clark b: 4/30/1947, Kansas City, KS BR/TR, 6'1", 190 lbs. Deb: 7/16/1971																							
1971 Cle-A	13	18	2	3	0	1	0	0	2	7	0	0	.167	.250	.278	.528	45	-1	1	1.86	0	/0-3(2-0-1),1-1	0	-0.2
• CLARK, Mel	Melvin Earl Clark b: 7/7/1926, Letart, WV BR/TR, 6', 180 lbs. Deb: 9/11/1951 Career OF: 37-0-134																							
1951 Phi-N	10	31	2	10	1	0	1	3	0	3	0	1	.323	.323	.452	.774	108	-0	4	5.11	-1	/0-7(1-0-6)	1	-0.1
1952 Phi-N	47	155	20	52	6	4	1	15	6	13	2	1	.335	.364	.445	.809	125	5	25	5.89	3	0-38(12-0-27)/3-1	6	0.6
1953 Phi-N	60	198	31	59	10	4	0	19	11	17	1	0	.298	.338	.389	.727	89	-3	24	4.30	-3	0-51(1-0-51)	4	-0.7
1954 Phi-N	83	233	26	56	9	7	1	24	17	21	0	1	.240	.292	.352	.644	67	-12	21	2.83	2	0-63(21-0-42)	2	-1.3
1955 Phi-N	10	32	3	5	3	0	0	1	3	4	0	0	.156	.229	.250	.479	27	-3	2	1.40	3	/0-8(0-0-8)	0	-0.1
1957 Det-A	5	7	0	0	0	0	0	1	0	3	0	0	.000	.000	.000	.000	-98	-2	0	.00	-0	/0-2(2-0-0)	0	-0.2
Total 6	215	656	82	182	29	15	3	63	37	61	3	3	.277	.318	.381	.699	85	-16	75	3.89	4	0-169/3-1	13	-1.8
• CLARK, Pep	Harry Clark b: 3/20/1883, Union City, OH d: 6/8/1965, Milwaukee, WI BR/TR, 5'7.5", 175 lbs. Deb: 9/11/1903																							
1903 Chi-A	15	65	7	20	4	2	0	9	2	....	5	....	.308	.338	.431	.769	135	3	11	6.74	1	3-15	3	0.4
• CLARK, Phil	Phillip Benjamin Clark b: 5/6/1968, Crockett, TX BR/TR, 6', 200 lbs. Deb: 5/27/1992 Career OF: 52-0-50																							
1992 Det-A	23	54	3	22	4	0	1	5	6	9	1	0	.407	.467	.537	1.004	179	6	13	10.30	-1	0-13(4-0-9)/D-7	4	0.5
1993 SD-N	102	240	33	75	17	0	9	33	8	31	2	0	.313	.348	.496	.844	121	6	42	6.64	4	0-36(22-0-15),1-24,C-11/3-5	6	0.7
1994 SD-N	61	149	14	32	6	0	5	20	5	17	1	2	.215	.255	.356	.610	59	-10	13	2.89	-1	1-24,0-17(12-0-5)/C-5,3-1	1	-1.3
1995 SD-N	75	97	12	21	3	0	2	7	8	18	0	2	.216	.283	.309	.592	59	-7	8	2.49	0	0-34(14-0-21)/1-2	0	-0.8
1996 Bos-A	3	3	0	0	0	0	0	0	0	1	0	0	.000	.000	.000	.000	-98	-1	0	.00	-0	/1-1,3-1,D-1	0	-0.1
Total 5	264	543	62	150	30	0	17	65	27	76	4	4	.276	.321	.425	.747	97	-6	76	4.94	2	0-100/1-51,C-16,D-8,3-7	11	-1.0
• CLARK, Ron	Ronald Bruce Clark b: 1/14/1943, Fort Worth, TX BR/TR, 5'10", 175 lbs. Deb: 9/11/1966 C																							
1966 Min-A	5	1	1	1	0	0	0	1	0	0	0	0	1.000	1.000	1.000	2.000	448	0	1	20.52	0	/3-1	0	0.0
1967 Min-A	20	60	7	10	3	1	2	11	4	9	0	0	.167	.219	.350	.569	61	-3	4	1.91	-1	3-16	0	-0.5
1968 Min-A	104	227	14	42	5	1	1	13	16	44	3	2	.185	.245	.229	.474	42	-16	14	1.88	-3	3-52,S-43,2-10	2	-1.7
1969 Min-A	5	8	0	1	0	0	0	0	0	0	0	0	.125	.125	.125	.250	-29	-1	0	.00	0	/3-2	0	-0.2
Sea-A	57	163	9	32	5	0	0	12	13	29	1	0	.196	.260	.227	.487	38	-13	11	2.11	-7	S-38,3-15/2-5,1-1	1	-1.7
Yr.	62	171	9	33	5	0	0	12	13	29	1	0	.193	.254	.222	.476	35	-15	11	1.99	-7	S-38,3-17/2-5,1-1	1	-1.9
1971 Oak-A	2	1	0	0	0	0	0	0	1	0	0	0	.000	.500	.000	.500	53	0	0	3.51	0	....	0	0.0
1972 Oak-A	14	15	1	4	2	0	0	1	2	4	0	0	.267	.353	.400	.753	130	1	2	4.06	1	2-11/3-3	1	0.2
Mil-A	22	54	8	10	1	1	2	5	5	11	0	0	.185	.254	.352	.606	81	-1	5	2.56	-2	2-11,3-10	1	-0.3
Yr.	36	69	9	14	3	1	2	6	7	15	0	0	.203	.276	.362	.639	92	-1	7	2.88	-1	2-22,3-13	2	-0.1
1975 Phi-N	1	1	0	0	0	0	0	0	0	1	0	0	.000	.000	.000	.000	-96	-0	0	.00	0	....	0	0.0
Total 7	230	530	40	100	16	3	5	43	41	98	4	2	.189	.251	.258	.509	50	-34	35	2.09	-12	/3-99,S-81,2-37,1-1	5	-4.2
• CLARK, Roy	Roy Elliott "Pepper" Clark b: 5/11/1874, New Haven, CT d: 11/1/1925, Bridgeport, CT BL/TR, 5'8", 170 lbs. Deb: 4/19/1902																							
1902 NY-N	21	76	4	11	1	0	0	3	1	....	5	....	.145	.156	.158	.314	-3	-9	3	1.11	0	0-20(2-9-9)	0	-1.0
• CLARK, Spider	Owen F. Clark b: 9/16/1867, Brooklyn, NY d: 2/8/1892, Brooklyn, NY TR, 5'10", 150 lbs. Deb: 5/2/1889 Career OF: 5-4-34 ♦																							
1889 Was-N	38	145	19	37	7	2	3	22	6	18	8	....	.255	.285	.393	.678	94	-2	19	4.66	5	C-14,S-13/0-9(0-0-9),2-2,3	3	0.4

YEAR TM-L	G	AB	R	H	2B	3B	HR	RBI	BB	SO	SB	CS	AVG	OBP	SLG	OPS	OPS+	BR/A	RC	RC/G	FR	G/POS	WS	TPW
1890 Buf-P	69	260	45	69	11	1	1	25	20	16	8	....	.265	.325	.327	.652	81	-6	31	4.38	2	0-34(5-4-25),C-14,2-13/1-6,3,P,S	4	-0.4
Total 2	107	405	64	106	18	3	4	47	26	34	16	....	.262	.311	.351	.662	86	-8	50	4.48	7	/0-43,C-28,2-15,S-14,1-6,3,P	7	0.0

• CLARK, Tony Anthony Christopher Clark b: 6/15/1972, Newton, KS BB/TR, 6'8", 240 lbs. Deb: 9/3/1995

YEAR TM-L	G	AB	R	H	2B	3B	HR	RBI	BB	SO	SB	CS	AVG	OBP	SLG	OPS	OPS+	BR/A	RC	RC/G	FR	G/POS	WS	TPW
1995 Det-A	27	101	10	24	5	1	3	11	8	30	0	0	.238	.294	.396	.690	78	-4	12	3.96	-2	1-27	2	-0.8
1996 Det-A	100	376	56	94	14	0	27	72	29	127	0	1	.250	.304	.503	.806	99	-4	56	5.09	-4	1-86,D-12	8	-1.5
1997 Det-A	159	580	105	160	28	3	32	117	93	144	1	3	.276	.379	.500	.879	128	24	112	6.88	-0	*1-158/D-1	24	0.9
1998 Det-A	157	602	84	175	37	0	34	103	63	128	3	3	.291	.361	.522	.882	125	20	110	6.60	-3	*1-142,D-15	15	0.4
1999 Det-A	143	536	74	150	29	0	31	99	64	133	2	1	.280	.363	.507	.870	118	14	98	6.55	4	*1-132,D-12	19	0.5
2000 Det-A	60	208	32	57	14	0	13	37	24	51	0	0	.274	.349	.529	.878	121	6	35	5.94	5	1-58/D-1	6	0.5
2001 Det-A★	126	428	67	123	29	3	16	75	62	108	0	1	.287	.379	.481	.860	130	19	77	6.35	0	1-78,D-41	16	1.0
2002 Bos-A	90	275	25	57	12	1	3	29	21	57	0	0	.207	.266	.291	.557	47	-21	20	2.31	3	1-85/D-2	1	-2.3
2003 NY-N	125	254	29	59	13	0	16	43	24	73	0	0	.232	.301	.472	.774	101	-1	34	4.54	-5	1-80/0-1	4	-1.0
Total 9	987	3360	482	899	181	8	175	586	388	851	6	9	.268	.346	.482	.828	113	55	553	5.77	-2	1-846/D-84,0-1	95	-2.3

• CLARK, Will William Nuschler "the Thrill" Clark b: 3/13/1964, New Orleans, LA BL/TL, 6'2", 190 lbs. Deb: 4/8/1986

YEAR TM-L	G	AB	R	H	2B	3B	HR	RBI	BB	SO	SB	CS	AVG	OBP	SLG	OPS	OPS+	BR/A	RC	RC/G	FR	G/POS	WS	TPW
1986 SF-N	111	408	66	117	27	2	11	41	34	76	4	7	.287	.346	.444	.790	122	9	62	5.32	3	*1-102	14	0.6
1987*SF-N	150	529	89	163	29	5	35	91	49	98	5	17	.308	.372	.580	.953	155	32	109	7.54	2	*1-139	25	2.6
1988 SF-N★	162	575	102	162	31	6	29	**109**	**100**	129	9	1	.282	.392	.508	.900	163	**51**	120	**7.46**	5	*1-158	**37**	4.8
1989*SF-N★	159	588	**104**	196	38	9	23	111	74	103	8	3	.333	.412	.546	.958	177	60	136	9.01	5	*1-158	**44**	5.7
1990 SF-N★	154	600	91	177	25	5	19	95	62	97	8	2	.295	.364	.448	.812	127	22	101	6.14	2	*1-153	25	1.3
1991 SF-N★	148	565	84	170	32	7	29	116	51	91	4	2	.301	.361	**.536**	.897	154	38	110	7.34	4	*1-144	34	3.3
1992 SF-N★	144	513	69	154	40	1	16	73	73	82	12	7	.300	.392	.476	.867	153	37	98	6.95	-3	*1-141	28	2.5
1993 SF-N	132	491	82	139	27	2	14	73	63	68	2	2	.283	.371	.432	.803	118	13	81	5.86	-2	*1-129	15	0.0
1994 Tex-A★	110	389	73	128	24	2	13	80	71	59	5	1	.329	.436	.501	.938	141	29	91	8.97	1	*1-107/D-1	19	1.8
1995 Tex-A	123	454	85	137	27	3	16	92	68	50	0	1	.302	.397	.480	.878	124	18	90	7.25	-3	*1-122/D-1	18	0.3
1996*Tex-A	117	436	69	124	25	1	13	72	64	67	2	1	.284	.382	.436	.818	101	2	75	6.15	1	*1-117	11	-0.6
1997 Tex-A	110	393	56	128	29	1	12	51	49	62	0	0	.326	.404	.496	.901	127	17	81	8.03	2	*1-100/D-7	14	0.9
1998*Tex-A	149	554	98	169	41	1	23	102	72	97	1	0	.305	.388	.507	.895	125	22	109	7.25	-8	*1-134,D-15	19	0.1
1999 Bal-A	77	251	40	76	15	0	10	29	38	42	2	2	.303	.399	.482	.881	128	11	49	7.22	1	1-63/D-4	8	0.6
2000 Bal-A	79	256	49	77	15	1	9	28	47	45	4	2	.301	.417	.473	.890	131	14	54	7.75	1	1-72/D-6	10	0.8
*StL-N	51	171	29	59	15	1	12	42	22	24	1	0	.345	.429	.655	1.084	168	18	49	11.44	0	1-50	10	1.4
Total 15	1976	7173	1186	2176	440	47	284	1205	937	1190	67	48	.303	.388	.497	.885	139	394	1417	7.27	10	*1-1889/D-34	331	26.2

• CLARK, Willie William Otis "Wee Willie" Clark b: 8/16/1872, Pittsburgh, PA d: 11/13/1932, Pittsburgh, PA BL, 6' Deb: 6/20/1895

YEAR TM-L	G	AB	R	H	2B	3B	HR	RBI	BB	SO	SB	CS	AVG	OBP	SLG	OPS	OPS+	BR/A	RC	RC/G	FR	G/POS	WS	TPW
1895 NY-N	23	88	9	23	3	2	0	16	5	6	1	....	.261	.301	.341	.642	67	-5	10	3.97	1	1-23	1	-0.3
1896 NY-N	72	247	38	72	12	4	0	33	15	12	8	....	.291	.352	.372	.724	93	-2	36	5.44	-4	1-65	5	-0.5
1897 NY-N	116	431	63	122	17	12	1	75	37	....	18	....	.283	.352	.385	.737	97	-1	67	5.67	5	*1-107/0-7(7-0-0),3-1	12	0.2
1898 Pit-N	57	209	29	64	9	7	1	31	22	....	0	....	.306	.378	.431	.808	134	9	35	6.31	4	1-57	9	1.2
1899 Pit-N	81	300	49	85	13	10	0	44	35	....	11	....	.283	.377	.393	.770	112	6	50	6.11	0	1-78	9	0.6
Total 5	349	1275	188	366	54	35	2	199	114	18	38	....	.287	.359	.389	.748	104	7	198	5.71	7	1-330/0-7,3-1	36	1.2

• CLARK, Win William Winfield Clark b: 4/11/1875, Circleville, OH d: 4/15/1959, Los Angeles, CA BR/TR, 5'10", 175 lbs. Deb: 7/12/1897

YEAR TM-L	G	AB	R	H	2B	3B	HR	RBI	BB	SO	SB	CS	AVG	OBP	SLG	OPS	OPS+	BR/A	RC	RC/G	FR	G/POS	WS	TPW
1897 Lou-N	4	16	2	3	0	0	0	2	1	....	1	....	.188	.235	.188	.423	13	-2	1	1.97	-2	/2-3,3-1	0	-0.3

• CLARKE, Artie Arthur Franklin Clarke b: 5/6/1865, Providence, RI d: 11/14/1949, Brookline, MA BR/TR, 5'8", 155 lbs. Deb: 4/19/1890 U Career OF: 3-2-31

YEAR TM-L	G	AB	R	H	2B	3B	HR	RBI	BB	SO	SB	CS	AVG	OBP	SLG	OPS	OPS+	BR/A	RC	RC/G	FR	G/POS	WS	TPW
1890 NY-N	101	395	55	89	12	8	0	49	32	38	44	....	.225	.290	.296	.586	71	-15	48	4.14	1	C-36,0-33(3-1-30),3-16,2-15/S	8	-0.9
1891 NY-N	48	174	17	33	2	2	0	21	15	16	5	....	.190	.254	.224	.478	41	-13	11	2.19	-1	C-42/3-5,0-2(0-1-1)	2	-0.9
Total 2	149	569	72	122	14	10	0	70	47	54	49	....	.214	.279	.274	.553	62	-28	59	3.53	0	/C-78,0-35,3-21,2-15,S-1	10	-1.9

• CLARKE, Boileryard William Jones Clarke b: 10/18/1868, New York, NY d: 7/29/1959, Princeton, NJ BR/TR, 5'11.5", 170 lbs. Deb: 5/1/1893 U

YEAR TM-L	G	AB	R	H	2B	3B	HR	RBI	BB	SO	SB	CS	AVG	OBP	SLG	OPS	OPS+	BR/A	RC	RC/G	FR	G/POS	WS	TPW
1893 Bal-N	49	183	23	32	1	3	1	24	19	14	2	....	.175	.274	.230	.504	34	-18	12	2.17	-2	C-38,1-11	2	-1.3
1894 Bal-N	28	100	18	24	8	0	1	19	16	14	2	....	.240	.361	.350	.711	69	-5	14	4.69	-2	C-23/1-5	2	-0.4
1895*Bal-N	67	241	38	70	15	3	0	35	13	18	8	....	.290	.350	.378	.727	85	-6	36	5.55	4	C-60/1-6	7	0.3
1896 Bal-N	80	300	48	89	14	7	2	71	14	12	7	....	.297	.345	.410	.755	97	-2	47	5.67	-6	C-67,1-14	8	-0.2
1897*Bal-N	64	241	32	65	7	1	1	38	9	....	5	....	.270	.320	.320	.640	69	-11	27	4.06	-6	C-59/1-4	4	-1.1
1898 Bal-N	82	285	26	69	5	2	0	27	4	....	2	....	.242	.289	.274	.563	60	-15	24	2.93	-5	C-70,1-10	4	-1.2
1899 Bos-N	60	223	25	50	3	2	2	32	10	....	2	....	.224	.270	.283	.553	47	-17	19	2.77	-3	C-60	2	-1.4
1900 Bos-N	81	270	35	85	5	2	1	30	9	....	0	....	.315	.344	.359	.703	84	-7	35	4.83	1	C-67/1-8	6	0.1
1901 Was-A	110	422	58	118	15	5	3	54	23	....	7	....	.280	.335	.360	.695	94	-3	56	4.72	-2	*C-107/1-3	12	0.5
1902 Was-A	87	291	31	78	15	0	6	40	23	....	1	....	.268	.330	.381	.712	96	-2	39	4.68	2	C-87	8	0.8
1903 Was-A	126	465	35	111	14	6	2	38	15	....	12	....	.239	.273	.308	.581	72	-16	44	3.24	-10	1-88,C-37	5	-2.5
1904 Was-A	85	275	23	58	8	1	0	17	17	....	5	....	.211	.269	.247	.517	65	-10	21	2.48	4	C-52,1-29	3	-0.1
1905 NY-N	31	50	2	9	0	0	1	4	4	....	1	....	.180	.241	.240	.481	42	-4	3	2.08	-2	1-15,C-12	0	-0.6
Total 13	950	3346	394	858	110	32	20	429	176	58	54	....	.256	.310	.326	.637	75	-116	377	3.93	-28	C-739,1-193	63	-7.1

• CLARKE, Fred Fred Clifford "Cap" Clarke
b: 10/3/1872, Winterset, IA d: 8/14/1960, Winfield, KS BL/TR, 5'10.5", 165 lbs. Deb: 6/30/1894 M/C HOF: 1945 Career OF: 2183-4-6

YEAR TM-L	G	AB	R	H	2B	3B	HR	RBI	BB	SO	SB	CS	AVG	OBP	SLG	OPS	OPS+	BR/A	RC	RC/G	FR	G/POS	WS	TPW
1894 Lou-N	76	314	55	86	11	7	7	48	26	27	26	....	.274	.337	.420	.758	88	-7	54	6.19	3	0-75(75-0-0)	5	-0.8
1895 Lou-N	132	550	96	191	21	5	4	82	34	24	40	....	.347	.396	.425	.821	119	17	111	8.31	8	*0-132(132-0-0)	16	1.1
1896 Lou-N	131	517	96	168	15	18	9	79	43	34	34	....	.325	.392	.476	.868	133	25	113	8.42	3	*0-131(131-0-0)	17	1.4
1897 Lou-N	130	526	122	205	30	13	6	67	45	....	59	....	.390	.461	.530	.991	**167**	**54**	159	12.99	9	*0-127(126-3-0)	30	4.3
1898 Lou-N	149	599	116	184	23	12	3	47	48	....	40	....	.307	.373	.401	.774	124	19	108	6.79	2	*0-149(148-0-2)	25	0.7
1899 Lou-N	149	606	122	206	23	9	5	70	49	....	49	....	.340	.404	.432	.836	129	26	130	8.39	0	*0-144(144-0-0)/S-3	25	1.2
1900 Pit-N	106	399	84	110	15	12	3	32	51	....	21	....	.276	.368	.396	.764	110	7	69	6.10	1	*0-104(104-0-0)	18	-0.2
1901 Pit-N	129	527	118	171	24	15	6	60	51	....	23	....	.324	.395	.461	.856	143	30	109	7.83	0	*0-127(127-0-0)/3-1,S-1	28	2.2
1902 Pit-N	113	459	103	145	27	14	2	53	51	....	29	....	.316	.401	.449	.850	157	33	97	8.05	-1	*0-113(110-0-4)	29	2.6
1903*Pit-N	104	427	88	150	**32**	15	5	70	41	....	21	....	.351	.414	**.532**	**.946**	**164**	35	106	9.73	-5	*0-101(101-0-0)/S-2	25	2.3
1904 Pit-N	72	278	51	85	7	11	0	25	22	....	11	....	.306	.367	.410	.777	136	12	48	6.21	-1	0-70(70-0-0)	14	0.7
1905 Pit-N	141	525	95	157	18	15	2	51	55	....	24	....	.299	.368	.402	.770	126	17	91	6.08	5	*0-137(137-0-0)	24	1.5
1906 Pit-N	118	417	69	129	14	**13**	1	39	40	....	18	....	.309	.371	.412	.784	138	18	75	6.30	5	*0-110(110-0-0)	21	1.8
1907 Pit-N	148	501	97	145	18	13	2	59	68	....	37	....	.289	.383	.389	.772	140	26	93	6.51	2	*0-144(144-0-0)	29	2.2
1908 Pit-N	151	551	83	146	18	15	2	53	65	....	24	....	.265	.349	.363	.712	127	19	79	4.79	5	*0-151(150-1-0)	28	1.8
1909*Pit-N	152	550	97	158	16	11	3	68	**80**	....	31	....	.287	.384	.373	.756	128	22	92	5.73	4	*0-152(152-0-0)	31	1.9
1910 Pit-N	123	429	57	113	23	9	2	63	53	23	12	....	.263	.350	.373	.723	104	3	62	4.68	-1	*0-118(118-0-0)	15	-0.6
1911 Pit-N	110	392	73	127	25	13	5	49	53	27	10	....	.324	.407	.492	.900	146	24	82	7.71	-4	*0-101(101-0-0)	20	1.7
1913 Pit-N	9	13	0	1	1	0	0	0	0	0	0	....	.077	.077	.154	.231	-37	-2	0	.30	0	/0-2(2-0-0)	0	-0.3
1914 Pit-N	2	2	0	0	0	0	0	0	0	0	0	....	.000	.000	.000	.000	-105	-0	0	.00	0	....	0	-0.1
1915 Pit-N	1	2	0	1	0	0	0	0	0	0	0	....	.500	.500	.500	1.000	206	0	1	13.25	0	/0-1	0	0.0
Total 21	2246	8584	1622	2678	361	220	67	1015	875	135	509	....	.312	.386	.429	.814	133	377	1679	7.21	35	*0-2189/S-6,3-1	400	25.6

• CLARKE, Grey Richard Grey "Noisy" Clarke b: 9/26/1912, Fulton, AL d: 11/25/1993, Kannapolis, NC BR/TR, 5'9", 183 lbs. Deb: 4/19/1944

YEAR TM-L	G	AB	R	H	2B	3B	HR	RBI	BB	SO	SB	CS	AVG	OBP	SLG	OPS	OPS+	BR/A	RC	RC/G	FR	G/POS	WS	TPW
1944 Chi-A	63	169	14	44	10	1	0	27	22	6	0	4	.260	.352	.331	.684	97	-1	19	3.72	0	3-45	5	-0.1

• CLARKE, Harry Harry Corson Clarke b: 1861, d: 3/3/1923, Long Beach, CA Deb: 8/28/1889

YEAR TM-L	G	AB	R	H	2B	3B	HR	RBI	BB	SO	SB	CS	AVG	OBP	SLG	OPS	OPS+	BR/A	RC	RC/G	FR	G/POS	WS	TPW
1889 Was-N	1	3	0	0	0	0	0	0	0	1	0	....	.000	.000	.000	.000	-106	-1	0	.00	1	/0-1	0	0.0

• CLARKE, Horace Horace Meredith Clarke b: 6/2/1940, Frederiksted, V.I. BB/TR, 5'9", 178 lbs. Deb: 5/13/1965

YEAR TM-L	G	AB	R	H	2B	3B	HR	RBI	BB	SO	SB	CS	AVG	OBP	SLG	OPS	OPS+	BR/A	RC	RC/G	FR	G/POS	WS	TPW
1965 NY-A	51	108	13	28	1	0	1	9	6	6	2	1	.259	.298	.296	.595	70	-4	10	3.03	2	3-17/2-7,S-1	2	-0.2
1966 NY-A	96	312	37	83	10	4	6	28	27	24	5	3	.266	.326	.381	.708	107	2	40	4.54	-10	S-63,2-16/3-4	9	-0.2
1967 NY-A	143	588	74	160	17	0	3	29	42	64	21	4	.272	.321	.316	.637	92	-2	64	3.91	1	*2-140	22	1.2

YEAR TM-L	G	AB	R	H	2B	3B	HR	RBI	BB	SO	SB	CS	AVG	OBP	SLG	OPS	OPS+	BR/A	RC	RC/G	FR	G/POS	WS	TPW
1968 NY-A	148	579	52	133	6	1	2	26	23	46	20	7	.230	.259	.254	.513	58	-29	39	2.23	10	*2-139	11	-0.8
1969 NY-A	156	641	82	183	26	7	4	48	53	41	33	13	.285	.340	.367	.707	101	2	83	4.60	-6	*2-156	23	0.8
1970 NY-A	158	686	81	172	24	2	4	46	35	35	23	7	.251	.289	.309	.598	68	-28	62	3.06	-11	*2-157	14	-2.9
1971 NY-A	159	625	76	156	23	7	2	41	64	43	17	7	.250	.321	.318	.640	87	-9	66	3.58	-15	*2-156	16	-1.4
1972 NY-A	147	547	65	132	20	2	3	37	56	44	18	6	.241	.316	.302	.618	87	-6	56	3.49	-1	*2-143	17	0.2
1973 NY-A	148	590	60	155	21	0	2	35	47	48	11	10	.263	.319	.308	.628	80	-17	56	3.18	2	*2-147	12	-0.5
1974 NY-A	24	47	3	11	1	0	0	1	4	5	1	0	.234	.294	.255	.549	61	-2	4	2.67	-1	2-20/D-1	1	-0.2
SD-N	42	90	5	17	1	0	0	4	8	6	0	0	.189	.255	.200	.455	30	-8	5	1.90	-2	2-21	0	-0.9
Total 10	1272	4813	548	1230	150	23	27	304	365	362	151	58	.256	.310	.313	.623	82	-101	482	3.45	-30	*2-1102/S-64,3-21,D-1	127	-4.9

• CLARKE, Josh Joshua Baldwin "Pepper" Clarke b: 3/8/1879, Winfield, KS d: 7/2/1962, Ventura, CA BL/TR, 5'10", 180 lbs. Deb: 6/15/1898 Career OF: 168-6-23

YEAR TM-L	G	AB	R	H	2B	3B	HR	RBI	BB	SO	SB	CS	AVG	OBP	SLG	OPS	OPS+	BR/A	RC	RC/G	FR	G/POS	WS	TPW
1898 Lou-N	6	18	0	3	0	0	0	0	1	....	0	....	.167	.211	.167	.377	9	-2	1	1.27	-1	/O-5(2-0-4)	0	-0.3
1905 StL-N	50	167	31	43	3	2	3	18	27	....	8	....	.257	.361	.353	.714	117	5	25	5.17	-8	O-26(2-5-19),2-16/S-4	7	-0.4
1908 Cle-A	131	492	70	119	8	4	1	21	76	....	37	....	.242	.348	.280	.628	104	7	61	4.12	-2	*O-131(130-1-0)	20	-0.3
1909 Cle-A	4	12	1	0	0	0	0	0	2	....	0	....	.000	.143	.000	.143	-52	-2	0	.00	-1	/O-4(4-0-0)	0	-0.4
1911 Bos-N	32	120	16	28	7	3	1	4	29	22	6	....	.233	.387	.367	.753	103	2	19	5.35	3	O-30(30-0-0)	4	0.3
Total 5	223	809	118	193	18	9	5	43	135	22	51	....	.239	.351	.302	.653	102	9	106	4.36	-8	O-196/2-16,S-4	31	-1.0

• CLARKE, Nig Jay Justin Clarke b: 12/15/1882, Amherstburg, Canada d: 6/15/1949, River Rouge, MI BL/TR, 5'8", 165 lbs. Deb: 4/26/1905

YEAR TM-L	G	AB	R	H	2B	3B	HR	RBI	BB	SO	SB	CS	AVG	OBP	SLG	OPS	OPS+	BR/A	RC	RC/G	FR	G/POS	WS	TPW
1905 Cle-A	5	9	2	1	1	0	0	1	1	....	0	....	.111	.200	.222	.422	33	-1	0	1.36	0	/C-5	0	-0.1
Det-A	3	7	1	3	0	0	1	1	0	....	0	....	.429	.500	.857	1.357	326	2	3	20.37	0	/C-2	1	0.2
Cle-A	37	114	9	23	5	1	0	8	10	....	0	....	.202	.266	.263	.529	67	-4	8	2.41	-4	C-37	2	-0.5
Yr.	45	130	12	27	6	1	1	10	11	....	0	....	.208	.275	.292	.567	79	-3	12	3.01	-4	C-44	3	-0.3
1906 Cle-A	57	179	22	64	12	4	1	21	13	....	3	....	.358	.404	.486	.890	180	16	38	8.49	-1	C-54	11	2.2
1907 Cle-A	120	390	44	105	19	6	3	33	35	....	3	....	.269	.333	.372	.704	124	10	51	4.68	-13	*C-115	17	0.9
1908 Cle-A	97	290	34	70	8	6	1	27	30	....	6	....	.241	.315	.321	.635	106	2	31	3.55	-5	C-90	10	0.6
1909 Cle-A	55	164	15	45	4	2	0	14	9	....	1	....	.274	.316	.323	.639	98	-1	17	3.58	-1	C-44	5	0.3
1910 Cle-A	21	58	4	9	2	0	0	2	8	....	0	....	.155	.258	.190	.447	40	-4	3	1.55	1	C-17	1	-0.1
1911 StL-A	82	256	22	55	10	1	0	18	26	....	2	....	.215	.287	.262	.549	56	-15	20	2.49	0	C-73/1-4	2	-0.9
1919 Phi-N	26	62	4	15	3	0	0	2	4	5	1	....	.242	.299	.290	.589	72	-2	5	2.94	1	C-22	1	0.0
1920 Pit-N	3	7	0	0	0	0	0	0	2	4	0	0	.000	.222	.000	.222	-32	-1	0	.42	0	/C-3	0	-0.1
Total 9	506	1536	157	390	64	20	6	127	138	9	16	0	.254	.318	.333	.652	103	3	177	3.95	-22	C-462/1-4	50	2.7

• CLARKE, Stu William Stuart Clarke b: 1/24/1906, San Francisco, CA d: 8/26/1985, Hayward, CA BR/TR, 5'8.5", 160 lbs. Deb: 7/17/1929

YEAR TM-L	G	AB	R	H	2B	3B	HR	RBI	BB	SO	SB	CS	AVG	OBP	SLG	OPS	OPS+	BR/A	RC	RC/G	FR	G/POS	WS	TPW
1929 Pit-N	57	178	20	47	5	7	2	21	19	21	3	....	.264	.338	.404	.743	81	-5	24	4.61	-6	S-41,3-15/2-1	5	-0.5
1930 Pit-N	4	9	2	4	0	1	0	2	1	0	0	....	.444	.500	.667	1.167	178	1	3	15.14	-1	/2-2	1	0.1
Total 2	61	187	22	51	5	8	2	23	20	21	3	....	.273	.346	.417	.763	86	-4	27	4.97	-6	/S-41,3-15,2-3	6	-0.5

• CLARKE, Sumpter Sumpter Mills Clarke b: 10/18/1897, Savannah, GA d: 3/16/1962, Knoxville, TN BR/TR, 5'11", 170 lbs. Deb: 9/27/1920 Career OF: 2-9-22

YEAR TM-L	G	AB	R	H	2B	3B	HR	RBI	BB	SO	SB	CS	AVG	OBP	SLG	OPS	OPS+	BR/A	RC	RC/G	FR	G/POS	WS	TPW
1920 Chi-N	1	3	0	1	0	0	0	0	0	1	0	0	.333	.333	.333	.667	90	-0	0	4.24	0	/3-1	0	0.0
1923 Cle-A	1	3	0	0	0	0	0	0	0	0	0	0	.000	.000	.000	.000	-100	-1	0	.00	-0	/O-1	0	-0.1
1924 Cle-A	35	104	17	24	6	1	0	11	6	12	0	0	.231	.273	.308	.580	49	-8	9	2.86	0	O-33(2-9-22)	0	-0.9
Total 3	37	110	17	25	6	1	0	11	6	13	0	0	.227	.267	.300	.567	46	-9	9	2.79	0	/O-34,3-1	0	-1.0

• CLARKE, Tommy Thomas Aloysius Clarke b: 5/9/1888, New York, NY d: 8/14/1945, Corona, NY BR/TR, 5'11", 175 lbs. Deb: 8/26/1909 C

YEAR TM-L	G	AB	R	H	2B	3B	HR	RBI	BB	SO	SB	CS	AVG	OBP	SLG	OPS	OPS+	BR/A	RC	RC/G	FR	G/POS	WS	TPW
1909 Cin-N	18	52	8	13	3	2	0	10	6	....	3	....	.250	.328	.385	.712	122	1	8	4.60	3	C-17	2	0.7
1910 Cin-N	64	151	19	42	6	5	1	20	19	17	1	....	.278	.370	.404	.774	131	6	23	5.22	-4	C-56	7	0.8
1911 Cin-N	86	203	20	49	6	7	1	25	25	22	4	....	.241	.328	.355	.682	94	-2	26	3.99	1	C-81/1-1	7	0.5
1912 Cin-N	72	146	19	41	7	2	0	22	28	14	9	....	.281	.400	.356	.756	111	4	25	5.73	0	C-63	8	0.8
1913 Cin-N	114	330	29	87	11	8	1	38	39	40	2	....	.264	.345	.355	.700	100	1	39	4.08	0	*C-100	10	0.9
1914 Cin-N	113	313	30	82	13	7	2	25	31	30	6	....	.262	.332	.367	.700	105	2	39	4.24	5	*C-106	11	1.5
1915 Cin-N	96	226	23	65	7	2	0	21	33	22	7	3	.288	.381	.336	.717	116	6	32	4.90	-1	C-72	10	1.2
1916 Cin-N	78	177	10	42	10	1	0	17	24	20	8	....	.237	.328	.305	.633	97	0	20	3.86	1	C-51	4	0.5
1917 Cin-N	58	110	11	32	3	3	1	13	11	12	2	....	.291	.361	.400	.761	139	5	16	5.22	-1	C-29	5	0.7
1918 Chi-N	1	0	0	0	0	0	0	0	0	0	0	....	....	....	....	....	-98	0	0	....	0	/C-1	0	0.0
Total 10	700	1708	169	453	66	37	6	191	216	177	42	3	.265	.351	.358	.709	109	25	227	4.51	5	C-576/1-1	64	7.5

• CLARKSON, Buzz James Buster Clarkson b: 3/13/1915, Hopkins, SC d: 1/18/1989, Jeannette, PA BR/TR, 5'11", 210 lbs. Deb: 4/30/1952

YEAR TM-L	G	AB	R	H	2B	3B	HR	RBI	BB	SO	SB	CS	AVG	OBP	SLG	OPS	OPS+	BR/A	RC	RC/G	FR	G/POS	WS	TPW
1952 Bos-N	14	25	3	5	0	0	0	1	3	3	0	0	.200	.286	.200	.486	38	-2	2	2.28	-1	/S-6,3-2	0	-0.3

• CLARY, Ellis Ellis "Cat" Clary b: 9/11/1916, Valdosta, GA d: 6/2/2000, Valdosta, GA BR/TR, 5'8", 160 lbs. Deb: 6/7/1942 C

YEAR TM-L	G	AB	R	H	2B	3B	HR	RBI	BB	SO	SB	CS	AVG	OBP	SLG	OPS	OPS+	BR/A	RC	RC/G	FR	G/POS	WS	TPW
1942 Was-A	76	240	34	66	9	0	0	16	45	25	2	0	.275	.394	.313	.706	101	4	35	5.20	-10	2-69/3-2	9	-0.1
1943 Was-A	73	254	36	65	19	1	0	19	44	31	8	4	.256	.370	.339	.709	112	6	35	4.58	-5	3-68/S-1	8	0.2
StL-A	23	69	15	19	2	0	0	5	11	6	1	2	.275	.375	.304	.679	98	-0	9	4.48	1	3-14/2-3	2	0.1
Yr.	96	323	51	84	21	1	0	24	55	37	9	6	.260	.371	.331	.702	109	6	43	4.56	-5	3-82/2-3,S-1	10	0.3
1944*StL-A	25	49	6	13	1	1	0	4	12	9	1	0	.265	.410	.327	.736	106	2	8	6.05	-1	3-11/2-6	3	0.1
1945 StL-A	26	38	6	8	1	0	1	2	2	3	0	2	.211	.250	.316	.566	61	-3	3	2.13	-2	3-16/2-3	0	-0.5
Total 4	223	650	97	171	32	2	1	46	114	74	12	8	.263	.376	.323	.699	103	9	89	4.74	-17	3-111/2-81,S-1	22	-0.2

• CLAY, Bill Frederick C. Clay b: 11/23/1874, Baltimore, MD d: 10/12/1917, York, PA TR Deb: 8/8/1902

YEAR TM-L	G	AB	R	H	2B	3B	HR	RBI	BB	SO	SB	CS	AVG	OBP	SLG	OPS	OPS+	BR/A	RC	RC/G	FR	G/POS	WS	TPW
1902 Phi-N	3	8	1	2	0	0	0	1	0	....	0	....	.250	.250	.250	.500	54	-0	1	2.26	-1	/O-3(3-0-0)	0	-0.1

• CLAY, Dain Dain Elmer "Sniffy,Ding-A-Ling" Clay
b: 7/10/1919, Hicksville, OH d: 8/28/1994, Chula Vista, CA BR/TR, 5'10.5", 160 lbs. Deb: 6/12/1943 Career OF: 17-381-5

YEAR TM-L	G	AB	R	H	2B	3B	HR	RBI	BB	SO	SB	CS	AVG	OBP	SLG	OPS	OPS+	BR/A	RC	RC/G	FR	G/POS	WS	TPW
1943 Cin-N	49	93	19	25	2	4	0	9	8	14	1	....	.269	.333	.376	.710	106	1	12	4.54	-1	O-33(1-29-3)	3	-0.2
1944 Cin-N	110	356	51	89	15	0	0	17	17	18	8	....	.250	.290	.292	.582	67	-16	31	2.89	-1	O-98(5-93-0)	7	-2.0
1945 Cin-N	153	656	81	184	29	2	1	50	37	58	19	....	.280	.321	.335	.656	84	-15	71	3.93	2	*O-152(0-152-0)	16	-1.7
1946 Cin-N	121	435	52	99	17	0	2	22	53	40	11	....	.228	.318	.280	.599	73	-14	43	3.31	1	*O-120(11-107-2)	8	-1.8
Total 4	433	1540	203	397	63	6	3	98	115	130	39	....	.258	.314	.312	.626	78	-44	157	3.53	1	O-403	34	-5.6

• CLAYTON, Royce Royce Spencer Clayton b: 1/2/1970, Burbank, CA BR/TR, 6', 183 lbs. Deb: 9/20/1991

YEAR TM-L	G	AB	R	H	2B	3B	HR	RBI	BB	SO	SB	CS	AVG	OBP	SLG	OPS	OPS+	BR/A	RC	RC/G	FR	G/POS	WS	TPW
1991 SF-N	9	26	0	3	1	0	0	2	1	6	0	0	.115	.148	.154	.302	-15	-4	0	.53	-3	/S-8	0	-0.7
1992 SF-N	98	321	31	72	7	4	4	24	26	63	8	4	.224	.282	.308	.591	71	-13	26	2.64	0	S-94/3-1	5	-0.6
1993 SF-N	153	549	54	155	21	5	6	70	38	91	11	10	.282	.334	.372	.706	91	-9	65	4.01	11	*S-153	15	1.4
1994 SF-N	108	385	38	91	14	6	3	30	30	74	23	3	.236	.297	.327	.624	66	-16	40	3.50	14	*S-108	9	0.7
1995 SF-N	138	509	56	124	29	3	5	58	38	109	24	9	.244	.300	.342	.642	71	-21	54	3.55	16	*S-136	12	0.6
1996*StL-N	129	491	64	136	20	4	6	35	33	89	33	15	.277	.324	.371	.694	83	-12	56	3.90	17	*S-113	12	1.3
1997 StL-N★	154	576	75	153	39	5	9	61	33	109	30	10	.266	.309	.398	.706	84	-13	66	3.90	9	*S-153	13	0.8
1998 StL-N	90	355	59	83	19	1	4	29	40	51	19	6	.234	.315	.327	.642	70	-14	38	3.48	12	S-89	7	0.5
*Tex-A	52	186	30	53	12	1	5	24	13	32	5	5	.285	.335	.441	.776	96	-3	25	4.47	-3	S-52	5	-0.1
1999*Tex-A	133	465	69	134	21	5	14	52	39	100	8	6	.288	.348	.445	.794	96	-4	72	5.51	-3	*S-133	15	0.3
2000 Tex-A	148	513	70	124	21	5	14	54	42	92	11	7	.242	.303	.384	.687	71	-25	55	3.41	1	*S-148	8	-1.1
2001 Chi-A	135	433	62	114	21	4	9	60	33	72	10	7	.263	.320	.393	.712	84	-12	50	3.80	-3	*S-133	10	-0.4
2002 Chi-A	112	342	51	86	14	2	7	35	20	67	5	1	.251	.299	.365	.664	73	-13	37	3.67	8	*S-109	8	0.3
2003 Mil-N	146	483	49	110	16	1	11	39	49	92	5	2	.228	.303	.333	.636	67	-23	44	2.94	-2	*S-141	7	-1.4
Total 13	1605	5634	708	1438	255	46	97	573	435	1047	192	85	.255	.312	.368	.681	78	-181	630	3.72	73	*S-1570/3-1	126	1.8

• CLEMENS, Bob Robert Baxter Clemens b: 8/9/1886, Odessa, MO d: 4/5/1964, Marshall, MO BR/TR, 5'9", 163 lbs. Deb: 9/17/1914

YEAR TM-L	G	AB	R	H	2B	3B	HR	RBI	BB	SO	SB	CS	AVG	OBP	SLG	OPS	OPS+	BR/A	RC	RC/G	FR	G/POS	WS	TPW
1914 StL-A	7	13	1	3	0	1	0	3	2	1	0	2	.231	.375	.385	.760	133	-0	1	2.76	0	/O-5(2-1-2)	0	-0.1

YEAR TM-L	G	AB	R	H	2B	3B	HR	RBI	BB	SO	SB	CS	AVG	OBP	SLG	OPS	OPS+	BR/A	RC	RC/G	FR	G/POS	WS	TPW
• CLEMENS, Chet																								
Chester Spurgeon Clemens b: 5/10/1917, San Fernando, CA d: 2/10/2002, San Clemente, CA BR/TR, 6', 175 lbs. Deb: 9/13/1939 Career OF: 14-0-0																								
1939 Bos-N	9	23	2	5	0	0	0	1	1	3	1	....	.217	.250	.217	.467	29	-2	1	1.97	-1	/O-7(7-0-0)	0	-0.3
1944 Bos-N	19	17	7	3	1	1	0	2	2	2	0	....	.176	.263	.353	.616	69	-1	2	3.31	0	/O-7(7-0-0)	0	-0.1
Total 2	28	40	9	8	1	1	0	3	3	5	1	....	.200	.256	.275	.531	47	-3	3	2.56	-1	/O-14	0	-0.4
• CLEMENS, Clem																								
Clement Lambert "Count" Clemens b: 11/2/1886, Chicago, IL d: 11/2/1967, St. Petersburg, FL BR/TR, 5'11", 176 lbs. Deb: 5/15/1914																								
1914 Chi-F	13	27	4	4	0	0	0	2	3	0	0	....	.148	.233	.148	.381	10	-3	1	1.07	0	/C-8	0	-0.3
1915 Chi-F	11	22	3	3	1	0	0	3	1	0	0	....	.136	.174	.182	.356	5	-3	1	.85	-1	/C-9,2-2	0	-0.4
1916 Chi-N	10	15	0	0	0	0	0	0	1	6	0	....	.000	.063	.000	.063	-72	-3	0	.00	-1	/C-9	0	-0.4
Total 3	34	64	7	7	1	0	0	5	5	6	0	....	.109	.174	.125	.299	-10	-9	2	.72	-3	/C-26,2-2	0	-1.1
• CLEMENS, Doug																								
Douglas Horace Clemens b: 6/9/1939, Leesport, PA BL/TR, 6', 180 lbs. Deb: 10/2/1960 Career OF: 109-18-142																								
1960 StL-N	1	0	0	0	0	0	0	0	0	0	0	0	....	....	....	....	-92	0	0	....	-0	/O-1	0	0.0
1961 StL-N	6	12	1	2	1	0	0	0	3	1	0	0	.167	.333	.250	.583	53	-1	1	3.40	-1	/O-3(2-0-2)	0	-0.1
1962 StL-N	48	93	12	22	1	1	1	12	17	19	0	0	.237	.355	.301	.656	71	-3	11	3.82	-2	O-34(7-1-27)	2	-0.7
1963 StL-N	5	6	1	1	0	0	1	2	1	2	0	0	.167	.286	.667	.952	151	0	1	5.38	1	/O-3(2-0-1)	0	0.1
1964 StL-N	33	78	8	16	4	3	1	9	6	16	0	0	.205	.271	.372	.642	73	-3	8	3.28	0	O-22(17-0-5)	1	-0.4
Chi-N	54	140	23	39	10	2	2	12	18	22	0	0	.279	.365	.421	.786	116	4	22	5.81	1	O-40(1-2-38)	5	0.2
Yr.	87	218	31	55	14	5	3	21	24	38	0	0	.252	.332	.404	.736	100	1	31	4.82	1	O-62(18-2-43)	6	-0.2
1965 Chi-N	128	340	36	75	11	0	4	26	38	53	5	8	.221	.303	.288	.591	66	-17	29	2.77	-1	*O-105(44-13-49)	4	-2.4
1966 Phi-N	79	121	10	31	1	0	1	15	16	25	1	0	.256	.353	.289	.642	81	-2	14	3.99	1	O-28(24-2-3)/1-1	3	-0.2
1967 Phi-N	69	73	2	13	5	0	0	4	8	15	0	0	.178	.268	.247	.515	48	-5	5	2.15	0	O-10(9-0-1)	0	-0.6
1968 Phi-N	29	57	6	12	1	1	2	8	7	13	0	0	.211	.297	.368	.665	99	0	6	3.67	0	O-17(3-0-15)	2	-0.1
Total 9	452	920	99	211	34	7	12	88	114	166	6	8	.229	.319	.321	.640	77	-26	98	3.52	-1	O-263/1-1	17	-4.2
• CLEMENT, Wally																								
Wallace Oakes Clement b: 7/21/1881, Auburn, ME d: 11/1/1953, Coral Gables, FL BL/TR, 5'11", 175 lbs. Deb: 8/17/1908 Career OF: 92-0-4																								
1908 Phi-N	16	36	0	8	3	0	0	1	0	....	2	....	.222	.222	.306	.528	66	-2	3	2.44	4	/O-8(8-0-0)	0	0.2
1909 Phi-N	3	3	0	0	0	0	0	0	0	....	0	....	.000	.000	.000	.000	-99	-1	0	.00	0	....	0	-0.1
Bro-N	92	340	35	88	8	4	0	17	18	....	11	....	.259	.296	.306	.602	90	-5	35	3.34	2	O-88(84-0-4)	6	-0.9
Yr.	95	343	35	88	8	4	0	17	18	....	11	....	.257	.294	.303	.597	88	-6	35	3.30	2	O-88(84-0-4)	6	-1.0
Total 2	111	379	35	96	11	4	0	18	18	....	13	....	.253	.287	.303	.591	86	-7	38	3.21	6	/O-96	6	-0.8
• CLEMENTE, Edgard																								
Edgard Alexis Velazquez Clemente b: 12/15/1975, Santurce, Puerto Rico BR/TR, 6', 188 lbs. Deb: 9/10/1998 Career OF: 17-51-22																								
1998 Col-N	11	17	2	6	0	1	0	2	2	8	0	0	.353	.421	.471	.892	110	0	4	8.81	-1	/O-7(0-1-6)	0	0.0
1999 Col-N	57	162	24	41	10	2	8	25	7	46	0	0	.253	.284	.488	.772	71	-8	21	4.34	-1	O-49(2-45-4)	2	-0.9
2000 Ana-A	46	78	4	17	2	0	0	5	0	27	0	1	.218	.228	.244	.471	19	-10	4	1.80	1	O-32(15-5-12),D-11	0	-1.0
Total 3	114	257	30	64	12	3	8	32	9	81	0	1	.249	.277	.412	.690	58	-18	28	3.79	-1	/O-88,D-11	2	-1.9
• CLEMENTE, Roberto																								
Roberto (Walker) "Arriba" Clemente b: 8/18/1934, Carolina, Puerto Rico d: 12/31/1972, At Sea BR/TR, 5'11", 175 lbs. Deb: 4/17/1955 HOF: 1973 Career OF: 27-63-2302																								
1955 Pit-N	124	474	48	121	23	11	5	47	18	60	2	5	.255	.285	.382	.667	76	-19	46	3.30	10	*O-118(1-10-111)	7	-1.3
1956 Pit-N	147	543	66	169	30	7	7	60	13	58	6	6	.311	.332	.431	.763	105	1	72	4.77	1	*O-139(26-22-101)/2-2,3-1	14	-0.3
1957 Pit-N	111	451	42	114	17	7	4	30	23	45	0	4	.253	.289	.348	.637	72	-20	41	3.14	7	*O-109(0-14-97)	5	-1.7
1958 Pit-N	140	519	69	150	24	10	6	50	31	41	8	2	.289	.329	.408	.738	96	-3	67	4.61	19	*O-135(0-0-135)	16	1.2
1959 Pit-N	105	432	60	128	17	7	4	50	15	51	2	3	.296	.324	.396	.720	91	-7	52	4.37	3	*O-104(0-0-104)	10	-0.8
1960*Pit-N★	144	570	89	179	22	6	16	94	39	72	4	5	.314	.360	.458	.818	121	15	87	5.50	1	*O-142(0-0-142)	20	1.1
1961 Pit-N★	146	572	100	201	30	10	23	89	35	59	4	1	**.351**	.392	.559	.951	148	39	119	8.14	11	*O-144(0-1-144)	26	4.0
1962 Pit-N★	144	538	95	168	28	9	10	74	35	73	6	4	.312	.355	.454	.809	115	10	81	5.46	10	*O-142(0-0-142)	20	0.9
1963 Pit-N★	152	600	77	192	23	8	17	76	31	64	12	2	.320	.357	.470	.827	135	28	94	5.74	-1	*O-151(0-8-143)	22	1.8
1964 Pit-N★	155	622	95	**211**	40	7	12	87	51	87	5	2	**.339**	.391	.484	.875	145	38	118	7.38	9	*O-154(0-0-154)	30	3.8
1965 Pit-N★	152	589	91	194	21	14	10	65	43	78	8	0	**.329**	.380	.463	.843	136	30	101	6.55	11	*O-145(0-5-143)	27	3.2
1966 Pit-N★	154	638	105	202	31	11	29	119	46	109	7	5	.317	.363	.536	.899	146	37	119	6.95	15	*O-154(0-1-154)	29	4.3
1967 Pit-N★	147	585	103	**209**	26	10	23	110	41	103	9	1	**.357**	.402	.554	.956	170	**54**	126	8.64	8	*O-145(0-2-144)	35	5.6
1968 Pit-N	132	502	74	146	18	12	18	57	51	77	2	3	.291	.357	.482	.839	152	31	82	5.91	11	*O-131(0-0-131)	25	3.7
1969 Pit-N★	138	507	87	175	20	**12**	19	91	56	73	4	1	.345	.413	.544	.958	170	48	109	8.30	7	*O-135(0-0-135)	28	5.1
1970*Pit-N★	108	412	65	145	22	10	14	60	38	66	3	0	.352	.409	.556	.965	161	35	93	9.11	6	*O-104(0-0-104)	23	3.6
1971*Pit-N★	132	522	82	178	29	8	13	86	26	65	1	2	.341	.372	.502	.874	144	27	90	6.53	6	*O-124(0-0-124)	24	2.8
1972*Pit-N★	102	378	68	118	19	7	10	60	29	49	0	0	.312	.361	.479	.840	140	19	61	5.83	3	O-94(0-0-94)	16	1.8
Total 18	2433	9454	1416	3000	440	166	240	1305	621	1230	83	46	.317	.362	.475	.837	131	363	1557	6.11	138	*O-2370/2-2,3-1	377	38.8
• CLEMENTS, Ed																								
Edward Clements b: Philadelphia, PA Deb: 6/24/1890																								
1890 Pit-N	1	1	0	0	0	0	0	0	0	0	0	....	.000	.000	.000	.000	-113	-0	0	.00	-2	/S-1	0	-0.2
• CLEMENTS, Jack																								
John J. Clements b: 7/24/1864, Philadelphia, PA d: 5/23/1941, Norristown, PA BL/TL, 5'8.5", 204 lbs. Deb: 4/22/1884 M/U Career OF: 8-7-26																								
1884 Phi-U	41	177	37	50	13	2	3	....	9	....	....	....	.282	.317	.429	.747	163	12	25	5.45	1	O-22(5-0-17),C-20/S-1	6	1.3
Phi-N	9	30	3	7	0	0	0	0	4	8	....	....	.233	.324	.233	.557	82	-0	2	2.78	-1	/C-9	1	0.0
1885 Phi-N	52	188	14	36	11	3	1	14	2	30	....	....	.191	.200	.298	.498	60	-8	11	2.04	-5	C-41,O-11(2-7-2)	2	-1.0
1886 Phi-N	54	185	15	38	5	1	0	11	7	34	4	....	.205	.234	.243	.478	45	-12	12	2.16	-6	C-47/O-7(1-0-6)	3	-1.3
1887 Phi-N	66	255	48	78	13	7	1	47	9	24	7	....	.306	.317	.402	.719	93	-3	34	5.15	-0	C-59/3-4,S-3	9	0.1
1888 Phi-N	86	326	26	80	8	4	1	32	10	36	3	....	.245	.276	.304	.580	81	-8	29	3.17	-8	C-85/O-1	7	-0.8
1889 Phi-N	78	310	51	88	17	1	4	35	29	21	3	....	.284	.347	.384	.731	96	-3	43	5.18	-12	C-78	9	-0.7
1890 Phi-N	97	381	64	120	23	8	7	74	45	30	10	....	.315	.392	.472	.864	148	23	76	7.74	-6	C-91/1-5	18	2.1
1891 Phi-N	107	423	58	131	29	4	4	75	43	19	3	....	.310	.380	.426	.806	131	17	71	6.59	-3	*C-107/1-2	19	2.0
1892 Phi-N	109	402	50	106	25	6	8	76	43	40	7	....	.264	.339	.415	.755	128	13	61	5.52	-10	*C-109	15	1.3
1893 Phi-N	94	376	64	107	20	3	17	80	39	29	3	....	.285	.360	.489	.849	125	11	69	6.79	-8	*C-92/1-1	12	1.0
1894 Phi-N	48	171	26	60	6	5	3	36	26	9	6	....	.351	.459	.497	.956	134	12	43	10.02	-6	C-45	7	0.8
1895 Phi-N	88	322	64	127	27	2	13	75	22	7	3	....	.394	.446	.612	1.058	170	32	92	12.50	1	*C-88	18	3.3
1896 Phi-N	57	184	35	66	5	7	5	45	17	14	2	....	.359	.427	.543	.971	157	15	45	9.67	2	C-53	9	1.9
1897 Phi-N	55	185	18	44	4	2	6	36	12	....	3	....	.238	.305	.378	.684	82	-5	23	4.26	-3	C-49	4	-0.3
1898 StL-N	99	335	39	86	19	5	3	41	21	....	1	....	.257	.314	.370	.684	94	-4	41	4.25	-1	C-86	6	0.2
1899 Cle-N	4	12	1	3	0	0	0	0	0	....	0	....	.250	.308	.250	.558	58	-1	1	2.79	1	/C-4	0	0.1
1900 Bos-N	16	42	6	13	1	0	1	10	3	....	0	....	.310	.370	.405	.774	101	0	6	5.88	0	C-10	1	0.1
Total 17	1160	4304	619	1240	226	60	77	687	341	301	55	....	.288	.348	.421	.769	117	89	686	5.94	-61	*C-1073/O-41,1-8,3-4,S-4	146	10.1
• CLEMONS, Verne																								
Verne James "Stinger,Tubby" Clemons b: 9/8/1891, Clemons, IA d: 5/5/1959, Bay Pines, FL BR/TR, 5'9.5", 190 lbs. Deb: 4/22/1916																								
1916 StL-A	4	7	0	1	1	0	0	0	0	1	0	....	.143	.143	.286	.429	30	-1	0	1.24	0	/C-2	0	-0.1
1919 StL-N	88	239	14	63	13	2	2	22	26	13	4	....	.264	.336	.360	.696	116	5	29	4.20	2	C-75	10	1.4
1920 StL-N	112	338	17	95	10	6	1	36	30	12	1	1	.281	.340	.355	.695	102	3	42	4.38	2	*C-103	11	1.3
1921 StL-N	117	341	29	109	16	2	2	48	33	17	0	0	.320	.380	.396	.776	108	6	53	5.84	1	*C-107	14	1.3
1922 StL-N	71	160	9	41	4	0	0	15	18	5	1	0	.256	.331	.281	.613	62	-7	16	3.54	5	C-63	4	0.0
1923 StL-N	57	130	6	37	9	1	0	13	10	11	0	0	.285	.345	.369	.714	90	-1	17	4.83	-2	C-41	4	0.0
1924 StL-N	25	56	3	18	3	0	0	6	2	3	0	0	.321	.345	.375	.720	94	-0	7	4.97	0	C-17	1	0.0
Total 7	474	1271	78	364	56	11	5	140	119	62	6	1	.286	.348	.360	.708	99	4	164	4.66	7	C-408	44	3.9
• CLENDENON, Donn																								
Donn Alvin Clendenon b: 7/15/1935, Neosho, MO BR/TR, 6'4", 210 lbs. Deb: 9/22/1961 Career OF: 27-2-10																								
1961 Pit-N	9	35	7	11	1	1	0	2	5	10	0	0	.314	.400	.400	.800	113	1	6	6.89	0	/O-8(1-0-7)	1	0.1
1962 Pit-N	80	222	39	67	8	5	7	28	26	58	16	4	.302	.378	.477	.855	128	11	42	6.94	-5	1-52,O-19(16-1-2)	10	0.2
1963 Pit-N	154	563	65	155	28	7	15	57	39	136	22	13	.275	.328	.430	.758	115	10	75	4.58	1	*1-151	15	0.2
1964 Pit-N	133	457	53	129	23	8	12	64	26	96	12	8	.282	.324	.446	.770	115	7	62	4.77	-2	*1-119	13	-0.2
1965 Pit-N	162	612	89	184	32	14	14	96	48	128	9	9	.301	.356	.467	.824	129	21	99	5.86	0	*1-158/3-1	22	1.3

YEAR TM-L	G	AB	R	H	2B	3B	HR	RBI	BB	SO	SB	CS	AVG	OBP	SLG	OPS	OPS+	BR/A	RC	RC/G	FR	G/POS	WS	TPW
1966 Pit-N	155	571	80	171	22	10	28	98	52	142	8	7	.299	.360	.520	.880	141	30	102	6.50	-4	*1-152	23	1.7
1967 Pit-N	131	478	46	119	15	2	13	56	34	107	4	4	.249	.300	.370	.670	90	-7	49	3.49	2	*1-123	9	-1.4
1968 Pit-N	158	584	63	150	20	6	17	87	47	163	10	3	.257	.313	.399	.712	114	10	72	4.19	8	*1-155	17	1.0
1969 Mon-N	38	129	14	31	6	1	4	14	6	32	0	2	.240	.274	.395	.669	85	-4	11	2.84	2	1-24,0-11(9-1-1)	1	-0.5
*NY-N	72	202	31	51	5	0	12	37	19	62	3	2	.252	.323	.455	.778	113	3	30	5.01	-3	1-58/0-1	7	-0.4
Yr.	110	331	45	82	11	1	16	51	25	94	3	4	.248	.304	.432	.736	103	-1	41	4.14	-1	1-82,0-12(10-1-1)	8	-0.9
1970 NY-N	121	396	65	114	18	3	22	97	39	91	4	1	.288	.353	.515	.868	129	15	68	6.04	1	*1-100	13	0.9
1971 NY-N	88	263	29	65	10	0	11	37	21	78	1	2	.247	.305	.411	.716	103	-1	29	3.66	-3	1-72	5	-1.0
1972 StL-N	61	136	13	26	4	0	4	9	17	37	1	2	.191	.281	.309	.590	68	-6	10	2.31	3	1-36	0	-0.6
Total 12	1362	4648	594	1273	192	57	159	682	379	1140	90	57	.274	.331	.442	.774	116	91	657	4.90	0	*1-1200/0-39,3-1	136	1.3

• CLEVELAND, Elmer Elmer Ellsworth Cleveland b: 9/15/1862, Washington, DC d: 10/8/1913, Zimmerman, PA BR/TR, 5'11" Deb: 8/29/1884

YEAR TM-L	G	AB	R	H	2B	3B	HR	RBI	BB	SO	SB	CS	AVG	OBP	SLG	OPS	OPS+	BR/A	RC	RC/G	FR	G/POS	WS	TPW
1884 Cin-U	29	115	24	37	9	2	0	....	4	....	....	....	.322	.345	.435	.779	150	5	18	6.34	5	3-29	6	1.0
1888 NY-N	9	34	6	8	0	2	2	5	3	1	1	....	.235	.297	.529	.827	161	2	6	6.01	-3	/3-9	2	0.0
Pit-N	30	108	10	24	2	1	2	11	5	23	3	....	.222	.270	.315	.584	93	-1	10	3.29	-6	3-30	3	-0.5
Yr.	39	142	16	32	2	3	4	16	8	24	4	....	.225	.276	.366	.643	109	2	16	3.93	-8	3-39	5	-0.6
1891 Col-a	12	41	12	7	0	0	0	4	12	9	4	....	.171	.370	.171	.541	59	-1	4	3.25	4	3-12	1	0.2
Total 3	80	298	52	76	11	5	4	20	24	33	8	....	.255	.317	.366	.683	116	6	38	4.67	0	/3-80	12	0.6

• CLIBURN, Stan Stanley Gene Cliburn b: 12/19/1956, Jackson, MS BR/TR, 6', 195 lbs. Deb: 5/6/1980

YEAR TM-L	G	AB	R	H	2B	3B	HR	RBI	BB	SO	SB	CS	AVG	OBP	SLG	OPS	OPS+	BR/A	RC	RC/G	FR	G/POS	WS	TPW
1980 Cal-A	54	56	7	10	2	0	2	6	3	9	0	0	.179	.220	.321	.542	48	-4	4	2.17	-2	C-54	1	-0.5

• CLIFT, Harlond Harlond Benton "Darkie" Clift b: 8/12/1912, El Reno, OK d: 4/27/1992, Yakima, WA BR/TR, 5'11", 180 lbs. Deb: 4/17/1934

YEAR TM-L	G	AB	R	H	2B	3B	HR	RBI	BB	SO	SB	CS	AVG	OBP	SLG	OPS	OPS+	BR/A	RC	RC/G	FR	G/POS	WS	TPW
1934 StL-A	147	572	104	149	30	10	14	56	84	100	7	2	.260	.357	.421	.778	92	-6	91	5.59	-16	*3-141	15	-1.6
1935 StL-A	137	475	101	140	26	4	11	69	83	39	0	3	.295	.406	.436	.842	113	12	89	6.86	-9	*3-127/2-6	17	0.7
1936 StL-A	152	576	145	174	40	11	20	73	115	68	12	4	.302	.424	.514	.938	127	29	134	8.69	2	*3-152	23	3.2
1937 StL-A★	155	571	103	175	36	7	29	118	98	80	8	5	.306	.413	.546	.960	139	36	134	8.75	30	*3-155	23	**6.5**
1938 StL-A	149	534	119	155	25	7	34	118	118	67	10	5	.290	.423	.554	.977	143	39	133	9.15	17	*3-149	25	**5.6**
1939 StL-A	151	526	90	142	25	2	15	84	**111**	55	4	3	.270	.402	.411	.813	106	10	97	6.47	-1	*3-149	18	1.3
1940 StL-A	150	523	92	143	29	5	20	87	104	62	9	8	.273	.396	.463	.859	119	17	103	7.00	-4	*3-147	23	1.8
1941 StL-A	154	584	108	149	33	9	17	84	113	93	6	4	.255	.376	.430	.806	109	10	102	6.06	3	*3-154	21	1.9
1942 StL-A	143	541	108	148	39	4	7	55	106	48	6	4	.274	.394	.399	.794	122	21	95	6.21	2	*3-141/S-1	24	2.9
1943 StL-A	105	379	43	88	11	3	3	25	54	37	5	4	.232	.329	.301	.630	83	-7	40	3.48	21	*3-104	12	1.8
Was-A	8	30	4	9	0	0	0	4	5	3	0	0	.300	.417	.300	.717	115	1	4	5.15	0	/3-8	1	0.1
Yr.	113	409	47	97	11	3	3	29	59	40	5	4	.237	.336	.301	.637	85	-5	44	3.59	21	*3-112	13	1.9
1944 Was-A	12	44	4	7	3	0	0	3	3	3	0	0	.159	.213	.227	.440	27	-4	2	1.50	-2	3-12	0	-0.6
1945 Was-A	119	375	49	79	12	0	8	53	76	58	2	1	.211	.349	.307	.656	99	4	48	4.28	-1	*3-111	14	0.5
Total 12	1582	5730	1070	1558	309	62	178	829	1070	713	69	43	.272	.390	.441	.831	115	164	1072	6.64	41	*3-1550/2-6,S-1	216	24.1

• CLIFTON, Flea Herman Earl Clifton b: 12/12/1909, Cincinnati, OH d: 12/22/1997, Cincinnati, OH BR/TR, 5'10", 160 lbs. Deb: 4/29/1934

YEAR TM-L	G	AB	R	H	2B	3B	HR	RBI	BB	SO	SB	CS	AVG	OBP	SLG	OPS	OPS+	BR/A	RC	RC/G	FR	G/POS	WS	TPW
1934 Det-A	16	16	3	1	0	0	0	1	1	2	0	0	.063	.118	.063	.180	-52	-4	0	.25	0	/3-4,2-1	0	-0.4
1935*Det-A	43	110	15	28	5	0	0	9	5	13	2	1	.255	.293	.300	.593	56	-7	10	3.03	-1	3-21/2-5,S-4	1	-0.7
1936 Det-A	13	26	5	5	1	0	0	1	4	3	0	1	.192	.300	.231	.531	33	-3	2	2.17	-1	/S-6,3-2,2-1	0	-0.4
1937 Det-A	15	43	4	5	1	0	0	2	7	10	3	0	.116	.240	.140	.380	-2	-6	2	1.53	-1	/3-7,S-4,2-3	0	-0.6
Total 4	87	195	27	39	7	0	0	13	17	28	5	2	.200	.268	.236	.504	30	-20	14	2.29	-4	/3-34,S-14,2-10	1	-2.0

• CLINE, Monk John P. Cline b: 3/3/1858, Louisville, KY d: 9/23/1916, Louisville, KY BL/TL, 5'4", 150 lbs. Deb: 7/4/1882 Career OF: 63-119-41

YEAR TM-L	G	AB	R	H	2B	3B	HR	RBI	BB	SO	SB	CS	AVG	OBP	SLG	OPS	OPS+	BR/A	RC	RC/G	FR	G/POS	WS	TPW
1882 Bal-a	44	172	18	38	6	2	0	....	3	....	....	....	.221	.234	.279	.513	78	-3	12	2.41	2	0-39(1-38-0)/S-8,2-2,3-1	3	-0.3
1884 Lou-a	94	396	91	115	16	7	2	39	27	....	....	....	.290	.342	.381	.723	142	19	53	5.18	8	*0-90(8-81-3)/S-6	18	2.2
1885 Lou-a	2	9	0	2	1	0	0	2	0	....	....	....	.222	.222	.333	.556	74	-0	1	2.64	0	/3-1,0-1	0	0.0
1888 KC-a	73	293	45	69	13	2	0	19	20	....	29	....	.235	.289	.294	.582	81	-7	34	4.10	8	0-70(32-0-38)/2-3,3-1	5	0.0
1891 Lou-a	19	70	11	21	3	1	0	11	16	2	2	....	.300	.430	.371	.802	131	4	12	6.68	-1	0-21(21-0-0)	3	0.3
Total 5	232	940	165	245	39	12	2	71	66	2	31	....	.261	.313	.334	.647	111	13	112	4.38	17	0-221/S-14,2-5,3-3	29	2.1

• CLINE, Ty Tyrone Alexander Cline b: 6/15/1939, Hampton, SC BL/TL, 6'.5", 170 lbs. Deb: 9/14/1960 Career OF: 112-402-44

YEAR TM-L	G	AB	R	H	2B	3B	HR	RBI	BB	SO	SB	CS	AVG	OBP	SLG	OPS	OPS+	BR/A	RC	RC/G	FR	G/POS	WS	TPW
1960 Cle-A	7	26	2	8	1	1	0	2	0	4	0	0	.308	.308	.423	.731	99	-0	3	4.03	1	/0-6(0-6-0)	1	0.0
1961 Cle-A	12	43	9	9	2	1	0	1	6	1	1	0	.209	.333	.302	.636	73	-1	5	4.13	0	0-12(0-12-0)	1	-0.1
1962 Cle-A	118	375	53	93	15	5	2	28	28	50	5	4	.248	.309	.331	.639	74	-14	39	3.57	-4	*0-107(0-107-0)	8	-2.1
1963 Mil-N	72	174	17	41	2	1	0	10	10	31	2	1	.236	.285	.259	.544	58	-9	14	2.67	4	0-62(0-62-0)	3	-0.7
1964 Mil-N	101	116	22	35	4	2	1	13	8	22	0	1	.302	.362	.397	.759	113	2	18	5.44	1	0-54(3-49-2)/1-6	5	0.2
1965 Mil-N	123	220	27	42	5	3	0	10	16	50	2	2	.191	.246	.241	.487	37	-19	14	2.00	0	0-86(17-58-12)/1-5	2	-2.2
1966 Chi-N	7	17	3	6	0	0	0	2	0	2	1	0	.353	.353	.353	.706	96	0	2	4.31	-0	/0-5(0-5-0)	0	0.0
Atl-N	42	71	12	18	0	0	0	6	3	11	2	1	.254	.303	.254	.556	56	-4	5	2.57	-1	0-19(7-5-10)/1-6	0	-0.6
Yr.	49	88	15	24	0	0	0	8	3	13	3	1	.273	.312	.273	.585	63	-4	7	2.87	-1	0-24(7-10-10)/1-6	0	-0.6
1967 Atl-N	10	8	0	0	0	0	0	0	0	3	0	0	.000	.111	.000	.111	-66	-2	0	.10	0	/0-1	0	-0.2
SF-N	64	122	18	33	5	5	0	4	9	13	2	1	.270	.326	.393	.719	106	1	16	4.72	0	0-37(17-21-3)	4	-0.1
Yr.	74	130	18	33	5	5	0	4	9	16	2	1	.254	.312	.369	.681	95	-1	16	4.35	-1	0-38(18-21-3)	4	-0.3
1968 SF-N	116	291	37	65	6	3	1	28	11	26	0	2	.223	.254	.275	.529	59	-16	20	2.24	1	0-70(48-13-10),1-24	3	-2.2
1969 Mon-N	101	209	26	50	5	3	2	12	32	22	4	3	.239	.346	.321	.666	87	-2	25	4.06	-1	0-41(7-35-0),1-17	4	-0.6
1970 Mon-N	2	2	0	1	0	0	0	0	0	0	0	0	.500	.500	.500	1.000	169	0	1	13.50	0	....	0	0.0
*Cin-N	48	63	13	17	7	1	0	8	12	11	1	2	.270	.387	.413	.799	110	1	11	5.67	0	0-20(6-8-6)/1-2	2	0.0
Yr.	50	65	13	18	7	1	0	8	12	11	1	2	.277	.390	.415	.805	111	1	11	5.82	0	0-20(6-8-6)/1-2	2	0.0
1971 Cin-N	69	97	12	19	1	0	0	1	18	16	2	2	.196	.333	.206	.540	59	-4	8	2.80	-1	0-28(6-21-1)/1-2	2	-0.6
Total 12	892	1834	251	437	53	25	6	125	153	262	22	19	.238	.304	.304	.609	72	-68	180	3.31	0	0-548/1-62	35	-9.2

• CLINES, Gene Eugene Anthony Clines b: 10/6/1946, San Pablo, CA BR/TR, 5'9", 170 lbs. Deb: 6/28/1970 C Career OF: 302-210-132

YEAR TM-L	G	AB	R	H	2B	3B	HR	RBI	BB	SO	SB	CS	AVG	OBP	SLG	OPS	OPS+	BR/A	RC	RC/G	FR	G/POS	WS	TPW
1970 Pit-N	31	37	4	15	2	0	0	3	2	5	2	1	.405	.436	.459	.895	145	2	7	7.20	0	/0-7(2-2-3)	1	0.2
1971*Pit-N	97	273	52	84	12	4	1	24	22	36	15	6	.308	.366	.392	.758	113	6	42	5.67	3	0-74(20-43-13)	11	0.7
1972*Pit-N	107	311	52	104	15	6	0	17	16	47	12	6	.334	.371	.421	.792	127	10	47	5.65	-1	0-83(38-17-39)	12	0.7
1973 Pit-N	110	304	42	80	11	3	1	23	26	36	8	7	.263	.327	.329	.656	84	-7	30	3.32	-2	0-77(7-45-25)	5	-1.2
1974*Pit-N	107	276	29	62	5	1	0	14	30	40	14	2	.225	.310	.250	.560	60	-11	23	2.67	1	0-78(19-51-11)	4	-1.4
1975 NY-N	82	203	25	46	6	3	0	10	11	21	4	4	.227	.270	.286	.555	57	-13	15	2.39	5	0-60(35-34-2)	2	-1.0
1976 Tex-A	116	446	52	123	12	3	0	38	16	52	11	9	.276	.307	.316	.623	81	-13	39	2.89	2	*0-103(96-5-4),D-10	6	-1.8
1977 Chi-N	101	239	27	70	12	2	3	41	25	25	1	2	.293	.362	.397	.760	93	-2	34	4.98	1	0-63(50-3-11)	5	-0.3
1978 Chi-N	109	229	31	59	10	2	0	17	21	28	4	3	.258	.323	.319	.641	71	-9	24	3.52	1	0-66(35-10-24)	4	-1.0
1979 Chi-N	10	10	0	2	0	0	0	0	0	1	0	0	.200	.200	.200	.400	9	-1	0	1.35	0	....	0	-0.1
Total 10	870	2328	314	645	85	24	5	187	169	291	71	40	.277	.331	.341	.672	88	-38	260	3.84	10	0-611/D-10	50	-5.4

• CLINGMAN, Billy William Frederick Clingman b: 11/21/1869, Cincinnati, OH d: 5/14/1958, Cincinnati, OH BB/TR, 5'11", 150 lbs. Deb: 9/9/1890

YEAR TM-L	G	AB	R	H	2B	3B	HR	RBI	BB	SO	SB	CS	AVG	OBP	SLG	OPS	OPS+	BR/A	RC	RC/G	FR	G/POS	WS	TPW
1890 Cin-N	7	27	2	7	1	0	0	5	1	0	0	....	.259	.286	.296	.582	70	-1	2	3.10	1	/S-6,2-1	1	0.0
1891 Cin-a	1	5	0	1	1	0	0	0	0	0	0	....	.200	.200	.400	.600	65	-0	0	2.72	0	/2-1	0	0.0
1895 Pit-N	107	386	69	99	16	4	0	45	41	43	19	....	.256	.331	.319	.650	72	-15	50	4.50	13	*3-106	11	0.0
1896 Lou-N	121	423	57	99	10	2	2	37	57	51	19	....	.234	.329	.281	.611	64	-19	47	3.81	17	*3-121	9	-0.1
1897 Lou-N	115	395	61	92	14	7	2	47	37	....	14	....	.233	.307	.319	.626	68	-18	45	3.84	21	*3-113	9	0.4
1898 Lou-N	154	538	65	138	12	6	0	50	51	....	15	....	.257	.327	.301	.628	81	-12	61	3.92	12	3-79,S-74/2-1,0-1	16	0.6
1899 Lou-N	110	369	68	97	15	5	2	45	46	....	13	....	.263	.349	.347	.696	91	-3	52	4.88	-4	*S-109	10	-0.2
1900 Chi-N	47	159	15	33	6	0	0	11	17	....	6	....	.208	.292	.245	.537	51	-10	14	2.84	-13	S-47	2	-1.8
1901 Was-A	137	480	66	116	10	7	2	55	42	....	10	....	.242	.308	.304	.612	71	-18	51	3.58	17	*S-137	13	0.4
1903 Cle-A	21	64	10	18	1	1	0	7	11	....	2	....	.281	.387	.328	.715	118	2	10	5.19	2	2-11/S-7,3-3	3	0.4
Total 10	820	2846	413	700	86	32	8	302	303	94	98	....	.246	.324	.307	.631	74	-94	331	3.99	66	3-422,S-380/2-14,0-1	74	-0.3

YEAR TM-L	G	AB	R	H	2B	3B	HR	RBI	BB	SO	SB	CS	AVG	OBP	SLG	OPS	OPS+	BR/A	RC	RC/G	FR	G/POS	WS	TPW
• CLINTON, Jim	James Lawrence "Big Jim" Clinton b: 8/10/1850, New York, NY d: 9/3/1921, Brooklyn, NY BR/TR, 5'8.5", 174 lbs. Deb: 5/18/1872 M/U NA OF: 0-9-10 Career OF: 150-196-18																							
1872 Eck-n	25	97	12	25	3	1	0	6	0	2	0	1	.258	.258	.309	.567	87	-0	8	3.37	-7	0-11(0-8-3),3-10/2-3,C-2,S	....	-0.5
1873 Res-n	9	38	5	9	1	0	0	4	0	0	0	0	.237	.237	.263	.500	52	-2	2	2.55	-2	/3-9	....	-0.2
1874 Atl-n	2	11	3	2	1	0	0	2	0	2	0	0	.182	.182	.273	.455	49	-0	1	1.86	-1	/2-1,0-1	....	-0.2
1875 Atl-n	22	81	3	10	0	0	0	0	0	0	0	0	.123	.123	.123	.247	-16	-7	1	.53	3	P-17/0-7(0-0-7),1-5,2-1	....	-0.6
1876 Lou-N	16	65	8	22	2	0	0	0	0	0	....	....	.338	.338	.369	.708	115	1	8	5.42	1	0-14(0-0-14)/1-1,P-1	2	-0.2
1882 Wor-N	26	98	9	16	2	0	0	3	7	13	....	....	.163	.219	.184	.403	30	-7	4	1.36	-4	0-26(21-1-4)	0	-1.1
1883 Bal-a	94	399	69	125	16	8	0	0	27	....	....	....	.313	.357	.393	.750	137	17	57	5.87	4	*0-92(92-0-0)/2-2	12	1.6
1884 Bal-a	104	437	82	118	12	6	4	0	29	....	....	....	.270	.334	.352	.686	119	10	53	4.55	-4	*0-104(37-67-0)/2-1	18	0.2
1885 Cin-a	105	408	48	97	5	5	0	34	15	....	....	....	.238	.277	.275	.551	73	-13	32	2.76	-6	*0-105(0-105-0)	8	-2.0
1886 Bal-a	23	83	8	15	1	0	0	6	4	....	3	....	.181	.227	.193	.420	33	-6	4	1.76	-1	0-23(0-23-0)	1	-0.7
Total 4 n	58	227	23	46	5	1	0	12	0	4	0	1	.203	.203	.233	.436	43	-9	12	2.05	-8	/3-19,0-19,P-17,1-5,2-5,C-2,S	....	-1.5
Total 6	368	1490	224	393	38	19	4	43	82	13	3	....	.264	.311	.323	.634	101	1	159	3.99	-9	0-364/2-3,1-1,P-1	41	-2.2
• CLINTON, Lou	Luciean Louis Clinton b: 10/13/1937, Ponca City, OK d: 12/6/1997, Wichita, KS BR/TR, 6'1", 185 lbs. Deb: 4/22/1960 Career OF: 16-2-603																							
1960 Bos-A	96	298	37	68	17	5	6	37	20	66	4	3	.228	.283	.379	.663	75	-12	29	3.00	0	0-89(0-0-89)	3	-1.5
1961 Bos-A	17	51	4	13	2	1	0	3	2	10	0	0	.255	.283	.333	.616	62	-3	5	3.47	2	0-13(0-0-13)	1	-0.2
1962 Bos-A	114	398	63	117	24	10	18	75	34	79	2	1	.294	.351	.540	.891	132	16	75	6.97	1	*0-103(0-0-103)	16	1.0
1963 Bos-A	148	560	71	130	23	7	22	77	49	118	0	0	.232	.295	.416	.711	94	-6	65	3.93	4	*0-146(0-0-146)	12	-1.3
1964 Bos-A	37	120	15	31	4	3	3	6	9	33	1	0	.258	.310	.417	.727	95	-1	15	4.23	2	0-35(0-0-35)	3	-0.1
LA-A	91	306	30	76	18	0	9	38	31	40	3	0	.248	.320	.395	.715	108	4	40	4.50	5	0-86(0-0-86)	11	0.3
Yr.	128	426	45	107	22	3	12	44	40	73	4	0	.251	.317	.401	.718	105	3	55	4.42	8	*0-121(0-0-121)	14	0.2
1965 Cal-A	89	222	29	54	12	3	1	8	23	37	2	3	.243	.317	.338	.655	88	-4	23	3.47	2	0-73(1-0-72)	5	-0.7
KC-A	1	1	0	0	0	0	0	0	0	0	0	0	.000	.000	.000	.000	-102	-0	0	.00	0	/0-1	0	0.0
Cle-A	12	34	2	6	1	0	1	2	3	7	0	0	.176	.243	.294	.537	51	-2	3	2.53	-1	/0-9(9-1-1)	0	-0.4
Yr.	102	257	31	60	13	3	2	10	26	44	2	3	.233	.306	.331	.637	83	-7	26	3.33	1	0-83(10-1-74)	5	-1.1
1966 NY-A	80	159	18	35	10	2	5	21	16	27	0	0	.220	.291	.403	.694	101	-0	19	3.87	-2	0-63(5-1-57)	4	-0.6
1967 NY-A	6	4	1	2	1	0	0	2	1	1	0	0	.500	.600	.750	1.350	308	1	2	24.30	0	/0-1	1	0.1
Total 8	691	2153	270	532	112	31	65	269	188	418	12	7	.247	.310	.418	.728	99	-7	275	4.34	14	0-619	56	-3.4
• CLOUGH, Ed	Edgar George "Big Ed,Spec" Clough b: 10/28/1906, Wiconisco, PA d: 1/30/1944, Harrisburg, PA BL/TL, 6', 188 lbs. Deb: 8/28/1924 ♦																							
1924 StL-N	7	14	0	1	0	0	0	1	0	3	0	0	.071	.071	.071	.143	-63	-3	0	.18	0	/0-6(5-0-1)	0	-0.3
1925 StL-N	3	4	0	1	0	0	0	0	0	0	0	0	.250	.250	.250	.500	28	-0	0	2.12	0	/P-3	0	-0.4
1926 StL-N	1	1	0	0	0	0	0	0	0	0	0	....	.000	.000	.000	.000	-96	-0	0	.00	0	/P-1	0	-0.4
Total 3	11	19	0	2	0	0	0	1	0	3	0	0	.105	.105	.105	.211	-46	-3	0	.50	0	/0-6,P-4	0	-1.1
• CLYBURN, Danny	Danny Clyburn b: 4/6/1974, Lancaster, SC BR/TR, 6'3", 220 lbs. Deb: 9/15/1997 Career OF: 20-0-15																							
1997 Bal-A	2	3	0	0	0	0	0	0	0	2	0	0	.000	.000	.000	.000	-103	-1	0	.00	0	/0-1	0	-0.1
1998 Bal-A	11	25	6	7	0	0	1	3	1	10	0	0	.280	.308	.400	.708	83	-1	3	4.74	0	/0-8(5-0-5),D-1	0	-0.1
1999 TB-A	28	81	8	16	4	0	3	5	7	21	0	0	.198	.270	.358	.628	58	-6	7	2.56	2	0-24(14-0-10)/D-4	0	-0.5
Total 3	41	109	14	23	4	0	4	8	8	33	0	0	.211	.271	.358	.629	59	-7	10	2.91	1	/0-33,D-5	0	-0.7
• CLYMER, Bill	William Johnston "Derby Day Bill" Clymer b: 12/18/1873, Philadelphia, PA d: 12/26/1936, Philadelphia, PA Deb: 6/25/1891 C																							
1891 Phi-a	3	11	0	0	0	0	0	0	1	2	1	....	.000	.154	.000	.154	-54	-2	0	.38	0	/S-3	0	-0.2
• CLYMER, Otis	Otis Edgar Clymer b: 1/27/1876, Pine Grove, PA d: 2/27/1926, St. Paul, MN BB/TR, 5'11", 180 lbs. Deb: 4/14/1905 Career OF: 33-33-262																							
1905 Pit-N	96	365	74	108	11	5	0	23	19	....	23	....	.296	.332	.353	.686	102	0	52	5.21	-2	0-89(4-0-85)/1-1	12	-0.6
1906 Pit-N	11	45	7	11	0	1	0	1	3	....	1	....	.244	.292	.289	.581	78	-1	4	3.20	-1	0-11(0-0-11)	1	-0.3
1907 Pit-N	22	66	8	15	2	0	0	4	5	....	4	....	.227	.311	.258	.568	77	-1	7	3.42	-3	0-15(0-0-15)/1-1	1	-0.6
Was-A	57	206	30	65	5	5	1	16	18	....	18	....	.316	.382	.403	.784	163	15	40	7.30	-5	0-51(27-1-24)/1-1	10	0.8
1908 Was-A	110	368	32	93	11	4	1	35	20	....	19	....	.253	.291	.313	.604	105	1	38	3.51	2	0-82(1-0-81),2-13/3-2	9	-0.1
1909 Was-A	45	138	11	27	5	2	0	6	17	....	7	....	.196	.284	.261	.545	76	-3	12	2.76	-3	0-41(0-1-40)	2	-1.0
1913 Chi-N	30	105	16	24	5	1	0	7	14	18	9	....	.229	.319	.295	.615	76	-3	12	3.67	-2	0-26(0-24-2)	2	-0.7
Bos-N	14	37	4	12	3	1	0	6	3	3	2	....	.324	.375	.459	.834	135	2	7	6.67	-2	0-11(1-7-4)	2	-0.1
Yr.	44	142	20	36	8	2	0	13	17	21	11	....	.254	.333	.338	.671	91	-1	19	4.40	-3	0-37(1-31-6)	4	-0.7
Total 6	385	1330	182	355	42	19	2	98	99	21	83	....	.267	.322	.332	.653	106	9	173	4.50	-16	0-326/2-13,1-3,3-2	39	-2.4
• COACHMAN, Pete	Bobby Dean Coachman b: 11/11/1961, Cottonwood, AL BR/TR, 5'9", 175 lbs. Deb: 8/18/1990																							
1990 Cal-A	16	45	3	14	3	0	0	5	1	7	0	1	.311	.354	.378	.732	107	-0	6	4.45	0	/3-9,2-2,D-2	2	0.0
• COAN, Gil	Gilbert Fitzgerald Coan b: 5/18/1922, Monroe, NC BL/TR, 6', 180 lbs. Deb: 4/27/1946 Career OF: 664-67-21																							
1946 Was-A	59	134	17	28	3	2	3	9	7	37	2	2	.209	.269	.328	.597	70	-6	12	2.98	-3	0-29(27-0-2)	2	-1.2
1947 Was-A	11	42	5	21	3	2	0	3	5	6	2	1	.500	.553	.667	1.220	244	8	17	20.26	1	0-11(0-0-11)	5	0.9
1948 Was-A	138	513	56	119	13	9	7	60	41	78	23	9	.232	.298	.333	.631	70	-23	55	3.58	9	*0-131(131-0-0)	10	-2.3
1949 Was-A	111	358	36	78	7	8	3	25	29	58	9	6	.218	.278	.307	.586	56	-25	32	2.94	-3	0-97(68-29-0)	2	-3.2
1950 Was-A	104	366	58	111	17	4	7	50	28	46	10	5	.303	.359	.429	.788	106	3	60	6.11	0	0-98(95-3-1)	11	-0.4
1951 Was-A	135	538	85	163	25	7	9	62	39	62	8	5	.303	.357	.426	.782	113	8	85	5.82	11	*0-132(132-0-0)	19	0.9
1952 Was-A	107	332	50	68	11	6	5	20	32	35	9	4	.205	.277	.319	.596	68	-15	32	3.17	-4	0-86(86-0-0)	5	-2.5
1953 Was-A	68	168	28	33	1	4	2	17	22	23	7	0	.196	.301	.286	.586	60	-7	17	3.28	1	0-46(45-1-0)	3	-0.9
1954 Bal-A	94	265	29	74	11	1	2	20	16	17	9	4	.279	.323	.351	.674	91	-3	31	4.21	-4	0-67(36-32-0)	5	-1.1
1955 Bal-A	61	130	18	31	7	1	1	11	13	15	4	2	.238	.313	.331	.643	78	-4	14	3.59	1	0-43(42-0-1)	2	-0.5
Chi-A	17	17	0	3	0	0	0	1	0	5	0	0	.176	.176	.176	.353	-5	-3	1	1.02	0	/0-3(1-0-2)	0	-0.3
Yr.	78	147	18	34	7	1	1	12	13	20	4	2	.231	.298	.313	.611	70	-6	15	3.29	0	0-46(43-0-3)	2	-0.8
NY-N	9	13	0	2	0	0	0	0	0	1	0	0	.154	.154	.154	.308	-18	-2	0	.76	0	/0-6(1-2-4)	0	-0.3
1956 NY-N	4	1	2	0	0	0	0	0	0	1	0	0	.000	.000	.000	.000	-101	-0	0	.00	0	....	0	0.0
Total 11	918	2877	384	731	98	44	39	278	232	384	83	38	.254	.316	.359	.675	84	-68	355	4.28	8	0-749	64	-10.9
• COBB, Joe	Joseph Stanley Cobb b: 1/24/1895, Hudson, PA d: 12/24/1947, Allentown, PA BR/TR, 5'9", 170 lbs. Deb: 4/25/1918																							
1918 Det-A	1	0	0	0	0	0	0	0	1	0	0	....	....	1.000	....	1.000	210	0	0	....	0	....	0	0.0
• COBB, Ty	Tyrus Raymond "The Georgia Peach" Cobb b: 12/18/1886, Narrows, GA d: 7/17/1961, Atlanta, GA BL/TR, 6'1", 175 lbs. Deb: 8/30/1905 M HOF: 1936 Career OF: 35-2194-706																							
1905 Det-A	41	150	19	36	6	0	1	15	10	....	2	....	.240	.288	.300	.588	86	-3	14	3.22	-1	0-41(2-39-0)	4	-0.6
1906 Det-A	98	358	45	113	15	5	1	34	19	....	23	....	.316	.355	.394	.749	131	12	61	6.26	2	0-96(18-55-24)	16	1.0
1907*Det-A	150	605	97	**212**	28	14	5	**119**	24	....	**49**	....	**.350**	.380	**.468**	**.848**	**164**	**40**	130	**8.53**	7	*0-150(0-0-150)	**41**	4.5
1908*Det-A	150	581	88	**188**	**36**	**20**	4	**108**	34	....	39	....	**.324**	.367	**.475**	**.842**	**166**	**40**	114	**7.26**	1	*0-150(0-0-150)	**36**	3.9
1909*Det-A	156	573	**116**	**216**	33	10	**9**	**107**	48	....	**76**	....	**.377**	**.431**	**.517**	**.947**	**190**	**59**	159	**10.82**	4	*0-156(0-0-156)	**44**	6.3
1910 Det-A	140	506	**106**	194	35	13	8	91	64	....	65	....	**.383**	**.456**	**.551**	**1.008**	**202**	61	156	**12.34**	5	*0-137(0-111-26)	45	6.6
1911 Det-A	146	591	**147**	**248**	**47**	**24**	8	**127**	44	....	**83**	....	**.420**	.467	**.621**	**1.088**	**193**	**72**	207	**15.19**	3	*0-146(0-146-0)	**47**	6.4
1912 Det-A	140	553	120	**226**	30	23	7	83	43	....	61	....	**.409**	.456	**.584**	**1.040**	**203**	**71**	173	**13.39**	7	*0-140(0-140-0)	40	7.0
1913 Det-A	122	428	70	167	18	16	4	67	58	31	51	....	**.390**	**.467**	.535	1.002	**196**	54	124	**11.62**	2	*0-118(0-116-2)/2-1	31	5.1
1914 Det-A	98	345	69	127	22	11	2	57	57	22	35	17	**.368**	.466	.513	.979	188	41	89	9.73	-9	0-96(0-96-0)	26	2.8
1915 Det-A	156	563	**144**	**208**	31	13	3	99	118	43	**96**	38	**.369**	**.486**	.487	**.973**	**182**	**70**	155	**10.19**	-4	*0-156(0-156-0)	**48**	6.0
1916 Det-A	145	542	**113**	201	31	10	5	68	78	39	**68**	24	.371	.452	.493	.944	177	**58**	136	**9.33**	-6	*0-143(0-143-0)/1-1	40	4.8
1917 Det-A	152	588	107	**225**	**44**	**24**	6	102	61	34	**55**	....	**.383**	**.444**	**.570**	**1.014**	**210**	**75**	164	**11.28**	10	*0-152(0-123-29)	**46**	**8.4**
1918 Det-A	111	421	83	161	19	**14**	3	64	41	21	34	....	**.382**	**.440**	.515	.955	196	48	105	9.94	-4	0-95(0-92-3),1-13/P-2,2-1,3	31	4.1
1919 Det-A	124	497	92	**191**	36	13	1	70	38	22	28	....	**.384**	.429	.515	.944	168	44	116	9.58	-9	*0-123(0-123-0)	32	2.9
1920 Det-A	112	428	86	143	28	8	2	63	58	28	15	10	.334	.416	.451	.867	133	23	82	7.22	-7	*0-112(0-112-0)	20	0.9
1921 Det-A	128	507	124	197	37	16	12	101	56	19	22	15	.389	.452	.596	1.048	167	51	134	10.43	6	*0-121(0-121-0)	26	4.8

YEAR TM-L	G	AB	R	H	2B	3B	HR	RBI	BB	SO	SB	CS	AVG	OBP	SLG	OPS	OPS+	BR/A	RC	RC/G	FR	G/POS	WS	TPW
1922 Det-A	137	526	99	211	42	16	4	99	55	24	9	13	.401	.462	.565	1.026	172	54	133	9.95	-2	*O-134(0-133-1)	29	4.4
1923 Det-A	145	556	103	189	40	7	6	88	66	14	9	10	.340	.413	.469	.882	134	28	108	7.20	5	*O-141(0-141-0)	24	2.7
1924 Det-A	155	625	115	211	38	10	4	79	85	18	23	14	.338	.418	.450	.867	126	27	121	7.22	7	*O-155(0-155-0)	27	2.7
1925 Det-A	121	415	97	157	31	12	12	102	65	12	13	9	.378	.468	.598	**1.066**	**171**	47	118	11.46	-6	*O-105(0-101-4)/P-1	25	3.5
1926 Det-A	79	233	48	79	18	5	4	62	26	2	9	4	.339	.408	.511	.918	137	13	49	7.63	-3	O-55(15-39-1)	10	0.7
1927 Phi-A	134	490	104	175	32	7	5	93	67	12	22	16	.357	.440	.482	.921	131	25	105	8.12	0	*O-127(0-52-75)	22	1.6
1928 Phi-A	95	353	54	114	27	4	1	40	34	16	5	8	.323	.389	.431	.819	112	5	58	6.19	2	O-85(0-0-85)	12	0.0
Total 24	**3035**	**11434**	**2246**	**4189**	**724**	**295**	**117**	**1938**	**1249**	**357**	**892**	**178**	**.366**	**.433**	**.512**	**.945**	**168**	**1015**	**2810**	**9.54**	**9**	***O-2934/1-14,P-3,2-2,3-1**	**722**	**90.6**

• COBLE, Dave David Lamar Coble b: 12/24/1912, Monroe, NC d: 10/15/1971, Orlando, FL BR/TR, 6'1", 183 lbs. Deb: 5/1/1939

YEAR TM-L	G	AB	R	H	2B	3B	HR	RBI	BB	SO	SB	CS	AVG	OBP	SLG	OPS	OPS+	BR/A	RC	RC/G	FR	G/POS	WS	TPW
1939 Phi-N	15	25	2	7	1	0	0	0	0	3	0	....	.280	.280	.320	.600	64	-1	2	2.73	-1	C-13	0	-0.2

• COCHRAN, George George Leslie Cochran b: 2/12/1889, Rusk, TX d: 5/21/1960, Harbor City, CA TR Deb: 7/29/1918

YEAR TM-L	G	AB	R	H	2B	3B	HR	RBI	BB	SO	SB	CS	AVG	OBP	SLG	OPS	OPS+	BR/A	RC	RC/G	FR	G/POS	WS	TPW
1918 Bos-A	24	60	7	7	0	0	0	3	10	6	3	....	.117	.264	.117	.381	15	-6	2	1.14	-1	3-22/S-1	1	-0.7

• COCHRANE, Dave David Carter Cochrane b: 1/31/1963, Riverside, CA BB/TR, 6'2", 180 lbs. Deb: 9/2/1986 Career OF: 42-0-12

YEAR TM-L	G	AB	R	H	2B	3B	HR	RBI	BB	SO	SB	CS	AVG	OBP	SLG	OPS	OPS+	BR/A	RC	RC/G	FR	G/POS	WS	TPW
1986 Chi-A	19	62	4	12	2	0	1	2	5	22	0	0	.194	.254	.274	.528	42	-5	4	2.09	-3	3-18/S-1	0	-0.8
1989 Sea-A	54	102	13	24	4	1	3	7	14	27	0	2	.235	.333	.382	.716	98	-1	13	4.23	-5	S-30/1-9,3-9,2-4,O-3(3-0-0),C	1	-0.5
1990 Sea-A	15	20	0	3	0	0	0	0	0	8	0	0	.150	.150	.150	.300	-16	-3	0	.71	-2	/S-5,1-3,3-3,C-1	0	-0.5
1991 Sea-A	65	178	16	44	13	0	2	22	9	38	0	1	.247	.287	.354	.641	76	-7	18	3.38	-4	O-26(23-0-3),C-19,3-13/1-4,D	4	-1.1
1992 Sea-A	65	152	10	38	5	0	2	12	12	34	1	0	.250	.309	.322	.631	77	-4	16	3.52	-1	O-25(16-0-9),C-21,3-10/1-3,S,D,2	1	-0.6
Total 5	**218**	**514**	**43**	**121**	**24**	**1**	**8**	**43**	**40**	**129**	**1**	**3**	**.235**	**.294**	**.333**	**.627**	**74**	**-20**	**50**	**3.31**	**-15**	**/O-54,3-53,C-43,S-39,1-19,2,D**	**6**	**-3.5**

• COCHRANE, Mickey Gordon Stanley "Black Mike" Cochrane
b: 4/6/1903, Bridgewater, MA d: 6/28/1962, Lake Forest, IL BL/TR, 5'10.5", 180 lbs. Deb: 4/14/1925 M/C HOF: 1947

YEAR TM-L	G	AB	R	H	2B	3B	HR	RBI	BB	SO	SB	CS	AVG	OBP	SLG	OPS	OPS+	BR/A	RC	RC/G	FR	G/POS	WS	TPW
1925 Phi-A	134	420	69	139	21	5	6	55	44	19	7	4	.331	.397	.448	.845	107	6	76	6.88	-7	*C-133	16	0.6
1926 Phi-A	120	370	50	101	8	9	8	47	56	15	5	2	.273	.369	.408	.777	97	0	60	5.33	0	*C-115	14	0.7
1927 Phi-A	126	432	80	146	20	6	12	80	50	7	9	6	.338	.409	.495	.904	127	18	89	7.46	-2	*C-123	23	2.2
1928 Phi-A	131	468	92	137	26	12	10	57	76	25	7	7	.293	.395	.464	.859	122	16	89	6.57	-6	*C-130	22	1.8
1929*Phi-A	135	514	113	170	37	8	7	95	69	8	7	6	.331	.412	.475	.887	123	20	103	7.36	-5	*C-135	27	2.3
1930*Phi-A	130	487	110	174	42	5	10	85	55	18	5	0	.357	.424	.526	.949	133	28	111	8.90	2	*C-130	31	3.4
1931*Phi-A	122	459	87	160	31	6	17	89	56	21	2	3	.349	.423	.553	.976	146	33	108	9.40	-3	*C-117	28	3.4
1932 Phi-A	139	518	118	152	35	4	23	112	100	22	0	1	.293	.412	.510	.921	132	29	115	8.21	8	*C-137/O-1	30	4.1
1933 Phi-A	130	429	104	138	30	4	15	60	106	22	8	6	.322	**.459**	.515	.974	156	42	109	9.60	1	*C-128	26	4.8
1934*Det-A★	129	437	74	140	32	1	2	76	78	26	8	4	.320	.428	.412	.840	117	16	83	7.20	-2	*C-124	23	2.0
1935*Det-A★	115	411	93	131	33	3	5	47	96	15	5	5	.319	.452	.450	.902	139	30	91	8.16	-3	*C-110	24	3.2
1936 Det-A	44	126	24	34	8	0	2	17	46	15	1	1	.270	.465	.381	.846	111	6	27	7.25	-5	C-42	6	0.3
1937 Det-A	27	98	27	30	10	1	2	12	25	4	0	1	.306	.452	.490	.941	134	6	23	8.73	0	C-27	5	0.7
Total 13	**1482**	**5169**	**1041**	**1652**	**333**	**64**	**119**	**832**	**857**	**217**	**64**	**46**	**.320**	**.419**	**.478**	**.897**	**127**	**249**	**1084**	**7.74**	**-24**	***C-1451/O-1**	**275**	**29.4**

• COCKMAN, Jim James Cockman b: 4/26/1873, Guelph, Canada d: 9/28/1947, Guelph, Canada BR/TR, 5'6", 145 lbs. Deb: 9/28/1905

YEAR TM-L	G	AB	R	H	2B	3B	HR	RBI	BB	SO	SB	CS	AVG	OBP	SLG	OPS	OPS+	BR/A	RC	RC/G	FR	G/POS	WS	TPW
1905 NY-A	13	38	5	4	0	0	0	2	4	....	2	....	.105	.190	.105	.296	-5	-4	1	.91	-1	3-13	0	-0.5

• COCKRELL, Alan Atlee Alan Cockrell b: 12/5/1962, Kansas City, KS BR/TR, 6'2", 210 lbs. Deb: 9/7/1996

YEAR TM-L	G	AB	R	H	2B	3B	HR	RBI	BB	SO	SB	CS	AVG	OBP	SLG	OPS	OPS+	BR/A	RC	RC/G	FR	G/POS	WS	TPW
1996 Col-N	9	8	0	2	1	0	0	2	0	4	0	0	.250	.250	.375	.625	50	-1	1	3.02	0	/O-1	0	-0.1

• COFFEY, Jack John Francis Coffey b: 1/28/1887, New York, NY d: 2/14/1966, Bronx, NY BR/TR, 5'11", 178 lbs. Deb: 6/23/1909

YEAR TM-L	G	AB	R	H	2B	3B	HR	RBI	BB	SO	SB	CS	AVG	OBP	SLG	OPS	OPS+	BR/A	RC	RC/G	FR	G/POS	WS	TPW
1909 Bos-N	73	257	21	48	4	4	0	20	11	....	2	....	.187	.229	.233	.462	41	-18	14	1.67	-14	S-73	2	-3.4
1918 Det-A	22	67	7	14	0	2	0	4	8	6	2	....	.209	.303	.269	.571	75	-2	6	2.76	-3	2-22	1	-0.5
Bos-A	15	44	5	7	1	0	1	2	3	2	2	....	.159	.213	.250	.463	40	-3	3	1.73	0	3-14/2-1	1	-0.4
Yr.	37	111	12	21	1	2	1	6	11	8	4	....	.189	.268	.261	.530	62	-5	9	2.34	-3	2-23,3-14	2	-0.9
Total 2	**110**	**368**	**33**	**69**	**5**	**6**	**1**	**26**	**22**	**8**	**6**	**....**	**.188**	**.241**	**.242**	**.483**	**48**	**-24**	**22**	**1.88**	**-18**	**/S-73,2-23,3-14**	**4**	**-4.2**

• COFFIE, Ivanon Ivanon Angelino Coffie b: 5/16/1977, Klein, Curacao BL/TR, 6'1", 192 lbs. Deb: 7/15/2000

YEAR TM-L	G	AB	R	H	2B	3B	HR	RBI	BB	SO	SB	CS	AVG	OBP	SLG	OPS	OPS+	BR/A	RC	RC/G	FR	G/POS	WS	TPW
2000 Bal-A	23	60	6	13	4	1	0	6	5	11	1	0	.217	.288	.317	.605	56	-4	5	2.73	0	3-15/S-4,D-1	1	-0.3

• COGGINS, Frank Franklin Coggins b: 5/22/1944, Griffin, GA BB/TR, 6'2", 187 lbs. Deb: 9/10/1967

YEAR TM-L	G	AB	R	H	2B	3B	HR	RBI	BB	SO	SB	CS	AVG	OBP	SLG	OPS	OPS+	BR/A	RC	RC/G	FR	G/POS	WS	TPW
1967 Was-A	19	75	9	23	3	0	1	8	2	17	1	0	.307	.325	.387	.711	114	1	9	4.16	2	2-19	3	0.6
1968 Was-A	62	171	15	30	6	1	0	7	9	33	1	1	.175	.217	.222	.439	34	-14	8	1.46	-4	2-52	1	-1.5
1972 Chi-N	6	1	1	0	0	0	0	0	1	0	0	0	.000	.500	.000	.500	48	0	0	3.51	0	....	0	0.0
Total 3	**87**	**247**	**25**	**53**	**9**	**1**	**1**	**15**	**12**	**50**	**2**	**1**	**.215**	**.251**	**.271**	**.522**	**58**	**-13**	**17**	**2.21**	**-1**	**/2-71**	**4**	**-1.0**

• COGGINS, Rich Richard Allen Coggins b: 12/7/1950, Indianapolis, IN BL/TL, 5'8", 170 lbs. Deb: 8/29/1972 Career OF: 20-106-203

YEAR TM-L	G	AB	R	H	2B	3B	HR	RBI	BB	SO	SB	CS	AVG	OBP	SLG	OPS	OPS+	BR/A	RC	RC/G	FR	G/POS	WS	TPW
1972 Bal-A	16	39	5	13	4	0	0	1	1	6	0	2	.333	.350	.436	.786	129	0	5	4.57	1	O-13(0-9-6)	2	0.1
1973*Bal-A	110	389	54	124	19	9	7	41	28	24	17	9	.319	.365	.468	.832	134	16	65	6.01	7	*O-101(0-39-76)/D-1	16	1.9
1974*Bal-A	113	411	53	100	13	3	4	32	29	31	26	6	.243	.301	.319	.620	81	-7	42	3.43	1	*O-105(2-30-87)	9	-1.1
1975 Mon-N	13	37	1	10	3	1	0	4	1	7	0	0	.270	.289	.405	.695	87	-1	4	4.17	0	O-10(9-0-2)	1	-0.1
NY-A	51	107	7	24	1	0	1	6	7	16	3	3	.224	.272	.262	.534	53	-7	8	2.26	1	O-36(3-25-8)/D-9	1	-0.8
1976 NY-A	7	4	1	1	0	0	0	1	0	1	1	0	.250	.250	.250	.500	47	-0	0	3.42	-0	/O-2(0-1-1)	0	0.0
Chi-A	32	96	4	15	2	0	0	5	6	15	3	1	.156	.206	.177	.383	13	-10	4	1.23	0	O-26(6-2-23)/D-1	0	-1.3
Yr.	39	100	5	16	2	0	0	6	6	16	4	1	.160	.208	.180	.388	14	-10	4	1.30	0	O-28(6-3-24)/D-1	0	-1.3
Total 5	**342**	**1083**	**125**	**287**	**42**	**13**	**12**	**90**	**72**	**100**	**50**	**21**	**.265**	**.314**	**.361**	**.675**	**93**	**-9**	**129**	**4.02**	**9**	**O-293/D-11**	**29**	**-1.2**

• COGSWELL, Ed Edward Cogswell b: 2/25/1854, England d: 7/27/1888, Fitchburg, MA BR/TR, 5'8", 150 lbs. Deb: 7/11/1879

YEAR TM-L	G	AB	R	H	2B	3B	HR	RBI	BB	SO	SB	CS	AVG	OBP	SLG	OPS	OPS+	BR/A	RC	RC/G	FR	G/POS	WS	TPW
1879 Bos-N	49	236	51	76	8	1	1	18	8	5	....	....	.322	.344	.377	.721	135	9	31	5.50	1	1-49	9	0.7
1880 Tro-N	47	209	41	63	7	3	0	13	11	10	....	....	.301	.336	.364	.700	130	6	26	4.94	-2	1-47	7	0.2
1882 Wor-N	13	51	10	7	1	0	0	1	6	6	....	....	.137	.228	.157	.385	26	-4	2	1.17	-1	1-13	0	-0.6
Total 3	**109**	**496**	**102**	**146**	**16**	**4**	**1**	**32**	**25**	**21**	**....**	**....**	**.294**	**.328**	**.349**	**.677**	**121**	**11**	**59**	**4.72**	**-2**	**1-109**	**16**	**0.3**

• COHEN, Alta Alta Albert "Schoolboy" Cohen b: 12/25/1908, New York, NY d: 3/11/2003, Maplewood, NJ BL/TL, 5'10.5", 170 lbs. Deb: 4/15/1931 Career OF: 12-3-1

YEAR TM-L	G	AB	R	H	2B	3B	HR	RBI	BB	SO	SB	CS	AVG	OBP	SLG	OPS	OPS+	BR/A	RC	RC/G	FR	G/POS	WS	TPW
1931 Bro-N	1	3	1	2	0	0	0	0	0	0	0	....	.667	.667	.667	1.333	261	1	1	33.76	1	/O-1	0	0.2
1932 Bro-N	9	32	1	5	1	0	0	1	3	7	0	....	.156	.229	.188	.416	14	-4	2	1.46	1	/O-8(5-3-0)	0	-0.3
1933 Phi-N	19	32	6	6	1	0	0	1	6	4	0	....	.188	.316	.219	.535	49	-2	2	2.22	0	/O-7(7-0-0)	0	-0.3
Total 3	**29**	**67**	**8**	**13**	**2**	**0**	**0**	**2**	**9**	**11**	**0**	**....**	**.194**	**.289**	**.224**	**.513**	**41**	**-5**	**5**	**2.40**	**2**	**/O-16**	**0**	**-0.4**

• COHEN, Andy Andrew Howard Cohen b: 10/25/1904, Baltimore, MD d: 10/29/1988, El Paso, TX BR/TR, 5'8", 155 lbs. Deb: 6/6/1926 M/C

YEAR TM-L	G	AB	R	H	2B	3B	HR	RBI	BB	SO	SB	CS	AVG	OBP	SLG	OPS	OPS+	BR/A	RC	RC/G	FR	G/POS	WS	TPW
1926 NY-N	32	35	4	9	0	1	0	8	1	2	0	....	.257	.278	.314	.592	60	-2	3	2.91	-2	2-10,S-10/3-2	0	-0.3
1928 NY-N	129	504	64	138	24	7	9	59	31	17	3	....	.274	.318	.403	.721	87	-11	63	4.34	-3	*2-126/S-3,3-1	14	-1.1
1929 NY-N	101	347	40	102	12	2	5	47	11	15	3	....	.294	.319	.383	.703	73	-15	41	4.20	6	2-94/3-1,S-1	9	-0.6
Total 3	**262**	**886**	**108**	**249**	**36**	**10**	**14**	**114**	**43**	**34**	**6**	**....**	**.281**	**.317**	**.392**	**.709**	**81**	**-29**	**106**	**4.23**	**1**	**2-230/S-14,3-4**	**23**	**-2.0**

• COKER, Jimmie Jimmie Goodwin Coker b: 3/28/1936, Holly Hill, SC d: 10/29/1991, Throckmorton, TX BR/TR, 5'11", 195 lbs. Deb: 9/11/1958

YEAR TM-L	G	AB	R	H	2B	3B	HR	RBI	BB	SO	SB	CS	AVG	OBP	SLG	OPS	OPS+	BR/A	RC	RC/G	FR	G/POS	WS	TPW
1958 Phi-N	2	6	0	1	0	0	0	0	0	0	0	0	.167	.167	.167	.333	-12	-1	0	.00	0	/C-2	0	-0.1
1960 Phi-N	81	252	18	54	5	3	6	34	23	45	0	3	.214	.290	.329	.620	69	-12	24	3.02	3	C-76	4	-0.6
1961 Phi-N	11	25	3	10	1	0	1	4	7	4	1	0	.400	.531	.560	1.091	193	4	9	14.43	-1	C-11	2	0.4
1962 Phi-N	5	3	0	0	0	0	0	1	1	2	0	0	.000	.250	.000	.250	-27	-0	0	1.05	0	....	0	0.0
1963 SF-N	4	5	0	1	0	0	0	0	1	2	0	0	.200	.333	.200	.533	58	-0	0	2.84	0	/C-2	0	-0.1
1964 Cin-N	11	32	3	10	2	0	1	4	3	5	0	0	.313	.371	.469	.840	130	1	5	6.25	1	C-11	2	0.3
1965 Cin-N	24	61	3	15	2	0	2	9	8	16	0	0	.246	.333	.377	.710	93	-0	8	4.48	1	C-19	2	0.1
1966 Cin-N	50	111	9	28	3	0	4	14	8	5	0	1	.252	.303	.387	.690	83	-3	13	4.00	2	C-39/O-2(2-0-0)	3	0.0

YEAR TM-L	G	AB	R	H	2B	3B	HR	RBI	BB	SO	SB	CS	AVG	OBP	SLG	OPS	OPS+	BR/A	RC	RC/G	FR	G/POS	WS	TPW
1967 Cin-N	45	97	8	18	2	1	2	4	4	20	0	1	.186	.218	.289	.506	39	-8	5	1.78	1	C-34	1	-0.7
Total 9	233	592	44	137	15	4	16	70	55	99	1	5	.231	.301	.351	.652	77	-19	64	3.61	5	C-194/0-2	14	-0.6

• COLANGELO, Mike Michael Gus Colangelo b: 10/22/1976, Teaneck, NJ BR/TR, 6'1", 185 lbs. Deb: 6/13/1999 Career OF: 40-15-9

YEAR TM-L	G	AB	R	H	2B	3B	HR	RBI	BB	SO	SB	CS	AVG	OBP	SLG	OPS	OPS+	BR/A	RC	RC/G	FR	G/POS	WS	TPW
1999 Ana-A	1	2	0	1	0	0	0	0	1	0	0	0	.500	.667	.500	1.167	205	1	1	22.68	1	/0-1	0	0.1
2001 SD-N	50	91	10	22	3	3	2	8	8	30	0	0	.242	.310	.407	.717	91	-1	11	4.13	-1	0-40(25-14-4)	1	-0.3
2002 Oak-A	20	23	2	4	1	0	0	0	1	2	0	0	.174	.240	.217	.457	23	-3	1	1.88	0	0-19(14-1-5)	0	-0.3
Total 3	71	116	12	27	4	3	2	8	10	32	0	0	.233	.305	.371	.675	80	-3	13	3.85	0	/0-60	1	-0.5

• COLAVITO, Rocky Rocco Domenico Colavito b: 8/10/1933, New York, NY BR/TR, 6'3", 190 lbs. Deb: 9/10/1955 C Career OF: 524-0-1285

YEAR TM-L	G	AB	R	H	2B	3B	HR	RBI	BB	SO	SB	CS	AVG	OBP	SLG	OPS	OPS+	BR/A	RC	RC/G	FR	G/POS	WS	TPW
1955 Cle-A	5	9	3	4	2	0	0	0	0	2	0	0	.444	.444	.667	1.111	188	1	3	14.40	2	/0-2(0-0-2)	1	0.3
1956 Cle-A	101	322	55	89	11	4	21	65	49	46	0	1	.276	.375	.531	.906	134	15	67	7.36	-3	0-98(0-0-98)	16	0.8
1957 Cle-A	134	461	66	116	26	0	25	84	71	80	1	6	.252	.353	.471	.823	124	14	76	5.46	5	*0-130(0-0-130)	18	1.5
1958 Cle-A	143	489	80	148	26	3	41	113	84	89	0	2	.303	.407	**.620**	1.027	183	56	122	9.07	0	*0-129(1-0-129),1-11/P-1	32	5.4
1959 Cle-A★	154	588	90	151	24	0	**42**	111	71	86	3	3	.257	.339	.512	.851	135	26	101	5.95	5	*0-154(0-0-154)	29	2.5
1960 Det-A	145	555	67	138	18	1	35	87	53	80	3	6	.249	.319	.474	.793	105	-0	78	4.76	2	*0-144(0-0-144)	13	-0.4
1961 Det-A★	163	583	129	169	30	2	45	140	113	75	1	2	.290	.407	.580	.987	155	47	141	8.67	2	*0-161(150-0-20)	33	4.0
1962 Det-A★	161	601	90	164	30	2	37	112	96	68	2	0	.273	.375	.514	.889	132	29	117	6.80	-3	*0-161(161-0-0)	26	1.6
1963 Det-A	160	597	91	162	29	2	22	91	84	78	0	0	.271	.362	.437	.799	119	17	95	5.52	-2	*0-159(142-0-23)	21	0.5
1964 KC-A★	160	588	89	161	31	2	34	102	83	56	3	1	.274	.368	.507	.875	136	31	110	6.64	-4	*0-159(3-0-157)	22	1.6
1965 Cle-A★	162	592	92	170	25	2	26	**108**	**93**	63	1	1	.287	.387	.468	.855	140	34	110	6.66	-2	*0-162(1-0-162)	28	2.2
1966 Cle-A★	151	533	68	127	13	0	30	72	76	81	2	1	.238	.337	.432	.768	119	15	74	4.59	2	*0-146(0-0-146)	18	0.7
1967 Cle-A	63	191	10	46	9	0	5	21	24	31	2	2	.241	.329	.366	.695	104	1	23	3.99	-2	0-50(28-0-31)	5	-0.4
Chi-A	60	190	20	42	4	1	3	29	25	10	1	1	.221	.312	.300	.612	84	-3	19	3.33	0	0-58(11-0-54)	5	-0.7
Yr.	123	381	30	88	13	1	8	50	49	41	3	3	.231	.320	.333	.654	94	-2	42	3.66	-2	*0-108(39-0-85)	10	-1.1
1968 LA-N	40	113	8	23	3	0	3	11	15	18	0	1	.204	.297	.310	.607	89	-2	9	2.59	1	0-33(21-0-13)	1	-0.2
NY-A	39	91	13	20	2	2	5	13	14	17	0	0	.220	.330	.451	.781	139	5	14	5.40	0	0-28(6-0-22)/P-1	5	0.5
Total 14	1841	6503	971	1730	283	21	374	1159	951	880	19	27	.266	.362	.489	.851	132	286	1157	6.18	1	*0-1774/1-11,P-2	273	19.9

• COLBERN, Mike Michael Malloy Colbern b: 4/19/1955, Santa Monica, CA BR/TR, 6'3", 205 lbs. Deb: 7/18/1978

YEAR TM-L	G	AB	R	H	2B	3B	HR	RBI	BB	SO	SB	CS	AVG	OBP	SLG	OPS	OPS+	BR/A	RC	RC/G	FR	G/POS	WS	TPW
1978 Chi-A	48	141	11	38	5	1	2	20	1	36	0	1	.270	.285	.362	.646	80	-5	14	3.56	-2	C-47/D-1	3	-0.5
1979 Chi-A	32	83	5	20	5	1	0	8	4	25	0	0	.241	.276	.325	.601	61	-5	8	3.02	0	C-32	1	-0.3
Total 2	80	224	16	58	10	2	2	28	5	61	0	1	.259	.281	.348	.630	73	-9	22	3.35	-2	/C-79,D-1	4	-0.8

• COLBERT, Craig Craig Charles Colbert b: 2/13/1965, Iowa City, IA BR/TR, 6', 190 lbs. Deb: 4/6/1992

YEAR TM-L	G	AB	R	H	2B	3B	HR	RBI	BB	SO	SB	CS	AVG	OBP	SLG	OPS	OPS+	BR/A	RC	RC/G	FR	G/POS	WS	TPW
1992 SF-N	49	126	10	29	5	2	1	16	9	22	1	0	.230	.281	.325	.607	76	-4	10	2.46	0	C-35/3-9,2-2	1	-0.3
1993 SF-N	23	37	2	6	2	0	1	5	3	13	0	0	.162	.225	.297	.522	40	-3	3	2.26	-1	C-10/2-2,3-1	2	-0.4
Total 2	72	163	12	35	7	2	2	21	12	35	1	0	.215	.269	.319	.588	68	-7	13	2.41	-2	/C-45,3-10,2-4	3	-0.7

• COLBERT, Nate Nathan Colbert b: 4/9/1946, St. Louis, MO BR/TR, 6'2", 209 lbs. Deb: 4/14/1966 Career OF: 58-5-3

YEAR TM-L	G	AB	R	H	2B	3B	HR	RBI	BB	SO	SB	CS	AVG	OBP	SLG	OPS	OPS+	BR/A	RC	RC/G	FR	G/POS	WS	TPW
1966 Hou-N	19	7	3	0	0	0	0	0	0	4	0	0	.000	.000	.000	.000	-107	-2	0	.00	0	....	0	-0.2
1968 Hou-N	20	53	5	8	1	0	0	4	1	23	1	1	.151	.167	.170	.336	1	-7	1	.63	-2	0-11(3-5-3)/1-5	0	-1.0
1969 SD-N	139	483	64	123	20	9	24	66	45	123	6	4	.255	.322	.482	.804	128	15	72	5.11	5	*1-134	16	1.0
1970 SD-N	156	572	84	148	17	6	38	86	56	150	3	5	.259	.329	.509	.838	126	16	93	5.66	-9	*1-153/3-1	18	-0.5
1971 SD-N★	156	565	81	149	25	3	27	84	63	119	5	2	.264	.342	.462	.804	135	25	87	5.33	-1	*1-153	19	1.2
1972 SD-N★	151	563	87	141	27	2	38	111	70	127	15	6	.250	.335	.508	.843	147	34	95	5.72	5	*1-150	28	2.9
1973 SD-N★	145	529	73	143	25	2	22	80	54	146	9	8	.270	.347	.450	.797	130	19	80	5.26	2	*1-144	20	1.0
1974 SD-N	119	368	53	76	16	0	14	54	62	108	10	2	.207	.323	.364	.687	96	0	46	3.98	4	1-79,0-48(48-0-0)	11	-0.3
1975 Det-A	45	156	16	23	4	2	4	18	17	52	0	2	.147	.231	.276	.507	41	-13	9	1.81	-4	1-44/D-1	0	-2.1
Mon-N	38	81	10	14	4	1	4	11	5	31	0	0	.173	.230	.395	.625	68	-4	7	2.84	-1	1-22	1	-0.7
1976 Mon-N	14	40	5	8	2	0	2	6	9	16	3	1	.200	.347	.400	.747	107	1	6	5.25	1	/0-7(7-0-0),1-6	1	0.1
Oak-A	2	5	0	0	0	0	0	0	1	3	0	0	.000	.167	.000	.167	-50	-1	0	.00	0	/D-2	0	-0.1
Total 10	1004	3422	481	833	141	25	173	520	383	902	52	31	.243	.324	.451	.775	120	83	497	4.90	1	1-890/0-66,D-3,3-1	114	1.3

• COLBRUNN, Greg Gregory Joseph Colbrunn b: 7/26/1969, Fontana, CA BR/TR, 6', 200 lbs. Deb: 7/9/1992

YEAR TM-L	G	AB	R	H	2B	3B	HR	RBI	BB	SO	SB	CS	AVG	OBP	SLG	OPS	OPS+	BR/A	RC	RC/G	FR	G/POS	WS	TPW
1992 Mon-N	52	168	12	45	8	0	2	18	6	34	3	2	.268	.301	.351	.652	85	-4	18	3.72	0	1-47	2	-0.8
1993 Mon-N	70	153	15	39	9	0	4	23	6	33	4	2	.255	.288	.392	.680	77	-6	17	3.85	1	1-61	3	-0.9
1994 Fla-N	47	155	17	47	10	0	6	31	9	27	1	1	.303	.349	.484	.833	111	2	26	6.05	-1	1-41	5	-0.2
1995 Fla-N	138	528	70	146	22	1	23	89	22	69	11	3	.277	.313	.453	.766	99	-3	70	4.71	-2	*1-134	14	-1.6
1996 Fla-N	141	511	60	146	26	2	16	69	25	76	4	5	.286	.336	.438	.775	106	1	68	4.62	2	*1-134	10	-0.8
1997 Min-A	70	217	24	61	14	0	5	26	8	38	1	2	.281	.310	.415	.724	86	-6	25	4.05	-1	1-64/D-2	3	-1.1
*Atl-N	28	54	3	15	3	0	2	9	2	11	0	0	.278	.316	.444	.760	94	-1	7	4.88	0	1-14/D-3	1	-0.1
1998 Col-N	62	122	12	38	8	2	2	13	8	23	3	3	.311	.359	.459	.818	93	-2	20	6.03	-1	1-27/0-5(0-0-5),C-1	2	-0.5
*Atl-N	28	44	6	13	3	0	1	10	2	11	1	0	.295	.367	.432	.799	109	1	8	6.66	-0	/1-9,D-3,0-1	2	0.0
Yr.	90	166	18	51	11	2	3	23	10	34	4	3	.307	.361	.452	.813	97	-1	27	6.20	-1	1-36/0-6(0-0-6),D-3,C-1	4	-0.5
1999*Ari-N	67	135	20	44	5	3	5	24	12	23	1	1	.326	.397	.519	.916	128	6	28	7.71	1	1-39/3-2,D-2	5	0.4
2000 Ari-N	116	329	48	103	22	1	15	57	43	45	0	1	.313	.408	.523	.931	129	16	69	7.66	1	1-99/D-2,3-1	12	0.8
2001*Ari-N	59	97	12	28	8	0	4	18	9	14	0	0	.289	.373	.495	.868	115	2	17	6.14	0	1-14,3-10	3	0.1
2002*Ari-N	72	171	30	57	16	2	10	27	13	19	0	0	.333	.380	.626	1.006	146	11	39	8.75	-3	1-40/3-5,D-3	7	0.5
2003 Sea-A	22	58	7	16	1	1	3	7	4	16	0	1	.276	.323	.483	.805	112	0	7	4.40	-1	1-14/D-4	1	-0.2
Total 12	972	2742	336	798	155	12	98	421	169	439	29	21	.291	.343	.464	.807	107	18	419	5.45	-4	1-737/D-19,3-18,0-6,C-1	70	-4.2

• COLE, Alex Alexander Cole b: 8/17/1965, Fayetteville, NC BL/TL, 6'2", 170 lbs. Deb: 7/27/1990 Career OF: 42-390-54

YEAR TM-L	G	AB	R	H	2B	3B	HR	RBI	BB	SO	SB	CS	AVG	OBP	SLG	OPS	OPS+	BR/A	RC	RC/G	FR	G/POS	WS	TPW
1990 Cle-A	63	227	43	68	5	4	0	13	28	38	40	9	.300	.379	.357	.736	107	8	37	5.83	0	0-59(0-59-0)/D-1	10	0.7
1991 Cle-A	122	387	58	114	17	3	0	21	58	47	27	17	.295	.388	.354	.742	106	5	55	4.91	-4	*0-107(8-101-0)/D-6	10	-0.1
1992 Cle-A	41	97	11	20	1	0	0	5	10	21	9	2	.206	.287	.216	.504	44	-6	7	2.37	0	0-24(18-5-2)/D-4	0	-0.7
*Pit-N	64	205	33	57	3	7	0	10	18	46	7	4	.278	.336	.361	.697	99	-1	25	4.41	1	0-53(0-1-52)	5	-0.1
1993 Col-N	126	348	50	89	9	4	0	24	43	58	30	13	.256	.341	.305	.646	64	-16	39	3.72	-4	0-93(0-93-0)	7	-1.9
1994 Min-A	105	345	68	102	15	5	4	23	44	60	29	8	.296	.377	.403	.780	101	5	58	5.97	1	*0-100(16-84-0)/D-1	9	0.5
1995 Min-A	28	79	10	27	3	2	1	14	8	15	1	3	.342	.409	.468	.877	127	2	15	7.10	-1	0-23(0-23-0)/D-2	4	0.1
1996 Bos-A	24	72	13	16	5	1	0	7	8	11	5	3	.222	.300	.319	.619	56	-5	7	2.82	0	0-24(0-24-0)	0	-0.5
Total 7	573	1760	286	493	58	26	5	117	217	296	148	59	.280	.361	.351	.713	92	-8	243	4.77	-9	0-483/D-14	45	-2.0

• COLE, Dick Richard Roy Cole b: 5/6/1926, Long Beach, CA BR/TR, 6'2", 175 lbs. Deb: 4/27/1951 C

YEAR TM-L	G	AB	R	H	2B	3B	HR	RBI	BB	SO	SB	CS	AVG	OBP	SLG	OPS	OPS+	BR/A	RC	RC/G	FR	G/POS	WS	TPW
1951 StL-N	15	36	4	7	1	0	0	3	6	5	0	0	.194	.310	.222	.532	45	-3	3	2.81	1	2-14	1	-0.1
Pit-N	42	106	9	25	4	0	1	11	15	9	0	1	.236	.331	.302	.632	69	-5	11	3.20	-4	2-34/S-8	2	-0.6
Yr.	57	142	13	32	5	0	1	14	21	14	0	1	.225	.325	.282	.607	63	-7	14	3.11	-3	2-48/S-8	3	-0.7
1953 Pit-N	97	235	29	64	13	1	0	23	38	26	2	2	.272	.374	.336	.710	87	-3	32	4.66	-14	S-77/2-7,1-1	5	-1.0
1954 Pit-N	138	486	40	131	22	5	1	40	41	48	0	0	.270	.326	.342	.668	75	-17	52	3.59	-17	S-66,3-55,2-17	7	-2.8
1955 Pit-N	77	239	16	54	8	3	0	21	18	22	0	0	.226	.286	.285	.570	53	-16	19	2.76	-5	3-33,2-24,S-12	3	-1.8
1956 Pit-N	72	99	7	21	2	1	0	9	11	9	0	0	.212	.291	.253	.543	49	-7	7	2.22	1	3-18,2-12/S-6	1	-0.6
1957 Mil-N	15	14	1	1	0	0	0	0	3	5	0	0	.071	.235	.071	.307	-13	-2	0	.68	-1	2-10/1-1,3-1	0	-0.3
Total 6	456	1215	106	303	50	10	2	107	132	124	2	3	.249	.324	.312	.636	69	-52	125	3.41	-39	S-169,2-118,3-107/1-2	19	-7.2

• COLE, Stu Stewart Bryan Cole b: 2/7/1966, Charlotte, NC BR/TR, 6'1", 175 lbs. Deb: 9/5/1991

YEAR TM-L	G	AB	R	H	2B	3B	HR	RBI	BB	SO	SB	CS	AVG	OBP	SLG	OPS	OPS+	BR/A	RC	RC/G	FR	G/POS	WS	TPW
1991 KC-A	9	7	1	1	0	0	0	0	2	2	0	0	.143	.333	.143	.476	37	-0	1	2.28	-1	/2-5,D-2,S-1	0	-0.2

• COLE, Willis Willis Russell Cole b: 1/6/1882, Milton Junction, WI d: 10/11/1965, Madison, WI BR/TR, 5'8", 170 lbs. Deb: 8/22/1909 Career OF: 0-68-0

YEAR TM-L	G	AB	R	H	2B	3B	HR	RBI	BB	SO	SB	CS	AVG	OBP	SLG	OPS	OPS+	BR/A	RC	RC/G	FR	G/POS	WS	TPW
1909 Chi-A	46	165	17	39	7	3	0	16	16	....	3	....	.236	.308	.315	.623	101	0	17	3.36	-3	0-46(0-46-0)	5	-0.5

YEAR TM-L	G	AB	R	H	2B	3B	HR	RBI	BB	SO	SB	CS	AVG	OBP	SLG	OPS	OPS+	BR/A	RC	RC/G	FR	G/POS	WS	TPW
1910 Chi-A	22	80	6	14	2	1	0	2	4	....	0	....	.175	.224	.225	.449	43	-5	4	1.56	1	0-22(0-22-0)	1	-0.6
Total 2	68	245	23	53	9	4	0	18	20	....	3	....	.216	.281	.286	.567	82	-5	21	2.73	-1	/0-68	6	-1.1
• COLEMAN, Bob	Robert Hunter Coleman b: 9/26/1890, Huntingburg, IN d: 7/16/1959, Boston, MA BR/TR, 6'2", 190 lbs. Deb: 6/13/1913 M																							
1913 Pit-N	24	50	5	9	2	0	0	9	7	8	0	....	.180	.281	.220	.501	46	-3	3	1.96	1	C-24	1	-0.1
1914 Pit-N	73	150	11	40	4	1	1	14	15	32	3	....	.267	.333	.327	.660	101	0	17	3.85	-1	C-72	5	0.3
1916 Cle-A	19	28	3	6	2	0	0	4	7	6	0	....	.214	.371	.286	.657	92	0	3	3.61	1	C-12	1	0.1
Total 3	116	228	19	55	8	1	1	27	29	46	3	....	.241	.327	.298	.625	87	-3	23	3.36	-0	C-108	7	0.3
• COLEMAN, Choo Choo	Clarence Coleman b: 8/25/1937, Orlando, FL BL/TR, 5'9", 165 lbs. Deb: 4/16/1961																							
1961 Phi-N	34	47	3	6	1	0	0	4	2	8	0	0	.128	.180	.149	.329	-12	-8	1	.80	0	C-14	0	-0.7
1962 NY-N	55	152	24	38	7	2	6	17	11	24	2	4	.250	.305	.441	.746	96	-3	19	4.34	2	C-44	3	0.1
1963 NY-N	106	247	22	44	0	0	3	9	24	49	5	5	.178	.264	.215	.479	39	-19	15	1.84	1	C-91/0-1	2	-1.5
1966 NY-N	6	16	2	3	0	0	0	0	0	4	0	0	.188	.188	.188	.375	5	-2	1	1.17	0	/C-5	0	-0.2
Total 4	201	462	51	91	8	2	9	30	37	85	7	9	.197	.267	.281	.548	51	-32	36	2.48	3	C-154/0-1	5	-2.4
• COLEMAN, Curt	Curtis Hancock Coleman b: 2/18/1887, Salem, OR d: 7/1/1980, Newport, OR BL/TR, 5'11", 180 lbs. Deb: 4/13/1912																							
1912 NY-A	12	37	8	9	4	0	0	4	7	....	0	....	.243	.364	.351	.715	99	0	5	4.29	0	3-10	1	0.0
• COLEMAN, Dave	David Lee Coleman b: 10/26/1950, Dayton, OH BR/TR, 6'3", 195 lbs. Deb: 4/13/1977																							
1977 Bos-A	11	12	1	0	0	0	0	0	1	3	0	0	.000	.077	.000	.077	-69	-3	0	.05	-1	/0-9(3-5-1)	0	-0.4
• COLEMAN, Ed	Parke Edward Coleman b: 12/1/1901, Canby, OR d: 8/5/1964, Oregon City, OR BL/TR, 6'2", 200 lbs. Deb: 4/15/1932 Career OF: 1-0-311																							
1932 Phi-A	26	73	13	25	7	1	1	13	1	6	1	0	.342	.351	.507	.858	116	1	13	7.04	3	0-16(0-0-16)	2	0.3
1933 Phi-A	102	388	48	109	26	3	6	68	19	51	0	0	.281	.318	.410	.728	91	-6	50	4.74	-2	0-89(1-0-88)	8	-1.3
1934 Phi-A	101	329	53	92	14	6	14	60	29	34	0	1	.280	.342	.486	.828	116	5	55	6.06	1	0-86(0-0-86)	9	0.2
1935 Phi-A	10	13	0	1	0	0	0	0	0	3	0	0	.077	.077	.077	.154	-61	-3	0	.16	0	/0-1	0	-0.3
StL-A	108	397	66	114	15	9	17	71	53	41	0	2	.287	.373	.499	.871	118	10	75	6.88	-4	*0-102(0-0-102)	12	0.0
Yr.	118	410	66	115	15	9	17	71	53	44	0	2	.280	.364	.485	.850	113	6	75	6.61	-4	*0-103(0-0-103)	12	-0.3
1936 StL-A	92	137	13	40	5	4	2	34	15	17	0	0	.292	.366	.431	.797	93	-1	22	6.06	-2	0-18(0-0-18)	3	-0.4
Total 5	439	1337	193	381	67	23	40	246	117	152	1	3	.285	.345	.459	.804	106	6	215	5.90	-4	0-312	34	-1.5
• COLEMAN, Gordy	Gordon Calvin Coleman b: 7/5/1934, Rockville, MD d: 3/12/1994, Cincinnati, OH BL/TR, 6'3", 218 lbs. Deb: 9/19/1959																							
1959 Cle-A	6	15	5	8	0	1	0	2	1	2	0	0	.533	.563	.667	1.229	245	3	6	22.26	1	/1-3	2	0.3
1960 Cin-N	66	251	26	68	10	1	6	32	12	32	1	1	.271	.309	.390	.700	88	-5	31	4.34	7	1-66	5	-0.1
1961*Cin-N	150	520	63	149	27	4	26	87	45	67	1	3	.287	.346	.504	.850	120	13	88	6.06	10	*1-150	19	1.4
1962 Cin-N	136	476	73	132	13	1	28	86	36	68	2	3	.277	.332	.485	.817	112	6	73	5.44	2	*1-128	16	0.1
1963 Cin-N	123	365	38	90	20	2	14	59	29	51	1	0	.247	.306	.427	.733	105	3	47	4.48	0	*1-107	11	-0.3
1964 Cin-N	89	198	18	48	6	2	5	27	13	30	2	0	.242	.292	.369	.661	82	-4	20	3.34	3	1-49	3	-0.4
1965 Cin-N	108	325	39	98	19	0	14	57	24	38	0	0	.302	.351	.489	.841	125	11	55	6.30	-2	1-89	11	0.4
1966 Cin-N	91	227	20	57	7	0	5	37	16	45	2	1	.251	.300	.348	.648	73	-8	24	3.65	0	1-65	4	-1.1
1967 Cin-N	4	7	0	0	0	0	0	0	1	0	0	0	.000	.125	.000	.125	-55	-1	0	.00	0	/1-2	0	-0.1
Total 9	773	2384	282	650	102	11	98	387	177	333	9	8	.273	.326	.448	.774	106	17	344	5.10	21	1-659	71	0.1
• COLEMAN, Jerry	Gerald Francis Coleman b: 9/14/1924, San Jose, CA BR/TR, 6', 170 lbs. Deb: 4/20/1949 M																							
1949*NY-A	128	447	54	123	21	5	2	42	63	44	8	6	.275	.367	.358	.725	92	-4	62	4.74	15	*2-122/S-4	17	1.7
1950*NY-A★	153	522	69	150	19	6	6	69	67	38	3	2	.287	.372	.381	.753	96	-2	79	5.42	0	*2-152/S-6	19	0.7
1951*NY-A	121	362	48	90	11	2	3	43	31	36	6	1	.249	.315	.315	.630	73	-12	37	3.44	6	*2-102,S-18	10	0.0
1952 NY-A	11	42	6	17	2	1	0	4	5	4	0	1	.405	.468	.500	.968	180	4	10	10.59	3	2-11	3	0.8
1953 NY-A	8	10	1	2	0	0	0	0	0	2	0	0	.200	.200	.200	.400	9	-1	0	1.40	0	/2-7,S-1	0	-0.1
1954 NY-A	107	300	39	65	7	1	3	21	26	29	3	0	.217	.279	.277	.556	54	-18	24	2.56	6	2-79,S-30/3-1	6	-0.6
1955*NY-A	43	96	12	22	5	0	0	8	11	11	0	2	.229	.321	.281	.602	64	-5	9	2.82	1	S-29,2-13/3-1	2	-0.2
1956*NY-A	80	183	15	47	5	1	0	18	12	33	1	2	.257	.306	.295	.601	61	-11	16	2.87	1	2-41,S-24,3-18	4	-0.6
1957*NY-A	72	157	23	42	7	2	2	12	20	21	1	1	.268	.354	.376	.730	101	1	20	4.36	1	2-45,3-21/S-4	5	0.4
Total 9	723	2119	267	558	77	18	16	217	235	218	22	15	.263	.341	.339	.680	83	-49	257	4.13	32	2-572,S-116/3-41	66	2.0
• COLEMAN, John	John Francis Coleman b: 3/6/1863, Saratoga Springs, NY d: 5/31/1922, Detroit, MI BL/TR, 5'9.5", 170 lbs. Deb: 5/1/1883 U Career OF: 47-71-393 ♦																							
1883 Phi-N	90	354	33	83	12	8	0	32	15	39	....	....	.234	.266	.314	.579	82	5	30	3.07	4	*P-65,0-31(19-12-0)/2-1	8	-4.5
1884 Phi-N	43	171	16	42	7	2	0	22	8	20	....	....	.246	.279	.310	.589	89	1	15	3.23	-1	0-27(3-19-5),P-21/1-2	6	-2.4
Phi-a	28	107	16	22	2	3	2	0	5	....	....	....	.206	.241	.336	.578	81	-2	9	2.88	-1	0-24(11-13-0)/P-3,1-2	2	-0.4
1885 Phi-a	96	398	71	119	15	11	3	70	25	....	....	....	.299	.345	.415	.760	131	14	58	5.65	1	*0-93(1-17-76)/P-8	17	1.4
1886 Phi-a	121	492	67	121	18	16	0	65	33	....	28	....	.246	.296	.348	.644	100	-1	60	4.39	-1	*0-115(0-5-110)/1-6,P-3,2	15	-0.1
Pit-a	11	43	3	15	2	1	0	9	2	....	1	....	.349	.378	.442	.820	157	3	8	7.47	-1	0-11(11-0-0)	2	0.1
Yr.	132	535	70	136	20	17	0	74	35	....	29	....	.254	.302	.355	.658	105	2	68	4.61	-2	*0-126(11-5-110)/1-6,P-3,2	17	0.0
1887 Pit-N	115	506	75	170	21	11	2	54	31	40	25	....	.336	.337	.396	.733	109	7	74	5.81	-2	*0-115(0-2-113)/1-2	12	0.3
1888 Pit-N	116	438	49	101	11	4	0	26	29	52	15	....	.231	.285	.274	.558	85	-5	39	3.15	-1	0-91(0-3-88),1-25	9	-1.0
1889 Phi-a	6	19	1	1	0	0	0	1	1	3	1	....	.053	.100	.053	.153	-57	-3	0	.30	0	/P-5,0-1	2	-0.1
1890 Pit-N	3	11	1	2	0	0	0	0	3	0	1	....	.182	.357	.182	.539	66	0	1	3.23	-1	/0-2(1-0-1),P-2	0	-0.8
Total 8	629	2539	332	676	88	56	7	279	152	154	71	....	.266	.302	.345	.648	100	18	295	4.27	-1	0-510,P-107/1-37,2-2	73	-7.6
• COLEMAN, Michael	Michael Donnell Coleman b: 8/16/1975, Nashville, TN BR/TR, 5'11", 180 lbs. Deb: 9/1/1997 Career OF: 2-15-3																							
1997 Bos-A	8	24	2	4	1	0	0	2	0	11	1	0	.167	.167	.208	.375	-3	-3	1	1.24	-1	/0-7(0-7-0)	0	-0.4
1999 Bos-A	2	5	1	1	0	0	0	0	1	0	0	0	.200	.333	.200	.533	39	-0	0	2.84	0	/0-2(1-1-0)	0	-0.1
2001 NY-A	12	38	5	8	0	0	1	7	0	15	0	1	.211	.211	.289	.500	30	-4	2	1.74	-2	/0-9(1-7-3),D-3	0	-0.6
Total 3	22	67	8	13	1	0	1	9	1	26	1	1	.194	.206	.254	.460	19	-8	3	1.64	-3	/0-18,D-3	0	-1.1
• COLEMAN, Ray	Raymond Leroy Coleman b: 6/4/1922, Dunsmuir, CA BL/TR, 5'11", 170 lbs. Deb: 4/22/1947 Career OF: 151-147-202																							
1947 StL-A	110	343	34	89	9	7	2	30	26	32	2	5	.259	.314	.344	.658	81	-11	33	3.30	-1	0-93(21-0-73)	4	-1.5
1948 StL-A	17	29	2	5	0	1	0	2	2	5	1	0	.172	.226	.241	.467	24	-3	1	1.36	-1	/0-5(0-0-5)	0	-0.4
Phi-A	68	210	32	51	6	6	0	21	31	17	4	3	.243	.340	.329	.669	78	-6	23	3.46	1	0-53(0-32-21)	3	-0.6
Yr.	85	239	34	56	6	7	0	23	33	22	5	3	.234	.327	.318	.645	72	-9	25	3.19	1	0-58(0-32-26)	3	-1.0
1950 StL-A	117	384	54	104	25	6	8	55	32	37	7	5	.271	.330	.430	.760	90	-8	52	4.67	-3	0-98(27-43-28)	8	-1.4
1951 StL-A	91	341	41	96	16	5	5	55	24	32	3	4	.282	.329	.402	.731	94	-5	43	4.46	-1	0-87(47-5-42)	8	-1.1
Chi-A	51	181	21	50	8	7	3	21	15	14	2	3	.276	.332	.448	.779	112	1	26	4.94	0	0-51(23-29-12)	5	-0.2
Yr.	142	522	62	146	24	12	8	76	39	46	5	7	.280	.330	.418	.747	100	-4	69	4.63	-2	*0-138(70-34-54)	13	-1.2
1952 Chi-A	85	195	19	42	7	1	2	14	13	17	0	0	.215	.264	.292	.557	54	-12	15	2.44	-2	0-73(28-33-15)	2	-1.7
StL-A	20	46	5	9	3	0	0	1	5	4	0	0	.196	.288	.261	.549	52	-3	4	2.92	0	0-16(5-5-6)	1	-0.4
Yr.	105	241	24	51	10	1	2	15	18	21	0	0	.212	.269	.286	.556	54	-15	19	2.53	-2	0-89(33-38-21)	3	-2.1
Total 5	559	1729	208	446	74	33	20	199	148	158	19	20	.258	.318	.374	.692	84	-47	198	3.85	-6	0-476	31	-7.3
• COLEMAN, Vince	Vincent Maurice "Vincent Van Go" Coleman b: 9/22/1961, Jacksonville, FL BB/TR, 6', 185 lbs. Deb: 4/18/1985 Career OF: 1154-155-25																							
1985*StL-N	151	636	107	170	20	10	1	40	50	115	**110**	25	.267	.321	.335	.656	84	-1	79	4.29	5	*0-150(138-17-10)	20	-0.3
1986 StL-N	154	600	94	139	13	8	0	29	60	98	**107**	14	.232	.304	.280	.584	63	-12	67	3.69	-3	*0-149(131-20-0)	14	-2.3
1987*StL-N	151	623	121	180	14	10	3	43	70	126	**109**	22	.289	.364	.358	.721	90	7	96	5.44	3	*0-150(150-0-0)	24	0.3
1988 StL-N★	153	616	77	160	20	10	3	38	49	111	**81**	27	.260	.315	.339	.655	87	-5	71	3.84	1	*0-150(127-24-0)	14	-1.0
1989 StL-N★	145	563	94	143	21	9	2	28	50	90	**65**	10	.254	.317	.334	.651	84	-2	70	4.24	-8	*0-142(142-0-0)	11	-1.6
1990 StL-N	124	497	73	145	18	9	6	39	35	88	**77**	17	.292	.341	.400	.741	103	10	74	5.26	2	*0-120(118-0-2)	14	0.8
1991 NY-N	72	278	45	71	7	5	1	17	39	47	37	14	.255	.347	.327	.674	91	0	35	4.24	-1	0-70(0-70-0)	7	-0.2
1992 NY-N	71	229	37	63	11	1	2	21	27	41	24	9	.275	.357	.358	.715	104	3	32	4.87	-1	0-61(42-21-0)	9	0.1
1993 NY-N	92	373	64	104	14	8	2	25	21	58	38	13	.279	.317	.375	.693	86	-6	46	4.32	-2	0-90(90-0-0)	6	-1.1

YEAR TM-L	G	AB	R	H	2B	3B	HR	RBI	BB	SO	SB	CS	AVG	OBP	SLG	OPS	OPS+	BR/A	RC	RC/G	FR	G/POS	WS	TPW
1994 KC-A	104	438	61	105	14	12	2	33	29	72	50	8	.240	.288	.340	.629	59	-21	49	3.77	0	O-99(99-0-0)/D-5	8	-2.4
1995 KC-A	75	293	39	84	13	4	4	20	27	48	26	9	.287	.349	.399	.748	93	-1	41	4.88	2	O-69(57-2-13)/D-4	8	-0.2
*Sea-A	40	162	27	47	10	2	1	9	10	32	16	7	.290	.335	.395	.730	88	-3	22	4.66	1	O-38(38-0-0)	3	-0.3
Yr.	115	455	66	131	23	6	5	29	37	80	42	16	.288	.344	.398	.742	91	-4	63	4.80	3	*O-107(95-2-13)/D-4	11	-0.5
1996 Cin-N	33	84	10	13	1	1	1	4	9	31	12	2	.155	.237	.226	.463	23	-8	6	2.18	0	O-20(20-0-0)	0	-0.8
1997 Det-A	6	14	0	1	0	0	0	0	1	3	0	0	.071	.133	.071	.205	-45	-3	0	.16	0	/O-3(2-1-0),D-1	0	-0.3
Total 13	1371	5406	849	1425	176	89	28	346	477	960	752	177	.264	.325	.345	.670	83	-41	689	4.35	-1	*O-1311/D-10	138	-9.4

• COLES, Cad
Cadwallader Coles b: 1/17/1886, Rock Hill, SC d: 6/30/1942, Miami, FL BL/TR, 6'.5", 174 lbs. Deb: 4/16/1914

YEAR TM-L	G	AB	R	H	2B	3B	HR	RBI	BB	SO	SB	CS	AVG	OBP	SLG	OPS	OPS+	BR/A	RC	RC/G	FR	G/POS	WS	TPW
1914 KC-F	78	194	17	49	7	3	1	25	5	30	6	....	.253	.271	.335	.606	76	-7	18	3.10	-2	O-39(3-31-6)/1-3	2	-1.2

• COLES, Chuck
Charles Edward Coles b: 6/27/1931, Fredericktown, PA d: 1/25/1996, Myrtle Beach, SC BL/TL, 5'9", 180 lbs. Deb: 9/19/1958

YEAR TM-L	G	AB	R	H	2B	3B	HR	RBI	BB	SO	SB	CS	AVG	OBP	SLG	OPS	OPS+	BR/A	RC	RC/G	FR	G/POS	WS	TPW
1958 Cin-N	5	11	0	2	1	0	0	2	2	6	0	0	.182	.308	.273	.580	52	-1	1	3.25	1	/O-4(3-1-0)	0	0.0

• COLES, Darnell
Darnell Coles b: 6/2/1962, San Bernardino, CA BR/TR, 6'1", 185 lbs. Deb: 9/4/1983 Career OF: 123-0-228

YEAR TM-L	G	AB	R	H	2B	3B	HR	RBI	BB	SO	SB	CS	AVG	OBP	SLG	OPS	OPS+	BR/A	RC	RC/G	FR	G/POS	WS	TPW
1983 Sea-A	27	92	9	26	7	0	1	6	7	12	0	3	.283	.333	.391	.725	95	-2	8	2.92	-3	3-26	1	-0.5
1984 Sea-A	48	143	15	23	3	1	0	6	17	26	2	1	.161	.259	.196	.455	28	-13	8	1.62	-5	3-42/D-3,O-3(3-0-0)	0	-1.9
1985 Sea-A	27	59	8	14	4	0	1	5	9	17	0	1	.237	.348	.356	.704	93	-1	8	4.49	-1	S-15/3-7,D-2,O-2(2-0-0)	2	-0.1
1986 Det-A	142	521	67	142	30	2	20	86	45	84	6	2	.273	.337	.453	.790	113	9	81	5.40	-2	*3-133/D-7,O-2(0-0-2),S-2	17	0.5
1987 Det-A	53	149	14	27	5	1	4	15	15	23	0	1	.181	.265	.309	.574	54	-11	13	2.73	-6	3-36/1-9,O-8(2-0-6),D-3,S	1	-1.6
Pit-N	40	119	20	27	8	0	6	24	19	20	1	3	.227	.338	.445	.784	105	-0	17	4.54	-2	O-26(1-0-26),3-10/1-1	3	-0.3
1988 Pit-N	68	211	20	49	13	1	5	36	20	41	1	1	.232	.308	.374	.682	96	-2	25	3.91	-4	O-55(0-0-55)/1-1,3-1	6	-0.8
Sea-A	55	195	32	57	10	1	10	34	17	26	3	2	.292	.361	.508	.869	134	9	35	6.28	0	O-47(43-0-4)/D-7,1-1	6	0.7
1989 Sea-A	146	535	54	135	21	3	10	59	27	61	5	4	.252	.296	.359	.655	81	-15	54	3.47	3	O-89(7-0-83),3-26,1-18,D-12	8	-1.7
1990 Sea-A	37	107	9	23	5	1	2	16	4	17	0	0	.215	.250	.336	.586	62	-6	9	2.82	1	O-20(0-0-20)/3-6,1-4,D-1	1	-0.6
Det-A	52	108	13	22	2	0	1	4	12	21	0	4	.204	.283	.250	.533	50	-9	7	1.94	1	D-30,O-11(4-0-9)/3-8	1	-0.9
Yr.	89	215	22	45	7	1	3	20	16	38	0	4	.209	.267	.293	.560	56	-15	16	2.36	2	D-31,O-31(4-0-29),3-14/1-4	2	-1.4
1991 SF-N	11	14	1	3	0	0	0	0	0	2	0	0	.214	.214	.214	.429	22	-1	0	.96	-1	/O-3(0-0-3),1-1	0	-0.2
1992 Cin-N	55	141	16	44	11	2	3	18	3	15	1	0	.312	.326	.482	.809	123	4	22	5.82	-1	3-23,1-20/O-5(3-0-2)	7	0.2
1993 Tor-A	64	194	26	49	9	1	4	26	16	29	1	1	.253	.322	.371	.694	85	-4	24	4.20	-5	O-44(31-0-13),3-16/1-1,D-1	4	-1.1
1994 Tor-A	48	143	15	30	6	1	4	15	10	25	0	0	.210	.266	.350	.616	57	-10	13	3.11	-4	O-29(24-0-5),1-10/3-7,D-1	1	-1.4
1995 StL-N	63	138	13	31	7	0	3	16	16	20	0	0	.225	.318	.341	.659	74	-5	16	4.01	-2	3-22,1-18/O-1	2	-0.8
1997 Col-N	21	22	1	7	1	0	1	2	0	6	0	0	.318	.348	.500	.848	97	-0	4	7.05	0	/3-3,O-2(2-0-0)	0	0.0
Total 14	957	2891	333	709	142	14	75	368	237	445	20	23	.245	.310	.382	.692	88	-58	345	4.01	-32	3-366,O-347/1-84,D-67,S-18	60	-10.6

• COLETTA, Chris
Christopher Michael Coletta b: 8/2/1944, Brooklyn, NY BL/TL, 5'11", 190 lbs. Deb: 8/15/1972

YEAR TM-L	G	AB	R	H	2B	3B	HR	RBI	BB	SO	SB	CS	AVG	OBP	SLG	OPS	OPS+	BR/A	RC	RC/G	FR	G/POS	WS	TPW
1972 Cal-A	14	30	5	9	1	0	1	7	1	4	0	0	.300	.323	.433	.756	131	1	4	4.72	0	/O-7(5-0-2)	1	0.0

• COLGAN, Ed
William H. Colgan b: East St. Louis, IL d: 8/8/1895, Great Falls, MT, 180 lbs. Deb: 5/3/1884

YEAR TM-L	G	AB	R	H	2B	3B	HR	RBI	BB	SO	SB	CS	AVG	OBP	SLG	OPS	OPS+	BR/A	RC	RC/G	FR	G/POS	WS	TPW
1884 Pit-a	48	161	10	25	4	1	0	0	3	....	....	....	.155	.171	.193	.363	18	-14	5	1.10	0	C-44/O-4(2-0-2)	2	-1.0

• COLLIER, Lou
Louis Keith Collier b: 8/21/1973, Chicago, IL BR/TR, 5'10", 170 lbs. Deb: 6/28/1997 Career OF: 30-22-2

YEAR TM-L	G	AB	R	H	2B	3B	HR	RBI	BB	SO	SB	CS	AVG	OBP	SLG	OPS	OPS+	BR/A	RC	RC/G	FR	G/POS	WS	TPW
1997 Pit-N	18	37	3	5	0	0	0	3	1	11	1	0	.135	.158	.135	.293	-22	-6	1	.62	2	S-18	1	-0.3
1998 Pit-N	110	334	30	82	13	6	2	34	31	70	2	2	.246	.321	.338	.659	73	-13	36	3.63	7	*S-107	8	0.1
1999 Mil-N	74	135	18	35	9	0	2	21	14	32	3	2	.259	.329	.370	.699	77	-5	17	4.24	-4	S-31,O-10(9-0-1)/3-7,2-4	2	-0.7
2000 Mil-N	14	32	9	7	1	0	1	2	6	4	0	0	.219	.342	.344	.686	75	-1	4	4.02	0	O-10(5-7-0)/3-1	0	-0.1
2001 Mil-N	50	127	19	32	8	1	2	14	17	30	5	1	.252	.345	.378	.723	89	-1	19	5.13	0	O-23(12-11-0),3-16/D-1	4	-0.1
2002 Mon-N	13	11	3	1	1	0	0	0	1	3	0	0	.091	.231	.182	.413	10	-1	1	1.46	-1	/O-7(3-3-1),2-2,3-1	0	-0.2
2003 Bos-A	4	1	0	0	0	0	0	0	0	0	0	1	.000	.000	.000	.000	-98	-1	0	.00	0	/3-2,O-2(1-1-0)	0	-0.1
Total 7	283	677	82	162	32	7	7	74	70	150	11	6	.239	.318	.338	.656	71	-29	77	3.80	6	S-156/O-52,3-27,2-6,D-1	15	-1.3

• COLLINS,
Collins Deb: 9/12/1892

YEAR TM-L	G	AB	R	H	2B	3B	HR	RBI	BB	SO	SB	CS	AVG	OBP	SLG	OPS	OPS+	BR/A	RC	RC/G	FR	G/POS	WS	TPW
1892 StL-N	1	2	0	0	0	0	0	0	0	0	0	....	.000	.000	.000	.000	-105	-0	0	.00	-0	/O-1	0	-0.1

• COLLINS, Bill
William J. Collins b: 1863, Dublin, Ireland d: 6/8/1893, Brooklyn, NY BR Deb: 8/1/1887

YEAR TM-L	G	AB	R	H	2B	3B	HR	RBI	BB	SO	SB	CS	AVG	OBP	SLG	OPS	OPS+	BR/A	RC	RC/G	FR	G/POS	WS	TPW
1887 NY-a	1	4	0	1	0	0	0	0	0	....	0	....	.250	.250	.250	.500	41	-0	0	2.31	-1	/C-1	0	-0.1
1889 Phi-a	1	4	0	1	0	0	0	1	1	0	1	....	.250	.400	.250	.650	88	0	1	7.24	0	/C-1	0	0.0
1890 Phi-a	1	1	0	0	0	0	0	0	0	....	0	....	.000	.000	.000	.000	-102	-0	0	.00	-1	/S-1	0	-0.1
1891 Cle-N	2	3	0	0	0	0	0	0	0	0	0	....	.000	.000	.000	.000	-96	-1	0	.00	1	/C-1,O-1	0	0.0
Total 4	5	12	0	2	0	0	0	1	1	0	1	....	.167	.231	.167	.397	16	-1	1	2.86	-1	/C-3,O-1,S-1	0	-0.2

• COLLINS, Bill
William Shirley Collins b: 3/27/1882, Chesterton, IN d: 6/26/1961, San Berardino, CA BB/TR, 6', 170 lbs. Deb: 4/14/1910 Career OF: 149-36-28

YEAR TM-L	G	AB	R	H	2B	3B	HR	RBI	BB	SO	SB	CS	AVG	OBP	SLG	OPS	OPS+	BR/A	RC	RC/G	FR	G/POS	WS	TPW
1910 Bos-N	151	584	67	141	6	7	3	40	43	48	36	....	.241	.308	.291	.599	72	-21	63	3.57	18	*O-151(129-10-13)	11	-1.2
1911 Bos-N	17	44	8	6	1	1	0	8	1	8	4	....	.136	.156	.205	.360		-6	2	1.26	0	O-13(3-8-2)/3-1	0	-0.7
Chi-N	7	3	2	1	1	0	0	0	1	0	0	....	.333	.500	.667	1.167	225	1	1	12.93	-1	/O-4(2-2-0)	0	0.0
Yr.	24	47	10	7	2	1	0	8	2	8	4	....	.149	.184	.234	.418	18	-6	3	1.80	-1	O-17(5-10-2)/3-1	0	-0.7
1913 Bro-N	32	95	8	18	1	0	0	4	8	11	2	....	.189	.267	.200	.467	33	-8	5	1.76	-4	O-27(13-15-0)	0	-1.4
1914 Buf-F	21	47	6	7	2	2	0	2	1	8	0	....	.149	.167	.277	.443	24	-5	2	1.26	1	O-15(2-1-13)	0	-0.5
Total 4	228	773	91	173	11	10	3	54	54	75	42	....	.224	.287	.276	.563	61	-40	74	3.06	14	O-210/3-1	11	-3.8

• COLLINS, Chub
Charles Augustine Collins b: 10/12/1857, Dundas, Canada d: 5/20/1914, Dundas, Canada BB, 5'11.5", 165 lbs. Deb: 5/1/1884

YEAR TM-L	G	AB	R	H	2B	3B	HR	RBI	BB	SO	SB	CS	AVG	OBP	SLG	OPS	OPS+	BR/A	RC	RC/G	FR	G/POS	WS	TPW
1884 Buf-N	45	169	24	30	6	0	0	20	14	36	....	....	.178	.240	.213	.453	42	-11	9	1.76	4	2-42/S-3	2	-0.5
Ind-a	38	138	18	31	3	1	0	0	9	....	....	....	.225	.272	.261	.533	77	-3	10	2.58	-7	2-38	2	-0.8
1885 Det-N	14	55	8	10	0	2	0	6	0	11	....	....	.182	.182	.255	.436	40	-4	3	1.57	-5	S-14	0	-0.8
Total 2	97	362	50	71	9	3	0	26	23	47	....	....	.196	.244	.238	.482	55	-18	22	2.03	-8	/2-80,S-17	4	-2.1

• COLLINS, Dan
Daniel Thomas Collins b: 7/12/1854, St. Louis, MO d: 9/21/1883, New Orleans, LA Deb: 6/8/1874 U

YEAR TM-L	G	AB	R	H	2B	3B	HR	RBI	BB	SO	SB	CS	AVG	OBP	SLG	OPS	OPS+	BR/A	RC	RC/G	FR	G/POS	WS	TPW
1874 Chi-n	3	12	1	1	1	0	0	0	0	2	1	0	.083	.083	.167	.250	-22	-1	0	.70	0	/O-2(0-0-2),P-2,S-1	....	-1.2
1876 Lou-N	7	28	3	4	1	0	0	9	0	2			.143	.143	.179	.321	5	-3	1	.85	1	/O-7(0-2-5)	0	-0.2

• COLLINS, Dave
David S. Collins b: 10/20/1952, Rapid City, SD BB/TL, 5'11", 175 lbs. Deb: 6/7/1975 C Career OF: 716-204-220

YEAR TM-L	G	AB	R	H	2B	3B	HR	RBI	BB	SO	SB	CS	AVG	OBP	SLG	OPS	OPS+	BR/A	RC	RC/G	FR	G/POS	WS	TPW
1975 Cal-A	93	319	41	85	13	4	3	29	36	55	24	10	.266	.343	.361	.703	106	4	42	4.44	3	O-75(74-1-0),D-12	10	0.2
1976 Cal-A	99	365	45	96	12	1	4	28	40	55	32	19	.263	.336	.334	.670	103	1	43	3.85	3	O-71(52-19-0),D-22	12	-0.1
1977 Sea-A	120	402	46	96	9	3	5	28	33	66	25	10	.239	.301	.313	.615	69	-16	41	3.39	2	O-73(67-3-3),D-40	6	-1.8
1978 Cin-N	102	102	13	22	1	0	0	7	15	18	7	7	.216	.316	.225	.542	54	-7	7	2.20	1	O-24(3-17-4)	0	-0.7
1979*Cin-N	122	396	59	126	16	4	3	35	27	48	16	9	.318	.365	.402	.766	108	4	58	5.38	-5	O-91(45-3-50),1-10	12	-0.6
1980 Cin-N	144	551	94	167	20	4	3	35	53	68	79	21	.303	.367	.370	.738	106	14	84	5.47	-3	*O-141(18-119-6)	22	0.9
1981 Cin-N	95	360	63	98	18	6	3	23	41	41	26	10	.272	.356	.381	.737	107	6	52	4.93	-2	O-94(1-0-93)	14	0.0
1982 NY-A	111	348	41	88	12	3	3	25	28	49	13	8	.253	.318	.330	.648	80	-10	37	3.49	-2	O-60(20-20-25),1-52/D-1	5	-1.7
1983 Tor-A	118	402	55	109	12	4	1	34	43	67	31	7	.271	.345	.328	.673	81	-5	50	4.36	2	*O-112(112-2-1)/1-5,D-1	10	-0.8
1984 Tor-A	128	441	59	136	24	**15**	2	44	33	41	60	14	.308	.369	.444	.813	119	19	81	6.66	-3	*O-108(106-2-0)/1-6,D-4	17	1.1
1985 Oak-A	112	379	52	95	16	4	4	29	29	37	29	8	.251	.306	.346	.651	84	-5	42	3.69	-6	O-91(91-0-0)	8	-1.5
1986 Det-A	124	419	44	113	18	2	1	27	44	49	27	12	.270	.342	.329	.671	84	-7	49	3.93	1	O-94(76-10-11),D-24	9	-1.1
1987 Cin-N	57	85	19	25	5	0	0	5	11	12	9	0	.294	.388	.353	.741	94	2	14	6.20	-1	O-21(18-2-1)	3	0.0
1988 Cin-N	99	174	12	41	6	2	0	14	11	27	7	2	.236	.289	.293	.582	65	-7	16	3.20	0	O-35(13-5-18)/1-3	3	-0.9
1989 Cin-N	78	106	12	25	4	0	0	7	10	17	3	1	.236	.302	.274	.575	63	-5	9	2.91	1	O-16(16-0-0)	1	-0.5
1990 StL-N	99	58	12	13	1	0	0	3	13	10	7	1	.224	.366	.241	.608	70	-0	7	3.86	-5	1-49,O-12(4-1-8)	1	-0.7
Total 16	1701	4907	667	1335	187	52	32	373	467	660	395	139	.272	.340	.351	.691	93	-13	633	4.42	-16	*O-1118,1-125,D-104	133	-8.3

• COLLINS, Eddie
Edward Trowbridge "Cocky" Collins, Sr. b: 5/2/1887, Millerton, NY d: 3/25/1951, Boston, MA BL/TR, 5'9", 175 lbs. Deb: 9/17/1906 M/C HOF: 1939

YEAR TM-L	G	AB	R	H	2B	3B	HR	RBI	BB	SO	SB	CS	AVG	OBP	SLG	OPS	OPS+	BR/A	RC	RC/G	FR	G/POS	WS	TPW
1906 Phi-A	6	15	2	3	0	0	0	0	0	....	1	....	.200	.200	.200	.400	25	-1	1	1.57	0	/S-3,2-1,3-1	0	-0.2
1907 Phi-A	14	23	0	8	0	1	0	2	0	....	0	....	.348	.348	.435	.783	146	1	4	6.07	-2	/S-6	0	0.0

YEAR TM-L	G	AB	R	H	2B	3B	HR	RBI	BB	SO	SB	CS	AVG	OBP	SLG	OPS	OPS+	BR/A	RC	RC/G	FR	G/POS	WS	TPW
1908 Phi-A	102	330	39	90	18	7	1	40	16	....	8	....	.273	.312	.379	.691	116	5	42	4.23	-7	2-47,S-28,0-10(2-3-5)	11	-0.2
1909 Phi-A	153	571	104	198	30	10	3	56	62	....	63	....	.347	.416	.450	.866	170	47	134	8.85	24	*2-152/S-1	43	**8.3**
1910*Phi-A	153	581	81	188	16	15	3	81	49	....	**81**	....	.324	.382	.418	.800	152	34	123	7.68	48	*2-153	39	**9.3**
1911*Phi-A	132	493	92	180	22	13	3	73	62	....	38	....	.365	.451	.481	.932	163	46	124	9.75	13	*2-132	35	5.9
1912 Phi-A	153	543	**137**	189	25	11	0	64	101	....	63	....	.348	.450	.435	.885	159	49	136	9.24	20	*2-153	36	**7.1**
1913*Phi-A	148	534	**125**	184	23	13	3	73	85	37	55	....	.345	.441	.453	.894	165	49	126	8.58	19	*2-148	**39**	**7.5**
1914*Phi-A	152	526	**122**	181	23	14	2	85	97	31	58	30	.344	**.452**	.452	.904	**179**	**57**	120	**7.91**	6	*2-152	43	**7.3**
1915 Chi-A	155	521	118	173	22	10	4	77	**119**	27	46	30	.332	.460	.436	.896	163	47	116	7.45	18	*2-155	40	**7.2**
1916 Chi-A	155	545	87	168	14	17	0	52	86	36	40	21	.308	.405	.396	.802	139	29	99	5.91	6	*2-155	31	4.3
1917*Chi-A	156	564	91	163	18	12	0	67	89	16	53	....	.289	.389	.363	.752	127	23	98	5.89	3	*2-156	32	3.2
1918 Chi-A	97	330	51	91	8	2	2	30	73	13	22	....	.276	.407	.330	.737	121	14	54	5.30	6	2-96	16	2.4
1919*Chi-A	140	518	87	165	19	7	4	80	68	27	**33**	....	.319	.400	.405	.805	126	21	97	6.44	10	*2-140	27	3.5
1920 Chi-A	153	602	117	224	38	13	3	76	69	19	20	8	.372	.438	.493	.932	146	45	134	8.45	24	*2-153	38	7.0
1921 Chi-A	139	526	79	177	20	10	2	58	66	11	12	10	.337	.412	.424	.836	115	14	94	6.71	14	*2-136	21	3.0
1922 Chi-A	154	598	92	194	20	12	1	69	73	16	20	12	.324	.401	.403	.804	110	13	101	6.02	-7	*2-154	23	1.0
1923 Chi-A	145	505	89	182	22	5	5	67	84	8	**48**	29	.360	.455	.453	.909	141	35	108	7.35	-1	*2-142	24	3.7
1924 Chi-A	152	556	108	194	27	7	6	86	89	16	**42**	17	.349	.441	.455	.896	136	38	119	7.78	-9	*2-150	25	3.1
1925 Chi-A	118	425	80	147	26	3	3	80	87	8	19	6	.346	.461	.442	.904	137	34	96	8.46	-8	*2-116	22	2.7
1926 Chi-A	106	375	66	129	32	4	1	62	62	8	13	8	.344	.441	.459	.900	140	26	80	7.86	-3	*2-101	17	2.4
1927 Phi-A	95	226	50	76	12	1	1	15	56	9	6	2	.336	.468	.412	.880	123	13	49	8.18	-3	2-56/S-1	11	1.1
1928 Phi-A	36	33	3	10	3	0	0	7	4	4	0	0	.303	.378	.394	.772	100	0	5	5.88	-1	/2-2,S-1	1	-0.1
1929 Phi-A	9	7	0	0	0	0	0	0	2	0	0	0	.000	.222	.000	.222	-37	-1	0	.42	0	....	0	-0.1
1930 Phi-A	3	2	1	1	0	0	0	0	0	0	0	0	.500	.500	.500	1.000	148	0	0	12.72	0	....	0	0.0
Total 25	2826	9949	1821	3315	438	187	47	1300	1499	286	741	173	.333	.424	.429	.853	143	637	2062	7.38	170	*2-2650/S-40,0-10,3-1	574	89.4

• COLLINS, Eddie Edward Trowbridge Collins, Jr. b: 11/23/1916, Lansdowne, PA d: 11/2/2000, Jennersville, PA BL/TR, 5'10", 175 lbs. Deb: 7/4/1939 Career OF: 5-12-50

YEAR TM-L	G	AB	R	H	2B	3B	HR	RBI	BB	SO	SB	CS	AVG	OBP	SLG	OPS	OPS+	BR/A	RC	RC/G	FR	G/POS	WS	TPW
1939 Phi-A	32	21	6	5	1	0	0	0	0	3	1	0	.238	.238	.286	.524	34	-2	2	2.62	-1	/0-6(0-0-6),2-1	0	-0.3
1941 Phi-A	80	219	29	53	6	3	0	12	20	24	2	1	.242	.305	.297	.602	61	-12	21	3.26	0	0-50(4-9-38)	2	-1.4
1942 Phi-A	20	34	6	8	2	0	0	4	4	2	1	0	.235	.316	.294	.610	72	-1	4	3.87	-1	/0-9(1-3-6)	1	-0.2
Total 3	132	274	41	66	9	3	0	16	24	29	4	1	.241	.302	.296	.598	61	-15	26	3.29	-2	/0-65,2-1	3	-1.9

• COLLINS, Hub Hubert B. Collins b: 4/15/1864, Louisville, KY d: 5/21/1892, Brooklyn, NY BR/TR, 5'8", 160 lbs. Deb: 9/4/1886 Career OF: 241-31-0

YEAR TM-L	G	AB	R	H	2B	3B	HR	RBI	BB	SO	SB	CS	AVG	OBP	SLG	OPS	OPS+	BR/A	RC	RC/G	FR	G/POS	WS	TPW
1886 Lou-a	27	101	12	29	3	2	0	10	5	....	7	....	.287	.321	.356	.677	106	0	14	5.30	0	0-24(22-2-0)/3-2,1-1,2-1,S	3	-0.1
1887 Lou-a	130	598	122	201	22	8	1	66	39	....	71	....	.336	.338	.363	.701	94	-6	95	6.46	0	*0-109(109-0-0),2-10/1-8,S,3	13	-0.8
1888 Lou-a	116	485	117	149	26	11	2	50	41	....	62	....	.307	.366	.419	.785	154	30	99	7.99	6	0-82(57-26-0),2-19,S-15	20	3.2
Bro-a	12	42	16	13	5	1	0	3	9	....	9	....	.310	.442	.476	.918	195	5	13	12.24	-1	2-12	3	0.4
Yr.	128	527	133	162	**31**	12	2	53	50	....	71	....	.307	.373	.423	.796	158	35	113	8.33	5	0-82(57-26-0),2-31,S-15	23	3.6
1889*Bro-a	138	560	139	149	18	3	2	73	80	41	65	....	.266	.365	.320	.684	95	0	91	5.88	9	*2-138	24	1.2
1890*Bro-N	129	510	**148**	142	32	7	3	69	85	47	85	....	.278	.385	.386	.771	124	19	111	8.01	12	*2-129	28	3.1
1891 Bro-N	107	435	82	120	16	5	3	31	59	63	32	....	.276	.365	.356	.721	111	8	70	6.00	-14	2-72,0-35(32-3-0)	12	-0.4
1892 Bro-N	21	87	17	26	5	1	0	17	14	13	4	....	.299	.396	.379	.775	140	5	15	6.65	-2	0-21(21-0-0)	3	0.1
Total 7	680	2818	653	829	127	38	11	319	332	164	335	....	.294	.365	.369	.734	116	61	509	6.86	9	2-381,0-271/S-20,1-9,3-3	106	6.6

• COLLINS, Jimmy James Joseph Collins b: 1/16/1870, Buffalo, NY d: 3/6/1943, Buffalo, NY BR/TR, 5'9", 178 lbs. Deb: 4/19/1895 M HOF: 1945

YEAR TM-L	G	AB	R	H	2B	3B	HR	RBI	BB	SO	SB	CS	AVG	OBP	SLG	OPS	OPS+	BR/A	RC	RC/G	FR	G/POS	WS	TPW
1895 Bos-N	11	38	10	8	3	0	1	8	4	4	0	....	.211	.302	.368	.671	69	-2	4	3.89	-1	0-10(0-0-10)	0	-0.3
Lou-N	96	373	65	104	17	5	6	49	33	16	12	....	.279	.352	.399	.751	100	1	58	5.80	15	3-77,0-18(0-7-11)/2-2,S-1	10	1.3
Yr.	107	411	75	112	20	5	7	57	37	20	12	....	.273	.347	.397	.744	97	-1	63	5.60	14	3-77,0-28(0-7-21)/2-2,S-1	10	1.0
1896 Bos-N	84	304	48	90	10	9	1	46	30	12	10	....	.296	.374	.398	.772	98	-1	51	6.12	17	3-80/S-4	11	1.5
1897*Bos-N	134	529	103	183	28	13	6	132	41	....	14	....	.346	.400	.482	.882	125	17	111	8.33	27	*3-134	26	4.0
1898 Bos-N	152	597	107	196	35	5	**15**	111	40	....	12	....	.328	.377	.479	.856	138	26	117	7.46	25	*3-152	**34**	5.0
1899 Bos-N	151	599	98	166	28	11	5	92	40	....	12	....	.277	.335	.386	.721	89	-12	84	5.07	33	*3-151	23	2.2
1900 Bos-N	142	586	104	178	25	5	6	95	34	....	23	....	.304	.352	.394	.747	94	-6	93	5.90	22	*3-141/S-1	18	1.6
1901 Bos-A	138	564	108	187	42	16	6	94	34	....	19	....	.332	.375	.495	.869	142	30	116	7.87	17	*3-138	28	4.6
1902 Bos-A	108	429	71	138	21	10	6	61	24	....	18	....	.322	.360	.459	.820	123	12	81	6.94	10	*3-107	20	2.4
1903*Bos-A	130	540	88	160	33	17	5	72	24	....	23	....	.296	.329	.448	.777	125	14	90	6.09	12	*3-130	26	3.1
1904 Bos-A	156	631	85	171	33	13	3	67	27	....	19	....	.271	.306	.379	.685	110	5	82	4.61	17	*3-156	28	3.0
1905 Bos-A	131	508	66	140	26	5	4	65	37	....	18	....	.276	.330	.370	.700	121	11	71	4.97	8	*3-131	23	2.5
1906 Bos-A	37	142	17	39	8	4	1	16	4	....	1	....	.275	.295	.408	.703	120	2	18	4.54	1	3-32	4	0.4
1907 Bos-A	41	158	13	46	8	0	0	10	10	....	4	....	.291	.333	.342	.675	116	3	21	4.62	-5	3-41	4	-0.2
Phi-A	99	364	38	99	21	0	0	35	24	....	4	....	.272	.331	.330	.660	108	4	43	4.19	-2	3-98	12	0.5
Yr.	140	522	51	145	29	0	0	45	34	....	8	....	.278	.332	.333	.665	111	6	64	4.32	-7	*3-139	16	0.4
1908 Phi-A	115	433	34	94	14	3	0	30	20	....	5	....	.217	.258	.263	.521	65	-17	31	2.26	-2	*3-115	7	-1.8
Total 14	1725	6795	1055	1999	352	116	65	983	426	32	194	....	.294	.343	.409	.752	112	87	1072	5.75	193	*3-1683/0-28,S-6,2-2	274	29.9

• COLLINS, Joe Joseph Edward Collins b: 12/3/1922, Scranton, PA d: 8/30/1989, Union, NJ BL/TL, 6', 185 lbs. Deb: 9/25/1948 Career OF: 27-9-83

YEAR TM-L	G	AB	R	H	2B	3B	HR	RBI	BB	SO	SB	CS	AVG	OBP	SLG	OPS	OPS+	BR/A	RC	RC/G	FR	G/POS	WS	TPW
1948 NY-A	5	5	0	1	1	0	0	2	0	1	0	0	.200	.200	.400	.600	58	-0	0	2.77	0	....	0	0.0
1949 NY-A	7	10	2	1	0	0	0	4	6	2	0	0	.100	.438	.100	.538	46	-0	1	3.39	-1	/1-5	0	-0.1
1950*NY-A	108	205	47	48	8	3	8	28	31	34	5	0	.234	.335	.420	.754	95	-1	31	5.19	-0	1-99/0-2(0-0-2)	6	-0.3
1951*NY-A	125	262	52	75	8	5	9	48	34	23	9	7	.286	.368	.458	.826	127	9	44	5.92	3	*1-114,0-15(0-0-15)	11	0.9
1952*NY-A	122	428	69	120	16	8	18	59	55	47	4	2	.280	.364	.481	.845	142	24	77	6.36	-2	*1-119	18	1.8
1953*NY-A	127	387	72	104	11	2	17	44	59	36	2	6	.269	.365	.439	.805	121	10	65	5.84	-1	*1-113/0-4(0-0-4)	14	0.3
1954 NY-A	130	343	67	93	20	2	12	46	51	37	2	2	.271	.365	.446	.812	126	12	58	6.03	-1	*1-117	15	0.7
1955*NY-A	105	278	40	65	9	1	13	45	44	32	0	2	.234	.343	.414	.756	104	1	40	4.74	6	1-73,0-27(0-0-27)	9	0.3
1956*NY-A	100	262	38	59	5	3	7	43	34	33	3	1	.225	.316	.347	.664	78	-8	30	3.83	3	0-51(25-7-24),1-43	6	-0.9
1957*NY-A	79	149	17	30	1	0	2	10	24	18	2	1	.201	.312	.248	.560	56	-8	12	2.69	-1	1-32,0-15(2-2-11)	2	-1.1
Total 10	908	2329	404	596	79	24	86	329	338	263	27	21	.256	.351	.421	.772	112	38	360	5.31	6	1-715,0-114	81	1.6

• COLLINS, Kevin Kevin Michael "Casey" Collins b: 8/4/1946, Springfield, MA BL/TR, 6'1", 190 lbs. Deb: 9/1/1965

YEAR TM-L	G	AB	R	H	2B	3B	HR	RBI	BB	SO	SB	CS	AVG	OBP	SLG	OPS	OPS+	BR/A	RC	RC/G	FR	G/POS	WS	TPW
1965 NY-N	11	23	3	4	1	0	0	0	1	9	0	1	.174	.208	.217	.426	21	-3	1	1.18	0	/3-7,S-3	0	-0.3
1967 NY-N	4	10	1	1	0	0	0	0	0	3	1	0	.100	.100	.100	.200	-43	-2	0	.00	0	/2-2	0	-0.1
1968 NY-N	58	154	12	31	5	2	1	13	7	37	0	1	.201	.236	.279	.515	54	-9	10	2.03	-1	3-40/2-6,S-1	1	-1.2
1969 NY-N	16	40	1	6	3	0	1	2	3	10	0	0	.150	.209	.300	.509	40	-3	3	2.08	0	3-14	0	-0.4
Mon-N	52	96	5	23	5	1	2	12	8	16	0	0	.240	.298	.375	.673	87	-2	11	3.75	-4	2-20,3-16	2	-0.6
Yr.	68	136	6	29	8	1	3	14	11	26	0	0	.213	.272	.353	.625	74	-5	13	3.24	-5	3-30,2-20	2	-1.0
1970 Det-A	25	24	2	5	1	0	1	3	1	10	0	0	.208	.240	.375	.615	67	-1	2	3.16	0	/1-1	0	-0.1
1971 Det-A	35	41	6	11	2	1	1	4	0	12	0	0	.268	.268	.439	.707	94	-1	4	3.82	0	/3-4,0-2(1-0-1),2-1	1	-0.1
Total 6	201	388	30	81	17	4	6	34	20	97	1	2	.209	.248	.320	.567	61	-21	31	2.57	-6	/3-81,2-29,S-4,0-2,1-1	4	-2.8

• COLLINS, Orth Orth Stein "Buck" Collins b: 4/27/1880, Lafayette, IN d: 12/13/1949, Fort Lauderdale, FL BL/TR, 6', 150 lbs. Deb: 6/1/1904 Career OF: 0-6-2

YEAR TM-L	G	AB	R	H	2B	3B	HR	RBI	BB	SO	SB	CS	AVG	OBP	SLG	OPS	OPS+	BR/A	RC	RC/G	FR	G/POS	WS	TPW
1904 NY-A	5	17	3	6	1	1	0	1	1	....	0	....	.353	.389	.529	.918	180	1	4	8.64	3	/0-5(0-5-1)	1	0.5
1909 Was-A	8	7	0	0	0	0	0	0	0	....	0	....	.000	.000	.000	.000	-105	-2	0	.00	0	/0-2(0-1-1),P-1	0	-0.2
Total 2	13	24	3	6	1	1	0	1	1	....	0	....	.250	.280	.375	.655	100	-0	4	5.28	3	/0-7,P-1	1	0.3

• COLLINS, Pat Tharon Leslie Collins b: 9/13/1896, Sweet Springs, MO d: 5/20/1960, Kansas City, KS BR/TR, 5'11.5", 178 lbs. Deb: 9/5/1919

YEAR TM-L	G	AB	R	H	2B	3B	HR	RBI	BB	SO	SB	CS	AVG	OBP	SLG	OPS	OPS+	BR/A	RC	RC/G	FR	G/POS	WS	TPW
1919 StL-A	11	21	2	3	1	0	0	1	4	2	0	....	.143	.280	.190	.470	32	-2	1	1.52	-1	/C-5	0	-0.2
1920 StL-A	23	28	5	6	1	0	0	6	3	5	0	0	.214	.290	.250	.540	43	-2	2	2.61	0	/C-7	0	-0.2
1921 StL-A	58	111	9	27	3	0	1	10	16	17	1	0	.243	.339	.297	.636	60	-6	12	3.79	-1	C-31	2	-0.5
1922 StL-A	63	127	14	39	6	0	8	23	21	21	0	1	.307	.405	.543	.949	140	8	28	8.39	-2	C-28/1-5	6	0.7
1923 StL-A	85	181	9	32	8	0	3	30	15	45	0	0	.177	.240	.271	.511	32	-18	13	2.13	1	C-47	2	-1.4
1924 StL-A	32	54	9	17	2	0	1	11	11	14	0	1	.315	.431	.407	.838	110	1	10	6.63	-1	C-20	2	0.1

YEAR TM-L	G	AB	R	H	2B	3B	HR	RBI	BB	SO	SB	CS	AVG	OBP	SLG	OPS	OPS+	BR/A	RC	RC/G	FR	G/POS	WS	TPW
1926*NY-A	102	290	41	83	11	3	7	35	73	57	3	2	.286	.433	.417	.850	124	16	59	7.16	2	*C-100	17	2.3
1927*NY-A	92	251	38	69	9	3	7	36	54	24	0	1	.275	.407	.418	.825	118	9	47	6.60	-5	C-89	12	0.9
1928*NY-A	70	136	18	30	5	0	6	14	35	16	0	0	.221	.380	.390	.770	106	3	23	5.55	0	C-70	7	0.5
1929 Bos-N	7	5	1	0	0	0	0	2	3	1	0	....	.000	.375	.000	.375	2	-1	1	1.78	0	/C-6	0	0.0
Total 10	543	1204	146	306	46	6	33	168	235	202	4	5	.254	.378	.385	.762	99	9	195	5.54	-8	C-403/1-5	48	2.1

• COLLINS, Rip Robert Joseph Collins b: 9/18/1909, Pittsburgh, PA d: 4/19/1969, Pittsburgh, PA BR/TR, 5'11", 176 lbs. Deb: 4/28/1940

YEAR TM-L	G	AB	R	H	2B	3B	HR	RBI	BB	SO	SB	CS	AVG	OBP	SLG	OPS	OPS+	BR/A	RC	RC/G	FR	G/POS	WS	TPW
1940 Chi-N	47	120	11	25	3	0	1	14	14	18	4	....	.208	.296	.258	.555	55	-7	9	2.44	-4	C-42	1	-0.9
1944 NY-A	3	3	0	1	0	0	0	0	1	0	0	0	.333	.500	.333	.833	136	0	1	8.67	0	/C-3	0	0.0
Total 2	50	123	11	26	3	0	1	14	15	18	4	0	.211	.302	.260	.562	58	-7	10	2.56	-4	/C-45	1	-0.8

• COLLINS, Ripper James Anthony Collins b: 3/30/1904, Altoona, PA d: 4/15/1970, New Haven, NY BB/TL, 5'9", 165 lbs. Deb: 4/18/1931 C Career OF: 17-0-58

YEAR TM-L	G	AB	R	H	2B	3B	HR	RBI	BB	SO	SB	CS	AVG	OBP	SLG	OPS	OPS+	BR/A	RC	RC/G	FR	G/POS	WS	TPW
1931*StL-N	89	279	34	84	20	10	4	59	18	24	1	....	.301	.350	.487	.837	118	6	48	6.39	4	1-68/0-3(1-0-2)	10	0.5
1932 StL-N	149	549	82	153	28	8	21	91	38	67	4	....	.279	.329	.474	.802	109	6	87	5.58	0	1-81,0-60(15-0-45)	15	-0.5
1933 StL-N	132	493	66	153	26	7	10	68	38	49	7	....	.310	.363	.452	.816	125	16	81	6.08	-4	*1-123	19	0.1
1934*StL-N	154	600	116	200	40	12	**35**	128	57	50	2	....	.333	.393	**.615**	**1.008**	155	46	148	9.65	-2	*1-154	32	2.8
1935 StL-N★	150	578	109	181	36	10	23	122	65	45	0	....	.313	.385	.529	.915	138	31	125	8.38	-4	*1-150	28	1.3
1936 StL-N★	103	277	48	81	15	3	13	48	48	30	1	....	.292	.399	.509	.908	143	18	61	8.17	-1	1-61/0-9(1-0-8)	15	1.1
1937 Chi-N★	115	456	77	125	16	5	16	71	32	46	2	....	.274	.329	.436	.765	102	-0	64	4.90	2	*1-111	12	-0.9
1938*Chi-N	143	490	78	131	22	8	13	61	54	48	1	....	.267	.344	.424	.768	107	5	73	5.20	3	*1-135	15	-0.5
1941 Pit-N	49	62	5	13	2	2	0	11	6	14	0	....	.210	.279	.306	.586	65	-3	6	3.10	1	1-11/0-3(0-0-3)	1	-0.3
Total 9	1084	3784	615	1121	205	65	135	659	356	373	18	....	.296	.360	.492	.852	124	125	694	6.72	-1	1-894/0-75	147	3.6

• COLLINS, Shano John Francis Collins b: 12/4/1885, Charlestown, MA d: 9/10/1955, Newton, MA BR/TR, 6', 185 lbs. Deb: 4/21/1910 M Career OF: 133-292-918

YEAR TM-L	G	AB	R	H	2B	3B	HR	RBI	BB	SO	SB	CS	AVG	OBP	SLG	OPS	OPS+	BR/A	RC	RC/G	FR	G/POS	WS	TPW
1910 Chi-A	97	315	29	62	10	8	1	24	25	....	10	....	.197	.258	.289	.547	75	-10	26	2.56	7	0-66(19-7-40),1-28	6	-0.8
1911 Chi-A	106	370	48	97	16	12	4	48	20	....	14	....	.262	.309	.403	.712	100	-2	50	4.47	3	1-98/2-3,0-3(2-0-0)	9	-0.1
1912 Chi-A	153	579	75	168	34	10	2	81	29	....	26	....	.290	.330	.394	.723	110	5	83	5.00	3	*0-105(1-17-85),1-46	18	0.1
1913 Chi-A	148	535	53	128	26	9	1	47	32	60	22	....	.239	.286	.327	.613	80	-16	55	3.25	5	*0-147(2-0-145)	11	-2.0
1914 Chi-A	154	598	61	164	34	9	3	65	27	49	30	24	.274	.312	.376	.688	108	-2	71	3.94	11	*0-154(7-45-103)	18	0.1
1915 Chi-A	153	576	73	148	24	17	2	85	28	50	38	19	.257	.298	.368	.666	96	-7	70	3.80	2	*0-104(20-21-64),1-47	15	-1.2
1916 Chi-A	143	527	74	128	28	12	0	42	59	51	16	....	.243	.323	.342	.664	98	-1	65	4.08	5	*0-137(23-2-112)/1-4	15	-0.4
1917*Chi-A	82	252	38	59	13	3	1	14	10	27	14	....	.234	.269	.321	.590	78	-8	24	3.13	-2	0-73(9-0-64)	5	-1.5
1918 Chi-A	103	365	30	100	18	11	1	56	17	19	7	....	.274	.310	.392	.702	111	2	45	4.12	7	0-93(16-34-42)/1-5	11	0.4
1919*Chi-A	63	179	21	50	6	3	1	16	7	11	3	....	.279	.317	.363	.681	90	-3	21	4.05	4	0-46(2-7-37)/1-8	5	-0.1
1920 Chi-A	133	495	70	150	21	10	1	63	23	24	12	9	.303	.339	.392	.731	93	-6	65	4.63	-6	*1-116,0-13(2-1-10)	12	-1.4
1921 Bos-A	141	542	63	155	29	12	4	69	18	38	15	8	.286	.314	.406	.720	85	-14	68	4.32	6	*0-139(1-44-94)/1-3	12	-1.7
1922 Bos-A	135	472	33	128	24	7	1	52	7	30	7	9	.271	.289	.358	.647	68	-25	46	3.30	-6	*0-117(11-45-63)/1-1	5	-3.7
1923 Bos-A	97	342	41	79	10	5	0	18	11	29	7	8	.231	.265	.289	.555	46	-29	25	2.40	-2	0-89(0-57-32)	2	-3.4
1924 Bos-A	89	240	37	70	17	5	0	28	18	17	4	6	.292	.349	.404	.753	94	-4	33	4.70	-7	0-56(18-11-27),1-12	5	-1.4
1925 Bos-A	2	3	1	1	0	0	0	1	0	0	0	0	.333	.333	.333	.667	70	-0	0	4.24	0	/0-1	0	0.0
Total 16	1799	6390	747	1687	310	133	22	709	331	405	225	83	.264	.306	.364	.671	91	-121	748	3.88	30	*0-1343,1-368/2-3	149	-17.2

• COLLINS, Wilson Cyril Wilson Collins b: 5/7/1889, Pulaski, TN d: 2/28/1941, Knoxville, TN BR/TR, 5'9.5", 165 lbs. Deb: 5/12/1913 Career OF: 14-6-8

YEAR TM-L	G	AB	R	H	2B	3B	HR	RBI	BB	SO	SB	CS	AVG	OBP	SLG	OPS	OPS+	BR/A	RC	RC/G	FR	G/POS	WS	TPW
1913 Bos-N	16	3	3	1	0	0	0	0	0	1	0	....	.333	.333	.333	.667	89	-0	0	4.00	-1	/0-9(5-3-1)	0	-0.1
1914 Bos-N	27	35	5	9	0	0	0	1	2	8	0	....	.257	.297	.257	.554	66	-1	3	2.51	-2	0-19(9-3-7)	1	-0.4
Total 2	43	38	8	10	0	0	0	1	2	9	0	....	.263	.300	.263	.563	67	-2	3	2.61	-3	/0-28	1	-0.5

• COLLINS, Zip John Edgar Collins b: 3/2/1892, Brooklyn, NY d: 12/19/1983, Manassas, VA BL/TL, 5'11", 152 lbs. Deb: 7/31/1914 Career OF: 31-147-71

YEAR TM-L	G	AB	R	H	2B	3B	HR	RBI	BB	SO	SB	CS	AVG	OBP	SLG	OPS	OPS+	BR/A	RC	RC/G	FR	G/POS	WS	TPW
1914 Pit-N	49	182	14	44	2	0	0	15	8	10	3	....	.242	.277	.253	.530	61	-9	13	2.42	-1	0-49(0-11-40)	2	-1.3
1915 Pit-N	101	354	51	104	8	5	1	23	24	38	6	7	.294	.340	.353	.693	112	3	44	4.31	-1	0-89(0-89-0)	11	-0.4
Bos-N	5	14	3	4	1	1	0	0	2	1	1	....	.286	.375	.500	.875	167	1	3	7.80	0	/0-4(4-0-0)	1	0.1
Yr.	106	368	54	108	9	6	1	23	26	39	7	7	.293	.342	.359	.700	114	4	47	4.43	-1	0-93(4-89-0)	12	-0.3
1916 Bos-N	93	268	39	56	1	6	1	18	18	42	4	....	.209	.261	.269	.530	66	-11	21	2.48	1	0-78(26-27-27)	4	-1.5
1917 Bos-N	9	27	3	4	0	1	0	2	0	4	0	....	.148	.148	.222	.370	14	-3	1	.87	0	/0-5(1-0-4)	0	-0.3
1921 Phi-A	24	71	14	20	5	1	0	5	6	5	1	2	.282	.354	.380	.735	87	-2	9	4.61	-1	0-20(0-20-0)	1	-0.3
Total 5	281	916	124	232	17	14	2	63	58	100	15	9	.253	.301	.309	.610	85	-21	92	3.34	-1	0-245	19	-3.7

• COLLVER, Bill William J. Collver b: 3/21/1867, Clyde, OH d: 3/24/1888, Detroit, MI Deb: 7/4/1885

YEAR TM-L	G	AB	R	H	2B	3B	HR	RBI	BB	SO	SB	CS	AVG	OBP	SLG	OPS	OPS+	BR/A	RC	RC/G	FR	G/POS	WS	TPW
1885 Bos-N	1	4	0	0	0	0	0	0	0	1	....	....	.000	.000	.000	.000	-104	-1	0	.00	0	/0-1	0	-0.1

• COLMAN, Frank Frank Lloyd Colman b: 3/2/1918, London, Canada d: 2/19/1983, London, Canada BL/TL, 5'11", 188 lbs. Deb: 9/12/1942 Career OF: 19-0-83

YEAR TM-L	G	AB	R	H	2B	3B	HR	RBI	BB	SO	SB	CS	AVG	OBP	SLG	OPS	OPS+	BR/A	RC	RC/G	FR	G/POS	WS	TPW
1942 Pit-N	10	37	2	5	0	0	1	2	2	2	0	....	.135	.179	.216	.396	15	-4	2	1.29	1	/0-8(0-0-8)	0	-0.4
1943 Pit-N	32	59	9	16	2	2	0	4	8	7	0	....	.271	.358	.373	.731	108	1	9	5.33	0	0-11(0-0-11)	2	0.0
1944 Pit-N	99	226	30	61	9	5	6	53	25	27	0	....	.270	.345	.434	.779	113	4	34	5.41	-1	0-53(3-0-50)/1-6	8	-0.1
1945 Pit-N	77	153	18	32	11	1	4	30	9	16	0	....	.209	.253	.373	.626	70	-7	14	2.93	1	1-22,0-12(6-0-5)	1	-0.7
1946 Pit-N	26	53	3	9	3	0	1	6	2	7	0	....	.170	.214	.283	.497	39	-5	3	2.07	0	/0-8(4-0-4),1-2	0	-0.5
NY-A	5	15	2	4	0	0	1	5	1	1	0	0	.267	.313	.467	.779	114	0	2	5.70	0	/0-5(0-0-5)	0	0.0
1947 NY-A	22	28	2	3	0	0	2	6	2	6	0	0	.107	.167	.321	.488	34	-3	2	1.75	1	/0-6(6-0-0)	0	-0.2
Total 6	271	571	66	130	25	8	15	106	49	66	0	0	.228	.291	.378	.669	85	-14	65	3.90	1	0-103/1-30	11	-2.0

• COLON, Cris Cristobal Colon b: 1/3/1969, La Guaira, Venezuela BB/TR, 6'2", 180 lbs. Deb: 9/18/1992

YEAR TM-L	G	AB	R	H	2B	3B	HR	RBI	BB	SO	SB	CS	AVG	OBP	SLG	OPS	OPS+	BR/A	RC	RC/G	FR	G/POS	WS	TPW
1992 Tex-A	14	36	5	6	0	0	0	1	1	8	0	0	.167	.189	.167	.356		-5	1	.73	-1	S-14	0	-0.5

• COLUCCIO, Bob Robert Pasquali Coluccio b: 10/2/1951, Centralia, WA BR/TR, 5'11", 183 lbs. Deb: 4/15/1973 Career OF: 46-150-161

YEAR TM-L	G	AB	R	H	2B	3B	HR	RBI	BB	SO	SB	CS	AVG	OBP	SLG	OPS	OPS+	BR/A	RC	RC/G	FR	G/POS	WS	TPW
1973 Mil-A	124	438	65	98	21	8	15	58	54	92	13	6	.224	.313	.411	.724	105	3	58	4.38	3	*0-108(18-14-79),D-11	12	0.0
1974 Mil-A	138	394	42	88	13	4	6	31	43	61	15	9	.223	.305	.322	.627	81	-10	40	3.23	0	*0-131(4-103-34)/D-2	9	-1.4
1975 Mil-A	22	62	8	12	0	1	1	5	11	11	1	4	.194	.324	.274	.599	70	-3	5	2.31	-2	0-22(0-22-0)	1	-0.6
Chi-A	61	161	22	33	4	2	4	13	13	34	4	0	.205	.269	.329	.598	67	-6	15	3.03	0	0-59(14-3-44)/D-1	2	-0.9
Yr.	83	223	30	45	4	3	5	18	24	45	5	4	.202	.285	.314	.599	68	-10	20	2.80	-2	0-81(14-25-44)/D-1	3	-1.5
1977 Chi-A	20	37	4	10	0	0	0	7	6	2	0	2	.270	.372	.270	.642	79	-2	4	3.07	0	0-19(9-8-3)	1	-0.2
1978 StL-N	5	3	0	0	0	0	0	0	1	2	0	0	.000	.250	.000	.250	-25	-0	0	.59	0	/0-2(1-0-1)	0	-0.1
Total 5	370	1095	141	241	38	15	26	114	128	202	33	21	.220	.306	.353	.660	87	-19	122	3.57	2	0-341/D-14	25	-3.1

• COMBS, Earle Earle Bryan "The Kentucky Colonel" Combs
b: 5/14/1899, Pebworth, KY d: 7/21/1976, Richmond, KY BL/TR, 6', 185 lbs. Deb: 4/16/1924 C HOF: 1970 Career OF: 211-1161-37

YEAR TM-L	G	AB	R	H	2B	3B	HR	RBI	BB	SO	SB	CS	AVG	OBP	SLG	OPS	OPS+	BR/A	RC	RC/G	FR	G/POS	WS	TPW
1924 NY-A	24	35	10	14	5	0	0	2	4	2	0	1	.400	.462	.543	1.004	159	3	8	10.10	0	0-11(5-3-3)	2	0.2
1925 NY-A	150	593	117	203	36	13	3	61	65	43	12	13	.342	.411	.462	.873	123	21	112	7.18	-9	*0-150(12-138-0)	20	0.5
1926*NY-A	145	606	113	181	31	12	8	55	47	23	8	6	.299	.352	.429	.781	105	2	92	5.46	-7	*0-145(0-145-0)	19	-1.0
1927*NY-A	152	648	137	**231**	36	**23**	6	64	62	31	15	6	.356	.414	.511	.925	143	42	138	8.44	-1	*0-152(0-152-0)	31	3.4
1928*NY-A	149	626	118	194	33	**21**	7	56	77	33	10	8	.310	.387	.463	.850	127	25	114	6.80	-3	*0-149(0-149-0)	28	1.5
1929 NY-A	142	586	119	202	33	15	3	65	69	32	11	7	.345	.414	.468	.881	135	33	115	7.60	-6	*0-141(0-141-0)	25	2.1
1930 NY-A	137	532	129	183	30	**22**	7	82	74	26	16	10	.344	.424	.523	.947	145	39	120	8.56	-6	*0-135(60-45-30)	23	2.2
1931 NY-A	138	563	120	179	31	13	5	58	68	34	11	3	.318	.394	.446	.840	128	28	103	7.02	-9	*0-129(0-129-0)	20	1.5
1932*NY-A	144	591	143	190	32	10	9	65	81	16	3	9	.321	.405	.455	.860	129	26	110	7.08	-13	*0-139(42-115-1)	25	0.7
1933 NY-A	122	417	86	125	22	16	5	64	47	19	6	4	.300	.372	.465	.837	128	17	73	6.49	-10	*0-104(23-80-2)	16	0.4
1934 NY-A	63	251	47	80	13	5	2	25	40	9	3	1	.319	.412	.434	.847	127	12	48	7.17	-3	0-62(12-51-0)	10	0.7
1935 NY-A	89	298	47	84	7	4	3	35	36	10	1	3	.282	.359	.362	.722	92	-3	40	4.83	-2	0-70(57-13-1)	8	-0.8
Total 12	1455	5746	1186	1866	309	154	58	632	670	278	96	71	.325	.397	.462	.859	127	245	1073	7.06	-68	*0-1387	227	11.3

• COMBS, Merl Merrill Russell Combs b: 12/11/1919, Los Angeles, CA d: 7/7/1981, Riverside, CA BL/TR, 6', 172 lbs. Deb: 9/12/1947 C

YEAR TM-L	G	AB	R	H	2B	3B	HR	RBI	BB	SO	SB	CS	AVG	OBP	SLG	OPS	OPS+	BR/A	RC	RC/G	FR	G/POS	WS	TPW
1947 Bos-A	17	68	8	15	1	0	1	6	9	9	0	0	.221	.329	.279	.609	65	-3	7	3.14	4	3-17	1	0.1

YEAR TM-L	G	AB	R	H	2B	3B	HR	RBI	BB	SO	SB	CS	AVG	OBP	SLG	OPS	OPS+	BR/A	RC	RC/G	FR	G/POS	WS	TPW
1949 Bos-A	14	24	5	5	1	0	0	1	9	0	0	0	.208	.424	.250	.674	75	-0	4	5.01	-1	/3-9,S-1	1	-0.1
1950 Bos-A	1	0	0	0	0	0	0	0	1	0	0	0	....	1.000	....	1.000	158	0	0	∞	0	....	0	0.0
Was-A	37	102	19	25	1	0	0	6	22	16	0	0	.245	.379	.255	.634	68	-3	12	3.82	0	S-30	2	-0.2
Yr.	38	102	19	25	1	0	0	6	23	16	0	0	.245	.384	.255	.639	69	-3	12	3.82	0	S-30	2	-0.1
1951 Cle-A	19	28	2	5	2	0	0	2	2	3	0	0	.179	.233	.250	.483	32	-3	2	2.09	1	S-16	1	-0.1
1952 Cle-A	52	139	11	23	1	1	1	10	14	15	0	1	.165	.242	.209	.450	28	-14	8	1.68	8	S-49/2-3	2	-0.3
Total 5	140	361	45	73	6	1	2	25	57	43	0	1	.202	.314	.241	.555	51	-22	32	2.79	11	/S-96,3-26,2-3	7	-0.6

• COMER, Wayne Harry Wayne Comer b: 2/3/1944, Shenandoah, VA BR/TR, 5'10", 175 lbs. Deb: 9/17/1967 Career OF: 80-117-70

YEAR TM-L	G	AB	R	H	2B	3B	HR	RBI	BB	SO	SB	CS	AVG	OBP	SLG	OPS	OPS+	BR/A	RC	RC/G	FR	G/POS	WS	TPW
1967 Det-A	4	3	0	1	0	0	0	0	0	0	0	0	.333	.333	.333	.667	95	-0	0	4.50	0	/0-1	0	0.0
1968*Det-A	48	48	8	6	0	1	1	3	2	7	0	0	.125	.160	.229	.389	16	-5	1	.54	-1	0-27(26-0-1)/C-1	0	-0.7
1969 Sea-A	147	481	88	118	18	1	15	54	82	79	18	7	.245	.356	.380	.737	108	8	70	4.87	0	*0-139(20-92-46)/3-1,C-1	16	0.3
1970 Mil-A	13	17	1	1	0	0	0	1	0	3	0	0	.059	.059	.059	.118	-67	-4	0	.00	0	/0-5(1-2-2)	0	-0.4
Was-A	77	129	21	30	4	0	0	8	22	16	4	1	.233	.349	.264	.612	75	-3	14	3.63	-1	0-58(18-21-20)/3-1	2	-0.6
Yr.	90	146	22	31	4	0	0	9	22	19	4	1	.212	.320	.240	.559	61	-6	14	3.12	-2	0-63(19-23-22)/3-1	2	-1.0
1972 Det-A	27	9	1	1	0	0	0	1	0	1	0	1	.111	.111	.111	.222	-33	-2	0	.00	-2	0-17(15-1-1)	0	-0.4
Total 5	316	687	119	157	22	2	16	67	106	106	22	9	.229	.333	.336	.670	90	-5	85	4.05	-4	0-247/3-2,C-2	18	-1.9

• COMISKEY, Charlie Charles Albert "Commy,The Old Roman" Comiskey
b: 8/15/1859, Chicago, IL d: 10/26/1931, Eagle River, WI BR/TR, 6', 180 lbs. Deb: 5/2/1882 M/U HOF: 1939 Career OF: 3-3-11

YEAR TM-L	G	AB	R	H	2B	3B	HR	RBI	BB	SO	SB	CS	AVG	OBP	SLG	OPS	OPS+	BR/A	RC	RC/G	FR	G/POS	WS	TPW
1882 StL-a	78	329	58	80	9	5	1	45	4	....	....	....	.243	.252	.310	.562	85	-6	26	2.97	6	*1-77/P-2	9	-0.3
1883 StL-a	96	401	87	118	17	9	2	64	11	....	....	....	.294	.313	.397	.710	120	7	51	5.05	4	*1-96/0-1	14	0.2
1884 StL-a	108	460	76	109	17	6	2	84	5	....	....	....	.237	.253	.313	.566	81	-11	37	2.93	5	*1-108/2-1,P-1	9	-1.4
1885*StL-a	83	340	68	87	15	7	2	44	14	....	....	....	.256	.293	.359	.652	100	-1	37	3.91	6	*1-83	13	-0.2
1886*StL-a	131	578	95	147	15	9	3	76	10	....	41	....	.254	.267	.327	.594	82	-16	63	3.94	2	*1-122/2-9,0-2(0-0-2)	10	-2.2
1887*StL-a	125	565	139	207	22	5	4	103	27	....	117	....	.366	.374	.416	.790	109	3	131	9.86	9	*1-116/2-9,0-3(0-0-3)	17	0.2
1888*StL-a	137	576	102	157	22	5	6	83	12	....	72	....	.273	.292	.359	.652	98	-6	84	5.39	1	*1-133/0-5(0-2-3),2-3	15	-1.5
1889 StL-a	137	587	105	168	28	10	3	102	19	19	65	....	.286	.312	.383	.695	86	-17	93	5.87	1	*1-134/2-3,0-3(0-1-2),P-1	15	-2.3
1890 Chi-P	88	377	53	92	11	3	0	59	14	17	34	....	.244	.277	.289	.566	49	-30	41	3.84	-1	1-88	3	-3.0
1891 StL-a	139	572	84	148	16	2	3	93	33	25	41	....	.259	.307	.309	.617	66	-30	69	4.29	12	*1-141/0-2(2-0-0)	11	-2.6
1892 Cin-N	141	551	61	125	14	6	3	71	32	16	30	....	.227	.274	.290	.565	72	-20	53	3.39	-5	*1-141	7	-2.4
1893 Cin-N	64	259	38	57	12	1	0	26	11	2	9	....	.220	.257	.274	.531	40	-24	21	2.77	-7	1-64	1	-2.5
1894 Cin-N	63	228	26	61	9	0	0	33	5	5	10	....	.268	.292	.307	.599	43	-22	24	3.73	-6	1-60/0-1	1	-2.2
Total 13	1390	5823	992	1556	207	68	29	883	197	84	419	....	.267	.293	.338	.631	82	-172	729	4.61	27	*1-1363/2-25,0-17,P-4	125	-20.2

• COMMAND, Jim James Dalton "Igor,Gor" Command b: 10/15/1928, Grand Rapids, MI BL/TR, 6'2", 200 lbs. Deb: 6/20/1954

YEAR TM-L	G	AB	R	H	2B	3B	HR	RBI	BB	SO	SB	CS	AVG	OBP	SLG	OPS	OPS+	BR/A	RC	RC/G	FR	G/POS	WS	TPW
1954 Phi-N	9	18	1	4	1	0	1	6	2	4	0	0	.222	.300	.444	.744	91	-0	3	4.93	0	/3-6	0	0.0
1955 Phi-N	5	5	0	0	0	0	0	0	0	0	0	0	.000	.000	.000	.000	-102	-1	0	.00	0	....	0	-0.1
Total 2	14	23	1	4	1	0	1	6	2	4	0	0	.174	.240	.348	.588	53	-2	3	3.63	0	/3-6	0	-0.2

• COMOROSKY, Adam Adam Anthony Comorosky b: 12/9/1905, Swoyersville, PA d: 3/2/1951, Swoyersville, PA BR/TR, 5'10", 167 lbs. Deb: 9/13/1926 Career OF: 575-77-77

YEAR TM-L	G	AB	R	H	2B	3B	HR	RBI	BB	SO	SB	CS	AVG	OBP	SLG	OPS	OPS+	BR/A	RC	RC/G	FR	G/POS	WS	TPW
1926 Pit-N	8	15	2	4	1	1	0	0	1	2	1	....	.267	.313	.467	.779	102	-0	2	4.99	0	/0-6(6-0-0)	0	-0.1
1927 Pit-N	18	61	5	14	1	0	0	4	3	1	0	....	.230	.266	.246	.512	35	-6	4	2.09	1	0-16(15-1-0)	1	-0.6
1928 Pit-N	51	176	22	52	6	3	2	34	15	6	1	....	.295	.354	.398	.752	92	-2	25	4.91	-1	0-49(38-9-5)	5	-0.6
1929 Pit-N	127	473	86	152	26	11	6	97	40	22	19	....	.321	.377	.461	.838	104	3	80	6.16	-3	*0-121(121-0-0)	15	-0.8
1930 Pit-N	152	597	112	187	47	**23**	12	119	51	33	14	....	.313	.371	.529	.900	114	12	114	6.66	-1	*0-152(130-30-0)	21	0.0
1931 Pit-N	99	350	37	85	12	1	1	48	34	28	11	....	.243	.310	.291	.601	63	-17	34	3.22	1	0-90(89-0-1)	5	-2.1
1932 Pit-N	108	370	54	106	18	4	4	46	25	20	7	....	.286	.337	.389	.726	96	-2	50	4.70	0	0-92(74-18-0)	11	-0.6
1933 Pit-N	64	162	18	46	8	1	1	15	4	9	2	....	.284	.301	.364	.665	89	-3	16	3.24	-2	0-30(30-0-0)	2	-0.7
1934 Cin-N	127	446	46	115	12	6	0	40	34	23	1	....	.258	.315	.312	.626	70	-18	44	3.36	-3	*0-122(47-9-66)	4	-2.8
1935 Cin-N	59	137	22	34	3	1	2	14	7	14	1	....	.248	.290	.328	.618	68	-6	13	3.38	-1	0-40(25-10-5)	2	-0.9
Total 10	813	2787	404	795	134	51	28	417	214	158	57	....	.285	.339	.400	.739	90	-39	382	4.72	-9	0-718	66	-9.2

• COMPTON, Mike Michael Lynn Compton b: 8/15/1944, Stamford, CT BR/TR, 5'10", 180 lbs. Deb: 4/17/1970

YEAR TM-L	G	AB	R	H	2B	3B	HR	RBI	BB	SO	SB	CS	AVG	OBP	SLG	OPS	OPS+	BR/A	RC	RC/G	FR	G/POS	WS	TPW
1970 Phi-N	47	110	8	18	0	1	1	7	9	22	0	0	.164	.240	.209	.449	22	-12	6	1.68	-2	C-40	2	-1.2

• COMPTON, Pete Anna Sebastian "Bash" Compton
b: 9/28/1889, San Marcos, TX d: 2/3/1978, Kansas City, MO BL/TL, 5'11", 170 lbs. Deb: 9/6/1911 Career OF: 73-55-80

YEAR TM-L	G	AB	R	H	2B	3B	HR	RBI	BB	SO	SB	CS	AVG	OBP	SLG	OPS	OPS+	BR/A	RC	RC/G	FR	G/POS	WS	TPW
1911 StL-A	28	107	9	29	4	0	0	5	8	....	2	....	.271	.322	.308	.630	79	-3	11	3.62	1	0-28(0-0-28)	2	-0.3
1912 StL-A	103	268	26	75	6	4	2	30	22	....	11	....	.280	.339	.354	.694	102	1	36	4.65	-1	0-72(50-0-22)	6	-0.4
1913 StL-A	63	100	14	18	5	2	2	17	13	13	2	....	.180	.274	.330	.604	79	-3	9	2.79	-2	0-21(8-5-8)	1	-0.6
1915 StL-F	2	8	0	2	0	0	0	3	0	0	0	....	.250	.250	.250	.500	45	-1	0	1.99	0	/0-2(0-2-0)	0	-0.1
Bos-N	35	116	10	28	7	1	1	12	8	11	4	1	.241	.290	.345	.635	94	-1	13	3.65	0	0-31(0-20-11)	3	-0.3
1916 Bos-N	34	98	13	20	2	0	0	8	7	7	5	....	.204	.264	.224	.489	54	-5	7	2.37	-1	0-30(3-26-1)	1	-0.8
Pit-N	5	16	1	1	0	0	0	0	2	5	0	....	.063	.211	.063	.273	-14	-2	0	.60	0	/0-5(0-0-5)	0	-0.3
Yr.	39	114	14	21	2	0	0	8	9	12	5	....	.184	.256	.202	.458	43	-7	8	2.08	-1	0-35(3-26-6)	1	-1.2
1918 NY-N	21	60	5	13	0	1	0	5	5	4	2	....	.217	.277	.250	.527	62	-3	4	2.42	1	0-19(12-2-5)	1	-0.2
Total 6	291	773	78	186	24	8	5	80	65	40	26	1	.241	.303	.312	.615	82	-17	81	3.49	-2	0-208	14	-3.0

• CONATSER, Clint Clinton Astor "Connie" Conatser b: 7/24/1921, Los Angeles, CA BR/TR, 5'11", 182 lbs. Deb: 4/21/1948 Career OF: 39-65-16

YEAR TM-L	G	AB	R	H	2B	3B	HR	RBI	BB	SO	SB	CS	AVG	OBP	SLG	OPS	OPS+	BR/A	RC	RC/G	FR	G/POS	WS	TPW
1948*Bos-N	90	224	30	62	9	3	3	23	32	27	0	....	.277	.370	.384	.754	106	3	34	5.40	-3	0-76(24-52-0)	7	-0.2
1949 Bos-N	53	152	10	40	6	0	3	16	14	19	0	....	.263	.325	.362	.687	89	-3	17	3.86	-1	0-44(15-13-16)	3	-0.5
Total 2	143	376	40	102	15	3	6	39	46	46	0	....	.271	.352	.375	.727	99	0	51	4.76	-3	0-120	10	-0.7

• CONCEPCION, Dave David Ismael (Benitez) Concepcion b: 6/17/1948, Aragua, Venezuela BR/TR, 6'2", 180 lbs. Deb: 4/6/1970 Career OF: 0-8-0

YEAR TM-L	G	AB	R	H	2B	3B	HR	RBI	BB	SO	SB	CS	AVG	OBP	SLG	OPS	OPS+	BR/A	RC	RC/G	FR	G/POS	WS	TPW
1970*Cin-N	101	265	38	69	6	3	1	19	23	45	10	2	.260	.326	.317	.643	70	-9	27	3.46	-6	S-93/2-3	5	-0.6
1971 Cin-N	130	327	24	67	4	4	1	20	18	51	9	3	.205	.246	.251	.497	43	-24	19	1.86	-6	*S-112,2-10/3-7,0-5(0-5-0)	4	-2.0
1972*Cin-N	119	378	40	79	13	2	2	29	32	65	13	6	.209	.274	.270	.544	58	-20	27	2.28	8	*S-114/3-9,2-1	6	0.1
1973 Cin-N★	89	328	39	94	18	3	8	46	21	55	22	5	.287	.331	.433	.764	116	9	47	5.04	11	S-88/0-2(0-2-0)	16	3.2
1974 Cin-N	160	594	70	167	25	1	14	82	44	79	41	6	.281	.337	.397	.734	106	10	80	4.66	25	*S-160/0-1	25	5.6
1975*Cin-N★	140	507	62	139	23	1	5	49	39	51	33	6	.274	.328	.353	.682	87	-4	59	4.00	31	*S-130/3-6	19	4.3
1976*Cin-N★	152	576	74	162	28	7	9	69	49	68	21	10	.281	.339	.401	.740	107	5	77	4.69	34	*S-150	23	6.0
1977 Cin-N★	156	572	59	155	26	3	8	64	46	77	29	7	.271	.325	.369	.694	84	-9	69	4.13	28	*S-156	19	3.5
1978 Cin-N★	153	565	75	170	33	4	6	67	51	83	23	10	.301	.360	.405	.765	113	11	82	5.17	9	*S-152	25	3.7
1979*Cin-N★	149	590	91	166	25	3	16	84	64	73	19	7	.281	.352	.415	.767	108	8	85	4.98	24	*S-148	24	4.9
1980 Cin-N★	156	622	72	162	31	8	5	77	37	107	12	2	.260	.303	.360	.663	84	-13	65	3.58	3	*S-155/2-1	17	0.7
1981 Cin-N★	106	421	57	129	28	0	5	67	37	61	4	5	.306	.364	.409	.772	117	8	60	5.08	16	*S-106	20	3.8
1982 Cin-N★	147	572	48	164	25	4	5	53	45	61	13	6	.287	.339	.371	.709	96	-3	68	4.19	12	*S-145/1-1,3-1	17	2.6
1983 Cin-N	143	528	54	123	22	0	1	47	56	81	14	9	.233	.307	.280	.587	61	-27	43	2.63	4	*S-139/3-6,1-1	8	-1.0
1984 Cin-N	154	531	46	130	26	1	4	58	52	72	22	6	.245	.312	.320	.632	75	-16	56	3.51	-7	*S-104,3-54/1-6	11	-1.4
1985 Cin-N	155	560	59	141	19	2	7	48	50	67	16	12	.252	.316	.330	.647	77	-19	54	3.15	-11	*S-151/3-5	12	-1.5
1986 Cin-N	90	311	42	81	13	2	3	30	26	43	13	2	.260	.318	.344	.662	79	-7	33	3.53	2	S-60,1-12,2-10,3-10	8	0.1
1987 Cin-N	104	279	32	89	15	0	1	33	28	24	4	3	.319	.381	.384	.765	99	0	39	5.11	8	2-59,1-26,3-13/S-2	8	0.9
1988 Cin-N	84	197	11	39	9	0	0	8	18	23	3	2	.198	.265	.244	.509	45	-14	13	2.07	4	2-46,1-16,S-13/3-9,P-1	2	-0.9
Total 19	2488	8723	993	2326	389	48	101	950	736	1186	321	109	.267	.325	.357	.682	88	-116	1005	3.91	188	*S-2178,2-130,3-120/1-62,0,P	269	32.1

• CONCEPCION, Onix Onix Cardona (Cardona) Concepcion b: 10/5/1957, Dorado, Puerto Rico BR/TR, 5'6", 180 lbs. Deb: 8/30/1980

YEAR TM-L	G	AB	R	H	2B	3B	HR	RBI	BB	SO	SB	CS	AVG	OBP	SLG	OPS	OPS+	BR/A	RC	RC/G	FR	G/POS	WS	TPW
1980*KC-A	12	15	1	2	0	0	0	2	0	1	0	0	.133	.133	.133	.267	-26	-3	0	.26	-2	/S-6	0	-0.4
1981 KC-A	2	0	0	0	0	0	0	0	0	0	0	0	....	....	....	....	-101	0	0	....	-1	/S-1	0	-0.1
1982 KC-A	74	205	17	48	9	1	0	15	5	18	2	1	.234	.256	.288	.544	49	-15	14	2.24	0	S-46,2-24/D-1	2	-0.9

YEAR TM-L	G	AB	R	H	2B	3B	HR	RBI	BB	SO	SB	CS	AVG	OBP	SLG	OPS	OPS+	BR/A	RC	RC/G	FR	G/POS	WS	TPW
1983 KC-A	80	219	22	53	11	3	0	20	12	12	10	3	.242	.284	.320	.604	66	-10	20	3.03	-1	3-31,2-28,S-21/D-1	4	-0.7
1984*KC-A	90	287	36	81	9	2	1	23	14	33	9	6	.282	.322	.338	.660	82	-7	31	3.82	5	S-85/2-6,3-1	8	0.6
1985*KC-A	131	314	32	64	5	1	2	20	16	29	4	4	.204	.256	.245	.501	38	-28	19	1.91	0	*S-128/2-2	5	-1.6
1987 Pit-N	1	1	0	1	0	0	0	0	0	0	0	0	1.000	1.000	1.000	2.000	429	0	1	∞	0	....	0	0.0
Total 7	**390**	**1041**	**108**	**249**	**34**	**7**	**3**	**80**	**47**	**93**	**25**	**14**	**.239**	**.279**	**.294**	**.573**	**58**	**-61**	**86**	**2.68**	**2**	**S-287/2-60,3-32,D-2**	**19**	**-3.0**

• CONDE, Ramon Ramon Luis (Roman) "Wito" Conde b: 12/29/1934, Juana Diaz, Puerto Rico BR/TR, 5'8", 172 lbs. Deb: 7/17/1962

YEAR TM-L	G	AB	R	H	2B	3B	HR	RBI	BB	SO	SB	CS	AVG	OBP	SLG	OPS	OPS+	BR/A	RC	RC/G	FR	G/POS	WS	TPW
1962 Chi-A	14	16	0	0	0	0	0	1	3	3	0	0	.000	.158	.000	.158	-54	-3	0	.06	-1	/3-7	0	-0.4

• CONE, Fred Joseph Frederick Cone b: 5/1848, Rockford, IL d: 4/13/1909, Chicago, IL, 5'9.5", 171 lbs. Deb: 5/5/1871 U

YEAR TM-L	G	AB	R	H	2B	3B	HR	RBI	BB	SO	SB	CS	AVG	OBP	SLG	OPS	OPS+	BR/A	RC	RC/G	FR	G/POS	WS	TPW
1871 Bos-n	19	77	17	20	3	1	0	16	8	2	12	1	.260	.329	.325	.654	86	1	12	6.78	0	O-18(18-0-1)	....	0.1

• CONGALTON, Bunk William Millar Congalton b: 1/24/1875, Guelph, Canada d: 8/19/1937, Cleveland, OH BL/TL, 5'11", 190 lbs. Deb: 4/18/1902 Career OF: 21-6-275

YEAR TM-L	G	AB	R	H	2B	3B	HR	RBI	BB	SO	SB	CS	AVG	OBP	SLG	OPS	OPS+	BR/A	RC	RC/G	FR	G/POS	WS	TPW
1902 Chi-N	47	188	16	45	3	0	1	27	7	....	3	....	.239	.267	.271	.538	68	-7	15	2.75	1	O-45(0-5-41)	2	-1.0
1905 Cle-A	12	47	4	17	0	0	0	5	2	....	4	....	.362	.388	.362	.749	136	2	8	7.02	-1	O-12(0-0-12)	2	0.0
1906 Cle-A	117	419	51	134	13	5	3	50	24	....	12	....	.320	.361	.396	.757	139	18	69	5.89	-8	*O-114(21-1-93)	15	0.5
1907 Cle-A	9	22	2	4	0	0	0	2	4	....	0	....	.182	.308	.182	.490	56	-1	1	1.86	0	/O-6(0-0-6)	1	-0.1
Bos-A	124	496	44	142	11	8	2	47	20	....	13	....	.286	.318	.353	.671	115	7	63	4.53	-2	*O-123(0-0-123)	12	-0.1
Yr.	133	518	46	146	11	8	2	49	24	....	13	....	.282	.317	.346	.663	112	6	64	4.41	-1	*O-129(0-0-129)	13	-0.2
Total 4	**309**	**1172**	**117**	**342**	**27**	**13**	**6**	**131**	**57**	**....**	**32**	**....**	**.292**	**.328**	**.352**	**.680**	**116**	**18**	**156**	**4.74**	**-9**	**O-300**	**32**	**-0.6**

• CONIGLIARO, Billy William Michael Conigliaro b: 8/15/1947, Revere, MA BR/TR, 6', 190 lbs. Deb: 4/11/1969 Career OF: 104-146-94

YEAR TM-L	G	AB	R	H	2B	3B	HR	RBI	BB	SO	SB	CS	AVG	OBP	SLG	OPS	OPS+	BR/A	RC	RC/G	FR	G/POS	WS	TPW
1969 Bos-A	32	80	14	23	6	2	4	7	9	23	1	1	.288	.367	.563	.929	149	5	17	7.59	-2	O-24(3-18-6)	4	0.2
1970 Bos-A	114	398	59	108	16	3	18	58	35	73	3	7	.271	.341	.462	.803	112	4	59	5.05	-3	*O-108(77-25-20)	12	-0.5
1971 Bos-A	101	351	42	92	26	1	11	33	25	68	3	2	.262	.311	.436	.747	102	-0	45	4.46	-3	*O-100(1-79-20)	11	-0.6
1972 Mil-A	52	191	22	44	6	2	7	16	8	54	1	0	.230	.261	.393	.654	94	-2	18	3.22	2	O-50(2-6-45)	4	-0.3
1973*Oak-A	48	110	5	22	2	2	0	14	9	26	1	0	.200	.261	.255	.515	48	-7	8	2.21	2	O-40(21-18-3)/2-1	1	-0.7
Total 5	**347**	**1130**	**142**	**289**	**56**	**10**	**40**	**128**	**86**	**244**	**9**	**10**	**.256**	**.313**	**.429**	**.742**	**102**	**-1**	**147**	**4.42**	**-3**	**O-322/2-1**	**32**	**-1.8**

• CONIGLIARO, Tony Anthony Richard Conigliaro b: 1/7/1945, Revere, MA d: 2/24/1990, Salem, MA BR/TR, 6'3", 185 lbs. Deb: 4/16/1964 Career OF: 81-27-733

YEAR TM-L	G	AB	R	H	2B	3B	HR	RBI	BB	SO	SB	CS	AVG	OBP	SLG	OPS	OPS+	BR/A	RC	RC/G	FR	G/POS	WS	TPW
1964 Bos-A	111	404	69	117	21	2	24	52	35	78	2	4	.290	.354	.530	.883	135	17	72	6.44	-1	*O-106(81-25-2)	16	1.2
1965 Bos-A	138	521	82	140	21	5	**32**	82	51	116	4	2	.269	.340	.512	.852	131	20	91	6.10	5	*O-137(0-2-135)	17	1.6
1966 Bos-A	150	558	77	148	26	7	28	93	52	112	0	2	.265	.333	.487	.821	120	14	91	5.73	-6	*O-146(0-0-146)	20	-0.2
1967 Bos-A★	95	349	59	100	11	5	20	67	27	58	4	6	.287	.346	.519	.865	141	16	62	6.26	-2	O-95(0-0-95)	16	0.7
1969 Bos-A	141	506	57	129	21	3	20	82	48	111	2	4	.255	.324	.427	.751	103	-0	68	4.62	-11	*O-137(0-0-137)	13	-1.9
1970 Bos-A	146	560	89	149	20	1	36	116	43	93	4	2	.266	.327	.498	.826	116	11	90	5.64	-7	*O-146(0-0-146)	18	-0.4
1971 Cal-A	74	266	23	59	18	0	4	15	23	52	3	3	.222	.286	.335	.621	81	-8	23	2.85	6	O-72(0-0-72)	5	-0.6
1975 Bos-A	21	57	8	7	1	0	2	9	8	9	1	0	.123	.231	.246	.476	32	-5	4	1.70	0	D-15	0	-0.5
Total 8	**876**	**3221**	**464**	**849**	**139**	**23**	**166**	**516**	**287**	**629**	**20**	**23**	**.264**	**.330**	**.476**	**.806**	**118**	**64**	**501**	**5.39**	**-16**	**O-839/D-15**	**105**	**-0.2**

• CONINE, Jeff Jeffrey Guy Conine b: 6/27/1966, Tacoma, WA BR/TR, 6'1", 220 lbs. Deb: 9/16/1990 Career OF: 636-0-68

YEAR TM-L	G	AB	R	H	2B	3B	HR	RBI	BB	SO	SB	CS	AVG	OBP	SLG	OPS	OPS+	BR/A	RC	RC/G	FR	G/POS	WS	TPW
1990 KC-A	9	20	3	5	2	0	0	2	2	5	0	0	.250	.318	.350	.668	88	-0	2	3.46	0	/1-9	0	0.0
1992 KC-A	28	91	10	23	5	2	0	9	8	23	0	0	.253	.313	.352	.665	84	-2	10	4.01	-1	O-23(22-0-1)/1-4	3	-0.4
1993 Fla-N	162	595	75	174	24	3	12	79	52	135	2	2	.292	.354	.403	.758	97	-2	84	5.15	1	*O-147(147-0-0),1-43	15	-0.8
1994 Fla-N★	115	451	60	144	27	6	18	82	40	92	1	2	.319	.376	.525	.902	128	17	88	7.40	0	O-97(97-0-0),1-46	15	1.1
1995 Fla-N★	133	483	72	146	26	2	25	105	66	94	2	0	.302	.387	.520	.907	136	26	98	7.28	-2	*O-118(118-0-0),1-14	20	1.8
1996 Fla-N	157	597	84	175	32	2	26	95	62	121	1	4	.293	.363	.484	.848	125	19	102	6.11	6	*O-128(128-0-0),1-48	17	1.7
1997*Fla-N	151	405	46	98	13	1	17	61	57	89	2	0	.242	.338	.405	.743	98	-0	57	4.78	7	*1-145/O-1	9	-0.4
1998 KC-A	93	309	30	79	26	0	8	43	26	68	3	0	.256	.318	.417	.735	87	-6	41	4.49	-4	O-80(50-0-31),1-12/D-3	6	-1.4
1999 Bal-A	139	444	54	129	31	1	13	75	30	40	0	3	.291	.340	.453	.792	104	-0	65	5.17	-3	1-99,D-22,O-13(7-0-6)/3-4	10	-1.2
2000 Bal-A	119	409	53	116	20	2	13	46	36	53	4	3	.284	.345	.438	.782	101	-0	59	5.04	5	3-44,1-39,D-20,O-19(7-0-12)	9	0.0
2001 Bal-A	139	524	75	163	23	2	14	97	64	75	12	8	.311	.391	.443	.834	126	21	91	6.34	-3	1-80,O-36(22-0-16),3-17,D-12	24	0.8
2002 Bal-A	116	451	44	123	26	4	15	63	25	66	8	0	.273	.314	.448	.762	104	3	62	4.83	-8	*1-103/D-7,O-6(6-0-0)	10	-1.4
2003 Bal-A	124	493	75	143	33	3	15	80	37	60	5	0	.290	.346	.460	.806	114	10	77	5.51	-2	*1-118/O-8(6-0-2),3-1	14	-0.2
*Fla-N	25	84	13	20	3	0	5	15	13	10	0	0	.238	.340	.452	.793	109	1	13	5.27	2	O-25(25-0-0)	2	0.2
Total 13	**1510**	**5356**	**694**	**1538**	**291**	**28**	**181**	**852**	**518**	**931**	**40**	**22**	**.287**	**.354**	**.453**	**.807**	**112**	**86**	**848**	**5.64**	**0**	**1-760,O-701/3-66,D-64**	**154**	**-0.2**

• CONLAN, Jocko John Bertrand Conlan
b: 12/6/1899, Chicago, IL d: 4/16/1989, Scottsdale, AZ BL/TL, 5'7.5", 165 lbs. Deb: 7/6/1934 U HOF: 1974 Career OF: 0-75-20

YEAR TM-L	G	AB	R	H	2B	3B	HR	RBI	BB	SO	SB	CS	AVG	OBP	SLG	OPS	OPS+	BR/A	RC	RC/G	FR	G/POS	WS	TPW
1934 Chi-A	63	225	35	56	11	3	0	16	19	7	2	2	.249	.310	.324	.635	62	-13	24	3.44	-4	O-54(0-54-4)	2	-1.7
1935 Chi-A	65	140	20	40	7	1	0	15	14	6	3	3	.286	.355	.350	.705	81	-4	18	4.31	1	O-37(0-21-16)	3	-0.4
Total 2	**128**	**365**	**55**	**96**	**18**	**4**	**0**	**31**	**33**	**13**	**5**	**5**	**.263**	**.328**	**.334**	**.662**	**69**	**-18**	**41**	**3.77**	**-3**	**/O-91**	**5**	**-2.2**

• CONLON, Jocko Arthur Joseph Conlon b: 12/10/1897, Woburn, MA d: 8/5/1987, Falmouth, MA BR/TR, 5'7", 145 lbs. Deb: 4/17/1923

YEAR TM-L	G	AB	R	H	2B	3B	HR	RBI	BB	SO	SB	CS	AVG	OBP	SLG	OPS	OPS+	BR/A	RC	RC/G	FR	G/POS	WS	TPW
1923 Bos-N	59	147	23	32	3	0	0	17	11	11	0	3	.218	.299	.238	.537	45	-12	11	2.35	-6	2-36/S-6,3-4	1	-1.6

• CONN, Bert Albert Thomas Conn b: 9/22/1879, Philadelphia, PA d: 11/2/1944, Philadelphia, PA TR, 6' Deb: 9/16/1898 ♦

YEAR TM-L	G	AB	R	H	2B	3B	HR	RBI	BB	SO	SB	CS	AVG	OBP	SLG	OPS	OPS+	BR/A	RC	RC/G	FR	G/POS	WS	TPW
1898 Phi-N	1	3	1	1	0	1	0	1	0	....	0	....	.333	.333	1.000	1.333	291	1	1	13.58	0	/P-1	0	-0.1
1900 Phi-N	6	9	4	3	1	0	0	1	0	....	0	....	.333	.333	.444	.778	114	1	1	6.04	-1	/P-4	0	-0.8
1901 Phi-N	5	18	2	4	1	0	0	0	0	....	0	....	.222	.263	.278	.541	56	-1	1	2.55	-1	/2-5	0	-0.2
Total 3	**12**	**30**	**7**	**8**	**2**	**1**	**0**	**2**	**0**	**....**	**0**	**....**	**.267**	**.290**	**.400**	**.690**	**96**	**0**	**4**	**4.51**	**-2**	**/2-5,P-5**	**0**	**-1.1**

• CONNALLY, Fritzie Fritzie Lee Connally b: 5/19/1958, Bryan, TX BR/TR, 6'3", 210 lbs. Deb: 9/9/1983

YEAR TM-L	G	AB	R	H	2B	3B	HR	RBI	BB	SO	SB	CS	AVG	OBP	SLG	OPS	OPS+	BR/A	RC	RC/G	FR	G/POS	WS	TPW
1983 Chi-N	8	10	0	1	0	0	0	0	0	5	0	0	.100	.100	.100	.200	-42	-2	0	.30	0	/3-3	0	-0.2
1985 Bal-A	50	112	16	26	4	0	3	15	19	21	0	0	.232	.348	.348	.697	94	-0	15	4.58	0	3-46/1-2,D-1	3	-0.1
Total 2	**58**	**122**	**16**	**27**	**4**	**0**	**3**	**15**	**19**	**26**	**0**	**0**	**.221**	**.331**	**.328**	**.659**	**85**	**-2**	**15**	**4.19**	**0**	**/3-49,1-2,D-1**	**3**	**-0.3**

• CONNALLY, Red John M. Connally b: 1863, New York, NY d: 3/2/1896, New York, NY BB Deb: 7/1/1886 U

YEAR TM-L	G	AB	R	H	2B	3B	HR	RBI	BB	SO	SB	CS	AVG	OBP	SLG	OPS	OPS+	BR/A	RC	RC/G	FR	G/POS	WS	TPW
1886 StL-N	2	7	0	0	0	0	0	0	0	3	0	....	.000	.000	.000	.000	-107	-2	0	.00	0	/O-2(0-2-0)	0	-0.2

• CONNATSER, Bruce Broadus Milburn Connatser b: 9/19/1902, Sevierville, TN d: 1/27/1971, Terre Haute, IN BR/TR, 5'11.5", 170 lbs. Deb: 9/15/1931

YEAR TM-L	G	AB	R	H	2B	3B	HR	RBI	BB	SO	SB	CS	AVG	OBP	SLG	OPS	OPS+	BR/A	RC	RC/G	FR	G/POS	WS	TPW
1931 Cle-A	12	49	5	14	3	0	0	4	2	3	0	0	.286	.327	.347	.674	73	-2	6	4.23	1	1-12	1	-0.2
1932 Cle-A	23	60	8	14	3	1	0	4	4	8	1	0	.233	.281	.317	.598	51	-4	6	3.20	1	1-14	0	-0.4
Total 2	**35**	**109**	**13**	**28**	**6**	**1**	**0**	**8**	**6**	**11**	**1**	**0**	**.257**	**.302**	**.330**	**.632**	**61**	**-6**	**11**	**3.64**	**2**	**/1-26**	**1**	**-0.6**

• CONNAUGHTON, Frank Frank Henry Connaughton b: 1/1/1869, Clinton, MA d: 12/1/1942, Boston, MA BR/TR, 5'9", 165 lbs. Deb: 5/28/1894 Career OF: 32-2-0

YEAR TM-L	G	AB	R	H	2B	3B	HR	RBI	BB	SO	SB	CS	AVG	OBP	SLG	OPS	OPS+	BR/A	RC	RC/G	FR	G/POS	WS	TPW
1894 Bos-N	46	171	42	59	9	2	2	33	16	8	3	....	.345	.407	.456	.864	96	-2	34	7.85	2	S-33/C-7,O-4(2-2-0)	6	0.2
1896 NY-N	88	315	53	82	3	2	2	43	25	7	22	....	.260	.319	.302	.620	66	-15	39	4.33	3	S-54,O-30(30-0-0)	6	-1.0
1906 Bos-N	12	44	3	9	0	0	0	1	3	....	1	....	.205	.271	.205	.475	50	-2	3	2.06	-1	S-11/2-1	0	-0.4
Total 3	**146**	**530**	**98**	**150**	**12**	**4**	**4**	**77**	**44**	**15**	**26**	**....**	**.283**	**.344**	**.343**	**.687**	**74**	**-19**	**75**	**5.15**	**5**	**/S-98,O-34,C-7,2-1**	**12**	**-1.1**

• CONNELL, Gene Eugene Joseph Connell b: 5/10/1906, Hazleton, PA d: 8/31/1937, Waverly, NY BR/TR, 6'.5", 180 lbs. Deb: 7/4/1931

YEAR TM-L	G	AB	R	H	2B	3B	HR	RBI	BB	SO	SB	CS	AVG	OBP	SLG	OPS	OPS+	BR/A	RC	RC/G	FR	G/POS	WS	TPW
1931 Phi-N	6	12	1	3	0	0	0	0	0	3	0	....	.250	.250	.250	.500	32	-1	1	2.11	0	/C-6	0	-0.1

• CONNELL, Joe Joseph Bernard Connell b: 1/16/1902, Bethlehem, PA d: 9/21/1977, Trexlertown, PA BL/TL, 5'8", 165 lbs. Deb: 6/15/1926

YEAR TM-L	G	AB	R	H	2B	3B	HR	RBI	BB	SO	SB	CS	AVG	OBP	SLG	OPS	OPS+	BR/A	RC	RC/G	FR	G/POS	WS	TPW
1926 NY-N	2	1	1	0	0	0	0	0	0	0	0	....	.000	.000	.000	.000	-101	-0	0	.00	0	....	0	0.0

• CONNELL, Pat Peter J. Connell b: 1862, Brooklyn, NY d: 5/5/1892, Brooklyn, NY, 6'1", 180 lbs. Deb: 9/3/1886

YEAR TM-L	G	AB	R	H	2B	3B	HR	RBI	BB	SO	SB	CS	AVG	OBP	SLG	OPS	OPS+	BR/A	RC	RC/G	FR	G/POS	WS	TPW
1886 NY-a	1	5	0	0	0	0	0	0	0	....	0	....	.000	.000	.000	.000	-105	-1	0	.00	0	/3-1	0	-0.1
1890 Bro-a	11	40	7	9	2	1	0	3	7	....	3	....	.225	.340	.325	.665	99	0	6	4.77	-2	3-10/1-1	1	-0.1
Total 2	**12**	**45**	**7**	**9**	**2**	**1**	**0**	**3**	**7**	**....**	**3**	**....**	**.200**	**.308**	**.289**	**.597**	**80**	**-1**	**6**	**4.11**	**-2**	**/3-11,1-1**	**1**	**-0.2**

• CONNELL, Terry

Terence G. Connell b: 6/17/1855, Philadelphia, PA d: 3/25/1924, Narberth, PA Deb: 6/20/1874 U

YEAR TM-L	G	AB	R	H	2B	3B	HR	RBI	BB	SO	SB	CS	AVG	OBP	SLG	OPS	OPS+	BR/A	RC	RC/G	FR	G/POS	WS	TPW
1874 Chi-n	1	4	0	0	0	0	0	0	0	0	0	0	.000	.000	.000	.000	-99	-1	0	.00	-1	/C-1	....	-0.1

• CONNELLY, Tom

Thomas Martin Connelly b: 10/20/1897, Chicago, IL d: 2/18/1941, Hines, IL BL/TR, 5'11.5", 165 lbs. Deb: 9/24/1920

YEAR TM-L	G	AB	R	H	2B	3B	HR	RBI	BB	SO	SB	CS	AVG	OBP	SLG	OPS	OPS+	BR/A	RC	RC/G	FR	G/POS	WS	TPW
1920 NY-A	1	1	0	0	0	0	0	0	0	0	0	0	.000	.000	.000	.000	-97	-0	0	.00	0	....	0	0.0
1921 NY-A	4	5	0	1	0	0	0	0	1	0	0	0	.200	.333	.200	.533	38	-0	0	2.67	-0	/0-3(0-1-2)	0	-0.1
Total 2	5	6	0	1	0	0	0	0	1	0	0	0	.167	.286	.167	.452	19	-1	0	2.14	-0	/0-3	0	-0.1

• CONNOLLY, Bud

Mervin Thomas "Mike" Connolly b: 5/25/1901, San Francisco, CA d: 6/12/1964, Berkeley, CA BR/TR, 5'8", 154 lbs. Deb: 5/3/1925

YEAR TM-L	G	AB	R	H	2B	3B	HR	RBI	BB	SO	SB	CS	AVG	OBP	SLG	OPS	OPS+	BR/A	RC	RC/G	FR	G/POS	WS	TPW
1925 Bos-A	43	107	12	28	7	1	0	21	23	9	0	3	.262	.392	.346	.738	89	-2	15	4.85	-1	S-34/3-2	2	0.0

• CONNOLLY, Ed

Edward Joseph Connolly, Sr. b: 7/17/1908, Brooklyn, NY d: 11/12/1963, Pittsfield, MA BR/TR, 5'8.5", 180 lbs. Deb: 9/20/1929

YEAR TM-L	G	AB	R	H	2B	3B	HR	RBI	BB	SO	SB	CS	AVG	OBP	SLG	OPS	OPS+	BR/A	RC	RC/G	FR	G/POS	WS	TPW
1929 Bos-A	5	8	0	0	0	0	0	0	0	2	0	0	.000	.000	.000	.000	-102	-2	0	.00	0	/C-5	0	-0.2
1930 Bos-A	27	48	1	9	2	0	0	7	4	3	0	0	.188	.250	.229	.479	23	-6	3	1.94	1	C-26	1	-0.3
1931 Bos-A	42	93	3	7	1	0	0	3	5	18	0	0	.075	.131	.086	.217	-44	-19	1	.38	-0	C-41	1	-1.6
1932 Bos-A	75	222	9	50	8	4	0	21	20	27	0	1	.225	.289	.297	.587	54	-15	20	2.97	3	C-75	1	-0.8
Total 4	149	371	13	66	11	4	0	31	29	50	0	1	.178	.239	.229	.469	22	-42	24	2.03	4	C-147	3	-2.9

• CONNOLLY, Joe

Joseph George "Coaster Joe" Connolly
b: 6/27/1896, San Francisco, CA d: 3/30/1960, San Francisco, CA BR/TR, 6', 170 lbs. Deb: 10/1/1921 Career OF: 3-15-37

YEAR TM-L	G	AB	R	H	2B	3B	HR	RBI	BB	SO	SB	CS	AVG	OBP	SLG	OPS	OPS+	BR/A	RC	RC/G	FR	G/POS	WS	TPW
1921 NY-N	2	4	0	0	0	0	0	0	1	1	0	0	.000	.200	.000	.200	-43	-1	0	.33	0	/0-1	0	-0.1
1922 Cle-A	12	45	6	11	2	1	0	6	5	8	1	0	.244	.320	.333	.653	70	-2	5	3.95	1	0-12(0-12-0)	1	-0.1
1923 Cle-A	52	109	25	33	10	1	3	25	13	7	1	2	.303	.377	.495	.872	129	4	20	6.27	-3	0-39(2-3-34)	3	-0.1
1924 Bos-A	14	10	1	1	0	0	0	1	2	2	0	0	.100	.250	.100	.350	-8	-2	0	1.19	0	/0-3(0-0-3)	0	-0.2
Total 4	80	168	32	45	12	2	3	32	21	18	2	2	.268	.349	.417	.766	100	-0	26	5.11	-2	/0-55	4	-0.5

• CONNOLLY, Joe

Joseph Aloysius Connolly
b: 2/1/1884, North Smithfield, RI d: 9/1/1943, North Smithfield, RI BL/TR, 5'7.5", 165 lbs. Deb: 4/10/1913 Career OF: 334-7-26

YEAR TM-L	G	AB	R	H	2B	3B	HR	RBI	BB	SO	SB	CS	AVG	OBP	SLG	OPS	OPS+	BR/A	RC	RC/G	FR	G/POS	WS	TPW
1913 Bos-N	126	427	79	120	18	11	5	57	66	47	18	....	.281	.379	.410	.788	123	15	72	5.62	-5	*0-124(124-0-0)	19	0.5
1914*Bos-N	120	399	64	122	28	10	9	65	49	36	12	....	.306	.393	.494	.886	164	32	80	7.14	1	*0-118(115-0-5)	25	3.0
1915 Bos-N	104	305	48	91	14	8	0	23	39	35	13	12	.298	.387	.397	.784	140	14	48	5.42	-3	0-93(81-3-9)	15	0.7
1916 Bos-N	62	110	11	25	5	2	0	12	14	13	5	....	.227	.320	.309	.629	99	0	13	3.78	1	0-31(14-4-12)	4	0.0
Total 4	412	1241	202	358	65	31	14	157	168	131	48	12	.288	.380	.425	.805	138	61	212	5.86	-7	0-366	63	4.3

• CONNOLLY, Tom

Thomas Francis "Blackie,Ham" Connolly b: 12/30/1892, Boston, MA d: 5/14/1966, Boston, MA BL/TR, 5'11", 175 lbs. Deb: 5/12/1915

YEAR TM-L	G	AB	R	H	2B	3B	HR	RBI	BB	SO	SB	CS	AVG	OBP	SLG	OPS	OPS+	BR/A	RC	RC/G	FR	G/POS	WS	TPW
1915 Was-A	50	141	14	26	3	2	0	7	14	19	5	4	.184	.268	.234	.502	49	-10	9	2.05	-1	3-24,0-19(11-0-8)/S-4	1	-1.0

• CONNOR, Jim

James Matthew Connor b: 5/11/1863, Port Jervis, NY d: 9/3/1950, Providence, RI BR/TR, 5'10.5" Deb: 7/11/1892

YEAR TM-L	G	AB	R	H	2B	3B	HR	RBI	BB	SO	SB	CS	AVG	OBP	SLG	OPS	OPS+	BR/A	RC	RC/G	FR	G/POS	WS	TPW
1892 Chi-N	9	34	0	2	0	0	0	0	1	7	0	....	.059	.111	.059	.170	-48	-6	0	.19	-4	/2-9	0	-0.9
1897 Chi-N	77	285	40	83	10	5	3	38	24	....	10	....	.291	.355	.393	.748	94	-3	45	5.76	5	2-76	8	0.5
1898 Chi-N	138	505	51	114	9	9	0	67	42	....	11	....	.226	.289	.279	.568	63	-24	47	3.07	-7	*2-138	8	-2.4
1899 Chi-N	69	234	26	48	7	1	0	24	18	....	6	....	.205	.265	.244	.508	41	-19	18	2.48	-2	2-44,3-25	2	-1.6
Total 4	293	1058	117	247	26	15	3	129	85	7	27	....	.233	.296	.295	.591	63	-52	110	3.48	-7	2-267/3-25	18	-4.4

• CONNOR, Joe

Joseph Francis Connor b: 12/8/1874, Waterbury, CT d: 11/8/1957, Waterbury, CT BR/TR, 6'2", 185 lbs. Deb: 9/9/1895

YEAR TM-L	G	AB	R	H	2B	3B	HR	RBI	BB	SO	SB	CS	AVG	OBP	SLG	OPS	OPS+	BR/A	RC	RC/G	FR	G/POS	WS	TPW
1895 StL-N	2	7	0	0	0	0	0	1	0	2	0	....	.000	.000	.000	.000	-101	-2	0	.00	1	/3-2	0	-0.1
1900 Bos-N	7	19	2	4	0	0	0	4	2	....	1	....	.211	.286	.211	.496	34	-2	1	2.59	1	/C-7	0	0.0
1901 Mil-A	38	102	10	28	3	1	1	9	6	....	4	....	.275	.321	.353	.674	91	-1	14	4.65	2	C-30/2-1,3-1,0-1	2	0.3
Cle-A	37	121	13	17	3	1	0	6	7	....	2	....	.140	.200	.182	.382	7	-15	5	1.30	1	C-32/0-4(0-0-4),S-1	1	-1.1
Yr.	75	223	23	45	6	2	1	15	13	....	6	....	.202	.255	.260	.515	45	-16	19	2.70	2	C-62/0-5(0-1-4),2-1,3-1,S	3	-0.8
1905 NY-A	8	22	4	5	1	0	0	2	3	....	1	....	.227	.320	.273	.593	79	-0	3	3.58	2	/C-6,1-2	0	0.3
Total 4	92	271	29	54	7	2	1	22	18	2	8	....	.199	.257	.251	.508	44	-20	23	2.69	6	/C-75,0-5,3-3,1-2,2-1,S-1	3	-0.7

• CONNOR, Roger

Roger Connor b: 7/1/1857, Waterbury, CT d: 1/4/1931, Waterbury, CT BL/TL, 6'3", 220 lbs. Deb: 5/1/1880 M HOF: 1976 Career OF: 5-56-1

YEAR TM-L	G	AB	R	H	2B	3B	HR	RBI	BB	SO	SB	CS	AVG	OBP	SLG	OPS	OPS+	BR/A	RC	RC/G	FR	G/POS	WS	TPW
1880 Tro-N	83	340	53	113	18	8	3	47	13	21	....	....	.332	.357	.459	.816	165	22	57	6.91	-8	*3-83	17	1.6
1881 Tro-N	85	367	55	107	17	6	2	31	15	20	....	....	.292	.319	.387	.706	115	5	46	4.83	-2	*1-85	11	-0.1
1882 Tro-N	81	349	65	115	22	**18**	4	42	13	20	....	....	.330	.354	.530	.884	188	34	67	7.88	1	1-43,0-24(5-19-0),3-14	19	2.8
1883 NY-N	98	409	80	146	28	15	1	50	25	16	....	....	.357	.394	.506	.900	173	36	84	8.74	2	*1-98	19	2.5
1884 NY-N	116	477	98	151	28	4	4	82	38	32	....	....	.317	.367	.417	.784	142	24	75	6.31	-3	2-67,0-37(0-37-0),3-12	23	2.0
1885 NY-N	110	455	102	**169**	23	15	1	65	51	8	....	....	**.371**	**.435**	.495	.929	**203**	**54**	100	9.47	6	*1-110	**30**	**4.7**
1886 NY-N	118	485	105	172	29	**20**	7	71	41	15	17	....	.355	.405	.540	.945	183	48	116	9.99	10	*1-118	**36**	4.3
1887 NY-N	127	546	113	209	26	22	17	104	75	50	43	....	.383	.392	.541	.933	164	44	120	9.41	6	*1-127	21	3.3
1888*NY-N	134	481	98	140	15	17	14	71	**73**	44	27	....	.291	.389	.480	.869	**178**	46	103	8.14	6	*1-133/2-1	32	3.9
1889*NY-N	131	496	117	157	32	17	13	**130**	93	46	21	....	.317	.426	**.528**	.955	**166**	47	124	9.67	-6	*1-131/3-1	26	2.5
1890 NY-P	123	484	133	169	24	15	**14**	103	88	32	22	....	.349	.450	**.548**	**.998**	152	37	132	11.35	20	*1-123	25	3.8
1891 NY-N	129	479	112	139	29	13	7	94	83	39	27	....	.290	.399	.449	.848	153	36	99	7.87	3	*1-129	23	2.5
1892 Phi-N	155	564	123	166	**37**	11	12	73	116	39	22	....	.294	.420	.463	.883	167	52	122	8.26	-11	*1-155	24	3.7
1893 NY-N	135	511	111	156	25	8	11	105	91	26	24	....	.305	.413	.450	.863	129	24	108	8.03	4	*1-135/3-1	16	2.2
1894 NY-N	22	82	10	24	7	0	1	14	8	0	2	....	.293	.356	.415	.770	86	-2	13	5.88	4	1-21/0-1	2	0.1
StL-N	99	380	83	122	28	25	7	79	51	17	17	....	.321	.410	.582	.991	137	22	100	10.07	4	*1-99	12	1.9
Yr.	121	462	93	146	35	25	8	93	59	17	19	....	.316	.400	.552	.952	128	19	113	9.30	7	*1-120/0-1	14	2.0
1895 StL-N	104	401	78	131	29	9	8	78	63	10	9	....	.327	.421	.504	.924	140	25	91	9.05	3	*1-103	12	2.3
1896 StL-N	126	483	71	137	21	9	11	72	52	14	10	....	.284	.356	.433	.788	112	8	80	6.12	10	*1-126	14	1.5
1897 StL-N	22	83	13	19	3	1	1	12	13	....	3	....	.229	.333	.325	.659	76	-3	10	4.24	-2	1-22	1	-0.4
Total 18	1998	7872	1620	2542	441	233	138	1323	1002	449	244	....	.323	.397	.486	.883	155	558	1647	8.30	46	*1-1758,3-111/2-68,0-62	363	45.1

• CONNORS, Chuck

Kevin Joseph Aloysius Connors b: 4/10/1921, Brooklyn, NY d: 11/10/1992, Los Angeles, CA BL/TL, 6'5", 190 lbs. Deb: 5/1/1949

YEAR TM-L	G	AB	R	H	2B	3B	HR	RBI	BB	SO	SB	CS	AVG	OBP	SLG	OPS	OPS+	BR/A	RC	RC/G	FR	G/POS	WS	TPW
1949 Bro-N	1	1	0	0	0	0	0	0	0	0	0	....	.000	.000	.000	.000	-96	-0	0	.00	0	....	0	0.0
1951 Chi-N	66	201	16	48	5	1	2	18	12	25	4	0	.239	.282	.303	.585	56	-12	19	3.35	-2	1-57	2	-1.6
Total 2	67	202	16	48	5	1	2	18	12	25	4	0	.238	.280	.302	.582	56	-12	19	3.31	-2	/1-57	2	-1.6

• CONNORS, Jerry

Jeremiah Connors b: Cleveland, OH Deb: 7/11/1892

YEAR TM-L	G	AB	R	H	2B	3B	HR	RBI	BB	SO	SB	CS	AVG	OBP	SLG	OPS	OPS+	BR/A	RC	RC/G	FR	G/POS	WS	TPW
1892 Phi-N	1	3	0	0	0	0	0	0	0	1	0	....	.000	.000	.000	.000	-100	-1	0	.00	0	/0-1	0	-0.1

• CONNORS, Joe

Joseph P. Connors b: 1862, Paterson, NJ d: 1/13/1891, Denver, CO Deb: 5/3/1884 ♦

YEAR TM-L	G	AB	R	H	2B	3B	HR	RBI	BB	SO	SB	CS	AVG	OBP	SLG	OPS	OPS+	BR/A	RC	RC/G	FR	G/POS	WS	TPW
1884 Alt-U	3	11	0	1	0	0	0	....	0	....	....	....	.091	.091	.091	.182	-38	-1	0	.26	-1	/3-1,0-1,P-1	0	-0.4
KC-U	3	11	2	1	0	0	0	....	1	....	....	....	.091	.167	.091	.258	-12	-1	0	.48	0	/0-2(0-2-0),P-2	0	-0.2
Yr.	6	22	2	2	0	0	0	....	1	....	....	....	.091	.130	.091	.221	-25	-2	0	.37	-1	/0-3(0-3-0),P-3,3-1	0	-0.7

• CONNORS, Merv

Mervin James Connors b: 1/23/1914, Berkeley, CA BR/TR, 6'2", 192 lbs. Deb: 9/4/1937

YEAR TM-L	G	AB	R	H	2B	3B	HR	RBI	BB	SO	SB	CS	AVG	OBP	SLG	OPS	OPS+	BR/A	RC	RC/G	FR	G/POS	WS	TPW
1937 Chi-A	28	103	12	24	4	1	2	12	14	19	2	1	.233	.325	.350	.674	70	-5	12	4.06	-1	3-28	2	-0.4
1938 Chi-A	24	62	14	22	4	0	6	13	9	17	0	0	.355	.437	.710	1.146	178	7	19	12.52	1	1-16	3	0.7
Total 2	52	165	26	46	8	1	8	25	23	36	2	1	.279	.367	.485	.852	111	3	32	6.90	0	/3-28,1-16	5	0.2

• CONNORS, Ned

Joseph P. Connors b: 1850, NY, 5'9", 156 lbs. Deb: 5/18/1871

YEAR TM-L	G	AB	R	H	2B	3B	HR	RBI	BB	SO	SB	CS	AVG	OBP	SLG	OPS	OPS+	BR/A	RC	RC/G	FR	G/POS	WS	TPW
1871 Tro-n	7	33	6	7	0	0	0	2	0	0	0	0	.212	.212	.212	.424	22	-3	2	1.84	0	/1-4,0-3(0-0-3)	....	-0.2

• CONROY, Ben

Bernard Patrick Conroy b: 3/14/1871, Philadelphia, PA d: 11/25/1937, Philadelphia, PA, 160 lbs. Deb: 4/21/1890

YEAR TM-L	G	AB	R	H	2B	3B	HR	RBI	BB	SO	SB	CS	AVG	OBP	SLG	OPS	OPS+	BR/A	RC	RC/G	FR	G/POS	WS	TPW
1890 Phi-a	117	404	45	69	13	1	0	21	45	....	17	....	.171	.262	.208	.470	39	-30	27	2.15	-15	S-74,2-42/0-1	4	-3.6

YEAR TM-L	G	AB	R	H	2B	3B	HR	RBI	BB	SO	SB	CS	AVG	OBP	SLG	OPS	OPS+	BR/A	RC	RC/G	FR	G/POS	WS	TPW
• CONROY, Bill	William Gordon Conroy b: 2/26/1915, Bloomington, IL d: 11/13/1997, Citrus Heights, CA BR/TR, 6', 185 lbs. Deb: 9/21/1935																							
1935 Phi-A	1	4	0	1	1	0	0	0	1	0	0	0	.250	.400	.500	.900	133	0	1	7.67	1	/C-1	0	0.1
1936 Phi-A	1	2	0	1	0	0	0	0	0	1	0	0	.500	.500	.500	1.000	151	0	0	12.72	0	/C-1	0	0.0
1937 Phi-A	26	60	4	12	1	1	0	3	7	9	1	0	.200	.284	.250	.534	36	-6	5	2.61	0	C-18/1-1	0	-0.5
1942 Bos-A	83	250	22	50	4	2	4	20	40	47	2	0	.200	.315	.280	.595	66	-10	26	3.30	-7	C-83	6	-1.1
1943 Bos-A	39	89	13	16	5	0	1	6	18	19	0	0	.180	.336	.270	.606	77	-1	9	3.28	-2	C-38	2	-0.1
1944 Bos-A	19	47	6	10	2	0	0	4	11	9	0	0	.213	.362	.255	.617	79	-1	5	3.71	0	C-19	2	0.0
Total 6	**169**	**452**	**45**	**90**	**13**	**3**	**5**	**33**	**77**	**85**	**3**	**0**	**.199**	**.322**	**.274**	**.596**	**67**	**-17**	**46**	**3.31**	**-8**	**C-160/1-1**	**10**	**-1.6**
• CONROY, Bill	William Frederick "Pep" Conroy b: 1/9/1899, Chicago, IL d: 1/23/1970, Chicago, IL BR/TR, 5'8.5", 160 lbs. Deb: 4/18/1923																							
1923 Was-A	18	60	6	8	2	2	0	2	4	9	0	0	.133	.188	.233	.421	11	-8	3	1.37	0	3-10/1-6,O-1	0	-0.8
• CONROY, Wid	William Edward Conroy b: 4/5/1877, Camden, NJ d: 12/6/1959, Mount Holly, NJ BR/TR, 5'9", 158 lbs. Deb: 4/25/1901 C Career OF: 224-76-10																							
1901 Mil-A	131	503	74	129	20	6	5	64	36	....	21	....	.256	.316	.350	.666	89	-7	65	4.48	10	*S-118,3-12	13	0.7
1902 Pit-N	99	365	55	89	10	6	1	47	24	....	10	....	.244	.299	.312	.612	86	-6	39	3.64	15	S-95/O-3(2-0-1)	12	1.2
1903 NY-A	126	503	74	137	23	12	1	45	32	....	33	....	.272	.322	.372	.694	101	1	74	5.21	3	*3-123/S-4	21	0.7
1904 NY-A	140	489	58	119	18	12	1	52	43	....	30	....	.243	.314	.335	.649	100	1	64	4.40	4	*3-110,S-27/O-3(0-3-0)	18	1.0
1905 NY-A	101	385	55	105	19	11	2	25	32	....	25	....	.273	.329	.395	.723	116	6	60	5.57	8	3-48,O-25(20-3-2),S-17,1-10/2	18	1.6
1906 NY-A	148	567	67	139	17	10	4	54	47	....	32	....	.245	.303	.332	.635	89	-7	70	4.18	-1	O-97(37-66-0),S-49/3-2	19	-1.3
1907 NY-A	140	530	58	124	12	11	3	51	30	....	41	....	.234	.279	.315	.594	83	-12	60	3.86	4	*O-100(100-0-0),S-38	15	-1.4
1908 NY-A	141	531	44	126	22	3	1	39	14	....	23	....	.237	.258	.296	.554	79	-14	46	2.81	13	*3-119,2-12,O-10(5-1-4)	11	0.2
1909 Was-A	139	488	44	119	13	4	1	20	37	....	24	....	.244	.298	.293	.592	91	-5	51	3.35	-2	*3-120,2-13/O-5(2-3-0),S-1	12	-0.5
1910 Was-A	103	351	36	89	11	3	1	27	30	....	11	....	.254	.314	.311	.625	100	0	38	3.59	-2	3-46,O-46(44-0-2)/2-5	9	-0.4
1911 Was-A	106	349	40	81	11	4	2	28	20	....	12	....	.232	.282	.304	.585	64	-18	33	3.07	0	3-85,O-15(14-0-1)/2-1	5	-1.6
Total 11	**1374**	**5061**	**605**	**1257**	**176**	**82**	**22**	**452**	**345**	**....**	**262**	**....**	**.248**	**.301**	**.329**	**.629**	**91**	**-61**	**601**	**4.01**	**51**	**3-665,S-349,O-304/2-34,1-10**	**153**	**0.2**
• CONSOLO, Billy	William Angelo Consolo b: 8/18/1934, Cleveland, OH BR/TR, 5'11", 180 lbs. Deb: 4/20/1953 C																							
1953 Bos-A	47	65	9	14	2	1	1	6	2	23	1	2	.215	.239	.323	.562	48	-6	5	2.40	-1	3-16,2-11	1	-0.6
1954 Bos-A	91	242	23	55	7	1	1	11	33	69	2	1	.227	.325	.277	.602	59	-12	24	3.31	-9	S-50,3-18,2-12	4	-1.7
1955 Bos-A	8	18	4	4	0	0	0	0	5	4	0	0	.222	.391	.222	.614	63	-1	2	3.32	-2	/2-4	0	-0.2
1956 Bos-A	48	11	13	2	0	0	0	1	3	5	0	0	.182	.357	.182	.539	41	-1	1	2.98	-7	2-25	0	-0.7
1957 Bos-A	68	196	26	53	6	1	4	19	23	48	1	3	.270	.347	.372	.719	91	-3	25	4.45	-4	S-42,2-16/3-2	5	-0.3
1958 Bos-A	46	72	13	9	2	1	0	5	6	14	0	0	.125	.192	.181	.373	3	-10	2	.92	-2	2-13,S-11/3-1	1	-1.0
1959 Bos-A	10	14	3	3	1	0	0	0	2	5	0	0	.214	.313	.286	.598	63	-1	1	3.34	-1	/S-2	0	-0.2
Was-A	79	202	25	43	5	3	0	10	36	54	1	0	.213	.332	.267	.599	67	-7	21	3.35	2	S-75/2-4	5	0.0
Yr.	89	216	28	46	6	3	0	10	38	59	1	0	.213	.331	.269	.599	67	-8	22	3.35	1	S-77/2-4	5	-0.2
1960 Was-A	100	174	23	36	4	2	3	15	25	29	1	1	.207	.310	.305	.615	66	-8	17	3.12	0	S-82,2-12/3-2	4	-0.4
1961 Min-A	11	5	1	0	0	0	0	0	0	1	0	0	.000	.000	.000	.000	-95	-1	0	.00	-2	/2-3,S-3,3-1	0	-0.4
1962 Phi-N	13	5	3	2	0	0	0	0	0	1	0	0	.400	.400	.400	.800	119	0	1	7.20	0	/3-1	0	0.0
LA-A	28	20	4	2	0	0	0	0	3	11	2	0	.100	.217	.100	.317	-12	-3	1	.94	-3	3-20/S-4,2-1	0	-0.6
KC-A	54	154	11	37	4	2	0	16	23	33	1	3	.240	.339	.292	.631	69	-7	16	3.43	-2	S-48	2	-0.5
Yr.	82	174	15	39	4	2	0	16	26	44	3	3	.224	.325	.270	.595	60	-10	17	3.11	-5	S-52,3-20/2-1	2	-1.1
Total 10	**603**	**1178**	**158**	**260**	**31**	**11**	**9**	**83**	**161**	**297**	**9**	**10**	**.221**	**.316**	**.289**	**.605**	**63**	**-59**	**116**	**3.22**	**-32**	**S-317,2-101/3-61**	**22**	**-6.6**
• CONTI, Jason	Stanley Jason Conti b: 1/27/1975, Pittsburgh, PA BL/TR, 5'11", 180 lbs. Deb: 6/29/2000 Career OF: 24-33-81																							
2000 Ari-N	47	91	11	21	4	3	1	15	7	30	3	0	.231	.293	.374	.667	65	-5	10	3.80	4	O-35(2-4-33)	3	-0.2
2001 Ari-N	5	4	1	1	0	0	0	0	1	2	0	0	.250	.400	.250	.650	70	-0	1	4.54	0	/O-1	0	0.0
2002 TB-A	78	222	26	57	15	2	3	21	18	55	4	2	.257	.315	.383	.698	86	-5	26	4.05	5	O-74(21-28-28)	4	-0.2
2003 Mil-N	30	48	3	11	2	0	2	7	2	18	0	1	.229	.260	.396	.656	69	-3	4	2.86	1	O-20(1-1-19)	1	-0.3
Total 4	**160**	**365**	**41**	**90**	**21**	**5**	**6**	**43**	**28**	**105**	**7**	**3**	**.247**	**.304**	**.381**	**.685**	**78**	**-12**	**41**	**3.83**	**9**	**O-130**	**8**	**-0.6**
• CONWAY, Bill	William F. Conway b: 11/28/1861, Lowell, MA d: 12/28/1943, Somerville, MA BR/TR, 5'8", 170 lbs. Deb: 7/28/1884																							
1884 Phi-N	1	4	0	0	0	0	0	0	0	1	....	....	.000	.000	.000	.000	-105	-1	0	.00	-0	/C-1	0	-0.1
1886 Bal-a	7	14	4	2	0	0	0	3	7	....	0	....	.143	.429	.143	.571	84	1	1	1.98	-2	/C-7	1	-0.1
Total 2	**8**	**18**	**4**	**2**	**0**	**0**	**0**	**3**	**7**	**1**	**0**	**....**	**.111**	**.360**	**.111**	**.471**	**54**	**-0**	**1**	**1.48**	**-2**	**/C-8**	**1**	**-0.2**
• CONWAY, Charlie	Charles Connell Conway b: 4/28/1886, Youngstown, OH d: 9/12/1968, Youngstown, OH BR/TR, 5'11" Deb: 4/15/1911																							
1911 Was-A	2	3	0	1	0	1	0	0	0	....	0	....	.333	.333	1.000	1.333	272	1	1	7.79	-1	/O-2(0-0-0)	0	0.0
• CONWAY, Jack	Jack Clements Conway b: 7/30/1919, Bryan, TX d: 6/11/1993, Waco, TX BR/TR, 5'11.5", 175 lbs. Deb: 9/9/1941																							
1941 Cle-A	2	2	0	1	0	0	0	1	0	0	0	0	.500	.500	.500	1.000	174	0	1	13.84	0	/S-2	0	0.0
1946 Cle-A	68	258	24	58	6	2	0	18	20	36	2	2	.225	.281	.264	.544	56	-15	20	2.51	-3	2-50,S-14/3-3	3	-1.6
1947 Cle-A	34	50	3	9	2	0	0	5	3	8	0	0	.180	.226	.220	.446	25	-5	2	1.09	-3	S-24/2-5,3-1	0	-0.7
1948 NY-N	24	49	8	12	2	1	1	3	5	10	0	....	.245	.315	.388	.703	89	-1	6	4.27	1	2-13/S-6,3-3	1	0.1
Total 4	**128**	**359**	**35**	**80**	**10**	**3**	**1**	**27**	**28**	**54**	**2**	**2**	**.223**	**.279**	**.276**	**.555**	**57**	**-21**	**28**	**2.55**	**-5**	**/2-68,S-46,3-7**	**4**	**-2.2**
• CONWAY, Owen	Owen Sylvester Conway b: 10/23/1890, New York, NY d: 3/12/1942, Philadelphia, PA TR Deb: 6/21/1915																							
1915 Phi-A	4	15	2	1	0	0	0	0	0	3	0	....	.067	.067	.067	.133	-62	-3	0	.13	1	/3-4	0	-0.2
• CONWAY, Rip	Richard Daniel Conway b: 4/18/1896, White Bear Lake, MN d: 12/2/1972, St. Paul, MN BL/TR, 5'6", 160 lbs. Deb: 4/16/1918																							
1918 Bos-N	14	24	4	4	0	0	0	2	2	4	1	....	.167	.231	.167	.397	23	-2	1	1.53	-3	/2-5,3-1	0	-0.6
• CONWELL, Ed	Edward James "Irish" Conwell b: 1/29/1890, Chicago, IL d: 5/1/1926, Chicago, IL BR/TR, 5'11", 155 lbs. Deb: 9/22/1911																							
1911 StL-N	1	1	0	0	0	0	0	0	0	1	0	....	.000	.000	.000	.000	-103	-0	0	.00	-1	/3-1	0	-0.1
• CONYERS, Herb	Herbert Leroy Conyers b: 1/8/1921, Cowgill, MO d: 9/16/1964, Cleveland, OH BL/TR, 6'5", 205 lbs. Deb: 4/18/1950																							
1950 Cle-A	7	9	2	3	0	0	1	1	1	2	1	0	.333	.400	.667	1.067	175	1	3	12.47	0	/1-1	0	0.1
• COOGAN, Dale	Dale Roger Coogan b: 8/14/1930, Los Angeles, CA d: 3/8/1989, Mission Viejo, CA BL/TL, 6'1", 190 lbs. Deb: 4/22/1950																							
1950 Pit-N	53	129	19	31	6	1	1	13	17	24	0	....	.240	.338	.326	.663	73	-5	15	3.86	1	1-32	1	-0.4
• COOGAN, Dan	Daniel George Coogan b: 2/16/1875, Philadelphia, PA d: 10/28/1942, Philadelphia, PA, 5'8", 128 lbs. Deb: 4/25/1895 U																							
1895 Was-N	26	77	9	17	2	1	0	7	13	6	1	....	.221	.333	.273	.606	58	-4	8	3.40	-11	S-18/C-5,O-2(0-0-2),3-1	0	-1.2
• COOK, Cliff	Raymond Clifford Cook b: 8/20/1936, Dallas, TX BR/TR, 6', 188 lbs. Deb: 9/9/1959 Career OF: 11-2-12																							
1959 Cin-N	9	21	3	8	2	1	0	5	2	8	1	0	.381	.435	.571	1.006	160	2	6	10.69	0	/3-9	1	0.2
1960 Cin-N	54	149	9	31	7	0	3	13	8	51	0	0	.208	.248	.315	.564	52	-10	12	2.64	3	3-47/O-4(3-1-0)	2	-0.8
1961 Cin-N	4	5	0	0	0	0	0	0	0	4	0	0	.000	.000	.000	.000	-99	-1	0	.00	0	/3-1	0	-0.1
1962 Cin-N	6	5	0	0	0	0	0	0	0	2	0	0	.000	.000	.000	.000	-97	-1	0	.00	-1	/3-4	0	-0.2
NY-N	40	112	12	26	6	1	2	9	4	34	1	0	.232	.277	.357	.634	68	-5	12	3.66	-4	3-16,O-10(0-0-10)	1	-0.9
Yr.	46	117	12	26	6	1	2	9	4	36	1	0	.222	.266	.342	.608	61	-7	12	3.46	-5	3-20,O-10(0-0-10)	1	-1.2
1963 NY-N	50	106	9	15	2	1	2	8	12	37	0	1	.142	.229	.236	.465	33	-9	6	1.67	2	O-21(8-1-2)/3-9,1-5	1	-0.9
Total 5	**163**	**398**	**33**	**80**	**17**	**3**	**7**	**35**	**26**	**136**	**2**	**1**	**.201**	**.255**	**.312**	**.567**	**54**	**-25**	**35**	**2.89**	**0**	**/3-86,O-35,1-5**	**5**	**-2.8**
• COOK, Doc	Luther Almus Cook b: 6/24/1886, Witt, TX d: 6/30/1973, Lawrenceburg, TN BL/TR, 6', 170 lbs. Deb: 8/7/1913 Career OF: 1-23-256																							
1913 NY-A	20	72	9	19	2	1	0	1	10	4	1	....	.264	.369	.319	.688	101	1	9	4.08	0	O-20(0-13-7)	2	0.0
1914 NY-A	132	470	59	133	11	3	1	40	44	60	26	32	.283	.356	.326	.681	105	-4	53	3.71	-5	*O-127(1-10-115)	13	-1.8
1915 NY-A	132	476	70	129	16	5	2	33	62	43	29	18	.271	.364	.338	.703	110	7	63	4.47	-1	*O-131(0-0-131)	15	-0.1
1916 NY-A	4	10	0	1	0	0	0	1	0	2	0	....	.100	.100	.100	.200	-39	-2	0	.29	0	/O-3(0-0-3)	0	-0.2
Total 4	**288**	**1028**	**138**	**282**	**29**	**9**	**3**	**75**	**116**	**109**	**56**	**50**	**.274**	**.359**	**.329**	**.687**	**106**	**1**	**125**	**4.04**	**-6**	**O-281**	**30**	**-2.2**

• COOK, Jim James Fitchie Cook b: 11/10/1879, Dundee, IL d: 6/17/1949, St. Louis, MO BR/TR, 5'9", 163 lbs. Deb: 7/2/1903

YEAR TM-L	G	AB	R	H	2B	3B	HR	RBI	BB	SO	SB	CS	AVG	OBP	SLG	OPS	OPS+	BR/A	RC	RC/G	FR	G/POS	WS	TPW
1903 Chi-N	8	26	3	4	1	0	0	2	2	....	1	....	.154	.241	.192	.434	25	-2	1	1.79	-1	/O-5(0-5-0),2-2,1-1	0	-0.4

• COOK, Paul Paul Cook b: 5/5/1863, Caledonia, NY d: 5/25/1905, Rochester, NY BR/TR, 5'10" Deb: 9/13/1884 Career OF: 2-2-10

YEAR TM-L	G	AB	R	H	2B	3B	HR	RBI	BB	SO	SB	CS	AVG	OBP	SLG	OPS	OPS+	BR/A	RC	RC/G	FR	G/POS	WS	TPW
1884 Phi-N	3	12	0	1	0	0	0	0	0	2	....	....	.083	.083	.083	.167	-50	-2	0	.21	-2	/C-3	0	-0.3
1886 Lou-a	66	262	28	54	5	2	0	14	10	....	6	....	.206	.235	.240	.476	47	-17	17	2.16	-4	1-43,C-21/O-2(1-0-1)	2	-2.0
1887 Lou-a	61	234	34	66	4	2	0	17	11	....	15	....	.282	.294	.283	.577	60	-12	24	3.78	1	C-55/1-6	4	-0.6
1888 Lou-a	57	185	20	34	2	0	0	13	5	....	9	....	.184	.222	.195	.416	34	-13	10	1.83	-1	C-53/O-4(1-0-3),S-1	1	-0.9
1889 Lou-a	81	286	34	65	10	1	0	15	15	48	11	....	.227	.287	.269	.556	60	-15	26	3.11	11	C-74/O-7(0-2-5),1-1,S-1	2	0.2
1890 Bro-P	58	218	32	55	3	3	0	31	14	18	7	....	.252	.303	.294	.597	56	-15	22	3.66	-1	C-36,1-21/O-1	4	-1.1
1891 Lou-a	45	153	21	35	3	1	0	23	11	17	4	....	.229	.285	.261	.546	57	-9	13	2.89	0	C-35,1-10	2	-0.6
StL-a	7	25	3	5	0	0	0	1	1	2	0	....	.200	.259	.200	.459	27	-3	1	1.76	0	/C-7	0	-0.2
Yr.	52	178	24	40	3	1	0	24	12	19	4	....	.225	.281	.253	.534	53	-11	14	2.72	-1	C-42,1-10	2	-0.8
Total 7	**378**	**1375**	**172**	**315**	**27**	**9**	**0**	**114**	**67**	**87**	**52**	**....**	**.229**	**.270**	**.256**	**.526**	**52**	**-86**	**113**	**2.85**	**5**	**C-284/1-81,O-14,S-2**	**15**	**-5.6**

• COOKE, Dusty Allen Lindsey Cooke b: 6/23/1907, Swepsonville, NC d: 11/21/1987, Raleigh, NC BL/TR, 6'1", 205 lbs. Deb: 4/15/1930 M/C Career OF: 161-148-199

YEAR TM-L	G	AB	R	H	2B	3B	HR	RBI	BB	SO	SB	CS	AVG	OBP	SLG	OPS	OPS+	BR/A	RC	RC/G	FR	G/POS	WS	TPW
1930 NY-A	92	216	43	55	12	3	6	29	32	61	4	6	.255	.353	.421	.775	100	-1	32	5.05	-3	O-73(21-28-24)	5	-0.7
1931 NY-A	27	39	10	13	1	0	1	6	8	11	4	1	.333	.447	.436	.883	141	4	9	8.48	0	O-11(7-0-6)	2	0.2
1932 NY-A	3	0	1	0	0	0	0	0	1	0	0	0	....	1.000	....	1.000	191	0	0	∞	0	....	0	0.0
1933 Bos-A	119	454	86	133	35	10	5	54	67	71	7	5	.293	.386	.447	.833	121	16	81	6.46	-2	*O-118(47-70-30)	15	0.9
1934 Bos-A	74	168	34	41	8	5	1	26	36	25	7	2	.244	.377	.369	.746	87	-1	26	5.44	-2	O-44(9-14-21)	5	-0.5
1935 Bos-A	100	294	51	90	18	6	3	34	46	24	6	8	.306	.400	.439	.839	109	4	52	6.35	-2	O-82(7-35-44)	10	-0.1
1936 Bos-A	111	341	58	93	20	3	6	47	72	48	4	3	.273	.401	.402	.803	93	-1	60	6.31	-2	O-91(24-1-67)	9	-0.8
1938 Cin-N	82	233	41	64	15	1	2	33	28	36	0	....	.275	.355	.373	.728	103	2	33	5.00	2	O-51(46-0-7)	7	0.1
Total 8	**608**	**1745**	**324**	**489**	**109**	**28**	**24**	**229**	**290**	**276**	**32**	**25**	**.280**	**.384**	**.416**	**.800**	**106**	**21**	**294**	**5.97**	**-9**	**O-470**	**53**	**-0.9**

• COOKE, Fred Frederick B. Cooke b: 10/1873, IL, 5'10" Deb: 7/30/1897

YEAR TM-L	G	AB	R	H	2B	3B	HR	RBI	BB	SO	SB	CS	AVG	OBP	SLG	OPS	OPS+	BR/A	RC	RC/G	FR	G/POS	WS	TPW
1897 Cle-N	5	17	2	5	2	0	0	3	3	....	0	....	.294	.400	.412	.812	109	0	3	6.15	1	/O-5(0-0-5)	0	0.1

• COOKSON, Brent Brent Adam Cookson b: 9/7/1969, Van Nuys, CA BR/TR, 5'11", 200 lbs. Deb: 8/12/1995 Career OF: 12-0-3

YEAR TM-L	G	AB	R	H	2B	3B	HR	RBI	BB	SO	SB	CS	AVG	OBP	SLG	OPS	OPS+	BR/A	RC	RC/G	FR	G/POS	WS	TPW
1995 KC-A	22	35	2	5	1	0	0	5	2	7	1	0	.143	.189	.171	.361	-5	-5	1	1.21	0	O-12(10-0-2)/D-2	0	-0.5
1999 LA-N	3	5	0	1	0	0	0	0	0	1	0	0	.200	.200	.200	.400	2	-1	0	1.35	-0	/O-3(2-0-1)	0	-0.1
Total 2	**25**	**40**	**2**	**6**	**1**	**0**	**0**	**5**	**2**	**8**	**1**	**0**	**.150**	**.190**	**.175**	**.365**	**-4**	**-6**	**2**	**1.23**	**0**	**/O-15,D-2**	**0**	**-0.6**

• COOLBAUGH, Mike Michael Robert Coolbaugh b: 6/5/1972, Binghamton, NY BR/TR, 6'1", 190 lbs. Deb: 7/16/2001

YEAR TM-L	G	AB	R	H	2B	3B	HR	RBI	BB	SO	SB	CS	AVG	OBP	SLG	OPS	OPS+	BR/A	RC	RC/G	FR	G/POS	WS	TPW
2001 Mil-N	39	70	10	14	6	0	2	7	5	16	0	0	.200	.273	.371	.644	66	-4	7	2.98	-2	3-27/S-3	0	-0.5
2002 StL-N	5	12	0	1	0	0	0	0	1	3	0	0	.083	.154	.083	.237	-36	-2	0	.26	1	/3-4	0	-0.1
Total 2	**44**	**82**	**10**	**15**	**6**	**0**	**2**	**7**	**6**	**19**	**0**	**0**	**.183**	**.256**	**.329**	**.585**	**50**	**-6**	**7**	**2.49**	**-1**	**/3-31,S-3**	**0**	**-0.6**

• COOLBAUGH, Scott Scott Robert Coolbaugh b: 6/13/1966, Binghamton, NY BR/TR, 5'10", 185 lbs. Deb: 9/2/1989

YEAR TM-L	G	AB	R	H	2B	3B	HR	RBI	BB	SO	SB	CS	AVG	OBP	SLG	OPS	OPS+	BR/A	RC	RC/G	FR	G/POS	WS	TPW
1989 Tex-A	25	51	7	14	1	0	2	7	4	12	0	0	.275	.327	.412	.739	105	0	6	4.27	3	3-23/D-2	2	0.3
1990 Tex-A	67	180	21	36	6	0	2	13	15	47	1	0	.200	.265	.267	.532	49	-12	14	2.46	5	3-66	2	-0.7
1991 SD-N	60	180	12	39	8	1	2	15	19	45	0	3	.217	.295	.306	.601	67	-9	15	2.51	2	3-54	2	-0.7
1994 StL-N	15	21	4	4	0	0	2	6	1	4	0	0	.190	.227	.476	.703	79	-1	1	1.21	0	/1-4,3-4	0	-0.1
Total 4	**167**	**432**	**44**	**93**	**15**	**1**	**8**	**41**	**39**	**108**	**1**	**3**	**.215**	**.283**	**.310**	**.593**	**65**	**-22**	**36**	**2.61**	**9**	**3-147/1-4,D-2**	**6**	**-1.2**

• COOLEY, Duff Duff Gordon "Sir Richard,Dick" Cooley
b: 3/29/1873, Leavenworth, KS d: 8/9/1937, Dallas, TX BL/TR, 5'11", 158 lbs. Deb: 7/27/1893 Career OF: 548-479-69

YEAR TM-L	G	AB	R	H	2B	3B	HR	RBI	BB	SO	SB	CS	AVG	OBP	SLG	OPS	OPS+	BR/A	RC	RC/G	FR	G/POS	WS	TPW
1893 StL-N	29	107	20	37	2	3	0	21	8	9	8	....	.346	.391	.421	.812	115	2	21	8.05	-1	O-15(0-0-15),C-10/S-5	3	0.1
1894 StL-N	54	206	35	61	3	1	1	21	12	16	7	....	.296	.335	.335	.670	62	-13	26	4.68	-10	O-39(8-4-28),3-13/1-1,S-1	2	-1.9
1895 StL-N	133	567	108	194	9	20	7	75	37	29	27	....	.342	.386	.466	.851	120	16	115	8.29	2	*O-124(115-8-1)/3-5,S-3,C	13	0.6
1896 StL-N	40	166	29	51	5	3	0	13	7	3	12	....	.307	.335	.373	.709	90	-3	26	5.73	-2	O-40(40-0-0)	3	-0.7
Phi-N	64	287	63	88	6	4	2	22	18	16	18	....	.307	.348	.376	.724	92	-4	46	5.84	-4	O-64(22-40-2)	6	-1.0
Yr.	104	453	92	139	11	7	2	35	25	19	30	....	.307	.343	.375	.718	91	-7	72	5.80	-6	*O-104(62-40-2)	9	-1.7
1897 Phi-N	133	566	124	186	14	13	4	40	51	....	31	....	.329	.386	.420	.807	116	14	108	7.31	-4	*O-131(0-108-23)/1-2	16	0.1
1898 Phi-N	149	629	123	196	24	12	4	55	48	....	17	....	.312	.364	.407	.771	126	20	103	6.16	-5	*O-149(0-149-0)	22	0.5
1899 Phi-N	94	406	75	112	15	8	1	31	29	....	15	....	.276	.330	.360	.690	92	-5	55	4.88	-4	1-79,O-14(0-14-0)/2-1	9	-0.9
1900 Pit-N	66	249	30	50	8	1	0	22	14	....	9	....	.201	.243	.241	.484	34	-23	19	2.33	-3	1-66	1	-2.4
1901 Bos-N	63	240	27	62	13	3	0	27	14	....	5	....	.258	.302	.338	.639	78	-7	28	3.93	1	O-53(29-24-0),1-10	5	-0.9
1902 Bos-N	135	548	73	162	26	8	0	58	34	....	27	....	.296	.339	.372	.711	118	11	82	5.44	-9	*O-127(94-33-0)/1-7	20	-0.6
1903 Bos-N	138	553	76	160	26	10	1	70	44	....	27	....	.289	.342	.378	.720	109	6	83	5.56	-4	*O-126(124-3-0),1-13	18	-0.5
1904 Bos-N	122	467	41	127	18	7	5	70	24	....	14	....	.272	.312	.373	.684	115	7	60	4.59	-8	*O-116(116-0-0)/1-6	14	-0.9
1905 Det-A	97	377	25	93	11	9	1	32	26	....	7	....	.247	.297	.332	.629	99	-1	42	3.72	1	O-96(0-96-0)	12	-0.6
Total 13	**1317**	**5368**	**849**	**1579**	**180**	**102**	**26**	**557**	**366**	**73**	**224**	**....**	**.294**	**.342**	**.380**	**.722**	**104**	**20**	**813**	**5.55**	**-50**	***O-1094,1-184/3-18,C-11,S-9,2**	**144**	**-9.2**

• COOMBS, Cecil Cecil Lysander Coombs b: 3/18/1888, Moweaqua, IL d: 11/25/1975, Fort Worth, TX BR/TR, 5'9", 160 lbs. Deb: 8/7/1914

YEAR TM-L	G	AB	R	H	2B	3B	HR	RBI	BB	SO	SB	CS	AVG	OBP	SLG	OPS	OPS+	BR/A	RC	RC/G	FR	G/POS	WS	TPW
1914 Chi-A	7	23	1	4	1	0	0	1	1	7	0	1	.174	.208	.217	.426	28	-3	1	1.10	1	/O-7(0-7-0)	0	-0.2

• COOMBS, Jack John Wesley "Colby Jack" Coombs
b: 11/18/1882, Le Grand, IA d: 4/15/1957, Palestine, TX BB/TR, 6', 185 lbs. Deb: 7/5/1906 M/C Career OF: 1-16-46 ♦

YEAR TM-L	G	AB	R	H	2B	3B	HR	RBI	BB	SO	SB	CS	AVG	OBP	SLG	OPS	OPS+	BR/A	RC	RC/G	FR	G/POS	WS	TPW
1906 Phi-A	24	67	9	16	2	0	0	3	1	....	2	....	.239	.261	.269	.530	64	1	5	2.78	0	P-23	11	0.7
1907 Phi-A	24	48	4	8	0	0	1	4	0	....	1	....	.167	.167	.229	.396	25	-1	2	1.39	0	P-23	6	-1.0
1908 Phi-A	78	220	24	56	9	5	1	23	9	....	6	....	.255	.287	.355	.642	101	3	24	3.60	4	O-47(1-11-35),P-26/1-1	17	2.0
1909 Phi-A	37	83	4	14	4	0	0	10	4	....	1	....	.169	.216	.217	.433	36	1	4	1.48	0	P-30	13	0.1
1910★Phi-A	46	132	20	29	3	0	0	9	7	....	3	....	.220	.270	.242	.512	61	3	9	2.28	-4	P-45	37	4.2
1911★Phi-A	52	141	31	45	6	1	2	23	8	....	5	....	.319	.356	.418	.774	118	13	22	5.88	-3	P-47	23	-0.3
1912 Phi-A	56	110	10	28	2	0	0	13	14	....	1	....	.255	.344	.273	.617	80	6	11	3.31	0	P-40	18	-0.4
1913 Phi-A	2	3	1	1	1	0	0	0	0	2	0	....	.333	.333	.667	1.000	195	1	1	7.99	0	/P-2	0	-0.4
1914 Phi-A	5	11	0	3	1	0	0	2	1	1	0	1	.273	.333	.364	.697	114	0	1	2.94	0	/O-2(0-2-0),P-2	0	-0.2
1915 Bro-N	29	75	8	21	1	1	0	5	2	17	0	1	.280	.299	.320	.619	86	4	7	3.32	-3	P-29	16	0.8
1916★Bro-N	27	61	2	11	2	0	0	3	2	10	0	....	.180	.206	.213	.419	28	-0	3	1.39	-5	P-27	11	-0.3
1917 Bro-N	32	44	4	10	0	1	0	2	4	9	1	....	.227	.292	.273	.564	72	2	4	2.72	-3	P-31	3	-2.0
1918 Bro-N	46	113	6	19	3	2	0	3	7	5	1	....	.168	.223	.230	.453	38	-2	6	1.54	-4	P-27,O-13(0-3-11)	5	-2.8
1920 Det-A	2	2	0	0	0	0	0	0	0	0	0	0	.000	.000	.000	.000	-103	-0	0	.00	0	/P-2	0	0.0
Total 14	**460**	**1110**	**123**	**261**	**34**	**10**	**4**	**100**	**59**	**44**	**21**	**2**	**.235**	**.278**	**.295**	**.573**	**74**	**29**	**98**	**2.94**	**-20**	**P-354/O-62,1-1**	**160**	**0.3**

• COOMER, Ron Ronald Bryan Coomer b: 11/18/1966, Crest Hill, IL BR/TR, 5'11", 195 lbs. Deb: 8/1/1995 Career OF: 0-0-35

YEAR TM-L	G	AB	R	H	2B	3B	HR	RBI	BB	SO	SB	CS	AVG	OBP	SLG	OPS	OPS+	BR/A	RC	RC/G	FR	G/POS	WS	TPW
1995 Min-A	37	101	15	26	3	1	5	19	9	11	0	1	.257	.324	.455	.780	100	-1	11	3.62	1	1-22,3-13/D-4,O-1	2	-0.1
1996 Min-A	95	233	34	69	12	1	12	41	17	24	3	0	.296	.344	.511	.855	110	3	38	5.79	5	1-57,O-23(0-0-23)/3-9,D-3	5	0.4
1997 Min-A	140	523	63	156	30	2	13	85	22	91	4	3	.298	.327	.438	.764	96	-5	71	4.97	1	*3-119/1-9,D-7,O-7(0-0-7)	14	-0.4
1998 Min-A	137	529	54	146	22	1	15	72	18	72	2	2	.276	.300	.406	.706	80	-18	57	3.69	1	3-75,1-54,D-13/O-3(0-0-3)	6	-1.9
1999 Min-A★	127	467	53	123	25	1	16	65	30	69	2	1	.263	.309	.424	.733	82	-15	57	4.18	11	1-71,3-57/D-7,O-1	8	-0.8
2000 Min-A	140	544	64	147	29	1	16	82	36	50	2	0	.270	.320	.415	.736	81	-17	66	4.17	8	*1-124/D-9,3-5	9	-1.9
2001 Chi-N	111	349	25	91	19	1	8	53	29	70	0	0	.261	.321	.390	.711	87	-7	38	3.54	0	3-76,1-36/D-1	6	-0.8
2002★NY-A	55	148	14	39	7	0	3	17	6	23	0	0	.264	.292	.372	.664	75	-6	14	3.09	-3	3-26,D-14,1-11	1	-0.9
2003 LA-N	69	125	11	30	4	0	4	15	10	19	0	0	.240	.301	.368	.669	78	-4	12	3.18	-1	1-24,3-11/D-4	0	-0.7
Total 9	**911**	**3019**	**333**	**827**	**151**	**8**	**92**	**449**	**177**	**429**	**13**	**7**	**.274**	**.316**	**.421**	**.737**	**87**	**-69**	**363**	**4.14**	**22**	**1-408,3-391/D-62,O-35**	**51**	**-7.2**

• COON, William William K. Coon b: 3/21/1855, Philadelphia, PA d: 8/30/1915, Burlington, NJ Deb: 9/4/1875

YEAR TM-L	G	AB	R	H	2B	3B	HR	RBI	BB	SO	SB	CS	AVG	OBP	SLG	OPS	OPS+	BR/A	RC	RC/G	FR	G/POS	WS	TPW
1875 Ath-n	4	12	1	2	0	0	0	1	0	0	1	0	.167	.167	.167	.333	15	-1	1	1.51	0	/C-4,O-1	....	-0.1

YEAR TM-L	G	AB	R	H	2B	3B	HR	RBI	BB	SO	SB	CS	AVG	OBP	SLG	OPS	OPS+	BR/A	RC	RC/G	FR	G/POS	WS	TPW
1876 Phi-N	54	222	30	50	5	1	0	22	2	4	....	....	.225	.234	.259	.493	65	-8	14	2.25	-14	0-29(0-2-29),C-18/2-4,3-4,P	1	-2.0
• COONEY, Bill	William A. "Cush" Cooney b: 4/7/1883, Boston, MA d: 11/6/1928, Roxbury, MA TR Deb: 9/22/1909																							
1909 Bos-N	5	10	0	3	0	0	0	0	0	....	0	....	.300	.300	.300	.600	82	-0	1	3.20	0	/P-3,2-1,S-1	1	0.1
1910 Bos-N	8	12	2	3	0	0	0	1	2	0	0	....	.250	.357	.250	.607	74	-0	1	3.02	0	/O-2(0-0-2)	0	-0.1
Total 2	13	22	2	6	0	0	0	1	2	0	0	....	.273	.333	.273	.606	78	-0	2	3.10	0	/P-3,0-2,2-1,S-1	1	0.1
• COONEY, Jimmy	James Edward "Scoops" Cooney b: 8/24/1894, Cranston, RI d: 8/7/1991, Warwick, RI BR/TR, 5'11", 160 lbs. Deb: 9/22/1917																							
1917 Bos-A	11	36	4	8	1	0	0	3	6	2	0	....	.222	.333	.250	.583	79	-1	4	2.98	5	2-10/S-1	2	0.5
1919 NY-N	5	14	3	3	0	0	0	1	0	0	0	....	.214	.214	.214	.429	29	-1	1	1.51	1	/S-4,2-1	0	0.0
1924 StL-N	110	383	44	113	20	8	1	57	20	20	12	10	.295	.330	.397	.727	96	-4	48	4.39	6	S-99/3-7,2-1	11	1.4
1925 StL-N	54	187	27	51	11	2	0	18	4	5	1	3	.273	.292	.353	.645	62	-12	18	3.27	2	S-37,2-15/O-1	3	-0.5
1926 Chi-N	141	513	52	129	18	5	1	47	23	10	11	....	.251	.288	.312	.599	61	-29	45	2.92	11	*S-141	12	-0.3
1927 Chi-N	33	132	16	32	2	0	0	6	8	7	1	....	.242	.286	.258	.543	46	-10	10	2.40	0	S-33	2	-0.6
Phi-N	76	259	33	70	12	1	0	15	13	9	4	....	.270	.305	.324	.629	68	-12	25	3.29	4	S-74	4	0.0
Yr.	109	391	49	102	14	1	0	21	21	16	5	....	.261	.299	.302	.600	60	-22	35	2.97	4	*S-107	6	-0.6
1928 Bos-N	18	51	2	7	0	0	0	3	2	5	1	....	.137	.170	.137	.307	-20	-9	1	.70	0	S-11/2-4	0	-0.8
Total 7	448	1575	181	413	64	16	2	150	76	58	30	13	.262	.298	.327	.625	67	-78	153	3.23	30	S-400/2-31,3-7,0-1	34	-0.4
• COONEY, Jimmy	James Joseph Cooney b: 7/9/1865, Cranston, RI d: 7/1/1903, Cranston, RI BB/TR, 5'9", 155 lbs. Deb: 4/19/1890																							
1890 Chi-N	135	574	114	156	19	10	4	52	73	23	45	....	.272	.360	.361	.721	106	5	93	5.89	6	*S-135/C-1	22	1.4
1891 Chi-N	118	465	84	114	15	3	0	42	48	17	21	....	.245	.318	.290	.609	78	-12	51	3.92	4	*S-118	14	-0.4
1892 Chi-N	65	238	18	41	1	0	0	20	23	5	10	....	.172	.248	.176	.425	28	-20	13	1.81	-3	S-65	2	-1.9
Was-N	6	25	5	4	0	1	0	4	4	3	1	....	.160	.276	.240	.516	58	-1	2	2.54	-2	/S-6	0	-0.2
Yr.	71	263	23	45	1	1	0	24	27	8	11	....	.171	.251	.183	.433	31	-21	15	1.88	-5	S-71	2	-2.1
Total 3	324	1302	221	315	35	14	4	118	148	48	77	....	.242	.324	.300	.623	81	-29	159	4.30	5	S-324/C-1	38	-1.2
• COONEY, Johnny	John Walter Cooney b: 3/18/1901, Cranston, RI d: 7/8/1986, Sarasota, FL BR/TL, 5'10", 165 lbs. Deb: 4/19/1921 M/C/U Career OF: 37-633-133 ♦																							
1921 Bos-N	8	5	0	1	0	0	0	0	0	1	0	0	.200	.200	.200	.400	6	-0	0	1.27	0	/P-8	1	-0.1
1922 Bos-N	4	8	0	0	0	0	0	0	0	1	0	0	.000	.000	.000	.000	-105	-1	0	.00	0	/P-4	2	0.4
1923 Bos-N	42	66	7	25	1	0	0	3	4	2	0	1	.379	.414	.394	.808	119	4	11	6.20	0	P-23,0-11(2-8-1)/1-1	9	1.3
1924 Bos-N	55	130	10	33	2	1	0	4	9	5	0	4	.254	.302	.285	.587	61	-3	11	2.65	-1	P-34,0-16(0-15-1)/1-1	16	1.1
1925 Bos-N	54	103	17	33	7	0	0	13	3	6	1	0	.320	.346	.388	.734	96	9	14	4.94	1	P-31/1-3,0-1	19	1.8
1926 Bos-N	64	126	17	38	3	2	0	18	13	7	6	....	.302	.367	.357	.724	105	4	17	4.55	2	1-31,P-19/0-1	6	0.1
1927 Bos-N	10	1	3	0	0	0	0	0	0	0	0	....	.000	.000	.000	.000	-108	-0	0	.00	0	....	0	0.0
1928 Bos-N	33	41	2	7	0	0	0	2	4	3	0	....	.171	.244	.171	.415	11	-1	2	1.40	2	P-24/1-3,0-2(0-1-1)	3	-0.3
1929 Bos-N	41	72	10	23	4	1	0	6	3	3	1	....	.319	.355	.403	.758	91	1	10	5.27	1	0-16(4-10-2),P-14	4	-0.1
1930 Bos-N	4	3	0	0	0	0	0	0	0	0	0	....	.000	.000	.000	.000	-103	-1	0	.00	0	/P-2	0	-0.9
1935 Bro-N	10	29	3	9	0	1	0	1	3	2	0	....	.310	.375	.379	.754	106	0	5	6.10	0	0-10(0-10-0)	1	0.0
1936 Bro-N	130	507	71	143	17	5	0	30	24	15	3	....	.282	.315	.335	.650	74	-19	54	3.76	8	*0-130(0-130-0)	11	-1.4
1937 Bro-N	120	430	61	126	18	5	0	37	22	10	5	....	.293	.327	.358	.686	85	-10	49	4.15	1	*0-111(5-104-3)/1-2	9	-1.1
1938 Bos-N	120	432	45	117	25	5	0	17	22	12	2	....	.271	.308	.352	.660	90	-7	47	3.80	1	*0-110(17-15-84),1-13	11	-1.3
1939 Bos-N	118	368	39	101	8	1	2	27	21	8	2	....	.274	.317	.318	.635	77	-12	37	3.46	6	*0-116(0-112-5)/1-2	7	-0.9
1940 Bos-N	108	365	40	116	14	3	0	21	25	9	4	....	.318	.363	.373	.736	109	5	50	5.01	0	0-99(0-98-1)/1-7	12	0.2
1941 Bos-N	123	442	52	141	25	2	0	29	27	15	3	....	.319	.358	.385	.743	114	7	59	4.93	5	*0-111(0-111-0)/1-4	14	0.9
1942 Bos-N	74	198	23	41	6	0	0	7	23	5	2	....	.207	.290	.237	.527	56	-10	15	2.35	-1	0-54(5-16-34),1-23	1	-1.6
1943 Bro-N	37	34	7	7	0	0	0	2	4	3	1	....	.206	.289	.206	.495	44	-2	2	2.04	0	/1-3,0-2(0-2-0)	0	-0.3
1944 Bro-N	7	4	0	3	0	0	0	1	0	0	0	....	.750	.750	.750	1.500	329	1	2	28.51	0	/0-2(1-1-0)	1	0.1
NY-A	10	8	1	1	0	0	0	1	1	0	0	0	.125	.222	.125	.347	1	-1	0	1.10	0	/0-2(2-0-0)	0	-0.1
Total 20	1172	3372	408	965	130	26	2	219	208	107	30	5	.286	.329	.342	.671	87	-36	383	4.01	25	0-794,P-159/1-93	127	-2.1
• COONEY, Phil	Philip Clarence Cooney b: 9/14/1882, New York, NY d: 10/6/1957, New York, NY BL/TR, 5'8", 155 lbs. Deb: 9/27/1905																							
1905 NY-A	1	3	0	0	0	0	0	0	0	....	0	....	.000	.000	.000	.000	-90	-1	0	.00	0	/3-1	0	-0.1
• COOPER, Cecil	Cecil Celester Cooper b: 12/20/1949, Brenham, TX BL/TL, 6'2", 190 lbs. Deb: 9/8/1971 C																							
1971 Bos-A	14	42	9	13	4	1	0	3	5	4	1	0	.310	.396	.452	.848	130	2	8	7.45	-1	1-11	2	0.1
1972 Bos-A	12	17	0	4	1	0	0	2	2	5	0	0	.235	.316	.294	.610	78	-0	2	3.45	-1	/1-3	1	-0.1
1973 Bos-A	30	101	12	24	2	0	3	11	7	12	1	2	.238	.287	.347	.634	73	-4	10	3.22	0	1-29	1	-0.7
1974 Bos-A	121	414	55	114	24	1	8	43	32	74	2	5	.275	.329	.396	.725	101	-1	54	4.63	0	1-74,D-41	10	-0.8
1975*Bos-A	106	305	49	95	17	6	14	44	19	33	1	4	.311	.358	.544	.902	140	13	57	6.95	3	D-54,1-35	13	1.3
1976 Bos-A	123	451	66	127	22	6	15	78	16	62	7	1	.282	.308	.457	.764	109	4	64	5.03	2	1-66,D-53	12	-0.1
1977 Mil-A	160	643	86	193	31	7	20	78	28	110	13	8	.300	.329	.463	.793	113	9	93	5.23	2	*1-148,D-10	18	0.1
1978 Mil-A	107	407	60	127	23	2	13	54	32	72	3	4	.312	.362	.474	.836	133	16	69	6.27	3	1-84,D-19	15	1.3
1979 Mil-A★	150	590	83	182	**44**	1	24	106	56	77	15	3	.308	.368	.508	.877	134	29	110	6.74	-3	*1-135,D-15	24	1.7
1980 Mil-A★	153	622	96	219	33	4	25	**122**	39	42	17	6	.352	.392	.539	.931	157	48	126	7.72	4	*1-142,D-11	27	4.2
1981*Mil-A	106	416	70	133	**35**	1	12	60	28	30	5	4	.320	.367	.495	.862	155	27	70	6.09	-2	*1-101/D-5	22	1.9
1982*Mil-A★	155	654	104	205	38	3	32	121	32	53	2	3	.313	.345	.528	.873	145	35	118	6.85	-2	*1-154/D-1	29	2.4
1983 Mil-A★	160	661	106	203	37	3	30	**126**	37	63	2	1	.307	.345	.508	.853	142	34	110	6.11	-7	*1-158/D-2	25	1.7
1984 Mil-A	148	603	63	166	28	3	11	67	27	59	8	2	.275	.309	.386	.695	95	-5	70	4.15	-2	*1-122,D-26	14	-1.6
1985 Mil-A★	154	631	82	185	39	8	16	99	30	77	10	3	.293	.327	.456	.784	112	9	86	4.82	-1	*1-123,D-30	17	-0.1
1986 Mil-A	134	542	46	140	24	1	12	75	41	87	1	2	.258	.312	.373	.684	83	-14	60	3.84	-2	1-90,D-44	8	-2.3
1987 Mil-A	63	250	25	62	13	0	6	36	17	51	1	1	.248	.296	.372	.668	74	-10	27	3.74	0	D-62	3	-1.2
Total 17	1896	7349	1012	2192	415	47	241	1125	448	911	89	49	.298	.340	.466	.806	122	191	1134	5.59	-9	*1-1475,D-373	241	7.7
• COOPER, Claude	Claude William Cooper b: 4/1/1892, Troup, TX d: 1/21/1974, Plainview, TX BL/TL, 5'9", 158 lbs. Deb: 4/14/1913 Career OF: 187-54-43																							
1913*NY-N	27	30	11	9	4	0	0	4	4	6	3	....	.300	.382	.433	.816	132	1	6	6.89	-1	0-15(6-10-0)	1	0.0
1914 Bro-F	113	399	56	96	14	11	2	25	26	60	25	....	.241	.294	.346	.640	81	-11	45	3.67	-5	*0-101(45-21-38)	8	-2.2
1915 Bro-F	153	527	75	155	26	12	2	63	77	78	31	....	.294	.388	.400	.789	135	26	90	6.09	15	*0-121(112-7-2),1-32	23	3.8
1916 Phi-N	56	104	9	20	2	0	0	11	7	15	1	....	.192	.250	.212	.462	41	-7	6	1.82	-1	0-29(15-13-1)/1-1	0	-1.1
1917 Phi-N	24	29	5	3	1	0	0	1	5	4	0	....	.103	.235	.138	.373	15	-3	1	.99	-2	0-12(9-3-2)	0	-0.6
Total 5	373	1089	156	283	47	23	4	104	119	163	60	....	.260	.338	.356	.694	104	7	148	4.59	6	0-278/1-33	32	0.0
• COOPER, Gary	Gary Nathaniel Cooper b: 12/22/1956, Savannah, GA BB/TR, 6'3", 175 lbs. Deb: 8/25/1980																							
1980 Atl-N	21	2	3	0	0	0	0	0	0	1	2	1	.000	.000	.000	.000	-97	-1	0	.00	0	0-13(11-2-0)	0	-0.1
• COOPER, Gary	Gary Clifton Cooper b: 8/13/1964, Lynwood, CA BR/TR, 6'1", 200 lbs. Deb: 9/15/1991																							
1991 Hou-N	9	16	1	4	1	0	0	2	3	6	0	0	.250	.368	.313	.681	99	0	2	4.79	-1	/3-4	1	0.0
• COOPER, Pat	Orge Patterson Cooper b: 11/26/1917, Albemarle, NC d: 3/15/1993, Charlotte, NC BR/TR, 6'3", 180 lbs. Deb: 5/11/1946 ♦																							
1946 Phi-A	1	0	0	0	0	0	0	0	0	0	0	0	....	....	....	....	-101	0	0	....	0	/P-1	0	0.0
1947 Phi-A	13	16	0	4	2	0	0	3	0	5	0	0	.250	.250	.375	.625	71	-1	2	3.46	0	/1-1	0	-0.1
Total 2	14	16	0	4	2	0	0	3	0	5	0	0	.250	.250	.375	.625	71	-1	2	3.46	0	/1-1,P-1	0	-0.1
• COOPER, Scott	Scott Kendrick Cooper b: 10/13/1967, St. Louis, MO BL/TR, 6'3", 205 lbs. Deb: 9/5/1990																							
1990 Bos-A	2	1	0	0	0	0	0	0	0	1	0	0	.000	.000	.000	.000	-96	-0	0	.00	0	....	0	0.0
1991 Bos-A	14	35	6	16	4	2	0	7	2	2	0	0	.457	.486	.686	1.172	210	5	12	16.95	0	3-13	3	0.5
1992 Bos-A	123	337	34	93	21	0	5	33	37	33	1	1	.276	.348	.383	.730	98	-0	46	4.92	-4	1-62,3-47/D-2,2-1,S-1	9	-0.8
1993 Bos-A★	156	526	67	147	29	3	9	63	58	81	5	2	.279	.357	.397	.754	96	-1	76	5.21	-16	*3-154/1-2,S-1	12	-1.4
1994 Bos-A★	104	369	49	104	16	4	13	53	30	65	0	3	.282	.338	.453	.790	97	-4	55	5.32	6	*3-104	10	0.3
1995 StL-N	118	374	29	86	18	2	3	40	49	85	0	3	.230	.324	.313	.637	69	-17	39	3.43	1	*3-110	5	-1.5

YEAR	TM-L	G	AB	R	H	2B	3B	HR	RBI	BB	SO	SB	CS	AVG	OBP	SLG	OPS	OPS+	BR/A	RC	RC/G	FR	G/POS	WS	TPW
1997	KC-A	75	159	12	32	6	1	3	15	17	32	1	1	.201	.287	.308	.595	54	-11	14	2.84	0	3-39/1-8,D-5	1	-1.0
Total	**7**	**592**	**1801**	**197**	**478**	**94**	**12**	**33**	**211**	**193**	**299**	**7**	**10**	**.265**	**.340**	**.386**	**.726**	**89**	**-29**	**243**	**4.71**	**-14**	**3-467/1-72,D-7,S-2,2-1**	**40**	**-4.0**

• COOPER, Walker

William Walker "Walk" Cooper b: 1/8/1915, Atherton, MO d: 4/11/1991, Scottsdale, AZ BR/TR, 6'3", 210 lbs. Deb: 9/25/1940 C

YEAR	TM-L	G	AB	R	H	2B	3B	HR	RBI	BB	SO	SB	CS	AVG	OBP	SLG	OPS	OPS+	BR/A	RC	RC/G	FR	G/POS	WS	TPW
1940	StL-N	6	19	3	6	1	0	0	2	2	2	1	....	.316	.381	.368	.749	102	0	3	5.95	0	/C-6	1	0.1
1941	StL-N	68	200	19	49	9	1	1	20	13	14	1	....	.245	.291	.315	.606	66	-9	17	2.91	1	C-63	4	-0.5
1942*	StL-N★	125	438	58	123	32	7	7	65	29	29	4	....	.281	.327	.434	.761	113	5	57	4.56	-5	*C-115	16	0.8
1943*	StL-N★	122	449	52	143	30	4	9	81	19	19	1	....	.318	.349	.463	.812	128	13	69	5.71	-10	*C-112	18	1.1
1944*	StL-N★	112	397	56	126	25	5	13	72	20	19	4	....	.317	.352	.504	.855	136	17	65	5.97	-4	C-97	18	1.9
1945	StL-N	4	18	3	7	0	0	0	1	0	1	0	....	.389	.389	.389	.778	114	0	3	6.68	1	/C-4	1	0.2
1946	NY-N★	87	280	29	75	10	1	8	46	17	12	0	....	.268	.310	.396	.706	99	-2	32	3.96	-1	C-73	6	0.1
1947	NY-N★	140	515	79	157	24	8	35	122	24	43	2	....	.305	.339	.586	.926	141	24	97	7.02	-7	*C-132	23	2.5
1948	NY-N★	91	290	40	77	12	0	16	54	28	29	1	....	.266	.332	.472	.805	115	5	42	4.90	-3	C-79	10	0.5
1949	NY-N	42	147	14	31	4	2	4	21	7	8	0	....	.211	.261	.347	.608	62	-9	11	2.27	0	C-40	2	-0.7
	Cin-N★	82	307	34	86	9	2	16	62	21	24	0	....	.280	.330	.479	.809	113	4	46	5.42	-1	C-77	11	0.8
	Yr.	124	454	48	117	13	4	20	83	28	32	0	....	.258	.308	.436	.744	97	-5	57	4.31	-1	*C-117	13	0.1
1950	Cin-N	15	47	3	9	3	0	0	4	0	5	0	....	.191	.191	.255	.447	16	-6	2	1.41	-1	C-13	0	-0.6
	Bos-N★	102	337	52	111	19	3	14	60	30	26	1	....	.329	.389	.528	.917	148	23	69	7.81	2	C-88	19	2.9
	Yr.	117	384	55	120	22	3	14	64	30	31	1	....	.313	.367	.495	.862	133	17	71	6.91	1	*C-101	19	2.3
1951	Bos-N	109	342	42	107	14	1	18	59	28	18	1	1	.313	.367	.518	.884	145	20	64	6.98	3	C-90	17	2.8
1952	Bos-N	102	349	33	82	12	1	10	55	22	32	1	0	.235	.282	.361	.643	80	-10	36	3.50	0	C-89	9	-0.5
1953	Mil-N	53	137	12	30	6	0	3	16	12	15	1	0	.219	.287	.328	.615	64	-7	12	2.93	-2	C-35	2	-0.7
1954	Pit-N	14	15	0	3	2	0	0	1	2	1	0	0	.200	.294	.333	.627	64	-1	1	2.70	-0	/C-2	0	-0.1
	Chi-N	57	158	21	49	10	2	7	32	21	23	0	0	.310	.398	.532	.929	138	9	32	7.52	1	C-48	7	1.2
	Yr.	71	173	21	52	12	2	7	33	23	24	0	0	.301	.389	.514	.903	132	9	34	7.04	1	C-50	7	1.1
1955	Chi-N	54	111	11	31	8	1	7	15	6	19	0	0	.279	.322	.559	.881	128	4	19	6.06	-1	C-31	5	0.4
1956	StL-N	40	68	5	18	5	1	2	14	3	8	0	0	.265	.296	.456	.752	98	-0	8	4.31	-1	C-16	2	-0.1
1957	StL-N	48	78	7	21	5	1	3	10	5	10	0	0	.269	.313	.474	.788	106	0	9	3.82	-1	C-13	2	0.0
Total	**18**	**1473**	**4702**	**573**	**1341**	**240**	**40**	**173**	**812**	**309**	**357**	**18**	**1**	**.285**	**.332**	**.464**	**.796**	**116**	**81**	**695**	**5.26**	**-26**	***C-1223**	**173**	**12.0**

• COQUILLETTE, Trace

Trace Robert Coquillette b: 6/4/1974, Carmichael, CA BR/TR, 6', 185 lbs. Deb: 9/7/1999

YEAR	TM-L	G	AB	R	H	2B	3B	HR	RBI	BB	SO	SB	CS	AVG	OBP	SLG	OPS	OPS+	BR/A	RC	RC/G	FR	G/POS	WS	TPW
1999	Mon-N	17	49	2	13	3	0	0	4	4	7	1	0	.265	.333	.327	.660	70	-2	5	3.38	-0	3-11/2-6	1	-0.2
2000	Mon-N	34	59	6	12	4	0	1	8	7	19	0	0	.203	.288	.322	.610	52	-4	5	2.92	-2	3-19/2-8,0-2(2-0-1)	0	-0.6
Total	**2**	**51**	**108**	**8**	**25**	**7**	**0**	**1**	**12**	**11**	**26**	**1**	**0**	**.231**	**.308**	**.324**	**.632**	**60**	**-6**	**10**	**3.12**	**-2**	**/3-30,2-14,0-2**	**1**	**-0.7**

• CORA, Alex

Jose Alexander Cora b: 10/18/1975, Caguas, Puerto Rico BL/TR, 6', 180 lbs. Deb: 6/7/1998

YEAR	TM-L	G	AB	R	H	2B	3B	HR	RBI	BB	SO	SB	CS	AVG	OBP	SLG	OPS	OPS+	BR/A	RC	RC/G	FR	G/POS	WS	TPW
1998	LA-N	29	33	1	4	0	1	0	0	2	8	0	0	.121	.194	.182	.376		-5	1	1.25	-1	S-21/2-4	1	-0.5
1999	LA-N	11	30	2	5	1	0	0	3	0	4	0	0	.167	.194	.200	.394		-5	1	1.05	-1	/S-8,2-3	0	-0.5
2000	LA-N	109	353	39	84	18	6	4	32	26	53	4	1	.238	.303	.357	.660	70	-16	39	3.71	-4	*S-101/2-8	6	-1.2
2001	LA-N	134	405	38	88	18	3	4	29	31	58	0	2	.217	.286	.306	.592	58	-27	33	2.61	-4	*S-132/2-1	6	-2.0
2002	LA-N	115	258	37	75	14	4	5	28	26	38	7	2	.291	.371	.434	.805	119	8	44	6.21	0	S-61,2-40	14	1.3
2003	LA-N	148	477	39	119	24	3	4	34	16	59	4	2	.249	.288	.338	.626	66	-25	47	3.37	14	*2-141,S-15	13	-0.4
Total	**6**	**546**	**1556**	**156**	**375**	**75**	**17**	**17**	**126**	**101**	**220**	**15**	**7**	**.241**	**.302**	**.344**	**.645**	**71**	**-69**	**165**	**3.57**	**3**	**S-338,2-197**	**40**	**-3.3**

• CORA, Joey

Jose Manuel (Amaro) Cora b: 5/14/1965, Caguas, Puerto Rico BB/TR, 5'7", 152 lbs. Deb: 4/6/1987 C

YEAR	TM-L	G	AB	R	H	2B	3B	HR	RBI	BB	SO	SB	CS	AVG	OBP	SLG	OPS	OPS+	BR/A	RC	RC/G	FR	G/POS	WS	TPW
1987	SD-N	77	241	23	57	7	2	0	13	28	26	15	11	.237	.319	.282	.601	63	-14	22	2.92	0	2-66/S-6	3	-1.0
1989	SD-N	12	19	5	6	1	0	0	1	1	0	1	0	.316	.350	.368	.718	105	0	3	5.66	-1	/S-7,3-2,2-1	1	0.0
1990	SD-N	51	100	12	27	3	0	0	2	6	9	8	3	.270	.311	.300	.611	68	-4	10	3.40	-5	S-21,2-15/C-1	1	-0.8
1991	Chi-A	100	228	37	55	2	3	0	18	20	21	11	6	.241	.316	.276	.593	67	-10	22	3.16	1	2-80/S-5,D-2	3	-0.7
1992	Chi-A	68	122	27	30	7	1	0	9	22	13	10	3	.246	.378	.320	.698	99	2	18	4.70	-1	2-28,D-18/S-6,3-5	4	0.2
1993*	Chi-A	153	579	95	155	15	13	2	51	67	63	20	8	.268	.353	.349	.702	91	-4	75	4.33	1	*2-151/3-3	16	0.4
1994	Chi-A	90	312	55	86	13	4	2	30	38	32	8	4	.276	.358	.362	.720	88	-5	42	4.47	6	2-84/D-1	8	0.5
1995*	Sea-A	120	427	64	127	19	2	3	39	37	31	18	7	.297	.362	.372	.734	91	-4	60	4.88	-17	*2-112/D-1,S-1	10	-1.5
1996	Sea-A	144	530	90	154	37	6	6	45	35	32	5	5	.291	.343	.417	.760	91	-9	75	5.04	0	*2-140/3-1	11	-0.3
1997*	Sea-A★	149	574	105	172	40	4	11	54	53	49	6	7	.300	.364	.441	.805	110	7	93	5.84	-13	*2-142	18	0.1
1998	Sea-A	131	519	95	147	23	6	6	26	62	50	13	5	.283	.364	.385	.749	95	-1	79	5.47	-30	*2-130	10	-2.4
	*Cle-A	24	83	16	19	4	0	0	6	11	9	2	1	.229	.326	.277	.603	57	-5	8	3.03	0	2-21	1	-0.4
	Yr.	155	602	111	166	27	6	6	32	73	59	15	6	.276	.359	.370	.729	90	-6	87	5.10	-30	*2-151	11	-2.8
Total	**11**	**1119**	**3734**	**624**	**1035**	**171**	**41**	**30**	**294**	**380**	**335**	**117**	**60**	**.277**	**.351**	**.369**	**.720**	**90**	**-46**	**508**	**4.67**	**-60**	**2-970/S-46,D-22,3-11,C-1**	**86**	**-6.1**

• CORBETT, Gene

Eugene Louis Corbett b: 10/25/1913, Winona, MN BL/TR, 6'1.5", 190 lbs. Deb: 9/19/1936

YEAR	TM-L	G	AB	R	H	2B	3B	HR	RBI	BB	SO	SB	CS	AVG	OBP	SLG	OPS	OPS+	BR/A	RC	RC/G	FR	G/POS	WS	TPW
1936	Phi-N	6	21	1	3	0	0	0	2	2	3	0	....	.143	.217	.143	.360	-1	-3	1	.89	0	/1-6	0	-0.4
1937	Phi-N	7	12	4	4	2	0	0	1	0	0	0	....	.333	.333	.500	.833	114	0	2	6.92	-1	/3-3,2-1	0	-0.1
1938	Phi-N	24	75	7	6	1	0	2	7	6	11	0	....	.080	.148	.173	.321	-12	-12	2	.78	-1	1-22	0	-1.5
Total	**3**	**37**	**108**	**12**	**13**	**3**	**0**	**2**	**10**	**8**	**14**	**0**	**....**	**.120**	**.181**	**.204**	**.385**	**3**	**-15**	**5**	**1.31**	**-3**	**/1-28,3-3,2-1**	**0**	**-1.9**

• CORBITT, Claude

Claude Elliott Corbitt b: 7/21/1915, Sunbury, NC d: 5/1/1978, Cincinnati, OH BR/TR, 5'10", 170 lbs. Deb: 9/23/1945

YEAR	TM-L	G	AB	R	H	2B	3B	HR	RBI	BB	SO	SB	CS	AVG	OBP	SLG	OPS	OPS+	BR/A	RC	RC/G	FR	G/POS	WS	TPW
1945	Bro-N	2	4	1	2	0	0	0	0	1	0	0	....	.500	.600	.500	1.100	209	1	1	18.31	0	/3-2	0	0.1
1946	Cin-N	82	274	25	68	10	1	1	16	23	13	3	....	.248	.309	.303	.612	77	-9	27	3.32	-4	S-77	6	-0.9
1948	Cin-N	87	258	24	66	11	0	0	18	14	16	4	....	.256	.297	.298	.595	64	-13	24	3.23	-2	2-52,3-16,S-11	4	-1.2
1949	Cin-N	44	94	10	17	1	0	0	3	9	1	1	....	.181	.252	.191	.444	20	-10	5	1.54	-4	S-18,2-17/3-1	1	-1.3
Total	**4**	**215**	**630**	**60**	**153**	**22**	**1**	**1**	**37**	**47**	**30**	**8**	**....**	**.243**	**.297**	**.286**	**.583**	**64**	**-32**	**57**	**3.05**	**-9**	**S-106/2-69,3-19**	**11**	**-3.3**

• CORCORAN, Art

Arthur Andrew "Bunny" Corcoran b: 11/23/1894, Roxbury, MA d: 7/27/1958, Chelsea, MA TR, 5'11", 185 lbs. Deb: 9/9/1915

YEAR	TM-L	G	AB	R	H	2B	3B	HR	RBI	BB	SO	SB	CS	AVG	OBP	SLG	OPS	OPS+	BR/A	RC	RC/G	FR	G/POS	WS	TPW
1915	Phi-A	1	4	0	0	0	0	0	0	0	2	0	....	.000	.000	.000	.000	-104	-1	0	.00	0	/3-1	0	-0.1

• CORCORAN, Jack

John H. Corcoran b: 1860, Lowell, MA Deb: 5/1/1884

YEAR	TM-L	G	AB	R	H	2B	3B	HR	RBI	BB	SO	SB	CS	AVG	OBP	SLG	OPS	OPS+	BR/A	RC	RC/G	FR	G/POS	WS	TPW
1884	Bro-a	52	185	17	39	4	3	0	0	8	....	....	....	.211	.251	.265	.516	68	-6	13	2.38	-5	C-38/0-9(4-2-3),2-4,S-2,P	3	-0.7

• CORCORAN, John

John A. Corcoran b: 1873, Cincinnati, OH d: 11/2/1901, Cincinnati, OH TL Deb: 9/17/1895

YEAR	TM-L	G	AB	R	H	2B	3B	HR	RBI	BB	SO	SB	CS	AVG	OBP	SLG	OPS	OPS+	BR/A	RC	RC/G	FR	G/POS	WS	TPW
1895	Pit-N	6	20	0	3	0	0	0	1	0	2	0	....	.150	.150	.150	.300	-24	-4	0	.73	0	/S-4,3-2	0	-0.3

• CORCORAN, Larry

Lawrence J. Corcoran b: 8/10/1859, Brooklyn, NY d: 10/14/1891, Newark, NJ BL/TR, 120 lbs. Deb: 5/1/1880 Career OF: 9-10-21 ♦

YEAR	TM-L	G	AB	R	H	2B	3B	HR	RBI	BB	SO	SB	CS	AVG	OBP	SLG	OPS	OPS+	BR/A	RC	RC/G	FR	G/POS	WS	TPW
1880	Chi-N	72	286	41	66	11	1	0	25	10	33	....	....	.231	.257	.276	.533	76	-2	21	2.60	6	*P-63/0-8(0-5-3),S-8	52	1.6
1881	Chi-N	47	189	25	42	8	0	0	9	5	22	....	....	.222	.242	.265	.507	55	-3	12	2.28	-1	P-45/S-2,0-1	30	0.6
1882	Chi-N	40	169	23	35	10	2	1	24	6	18	....	....	.207	.234	.308	.542	71	-2	12	2.56	1	P-39/3-1	28	1.3
1883	Chi-N	68	263	40	55	12	7	0	25	6	62	....	....	.209	.227	.308	.535	56	-5	19	2.49	-2	P-56,0-13(8-4-1)/S-3,2-1	38	1.9
1884	Chi-N	64	251	43	61	3	4	1	19	10	33	....	....	.243	.272	.299	.571	73	1	21	3.03	8	P-60/0-4(0-0-4),S-2	37	2.2
1885	Chi-N	7	22	6	6	1	0	0	4	6	1	....	....	.273	.429	.318	.747	126	2	3	5.19	0	/P-7,S-1	5	-0.4
	NY-N	3	14	3	5	0	0	0	2	0	1	....	....	.357	.357	.357	.714	133	1	2	5.49	1	/P-3	3	-0.1
	Yr.	10	36	9	11	1	0	0	6	6	2	....	....	.306	.405	.333	.738	128	3	5	5.30	1	P-10/S-1	8	-0.4
1886	NY-N	1	4	0	0	0	0	0	0	0	2	0	....	.000	.000	.000	.000	-99	-1	0	.00	0	/0-1	0	-0.1
	Was-N	21	81	9	15	2	1	0	3	7	14	3	....	.185	.250	.235	.485	51	-4	6	2.31	-4	0-11(0-0-11)/S-9,P-2	0	-1.0
	Yr.	22	85	9	15	2	1	0	3	7	16	3	....	.176	.239	.224	.463	44	-5	6	2.17	-4	0-12(0-0-12)/S-9,P-2	0	-1.2
1887	Ind-N	3	12	2	4	0	0	0	0	2	1	2	....	.333	.333	.200	.533	53	-0	1	4.53	0	/0-2(0-1-1),P-2	0	-1.2
Total	**8**	**326**	**1291**	**192**	**289**	**47**	**15**	**2**	**111**	**52**	**187**	**5**	**....**	**.224**	**.253**	**.287**	**.540**	**67**	**-14**	**97**	**2.66**	**9**	**P-277/0-40,S-25,2-1,3-1**	**193**	**4.8**

• CORCORAN, Mickey

Michael Joseph Corcoran b: 8/26/1882, Buffalo, NY d: 12/9/1950, Buffalo, NY BR/TR, 5'8", 165 lbs. Deb: 9/15/1910

YEAR	TM-L	G	AB	R	H	2B	3B	HR	RBI	BB	SO	SB	CS	AVG	OBP	SLG	OPS	OPS+	BR/A	RC	RC/G	FR	G/POS	WS	TPW
1910	Cin-N	14	46	3	10	3	0	0	7	5	9	0	....	.217	.308	.283	.590	76	-1	4	2.83	0	2-14	1	-0.1

YEAR TM-L	G	AB	R	H	2B	3B	HR	RBI	BB	SO	SB	CS	AVG	OBP	SLG	OPS	OPS+	BR/A	RC	RC/G	FR	G/POS	WS	TPW
• CORCORAN, Tim				Timothy Michael Corcoran				b: 3/19/1953, Glendale, CA			BL/TL, 5'11", 175 lbs.				Deb: 5/18/1977		Career OF: 20-8-147						
1977 Det-A	55	103	13	29	3	0	3	15	6	9	0	1	.282	.321	.398	.719	90	-2	12	4.09	-1	0-18(4-6-8)/D-3	2	-0.3
1978 Det-A	116	324	37	86	13	1	1	27	24	27	3	2	.265	.326	.321	.647	80	-8	33	3.47	-5	*0-109(0-2-107)/D-1	5	-1.9
1979 Det-A	18	22	4	5	1	0	0	6	4	2	1	1	.227	.346	.273	.619	67	-1	2	2.74	0	/0-9(3-0-6),1-5,D-2	0	-0.2
1980 Det-A	84	153	20	44	7	1	3	18	22	10	0	2	.288	.381	.405	.786	113	3	23	5.45	0	1-48,0-18(7-0-11)/D-5	5	0.0
1981 Min-A	22	51	4	9	3	0	0	4	6	7	0	0	.176	.263	.235	.498	42	-4	3	1.71	0	1-16/D-3	0	-0.4
1983 Phi-N	3	0	0	0	0	0	0	0	0	0	0	0	....	....	....	....	-101	0	0	.00	0	/1-3	0	0.0
1984 Phi-N	102	208	30	71	13	1	5	36	37	27	0	1	.341	.443	.486	.929	158	18	45	8.41	0	1-51,0-17(4-0-13)	10	1.6
1985 Phi-N	103	182	11	39	6	1	0	22	29	20	0	0	.214	.322	.258	.581	63	-8	16	2.81	-3	1-59/0-3(2-0-2)	2	-1.4
1986 NY-N	6	7	1	0	0	0	0	0	2	0	0	0	.000	.222	.000	.222	-34	-1	0	.22	0	/1-1	0	-0.1
Total 9	509	1050	120	283	46	4	12	128	130	102	4	7	.270	.354	.355	.709	95	-3	136	4.40	-9	1-183,0-174/D-14	24	-2.8
• CORCORAN, Tommy				Thomas William "Corky, Tommy the Cork" Corcoran				b: 1/4/1869, New Haven, CT			d: 6/25/1960, Plainfield, CT			BR/TR, 5'9", 164 lbs.			Deb: 4/19/1890					
1890 Pit-P	123	503	80	117	14	13	1	61	38	45	43	....	.233	.289	.318	.607	68	-22	60	4.21	11	*S-123	11	-0.6
1891 Phi-a	133	511	84	130	11	15	7	71	29	56	30	....	.254	.307	.376	.683	92	-9	74	4.86	24	*S-133	19	1.6
1892 Bro-N	151	613	77	145	11	6	1	74	34	51	39	....	.237	.281	.279	.560	72	-21	61	3.49	2	*S-151	14	-1.1
1893 Bro-N	115	459	61	126	11	10	2	58	27	12	14	....	.275	.318	.355	.673	82	-13	58	4.59	21	*S-115	16	1.2
1894 Bro-N	129	576	123	173	21	20	5	92	25	17	33	....	.300	.329	.432	.762	89	-12	95	6.14	9	*S-129	16	0.3
1895 Bro-N	128	540	83	145	17	10	2	69	23	11	17	....	.269	.302	.348	.650	73	-22	65	4.28	24	*S-127	15	0.8
1896 Bro-N	132	532	63	154	15	7	3	73	15	13	16	....	.289	.310	.361	.671	81	-16	67	4.58	20	*S-132	15	0.9
1897 Cin-N	109	445	76	128	30	5	3	57	13	....	15	....	.288	.311	.398	.709	81	-16	52	5.02	8	S-63,2-47	12	-0.2
1898 Cin-N	153	619	80	155	28	15	2	87	26	....	19	....	.250	.283	.354	.637	77	-23	71	3.90	19	*S-153	18	0.4
1899 Cin-N	138	540	93	150	11	9	0	81	29	....	32	....	.278	.317	.328	.645	76	-19	70	4.56	13	*S-123,2-14	16	0.0
1900 Cin-N	127	523	64	128	21	9	1	54	22	....	27	....	.245	.278	.325	.603	68	-25	58	3.73	-13	*S-124/2-5	9	-2.8
1901 Cin-N	31	115	14	24	3	3	0	15	11	....	6	....	.209	.278	.287	.565	68	-4	11	3.23	3	S-30	2	-0.1
1902 Cin-N	138	538	54	136	18	4	0	54	11	....	20	....	.253	.268	.301	.569	69	-22	51	3.28	-12	*S-137/2-1	7	-3.1
1903 Cin-N	115	459	61	113	18	7	2	73	12	....	12	....	.246	.267	.329	.596	63	-26	45	3.41	12	*S-115	8	-1.0
1904 Cin-N	150	578	55	133	17	9	2	74	19	....	19	....	.230	.257	.301	.558	66	-25	52	2.96	13	*S-150	12	-0.8
1905 Cin-N	151	605	70	150	21	11	2	85	23	....	28	....	.248	.277	.329	.606	72	-24	66	3.64	2	*S-151	14	-1.7
1906 Cin-N	117	430	29	89	13	1	1	33	19	....	8	....	.207	.242	.249	.491	51	-26	30	2.20	4	*S-117	6	-2.0
1907 NY-N	62	226	21	60	9	2	0	24	7	....	9	....	.265	.288	.323	.611	88	-4	25	3.75	-6	2-62	4	-1.1
Total 18	2202	8812	1188	2256	289	155	34	1135	383	205	387	....	.256	.290	.336	.625	74	-330	1017	4.01	154	*S-2073,2-129	214	-9.4
• CORDERO, Wil				Wilfredo (Nieva) Cordero				b: 10/3/1971, Mayagüez, Puerto Rico			BR/TR, 6'2", 190 lbs.			Deb: 7/24/1992		Career OF: 396-0-18						
1992 Mon-N	45	126	17	38	4	1	2	8	9	31	0	0	.302	.353	.397	.750	113	2	17	5.12	-5	S-35/2-9	4	-0.1
1993 Mon-N	138	475	56	118	32	2	10	58	34	60	12	3	.248	.308	.387	.696	81	-12	56	3.99	-19	*S-134/3-2	13	-2.1
1994 Mon-N★	110	415	65	122	30	3	15	63	41	62	16	3	.294	.366	.489	.855	119	14	76	6.66	-1	*S-109	17	2.1
1995 Mon-N	131	514	64	147	35	2	10	49	36	88	9	5	.286	.343	.420	.764	97	-3	73	5.08	-21	*S-105,0-26(26-0-0)	12	-1.6
1996 Bos-A	59	198	29	57	14	0	3	37	11	31	2	1	.288	.332	.404	.736	83	-5	24	4.29	-2	2-37,D-13/1-1	5	-0.6
1997 Bos-A	140	570	82	160	26	3	18	72	31	122	1	3	.281	.322	.432	.754	93	-9	76	4.80	-4	*0-137(137-0-0)/D-2,2-1	11	-1.7
1998 Chi-A	96	341	58	91	18	2	13	49	22	66	2	1	.267	.317	.446	.763	98	-2	47	4.85	5	1-83,0-11(4-0-8)	8	-0.4
1999★Cle-A	54	194	35	58	15	0	8	32	15	37	2	0	.299	.367	.500	.867	113	4	35	6.46	-2	0-29(29-0-0),D-26	5	-0.1
2000 Pit-N	89	348	46	98	24	3	16	51	25	58	1	2	.282	.337	.506	.843	110	3	56	5.69	-7	0-85(85-0-0)/D-1	8	-0.8
Cle-A	38	148	18	39	11	2	0	17	7	18	0	0	.264	.310	.365	.675	69	-7	15	3.50	3	0-38(38-0-0)	2	-0.6
2001★Cle-A	89	268	30	67	11	1	4	21	22	50	0	1	.250	.316	.343	.660	73	-10	29	3.62	-5	0-51(48-0-5),1-22,D-11	1	-1.9
2002 Cle-A	6	18	1	4	0	0	1	1	0	3	0	0	.222	.222	.222	.444	19	-2	1	1.20	2	/0-4(4-0-0),1-1	0	0.0
Mon-N	66	143	21	39	9	0	6	29	17	26	2	0	.273	.358	.462	.820	110	3	25	5.97	1	0-28(24-0-5),1-10/D-2	6	0.2
2003 Mon-N	130	436	57	121	27	0	16	71	49	90	1	1	.278	.356	.450	.805	92	-5	69	5.67	0	*1-123/D-2,0-1	10	-1.5
Total 12	1191	4194	579	1159	256	19	121	558	319	742	48	19	.276	.336	.433	.769	96	-31	598	5.04	-56	0-410,S-383,1-240/D-57,2-47,3	102	-9.1
• CORDOVA, Marty				Martin Kevin Cordova				b: 7/10/1969, Las Vegas, NV			BR/TR, 6', 206 lbs.			Deb: 4/26/1995		Career OF: 682-13-72						
1995 Min-A	137	512	81	142	27	4	24	84	52	111	20	7	.277	.355	.486	.842	116	13	90	6.18	8	*0-137(132-11-0)	17	1.4
1996 Min-A	145	569	97	176	46	1	16	111	53	96	11	5	.309	.376	.478	.854	112	11	100	6.32	0	*0-145(145-0-0)	18	0.4
1997 Min-A	103	378	44	93	18	4	15	51	30	92	5	3	.246	.307	.434	.740	89	-7	47	4.17	7	*0-101(101-0-0)/D-2	6	-0.5
1998 Min-A	119	438	52	111	20	2	10	69	50	103	3	6	.253	.337	.377	.713	84	-12	54	4.10	-3	*0-115(115-0-0)/D-4	8	-1.9
1999 Min-A	124	425	62	121	28	3	14	70	48	96	13	4	.285	.369	.464	.833	107	6	69	5.54	-2	D-88,0-29(6-0-25)	9	-0.3
2000 Tor-A	62	200	23	49	7	0	4	18	18	35	3	2	.245	.317	.340	.657	64	-11	21	3.57	-7	0-41(23-0-18),D-15	1	-1.9
2001★Cle-A	122	409	61	123	20	2	20	69	23	81	0	3	.301	.350	.506	.856	120	10	69	6.25	1	*0-107(100-0-7)/D-7	11	1.1
2002 Bal-A	131	458	55	116	25	2	18	64	47	111	1	6	.253	.327	.434	.761	105	0	60	4.36	-3	0-72(72-0-0),D-56	9	-0.9
2003 Bal-A	9	30	5	7	1	0	1	4	8	5	1	0	.233	.410	.367	.777	111	1	5	5.88	1	/D-5,0-4(4-0-0)	1	0.2
Total 9	952	3419	480	938	192	18	122	540	329	730	57	36	.274	.347	.448	.795	103	10	514	5.21	7	0-751,D-177	80	-2.4
• COREY, Fred				Frederick Harrison Corey				b: 1857, South Kingston, RI			d: 11/27/1912, Providence, RI			BR/TR, 5'7"			Deb: 5/1/1878		Career OF: 8-29-46 ◆			
1878 Pro-N	7	21	3	3	0	0	0	1	0	2	....	....	.143	.143	.143	.286	-6	-2	0	.67	0	/P-5,2-2,1-1	1	-0.2
1880 Wor-N	41	138	11	24	8	1	0	6	4	27	....	....	.174	.197	.246	.444	45	-7	7	1.66	-8	0-29(2-6-21),P-25/S-3,1-1,3	10	-1.2
1881 Wor-N	51	203	22	45	8	4	0	10	5	10	....	....	.222	.240	.300	.541	65	-6	15	2.57	-0	0-25(1-0-24),P-23/S-7	10	-1.3
1882 Wor-N	64	255	33	63	7	12	0	29	5	31	....	....	.247	.262	.369	.630	97	-0	25	3.61	-11	S-26,P-21,0-15(5-10-0)/3-6,1	6	-1.0
1883 Phi-a	71	298	45	77	16	2	1	40	12	....	....	....	.258	.287	.336	.623	92	-1	29	3.73	1	3-34,P-18,0-14(0-13-1)/2-9,C,S	18	0.1
1884 Phi-a	104	439	64	121	17	16	5	0	17	....	....	....	.276	.306	.421	.727	127	11	58	5.01	10	*3-104	16	2.1
1885 Phi-a	94	384	61	94	14	8	1	38	17	....	....	....	.245	.282	.331	.613	88	-6	37	3.42	1	*3-92/P-1,S-1	9	-0.7
Total 7	432	1738	239	427	70	43	7	124	60	70	....	....	.246	.273	.348	.620	93	-11	172	3.59	-7	3-237/P-93,0-83,S-38,2-11,1,C	70	-1.8
• COREY, Mark				Mark Mundell Corey				b: 11/3/1955, Tucumcari, NM			BR/TR, 6'2", 200 lbs.			Deb: 9/1/1979		Career OF: 22-0-32				
1979 Bal-A	13	13	1	2	0	0	0	0	4	1	0	1	.154	.154	.154	.308	-17	-2	0	.44	0	0-11(0-0-11)/D-1	0	-0.2
1980 Bal-A	36	36	7	10	2	0	1	2	5	7	0	1	.278	.366	.417	.783	115	0	6	5.57	-1	0-34(15-0-19)	1	-0.2
1981 Bal-A	10	8	2	0	0	0	0	0	2	2	0	0	.000	.200	.000	.200	-38	-1	0	.35	0	/0-9(7-0-2)	0	-0.1
Total 3	59	57	10	12	2	0	1	3	7	13	1	1	.211	.297	.298	.595	64	-3	6	3.37	-1	/0-54,D-1	1	-0.5
• CORGAN, Chuck				Charles Howard Corgan				b: 12/4/1902, Wagoner, OK			d: 6/13/1928, Wagoner, OK			BB/TR, 5'11", 180 lbs.			Deb: 9/19/1925					
1925 Bro-N	14	47	4	8	1	1	0	3	0	9	0	0	.170	.220	.234	.454	16	-6	3	1.69	-2	S-14	0	-0.5
1927 Bro-N	19	57	3	15	1	0	0	1	4	4	0	0	.263	.311	.281	.592	59	-3	5	3.02	1	2-13/S-3	1	-0.2
Total 2	33	104	7	23	2	1	0	7	13	0	0	0	.221	.270	.260	.530	40	-9	8	2.37	-1	/S-17,2-13	1	-0.7
• CORHAN, Roy				Roy George "Irish" Corhan				b: 10/21/1887, Indianapolis, IN			d: 11/24/1958, San Francisco, CA			BR/TR, 5'9.5", 165 lbs.			Deb: 4/20/1911			
1911 Chi-A	43	131	14	28	6	2	0	8	15	....	6	....	.214	.304	.290	.594	68	-5	12	2.98	4	S-43	4	0.5
1916 StL-N	92	295	30	62	6	3	0	18	20	31	15	....	.210	.265	.251	.516	59	-14	24	2.59	-12	S-84	3	-2.3
Total 2	135	426	44	90	12	5	0	26	35	31	17	....	.211	.277	.263	.540	62	-20	36	2.72	-4	S-127	7	-1.8
• CORIDAN, Phil				Philip F. Coridan				b: 8/19/1858, Walpole, IN			d: 7/1/1915, Indianapolis, IN			BL			Deb: 7/16/1884					
1884 CP-U	2	7	1	1	0	0	0	....	0	....	....	....	.143	.143	.143	.286	-3	-1	0	.68	-1	/2-2,0-1	0	-0.1
• CORKHILL, Pop				John Stewart Corkhill				b: 4/11/1858, Parkesburg, PA			d: 4/3/1921, Pennsauken, NJ			BL/TL, 5'10", 180 lbs.			Deb: 5/1/1883		Career OF: 6-615-420 ◆	
1883 Cin-a	88	375	53	81	10	8	2	46	3	....	....	....	.216	.222	.301	.524	63	-17	26	2.45	-1	*0-85(0-15-70)/1-2,2-2,S-2	8	-1.7
1884 Cin-a	110	452	85	124	13	11	4	70	6	....	....	....	.274	.290	.378	.668	111	3	51	4.26	4	*0-92(0-0-92),S-11/1-6,3-3,P	16	0.6
1885 Cin-a	112	440	64	111	10	8	1	53	7	....	....	....	.252	.275	.318	.594	85	-8	40	3.24	13	*0-110(0-0-110)/P-8,1-3	13	-0.5
1886 Cin-a	129	540	81	143	9	7	5	97	23	....	24	....	.265	.302	.335	.637	97	-4	64	4.32	2	*0-112(0-0-112),3-12/1-7,S,P	13	-0.5
1887 Cin-a	128	555	79	182	19	11	5	97	14	....	30	....	.328	.333	.414	.747	105	1	87	6.27	14	*0-128(0-121-7)/P-5	16	0.6
1888 Cin-a	118	490	68	133	11	9	1	74	15	....	27	....	.271	.299	.337	.635	98	-3	59	4.44	1	*0-116(4-112-0)/P-2,1-1,2	16	-0.9
Bro-a	19	71	17	27	4	3	1	19	4	....	3	....	.380	.429	.563	.992	217	9	19	11.59	1	0-19(0-19-0)	5	0.8
Yr.	137	561	85	160	15	12	2	93	19	....	30	....	.285	.316	.365	.681	114	6	78	5.23	2	*0-135(4-131-0)/P-2,1-1,2	21	-0.1

YEAR TM-L	G	AB	R	H	2B	3B	HR	RBI	BB	SO	SB	CS	AVG	OBP	SLG	OPS	OPS+	BR/A	RC	RC/G	FR	G/POS	WS	TPW
1889*Bro-a	138	537	91	134	21	9	8	78	42	24	22	....	.250	.308	.367	.674	91	-8	69	4.54	8	*0-138(0-138-0)/1-1,S-1	17	-0.4
1890 Bro-N	51	204	23	46	4	2	1	21	15	11	6	....	.225	.279	.279	.558	62	-10	18	3.02	2	0-48(0-48-0)/1-6	4	-0.9
1891 Phi-a	83	349	50	73	7	7	0	31	26	15	12	....	.209	.268	.269	.537	52	-24	29	2.79	1	0-83(0-73-10)	4	-2.2
Cin-N	1	4	0	0	0	0	0	0	0	1	0	....	.000	.000	.000	.000	-99	-1	0	.00	1	/0-1	0	0.0
Pit-N	41	145	16	33	1	1	3	20	7	10	7	....	.228	.268	.310	.578	70	-6	14	3.44	1	0-41(1-40-0)	3	-0.6
Yr.	42	149	16	33	1	1	3	20	7	11	7	....	.221	.261	.302	.563	66	-7	14	3.32	2	0-42(1-41-0)	3	-0.6
1892 Pit-N	68	256	23	47	1	4	0	25	12	19	6	....	.184	.229	.219	.448	35	-21	15	1.88	8	0-68(1-48-19)	2	-1.6
Total 10	**1086**	**4418**	**650**	**1134**	**110**	**80**	**31**	**631**	**174**	**80**	**137**	**....**	**.257**	**.288**	**.337**	**.625**	**87**	**-89**	**489**	**4.02**	**54**	***0-1041/1-26,P-17,S-17,3-15,2**	**120**	**-6.8**

• CORRALES, Pat Patrick "Ike" Corrales b: 3/20/1941, Los Angeles, CA BR/TR, 6', 195 lbs. Deb: 8/2/1964 M/C

YEAR TM-L	G	AB	R	H	2B	3B	HR	RBI	BB	SO	SB	CS	AVG	OBP	SLG	OPS	OPS+	BR/A	RC	RC/G	FR	G/POS	WS	TPW
1964 Phi-N	2	1	1	0	0	0	0	0	1	0	0	0	.000	.500	.000	.500	55	0	0	3.51	0	....	0	0.0
1965 Phi-N	63	174	16	39	8	1	2	15	25	42	0	0	.224	.325	.316	.641	83	-3	19	3.57	0	C-62	5	0.0
1966 StL-N	28	72	5	13	2	0	0	3	2	17	1	0	.181	.224	.208	.432	21	-7	3	1.33	1	C-27	1	-0.5
1968 Cin-N	20	56	3	15	4	0	0	6	6	16	0	0	.268	.349	.339	.688	101	0	7	4.40	1	C-20	2	0.2
1969 Cin-N	29	72	10	19	5	0	1	5	8	17	0	1	.264	.346	.375	.721	97	-0	9	4.37	0	C-29	3	0.1
1970*Cin-N	43	106	9	25	5	1	1	10	8	22	0	0	.236	.289	.330	.620	63	-6	9	2.98	1	C-42	2	-0.4
1971 Cin-N	40	94	6	17	2	0	0	6	6	17	0	0	.181	.230	.202	.432	25	-9	5	1.55	-2	C-39	1	-1.0
1972 Cin-N	2	1	0	0	0	0	0	0	2	0	0	0	.000	.667	.000	.667	110	0	0	4.68	0	/C-2	0	0.1
SD-N	44	119	6	23	0	0	0	6	11	26	0	0	.193	.267	.193	.460	35	-10	7	1.87	1	C-43	2	-0.7
Yr.	46	120	6	23	0	0	0	6	13	26	0	0	.192	.276	.192	.468	37	-9	7	1.90	2	C-45	2	-0.6
1973 SD-N	29	72	7	15	2	1	0	3	6	10	0	0	.208	.278	.264	.542	55	-4	6	2.52	-2	C-28	1	-0.5
Total 9	**300**	**767**	**63**	**166**	**28**	**3**	**4**	**54**	**75**	**167**	**1**	**1**	**.216**	**.292**	**.276**	**.569**	**60**	**-39**	**64**	**2.77**	**1**	**C-292**	**17**	**-2.8**

• CORREIA, Rod Ronald Douglas Correia b: 9/13/1967, Providence, RI BR/TR, 5'11", 180 lbs. Deb: 6/20/1993

YEAR TM-L	G	AB	R	H	2B	3B	HR	RBI	BB	SO	SB	CS	AVG	OBP	SLG	OPS	OPS+	BR/A	RC	RC/G	FR	G/POS	WS	TPW
1993 Cal-A	64	128	12	34	5	0	0	9	6	20	2	4	.266	.319	.305	.624	66	-7	12	3.20	-2	S-40,2-11/D-6,3-3	3	-0.6
1994 Cal-A	6	17	4	4	1	0	0	0	0	0	0	0	.235	.316	.294	.610	58	-1	2	3.62	-1	/2-5,S-1	0	-0.2
1995 Cal-A	14	21	3	5	1	1	0	3	0	5	0	0	.238	.238	.381	.619	58	-1	2	2.32	-1	/S-7,2-3,3-2,D-1	1	-0.2
Total 3	**84**	**166**	**19**	**43**	**7**	**1**	**0**	**12**	**6**	**25**	**2**	**4**	**.259**	**.309**	**.313**	**.622**	**64**	**-10**	**16**	**3.13**	**-4**	**/S-48,2-19,D-7,3-5**	**4**	**-1.0**

• CORRELL, Vic Victor Crosby Correll b: 2/5/1946, Washington, DC BR/TR, 5'10", 185 lbs. Deb: 10/4/1972

YEAR TM-L	G	AB	R	H	2B	3B	HR	RBI	BB	SO	SB	CS	AVG	OBP	SLG	OPS	OPS+	BR/A	RC	RC/G	FR	G/POS	WS	TPW
1972 Bos-A	1	4	1	2	0	0	0	1	0	1	0	0	.500	.500	.500	1.000	188	0	1	13.50	1	/C-1	0	0.1
1974 Atl-N	73	202	20	48	15	1	4	29	21	38	0	0	.238	.322	.381	.703	92	-2	25	4.13	2	C-59	7	0.3
1975 Atl-N	103	325	37	70	12	1	11	39	42	66	0	2	.215	.307	.360	.667	82	-9	34	3.32	0	C-97	6	-0.5
1976 Atl-N	69	200	26	45	6	2	5	16	21	37	0	1	.225	.302	.350	.652	79	-6	20	3.25	-1	C-65	4	-0.4
1977 Atl-N	54	144	16	30	7	0	7	16	22	33	2	3	.208	.317	.403	.720	82	-4	18	4.02	1	C-49	4	-0.1
1978 Cin-N	52	105	9	25	7	0	1	6	8	17	0	2	.238	.292	.333	.625	74	-5	8	2.44	0	C-52	2	-0.4
1979 Cin-N	48	133	14	31	12	0	1	15	14	26	0	0	.233	.311	.346	.657	78	-4	14	3.65	-1	C-47	4	-0.3
1980 Cin-N	10	19	1	8	1	0	0	3	0	2	0	0	.421	.421	.474	.895	149	1	4	9.30	-2	C-10	1	0.0
Total 8	**410**	**1132**	**124**	**259**	**60**	**4**	**29**	**125**	**128**	**220**	**2**	**8**	**.229**	**.312**	**.366**	**.677**	**83**	**-29**	**125**	**3.59**	**-1**	**C-380**	**28**	**-1.4**

• CORRIDEN, John John Michael Corriden, Jr. b: 1/6/1918, Logansport, IN d: 6/4/2001, Indianapolis, IN BB/TR, 5'6", 160 lbs. Deb: 4/20/1946

YEAR TM-L	G	AB	R	H	2B	3B	HR	RBI	BB	SO	SB	CS	AVG	OBP	SLG	OPS	OPS+	BR/A	RC	RC/G	FR	G/POS	WS	TPW
1946 Bro-N	1	0	1	0	0	0	0	0	0	0	0	....	....	....	....	....	-99	0	0	....	0	....	0	0.0

• CORRIDEN, Red John Michael Corriden, Sr. b: 9/4/1887, Logansport, IN d: 9/28/1959, Indianapolis, IN BR/TR, 5'9", 165 lbs. Deb: 9/8/1910 M/C

YEAR TM-L	G	AB	R	H	2B	3B	HR	RBI	BB	SO	SB	CS	AVG	OBP	SLG	OPS	OPS+	BR/A	RC	RC/G	FR	G/POS	WS	TPW
1910 StL-A	26	84	19	13	3	0	1	4	13	....	5	....	.155	.297	.226	.523	68	-2	8	2.62	3	S-14,3-12	2	0.1
1912 Det-A	38	138	22	28	6	0	0	5	15	....	4	....	.203	.286	.246	.532	54	-8	11	2.49	-4	3-25/2-7,S-3	1	-1.1
1913 Chi-N	46	97	13	17	3	0	2	9	10	14	4	....	.175	.252	.268	.520	48	-7	7	2.22	-2	S-37/2-2,3-1	1	-0.7
1914 Chi-N	107	318	42	73	9	5	3	29	35	33	13	....	.230	.323	.318	.641	91	-3	37	3.66	-25	S-91/3-8,2-3	7	-2.2
1915 Chi-N	6	3	1	0	0	0	0	0	2	1	0	....	.000	.571	.000	.571	79	1	0	.00	-1	/3-1,0-1	0	0.0
Total 5	**223**	**640**	**97**	**131**	**21**	**5**	**6**	**47**	**75**	**48**	**26**	**....**	**.205**	**.304**	**.281**	**.585**	**74**	**-19**	**63**	**3.03**	**-29**	**S-145/3-47,2-12,0-1**	**11**	**-4.0**

• CORTAZZO, Jess John Francis Cortazzo b: 9/26/1904, Wilmerding, PA d: 3/4/1963, Pittsburgh, PA BR/TR, 5'3.5", 142 lbs. Deb: 9/1/1923

YEAR TM-L	G	AB	R	H	2B	3B	HR	RBI	BB	SO	SB	CS	AVG	OBP	SLG	OPS	OPS+	BR/A	RC	RC/G	FR	G/POS	WS	TPW
1923 Chi-A	1	1	0	0	0	0	0	0	0	0	0	0	.000	.000	.000	.000	-101	-0	0	.00	0	....	0	0.0

• COSCARART, Joe Joseph Marvin Coscarart b: 11/18/1909, Escondido, CA d: 4/5/1993, Sequim, WA BR/TR, 6', 185 lbs. Deb: 4/26/1935

YEAR TM-L	G	AB	R	H	2B	3B	HR	RBI	BB	SO	SB	CS	AVG	OBP	SLG	OPS	OPS+	BR/A	RC	RC/G	FR	G/POS	WS	TPW
1935 Bos-N	86	284	30	67	11	2	1	29	16	28	2	....	.236	.277	.299	.576	59	-16	23	2.71	-7	3-41,S-27,2-15	2	-1.9
1936 Bos-N	104	367	28	90	11	2	2	44	19	37	0	....	.245	.292	.302	.594	64	-18	31	2.84	-6	3-97/S-6,2-1	5	-2.0
Total 2	**190**	**651**	**58**	**157**	**22**	**4**	**3**	**73**	**35**	**65**	**2**	**....**	**.241**	**.285**	**.301**	**.586**	**62**	**-35**	**55**	**2.79**	**-13**	**3-138/S-33,2-16**	**7**	**-3.9**

• COSCARART, Pete Peter Joseph Coscarart b: 6/16/1913, Escondido, CA d: 7/24/2002, Escondido, CA BR/TR, 5'11.5", 175 lbs. Deb: 4/26/1938

YEAR TM-L	G	AB	R	H	2B	3B	HR	RBI	BB	SO	SB	CS	AVG	OBP	SLG	OPS	OPS+	BR/A	RC	RC/G	FR	G/POS	WS	TPW
1938 Bro-N	32	79	10	12	3	0	0	6	9	18	0	....	.152	.256	.190	.445	24	-8	5	1.89	0	2-27	1	-0.6
1939 Bro-N	115	419	59	116	22	2	4	43	46	56	10	....	.277	.354	.368	.721	91	-4	58	4.95	1	*2-107/3-4,S-2	13	0.4
1940 Bro-N★	143	506	55	120	24	4	9	58	53	59	5	....	.237	.311	.354	.664	78	-15	56	3.74	-2	*2-140	10	-0.9
1941*Bro-N	43	62	13	8	1	0	0	5	7	12	1	....	.129	.217	.145	.363	3	-8	2	1.01	-1	2-19/S-1	0	-0.8
1942 Pit-N	133	487	57	111	12	4	3	29	38	56	2	....	.228	.288	.287	.575	67	-21	42	2.86	-18	*S-108,2-25	7	-3.1
1943 Pit-N	133	491	57	119	19	6	0	48	46	48	4	....	.242	.307	.305	.613	75	-16	47	3.27	-4	2-85,S-47/3-1	10	-1.2
1944 Pit-N	139	554	89	146	30	4	4	42	41	57	10	....	.264	.315	.354	.669	84	-12	62	3.86	-3	*2-136/S-4,0-1	14	-0.8
1945 Pit-N	123	392	59	95	17	2	8	38	55	55	2	....	.242	.341	.357	.699	91	-4	50	4.33	10	*2-122/S-1	13	1.2
1946 Pit-N	3	2	0	1	1	0	0	0	0	0	0	....	.500	.500	1.000	1.500	312	1	1	27.00	-1	/S-1	0	0.0
Total 9	**864**	**2992**	**399**	**728**	**129**	**22**	**28**	**269**	**295**	**361**	**34**	**....**	**.243**	**.314**	**.329**	**.644**	**77**	**-87**	**322**	**3.66**	**-18**	**2-661,S-164/3-5,0-1**	**68**	**-5.9**

• COSEY, Ray Donald Ray Cosey b: 2/15/1956, San Rafael, CA BL/TL, 5'10", 185 lbs. Deb: 4/14/1980

YEAR TM-L	G	AB	R	H	2B	3B	HR	RBI	BB	SO	SB	CS	AVG	OBP	SLG	OPS	OPS+	BR/A	RC	RC/G	FR	G/POS	WS	TPW
1980 Oak-A	9	9	0	1	0	0	0	0	0	0	0	0	.111	.111	.111	.222	-42	-2	0	.38	0	....	0	-0.2

• COSTELLO, Dan Daniel Francis "Dashing Dan" Costello b: 9/9/1891, Jessup, PA d: 3/26/1936, Pittsburgh, PA BL/TR, 6'.5", 185 lbs. Deb: 7/2/1913 Career OF: 38-13-32

YEAR TM-L	G	AB	R	H	2B	3B	HR	RBI	BB	SO	SB	CS	AVG	OBP	SLG	OPS	OPS+	BR/A	RC	RC/G	FR	G/POS	WS	TPW
1913 NY-A	2	2	1	1	0	0	0	0	0	0	0	....	.500	.500	.500	1.000	192	0	0	12.24	0	....	0	0.0
1914 Pit-N	21	64	7	19	1	0	0	5	8	16	2	....	.297	.375	.313	.688	110	1	8	4.49	0	0-20(0-0-20)	2	0.1
1915 Pit-N	71	125	16	27	4	1	0	11	7	23	7	1	.216	.258	.264	.522	59	-5	10	2.62	-2	0-22(5-12-5)/1-1	1	-0.9
1916 Pit-N	60	159	11	38	1	3	0	8	6	23	3	....	.239	.267	.283	.550	68	-6	13	2.76	-4	0-41(33-1-7)	2	-1.4
Total 4	**154**	**350**	**35**	**85**	**6**	**4**	**0**	**24**	**21**	**62**	**12**	**1**	**.243**	**.286**	**.283**	**.569**	**74**	**-10**	**32**	**3.03**	**-6**	**/0-83,1-1**	**5**	**-2.2**

• COSTO, Tim Timothy Roger Costo b: 2/16/1969, Melrose Park, IL BR/TR, 6'5", 220 lbs. Deb: 9/18/1992

YEAR TM-L	G	AB	R	H	2B	3B	HR	RBI	BB	SO	SB	CS	AVG	OBP	SLG	OPS	OPS+	BR/A	RC	RC/G	FR	G/POS	WS	TPW
1992 Cin-N	12	36	3	8	2	0	0	2	5	6	0	0	.222	.317	.278	.595	68	-1	3	2.07	0	1-12	0	-0.2
1993 Cin-N	31	98	13	22	5	0	3	12	4	17	0	0	.224	.255	.367	.622	64	-5	9	3.13	-0	0-26(11-0-16)/1-2,3-2	1	-0.7
Total 2	**43**	**134**	**16**	**30**	**7**	**0**	**3**	**14**	**9**	**23**	**0**	**0**	**.224**	**.273**	**.343**	**.616**	**65**	**-7**	**12**	**2.82**	**0**	**/0-26,1-14,3-2**	**1**	**-0.9**

• COTA, Humberto Humberto Figueroa Cota b: 2/7/1979, San Luis Rio Colorado, Mexico BR/TR, 6', 175 lbs. Deb: 9/9/2001

YEAR TM-L	G	AB	R	H	2B	3B	HR	RBI	BB	SO	SB	CS	AVG	OBP	SLG	OPS	OPS+	BR/A	RC	RC/G	FR	G/POS	WS	TPW
2001 Pit-N	7	9	0	2	0	0	0	1	0	5	0	0	.222	.222	.222	.444	15	-1	0	1.71	1	/C-3	0	0.0
2002 Pit-N	7	17	2	5	1	0	0	0	1	4	0	0	.294	.333	.353	.686	80	-0	2	4.50	1	/C-7	0	0.1
2003 Pit-N	10	16	1	4	1	0	0	1	1	5	0	0	.250	.294	.313	.607	57	-1	2	3.48	0	/C-4	0	-0.1
Total 3	**24**	**42**	**3**	**11**	**2**	**0**	**0**	**2**	**2**	**14**	**0**	**0**	**.262**	**.295**	**.310**	**.605**	**58**	**-3**	**4**	**3.48**	**2**	**/C-14**	**0**	**-0.1**

• COTE, Henry Henry Joseph Cote b: 2/19/1864, Troy, NY d: 4/28/1940, Troy, NY, 5'9.5", 165 lbs. Deb: 9/16/1894

YEAR TM-L	G	AB	R	H	2B	3B	HR	RBI	BB	SO	SB	CS	AVG	OBP	SLG	OPS	OPS+	BR/A	RC	RC/G	FR	G/POS	WS	TPW
1894 Lou-N	10	31	7	9	2	2	0	3	5	6	2	....	.290	.389	.484	.873	118	1	7	8.01	2	C-10	1	0.3
1895 Lou-N	10	33	10	10	0	0	0	5	3	3	2	....	.303	.361	.303	.664	77	-1	5	5.10	-2	C-10	1	-0.2
Total 2	**20**	**64**	**17**	**19**	**2**	**2**	**0**	**8**	**8**	**9**	**4**	**....**	**.297**	**.375**	**.391**	**.766**	**97**	**0**	**11**	**6.46**	**0**	**/C-20**	**2**	**0.1**

• COTE, Pete Warren Peter Cote b: 8/30/1902, Cambridge, MA d: 10/17/1987, Middleton, MA BR/TR, 5'6", 148 lbs. Deb: 6/18/1926

YEAR TM-L	G	AB	R	H	2B	3B	HR	RBI	BB	SO	SB	CS	AVG	OBP	SLG	OPS	OPS+	BR/A	RC	RC/G	FR	G/POS	WS	TPW
1926 NY-N	2	1	0	0	0	0	0	0	0	0	0	....	.000	.000	.000	.000	-101	-0	0	.00	0	....	0	0.0

YEAR TM-L	G	AB	R	H	2B	3B	HR	RBI	BB	SO	SB	CS	AVG	OBP	SLG	OPS	OPS+	BR/A	RC	RC/G	FR	G/POS	WS	TPW
• COTTER, Dick	Richard Raphael Cotter b: 10/12/1889, Manchester, NH d: 4/4/1945, Brooklyn, NY BR/TR, 5'11", 172 lbs. Deb: 8/17/1911																							
1911 Phi-N	20	46	2	13	0	0	0	5	5	7	1	....	.283	.353	.283	.636	78	-1	5	3.79	2	C-17	1	0.2
1912 Chi-N	26	54	6	15	0	2	0	10	6	13	1	....	.278	.361	.352	.713	96	-0	7	4.60	-2	C-24	2	0.0
Total 2	46	100	8	28	0	2	0	15	11	20	2	....	.280	.357	.320	.677	87	-1	12	4.22	0	/C-41	3	0.1
• COTTER, Ed	Edward Christopher Cotter b: 7/4/1904, Hartford, CT d: 6/14/1959, Hartford, CT BR/TR, 6', 185 lbs. Deb: 6/12/1926																							
1926 Phi-N	17	26	3	8	0	1	0	1	1	4	1	....	.308	.333	.385	.718	88	-0	3	4.59	-2	/3-8,S-5	0	-0.2
• COTTER, Hooks	Harvey Louis Cotter b: 5/22/1900, Holden, MO d: 8/6/1955, Los Angeles, CA BL/TL, 5'10", 160 lbs. Deb: 4/15/1922																							
1922 Chi-N	1	1	0	1	1	0	0	0	0	0	0	0	1.000	1.000	2.000	3.000	643	1	2	∞	0	....	0	0.1
1924 Chi-N	98	310	39	81	16	4	4	33	36	31	3	5	.261	.338	.377	.716	91	-4	40	4.40	3	1-90	8	-0.7
Total 2	99	311	39	82	17	4	4	33	36	31	3	5	.264	.340	.383	.723	92	-3	42	4.40	3	/1-90	8	-0.6
• COTTER, Tom	Thomas B. Cotter b: 9/30/1866, Waltham, MA d: 11/22/1906, Brookline, MA BR/TR, 5'10.5", 149 lbs. Deb: 9/3/1891																							
1891 Bos-a	6	12	1	3	0	0	0	4	1	2	0	....	.250	.308	.250	.558	61	-1	1	2.79	-0	/C-5,0-1	0	0.0
• COTTIER, Chuck	Charles Keith Cottier b: 1/18/1936, Delta, CO BR/TR, 5'10.5", 175 lbs. Deb: 4/17/1959 M/C																							
1959 Mil-N	10	24	1	3	1	0	0	1	3	7	0	0	.125	.222	.167	.389	6	-3	1	1.39	-1	2-10	0	-0.4
1960 Mil-N	95	229	29	52	8	0	3	19	14	21	1	0	.227	.278	.301	.579	63	-11	20	2.84	-3	2-92	4	-0.8
1961 Det-A	10	7	2	2	0	0	0	1	1	1	0	0	.286	.375	.286	.661	77	-0	1	4.17	-1	/S-8,2-2	0	-0.1
Was-A	101	337	37	79	14	4	2	34	30	51	9	1	.234	.299	.318	.616	68	-14	34	3.38	4	*2-100	7	-0.1
Yr.	111	344	39	81	14	4	2	35	31	52	9	1	.235	.301	.317	.617	68	-14	35	3.40	3	*2-102/S-8	7	-0.2
1962 Was-A	136	443	50	107	14	6	6	40	44	57	14	8	.242	.313	.341	.654	76	-15	49	3.64	10	*2-134	9	0.6
1963 Was-A	113	337	30	69	16	4	5	21	24	63	2	1	.205	.258	.320	.578	61	-18	28	2.68	-6	2-85,S-24/3-1	4	-1.6
1964 Was-A	73	137	16	23	6	2	3	10	19	33	2	0	.168	.269	.307	.576	60	-7	12	2.80	-4	2-53/3-3,S-2	2	-0.8
1965 Was-A	7	1	1	0	0	0	0	0	0	0	0	0	.000	.000	.000	.000	-101	-0	0	.00	0	....	0	0.0
1968 Cal-A	33	67	2	13	4	1	0	1	2	15	0	0	.194	.217	.284	.501	53	-4	4	2.12	1	3-27/2-4	1	-0.4
1969 Cal-A	2	2	0	0	0	0	0	0	0	0	0	0	.000	.000	.000	.000	-105	-1	0	.00	-1	/2-2	0	-0.1
Total 9	580	1584	168	348	63	17	19	127	137	248	28	10	.220	.284	.317	.601	66	-74	150	3.08	0	2-482/S-34,3-31	27	-3.6
• COTTO, Henry	Henry Cotto b: 1/5/1961, New York, NY BR/TR, 6'2", 178 lbs. Deb: 4/5/1984 Career OF: 322-355-133																							
1984*Chi-N	105	146	24	40	5	0	0	8	10	23	9	3	.274	.325	.308	.633	72	-5	16	3.76	1	O-88(47-34-10)	3	-0.6
1985 NY-A	34	56	4	17	1	0	1	6	3	12	1	1	.304	.339	.375	.714	98	-0	7	4.40	1	O-30(14-20-1)	2	0.0
1986 NY-A	35	80	11	17	3	0	1	6	2	17	3	0	.213	.232	.288	.519	41	-6	5	1.99	0	O-29(11-19-0)/D-1	1	-0.6
1987 NY-A	68	149	21	35	10	0	5	20	6	35	4	2	.235	.269	.403	.672	76	-6	14	2.97	0	O-57(15-41-2)	2	-0.6
1988 Sea-A	133	386	50	100	18	1	8	33	23	53	27	3	.259	.304	.373	.677	85	-4	46	4.07	-1	*O-120(0-120-0)/D-2	7	-0.7
1989 Sea-A	100	295	44	78	11	2	9	33	12	44	10	4	.264	.300	.407	.707	94	-3	35	4.22	5	O-90(57-30-14)/D-2	8	0.0
1990 Sea-A	127	355	40	92	14	3	4	33	22	52	21	3	.259	.310	.349	.659	83	-5	38	3.58	-2	*O-118(41-18-67)/D-3	5	-1.1
1991 Sea-A	66	177	35	54	6	2	6	23	10	27	16	3	.305	.349	.463	.812	123	7	28	5.50	0	O-56(38-19-8)/D-6	7	0.6
1992 Sea-A	108	294	42	76	11	1	5	27	14	49	23	2	.259	.294	.354	.648	80	-4	34	4.02	-2	O-92(63-30-6)/D-3	6	-0.9
1993 Sea-A	54	105	10	20	1	0	2	7	2	22	5	4	.190	.213	.257	.470	25	-12	5	1.62	-2	O-34(23-9-4),D-15	1	-1.5
Fla-N	54	135	15	40	7	0	3	14	3	18	11	1	.296	.317	.415	.731	89	-1	18	4.80	-2	O-46(13-15-21)	4	-0.4
Total 10	884	2178	296	569	87	9	44	210	107	352	130	26	.261	.301	.370	.671	83	-39	245	3.86	-1	O-760/D-32	46	-5.7
• COUGHLIN, Bill	William Paul "Scranton Bill" Coughlin b: 7/12/1878, Scranton, PA d: 5/7/1943, Scranton, PA BR/TR, 5'9", 140 lbs. Deb: 8/9/1899 U																							
1899 Was-N	6	24	2	3	0	1	0	3	1	....	1	....	.125	.160	.208	.368	1	-3	1	1.24	-1	/3-6	0	-0.4
1901 Was-A	137	506	75	139	17	13	6	68	25	....	16	....	.275	.317	.395	.712	98	-3	71	4.99	0	*3-137	15	0.1
1902 Was-A	123	469	84	141	27	4	6	71	26	....	29	....	.301	.348	.414	.762	110	5	80	6.39	4	3-66,S-31,2-26	17	1.2
1903 Was-A	125	473	56	116	18	3	1	31	9	....	30	....	.245	.267	.302	.569	69	-19	48	3.51	1	*3-119/S-4,2-2	9	-1.4
1904 Was-A	65	265	28	73	15	4	0	17	9	....	10	....	.275	.307	.362	.669	113	3	35	4.49	-1	3-64	8	0.5
Det-A	56	206	22	47	6	0	0	17	5	....	1	....	.228	.257	.257	.514	65	-8	14	2.37	-7	3-56	2	-1.5
Yr.	121	471	50	120	21	4	0	34	14	....	11	....	.255	.285	.316	.601	92	-5	49	3.56	-8	*3-120	10	-1.0
1905 Det-A	137	489	48	123	20	6	0	44	34	....	16	....	.252	.309	.317	.626	98	-1	57	3.90	-7	*3-136	17	-0.4
1906 Det-A	147	498	54	117	15	5	2	60	36	....	31	....	.235	.293	.297	.590	83	-10	58	3.68	-13	*3-147	12	-2.0
1907*Det-A	134	519	80	126	10	2	0	46	35	....	15	....	.243	.301	.270	.570	79	-11	51	3.24	-3	*3-133	13	-1.2
1908*Det-A	119	405	32	87	5	1	0	23	23	....	10	....	.215	.269	.232	.501	60	-17	29	2.23	-13	*3-119	6	-3.1
Total 9	1049	3854	481	972	133	39	15	380	203	....	159	....	.252	.299	.319	.617	86	-64	442	3.90	-40	3-983/S-35,2-28	99	-8.4
• COUGHLIN, Dennis	Dennis H. Coughlin b: 1/1844, NY d: 5/14/1913, Washington, DC Deb: 4/27/1872																							
1872 Nat-n	8	37	5	12	1	0	0	7	0	0	0	0	.324	.324	.351	.676	92	-1	4	5.36	0	/O-5(0-5-0),1-1,2-1,S-1	....	-0.1
• COUGHLIN, Ed	Edward E. Coughlin b: 8/5/1861, Hartford, CT d: 12/25/1952, Hartford, CT Deb: 5/15/1884																							
1884 Buf-N	1	4	0	1	0	0	0	1	0	2	....	....	.250	.250	.250	.500	56	-0	0	2.35	0	/O-1,P-1	0	0.0
• COUGHTRY, Marlan	James Marlan Coughtry b: 9/11/1934, Hollywood, CA BL/TR, 6'1", 170 lbs. Deb: 9/2/1960																							
1960 Bos-A	15	19	3	3	0	0	0	0	5	8	0	0	.158	.333	.158	.491	36	-1	1	2.42	-2	2-13/3-1	0	-0.3
1962 LA-A	11	22	0	4	0	0	0	2	0	6	0	0	.182	.182	.182	.364	-2	-3	1	1.09	0	/3-5,2-2	0	-0.3
KC-A	6	11	1	2	0	0	0	1	4	3	0	0	.182	.400	.182	.582	61	-0	1	3.60	1	/3-3	0	0.1
Cle-A	3	2	1	1	0	0	0	1	1	1	0	0	.500	.667	.500	1.167	226	1	1	22.68	0	....	0	0.1
Yr.	20	35	2	7	0	0	0	4	5	10	0	0	.200	.300	.200	.500	39	-3	3	2.70	1	/3-8,2-2	0	-0.1
Total 2	35	54	5	10	0	0	0	4	10	18	0	0	.185	.313	.185	.498	38	-4	4	2.60	-1	/2-15,3-9	0	-0.5
• COULSON, Bob	Robert Jackson Coulson b: 6/17/1887, Courtney, PA d: 9/11/1953, Washington, PA BR/TR, 5'10.5", 175 lbs. Deb: 8/4/1908 Career OF: 15-3-177																							
1908 Cin-N	8	18	3	6	1	1	0	1	3	....	0	....	.333	.429	.500	.929	202	2	4	8.22	1	/O-6(4-1-1)	2	0.3
1910 Bro-N	25	89	14	22	3	4	1	13	6	14	9	....	.247	.302	.404	.707	109	0	13	5.03	0	O-25(0-0-25)	2	-0.1
1911 Bro-N	146	521	52	122	23	7	0	50	42	78	32	....	.234	.301	.305	.606	73	-19	57	3.58	0	*O-145(0-2-144)	8	-2.7
1914 Pit-F	18	64	7	13	1	0	0	3	7	10	2	....	.203	.282	.219	.500	46	-4	5	2.18	-1	O-18(11-0-7)	0	-0.7
Total 4	197	692	76	163	28	12	1	67	58	102	43	....	.236	.303	.315	.618	78	-21	79	3.73	-1	O-194	12	-3.2
• COULTER, Chip	Thomas Lee Coulter b: 6/5/1945, Steubenville, OH BB/TR, 5'10", 172 lbs. Deb: 9/18/1969																							
1969 StL-N	6	19	3	6	1	1	0	4	2	6	0	1	.316	.381	.474	.855	138	1	3	6.12	0	/2-6	1	0.1
• COUNSELL, Craig	Craig John Counsell b: 8/21/1970, South Bend, IN BL/TR, 6', 180 lbs. Deb: 9/17/1995																							
1995 Col-N	3	1	0	0	0	0	0	0	1	0	0	0	.000	.500	.000	.500	36	-0	0	3.51	-1	/S-3	0	-0.1
1997 Col-N	1	0	0	0	0	0	0	0	0	0	0	0	....	....	....	....	-81	0	0	....	0	....	0	0.0
*Fla-N	51	164	20	49	9	2	1	16	18	17	1	1	.299	.378	.396	.775	108	2	25	5.31	8	2-51	8	1.2
Yr.	52	164	20	49	9	2	1	16	18	17	1	1	.299	.378	.396	.775	108	2	25	5.31	8	2-51	8	1.2
1998 Fla-N	107	335	43	84	19	5	4	40	51	47	3	0	.251	.356	.373	.730	96	0	48	4.92	2	*2-104	13	0.7
1999 Fla-N	37	66	4	10	1	0	0	2	5	10	0	0	.152	.211	.167	.378	-3	-10	3	1.17	-1	2-12	0	-1.0
LA-N	50	108	20	28	6	0	0	9	9	14	1	0	.259	.316	.315	.631	64	-6	12	3.66	0	2-38/S-2	2	-0.4
Yr.	87	174	24	38	7	0	0	11	14	24	1	0	.218	.277	.259	.535	39	-16	14	2.64	0	2-50/S-2	2	-1.4
2000 Ari-N	67	152	23	48	8	1	2	11	20	18	3	3	.316	.402	.421	.823	105	1	26	6.19	3	2-25,3-23/S-6	5	0.6
2001*Ari-N	141	458	76	126	22	3	4	38	61	76	6	8	.275	.363	.362	.725	83	-11	62	4.61	20	S-58,2-55,3-38/1-2	14	1.5
2002 Ari-N	112	436	63	123	22	1	2	51	45	52	7	5	.282	.351	.351	.702	78	-13	54	4.35	22	3-94,S-22,2-13	15	1.2
2003 Ari-N	89	303	40	71	6	3	3	21	41	32	11	4	.234	.329	.304	.633	61	-16	34	3.71	7	3-57,S-26,2-10/1-2	4	-0.6
Total 8	658	2023	289	539	93	15	16	188	251	266	32	21	.266	.351	.351	.702	81	-52	262	4.45	60	2-308,3-212,S-117/1-4	61	3.1
• COURTNEY, Clint	Clinton Dawson "Scrap Iron,The Toy Bulldog" Courtney b: 3/16/1927, Hall Summit, LA d: 6/16/1975, Rochester, NY BL/TR, 5'8", 180 lbs. Deb: 9/29/1951 C																							
1951 NY-A	1	2	0	0	0	0	0	0	0	1	0	0	.000	.333	.000	.333	-5	-0	0	1.17	0	/C-1	0	0.0
1952 StL-A	119	413	38	118	24	3	5	50	39	26	0	2	.286	.349	.395	.743	104	1	58	5.02	4	*C-113	14	1.2

YEAR TM-L	G	AB	R	H	2B	3B	HR	RBI	BB	SO	SB	CS	AVG	OBP	SLG	OPS	OPS+	BR/A	RC	RC/G	FR	G/POS	WS	TPW
1953 StL-A	106	355	28	89	12	2	4	19	25	20	0	1	.251	.302	.330	.631	69	-16	33	3.18	-2	*C-103	3	-1.4
1954 Bal-A	122	397	25	107	18	3	4	37	30	7	2	1	.270	.326	.360	.686	95	-3	46	4.04	1	*C-111	10	0.3
1955 Chi-A	19	37	7	14	3	0	1	10	7	0	0	0	.378	.477	.541	1.018	168	4	9	9.57	0	C-17	3	0.5
Was-A	75	238	26	71	8	4	2	30	19	9	0	0	.298	.353	.391	.743	105	2	33	5.04	0	C-67	7	0.4
Yr.	94	275	33	85	11	4	3	40	26	9	0	0	.309	.371	.411	.782	114	6	42	5.62	0	C-84	10	0.9
1956 Was-A	101	283	31	85	20	3	5	44	20	10	0	5	.300	.365	.445	.811	113	3	43	5.32	1	C-76	9	0.7
1957 Was-A	91	232	23	62	14	1	6	27	16	11	0	0	.267	.346	.414	.760	108	3	33	5.05	1	C-59	8	0.7
1958 Was-A	134	450	46	113	18	0	8	62	48	23	1	5	.251	.335	.344	.680	89	-7	52	3.89	4	*C-128	13	0.4
1959 Was-A	72	189	19	44	4	1	2	18	20	19	0	1	.233	.310	.296	.606	67	-8	18	3.19	-4	C-53	3	-1.0
1960 Bal-A	83	154	14	35	3	0	1	12	30	14	0	1	.227	.380	.266	.646	79	-2	18	3.73	-2	C-58	4	-0.2
1961 KC-A	1	1	0	0	0	0	0	0	0	0	0	0	.000	.000	.000	.000	-100	-0	0	.00	0	....	0	0.0
Bal-A	22	45	3	12	2	0	0	4	10	3	0	0	.267	.400	.311	.711	95	0	6	5.03	1	C-16	2	0.2
Yr.	23	46	3	12	2	0	0	4	10	3	0	0	.261	.393	.304	.697	91	0	6	4.89	1	C-16	2	0.1
Total 11	946	2796	260	750	126	17	38	313	264	143	3	16	.268	.341	.366	.708	94	-24	349	4.33	3	C-802	76	1.7

• COURTNEY, Ernie Edward Ernest Courtney b: 1/20/1875, Des Moines, IA d: 2/29/1920, Buffalo, NY BL/TR, 5'8" Deb: 4/17/1902 Career OF: 40-1-6

YEAR TM-L	G	AB	R	H	2B	3B	HR	RBI	BB	SO	SB	CS	AVG	OBP	SLG	OPS	OPS+	BR/A	RC	RC/G	FR	G/POS	WS	TPW
1902 Bos-N	48	165	23	36	3	0	0	17	13	....	3	....	.218	.291	.236	.528	62	-7	13	2.59	-1	O-39(36-1-3)/S-3	2	-1.0
Bal-A	1	4	3	2	0	1	0	1	1	....	0	....	.500	.600	1.000	1.600	324	1	2	32.60	0	/3-1	1	0.2
1903 NY-A	25	79	7	21	3	3	1	8	7	....	1	....	.266	.341	.418	.759	119	2	12	5.31	2	S-19/2-4,1-1	4	0.5
Det-A	23	74	7	17	0	0	0	6	5	....	1	....	.230	.305	.230	.535	64	-3	6	2.64	-1	3-13/S-9	1	-0.4
Yr.	48	153	14	38	3	3	1	14	12	....	2	....	.248	.324	.327	.650	93	-1	18	4.01	1	S-28,3-13/2-4,1-1	5	0.1
1905 Phi-N	155	601	77	165	14	7	2	77	47	....	17	....	.275	.334	.331	.665	102	2	77	4.36	-6	*3-155	17	0.1
1906 Phi-N	116	398	53	94	12	2	0	42	45	....	6	....	.236	.315	.276	.592	85	-6	38	3.22	-4	3-96,1-13/O-3(0-0-3),S-1	10	-0.9
1907 Phi-N	130	440	42	107	17	4	2	43	55	....	6	....	.243	.335	.314	.649	105	4	51	3.87	-4	3-75,1-48/O-4(4-0-0),2-2,S	15	0.2
1908 Phi-N	60	160	14	29	3	0	0	6	15	....	1	....	.181	.260	.200	.460	46	-9	9	1.69	-5	3-22,1-13/2-5,S-2	1	-1.6
Total 6	558	1921	226	471	52	17	5	200	188	....	35	....	.245	.321	.298	.618	91	-14	208	3.63	-18	3-362/1-75,O-46,S-36,2-11	51	-2.9

• COUSINEAU, Dee Edward Thomas Cousineau b: 12/16/1898, Watertown, MA d: 7/14/1951, Watertown, MA BR/TR, 6', 170 lbs. Deb: 10/6/1923

YEAR TM-L	G	AB	R	H	2B	3B	HR	RBI	BB	SO	SB	CS	AVG	OBP	SLG	OPS	OPS+	BR/A	RC	RC/G	FR	G/POS	WS	TPW
1923 Bos-N	1	2	1	2	0	0	0	2	0	0	0	0	1.000	1.000	1.000	2.000	447	1	2	∞	0	/C-1	0	0.1
1924 Bos-N	3	2	0	0	0	0	0	0	0	0	0	0	.000	.000	.000	.000	-104	-1	0	.00	-1	/C-3	0	-0.2
1925 Bos-N	1	0	0	0	0	0	0	0	0	0	0	0	....	....	....	....	-110	0	0	....	0	/C-1	0	0.0
Total 3	5	4	1	2	0	0	0	2	0	0	0	0	.500	.500	.500	1.000	171	0	2	.00	-2	/C-5	0	-0.1

• COVENEY, Jack John Patrick Coveney b: 6/10/1880, South Natick, MA d: 3/28/1961, Wayland, MA BR/TR, 5'9", 175 lbs. Deb: 9/19/1903

YEAR TM-L	G	AB	R	H	2B	3B	HR	RBI	BB	SO	SB	CS	AVG	OBP	SLG	OPS	OPS+	BR/A	RC	RC/G	FR	G/POS	WS	TPW
1903 StL-N	4	14	0	2	0	0	0	0	0	....	0	....	.143	.143	.143	.286	-19	-2	0	.65	1	/C-4	0	-0.1

• COVINGTON, Sam Clarence Calvert Covington b: 11/18/1894, Denison, TX d: 1/4/1963, Denison, TX BL/TR, 6'1", 190 lbs. Deb: 8/25/1913

YEAR TM-L	G	AB	R	H	2B	3B	HR	RBI	BB	SO	SB	CS	AVG	OBP	SLG	OPS	OPS+	BR/A	RC	RC/G	FR	G/POS	WS	TPW
1913 StL-A	20	60	3	9	0	1	0	4	4	6	3	....	.150	.203	.183	.386	14	-7	3	1.31	3	1-16	0	-0.4
1917 Bos-N	17	66	8	13	2	0	1	10	5	5	1	....	.197	.264	.273	.537	69	-2	5	2.34	1	1-17	1	-0.2
1918 Bos-N	3	3	0	1	0	0	0	0	0	0	0	....	.333	.333	.333	.667	108	0	0	4.07	0	....	0	0.0
Total 3	40	129	11	23	2	1	1	14	9	11	4	....	.178	.237	.233	.470	44	-9	8	1.88	4	/1-33	1	-0.6

• COVINGTON, Wes John Wesley Covington b: 3/27/1932, Laurinburg, NC BL/TR, 6'1", 205 lbs. Deb: 4/19/1956 Career OF: 761-1-43

YEAR TM-L	G	AB	R	H	2B	3B	HR	RBI	BB	SO	SB	CS	AVG	OBP	SLG	OPS	OPS+	BR/A	RC	RC/G	FR	G/POS	WS	TPW
1956 Mil-N	75	138	17	39	4	0	2	16	16	20	1	0	.283	.361	.355	.716	100	1	19	4.89	1	O-35(34-0-1)	4	0.0
1957*Mil-N	96	328	51	93	4	8	21	65	29	44	4	1	.284	.345	.537	.882	143	19	61	6.47	3	O-89(89-0-0)	15	1.7
1958*Mil-N	90	294	43	97	12	1	24	74	20	35	0	0	.330	.382	.622	1.005	175	30	68	8.72	1	O-82(82-0-0)	17	2.7
1959 Mil-N	103	373	38	104	17	3	7	45	26	41	0	1	.279	.331	.397	.728	101	-0	46	4.30	-2	O-94(94-0-0)	8	-0.8
1960 Mil-N	95	281	25	70	16	1	10	35	15	37	1	2	.249	.290	.420	.709	99	-2	31	3.73	-2	O-72(72-0-0)	6	-0.8
1961 Mil-N	9	21	3	4	1	0	0	0	2	4	0	0	.190	.261	.238	.499	36	-2	1	2.29	0	/O-5(5-0-0)	0	-0.2
Chi-A	22	59	5	17	1	0	4	15	4	5	0	0	.288	.333	.508	.842	123	2	9	5.46	0	O-14(11-0-3)	2	0.1
KC-A	17	44	3	7	0	0	1	6	4	7	0	0	.159	.260	.227	.487	31	-4	3	1.76	0	O-12(11-0-1)	0	-0.5
Yr.	39	103	8	24	1	0	5	21	8	12	0	0	.233	.301	.388	.689	83	-3	12	3.76	0	O-26(22-0-4)	2	-0.4
Phi-N	57	165	23	50	9	0	7	26	15	17	0	0	.303	.361	.485	.846	124	5	28	6.29	1	O-45(10-0-36)	5	0.4
Yr.	66	186	26	54	10	0	7	26	17	21	0	0	.290	.350	.457	.807	114	4	30	5.80	1	O-50(15-0-36)	5	0.2
1962 Phi-N	116	304	36	86	12	1	9	44	19	44	0	0	.283	.329	.418	.747	102	0	40	4.64	-1	O-88(88-0-0)	7	-0.4
1963 Phi-N	119	353	46	107	24	1	17	64	26	56	1	0	.303	.354	.521	.876	150	22	63	6.68	1	*O-101(101-0-0)	17	2.1
1964 Phi-N	129	339	37	95	18	0	13	58	38	50	0	0	.280	.358	.448	.806	127	13	55	5.89	-1	O-99(97-1-2)	14	0.9
1965 Phi-N	101	235	27	58	10	1	15	45	26	47	0	0	.247	.324	.489	.814	128	8	37	5.38	0	O-64(64-0-0)	9	0.5
1966 Chi-N	9	11	0	1	0	0	0	0	1	2	0	0	.091	.167	.091	.258	-26	-2	0	.45	0	/O-1	0	-0.2
*LA-N	37	33	1	4	0	1	1	6	6	5	0	0	.121	.293	.273	.565	63	-1	3	2.68	-0	/O-2(2-0-0)	0	-0.1
Yr.	46	44	1	5	0	1	1	6	7	7	0	0	.114	.264	.227	.491	43	-3	3	2.12	-0	/O-3(3-0-0)	0	-0.3
Total 11	1075	2978	355	832	128	17	131	499	247	414	7	4	.279	.339	.466	.805	123	88	463	5.52	-1	O-803	104	5.4

• COWAN, Billy Billy Rolland Cowan b: 8/28/1938, Calhoun City, MS BR/TR, 6', 170 lbs. Deb: 9/9/1963 Career OF: 78-210-41

YEAR TM-L	G	AB	R	H	2B	3B	HR	RBI	BB	SO	SB	CS	AVG	OBP	SLG	OPS	OPS+	BR/A	RC	RC/G	FR	G/POS	WS	TPW
1963 Chi-N	14	36	1	9	1	1	1	2	0	11	0	1	.250	.250	.417	.667	84	-1	3	3.21	0	O-10(1-7-2)	0	-0.2
1964 Chi-N	139	497	52	120	16	4	19	50	18	128	12	3	.241	.269	.404	.674	83	-11	53	3.69	-1	*O-134(0-134-0)	10	-1.8
1965 NY-N	82	156	16	28	8	2	3	9	4	45	3	2	.179	.205	.314	.519	45	-12	9	1.89	-1	O-61(2-59-0)/2-2,S-1	1	-1.5
Mil-N	19	27	4	5	1	0	0	0	0	9	0	0	.185	.185	.222	.407	14	-3	1	1.36	0	O-10(7-3-0)	0	-0.4
Yr.	101	183	20	33	9	2	3	9	4	54	3	2	.180	.202	.301	.503	41	-15	10	1.82	-1	O-71(9-62-0)/2-2,S-1	1	-1.8
1967 Phi-N	34	59	11	9	0	0	3	6	4	14	1	0	.153	.206	.305	.511	44	-4	4	1.92	-1	O-20(16-0-4)/2-1,3-1	0	-0.6
1969 NY-A	32	48	5	8	0	0	1	3	3	9	0	0	.167	.216	.229	.445	25	-5	2	1.16	0	O-14(8-4-2)	0	-0.5
Cal-A	28	56	10	17	1	0	4	10	3	9	0	0	.304	.350	.536	.886	152	3	10	6.93	1	O-13(3-2-8)/1-6	3	0.4
Yr.	60	104	15	25	1	0	5	13	6	18	0	0	.240	.288	.394	.683	94	-1	12	3.94	2	O-27(11-6-10)/1-6	3	-0.1
1970 Cal-A	68	134	20	37	9	1	5	25	11	29	0	1	.276	.336	.470	.806	124	4	21	5.58	-1	O-27(3-1-23),1-14/3-2	5	0.1
1971 Cal-A	74	174	12	48	8	0	4	20	7	41	1	1	.276	.304	.391	.695	103	-1	20	4.19	-1	O-40(38-0-2)/1-5	5	-0.4
1972 Cal-A	3	3	0	0	0	0	0	0	0	2	0	0	.000	.000	.000	.000	-106	-1	0	.00	0	....	0	-0.1
Total 8	493	1190	131	281	44	8	40	125	50	297	17	8	.236	.269	.387	.657	83	-31	124	3.54	-3	O-329/1-25,2-3,3-3,S-1	24	-4.8

• COWENS, Al Alfred Edward "A. C." Cowens b: 10/25/1951, Los Angeles, CA d: 3/11/2002, Downey, CA BR/TR, 6'1", 200 lbs. Deb: 4/6/1974 Career OF: 34-195-1288

YEAR TM-L	G	AB	R	H	2B	3B	HR	RBI	BB	SO	SB	CS	AVG	OBP	SLG	OPS	OPS+	BR/A	RC	RC/G	FR	G/POS	WS	TPW
1974 KC-A	110	269	28	65	7	1	1	25	23	38	5	0	.242	.304	.286	.590	67	-10	23	2.90	3	*O-102(6-24-75)/D-4,3-2	4	-1.1
1975 KC-A	120	328	44	91	13	8	4	42	28	36	12	7	.277	.342	.402	.744	107	3	44	4.54	-4	*O-113(22-35-65)/D-2	10	-0.6
1976*KC-A	152	581	71	154	23	6	3	59	26	50	23	16	.265	.300	.341	.641	87	-13	57	3.34	2	*O-148(0-12-142)/D-1	12	-2.1
1977*KC-A	162	606	98	189	32	14	23	112	41	64	16	12	.312	.363	.525	.888	138	29	109	6.58	2	*O-159(0-26-141)/D-1	27	2.4
1978*KC-A	132	485	63	133	24	8	5	63	31	54	14	6	.274	.326	.388	.713	97	-2	62	4.43	-1	*O-127(0-16-119)/3-5,D-2	15	-0.9
1979 KC-A	136	516	69	152	18	7	9	73	40	44	10	8	.295	.349	.409	.758	102	0	71	4.89	-12	*O-134(0-1-134)/D-1	14	-1.8
1980 Cal-A	34	119	11	27	5	0	1	17	12	21	1	2	.227	.303	.294	.597	66	-6	11	2.96	1	O-30(3-10-19)/D-1	1	-0.6
Det-A	108	403	58	113	15	3	5	42	37	40	5	6	.280	.342	.370	.712	93	-5	51	4.41	-4	*O-107(0-0-107)/D-1	9	-1.4
Yr.	142	522	69	140	20	3	6	59	49	61	6	8	.268	.333	.352	.686	87	-11	62	4.07	-3	*O-137(3-10-126)/D-2	10	-2.0
1981 Det-A	85	253	27	66	11	4	1	18	22	36	3	3	.261	.322	.348	.670	90	-4	29	3.88	-1	O-83(0-65-18)	7	-0.7
1982 Sea-A	146	560	72	151	39	8	20	78	46	81	11	7	.270	.326	.475	.801	114	9	84	5.22	2	*O-145(0-0-145)/D-1	17	0.3
1983 Sea-A	110	356	39	73	19	2	7	35	23	38	10	2	.205	.257	.329	.586	58	-20	28	2.53	3	O-70(2-4-65),D-34	1	-2.1
1984 Sea-A	139	524	60	145	34	2	15	78	27	83	9	5	.277	.315	.435	.750	106	3	66	4.34	-4	*O-130(0-2-130)/D-7	11	-0.8
1985 Sea-A	122	452	59	120	32	5	14	69	30	56	0	2	.265	.313	.451	.764	105	2	56	4.22	5	*O-110(0-0-110)/D-5	10	0.2
1986 Sea-A	28	82	5	15	4	0	0	6	3	18	1	0	.183	.212	.232	.443	20	-9	4	1.38	0	O-19(1-0-18)/D-1	0	-1.0
Total 13	1584	5534	704	1494	276	68	108	717	389	659	120	74	.270	.322	.403	.725	98	-23	694	4.32	-8	*O-1477/D-61,3-7	138	-10.1

• COX, Billy William Richard Cox b: 8/29/1919, Newport, PA d: 3/30/1978, Harrisburg, PA BR/TR, 5'10", 150 lbs. Deb: 9/20/1941

YEAR TM-L	G	AB	R	H	2B	3B	HR	RBI	BB	SO	SB	CS	AVG	OBP	SLG	OPS	OPS+	BR/A	RC	RC/G	FR	G/POS	WS	TPW
1941 Pit-N	10	37	4	10	3	1	0	2	3	2	1	....	.270	.325	.405	.730	105	0	5	4.56	0	S-10	1	0.1
1946 Pit-N	121	411	32	119	22	6	2	36	26	15	4	....	.290	.333	.387	.720	101	-1	54	4.79	-14	*S-114	11	-0.8
1947 Pit-N	132	529	75	145	30	7	15	54	29	28	5	....	.274	.313	.442	.755	96	-6	74	5.08	-1	*S-129	14	0.1

YEAR TM-L	G	AB	R	H	2B	3B	HR	RBI	BB	SO	SB	CS	AVG	OBP	SLG	OPS	OPS+	BR/A	RC	RC/G	FR	G/POS	WS	TPW
1948 Bro-N	88	237	36	59	13	2	3	15	38	19	3	....	.249	.353	.359	.711	90	-2	31	4.40	0	3-70/S-6,2-1	6	-0.2
1949*Bro-N	100	390	48	91	18	2	8	40	30	18	5	....	.233	.290	.351	.641	68	-19	39	3.38	11	*3-100	8	-0.8
1950 Bro-N	119	451	62	116	17	2	8	44	35	24	6	....	.257	.311	.357	.668	74	-18	48	3.62	11	*3-107,2-13/S-9	10	-0.6
1951 Bro-N	142	455	62	127	25	4	9	51	37	30	5	5	.279	.336	.411	.747	98	-3	64	4.86	-2	*3-139/S-1	14	-0.5
1952*Bro-N	116	455	56	118	12	3	6	34	25	32	10	12	.259	.301	.338	.639	76	-18	43	3.11	1	*3-100,S-10/2-9	9	-1.7
1953*Bro-N	100	327	44	95	18	1	10	44	37	21	2	2	.291	.363	.443	.806	106	3	54	5.88	-2	3-89/S-6,2-1	12	0.1
1954 Bro-N	77	226	26	53	9	2	2	17	21	13	0	0	.235	.300	.319	.618	59	-13	21	3.04	0	3-58,2-11/S-8	3	-1.2
1955 Bal-A	53	194	25	41	7	2	3	14	17	16	1	2	.211	.275	.314	.589	62	-11	16	2.67	-2	3-37,2-18/S-6	2	-1.3
Total 11	**1058**	**3712**	**470**	**974**	**174**	**32**	**66**	**351**	**298**	**218**	**42**	**21**	**.262**	**.318**	**.380**	**.698**	**85**	**-88**	**448**	**4.16**	**2**	**3-700,S-299/2-53**	**90**	**-6.9**
• COX, Bobby	Robert Joseph Cox b: 5/21/1941, Tulsa, OK BR/TR, 5'11", 180 lbs. Deb: 4/14/1968 M/C																							
1968 NY-A	135	437	33	100	15	1	7	41	41	85	3	2	.229	.302	.316	.618	90	-5	42	3.21	-15	*3-132	12	-2.2
1969 NY-A	85	191	17	41	7	1	2	17	34	41	0	1	.215	.336	.293	.629	80	-4	19	3.16	7	3-56/2-6	4	0.3
Total 2	**220**	**628**	**50**	**141**	**22**	**2**	**9**	**58**	**75**	**126**	**3**	**3**	**.225**	**.313**	**.309**	**.622**	**87**	**-9**	**61**	**3.20**	**-8**	**3-188/2-6**	**16**	**-1.9**
• COX, Darron	James Darron Cox b: 11/21/1967, Oklahoma City, OK BR/TR, 6'1", 205 lbs. Deb: 4/6/1999																							
1999 Mon-N	15	25	2	6	1	0	1	2	0	5	0	0	.240	.296	.400	.696	76	-1	3	4.43	0	C-14	0	-0.1
• COX, Dick	Elmer Joseph Cox b: 9/30/1895, Pasadena, CA d: 6/1/1966, Morro Bay, CA BR/TR, 5'7.5", 158 lbs. Deb: 4/16/1925 Career OF: 3-1-224																							
1925 Bro-N	122	434	68	143	23	10	7	64	37	29	4	3	.329	.382	.477	.859	121	14	79	6.98	-2	*O-111(3-0-108)	15	0.4
1926 Bro-N	124	398	53	118	17	4	1	45	46	20	6	....	.296	.375	.367	.742	102	3	56	4.99	-5	*O-117(0-1-116)	12	-1.0
Total 2	**246**	**832**	**121**	**261**	**40**	**14**	**8**	**109**	**83**	**49**	**10**	**3**	**.314**	**.379**	**.424**	**.803**	**112**	**17**	**135**	**6.00**	**-7**	**O-228**	**27**	**-0.6**
• COX, Frank	Francis Bernard "Runt" Cox b: 8/29/1857, Waltham, MA d: 6/24/1928, Hartford, CT, 5'6" Deb: 8/13/1884																							
1884 Det-N	27	102	6	13	3	1	0	4	2	36	....	....	.127	.144	.176	.321		-11	3	.82	-3	S-27	1	-1.2
• COX, Jeff	Jeffrey Lindon Cox b: 11/9/1955, Los Angeles, CA BR/TR, 5'11", 170 lbs. Deb: 7/1/1980 C																							
1980 Oak-A	59	169	20	36	3	0	0	9	14	23	8	5	.213	.273	.231	.504	43	-13	12	2.08	1	2-58	1	-0.9
1981 Oak-A	2	0	0	0	0	0	0	0	0	0	0	0	....	....	....	....	-105	0	0	....	0	/2-1	0	0.0
Total 2	**61**	**169**	**20**	**36**	**3**	**0**	**0**	**9**	**14**	**23**	**8**	**5**	**.213**	**.273**	**.231**	**.504**	**43**	**-13**	**12**	**2.08**	**1**	**/2-59**	**1**	**-0.9**
• COX, Jim	James Charles Cox b: 5/28/1950, Bloomington, IL BR/TR, 5'11", 175 lbs. Deb: 7/19/1973																							
1973 Mon-N	9	15	1	2	1	0	0	0	1	4	0	0	.133	.188	.200	.388	7	-2	1	1.29	-1	/2-7	0	-0.3
1974 Mon-N	77	236	29	52	9	1	2	26	23	36	2	3	.220	.292	.292	.585	60	-13	20	2.62	-1	2-72	3	-1.1
1975 Mon-N	11	27	1	7	1	0	1	5	1	2	1	0	.259	.286	.407	.693	87	-0	2	2.92	2	/2-8	1	0.2
1976 Mon-N	13	29	2	5	0	1	0	2	2	2	0	0	.172	.226	.241	.467	31	-3	1	1.57	-2	2-11	0	-0.4
Total 4	**110**	**307**	**33**	**66**	**11**	**2**	**3**	**33**	**27**	**44**	**3**	**3**	**.215**	**.281**	**.293**	**.574**	**57**	**-18**	**24**	**2.48**	**-3**	**/2-98**	**4**	**-1.6**
• COX, Larry	Larry Eugene Cox b: 9/11/1947, Bluffton, OH d: 2/17/1990, Bellefontaine, OH BR/TR, 5'10", 190 lbs. Deb: 4/18/1973 C																							
1973 Phi-N	1	0	0	0	0	0	0	0	0	0	0	0	....	....	....	....	-97	0	0	....	0	/C-1	0	0.0
1974 Phi-N	30	53	5	9	2	0	0	4	4	9	0	0	.170	.241	.208	.449	25	-5	3	1.65	0	C-29	0	-0.5
1975 Phi-N	11	5	0	1	0	0	0	1	1	0	1	0	.200	.333	.200	.533	49	-0	0	1.48	-3	C-10	0	-0.3
1977 Sea-A	35	93	6	23	6	0	2	6	10	12	1	1	.247	.320	.376	.697	90	-1	11	4.07	0	C-35	3	0.0
1978 Chi-N	59	121	10	34	5	0	2	18	12	16	0	0	.281	.346	.372	.718	90	-1	15	4.51	-1	C-58	4	0.0
1979 Sea-A	100	293	32	63	11	3	4	36	22	39	2	1	.215	.270	.314	.584	56	-18	24	2.60	0	C-99	3	-1.4
1980 Sea-A	105	243	18	49	6	2	4	20	19	36	1	2	.202	.260	.292	.552	50	-17	17	2.15	0	*C-104	4	-1.3
1981 Tex-A	5	13	0	3	1	0	0	0	0	4	0	0	.231	.231	.308	.538	57	-1	1	2.49	1	/C-5	0	0.1
1982 Chi-N	2	4	1	0	0	0	0	0	2	1	0	0	.000	.333	.000	.333	1	-0	0	.59	1	/C-2	0	0.0
Total 9	**348**	**825**	**72**	**182**	**31**	**5**	**12**	**85**	**70**	**117**	**5**	**4**	**.221**	**.282**	**.314**	**.596**	**61**	**-45**	**71**	**2.79**	**-2**	**C-343**	**14**	**-3.3**
• COX, Steve	Charles Steven Cox b: 10/31/1974, Delano, CA BL/TL, 6'4", 222 lbs. Deb: 9/19/1999 Career OF: 34-0-32																							
1999 TB-A	6	19	0	4	1	0	0	0	0	2	0	0	.211	.211	.263	.474	20	-2	1	.84	0	/1-4,O-2(2-0-0)	0	-0.3
2000 TB-A	116	318	44	90	19	1	11	35	46	47	1	2	.283	.380	.453	.833	111	6	55	6.20	0	O-56(26-0-30),1-24,D-17	8	0.1
2001 TB-A	108	342	37	88	22	0	12	51	24	75	2	2	.257	.324	.427	.751	97	-2	45	4.54	-1	1-78/O-8(6-0-2),D-4	5	-1.0
2002 TB-A	148	560	65	142	30	1	16	72	60	116	5	0	.254	.333	.396	.730	95	-3	75	4.60	1	*1-110,D-35	8	-1.4
Total 4	**378**	**1239**	**146**	**324**	**72**	**2**	**39**	**158**	**130**	**240**	**8**	**4**	**.262**	**.342**	**.417**	**.759**	**99**	**-2**	**176**	**4.91**	**-1**	**1-216/O-66,D-56**	**21**	**-2.6**
• COX, Ted	William Ted Cox b: 1/24/1955, Oklahoma City, OK BR/TR, 6'3", 195 lbs. Deb: 9/18/1977 Career OF: 49-0-5																							
1977 Bos-A	13	58	11	21	3	1	1	6	3	6	0	0	.362	.393	.500	.893	127	2	12	8.33	0	D-13	2	0.2
1978 Cle-A	82	227	14	53	7	0	1	19	16	30	0	1	.233	.287	.278	.564	60	-12	18	2.65	2	O-38(33-0-5),3-20,D-12/1-7,S	2	-1.2
1979 Cle-A	78	189	17	40	6	0	4	22	14	27	3	4	.212	.273	.307	.580	56	-13	14	2.33	-7	3-52,O-16(16-0-0)/2-4,D-1	1	-2.1
1980 Sea-A	83	247	17	60	9	0	2	23	19	25	0	0	.243	.297	.304	.601	64	-12	21	2.91	0	3-80	3	-1.2
1981 Tor-A	16	50	6	15	4	0	2	9	5	10	0	1	.300	.364	.500	.864	138	2	9	6.81	-1	3-14/1-1,D-1	2	0.1
Total 5	**272**	**771**	**65**	**189**	**29**	**1**	**10**	**79**	**57**	**98**	**3**	**6**	**.245**	**.300**	**.324**	**.624**	**70**	**-33**	**75**	**3.23**	**-6**	**3-166/O-54,D-27,1-8,2-4,S-1**	**10**	**-4.3**
• COYNE, Toots	Martin Albert Coyne b: 10/20/1894, St. Louis, MO d: 9/18/1939, St. Louis, MO TR Deb: 9/28/1914																							
1914 Phi-A	1	2	0	0	0	0	0	0	0	2	0	....	.000	.000	.000	.000	-104	-0	0	.00	0	/3-1	0	0.0
• CRABTREE, Estel	Estel Crayton "Crabby" Crabtree b: 8/19/1903, Crabtree, OH d: 1/4/1967, Logan, OH BL/TR, 6', 168 lbs. Deb: 4/18/1929 C Career OF: 57-156-125																							
1929 Cin-N	1	1	0	0	0	0	0	0	0	0	0	....	.000	.000	.000	.000	-105	-0	0	.00	0	....	0	0.0
1931 Cin-N	117	443	70	119	12	12	4	37	23	33	3	....	.269	.309	.377	.686	89	-8	53	4.13	9	*O-101(9-16-76)/3-4,1-2	9	-0.5
1932 Cin-N	108	402	38	110	14	9	2	35	23	26	2	....	.274	.316	.368	.684	86	-8	48	4.13	4	O-95(14-73-9)	9	-0.7
1933 StL-N	23	34	6	9	3	0	0	3	2	3	1	....	.265	.306	.353	.658	83	-1	4	4.23	0	/O-7(0-4-3)	1	-0.2
1941 StL-N	77	167	27	57	6	3	5	28	26	24	1	....	.341	.439	.503	.942	154	14	39	9.11	-1	O-50(17-16-19)/3-1	10	1.1
1942 StL-N	10	9	1	3	2	0	0	2	1	3	0	....	.333	.400	.556	.956	166	1	2	9.47	0	....	1	0.1
1943 Cin-N	95	254	25	70	12	0	2	26	25	17	1	....	.276	.345	.346	.692	101	1	29	3.91	-5	O-65(2-44-17)	7	-0.7
1944 Cin-N	58	98	7	28	4	1	0	11	13	3	0	....	.286	.369	.347	.716	106	1	12	4.36	0	O-19(15-3-1)/1-2	3	0.1
Total 8	**489**	**1408**	**174**	**396**	**53**	**25**	**13**	**142**	**113**	**109**	**8**	**....**	**.281**	**.339**	**.382**	**.721**	**100**	**-1**	**186**	**4.68**	**6**	**O-337/3-5,1-4**	**40**	**-0.8**
• CRADLE, Rickey	Rickey Nelson Cradle b: 6/20/1973, Norfolk, VA BR/TR, 6'2" Deb: 7/1/1998																							
1998 Sea-A	5	7	0	1	0	0	0	2	1	5	1	0	.143	.250	.143	.393	6	-1	0	2.00	0	/O-4(1-2-1)	0	-0.1
• CRAFT, Harry	Harry Francis "Wildfire" Craft b: 4/19/1915, Ellisville, MS d: 8/3/1995, Conroe, TX BR/TR, 6'1", 185 lbs. Deb: 9/19/1937 M/C Career OF: 0-549-3																							
1937 Cin-N	10	42	7	13	2	1	0	4	1	3	0	....	.310	.326	.405	.730	102	-0	5	4.81	0	O-10(0-10-0)	1	0.0
1938 Cin-N	151	612	70	165	28	9	15	83	29	46	3	....	.270	.305	.418	.723	100	-3	77	4.54	10	*O-151(0-151-0)	19	0.3
1939*Cin-N	134	502	58	129	20	7	13	67	27	54	5	....	.257	.299	.402	.701	86	-12	61	4.26	2	*O-134(0-134-0)	14	-1.3
1940*Cin-N	115	422	47	103	18	5	6	48	17	46	2	....	.244	.277	.353	.630	72	-18	41	3.33	1	*O-109(0-106-3)/1-2	10	-2.0
1941 Cin-N	119	413	48	103	15	2	10	59	33	43	4	....	.249	.308	.368	.676	90	-7	46	3.91	-3	*O-115(0-115-0)	14	-1.3
1942 Cin-N	37	113	7	20	2	1	0	6	3	11	0	....	.177	.205	.212	.418	22	-11	5	1.34	3	O-33(0-33-0)	1	-1.0
Total 6	**566**	**2104**	**237**	**533**	**85**	**25**	**44**	**267**	**110**	**203**	**14**	**....**	**.253**	**.294**	**.380**	**.674**	**85**	**-51**	**236**	**3.91**	**13**	**O-552/1-2**	**59**	**-5.3**
• CRAIG, Rod	Rodney Paul Craig b: 1/12/1958, Los Angeles, CA BB/TR, 6'1", 195 lbs. Deb: 9/11/1979 Career OF: 15-62-26																							
1979 Sea-A	16	52	9	20	8	1	0	6	1	5	1	1	.385	.396	.577	.973	156	4	12	9.50	-1	O-15(0-0-16)	2	0.2
1980 Sea-A	70	240	30	57	15	1	3	20	17	35	3	6	.238	.293	.346	.639	74	-11	22	3.05	-2	O-63(3-58-2)	2	-1.4
1982 Cle-A	49	65	7	15	2	0	0	1	4	6	3	1	.231	.275	.262	.537	49	-4	4	1.76	-1	O-22(11-4-7)/D-4	0	-0.6
1986 Chi-A	10	10	3	2	0	0	0	0	2	2	0	0	.200	.333	.200	.533	48	-1	1	2.84	0	/O-2(1-0-1)	0	-0.1
Total 4	**145**	**367**	**49**	**94**	**25**	**2**	**3**	**27**	**24**	**48**	**7**	**8**	**.256**	**.305**	**.360**	**.665**	**79**	**-12**	**39**	**3.51**	**-4**	**O-102/D-4**	**4**	**-1.8**
• CRAMER, Dick	William B. Cramer b: Brooklyn, NY d: 8/11/1885, Camden, NJ Deb: 5/12/1883																							
1883 NY-N	2	6	0	0	0	0	0	0	1	5	....	....	.000	.143	.000	.143	-52	-1	0	.00	0	/O-2(0-1-1)	0	-0.1

YEAR TM-L	G	AB	R	H	2B	3B	HR	RBI	BB	SO	SB	CS	AVG	OBP	SLG	OPS	OPS+	BR/A	RC	RC/G	FR	G/POS	WS	TPW
• CRAMER, Doc	Roger Maxwell "Flit" Cramer b: 7/22/1905, Beach Haven, NJ d: 9/9/1990, Manahawkin, NJ BL/TR, 6'2", 185 lbs. Deb: 9/18/1929 C Career OF: 25-2031-87																							
1929 Phi-A	2	6	0	0	0	0	0	0	0	2	0	0	.000	.000	.000	.000	-97	-2	0	.00	1	/O-1	0	-0.1
1930 Phi-A	30	82	12	19	1	1	0	6	2	8	0	0	.232	.250	.268	.518	30	-9	5	2.26	-1	O-21(6-13-2)/S-1	0	-0.9
1931*Phi-A	65	223	37	58	8	2	2	20	11	15	2	1	.260	.301	.341	.642	64	-11	23	3.57	-1	O-55(2-47-6)	4	-1.3
1932 Phi-A	92	384	73	129	27	6	3	46	17	27	3	1	.336	.367	.461	.828	109	5	64	6.56	5	O-86(0-45-42)	13	0.6
1933 Phi-A	152	661	109	195	27	8	8	75	36	24	5	4	.295	.331	.396	.728	91	-10	86	4.67	-4	*O-152(0-152-0)	14	-1.7
1934 Phi-A	153	649	99	202	29	9	6	46	40	35	1	5	.311	.353	.411	.765	100	-3	93	5.31	3	*O-152(0-152-0)	17	-0.3
1935 Phi-A★	149	644	96	214	37	4	3	70	37	34	6	7	.332	.373	.416	.789	105	3	99	5.79	-5	*O-149(0-149-0)	16	-0.6
1936 Bos-A	154	643	99	188	31	7	0	41	49	20	4	6	.292	.347	.362	.710	71	-31	82	4.54	8	*O-154(0-154-0)	15	-2.3
1937 Bos-A★	133	560	90	171	22	11	0	51	35	14	8	6	.305	.351	.384	.735	82	-16	76	4.87	-1	*O-133(0-133-0)	14	-1.9
1938 Bos-A★	148	658	116	198	36	8	0	71	51	19	4	9	.301	.354	.380	.734	80	-23	87	4.89	6	*O-148(0-148-0)/P-1	17	-1.8
1939 Bos-A★	137	589	110	183	30	6	0	56	36	17	3	3	.311	.352	.382	.734	85	-14	77	4.72	-2	*O-135(0-135-0)	14	-1.8
1940 Bos-A★	150	661	94	**200**	27	12	1	51	36	29	3	5	.303	.340	.384	.724	84	-17	86	4.70	-6	*O-149(16-96-37)	12	-2.7
1941 Was-A	154	660	93	180	25	6	2	66	37	15	4	1	.273	.317	.338	.655	77	-22	71	3.83	-13	*O-152(0-152-0)	11	-3.7
1942 Det-A	151	630	71	166	26	4	0	43	43	18	4	4	.263	.314	.317	.631	72	-24	63	3.47	0	*O-150(0-150-0)	12	-2.8
1943 Det-A	140	606	79	182	18	4	1	43	31	13	4	3	.300	.335	.348	.684	93	-6	73	4.39	-1	*O-138(0-138-0)	18	-1.1
1944 Det-A	143	578	69	169	20	9	2	42	37	21	6	5	.292	.337	.369	.706	96	-4	74	4.64	-4	*O-141(0-141-0)	19	-1.2
1945*Det-A	141	541	62	149	22	8	6	58	36	21	2	9	.275	.324	.379	.703	97	-6	65	4.16	-10	*O-140(0-140-0)	16	-2.1
1946 Det-A	68	204	26	60	8	2	1	26	15	8	3	0	.294	.342	.368	.710	93	-1	26	4.56	-4	O-50(0-50-0)	5	-0.6
1947 Det-A	73	157	21	42	2	2	2	30	20	5	0	4	.268	.350	.344	.694	91	-3	17	3.50	0	O-35(0-35-0)	2	-0.4
1948 Det-A	4	4	1	0	0	0	0	1	3	0	0	0	.000	.429	.000	.429	19	-0	0	2.26	0	/O-1	0	0.0
Total 20	**2239**	**9140**	**1357**	**2705**	**396**	**109**	**37**	**842**	**572**	**345**	**62**	**73**	**.296**	**.340**	**.375**	**.715**	**87**	**-195**	**1168**	**4.60**	**-27**	***O-2142/P-1,S-1**	**219**	**-26.8**
• CRANDALL, Del	Delmar Wesley Crandall b: 3/5/1930, Ontario, CA BR/TR, 6'1.5", 195 lbs. Deb: 6/17/1949 M/C																							
1949 Bos-N	67	228	21	60	10	1	4	34	9	18	2	....	.263	.291	.368	.660	80	-7	22	3.38	3	C-63	6	-0.1
1950 Bos-N	79	255	21	56	11	0	4	37	13	24	0	....	.220	.257	.310	.567	52	-19	20	2.52	1	C-75/1-1	3	-1.3
1953 Mil-N★	116	382	55	104	13	1	15	51	33	47	2	1	.272	.330	.429	.759	102	1	53	4.80	4	*C-108	16	0.9
1954 Mil-N★	138	463	60	112	18	2	21	64	40	56	0	3	.242	.306	.425	.732	94	-7	57	4.09	6	*C-136	17	0.6
1955 Mil-N★	133	440	61	104	15	2	26	62	40	56	2	1	.236	.303	.457	.760	103	1	58	4.36	-1	*C-131	16	0.6
1956 Mil-N★	112	311	37	74	14	2	16	48	35	30	1	2	.238	.317	.450	.767	110	3	44	4.62	3	*C-109	15	1.1
1957*Mil-N	118	383	45	97	11	2	15	46	30	38	1	2	.253	.309	.410	.719	98	-2	45	3.94	5	*C-102/O-9(1-0-9),1-1	13	0.7
1958*Mil-N★	131	427	50	116	23	1	18	63	48	38	4	1	.272	.351	.457	.807	122	14	66	5.36	2	*C-124	22	2.2
1959 Mil-N★	150	518	65	133	19	2	21	72	46	48	5	1	.257	.321	.423	.744	105	3	65	4.12	5	*C-146	20	1.6
1960 Mil-N★	142	537	81	158	14	1	19	77	34	36	4	6	.294	.341	.430	.771	118	10	74	4.75	-4	*C-141	23	1.4
1961 Mil-N	15	30	3	6	3	0	0	1	1	0	0	0	.200	.226	.300	.526	40	-3	2	1.90	0	/C-5	0	-0.2
1962 Mil-N★	107	350	35	104	12	3	8	45	27	24	3	4	.297	.351	.417	.768	108	3	46	4.55	4	C-90/1-5	13	1.1
1963 Mil-N	86	259	18	52	4	0	3	28	18	22	1	4	.201	.253	.251	.504	46	-19	14	1.70	0	C-75/1-7	3	-1.8
1964 SF-N	69	195	12	45	8	1	3	11	22	21	0	3	.231	.309	.328	.637	78	-6	18	3.11	3	C-65	6	0.0
1965 Pit-N	60	140	11	30	2	0	2	10	14	10	1	0	.214	.290	.271	.562	59	-7	11	2.62	0	C-60	3	-0.5
1966 Cle-A	50	108	10	25	2	0	4	8	14	9	0	0	.231	.320	.361	.681	95	-0	12	3.83	-1	C-49	3	0.1
Total 16	**1573**	**5026**	**585**	**1276**	**179**	**18**	**179**	**657**	**424**	**477**	**26**	**28**	**.254**	**.315**	**.404**	**.718**	**97**	**-37**	**607**	**4.05**	**30**	***C-1479/1-14,O-9**	**179**	**6.4**
• CRANDALL, Doc	James Otis Crandall b: 10/8/1887, Wadena, IN d: 8/17/1951, Bell, CA BR/TR, 5'10.5", 180 lbs. Deb: 4/24/1908 C Career OF: 0-1-2 ♦																							
1908 NY-N	34	72	8	16	4	0	2	6	4	....	0	....	.222	.273	.361	.634	97	5	7	3.08	-2	P-32/2-1	11	-0.7
1909 NY-N	30	41	4	10	0	1	1	1	1	....	0	....	.244	.262	.366	.628	93	3	4	3.08	2	P-30	7	-0.1
1910 NY-N	45	73	10	25	2	4	1	13	5	7	0	....	.342	.385	.521	.905	163	10	15	7.40	-2	P-42/S-1	19	2.3
1911*NY-N	61	113	12	27	1	4	2	21	8	16	2	....	.239	.295	.372	.667	84	5	13	3.71	1	P-41/S-6,2-3	20	2.4
1912*NY-N	50	80	9	25	6	2	0	19	6	7	0	....	.313	.360	.438	.798	114	7	13	5.54	0	P-37/2-2,1-1	12	0.3
1913*NY-N	31	25	4	7	2	1	0	2	1	5	0	....	.280	.308	.440	.748	111	2	3	4.50	1	P-24/2-2	8	0.2
StL-N	2	2	0	0	0	0	0	0	0	2	0	....	.000	.000	.000	.000	-101	-0	0	.00	0	....	0	-0.1
*NY-N	15	22	3	8	2	0	0	2	2	3	0	....	.364	.417	.455	.871	147	3	4	7.26	1	P-11	0	0.6
Yr.	48	49	7	15	4	1	0	4	3	10	0	....	.306	.346	.429	.775	120	4	7	5.37	1	P-35/2-2	8	0.7
1914 StL-F	118	278	40	86	16	5	2	41	58	32	3	....	.309	.429	.424	.853	135	23	51	6.56	-11	2-63,P-27/O-1,S-1	26	1.7
1915 StL-F	84	141	18	40	2	2	1	19	27	15	4	....	.284	.406	.348	.753	117	15	20	5.25	0	P-51	29	3.0
1916 StL-A	16	12	0	1	0	0	0	0	2	4	0	....	.083	.214	.083	.298	-11	-0	0	.51	0	/P-2	0	-0.4
1918 Bos-N	14	28	1	8	0	0	0	2	4	3	0	....	.286	.375	.286	.661	107	2	3	3.72	0	/P-5,O-3(0-0-2)	3	0.4
Total 10	**500**	**887**	**109**	**253**	**35**	**19**	**9**	**126**	**118**	**94**	**9**	**....**	**.285**	**.372**	**.398**	**.770**	**118**	**74**	**133**	**5.19**	**-11**	**P-302/2-71,S-8,O-4,1-1**	**135**	**9.7**
• CRANE, Ed	Edward Nicholas "Cannonball" Crane b: 5/27/1862, Boston, MA d: 9/20/1896, Rochester, NY BR/TR, 5'10.5", 204 lbs. Deb: 4/17/1884 U Career OF: 37-13-95 ♦																							
1884 Bos-U	101	428	83	122	23	6	12	....	14	....	....	....	.285	.308	.451	.759	156	24	61	5.57	3	O-57(18-0-39),C-42/1-5,P-4	22	2.3
1885 Pro-N	1	2	0	0	0	0	0	0	1	1	....	....	.000	.333	.000	.333	16	-0	0	.00	0	/O-1	0	0.0
Buf-N	13	51	5	14	0	1	2	9	3	8	....	....	.275	.315	.431	.746	135	2	7	5.18	-3	O-13(10-3-0)	2	-0.2
Yr.	14	53	5	14	0	1	2	9	4	9	....	....	.264	.316	.415	.731	128	2	7	4.91	-3	O-14(11-3-0)	2	-0.2
1886 Was-N	80	292	20	50	11	3	0	20	13	54	8	....	.171	.207	.229	.436	34	-20	16	1.77	1	O-68(8-9-51),P-10/C-4	1	-4.6
1888*NY-N	12	37	3	6	2	0	1	2	3	11	1	....	.162	.225	.297	.522	66	1	3	2.41	1	P-12	5	0.2
1889*NY-N	29	103	16	21	1	0	2	11	13	21	6	....	.204	.293	.272	.565	58	3	10	3.30	-4	P-29/1-1	15	0.8
1890 NY-P	43	146	27	46	5	4	0	16	10	26	5	....	.315	.363	.404	.767	96	8	24	6.43	-3	P-43	22	0.1
1891 Cin-a	34	110	13	17	0	0	1	7	8	28	4	....	.155	.212	.182	.394	12	-7	5	1.49	-2	P-32/O-3(0-1-2)	20	3.4
Cin-N	15	46	3	5	0	0	0	2	3	12	3	....	.109	.163	.109	.272	-20	-3	1	.88	-0	P-15	3	-1.2
1892 NY-N	48	163	20	40	1	1	0	14	11	30	2	....	.245	.297	.264	.561	71	4	14	3.01	-2	P-47/O-1	14	-1.4
1893 NY-N	12	26	8	12	1	0	0	3	7	0	0	....	.462	.576	.500	1.076	186	5	8	14.52	-1	P-10/1-1,O-1	4	-0.4
Bro-N	3	5	1	2	1	0	0	0	0	0	0	....	.400	.400	.600	1.000	172	1	1	10.87	-1	/P-2,O-1	0	-0.8
Yr.	15	31	9	14	2	0	0	3	7	0	0	....	.452	.553	.516	1.069	184	6	9	13.88	-1	P-12/O-2(0-0-2),1-1	4	-1.2
Total 9	**391**	**1409**	**199**	**335**	**45**	**15**	**18**	**84**	**86**	**191**	**29**	**....**	**.238**	**.283**	**.329**	**.612**	**87**	**17**	**150**	**3.81**	**-9**	**P-204,O-145/C-46,1-7**	**108**	**-1.8**
• CRANE, Fred	Frederic William Hotchkiss Crane b: 11/4/1840, Saybrook, CT d: 4/27/1925, Brooklyn, NY, 5'9", 135 lbs. Deb: 5/26/1873																							
1873 Res-n	1	4	0	1	0	0	0	1	0	0	0	0	.250	.250	.250	.500	53	-0	0	2.61	-1	/2-1	....	-0.1
1875 Atl-n	21	81	7	17	1	0	0	4	0	4	0	0	.210	.210	.222	.432	58	-2	4	1.78	2	1-20/O-1,S-1	....	0.0
Total 2 n	**22**	**85**	**7**	**18**	**1**	**0**	**0**	**5**	**0**	**4**	**0**	**0**	**.212**	**.212**	**.224**	**.435**	**57**	**-3**	**4**	**1.82**	**2**	**/1-20,2-1,O-1,S-1**	**....**	**0.0**
• CRANE, Sam	Samuel Byren "Lucky,Red" Crane b: 9/13/1894, Harrisburg, PA d: 11/12/1955, Philadelphia, PA BR/TR, 5'11.5", 154 lbs. Deb: 10/2/1914 Career OF: 0-0-4																							
1914 Phi-A	2	6	0	0	0	0	0	0	2	3	0	....	.000	.250	.000	.250	-25	-1	0	.00	1	/S-2	0	0.0
1915 Phi-A	8	23	3	2	2	0	0	1	0	4	0	....	.087	.087	.174	.261	-23	-4	0	.49	0	/S-6,2-1	0	-0.3
1916 Phi-A	2	4	1	1	0	0	0	0	2	1	0	....	.250	.500	.250	.750	132	0	1	5.15	0	/S-2	0	0.1
1917 Was-A	32	95	6	17	2	0	0	4	4	14	0	....	.179	.212	.200	.412	26	-9	4	1.34	-3	S-32	1	-1.1
1920 Cin-N	54	144	20	31	4	0	0	9	7	9	5	4	.215	.261	.243	.504	46	-10	9	2.03	-5	S-25,3-10/2-4,O-3(0-0-3)	1	-1.4
1921 Cin-N	73	215	20	50	10	2	0	16	14	14	2	5	.233	.292	.298	.590	59	-13	19	2.75	-11	S-63/3-2,O-1	3	-1.8
1922 Bro-N	3	8	1	2	1	0	0	0	0	1	0	0	.250	.333	.375	.708	83	-0	1	4.61	1	/S-3	0	0.1
Total 7	**174**	**495**	**51**	**103**	**19**	**2**	**0**	**30**	**29**	**46**	**7**	**9**	**.208**	**.262**	**.255**	**.516**	**46**	**-36**	**34**	**2.16**	**-17**	**S-133/3-12,2-5,O-4**	**5**	**-4.4**
• CRANE, Sam	Samuel Newhall Crane b: 1/2/1854, Springfield, MA d: 6/26/1925, New York, NY BR/TR, 6', 190 lbs. Deb: 5/1/1880 M/U Career OF: 1-2-5																							
1880 Buf-N	10	31	4	4	0	0	0	2	1	8	....	....	.129	.156	.129	.285	-2	-3	1	.65	-2	2-10/O-1	0	-0.5
1883 NY-a	96	349	57	82	8	5	0	0	13	....	....	....	.235	.262	.287	.549	73	-11	27	2.82	-6	*2-96/O-1	6	-1.2
1884 Cin-U	80	309	56	72	9	3	1	....	11	....	....	....	.233	.259	.291	.551	79	-8	24	2.83	1	*2-80	6	-0.4
1885 Det-N	68	245	23	47	4	6	1	20	13	45	....	....	.192	.233	.269	.502	62	-10	16	2.15	-5	2-68	3	-1.2
1886 Det-N	47	185	24	26	2	2	1	12	8	34	8	....	.141	.176	.189	.365	11	-20	8	1.32	2	2-38/S-8,O-4(1-0-3)	2	-1.5
StL-N	39	116	10	20	3	1	0	7	13	27	6	....	.172	.256	.216	.471	47	-6	8	2.29	-3	2-39	1	-0.7

YEAR TM-L	G	AB	R	H	2B	3B	HR	RBI	BB	SO	SB	CS	AVG	OBP	SLG	OPS	OPS+	BR/A	RC	RC/G	FR	G/POS	WS	TPW
Yr.	86	301	34	46	5	3	1	19	21	61	14	....	.153	.208	.199	.407	25	-26	16	1.68	-1	2-77/S-8,0-4(1-0-3)	3	-2.2
1887 Was-N	7	31	6	10	1	1	0	1	1	6	5	....	.323	.323	.400	.723	105	0	6	7.09	0	/S-7	1	0.0
1890 NY-N	2	6	0	0	0	0	0	0	0	1	1	....	.000	.000	.000	.000	-100	-2	0	.00	-1	/1-1,0-1	0	-0.2
Pit-N	22	82	3	16	3	0	0	3	0	5	5	....	.195	.205	.232	.437	31	-7	5	2.02	-3	2-15/S-7,0-1	0	-0.8
NY-N	2	6	0	0	0	0	0	0	0	1	0	....	.000	.000	.000	.000	-100	-2	0	.00	0	/2-2	0	-0.1
Yr.	26	94	3	16	3	0	0	3	0	7	6	....	.170	.179	.202	.381	14	-10	5	1.71	-3	2-17/S-7,0-2(0-0-2),1-1	0	-1.2
Total 7	**373**	**1360**	**183**	**277**	**30**	**18**	**3**	**45**	**60**	**127**	**25**	**....**	**.204**	**.237**	**.258**	**.496**	**57**	**-69**	**94**	**2.38**	**-17**	**2-348/S-22,0-8,1-1**	**19**	**-6.7**

• CRAVATH, Gavvy Clifford Carlton "Cactus Gavvy" Cravath
b: 3/23/1881, Poway, CA d: 5/23/1963, Laguna Beach, CA BR/TR, 5'10.5", 186 lbs. Deb: 4/18/1908 M/C Career OF: 108-40-947

YEAR TM-L	G	AB	R	H	2B	3B	HR	RBI	BB	SO	SB	CS	AVG	OBP	SLG	OPS	OPS+	BR/A	RC	RC/G	FR	G/POS	WS	TPW
1908 Bos-A	94	277	43	71	10	11	1	34	38	....	6	....	.256	.354	.383	.737	136	12	40	4.82	-1	0-77(62-0-15)/1-5	12	0.8
1909 Chi-A	19	50	7	9	0	0	1	8	19	....	3	....	.180	.406	.240	.646	109	3	6	3.85	-2	0-18(0-18-0)	2	0.0
Was-A	4	6	0	0	0	0	0	1	1	....	0	....	.000	.143	.000	.143	-57	-1	0	.00	1	/0-1	0	-0.1
Yr.	23	56	7	9	0	0	1	9	20	....	3	....	.161	.382	.214	.596	94	2	6	3.37	-1	0-19(0-18-1)	2	-0.1
1912 Phi-N	130	436	63	124	30	9	11	70	47	77	15	....	.284	.358	.470	.828	118	9	78	6.08	8	*0-113(30-14-73)	15	1.1
1913 Phi-N	147	525	78	**179**	34	14	**19**	**128**	55	63	10	....	.341	.407	**.568**	**.974**	**169**	**46**	120	**8.60**	-4	*0-141(3-7-133)	**29**	**3.6**
1914 Phi-N	149	499	76	149	27	8	**19**	100	83	72	14	....	.299	.402	.499	**.901**	**157**	37	103	7.27	-0	*0-143(1-0-142)	28	3.2
1915*Phi-N	150	522	**89**	149	31	7	**24**	**115**	**86**	77	11	9	.285	**.393**	**.510**	**.902**	**170**	**45**	105	**7.16**	11	*0-149(0-0-149)	**35**	**5.4**
1916 Phi-N	137	448	70	127	21	8	11	70	64	89	9	....	.283	**.379**	.440	.819	146	27	80	6.20	-4	*0-130(0-0-130)	26	1.8
1917 Phi-N	140	503	70	141	29	16	**12**	83	70	57	6	....	.280	.369	.473	.842	151	32	88	6.04	-3	*0-139(0-0-139)	26	2.5
1918 Phi-N	121	426	43	99	27	5	**8**	54	54	46	7	....	.232	.320	.376	.696	105	3	51	3.99	-7	*0-118(7-0-110)	11	-1.2
1919 Phi-N	83	214	34	73	18	5	**12**	45	35	21	8	....	.341	.438	.640	1.078	207	29	61	10.94	-2	0-56(2-1-53)	16	2.7
1920 Phi-N	46	45	2	13	5	0	1	11	9	12	0	0	.289	.407	.467	.874	144	3	9	7.56	-1	/0-5(3-0-2)	2	0.3
Total 11	**1220**	**3951**	**575**	**1134**	**232**	**83**	**119**	**719**	**561**	**514**	**89**	**9**	**.287**	**.380**	**.478**	**.858**	**149**	**245**	**742**	**6.57**	**-3**	***0-1090/1-5**	**202**	**20.2**

• CRAVER, Bill William H. Craver b: 6/1844, Troy, NY d: 6/17/1901, Troy, NY BR/TR, 5'9", 160 lbs. Deb: 5/9/1871 M/U NA OF: 0-7-5

YEAR TM-L	G	AB	R	H	2B	3B	HR	RBI	BB	SO	SB	CS	AVG	OBP	SLG	OPS	OPS+	BR/A	RC	RC/G	FR	G/POS	WS	TPW
1871 Tro-n	27	118	26	38	8	1	0	26	3	0	6	3	.322	.339	.407	.746	111	1	19	7.12	2	2-18/S-4,C-3,1-2,0-1	....	0.2
1872 Bal-n	35	179	55	50	3	2	0	23	5	2	7	1	.279	.299	.318	.617	86	-2	20	4.68	-1	C-27/0-4(0-0-4),2-2,3-2	....	-0.2
1873 Bal-n	41	196	45	57	9	2	0	28	2	3	2	3	.291	.298	.357	.655	94	-2	22	4.72	4	C-22,S-15/0-7(0-7-0),1-3	....	0.1
1874 Phi-n	55	265	68	91	19	11	0	56	4	2	11	3	.343	.353	.498	.851	164	18	52	8.77	6	*2-54/C-5,1-1	....	1.7
1875 Cen-n	14	65	8	18	4	2	0	5	2	4	1	0	.277	.299	.400	.699	153	4	8	5.19	2	/S-9,3-4,1-1	....	0.5
Ath-n	54	260	71	83	11	11	2	40	4	5	8	4	.319	.330	.469	.799	157	13	44	7.16	-4	*2-54/C-2,3-1	....	0.5
Yr.	68	325	79	101	15	**13**	2	45	6	9	9	4	.311	.323	.455	.779	156	17	52	6.75	-2	*2-54/S-9,3-5,C-2,1-1	....	1.0
1876 NY-N	56	248	24	55	4	0	0	22	2	7	....	....	.222	.230	.240	.470	65	-7	14	2.04	-20	2-42,C-11/S-6	4	-2.2
1877 Lou-N	57	238	33	63	5	2	0	29	5	11	....	....	.265	.280	.303	.582	71	-9	21	3.25	-4	*S-57	4	-1.0
Total 5 n	**226**	**1083**	**273**	**337**	**54**	**29**	**2**	**178**	**20**	**16**	**35**	**14**	**.311**	**.324**	**.420**	**.744**	**130**	**32**	**164**	**6.53**	**10**	**2-128/C-59,S-28,0-12,1-7,3**	**....**	**2.8**
Total 2	**113**	**486**	**57**	**118**	**9**	**2**	**0**	**51**	**7**	**18**	**....**	**....**	**.243**	**.255**	**.271**	**.525**	**68**	**-16**	**35**	**2.62**	**-25**	**/S-63,2-42,C-11**	**8**	**-3.1**

• CRAWFORD, Carl Carl Demonte Crawford b: 8/5/1981, Houston, TX BL/TL, 6'2", 219 lbs. Deb: 7/20/2002 Career OF: 200-13-0

YEAR TM-L	G	AB	R	H	2B	3B	HR	RBI	BB	SO	SB	CS	AVG	OBP	SLG	OPS	OPS+	BR/A	RC	RC/G	FR	G/POS	WS	TPW
2002 TB-A	63	259	23	67	11	6	2	30	9	41	9	5	.259	.292	.371	.662	76	-10	29	3.79	5	0-63(63-0-0)	6	-0.8
2003 TB-A	151	630	80	177	18	9	5	54	26	102	**55**	10	.281	.311	.362	.672	78	-13	76	4.33	6	*0-146(137-13-0)/D-1	13	-1.2
Total 2	**214**	**889**	**103**	**244**	**29**	**15**	**7**	**84**	**35**	**143**	**64**	**15**	**.274**	**.305**	**.364**	**.669**	**77**	**-23**	**104**	**4.16**	**11**	**0-209/D-1**	**19**	**-2.0**

• CRAWFORD, Forrest Forrest A. Crawford b: 5/10/1881, Rockdale, TX d: 3/29/1908, Austin, TX BL/TR Deb: 7/30/1906

YEAR TM-L	G	AB	R	H	2B	3B	HR	RBI	BB	SO	SB	CS	AVG	OBP	SLG	OPS	OPS+	BR/A	RC	RC/G	FR	G/POS	WS	TPW
1906 StL-N	45	145	8	30	3	1	0	11	7	....	1	....	.207	.248	.241	.490	55	-8	10	2.11	-10	S-39/3-6	1	-1.9
1907 StL-N	7	22	0	5	0	0	0	3	2	....	0	....	.227	.292	.227	.519	65	-1	2	2.44	-1	/S-7	0	-0.1
Total 2	**52**	**167**	**8**	**35**	**3**	**1**	**0**	**14**	**9**	**....**	**1**	**....**	**.210**	**.254**	**.240**	**.494**	**56**	**-9**	**11**	**2.16**	**-11**	**/S-46,3-6**	**1**	**-2.0**

• CRAWFORD, George George Crawford Deb: 10/8/1890

YEAR TM-L	G	AB	R	H	2B	3B	HR	RBI	BB	SO	SB	CS	AVG	OBP	SLG	OPS	OPS+	BR/A	RC	RC/G	FR	G/POS	WS	TPW
1890 Phi-a	5	17	1	2	0	0	0	3	0	....	1	....	.118	.118	.118	.235	-31	-3	0	.64	0	/0-4(0-0-4),S-1	0	-0.2

• CRAWFORD, Glenn Glenn Martin "Shorty" Crawford b: 12/2/1913, North Branch, MI d: 1/2/1972, Saginaw, MI BL/TR, 5'9", 165 lbs. Deb: 4/22/1945

YEAR TM-L	G	AB	R	H	2B	3B	HR	RBI	BB	SO	SB	CS	AVG	OBP	SLG	OPS	OPS+	BR/A	RC	RC/G	FR	G/POS	WS	TPW
1945 StL-N	4	3	0	0	0	0	0	0	1	0	0	....	.000	.250	.000	.250	-26	-0	0	.59	0	/0-1	0	-0.1
Phi-N	82	302	41	89	13	2	2	24	36	15	5	....	.295	.372	.371	.743	110	5	45	5.48	1	0-38(6-0-32),S-34,2-14	11	0.6
Yr.	86	305	41	89	13	2	2	24	37	15	5	....	.292	.370	.367	.737	108	5	45	5.41	1	0-39(7-0-32),S-34,2-14	11	0.6
1946 Phi-N	1	1	0	0	0	0	0	0	0	0	0	....	.000	.000	.000	.000	-103	-0	0	.00	0	....	0	0.0
Total 2	**87**	**306**	**41**	**89**	**13**	**2**	**2**	**24**	**37**	**15**	**5**	**....**	**.291**	**.369**	**.366**	**.735**	**108**	**4**	**45**	**5.36**	**1**	**/0-39,S-34,2-14**	**11**	**0.5**

• CRAWFORD, Jake Rufus Crawford b: 3/20/1928, Campbell, MO BR/TR, 6'1.5", 185 lbs. Deb: 9/7/1952

YEAR TM-L	G	AB	R	H	2B	3B	HR	RBI	BB	SO	SB	CS	AVG	OBP	SLG	OPS	OPS+	BR/A	RC	RC/G	FR	G/POS	WS	TPW
1952 StL-A	7	11	1	2	1	0	0	0	1	5	1	0	.182	.250	.273	.523	44	-1	1	2.89	-0	/0-3(0-2-1)	0	-0.1

• CRAWFORD, Ken Kenneth Daniel Crawford b: 10/31/1894, South Bend, IN d: 11/11/1976, Pittsburgh, PA BL/TR, 5'9", 145 lbs. Deb: 9/6/1915

YEAR TM-L	G	AB	R	H	2B	3B	HR	RBI	BB	SO	SB	CS	AVG	OBP	SLG	OPS	OPS+	BR/A	RC	RC/G	FR	G/POS	WS	TPW
1915 Bal-F	23	82	4	20	2	1	0	7	1	18	0	....	.244	.253	.293	.546	56	-5	6	2.35	-2	1-14/0-4(1-0-3)	0	-0.8

• CRAWFORD, Pat Clifford Rankin Crawford b: 1/28/1902, Society Hill, SC d: 1/25/1994, Morehead City, NC BL/TR, 5'11", 170 lbs. Deb: 4/18/1929

YEAR TM-L	G	AB	R	H	2B	3B	HR	RBI	BB	SO	SB	CS	AVG	OBP	SLG	OPS	OPS+	BR/A	RC	RC/G	FR	G/POS	WS	TPW
1929 NY-N	65	57	13	17	3	0	3	24	11	5	1	....	.298	.412	.509	.921	127	3	12	6.74	0	/1-7,3-1	2	0.2
1930 NY-N	25	76	11	21	3	2	3	17	7	2	0	....	.276	.345	.487	.832	100	-0	13	5.82	0	2-18/1-1	2	0.0
Cin-N	76	224	24	65	7	1	3	26	23	10	2	....	.290	.359	.371	.729	81	-6	30	4.70	-2	2-54,1-13	5	-0.7
Yr.	101	300	35	86	10	3	6	43	30	12	2	....	.287	.355	.400	.755	86	-6	43	4.98	-2	2-72,1-14	7	-0.7
1933 StL-N	91	224	24	60	8	2	0	21	14	9	1	....	.268	.317	.321	.638	78	-6	23	3.60	0	1-29,2-15/3-7	4	-0.8
1934*StL-N	61	70	3	19	2	0	0	16	5	3	0	....	.271	.320	.300	.620	63	-4	7	3.38	1	/3-9,2-4	1	-0.2
Total 4	**318**	**651**	**75**	**182**	**23**	**5**	**9**	**104**	**60**	**29**	**4**	**....**	**.280**	**.344**	**.372**	**.716**	**85**	**-13**	**85**	**4.49**	**-2**	**/2-91,1-50,3-17**	**14**	**-1.6**

• CRAWFORD, Sam Samuel Earl "Wahoo Sam" Crawford
b: 4/18/1880, Wahoo, NE d: 6/15/1968, Hollywood, CA BL/TL, 6', 190 lbs. Deb: 9/10/1899 HOF: 1957 Career OF: 134-479-1687

YEAR TM-L	G	AB	R	H	2B	3B	HR	RBI	BB	SO	SB	CS	AVG	OBP	SLG	OPS	OPS+	BR/A	RC	RC/G	FR	G/POS	WS	TPW
1899 Cin-N	31	127	25	39	3	7	1	20	2	....	6	....	.307	.318	.465	.782	111	1	21	6.18	1	0-31(9-22-0)	4	0.0
1900 Cin-N	101	389	68	101	15	15	7	59	28	....	14	....	.260	.314	.429	.744	107	2	59	5.33	12	0-95(70-12-12)	12	0.5
1901 Cin-N	131	515	91	170	20	16	**16**	104	37	....	13	....	.330	.378	.524	.903	172	44	110	8.36	1	*0-127(1-0-126)	24	3.9
1902 Cin-N	140	555	92	185	18	**22**	3	78	47	....	16	....	.333	.386	.461	.848	147	30	108	7.64	4	*0-140(7-0-133)	23	2.9
1903 Det-A	137	550	88	184	23	**25**	4	89	25	....	18	....	.335	.366	.489	.855	159	37	110	7.43	2	*0-137(45-0-92)	25	3.4
1904 Det-A	150	562	49	143	22	16	2	73	44	....	20	....	.254	.309	.361	.670	115	9	72	4.42	5	*0-150(1-0-149)	21	0.8
1905 Det-A	154	575	73	171	38	10	6	75	50	....	22	....	.297	.357	.430	.786	148	30	99	6.43	6	*0-103(0-0-103),1-51	**36**	3.4
1906 Det-A	145	563	65	166	25	16	2	72	38	....	24	....	.295	.341	.407	.747	130	18	89	5.83	0	*0-116(0-2-116),1-32	23	1.3
1907*Det-A	144	582	**102**	188	34	17	4	81	37	....	18	....	.323	.366	.460	.826	157	35	108	7.08	-2	*0-144(0-144-0)/1-2	36	2.9
1908*Det-A	152	591	102	184	33	16	**7**	80	37	....	15	....	.311	.355	.457	.812	157	34	100	6.07	-13	*0-134(0-134-0),1-17	32	1.7
1909*Det-A	156	589	83	185	**35**	14	6	97	47	....	30	....	.314	.366	.452	.817	151	33	108	6.52	-11	*0-139(0-139-0),1-18	32	1.7
1910 Det-A	154	588	83	170	26	**19**	5	**120**	37	....	20	....	.289	.332	.423	.756	128	16	89	5.22	-8	*0-153(0-26-127)/1-1	23	0.1
1911 Det-A	146	574	109	217	36	14	7	115	61	....	37	....	.378	.438	.526	.964	160	47	147	10.32	-17	*0-146(0-0-146)	32	2.2
1912 Det-A	149	581	81	189	30	21	4	109	42	....	41	....	.325	.373	.470	.843	145	31	116	7.31	-9	*0-149(0-0-149)	24	1.4
1913 Det-A	153	609	78	193	32	**23**	9	83	52	28	13	....	.317	.371	.489	.860	153	37	110	6.60	-8	*0-140(0-0-140),1-13	27	2.3
1914 Det-A	157	582	74	183	22	**26**	8	**104**	69	31	25	16	.314	.388	.483	.871	157	37	113	6.84	-3	*0-157(0-0-157)	31	2.9
1915 Det-A	156	612	81	183	31	**19**	4	**112**	66	29	24	14	.299	.367	.431	.799	132	22	101	5.83	-13	*0-156(0-0-156)	28	0.0
1916 Det-A	100	322	41	92	11	13	0	42	37	10	10	....	.286	.359	.401	.760	124	9	51	5.54	-9	0-79(1-0-78)/1-2	13	-0.4
1917 Det-A	61	104	6	18	4	0	2	12	4	6	0	....	.173	.204	.269	.473	44	-8	6	1.61	-2	1-15/0-3(0-0-3)	0	-1.2
Total 19	**2517**	**9570**	**1391**	**2961**	**458**	**309**	**97**	**1525**	**760**	**104**	**366**	**30**	**.309**	**.362**	**.452**	**.814**	**143**	**465**	**1716**	**6.55**	**-64**	***0-2299,1-151**	**446**	**29.8**

• CRAWFORD, Willie Willie Murphy Crawford b: 9/7/1946, Los Angeles, CA BL/TL, 6'1", 205 lbs. Deb: 9/16/1964 Career OF: 323-40-653

YEAR TM-L	G	AB	R	H	2B	3B	HR	RBI	BB	SO	SB	CS	AVG	OBP	SLG	OPS	OPS+	BR/A	RC	RC/G	FR	G/POS	WS	TPW
1964 LA-N	10	16	3	5	1	0	0	0	1	7	1	1	.313	.353	.375	.728	113	0	2	4.49	0	/0-4(1-0-3)	0	0.0
1965*LA-N	52	27	10	4	0	0	0	0	2	8	2	0	.148	.207	.148	.355	2	-3	1	1.35	0	/0-8(2-1-5)	0	-0.4
1966 LA-N	6	0	1	0	0	0	0	0	0	0	0	0	....	....	....	....	-109	0	0	....	0	....	0	0.0
1967 LA-N	4	4	0	1	0	0	0	0	1	3	0	0	.250	.400	.250	.650	98	0	1	4.54	0	/0-1	0	0.0

YEAR	TM-L	G	AB	R	H	2B	3B	HR	RBI	BB	SO	SB	CS	AVG	OBP	SLG	OPS	OPS+	BR/A	RC	RC/G	FR	G/POS	WS	TPW
1968	LA-N	61	175	25	44	12	1	4	14	20	64	1	3	.251	.335	.400	.735	130	5	24	4.88	3	O-48(45-1-4)	7	0.7
1969	LA-N	129	389	64	96	17	5	11	41	49	85	4	5	.247	.331	.401	.732	112	5	52	4.65	-1	*O-113(56-22-38)	12	-0.1
1970	LA-N	109	299	48	70	8	6	8	40	33	88	4	4	.234	.314	.381	.696	89	-6	36	4.02	2	O-94(34-4-64)	8	-0.8
1971	LA-N	114	342	64	96	16	6	9	40	28	49	5	2	.281	.337	.442	.778	126	11	51	5.31	-1	O-97(63-5-35)	13	0.6
1972	LA-N	96	243	28	61	7	3	8	27	35	55	4	2	.251	.350	.403	.753	116	6	34	4.76	-2	O-74(51-0-28)	9	0.0
1973	LA-N	145	457	75	135	26	2	14	66	78	91	12	5	.295	.399	.453	.852	142	30	88	6.96	3	*O-138(11-5-125)	24	2.6
1974*	LA-N	139	468	73	138	23	4	11	61	64	88	7	8	.295	.380	.432	.811	132	19	77	5.84	-6	*O-133(0-2-132)	20	0.6
1975	LA-N	124	373	46	98	15	2	9	46	49	43	5	5	.263	.348	.386	.734	108	3	52	4.84	-2	*O-113(25-0-93)	12	-0.4
1976	StL-N	120	392	49	119	17	5	9	50	37	53	2	1	.304	.365	.441	.806	127	14	62	5.75	-1	*O-107(3-0-105)	14	0.8
1977	Hou-N	42	114	14	29	3	0	2	18	16	10	0	0	.254	.346	.333	.679	91	-1	14	4.39	-1	O-30(30-0-0)	3	-0.3
	Oak-A	59	136	7	25	7	1	1	16	18	20	0	0	.184	.279	.272	.551	52	-9	10	2.32	2	O-22(2-0-20),D-18	1	-0.8
Total	**14**	**1210**	**3435**	**507**	**921**	**152**	**35**	**86**	**419**	**431**	**664**	**47**	**36**	**.268**	**.351**	**.408**	**.759**	**117**	**75**	**505**	**5.13**	**-4**	**O-982/D-18**	**123**	**2.6**
• CREAMER, George	George W. Creamer b: 1855, Philadelphia, PA d: 6/27/1886, Philadelphia, PA BR/TR, 6'2" Deb: 5/1/1878 M Career OF: 0-17-5																								
1878	Mil-N	50	193	30	41	7	3	0	15	5	15	....	....	.212	.232	.280	.512	63	-8	13	2.33	-2	2-28,O-17(0-16-4)/3-6	1	-0.9
1879	Syr-N	15	60	3	13	2	0	0	3	1	2	....	....	.217	.230	.250	.480	65	-2	4	2.10	-4	2-10/S-3,O-2(0-1-1)	1	-0.5
1880	Wor-N	85	306	40	61	6	3	0	27	4	21	....	....	.199	.210	.239	.448	47	-17	16	1.76	-8	*2-85	3	-2.1
1881	Wor-N	80	309	42	64	9	2	0	25	11	27	....	....	.207	.234	.249	.484	49	-18	18	2.04	-15	*2-80	2	-2.8
1882	Wor-N	81	286	27	65	16	6	1	29	14	24	....	....	.227	.263	.336	.599	88	-4	26	3.22	-8	*2-81	5	-0.8
1883	Pit-a	91	369	54	94	7	9	0	0	20	....	....	....	.255	.293	.322	.616	103	2	36	3.64	-11	*2-91	8	-0.5
1884	Pit-a	98	339	38	62	8	5	0	0	16	....	....	....	.183	.224	.236	.460	49	-19	18	1.82	10	*2-98	3	-0.5
Total	**7**	**500**	**1862**	**234**	**400**	**55**	**28**	**1**	**99**	**71**	**89**	**....**	**....**	**.215**	**.244**	**.276**	**.520**	**68**	**-66**	**131**	**2.46**	**-38**	**2-473/O-19,3-6,S-3**	**23**	**-8.0**
• CREDE, Joe	Joseph Crede b: 4/26/1978, Jefferson City, MO BR/TR, 6'3", 195 lbs. Deb: 9/12/2000																								
2000	Chi-A	7	14	2	5	1	0	0	3	0	3	0	0	.357	.357	.429	.786	96	-0	2	5.87	1	/3-6,D-1	0	0.1
2001	Chi-A	17	50	1	11	1	1	0	7	3	11	1	0	.220	.278	.280	.558	46	-4	4	2.70	-1	3-15	1	-0.5
2002	Chi-A	53	200	28	57	10	0	12	35	8	40	0	2	.285	.313	.515	.828	112	1	31	5.75	-4	3-53	6	-0.2
2003	Chi-A	151	536	68	140	31	2	19	75	32	75	1	1	.261	.310	.433	.743	94	-7	70	4.58	2	*3-151	14	-0.3
Total	**4**	**228**	**800**	**99**	**213**	**43**	**3**	**31**	**120**	**43**	**129**	**2**	**3**	**.266**	**.309**	**.444**	**.753**	**95**	**-9**	**108**	**4.76**	**-2**	**3-225/D-1**	**21**	**-0.8**
• CREE, Birdie	William Franklin Cree b: 10/23/1882, Khedive, PA d: 11/8/1942, Sunbury, PA BR/TR, 5'6", 150 lbs. Deb: 9/17/1908 Career OF: 389-258-44																								
1908	NY-A	21	78	5	21	0	2	0	4	7	....	1	....	.269	.345	.321	.665	115	2	9	3.97	2	O-21(0-21-0)	3	0.3
1909	NY-A	104	343	48	90	6	3	2	27	30	....	10	....	.262	.338	.315	.653	105	3	40	3.95	-6	O-79(24-32-25)/S-6,2-4,3-1	12	-0.7
1910	NY-A	134	467	58	134	19	16	4	73	40	....	28	....	.287	.353	.422	.775	135	18	79	5.92	-18	*O-134(49-85-0)	22	-0.7
1911	NY-A	137	520	90	181	30	22	4	88	56	....	48	....	.348	.415	.513	.928	149	34	129	9.62	-3	*O-132(122-7-3)/S-4,2-2	25	2.4
1912	NY-A	50	190	25	63	11	6	0	22	20	....	12	....	.332	.409	.453	.862	138	10	39	8.01	2	O-50(50-0-0)	8	1.0
1913	NY-A	145	534	51	145	25	6	1	63	50	51	22	....	.272	.338	.346	.685	100	-0	68	4.26	-5	*O-144(144-0-0)	14	-1.1
1914	NY-A	77	275	45	85	18	5	0	40	30	24	4	9	.309	.389	.411	.800	141	11	43	5.53	3	O-76(0-76-0)	15	1.1
1915	NY-A	74	196	23	42	8	2	0	15	36	22	7	8	.214	.353	.276	.628	88	-3	20	3.19	-4	O-53(0-37-16)	4	-1.0
Total	**8**	**742**	**2603**	**345**	**761**	**117**	**62**	**11**	**332**	**269**	**97**	**132**	**17**	**.292**	**.368**	**.398**	**.766**	**123**	**75**	**427**	**5.77**	**-28**	**O-689/S-10,2-6,3-1**	**103**	**1.2**
• CREEDEN, Connie	Cornelius Stephen Creeden b: 7/21/1915, Danvers, MA d: 11/30/1969, Santa Ana, CA BL/TL, 6'1", 200 lbs. Deb: 4/28/1943																								
1943	Bos-N	5	4	0	1	0	0	0	1	1	0	0	....	.250	.400	.250	.650	91	0	1	4.54	0	....	0	0.0
• CREEDEN, Pat	Patrick Francis "Whoops" Creeden b: 5/23/1906, Newburyport, MA d: 4/20/1992, Brockton, MA BL/TR, 5'8", 175 lbs. Deb: 4/14/1931																								
1931	Bos-A	5	8	0	0	0	0	0	0	1	3	0	0	.000	.111	.000	.111	-73	-2	0	.09	-1	/2-2	0	-0.3
• CREEGAN, Mark	Marcus Creegan b: 1864, San Francisco, CA d: 9/29/1920, San Francisco, CA, 161 lbs. Deb: 4/17/1884																								
1884	Was-U	9	33	4	5	0	0	0	....	1	....	....	....	.152	.176	.152	.328	12	-3	1	.90	-2	/O-6(0-5-1),C-3,3-2,1-1	0	-0.4
• CREELY, Gus	August L. Creely b: 6/6/1870, St. Louis, MO d: 4/22/1934, St. Louis, MO, 5'6", 150 lbs. Deb: 10/9/1890																								
1890	StL-a	4	15	0	0	0	0	0	0	0	....	1	....	.000	.000	.000	.000	-88	-4	0	.00	0	/S-4	0	-0.4
• CREGAN, Pete	Peter James "Peeksill Pete" Cregan b: 4/13/1875, Kingston, NY d: 5/18/1945, New York, NY BR/TR, 5'7.5", 150 lbs. Deb: 9/8/1899 Career OF: 5-0-2																								
1899	NY-N	1	2	0	0	0	0	0	0	0	....	0	....	.000	.000	.000	.000	-104	-1	0	.00	0	/O-1	0	-0.1
1903	Cin-N	6	19	0	2	0	0	0	0	1	....	0	....	.105	.190	.105	.296	-13	-3	1	.75	-1	/O-6(5-0-1)	0	-0.4
Total	**2**	**7**	**21**	**0**	**2**	**0**	**0**	**0**	**0**	**1**	**....**	**0**	**....**	**.095**	**.174**	**.095**	**.269**	**-21**	**-3**	**1**	**.67**	**-1**	**/O-7**	**0**	**-0.5**
• CREGER, Bernie	Bernard Odell Creger b: 3/21/1927, Wytheville, VA d: 11/30/1997, Lynchburg, VA BR/TR, 6', 175 lbs. Deb: 4/29/1947																								
1947	StL-N	15	16	3	3	1	0	0	0	1	3	1	....	.188	.235	.250	.485	28	-2	1	1.43	-1	S-13	0	-0.3
• CRESPI, Creepy	Frank Angelo Joseph Crespi b: 2/16/1918, St. Louis, MO d: 3/1/1990, Florissant, MO BR/TR, 5'8.5", 175 lbs. Deb: 9/14/1938																								
1938	StL-N	7	19	2	5	2	0	0	1	2	7	0	....	.263	.333	.368	.702	88	-0	2	3.96	-3	/S-7	0	-0.3
1939	StL-N	15	29	3	5	1	0	0	6	3	6	0	....	.172	.250	.207	.457	23	-3	2	1.91	0	/2-6,S-4	0	-0.2
1940	StL-N	3	11	2	3	1	0	0	0	1	2	1	....	.273	.333	.364	.697	87	-0	1	4.79	-1	/3-2,S-1	0	-0.1
1941	StL-N	146	560	85	156	24	2	4	46	57	58	3	....	.279	.355	.350	.705	93	-4	72	4.61	3	*2-145	18	0.9
1942*	StL-N	93	292	33	71	4	2	0	35	27	29	4	....	.243	.309	.271	.580	65	-12	26	2.92	-3	2-83/S-5	5	-1.0
Total	**5**	**264**	**911**	**125**	**240**	**32**	**4**	**4**	**88**	**90**	**102**	**8**	**....**	**.263**	**.336**	**.321**	**.657**	**81**	**-19**	**104**	**3.93**	**-2**	**2-234/S-17,3-2**	**23**	**-0.6**
• CRESPO, Cesar	Cesar Antonio (Claudio) Crespo b: 5/23/1979, Rio Piedras, Puerto Rico BB/TR, 5'11", 170 lbs. Deb: 5/29/2001 Career OF: 12-12-3																								
2001	SD-N	55	153	27	32	6	0	4	12	25	50	6	2	.209	.320	.327	.647	74	-5	18	3.82	-4	2-34,O-18(6-11-2)/3-2,S-1	3	-0.8
2002	SD-N	25	29	5	5	2	0	0	0	3	6	3	2	.172	.250	.241	.491	33	-3	2	1.79	-1	/O-7(6-1-1),2-4,3-4,S-1	0	-0.4
Total	**2**	**80**	**182**	**32**	**37**	**8**	**0**	**4**	**12**	**28**	**56**	**9**	**4**	**.203**	**.310**	**.313**	**.623**	**68**	**-8**	**20**	**3.46**	**-6**	**/2-38,O-25,3-6,S-2**	**3**	**-1.2**
• CRESPO, Felipe	Felipe Javier (Claudio) Crespo b: 3/5/1973, Rio Piedras, Puerto Rico BB/TR, 5'11", 195 lbs. Deb: 4/28/1996 Career OF: 41-0-35																								
1996	Tor-A	22	49	6	9	4	0	0	4	12	13	1	0	.184	.375	.265	.640	66	-2	7	4.41	1	2-10/3-6,1-2	2	0.0
1997	Tor-A	12	28	3	8	0	1	1	5	2	4	0	0	.286	.333	.464	.798	105	0	4	5.00	-1	/3-7,D-2,2-1	1	-0.1
1998	Tor-A	66	130	11	34	8	1	1	15	15	27	4	3	.262	.347	.362	.708	84	-3	17	4.41	-1	O-42(19-0-25)/2-8,3-2,D-2,1	4	-0.5
2000*	SF-N	89	131	17	38	6	1	4	29	10	23	3	2	.290	.359	.443	.801	109	1	20	5.36	-2	O-26(18-0-9),1-11/2-7,D-1	3	-0.2
2001	SF-N	40	66	8	13	1	0	4	10	7	26	1	1	.197	.293	.394	.687	81	-2	7	3.36	-2	1-16/2-2,O-1	0	-0.5
	Phi-N	33	41	1	7	3	1	0	5	4	8	0	0	.171	.244	.293	.537	39	-4	3	2.47	1	/O-4(4-0-0),1-2,2-1	0	-0.3
	Yr.	73	107	9	20	4	1	4	15	11	34	1	1	.187	.275	.355	.630	65	-6	11	3.02	-1	1-18/O-5(4-0-1),2-3	0	-0.8
Total	**5**	**262**	**445**	**46**	**109**	**22**	**4**	**10**	**68**	**50**	**101**	**9**	**6**	**.245**	**.336**	**.380**	**.716**	**86**	**-9**	**59**	**4.35**	**-4**	**/O-73,1-32,2-29,3-15,D-5**	**10**	**-1.6**
• CRIGER, Lou	Louis Criger b: 2/3/1872, Elkhart, IN d: 5/14/1934, Tucson, AZ BR/TR, 5'10", 165 lbs. Deb: 9/21/1896																								
1896	Cle-N	2	5	0	0	0	0	0	0	1	0	1	....	.000	.167	.000	.167	-51	-1	0	.91	0	/C-1	0	0.0
1897	Cle-N	39	138	15	31	4	1	0	22	23	....	5	....	.225	.340	.268	.608	58	-8	15	3.64	-2	C-37/1-2	3	-0.5
1898	Cle-N	84	287	43	80	13	4	1	32	40	....	2	....	.279	.377	.362	.739	113	7	42	5.21	5	C-82	15	1.9
1899	StL-N	77	258	39	66	4	5	2	44	28	....	14	....	.256	.333	.333	.667	81	-6	35	4.68	1	C-75	7	0.1
1900	StL-N	80	288	31	78	8	6	2	38	4	....	5	....	.271	.286	.361	.647	78	-10	32	4.03	3	C-75/3-1	6	0.0
1901	Bos-A	76	268	26	62	6	3	0	24	11	....	7	....	.231	.270	.276	.546	52	-17	23	2.89	12	C-68/1-8	6	0.2
1902	Bos-A	83	266	32	68	16	6	0	28	27	....	7	....	.256	.324	.361	.685	87	-5	35	4.55	4	C-80/O-1	10	0.8
1903*	Bos-A	96	317	41	61	7	10	3	31	26	....	5	....	.192	.256	.306	.562	64	-14	28	2.78	14	C-96	9	1.0
1904	Bos-A	98	299	34	63	10	5	2	34	27	....	1	....	.211	.283	.298	.580	79	-7	27	2.94	9	C-95	11	1.3
1905	Bos-A	109	313	33	62	6	7	1	36	54	....	5	....	.198	.322	.272	.593	88	-1	31	3.16	4	*C-109	11	1.5
1906	Bos-A	7	17	0	3	1	0	0	1	1	....	1	....	.176	.222	.235	.458	43	-1	1	2.19	3	/C-6	0	0.3
1907	Bos-A	75	226	12	41	4	0	0	14	19	....	2	....	.181	.251	.199	.450	44	-13	13	1.83	9	C-75	4	0.2
1908	Bos-A	84	237	12	45	4	2	0	25	13	....	1	....	.190	.232	.224	.456	47	-14	13	1.64	11	C-84	5	0.6
1909	StL-A	74	212	15	36	1	1	0	9	25	....	2	....	.170	.261	.184	.444	44	-12	12	1.63	6	C-73	4	0.2
1910	NY-A	27	69	3	13	2	0	0	4	10	....	0	....	.188	.291	.217	.509	56	-3	4	1.95	-2	C-27	1	-0.3

YEAR TM-L	G	AB	R	H	2B	3B	HR	RBI	BB	SO	SB	CS	AVG	OBP	SLG	OPS	OPS+	BR/A	RC	RC/G	FR	G/POS	WS	TPW
1912 StL-A	1	2	1	0	0	0	0	0	0	....	0	....	.000	.000	.000	.000	-104	-1	0	.00	0	/C-1	0	0.0
Total 16	**1012**	**3202**	**337**	**709**	**86**	**50**	**11**	**342**	**309**	**0**	**58**	**....**	**.221**	**.295**	**.290**	**.584**	**71**	**-107**	**311**	**3.19**	**79**	**C-984/1-10,3-1,0-1**	**92**	**7.2**
• CRIPE, Dave	David Gordon Cripe b: 4/7/1951, Ramona, CA BR/TR, 6', 180 lbs. Deb: 9/10/1978																							
1978 KC-A	7	13	1	2	0	0	0	1	0	2	0	0	.154	.154	.154	.308	-13	-2	0	.76	-1	/3-5	0	-0.3
• CRISCIONE, Dave	David Gerald Criscione b: 9/2/1951, Dunkirk, NY BR/TR, 5'8", 185 lbs. Deb: 7/17/1977																							
1977 Bal-A	7	9	1	3	0	0	1	1	0	1	0	0	.333	.333	.667	1.000	175	1	2	7.54	0	/C-7	1	0.1
• CRISCOLA, Tony	Anthony Paul Criscola b: 7/9/1915, Walla Walla, WA d: 7/10/2001, La Jolla, CA BL/TR, 5'11.5", 180 lbs. Deb: 4/15/1942 Career OF: 50-15-35																							
1942 StL-A	91	158	17	47	9	2	1	13	8	13	2	2	.297	.331	.399	.730	103	-0	22	5.13	-4	0-52(37-13-2)	4	-0.6
1943 StL-A	29	52	4	8	0	0	0	1	8	7	0	0	.154	.267	.154	.421	24	-5	3	1.68	-1	0-13(10-2-1)	0	-0.7
1944 Cin-N	64	157	14	36	3	2	0	14	14	12	0	....	.229	.297	.274	.570	64	-7	13	2.83	2	0-35(3-0-32)	2	-0.8
Total 3	**184**	**367**	**35**	**91**	**12**	**4**	**1**	**28**	**30**	**32**	**2**	**2**	**.248**	**.307**	**.311**	**.617**	**74**	**-12**	**38**	**3.57**	**-3**	**0-100**	**6**	**-2.1**
• CRISHAM, Pat	Patrick J. Crisham b: 6/4/1877, Amesbury, MA d: 6/12/1915, Syracuse, NY, 6', 168 lbs. Deb: 5/5/1899																							
1899 Bal-N	53	172	23	50	5	3	0	20	4	....	4	....	.291	.311	.355	.665	78	-6	21	4.49	-3	1-26,C-22	2	-0.7
• CRISP, Coco	Covelli Loyce Crisp b: 11/1/1979, Los Angeles, CA BB/TR, 6', 185 lbs. Deb: 8/15/2002 Career OF: 41-84-0																							
2002 Cle-A	32	127	16	33	9	2	1	9	11	19	4	1	.260	.319	.386	.705	88	-2	17	4.59	0	0-32(2-31-0)	3	-0.1
2003 Cle-A	99	414	55	110	15	6	3	27	23	51	15	9	.266	.304	.353	.657	75	-16	44	3.65	2	0-90(39-53-0)/D-7	7	-1.6
Total 2	**131**	**541**	**71**	**143**	**24**	**8**	**4**	**36**	**34**	**70**	**19**	**10**	**.264**	**.308**	**.360**	**.668**	**78**	**-18**	**61**	**3.87**	**2**	**0-122/D-7**	**10**	**-1.7**
• CRISP, Joe	Joseph Shelby Crisp b: 7/8/1889, Higginsville, MO d: 2/5/1939, Kansas City, MO BR/TR, 6'4", 200 lbs. Deb: 9/2/1910																							
1910 StL-A	1	1	0	0	0	0	0	0	0	....	0	....	.000	.000	.000	.000	-107	-0	0	.00	0	/C-1	0	0.0
1911 StL-A	1	1	0	1	0	0	0	0	0	....	0	....	1.000	1.000	1.000	2.000	477	0	1	∞	0	....	0	0.0
Total 2	**2**	**2**	**0**	**1**	**0**	**0**	**0**	**0**	**0**	**....**	**0**	**....**	**.500**	**.500**	**.500**	**1.000**	**185**	**0**	**1**	**.00**	**0**	**/C-1**	**0**	**0.0**
• CRISS, Dode	Dode Criss b: 3/12/1885, Sherman, MS d: 9/8/1955, Sherman, MS BL/TR, 6'2", 200 lbs. Deb: 4/20/1908 ♦																							
1908 StL-A	64	82	15	28	6	0	0	14	9	....	1	....	.341	.407	.415	.821	166	7	14	6.71	0	0-11(0-0-11)/P-9,1-1	5	-0.2
1909 StL-A	35	48	2	14	6	1	0	7	0	....	0	....	.292	.306	.458	.764	152	6	6	4.94	-1	P-11	3	-0.1
1910 StL-A	70	91	11	21	4	2	1	11	11	....	2	....	.231	.320	.352	.672	118	3	11	3.92	-1	1-11/P-6	4	0.4
1911 StL-A	58	83	10	21	3	1	2	15	11	....	0	....	.253	.347	.386	.733	109	2	11	4.52	-2	1-14/P-4	2	-1.0
Total 4	**227**	**304**	**38**	**84**	**19**	**4**	**3**	**47**	**31**	**....**	**3**	**....**	**.276**	**.349**	**.395**	**.744**	**133**	**18**	**42**	**4.93**	**-4**	**/P-30,1-26,0-11**	**14**	**-0.8**
• CRIST, Ches	Chester Arthur "Squak" Crist b: 2/10/1882, Cozaddale, OH d: 1/7/1957, Cincinnati, OH BR/TR, 5'11", 165 lbs. Deb: 5/18/1906																							
1906 Phi-N	6	11	1	0	0	0	0	0	0	....	0	....	.000	.083	.000	.083	-74	-2	0	.00	-1	/C-6	0	-0.4
• CRITZ, Hughie	Hugh Melville Critz b: 9/17/1900, Starkville, MS d: 1/10/1980, Greenwood, MS BR/TR, 5'8", 147 lbs. Deb: 5/31/1924																							
1924 Cin-N	102	413	67	133	15	14	3	35	19	18	19	11	.322	.352	.448	.800	115	8	63	5.50	-2	2-96/S-1	14	0.8
1925 Cin-N	144	541	74	150	14	8	2	51	34	17	13	13	.277	.321	.344	.665	72	-25	59	3.66	15	*2-144	13	-0.5
1926 Cin-N	155	607	96	164	24	14	3	79	39	25	7	....	.270	.316	.371	.687	87	-13	70	3.90	18	*2-155	19	1.0
1927 Cin-N	113	396	50	110	10	8	4	49	16	18	7	....	.278	.306	.374	.680	84	-10	44	3.75	-5	*2-113	10	-1.2
1928 Cin-N	153	641	95	190	21	11	5	52	37	24	18	....	.296	.335	.387	.722	90	-11	81	4.45	-15	*2-153	20	-2.1
1929 Cin-N	107	425	55	105	17	9	1	50	27	21	9	....	.247	.292	.336	.629	58	-29	41	3.15	8	*2-106/S-1	5	-1.6
1930 Cin-N	28	104	15	24	3	2	0	11	6	6	1	....	.231	.273	.298	.571	40	-10	8	2.59	1	2-28	1	-0.8
NY-N	124	558	93	148	17	11	4	50	24	26	7	....	.265	.296	.357	.652	58	-39	57	3.51	-5	*2-124	8	-3.6
Yr.	152	662	108	172	20	13	4	61	30	32	8	....	.260	.292	.347	.639	55	-49	65	3.35	-4	*2-152	9	-4.4
1931 NY-N	66	238	33	69	7	2	4	17	8	17	4	....	.290	.313	.387	.700	89	-4	29	4.35	3	2-54	6	0.2
1932 NY-N	151	659	90	182	32	7	2	50	34	27	3	....	.276	.313	.355	.668	81	-18	74	4.00	-9	*2-151	15	-1.7
1933*NY-N	133	558	68	137	18	5	2	33	23	24	4	....	.246	.279	.306	.586	68	-24	48	2.89	31	*2-133	16	1.7
1934 NY-N	137	571	77	138	17	1	6	40	19	24	3	....	.242	.269	.306	.575	55	-37	47	2.72	16	*2-137	11	-1.2
1935 NY-N	65	219	19	41	0	3	2	14	3	10	2	....	.187	.198	.242	.440	18	-26	10	1.47	-1	2-59	3	-2.2
Total 12	**1478**	**5930**	**832**	**1591**	**195**	**95**	**38**	**531**	**289**	**257**	**97**	**24**	**.268**	**.303**	**.352**	**.656**	**74**	**-238**	**631**	**3.62**	**55**	***2-1453/S-2**	**141**	**-11.3**
• CROCKETT, Davey	Daniel Solomon Crockett b: 10/5/1875, Roanoke, VA d: 2/23/1961, Charlottesville, VA BL/TR, 6'1", 175 lbs. Deb: 7/11/1901																							
1901 Det-A	28	102	10	29	2	2	0	14	6	....	1	....	.284	.336	.343	.680	85	-2	13	4.47	-1	1-27	2	-0.4
• CROFT, Art	Arthur F. Croft b: 1/23/1855, St. Louis, MO d: 3/16/1884, St. Louis, MO Deb: 5/4/1875 Career OF: 34-1-1																							
1875 RS-n	19	75	5	15	3	0	0	2	0	2	5	1	.200	.200	.240	.440	58	-2	5	2.28	-3	0-19(10-7-2)	....	-0.4
1877 StL-N	54	220	23	51	5	2	0	27	1	15	....	....	.232	.235	.273	.508	63	-9	14	2.35	-4	1-28,0-25(25-1-1)/2-1	3	-1.4
1878 Ind-N	60	222	22	35	6	0	0	16	5	23	....	....	.158	.176	.185	.361	22	-16	7	1.09	-1	*1-51/0-9(9-0-0)	1	-1.9
Total 2	**114**	**442**	**45**	**86**	**11**	**2**	**0**	**43**	**6**	**38**	**....**	**....**	**.195**	**.205**	**.229**	**.434**	**42**	**-25**	**22**	**1.69**	**-5**	**/1-79,0-34,2-1**	**4**	**-3.3**
• CROFT, Harry	Henry T. Croft b: 8/1/1875, Chicago, IL d: 12/11/1933, Oak Park, IL Deb: 5/19/1899																							
1899 Lou-N	2	2	0	0	0	0	0	0	0	....	0	....	.000	.000	.000	.000	-100	-1	0	.00	0	....	0	0.0
Phi-N	2	7	0	1	0	0	0	0	1	....	0	....	.143	.250	.143	.393	9	-1	0	1.13	1	/2-2	0	0.0
Yr.	4	9	0	1	0	0	0	0	1	....	0	....	.111	.200	.111	.311	-13	-1	0	.85	1	/2-2	0	-0.1
1901 Chi-N	3	12	1	4	0	0	0	4	0	....	0	....	.333	.333	.333	.667	97	-0	1	4.53	2	/0-3(0-0-3)	0	0.2
Total 2	**7**	**21**	**1**	**5**	**0**	**0**	**0**	**4**	**1**	**....**	**0**	**....**	**.238**	**.273**	**.238**	**.511**	**47**	**-1**	**2**	**2.69**	**3**	**/0-3,2-2**	**0**	**0.1**
• CROLIUS, Fred	Fred Joseph Crolius b: 12/16/1876, Jersey City, NJ d: 8/25/1960, Ormond Beach, FL Deb: 4/19/1901 U Career OF: 0-3-55																							
1901 Bos-N	49	200	22	48	4	1	1	13	9	....	6	....	.240	.306	.285	.591	66	-9	20	3.45	-8	0-49(0-3-46)	2	-1.8
1902 Pit-N	9	38	4	10	2	1	0	7	0	....	0	....	.263	.263	.368	.632	91	-1	4	3.57	0	/0-9(0-0-9)	1	-0.1
Total 2	**58**	**238**	**26**	**58**	**6**	**2**	**1**	**20**	**9**	**....**	**6**	**....**	**.244**	**.300**	**.298**	**.598**	**70**	**-9**	**24**	**3.47**	**-8**	**/0-58**	**3**	**-2.0**
• CROMARTIE, Warren	Warren Livingston Cromartie b: 9/29/1953, Miami Beach, FL BL/TL, 6', 192 lbs. Deb: 9/6/1974 Career OF: 487-1-296																							
1974 Mon-N	8	17	2	3	0	0	0	0	3	3	1	0	.176	.300	.176	.476	34	-1	1	2.49	0	/0-6(6-0-0)	0	-0.2
1976 Mon-N	33	81	8	17	1	0	0	2	1	5	1	2	.210	.220	.222	.442	24	-9	3	1.27	0	0-20(5-0-16)	0	-1.1
1977 Mon-N	155	620	64	175	41	7	5	50	33	40	10	3	.282	.323	.395	.718	94	-6	77	4.42	7	*0-155(153-0-4)	14	-0.6
1978 Mon-N	159	607	77	180	32	6	10	56	33	60	8	8	.297	.340	.418	.758	112	6	82	4.81	17	*0-158(157-0-1)/1-4	20	1.6
1979 Mon-N	158	659	84	181	46	5	8	46	38	78	8	7	.275	.315	.396	.711	94	-9	79	4.18	6	*0-158(158-0-0)	17	-1.2
1980 Mon-N	162	597	74	172	33	5	14	70	51	64	8	8	.288	.346	.430	.777	115	10	80	4.66	2	*1-158/0-2(2-0-0)	17	0.1
1981*Mon-N	99	358	41	109	19	2	6	42	39	27	2	3	.304	.373	.419	.792	123	10	55	5.61	-2	1-62,0-38(0-0-38)	14	0.3
1982 Mon-N	144	497	59	126	24	3	14	62	69	60	3	0	.254	.348	.398	.746	106	6	71	4.97	-2	*0-136(2-0-135)/1-9	14	-0.3
1983 Mon-N	120	360	37	100	26	2	3	43	43	48	8	3	.278	.356	.386	.743	106	4	49	4.77	5	*0-101(0-0-101)/1-1	10	0.4
1991 KC-A	69	131	13	41	7	2	1	20	15	18	1	3	.313	.384	.420	.803	122	3	20	5.63	-3	1-29/0-6(4-1-1),D-1	5	-0.1
Total 10	**1107**	**3927**	**459**	**1104**	**229**	**32**	**61**	**391**	**325**	**403**	**50**	**37**	**.281**	**.339**	**.402**	**.741**	**105**	**15**	**517**	**4.64**	**28**	**0-780,1-263/D-1**	**111**	**-1.0**
• CROMER, D.T.	David Thomas Cromer b: 3/19/1971, Lake City, SC BL/TL, 6'2", 220 lbs. Deb: 4/5/2000																							
2000 Cin-N	35	47	7	16	4	0	2	8	1	14	0	0	.340	.367	.553	.921	126	2	10	7.88	-1	1-13	2	0.0
2001 Cin-N	50	57	7	16	3	0	5	12	3	19	0	0	.281	.317	.596	.913	123	2	11	6.73	0	/1-8,D-1	2	0.1
Total 2	**85**	**104**	**14**	**32**	**7**	**0**	**7**	**20**	**4**	**33**	**0**	**0**	**.308**	**.339**	**.577**	**.916**	**124**	**3**	**21**	**7.22**	**0**	**/1-21,D-1**	**4**	**0.2**
• CROMER, Tripp	Roy Bunyan Cromer, III b: 11/21/1967, Lake City, SC BR/TR, 6'2", 165 lbs. Deb: 9/7/1993																							
1993 StL-N	10	23	1	2	0	0	0	0	1	6	0	0	.087	.125	.087	.212	-43	-5	0	.36	-1	/S-9	0	-0.5
1994 StL-N	2	0	1	0	0	0	0	0	0	0	0	0	....	....	....	....	-102	0	0	....	-1	/S-2	0	-0.1
1995 StL-N	105	345	36	78	19	0	5	18	14	66	0	0	.226	.264	.325	.589	54	-24	27	2.49	1	S-95,2-11	4	-1.5
1997 LA-N	28	86	8	25	3	0	4	20	6	16	0	1	.291	.337	.465	.802	116	1	12	5.03	-2	2-17,S-10/3-1	5	0.1
1998 LA-N	6	6	1	1	0	0	1	1	0	2	0	0	.167	.167	.667	.833	113	0	1	3.60	0	....	0	0.0
1999 LA-N	33	52	5	10	0	0	2	8	5	10	0	0	.192	.263	.308	.571	46	-4	3	1.96	1	/2-9,S-9,3-2,0-2(1-0-1),1-1	1	-0.3

YEAR TM-L	G	AB	R	H	2B	3B	HR	RBI	BB	SO	SB	CS	AVG	OBP	SLG	OPS	OPS+	BR/A	RC	RC/G	FR	G/POS	WS	TPW
2000 Hou-N	9	8	2	1	0	0	0	0	1	1	0	0	.125	.222	.125	.347	-9	-1	0	1.20	-1	/3-2,2-1,S-1	0	-0.2
2003 Hou-N	3	4	0	1	0	1	0	1	0	0	0	0	.250	.250	.750	1.000	141	0	1	6.75	1	/2-1	0	0.1
Total 8	196	524	54	118	22	1	12	48	27	101	0	1	.225	.268	.340	.608	60	-33	44	2.74	-2	S-126/2-39,3-5,0-2,1-1	10	-2.4
• CROMPTON, Herb	Herbert Bryan “Workhorse” Crompton b: 11/7/1911, Taylor Ridge, IL d: 8/5/1963, Moline, IL BR/TR, 6', 185 lbs. Deb: 4/26/1937																							
1937 Was-A	2	3	0	1	0	0	0	0	0	0	0	0	.333	.333	.333	.667	72	-0	0	4.24	0	/C-2	0	0.0
1945 NY-A	36	99	6	19	3	0	0	12	2	7	0	0	.192	.208	.222	.430	24	-10	4	1.34	-1	C-33	1	-1.0
Total 2	38	102	6	20	3	0	0	12	2	7	0	0	.196	.212	.225	.437	25	-10	5	1.40	-1	/C-35	1	-1.0
• CROMPTON, Ned	Edward Crompton b: 2/12/1889, Liverpool, England d: 9/28/1950, Aspinwall, PA BL/TL, 5'10.5", 175 lbs. Deb: 9/13/1909 Career OF: 17-1-0																							
1909 StL-A	17	63	7	10	2	1	0	2	7	....	1	....	.159	.254	.222	.476	54	-3	4	1.81	1	0-17(17-0-0)	0	-0.4
1910 Cin-N	1	2	0	0	0	0	0	0	0	2	0	....	.000	.000	.000	.000	-105	-1	0	.00	0	/0-1	0	-0.1
Total 2	18	65	7	10	2	1	0	2	7	2	1	....	.154	.247	.215	.462	50	-4	4	1.74	0	/0-18	0	-0.5
• CRON, Chris	Christopher John Cron b: 3/31/1964, Albuquerque, NM BR/TR, 6'2", 200 lbs. Deb: 8/15/1991																							
1991 Cal-A	6	15	0	2	0	0	0	0	2	5	0	0	.133	.235	.133	.369	5	-2	1	1.23	1	/1-5,D-1	0	-0.1
1992 Chi-A	6	10	0	0	0	0	0	0	0	4	0	0	.000	.000	.000	.000	-101	-3	0	.00	-0	/1-5,0-1	0	-0.3
Total 2	12	25	0	2	0	0	0	0	2	9	0	0	.080	.148	.080	.228	-35	-5	1	.70	1	/1-10,D-1,0-1	0	-0.4
• CRONIN, Bill	William Patrick “Crungy” Cronin b: 12/26/1902, West Newton, MA d: 10/26/1966, Newton, MA BR/TR, 5'9", 167 lbs. Deb: 7/4/1928																							
1928 Bos-N	3	2	1	0	0	0	0	0	1	0	0	....	.000	.333	.000	.333	-6	-0	0	1.05	0	/C-3	0	0.0
1929 Bos-N	6	9	0	1	0	0	0	0	0	0	0	....	.111	.111	.111	.222	-47	-2	0	.34	0	/C-6	0	-0.1
1930 Bos-N	66	178	19	45	9	1	0	17	4	8	0	....	.253	.277	.315	.592	44	-16	15	2.83	0	C-64	2	-1.1
1931 Bos-N	51	107	8	22	6	1	0	10	7	5	0	....	.206	.267	.280	.548	49	-8	8	2.57	-1	C-50	1	-0.6
Total 4	126	296	28	68	15	2	0	27	12	13	0	....	.230	.269	.294	.563	43	-26	24	2.63	-2	C-123	3	-2.0
• CRONIN, Dan	Daniel T. Cronin b: 4/1/1857, Boston, MA d: 11/30/1885, Boston, MA, 5'8", 170 lbs. Deb: 7/9/1884																							
1884 CP-U	1	4	1	1	0	0	0	....	0	....	....	....	.250	.250	.250	.500	74	-0	0	2.39	-2	/2-1	0	-0.2
StL-U	1	5	0	0	0	0	0	....	0	....	....	....	.000	.000	.000	.000	-96	-1	0	.00	-1	/0-1	0	-0.2
Yr.	2	9	1	1	0	0	0	....	0	....	....	....	.111	.111	.111	.222	-21	-1	0	.90	-3	/2-1,0-1	0	-0.3
• CRONIN, Jim	James John Cronin b: 8/7/1905, Richmond, CA d: 6/10/1983, Concord, CA BB/TR, 5'10.5", 150 lbs. Deb: 7/4/1929																							
1929 Phi-A	25	56	7	13	2	1	0	4	5	7	0	0	.232	.295	.304	.599	52	-4	5	3.12	2	2-10/S-9,3-4	1	-0.1
• CRONIN, Joe	Joseph Edward Cronin b: 10/12/1906, San Francisco, CA d: 9/7/1984, Barnstable, MA BR/TR, 5'11.5", 180 lbs. Deb: 4/29/1926 M HOF: 1956																							
1926 Pit-N	38	83	9	22	2	2	0	11	6	15	0	....	.265	.315	.337	.652	72	-3	9	3.56	3	2-27/S-7	2	0.0
1927 Pit-N	12	22	2	5	1	0	0	3	2	3	0	....	.227	.292	.273	.564	48	-2	2	2.70	-4	/2-7,S-4,1-1	0	-0.5
1928 Was-A	63	227	23	55	10	4	0	25	22	27	4	0	.242	.309	.322	.631	66	-10	25	3.57	4	S-63	4	0.1
1929 Was-A	145	494	72	139	29	8	8	61	85	37	5	9	.281	.388	.421	.809	107	6	84	5.79	1	*S-143/2-1	19	2.2
1930 Was-A	154	587	127	203	41	9	13	126	72	36	17	10	.346	.422	.513	.934	135	34	129	8.21	35	*S-154	33	7.7
1931 Was-A	156	611	103	187	44	13	12	126	81	52	10	9	.306	.391	.480	.870	127	26	116	7.05	28	*S-155	35	6.2
1932 Was-A	143	557	95	177	43	**18**	6	116	66	45	7	5	.318	.393	.492	.885	129	25	109	7.46	20	*S-141	31	5.1
1933*Was-A★	152	602	89	186	**45**	11	5	118	87	49	5	4	.309	.398	.445	.843	124	24	111	6.91	20	*S-152	34	5.3
1934 Was-A★	127	504	68	143	30	9	7	101	53	28	8	0	.284	.353	.421	.774	103	4	78	5.61	8	*S-127	17	1.9
1935 Bos-A★	144	556	70	164	37	14	9	95	63	40	3	3	.295	.370	.460	.830	106	5	96	6.34	-19	*S-139/1-2	16	-0.3
1936 Bos-A	81	295	36	83	22	4	2	43	32	21	1	3	.281	.354	.403	.757	82	-10	43	5.11	0	S-60,3-21	7	-0.4
1937 Bos-A★	148	570	102	175	40	4	18	110	84	73	5	3	.307	.402	.486	.887	118	18	116	7.50	-6	*S-148	24	2.0
1938 Bos-A★	143	530	98	172	**51**	5	17	94	91	60	7	5	.325	.428	.536	.964	134	30	126	8.94	10	*S-142	30	4.5
1939 Bos-A★	143	520	97	160	33	3	19	107	87	48	6	6	.308	.407	.492	.899	124	20	104	6.94	-9	*S-142	22	1.9
1940 Bos-A	149	548	104	156	35	6	24	111	83	65	7	5	.285	.380	.502	.882	121	18	112	7.24	-7	*S-146/3-2	24	2.1
1941 Bos-A★	143	518	98	161	38	8	16	95	82	55	1	4	.311	.406	.508	.914	137	28	107	7.31	0	*S-119,3-22/0-1	23	3.6
1942 Bos-A	45	79	7	24	3	0	4	24	15	21	0	1	.304	.415	.494	.909	150	5	16	7.36	-1	3-11/1-5,S-1	3	0.5
1943 Bos-A	59	77	8	24	4	0	5	29	11	4	0	0	.312	.398	.558	.956	175	7	17	8.23	-1	3-10	4	0.7
1944 Bos-A	76	191	24	46	7	0	5	28	34	19	1	4	.241	.358	.356	.714	106	1	25	4.16	-1	1-49	4	-0.2
1945 Bos-A	3	8	1	3	0	0	0	1	3	2	0	0	.375	.545	.375	.920	165	1	2	11.35	1	/3-3	1	0.2
Total 20	2124	7579	1233	2285	515	118	170	1424	1059	700	87	71	.301	.390	.468	.857	119	228	1426	6.80	83	*S-1843/3-69,1-57,2-35,0-1	333	42.6
• CROOKE, Tom	Thomas Aloysius Crooke b: 7/26/1884, Washington, DC d: 4/5/1929, Quantico, VA BR/TR, 6', 180 lbs. Deb: 9/29/1909																							
1909 Was-A	3	7	2	2	1	0	0	2	2	....	1	....	.286	.444	.429	.873	184	1	2	7.30	-1	/1-3	1	0.0
1910 Was-A	8	21	1	4	1	0	0	1	1	....	0	....	.190	.227	.238	.465	48	-1	1	1.63	0	/1-5	0	-0.2
Total 2	11	28	3	6	2	0	0	3	3	....	1	....	.214	.290	.286	.576	93	-0	3	3.28	-1	/1-8	1	-0.2
• CROOKS, Jack	John Charles Crooks b: 11/9/1865, St. Paul, MN d: 2/2/1918, St. Louis, MO BR/TR, 5'10", 170 lbs. Deb: 9/26/1889 M Career OF: 2-1-2																							
1889 Col-a	12	43	13	14	2	3	0	7	10	4	10	....	.326	.463	.512	.975	187	6	15	13.88	3	2-12	4	0.8
1890 Col-a	135	485	86	107	5	4	1	62	96	....	57	....	.221	.357	.254	.611	86	0	66	4.62	4	*2-134/3-1,0-1	14	0.7
1891 Col-a	138	519	110	127	19	13	0	46	103	47	50	....	.245	.379	.331	.710	110	14	86	5.83	16	*2-138	23	2.9
1892 StL-N	128	445	82	95	7	4	7	38	**136**	52	23	....	.213	.400	.294	.694	116	22	63	4.87	-10	*2-101,3-25/0-2(0-0-2)	18	1.6
1893 StL-N	128	448	93	106	10	9	1	48	**121**	37	31	....	.237	.408	.306	.714	91	3	70	5.45	14	*3-123/S-4,C-1	15	1.6
1895 Was-N	118	412	81	117	19	8	6	58	70	39	36	....	.284	.398	.413	.811	111	10	86	7.47	2	*2-117	11	1.3
1896 Was-N	25	84	20	24	3	0	3	20	16	8	2	....	.286	.406	.429	.835	120	3	17	6.73	-3	2-20/3-4	3	0.1
Lou-N	39	122	19	29	5	1	2	15	20	8	8	....	.238	.354	.344	.698	88	-1	18	5.17	-6	2-39	3	-0.5
Yr.	64	206	39	53	8	1	5	35	36	16	10	....	.257	.376	.379	.754	101	2	35	5.81	-9	2-59/3-4	6	-0.4
1898 StL-N	72	225	33	52	4	2	1	20	40	....	3	....	.231	.359	.280	.639	82	-3	26	3.77	-4	2-66/3-3,S-2,0-1	4	-0.4
Total 8	795	2783	537	671	74	44	21	314	612	195	220	....	.241	.386	.322	.708	102	53	448	5.57	16	2-627,3-156/S-6,0-4,C-1	95	8.3
• CROSBY, Bobby	Robert Edward Crosby b: 1/12/1980, Lakewood, CA BR/TR, 6'3", 195 lbs. Deb: 9/2/2003																							
2003 Oak-A	11	12	1	0	0	0	0	0	1	5	0	0	.000	.143	.000	.143	-57	-3	0	.17	2	/S-9,D-2	0	-0.1
• CROSBY, Bubba	Richard Stephen Crosby b: 8/11/1976, Houston, TX BL/TL, 5'11", 185 lbs. Deb: 5/29/2003																							
2003 LA-N	9	12	0	1	0	0	0	1	0	3	0	0	.083	.083	.083	.167	-60	-3	0	.20	0	/0-1	0	-0.3
• CROSBY, Ed	Edward Carlton Crosby b: 5/26/1949, Long Beach, CA BL/TR, 6'2", 180 lbs. Deb: 7/12/1970																							
1970 StL-N	38	95	9	24	4	1	0	6	7	5	0	1	.253	.311	.316	.626	67	-4	10	3.57	3	S-35/3-3,2-2	2	0.1
1972 StL-N	101	276	27	60	9	1	0	19	18	27	1	1	.217	.270	.257	.528	51	-18	18	2.11	1	S-43,2-38,3-14	3	-1.2
1973 StL-N	22	39	4	5	2	1	0	1	4	4	0	0	.128	.209	.231	.440	22	-4	2	1.63	-1	/S-7,2-5,3-4	0	-0.5
*Cin-N	36	51	4	11	1	1	0	5	7	12	0	1	.216	.333	.275	.608	74	-2	5	3.10	2	S-29/2-5	2	0.2
Yr.	58	90	8	16	3	2	0	6	11	16	0	1	.178	.282	.256	.537	52	-6	7	2.44	1	S-36,2-10/3-4	2	-0.2
1974 Cle-A	37	86	11	18	3	0	0	6	6	12	0	1	.209	.261	.244	.505	46	-6	6	2.07	1	3-18,S-13/2-3	1	-0.7
1975 Cle-A	61	128	12	30	3	0	0	7	13	14	0	4	.234	.305	.258	.563	60	-8	9	2.28	0	S-30,2-19,3-13	2	-0.5
1976 Cle-A	2	2	0	1	0	0	0	0	0	0	0	0	.500	.500	.500	1.000	195	0	1	13.50	0	/3-1,D-1	0	0.0
Total 6	297	677	67	149	22	4	0	44	55	74	1	7	.220	.284	.264	.548	55	-42	50	2.39	4	S-157/2-72,3-53,D-1	10	-2.5
• CROSETTI, Frankie	Frank Peter Joseph “Crow” Crosetti b: 10/4/1910, San Francisco, CA d: 2/11/2002, Stockton, CA BR/TR, 5'10", 165 lbs. Deb: 4/12/1932 C																							
1932*NY-A	116	398	47	96	20	9	5	57	51	51	3	2	.241	.335	.374	.709	88	-6	53	4.49	4	S-84,3-33/2-1	13	0.4
1933 NY-A	136	451	71	114	20	5	9	60	55	40	4	1	.253	.337	.379	.716	95	-1	61	4.68	-5	*S-133	15	0.3
1934 NY-A	138	554	85	147	22	10	11	67	61	58	5	6	.265	.344	.401	.744	98	-3	78	4.86	13	*S-119,3-23/2-1	18	1.8
1935 NY-A	87	305	49	78	17	6	8	50	41	27	3	1	.256	.351	.430	.781	107	4	48	5.59	5	S-87	12	1.4
1936*NY-A★	151	632	137	182	35	7	15	78	90	83	18	7	.288	.387	.437	.824	107	10	113	6.48	6	*S-151	24	2.4
1937*NY-A	149	611	127	143	29	5	11	49	86	105	13	7	.234	.340	.352	.692	74	-23	79	4.30	11	*S-147	16	-0.1
1938*NY-A	157	631	113	166	35	3	9	55	106	97	**27**	12	.263	.382	.371	.752	90	-5	98	5.41	8	*S-157	23	1.3
1939*NY-A★	152	656	109	153	25	5	10	56	65	81	11	7	.233	.315	.332	.647	67	-33	71	3.63	28	*S-152	17	0.5

YEAR TM-L	G	AB	R	H	2B	3B	HR	RBI	BB	SO	SB	CS	AVG	OBP	SLG	OPS	OPS+	BR/A	RC	RC/G	FR	G/POS	WS	TPW
1940 NY-A	145	546	84	106	23	4	4	31	72	77	14	8	.194	.299	.273	.572	51	-38	47	2.72	-7	*S-145	8	-3.2
1941 NY-A	50	148	13	33	2	2	1	22	18	14	0	2	.223	.320	.284	.603	61	-8	13	2.90	3	S-32,3-13	3	-0.3
1942*NY-A	74	285	50	69	5	5	4	23	31	31	1	1	.242	.335	.337	.672	91	-2	35	4.18	3	3-62/S-8,2-2	9	0.3
1943*NY-A	95	348	36	81	8	1	2	20	36	47	4	4	.233	.317	.279	.596	74	-11	33	3.14	3	S-90	9	0.0
1944 NY-A	55	197	20	47	4	2	5	30	11	21	3	0	.239	.299	.355	.654	84	-4	20	3.23	2	S-55	5	0.3
1945 NY-A	130	441	57	105	12	0	4	48	59	65	7	1	.238	.341	.293	.634	81	-6	52	3.99	1	*S-126	14	0.5
1946 NY-A	28	59	4	17	3	0	0	3	8	2	0	3	.288	.382	.339	.721	101	-1	8	4.57	2	S-24	2	0.3
1947 NY-A	3	1	0	0	0	0	0	0	0	0	0	0	.000	.000	.000	.000	-101	-0	0	.00	-1	/2-1,S-1	0	-0.1
1948 NY-A	17	14	4	4	0	1	0	0	2	0	0	0	.286	.375	.429	.804	114	0	3	6.75	-2	/2-6,S-5	1	-0.1
Total 17	**1683**	**6277**	**1006**	**1541**	**260**	**65**	**98**	**649**	**792**	**799**	**113**	**62**	**.245**	**.341**	**.354**	**.695**	**84**	**-128**	**812**	**4.38**	**73**	***S-1516,3-131/2-11**	**189**	**5.7**
• CROSS, Amos	Amos C. Cross b: 1861, Czechoslovakia d: 7/16/1888, Cleveland, OH Deb: 4/22/1885 Career OF: 1-0-1																							
1885 Lou-a	35	130	11	37	2	1	0	14	0	....	....	....	.285	.290	.315	.605	91	-2	12	3.54	0	C-35	3	0.1
1886 Lou-a	74	283	51	78	14	6	1	42	44	....	13	....	.276	.375	.378	.753	129	11	46	6.08	0	C-51,1-20/S-2,0-1	10	1.1
1887 Lou-a	8	29	0	4	0	0	0	0	1	....	0	....	.138	.138	.107	.245	-31	-5	0	.46	0	/C-5,1-2,0-1	0	-0.4
Total 3	**117**	**442**	**62**	**119**	**16**	**7**	**1**	**56**	**45**	**....**	**13**	**....**	**.269**	**.338**	**.342**	**.681**	**109**	**4**	**59**	**4.91**	**-1**	**/C-91,1-22,0-2,S-2**	**13**	**0.8**
• CROSS, Clarence	Clarence Cross b: 3/4/1856, St. Louis, MO d: 6/23/1931, Seattle, WA Deb: 5/5/1884																							
1884 Alt-U	2	7	1	4	1	0	0	....	2	....	....	....	.571	.667	.714	1.381	363	2	3	31.89	-2	/3-2	1	0.1
Phi-U	2	9	0	2	0	0	0	....	0	....	....	....	.222	.222	.222	.444	55	-0	0	1.82	-2	/S-2	0	-0.2
KC-U	25	93	13	20	1	0	0	....	6	....	....	....	.215	.263	.226	.488	77	-1	6	2.17	0	S-24/3-1	1	0.0
Yr.	29	109	14	26	2	0	0	....	8	....	....	....	.239	.291	.257	.547	97	1	10	3.21	-3	S-26/3-3	2	-0.1
1887 NY-a	16	57	9	13	2	1	0	5	2	....	0	....	.228	.267	.273	.539	53	-3	4	2.52	-1	S-13/3-4	0	-0.3
Total 2	**45**	**166**	**23**	**39**	**4**	**1**	**0**	**5**	**10**	**....**	**0**	**....**	**.235**	**.282**	**.262**	**.545**	**82**	**-3**	**14**	**2.97**	**-4**	**/S-39,3-7**	**2**	**-0.4**
• CROSS, Frank	Frank Atwell "Mickey" Cross b: 1/20/1873, Cleveland, OH d: 11/2/1932, Geauga Lake, OH TR, 5'9" Deb: 5/20/1901																							
1901 Cle-A	1	5	0	3	0	0	0	0	0	....	0	....	.600	.600	.600	1.200	243	1	2	24.45	0	/0-1	0	0.1
• CROSS, Jeff	Joffre James Cross b: 8/28/1918, Tulsa, OK d: 7/23/1997, Huntsville, TX BR/TR, 5'11", 160 lbs. Deb: 9/27/1942																							
1942 StL-N	1	4	0	1	0	0	0	1	0	0	0	....	.250	.250	.250	.500	43	-0	0	2.25	0	/S-1	0	0.0
1946 StL-N	49	69	17	15	3	0	0	6	10	8	4	....	.217	.316	.261	.577	62	-3	6	3.05	0	S-17/2-8,3-1	2	-0.3
1947 StL-N	51	49	4	5	1	0	0	3	10	6	0	....	.102	.254	.122	.377	3	-7	2	1.11	0	3-15,S-14/2-2	1	-0.6
1948 StL-N	2	0	0	0	0	0	0	0	0	0	0	....	....	....	....	....	-95	0	0	....	0	....	0	0.0
Chi-N	16	20	1	2	0	0	0	0	0	4	0	....	.100	.100	.100	.200	-48	-4	0	.30	-3	/S-9,2-1	0	-0.7
Yr.	18	20	1	2	0	0	0	0	0	4	0	....	.100	.100	.100	.200	-48	-4	0	.30	-3	/S-9,2-1	0	-0.7
Total 4	**119**	**142**	**22**	**23**	**4**	**0**	**0**	**10**	**20**	**18**	**4**	**....**	**.162**	**.265**	**.190**	**.456**	**27**	**-14**	**9**	**1.91**	**-3**	**/S-41,3-16,2-11**	**3**	**-1.5**
• CROSS, Lave	Lafayette Napoleon Cross b: 5/12/1866, Milwaukee, WI d: 9/6/1927, Toledo, OH BR/TR, 5'8.5", 155 lbs. Deb: 4/23/1887 M/U Career OF: 13-34-72																							
1887 Lou-a	54	218	32	69	8	3	0	26	15	....	15	....	.317	.320	.335	.655	81	-6	27	4.93	-7	C-44,0-10(3-1-6)	5	-0.7
1888 Lou-a	47	181	20	41	3	0	0	15	2	....	10	....	.227	.239	.243	.482	56	-9	13	2.55	1	C-37,0-12(2-0-10)/S-2	2	-0.5
1889 Phi-a	55	199	22	44	8	2	0	23	14	9	11	....	.221	.272	.281	.554	58	-11	19	3.20	7	C-55	5	0.1
1890 Phi-P	63	245	42	73	7	8	3	47	12	6	5	....	.298	.331	.429	.759	100	-2	37	5.85	2	C-49,0-15(0-5-10)	8	0.3
1891 Phi-a	110	402	66	121	20	14	5	52	38	23	14	....	.301	.366	.458	.823	131	14	74	7.00	-3	C-43,0-43(0-0-43),3-24/2-1,S	16	1.2
1892 Phi-N	140	541	84	149	15	10	4	69	39	16	18	....	.275	.328	.362	.690	109	4	72	4.95	10	3-65,C-39,0-25(8-17-0),2-14/S	17	1.7
1893 Phi-N	96	415	81	124	17	6	4	78	26	7	18	....	.299	.342	.398	.739	96	-4	64	5.84	14	C-40,3-30,0-10(0-9-1),S-10/1	11	1.2
1894 Phi-N	122	542	128	210	35	10	7	132	31	7	23	....	.387	.424	.528	.951	132	27	133	10.44	25	*3-100,C-16/S-7,2-1	22	4.2
1895 Phi-N	125	535	95	145	26	9	2	101	35	8	21	....	.271	.319	.364	.684	76	-21	73	4.82	33	*3-125	14	1.1
1896 Phi-N	106	406	63	104	23	5	1	73	32	14	8	....	.256	.312	.345	.657	74	-16	49	4.11	8	3-61,S-37/2-6,0-2(0-2-0),C	8	-0.4
1897 Phi-N	88	344	37	89	17	5	3	51	10	....	10	....	.259	.282	.363	.645	71	-16	40	3.99	3	3-47,2-38/0-2(0-0-2),S-1	5	-0.9
1898 StL-N	151	602	71	191	28	8	3	79	28	....	14	....	.317	.348	.405	.753	113	7	94	5.82	11	*3-149/S-2	17	1.9
1899 Cle-N	38	154	15	44	5	0	1	20	8	....	2	....	.286	.325	.338	.663	88	-2	18	4.32	-2	3-38	2	-0.3
StL-N	103	403	61	122	14	5	4	64	17	....	11	....	.303	.333	.392	.725	96	-4	58	5.38	26	*3-103	15	2.1
Yr.	141	557	76	166	19	5	5	84	25	....	13	....	.298	.330	.377	.707	94	-7	77	5.08	24	*3-141	17	1.8
1900 StL-N	16	61	6	18	1	0	0	6	1	....	1	....	.295	.306	.311	.618	71	-3	7	3.83	2	3-16	1	0.0
*Bro-N	117	461	73	135	14	6	4	67	25	....	20	....	.293	.332	.375	.707	89	-8	66	5.31	5	*3-117	15	-0.1
Yr.	133	522	79	153	15	6	4	73	26	....	21	....	.293	.329	.368	.697	87	-11	73	5.13	7	*3-133	16	-0.1
1901 Phi-A	100	424	82	139	28	12	2	73	19	....	23	....	.328	.358	.465	.823	121	10	81	7.40	3	*3-100	19	1.4
1902 Phi-A	137	559	90	191	39	8	0	108	27	....	25	....	.342	.374	.440	.814	120	14	105	7.40	4	*3-137	26	2.1
1903 Phi-A	137	559	60	163	22	4	2	90	10	....	14	....	.292	.304	.356	.660	93	-6	67	4.41	-2	*3-136/1-1	16	-0.5
1904 Phi-A	155	607	73	176	31	10	1	71	13	....	10	....	.290	.310	.379	.689	112	6	78	4.64	-9	*3-155	21	0.2
1905*Phi-A	147	587	69	156	29	5	0	77	26	....	8	....	.266	.299	.332	.631	99	-3	64	3.81	-4	*3-147	15	-0.2
1906 Was-A	130	494	55	130	14	6	1	46	28	....	19	....	.263	.303	.322	.625	100	-1	57	3.98	-8	*3-130	16	-0.5
1907 Was-A	41	161	13	32	8	0	0	10	10	....	3	....	.199	.246	.248	.494	62	-7	11	2.26	7	3-41	2	0.1
Total 21	**2278**	**9100**	**1338**	**2666**	**412**	**136**	**47**	**1378**	**466**	**90**	**303**	**....**	**.293**	**.329**	**.383**	**.711**	**99**	**-38**	**1308**	**5.28**	**128**	***3-1721,C-324,0-119/S-65,2,1**	**278**	**13.4**
• CROSS, Monte	Montford Montgomery Cross b: 8/31/1869, Philadelphia, PA d: 6/21/1934, Philadelphia, PA BR/TR, 5'8.5", 148 lbs. Deb: 9/27/1892 U																							
1892 Bal-N	15	50	5	8	0	0	0	2	4	10	2	....	.160	.222	.160	.382	16	-5	2	1.46	-2	S-15	0	-0.7
1894 Pit-N	13	43	14	19	1	5	2	13	5	4	6	....	.442	.520	.837	1.357	225	9	22	24.25	-2	S-13	3	0.6
1895 Pit-N	109	397	67	101	14	13	3	54	38	38	39	....	.254	.324	.378	.702	85	-9	63	5.67	-16	*S-107/2-1	9	-1.5
1896 StL-N	125	427	66	104	10	6	6	52	58	48	40	....	.244	.342	.337	.679	83	-9	66	5.23	-18	*S-125	9	-1.7
1897 StL-N	132	465	60	133	17	11	4	55	62	....	38	....	.286	.378	.396	.774	107	7	88	6.73	6	*S-131	13	1.6
1898 Phi-N	149	525	68	135	25	5	1	50	55	....	20	....	.257	.337	.330	.666	95	-2	68	4.50	19	*S-149	20	2.3
1899 Phi-N	154	557	85	143	25	6	3	65	56	....	26	....	.257	.335	.339	.675	88	-8	77	4.65	15	*S-154	18	1.4
1900 Phi-N	131	466	59	94	11	3	3	62	51	....	19	....	.202	.289	.258	.546	52	-30	42	2.94	-9	*S-131	8	-2.9
1901 Phi-N	139	483	49	95	14	1	1	44	52	....	24	....	.197	.281	.236	.518	50	-29	41	2.73	-5	*S-139	7	-2.9
1902 Phi-A	137	497	72	115	22	2	3	59	32	....	17	....	.231	.289	.302	.590	61	-27	52	3.41	7	*S-137	10	-1.5
1903 Phi-A	137	470	44	116	21	2	3	45	49	....	31	....	.247	.326	.319	.645	90	-4	62	4.49	9	*S-137/2-1	18	1.0
1904 Phi-A	153	503	33	95	23	4	1	38	46	....	19	....	.189	.266	.256	.523	63	-20	42	2.65	-15	*S-153	10	-3.4
1905*Phi-A	79	252	28	67	17	2	0	24	19	....	8	....	.266	.332	.349	.681	114	4	36	4.51	-7	S-77/2-2	9	0.0
1906 Phi-A	134	445	32	89	23	3	1	40	50	....	22	....	.200	.291	.272	.563	74	-12	46	3.19	3	*S-134	10	-0.4
1907 Phi-A	77	248	37	51	9	5	0	18	39	....	17	....	.206	.316	.282	.598	89	-1	30	3.77	7	S-74	9	0.9
Total 15	**1684**	**5828**	**719**	**1365**	**232**	**68**	**31**	**621**	**616**	**100**	**328**	**....**	**.234**	**.316**	**.313**	**.629**	**80**	**-135**	**737**	**4.20**	**-8**	***S-1676/2-4**	**153**	**-7.2**
• CROSSIN, Frank	Frank Patrick Crossin b: 6/15/1891, Avondale, PA d: 12/6/1965, Kingston, PA BR/TR, 5'10", 160 lbs. Deb: 9/24/1912																							
1912 StL-A	8	22	2	5	0	0	0	2	1	....	1	....	.227	.261	.227	.488	41	-2	1	2.27	0	/C-8	0	-0.2
1913 StL-A	4	4	1	1	0	0	0	0	1	1	0	....	.250	.500	.250	.750	124	0	1	4.92	0	/C-2	0	0.0
1914 StL-A	43	90	5	11	1	1	0	5	10	10	3	....	.122	.225	.156	.381	15	-9	4	1.35	-3	C-41	1	-1.0
Total 3	**55**	**116**	**8**	**17**	**1**	**1**	**0**	**7**	**12**	**11**	**4**	**....**	**.147**	**.244**	**.172**	**.417**	**25**	**-10**	**6**	**1.64**	**-4**	**/C-51**	**1**	**-1.2**
• CROTTY, Joe	Joseph P. Crotty b: 12/24/1860, Cincinnati, OH d: 6/22/1926, Minneapolis, MN BR/TR Deb: 5/4/1882																							
1882 Lou-a	5	20	1	2	0	0	0	....	0	....	....	....	.100	.100	.100	.200	-34	-3	0	.32	0	/C-5	0	-0.2
StL-a	8	28	2	4	1	0	0	....	3	....	....	....	.143	.226	.179	.404	36	-2	1	1.35	-1	/C-7,0-1	0	-0.2
Yr.	13	48	3	6	1	0	0	....	3	....	....	....	.125	.176	.146	.322	9	-4	1	.91	-1	C-12/0-1	0	-0.4
1884 Cin-U	21	84	11	22	4	2	1	....	1	....	....	....	.262	.271	.393	.663	113	1	9	4.13	-1	C-21	3	0.1
1885 Lou-a	39	129	14	20	2	0	0	7	3	....	....	....	.155	.193	.171	.363	15	-12	4	1.08	-2	C-38/1-1	1	-1.0
1886 NY-a	14	47	6	8	0	1	0	2	4	....	3	....	.170	.250	.213	.463	48	-3	3	2.31	1	C-14	1	0.0
Total 4	**87**	**308**	**34**	**56**	**7**	**3**	**1**	**9**	**11**	**....**	**3**	**....**	**.182**	**.220**	**.234**	**.454**	**45**	**-19**	**18**	**1.99**	**-2**	**/C-85,1-1,0-1**	**5**	**-1.3**
• CROUCH, Jack	Jack Albert "Roxy" Crouch b: 6/12/1903, Salisbury, NC d: 8/25/1972, Leesburg, FL BR/TR, 5'9", 165 lbs. Deb: 9/18/1930																							
1930 StL-A	6	14	1	2	1	0	0	1	1	3	0	0	.143	.200	.214	.414	5	-2	1	1.38	0	/C-5	0	-0.1

YEAR TM-L	G	AB	R	H	2B	3B	HR	RBI	BB	SO	SB	CS	AVG	OBP	SLG	OPS	OPS+	BR/A	RC	RC/G	FR	G/POS	WS	TPW
1931 StL-A	8	12	0	0	0	0	0	1	0	4	0	0	.000	.000	.000	.000	-97	-3	0	.00	-1	/C-7	0	-0.4
1933 StL-A	19	30	1	5	0	0	1	5	2	6	0	0	.167	.219	.267	.485	26	-3	2	1.90	1	/C-9	0	-0.2
Cin-N	10	16	5	2	0	0	0	1	0	0	1	....	.125	.222	.125	.347	1	-2	1	1.10	0	/C-6	0	-0.2
Total 3	**43**	**72**	**7**	**9**	**1**	**0**	**1**	**8**	**3**	**13**	**1**	**0**	**.125**	**.182**	**.181**	**.362**	**-3**	**-11**	**3**	**1.26**	**0**	**/C-27**	**0**	**-0.9**
• CROUCHER, Frank	Frank Donald "Dingle" Croucher b: 7/23/1914, San Antonio, TX d: 5/21/1980, Houston, TX BR/TR, 5'11", 165 lbs. Deb: 4/18/1939																							
1939 Det-A	97	324	38	87	15	0	5	40	16	42	2	2	.269	.303	.361	.664	64	-19	33	3.44	-4	S-93/2-3	5	-1.5
1940*Det-A	37	57	3	6	0	0	0	2	4	5	0	0	.105	.164	.105	.269	-26	-11	1	.62	-3	S-26/2-7,3-1	0	-1.3
1941 Det-A	136	489	51	124	21	4	2	39	33	72	2	0	.254	.305	.325	.630	61	-28	50	3.54	-11	*S-136	6	-2.8
1942 Was-A	26	65	2	18	1	1	0	5	3	9	0	0	.277	.309	.323	.632	79	-2	6	2.95	-2	2-18	1	-0.3
Total 4	**296**	**935**	**94**	**235**	**37**	**5**	**7**	**86**	**56**	**128**	**4**	**2**	**.251**	**.296**	**.324**	**.620**	**58**	**-59**	**90**	**3.27**	**-20**	**S-255/2-28,3-1**	**12**	**-5.8**
• CROUSE, Buck	Clyde Elsworth Crouse b: 1/6/1897, Anderson, IN d: 10/23/1983, Muncie, IN BL/TR, 5'8", 158 lbs. Deb: 8/1/1923																							
1923 Chi-A	23	70	6	18	2	1	1	7	3	4	0	0	.257	.297	.357	.654	73	-3	7	3.74	-1	C-22	1	-0.2
1924 Chi-A	94	305	30	79	10	1	1	44	23	12	3	2	.259	.319	.308	.627	64	-16	32	3.47	7	C-90	6	-0.2
1925 Chi-A	54	131	18	46	7	0	2	25	12	4	1	2	.351	.410	.450	.860	125	5	24	7.20	0	C-48	6	0.7
1926 Chi-A	49	135	10	32	4	1	0	17	14	7	0	0	.237	.309	.281	.590	57	-8	13	3.08	-2	C-45	2	-0.7
1927 Chi-A	85	222	22	53	11	0	0	20	21	10	4	1	.239	.307	.288	.596	57	-13	22	3.16	5	C-81	4	-0.4
1928 Chi-A	78	218	17	55	5	2	2	20	19	14	3	4	.252	.315	.321	.636	68	-11	22	3.47	1	C-76	5	-0.5
1929 Chi-A	45	107	11	29	7	0	2	12	5	7	2	0	.271	.316	.393	.708	82	-3	14	4.48	1	C-40	3	0.1
1930 Chi-A	42	118	14	30	8	1	0	15	17	10	1	1	.254	.348	.339	.687	78	-3	15	4.38	3	C-38	3	0.2
Total 8	**470**	**1306**	**128**	**342**	**54**	**6**	**8**	**160**	**114**	**68**	**14**	**10**	**.262**	**.326**	**.331**	**.657**	**72**	**-52**	**148**	**3.87**	**14**	**C-440**	**30**	**-1.2**
• CROW, Don	Donald Le Roy Crow b: 8/18/1958, Yakima, WA BR/TR, 6'4", 200 lbs. Deb: 7/25/1982																							
1982 LA-N	4	4	0	0	0	0	0	0	0	3	0	0	.000	.000	.000	.000	-103	-1	0	.00	0	/C-4	0	-0.1
• CROWE, George	George Daniel "Big George" Crowe b: 3/22/1921, Whiteland, IN BL/TL, 6'2", 212 lbs. Deb: 4/16/1952																							
1952 Bos-N	73	217	25	56	13	1	4	20	18	25	0	1	.258	.329	.382	.712	100	-0	28	4.48	1	1-55	6	-0.1
1953 Mil-N	47	42	6	12	2	0	2	6	2	7	0	0	.286	.333	.476	.810	115	1	7	5.77	0	/1-9	1	0.1
1955 Mil-N	104	303	41	85	12	4	15	55	45	44	1	0	.281	.375	.495	.870	135	17	59	7.13	-1	1-79	14	1.1
1956 Cin-N	77	144	22	36	2	1	10	23	11	28	0	0	.250	.312	.486	.798	104	0	22	5.54	2	1-32	4	0.0
1957 Cin-N	133	494	71	134	20	1	31	92	32	62	1	1	.271	.317	.504	.821	108	4	77	5.52	-5	*1-120	14	-0.8
1958 Cin-N★	111	345	31	95	12	5	7	61	41	51	1	0	.275	.352	.400	.752	94	-2	50	5.12	-2	1-93/2-1	9	-0.8
1959 StL-N	77	103	14	31	6	0	8	29	5	12	0	0	.301	.333	.592	.926	132	4	18	6.41	2	1-14	3	0.5
1960 StL-N	73	72	5	17	3	0	4	13	5	16	0	0	.236	.286	.444	.730	89	-1	8	3.44	0	/1-5	1	-0.1
1961 StL-N	7	7	0	1	0	0	0	0	0	1	0	0	.143	.143	.143	.286	-22	-1	0	.64	0	....	0	-0.1
Total 9	**702**	**1727**	**215**	**467**	**70**	**12**	**81**	**299**	**159**	**246**	**3**	**2**	**.270**	**.335**	**.466**	**.801**	**109**	**21**	**269**	**5.52**	**-2**	**1-407/2-1**	**52**	**-0.2**
• CROWLEY, Bill	William Michael Crowley b: 4/8/1857, Philadelphia, PA d: 7/14/1891, Gloucester, NJ BR/TR, 5'7.5", 159 lbs. Deb: 4/26/1875 Career OF: 82-150-254																							
1875 Phi-n	9	37	4	3	0	0	0	3	1	0	0	0	.081	.105	.081	.186	-33	-5	0	.28	0	/3-4,0-4(0-4-0),1-1	....	-0.4
1877 Lou-N	61	238	30	67	9	3	1	23	4	13	....	....	.282	.293	.357	.651	88	-5	26	4.11	9	*0-58(0-57-2)/C-2,S-2,2-1,3	6	0.1
1879 Buf-N	60	261	41	75	9	5	0	30	6	14	....	....	.287	.303	.360	.664	115	4	29	4.40	0	0-43(3-1-39),C-10/1-7,2-3	8	0.4
1880 Buf-N	85	354	57	95	16	4	0	20	19	23	....	....	.268	.306	.336	.642	115	6	37	3.96	-5	*0-74(8-21-48),C-22	10	0.0
1881 Bos-N	72	279	33	71	12	0	0	31	14	15	....	....	.254	.290	.297	.588	89	-3	25	3.20	-3	*0-72(0-47-26)	6	-0.8
1883 Phi-a	23	96	16	24	4	3	0	16	3	....	....	....	.250	.273	.354	.627	93	-1	10	3.70	-2	0-22(0-21-1)/1-1	3	-0.3
Cle-N	11	41	3	12	5	0	0	5	1	7	....	....	.293	.310	.415	.724	119	1	5	5.11	-1	0-11(0-0-11)	1	-0.1
1884 Bos-N	108	407	50	110	14	6	6	61	33	74	....	....	.270	.325	.378	.703	121	10	51	4.75	-4	*0-108(0-2-107)	14	0.4
1885 Buf-N	92	344	29	83	14	1	1	36	21	32	....	....	.241	.285	.297	.581	85	-6	30	3.08	-9	*0-92(71-1-20)	5	-1.7
Total 7	**512**	**2020**	**259**	**537**	**83**	**22**	**8**	**222**	**101**	**178**	**....**	**....**	**.266**	**.301**	**.341**	**.641**	**103**	**6**	**213**	**3.94**	**-15**	**0-480/C-34,1-8,2-4,S-2,3-1**	**53**	**-2.0**
• CROWLEY, Ed	Edgar Jewel Crowley b: 8/6/1906, Watkinsville, GA d: 4/14/1970, Birmingham, AL BR/TR, 6'1", 180 lbs. Deb: 6/21/1928																							
1928 Was-A	2	1	0	0	0	0	0	0	0	0	0	0	.000	.000	.000	.000	-101	-0	0	.00	-1	/3-2	0	-0.1
• CROWLEY, John	John A. Crowley b: 1/12/1862, Lawrence, MA d: 9/23/1896, Lawrence, MA, 5'10", 164 lbs. Deb: 5/1/1884																							
1884 Phi-N	48	168	26	41	7	3	0	19	15	21	....	....	.244	.306	.321	.627	102	1	17	3.67	-11	C-48	5	-0.5
• CROWLEY, Terry	Terrence Michael Crowley b: 2/16/1947, Staten Island, NY BL/TL, 6', 180 lbs. Deb: 9/4/1969 C Career OF: 20-0-122																							
1969 Bal-A	7	18	2	6	0	0	0	3	1	4	0	0	.333	.368	.333	.702	97	-0	2	4.93	0	/1-3,0-2(2-0-0)	0	0.0
1970*Bal-A	83	152	25	39	5	0	5	20	35	26	2	0	.257	.396	.388	.784	116	6	25	5.67	-2	0-27(6-0-22),1-23	6	0.2
1971 Bal-A	18	23	2	4	0	0	0	1	3	4	0	0	.174	.269	.174	.443	28	-2	1	1.18	0	/0-6(1-0-5),1-2	0	-0.3
1972 Bal-A	97	247	30	57	10	0	11	29	32	26	0	0	.231	.321	.405	.726	112	4	32	4.24	-1	0-68(3-0-65),1-15	8	0.0
1973*Bal-A	54	131	16	27	4	0	3	15	16	14	0	0	.206	.297	.305	.603	71	-5	12	2.98	1	D-23,0-10(2-0-8)/1-7	1	-0.5
1974 Cin-N	84	125	11	30	12	0	1	20	10	16	1	0	.240	.301	.360	.661	86	-3	13	3.50	0	0-22(1-0-21)/1-7	2	-0.3
1975*Cin-N	66	71	8	19	6	0	1	11	7	6	0	0	.268	.333	.394	.728	99	-0	8	3.53	1	/1-4,0-4(3-0-1)	1	0.0
1976 Atl-N	7	6	0	0	0	0	0	1	0	0	0	0	.000	.000	.000	.000	-94	-1	0	.00	0	....	0	- -0.2
Bal-A	33	61	5	15	1	0	0	5	7	11	0	0	.246	.333	.262	.596	81	-1	6	3.26	0	D-17/1-1	1	-0.1
1977 Bal-A	18	22	3	8	1	0	1	9	1	3	0	0	.364	.391	.545	.937	162	2	5	9.25	0	/D-2,1-1	1	0.2
1978 Bal-A	62	95	9	24	2	0	0	12	8	12	0	0	.253	.317	.274	.591	72	-3	8	2.83	0	D-17/0-2(2-0-0),1-1	1	-0.3
1979*Bal-A	61	63	8	20	5	1	1	8	14	13	0	0	.317	.449	.476	.925	155	6	14	8.47	0	D-15/1-2	3	0.6
1980 Bal-A	92	233	33	67	8	0	12	50	29	21	0	0	.288	.366	.476	.843	130	10	40	6.03	1	D-65/1-3	8	1.0
1981 Bal-A	68	134	12	33	6	0	4	25	29	12	0	0	.246	.380	.381	.761	120	5	21	5.27	0	D-42/1-4	5	0.4
1982 Bal-A	65	93	8	22	2	0	3	17	21	9	0	0	.237	.377	.355	.732	103	2	13	4.52	0	D-14,1-10	2	0.1
1983 Mon-N	50	44	2	8	0	0	0	3	9	4	0	0	.182	.333	.182	.515	47	-3	3	2.24	-1	/1-4	0	-0.3
Total 15	**865**	**1518**	**174**	**379**	**62**	**1**	**42**	**229**	**222**	**181**	**3**	**0**	**.250**	**.348**	**.375**	**.723**	**104**	**16**	**202**	**4.49**	**0**	**D-195,0-141/1-87**	**39**	**0.3**
• CRUISE, Walton	Walton Edwin Cruise b: 5/6/1890, Childersburg, AL d: 1/9/1975, Sylacauga, AL BL/TR, 6', 175 lbs. Deb: 4/14/1914 Career OF: 317-153-205																							
1914 StL-N	95	256	20	58	9	3	4	28	25	42	3	....	.227	.303	.332	.635	90	-3	26	3.29	-4	0-81(43-38-0)	6	-1.2
1916 StL-N	3	3	0	2	0	0	0	0	1	0	0	....	.667	.750	.667	1.417	338	1	2	39.00	0	/0-2(1-1-0)	0	0.1
1917 StL-N	153	529	70	156	20	10	5	59	38	73	16	....	.295	.343	.399	.742	131	18	76	5.01	-4	*0-152(49-85-26)	23	0.7
1918 StL-N	70	240	34	65	5	4	6	39	30	26	2	....	.271	.359	.400	.759	136	11	35	4.93	-4	0-65(48-0-17)	9	0.4
1919 StL-N	9	21	0	2	1	0	0	0	1	6	0	....	.095	.136	.143	.279	-17	-3	0	.48	0	/0-5(0-4-1),1-2	0	-0.4
Bos-N	73	241	23	52	7	0	1	21	17	29	8	....	.216	.267	.257	.525	61	-11	18	2.41	-2	0-66(31-23-14)	1	-1.8
Yr.	82	262	23	54	8	0	1	21	18	35	8	....	.206	.257	.248	.505	55	-14	19	2.24	-2	0-71(31-27-15)/1-2	1	-2.2
1920 Bos-N	91	288	40	80	7	5	1	21	31	26	5	3	.278	.352	.347	.699	106	4	37	4.45	-6	0-82(0-0-82)	8	-0.6
1921 Bos-N	108	344	47	119	16	7	8	55	48	24	10	8	.346	.429	.503	.932	154	29	75	8.22	-3	*0-102(100-2-0)/1-2	19	1.8
1922 Bos-N	104	352	51	98	15	10	4	46	44	20	4	4	.278	.360	.412	.772	103	3	54	5.22	0	*0-100(37-0-64)/1-2	10	-0.5
1923 Bos-N	21	38	4	8	2	0	0	0	3	2	1	0	.211	.268	.263	.531	42	-3	3	2.50	-1	/0-9(8-0-1)	0	-0.4
1924 Bos-N	9	9	4	4	1	0	1	3	0	2	0	0	.444	.444	.889	1.333	260	2	3	18.09	0	....	1	0.2
Total 10	**736**	**2321**	**293**	**644**	**83**	**39**	**30**	**272**	**238**	**250**	**49**	**15**	**.277**	**.348**	**.386**	**.733**	**114**	**48**	**329**	**4.88**	**-24**	**0-664/1-6**	**77**	**-1.7**
• CRUMLING, Gene	Eugene Leon Crumling b: 4/5/1922, Wrightsville, PA BR/TR, 6', 180 lbs. Deb: 9/11/1945																							
1945 StL-N	6	12	0	1	0	0	0	1	0	1	0	....	.083	.083	.083	.167	-52	-2	0	.30	1	/C-6	0	-0.2
• CRUMP, Buddy	Arthur Elliott Crump b: 11/29/1901, Norfolk, VA d: 9/7/1976, Raleigh, NC BL/TL, 5'10", 156 lbs. Deb: 9/28/1924																							
1924 NY-N	1	4	0	0	0	0	0	1	0	1	0	0	.000	.000	.000	.000	-103	-1	0	.00	-1	/0-1	0	-0.2
• CRUTHERS, Press	Charles Preston Cruthers b: 9/8/1890, Marshallton, DE d: 12/27/1976, Kenosha, WI BR/TR, 5'9", 152 lbs. Deb: 9/29/1913																							
1913 Phi-A	3	12	0	3	1	0	0	0	0	0	0	....	.250	.250	.333	.583	72	-1	1	2.61	0	/2-3	0	-0.1
1914 Phi-A	4	15	1	3	0	1	0	0	0	4	0	1	.200	.200	.333	.533	63	-1	1	1.38	1	/2-4	0	0.0
Total 2	**7**	**27**	**1**	**6**	**1**	**1**	**0**	**0**	**0**	**4**	**0**	**1**	**.222**	**.222**	**.333**	**.556**	**67**	**-2**	**2**	**1.86**	**1**	**/2-7**	**0**	**-0.1**

YEAR TM-L	G	AB	R	H	2B	3B	HR	RBI	BB	SO	SB	CS	AVG	OBP	SLG	OPS	OPS+	BR/A	RC	RC/G	FR	G/POS	WS	TPW
• CRUZ, Deivi	Deivi (Garcia) Cruz b: 11/6/1972, Bani, Dominican Republic BR/TR, 5'11", 184 lbs. Deb: 4/1/1997																							
1997 Det-A	147	436	35	105	26	0	2	40	14	55	3	6	.241	.264	.314	.579	51	-35	34	2.50	4	*S-147	7	-1.8
1998 Det-A	135	454	52	118	22	3	5	45	13	55	3	4	.260	.285	.355	.640	65	-26	43	3.21	3	*S-135	7	-1.1
1999 Det-A	155	518	64	147	35	0	13	58	12	57	1	4	.284	.305	.427	.732	84	-17	63	4.24	11	*S-155	13	0.6
2000 Det-A	156	583	68	176	46	5	10	82	13	43	1	4	.302	.322	.449	.771	95	-9	73	4.38	-6	*S-156	15	-0.2
2001 Det-A	110	414	39	106	28	1	7	52	17	46	4	1	.256	.292	.379	.671	78	-14	43	3.56	-19	*S-109/3-7	8	-2.3
2002 SD-N	151	514	49	135	28	2	7	47	22	58	2	3	.263	.297	.366	.663	81	-18	50	3.29	-16	*S-147/1-1	7	-2.3
2003 Bal-A	152	548	61	137	24	2	14	65	13	49	1	2	.250	.270	.378	.648	71	-26	52	3.21	-6	*S-147/D-4	10	-1.9
Total 7	**1006**	**3467**	**368**	**924**	**209**	**13**	**58**	**389**	**104**	**363**	**15**	**24**	**.267**	**.292**	**.384**	**.676**	**76**	**-143**	**357**	**3.51**	**-29**	**S-996/3-7,D-4,1-1**	**67**	**-9.0**
• CRUZ, Enrique	Enrique Manuel Cruz b: 11/21/1981, Santo Domingo, Dominican Republic BR/TR, 6'1", 180 lbs. Deb: 4/2/2003																							
2003 Mil-N	60	71	6	6	1	0	0	2	4	30	0	0	.085	.145	.099	.243	-36	-14	1	.40	-3	S-13/2-6,3-2	0	-1.7
• CRUZ, Fausto	Fausto Santiago Cruz b: 5/1/1972, Monte Cristi, Dominican Republic BR/TR, 5'10", 165 lbs. Deb: 4/10/1994																							
1994 Oak-A	17	28	2	3	0	0	0	0	4	6	0	0	.107	.219	.107	.326	-14	-5	1	.95	0	S-10/3-4,2-1	1	-0.4
1995 Oak-A	8	23	0	5	0	0	0	5	3	5	1	1	.217	.308	.217	.525	42	-2	2	1.89	0	/S-8	1	-0.1
1996 Det-A	14	38	5	9	2	0	0	0	1	11	0	0	.237	.256	.289	.546	38	-4	3	2.31	-4	/2-8,S-4,D-1	0	-0.6
Total 3	**39**	**89**	**7**	**17**	**2**	**0**	**0**	**5**	**8**	**22**	**1**	**1**	**.191**	**.258**	**.213**	**.471**	**23**	**-10**	**5**	**1.76**	**-4**	**/S-22,2-9,3-4,D-1**	**2**	**-1.1**
• CRUZ, Hector	Hector Louis (Dilan) "Heity" Cruz b: 4/2/1953, Arroyo, Puerto Rico BR/TR, 5'11", 170 lbs. Deb: 8/11/1973 Career OF: 109-59-177																							
1973 StL-N	11	11	1	0	0	0	0	0	1	3	0	0	.000	.083	.000	.083	-75	-3	0	.05	0	/O-5(1-4-0)	0	-0.3
1975 StL-N	23	48	7	7	2	2	0	6	2	4	0	0	.146	.180	.271	.451	23	-5	2	1.37	-2	3-12/O-6(4-0-2)	0	-0.8
1976 StL-N	151	526	54	120	17	1	13	71	42	119	1	0	.228	.288	.338	.626	76	-17	50	3.18	-18	*3-148	6	-3.8
1977 StL-N	118	339	50	80	19	2	6	42	46	56	4	3	.236	.329	.357	.686	85	-7	41	4.01	0	*O-106(27-0-85)/3-2	9	-1.1
1978 Chi-N	30	76	8	18	5	0	2	9	3	6	0	0	.237	.266	.382	.647	70	-3	6	2.74	-0	O-14(1-14-0)/3-7	1	-0.4
SF-N	79	197	19	44	8	1	6	24	21	39	0	2	.223	.301	.365	.667	89	-4	20	3.41	3	O-53(31-17-14),3-14	4	-0.4
Yr.	109	273	27	62	13	1	8	33	24	45	0	2	.227	.292	.370	.662	84	-8	27	3.22	2	O-67(32-31-14),3-21	5	-0.7
1979 SF-N	16	25	2	3	0	0	0	1	3	7	0	0	.120	.214	.120	.334	-7	-4	1	.61	-1	/O-6(5-0-1),3-2	0	-0.5
*Cin-N	74	182	24	44	10	2	4	27	31	39	0	1	.242	.352	.385	.737	100	1	24	4.36	2	O-69(13-23-49)	5	0.0
Yr.	90	207	26	47	10	2	4	28	34	46	0	1	.227	.336	.353	.689	88	-3	25	3.84	1	O-75(18-23-50)/3-2	5	-0.4
1980 Cin-N	52	75	5	16	4	1	1	5	8	16	0	0	.213	.289	.333	.622	73	-3	7	3.34	-2	O-29(15-1-15)	1	-0.6
1981 Chi-N	53	109	15	25	5	0	7	15	17	24	2	2	.229	.333	.468	.801	120	2	17	4.98	-2	3-18,O-16(8-0-10)	3	0.0
1982 Chi-N	17	19	1	4	1	0	0	0	2	4	0	0	.211	.286	.263	.549	53	-1	1	2.22	-1	/O-4(4-0-1)	0	-0.2
Total 9	**624**	**1607**	**186**	**361**	**71**	**9**	**39**	**200**	**176**	**317**	**7**	**8**	**.225**	**.303**	**.353**	**.656**	**81**	**-44**	**170**	**3.48**	**-21**	**O-308,3-203**	**29**	**-8.0**
• CRUZ, Henry	Henry (Acosta) Cruz b: 2/27/1952, Christiansted, V.I. BL/TL, 6', 175 lbs. Deb: 4/18/1975 Career OF: 33-54-33																							
1975 LA-N	53	94	8	25	3	1	0	5	7	6	1	1	.266	.317	.319	.636	80	-3	10	3.83	-2	O-41(17-23-4)	2	-0.6
1976 LA-N	49	88	8	16	2	1	4	14	9	11	0	2	.182	.258	.364	.621	76	-4	8	2.72	0	O-23(5-5-17)	1	-0.5
1977 Chi-A	16	21	3	6	0	0	2	5	1	3	0	0	.286	.318	.571	.890	137	1	4	6.87	-1	/O-9(1-2-6)	1	0.0
1978 Chi-A	53	77	13	17	2	1	2	10	8	11	0	1	.221	.302	.351	.653	82	-2	8	3.27	2	O-40(10-24-6)/D-1	2	0.0
Total 4	**171**	**280**	**32**	**64**	**7**	**3**	**8**	**34**	**25**	**31**	**1**	**4**	**.229**	**.294**	**.361**	**.655**	**84**	**-8**	**29**	**3.49**	**0**	**O-113/D-1**	**6**	**-1.1**
• CRUZ, Ivan	Luis Ivan Cruz b: 5/3/1968, Fajardo, Puerto Rico BL/TL, 6'3", 210 lbs. Deb: 7/18/1997 Career OF: 1-0-1																							
1997 NY-A	11	20	0	5	1	0	0	3	2	4	0	0	.250	.318	.300	.618	63	-1	2	3.73	0	/D-4,1-3,O-1	0	-0.1
1999 Pit-N	5	10	3	4	0	0	1	2	0	2	0	0	.400	.400	.700	1.100	171	1	3	12.60	0	/1-1,0-1	0	0.1
2000 Pit-N	8	11	0	1	0	0	0	0	0	8	0	0	.091	.091	.091	.182	-55	-3	0	.00	0	/1-1	0	-0.3
2002 StL-N	17	14	2	5	0	0	1	3	1	3	0	0	.357	.400	.571	.971	156	1	3	9.91	0	/1-7	1	0.1
Total 4	**41**	**55**	**5**	**15**	**1**	**0**	**2**	**8**	**3**	**17**	**0**	**0**	**.273**	**.310**	**.400**	**.710**	**84**	**-2**	**8**	**5.39**	**0**	**/1-12,D-4,O-2**	**1**	**-0.2**
• CRUZ, Jacob	Jacob Cruz b: 1/28/1973, Oxnard, CA BL/TL, 6', 175 lbs. Deb: 7/18/1996 Career OF: 44-39-49																							
1996 SF-N	33	77	10	18	3	0	3	10	12	24	0	1	.234	.352	.390	.741	99	-0	11	4.61	-1	O-23(6-0-17)	2	-0.3
1997 SF-N	16	25	3	4	1	0	0	3	3	4	0	0	.160	.250	.200	.450	20	-3	1	.94	1	O-11(2-0-10)	0	-0.2
1998 SF-N	3	3	0	0	0	0	0	0	0	2	0	0	.000	.000	.000	.000	-106	-1	0	.00	0	....	0	-0.1
Cle-A	1	1	0	0	0	0	0	0	0	1	0	0	.000	.000	.000	.000	-97	-0	0	.00	0	....	0	0.0
1999 Cle-A	32	88	14	29	5	1	3	17	5	13	0	2	.330	.372	.511	.884	117	1	14	5.79	-1	O-23(11-15-2)/D-3	3	0.0
2000 Cle-A	11	29	3	7	3	0	0	5	5	4	1	0	.241	.371	.345	.716	81	-0	5	5.34	1	/O-9(1-8-0),D-2	1	0.0
2001 Cle-A	28	68	12	15	4	0	3	11	5	23	0	2	.221	.303	.412	.714	85	-3	7	3.32	0	O-22(3-15-5)	1	-0.2
Col-N	44	76	7	16	1	0	1	7	10	27	0	2	.211	.310	.263	.574	41	-7	7	2.66	-2	O-24(18-1-6)	0	-0.9
2002 Det-A	35	88	12	24	3	1	2	6	13	20	3	1	.273	.385	.398	.782	115	3	15	5.64	-2	D-15,O-12(3-0-9)/1-4	2	-0.1
Total 7	**203**	**455**	**61**	**113**	**20**	**2**	**12**	**59**	**53**	**118**	**4**	**8**	**.248**	**.341**	**.380**	**.721**	**87**	**-10**	**59**	**4.22**	**-4**	**O-124/D-20,1-4**	**9**	**-1.8**
• CRUZ, Jose	Jose L. Cruz b: 4/19/1974, Arroyo, Puerto Rico BB/TR, 6', 190 lbs. Deb: 5/31/1997 Career OF: 234-523-204																							
1997 Sea-A	49	183	28	49	12	1	12	34	13	45	1	0	.268	.316	.541	.857	119	4	31	6.02	-3	O-49(49-0-0)	6	-0.1
Tor-A	55	212	31	49	7	0	14	34	28	72	6	2	.231	.321	.462	.783	101	0	33	5.19	7	O-55(100-4-0)	5	0.4
Yr.	104	395	59	98	19	1	26	68	41	117	7	2	.248	.319	.499	.818	109	4	64	5.56	4	*O-104(149-4-0)	11	0.3
1998 Tor-A	105	352	55	89	14	3	11	42	57	99	11	4	.253	.357	.403	.760	97	0	56	5.62	-3	*O-105(6-103-0)	12	-0.2
1999 Tor-A	106	349	63	84	19	3	14	45	64	91	14	4	.241	.358	.433	.791	99	2	58	5.74	4	*O-106(9-97-0)	11	0.6
2000 Tor-A	162	603	91	146	32	5	31	76	71	129	15	5	.242	.324	.466	.790	94	-7	92	5.21	-5	*O-162(0-162-0)	15	-1.0
2001 Tor-A	146	577	92	158	38	4	34	88	45	138	32	5	.274	.327	.530	.858	118	17	102	6.33	-11	*O-143(14-133-0)	16	0.6
2002 Tor-A	124	466	64	114	26	5	18	70	51	106	7	1	.245	.319	.438	.757	95	-3	67	4.92	2	*O-119(56-21-47)/D-2	14	-0.5
2003*SF-N	158	539	90	135	26	1	20	68	102	121	5	8	.250	.370	.414	.783	107	6	84	5.24	14	*O-158(0-3-157)	16	1.2
Total 7	**905**	**3281**	**514**	**824**	**174**	**22**	**154**	**457**	**431**	**801**	**91**	**29**	**.251**	**.339**	**.458**	**.797**	**103**	**20**	**524**	**5.51**	**5**	**O-897/D-2**	**95**	**1.0**
• CRUZ, Jose	Jose (Dilan) Cruz b: 8/8/1947, Arroyo, Puerto Rico BL/TL, 6', 175 lbs. Deb: 9/19/1970 C Career OF: 1411-284-474																							
1970 StL-N	6	17	2	6	1	0	0	1	4	0	0	0	.353	.500	.412	.912	144	2	4	8.49	1	/O-4(1-0-3)	1	0.3
1971 StL-N	83	292	46	80	13	2	9	27	49	35	6	3	.274	.380	.425	.805	123	11	49	5.90	-2	O-83(1-82-0)	14	0.7
1972 StL-N	117	332	33	78	14	4	2	23	36	54	9	3	.235	.312	.319	.631	81	-7	35	3.58	2	*O-102(10-87-7)	8	-0.9
1973 StL-N	132	406	51	92	22	5	10	57	51	66	10	4	.227	.314	.379	.694	92	-4	50	3.98	-3	*O-118(1-85-37)	12	-1.1
1974 StL-N	107	161	24	42	4	3	5	20	20	27	4	2	.261	.343	.416	.759	112	3	23	4.97	0	O-53(21-8-24)/1-1	5	0.0
1975 Hou-N	120	315	44	81	15	2	9	49	52	44	6	3	.257	.364	.403	.767	121	10	49	5.22	1	O-94(27-2-65)	11	0.6
1976 Hou-N	133	439	49	133	21	5	4	61	53	46	28	11	.303	.378	.401	.779	133	21	70	5.77	2	*O-125(85-13-27)	22	1.8
1977 Hou-N	157	579	87	173	31	10	17	87	69	67	44	23	.299	.373	.475	.848	138	31	104	6.29	-2	*O-155(0-6-155)	24	2.1
1978 Hou-N	153	565	79	178	34	9	10	83	57	57	37	9	.315	.378	.460	.838	144	37	102	6.71	-8	*O-152(0-0-152)/1-2	26	2.2
1979 Hou-N	157	558	73	161	33	7	9	72	72	66	36	14	.289	.370	.421	.791	122	20	91	5.84	0	*O-156(156-0-0)	27	1.4
1980*Hou-N★	160	612	79	185	29	7	11	91	60	66	36	11	.302	.365	.426	.791	130	27	97	5.74	4	*O-158(158-0-0)	25	2.5
1981*Hou-N	107	409	53	109	16	5	13	55	35	49	5	7	.267	.324	.425	.750	117	5	54	4.57	3	*O-105(105-0-0)	14	0.3
1982 Hou-N	155	570	62	157	27	2	9	68	60	67	21	11	.275	.345	.377	.723	110	8	75	4.53	4	*O-155(155-0-0)	18	0.5
1983 Hou-N	160	594	85	**189**	28	8	14	92	65	86	30	16	.318	.386	.463	.849	143	34	109	6.84	2	*O-160(160-0-0)	30	3.0
1984 Hou-N	160	600	96	187	28	13	12	95	73	68	22	8	.312	.386	.462	.848	148	40	111	6.78	5	*O-160(160-0-0)	29	3.9
1985 Hou-N★	141	544	69	163	34	4	9	79	43	74	16	5	.300	.351	.426	.777	120	14	81	5.44	2	*O-137(136-1-0)	21	1.0
1986*Hou-N	141	479	48	133	22	4	10	72	55	86	3	4	.278	.352	.403	.755	111	6	68	5.05	2	*O-134(134-0-0)	17	0.3
1987 Hou-N	126	365	47	88	17	4	11	38	36	65	4	1	.241	.309	.400	.709	89	-6	47	4.40	2	O-97(97-0-0)	9	-0.9
1988 NY-A	38	80	9	16	2	0	1	7	8	8	0	1	.200	.273	.263	.535	51	-6	5	2.19	-1	D-12/O-8(4-0-4)	0	-0.7
Total 19	**2353**	**7917**	**1036**	**2251**	**391**	**94**	**165**	**1077**	**898**	**1031**	**317**	**136**	**.284**	**.358**	**.420**	**.778**	**122**	**246**	**1223**	**5.47**	**16**	***O-2156/D-12,1-3**	**313**	**17.0**
• CRUZ, Julio	Julio Luis Cruz b: 12/2/1954, Brooklyn, NY BB/TR, 5'9", 165 lbs. Deb: 7/4/1977																							
1977 Sea-A	60	199	25	51	3	1	1	7	24	29	15	6	.256	.336	.296	.633	75	-5	22	3.69	3	2-54/D-1	5	0.1
1978 Sea-A	147	550	77	129	14	1	1	25	69	66	59	10	.235	.321	.269	.590	68	-12	58	3.47	11	*2-141/S-5,D-1	12	0.7
1979 Sea-A	107	414	70	112	16	2	1	29	62	61	49	9	.271	.366	.326	.692	87	2	59	4.90	6	*2-107	13	1.4
1980 Sea-A	119	422	66	88	9	3	2	16	59	49	45	7	.209	.307	.258	.565	56	-17	42	3.16	-4	*2-115/D-3	8	-1.5

YEAR TM-L	G	AB	R	H	2B	3B	HR	RBI	BB	SO	SB	CS	AVG	OBP	SLG	OPS	OPS+	BR/A	RC	RC/G	FR	G/POS	WS	TPW
1981 Sea-A	94	352	57	90	12	3	2	24	39	40	43	8	.256	.335	.324	.659	87	1	45	4.34	9	2-92/S-1	12	1.6
1982 Sea-A	154	549	83	133	22	5	8	49	57	71	46	13	.242	.317	.344	.661	79	-10	66	3.99	0	*2-151/D-2,S-2,3-1	16	-0.2
1983 Sea-A	61	181	24	46	10	1	2	12	20	22	33	6	.254	.335	.354	.689	87	2	25	4.64	-6	2-60/D-1	6	-0.2
*Chi-A	99	334	47	84	9	4	1	40	29	44	24	6	.251	.315	.311	.626	71	-10	35	3.40	2	2-97	9	-0.3
Yr.	160	515	71	130	19	5	3	52	49	66	57	12	.252	.322	.326	.648	76	-9	60	3.84	-4	*2-157/D-1	15	-0.5
1984 Chi-A	143	415	42	92	14	4	5	43	45	58	14	6	.222	.298	.311	.609	66	-18	40	3.09	19	*2-141	9	0.8
1985 Chi-A	91	234	28	46	2	3	0	15	32	40	8	5	.197	.299	.231	.529	46	-17	17	2.34	1	2-87/D-2	4	-1.2
1986 Chi-A	81	209	38	45	2	0	0	19	42	28	7	2	.215	.347	.225	.571	58	-9	20	3.13	1	2-78/D-3	4	-0.5
Total 10	**1156**	**3859**	**557**	**916**	**113**	**27**	**23**	**279**	**478**	**508**	**343**	**78**	**.237**	**.324**	**.299**	**.622**	**71**	**-94**	**430**	**3.66**	**42**	***2-1123/D-13,S-8,3-1**	**98**	**0.8**

• CRUZ, Todd Todd Ruben Cruz b: 11/23/1955, Highland Park, MI BR/TR, 6', 175 lbs. Deb: 9/4/1978

YEAR TM-L	G	AB	R	H	2B	3B	HR	RBI	BB	SO	SB	CS	AVG	OBP	SLG	OPS	OPS+	BR/A	RC	RC/G	FR	G/POS	WS	TPW
1978 Phi-N	3	4	0	2	0	0	0	2	0	0	0	1	.500	.500	.500	1.000	179	-0	1	4.50	0	/S-2	0	0.0
1979 KC-A	55	118	9	24	7	0	2	15	3	19	0	1	.203	.230	.314	.543	44	-10	8	2.13	-1	S-48/3-9	1	-0.7
1980 Cal-A	18	40	5	11	3	0	1	5	5	8	0	0	.275	.356	.425	.781	116	1	6	5.97	-4	S-12/3-4,2-1,O-1	1	-0.2
Chi-A	90	293	23	68	11	1	2	18	9	54	2	1	.232	.260	.297	.557	52	-20	22	2.52	0	S-90	4	-1.0
Yr.	108	333	28	79	14	1	3	23	14	62	2	1	.237	.272	.312	.585	60	-19	29	2.89	-4	*S-102/3-4,2-1,O-1	5	-1.2
1982 Sea-A	136	492	44	113	20	2	16	57	12	95	2	10	.230	.248	.376	.624	67	-28	37	2.35	9	*S-136	8	-0.4
1983 Sea-A	65	216	21	41	4	2	7	21	7	56	1	3	.190	.222	.324	.546	46	-18	15	2.15	4	S-63	3	-0.7
*Bal-A	81	221	16	46	9	1	3	27	15	52	3	4	.208	.262	.299	.560	55	-15	14	1.92	0	3-79/2-2	2	-1.6
Yr.	146	437	37	87	13	3	10	48	22	108	4	7	.199	.242	.311	.554	51	-33	29	2.03	4	3-79,S-63/2-2	5	-2.3
1984 Bal-A	96	142	15	31	4	0	3	9	8	33	1	4	.218	.265	.310	.575	60	-9	11	2.41	4	3-89/D-1,P-1	1	-0.6
Total 6	**544**	**1526**	**133**	**336**	**58**	**6**	**34**	**154**	**59**	**317**	**9**	**24**	**.220**	**.253**	**.333**	**.585**	**59**	**-99**	**113**	**2.36**	**13**	**S-351,3-181/2-3,D-1,O-1,P-1**	**20**	**-5.2**

• CRUZ, Tommy Cirilo (Dilan) Cruz b: 2/15/1951, Arroyo, Puerto Rico BL/TL, 5'9", 165 lbs. Deb: 9/4/1973 Career OF: 3-0-0

YEAR TM-L	G	AB	R	H	2B	3B	HR	RBI	BB	SO	SB	CS	AVG	OBP	SLG	OPS	OPS+	BR/A	RC	RC/G	FR	G/POS	WS	TPW
1973 StL-N	3	0	1	0	0	0	0	0	0	0	0	0	....	....	....	....	-100	0	0	....	0	/O-1	0	0.0
1977 Chi-A	4	2	1	0	0	0	0	0	0	0	0	0	.000	.000	.000	.000	-100	-1	0	.00	0	/O-2(2-0-0)	0	-0.1
Total 2	**7**	**2**	**2**	**0**	**0**	**0**	**0**	**0**	**0**	**0**	**0**	**0**	**.000**	**.000**	**.000**	**.000**	**-100**	**-1**	**0**	**.00**	**0**	**/O-3**	**0**	**-0.1**

• CUBBAGE, Mike Michael Lee Cubbage b: 7/21/1950, Charlottesville, VA BL/TR, 6', 180 lbs. Deb: 4/7/1974 M/C

YEAR TM-L	G	AB	R	H	2B	3B	HR	RBI	BB	SO	SB	CS	AVG	OBP	SLG	OPS	OPS+	BR/A	RC	RC/G	FR	G/POS	WS	TPW
1974 Tex-A	9	15	0	0	0	0	0	0	0	4	0	0	.000	.000	.000	.000	-103	-4	0	.00	1	/3-3,2-2	0	-0.3
1975 Tex-A	58	143	12	32	6	0	4	21	18	14	0	0	.224	.311	.350	.660	87	-2	17	3.72	1	2-37/3-3,D-2	4	0.1
1976 Tex-A	14	32	2	7	0	0	0	0	7	7	0	0	.219	.359	.219	.578	70	-1	3	3.05	0	/D-6,2-5,3-1	0	-0.1
Min-A	104	342	40	89	19	5	3	49	42	37	1	1	.260	.346	.371	.718	107	4	44	4.44	0	3-99/2-2,D-2	12	0.4
Yr.	118	374	42	96	19	5	3	49	49	44	1	1	.257	.347	.358	.706	104	3	47	4.32	0	*3-100/D-8,2-7	12	0.3
1977 Min-A	129	417	60	110	16	5	9	55	37	49	1	4	.264	.324	.391	.715	95	-4	53	4.40	1	*3-126/D-1	11	-0.4
1978 Min-A	125	394	40	111	12	7	7	57	40	44	3	1	.282	.349	.401	.750	108	5	56	5.08	3	*3-115/2-5	12	0.8
1979 Min-A	94	243	26	67	10	1	2	23	39	26	1	8	.276	.376	.350	.726	94	-3	33	4.56	-6	3-63,D-21/1-1,2-1	5	-1.1
1980 Min-A	103	285	29	70	9	0	8	42	23	37	0	1	.246	.304	.361	.666	76	-10	32	3.72	3	1-72,3-32/2-1,D-1	6	-1.0
1981 NY-N	67	80	9	17	2	2	1	4	9	15	0	0	.213	.292	.325	.617	76	-3	8	3.12	1	3-12	1	-0.2
Total 8	**703**	**1951**	**218**	**503**	**74**	**20**	**34**	**251**	**215**	**233**	**6**	**15**	**.258**	**.333**	**.369**	**.702**	**94**	**-17**	**245**	**4.29**	**3**	**3-454/1-73,2-53,D-33**	**51**	**-1.9**

• CUCCINELLO, Al Alfred Edward Cuccinello b: 11/26/1914, Long Island City, NY BR/TR, 5'10", 165 lbs. Deb: 5/17/1935

YEAR TM-L	G	AB	R	H	2B	3B	HR	RBI	BB	SO	SB	CS	AVG	OBP	SLG	OPS	OPS+	BR/A	RC	RC/G	FR	G/POS	WS	TPW
1935 NY-N	54	165	27	41	7	1	4	20	1	20	0	....	.248	.262	.376	.638	70	-8	15	2.94	-3	2-48/3-2	3	-0.8

• CUCCINELLO, Tony Anthony Francis "Cooch,Chick" Cuccinello b: 11/8/1907, Long Island City, NY d: 9/21/1995, Tampa, FL BR/TR, 5'7", 160 lbs. Deb: 4/15/1930 C

YEAR TM-L	G	AB	R	H	2B	3B	HR	RBI	BB	SO	SB	CS	AVG	OBP	SLG	OPS	OPS+	BR/A	RC	RC/G	FR	G/POS	WS	TPW
1930 Cin-N	125	443	64	138	22	5	10	78	47	44	5	....	.312	.380	.451	.832	105	5	75	6.14	-12	*3-109,2-15/S-4	12	-0.1
1931 Cin-N	154	575	67	181	39	11	2	93	54	28	1	....	.315	.374	.431	.805	123	19	96	6.15	7	*2-154	23	3.6
1932 Bro-N	154	597	76	168	32	6	12	77	46	47	5	....	.281	.337	.415	.752	103	2	86	5.10	-2	*2-154	20	1.0
1933 Bro-N★	134	485	58	122	31	4	9	65	44	40	4	....	.252	.316	.388	.704	105	3	57	3.97	-13	*2-120,3-14	12	-0.2
1934 Bro-N	140	528	59	138	32	2	14	94	49	45	0	....	.261	.325	.409	.734	100	-0	73	4.86	-3	*2-101,3-43	15	0.5
1935 Bro-N	102	360	49	105	20	3	8	53	40	35	3	....	.292	.366	.431	.796	116	9	57	5.67	4	2-64,3-36	14	1.8
1936 Bos-N	150	565	68	174	26	3	7	86	58	49	1	....	.308	.374	.402	.776	116	15	89	5.73	11	*2-150	23	3.5
1937 Bos-N	152	575	77	156	36	4	11	80	61	40	2	....	.271	.341	.405	.746	112	10	83	5.08	0	*2-151	23	1.9
1938 Bos-N★	147	555	62	147	25	2	9	76	52	32	4	....	.265	.331	.366	.697	102	1	67	4.18	-18	*2-147	17	-0.7
1939 Bos-N	81	310	42	95	17	1	2	40	26	26	5	....	.306	.360	.387	.747	109	4	43	4.99	-7	2-80	10	0.2
1940 Bos-N	34	126	14	34	9	0	0	19	8	9	1	....	.270	.319	.341	.660	87	-2	13	3.68	2	3-33	3	0.1
NY-N	88	307	26	64	9	2	5	36	16	42	1	....	.208	.248	.300	.547	50	-22	21	2.26	-2	2-47,3-37	3	-2.0
Yr.	122	433	40	98	18	2	5	55	24	51	2	....	.226	.269	.312	.580	61	-24	34	2.65	1	3-70,2-47	6	-1.9
1942 Bos-N	40	104	8	21	3	0	1	8	9	11	1	....	.202	.265	.260	.525	55	-6	7	2.19	1	3-20,2-14	1	-0.4
1943 Bos-N	13	19	0	0	0	0	0	2	3	1	0	....	.000	.136	.000	.136	-60	-4	0	.15	-1	/3-4,2-2,S-1	0	-0.5
Chi-A	34	103	5	28	5	0	2	11	13	13	3	1	.272	.353	.379	.732	114	2	15	4.99	-2	3-30	5	0.1
1944 Chi-A	38	130	5	34	3	0	0	17	8	16	0	0	.262	.304	.285	.589	70	-5	12	3.18	-1	3-30/2-6	3	-0.6
1945 Chi-A★	118	402	50	124	25	3	2	49	45	19	6	2	.308	.379	.400	.780	130	17	64	5.94	-7	*3-112	19	1.2
Total 15	**1704**	**6184**	**730**	**1729**	**334**	**46**	**94**	**884**	**579**	**497**	**42**	**3**	**.280**	**.343**	**.394**	**.737**	**105**	**47**	**857**	**4.90**	**-42**	***2-1205,3-468/S-5**	**203**	**9.3**

• CUDDYER, Mike Michael Brent Cuddyer b: 3/27/1979, Norfolk, VA BR/TR, 6'2", 202 lbs. Deb: 9/23/2001 Career OF: 1-0-42

YEAR TM-L	G	AB	R	H	2B	3B	HR	RBI	BB	SO	SB	CS	AVG	OBP	SLG	OPS	OPS+	BR/A	RC	RC/G	FR	G/POS	WS	TPW
2001 Min-A	8	18	1	4	2	0	0	1	2	6	1	0	.222	.300	.333	.633	65	-1	2	3.17	0	/1-5,3-2,D-1	0	-0.2
2002*Min-A	41	112	12	29	7	0	4	13	8	30	2	0	.259	.314	.429	.743	94	-1	15	4.58	2	O-25(O-0-25),3-10/1-6,D-3	3	0.0
2003*Min-A	35	102	14	25	1	3	4	8	12	19	1	1	.245	.325	.431	.756	96	-1	13	4.03	-4	O-18(1-0-17)/3-7,1-5,D-2,2	1	-0.6
Total 3	**84**	**232**	**27**	**58**	**10**	**3**	**8**	**22**	**22**	**55**	**4**	**1**	**.250**	**.318**	**.422**	**.740**	**93**	**-2**	**29**	**4.22**	**-3**	**/O-43,3-19,1-16,D-6,2-1**	**4**	**-0.8**

• CUDWORTH, Jim James Alaric "Cuddy" Cudworth b: 8/22/1858, Fairhaven, MA d: 12/21/1943, Middleboro, MA BR/TR, 6', 165 lbs. Deb: 7/27/1884

YEAR TM-L	G	AB	R	H	2B	3B	HR	RBI	BB	SO	SB	CS	AVG	OBP	SLG	OPS	OPS+	BR/A	RC	RC/G	FR	G/POS	WS	TPW
1884 KC-U	32	116	7	17	3	1	0	....	2	....	....	....	.147	.161	.190	.351	21	-8	4	1.03	1	1-19,O-12(O-12-0)/P-2	0	-1.0

• CUETO, Manuel Manuel "Potato" Cueto b: 2/8/1892, Guanajay, Cuba d: 6/29/1942, Regla, Cuba BR/TR, 5'5", 157 lbs. Deb: 6/25/1914 Career OF: 51-6-22

YEAR TM-L	G	AB	R	H	2B	3B	HR	RBI	BB	SO	SB	CS	AVG	OBP	SLG	OPS	OPS+	BR/A	RC	RC/G	FR	G/POS	WS	TPW
1914 StL-F	19	43	2	4	0	0	0	2	5	0	0	....	.093	.188	.093	.281	-18	-7	1	.73	-2	3-10/S-5,2-2	0	-0.8
1917 Cin-N	56	140	10	28	3	0	1	11	16	17	4	....	.200	.287	.243	.529	66	-5	11	2.38	0	O-38(32-4-3)/2-6,C-5	2	-0.7
1918 Cin-N	47	108	14	32	5	1	0	14	19	5	4	....	.296	.406	.361	.767	137	6	18	5.60	-5	O-19(12-2-1),2-10/S-9,C-6	6	0.2
1919 Cin-N	29	88	10	22	2	0	0	4	10	4	5	....	.250	.340	.273	.613	88	-1	10	3.65	3	O-25(7-0-18)/3-1	3	0.2
Total 4	**151**	**379**	**36**	**86**	**10**	**1**	**1**	**31**	**50**	**26**	**13**	**....**	**.227**	**.323**	**.266**	**.590**	**82**	**-6**	**39**	**3.29**	**-3**	**/O-82,2-18,S-14,3-11,C-11**	**11**	**-1.2**

• CUFF, John John Patrick Cuff b: 6/1864, Jersey City, NJ d: 12/5/1916, Hoboken, NJ Deb: 9/11/1884

YEAR TM-L	G	AB	R	H	2B	3B	HR	RBI	BB	SO	SB	CS	AVG	OBP	SLG	OPS	OPS+	BR/A	RC	RC/G	FR	G/POS	WS	TPW
1884 Bal-U	3	11	1	1	1	0	0	....	1	....	....	....	.091	.167	.182	.348	16	-1	0	.96	2	/C-3	0	0.1

• CULBERSON, Leon Delbert Leon "Lee" Culberson b: 8/6/1919, Hall's Station, GA d: 9/17/1989, Rome, GA BR/TR, 5'11", 180 lbs. Deb: 5/16/1943 Career OF: 40-245-43

YEAR TM-L	G	AB	R	H	2B	3B	HR	RBI	BB	SO	SB	CS	AVG	OBP	SLG	OPS	OPS+	BR/A	RC	RC/G	FR	G/POS	WS	TPW
1943 Bos-A	80	312	36	85	16	6	3	34	30	35	13	0	.272	.336	.391	.727	111	7	45	5.15	5	O-79(28-51-0)	11	1.0
1944 Bos-A	75	282	41	67	11	5	2	21	20	20	6	4	.238	.288	.333	.621	78	-9	27	3.25	0	O-72(0-72-0)	5	-1.1
1945 Bos-A	97	331	26	91	21	6	6	45	20	37	4	3	.275	.316	.429	.745	113	3	41	4.24	5	O-91(1-89-1)	10	0.7
1946*Bos-A	59	179	34	56	10	1	3	18	16	19	3	2	.313	.369	.430	.799	116	4	29	5.65	-3	O-49(6-18-26)/3-4	7	0.0
1947 Bos-A	47	84	10	20	1	0	0	11	12	10	1	1	.238	.354	.250	.604	65	-3	9	3.33	0	O-25(5-4-16)/3-4	1	-0.4
1948 Was-A	12	29	1	5	0	0	0	2	8	5	0	0	.172	.351	.172	.524	43	-2	2	2.22	0	O-11(0-11-0)	0	-0.2
Total 6	**370**	**1217**	**148**	**324**	**59**	**18**	**14**	**131**	**106**	**126**	**27**	**10**	**.266**	**.327**	**.379**	**.705**	**99**	**-0**	**153**	**4.32**	**8**	**O-327/3-8**	**34**	**-0.1**

• CULLEN, John John J. Cullen b: 7/9/1852, New Orleans, LA d: 2/11/1921, Ukiah, CA Deb: 8/18/1884

YEAR TM-L	G	AB	R	H	2B	3B	HR	RBI	BB	SO	SB	CS	AVG	OBP	SLG	OPS	OPS+	BR/A	RC	RC/G	FR	G/POS	WS	TPW
1884 Wil-U	9	31	2	6	0	0	0	....	1	....	....	....	.194	.219	.194	.412	39	-2	1	1.51	-2	/O-6(4-0-2),S-3	0	-0.3

• CULLEN, Tim Timothy Leo Cullen b: 2/16/1942, San Francisco, CA BR/TR, 6'1", 185 lbs. Deb: 8/8/1966

YEAR TM-L	G	AB	R	H	2B	3B	HR	RBI	BB	SO	SB	CS	AVG	OBP	SLG	OPS	OPS+	BR/A	RC	RC/G	FR	G/POS	WS	TPW
1966 Was-A	18	34	8	8	1	0	0	0	2	8	0	0	.235	.278	.265	.542	57	-2	3	2.75	-1	/3-8,2-5	1	-0.2
1967 Was-A	124	402	35	95	7	0	2	31	40	47	4	5	.236	.307	.269	.576	74	-13	35	2.88	-1	S-69,2-46,3-15/O-1	11	-0.4
1968 Chi-A	72	155	16	31	7	0	2	13	15	23	0	0	.200	.275	.284	.559	69	-6	12	2.53	-11	2-71	2	-1.3
Was-A	47	114	8	31	4	2	1	16	7	12	0	0	.272	.325	.368	.694	113	2	14	4.22	-3	S-33,2-16/3-3	5	0.2

YEAR TM-L	G	AB	R	H	2B	3B	HR	RBI	BB	SO	SB	CS	AVG	OBP	SLG	OPS	OPS+	BR/A	RC	RC/G	FR	G/POS	WS	TPW
Yr.	119	269	24	62	11	2	3	29	22	35	0	0	.230	.296	.320	.616	87	-4	26	3.21	-14	2-87,S-33/3-3	7	-1.2
1969 Was-A	119	249	22	52	7	0	1	15	14	27	1	1	.209	.257	.249	.506	44	-19	14	1.72	3	*2-105/S-9,3-1	3	-1.2
1970 Was-A	123	262	22	56	10	2	1	18	31	38	3	2	.214	.304	.279	.583	65	-12	22	2.65	7	*2-112/S-6	4	0.1
1971 Was-A	125	403	34	77	13	4	2	26	33	47	2	0	.191	.252	.258	.510	47	-28	26	2.04	10	2-78,S-62	5	-0.7
1972*Oak-A	72	142	10	37	8	1	0	15	5	17	0	1	.261	.286	.331	.617	88	-3	13	3.06	-2	2-65/3-4,S-1	3	-0.2
Total 7	700	1761	155	387	57	9	9	134	147	219	10	9	.220	.283	.278	.561	65	-80	138	2.53	3	2-498,S-180/3-31,0-1	34	-3.9

• CULLENBINE, Roy Roy Joseph Cullenbine b: 10/18/1913, Nashville, TN d: 5/28/1991, Mount Clemens, MI BB/TR, 6'1", 190 lbs. Deb: 4/19/1938 Career OF: 236-12-600

YEAR TM-L	G	AB	R	H	2B	3B	HR	RBI	BB	SO	SB	CS	AVG	OBP	SLG	OPS	OPS+	BR/A	RC	RC/G	FR	G/POS	WS	TPW
1938 Det-A	25	67	12	19	1	3	0	9	12	9	2	0	.284	.392	.388	.780	91	-0	11	6.27	0	0-17(17-0-0)	2	0.0
1939 Det-A	75	179	31	43	9	2	6	23	34	29	0	1	.240	.362	.413	.775	91	-2	29	5.56	-2	0-46(24-4-19)/1-2	4	-0.7
1940 Bro-N	22	61	8	11	1	0	1	9	23	11	2	....	.180	.405	.246	.651	78	-0	8	4.36	0	0-19(0-0-19)	2	-0.1
StL-A	86	257	41	59	11	2	7	31	50	34	0	1	.230	.359	.370	.729	87	-3	38	5.11	-1	0-57(11-0-49)/1-6	6	-0.8
1941 StL-A★	149	501	82	159	29	9	9	98	121	43	6	4	.317	.452	.465	.917	138	36	120	9.16	-3	*0-120(108-7-5),1-22	23	2.4
1942 StL-A	38	109	15	21	7	1	2	14	30	20	0	1	.193	.367	.330	.697	95	1	16	4.49	1	0-27(27-0-0)/1-5	3	-0.1
Was-A	64	241	30	69	19	0	2	35	44	18	1	2	.286	.396	.390	.787	123	9	41	6.26	6	0-35(35-0-0),3-28	11	1.4
*NY-A	21	77	16	28	7	0	2	17	18	2	0	1	.364	.484	.532	1.017	190	10	22	11.03	2	0-19(0-0-19)/1-1	6	1.1
Yr.	123	427	61	118	33	1	6	66	92	40	1	4	.276	.405	.400	.805	128	20	78	6.53	9	0-81(62-0-19),3-28/1-6	20	2.5
1943 Cle-A	138	488	66	141	24	4	8	56	96	58	3	4	.289	.407	.404	.811	146	33	89	6.46	6	*0-121(0-0-121),1-13	27	3.3
1944 Cle-A★	154	571	98	162	34	5	16	80	87	49	4	4	.284	.380	.445	.825	141	32	102	6.42	1	*0-151(0-1-150)	21	2.3
1945 Cle-A	8	13	3	1	1	0	0	0	11	0	0	0	.077	.500	.154	.654	97	2	2	5.52	-1	/0-4(0-0-4),3-3	1	0.1
*Det-A	146	523	80	145	27	5	18	93	102	36	2	0	.277	.398	.451	.849	137	30	103	7.06	15	*0-146(2-0-145)	30	3.7
Yr.	154	536	83	146	28	5	18	93	**113**	36	2	0	.272	.402	.444	.846	136	32	105	**7.01**	14	*0-150(2-0-149)/3-3	31	3.8
1946 Det-A	113	328	63	110	21	0	15	56	88	39	3	0	.335	.477	.537	1.014	172	40	95	11.45	6	0-81(12-0-69),1-21	25	4.4
1947 Det-A	142	464	82	104	18	1	24	78	137	51	3	2	.224	.401	.422	.823	125	23	91	6.50	13	*1-138	21	3.2
Total 10	1181	3879	627	1072	209	32	110	599	853	399	26	20	.276	.408	.432	.840	132	210	769	7.08	42	0-843,1-208/3-31	182	20.3

• CULLER, Dick Richard Broadus Culler b: 1/15/1915, High Point, NC d: 6/16/1964, Chapel Hill, NC BR/TR, 5'9.5", 155 lbs. Deb: 9/19/1936 U

YEAR TM-L	G	AB	R	H	2B	3B	HR	RBI	BB	SO	SB	CS	AVG	OBP	SLG	OPS	OPS+	BR/A	RC	RC/G	FR	G/POS	WS	TPW
1936 Phi-A	9	38	3	9	0	0	0	1	1	3	0	0	.237	.256	.237	.493	23	-5	2	2.07	-1	/2-7,S-2	0	-0.4
1943 Chi-A	53	148	9	32	5	1	0	11	16	11	4	5	.216	.297	.264	.560	64	-7	11	2.42	1	3-26,2-19/S-3	2	-0.5
1944 Bos-N	8	28	2	2	0	0	0	0	4	2	0	....	.071	.188	.071	.259	-24	-5	0	.48	1	/S-8	0	-0.3
1945 Bos-N	136	527	87	138	12	1	2	30	50	35	7	....	.262	.328	.300	.628	75	-17	54	3.63	0	*S-126/3-6	10	-0.6
1946 Bos-N	134	482	70	123	15	3	0	33	62	18	7	....	.255	.342	.299	.641	82	-9	51	3.62	2	*S-132	14	0.1
1947 Bos-N	77	214	20	53	5	1	0	19	19	15	1	....	.248	.309	.280	.589	59	-12	19	2.98	2	S-77	3	-0.7
1948 Chi-N	48	89	4	15	2	0	0	5	13	3	0	....	.169	.275	.191	.466	29	-8	5	1.67	0	S-43/2-2	1	-0.6
1949 NY-N	7	1	0	0	0	0	0	0	1	0	0	....	.000	.500	.000	.500	45	0	0	3.51	-1	/S-7	0	-0.1
Total 8	472	1527	195	372	39	6	2	99	166	87	19	5	.244	.320	.281	.601	68	-64	144	3.17	5	S-398/3-32,2-28	30	-3.1

• CULLOP, Nick Henry Nicholas "Tomato Face" Cullop
b: 10/16/1900, St. Louis, MO d: 12/1/1978, Gahanna, OH BR/TR, 6', 200 lbs. Deb: 4/14/1926 Career OF: 90-24-12 ♦

YEAR TM-L	G	AB	R	H	2B	3B	HR	RBI	BB	SO	SB	CS	AVG	OBP	SLG	OPS	OPS+	BR/A	RC	RC/G	FR	G/POS	WS	TPW
1926 NY-A	2	2	0	1	0	0	0	0	0	1	0	0	.500	.500	.500	1.000	164	0	0	12.72	0	....	0	0.0
1927 Was-A	15	23	2	5	2	0	0	1	1	6	0	0	.217	.250	.304	.554	44	-2	2	2.57	0	/0-5(2-0-3),1-1	0	-0.2
Cle-A	32	68	9	16	2	3	1	8	9	19	0	4	.235	.333	.397	.730	88	-3	8	3.69	2	0-20(0-13-7)/P-1	1	-0.3
Yr.	47	91	11	21	4	3	1	9	10	25	0	4	.231	.314	.374	.687	78	-5	10	3.43	2	0-25(2-13-10)/1-1,P-1	1	-0.5
1929 Bro-N	13	41	7	8	2	2	1	5	8	7	0	....	.195	.327	.415	.741	84	-1	6	4.45	1	0-11(5-6-2)/1-1	1	-0.1
1930 Cin-N	7	22	2	4	0	0	1	5	1	9	0	....	.182	.217	.318	.536	29	-3	1	2.12	1	/0-5(0-5-0)	0	-0.2
1931 Cin-N	104	334	29	88	23	7	8	48	21	86	1	....	.263	.309	.446	.755	107	2	47	4.86	-1	0-83(83-0-0)	8	-0.5
Total 5	173	490	49	122	29	12	11	67	40	128	1	4	.249	.308	.424	.733	96	-7	64	4.43	2	0-124/1-2,P-1	10	-1.2

• CULMER, Wil Wilfred Hillard Culmer b: 11/11/1958, Nassau, Bahamas BR/TR, 6'4", 210 lbs. Deb: 4/12/1983

YEAR TM-L	G	AB	R	H	2B	3B	HR	RBI	BB	SO	SB	CS	AVG	OBP	SLG	OPS	OPS+	BR/A	RC	RC/G	FR	G/POS	WS	TPW
1983 Cle-A	7	19	0	2	0	0	0	1	0	4	0	1	.105	.105	.105	.211	-40	-4	0	.00	0	/0-4(0-0-4),D-2	0	-0.4

• CULP, Benny Benjamin Baldy Culp b: 1/19/1914, Philadelphia, PA d: 10/23/2000, Philadelphia, PA BR/TR, 5'9", 175 lbs. Deb: 9/17/1942 C

YEAR TM-L	G	AB	R	H	2B	3B	HR	RBI	BB	SO	SB	CS	AVG	OBP	SLG	OPS	OPS+	BR/A	RC	RC/G	FR	G/POS	WS	TPW
1942 Phi-N	1	0	0	0	0	0	0	0	0	0	0	....	....	....	....	....	-105	0	0	....	0	/C-1	0	0.0
1943 Phi-N	10	24	4	5	1	0	0	2	3	3	0	....	.208	.296	.250	.546	61	-1	2	2.35	0	C-10	0	-0.1
1944 Phi-N	4	2	1	0	0	0	0	0	0	0	0	....	.000	.000	.000	.000	-103	-1	0	.00	0	/C-1	0	-0.1
Total 3	15	26	5	5	1	0	0	2	3	3	0	....	.192	.276	.231	.507	50	-2	2	2.14	-1	/C-12	0	-0.2

• CUMMINGS, Jack John William Cummings b: 4/1/1904, Pittsburgh, PA d: 10/5/1962, West Mifflin, PA BR/TR, 6', 195 lbs. Deb: 9/11/1926

YEAR TM-L	G	AB	R	H	2B	3B	HR	RBI	BB	SO	SB	CS	AVG	OBP	SLG	OPS	OPS+	BR/A	RC	RC/G	FR	G/POS	WS	TPW
1926 NY-N	7	16	3	5	3	0	0	4	4	2	0	....	.313	.450	.500	.950	157	2	4	8.20	0	/C-6	1	0.2
1927 NY-N	43	80	8	29	6	1	2	14	5	10	0	....	.363	.407	.538	.944	151	6	17	8.09	-1	C-34	4	0.5
1928 NY-N	33	27	4	9	2	0	2	9	3	4	0	....	.333	.400	.630	1.030	165	2	7	8.48	-1	/C-4	1	0.2
1929 NY-N	3	3	0	1	0	0	0	0	0	0	0	....	.333	.333	.333	.667	66	-0	0	4.03	0	/C-1	0	0.0
Bos-N	3	6	0	1	0	0	0	1	0	2	0	....	.167	.167	.167	.333	-18	-1	0	.81	-1	/C-3	0	-0.2
Yr.	6	9	0	2	0	0	0	1	0	2	0	....	.222	.222	.222	.444	10	-1	0	1.73	-1	/C-4	0	-0.2
Total 4	89	132	15	45	11	1	4	28	12	18	0	....	.341	.400	.530	.930	147	8	28	7.71	-2	/C-48	6	0.8

• CUMMINGS, Midre Midre Almeric Cummings b: 10/14/1971, St. Croix, V.I. BL/TR, 6'1", 196 lbs. Deb: 9/10/1993 Career OF: 56-95-101

YEAR TM-L	G	AB	R	H	2B	3B	HR	RBI	BB	SO	SB	CS	AVG	OBP	SLG	OPS	OPS+	BR/A	RC	RC/G	FR	G/POS	WS	TPW
1993 Pit-N	13	36	5	4	1	0	0	3	4	9	0	0	.111	.200	.139	.339	-7	-6	1	.89	0	0-11(5-5-1)	0	-0.6
1994 Pit-N	24	86	11	21	4	0	1	12	4	18	0	0	.244	.286	.326	.611	58	-5	8	3.45	-1	0-24(18-5-4)	2	-0.7
1995 Pit-N	59	152	13	37	7	1	2	15	13	30	1	0	.243	.303	.342	.645	68	-7	16	3.81	0	0-41(8-20-14)	2	-0.7
1996 Pit-N	24	85	11	19	3	1	3	7	0	16	0	0	.224	.224	.388	.612	56	-6	7	2.95	0	0-21(0-11-10)	1	-0.6
1997 Pit-N	52	106	11	20	6	2	3	8	8	26	0	0	.189	.252	.368	.620	59	-7	10	3.10	-1	0-25(14-0-11)	0	-0.9
Phi-N	63	208	24	63	16	4	1	23	23	30	2	3	.303	.372	.433	.805	110	2	34	6.02	-0	0-54(0-53-2)	9	0.3
Yr.	115	314	35	83	22	6	4	31	31	56	2	3	.264	.332	.411	.743	93	-5	44	4.96	-1	0-79(14-53-13)	9	-0.6
1998*Bos-A	67	120	20	34	8	0	5	15	17	19	3	3	.283	.381	.475	.856	119	3	22	6.44	-1	D-29,0-17(0-0-17)	3	0.1
1999 Min-A	16	38	1	10	0	0	1	9	3	7	2	0	.263	.317	.342	.659	66	-2	5	4.42	0	/D-5,0-5(1-0-5)	1	-0.2
2000 Min-A	77	181	28	50	10	0	4	22	11	25	0	0	.276	.328	.398	.726	79	-6	23	4.61	3	0-40(7-0-33),D-15	1	-0.5
Bos-A	21	25	1	7	0	0	0	2	6	3	0	0	.280	.419	.280	.699	80	-0	3	4.71	-0	/0-4(0-1-3),D-1	0	-0.1
Yr.	98	206	29	57	10	0	4	24	17	28	0	0	.277	.341	.383	.724	80	-6	27	4.62	3	0-44(7-1-36),D-16	1	-0.5
2001*Ari-N	20	20	1	6	1	0	0	1	0	4	0	0	.300	.300	.350	.650	63	-1	1	2.27	0	/0-4(3-0-1)	0	-0.1
Total 9	436	1057	126	271	56	8	20	117	89	187	8	6	.256	.318	.381	.700	79	-34	132	4.37	0	0-246/D-50	19	-4.0

• CUNNINGHAM, Bill William John Cunningham b: 6/9/1888, Schenectady, NY d: 2/21/1946, Schenectady, NY BR/TR, 5'9", 170 lbs. Deb: 9/12/1910

YEAR TM-L	G	AB	R	H	2B	3B	HR	RBI	BB	SO	SB	CS	AVG	OBP	SLG	OPS	OPS+	BR/A	RC	RC/G	FR	G/POS	WS	TPW
1910 Was-A	21	74	3	22	5	1	0	14	12	....	4	....	.297	.402	.392	.794	156	6	14	6.30	-1	2-21	4	0.5
1911 Was-A	94	331	34	63	10	5	3	37	19	....	10	....	.190	.239	.278	.517	45	-26	25	2.24	-18	2-93	2	-4.1
1912 Was-A	8	27	5	5	1	0	1	8	3	....	2	....	.185	.267	.333	.600	71	-1	3	3.27	-1	/2-7,S-1	0	-0.2
Total 3	123	432	42	90	16	6	4	59	34	....	16	....	.208	.271	.301	.572	67	-22	41	2.93	-19	2-121/S-1	6	-3.8

• CUNNINGHAM, Bill William Aloysius Cunningham
b: 7/30/1895, San Francisco, CA d: 9/26/1953, Colusa, CA BR/TR, 5'8", 155 lbs. Deb: 7/14/1921 C Career OF: 108-159-1

YEAR TM-L	G	AB	R	H	2B	3B	HR	RBI	BB	SO	SB	CS	AVG	OBP	SLG	OPS	OPS+	BR/A	RC	RC/G	FR	G/POS	WS	TPW
1921 NY-N	40	76	10	21	2	1	1	12	3	3	0	1	.276	.313	.368	.681	79	-2	8	3.81	0	0-20(1-18-1)	2	-0.3
1922*NY-N	85	229	37	75	15	2	2	33	7	9	4	5	.328	.350	.437	.787	101	-1	33	5.30	1	0-71(2-68-0)/3-1	7	-0.2
1923*NY-N	79	203	22	55	7	1	5	27	10	9	5	2	.271	.305	.389	.694	83	-5	24	4.05	-1	0-68(10-58-0)/2-4	5	-0.8
1924 Bos-N	114	437	44	119	15	8	1	40	32	27	8	5	.272	.326	.350	.676	85	-8	51	4.10	5	*0-109(95-15-0)	9	-1.1
Total 4	318	945	113	270	39	12	9	112	52	48	17	13	.286	.326	.381	.707	88	-17	116	4.34	5	0-268/2-4,3-1	23	-2.5

• CUNNINGHAM, George George Harold Cunningham
b: 7/13/1894, Sturgeon Lake, MN d: 3/10/1972, Chattanooga, TN BR/TR, 5'11", 185 lbs. Deb: 4/14/1916 Career OF: 0-2-19 ♦

YEAR TM-L	G	AB	R	H	2B	3B	HR	RBI	BB	SO	SB	CS	AVG	OBP	SLG	OPS	OPS+	BR/A	RC	RC/G	FR	G/POS	WS	TPW
1916 Det-A	35	41	7	11	2	2	0	3	8	12	0	....	.268	.388	.415	.802	136	5	7	5.69	1	P-35	9	1.1
1917 Det-A	44	34	5	6	0	0	1	3	3	13	0	....	.176	.243	.265	.508	55	1	2	1.98	0	P-44	4	-0.1

YEAR TM-L	G	AB	R	H	2B	3B	HR	RBI	BB	SO	SB	CS	AVG	OBP	SLG	OPS	OPS+	BR/A	RC	RC/G	FR	G/POS	WS	TPW
1918 Det-A	56	112	11	25	4	1	0	2	16	34	2	....	.223	.320	.277	.597	84	3	11	2.97	-2	P-27,0-20(0-2-18)	7	0.0
1919 Det-A	26	23	4	5	0	0	0	5	9	8	0	....	.217	.438	.217	.655	89	3	2	3.06	0	P-17	1	-0.6
1921 Det-A	1	0	0	0	0	0	0	0	0	0	0	0	....	....	....	....	-101	0	0	....	0	/0-1	0	0.0
Total 5	162	210	27	47	6	3	1	13	36	67	2	0	.224	.337	.295	.633	90	12	22	3.30	0	P-123/0-21	21	0.4

• CUNNINGHAM, Joe Joseph Robert Cunningham b: 8/27/1931, Paterson, NJ BL/TL, 6', 190 lbs. Deb: 6/30/1954 C Career OF: 46-1-403

YEAR TM-L	G	AB	R	H	2B	3B	HR	RBI	BB	SO	SB	CS	AVG	OBP	SLG	OPS	OPS+	BR/A	RC	RC/G	FR	G/POS	WS	TPW
1954 StL-N	85	310	40	88	11	3	11	50	43	40	1	1	.284	.375	.445	.820	112	6	55	6.50	-6	1-85	10	-0.4
1956 StL-N	4	3	1	0	0	0	0	0	1	1	0	0	.000	.250	.000	.250	-25	-1	0	.59	0	/1-1	0	-0.1
1957 StL-N	122	261	50	83	15	0	9	52	56	29	3	3	.318	.447	.479	.926	146	21	61	8.57	-3	1-57,0-46(0-0-46)	14	1.4
1958 StL-N	131	337	61	105	20	3	12	57	82	23	4	4	.312	.450	.496	.946	144	27	80	8.74	-2	1-67,0-66(24-0-42)	17	2.0
1959 StL-N★	144	458	65	158	28	6	7	60	88	47	2	6	.345	**.456**	.478	.934	140	31	104	8.76	0	*0-121(20-0-109),1-35	20	2.7
1960 StL-N	139	492	68	138	28	3	6	39	59	59	1	7	.280	.364	.386	.751	97	-2	70	5.04	-5	*0-116(1-0-116),1-15	14	-1.2
1961 StL-N	113	322	60	92	11	2	7	40	53	32	1	0	.286	.404	.398	.802	104	6	58	6.69	-5	0-86(1-1-85),1-10	12	-0.5
1962 Chi-A	149	526	91	155	32	7	8	70	101	59	3	3	.295	.415	.428	.843	128	26	102	6.87	-2	*1-143/0-5(0-0-5)	24	1.5
1963 Chi-A	67	210	32	60	12	1	1	31	33	23	1	0	.286	.393	.367	.759	116	7	33	5.59	-7	1-58	8	-0.4
1964 Chi-A	40	108	13	27	7	0	0	10	14	15	0	1	.250	.352	.315	.667	90	-1	13	4.29	-1	1-33	3	-0.4
Was-A	49	126	15	27	4	0	0	7	23	13	0	1	.214	.344	.246	.590	68	-5	12	3.02	-3	1-41	2	-1.0
Yr.	89	234	28	54	11	0	0	17	37	28	0	2	.231	.348	.278	.626	78	-6	25	3.58	-3	1-74	5	-1.3
1965 Was-A	95	201	29	46	9	1	3	20	46	27	0	1	.229	.375	.328	.703	103	3	27	4.43	-3	1-59	7	-0.3
1966 Was-A	3	8	0	1	0	0	0	0	0	1	0	0	.125	.125	.125	.250	-28	-1	0	.48	1	/1-3	0	0.0
Total 12	1141	3362	525	980	177	26	64	436	599	369	16	27	.291	.406	.417	.823	119	117	614	6.59	-35	1-607,0-440	131	3.4

• CUNNINGHAM, Ray Raymond Lee Cunningham b: 1/17/1905, Mesquite, TX BR/TR, 5'7.5", 150 lbs. Deb: 9/16/1931

YEAR TM-L	G	AB	R	H	2B	3B	HR	RBI	BB	SO	SB	CS	AVG	OBP	SLG	OPS	OPS+	BR/A	RC	RC/G	FR	G/POS	WS	TPW
1931 StL-N	3	4	0	0	0	0	0	1	0	0	0	....	.000	.000	.000	.000	-96	-1	0	.00	0	/3-3	0	-0.1
1932 StL-N	11	22	4	4	1	0	0	0	3	4	0	....	.182	.280	.227	.507	37	-2	2	2.25	0	/3-8,2-2	0	-0.2
Total 2	14	26	4	4	1	0	0	1	3	4	0	....	.154	.241	.192	.434	19	-3	2	1.86	0	/3-11,2-2	0	-0.3

• CURLEY, Doc Walter James Curley b: 3/12/1874, Upton, MA d: 9/23/1920, Worcester, MA BR/TR Deb: 9/12/1899

YEAR TM-L	G	AB	R	H	2B	3B	HR	RBI	BB	SO	SB	CS	AVG	OBP	SLG	OPS	OPS+	BR/A	RC	RC/G	FR	G/POS	WS	TPW
1899 Chi-N	10	37	7	4	0	1	0	2	3	....	0	....	.108	.233	.162	.395	9	-5	2	1.22	-1	2-10	0	-0.4

• CURREN, Pete Peter Curren b: Baltimore, MD, 175 lbs. Deb: 9/12/1876

YEAR TM-L	G	AB	R	H	2B	3B	HR	RBI	BB	SO	SB	CS	AVG	OBP	SLG	OPS	OPS+	BR/A	RC	RC/G	FR	G/POS	WS	TPW
1876 Phi-N	3	12	5	4	1	0	0	2	0	0	....	....	.333	.333	.417	.750	150	1	2	5.98	-1	/C-2,0-1	0	0.0

• CURRIN, Perry Perry Gilmore Currin b: 9/27/1928, Washington, DC BL/TR, 6', 175 lbs. Deb: 6/29/1947

YEAR TM-L	G	AB	R	H	2B	3B	HR	RBI	BB	SO	SB	CS	AVG	OBP	SLG	OPS	OPS+	BR/A	RC	RC/G	FR	G/POS	WS	TPW
1947 StL-A	3	2	0	0	0	0	0	0	1	0	0	0	.000	.333	.000	.333	-3	-0	0	1.17	0	/S-1	0	0.0

• CURRY, Jim James L. Curry b: 3/10/1893, Camden, NJ d: 8/2/1938, Grenloch, NJ BR/TR, 5'11", 160 lbs. Deb: 10/2/1909

YEAR TM-L	G	AB	R	H	2B	3B	HR	RBI	BB	SO	SB	CS	AVG	OBP	SLG	OPS	OPS+	BR/A	RC	RC/G	FR	G/POS	WS	TPW
1909 Phi-A	1	4	1	1	0	0	0	0	0	....	0	....	.250	.250	.250	.500	57	-0	0	2.04	-1	/2-1	0	-0.1
1911 NY-A	4	11	3	2	0	0	0	0	1	....	0	....	.182	.250	.182	.432	20	-1	1	1.56	-3	/2-4	0	-0.4
1918 Det-A	5	20	1	5	1	0	0	0	0	0	0	....	.250	.286	.300	.586	80	-1	2	2.72	0	/2-5	0	-0.1
Total 3	10	35	5	8	1	0	0	0	1	0	0	....	.229	.270	.257	.527	57	-2	2	2.23	-4	/2-10	0	-0.5

• CURRY, Tony George Anthony Curry b: 12/22/1938, Nassau, Bahamas BL/TL, 5'11", 185 lbs. Deb: 4/12/1960 Career OF: 59-3-14

YEAR TM-L	G	AB	R	H	2B	3B	HR	RBI	BB	SO	SB	CS	AVG	OBP	SLG	OPS	OPS+	BR/A	RC	RC/G	FR	G/POS	WS	TPW
1960 Phi-N	95	245	26	64	14	2	6	34	16	53	0	2	.261	.309	.408	.717	94	-3	31	4.50	-4	0-64(51-3-14)	5	-1.0
1961 Phi-N	15	36	3	7	2	0	0	3	1	8	0	0	.194	.216	.250	.466	24	-4	2	1.86	0	/0-8(8-0-0)	0	-0.4
1966 Cle-A	19	16	4	2	0	0	0	3	3	8	0	0	.125	.263	.125	.388	16	-1	1	1.41	0	....	0	-0.2
Total 3	129	297	33	73	16	2	6	40	20	69	0	2	.246	.296	.374	.669	81	-9	34	3.98	-3	/0-72	5	-1.6

• CURTIS, Chad Chad David Curtis b: 11/6/1968, Marion, IN BR/TR, 5'10", 175 lbs. Deb: 4/8/1992 Career OF: 388-698-126

YEAR TM-L	G	AB	R	H	2B	3B	HR	RBI	BB	SO	SB	CS	AVG	OBP	SLG	OPS	OPS+	BR/A	RC	RC/G	FR	G/POS	WS	TPW
1992 Cal-A	139	441	59	114	16	2	10	46	51	71	43	18	.259	.343	.372	.715	100	2	58	4.30	6	*0-135(48-35-62)/D-1	13	0.5
1993 Cal-A	152	583	94	166	25	3	6	59	70	89	48	24	.285	.365	.369	.734	95	-2	79	4.54	5	*0-151(0-151-0)/2-3	14	0.4
1994 Cal-A	114	453	67	116	23	4	11	50	37	69	25	11	.256	.319	.397	.717	82	-12	57	4.15	7	*0-114(0-114-0)	8	-0.4
1995 Det-A	144	586	96	157	29	3	21	67	70	93	27	15	.268	.353	.435	.788	104	3	90	5.26	-8	*0-144(0-144-0)	15	-0.4
1996 Det-A	104	400	65	105	20	1	10	37	53	73	16	10	.263	.350	.393	.743	88	-8	54	4.39	0	*0-104(48-80-0)	6	-0.8
*LA-N	43	104	20	22	5	0	2	9	17	15	2	1	.212	.322	.317	.640	75	-3	12	3.78	0	0-40(0-40-0)	2	-0.3
1997 Cle-A	22	29	8	6	1	0	3	5	7	10	0	0	.207	.361	.552	.913	129	1	6	6.68	-1	0-19(3-12-4)	1	0.1
*NY-A	93	320	51	93	21	1	12	50	36	49	12	6	.291	.371	.475	.846	120	10	57	6.18	-3	0-92(56-55-9)	11	0.5
Yr.	115	349	59	99	22	1	15	55	43	59	12	6	.284	.370	.481	.852	121	11	63	6.22	-3	*0-111(59-67-13)	12	0.5
1998*NY-A	151	456	79	111	21	1	10	56	75	80	21	5	.243	.359	.360	.718	91	-1	65	4.74	1	*0-148(100-45-9)/D-2	14	-0.3
1999*NY-A	96	195	37	51	6	0	5	24	43	35	8	4	.262	.402	.369	.772	100	3	32	5.47	-1	0-81(72-6-3),D-14	5	-0.1
2000 Tex-A	108	335	48	91	25	1	8	48	37	71	3	3	.272	.346	.424	.770	92	-5	47	4.77	-4	0-80(51-0-30),D-16	6	-1.2
2001 Tex-A	38	115	24	29	3	0	3	10	14	21	7	1	.252	.338	.357	.695	81	-2	15	4.48	2	0-33(10-16-9)/D-2	3	0.0
Total 10	1204	4017	648	1061	195	16	101	461	510	676	212	98	.264	.353	.396	.749	96	-14	572	4.76	3	*0-1141/D-35,2-3	98	-2.2

• CURTIS, Fred Frederick Marion Curtis b: 10/30/1880, Beaver Lake, MI d: 4/5/1939, Minneapolis, MN BR/TR, 6'1" Deb: 7/24/1905

YEAR TM-L	G	AB	R	H	2B	3B	HR	RBI	BB	SO	SB	CS	AVG	OBP	SLG	OPS	OPS+	BR/A	RC	RC/G	FR	G/POS	WS	TPW
1905 NY-A	2	9	0	2	1	0	0	2	1	....	1	....	.222	.300	.333	.633	90	-0	1	4.66	0	/1-2	0	0.0

• CURTIS, Gene Eugene Holmes "Eude" Curtis b: 5/5/1883, Bethany, WV d: 1/1/1919, Steubenville, OH BR/TR, 6'3", 220 lbs. Deb: 9/21/1903

YEAR TM-L	G	AB	R	H	2B	3B	HR	RBI	BB	SO	SB	CS	AVG	OBP	SLG	OPS	OPS+	BR/A	RC	RC/G	FR	G/POS	WS	TPW
1903 Pit-N	5	19	2	8	1	0	0	3	1	....	0	....	.421	.450	.474	.924	158	1	4	10.00	0	/0-5(5-0-0)	1	0.1

• CURTIS, Harry Harry Albert Curtis b: 2/19/1883, Portland, ME d: 8/1/1951, Evanston, IL TR, 5'10.5", 170 lbs. Deb: 8/28/1907

YEAR TM-L	G	AB	R	H	2B	3B	HR	RBI	BB	SO	SB	CS	AVG	OBP	SLG	OPS	OPS+	BR/A	RC	RC/G	FR	G/POS	WS	TPW
1907 NY-N	6	9	2	2	0	0	0	1	2	....	....	....	.222	.364	.222	.586	81	-0	1	5.54	-1	/C-6	0	-0.1

• CURTISS, Ervin Ervin Duane Curtiss b: 12/27/1861, Coldwater, MI d: 2/14/1945, North Adams, MA BL/TL, 5'8.5", 157 lbs. Deb: 7/15/1891

YEAR TM-L	G	AB	R	H	2B	3B	HR	RBI	BB	SO	SB	CS	AVG	OBP	SLG	OPS	OPS+	BR/A	RC	RC/G	FR	G/POS	WS	TPW
1891 Cin-N	27	108	11	29	3	3	1	13	9	19	3	....	.269	.331	.380	.710	106	0	15	5.09	0	0-27(0-24-3)	3	-0.1
Was-a	29	103	17	26	3	2	0	12	13	16	2	....	.252	.347	.320	.668	95	-0	12	4.29	-3	0-29(0-20-9)	2	-0.3

• CURTRIGHT, Guy Guy Paxton Curtright b: 10/18/1912, Holliday, MO d: 8/23/1997, Sun City Center, FL BR/TR, 5'11", 200 lbs. Deb: 4/21/1943 Career OF: 191-48-41

YEAR TM-L	G	AB	R	H	2B	3B	HR	RBI	BB	SO	SB	CS	AVG	OBP	SLG	OPS	OPS+	BR/A	RC	RC/G	FR	G/POS	WS	TPW
1943 Chi-A	138	488	67	142	20	7	3	48	69	60	13	12	.291	.382	.379	.761	123	15	74	5.24	-2	*0-128(128-0-0)	21	0.5
1944 Chi-A	72	198	22	50	8	2	2	23	23	21	4	3	.253	.330	.343	.674	94	-2	23	3.96	2	0-51(35-0-17)	5	-0.3
1945 Chi-A	98	324	51	91	15	7	4	32	39	29	3	4	.281	.358	.407	.766	125	10	49	5.33	1	0-84(26-46-13)	13	0.7
1946 Chi-A	23	55	7	11	2	0	0	5	11	14	0	1	.200	.333	.236	.570	63	-3	4	2.47	1	0-15(2-2-11)	1	-0.2
Total 4	331	1065	147	294	45	16	9	108	142	124	20	20	.276	.363	.374	.737	115	21	150	4.86	1	0-278	40	0.7

• CUSICK, Jack John Peter Cusick b: 6/12/1928, Weehawken, NJ d: 11/17/1989, Englewood, NJ BR/TR, 6', 170 lbs. Deb: 4/24/1951

YEAR TM-L	G	AB	R	H	2B	3B	HR	RBI	BB	SO	SB	CS	AVG	OBP	SLG	OPS	OPS+	BR/A	RC	RC/G	FR	G/POS	WS	TPW
1951 Chi-N	65	164	16	29	3	2	2	16	17	29	2	1	.177	.254	.256	.510	37	-15	11	2.10	-5	S-56	2	-1.6
1952 Bos-N	49	78	5	13	1	0	0	6	6	9	0	1	.167	.226	.179	.406	14	-9	2	.85	-4	S-28/3-3	1	-1.3
Total 2	114	242	21	42	4	2	2	22	23	38	2	2	.174	.245	.231	.477	30	-24	13	1.69	-9	/S-84,3-3	3	-2.9

• CUSICK, Tony Andrew Daniel "Andy" Cusick b: 12/1857, Limerick, Ireland d: 8/6/1929, Chicago, IL BR/TR, 5'9.5", 190 lbs. Deb: 8/21/1884 U Career OF: 2-2-3

YEAR TM-L	G	AB	R	H	2B	3B	HR	RBI	BB	SO	SB	CS	AVG	OBP	SLG	OPS	OPS+	BR/A	RC	RC/G	FR	G/POS	WS	TPW
1884 Wil-U	11	34	0	5	0	0	0	....	1	....	....	....	.147	.171	.147	.318	8	-3	1	.85	-1	/C-6,0-3(1-1-1),S-3,2-1,3-1	0	-0.3
Phi-N	9	29	2	4	0	0	0	1	0	3	....	....	.138	.138	.138	.276	-14	-4	1	.62	1	/C-9	0	-0.1
1885 Phi-N	39	141	12	25	1	0	0	5	1	24	....	....	.177	.183	.184	.367	19	-12	5	1.14	-4	C-38/0-1	1	-1.2
1886 Phi-N	29	104	10	23	5	1	0	4	3	14	1	....	.221	.243	.288	.531	60	-5	8	2.57	-1	C-25/0-3(1-0-2),1-1	2	-0.4
1887 Phi-N	7	27	3	10	1	0	0	5	3	1	0	....	.370	.393	.333	.726	98	0	3	5.02	-2	/C-4,1-3,2-1	1	-0.2
Total 4	95	335	27	67	7	1	0	15	8	42	1	....	.200	.214	.220	.434	35	-24	17	1.74	-7	/C-82,0-7,1-4,S-3,2-2,3-1	4	-2.2

• CUST, Jack John Joseph Cust b: 1/16/1979, Flemington, NJ BL/TR, 6'2", 205 lbs. Deb: 9/26/2001 Career OF: 20-0-0

YEAR TM-L	G	AB	R	H	2B	3B	HR	RBI	BB	SO	SB	CS	AVG	OBP	SLG	OPS	OPS+	BR/A	RC	RC/G	FR	G/POS	WS	TPW
2001 Ari-N	3	2	0	1	0	0	0	0	1	0	0	0	.500	.667	.500	1.167	197	0	1	22.68	0	/0-1	0	0.0
2002 Col-N	35	65	8	11	2	0	1	8	12	32	0	1	.169	.299	.246	.545	39	-6	5	2.19	-1	0-18(18-0-0)	0	-0.8
2003 Bal-A	27	73	7	19	7	0	4	11	10	25	0	0	.260	.357	.521	.878	132	3	15	7.30	0	D-21/0-1	4	0.3
Total 3	65	140	15	31	9	0	5	19	23	57	0	1	.221	.335	.393	.728	90	-2	20	4.79	-1	/D-21,0-20	4	-0.5

YEAR TM-L	G	AB	R	H	2B	3B	HR	RBI	BB	SO	SB	CS	AVG	OBP	SLG	OPS	OPS+	BR/A	RC	RC/G	FR	G/POS	WS	TPW
• CUTHBERT, Ned	Edgar Edward Cuthbert b: 6/20/1845, Philadelphia, PA d: 2/6/1905, St. Louis, MO BR/TR, 5'6", 140 lbs. Deb: 5/20/1871 M/U NA OF: 245-4-0 Career OF: 153-45-1																							
1871 Ath-n	28	150	47	37	7	5	3	30	10	2	16	2	.247	.294	.420	.714	103	3	24	6.52	3	*0-27(27-0-0)/C-1	....	0.4
1872 Ath-n	47	260	83	88	10	0	1	47	6	10	14	4	.338	.353	.388	.742	127	9	42	7.34	-2	*0-47(47-0-0)	....	0.6
1873 Phi-n	51	278	78	77	5	3	2	33	2	4	**13**	2	.277	.282	.338	.620	80	-6	31	4.65	-4	*0-51(51-0-0)	....	-0.6
1874 Chi-n	58	295	65	79	6	1	2	22	5	5	8	0	.268	.280	.315	.595	90	-2	29	4.03	0	*0-55(55-2-0)/C-4	....	0.0
1875 StL-n	68	319	68	78	9	2	0	17	3	8	18	1	.245	.252	.285	.537	95	4	28	3.43	-8	*0-67(65-2-0)/C-3,2-1	....	-0.2
1876 StL-N	63	290	46	70	10	1	0	25	7	4	....	....	.241	.266	.290	.555	89	-2	22	2.93	-5	*0-63(63-0-0)	8	-1.0
1877 Cin-N	12	56	6	10	5	0	0	2	1	2	....	....	.179	.193	.268	.461	49	-3	3	1.77	4	0-12(12-0-0)	0	0.0
1882 StL-a	60	233	28	52	16	5	0	....	17	....	....	....	.223	.276	.335	.611	101	0	22	3.41	-5	*0-60(60-0-0)	7	-0.6
1883 StL-a	21	71	3	12	1	0	0	3	4	....	....	....	.169	.213	.183	.396	27	-6	3	1.35	0	0-20(18-1-1)/1-1	1	-0.6
1884 Bal-U	44	168	29	34	5	0	0	....	10	....	....	....	.202	.247	.232	.479	57	-8	10	2.06	-5	0-44(0-44-0)	2	-1.3
Total 5 n	252	1302	341	359	37	11	8	149	26	29	69	9	.276	.290	.339	.629	98	9	153	4.92	-11	0-247/C-8,2-1	....	0.2
Total 5	200	818	112	178	37	6	0	30	39	6	....	....	.218	.255	.280	.535	78	-18	60	2.65	-12	0-199/1-1	18	-3.4
• CUTSHAW, George	George William "Clancy,Cutty" Cutshaw b: 7/29/1886, Wilmington, IL d: 8/22/1973, San Diego, CA BR/TR, 5'9", 160 lbs. Deb: 4/25/1912																							
1912 Bro-N	102	357	41	100	14	4	0	28	31	16	16	....	.280	.341	.342	.683	91	-4	47	4.45	-1	2-91/3-5,S-1	8	-0.4
1913 Bro-N	147	592	72	158	23	13	7	80	39	22	39	....	.267	.315	.385	.701	97	-4	80	4.50	28	*2-147	15	2.7
1914 Bro-N	153	583	69	150	22	12	2	78	30	32	34	....	.257	.297	.346	.644	89	-10	67	3.84	31	*2-153	15	2.5
1915 Bro-N	154	566	68	139	18	9	0	62	34	35	28	23	.246	.293	.309	.602	81	-18	53	3.00	24	*2-154	16	1.0
1916*Bro-N	154	581	58	151	21	4	2	63	25	32	27	20	.260	.292	.320	.612	85	-14	58	3.13	27	*2-154	16	1.8
1917 Bro-N	135	487	42	126	17	7	4	49	21	26	22	....	.259	.292	.347	.639	93	-5	54	3.67	-4	*2-134	12	-0.8
1918 Pit-N	126	463	56	132	16	10	5	68	27	18	25	....	.285	.326	.395	.721	115	7	66	4.79	4	*2-126	17	1.5
1919 Pit-N	139	512	49	124	15	8	3	51	30	22	36	....	.242	.287	.320	.607	79	-13	54	3.49	17	*2-139	13	0.6
1920 Pit-N	131	488	56	123	16	8	0	47	23	10	17	14	.252	.287	.318	.605	71	-19	44	2.80	18	*2-129	9	0.2
1921 Pit-N	98	350	46	119	18	4	0	53	11	11	14	5	.340	.362	.414	.776	102	3	52	5.58	2	2-84	11	0.8
1922 Det-A	132	499	57	133	14	8	2	61	20	13	11	5	.267	.300	.339	.639	68	-23	52	3.40	-2	*2-132	7	-2.1
1923 Det-A	45	143	15	32	1	2	0	13	9	5	2	1	.224	.279	.259	.538	43	-11	12	2.39	3	2-43/3-2	1	-0.7
Total 12	1516	5621	629	1487	195	89	25	653	300	242	271	68	.265	.305	.344	.649	87	-113	639	3.73	148	*2-1486/3-7,S-1	140	7.2
• CUYLER, Kiki	Hazen Shirley Cuyler b: 8/30/1898, Harrisville, MI d: 2/11/1950, Ann Arbor, MI BR/TR, 5'10.5", 180 lbs. Deb: 9/29/1921 C HOF: 1968 Career OF: 331-700-796																							
1921 Pit-N	1	3	0	0	0	0	0	0	0	1	0	0	.000	.000	.000	.000	-98	-1	0	.00	-0	/0-1	0	-0.1
1922 Pit-N	1	0	0	0	0	0	0	0	0	0	0	0	....	....	....	....	-99	0	0	....	0	....	0	0.0
1923 Pit-N	11	40	4	10	1	1	0	2	5	3	2	3	.250	.348	.325	.673	77	-2	4	3.39	0	0-11(10-3-0)	0	-0.3
1924 Pit-N	117	466	94	165	27	16	9	85	30	62	32	11	.354	.402	.539	.940	147	34	101	8.24	6	*0-114(78-4-35)	24	3.0
1925*Pit-N	153	617	**144**	220	43	**26**	18	102	58	56	41	13	.357	.423	.598	1.021	148	49	158	9.92	0	*0-153(0-25-129)	34	3.4
1926 Pit-N	157	614	**113**	197	31	15	8	92	50	66	**35**	....	.321	.380	.459	.840	119	16	105	6.25	5	*0-157(62-79-18)	26	1.2
1927 Pit-N	85	285	60	88	13	7	3	31	37	36	20	....	.309	.394	.435	.829	114	7	49	6.35	-4	0-73(12-49-13)	12	-0.1
1928 Chi-N	133	499	92	142	25	9	17	79	51	61	**37**	....	.285	.359	.473	.832	117	12	84	5.73	6	*0-127(13-7-108)	18	0.8
1929*Chi-N	139	509	111	183	29	7	15	102	66	56	**43**	....	.360	.438	.532	.970	139	34	118	8.94	3	*0-129(16-8-114)	25	2.4
1930 Chi-N	156	642	155	228	50	17	13	134	72	49	**37**	....	.355	.428	.547	.975	133	36	148	8.92	10	*0-156(29-0-131)	29	3.0
1931 Chi-N	154	613	110	202	37	12	9	88	72	54	13	....	.330	.404	.473	.877	133	31	122	7.38	-8	*0-153(0-66-84)	26	1.6
1932*Chi-N	110	446	58	130	19	9	10	77	29	43	9	....	.291	.340	.442	.782	109	5	68	5.45	-6	*0-109(0-49-60)	15	-0.6
1933 Chi-N	70	262	37	83	13	3	5	35	21	29	4	....	.317	.376	.447	.823	135	12	43	5.97	-2	0-69(35-15-19)	11	0.8
1934 Chi-N★	142	559	80	189	**42**	8	6	69	31	62	15	....	.338	.377	.474	.851	129	22	101	6.96	1	*0-142(0-136-6)	23	1.9
1935 Chi-N	45	157	22	42	5	1	4	18	10	16	3	....	.268	.331	.389	.720	92	-2	21	4.62	1	0-42(0-41-2)	5	-0.2
Cin-N	62	223	36	56	8	3	2	22	27	18	5	....	.251	.337	.341	.678	85	-4	28	4.48	-3	0-57(5-49-3)	6	-0.8
Yr.	107	380	58	98	13	4	6	40	37	34	8	....	.258	.335	.361	.695	88	-5	49	4.54	-3	0-99(5-90-5)	11	-1.1
1936 Cin-N	144	567	96	185	29	11	7	74	47	67	16	....	.326	.380	.453	.833	132	25	102	6.95	-2	*0-140(22-105-14)	24	1.8
1937 Cin-N	117	406	48	110	12	4	0	32	36	50	10	....	.271	.333	.320	.654	82	-9	43	3.69	-3	*0-106(41-47-16)	6	-1.5
1938 Bro-N	82	253	45	69	10	8	2	23	34	23	6	....	.273	.363	.399	.763	107	3	39	5.47	2	0-68(8-17-43)	8	0.2
Total 18	1879	7161	1305	2299	394	157	128	1065	676	752	328	27	.321	.386	.474	.860	124	269	1336	6.88	6	*0-1807	292	16.5
• CUYLER, Milt	Milton Cuyler b: 10/7/1968, Macon, GA BB/TR, 5'10", 185 lbs. Deb: 9/6/1990 Career OF: 48-398-33																							
1990 Det-A	19	51	8	13	3	1	0	8	5	10	1	2	.255	.321	.353	.674	88	-1	5	3.34	1	0-17(0-17-1)	2	-0.1
1991 Det-A	154	475	77	122	15	7	3	33	52	92	41	10	.257	.336	.337	.673	86	-3	61	4.36	5	*0-151(1-150-0)	9	-0.1
1992 Det-A	89	291	39	70	11	1	3	28	10	62	8	5	.241	.275	.316	.592	65	-15	25	2.83	-1	0-89(0-88-1)	4	-1.7
1993 Det-A	82	249	46	53	11	7	0	19	19	53	13	2	.213	.277	.313	.590	59	-13	24	3.15	0	0-80(0-80-0)	2	-1.2
1994 Det-A	48	116	20	28	3	1	1	11	13	21	5	3	.241	.323	.310	.633	64	-6	12	3.28	-2	0-45(13-29-8)	1	-0.8
1995 Det-A	41	88	15	18	1	4	0	5	8	16	2	1	.205	.271	.307	.578	50	-7	8	2.94	-2	0-36(34-1-1)/D-2	0	-0.9
1996 Bos-A	50	110	19	22	1	2	2	12	13	19	7	3	.200	.302	.300	.602	52	-8	11	3.08	-4	0-45(0-30-22)/D-2	2	-1.1
1998 Tex-A	7	6	3	3	2	0	1	3	1	0	0	0	.500	.571	1.333	1.905	360	2	5	42.48	-0	/D-3,0-3(0-3-0)	1	0.2
Total 8	490	1386	227	329	47	23	10	119	121	273	77	26	.237	.306	.326	.632	71	-51	152	3.59	-4	0-466/D-7	21	-5.8
• CYPERT, Al	Alfred Boyd "Cy" Cypert b: 8/8/1889, Little Rock, AR d: 1/9/1973, Washington, DC BR/TR, 5'10.5", 150 lbs. Deb: 6/27/1914																							
1914 Cle-A	1	1	0	0	0	0	0	0	0	1	0	....	.000	.000	.000	.000	-96	-0	0	.00	0	/3-1	0	-0.1
• DADE, Paul	Lonnie Paul Dade b: 12/7/1951, Seattle, WA BR/TR, 6'1", 195 lbs. Deb: 9/12/1975 Career OF: 62-41-142																							
1975 Cal-A	11	30	5	6	4	0	0	1	6	7	0	0	.200	.333	.333	.667	96	0	4	4.34	0	/D-7,0-3(1-0-2),3-1	1	0.0
1976 Cal-A	13	9	2	1	0	0	0	1	3	3	0	0	.111	.333	.111	.444	36	-0	0	1.34	0	/0-4(3-0-1),2-2,3-1,D-1	0	-0.1
1977 Cle-A	134	461	65	134	15	3	3	45	32	58	16	8	.291	.339	.356	.695	93	-4	54	4.08	0	0-99(32-28-46),3-26/D-7,2	10	-0.7
1978 Cle-A	93	307	37	78	12	1	3	20	34	45	12	9	.254	.332	.329	.661	88	-5	35	3.82	0	0-81(1-7-75)/D-9	7	-0.9
1979 Cle-A	44	170	22	48	4	1	3	18	12	22	12	6	.282	.330	.371	.700	88	-3	21	4.32	0	0-37(20-0-17)/D-4,3-2	4	-0.5
SD-N	76	283	38	78	19	2	1	19	14	48	13	5	.276	.314	.367	.682	91	-4	32	3.85	4	3-70/0-4(1-3-0)	7	0.0
1980 SD-N	68	53	17	10	0	0	0	3	12	10	4	5	.189	.338	.189	.527	54	-4	4	1.89	-2	3-21/0-8(4-3-1),2-1	0	-0.6
Total 6	439	1313	186	355	54	7	10	107	113	193	57	33	.270	.331	.345	.676	88	-20	151	3.88	3	0-236,3-121/D-28,2-4	29	-2.9
• DAGRES, Angelo	Angelo George "Junior" Dagres b: 8/22/1934, Newburyport, MA BL/TL, 5'11", 175 lbs. Deb: 9/11/1955																							
1955 Bal-A	8	15	5	4	0	0	0	3	1	2	0	0	.267	.313	.267	.579	61	-1	2	2.95	-1	/0-5(1-0-4)	0	-0.2
• DAHLEN, Bill	William Frederick "Bad Bill" Dahlen b: 1/5/1870, Nelliston, NY d: 12/5/1950, Brooklyn, NY BR/TR, 5'9", 180 lbs. Deb: 4/22/1891 M Career OF: 36-11-11																							
1891 Chi-N	135	549	114	143	18	13	9	76	67	60	21	....	.260	.348	.390	.738	115	11	84	5.58	5	3-84,0-37(30-0-7),S-15	21	1.5
1892 Chi-N	143	581	114	169	23	19	5	58	45	56	60	....	.291	.347	.422	.769	131	19	109	7.11	21	S-72,3-68/0-2(0-2-0),2-1	32	4.2
1893 Chi-N	116	485	113	146	28	15	5	64	58	30	31	....	.301	.381	.452	.833	123	15	98	7.64	6	*S-88,0-17(5-8-4),2-10/3-3	17	2.1
1894 Chi-N	122	507	150	182	32	14	15	108	76	33	42	....	.359	.445	.566	1.011	135	30	150	12.02	16	S-66,3-55	21	3.9
1895 Chi-N	129	516	106	131	19	10	7	62	61	51	38	....	.254	.344	.370	.714	79	-17	81	5.63	27	*S-129/0-1	20	1.3
1896 Chi-N	125	474	137	167	30	19	9	74	64	36	51	....	.352	.438	.553	.990	154	38	142	11.29	24	*S-125	31	5.8
1897 Chi-N	75	276	67	80	18	8	6	40	43	....	15	....	.290	.399	.478	.877	126	11	62	7.80	10	S-75	14	2.1
1898 Chi-N	142	521	96	151	35	8	1	79	58	....	27	....	.290	.385	.393	.779	124	19	94	6.43	22	*S-142	27	4.5
1899 Bro-N	121	428	87	121	22	7	4	76	67	....	29	....	.283	.398	.395	.793	115	13	81	6.93	15	*S-110,3-11	23	3.1
1900*Bro-N	133	483	87	125	16	11	1	69	73	....	31	....	.259	.364	.344	.708	90	-4	74	5.43	27	*S-133	21	2.7
1901 Bro-N	131	511	69	136	17	9	4	82	30	....	23	....	.266	.313	.358	.671	92	-6	67	4.64	15	*S-129/2-2	18	1.3
1902 Bro-N	138	527	67	139	25	8	2	74	43	....	20	....	.264	.329	.353	.682	110	6	71	4.71	12	*S-138	23	2.4
1903 Bro-N	138	474	71	124	17	9	1	64	82	....	34	....	.262	.373	.342	.715	107	9	76	5.63	-26	*S-138	23	-1.2
1904 NY-N	145	523	70	140	26	2	2	**80**	44	....	47	....	.268	.326	.337	.662	100	0	76	4.99	19	*S-145	25	2.6
1905*NY-N	148	520	67	126	20	4	7	81	62	....	37	....	.242	.337	.337	.673	99	1	74	4.80	10	*S-147/0-1	24	1.6
1906 NY-N	143	471	63	113	18	3	1	49	76	....	16	....	.240	.357	.297	.655	102	6	58	4.15	-21	*S-143	19	-1.1
1907 NY-N	143	464	40	96	20	1	0	34	51	....	11	....	.207	.291	.254	.545	69	-16	40	2.74	8	*S-143	13	-0.3

YEAR TM-L	G	AB	R	H	2B	3B	HR	RBI	BB	SO	SB	CS	AVG	OBP	SLG	OPS	OPS+	BR/A	RC	RC/G	FR	G/POS	WS	TPW
1908 Bos-N	144	524	50	125	23	2	3	48	35	....	10	....	.239	.296	.307	.604	94	-4	51	3.17	26	*S-144	16	3.1
1909 Bos-N	69	197	22	46	6	1	2	16	29	....	4	....	.234	.332	.305	.636	93	-1	21	3.56	2	S-49/2-6,3-2	6	0.3
1910 Bro-N	3	2	0	0	0	0	0	0	0	0	0	....	.000	.000	.000	.000	-103	-0	0	.00	0	....	0	-0.1
1911 Bro-N	1	3	0	0	0	0	0	0	0	3	0	....	.000	.000	.000	.000	-104	-1	0	.00	1	/S-1	0	0.0
Total 21	2444	9036	1590	2460	413	163	84	1234	1064	269	547	....	.272	.358	.382	.740	109	129	1509	5.92	219	*S-2132,3-223/0-58,2-19	394	39.8

• DAHLGREN, Babe

Ellsworth Tenney Dahlgren b: 6/15/1912, San Francisco, CA d: 9/4/1996, Arcadia, CA BR/TR, 6', 190 lbs. Deb: 4/16/1935 C

YEAR TM-L	G	AB	R	H	2B	3B	HR	RBI	BB	SO	SB	CS	AVG	OBP	SLG	OPS	OPS+	BR/A	RC	RC/G	FR	G/POS	WS	TPW
1935 Bos-A	149	525	77	138	27	7	9	63	56	67	6	5	.263	.337	.392	.730	83	-15	71	4.68	-7	*1-149	8	-3.3
1936 Bos-A	16	57	6	16	3	1	1	7	7	1	2	1	.281	.359	.421	.780	87	-1	9	5.48	0	1-16	1	-0.2
1937 NY-A	1	1	0	0	0	0	0	0	0	0	0	0	.000	.000	.000	.000	-99	-0	0	.00	0	....	0	0.0
1938 NY-A	27	43	8	8	1	0	0	1	1	7	0	0	.186	.205	.209	.414	4	-6	2	1.38	-3	/3-8,1-6	0	-0.9
1939★NY-A	144	531	71	125	18	6	15	89	57	54	2	3	.235	.312	.377	.689	76	-21	61	3.80	-1	*1-144	8	-3.3
1940 NY-A	155	568	51	150	24	4	12	73	46	54	1	1	.264	.325	.384	.709	86	-12	69	4.22	-0	*1-155	11	-2.5
1941 Bos-N	44	166	20	39	8	1	7	30	16	13	0	....	.235	.306	.422	.728	108	1	20	4.02	1	1-39/3-5	4	-0.1
Chi-N	99	359	50	101	20	1	16	59	43	39	2	....	.281	.360	.476	.836	139	18	62	6.30	-3	1-98	15	0.6
Yr.	143	525	70	140	28	2	23	89	59	52	2	....	.267	.343	.459	.802	129	19	82	5.53	-2	*1-137/3-5	19	0.5
1942 Chi-N	17	56	4	12	1	0	0	6	4	2	0	....	.214	.267	.232	.499	48	-4	3	1.75	0	1-14	0	-0.5
StL-A	2	2	0	0	0	0	0	0	0	0	0	0	.000	.000	.000	.000	-99	-0	0	.00	0	....	0	-0.1
Bro-N	17	19	2	1	0	0	0	0	4	5	0	....	.053	.217	.053	.270	-19	-3	0	.50	1	1-10	0	-0.3
Yr.	34	75	6	13	1	0	0	6	8	7	0	....	.173	.253	.187	.440	30	-6	3	1.39	1	1-24	0	-0.8
1943 Phi-N★	136	508	55	146	19	2	5	56	50	39	2	....	.287	.354	.362	.716	111	8	62	4.33	-7	1-73,3-35,S-25/C-1	14	-0.1
1944 Pit-N	158	599	67	173	28	7	12	101	47	56	2	....	.289	.347	.419	.766	110	7	84	5.00	6	*1-158	19	0.5
1945 Pit-N	144	531	57	133	24	8	5	75	51	51	1	....	.250	.318	.354	.673	84	-12	57	3.57	-5	*1-144	9	-2.5
1946 StL-A	28	80	2	14	1	0	0	9	8	13	0	1	.175	.250	.188	.438	22	-9	4	1.48	0	1-24	0	-0.9
Total 12	1137	4045	470	1056	174	37	82	569	390	401	18	11	.261	.329	.383	.713	93	-49	505	4.29	-19	*1-1030/3-48,S-25,C-1	89	-13.7

• DAILEY, John

John G. Dailey b: Brooklyn, NY Deb: 4/29/1875

YEAR TM-L	G	AB	R	H	2B	3B	HR	RBI	BB	SO	SB	CS	AVG	OBP	SLG	OPS	OPS+	BR/A	RC	RC/G	FR	G/POS	WS	TPW
1875 Was-n	27	110	16	20	5	4	0	13	0	1	3	2	.182	.182	.300	.482	67	-3	7	2.15	-5	S-20/3-5,2-2	....	-0.7
Atl-n	2	8	3	1	0	0	0	0	0	1	0	0	.125	.125	.125	.250	-15	-1	0	.54	-1	/O-2(0-0-2),1-1,S-1	....	-0.2
Yr.	29	118	19	21	5	4	0	13	0	2	3	2	.178	.178	.288	.466	61	-4	7	2.04	-6	S-21/3-5,2-2,O-2(0-0-2),1	....	-0.9

• DAILEY, Vince

Vincent Perry Dailey b: 12/25/1864, Osceola, NY d: 11/14/1919, Hornell, NY, 6', 200 lbs. Deb: 4/21/1890

YEAR TM-L	G	AB	R	H	2B	3B	HR	RBI	BB	SO	SB	CS	AVG	OBP	SLG	OPS	OPS+	BR/A	RC	RC/G	FR	G/POS	WS	TPW
1890 Cle-N	64	246	41	71	5	7	0	32	33	23	17	....	.289	.373	.366	.739	118	7	41	6.19	1	O-64(0-0-64)/P-2	7	0.2

• DAILY, Con

Cornelius F. Daily b: 9/11/1864, Blackstone, MA d: 6/14/1928, Brooklyn, NY BL, 6', 192 lbs. Deb: 6/9/1884 U Career OF: 8-9-28

YEAR TM-L	G	AB	R	H	2B	3B	HR	RBI	BB	SO	SB	CS	AVG	OBP	SLG	OPS	OPS+	BR/A	RC	RC/G	FR	G/POS	WS	TPW
1884 Phi-U	2	8	0	0	0	0	0	....	0	....	....	....	.000	.000	.000	.000	-108	-2	0	.00	-1	/C-2	0	-0.2
1885 Pro-N	60	223	20	58	6	1	0	19	12	20	....	....	.260	.298	.296	.594	96	-0	20	3.30	1	C-48/1-7,O-6(1-3-2)	8	0.4
1886 Bos-N	50	180	25	43	4	2	0	21	19	29	2	....	.239	.312	.283	.595	85	-2	17	3.34	-7	C-49/O-1	4	-0.4
1887 Bos-N	36	129	12	28	5	0	0	13	9	8	7	....	.217	.229	.200	.429	21	-13	7	1.91	-2	C-36	1	-1.0
1888 Ind-N	57	202	14	44	6	1	0	14	10	28	15	....	.218	.255	.257	.512	62	-9	17	2.99	-4	C-42/1-5,3-5,O-5(0-0-5),2	3	-0.9
1889 Ind-N	62	219	35	55	6	2	0	26	28	21	14	....	.251	.347	.297	.643	79	-5	28	4.54	-11	C-51/1-6,O-6(1-3-2),3-1	4	-1.0
1890 Bro-P	46	168	20	42	6	3	0	35	15	14	6	....	.250	.315	.321	.637	66	-9	19	4.15	-4	C-40/1-6,O-1	4	-0.9
1891 Bro-N	60	206	25	66	10	1	0	30	15	13	7	....	.320	.378	.379	.756	121	6	33	6.35	2	C-55/O-3(0-0-3),S-2,1-1	8	1.1
1892 Bro-N	80	278	38	65	10	1	0	28	38	21	18	....	.234	.328	.277	.605	86	-3	32	4.05	0	C-68,O-13(2-3-8)	10	0.3
1893 Bro-N	61	215	33	57	4	2	1	32	20	12	13	....	.265	.342	.316	.658	79	-6	28	4.76	-5	C-51/O-9(2-0-7)	6	-0.5
1894 Bro-N	67	234	40	60	14	7	0	32	31	22	8	....	.256	.351	.376	.727	81	-6	35	5.16	0	C-60/1-7	6	-0.1
1895 Bro-N	40	142	17	30	3	2	1	11	10	18	3	....	.211	.268	.282	.550	45	-11	12	2.86	-4	C-39/O-1	2	-0.9
1896 Chi-N	9	27	1	2	0	0	0	1	1	2	1	....	.074	.107	.074	.181	-50	-6	0	.40	-0	/C-9	0	-0.5
Total 13	630	2231	280	550	74	22	2	262	208	208	94	....	.247	.314	.299	.613	76	-65	250	3.96	-34	C-550/O-45,1-32,3-6,S-2,2-1	56	-4.6

• DAILY, Ed

Edward M. Daily b: 9/7/1862, Providence, RI d: 10/21/1891, Washington, DC BR/TR, 5'10.5", 174 lbs. Deb: 5/4/1885 Career OF: 153-33-311 ♦

YEAR TM-L	G	AB	R	H	2B	3B	HR	RBI	BB	SO	SB	CS	AVG	OBP	SLG	OPS	OPS+	BR/A	RC	RC/G	FR	G/POS	WS	TPW
1885 Phi-N	50	184	22	38	8	2	1	13	0	25	....	....	.207	.207	.288	.495	60	-0	11	2.07	-3	P-50	35	2.4
1886 Phi-N	79	309	40	70	17	1	4	50	7	34	23	....	.227	.244	.327	.571	71	-6	31	3.50	3	O-56(13-11-32),P-27	22	0.5
1887 Phi-N	26	109	18	33	11	1	1	17	3	9	8	....	.303	.303	.434	.737	97	0	17	5.84	-4	O-22(1-20-1)/P-6	3	-1.6
Was-N	78	325	39	92	6	10	2	36	14	27	26	....	.283	.285	.354	.639	80	-8	40	4.52	-4	O-77(0-0-77)/P-1	5	-1.4
Yr.	104	434	57	125	17	11	3	53	17	36	34	....	.288	.290	.374	.664	85	-8	57	4.85	-9	*O-99(1-20-78)/P-7	8	-3.0
1888 Was-N	110	453	56	102	8	4	7	39	7	42	44	....	.225	.239	.307	.545	77	-10	45	3.44	-1	*O-100(0-0-100)/P-9,1-1	8	-2.9
1889 Col-a	136	578	105	148	22	8	3	70	38	65	60	....	.256	.303	.337	.640	87	-11	79	4.88	-1	*O-136(136-0-0)/P-2	11	-1.7
1890 Bro-a	91	394	68	94	15	7	1	39	24	....	49	....	.239	.284	.320	.604	81	-4	51	4.50	4	O-64(0-0-64),P-27	13	-0.3
NY-N	4	15	1	2	1	0	0	1	0	4	0	....	.133	.133	.200	.333	-3	-2	0	.84	1	/O-3(1-0-2),P-2	1	0.1
*Lou-a	23	80	24	20	0	2	0	9	13	....	13	....	.250	.355	.300	.655	95	3	13	5.94	2	P-12,O-11(0-2-9)	12	1.9
Yr.	114	474	92	114	15	9	1	48	37	....	62	....	.241	.297	.316	.613	83	-1	64	4.74	6	O-75(0-2-73),P-39	25	1.5
1891 Lou-a	22	64	10	16	2	0	0	8	8	6	4	....	.250	.342	.281	.624	80	1	8	4.26	0	P-15/O-7(2-0-5)	2	-2.2
Was-a	21	79	13	18	2	0	0	6	11	10	8	....	.228	.322	.253	.575	68	-3	9	4.02	-4	O-21(0-0-21)	1	-0.6
Yr.	43	143	23	34	4	0	0	14	19	16	12	....	.238	.331	.266	.597	73	-2	17	4.13	-4	O-28(2-0-26),P-15	3	-2.8
Total 7	640	2590	396	633	92	35	19	288	125	222	235	....	.244	.276	.325	.601	79	-39	304	4.15	-8	O-497,P-151/1-1	113	-5.7

• DAISY, George

George R. Daisy b: 1857, Gloucester, NJ d: 4/17/1931, Cumberland, MD, 5'11", 190 lbs. Deb: 5/31/1884

YEAR TM-L	G	AB	R	H	2B	3B	HR	RBI	BB	SO	SB	CS	AVG	OBP	SLG	OPS	OPS+	BR/A	RC	RC/G	FR	G/POS	WS	TPW
1884 Alt-U	1	4	0	0	0	0	0	....	0	....	....	....	.000	.000	.000	.000	-99	-1	0	.00	0	/O-1	0	-0.1

• DALENA, Pete

Peter Martin Dalena b: 6/26/1960, Fresno, CA BL/TR, 5'11", 200 lbs. Deb: 7/7/1989

YEAR TM-L	G	AB	R	H	2B	3B	HR	RBI	BB	SO	SB	CS	AVG	OBP	SLG	OPS	OPS+	BR/A	RC	RC/G	FR	G/POS	WS	TPW
1989 Cle-A	5	7	0	1	1	0	0	0	0	3	0	0	.143	.143	.286	.429	18	-1	0	1.29	0	/D-1	0	-0.1

• DALESANDRO, Mark

Mark Anthony Dalesandro b: 5/14/1968, Chicago, IL BR/TR, 6', 185 lbs. Deb: 6/6/1994 Career OF: 3-0-1

YEAR TM-L	G	AB	R	H	2B	3B	HR	RBI	BB	SO	SB	CS	AVG	OBP	SLG	OPS	OPS+	BR/A	RC	RC/G	FR	G/POS	WS	TPW
1994 Cal-A	19	25	5	5	1	0	1	2	2	4	0	0	.200	.259	.360	.619	57	-2	2	2.16	-2	C-11/3-5,O-2(2-0-0)	0	-0.4
1995 Cal-A	11	10	1	1	1	0	0	0	0	2	0	0	.100	.100	.200	.300	-25	-2	0	.60	-2	/C-8,D-1,O-1	0	-0.3
1998 Tor-A	32	67	8	20	5	0	2	14	1	6	0	0	.299	.309	.463	.772	97	-1	8	4.39	-1	C-18/3-8,1-2,O-1	2	-0.1
1999 Tor-A	16	27	3	5	0	0	0	1	0	2	1	0	.185	.214	.185	.399	3	-4	1	1.22	0	/C-8,D-5,3-2	0	-0.3
2001 Chi-A	1	0	0	0	0	0	0	0	0	0	0	0	....	....	....	....	-97	0	0	....	0	/C-1	0	0.0
Total 5	79	129	17	31	7	0	3	17	3	14	1	0	.240	.263	.364	.627	60	-8	11	2.89	-6	/C-46,3-15,D-6,O-4,1-2	2	-1.2

• DALEY, John

John Francis Daley b: 5/25/1887, Pittsburgh, PA d: 8/31/1988, Mansfield, OH BR/TR, 5'7.5", 155 lbs. Deb: 7/19/1912

YEAR TM-L	G	AB	R	H	2B	3B	HR	RBI	BB	SO	SB	CS	AVG	OBP	SLG	OPS	OPS+	BR/A	RC	RC/G	FR	G/POS	WS	TPW
1912 StL-A	18	52	7	9	0	0	1	3	9	....	4	....	.173	.317	.231	.548	60	-2	5	3.00	-3	S-17	1	-0.4

• DALEY, Jud

Judson Lawrence Daley b: 3/14/1884, South Coventry, CT d: 1/26/1967, Gadsden, AL BL/TR, 5'8", 172 lbs. Deb: 9/19/1911 Career OF: 40-24-7

YEAR TM-L	G	AB	R	H	2B	3B	HR	RBI	BB	SO	SB	CS	AVG	OBP	SLG	OPS	OPS+	BR/A	RC	RC/G	FR	G/POS	WS	TPW
1911 Bro-N	19	65	8	15	2	1	0	7	2	8	2	....	.231	.286	.292	.578	65	-3	6	2.99	1	O-16(16-0-0)	1	-0.3
1912 Bro-N	61	199	22	51	9	1	1	13	24	17	2	....	.256	.342	.327	.669	87	-3	24	3.81	1	O-55(24-24-7)	4	-0.5
Total 2	80	264	30	66	11	2	1	20	26	25	4	....	.250	.329	.318	.647	82	-6	30	3.61	2	/O-71	5	-0.7

• DALEY, Pete

Peter Harvey Daley b: 1/14/1930, Grass Valley, CA BR/TR, 6', 195 lbs. Deb: 5/3/1955

YEAR TM-L	G	AB	R	H	2B	3B	HR	RBI	BB	SO	SB	CS	AVG	OBP	SLG	OPS	OPS+	BR/A	RC	RC/G	FR	G/POS	WS	TPW
1955 Bos-A	17	50	4	11	2	1	0	5	3	6	0	0	.220	.264	.300	.564	47	-4	4	2.89	0	C-14	1	-0.3
1956 Bos-A	59	187	22	50	11	3	5	29	18	30	1	0	.267	.338	.439	.777	92	-2	25	4.47	-4	C-57	4	-0.4
1957 Bos-A	78	191	17	43	10	0	3	25	16	31	0	0	.225	.288	.325	.613	63	-10	16	2.75	-3	C-77	3	-1.0
1958 Bos-A	27	56	10	18	2	1	2	8	7	11	0	0	.321	.397	.500	.897	136	3	10	6.65	0	C-27	3	0.4
1959 Bos-A	65	169	9	38	7	0	1	11	13	31	1	1	.225	.280	.284	.564	53	-11	14	2.89	2	C-58	3	-0.6
1960 KC-A	73	228	19	60	10	2	5	25	16	41	0	0	.263	.311	.390	.702	88	-4	26	3.96	1	C-61/O-1	5	0.0
1961 Was-A	72	203	12	39	7	1	2	17	14	37	0	1	.192	.244	.266	.510	38	-19	11	1.64	0	C-72	2	-1.5
Total 7	391	1084	93	259	49	8	18	120	87	187	2	2	.239	.297	.349	.646	70	-47	106	3.28	-4	C-366/O-1	21	-3.5

• DALEY, Tom

Thomas Francis "Pete" Daley b: 11/13/1884, Du Bois, PA d: 12/2/1934, Los Angeles, CA BL/TR, 5'5", 168 lbs. Deb: 8/29/1908 Career OF: 43-77-14

YEAR TM-L	G	AB	R	H	2B	3B	HR	RBI	BB	SO	SB	CS	AVG	OBP	SLG	OPS	OPS+	BR/A	RC	RC/G	FR	G/POS	WS	TPW
1908 Cin-N	14	46	5	5	0	0	0	1	3	....	1	....	.109	.196	.109	.305	-2	-5	1	.69	1	O-13(0-0-13)	0	-0.6

YEAR TM-L	G	AB	R	H	2B	3B	HR	RBI	BB	SO	SB	CS	AVG	OBP	SLG	OPS	OPS+	BR/A	RC	RC/G	FR	G/POS	WS	TPW
1913 Phi-A	62	141	13	36	2	1	0	11	13	28	4	....	.255	.327	.284	.611	81	-3	14	3.31	0	O-39(0-38-0)	4	-0.6
1914 Phi-A	28	86	17	22	1	3	0	7	12	14	4	7	.256	.347	.337	.684	110	-1	9	3.35	1	O-24(14-10-0)	3	-0.1
NY-A	69	191	36	48	6	4	0	9	38	13	8	8	.251	.378	.325	.703	112	3	25	4.18	3	O-58(28-29-0)	8	0.4
Yr.	97	277	53	70	7	7	0	16	50	27	12	15	.253	.369	.329	.697	111	2	35	3.92	4	O-82(42-39-0)	11	0.2
1915 NY-A	10	8	2	2	0	0	0	1	2	2	1	....	.250	.400	.250	.650	95	0	1	5.04	0	/O-2(1-0-1)	0	0.0
Total 4	**183**	**472**	**73**	**113**	**9**	**8**	**0**	**29**	**68**	**57**	**18**	**15**	**.239**	**.341**	**.292**	**.634**	**92**	**-6**	**51**	**3.42**	**4**	**O-136**	**15**	**-0.9**

• DALLESSANDRO, Dom Nicholas Dominic "Dim Dom" Dallessandro
b: 10/3/1913, Reading, PA d: 4/29/1988, Indianapolis, IN BL/TL, 5'6", 168 lbs. Deb: 4/24/1937 Career OF: 370-125-12

YEAR TM-L	G	AB	R	H	2B	3B	HR	RBI	BB	SO	SB	CS	AVG	OBP	SLG	OPS	OPS+	BR/A	RC	RC/G	FR	G/POS	WS	TPW
1937 Bos-A	68	147	18	34	7	1	0	11	27	16	2	1	.231	.351	.293	.643	61	-8	17	3.91	-3	O-35(30-1-4)	2	-1.2
1940 Chi-N	107	287	33	77	19	6	1	36	34	13	4	....	.268	.348	.387	.735	104	2	40	4.93	0	O-74(74-0-0)	7	-0.1
1941 Chi-N	140	486	73	132	36	2	6	85	68	37	3	....	.272	.362	.391	.753	116	12	72	5.27	-10	*O-131(69-62-0)	16	-0.3
1942 Chi-N	96	264	30	69	12	4	4	43	36	18	4	....	.261	.350	.383	.733	119	7	35	4.50	0	O-66(31-32-4)	7	0.4
1943 Chi-N	87	176	13	39	8	3	1	31	40	14	1	....	.222	.369	.318	.687	101	3	24	4.64	-4	O-45(31-14-0)	5	-0.4
1944 Chi-N	117	381	53	116	19	4	8	74	61	29	1	....	.304	.400	.438	.839	137	21	70	6.87	-2	*O-106(91-16-0)	16	1.3
1946 Chi-N	65	89	4	20	2	2	1	9	23	12	1	....	.225	.384	.326	.710	104	2	12	4.16	-1	O-20(16-0-4)	3	0.0
1947 Chi-N	66	115	18	33	7	1	1	14	21	11	0	....	.287	.397	.391	.788	115	3	18	5.64	0	O-28(28-0-0)	3	0.2
Total 8	**746**	**1945**	**242**	**520**	**110**	**23**	**22**	**303**	**310**	**150**	**16**	**1**	**.267**	**.369**	**.381**	**.750**	**112**	**42**	**287**	**5.21**	**-20**	**O-505**	**59**	**-0.1**

• DALRYMPLE, Abner Abner Frank Dalrymple b: 9/9/1857, Warren, IL d: 1/25/1939, Warren, IL BL/TR, 5'10.5", 175 lbs. Deb: 5/1/1878 Career OF: 944-2-5

YEAR TM-L	G	AB	R	H	2B	3B	HR	RBI	BB	SO	SB	CS	AVG	OBP	SLG	OPS	OPS+	BR/A	RC	RC/G	FR	G/POS	WS	TPW
1878 Mil-N	61	271	52	96	10	4	0	15	6	29	....	....	**.354**	.368	.421	.789	149	13	43	6.76	5	*O-61(61-0-0)	8	1.4
1879 Chi-N	71	333	47	97	25	1	0	23	4	29	....	....	.291	.300	.372	.672	113	4	38	4.52	-11	*O-71(66-1-4)	9	-1.0
1880 Chi-N	86	382	**91**	**126**	25	12	0	36	3	18	....	....	.330	.335	.458	.793	156	20	60	6.46	8	*O-86(86-0-0)	23	2.3
1881 Chi-N	82	362	72	117	22	4	1	37	15	22	....	....	.323	.350	.414	.764	130	12	54	5.93	-4	*O-82(82-0-0)	15	0.3
1882 Chi-N	84	397	96	117	25	11	1	36	14	18	....	....	.295	.319	.421	.739	133	14	55	5.36	1	*O-84(84-0-0)	16	1.1
1883 Chi-N	80	363	78	108	24	4	2	37	11	29	....	....	.298	.318	.402	.720	108	2	48	5.14	1	*O-80(80-0-0)	13	0.0
1884 Chi-N	111	521	111	161	18	9	22	69	14	39	....	....	.309	.327	.505	.832	146	24	88	6.74	8	*O-111(111-0-0)	17	2.5
1885*Chi-N	113	492	109	135	27	12	**11**	61	46	42	....	....	.274	.336	.445	.782	131	15	76	5.71	6	*O-113(112-1-0)	25	1.7
1886*Chi-N	82	331	62	77	7	12	3	26	33	44	16	....	.233	.302	.353	.656	86	-7	41	4.38	8	O-82(82-0-0)	10	-0.2
1887 Pit-N	92	403	45	121	18	5	2	31	45	43	29	....	.300	.311	.307	.618	77	-9	44	4.16	2	O-92(92-0-0)	6	-0.8
1888 Pit-N	57	227	19	50	9	2	0	14	6	28	7	....	.220	.247	.278	.524	72	-7	18	2.70	-4	O-57(56-0-1)	3	-1.3
1891 Mil-a	32	135	31	42	7	5	1	22	7	18	6	....	.311	.345	.459	.804	108	-0	24	6.85	-1	O-32(32-0-0)	5	-0.2
Total 12	**951**	**4217**	**813**	**1247**	**217**	**81**	**43**	**407**	**204**	**359**	**58**	**....**	**.296**	**.323**	**.410**	**.732**	**120**	**82**	**588**	**5.40**	**20**	**O-951**	**150**	**5.8**

• DALRYMPLE, Bill William Dunn Dalrymple b: 2/7/1891, Baltimore, MD d: 7/14/1967, San Diego, CA TR Deb: 7/6/1915

YEAR TM-L	G	AB	R	H	2B	3B	HR	RBI	BB	SO	SB	CS	AVG	OBP	SLG	OPS	OPS+	BR/A	RC	RC/G	FR	G/POS	WS	TPW
1915 StL-A	3	2	0	0	0	0	0	0	0	0	0	....	.000	.000	.000	.000	-104	-0	0	.00	0	/3-1	0	0.0

• DALRYMPLE, Clay Clayton Errol Dalrymple b: 12/3/1936, Chico, CA BL/TR, 6', 199 lbs. Deb: 4/24/1960

YEAR TM-L	G	AB	R	H	2B	3B	HR	RBI	BB	SO	SB	CS	AVG	OBP	SLG	OPS	OPS+	BR/A	RC	RC/G	FR	G/POS	WS	TPW
1960 Phi-N	82	158	11	43	6	2	4	21	15	21	0	0	.272	.347	.411	.758	106	2	22	4.92	1	C-48	5	0.4
1961 Phi-N	129	378	23	83	11	1	5	42	30	30	0	2	.220	.284	.294	.578	54	-25	30	2.56	9	*C-122	4	-1.0
1962 Phi-N	123	370	40	102	13	3	11	54	70	32	1	3	.276	.396	.416	.813	122	14	65	6.12	0	*C-119	19	2.0
1963 Phi-N	142	452	40	114	15	3	10	40	45	55	0	2	.252	.327	.365	.692	100	0	54	4.07	3	*C-142	16	1.1
1964 Phi-N	127	382	36	91	16	3	6	46	39	40	0	1	.238	.309	.343	.652	84	-8	41	3.53	4	*C-124	13	0.2
1965 Phi-N	103	301	14	64	5	5	4	23	34	37	0	1	.213	.293	.302	.595	69	-12	27	2.87	9	*C-102	8	0.2
1966 Phi-N	114	331	30	81	13	3	4	39	60	57	0	0	.245	.365	.338	.704	97	2	46	4.69	-3	*C-110	14	0.5
1967 Phi-N	101	268	12	46	7	1	3	21	36	49	1	2	.172	.272	.239	.511	47	-18	18	1.98	6	C-97	5	-0.8
1968 Phi-N	85	241	19	50	9	1	3	26	22	57	1	2	.207	.277	.290	.567	70	-9	19	2.56	-4	C-80	5	-1.0
1969*Bal-A	37	80	8	19	1	1	3	6	13	8	0	0	.238	.344	.388	.732	103	1	10	3.80	1	C-30	3	0.3
1970 Bal-A	13	32	4	7	1	0	1	3	7	4	0	0	.219	.359	.344	.703	94	0	4	4.66	3	C-11	2	0.4
1971 Bal-A	23	49	6	10	1	0	1	6	16	13	0	0	.204	.409	.286	.695	101	1	8	5.08	-1	C-18	2	0.1
Total 12	**1079**	**3042**	**243**	**710**	**98**	**23**	**55**	**327**	**387**	**403**	**3**	**13**	**.233**	**.324**	**.335**	**.659**	**85**	**-52**	**343**	**3.72**	**29**	***C-1003**	**96**	**2.4**

• DALTON, Jack Talbot Percy Dalton b: 7/3/1885, Henderson, TN BR/TR, 5'10.5", 187 lbs. Deb: 6/20/1910 Career OF: 16-169-129

YEAR TM-L	G	AB	R	H	2B	3B	HR	RBI	BB	SO	SB	CS	AVG	OBP	SLG	OPS	OPS+	BR/A	RC	RC/G	FR	G/POS	WS	TPW
1910 Bro-N	77	273	33	62	9	4	1	21	26	30	5	....	.227	.304	.300	.604	79	-7	27	3.14	1	O-72(0-0-72)	4	-1.0
1914 Bro-N	128	442	65	141	13	8	1	45	53	39	19	....	.319	.396	.391	.787	131	19	74	6.08	-13	*O-116(5-109-2)	19	-0.1
1915 Buf-F	132	437	68	128	17	3	2	46	50	38	28	....	.293	.368	.359	.727	114	9	66	5.27	-2	*O-119(10-60-52)	18	0.1
1916 Det-A	8	11	1	2	0	0	0	0	0	5	0	....	.182	.182	.182	.364	9	-1	0	1.05	0	/O-4(1-0-3)	0	-0.2
Total 4	**345**	**1163**	**167**	**333**	**39**	**15**	**4**	**112**	**129**	**112**	**52**	**....**	**.286**	**.362**	**.356**	**.718**	**112**	**20**	**168**	**4.98**	**-15**	**O-311**	**41**	**-1.3**

• DALY, Bert Albert Joseph Daly b: 4/8/1881, Bayonne, NJ d: 9/3/1952, Bayonne, NJ BR/TR, 5'9", 170 lbs. Deb: 8/7/1903

YEAR TM-L	G	AB	R	H	2B	3B	HR	RBI	BB	SO	SB	CS	AVG	OBP	SLG	OPS	OPS+	BR/A	RC	RC/G	FR	G/POS	WS	TPW
1903 Phi-A	10	21	2	4	0	2	0	4	1	....	0	....	.190	.227	.381	.608	76	-1	2	2.91	-2	/2-4,3-3,S-1	0	-0.2

• DALY, Joe Joseph John Daly b: 9/21/1868, Conshohocken, PA d: 3/21/1943, Philadelphia, PA TR, 5'8", 157 lbs. Deb: 9/19/1890 Career OF: 3-8-4

YEAR TM-L	G	AB	R	H	2B	3B	HR	RBI	BB	SO	SB	CS	AVG	OBP	SLG	OPS	OPS+	BR/A	RC	RC/G	FR	G/POS	WS	TPW
1890 Phi-a	21	75	8	21	4	1	0	7	3	....	1	....	.280	.308	.360	.668	99	-1	9	4.33	1	O-14(3-8-3)/C-9	2	0.0
1891 Cle-N	1	3	0	0	0	0	0	0	0	2	0	....	.000	.000	.000	.000	-96	-1	0	.00	0	/O-1	0	-0.1
1892 Bos-N	1	0	0	0	0	0	0	0	0	0	0	....	....	....	....	....	-92	0	0	....	0	/C-1	0	0.0
Total 3	**23**	**78**	**8**	**21**	**4**	**1**	**0**	**7**	**3**	**2**	**1**	**....**	**.269**	**.296**	**.346**	**.642**	**92**	**-1**	**9**	**4.11**	**0**	**/O-15,C-10**	**2**	**-0.1**

• DALY, Sun James J. Daly b: 1/6/1865, Port Henry, NY d: 4/30/1938, Albany, NY BL Deb: 9/30/1892

YEAR TM-L	G	AB	R	H	2B	3B	HR	RBI	BB	SO	SB	CS	AVG	OBP	SLG	OPS	OPS+	BR/A	RC	RC/G	FR	G/POS	WS	TPW
1892 Bal-N	13	48	5	12	0	2	0	7	1	4	0	....	.250	.265	.333	.599	79	-2	4	3.26	0	O-13(10-3-0)	0	-0.2

• DALY, Tom Thomas Daniel Daly b: 12/12/1891, St. John, Canada d: 11/7/1946, Medford, MA BR/TR, 5'11.5", 171 lbs. Deb: 9/23/1913 C Career OF: 14-0-11

YEAR TM-L	G	AB	R	H	2B	3B	HR	RBI	BB	SO	SB	CS	AVG	OBP	SLG	OPS	OPS+	BR/A	RC	RC/G	FR	G/POS	WS	TPW
1913 Chi-A	1	3	0	0	0	0	0	0	0	0	0	....	.000	.000	.000	.000	-101	-1	0	.00	0	/C-1	0	-0.1
1914 Chi-A	62	133	13	31	2	0	0	8	7	13	3	4	.233	.271	.248	.520	57	-8	9	2.19	-2	O-23(14-0-10)/3-5,C-4,1-2	1	-1.3
1915 Chi-A	29	47	5	9	1	0	0	3	5	9	0	....	.191	.269	.213	.482	43	-3	3	1.95	-3	C-19/1-1	0	-0.6
1916 Cle-A	31	73	3	16	1	1	0	8	1	2	0	....	.219	.230	.260	.490	45	-5	4	2.02	0	C-25/O-1	1	-0.4
1918 Chi-N	1	1	0	0	0	0	0	0	0	0	0	....	.000	.000	.000	.000	-98	-0	0	.00	-1	/C-1	0	-0.1
1919 Chi-N	25	50	4	11	0	1	0	1	2	5	0	....	.220	.250	.260	.510	53	-3	3	2.04	-2	C-18	1	-0.4
1920 Chi-N	44	90	12	28	6	0	0	13	2	6	1	1	.311	.333	.378	.711	102	0	11	4.54	-1	C-29	4	0.1
1921 Chi-N	51	143	12	34	7	1	0	22	8	8	1	2	.238	.278	.301	.579	53	-10	12	2.74	2	C-47	2	-0.5
Total 8	**244**	**540**	**49**	**129**	**17**	**3**	**0**	**55**	**25**	**43**	**5**	**7**	**.239**	**.274**	**.281**	**.555**	**59**	**-30**	**42**	**2.61**	**-6**	**C-144/O-24,3-5,1-3**	**9**	**-3.1**

• DALY, Tom Thomas Peter "Tido" Daly b: 2/7/1866, Philadelphia, PA d: 10/29/1938, Brooklyn, NY BB/TR, 5'7", 170 lbs. Deb: 4/30/1887 U Career OF: 9-17-29

YEAR TM-L	G	AB	R	H	2B	3B	HR	RBI	BB	SO	SB	CS	AVG	OBP	SLG	OPS	OPS+	BR/A	RC	RC/G	FR	G/POS	WS	TPW
1887 Chi-N	74	278	45	75	10	4	2	17	22	25	29	....	.270	.270	.301	.571	51	-19	29	3.83	21	C-64/O-8(2-3-3),1-2,2-2,S	8	0.7
1888 Chi-N	65	219	34	42	2	6	0	29	10	26	10	....	.192	.230	.256	.486	51	-13	16	2.38	6	C-62/O-4(0-1-3)	5	-0.1
1889 Was-N	71	250	39	75	13	5	1	40	38	28	18	....	.300	.394	.404	.798	131	13	48	7.29	3	C-57/1-8,2-4,O-3(1-0-2),S	11	1.7
1890*Bro-N	82	292	55	71	9	4	5	43	32	43	20	....	.243	.326	.353	.679	97	-1	41	4.93	1	C-69,1-12/O-1	11	0.4
1891 Bro-N	58	200	29	50	11	5	2	27	21	34	7	....	.250	.327	.385	.712	108	2	28	5.07	-7	C-26,1-15,S-11/O-7(0-0-7)	5	-0.4
1892 Bro-N	124	446	76	114	15	6	4	51	64	62	34	....	.256	.355	.343	.698	115	11	68	5.54	-3	3-57,O-30(5-13-12),C-27,2-10	16	0.9
1893 Bro-N	126	470	94	136	21	14	8	70	76	65	32	....	.289	.388	.445	.833	127	20	96	7.61	-9	2-82,3-45	20	1.2
1894 Bro-N	124	496	135	168	22	10	8	82	77	42	51	....	.339	.433	.472	.904	129	28	127	10.21	-10	*2-123	20	1.8
1895 Bro-N	121	460	90	129	17	8	2	68	52	52	28	....	.280	.357	.365	.722	94	-1	73	5.78	-15	*2-120	14	-0.9
1896 Bro-N	67	224	43	63	13	6	3	29	33	25	19	....	.281	.385	.433	.819	122	9	46	7.54	-12	2-66/C-1	9	0.0
1898 Bro-N	23	73	11	24	3	1	0	11	14	....	6	....	.329	.443	.397	.840	142	5	16	8.60	1	2-23	5	0.7
1899 Bro-N	141	498	95	156	24	9	5	88	69	....	43	....	.313	.409	.428	.837	127	22	108	8.20	14	*2-141	28	3.8
1900*Bro-N	97	343	72	107	17	3	4	55	46	....	27	....	.312	.403	.414	.817	118	10	70	7.74	-3	2-93/1-3,O-2(1-0-1)	15	1.0
1901 Bro-N	133	520	88	164	**38**	10	3	90	42	....	31	....	.315	.371	.444	.815	132	21	101	7.29	12	*2-133	25	3.4
1902 Chi-A	137	489	57	110	22	3	1	54	55	....	19	....	.225	.303	.288	.592	67	-20	52	3.48	-12	*2-137	11	-2.9
1903 Chi-A	43	150	20	31	11	0	0	19	20	....	6	....	.207	.304	.280	.584	80	-3	16	3.34	-11	2-43	4	-1.4

YEAR TM-L	G	AB	R	H	2B	3B	HR	RBI	BB	SO	SB	CS	AVG	OBP	SLG	OPS	OPS+	BR/A	RC	RC/G	FR	G/POS	WS	TPW
Cin-N	80	307	42	90	14	9	1	38	16	....	5	....	.293	.332	.407	.739	99	-2	45	5.33	-3	2-79	8	-0.5
Total 16	1566	5715	1025	1605	262	103	49	811	687	402	385	....	.281	.361	.386	.747	108	82	980	6.24	-28	*2-1056,C-306,3-102/0-55,1,S	215	9.4
• **DAM, Bill**	Elbridge Rust Dam b: 4/4/1885, Cambridge, MA d: 6/22/1930, Quincy, MA BL Deb: 8/23/1909																							
1909 Bos-N	1	2	1	1	1	0	0	0	1	....	0	....	.500	.667	1.000	1.667	398	1	1	34.82	-0	/0-1	0	0.1
• **DAMASKA, Jack**	Jack Lloyd Damaska b: 8/21/1937, Beaver Falls, PA BR/TR, 5'11", 168 lbs. Deb: 7/3/1963																							
1963 StL-N	5	5	1	1	0	0	0	1	0	4	0	0	.200	.200	.200	.400	14	-1	0	1.35	-1	/2-1,0-1	0	-0.1
• **DAMON, Johnny**	Johnny David Damon b: 11/5/1973, Fort Riley, KS BL/TL, 6', 175 lbs. Deb: 8/12/1995 Career OF: 328-786-146																							
1995 KC-A	47	188	32	53	11	5	3	23	12	22	7	0	.282	.328	.441	.770	97	-0	29	5.47	-1	0-47(0-44-4)	6	0.0
1996 KC-A	145	517	61	140	22	5	6	50	31	64	25	5	.271	.316	.368	.683	72	-20	64	4.30	-3	*0-144(0-89-63)/D-1	9	-2.3
1997 KC-A	146	472	70	130	12	8	8	48	42	70	16	10	.275	.338	.386	.724	86	-10	63	4.73	-1	*0-136(48-65-47)/D-5	11	-1.3
1998 KC-A	161	642	104	178	30	10	18	66	58	84	26	12	.277	.341	.439	.780	98	-2	99	5.50	-1	*0-158(14-130-24)	17	-0.3
1999 KC-A	145	583	101	179	39	9	14	77	67	50	36	6	.307	.381	.477	.858	115	19	111	6.94	0	*0-140(132-8-3)/D-4	18	1.2
2000 KC-A	159	655	**136**	214	42	10	16	88	65	60	**46**	9	.327	.388	.495	.883	117	24	133	7.55	5	*0-133(67-69-0),D-25	26	2.3
2001*Oak-A	155	644	108	165	34	4	9	49	61	70	27	12	.256	.325	.363	.689	81	-17	79	4.23	2	*0-154(67-86-5)	17	-1.7
2002 Bos-A★	154	623	118	178	34	**11**	14	63	65	70	31	6	.286	.359	.443	.802	109	13	107	6.22	0	*0-151(0-151-0)/D-1	21	1.3
2003*Bos-A	145	608	103	166	32	6	12	67	68	74	30	6	.273	.348	.405	.753	96	1	93	5.40	3	*0-144(0-144-0)/D-1	18	0.5
Total 9	1257	4932	833	1403	256	68	100	531	469	564	244	66	.284	.350	.425	.775	98	8	778	5.63	4	*0-1207/D-37	143	-0.5
• **DAMRAU, Harry**	Harry Robert Damrau b: 9/11/1890, Newburgh, NY d: 8/21/1957, Staten Island, NY BR/TR, 5'10", 178 lbs. Deb: 9/17/1915																							
1915 Phi-A	16	56	4	11	1	0	0	3	5	17	1	1	.196	.262	.214	.477	44	-4	3	1.87	-2	3-16	0	-0.6
• **DANIEL, Jake**	Handley Jacob Daniel b: 4/22/1912, Roanoke, AL d: 4/23/1996, LaGrange, GA BL/TL, 5'11", 175 lbs. Deb: 7/24/1937																							
1937 Bro-N	12	27	3	5	1	0	0	3	3	4	0	....	.185	.267	.222	.489	33	-2	2	2.27	0	/1-7	0	-0.3
• **DANIELS, Bert**	Bernard Elmer Daniels b: 10/31/1882, Danville, IL d: 6/6/1958, Cedar Grove, NJ BR/TR, 5'9.5", 170 lbs. Deb: 6/25/1910 Career OF: 190-118-190																							
1910 NY-A	95	356	68	90	13	8	1	17	41	....	41	....	.253	.356	.343	.699	112	7	58	5.46	1	0-85(79-6-0)/3-6,1-4	17	0.3
1911 NY-A	131	462	74	132	16	9	2	31	48	....	40	....	.286	.375	.372	.747	102	3	80	5.95	-5	*0-120(8-86-26)	15	-0.9
1912 NY-A	135	496	72	136	25	11	2	41	51	....	37	....	.274	.363	.381	.744	106	5	82	5.63	1	*0-131(92-0-39)	14	0.0
1913 NY-A	94	320	52	69	13	5	0	22	44	36	27	....	.216	.343	.288	.630	85	-3	38	3.82	1	0-87(0-0-87)	7	-0.7
1914 Cin-N	71	269	29	59	9	7	0	19	19	40	14	....	.219	.276	.305	.581	70	-10	25	3.01	-1	0-71(11-26-38)	5	-1.7
Total 5	526	1903	295	486	76	40	5	130	203	76	159	....	.255	.349	.345	.695	98	2	283	4.97	-3	0-494/3-6,1-4	58	-2.9
• **DANIELS, Jack**	Harold Jack "Sour Mash Jack" Daniels b: 12/21/1927, Chester, PA BL/TL, 5'10", 165 lbs. Deb: 4/18/1952																							
1952 Bos-N	106	219	31	41	5	1	2	14	28	30	3	3	.187	.288	.247	.535	51	-14	18	2.60	-2	0-87(13-0-75)	2	-1.9
• **DANIELS, Kal**	Kalvoski Daniels b: 8/20/1963, Vienna, GA BL/TR, 5'11", 195 lbs. Deb: 4/9/1986 Career OF: 636-0-0																							
1986 Cin-N	74	181	34	58	10	4	6	23	22	30	15	2	.320	.400	.519	.919	145	14	40	8.23	-1	0-47(47-0-0)	10	1.1
1987 Cin-N	108	368	73	123	24	1	26	64	60	62	26	8	.334	.429	.617	1.046	166	38	100	10.43	-6	0-94(94-0-0)	22	2.8
1988 Cin-N	140	495	95	144	29	1	18	64	87	94	27	6	.291	**.400**	.463	.863	141	33	98	7.11	4	*0-137(138-0-0)	26	3.5
1989 Cin-N	44	133	26	29	11	0	2	9	36	28	6	4	.218	.392	.346	.738	109	3	21	5.24	1	0-38(38-0-0)	4	0.4
LA-N	11	38	7	13	2	0	2	8	7	5	3	0	.342	.444	.553	.997	187	5	10	10.28	0	0-11(11-0-0)	3	0.5
Yr.	55	171	33	42	13	0	4	17	43	33	9	4	.246	.403	.392	.795	125	9	32	6.24	1	0-49(49-0-0)	7	0.9
1990 LA-N	130	450	81	133	23	1	27	94	68	104	4	3	.296	.392	.531	.923	156	34	96	7.73	0	*0-127(127-0-0)	26	3.1
1991 LA-N	137	461	54	115	15	1	17	73	63	116	6	1	.249	.341	.397	.738	109	7	65	4.86	2	*0-132(132-0-0)	18	0.5
1992 LA-N	35	104	9	24	5	0	2	8	10	30	0	0	.231	.304	.337	.641	83	-2	9	2.84	-1	0-21(21-0-0)/1-8	0	-0.5
Chi-N	48	108	12	27	6	0	4	17	12	24	0	2	.250	.331	.417	.747	108	0	14	4.35	2	0-28(28-0-0)	3	0.1
Yr.	83	212	21	51	11	0	6	25	22	54	0	2	.241	.318	.377	.695	95	-2	23	3.59	1	0-49(49-0-0)/1-8	3	-0.3
Total 7	727	2338	391	666	125	8	104	360	365	493	87	26	.285	.385	.479	.863	137	134	454	6.92	1	0-635/1-8	112	11.6
• **DANIELS, Law**	Lawrence Long Daniels b: 7/14/1862, Newton, MA d: 1/7/1929, Waltham, MA BR/TR, 5'10", 170 lbs. Deb: 4/25/1887 Career OF: 24-14-7																							
1887 Bal-a	48	173	23	49	5	1	0	32	8	....	7	....	.283	.287	.291	.578	65	-7	16	3.53	-10	C-26,0-15(10-5-0)/1-4,2-2,3,S	3	-1.2
1888 KC-a	61	218	32	45	2	0	2	28	14	....	20	....	.206	.264	.243	.507	59	-10	20	3.08	2	0-30(14-9-7),C-29/3-2,S-1	3	-0.7
Total 2	109	391	55	94	7	1	2	60	22	....	27	....	.240	.274	.264	.538	62	-18	36	3.27	-8	/C-55,0-45,1-4,3-3,2-2,S-2	6	-1.9
• **DANIELS, Tony**	Frederick Clinton Daniels b: 12/28/1924, Gastonia, NC BR/TR, 5'9.5", 185 lbs. Deb: 6/12/1945																							
1945 Phi-N	76	230	15	46	3	2	0	10	12	22	1	....	.200	.249	.230	.479	35	-20	13	1.73	-9	2-75/3-1	1	-2.6
• **DANNER, Buck**	Henry Frederick Danner b: 6/8/1891, Dedham, MA d: 9/21/1949, Boston, MA BR/TR, 5'6", 140 lbs. Deb: 9/17/1915																							
1915 Phi-A	3	12	1	3	0	0	0	0	0	1	1	....	.250	.250	.250	.500	51	-1	1	2.83	-2	/S-3	0	-0.3
• **DANNING, Harry**	Harry "Harry The Horse" Danning b: 9/6/1911, Los Angeles, CA BR/TR, 6'1", 190 lbs. Deb: 7/30/1933																							
1933 NY-N	3	2	0	0	0	0	0	0	1	0	0	....	.000	.333	.000	.333	2	-0	0	.00	0	/C-1	0	0.0
1934 NY-N	53	97	8	32	7	0	1	7	1	9	1	....	.330	.337	.433	.770	107	1	12	4.71	0	C-37	3	0.2
1935 NY-N	65	152	16	37	11	1	2	20	9	16	0	....	.243	.286	.368	.654	76	-6	16	3.49	0	C-44	4	-0.3
1936*NY-N	32	69	3	11	2	2	0	4	1	5	0	....	.159	.183	.246	.429	15	-8	2	.86	0	C-24	1	-0.7
1937*NY-N	93	292	30	84	12	4	8	51	18	20	0	....	.288	.331	.438	.770	106	1	42	5.18	-1	C-86	12	0.5
1938 NY-N★	120	448	59	137	26	3	9	60	23	40	1	....	.306	.345	.438	.783	113	7	66	5.44	-5	*C-114	17	0.9
1939 NY-N★	135	520	79	163	28	5	16	74	35	42	4	....	.313	.359	.479	.838	122	15	87	6.29	9	*C-132	27	3.1
1940 NY-N★	140	524	65	157	34	4	13	91	35	31	3	....	.300	.349	.454	.803	119	12	79	5.50	2	*C-131	21	2.3
1941 NY-N★	130	459	58	112	22	4	7	56	30	25	1	....	.244	.292	.355	.647	80	-14	46	3.42	8	*C-116/1-1	12	0.1
1942 NY-N	119	408	45	114	20	3	1	34	34	29	3	....	.279	.335	.350	.685	100	-0	46	3.97	-4	*C-116	14	0.3
Total 10	890	2971	363	847	162	26	57	397	187	217	13	....	.285	.330	.415	.745	104	7	395	4.77	9	C-801/1-1	111	6.5
• **DANNING, Ike**	Isaac Danning b: 1/20/1905, Los Angeles, CA d: 3/30/1983, Santa Monica, CA BR/TR, 5'10", 160 lbs. Deb: 9/21/1928																							
1928 StL-A	2	6	0	3	0	0	0	1	1	2	0	0	.500	.571	.500	1.071	178	1	2	15.80	0	/C-2	1	0.1
• **DANTONIO, Fats**	John James Dantonio b: 12/31/1918, New Orleans, LA d: 5/28/1993, New Orleans, LA BR/TR, 5'8", 165 lbs. Deb: 9/18/1944																							
1944 Bro-N	3	7	0	1	0	0	0	0	0	1	0	....	.143	.143	.143	.286	-20	-1	0	.00	-1	/C-3	0	-0.2
1945 Bro-N	47	128	12	32	6	1	0	12	11	6	3	....	.250	.309	.313	.622	74	-5	13	3.31	-4	C-45	2	-0.7
Total 2	50	135	12	33	6	1	0	12	11	7	3	....	.244	.301	.304	.605	69	-6	13	3.10	-5	/C-48	2	-0.9
• **DANZIG, Babe**	Harold P. Danzig b: 4/30/1887, Binghamton, NY d: 7/14/1931, San Francisco, CA BR/TR, 6'2", 205 lbs. Deb: 4/12/1909																							
1909 Bos-A	6	13	0	2	0	0	0	0	2	....	0	....	.154	.313	.154	.466	47	-1	1	1.44	-1	/1-3	0	-0.1
• **DAPPER, Cliff**	Clifford Roland Dapper b: 1/2/1920, Los Angeles, CA BR/TR, 6'2", 190 lbs. Deb: 4/19/1942																							
1942 Bro-N	8	17	2	8	1	0	1	9	2	2	0	....	.471	.526	.706	1.232	255	3	7	19.77	0	/C-8	2	0.4
• **DARINGER, Cliff**	Clifford Clarence "Shanty" Daringer b: 4/10/1885, Hayden, IN d: 12/26/1971, Sacramento, CA BL/TR, 5'7.5", 155 lbs. Deb: 4/20/1914																							
1914 KC-F	64	160	12	42	2	1	0	16	11	7	9	....	.263	.322	.288	.609	78	-4	18	3.55	-2	S-24,3-19,2-14	4	-0.4
• **DARINGER, Rolla**	Rolla Harrison Daringer b: 11/15/1888, North Vernon, IN d: 5/23/1974, Seymour, IN BL/TR, 5'10", 155 lbs. Deb: 9/19/1914																							
1914 StL-N	2	4	1	2	1	0	0	0	1	2	0	....	.500	.600	.750	1.350	304	1	2	22.78	0	/S-1	1	0.1
1915 StL-N	10	23	3	2	0	0	0	0	9	5	0	1	.087	.344	.087	.431	33	-2	1	1.00	-1	S-10	0	-0.2
Total 2	12	27	4	4	1	0	0	0	10	7	0	1	.148	.378	.185	.564	69	-0	3	2.74	-1	/S-11	1	-0.1
• **DARK, Alvin**	Alvin Ralph "Blackie" Dark b: 1/7/1922, Comanche, OK BR/TR, 5'11", 185 lbs. Deb: 7/14/1946 M/C Career OF: 39-0-4																							
1946 Bos-N	15	13	0	3	3	0	0	1	0	3	0	....	.231	.231	.462	.692	93	-0	1	3.74	0	S-12/0-1	0	0.0
1948*Bos-N	137	543	85	175	39	6	3	48	24	36	4	....	.322	.353	.433	.786	114	8	84	5.94	-2	*S-133	20	1.5
1949 Bos-N	130	529	74	146	23	5	3	53	31	43	5	....	.276	.317	.355	.673	85	-13	59	3.97	-5	*S-125/3-4	12	-0.9
1950 NY-N	154	587	79	164	36	5	16	67	39	60	9	....	.279	.331	.440	.770	100	-2	85	5.18	-6	*S-154	19	0.2

YEAR TM-L	G	AB	R	H	2B	3B	HR	RBI	BB	SO	SB	CS	AVG	OBP	SLG	OPS	OPS+	BR/A	RC	RC/G	FR	G/POS	WS	TPW
1951*NY-N★	156	646	114	196	**41**	7	14	69	42	39	12	7	.303	.352	.454	.805	114	11	104	5.92	6	*S-156	27	2.7
1952 NY-N★	151	589	92	177	29	3	14	73	47	39	6	6	.301	.357	.431	.788	117	12	92	5.71	1	*S-150	28	2.3
1953 NY-N	155	647	126	194	41	6	23	88	28	34	7	2	.300	.335	.488	.823	109	7	102	5.69	3	*S-110,2-26,O-17(13-0-4)/3,P	21	1.8
1954*NY-N★	154	644	98	189	26	6	20	70	27	40	5	3	.293	.327	.446	.773	98	-4	89	4.92	8	*S-154	23	1.7
1955 NY-N	115	475	77	134	20	3	9	45	22	32	2	1	.282	.321	.394	.714	88	-9	60	4.61	-10	*S-115	13	-0.9
1956 NY-N	48	206	19	52	12	0	2	17	8	13	0	0	.252	.284	.340	.624	67	-10	19	3.12	-6	S-48	3	-1.2
StL-N	100	413	54	118	14	7	4	37	21	33	3	1	.286	.323	.383	.706	89	-7	50	4.34	-6	S-99	10	-0.5
Yr.	148	619	73	170	26	7	6	54	29	46	3	1	.275	.310	.368	.679	82	-16	69	3.91	-12	*S-147	13	-1.6
1957 StL-N	140	583	80	169	25	8	4	64	29	56	3	4	.290	.328	.381	.709	88	-11	72	4.48	4	*S-139/3-1	18	0.4
1958 StL-N	18	64	7	19	0	0	1	5	2	6	0	0	.297	.318	.344	.662	72	-3	6	3.45	0	/3-8,S-8	1	-0.2
Chi-N	114	464	54	137	16	4	3	43	29	23	1	1	.295	.343	.366	.710	89	-7	57	4.40	2	*3-111	10	-0.6
Yr.	132	528	61	156	16	4	4	48	31	29	1	1	.295	.340	.364	.704	87	-9	63	4.28	1	*3-119/S-8	11	-0.8
1959 Chi-N	136	477	60	126	22	9	6	45	55	50	1	1	.264	.344	.386	.730	95	-3	66	4.91	0	*3-131/1-4,S-1	14	-0.3
1960 Phi-N	55	198	29	48	5	1	3	14	19	14	1	1	.242	.315	.323	.638	75	-7	20	3.43	-4	3-53/1-1	3	-1.1
Mil-N	50	141	16	42	6	2	1	18	7	13	0	0	.298	.336	.390	.726	106	1	18	4.62	-3	O-25(25-0-0),1-10/3-4,2-3	4	-0.4
Yr.	105	339	45	90	11	3	4	32	26	27	1	1	.265	.323	.351	.674	87	-6	38	3.91	-6	3-57,O-25(25-0-0),1-11/2-3	7	-1.4
Total 14	1828	7219	1064	2089	358	72	126	757	430	534	59	27	.289	.334	.411	.745	98	-34	987	4.92	-18	*S-1404,3-320/O-43,2-29,1,P	226	4.7

• DARLING, Dell Conrad Darling b: 12/21/1861, Erie, PA d: 11/20/1904, Erie, PA BR/TR, 5'8", 170 lbs. Deb: 7/3/1883 U Career OF: 0-0-27

YEAR TM-L	G	AB	R	H	2B	3B	HR	RBI	BB	SO	SB	CS	AVG	OBP	SLG	OPS	OPS+	BR/A	RC	RC/G	FR	G/POS	WS	TPW
1883 Buf-N	6	18	1	3	0	0	0	1	2	5	....	....	.167	.250	.167	.417	29	-1	1	1.41	-1	/C-6	0	-0.2
1887 Chi-N	38	163	28	67	7	4	3	20	22	18	19	....	.411	.411	.489	.900	132	6	37	10.23	1	C-20,O-20(0-0-20)	7	0.8
1888 Chi-N	20	75	12	16	3	1	2	7	3	12	0	....	.213	.253	.360	.613	87	-1	7	3.21	-3	C-20	2	-0.2
1889 Chi-N	36	120	14	23	1	1	0	7	25	22	5	....	.192	.331	.217	.548	52	-7	11	2.87	-1	C-36	2	-0.4
1890 Chi-P	58	221	45	57	12	4	2	39	29	28	5	....	.258	.352	.376	.727	90	-3	32	5.22	-6	1-29,S-15/C-9,O-7(0-0-7),2,3	5	-0.9
1891 StL-a	17	53	9	7	1	3	0	9	10	11	0	....	.132	.270	.264	.534	46	-4	4	2.23	-1	C-17/2-2,S-1	1	-0.4
Total 6	175	650	109	173	24	13	7	83	91	96	29	....	.266	.340	.354	.694	86	-11	91	5.10	-11	C-108/1-29,O-27,S-16,2-5,3	17	-1.3

• DARR, Mike Michael Curtis Darr b: 3/21/1976, Corona, CA d: 2/15/2002, Phoenix, AZ BL/TR, 6'3", 205 lbs. Deb: 5/23/1999 Career OF: 13-51-137

YEAR TM-L	G	AB	R	H	2B	3B	HR	RBI	BB	SO	SB	CS	AVG	OBP	SLG	OPS	OPS+	BR/A	RC	RC/G	FR	G/POS	WS	TPW
1999 SD-N	25	48	6	13	1	0	2	3	5	18	2	1	.271	.340	.417	.756	98	-0	7	4.92	-1	O-22(0-3-21)	1	-0.2
2000 SD-N	58	205	21	55	14	4	1	30	23	45	9	1	.268	.342	.390	.732	91	-1	27	4.55	5	O-57(8-19-47)	6	0.2
2001 SD-N	105	289	36	80	13	1	2	34	39	72	6	2	.277	.365	.349	.714	94	-0	38	4.66	4	O-93(5-29-69)	7	0.0
Total 3	188	542	63	148	28	5	5	67	67	135	17	4	.273	.354	.371	.725	93	-2	72	4.64	8	O-172	14	0.0

• DARRAGH, Jack James S. Darragh b: 7/17/1866, Ebensburg, PA d: 8/12/1939, Rochester, PA, 6'2.5" Deb: 5/13/1891

YEAR TM-L	G	AB	R	H	2B	3B	HR	RBI	BB	SO	SB	CS	AVG	OBP	SLG	OPS	OPS+	BR/A	RC	RC/G	FR	G/POS	WS	TPW
1891 Lou-a	1	2	0	1	0	0	0	0	0	0	0	....	.500	.500	.500	1.000	189	0	1	13.58	0	/1-1	0	0.0

• DARWIN, Bobby Arthur Bobby Lee Darwin b: 2/16/1943, Los Angeles, CA BR/TR, 6'2", 200 lbs. Deb: 9/30/1962 Career OF: 37-87-417

YEAR TM-L	G	AB	R	H	2B	3B	HR	RBI	BB	SO	SB	CS	AVG	OBP	SLG	OPS	OPS+	BR/A	RC	RC/G	FR	G/POS	WS	TPW
1962 LA-A	1	1	0	0	0	0	0	0	0	1	0	0	.000	.000	.000	.000	-103	-0	0	.00	0	/P-1	0	-0.3
1969 LA-N	6	0	1	0	0	0	0	0	0	0	0	0	....	....	....	....	-108	0	0	....	0	/P-3	0	-0.3
1971 LA-N	11	20	2	5	1	0	1	4	2	9	0	0	.250	.318	.450	.768	123	1	3	5.45	0	/O-4(0-0-4)	1	0.0
1972 Min-A	145	513	48	137	20	2	22	80	38	145	2	3	.267	.327	.442	.770	121	12	67	4.44	-2	*O-142(9-86-47)	18	0.6
1973 Min-A	145	560	69	141	20	2	18	90	46	137	5	2	.252	.312	.391	.703	93	-5	64	3.84	-3	*O-140(0-0-140)/D-1	10	-1.5
1974 Min-A	152	575	67	152	13	7	25	94	37	127	1	3	.264	.324	.442	.766	114	8	80	4.91	-6	*O-142(0-0-142)	16	-0.5
1975 Min-A	48	169	26	37	6	0	5	18	18	44	2	0	.219	.309	.343	.652	82	-3	17	3.31	0	O-27(0-0-27),D-19	2	-0.5
Mil-A	55	186	19	46	6	2	8	23	11	54	4	1	.247	.300	.430	.730	104	1	24	4.36	2	O-43(25-0-20)/D-9	5	0.0
Yr.	103	355	45	83	12	2	13	41	29	98	6	1	.234	.304	.389	.693	93	-3	41	3.84	2	O-70(25-0-47),D-28	7	-0.5
1976 Mil-A	25	73	6	18	3	1	1	5	6	16	0	0	.247	.321	.356	.677	100	0	8	3.90	0	O-21(0-1-21)/D-1	2	-0.1
Bos-A	43	106	9	19	5	2	3	13	2	35	1	0	.179	.216	.349	.565	57	-6	8	2.32	0	O-17(3-0-14),D-16	0	-0.8
Yr.	68	179	15	37	8	3	4	18	8	51	1	0	.207	.260	.352	.612	75	-6	16	2.93	-0	O-38(3-1-35),D-17	2	-0.8
1977 Bos-A	4	9	1	2	1	0	0	1	0	4	0	0	.222	.222	.333	.556	44	-1	0	1.13	0	/D-2,O-1	0	-0.1
Chi-N	11	12	2	2	1	0	0	0	0	5	0	0	.167	.167	.250	.417	9	-2	1	1.35	0	/O-1	0	-0.2
Total 9	646	2224	250	559	76	16	83	328	160	577	15	9	.251	.312	.412	.724	103	4	272	4.16	-9	O-538/D-48,P-4	54	-3.5

• DASCENZO, Doug Douglas Craig Dascenzo b: 6/30/1964, Cleveland, OH BB/TL, 5'7", 160 lbs. Deb: 9/2/1988 Career OF: 146-270-101

YEAR TM-L	G	AB	R	H	2B	3B	HR	RBI	BB	SO	SB	CS	AVG	OBP	SLG	OPS	OPS+	BR/A	RC	RC/G	FR	G/POS	WS	TPW
1988 Chi-N	26	75	9	16	3	0	0	4	9	4	6	1	.213	.298	.253	.551	57	-3	6	2.74	1	O-20(0-20-0)	1	-0.3
1989 Chi-N	47	139	20	23	1	0	1	12	13	13	6	3	.165	.237	.194	.431	23	-14	7	1.53	-1	O-45(8-37-1)	1	-1.7
1990 Chi-N	113	241	27	61	9	5	1	26	21	18	15	6	.253	.316	.344	.660	76	-7	27	3.75	-1	*O-107(65-38-22)/P-1	7	-1.0
1991 Chi-N	118	239	40	61	11	0	1	18	24	26	14	7	.255	.328	.314	.642	78	-6	26	3.61	-5	O-86(32-59-16)/P-3	3	-1.1
1992 Chi-N	139	376	37	96	13	4	0	20	27	32	6	8	.255	.305	.311	.616	73	-16	36	3.23	-9	*O-122(25-80-28)	6	-2.9
1993 Tex-A	76	146	20	29	5	1	2	10	8	22	2	0	.199	.240	.288	.528	43	-12	11	2.38	3	O-68(16-35-25)/D-2	1	-1.0
1996 SD-N	21	9	3	1	0	0	0	0	1	2	0	1	.111	.200	.111	.311	-16	-2	0	.38	-1	O-10(0-1-9)	0	-0.3
Total 7	540	1225	156	287	42	10	5	90	103	117	49	26	.234	.295	.297	.592	64	-60	113	3.03	-13	O-458/P-4,D-2	19	-8.3

• DASHIELL, Wally John Wallace Dashiell b: 5/9/1902, Jewett, TX d: 5/20/1972, Pensacola, FL BR/TR, 5'9.5", 170 lbs. Deb: 4/20/1924

YEAR TM-L	G	AB	R	H	2B	3B	HR	RBI	BB	SO	SB	CS	AVG	OBP	SLG	OPS	OPS+	BR/A	RC	RC/G	FR	G/POS	WS	TPW
1924 Chi-A	1	2	0	0	0	0	0	0	0	0	0	0	.000	.000	.000	.000	-103	-1	0	.00	-1	/S-1	0	-0.1

• DATZ, Jeff Jeffrey William Datz b: 11/28/1959, Camden, NJ BR/TR, 6'4", 220 lbs. Deb: 9/5/1989 C

YEAR TM-L	G	AB	R	H	2B	3B	HR	RBI	BB	SO	SB	CS	AVG	OBP	SLG	OPS	OPS+	BR/A	RC	RC/G	FR	G/POS	WS	TPW
1989 Det-A	7	10	0	2	0	0	0	0	1	1	0	0	.200	.333	.200	.533	55	-0	1	1.89	0	/C-6,D-1	0	0.0

• DAUBACH, Brian Brian Michael Daubach b: 2/11/1972, Belleville, IL BL/TR, 6'1", 201 lbs. Deb: 9/10/1998 Career OF: 53-0-31

YEAR TM-L	G	AB	R	H	2B	3B	HR	RBI	BB	SO	SB	CS	AVG	OBP	SLG	OPS	OPS+	BR/A	RC	RC/G	FR	G/POS	WS	TPW
1998 Fla-N	10	15	0	3	1	0	0	3	1	5	0	0	.200	.294	.267	.561	51	-1	1	2.99	-1	/1-4	0	-0.2
1999*Bos-A	110	381	61	112	33	3	21	73	36	92	0	1	.294	.360	.562	.921	126	13	77	7.60	1	1-61,D-48/O-2(2-0-0),3-1	14	0.6
2000 Bos-A	142	495	55	123	32	2	21	76	44	130	1	1	.248	.317	.448	.766	88	-11	72	5.05	2	1-83,D-41/O-8(7-0-1),3-1	10	-1.7
2001 Bos-A	122	407	54	107	28	3	22	71	53	108	1	0	.263	.355	.509	.863	123	14	74	6.28	2	*1-106,O-14(6-0-8)	13	0.5
2002 Bos-A	137	444	62	118	24	2	20	78	51	126	2	1	.266	.351	.464	.815	112	8	73	5.76	-3	1-60,O-48(35-0-13),D-28	14	-0.3
2003 Chi-A	95	183	26	42	11	0	6	21	34	54	1	0	.230	.353	.388	.741	96	0	27	5.09	-2	1-45,D-14,O-12(3-0-9)	4	-0.5
Total 6	616	1925	258	505	129	10	90	322	219	515	5	3	.262	.345	.480	.825	109	23	324	5.94	-1	1-359,D-131/O-84,3-2	55	-1.6

• DAUBERT, Harry Harry "Jake" Daubert b: 6/19/1892, Columbus, OH d: 1/8/1944, Detroit, MI BR/TR, 6', 160 lbs. Deb: 9/4/1915

YEAR TM-L	G	AB	R	H	2B	3B	HR	RBI	BB	SO	SB	CS	AVG	OBP	SLG	OPS	OPS+	BR/A	RC	RC/G	FR	G/POS	WS	TPW
1915 Pit-N	1	1	0	0	0	0	0	0	0	1	0	....	.000	.000	.000	.000	-101	-0	0	.00	0	....	0	0.0

• DAUBERT, Jake Jacob Ellsworth Daubert b: 4/17/1884, Shamokin, PA d: 10/9/1924, Cincinnati, OH BL/TL, 5'10.5", 160 lbs. Deb: 4/14/1910

YEAR TM-L	G	AB	R	H	2B	3B	HR	RBI	BB	SO	SB	CS	AVG	OBP	SLG	OPS	OPS+	BR/A	RC	RC/G	FR	G/POS	WS	TPW
1910 Bro-N	144	552	67	146	15	15	8	50	47	53	23	....	.264	.328	.389	.717	112	6	79	4.68	4	*1-144	17	0.8
1911 Bro-N	149	573	89	176	17	8	5	45	51	56	32	....	.307	.366	.391	.757	117	12	94	5.78	9	*1-149	20	1.9
1912 Bro-N	145	559	81	172	19	16	3	66	48	45	29	....	.308	.369	.415	.784	119	14	95	6.06	3	*1-143	17	1.5
1913 Bro-N	139	508	76	178	17	7	2	52	44	40	25	....	**.350**	.405	.423	.829	133	23	94	6.92	-1	*1-139	17	2.0
1914 Bro-N	126	474	89	156	17	7	6	45	30	34	25	....	**.329**	.375	.432	.808	137	20	85	6.31	-14	*1-126	19	0.5
1915 Bro-N	150	544	62	164	21	8	2	47	57	48	11	13	.301	.369	.381	.749	125	14	81	4.99	2	*1-150	27	1.5
1916*Bro-N	127	478	75	151	16	7	3	33	38	39	21	7	.316	.371	.397	.769	132	20	80	5.61	-2	*1-126	21	1.9
1917 Bro-N	125	468	59	122	4	4	2	30	51	30	11	....	.261	.341	.299	.640	94	-0	53	3.69	-1	*1-125	12	-0.4
1918 Bro-N	108	396	50	122	12	**15**	2	47	27	18	10	....	.308	.360	.429	.789	141	18	63	5.66	0	*1-105	15	1.9
1919*Cin-N	140	537	79	148	10	12	2	44	35	23	11	....	.276	.322	.350	.672	105	3	66	3.98	0	*1-140	17	0.0
1920 Cin-N	142	553	97	168	28	13	4	48	47	29	11	13	.304	.362	.423	.785	126	18	83	5.19	-2	*1-140	24	1.4
1921 Cin-N	136	516	69	158	18	12	2	64	24	16	12	6	.306	.341	.399	.740	100	1	70	4.70	2	*1-136	12	-0.6
1922 Cin-N	156	610	114	205	15	**22**	12	66	56	21	14	17	.336	.395	.492	.886	130	24	115	6.70	-1	*1-156	24	1.2
1923 Cin-N	125	500	63	146	27	10	2	54	40	20	11	12	.292	.349	.398	.747	99	-3	68	4.79	3	*1-121	13	-0.8
1924 Cin-N	102	405	47	114	14	9	1	31	28	17	5	10	.281	.331	.368	.699	88	-9	48	4.02	7	*1-102	8	-0.8
Total 15	2014	7673	1117	2326	250	165	56	722	623	489	251	78	.303	.360	.401	.760	117	163	1174	5.27	11	*1-2002	263	11.9

• DAUER, Rich Richard Fremont Dauer b: 7/27/1952, San Bernardino, CA BR/TR, 6', 180 lbs. Deb: 9/11/1976 C

YEAR TM-L	G	AB	R	H	2B	3B	HR	RBI	BB	SO	SB	CS	AVG	OBP	SLG	OPS	OPS+	BR/A	RC	RC/G	FR	G/POS	WS	TPW
1976 Bal-A	11	39	0	4	0	0	0	3	1	3	0	0	.103	.146	.103	.249	-28	-6	1	.54	1	2-10	0	-0.5

YEAR TM-L	G	AB	R	H	2B	3B	HR	RBI	BB	SO	SB	CS	AVG	OBP	SLG	OPS	OPS+	BR/A	RC	RC/G	FR	G/POS	WS	TPW
1977 Bal-A	96	304	38	74	15	1	5	25	20	28	1	0	.243	.294	.349	.643	79	-9	30	3.31	6	2-83/3-9,D-2	8	0.1
1978 Bal-A	133	459	57	121	23	0	6	46	26	22	0	4	.264	.303	.353	.656	89	-9	44	3.30	-4	2-87,3-52/D-1	10	-0.9
1979*Bal-A	142	479	63	123	20	0	9	61	36	36	0	1	.257	.310	.355	.665	82	-13	51	3.55	3	*2-103,3-44	11	-0.5
1980 Bal-A	152	557	71	158	32	0	2	63	46	19	3	2	.284	.342	.352	.693	91	-6	64	3.98	11	*2-137,3-35	17	1.2
1981 Bal-A	96	369	41	97	27	0	4	38	27	18	0	0	.263	.318	.369	.687	98	-1	44	4.18	-11	2-94/3-4	12	-0.7
1982 Bal-A	158	558	75	156	24	2	8	57	50	34	0	1	.280	.340	.373	.713	96	-3	70	4.35	-10	*2-123,3-61	15	-0.7
1983*Bal-A	140	459	49	108	19	0	5	41	47	29	1	1	.235	.309	.309	.618	72	-17	42	2.96	-16	*2-131,3-17	8	-2.6
1984 Bal-A	127	397	29	101	26	0	2	24	24	23	1	3	.254	.297	.335	.632	76	-14	36	3.02	-17	*2-123/3-3	7	-2.6
1985 Bal-A	85	208	25	42	7	0	2	14	20	7	0	1	.202	.275	.264	.540	50	-15	14	2.13	-4	2-73,3-17/1-1	1	-1.6
Total 10	**1140**	**3829**	**448**	**984**	**193**	**3**	**43**	**372**	**297**	**219**	**6**	**13**	**.257**	**.313**	**.343**	**.655**	**83**	**-92**	**396**	**3.49**	**-41**	**2-964,3-242/D-3,1-1**	**89**	**-8.8**

• DAUGHERTY, Doc Harold Ray Daugherty b: 10/12/1927, Paris, PA BR/TR, 6', 180 lbs. Deb: 4/22/1951

YEAR TM-L	G	AB	R	H	2B	3B	HR	RBI	BB	SO	SB	CS	AVG	OBP	SLG	OPS	OPS+	BR/A	RC	RC/G	FR	G/POS	WS	TPW
1951 Det-A	1	1	0	0	0	0	0	0	0	1	0	0	.000	.000	.000	.000	-100	-0	0	.00	0	....	0	0.0

• DAUGHERTY, Jack John Michael Daugherty b: 7/3/1960, Hialeah, FL BB/TL, 6', 195 lbs. Deb: 9/1/1987 Career OF: 104-1-25

YEAR TM-L	G	AB	R	H	2B	3B	HR	RBI	BB	SO	SB	CS	AVG	OBP	SLG	OPS	OPS+	BR/A	RC	RC/G	FR	G/POS	WS	TPW
1987 Mon-N	11	10	1	1	1	0	0	1	0	3	0	0	.100	.100	.200	.300	-22	-2	0	.62	0	/1-1	0	-0.1
1989 Tex-A	52	106	15	32	4	2	1	10	11	21	2	1	.302	.373	.406	.779	117	3	17	5.78	2	1-23/D-8,0-5(4-0-1)	3	0.3
1990 Tex-A	125	310	36	93	20	2	6	47	22	49	0	0	.300	.350	.435	.786	118	7	48	5.73	2	0-42(39-0-4),1-30,D-21	10	0.6
1991 Tex-A	58	144	8	28	3	2	1	11	16	23	1	0	.194	.275	.264	.539	51	-9	12	2.50	-1	0-37(34-0-3),1-11/D-1	0	-1.2
1992 Tex-A	59	127	13	26	9	0	0	9	16	21	2	1	.205	.299	.276	.574	64	-6	11	2.78	0	0-26(16-1-11),D-13/1-8	1	-0.7
1993 Hou-N	4	3	0	1	0	0	0	0	0	0	0	0	.333	.333	.333	.667	82	-0	0	4.50	0	/1-1,0-1	0	0.0
Cin-N	46	59	7	13	2	0	2	9	11	15	0	0	.220	.343	.356	.699	87	-1	8	4.73	0	0-16(11-0-5)/1-2	2	-0.2
Yr.	50	62	7	14	2	0	2	9	11	15	0	0	.226	.342	.355	.697	87	-1	9	4.72	-1	0-17(11-0-6)/1-3	2	-0.2
Total 6	**355**	**759**	**80**	**194**	**39**	**6**	**10**	**87**	**76**	**132**	**5**	**2**	**.256**	**.327**	**.362**	**.689**	**91**	**-8**	**96**	**4.35**	**3**	**0-127/1-76,D-43**	**16**	**-1.3**

• DAUGHTERS, Bob Robert Francis "Red" Daughters b: 8/5/1914, Cincinnati, OH d: 8/22/1988, Southbury, CT BR/TR, 6'2", 185 lbs. Deb: 4/24/1937

YEAR TM-L	G	AB	R	H	2B	3B	HR	RBI	BB	SO	SB	CS	AVG	OBP	SLG	OPS	OPS+	BR/A	RC	RC/G	FR	G/POS	WS	TPW
1937 Bos-A	1	0	1	0	0	0	0	0	0	0	0	0	....	....	....	....	-96	0	0	....	0	....	0	0.0

• DAULTON, Darren Darren Arthur "Dutch" Daulton b: 1/3/1962, Arkansas City, KS BL/TR, 6'2", 190 lbs. Deb: 9/25/1983 C Career OF: 6-0-73

YEAR TM-L	G	AB	R	H	2B	3B	HR	RBI	BB	SO	SB	CS	AVG	OBP	SLG	OPS	OPS+	BR/A	RC	RC/G	FR	G/POS	WS	TPW
1983 Phi-N	2	3	1	1	0	0	0	0	1	1	0	0	.333	.500	.333	.833	137	0	1	8.51	0	/C-2	0	0.0
1985 Phi-N	36	103	14	21	3	1	4	11	16	37	3	0	.204	.311	.369	.680	87	-1	13	4.30	0	C-28	4	0.0
1986 Phi-N	49	138	18	31	4	0	8	21	38	41	2	3	.225	.395	.428	.823	123	5	26	6.12	-1	C-48	7	0.7
1987 Phi-N	53	129	10	25	6	0	3	13	16	37	0	0	.194	.283	.310	.593	55	-9	13	3.15	0	C-40/1-1	3	-0.7
1988 Phi-N	58	144	13	30	6	0	1	12	17	26	2	1	.208	.292	.271	.563	61	-7	12	2.77	-2	C-44/1-1	1	-0.7
1989 Phi-N	131	368	29	74	12	2	8	44	52	58	2	1	.201	.303	.310	.613	76	-11	37	3.33	1	*C-126	11	-0.3
1990 Phi-N	143	459	62	123	30	1	12	57	72	72	7	1	.268	.370	.416	.786	116	13	76	5.84	2	*C-139	23	2.4
1991 Phi-N	89	285	36	56	12	0	12	42	41	66	5	0	.196	.302	.365	.667	88	-3	34	3.84	-6	C-88	9	-0.4
1992 Phi-N★	145	485	80	131	32	5	27	**109**	88	103	11	2	.270	.389	.524	.912	157	40	107	7.91	-3	*C-141	31	5.0
1993*Phi-N★	147	510	90	131	35	4	24	105	117	111	5	0	.257	.397	.482	.880	136	32	109	7.58	-4	*C-146	29	3.9
1994 Phi-N	69	257	43	77	17	1	15	56	33	43	4	1	.300	.381	.549	.930	136	14	56	8.12	3	C-68	13	2.1
1995 Phi-N★	98	342	44	85	19	3	9	55	55	52	3	0	.249	.361	.401	.761	100	2	54	5.54	-3	C-95	12	0.6
1996 Phi-N	5	12	3	2	0	0	0	0	7	5	0	0	.167	.500	.167	.667	85	1	2	4.51	0	/0-5(5-0-0)	0	0.0
1997 Phi-N	84	269	46	71	13	6	11	42	54	57	4	0	.264	.389	.480	.868	126	13	55	7.14	2	0-70(0-0-70)/D-6,1-3	11	1.1
*Fla-N	52	126	22	33	8	2	3	21	22	17	2	1	.262	.376	.429	.804	115	3	22	6.15	-3	1-39/0-3(1-0-3),D-1	5	-0.2
Yr.	136	395	68	104	21	8	14	63	76	74	6	1	.263	.385	.463	.848	123	16	77	6.82	-1	0-73(1-0-73),1-42/D-7	16	0.9
Total 14	**1161**	**3630**	**511**	**891**	**197**	**25**	**137**	**588**	**629**	**726**	**50**	**10**	**.245**	**.360**	**.427**	**.787**	**114**	**93**	**617**	**5.87**	**-14**	**C-965/0-78,1-44,D-7**	**159**	**13.4**

• DAVALILLO, Vic Victor Jose (Romero) Davalillo b: 7/31/1936, Cabimas, Venezuela BL/TL, 5'7", 155 lbs. Deb: 4/9/1963 Career OF: 131-752-196 ♦

YEAR TM-L	G	AB	R	H	2B	3B	HR	RBI	BB	SO	SB	CS	AVG	OBP	SLG	OPS	OPS+	BR/A	RC	RC/G	FR	G/POS	WS	TPW
1963 Cle-A	90	370	44	108	18	5	7	36	16	41	3	3	.292	.323	.424	.747	108	2	50	4.88	9	0-89(0-89-0)	14	0.9
1964 Cle-A	150	577	64	156	26	2	6	51	34	77	21	11	.270	.312	.354	.666	85	-12	65	3.92	5	*0-143(0-143-0)	13	-1.3
1965 Cle-A★	142	505	67	152	19	1	5	40	35	50	26	7	.301	.346	.372	.719	103	5	68	4.93	4	*0-134(0-134-0)	18	0.5
1966 Cle-A	121	344	42	86	6	4	3	19	24	37	8	6	.250	.299	.317	.616	77	-11	32	3.12	-5	*0-108(0-108-0)	7	-2.0
1967 Cle-A	139	359	47	103	17	5	2	22	10	30	6	7	.287	.308	.379	.687	101	-2	39	3.89	-2	*0-125(1-125-0)	9	-0.8
1968 Cle-A	51	180	15	43	2	3	2	13	3	19	8	6	.239	.255	.317	.572	74	-7	13	2.44	0	0-49(3-2-48)	3	-1.3
Cal-A	93	339	34	101	15	4	1	18	15	34	17	10	.298	.328	.375	.702	117	5	41	4.36	1	0-86(0-70-17)	13	0.2
Yr.	144	519	49	144	17	7	3	31	18	53	25	16	.277	.303	.355	.658	102	-3	54	3.66	1	*0-135(3-72-65)	16	-1.0
1969 Cal-A	33	71	10	11	1	1	0	1	6	5	3	0	.155	.231	.197	.428	22	-7	4	1.78	0	0-22(0-2-20)/1-3	0	-0.8
StL-N	63	98	15	26	3	0	2	10	7	8	1	1	.265	.314	.357	.671	87	-2	10	3.66	0	0-23(2-10-11)/P-2	2	-0.4
1970 StL-N	111	183	29	57	14	3	1	33	13	19	4	1	.311	.357	.437	.794	109	3	28	5.71	-1	0-54(12-33-13)	5	0.1
1971*Pit-N	99	295	48	84	14	6	1	33	11	31	10	2	.285	.315	.383	.698	96	-1	36	4.40	0	0-61(11-20-31),1-16	8	-0.6
1972*Pit-N	117	368	59	117	19	2	4	28	26	44	14	1	.318	.368	.413	.781	124	14	59	6.14	-2	0-97(64-7-26)/1-8	16	0.8
1973 Pit-N	59	83	9	15	1	0	1	3	2	7	0	2	.181	.200	.229	.429	19	-10	3	1.22	1	1-10,0-10(7-0-3)	0	-1.1
*Oak-A	38	64	5	12	1	0	0	4	3	4	0	0	.188	.224	.203	.427	22	-7	3	1.57	0	0-19(8-1-10)/1-8,D-2	0	-0.8
1974 Oak-A	17	23	0	4	0	0	0	1	2	2	0	0	.174	.240	.174	.414	22	-2	1	1.49	0	/0-6(2-2-2),D-4	0	-0.3
1977*LA-N	24	48	3	15	2	0	0	4	0	6	0	0	.313	.313	.354	.667	79	-2	5	4.35	-1	0-12(2-4-8)	1	-0.2
1978*LA-N	75	77	15	24	1	1	1	11	3	7	2	1	.312	.338	.390	.727	103	0	10	4.81	0	0-25(16-2-7)/1-1	2	-0.1
1979 LA-N	29	27	2	7	1	0	0	2	2	0	2	0	.259	.310	.296	.607	67	-1	3	4.01	0	/0-3(3-0-0)	0	-0.1
1980 LA-N	7	6	1	1	0	0	0	0	0	1	0	0	.167	.167	.167	.333	-7	-1	0	.90	0	/1-1	0	-0.1
Total 16	**1458**	**4017**	**509**	**1122**	**160**	**37**	**36**	**329**	**212**	**422**	**125**	**58**	**.279**	**.317**	**.364**	**.682**	**94**	**-36**	**472**	**4.17**	**8**	***0-1066/1-47,D-6,P-2**	**111**	**-7.3**

• DAVALILLO, Yo-Yo Pompeyo Antonio (Romero) Davalillo b: 6/30/1931, Caracas, Venezuela BR/TR, 5'3", 140 lbs. Deb: 8/1/1953

YEAR TM-L	G	AB	R	H	2B	3B	HR	RBI	BB	SO	SB	CS	AVG	OBP	SLG	OPS	OPS+	BR/A	RC	RC/G	FR	G/POS	WS	TPW
1953 Was-A	19	58	10	17	1	0	0	2	1	7	1	0	.293	.305	.310	.615	68	-2	6	3.33	-2	S-17	1	-0.3

• DAVANON, Jeff Jeffrey Graham DaVanon b: 12/8/1973, San Diego, CA BB/TR, 6', 185 lbs. Deb: 9/7/1999 Career OF: 13-48-114

YEAR TM-L	G	AB	R	H	2B	3B	HR	RBI	BB	SO	SB	CS	AVG	OBP	SLG	OPS	OPS+	BR/A	RC	RC/G	FR	G/POS	WS	TPW
1999 Ana-A	7	20	4	4	0	1	1	4	2	7	0	1	.200	.273	.450	.723	81	-1	2	3.44	0	/0-5(3-0-2),D-2	0	-0.2
2001 Ana-A	40	88	7	17	2	1	5	9	11	29	1	3	.193	.283	.409	.692	77	-4	10	3.40	0	0-29(0-13-17)/D-6	1	-0.5
2002 Ana-A	16	30	3	5	3	0	1	4	2	6	1	0	.167	.219	.367	.585	52	-2	3	2.77	0	0-10(2-4-4)/D-3	1	-0.2
2003 Ana-A	123	330	56	93	16	1	12	43	42	59	17	5	.282	.365	.445	.810	117	10	56	5.90	1	*0-115(8-31-91)/D-1	12	0.8
Total 4	**186**	**468**	**70**	**119**	**21**	**3**	**19**	**60**	**57**	**101**	**19**	**9**	**.254**	**.337**	**.434**	**.770**	**104**	**3**	**71**	**5.07**	**1**	**0-159/D-12**	**14**	**-0.1**

• DAVANON, Jerry Frank Gerald DaVanon b: 8/21/1945, Oceanside, CA BR/TR, 5'11", 175 lbs. Deb: 4/11/1969

YEAR TM-L	G	AB	R	H	2B	3B	HR	RBI	BB	SO	SB	CS	AVG	OBP	SLG	OPS	OPS+	BR/A	RC	RC/G	FR	G/POS	WS	TPW
1969 SD-N	24	59	4	8	1	0	0	3	3	12	0	3	.136	.177	.153	.330	-7	-10	1	.46	-3	2-15/S-7	0	-1.2
StL-N	16	40	7	12	3	0	1	7	6	8	0	0	.300	.391	.450	.841	135	2	7	6.04	1	S-16	2	0.5
Yr.	40	99	11	20	4	0	1	10	9	20	0	3	.202	.269	.273	.541	53	-8	8	2.40	-2	S-23,2-15	2	-0.7
1970 StL-N	11	18	2	2	1	0	0	0	2	5	0	0	.111	.200	.167	.367	-1	-3	1	.84	0	/3-5,2-3	0	-0.3
1971 Bal-A	38	81	14	19	5	0	0	4	12	20	0	0	.235	.340	.296	.637	82	-1	8	3.17	0	2-20,S-11/3-3,1-1	2	0.0
1973 Cal-A	41	49	6	12	3	0	0	2	3	9	1	2	.245	.288	.306	.595	73	-2	4	2.82	-3	S-14,2-12/3-7	1	-0.4
1974 StL-N	30	40	4	6	1	0	0	4	4	5	0	1	.150	.261	.175	.436	24	-4	2	1.41	-1	S-14/3-8,2-7,0-1	1	-0.5
1975 Hou-N	32	97	15	27	4	2	1	10	16	7	2	0	.278	.386	.392	.778	125	4	16	5.75	-2	S-21/2-9,3-3	4	0.5
1976 Hou-N	61	107	19	31	3	3	1	20	21	12	0	2	.290	.411	.402	.813	144	7	18	6.15	0	2-17,S-17/3-9	6	1.0
1977 StL-N	9	8	2	0	0	0	0	0	1	2	0	0	.000	.111	.000	.111	-68	-2	0	.10	0	/2-5	0	-0.2
Total 8	**262**	**499**	**73**	**117**	**21**	**5**	**3**	**50**	**68**	**80**	**3**	**8**	**.234**	**.332**	**.315**	**.647**	**88**	**-9**	**56**	**3.71**	**-9**	**S-100/2-88,3-35,1-1,0-1**	**16**	**-0.6**

• DAVENPORT, Jim James Houston Davenport b: 8/17/1933, Siluria, AL BR/TR, 5'11", 175 lbs. Deb: 4/15/1958 M/C

YEAR TM-L	G	AB	R	H	2B	3B	HR	RBI	BB	SO	SB	CS	AVG	OBP	SLG	OPS	OPS+	BR/A	RC	RC/G	FR	G/POS	WS	TPW
1958 SF-N	134	434	70	111	22	3	12	41	33	64	1	3	.256	.319	.403	.722	91	-7	57	4.42	-4	*3-130/S-5	11	-1.1
1959 SF-N	123	469	65	121	16	3	6	38	28	65	0	1	.258	.303	.342	.646	73	-19	50	3.71	8	*3-121/S-1	9	-1.1
1960 SF-N	112	363	43	91	15	3	6	38	26	58	0	2	.251	.308	.358	.666	87	-8	39	3.63	6	*3-103/S-7	9	-0.2
1961 SF-N	137	436	64	121	28	4	12	65	45	65	4	3	.278	.348	.443	.790	112	7	67	5.20	14	*3-132	18	2.1
1962*SF-N★	144	485	83	144	25	5	14	58	45	76	2	5	.297	.359	.456	.815	119	11	76	5.56	11	*3-141	20	2.1
1963 SF-N	147	460	40	116	19	3	4	36	32	87	5	2	.252	.301	.333	.633	83	-9	46	3.29	-2	*3-127,2-22/S-1	9	-1.1
1964 SF-N	116	297	24	70	10	6	2	26	29	46	2	0	.236	.304	.330	.634	77	-8	29	3.13	3	S-64,3-41,2-30	7	0.0

YEAR TM-L	G	AB	R	H	2B	3B	HR	RBI	BB	SO	SB	CS	AVG	OBP	SLG	OPS	OPS+	BR/A	RC	RC/G	FR	G/POS	WS	TPW
1965 SF-N	106	271	29	68	14	3	4	31	21	47	0	0	.251	.307	.369	.676	87	-5	30	3.66	-11	3-39,S-37,2-26	6	-1.2
1966 SF-N	111	305	42	76	6	2	9	30	22	40	1	1	.249	.302	.370	.672	83	-7	33	3.62	-4	S-58,3-36,2-21/1-2	8	-0.7
1967 SF-N	124	295	42	81	10	3	5	30	39	50	1	4	.275	.367	.380	.747	115	6	41	4.77	3	3-64,S-28,2-12	11	1.3
1968 SF-N	113	272	27	61	1	1	1	17	26	32	0	3	.224	.292	.246	.538	63	-13	19	2.27	-2	3-82,S-17/2-1	3	-1.6
1969 SF-N	112	303	20	73	10	1	2	42	29	37	0	1	.241	.307	.300	.608	72	-11	27	2.89	-2	*3-104/1-1,0-1,S-1	4	-1.4
1970 SF-N	22	37	3	9	1	0	0	4	7	6	0	0	.243	.364	.270	.634	73	-1	4	3.94	-1	3-10	1	-0.2
Total 13	1501	4427	552	1142	177	37	77	456	382	673	16	25	.258	.320	.367	.687	90	-63	519	3.94	19	*3-1130,S-219,2-112/1-3,0-1	116	-3.1
• DAVID, Andre	Andre Anter David b: 5/18/1958, Hollywood, CA BL/TL, 6', 170 lbs. Deb: 6/29/1984																							
1984 Min-A	33	48	5	12	2	0	1	5	7	11	0	0	.250	.357	.354	.711	93	-0	6	4.17	0	0-14(10-0-4)/D-2	1	-0.1
1986 Min-A	5	5	0	1	0	0	0	0	0	2	0	0	.200	.333	.200	.533	48	-0	0	2.84	0	/D-1	0	0.0
Total 2	38	53	5	13	2	0	1	5	7	13	0	0	.245	.355	.340	.694	89	-0	6	4.05	0	/0-14,D-3	1	-0.1
• DAVIDSON, Bill	William Simpson Davidson b: 5/10/1887, Lafayette, IN d: 5/23/1954, Lincoln, NE BR/TR, 5'10", 170 lbs. Deb: 9/29/1909 Career OF: 1-202-4																							
1909 Chi-N	2	7	2	1	0	0	0	0	1	....	1	....	.143	.250	.143	.393	22	-1	0	2.07	0	/0-2(1-1-0)	0	-0.1
1910 Bro-N	136	509	48	121	13	7	0	34	24	54	27	....	.238	.277	.291	.568	68	-23	48	3.10	-14	*0-131(0-127-4)	6	-4.6
1911 Bro-N	87	292	33	68	3	4	1	26	16	21	18	....	.233	.275	.281	.556	58	-17	27	3.04	-7	0-74(0-74-0)	3	-2.9
Total 3	225	808	83	190	16	11	1	60	41	75	46	....	.235	.276	.286	.562	64	-40	75	3.06	-21	0-207	9	-7.5
• DAVIDSON, Claude	Claude Boucher "Davey" Davidson b: 10/13/1896, Boston, MA d: 4/18/1956, Weymouth, MA BL/TR, 5'11", 155 lbs. Deb: 4/25/1918																							
1918 Phi-A	31	81	4	15	1	0	0	4	5	9	0	....	.185	.233	.198	.430	29	-7	4	1.44	-1	2-15/0-8(1-0-7),3-1	0	-0.9
1919 Was-A	2	7	1	3	0	0	0	0	1	1	0	....	.429	.500	.429	.929	163	1	2	8.59	0	/3-2	0	0.1
Total 2	33	88	5	18	1	0	0	4	6	10	0	....	.205	.255	.216	.471	42	-6	6	1.92	-1	/2-15,0-8,3-3	0	-0.8
• DAVIDSON, Cleatus	Cleatus Lavon Davidson b: 11/1/1976, Bartow, FL BB/TR, 5'10", 180 lbs. Deb: 5/30/1999																							
1999 Min-A	12	22	3	3	0	0	0	3	0	4	2	0	.136	.136	.136	.273	-29	-4	0	.25	2	/2-6,S-4	0	-0.1
• DAVIDSON, Homer	Homer Hurd "Divvy" Davidson b: 10/14/1884, Cleveland, OH d: 7/26/1948, Detroit, MI BR/TR, 5'10.5", 155 lbs. Deb: 4/25/1908																							
1908 Cle-A	9	4	2	0	0	0	0	0	0	....	1	....	.000	.000	.000	.000	-100	-1	0	.00	-1	/C-5,0-1	0	-0.1
• DAVIDSON, Mark	John Mark Davidson b: 2/15/1961, Knoxville, TN BR/TR, 6'2", 190 lbs. Deb: 6/20/1986 Career OF: 125-37-198																							
1986 Min-A	36	68	5	8	3	0	0	2	6	22	2	3	.118	.189	.162	.351	-3	-11	2	.79	-1	0-31(20-5-7)/D-3	0	-1.3
1987*Min-A	102	150	32	40	4	1	1	14	13	26	9	2	.267	.325	.327	.652	71	-5	17	3.69	0	0-86(36-20-33)/D-9	3	-0.7
1988 Min-A	100	106	22	23	7	0	1	10	10	20	3	3	.217	.291	.311	.602	67	-5	9	2.68	-2	0-91(4-4-84)/D-3,3-1	1	-0.9
1989 Hou-N	33	65	7	13	2	1	1	5	7	14	1	0	.200	.278	.308	.585	70	-2	6	2.97	-1	0-23(7-3-15)	1	-0.4
1990 Hou-N	57	130	12	38	5	1	1	11	10	18	0	3	.292	.343	.369	.712	99	-2	16	4.39	-1	0-51(26-1-27)	4	-0.4
1991 Hou-N	85	142	10	27	6	0	2	15	12	28	0	0	.190	.263	.275	.537	54	-9	11	2.46	0	0-63(32-4-32)	1	-1.0
Total 6	413	661	88	149	27	3	6	57	58	128	15	11	.225	.291	.303	.593	64	-34	60	2.96	-4	0-345/D-15,3-1	10	-4.6
• DAVIES, Chick	Lloyd Garrison Davies b: 3/6/1892, Peabody, MA d: 9/5/1973, Middletown, CT BL/TL, 5'8", 145 lbs. Deb: 7/11/1914 Career OF: 16-21-6 ♦																							
1914 Phi-A	19	46	6	11	3	1	0	5	5	13	1	....	.239	.314	.348	.662	103	0	6	4.01	0	0-10(9-0-1)/P-1	2	0.2
1915 Phi-A	56	132	13	24	5	3	0	11	14	31	2	4	.182	.270	.265	.535	62	-7	10	2.18	4	0-32(7-21-4)/P-4	0	-1.6
1925 NY-N	4	6	1	0	0	0	0	0	0	1	0	0	.000	.000	.000	.000	-104	-1	0	.00	0	/P-2,0-1	0	-0.3
1926 NY-N	38	18	4	4	0	0	0	1	3	5	0	....	.222	.333	.222	.556	53	1	1	2.75	1	P-38	4	-0.2
Total 4	117	202	24	39	8	4	0	17	22	50	3	4	.193	.279	.272	.551	67	-7	17	2.55	5	/P-45,0-43	6	-2.0
• DAVIS, Alvin	Alvin Glenn Davis b: 9/9/1960, Riverside, CA BL/TR, 6'1", 195 lbs. Deb: 4/11/1984																							
1984 Sea-A★	152	567	80	161	34	3	27	116	97	78	5	4	.284	.395	.497	.892	147	40	117	7.42	-4	*1-147/D-7	27	2.6
1985 Sea-A	155	578	78	166	33	1	18	78	90	71	1	2	.287	.385	.441	.826	125	23	101	6.24	-7	*1-154	22	0.6
1986 Sea-A	135	479	66	130	18	1	18	72	76	68	0	3	.271	.375	.426	.800	116	12	78	5.72	-5	*1-101,D-32	13	0.0
1987 Sea-A	157	580	86	171	37	2	29	100	72	84	0	0	.295	.375	.516	.890	126	23	111	6.87	-7	*1-157	20	0.6
1988 Sea-A	140	478	67	141	24	1	18	69	95	53	1	1	.295	.416	.462	.878	139	30	95	7.21	-1	*1-115,D-25	18	2.1
1989 Sea-A	142	498	84	152	30	1	21	95	101	49	0	1	.305	.428	.496	.924	155	42	109	**8.00**	-3	*1-125,D-14	26	3.0
1990 Sea-A	140	494	63	140	21	0	17	68	85	68	0	2	.283	.393	.429	.822	128	22	87	6.31	-1	D-87,1-52	16	1.5
1991 Sea-A	145	462	39	102	15	1	12	69	56	78	0	3	.221	.305	.335	.641	77	-15	48	3.40	-1	*D-126,1-14	7	-2.1
1992 Cal-A	40	104	5	26	8	0	0	16	13	9	0	0	.250	.333	.327	.660	85	-2	12	3.91	-1	1-22/D-9	4	-0.4
Total 9	1206	4240	568	1189	220	10	160	683	685	558	7	16	.280	.384	.450	.834	127	174	757	6.34	-30	1-887,D-300	153	7.7
• DAVIS, Ben	Mark Christopher Davis b: 3/10/1977, Chester, PA BB/TR, 6'4", 215 lbs. Deb: 9/25/1998																							
1998 SD-N	1	1	0	0	0	0	0	0	0	0	0	0	.000	.000	.000	.000	-108	-0	0	.00	0	/C-1	0	0.0
1999 SD-N	76	266	29	65	14	1	5	30	25	70	2	1	.244	.309	.361	.670	75	-11	28	3.59	-3	C-74	3	-0.9
2000 SD-N	43	130	12	29	6	0	3	14	14	35	1	1	.223	.299	.338	.637	65	-7	14	3.38	1	C-38/D-1	3	-0.3
2001 SD-N	138	448	56	107	20	0	11	57	66	112	4	4	.239	.342	.357	.699	89	-7	56	4.11	1	*C-135/1-2	15	0.3
2002 Sea-A	80	228	24	59	10	1	7	43	18	58	1	1	.259	.319	.404	.722	94	-3	28	4.25	0	C-77/1-2	10	0.2
2003 Sea-A	80	246	25	58	18	0	6	42	18	61	0	0	.236	.288	.382	.670	77	-9	27	3.63	-2	C-73/D-1	7	-0.6
Total 6	418	1319	146	318	68	2	32	186	141	336	8	7	.241	.317	.368	.686	82	-37	153	3.86	-3	C-398/1-4,D-2	38	-1.3
• DAVIS, Bill	Arthur Willard Davis b: 6/6/1942, Graceville, MN BL/TL, 6'7", 215 lbs. Deb: 9/16/1965																							
1965 Cle-A	10	10	0	3	1	0	0	0	0	1	0	0	.300	.300	.400	.700	96	-0	1	4.63	0	....	0	0.0
1966 Cle-A	23	38	2	6	1	0	1	4	6	9	0	0	.158	.273	.263	.536	55	-2	3	2.34	1	/1-9	0	-0.2
1969 SD-N	31	57	1	10	1	0	0	1	8	18	0	0	.175	.288	.193	.481	39	-4	3	1.89	-1	1-14	0	-0.6
Total 3	64	105	3	19	3	0	1	5	14	28	0	0	.181	.283	.238	.521	49	-6	8	2.28	0	/1-23	0	-0.8
• DAVIS, Bob	Robert John Eugene Davis b: 3/1/1952, Pryor, OK BR/TR, 6', 180 lbs. Deb: 4/6/1973																							
1973 SD-N	5	11	1	1	0	0	0	0	0	5	0	0	.091	.091	.091	.182	-54	-2	0	.31	-1	/C-5	0	-0.3
1975 SD-N	43	128	6	30	3	2	0	7	11	31	0	0	.234	.310	.289	.599	71	-5	12	3.06	0	C-43	3	-0.3
1976 SD-N	51	83	7	17	0	1	0	5	5	13	0	0	.205	.250	.229	.479	40	-7	5	2.05	-2	C-47	1	-0.7
1977 SD-N	48	94	9	17	2	0	1	10	5	24	0	0	.181	.238	.234	.472	30	-9	5	1.73	0	C-46	1	-0.8
1978 SD-N	19	40	3	8	1	0	0	2	1	5	0	1	.200	.220	.225	.445	26	-4	1	.83	-1	C-16	0	-0.5
1979 Tor-A	32	89	6	11	2	0	1	8	6	15	0	0	.124	.188	.180	.367		-13	2	.67	-1	C-32	1	-1.2
1980 Tor-A	91	218	18	47	11	0	4	19	12	25	0	0	.216	.260	.321	.581	56	-14	17	2.37	0	C-89	3	-1.1
1981 Cal-A	1	2	0	0	0	0	0	0	0	0	0	0	.000	.000	.000	.000	-100	-1	0	.00	-0	/C-1	0	-0.1
Total 8	290	665	50	131	19	3	6	51	40	118	0	1	.197	.250	.262	.512	42	-54	42	1.95	-4	C-279	9	-4.9
• DAVIS, Brandy	Robert Brandon Davis b: 9/10/1928, Newark, DE BR/TR, 6', 170 lbs. Deb: 4/15/1952 C Career OF: 18-9-12																							
1952 Pit-N	55	95	14	17	1	1	0	1	11	28	9	2	.179	.264	.211	.475	32	-7	7	2.31	-3	0-29(9-9-12)	0	-1.2
1953 Pit-N	12	39	5	8	2	0	0	2	0	3	0	2	.205	.205	.256	.462	19	-6	2	1.29	0	/0-9(9-0-0)	0	-0.6
Total 2	67	134	19	25	3	1	0	3	11	31	9	4	.187	.248	.224	.472	29	-13	9	2.01	-3	/0-38	0	-1.8
• DAVIS, Brock	Bryshear Barnett Davis b: 10/19/1943, Oakland, CA BL/TL, 5'10", 168 lbs. Deb: 4/9/1963 Career OF: 28-118-13																							
1963 Hou-N	34	55	7	11	2	0	1	2	4	10	0	0	.200	.254	.291	.545	60	-3	4	2.37	-1	0-14(5-6-3)	0	-0.5
1964 Hou-N	1	3	0	0	0	0	0	0	1	1	0	0	.000	.250	.000	.250	-24	-0	0	.59	0	/0-1	0	-0.1
1966 Hou-N	10	27	2	4	1	0	0	1	5	4	1	0	.148	.281	.185	.466	35	-2	2	2.25	0	/0-7(0-7-0)	0	-0.3
1970 Chi-N	6	3	0	0	0	0	0	0	0	1	0	0	.000	.000	.000	.000	-89	-1	0	.00	0	/0-1	0	-0.1
1971 Chi-N	106	301	22	77	7	5	0	28	35	34	0	6	.256	.337	.312	.650	74	-11	33	3.78	-2	0-93(3-85-5)	7	-1.7
1972 Mil-A	85	154	17	49	2	0	0	12	12	23	6	4	.318	.367	.331	.699	111	2	18	4.32	0	0-43(19-19-5)	5	0.0
Total 6	242	543	48	141	12	5	1	43	57	73	7	10	.260	.332	.306	.638	79	-15	58	3.64	-4	0-159	12	-2.5
• DAVIS, Butch	Wallace McArthur Davis b: 6/19/1958, Williamston, NC BR/TR, 6', 190 lbs. Deb: 8/23/1983 Career OF: 95-11-31																							
1983 KC-A	33	122	13	42	2	6	2	18	4	19	4	3	.344	.365	.508	.873	137	5	21	6.20	-1	0-33(33-0-0)	5	0.2
1984 KC-A	41	116	11	17	3	0	2	12	10	19	4	3	.147	.214	.224	.438	21	-13	5	1.39	0	0-35(34-1-1)/D-2	1	-1.5

YEAR TM-L	G	AB	R	H	2B	3B	HR	RBI	BB	SO	SB	CS	AVG	OBP	SLG	OPS	OPS+	BR/A	RC	RC/G	FR	G/POS	WS	TPW
1987 Pit-N	7	7	3	1	1	0	0	0	1	3	0	0	.143	.250	.286	.536	41	-1	1	2.54	0	/0-1	0	-0.1
1988 Bal-A	13	25	2	6	1	0	0	0	0	8	1	0	.240	.240	.280	.520	46	-2	1	1.55	1	0-10(2-0-8)/D-1	0	-0.1
1989 Bal-A	5	6	1	1	1	0	0	0	0	3	0	0	.167	.167	.333	.500	39	-1	0	1.80	-0	/0-3(2-0-1),D-1	0	-0.1
1991 LA-N	1	1	0	0	0	0	0	0	0	0	0	0	.000	.000	.000	.000	-102	-0	0	.00	0	....	0	0.0
1993 Tex-A	62	159	24	39	10	4	3	20	5	28	3	1	.245	.273	.415	.688	85	-4	18	3.96	-1	0-44(23-10-17),D-11	5	-0.7
1994 Tex-A	4	17	2	4	3	0	0	0	0	3	1	0	.235	.235	.412	.647	63	-1	2	3.67	1	/0-4(0-0-4)	0	0.0
Total 8	166	453	56	110	21	10	7	50	20	83	13	7	.243	.276	.380	.656	78	-16	48	3.56	0	0-130/D-15	11	-2.2

• DAVIS, Chili

Charles Theodore Davis b: 1/17/1960, Kingston, Jamaica BB/TR, 6'3", 210 lbs. Deb: 4/10/1981 Career OF: 231-538-481

YEAR TM-L	G	AB	R	H	2B	3B	HR	RBI	BB	SO	SB	CS	AVG	OBP	SLG	OPS	OPS+	BR/A	RC	RC/G	FR	G/POS	WS	TPW
1981 SF-N	8	15	1	2	0	0	0	0	1	2	2	0	.133	.188	.133	.321	-8	-2	0	.80	0	/0-6(1-2-3)	0	-0.2
1982 SF-N	154	641	86	167	27	6	19	76	45	115	24	13	.261	.311	.410	.721	100	-3	79	4.15	6	*0-153(13-142-1)	19	0.1
1983 SF-N	137	486	54	113	21	2	11	59	55	108	10	12	.233	.311	.352	.662	86	-13	52	3.45	4	*0-133(0-121-12)	11	-1.1
1984 SF-N★	137	499	87	157	21	6	21	81	42	74	12	8	.315	.369	.507	.876	149	29	89	6.53	0	*0-123(1-67-57)	21	2.7
1985 SF-N	136	481	53	130	25	2	13	56	62	74	15	7	.270	.354	.412	.765	119	13	68	4.83	5	*0-126(0-36-91)	16	1.4
1986 SF-N★	153	526	71	146	28	3	13	70	84	96	16	13	.278	.378	.416	.794	125	18	83	5.44	1	*0-148(0-53-117)	21	1.4
1987*SF-N	149	500	80	125	22	1	24	76	72	109	16	9	.250	.347	.442	.789	113	8	78	5.30	-2	*0-135(18-114-36)	16	0.3
1988 Cal-A	158	600	81	161	29	3	21	93	56	118	9	10	.268	.331	.432	.762	115	8	82	4.65	-5	*0-153(0-3-154)/D-3	16	-0.2
1989 Cal-A	154	560	81	152	24	1	22	90	61	109	3	0	.271	.343	.436	.779	120	15	80	4.94	-4	*0-147(147-0-0)/D-6	22	0.5
1990 Cal-A	113	412	58	109	17	1	12	58	61	89	1	2	.265	.359	.398	.757	114	9	59	4.91	1	D-60,0-52(46-0-7)	10	0.5
1991*Min-A	153	534	84	148	34	1	29	93	95	117	5	6	.277	.387	.507	.895	139	29	107	7.16	-0	*D-150/0-2(2-0-0)	22	2.4
1992 Min-A	138	444	63	128	27	2	12	66	73	76	4	5	.288	.392	.439	.831	128	19	78	6.15	0	*D-125/0-4(1-0-3),1-1	14	1.4
1993 Cal-A	153	573	74	139	32	0	27	112	71	135	4	1	.243	.327	.440	.767	101	38	80	4.78	0	*D-150/P-1	16	2.8
1994 Cal-A★	108	392	72	122	18	1	26	84	69	84	3	2	.311	.416	.561	.977	147	29	91	8.50	0	*D-106/0-2(2-0-0)	15	2.0
1995 Cal-A	119	424	81	135	23	0	20	86	89	79	3	3	.318	.437	.514	.951	148	34	98	8.44	0	*D-119	18	2.4
1996 Cal-A	145	530	73	155	24	0	28	95	86	99	5	2	.292	.391	.496	.887	125	22	102	6.88	0	*D-143	18	1.2
1997 KC-A	140	477	71	133	20	0	30	90	85	96	6	3	.279	.389	.509	.898	129	23	94	6.97	0	*D-133	15	1.4
1998*NY-A	35	103	11	30	7	0	3	9	14	18	0	1	.291	.376	.447	.823	117	2	16	5.22	0	D-34	2	0.1
1999*NY-A	146	476	59	128	25	1	19	78	73	100	4	1	.269	.368	.445	.814	108	7	80	5.94	0	*D-141	13	-0.1
Total 19	2436	8673	1240	2380	424	30	350	1372	1194	1698	142	98	.274	.363	.451	.814	121	287	1416	5.67	6	*0-1184,D-1170/1-1,P-1	285	19.0

• DAVIS, Crash

Lawrence Columbus Davis b: 7/14/1919, Canon, GA d: 8/31/2001, Greensboro, NC BR/TR, 6', 173 lbs. Deb: 6/15/1940

YEAR TM-L	G	AB	R	H	2B	3B	HR	RBI	BB	SO	SB	CS	AVG	OBP	SLG	OPS	OPS+	BR/A	RC	RC/G	FR	G/POS	WS	TPW
1940 Phi-A	23	67	4	18	1	1	0	9	3	10	1	0	.269	.310	.313	.623	63	-3	7	3.37	-2	2-19/S-1	1	-0.4
1941 Phi-A	39	105	8	23	3	0	0	8	11	16	0	0	.219	.293	.248	.541	45	-8	9	2.71	0	2-20,1-12	1	-0.8
1942 Phi-A	86	272	31	61	8	1	2	26	21	30	1	0	.224	.282	.283	.565	59	-14	22	2.64	-9	2-57,S-26/1-3	2	-1.9
Total 3	148	444	43	102	12	2	2	43	35	56	2	0	.230	.289	.279	.568	57	-26	37	2.76	-11	/2-96,S-27,1-15	4	-3.0

• DAVIS, Dick

Richard Earl Davis b: 9/25/1953, Long Beach, CA BR/TR, 6'3", 195 lbs. Deb: 7/12/1977 Career OF: 78-4-112

YEAR TM-L	G	AB	R	H	2B	3B	HR	RBI	BB	SO	SB	CS	AVG	OBP	SLG	OPS	OPS+	BR/A	RC	RC/G	FR	G/POS	WS	TPW
1977 Mil-A	22	51	7	14	2	0	0	6	1	8	0	0	.275	.288	.314	.602	64	-3	4	3.03	0	0-12(12-0-0)/D-6	0	-0.3
1978 Mil-A	69	218	28	54	10	1	5	26	7	23	2	5	.248	.278	.372	.649	81	-8	20	2.96	0	D-34,0-28(18-4-8)	2	-1.0
1979 Mil-A	91	335	51	89	13	1	12	41	16	46	3	3	.266	.299	.418	.717	91	-6	38	3.96	-1	D-53,0-35(32-0-3)	5	-1.1
1980 Mil-A	106	365	50	99	26	2	4	30	11	43	5	3	.271	.298	.386	.684	89	-7	40	3.84	1	D-63,0-38(13-0-27)	5	-1.0
1981*Phi-N	45	96	12	32	6	1	2	19	8	13	1	2	.333	.390	.479	.870	139	4	18	7.03	-1	0-32(1-0-31)	5	0.3
1982 Phi-N	28	68	5	19	3	1	2	7	2	9	1	0	.279	.300	.441	.741	103	0	8	3.78	0	0-16(0-0-16)	2	-0.1
Tor-A	3	7	0	2	0	0	0	2	0	1	0	0	.286	.286	.286	.571	53	-0	0	1.22	0	/D-1,0-1	0	-0.1
Pit-N	39	77	7	14	2	1	2	10	5	9	1	0	.182	.232	.312	.543	49	-5	6	2.32	-1	0-28(1-0-27)	0	-0.7
Yr.	67	145	12	33	5	2	4	17	7	18	2	0	.228	.263	.372	.636	73	-5	13	2.96	-1	0-44(1-0-43)	2	-0.8
Total 6	403	1217	160	323	62	7	27	141	50	152	13	13	.265	.298	.394	.692	89	-25	134	3.77	-1	0-190,D-157	19	-3.9

• DAVIS, Doug

Douglas Raymond Davis b: 9/24/1962, Bloomsburg, PA BR/TR, 6', 180 lbs. Deb: 7/8/1988 C

YEAR TM-L	G	AB	R	H	2B	3B	HR	RBI	BB	SO	SB	CS	AVG	OBP	SLG	OPS	OPS+	BR/A	RC	RC/G	FR	G/POS	WS	TPW
1988 Cal-A	6	12	1	0	0	0	0	0	0	3	0	0	.000	.077	.000	.077	-79	-3	0	.05	-1	/3-3,C-3	0	-0.4
1992 Tex-A	1	1	0	1	0	0	0	0	0	0	0	0	1.000	1.000	1.000	2.000	479	0	1	∞	-1	/C-1	0	0.0
Total 2	7	13	1	1	0	0	0	0	0	3	0	0	.077	.143	.077	.220	-39	-2	1	.05	-2	/C-4,3-3	0	-0.4

• DAVIS, Eric

Eric Keith Davis b: 5/29/1962, Los Angeles, CA BR/TR, 6'2", 185 lbs. Deb: 5/19/1984 Career OF: 353-845-304

YEAR TM-L	G	AB	R	H	2B	3B	HR	RBI	BB	SO	SB	CS	AVG	OBP	SLG	OPS	OPS+	BR/A	RC	RC/G	FR	G/POS	WS	TPW
1984 Cin-N	57	174	33	39	10	1	10	30	24	48	10	2	.224	.322	.466	.787	114	4	28	5.52	3	0-51(2-46-10)	7	0.6
1985 Cin-N	56	122	26	30	3	3	8	18	7	39	16	3	.246	.287	.516	.803	114	3	19	5.15	2	0-47(24-28-5)	5	0.4
1986 Cin-N	132	415	97	115	15	3	27	71	68	100	80	11	.277	.380	.523	.903	140	36	95	8.01	-2	*0-121(72-71-16)	25	3.1
1987 Cin-N★	129	474	120	139	23	4	37	100	84	134	50	6	.293	.401	.593	.994	152	45	124	9.56	9	*0-128(4-124-0)	30	5.2
1988 Cin-N	135	472	81	129	18	3	26	93	65	124	35	3	.273	.365	.489	.854	138	30	90	6.72	-5	*0-130(0-125-5)	27	2.5
1989 Cin-N★	131	462	74	130	14	2	34	101	68	116	21	7	.281	.375	.541	.916	154	34	91	6.74	-4	*0-125(4-118-3)	26	3.0
1990*Cin-N	127	453	84	118	26	2	24	86	60	100	21	3	.260	.350	.486	.835	122	16	81	6.29	5	*0-122(56-66-0)	17	1.9
1991 Cin-N	89	285	39	67	10	0	11	33	48	92	14	2	.235	.355	.386	.741	104	5	44	5.24	-1	0-81(7-77-0)	8	0.4
1992 LA-N	76	267	21	61	8	1	5	32	36	71	19	1	.228	.327	.322	.649	86	-0	31	3.86	-5	0-74(69-5-4)	6	-0.9
1993 LA-N	108	376	57	88	17	0	14	53	41	88	33	5	.234	.311	.391	.702	92	0	49	4.31	5	*0-103(101-3-0)	9	0.1
Det-A	23	75	14	19	1	1	6	15	14	18	2	2	.253	.371	.533	.904	141	4	13	5.87	0	0-18(0-18-0)/D-5	3	0.4
1994 Det-A	37	120	19	22	4	0	3	13	18	45	5	0	.183	.290	.292	.582	50	-8	11	2.92	-3	0-35(0-35-0)	1	-1.0
1996 Cin-N	129	415	81	119	20	0	26	83	70	121	23	9	.287	.397	.523	.920	141	28	90	7.63	-3	*0-126(14-115-0)/1-1	22	2.4
1997*Bal-A	42	158	29	48	11	0	8	25	14	47	6	0	.304	.364	.525	.889	132	8	32	7.45	-1	0-30(0-0-30),D-12	6	0.6
1998 Bal-A	131	452	81	148	29	1	28	89	44	108	7	6	.327	.393	.582	.975	151	32	99	8.11	1	0-72(0-11-64),D-53	18	2.6
1999 StL-N	58	191	27	49	9	2	5	30	30	49	5	4	.257	.360	.403	.764	92	-2	30	5.39	0	0-51(0-3-50)/D-2	5	-0.4
2000*StL-N	92	254	38	77	14	0	6	40	36	60	1	1	.303	.392	.429	.821	107	4	43	6.28	-3	0-69(0-0-69)/D-4	8	-0.2
2001 SF-N	74	156	17	32	7	3	4	22	13	38	1	1	.205	.271	.365	.636	67	-8	15	3.07	-1	0-48(0-0-48)/D-1	1	-1.1
Total 17	1626	5321	938	1430	239	26	282	934	740	1398	349	66	.269	.362	.482	.844	125	231	985	6.45	-2	*0-1431/D-77,1-1	224	19.5

• DAVIS, George

George Stacey Davis
b: 8/23/1870, Cohoes, NY d: 10/17/1940, Philadelphia, PA BB/TR, 5'9", 180 lbs. Deb: 4/19/1890 M HOF: 1998 Career OF: 12-243-48

YEAR TM-L	G	AB	R	H	2B	3B	HR	RBI	BB	SO	SB	CS	AVG	OBP	SLG	OPS	OPS+	BR/A	RC	RC/G	FR	G/POS	WS	TPW
1890 Cle-N	136	526	98	139	22	9	6	73	53	34	22	....	.264	.336	.375	.711	109	6	75	5.17	9	*0-133(0-129-4)/2-2,S-1	14	0.9
1891 Cle-N	136	570	115	165	35	12	3	89	53	29	42	....	.289	.354	.409	.763	117	11	100	6.65	7	*0-116(4-111-1),3-22/P-3	21	0.8
1892*Cle-N	144	597	95	144	27	12	5	82	58	51	36	....	.241	.312	.352	.663	96	-4	79	4.68	2	3-79,0-44(0-3-41),S-20/2-3	19	-0.2
1893 NY-N	133	549	112	195	22	27	11	119	42	20	37	....	.355	.410	.554	.964	155	39	143	10.73	-3	*3-133/S-1	22	3.2
1894*NY-N	124	486	125	171	27	19	9	93	67	10	40	....	.352	.434	.541	.976	135	29	135	11.14	3	*3-122	25	2.6
1895 NY-N	110	430	108	146	36	9	5	101	55	12	48	....	.340	.417	.500	.917	139	26	113	10.59	6	3-80,1-14,2-10/0-7(5-0-2)	21	2.7
1896 NY-N	124	494	98	158	25	12	5	99	50	24	48	....	.320	.387	.449	.836	123	17	108	8.34	15	3-74,S-45/1-3,0-3(3-0-0)	21	3.0
1897 NY-N	131	521	112	184	31	10	10	**136**	43	....	65	....	.353	.410	.509	.918	146	34	139	10.77	13	*S-129	31	4.6
1898 NY-N	121	486	80	149	20	5	2	86	32	....	26	....	.307	.351	.381	.731	113	7	77	5.88	9	*S-121	20	2.1
1899 NY-N	109	419	69	141	22	5	1	57	38	....	34	....	.337	.394	.420	.814	128	17	86	7.95	22	*S-108	20	4.0
1900 NY-N	114	426	69	136	20	4	3	61	35	....	29	....	.319	.376	.406	.782	121	13	79	7.02	10	*S-114	18	2.6
1901 NY-N	130	491	69	148	26	7	7	65	40	....	27	....	.301	.356	.426	.782	131	19	87	6.61	2	*S-113,3-17	24	2.5
1902 Chi-A	132	485	76	145	27	7	3	93	65	....	31	....	.299	.386	.402	.788	124	19	91	6.85	-1	*S-129/1-3	26	2.1
1903 NY-N	4	15	2	4	0	0	0	1	1	....	0	....	.267	.313	.267	.579	63	-1	1	3.09	-1	/S-4	0	-0.2
1904 Chi-A	152	563	75	142	27	15	1	69	43	....	32	....	.252	.311	.359	.670	116	10	76	4.63	17	*S-152	28	3.6
1905 Chi-A	151	550	74	153	29	1	1	55	60	....	31	....	.278	.353	.340	.693	125	18	84	5.10	8	*S-151	28	3.4
1906*Chi-A	133	484	63	134	26	6	0	80	41	....	27	....	.277	.338	.355	.694	120	12	70	5.16	8	*S-129/2-1	29	2.7
1907 Chi-A	132	466	59	111	16	2	1	52	47	....	15	....	.238	.313	.288	.601	95	-1	50	3.58	-16	*S-132	17	-1.4
1908 Chi-A	128	419	41	91	14	1	0	26	41	....	22	....	.217	.298	.255	.553	81	-7	41	2.95	-8	2-95,S-23/1-4	14	-1.6
1909 Chi-A	28	68	5	9	1	0	0	2	10	....	4	....	.132	.253	.147	.400	28	-5	4	1.63	2	1-17/2-2	0	-0.4
Total 20	2372	9045	1545	2665	453	163	73	1439	874	180	616	....	.295	.362	.405	.767	120	258	1637	6.63	103	*S-1372,3-527,0-303,2-113/1,P	398	37.0

• DAVIS, Gerry

Gerald Edward Davis b: 12/25/1958, Trenton, NJ BR/TR, 6', 185 lbs. Deb: 9/20/1983 Career OF: 7-1-19

YEAR TM-L	G	AB	R	H	2B	3B	HR	RBI	BB	SO	SB	CS	AVG	OBP	SLG	OPS	OPS+	BR/A	RC	RC/G	FR	G/POS	WS	TPW
1983 SD-N	5	15	3	5	2	0	0	1	3	4	1	0	.333	.444	.467	.911	158	2	3	7.92	1	/0-5(0-0-5)	1	0.2

YEAR TM-L	G	AB	R	H	2B	3B	HR	RBI	BB	SO	SB	CS	AVG	OBP	SLG	OPS	OPS+	BR/A	RC	RC/G	FR	G/POS	WS	TPW
1985 SD-N	44	58	10	17	3	1	0	2	5	7	0	0	.293	.349	.379	.729	105	0	7	4.57	0	0-23(7-1-14)	1	0.0
Total 2	49	73	13	22	5	1	0	3	8	11	1	0	.301	.370	.397	.768	117	2	11	5.24	1	/0-28	2	0.2

• DAVIS, Glenn Glenn Earle Davis b: 3/28/1961, Jacksonville, FL BR/TR, 6'3", 210 lbs. Deb: 9/2/1984

YEAR TM-L	G	AB	R	H	2B	3B	HR	RBI	BB	SO	SB	CS	AVG	OBP	SLG	OPS	OPS+	BR/A	RC	RC/G	FR	G/POS	WS	TPW
1984 Hou-N	18	61	6	13	5	0	2	8	4	12	0	0	.213	.262	.393	.655	88	-1	7	3.52	1	1-16	1	-0.1
1985 Hou-N	100	350	51	95	11	0	20	64	27	68	0	0	.271	.336	.474	.810	128	12	53	5.23	-3	1-89/0-9(0-0-9)	13	0.3
1986*Hou-N★	158	574	91	152	32	3	31	101	64	72	3	1	.265	.348	.493	.841	133	25	100	6.09	6	*1-156	24	2.2
1987 Hou-N	151	578	70	145	35	2	27	93	47	84	4	1	.251	.313	.458	.771	105	2	80	4.72	6	*1-151	14	-0.2
1988 Hou-N	152	561	78	152	26	0	30	99	53	77	4	3	.271	.346	.478	.823	140	27	91	5.70	3	*1-151	23	2.0
1989 Hou-N★	158	581	87	156	26	1	34	89	69	123	4	2	.269	.353	.492	.845	144	33	102	6.24	6	*1-156	30	2.9
1990 Hou-N	93	327	44	82	15	4	22	64	46	54	8	3	.251	.357	.523	.880	143	19	62	6.62	2	1-91	15	1.5
1991 Bal-A	49	176	29	40	9	1	10	28	16	29	4	0	.227	.310	.460	.770	115	4	27	5.12	3	1-36,D-12	4	0.4
1992 Bal-A	106	398	46	110	15	2	13	48	37	65	1	0	.276	.341	.422	.763	110	5	56	4.96	0	*D-103/1-2	8	0.1
1993 Bal-A	30	113	8	20	3	0	1	9	7	29	0	1	.177	.231	.230	.461	24	-13	6	1.63	-1	1-22/D-7	0	-1.6
Total 10	1015	3719	510	965	177	13	190	603	370	613	28	11	.259	.335	.467	.803	125	111	583	5.44	23	1-870,D-122/0-9	132	7.6

• DAVIS, Harry Harry H "Jasper" Davis
b: 7/19/1873, Philadelphia, PA d: 8/11/1947, Philadelphia, PA BR/TR, 5'10", 180 lbs. Deb: 9/21/1895 M/C/U Career OF: 50-19-11

YEAR TM-L	G	AB	R	H	2B	3B	HR	RBI	BB	SO	SB	CS	AVG	OBP	SLG	OPS	OPS+	BR/A	RC	RC/G	FR	G/POS	WS	TPW
1895 NY-N	7	24	1	7	0	1	0	6	2	0	1	....	.292	.346	.375	.721	88	-0	4	5.64	-0	/1-7	0	0.0
1896 NY-N	64	233	43	64	11	10	2	50	31	20	16	....	.275	.372	.433	.805	115	6	45	6.87	-5	0-40(39-1-0),1-23	7	-0.3
Pit-N	44	168	24	32	5	6	0	23	13	21	9	....	.190	.257	.292	.548	46	-13	16	2.97	1	1-35,0-10(9-0-1)/S-1	1	-1.1
Yr.	108	401	67	96	16	16	2	73	44	41	25	....	.239	.325	.374	.699	87	-8	61	5.13	-4	1-58,0-50(48-1-1)/S-1	8	-1.4
1897 Pit-N	111	429	70	131	10	**28**	2	63	26	....	21	....	.305	.359	.473	.832	123	13	83	7.17	-11	1-64,3-32,0-14(0-7-9)/S-1	14	0.1
1898 Pit-N	58	222	31	65	9	13	1	24	12	....	7	....	.293	.332	.464	.796	130	7	38	6.17	2	1-53/0-6(0-6-0)	9	0.8
Lou-N	37	138	18	30	5	2	1	16	7	....	6	....	.217	.255	.304	.560	61	-8	13	3.07	0	1-34/2-2,0-1	1	-0.7
Was-N	1	3	0	0	0	0	0	0	0	....	0	....	.000	.000	.000	.000	-100	-1	0	.00	0	/1-1	0	-0.1
Yr.	96	363	49	95	14	15	2	40	19	....	13	....	.262	.300	.399	.700	102	-2	51	4.86	2	1-88/0-7(0-6-1),2-2	10	0.0
1899 Was-N	18	64	3	12	2	3	0	8	8	....	2	....	.188	.288	.313	.600	65	-3	7	3.30	-1	1-18	1	-0.4
1901 Phi-A	117	496	92	152	28	10	8	76	23	....	21	....	.306	.340	.452	.791	113	6	86	6.52	6	*1-117	17	0.9
1902 Phi-A	133	561	89	172	**43**	8	6	92	30	....	28	....	.307	.343	.444	.787	112	7	98	6.56	3	*1-128/0-5(0-5-0)	19	0.7
1903 Phi-A	106	420	77	125	28	7	6	55	24	....	24	....	.298	.343	.440	.783	128	13	74	6.52	-2	*1-104/0-2(2-0-0)	17	1.0
1904 Phi-A	102	404	54	125	21	11	**10**	62	23	....	12	....	.309	.350	.490	.840	156	24	76	7.05	1	*1-102	21	2.6
1905*Phi-A	150	607	**93**	173	**47**	6	**8**	**83**	43	....	36	....	.285	.334	.422	.756	137	23	101	6.07	7	*1-150	26	3.0
1906 Phi-A	145	551	94	161	42	7	**12**	**96**	49	....	23	....	.292	.355	.459	.815	150	31	101	6.74	-4	*1-145	31	2.6
1907 Phi-A	149	582	84	155	**35**	8	**8**	87	42	....	20	....	.266	.318	.395	.713	124	14	83	4.99	-1	*1-149	21	1.1
1908 Phi-A	147	513	65	127	23	9	5	62	61	....	20	....	.248	.332	.357	.689	116	10	68	4.34	1	*1-147	18	1.0
1909 Phi-A	149	530	73	142	22	11	4	75	51	....	20	....	.268	.338	.374	.711	122	14	73	4.71	-6	*1-149	19	0.5
1910*Phi-A	139	492	61	122	19	4	1	41	53	....	17	....	.248	.332	.309	.641	102	3	57	3.81	-9	*1-139	13	-1.0
1911*Phi-A	57	183	27	36	9	1	1	22	24	....	2	....	.197	.297	.273	.570	60	-9	16	2.66	2	1-53	2	-0.8
1912 Cle-A	2	5	0	0	0	0	0	0	0	....	0	....	.000	.000	.000	.000	-97	-1	0	.00	0	/1-2	0	-0.1
1913 Phi-A	7	17	2	6	2	0	0	4	1	4	0	....	.353	.389	.471	.859	155	1	3	6.86	1	/1-6	1	0.2
1914 Phi-A	5	7	0	3	0	0	0	2	1	0	0	2	.429	.556	.429	.984	204	0	1	4.42	0	/1-1	0	0.0
1915 Phi-A	5	3	0	1	0	0	0	4	0	0	0	....	.333	.333	.333	.667	103	-0	0	4.09	0	/1-1	0	0.0
1916 Phi-A	1	0	0	0	0	0	0	0	1	0	0	....	....	1.000	....	1.000	213	0	0	....	0	....	0	0.0
1917 Phi-A	1	1	0	0	0	0	0	0	0	0	0	....	.000	.000	.000	.000	-101	-0	0	.00	0	....	0	0.0
Total 22	1755	6653	1001	1841	361	145	75	951	525	45	285	2	.277	.335	.408	.743	119	136	1042	5.55	-16	*1-1628/0-78,3-32,2-2,S-2	238	10.0

• DAVIS, Harry Harry Albert "Stinky" Davis b: 3/7/1908, Shreveport, LA d: 3/3/1997, Shreveport, LA BL/TL, 5'10.5", 160 lbs. Deb: 4/13/1932

YEAR TM-L	G	AB	R	H	2B	3B	HR	RBI	BB	SO	SB	CS	AVG	OBP	SLG	OPS	OPS+	BR/A	RC	RC/G	FR	G/POS	WS	TPW
1932 Det-A	141	590	92	159	32	13	4	74	60	53	12	7	.269	.339	.388	.727	84	-14	80	4.65	-7	*1-141	12	-3.1
1933 Det-A	66	173	24	37	8	2	0	14	22	8	2	3	.214	.303	.283	.586	55	-12	16	2.88	-4	1-44	1	-1.8
1937 StL-A	120	450	89	124	25	3	3	35	71	26	7	6	.276	.374	.364	.739	86	-8	65	5.10	-7	*1-112/0-1	6	-2.3
Total 3	327	1213	205	320	65	18	7	123	153	87	21	16	.264	.347	.364	.712	81	-33	161	4.54	-17	1-297/0-1	19	-7.2

• DAVIS, Ike Isaac Marion Davis b: 6/14/1895, Pueblo, CO d: 4/2/1984, Tucson, AZ BR/TR, 5'7", 140 lbs. Deb: 4/23/1919

YEAR TM-L	G	AB	R	H	2B	3B	HR	RBI	BB	SO	SB	CS	AVG	OBP	SLG	OPS	OPS+	BR/A	RC	RC/G	FR	G/POS	WS	TPW
1919 Was-A	8	14	0	0	0	0	0	0	0	6	0	....	.000	.000	.000	.000	-101	-4	0	.00	-2	/S-4	0	-0.5
1924 Chi-A	10	33	5	8	1	1	0	4	2	5	0	0	.242	.286	.333	.619	61	-2	3	3.19	0	S-10	0	-0.1
1925 Chi-A	146	562	105	135	31	9	0	61	71	58	19	14	.240	.333	.327	.660	72	-23	66	3.63	8	*S-144	13	0.1
Total 3	164	609	110	143	32	10	0	65	73	69	19	14	.235	.324	.320	.644	68	-29	69	3.51	6	S-158	13	-0.6

• DAVIS, Ira J. Ira "Slats" Davis b: 7/8/1870, Philadelphia, PA d: 12/21/1942, Brooklyn, NY, 162 lbs. Deb: 4/22/1899

YEAR TM-L	G	AB	R	H	2B	3B	HR	RBI	BB	SO	SB	CS	AVG	OBP	SLG	OPS	OPS+	BR/A	RC	RC/G	FR	G/POS	WS	TPW
1899 NY-N	6	17	3	4	1	1	0	2	0	....	1	....	.235	.235	.412	.647	79	-1	2	3.93	-1	/S-3,1-2	0	-0.2

• DAVIS, J.J. Jerry C. Davis b: 10/25/1978, Glendora, CA BR/TR, 6'4", 250 lbs. Deb: 9/4/2002 Career OF: 0-0-14

YEAR TM-L	G	AB	R	H	2B	3B	HR	RBI	BB	SO	SB	CS	AVG	OBP	SLG	OPS	OPS+	BR/A	RC	RC/G	FR	G/POS	WS	TPW
2002 Pit-N	9	10	1	1	0	0	0	0	0	4	0	0	.100	.182	.100	.282	-23	-2	0	.31	0	/0-4(0-0-4)	0	-0.2
2003 Pit-N	19	35	1	7	0	0	1	4	3	13	0	1	.200	.263	.286	.549	42	-3	3	2.38	0	0-10(0-0-10)	0	-0.4
Total 2	28	45	2	8	0	0	1	4	3	17	0	1	.178	.245	.244	.489	28	-5	3	1.85	0	/0-14	0	-0.6

• DAVIS, Jacke Jacke Sylvesta Davis b: 3/5/1936, Carthage, TX BR/TR, 5'11", 160 lbs. Deb: 4/19/1962

YEAR TM-L	G	AB	R	H	2B	3B	HR	RBI	BB	SO	SB	CS	AVG	OBP	SLG	OPS	OPS+	BR/A	RC	RC/G	FR	G/POS	WS	TPW
1962 Phi-N	48	75	9	16	0	1	1	6	4	20	1	0	.213	.253	.280	.533	44	-6	5	2.26	-1	0-26(16-5-7)	0	-0.8

• DAVIS, Jody Jody Richard Davis b: 11/12/1956, Gainesville, GA BR/TR, 6'4", 210 lbs. Deb: 4/21/1981

YEAR TM-L	G	AB	R	H	2B	3B	HR	RBI	BB	SO	SB	CS	AVG	OBP	SLG	OPS	OPS+	BR/A	RC	RC/G	FR	G/POS	WS	TPW
1981 Chi-N	56	180	14	46	5	1	4	21	21	28	0	1	.256	.337	.361	.698	94	-1	21	3.95	2	C-56	5	0.3
1982 Chi-N	130	418	41	109	20	2	12	52	36	92	0	1	.261	.321	.404	.725	99	-2	55	4.51	9	*C-129	15	1.3
1983 Chi-N	151	510	56	138	31	2	24	84	33	93	0	2	.271	.317	.480	.798	113	5	72	4.92	-7	*C-150	16	0.6
1984*Chi-N★	150	523	55	134	25	2	19	94	47	99	5	6	.256	.319	.421	.739	97	-4	63	4.05	3	*C-146	18	0.6
1985 Chi-N	142	482	47	112	30	0	17	58	48	83	1	0	.232	.302	.400	.702	85	-10	57	3.92	6	*C-138	13	0.2
1986 Chi-N★	148	528	61	132	27	2	21	74	41	110	0	1	.250	.304	.428	.732	92	-8	66	4.20	5	*C-145/1-1	16	0.5
1987 Chi-N	125	428	57	106	12	2	19	51	52	91	1	2	.248	.332	.418	.750	94	-5	58	4.57	4	*C-123	13	0.5
1988 Chi-N	88	249	19	57	9	0	6	33	29	51	0	3	.229	.312	.337	.649	83	-7	25	3.31	-2	C-74	6	-0.4
Atl-N	2	8	2	2	0	0	1	3	0	1	0	0	.250	.250	.625	.875	137	0	1	5.63	1	/C-2	1	0.1
Yr.	90	257	21	59	9	0	7	36	29	52	0	3	.230	.310	.346	.656	84	-6	27	3.38	-1	C-76	7	-0.3
1989 Atl-N	78	231	12	39	5	0	4	19	23	61	0	0	.169	.247	.242	.489	39	-18	13	1.79	0	C-72/1-2	3	-1.5
1990 Atl-N	12	28	0	2	0	0	0	1	3	3	0	0	.071	.161	.071	.233	-32	-5	0	.36	0	/1-6,C-4	0	-0.5
Total 10	1082	3585	364	877	164	11	127	490	333	712	7	16	.245	.310	.403	.713	91	-55	432	4.04	21	*C-1039/1-9	106	1.6

• DAVIS, John John Humphrey "Red" Davis b: 7/15/1915, Wilkes-Barre, PA d: 4/26/2002, Laurel, MS BR/TR, 5'11", 172 lbs. Deb: 9/9/1941

YEAR TM-L	G	AB	R	H	2B	3B	HR	RBI	BB	SO	SB	CS	AVG	OBP	SLG	OPS	OPS+	BR/A	RC	RC/G	FR	G/POS	WS	TPW
1941 NY-N	21	70	8	15	3	0	0	5	8	12	0	....	.214	.295	.257	.552	55	-4	6	2.91	1	3-21	1	-0.2

• DAVIS, Jumbo James J. Davis b: 9/5/1861, New York, NY d: 2/14/1921, St. Louis, MO BL/TR, 5'11", 195 lbs. Deb: 7/27/1884 U

YEAR TM-L	G	AB	R	H	2B	3B	HR	RBI	BB	SO	SB	CS	AVG	OBP	SLG	OPS	OPS+	BR/A	RC	RC/G	FR	G/POS	WS	TPW
1884 KC-U	7	29	3	6	0	0	0	....	0	....	....	....	.207	.207	.207	.414	46	-1	1	1.55	-1	/3-7	0	-0.2
1886 Bal-a	60	216	23	42	5	2	1	20	11	....	12	....	.194	.240	.250	.490	55	-11	16	2.52	-1	3-60	4	-0.9
1887 Bal-a	130	513	81	178	23	**19**	8	109	28	....	49	....	.347	.353	.485	.838	140	25	103	8.29	4	*3-87,S-43	20	2.6
1888 KC-a	121	491	70	131	22	8	3	61	20	....	42	....	.267	.304	.363	.666	106	1	68	5.14	8	*3-113/S-8	15	1.0
1889 KC-a	62	241	40	64	4	3	0	30	17	35	25	....	.266	.319	.307	.626	74	-9	32	4.85	-5	3-62	5	-1.1
StL-a	2	4	1	0	0	0	0	0	1	1	0	....	.000	.200	.000	.200	-36	-1	0	.00	0	/0-1,S-1	0	-0.1
Yr.	64	245	41	64	4	3	0	30	18	36	25	....	.261	.317	.302	.619	72	-10	32	4.74	-5	3-62/0-1,S-1	5	-1.1
1890 StL-a	21	71	8	18	3	1	0	13	9	....	5	....	.254	.338	.324	.661	83	-2	10	4.84	-1	3-21	2	-0.2
Bro-a	38	142	33	43	9	2	2	28	15	....	10	....	.303	.385	.437	.822	147	9	28	7.61	-5	3-38	5	0.4
Yr.	59	213	41	61	12	3	2	41	24	....	15	....	.286	.369	.399	.768	126	7	38	6.64	-7	3-59	7	0.1

YEAR TM-L	G	AB	R	H	2B	3B	HR	RBI	BB	SO	SB	CS	AVG	OBP	SLG	OPS	OPS+	BR/A	RC	RC/G	FR	G/POS	WS	TPW
1891 Was-a	12	44	7	14	3	2	0	9	7	5	8	....	.318	.412	.477	.889	161	4	12	10.81	-1	3-12	3	0.3
Total 7	**453**	**1751**	**266**	**496**	**69**	**37**	**14**	**270**	**108**	**41**	**151**	**....**	**.283**	**.322**	**.379**	**.701**	**108**	**14**	**272**	**5.81**	**-3**	**3-400/S-52,O-1**	**54**	**1.7**
• DAVIS, Kiddo	George Willis Davis b: 2/12/1902, Bridgeport, CT d: 3/4/1983, Bridgeport, CT BR/TR, 5'11", 178 lbs. Deb: 6/15/1926 Career OF: 31-425-29																							
1926 NY-A	1	0	0	0	0	0	0	0	0	0	0	0	....	....	....	....	-102	0	0	....	0	/O-1	0	0.0
1932 Phi-N	137	576	100	178	39	6	5	57	44	56	16	....	.309	.359	.424	.783	98	-1	90	5.74	4	*O-133(1-132-0)	17	0.0
1933*NY-N	126	434	61	112	20	4	7	37	25	30	10	....	.258	.298	.371	.669	92	-6	47	3.74	1	*O-120(0-120-0)	13	-0.8
1934 StL-N	16	33	6	10	3	0	1	4	3	1	1	....	.303	.361	.485	.846	117	1	6	6.44	0	/O-9(0-9-0)	1	0.0
Phi-N	100	393	50	115	25	5	3	48	27	28	1	....	.293	.338	.405	.743	86	-8	55	5.12	10	*O-100(0-100-0)	11	0.0
Yr.	116	426	56	125	28	5	4	52	30	29	2	....	.293	.340	.411	.751	89	-7	61	5.22	10	*O-109(0-109-0)	12	0.0
1935 NY-N	47	91	16	24	7	1	2	6	10	4	2	....	.264	.343	.429	.772	108	1	14	5.23	-1	O-21(2-2-17)	3	-0.1
1936*NY-N	47	67	6	16	1	0	0	5	6	5	0	....	.239	.301	.254	.555	51	-4	6	2.82	1	O-22(6-11-6)	1	-0.4
1937 NY-N	56	76	20	20	10	0	0	9	10	7	1	....	.263	.356	.395	.751	102	1	11	5.15	-2	O-37(11-25-0)	2	-0.2
Cin-N	40	136	19	35	6	0	1	5	16	6	1	....	.257	.340	.324	.663	85	-2	16	3.93	0	O-35(9-26-0)	3	-0.3
Yr.	96	212	39	55	16	0	1	14	26	13	2	....	.259	.346	.349	.695	91	-2	27	4.36	-2	O-72(20-51-0)	5	-0.6
1938 Cin-N	5	18	3	5	1	0	0	0	1	4	0	....	.278	.316	.333	.649	81	-0	2	4.01	1	/O-5(2-0-5)	0	0.0
Total 8	**575**	**1824**	**281**	**515**	**112**	**16**	**19**	**171**	**142**	**141**	**32**	**0**	**.282**	**.336**	**.393**	**.728**	**92**	**-19**	**246**	**4.79**	**14**	**O-483**	**51**	**-1.8**
• DAVIS, Lefty	Alphonzo De Ford Davis b: 2/4/1875, Nashville, TN d: 2/7/1919, Collins, NY BL/TL, 5'10", 170 lbs. Deb: 4/18/1901 Career OF: 107-72-162																							
1901 Bro-N	25	91	11	19	2	0	0	7	10	....	4	....	.209	.287	.231	.518	50	-6	7	2.72	-5	O-24(12-2-10)/2-1	0	-1.1
Pit-N	87	335	87	105	8	11	2	33	56	....	22	....	.313	.415	.421	.836	138	20	70	7.83	7	O-86(0-0-86)	19	2.2
Yr.	112	426	98	124	10	11	2	40	66	....	26	....	.291	.389	.380	.769	120	14	78	6.63	2	*O-110(12-2-96)/2-1	19	1.1
1902 Pit-N	59	232	52	65	7	3	0	20	35	....	19	....	.280	.377	.336	.713	116	6	38	5.87	-3	O-59(0-0-59)	10	0.1
1903 NY-A	104	372	54	88	10	0	0	25	43	....	11	....	.237	.319	.263	.582	72	-11	38	3.36	-7	*O-102(95-1-6)/S-1	7	-2.5
1907 Cin-N	73	266	28	61	5	5	1	25	23	....	9	....	.229	.293	.297	.590	81	-6	27	3.35	-1	O-70(0-69-1)	6	-1.2
Total 4	**348**	**1296**	**232**	**338**	**32**	**19**	**3**	**110**	**167**	**....**	**65**	**....**	**.261**	**.348**	**.322**	**.670**	**98**	**4**	**182**	**4.81**	**-10**	**O-341/2-1,S-1**	**42**	**-2.5**
• DAVIS, Mark	Mark Anthony Davis b: 11/25/1964, San Diego, CA BR/TR, 6', 180 lbs. Deb: 7/2/1991																							
1991 Cal-A	3	2	0	0	0	0	0	0	0	0	0	0	.000	.000	.000	.000	-100	-1	0	.00	0	/O-3(0-0-3)	0	-0.1
• DAVIS, Mike	Michael Dwayne Davis b: 6/11/1959, San Diego, CA BL/TL, 6'2", 185 lbs. Deb: 4/10/1980 Career OF: 33-128-728																							
1980 Oak-A	51	95	11	20	2	1	1	8	7	14	2	1	.211	.265	.284	.549	54	-6	7	2.37	2	O-18(5-0-13)/1-7,D-6	1	-0.5
1981*Oak-A	17	20	0	1	1	0	0	0	2	4	0	0	.050	.136	.100	.236	-33	-3	0	.31	-0	/D-3,O-2(2-0-0),1-1	0	-0.4
1982 Oak-A	23	75	12	30	4	0	1	10	2	8	3	2	.400	.416	.493	.909	155	5	15	8.75	-1	O-13(8-3-5)/1-7	4	0.3
1983 Oak-A	128	443	61	122	24	4	8	62	27	74	32	15	.275	.324	.402	.726	105	2	56	4.25	6	*O-121(0-21-110)/D-3	13	0.3
1984 Oak-A	134	382	47	88	18	3	9	46	31	66	14	9	.230	.290	.364	.654	85	-9	40	3.39	-6	*O-127(1-16-121)/D-4	7	-2.1
1985 Oak-A	154	547	92	157	34	1	24	82	50	99	24	10	.287	.349	.484	.833	135	26	91	5.93	-6	*O-151(0-31-138)	23	1.4
1986 Oak-A	142	489	77	131	28	3	19	55	34	91	27	4	.268	.317	.454	.771	115	13	72	5.18	4	*O-139(0-34-120)	18	1.2
1987 Oak-A	139	494	69	131	32	1	22	72	42	94	19	7	.265	.324	.468	.792	114	10	72	4.95	-9	*O-124(0-0-124),D-14	14	-0.5
1988*LA-N	108	281	29	55	11	2	2	17	25	59	7	3	.196	.261	.270	.532	55	-17	20	2.28	-2	O-76(1-23-63)	2	-2.2
1989 LA-N	67	173	21	43	7	1	5	19	16	28	6	5	.249	.312	.387	.699	101	-1	20	3.97	0	O-48(16-0-34)	3	-0.3
Total 10	**963**	**2999**	**419**	**778**	**161**	**16**	**91**	**371**	**236**	**537**	**134**	**56**	**.259**	**.316**	**.415**	**.730**	**105**	**20**	**395**	**4.47**	**-12**	**O-819/D-30,1-15**	**85**	**-2.8**
• DAVIS, Odie	Odie Ernest Davis b: 8/13/1955, San Antonio, TX BR/TR, 6'1", 178 lbs. Deb: 9/3/1980																							
1980 Tex-A	17	8	0	1	0	0	0	0	0	2	0	0	.125	.125	.125	.250	-32	-1	0	.48	-2	S-13/3-1	0	-0.3
• DAVIS, Otis	Otis Allen "Scat" Davis b: 9/24/1920, Charleston, AR BL/TR, 6', 160 lbs. Deb: 4/22/1946																							
1946 Bro-N	1	0	1	0	0	0	0	0	0	0	0	....	....	....	....	....	-99	0	0	....	0	....	0	0.0
• DAVIS, Ron	Ronald Everette Davis b: 10/21/1941, Roanoke Rapids, NC d: 9/5/1992, Houston, TX BR/TR, 6', 180 lbs. Deb: 8/1/1962 Career OF: 87-138-42																							
1962 Hou-N	6	14	1	3	0	0	0	1	1	7	1	0	.214	.267	.214	.481	33	-1	1	1.70	0	/O-5(0-5-0)	0	-0.1
1966 Hou-N	48	194	21	48	10	1	2	19	13	26	2	2	.247	.308	.340	.648	86	-4	20	3.48	2	O-48(0-48-0)	4	-0.4
1967 Hou-N	94	285	31	73	19	1	7	38	17	48	5	3	.256	.303	.404	.706	104	0	34	4.18	-1	O-80(63-11-8)	8	-0.5
1968 Hou-N	52	217	22	46	10	1	1	12	13	48	0	4	.212	.269	.281	.550	67	-10	16	2.48	2	O-52(0-52-0)	3	-1.2
*StL-N	33	79	11	14	4	2	0	5	5	17	1	0	.177	.226	.278	.505	51	-5	5	1.91	1	O-25(2-10-14)	1	-0.5
Yr.	85	296	33	60	14	3	1	17	18	65	1	4	.203	.258	.280	.538	63	-15	21	2.32	3	O-77(2-62-14)	4	-1.7
1969 Pit-N	62	64	10	15	1	1	0	4	7	14	0	0	.234	.310	.281	.591	68	-3	6	3.33	-1	O-51(22-12-20)	1	-0.5
Total 5	**295**	**853**	**96**	**199**	**44**	**6**	**10**	**79**	**56**	**160**	**9**	**9**	**.233**	**.288**	**.334**	**.622**	**81**	**-22**	**83**	**3.24**	**2**	**O-261**	**17**	**-3.2**
• DAVIS, Russ	Russell Stuart Davis b: 9/13/1969, Birmingham, AL BR/TR, 6', 170 lbs. Deb: 7/6/1994																							
1994 NY-A	4	14	0	2	0	0	0	1	0	4	0	0	.143	.143	.143	.286	-27	-3	0	.30	0	/3-4	0	-0.2
1995*NY-A	40	98	14	27	5	2	2	12	10	26	0	0	.276	.349	.429	.777	102	0	16	5.95	0	3-34/D-4,1-2	3	0.0
1996 Sea-A	51	167	24	39	9	0	5	18	17	50	2	0	.234	.312	.377	.689	73	-7	21	4.31	-2	3-51	2	-0.7
1997 Sea-A	119	420	57	114	29	1	20	63	27	100	6	2	.271	.318	.488	.807	108	3	62	5.20	0	*3-117/D-1	11	0.5
1998 Sea-A	141	502	68	130	30	1	20	82	34	134	4	3	.259	.310	.442	.752	93	-8	67	4.57	2	*3-137/O-3(3-0-0)	11	-0.4
1999 Sea-A	124	432	55	106	17	1	21	59	32	111	3	3	.245	.305	.435	.740	84	-13	54	4.16	-5	*3-124/S-2	6	-1.5
2000*SF-N	80	180	27	47	5	0	9	24	9	29	0	3	.261	.304	.439	.743	91	-5	23	4.53	-10	3-43/1-6,D-3	4	-1.4
2001 SF-N	53	167	16	43	13	1	7	17	17	49	1	0	.257	.330	.473	.803	112	3	25	5.16	-9	3-46/D-1	2	-0.5
Total 8	**612**	**1980**	**261**	**508**	**108**	**6**	**84**	**276**	**146**	**503**	**16**	**11**	**.257**	**.313**	**.444**	**.757**	**93**	**-29**	**269**	**4.66**	**-24**	**3-556/D-9,1-8,O-3,S-2**	**39**	**-4.3**
• DAVIS, Spud	Virgil Lawrence Davis b: 12/20/1904, Birmingham, AL d: 8/14/1984, Birmingham, AL BR/TR, 6'1", 197 lbs. Deb: 4/30/1928 M/C																							
1928 StL-N	2	5	1	1	0	0	0	1	1	0	0	....	.200	.333	.200	.533	42	-0	0	2.38	-1	/C-2	0	-0.1
Phi-N	67	163	16	46	2	0	3	18	15	11	0	....	.282	.343	.350	.692	79	-5	19	4.26	5	C-49	3	0.3
Yr.	69	168	17	47	2	0	3	19	16	11	0	....	.280	.342	.345	.688	77	-5	20	4.18	3	C-51	3	0.1
1929 Phi-N	98	263	31	90	18	0	7	48	19	17	1	....	.342	.391	.490	.881	110	4	49	7.14	0	C-89	9	0.7
1930 Phi-N	106	329	41	103	16	1	14	65	17	20	1	....	.313	.349	.495	.844	94	-4	54	5.98	4	C-96	8	0.5
1931 Phi-N	120	393	30	128	32	1	4	51	36	28	0	....	.326	.382	.443	.825	112	8	68	6.60	6	*C-114	16	2.0
1932 Phi-N	125	402	44	135	23	5	14	70	40	39	1	....	.336	.399	.522	.921	130	18	86	8.22	-2	*C-120	17	2.3
1933 Phi-N	141	495	51	173	28	3	9	65	32	24	2	....	.349	.395	.473	.867	130	21	89	6.83	2	*C-132	18	3.2
1934*StL-N	107	347	45	104	22	4	9	65	34	27	0	....	.300	.366	.464	.830	113	7	58	6.15	-1	C-94	15	1.1
1935 StL-N	102	315	28	100	24	2	1	60	33	30	0	....	.317	.386	.416	.802	111	6	54	6.52	-6	C-81/1-5	14	0.4
1936 StL-N	112	363	24	99	26	2	4	59	35	34	0	....	.273	.342	.388	.730	96	-1	48	4.70	2	*C-103/3-2	13	0.6
1937 Cin-N	76	209	19	56	10	1	3	33	23	15	0	....	.268	.341	.368	.709	97	-0	26	4.45	3	C-59	5	0.6
1938 Cin-N	12	36	3	6	1	0	0	1	5	6	0	....	.167	.286	.194	.480	35	-3	2	1.75	-1	C-11	0	-0.3
Phi-N	70	215	11	53	7	0	2	23	14	14	1	....	.247	.293	.307	.600	65	-10	17	2.65	1	C-63	2	-0.6
Yr.	82	251	14	59	8	0	2	24	19	20	1	....	.235	.292	.291	.582	60	-13	19	2.51	0	C-74	2	-0.9
1939 Phi-N	87	202	10	62	8	1	0	23	24	20	0	....	.307	.383	.356	.740	104	2	29	5.11	4	C-85	6	1.1
1940 Pit-N	99	285	23	93	14	1	5	39	35	20	0	....	.326	.404	.435	.839	132	14	48	6.17	4	C-87	14	2.3
1941 Pit-N	57	107	3	27	4	1	0	6	11	11	0	....	.252	.322	.308	.630	78	-3	10	3.05	1	C-49	3	-0.1
1944 Pit-N	54	93	6	28	7	0	2	14	10	8	0	....	.301	.369	.441	.810	122	3	15	6.14	1	C-35	5	0.5
1945 Pit-N	23	33	2	8	2	0	0	6	2	2	0	....	.242	.306	.303	.609	67	-1	3	2.70	0	C-13	1	-0.1
Total 16	**1458**	**4255**	**388**	**1312**	**244**	**22**	**77**	**647**	**386**	**326**	**6**	**....**	**.308**	**.369**	**.430**	**.799**	**108**	**53**	**676**	**5.81**	**19**	***C-1282/1-5,3-2**	**149**	**14.2**
• DAVIS, Steve	Steven Michael Davis b: 12/30/1953, Oakland, CA BR/TR, 6'1", 200 lbs. Deb: 9/23/1979																							
1979 Chi-N	3	4	0	0	0	0	0	1	0	0	0	0	.000	.000	.000	.000	-91	-1	0	.00	-1	/2-2,3-1	0	-0.2
• DAVIS, Tod	Thomas Oscar Davis b: 7/24/1924, Los Angeles, CA d: 12/31/1978, West Covina, CA BR/TR, 6'2", 190 lbs. Deb: 4/27/1949																							
1949 Phi-A	31	75	7	20	0	1	1	6	9	16	0	0	.267	.345	.333	.679	83	-2	10	4.35	0	S-14,3-12/2-1	2	-0.1
1951 Phi-A	11	15	0	1	0	0	0	0	1	3	0	0	.067	.125	.067	.192	-46	-3	0	.14	-1	/2-2,3-1	0	-0.4
Total 2	**42**	**90**	**7**	**21**	**0**	**1**	**1**	**6**	**10**	**19**	**0**	**0**	**.233**	**.310**	**.289**	**.599**	**63**	**-5**	**10**	**3.50**	**-1**	**/S-14,3-13,2-3**	**2**	**-0.5**

• DAVIS, Tommy Thomas James Davis b: 5/21/1973, Mobile, AL BR/TR, 6'1", 210 lbs. Deb: 5/14/1999

YEAR TM-L	G	AB	R	H	2B	3B	HR	RBI	BB	SO	SB	CS	AVG	OBP	SLG	OPS	OPS+	BR/A	RC	RC/G	FR	G/POS	WS	TPW
1999 Bal-A	5	6	0	1	0	0	0	0	0	2	0	0	.167	.167	.167	.333	-15	-1	0	.00	0	/C-4,1-1	0	-0.1

• DAVIS, Tommy Herman Thomas Davis b: 3/21/1939, Brooklyn, NY BR/TR, 6'2", 205 lbs. Deb: 9/22/1959 Career OF: 1101-122-56

YEAR TM-L	G	AB	R	H	2B	3B	HR	RBI	BB	SO	SB	CS	AVG	OBP	SLG	OPS	OPS+	BR/A	RC	RC/G	FR	G/POS	WS	TPW
1959 LA-N	1	1	0	0	0	0	0	0	0	1	0	0	.000	.000	.000	.000	-93	-0	0	.00	0	....	0	0.0
1960 LA-N	110	352	43	97	18	1	11	44	13	35	6	2	.276	.305	.426	.731	92	-5	45	4.45	1	0-87(24-55-10)/3-5	9	-0.9
1961 LA-N	132	460	60	128	13	2	15	58	32	53	10	4	.278	.328	.413	.741	87	-8	59	4.34	-2	0-86(44-39-30),3-59	11	-1.3
1962 LA-N★	163	665	120	**230**	27	9	27	**153**	33	65	18	6	**.346**	.379	.535	.914	151	46	129	7.42	-1	*O-146(134-13-5),3-39	36	3.6
1963*LA-N★	146	556	69	181	19	3	16	88	29	59	15	10	**.326**	.363	.457	.820	144	29	86	5.64	-2	*O-129(120-14-3),3-40	29	2.2
1964 LA-N	152	592	70	163	20	5	14	86	29	68	11	8	.275	.314	.397	.711	106	2	69	4.09	3	*O-148(148-0-0)	17	-0.4
1965 LA-N	17	60	3	15	1	1	0	9	2	4	2	1	.250	.274	.300	.574	66	-3	3	1.78	1	O-16(16-0-0)	0	-0.3
1966*LA-N	100	313	27	98	11	1	3	27	16	36	3	3	.313	.347	.383	.730	111	4	38	4.45	2	O-79(79-0-0)/3-2	9	0.2
1967 NY-N	154	577	72	174	32	0	16	73	31	71	9	3	.302	.345	.440	.785	125	18	84	5.28	4	*O-149(149-0-0)/1-1	19	1.7
1968 Chi-A	132	456	30	122	5	3	8	50	16	48	4	2	.268	.292	.344	.637	91	-6	42	3.11	0	*O-116(115-0-4)/1-6	8	-1.4
1969 Sea-A	123	454	52	123	29	1	6	80	30	46	19	4	.271	.322	.379	.701	97	-0	53	4.00	-6	*O-112(112-0-0)/1-1	10	-1.3
Hou-N	24	79	2	19	3	0	1	9	8	9	1	1	.241	.318	.316	.635	80	-2	8	3.39	0	O-21(20-1-0)	1	-0.3
1970 Hou-N	57	213	24	60	12	2	3	30	7	25	8	3	.282	.305	.399	.704	91	-3	25	4.27	0	O-53(53-0-0)	5	-0.6
Oak-A	66	200	17	58	9	1	1	27	8	18	2	4	.290	.321	.360	.681	91	-4	21	3.75	-1	O-45(10-0-0)/1-8	4	-0.8
Chi-N	11	42	4	11	2	0	2	8	1	1	0	0	.262	.279	.452	.731	83	-1	5	4.68	-3	O-10(43-0-2)	1	-0.5
Yr.	68	255	28	71	14	2	5	38	8	26	8	3	.278	.300	.408	.708	89	-5	31	4.34	-3	O-63(96-0-2)	6	-1.1
1971*Oak-A	79	219	26	71	8	1	3	42	15	19	7	1	.324	.368	.411	.778	123	7	31	5.19	2	1-35,O-16(16-0-0)/2-3,3-2	9	0.6
1972 Chi-N	15	26	3	7	1	0	0	6	2	3	0	1	.269	.321	.308	.629	72	-1	2	3.29	0	/1-3,O-2(1-0-1)	0	-0.2
Bal-A	26	82	9	21	3	0	0	6	6	18	2	0	.256	.307	.293	.600	77	-2	7	3.06	0	O-18(17-0-1)/1-3	1	-0.4
1973*Bal-A	137	552	53	169	20	3	7	89	30	56	11	3	.306	.343	.391	.734	107	6	72	4.75	0	*D-127/1-4	12	0.0
1974*Bal-A	158	626	67	181	20	1	11	84	34	49	6	2	.289	.329	.377	.706	106	4	73	4.15	0	*D-155	15	-0.1
1975 Bal-A	116	460	43	130	14	1	6	57	23	52	2	0	.283	.317	.357	.673	96	-3	49	3.81	0	*D-111	8	-0.7
1976 Cal-A	72	219	16	58	5	0	3	26	15	18	0	1	.265	.315	.329	.644	95	-2	20	3.02	0	D-54/1-1	3	-0.4
KC-A	8	19	1	5	0	0	0	0	1	0	0	0	.263	.300	.263	.563	65	-1	1	2.37	0	/D-3	0	-0.1
Yr.	80	238	17	63	5	0	3	26	16	18	0	1	.265	.314	.324	.637	92	-3	21	2.97	0	D-57/1-1	3	-0.5
Total 18	1999	7223	811	2121	272	35	153	1052	381	754	136	59	.294	.332	.405	.736	109	74	923	4.54	-4	*O-1233,D-450,3-147/1-62,2	207	-1.4

• DAVIS, Trench Trench Neal Davis b: 9/12/1960, Baltimore, MD BL/TL, 6'3", 171 lbs. Deb: 6/4/1985 Career OF: 0-9-0

YEAR TM-L	G	AB	R	H	2B	3B	HR	RBI	BB	SO	SB	CS	AVG	OBP	SLG	OPS	OPS+	BR/A	RC	RC/G	FR	G/POS	WS	TPW
1985 Pit-N	2	7	1	1	0	0	0	0	0	0	1	0	.143	.143	.143	.286	-20	-1	0	.00	0	/O-2(0-2-0)	0	-0.1
1986 Pit-N	15	23	2	3	0	0	0	1	0	4	0	0	.130	.130	.130	.261	-27	-4	0	.36	0	/O-7(0-7-0)	0	-0.4
1987 Atl-N	6	3	0	0	0	0	0	0	0	1	0	0	.000	.000	.000	.000	-95	-1	0	.00	0	....	0	-0.1
Total 3	23	33	3	4	0	0	0	1	0	5	1	0	.121	.121	.121	.242	-32	-6	0	.25	0	/O-9	0	-0.6

• DAVIS, Willie William Henry Davis b: 4/15/1940, Mineral Springs, AR BL/TL, 5'11", 181 lbs. Deb: 9/8/1960 Career OF: 10-2237-81

YEAR TM-L	G	AB	R	H	2B	3B	HR	RBI	BB	SO	SB	CS	AVG	OBP	SLG	OPS	OPS+	BR/A	RC	RC/G	FR	G/POS	WS	TPW
1960 LA-N	22	88	12	28	6	1	2	10	4	12	3	5	.318	.348	.477	.825	116	0	12	4.96	1	O-22(0-22-0)	3	0.0
1961 LA-N	128	339	56	86	19	6	12	45	27	46	12	5	.254	.318	.451	.769	93	-4	49	4.83	-2	*O-114(0-114-0)	10	-0.9
1962 LA-N	157	600	103	171	18	**10**	21	85	42	72	32	7	.285	.338	.453	.791	117	17	92	5.28	6	*O-156(1-155-0)	26	1.8
1963*LA-N	156	515	60	126	19	8	9	60	25	61	25	11	.245	.284	.365	.649	91	-6	51	3.30	12	*O-153(0-153-0)	17	0.2
1964 LA-N	157	613	91	180	23	7	12	77	22	59	42	13	.294	.319	.413	.732	112	12	82	4.77	16	*O-155(0-155-0)	26	2.4
1965*LA-N	142	558	52	133	24	3	10	57	14	81	25	9	.238	.266	.346	.612	76	-18	51	3.00	5	*O-141(0-141-0)	15	-1.8
1966*LA-N	153	624	74	177	31	6	11	61	15	68	21	10	.284	.305	.405	.710	103	1	76	4.37	5	*O-152(0-152-0)	20	0.1
1967 LA-N	143	569	65	146	27	9	6	41	29	65	20	6	.257	.296	.367	.663	97	-2	62	3.76	-1	*O-138(0-138-0)	15	-0.8
1968 LA-N	160	643	86	161	24	10	7	31	31	88	36	10	.250	.286	.351	.637	98	0	68	3.61	-1	*O-158(0-158-0)	19	-0.6
1969 LA-N	129	498	66	155	23	8	11	59	33	39	24	10	.311	.359	.456	.815	136	24	79	5.80	2	*O-125(0-125-0)	22	2.3
1970 LA-N	146	593	92	181	23	**16**	8	93	29	54	38	14	.305	.339	.438	.777	111	9	88	5.34	11	*O-143(0-139-4)	24	1.6
1971 LA-N★	158	641	84	198	33	10	10	74	23	47	20	8	.309	.333	.438	.771	124	17	88	4.98	5	*O-157(0-157-0)	25	1.9
1972 LA-N	149	615	81	178	22	7	19	79	27	61	20	3	.289	.320	.441	.761	117	14	87	5.11	8	*O-146(0-146-0)	25	1.9
1973 LA-N★	152	599	82	171	29	9	16	77	29	62	17	5	.285	.324	.444	.768	116	11	86	5.17	1	*O-146(0-146-0)	23	0.9
1974 Mon-N	153	611	86	180	27	9	12	89	27	69	25	7	.295	.328	.427	.755	104	3	85	5.02	4	*O-151(0-151-0)	20	0.3
1975 Tex-A	42	169	16	42	8	2	5	17	4	25	13	5	.249	.270	.408	.678	90	-3	18	3.57	0	O-42(0-42-0)	4	-0.4
StL-N	98	350	41	102	19	6	6	50	14	27	10	1	.291	.326	.431	.758	105	2	50	5.15	0	O-89(8-15-71)	11	-0.2
1976 SD-N	141	493	61	132	18	10	5	46	19	34	14	2	.268	.298	.375	.673	98	-2	56	4.01	2	*O-128(0-128-0)	16	-0.3
1979*Cal-A	43	56	9	14	2	1	0	2	4	7	1	0	.250	.300	.321	.621	70	-2	5	3.16	0	/O-7(1-0-6),D-6	1	-0.2
Total 18	2429	9174	1217	2561	395	138	182	1053	418	977	398	131	.279	.314	.412	.726	106	74	1186	4.54	72	*O-2323/D-6	322	8.0

• DAWKINS, Travis Travis Sentell Dawkins b: 5/12/1979, Newberry, SC BR/TR, 6'1", 180 lbs. Deb: 9/3/1999

YEAR TM-L	G	AB	R	H	2B	3B	HR	RBI	BB	SO	SB	CS	AVG	OBP	SLG	OPS	OPS+	BR/A	RC	RC/G	FR	G/POS	WS	TPW
1999 Cin-N	7	7	1	1	0	0	0	0	0	4	0	0	.143	.250	.143	.393	3	-1	0	1.42	-1	/S-7	0	-0.2
2000 Cin-N	14	41	5	9	2	0	0	3	2	7	0	0	.220	.256	.268	.524	32	-4	2	1.61	2	S-14	1	-0.1
2002 Cin-N	31	48	2	6	2	0	0	0	6	21	2	1	.125	.222	.167	.389	4	-7	2	1.21	-7	S-21/2-3	0	-1.3
2003 KC-A	3	2	0	0	0	0	0	0	1	2	0	0	.000	.333	.000	.333	-1	-0	0	1.17	0	/2-3	0	0.0
Total 4	55	98	8	16	4	0	0	3	9	34	2	1	.163	.241	.204	.445	15	-12	5	1.38	-6	/S-42,2-6	1	-1.6

• DAWSON, Andre Andre Nolan "Hawk" Dawson b: 7/10/1954, Miami, FL BR/TR, 6'3", 195 lbs. Deb: 9/11/1976 Career OF: 39-1027-1284

YEAR TM-L	G	AB	R	H	2B	3B	HR	RBI	BB	SO	SB	CS	AVG	OBP	SLG	OPS	OPS+	BR/A	RC	RC/G	FR	G/POS	WS	TPW
1976 Mon-N	24	85	9	20	4	1	0	7	5	13	1	2	.235	.278	.306	.584	63	-5	7	2.80	1	O-24(8-14-2)	1	-0.5
1977 Mon-N	139	525	64	148	26	9	19	65	34	93	21	7	.282	.328	.474	.802	116	11	82	5.59	-2	*O-136(13-129-3)	18	0.6
1978 Mon-N	157	609	84	154	24	8	25	72	30	128	28	11	.253	.301	.442	.743	106	3	80	4.51	7	*O-153(0-153-0)	21	0.9
1979 Mon-N	155	639	90	176	24	12	25	92	27	115	35	10	.275	.311	.468	.779	111	9	91	4.98	-10	*O-153(0-153-0)	24	-0.4
1980 Mon-N	151	577	96	178	41	7	17	87	44	69	34	9	.308	.364	.492	.856	137	30	105	6.62	5	*O-147(0-147-0)	29	3.5
1981*Mon-N★	103	394	71	119	21	3	24	64	35	50	26	4	.302	.369	.553	.923	157	32	83	7.70	7	*O-103(0-103-0)	25	4.0
1982 Mon-N★	148	608	107	183	37	7	23	83	34	96	39	10	.301	.346	.498	.845	131	26	106	6.33	1	*O-147(0-147-0)	26	2.7
1983 Mon-N★	159	633	104	**189**	36	10	32	113	38	81	25	11	.299	.347	.539	.886	143	33	113	6.24	-4	*O-157(0-157-0)	28	2.9
1984 Mon-N	138	533	73	132	23	6	17	86	41	80	13	5	.248	.304	.409	.713	103	1	65	4.12	4	*O-134(0-0-134)	12	-0.3
1985 Mon-N	139	529	65	135	27	2	23	91	29	92	13	4	.255	.299	.444	.743	112	6	67	4.35	2	*O-131(0-24-123)	16	0.3
1986 Mon-N	130	496	65	141	32	2	20	78	37	79	18	12	.284	.341	.478	.819	125	13	75	5.25	2	*O-127(0-0-127)	16	0.9
1987 Chi-N★	153	621	90	178	24	2	**49**	**137**	32	103	11	3	.287	.329	.568	.897	127	21	111	6.45	2	*O-152(0-0-152)	20	1.5
1988 Chi-N★	157	591	78	179	31	8	24	79	37	73	12	4	.303	.348	.504	.852	136	25	100	6.19	1	*O-147(0-0-147)	19	2.5
1989*Chi-N★	118	416	62	105	18	6	21	77	35	62	8	5	.252	.312	.476	.788	114	5	55	4.41	2	*O-112(0-0-112)	13	0.4
1990 Chi-N★	147	529	72	164	28	5	27	100	42	65	16	2	.310	.363	.535	.898	134	25	101	7.02	-3	*O-139(0-0-140)	22	1.9
1991 Chi-N★	149	563	69	153	21	4	31	104	22	80	4	5	.272	.305	.488	.794	114	6	79	4.97	-1	*O-137(0-0-138)	20	0.1
1992 Chi-N	143	542	60	150	27	2	22	90	30	70	6	2	.277	.319	.456	.775	114	8	75	4.94	4	*O-139(0-0-139)	16	0.9
1993 Bos-A	121	461	44	126	29	1	13	67	17	49	2	1	.273	.318	.425	.743	92	-6	57	4.27	0	D-97,O-20(0-0-20)	7	-1.4
1994 Bos-A	75	292	34	70	18	0	16	48	9	53	2	2	.240	.272	.466	.738	82	-11	30	3.40	0	D-74	1	-1.5
1995 Fla-N	79	226	30	58	10	3	8	37	9	45	0	0	.257	.309	.434	.742	93	-3	29	4.35	-2	O-59(12-0-47)	4	-0.8
1996 Fla-N	42	58	6	16	2	0	2	14	2	13	0	0	.276	.311	.414	.725	92	-1	7	4.59	0	/O-6(6-0-0)	2	-0.2
Total 21	2627	9927	1373	2774	503	98	438	1591	589	1509	314	109	.279	.327	.482	.809	119	228	1519	5.38	15	*O-2323,D-171	340	18.1

• DAY, Boots Charles Frederick Day b: 8/31/1947, Ilion, NY BL/TL, 5'9", 160 lbs. Deb: 6/15/1969 Career OF: 34-304-23

YEAR TM-L	G	AB	R	H	2B	3B	HR	RBI	BB	SO	SB	CS	AVG	OBP	SLG	OPS	OPS+	BR/A	RC	RC/G	FR	G/POS	WS	TPW
1969 StL-N	11	6	1	0	0	0	0	0	1	1	0	0	.000	.143	.000	.143	-57	-1	0	.00	0	/O-1	0	-0.2
1970 Chi-N	11	8	2	2	0	0	0	0	0	3	0	0	.250	.250	.250	.500	31	-1	0	.96	0	/O-7(0-7-0)	0	-0.1
Mon-N	41	108	14	29	4	0	0	5	6	18	3	2	.269	.307	.306	.613	65	-6	10	3.07	-1	O-35(5-30-0)	2	-0.8
Yr.	52	116	16	31	4	0	0	5	6	21	3	2	.267	.303	.302	.605	63	-6	10	2.92	-1	O-42(5-37-0)	2	-0.9
1971 Mon-N	127	371	53	105	10	2	4	33	33	39	9	4	.283	.343	.353	.696	97	-1	47	4.38	3	*O-120(3-118-0)	13	-0.1
1972 Mon-N	128	386	32	90	7	4	0	30	29	44	3	6	.233	.288	.272	.560	59	-22	31	2.58	-2	*O-117(0-103-15)	5	-2.9
1973 Mon-N	101	207	36	57	7	0	4	28	21	28	0	3	.275	.342	.367	.709	93	-3	26	4.32	-3	O-51(12-45-6)	5	-0.7

YEAR TM-L	G	AB	R	H	2B	3B	HR	RBI	BB	SO	SB	CS	AVG	OBP	SLG	OPS	OPS+	BR/A	RC	RC/G	FR	G/POS	WS	TPW
1974 Mon-N	52	65	8	12	0	0	0	2	5	8	0	0	.185	.243	.185	.427	20	-7	3	1.42	0	O-16(14-0-2)	0	-0.8
Total 6	471	1151	146	295	28	6	8	98	95	141	15	15	.256	.314	.312	.626	75	-40	117	3.39	-3	O-347	25	-5.6
• DAYETT, Brian	Brian Kelly Dayett b: 1/22/1957, New London, CT BR/TR, 5'10", 180 lbs. Deb: 9/11/1983 Career OF: 158-1-34																							
1983 NY-A	11	29	3	6	0	1	0	5	2	4	0	0	.207	.258	.276	.534	49	-2	2	2.54	1	/O-9(9-0-0)	0	-0.2
1984 NY-A	64	127	14	31	8	0	4	23	9	14	0	0	.244	.299	.402	.701	96	-1	15	3.99	1	O-62(55-0-10)/D-1	3	-0.2
1985 Chi-N	22	26	1	6	0	0	1	4	0	6	0	0	.231	.259	.346	.605	61	-1	2	2.65	0	O-10(11-0-0)	0	-0.2
1986 Chi-N	24	67	7	18	4	0	4	11	6	10	0	1	.269	.329	.507	.836	118	1	10	5.04	-1	O-24(15-1-12)	2	-0.1
1987 Chi-N	97	177	20	49	14	1	5	25	20	37	0	0	.277	.350	.452	.802	106	1	29	5.84	-1	O-78(68-0-12)	5	-0.2
Total 5	218	426	45	110	26	2	14	68	37	71	0	1	.258	.320	.427	.748	99	-2	58	4.71	-1	O-183/D-1	10	-0.8
• DE LA HOZ, Mike	Miguel Angel (Piloto) de la Hoz b: 10/2/1938, Havana, Cuba BR/TR, 5'11" Deb: 7/22/1960																							
1960 Cle-A	49	160	20	41	6	2	6	23	9	12	0	0	.256	.300	.431	.731	98	-1	19	3.77	-2	S-38/3-8	5	-0.1
1961 Cle-A	61	173	20	45	10	0	3	23	7	10	0	0	.260	.297	.370	.667	79	-6	18	3.71	2	2-17,S-17,3-16	4	-0.1
1962 Cle-A	12	12	0	1	0	0	0	0	0	3	0	0	.083	.083	.083	.167	-57	-3	0	.20	0	/2-2	0	-0.3
1963 Cle-A	67	150	15	40	10	0	5	25	9	29	0	0	.267	.313	.433	.746	107	1	20	4.71	2	2-34/3-6,O-2(2-0-0),S-2	6	0.6
1964 Mil-N	78	189	25	55	7	1	4	12	14	22	1	1	.291	.346	.402	.748	109	2	25	4.84	-2	2-25,3-25/S-8	7	0.3
1965 Mil-N	81	176	15	45	3	2	2	11	8	21	0	1	.256	.296	.330	.625	75	-6	16	3.02	1	S-41,3-22,2-10/1-1	3	-0.4
1966 Atl-N	71	110	11	24	3	0	2	7	5	18	0	1	.218	.252	.300	.552	52	-8	8	2.43	-4	3-30/2-8,S-1	1	-1.2
1967 Atl-N	74	143	10	29	3	0	3	14	4	14	1	0	.203	.224	.287	.511	46	-10	8	1.89	1	2-23,3-22/S-1	1	-0.9
1969 Cin-N	1	1	0	0	0	0	0	0	0	1	0	0	.000	.000	.000	.000	-95	-0	0	.00	0	....	0	0.0
Total 9	494	1114	116	280	42	5	25	115	56	130	2	3	.251	.292	.365	.657	82	-30	114	3.50	-3	3-129,2-119,S-108/O-2,1-1	27	-2.2
• DE LA ROSA, Jesus	Jesus de la Rosa b: 8/5/1953, Santo Domingo, Dominican Republic BR/TR, 6'1" Deb: 8/2/1975																							
1975 Hou-N	3	3	1	1	1	0	0	0	0	0	0	0	.333	.333	.667	1.000	186	0	1	9.00	0	....	0	0.0
• DE LA ROSA, Tomas	Tomas Agramonte De La Rosa b: 1/28/1978, La Victoria, Dominican Republic BR/TR, 5'10", 155 lbs. Deb: 7/17/2000																							
2000 Mon-N	32	66	7	19	3	1	2	9	7	11	2	1	.288	.365	.455	.819	103	0	11	5.51	0	S-29	3	0.2
2001 Mon-N	1	1	0	0	0	0	0	0	0	0	0	0	.000	.000	.000	.000	-98	-0	0	.00	0	....	0	0.0
Total 2	33	67	7	19	3	1	2	9	7	11	2	1	.284	.360	.448	.808	100	-0	11	5.40	0	/S-29	3	0.2
• DE LOS SANTOS, Luis	Luis Manuel (Martinez) de los Santos b: 12/29/1966, San Cristobal, Dominican Republic BR/TR, 6'5" Deb: 9/7/1988																							
1988 KC-A	11	22	1	2	1	1	0	1	4	4	0	0	.091	.231	.227	.458	28	-2	1	.82	0	/1-5,D-3	0	-0.3
1989 KC-A	28	87	6	22	3	1	0	6	5	14	0	0	.253	.293	.310	.604	71	-3	8	3.10	0	1-27	1	-0.5
1991 Det-A	16	30	1	5	2	0	0	0	2	4	0	0	.167	.219	.233	.452	25	-3	1	1.18	-1	/D-9,O-3(3-0-0),1-2,3-2	0	-0.4
Total 3	55	139	8	29	6	2	0	7	11	22	0	0	.209	.267	.281	.547	54	-9	10	2.21	-1	/1-34,D-12,O-3,3-2	1	-1.2
• DEAL, Charlie	Charles Albert Deal b: 10/30/1891, Wilkinsburg, PA d: 9/16/1979, Covina, CA BR/TR, 6', 160 lbs. Deb: 7/19/1912																							
1912 Det-A	42	142	13	32	4	2	0	11	9	....	4	....	.225	.272	.282	.553	60	-8	12	2.70	4	3-41	2	-0.2
1913 Det-A	16	50	3	11	0	2	0	3	1	7	2	....	.220	.235	.300	.535	57	-3	4	2.38	0	3-15	0	-0.3
Bos-N	10	36	6	11	1	0	0	3	2	1	1	....	.306	.359	.333	.692	96	-0	5	4.45	0	2-10	1	0.0
1914*Bos-N	79	257	17	54	13	2	0	23	20	23	4	....	.210	.270	.276	.546	63	-12	21	2.48	-6	3-74/S-1	4	-1.7
1915 StL-F	65	223	21	72	12	4	1	27	12	16	10	....	.323	.357	.426	.783	124	6	37	5.79	6	3-65	10	1.4
1916 StL-A	23	74	7	10	1	0	0	10	6	8	4	....	.135	.200	.149	.349	5	-9	3	1.20	-2	3-22/2-1	1	-1.1
Chi-N	2	8	2	2	1	0	0	3	0	0	0	....	.250	.250	.375	.625	82	-0	1	3.25	2	/3-2	0	0.2
1917 Chi-N	135	449	46	114	11	3	0	47	19	18	10	....	.254	.284	.292	.576	71	-16	41	2.93	4	*3-130	13	-0.9
1918*Chi-N	119	414	43	99	9	3	2	34	21	13	11	....	.239	.279	.290	.569	72	-14	37	2.83	2	*3-118	10	-1.0
1919 Chi-N	116	405	37	117	23	5	2	52	12	12	11	....	.289	.316	.385	.701	110	3	52	4.35	4	*3-116	15	1.2
1920 Chi-N	129	450	48	108	10	5	3	39	20	14	5	8	.240	.285	.304	.589	68	-19	39	2.72	3	*3-128	10	-1.3
1921 Chi-N	115	422	52	122	19	8	3	66	13	9	3	5	.289	.310	.393	.704	85	-10	50	4.06	7	*3-112	11	0.4
Total 10	851	2930	295	752	104	34	11	318	135	121	65	13	.257	.293	.327	.620	79	-82	301	3.33	23	3-823/2-11,S-1	77	-3.4
• DEAL, Lindsay	Fred Lindsay Deal b: 9/3/1911, Lenoir, NC d: 4/18/1979, Little Rock, AR BL/TR, 6', 175 lbs. Deb: 9/13/1939																							
1939 Bro-N	4	7	0	0	0	0	0	0	0	2	0	....	.000	.000	.000	.000	-97	-2	0	.00	0	/O-1	0	-0.2
• DEAL, Snake	John Wesley Deal b: 1/21/1879, Lancaster, PA d: 5/9/1944, Harrisburg, PA BR/TR, 6', 164 lbs. Deb: 7/9/1906																							
1906 Cin-N	65	231	13	48	4	3	0	21	6	....	15	....	.208	.228	.251	.479	47	-15	18	2.42	1	1-65	1	-1.7
• DEALY, Pat	Patrick E. Dealy b: Burlington, VT d: 12/17/1924, Buffalo, NY BR/TR, 5'8", 145 lbs. Deb: 9/30/1884 U Career OF: 6-3-2																							
1884 StP-U	5	15	2	2	0	0	0	....	0	....	....	....	.133	.133	.133	.267	-10	-2	0	.59	2	/C-4,O-1	0	0.0
1885 Bos-N	35	130	18	29	4	1	1	9	2	14	....	....	.223	.235	.292	.527	72	-4	9	2.45	-2	C-29/3-3,O-2(1-1-0),S-2,1	3	-0.3
1886 Bos-N	15	46	9	15	1	1	0	3	4	4	5	....	.326	.380	.391	.771	140	2	9	7.80	-2	C-14/O-1	2	0.1
1887 Was-N	58	220	33	63	8	2	1	18	8	8	36	....	.286	.293	.330	.623	77	-6	32	5.37	-3	C-28,S-23/3-5,O-5(4-1-0)	5	-0.5
1890 Syr-a	18	66	9	12	1	0	0	4	5	....	4	....	.182	.250	.197	.447	35	-5	4	2.14	-2	C-10/3-6,O-2(0-1-1)	0	-0.5
Total 5	131	477	71	121	14	4	2	34	19	26	45	....	.254	.275	.301	.576	73	-15	55	4.09	-7	/C-85,S-25,3-14,O-11,1-1	10	-1.3
• DEAN, Chubby	Alfred Lovill Dean b: 8/24/1915, Mount Airy, NC d: 12/21/1970, Riverside, NJ BL/TL, 5'11", 181 lbs. Deb: 4/14/1936 ♦																							
1936 Phi-A	111	342	41	98	21	3	1	48	24	24	3	2	.287	.337	.374	.711	77	-13	44	4.58	-1	1-77	5	-1.8
1937 Phi-A	104	309	36	81	14	4	2	31	42	10	2	1	.262	.350	.353	.703	79	-9	41	4.58	-1	1-78/P-2	5	-1.5
1938 Phi-A	16	20	3	6	2	0	0	1	1	4	0	0	.300	.333	.400	.733	85	2	3	5.00	1	/P-6	3	0.5
1939 Phi-A	80	77	12	27	4	0	0	19	8	4	0	0	.351	.412	.403	.814	111	9	12	5.50	1	P-54	7	0.5
1940 Phi-A	67	90	6	26	2	0	0	6	16	9	0	0	.289	.396	.311	.707	88	8	13	5.19	0	P-30/1-1	2	-2.6
1941 Phi-A	27	37	0	9	2	0	0	9	4	3	0	0	.243	.317	.297	.614	65	2	4	3.70	0	P-18/1-1	1	-1.5
Cle-A	17	25	2	4	1	0	0	2	3	2	0	0	.160	.250	.200	.450	21	0	1	1.25	1	/P-8	2	-0.2
Yr.	44	62	2	13	3	0	0	11	7	5	0	0	.210	.290	.258	.548	47	3	5	2.59	1	P-26/1-1	3	-1.7
1942 Cle-A	70	101	4	27	1	0	0	7	11	7	0	0	.267	.339	.277	.617	79	8	10	3.46	-3	P-27	10	-0.2
1943 Cle-A	41	46	2	9	0	0	0	5	6	2	0	0	.196	.288	.196	.484	45	1	3	1.69	-1	P-17	0	-1.3
Total 8	533	1047	106	287	47	7	3	128	115	65	5	3	.274	.347	.341	.688	78	10	129	4.31	-4	P-162,1-157	35	-8.1
• DEAN, Tommy	Tommy Douglas Dean b: 8/30/1945, Iuka, MS BR/TR, 6', 165 lbs. Deb: 9/17/1967																							
1967 LA-N	12	28	1	4	1	0	0	2	0	9	0	0	.143	.143	.179	.321	-9	-4	1	.82	1	S-12	0	-0.3
1969 SD-N	101	273	14	48	9	2	2	9	27	54	0	3	.176	.252	.245	.498	42	-22	17	1.95	-8	S-97/2-2	2	-2.1
1970 SD-N	61	158	18	35	5	1	2	13	11	29	2	0	.222	.272	.304	.576	56	-10	13	2.62	3	S-55	2	-0.2
1971 SD-N	41	70	2	8	0	0	0	1	4	13	1	0	.114	.162	.114	.276	-22	-11	2	.61	-1	S-28,3-11/2-1	1	-1.1
Total 4	215	529	35	95	15	3	4	25	42	105	3	3	.180	.241	.242	.483	35	-47	33	1.88	-5	S-192/3-11,2-3	5	-3.6
• DEANE, Harry	John Henry Deane b: 5/6/1846, Trenton, NJ d: 5/31/1925, Indianapolis, IN, 5'7", 150 lbs. Deb: 7/20/1871 M/U NA OF: 6-46-0																							
1871 Kek-n	6	22	3	4	0	1	0	2	2	0	0	0	.182	.250	.273	.523	49	-2	2	2.69	1	/O-6(6-0-0)	....	0.0
1874 Bal-n	47	203	29	50	8	1	0	13	5	3	2	1	.246	.264	.296	.560	80	-4	17	3.27	-3	*O-46(0-46-0)/2-2,S-1	....	-0.6
Total 2 n	53	225	32	54	8	2	0	15	7	3	2	1	.240	.263	.293	.556	76	-6	18	3.21	-3	/O-52,2-2,S-1	....	-0.7
• DEAR, Buddy	Paul Stanford Dear b: 12/1/1905, Norfolk, VA d: 8/29/1989, Radford, VA BR/TR, 5'8", 143 lbs. Deb: 9/9/1927																							
1927 Was-A	2	1	1	0	0	0	0	0	0	0	0	0	.000	.000	.000	.000	-101	-0	0	.00	-1	/2-1	0	-0.1
• DEARMOND, Charlie	Charles Hommer "Hummer" DeArmond b: 2/13/1877, Okeana, OH d: 12/17/1933, Morning Sun, OH BR/TR, 5'10", 165 lbs. Deb: 9/19/1903																							
1903 Cin-N	11	39	10	11	2	1	0	7	3	....	1	....	.282	.349	.385	.733	98	-0	6	5.34	-1	3-11	1	-0.1
• DEASLEY, John	John Deasley b: 1/1861, Philadelphia, PA d: 12/25/1910, Philadelphia, PA Deb: 6/17/1884																							
1884 Was-U	31	134	20	29	1	1	0	....	3	....	....	....	.216	.234	.239	.472	62	-5	8	2.04	-1	S-31	3	-0.4
KC-U	13	40	3	7	2	0	0	....	2	....	....	....	.175	.214	.225	.439	56	-1	2	1.68	-1	S-13	0	-0.2
Yr.	44	174	23	36	3	1	0	....	5	....	....	....	.207	.229	.236	.465	61	-6	10	1.96	-2	S-44	3	-0.6

YEAR TM-L	G	AB	R	H	2B	3B	HR	RBI	BB	SO	SB	CS	AVG	OBP	SLG	OPS	OPS+	BR/A	RC	RC/G	FR	G/POS	WS	TPW
• DEASLEY, Pat	Thomas H. Deasley b: 11/17/1857, Philadelphia, PA d: 4/1/1943, Philadelphia, PA BR/TR, 5'8.5", 154 lbs. Deb: 5/18/1881 Career OF: 3-12-29																							
1881 Bos-N	43	147	13	35	5	2	0	8	5	10	....	....	.238	.263	.299	.562	80	-3	12	2.86	-2	C-28/O-7(0-2-6),S-7,1-2	3	-0.4
1882 Bos-N	67	264	36	70	8	0	0	29	7	22	....	....	.265	.284	.295	.580	86	-4	23	3.22	0	*C-56,O-14(1-0-13)/S-1	7	0.0
1883 StL-a	58	206	27	53	2	1	0	15	6	....	....	....	.257	.278	.277	.555	75	-6	16	2.98	2	C-56/O-2(0-2-0)	6	0.0
1884 StL-a	75	254	27	52	5	4	0	0	7	....	....	....	.205	.235	.256	.491	58	-12	16	2.13	7	*C-75/O-2(1-0-1),1-1	6	0.1
1885 NY-N	54	207	22	53	5	1	0	24	9	20	....	....	.256	.287	.290	.577	88	-3	18	3.09	5	C-54/O-2(0-2-0),S-1	7	0.7
1886 NY-N	41	143	18	38	6	1	0	17	4	12	2	....	.266	.286	.322	.607	83	-3	14	3.61	-1	C-30,O-15(1-6-8)	5	-0.2
1887 NY-N	30	127	12	46	5	0	0	23	9	7	3	....	.362	.367	.356	.723	106	2	17	5.54	-5	C-24/3-7,S-1	3	-0.1
1888 Was-N	34	127	6	20	1	0	0	4	2	18	2	....	.157	.171	.165	.336	8	-13	4	1.01	4	C-31/2-1,O-1,S-1	2	-0.6
Total 8	402	1475	161	367	37	9	0	120	49	89	7	....	.249	.271	.282	.552	74	-42	119	2.93	11	C-354/O-43,S-11,3-7,1-3,2-1	39	-0.5
• DEBERRY, Hank	John Herman DeBerry b: 12/29/1894, Savannah, TN d: 9/10/1951, Savannah, TN BR/TR, 5'11", 195 lbs. Deb: 9/12/1916																							
1916 Cle-A	15	33	7	9	4	0	0	4	6	9	0	....	.273	.385	.394	.779	126	1	5	5.42	1	C-14	2	0.3
1917 Cle-A	25	33	3	9	2	0	0	1	2	7	0	....	.273	.333	.333	.667	96	-0	3	3.75	-0	/C-9	1	0.0
1922 Bro-N	85	259	29	78	10	1	3	35	20	9	4	1	.301	.354	.382	.736	90	-2	36	5.02	0	C-81	9	0.2
1923 Bro-N	78	235	21	67	11	6	1	48	20	12	2	1	.285	.346	.396	.742	98	0	33	5.07	5	C-60	8	0.9
1924 Bro-N	77	218	20	53	10	3	3	26	20	21	0	1	.243	.307	.358	.665	80	-6	24	3.76	12	C-63	10	1.0
1925 Bro-N	67	193	26	50	8	1	2	24	16	8	2	2	.259	.322	.342	.664	72	-8	22	3.81	15	C-55	6	1.0
1926 Bro-N	48	115	6	33	11	0	0	13	8	5	0	....	.287	.333	.383	.716	94	-1	14	4.31	1	C-37	5	0.2
1927 Bro-N	68	201	15	47	3	2	1	21	17	8	1	....	.234	.294	.284	.577	55	-13	17	2.77	10	C-67	6	0.2
1928 Bro-N	82	258	19	65	8	2	0	23	18	15	3	....	.252	.301	.298	.599	58	-16	23	3.05	2	C-80	5	-0.9
1929 Bro-N	68	210	13	55	11	1	1	25	17	15	1	....	.262	.317	.338	.655	64	-12	23	3.61	1	C-68	5	-0.6
1930 Bro-N	35	95	11	28	3	0	0	14	4	10	0	....	.295	.323	.326	.650	58	-6	10	3.70	-1	C-35	2	-0.5
Total 11	648	1850	170	494	81	16	11	234	148	119	13	5	.267	.323	.346	.669	76	-63	210	3.93	44	C-569	59	1.9
• DEBUS, Adam	Adam Joseph DeBus b: 10/7/1892, Chicago, IL d: 5/13/1977, Chicago, IL BR/TR, 5'10.5", 150 lbs. Deb: 7/14/1917																							
1917 Pit-N	38	131	9	30	5	4	0	7	7	14	2	....	.229	.279	.328	.607	83	-3	12	3.00	-4	S-21,3-18	2	-0.5
• DECINCES, Doug	Douglas Vernon DeCinces b: 8/29/1950, Burbank, CA BR/TR, 6'2", 194 lbs. Deb: 9/9/1973																							
1973 Bal-A	10	18	2	2	0	0	0	3	1	5	0	0	.111	.158	.111	.269	-23	-3	0	.60	0	/3-8,2-2,S-1	0	-0.3
1974 Bal-A	1	1	0	0	0	0	0	0	1	0	0	0	.000	.500	.000	.500	55	0	0	3.51	0	/3-1	0	0.0
1975 Bal-A	61	167	20	42	6	3	4	23	13	32	0	1	.251	.309	.395	.705	105	0	20	4.11	-1	3-34,S-13,2-11/1-2	5	0.1
1976 Bal-A	129	440	36	103	17	2	11	42	29	68	8	4	.234	.285	.357	.641	93	-6	43	3.25	-4	*3-109,2-17,1-11/S-2,D-1	10	-1.0
1977 Bal-A	150	522	63	135	28	3	19	69	64	86	8	8	.259	.342	.433	.775	117	11	75	4.89	9	*3-148/1-1,2-1,D-1	21	1.9
1978 Bal-A	142	511	72	146	37	1	28	80	46	81	7	7	.286	.347	.526	.873	152	31	89	6.23	5	*3-130,2-12	27	3.6
1979*Bal-A	120	422	67	97	27	1	16	61	54	68	5	3	.230	.322	.412	.734	100	-0	56	4.38	6	*3-120	13	0.5
1980 Bal-A	145	489	64	122	23	2	16	64	49	83	11	6	.249	.322	.403	.724	98	-2	59	3.98	24	*3-142/1-1	16	2.1
1981 Bal-A	100	346	49	91	23	2	13	55	41	32	0	3	.263	.343	.454	.797	128	11	51	5.04	-2	*3-100/1-1,O-1	15	0.8
1982*Cal-A	153	575	94	173	42	5	30	97	66	80	7	5	.301	.374	.548	.922	149	38	113	6.96	11	*3-153/S-2	28	4.8
1983 Cal-A★	95	370	49	104	19	3	18	65	32	56	2	0	.281	.338	.495	.833	127	13	59	5.51	4	3-84,D-10	13	1.6
1984 Cal-A	146	547	77	147	23	3	20	82	53	79	4	1	.269	.333	.431	.765	111	8	77	4.84	-5	*3-140/D-5	17	0.1
1985 Cal-A	120	427	50	104	22	1	20	78	47	71	1	4	.244	.321	.440	.762	107	2	55	4.15	-8	*3-111/D-3	12	-0.7
1986*Cal-A	140	512	69	131	20	3	26	96	52	74	2	2	.256	.327	.459	.786	112	7	72	4.78	-8	*3-132/D-3,S-1	16	-0.2
1987 Cal-A	133	453	65	106	23	0	16	63	70	87	3	4	.234	.339	.391	.730	96	-2	61	4.53	1	*3-128/1-4,D-1,S-1	12	-0.3
StL-N	4	9	1	2	2	0	0	1	0	2	0	0	.222	.222	.444	.667	70	-0	1	3.43	0	/3-3	0	-0.1
Total 15	1649	5809	778	1505	312	29	237	879	618	904	58	48	.259	.333	.445	.778	116	109	831	4.86	36	*3-1543/2-43,D-24,1-20,S-20,O	205	13.1
• DECKER, Frank	Frank Decker b: 2/26/1856, St. Louis, MO d: 2/5/1940, St. Louis, MO BR/TR Deb: 6/25/1879																							
1879 Syr-N	3	10	0	1	0	0	0	0	0	3	....	....	.100	.100	.100	.200	-38	-1	0	.32	-2	/C-2,1-1,O-1	0	-0.3
1882 StL-a	2	8	0	2	0	0	0	1	0	....	....	....	.250	.250	.250	.500	66	-0	1	2.39	0	/2-2	0	0.0
Total 2	5	18	0	3	0	0	0	1	0	3	....	....	.167	.167	.167	.333	8	-2	1	1.15	-2	/2-2,C-2,1-1,O-1	0	-0.3
• DECKER, George	George A. "Gentleman George" Decker b: 6/1/1869, York, PA d: 6/7/1909, Patton, CA BL/TL, 6'1", 180 lbs. Deb: 7/11/1892 Career OF: 189-34-111																							
1892 Chi-N	78	291	32	66	6	7	1	28	20	49	9	....	.227	.277	.306	.582	75	-10	28	3.33	-11	O-62(0-0-62),2-16	4	-2.2
1893 Chi-N	81	328	57	89	9	8	2	48	24	22	22	....	.271	.325	.366	.691	85	-8	47	5.24	-6	O-33(23-0-10),1-27,2-20/S-2	5	-1.3
1894 Chi-N	93	393	76	122	17	7	8	93	24	20	23	....	.310	.358	.450	.808	89	-10	73	7.04	-9	1-48,O-29(0-23-6)/3-7,2-2,S	7	-1.5
1895 Chi-N	73	297	51	82	9	7	2	41	17	22	11	....	.276	.324	.374	.698	75	-13	41	5.06	-5	O-57(25-8-24),1-11/3-3,2-1,S	5	-1.7
1896 Chi-N	107	421	68	118	23	11	5	61	23	14	20	....	.280	.318	.423	.740	91	-9	65	5.55	-5	O-71(67-3-1),1-36	9	-1.7
1897 Chi-N	111	428	72	124	12	7	5	63	24	....	11	....	.290	.333	.386	.719	86	-10	61	5.18	-5	O-75(74-0-1),1-38/2-1	8	-1.8
1898 StL-N	76	286	26	74	10	0	1	45	20	....	4	....	.259	.314	.304	.618	75	-9	30	3.66	-2	1-75	3	-1.1
Lou-N	42	148	27	44	4	3	0	19	9	....	9	....	.297	.342	.365	.707	104	1	22	5.55	1	1-32/O-6(0-0-6)	4	0.1
Yr.	118	434	53	118	14	3	1	64	29	....	13	....	.272	.323	.325	.648	85	-9	52	4.28	-2	*1-107/O-6(0-0-6)	7	-1.1
1899 Lou-N	39	138	14	37	8	1	1	18	12	....	3	....	.268	.336	.362	.698	91	-2	20	4.62	-1	1-38	2	-0.3
Was-N	4	9	0	0	0	0	0	0	0	....	0	....	.000	.000	.000	.000	-101	-2	0	.00	0	/1-2,O-1	0	-0.3
Yr.	43	147	14	37	8	1	1	18	12	....	3	....	.252	.317	.340	.657	81	-4	20	4.28	-2	1-40/O-1	2	-0.6
Total 8	704	2739	423	756	98	51	25	416	173	127	112	....	.276	.324	.376	.700	84	-73	388	5.08	-43	O-334,1-307/2-40,3-10,S-4	47	-11.9
• DECKER, Harry	Earle Harry Decker b: 9/3/1864, Lockport, IL BR/TR, 5'11", 180 lbs. Deb: 8/23/1884 Career OF: 12-4-8																							
1884 Ind-a	4	15	1	4	1	0	0	0	1	....	....	....	.267	.313	.333	.646	114	0	2	4.00	-1	/C-4	0	-0.1
KC-U	23	75	8	10	2	0	0	....	5	....	....	....	.133	.188	.160	.348	21	-5	2	.99	0	O-16(6-4-6),C-11	0	-0.4
1886 Det-N	14	54	2	12	1	0	0	5	2	9	0	....	.222	.250	.241	.491	48	-3	3	2.14	2	C-14/O-1	1	0.0
Was-N	7	23	0	5	1	1	0	2	1	5	0	....	.217	.250	.348	.598	85	-0	2	3.08	0	/C-4,3-2,S-1	1	0.0
Yr.	21	77	2	17	2	1	0	7	3	14	0	....	.221	.250	.273	.523	59	-4	5	2.42	2	C-18/3-2,O-1,S-1	2	0.0
1889 Phi-N	11	30	4	3	0	0	0	2	2	5	1	....	.100	.156	.100	.256	-25	-5	1	.63	-3	/2-7,C-3,O-1	0	-0.7
1890 Phi-N	5	19	5	7	1	0	0	2	4	1	4	....	.368	.478	.421	.899	159	2	6	12.99	-2	/1-2,O-2(2-0-0),C-1	1	0.0
Pit-N	92	354	52	97	14	3	5	38	26	36	8	....	.274	.324	.373	.697	116	7	46	4.79	-5	C-70,1-16/O-4(2-0-2),2-1,S	7	0.6
Yr.	97	373	57	104	15	3	5	40	30	37	12	....	.279	.333	.375	.708	119	9	52	5.16	-6	C-71,1-18/O-6(4-0-2),2-1,S	8	0.6
Total 4	156	570	72	138	20	4	5	49	41	56	13	....	.242	.293	.318	.611	90	-5	62	3.84	-8	C-107/O-24,1-18,2-8,3-2,S-2	10	-0.5
• DECKER, Steve	Steven Michael Decker b: 10/25/1965, Rock Island, IL BR/TR, 6'3", 205 lbs. Deb: 9/18/1990																							
1990 SF-N	15	54	5	16	2	0	3	8	1	10	0	0	.296	.309	.500	.809	123	1	8	5.36	1	C-15	2	0.3
1991 SF-N	79	233	11	48	7	1	5	24	16	44	0	1	.206	.266	.309	.575	63	-12	18	2.48	0	C-78	3	-0.8
1992 SF-N	15	43	3	7	1	0	0	1	6	7	0	0	.163	.280	.186	.466	36	-3	3	2.06	-1	C-15	1	-0.3
1993 Fla-N	8	15	0	0	0	0	0	1	3	3	0	0	.000	.167	.000	.167	-48	-3	0	.10	0	/C-5	0	-0.3
1995 Fla-N	51	133	12	30	2	1	3	13	19	22	1	0	.226	.322	.323	.646	71	-5	15	3.91	-1	C-46/1-2	4	-0.3
1996 SF-N	57	122	16	28	1	0	1	12	15	26	0	0	.230	.314	.262	.576	56	-7	11	2.79	2	C-30/1-3,3-2	2	-0.3
Col-N	10	25	8	8	2	0	1	8	3	3	1	0	.320	.393	.520	.913	112	1	6	8.43	0	C-10	2	0.2
Yr.	67	147	24	36	3	0	2	20	18	29	1	0	.245	.327	.306	.633	66	-7	16	3.64	2	C-40/1-3,3-2	4	-0.2
1999 Ana-A	28	63	5	15	6	0	0	5	13	9	0	0	.238	.377	.333	.710	84	-1	8	4.06	-1	C-17/1-6,D-3	1	-0.1
Total 7	263	688	60	152	21	2	13	72	76	124	2	1	.221	.303	.314	.617	67	-30	69	3.23	1	C-216/1-11,D-3,3-2	15	-1.7
• DEDE, Artie	Arthur Richard Dede b: 7/12/1895, Brooklyn, NY d: 9/6/1971, Keene, NH BR/TR, 5'9", 155 lbs. Deb: 10/4/1916																							
1916 Bro-N	1	1	0	0	0	0	0	0	0	0	0	....	.000	.000	.000	.000	-97	-0	0	.00	-1	/C-1	0	-0.1
• DEDEAUX, Rod	Raoul Martial Dedeaux b: 2/17/1915, New Orleans, LA BR/TR, 5'11", 160 lbs. Deb: 9/28/1935																							
1935 Bro-N	2	4	0	1	0	0	0	1	0	0	0	....	.250	.250	.250	.500	36	-0	0	2.31	0	/S-2	0	0.0
• DEE, Jim	James D. Dee b: Buffalo, NY Deb: 7/30/1884																							
1884 Pit-a	12	40	0	5	0	0	0	0	1	....	....	....	.125	.146	.125	.271	-11	-5	1	.59	-1	S-12	0	-0.5

YEAR	TM-L	G	AB	R	H	2B	3B	HR	RBI	BB	SO	SB	CS	AVG	OBP	SLG	OPS	OPS+	BR/A	RC	RC/G	FR	G/POS	WS	TPW
• DEE, Shorty	Maurice Leo Dee b: 10/4/1889, Halifax, Canada d: 8/12/1971, Jamaica Plain, MA BR/TR, 5'6", 155 lbs. Deb: 9/14/1915																								
1915	StL-A	1	3	1	0	0	0	0	0	1	0	0	1	.000	.250	.000	.250	-26	-1	0	.00	-1	/S-1	0	-0.2
• DEER, Rob	Robert George Deer b: 9/29/1960, Orange, CA BR/TR, 6'3", 210 lbs. Deb: 9/4/1984 Career OF: 186-5-871																								
1984	SF-N	13	24	5	4	0	0	3	3	7	10	1	1	.167	.375	.542	.917	160	2	5	6.89	-1	/O-9(9-0-0)	1	0.1
1985	SF-N	78	162	22	30	5	1	8	20	23	71	0	1	.185	.286	.377	.663	88	-3	19	3.78	-3	O-37(21-0-17),1-10	3	-0.8
1986	Mil-A	134	466	75	108	17	3	33	86	72	179	5	2	.232	.338	.494	.832	119	13	82	6.02	-2	*O-131(1-0-131)/1-4	17	0.3
1987	Mil-A	134	474	71	113	15	2	28	80	86	186	12	4	.238	.361	.456	.817	112	11	85	6.19	4	*O-123(98-0-29),1-12/D-4	17	0.8
1988	Mil-A	135	492	71	124	24	0	23	85	51	153	9	5	.252	.331	.441	.772	113	8	74	5.25	2	*O-133(54-2-79)/D-1	19	0.6
1989	Mil-A	130	466	72	98	18	2	26	65	60	158	4	8	.210	.306	.425	.731	105	-1	59	4.16	1	*O-125(2-1-123)/D-5	12	-0.3
1990	Mil-A	134	440	57	92	15	1	27	69	64	147	2	3	.209	.315	.432	.747	108	3	64	4.89	7	*O-117(0-0-117),1-21/D-1	15	0.7
1991	Det-A	134	448	64	80	14	2	25	64	89	175	1	3	.179	.315	.386	.701	91	-5	60	4.29	3	*O-132(0-0-132)/D-2	11	-0.6
1992	Det-A	110	393	66	97	20	1	32	64	51	131	4	2	.247	.338	.547	.885	143	21	73	6.40	2	*O-106(0-0-106)/D-2	14	2.0
1993	Det-A	90	323	48	70	11	0	14	39	38	120	3	2	.217	.305	.381	.686	84	-8	39	4.03	0	O-86(0-2-84)/D-4	5	-1.3
	Bos-A	38	143	18	28	6	1	7	16	20	49	2	0	.196	.303	.399	.702	82	-3	19	4.28	3	O-36(0-0-36)/D-2	2	-0.3
	Yr.	128	466	66	98	17	1	21	55	58	169	5	2	.210	.304	.386	.691	83	-11	58	4.10	2	*O-122(0-2-120)/D-6	7	-1.6
1996	SD-N	25	50	9	9	3	0	4	9	14	30	0	0	.180	.359	.480	.839	126	2	10	6.11	-1	O-18(1-0-17)	2	0.0
Total	**11**	**1155**	**3881**	**578**	**853**	**148**	**13**	**230**	**600**	**575**	**1409**	**43**	**31**	**.220**	**.325**	**.442**	**.768**	**108**	**40**	**589**	**5.09**	**15**	***O-1053/1-47,D-21**	**118**	**1.2**
• DEES, Charlie	Charles Henry Dees b: 6/24/1935, Birmingham, AL BL/TL, 6'1", 173 lbs. Deb: 5/26/1963																								
1963	LA-A	60	202	23	62	11	1	3	27	11	31	3	3	.307	.367	.416	.782	126	6	30	5.16	-2	1-56	7	0.1
1964	LA-A	26	26	3	2	1	0	0	1	1	4	1	2	.077	.143	.115	.258	-30	-5	0	.30	0	1-12	0	-0.6
1965	Cal-A	12	32	1	5	0	0	0	1	1	8	1	2	.156	.182	.156	.338	-3	-5	1	.62	-1	/1-8	0	-0.7
Total	**3**	**98**	**260**	**27**	**69**	**12**	**1**	**3**	**29**	**13**	**43**	**5**	**7**	**.265**	**.323**	**.354**	**.677**	**96**	**-4**	**31**	**3.93**	**-3**	**/1-76**	**7**	**-1.2**
• DEFATE, Tony	Clyde Herbert DeFate b: 2/22/1895, Kansas City, MO d: 9/3/1963, New Orleans, LA BR/TR, 5'8.5", 158 lbs. Deb: 4/18/1917																								
1917	StL-N	14	14	0	2	0	0	0	1	4	5	0	....	.143	.333	.143	.476	50	-1	1	1.38	0	/3-5,2-1	0	-0.1
	Det-A	3	2	1	0	0	0	0	0	0	1	0	....	.000	.000	.000	.000	-100	-0	0	.00	0	/2-1	0	-0.1
• DEFREITES, Arturo	Arturo Marcelino (Simon) DeFreites b: 4/26/1953, San Pedro de Macoris, Dominican Republic BR/TR, 6'2", 195 lbs. Deb: 9/7/1978																								
1978	Cin-N	9	19	1	4	1	0	1	2	1	4	0	0	.211	.250	.421	.671	84	-1	2	3.53	0	/1-6	0	-0.1
1979	Cin-N	23	34	2	7	2	0	0	4	0	16	0	0	.206	.206	.265	.471	27	-4	2	1.52	-1	/1-6,0-1	0	-0.5
Total	**2**	**32**	**53**	**3**	**11**	**3**	**0**	**1**	**6**	**1**	**20**	**0**	**0**	**.208**	**.222**	**.321**	**.543**	**49**	**-4**	**4**	**2.23**	**-1**	**/1-12,0-1**	**0**	**-0.6**
• DEGROFF, Rube	Edward Arthur DeGroff b: 9/2/1879, Hyde Park, NY d: 12/17/1955, Poughkeepsie, NY BL/TL, 5'11" Deb: 9/22/1905 Career OF: 0-8-8																								
1905	StL-N	15	56	3	14	2	1	0	5	5	....	1	....	.250	.311	.321	.633	91	-1	6	3.75	0	O-15(0-8-7)	1	-0.2
1906	StL-N	1	4	1	0	0	0	0	0	0	....	0	....	.000	.000	.000	.000	-104	-1	0	.00	0	/O-1	0	-0.1
Total	**2**	**16**	**60**	**4**	**14**	**2**	**1**	**0**	**5**	**5**	**....**	**1**	**....**	**.233**	**.292**	**.300**	**.592**	**80**	**-2**	**6**	**3.43**	**-1**	**/O-16**	**1**	**-0.3**
• DEHAAN, Kory	Korwin Jay DeHaan b: 7/16/1976, Pella, IA BL/TR, 6'2", 187 lbs. Deb: 4/25/2000 Career OF: 16-6-50																								
2000	SD-N	90	103	19	21	7	0	2	13	5	39	4	2	.204	.241	.330	.571	45	-9	8	2.36	2	O-60(10-4-49)/D-1	1	-0.8
2002	SD-N	12	11	1	1	0	0	0	0	0	6	0	0	.091	.091	.091	.182	-57	-2	0	.25	-0	/O-9(6-2-1)	0	-0.3
Total	**2**	**102**	**114**	**20**	**22**	**7**	**0**	**2**	**13**	**5**	**45**	**4**	**2**	**.193**	**.227**	**.307**	**.534**	**36**	**-12**	**8**	**2.14**	**1**	**/O-69,D-1**	**1**	**-1.1**
• DEHLMAN, Herman	Herman J. "Dutch" Dehlman b: 1852, Brooklyn, NY d: 3/13/1885, Wilkes-Barre, PA Deb: 5/2/1872 U																								
1872	Atl-n	37	165	30	36	3	1	0	14	3	1	4	2	.218	.232	.248	.481	41	-14	11	2.53	1	*1-37	....	-0.9
1873	Atl-n	54	221	50	52	4	1	0	17	9	7	5	0	.235	.265	.262	.528	64	-5	17	3.09	-1	*1-54/S-1	....	-0.4
1874	Atl-n	53	218	40	49	3	1	0	18	7	5	2	0	.225	.249	.248	.497	67	-4	14	2.54	9	*1-53	....	0.4
1875	StL-n	67	254	42	57	12	2	0	14	**11**	21	23	9	.224	.257	.287	.544	98	3	25	3.62	10	*1-67/O-2(0-0-2)	....	1.2
1876	StL-N	64	254	40	45	6	0	0	9	9	10	....	....	.177	.213	.208	.421	43	-13	11	1.56	7	*1-64	2	-0.8
1877	StL-N	32	119	24	22	4	0	0	11	7	21	....	....	.185	.230	.218	.449	44	-7	6	1.74	-5	1-31/O-1	1	-1.2
Total	**4 n**	**211**	**858**	**162**	**194**	**22**	**5**	**0**	**63**	**30**	**34**	**34**	**11**	**.226**	**.252**	**.263**	**.516**	**71**	**-20**	**67**	**3.00**	**19**	**1-211/O-2,S-1**	**....**	**0.4**
Total	**2**	**96**	**373**	**64**	**67**	**10**	**0**	**0**	**20**	**16**	**31**	**....**	**....**	**.180**	**.218**	**.212**	**.430**	**43**	**-20**	**17**	**1.62**	**2**	**/1-95,O-1**	**3**	**-2.0**
• DEIDEL, Jim	James Lawrence Deidel b: 6/6/1949, Denver, CO BR/TR, 6'2", 195 lbs. Deb: 5/31/1974																								
1974	NY-A	2	2	0	0	0	0	0	0	0	0	0	0	.000	.000	.000	.000	-103	-1	0	.00	0	/C-2	0	0.0
• DEININGER, Pep	Otto Charles Deininger b: 10/10/1877, Wasseralfingen, Germany d: 9/25/1950, Boston, MA BL/TL, 5'8.5", 180 lbs. Deb: 4/26/1902 Career OF: 1-39-6																								
1902	Bos-A	2	6	0	2	1	1	0	0	0	....	0	....	.333	.333	.833	1.167	210	1	2	11.32	-1	/P-2	1	-0.7
1908	Phi-N	1	0	0	0	0	0	0	0	0	....	0	....	....	....	....	....	-97	0	0	....	0	/O-1	0	0.0
1909	Phi-N	55	169	22	44	9	0	0	16	11	....	5	....	.260	.309	.314	.623	93	-2	18	3.58	-2	O-45(1-38-6)/2-1	4	-0.7
Total	**3**	**58**	**175**	**22**	**46**	**10**	**1**	**0**	**16**	**11**	**....**	**5**	**....**	**.263**	**.310**	**.331**	**.642**	**96**	**-1**	**19**	**3.81**	**-3**	**/O-46,P-2,2-1**	**5**	**-1.4**
• DEISEL, Pat	Edward Deisel b: 4/29/1876, Ripley, OH d: 4/17/1948, Cincinnati, OH BR/TR, 5'5", 145 lbs. Deb: 8/21/1902																								
1902	Bro-N	1	3	0	2	0	0	0	1	1	....	0	....	.667	.800	.667	1.467	351	1	2	43.46	0	/C-1	1	0.2
1903	Cin-N	2	0	0	0	0	0	0	0	1	....	0	....	....	1.000	....	1.000	174	0	0	....	-1	/C-1	0	0.0
Total	**2**	**3**	**3**	**0**	**2**	**0**	**0**	**0**	**1**	**2**	**....**	**0**	**....**	**.667**	**.833**	**.667**	**1.500**	**321**	**2**	**2**	**43.46**	**0**	**/C-2**	**1**	**0.1**
• DEITRICK, Bill	William Alexander Deitrick b: 4/20/1902, Hanover County, VA d: 5/6/1946, Bethesda, MD BR/TR, 5'10", 160 lbs. Deb: 9/19/1927																								
1927	Phi-N	5	6	1	1	0	0	0	0	0	0	0	....	.167	.167	.167	.333	-10	-1	0	.81	-2	/S-5	0	-0.2
1928	Phi-N	52	100	13	20	6	0	0	7	17	10	1	....	.200	.322	.260	.582	52	-7	9	2.95	0	O-21(17-1-3)/S-8	0	-0.7
Total	**2**	**57**	**106**	**14**	**21**	**6**	**0**	**0**	**7**	**17**	**10**	**1**	**....**	**.198**	**.315**	**.255**	**.569**	**49**	**-7**	**9**	**2.83**	**-2**	**/O-21,S-13**	**0**	**-1.0**
• DEJAN, Mike	Michael Dan Dejan b: 1/13/1915, Cleveland, OH d: 2/2/1953, West Los Angeles, CA BL/TL, 6'1", 185 lbs. Deb: 7/13/1940																								
1940	Cin-N	12	16	1	3	0	1	0	2	3	3	0	....	.188	.316	.313	.628	73	-1	2	2.93	-0	/O-2(2-0-0)	0	-0.1
• DEJESUS, David	David Christopher DeJesus b: 12/20/1979, Brooklyn, NY BL/TL, 6', 175 lbs. Deb: 9/4/2003																								
2003	KC-A	12	7	0	2	0	1	0	0	1	2	0	0	.286	.444	.571	1.016	146	1	2	9.07	-1	/O-9(0-8-1)	0	0.0
• DEJESUS, Ivan	Ivan (Alvarez) DeJesus b: 1/9/1953, Santurce, Puerto Rico BR/TR, 5'11", 175 lbs. Deb: 9/13/1974																								
1974	LA-N	3	3	1	1	0	0	0	0	0	2	0	0	.333	.333	.333	.667	91	-0	0	4.50	-1	/S-2	0	-0.1
1975	LA-N	63	87	10	16	2	1	0	2	11	15	1	2	.184	.276	.230	.505	43	-7	6	2.20	2	S-63	2	-0.1
1976	LA-N	22	41	4	7	2	1	0	2	4	9	0	1	.171	.244	.268	.513	46	-3	2	1.54	1	S-13/3-7	1	-0.1
1977	Chi-N	155	624	91	166	31	7	3	40	56	90	24	12	.266	.330	.353	.683	75	-21	75	4.14	-1	*S-154	15	-0.5
1978	Chi-N	160	619	**104**	172	24	7	3	35	74	78	41	12	.278	.357	.354	.711	88	-4	84	4.66	-15	*S-160	19	-0.2
1979	Chi-N	160	636	92	180	26	10	5	52	59	82	24	20	.283	.346	.379	.725	89	-12	83	4.42	-23	*S-160	16	-1.8
1980	Chi-N	157	618	78	160	26	3	3	33	60	81	44	16	.259	.328	.325	.654	77	-15	72	4.00	-16	*S-156	14	-1.5
1981	Chi-N	106	403	49	78	8	4	0	13	46	61	21	9	.194	.276	.233	.509	44	-28	30	2.33	-1	*S-106	4	-2.0
1982	Phi-N	161	536	53	128	21	5	3	59	54	70	14	4	.239	.311	.313	.624	73	-17	55	3.44	-13	*S-154/3-7	14	-1.4
1983*	Phi-N	158	497	60	126	15	7	4	45	53	77	11	4	.254	.325	.336	.661	85	-9	56	3.83	-27	*S-158	12	-2.0
1984	Phi-N	144	435	40	112	15	3	0	35	43	76	12	5	.257	.327	.306	.633	77	-12	43	3.40	-5	*S-141	8	-0.4
1985*	StL-N	59	72	11	16	5	0	0	7	4	16	2	2	.222	.263	.292	.555	55	-5	6	2.50	2	3-20,S-13	1	-0.3
1986	NY-A	7	4	1	0	0	0	0	0	1	1	0	0	.000	.200	.000	.200	-40	-1	0	.35	-1	/S-7	0	-0.2
1987	SF-N	9	10	0	2	0	0	0	1	0	2	0	1	.200	.200	.200	.400	7	-2	0	.60	-1	/S-9	0	-0.3
1988	Det-A	7	17	1	3	0	0	0	0	1	4	0	0	.176	.222	.176	.399	14	-2	1	1.46	-1	/S-7	0	-0.2
Total	**15**	**1371**	**4602**	**595**	**1167**	**175**	**48**	**21**	**324**	**466**	**664**	**194**	**88**	**.254**	**.324**	**.326**	**.651**	**76**	**-138**	**514**	**3.76**	**-100**	***S-1303/3-34**	**106**	**-11.1**
• DEJOHN, Mark	Mark Stephen DeJohn b: 9/18/1953, Middletown, CT BB/TR, 5'11", 170 lbs. Deb: 4/28/1982 C																								
1982	Det-A	24	21	1	4	2	0	0	1	4	4	1	0	.190	.320	.286	.606	68	-1	3	3.52	0	S-20/3-4,2-1	1	0.0

Player Register DELGADO • 1155

YEAR TM-L	G	AB	R	H	2B	3B	HR	RBI	BB	SO	SB	CS	AVG	OBP	SLG	OPS	OPS+	BR/A	RC	RC/G	FR	G/POS	WS	TPW

• DEKONING, Bill William Callahan DeKoning b: 12/19/1919, Brooklyn, NY d: 7/26/1979, Palm Harbor, FL BR/TR, 5'11", 185 lbs. Deb: 5/27/1945

YEAR TM-L	G	AB	R	H	2B	3B	HR	RBI	BB	SO	SB	CS	AVG	OBP	SLG	OPS	OPS+	BR/A	RC	RC/G	FR	G/POS	WS	TPW
1945 NY-N	3	1	0	0	0	0	0	0	0	1	0	....	.000	.000	.000	.000	-98	-0	0	.00	-1	/C-2	0	-0.1

• DEL GRECO, Bobby Robert George Del Greco b: 4/7/1933, Pittsburgh, PA BR/TR, 5'10.5", 190 lbs. Deb: 4/16/1952 Career OF: 74-588-16

YEAR TM-L	G	AB	R	H	2B	3B	HR	RBI	BB	SO	SB	CS	AVG	OBP	SLG	OPS	OPS+	BR/A	RC	RC/G	FR	G/POS	WS	TPW
1952 Pit-N	99	341	34	74	14	2	1	20	38	70	6	5	.217	.301	.279	.580	60	-18	30	2.81	1	0-93(1-88-4)	3	-2.0
1956 Pit-N	14	20	4	4	0	0	2	3	3	3	0	0	.200	.304	.500	.804	114	0	3	4.24	0	/O-7(0-7-0),3-3	1	0.0
StL-N	102	270	29	58	16	2	5	18	32	50	1	1	.215	.312	.344	.656	76	-9	31	3.82	-7	O-99(0-99-0)	6	-2.0
Yr.	116	290	33	62	16	2	7	21	35	53	1	1	.214	.311	.355	.666	79	-8	34	3.85	-7	*O-106(0-106-0)/3-3	7	-2.0
1957 Chi-N	20	40	2	8	2	0	0	3	10	17	1	0	.200	.360	.250	.610	69	-1	5	3.61	-1	O-16(0-16-0)	1	-0.3
NY-A	8	7	3	3	0	0	0	0	2	2	1	0	.429	.556	.429	.984	175	1	2	15.15	0	/O-6(0-6-0)	1	0.1
1958 NY-A	12	5	1	1	0	0	0	0	1	1	0	1	.200	.333	.200	.533	52	-1	0	1.13	-1	O-12(11-1-0)	0	-0.2
1960 Phi-N	100	300	48	71	16	4	10	26	54	64	1	5	.237	.355	.417	.772	110	4	46	5.09	2	O-89(0-87-2)	10	0.2
1961 Phi-N	41	112	14	29	5	0	2	11	12	17	0	0	.259	.346	.357	.704	88	-1	14	4.36	-2	O-32(1-31-0)/2-1,3-1	2	-0.4
KC-A	74	239	34	55	14	1	5	21	30	31	1	0	.230	.319	.360	.678	81	-6	29	4.02	2	O-73(0-73-0)	5	-0.6
1962 KC-A	132	338	61	86	21	1	9	38	49	62	4	1	.254	.370	.402	.772	104	5	55	5.68	3	*O-124(33-95-4)	12	0.4
1963 KC-A	121	306	40	65	7	1	8	29	40	52	1	2	.212	.313	.320	.634	75	-10	32	3.41	-6	*O-110(24-85-6)/3-2	6	-2.0
1965 Phi-N	8	4	1	0	0	0	0	0	0	3	0	0	.000	.000	.000	.000	-102	-1	0	.00	0	/O-4(4-0-0)	0	-0.2
Total 9	731	1982	271	454	95	11	42	169	271	372	16	15	.229	.331	.352	.683	85	-37	247	4.14	-7	O-665/3-6,2-1	47	-7.0

• DEL SAVIO, Garton Garton Orville Del Savio b: 11/26/1913, New York, NY BR/TR, 5'9.5", 165 lbs. Deb: 4/24/1943

YEAR TM-L	G	AB	R	H	2B	3B	HR	RBI	BB	SO	SB	CS	AVG	OBP	SLG	OPS	OPS+	BR/A	RC	RC/G	FR	G/POS	WS	TPW
1943 Phi-N	4	11	0	1	0	0	0	0	1	0	0	....	.091	.167	.091	.258	-26	-2	0	.57	-1	/S-4	0	-0.3

• DELAHANTY, Ed Edward James "Big Ed" Delahanty b: 10/30/1867, Cleveland, OH d: 7/2/1903, Niagara Falls, Canada BR/TR, 6'1", 170 lbs. Deb: 5/22/1888 HOF: 1945 Career OF: 1054-250-40

YEAR TM-L	G	AB	R	H	2B	3B	HR	RBI	BB	SO	SB	CS	AVG	OBP	SLG	OPS	OPS+	BR/A	RC	RC/G	FR	G/POS	WS	TPW
1888 Phi-N	74	290	40	66	12	2	1	31	12	26	38	....	.228	.261	.293	.554	72	-10	33	3.96	-11	2-56,O-17(10-1-6)	7	-1.8
1889 Phi-N	56	246	37	72	13	3	0	27	14	17	19	....	.293	.333	.370	.703	89	-5	38	5.72	-7	O-31(30-0-1),2-24/S-1	5	-1.1
1890 Cle-P	115	517	107	153	26	13	3	64	24	30	25	....	.296	.337	.414	.751	109	5	83	6.12	-7	S-76,2-20,O-18(4-11-3)/3-3,1	13	0.1
1891 Phi-N	128	543	92	132	19	9	5	86	33	50	25	....	.243	.296	.339	.635	83	-14	63	4.17	-4	*O-99(2-95-2),1-27/2-3	12	-2.2
1892 Phi-N	123	477	79	146	30	**21**	6	91	31	32	29	....	.306	.360	**.495**	.855	158	30	98	7.97	2	*O-121(1-120-0)/3-4	20	2.2
1893 Phi-N	132	595	145	219	35	18	**19**	**146**	47	20	37	....	.368	.423	**.583**	1.007	167	**53**	167	11.74	22	*O-117(100-17-0),2-15/1-6	**28**	**5.4**
1894 Phi-N	116	495	148	200	39	19	4	133	60	16	21	....	.404	.475	.584	1.059	159	50	151	13.30	10	*O-88(82-0-6),1-12/2-9,S-8,2	22	4.0
1895 Phi-N	116	480	149	194	**49**	10	11	106	86	31	46	....	.404	**.500**	.617	**1.117**	**186**	**67**	176	**16.24**	-2	*O-103(98-5-0)/S-9,2-6,3-1	31	4.5
1896 Phi-N	123	499	131	198	**44**	17	**13**	**126**	62	22	37	....	.397	.472	**.631**	**1.103**	**191**	**67**	170	**14.81**	8	*O-99(99-0-0),1-22/2-1	31	5.6
1897 Phi-N	129	530	109	200	40	15	5	96	60	....	26	....	.377	.444	.538	.981	163	49	142	11.22	2	*O-129(128-0-1)/1-1	23	3.3
1898 Phi-N	144	548	115	183	36	9	4	92	77	....	**58**	....	.334	.426	.454	.880	159	**46**	135	9.66	1	*O-144(144-0-0)	33	3.2
1899 Phi-N	146	581	135	**238**	**55**	9	9	**137**	55	....	30	....	**.410**	.464	**.582**	**1.046**	**193**	**73**	175	13.36	-1	*O-143(143-0-0)	**41**	5.4
1900 Phi-N	131	539	82	174	32	10	2	109	41	....	16	....	.323	.378	.430	.809	124	17	98	6.84	-4	*1-130	19	1.2
1901 Phi-N	139	542	106	192	**38**	16	8	108	65	....	29	....	.354	.427	.528	**.955**	172	51	139	10.22	-3	O-84(82-1-1),1-58	33	4.1
1902 Was-A	123	473	103	178	**43**	14	10	93	62	....	16	....	**.376**	**.453**	**.590**	**1.043**	**186**	**57**	137	**12.30**	-2	*O-111(111-0-0),1-13	**31**	4.6
1903 Was-A	42	156	22	52	11	1	1	21	12	....	3	....	.333	.388	.436	.824	144	9	28	7.16	1	O-40(20-0-20)/1-1	6	0.8
Total 16	1837	7511	1600	2597	522	186	101	1466	741	244	455	....	.346	.411	.505	.916	152	546	1832	9.81	4	*O-1344,1-271,2-131/S-94,3	355	39.2

• DELAHANTY, Frank Frank George "Pudgie" Delahanty b: 1/29/1883, Cleveland, OH d: 7/22/1966, Cleveland, OH BR/TR, 5'9", 160 lbs. Deb: 8/23/1905 Career OF: 236-1-29

YEAR TM-L	G	AB	R	H	2B	3B	HR	RBI	BB	SO	SB	CS	AVG	OBP	SLG	OPS	OPS+	BR/A	RC	RC/G	FR	G/POS	WS	TPW
1905 NY-A	9	27	0	6	1	0	0	2	1	....	0	....	.222	.250	.259	.509	55	-1	2	2.30	-1	/1-5,O-3(3-0-0)	0	-0.3
1906 NY-A	92	307	37	73	11	8	2	41	16	....	11	....	.238	.282	.345	.627	87	-5	35	3.77	2	O-86(86-0-0)	8	-1.0
1907 Cle-A	15	52	3	9	0	1	0	4	4	....	2	....	.173	.232	.212	.444	41	-3	3	1.91	0	O-15(9-0-6)	0	-0.4
1908 NY-A	37	125	12	32	1	2	0	10	10	....	9	....	.256	.316	.296	.612	98	-0	14	3.92	-2	O-36(36-0-0)	4	-0.5
1914 Buf-F	79	274	29	55	4	7	2	27	23	19	21	....	.201	.265	.288	.553	55	-17	25	2.80	-4	O-78(78-0-0)	4	-2.5
Pit-F	41	159	25	38	4	4	1	7	11	11	7	....	.239	.297	.333	.630	84	-4	17	3.46	-2	O-36(13-1-23)/2-4	2	-0.7
Yr.	120	433	54	93	8	11	3	34	34	30	28	....	.215	.277	.305	.581	65	-20	42	3.03	-6	*O-114(91-1-23)/2-4	6	-3.2
1915 Pit-F	14	42	3	10	1	0	0	3	1	0	0	....	.238	.256	.262	.518	50	-3	3	2.16	1	O-11(11-0-0)	1	-0.2
Total 6	287	986	109	223	22	22	5	94	66	30	50	....	.226	.280	.308	.588	74	-34	100	3.25	-6	O-265/1-5,2-4	19	-5.7

• DELAHANTY, Jim James Christopher Delahanty b: 6/20/1879, Cleveland, OH d: 10/17/1953, Cleveland, OH BR/TR, 5'10.5", 170 lbs. Deb: 4/19/1901 Career OF: 173-1-12

YEAR TM-L	G	AB	R	H	2B	3B	HR	RBI	BB	SO	SB	CS	AVG	OBP	SLG	OPS	OPS+	BR/A	RC	RC/G	FR	G/POS	WS	TPW
1901 Chi-N	17	63	4	12	2	0	0	4	3	....	5	....	.190	.239	.222	.461	35	-5	5	2.44	-3	3-17/2-1	0	-0.7
1902 NY-N	7	26	3	6	1	0	0	3	1	....	0	....	.231	.259	.269	.528	64	-1	2	2.50	-1	/O-7(0-0-7)	0	-0.2
1904 Bos-N	142	499	56	142	27	8	3	60	27	....	16	....	.285	.333	.389	.721	127	15	72	5.18	-7	*3-113,2-18/O-9(5-1-0),P-1	20	1.3
1905 Bos-N	125	461	50	119	11	8	5	55	28	....	12	....	.258	.315	.349	.664	100	-1	57	4.22	-7	*O-124(123-0-1)/P-1	10	-1.5
1906 Cin-N	115	379	63	106	21	4	1	39	45	....	21	....	.280	.371	.364	.735	124	12	62	5.66	-15	*3-105/S-5,O-2(2-0-0)	13	0.0
1907 StL-A	33	95	8	21	3	0	0	6	5	....	6	....	.221	.275	.253	.527	69	-3	9	3.03	-2	3-21/O-4(0-0-4),2-2	1	-0.6
Was-A	108	404	44	118	18	7	2	54	36	....	18	....	.292	.367	.386	.753	152	25	67	5.98	-13	2-68,3-27/O-9(10-0-0),1-4	17	1.4
Yr.	141	499	52	139	21	7	2	60	41	....	24	....	.279	.350	.361	.711	137	22	76	5.36	-16	2-70,3-48,O-13(10-0-4)/1-4	18	0.8
1908 Was-A	83	287	33	91	11	4	1	30	24	....	16	....	.317	.376	.394	.770	164	20	48	6.13	-3	2-80	16	2.0
1909 Was-A	90	302	18	67	13	5	1	21	23	....	4	....	.222	.290	.308	.598	93	-2	28	2.99	-7	2-85	7	-1.0
*Det-A	46	150	29	38	10	1	0	20	17	....	9	....	.253	.364	.333	.697	115	4	22	4.76	0	2-46	7	0.5
Yr.	136	452	47	105	23	6	1	41	40	....	13	....	.232	.316	.316	.632	101	2	51	3.58	-7	*2-131	14	-0.5
1910 Det-A	106	378	67	111	16	2	3	45	43	....	15	....	.294	.379	.370	.749	126	13	59	5.49	-12	*2-106	16	0.2
1911 Det-A	144	542	83	184	30	14	3	94	56	....	15	....	.339	.411	.463	.874	137	28	110	7.53	-7	1-71,2-59,3-13	24	2.0
1912 Det-A	79	266	34	76	14	1	0	41	42	....	9	....	.286	.397	.346	.743	117	9	41	5.33	-2	2-44,O-33(33-0-0)	10	0.6
1914 Bro-F	74	214	28	62	13	5	0	15	25	21	4	....	.290	.372	.397	.769	118	6	33	5.17	-5	2-55/1-5	7	0.2
1915 Bro-F	17	25	0	6	1	0	0	2	3	3	1	....	.240	.345	.280	.625	86	-0	3	3.52	-1	/2-4	1	-0.1
Total 13	1186	4091	520	1159	191	59	19	489	378	24	151	....	.283	.357	.373	.730	123	119	618	5.26	-85	2-568,3-296,O-188/1-80,S-5,P	149	4.1

• DELAHANTY, Joe Joseph Nicholas Delahanty b: 10/18/1875, Cleveland, OH d: 1/29/1936, Cleveland, OH BR/TR, 5'9", 168 lbs. Deb: 9/30/1907 Career OF: 159-45-7

YEAR TM-L	G	AB	R	H	2B	3B	HR	RBI	BB	SO	SB	CS	AVG	OBP	SLG	OPS	OPS+	BR/A	RC	RC/G	FR	G/POS	WS	TPW
1907 StL-N	7	22	3	7	0	0	1	2	0	....	3	....	.318	.318	.455	.773	147	1	4	7.35	0	/O-7(7-0-0)	1	0.0
1908 StL-N	140	499	37	127	14	11	1	44	32	....	11	....	.255	.309	.333	.641	110	5	54	3.65	-5	*O-138(138-0-0)	14	-1.0
1909 StL-N	123	411	28	88	16	4	2	54	42	....	10	....	.214	.292	.287	.579	85	-7	37	2.90	-12	O-63(14-45-7),2-48	6	-2.4
Total 3	270	932	68	222	30	15	4	100	74	....	24	....	.238	.301	.315	.617	99	-1	96	3.39	-17	O-208/2-48	21	-3.4

• DELAHANTY, Tom Thomas James Delahanty b: 3/9/1872, Cleveland, OH d: 1/10/1951, Sanford, FL BL/TR, 5'8", 175 lbs. Deb: 9/29/1894

YEAR TM-L	G	AB	R	H	2B	3B	HR	RBI	BB	SO	SB	CS	AVG	OBP	SLG	OPS	OPS+	BR/A	RC	RC/G	FR	G/POS	WS	TPW
1894 Phi-N	1	4	0	1	0	0	0	0	0	1	0	....	.250	.250	.250	.500	22	-1	0	2.22	0	/2-1	0	0.0
1896 Cle-N	16	56	11	13	4	0	0	4	8	4	4	....	.232	.338	.304	.642	66	-3	7	4.47	-3	3-16	1	-0.4
Pit-N	1	3	1	1	0	0	0	0	0	0	0	....	.333	.333	.333	.667	79	-0	0	4.53	0	/S-1	0	0.0
Yr.	17	59	12	14	4	0	0	4	8	4	4	....	.237	.338	.305	.643	67	-3	8	4.47	-3	3-16/S-1	1	-0.5
1897 Lou-N	1	4	1	1	1	0	0	2	0	....	0	....	.250	.250	.500	.750	99	-0	1	4.53	-1	/2-1	0	-0.1
Total 3	19	67	13	16	5	0	0	6	8	5	4	....	.239	.329	.313	.642	66	-3	9	4.35	-4	/3-16,2-2,S-1	1	-0.6

• DELANCEY, Bill William Pinkney DeLancey b: 11/28/1911, Greensboro, NC d: 11/28/1946, Phoenix, AZ BL/TR, 5'11.5", 185 lbs. Deb: 9/11/1932

YEAR TM-L	G	AB	R	H	2B	3B	HR	RBI	BB	SO	SB	CS	AVG	OBP	SLG	OPS	OPS+	BR/A	RC	RC/G	FR	G/POS	WS	TPW
1932 StL-N	8	26	1	5	0	2	0	2	2	1	0	....	.192	.250	.346	.596	57	-2	2	2.87	0	/C-8	0	-0.1
1934*StL-N	93	253	41	80	18	3	13	40	41	37	1	....	.316	.414	.565	.979	150	19	62	9.47	-3	C-77	16	2.0
1935 StL-N	103	301	37	84	14	5	6	41	42	34	0	....	.279	.369	.419	.788	107	4	50	6.03	-10	C-83	13	0.0
1940 StL-N	15	18	0	4	0	0	0	2	0	2	0	....	.222	.222	.222	.444	22	-2	1	1.20	-1	C-12	0	-0.3
Total 4	219	598	79	173	32	10	19	85	85	74	1	....	.289	.380	.472	.851	121	20	115	7.12	-13	C-180	29	1.7

• DELANEY, Bill William L. Delaney b: 3/5/1863, Cincinnati, OH d: 3/1/1942, Canton, OH BR/TR, 5'10" Deb: 8/21/1890

YEAR TM-L	G	AB	R	H	2B	3B	HR	RBI	BB	SO	SB	CS	AVG	OBP	SLG	OPS	OPS+	BR/A	RC	RC/G	FR	G/POS	WS	TPW
1890 Cle-N	36	116	16	22	1	1	1	7	21	19	5	....	.190	.314	.241	.555	64	-4	11	2.99	-7	2-36	2	-0.9

• DELGADO, Alex Alexander Delgado b: 1/11/1971, Palmerejo, Venezuela BR/TR, 6', 160 lbs. Deb: 4/4/1996

YEAR TM-L	G	AB	R	H	2B	3B	HR	RBI	BB	SO	SB	CS	AVG	OBP	SLG	OPS	OPS+	BR/A	RC	RC/G	FR	G/POS	WS	TPW
1996 Bos-A	26	20	5	5	0	0	0	1	3	3	0	0	.250	.348	.250	.598	54	-1	2	3.54	-5	C-14/O-6(5-0-2),3-4,1-1,2	0	-0.6

YEAR TM-L	G	AB	R	H	2B	3B	HR	RBI	BB	SO	SB	CS	AVG	OBP	SLG	OPS	OPS+	BR/A	RC	RC/G	FR	G/POS	WS	TPW
• DELGADO, Carlos	Carlos Juan (Hernandez) Delgado b: 6/25/1972, Mayaguez, Puerto Rico BL/TR, 6'3", 220 lbs. Deb: 10/1/1993 Career OF: 58-0-0																							
1993 Tor-A	2	1	0	0	0	0	0	0	1	0	0	0	.000	.500	.000	.500	47	0	0	3.51	0	/C-1,D-1	0	0.0
1994 Tor-A	43	130	17	28	2	0	9	24	25	46	1	1	.215	.354	.438	.793	103	1	20	5.01	-3	0-41(41-0-0)/C-1	3	-0.3
1995 Tor-A	37	91	7	15	3	0	3	11	6	26	0	0	.165	.216	.297	.513	32	-10	6	2.04	0	0-17(17-0-0)/D-7,1-4	0	-1.1
1996 Tor-A	138	488	68	132	28	2	25	92	58	139	0	0	.270	.359	.490	.848	112	9	86	6.15	-2	*D-108,1-27	12	-0.3
1997 Tor-A	153	519	79	136	42	3	30	91	64	133	0	3	.262	.352	.528	.880	125	17	98	6.67	-3	*1-119,D-32	18	0.1
1998 Tor-A	142	530	94	155	43	1	38	115	73	139	3	0	.292	.389	.592	.982	150	40	126	8.72	1	*1-141/D-1	24	2.6
1999 Tor-A	152	573	113	156	39	0	44	134	86	141	1	1	.272	.381	.571	.952	136	32	128	7.92	-6	*1-147/D-5	21	1.1
2000 Tor-A★	162	569	115	196	**57**	1	41	137	123	104	0	1	.344	.472	.664	1.137	178	75	186	12.86	-11	*1-162	36	4.5
2001 Tor-A	162	574	102	160	31	1	39	102	111	136	3	0	.279	.409	.540	.949	144	42	134	8.52	-8	*1-161	23	1.8
2002 Tor-A	143	505	103	140	34	2	33	108	102	126	1	0	.277	.411	.549	.960	147	39	121	8.55	5	*1-140/D-3	26	3.0
2003 Tor-A★	161	570	117	172	38	1	42	**145**	109	137	0	0	.302	.430	.593	**1.023**	**163**	**58**	152	**9.93**	-1	*1-147,D-14	**33**	4.1
Total 11	1295	4550	815	1290	317	11	304	959	758	1127	9	6	.284	.398	.558	.957	142	302	1057	8.40	-28	*1-1048,D-171/0-58,C-2	196	15.6
• DELGADO, Puchy	Luis Felipe (Robles) Delgado b: 2/2/1954, Hatillo, Puerto Rico BB/TL, 5'11", 170 lbs. Deb: 9/6/1977																							
1977 Sea-A	13	22	4	4	0	0	0	2	1	8	0	0	.182	.217	.182	.399	10	-3	1	1.39	1	0-13(1-2-10)	0	-0.2
• DELGADO, Wilson	Wilson (Duran) Delgado b: 7/15/1972, San Cristobal, Dominican Republic BB/TR, 5'11", 165 lbs. Deb: 9/24/1996																							
1996 SF-N	6	22	3	8	0	0	0	2	1	5	1	0	.364	.440	.364	.804	120	1	4	7.89	-1	/S-6	1	0.1
1997 SF-N	8	7	1	1	1	0	0	0	0	2	0	0	.143	.143	.286	.429	9	-1	0	1.22	-1	/2-3,S-1	0	-0.1
1998 SF-N	10	12	1	2	1	0	0	1	1	3	0	0	.167	.231	.250	.481	28	-1	1	2.03	0	/S-6	0	-0.1
1999 SF-N	35	71	7	18	2	1	0	3	5	9	1	0	.254	.312	.310	.622	62	-4	7	3.35	-2	S-20,2-15	1	-0.4
2000 NY-A	31	45	6	11	1	0	1	4	5	9	1	0	.244	.320	.333	.653	66	-2	5	3.83	-1	2-14,S-11/3-5	1	-0.2
KC-A	33	83	15	22	1	0	0	7	6	17	1	1	.265	.315	.277	.592	50	-6	7	3.12	12	2-19,S-12/3-3	2	0.6
Yr.	64	128	21	33	2	0	1	11	11	26	2	1	.258	.317	.297	.613	56	-9	12	3.37	11	2-33,S-23/3-8	3	0.4
2001 KC-A	14	25	1	3	0	0	0	1	3	10	0	0	.120	.214	.120	.334	-8	-4	1	.79	0	/S-6,3-3,2-2	0	-0.3
2002 StL-N	12	20	2	4	2	0	2	5	0	6	0	0	.200	.200	.600	.800	103	-0	2	3.79	-2	/S-8	0	-0.2
2003 StL-N	43	77	8	13	3	0	0	3	3	10	0	0	.169	.210	.208	.418	10	-10	3	1.09	-1	2-12,3-11,S-11	0	-1.1
Ana-A	19	50	4	16	0	0	0	4	8	8	0	0	.320	.414	.320	.734	102	1	7	5.53	1	/3-9,S-9,2-1	1	0.3
Total 8	211	412	48	98	11	1	3	30	32	79	4	1	.238	.299	.291	.590	55	-27	38	3.07	5	/S-90,2-66,3-31	6	-1.5
• DELIS, Juan	Juan Francisco Delis b: 2/27/1928, Santiago de Cuba, Cuba BR/TR, 5'11", 170 lbs. Deb: 4/16/1955																							
1955 Was-A	54	132	12	25	3	1	0	11	3	15	1	2	.189	.219	.227	.446	21	-16	6	1.47	-1	3-24/0-8(2-0-6),2-1	0	-1.7
• DELKER, Eddie	Edward Alberts Delker b: 4/17/1906, Palo Alto, PA d: 5/14/1997, Pottsville, PA BR/TR, 5'10.5", 170 lbs. Deb: 4/28/1929																							
1929 StL-N	22	40	5	6	0	1	0	3	2	12	0	....	.150	.227	.200	.427	7	-6	2	1.45	-3	/S-9,2-7,3-3	0	-0.8
1931 StL-N	1	2	0	1	1	0	0	2	0	0	0	....	.500	.500	1.000	1.500	283	0	1	25.32	0	/3-1	0	0.0
1932 StL-N	20	42	1	5	4	0	0	2	8	7	0	....	.119	.260	.214	.474	28	-4	3	1.96	1	2-10/3-5,S-4	1	-0.3
Phi-N	30	62	7	10	1	1	1	7	6	14	0	....	.161	.235	.258	.493	29	-6	4	1.96	-6	2-27	0	-1.1
Yr.	50	104	8	15	5	1	1	9	14	21	0	....	.144	.246	.240	.486	29	-11	7	1.96	-6	2-37/3-5,S-4	1	-1.4
1933 Phi-N	25	41	6	7	3	1	0	1	0	12	0	....	.171	.171	.293	.463	27	-4	2	1.57	-1	2-17/3-4	0	-0.4
Total 4	98	187	19	29	9	3	1	15	16	45	0	....	.155	.229	.251	.481	26	-20	12	1.90	-10	/2-61,3-13,S-13	1	-2.6
• DELLAERO, Jason	Jason Christopher Dellaero b: 12/17/1976, Mount Kisco, NY BB/TR, 6'2", 195 lbs. Deb: 9/7/1999																							
1999 Chi-A	11	33	1	3	0	0	0	2	1	13	0	0	.091	.118	.091	.209	-46	-7	0	.38	-2	S-11	0	-0.8
• DELLUCCI, David	David Michael Dellucci b: 10/31/1973, Baton Rouge, LA BL/TL, 5'10", 180 lbs. Deb: 6/3/1997 Career OF: 146-53-190																							
1997 Bal-A	17	27	3	6	1	0	1	3	4	7	0	0	.222	.344	.370	.714	89	-0	3	3.65	2	/0-9(3-0-6),D-5	1	0.1
1998 Ari-N	124	416	43	108	19	**12**	5	51	33	103	3	5	.260	.319	.399	.718	87	-10	52	4.38	1	*0-117(95-19-15)	10	-1.3
1999 Ari-N	63	109	27	43	7	1	1	15	11	24	2	0	.394	.463	.505	.968	144	9	26	10.25	0	0-31(13-4-19)/D-1	5	0.7
2000 Ari-N	34	50	2	15	3	0	0	2	4	9	0	2	.300	.352	.360	.712	78	-2	6	4.01	0	0-12(1-0-11)	1	-0.3
2001*Ari-N	115	217	28	60	10	2	10	40	22	52	2	1	.276	.349	.479	.828	105	1	37	6.25	-2	0-58(8-18-35)	7	-0.2
2002*Ari-N	97	229	34	56	11	2	7	29	28	55	2	4	.245	.329	.402	.731	84	-7	29	4.13	-4	0-64(20-2-45)/D-3	4	-1.4
2003 Ari-N	70	165	18	40	11	3	2	19	19	45	9	0	.242	.332	.382	.713	78	-3	23	4.66	0	0-53(4-9-43)	4	-0.6
*NY-A	21	51	8	9	1	0	1	4	4	13	3	0	.176	.263	.255	.518	38	-4	4	2.24	1	0-18(2-1-16)/D-2	0	-0.4
Total 7	541	1264	163	337	63	20	27	163	125	308	21	12	.267	.340	.412	.752	91	-16	179	4.96	-4	0-362/D-11	32	-3.4
• DELMAS, Bert	Albert Charles Delmas b: 5/20/1911, San Francisco, CA d: 12/4/1979, Huntington Beach, CA BL/TR, 5'11", 165 lbs. Deb: 9/10/1933																							
1933 Bro-N	12	28	4	7	0	0	0	0	1	7	0	....	.250	.276	.250	.526	53	-2	2	2.64	-2	2-10	0	-0.3
• DELSING, Jim	James Henry Delsing b: 11/13/1925, Rudolph, WI BL/TR, 5'10", 175 lbs. Deb: 4/21/1948 Career OF: 284-383-39																							
1948 Chi-A	20	63	5	12	0	0	0	5	5	12	0	0	.190	.261	.190	.451	22	-7	3	1.64	1	0-15(0-15-0)	0	-0.6
1949 NY-A	9	20	5	7	1	0	1	3	1	2	0	0	.350	.381	.550	.931	145	1	4	9.13	0	/0-5(0-5-0)	1	0.1
1950 NY-A	12	10	2	4	0	0	0	2	2	0	0	0	.400	.500	.400	.900	137	1	2	10.40	0	....	0	0.1
StL-A	69	209	25	55	5	2	0	15	20	23	1	4	.263	.328	.306	.634	61	-14	21	3.47	0	0-53(0-53-0)	3	-1.4
Yr.	81	219	27	59	5	2	0	17	22	23	1	4	.269	.336	.311	.647	64	-13	23	3.71	0	0-53(0-53-0)	3	-1.3
1951 StL-A	131	449	59	112	20	2	8	45	56	39	2	9	.249	.338	.356	.694	85	-12	52	3.87	4	*0-124(4-118-4)	10	-1.1
1952 StL-A	93	298	34	76	13	6	1	34	25	29	3	3	.255	.323	.349	.672	85	-7	33	3.74	1	0-85(34-44-10)	5	-1.0
Det-A	33	113	14	31	2	1	3	15	11	8	1	0	.274	.344	.389	.733	103	1	16	5.23	-1	0-32(32-0-0)	3	-0.3
Yr.	126	411	48	107	15	7	4	49	36	37	4	3	.260	.329	.360	.689	90	-6	50	4.13	0	*0-117(66-44-10)	8	-1.2
1953 Det-A	138	479	77	138	26	6	11	62	66	39	1	3	.288	.380	.436	.816	121	15	84	6.41	-9	*0-133(0-133-0)	18	0.0
1954 Det-A	122	371	39	92	24	2	6	38	49	38	4	4	.248	.337	.372	.709	96	-2	48	4.43	2	*0-108(90-5-16)	10	-0.6
1955 Det-A	114	356	49	85	15	2	10	60	48	40	2	0	.239	.331	.376	.707	92	-3	47	4.49	-3	*0-101(98-3-0)	9	-1.1
1956 Det-A	10	12	0	0	0	0	0	0	3	3	0	0	.000	.250	.000	.250	-29	-2	0	.59	-0	/0-3(0-0-0)	0	-0.2
Chi-A	55	41	11	5	3	0	0	2	10	13	1	0	.122	.294	.195	.489	31	-4	3	2.45	0	0-29(13-7-9)	0	-0.5
Yr.	65	53	11	5	3	0	0	2	13	16	1	0	.094	.284	.151	.435	17	-6	4	1.99	-1	0-32(16-7-9)	0	-0.7
1960 KC-A	16	40	2	10	3	0	0	5	3	5	0	0	.250	.302	.325	.627	69	-2	4	3.75	0	0-10(10-0-0)	1	-0.3
Total 10	822	2461	322	627	112	21	40	286	299	251	15	23	.255	.340	.366	.706	91	-34	320	4.46	-7	0-698	60	-6.9
• DEMAESTRI, Joe	Joseph Paul "Oats" DeMaestri b: 12/9/1928, San Francisco, CA BR/TR, 6', 174 lbs. Deb: 4/19/1951																							
1951 Chi-A	56	74	8	15	0	2	1	3	5	11	0	4	.203	.253	.297	.550	49	-7	5	1.91	-2	S-27,2-11/3-8	1	-0.8
1952 StL-A	81	186	13	42	9	1	1	18	8	25	0	1	.226	.258	.301	.559	54	-13	14	2.47	-7	S-77/2-1,3-1	2	-1.7
1953 Phi-A	111	420	53	107	17	3	6	35	24	39	0	1	.255	.297	.352	.649	72	-18	42	3.34	-9	*S-108	5	-1.8
1954 Phi-A	146	539	49	124	16	3	8	40	20	63	1	4	.230	.262	.315	.577	57	-35	42	2.60	-11	*S-142/2-1,3-1	5	-3.5
1955 KC-A	123	457	42	114	14	1	6	37	20	47	3	5	.249	.285	.324	.609	63	-27	39	2.89	-12	*S-122	4	-2.9
1956 KC-A	133	434	41	101	16	1	6	39	25	73	3	3	.233	.279	.316	.595	57	-29	37	2.89	2	*S-132/2-2	6	-1.7
1957 KC-A★	135	461	44	113	14	6	9	33	22	82	6	1	.245	.282	.360	.643	73	-17	44	3.23	-5	*S-134	9	-1.2
1958 KC-A	139	442	32	97	11	1	6	38	16	84	1	0	.219	.248	.290	.538	47	-32	29	2.15	-2	*S-137	6	-2.4
1959 KC-A	118	352	31	86	16	5	6	34	28	65	1	0	.244	.307	.369	.677	83	-8	38	3.64	-4	*S-115	8	-0.4
1960*NY-A	49	35	8	8	1	0	0	2	0	9	0	0	.229	.229	.257	.486	33	-3	2	2.06	-5	2-19,S-17	0	-0.8
1961 NY-A	30	41	1	6	0	0	0	2	0	13	0	0	.146	.146	.146	.293	-23	-7	1	.55	1	S-18/2-5,3-4	1	-0.4
Total 11	1121	3441	322	813	114	23	49	281	168	511	15	19	.236	.275	.325	.601	62	-197	293	2.84	-54	*S-1029/2-39,3-14	47	-17.6
• DEMAREE, Frank	Joseph Franklin Demaree b: 6/10/1910, Winters, CA d: 8/30/1958, Los Angeles, CA BR/TR, 5'11.5", 185 lbs. Deb: 7/22/1932 Career OF: 133-406-545																							
1932*Chi-N	23	56	4	14	3	0	0	6	2	7	0	....	.250	.288	.304	.592	60	-3	5	3.01	1	0-17(4-9-4)	1	-0.3
1933 Chi-N	134	515	68	140	24	6	6	51	22	42	4	....	.272	.304	.377	.681	94	-5	59	3.99	-2	*0-133(10-123-0)	14	-1.2
1935*Chi-N	107	385	60	125	19	4	2	66	26	23	6	....	.325	.369	.410	.779	109	5	58	5.62	3	0-98(0-69-29)	13	0.4
1936 Chi-N★	154	605	93	212	34	3	16	96	49	30	4	....	.350	.400	.496	.896	137	31	119	7.45	-1	*0-154(36-0-118)	24	2.1
1937 Chi-N★	154	615	104	199	36	6	17	115	57	31	6	....	.324	.382	.485	.866	129	24	112	6.65	0	*0-154(0-0-154)	26	1.5
1938*Chi-N	129	476	63	130	15	7	8	62	45	34	1	....	.273	.341	.384	.725	96	-2	62	4.53	-6	*0-125(9-0-119)	13	-1.5
1939 NY-N	150	560	68	170	27	2	11	79	66	40	2	....	.304	.381	.418	.799	113	13	89	5.66	-4	*0-150(1-116-36)	19	0.3

YEAR TM-L	G	AB	R	H	2B	3B	HR	RBI	BB	SO	SB	CS	AVG	OBP	SLG	OPS	OPS+	BR/A	RC	RC/G	FR	G/POS	WS	TPW
1940 NY-N	121	460	68	139	18	6	7	61	45	39	5	....	.302	.364	.413	.777	113	9	71	5.50	-3	*O-119(9-74-37)	14	0.2
1941 NY-N	16	35	3	6	0	0	0	1	4	1	0	....	.171	.256	.171	.428	22	-4	1	1.08	0	O-10(1-8-1)	0	-0.4
Bos-N	48	113	20	26	5	2	2	15	12	5	2	....	.230	.304	.363	.667	91	-2	12	3.51	0	O-28(9-7-12)	2	-0.2
Yr.	64	148	23	32	5	2	2	16	16	6	2	....	.216	.293	.318	.610	74	-5	13	2.87	1	O-38(10-15-13)	2	-0.6
1942 Bos-N	64	187	18	42	5	0	3	24	17	10	2	....	.225	.289	.299	.589	74	-6	15	2.64	3	O-49(27-0-22)	2	-0.7
1943*StL-N	39	86	5	25	2	0	0	9	8	4	1	....	.291	.351	.314	.665	89	-1	9	3.29	0	O-23(12-0-12)	1	-0.2
1944 StL-A	16	51	4	13	2	0	0	6	6	3	0	0	.255	.333	.294	.627	76	-1	6	3.96	0	O-16(15-0-1)	1	-0.3
Total 12	1155	4144	578	1241	190	36	72	591	359	269	33	0	.299	.357	.415	.772	109	58	616	5.31	-8	*O-1076	130	-0.2

• DEMARS, Billy William Lester "Kid" DeMars b: 8/26/1925, Brooklyn, NY BR/TR, 5'10", 160 lbs. Deb: 5/18/1948 C

YEAR TM-L	G	AB	R	H	2B	3B	HR	RBI	BB	SO	SB	CS	AVG	OBP	SLG	OPS	OPS+	BR/A	RC	RC/G	FR	G/POS	WS	TPW
1948 Phi-A	18	29	3	5	0	0	0	1	5	3	0	0	.172	.294	.172	.467	26	-3	2	2.14	0	/S-9,2-1,3-1	0	-0.2
1950 StL-A	61	178	25	44	5	1	0	13	22	13	0	1	.247	.330	.287	.617	57	-11	17	3.24	-10	S-54/3-5	2	-1.7
1951 StL-A	1	4	1	1	0	0	0	0	1	0	0	0	.250	.400	.250	.650	76	-0	1	4.63	0	/S-1	0	0.0
Total 3	80	211	29	50	5	1	0	14	28	16	0	1	.237	.326	.270	.597	53	-14	20	3.10	-9	/S-64,3-6,2-1	2	-1.9

• DEMERIT, John John Stephen "Thumper" DeMerit b: 1/8/1936, West Bend, WI BR/TR, 6'1.5", 195 lbs. Deb: 6/18/1957 Career OF: 10-20-20

YEAR TM-L	G	AB	R	H	2B	3B	HR	RBI	BB	SO	SB	CS	AVG	OBP	SLG	OPS	OPS+	BR/A	RC	RC/G	FR	G/POS	WS	TPW
1957*Mil-N	33	34	8	5	0	0	0	1	0	8	1	0	.147	.147	.147	.294	-22	-6	1	.76	0	O-13(2-11-0)	0	-0.6
1958 Mil-N	3	3	1	2	0	0	0	0	0	0	0	0	.667	.667	.667	1.333	278	1	1	36.00	-0	/O-2(0-1-1)	0	0.1
1959 Mil-N	11	5	4	1	0	0	0	0	1	2	0	0	.200	.333	.200	.533	50	-0	0	2.84	0	/O-4(3-1-0)	0	-0.1
1961 Mil-N	32	74	5	12	3	0	2	5	5	19	0	0	.162	.225	.284	.509	36	-7	5	1.90	1	O-21(2-5-15)	1	-0.7
1962 NY-N	14	16	3	3	0	0	1	1	2	4	0	0	.188	.278	.375	.653	72	-1	2	3.76	-1	/O-9(3-2-4)	0	-0.1
Total 5	93	132	21	23	3	0	3	7	8	33	1	0	.174	.227	.265	.492	32	-13	9	2.16	-0	/O-49	1	-1.5

• DEMETER, Don Donald Lee Demeter b: 6/25/1935, Oklahoma City, OK BR/TR, 6'4", 190 lbs. Deb: 9/18/1956 Career OF: 143-592-92

YEAR TM-L	G	AB	R	H	2B	3B	HR	RBI	BB	SO	SB	CS	AVG	OBP	SLG	OPS	OPS+	BR/A	RC	RC/G	FR	G/POS	WS	TPW
1956 Bro-N	3	3	1	1	0	0	1	1	0	1	0	0	.333	.333	1.333	1.667	297	1	1	18.00	0	/O-1	0	0.1
1958 LA-N	43	106	11	20	2	0	5	8	5	32	2	3	.189	.225	.349	.574	48	-9	8	2.35	-2	O-39(11-25-4)	1	-1.3
1959*LA-N	139	371	55	95	11	1	18	70	16	87	5	6	.256	.298	.437	.734	86	-10	45	4.11	0	*O-124(0-124-0)	9	-1.6
1960 LA-N	64	168	23	46	7	1	9	29	8	34	0	1	.274	.311	.488	.799	108	1	25	5.32	-2	O-62(0-61-1)	5	-0.3
1961 LA-N	15	29	3	5	0	0	1	2	3	6	0	0	.172	.250	.276	.526	36	-3	2	1.69	0	O-14(0-3-12)	0	-0.3
Phi-N	106	382	54	98	18	4	20	68	19	74	2	1	.257	.300	.482	.782	105	1	54	4.88	4	O-79(23-44-17),1-22	9	0.0
Yr.	121	411	57	103	18	4	21	70	22	80	2	1	.251	.297	.467	.764	100	-2	55	4.61	4	O-93(23-47-29),1-22	9	-0.3
1962 Phi-N	153	550	85	169	24	3	29	107	41	93	2	7	.307	.366	.520	.886	139	26	101	6.54	-6	*3-105,O-63(23-42-4)/1-1	25	1.7
1963 Phi-N	154	515	63	133	20	2	22	83	31	93	1	4	.258	.308	.433	.741	112	6	66	4.45	-1	*O-119(41-80-0),3-43,1-26	17	0.0
1964 Det-A	134	441	57	113	22	1	22	80	17	85	4	1	.256	.292	.460	.752	104	0	58	4.58	-3	O-88(24-52-13),1-23	12	-0.8
1965 Det-A	122	389	50	108	16	4	16	58	23	65	4	2	.278	.328	.463	.790	121	9	56	5.05	-6	O-82(1-56-25),1-34	13	-0.2
1966 Det-A	32	99	12	21	5	0	5	12	3	19	1	0	.212	.235	.414	.649	81	-3	8	2.54	3	O-27(4-20-3)/1-4	1	-0.1
Bos-A	73	226	31	66	13	1	9	29	5	42	1	0	.292	.310	.478	.788	111	3	33	5.23	-4	O-57(0-55-3)/1-2	7	-0.3
Yr.	105	325	43	87	18	1	14	41	8	61	2	0	.268	.287	.458	.746	102	-0	41	4.34	-1	O-84(4-75-6)/1-6	8	-0.5
1967 Bos-A	20	43	7	12	5	0	1	4	3	11	0	0	.279	.326	.465	.791	121	1	7	5.74	0	O-12(3-1-9)/3-1	2	0.1
Cle-A	51	121	15	25	4	0	5	12	6	16	0	0	.207	.256	.364	.619	80	-3	10	2.76	0	O-35(13-28-1)/3-1	2	-0.5
Yr.	71	164	22	37	9	0	6	16	9	27	0	0	.226	.274	.390	.665	91	-2	17	3.48	0	O-47(16-29-10)/3-2	4	-0.4
Total 11	1109	3443	467	912	147	17	163	563	180	658	22	25	.265	.309	.459	.769	108	19	474	4.76	-18	O-802,3-150,1-112	103	-3.7

• DEMETER, Steve Stephen Demeter b: 1/27/1935, Homer City, PA BR/TR, 5'9.5", 185 lbs. Deb: 7/29/1959 C

YEAR TM-L	G	AB	R	H	2B	3B	HR	RBI	BB	SO	SB	CS	AVG	OBP	SLG	OPS	OPS+	BR/A	RC	RC/G	FR	G/POS	WS	TPW
1959 Det-A	11	18	1	2	1	0	0	1	0	1	0	0	.111	.111	.167	.278	-24	-3	0	.26	0	/3-4	0	-0.3
1960 Cle-A	4	5	0	0	0	0	0	0	0	1	0	0	.000	.000	.000	.000	-103	-1	0	.00	0	/3-3	0	-0.2
Total 2	15	23	1	2	1	0	0	1	0	2	0	0	.087	.087	.130	.217	-41	-4	0	.20	0	/3-7	0	-0.5

• DEMMITT, Ray Charles Raymond Demmitt b: 2/2/1884, Illiopolis, IL d: 2/19/1956, Glen Ellyn, IL BL/TR, 5'8", 170 lbs. Deb: 4/12/1909 Career OF: 128-74-238

YEAR TM-L	G	AB	R	H	2B	3B	HR	RBI	BB	SO	SB	CS	AVG	OBP	SLG	OPS	OPS+	BR/A	RC	RC/G	FR	G/POS	WS	TPW
1909 NY-A	123	427	68	105	12	12	4	30	55	....	16	....	.246	.340	.358	.698	120	11	57	4.48	0	*O-109(0-70-39)	18	0.7
1910 StL-A	10	23	4	4	1	0	0	2	3	....	0	....	.174	.296	.217	.514	65	-1	2	2.13	1	/O-8(0-0-8)	0	0.0
1914 Det-A	1	0	0	0	0	0	0	0	0	0	0	....	....	....	....	....	-97	0	0	....	0		0	0.0
Chi-A	146	515	63	133	13	12	2	46	61	48	12	20	.258	.344	.342	.685	108	-1	60	3.81	3	*O-142(127-4-12)	16	-0.5
Yr.	147	515	63	133	13	12	2	46	61	48	12	20	.258	.344	.342	.685	108	-1	60	3.81	3	*O-142(127-4-12)	16	-0.5
1915 Chi-A	9	6	0	0	0	0	0	0	1	2	0	....	.000	.143	.000	.143	-55	-1	0	.00	0	/O-3(1-0-2)	0	-0.2
1917 StL-A	14	53	6	15	1	2	0	7	0	8	1	....	.283	.296	.377	.674	109	0	6	3.95	-1	O-14(0-0-14)	1	-0.1
1918 StL-A	116	405	45	114	23	5	1	61	38	35	10	....	.281	.346	.370	.716	120	9	55	4.52	11	*O-114(0-0-114)	14	1.6
1919 StL-A	79	202	19	48	11	2	1	19	14	27	3	....	.238	.290	.327	.617	71	-8	19	3.16	-6	O-49(0-0-49)	2	-1.7
Total 7	498	1631	205	419	61	33	8	165	172	120	42	20	.257	.334	.349	.684	108	10	199	4.03	7	O-439	51	-0.2

• DEMONTREVILLE, Gene Eugene Napoleon DeMontreville b: 3/26/1874, St. Paul, MN d: 2/18/1935, Memphis, TN BR/TR, 5'8", 165 lbs. Deb: 8/20/1894

YEAR TM-L	G	AB	R	H	2B	3B	HR	RBI	BB	SO	SB	CS	AVG	OBP	SLG	OPS	OPS+	BR/A	RC	RC/G	FR	G/POS	WS	TPW
1894 Pit-N	2	8	0	2	0	0	0	0	1	4	0	....	.250	.333	.250	.583	43	-1	1	2.96	0	/S-2	0	0.0
1895 Was-N	12	46	7	10	1	3	0	9	3	4	5	....	.217	.265	.370	.635	63	-3	6	4.49	1	S-12	1	-0.1
1896 Was-N	133	533	94	183	24	5	8	77	29	27	28	....	.343	.381	.452	.833	119	13	106	7.71	9	*S-133	21	2.5
1897 Was-N	133	566	92	193	27	8	3	93	21	....	30	....	.341	.366	.433	.799	111	6	104	7.15	-4	*S-99,2-33	18	0.8
1898 Bal-N	151	567	93	186	19	2	0	86	52	....	49	....	.328	.394	.369	.763	117	15	106	7.13	19	*2-123,S-28	24	3.8
1899 Chi-N	82	310	43	87	6	3	0	40	17	....	26	....	.281	.328	.319	.648	80	-8	44	4.88	2	S-82	9	-0.2
Bal-N	60	240	40	67	13	4	1	36	10	....	21	....	.279	.313	.379	.693	85	-6	36	5.43	12	2-60	6	0.8
Yr.	142	550	83	154	19	7	1	76	27	....	47	....	.280	.322	.345	.667	82	-15	80	5.12	14	S-82,2-60	15	0.6
1900 Bro-N	69	234	34	57	8	1	0	28	10	....	21	....	.244	.283	.286	.570	54	-15	26	3.79	-2	2-48,S-12/3-7,1-1,O-1	3	-1.3
1901 Bos-N	140	577	83	173	14	4	5	72	17	....	25	....	.300	.321	.364	.685	90	-9	80	4.95	15	*2-120,3-20	15	0.8
1902 Bos-N	124	481	51	125	16	5	0	53	12	....	23	....	.260	.278	.314	.592	82	-12	52	3.62	-16	*2-112,S-10	10	-2.9
1903 Was-A	12	44	0	12	2	0	0	3	0	....	0	....	.273	.273	.318	.591	75	-1	4	3.23	-2	2-11/S-1	0	-0.4
1904 StL-A	4	9	0	1	0	0	0	0	2	....	0	....	.111	.273	.111	.384	25	-1	0	.93	0	/2-3	0	-0.1
Total 11	922	3615	537	1096	130	35	17	497	174	35	228	....	.303	.340	.373	.712	96	-23	566	5.69	34	2-510,S-379/3-27,1-1,O-1	107	3.5

• DEMONTREVILLE, Lee Leon DeMontreville b: 9/23/1875, Washington County, MN d: 3/22/1962, Pelham Manor, NY BR/TR, 5'7", 140 lbs. Deb: 7/10/1903

YEAR TM-L	G	AB	R	H	2B	3B	HR	RBI	BB	SO	SB	CS	AVG	OBP	SLG	OPS	OPS+	BR/A	RC	RC/G	FR	G/POS	WS	TPW
1903 StL-N	26	70	8	17	3	1	0	7	8	....	3	....	.243	.338	.314	.652	89	-1	9	4.30	-3	S-15/2-4,O-1	2	-0.3

• DEMPSEY, Rick John Rikard Dempsey b: 9/13/1949, Fayetteville, TN BR/TR, 6', 190 lbs. Deb: 9/23/1969 C Career OF: 6-0-17

YEAR TM-L	G	AB	R	H	2B	3B	HR	RBI	BB	SO	SB	CS	AVG	OBP	SLG	OPS	OPS+	BR/A	RC	RC/G	FR	G/POS	WS	TPW
1969 Min-A	5	6	1	3	1	0	0	0	1	0	0	0	.500	.571	.667	1.238	240	1	2	21.91	-1	/C-3	1	0.1
1970 Min-A	5	7	1	0	0	0	0	0	1	1	0	0	.000	.125	.000	.125	-62	-2	0	.00	-1	/C-3	0	-0.2
1971 Min-A	6	13	2	4	1	0	0	0	1	1	0	0	.308	.357	.385	.742	107	0	2	4.06	0	/C-6	1	0.0
1972 Min-A	25	40	0	8	1	0	0	0	6	8	0	0	.200	.304	.225	.529	56	-2	3	2.18	0	C-23	0	-0.2
1973 NY-A	6	11	0	2	0	0	0	0	1	3	0	0	.182	.250	.182	.432	24	-1	0	1.05	-1	/C-5	0	-0.2
1974 NY-A	43	109	12	26	3	0	2	12	8	7	1	0	.239	.291	.321	.612	78	-3	9	2.82	1	C-31/O-2(1-0-1),D-1	2	0.0
1975 NY-A	71	145	18	38	8	0	1	11	21	15	0	0	.262	.355	.338	.693	100	1	18	4.16	1	C-19,D-18/O-8(1-0-7),3-1	3	0.1
1976 NY-A	21	42	1	5	0	0	0	2	5	4	0	0	.119	.213	.119	.332	-1	-5	1	1.01	1	/C-9,O-4(0-0-4)	1	-0.4
Bal-A	59	174	11	37	2	0	0	10	13	17	1	1	.213	.275	.224	.499	50	-11	11	2.17	0	C-58/O-3(1-0-2)	3	-0.8
Yr.	80	216	12	42	2	0	0	12	18	21	1	1	.194	.263	.204	.466	40	-16	13	1.92	1	C-67/O-7(1-0-6)	4	-1.3
1977 Bal-A	91	270	27	61	7	4	3	34	34	34	2	3	.226	.317	.315	.632	78	-8	27	3.17	0	C-91	8	-0.3
1978 Bal-A	136	441	41	114	25	0	6	32	48	54	7	3	.259	.331	.356	.687	99	1	53	4.06	1	*C-135	17	0.9
1979*Bal-A	124	368	48	88	23	0	6	41	38	37	0	1	.239	.310	.351	.661	81	-10	39	3.50	8	*C-124	14	0.4
1980 Bal-A	119	362	51	95	26	3	9	40	36	45	3	1	.262	.334	.425	.760	108	4	50	4.80	4	*C-112/O-6(3-0-3),1-2,D-1	15	1.3
1981 Bal-A	92	251	24	54	10	1	6	15	32	36	0	1	.215	.306	.335	.641	85	-5	26	3.47	1	C-90/D-1	9	0.1
1982 Bal-A	125	344	35	88	15	1	5	36	46	37	0	3	.256	.344	.349	.692	91	-4	42	3.99	1	*C-124/D-1	11	0.2
1983*Bal-A	128	347	33	80	16	2	4	32	40	54	1	1	.231	.315	.323	.638	78	-10	36	3.42	8	*C-128	13	0.4
1984 Bal-A	109	330	37	76	11	0	11	34	40	58	1	2	.230	.315	.364	.679	89	-5	37	3.64	1	*C-108	10	0.1
1985 Bal-A	132	362	54	92	19	0	12	52	50	87	0	1	.254	.346	.406	.752	108	5	55	5.27	-2	*C-131	14	0.8
1986 Bal-A	122	327	42	68	15	1	13	29	45	78	1	0	.208	.309	.379	.689	87	-5	41	4.07	3	*C-121	9	0.3

YEAR	TM-L	G	AB	R	H	2B	3B	HR	RBI	BB	SO	SB	CS	AVG	OBP	SLG	OPS	OPS+	BR/A	RC	RC/G	FR	G/POS	WS	TPW
1987	Cle-A	60	141	16	25	10	0	1	9	23	29	0	0	.177	.297	.270	.566	51	-10	12	2.68	-1	C-59	2	-0.7
1988*	LA-N	77	167	25	42	13	0	7	30	25	44	1	0	.251	.349	.455	.804	133	7	27	5.48	2	C-74	11	1.3
1989	LA-N	79	151	16	27	7	0	4	16	30	37	1	0	.179	.319	.305	.623	80	-3	16	3.27	4	C-62	6	0.4
1990	LA-N	62	128	13	25	5	0	2	15	23	29	1	0	.195	.318	.281	.599	68	-5	11	2.74	3	C-53	3	0.1
1991	Mil-A	61	147	15	34	5	0	4	21	23	20	0	2	.231	.335	.347	.682	91	-2	16	3.48	1	C-56/P-2,1-1	5	0.2
1992	Bal-A	8	9	2	1	0	0	0	0	2	1	0	0	.111	.273	.111	.384	11	-1	0	.83	-1	/C-8	0	-0.1
Total	**24**	**1766**	**4692**	**525**	**1093**	**223**	**12**	**96**	**471**	**592**	**736**	**20**	**19**	**.233**	**.321**	**.347**	**.668**	**88**	**-71**	**537**	**3.76**	**34**	***C-1633/0-23,D-22,1-3,P-2,3**	**158**	**3.5**
• DENNEHEY, Tod		Thomas Francis Dennehey b: 5/12/1899, Philadelphia, PA d: 8/8/1977, Philadelphia, PA BL/TL, 5'10", 180 lbs. Deb: 4/21/1923																							
1923	Phi-N	9	24	4	7	2	0	0	2	1	3	0	0	.292	.320	.375	.695	74	-1	3	4.43	0	/0-9(7-0-2)	0	-0.2
• DENNING, Otto		Otto George "Dutch" Denning b: 12/28/1912, Hays, KS d: 5/25/1992, Chicago, IL BR/TR, 6', 180 lbs. Deb: 4/15/1942																							
1942	Cle-A	92	214	15	45	14	0	1	19	18	14	0	0	.210	.275	.290	.564	62	-11	18	2.75	3	C-78/0-2(2-0-0)	4	-0.4
1943	Cle-A	37	129	8	31	6	0	0	13	5	1	3	1	.240	.269	.287	.555	67	-6	9	2.34	-4	1-34	1	-1.2
Total	**2**	**129**	**343**	**23**	**76**	**20**	**0**	**1**	**32**	**23**	**15**	**3**	**1**	**.222**	**.272**	**.289**	**.561**	**64**	**-16**	**27**	**2.59**	**-1**	**/C-78,1-34,0-2**	**5**	**-1.7**
• DENNY, Jerry		Jeremiah Dennis Denny b: 3/16/1859, New York, NY d: 8/16/1927, Houston, TX BR/TR, 5'11.5", 180 lbs. Deb: 5/2/1881 Career OF: 1-2-7																							
1881	Pro-N	85	320	38	77	16	2	1	24	5	44	....	....	.241	.252	.313	.565	78	-8	26	2.87	6	*3-85	8	0.0
1882	Pro-N	84	329	54	81	10	9	2	42	4	46	....	....	.246	.255	.350	.605	92	-3	30	3.34	15	*3-84	10	1.2
1883	Pro-N	98	393	73	108	26	8	8	55	9	48	....	....	.275	.291	.443	.734	116	6	52	5.01	10	*3-98	15	1.6
1884*	Pro-N	110	439	57	109	22	9	6	59	14	58	....	....	.248	.272	.380	.652	105	2	46	3.87	9	*3-99/1-9,2-3,C-1	16	1.1
1885	Pro-N	83	318	40	71	14	4	3	24	12	53	....	....	.223	.252	.321	.572	88	-4	26	2.87	1	*3-83	9	-0.1
1886	StL-N	119	475	58	122	24	6	9	62	14	68	16	....	.257	.278	.389	.668	108	4	57	4.38	23	*3-117/S-3	14	2.7
1887	Ind-N	122	523	86	178	34	12	11	97	13	22	29	....	.340	.344	.502	.846	137	23	101	7.72	11	*3-116/S-4,2-1,0-1	19	3.1
1888	Ind-N	126	524	92	137	27	7	12	63	9	79	32	....	.261	.277	.408	.685	114	6	70	4.87	18	*3-96,S-25/2-5,0-1,P-1	19	2.4
1889	Ind-N	133	578	96	163	24	0	18	112	27	63	22	....	.282	.314	.417	.731	101	-3	85	5.41	7	*3-123/2-7,S-5	15	0.6
1890	NY-N	114	437	50	93	18	7	3	42	28	62	11	....	.213	.270	.307	.576	68	-20	40	3.09	1	*3-106/S-7,2-1	6	-1.5
1891	NY-N	4	16	0	4	1	0	0	1	0	3	2	....	.250	.250	.313	.563	66	-1	2	4.04	-2	/3-4	0	-0.2
	Cle-N	36	138	17	31	5	0	0	21	12	23	3	....	.225	.291	.261	.552	59	-7	12	2.94	1	3-29/0-7(1-1-6)	1	-0.6
	Phi-N	19	73	5	21	1	1	0	11	4	6	1	....	.288	.325	.329	.653	88	-1	8	4.32	-1	1-12/3-7	2	-0.3
	Yr.	59	227	22	56	7	1	0	33	16	32	6	....	.247	.299	.286	.586	68	-9	22	3.44	-2	3-40,1-12/0-7(1-1-6)	3	-1.1
1893	Lou-N	44	175	22	43	5	4	1	22	9	15	4	....	.246	.283	.337	.620	70	-8	18	3.66	-3	S-42/3-2	3	-0.8
1894	Lou-N	60	221	26	61	11	7	0	32	13	12	10	....	.276	.325	.389	.714	77	-8	32	5.20	-2	3-60	3	-0.8
Total	**13**	**1237**	**4959**	**714**	**1299**	**238**	**76**	**74**	**667**	**173**	**602**	**130**	**....**	**.262**	**.287**	**.384**	**.671**	**98**	**-25**	**605**	**4.44**	**93**	***3-1109/S-86,1-21,2-17,0,C,P**	**140**	**8.5**
• DENSON, Drew		Andrew Denson b: 11/16/1965, Cincinnati, OH BB/TR, 6'5", 210 lbs. Deb: 9/13/1989																							
1989	Atl-N	12	36	1	9	1	0	0	5	3	9	1	0	.250	.308	.278	.585	67	-1	3	3.48	2	1-12	1	0.0
1993	Chi-A	4	5	0	1	0	0	0	0	0	2	0	0	.200	.200	.200	.400	8	-1	0	1.35	0	/1-3	0	-0.1
Total	**2**	**16**	**41**	**1**	**10**	**1**	**0**	**0**	**5**	**3**	**11**	**1**	**0**	**.244**	**.295**	**.268**	**.564**	**60**	**-2**	**4**	**3.20**	**1**	**/1-15**	**1**	**-0.2**
• DENT, Bucky		Russell Earl Dent b: 11/25/1951, Savannah, GA BR/TR, 5'9", 181 lbs. Deb: 6/1/1973 M/C																							
1973	Chi-A	40	117	17	29	2	0	0	10	10	18	2	3	.248	.313	.265	.577	62	-6	10	2.84	-2	S-36/2-3,3-1	2	-0.4
1974	Chi-A	154	496	55	136	15	3	5	45	28	48	3	4	.274	.317	.347	.664	89	-8	54	3.68	14	*S-154	16	2.4
1975	Chi-A★	157	602	52	159	29	4	3	58	36	48	2	4	.264	.306	.341	.646	81	-17	60	3.33	18	*S-157	16	2.0
1976	Chi-A	158	562	44	138	18	4	2	52	43	45	3	5	.246	.301	.302	.604	77	-18	52	3.04	-11	*S-158	9	-1.0
1977*	NY-A	158	477	54	118	18	4	8	49	39	28	1	1	.247	.306	.352	.658	80	-13	52	3.60	9	*S-158	14	1.1
1978*	NY-A	123	379	40	92	11	1	5	40	23	24	3	1	.243	.290	.317	.606	72	-14	34	2.98	5	*S-123	9	0.3
1979	NY-A	141	431	47	99	14	2	2	32	37	30	0	0	.230	.292	.285	.577	58	-25	39	2.92	15	*S-141	12	0.5
1980*	NY-A★	141	489	57	128	26	2	5	52	48	37	0	3	.262	.330	.354	.684	89	-8	59	4.15	13	*S-141	19	2.1
1981	NY-A★	73	227	20	54	11	0	7	27	19	17	0	1	.238	.302	.379	.681	97	-2	27	3.99	-2	S-73	8	0.5
1982	NY-A	59	160	11	27	1	1	0	9	8	11	0	0	.169	.208	.188	.396	10	-20	6	1.05	0	S-58	3	-1.4
	Tex-A	46	146	16	32	9	0	1	14	13	10	0	0	.219	.283	.301	.584	64	-7	13	2.92	0	S-45	2	-0.2
	Yr.	105	306	27	59	10	1	1	23	21	21	0	0	.193	.245	.242	.486	36	-27	19	1.90	0	*S-103	5	-1.6
1983	Tex-A	131	417	36	99	15	2	2	34	23	31	3	7	.237	.279	.297	.576	60	-26	34	2.75	-12	*S-129/D-1	6	-2.5
1984	KC-A	11	9	2	3	0	0	0	1	1	2	0	0	.333	.400	.333	.733	105	0	1	5.87	-3	/S-9,3-2	0	-0.3
Total	**12**	**1392**	**4512**	**451**	**1114**	**169**	**23**	**40**	**423**	**328**	**349**	**17**	**29**	**.247**	**.300**	**.321**	**.621**	**74**	**-164**	**442**	**3.24**	**44**	***S-1382/2-3,3-3,D-1**	**116**	**3.1**
• DENTE, Sam		Samuel Joseph "Blackie" Dente b: 4/26/1922, Harrison, NJ d: 4/21/2002, Montclair, NJ BR/TR, 5'11", 175 lbs. Deb: 7/10/1947																							
1947	Bos-A	46	168	14	39	4	2	0	11	19	15	0	1	.232	.310	.280	.590	60	-9	15	2.86	-3	3-46	2	-1.3
1948	StL-A	98	267	26	72	11	2	0	22	22	8	1	3	.270	.328	.326	.653	72	-12	29	3.75	2	S-76/3-6	6	-0.5
1949	Was-A	153	590	48	161	24	4	1	53	31	24	4	4	.273	.309	.332	.641	71	-27	58	3.47	-16	*S-153	8	-3.3
1950	Was-A	155	603	56	144	20	5	2	59	39	19	1	1	.239	.286	.299	.585	52	-44	49	2.65	-8	*S-128,2-29	7	-4.0
1951	Was-A	88	273	21	65	8	1	0	29	25	10	3	0	.238	.302	.275	.577	58	-15	22	2.71	4	S-65,2-10/3-5	4	-0.6
1952	Chi-A	62	145	12	32	0	1	0	11	5	8	0	0	.221	.257	.234	.491	37	-12	8	1.80	4	S-27,3-18/2-6,0-6(4-0-2),1	2	-0.7
1953	Chi-A	2	0	0	0	0	0	0	0	0	0	0	0	....	....	....	....	-97	0	0	....	-1	/S-1	0	-0.1
1954*	Cle-A	68	169	18	45	7	1	1	19	14	4	0	0	.266	.322	.337	.660	79	-5	18	3.56	5	S-60/2-7	5	0.5
1955	Cle-A	73	105	10	27	4	0	0	10	12	8	0	0	.257	.333	.295	.629	67	-4	11	3.53	5	S-53,3-13/2-4	3	0.3
Total	**9**	**745**	**2320**	**205**	**585**	**78**	**16**	**4**	**214**	**167**	**96**	**9**	**9**	**.252**	**.303**	**.305**	**.608**	**62**	**-129**	**211**	**3.05**	**-7**	**S-563/3-88,2-56,0-6,1-2**	**37**	**-9.7**
• DEPANGHER, Mike		Michael Anthony DePangher b: 9/11/1858, Marysville, CA d: 7/7/1915, San Francisco, CA BL, 5'8", 190 lbs. Deb: 8/8/1884																							
1884	Phi-N	4	10	0	2	0	0	0	0	1	3	....	....	.200	.273	.200	.473	54	-0	1	1.92	0	/C-4	0	0.0
• DEPASTINO, Joe		Joseph Bernard Depastino b: 9/4/1973, Philadelphia, PA BR/TR, 6'2", 210 lbs. Deb: 8/5/2003																							
2003	NY-N	2	2	0	0	0	0	0	0	0	1	0	0	.000	.000	.000	.000	-104	-1	0	.00	0	/C-1	0	-0.1
• DEPHILLIPS, Tony		Anthony Andrew DePhillips b: 9/20/1912, New York, NY d: 5/5/1994, Port Jefferson, NY BR/TR, 6'2", 185 lbs. Deb: 4/25/1943																							
1943	Cin-N	35	20	0	2	1	0	0	2	1	5	0	....	.100	.143	.150	.293	-16	-3	1	.73	-1	C-35	1	-0.3
• DERBY, Gene		Eugene A. Derby b: 2/3/1860, Fitchburg, MA d: 9/13/1917, Waterbury, CT, 5'7", 160 lbs. Deb: 9/3/1885																							
1885	Bal-a	10	31	4	4	0	0	0	2	1	....	....	....	.129	.182	.129	.311	-1	-3	1	.75	-1	/C-9,0-1	0	-0.3
• DERNIER, Bob		Robert Eugene Dernier b: 1/5/1957, Kansas City, MO BR/TR, 6', 165 lbs. Deb: 9/7/1980 Career OF: 41-660-114																							
1980	Phi-N	10	7	5	4	0	0	0	1	1	0	3	0	.571	.625	.571	1.196	224	2	4	32.74	0	/0-3(0-3-0)	1	0.2
1981	Phi-N	10	4	0	3	0	0	0	0	0	0	2	1	.750	.750	.750	1.500	313	1	2	27.27	-1	/0-5(0-5-0)	1	0.1
1982	Phi-N	122	370	56	92	10	2	4	21	36	69	42	12	.249	.317	.319	.636	77	-7	41	3.67	1	*0-119(0-70-62)	9	-1.0
1983*	Phi-N	122	221	41	51	10	0	1	15	18	21	35	7	.231	.289	.290	.578	61	-7	22	3.22	-0	*0-107(12-68-31)	5	-1.0
1984*	Chi-N	143	536	94	149	26	5	3	32	63	60	45	17	.278	.356	.362	.718	94	-1	75	4.84	1	*0-140(1-139-0)	18	-0.2
1985	Chi-N	121	469	63	119	20	3	1	21	40	44	31	8	.254	.316	.316	.632	70	-16	51	3.66	2	*0-116(0-116-0)	9	-1.6
1986	Chi-N	108	324	32	73	14	1	4	18	22	41	27	2	.225	.275	.312	.586	57	-15	30	3.07	-1	*0-105(0-105-0)	3	-1.8
1987	Chi-N	93	199	38	63	4	4	8	21	19	19	16	7	.317	.379	.497	.876	125	7	37	6.75	-1	0-71(0-72-0)	7	0.6
1988	Phi-N	68	166	19	48	3	1	1	10	9	19	13	6	.289	.330	.337	.667	90	-2	19	3.91	0	0-54(0-53-1)	4	-0.3
1989	Phi-N	107	187	26	32	5	0	1	13	14	28	4	3	.171	.229	.214	.443	27	-18	10	1.62	-2	0-74(28-29-20)	1	-2.3
Total	**10**	**904**	**2483**	**374**	**634**	**92**	**16**	**23**	**152**	**222**	**301**	**218**	**63**	**.255**	**.318**	**.333**	**.652**	**77**	**-56**	**290**	**3.94**	**0**	**0-794**	**58**	**-7.3**
• DEROSA, Mark		Mark Thomas DeRosa b: 2/26/1975, Passaic, NJ BR/TR, 6'1", 195 lbs. Deb: 9/2/1998 Career OF: 5-0-5																							
1998	Atl-N	5	3	2	1	0	0	0	0	0	1	0	0	.333	.333	.333	.667	76	-0	0	4.50	-1	/S-4	0	-0.1
1999	Atl-N	7	8	0	0	0	0	0	0	0	2	0	0	.000	.000	.000	.000	-100	-2	0	.00	0	/S-2	0	-0.2
2000	Atl-N	22	13	9	4	1	0	0	3	2	1	0	0	.308	.400	.385	.785	99	0	2	6.62	-2	S-10	1	-0.2
2001*	Atl-N	66	164	27	47	8	0	3	20	12	19	2	1	.287	.354	.390	.744	90	-2	23	4.93	1	S-48/2-5,D-3,3-1,0-1	6	0.3
2002*	Atl-N	72	212	24	63	9	2	5	23	12	24	2	3	.297	.344	.429	.773	101	-1	29	4.92	6	2-32,S-19/0-7(2-0-5),3-4	7	0.8

YEAR TM-L	G	AB	R	H	2B	3B	HR	RBI	BB	SO	SB	CS	AVG	OBP	SLG	OPS	OPS+	BR/A	RC	RC/G	FR	G/POS	WS	TPW
2003*Atl-N	103	266	40	70	14	0	6	22	16	49	1	0	.263	.317	.383	.701	82	-7	32	4.26	1	2-29,3-25,S-20/D-2,O-2(2-0-0),1	5	-0.4
Total 6	**275**	**666**	**102**	**185**	**32**	**2**	**14**	**68**	**42**	**96**	**5**	**4**	**.278**	**.333**	**.395**	**.728**	**88**	**-13**	**87**	**4.61**	**5**	**S-103/2-66,3-30,O-10,D-5,1**	**19**	**0.1**
• DERRICK, Claud	Claud Lester "Deek" Derrick b: 6/11/1886, Burton, GA d: 7/15/1974, Clayton, GA BR/TR, 6', 175 lbs. Deb: 9/8/1910																							
1910 Phi-A	2	1	0	0	0	0	0	0	0	....	0	....	.000	.000	.000	.000	-101	-0	0	.00	-1	/S-1	0	-0.1
1911 Phi-A	36	100	14	23	1	2	0	5	7	....	7	....	.230	.294	.280	.574	61	-5	11	3.29	3	2-21/S-6,1-3,3-2	2	-0.1
1912 Phi-A	21	58	7	14	0	1	0	7	5	....	1	....	.241	.313	.276	.588	71	-2	6	3.06	-2	S-18	1	-0.3
1913 NY-A	23	65	7	19	1	0	1	7	5	8	2	....	.292	.352	.354	.706	106	1	8	4.57	-4	S-17/3-4,2-1	2	-0.2
1914 Cin-N	3	6	2	2	1	0	0	1	0	0	1	....	.333	.333	.500	.833	142	0	1	7.84	0	/S-2	0	0.0
Chi-N	28	96	5	21	3	1	0	13	5	13	2	....	.219	.257	.271	.528	57	-5	7	2.33	2	S-28	1	-0.2
Yr.	31	102	7	23	4	1	0	14	5	13	3	....	.225	.262	.284	.546	62	-5	8	2.60	2	S-30	1	-0.1
Total 5	**113**	**326**	**35**	**79**	**6**	**4**	**1**	**33**	**22**	**21**	**13**	**....**	**.242**	**.298**	**.294**	**.593**	**72**	**-12**	**33**	**3.25**	**-2**	**/S-72,2-22,3-6,1-3**	**6**	**-0.9**
• DERRICK, Mike	James Michael Derrick b: 9/19/1943, Columbia, SC BL/TR, 6', 190 lbs. Deb: 4/9/1970																							
1970 Bos-A	24	33	3	7	1	0	0	5	0	11	0	1	.212	.212	.242	.455	23	-4	1	1.17	-0	/O-2(2-0-0),1-1	0	-0.4
• DERRY, Russ	Alva Russell Derry b: 10/7/1916, Princeton, MO BL/TR, 6'1", 180 lbs. Deb: 7/4/1944 Career OF: 71-46-32																							
1944 NY-A	38	114	14	29	3	0	4	14	20	19	1	0	.254	.366	.386	.752	111	3	19	5.85	-2	O-28(16-0-12)	4	-0.1
1945 NY-A	78	253	37	57	6	2	13	45	31	49	1	0	.225	.312	.419	.731	107	2	34	4.48	0	O-68(10-44-15)	7	-0.1
1946 Phi-A	69	184	17	38	8	5	0	14	27	54	0	0	.207	.311	.304	.616	73	-6	20	3.54	1	O-50(45-2-5)	3	-0.9
1949 StL-N	2	2	0	0	0	0	0	0	0	2	0	....	.000	.000	.000	.000	-96	-1	0	.00	0	....	0	-0.1
Total 4	**187**	**553**	**68**	**124**	**17**	**7**	**17**	**73**	**78**	**124**	**2**	**0**	**.224**	**.322**	**.373**	**.695**	**96**	**-2**	**72**	**4.41**	**-1**	**O-146**	**14**	**-1.2**
• DESA, Joe	Joseph DeSa b: 7/27/1959, Honolulu, HI d: 12/20/1986, San Juan, Puerto Rico BL/TL, 5'11", 170 lbs. Deb: 9/6/1980 Career OF: 1-0-1																							
1980 StL-N	7	11	0	3	0	0	0	0	0	2	0	0	.273	.273	.273	.545	51	-1	1	1.64	0	/1-1,O-1	0	-0.1
1985 Chi-A	28	44	5	8	2	0	2	7	3	6	0	0	.182	.234	.364	.598	58	-3	4	2.85	0	/1-9,D-4,O-1	0	-0.3
Total 2	**35**	**55**	**5**	**11**	**2**	**0**	**2**	**7**	**3**	**8**	**0**	**0**	**.200**	**.241**	**.345**	**.587**	**57**	**-3**	**4**	**2.61**	**-0**	**/1-10,D-4,O-2**	**0**	**-0.4**
• DESAUTELS, Gene	Eugene Abraham "Red" Desautels b: 6/13/1907, Worcester, MA d: 11/5/1994, Flint, MI BR/TR, 5'11", 170 lbs. Deb: 6/22/1930																							
1930 Det-A	42	126	13	24	4	2	0	9	7	9	2	0	.190	.239	.254	.493	25	-14	8	2.07	0	C-42	2	-1.0
1931 Det-A	3	11	1	1	0	0	0	1	0	1	0	0	.091	.091	.091	.182	-50	-2	0	.23	0	/C-3	0	-0.2
1932 Det-A	28	72	8	17	2	0	0	2	13	11	0	0	.236	.360	.264	.624	62	-3	8	3.75	-1	C-24	2	-0.2
1933 Det-A	30	42	5	6	1	0	0	4	4	6	0	0	.143	.234	.167	.401	8	-6	2	1.37	-2	C-30	1	-0.6
1937 Bos-A	96	305	33	74	10	3	0	27	36	26	1	2	.243	.325	.295	.620	55	-21	31	3.44	0	C-94	8	-1.4
1938 Bos-A	108	333	47	97	16	2	2	48	57	31	1	1	.291	.396	.369	.766	89	-3	53	5.67	-4	*C-108	12	-0.1
1939 Bos-A	76	226	26	55	14	0	0	21	33	13	3	1	.243	.340	.305	.645	64	-11	27	3.91	4	C-73	8	-0.2
1940 Bos-A	71	222	19	50	7	1	0	17	32	13	0	1	.225	.328	.266	.594	54	-14	21	3.06	-5	C-70	4	-1.4
1941 Cle-A	66	189	20	38	5	1	1	17	14	12	1	0	.201	.260	.254	.514	38	-17	14	2.34	2	C-66	4	-1.0
1942 Cle-A	62	162	14	40	5	0	0	9	12	13	1	0	.247	.303	.278	.581	68	-6	15	3.03	-2	C-61	3	-0.6
1943 Cle-A	68	185	14	38	6	1	0	19	11	16	2	0	.205	.250	.249	.499	49	-12	12	2.15	0	C-66	2	-0.8
1945 Cle-A	10	9	1	1	0	0	0	0	1	1	0	0	.111	.200	.111	.311	-9	-1	0	.87	-1	C-10	0	-0.2
1946 Phi-A	52	130	10	28	3	1	0	13	12	16	1	1	.215	.282	.254	.536	51	-9	10	2.40	4	C-52	2	-0.2
Total 13	**712**	**2012**	**211**	**469**	**73**	**11**	**3**	**187**	**232**	**168**	**12**	**6**	**.233**	**.315**	**.285**	**.600**	**57**	**-119**	**201**	**3.30**	**-3**	**C-699**	**48**	**-8.0**
• DESHIELDS, Delino	Delino Lamont DeShields b: 1/15/1969, Seaford, DE BL/TR, 6'1", 170 lbs. Deb: 4/9/1990 Career OF: 118-3-1																							
1990 Mon-N	129	499	69	144	28	6	4	45	66	96	42	22	.289	.376	.393	.769	116	12	75	5.22	3	*2-128	19	1.9
1991 Mon-N	151	563	83	134	15	4	10	51	95	151	56	23	.238	.350	.332	.682	94	2	74	4.26	-23	*2-148	15	-1.8
1992 Mon-N	135	530	82	155	19	8	7	56	54	108	46	15	.292	.361	.398	.759	116	15	80	5.22	-18	*2-134	19	0.1
1993 Mon-N	123	481	75	142	17	7	2	29	72	64	43	10	.295	.390	.372	.762	101	9	80	5.97	3	*2-123	21	1.8
1994 LA-N	89	320	51	80	11	3	2	33	54	53	27	7	.250	.358	.322	.680	85	-2	41	4.34	4	2-88,S-10	10	0.6
1995*LA-N	127	425	66	109	18	3	8	37	63	83	39	14	.256	.354	.369	.723	100	4	61	4.80	7	*2-113	16	1.6
1996*LA-N	154	581	75	130	12	8	5	41	53	124	48	11	.224	.290	.298	.588	60	-28	54	3.01	-9	*2-154	11	-2.8
1997 StL-N	150	572	92	169	26	**14**	11	58	55	72	55	14	.295	.360	.448	.808	111	15	99	6.15	-5	*2-147	21	1.6
1998 StL-N	117	420	74	122	21	8	7	44	56	61	26	10	.290	.374	.429	.803	111	10	71	5.94	-1	*2-111/1-1	15	1.4
1999 Bal-A	96	330	46	87	11	2	6	34	37	52	11	8	.264	.340	.364	.703	83	-9	42	4.28	-3	2-93	7	-0.8
2000 Bal-A	151	561	84	166	43	5	10	86	69	82	37	10	.296	.374	.444	.818	111	15	95	5.95	-9	2-96,O-41(39-2-0),D-10	21	0.7
2001 Bal-A	58	188	29	37	8	2	3	21	31	42	11	1	.197	.314	.309	.622	69	-6	21	3.68	-4	O-47(46-1-0)/D-8	3	-1.2
Chi-N	68	163	26	45	9	3	2	16	28	35	12	1	.276	.382	.405	.787	109	6	28	5.91	-3	O-33(33-0-0),2-16/3-5,1-1	5	0.2
2002 Chi-N	67	146	20	28	6	1	3	10	21	38	10	1	.192	.293	.308	.602	60	-7	16	3.47	4	2-41/O-1	3	-0.1
Total 13	**1615**	**5779**	**872**	**1548**	**244**	**74**	**80**	**561**	**754**	**1061**	**463**	**147**	**.268**	**.354**	**.377**	**.732**	**98**	**36**	**837**	**4.94**	**-55**	***2-1392,O-122/D-18,S-10,3-5,1**	**186**	**3.1**
• DESTRADE, Orestes	Orestes (Cucuas) Destrade b: 5/8/1962, Santiago de Cuba, Cuba BB/TR, 6'4", 210 lbs. Deb: 9/11/1987																							
1987 NY-A	9	19	5	5	0	0	0	1	5	5	0	0	.263	.417	.263	.680	87	0	2	4.25	0	/1-3,D-2	1	0.0
1988 Pit-N	36	47	2	7	1	0	1	3	5	17	0	0	.149	.231	.234	.465	34	-4	3	1.91	-1	/1-8	0	-0.6
1993 Fla-N	153	569	61	145	20	3	20	87	58	130	0	2	.255	.327	.406	.733	90	-9	73	4.38	0	*1-152	12	-2.2
1994 Fla-N	39	130	12	27	4	0	5	15	19	32	1	0	.208	.318	.354	.672	73	-5	16	4.03	-3	1-37	1	-1.0
Total 4	**237**	**765**	**80**	**184**	**25**	**3**	**26**	**106**	**87**	**184**	**1**	**2**	**.241**	**.322**	**.383**	**.705**	**83**	**-18**	**94**	**4.15**	**-3**	**1-200/D-2**	**14**	**-3.9**
• DETHERAGE, Bob	Robert Wayne Detherage b: 9/20/1954, Springfield, MO BR/TR, 6', 180 lbs. Deb: 4/11/1980																							
1980 KC-A	20	26	2	8	2	0	1	7	1	4	1	1	.308	.333	.500	.833	124	0	4	5.80	-1	O-20(12-0-11)	1	-0.1
• DETORE, George	George Francis Detore b: 11/11/1906, Utica, NY d: 2/7/1991, Utica, NY BR/TR, 5'8", 170 lbs. Deb: 9/14/1930 C																							
1930 Cle-A	3	12	0	2	1	0	0	2	0	2	0	0	.167	.167	.250	.417	4	-2	1	1.25	0	/3-3	0	-0.2
1931 Cle-A	30	56	3	15	6	0	0	7	8	2	0	2	.268	.359	.375	.734	88	-1	7	4.48	-2	3-13,S-10/2-3	1	-0.3
Total 2	**33**	**68**	**3**	**17**	**7**	**0**	**0**	**9**	**8**	**4**	**0**	**2**	**.250**	**.329**	**.353**	**.682**	**74**	**-3**	**8**	**3.82**	**-3**	**/3-16,S-10,2-3**	**1**	**-0.4**
• DETWEILER, Ducky	Robert Sterling Detweiler b: 2/15/1919, Trumbauersville, PA BR/TR, 5'11", 178 lbs. Deb: 9/12/1942																							
1942 Bos-N	12	44	3	14	2	1	0	5	2	7	0	....	.318	.348	.409	.757	123	1	6	5.26	-1	3-12	2	0.0
1946 Bos-N	1	1	0	0	0	0	0	0	0	0	0	....	.000	.000	.000	.000	-99	-0	0	.00	0	....	0	0.0
Total 2	**13**	**45**	**3**	**14**	**2**	**1**	**0**	**5**	**2**	**7**	**0**	**....**	**.311**	**.340**	**.400**	**.740**	**119**	**1**	**6**	**5.10**	**-1**	**/3-12**	**2**	**0.0**
• DEVAREZ, Cesar	Cesar Salvatore (Santana) Devarez b: 9/22/1969, San Francisco de Macoris, Dominican Republic BR/TR, 5'10", 175 lbs. Deb: 6/2/1995																							
1995 Bal-A	6	4	0	0	0	0	0	0	0	0	0	0	.000	.000	.000	.000	-98	-1	0	.00	0	/C-6	0	-0.1
1996 Bal-A	10	18	3	2	0	1	0	0	1	3	0	0	.111	.158	.222	.380	-5	-3	1	1.14	0	C-10	0	-0.3
Total 2	**16**	**22**	**3**	**2**	**0**	**1**	**0**	**0**	**1**	**3**	**0**	**0**	**.091**	**.130**	**.182**	**.312**	**-25**	**-4**	**1**	**.86**	**-1**	**/C-16**	**0**	**-0.4**
• DEVEREAUX, Mike	Michael Devereaux b: 4/10/1963, Casper, WY BR/TR, 6', 195 lbs. Deb: 9/2/1987 Career OF: 71-774-226																							
1987 LA-N	19	54	7	12	3	0	0	4	3	10	3	1	.222	.263	.278	.541	45	-4	4	2.65	0	O-18(11-2-5)	0	-0.5
1988 LA-N	30	43	4	5	1	0	0	2	2	10	0	1	.116	.156	.140	.295	-15	-7	1	.60	0	O-26(0-17-8)	0	-0.8
1989 Bal-A	122	391	55	104	14	3	8	46	36	60	22	11	.266	.331	.379	.710	103	1	49	4.28	-6	*O-112(4-80-35)/D-5	12	-0.7
1990 Bal-A	108	367	48	88	18	1	12	49	28	48	13	12	.240	.294	.392	.686	93	-7	38	3.31	0	*O-104(0-104-0)/D-3	8	-0.9
1991 Bal-A	149	608	82	158	27	10	19	59	47	115	16	9	.260	.315	.431	.746	109	5	80	4.46	2	*O-149(1-148-0)	15	0.4
1992 Bal-A	156	653	76	180	29	11	24	107	44	94	10	8	.276	.325	.464	.789	116	10	94	5.05	-8	*O-155(0-155-0)	22	0.0
1993 Bal-A	131	527	72	132	31	3	14	75	43	99	3	3	.250	.308	.400	.709	85	-13	63	4.08	0	*O-130(0-130-0)	13	-1.2
1994 Bal-A	85	301	35	61	8	2	9	33	22	72	1	2	.203	.259	.332	.591	49	-25	25	2.68	-2	O-84(0-84-0)/D-1	3	-2.4
1995 Chi-A	92	333	48	102	21	1	10	55	25	51	6	6	.306	.355	.465	.820	117	6	51	5.49	0	O-90(0-9-87)	8	0.1
*Atl-N	29	55	7	14	3	0	1	8	2	11	2	0	.255	.281	.364	.644	66	-2	6	3.65	-1	O-27(14-9-4)	2	-0.4
1996*Bal-A	127	323	49	74	11	2	8	34	34	53	8	2	.229	.306	.350	.656	66	-16	35	3.64	2	*O-112(35-30-62),D-10	3	-1.6
1997 Tex-A	29	72	8	15	3	0	0	7	7	10	1	0	.208	.278	.250	.528	37	-6	6	2.67	-2	O-28(5-3-24)	1	-0.9

YEAR TM-L	G	AB	R	H	2B	3B	HR	RBI	BB	SO	SB	CS	AVG	OBP	SLG	OPS	OPS+	BR/A	RC	RC/G	FR	G/POS	WS	TPW
1998 LA-N	9	13	0	4	1	0	0	1	3	2	0	1	.308	.438	.385	.822	126	0	1	3.25	0	/0-5(1-3-1)	0	0.1
Total 12	**1086**	**3740**	**491**	**949**	**170**	**33**	**105**	**480**	**296**	**635**	**85**	**56**	**.254**	**.311**	**.401**	**.712**	**92**	**-60**	**454**	**4.10**	**-16**	***0-1040/D-19**	**87**	**-8.9**
• DEVINE, Mickey	William Patrick Devine b: 5/9/1892, Albany, NY d: 10/1/1937, Albany, NY BR/TR, 5'10", 165 lbs. Deb: 8/2/1918																							
1918 Phi-N	4	8	0	1	1	0	0	0	0	1	0	....	.125	.125	.250	.375	13	-1	0	.78	0	/C-3	0	-0.1
1920 Bos-A	8	12	1	2	0	0	0	0	1	2	1	0	.167	.231	.167	.397	7	-1	1	1.63	-1	/C-5	0	-0.2
1925 NY-N	21	33	6	9	3	0	0	4	2	3	0	0	.273	.314	.364	.678	76	-1	4	4.17	-1	C-11/3-1	1	-0.2
Total 3	**33**	**53**	**7**	**12**	**4**	**0**	**0**	**4**	**3**	**6**	**1**	**0**	**.226**	**.268**	**.302**	**.570**	**50**	**-3**	**5**	**2.94**	**-2**	**/C-19,3-1**	**1**	**-0.4**
• DEVIVEIROS, Bernie	Bernard John DeViveiros b: 4/19/1901, Oakland, CA d: 7/5/1994, Oakland, CA BR/TR, 5'7", 160 lbs. Deb: 9/13/1924																							
1924 Chi-A	1	1	0	0	0	0	0	0	0	0	0	0	.000	.000	.000	.000	-103	-0	0	.00	-1	/S-1	0	-0.1
1927 Det-A	24	22	4	5	1	0	0	2	2	8	1	0	.227	.292	.273	.564	46	-1	2	2.90	-1	S-14/3-1	0	-0.2
Total 2	**25**	**23**	**4**	**5**	**1**	**0**	**0**	**2**	**2**	**8**	**1**	**0**	**.217**	**.280**	**.261**	**.541**	**41**	**-2**	**2**	**2.76**	**-2**	**/S-15,3-1**	**0**	**-0.3**
• DEVLIN, Art	Arthur McArthur Devlin b: 10/16/1879, Washington, DC d: 9/18/1948, Jersey City, NJ BR/TR, 6', 175 lbs. Deb: 4/14/1904 C																							
1904 NY-N	130	474	81	133	16	8	1	66	62	....	33	....	.281	.371	.354	.725	119	14	79	5.69	2	*3-130	25	2.0
1905*NY-N	153	525	74	129	14	7	2	61	66	....	**59**	....	.246	.344	.310	.655	94	-1	80	5.09	1	*3-153	23	0.5
1906 NY-N	148	498	76	149	23	8	2	65	74	....	54	....	.299	.396	.390	.786	142	28	102	7.35	15	*3-148	36	5.3
1907 NY-N	143	491	61	136	16	2	1	54	63	....	38	....	.277	.376	.324	.700	116	13	81	5.38	0	*3-140/S-3	22	2.0
1908 NY-N	157	534	59	135	18	4	2	45	62	....	19	....	.253	.346	.313	.659	105	7	65	4.06	9	*3-157	24	2.3
1909 NY-N	143	491	61	130	19	8	0	56	65	....	26	....	.265	.362	.336	.698	115	12	70	4.80	14	*3-143	23	3.3
1910 NY-N	147	493	71	128	17	5	2	67	62	32	28	....	.260	.353	.327	.679	98	1	69	4.54	6	*3-147	19	1.2
1911 NY-N	95	260	42	71	16	2	0	25	42	19	9	....	.273	.386	.350	.736	104	4	40	5.14	0	3-79/1-6,2-6,S-6	11	0.6
1912 Bos-N	124	436	59	126	18	8	0	54	51	37	11	....	.289	.367	.367	.734	99	1	62	5.00	0	1-69,3-26,S-26/0-1	9	0.2
1913 Bos-N	73	210	19	48	7	5	0	12	29	17	8	....	.229	.328	.310	.637	81	-4	23	3.53	0	3-69	6	-0.2
Total 10	**1313**	**4412**	**603**	**1185**	**164**	**57**	**10**	**505**	**576**	**105**	**285**	**....**	**.269**	**.364**	**.338**	**.702**	**109**	**74**	**671**	**5.12**	**47**	***3-1192/1-75,S-35,2-6,0-1**	**198**	**17.1**
• DEVLIN, Jim	James Raymond Devlin b: 8/25/1922, Plains, PA BL/TR, 5'11.5", 165 lbs. Deb: 4/27/1944																							
1944 Cle-A	1	1	0	0	0	0	0	0	0	0	0	0	.000	.000	.000	.000	-104	-0	0	.00	0	/C-1	0	0.0
• DEVLIN, Jim	James Alexander Devlin b: 1849, Philadelphia, PA d: 10/10/1883, Philadelphia, PA BR/TR, 5'11", 175 lbs. Deb: 4/21/1873 NA OF: 0-3-19 ♦																							
1873 Phi-n	23	99	18	24	4	4	0	10	2	4	0	0	.242	.257	.364	.621	79	-3	9	3.86	-2	1-12/3-6,S-5,0-1	....	-0.4
1874 Chi-n	45	203	26	58	5	0	0	27	2	9	2	1	.286	.293	.310	.603	92	-2	20	4.01	-4	1-24,0-17(0-0-17)/3-5	....	-0.3
1875 Chi-n	69	318	60	92	17	6	0	40	4	4	6	1	.289	.298	.381	.679	133	13	39	5.04	2	1-42,P-28/0-4(0-3-1)	....	0.3
1876 Lou-N	68	299	38	94	14	1	0	28	1	11	....	....	.314	.318	.369	.687	109	4	36	4.92	4	*P-68/1-1	53	**5.3**
1877 Lou-N	61	268	38	72	6	3	1	27	7	27	....	....	.269	.287	.325	.612	78	1	26	3.59	3	*P-61	**60**	**3.8**
Total 3 n	**137**	**620**	**104**	**174**	**26**	**10**	**0**	**77**	**8**	**17**	**8**	**2**	**.281**	**.290**	**.355**	**.645**	**111**	**9**	**68**	**4.51**	**-4**	**/1-78,P-28,0-22,3-11,S-5**	**....**	**-0.4**
Total 2	**129**	**567**	**76**	**166**	**20**	**4**	**1**	**55**	**8**	**38**	**....**	**....**	**.293**	**.303**	**.348**	**.651**	**94**	**5**	**61**	**4.27**	**6**	**P-129/1-1**	**113**	**9.1**
• DEVOGT, Rex	Rex Eugene DeVogt b: 1/4/1888, Clare, MI d: 11/9/1935, Alma, MI BR/TR, 5'9", 170 lbs. Deb: 4/17/1913																							
1913 Bos-N	3	6	0	0	0	0	0	0	0	3	0	....	.000	.000	.000	.000	-98	-2	0	.00	0	/C-3	0	-0.2
• DEVORE, Josh	Joshua D. Devore b: 11/13/1887, Murray City, OH d: 10/6/1954, Chillicothe, OH BL/TL, 5'6", 160 lbs. Deb: 9/25/1908 Career OF: 328-103-95																							
1908 NY-N	5	6	1	1	0	0	0	2	1	....	1	....	.167	.286	.167	.452	43	-0	1	2.86	0	/0-2(0-0-2)	0	0.0
1909 NY-N	22	28	6	4	1	0	0	1	2	....	3	....	.143	.250	.179	.429	33	-2	2	2.07	-1	0-12(3-10-1)	0	-0.4
1910 NY-N	133	490	92	149	11	10	2	27	46	67	43	....	.304	.371	.380	.750	119	12	84	6.24	-5	*0-130(106-2-22)	17	0.0
1911*NY-N	149	565	96	158	19	10	3	50	81	69	61	....	.280	.376	.365	.740	105	7	99	6.20	4	*0-149(104-0-48)	18	0.4
1912*NY-N	106	327	66	90	14	6	2	37	51	43	27	....	.275	.381	.373	.754	103	4	56	5.90	-4	0-96(76-1-19)	12	-0.5
1913 NY-N	16	21	4	4	0	1	0	1	3	4	6	....	.190	.320	.286	.606	73	-1	3	5.05	0	/0-8(1-5-2)	0	-0.1
Cin-N	66	217	30	58	6	4	3	14	12	21	17	....	.267	.309	.373	.682	95	-2	29	4.36	-1	0-57(0-57-1)	4	-0.6
Phi-N	23	39	9	11	1	0	0	5	4	7	0	....	.282	.364	.308	.671	89	-0	4	3.78	0	0-14(8-6-0)	1	-0.1
Yr.	105	277	43	73	7	5	3	20	19	32	23	....	.264	.318	.357	.675	92	-3	36	4.34	0	0-79(9-68-3)	5	-0.7
1914 Phi-N	30	53	5	16	2	0	0	7	4	5	0	....	.302	.351	.340	.691	99	-0	6	4.22	3	/0-9(7-2-0)	1	0.3
*Bos-N	51	128	22	29	4	0	1	5	18	14	2	....	.227	.327	.281	.608	82	-2	12	3.12	-1	0-42(23-20-0)	3	-0.5
Yr.	81	181	27	45	6	0	1	12	22	19	2	....	.249	.333	.298	.632	87	-2	19	3.43	2	0-51(30-22-0)	4	-0.2
Total 7	**601**	**1874**	**331**	**520**	**58**	**31**	**11**	**149**	**222**	**230**	**160**	**....**	**.277**	**.361**	**.359**	**.720**	**103**	**14**	**297**	**5.51**	**-5**	**0-519**	**56**	**-1.4**
• DEVORMER, Al	Albert E. DeVormer b: 8/19/1891, Grand Rapids, MI d: 8/29/1966, Grand Rapids, MI BR/TR, 6'.5", 175 lbs. Deb: 8/4/1918																							
1918 Chi-A	8	19	2	5	2	0	0	0	0	4	1	....	.263	.263	.368	.632	90	-0	2	3.48	0	/C-6,0-1	0	-0.1
1921*NY-A	22	49	6	17	4	0	0	7	2	4	2	0	.347	.373	.429	.801	102	1	8	6.32	-2	C-17	2	0.0
1922 NY-A	24	59	8	12	4	1	0	11	1	6	0	0	.203	.217	.305	.522	34	-6	4	2.06	-2	C-17/1-1	0	-0.7
1923 Bos-A	74	209	20	54	7	3	0	18	6	21	3	0	.258	.282	.321	.603	58	-12	19	3.19	1	C-55/1-2	3	-0.7
1927 NY-N	68	141	14	35	3	1	2	21	11	11	1	....	.248	.312	.326	.638	71	-6	14	3.42	-2	C-54/1-3	3	-0.6
Total 5	**196**	**477**	**50**	**123**	**20**	**5**	**2**	**57**	**20**	**46**	**7**	**0**	**.258**	**.292**	**.333**	**.625**	**65**	**-24**	**48**	**3.40**	**-5**	**C-149/1-6,0-1**	**8**	**-2.1**
• DEVOY, Walt	Walter Joseph Devoy b: 3/14/1885, St. Louis, MO d: 12/17/1953, St. Louis, MO BR/TR, 5'11", 165 lbs. Deb: 9/13/1909																							
1909 StL-A	19	69	7	17	3	1	0	8	3	....	4	....	.246	.278	.319	.597	95	-1	7	3.43	-1	0-16(0-0-16)/1-3	2	-0.3
• DEWILLIS, Jeff	Jeffrey Allen DeWillis b: 4/13/1965, Houston, TX BR/TR, 6'2", 170 lbs. Deb: 4/19/1987																							
1987 Tor-A	13	25	2	3	1	0	1	2	2	12	0	0	.120	.185	.280	.465	21	-3	1	1.69	0	C-13	1	-0.2
• DEXTER, Charlie	Charles Dana Dexter b: 6/15/1876, Evansville, IN d: 6/9/1934, Cedar Rapids, IA BR/TR, 5'7", 155 lbs. Deb: 4/17/1896 U Career OF: 8-159-235																							
1896 Lou-N	107	402	65	112	18	7	3	37	17	34	21	....	.279	.318	.381	.698	87	-9	57	5.16	1	C-55,0-47(0-46-1)	7	-0.5
1897 Lou-N	76	257	43	72	12	5	2	46	21	....	12	....	.280	.342	.389	.731	96	-2	39	5.59	1	0-32(3-14-16),C-23,3-14/S-2	7	0.0
1898 Lou-N	112	421	76	132	13	5	1	66	26	....	44	....	.314	.363	.375	.739	114	7	77	6.72	-5	0-95(0-0-95)/2-8,C-7	16	-0.1
1899 Lou-N	81	298	47	76	7	1	1	34	21	....	21	....	.255	.315	.295	.610	68	-13	38	4.11	3	0-71(1-0-70)/S-6	4	-1.3
1900 Chi-N	40	125	7	25	5	0	2	20	1	....	2	....	.200	.213	.288	.501	39	-11	9	2.20	4	C-22,0-13(0-0-13)/2-1	1	-0.5
1901 Chi-N	116	460	46	123	9	5	1	66	16	....	22	....	.267	.302	.315	.617	82	-11	52	4.06	1	1-54,3-25,0-21(1-9-11),2-13/C	7	-1.1
1902 Chi-N	71	273	31	62	13	0	2	26	19	....	13	....	.227	.290	.297	.586	83	-5	30	3.48	-12	3-39,1-22,0-10(1-4-5)	4	-1.8
Bos-N	48	183	33	47	3	0	1	18	16	....	16	....	.257	.323	.290	.613	88	-2	24	4.41	-1	S-22,2-19/0-7(0-4-3),3-1	6	-0.3
Yr.	119	456	64	109	16	0	3	44	35	....	29	....	.239	.303	.294	.597	85	-7	53	3.84	-13	3-40,1-22,S-22,2-19,0-17(1-8-8)	10	-2.1
1903 Bos-N	123	457	82	102	15	1	3	34	61	....	32	....	.223	.323	.280	.603	75	-12	55	3.94	-4	*0-106(2-82-21)/S-9,C-6	9	-1.9
Total 8	**774**	**2876**	**430**	**751**	**95**	**24**	**16**	**347**	**198**	**34**	**183**	**....**	**.261**	**.318**	**.328**	**.646**	**85**	**-57**	**379**	**4.56**	**-13**	**0-402,C-116/3-79,1-76,2-41,S**	**61**	**-7.5**
• DIAZ, Alex	Alexis Diaz b: 10/5/1968, Brooklyn, NY BB/TR, 5'11", 180 lbs. Deb: 7/25/1992 Career OF: 56-169-66																							
1992 Mil-A	22	9	5	1	0	0	0	1	0	0	3	2	.111	.111	.111	.222	-38	-2	0	.00	0	0-11(2-10-0)/D-2	0	-0.2
1993 Mil-A	32	69	9	22	2	0	0	1	0	12	5	3	.319	.319	.348	.667	80	-2	6	3.02	0	0-28(4-12-13)/D-1	0	-0.3
1994 Mil-A	79	187	17	47	5	7	1	17	10	19	5	5	.251	.289	.369	.658	65	-11	18	3.09	1	0-73(0-58-20)/2-2,D-1	2	-1.0
1995*Sea-A	103	270	44	67	14	0	3	27	13	27	18	8	.248	.288	.333	.621	60	-16	26	3.16	-3	0-88(17-69-4)	3	-1.8
1996 Sea-A	38	79	11	19	2	0	1	5	2	8	6	3	.241	.277	.304	.581	47	-7	6	2.51	0	0-28(19-5-5)/D-1	1	-0.7
1997 Tex-A	28	90	8	20	4	0	2	12	5	13	1	1	.222	.271	.333	.604	54	-7	7	2.66	-1	0-23(3-0-20)/1-1,2-1	0	-0.8
1998 SF-N	34	62	5	8	2	0	0	5	0	15	1	1	.129	.129	.161	.290	-26	-12	1	.58	0	0-21(4-15-3)	0	-1.2
1999 Hou-N	30	50	3	11	2	0	1	7	3	13	2	2	.220	.264	.320	.584	48	-5	4	2.66	0	/0-8(7-0-1)	0	-0.4
Total 8	**366**	**816**	**102**	**195**	**31**	**7**	**8**	**75**	**33**	**107**	**41**	**25**	**.239**	**.273**	**.324**	**.596**	**53**	**-61**	**69**	**2.73**	**-4**	**0-280/D-5,2-3,1-1**	**6**	**-6.5**
• DIAZ, Bo	Baudilio Jose (Seijas) Diaz b: 3/23/1953, Cua, Venezuela d: 11/23/1990, Caracas, Venezuela BR/TR, 5'11", 190 lbs. Deb: 9/6/1977																							
1977 Bos-A	2	1	0	0	0	0	0	0	0	1	0	0	.000	.000	.000	.000	-89	-0	0	.00	0	/C-2	0	0.0
1978 Cle-A	44	127	12	30	4	0	2	11	4	17	0	0	.236	.260	.315	.575	61	-7	10	2.71	-3	C-44	1	-0.8
1979 Cle-A	15	32	0	5	2	0	0	1	2	6	0	0	.156	.206	.219	.425	15	-4	1	1.28	-1	C-15	0	-0.4
1980 Cle-A	76	207	15	47	11	2	3	32	7	27	1	0	.227	.252	.343	.595	61	-12	14	2.18	1	C-75	3	-0.7
1981 Cle-A★	63	182	25	57	19	0	7	38	13	23	2	2	.313	.362	.533	.895	157	12	32	6.31	0	C-51/D-3	10	1.5

YEAR TM-L	G	AB	R	H	2B	3B	HR	RBI	BB	SO	SB	CS	AVG	OBP	SLG	OPS	OPS+	BR/A	RC	RC/G	FR	G/POS	WS	TPW
1982 Phi-N	144	525	69	151	29	1	18	85	36	87	3	6	.288	.337	.450	.786	116	7	72	4.75	-3	*C-144	21	1.1
1983*Phi-N	136	471	49	111	17	0	15	64	38	57	1	4	.236	.295	.367	.663	84	-13	49	3.51	5	*C-134	15	-0.2
1984 Phi-N	27	75	5	16	4	0	1	9	5	13	0	0	.213	.263	.307	.569	58	-4	5	2.17	-1	C-23	1	-0.4
1985 Phi-N	26	76	9	16	5	1	2	16	6	7	0	0	.211	.268	.382	.650	78	-3	6	2.63	-1	C-24	1	-0.3
Cin-N	51	161	12	42	8	0	3	15	15	18	0	0	.261	.328	.366	.694	89	-2	19	3.92	3	C-51	5	0.3
Yr.	77	237	21	58	13	1	5	31	21	25	0	0	.245	.309	.371	.680	86	-5	25	3.49	1	C-75	6	0.0
1986 Cin-N	134	474	50	129	21	0	10	56	40	52	1	1	.272	.329	.380	.709	91	-6	59	4.37	0	*C-134	15	-0.1
1987 Cin-N★	140	496	49	134	28	1	15	82	19	73	1	0	.270	.304	.421	.725	86	-12	59	4.11	1	*C-137	15	-0.5
1988 Cin-N	92	315	26	69	9	0	10	35	7	41	0	2	.219	.238	.343	.581	63	-18	20	2.02	2	C-88	5	-1.2
1989 Cin-N	43	132	6	27	5	0	1	8	6	7	0	2	.205	.239	.265	.504	43	-11	7	1.78	-2	C-43	2	-1.1
Total 13	**993**	**3274**	**327**	**834**	**162**	**5**	**87**	**452**	**198**	**429**	**9**	**17**	**.255**	**.300**	**.387**	**.687**	**87**	**-73**	**354**	**3.65**	**-1**	**C-965/D-3**	**94**	**-2.9**
• DIAZ, Carlos	Carlos Francisco Diaz b: 12/24/1964, Jersey City, NJ BR/TR, 6'3", 195 lbs. Deb: 5/8/1990																							
1990 Tor-A	9	3	1	1	0	0	0	0	0	2	0	0	.333	.333	.333	.667	82	-0	0	3.42	0	/C-9	0	0.0
• DIAZ, Eddy	Eddy Javier Diaz b: 9/29/1971, Barquisimeto, Venezuela BR/TR, 5'10", 160 lbs. Deb: 4/17/1997																							
1997 Mil-A	16	50	4	11	2	1	0	7	1	5	0	0	.220	.235	.300	.535	38	-5	3	1.73	1	2-14/3-1,S-1	1	-0.3
• DIAZ, Edgar	Edgar (Serrano) Diaz b: 2/8/1964, Santurce, Puerto Rico BR/TR, 6', 155 lbs. Deb: 9/16/1986																							
1986 Mil-A	5	13	0	3	0	0	0	0	1	3	0	0	.231	.286	.231	.516	41	-1	1	2.51	-1	/S-5	0	-0.2
1990 Mil-A	86	218	27	59	2	2	0	14	21	32	3	2	.271	.338	.298	.636	80	-5	23	3.71	-9	S-65,2-15/3-7,D-1	3	-1.0
Total 2	**91**	**231**	**27**	**62**	**2**	**2**	**0**	**14**	**22**	**35**	**3**	**2**	**.268**	**.335**	**.294**	**.629**	**78**	**-6**	**24**	**3.64**	**-11**	**/S-70,2-15,3-7,D-1**	**3**	**-1.2**
• DIAZ, Edwin	Edwin (Rosario) Diaz b: 1/15/1975, Bayamon, Puerto Rico BR/TR, 5'11", 172 lbs. Deb: 3/31/1998																							
1998 Ari-N	3	7	0	0	0	0	0	0	0	2	0	0	.000	.000	.000	.000	-100	-2	0	.00	-1	/2-3	0	-0.2
1999 Ari-N	4	5	2	2	2	0	0	1	3	1	0	0	.400	.625	.800	1.425	256	2	3	25.43	0	/2-2,S-2	1	0.1
Total 2	**7**	**12**	**2**	**2**	**2**	**0**	**0**	**1**	**3**	**3**	**0**	**0**	**.167**	**.333**	**.333**	**.667**	**90**	**-0**	**3**	**7.63**	**-1**	**/2-5,S-2**	**1**	**-0.1**
• DIAZ, Einar	Einar Antonio Diaz b: 12/28/1972, Chiriqui, Panama BR/TR, 5'10", 165 lbs. Deb: 9/9/1996																							
1996 Cle-A	4	1	0	0	0	0	0	0	0	0	0	0	.000	.000	.000	.000	-101	-0	0	.00	-1	/C-4	0	-0.1
1997 Cle-A	5	7	1	1	1	0	0	1	0	2	0	0	.143	.143	.286	.429	8	-1	0	1.29	0	/C-5	0	-0.1
1998*Cle-A	17	48	8	11	1	0	2	9	3	2	0	0	.229	.302	.375	.677	72	-2	5	3.35	0	C-17	1	-0.1
1999*Cle-A	119	392	43	110	21	1	3	32	23	41	11	4	.281	.329	.362	.691	73	-16	46	4.11	6	*C-119	8	-0.1
2000 Cle-A	75	250	29	68	14	2	4	25	11	29	4	2	.272	.323	.392	.715	78	-9	31	4.20	15	C-74/3-1	6	1.0
2001*Cle-A	134	437	54	121	34	1	4	56	17	44	1	2	.277	.328	.387	.714	86	-10	54	4.31	12	*C-134/2-1	15	1.1
2002 Cle-A	102	320	34	66	19	0	2	16	17	27	0	1	.206	.259	.284	.544	45	-26	22	2.11	12	*C-100	4	-0.7
2003 Tex-A	101	334	30	86	14	1	4	35	9	32	3	1	.257	.297	.341	.639	63	-18	32	3.19	10	*C-101	5	-0.1
Total 8	**557**	**1789**	**199**	**463**	**104**	**5**	**19**	**174**	**80**	**177**	**19**	**10**	**.259**	**.308**	**.354**	**.662**	**70**	**-81**	**189**	**3.57**	**53**	**C-554/2-1,3-1**	**39**	**0.9**
• DIAZ, Juan	Juan Carlos Diaz b: 2/19/1974, San Jose de las Lajas, Cuba BR/TR, 6'2", 228 lbs. Deb: 6/12/2002																							
2002 Bos-A	4	7	2	2	1	0	1	2	1	2	0	0	.286	.375	.857	1.232	210	1	2	12.68	0	/1-1,D-1	1	0.1
• DIAZ, Mario	Mario Rafael (Torres) Diaz b: 1/10/1962, Humacao, Puerto Rico BR/TR, 5'10", 160 lbs. Deb: 9/12/1987																							
1987 Sea-A	11	23	4	7	0	1	0	3	0	4	0	0	.304	.304	.391	.696	79	-1	3	4.62	1	S-10	1	0.1
1988 Sea-A	28	72	6	22	5	0	0	9	3	5	0	0	.306	.333	.375	.708	94	-1	8	4.10	0	S-21/2-4,1-1,3-1	2	0.1
1989 Sea-A	52	74	9	10	0	0	1	7	7	7	0	0	.135	.210	.176	.386	9	-9	3	1.16	-6	S-37,2-14/3-3	0	-1.3
1990 NY-N	16	22	0	3	1	0	0	1	0	3	0	0	.136	.136	.182	.318	-13	-3	1	.80	0	S-10/2-1	0	-0.3
1991 Tex-A	96	182	24	48	7	0	1	22	15	18	0	1	.264	.320	.319	.638	79	-6	18	3.39	-1	S-65,2-20/3-8,D-1	4	-0.3
1992 Tex-A	19	31	2	7	1	0	0	1	1	2	0	1	.226	.250	.258	.508	44	-3	1	1.24	-2	S-16/2-3,3-1	0	-0.4
1993 Tex-A	71	205	24	56	10	1	2	24	8	13	1	0	.273	.304	.361	.665	81	-6	22	3.51	0	S-57,3-12/1-1	5	-0.2
1994 Fla-N	32	77	10	25	4	2	0	11	6	6	0	0	.325	.381	.429	.810	108	1	13	6.44	2	3-11/2-7,S-7	3	0.3
1995 Fla-N	49	87	5	20	3	0	1	6	1	12	0	0	.230	.239	.299	.537	41	-8	5	1.92	1	/2-9,S-5,3-3	0	-0.6
Total 9	**374**	**773**	**84**	**198**	**31**	**4**	**5**	**84**	**41**	**70**	**1**	**2**	**.256**	**.295**	**.326**	**.621**	**69**	**-35**	**74**	**3.18**	**-4**	**S-228/2-58,3-39,1-2,D-1**	**15**	**-2.7**
• DIAZ, Matt	Matthew E. Diaz b: 3/3/1978, Portland, OR BR/TR, 6'1", 206 lbs. Deb: 7/19/2003																							
2003 TB-A	4	9	2	1	0	0	0	0	1	3	0	0	.111	.200	.111	.311	-15	-1	0	.85	0	/D-1,O-1	0	-0.1
• DIAZ, Mike	Michael Anthony Diaz b: 4/15/1960, San Francisco, CA BR/TR, 6'2", 195 lbs. Deb: 9/15/1983 Career OF: 73-0-20																							
1983 Chi-N	6	7	2	2	1	0	0	1	0	0	0	0	.286	.286	.429	.714	91	-0	1	4.63	0	/C-3	0	-0.1
1986 Pit-N	97	209	22	56	9	0	12	36	19	43	0	1	.268	.335	.483	.818	120	5	33	5.49	-5	O-38(37-0-1),1-20/3-5,C-1	6	-0.3
1987 Pit-N	103	241	28	58	8	2	16	48	31	42	1	0	.241	.335	.490	.824	114	4	40	5.47	0	O-37(27-0-10),1-32/C-8	7	0.2
1988 Pit-N	47	74	6	17	3	0	0	5	16	13	0	0	.230	.367	.270	.637	87	-0	8	3.77	-1	O-19(9-0-9)/1-6,C-1	2	-0.2
Chi-A	40	152	12	36	6	0	3	12	5	30	0	1	.237	.266	.336	.601	68	-8	12	2.65	-3	1-39/D-1	1	-1.3
Total 4	**293**	**683**	**70**	**169**	**27**	**2**	**31**	**102**	**71**	**128**	**1**	**2**	**.247**	**.324**	**.429**	**.753**	**103**	**1**	**94**	**4.65**	**-9**	**/1-97,O-94,C-13,3-5,D-1**	**16**	**-1.6**
• DICKEN, Paul	Paul Franklin Dicken b: 10/2/1943, Deland, FL BR/TR, 6'5", 195 lbs. Deb: 6/7/1964																							
1964 Cle-A	11	11	0	0	0	0	0	0	0	5	0	0	.000	.000	.000	.000	-101	-3	0	.00	0	....	0	-0.3
1966 Cle-A	2	2	0	0	0	0	0	0	0	1	0	0	.000	.000	.000	.000	-100	-0	0	.00	0	....	0	-0.1
• DICKERSON, Buttercup	Lewis Pessano Dickerson b: 10/11/1858, Tyaskin, MD d: 7/23/1920, Baltimore, MD BL/TR, 5'6", 140 lbs. Deb: 7/15/1878 Career OF: 216-117-64																							
1878 Cin-N	29	123	17	38	5	1	0	9	0	7	....	....	.309	.309	.366	.675	133	4	14	4.61	-2	O-29(10-19-0)	5	0.1
1879 Cin-N	81	350	73	102	18	**14**	2	57	3	27	....	....	.291	.297	.440	.737	147	17	47	5.30	-4	*O-81(81-0-0)	14	0.8
1880 Tro-N	30	119	15	23	2	2	0	10	2	3	....	....	.193	.207	.244	.450	49	-6	6	1.76	4	O-30(0-29-1)/S-1	2	-0.3
Wor-N	31	133	22	39	8	6	0	20	1	2	....	....	.293	.299	.444	.742	136	4	18	5.28	-2	O-31(0-31-0)	5	0.0
Yr.	61	252	37	62	10	8	0	30	3	5	....	....	.246	.255	.349	.604	95	-2	24	3.50	2	*O-61(0-60-1)/S-1	7	-0.3
1881 Wor-N	80	367	48	116	18	6	1	31	8	8	....	....	.316	.331	.406	.737	123	8	51	5.43	9	*O-80(79-0-1)	12	1.2
1883 Pit-a	85	354	62	88	15	1	0	0	18	....	....	....	.249	.285	.297	.582	92	-2	31	3.23	-1	*O-78(1-30-47)/S-8,2-2	6	-0.4
1884 StL-U	46	211	49	77	15	1	0	....	8	....	....	....	.365	.388	.445	.834	174	16	37	7.81	5	O-42(42-0-0)/3-4	12	1.7
Bal-a	13	56	9	12	2	1	0	0	4	....	....	....	.214	.290	.286	.576	85	-1	5	2.98	-2	O-12(0-0-12)/3-1	2	-0.3
Lou-a	8	28	6	4	0	2	1	0	3	....	....	....	.143	.226	.393	.619	102	0	3	2.92	0	/O-8(1-5-3)	1	0.0
Yr.	21	84	15	16	2	3	1	0	7	....	....	....	.190	.269	.321	.590	91	-1	7	2.96	-2	O-20(1-5-15)/3-1	3	-0.3
1885 Buf-N	5	21	1	1	1	0	0	0	1	4	....	....	.048	.091	.095	.186	-38	-3	0	.25	1	/O-5(2-3-0)	0	-0.2
Total 7	**408**	**1762**	**302**	**500**	**84**	**34**	**4**	**127**	**48**	**51**	**....**	**....**	**.284**	**.304**	**.377**	**.680**	**120**	**38**	**211**	**4.63**	**7**	**O-396/S-9,3-5,2-2**	**59**	**2.5**
• DICKEY, Bill	William Malcolm Dickey b: 6/6/1907, Bastrop, LA d: 11/12/1993, Little Rock, AR BL/TR, 6'1.5", 185 lbs. Deb: 8/15/1928 M/C HOF: 1954																							
1928 NY-A	10	15	1	3	1	1	0	2	0	2	0	0	.200	.200	.400	.600	56	-1	1	2.54	0	/C-6	0	-0.1
1929 NY-A	130	447	60	145	30	6	10	65	14	16	4	3	.324	.346	.485	.832	120	10	73	6.11	3	*C-127	18	2.0
1930 NY-A	109	366	55	124	25	7	5	65	21	14	7	1	.339	.375	.486	.861	122	13	67	7.03	0	*C-101	15	1.7
1931 NY-A	130	477	65	156	17	10	6	78	39	20	2	1	.327	.378	.442	.820	122	17	80	6.48	2	*C-125	20	2.5
1932*NY-A	108	423	66	131	20	4	15	84	34	13	2	4	.310	.361	.482	.843	123	12	72	6.44	-5	*C-108	18	1.3
1933 NY-A★	130	478	58	152	24	8	14	97	47	14	3	4	.318	.381	.490	.871	138	25	89	7.06	5	*C-127	25	3.5
1934 NY-A★	104	395	56	127	24	4	12	72	38	18	0	3	.322	.384	.494	.878	134	18	74	7.19	0	*C-104	20	2.2
1935 NY-A	120	448	54	125	26	6	14	81	35	11	1	1	.279	.339	.458	.797	111	5	70	5.70	-3	*C-118	20	0.9
1936*NY-A★	112	423	99	153	26	8	22	107	46	16	0	2	.362	.428	.617	1.045	161	38	111	10.85	-2	*C-107	25	3.8
1937*NY-A★	140	530	87	176	35	2	29	133	73	22	3	2	.332	.417	.570	.987	145	37	128	9.53	3	*C-137	33	4.5
1938*NY-A★	132	454	84	142	27	4	27	115	75	22	3	0	.313	.412	.568	.981	144	32	111	9.37	-3	*C-126	27	3.3
1939*NY-A★	128	480	98	145	23	3	24	105	77	37	5	0	.302	.403	.513	.915	135	28	104	8.10	-1	*C-126	27	3.2
1940 NY-A★	106	372	45	92	11	1	9	54	48	32	0	3	.247	.336	.355	.691	83	-10	46	4.30	0	*C-102	13	-0.3
1941*NY-A★	109	348	35	99	15	5	7	71	45	17	2	1	.284	.371	.417	.788	109	6	56	5.76	-3	*C-104	17	0.8
1942*NY-A★	82	268	28	79	13	1	2	37	26	11	2	2	.295	.359	.373	.732	108	3	34	4.59	0	C-80	11	0.8
1943*NY-A★	85	242	29	85	18	2	4	33	41	12	2	1	.351	.445	.492	.937	173	25	57	9.34	-1	C-71	20	3.0

YEAR TM-L	G	AB	R	H	2B	3B	HR	RBI	BB	SO	SB	CS	AVG	OBP	SLG	OPS	OPS+	BR/A	RC	RC/G	FR	G/POS	WS	TPW
1946 NY-A★	54	134	10	35	8	0	2	10	19	12	0	1	.261	.357	.366	.723	101	0	17	4.34	4	C-39	5	0.7
Total 17	**1789**	**6300**	**930**	**1969**	**343**	**72**	**202**	**1209**	**678**	**289**	**36**	**29**	**.313**	**.382**	**.486**	**.868**	**128**	**259**	**1193**	**7.12**	**-2**	***C-1708**	**314**	**33.8**

• DICKEY, George George Willard "Skeets" Dickey b: 7/10/1915, Kensett, AR d: 7/16/1976, DeWitt, AR BB/TR, 6'2", 180 lbs. Deb: 9/21/1935

YEAR TM-L	G	AB	R	H	2B	3B	HR	RBI	BB	SO	SB	CS	AVG	OBP	SLG	OPS	OPS+	BR/A	RC	RC/G	FR	G/POS	WS	TPW
1935 Bos-A	5	11	1	0	0	0	0	1	1	3	0	0	.000	.083	.000	.083	-72	-3	0	.05	0	/C-4	0	-0.3
1936 Bos-A	10	23	0	1	1	0	0	0	2	3	0	0	.043	.120	.087	.207	-46	-6	0	.35	0	C-10	0	-0.5
1941 Chi-A	32	55	6	11	1	0	2	8	5	7	0	0	.200	.267	.327	.594	57	-4	5	2.96	0	C-17	1	-0.2
1942 Chi-A	59	116	6	27	3	0	1	17	9	11	0	0	.233	.288	.284	.572	63	-6	10	2.79	-4	C-29	1	-0.8
1946 Chi-A	37	78	8	15	1	0	0	1	12	13	0	2	.192	.300	.205	.505	45	-6	5	2.01	2	C-30	2	-0.3
1947 Chi-A	83	211	15	47	6	0	1	27	34	25	4	2	.223	.331	.265	.596	69	-7	22	3.44	-2	C-80	4	-0.5
Total 6	**226**	**494**	**36**	**101**	**12**	**0**	**4**	**54**	**63**	**62**	**4**	**4**	**.204**	**.294**	**.253**	**.547**	**54**	**-31**	**41**	**2.74**	**-4**	**C-170**	**8**	**-2.6**

• DICKSHOT, Johnny John Oscar "Ugly" Dickshot b: 1/24/1910, Waukegan, IL d: 11/4/1997, Waukegan, IL BR/TR, 6', 195 lbs. Deb: 4/16/1936 Career OF: 222-1-26

YEAR TM-L	G	AB	R	H	2B	3B	HR	RBI	BB	SO	SB	CS	AVG	OBP	SLG	OPS	OPS+	BR/A	RC	RC/G	FR	G/POS	WS	TPW
1936 Pit-N	9	9	2	2	0	0	0	1	1	2	0	....	.222	.300	.222	.522	42	-1	1	2.67	0	/0-1	0	-0.1
1937 Pit-N	82	264	42	67	8	4	3	33	26	36	0	....	.254	.323	.348	.672	82	-6	29	3.68	0	0-64(58-0-6)	4	-0.9
1938 Pit-N	29	35	3	8	0	0	0	4	8	5	3	....	.229	.372	.229	.601	68	-1	4	3.83	0	0-10(5-0-5)	1	-0.2
1939 NY-N	10	34	3	8	0	0	0	5	5	3	0	....	.235	.333	.235	.569	55	-2	3	2.53	1	0-10(0-0-10)	0	-0.2
1944 Chi-A	62	162	18	41	8	5	0	15	13	10	2	0	.253	.313	.364	.677	94	-1	20	4.35	0	0-40(35-0-5)	5	-0.3
1945 Chi-A	130	486	74	147	19	10	4	58	48	41	18	3	.302	.366	.407	.774	128	20	75	5.52	-1	*0-124(124-0-0)	20	1.3
Total 6	**322**	**990**	**142**	**273**	**35**	**19**	**7**	**116**	**101**	**97**	**23**	**3**	**.276**	**.345**	**.371**	**.715**	**105**	**9**	**131**	**4.62**	**-1**	**0-249**	**30**	**-0.5**

• DIDIER, Bob Robert Daniel Didier b: 2/16/1949, Hattiesburg, MS BB/TR, 6', 190 lbs. Deb: 4/7/1969 C

YEAR TM-L	G	AB	R	H	2B	3B	HR	RBI	BB	SO	SB	CS	AVG	OBP	SLG	OPS	OPS+	BR/A	RC	RC/G	FR	G/POS	WS	TPW
1969*Atl-N	114	352	30	90	16	1	0	32	34	39	1	3	.256	.321	.307	.628	76	-11	36	3.42	-7	*C-114	10	-1.3
1970 Atl-N	57	168	9	25	2	1	0	7	12	11	1	0	.149	.210	.173	.383	3	-23	6	1.15	-2	C-57	1	-2.2
1971 Atl-N	51	155	9	34	4	1	0	5	6	17	0	0	.219	.248	.258	.507	41	-12	10	1.98	1	C-50	2	-0.9
1972 Atl-N	13	40	5	12	2	1	0	5	2	4	0	0	.300	.349	.400	.749	103	0	6	4.95	1	C-11	1	0.2
1973 Det-A	7	22	3	10	1	0	0	1	3	0	0	0	.455	.520	.500	1.020	177	3	6	13.78	1	/C-7	2	0.4
1974 Bos-A	5	14	0	1	0	0	0	1	2	1	0	0	.071	.188	.071	.259	-22	-2	0	.52	0	/C-5	0	-0.2
Total 6	**247**	**751**	**56**	**172**	**25**	**4**	**0**	**51**	**59**	**72**	**2**	**3**	**.229**	**.287**	**.273**	**.560**	**56**	**-46**	**64**	**2.77**	**-5**	**C-244**	**16**	**-4.1**

• DIEHL, Ernie Ernest Guy Diehl b: 10/2/1877, Cincinnati, OH d: 11/6/1958, Miami, FL BR/TR, 6'1", 190 lbs. Deb: 5/31/1903 Career OF: 6-0-5

YEAR TM-L	G	AB	R	H	2B	3B	HR	RBI	BB	SO	SB	CS	AVG	OBP	SLG	OPS	OPS+	BR/A	RC	RC/G	FR	G/POS	WS	TPW
1903 Pit-N	1	3	0	1	0	0	0	0	0	....	0	....	.333	.333	.333	.667	87	-0	0	4.53	0	/0-1	0	0.0
1904 Pit-N	12	37	6	6	0	0	0	4	6	....	3	....	.162	.311	.162	.473	46	-2	3	2.41	2	/0-7(2-0-5),S-4	1	0.0
1906 Bos-N	3	11	1	5	0	1	0	0	0	....	0	....	.455	.455	.636	1.091	247	2	3	14.13	-0	/0-2(2-0-0),S-1	1	0.2
1909 Bos-N	1	4	1	2	1	0	0	0	0	....	0	....	.500	.500	.750	1.250	275	1	1	19.19	1	/0-1	0	0.2
Total 4	**17**	**55**	**8**	**14**	**1**	**1**	**0**	**4**	**6**	**....**	**3**	**....**	**.255**	**.349**	**.309**	**.658**	**98**	**1**	**8**	**5.05**	**2**	**/0-11,S-5**	**2**	**0.2**

• DIERING, Chuck Charles Edward Allen Diering b: 2/5/1923, St. Louis, MO BR/TR, 5'10", 165 lbs. Deb: 4/15/1947 Career OF: 60-527-47

YEAR TM-L	G	AB	R	H	2B	3B	HR	RBI	BB	SO	SB	CS	AVG	OBP	SLG	OPS	OPS+	BR/A	RC	RC/G	FR	G/POS	WS	TPW
1947 StL-N	105	74	22	16	3	1	2	11	19	22	3	....	.216	.383	.365	.748	95	0	12	5.30	0	0-75(13-31-31)	3	0.0
1948 StL-N	7	7	2	0	0	0	0	0	2	2	1	....	.000	.222	.000	.222	-33	-1	0	.20	0	/0-5(5-0-0)	0	-0.1
1949 StL-N	131	369	60	97	21	8	3	38	35	49	1	....	.263	.328	.388	.716	87	-7	49	4.70	1	*0-124(0-123-1)	11	-0.9
1950 StL-N	89	204	34	51	12	0	3	18	35	38	1	....	.250	.360	.353	.713	84	-4	28	4.87	2	0-81(0-78-3)	6	-0.3
1951 StL-N	64	85	9	22	5	1	0	8	6	15	0	1	.259	.308	.341	.649	74	-4	9	3.71	-2	0-44(6-33-5)	2	-0.6
1952 NY-N	41	23	2	4	1	1	0	2	4	3	0	2	.174	.296	.304	.601	66	-2	2	2.35	-0	0-36(27-4-5)	0	-0.3
1954 Bal-A	128	418	35	108	14	1	2	29	56	57	3	7	.258	.351	.311	.662	89	-6	46	3.65	8	*0-119(0-119-0)	9	-0.4
1955 Bal-A	137	371	38	95	16	2	3	31	57	45	5	8	.256	.355	.334	.689	93	-4	45	4.11	-1	*0-107(2-105-0),3-34,S-12	10	-0.9
1956 Bal-A	50	97	15	18	4	0	1	4	23	19	2	5	.186	.342	.258	.599	65	-6	10	2.91	0	0-40(7-34-2)/3-2	1	-0.7
Total 9	**752**	**1648**	**217**	**411**	**76**	**14**	**14**	**141**	**237**	**250**	**16**	**23**	**.249**	**.346**	**.338**	**.684**	**86**	**-33**	**201**	**4.11**	**10**	**0-631/3-36,S-12**	**42**	**-4.2**

• DIETZ, Dick Richard Allen Dietz b: 9/18/1941, Crawfordsville, IN BR/TR, 6'1", 195 lbs. Deb: 6/18/1966

YEAR TM-L	G	AB	R	H	2B	3B	HR	RBI	BB	SO	SB	CS	AVG	OBP	SLG	OPS	OPS+	BR/A	RC	RC/G	FR	G/POS	WS	TPW
1966 SF-N	13	23	1	1	0	0	0	0	0	9	0	0	.043	.083	.043	.127	-62	-5	0	.06	0	/C-6	0	-0.5
1967 SF-N	56	120	10	27	3	0	4	19	25	44	0	1	.225	.363	.350	.713	106	2	16	4.50	-2	C-43	5	0.2
1968 SF-N	98	301	21	82	14	2	6	38	34	68	1	1	.272	.348	.392	.740	122	9	42	5.00	-4	C-90	14	1.0
1969 SF-N	79	244	28	56	8	1	11	35	53	53	0	0	.230	.373	.406	.779	120	9	38	5.09	-6	C-73	9	0.7
1970 SF-N★	148	493	82	148	36	2	22	107	109	106	0	1	.300	.430	.515	.945	154	43	113	8.26	-4	*C-139	29	4.5
1971*SF-N	142	453	58	114	19	0	19	72	97	86	1	3	.252	.388	.419	.808	131	22	79	6.04	-11	*C-135	19	1.9
1972 LA-N	27	56	4	9	1	0	1	6	14	11	2	0	.161	.329	.232	.561	63	-1	5	3.03	0	C-22	2	-0.1
1973 Atl-N	83	139	22	41	8	1	3	24	49	25	0	0	.295	.479	.432	.910	143	13	32	8.13	1	1-36,C-20	6	1.3
Total 8	**646**	**1829**	**226**	**478**	**89**	**6**	**66**	**301**	**381**	**402**	**4**	**6**	**.261**	**.392**	**.425**	**.817**	**130**	**92**	**326**	**6.17**	**-26**	**C-528/1-36**	**84**	**9.1**

• DIETZEL, Roy Leroy Louis Dietzel b: 1/9/1931, Baltimore, MD BR/TR, 6', 190 lbs. Deb: 9/2/1954

YEAR TM-L	G	AB	R	H	2B	3B	HR	RBI	BB	SO	SB	CS	AVG	OBP	SLG	OPS	OPS+	BR/A	RC	RC/G	FR	G/POS	WS	TPW
1954 Was-A	9	21	1	5	0	0	0	1	5	4	0	0	.238	.385	.238	.623	78	-0	2	3.46	0	/2-7,3-2	0	0.0

• DIFANI, Jay Clarence Joseph Difani b: 12/21/1923, Crystal City, MO BR/TR, 6', 170 lbs. Deb: 4/23/1948

YEAR TM-L	G	AB	R	H	2B	3B	HR	RBI	BB	SO	SB	CS	AVG	OBP	SLG	OPS	OPS+	BR/A	RC	RC/G	FR	G/POS	WS	TPW
1948 Was-A	2	2	0	0	0	0	0	0	0	2	0	0	.000	.000	.000	.000	-103	-1	0	.00	0	....	0	-0.1
1949 Was-A	2	1	0	1	1	0	0	0	0	0	0	0	1.000	1.000	2.000	3.000	699	1	2	∞	0	/2-1	0	0.1
Total 2	**4**	**3**	**0**	**1**	**1**	**0**	**0**	**0**	**0**	**2**	**0**	**0**	**.333**	**.333**	**.667**	**1.000**	**164**	**0**	**2**	**.00**	**0**	**/2-1**	**0**	**0.0**

• DIFELICE, Mike Michael William Difelice b: 5/28/1969, Philadelphia, PA BR/TR, 6'2", 205 lbs. Deb: 9/1/1996

YEAR TM-L	G	AB	R	H	2B	3B	HR	RBI	BB	SO	SB	CS	AVG	OBP	SLG	OPS	OPS+	BR/A	RC	RC/G	FR	G/POS	WS	TPW
1996 StL-N	4	7	0	2	1	0	0	2	0	1	0	0	.286	.286	.429	.714	86	-0	1	4.63	0	/C-4	0	0.0
1997 StL-N	93	260	16	62	10	1	4	30	19	61	1	1	.238	.298	.331	.629	65	-14	24	2.97	5	C-91/1-1	6	-0.2
1998 TB-A	84	248	17	57	12	3	3	23	15	56	0	0	.230	.277	.339	.615	58	-16	21	2.67	3	C-84	5	-0.7
1999 TB-A	51	179	21	55	11	0	6	27	8	23	0	0	.307	.347	.469	.817	105	1	30	6.37	0	C-51	8	0.4
2000 TB-A	60	204	23	49	13	1	6	19	12	40	0	0	.240	.282	.402	.684	71	-10	21	3.35	5	C-59	2	-0.1
2001 TB-A	48	149	13	31	5	1	2	9	8	39	1	1	.208	.263	.295	.558	47	-12	11	2.46	4	C-48	1	-0.5
Ari-N	12	21	1	1	0	0	0	1	0	10	0	0	.048	.091	.048	.139	-59	-5	0	.20	-1	C-12	0	-0.5
2002*StL-N	70	174	17	40	11	0	4	19	17	42	0	0	.230	.302	.362	.664	76	-6	19	3.60	3	C-61	4	0.0
2003 KC-A	62	189	29	48	16	1	3	25	9	30	1	0	.254	.302	.397	.699	73	-8	22	3.89	6	C-58	6	0.2
Total 8	**484**	**1431**	**137**	**345**	**79**	**7**	**28**	**155**	**88**	**302**	**3**	**2**	**.241**	**.293**	**.365**	**.657**	**68**	**-70**	**148**	**3.44**	**25**	**C-468/1-1**	**32**	**-1.4**

• DIGNAN, Steve Stephen E. Dignan b: 4/16/1859, Boston, MA d: 7/11/1881, Boston, MA Deb: 6/1/1880

YEAR TM-L	G	AB	R	H	2B	3B	HR	RBI	BB	SO	SB	CS	AVG	OBP	SLG	OPS	OPS+	BR/A	RC	RC/G	FR	G/POS	WS	TPW
1880 Bos-N	8	34	4	11	1	0	0	4	0	3	....	....	.324	.324	.353	.676	133	1	4	4.76	0	/0-8(1-0-7)	1	0.1
Wor-N	3	10	1	3	0	1	0	2	0	1	....	....	.300	.300	.500	.800	152	0	2	6.04	-1	/0-3(0-3-0)	1	0.0
Yr.	11	44	5	14	1	1	0	6	0	4	....	....	.318	.318	.386	.705	138	2	6	5.06	-1	0-11(1-3-7)	2	0.1

• DILLARD, Don David Donald Dillard b: 1/8/1937, Greenville, SC BL/TR, 6'1", 200 lbs. Deb: 4/24/1959 Career OF: 67-49-7

YEAR TM-L	G	AB	R	H	2B	3B	HR	RBI	BB	SO	SB	CS	AVG	OBP	SLG	OPS	OPS+	BR/A	RC	RC/G	FR	G/POS	WS	TPW
1959 Cle-A	10	10	0	4	0	0	0	1	0	2	0	0	.400	.400	.400	.800	125	0	2	7.20	0	....	0	0.0
1960 Cle-A	6	7	0	1	0	0	0	0	1	3	0	0	.143	.250	.143	.393	9	-1	0	.61	0	/0-1	0	-0.1
1961 Cle-A	74	147	27	40	5	0	7	17	15	28	0	0	.272	.340	.449	.788	112	2	23	5.80	0	0-39(14-24-1)	5	0.1
1962 Cle-A	95	174	22	40	5	1	5	14	11	25	0	1	.230	.276	.356	.632	71	-8	16	3.21	-1	0-50(28-20-4)	2	-1.1
1963 Mil-N	67	119	9	28	6	4	1	12	5	21	0	2	.235	.272	.378	.650	86	-3	11	2.99	2	0-30(24-5-1)	2	-0.3
1965 Mil-N	20	19	1	3	0	0	1	3	0	6	0	0	.158	.158	.316	.474	30	-2	0	.47	0	/0-1	0	-0.2
Total 6	**272**	**476**	**59**	**116**	**16**	**5**	**14**	**47**	**32**	**85**	**0**	**3**	**.244**	**.293**	**.387**	**.679**	**86**	**-12**	**53**	**3.78**	**0**	**0-121**	**9**	**-1.6**

• DILLARD, Pat Robert Lee Dillard b: 6/12/1873, Chattanooga, TN d: 7/22/1907, Denver, CO BL/TR, 6', 180 lbs. Deb: 4/21/1900

YEAR TM-L	G	AB	R	H	2B	3B	HR	RBI	BB	SO	SB	CS	AVG	OBP	SLG	OPS	OPS+	BR/A	RC	RC/G	FR	G/POS	WS	TPW
1900 StL-N	57	183	24	42	5	2	0	12	13	....	7	....	.230	.284	.279	.563	56	-11	17	3.18	-4	0-26(0-20-6),3-21/S-3	2	-1.5

• DILLARD, Steve Stephen Bradley Dillard b: 2/8/1951, Memphis, TN BR/TR, 6'1", 180 lbs. Deb: 9/28/1975

YEAR TM-L	G	AB	R	H	2B	3B	HR	RBI	BB	SO	SB	CS	AVG	OBP	SLG	OPS	OPS+	BR/A	RC	RC/G	FR	G/POS	WS	TPW
1975 Bos-A	1	5	2	2	0	0	0	0	0	0	1	0	.400	.400	.400	.800	117	0	1	9.07	1	/2-1	0	0.1
1976 Bos-A	57	167	22	46	14	0	1	15	17	20	6	4	.275	.342	.377	.720	99	-0	20	4.00	-4	3-18,2-17,S-12/D-7	4	-0.2
1977 Bos-A	66	141	22	34	7	0	1	13	7	13	4	3	.241	.277	.312	.589	54	-9	12	2.83	-3	2-45/S-9,D-6	2	-1.0

YEAR TM-L	G	AB	R	H	2B	3B	HR	RBI	BB	SO	SB	CS	AVG	OBP	SLG	OPS	OPS+	BR/A	RC	RC/G	FR	G/POS	WS	TPW
1978 Det-A	56	130	21	29	5	2	0	7	6	11	1	2	.223	.257	.292	.550	53	-9	9	2.01	5	2-41/D-4	2	-0.3
1979 Chi-N	89	166	31	47	6	1	5	24	17	24	1	0	.283	.353	.422	.775	101	1	25	5.19	3	2-60/3-9	7	0.6
1980 Chi-N	100	244	31	55	8	1	4	27	20	54	2	2	.225	.287	.316	.602	63	-13	22	3.08	-5	3-51,2-38/S-2	3	-1.7
1981 Chi-N	53	119	18	26	7	1	2	11	8	20	0	0	.218	.268	.345	.612	70	-5	11	3.22	0	2-32/3-7,S-2	2	-0.4
1982 Chi-A	16	41	1	7	3	1	0	5	1	5	0	1	.171	.190	.293	.483	30	-4	2	1.31	0	2-16	1	-0.4
Total 8	438	1013	148	246	50	6	13	102	76	147	15	12	.243	.297	.343	.640	73	-40	102	3.33	-3	2-250/3-85,S-25,D-17	21	-3.2

• DILLHOEFER, Pickles William Martin Dillhoefer b: 10/13/1894, Cleveland, OH d: 2/23/1922, St. Louis, MO BR/TR, 5'7", 154 lbs. Deb: 4/16/1917

YEAR TM-L	G	AB	R	H	2B	3B	HR	RBI	BB	SO	SB	CS	AVG	OBP	SLG	OPS	OPS+	BR/A	RC	RC/G	FR	G/POS	WS	TPW
1917 Chi-N	42	95	3	12	1	1	0	8	2	9	1	....	.126	.144	.158	.302	-7	-12	3	.73	4	C-37	2	-0.7
1918 Phi-N	8	11	0	1	0	0	0	0	1	1	2	....	.091	.167	.091	.258	-19	-2	0	1.04	0	/C-6	0	-0.2
1919 StL-N	45	108	11	23	3	2	0	12	8	6	5	....	.213	.267	.278	.545	68	-4	9	2.64	0	C-39	2	-0.3
1920 StL-N	76	224	26	59	8	3	0	13	13	7	2	1	.263	.304	.326	.630	83	-4	22	3.51	-4	C-74	5	-0.3
1921 StL-N	76	162	19	39	4	4	0	15	11	7	2	1	.241	.289	.315	.604	61	-8	15	3.16	-2	C-69	3	-0.7
Total 5	247	600	59	134	16	10	0	48	35	30	12	2	.223	.266	.283	.549	58	-30	49	2.69	-3	C-225	12	-2.2

• DILLINGER, Bob Robert Bernard "Duke" Dillinger b: 9/17/1918, Glendale, CA BR/TR, 5'11.5", 170 lbs. Deb: 4/16/1946

YEAR TM-L	G	AB	R	H	2B	3B	HR	RBI	BB	SO	SB	CS	AVG	OBP	SLG	OPS	OPS+	BR/A	RC	RC/G	FR	G/POS	WS	TPW
1946 StL-A	83	225	33	63	6	3	0	11	19	30	8	1	.280	.341	.333	.675	85	-3	27	4.12	-4	3-54/S-1	6	-0.7
1947 StL-A	137	571	70	168	23	6	3	37	56	38	**34**	13	.294	.361	.371	.733	102	5	80	5.01	0	*3-137	16	0.4
1948 StL-A	153	644	110	**207**	34	10	2	44	65	34	**28**	11	.321	.385	.415	.799	110	11	105	5.95	-19	*3-153	17	-0.8
1949 StL-A★	137	544	68	176	22	13	1	51	51	40	**20**	14	.324	.385	.417	.802	108	4	87	5.83	-19	*3-133	14	-1.4
1950 Phi-A	84	356	55	110	21	9	3	41	31	20	5	3	.309	.366	.444	.810	109	4	57	5.90	0	3-84	9	0.3
Pit-N	58	222	23	64	8	2	1	9	13	22	4	....	.288	.328	.356	.684	77	-8	24	3.82	2	3-51	3	-0.6
1951 Pit-N	12	43	3	10	3	0	0	0	1	0	2	0	.233	.250	.302	.552	46	-3	2	1.70	0	3-10	0	-0.3
Chi-A	89	299	39	90	6	4	0	20	15	17	5	5	.301	.337	.348	.684	87	-7	34	4.13	-1	3-70	5	-0.8
Total 6	753	2904	401	888	123	47	10	213	251	201	106	47	.306	.363	.391	.754	100	4	417	5.16	-42	3-692/S-1	70	-4.0

• DILLON, John John Dillon b: St. Louis, MO Deb: 5/8/1875

YEAR TM-L	G	AB	R	H	2B	3B	HR	RBI	BB	SO	SB	CS	AVG	OBP	SLG	OPS	OPS+	BR/A	RC	RC/G	FR	G/POS	WS	TPW
1875 RS-n	1	1	0	0	0	0	0	0	0	0	0	0	.000	.000	.000	.000	-111	-0	0	.00	0	/S-1	....	-0.1

• DILLON, Packy Packard Andrew Dillon b: St. Louis, MO d: 1/9/1890, Guelph, Canada Deb: 5/4/1875

YEAR TM-L	G	AB	R	H	2B	3B	HR	RBI	BB	SO	SB	CS	AVG	OBP	SLG	OPS	OPS+	BR/A	RC	RC/G	FR	G/POS	WS	TPW
1875 RS-n	3	13	1	3	1	0	0	1	0	0	0	0	.231	.231	.308	.538	94	0	1	2.79	0	/C-3	....	0.0

• DILLON, Pop Frank Edward Dillon b: 10/17/1873, Normal, IL d: 9/12/1931, Pasadena, CA BL/TR, 6'1", 185 lbs. Deb: 9/8/1899

YEAR TM-L	G	AB	R	H	2B	3B	HR	RBI	BB	SO	SB	CS	AVG	OBP	SLG	OPS	OPS+	BR/A	RC	RC/G	FR	G/POS	WS	TPW
1899 Pit-N	30	121	21	31	5	0	0	20	5	....	5	....	.256	.286	.298	.583	60	-7	12	3.52	2	1-30	1	-0.5
1900 Pit-N	5	18	3	2	1	0	0	1	0	....	0	....	.111	.111	.167	.278	-24	-3	0	.57	1	/1-5	0	-0.2
1901 Det-A	74	281	40	81	14	6	1	42	15	....	14	....	.288	.324	.391	.716	94	-3	42	5.35	0	1-74	6	-0.4
1902 Det-A	66	243	21	50	6	3	0	22	16	....	2	....	.206	.255	.255	.510	41	-20	17	2.31	1	1-66	1	-1.9
Bal-A	2	7	1	2	0	1	0	0	2	....	0	....	.286	.444	.571	1.016	173	1	2	9.66	0	/1-2	0	0.1
Yr.	68	250	22	52	6	4	0	22	18	....	2	....	.208	.261	.264	.525	45	-19	19	2.49	1	1-68	1	-1.8
1904 Bro-N	135	511	60	132	18	6	0	31	40	....	13	....	.258	.313	.317	.630	97	-1	57	3.85	12	*1-134	10	0.9
Total 5	312	1181	146	298	44	16	1	116	78	....	34	....	.252	.299	.319	.618	80	-34	131	3.80	16	1-311	18	-2.1

• DILONE, Miguel Miguel Angel (Reyes) Dilone b: 11/1/1954, Santiago, Dominican Republic BB/TR, 6', 160 lbs. Deb: 9/2/1974 Career OF: 380-103-75

YEAR TM-L	G	AB	R	H	2B	3B	HR	RBI	BB	SO	SB	CS	AVG	OBP	SLG	OPS	OPS+	BR/A	RC	RC/G	FR	G/POS	WS	TPW
1974 Pit-N	12	2	3	0	0	0	0	0	1	0	2	0	.000	.333	.000	.333	-1	0	0	5.85	0	/O-2(0-1-1)	0	0.0
1975 Pit-N	18	6	8	0	0	0	0	0	0	1	2	2	.000	.000	.000	.000	-101	-2	0	.00	-0	/O-2(0-2-0)	0	-0.2
1976 Pit-N	16	17	7	4	0	0	0	0	0	0	5	1	.235	.235	.235	.471	34	-1	1	2.25	1	/O-3(1-2-0)	0	0.0
1977 Pit-N	29	44	5	6	0	0	0	0	2	3	12	0	.136	.174	.136	.310	-15	-5	2	1.54	0	O-17(9-7-2)	0	-0.5
1978 Oak-A	135	258	34	59	8	0	1	14	23	30	50	23	.229	.294	.271	.566	63	-11	21	2.46	-2	O-99(47-25-36),D-11/3-3	4	-1.7
1979 Oak-A	30	91	15	17	1	2	1	6	6	7	6	5	.187	.237	.275	.512	40	-9	5	1.62	-2	O-25(5-0-20)	0	-1.1
Chi-N	43	36	14	11	0	0	0	1	2	5	15	5	.306	.342	.306	.648	71	-0	4	3.66	0	O-22(4-18-0)	1	-0.1
1980 Cle-A	132	528	82	180	30	9	0	40	28	45	61	18	.341	.376	.432	.808	120	20	89	6.29	-3	*O-118(90-23-13),D-11	21	1.1
1981 Cle-A	72	269	33	78	5	5	0	19	18	28	29	10	.290	.334	.346	.680	98	1	31	4.06	3	O-56(56-0-0),D-11	7	0.1
1982 Cle-A	104	379	50	89	12	3	3	25	25	36	33	5	.235	.286	.306	.592	63	-14	35	3.01	-2	O-97(96-1-0)/D-1	3	-2.0
1983 Cle-A	32	68	15	13	3	1	0	7	10	5	5	1	.191	.295	.265	.560	53	-3	6	2.96	-1	O-19(19-0-0)	1	-0.5
Chi-A	4	3	1	0	0	0	0	0	0	0	1	0	.000	.000	.000	.000	-96	-1	0	.00	0	/D-2,O-2(0-2-0)	0	-0.1
Yr.	36	71	16	13	3	1	0	7	10	5	6	1	.183	.284	.254	.537	48	-4	6	2.81	-1	O-21(19-2-0)/D-2	1	-0.6
Pit-N	7	0	1	0	0	0	0	0	0	0	2	0	....	....	....	....	-98	0	0	....	0	....	0	0.0
1984 Mon-N	88	169	28	47	8	2	1	10	17	18	27	2	.278	.348	.367	.714	106	7	26	5.30	-2	O-41(41-0-0)	6	0.3
1985 Mon-N	51	84	10	16	0	2	0	6	6	11	7	3	.190	.244	.238	.483	38	-7	4	1.51	0	O-22(8-13-2)	0	-0.8
SD-N	27	46	8	10	0	1	0	1	4	8	10	3	.217	.280	.261	.541	53	-2	4	2.78	0	O-14(4-9-1)	1	-0.3
Yr.	78	130	18	26	0	3	0	7	10	19	17	6	.200	.257	.246	.503	43	-9	8	1.94	-1	O-36(12-22-3)	1	-1.1
Total 12	800	2000	314	530	67	25	6	129	142	197	267	78	.265	.316	.333	.648	81	-26	229	3.82	-9	O-539/D-36,3-3	44	-5.8

• DIMAGGIO, Dom Dominic Paul "The Little Professor" DiMaggio b: 2/12/1917, San Francisco, CA BR/TR, 5'9", 168 lbs. Deb: 4/16/1940 Career OF: 11-1338-26

YEAR TM-L	G	AB	R	H	2B	3B	HR	RBI	BB	SO	SB	CS	AVG	OBP	SLG	OPS	OPS+	BR/A	RC	RC/G	FR	G/POS	WS	TPW
1940 Bos-A	108	418	81	126	32	6	8	46	41	46	7	6	.301	.367	.464	.831	109	5	73	6.43	9	O-94(11-59-26)	14	1.0
1941 Bos-A★	144	584	117	165	37	6	8	58	90	57	13	6	.283	.385	.408	.792	107	10	101	6.22	5	*O-144(0-144-0)	21	1.1
1942 Bos-A★	151	622	110	178	36	8	14	48	70	52	16	10	.286	.364	.437	.801	121	17	103	5.98	18	*O-151(0-151-0)	28	3.1
1946*Bos-A★	142	534	85	169	24	7	7	73	66	58	10	6	.316	.393	.427	.820	122	18	92	6.24	4	*O-142(0-142-0)	26	1.9
1947 Bos-A	136	513	75	145	21	5	8	71	74	62	10	6	.283	.376	.390	.766	105	6	80	5.47	15	*O-134(0-134-0)	20	1.8
1948 Bos-A	155	648	127	185	40	4	9	87	101	58	10	2	.285	.383	.401	.785	104	8	110	6.15	12	*O-155(0-155-0)	26	1.5
1949 Bos-A★	145	605	126	186	34	5	8	60	96	55	9	7	.307	.404	.420	.824	110	11	110	6.79	7	*O-144(0-144-0)	24	1.4
1950 Bos-A★	141	588	**131**	193	30	**11**	7	70	82	68	**15**	4	.328	.414	.452	.866	111	14	117	7.55	7	*O-140(0-140-0)	24	1.6
1951 Bos-A★	146	639	**113**	189	34	4	12	72	73	53	4	7	.296	.370	.418	.788	103	2	101	5.76	-1	*O-146(0-146-0)	21	-0.4
1952 Bos-A★	128	486	81	143	20	1	6	33	57	61	6	8	.294	.371	.377	.747	100	0	70	5.16	0	*O-123(0-123-0)	16	-0.3
1953 Bos-A	3	3	0	1	0	0	0	0	0	1	0	0	.333	.333	.333	.667	76	-0	0	4.61	0	....	0	0.0
Total 11	1399	5640	1046	1680	308	57	87	618	750	571	100	62	.298	.383	.419	.802	109	91	958	6.18	74	*O-1373	220	12.7

• DIMAGGIO, Joe Joseph Paul "Joltin' Joe,The Yankee Clipper" DiMaggio
b: 11/25/1914, Martinez, CA d: 3/8/1999, Hollywood, FL BR/TR, 6'2", 193 lbs. Deb: 5/3/1936 C HOF: 1955 Career OF: 66-1638-18

YEAR TM-L	G	AB	R	H	2B	3B	HR	RBI	BB	SO	SB	CS	AVG	OBP	SLG	OPS	OPS+	BR/A	RC	RC/G	FR	G/POS	WS	TPW
1936*NY-A★	138	637	132	206	44	**15**	29	125	24	39	4	0	.323	.352	.576	.928	130	24	127	7.76	10	*O-138(66-55-18)	25	2.5
1937*NY-A★	151	621	**151**	215	35	15	**46**	167	64	37	3	0	.346	.412	**.673**	1.085	168	61	173	11.22	7	*O-150(0-150-0)	**39**	5.9
1938*NY-A★	145	599	129	194	32	13	32	140	59	21	6	1	.324	.386	.581	.967	140	34	136	8.85	6	*O-145(0-145-0)	30	3.3
1939*NY-A★	120	462	108	176	32	6	30	126	52	20	3	0	**.381**	.448	.671	1.119	**185**	59	139	12.37	5	*O-117(0-117-0)	**34**	**5.7**
1940 NY-A★	132	508	93	179	28	9	31	133	61	30	1	2	**.352**	.425	.626	1.051	**175**	56	135	10.50	-4	*O-130(0-130-0)	**31**	4.6
1941*NY-A★	139	541	122	193	43	11	30	**125**	76	13	4	2	.357	.440	.643	1.083	186	67	162	12.28	8	*O-139(0-139-0)	41	6.9
1942*NY-A★	154	610	123	186	29	13	21	114	68	36	4	2	.305	.376	.498	.875	148	38	120	7.42	0	*O-154(0-154-0)	32	3.4
1946 NY-A★	132	503	81	146	20	8	25	95	59	24	1	0	.290	.367	.511	.878	142	28	96	6.97	6	*O-131(0-131-0)	24	3.2
1947*NY-A★	141	534	97	168	31	10	20	97	64	32	3	0	.315	.391	.522	.913	154	39	112	7.97	-20	*O-139(0-139-0)	30	1.5
1948 NY-A★	153	594	110	190	26	11	**39**	**155**	67	30	1	1	.320	.396	.598	.994	164	50	140	8.90	-5	*O-152(0-152-0)	34	4.0
1949*NY-A★	76	272	58	94	14	6	14	67	55	18	0	1	.346	.459	.596	1.055	178	32	76	10.86	-3	O-76(0-76-0)	21	2.6
1950*NY-A★	139	525	114	158	33	10	32	122	80	33	0	0	.301	.394	**.585**	.979	152	40	125	8.83	-7	*O-137(0-137-0)/1-1	29	2.8
1951*NY-A★	116	415	72	109	22	4	12	71	61	36	0	0	.263	.365	.422	.787	117	11	65	5.48	0	*O-113(0-113-0)	17	0.8
Total 13	1736	6821	1390	2214	389	131	361	1537	790	369	30	9	.325	.398	.579	.977	156	539	1606	9.06	3	*O-1721/1-1	387	47.3

• DIMAGGIO, Vince Vincent Paul DiMaggio b: 9/6/1912, Martinez, CA d: 10/3/1986, North Hollywood, CA BR/TR, 5'11", 183 lbs. Deb: 4/19/1937 Career OF: 4-1070-7

YEAR TM-L	G	AB	R	H	2B	3B	HR	RBI	BB	SO	SB	CS	AVG	OBP	SLG	OPS	OPS+	BR/A	RC	RC/G	FR	G/POS	WS	TPW
1937 Bos-N	132	493	56	126	18	4	13	69	39	111	8	....	.256	.311	.387	.699	97	-3	61	4.31	10	*O-130(0-129-1)	17	0.3
1938 Bos-N	150	540	71	123	28	3	14	61	65	134	11	....	.228	.313	.369	.682	96	-2	68	4.32	14	*O-149(0-149-0)/2-1	20	0.8
1939 Cin-N	8	14	1	1	1	0	0	2	2	10	0	....	.071	.188	.143	.330	-10	-2	0	.98	1	/O-7(3-3-1)	0	-0.2
1940 Cin-N	2	4	2	1	0	0	0	0	1	0	0	....	.250	.400	.250	.650	82	-0	0	1.70	-0	/O-1	0	0.0
Pit-N	110	356	59	103	26	0	19	54	37	83	11	....	.289	.364	.522	.887	143	20	68	7.04	2	*O-108(1-103-4)	17	2.0

YEAR TM-L	G	AB	R	H	2B	3B	HR	RBI	BB	SO	SB	CS	AVG	OBP	SLG	OPS	OPS+	BR/A	RC	RC/G	FR	G/POS	WS	TPW
Yr.	112	360	61	104	26	0	19	54	38	83	11	....	.289	.365	.519	.884	142	20	69	6.96	2	*0-109(1-103-5)	17	2.0
1941 Pit-N	151	528	73	141	27	5	21	100	68	100	10	....	.267	.354	.456	.810	128	19	88	5.92	0	*0-151(0-151-0)	24	1.6
1942 Pit-N	143	496	57	118	22	3	15	75	52	87	10	....	.238	.311	.385	.697	101	-1	59	3.99	8	*0-138(0-138-0)	15	0.4
1943 Pit-N★	157	580	64	144	41	2	15	88	70	126	11	....	.248	.329	.403	.733	107	5	80	4.85	9	*0-156(0-156-0)/S-1	20	1.1
1944 Pit-N★	109	342	41	82	20	4	9	50	33	83	6	....	.240	.307	.401	.707	94	-4	42	4.25	-1	*0-101(0-101-0)/3-1	10	-0.7
1945 Phi-N	127	452	64	116	25	3	19	84	43	91	12	....	.257	.321	.451	.773	117	7	67	5.22	7	*0-121(0-121-0)	15	1.2
1946 Phi-N	6	19	1	4	1	0	0	1	0	7	0	....	.211	.211	.263	.474	35	-2	1	1.33	0	/0-6(0-6-0)	0	-0.2
NY-N	15	25	2	0	0	0	0	0	2	5	0	....	.000	.074	.000	.074	-78	-6	0	.00	-1	0-13(0-13-0)	0	-0.8
Yr.	21	44	3	4	1	0	0	1	2	12	0	....	.091	.130	.114	.244	-32	-8	1	.48	-2	0-19(0-19-0)	0	-1.0
Total 10	**1110**	**3849**	**491**	**959**	**209**	**24**	**125**	**584**	**412**	**837**	**79**	**....**	**.249**	**.324**	**.413**	**.737**	**108**	**32**	**535**	**4.83**	**48**	***0-1081/2-1,3-1,S-1**	**138**	**5.5**
• DIMMEL, Mike	Michael Wayne Dimmel b: 10/16/1954, Albert Lea, MN BR/TR, 6', 180 lbs. Deb: 9/2/1977 Career OF: 6-3-27																							
1977 Bal-A	25	5	8	0	0	0	0	0	0	1	1	0	.000	.000	.000	.000	-107	-1	0	.00	0	0-23(0-1-22)	0	-0.1
1978 Bal-A	8	0	2	0	0	0	0	0	0	0	0	1	....	....	....	....	-107	-0	0	.00	-1	/0-7(1-1-5)	0	-0.2
1979 StL-N	6	3	1	1	0	0	0	0	0	0	0	1	.333	.333	.333	.667	82	-1	0	.00	0	/0-5(5-1-0)	0	-0.1
Total 3	**39**	**8**	**11**	**1**	**0**	**0**	**0**	**0**	**0**	**1**	**1**	**2**	**.125**	**.125**	**.125**	**.250**	**-44**	**-2**	**0**	**.00**	**-1**	**/0-35**	**0**	**-0.4**
• DINEEN, Kerry	Kerry Michael Dineen b: 7/1/1952, Englewood, NJ BL/TL, 5'11", 165 lbs. Deb: 6/14/1975 Career OF: 1-9-2																							
1975 NY-A	7	22	3	8	1	0	0	1	2	1	0	0	.364	.417	.409	.826	138	1	4	7.65	0	/0-7(0-7-0)	1	0.1
1976 NY-A	4	7	0	2	0	0	0	1	1	2	1	1	.286	.375	.286	.661	96	-0	1	3.13	0	/0-4(0-2-2)	0	-0.1
1978 Phi-N	5	8	0	2	1	0	0	0	1	0	0	0	.250	.333	.375	.708	97	-0	1	2.79	-0	/0-1	0	0.0
Total 3	**16**	**37**	**3**	**12**	**2**	**0**	**0**	**2**	**4**	**3**	**1**	**1**	**.324**	**.390**	**.378**	**.769**	**121**	**1**	**5**	**5.39**	**-1**	**/0-12**	**1**	**0.0**
• DINGES, Vance	Vance George Dinges b: 5/29/1915, Elizabeth, NJ d: 10/4/1990, Harrisonburg, VA BL/TL, 6'2", 175 lbs. Deb: 4/17/1945 Career OF: 17-18-33																							
1945 Phi-N	109	397	46	114	15	4	1	36	35	17	5	....	.287	.346	.353	.699	97	-1	49	4.47	0	0-65(16-18-33),1-42	10	-0.7
1946 Phi-N	50	104	7	32	5	1	1	10	9	12	2	....	.308	.363	.404	.767	121	3	15	5.16	1	1-26/0-1	4	0.3
Total 2	**159**	**501**	**53**	**146**	**20**	**5**	**2**	**46**	**44**	**29**	**7**	**....**	**.291**	**.350**	**.363**	**.713**	**102**	**1**	**64**	**4.61**	**0**	**/1-68,0-66**	**14**	**-0.5**
• DIPIETRO, Bob	Robert Louis Paul DiPietro b: 9/1/1927, San Francisco, CA BR/TR, 5'11", 185 lbs. Deb: 9/23/1951																							
1951 Bos-A	4	11	0	1	0	0	0	0	1	1	0	0	.091	.167	.091	.258	-26	-2	0	.26	1	/0-3(0-0-3)	0	-0.2
• DISARCINA, Gary	Gary Thomas Disarcina b: 11/19/1967, Malden, MA BR/TR, 6'1", 178 lbs. Deb: 9/23/1989																							
1989 Cal-A	2	0	0	0	0	0	0	0	0	0	0	0	....	....	....	....	-102	0	0	....	-1	/S-1	0	-0.1
1990 Cal-A	18	57	8	8	1	1	0	0	3	10	1	0	.140	.183	.193	.376	5	-7	2	.86	0	S-14/2-3	0	-0.6
1991 Cal-A	18	57	5	12	2	0	0	3	3	4	0	0	.211	.274	.246	.520	45	-4	4	2.49	-2	S-10/2-7,3-2	1	-0.6
1992 Cal-A	157	518	48	128	19	0	3	42	20	50	9	7	.247	.284	.301	.586	64	-27	41	2.66	-3	*S-157	9	-1.8
1993 Cal-A	126	416	44	99	20	1	3	45	15	38	5	7	.238	.275	.313	.587	56	-29	32	2.50	6	*S-126	6	-1.3
1994 Cal-A	112	389	53	101	14	2	3	33	18	28	3	7	.260	.296	.329	.625	60	-26	35	2.97	6	*S-110	6	-1.0
1995 Cal-A★	99	362	61	111	28	6	5	41	20	25	7	4	.307	.346	.459	.805	108	3	55	5.35	3	S-98	12	1.3
1996 Cal-A	150	536	62	137	26	4	5	48	21	36	2	1	.256	.286	.347	.633	60	-34	50	3.12	-2	*S-150	6	-2.1
1997 Ana-A	154	549	52	135	28	2	4	47	17	29	7	8	.246	.274	.326	.600	55	-39	43	2.59	-1	*S-153	6	-2.6
1998 Ana-A	157	551	73	158	39	3	3	56	21	51	11	7	.287	.322	.385	.707	82	-16	66	4.20	-8	*S-157	15	-1.0
1999 Ana-A	81	271	32	62	7	1	1	29	15	32	2	2	.229	.274	.273	.547	41	-25	20	2.31	0	S-81	2	-1.7
2000 Ana-A	12	38	6	15	2	0	1	11	1	3	0	1	.395	.425	.526	.951	135	2	8	7.70	6	S-12	2	0.8
Total 12	**1086**	**3744**	**444**	**966**	**186**	**20**	**28**	**355**	**154**	**306**	**47**	**44**	**.258**	**.294**	**.341**	**.635**	**66**	**-203**	**356**	**3.18**	**5**	***S-1069/2-10,3-2**	**65**	**-10.6**
• DISTEFANO, Benny	Benito James Distefano b: 1/23/1962, Brooklyn, NY BL/TL, 6'1", 195 lbs. Deb: 5/18/1984 Career OF: 14-0-32																							
1984 Pit-N	45	78	10	13	1	2	3	9	5	13	0	1	.167	.226	.346	.572	59	-5	5	1.95	2	0-20(7-0-15),1-17	0	-0.4
1986 Pit-N	31	39	3	7	1	0	1	5	1	5	0	0	.179	.200	.282	.482	31	-4	2	1.86	0	/0-9(0-0-9),1-1	0	-0.5
1988 Pit-N	16	29	6	10	3	1	1	6	3	4	0	0	.345	.406	.621	1.027	194	3	7	8.90	0	/1-5,0-2(0-0-2)	2	0.3
1989 Pit-N	96	154	12	38	8	0	2	15	17	30	1	0	.247	.333	.338	.671	96	-0	17	3.73	-3	1-48/C-3,0-1	2	-0.6
1992 Hou-N	52	60	4	14	0	2	0	7	5	14	0	0	.233	.303	.300	.603	75	-2	6	3.19	1	0-12(7-0-5)/1-6	1	-0.2
Total 5	**240**	**360**	**35**	**82**	**13**	**5**	**7**	**42**	**31**	**66**	**1**	**1**	**.228**	**.298**	**.350**	**.648**	**86**	**-8**	**37**	**3.37**	**-1**	**/1-77,0-44,C-3**	**5**	**-1.4**
• DISTEL, Dutch	George Adam Distel b: 4/15/1896, Madison, IN d: 2/12/1967, Madison, IN BR/TR, 5'9", 165 lbs. Deb: 6/21/1918																							
1918 StL-N	8	17	3	3	1	1	0	1	2	3	0	....	.176	.263	.353	.616	90	-0	2	2.78	-2	/2-5,S-2,0-1	0	-0.2
• DITTMER, Jack	John Douglas Dittmer b: 1/10/1928, Elkader, IA BL/TR, 6'1", 175 lbs. Deb: 6/17/1952																							
1952 Bos-N	93	326	26	63	7	2	7	41	26	26	1	0	.193	.255	.291	.546	53	-21	24	2.38	1	2-90	4	-1.5
1953 Mil-N	138	504	54	134	22	1	9	63	18	35	1	0	.266	.293	.367	.660	75	-19	53	3.74	-19	*2-138	11	-2.7
1954 Mil-N	66	192	22	47	8	0	6	20	19	17	0	1	.245	.322	.380	.703	88	-4	24	4.14	-1	2-55	6	-0.1
1955 Mil-N	38	72	4	9	1	1	1	4	4	15	0	0	.125	.171	.208	.379		-10	3	1.06	0	2-28	1	-0.9
1956 Mil-N	44	102	8	25	4	0	1	6	8	8	0	0	.245	.300	.314	.614	69	-4	10	3.54	-2	2-42	3	-0.4
1957 Det-A	16	22	3	5	1	0	0	2	2	1	0	0	.227	.292	.273	.564	54	-1	2	2.90	0	/3-3,2-1	0	-0.2
Total 6	**395**	**1218**	**117**	**283**	**43**	**4**	**24**	**136**	**77**	**102**	**2**	**1**	**.232**	**.281**	**.333**	**.614**	**66**	**-60**	**116**	**3.21**	**-21**	**2-354/3-3**	**25**	**-5.8**
• DIVEN, Jim	Frank Robert Diven b: 8/29/1859, Brooklyn, NY d: 5/30/1914, Nutley, NJ TL Deb: 5/9/1883 U Career OF: 0-0-2 ♦																							
1883 Bal-a	2	9	4	2	0	0	0	0	0	....	....	....	.222	.222	.222	.444	42	-0	0	1.82	-1	/P-2,0-1	0	-0.4
1886 NY-N	1	3	0	0	0	0	0	0	0	1	0	....	.000	.000	.000	.000	-99	-1	0	.00	0	/0-1	0	-0.1
Total 2	**3**	**12**	**4**	**2**	**0**	**0**	**0**	**0**	**0**	**1**	**0**	**....**	**.167**	**.167**	**.167**	**.333**	**7**	**-1**	**0**	**1.28**	**-1**	**/0-2,P-2**	**0**	**-0.5**
• DIVIS, Moxie	Edward George Divis b: 1/16/1894, Cleveland, OH d: 12/19/1955, Lakewood, OH Deb: 8/4/1916																							
1916 Phi-A	3	6	0	1	0	0	0	1	0	2	0	....	.167	.167	.167	.333		-1	0	.87	1	/0-1	0	0.0
• DIXON, Leo	Leo Moses Dixon b: 9/4/1894, Chicago, IL d: 4/11/1984, Chicago, IL BR/TR, 5'11", 170 lbs. Deb: 4/14/1925																							
1925 StL-A	76	205	27	46	11	1	1	19	24	42	3	2	.224	.318	.302	.620	55	-14	21	3.39	5	C-75	5	-0.4
1926 StL-A	33	89	7	17	3	1	0	8	11	14	1	4	.191	.294	.247	.541	40	-9	7	2.14	2	C-33	2	-0.5
1927 StL-A	36	103	6	20	3	1	0	12	7	6	0	1	.194	.245	.243	.488	26	-12	6	1.92	-2	C-35	1	-1.1
1929 Cin-N	14	30	0	5	2	0	0	2	3	7	0	....	.167	.242	.233	.476	19	-4	2	1.80	0	C-14	1	-0.3
Total 4	**159**	**427**	**40**	**88**	**19**	**3**	**1**	**41**	**45**	**69**	**4**	**7**	**.206**	**.291**	**.272**	**.562**	**43**	**-38**	**36**	**2.64**	**5**	**C-157**	**9**	**-2.3**
• DOANE, Walt	Walter Rudolph Doane b: 3/12/1887, Bellevue, ID d: 10/19/1935, West Brandywine, PA BL/TR, 6', 165 lbs. Deb: 9/20/1909 ♦																							
1909 Cle-A	4	9	1	1	0	0	0	0	1	....	0	....	.111	.200	.111	.311	-1	-1	0	.61	0	/0-2(2-0-0),P-1	0	-0.2
1910 Cle-A	6	7	0	2	1	0	0	2	1	....	0	....	.286	.375	.429	.804	150	1	1	5.72	-1	/P-6	0	-0.6
Total 2	**10**	**16**	**1**	**3**	**1**	**0**	**0**	**2**	**2**	**....**	**0**	**....**	**.188**	**.278**	**.250**	**.528**	**66**	**0**	**1**	**2.57**	**-1**	**/P-7,0-2**	**0**	**-0.8**
• DOBBEK, Dan	Daniel John Dobbek b: 12/6/1934, Ontonagon, MI BL/TR, 6', 195 lbs. Deb: 9/9/1959 Career OF: 44-68-46																							
1959 Was-A	16	60	8	15	1	2	1	5	5	13	0	0	.250	.308	.383	.691	89	-1	7	4.30	0	0-16(0-0-16)	1	-0.1
1960 Was-A	110	248	32	54	8	2	10	30	35	41	4	3	.218	.317	.387	.704	88	-4	31	4.02	-2	0-78(12-58-17)	6	-0.9
1961 Min-A	72	125	12	21	3	1	4	14	13	18	1	2	.168	.257	.304	.561	47	-11	10	2.40	0	0-48(32-10-13)	1	-1.2
Total 3	**198**	**433**	**52**	**90**	**12**	**5**	**15**	**49**	**53**	**72**	**5**	**5**	**.208**	**.299**	**.363**	**.661**	**77**	**-16**	**48**	**3.57**	**-2**	**0-142**	**8**	**-2.3**
• DOBBS, John	John Gordon Dobbs b: 6/3/1875, Chattanooga, TN d: 9/9/1934, Charlotte, NC BL/TR, 5'9.5", 170 lbs. Deb: 4/20/1901 Career OF: 65-494-3																							
1901 Cin-N	109	435	71	119	17	4	2	27	36	....	19	....	.274	.338	.345	.682	105	4	60	4.85	-7	*0-100(0-100-0)/3-8	10	-0.8
1902 Cin-N	63	256	39	76	7	3	1	16	19	....	7	....	.297	.348	.359	.707	108	2	37	5.04	7	0-63(63-0-0)	8	0.6
Chi-N	59	235	31	71	8	2	0	35	18	....	3	....	.302	.352	.353	.705	121	6	32	4.93	3	0-59(0-59-0)	8	0.7
Yr.	122	491	70	147	15	5	1	51	37	....	10	....	.299	.350	.356	.706	114	8	70	4.99	10	*0-122(63-59-0)	16	1.3
1903 Chi-N	16	61	8	14	1	1	0	4	7	....	0	....	.230	.329	.279	.607	76	-2	6	3.29	0	0-16(0-16-0)	2	-0.2
Bro-N	111	414	61	98	15	7	2	59	48	....	23	....	.237	.323	.321	.645	86	-6	53	4.30	-11	*0-110(0-110-0)	10	-2.1
Yr.	127	475	69	112	16	8	2	63	55	....	23	....	.236	.324	.316	.640	85	-8	60	4.17	-11	*0-126(0-126-0)	12	-2.4
1904 Bro-N	101	363	36	90	16	2	0	30	28	....	11	....	.248	.304	.303	.607	90	-4	39	3.58	-5	0-92(2-86-3)/2-2,S-2	6	-1.4

YEAR TM-L	G	AB	R	H	2B	3B	HR	RBI	BB	SO	SB	CS	AVG	OBP	SLG	OPS	OPS+	BR/A	RC	RC/G	FR	G/POS	WS	TPW
1905 Bro-N	123	460	59	117	21	4	2	36	31	....	15	....	.254	.304	.330	.635	96	-3	54	3.91	-9	*0-123(0-123-0)	8	-1.8
Total 5	582	2224	305	585	85	23	7	207	187	....	78	....	.263	.325	.331	.656	98	-2	282	4.32	-22	0-563/3-8,2-2,S-2	52	-5.0

• DOBY, Larry Lawrence Eugene Doby b: 12/13/1923, Camden, SC d: 6/18/2003, Montclair, NJ BL/TR, 6'1", 182 lbs. Deb: 7/5/1947 M/C HOF: 1998 Career OF: 20-1329-101

YEAR TM-L	G	AB	R	H	2B	3B	HR	RBI	BB	SO	SB	CS	AVG	OBP	SLG	OPS	OPS+	BR/A	RC	RC/G	FR	G/POS	WS	TPW
1947 Cle-A	29	32	3	5	1	0	0	2	1	11	0	0	.156	.182	.188	.369	3	-4	1	.72	-1	/2-4,1-1,S-1	0	-0.6
1948*Cle-A	121	439	83	132	23	9	14	66	54	77	9	9	.301	.384	.490	.873	135	19	84	6.96	5	*0-114(0-68-46)	18	2.0
1949 Cle-A★	147	547	106	153	25	3	24	85	91	90	10	9	.280	.389	.468	.857	129	22	104	6.64	-6	*0-147(0-117-39)	24	1.1
1950 Cle-A★	142	503	110	164	25	5	25	102	98	71	8	6	.326	**.442**	.545	**.986**	**157**	**46**	130	**9.86**	-9	*0-140(0-140-0)	30	3.2
1951 Cle-A★	134	447	84	132	27	5	20	69	101	81	4	1	.295	.428	.512	.941	**163**	45	108	8.92	-2	*0-132(0-132-0)	29	3.9
1952 Cle-A★	140	519	**104**	143	26	8	**32**	104	90	111	5	2	.276	.383	**.541**	.924	**166**	47	116	8.12	4	*0-136(0-136-0)	**34**	**4.8**
1953 Cle-A★	149	513	92	135	18	5	29	102	96	121	3	2	.263	.385	.487	.873	138	30	105	7.32	-5	*0-146(0-146-0)	26	1.8
1954*Cle-A★	153	577	94	157	18	4	**32**	**126**	85	94	3	1	.272	.368	.484	.852	130	24	108	6.68	1	*0-153(0-153-0)	33	1.9
1955 Cle-A★	131	491	91	143	17	5	26	75	61	100	2	0	.291	.372	.505	.877	129	20	95	7.14	-5	*0-129(0-129-0)	22	0.8
1956 Chi-A	140	504	89	135	22	3	24	102	102	105	0	1	.268	.395	.466	.861	125	21	100	7.00	-3	*0-137(0-137-0)	23	1.1
1957 Chi-A	119	416	57	120	27	2	14	79	56	79	2	3	.288	.376	.464	.839	127	16	71	6.11	-5	*0-110(0-110-0)	18	0.6
1958 Cle-A	89	247	41	70	10	1	13	45	26	49	0	2	.283	.352	.490	.842	132	10	41	5.80	3	0-68(8-59-1)	10	1.1
1959 Det-A	18	55	5	12	3	1	0	4	8	9	0	0	.218	.317	.309	.627	69	-2	6	3.76	0	0-16(11-0-5)	1	-0.3
Chi-A	21	58	1	14	1	1	0	9	2	13	1	0	.241	.267	.293	.560	54	-4	5	2.71	0	0-12(1-2-10)/1-2	0	-0.4
Yr.	39	113	6	26	4	2	0	13	10	22	1	0	.230	.293	.301	.594	62	-6	11	3.23	-0	0-28(12-2-15)/1-2	1	-0.7
Total 13	1533	5348	960	1515	243	52	253	970	871	1011	47	36	.283	.387	.490	.877	137	290	1074	7.23	-23	*0-1440/2-4,1-3,S-1	268	21.2

• DODD, Ona Ona Melvin Dodd b: 10/14/1886, Springtown, TX d: 12/17/1956, Carter, OK BR/TR, 5'8", 150 lbs. Deb: 7/26/1912

YEAR TM-L	G	AB	R	H	2B	3B	HR	RBI	BB	SO	SB	CS	AVG	OBP	SLG	OPS	OPS+	BR/A	RC	RC/G	FR	G/POS	WS	TPW
1912 Pit-N	5	9	0	0	0	0	0	1	1	3	0	....	.000	.100	.000	.100	-73	-2	0	.00	-1	/3-4,2-1	0	-0.3

• DODD, Tom Thomas Marion Dodd b: 8/15/1958, Portland, OR BR/TR, 6', 190 lbs. Deb: 7/25/1986

YEAR TM-L	G	AB	R	H	2B	3B	HR	RBI	BB	SO	SB	CS	AVG	OBP	SLG	OPS	OPS+	BR/A	RC	RC/G	FR	G/POS	WS	TPW
1986 Bal-A	8	13	1	3	0	0	1	2	2	2	0	0	.231	.375	.462	.837	128	1	2	5.20	0	/D-6,3-1	0	0.0

• DODGE, John John Lewis Dodge b: 4/27/1889, Bolivar, TN d: 6/19/1916, Mobile, AL BR/TR, 5'11.5", 165 lbs. Deb: 8/29/1912

YEAR TM-L	G	AB	R	H	2B	3B	HR	RBI	BB	SO	SB	CS	AVG	OBP	SLG	OPS	OPS+	BR/A	RC	RC/G	FR	G/POS	WS	TPW
1912 Phi-N	30	92	3	11	1	0	0	3	4	11	2	....	.120	.156	.130	.287	-20	-16	2	.71	2	3-23/2-5,S-1	1	-1.3
1913 Phi-N	3	3	0	1	0	0	0	0	2	0	0	....	.333	.600	.333	.933	164	1	1	7.50	0	/S-3	0	0.1
Cin-N	94	323	35	78	8	8	4	45	10	34	11	....	.241	.269	.353	.622	77	-11	32	3.19	-3	3-91	5	-1.2
Yr.	97	326	35	79	8	8	4	45	12	34	11	....	.242	.274	.353	.626	78	-11	32	3.23	-3	3-91/S-3	5	-1.2
Total 2	127	418	38	90	9	8	4	48	16	45	13	....	.215	.248	.304	.552	56	-26	35	2.59	-1	3-114/2-5,S-4	6	-2.5

• DODSON, Pat Patrick Neal Dodson b: 10/11/1959, Santa Monica, CA BL/TL, 6'4", 210 lbs. Deb: 9/5/1986

YEAR TM-L	G	AB	R	H	2B	3B	HR	RBI	BB	SO	SB	CS	AVG	OBP	SLG	OPS	OPS+	BR/A	RC	RC/G	FR	G/POS	WS	TPW
1986 Bos-A	9	12	3	5	2	0	1	3	3	3	0	0	.417	.533	.833	1.367	264	3	6	22.18	-1	/1-7	2	0.2
1987 Bos-A	26	42	4	7	3	0	2	6	8	13	0	0	.167	.300	.381	.681	77	-1	5	3.97	-2	1-21/D-1	0	-0.4
1988 Bos-A	17	45	5	8	3	1	1	1	6	17	0	0	.178	.275	.356	.630	72	-2	5	3.52	2	1-17	0	-0.1
Total 3	52	99	12	20	8	1	4	10	17	33	0	0	.202	.319	.424	.743	99	-0	16	5.34	-1	/1-45,D-1	2	-0.3

• DOERR, Bobby Robert Pershing Doerr b: 4/7/1918, Los Angeles, CA BR/TR, 5'11", 175 lbs. Deb: 4/20/1937 C HOF: 1986

YEAR TM-L	G	AB	R	H	2B	3B	HR	RBI	BB	SO	SB	CS	AVG	OBP	SLG	OPS	OPS+	BR/A	RC	RC/G	FR	G/POS	WS	TPW
1937 Bos-A	55	147	22	33	5	1	2	14	18	25	2	4	.224	.313	.313	.626	56	-11	15	3.18	2	2-47	2	-0.6
1938 Bos-A	145	509	70	147	26	7	5	80	59	39	5	10	.289	.363	.397	.760	86	-14	74	4.96	8	*2-145	14	0.2
1939 Bos-A	127	525	75	167	28	2	12	73	38	32	1	10	.318	.365	.448	.813	103	-3	78	5.35	13	*2-126	17	1.7
1940 Bos-A	151	595	87	173	37	10	22	105	57	53	10	5	.291	.353	.497	.850	113	10	104	6.24	1	*2-151	21	2.0
1941 Bos-A★	132	500	74	141	28	4	16	93	43	43	1	3	.282	.339	.450	.789	105	1	78	5.65	-9	*2-132	15	0.0
1942 Bos-A★	144	545	71	158	35	5	15	102	67	55	4	4	.290	.369	.455	.824	127	19	95	6.17	13	*2-142	24	4.2
1943 Bos-A★	155	604	78	163	32	3	16	75	62	59	8	8	.270	.339	.412	.751	117	11	86	4.94	7	*2-155	24	2.9
1944 Bos-A★	125	468	95	152	30	10	15	81	58	31	5	2	.325	.399	**.528**	.927	166	40	106	8.61	3	*2-125	27	5.2
1946*Bos-A★	151	583	95	158	34	9	18	116	66	67	5	6	.271	.346	.453	.799	115	10	90	5.31	27	*2-151	27	4.8
1947 Bos-A★	146	561	79	145	23	10	17	95	59	47	3	3	.258	.329	.426	.755	101	-1	74	4.49	20	*2-146	19	2.9
1948 Bos-A★	140	527	94	150	23	6	27	111	83	49	3	2	.285	.386	.505	.891	129	22	107	7.32	1	*2-138	27	3.0
1949 Bos-A	139	541	91	167	30	9	18	109	75	33	2	2	.309	.393	.497	.890	126	19	101	6.56	22	*2-139	25	4.8
1950 Bos-A★	149	586	103	172	29	**11**	27	120	67	42	3	4	.294	.367	.519	.886	114	9	109	6.56	0	*2-149	23	1.6
1951 Bos-A★	106	402	60	116	21	2	13	73	57	33	2	1	.289	.378	.448	.826	112	8	71	6.41	-4	*2-106	16	1.0
Total 14	1865	7093	1094	2042	381	89	223	1247	809	608	54	64	.288	.362	.461	.823	115	120	1187	5.91	104	*2-1852	281	33.7

• DOHERTY, John John Michael Doherty b: 8/22/1951, Woburn, MA BL/TL, 5'11", 185 lbs. Deb: 6/1/1974

YEAR TM-L	G	AB	R	H	2B	3B	HR	RBI	BB	SO	SB	CS	AVG	OBP	SLG	OPS	OPS+	BR/A	RC	RC/G	FR	G/POS	WS	TPW
1974 Cal-A	74	223	20	57	14	1	3	15	8	13	2	1	.256	.281	.368	.649	91	-4	23	3.49	-2	1-70/D-2	4	-1.1
1975 Cal-A	30	94	7	19	3	0	1	12	8	12	1	1	.202	.265	.266	.531	54	-6	7	2.20	-1	1-26/D-1	0	-0.9
Total 2	104	317	27	76	17	1	4	27	16	25	3	2	.240	.276	.338	.614	79	-10	29	3.08	-4	/1-96,D-3	4	-2.1

• DOLAN, Biddy Leon Mark Dolan b: 7/9/1881, Onalaska, WI d: 7/15/1950, Indianapolis, IN BR/TR, 6' Deb: 4/16/1914

YEAR TM-L	G	AB	R	H	2B	3B	HR	RBI	BB	SO	SB	CS	AVG	OBP	SLG	OPS	OPS+	BR/A	RC	RC/G	FR	G/POS	WS	TPW
1914 Ind-F	32	103	13	23	4	2	1	15	12	13	5	....	.223	.316	.330	.646	76	-3	13	3.65	-1	1-31	2	-0.5

• DOLAN, Cozy Patrick Henry Dolan b: 12/3/1872, Cambridge, MA d: 3/29/1907, Louisville, KY BL/TL, 5'10", 160 lbs. Deb: 4/26/1895 Career OF: 8-207-509 ♦

YEAR TM-L	G	AB	R	H	2B	3B	HR	RBI	BB	SO	SB	CS	AVG	OBP	SLG	OPS	OPS+	BR/A	RC	RC/G	FR	G/POS	WS	TPW
1895 Bos-N	26	83	12	20	4	1	0	7	6	7	3	....	.241	.300	.313	.613	55	-1	9	3.81	4	P-25/O-1	14	1.1
1896 Bos-N	6	14	4	2	0	0	0	0	0	1	0	....	.143	.143	.143	.286	-23	-1	0	.84	0	/P-6	1	-0.3
1900 Chi-N	13	48	5	13	1	0	0	2	2	....	2	....	.271	.300	.292	.592	66	-2	5	3.73	-1	0-13(0-0-13)	1	-0.4
1901 Chi-N	43	171	29	45	1	2	0	16	7	....	3	....	.263	.296	.292	.588	74	-6	16	3.38	2	0-41(0-0-41)	2	-0.5
Bro-N	66	253	33	66	11	1	0	29	17	....	7	....	.261	.313	.312	.625	79	-7	28	3.89	-2	0-64(2-57-5)	5	-1.2
Yr.	109	424	62	111	12	3	0	45	24	....	10	....	.262	.306	.304	.610	77	-12	44	3.69	0	*0-105(2-57-46)	7	-1.7
1902 Bro-N	141	592	72	166	16	7	1	54	33	....	24	....	.280	.324	.336	.660	103	1	75	4.57	-14	*0-141(1-140-0)	19	-2.1
1903 Chi-A	27	104	16	27	5	1	0	7	6	....	5	....	.260	.313	.327	.639	96	-0	12	4.30	2	1-19/0-4(2-2-0)	3	0.1
Cin-N	93	385	64	111	20	3	0	58	28	....	11	....	.288	.340	.356	.696	88	-7	52	4.95	-6	0-93(0-0-93)	8	-1.6
1904 Cin-N	129	465	88	132	8	10	6	51	39	....	19	....	.284	.342	.383	.725	113	7	71	5.28	-6	*0-102(0-7-95),1-24	16	-0.4
1905 Cin-N	22	77	7	18	2	1	0	4	7	....	2	....	.234	.306	.286	.592	69	-3	8	3.32	-4	1-13/0-9(1-0-8)	1	-0.8
Bos-N	112	433	44	119	11	7	3	48	27	....	21	....	.275	.322	.353	.675	103	1	58	4.70	4	*0-111(0-0-111)/1-2,P-2	10	-0.3
Yr.	134	510	51	137	13	8	3	52	34	....	23	....	.269	.319	.343	.662	98	-2	66	4.48	0	*0-120(1-0-119),1-15/P-2	11	-1.1
1906 Bos-N	152	549	54	136	20	4	0	39	55	....	17	....	.248	.318	.299	.617	95	-2	61	3.72	1	*0-144(2-0-143)/2-7,P-2,1	11	-1.0
Total 9	830	3174	428	855	99	37	10	315	227	8	114	....	.269	.322	.333	.656	95	-19	397	4.37	-21	0-723/1-59,P-35,2-7	91	-7.2

• DOLAN, Cozy Albert J. Dolan b: 12/23/1889, Chicago, IL d: 12/10/1958, Chicago, IL BR/TR, 5'10", 160 lbs. Deb: 8/15/1909 C Career OF: 126-48-33

YEAR TM-L	G	AB	R	H	2B	3B	HR	RBI	BB	SO	SB	CS	AVG	OBP	SLG	OPS	OPS+	BR/A	RC	RC/G	FR	G/POS	WS	TPW
1909 Cin-N	3	6	2	1	0	0	0	0	2	....	0	....	.167	.375	.167	.542	69	-0	1	2.46	-1	/3-3	0	-0.1
1911 NY-A	19	69	19	21	1	2	0	6	8	....	12	....	.304	.385	.377	.761	106	1	14	7.63	-1	3-19	3	0.0
1912 NY-A	18	60	15	12	1	3	0	11	5	....	5	....	.200	.273	.317	.589	64	-3	7	3.31	-4	3-17	0	-0.6
Phi-N	11	50	8	14	2	2	0	7	1	10	3	....	.280	.294	.400	.694	83	-2	6	4.58	-1	3-11	1	-0.2
1913 Phi-N	55	126	15	33	4	0	0	8	1	21	9	....	.262	.273	.294	.567	59	-7	12	3.11	-6	0-12(8-0-4),S-10/2-9,3-4,1	1	-1.3
Pit-N	35	133	22	27	5	2	0	9	15	14	14	....	.203	.289	.271	.559	63	-6	13	3.13	1	3-35	2	-0.4
Yr.	90	259	37	60	9	2	0	17	16	35	23	....	.232	.282	.282	.563	61	-13	25	3.12	-4	3-39,0-12(8-0-4),S-10/2-9,1	3	-1.7
1914 StL-N	126	421	76	101	16	3	4	32	55	74	42	....	.240	.335	.321	.655	96	-0	57	4.37	-9	0-96(90-1-5),3-27	11	-1.3
1915 StL-N	111	322	53	90	14	9	2	38	34	37	17	11	.280	.356	.398	.753	127	10	49	4.95	-7	0-98(28-47-24)	12	-0.2
1922 NY-N	1	0	0	0	0	0	0	0	0	0	0	0	....	....	....	....	-99	0	0	....	0		0	0.0
Total 7	379	1187	210	299	43	21	6	111	121	156	102	11	.252	.328	.339	.666	96	-7	159	4.37	-27	0-206,3-116/S-10,2-9,1-1	30	-4.1

• DOLAN, Joe Joseph Dolan b: 2/24/1873, Baltimore, MD d: 3/24/1938, Omaha, NE TR, 5'10", 155 lbs. Deb: 8/11/1896

YEAR TM-L	G	AB	R	H	2B	3B	HR	RBI	BB	SO	SB	CS	AVG	OBP	SLG	OPS	OPS+	BR/A	RC	RC/G	FR	G/POS	WS	TPW
1896 Lou-N	44	165	14	35	2	1	3	18	9	12	6	....	.212	.253	.291	.544	45	-14	14	2.85	-1	S-44	1	-1.0
1897 Lou-N	36	133	10	28	2	2	0	7	8	....	6	....	.211	.271	.256	.526	41	-11	11	2.80	-9	2-18,S-18	0	-1.6
1899 Phi-N	61	222	27	57	6	3	1	30	11	....	3	....	.257	.298	.324	.622	73	-9	23	3.67	-3	2-61	3	-0.8
1900 Phi-N	74	257	39	51	7	3	1	27	16	....	10	....	.198	.259	.261	.520	44	-20	21	2.65	0	3-31,2-29,S-12	3	-1.6

YEAR TM-L	G	AB	R	H	2B	3B	HR	RBI	BB	SO	SB	CS	AVG	OBP	SLG	OPS	OPS+	BR/A	RC	RC/G	FR	G/POS	WS	TPW
1901 Phi-N	10	37	0	3	0	0	0	2	2	....	0	....	.081	.128	.081	.209	-38	-7	0	.31	1	2-10	0	-0.6
Phi-A	98	338	50	73	21	2	1	38	26	....	3	....	.216	.282	.299	.581	58	-20	31	3.01	3	S-61,3-35/2-1,O-1	6	-1.2
Total 5	323	1152	140	247	38	11	6	122	72	12	28	....	.214	.270	.282	.552	51	-80	101	2.90	-9	S-135,2-119/3-66,O-1	13	-6.8

• DOLAN, Tom Thomas J. Dolan b: 1/10/1859, New York, NY d: 1/16/1913, St. Louis, MO BR/TR, 5'11" Deb: 9/30/1879 U Career OF: 24-23-4

YEAR TM-L	G	AB	R	H	2B	3B	HR	RBI	BB	SO	SB	CS	AVG	OBP	SLG	OPS	OPS+	BR/A	RC	RC/G	FR	G/POS	WS	TPW
1879 Chi-N	1	4	0	0	0	0	0	0	0	2	....	....	.000	.000	.000	.000	-94	-1	0	.00	1	/C-1	0	0.0
1882 Buf-N	22	89	12	14	0	1	0	8	2	11	....	....	.157	.176	.180	.356	14	-8	3	1.06	-4	C-18/O-4(1-2-1),3-2	1	-1.0
1883 StL-a	81	295	32	63	9	2	1	18	9	....	....	....	.214	.237	.268	.505	59	-14	19	2.31	8	C-42,O-40(19-19-2)/P-1	6	-0.5
1884 StL-a	35	137	19	36	6	2	0	0	6	....	....	....	.263	.299	.336	.634	103	0	14	3.83	-4	C-34/O-2(1-1-0)	5	-0.1
StL-U	19	69	9	13	3	0	0	....	4	....	....	....	.188	.233	.232	.465	55	-3	4	1.91	2	C-14/3-3,O-2(0-1-1)	2	0.0
1885 StL-N	3	9	1	2	0	0	0	0	2	1	....	....	.222	.364	.222	.586	99	0	1	2.88	0	/C-3	0	0.1
1886 StL-N	15	44	8	11	3	0	0	1	7	9	2	....	.250	.353	.318	.671	112	1	6	4.74	6	C-15	1	0.7
Bal-a	38	125	13	19	3	2	0	12	8	....	8	....	.152	.203	.208	.411	30	-10	7	1.80	4	C-35/O-3(3-0-0)	1	-0.3
1888 StL-a	11	36	1	7	1	0	0	1	1	....	1	....	.194	.216	.222	.438	36	-3	2	1.86	-1	C-11	1	-0.2
Total 7	225	808	95	165	25	7	1	40	39	23	11	....	.204	.242	.256	.498	59	-38	56	2.38	12	C-173/O-51,3-5,P-1	17	-1.2

• DOLE, Lester Lester Carrington Dole b: 7/8/1855, Meriden, CT d: 12/10/1918, Concord, NH, 5'11" Deb: 5/27/1875 U

YEAR TM-L	G	AB	R	H	2B	3B	HR	RBI	BB	SO	SB	CS	AVG	OBP	SLG	OPS	OPS+	BR/A	RC	RC/G	FR	G/POS	WS	TPW
1875 NH-n	1	4	1	2	0	0	0	0	0	0	0	0	.500	.500	.500	1.000	285	1	1	15.12	0	/O-1	....	0.1

• DOLJACK, Frank Frank Joseph "Dolie" Doljack b: 10/5/1907, Cleveland, OH d: 1/23/1948, Cleveland, OH BR/TR, 5'11", 175 lbs. Deb: 9/4/1930 Career OF: 48-60-42

YEAR TM-L	G	AB	R	H	2B	3B	HR	RBI	BB	SO	SB	CS	AVG	OBP	SLG	OPS	OPS+	BR/A	RC	RC/G	FR	G/POS	WS	TPW
1930 Det-A	20	74	10	19	5	1	3	17	2	11	0	1	.257	.286	.473	.759	87	-2	9	4.43	0	O-20(0-4-16)	1	-0.3
1931 Det-A	63	187	20	52	13	3	4	20	15	17	3	2	.278	.335	.444	.779	100	-0	28	5.29	0	O-54(3-44-8)	5	-0.2
1932 Det-A	8	26	5	10	1	0	1	7	2	2	1	0	.385	.429	.538	.967	143	2	6	10.25	-0	/O-6(6-0-0)	1	0.2
1933 Det-A	42	147	18	42	5	2	0	22	14	13	2	6	.286	.348	.347	.695	83	-5	17	3.87	1	O-37(32-0-5)	2	-0.6
1934*Det-A	56	120	15	28	7	1	1	19	13	15	2	1	.233	.313	.333	.647	67	-6	13	3.69	0	O-30(6-12-12)/1-3	2	-0.7
1943 Cle-A	3	7	0	0	0	0	0	0	1	2	0	0	.000	.125	.000	.125	-66	-1	0	.13	0	/O-2(1-0-1)	0	-0.2
Total 6	192	561	68	151	31	7	9	85	47	60	8	10	.269	.329	.398	.726	86	-13	73	4.54	2	O-149/1-3	11	-1.7

• DOLL, Art Arthur James "Moose" Doll b: 5/7/1913, Chicago, IL d: 4/28/1978, Calumet City, IL BR/TR, 6'1", 190 lbs. Deb: 9/21/1935 ♦

YEAR TM-L	G	AB	R	H	2B	3B	HR	RBI	BB	SO	SB	CS	AVG	OBP	SLG	OPS	OPS+	BR/A	RC	RC/G	FR	G/POS	WS	TPW
1935 Bos-N	3	10	0	1	0	0	0	0	0	1	0	....	.100	.100	.100	.200	-50	-2	0	.31	0	/C-3	0	-0.2
1936 Bos-N	1	2	0	0	0	0	0	0	0	2	0	....	.000	.000	.000	.000	-107	-0	0	.00	0	/P-1	0	0.0
1938 Bos-N	3	1	0	1	0	0	0	0	0	0	0	....	1.000	1.000	1.000	2.000	501	1	1	∞	0	/P-3	1	0.1
Total 3	7	13	0	2	0	0	0	0	0	3	0	....	.154	.154	.154	.308	-16	-2	1	.25	0	/P-4,C-3	1	-0.1

• DONAHUE, Jiggs John Augustus Donahue b: 7/13/1879, Springfield, OH d: 7/19/1913, Columbus, OH BL/TL, 6'1", 178 lbs. Deb: 9/10/1900 Career OF: 1-0-1

YEAR TM-L	G	AB	R	H	2B	3B	HR	RBI	BB	SO	SB	CS	AVG	OBP	SLG	OPS	OPS+	BR/A	RC	RC/G	FR	G/POS	WS	TPW
1900 Pit-N	3	10	1	2	0	1	0	3	0	....	1	....	.200	.200	.400	.600	63	-1	1	3.40	-1	/C-2,O-1	0	-0.1
1901 Pit-N	2	0	0	0	0	0	0	0	0	....	0	....	....	....	....	....	-97	0	0	....	-1	/C-1,O-1	0	-0.1
Mil-A	37	107	10	34	5	4	0	16	10	....	4	....	.318	.387	.439	.826	135	5	20	7.28	-2	C-19,1-13	4	0.5
1902 StL-A	30	89	11	21	1	1	1	7	12	....	2	....	.236	.327	.303	.630	76	-2	10	3.79	-3	C-23/1-5	2	-0.3
1904 Chi-A	102	367	46	91	9	7	1	48	25	....	18	....	.248	.298	.319	.617	99	-1	43	3.91	4	*1-101	11	0.2
1905 Chi-A	149	533	71	153	22	4	1	76	44	....	32	....	.287	.346	.349	.695	126	16	81	5.25	4	*1-149	22	1.9
1906*Chi-A	154	556	70	143	17	7	1	57	48	....	36	....	.257	.320	.318	.638	103	2	74	4.37	6	*1-154	21	0.6
1907 Chi-A	157	609	75	158	16	4	0	68	28	....	27	....	.259	.295	.299	.594	93	-6	65	3.70	23	*1-157	17	1.5
1908 Chi-A	93	304	22	62	8	2	0	22	25	....	14	....	.204	.271	.243	.515	68	-10	24	2.47	8	1-83	6	-0.4
1909 Chi-A	2	4	0	0	0	0	0	2	1	....	0	....	.000	.200	.000	.200	-38	-1	0	.00	0	/1-2	0	-0.1
Was-A	84	283	13	67	12	1	0	28	22	....	9	....	.237	.294	.286	.580	87	-4	27	3.06	-6	1-81	5	-1.3
Yr.	86	287	13	67	12	1	0	30	23	....	9	....	.233	.293	.282	.575	85	-5	27	3.01	-6	1-83	5	-1.4
Total 9	813	2862	319	731	90	31	4	327	215	....	143	....	.255	.311	.313	.624	99	-0	345	4.05	33	1-745/C-45,O-2	88	2.5

• DONAHUE, Jim James Augustus Donahue b: 1/8/1862, Lockport, IL d: 4/19/1935, Lockport, IL BR/TR, 6', 175 lbs. Deb: 4/19/1886 U Career OF: 38-28-6

YEAR TM-L	G	AB	R	H	2B	3B	HR	RBI	BB	SO	SB	CS	AVG	OBP	SLG	OPS	OPS+	BR/A	RC	RC/G	FR	G/POS	WS	TPW
1886 NY-a	49	186	14	37	0	0	0	9	10	....	1	....	.199	.251	.199	.450	44	-11	10	1.77	-1	O-32(12-21-1),C-19	2	-1.1
1887 NY-a	60	241	33	83	4	1	1	29	21	....	6	....	.344	.350	.323	.673	92	-1	28	4.72	-2	C-51/O-5(0-2-3),1-4,2-1,3	6	0.0
1888 KC-a	88	337	29	79	11	3	1	28	21	....	12	....	.234	.281	.294	.575	79	-9	32	3.35	1	C-67,O-18(12-5-1)/3-5,2-1	7	-0.3
1889 KC-a	67	252	30	59	5	4	0	32	21	20	12	....	.234	.293	.286	.579	61	-14	25	3.46	-2	C-46,O-14(14-0-0),3-10	3	-1.0
1891 Col-a	77	280	27	61	4	3	0	35	31	18	2	....	.218	.298	.254	.552	62	-13	22	2.70	7	C-75/1-1,O-1	5	0.1
Total 5	341	1296	133	319	24	11	2	133	104	38	33	....	.246	.295	.275	.570	69	-48	117	3.21	3	C-258/O-70,3-16,1-5,2-2	23	-2.3

• DONAHUE, John John Frederick "Jiggs" Donahue b: 4/19/1894, Roxbury, MA d: 10/3/1949, Boston, MA BB/TR, 5'8", 170 lbs. Deb: 9/25/1923

YEAR TM-L	G	AB	R	H	2B	3B	HR	RBI	BB	SO	SB	CS	AVG	OBP	SLG	OPS	OPS+	BR/A	RC	RC/G	FR	G/POS	WS	TPW
1923 Bos-A	10	36	5	10	4	0	0	1	4	5	0	1	.278	.350	.389	.739	94	-1	5	4.36	3	/O-9(0-0-9)	1	0.2

• DONAHUE, Pat Patrick William Donahue b: 11/3/1884, Springfield, OH d: 1/31/1966, Springfield, OH BR/TR, 6', 175 lbs. Deb: 5/29/1908

YEAR TM-L	G	AB	R	H	2B	3B	HR	RBI	BB	SO	SB	CS	AVG	OBP	SLG	OPS	OPS+	BR/A	RC	RC/G	FR	G/POS	WS	TPW
1908 Bos-A	35	86	8	17	2	0	1	6	9	....	0	....	.198	.289	.256	.544	75	-2	6	2.34	2	C-32/1-3	3	0.2
1909 Bos-A	64	176	14	42	4	1	2	25	17	....	2	....	.239	.309	.307	.616	93	-1	18	3.25	-1	C-58	6	0.3
1910 Bos-A	2	4	0	0	0	0	0	0	0	....	0	....	.000	.000	.000	.000	-98	-1	0	.00	0	/C-1	0	-0.1
Phi-A	14	34	2	5	0	0	0	4	3	....	1	....	.147	.237	.147	.384	21	-3	2	1.43	3	C-13	0	0.1
Cle-A	2	6	0	1	0	0	0	0	0	....	0	....	.167	.167	.167	.333	4	-1	0	.78	0	/C-2,1-1	0	-0.1
Phi-A	1	1	0	0	0	0	0	0	0	....	0	....	.000	.000	.000	.000	-101	-0	0	.00	0	/C-1	1	0.0
Yr.	19	45	2	6	0	0	0	4	3	....	1	....	.133	.204	.133	.337	8	-5	2	1.19	3	C-17/1-1	1	-0.1
Total 3	118	307	24	65	6	1	3	35	29	....	3	....	.212	.288	.267	.555	75	-8	26	2.65	3	C-107/1-4	10	0.5

• DONAHUE, She Charles Michael Donahue b: 6/29/1877, Oswego, NY d: 8/28/1947, New York, NY BR/TR, 5'9" Deb: 4/29/1904

YEAR TM-L	G	AB	R	H	2B	3B	HR	RBI	BB	SO	SB	CS	AVG	OBP	SLG	OPS	OPS+	BR/A	RC	RC/G	FR	G/POS	WS	TPW
1904 StL-N	4	15	1	4	0	0	0	2	0	....	3	....	.267	.267	.267	.533	68	-1	2	4.52	-2	/2-3,S-1	0	-0.2
Phi-N	58	200	21	43	4	0	0	14	3	....	7	....	.215	.227	.235	.462	44	-14	13	2.09	-15	S-29,3-24/1-3,2-2	0	-2.8
Yr.	62	215	22	47	4	0	0	16	3	....	10	....	.219	.229	.237	.467	46	-14	15	2.24	-16	S-30,3-24/2-5,1-3	0	-3.0

• DONAHUE, Tim Timothy Cornelius "Bridget" Donahue b: 6/8/1870, Raynham, MA d: 6/12/1902, Taunton, MA BL/TR, 5'11", 180 lbs. Deb: 7/28/1891 U

YEAR TM-L	G	AB	R	H	2B	3B	HR	RBI	BB	SO	SB	CS	AVG	OBP	SLG	OPS	OPS+	BR/A	RC	RC/G	FR	G/POS	WS	TPW
1891 Bos-a	4	7	0	0	0	0	0	0	0	5	0	....	.000	.000	.000	.000	-101	-2	0	.00	0	/C-4	0	-0.2
1895 Chi-N	63	219	29	59	9	1	2	36	20	25	5	....	.269	.339	.347	.686	72	-10	29	4.73	-9	C-63	5	-1.0
1896 Chi-N	57	188	27	41	10	1	0	20	11	15	11	....	.218	.276	.282	.558	45	-16	19	3.26	-1	C-57	3	-0.9
1897 Chi-N	58	188	28	45	7	3	0	21	9	....	3	....	.239	.281	.309	.590	54	-13	18	3.26	3	C-55/S-2,1-1	3	-0.4
1898 Chi-N	122	396	52	87	12	3	0	39	49	....	17	....	.220	.318	.265	.583	68	-15	42	3.43	-10	*C-122	10	-1.2
1899 Chi-N	92	278	39	69	9	3	0	29	34	....	10	....	.248	.345	.302	.647	80	-6	35	4.19	-5	C-91/1-1	8	-0.2
1900 Chi-N	67	216	21	51	10	1	0	17	19	....	8	....	.236	.313	.292	.604	70	-8	24	3.65	-8	C-66/2-1	4	-1.0
1902 Was-A	3	8	0	2	0	0	0	1	0	....	0	....	.250	.250	.250	.500	39	-1	1	2.26	0	/C-3	0	0.0
Total 8	466	1500	196	354	57	12	2	163	142	45	54	....	.236	.314	.294	.608	66	-70	166	3.71	-30	C-461/1-2,S-2,2-1	33	-4.9

• DONALDSON, John John David Donaldson b: 5/5/1943, Charlotte, NC BL/TR, 5'11", 165 lbs. Deb: 8/26/1966

YEAR TM-L	G	AB	R	H	2B	3B	HR	RBI	BB	SO	SB	CS	AVG	OBP	SLG	OPS	OPS+	BR/A	RC	RC/G	FR	G/POS	WS	TPW
1966 KC-A	15	30	4	4	0	0	0	1	3	4	1	0	.133	.212	.133	.345	2	-3	1	1.20	-1	/2-9	0	-0.4
1967 KC-A	105	377	27	104	16	5	0	28	37	39	6	3	.276	.344	.345	.689	107	4	47	4.44	-3	*2-101/S-1	13	1.1
1968 Oak-A	127	363	37	80	9	2	2	27	45	44	5	5	.220	.310	.273	.582	82	-8	32	2.85	9	2-98/3-5,S-1	9	1.0
1969 Oak-A	12	13	1	1	0	0	0	0	2	4	0	0	.077	.200	.077	.277	-21	-2	0	.57	0	/2-1	0	-0.2
Sea-A	95	338	22	79	8	3	1	19	36	36	6	1	.234	.307	.284	.592	67	-13	32	3.16	-10	2-90/3-2,S-1	5	-1.8
Yr.	107	351	23	80	8	3	1	19	38	40	6	1	.228	.303	.276	.580	64	-15	32	3.05	-10	2-91/3-2,S-1	5	-2.0
1970 Oak-A	41	89	4	22	2	1	1	11	9	6	1	0	.247	.316	.326	.642	80	-2	9	3.43	4	2-21/S-6,3-1	2	0.3
1974 Oak-A	10	15	1	2	0	0	0	0	0	0	0	0	.133	.133	.133	.267	-25	-2	0	.55	0	/2-7,3-3	0	-0.2
Total 6	405	1225	96	292	35	11	4	86	132	133	19	9	.238	.314	.295	.609	81	-26	121	3.34	-2	2-327/3-11,S-9	29	-0.2

• DONDERO, Len Leonard Peter "Mike" Dondero b: 9/12/1903, Newark, CA d: 1/1/1999, Fremont, CA BR/TR, 5'11", 178 lbs. Deb: 4/21/1929

YEAR TM-L	G	AB	R	H	2B	3B	HR	RBI	BB	SO	SB	CS	AVG	OBP	SLG	OPS	OPS+	BR/A	RC	RC/G	FR	G/POS	WS	TPW
1929 StL-A	19	31	2	6	0	0	1	8	0	4	0	0	.194	.194	.290	.484	22	-4	2	1.66	-3	3-10/2-5	0	-0.6

• DONLIN, Mike Michael Joseph "Turkey Mike" Donlin
b: 5/30/1878, Peoria, IL d: 9/24/1933, Hollywood, CA BL/TL, 5'9", 170 lbs. Deb: 7/19/1899 U Career OF: 286-341-243

YEAR	TM-L	G	AB	R	H	2B	3B	HR	RBI	BB	SO	SB	CS	AVG	OBP	SLG	OPS	OPS+	BR/A	RC	RC/G	FR	G/POS	WS	TPW
1899	StL-N	66	266	49	86	9	6	6	27	17	....	20	....	.323	.366	.470	.836	126	8	55	7.92	-5	0-51(1-50-0),1-13/P-3,S-3	9	-0.7
1900	StL-N	78	276	40	90	8	6	10	48	14	....	14	....	.326	.361	.507	.868	139	13	57	7.92	-2	0-47(2-35-10),1-21	10	0.7
1901	Bal-A	121	476	107	162	23	13	5	67	53	....	33	....	.340	.409	.475	.883	138	26	109	8.99	3	0-74(73-1-0),1-47	21	2.1
1902	Cin-N	34	143	30	41	5	4	0	9	9	....	9	....	.287	.333	.378	.711	109	1	22	5.59	-1	0-32(30-0-2)/P-1,S-1	4	-0.1
1903	Cin-N	126	496	110	174	25	18	7	67	56	....	26	....	.351	.420	.516	.936	150	32	122	9.81	-3	*0-118(70-0-48)/1-7	24	2.2
1904	Cin-N	60	236	42	84	11	7	1	38	18	....	21	....	.356	.406	.475	.881	158	16	56	9.20	-2	0-53(52-0-1)/1-6	13	1.2
	NY-N	42	132	17	37	7	3	2	14	10	....	1	....	.280	.340	.424	.765	130	4	20	5.42	-1	0-37(23-11-3)	5	0.2
	Yr.	102	368	59	121	18	10	3	52	28	....	22	....	.329	.383	.457	.839	148	20	76	7.77	-3	0-90(75-11-4)/1-6	18	1.4
1905*	NY-N	150	606	**124**	216	31	16	7	80	56	....	33	....	.356	.413	.495	.908	166	49	142	9.18	-4	*0-150(4-147-0)	36	4.0
1906	NY-N	37	121	15	38	5	1	1	14	11	....	9	....	.314	.371	.397	.768	136	5	22	6.57	-2	0-29(0-29-0)/1-1	5	0.2
1908	NY-N	155	593	71	198	26	13	6	106	23	....	30	....	.334	.364	.452	.816	153	32	108	6.57	5	*0-155(29-0-127)	31	3.4
1911	NY-N	12	12	3	4	0	0	1	1	0	1	2	....	.333	.333	.583	.917	151	1	3	9.39	0	/0-3(0-2-1)	0	0.0
	Bos-N	56	222	33	70	16	1	2	34	22	17	7	....	.315	.377	.423	.800	115	4	38	6.27	-4	0-56(0-56-0)	7	-0.3
	Yr.	68	234	36	74	16	1	3	35	22	18	9	....	.316	.375	.432	.807	116	5	41	6.42	-4	0-59(0-58-1)	7	-0.3
1912	Pit-N	77	244	27	77	9	8	2	35	20	16	8	....	.316	.370	.443	.812	124	7	43	6.17	-1	0-62(2-10-51)	9	0.4
1914	NY-N	35	31	1	5	1	1	1	3	3	5	0	....	.161	.235	.355	.590	77	-1	2	2.39	0	....	0	-0.1
Total	**12**	**1049**	**3854**	**669**	**1282**	**176**	**97**	**51**	**543**	**312**	**39**	**213**	**....**	**.333**	**.386**	**.468**	**.854**	**143**	**197**	**799**	**7.85**	**-16**	**0-867/1-95,P-4,S-4**	**174**	**13.2**

• DONNELLY, Jim James B. Donnelly b: 7/19/1865, New Haven, CT d: 3/15/1915, New Haven, CT BR/TR, 5'10.5", 155 lbs. Deb: 8/11/1884 U

YEAR	TM-L	G	AB	R	H	2B	3B	HR	RBI	BB	SO	SB	CS	AVG	OBP	SLG	OPS	OPS+	BR/A	RC	RC/G	FR	G/POS	WS	TPW
1884	Ind-a	40	134	22	34	2	2	0	0	5	....	....	....	.254	.301	.299	.599	99	0	12	3.39	-4	3-24/S-8,0-6(2-2-2),2-2	3	-0.3
1885	Det-N	56	211	24	49	4	3	1	22	10	29	....	....	.232	.267	.294	.561	81	-4	17	2.83	-3	3-56/1-1	3	-0.6
1886	KC-N	113	438	51	88	11	3	0	38	36	57	16	....	.201	.262	.240	.501	50	-27	32	2.50	-11	*3-113	3	-3.2
1887	Was-N	117	441	51	101	9	6	1	46	16	26	42	....	.229	.234	.256	.491	38	-35	36	2.83	12	*3-115/S-2	5	-1.7
1888	Was-N	122	428	43	86	9	4	0	23	20	16	44	....	.201	.242	.241	.482	57	-19	36	2.87	-3	*3-117/S-5	7	-1.9
1889	Was-N	4	13	3	2	0	0	0	0	2	0	1	....	.154	.267	.154	.421	20	-1	1	1.98	-1	/3-4	0	-0.2
1890	StL-a	11	42	11	14	0	0	0	3	8	....	5	....	.333	.451	.333	.784	115	1	9	8.31	-2	3-11	1	0.0
1891	Col-a	17	54	6	13	0	0	0	9	13	5	7	....	.241	.388	.241	.629	85	0	8	5.14	1	3-17	2	0.2
1896	Bal-N	106	396	70	130	14	10	0	71	34	11	38	....	.328	.387	.414	.801	110	6	82	7.61	4	*3-106	14	1.0
1897	Pit-N	44	161	22	31	4	0	0	14	16	....	14	....	.193	.270	.217	.487	31	-16	14	2.77	1	3-44	1	-1.2
	NY-N	23	85	19	16	3	0	0	11	9	....	6	....	.188	.266	.224	.489	31	-8	7	2.63	-3	3-23	0	-1.0
	Yr.	67	246	41	47	7	0	0	25	25	....	20	....	.191	.268	.220	.488	31	-24	21	2.72	-2	3-67	1	-2.1
1898	StL-N	1	1	0	1	0	0	0	0	0	....	0	....	1.000	1.000	1.000	2.000	463	0	1	∞	0	/3-1	0	0.0
Total	**11**	**654**	**2404**	**322**	**565**	**56**	**28**	**2**	**237**	**169**	**144**	**173**	**....**	**.235**	**.285**	**.279**	**.565**	**65**	**-102**	**256**	**3.66**	**-8**	**3-631/S-15,0-6,2-2,1-1**	**39**	**-8.8**

• DONNELLY, Jim James J. Donnelly b: Boston, MA, 155 lbs. Deb: 7/11/1884

YEAR	TM-L	G	AB	R	H	2B	3B	HR	RBI	BB	SO	SB	CS	AVG	OBP	SLG	OPS	OPS+	BR/A	RC	RC/G	FR	G/POS	WS	TPW
1884	KC-U	6	23	2	3	1	0	0	....	1	....	....	....	.130	.167	.174	.341	18	-2	1	.96	-4	/3-5,C-1	0	-0.4

• DONNELLY, John John Donnelly NA OF: 0-6-3

YEAR	TM-L	G	AB	R	H	2B	3B	HR	RBI	BB	SO	SB	CS	AVG	OBP	SLG	OPS	OPS+	BR/A	RC	RC/G	FR	G/POS	WS	TPW
1873	Was-n	30	137	15	35	1	0	0	20	1	0	0	0	.255	.261	.263	.524	58	-6	10	2.88	-2	S-13,2-12/0-6(0-6-0),3-1	....	-0.6
1874	Phi-n	6	22	2	5	0	0	0	2	0	0	0	0	.227	.227	.227	.455	45	-1	1	2.06	-2	/0-3(0-0-3),S-2,2-1	....	-0.2
Total	**2 n**	**36**	**159**	**17**	**40**	**1**	**0**	**0**	**22**	**1**	**0**	**0**	**0**	**.252**	**.256**	**.258**	**.514**	**56**	**-8**	**11**	**2.76**	**-3**	**/S-15,2-13,0-9,3-1**	**....**	**-0.9**

• DONNELLY, Pete Peter J. Donnelly b: 10/8/1849, Philadelphia, PA d: 10/1/1890, Jersey City, NJ Deb: 5/13/1871

YEAR	TM-L	G	AB	R	H	2B	3B	HR	RBI	BB	SO	SB	CS	AVG	OBP	SLG	OPS	OPS+	BR/A	RC	RC/G	FR	G/POS	WS	TPW
1871	Kek-n	9	34	7	7	1	1	0	3	1	2	0	0	.206	.229	.294	.523	48	-3	2	2.73	-4	/0-9(2-1-6),3-2	....	-0.4

• DONNELS, Chris Chris Barton Donnels b: 4/21/1966, Los Angeles, CA BL/TR, 6', 185 lbs. Deb: 5/7/1991

YEAR	TM-L	G	AB	R	H	2B	3B	HR	RBI	BB	SO	SB	CS	AVG	OBP	SLG	OPS	OPS+	BR/A	RC	RC/G	FR	G/POS	WS	TPW
1991	NY-N	37	89	7	20	2	0	0	5	14	19	1	1	.225	.330	.247	.577	65	-4	8	3.19	0	1-15,3-11	1	-0.4
1992	NY-N	45	121	8	21	4	0	0	6	17	25	1	0	.174	.275	.207	.482	39	-9	8	2.15	-4	3-29,2-12	1	-1.3
1993	Hou-N	88	179	18	46	14	2	2	24	19	33	2	0	.257	.328	.391	.719	95	-1	23	4.37	1	3-31,1-23/2-1	4	-0.2
1994	Hou-N	54	86	12	23	5	0	3	5	13	18	1	0	.267	.364	.430	.794	112	2	14	6.10	0	3-14/1-4,2-4	2	0.2
1995	Hou-N	19	30	4	9	0	0	0	2	3	6	0	0	.300	.364	.300	.664	83	-1	3	3.79	-1	/3-9,2-1	0	-0.2
	Bos-A	40	91	13	23	2	2	2	11	9	18	0	0	.253	.320	.385	.705	80	-3	12	4.48	-1	3-27/1-8,2-3	1	-0.4
2000	LA-N	27	34	8	10	3	0	4	9	6	7	0	0	.294	.400	.735	1.135	190	5	9	8.20	-1	/0-6(6-0-0),1-4,3-2,2-1	2	0.3
2001	LA-N	66	88	8	15	2	0	3	8	12	25	0	0	.170	.277	.295	.573	52	-6	7	2.67	0	3-14/1-7,P-1	0	-0.6
2002*	Ari-N	74	80	5	19	4	1	3	16	10	14	0	0	.238	.322	.425	.747	87	-2	11	4.50	-2	3-26/1-1	2	-0.3
Total	**8**	**450**	**798**	**83**	**186**	**36**	**5**	**17**	**86**	**103**	**165**	**5**	**1**	**.233**	**.322**	**.355**	**.676**	**81**	**-18**	**95**	**4.03**	**-8**	**3-163/1-62,2-22,0-6,P-1**	**13**	**-2.9**

• DONOHUE, Joe Joseph F. Donohue b: 1869, Altoona, PA Deb: 8/24/1891

YEAR	TM-L	G	AB	R	H	2B	3B	HR	RBI	BB	SO	SB	CS	AVG	OBP	SLG	OPS	OPS+	BR/A	RC	RC/G	FR	G/POS	WS	TPW
1891	Phi-N	6	22	2	7	1	0	0	2	1	3	0	....	.318	.375	.364	.739	112	0	3	5.54	-1	/0-4(0-4-0),S-2	1	0.0

• DONOHUE, Tom Thomas James Donohue b: 11/15/1952, Mineola, NY BR/TR, 6', 185 lbs. Deb: 4/6/1979

YEAR	TM-L	G	AB	R	H	2B	3B	HR	RBI	BB	SO	SB	CS	AVG	OBP	SLG	OPS	OPS+	BR/A	RC	RC/G	FR	G/POS	WS	TPW
1979	Cal-A	38	107	13	24	3	1	3	14	3	29	2	0	.224	.259	.355	.614	66	-5	10	3.22	-1	C-38	2	-0.5
1980	Cal-A	84	218	18	41	4	1	2	14	7	63	5	1	.188	.217	.243	.460	26	-22	12	1.85	-1	C-84	2	-1.9
Total	**2**	**122**	**325**	**31**	**65**	**7**	**2**	**5**	**28**	**10**	**92**	**7**	**1**	**.200**	**.231**	**.280**	**.511**	**39**	**-27**	**23**	**2.29**	**-2**	**C-122**	**4**	**-2.4**

• DONOVAN, Bill William Edward "Wild Bill" Donovan
b: 10/13/1876, Lawrence, MA d: 12/9/1923, Forsyth, NY BR/TR, 5'11", 190 lbs. Deb: 4/22/1898 M/U Career OF: 17-8-12 ♦

YEAR	TM-L	G	AB	R	H	2B	3B	HR	RBI	BB	SO	SB	CS	AVG	OBP	SLG	OPS	OPS+	BR/A	RC	RC/G	FR	G/POS	WS	TPW
1898	Was-N	39	103	11	17	2	2	2	8	4	....	2	....	.165	.211	.282	.493	41	-6	7	2.07	-1	0-20(6-6-8),P-17/2-1,S-1	2	-1.1
1899	Bro-N	5	13	2	3	1	0	0	0	0	....	0	....	.231	.231	.308	.538	46	-0	1	2.51	0	/P-5	1	-0.1
1900	Bro-N	5	13	0	0	0	0	0	2	0	....	0	....	.000	.000	.000	.000	-94	-2	0	.00	1	/P-5	0	-1.1
1901	Bro-N	46	135	16	23	3	0	2	13	8	....	1	....	.170	.217	.237	.454	31	-1	8	1.81	-1	P-45	27	1.9
1902	Bro-N	48	161	16	28	3	2	1	16	9	....	7	....	.174	.227	.236	.463	43	-3	11	2.10	2	P-35/1-8,0-4(2-0-2),2-1	18	-0.3
1903	Det-A	40	124	11	30	3	2	0	12	4	....	3	....	.242	.266	.298	.564	71	4	12	3.05	-2	P-35/S-2,2-1,0-1	22	2.7
1904	Det-A	46	140	12	38	2	1	1	6	3	....	2	....	.271	.287	.321	.608	95	5	14	3.56	-2	P-34/1-8,0-1	19	0.3
1905	Det-A	44	130	16	25	4	0	0	5	12	....	8	....	.192	.266	.223	.489	55	1	12	2.61	-1	P-34/0-8(5-0-0),2-2	20	0.4
1906	Det-A	28	91	5	11	0	1	0	0	1	....	6	....	.121	.130	.143	.273	-14	-6	3	.89	-2	P-25/2-3,0-1	11	-1.8
1907*	Det-A	37	109	20	29	7	2	0	19	6	....	4	....	.266	.304	.367	.671	110	7	14	4.46	-5	P-32	23	2.2
1908*	Det-A	30	82	5	13	1	0	0	2	10	....	2	....	.159	.250	.171	.421	36	0	4	1.46	-6	P-29	18	1.5
1909*	Det-A	22	45	6	9	0	0	0	1	2	....	0	....	.200	.250	.200	.450	41	1	3	1.72	-2	P-21	10	0.4
1910	Det-A	26	69	6	10	1	0	0	2	5	....	0	....	.145	.203	.159	.362	13	-2	2	.98	-6	P-26	15	0.3
1911	Det-A	24	60	11	12	3	1	1	6	11	....	1	....	.200	.324	.333	.657	79	4	7	3.58	-4	P-20	14	0.8
1912	Det-A	6	13	3	1	0	0	0	0	1	....	0	....	.077	.143	.077	.220	-38	-2	0	.28	-1	/P-3,1-2,0-2(0-0-2)	1	0.0
1915	NY-A	10	12	1	1	0	0	0	0	1	6	0	....	.083	.154	.083	.237	-29	-1	0	.37	-1	/P-9	0	-0.9
1916	NY-A	1	0	0	0	0	0	0	0	0	0	0	0	....	....	....	....	-98	0	0	....	0	/P-1	0	0.0
1918	Det-A	2	2	1	1	0	0	0	1	0	0	0	....	.500	.500	.500	1.000	210	0	0	12.24	0	/P-2	1	0.2
Total	**18**	**459**	**1302**	**142**	**251**	**30**	**11**	**7**	**93**	**77**	**6**	**36**	**0**	**.193**	**.241**	**.249**	**.490**	**50**	**-3**	**98**	**2.34**	**-33**	**P-378/0-37,1-18,2-8,S-3**	**202**	**5.4**

• DONOVAN, Fred Frederick Maurice Donovan b: 7/4/1864, Auburn, NH d: 3/7/1916, Springfield, IL BR/TR Deb: 6/23/1895

YEAR	TM-L	G	AB	R	H	2B	3B	HR	RBI	BB	SO	SB	CS	AVG	OBP	SLG	OPS	OPS+	BR/A	RC	RC/G	FR	G/POS	WS	TPW
1895	Cle-N	3	12	1	1	0	0	0	1	1	2	0	....	.083	.154	.083	.237	-36	-3	0	.39	-1	/C-3	0	-0.3

• DONOVAN, Jerry Jeremiah Francis Donovan b: 9/3/1876, Lock Haven, PA d: 6/27/1938, St. Petersburg, FL BR/TR Deb: 4/12/1906

YEAR	TM-L	G	AB	R	H	2B	3B	HR	RBI	BB	SO	SB	CS	AVG	OBP	SLG	OPS	OPS+	BR/A	RC	RC/G	FR	G/POS	WS	TPW
1906	Phi-N	61	166	11	33	4	0	0	15	6	....	2	....	.199	.236	.223	.459	43	-11	10	1.87	-5	C-53/0-1,S-1	1	-1.2

• DONOVAN, Mike Michael Berchman Donovan b: 10/18/1881, Brooklyn, NY d: 2/3/1938, New York, NY BR/TR, 5'8", 155 lbs. Deb: 5/29/1904

YEAR	TM-L	G	AB	R	H	2B	3B	HR	RBI	BB	SO	SB	CS	AVG	OBP	SLG	OPS	OPS+	BR/A	RC	RC/G	FR	G/POS	WS	TPW
1904	Cle-A	2	2	0	0	0	0	0	0	0	....	0	....	.000	.000	.000	.000	-101	-0	0	.00	-1	/S-1	0	-0.1
1908	NY-A	5	19	2	5	1	0	0	2	0	....	0	....	.263	.263	.316	.579	87	-0	1	2.78	1	/3-5	0	0.1
Total	**2**	**7**	**21**	**2**	**5**	**1**	**0**	**0**	**2**	**0**	**....**	**0**	**....**	**.238**	**.238**	**.286**	**.524**	**69**	**-1**	**1**	**2.43**	**0**	**/3-5,S-1**	**0**	**0.0**

YEAR TM-L	G	AB	R	H	2B	3B	HR	RBI	BB	SO	SB	CS	AVG	OBP	SLG	OPS	OPS+	BR/A	RC	RC/G	FR	G/POS	WS	TPW
• DONOVAN, Patsy	Patrick Joseph Donovan b: 3/16/1865, Queenstown, Ireland d: 12/25/1953, Lawrence, MA BL/TL, 5'11.5", 175 lbs. Deb: 4/19/1890 M Career OF: 121-74-1620																							
1890 Bos-N	32	140	17	36	0	0	0	9	8	17	10	....	.257	.307	.257	.564	60	-7	14	3.68	-5	O-32(0-32-0)	2	-1.2
*Bro-N	28	105	17	23	5	1	0	8	5	5	3	....	.219	.268	.286	.554	61	-6	9	2.93	1	O-28(1-24-3)	2	-0.5
Yr.	60	245	34	59	5	1	0	17	13	22	13	....	.241	.290	.269	.559	60	-13	24	3.35	-4	O-60(1-56-3)	4	-1.7
1891 Lou-a	105	439	73	141	10	3	2	53	30	18	27	....	.321	.375	.371	.747	115	8	73	6.50	2	*O-105(105-0-0)	14	0.5
Was-a	17	70	9	14	1	0	0	3	4	5	1	....	.200	.243	.214	.458	32	-6	4	1.89	-2	O-17(0-13-4)	0	-0.7
Yr.	122	509	82	155	11	3	2	56	34	23	28	....	.305	.358	.350	.707	104	2	77	5.77	0	*O-122(105-13-4)	14	-0.2
1892 Was-N	40	163	29	39	3	3	0	12	11	13	16	....	.239	.295	.294	.590	81	-4	19	4.22	1	O-40(14-0-26)	3	-0.5
Pit-N	90	388	77	114	15	3	2	26	20	16	40	....	.294	.333	.363	.697	110	3	62	6.09	1	O-90(1-1-90)	16	0.0
Yr.	130	551	106	153	18	6	2	38	31	29	56	....	.278	.322	.343	.665	101	-1	81	5.51	2	*O-130(15-1-116)	19	-0.5
1893 Pit-N	113	499	114	158	5	8	2	56	42	8	46	....	.317	.373	.371	.744	100	0	88	6.87	2	*O-112(0-0-112)	14	-0.3
1894 Pit-N	133	577	147	175	21	10	4	76	36	12	41	....	.303	.350	.395	.745	80	-20	96	6.23	7	*O-132(0-0-132)	10	-1.5
1895 Pit-N	126	522	115	162	18	6	1	58	48	19	36	....	.310	.377	.374	.751	99	2	90	6.64	-1	*O-125(0-1-124)	15	-0.4
1896 Pit-N	131	573	113	183	20	5	3	59	35	18	48	....	.319	.370	.387	.757	104	4	103	6.91	5	*O-131(0-0-131)	17	0.2
1897 Pit-N	120	479	82	154	16	7	0	57	25	....	34	....	.322	.360	.384	.744	100	0	81	6.46	-3	*O-120(0-0-120)	13	-0.8
1898 Pit-N	147	610	112	184	16	9	0	37	34	....	41	....	.302	.346	.357	.703	104	2	93	5.65	1	*O-147(0-0-147)	19	-0.5
1899 Pit-N	122	536	82	156	11	7	1	56	17	....	26	....	.291	.319	.343	.662	82	-15	70	4.75	-11	*O-121(0-1-120)	9	-2.9
1900 StL-N	126	503	78	159	11	1	0	61	38	....	**45**	....	.316	.368	.342	.710	97	-1	83	6.25	-7	*O-124(0-0-124)	13	-1.2
1901 StL-N	130	531	92	161	23	5	1	73	27	....	28	....	.303	.344	.371	.715	113	8	81	5.59	5	*O-129(0-0-129)	17	0.8
1902 StL-N	126	502	70	158	12	4	0	35	28	....	34	....	.315	.363	.355	.718	127	16	80	5.99	11	*O-126(0-0-126)	21	2.2
1903 StL-N	105	410	63	134	15	3	0	39	25	....	25	....	.327	.370	.378	.748	117	9	70	6.39	4	*O-105(0-0-105)	13	0.8
1904 Was-A	125	436	30	100	6	0	0	19	24	....	17	....	.229	.271	.243	.514	64	-17	36	2.73	4	*O-122(0-2-120)	3	-2.1
1906 Bro-N	7	21	1	5	0	0	0	0	0	....	0	....	.238	.238	.238	.476	53	-1	1	1.98	0	/O-6(0-0-6)	0	-0.2
1907 Bro-N	1	1	0	0	0	0	0	0	0	....	0	....	.000	.000	.000	.000	-109	-0	0	.00	0	/O-1	0	0.0
Total 17	1824	7505	1321	2256	208	75	16	737	457	131	518	....	.301	.348	.355	.702	98	-23	1155	5.73	16	*O-1813	201	-8.4
• DONOVAN, Tom	Thomas Joseph Donovan b: 1/1/1873, West Troy, NY d: 3/25/1933, Watervliet, NY BR/TR, 6'2", 168 lbs. Deb: 9/10/1901																							
1901 Cle-A	18	71	9	18	3	1	0	5	0	....	1	....	.254	.254	.324	.577	62	-4	6	3.11	0	O-18(0-0-18)/P-1	0	-0.5
• DOOIN, Red	Charles Sebastian Dooin b: 6/12/1879, Cincinnati, OH d: 5/12/1952, Rochester, NY BR/TR, 5'9.5", 165 lbs. Deb: 4/18/1902 M/U Career OF: 11-3-2																							
1902 Phi-N	94	333	20	77	7	3	0	35	10	....	8	....	.231	.262	.270	.533	64	-15	27	2.74	0	C-84/O-6(6-0-0)	4	-0.6
1903 Phi-N	62	188	18	41	5	1	0	14	8	....	9	....	.218	.254	.255	.509	47	-13	15	2.68	2	C-51/1-1,O-1	2	-0.6
1904 Phi-N	108	355	41	86	11	4	6	36	8	....	15	....	.242	.261	.346	.607	90	-6	37	3.56	6	C-96/1-4,O-3(1-2-0),3-1	8	1.0
1905 Phi-N	113	380	45	95	13	5	0	36	10	....	12	....	.250	.269	.311	.580	75	-13	37	3.26	6	*C-107/3-1	10	0.4
1906 Phi-N	113	351	25	86	19	1	0	32	13	....	15	....	.245	.274	.305	.579	80	-10	35	3.34	-10	*C-107	6	-1.0
1907 Phi-N	101	313	18	66	8	4	0	14	15	....	10	....	.211	.252	.262	.513	62	-15	24	2.51	3	C-94/2-1,O-1	8	-0.3
1908 Phi-N	133	435	28	108	17	4	0	41	17	....	20	....	.248	.283	.306	.589	85	-9	43	3.27	11	*C-132	16	1.8
1909 Phi-N	141	468	42	105	14	1	2	38	21	....	14	....	.224	.264	.271	.535	65	-20	37	2.55	3	*C-140	9	-0.4
1910 Phi-N	103	331	30	80	13	4	0	30	22	17	10	....	.242	.289	.305	.594	71	-13	31	3.18	-6	C-91/O-3(1-1-1)	7	-1.1
1911 Phi-N	74	247	18	81	15	1	1	16	14	12	6	....	.328	.366	.409	.775	115	4	39	5.85	-2	C-74	11	0.9
1912 Phi-N	69	184	20	43	9	0	0	22	5	12	8	....	.234	.262	.283	.544	46	-14	15	2.69	-1	C-58	3	-1.1
1913 Phi-N	55	129	6	33	4	1	0	13	3	9	1	....	.256	.273	.302	.575	61	-7	10	2.70	0	C-50	3	-0.4
1914 Phi-N	53	118	10	21	2	0	1	8	4	14	4	....	.178	.205	.220	.425	25	-11	6	1.53	2	C-40/O-2(2-0-0)	2	-0.7
1915 Cin-N	10	31	2	10	0	0	0	0	2	5	1	....	.323	.364	.323	.686	106	0	4	4.98	-2	C-10	1	-0.2
NY-N	46	124	9	27	2	2	0	9	3	15	0	2	.218	.236	.266	.502	55	-8	8	1.98	-1	C-46	1	-0.7
Yr.	56	155	11	37	2	2	0	9	5	20	1	2	.239	.263	.277	.540	66	-8	11	2.49	-4	C-56	2	-0.9
1916 NY-N	15	17	1	2	0	0	0	0	0	3	0	....	.118	.118	.118	.235	-29	-3	0	.41	-1	C-15	0	-0.4
Total 15	1290	4004	333	961	139	31	10	344	155	87	133	2	.240	.272	.298	.570	72	-153	370	3.07	10	*C-1195/O-16,1-5,3-2,2-1	91	-3.4
• DOOLAN, Mickey	Michael Joseph "Doc" Doolan b: 5/7/1880, Ashland, PA d: 11/1/1951, Orlando, FL BR/TR, 5'10.5", 170 lbs. Deb: 4/14/1905 C																							
1905 Phi-N	136	492	53	125	27	11	1	48	24	....	17	....	.254	.292	.360	.651	97	-4	59	4.08	3	*S-135	17	0.4
1906 Phi-N	154	535	41	123	19	7	1	55	27	....	16	....	.230	.270	.297	.567	77	-17	51	3.04	26	*S-154	15	1.6
1907 Phi-N	145	509	33	104	19	7	1	47	25	....	18	....	.204	.243	.275	.518	63	-24	40	2.53	19	*S-145	12	0.0
1908 Phi-N	129	445	29	104	25	4	2	49	17	....	5	....	.234	.267	.321	.588	85	-10	39	2.85	-1	*S-129	11	-0.7
1909 Phi-N	147	493	39	108	12	10	1	35	37	....	10	....	.219	.276	.290	.566	75	-15	43	2.74	19	*S-147	13	1.0
1910 Phi-N	148	536	58	141	31	6	2	57	35	56	16	....	.263	.315	.354	.670	92	-7	64	4.09	23	*S-148	22	2.2
1911 Phi-N	146	512	51	122	23	6	1	49	44	65	14	....	.238	.301	.313	.614	71	-21	52	3.35	18	*S-145	15	0.7
1912 Phi-N	146	532	47	137	26	6	1	62	34	59	6	....	.258	.305	.335	.639	70	-24	56	3.45	5	*S-146	13	-0.8
1913 Phi-N	151	518	32	113	12	6	1	43	29	68	17	....	.218	.262	.270	.533	50	-35	40	2.41	13	*S-148/2-3	9	-1.2
1914 Bal-F	145	486	58	119	23	6	1	53	40	47	30	....	.245	.311	.323	.634	81	-12	57	3.71	16	*S-145	18	1.5
1915 Bal-F	119	404	41	75	13	7	2	21	24	39	10	....	.186	.238	.267	.506	45	-29	28	2.09	23	*S-119	7	0.3
Chi-F	24	86	9	23	1	1	0	9	2	7	5	....	.267	.292	.302	.594	79	-3	9	3.41	2	S-24	2	0.2
Yr.	143	490	50	98	14	8	2	30	26	46	15	....	.200	.248	.273	.521	51	-32	37	2.30	25	*S-143	9	0.4
1916 Chi-N	28	70	4	15	2	1	0	5	8	7	0	....	.214	.295	.271	.566	67	-2	6	2.77	-4	S-24	1	-0.6
NY-N	18	51	4	12	3	1	1	3	2	4	1	....	.235	.264	.392	.656	106	-0	6	3.62	1	S-16/2-2	2	0.2
Yr.	46	121	8	27	5	2	1	8	10	11	1	....	.223	.282	.322	.605	83	-2	12	3.12	-3	S-40/2-2	3	-0.4
1918 Bro-N	92	308	14	55	8	2	0	18	22	24	8	....	.179	.233	.218	.451	38	-23	18	1.71	8	2-91	4	-1.5
Total 13	1728	5977	513	1376	244	81	15	554	370	376	173	....	.230	.279	.306	.585	72	-224	569	3.05	170	*S-1625/2-96	161	3.3
• DOOMS, Harry	Henry E. "Jack" Dooms b: 1/30/1867, St. Louis, MO d: 12/14/1899, St. Louis, MO Deb: 8/7/1892																							
1892 Lou-N	1	4	0	0	0	0	0	0	1	3	0	....	.000	.200	.000	.200	-42	-1	0	.00	0	/O-1	0	-0.1
• DORAN, Bill	William James Doran b: 6/14/1898, San Francisco, CA d: 3/9/1978, Santa Monica, CA BL/TR, 5'11.5", 175 lbs. Deb: 6/23/1922																							
1922 Cle-A	3	2	0	1	0	0	0	0	1	0	0	0	.500	.667	.500	1.167	206	1	1	21.37	-1	/3-2	0	0.0
• DORAN, Bill	William Donald Doran b: 5/28/1958, Cincinnati, OH BB/TR, 5'11", 175 lbs. Deb: 9/6/1982																							
1982 Hou-N	26	97	11	27	3	0	0	6	4	11	5	0	.278	.307	.309	.616	79	-2	10	3.95	-1	2-26	3	-0.1
1983 Hou-N	154	535	70	145	12	7	8	39	86	67	12	12	.271	.372	.364	.736	112	9	76	4.94	6	*2-153	22	2.5
1984 Hou-N	147	548	92	143	18	11	4	41	66	69	21	12	.261	.343	.356	.698	104	3	70	4.36	6	*2-139,S-13	18	1.8
1985 Hou-N	148	578	84	166	31	6	14	59	71	69	23	15	.287	.365	.434	.799	126	19	92	5.56	9	*2-147	28	3.8
1986*Hou-N	145	550	92	152	29	3	6	37	81	57	42	19	.276	.371	.373	.744	109	10	81	4.99	-13	*2-144	19	0.5
1987 Hou-N	162	625	82	177	23	3	16	79	82	64	31	11	.283	.369	.406	.775	109	12	99	5.57	-5	*2-162/S-3	24	1.5
1988 Hou-N	132	480	66	119	18	1	7	53	65	60	17	4	.248	.339	.333	.672	97	2	59	4.24	3	*2-130	19	1.0
1989 Hou-N	142	507	65	111	25	2	8	58	59	63	22	3	.219	.303	.323	.626	82	-8	54	3.56	-6	*2-138	17	-1.1
1990 Hou-N	109	344	49	99	21	2	6	32	71	53	18	9	.288	.410	.413	.822	131	18	65	6.72	3	2-99	18	2.4
Cin-N	17	59	10	22	8	0	1	5	8	5	5	0	.373	.448	.559	1.007	168	7	16	11.51	1	2-12/3-4	3	0.8
Yr.	126	403	59	121	29	2	7	37	79	58	23	9	.300	.415	.434	.849	136	25	81	7.33	4	*2-111/3-4	21	3.3
1991 Cin-N	111	361	51	101	12	2	6	35	46	39	5	4	.280	.361	.374	.735	103	2	51	5.10	-4	2-88/O-6(6-0-0),1-4	9	0.0
1992 Cin-N	132	387	48	91	16	2	8	47	64	40	7	4	.235	.344	.349	.693	94	-1	48	4.08	-7	*2-104,1-25	12	-0.7
1993 Mil-A	28	60	7	13	4	0	0	6	6	3	1	0	.217	.288	.283	.571	55	-4	5	2.45	-1	2-17/1-4	1	-0.4
Total 12	1453	5131	727	1366	220	39	84	497	709	600	209	93	.266	.356	.373	.730	106	68	726	4.89	-9	*2-1359/1-33,S-16,O-6,3-4	193	11.9
• DORAN, Tom	Thomas J. "Long Tom" Doran b: 12/2/1880, Westchester County, NY d: 6/22/1910, New York, NY BL/TR, 5'11", 152 lbs. Deb: 4/19/1904																							
1904 Bos-A	12	32	1	4	0	1	0	0	4	....	1	....	.125	.243	.188	.431	35	-2	2	1.72	-3	C-11	0	-0.5
1905 Bos-A	3	3	0	0	0	0	0	0	0	....	0	....	.000	.000	.000	.000	-99	-1	0	.00	0	/C-1	0	-0.1
Det-A	34	94	8	15	3	0	0	4	8	....	2	....	.160	.248	.191	.439	40	-6	6	1.83	0	C-32	1	-0.4
Yr.	37	97	8	15	3	0	0	4	8	....	2	....	.155	.241	.186	.426	36	-7	6	1.76	0	C-33	1	-0.5
1906 Bos-A	2	3	1	0	0	0	0	0	0	....	0	....	.000	.000	.000	.000	-100	-1	0	.00	0	/C-2	0	-0.1
Total 3	51	132	10	19	3	1	0	4	12	....	3	....	.144	.236	.182	.418	33	-10	8	1.71	-3	/C-46	1	-1.0

YEAR	TM-L	G	AB	R	H	2B	3B	HR	RBI	BB	SO	SB	CS	AVG	OBP	SLG	OPS	OPS+	BR/A	RC	RC/G	FR	G/POS	WS	TPW
• DORGAN, Jerry	Jeremiah F. Dorgan b: 1856, Meriden, CT d: 6/10/1891, New Haven, CT BL/TR, 165 lbs. Deb: 7/8/1880 Career OF: 1-2-96																								
1880	Wor-N	10	35	2	7	1	0	0	1	0	1	....	....	.200	.200	.229	.429	41	-2	2	1.61	-2	/0-9(0-0-9),C-1	0	-0.4
1882	Phi-a	44	181	25	51	9	1	0	24	4	....	....	....	.282	.297	.343	.640	103	-0	19	4.07	-2	C-25,0-22(1-1-20)/3-1	7	-0.1
1884	Ind-a	34	141	22	42	6	1	0	0	2	....	....	....	.298	.317	.355	.672	122	3	16	4.52	-3	0-29(0-0-29)/C-5	4	0.0
	Bro-a	4	13	2	4	0	0	0	0	0	....	....	....	.308	.308	.308	.615	101	-0	1	3.85	1	/C-4	0	0.1
	Yr.	38	154	24	46	6	1	0	0	2	....	....	....	.299	.316	.351	.667	120	3	18	4.46	-2	0-29(0-0-29)/C-9	4	0.1
1885	Det-N	39	161	23	46	6	2	0	24	8	10	....	....	.286	.320	.348	.667	115	3	18	4.31	-3	0-39(0-1-38)	4	-0.1
Total	**4**	**131**	**531**	**74**	**150**	**22**	**4**	**0**	**49**	**14**	**11**	**....**	**....**	**.282**	**.303**	**.339**	**.642**	**108**	**3**	**56**	**4.07**	**-9**	**/0-99,C-35,3-1**	**15**	**-0.4**
• DORGAN, Mike	Michael Cornelius Dorgan b: 10/2/1853, Middletown, CT d: 4/26/1909, Hartford, CT BR/TR, 5'9", 180 lbs. Deb: 5/8/1877 M Career OF: 29-17-556																								
1877	StL-N	60	266	45	82	9	7	0	23	9	13	....	....	.308	.331	.395	.726	135	11	36	5.32	-7	*0-50(20-1-29),C-12/3-2,2,S	10	0.3
1879	Syr-N	59	270	38	72	11	5	1	17	4	13	....	....	.267	.277	.356	.633	120	7	27	3.86	-2	1-21,0-16(0-0-16),3-11/S-6,C,P,2	9	0.5
1880	Pro-N	79	321	45	79	10	1	0	31	10	18	....	....	.246	.269	.283	.552	90	-3	25	2.85	5	*0-77(0-0-77)/3-2,P-1	9	0.2
1881	Wor-N	51	220	36	61	5	0	0	18	8	4	....	....	.277	.303	.300	.603	85	-4	20	3.48	1	1-26,0-23(0-0-23)/S-2	4	-0.5
	Det-N	8	34	5	8	1	0	0	5	1	0	....	....	.235	.257	.265	.522	61	-2	2	2.46	0	/0-5(0-4-1),3-2,1-1	1	-0.2
	Yr.	59	254	41	69	6	0	0	23	9	4	....	....	.272	.297	.295	.592	82	-6	23	3.33	0	0-28(0-4-24),1-27/3-2,S-2	5	-0.7
1883	NY-N	64	261	32	61	11	3	0	27	2	23	....	....	.234	.240	.299	.538	63	-11	19	2.63	-9	0-59(0-9-51)/C-6,P-1	3	-1.9
1884	NY-N	83	341	61	94	11	6	1	48	13	27	....	....	.276	.302	.352	.654	102	2	37	4.14	-3	0-64(2-2-60),P-14/C-6,2-3	16	-0.7
1885	NY-N	89	347	60	113	17	8	0	46	11	24	....	....	.326	.346	.421	.767	149	18	52	5.98	-3	*0-88(0-0-88)/1-1	16	1.2
1886	NY-N	118	442	61	129	19	4	2	79	29	37	9	....	.292	.335	.367	.702	112	6	59	5.07	-9	*0-116(6-1-110)/1-3	16	-0.5
1887	NY-N	71	298	41	88	10	0	0	34	15	20	22	....	.295	.302	.293	.596	69	-11	33	4.11	-2	0-69(1-0-68)/1-2	4	-1.2
1890	Syr-a	33	139	19	30	8	0	0	18	16	....	8	....	.216	.301	.273	.575	77	-3	14	3.45	-3	0-33(0-0-33)	2	-0.6
Total	**10**	**715**	**2939**	**443**	**817**	**112**	**34**	**4**	**346**	**118**	**179**	**39**	**....**	**.278**	**.303**	**.340**	**.643**	**103**	**11**	**325**	**4.16**	**-32**	**0-600/1-54,C-28,P-18,3-17,S,2**	**90**	**-3.3**
• DORMAN, Charlie	Charles William "Slats" Dorman b: 4/23/1898, San Francisco, CA d: 11/15/1928, San Francisco, CA BR/TR, 6'2", 185 lbs. Deb: 5/14/1923																								
1923	Chi-A	1	2	0	1	0	0	0	0	0	0	0	0	.500	.500	.500	1.000	166	0	0	12.72	0	/C-1	0	0.0
• DORMAN, Red	Charles Dwight "Curlie" Dorman b: 10/3/1900, Jacksonville, IL d: 12/7/1974, Anaheim, CA BR/TR, 5'10.5", 180 lbs. Deb: 8/21/1928																								
1928	Cle-A	25	77	12	28	6	0	0	11	9	6	1	0	.364	.430	.442	.872	128	4	15	8.08	-2	0-24(5-19-0)	3	0.1
• DORSETT, Brian	Brian Richard Dorsett b: 4/9/1961, Terre Haute, IN BR/TR, 6'3", 220 lbs. Deb: 9/8/1987																								
1987	Cle-A	5	11	2	3	0	0	1	3	0	3	0	0	.273	.333	.545	.879	127	0	2	7.04	0	/C-4	0	0.0
1988	Cal-A	7	11	0	1	0	0	0	2	1	5	0	0	.091	.167	.091	.258	-26	-2	0	.57	0	/C-7	0	-0.1
1989	NY-A	8	22	3	8	1	0	0	4	1	3	0	0	.364	.391	.409	.800	127	1	4	6.99	1	/C-8	2	0.2
1990	NY-A	14	35	2	5	2	0	0	0	2	4	0	0	.143	.189	.200	.389	9	-4	1	.86	0	/C-9,D-5	0	-0.4
1991	SD-N	11	12	0	1	0	0	0	1	0	3	0	0	.083	.083	.083	.167	-51	-2	0	.20	0	/1-2	0	-0.2
1993	Cin-N	25	63	7	16	4	0	2	12	3	14	0	0	.254	.288	.413	.701	85	-2	7	4.11	-1	C-18/1-3	2	-0.1
1994	Cin-N	76	216	21	53	8	0	5	26	21	33	0	0	.245	.315	.352	.667	74	-8	22	3.37	-1	C-73/1-1	4	-0.5
1996	Chi-N	17	41	3	5	0	0	1	3	4	8	0	0	.122	.200	.195	.395	5	-6	1	1.01	0	C-15	1	-0.5
Total	**8**	**163**	**411**	**38**	**92**	**15**	**0**	**9**	**51**	**32**	**73**	**0**	**0**	**.224**	**.283**	**.326**	**.609**	**61**	**-23**	**38**	**3.02**	**-1**	**C-134/1-6,D-5**	**9**	**-1.7**
• DORSEY, Jerry	Jeremiah Dorsey b: 1885, Oakland, CA BL/TL, 5'11", 175 lbs. Deb: 9/23/1911																								
1911	Pit-N	2	6	0	0	0	0	0	0	0	1	0	....	.000	.000	.000	.000	-96	-2	0	.00	0	/0-1	0	-0.1
• DORSEY, Jerry	Michael Jeremiah Dorsey b: 1854, Canada d: 11/3/1938, Auburn, NY BL Deb: 7/9/1884																								
1884	Bal-U	1	3	0	0	0	0	0	....	0	....	....	....	.000	.000	.000	.000	-91	-1	0	.00	0	/0-1,P-1	0	-0.3
• DOSCHER, Herm	John Henry Doscher, Sr. b: 12/20/1852, New York, NY d: 3/20/1934, Buffalo, NY BR/TR, 5'10", 182 lbs. Deb: 9/4/1872 U NA OF: 0-1-6																								
1872	Atl-n	6	25	4	9	0	0	0	5	0	1	0	0	.360	.360	.360	.720	104	-0	3	6.43	1	/0-6(0-0-6)	....	0.1
1873	Atl-n	1	6	1	1	0	0	0	1	0	0	0	0	.167	.167	.167	.333	-1	-1	0	1.04	0	/0-1	....	-0.1
1875	Was-n	22	81	5	15	4	0	0	5	0	6	1	0	.185	.185	.235	.420	46	-4	4	1.70	-1	3-22	....	-0.4
1879	Tro-N	47	191	16	42	8	0	0	18	2	10	....	....	.220	.228	.262	.490	65	-6	12	2.20	-9	3-47	2	-1.3
	Chi-N	3	11	1	2	0	0	0	1	0	3	....	....	.182	.182	.182	.364	19	-1	0	1.16	-1	/3-3	0	-0.2
	Yr.	50	202	17	44	8	0	0	19	2	13	....	....	.218	.225	.257	.483	63	-7	12	2.14	-10	3-50	2	-1.5
1881	Cle-N	5	19	2	4	0	0	0	0	0	2	....	....	.211	.211	.211	.421	34	-1	1	1.55	0	/3-5	0	-0.1
1882	Cle-N	25	104	7	25	2	0	0	10	0	11	....	....	.240	.240	.260	.500	62	-4	7	2.32	-2	3-22/0-2(2-0-0),S-1	2	-0.5
Total	**3 n**	**29**	**112**	**10**	**25**	**4**	**0**	**0**	**11**	**0**	**7**	**1**	**0**	**.223**	**.223**	**.259**	**.482**	**57**	**-4**	**7**	**2.53**	**0**	**/3-22,0-7**	**....**	**-0.4**
Total	**3**	**80**	**325**	**26**	**73**	**10**	**0**	**0**	**29**	**2**	**26**	**....**	**....**	**.225**	**.229**	**.255**	**.485**	**61**	**-13**	**20**	**2.16**	**-12**	**/3-77,0-2,S-1**	**4**	**-2.1**
• DOSTER, David	David Eric Doster b: 10/8/1970, Fort Wayne, IN BR/TR, 5'10", 185 lbs. Deb: 6/16/1996																								
1996	Phi-N	39	105	14	28	8	0	1	8	7	21	0	0	.267	.313	.371	.684	79	-3	12	4.25	-1	2-24/3-1	2	-0.3
1999	Phi-N	99	97	9	19	2	0	3	10	12	23	1	0	.196	.284	.309	.594	49	-8	9	2.94	4	2-77/3-6,S-5	1	-0.2
Total	**2**	**138**	**202**	**23**	**47**	**10**	**0**	**4**	**18**	**19**	**44**	**1**	**0**	**.233**	**.299**	**.342**	**.640**	**64**	**-11**	**21**	**3.58**	**3**	**2-101/3-7,S-5**	**3**	**-0.5**
• DOTTERER, Dutch	Henry John Dotterer b: 11/11/1931, Syracuse, NY d: 10/9/1999, Syracuse, NY BR/TR, 6', 209 lbs. Deb: 9/25/1957																								
1957	Cin-N	4	12	0	1	0	0	0	2	1	2	0	0	.083	.154	.083	.237	-32	-2	0	.48	0	/C-4	0	-0.2
1958	Cin-N	11	28	1	7	1	0	1	2	2	4	0	0	.250	.300	.393	.693	77	-1	3	4.44	2	/C-8	1	0.1
1959	Cin-N	52	161	21	43	7	0	2	17	16	23	0	0	.267	.333	.348	.681	79	-4	19	4.14	1	C-51	5	-0.1
1960	Cin-N	33	79	4	18	5	0	2	11	13	10	0	1	.228	.337	.367	.704	91	-1	10	4.07	0	C-31	2	0.0
1961	Was-A	7	19	1	5	2	0	0	1	3	5	0	0	.263	.364	.368	.732	101	0	3	5.46	1	/C-7	1	0.1
Total	**5**	**107**	**299**	**27**	**74**	**15**	**0**	**5**	**33**	**35**	**44**	**0**	**1**	**.247**	**.326**	**.348**	**.674**	**79**	**-8**	**36**	**4.06**	**3**	**C-101**	**9**	**-0.1**
• DOUGHERTY, Charlie	Charles William Dougherty b: 2/7/1862, Darlington, WI d: 2/18/1925, Milwaukee, WI Deb: 4/17/1884																								
1884	Alt-U	23	85	6	22	5	0	0	....	2	....	....	....	.259	.276	.318	.594	99	-0	8	3.39	-2	2-16/0-8(2-2-4),S-1	1	-0.1
• DOUGHERTY, Patsy	Patrick Henry Dougherty b: 10/27/1876, Andover, NY d: 4/30/1940, Bolivar, NY BL/TR, 6'2", 190 lbs. Deb: 4/19/1902 Career OF: 1181-0-0																								
1902	Bos-A	108	438	77	150	12	6	0	34	42	....	20	....	.342	.407	.397	.805	120	14	81	7.42	-8	*0-102(102-0-0)/3-1	17	0.1
1903*	Bos-A	139	590	**107**	**195**	19	12	4	59	33	....	35	....	.331	.372	.424	.796	131	22	111	7.09	5	*0-139(139-0-0)	28	2.0
1904	Bos-A	49	195	33	53	5	4	0	4	25	....	10	....	.272	.355	.338	.693	113	4	28	5.12	0	0-49(49-0-0)	9	0.1
	NY-A	106	452	80	128	13	10	6	22	19	....	11	....	.283	.316	.396	.712	119	8	62	5.01	-5	*0-106(106-0-0)	15	-0.3
	Yr.	155	647	**113**	181	18	14	6	26	44	....	21	....	.280	.329	.379	.707	117	12	90	5.05	-5	*0-155(155-0-0)	24	-0.2
1905	NY-A	116	418	56	110	9	6	3	29	28	....	17	....	.263	.319	.335	.654	96	-2	52	4.39	-10	*0-108(108-0-0)/3-1	12	-2.0
1906	NY-A	12	52	3	10	2	0	0	4	0	....	0	....	.192	.192	.231	.423	29	-4	2	1.49	2	0-12(12-0-0)	1	-0.3
	*Chi-A	75	253	30	59	9	4	1	27	19	....	11	....	.233	.295	.312	.607	92	-2	29	3.67	3	0-74(74-0-0)	8	-0.4
	Yr.	87	305	33	69	11	4	1	31	19	....	11	....	.226	.278	.298	.577	83	-7	31	3.30	5	0-86(86-0-0)	9	-0.8
1907	Chi-A	148	533	69	144	17	2	1	59	36	....	33	....	.270	.322	.315	.637	107	4	68	4.47	5	*0-148(148-0-0)	20	0.1
1908	Chi-A	138	482	68	134	11	6	0	45	58	....	**47**	....	.278	.367	.326	.693	128	18	76	5.35	-6	*0-128(128-0-0)	29	0.6
1909	Chi-A	139	491	71	140	23	13	1	55	51	....	36	....	.285	.359	.391	.751	143	25	82	5.74	-9	*0-138(138-0-0)	25	0.9
1910	Chi-A	127	443	45	110	8	6	1	43	41	....	22	....	.248	.318	.300	.618	99	-0	48	3.71	-8	*0-121(121-0-0)	14	-1.7
1911	Chi-A	76	211	39	61	10	9	0	32	26	....	19	....	.289	.380	.422	.802	126	8	41	6.69	-4	0-56(56-0-0)	9	0.2
Total	**10**	**1233**	**4558**	**678**	**1294**	**138**	**78**	**17**	**413**	**378**	**....**	**261**	**....**	**.284**	**.346**	**.360**	**.705**	**117**	**97**	**681**	**5.29**	**-35**	***0-1181/3-2**	**187**	**-1.0**
• DOUGLAS, John	John Franklin Douglas b: 9/14/1917, Thayer, WV d: 2/11/1984, Miami, FL BL/TL, 6'2.5", 195 lbs. Deb: 4/21/1945																								
1945	Bro-N	5	9	0	0	0	0	0	0	2	4	0	....	.000	.182	.000	.182	-47	-2	0	.28	-1	/1-4	0	-0.3
• DOUGLASS, Astyanax	Astyanax Saunders Douglass b: 9/19/1899, Covington, TX d: 1/26/1975, El Paso, TX BL/TR, 6'1", 190 lbs. Deb: 7/30/1921																								
1921	Cin-N	4	7	1	1	0	0	0	0	0	1	0	0	.143	.143	.143	.286	-25	-1	0	.61	0	/C-4	0	-0.1
1925	Cin-N	7	17	1	3	0	0	0	1	1	3	0	0	.176	.222	.176	.399	3	-2	1	1.32	0	/C-7	0	-0.2
Total	**2**	**11**	**24**	**2**	**4**	**0**	**0**	**0**	**1**	**1**	**4**	**0**	**0**	**.167**	**.200**	**.167**	**.367**	**-5**	**-4**	**1**	**1.10**	**0**	**/C-11**	**0**	**-0.3**

YEAR TM-L	G	AB	R	H	2B	3B	HR	RBI	BB	SO	SB	CS	AVG	OBP	SLG	OPS	OPS+	BR/A	RC	RC/G	FR	G/POS	WS	TPW

• DOUGLASS, Klondike William Bingham Douglass b: 5/10/1872, Boston, PA d: 12/13/1953, Bend, OR BL/TR, 6', 200 lbs. Deb: 4/23/1896 U Career OF: 68-9-54

YEAR TM-L	G	AB	R	H	2B	3B	HR	RBI	BB	SO	SB	CS	AVG	OBP	SLG	OPS	OPS+	BR/A	RC	RC/G	FR	G/POS	WS	TPW
1896 StL-N	81	296	42	78	6	4	1	28	35	15	18	....	.264	.351	.321	.672	81	-6	41	4.92	-3	O-74(29-5-41)/C-6,S-2	6	-1.2
1897 StL-N	126	519	77	170	15	3	6	50	52	....	12	....	.328	.401	.403	.804	115	14	91	6.88	1	C-61,O-43(28-2-13),1-17/3-7,S	15	1.5
1898 Phi-N	146	582	105	150	26	4	2	48	55	....	18	....	.258	.333	.326	.660	93	-4	74	4.32	-7	*1-146	11	-1.1
1899 Phi-N	77	275	26	70	6	6	0	27	10	....	7	....	.255	.296	.320	.616	71	-11	29	3.71	3	C-66/1-4,3-4,O-1	6	-0.3
1900 Phi-N	50	160	23	48	9	4	0	25	13	....	7	....	.300	.360	.406	.766	112	3	27	6.26	-4	C-47/3-2	6	0.3
1901 Phi-N	51	173	14	56	6	1	0	23	11	....	10	....	.324	.371	.370	.741	113	3	29	6.30	-4	C-41/1-6,O-2(1-1-0)	7	0.3
1902 Phi-N	109	408	37	95	12	3	0	37	23	....	6	....	.233	.274	.277	.551	70	-15	35	2.84	-3	1-69,C-29,O-10(10-0-0)	5	-1.8
1903 Phi-N	105	377	43	96	5	4	1	36	28	....	6	....	.255	.308	.297	.605	75	-12	39	3.51	-2	1-97	5	-1.5
1904 Phi-N	3	10	1	3	0	0	0	1	0	....	0	....	.300	.364	.300	.664	109	0	1	4.15	-1	/1-3	0	-0.1
Total 9	**748**	**2800**	**368**	**766**	**85**	**29**	**10**	**275**	**227**	**15**	**84**	**....**	**.274**	**.337**	**.335**	**.672**	**90**	**-29**	**366**	**4.63**	**-20**	**1-342,C-250,O-130/3-13,S-3**	**61**	**-3.8**

• DOUTHIT, Taylor Taylor Lee Douthit b: 4/22/1901, Little Rock, AR d: 5/28/1986, Fremont, CA BR/TR, 5'11.5", 175 lbs. Deb: 9/14/1923 Career OF: 25-984-26

YEAR TM-L	G	AB	R	H	2B	3B	HR	RBI	BB	SO	SB	CS	AVG	OBP	SLG	OPS	OPS+	BR/A	RC	RC/G	FR	G/POS	WS	TPW
1923 StL-N	9	27	3	5	0	2	0	0	0	4	1	0	.185	.185	.333	.519	35	-2	2	2.04	0	/O-7(3-0-4)	0	-0.2
1924 StL-N	53	173	24	48	13	1	0	13	16	19	4	3	.277	.349	.364	.713	93	-1	23	4.41	0	O-50(9-22-19)	4	-0.4
1925 StL-N	30	73	13	20	3	1	1	8	2	6	0	0	.274	.312	.384	.695	75	-3	9	4.17	-1	O-21(4-16-1)	1	-0.4
1926*StL-N	139	530	96	163	20	4	3	52	55	46	23	....	.308	.375	.377	.752	99	1	76	4.89	5	*O-138(1-137-0)	19	0.0
1927 StL-N	130	488	81	128	29	6	5	50	52	45	6	....	.262	.336	.377	.713	88	-8	62	4.34	4	*O-125(1-122-1)	16	-1.0
1928*StL-N	154	648	111	191	35	3	3	43	84	36	11	....	.295	.384	.372	.756	97	1	95	5.30	11	*O-154(0-154-0)	24	0.5
1929 StL-N	150	613	128	206	42	7	9	62	79	49	8	....	.336	.416	.471	.888	118	21	120	7.49	-8	*O-150(0-150-0)	22	0.6
1930*StL-N	154	664	109	201	41	10	7	93	60	38	4	....	.303	.364	.426	.790	87	-13	102	5.48	0	*O-154(0-154-0)	17	-1.7
1931 StL-N	36	133	21	44	11	2	1	21	11	9	1	....	.331	.386	.466	.852	123	4	25	6.86	-1	O-36(0-35-1)	6	0.2
Cin-N	95	374	42	98	9	1	0	24	42	24	4	....	.262	.340	.291	.631	76	-11	40	3.71	-3	O-95(0-95-0)	7	-1.6
Yr.	131	507	63	142	20	3	1	45	53	33	5	....	.280	.352	.337	.689	88	-6	65	4.49	-4	*O-131(0-130-1)	13	-1.4
1932 Cin-N	96	333	28	81	12	1	0	25	31	29	3	....	.243	.311	.285	.597	64	-16	32	3.18	1	O-88(2-86-0)	4	-1.7
1933 Cin-N	1	0	1	0	0	0	0	0	0	0	0	....	....	....	....	....	-102	0	0	....	0	....	0	0.0
Chi-N	27	71	8	16	5	0	0	5	11	7	2	....	.225	.329	.296	.625	80	-1	6	2.70	0	O-18(5-13-0)	1	-0.2
Yr.	28	71	9	16	5	0	0	5	11	7	2	....	.225	.329	.296	.625	80	-1	6	2.70	0	O-18(5-13-0)	1	-0.2
Total 11	**1074**	**4127**	**665**	**1201**	**220**	**38**	**29**	**396**	**443**	**312**	**67**	**3**	**.291**	**.364**	**.384**	**.748**	**93**	**-28**	**592**	**5.04**	**8**	***O-1036**	**121**	**-5.9**

• DOW, Clarence Clarence G. Dow b: 10/2/1854, Charlestown, MA d: 3/11/1893, West Somerville, MA Deb: 9/22/1884 U

YEAR TM-L	G	AB	R	H	2B	3B	HR	RBI	BB	SO	SB	CS	AVG	OBP	SLG	OPS	OPS+	BR/A	RC	RC/G	FR	G/POS	WS	TPW
1884 Bos-U	1	6	1	2	0	0	0	....	0	....	....	....	.333	.333	.333	.667	128	0	1	4.78	1	/O-1	0	0.1

• DOWD, John John Leo Dowd b: 1/3/1891, Weymouth, MA d: 1/31/1981, Fort Lauderdale, FL BR/TR, 5'8", 170 lbs. Deb: 7/3/1912

YEAR TM-L	G	AB	R	H	2B	3B	HR	RBI	BB	SO	SB	CS	AVG	OBP	SLG	OPS	OPS+	BR/A	RC	RC/G	FR	G/POS	WS	TPW
1912 NY-A	10	31	1	6	1	0	0	0	6	....	0	....	.194	.342	.226	.568	60	-1	2	2.43	-3	S-10	0	-0.4

• DOWD, Snooks Raymond Bernard Dowd b: 12/20/1897, Springfield, MA d: 4/4/1962, Northampton, MA BR/TR, 5'8", 163 lbs. Deb: 4/27/1919

YEAR TM-L	G	AB	R	H	2B	3B	HR	RBI	BB	SO	SB	CS	AVG	OBP	SLG	OPS	OPS+	BR/A	RC	RC/G	FR	G/POS	WS	TPW
1919 Det-A	1	0	0	0	0	0	0	0	0	0	0	....	....	....	....	....	-102	0	0	....	0	....	0	0.0
Phi-A	13	18	4	3	0	0	0	6	0	5	2	....	.167	.167	.167	.333	-6	-3	1	1.19	0	/2-3,S-2,3-1,O-1	0	-0.3
Yr.	14	18	4	3	0	0	0	6	0	5	2	....	.167	.167	.167	.333	-6	-3	1	1.19	0	/2-3,S-2,3-1,O-1	0	-0.3
1926 Bro-N	2	8	0	0	0	0	0	0	0	0	0	....	.000	.000	.000	.000	-102	-2	0	.00	0	/2-2	0	-0.3
Total 2	**16**	**26**	**4**	**3**	**0**	**0**	**0**	**6**	**0**	**5**	**2**	**....**	**.115**	**.115**	**.115**	**.231**	**-36**	**-5**	**1**	**.78**	**-1**	**/2-5,S-2,3-1,O-1**	**0**	**-0.6**

• DOWD, Tommy Thomas Jefferson "Buttermilk Tommy" Dowd b: 4/20/1869, Holyoke, MA d: 7/2/1933, Holyoke, MA BR/TR, 5'8", 173 lbs. Deb: 4/8/1891 M Career OF: 284-331-349

YEAR TM-L	G	AB	R	H	2B	3B	HR	RBI	BB	SO	SB	CS	AVG	OBP	SLG	OPS	OPS+	BR/A	RC	RC/G	FR	G/POS	WS	TPW
1891 Bos-a	4	11	1	1	0	0	0	0	0	1	0	....	.091	.091	.091	.182	-49	-2	0	.25	0	/O-4(0-0-4)	0	-0.2
Was-a	112	464	66	120	9	10	1	44	19	44	39	....	.259	.291	.328	.618	80	-14	57	4.38	-28	*2-107/O-5(5-0-0)	7	-3.3
Yr.	116	475	67	121	9	10	1	44	19	45	39	....	.255	.286	.322	.608	78	-16	57	4.27	-28	*2-107/O-9(5-0-4)	7	-3.5
1892 Was-N	144	584	94	142	9	10	1	50	34	49	49	....	.243	.286	.298	.584	79	-16	65	3.99	-31	2-98,O-23(7-0-16),3-18/S-6	8	-4.0
1893 StL-N	132	581	114	164	18	7	1	54	49	23	59	....	.282	.340	.343	.683	81	-16	90	5.72	-1	*O-132(64-5-63)/2-1	11	-2.1
1894 StL-N	123	524	92	142	16	8	4	62	54	33	31	....	.271	.341	.355	.696	68	-27	76	5.17	-4	*O-117(48-0-69)/2-7,3-1	7	-3.0
1895 StL-N	130	508	95	164	19	17	7	74	31	31	32	....	.323	.365	.469	.834	116	9	101	7.81	-8	*O-115(14-36-65),3-17/2-2	10	-0.4
1896 StL-N	126	521	93	138	17	11	5	46	42	19	40	....	.265	.322	.369	.691	85	-12	78	5.23	-16	2-78,O-48(0-48-0)	10	-2.4
1897 StL-N	35	145	25	38	9	1	0	9	6	....	11	....	.262	.291	.338	.629	67	-7	18	4.34	-5	O-30(0-30-0)/2-5	1	-1.2
Phi-N	91	391	68	114	14	4	0	43	19	....	30	....	.292	.324	.348	.672	80	-12	56	5.21	-4	O-73(0-23-50),2-19	6	-1.6
Yr.	126	536	93	152	23	5	0	52	25	....	41	....	.284	.316	.345	.661	76	-20	75	4.96	-9	*O-103(0-53-50),2-24	7	-2.8
1898 StL-N	139	586	70	143	17	7	0	32	30	....	16	....	.244	.287	.297	.584	66	-28	58	3.34	-11	*O-129(9-42-82),2-11	3	-4.2
1899 Cle-N	147	605	81	168	17	6	2	35	48	....	28	....	.278	.333	.336	.668	90	-7	79	4.77	-9	*O-147(0-147-0)	4	-2.3
1901 Bos-A	138	594	104	159	18	7	3	52	38	....	33	....	.268	.315	.337	.652	82	-14	76	4.56	5	*O-137(137-0-0)/1-2,3-1	15	-1.5
Total 10	**1321**	**5514**	**903**	**1493**	**163**	**88**	**24**	**501**	**370**	**200**	**368**	**....**	**.271**	**.319**	**.345**	**.664**	**82**	**-147**	**754**	**4.92**	**-111**	**O-960,2-328/3-37,S-6,1-2**	**82**	**-26.3**

• DOWELL, Ken Kenneth Allen Dowell b: 1/19/1961, Sacramento, CA BR/TR, 5'9", 160 lbs. Deb: 6/24/1987

YEAR TM-L	G	AB	R	H	2B	3B	HR	RBI	BB	SO	SB	CS	AVG	OBP	SLG	OPS	OPS+	BR/A	RC	RC/G	FR	G/POS	WS	TPW
1987 Phi-N	15	39	4	5	0	0	0	1	2	5	0	0	.128	.171	.128	.299	-19	-7	1	.65	2	S-15	1	-0.3

• DOWIE, Joe Joseph E. Dowie b: 7/15/1865, New Orleans, LA d: 3/4/1917, New Orleans, LA, 5'8", 150 lbs. Deb: 7/10/1889

YEAR TM-L	G	AB	R	H	2B	3B	HR	RBI	BB	SO	SB	CS	AVG	OBP	SLG	OPS	OPS+	BR/A	RC	RC/G	FR	G/POS	WS	TPW
1889 Bal-a	20	75	12	17	5	0	0	8	2	10	5	....	.227	.266	.293	.559	60	-4	7	3.36	0	O-20(0-0-20)	1	-0.4

• DOWNEY, Red Alexander Cummings Downey b: 2/6/1889, Aurora, IN d: 7/10/1949, Detroit, MI BL/TL, 5'11", 174 lbs. Deb: 9/14/1909

YEAR TM-L	G	AB	R	H	2B	3B	HR	RBI	BB	SO	SB	CS	AVG	OBP	SLG	OPS	OPS+	BR/A	RC	RC/G	FR	G/POS	WS	TPW
1909 Bro-N	19	78	7	20	1	0	0	8	2	....	4	....	.256	.275	.269	.544	71	-3	7	2.93	-1	O-19(0-3-16)	1	-0.5

• DOWNEY, Tom Thomas Edward Downey b: 1/1/1884, Lewiston, ME d: 8/3/1961, Passaic, NJ BR/TR, 5'10", 178 lbs. Deb: 5/7/1909

YEAR TM-L	G	AB	R	H	2B	3B	HR	RBI	BB	SO	SB	CS	AVG	OBP	SLG	OPS	OPS+	BR/A	RC	RC/G	FR	G/POS	WS	TPW
1909 Cin-N	119	416	39	96	9	6	1	32	32	....	16	....	.231	.287	.288	.576	79	-11	40	3.04	-1	*S-119/C-1	10	-0.8
1910 Cin-N	111	378	43	102	9	3	2	32	34	28	12	....	.270	.335	.325	.660	97	-1	46	4.08	-3	S-68,3-41	12	-0.1
1911 Cin-N	111	360	50	94	16	7	0	36	44	38	10	....	.261	.345	.344	.689	97	-1	46	4.36	-4	S-93/2-6,3-5,1-2,O-1	10	0.2
1912 Phi-N	54	171	27	50	6	3	1	23	21	20	3	....	.292	.370	.380	.750	99	0	26	4.96	-6	3-46/S-3	5	-0.4
Chi-N	13	22	4	4	0	2	0	4	1	5	0	....	.182	.217	.364	.581	58	-2	2	2.28	-2	/S-5,3-3,2-1	0	-0.3
Yr.	67	193	31	54	6	5	1	27	22	25	3	....	.280	.353	.378	.732	94	-1	28	4.63	-8	3-49/S-8,2-1	5	-0.7
1914 Buf-F	151	541	69	118	20	3	2	42	40	55	35	....	.218	.273	.277	.550	54	-33	49	2.79	21	*2-129,S-16/3-5	10	-0.9
1915 Buf-F	92	282	24	56	9	1	1	19	26	26	11	....	.199	.269	.248	.517	52	-17	21	2.33	-5	2-48,3-35/S-2,1-1	3	-2.2
Total 6	**651**	**2170**	**256**	**520**	**69**	**25**	**7**	**188**	**198**	**172**	**87**	**....**	**.240**	**.306**	**.304**	**.610**	**77**	**-64**	**230**	**3.41**	**0**	**S-306,2-184,3-135/1-3,C-1,O-1**	**50**	**-4.5**

• DOWNING, Brian Brian Jay Downing b: 10/9/1950, Los Angeles, CA BR/TR, 5'10", 194 lbs. Deb: 5/31/1973 Career OF: 737-0-41

YEAR TM-L	G	AB	R	H	2B	3B	HR	RBI	BB	SO	SB	CS	AVG	OBP	SLG	OPS	OPS+	BR/A	RC	RC/G	FR	G/POS	WS	TPW
1973 Chi-A	34	73	5	13	1	0	2	4	10	17	0	0	.178	.277	.274	.551	54	-4	6	2.29	-1	O-13(8-0-6),C-11/3-8,D-1	1	-0.5
1974 Chi-A	108	293	41	66	12	1	10	39	51	72	0	1	.225	.344	.375	.719	104	3	38	4.25	2	C-63,O-39(5-0-34)/D-9	10	0.6
1975 Chi-A	138	420	58	101	12	1	7	41	76	75	13	4	.240	.361	.324	.685	93	2	54	4.16	2	*C-137/D-1	16	1.1
1976 Chi-A	104	317	38	81	14	0	3	30	40	55	7	3	.256	.341	.328	.669	96	-0	39	4.26	0	C-93,D-11	10	0.3
1977 Chi-A	69	169	28	48	4	2	4	25	34	21	1	2	.284	.410	.402	.812	123	7	30	6.10	2	C-61/O-3(2-0-1),D-2	9	1.1
1978 Cal-A	133	412	42	105	15	0	7	46	52	47	3	2	.255	.347	.342	.689	98	1	49	4.06	7	*C-128/D-2	18	1.4
1979*Cal-A★	148	509	87	166	27	3	12	75	77	57	3	3	.326	.420	.462	.881	142	34	99	7.28	-14	*C-129,D-18	25	2.5
1980 Cal-A	30	93	5	27	6	0	2	25	12	12	0	2	.290	.371	.419	.791	119	2	13	4.57	0	C-16,D-13	2	0.2
1981 Cal-A	93	317	47	79	14	0	9	41	46	35	1	1	.249	.351	.379	.730	110	6	43	4.55	-2	O-56(56-0-0),C-37/D-5	10	0.3
1982*Cal-A	158	623	109	175	37	2	28	84	86	58	2	1	.281	.373	.482	.854	132	30	114	6.51	8	*O-158(158-0-0)	25	3.1
1983 Cal-A	113	403	68	99	15	1	19	53	62	59	1	2	.246	.353	.429	.782	115	9	63	5.38	4	O-84(84-0-0),D-26	13	0.9
1984 Cal-A	156	539	65	148	28	2	23	91	70	66	0	4	.275	.365	.462	.827	128	20	89	5.64	-1	*O-131(131-0-0),D-21	20	1.3
1985 Cal-A	150	520	80	137	23	1	20	85	78	61	5	3	.263	.373	.427	.800	119	17	87	5.75	-2	*O-121(121-0-0),D-25	21	0.8
1986*Cal-A	152	513	90	137	27	4	20	95	90	84	4	4	.267	.394	.452	.846	131	26	96	6.38	0	*O-138(138-0-0),D-10	23	2.0
1987 Cal-A	155	567	110	154	29	3	29	77	**106**	85	5	5	.272	.401	.487	.888	139	36	117	7.33	-1	*D-118,O-34(34-0-0)	23	2.8
1988 Cal-A	135	484	80	117	18	2	25	64	81	63	3	4	.242	.366	.442	.808	129	20	81	5.57	0	*D-132	15	1.6
1989 Cal-A	142	544	59	154	25	2	14	59	56	87	0	2	.283	.356	.414	.770	118	13	83	5.55	0	*D-141	17	0.7
1990 Cal-A	96	330	47	90	18	2	14	51	50	45	0	0	.273	.378	.467	.845	138	18	59	6.24	0	D-87	13	1.5
1991 Tex-A	123	407	76	113	17	2	17	49	58	70	1	1	.278	.378	.455	.833	132	19	73	6.44	0	*D-109	14	1.5

YEAR	TM-L	G	AB	R	H	2B	3B	HR	RBI	BB	SO	SB	CS	AVG	OBP	SLG	OPS	OPS+	BR/A	RC	RC/G	FR	G/POS	WS	TPW
1992	Tex-A	107	320	53	89	18	0	10	39	62	58	1	0	.278	.408	.428	.836	139	21	61	6.84	0	D-93	13	1.8
Total 20		2344	7853	1188	2099	360	28	275	1073	1197	1127	50	44	.267	.373	.425	.798	122	280	1294	5.70	5	D-824,0-777,C-675/3-8	298	25.1

• DOWNS, Red Jerome Willis Downs b: 8/22/1883, Neola, IA d: 10/19/1939, Council Bluffs, IA BR/TR, 5'11", 155 lbs. Deb: 5/2/1907

YEAR	TM-L	G	AB	R	H	2B	3B	HR	RBI	BB	SO	SB	CS	AVG	OBP	SLG	OPS	OPS+	BR/A	RC	RC/G	FR	G/POS	WS	TPW
1907	Det-A	105	374	28	82	13	5	1	42	13	....	3	....	.219	.249	.289	.538	69	-14	30	2.59	-17	2-80,0-20(12-8-0)/3-1,S-1	4	-3.5
1908*	Det-A	84	289	28	64	10	3	1	35	5	....	2	....	.221	.237	.287	.524	67	-12	20	2.20	0	2-82/3-1	4	-1.2
1912	Bro-N	9	32	2	8	3	0	0	3	1	5	3	....	.250	.273	.344	.616	71	-1	4	3.79	-2	/2-9	0	-0.3
	Chi-N	43	95	9	25	4	3	1	14	9	17	5	....	.263	.327	.400	.727	98	-1	14	4.89	3	2-16/S-9,3-5	3	0.3
	Yr.	52	127	11	33	7	3	1	17	10	22	8	....	.260	.314	.386	.700	92	-2	18	4.60	1	2-25/S-9,3-5	3	0.0
Total 3		241	790	67	179	30	11	3	94	28	22	13	....	.227	.256	.304	.560	72	-28	67	2.76	-16	2-187/0-20,S-10,3-7	11	-4.7

• DOWSE, Tom Thomas Joseph Dowse b: 8/12/1866, Mohill, Ireland d: 12/14/1946, Riverside, CA BR/TR, 5'11", 175 lbs. Deb: 4/21/1890 U Career OF: 12-3-25

YEAR	TM-L	G	AB	R	H	2B	3B	HR	RBI	BB	SO	SB	CS	AVG	OBP	SLG	OPS	OPS+	BR/A	RC	RC/G	FR	G/POS	WS	TPW
1890	Cle-N	40	159	20	33	2	1	0	9	12	22	3	....	.208	.267	.233	.500	47	-10	11	2.31	-2	0-26(6-3-19),1-10/C-3,P-1	1	-1.1
1891	Col-a	55	201	24	45	7	0	0	22	13	22	2	....	.224	.278	.259	.536	57	-11	15	2.61	-8	C-51/0-5(2-0-3)	3	-1.3
1892	Lou-N	41	145	10	21	2	0	0	7	2	15	1	....	.145	.173	.159	.332	1	-17	4	.93	2	C-29,1-11/0-3(0-0-3),2-1	1	-1.2
	Cin-N	1	4	0	0	0	0	0	0	0	0	0	....	.000	.000	.000	.000	-101	-1	0	.00	0	/C-1	0	-0.1
	Phi-N	16	54	3	10	0	0	0	6	2	4	1	....	.185	.228	.185	.413	25	-5	3	1.58	0	C-15	1	-0.4
	Was-N	7	27	5	7	1	0	0	2	0	3	0	....	.259	.259	.296	.556	70	-1	2	2.87	0	/0-4(4-0-0),C-3	0	-0.1
	Yr.	65	230	18	38	3	0	0	15	4	22	2	....	.165	.193	.178	.372	13	-24	9	1.26	2	C-48,1-11/0-7(4-0-3),2-1	2	-1.7
Total 3		160	590	62	116	12	1	0	46	29	66	7	....	.197	.243	.220	.463	37	-46	35	1.98	-6	C-102/0-38,1-21,2-1,P-1	6	-4.1

• DOYLE, Brian Brian Reed Doyle b: 1/26/1955, Glasgow, KY BL/TR, 5'10", 160 lbs. Deb: 4/30/1978

YEAR	TM-L	G	AB	R	H	2B	3B	HR	RBI	BB	SO	SB	CS	AVG	OBP	SLG	OPS	OPS+	BR/A	RC	RC/G	FR	G/POS	WS	TPW
1978*	NY-A	39	52	6	10	0	0	0	0	3	3	0	3	.192	.192	.192	.385	9	-8	1	.56	2	2-29/S-7,3-5	1	-0.5
1979	NY-A	20	32	2	4	2	0	0	5	3	1	0	0	.125	.200	.188	.388	5	-4	1	1.10	-1	2-13/3-6	0	-0.5
1980	NY-A	34	75	8	13	1	0	1	5	6	7	1	1	.173	.235	.227	.461	27	-8	4	1.69	0	2-20,S-12/3-2	1	-0.6
1981	Oak-A	17	40	2	5	0	0	0	3	1	2	0	1	.125	.146	.125	.271	-22	-7	1	.41	2	2-17	0	-0.5
Total 4		110	199	18	32	3	0	1	13	10	13	1	5	.161	.201	.191	.392	9	-26	7	1.01	3	/2-79,S-19,3-13	2	-2.0

• DOYLE, Conny Cornelius J. Doyle b: 1862, Ireland d: 7/29/1931, El Paso, TX, 5'10", 185 lbs. Deb: 6/23/1883 Career OF: 30-0-0

YEAR	TM-L	G	AB	R	H	2B	3B	HR	RBI	BB	SO	SB	CS	AVG	OBP	SLG	OPS	OPS+	BR/A	RC	RC/G	FR	G/POS	WS	TPW
1883	Phi-N	16	68	3	15	3	0	0		0	15	....	....	.221	.221	.324	.544	69	-2	5	2.58	-2	0-16(16-0-0)	0	-0.4
1884	Pit-a	15	58	8	17	3	2	0	0	2	....	....	....	.293	.317	.414	.730	134	2	8	5.23	0	0-14(14-0-0)/S-1	2	0.1
Total 2		31	126	11	32	6	4	0	0	2	15	....	....	.254	.266	.365	.631	99	-0	13	3.73	-2	/0-30,S-1	2	-0.3

• DOYLE, Danny Howard James Doyle b: 6/24/1917, McLoud, OK BB/TR, 6'1", 195 lbs. Deb: 9/14/1943

YEAR	TM-L	G	AB	R	H	2B	3B	HR	RBI	BB	SO	SB	CS	AVG	OBP	SLG	OPS	OPS+	BR/A	RC	RC/G	FR	G/POS	WS	TPW
1943	Bos-A	13	43	2	9	1	0	0	6	7	9	0	1	.209	.320	.233	.553	62	-2	3	2.29	-1	C-13	0	-0.2

• DOYLE, Denny Robert Dennis Doyle b: 1/17/1944, Glasgow, KY BL/TR, 5'9", 175 lbs. Deb: 4/7/1970

YEAR	TM-L	G	AB	R	H	2B	3B	HR	RBI	BB	SO	SB	CS	AVG	OBP	SLG	OPS	OPS+	BR/A	RC	RC/G	FR	G/POS	WS	TPW
1970	Phi-N	112	413	43	86	10	7	2	16	33	64	6	5	.208	.267	.281	.548	48	-32	31	2.45	-7	*2-103	4	-3.2
1971	Phi-N	95	342	34	79	12	1	3	24	19	31	4	2	.231	.281	.298	.580	64	-16	29	2.84	-3	2-91	5	-1.4
1972	Phi-N	123	442	33	110	14	2	1	26	31	33	6	7	.249	.298	.296	.594	68	-20	38	2.86	-13	*2-119	6	-2.8
1973	Phi-N	116	370	45	101	9	3	3	26	31	32	1	3	.273	.329	.338	.667	89	-9	41	3.94	3	*2-114	9	0.0
1974	Cal-A	147	511	47	133	19	2	1	34	25	49	6	7	.260	.296	.311	.607	79	-16	46	3.09	10	*2-146/S-2	11	0.4
1975	Cal-A	8	15	0	1	0	0	0	1	1	1	0	0	.067	.125	.067	.192	-48	-3	0	.30	-2	/2-6,3-1	0	-0.4
	*Bos-A	89	310	50	96	21	2	4	36	14	11	5	7	.310	.342	.429	.771	107	1	43	4.86	-8	2-84/3-6,S-2	9	-0.3
	Yr.	97	325	50	97	21	2	4	36	15	12	5	7	.298	.331	.412	.744	100	-2	43	4.60	-9	2-90/3-7,S-2	9	-0.7
1976	Bos-A	117	432	51	108	15	5	0	26	22	39	8	5	.250	.286	.308	.594	66	-19	37	2.89	-10	*2-112	6	-2.3
1977	Bos-A	137	455	54	109	13	6	2	49	29	50	2	4	.240	.291	.308	.599	57	-28	40	2.94	2	*2-137	6	-1.9
Total 8		944	3290	357	823	113	28	16	237	205	310	38	40	.250	.296	.316	.612	70	-143	305	3.14	-27	2-912/3-7,S-4	56	-11.8

• DOYLE, Jack John Joseph "Dirty Jack" Doyle b: 10/25/1869, Killorgin, Ireland d: 12/31/1958, Holyoke, MA BR/TR, 5'9", 155 lbs. Deb: 8/27/1889 M/U Career OF: 13-45-76

YEAR	TM-L	G	AB	R	H	2B	3B	HR	RBI	BB	SO	SB	CS	AVG	OBP	SLG	OPS	OPS+	BR/A	RC	RC/G	FR	G/POS	WS	TPW
1889	Col-a	11	36	6	10	1	1	0	3	6	6	9	....	.278	.381	.361	.742	118	1	9	8.76	0	/C-7,0-3(0-0-3),2-2	2	0.1
1890	Col-a	77	298	47	80	17	7	1	44	13		27	....	.268	.299	.393	.692	111	2	44	5.37	-2	C-38,S-25/0-9(2-6-1),2-6,3	9	0.3
1891	Cle-N	69	250	43	69	14	4	0	43	26	44	24	....	.276	.351	.364	.715	104	1	41	6.18	-4	C-29,0-21(4-8-10),3-20/S-1	9	-0.1
1892	Cle-N	24	88	17	26	4	1	1	14	6	10	5	....	.295	.340	.398	.738	118	1	14	6.08	-1	0-12(1-0-11)/C-9,1-1,S-1	3	0.1
	NY-N	90	366	61	109	22	1	5	55	18	30	42	....	.298	.336	.404	.740	126	9	65	6.87	-6	2-31,C-26,0-17(0-10-7),3-13/S	14	0.6
	Yr.	114	454	78	135	26	2	6	69	24	40	47	....	.297	.337	.403	.740	124	11	79	6.72	-7	C-35,2-31,0-29(1-10-18),3-13/S,1	17	0.6
1893	NY-N	82	318	56	102	17	5	1	51	27	12	40	....	.321	.383	.415	.798	112	5	67	8.24	3	C-48,0-29(0-21-8)/S-4,3-3,1	10	0.9
1894*	NY-N	107	427	94	157	30	8	3	102	37	3	43	....	.368	.422	.496	.918	122	16	110	10.58	7	*1-99/C-6	17	1.7
1895	NY-N	82	319	52	100	21	3	1	66	24	12	35	....	.313	.365	.408	.773	101	1	62	7.62	-3	1-58,2-13/3-6,C-4	10	-0.1
1896*	Bal-N	118	487	116	165	29	4	1	101	42	15	73	....	.339	.394	.421	.821	115	12	115	9.20	-9	*1-118/2-1	17	0.2
1897*	Bal-N	114	460	91	163	29	4	2	87	29		62	....	.354	.394	.448	.842	122	14	108	9.60	3	*1-114	18	1.3
1898	Was-N	43	177	26	54	2	2	2	26	7		9	....	.305	.335	.373	.708	103	-0	26	5.55	-3	1-38/2-5	4	-0.3
	NY-N	82	297	42	84	15	3	1	43	12		14	....	.283	.317	.364	.681	98	-2	40	4.90	1	0-38(6-0-32),1-24,S-15/3-5,C	8	-0.2
	Yr.	125	474	68	138	17	5	3	69	19		23	....	.291	.324	.367	.691	100	-2	66	5.13	-2	1-62,0-38(6-0-32),S-15/2-5,3,C	12	-0.5
1899	NY-N	119	452	56	135	16	7	3	77	33		35	....	.299	.352	.385	.737	106	3	76	6.27	-1	*1-113/C-5	12	0.2
1900	NY-N	133	505	69	135	24	1	1	66	34		34	....	.267	.317	.325	.642	81	-13	65	4.60	-5	*1-133	9	-1.6
1901	Chi-N	75	285	21	66	9	2	0	39	7		8	....	.232	.263	.277	.540	59	-15	24	2.84	4	1-75	1	-1.3
1902	NY-N	51	193	22	58	13	0	0	18	11		12	....	.301	.341	.368	.709	125	5	30	5.86	6	1-49	5	1.0
	Was-N	78	312	52	77	15	2	1	20	29		6	....	.247	.311	.317	.628	74	-11	34	3.77	-6	2-68/1-7,0-4(0-0-4),C-2	5	-1.6
	Yr.	129	505	74	135	28	2	1	38	40		18	....	.267	.321	.337	.658	93	-6	64	4.57	-0	2-68,1-56/0-4(0-0-4),C-4	10	-0.6
1903	Bro-N	139	524	84	164	27	6	0	91	54		34	....	.313	.383	.387	.770	123	18	94	6.75	3	*1-139	19	1.7
1904	Bro-N	8	22	2	5	1	0	0	2	6		1	....	.227	.414	.273	.687	116	1	3	4.54	1	/1-8	1	0.3
	Phi-N	66	236	20	52	10	3	1	22	19		4	....	.220	.281	.301	.582	83	-5	22	3.06	1	1-65/2-1	3	-0.5
	Yr.	74	258	22	57	11	3	1	24	25		5	....	.221	.295	.298	.593	86	-4	25	3.18	2	1-73/2-1	4	-0.3
1905	NY-A	1	3	0	0	0	0	0	0	0		0	....	.000	.000	.000	.000	-90	-1	0	.00	-1	/1-1	0	-0.1
Total 17		1569	6055	977	1811	316	64	25	970	440	132	517	....	.299	.351	.385	.736	105	42	1049	6.49	-12	*1-1043,C-176,0-133,2-127/S,3	176	2.6

• DOYLE, Jeff Jeffrey Donald Doyle b: 10/2/1956, Havre, MT BB/TR, 5'9", 160 lbs. Deb: 9/13/1983

YEAR	TM-L	G	AB	R	H	2B	3B	HR	RBI	BB	SO	SB	CS	AVG	OBP	SLG	OPS	OPS+	BR/A	RC	RC/G	FR	G/POS	WS	TPW
1983	StL-N	13	37	4	11	1	2	0	2	1				.297	.316	.432	.748	105	0	4	3.83	-2	2-12	1	-0.1

• DOYLE, Jim James Francis Doyle b: 12/25/1881, Detroit, MI d: 2/1/1912, Syracuse, NY BR/TR, 5'10", 168 lbs. Deb: 5/4/1910

YEAR	TM-L	G	AB	R	H	2B	3B	HR	RBI	BB	SO	SB	CS	AVG	OBP	SLG	OPS	OPS+	BR/A	RC	RC/G	FR	G/POS	WS	TPW
1910	Cin-N	7	13	1	2	0	0	0		0	2	0	....	.154	.154	.308	.462	36	-1	1	1.30	-1	/3-3,0-1	0	-0.2
1911	Chi-N	130	472	69	133	23	12	5	62	40	54	19	....	.282	.340	.413	.754	110	4	73	5.27	9	*3-127	19	1.8
Total 2		137	485	70	135	25	12	5	63	40	56	19	....	.278	.336	.410	.746	108	3	73	5.13	8	3-130/0-1	19	1.6

• DOYLE, Joe Joseph K. Doyle b: Cincinnati, OH Deb: 4/20/1872

YEAR	TM-L	G	AB	R	H	2B	3B	HR	RBI	BB	SO	SB	CS	AVG	OBP	SLG	OPS	OPS+	BR/A	RC	RC/G	FR	G/POS	WS	TPW
1872	Nat-n	9	41	6	12	1	0	0		0	0	....	....	.293	.293	.317	.610	75	-2	4	4.17	-5	/S-8,2-1	....	-0.5

• DOYLE, Larry Lawrence Joseph "Laughing Larry" Doyle b: 7/31/1886, Caseyville, IL d: 3/1/1974, Saranac Lake, NY BL/TR, 5'10", 165 lbs. Deb: 7/22/1907

YEAR	TM-L	G	AB	R	H	2B	3B	HR	RBI	BB	SO	SB	CS	AVG	OBP	SLG	OPS	OPS+	BR/A	RC	RC/G	FR	G/POS	WS	TPW
1907	NY-N	69	227	16	59	9	3	0	16	20		3	....	.260	.320	.273	.593	83	-4	22	3.31	-20	2-69	4	-2.7
1908	NY-N	104	377	65	116	16	9	0	33	22		17	....	.308	.354	.398	.752	134	14	60	5.45	-11	*2-102	17	0.4
1909	NY-N	147	570	86	172	27	11	6	49	45		31	....	.302	.360	.419	.779	140	25	96	6.08	-19	*2-144	27	0.8
1910	NY-N	151	575	97	164	21	14	8	69	70	26	39	....	.285	.372	.412	.784	128	20	101	6.13	-19	*2-151	25	0.3
1911*	NY-N	143	526	102	163	25	**25**	13	77	71	39	38	....	.310	.397	.527	.924	154	37	124	8.43	-27	*2-141	28	1.2
1912*	NY-N	143	558	98	184	33	8	10	90	56	20	36	....	.330	.393	.471	.864	131	24	116	7.65	-2	*2-143	29	2.4
1913*	NY-N	132	482	67	135	25	5	5	73	59	29	38	....	.280	.364	.388	.752	114	10	78	5.53	-1	*2-130	21	1.2
1914	NY-N	145	539	87	140	19	8	5	63	58	25	19	....	.260	.343	.353	.695	110	8	69	4.32	-17	*2-145	19	-0.6
1915	NY-N	150	591	86	**189**	**40**	10	4	70	32	28	22	18	**.320**	.358	.442	.799	150	29	94	5.73	-17	*2-113	33	1.7
1916	NY-N	113	441	53	118	24	10	2	47	27	23	17	....	.268	.316	.381	.697	120	9	68	4.59	14	*2-113	18	2.9
	Chi-N	9	38	6	15	5	1	1	7	1	1	2	....	.395	.410	.658	1.068	204	4	11	12.38	4	/2-9	2	1.0
	Yr.	122	4"9	61	133	29	11	3	54	28	24	19	....	.278	.323	.403	.726	126	13	71	5.09	18	*2-122	20	3.9

YEAR TM-L	G	AB	R	H	2B	3B	HR	RBI	BB	SO	SB	CS	AVG	OBP	SLG	OPS	OPS+	BR/A	RC	RC/G	FR	G/POS	WS	TPW
1917 Chi-N	135	476	48	121	19	5	6	61	48	28	5	....	.254	.323	.353	.675	99	0	56	3.85	0	*2-128	18	0.3
1918 NY-N	75	257	38	67	7	4	3	36	37	10	10	....	.261	.354	.354	.708	118	7	34	4.58	1	2-73	12	1.0
1919 NY-N	113	381	61	110	14	10	7	52	31	17	12	....	.289	.350	.433	.783	136	16	59	5.56	11	*2-100	20	3.3
1920 NY-N	137	471	48	134	21	2	4	50	47	28	11	9	.285	.352	.363	.715	107	6	61	4.56	-24	*2-133	16	-1.7
Total 14	**1766**	**6509**	**960**	**1887**	**299**	**123**	**74**	**793**	**625**	**274**	**298**	**27**	**.290**	**.357**	**.408**	**.765**	**126**	**206**	**1041**	**5.58**	**-126**	***2-1728**	**289**	**11.3**

• DOZIER, D.J. William Henry Dozier b: 9/21/1965, Norfolk, VA BR/TR, 6', 202 lbs. Deb: 5/6/1992

YEAR TM-L	G	AB	R	H	2B	3B	HR	RBI	BB	SO	SB	CS	AVG	OBP	SLG	OPS	OPS+	BR/A	RC	RC/G	FR	G/POS	WS	TPW
1992 NY-N	25	47	4	9	2	0	0	2	4	19	4	0	.191	.269	.234	.503	44	-2	4	2.70	-1	0-17(17-0-0)	1	-0.4

• DRAKE, Delos Delos Daniel Drake b: 12/3/1886, Girard, OH d: 10/3/1965, Findlay, OH BR/TL, 5'11.5", 170 lbs. Deb: 4/30/1911 Career OF: 150-103-49

YEAR TM-L	G	AB	R	H	2B	3B	HR	RBI	BB	SO	SB	CS	AVG	OBP	SLG	OPS	OPS+	BR/A	RC	RC/G	FR	G/POS	WS	TPW
1911 Det-A	95	315	37	88	9	9	1	36	17	....	20	....	.279	.324	.375	.699	90	-5	44	4.88	-7	0-83(74-5-5)/1-2	7	-1.6
1914 StL-F	138	514	51	129	18	8	3	42	31	57	17	....	.251	.295	.335	.630	75	-19	54	3.41	-4	*0-116(69-36-11),1-18	8	-3.0
1915 StL-F	102	343	32	91	23	4	1	41	23	27	6	....	.265	.313	.364	.678	94	-3	40	3.95	-3	0-97(7-62-33)/1-1	8	-1.3
Total 3	**335**	**1172**	**120**	**308**	**50**	**21**	**5**	**119**	**71**	**84**	**43**	**....**	**.263**	**.308**	**.354**	**.662**	**85**	**-27**	**137**	**3.95**	**-14**	**0-296/1-21**	**23**	**-5.8**

• DRAKE, Larry Larry Francis Drake b: 5/4/1921, McKinney, TX d: 7/14/1985, Houston, TX BL/TR, 6'1.5", 195 lbs. Deb: 7/20/1945 Career OF: 1-0-2

YEAR TM-L	G	AB	R	H	2B	3B	HR	RBI	BB	SO	SB	CS	AVG	OBP	SLG	OPS	OPS+	BR/A	RC	RC/G	FR	G/POS	WS	TPW
1945 Phi-A	1	2	0	0	0	0	0	0	0	2	0	0	.000	.000	.000	.000	-100	-1	0	.00	0	/0-1	0	-0.1
1948 Was-A	4	7	0	2	0	0	0	1	1	3	0	0	.286	.375	.286	.661	79	-0	1	4.25	-0	/0-2(0-0-2)	0	0.0
Total 2	**5**	**9**	**0**	**2**	**0**	**0**	**0**	**1**	**1**	**5**	**0**	**0**	**.222**	**.300**	**.222**	**.522**	**47**	**-1**	**1**	**3.18**	**0**	**/0-3**	**0**	**-0.1**

• DRAKE, Lyman Lyman Daniel Drake b: 2/9/1852, Berea, OH d: 2/6/1932, Muskegon, MI, 6' Deb: 6/29/1884

YEAR TM-L	G	AB	R	H	2B	3B	HR	RBI	BB	SO	SB	CS	AVG	OBP	SLG	OPS	OPS+	BR/A	RC	RC/G	FR	G/POS	WS	TPW
1884 Was-a	2	7	0	2	1	0	0	2	0	....	....	....	.286	.286	.429	.714	147	0	1	4.83	-1	/0-2(0-0-2)	0	0.0

• DRAKE, Sammy Samuel Harrison Drake b: 10/7/1934, Little Rock, AR BB/TR, 5'11", 175 lbs. Deb: 4/17/1960

YEAR TM-L	G	AB	R	H	2B	3B	HR	RBI	BB	SO	SB	CS	AVG	OBP	SLG	OPS	OPS+	BR/A	RC	RC/G	FR	G/POS	WS	TPW
1960 Chi-N	15	15	5	1	0	0	0	0	1	4	0	0	.067	.125	.067	.192	-46	-3	0	.30	-1	/3-6,2-2	0	-0.5
1961 Chi-N	13	5	1	0	0	0	0	0	1	1	0	0	.000	.167	.000	.167	-50	-1	0	.23	-0	/0-1	0	-0.1
1962 NY-N	25	52	2	10	0	0	0	7	6	12	0	0	.192	.276	.192	.468	28	-5	3	2.01	-1	2-10/3-6	0	-0.6
Total 3	**53**	**72**	**8**	**11**	**0**	**0**	**0**	**7**	**8**	**17**	**0**	**0**	**.153**	**.238**	**.153**	**.390**	**7**	**-9**	**3**	**1.48**	**-3**	**/2-12,3-12,0-1**	**0**	**-1.1**

• DRAKE, Solly Solomon Louis Drake b: 10/23/1930, Little Rock, AR BB/TR, 6', 170 lbs. Deb: 4/17/1956 Career OF: 22-64-13

YEAR TM-L	G	AB	R	H	2B	3B	HR	RBI	BB	SO	SB	CS	AVG	OBP	SLG	OPS	OPS+	BR/A	RC	RC/G	FR	G/POS	WS	TPW
1956 Chi-N	65	215	29	55	9	1	2	15	23	35	9	5	.256	.331	.335	.665	81	-5	26	4.15	-1	0-53(0-53-0)	5	-0.9
1959 LA-N	9	8	2	2	0	0	0	0	1	3	1	0	.250	.333	.250	.583	54	-0	1	4.17	0	/0-4(0-0-4)	0	-0.1
Phi-N	67	62	10	9	1	0	0	3	8	15	5	5	.145	.243	.161	.404	10	-9	3	1.17	-1	0-37(22-11-9)	0	-1.0
Yr.	76	70	12	11	1	0	0	3	9	18	6	5	.157	.253	.171	.425	15	-9	3	1.45	-1	0-41(22-11-13)	0	-1.1
Total 2	**141**	**285**	**41**	**66**	**10**	**1**	**2**	**18**	**32**	**53**	**15**	**10**	**.232**	**.311**	**.295**	**.606**	**65**	**-15**	**29**	**3.41**	**-2**	**/0-94**	**5**	**-2.0**

• DRANSFELDT, Kelly Kelly Daniel Dransfeldt b: 4/16/1975, Joliet, IL BR/TR, 6'2", 195 lbs. Deb: 5/1/1999

YEAR TM-L	G	AB	R	H	2B	3B	HR	RBI	BB	SO	SB	CS	AVG	OBP	SLG	OPS	OPS+	BR/A	RC	RC/G	FR	G/POS	WS	TPW
1999 Tex-A	16	53	3	10	1	0	1	5	3	12	0	0	.189	.232	.264	.496	25	-6	3	1.73	2	S-16	1	-0.3
2000 Tex-A	16	26	2	3	2	0	0	2	1	14	0	0	.115	.148	.192	.340	-14	-5	1	.91	3	S-14/2-2	1	-0.1
2001 Tex-A	4	3	0	0	0	0	0	0	0	0	0	0	.000	.000	.000	.000	-97	-1	0	.00	0	/S-3,3-1	0	-0.1
Total 3	**36**	**82**	**5**	**13**	**3**	**0**	**1**	**7**	**4**	**26**	**0**	**0**	**.159**	**.198**	**.232**	**.429**	**9**	**-12**	**4**	**1.40**	**5**	**/S-33,2-2,3-1**	**2**	**-0.4**

• DRAUBY, Jake Jacob C. Drauby b: 1865, Harrisburg, PA, 5'10", 163 lbs. Deb: 10/3/1892

YEAR TM-L	G	AB	R	H	2B	3B	HR	RBI	BB	SO	SB	CS	AVG	OBP	SLG	OPS	OPS+	BR/A	RC	RC/G	FR	G/POS	WS	TPW
1892 Was-N	10	34	3	7	0	1	0	3	2	12	0	....	.206	.250	.265	.515	57	-2	2	2.31	-3	3-10	0	-0.4

• DREESEN, Bill William Richard Dreesen b: 7/26/1904, New York, NY d: 11/9/1971, Mount Vernon, NY BL/TR, 5'7.5", 160 lbs. Deb: 5/1/1931

YEAR TM-L	G	AB	R	H	2B	3B	HR	RBI	BB	SO	SB	CS	AVG	OBP	SLG	OPS	OPS+	BR/A	RC	RC/G	FR	G/POS	WS	TPW
1931 Bos-N	48	180	38	40	10	4	1	10	23	23	1	....	.222	.310	.339	.649	77	-6	20	3.73	-2	3-47	3	-0.6

• DRESCHER, Bill William Clayton "Dutch" Drescher b: 5/23/1921, Congers, NY d: 5/15/1968, Haverstraw, NY BL/TR, 6'2", 190 lbs. Deb: 4/19/1944

YEAR TM-L	G	AB	R	H	2B	3B	HR	RBI	BB	SO	SB	CS	AVG	OBP	SLG	OPS	OPS+	BR/A	RC	RC/G	FR	G/POS	WS	TPW
1944 NY-A	4	7	0	1	0	0	0	0	0	0	0	0	.143	.143	.143	.286	-18	-1	0	.00	0	/C-1	0	-0.1
1945 NY-A	48	126	10	34	3	1	0	15	8	5	0	2	.270	.313	.310	.623	77	-4	12	3.16	-2	C-33	2	-0.5
1946 NY-A	5	6	0	2	1	0	0	1	0	0	0	0	.333	.333	.500	.833	129	0	1	6.92	0	/C-3	0	0.1
Total 3	**57**	**139**	**10**	**37**	**4**	**1**	**0**	**16**	**8**	**5**	**0**	**2**	**.266**	**.306**	**.309**	**.615**	**75**	**-5**	**13**	**3.10**	**-1**	**/C-37**	**2**	**-0.5**

• DRESSEN, Chuck Charles Walter Dressen b: 9/20/1898, Decatur, IL d: 8/10/1966, Detroit, MI BR/TR, 5'5.5", 146 lbs. Deb: 4/17/1925 M/C Career OF: 4-0-1

YEAR TM-L	G	AB	R	H	2B	3B	HR	RBI	BB	SO	SB	CS	AVG	OBP	SLG	OPS	OPS+	BR/A	RC	RC/G	FR	G/POS	WS	TPW
1925 Cin-N	76	215	35	59	8	2	3	19	12	4	5	3	.274	.319	.372	.691	78	-7	26	4.06	3	3-47/2-5,0-4(3-0-1)	6	-0.2
1926 Cin-N	127	474	76	126	27	11	4	48	49	31	0	....	.266	.338	.395	.733	99	-0	63	4.57	14	*3-123/0-1,S-1	18	2.1
1927 Cin-N	144	548	78	160	36	10	2	55	71	32	7	....	.292	.376	.405	.781	113	12	85	5.35	12	*3-142/S-2	23	3.3
1928 Cin-N	135	498	72	145	26	3	1	59	43	22	10	....	.291	.355	.361	.716	89	-7	64	4.44	-1	*3-135	16	0.0
1929 Cin-N	110	401	49	98	22	3	1	36	41	21	8	....	.244	.321	.322	.642	63	-23	42	3.50	-11	3-98/2-8	6	-2.5
1930 Cin-N	33	19	0	4	0	0	0	1	1	3	0	....	.211	.250	.211	.461	14	-3	1	1.72	-2	3-10/2-3	0	-0.4
1931 Cin-N	5	15	0	1	0	0	0	0	1	1	0	....	.067	.125	.067	.192	-50	-3	0	.28	-1	/3-4	0	-0.4
1933 NY-N	16	45	3	10	4	0	0	3	1	4	0	....	.222	.239	.311	.550	57	-3	3	2.06	-2	3-16	0	-0.4
Total 8	**646**	**2215**	**313**	**603**	**123**	**29**	**11**	**221**	**219**	**118**	**30**	**3**	**.272**	**.343**	**.369**	**.711**	**89**	**-34**	**285**	**4.37**	**12**	**3-575/2-16,0-5,S-3**	**69**	**1.6**

• DRESSEN, Lee Lee August Dressen b: 7/23/1889, Ellinwood, KS d: 6/30/1931, Diller, NE BL/TL, 6', 165 lbs. Deb: 4/21/1914

YEAR TM-L	G	AB	R	H	2B	3B	HR	RBI	BB	SO	SB	CS	AVG	OBP	SLG	OPS	OPS+	BR/A	RC	RC/G	FR	G/POS	WS	TPW
1914 StL-N	46	103	16	24	2	1	0	7	11	20	2	....	.233	.307	.272	.579	73	-3	9	2.88	0	1-38	2	-0.3
1918 Det-A	31	107	10	19	1	2	0	3	21	10	2	....	.178	.323	.224	.547	68	-3	9	2.40	-1	1-30	2	-0.5
Total 2	**77**	**210**	**26**	**43**	**3**	**3**	**0**	**10**	**32**	**30**	**4**	**....**	**.205**	**.316**	**.248**	**.563**	**70**	**-6**	**18**	**2.63**	**-1**	**/1-68**	**4**	**-0.9**

• DREW, Cameron Cameron Steward Drew b: 2/12/1964, Boston, MA BL/TR, 6'5", 230 lbs. Deb: 9/9/1988

YEAR TM-L	G	AB	R	H	2B	3B	HR	RBI	BB	SO	SB	CS	AVG	OBP	SLG	OPS	OPS+	BR/A	RC	RC/G	FR	G/POS	WS	TPW
1988 Hou-N	7	16	1	3	0	1	0	1	0	1	0	0	.188	.188	.313	.500	43	-1	1	1.95	0	/0-5(3-0-2)	0	-0.2

• DREW, Dave David Drew Deb: 5/14/1884

YEAR TM-L	G	AB	R	H	2B	3B	HR	RBI	BB	SO	SB	CS	AVG	OBP	SLG	OPS	OPS+	BR/A	RC	RC/G	FR	G/POS	WS	TPW
1884 Phi-U	2	9	1	4	0	0	0	....	0	....	....	....	.444	.444	.444	.889	218	1	2	10.20	0	/2-1,P-1,S-1	1	0.1
Was-U	13	53	8	16	1	2	0	....	1	....	....	....	.302	.315	.396	.711	144	2	7	5.13	1	/S-8,1-5,0-1	2	0.2
Yr.	15	62	9	20	1	2	0	....	1	....	....	....	.323	.333	.403	.737	154	3	9	5.73	1	/S-9,1-5,2-1,0-1,P-1	3	0.3

• DREW, J.D. David Jonathan Drew b: 11/20/1975, Tallahassee, FL BL/TR, 6'1", 195 lbs. Deb: 9/8/1998 Career OF: 33-177-372

YEAR TM-L	G	AB	R	H	2B	3B	HR	RBI	BB	SO	SB	CS	AVG	OBP	SLG	OPS	OPS+	BR/A	RC	RC/G	FR	G/POS	WS	TPW
1998 StL-N	14	36	9	15	3	1	5	13	4	10	0	0	.417	.475	.972	1.447	271	9	13	13.89	0	0-11(6-2-5)	3	0.8
1999 StL-N	104	368	72	89	16	6	13	39	50	77	19	3	.242	.342	.424	.766	92	-2	59	5.45	0	0-98(1-97-0)	10	-0.1
2000*StL-N	135	407	73	120	17	2	18	57	67	99	17	9	.295	.402	.479	.881	121	15	84	7.41	-2	*0-127(24-26-98)	18	0.8
2001*StL-N	109	375	80	121	18	5	27	73	57	75	13	3	.323	.417	.613	1.031	163	38	100	9.97	0	*0-107(1-20-97)	22	3.2
2002*StL-N	135	424	61	107	19	1	18	56	57	104	8	2	.252	.352	.429	.781	107	6	69	5.63	-3	*0-120(0-6-119)	15	-0.2
2003 StL-N	100	287	60	83	13	3	15	42	36	48	2	2	.289	.374	.512	.886	134	14	55	6.98	1	0-75(1-26-53)	13	1.2
Total 6	**597**	**1897**	**355**	**535**	**86**	**18**	**96**	**280**	**271**	**413**	**59**	**19**	**.282**	**.379**	**.498**	**.878**	**125**	**80**	**380**	**7.14**	**-2**	**0-538**	**81**	**5.8**

• DREWS, Frank Frank John Drews b: 5/25/1916, Buffalo, NY d: 4/22/1972, Buffalo, NY BR/TR, 5'10", 175 lbs. Deb: 8/13/1944

YEAR TM-L	G	AB	R	H	2B	3B	HR	RBI	BB	SO	SB	CS	AVG	OBP	SLG	OPS	OPS+	BR/A	RC	RC/G	FR	G/POS	WS	TPW
1944 Bos-N	46	141	14	29	9	1	0	10	25	14	0	....	.206	.329	.284	.613	71	-5	15	3.39	0	2-46	4	-0.2
1945 Bos-N	49	147	13	30	4	1	0	19	16	18	0	....	.204	.282	.245	.527	47	-10	12	2.59	2	2-48	1	-0.6
Total 2	**95**	**288**	**27**	**59**	**13**	**2**	**0**	**29**	**41**	**32**	**0**	**....**	**.205**	**.306**	**.264**	**.570**	**59**	**-15**	**26**	**2.98**	**3**	**/2-94**	**5**	**-0.8**

• DRIESSEN, Dan Daniel Driessen b: 7/29/1951, Hilton Head Island, SC BL/TR, 5'11", 190 lbs. Deb: 6/9/1973 Career OF: 30-0-23

YEAR TM-L	G	AB	R	H	2B	3B	HR	RBI	BB	SO	SB	CS	AVG	OBP	SLG	OPS	OPS+	BR/A	RC	RC/G	FR	G/POS	WS	TPW
1973*Cin-N	102	366	49	110	15	2	4	47	24	37	8	3	.301	.347	.385	.732	108	4	48	4.84	4	3-87,1-35/0-1	12	0.7
1974 Cin-N	150	470	63	132	23	6	7	56	48	62	10	5	.281	.349	.400	.749	111	6	66	5.01	-5	*3-126,1-47/0-3(0-0-3)	14	0.0
1975*Cin-N	88	210	38	59	8	1	7	38	35	30	10	3	.281	.389	.429	.817	124	9	36	5.92	-1	1-41,0-29(10-0-19)	8	0.5
1976*Cin-N	98	219	32	54	11	1	7	44	43	32	14	1	.247	.370	.402	.772	116	9	35	5.10	1	1-40,0-20(20-0-0)	7	0.6
1977 Cin-N	151	536	75	161	31	4	17	91	64	85	31	13	.300	.378	.468	.846	123	20	95	6.35	-4	*1-148	19	0.7
1978 Cin-N	153	524	68	131	23	3	16	70	75	79	28	9	.250	.348	.397	.745	108	9	76	4.81	4	*1-151	18	0.5
1979*Cin-N	150	515	72	129	24	3	18	75	62	77	11	5	.250	.334	.414	.748	102	2	74	4.91	3	*1-143	15	-0.4
1980 Cin-N	154	524	81	139	36	1	14	74	**93**	68	19	6	.265	.382	.418	.800	123	22	88	5.73	2	*1-151	21	1.5
1981 Cin-N	82	233	35	55	14	0	7	33	40	31	2	4	.236	.353	.386	.739	108	2	33	4.59	-4	1-74	8	-0.6

YEAR TM-L	G	AB	R	H	2B	3B	HR	RBI	BB	SO	SB	CS	AVG	OBP	SLG	OPS	OPS+	BR/A	RC	RC/G	FR	G/POS	WS	TPW
1982 Cin-N	149	516	64	139	25	1	17	57	82	62	11	6	.269	.372	.421	.792	119	15	85	5.76	-11	*1-144	15	-0.5
1983 Cin-N	122	386	57	107	17	1	12	57	75	51	6	4	.277	.395	.420	.814	121	14	66	5.90	1	*1-112	16	0.9
1984 Cin-N	81	218	27	61	13	0	7	28	37	25	2	1	.280	.384	.436	.820	124	8	38	6.16	-3	1-70	8	0.1
Mon-N	51	169	20	43	11	0	9	32	17	15	0	1	.254	.323	.479	.802	128	5	24	4.91	0	1-45	5	0.2
Yr.	132	387	47	104	24	0	16	60	54	40	2	2	.269	.358	.455	.813	126	13	62	5.60	-4	*1-115	13	0.4
1985 Mon-N	91	312	31	78	18	0	6	25	33	29	2	2	.250	.326	.365	.691	99	-1	36	3.97	2	1-88	8	-0.5
SF-N	54	181	22	42	8	0	3	22	17	22	0	0	.232	.302	.326	.627	79	-5	19	3.47	0	1-49	3	-0.8
Yr.	145	493	53	120	26	0	9	47	50	51	2	2	.243	.317	.351	.668	92	-6	55	3.78	2	*1-137	11	-1.3
1986 SF-N	15	16	2	3	2	0	0	0	4	4	0	0	.188	.350	.313	.663	88	-0	2	4.20	1	/1-4	0	0.0
Hou-N	17	24	5	7	1	0	1	3	5	2	0	0	.292	.414	.458	.872	144	2	5	7.91	0	1-12	1	0.1
Yr.	32	40	7	10	3	0	1	3	9	6	0	0	.250	.388	.400	.788	121	2	7	6.30	0	1-16	1	0.1
1987*StL-N	24	60	5	14	2	0	1	11	7	8	0	0	.233	.313	.317	.630	66	-3	6	3.25	-1	1-21	1	-0.5
Total 15	1732	5479	746	1464	282	23	153	763	761	719	154	63	.267	.359	.411	.770	113	119	830	5.24	-13	*1-1375,3-213/0-53	179	2.6

• DRILL, Lew Lewis L. Drill b: 5/9/1877, Browerville, MN d: 7/4/1969, St. Paul, MN BR/TR, 5'6", 186 lbs. Deb: 4/23/1902 U Career OF: 1-3-18

YEAR TM-L	G	AB	R	H	2B	3B	HR	RBI	BB	SO	SB	CS	AVG	OBP	SLG	OPS	OPS+	BR/A	RC	RC/G	FR	G/POS	WS	TPW
1902 Was-A	38	123	21	34	7	2	1	16	16	....	0	....	.276	.369	.390	.759	110	2	19	5.33	-5	C-28/2-4,0-4(1-0-3),3-1	0	-0.1
Bal-A	2	8	2	2	0	0	0	0	0	....	0	....	.250	.250	.250	.500	37	-1	1	2.26	0	/1-1,C-1	0	0.0
Was-A	33	98	12	24	3	2	0	13	10	....	5	....	.245	.327	.316	.644	78	-1	12	4.29	-3	C-25/0-4(0-0-4),2-1	6	-0.2
Yr.	73	229	35	60	10	4	1	29	26	....	5	....	.262	.347	.354	.701	94	0	32	4.77	-8	C-54/0-8(1-0-7),2-5,1-1,3	6	-0.3
1903 Was-A	51	154	11	39	9	3	0	23	15	....	4	....	.253	.331	.351	.682	103	1	20	4.52	-2	C-47/1-3	4	0.4
1904 Was-A	46	142	17	38	7	2	1	11	21	....	3	....	.268	.385	.366	.751	140	8	22	5.51	-1	C-29,0-14(0-3-11)	8	1.1
Det-A	51	160	7	39	6	1	0	13	20	....	2	....	.244	.335	.294	.629	103	2	17	3.70	-1	C-49/1-2	6	0.5
Yr.	97	302	24	77	13	3	1	24	41	....	5	....	.255	.359	.328	.687	121	10	39	4.53	-2	C-78,0-14(0-3-11)/1-2	14	1.6
1905 Det-A	72	211	17	55	9	0	0	24	32	....	7	....	.261	.366	.303	.669	112	5	28	4.51	-1	C-71	12	1.3
Total 4	293	896	87	231	41	10	2	100	114	....	21	....	.258	.353	.333	.686	109	16	119	4.59	-13	C-250/0-22,1-6,2-5,3-1	36	3.0

• DRISCOLL, Dennis Dennis F. Driscoll d: 2/21/1901, Providence, RI, 160 lbs. Deb: 7/25/1885

YEAR TM-L	G	AB	R	H	2B	3B	HR	RBI	BB	SO	SB	CS	AVG	OBP	SLG	OPS	OPS+	BR/A	RC	RC/G	FR	G/POS	WS	TPW
1885 Buf-N	7	19	2	3	0	0	0	0	2	5	....	....	.158	.238	.158	.396	29	-1	1	1.24	-3	/2-7	0	-0.4

• DRISCOLL, Denny John F. Driscoll b: 11/19/1855, Lowell, MA d: 7/11/1886, Lowell, MA BL/TL, 5'10.5", 160 lbs. Deb: 7/1/1880 Career OF: 1-17-2 ♦

YEAR TM-L	G	AB	R	H	2B	3B	HR	RBI	BB	SO	SB	CS	AVG	OBP	SLG	OPS	OPS+	BR/A	RC	RC/G	FR	G/POS	WS	TPW
1880 Buf-N	18	65	1	10	1	0	0	4	1	7	....	....	.154	.167	.169	.336	14	-5	2	.94	0	0-14(0-14-0)/P-6	0	-0.9
1882 Pit-a	23	80	12	11	2	0	1	....	3	....	....	....	.138	.169	.200	.369	25	-2	3	1.12	-3	P-23	17	2.8
1883 Pit-a	41	148	19	27	2	1	0	0	4	....	....	....	.182	.204	.209	.413	35	-5	6	1.50	4	P-41/0-4(0-2-2),3-1	10	-2.4
1884 Lou-a	13	48	5	9	1	0	0	1	2	....	....	....	.188	.220	.208	.428	42	-1	2	1.59	2	P-13/0-2(1-1-0)	4	-0.8
Total 4	95	341	37	57	6	1	1	5	10	7	....	....	.167	.191	.199	.390	30	-13	13	1.31	3	/P-83,0-20,3-1	31	-1.4

• DRISCOLL, Jim James Bernard Driscoll b: 5/14/1944, Medford, MA BL/TR, 5'11", 175 lbs. Deb: 6/17/1970

YEAR TM-L	G	AB	R	H	2B	3B	HR	RBI	BB	SO	SB	CS	AVG	OBP	SLG	OPS	OPS+	BR/A	RC	RC/G	FR	G/POS	WS	TPW
1970 Oak-A	21	52	2	10	0	0	1	2	2	15	0	0	.192	.236	.250	.486	35	-5	3	1.88	-2	/2-7,S-7	0	-0.6
1972 Tex-A	15	18	0	0	0	0	0	0	2	3	0	0	.000	.100	.000	.100	-72	-4	0	.02	0	/2-4,3-2	0	-0.4
Total 2	36	70	2	10	0	0	1	2	4	18	0	0	.143	.200	.186	.386	7	-8	3	1.32	-3	/2-11,S-7,3-2	0	-1.0

• DRISCOLL, Paddy John Leo Driscoll b: 1/11/1895, Evanston, IL d: 6/28/1968, Chicago, IL BR/TR, 5'8.5", 155 lbs. Deb: 6/12/1917

YEAR TM-L	G	AB	R	H	2B	3B	HR	RBI	BB	SO	SB	CS	AVG	OBP	SLG	OPS	OPS+	BR/A	RC	RC/G	FR	G/POS	WS	TPW
1917 Chi-N	13	28	2	3	1	0	0	3	2	6	2	....	.107	.167	.143	.310	-4	-3	1	.99	-1	/2-8,3-2,S-1	0	-0.5

• DRISSEL, Mike Michael F. Drissel b: 12/19/1864, St. Louis, MO d: 2/26/1913, St. Louis, MO BR/TR, 5'11" Deb: 9/5/1885

YEAR TM-L	G	AB	R	H	2B	3B	HR	RBI	BB	SO	SB	CS	AVG	OBP	SLG	OPS	OPS+	BR/A	RC	RC/G	FR	G/POS	WS	TPW
1885 StL-a	6	20	0	1	0	0	0	0	0	....	....	....	.050	.050	.050	.100	-65	-4	0	.07	0	/C-6	0	-0.3

• DROPO, Walt Walter "Moose" Dropo b: 1/30/1923, Moosup, CT BR/TR, 6'5", 220 lbs. Deb: 4/19/1949

YEAR TM-L	G	AB	R	H	2B	3B	HR	RBI	BB	SO	SB	CS	AVG	OBP	SLG	OPS	OPS+	BR/A	RC	RC/G	FR	G/POS	WS	TPW
1949 Bos-A	11	41	3	6	2	0	0	1	3	7	0	0	.146	.205	.195	.400	6	-6	1	1.04	-2	1-11	0	-0.7
1950 Bos-A★	136	559	101	180	28	8	34	**144**	45	75	0	0	.322	.378	.583	.961	130	22	122	8.34	-5	*1-134	21	1.2
1951 Bos-A	99	360	37	86	14	0	11	57	38	52	0	0	.239	.312	.369	.681	76	-13	40	3.69	-3	1-93	5	-1.9
1952 Bos-A	37	132	13	35	7	1	6	27	11	22	0	0	.265	.331	.470	.801	112	2	18	4.59	-2	1-35	3	-0.2
Det-A	115	459	56	128	17	3	23	70	26	63	2	2	.279	.320	.479	.800	120	9	66	5.06	-3	*1-115	11	0.2
Yr.	152	591	69	163	24	4	29	97	37	85	2	2	.276	.323	.477	.800	118	10	84	4.95	-5	*1-150	14	0.0
1953 Det-A	152	606	61	150	30	3	13	96	29	69	2	0	.248	.289	.371	.660	78	-20	61	3.44	7	*1-150	8	-2.2
1954 Det-A	107	320	27	90	14	2	4	44	24	41	0	1	.281	.331	.375	.706	95	-3	37	3.95	1	1-95	6	-0.6
1955 Chi-A	141	453	55	127	15	2	19	79	42	71	0	1	.280	.344	.448	.792	109	4	66	5.16	-5	*1-140	13	-0.8
1956 Chi-A	125	361	42	96	13	1	8	52	37	51	1	0	.266	.339	.374	.713	87	-6	44	4.12	-6	*1-117	7	-1.8
1957 Chi-A	93	223	24	57	2	0	13	49	16	40	0	1	.256	.305	.439	.745	101	-1	26	3.93	1	1-69	5	-0.3
1958 Chi-A	28	52	3	10	1	0	2	8	5	11	0	0	.192	.276	.327	.603	66	-2	4	2.47	1	1-16	0	-0.2
Cin-N	63	162	18	47	7	2	7	31	12	31	0	0	.290	.343	.488	.831	111	2	25	5.36	2	1-43	4	0.2
1959 Cin-N	26	39	4	4	1	0	1	2	4	7	0	0	.103	.205	.205	.410	9	-5	1	.90	1	1-23	0	-0.5
Bal-A	62	151	17	42	9	0	6	21	12	20	0	0	.278	.331	.457	.788	117	3	21	4.87	-2	1-54/3-2	4	-0.2
1960 Bal-A	79	179	16	48	8	0	4	21	20	19	0	1	.268	.345	.380	.725	97	-1	22	4.13	-2	1-67/3-1	4	-0.6
1961 Bal-A	14	27	1	7	0	0	1	2	4	3	0	0	.259	.355	.370	.725	96	-0	3	3.34	1	1-12	1	0.0
Total 13	1288	4124	478	1113	168	22	152	704	328	582	5	6	.270	.327	.432	.759	99	-17	559	4.68	-16	*1-1174/3-3	92	-8.5

• DRUMRIGHT, Keith Keith Alan Drumright b: 10/21/1954, Springfield, MO BL/TR, 5'10", 170 lbs. Deb: 9/1/1978

YEAR TM-L	G	AB	R	H	2B	3B	HR	RBI	BB	SO	SB	CS	AVG	OBP	SLG	OPS	OPS+	BR/A	RC	RC/G	FR	G/POS	WS	TPW
1978 Hou-N	17	55	5	9	0	0	0	2	3	4	0	1	.164	.207	.164	.371	5	-7	2	.85	-1	2-17	0	-0.8
1981*Oak-A	31	86	8	25	1	1	0	11	4	4	0	0	.291	.322	.326	.648	91	-1	9	3.48	1	2-19/D-5	2	0.1
Total 2	48	141	13	34	1	1	0	13	7	8	0	1	.241	.277	.262	.539	58	-8	10	2.34	1	/2-36,D-5	2	-0.7

• DUCEY, Rob Robert Thomas Ducey b: 5/24/1965, Toronto, Canada BL/TR, 6'2", 180 lbs. Deb: 5/1/1987 Career OF: 237-89-160

YEAR TM-L	G	AB	R	H	2B	3B	HR	RBI	BB	SO	SB	CS	AVG	OBP	SLG	OPS	OPS+	BR/A	RC	RC/G	FR	G/POS	WS	TPW
1987 Tor-A	34	48	12	9	1	0	1	6	8	10	2	0	.188	.304	.271	.574	53	-3	5	3.35	-1	0-28(17-11-3)/D-1	1	-0.4
1988 Tor-A	27	54	15	17	4	1	0	6	5	7	1	0	.315	.373	.426	.799	123	2	9	5.76	0	0-26(1-25-0)/D-1	2	0.1
1989 Tor-A	41	76	5	16	4	0	0	7	9	25	2	1	.211	.294	.263	.557	62	-4	6	2.55	2	0-35(16-2-18)/D-1	2	-0.3
1990 Tor-A	19	53	7	16	5	0	0	7	7	15	1	1	.302	.393	.396	.790	115	1	9	6.19	0	0-19(19-0-0)	3	0.0
1991*Tor-A	39	68	8	16	2	2	1	4	6	26	2	0	.235	.297	.368	.665	80	-2	8	3.94	-2	0-24(18-1-6)/D-2	1	-0.4
1992 Tor-A	23	21	3	1	1	0	0	0	0	10	0	1	.048	.048	.095	.143	-58	-5	0	.00	0	0-13(3-2-8)/D-4	0	-0.5
Cal-A	31	59	4	14	3	0	0	2	5	12	2	3	.237	.297	.288	.585	64	-4	5	2.47	0	0-20(17-1-2)/D-1	0	-0.5
Yr.	54	80	7	15	4	0	0	2	5	22	2	4	.188	.235	.238	.473	34	-9	5	1.74	0	0-33(20-3-10)/D-5	0	-1.0
1993 Tex-A	27	85	15	24	6	3	2	9	10	17	2	3	.282	.358	.494	.852	132	3	14	5.60	0	0-26(1-14-13)	3	0.2
1994 Tex-A	11	29	1	5	1	0	0	1	2	1	0	0	.172	.226	.207	.433	13	-4	1	1.36	-1	0-10(0-0-10)	0	-0.5
1997*Sea-A	76	143	25	41	15	2	5	10	6	31	3	3	.287	.315	.524	.840	115	2	21	5.28	0	0-69(43-12-19)	2	0.0
1998 Sea-A	97	217	30	52	18	2	5	23	23	61	4	3	.240	.337	.410	.747	93	-2	31	4.78	-1	0-83(23-6-61)	4	-0.6
1999 Phi-N	104	188	29	49	10	2	8	33	38	57	2	1	.261	.385	.463	.848	110	4	37	6.99	-1	0-58(39-9-11)/D-2	7	0.1
2000 Phi-N	70	106	16	20	3	1	6	20	20	36	1	0	.189	.317	.406	.723	80	-3	15	4.64	-2	0-25(24-1-1)/D-5	0	-0.5
Tor-A	5	13	2	2	1	0	0	1	2	2	0	0	.154	.267	.231	.497	27	-1	1	2.30	0	/0-3(2-0-1)	0	-0.1
Phi-N	42	46	8	10	1	0	0	5	9	11	0	0	.217	.345	.239	.585	51	-3	5	3.37	0	/0-8(4-1-3)	0	-0.3
Yr.	112	152	24	30	4	1	6	25	29	47	1	0	.197	.326	.355	.681	71	-6	20	4.26	-2	0-33(28-2-4)/D-5	0	-0.9
2001 Phi-N	30	27	4	6	1	0	1	4	6	11	0	0	.222	.364	.370	.734	93	-0	4	5.23	0	/0-3(1-1-1)	1	0.0
Mon-N	27	46	6	11	2	0	2	8	10	14	0	1	.239	.386	.413	.799	105	0	8	5.79	1	0-14(9-3-3)/D-2	2	0.1
Yr.	57	73	10	17	3	0	3	12	16	25	0	1	.233	.378	.397	.775	101	0	12	5.59	1	0-17(10-4-4)/D-2	3	0.1
Total 13	703	1279	190	309	78	13	31	146	166	346	22	17	.242	.334	.396	.729	91	-19	179	4.71	-5	0-464/D-19	28	-3.5

• DUDRA, John John Joseph Dudra b: 5/27/1916, Assumption, IL d: 10/24/1965, Pana, IL BR/TR, 5'11.5", 175 lbs. Deb: 9/7/1941

YEAR TM-L	G	AB	R	H	2B	3B	HR	RBI	BB	SO	SB	CS	AVG	OBP	SLG	OPS	OPS+	BR/A	RC	RC/G	FR	G/POS	WS	TPW
1941 Bos-N	14	25	3	9	3	1	0	3	3	4	0	....	.360	.429	.560	.989	185	3	6	10.69	0	/2-5,3-5,1-1,S-1	2	0.3

• DUFF, Pat Patrick Henry Duff b: 5/6/1875, Providence, RI d: 9/11/1925, Providence, RI TR, 5'10" Deb: 4/16/1906

YEAR TM-L	G	AB	R	H	2B	3B	HR	RBI	BB	SO	SB	CS	AVG	OBP	SLG	OPS	OPS+	BR/A	RC	RC/G	FR	G/POS	WS	TPW
1906 Was-A	1	1	0	0	0	0	0	0	0	....	0	....	.000	.000	.000	.000	-105	-0	0	.00	0	....	0	0.0

YEAR TM-L	G	AB	R	H	2B	3B	HR	RBI	BB	SO	SB	CS	AVG	OBP	SLG	OPS	OPS+	BR/A	RC	RC/G	FR	G/POS	WS	TPW
• DUFFEE, Charlie	Charles Edward "Home Run" Duffee b: 1/27/1866, Mobile, AL d: 12/24/1894, Mobile, AL BR/TR Deb: 4/17/1889 Career OF: 152-257-48																							
1889 StL-a	137	509	93	124	15	11	16	86	60	81	21	....	.244	.327	.411	.738	97	-7	77	5.30	13	*O-132(1-132-0)/3-5,2-2	19	0.1
1890 StL-a	98	378	68	104	11	7	3	54	37	....	20	....	.275	.344	.365	.710	96	-4	56	5.40	7	O-66(1-65-0),3-33/S-1	11	0.0
1891 Col-a	137	552	86	166	28	4	10	90	42	36	41	....	.301	.353	.420	.774	129	18	99	6.79	12	*O-128(73-55-0)/3-7,S-2	22	2.2
1892 Was-N	132	492	64	122	12	11	6	51	36	33	28	....	.248	.302	.354	.656	101	-1	63	4.56	16	*O-125(73-5-48)/3-6,1-4	12	0.5
1893 Cin-N	4	12	3	2	1	0	0	0	5	0	0	....	.167	.412	.250	.662	76	-0	1	3.36	-1	/O-4(4-0-0)	0	-0.1
Total 5	508	1943	314	518	67	33	35	281	180	150	110	....	.267	.332	.389	.721	106	6	296	5.52	46	O-455/3-51,1-4,S-3,2-2	64	2.8
• DUFFY, Ed	Edward Charles Duffy b: 1844, Ireland d: 6/21/1889, Brooklyn, NY TR, 5'7.5", 152 lbs. Deb: 5/8/1871																							
1871 Chi-n	26	121	30	28	5	0	0	15	3	2	11	4	.231	.250	.273	.523	45	-10	11	3.66	-5	*S-26/3-1	....	-1.0
• DUFFY, Frank	Frank Thomas Duffy b: 10/14/1946, Oakland, CA BR/TR, 6'1", 180 lbs. Deb: 9/4/1970																							
1970 Cin-N	6	11	1	2	2	0	0	0	1	2	1	0	.182	.250	.364	.614	60	-0	1	3.59	1	/S-5	0	0.1
1971 Cin-N	13	16	0	3	1	0	0	1	1	2	0	0	.188	.235	.250	.485	40	-1	1	2.08	-1	S-10	0	-0.1
*SF-N	21	28	4	5	0	0	0	2	0	10	0	0	.179	.179	.179	.357	1	-4	1	.82	0	/S-6,2-1,3-1	0	-0.3
Yr.	34	44	4	8	1	0	0	3	1	12	0	0	.182	.200	.205	.405	15	-5	2	1.25	0	S-16/2-1,3-1	0	-0.4
1972 Cle-A	130	385	23	92	16	4	3	27	31	54	6	2	.239	.297	.325	.622	82	-8	36	3.07	-5	*S-126	9	0.1
1973 Cle-A	116	361	34	95	16	4	8	50	25	41	6	6	.263	.314	.396	.711	97	-3	41	3.83	-8	*S-115	11	0.3
1974 Cle-A	158	549	62	128	18	0	8	48	30	64	7	8	.233	.273	.310	.583	68	-25	45	2.65	-7	*S-158	9	-1.5
1975 Cle-A	146	482	44	117	22	2	1	47	27	60	10	10	.243	.286	.303	.589	66	-24	39	2.65	19	*S-145	12	1.2
1976 Cle-A	133	392	38	83	11	2	2	30	29	50	10	0	.212	.270	.265	.535	58	-19	29	2.30	-6	*S-132	6	-1.1
1977 Cle-A	122	334	30	67	13	2	4	31	21	47	8	3	.201	.248	.287	.535	47	-24	24	2.18	-7	*S-121	4	-2.0
1978 Bos-A	64	104	12	27	5	0	0	4	6	11	1	1	.260	.306	.308	.614	66	-5	10	3.25	-2	3-22,S-21,2-12/D-6	3	-0.4
1979 Bos-A	6	3	0	0	0	0	0	0	0	1	0	0	.000	.000	.000	.000	-95	-1	0	.00	-1	/2-3,1-1	0	-0.1
Total 10	915	2665	248	619	104	14	26	240	171	342	49	30	.232	.281	.311	.592	68	-114	227	2.75	-16	S-839/3-23,2-16,D-6,1-1	54	-3.8
• DUFFY, Hugh	Hugh Duffy b: 11/26/1866, Cranston, RI d: 10/19/1954, Boston, MA BR/TR, 5'7", 168 lbs. Deb: 6/23/1888 M/C HOF: 1945 Career OF: 574-676-437																							
1888 Chi-N	71	298	60	84	10	4	7	41	9	32	13	....	.282	.305	.413	.718	118	5	43	5.37	6	O-67(3-0-64)/S-3,3-1	10	0.9
1889 Chi-N	136	584	144	172	21	7	12	89	46	30	52	....	.295	.348	.416	.764	108	3	105	6.77	-13	*O-126(0-0-126),S-10	17	-1.0
1890 Chi-P	138	596	**161**	**191**	36	16	7	82	59	20	78	....	.320	.384	.470	.853	122	16	141	9.38	14	*O-137(0-17-120)	26	2.2
1891 Bos-a	127	536	134	180	20	8	9	**110**	61	29	85	....	.336	.408	.453	.861	148	34	137	10.20	4	*O-124(7-2-118)/3-3,S-1	28	3.1
1892*Bos-N	147	612	125	184	28	12	5	81	60	37	51	....	.301	.364	.410	.774	123	15	113	7.11	-8	*O-146(0-146-0)/3-2	29	-0.3
1893 Bos-N	131	560	147	203	23	7	6	118	50	13	44	....	**.363**	.416	.461	.876	123	17	129	9.55	-7	*O-131(0-128-3)	**28**	0.2
1894 Bos-N	125	539	160	**237**	**51**	16	**18**	145	66	15	48	....	**.440**	.502	.694	**1.196**	165	57	217	**18.68**	3	*O-124(4-121-0)/S-2	**33**	4.0
1895 Bos-N	131	533	112	188	30	6	9	100	65	17	42	....	.353	.427	.482	.909	127	23	132	9.91	3	*O-130(0-130-0)	23	1.4
1896 Bos-N	131	527	97	158	16	8	5	113	52	19	39	....	.300	.365	.389	.754	93	-6	94	6.37	0	*O-120(114-6-0)/2-9,S-2	17	-1.4
1897*Bos-N	134	550	130	187	25	10	**11**	129	52	....	41	....	.340	.403	.482	.885	125	19	128	8.99	0	*O-129(129-0-0)/2-6,S-2	25	0.7
1898 Bos-N	152	568	97	169	13	3	8	108	59	....	29	....	.298	.365	.373	.738	106	5	92	5.88	2	*O-152(115-39-0)/1-1,3-1,C	25	-0.7
1899 Bos-N	147	588	103	164	29	7	5	102	39	....	26	....	.279	.327	.378	.705	85	-15	84	5.14	-5	*O-147(138-8-1)	17	-3.1
1900 Bos-N	55	181	27	55	5	4	2	31	16	....	11	....	.304	.360	.409	.769	100	-1	32	6.46	-3	O-49(44-5-0)/2-1	5	-0.7
1901 Mil-A	79	285	40	86	15	9	2	45	16	....	12	....	.302	.341	.439	.780	121	7	49	6.16	-7	O-77(12-65-0)	8	-0.3
1904 Phi-N	18	46	10	13	1	1	0	5	13	....	3	....	.283	.441	.348	.789	150	4	9	6.76	-1	O-14(8-6-0)	3	0.3
1905 Phi-N	15	40	7	12	2	1	0	3	1	....	0	....	.300	.317	.400	.717	117	1	5	4.83	0	/O-8(0-3-5)	1	0.0
1906 Phi-N	1	1	0	0	0	0	0	0	0	....	0	....	.000	.000	.000	.000	-100	-0	0	.00	0	....	0	0.0
Total 17	1738	7044	1554	2283	325	119	106	1302	664	212	574	....	.324	.385	.449	.834	120	184	1509	8.26	-11	*O-1681/S-20,2-16,3-7,1-1,C	295	5.3
• DUGAN, Bill	William H. Dugan b: 1864, New York, NY d: 7/24/1921, New York, NY Deb: 8/5/1884																							
1884 Ric-a	9	28	4	3	1	0	0	0	0	....	....	....	.107	.138	.143	.281	-8	-3	1	.62	-1	/C-9	0	-0.4
KC-U	3	6	0	0	0	0	0	....	0	....	....	....	.000	.000	.000	.000	-115	-1	0	.00	-1	/O-3(1-2-0)	0	-0.2
• DUGAN, Joe	Joseph Anthony "Jumping Joe" Dugan b: 5/12/1897, Mahanoy City, PA d: 7/7/1982, Norwood, PA BR/TR, 5'11", 160 lbs. Deb: 7/5/1917																							
1917 Phi-A	43	134	9	26	8	0	0	16	3	16	0	....	.194	.229	.254	.482	48	-9	8	1.80	-5	S-39/2-2	1	-1.2
1918 Phi-A	121	411	26	80	11	3	3	34	16	55	4	....	.195	.230	.258	.488	47	-29	25	1.84	2	S-86,2-34	4	-2.2
1919 Phi-A	104	387	25	105	17	2	1	30	11	30	9	....	.271	.300	.333	.634	77	-13	40	3.54	-15	S-98/2-4,3-2	6	-2.2
1920 Phi-A	123	491	65	158	40	5	3	60	19	51	5	8	.322	.351	.442	.793	108	3	73	5.52	-11	3-60,S-32,2-31	14	-0.4
1921 Phi-A	119	461	54	136	22	6	10	58	28	45	5	1	.295	.342	.434	.776	96	-3	69	5.41	-26	*3-119	9	-1.9
1922 Bos-A	84	341	45	98	22	3	3	38	9	28	2	3	.287	.308	.396	.704	83	-10	40	4.15	-7	3-64,S-21	7	-1.1
*NY-A	60	252	44	72	9	1	3	25	13	21	1	0	.286	.331	.365	.696	79	-7	31	4.32	-7	3-60	7	-1.0
Yr.	144	593	89	170	31	4	6	63	22	49	3	3	.287	.318	.383	.701	81	-18	71	4.23	-14	*3-124,S-21	14	-2.1
1923*NY-A	146	644	111	182	30	7	7	67	25	41	4	2	.283	.311	.384	.695	81	-19	76	4.24	-4	*3-146	17	-1.3
1924 NY-A	148	610	105	184	31	7	3	56	31	33	1	2	.302	.341	.390	.731	88	-12	81	4.76	-8	*3-148/2-2	17	-1.0
1925 NY-A	102	404	50	118	19	4	0	31	19	20	2	4	.292	.330	.359	.689	76	-16	47	4.14	8	3-96	9	-0.1
1926*NY-A	123	434	39	125	19	5	1	64	25	16	2	4	.288	.328	.362	.690	81	-14	52	4.07	-7	*3-122	10	-1.3
1927*NY-A	112	387	44	104	24	3	2	43	27	37	1	4	.269	.321	.362	.683	79	-14	45	3.98	-15	*3-111	6	-2.1
1928*NY-A	94	312	33	86	15	0	6	34	16	15	1	0	.276	.317	.381	.699	85	-7	38	4.33	-9	3-91/2-1	7	-1.0
1929 Bos-N	60	125	14	38	10	0	0	15	8	8	0	....	.304	.346	.384	.730	84	-3	16	4.55	-5	3-24/S-5,2-2,O-2(2-0-0)	2	-0.6
1931 Det-A	8	17	1	4	0	0	0	0	0	3	0	0	.235	.235	.235	.471	23	-2	1	1.84	-1	/3-5	0	-0.2
Total 14	1447	5410	665	1516	277	46	42	571	250	419	37	28	.280	.317	.372	.689	81	-154	643	4.14	-107	*3-1048,S-281/2-76,O-2	116	-17.6
• DUGAS, Gus	Augustin Joseph Dugas b: 3/24/1907, St. Jean de Matha, Canada d: 4/14/1997, Colchester, CT BL/TL, 5'9", 165 lbs. Deb: 9/17/1930 Career OF: 6-3-23																							
1930 Pit-N	9	31	8	9	2	0	0	1	7	4	0	....	.290	.421	.355	.776	90	-0	5	5.73	-1	/O-9(0-0-9)	1	-0.2
1932 Pit-N	55	97	13	23	3	3	3	12	7	11	0	....	.237	.288	.423	.711	90	-2	12	4.22	-2	O-20(6-1-13)	2	-0.4
1933 Phi-N	37	71	4	12	3	0	0	9	1	9	0	....	.169	.181	.211	.392	10	-8	2	1.06	-1	1-11/O-1	0	-1.1
1934 Was-A	24	19	2	1	1	0	0	1	3	3	0	0	.053	.182	.105	.287	-25	-4	0	.71	-0	/O-2(0-1-1)	0	-0.3
Total 4	125	218	27	45	9	3	3	23	18	27	0	0	.206	.267	.317	.583	55	-14	20	2.94	-3	/O-32,1-11	3	-2.0
• DUGDALE, Dan	Daniel Edward Dugdale b: 10/28/1864, Peoria, IL d: 3/9/1934, Seattle, WA, 5'8", 180 lbs. Deb: 5/20/1886 Career OF: 2-1-5																							
1886 KC-N	12	40	4	7	0	0	0	2	2	13	1	....	.175	.214	.175	.389	18	-4	2	1.44	-1	/C-7,O-6(0-1-5)	0	-0.4
1894 Was-N	38	134	19	32	4	2	0	16	13	14	7	....	.239	.306	.299	.605	48	-11	15	3.76	0	C-33/3-3,O-2(2-0-0)	1	-0.7
Total 2	50	174	23	39	4	2	0	18	15	27	8	....	.224	.286	.270	.556	41	-15	17	3.19	-1	/C-40,O-8,3-3	1	-1.1
• DUGEY, Oscar	Oscar Joseph "Jake" Dugey b: 10/25/1887, Palestine, TX d: 1/1/1966, Dallas, TX BR/TR, 5'8", 160 lbs. Deb: 9/13/1913 C Career OF: 1-2-16																							
1913 Bos-N	5	8	1	2	0	0	0	0	1	1	0	....	.250	.333	.250	.583	67	-0	1	2.68	-1	/3-2,2-1,S-1	0	-0.1
1914 Bos-N	58	109	17	21	2	0	1	10	10	15	10	....	.193	.267	.239	.505	51	-7	9	2.56	-4	2-16,O-16(0-0-16)/3-1	1	-1.3
1915*Phi-N	42	39	4	6	1	0	0	0	7	5	2	1	.154	.283	.179	.462	41	-2	2	1.85	0	2-14	0	-0.2
1916 Phi-N	41	50	9	11	3	0	0	1	9	8	3	....	.220	.339	.280	.619	88	-0	6	3.81	1	2-12	2	0.1
1917 Phi-N	44	72	12	14	4	1	0	9	4	9	2	....	.194	.237	.278	.515	55	-4	5	2.15	-3	2-15/O-4(1-2-0)	1	-0.8
1920 Bos-N	5	0	2	0	0	0	0	0	0	0	0	0	....	....	....	....	-105	0	0	....	0	....	0	0.0
Total 6	195	278	45	54	10	1	1	20	31	38	17	1	.194	.277	.248	.526	58	-13	23	2.58	-8	/2-58,O-20,3-3,S-1	4	-2.4
• DUGGAN, Jim	James Elmer "Mer" Duggan b: 6/1/1885, Whiteland, IN d: 12/5/1951, Indianapolis, IN BL/TL, 5'10", 165 lbs. Deb: 6/29/1911																							
1911 StL-A	1	4	1	0	0	0	0	1	1	....	0	....	.000	.200	.000	.200	-44	-1	0	.00	0	/1-1	0	-0.1
• DUNBAR, Tom	Thomas Jerome Dunbar b: 11/24/1959, Graniteville, SC BL/TL, 6'2", 192 lbs. Deb: 9/7/1983 Career OF: 23-0-21																							
1983 Tex-A	12	24	3	6	0	0	0	3	5	7	3	1	.250	.379	.250	.629	79	-0	3	3.71	-1	/O-9(2-0-7),D-1	0	-0.1
1984 Tex-A	34	97	9	25	2	0	2	10	6	16	1	0	.258	.301	.340	.641	75	-3	10	3.75	-1	O-20(9-0-11)/D-6	1	-0.6
1985 Tex-A	45	104	7	21	4	0	1	5	12	9	0	3	.202	.291	.269	.560	54	-8	7	2.02	-1	D-18,O-14(12-0-3)	0	-0.9
Total 3	91	225	19	52	6	0	3	18	23	32	4	4	.231	.305	.298	.603	65	-11	20	2.89	-3	/O-43,D-25	1	-1.6
• DUNCAN, Dave	David Edwin Duncan b: 9/26/1945, Dallas, TX BR/TR, 6'2", 200 lbs. Deb: 5/6/1964 C																							
1964 KC-A	25	53	2	9	0	1	1	5	2	20	0	0	.170	.200	.264	.464	27	-5	3	1.58	1	C-22	1	-0.4

YEAR TM-L	G	AB	R	H	2B	3B	HR	RBI	BB	SO	SB	CS	AVG	OBP	SLG	OPS	OPS+	BR/A	RC	RC/G	FR	G/POS	WS	TPW
1967 KC-A	34	101	9	19	4	0	5	11	4	50	0	1	.188	.219	.376	.595	75	-4	8	2.49	-1	C-32	1	-0.4
1968 Oak-A	82	246	15	47	4	0	7	28	25	68	1	2	.191	.268	.293	.561	73	-8	19	2.43	-5	C-79	3	-1.1
1969 Oak-A	58	127	11	16	3	0	3	22	19	41	0	0	.126	.240	.220	.460	31	-12	7	1.73	-3	C-56	1	-1.3
1970 Oak-A	86	232	21	60	7	0	10	29	22	38	0	0	.259	.323	.418	.741	107	2	31	4.64	0	C-73	9	0.5
1971*Oak-A★	103	363	39	92	13	1	15	40	28	77	1	1	.253	.309	.419	.727	106	2	47	4.43	-4	*C-102	14	0.3
1972*Oak-A	121	403	39	88	13	0	19	59	34	68	0	2	.218	.287	.392	.679	106	1	43	3.40	-4	*C-113	14	0.3
1973 Cle-A	95	344	43	80	11	1	17	43	35	86	3	3	.233	.309	.419	.728	101	-1	44	4.37	4	C-86/D-9	11	0.8
1974 Cle-A	136	425	45	85	10	1	16	46	42	91	0	4	.200	.275	.341	.616	77	-15	38	2.82	-7	*C-134/1-3,D-1	7	-1.6
1975 Bal-A	96	307	30	63	7	0	12	41	16	82	0	0	.205	.247	.345	.592	70	-13	25	2.62	-6	C-95	5	-1.6
1976 Bal-A	93	284	20	58	7	0	4	17	25	56	0	0	.204	.271	.271	.542	63	-13	21	2.36	-7	C-93	5	-1.7
Total 11	**929**	**2885**	**274**	**617**	**79**	**4**	**109**	**341**	**252**	**677**	**5**	**13**	**.214**	**.280**	**.357**	**.638**	**85**	**-67**	**285**	**3.22**	**-30**	**C-885/D-10,1-3**	**71**	**-6.0**

• DUNCAN, Jeff
Jeffrey Matthew Duncan b: 12/9/1978, Harvey, IL BL/TL, 6'2", 188 lbs. Deb: 5/20/2003

YEAR TM-L	G	AB	R	H	2B	3B	HR	RBI	BB	SO	SB	CS	AVG	OBP	SLG	OPS	OPS+	BR/A	RC	RC/G	FR	G/POS	WS	TPW
2003 NY-N	56	139	13	27	0	2	1	10	17	41	4	2	.194	.291	.245	.536	43	-11	12	2.52	3	O-52(1-52-0)	2	-0.8

• DUNCAN, Jim
James William Duncan b: 7/1/1871, Saltsburg, PA d: 10/16/1901, Foxburg, PA BR/TR, 5'8", 140 lbs. Deb: 7/18/1899

YEAR TM-L	G	AB	R	H	2B	3B	HR	RBI	BB	SO	SB	CS	AVG	OBP	SLG	OPS	OPS+	BR/A	RC	RC/G	FR	G/POS	WS	TPW
1899 Was-N	15	47	5	11	2	0	0	5	4	....	1	....	.234	.294	.277	.571	57	-3	4	3.12	1	C-14	1	-0.1
Cle-N	31	105	9	24	2	3	2	9	4	....	0	....	.229	.257	.362	.619	74	-4	10	3.27	-1	1-17,C-14	1	-0.4
Yr.	46	152	14	35	4	3	2	14	8	....	1	....	.230	.269	.336	.604	69	-7	14	3.23	-0	C-28,1-17	2	-0.4

• DUNCAN, Mariano
Mariano (Nalasco) Duncan b: 3/13/1963, San Pedro de Macoris, Dominican Republic BR/TR, 6', 185 lbs. Deb: 4/9/1985 Career OF: 88-2-6

YEAR TM-L	G	AB	R	H	2B	3B	HR	RBI	BB	SO	SB	CS	AVG	OBP	SLG	OPS	OPS+	BR/A	RC	RC/G	FR	G/POS	WS	TPW
1985*LA-N	142	562	74	137	24	6	6	39	38	113	38	8	.244	.295	.340	.635	80	-12	60	3.50	-9	*S-123,2-19	13	-0.7
1986 LA-N	109	407	47	93	7	0	8	30	30	78	48	13	.229	.285	.305	.589	67	-14	38	3.04	-7	*S-106	7	-0.9
1987 LA-N	76	261	31	56	8	1	6	18	17	62	11	1	.215	.268	.322	.590	57	-15	24	2.98	-3	S-67/2-7,O-2(1-0-1)	4	-1.1
1989 LA-N	49	84	9	21	5	1	0	8	0	15	3	3	.250	.267	.333	.601	72	-4	7	2.65	-2	S-16/2-8,O-7(4-0-4)	2	-0.6
Cin-N	45	174	23	43	10	1	3	13	8	36	6	2	.247	.292	.368	.660	85	-4	19	3.76	-2	S-44/2-5	5	-0.2
Yr.	94	258	32	64	15	2	3	21	8	51	9	5	.248	.284	.357	.641	81	-8	26	3.39	-4	S-60,2-13/O-7(4-0-4)	7	-0.8
1990*Cin-N	125	435	67	133	22	**11**	10	55	24	67	13	7	.306	.348	.476	.824	119	9	69	5.66	-3	*2-115,S-12/O-1	15	1.0
1991 Cin-N	100	333	46	86	7	4	12	40	12	57	5	4	.258	.290	.411	.702	92	-6	40	4.19	-2	2-62,S-32/O-7(6-2-0)	10	-0.4
1992 Phi-N	142	574	71	153	40	3	8	50	17	108	23	3	.267	.294	.389	.682	92	-5	64	3.84	2	O-65(65-0-0),2-52,S-42/3-4	12	-0.3
1993*Phi-N	124	496	68	140	26	4	11	73	12	88	6	5	.282	.305	.417	.722	92	-9	58	4.12	5	2-65,S-59	13	0.3
1994 Phi-N★	88	347	49	93	22	1	8	48	17	72	10	2	.268	.310	.406	.716	83	-8	42	4.18	2	2-37,3-28,S-19/1-6	10	-0.3
1995 Phi-N	52	196	20	56	12	1	3	23	0	43	1	2	.286	.289	.403	.692	80	-7	20	3.54	2	2-24,S-14,1-12/3-1	5	-0.4
*Cin-N	29	69	16	20	2	1	3	13	5	19	0	1	.290	.338	.478	.816	113	1	11	5.45	-2	/2-7,1-6,S-6,O-3(3-0-0)	2	-0.1
Yr.	81	265	36	76	14	2	6	36	5	62	1	3	.287	.303	.423	.725	89	-7	31	4.04	1	2-31,S-20,1-18/O-3(3-0-0),3	7	-0.5
1996*NY-A	109	400	62	136	34	3	8	56	9	77	4	3	.340	.356	.500	.856	113	6	66	6.31	-10	*2-104/3-3,O-3(2-0-1),D-2	12	0.0
1997 NY-A	50	172	16	42	8	0	1	13	6	39	2	1	.244	.270	.308	.578	51	-13	14	2.84	0	2-41/O-6(6-0-0),D-2	3	-1.1
Tor-A	39	167	20	38	6	0	0	12	6	39	4	2	.228	.267	.263	.531	39	-15	11	2.26	2	2-39	2	-1.0
Yr.	89	339	36	80	14	0	1	25	12	78	6	3	.236	.268	.286	.554	45	-28	25	2.55	2	2-80/O-6(6-0-0),D-2	5	-2.2
Total 12	**1279**	**4677**	**619**	**1247**	**233**	**37**	**87**	**491**	**201**	**913**	**174**	**57**	**.267**	**.302**	**.388**	**.690**	**86**	**-96**	**542**	**4.00**	**-26**	**2-585,S-540/O-94,3-36,1-24,D**	**115**	**-5.9**

• DUNCAN, Pat
Louis Baird Duncan b: 10/6/1893, Coalton, OH d: 7/17/1960, Jackson, OH BR/TR, 5'9", 170 lbs. Deb: 7/16/1915 Career OF: 687-20-2

YEAR TM-L	G	AB	R	H	2B	3B	HR	RBI	BB	SO	SB	CS	AVG	OBP	SLG	OPS	OPS+	BR/A	RC	RC/G	FR	G/POS	WS	TPW
1915 Pit-N	3	5	0	1	0	0	0	0	0	1	0	....	.200	.200	.200	.400	21	-0	0	1.33	-0	/O-1	0	-0.1
1919*Cin-N	31	90	9	22	3	3	2	17	8	7	2	....	.244	.306	.411	.717	118	2	12	4.19	0	O-27(27-0-0)	4	0.0
1920 Cin-N	154	576	75	170	16	11	2	83	42	42	18	18	.295	.350	.372	.722	109	6	74	4.34	-4	*O-154(154-0-0)	21	-0.5
1921 Cin-N	145	532	57	164	27	10	2	60	44	33	7	18	.308	.367	.408	.775	110	4	76	4.97	1	*O-145(129-16-1)	15	-0.6
1922 Cin-N	151	607	94	199	44	12	8	94	40	31	12	28	.328	.370	.479	.850	120	8	97	5.61	5	*O-151(151-0-0)	21	0.1
1923 Cin-N	147	566	92	185	26	8	7	83	30	27	15	13	.327	.363	.438	.801	113	8	87	5.47	-1	*O-146(144-3-0)	20	-0.4
1924 Cin-N	96	319	34	86	21	6	2	37	20	23	1	7	.270	.313	.392	.705	89	-8	37	3.88	-9	O-83(82-0-1)	5	-2.2
Total 7	**727**	**2695**	**361**	**827**	**137**	**50**	**23**	**374**	**184**	**164**	**55**	**84**	**.307**	**.355**	**.420**	**.775**	**110**	**19**	**383**	**4.91**	**-7**	**O-707**	**86**	**-3.6**

• DUNCAN, Taylor
Taylor McDowell Duncan b: 5/12/1953, Memphis, TN BR/TR, 6', 170 lbs. Deb: 9/15/1977

YEAR TM-L	G	AB	R	H	2B	3B	HR	RBI	BB	SO	SB	CS	AVG	OBP	SLG	OPS	OPS+	BR/A	RC	RC/G	FR	G/POS	WS	TPW
1977 StL-N	8	12	2	4	0	0	1	2	2	1	0	0	.333	.429	.583	1.012	171	1	3	9.65	-1	/3-5	1	0.0
1978 Oak-A	104	319	25	82	15	2	2	37	19	38	1	2	.257	.299	.335	.634	82	-9	32	3.38	-4	3-84,2-11/D-7,S-1	6	-1.4
Total 2	**112**	**331**	**27**	**86**	**15**	**2**	**3**	**39**	**21**	**39**	**1**	**2**	**.260**	**.304**	**.344**	**.648**	**86**	**-7**	**35**	**3.59**	**-5**	**/3-89,2-11,D-7,S-1**	**7**	**-1.4**

• DUNCAN, Vern
Vernon Van Duke Duncan b: 1/6/1890, Clayton, NC d: 6/1/1954, Daytona Beach, FL BL/TR, 5'9", 155 lbs. Deb: 9/11/1913 Career OF: 97-165-13

YEAR TM-L	G	AB	R	H	2B	3B	HR	RBI	BB	SO	SB	CS	AVG	OBP	SLG	OPS	OPS+	BR/A	RC	RC/G	FR	G/POS	WS	TPW
1913 Phi-N	8	12	3	5	1	0	0	1	0	3	0	....	.417	.417	.500	.917	155	1	2	8.67	0	/O-3(1-0-2)	1	0.1
1914 Bal-F	157	557	99	160	20	8	2	53	67	55	13	....	.287	.375	.363	.737	111	11	81	4.86	-3	*O-148(36-101-11)/3-8,2-1	19	0.0
1915 Bal-F	146	531	68	142	18	4	2	43	54	40	19	....	.267	.337	.328	.665	89	-6	66	4.06	-6	*O-124(60-64-0),3-21/2-1	10	-2.0
Total 3	**311**	**1100**	**170**	**307**	**39**	**12**	**4**	**97**	**121**	**98**	**32**	**....**	**.279**	**.357**	**.347**	**.705**	**101**	**6**	**149**	**4.50**	**-10**	**O-275/3-29,2-2**	**30**	**-1.9**

• DUNDON, Ed
Edward Joseph "Dummy" Dundon b: 7/10/1859, Columbus, OH d: 8/18/1893, Columbus, OH TR, 6' Deb: 6/2/1883 Career OF: 20-3-2 ♦

YEAR TM-L	G	AB	R	H	2B	3B	HR	RBI	BB	SO	SB	CS	AVG	OBP	SLG	OPS	OPS+	BR/A	RC	RC/G	FR	G/POS	WS	TPW
1883 Col-a	26	93	8	15	1	0	0	0	3	....	....	....	.161	.188	.172	.360	18	-5	3	1.10	0	P-20/O-9(6-2-1),2-1	2	-2.7
1884 Col-a	26	86	6	12	2	2	0	0	5	....	....	....	.140	.196	.209	.405	35	-4	4	1.34	3	O-16(14-1-1),P-11/1-3	5	-1.0
Total 2	**52**	**179**	**14**	**27**	**3**	**2**	**0**	**0**	**8**	**....**	**....**	**....**	**.151**	**.191**	**.190**	**.381**	**26**	**-9**	**7**	**1.22**	**3**	**/P-31,O-25,1-3,2-1**	**7**	**-3.8**

• DUNDON, Gus
Augustus Joseph Dundon b: 7/10/1874, Columbus, OH d: 9/1/1940, Pittsburgh, PA BR/TR, 5'10", 165 lbs. Deb: 4/14/1904

YEAR TM-L	G	AB	R	H	2B	3B	HR	RBI	BB	SO	SB	CS	AVG	OBP	SLG	OPS	OPS+	BR/A	RC	RC/G	FR	G/POS	WS	TPW
1904 Chi-A	108	373	40	85	9	3	0	36	30	....	19	....	.228	.292	.268	.560	81	-7	37	3.29	-15	*2-103/3-3,S-2	10	-2.3
1905 Chi-A	106	364	30	70	7	3	0	22	23	....	14	....	.192	.248	.228	.476	53	-19	26	2.27	4	*2-100/S-6	6	-1.5
1906 Chi-A	33	96	7	13	1	0	0	4	11	....	4	....	.135	.224	.146	.370	17	-9	4	1.37	-2	2-18,S-14	1	-1.1
Total 3	**247**	**833**	**77**	**168**	**17**	**6**	**0**	**62**	**64**	**....**	**37**	**....**	**.202**	**.265**	**.236**	**.502**	**61**	**-35**	**68**	**2.59**	**-13**	**2-221/S-22,3-3**	**17**	**-4.9**

• DUNGAN, Sam
Samuel Morrison Dungan b: 7/29/1866, Ferndale, CA d: 3/16/1939, Santa Ana, CA BR, 5'11", 180 lbs. Deb: 4/12/1892 Career OF: 39-3-303

YEAR TM-L	G	AB	R	H	2B	3B	HR	RBI	BB	SO	SB	CS	AVG	OBP	SLG	OPS	OPS+	BR/A	RC	RC/G	FR	G/POS	WS	TPW
1892 Chi-N	113	433	46	123	19	7	0	53	35	19	15	....	.284	.346	.360	.706	112	6	61	5.28	-7	*O-113(37-0-76)	14	-0.8
1893 Chi-N	107	465	86	138	23	7	2	64	29	8	11	....	.297	.350	.389	.739	98	-3	69	5.58	1	*O-107(1-0-106)	9	-0.6
1894 Chi-N	10	39	5	9	2	0	0	3	7	1	1	....	.231	.348	.282	.630	51	-3	4	3.71	1	O-10(0-0-10)	0	-0.2
Lou-N	8	32	6	11	1	0	0	3	4	1	2	....	.344	.417	.375	.792	99	0	6	7.40	0	/O-8(0-0-8)	1	0.0
Yr.	18	71	11	20	3	0	0	6	11	2	3	....	.282	.378	.324	.702	72	-3	10	5.23	1	O-18(0-0-18)	1	-0.2
1900 Chi-N	6	15	1	4	0	0	0	1	1	....	0	....	.267	.313	.267	.579	63	-1	1	3.09	0	/O-3(0-3-0)	0	-0.1
1901 Was-A	138	559	70	179	26	12	1	73	40	....	9	....	.320	.368	.415	.783	119	14	92	6.26	-5	*O-104(1-0-103),1-35	17	0.4
Total 5	**382**	**1543**	**214**	**464**	**71**	**26**	**3**	**197**	**116**	**29**	**38**	**....**	**.301**	**.356**	**.386**	**.742**	**108**	**14**	**233**	**5.70**	**-11**	**O-345/1-35**	**41**	**-1.4**

• DUNHAM, Lee
Leland Huffield Dunham b: 6/9/1902, Atlanta, IL d: 5/11/1961, Atlanta, IL BL/TL, 5'11", 185 lbs. Deb: 4/17/1926

YEAR TM-L	G	AB	R	H	2B	3B	HR	RBI	BB	SO	SB	CS	AVG	OBP	SLG	OPS	OPS+	BR/A	RC	RC/G	FR	G/POS	WS	TPW
1926 Phi-N	5	4	0	1	0	0	0	1	0	1	0	....	.250	.250	.250	.500	33	-0	0	2.02	0	/1-2	0	-0.1

• DUNLAP, Bill
William James Dunlap b: 5/1/1909, Palmer, MA d: 11/29/1980, Reading, PA BR/TR, 5'11", 170 lbs. Deb: 9/2/1929 Career OF: 8-2-6

YEAR TM-L	G	AB	R	H	2B	3B	HR	RBI	BB	SO	SB	CS	AVG	OBP	SLG	OPS	OPS+	BR/A	RC	RC/G	FR	G/POS	WS	TPW
1929 Bos-N	10	29	6	12	0	1	1	4	4	4	0	....	.414	.485	.586	1.071	171	3	8	12.44	-1	/O-9(8-0-1)	2	0.2
1930 Bos-N	16	29	3	2	1	0	0	0	0	6	0	....	.069	.069	.103	.172	-61	-8	0	.19	0	/O-7(0-2-5)	0	-0.7
Total 2	**26**	**58**	**9**	**14**	**1**	**1**	**1**	**4**	**4**	**10**	**0**	**....**	**.241**	**.290**	**.345**	**.635**	**62**	**-4**	**8**	**4.92**	**-1**	**/O-16**	**2**	**-0.5**

• DUNLAP, Fred
Frederick C. "Sure Shot" Dunlap
b: 5/21/1859, Philadelphia, PA d: 12/1/1902, Philadelphia, PA BR/TR, 5'8", 165 lbs. Deb: 5/1/1880 M/U Career OF: 0-1-2

YEAR TM-L	G	AB	R	H	2B	3B	HR	RBI	BB	SO	SB	CS	AVG	OBP	SLG	OPS	OPS+	BR/A	RC	RC/G	FR	G/POS	WS	TPW
1880 Cle-N	85	373	61	103	**27**	9	4	30	7	32	....	....	.276	.289	.429	.718	143	16	47	4.84	13	*2-85	17	**3.2**
1881 Cle-N	80	351	60	114	25	4	3	24	18	24	....	....	.325	.358	.444	.802	159	24	57	6.52	15	*2-79/3-1	15	**4.0**
1882 Cle-N	84	364	68	102	19	4	0	28	23	26	....	....	.280	.323	.354	.677	121	10	43	4.48	13	*2-84	14	2.3
1883 Cle-N	93	396	81	129	34	2	4	37	22	21	....	....	.326	.361	.452	.813	147	22	66	6.83	12	*2-93/O-1	16	3.2
1884 StL-U	101	449	**160**	**185**	39	8	**13**	....	29	....	....	....	**.412**	**.448**	**.621**	**1.069**	**248**	**68**	128	**13.58**	36	*2-100/O-1,P-1	38	**9.4**
1885 StL-N	106	423	70	114	11	5	2	25	41	24	....	....	.270	.334	.333	.667	124	14	48	4.22	22	*2-106	14	3.7
1886 StL-N	71	285	53	76	15	2	3	32	28	30	7	....	.267	.332	.365	.697	119	8	38	4.88	10	2-71/O-1	9	1.8
Det-N	51	196	32	56	8	3	4	37	16	21	13	....	.286	.340	.418	.758	126	6	33	6.38	9	2-51	8	1.5

YEAR TM-L	G	AB	R	H	2B	3B	HR	RBI	BB	SO	SB	CS	AVG	OBP	SLG	OPS	OPS+	BR/A	RC	RC/G	FR	G/POS	WS	TPW
Yr.	122	481	85	132	23	5	7	69	44	51	20	....	.274	.335	.387	.722	122	14	71	5.48	18	*2-122/O-1	17	3.3
1887*Det-N	65	297	60	97	13	10	5	45	25	12	15	....	.327	.327	.441	.768	108	2	45	5.99	23	2-65/P-1	10	2.3
1888 Pit-N	82	321	41	84	12	4	1	36	16	30	24	....	.262	.303	.333	.636	111	4	41	4.63	9	2-82	13	1.6
1889 Pit-N	121	451	59	106	19	0	2	65	46	33	21	....	.235	.309	.290	.599	75	-12	48	3.69	1	*2-121	10	-0.6
1890 Pit-N	17	64	9	11	1	1	0	3	7	6	2	....	.172	.264	.219	.483	46	-4	4	2.16	-2	2-17	0	-0.5
NY-P	1	4	1	2	0	0	0	0	0	0	0	....	.500	.500	.500	1.000	154	0	1	13.84	0	/2-1	0	0.0
1891 Was-a	8	25	4	5	1	1	0	4	5	4	3	....	.200	.355	.320	.675	98	0	4	5.30	-2	/2-8	1	-0.1
Total 12	965	3999	759	1184	224	53	41	366	283	263	85	....	.296	.340	.406	.745	135	158	604	5.85	159	2-963/O-3,P-2,3-1	165	31.9

• DUNLAP, Grant
Grant Lester "Snap" Dunlap b: 12/20/1923, Stockton, CA BR/TR, 6'2", 180 lbs. Deb: 4/21/1953

YEAR TM-L	G	AB	R	H	2B	3B	HR	RBI	BB	SO	SB	CS	AVG	OBP	SLG	OPS	OPS+	BR/A	RC	RC/G	FR	G/POS	WS	TPW
1953 StL-N	16	17	2	6	0	1	1	3	0	2	0	0	.353	.353	.647	1.000	154	1	3	7.46	0	/O-1	1	0.1

• DUNLEAVY, Jack
John Francis Dunleavy b: 9/14/1879, Harrison, NJ d: 4/11/1944, South Norwalk, CT BL/TL, 5'6", 167 lbs. Deb: 5/30/1903 Career OF: 24-3-183 ♦

YEAR TM-L	G	AB	R	H	2B	3B	HR	RBI	BB	SO	SB	CS	AVG	OBP	SLG	OPS	OPS+	BR/A	RC	RC/G	FR	G/POS	WS	TPW
1903 StL-N	61	193	23	48	3	3	0	10	13	....	10	....	.249	.306	.295	.602	74	-3	22	3.82	8	O-38(6-0-32),P-14	7	-0.8
1904 StL-N	51	172	23	40	7	3	1	14	16	....	8	....	.233	.305	.326	.631	99	2	20	3.94	1	O-44(5-3-36)/P-7	6	-1.0
1905 StL-N	119	435	52	105	8	8	1	25	55	....	15	....	.241	.328	.303	.631	91	-3	51	3.89	5	*O-118(13-0-115)/2-1	11	-0.3
Total 3	231	800	98	193	18	14	2	49	84	....	33	....	.241	.318	.306	.624	89	-4	93	3.88	14	O-200/P-21,2-1	24	-2.0

• DUNLOP, George
George Henry Dunlop b: 7/19/1888, Meriden, CT d: 12/12/1972, Meriden, CT BR/TR, 5'10", 170 lbs. Deb: 9/9/1913

YEAR TM-L	G	AB	R	H	2B	3B	HR	RBI	BB	SO	SB	CS	AVG	OBP	SLG	OPS	OPS+	BR/A	RC	RC/G	FR	G/POS	WS	TPW
1913 Cle-A	7	17	3	4	1	0	0	0	0	5	0	....	.235	.235	.294	.529	53	-1	1	2.11	0	/S-4,3-3	0	-0.1
1914 Cle-A	1	3	0	0	0	0	0	0	1	1	0	....	.000	.250	.000	.250	-23	-0	0	.00	0	/S-1	0	-0.1
Total 2	8	20	3	4	1	0	0	0	1	6	0	....	.200	.238	.250	.488	39	-2	1	1.72	0	/S-5,3-3	0	-0.2

• DUNN, Adam
Adam Troy Dunn b: 11/9/1979, Houston, TX BL/TR, 6'6", 240 lbs. Deb: 7/20/2001 Career OF: 242-0-59

YEAR TM-L	G	AB	R	H	2B	3B	HR	RBI	BB	SO	SB	CS	AVG	OBP	SLG	OPS	OPS+	BR/A	RC	RC/G	FR	G/POS	WS	TPW
2001 Cin-N	66	244	54	64	18	1	19	43	38	74	4	2	.262	.371	.578	.948	134	13	54	7.79	1	O-63(30-0-38)	10	1.0
2002 Cin-N★	158	535	84	133	28	2	26	71	128	170	19	9	.249	.402	.454	.856	122	23	107	6.86	-2	*O-119(113-0-17),1-44/D-1	21	1.3
2003 Cin-N	116	381	70	82	12	1	27	57	74	126	8	2	.215	.357	.465	.822	114	10	69	6.05	1	*O-102(99-0-4),1-19/D-2	13	0.6
Total 3	340	1160	208	279	58	4	72	171	240	370	31	13	.241	.381	.484	.865	122	46	230	6.78	1	O-284/1-63,D-3	44	2.9

• DUNN, Jack
John Joseph Dunn b: 10/6/1872, Meadville, PA d: 10/22/1928, Towson, MD BR/TR, 5'9" Deb: 5/6/1897 Career OF: 9-10-41 ♦

YEAR TM-L	G	AB	R	H	2B	3B	HR	RBI	BB	SO	SB	CS	AVG	OBP	SLG	OPS	OPS+	BR/A	RC	RC/G	FR	G/POS	WS	TPW
1897 Bro-N	36	131	20	29	4	0	0	17	4	....	2	....	.221	.244	.252	.496	33	-6	9	2.31	-1	P-25/2-4,3-3,O-3(3-0-0),S	13	-1.4
1898 Bro-N	51	167	21	41	0	1	0	19	7	....	3	....	.246	.280	.257	.537	54	-2	13	2.78	-1	P-41/O-4(1-2-1),S-4,3-2	17	0.2
1899 Bro-N	43	122	21	30	2	1	0	16	3	....	3	....	.246	.270	.279	.549	49	0	10	2.95	2	P-41/S-1	24	0.1
1900 Bro-N	10	26	2	6	0	0	0	1	1	....	0	....	.231	.259	.231	.490	34	-0	2	2.11	1	P-10	2	-1.2
Phi-N	10	33	3	10	1	0	0	5	0	....	1	....	.303	.303	.333	.636	76	1	4	4.29	0	P-10	4	-0.8
Yr.	20	59	5	16	1	0	0	6	1	....	1	....	.271	.283	.288	.571	57	1	5	3.28	0	P-20	6	-2.0
1901 Phi-N	2	1	1	1	0	0	0	0	1	....	0	....	1.000	1.000	1.000	2.000	471	1	1	∞	0	/P-2	0	-0.8
Bal-A	96	362	41	90	9	4	0	36	21	....	10	....	.249	.301	.296	.596	63	-17	38	3.51	-5	3-67,S-19/P-9,2-1,O-1	8	-1.4
1902 NY-N	100	342	26	72	11	1	0	14	20	....	13	....	.211	.256	.249	.505	56	-17	28	2.56	-7	O-43(1-3-40),S-36,3-18/P-3,2	3	-2.9
1903 NY-N	78	257	35	62	15	1	0	37	15	....	12	....	.241	.291	.307	.598	68	-11	28	3.66	7	S-27,3-25,2-19/O-1	6	-0.3
1904 NY-N	64	181	27	56	12	2	1	19	11	....	11	....	.309	.356	.414	.770	132	6	32	6.37	-2	3-28,S-10/2-9,O-7(3-4-0),P	9	0.5
Total 8	490	1622	197	397	54	10	1	164	83	....	55	....	.245	.287	.292	.580	66	-45	165	3.39	-7	3-143,P-142/S-98,O-59,2-35	86	-8.0

• DUNN, Joe
Joseph Edward Dunn b: 3/11/1885, Springfield, OH d: 3/19/1944, Springfield, OH BR/TR, 5'9", 160 lbs. Deb: 9/12/1908

YEAR TM-L	G	AB	R	H	2B	3B	HR	RBI	BB	SO	SB	CS	AVG	OBP	SLG	OPS	OPS+	BR/A	RC	RC/G	FR	G/POS	WS	TPW
1908 Bro-N	20	64	3	11	3	0	0	5	0	....	0	....	.172	.172	.219	.391	26	-6	2	1.10	6	C-20	1	0.2
1909 Bro-N	10	25	1	4	1	0	0	2	0	....	0	....	.160	.192	.200	.392	22	-2	1	1.16	0	/C-7	0	-0.2
Total 2	30	89	4	15	4	0	0	7	0	....	0	....	.169	.178	.213	.391	25	-8	3	1.12	6	/C-27	1	0.0

• DUNN, Ron
Ronald Ray Dunn b: 1/24/1950, Oklahoma City, OK BR/TR, 5'11", 180 lbs. Deb: 9/3/1974

YEAR TM-L	G	AB	R	H	2B	3B	HR	RBI	BB	SO	SB	CS	AVG	OBP	SLG	OPS	OPS+	BR/A	RC	RC/G	FR	G/POS	WS	TPW
1974 Chi-N	23	68	6	20	7	0	2	15	12	8	0	0	.294	.400	.485	.885	141	4	12	6.08	-5	2-21/3-6	3	0.0
1975 Chi-N	32	44	2	7	3	0	1	6	6	17	0	0	.159	.260	.295	.555	52	-3	4	2.70	-2	3-11/O-2(2-0-0),2-1	1	-0.5
Total 2	55	112	8	27	10	0	3	21	18	25	0	0	.241	.346	.411	.757	106	1	16	4.64	-7	/2-22,3-17,O-2	4	-0.5

• DUNN, Steve
Steven Robert Dunn b: 4/18/1970, Champaign, IL BL/TL, 6'4", 225 lbs. Deb: 5/3/1994

YEAR TM-L	G	AB	R	H	2B	3B	HR	RBI	BB	SO	SB	CS	AVG	OBP	SLG	OPS	OPS+	BR/A	RC	RC/G	FR	G/POS	WS	TPW
1994 Min-A	14	35	2	8	5	0	0	4	1	12	0	0	.229	.250	.371	.621	57	-2	3	2.84	0	1-12	0	-0.3
1995 Min-A	5	6	0	0	0	0	0	0	1	3	0	0	.000	.143	.000	.143	-59	-1	0	.17	0	/1-3	0	-0.2
Total 2	19	41	2	8	5	0	0	4	2	15	0	0	.195	.233	.317	.550	39	-4	3	2.37	0	/1-15	0	-0.5

• DUNN, Steve
Stephen B. Dunn b: 12/21/1858, London, Canada d: 5/5/1933, London, Canada BL, 5'9.5", 173 lbs. Deb: 9/27/1884

YEAR TM-L	G	AB	R	H	2B	3B	HR	RBI	BB	SO	SB	CS	AVG	OBP	SLG	OPS	OPS+	BR/A	RC	RC/G	FR	G/POS	WS	TPW
1884 StP-U	9	32	2	8	2	0	0	....	0	....	....	....	.250	.250	.313	.563	89	-0	3	2.99	0	/1-9,3-1	1	-0.1

• DUNN, Todd
Todd Kent Dunn b: 7/29/1970, Tulsa, OK BR/TR, 6'5", 220 lbs. Deb: 9/8/1996 Career OF: 20-3-11

YEAR TM-L	G	AB	R	H	2B	3B	HR	RBI	BB	SO	SB	CS	AVG	OBP	SLG	OPS	OPS+	BR/A	RC	RC/G	FR	G/POS	WS	TPW
1996 Mil-A	6	10	2	3	1	0	0	1	0	3	0	0	.300	.300	.400	.700	72	-0	1	2.70	0	/O-6(1-1-4)	0	-0.1
1997 Mil-A	44	118	17	27	5	0	3	9	2	39	3	0	.229	.242	.347	.589	51	-8	10	2.81	-2	O-27(19-2-7),D-14	1	-1.1
Total 2	50	128	19	30	6	0	3	10	2	42	3	0	.234	.246	.352	.598	53	-9	10	2.81	-2	/O-33,D-14	1	-1.2

• DUNSTON, Shawon
Shawon Donnell Dunston b: 3/21/1963, Brooklyn, NY BR/TR, 6'1", 175 lbs. Deb: 4/9/1985 Career OF: 107-75-70

YEAR TM-L	G	AB	R	H	2B	3B	HR	RBI	BB	SO	SB	CS	AVG	OBP	SLG	OPS	OPS+	BR/A	RC	RC/G	FR	G/POS	WS	TPW
1985 Chi-N	74	250	40	65	12	4	4	18	19	42	11	3	.260	.312	.388	.700	85	-4	31	4.33	1	S-73	8	0.4
1986 Chi-N	150	581	66	145	37	3	17	68	21	114	13	11	.250	.279	.411	.691	82	-20	64	3.75	12	*S-149	14	0.9
1987 Chi-N	95	346	40	85	18	3	5	22	10	68	12	3	.246	.269	.358	.627	62	-19	32	3.22	-6	S-94	5	-1.5
1988 Chi-N★	155	575	69	143	23	6	9	56	16	108	30	9	.249	.272	.357	.628	76	-18	55	3.29	3	*S-151	13	-0.4
1989*Chi-N	138	471	52	131	20	6	9	60	30	86	19	11	.278	.323	.403	.726	99	-2	59	4.32	10	*S-138	18	1.9
1990 Chi-N★	146	545	73	143	22	8	17	66	15	87	25	5	.262	.286	.426	.712	87	-10	65	4.14	-4	*S-144	15	-0.3
1991 Chi-N	142	492	59	128	22	7	12	50	23	64	21	6	.260	.299	.407	.705	92	-5	59	4.03	-11	*S-142	14	-0.6
1992 Chi-N	18	73	8	23	3	1	0	2	3	13	2	3	.315	.342	.384	.726	103	-1	9	4.60	0	S-18	1	0.0
1993 Chi-N	7	10	3	4	2	0	0	2	0	1	0	0	.400	.400	.600	1.000	166	1	2	10.80	-1	/S-2	1	0.0
1994 Chi-N	88	331	38	92	19	0	11	35	16	48	3	8	.278	.315	.435	.750	94	-7	42	4.41	2	S-84	8	0.1
1995 Chi-N	127	477	58	141	30	6	14	69	10	75	10	5	.296	.318	.472	.790	107	2	68	5.14	-3	*S-125	16	0.8
1996 SF-N	82	287	27	86	12	2	5	25	13	40	8	0	.300	.332	.408	.740	98	-0	38	4.81	3	S-78	8	0.9
1997 Chi-N	114	419	57	119	18	4	9	41	8	64	29	7	.284	.302	.411	.713	82	-9	51	4.32	-5	*S-108/O-7(7-0-0)	7	-0.7
Pit-N	18	71	14	28	4	1	5	16	0	11	3	1	.394	.394	.690	1.085	174	7	18	9.70	-1	S-18	4	0.8
Yr.	132	490	71	147	22	5	14	57	8	75	32	8	.300	.315	.451	.766	96	-2	69	5.03	-6	*S-126/O-7(7-0-0)	11	0.0
1998 Cle-A	62	156	26	37	11	3	3	12	6	18	9	2	.237	.270	.404	.674	70	-7	17	3.67	0	2-24,S-14,O-12(11-1-0)/D-7	2	-0.6
SF-N	36	51	10	9	2	0	3	8	0	10	0	2	.176	.222	.392	.614	61	-4	3	2.05	-2	/S-9,O-6(0-6-0),2-1	1	-0.6
1999 StL-N	62	150	23	46	5	2	5	25	2	23	6	3	.307	.329	.467	.796	98	-1	21	5.01	0	O-23(9-11-4)/1-8,S-7,3-5,D	4	-0.1
*NY-N	42	93	12	32	6	1	0	16	0	16	4	1	.344	.358	.430	.788	101	0	13	5.18	-2	O-27(9-16-5)/3-1	4	-0.2
Yr.	104	243	35	78	11	3	5	41	2	39	10	4	.321	.340	.453	.793	99	-1	34	5.07	-2	O-50(18-27-9)/1-8,S-7,3-6,D	8	-0.3
2000*StL-N	98	216	28	54	11	2	12	43	6	47	3	1	.250	.280	.486	.766	88	-5	25	3.71	0	O-58(41-9-13)/S-8,1-6,3-5,D	4	-0.6
2001 SF-N	88	186	26	52	10	3	9	25	2	32	3	1	.280	.295	.511	.805	110	2	27	5.25	2	O-60(12-23-26)/1-1,D-1	4	0.2
2002*SF-N	72	147	7	34	5	0	1	9	3	33	1	0	.231	.252	.286	.537	43	-12	11	2.60	-5	O-49(18-9-22)/D-3,1-1,S-1	1	-1.9
Total 18	1814	5927	736	1597	292	62	150	668	203	1000	212	82	.269	.298	.416	.714	88	-114	712	4.17	-8	*S-1363,O-242/2-25,1-16,D,3	152	-1.4

• DUNWOODY, Todd
Todd Franklin Dunwoody b: 4/11/1975, Lafayette, IN BL/TL, 6'1", 190 lbs. Deb: 5/10/1997 Career OF: 44-188-22

YEAR TM-L	G	AB	R	H	2B	3B	HR	RBI	BB	SO	SB	CS	AVG	OBP	SLG	OPS	OPS+	BR/A	RC	RC/G	FR	G/POS	WS	TPW
1997 Fla-N	19	50	7	13	2	2	2	7	7	21	2	0	.260	.362	.500	.862	129	3	10	6.89	-1	O-14(6-8-0)	2	0.2
1998 Fla-N	116	434	53	109	27	7	5	28	21	113	5	1	.251	.292	.380	.672	78	-15	48	3.89	7	*O-111(0-111-0)	6	-0.6
1999 Fla-N	64	186	20	41	6	3	2	20	12	41	3	4	.220	.271	.317	.589	51	-16	16	2.82	0	O-55(8-44-5)	1	-1.4
2000 KC-A	61	178	12	37	9	0	1	23	8	42	3	0	.208	.246	.275	.521	31	-19	12	2.17	-1	O-40(14-19-9),D-11	1	-1.9
2001 Chi-N	33	61	6	13	4	0	1	3	3	14	0	1	.213	.250	.328	.578	50	-5	5	2.68	1	O-26(15-6-7)	0	-0.5
2002 Cle-A	2	6	0	0	0	0	0	0	0	3	0	0	.000	.000	.000	.000	-102	-2	0	.00	0	/O-2(1-0-1)	0	-0.2
Total 6	295	915	98	213	48	12	11	81	51	234	13	6	.233	.279	.348	.626	63	-53	91	3.35	6	O-248/D-11	10	-4.5

YEAR TM-L	G	AB	R	H	2B	3B	HR	RBI	BB	SO	SB	CS	AVG	OBP	SLG	OPS	OPS+	BR/A	RC	RC/G	FR	G/POS	WS	TPW
• DURAN, Dan	Daniel James Duran b: 3/16/1954, Palo Alto, CA BL/TL, 5'11", 190 lbs. Deb: 4/17/1981																							
1981 Tex-A	13	16	1	4	0	0	0	0	1	1	0	0	.250	.294	.250	.544	61	-1	1	2.08	0	/0-7(7-0-0),1-1	0	-0.1
• DURANT, Mike	Michael Joseph Durant b: 9/14/1969, Columbus, OH BR/TR, 6'2", 200 lbs. Deb: 4/3/1996																							
1996 Min-A	40	81	15	17	3	0	0	5	10	15	3	0	.210	.297	.247	.544	39	-7	7	2.65	-1	C-37	1	-0.5
• DURAZO, Erubiel	Erubiel Cardenas Durazo b: 1/23/1974, Hermosillo, Mexico BL/TL, 6'3", 240 lbs. Deb: 7/26/1999 Career OF: 0-0-4																							
1999*Ari-N	52	155	31	51	4	2	11	30	26	43	1	1	.329	.429	.594	1.022	154	13	41	10.26	0	1-44	9	0.9
2000 Ari-N	67	196	35	52	11	0	8	33	34	43	1	0	.265	.377	.444	.821	103	2	35	6.35	-4	1-60	5	-0.7
2001*Ari-N	92	175	34	47	11	0	12	38	28	49	0	0	.269	.376	.537	.913	124	7	38	7.76	1	1-38/D-7,0-2(0-0-2)	7	0.4
2002*Ari-N	76	222	46	58	12	2	16	48	49	60	0	1	.261	.399	.550	.949	135	12	53	8.44	-1	1-56/D-5,0-2(0-0-2)	10	0.6
2003*Oak-A	154	537	92	139	29	0	21	77	100	105	1	1	.259	.377	.430	.807	111	12	92	5.95	-6	*D-121,1-33	17	-0.4
Total 5	441	1285	238	347	67	4	68	226	237	300	3	3	.270	.387	.487	.874	121	46	259	7.17	-11	1-231,D-133/0-4	48	0.8
• DURBIN, Kid	Blaine Alphonsus Durbin b: 9/10/1886, Lamar, MO d: 9/11/1943, Kirkwood, MO BL/TL, 5'8", 155 lbs. Deb: 4/24/1907 Career OF: 1-11-4 ♦																							
1907 Chi-N	11	18	2	6	0	0	0	0	1	....	0	....	.333	.368	.333	.702	113	1	2	4.91	1	/0-5(1-0-4),P-5	1	-0.5
1908 Chi-N	14	28	3	7	1	0	0	0	2	....	0	....	.250	.323	.286	.608	91	-0	3	3.12	-1	0-14(0-11-0)	1	-0.1
1909 Cin-N	6	5	1	1	0	0	0	0	1	....	0	....	.200	.333	.200	.533	66	-0	0	2.11	0	....	0	0.0
Pit-N	1	0	0	0	0	0	0	0	0	....	0	....	....	....	....	....	-95	0	0	....	0	....	0	0.0
Yr.	7	5	1	1	0	0	0	0	1	....	0	....	.200	.333	.200	.533	66	-0	0	2.11	0	....	0	0.0
Total 3	32	51	6	14	1	0	0	0	4	....	0	....	.275	.339	.294	.633	95	0	5	3.58	0	/0-19,P-5	2	-0.6
• DURHAM, Joe	Joseph Vann "Pop" Durham b: 7/31/1931, Newport News, VA BR/TR, 6'1", 186 lbs. Deb: 9/10/1954 Career OF: 46-6-26																							
1954 Bal-A	10	40	4	9	0	0	1	3	4	7	0	0	.225	.295	.300	.595	68	-2	4	3.36	-1	0-10(10-1-0)	0	-0.4
1957 Bal-A	77	157	19	29	2	0	4	17	16	42	1	1	.185	.260	.274	.534	49	-11	11	2.20	0	0-59(36-5-25)	1	-1.3
1959 StL-N	6	5	2	0	0	0	0	0	0	1	0	0	.000	.000	.000	.000	-94	-1	0	.00	0	/0-1	0	-0.1
Total 3	93	202	25	38	2	0	5	20	20	50	1	1	.188	.261	.272	.534	50	-14	15	2.35	-1	/0-70	1	-1.8
• DURHAM, Leon	Leon Durham b: 7/31/1957, Cincinnati, OH BL/TL, 6'1", 210 lbs. Deb: 5/27/1980 Career OF: 86-116-219																							
1980 StL-N	96	303	42	82	15	4	8	42	18	55	8	5	.271	.314	.426	.739	101	-1	40	4.56	8	0-78(35-2-43)/1-8	8	0.3
1981 Chi-N	87	328	42	95	14	6	10	35	27	53	25	11	.290	.344	.460	.804	121	9	50	5.41	-3	0-83(0-0-83)/1-3	10	0.2
1982 Chi-N★	148	539	84	168	33	7	22	90	66	77	28	14	.312	.389	.521	.910	148	35	108	7.30	-4	*0-143(0-74-89)/1-1	25	2.8
1983 Chi-N★	100	337	58	87	18	8	12	55	66	83	12	6	.258	.384	.466	.850	128	15	64	6.58	-5	0-95(51-40-4)/1-6	13	0.7
1984*Chi-N	137	473	86	132	30	4	23	96	69	86	16	8	.279	.372	.505	.877	132	21	90	6.72	5	*1-130	22	1.9
1985 Chi-N	153	542	58	153	32	2	21	75	64	99	7	6	.282	.358	.465	.823	116	11	90	6.09	1	*1-151	18	0.3
1986 Chi-N	141	484	66	127	18	7	20	65	67	98	8	7	.262	.353	.452	.806	112	7	78	5.63	-6	*1-141	15	-0.7
1987 Chi-N	131	439	70	120	22	1	27	63	51	92	2	2	.273	.349	.513	.862	120	11	79	6.47	-12	*1-123	14	-0.8
1988 Chi-N	24	73	10	16	6	1	3	6	9	20	0	1	.219	.305	.452	.757	110	0	10	4.74	1	1-20	1	-0.1
Cin-N	21	51	4	11	3	0	1	2	5	12	0	0	.216	.286	.333	.619	74	-2	5	3.48	-2	1-17	0	-0.5
Yr.	45	124	14	27	9	1	4	8	14	32	0	1	.218	.297	.403	.700	95	-2	15	4.23	-1	1-37	1	-0.5
1989 StL-N	29	18	2	1	1	0	0	1	2	4	0	1	.056	.190	.111	.302	-11	-3	0	.64	0	1-18	0	-0.4
Total 10	1067	3587	522	992	192	40	147	530	444	679	106	61	.277	.358	.475	.833	122	103	615	6.08	-16	1-618,0-399	126	3.8
• DURHAM, Ray	Ray Durham b: 11/30/1971, Charlotte, NC BB/TR, 5'8", 170 lbs. Deb: 4/26/1995																							
1995 Chi-A	125	471	68	121	27	6	7	51	31	83	18	5	.257	.311	.384	.695	83	-11	57	4.16	-16	*2-122/D-1	8	-1.9
1996 Chi-A	156	557	79	153	33	5	10	65	58	95	30	4	.275	.354	.406	.759	96	2	88	5.53	-5	*2-150/D-3	17	0.4
1997 Chi-A	155	634	106	172	27	5	11	53	61	96	33	16	.271	.341	.382	.723	92	-7	83	4.45	-5	*2-153/D-1	13	-0.4
1998 Chi-A★	158	635	126	181	35	8	19	67	73	105	36	9	.285	.364	.455	.819	115	18	113	6.40	-4	*2-158	25	2.1
1999 Chi-A	153	612	109	181	30	8	13	60	73	105	34	11	.296	.374	.435	.809	105	9	105	6.21	0	*2-148/D-4	20	1.4
2000*Chi-A★	151	614	121	172	35	9	17	75	75	105	25	13	.280	.365	.450	.814	103	3	102	5.72	0	*2-151	19	1.0
2001 Chi-A	152	611	104	163	42	10	20	65	64	110	23	10	.267	.340	.466	.807	106	5	98	5.50	1	*2-150/D-1	21	1.3
2002 Chi-A	96	345	71	103	20	2	9	48	49	59	20	5	.299	.393	.446	.840	120	14	62	6.20	7	2-92	13	2.4
*Oak-A	54	219	43	60	14	4	6	22	24	34	6	2	.274	.351	.457	.808	112	4	37	5.98	2	D-43,2-11	7	0.3
Yr.	150	564	114	163	34	6	15	70	73	93	26	7	.289	.377	.450	.828	117	18	99	6.12	8	*2-103,D-43	20	2.7
2003*SF-N	110	410	61	117	30	5	8	33	50	82	7	7	.285	.367	.441	.809	113	7	68	5.94	9	*2-105	15	2.0
Total 9	1310	5108	888	1423	293	62	120	539	558	874	232	82	.279	.356	.431	.786	104	45	813	5.56	-11	*2-1240/D-53	158	8.6
• DURNBAUGH, Bobby	Robert Eugene "Scroggy" Durnbaugh b: 1/15/1933, Dayton, OH BR/TR, 5'8", 170 lbs. Deb: 9/22/1957																							
1957 Cin-N	2	1	0	0	0	0	0	0	0	0	0	0	.000	.000	.000	.000	-93	-0	0	.00	-1	/S-2	0	-0.1
• DURNING, George	George Dewey Durning b: 5/9/1898, Philadelphia, PA d: 4/18/1986, Tampa, FL BR/TR, 5'11", 175 lbs. Deb: 9/12/1925																							
1925 Phi-N	5	14	3	5	0	0	0	1	2	1	0	0	.357	.438	.357	.795	97	0	2	6.83	2	/0-4(0-0-4)	1	0.2
• DUROCHER, Leo	Leo Ernest "The Lip" Durocher b: 7/27/1905, West Springfield, MA d: 10/7/1991, Palm Springs, CA BR/TR, 5'10", 160 lbs. Deb: 10/2/1925 M/C HOF: 1994																							
1925 NY-A	2	1	1	0	0	0	0	0	0	0	0	0	.000	.000	.000	.000	-102	-0	0	.00	0	....	0	0.0
1928*NY-A	102	296	46	80	8	6	0	31	22	52	1	4	.270	.327	.338	.665	77	-11	33	3.82	7	2-66,S-29	7	0.1
1929 NY-A	106	341	53	84	4	5	0	32	34	33	3	1	.246	.320	.287	.607	61	-17	34	3.37	19	S-93,2-12	9	1.1
1930 Cin-N	119	354	31	86	15	3	3	32	20	45	0	....	.243	.287	.328	.615	51	-29	33	3.08	4	*S-103,2-13	6	-1.2
1931 Cin-N	121	361	26	82	11	5	1	29	18	32	0	....	.227	.264	.294	.557	53	-24	29	2.62	-0	*S-120	5	-1.7
1932 Cin-N	143	457	43	99	22	5	1	33	36	40	3	....	.217	.275	.293	.569	55	-29	39	2.76	-5	*S-142	6	-2.3
1933 Cin-N	16	51	6	11	1	0	1	3	4	5	0	....	.216	.273	.294	.567	63	-2	4	2.18	4	S-16	1	0.3
StL-N	123	395	45	102	18	4	2	41	26	32	3	....	.258	.306	.339	.645	80	-10	40	3.45	5	*S-123	11	0.4
Yr.	139	446	51	113	19	4	3	44	30	37	3	....	.253	.302	.334	.636	78	-13	44	3.28	9	*S-139	12	0.6
1934*StL-N	146	500	62	130	26	5	3	70	33	40	2	....	.260	.308	.350	.658	71	-21	53	3.63	7	*S-146	13	-0.3
1935 StL-N	143	513	62	136	23	5	8	78	29	46	4	....	.265	.304	.376	.681	79	-16	57	3.85	25	*S-142	18	1.9
1936 StL-N★	136	510	57	146	22	3	1	58	29	47	3	....	.286	.327	.347	.674	82	-13	56	3.88	2	*S-136	14	-0.1
1937 StL-N	135	477	46	97	11	3	1	47	38	36	6	....	.203	.262	.245	.507	38	-41	30	2.02	0	*S-134	6	-3.2
1938 Bro-N★	141	479	41	105	18	5	1	56	47	30	3	....	.219	.293	.284	.577	58	-27	42	2.96	0	*S-141	9	-1.8
1939 Bro-N	116	390	42	108	21	6	1	34	27	24	2	....	.277	.325	.369	.695	83	-10	46	4.23	-4	*S-113/3-1	11	-0.6
1940 Bro-N★	62	160	10	37	9	1	1	14	12	13	1	....	.231	.285	.319	.604	62	-8	14	2.80	5	S-53/2-4	4	0.0
1941 Bro-N	18	42	2	12	1	0	0	6	1	3	0	....	.286	.302	.310	.612	69	-2	4	3.22	1	S-12/2-1	1	-0.1
1943 Bro-N	6	18	1	4	0	0	0	1	1	2	0	....	.222	.263	.222	.485	41	-1	1	1.61	0	/S-6	0	-0.1
1945 Bro-N	2	5	1	1	0	0	0	2	0	0	0	....	.200	.200	.200	.400	11	-1	0	1.35	0	/2-2	0	0.0
Total 17	1637	5350	575	1320	210	56	24	567	377	480	31	5	.247	.299	.320	.619	65	-263	513	3.25	69	*S-1509/2-98,3-1	121	-7.7
• DURRETT, Red	Elmer Cable Durrett b: 2/3/1921, Sherman, TX d: 1/17/1992, Waxahachie, TX BL/TL, 5'10", 170 lbs. Deb: 9/14/1944 Career OF: 0-9-4																							
1944 Bro-N	11	32	3	5	1	0	1	1	7	10	0	....	.156	.308	.281	.589	68	-1	3	2.94	0	/0-9(0-5-4)	0	-0.1
1945 Bro-N	8	16	2	2	0	0	0	0	3	3	0	....	.125	.263	.125	.388	10	-2	1	1.41	0	/0-4(0-4-0)	0	-0.2
Total 2	19	48	5	7	1	0	1	1	10	13	0	....	.146	.293	.229	.522	49	-3	4	2.43	-0	/0-13	0	-0.4
• DURRINGTON, Trent	Trent John Durrington b: 8/27/1975, Sydney, Australia BR/TR, 5'10", 188 lbs. Deb: 8/6/1999																							
1999 Ana-A	43	122	14	22	2	0	0	2	9	28	4	3	.180	.237	.197	.433	12	-17	6	1.53	-3	2-41	1	-1.7
2000 Ana-A	4	3	0	0	0	0	0	0	0	0	0	0	.000	.000	.000	.000	-97	-1	0	.00	-1	/2-1	0	-0.1
2003 Ana-A	12	14	5	2	0	0	0	1	3	0	1	1	.143	.294	.143	.437	22	-2	1	1.61	-2	/2-5,3-4,D-2,0-1	0	-0.3
Total 3	59	139	19	24	2	0	0	3	12	28	5	4	.173	.238	.187	.425	11	-19	7	1.49	-5	/2-47,3-4,D-2,0-1	1	-2.1
• DURST, Cedric	Cedric Montgomery Durst b: 8/23/1896, Austin, TX d: 2/16/1971, San Diego, CA BL/TL, 5'11", 160 lbs. Deb: 5/30/1922 Career OF: 134-68-93																							
1922 StL-A	15	12	5	4	1	0	0	0	0	1	0	0	.333	.333	.417	.750	91	-0	2	4.79	-1	/0-6(1-4-1)	0	-0.1
1923 StL-A	45	85	12	18	2	0	5	11	8	14	0	0	.212	.280	.412	.691	76	-3	10	3.84	-2	0-10(4-5-1)/1-8	1	-0.7
1926 StL-A	80	219	32	52	7	5	3	16	22	19	0	5	.237	.310	.356	.666	70	-12	24	3.46	0	0-57(5-42-10)/1-4	3	-1.5

YEAR TM-L	G	AB	R	H	2B	3B	HR	RBI	BB	SO	SB	CS	AVG	OBP	SLG	OPS	OPS+	BR/A	RC	RC/G	FR	G/POS	WS	TPW
1927*NY-A	65	129	18	32	4	3	0	25	6	7	0	3	.248	.281	.326	.607	59	-9	11	2.76	0	0-36(13-6-17)/1-2	1	-1.1
1928*NY-A	74	135	18	34	2	1	2	10	7	9	1	0	.252	.289	.326	.615	63	-7	13	3.29	0	0-33(13-5-15)/1-3	2	-0.9
1929 NY-A	92	202	32	52	3	3	4	31	15	25	3	2	.257	.309	.361	.670	77	-7	23	3.84	0	0-72(46-6-20)/1-1	3	-1.1
1930 NY-A	8	19	0	3	1	0	0	5	0	1	0	0	.158	.158	.211	.368	-8	-3	1	1.00	0	/0-6(6-0-0)	0	-0.3
Bos-A	102	302	29	74	19	5	1	24	17	24	3	1	.245	.290	.351	.641	64	-16	31	3.49	-1	0-75(46-0-29)	3	-2.1
Yr.	110	321	29	77	20	5	1	29	17	25	3	1	.240	.282	.343	.625	60	-20	32	3.33	-2	0-81(52-0-29)	3	-2.4
Total 7	**481**	**1103**	**146**	**269**	**39**	**17**	**15**	**122**	**75**	**100**	**7**	**11**	**.244**	**.294**	**.351**	**.645**	**67**	**-59**	**114**	**3.43**	**-5**	**0-295/1-18**	**13**	**-7.8**

• DUSAK, Erv — Ervin Frank "Four Sack" Dusak
b: 7/29/1920, Chicago, IL d: 11/6/1994, Glendale Heights, IL BR/TR, 6'2", 185 lbs. Deb: 9/18/1941 Career OF: 105-106-67 ♦

YEAR TM-L	G	AB	R	H	2B	3B	HR	RBI	BB	SO	SB	CS	AVG	OBP	SLG	OPS	OPS+	BR/A	RC	RC/G	FR	G/POS	WS	TPW
1941 StL-N	6	14	1	2	0	0	0	3	2	6	1	....	.143	.250	.143	.393	12	-2	1	1.42	1	/0-4(1-2-1)	0	-0.1
1942 StL-N	12	27	4	5	3	0	0	3	3	7	0	....	.185	.267	.296	.563	60	-1	2	2.40	1	/0-8(5-0-3),3-1	0	-0.1
1946*StL-N	100	275	38	66	9	1	9	42	33	63	7	....	.240	.321	.378	.700	94	-3	34	4.20	5	0-77(72-5-0),3-11/2-2	8	-0.3
1947 StL-N	111	328	56	93	7	3	6	28	50	34	1	....	.284	.378	.378	.756	97	0	50	5.54	3	0-89(22-28-47)/3-7	11	0.0
1948 StL-N	114	311	60	65	9	2	6	19	49	55	3	....	.209	.317	.309	.625	66	-14	34	3.65	-2	0-68(2-55-12),2-29/3-9,P-1,S	7	-1.5
1949 StL-N	1	0	1	0	0	0	0	0	0	0	0	....	....	....	....	....	-96	0	0	....	0	....	0	0.0
1950 StL-N	23	12	0	1	1	0	0	0	0	3	0	....	.083	.083	.167	.250	-34	-1	0	.41	0	P-14/0-2(0-2-0)	2	0.1
1951 StL-N	5	2	1	1	0	0	1	1	0	1	0	0	.500	.500	2.000	2.500	537	1	2	55.35	0	/P-5	0	-0.2
Pit-N	21	39	6	12	3	0	1	7	3	11	0	0	.308	.357	.462	.819	115	1	7	6.87	-2	0-12(1-10-1)/P-3,2-2,3-2	1	-0.6
Yr.	26	41	7	13	3	0	2	8	3	12	0	0	.317	.364	.537	.900	134	2	9	8.60	-2	0-12(1-10-1)/P-8,2-2,3-2	1	-0.9
1952 Pit-N	20	27	1	6	0	0	1	3	2	8	0	0	.222	.276	.333	.609	66	-1	2	2.37	0	0-11(2-4-3)	0	-0.1
Total 9	**413**	**1035**	**168**	**251**	**32**	**6**	**24**	**106**	**142**	**188**	**12**	**0**	**.243**	**.334**	**.355**	**.688**	**84**	**-19**	**132**	**4.39**	**7**	**0-271/2-33,3-30,P-23,S-1**	**29**	**-2.8**

• DWIGHT, Al — Albert Ward Dwight b: 1/4/1856, New York, NY d: 2/20/1903, San Francisco, CA Deb: 6/19/1884

YEAR TM-L	G	AB	R	H	2B	3B	HR	RBI	BB	SO	SB	CS	AVG	OBP	SLG	OPS	OPS+	BR/A	RC	RC/G	FR	G/POS	WS	TPW
1884 KC-U	12	43	8	10	2	0	0	....	2	....	....	....	.233	.267	.279	.546	97	0	3	2.78	2	C-10/2-1,0-1	1	0.2

• DWYER, Double Joe — Joseph Michael Dwyer b: 3/27/1903, Orange, NJ d: 10/21/1992, Glen Ridge, NJ BL/TL, 5'9", 186 lbs. Deb: 4/20/1937

YEAR TM-L	G	AB	R	H	2B	3B	HR	RBI	BB	SO	SB	CS	AVG	OBP	SLG	OPS	OPS+	BR/A	RC	RC/G	FR	G/POS	WS	TPW
1937 Cin-N	12	11	2	3	0	0	0	1	1	0	0	....	.273	.333	.273	.606	70	-0	1	3.75	0	....	0	0.0

• DWYER, Jim — James Edward "Pig Pen" Dwyer b: 6/3/1950, Evergreen Park, IL BL/TL, 5'10", 175 lbs. Deb: 6/10/1973 Career OF: 250-75-329

YEAR TM-L	G	AB	R	H	2B	3B	HR	RBI	BB	SO	SB	CS	AVG	OBP	SLG	OPS	OPS+	BR/A	RC	RC/G	FR	G/POS	WS	TPW
1973 StL-N	28	57	7	11	1	1	0	0	1	5	0	0	.193	.207	.246	.453	25	-6	2	1.06	0	0-20(9-10-1)	0	-0.7
1974 StL-N	74	86	13	24	1	0	2	11	11	16	0	0	.279	.367	.360	.728	105	1	12	5.04	1	0-25(8-1-16)/1-3	3	0.1
1975 StL-N	21	31	4	6	1	0	0	1	4	6	0	0	.194	.286	.226	.512	42	-2	2	2.14	0	/0-9(5-3-2)	0	-0.3
Mon-N	60	175	22	50	7	1	3	20	23	30	4	1	.286	.369	.389	.757	106	2	28	5.49	3	0-52(46-3-3)	6	0.3
Yr.	81	206	26	56	8	1	3	21	27	36	4	1	.272	.356	.364	.720	96	0	30	4.94	3	0-61(51-6-5)	6	0.0
1976 Mon-N	50	92	7	17	3	1	0	5	11	10	0	0	.185	.272	.239	.511	44	-7	6	2.06	0	0-19(15-0-5)	0	-0.8
NY-N	11	13	2	2	0	0	0	0	2	1	0	0	.154	.267	.154	.421	23	-1	1	1.48	-0	/0-2(0-0-2)	0	-0.1
Yr.	61	105	9	19	3	1	0	5	13	11	0	0	.181	.271	.229	.500	41	-8	7	1.99	0	0-21(15-0-7)	0	-1.0
1977 StL-N	13	31	3	7	1	0	0	2	4	5	0	0	.226	.351	.258	.609	68	-1	3	3.78	0	0-12(3-0-10)	1	-0.2
1978 StL-N	34	65	8	14	3	0	1	4	9	3	1	0	.215	.320	.308	.628	77	-2	7	3.64	0	0-22(18-0-5)	1	-0.2
SF-N	73	173	22	39	9	2	5	22	28	29	6	0	.225	.333	.387	.721	105	3	25	4.84	3	0-36(3-26-9),1-29	6	0.4
Yr.	107	238	30	53	12	2	6	26	37	32	7	0	.223	.330	.366	.695	98	1	32	4.52	3	0-58(21-26-14),1-29	7	0.2
1979 Bos-A	76	113	19	30	7	0	2	14	17	9	3	1	.265	.366	.381	.747	96	0	15	4.37	1	1-25,0-19(6-1-12)/D-4	2	0.0
1980 Bos-A	93	260	41	74	11	1	9	38	28	23	3	2	.285	.359	.438	.797	111	4	41	5.75	4	0-65(11-29-27),D-12/1-9	8	0.5
1981 Bal-A	68	134	16	30	0	1	3	10	20	19	0	2	.224	.325	.306	.631	83	-3	14	3.40	-2	0-59(43-2-19)/1-3,D-1	3	-0.7
1982 Bal-A	71	148	28	45	4	3	6	15	27	24	2	0	.304	.411	.493	.905	148	11	33	8.41	-1	0-49(16-0-37)/1-1,D-1	8	0.8
1983*Bal-A	100	196	37	56	17	1	8	38	31	29	1	1	.286	.383	.505	.888	145	13	39	7.23	-2	0-56(7-0-49),D-10/1-4	9	0.8
1984 Bal-A	76	161	22	41	9	1	2	21	23	24	0	2	.255	.348	.360	.708	98	-0	21	4.29	1	0-52(1-0-51)/D-3	4	-0.2
1985 Bal-A	101	233	35	58	8	3	7	36	37	31	0	3	.249	.354	.399	.753	109	3	33	4.84	1	0-78(46-0-33)/D-3	7	0.1
1986 Bal-A	94	160	18	39	13	1	8	31	23	31	0	2	.244	.346	.488	.833	126	5	27	5.74	2	D-24,0-24(8-0-16)/1-1	5	0.6
1987 Bal-A	92	241	54	66	7	1	15	33	37	57	4	1	.274	.373	.498	.871	132	12	46	6.90	0	D-41,0-30(3-0-29)	9	0.9
1988 Bal-A	35	53	3	12	0	0	0	3	12	11	0	0	.226	.369	.226	.596	73	-1	5	3.47	-0	D-17/0-2(1-0-1)	1	-0.1
Min-A	20	41	6	12	1	0	2	15	13	8	0	0	.293	.473	.463	.936	159	4	10	8.90	0	D-13	3	0.4
Yr.	55	94	9	24	1	0	2	18	25	19	0	0	.255	.417	.330	.746	112	3	16	5.78	-0	D-30/0-2(1-0-1)	4	0.3
1989 Min-A	88	225	34	71	11	0	3	23	28	23	2	0	.316	.391	.404	.796	117	7	36	6.11	0	D-74/0-1	6	0.4
Mon-N	13	10	1	3	1	0	0	2	1	1	0	0	.300	.364	.400	.764	116	0	2	5.98	0	....	1	0.0
1990 Min-A	37	63	7	12	0	0	1	5	12	7	0	0	.190	.320	.238	.558	55	-3	5	2.67	-0	D-23/0-2(1-0-1)	0	-0.4
Total 18	**1328**	**2761**	**409**	**719**	**115**	**17**	**77**	**349**	**402**	**402**	**26**	**15**	**.260**	**.357**	**.398**	**.755**	**107**	**39**	**417**	**5.20**	**9**	**0-634,D-226/1-75**	**83**	**1.7**

• DWYER, John — John E. Dwyer b: Lisbon, IL Deb: 5/16/1882

YEAR TM-L	G	AB	R	H	2B	3B	HR	RBI	BB	SO	SB	CS	AVG	OBP	SLG	OPS	OPS+	BR/A	RC	RC/G	FR	G/POS	WS	TPW
1882 Cle-N	1	3	0	0	0	0	0	1	0	0	....	....	.000	.000	.000	.000	-104	-1	0	.00	0	/C-1,0-1	0	-0.1

• DYBZINSKI, Jerry — Jerome Matthew Dybzinski b: 7/7/1955, Cleveland, OH BR/TR, 6'2", 180 lbs. Deb: 4/11/1980

YEAR TM-L	G	AB	R	H	2B	3B	HR	RBI	BB	SO	SB	CS	AVG	OBP	SLG	OPS	OPS+	BR/A	RC	RC/G	FR	G/POS	WS	TPW
1980 Cle-A	114	248	32	57	11	1	1	23	13	35	4	1	.230	.274	.294	.568	55	-15	21	2.62	2	S-73,2-29/3-4,D-2	4	-0.5
1981 Cle-A	48	57	10	17	0	0	0	6	5	8	7	1	.298	.355	.298	.653	91	1	8	4.51	-3	S-34/2-3,3-3,D-1	2	0.0
1982 Cle-A	80	212	19	49	6	2	0	22	21	25	3	5	.231	.309	.278	.588	63	-12	18	2.61	3	S-77/3-3	3	0.0
1983*Chi-A	127	256	30	59	10	1	1	32	18	29	11	4	.230	.286	.289	.575	57	-14	21	2.58	-1	*S-118/3-9	5	-0.7
1984 Chi-A	94	132	17	31	5	1	1	10	13	12	7	2	.235	.313	.311	.624	70	-4	14	3.36	4	S-76,3-14/2-1,D-1	4	0.4
1985 Pit-N	5	4	0	0	0	0	0	0	0	0	0	0	.000	.000	.000	.000	-101	-1	0	.00	-1	/S-5	0	-0.2
Total 6	**468**	**909**	**108**	**213**	**32**	**5**	**3**	**93**	**70**	**109**	**32**	**13**	**.234**	**.296**	**.290**	**.586**	**61**	**-46**	**81**	**2.81**	**5**	**S-383/2-33,3-33,D-4**	**18**	**-0.9**

• DYCK, Jim — James Robert Dyck b: 2/3/1922, Omaha, NE d: 1/11/1999, Cheney, WA BR/TR, 6'2", 205 lbs. Deb: 9/27/1951 Career OF: 125-27-10

YEAR TM-L	G	AB	R	H	2B	3B	HR	RBI	BB	SO	SB	CS	AVG	OBP	SLG	OPS	OPS+	BR/A	RC	RC/G	FR	G/POS	WS	TPW
1951 StL-A	4	15	1	1	0	0	0	0	1	1	0	0	.067	.125	.067	.192	-46	-3	0	.31	0	/3-4	0	-0.3
1952 StL-A	122	402	60	108	22	3	15	64	50	68	0	4	.269	.354	.450	.804	119	9	67	5.94	9	3-74,0-48(39-8-2)	15	1.5
1953 StL-A	112	334	38	71	15	1	9	27	38	40	3	2	.213	.299	.344	.643	72	-13	33	3.14	-2	0-55(32-19-8),3-51	3	-1.8
1954 Cle-A	2	1	0	1	0	0	0	1	1	0	0	0	1.000	1.000	1.000	2.000	441	1	1	∞	0	....	0	0.1
1955 Bal-A	61	197	32	55	13	1	2	22	28	21	1	0	.279	.372	.386	.757	112	4	29	5.12	-3	0-45(45-0-0),3-17	7	-0.2
1956 Bal-A	11	23	3	5	2	0	0	0	10	5	0	0	.217	.455	.304	.759	112	1	4	6.34	1	/0-9(9-0-0)	1	0.2
Cin-N	18	11	5	1	0	0	0	0	3	5	0	0	.091	.286	.091	.377	7	-1	0	1.04	0	/1-1,3-1	0	-0.1
Total 6	**330**	**983**	**139**	**242**	**52**	**5**	**26**	**114**	**131**	**140**	**4**	**6**	**.246**	**.339**	**.389**	**.728**	**98**	**-2**	**135**	**4.60**	**5**	**0-157,3-147/1-1**	**26**	**-0.6**

• DYE, Jermaine — Jermaine Terrell Dye b: 1/28/1974, Oakland, CA BR/TR, 6'4", 210 lbs. Deb: 5/17/1996 Career OF: 27-9-832

YEAR TM-L	G	AB	R	H	2B	3B	HR	RBI	BB	SO	SB	CS	AVG	OBP	SLG	OPS	OPS+	BR/A	RC	RC/G	FR	G/POS	WS	TPW
1996*Atl-N	98	292	32	82	16	0	12	37	8	67	1	4	.281	.307	.459	.766	93	-6	35	4.19	2	0-92(25-4-71)	5	-0.7
1997 KC-A	75	263	26	62	14	0	7	22	17	51	2	1	.236	.285	.369	.654	67	-13	27	3.44	5	0-75(1-0-75)	2	-1.1
1998 KC-A	60	214	24	50	5	1	5	23	11	46	2	2	.234	.274	.336	.611	56	-15	18	2.67	7	0-59(0-0-59)	2	-1.1
1999 KC-A	158	608	96	179	44	8	27	119	58	119	2	3	.294	.357	.526	.883	119	15	110	6.51	13	*0-157(0-0-157)/D-1	16	1.8
2000 KC-A★	157	601	107	193	41	2	33	118	69	99	0	1	.321	.394	.561	.954	133	30	133	8.38	-2	*0-146(0-0-146),D-10	21	1.8
2001 KC-A	97	367	50	100	14	0	13	47	30	68	7	1	.272	.337	.417	.754	90	-5	55	5.34	-1	0-93(0-2-92)/D-4	7	-1.0
*Oak-A	61	232	41	69	17	1	13	59	27	44	2	0	.297	.373	.547	.920	138	13	47	7.31	0	0-61(0-0-61)	11	0.9
Yr.	158	599	91	169	31	1	26	106	57	112	9	1	.282	.351	.467	.819	109	8	102	6.10	-1	*0-154(0-2-153)/D-4	18	-0.1
2002*Oak-A	131	488	74	123	27	1	24	86	52	108	2	0	.252	.336	.459	.795	108	6	75	5.23	-9	*0-111(0-0-111),D-19	13	-0.9
2003*Oak-A	65	221	28	38	6	0	4	20	25	42	1	0	.172	.265	.253	.518	37	-20	14	1.94	-1	0-61(1-3-60)/D-3	2	-2.3
Total 8	**902**	**3286**	**478**	**896**	**184**	**13**	**138**	**531**	**297**	**644**	**19**	**12**	**.273**	**.338**	**.463**	**.801**	**102**	**5**	**513**	**5.47**	**15**	**0-855/D-37**	**79**	**-2.7**

• DYER, Ben — Benjamin Franklin Dyer b: 2/13/1893, Chicago, IL d: 8/7/1959, Kenosha, WI BR/TR, 5'10", 170 lbs. Deb: 5/23/1914 Career OF: 1-0-2

YEAR TM-L	G	AB	R	H	2B	3B	HR	RBI	BB	SO	SB	CS	AVG	OBP	SLG	OPS	OPS+	BR/A	RC	RC/G	FR	G/POS	WS	TPW
1914 NY-N	7	4	1	1	0	0	0	0	0	1	1	....	.250	.250	.250	.500	50	-0	0	3.69	-2	/S-6,2-1	0	-0.2
1915 NY-N	7	19	4	4	0	1	0	0	4	3	0	....	.211	.375	.316	.691	117	1	2	3.98	-1	/3-6,S-1	1	0.0
1916 Det-A	4	14	4	4	1	0	0	1	1	1	0	....	.286	.333	.357	.690	104	0	2	4.33	-3	/S-4	1	-0.3
1917 Det-A	30	67	6	14	5	0	0	0	2	17	3	....	.209	.232	.284	.515	57	-4	5	2.27	-2	S-14/3-8	1	-0.6
1918 Det-A	13	18	1	5	0	0	0	2	0	6	0	....	.278	.278	.278	.556	70	-1	1	2.53	1	/1-2,0-2(1-0-1),P-2,2-1	0	0.0

YEAR TM-L	G	AB	R	H	2B	3B	HR	RBI	BB	SO	SB	CS	AVG	OBP	SLG	OPS	OPS+	BR/A	RC	RC/G	FR	G/POS	WS	TPW
1919 Det-A	44	85	11	21	4	0	0	15	8	19	0	....	.247	.312	.294	.606	72	-3	8	3.00	-2	3-23,S-11/O-1	2	-0.4
Total 6	105	207	27	49	10	1	0	18	15	47	4	....	.237	.291	.295	.586	74	-7	18	2.90	-10	/3-37,S-36,O-3,1-2,2-2,P-2	5	-1.5

• DYER, Duffy Don Robert Dyer b: 8/15/1945, Dayton, OH BR/TR, 6', 195 lbs. Deb: 9/21/1968 C

YEAR TM-L	G	AB	R	H	2B	3B	HR	RBI	BB	SO	SB	CS	AVG	OBP	SLG	OPS	OPS+	BR/A	RC	RC/G	FR	G/POS	WS	TPW
1968 NY-N	1	3	0	1	0	0	0	0	1	1	0	0	.333	.500	.333	.833	153	0	1	8.51	0	/C-1	0	0.0
1969*NY-N	29	74	5	19	3	1	3	12	4	22	0	0	.257	.295	.446	.741	103	-0	9	4.00	0	C-19	3	0.1
1970 NY-N	59	148	8	31	1	0	2	12	21	32	1	1	.209	.308	.257	.564	53	-10	12	2.56	1	C-57	3	-0.6
1971 NY-N	59	169	13	39	7	1	2	18	14	45	1	0	.231	.293	.320	.613	75	-5	16	3.13	-0	C-53	4	-0.3
1972 NY-N	94	325	33	75	17	3	8	36	28	71	0	1	.231	.302	.375	.677	94	-3	36	3.65	15	C-91/O-1	16	1.7
1973 NY-N	70	189	9	35	6	1	1	9	13	40	0	1	.185	.245	.243	.488	36	-17	11	1.81	2	C-60	3	-1.3
1974 NY-N	63	142	14	30	1	1	0	10	18	15	0	0	.211	.304	.232	.537	52	-8	10	2.28	-1	C-45	0	-0.8
1975*Pit-N	48	132	8	30	5	2	3	16	6	22	0	0	.227	.266	.364	.630	74	-5	12	2.99	-2	C-36	3	-0.5
1976 Pit-N	69	184	12	41	8	0	3	9	29	35	0	0	.223	.338	.315	.653	85	-2	21	3.77	2	C-58	7	0.2
1977 Pit-N	94	270	27	65	11	1	3	19	54	49	6	0	.241	.373	.322	.695	86	-1	36	4.52	-3	C-93	11	0.1
1978 Pit-N	58	175	7	37	8	1	0	13	18	32	2	1	.211	.296	.269	.564	56	-10	14	2.61	-2	C-55	3	-1.0
1979 Mon-N	28	74	4	18	6	0	1	8	9	17	0	0	.243	.325	.365	.690	89	-1	9	4.20	1	C-27	3	0.1
1980 Det-A	48	108	11	20	1	0	4	11	13	34	0	0	.185	.273	.306	.578	57	-6	9	2.59	0	C-37,D-10	1	-0.6
1981 Det-A	2	0	0	0	0	0	0	0	0	0	0	0	....	....	....	....	-96	0	0	....	-1	/C-2	0	-0.1
Total 14	722	1993	151	441	74	11	30	173	228	415	10	4	.221	.307	.315	.622	73	-70	195	3.21	12	C-634/D-10,O-1	57	-3.0

• DYER, Eddie Edwin Hawley Dyer b: 10/11/1900, Morgan City, LA d: 4/20/1964, Houston, TX BL/TL, 5'11.5", 168 lbs. Deb: 7/8/1922 M Career OF: 7-3-0 ♦

YEAR TM-L	G	AB	R	H	2B	3B	HR	RBI	BB	SO	SB	CS	AVG	OBP	SLG	OPS	OPS+	BR/A	RC	RC/G	FR	G/POS	WS	TPW
1922 StL-N	6	3	1	1	1	0	0	0	0	0	0	0	.333	.333	.667	1.000	159	1	1	8.48	0	/P-2	1	0.1
1923 StL-N	35	45	17	12	3	0	2	5	3	5	1	0	.267	.313	.467	.779	105	2	7	5.37	0	/O-8(7-2-0),P-4	3	0.1
1924 StL-N	50	76	8	18	2	3	0	8	3	8	1	0	.237	.266	.342	.608	63	2	7	3.08	1	P-29/O-1	5	-1.0
1925 StL-N	31	31	4	3	1	0	0	0	3	1	1	1	.097	.176	.129	.306	-20	-2	1	.70	0	P-27	4	-0.1
1926 StL-N	6	2	1	1	0	0	0	0	0	0	0	....	.500	.500	.500	1.000	163	0	0	12.09	0	/P-6	0	-0.8
1927 StL-N	1	0	0	0	0	0	0	0	1	0	0	....	....	1.000	....	1.000	181	0	0	∞	0	/P-1	0	-0.3
Total 6	129	157	31	35	7	3	2	13	10	14	3	1	.223	.269	.344	.613	61	3	16	3.27	0	/P-69,O-9	13	-2.0

• DYKES, Jimmie James Joseph Dykes b: 11/10/1896, Philadelphia, PA d: 6/15/1976, Philadelphia, PA BR/TR, 5'9", 185 lbs. Deb: 5/6/1918 M/C Career OF: 2-4-1

YEAR TM-L	G	AB	R	H	2B	3B	HR	RBI	BB	SO	SB	CS	AVG	OBP	SLG	OPS	OPS+	BR/A	RC	RC/G	FR	G/POS	WS	TPW
1918 Phi-A	59	186	13	35	3	3	0	13	19	32	3	....	.188	.267	.237	.504	51	-11	13	2.04	0	2-56/3-1	1	-1.1
1919 Phi-A	17	49	4	9	1	0	0	1	7	11	0	....	.184	.286	.204	.490	38	-4	3	1.74	-1	2-16	0	-0.5
1920 Phi-A	142	546	81	140	25	4	8	35	55	73	6	9	.256	.334	.361	.695	83	-13	68	4.06	-1	*2-108,3-34	12	-1.1
1921 Phi-A	155	613	88	168	32	13	16	77	60	75	6	5	.274	.353	.447	.800	102	2	99	5.66	25	*2-155	16	2.9
1922 Phi-A	145	501	66	138	23	7	12	68	55	98	6	2	.275	.359	.421	.780	100	2	79	5.53	-9	*3-141/2-5	17	0.2
1923 Phi-A	124	416	50	105	28	1	4	43	35	40	6	4	.252	.318	.353	.671	75	-15	48	3.87	1	*2-102,S-20/3-2	9	-0.9
1924 Phi-A	110	410	68	128	26	6	3	50	38	60	1	3	.312	.372	.427	.799	105	2	65	5.86	2	2-77,3-27/S-4	16	0.9
1925 Phi-A	122	465	93	150	32	11	5	55	46	49	3	2	.323	.393	.471	.864	111	9	88	7.04	7	3-64,2-58/S-2	18	2.0
1926 Phi-A	124	429	54	123	32	5	1	44	49	34	6	2	.287	.370	.392	.762	94	-2	66	5.44	6	3-82,2-44/S-1	15	1.1
1927 Phi-A	121	417	61	135	33	6	3	60	44	23	2	3	.324	.394	.453	.847	113	8	76	6.68	-1	1-82,3-25/O-5(0-4-1),S-5,2,P	16	0.3
1928 Phi-A	85	242	39	67	11	0	5	30	27	21	2	1	.277	.361	.384	.746	93	-1	36	5.03	1	2-32,S-22,3-20/1-8,O-1	8	0.3
1929*Phi-A	119	401	76	131	34	6	13	79	51	25	8	3	.327	.412	.539	.950	138	25	91	8.36	-5	S-60,3-48,2-12	21	2.8
1930*Phi-A	125	435	69	131	28	4	6	73	74	53	3	3	.301	.414	.425	.840	109	10	82	6.76	-8	*3-123/O-1	18	0.8
1931*Phi-A	101	355	48	97	28	2	3	46	49	47	1	2	.273	.371	.389	.759	94	-0	54	5.41	7	3-87,S-15	13	1.0
1932 Phi-A	153	558	71	148	29	5	7	90	77	65	8	2	.265	.358	.373	.731	87	-8	80	5.04	-3	*3-141,S-10/2-1	14	-0.4
1933 Chi-A★	151	554	49	144	22	6	1	68	69	37	3	7	.260	.354	.327	.681	85	-10	67	4.23	-5	*3-151	15	-1.0
1934 Chi-A★	127	456	52	122	17	4	7	82	64	28	1	1	.268	.363	.368	.731	86	-8	65	4.97	-6	3-74,1-27,2-27	11	-1.1
1935 Chi-A	117	403	45	116	24	2	4	61	59	28	4	3	.288	.381	.387	.769	97	0	63	5.59	-11	3-98,1-16/2-3	11	-0.8
1936 Chi-A	127	435	62	116	16	3	7	60	61	36	1	3	.267	.362	.366	.728	77	-15	61	4.85	-14	*3-125	9	-2.2
1937 Chi-A	30	85	10	26	5	0	1	23	9	7	0	0	.306	.372	.400	.772	95	-0	13	5.68	-1	1-15,3-11	2	-0.2
1938 Chi-A	26	89	9	27	4	2	2	13	10	8	0	0	.303	.374	.461	.834	105	1	16	6.69	-1	2-23/3-1,S-1	3	0.1
1939 Chi-A	2	1	0	0	0	0	0	0	0	0	0	0	.000	.000	.000	.000	-97	-0	0	.00	-1	/3-2	0	-0.1
Total 22	2282	8046	1108	2256	453	90	108	1071	958	850	70	55	.280	.365	.399	.764	95	-30	1233	5.38	-16	*3-1257,2-722,1-148,S-140/O,P	245	3.1

• DYKSTRA, Lenny Leonard Kyle "Nails,Dude" Dykstra b: 2/10/1963, Santa Ana, CA BL/TL, 5'10", 167 lbs. Deb: 5/3/1985 Career OF: 10-1213-0

YEAR TM-L	G	AB	R	H	2B	3B	HR	RBI	BB	SO	SB	CS	AVG	OBP	SLG	OPS	OPS+	BR/A	RC	RC/G	FR	G/POS	WS	TPW
1985 NY-N	83	236	40	60	9	3	1	19	30	24	15	2	.254	.341	.331	.671	91	0	30	4.34	4	O-74(0-74-0)	8	0.4
1986*NY-N	147	431	77	127	27	7	8	45	58	55	31	7	.295	.378	.445	.824	130	22	80	6.63	6	*O-139(1-138-0)	23	2.8
1987 NY-N	132	431	86	123	37	3	10	43	40	67	27	7	.285	.352	.455	.806	118	13	74	6.24	2	*O-118(0-118-0)	17	1.4
1988*NY-N	126	429	57	116	19	3	8	33	30	43	30	8	.270	.323	.385	.707	108	6	56	4.65	2	*O-112(0-112-0)	15	0.7
1989 NY-N	56	159	27	43	12	1	3	13	23	15	13	1	.270	.370	.415	.785	130	9	28	6.00	-1	O-51(0-51-0)	8	0.8
Phi-N	90	352	39	78	20	3	4	19	37	38	17	11	.222	.297	.330	.627	79	-11	35	3.20	5	O-88(0-89-0)	6	-0.8
Yr.	146	511	66	121	32	4	7	32	60	53	30	12	.237	.321	.356	.677	96	-1	63	4.05	4	*O-139(0-140-0)	14	0.0
1990 Phi-N★	149	590	106	**192**	35	3	9	60	89	48	33	5	.325	.420	.441	.861	137	40	121	7.92	9	*O-149(0-149-0)	35	4.8
1991 Phi-N	63	246	48	73	13	5	3	12	37	20	24	4	.297	.391	.427	.818	131	15	47	7.20	0	O-63(0-63-0)	13	1.5
1992 Phi-N	85	345	53	104	18	0	6	39	40	32	30	5	.301	.379	.406	.785	123	16	60	6.49	3	O-85(0-85-0)	17	1.8
1993*Phi-N	161	637	**143**	**194**	44	6	19	66	**129**	64	37	12	.305	.423	.482	.905	144	49	142	8.21	-1	*O-160(0-160-0)	32	4.9
1994 Phi-N★	84	315	68	86	26	5	5	24	68	44	15	4	.273	.405	.435	.840	116	13	62	7.07	0	O-82(0-83-0)	14	1.3
1995 Phi-N★	62	254	37	67	15	1	2	18	33	28	10	5	.264	.355	.354	.710	87	-4	35	4.83	1	O-61(9-52-0)	8	-0.2
1996 Phi-N	40	134	21	35	6	3	3	13	26	25	3	1	.261	.389	.418	.807	112	4	24	6.37	2	O-39(0-39-0)	5	0.6
Total 12	1278	4559	802	1298	281	43	81	404	640	503	285	72	.285	.376	.419	.795	120	173	795	6.27	32	*O-1221	201	19.9

• DYLER, John John F. Dyler b: 6/5/1852, Louisville, KY d: 8/15/1916, Fort Myers, FL Deb: 7/22/1882 U

YEAR TM-L	G	AB	R	H	2B	3B	HR	RBI	BB	SO	SB	CS	AVG	OBP	SLG	OPS	OPS+	BR/A	RC	RC/G	FR	G/POS	WS	TPW
1882 Lou-a	1	4	0	0	0	0	0	....	0	....	....	....	.000	.000	.000	.000	-106	-1	0	.00	0	/O-1	0	-0.1

• EADDY, Don Donald Johnson Eaddy b: 2/16/1934, Grand Rapids, MI BR/TR, 5'11", 165 lbs. Deb: 4/24/1959

YEAR TM-L	G	AB	R	H	2B	3B	HR	RBI	BB	SO	SB	CS	AVG	OBP	SLG	OPS	OPS+	BR/A	RC	RC/G	FR	G/POS	WS	TPW
1959 Chi-N	15	1	3	0	0	0	0	0	0	1	0	0	.000	.000	.000	.000	-101	-0	0	.00	0	/3-1	0	-0.1

• EAGAN, Bill William "Bad Bill" Eagan b: 6/1/1869, Camden, NJ d: 2/13/1905, Denver, CO Deb: 4/8/1891

YEAR TM-L	G	AB	R	H	2B	3B	HR	RBI	BB	SO	SB	CS	AVG	OBP	SLG	OPS	OPS+	BR/A	RC	RC/G	FR	G/POS	WS	TPW
1891 StL-a	82	297	49	65	11	4	4	43	44	53	21	....	.219	.326	.323	.649	74	-12	39	4.46	21	2-83	9	1.1
1893 Chi-N	6	19	3	5	0	0	0	2	5	5	4	....	.263	.417	.263	.680	83	0	4	7.28	-1	/2-6	0	0.0
1898 Pit-N	19	61	14	20	2	3	0	5	8	....	1	....	.328	.453	.459	.912	165	6	14	8.60	1	2-17	4	0.8
Total 3	107	377	66	90	13	7	4	50	57	58	26	....	.239	.352	.342	.694	90	-5	57	5.20	22	2-106	13	1.8

• EAGAN, Truck Charles Eugene Eagan b: 8/10/1877, San Francisco, CA d: 3/19/1949, San Francisco, CA BR/TR, 5'11", 190 lbs. Deb: 5/1/1901

YEAR TM-L	G	AB	R	H	2B	3B	HR	RBI	BB	SO	SB	CS	AVG	OBP	SLG	OPS	OPS+	BR/A	RC	RC/G	FR	G/POS	WS	TPW
1901 Pit-N	4	12	0	1	0	0	0	2	0	....	1	....	.083	.083	.083	.167	-50	-2	0	.41	0	/S-3	0	-0.2
Cle-A	5	18	2	3	0	1	0	2	1	....	0	....	.167	.211	.278	.488	36	-2	1	1.91	1	/2-5,3-1	0	-0.1

• EAGLE, Bill William Lycurgus Eagle b: 7/25/1877, Rockville, MD d: 4/27/1951, Churchton, MD Deb: 8/20/1898

YEAR TM-L	G	AB	R	H	2B	3B	HR	RBI	BB	SO	SB	CS	AVG	OBP	SLG	OPS	OPS+	BR/A	RC	RC/G	FR	G/POS	WS	TPW
1898 Was-N	4	13	0	4	1	0	0	2	0	....	0	....	.308	.308	.385	.692	98	-0	2	4.64	0	/O-4(1-0-1)	0	0.0

• EAKLE, Charlie Charles Emory Eakle b: 9/27/1887, Baltimore, MD d: 6/15/1959, Baltimore, MD Deb: 8/20/1915

YEAR TM-L	G	AB	R	H	2B	3B	HR	RBI	BB	SO	SB	CS	AVG	OBP	SLG	OPS	OPS+	BR/A	RC	RC/G	FR	G/POS	WS	TPW
1915 Bal-F	2	7	0	2	1	0	0	0	0	0	1	....	.286	.286	.429	.714	102	-0	1	5.32	-1	/2-2	0	-0.1

• EARL, Howard Howard J. "Slim Jim" Earl b: 2/25/1867, Palmyra, NY d: 12/23/1916, North Bay, NY, 6'2", 180 lbs. Deb: 4/19/1890 Career OF: 0-0-79

YEAR TM-L	G	AB	R	H	2B	3B	HR	RBI	BB	SO	SB	CS	AVG	OBP	SLG	OPS	OPS+	BR/A	RC	RC/G	FR	G/POS	WS	TPW
1890 Chi-N	92	384	57	95	10	3	7	51	18	47	17	....	.247	.285	.344	.628	80	-13	43	3.99	1	O-49(0-0-49),2-39/S-4,1-3	7	-1.0
1891 Mil-a	31	129	21	32	5	2	1	17	5	13	3	....	.248	.281	.341	.623	65	-8	14	3.70	-2	O-30(0-0-30)/1-2	2	-0.9
Total 2	123	513	78	127	15	5	8	68	23	60	20	....	.248	.284	.343	.627	76	-20	57	3.92	-1	/O-79,2-39,1-5,S-4	9	-1.9

• EARL, Scott William Scott Earl b: 9/18/1960, Seymour, IN BR/TR, 5'11", 165 lbs. Deb: 9/10/1984

YEAR TM-L	G	AB	R	H	2B	3B	HR	RBI	BB	SO	SB	CS	AVG	OBP	SLG	OPS	OPS+	BR/A	RC	RC/G	FR	G/POS	WS	TPW
1984 Det-A	14	35	3	4	0	1	0	1	0	9	1	0	.114	.114	.171	.286	-22	-6	1	.67	0	2-14	0	-0.5

YEAR TM-L	G	AB	R	H	2B	3B	HR	RBI	BB	SO	SB	CS	AVG	OBP	SLG	OPS	OPS+	BR/A	RC	RC/G	FR	G/POS	WS	TPW
• EARLE, Billy					William Moffat "The Little Globetrotter" Earle b: 11/10/1867, Philadelphia, PA d: 5/30/1946, Omaha, NE BR/TR, 5'10.5", 170 lbs. Deb: 4/27/1889 U Career OF: 3-1-26																			
1889 Cin-a	53	169	37	45	4	7	4	31	30	24	26	....	.266	.386	.444	.830	132	8	40	8.54	-8	0-26(2-1-23),C-23/1-5	7	0.1
1890 StL-a	22	73	16	17	3	1	0	12	7	....	6	....	.233	.317	.301	.618	72	-3	9	4.31	0	C-18/0-3(0-0-3),2-1,3-1,S	2	-0.1
1892 Pit-N	5	13	5	7	2	0	0	3	4	1	2	....	.538	.647	.692	1.339	304	4	7	32.83	0	/C-5	2	0.4
1893 Pit-N	27	95	21	24	4	4	2	15	7	6	1	....	.253	.304	.442	.746	99	-1	13	5.00	-3	C-27	3	-0.1
1894 Lou-N	21	65	10	23	1	0	0	7	9	3	2	....	.354	.432	.369	.802	102	1	12	7.13	5	C-18/1-1,2-1,3-1,0-1	2	0.6
Bro-N	14	50	13	17	6	0	0	6	6	2	4	....	.340	.421	.460	.881	121	2	12	9.18	1	C-12/2-1	2	0.4
Yr.	35	115	23	40	7	0	0	13	15	5	6	....	.348	.427	.409	.836	110	3	23	8.03	6	C-30/2-2,1-1,3-1,0-1	4	0.9
Total 5	142	465	102	133	20	12	6	74	63	36	41	....	.286	.378	.419	.798	117	11	93	7.39	-4	C-103/0-30,1-6,2-3,3-2,S-1	18	1.2
• EARLY, Jake					Jacob Willard Early b: 5/19/1915, King's Mountain, NC d: 5/31/1985, Melbourne, FL BL/TR, 5'11", 168 lbs. Deb: 5/4/1939																			
1939 Was-A	32	84	8	22	7	2	0	14	5	14	0	0	.262	.303	.393	.696	83	-2	10	4.19	-1	C-24	2	-0.2
1940 Was-A	80	206	26	53	8	4	5	14	23	22	0	1	.257	.335	.408	.743	98	-1	29	5.01	1	C-56	6	0.4
1941 Was-A	104	355	42	102	20	7	10	54	24	38	0	1	.287	.338	.468	.805	116	6	57	5.83	-3	*C-100	11	0.8
1942 Was-A	104	353	31	72	14	2	3	46	37	37	0	0	.204	.281	.280	.562	59	-19	30	2.81	8	C-98	7	-0.6
1943 Was-A★	126	423	37	109	23	3	5	60	53	43	5	3	.258	.346	.362	.708	111	7	57	4.72	-4	*C-122	17	1.2
1946 Was-A	64	189	13	38	6	0	4	18	23	27	0	0	.201	.288	.296	.584	67	-8	17	3.04	1	C-64	3	-0.4
1947 StL-A	87	214	25	48	9	3	3	19	54	34	0	1	.224	.381	.336	.717	98	2	32	5.10	1	C-85	8	0.7
1948 Was-A	97	246	22	54	7	2	1	28	36	33	2	1	.220	.322	.276	.598	62	-12	25	3.49	4	C-92	7	-0.4
1949 Was-A	53	138	12	34	4	0	1	11	26	11	0	1	.246	.370	.297	.667	79	-3	17	3.96	-2	C-53	3	-0.3
Total 9	747	2208	216	532	98	23	32	264	281	259	7	8	.241	.330	.350	.679	89	-30	275	4.28	3	C-694	64	1.2
• EASLER, Mike					Michael Anthony Easler b: 11/29/1950, Cleveland, OH BL/TR, 6', 196 lbs. Deb: 9/5/1973 C Career OF: 479-0-82																			
1973 Hou-N	6	7	1	0	0	0	0	0	2	4	0	0	.000	.222	.000	.222	-34	-1	0	.22	-1	/0-2(1-0-1)	0	-0.2
1974 Hou-N	15	15	0	1	0	0	0	0	0	5	0	0	.067	.067	.067	.133	-65	-3	0	.00	0	....	0	-0.3
1975 Hou-N	5	5	0	0	0	0	0	0	0	1	0	0	.000	.000	.000	.000	-108	-1	0	.00	0	....	0	-0.1
1976 Cal-A	21	54	6	13	1	1	0	4	2	11	1	1	.241	.268	.296	.564	69	-2	4	2.37	0	D-16	0	-0.3
1977 Pit-N	10	18	3	8	2	0	1	5	0	1	0	0	.444	.444	.722	1.167	201	2	6	13.97	0	/0-4(1-0-3)	2	0.2
1979★Pit-N	55	54	8	15	1	1	2	11	8	13	0	1	.278	.371	.444	.815	116	1	9	6.25	-1	/0-4(2-0-2)	2	0.0
1980 Pit-N	132	393	66	133	27	3	21	74	43	65	5	9	.338	.404	.583	.986	169	33	88	8.38	0	*0-119(91-0-42)	22	3.0
1981 Pit-N★	95	339	43	97	18	5	7	42	24	45	4	7	.286	.333	.431	.764	112	2	44	4.47	5	0-90(72-0-25)	9	0.2
1982 Pit-N	142	475	52	131	27	2	15	58	40	85	1	1	.276	.340	.436	.776	112	7	69	5.14	-2	*0-138(137-0-3)	14	-0.1
1983 Pit-N	115	381	44	117	17	2	10	54	22	64	4	2	.307	.350	.441	.791	115	7	57	5.49	-3	*0-105(105-0-0)	11	-0.1
1984 Bos-A	156	601	87	188	31	5	27	91	58	134	1	1	.313	.377	.516	.893	138	31	118	7.52	2	*D-126,1-29	23	2.7
1985 Bos-A	155	568	71	149	29	4	16	74	53	129	0	1	.262	.329	.412	.740	97	-3	75	4.61	-2	*D-130,0-20(18-0-2)	9	-1.0
1986 NY-A	146	490	64	148	26	2	14	78	49	87	3	2	.302	.365	.449	.814	122	15	76	5.61	-1	*D-129,0-11(8-0-3)	13	0.9
1987 Phi-N	33	110	7	31	4	0	1	10	6	20	0	1	.282	.319	.345	.664	74	-5	12	3.95	1	0-30(30-0-0)	2	-0.5
NY-A	65	167	13	47	6	0	4	21	14	32	1	0	.281	.341	.389	.730	94	-1	22	4.76	0	D-32,0-15(14-0-1)	3	-0.2
Total 14	1151	3677	465	1078	189	25	118	522	321	696	20	26	.293	.353	.454	.807	119	81	581	5.69	-1	0-538,D-433/1-29	110	4.2
• EASLEY, Damion					Jacinto Damion Easley b: 11/11/1969, New York, NY BR/TR, 5'11", 185 lbs. Deb: 8/13/1992																			
1992 Cal-A	47	151	14	39	5	0	1	12	8	26	9	5	.258	.309	.311	.620	74	-6	15	3.24	7	3-45/S-3	4	0.1
1993 Cal-A	73	230	33	72	13	2	2	22	28	35	6	6	.313	.395	.413	.808	114	4	37	5.87	-4	2-54,3-14/D-1	7	0.3
1994 Cal-A	88	316	41	68	16	1	6	30	29	48	4	5	.215	.289	.329	.619	58	-22	29	2.95	-5	3-47,2-40	3	-2.3
1995 Cal-A	114	357	35	77	14	2	4	35	32	47	5	2	.216	.291	.300	.591	55	-24	31	2.79	-2	2-88,S-25	4	-1.9
1996 Cal-A	28	45	4	7	1	0	2	7	6	12	0	0	.156	.255	.311	.566	43	-4	4	2.71	-1	S-13/2-9,3-3,D-2,0-2(0-2-0)	1	-0.4
Det-A	21	67	10	23	1	0	2	10	4	13	3	1	.343	.389	.448	.837	111	1	12	6.97	-1	/2-8,S-8,3-2,D-1	2	0.1
Yr.	49	112	14	30	2	0	4	17	10	25	3	1	.268	.333	.393	.726	83	-3	17	5.01	-2	S-21,2-17/3-5,D-3,0-2(0-2-0)	3	-0.3
1997 Det-A	151	527	97	139	37	3	22	72	68	102	28	13	.264	.365	.471	.836	117	15	89	5.63	-3	*2-137,S-21/D-4	18	1.8
1998 Det-A★	153	594	84	161	38	2	27	100	39	112	15	5	.271	.333	.478	.811	107	5	96	5.76	12	*2-140,S-30/D-2	23	2.4
1999 Det-A	151	549	83	146	30	1	20	65	51	124	11	3	.266	.349	.434	.782	98	-1	84	5.28	10	*2-147,S-19	13	1.5
2000 Det-A	126	464	76	120	27	2	14	58	55	79	13	4	.259	.351	.416	.767	96	-1	70	5.20	7	*2-125	14	1.1
2001 Det-A	154	585	77	146	27	7	11	65	52	90	10	5	.250	.325	.376	.701	88	-10	73	4.27	2	*2-153	15	-0.1
2002 Det-A	85	304	29	68	14	1	8	30	27	43	1	3	.224	.310	.355	.665	81	-9	34	3.74	-3	2-84	5	-0.8
2003 TB-A	36	107	8	20	3	1	1	7	2	18	0	0	.187	.202	.262	.464	21	-12	5	1.49	-3	3-23/D-6,2-4	0	-1.5
Total 12	1227	4296	591	1086	226	22	120	513	401	749	105	52	.253	.331	.399	.731	90	-63	580	4.58	15	2-989,3-134,S-119/D-16,0-2	109	0.4
• EAST, Carl					Carlton William East b: 8/27/1894, Marietta, GA d: 1/15/1953, Whitesburg, GA BL/TR, 6'2", 178 lbs. Deb: 8/24/1915 ♦																			
1915 StL-A	1	1	0	0	0	0	0	0	0	0	0	....	.000	.000	.000	.000	-104	-0	0	.00	0	/P-1	0	-0.5
1924 Was-A	2	6	1	2	1	0	0	2	2	1	0	0	.333	.500	.500	1.000	163	1	2	11.19	0	/0-2(0-0-2)	0	0.0
Total 2	3	7	1	2	1	0	0	2	2	1	0	0	.286	.444	.429	.873	134	1	2	8.95	-1	/0-2,P-1	0	-0.5
• EAST, Harry					Harry H. East b: 4/1863, St. Louis, MO d: 6/2/1905, St. Louis, MO Deb: 6/17/1882																			
1882 Bal-a	1	4	0	0	0	0	0	....	0	....	....	....	.000	.000	.000	.000	-108	-1	0	.00	0	/3-1	0	-0.1
• EASTER, Luke					Luscious Luke Easter b: 8/4/1915, Jonestown, MS d: 3/29/1979, Euclid, OH BL/TR, 6'4.5", 240 lbs. Deb: 8/11/1949 C Career OF: 0-0-25																			
1949 Cle-A	21	45	6	10	3	0	0	2	8	6	0	1	.222	.340	.289	.629	68	-2	4	3.06	0	0-12(0-0-12)	0	-0.2
1950 Cle-A	141	540	96	151	20	4	28	107	70	95	0	3	.280	.373	.487	.860	123	16	100	6.57	7	*1-128,0-13(0-0-13)	20	1.8
1951 Cle-A	128	486	65	131	12	5	27	103	37	71	0	1	.270	.333	.481	.814	125	14	77	5.60	0	*1-125	17	0.9
1952 Cle-A	127	437	63	115	10	3	31	97	44	84	1	1	.263	.337	.513	.850	144	23	79	6.50	7	*1-118	20	2.7
1953 Cle-A	68	211	26	64	9	0	7	31	15	35	0	2	.303	.361	.445	.806	120	5	30	4.99	0	1-56	6	0.2
1954 Cle-A	6	6	0	1	0	0	0	0	0	2	0	0	.167	.167	.167	.333	-8	-1	0	.90	0	....	0	-0.1
Total 6	491	1725	256	472	54	12	93	340	174	293	1	8	.274	.350	.481	.830	126	55	290	5.96	14	1-427/0-25	63	5.3
• EASTERDAY, Henry					Henry P. Easterday b: 9/16/1864, Philadelphia, PA d: 3/30/1895, Philadelphia, PA BR/TR, 5'6", 145 lbs. Deb: 6/23/1884																			
1884 Phi-U	28	115	12	28	5	0	0	....	5	....	....	....	.243	.275	.287	.562	98	0	9	2.99	4	S-28	3	0.5
1888 KC-a	115	401	42	76	7	6	3	37	31	....	23	....	.190	.256	.259	.516	61	-18	33	2.77	1	*S-115	7	-1.3
1889 Col-a	95	324	43	56	5	8	4	34	41	57	10	....	.173	.270	.275	.544	58	-17	27	2.71	6	S-89/2-5,3-1	5	-0.7
1890 Col-a	58	197	25	31	5	1	1	17	23	....	5	....	.157	.249	.208	.457	37	-15	12	1.87	6	S-58	3	-0.6
Phi-a	19	68	17	10	1	0	1	3	10	....	4	....	.147	.256	.206	.462	37	-5	5	2.16	-3	S-19	1	-0.7
Lou-a	7	24	2	2	0	0	0	1	2	....	1	....	.083	.185	.083	.269	-21	-4	1	.69	0	/S-6,3-1	0	-0.3
Yr.	84	289	44	43	6	1	2	21	35	....	10	....	.149	.245	.197	.443	32	-23	17	1.84	3	S-83/3-1	4	-1.6
Total 4	322	1129	141	203	23	15	9	92	112	57	43	....	.180	.259	.251	.510	56	-58	87	2.52	14	S-315/2-5,3-2	19	-3.0
• EASTERLING, Paul					Paul Easterling b: 9/28/1905, Reidsville, GA d: 3/15/1993, Reidsville, GA BR/TR, 5'11", 180 lbs. Deb: 4/11/1928 Career OF: 40-2-18																			
1928 Det-A	43	114	17	37	7	1	3	12	8	24	2	1	.325	.374	.482	.856	122	3	21	6.88	-3	0-34(32-0-2)	4	-0.2
1930 Det-A	29	79	7	16	6	0	1	14	6	18	0	1	.203	.259	.316	.575	44	-7	6	2.57	2	0-25(8-1-16)	0	-0.6
1938 Phi-A	4	7	1	2	0	0	0	0	1	2	0	0	.286	.375	.286	.661	70	-0	1	4.31	0	/0-1	0	-0.1
Total 3	76	200	25	55	13	1	4	26	15	44	2	2	.275	.329	.410	.739	89	-4	28	4.90	-1	/0-60	4	-0.8
• EASTERLY, Ted					Theodore Harrison Easterly b: 4/20/1885, Lincoln, NE d: 7/6/1951, Clearlake Highlands, CA BL/TR, 5'8", 165 lbs. Deb: 4/17/1909 Career OF: 1-2-84																			
1909 Cle-A	98	287	32	75	14	10	1	27	13	....	8	....	.261	.293	.390	.684	111	2	34	4.07	2	C-76	10	1.3
1910 Cle-A	110	363	34	111	16	6	0	55	21	....	10	....	.306	.344	.383	.727	126	9	51	5.00	-0	C-65,0-32(0-0-32)	15	1.6
1911 Cle-A	99	287	34	93	19	5	1	37	8	....	6	....	.324	.345	.436	.780	116	4	45	5.68	-1	0-54(0-2-52),C-22	8	0.2
1912 Cle-A	65	186	17	55	4	0	2	21	7	....	3	....	.296	.328	.349	.678	91	-3	22	4.24	2	C-51	5	0.3
Chi-A	30	55	5	20	2	0	0	14	2	....	1	....	.364	.386	.400	.786	129	2	9	6.33	0	C-10/0-1	3	0.3
Yr.	95	241	22	75	6	0	2	35	9	....	4	....	.311	.341	.361	.702	99	-1	31	4.68	3	C-61/0-1	8	0.6
1913 Chi-A	60	97	3	23	1	0	0	8	4	9	2	....	.237	.267	.247	.515	51	-6	7	2.25	-2	C-19	1	-0.7
1914 KC-F	134	436	58	146	20	12	1	67	31	25	10	....	.335	.384	.443	.827	142	23	75	6.43	-8	*C-128	19	2.5

YEAR TM-L	G	AB	R	H	2B	3B	HR	RBI	BB	SO	SB	CS	AVG	OBP	SLG	OPS	OPS+	BR/A	RC	RC/G	FR	G/POS	WS	TPW
1915 KC-F	110	309	32	84	12	5	3	32	21	15	2	....	.272	.320	.372	.692	107	2	36	4.06	1	C-88	14	1.1
Total 7	**706**	**2020**	**215**	**607**	**88**	**38**	**8**	**261**	**107**	**49**	**42**	**....**	**.300**	**.338**	**.394**	**.732**	**116**	**33**	**279**	**4.91**	**-5**	**C-459/0-87**	**75**	**6.6**
• EASTERWOOD, Roy	Roy Charles "Shag" Easterwood b: 1/12/1915, Waxahachie, TX d: 8/24/1984, Graham, TX BR/TR, 6'.5", 196 lbs. Deb: 4/21/1944																							
1944 Chi-N	17	33	1	7	2	0	1	2	1	11	0	....	.212	.235	.364	.599	67	-2	2	2.09	0	C-12	0	-0.1
• EASTON, John	John David "Goose" Easton b: 3/4/1933, Trenton, NJ d: 7/28/2001, Princeton, NJ BR/TR, 6'2", 185 lbs. Deb: 6/19/1955																							
1955 Phi-N	1	0	0	0	0	0	0	0	0	0	0	0	....	....	....	....	-102	0	0	....	0	....	0	0.0
1959 Phi-N	3	3	0	0	0	0	0	0	0	3	0	0	.000	.000	.000	.000	-98	-1	0	.00	0	....	0	-0.1
• EAYRS, Eddie	Edwin Eayrs b: 11/10/1890, Blackstone, MA d: 11/30/1969, Warwick, RI BL/TL, 5'7", 160 lbs. Deb: 6/30/1913 Career OF: 43-7-14 ♦																							
1913 Pit-N	4	6	0	1	0	0	0	0	0	1	0	....	.167	.167	.167	.333	-5	-0	0	.75	0	/P-2	0	0.1
1920 Bos-N	87	244	31	80	5	2	1	24	30	18	4	3	.328	.410	.377	.787	133	14	40	6.09	0	0-63(43-7-13)/P-7	11	0.3
1921 Bos-N	15	15	0	1	0	0	0	1	0	4	0	0	.067	.067	.067	.133	-68	-2	0	.12	0	/P-2	0	-0.9
Bro-N	8	6	1	1	0	0	0	1	2	0	0	0	.167	.375	.167	.542	47	-0	1	2.90	0	/0-1	0	0.0
Yr.	23	21	1	2	0	0	0	2	2	4	0	0	.095	.174	.095	.269	-28	-2	1	.85	0	/P-2,0-1	0	-0.9
Total 3	**114**	**271**	**32**	**83**	**5**	**2**	**1**	**26**	**32**	**23**	**4**	**3**	**.306**	**.388**	**.351**	**.738**	**118**	**11**	**41**	**5.45**	**0**	**/0-64,P-11**	**11**	**-0.5**
• EBRIGHT, Hi	Hiram C. "Buck" Ebright b: 6/12/1859, Lancaster County, PA d: 10/24/1916, Milwaukee, WI BR/TR Deb: 4/24/1889																							
1889 Was-N	16	59	7	15	2	2	1	6	3	8	1	....	.254	.302	.407	.708	103	0	8	4.65	3	/C-9,0-4(0-0-4),S-3	2	0.3
• ECHEVARRIA, Angel	Angel Santos Echevarria b: 5/25/1971, Bridgeport, CT BR/TR, 6'4", 215 lbs. Deb: 7/15/1996 Career OF: 59-2-61																							
1996 Col-N	26	21	2	6	0	0	0	6	2	5	0	0	.286	.375	.286	.661	63	-1	3	4.30	-1	0-11(4-0-7)	0	-0.2
1997 Col-N	15	20	4	5	2	0	0	0	2	5	0	0	.250	.318	.350	.668	61	-1	2	4.31	0	/0-7(2-2-3)	0	-0.1
1998 Col-N	19	29	7	11	3	0	1	9	2	3	0	0	.379	.455	.586	1.041	141	2	6	7.38	0	/1-4,0-4(3-0-1)	1	0.2
1999 Col-N	102	191	28	56	7	0	11	35	17	34	1	3	.293	.360	.503	.863	91	-4	30	5.42	0	0-49(20-0-31),1-10	4	-0.5
2000 Col-N	10	9	0	1	0	0	0	2	0	2	0	0	.111	.111	.111	.222	-35	-2	0	.38	0	/1-2,0-1	0	-0.2
Mil-N	31	42	3	9	2	0	1	4	7	9	0	0	.214	.327	.333	.660	69	-2	5	3.85	0	/1-9,0-5(2-0-3)	1	-0.2
Yr.	41	51	3	10	2	0	1	6	7	11	0	0	.196	.293	.294	.587	53	-4	5	3.18	0	1-11/0-6(3-0-3)	1	-0.4
2001 Mil-N	75	133	12	34	11	0	5	13	8	29	0	1	.256	.313	.451	.764	96	-2	18	4.81	-3	0-23(19-0-5),1-10/D-1	1	-0.6
2002 Chi-N	50	98	14	30	7	0	3	21	8	17	0	0	.306	.364	.469	.834	120	3	16	5.65	2	0-19(8-0-11),1-13	3	0.3
Total 7	**328**	**543**	**70**	**152**	**32**	**0**	**21**	**90**	**46**	**104**	**1**	**4**	**.280**	**.347**	**.455**	**.802**	**94**	**-7**	**80**	**5.11**	**-2**	**0-119/1-48,D-1**	**10**	**-1.4**
• ECHOLS, Johnny	John Gresham Echols b: 1/9/1917, Atlanta, GA d: 11/13/1972, Atlanta, GA BR/TR, 5'10.5", 175 lbs. Deb: 5/24/1939																							
1939 StL-N	2	0	0	0	0	0	0	0	0	0	0	....	....	....	....	....	-94	0	0	....	0	....	0	0.0
• ECKHARDT, Ox	Oscar George Eckhardt b: 12/23/1901, Yorktown, TX d: 4/22/1951, Yorktown, TX BL/TR, 6'1", 185 lbs. Deb: 4/16/1932																							
1932 Bos-N	8	8	1	2	0	0	0	1	0	1	0	....	.250	.250	.250	.500	36	-1	0	2.11	0	....	0	-0.1
1936 Bro-N	16	44	5	8	1	0	1	6	5	2	0	....	.182	.265	.273	.538	45	-3	4	2.71	1	0-10(0-0-10)	1	-0.3
Total 2	**24**	**52**	**6**	**10**	**1**	**0**	**1**	**7**	**5**	**3**	**0**	**....**	**.192**	**.263**	**.269**	**.532**	**43**	**-4**	**4**	**2.62**	**1**	**/0-10**	**1**	**-0.4**
• ECKSTEIN, David	David Mark Eckstein b: 1/20/1975, Sanford, FL BR/TR, 5'6.5", 170 lbs. Deb: 4/3/2001																							
2001 Ana-A	153	582	82	166	26	2	4	41	43	60	29	4	.285	.356	.357	.713	87	-5	81	4.85	-10	*S-126,2-14,D-14	12	-0.5
2002*Ana-A	152	608	107	178	22	6	8	63	45	44	21	13	.293	.368	.388	.756	101	2	91	5.19	2	*S-147/D-3	20	1.6
2003 Ana-A	120	452	59	114	22	1	3	31	36	45	16	5	.252	.328	.325	.653	76	-13	51	3.79	5	*S-116/D-3	11	0.1
Total 3	**425**	**1642**	**248**	**458**	**70**	**9**	**15**	**135**	**124**	**149**	**66**	**22**	**.279**	**.353**	**.360**	**.713**	**89**	**-16**	**223**	**4.67**	**-3**	**S-389/D-20,2-14**	**43**	**1.1**
• EDEN, Charlie	Charles M. Eden b: 1/18/1855, Lexington, KY d: 9/17/1920, Cincinnati, OH BL/TL, 168 lbs. Deb: 8/17/1877 Career OF: 96-32-94 ♦																							
1877 Chi-N	15	55	9	12	0	1	0	5	3	6	....	....	.218	.259	.255	.513	55	-3	4	2.37	-2	0-15(0-0-15)	0	-0.4
1879 Cle-N	81	353	40	96	**31**	7	3	34	6	20	....	....	.272	.284	.425	.709	131	11	44	4.76	-6	*0-80(0-1-79)/1-3,C-1	9	0.4
1884 Pit-a	32	122	12	33	7	4	1	0	7	....	....	....	.270	.341	.418	.759	144	6	18	5.50	-5	0-31(0-31-0)/P-2	5	-0.2
1885 Pit-a	98	405	57	103	18	6	0	38	17	....	....	....	.254	.298	.328	.626	99	0	41	3.63	-15	*0-96(96-0-0)/P-4,3-2	8	-1.9
Total 4	**226**	**935**	**118**	**244**	**56**	**18**	**4**	**77**	**33**	**' 26**	**....**	**....**	**.261**	**.296**	**.372**	**.669**	**114**	**15**	**106**	**4.21**	**-28**	**0-222/P-6,1-3,3-2,C-1**	**22**	**-2.1**
• EDEN, Mike	Edward Michael Eden b: 5/22/1949, Fort Clayton, Panama BB/TR, 5'10", 170 lbs. Deb: 8/2/1976																							
1976 Atl-N	5	8	0	0	0	0	0	1	0	0	0	0	.000	.000	.000	.000	-94	-2	0	.00	0	/2-2	0	-0.2
1978 Chi-A	10	17	1	2	0	0	0	0	4	0	0	0	.118	.286	.118	.403	17	-2	1	1.22	-1	/S-5,2-4	0	-0.3
Total 2	**15**	**25**	**1**	**2**	**0**	**0**	**0**	**1**	**4**	**0**	**0**	**0**	**.080**	**.207**	**.080**	**.287**	**-13**	**-4**	**1**	**.78**	**-1**	**/2-6,S-5**	**0**	**-0.4**
• EDINGTON, Stump	Jacob Frank Edington b: 7/4/1891, Koleen, IN d: 11/11/1969, Bastrop, LA BL/TL, 5'8", 170 lbs. Deb: 6/20/1912																							
1912 Pit-N	15	53	4	16	0	2	0	12	3	1	0	....	.302	.339	.377	.717	97	-0	7	4.41	1	0-14(0-0-14)	1	0.0
• EDLER, Dave	David Delmar Edler b: 8/5/1956, Sioux City, IA BR/TR, 6', 185 lbs. Deb: 9/4/1980 Career OF: 1-0-2																							
1980 Sea-A	28	89	11	20	1	0	3	9	8	16	2	3	.225	.289	.337	.626	70	-5	8	2.64	1	3-28	1	-0.4
1981 Sea-A	29	78	7	11	3	0	0	5	11	13	3	3	.141	.256	.179	.435	26	-8	4	1.51	-4	3-26/S-1	0	-1.3
1982 Sea-A	40	104	14	29	2	2	2	18	11	13	4	2	.279	.348	.394	.742	100	0	14	4.60	-3	3-31/D-2,0-2(1-0-1)	3	-0.3
1983 Sea-A	29	63	2	12	1	1	1	4	5	11	3	3	.190	.261	.286	.547	49	-5	4	1.87	-1	3-13/D-6,1-5,0-1	0	-0.7
Total 4	**126**	**334**	**34**	**72**	**7**	**3**	**6**	**36**	**35**	**53**	**12**	**11**	**.216**	**.294**	**.308**	**.602**	**65**	**-17**	**30**	**2.75**	**-7**	**/3-98,D-8,1-5,0-3,S-1**	**4**	**-2.6**
• EDMONDS, Jim	James Patrick Edmonds b: 6/27/1970, Fullerton, CA BL/TL, 6'1", 190 lbs. Deb: 9/9/1993 Career OF: 61-1126-34																							
1993 Cal-A	18	61	5	15	4	1	0	4	2	16	0	2	.246	.270	.344	.614	62	-4	5	2.60	4	0-17(1-1-15)	1	-0.1
1994 Cal-A	94	289	35	79	13	1	5	37	30	72	4	2	.273	.344	.377	.721	85	-6	39	4.84	4	0-77(59-5-19),1-22	7	-0.6
1995 Cal-A★	141	558	120	162	30	4	33	107	51	130	1	4	.290	.355	.536	.891	129	20	104	6.75	10	*0-139(0-139-0)	21	2.9
1996 Cal-A	114	431	73	131	28	3	27	66	46	101	4	0	.304	.376	.571	.947	138	25	94	8.16	2	*0-111(0-111-0)/D-1	18	2.5
1997 Ana-A	133	502	82	146	27	0	26	80	60	80	5	7	.291	.371	.500	.871	123	15	93	6.66	7	*0-115(0-115-0),1-11/D-8	19	2.1
1998 Ana-A	154	599	115	184	42	1	25	91	57	114	7	5	.307	.368	.506	.874	124	19	108	6.63	2	*0-153(0-153-0)	24	2.2
1999 Ana-A	55	204	34	51	17	2	5	23	28	45	5	4	.250	.341	.426	.767	95	-2	30	5.05	3	0-42(0-42-0)/D-9,1-2	5	0.0
2000*StL-N★	152	525	129	155	25	0	42	108	103	167	10	3	.295	.416	.583	.999	148	43	137	9.54	-1	*0-146(0-146-0)/1-6	29	4.0
2001*StL-N	150	500	95	152	38	1	30	110	93	136	5	5	.304	.417	.564	.981	152	41	121	8.80	-2	*0-147(0-147-0)/1-2	30	3.9
2002*StL-N	144	476	96	148	31	2	28	83	86	134	4	3	.311	.425	.561	.985	161	45	117	9.13	5	*0-139(0-139-0)	29	5.2
2003 StL-N★	137	447	89	123	32	2	39	89	77	127	1	3	.275	.386	.617	1.004	163	40	106	8.43	9	*0-129(1-128-0)/D-2	22	4.9
Total 11	**1292**	**4592**	**873**	**1346**	**287**	**17**	**260**	**798**	**633**	**1122**	**46**	**38**	**.293**	**.383**	**.533**	**.916**	**135**	**235**	**953**	**7.54**	**44**	***0-1215/1-43,D-20**	**205**	**26.9**
• EDMONSON, Eddie	Earl Edward Edmonson b: 11/20/1889, Hopewell, PA d: 5/10/1971, Leesburg, FL BL/TR, 6', 175 lbs. Deb: 10/4/1913																							
1913 Cle-A	2	5	0	0	0	0	0	0	0	0	0	....	.000	.000	.000	.000	-97	-1	0	.00	-1	/1-1,0-1	0	-0.2
• EDMUNDSON, Bob	Robert E. Edmundson b: 4/30/1879, Paris, KY d: 8/14/1931, Lawrence, KS BR/TR, 5'11", 185 lbs. Deb: 7/30/1908 Career OF: 1-9-15 ♦																							
1906 Was-A	3	3	1	1	0	0	0	0	0	....	0	....	.333	.333	.333	.667	114	0	0	4.53	0	/P-2,0-1	0	-0.2
1908 Was-A	26	80	5	15	4	1	0	2	7	....	0	....	.188	.261	.263	.524	77	-2	5	2.09	-2	0-24(1-9-14)	0	-0.6
Total 2	**29**	**83**	**6**	**16**	**4**	**1**	**0**	**2**	**7**	**....**	**0**	**....**	**.193**	**.264**	**.265**	**.529**	**78**	**-2**	**6**	**2.17**	**-2**	**/0-25,P-2**	**0**	**-0.8**
• EDWARDS, Bruce	Charles Bruce "Bull" Edwards b: 7/15/1923, Quincy, IL d: 4/25/1975, Sacramento, CA BR/TR, 5'8", 194 lbs. Deb: 6/23/1946 Career OF: 25-0-0																							
1946 Bro-N	92	292	24	78	13	5	1	25	34	20	1	....	.267	.348	.356	.704	99	0	37	4.27	2	C-91	11	0.7
1947*Bro-N★	130	471	53	139	15	8	9	80	49	55	2	....	.295	.364	.418	.782	103	2	73	5.64	1	*C-128	20	1.0
1948 Bro-N	96	286	36	79	17	2	8	54	26	28	4	....	.276	.341	.434	.774	105	1	41	4.97	-4	C-48,0-21(21-0-0),3-14/1-1	9	-0.2
1949*Bro-N	64	148	24	31	3	0	8	25	25	15	0	....	.209	.324	.392	.716	87	-3	19	4.09	-2	C-41/0-4(4-0-0),3-1	4	-0.3
1950 Bro-N	50	142	16	26	4	1	8	16	13	22	1	....	.183	.256	.394	.651	67	-8	13	2.88	-1	C-38/1-2	2	-0.7
1951 Bro-N	17	36	6	9	2	0	1	8	1	3	0	0	.250	.270	.389	.659	74	-2	4	3.43	0	/C-9	1	-0.1
Chi-N★	51	141	19	33	9	2	3	17	16	14	1	2	.234	.316	.390	.707	87	-3	17	4.04	-1	C-28/1-9	3	-0.3
Yr.	68	177	25	42	11	2	4	25	17	17	1	2	.237	.308	.390	.698	85	-5	21	3.92	-1	C-37/1-9	4	-0.4
1952 Chi-N	50	94	7	23	2	2	1	12	8	12	0	0	.245	.304	.340	.644	77	-3	9	3.30	-1	C-22/2-1	1	-0.3
1954 Chi-N	4	3	1	0	0	0	0	1	2	2	0	0	.000	.400	.000	.400	15	-0	0	1.87	0	....	0	0.0

YEAR TM-L	G	AB	R	H	2B	3B	HR	RBI	BB	SO	SB	CS	AVG	OBP	SLG	OPS	OPS+	BR/A	RC	RC/G	FR	G/POS	WS	TPW
1955 Was-A	30	57	5	10	2	0	0	3	16	6	0	1	.175	.356	.211	.567	58	-3	5	2.58	-0	C-22/3-5	1	-0.2
1956 Cin-N	7	5	0	1	0	0	0	0	0	2	0	0	.200	.200	.200	.400	7	-1	0	1.35	-2	/C-2,2-1,3-1	0	-0.2
Total 10	591	1675	191	429	67	20	39	241	190	179	9	3	.256	.335	.390	.725	93	-18	217	4.43	-8	C-429/O-25,3-21,1-12,2-2	52	-0.6

• EDWARDS, Dave David Leonard Edwards b: 2/24/1954, Los Angeles, CA BR/TR, 6', 177 lbs. Deb: 9/11/1978 Career OF: 103-113-67

YEAR TM-L	G	AB	R	H	2B	3B	HR	RBI	BB	SO	SB	CS	AVG	OBP	SLG	OPS	OPS+	BR/A	RC	RC/G	FR	G/POS	WS	TPW
1978 Min-A	15	44	7	11	3	0	1	3	7	13	1	1	.250	.377	.386	.764	113	1	7	5.65	1	O-15(10-8-0)	2	0.2
1979 Min-A	96	229	42	57	8	0	8	35	24	45	6	3	.249	.323	.389	.711	88	-4	29	4.24	1	O-86(37-31-23)/D-3	5	-0.6
1980 Min-A	81	200	26	50	9	1	2	20	12	51	2	1	.250	.296	.335	.631	67	-9	19	3.19	-2	O-72(27-47-2)/D-3	3	-1.3
1981 SD-N	58	112	13	24	4	1	2	13	11	24	3	1	.214	.285	.321	.606	77	-3	10	2.95	3	O-49(11-2-40)	1	-0.1
1982 SD-N	71	55	7	10	2	0	1	2	1	14	0	0	.182	.196	.273	.469	32	-5	2	1.41	-2	O-45(18-25-2)/1-1	0	-0.8
Total 5	321	640	95	152	26	2	14	73	55	147	12	6	.238	.302	.350	.652	77	-20	67	3.52	2	O-267/D-6,1-1	11	-2.7

• EDWARDS, Doc Howard Rodney Edwards b: 12/10/1936, Red Jacket, WV BR/TR, 6'2", 215 lbs. Deb: 4/21/1962 M/C

YEAR TM-L	G	AB	R	H	2B	3B	HR	RBI	BB	SO	SB	CS	AVG	OBP	SLG	OPS	OPS+	BR/A	RC	RC/G	FR	G/POS	WS	TPW
1962 Cle-A	53	143	13	39	6	0	3	9	9	14	0	0	.273	.325	.378	.702	91	-2	18	4.51	2	C-39	6	0.2
1963 Cle-A	10	31	6	8	2	0	0	0	2	6	0	0	.258	.303	.323	.626	76	-1	3	3.56	2	C-10	1	0.2
KC-A	71	240	16	60	12	0	6	35	11	23	0	1	.250	.289	.375	.664	81	-7	24	3.50	1	C-63	5	-0.4
Yr.	81	271	22	68	14	0	6	35	13	29	0	1	.251	.290	.369	.659	80	-8	27	3.51	3	C-73	6	-0.2
1964 KC-A	97	294	25	66	10	0	5	28	13	40	0	1	.224	.265	.310	.574	57	-18	21	2.37	1	C-79/1-7	3	-1.4
1965 KC-A	6	20	1	3	0	0	0	0	1	2	0	0	.150	.190	.150	.340	-2	-3	0	.44	0	/C-6	0	-0.2
NY-A	45	100	3	19	3	0	1	9	13	14	1	2	.190	.289	.250	.539	55	-6	6	1.84	0	C-43	2	-0.5
Yr.	51	120	4	22	3	0	1	9	14	16	1	2	.183	.274	.233	.507	46	-9	6	1.59	1	C-49	2	-0.7
1970 Phi-N	35	78	5	21	0	0	0	6	4	10	0	0	.269	.313	.269	.582	59	-4	6	2.49	0	C-34	2	-0.3
Total 5	317	906	69	216	33	0	15	87	53	109	1	4	.238	.287	.325	.612	68	-41	79	2.91	7	C-274/1-7	19	-2.3

• EDWARDS, Hank Henry Albert Edwards b: 1/29/1919, Elmwood Place, OH d: 6/22/1988, Santa Ana, CA BL/TL, 6', 190 lbs. Deb: 9/10/1941 Career OF: 132-91-345

YEAR TM-L	G	AB	R	H	2B	3B	HR	RBI	BB	SO	SB	CS	AVG	OBP	SLG	OPS	OPS+	BR/A	RC	RC/G	FR	G/POS	WS	TPW
1941 Cle-A	16	68	10	15	1	1	1	6	2	4	0	0	.221	.243	.309	.552	47	-5	5	2.68	0	O-16(2-0-14)	0	-0.6
1942 Cle-A	13	48	6	12	2	1	0	7	5	8	2	1	.250	.321	.333	.654	89	-1	6	4.13	0	O-12(0-12-0)	1	-0.1
1943 Cle-A	92	297	38	82	18	6	3	28	30	34	4	8	.276	.343	.407	.750	127	7	41	4.77	-4	O-74(0-74-0)	11	0.1
1946 Cle-A	124	458	62	138	33	**16**	10	54	43	48	1	3	.301	.361	.509	.870	151	28	88	7.23	1	*O-123(0-1-122)	23	2.7
1947 Cle-A	108	393	54	102	12	3	15	59	31	55	1	3	.260	.315	.420	.735	106	0	53	4.79	-2	*O-100(39-0-67)	11	-0.6
1948 Cle-A	55	160	27	43	9	2	3	18	18	18	1	1	.269	.346	.406	.753	102	0	24	5.35	0	O-41(0-0-41)	5	-0.1
1949 Cle-A	5	15	3	4	0	0	1	1	1	2	0	0	.267	.313	.467	.779	107	-0	2	4.18	0	/O-5(0-0-5)	0	0.0
Chi-N	58	176	25	51	8	4	7	21	19	22	0	....	.290	.359	.500	.859	131	7	31	6.54	0	O-51(18-0-34)	7	0.6
1950 Chi-N	41	110	13	40	11	1	2	21	10	13	0	....	.364	.417	.536	.953	150	8	25	9.24	-2	O-29(0-0-29)	5	0.5
1951 Bro-N	35	31	1	7	3	0	0	3	4	9	0	0	.226	.314	.323	.637	70	-1	3	3.01	0	....	0	-0.1
Cin-N	41	127	14	40	9	1	3	20	13	17	0	2	.315	.379	.472	.851	126	4	22	6.53	-1	O-34(26-0-8)	5	0.1
Yr.	76	158	15	47	12	1	3	23	17	26	0	2	.297	.366	.443	.809	114	3	25	5.75	-1	O-34(26-0-8)	5	0.0
1952 Cin-N	74	184	24	52	7	6	6	28	19	22	0	3	.283	.350	.484	.833	129	6	31	6.16	0	O-51(33-0-18)	7	0.4
Chi-A	8	18	2	6	0	0	0	1	0	2	0	0	.333	.333	.333	.667	85	-0	2	3.55	0	/O-3(3-0-0)	0	0.0
1953 StL-A	65	106	6	21	3	0	0	9	13	10	0	1	.198	.286	.226	.512	39	-9	8	2.34	0	O-21(11-4-7)	0	-1.0
Total 11	735	2191	285	613	116	41	51	276	208	264	9	22	.280	.343	.440	.783	119	43	340	5.60	-7	O-560	75	1.7

• EDWARDS, Johnny John Alban Edwards b: 6/10/1938, Columbus, OH BL/TR, 6'4", 220 lbs. Deb: 6/27/1961

YEAR TM-L	G	AB	R	H	2B	3B	HR	RBI	BB	SO	SB	CS	AVG	OBP	SLG	OPS	OPS+	BR/A	RC	RC/G	FR	G/POS	WS	TPW
1961*Cin-N	52	145	14	27	5	0	2	14	18	28	1	0	.186	.280	.262	.543	44	-11	11	2.48	-2	C-52	2	-1.1
1962 Cin-N	133	452	47	115	28	5	8	50	45	70	1	1	.254	.323	.392	.715	88	-8	58	4.55	10	*C-130	18	0.8
1963 Cin-N★	148	495	46	128	19	4	11	67	45	93	1	5	.259	.325	.380	.705	99	-1	61	4.23	10	*C-148	21	1.7
1964 Cin-N★	126	423	47	119	23	1	7	55	34	65	1	2	.281	.336	.390	.726	100	0	56	4.69	8	*C-120	19	1.5
1965 Cin-N★	114	371	47	99	22	2	17	51	50	45	0	0	.267	.355	.474	.830	123	12	64	6.10	8	*C-110	17	2.7
1966 Cin-N	98	282	24	54	8	0	6	39	31	42	1	3	.191	.272	.284	.555	50	-19	21	2.37	3	C-98	4	-1.3
1967 Cin-N	80	209	10	43	6	0	2	20	16	28	1	4	.206	.262	.263	.525	46	-16	14	2.06	0	C-73	4	-1.3
1968*StL-N	85	230	14	55	9	1	3	29	16	20	1	1	.239	.291	.326	.618	86	-4	21	3.07	-1	C-54	6	-0.2
1969 Hou-N	151	496	52	115	20	6	6	50	53	69	2	1	.232	.309	.333	.641	81	-12	49	3.27	4	*C-151	14	0.0
1970 Hou-N	140	458	46	101	16	4	7	49	51	63	1	0	.221	.300	.319	.619	69	-20	44	3.22	12	*C-139	12	-0.1
1971 Hou-N	106	317	18	74	13	4	1	23	26	38	1	1	.233	.292	.309	.601	72	-12	30	3.27	4	*C-104	10	-0.4
1972 Hou-N	108	332	33	89	16	2	5	40	50	39	2	4	.268	.366	.373	.739	113	6	47	4.84	-4	*C-105	12	0.8
1973 Hou-N	79	250	24	61	10	2	5	27	19	23	1	0	.244	.303	.360	.663	83	-6	27	3.73	-3	C-76	7	-0.6
1974 Hou-N	50	117	8	26	7	1	1	10	11	12	1	1	.222	.295	.325	.619	76	-4	11	3.29	1	C-32	3	-0.2
Total 14	1470	4577	430	1106	202	32	81	524	465	635	15	23	.242	.314	.353	.667	85	-95	515	3.82	49	*C-1392	149	2.3

• EDWARDS, Marshall Marshall Lynn Edwards b: 8/27/1952, Fort Lewis, WA BL/TL, 5'9", 157 lbs. Deb: 4/11/1981 Career OF: 18-46-68

YEAR TM-L	G	AB	R	H	2B	3B	HR	RBI	BB	SO	SB	CS	AVG	OBP	SLG	OPS	OPS+	BR/A	RC	RC/G	FR	G/POS	WS	TPW
1981*Mil-A	40	58	10	14	1	1	0	4	0	2	6	2	.241	.241	.293	.534	56	-3	4	2.19	0	O-36(2-21-14)/D-1	1	-0.4
1982*Mil-A	69	178	24	44	4	1	2	14	4	8	10	4	.247	.264	.315	.578	62	-9	14	2.45	0	O-54(4-13-41)/D-6	1	-1.2
1983 Mil-A	51	74	14	22	1	1	0	5	1	9	5	5	.297	.307	.338	.645	84	-3	6	2.81	2	O-35(12-12-13)/D-4	1	-0.3
Total 3	160	310	48	80	6	3	2	23	5	19	21	11	.258	.270	.316	.586	66	-15	24	2.49	1	O-125/D-11	3	-1.8

• EDWARDS, Mike Michael Lewis Edwards b: 8/27/1952, Fort Lewis, WA BR/TR, 5'10", 154 lbs. Deb: 9/10/1977

YEAR TM-L	G	AB	R	H	2B	3B	HR	RBI	BB	SO	SB	CS	AVG	OBP	SLG	OPS	OPS+	BR/A	RC	RC/G	FR	G/POS	WS	TPW
1977 Pit-N	7	6	1	0	0	0	0	0	0	3	0	2	.000	.143	.000	.143	-56	-2	0	.00	0	/2-4	0	-0.2
1978 Oak-A	142	414	48	113	16	2	1	23	16	32	27	21	.273	.303	.329	.632	82	-14	37	2.95	-5	*2-133/S-9,D-4	6	-1.4
1979 Oak-A	122	400	35	93	12	2	1	23	15	37	10	6	.233	.264	.280	.544	49	-29	27	2.25	-17	*2-113/S-3,D-2	1	-3.9
1980 Oak-A	46	59	10	14	0	0	0	3	1	5	1	1	.237	.250	.237	.487	37	-5	3	1.82	1	2-23/D-5,O-1	0	-0.3
Total 4	317	879	94	220	28	4	2	49	32	77	38	30	.250	.281	.298	.579	63	-51	68	2.52	-21	2-273/S-12,D-11,O-1	7	-5.8

• EDWARDS, Mike Michael Donald Edwards b: 11/24/1976, Goshen, NY BR/TR, 6'1", 185 lbs. Deb: 9/20/2003

YEAR TM-L	G	AB	R	H	2B	3B	HR	RBI	BB	SO	SB	CS	AVG	OBP	SLG	OPS	OPS+	BR/A	RC	RC/G	FR	G/POS	WS	TPW
2003 Oak-A	4	4	0	1	0	0	0	0	2	1	0	0	.250	.500	.250	.750	106	0	1	6.84	0	/D-2,O-2(2-0-0)	0	0.0

• EDWARDS, Ralph Ralph Strunk Edwards b: 12/14/1882, Brewster, NY d: 1/5/1949, White Plains, NY BR/TR, 5'9", 165 lbs. Deb: 9/17/1915

YEAR TM-L	G	AB	R	H	2B	3B	HR	RBI	BB	SO	SB	CS	AVG	OBP	SLG	OPS	OPS+	BR/A	RC	RC/G	FR	G/POS	WS	TPW
1915 Phi-A	2	5	0	0	0	0	0	0	0	3	0	....	.000	.000	.000	.000	-104	-1	0	.00	0	/2-1	0	-0.2

• EENHOORN, Robert Robert Franciscus Eenhoorn b: 2/9/1968, Rotterdam, Holland BR/TR, 6'3", 170 lbs. Deb: 4/27/1994

YEAR TM-L	G	AB	R	H	2B	3B	HR	RBI	BB	SO	SB	CS	AVG	OBP	SLG	OPS	OPS+	BR/A	RC	RC/G	FR	G/POS	WS	TPW
1994 NY-A	3	4	1	2	1	0	0	0	0	0	0	0	.500	.500	.750	1.250	225	1	2	20.25	-1	/S-3	0	0.0
1995 NY-A	5	14	1	2	1	0	0	2	1	3	0	0	.143	.200	.214	.414	8	-2	0	.90	-1	/2-3,S-2	0	-0.2
1996 NY-A	12	14	2	1	0	0	0	2	2	3	0	0	.071	.188	.071	.259	-31	-3	0	.82	-1	2-10/3-2	0	-0.3
Cal-A	6	15	1	4	0	0	0	0	0	2	0	0	.267	.267	.267	.533	36	-1	1	2.62	-1	/S-4,2-2	0	-0.2
Yr.	18	29	3	5	0	0	0	2	2	5	0	0	.172	.226	.172	.398	-1	-4	2	1.55	-2	2-12/S-4,3-2	0	-0.5
1997 Ana-A	11	20	2	7	1	0	1	6	0	2	0	0	.350	.350	.550	.900	129	1	4	7.41	-2	/3-5,2-3,S-2	1	-0.1
Total 4	37	67	7	16	3	0	1	10	3	10	0	0	.239	.271	.328	.600	50	-5	7	3.53	-6	/2-18,S-11,3-7	1	-0.9

• EGAN, Ben Arthur Augustus Egan b: 11/20/1883, Augusta, NY d: 2/18/1968, Sherrill, NY BR/TR, 6', 195 lbs. Deb: 9/29/1908 C

YEAR TM-L	G	AB	R	H	2B	3B	HR	RBI	BB	SO	SB	CS	AVG	OBP	SLG	OPS	OPS+	BR/A	RC	RC/G	FR	G/POS	WS	TPW
1908 Phi-A	2	6	1	1	1	0	0	0	1	....	0	....	.167	.286	.333	.619	95	-0	1	2.86	0	/C-2	0	0.0
1912 Phi-A	49	138	9	24	3	4	0	13	6	....	3	....	.174	.208	.254	.462	33	-13	7	1.69	0	C-46	2	-0.9
1914 Cle-A	29	88	7	20	2	1	0	11	3	20	0	1	.227	.277	.273	.549	63	-5	7	2.48	2	C-27	1	0.0
1915 Cle-A	42	120	4	13	3	0	0	6	8	14	0	....	.108	.164	.133	.297	-11	-17	3	.74	2	C-40	2	-1.2
Total 4	122	352	21	58	9	5	0	30	18	34	3	1	.165	.212	.219	.431	26	-34	18	1.54	5	C-115	5	-2.1

• EGAN, Dick Richard Joseph Egan b: 6/23/1884, Portland, OR d: 7/7/1947, Oakland, CA BR/TR, 5'11", 162 lbs. Deb: 9/15/1908 Career OF: 11-2-14

YEAR TM-L	G	AB	R	H	2B	3B	HR	RBI	BB	SO	SB	CS	AVG	OBP	SLG	OPS	OPS+	BR/A	RC	RC/G	FR	G/POS	WS	TPW
1908 Cin-N	18	68	8	14	3	1	0	5	2	....	7	....	.206	.229	.279	.508	64	-3	6	2.60	-1	2-18	1	-0.4
1909 Cin-N	127	480	59	132	14	3	2	53	37	....	39	....	.275	.329	.329	.659	105	2	66	4.54	32	*2-116,S-10	19	4.0
1910 Cin-N	135	474	70	116	11	5	0	46	53	38	41	....	.245	.322	.289	.611	82	-10	59	3.94	-10	*2-131/S-3	10	-2.0
1911 Cin-N	153	558	80	139	11	5	1	56	59	50	37	....	.249	.322	.292	.614	75	-18	65	3.83	12	*2-152	11	-0.2
1912 Cin-N	149	507	69	125	14	5	0	52	56	26	24	....	.247	.324	.294	.618	72	-18	58	3.59	5	*2-149	13	-1.1
1913 Cin-N	60	195	15	55	7	3	0	22	15	13	6	....	.282	.333	.349	.682	95	-1	25	4.16	-1	2-37,S-17/3-2	5	-0.1

YEAR TM-L	G	AB	R	H	2B	3B	HR	RBI	BB	SO	SB	CS	AVG	OBP	SLG	OPS	OPS+	BR/A	RC	RC/G	FR	G/POS	WS	TPW
1914 Bro-N	106	337	30	76	10	3	1	21	22	25	8	....	.226	.273	.282	.555	64	-16	28	2.64	-10	S-83,3-10/O-3(0-2-1),2-2,1	5	-2.2
1915 Bro-N	3	3	0	0	0	0	0	0	0	0	0	....	.000	.000	.000	.000	-98	-1	0	.00	0	....	0	-0.1
Bos-N	83	220	20	57	9	1	0	21	28	18	3	4	.259	.343	.309	.652	100	-0	24	3.71	-1	O-24(11-0-13),2-22,S-10/1-9,3	7	-0.1
Yr.	86	223	20	57	9	1	0	21	28	18	3	4	.256	.339	.305	.644	97	-1	24	3.64	-1	O-24(11-0-13),2-22,S-10/1-9,3	7	-0.2
1916 Bos-N	83	238	23	53	8	3	0	16	19	21	2	....	.223	.280	.282	.562	77	-7	21	2.80	-17	2-59,S-12/3-8	5	-2.5
Total 9	917	3080	374	767	87	29	4	292	291	191	167	4	.249	.315	.300	.615	82	-71	353	3.68	9	2-686,S-135/O-27,3-24,1-10	76	-4.7
• EGAN, Jim	James K. "Troy Terrier" Egan b: 1858, Derby, CT d: 9/26/1884, New Haven, CT TL Deb: 5/15/1882 ♦																							
1882 Tro-N	30	115	15	23	3	2	0	10	1	21	....	....	.200	.207	.261	.468	51	-5	6	1.90	-8	O-18(2-16-0),P-12/C-2	3	-2.3
• EGAN, Tom	Thomas Patrick Egan b: 6/9/1946, Los Angeles, CA BR/TR, 6'4", 218 lbs. Deb: 5/27/1965																							
1965 Cal-A	18	38	3	10	0	1	0	1	3	12	0	0	.263	.317	.316	.633	82	-1	4	3.48	-1	C-16	1	-0.1
1966 Cal-A	7	11	0	0	0	0	0	0	1	5	0	0	.000	.083	.000	.083	-76	-2	0	.05	0	/C-6	0	-0.3
1967 Cal-A	1	1	0	0	0	0	0	0	0	0	0	0	.000	.000	.000	.000	-104	-0	0	.00	0	/C-1	0	0.0
1968 Cal-A	16	43	2	5	1	0	1	4	2	15	0	0	.116	.156	.209	.365	10	-5	1	.56	1	C-14	0	-0.4
1969 Cal-A	46	120	7	17	1	0	5	16	17	41	0	1	.142	.254	.275	.529	50	-9	9	2.18	2	C-46	2	-0.5
1970 Cal-A	79	210	14	50	6	0	4	20	14	67	0	0	.238	.289	.324	.613	71	-8	20	3.17	-4	C-79	5	-0.9
1971 Chi-A	85	251	29	60	11	1	10	34	26	94	1	0	.239	.320	.410	.731	102	1	35	4.87	1	C-77/1-1	9	0.5
1972 Chi-A	50	141	8	27	3	0	2	9	4	48	0	0	.191	.224	.255	.480	42	-10	7	1.62	1	C-46	2	-0.8
1974 Cal-A	43	94	4	11	0	0	0	4	8	40	1	0	.117	.194	.117	.311	-9	-13	3	.78	2	C-41	2	-1.0
1975 Cal-A	28	70	7	16	3	1	0	3	5	14	0	0	.229	.280	.300	.580	69	-3	6	2.46	0	C-28	1	-0.2
Total 10	373	979	74	196	25	3	22	91	80	336	2	1	.200	.267	.299	.566	60	-50	83	2.73	0	C-354/1-1	22	-3.7
• EGGERT, Elmer	Elmer Albert "Moose" Eggert b: 1/29/1902, Rochester, NY d: 4/9/1971, Rochester, NY BR/TR, 5'9", 160 lbs. Deb: 4/27/1927																							
1927 Bos-A	5	3	0	0	0	0	0	0	1	1	0	0	.000	.250	.000	.250	-31	-1	0	.55	-1	/2-1	0	-0.1
• EGGLER, Dave	David Daniel Eggler b: 4/30/1851, Brooklyn, NY d: 4/5/1902, Buffalo, NY BR/TR, 5'9", 165 lbs. Deb: 5/18/1871 NA OF: 10-256-0 Career OF: 4-305-1																							
1871 Mut-n	33	147	37	47	7	3	0	18	4	3	14	3	.320	.338	.408	.746	124	7	26	7.83	4	*O-33(0-33-0)	....	0.8
1872 Mut-n	56	290	**94**	98	20	0	0	20	8	9	**18**	5	.338	.356	.407	.763	143	18	50	7.80	13	*O-56(1-55-0)	....	2.2
1873 Mut-n	53	268	82	90	13	4	0	34	5	2	4	1	.336	.348	.414	.762	126	9	41	6.99	1	*O-53(0-53-0)/3-1	....	0.7
1874 Phi-n	58	299	70	95	13	8	0	31	5	1	5	6	.318	.329	.415	.744	132	8	43	6.21	5	*O-57(7-50-0)/2-2	....	1.0
1875 Ath-n	66	295	66	89	13	7	0	33	1	10	6	5	.302	.304	.393	.697	126	5	38	5.32	2	*O-66(2-65-0)	....	0.5
1876 Phi-N	39	176	28	52	4	0	0	19	2	4	....	....	.295	.307	.322	.629	110	2	18	4.04	3	O-39(1-37-1)	3	0.3
1877 Chi-N	33	136	20	36	3	0	0	20	1	5	....	....	.265	.270	.287	.557	67	-6	11	2.97	2	O-33(0-33-0)	3	-0.4
1879 Buf-N	78	317	41	66	5	7	0	27	11	41	....	....	.208	.235	.268	.503	64	-12	20	2.28	-6	*O-78(0-78-0)	4	-2.0
1883 Bal-a	53	202	15	38	2	0	0	7	1	....	....	....	.188	.192	.198	.390	25	-17	8	1.34	-1	O-53(0-53-0)	1	-1.7
Buf-N	38	153	13	38	2	1	0	13	2	29	....	....	.248	.258	.275	.533	61	-7	11	2.66	-3	O-38(1-37-0)	2	-1.0
1884 Buf-N	63	241	25	47	3	1	0	20	6	54	....	....	.195	.215	.216	.430	34	-18	11	1.62	-1	O-63(2-61-0)	2	-1.9
1885 Buf-N	6	24	0	2	0	0	0	0	2	4	....	....	.083	.154	.083	.237	-21	-3	0	.39	0	/O-6(0-6-0)	0	-0.3
Total 5 n	266	1299	349	419	66	22	0	136	23	25	47	20	.323	.334	.407	.742	131	47	198	6.69	25	O-265/2-2,3-1	....	5.2
Total 6	310	1249	142	279	19	9	0	106	25	137	....	....	.223	.239	.253	.492	57	-62	80	2.28	-6	O-310	15	-7.2
• EHRET, Red	Philip Sydney Ehret b: 8/31/1868, Louisville, KY d: 7/28/1940, Cincinnati, OH BR/TR, 6', 175 lbs. Deb: 7/7/1888 U Career OF: 11-3-18 ♦																							
1888 KC-a	17	63	4	12	4	0	0	4	1	....	1	....	.190	.203	.254	.457	43	-3	4	1.87	-2	O-10(5-2-3)/P-7,1-1,2-1	3	-0.8
1889 Lou-a	67	258	27	65	6	6	1	31	4	23	4	....	.252	.263	.333	.597	71	-2	24	3.34	-1	P-45,O-22(6-1-15)/2-1,3-1,S	11	-3.1
1890*Lou-a	43	146	11	31	2	1	0	10	1	....	1	....	.212	.218	.240	.457	36	-3	8	1.85	-2	P-43	34	4.3
1891 Lou-a	26	91	9	22	2	1	0	9	5	15	3	....	.242	.281	.286	.567	63	1	8	3.21	0	P-26	13	0.4
1892 Pit-N	40	132	12	34	2	0	0	19	7	22	1	....	.258	.295	.273	.568	72	3	11	3.08	-3	P-39	20	1.5
1893 Pit-N	40	136	16	24	3	0	1	17	10	18	1	....	.176	.233	.221	.453	21	-6	7	1.75	2	P-39	24	2.0
1894 Pit-N	46	135	6	23	4	1	0	11	8	22	0	....	.170	.217	.215	.432	4	-11	6	1.50	-2	P-46	21	-0.4
1895 StL-N	37	96	13	21	2	1	1	9	6	12	0	....	.219	.265	.292	.556	44	-2	8	2.75	-1	P-37	7	-2.1
1896 Cin-N	34	102	10	20	2	0	1	20	10	12	2	....	.196	.268	.245	.513	33	-3	8	2.45	0	P-34/1-1	24	2.4
1897 Cin-N	34	66	6	13	2	0	0	6	4	....	2	....	.197	.254	.227	.481	26	-3	5	2.25	-2	P-34	11	-0.6
1898 Lou-N	13	40	3	9	3	1	0	4	1	....	0	....	.225	.262	.350	.612	76	1	4	3.21	-2	P-12	1	-1.9
Total 11	397	1265	117	274	32	11	4	140	57	124	15	....	.217	.252	.269	.520	45	-28	94	2.49	-13	P-362/O-32,1-2,2-2,3-1,S-1	169	1.6
• EIBEL, Hack	Henry Hack Eibel b: 12/6/1893, Brooklyn, NY d: 10/16/1945, Macon, GA BL/TL, 5'11", 220 lbs. Deb: 6/13/1912 Career OF: 3-0-3 ♦																							
1912 Cle-A	1	3	0	0	0	0	0	0	0	....	0	....	.000	.000	.000	.000	-97	-1	0	.00	0	/O-1	0	-0.1
1920 Bos-A	29	43	4	8	2	0	0	6	3	6	1	1	.186	.239	.233	.472	26	-3	2	1.73	-1	/O-5(3-0-2),P-3,1-1	0	-0.4
Total 2	30	46	4	8	2	0	0	6	3	6	1	1	.174	.224	.217	.442	19	-4	2	1.60	-1	/O-6,P-3,1-1	0	-0.5
• EICHRODT, Ike	Frederick George Eichrodt b: 1/6/1903, Chicago, IL d: 7/14/1965, Indianapolis, IN BR/TR, 5'11.5", 167 lbs. Deb: 9/7/1925 Career OF: 32-113-10																							
1925 Cle-A	15	52	4	12	3	1	0	4	2	7	0	0	.231	.259	.327	.586	48	-4	4	2.85	-1	O-13(0-13-0)	0	-0.6
1926 Cle-A	37	80	14	25	7	1	0	7	2	11	1	0	.313	.329	.425	.754	95	-1	11	5.09	1	O-27(19-6-2)	2	-0.1
1927 Cle-A	85	267	24	59	19	2	0	25	16	25	2	3	.221	.265	.307	.572	48	-22	22	2.61	6	O-81(13-64-5)	2	-1.9
1931 Chi-A	34	117	9	25	5	1	0	15	1	8	0	0	.214	.220	.274	.494	31	-11	7	1.93	0	O-32(0-30-3)	0	-1.1
Total 4	171	516	51	121	34	5	0	51	21	51	3	3	.234	.264	.320	.584	51	-39	44	2.82	6	O-153	4	-3.6
• EISENREICH, Jim	James Michael Eisenreich b: 4/18/1959, St. Cloud, MN BL/TL, 5'11", 195 lbs. Deb: 4/6/1982 Career OF: 361-167-625																							
1982 Min-A	34	99	10	30	6	0	2	9	11	13	0	0	.303	.378	.424	.803	117	3	17	6.43	0	O-30(0-30-0)	4	0.2
1983 Min-A	2	7	1	2	1	0	0	0	1	1	0	0	.286	.375	.429	.804	116	0	1	6.60	1	/O-2(0-2-0)	0	0.1
1984 Min-A	12	32	1	7	1	0	0	3	2	4	2	0	.219	.265	.250	.515	41	-2	2	2.22	-0	/D-6,O-3(0-2-1)	0	-0.2
1987 KC-A	44	105	10	25	8	2	4	21	7	13	1	1	.238	.286	.467	.752	93	-2	13	4.15	0	D-26	1	-0.2
1988 KC-A	82	202	26	44	8	1	1	19	6	31	9	3	.218	.240	.282	.523	45	-15	14	2.22	-3	O-64(30-15-21),D-13	1	-2.0
1989 KC-A	134	475	64	139	33	7	9	59	37	44	27	8	.293	.344	.448	.792	122	15	73	5.52	-3	*O-123(26-67-58),D-10	21	0.9
1990 KC-A	142	496	61	139	29	7	5	51	42	51	12	14	.280	.338	.397	.735	106	0	64	4.51	-4	*O-138(70-19-78)/D-2	12	-0.8
1991 KC-A	135	375	47	113	22	3	2	47	20	35	5	3	.301	.338	.392	.730	101	-0	48	4.53	-5	*O-105(59-13-42),1-15/D-1	9	-0.8
1992 KC-A	113	353	31	95	13	3	2	28	24	36	11	6	.269	.316	.340	.656	81	-9	37	3.69	-2	O-88(24-1-66)/D-8	4	-1.4
1993*Phi-N	153	362	51	115	17	4	7	54	26	36	5	0	.318	.365	.445	.810	117	9	59	6.21	0	*O-137(1-3-133)/1-1	13	0.4
1994 Phi-N	104	290	42	87	15	4	4	43	33	31	6	2	.300	.373	.421	.794	104	3	46	5.67	-3	O-93(0-5-90)	10	-0.4
1995 Phi-N	129	377	46	119	22	2	10	55	38	44	10	0	.316	.380	.464	.844	120	13	69	6.84	-2	*O-111(39-6-68)	13	0.7
1996 Phi-N	113	338	45	122	24	3	3	41	31	32	11	1	.361	.416	.476	.893	133	19	68	8.11	-3	O-91(43-3-50)	14	1.2
1997*Fla-N	120	293	36	82	19	1	2	34	30	28	0	0	.280	.349	.372	.721	93	-3	38	4.60	-2	O-55(42-1-13),1-29/D-4	6	-0.8
1998 Fla-N	30	64	9	16	1	0	1	7	4	14	2	0	.250	.294	.313	.607	62	-3	6	3.36	-2	1-10/O-8(5-0-3)	0	-0.6
LA-N	75	127	12	25	2	2	0	6	12	22	4	0	.197	.266	.244	.510	38	-11	9	2.34	0	O-24(22-0-2)/1-9,D-2	0	-1.1
Yr.	105	191	21	41	3	2	1	13	16	36	6	0	.215	.275	.267	.542	46	-14	15	2.67	-1	O-32(27-0-5),1-19/D-2	0	-1.7
Total 15	1422	3995	492	1160	221	39	52	477	324	435	105	38	.290	.345	.404	.749	103	18	565	5.07	-26	*O-1072/D-72,1-64	108	-4.9
• ELAND,	Eland Deb: 4/14/1873																							
1873 Mar-n	1	3	0	0	0	0	0	0	0	0	0	0	.000	.000	.000	.000	-130	-1	0	.00	0	/O-1	....	-0.1
• ELBERFELD, Kid	Norman Arthur "The Tabasco Kid" Elberfeld b: 4/13/1875, Pomeroy, OH d: 1/13/1944, Chattanooga, TN BR/TR, 5'7", 158 lbs. Deb: 5/30/1898 M																							
1898 Phi-N	14	38	1	9	4	0	0	7	5	....	0	....	.237	.420	.342	.762	124	2	6	5.12	-3	3-14	1	-0.1
1899 Cin-N	41	138	23	36	4	2	0	22	15	....	5	....	.261	.378	.319	.697	90	-0	19	4.92	-2	S-24,3-18	4	-0.1
1901 Det-A	121	432	76	133	21	11	3	76	57	....	23	....	.308	.397	.428	.825	123	16	86	7.34	12	*S-121	22	2.9
1902 Det-A	130	488	70	127	17	6	1	64	55	....	19	....	.260	.348	.326	.674	86	-7	65	4.65	7	*S-130	15	0.4
1903 Det-A	35	132	29	45	5	3	0	19	11	....	6	....	.341	.412	.424	.836	156	10	26	7.93	5	S-34/3-1	8	1.6
NY-A	90	349	49	100	18	5	0	45	22	....	16	....	.287	.346	.367	.713	107	4	52	5.41	5	S-90	17	1.3
Yr.	125	481	78	145	23	8	0	64	33	....	22	....	.301	.365	.383	.747	121	14	78	6.06	10	*S-124/3-1	25	2.9
1904 NY-A	122	445	55	117	13	5	2	46	37	....	18	....	.263	.337	.328	.665	106	5	59	4.53	10	*S-122	18	2.1
1905 NY-A	111	390	48	102	18	2	0	53	23	....	18	....	.262	.329	.318	.647	95	-2	50	4.34	5	*S-108	15	0.7

YEAR TM-L	G	AB	R	H	2B	3B	HR	RBI	BB	SO	SB	CS	AVG	OBP	SLG	OPS	OPS+	BR/A	RC	RC/G	FR	G/POS	WS	TPW
1906 NY-A	99	346	59	106	11	5	2	31	30	....	19	....	.306	.378	.384	.763	126	12	60	6.42	-4	S-98	18	1.2
1907 NY-A	120	447	61	121	17	6	0	51	36	....	22	....	.271	.343	.336	.678	108	5	62	4.87	14	*S-118	21	2.6
1908 NY-A	19	56	11	11	3	0	0	5	6	....	1	....	.196	.328	.250	.578	87	-0	5	2.82	-1	S-17	2	-0.1
1909 NY-A	106	379	47	90	9	5	0	26	28	....	23	....	.237	.314	.288	.601	89	-3	41	3.58	9	S-61,3-44	13	0.9
1910 Was-A	127	455	53	114	9	2	2	42	35	....	19	....	.251	.322	.292	.614	97	-0	49	3.60	-9	*3-113,2-10/S-3	12	-0.7
1911 Was-A	127	404	58	110	19	4	0	47	65	....	24	....	.272	.405	.339	.744	110	12	66	5.60	-5	2-68,3-52	17	0.9
1914 Bro-N	30	62	7	14	1	0	0	1	2	4	0	....	.226	.304	.242	.546	62	-3	4	2.37	-3	S-18/2-1	1	-0.5
Total 14	**1292**	**4561**	**647**	**1235**	**169**	**56**	**10**	**535**	**427**	**4**	**213**	**....**	**.271**	**.355**	**.339**	**.694**	**105**	**50**	**651**	**4.98**	**39**	**S-944,3-242/2-79**	**184**	**13.3**

• ELDER, George George Rezin Elder b: 3/10/1921, Lebanon, KY BL/TR, 5'11", 180 lbs. Deb: 7/22/1949

YEAR TM-L	G	AB	R	H	2B	3B	HR	RBI	BB	SO	SB	CS	AVG	OBP	SLG	OPS	OPS+	BR/A	RC	RC/G	FR	G/POS	WS	TPW
1949 StL-A	41	44	9	11	3	0	0	2	4	11	0	0	.250	.313	.318	.631	64	-2	5	3.68	-1	0-10(10-0-0)	1	-0.3

• ELIA, Lee Lee Constantine Elia b: 7/16/1937, Philadelphia, PA BR/TR, 5'11", 175 lbs. Deb: 4/23/1966 M/C

YEAR TM-L	G	AB	R	H	2B	3B	HR	RBI	BB	SO	SB	CS	AVG	OBP	SLG	OPS	OPS+	BR/A	RC	RC/G	FR	G/POS	WS	TPW
1966 Chi-A	80	195	16	40	5	2	3	22	15	39	0	1	.205	.269	.297	.566	67	-9	14	2.34	-3	S-75	3	-0.7
1968 Chi-N	15	17	1	3	0	0	0	3	0	6	0	0	.176	.222	.176	.399	19	-2	1	1.40	-1	/S-2,2-1,3-1	0	-0.3
Total 2	**95**	**212**	**17**	**43**	**5**	**2**	**3**	**25**	**15**	**45**	**0**	**1**	**.203**	**.265**	**.288**	**.553**	**63**	**-10**	**15**	**2.26**	**-4**	**/S-77,2-1,3-1**	**3**	**-1.0**

• ELKO, Pete Peter "Piccolo Pete" Elko b: 6/17/1918, Wilkes-Barre, PA d: 9/17/1993, Wilkes-Barre, NC BR/TR, 5'11", 185 lbs. Deb: 9/17/1943

YEAR TM-L	G	AB	R	H	2B	3B	HR	RBI	BB	SO	SB	CS	AVG	OBP	SLG	OPS	OPS+	BR/A	RC	RC/G	FR	G/POS	WS	TPW
1943 Chi-N	9	30	1	4	0	0	0	0	4	5	0	....	.133	.235	.133	.369	8	-3	1	.86	-2	/3-9	0	-0.6
1944 Chi-N	7	22	2	5	1	0	0	0	0	0	0	....	.227	.227	.273	.500	40	-2	1	2.17	0	/3-6	0	-0.1
Total 2	**16**	**52**	**3**	**9**	**1**	**0**	**0**	**0**	**4**	**5**	**0**	**....**	**.173**	**.232**	**.192**	**.424**	**21**	**-5**	**2**	**1.35**	**-2**	**/3-15**	**0**	**-0.7**

• ELLAM, Roy Roy "Whitey,Slippery" Ellam b: 2/8/1886, Conshohocken, PA d: 10/28/1948, Conshohocken, PA BR/TR, 5'10.5", 203 lbs. Deb: 9/18/1909

YEAR TM-L	G	AB	R	H	2B	3B	HR	RBI	BB	SO	SB	CS	AVG	OBP	SLG	OPS	OPS+	BR/A	RC	RC/G	FR	G/POS	WS	TPW
1909 Cin-N	10	21	4	4	0	1	1	4	7	....	1	....	.190	.393	.429	.821	156	2	4	5.80	0	/S-9	1	0.2
1918 Pit-N	26	77	9	10	1	1	0	2	17	17	2	....	.130	.302	.169	.471	43	-4	5	1.86	-3	S-26	1	-0.6
Total 2	**36**	**98**	**13**	**14**	**1**	**2**	**1**	**6**	**24**	**17**	**3**	**....**	**.143**	**.323**	**.224**	**.547**	**68**	**-2**	**9**	**2.65**	**-3**	**/S-35**	**2**	**-0.4**

• ELLERBE, Frank Francis Rogers "Governor" Ellerbe b: 12/25/1895, Marion County, SC d: 7/8/1988, Latta, SC BR/TR, 5'10.5", 165 lbs. Deb: 8/28/1919

YEAR TM-L	G	AB	R	H	2B	3B	HR	RBI	BB	SO	SB	CS	AVG	OBP	SLG	OPS	OPS+	BR/A	RC	RC/G	FR	G/POS	WS	TPW
1919 Was-A	28	105	13	29	4	1	0	16	2	15	5	....	.276	.290	.333	.623	75	-4	12	3.57	-2	S-28	2	-0.4
1920 Was-A	101	336	38	98	14	2	0	36	19	23	5	4	.292	.331	.345	.677	82	-9	39	3.94	-2	3-75,S-19/0-1	7	-0.7
1921 Was-A	10	10	1	2	0	1	0	1	0	2	0	0	.200	.200	.400	.600	52	-1	1	2.54	0	....	0	-0.1
StL-A	105	430	65	124	20	12	2	49	22	42	1	6	.288	.327	.405	.732	81	-15	56	4.31	5	*3-105	10	-0.3
Yr.	115	440	66	126	20	13	2	50	22	44	1	6	.286	.325	.405	.729	80	-16	56	4.27	5	*3-105	10	-0.4
1922 StL-A	91	342	42	84	16	3	1	33	25	36	1	1	.246	.303	.319	.621	60	-20	35	3.30	20	3-91	6	0.6
1923 StL-A	18	49	6	9	0	0	0	1	1	5	0	1	.184	.200	.184	.384	1	-7	2	1.03	0	3-14	0	-0.6
1924 StL-A	21	61	7	12	3	0	0	2	2	3	0	1	.197	.222	.246	.468	19	-8	3	1.60	-1	3-21	1	-0.7
Cle-A	46	120	7	31	1	3	1	14	1	10	0	0	.258	.270	.342	.612	56	-8	11	3.10	4	3-39/2-2	1	-0.2
Yr.	67	181	14	43	4	3	1	16	3	13	0	1	.238	.254	.309	.563	44	-16	14	2.54	4	3-60/2-2	2	-0.9
Total 6	**420**	**1453**	**179**	**389**	**58**	**22**	**4**	**152**	**72**	**136**	**12**	**13**	**.268**	**.306**	**.346**	**.652**	**69**	**-72**	**158**	**3.58**	**25**	**3-345/S-47,2-2,0-1**	**27**	**-2.4**

• ELLICK, Joe Joseph J. Ellick b: 4/3/1854, Cincinnati, OH d: 4/21/1923, Kansas City, MO, 5'10", 162 lbs. Deb: 5/13/1875 M/U

YEAR TM-L	G	AB	R	H	2B	3B	HR	RBI	BB	SO	SB	CS	AVG	OBP	SLG	OPS	OPS+	BR/A	RC	RC/G	FR	G/POS	WS	TPW
1875 RS-n	7	27	1	6	1	0	0	1	0	1	1	0	.222	.222	.259	.481	74	-0	2	2.56	-3	/3-5,0-2(0-2-0)	....	-0.3
1878 Mil-N	3	13	2	2	0	0	0	1	0	1	....	....	.154	.154	.154	.308	1	-1	0	.79	-1	/C-2,3-1,P-1	0	-0.2
1880 Wor-N	5	18	1	1	0	0	0	0	1	2	....	....	.056	.105	.056	.161	-40	-3	0	.17	0	/3-5	0	-0.2
1884 CP-U	92	394	71	93	11	0	0	....	16	....	....	....	.236	.266	.264	.530	85	-4	28	2.64	2	0-57(3-0-54),S-33/2-4	8	-0.2
KC-U	2	8	0	0	0	0	0	....	0	....	....	....	.000	.000	.000	.000	-115	-2	0	.00	-1	/2-1,0-1	0	-0.2
Bal-U	7	27	2	4	0	0	0	....	2	....	....	....	.148	.207	.148	.355	20	-2	1	1.03	-1	/S-6,0-1	0	-0.2
Yr.	101	429	73	97	11	0	0	....	18	....	....	....	.226	.257	.252	.509	77	-8	29	2.46	1	0-59(3-0-56),S-39/2-5	8	-0.6
Total 3	**109**	**460**	**76**	**100**	**11**	**0**	**0**	**1**	**19**	**3**	**....**	**....**	**.217**	**.248**	**.241**	**.490**	**70**	**-12**	**30**	**2.30**	**0**	**/0-59,S-39,3-6,2-5,C-2,P-1**	**8**	**-1.1**

• ELLIOT, Larry Lawrence Lee Elliot b: 3/5/1938, San Diego, CA BL/TL, 6'2", 200 lbs. Deb: 4/19/1962 Career OF: 29-57-38

YEAR TM-L	G	AB	R	H	2B	3B	HR	RBI	BB	SO	SB	CS	AVG	OBP	SLG	OPS	OPS+	BR/A	RC	RC/G	FR	G/POS	WS	TPW
1962 Pit-N	8	10	2	3	0	0	1	2	0	1	0	0	.300	.300	.600	.900	135	0	2	6.94	-1	/0-3(0-0-3)	1	0.0
1963 Pit-N	4	4	0	0	0	0	0	0	0	3	0	0	.000	.000	.000	.000	-99	-1	0	.00	0	....	0	-0.1
1964 NY-N	80	224	27	51	8	0	9	22	28	55	1	2	.228	.322	.384	.705	100	0	27	4.06	-3	0-63(4-57-4)	6	-0.5
1966 NY-N	65	199	24	49	14	2	5	32	17	46	0	1	.246	.306	.412	.718	99	-1	25	4.34	2	0-54(25-0-31)	6	-0.2
Total 4	**157**	**437**	**53**	**103**	**22**	**2**	**15**	**56**	**45**	**105**	**1**	**3**	**.236**	**.311**	**.398**	**.710**	**99**	**-1**	**54**	**4.19**	**-1**	**0-120**	**13**	**-0.8**

• ELLIOTT, Allen Allen Clifford "Ace" Elliott b: 12/25/1897, St. Louis, MO d: 5/6/1979, St. Louis, MO BL/TR, 6', 170 lbs. Deb: 6/14/1923

YEAR TM-L	G	AB	R	H	2B	3B	HR	RBI	BB	SO	SB	CS	AVG	OBP	SLG	OPS	OPS+	BR/A	RC	RC/G	FR	G/POS	WS	TPW
1923 Chi-N	53	168	21	42	8	2	2	29	2	12	3	3	.250	.267	.357	.625	63	-10	15	2.94	-1	1-52	1	-1.3
1924 Chi-N	10	14	0	2	0	0	0	0	0	1	0	0	.143	.143	.143	.286	-23	-2	0	.65	-1	1-10	0	-0.3
Total 2	**63**	**182**	**21**	**44**	**8**	**2**	**2**	**29**	**2**	**13**	**3**	**3**	**.242**	**.258**	**.341**	**.599**	**57**	**-12**	**16**	**2.74**	**-1**	**/1-62**	**1**	**-1.6**

• ELLIOTT, Bob Robert Irving "Mr. Team" Elliott
b: 11/26/1916, San Francisco, CA d: 5/4/1966, San Francisco, CA BR/TR, 6', 185 lbs. Deb: 9/2/1939 M/C Career OF: 63-63-415

YEAR TM-L	G	AB	R	H	2B	3B	HR	RBI	BB	SO	SB	CS	AVG	OBP	SLG	OPS	OPS+	BR/A	RC	RC/G	FR	G/POS	WS	TPW
1939 Pit-N	32	129	18	43	10	3	3	19	9	4	0	....	.333	.377	.527	.904	143	7	24	7.18	0	0-30(0-30-0)	5	0.6
1940 Pit-N	148	551	88	161	34	11	5	64	45	28	13	....	.292	.348	.421	.769	112	8	81	5.28	1	*0-147(4-31-113)	18	0.2
1941 Pit-N★	141	527	74	144	24	10	3	76	64	52	6	....	.273	.353	.374	.727	105	5	72	4.81	-1	*0-139(4-2-134)	16	-0.4
1942 Pit-N★	143	560	75	166	26	7	9	89	52	35	2	....	.296	.358	.416	.774	123	16	84	5.49	0	*3-142/0-1	22	2.2
1943 Pit-N	156	581	82	183	30	12	7	101	56	24	4	....	.315	.376	.444	.820	132	24	96	6.18	-5	*3-151/2-2,S-1	25	2.2
1944 Pit-N★	143	538	85	160	28	16	10	108	75	42	9	....	.297	.383	.465	.848	132	24	100	6.92	-1	*3-140/S-1	27	2.6
1945 Pit-N★	144	541	80	157	36	6	8	108	64	38	5	....	.290	.366	.423	.790	115	11	84	5.62	7	3-81,0-61(0-0-61)	20	1.5
1946 Pit-N	140	486	50	128	25	3	5	68	64	44	6	....	.263	.351	.358	.709	99	1	62	4.43	6	0-92(0-0-92),3-43	12	0.5
1947 Bos-N★	150	555	93	176	35	5	22	113	87	60	3	....	.317	.410	.517	.927	148	40	120	8.14	2	*3-148	29	4.1
1948*Bos-N★	151	540	99	153	24	5	23	100	**131**	57	6	....	.283	.423	.474	.897	145	41	117	7.79	-4	*3-150	27	3.7
1949 Bos-N	139	482	77	135	29	5	17	76	90	38	0	....	.280	.395	.467	.862	138	29	92	6.74	10	*3-130	23	3.8
1950 Bos-N	142	531	94	162	28	5	24	107	68	67	2	....	.305	.386	.512	.898	143	33	103	7.19	-10	*3-137	27	2.3
1951 Bos-N★	136	480	73	137	29	2	15	70	65	56	2	0	.285	.371	.448	.819	128	20	81	6.09	-3	*3-127	18	1.7
1952 NY-N	98	272	33	62	6	2	10	35	36	20	1	0	.228	.323	.375	.698	92	-2	35	4.25	1	0-65(52-0-15),3-13	7	-0.4
1953 StL-A	48	160	19	40	7	1	5	29	30	18	0	1	.250	.368	.400	.768	105	2	25	5.39	1	3-45	4	0.3
Chi-A	67	208	24	54	11	1	4	32	31	21	1	1	.260	.358	.380	.738	96	-0	31	5.22	-2	3-58/0-2(2-0-0)	7	-0.3
Yr.	115	368	43	94	18	2	9	61	61	39	1	2	.255	.363	.389	.751	100	2	56	5.30	-1	*3-103/0-2(2-0-0)	11	0.0
Total 15	**1978**	**7141**	**1064**	**2061**	**382**	**94**	**170**	**1195**	**967**	**604**	**60**	**2**	**.289**	**.375**	**.440**	**.815**	**125**	**259**	**1206**	**6.10**	**3**	***3-1365,0-537/2-2,S-2**	**287**	**24.5**

• ELLIOTT, Carter Carter Ward Elliott b: 11/29/1893, Atchison, KS d: 5/21/1959, Palm Springs, CA BL/TR, 5'11", 165 lbs. Deb: 9/10/1921

YEAR TM-L	G	AB	R	H	2B	3B	HR	RBI	BB	SO	SB	CS	AVG	OBP	SLG	OPS	OPS+	BR/A	RC	RC/G	FR	G/POS	WS	TPW
1921 Chi-N	12	28	5	7	2	0	0	0	5	3	0	0	.250	.364	.321	.685	83	-0	4	4.29	-1	S-10	1	0.0

• ELLIOTT, Gene Eugene Birminghouse Elliott b: 2/8/1889, Fayette City, PA d: 1/5/1976, Huntingdon, PA BL/TR, 5'7", 150 lbs. Deb: 4/13/1911

YEAR TM-L	G	AB	R	H	2B	3B	HR	RBI	BB	SO	SB	CS	AVG	OBP	SLG	OPS	OPS+	BR/A	RC	RC/G	FR	G/POS	WS	TPW
1911 NY-A	5	13	1	1	1	0	0	1	2	....	0	....	.077	.200	.154	.354	-1	-2	0	.96	-1	/0-2(0-0-2),3-1	0	-0.3

• ELLIOTT, Harry Harry Lewis Elliott b: 10/30/1923, San Francisco, CA BR/TR, 5'9", 175 lbs. Deb: 8/1/1953 Career OF: 23-0-22

YEAR TM-L	G	AB	R	H	2B	3B	HR	RBI	BB	SO	SB	CS	AVG	OBP	SLG	OPS	OPS+	BR/A	RC	RC/G	FR	G/POS	WS	TPW
1953 StL-N	24	59	6	15	6	1	1	6	3	8	0	0	.254	.302	.441	.742	90	-1	7	4.04	0	0-17(15-0-2)	1	-0.2
1955 StL-N	68	117	9	30	4	0	1	12	11	9	0	2	.256	.326	.316	.642	71	-5	10	2.69	-1	0-28(8-0-20)	0	-0.7
Total 2	**92**	**176**	**15**	**45**	**10**	**1**	**2**	**18**	**14**	**17**	**0**	**2**	**.256**	**.318**	**.358**	**.676**	**78**	**-6**	**17**	**3.12**	**0**	**/0-45**	**1**	**-0.9**

• ELLIOTT, Randy Randy Lee Elliott b: 6/5/1951, Oxnard, CA BR/TR, 6'2", 190 lbs. Deb: 9/10/1972 Career OF: 53-0-17

YEAR TM-L	G	AB	R	H	2B	3B	HR	RBI	BB	SO	SB	CS	AVG	OBP	SLG	OPS	OPS+	BR/A	RC	RC/G	FR	G/POS	WS	TPW
1972 SD-N	14	49	5	10	3	1	0	6	2	11	0	0	.204	.235	.306	.541	57	-3	3	2.26	-0	0-13(0-0-13)	0	-0.4
1974 SD-N	13	33	5	7	1	0	1	2	7	9	0	1	.212	.350	.333	.683	96	-0	4	4.00	0	0-11(7-0-4)/1-1	1	-0.1
1977 SF-N	73	167	17	40	5	1	7	26	8	24	0	2	.240	.278	.407	.686	82	-6	17	3.33	3	0-46(46-0-0)	2	-0.4
1980 Oak-A	14	39	4	5	3	0	0	1	1	13	0	0	.128	.150	.205	.355	-4	-6	1	.80	0	D-11	0	-0.6
Total 4	**114**	**288**	**31**	**62**	**12**	**2**	**8**	**35**	**18**	**57**	**0**	**3**	**.215**	**.264**	**.354**	**.618**	**68**	**-15**	**25**	**2.86**	**3**	**/0-70,D-11,1-1**	**3**	**-1.5**

YEAR TM-L	G	AB	R	H	2B	3B	HR	RBI	BB	SO	SB	CS	AVG	OBP	SLG	OPS	OPS+	BR/A	RC	RC/G	FR	G/POS	WS	TPW
• ELLIOTT, Rowdy	Harold Bell Elliott b: 7/8/1890, Kokomo, IN d: 2/12/1934, San Francisco, CA BR/TR, 5'9", 160 lbs. Deb: 9/24/1910																							
1910 Bos-N	3	2	0	0	0	0	0	0	0	0	0	....	.000	.000	.000	.000	-96	-1	0	.00	0	/C-1	0	-0.1
1916 Chi-N	23	55	5	14	3	0	0	3	3	5	1	....	.255	.293	.309	.602	77	-2	6	3.37	-2	C-18	1	-0.2
1917 Chi-N	85	223	18	56	8	5	0	28	11	11	4	....	.251	.292	.332	.624	85	-4	22	3.31	5	C-73	8	0.6
1918 Chi-N	5	10	0	0	0	0	0	0	2	1	0	....	.000	.167	.000	.167	-47	-2	0	.00	0	/C-5	0	-0.2
1920 Bro-N	41	112	13	27	4	0	1	13	3	6	0	0	.241	.267	.304	.571	62	-5	9	2.74	-2	C-39	2	-0.4
Total 5	**157**	**402**	**36**	**97**	**15**	**5**	**1**	**44**	**19**	**23**	**5**	**0**	**.241**	**.281**	**.311**	**.592**	**73**	**-13**	**37**	**3.04**	**1**	**C-136**	**11**	**-0.3**
• ELLIS, Ben	Alfred Benjamin Ellis b: 7/1870, New York, NY d: 7/26/1931, Schenectady, NY, 5'10", 165 lbs. Deb: 7/16/1896																							
1896 Phi-N	4	16	0	1	0	0	0	0	3	6	0	....	.063	.211	.063	.273	-26	-3	0	.38	-1	/3-2,S-2	0	-0.3
• ELLIS, John	John Charles Ellis b: 8/21/1948, New London, CT BR/TR, 6'2.5", 225 lbs. Deb: 5/17/1969																							
1969 NY-A	22	62	2	18	4	0	1	8	1	11	0	2	.290	.313	.403	.716	103	-1	7	4.14	-1	C-15	2	-0.1
1970 NY-A	78	226	24	56	12	1	7	29	18	47	0	1	.248	.309	.403	.712	100	-1	27	4.15	1	1-53/3-5,C-2	6	-0.4
1971 NY-A	83	238	16	58	12	1	3	34	23	42	0	0	.244	.326	.340	.666	95	-1	25	3.41	-4	1-65/C-2	5	-1.1
1972 NY-A	52	136	13	40	5	1	5	25	8	22	0	0	.294	.333	.456	.789	138	6	17	4.46	0	C-25/1-8	5	0.7
1973 Cle-A	127	437	59	118	12	2	14	68	46	57	0	0	.270	.344	.403	.746	108	5	60	4.76	-13	C-72,D-38,1-12	14	-0.6
1974 Cle-A	128	477	58	136	23	6	10	64	32	53	1	2	.285	.331	.421	.753	116	8	62	4.63	1	1-69,C-42,D-21	16	0.5
1975 Cle-A	92	296	22	68	11	1	7	32	14	33	0	1	.230	.269	.345	.614	72	-12	24	2.62	-3	C-84/D-3,1-2	4	-1.2
1976 Tex-A	11	31	4	13	2	0	1	8	0	4	0	0	.419	.419	.581	1.000	187	3	7	9.90	0	/C-7,D-3	2	0.3
1977 Tex-A	49	119	7	28	7	0	4	15	8	26	0	0	.235	.283	.395	.678	82	-3	13	3.93	0	C-16,D-15/1-8	2	-0.3
1978 Tex-A	34	94	7	23	4	0	3	17	6	20	0	1	.245	.290	.383	.673	88	-2	11	3.79	-1	C-22/D-7	2	-0.3
1979 Tex-A	111	316	33	90	12	0	12	61	15	55	2	2	.285	.321	.437	.758	103	0	44	5.05	-2	D-62,1-30/C-7	7	-0.4
1980 Tex-A	73	182	12	43	9	1	1	23	14	23	3	0	.236	.294	.313	.608	69	-7	17	3.02	-3	1-39,D-20/C-3	1	-1.2
1981 Tex-A	23	58	2	8	3	0	1	7	5	10	0	1	.138	.219	.241	.460	34	-5	2	1.20	-1	1-18/D-1	0	-0.8
Total 13	**883**	**2672**	**259**	**699**	**116**	**13**	**69**	**391**	**190**	**403**	**6**	**10**	**.262**	**.315**	**.392**	**.707**	**99**	**-11**	**317**	**4.07**	**-24**	**1-304,C-297,D-170/3-5**	**66**	**-4.8**
• ELLIS, Mark	Mark William Ellis b: 6/6/1977, Rapid City, SD BR/TR, 5'11", 180 lbs. Deb: 4/9/2002																							
2002*Oak-A	98	345	58	94	16	4	6	35	44	54	4	2	.272	.361	.394	.756	101	2	53	5.35	-5	2-85/S-8,3-7,D-1	14	0.1
2003*Oak-A	154	553	78	137	31	5	9	52	48	94	6	2	.248	.316	.371	.686	79	-16	67	4.14	9	*2-153	18	0.1
Total 2	**252**	**898**	**136**	**231**	**47**	**9**	**15**	**87**	**92**	**148**	**10**	**4**	**.257**	**.334**	**.380**	**.713**	**88**	**-14**	**120**	**4.60**	**5**	**2-238/S-8,3-7,D-1**	**32**	**0.2**
• ELLIS, Rob	Robert Walter Ellis b: 7/3/1950, Grand Rapids, MI BR/TR, 5'11", 180 lbs. Deb: 6/18/1971 Career OF: 10-1-21																							
1971 Mil-A	36	111	9	22	2	0	0	6	12	24	0	2	.198	.282	.216	.498	43	-9	7	1.74	-2	3-19,O-15(1-1-13)	1	-1.2
1974 Mil-A	22	48	4	14	2	0	0	4	4	11	0	0	.292	.346	.333	.679	97	-0	6	4.68	1	O-11(4-0-8)/D-9,3-1	1	0.1
1975 Mil-A	6	7	3	2	0	0	0	0	0	0	0	0	.286	.286	.286	.571	62	-0	0	1.22	-1	/O-5(5-0-0),D-1	0	-0.1
Total 3	**64**	**166**	**16**	**38**	**4**	**0**	**0**	**10**	**16**	**35**	**0**	**2**	**.229**	**.301**	**.253**	**.554**	**59**	**-9**	**13**	**2.42**	**-1**	**/O-31,3-20,D-10**	**2**	**-1.3**
• ELLIS, Rube	George William Ellis b: 11/17/1885, Downey, CA d: 3/13/1938, Rivera, CA BL/TL, 6', 170 lbs. Deb: 4/15/1909 Career OF: 498-4-8																							
1909 StL-N	149	575	76	154	10	9	3	46	54	....	16	....	.268	.334	.332	.666	114	9	68	4.13	9	*O-145(144-0-1)	16	1.1
1910 StL-N	142	550	87	142	18	8	4	54	62	70	25	....	.258	.339	.342	.681	102	2	72	4.42	1	*O-141(141-0-0)	15	-0.5
1911 StL-N	155	555	69	139	20	11	2	66	66	64	9	....	.250	.332	.337	.669	90	-7	66	3.92	0	*O-148(148-0-0)	14	-1.4
1912 StL-N	109	305	47	82	18	2	4	33	34	36	6	....	.269	.342	.380	.723	100	-0	42	4.55	2	O-76(65-4-7)	8	-0.1
Total 4	**555**	**1985**	**279**	**517**	**66**	**30**	**13**	**199**	**216**	**170**	**56**	**....**	**.260**	**.336**	**.344**	**.680**	**102**	**4**	**248**	**4.21**	**12**	**O-510**	**53**	**-0.9**
• ELLISON, Babe	Herbert Spencer "Bert" Ellison b: 11/15/1895, Rutland, AR d: 8/11/1955, San Francisco, CA BR/TR, 5'11", 170 lbs. Deb: 9/18/1916 Career OF: 1-3-14																							
1916 Det-A	2	7	0	1	0	0	0	1	0	1	0	....	.143	.143	.143	.286	-14	-1	0	.62	-1	/3-2	0	-0.2
1917 Det-A	9	29	2	5	1	2	1	4	6	3	0	....	.172	.333	.448	.782	139	1	4	4.45	-2	/1-9	1	0.0
1918 Det-A	7	23	1	6	1	0	0	2	3	1	1	....	.261	.346	.304	.651	100	0	3	3.87	1	/O-4(0-0-4),2-3	1	0.1
1919 Det-A	56	134	18	29	4	0	0	11	13	24	4	....	.216	.291	.246	.537	53	-8	11	2.55	2	2-25,O-10(1-1-8)/S-1	1	-0.7
1920 Det-A	61	155	11	34	7	2	0	21	8	26	4	1	.219	.258	.290	.548	46	-11	12	2.50	3	1-38/O-4(0-2-2),3-1	1	-0.9
Total 5	**135**	**348**	**32**	**75**	**13**	**4**	**1**	**39**	**30**	**55**	**9**	**1**	**.216**	**.282**	**.284**	**.566**	**60**	**-19**	**30**	**2.73**	**3**	**/1-47,2-28,O-18,3-3,S-1**	**4**	**-1.7**
• ELLISON, Jason	Jason Jerome Ellison b: 4/4/1978, Quincy, CA BR/TR, 5'10", 180 lbs. Deb: 5/9/2003																							
2003 SF-N	7	10	1	1	0	0	0	0	0	1	0	0	.100	.100	.100	.200	-49	-2	0	.30	0	/O-4(3-1-0)	0	-0.2
• ELMORE, Verdo	Verdo Wilson "Ellie" Elmore b: 12/10/1899, Gordo, AL d: 8/5/1969, Birmingham, AL BL/TR, 5'11", 185 lbs. Deb: 9/11/1924																							
1924 StL-A	7	17	2	3	3	0	0	0	1	3	0	0	.176	.222	.353	.575	44	-2	1	2.53	-1	/O-3(0-0-3)	0	-0.2
• ELSH, Roy	Eugene Reybold Elsh b: 3/1/1892, Pennsgrove, NJ d: 11/12/1978, Philadelphia, PA BR/TR, 5'9", 165 lbs. Deb: 4/19/1923 Career OF: 54-14-43																							
1923 Chi-A	81	209	28	52	7	2	0	24	16	23	16	8	.249	.305	.301	.607	61	-11	20	3.09	0	O-57(50-6-1)	2	-1.5
1924 Chi-A	60	147	21	45	9	1	0	11	10	14	6	1	.306	.350	.381	.731	91	-1	21	5.04	-1	O-38(2-5-31)/1-2	3	-0.4
1925 Chi-A	32	48	6	9	1	0	0	4	5	7	2	0	.188	.264	.208	.472	22	-5	3	2.12	1	O-16(2-3-11)/1-3	0	-0.5
Total 3	**173**	**404**	**55**	**106**	**17**	**3**	**0**	**39**	**31**	**44**	**24**	**9**	**.262**	**.317**	**.319**	**.636**	**67**	**-17**	**44**	**3.63**	**-0**	**O-111/1-5**	**5**	**-2.3**
• ELSTER, Kevin	Kevin Daniel Elster b: 8/3/1964, San Pedro, CA BR/TR, 6'2", 200 lbs. Deb: 9/2/1986																							
1986*NY-N	19	30	3	5	1	0	0	0	3	8	0	0	.167	.242	.200	.442	24	-3	2	1.71	1	S-19	1	0.0
1987 NY-N	5	10	1	4	2	0	0	1	0	1	0	0	.400	.400	.600	1.000	169	1	2	6.94	-1	/S-3	1	0.0
1988*NY-N	149	406	41	87	11	1	9	37	35	47	2	0	.214	.282	.313	.594	74	-14	37	3.01	-1	*S-148	12	-0.5
1989 NY-N	151	458	52	106	25	2	10	55	34	77	4	3	.231	.287	.360	.648	88	-9	45	3.17	19	*S-150	18	2.3
1990 NY-N	92	314	36	65	20	1	9	45	30	54	2	0	.207	.278	.363	.641	75	-11	33	3.43	4	S-92	10	0.0
1991 NY-N	115	348	33	84	16	2	6	36	40	53	2	3	.241	.321	.351	.672	90	-5	40	3.95	3	*S-107	10	0.6
1992 NY-N	6	18	0	4	0	0	0	0	0	2	0	0	.222	.222	.222	.444	27	-2	1	1.20	0	/S-5	0	-0.1
1994 NY-A	7	20	0	0	0	0	0	0	1	6	0	0	.000	.048	.000	.048	-90	-6	0	.05	3	/S-7	0	-0.2
1995 NY-A	10	17	1	2	1	0	0	0	1	5	0	0	.118	.167	.176	.343	-11	-3	1	.98	-1	S-10/2-1	0	-0.3
Phi-N	26	53	10	11	4	1	1	9	7	14	0	0	.208	.311	.377	.689	80	-2	7	3.80	1	S-19/1-4,3-2	1	0.0
1996*Tex-A	157	515	79	130	32	2	24	99	52	138	4	1	.252	.323	.462	.786	91	-9	79	5.04	8	*S-157	14	1.1
1997 Pit-N	39	138	14	31	6	2	7	25	21	39	0	2	.225	.331	.449	.781	100	-1	21	5.04	4	S-39	5	0.6
1998 Tex-A	84	297	33	69	10	1	8	37	33	66	0	2	.232	.313	.354	.667	70	-14	33	3.68	-2	S-84	7	-0.8
2000 LA-N	80	220	29	50	8	0	14	32	38	52	0	0	.227	.341	.455	.796	105	2	37	5.85	-13	S-55/3-8,1-1	7	-0.7
Total 13	**940**	**2844**	**332**	**648**	**136**	**12**	**88**	**376**	**295**	**562**	**14**	**11**	**.228**	**.303**	**.377**	**.680**	**83**	**-76**	**336**	**3.90**	**26**	**S-895/3-10,1-5,2-1**	**86**	**1.8**
• ELY, Bones	William Frederick Ely b: 6/7/1863, North Girard, PA d: 1/10/1952, Imola, CA BR/TR, 6'1", 155 lbs. Deb: 6/19/1884 Career OF: 74-9-1																							
1884 Buf-N	1	4	0	0	0	0	0	0	0	2	....	....	.000	.000	.000	.000	-97	-1	0	.00	-1	/O-1,P-1	0	-0.7
1886 Lou-a	10	32	5	5	0	0	0	6	2	....	1	....	.156	.206	.156	.362	13	-3	1	1.27	0	/P-6,O-5(4-1-0)	1	-1.1
1890 Syr-a	119	496	72	130	16	6	0	64	31	....	44	....	.262	.308	.319	.627	94	-3	64	4.62	13	O-78(70-8-0),S-36/1-4,2-2,3,P	13	0.3
1891 Bro-N	31	111	9	17	0	1	0	11	7	9	4	....	.153	.203	.171	.375	9	-13	5	1.38	6	S-28/3-2,2-1	2	-0.5
1893 StL-N	44	178	25	45	1	6	0	16	17	13	2	....	.253	.318	.326	.644	71	-8	20	3.90	0	S-44	4	-0.4
1894 StL-N	127	510	85	156	20	12	12	89	30	34	23	....	.306	.344	.463	.807	93	-9	91	6.72	8	*S-126/2-1,P-1	14	0.4
1895 StL-N	118	471	122	122	16	2	1	47	19	18	29	....	.259	.288	.308	.596	53	-34	52	3.85	4	*S-117	7	-1.9
1896 Pit-N	128	537	85	153	15	9	3	77	33	33	18	....	.285	.326	.363	.689	85	-12	74	4.79	3	*S-128	14	-0.3
1897 Pit-N	133	516	63	146	20	8	2	74	25	....	10	....	.283	.317	.364	.682	83	-14	66	4.55	7	*S-133	14	-0.1
1898 Pit-N	148	519	49	110	14	5	2	44	24	....	6	....	.212	.247	.270	.517	49	-36	38	2.41	9	*S-148	10	-1.9
1899 Pit-N	139	526	66	146	18	6	3	72	22	....	8	....	.278	.313	.352	.665	83	-14	65	4.24	3	*S-132/2-6	10	-0.3
1900*Pit-N	130	475	60	116	6	6	0	51	17	....	6	....	.244	.272	.282	.554	53	-32	40	2.89	19	*S-130	11	-0.6
1901 Pit-N	65	240	18	50	6	3	0	28	6	....	5	....	.208	.234	.258	.492	41	-19	17	2.26	-5	S-64/3-1	3	-2.1
Phi-A	45	171	11	37	6	2	0	16	3	....	6	....	.216	.230	.275	.505	38	-15	13	2.47	-2	S-45	2	-1.4
1902 Was-A	105	381	39	100	11	2	1	62	21	....	3	....	.262	.301	.310	.611	69	-16	39	3.51	-8	*S-105	5	-1.9
Total 14	**1343**	**5167**	**709**	**1333**	**149**	**68**	**24**	**657**	**257**	**109**	**165**	**....**	**.258**	**.295**	**.327**	**.622**	**69**	**-229**	**586**	**3.91**	**55**	***S-1236/O-84,2-10,P-9,1-4,3**	**110**	**-12.4**

YEAR TM-L	G	AB	R	H	2B	3B	HR	RBI	BB	SO	SB	CS	AVG	OBP	SLG	OPS	OPS+	BR/A	RC	RC/G	FR	G/POS	WS	TPW
• EMERSON, Chester	Chester Arthur "Chuck" Emerson b: 10/27/1889, Stow, ME d: 7/2/1971, Augusta, ME BL/TR, 5'8", 165 lbs. Deb: 9/27/1911																							
1911 Phi-A	7	18	2	4	0	0	0	0	6	....	1	....	.222	.417	.222	.639	82	0	2	3.99	0	/0-7(0-1-6)	1	0.0
1912 Phi-A	1	1	0	0	0	0	0	0	0	....	0	....	.000	.000	.000	.000	-104	-0	0	.00	0	....	0	0.0
Total 2	8	19	2	4	0	0	0	0	6	....	1	....	.211	.400	.211	.611	75	-0	2	3.76	0	/0-7	1	0.0
• EMERY, Cal	Calvin Wayne Emery b: 6/28/1937, Centre Hall, PA BL/TL, 6'2", 205 lbs. Deb: 7/15/1963 C																							
1963 Phi-N	16	19	0	3	1	0	0	0	0	2	0	0	.158	.158	.211	.368	5	-2	1	1.07	0	/1-2	0	-0.3
• EMERY, Spoke	Herrick Smith Emery b: 12/10/1896, Bay City, MI d: 1/2/1975, Cape Canaveral, FL BR/TR, 5'9", 165 lbs. Deb: 7/18/1924																							
1924 Phi-N	5	3	3	2	0	0	0	0	0	0	0	1	.667	.667	.667	1.333	230	0	1	8.48	0	/0-1	0	0.0
• EMMER, Frank	Frank William Emmer b: 2/17/1896, Crestline, OH d: 10/18/1963, Homestead, FL BR/TR, 5'8", 150 lbs. Deb: 4/25/1916																							
1916 Cin-N	42	89	8	13	3	1	0	2	7	27	1	....	.146	.208	.202	.411	27	-8	4	1.34	-7	S-29/0-2(2-0-0),2-1,3-1	1	-1.4
1926 Cin-N	80	224	22	44	7	6	0	18	13	30	1	....	.196	.244	.281	.525	42	-19	16	2.08	-13	S-79	1	-2.4
Total 2	122	313	30	57	10	7	0	20	20	57	2	....	.182	.234	.259	.492	38	-26	20	1.87	-20	S-108/0-2,2-1,3-1	2	-3.8
• EMMERICH, Bob	Robert George Emmerich b: 8/1/1897, New York, NY d: 11/22/1948, Bridgeport, CT BR/TR, 5'3", 155 lbs. Deb: 9/22/1923																							
1923 Bos-N	13	24	3	2	0	0	0	0	2	3	1	1	.083	.154	.083	.237	-37	-5	0	.42	0	/0-8(0-8-0)	0	-0.5
• ENCARNACION, Angelo	Angelo Benjamin Encarnacion b: 4/18/1969, Santo Domingo, Dominican Republic BR/TR, 5'8", 180 lbs. Deb: 5/2/1995																							
1995 Pit-N	58	159	18	36	7	2	2	10	13	28	1	1	.226	.285	.333	.618	61	-10	15	3.05	3	C-55	3	-0.3
1996 Pit-N	7	22	3	7	2	0	0	1	0	5	0	0	.318	.318	.409	.727	88	-0	3	5.15	0	/C-7	0	-0.1
1997 Ana-A	11	17	2	7	1	0	1	4	0	1	2	0	.412	.412	.647	1.059	169	2	4	10.43	-1	C-11	1	0.2
Total 3	76	198	23	50	10	2	3	15	13	34	3	1	.253	.299	.369	.667	72	-8	22	3.78	1	/C-73	4	-0.2
• ENCARNACION, Juan	Juan De Dios Encarnacion b: 3/8/1976, Las Matas de Faran, Dominican Republic BR/TR, 6'2", 160 lbs. Deb: 9/2/1997 Career OF: 126-305-342																							
1997 Det-A	11	33	3	7	1	1	1	5	3	12	3	1	.212	.316	.394	.710	85	-1	4	4.02	0	0-10(0-2-10)	1	-0.1
1998 Det-A	40	164	30	54	9	4	7	21	7	31	7	4	.329	.360	.561	.921	134	7	32	7.21	2	0-39(8-13-21)/D-1	4	0.7
1999 Det-A	132	509	62	130	30	6	19	74	14	113	33	12	.255	.288	.450	.737	84	-14	61	4.04	-0	*0-131(118-22-1)	8	-1.7
2000 Det-A	141	547	75	158	25	6	14	72	29	90	16	4	.289	.333	.433	.766	94	-4	77	4.98	-1	*0-141(0-141-0)	14	-0.4
2001 Det-A	120	417	52	101	19	7	12	52	25	93	9	5	.242	.295	.408	.702	86	-10	48	3.85	-7	*0-116(0-56-63)/D-1	5	-1.9
2002 Cin-N	83	321	43	89	11	2	16	51	26	63	9	4	.277	.333	.474	.807	107	2	49	5.37	5	0-82(0-59-31)	8	0.7
Fla-N	69	263	34	69	11	3	8	34	20	50	12	5	.262	.322	.418	.740	97	-2	33	4.11	-1	0-67(0-12-61)	6	-0.6
Yr.	152	584	77	158	22	5	24	85	46	113	21	9	.271	.328	.449	.777	102	1	82	4.79	4	*0-149(0-71-92)	14	0.0
2003*Fla-N	156	601	80	162	37	6	19	94	37	82	19	8	.270	.316	.446	.762	100	-2	80	4.56	1	*0-155(0-0-155)	15	-0.9
Total 7	752	2855	379	770	143	35	96	403	161	534	108	43	.270	.316	.445	.761	96	-22	384	4.61	-2	0-741/D-2	61	-4.3
• ENCARNACION, Mario	Mario (Gonzalez) Encarnacion b: 9/24/1975, Bani, Dominican Republic BR/TR, 6'2", 205 lbs. Deb: 8/26/2001 Career OF: 16-0-6																							
2001 Col-N	20	62	3	14	1	0	0	3	5	14	2	1	.226	.284	.242	.526	31	-6	4	2.02	2	0-20(14-0-6)	1	-0.5
2002 Chi-N	3	7	0	0	0	0	0	0	2	3	0	0	.000	.222	.000	.222	-36	-1	0	.45	0	/0-2(2-0-0)	0	-0.1
Total 2	23	69	3	14	1	0	0	3	7	17	2	1	.203	.276	.217	.494	23	-8	4	1.83	2	/0-22	1	-0.6
• ENDICOTT, Bill	William Franklin Endicott b: 9/4/1918, Acorn, MO BL/TL, 5'11.5", 175 lbs. Deb: 4/21/1946																							
1946 StL-N	20	20	2	4	3	0	0	3	4	4	0	....	.200	.333	.350	.683	90	-0	2	3.72	0	/0-2(2-0-0)	0	0.0
• ENGLE, Charlie	Charlie August "Cholly" Engle b: 8/27/1903, New York, NY d: 10/12/1983, San Antonio, TX BR/TR, 5'8", 145 lbs. Deb: 9/14/1925																							
1925 Phi-A	1	0	0	0	0	0	0	0	0	0	0	0	....	....	....	....	-94	0	0	....	-1	/S-1	0	0.0
1926 Phi-A	19	19	7	2	0	0	0	0	10	6	0	0	.105	.433	.105	.539	43	-1	2	3.18	0	S-16	1	0.1
1930 Pit-N	67	216	34	57	10	1	0	15	22	20	1	....	.264	.335	.319	.654	59	-14	24	3.70	-1	3-24,S-23,2-10	4	-0.9
Total 3	87	235	41	59	10	1	0	15	32	26	1	0	.251	.346	.302	.648	57	-14	26	3.65	-1	/S-40,3-24,2-10	5	-0.9
• ENGLE, Clyde	Arthur Clyde "Hack" Engle b: 3/19/1884, Dayton, OH d: 12/26/1939, Boston, MA BR/TR, 5'10", 190 lbs. Deb: 4/12/1909 Career OF: 142-111-25																							
1909 NY-A	135	492	66	137	20	5	3	71	47	....	18	....	.278	.347	.358	.705	122	13	68	4.71	11	*0-134(119-16-0)	23	1.8
1910 NY-A	5	13	0	3	0	0	0	0	2	....	1	....	.231	.333	.231	.564	73	-0	1	3.37	0	/0-3(3-0-0)	0	-0.1
Bos-A	106	363	59	96	18	7	2	38	31	....	12	....	.264	.326	.369	.695	115	5	47	4.41	-1	3-51,2-27,0-15(0-13-2)/S-7	12	0.6
Yr.	111	376	59	99	18	7	2	38	33	....	13	....	.263	.326	.364	.690	113	5	49	4.38	-1	3-51,2-27,0-18(3-13-2)/S-7	12	0.5
1911 Bos-A	146	514	58	139	13	3	2	48	51	....	24	....	.270	.343	.319	.662	86	-8	65	4.31	0	1-65,3-51,2-13,0-10(3-7-0)	10	-0.8
1912*Bos-A	58	171	32	40	5	3	0	18	28	....	12	....	.234	.348	.298	.647	81	-3	22	4.22	-3	1-25,2-15,3-11/S-2,0-1	5	-0.6
1913 Bos-A	143	498	75	144	17	12	2	50	53	41	28	....	.289	.363	.384	.747	116	10	76	5.30	-7	*1-133/0-2(0-1-1)	16	0.1
1914 Bos-A	59	134	14	26	2	0	0	9	14	11	4	9	.194	.275	.209	.484	46	-12	7	1.56	-3	1-29/2-5,3-3,0-1	0	-1.7
Buf-F	32	110	12	28	4	1	0	12	11	18	5	....	.255	.328	.309	.637	78	-3	13	3.71	-3	3-23/0-9(3-0-7)	3	-0.6
1915 Buf-F	141	501	56	131	22	8	3	71	34	43	24	....	.261	.312	.355	.668	96	-4	60	4.08	-7	*0-100(14-74-13),2-21,3-17/1	15	-1.8
1916 Cle-A	11	26	1	4	0	0	0	1	0	6	0	....	.154	.154	.154	.308	-7	-3	1	.88	-2	/3-7,1-2,0-1	0	-0.6
Total 8	836	2822	373	748	101	39	12	318	271	119	128	9	.265	.335	.341	.676	100	-5	360	4.29	-16	0-276,1-255,3-163/2-81,S-9	84	-3.6
• ENGLE, Dave	Ralph David Engle b: 11/30/1956, San Diego, CA BR/TR, 6'3", 216 lbs. Deb: 4/14/1981 C Career OF: 17-1-119																							
1981 Min-A	82	248	29	64	14	4	5	32	13	37	0	1	.258	.298	.407	.705	95	-3	27	3.73	0	0-76(0-0-76)/3-1,D-1	5	-0.6
1982 Min-A	58	186	20	42	7	2	4	16	10	22	0	0	.226	.269	.349	.618	67	-9	16	2.91	1	0-34(2-1-32),D-20	1	-1.0
1983 Min-A	120	374	46	114	22	4	8	43	28	39	2	1	.305	.355	.449	.804	115	8	57	5.47	0	C-73,D-29/0-4(0-0-4)	12	0.9
1984 Min-A★	109	391	56	104	20	1	4	38	26	22	0	1	.266	.312	.353	.665	80	-11	39	3.33	0	C-86,D-22	6	-0.8
1985 Min-A	70	172	28	44	8	2	7	25	21	28	2	2	.256	.337	.448	.784	106	1	26	5.19	1	D-38,C-17/0-3(3-0-0)	5	0.1
1986 Det-A	35	86	6	22	7	0	0	4	7	13	0	0	.256	.312	.337	.649	77	-3	9	3.66	-2	1-23/D-5,0-4(2-0-2),C-3	1	-0.6
1987 Mon-N	59	84	7	19	4	0	1	14	6	11	1	0	.226	.278	.310	.587	54	-6	6	2.38	0	0-11(9-0-2)/C-6,1-2,3-1	1	-0.6
1988 Mon-N	34	37	4	8	3	0	0	1	5	5	0	0	.216	.310	.297	.607	72	-1	3	2.81	0	/C-9,0-4(1-0-3),3-1	0	-0.2
1989 Mil-A	27	65	5	14	3	0	2	8	4	13	0	0	.215	.261	.354	.615	72	-3	6	3.04	-1	1-18/C-3,D-3	1	-0.5
Total 9	594	1643	201	431	88	13	31	181	120	190	5	5	.262	.314	.388	.702	90	-26	189	3.94	-2	C-197,0-136,D-118/1-43,3-3	32	-3.2
• ENGLISH, Charlie	Charles Dewie English b: 4/8/1910, Darlington, SC d: 6/25/1999, Pasadena, CA BR/TR, 5'9.5", 160 lbs. Deb: 7/23/1932																							
1932 Chi-A	24	63	7	20	3	1	1	8	3	7	0	0	.317	.348	.444	.793	111	1	10	5.93	-3	3-13/S-1	2	-0.2
1933 Chi-A	3	9	2	4	2	0	0	1	1	1	0	0	.444	.500	.667	1.167	216	2	3	15.93	0	/2-3	1	0.1
1936 NY-N	6	1	0	0	0	0	0	0	0	0	0	....	.000	.000	.000	.000	-101	-0	0	.00	-1	/2-1	0	-0.1
1937 Cin-N	17	63	1	15	3	1	0	4	0	2	0	....	.238	.238	.317	.556	52	-4	4	2.07	2	3-15/2-2	1	-0.2
Total 4	50	136	10	39	8	2	1	13	4	10	0	0	.287	.307	.397	.704	91	-2	17	4.40	-3	/3-28,2-6,S-1	4	-0.3
• ENGLISH, Gil	Gilbert Raymond English b: 7/2/1909, Glenola, NC d: 8/31/1996, Trinity, NC BR/TR, 5'11", 180 lbs. Deb: 9/20/1931																							
1931 NY-N	3	8	0	0	0	0	0	0	1	3	0	....	.000	.111	.000	.111	-69	-2	0	.09	0	/3-3	0	-0.2
1932 NY-N	59	204	22	46	7	5	2	19	5	20	0	....	.225	.244	.338	.582	56	-13	17	2.71	0	3-39,S-23	2	-1.1
1936 Det-A	1	1	0	0	0	0	0	0	0	1	0	0	.000	.000	.000	.000	-100	-0	0	.00	-0	/3-1	0	0.0
1937 Det-A	18	65	6	17	1	0	1	6	6	4	1	1	.262	.333	.323	.656	65	-4	7	3.87	-1	2-12/3-6	1	-0.4
Bos-N	79	269	25	78	5	2	2	37	23	27	3	....	.290	.348	.346	.694	98	-0	32	4.19	-3	3-71	8	-0.1
1938 Bos-N	53	165	17	41	6	0	2	21	15	16	1	....	.248	.315	.321	.636	84	-3	16	3.32	-1	3-43/0-3(3-0-0),2-2,S-2	4	-0.4
1944 Bro-N	27	79	4	12	3	0	1	7	6	7	0	....	.152	.212	.228	.440	24	-8	4	1.44	-2	S-13,3-11/2-2	1	-0.9
Total 6	240	791	74	194	22	7	8	90	56	78	5	1	.245	.298	.321	.619	72	-31	76	3.23	-7	3-174/S-38,2-16,0-3	16	-3.0
• ENGLISH, Woody	Elwood George English b: 3/2/1906, Fredonia, OH d: 9/26/1997, Newark, OH BR/TR, 5'10", 155 lbs. Deb: 4/26/1927																							
1927 Chi-N	87	334	46	97	14	4	1	28	16	26	1	....	.290	.325	.365	.690	84	-8	39	3.88	0	S-84/3-1	8	0.1
1928 Chi-N	116	475	68	142	22	4	2	34	30	28	4	....	.299	.343	.375	.718	89	-8	60	4.48	-1	*S-114/3-2	14	0.4
1929*Chi-N	144	608	131	168	29	3	1	52	68	50	13	....	.276	.352	.339	.691	72	-25	74	4.19	11	*S-144	17	0.2
1930 Chi-N	156	638	152	214	36	17	14	59	100	72	3	....	.335	.430	.511	.941	125	31	141	8.45	-6	3-83,S-78	28	3.4
1931 Chi-N	156	634	117	202	38	8	2	53	68	80	12	....	.319	.391	.413	.804	114	16	108	6.22	-2	*S-138,3-18	24	2.5
1932*Chi-N	127	522	70	142	23	7	3	47	55	73	5	....	.272	.344	.360	.704	90	-5	68	4.54	2	3-93,S-38	16	0.2

YEAR TM-L	G	AB	R	H	2B	3B	HR	RBI	BB	SO	SB	CS	AVG	OBP	SLG	OPS	OPS+	BR/A	RC	RC/G	FR	G/POS	WS	TPW
1933 Chi-N★	105	398	54	104	19	2	3	41	53	44	5	....	.261	.348	.342	.690	98	1	51	4.51	-13	*3-103/S-1	14	-0.8
1934 Chi-N	109	421	65	117	26	5	3	31	48	65	6	....	.278	.353	.385	.738	99	1	61	5.24	-12	S-56,3-46/2-7	15	-0.4
1935 Chi-N	34	84	11	17	2	0	2	8	20	4	1	....	.202	.368	.298	.666	81	-1	12	4.54	-3	3-16,S-12	3	-0.2
1936 Chi-N	64	182	33	45	9	0	0	20	40	28	1	....	.247	.394	.297	.691	86	-0	26	4.79	9	S-42,3-17/2-1	7	1.1
1937 Bro-N	129	378	45	90	16	2	1	42	65	55	4	....	.238	.350	.299	.649	76	-9	42	3.76	-11	*S-116,2-11	8	-1.2
1938 Bro-N	34	72	9	18	2	0	0	7	8	11	2	....	.250	.333	.278	.611	68	-3	7	3.40	-1	3-21/2-3,S-3	1	-0.3
Total 12	**1261**	**4746**	**801**	**1356**	**236**	**52**	**32**	**422**	**571**	**536**	**57**	**....**	**.286**	**.366**	**.378**	**.743**	**95**	**-11**	**690**	**5.12**	**-26**	**S-826,3-400/2-22**	**155**	**4.9**

• ENNIS, Del Delmer Ennis b: 6/8/1925, Philadelphia, PA d: 2/8/1996, Huntingdon Valley, PA BR/TR, 6', 195 lbs. Deb: 4/28/1946 Career OF: 1291-1-568

YEAR TM-L	G	AB	R	H	2B	3B	HR	RBI	BB	SO	SB	CS	AVG	OBP	SLG	OPS	OPS+	BR/A	RC	RC/G	FR	G/POS	WS	TPW
1946 Phi-N★	141	540	70	169	30	6	17	73	39	65	5	....	.313	.364	.485	.849	144	28	96	6.81	5	*O-138(138-0-1)	26	2.4
1947 Phi-N	139	541	71	149	25	6	12	81	37	51	9	....	.275	.325	.410	.736	98	-4	69	4.54	3	*O-135(135-0-2)	11	-1.1
1948 Phi-N	152	589	86	171	40	4	30	95	47	58	2	....	.290	.345	.525	.869	135	25	106	6.64	-2	*O-151(0-0-151)	24	1.8
1949 Phi-N	154	610	92	184	39	11	25	110	59	61	2	....	.302	.367	.525	.892	140	32	118	7.32	-3	*O-154(154-0-0)	27	1.7
1950*Phi-N	153	595	92	185	34	8	31	**126**	56	59	2	....	.311	.372	.551	.923	142	34	115	7.09	-2	*O-149(14-1-140)	26	2.6
1951 Phi-N★	144	532	76	142	20	5	15	73	68	42	4	2	.267	.352	.408	.760	105	5	77	5.10	-6	*O-135(26-0-116)	14	-0.6
1952 Phi-N	151	592	90	171	30	10	20	107	47	65	6	4	.289	.341	.475	.816	125	18	94	5.65	-5	*O-149(120-0-31)	21	0.4
1953 Phi-N	152	578	79	165	22	3	29	125	57	53	1	3	.285	.355	.484	.839	117	13	100	6.22	-6	*O-150(150-0-0)	19	-0.2
1954 Phi-N	145	556	73	145	23	2	25	119	50	60	2	1	.261	.324	.444	.768	98	-3	75	4.51	-7	*O-142(72-0-71)/1-1	11	-1.7
1955 Phi-N★	146	564	82	167	24	7	29	120	46	46	4	2	.296	.351	.518	.869	129	22	99	6.31	-6	*O-145(143-0-3)	21	0.7
1956 Phi-N	153	630	80	164	23	3	26	95	33	62	7	3	.260	.300	.430	.730	95	-6	77	4.25	-17	*O-153(153-0-0)	15	-3.3
1957 StL-N	136	490	61	140	24	3	24	105	37	50	1	3	.286	.337	.494	.831	117	10	73	5.13	-8	*O-127(74-0-53)	14	-0.4
1958 StL-N	106	329	22	86	18	1	3	47	15	35	0	1	.261	.296	.350	.645	67	-16	29	2.93	1	O-84(84-0-0)	3	-2.1
1959 Cin-N	5	12	1	4	0	0	0	1	2	2	0	0	.333	.429	.333	.762	103	0	2	6.16	0	/O-3(3-0-0)	0	0.0
Chi-A	26	96	10	21	6	0	2	7	4	10	0	0	.219	.250	.344	.594	62	-5	8	2.75	-1	O-25(25-0-0)	1	-0.8
Total 14	**1903**	**7254**	**985**	**2063**	**358**	**69**	**288**	**1284**	**597**	**719**	**45**	**19**	**.284**	**.341**	**.472**	**.813**	**117**	**152**	**1137**	**5.60**	**-55**	***O-1840/1-1**	**233**	**-0.7**

• ENNIS, Russ Russell Elwood "Hack" Ennis b: 3/10/1897, Superior, WI d: 1/21/1949, Superior, WI BR/TR, 5'11.5", 160 lbs. Deb: 9/19/1926

YEAR TM-L	G	AB	R	H	2B	3B	HR	RBI	BB	SO	SB	CS	AVG	OBP	SLG	OPS	OPS+	BR/A	RC	RC/G	FR	G/POS	WS	TPW
1926 Was-A	1	0	0	0	0	0	0	0	0	0	0	0	....	....	....	....	-102	0	0	....	0	/C-1	0	0.0

• ENRIGHT, George George Albert Enright b: 5/9/1954, New Britain, CT BR/TR, 5'11", 175 lbs. Deb: 8/8/1976

YEAR TM-L	G	AB	R	H	2B	3B	HR	RBI	BB	SO	SB	CS	AVG	OBP	SLG	OPS	OPS+	BR/A	RC	RC/G	FR	G/POS	WS	TPW
1976 Chi-A	2	1	0	0	0	0	0	0	0	0	0	0	.000	.000	.000	.000	-99	-0	0	.00	0	/C-2	0	0.0

• ENS, Jewel Jewel Winklemeyer Ens b: 8/24/1889, St. Louis, MO d: 1/17/1950, Syracuse, NY BR/TR, 5'10.5", 165 lbs. Deb: 4/29/1922 M/C

YEAR TM-L	G	AB	R	H	2B	3B	HR	RBI	BB	SO	SB	CS	AVG	OBP	SLG	OPS	OPS+	BR/A	RC	RC/G	FR	G/POS	WS	TPW
1922 Pit-N	47	142	18	42	7	3	0	17	7	9	3	0	.296	.338	.387	.725	86	-2	19	4.76	-9	2-29/3-3,1-2,S-1	3	-1.0
1923 Pit-N	12	29	3	8	1	1	0	5	0	3	2	0	.276	.276	.379	.655	70	-1	3	4.02	0	/1-4,3-3	0	-0.1
1924 Pit-N	5	10	2	3	0	0	0	0	0	3	0	0	.300	.300	.300	.600	60	-1	1	3.04	0	/1-5	0	-0.1
1925 Pit-N	3	5	2	1	0	0	1	2	0	1	0	0	.200	.200	.800	1.000	133	0	1	3.82	0	/1-3	0	0.0
Total 4	**67**	**186**	**25**	**54**	**8**	**4**	**1**	**24**	**7**	**16**	**5**	**0**	**.290**	**.323**	**.392**	**.716**	**83**	**-3**	**24**	**4.52**	**-10**	**/2-29,1-14,3-6,S-1**	**3**	**-1.2**

• ENS, Mutz Anton Ens b: 11/8/1884, St. Louis, MO d: 6/28/1950, St. Louis, MO BL/TL, 6'1", 180 lbs. Deb: 9/2/1912

YEAR TM-L	G	AB	R	H	2B	3B	HR	RBI	BB	SO	SB	CS	AVG	OBP	SLG	OPS	OPS+	BR/A	RC	RC/G	FR	G/POS	WS	TPW
1912 Chi-A	3	6	0	0	0	0	0	0	0	....	0	....	.000	.000	.000	.000	-103	-2	0	.00	-1	/1-3	0	-0.2

• ENSBERG, Morgan Morgan Paul Ensberg b: 8/26/1975, Redondo Beach, CA BR/TR, 6'2", 210 lbs. Deb: 9/20/2000

YEAR TM-L	G	AB	R	H	2B	3B	HR	RBI	BB	SO	SB	CS	AVG	OBP	SLG	OPS	OPS+	BR/A	RC	RC/G	FR	G/POS	WS	TPW
2000 Hou-N	4	7	0	2	0	0	0	0	0	1	0	0	.286	.286	.286	.571	43	-1	1	3.09	-1	/3-1	0	-0.1
2002 Hou-N	49	132	14	32	7	2	3	19	18	25	2	0	.242	.346	.394	.740	90	-1	17	4.30	1	3-43	2	0.0
2003 Hou-N	127	385	69	112	15	1	25	60	48	60	7	2	.291	.378	.530	.908	128	17	78	7.31	5	*3-111/D-1	15	2.3
Total 3	**180**	**524**	**83**	**146**	**22**	**3**	**28**	**79**	**66**	**86**	**9**	**2**	**.279**	**.369**	**.492**	**.861**	**117**	**15**	**95**	**6.44**	**5**	**3-155/D-1**	**17**	**2.2**

• ENWRIGHT, Charlie Charles Massey Enwright b: 10/6/1887, Sacramento, CA d: 1/19/1917, Sacramento, CA BL/TR, 5'10" Deb: 4/19/1909

YEAR TM-L	G	AB	R	H	2B	3B	HR	RBI	BB	SO	SB	CS	AVG	OBP	SLG	OPS	OPS+	BR/A	RC	RC/G	FR	G/POS	WS	TPW
1909 StL-N	3	7	1	1	0	0	0	1	2	....	0	....	.143	.333	.143	.476	51	-0	0	1.41	-3	/S-2	0	-0.4

• ENZENROTH, Jack Clarence Herman Enzenroth b: 11/4/1885, Mineral Point, WI d: 2/21/1944, Detroit, MI BR/TR, 5'10", 160 lbs. Deb: 5/1/1914

YEAR TM-L	G	AB	R	H	2B	3B	HR	RBI	BB	SO	SB	CS	AVG	OBP	SLG	OPS	OPS+	BR/A	RC	RC/G	FR	G/POS	WS	TPW
1914 StL-A	3	6	0	1	0	0	0	0	2	3	0	1	.167	.444	.167	.611	88	-0	0	1.47	0	/C-3	0	0.0
KC-F	26	67	7	12	4	1	0	5	5	19	0	....	.179	.236	.269	.505	46	-5	4	1.82	0	C-24	0	-0.4
1915 KC-F	14	19	3	3	0	0	0	3	6	0	0	....	.158	.360	.158	.518	56	-1	1	1.68	1	/C-8	1	0.1
Total 2	**43**	**92**	**10**	**16**	**4**	**1**	**0**	**8**	**13**	**22**	**0**	**1**	**.174**	**.283**	**.239**	**.522**	**52**	**-6**	**5**	**1.76**	**0**	**/C-35**	**1**	**-0.3**

• EPPARD, Jim James Gerhard Eppard b: 4/27/1960, South Bend, IN BL/TL, 6'2", 180 lbs. Deb: 9/8/1987 Career OF: 17-0-1

YEAR TM-L	G	AB	R	H	2B	3B	HR	RBI	BB	SO	SB	CS	AVG	OBP	SLG	OPS	OPS+	BR/A	RC	RC/G	FR	G/POS	WS	TPW
1987 Cal-A	8	9	2	3	0	0	0	0	2	0	0	0	.333	.455	.333	.788	118	0	1	4.94	0	/O-1	0	0.0
1988 Cal-A	56	113	7	32	3	1	0	14	11	15	0	0	.283	.347	.327	.674	92	-1	13	3.93	0	O-17(17-0-0),D-10/1-6	2	-0.2
1989 Cal-A	12	12	0	3	0	0	0	2	1	4	0	0	.250	.308	.250	.558	60	-1	1	3.01	0	/1-4	0	-0.1
1990 Tor-A	6	5	0	1	0	0	0	0	0	2	0	0	.200	.333	.200	.533	50	-0	0	2.84	0	....	0	0.0
Total 4	**82**	**139**	**9**	**39**	**3**	**1**	**0**	**16**	**14**	**21**	**0**	**0**	**.281**	**.351**	**.317**	**.667**	**90**	**-1**	**15**	**3.88**	**0**	**/O-18,1-10,D-10**	**2**	**-0.3**

• EPPS, Aubrey Aubrey Lee "Yo-Yo" Epps b: 3/3/1912, Memphis, TN d: 11/13/1984, Ackerman, MS BR/TR, 5'10", 170 lbs. Deb: 9/29/1935

YEAR TM-L	G	AB	R	H	2B	3B	HR	RBI	BB	SO	SB	CS	AVG	OBP	SLG	OPS	OPS+	BR/A	RC	RC/G	FR	G/POS	WS	TPW
1935 Pit-N	1	4	1	3	0	1	0	3	0	0	0	....	.750	.750	1.250	2.000	414	2	4	103.78	0	/C-1	1	0.1

• EPPS, Hal Harold Franklin Epps b: 3/26/1914, Athens, GA BL/TL, 6', 175 lbs. Deb: 9/9/1938 Career OF: 0-83-16

YEAR TM-L	G	AB	R	H	2B	3B	HR	RBI	BB	SO	SB	CS	AVG	OBP	SLG	OPS	OPS+	BR/A	RC	RC/G	FR	G/POS	WS	TPW
1938 StL-N	17	50	8	15	0	0	1	3	2	4	2	....	.300	.327	.360	.687	84	-1	6	4.69	-1	O-10(0-10-0)	1	-0.2
1940 StL-N	11	15	6	3	0	0	0	1	0	3	0	....	.200	.200	.200	.400	10	-2	1	1.35	0	/O-3(0-3-0)	0	-0.2
1943 StL-A	8	35	2	10	4	0	0	1	3	4	1	1	.286	.342	.400	.742	114	0	4	3.97	-1	/O-8(0-8-0)	1	-0.1
1944 StL-A	22	62	15	11	1	1	0	3	14	14	0	1	.177	.338	.226	.563	59	-3	6	2.90	1	O-18(0-18-0)	1	-0.3
Phi-A	67	229	27	60	8	8	0	13	18	18	2	1	.262	.316	.367	.683	96	-2	28	4.21	-4	O-60(0-44-16)	6	-0.8
Yr.	89	291	42	71	9	9	0	16	32	32	2	2	.244	.321	.337	.658	87	-4	33	3.91	-3	O-78(0-62-16)	7	-1.0
Total 4	**125**	**391**	**58**	**99**	**13**	**9**	**1**	**21**	**37**	**43**	**5**	**3**	**.253**	**.319**	**.340**	**.660**	**87**	**-7**	**44**	**3.90**	**-6**	**/O-99**	**9**	**-1.6**

• EPSTEIN, Mike Michael Peter "Superjew" Epstein b: 4/4/1943, Bronx, NY BL/TL, 6'3.5", 230 lbs. Deb: 9/16/1966

YEAR TM-L	G	AB	R	H	2B	3B	HR	RBI	BB	SO	SB	CS	AVG	OBP	SLG	OPS	OPS+	BR/A	RC	RC/G	FR	G/POS	WS	TPW
1966 Bal-A	6	11	1	2	0	1	0	3	1	3	0	0	.182	.250	.364	.614	75	-0	1	3.20	0	/1-4	0	-0.1
1967 Bal-A	9	13	0	2	0	0	0	0	3	5	0	0	.154	.313	.154	.466	42	-1	1	1.56	0	/1-3	0	-0.2
Was-A	96	284	32	65	7	4	9	29	38	74	1	4	.229	.332	.377	.709	113	4	37	4.36	-3	1-80	10	-0.4
Yr.	105	297	32	67	7	4	9	29	41	79	1	4	.226	.331	.367	.698	110	4	37	4.22	-4	1-83	10	-0.5
1968 Was-A	123	385	40	90	8	2	13	33	48	91	1	1	.234	.339	.366	.705	117	10	48	4.17	-4	*1-110	14	0.0
1969 Was-A	131	403	73	112	18	1	30	85	85	99	2	5	.278	.416	.551	.967	177	44	96	8.43	-5	*1-118	24	3.2
1970 Was-A	140	430	55	110	15	3	20	56	73	117	2	3	.256	.375	.444	.819	131	20	76	6.07	-10	*1-122	16	0.1
1971 Was-A	24	85	6	21	1	1	1	9	12	31	1	0	.247	.366	.318	.684	101	1	12	4.86	-2	1-24	3	-0.3
*Oak-A	104	329	43	77	13	0	18	51	62	71	0	3	.234	.368	.438	.806	130	14	57	5.89	-3	1-96	17	0.4
Yr.	128	414	49	98	14	1	19	60	74	102	1	3	.237	.368	.413	.781	124	15	68	5.69	-6	*1-120	20	0.1
1972*Oak-A	138	455	63	123	18	2	26	70	68	68	0	1	.270	.378	.490	.868	165	38	88	6.90	-1	*1-137	27	3.1
1973 Tex-A	27	85	9	16	3	0	1	6	14	19	0	0	.188	.324	.259	.582	69	-3	8	3.03	-1	1-25	1	-0.6
Cal-A	91	312	30	67	8	2	8	32	34	54	0	0	.215	.302	.330	.632	84	-6	31	3.29	1	1-86	6	-1.2
Yr.	118	397	39	83	11	2	9	38	48	73	0	0	.209	.307	.315	.622	81	-9	39	3.23	0	*1-111	7	-1.7
1974 Cal-A	18	62	10	10	2	0	4	6	10	13	0	0	.161	.288	.387	.675	98	-0	8	4.01	1	1-18	2	0.0
Total 9	**907**	**2854**	**362**	**695**	**93**	**16**	**130**	**380**	**448**	**645**	**7**	**17**	**.244**	**.360**	**.424**	**.784**	**131**	**122**	**461**	**5.53**	**-27**	**1-823**	**120**	**4.1**

• ERAUTT, Joe Joseph Michael "Stubby" Erautt b: 9/1/1921, Vibank, Canada d: 10/6/1976, Portland, OR BR/TR, 5'9", 175 lbs. Deb: 5/9/1950

YEAR TM-L	G	AB	R	H	2B	3B	HR	RBI	BB	SO	SB	CS	AVG	OBP	SLG	OPS	OPS+	BR/A	RC	RC/G	FR	G/POS	WS	TPW
1950 Chi-A	16	18	0	4	0	0	0	1	1	3	0	0	.222	.263	.222	.485	26	-2	1	2.21	0	/C-5	0	-0.1
1951 Chi-A	16	25	3	4	1	0	0	0	3	2	0	0	.160	.276	.200	.476	31	-2	1	1.20	0	C-12	1	-0.1
Total 2	**32**	**43**	**3**	**8**	**1**	**0**	**0**	**1**	**4**	**5**	**0**	**0**	**.186**	**.271**	**.209**	**.480**	**29**	**-4**	**2**	**1.57**	**1**	**/C-17**	**1**	**-0.3**

• ERICKSON, Hank Henry Nels "Popeye" Erickson b: 11/11/1907, Chicago, IL d: 12/13/1964, Louisville, KY BR/TR, 6'1", 185 lbs. Deb: 4/17/1935

YEAR TM-L	G	AB	R	H	2B	3B	HR	RBI	BB	SO	SB	CS	AVG	OBP	SLG	OPS	OPS+	BR/A	RC	RC/G	FR	G/POS	WS	TPW
1935 Cin-N	37	88	9	23	3	2	1	4	6	4	0	....	.261	.323	.375	.698	90	-1	11	4.54	2	C-25	3	0.2

YEAR TM-L	G	AB	R	H	2B	3B	HR	RBI	BB	SO	SB	CS	AVG	OBP	SLG	OPS	OPS+	BR/A	RC	RC/G	FR	G/POS	WS	TPW
• ERMER, Cal	Calvin Coolidge Ermer b: 11/10/1923, Baltimore, MD BR/TR, 6'.5", 175 lbs. Deb: 9/26/1947 M/C																							
1947 Was-A	1	3	0	0	0	0	0	0	0	0	0	0	.000	.000	.000	.000	-103	-1	0	.00	0	/2-1	0	-0.1
• ERNAGA, Frank	Frank John Ernaga b: 8/22/1930, Susanville, CA BR/TR, 6'1", 195 lbs. Deb: 5/24/1957																							
1957 Chi-N	20	35	9	11	3	2	2	7	9	14	0	0	.314	.455	.686	1.140	204	6	12	13.47	0	O-10(3-0-7)	3	0.5
1958 Chi-N	9	8	0	1	0	0	0	0	0	2	0	0	.125	.125	.125	.250	-34	-1	0	.48	0	....	0	-0.1
Total 2	**29**	**43**	**9**	**12**	**3**	**2**	**2**	**7**	**9**	**16**	**0**	**0**	**.279**	**.404**	**.581**	**.985**	**167**	**4**	**12**	**10.54**	**0**	**/O-10**	**3**	**0.3**
• ERSTAD, Darin	Darin Charles Erstad b: 6/4/1974, Jamestown, ND BL/TL, 6'2", 195 lbs. Deb: 6/14/1996 Career OF: 260-427-1																							
1996 Cal-A	57	208	34	59	5	1	4	20	17	29	3	3	.284	.338	.375	.713	82	-7	26	4.45	1	O-48(11-36-1)	3	-0.5
1997 Ana-A	139	539	99	161	34	4	16	77	51	86	23	8	.299	.364	.466	.829	113	12	95	6.35	-6	*1-126/D-9,O-1	19	-0.5
1998 Ana-A★	133	537	84	159	39	3	19	82	43	77	20	6	.296	.355	.486	.841	115	13	96	6.67	0	O-72(70-3-0),1-70/D-2	21	0.4
1999 Ana-A	142	585	84	148	22	5	13	53	47	101	13	7	.253	.310	.374	.684	74	-24	65	3.78	12	1-78,O-69(67-2-0)/D-2	9	-2.1
2000 Ana-A★	157	676	121	**240**	39	6	25	100	64	82	28	8	.355	.412	.541	.953	135	39	154	9.08	11	*O-136(112-30-0),D-20/1-4	30	4.0
2001 Ana-A	157	631	89	163	35	1	9	63	62	113	24	10	.258	.334	.360	.694	81	-16	80	4.35	8	*O-146(0-146-0),1-12/D-4	14	-0.7
2002*Ana-A	150	625	99	177	28	4	10	73	27	67	23	3	.283	.315	.389	.704	86	-10	78	4.48	19	*O-143(0-143-0)/1-5,D-4	17	0.9
2003 Ana-A	67	258	35	65	7	1	4	17	18	40	9	1	.252	.311	.333	.644	73	-8	27	3.54	2	O-66(0-66-0)	3	-0.6
Total 8	**1002**	**4059**	**645**	**1172**	**209**	**25**	**100**	**485**	**329**	**595**	**143**	**46**	**.289**	**.346**	**.426**	**.773**	**98**	**-2**	**621**	**5.51**	**46**	**O-681,1-295/D-41**	**116**	**0.9**
• ERWIN, Tex	Ross Emil Erwin b: 12/22/1885, Forney, TX d: 4/5/1953, Rochester, NY BL/TR, 6', 185 lbs. Deb: 8/26/1907																							
1907 Det-A	4	5	0	1	0	0	0	1	1	....	0	....	.200	.333	.200	.533	68	-0	0	2.26	0	/C-4	0	0.0
1910 Bro-N	81	202	15	38	3	1	1	10	24	12	3	....	.188	.278	.228	.505	49	-13	14	2.14	7	C-68	4	0.1
1911 Bro-N	91	218	30	59	13	2	7	34	31	23	5	....	.271	.367	.445	.811	132	9	37	5.88	4	C-74	11	1.8
1912 Bro-N	59	133	14	28	3	0	2	14	18	16	1	....	.211	.305	.278	.583	62	-7	12	2.74	-1	C-41	2	-0.4
1913 Bro-N	20	31	6	8	1	0	0	3	4	5	0	....	.258	.343	.290	.633	80	-1	3	3.31	-1	C-13	1	-0.1
1914 Bro-N	9	11	0	5	0	0	0	1	2	1	1	....	.455	.538	.455	.993	192	1	3	13.22	0	/C-4	1	0.2
Cin-N	12	35	5	11	3	0	1	7	2	3	0	....	.314	.351	.486	.837	144	2	6	6.12	-2	C-12	2	0.1
Yr.	21	46	5	16	3	0	1	8	4	4	1	....	.348	.400	.478	.878	156	3	9	7.54	-1	C-16	3	0.3
Total 6	**276**	**635**	**70**	**150**	**23**	**3**	**11**	**70**	**82**	**60**	**10**	**....**	**.236**	**.326**	**.334**	**.660**	**90**	**-7**	**75**	**3.87**	**8**	**C-216**	**21**	**1.6**
• ESASKY, Nick	Nicholas Andrew Esasky b: 2/24/1960, Hialeah, FL BR/TR, 6'3", 205 lbs. Deb: 6/19/1983 Career OF: 98-0-0																							
1983 Cin-N	85	302	41	80	10	5	12	46	27	99	6	2	.265	.331	.450	.782	111	4	46	5.30	-5	3-84	11	-0.2
1984 Cin-N	113	322	30	62	10	5	10	45	52	103	1	2	.193	.305	.348	.653	79	-9	36	3.51	-3	3-82,1-25	6	-1.5
1985 Cin-N	125	413	61	108	21	0	21	66	41	102	3	4	.262	.334	.465	.799	115	6	63	5.22	1	3-62,O-54(54-0-0),1-12	15	0.4
1986 Cin-N	102	330	35	76	17	2	12	41	47	97	0	2	.230	.328	.403	.731	96	-2	44	4.42	-4	1-70,O-42(42-0-0)/3-1	8	-1.2
1987 Cin-N	100	346	48	94	19	2	22	59	29	76	0	0	.272	.328	.529	.857	117	7	57	5.83	-9	1-93/3-1,O-1	11	-0.8
1988 Cin-N	122	391	40	95	17	2	15	62	48	104	7	2	.243	.332	.412	.744	108	5	56	4.85	-9	*1-116	10	-1.3
1989 Bos-A	154	564	79	156	26	5	30	108	66	117	1	2	.277	.355	.500	.855	130	22	100	6.40	5	*1-153/O-1	24	1.6
1990 Atl-N	9	35	2	6	0	0	0	0	4	14	0	0	.171	.256	.171	.428	19	-4	2	1.68	-2	/1-9	0	-0.7
Total 8	**810**	**2703**	**336**	**677**	**120**	**21**	**122**	**427**	**314**	**712**	**18**	**14**	**.250**	**.332**	**.446**	**.778**	**109**	**28**	**403**	**5.11**	**-27**	**1-478,3-230/O-98**	**85**	**-3.6**
• ESCALERA, Nino	Saturnino Cuadrado Escalera b: 12/1/1929, Santurce, Puerto Rico BL/TR, 5'10", 165 lbs. Deb: 4/17/1954																							
1954 Cin-N	73	69	15	11	1	1	0	3	7	11	1	0	.159	.237	.203	.440	15	-8	4	1.68	0	O-14(1-3-10)/1-8,S-1	0	-0.9
• ESCALONA, Felix	Felix Eduardo Escalona b: 3/12/1979, Puerto Cabello, Venezuela BR/TR, 6', 196 lbs. Deb: 4/4/2002																							
2002 TB-A	59	157	17	34	8	2	0	9	3	44	7	2	.217	.263	.293	.556	49	-11	13	2.62	1	S-26,2-25/3-4,D-1	1	-0.7
2003 TB-A	10	27	2	5	2	0	0	2	2	6	1	0	.185	.241	.259	.501	33	-2	2	2.38	2	/S-8,2-1,3-1	1	0.1
Total 2	**69**	**184**	**19**	**39**	**10**	**2**	**0**	**11**	**5**	**50**	**8**	**2**	**.212**	**.260**	**.288**	**.548**	**46**	**-14**	**15**	**2.58**	**4**	**/S-34,2-26,3-5,D-1**	**2**	**-0.6**
• ESCHEN, Jim	James Godrich Eschen b: 8/21/1891, Brooklyn, NY d: 9/27/1960, Sloatsburg, NY BR/TR, 5'10.5", 160 lbs. Deb: 7/10/1915																							
1915 Cle-A	15	42	11	10	1	0	0	2	5	9	0	1	.238	.319	.262	.581	73	-2	4	2.79	1	O-10(0-10-0)	1	-0.2
• ESCHEN, Larry	Lawrence Edward Eschen b: 9/22/1920, Suffern, NY BR/TR, 6', 180 lbs. Deb: 6/16/1942																							
1942 Phi-A	12	11	0	0	0	0	0	0	4	6	0	0	.000	.267	.000	.267	-22	-2	0	.68	-3	/S-7,2-1	0	-0.4
• ESCOBAR, Alex	Alexander Jose Escobar b: 9/6/1978, Valencia, Venezuela BR/TR, 6'1", 180 lbs. Deb: 5/8/2001 Career OF: 0-9-32																							
2001 NY-N	18	50	3	10	1	0	3	8	3	19	1	0	.200	.245	.400	.645	66	-3	5	3.18	1	O-15(0-9-7)	1	-0.2
2003 Cle-A	28	99	16	27	2	0	5	14	7	33	1	0	.273	.327	.444	.772	104	1	15	5.62	4	O-25(0-0-25)	1	0.3
Total 2	**46**	**149**	**19**	**37**	**3**	**0**	**8**	**22**	**10**	**52**	**2**	**0**	**.248**	**.300**	**.430**	**.730**	**92**	**-2**	**20**	**4.74**	**5**	**/O-40**	**2**	**0.1**
• ESCOBAR, Angel	Angel Rubenque (Rivas) Escobar b: 5/12/1965, La Sabana, Venezuela BB/TR, 6', 160 lbs. Deb: 5/17/1988																							
1988 SF-N	3	3	1	1	0	0	0	0	0	0	0	0	.333	.333	.333	.667	96	-0	0	4.50	0	/3-1,S-1	0	0.0
• ESCOBAR, Jose	Jose Elias (Sanchez) Escobar b: 10/30/1960, Las Flores, Venezuela BR/TR, 5'10", 140 lbs. Deb: 4/13/1991																							
1991 Cle-A	10	15	0	3	0	0	0	1	1	4	0	0	.200	.250	.200	.450	26	-1	1	1.85	-1	/S-5,2-4,3-1	0	-0.2
• ESMOND, Jimmy	James Joseph Esmond b: 8/8/1889, Albany, NY d: 6/26/1948, Troy, NY BR/TR, 5'11", 167 lbs. Deb: 4/20/1911																							
1911 Cin-N	73	198	27	54	4	6	1	11	17	30	7	....	.273	.330	.369	.699	99	-1	26	4.59	-4	S-44,3-14/2-2	6	-0.2
1912 Cin-N	82	231	24	45	5	3	1	40	20	31	11	....	.195	.259	.255	.514	42	-19	19	2.39	-6	S-74	2	-2.0
1914 Ind-F	151	542	74	160	23	**15**	2	49	40	48	25	....	.295	.344	.404	.748	101	-0	81	5.11	-10	*S-151	18	0.1
1915 New-F	155	569	79	147	20	10	5	62	59	54	18	....	.258	.329	.355	.684	107	5	73	4.14	6	*S-155	22	2.4
Total 4	**461**	**1540**	**204**	**406**	**52**	**34**	**9**	**162**	**136**	**163**	**61**	**....**	**.264**	**.324**	**.359**	**.683**	**94**	**-14**	**198**	**4.24**	**-14**	**S-424/3-14,2-2**	**48**	**0.4**
• ESPINO, Juan	Juan (Reyes) Espino b: 3/16/1956, Bonao, Dominican Republic BR/TR, 6'1", 190 lbs. Deb: 6/25/1982																							
1982 NY-A	3	2	0	0	0	0	0	0	0	1	0	0	.000	.000	.000	.000	-102	-1	0	.00	-1	/C-3	0	-0.1
1983 NY-A	10	23	1	6	0	0	1	3	1	5	0	0	.261	.292	.391	.683	89	-0	3	4.11	-1	C-10	1	-0.1
1985 NY-A	9	11	0	4	0	0	0	0	0	0	0	0	.364	.364	.364	.727	102	0	1	5.61	1	/C-9	0	0.1
1986 NY-A	27	37	1	6	2	0	0	5	2	9	0	0	.162	.205	.216	.421	15	-4	2	1.53	0	C-27	0	-0.4
Total 4	**49**	**73**	**2**	**16**	**2**	**0**	**1**	**8**	**3**	**15**	**0**	**0**	**.219**	**.250**	**.288**	**.538**	**48**	**-5**	**6**	**2.75**	**-1**	**/C-49**	**1**	**-0.5**
• ESPINOZA, Alvaro	Alvaro Alberto Espinoza b: 2/19/1962, Valencia, Venezuela BR/TR, 6', 181 lbs. Deb: 9/14/1984 C																							
1984 Min-A	1	0	0	0	0	0	0	0	0	0	0	0	....	....	....	....	-96	0	0	....	-1	/S-1	0	-0.1
1985 Min-A	32	57	5	15	2	0	0	9	1	9	0	1	.263	.288	.298	.586	58	-4	4	2.42	0	S-31	1	-0.2
1986 Min-A	37	42	4	9	1	0	0	1	1	10	0	1	.214	.233	.238	.471	28	-5	2	1.70	0	2-19,S-18	1	-0.4
1988 NY-A	3	3	0	0	0	0	0	0	0	0	0	0	.000	.000	.000	.000	-101	-1	0	.00	0	/2-2,S-1	0	-0.1
1989 NY-A	146	503	51	142	23	1	0	41	14	60	3	3	.282	.303	.332	.635	80	-16	48	3.19	17	*S-146	12	1.3
1990 NY-A	150	438	31	98	12	2	2	20	16	54	1	2	.224	.259	.274	.533	49	-31	29	2.15	24	*S-150	7	0.4
1991 NY-A	148	480	51	123	23	2	5	33	16	57	4	1	.256	.283	.344	.627	72	-19	45	3.23	16	*S-147/3-2,P-1	11	0.8
1993 Cle-A	129	263	34	73	15	0	4	27	8	36	2	2	.278	.301	.380	.682	82	-8	28	3.62	-3	3-99,S-35/2-2	5	-0.8
1994 Cle-A	90	231	27	55	13	0	1	19	6	33	1	3	.238	.261	.307	.568	46	-20	16	2.29	1	3-37,S-36,2-20/1-3	3	-1.4
1995*Cle-A	66	143	15	36	4	0	2	17	2	16	0	2	.252	.267	.322	.589	52	-12	11	2.58	-2	2-22,3-22,S-19/D-3,1-2	2	-1.1
1996 Cle-A	59	112	12	25	4	2	4	11	6	18	1	1	.223	.281	.402	.683	70	-6	12	3.26	0	3-20,1-18,S-16/2-5,D-1	1	-0.5
NY-N	48	134	19	41	7	2	4	16	4	19	0	2	.306	.326	.478	.804	114	1	18	4.75	-1	3-38/S-7,2-2,1-1	3	0.1
1997 Sea-A	33	72	3	13	1	0	0	7	2	12	1	1	.181	.213	.194	.408	7	-10	3	1.17	-1	S-17,2-14/3-1	1	-0.9
Total 12	**942**	**2478**	**252**	**630**	**105**	**9**	**22**	**201**	**76**	**324**	**13**	**19**	**.254**	**.281**	**.331**	**.611**	**66**	**-130**	**217**	**2.90**	**51**	**S-624,3-219/2-86,1-24,D-4,P**	**47**	**-2.9**
• ESPOSITO, Sammy	Samuel Esposito b: 12/15/1931, Chicago, IL BR/TR, 5'9", 165 lbs. Deb: 9/28/1952 Career OF: 1-1-0																							
1952 Chi-A	1	4	0	1	0	0	0	0	0	2	0	1	.250	.250	.250	.500	39	-1	0	.00	-1	/S-1	0	-0.2
1955 Chi-A	3	4	3	0	0	0	0	0	1	0	0	0	.000	.200	.000	.200	-41	-1	0	.35	-1	/3-2	0	-0.1
1956 Chi-A	81	184	30	42	8	2	3	25	41	19	1	2	.228	.374	.342	.717	89	-2	26	4.61	4	3-61,S-19/2-3	6	0.2
1957 Chi-A	94	176	26	36	3	0	2	15	38	27	5	1	.205	.346	.256	.601	66	-5	19	3.23	4	3-53,S-22/2-4,O-1	5	0.1

YEAR TM-L	G	AB	R	H	2B	3B	HR	RBI	BB	SO	SB	CS	AVG	OBP	SLG	OPS	OPS+	BR/A	RC	RC/G	FR	G/POS	WS	TPW
1958 Chi-A	98	81	16	20	3	0	0	3	12	6	1	1	.247	.358	.284	.642	81	-2	9	3.83	-6	3-63,S-22/2-2,O-1	3	-0.7
1959*Chi-A	69	66	12	11	1	0	1	5	11	16	0	1	.167	.286	.227	.513	43	-5	5	2.15	-2	3-45,S-14/2-2	1	-0.7
1960 Chi-A	57	77	14	14	5	0	1	11	10	20	0	0	.182	.276	.286	.562	53	-5	6	2.39	-5	3-37,S-11/2-5	1	-1.0
1961 Chi-A	63	94	12	16	5	0	1	8	12	21	0	0	.170	.264	.255	.519	40	-8	7	2.11	-1	3-28,S-20,2-11	1	-0.7
1962 Chi-A	75	81	14	19	1	0	0	4	17	13	0	1	.235	.367	.247	.614	69	-3	8	3.20	-6	3-41,S-20/2-7	2	-0.8
1963 Chi-A	1	0	0	0	0	0	0	0	0	0	0	0	....	....	....	....	-102	0	0	....	0	....	0	0.0
KC-A	18	25	3	5	1	0	0	2	3	3	0	0	.200	.286	.240	.526	47	-2	2	1.77	-2	/2-7,S-4,3-3	0	-0.4
Yr.	19	25	3	5	1	0	0	2	3	3	0	0	.200	.286	.240	.526	47	-2	2	1.77	-2	/2-7,S-4,3-3	0	-0.4
Total 10	560	792	130	164	27	2	8	73	145	127	7	7	.207	.333	.277	.609	66	-33	81	3.20	-16	3-333,S-133/2-41,O-2	19	-4.2

• ESPY, Cecil Cecil Edward Espy b: 1/20/1963, San Diego, CA BB/TR, 6'3", 195 lbs. Deb: 9/2/1983 Career OF: 95-263-89

YEAR TM-L	G	AB	R	H	2B	3B	HR	RBI	BB	SO	SB	CS	AVG	OBP	SLG	OPS	OPS+	BR/A	RC	RC/G	FR	G/POS	WS	TPW
1983 LA-N	20	11	4	3	1	0	0	1	1	2	0	0	.273	.333	.364	.697	93	-0	1	4.79	0	O-15(0-15-0)	0	-0.1
1987 Tex-A	14	8	1	0	0	0	0	0	1	3	2	0	.000	.111	.000	.111	-67	-2	0	.00	1	/O-8(5-0-3)	0	-0.1
1988 Tex-A	123	347	46	86	17	6	2	39	20	83	33	10	.248	.291	.349	.639	76	-9	37	3.58	0	O-98(52-46-8),D-12/S-3,C-2,1,2	11	-1.2
1989 Tex-A	142	475	65	122	12	7	3	31	38	99	45	20	.257	.315	.331	.645	81	-11	52	3.64	4	*O-133(3-131-1)/D-3	10	-0.9
1990 Tex-A	52	71	10	9	0	0	0	1	10	20	11	5	.127	.235	.127	.361	4	-9	3	1.11	0	O-39(4-28-9)/D-4,2-1	1	-1.0
1991*Pit-N	43	82	7	20	4	0	1	11	5	17	4	0	.244	.287	.329	.617	74	-2	9	3.61	1	O-35(2-25-11)	2	-0.2
1992*Pit-N	112	194	21	50	7	3	1	20	15	40	6	3	.258	.311	.340	.651	85	-4	21	3.65	-2	O-82(11-18-56)	4	-0.8
1993 Cin-N	40	60	6	14	2	0	0	5	14	13	2	2	.233	.378	.267	.645	76	-2	7	3.56	1	O-18(18-0-1)	1	-0.2
Total 8	546	1248	160	304	43	16	7	108	104	277	103	40	.244	.303	.321	.624	74	-38	130	3.43	3	O-428/D-19,S-3,2-2,C-2,1-1	29	-4.4

• ESSEGIAN, Chuck Charles Abraham Essegian b: 8/9/1931, Boston, MA BR/TR, 5'11", 202 lbs. Deb: 4/15/1958 Career OF: 212-22-28

YEAR TM-L	G	AB	R	H	2B	3B	HR	RBI	BB	SO	SB	CS	AVG	OBP	SLG	OPS	OPS+	BR/A	RC	RC/G	FR	G/POS	WS	TPW
1958 Phi-N	39	114	15	28	5	2	5	16	12	34	0	0	.246	.317	.456	.774	103	0	17	5.00	-4	O-30(28-2-0)	3	-0.6
1959 StL-N	17	39	2	7	2	1	0	5	1	13	0	0	.179	.200	.282	.482	25	-4	1	1.09	1	/O-9(9-0-0)	0	-0.4
*LA-N	24	46	6	14	6	0	1	5	4	11	0	0	.304	.360	.500	.860	117	1	8	6.62	0	O-10(4-0-6)	2	0.0
Yr.	41	85	8	21	8	1	1	10	5	24	0	0	.247	.289	.400	.689	76	-3	9	3.77	0	O-19(13-0-6)	2	-0.3
1960 LA-N	52	79	8	17	3	0	3	11	8	24	0	0	.215	.287	.367	.654	73	-3	9	3.82	0	O-18(13-0-5)	1	-0.4
1961 Bal-A	1	1	0	0	0	0	0	0	0	0	0	0	.000	.000	.000	.000	-102	-0	0	.00	0	....	0	0.0
KC-A	4	6	1	2	1	0	0	1	1	2	0	0	.333	.429	.500	.929	147	0	1	9.43	0	/O-1	0	0.1
Cle-A	60	166	25	48	7	1	12	35	10	33	0	0	.289	.333	.560	.894	138	8	29	6.05	1	O-49(16-19-16)	6	0.7
Yr.	65	173	26	50	8	1	12	36	11	35	0	0	.289	.335	.555	.890	137	8	30	6.11	2	O-50(17-19-16)	6	0.7
1962 Cle-A	106	336	59	92	12	0	21	50	42	68	0	0	.274	.366	.497	.863	134	16	62	6.42	-3	O-90(88-1-1)	16	0.9
1963 KC-A	101	231	23	52	9	0	5	27	19	48	0	0	.225	.287	.329	.616	69	-10	21	3.03	0	O-53(53-0-0)	3	-1.3
Total 6	404	1018	139	260	45	4	47	150	97	233	0	0	.255	.326	.446	.772	107	8	148	4.98	-5	O-260	31	-1.0

• ESSIAN, Jim James Sarkis Essian b: 1/2/1951, Detroit, MI BR/TR, 6'2", 195 lbs. Deb: 9/15/1973 M

YEAR TM-L	G	AB	R	H	2B	3B	HR	RBI	BB	SO	SB	CS	AVG	OBP	SLG	OPS	OPS+	BR/A	RC	RC/G	FR	G/POS	WS	TPW
1973 Phi-N	2	3	0	0	0	0	0	0	0	1	0	0	.000	.000	.000	.000	-97	-1	0	.00	0	/C-1	0	-0.1
1974 Phi-N	17	20	1	2	0	0	0	0	2	1	0	0	.100	.182	.100	.282	-19	-3	0	.49	0	C-15/1-1,3-1	0	-0.3
1975 Phi-N	2	1	1	1	0	0	0	1	1	0	0	0	1.000	1.000	1.000	2.000	439	1	1	∞	0	/C-2	0	0.0
1976 Chi-A	78	199	20	49	7	0	0	21	23	28	2	1	.246	.327	.281	.609	79	-4	19	3.17	3	C-77/1-2,3-1	5	0.2
1977 Chi-A	114	322	50	88	18	2	10	44	52	35	1	4	.273	.376	.435	.811	120	10	53	5.63	6	*C-111/3-2	16	2.0
1978 Oak-A	126	278	21	62	9	1	3	26	44	22	2	1	.223	.329	.295	.624	81	-5	28	3.10	13	*C-119/1-3,2-1,D-1	10	1.3
1979 Oak-A	98	313	34	76	16	0	8	40	25	29	0	1	.243	.303	.371	.674	85	-7	33	3.40	9	C-70,3-10/1-4,O-4(3-0-1),D	9	0.5
1980 Oak-A	87	285	19	66	11	0	5	29	30	18	1	3	.232	.305	.323	.628	77	-10	25	2.84	3	C-68,D-11/1-1	6	-0.4
1981 Chi-A	27	52	6	16	3	0	0	5	4	5	0	1	.308	.357	.365	.723	111	0	6	4.14	0	C-25/3-2	2	0.1
1982 Sea-A	48	153	14	42	8	0	3	20	11	7	2	0	.275	.327	.386	.713	92	-1	20	4.62	1	C-48	5	0.2
1983 Cle-A	48	93	11	19	4	0	2	11	16	8	0	1	.204	.321	.312	.633	72	-4	10	3.50	-1	C-47/3-1	3	-0.2
1984 Oak-A	63	136	17	32	9	0	2	10	23	17	1	1	.235	.350	.346	.696	100	1	18	4.32	3	C-59/3-1,D-1	6	0.7
Total 12	710	1855	194	453	85	3	33	207	231	171	9	13	.244	.330	.347	.676	90	-23	214	3.75	36	C-642/3-18,D-16,1-11,O-4,2	62	3.9

• ESTALELLA, Bobby Roberto (Ventoza) Estalella b: 4/25/1911, Cardenas, Cuba d: 1/6/1991, Hialeah, FL BR/TR, 5'8", 180 lbs. Deb: 9/7/1935 Career OF: 211-224-55

YEAR TM-L	G	AB	R	H	2B	3B	HR	RBI	BB	SO	SB	CS	AVG	OBP	SLG	OPS	OPS+	BR/A	RC	RC/G	FR	G/POS	WS	TPW
1935 Was-A	15	51	7	16	2	0	2	10	17	7	1	0	.314	.485	.471	.956	153	6	13	10.21	1	3-15	3	0.7
1936 Was-A	13	9	2	2	0	2	0	0	4	5	0	0	.222	.462	.667	1.128	186	2	3	11.81	0	....	1	0.1
1939 Was-A	82	280	51	77	18	6	8	41	40	27	2	3	.275	.368	.468	.835	121	8	48	5.93	-3	O-74(70-0-4)	8	0.1
1941 StL-A	46	83	7	20	6	1	0	14	18	13	0	0	.241	.376	.337	.714	87	-1	12	4.73	-1	O-17(15-0-2)	1	-0.2
1942 Was-A	133	429	68	119	24	5	8	65	85	42	5	2	.277	.400	.413	.813	130	22	74	6.07	-5	3-78,O-36(17-2-17)	20	1.8
1943 Phi-A	117	367	43	95	14	4	11	63	52	44	1	3	.259	.352	.409	.761	123	11	52	4.74	-5	O-97(95-1-1)	13	0.0
1944 Phi-A	140	506	54	151	17	9	7	60	59	60	3	3	.298	.374	.409	.783	125	17	80	5.69	-3	*O-128(5-103-25)/1-6	20	1.1
1945 Phi-A	126	451	45	135	25	6	8	52	74	46	1	6	.299	.399	.435	.834	142	25	79	6.34	-2	*O-124(9-118-0)	18	2.1
1949 Phi-A	8	20	2	5	0	0	0	3	1	2	0	0	.250	.286	.250	.536	44	-2	0	.35	1	/O-6(0-0-6)	0	-0.1
Total 9	680	2196	279	620	106	33	44	308	350	246	13	17	.282	.383	.421	.804	128	89	361	5.78	-17	O-482/3-93,1-6	84	5.6

• ESTALELLA, Bobby Robert M. Estalella b: 8/23/1974, Hialeah, FL BR/TR, 6'1", 200 lbs. Deb: 9/17/1996

YEAR TM-L	G	AB	R	H	2B	3B	HR	RBI	BB	SO	SB	CS	AVG	OBP	SLG	OPS	OPS+	BR/A	RC	RC/G	FR	G/POS	WS	TPW
1996 Phi-N	7	17	5	6	0	0	2	4	1	6	1	0	.353	.389	.706	1.095	179	2	5	12.20	0	/C-4	1	0.2
1997 Phi-N	13	29	9	10	1	0	4	9	7	7	0	0	.345	.472	.793	1.265	224	6	10	13.30	0	C-11	2	0.6
1998 Phi-N	47	165	16	31	6	1	8	20	13	49	0	0	.188	.251	.382	.633	63	-10	15	2.94	-5	C-47	1	-1.2
1999 Phi-N	9	18	2	3	0	0	0	1	4	7	0	1	.167	.318	.167	.485	27	-2	1	1.86	-1	/C-7	0	-0.2
2000*SF-N	106	299	45	70	22	3	14	53	57	92	3	0	.234	.360	.468	.829	116	9	54	6.18	13	*C-106	15	2.6
2001 SF-N	29	93	11	19	5	1	3	10	11	28	0	0	.204	.295	.376	.672	78	-3	10	3.69	3	C-28	3	0.2
NY-A	3	4	1	0	0	0	0	0	1	2	0	0	.000	.333	.000	.333	-1	-0	0	1.17	0	/C-3	0	0.0
2002 Col-N	38	112	17	23	8	0	8	25	14	33	0	1	.205	.294	.491	.785	88	-3	16	4.65	-1	C-38	4	-0.2
2003 Col-N	46	140	17	28	7	0	7	21	19	55	2	0	.200	.300	.400	.700	71	-6	17	3.86	1	C-46	4	-0.1
Total 8	298	877	123	190	49	5	46	143	127	279	6	2	.217	.320	.441	.761	94	-9	130	4.87	10	C-290	30	1.8

• ESTERBROOK, Dude Thomas John Esterbrook b: 6/9/1857, Staten Island, NY d: 4/30/1901, Middletown, NY BR/TR, 5'11", 167 lbs. Deb: 5/1/1880 M Career OF: 40-24-12

YEAR TM-L	G	AB	R	H	2B	3B	HR	RBI	BB	SO	SB	CS	AVG	OBP	SLG	OPS	OPS+	BR/A	RC	RC/G	FR	G/POS	WS	TPW
1880 Buf-N	64	253	20	61	12	1	0	35	0	15	....	....	.241	.241	.296	.538	79	-6	19	2.65	-3	1-47,O-15(1-14-0)/2-6,C-1,S	4	-1.2
1882 Cle-N	45	179	13	44	4	3	0	19	5	12	....	....	.246	.266	.302	.568	85	-3	15	3.00	12	O-45(38-7-0)/1-1	5	0.7
1883 NY-a	97	407	55	103	9	7	0	0	15	....	....	....	.253	.280	.310	.589	86	-7	36	3.33	-3	*3-97	9	-0.7
1884*NY-a	112	477	110	150	29	11	1	0	12	....	....	....	.314	.345	.428	.772	154	27	72	6.06	12	*3-112	26	3.8
1885 NY-N	88	359	48	92	14	5	2	44	4	28	....	....	.256	.264	.340	.604	96	-3	33	3.34	6	*3-84/O-4(1-0-3)	11	0.4
1886 NY-N	123	473	62	125	20	6	3	43	8	43	13	....	.264	.277	.351	.627	89	-8	51	3.94	-5	*3-123	16	-1.0
1887 NY-a	26	107	11	23	1	0	0	7	6	....	8	....	.215	.222	.178	.400	13	-11	6	1.90	-6	/1-9,O-7(0-3-5),2-5,S-5	0	-1.4
1888 Ind-N	64	246	21	54	8	0	0	17	2	20	11	....	.220	.232	.252	.484	53	-13	17	2.44	-3	1-61/3-3	1	-2.1
Lou-a	23	93	9	21	6	0	0	7	3	....	5	....	.226	.265	.290	.556	80	-2	9	3.26	0	1-23	1	-0.4
1889 Lou-a	11	44	8	14	3	0	0	9	5	2	6	....	.318	.400	.386	.786	126	2	9	8.33	0	/1-8,O-2(0-0-2),S-1	1	0.1
1890 NY-N	45	197	29	57	14	1	0	29	10	8	12	....	.289	.333	.371	.704	105	0	29	5.50	1	1-45	5	-0.2
1891 Bro-N	3	8	1	3	0	0	0	0	0	1	0	....	.375	.444	.375	.819	140	0	1	7.38	-1	/O-2(0-0-2),2-1	0	0.0
Total 11	701	2843	387	747	120	34	6	210	70	129	55	....	.263	.284	.334	.618	95	-24	297	3.86	8	3-419,1-194/O-75,2-12,S-7,C	79	-2.1

• ESTRADA, Frank Francisco (Soto) Estrada b: 2/12/1948, Navojoa, Mexico BR/TR, 5'8", 182 lbs. Deb: 9/14/1971

YEAR TM-L	G	AB	R	H	2B	3B	HR	RBI	BB	SO	SB	CS	AVG	OBP	SLG	OPS	OPS+	BR/A	RC	RC/G	FR	G/POS	WS	TPW
1971 NY-N	1	2	0	1	0	0	0	0	0	0	0	0	.500	.500	.500	1.000	187	0	1	13.50	0	/C-1	0	0.0

• ESTRADA, Johnny Johnny P. Estrada b: 6/27/1976, Hayward, CA BB/TR, 5'11", 195 lbs. Deb: 5/15/2001

YEAR TM-L	G	AB	R	H	2B	3B	HR	RBI	BB	SO	SB	CS	AVG	OBP	SLG	OPS	OPS+	BR/A	RC	RC/G	FR	G/POS	WS	TPW
2001 Phi-N	89	298	26	68	15	0	8	37	16	32	0	0	.228	.277	.359	.636	64	-17	26	2.76	-6	C-89	5	-1.7
2002 Phi-N	10	17	0	2	1	0	0	2	2	2	0	0	.118	.211	.176	.387	3	-2	1	1.24	0	C-10	0	-0.2
2003 Atl-N	16	36	2	11	0	0	0	2	0	3	0	0	.306	.359	.306	.665	76	-1	4	4.08	-3	C-14	0	-0.3
Total 3	115	351	28	81	16	0	8	41	18	37	0	0	.231	.282	.345	.627	62	-20	30	2.80	-9	C-113	5	-2.1

• ETCHEBARREN, Andy Andrew Auguste Etchebarren b: 6/20/1943, Whittier, CA BR/TR, 6'1", 197 lbs. Deb: 9/26/1962 C

YEAR TM-L	G	AB	R	H	2B	3B	HR	RBI	BB	SO	SB	CS	AVG	OBP	SLG	OPS	OPS+	BR/A	RC	RC/G	FR	G/POS	WS	TPW
1962 Bal-A	2	6	0	2	0	0	0	1	0	2	0	0	.333	.333	.333	.667	84	-0	1	4.50	0	/C-2	0	-0.1

YEAR	TM-L	G	AB	R	H	2B	3B	HR	RBI	BB	SO	SB	CS	AVG	OBP	SLG	OPS	OPS+	BR/A	RC	RC/G	FR	G/POS	WS	TPW
1965	Bal-A	5	6	1	1	0	0	1	4	0	2	0	0	.167	.167	.667	.833	123	0	1	3.60	0	/C-5	0	0.0
1966*	Bal-A★	121	412	49	91	14	6	11	50	38	106	0	1	.221	.295	.364	.659	89	-6	42	3.38	-3	*C-121	12	-0.3
1967	Bal-A★	112	330	29	71	13	0	7	35	38	80	1	0	.215	.300	.318	.618	83	-6	31	3.01	1	*C-110	8	0.1
1968	Bal-A	74	189	20	44	11	2	5	20	19	46	0	0	.233	.313	.392	.704	112	3	23	4.13	-3	C-70	8	0.4
1969*	Bal-A	73	217	29	54	9	2	3	26	28	42	1	2	.249	.353	.350	.703	96	-1	25	3.83	-3	C-72	8	0.0
1970*	Bal-A	78	230	19	56	10	1	4	28	21	41	4	1	.243	.315	.348	.663	82	-5	24	3.46	-5	C-76	6	-0.7
1971*	Bal-A	70	222	21	60	8	0	9	29	16	40	1	4	.270	.322	.428	.750	112	1	28	4.38	-3	C-70	8	0.2
1972	Bal-A	71	188	11	38	6	1	2	21	17	43	0	2	.202	.279	.277	.555	64	-9	14	2.38	-2	C-70	4	-0.9
1973*	Bal-A	54	152	16	39	9	1	2	23	12	21	1	1	.257	.319	.368	.688	94	-1	16	3.58	-1	C-51	4	-0.1
1974*	Bal-A	62	180	13	40	8	0	2	15	6	26	1	0	.222	.251	.300	.551	60	-9	13	2.48	-5	C-60	3	-1.2
1975	Bal-A	8	20	0	4	1	0	0	3	0	3	0	0	.200	.200	.250	.450	28	-2	1	1.69	0	/C-7	0	-0.2
	Cal-A	31	100	10	28	0	1	3	17	14	19	1	0	.280	.368	.390	.758	123	4	15	5.18	-1	C-31	4	0.4
	Yr.	39	120	10	32	1	1	3	20	14	22	1	0	.267	.343	.367	.710	109	2	16	4.58	-2	C-38	4	0.2
1976	Cal-A	103	247	15	56	9	1	0	21	24	37	0	2	.227	.305	.271	.577	74	-8	20	2.61	-2	*C-102	5	-0.6
1977	Cal-A	80	114	11	29	2	2	0	14	12	19	3	1	.254	.325	.307	.632	77	-3	12	3.43	-3	C-80	3	-0.3
1978	Mil-A	4	5	1	2	1	0	0	2	1	2	0	0	.400	.500	.600	1.100	207	1	2	14.67	0	/C-4	0	0.1
Total	15	948	2618	245	615	101	17	49	309	246	529	13	14	.235	.308	.343	.651	88	-42	268	3.38	-29	C-931	73	-3.2

• ETCHISON, Buck

Clarence Hampton Etchison b: 1/27/1915, Baltimore, MD d: 1/24/1980, Cambridge, MD BL/TL, 6'1", 190 lbs. Deb: 9/22/1943

YEAR	TM-L	G	AB	R	H	2B	3B	HR	RBI	BB	SO	SB	CS	AVG	OBP	SLG	OPS	OPS+	BR/A	RC	RC/G	FR	G/POS	WS	TPW
1943	Bos-N	10	19	2	6	3	0	0	2	2	2	0	....	.316	.381	.474	.855	148	1	4	7.53	-1	/1-6	1	0.0
1944	Bos-N	109	308	30	66	16	0	8	33	33	50	1	....	.214	.292	.344	.637	76	-10	32	3.39	-1	1-85	4	-1.6
Total	2	119	327	32	72	19	0	8	35	35	52	1	....	.220	.298	.352	.649	80	-9	35	3.59	-2	/1-91	5	-1.6

• ETHERIDGE, Bobby

Bobby Lamar "Luke" Etheridge b: 11/25/1942, Greenville, MS BR/TR, 5'9", 170 lbs. Deb: 7/16/1967

YEAR	TM-L	G	AB	R	H	2B	3B	HR	RBI	BB	SO	SB	CS	AVG	OBP	SLG	OPS	OPS+	BR/A	RC	RC/G	FR	G/POS	WS	TPW
1967	SF-N	40	115	13	26	7	2	1	15	7	12	0	0	.226	.299	.348	.647	86	-2	12	3.31	-3	3-37	2	-0.5
1969	SF-N	56	131	13	34	9	0	1	10	19	26	0	0	.260	.358	.351	.709	101	1	15	3.86	-3	3-39/S-1	3	-0.3
Total	2	96	246	26	60	16	2	2	25	26	38	0	0	.244	.331	.350	.681	94	-1	27	3.60	-6	/3-76,S-1	5	-0.8

• ETTEN, Nick

Nicholas Raymond Thomas Etten b: 9/19/1913, Spring Grove, IL d: 10/18/1990, Hinsdale, IL BL/TL, 6'2", 198 lbs. Deb: 9/8/1938

YEAR	TM-L	G	AB	R	H	2B	3B	HR	RBI	BB	SO	SB	CS	AVG	OBP	SLG	OPS	OPS+	BR/A	RC	RC/G	FR	G/POS	WS	TPW
1938	Phi-A	22	81	6	21	6	2	0	11	9	7	1	0	.259	.333	.383	.716	81	-2	11	4.79	-1	1-22	1	-0.5
1939	Phi-A	43	155	20	39	11	2	3	29	16	11	0	0	.252	.322	.406	.728	87	-3	20	4.42	-1	1-41	3	-0.8
1941	Phi-N	151	540	78	168	27	4	14	79	82	33	9	....	.311	.405	.454	.859	147	37	104	7.31	-13	*1-150	20	1.0
1942	Phi-N	139	459	37	121	21	3	8	41	67	26	3	....	.264	.357	.375	.732	120	13	65	5.01	-9	*1-135	12	-0.8
1943*	NY-A	154	583	78	158	35	5	14	107	76	31	3	7	.271	.355	.420	.775	125	17	89	5.31	-14	*1-154	22	-0.5
1944	NY-A	154	573	88	168	25	4	**22**	91	**97**	29	4	2	.293	.399	.466	.865	142	35	114	7.18	1	*1-154	25	3.0
1945	NY-A★	152	565	77	161	24	4	18	**111**	90	23	2	3	.285	.387	.437	.824	133	26	98	6.11	-10	*1-152	22	1.0
1946	NY-A	108	323	37	75	14	1	9	49	38	35	0	1	.232	.315	.365	.680	88	-5	39	4.13	-2	1-84	6	-1.0
1947	Phi-N	14	41	5	10	4	0	1	8	5	4	0	....	.244	.326	.415	.741	99	-0	5	4.23	1	1-11	1	0.1
Total	9	937	3320	426	921	167	25	89	526	480	199	22	13	.277	.371	.423	.794	126	118	544	5.84	-47	1-903	112	1.4

• EUNICK, Ferd

Fernandas Bowen Eunick b: 4/22/1892, Baltimore, MD d: 12/9/1959, Baltimore, MD BR/TR, 5'6", 148 lbs. Deb: 8/29/1917

YEAR	TM-L	G	AB	R	H	2B	3B	HR	RBI	BB	SO	SB	CS	AVG	OBP	SLG	OPS	OPS+	BR/A	RC	RC/G	FR	G/POS	WS	TPW
1917	Cle-A	1	2	0	0	0	0	0	0	0	0	0	....	.000	.000	.000	.000	-93	-0	0	.00	0	/3-1	0	0.0

• EUSEBIO, Tony

Raul Antonio Bare Eusebio b: 4/27/1967, San Jose de los Llamos, Dominican Republic BR/TR, 6'2", 180 lbs. Deb: 8/8/1991

YEAR	TM-L	G	AB	R	H	2B	3B	HR	RBI	BB	SO	SB	CS	AVG	OBP	SLG	OPS	OPS+	BR/A	RC	RC/G	FR	G/POS	WS	TPW
1991	Hou-N	10	19	4	2	1	0	0	0	6	8	0	0	.105	.320	.158	.478	41	-1	1	1.92	0	/C-9	0	-0.1
1994	Hou-N	55	159	18	47	9	1	5	30	8	33	0	1	.296	.329	.459	.788	108	1	23	4.93	0	C-52	6	0.3
1995	Hou-N	113	368	46	110	21	1	6	58	31	59	0	2	.299	.358	.410	.769	110	4	52	5.03	1	*C-103	14	1.1
1996	Hou-N	58	152	15	41	7	2	1	19	18	20	0	1	.270	.347	.362	.709	95	-1	19	4.21	2	C-47	5	0.3
1997*	Hou-N	60	164	12	45	2	0	1	18	19	27	0	1	.274	.364	.305	.669	80	-4	19	4.09	-2	C-43	4	-0.3
1998*	Hou-N	66	182	13	46	6	1	1	36	18	31	1	0	.253	.323	.313	.637	70	-7	18	3.27	-2	C-54	5	-0.6
1999*	Hou-N	103	323	31	88	15	0	4	33	40	67	0	0	.272	.353	.356	.709	81	-9	40	4.46	-3	C-98	10	-0.5
2000	Hou-N	74	218	24	61	18	0	7	33	25	45	0	0	.280	.364	.459	.823	101	0	36	5.75	-5	C-68	5	0.0
2001*	Hou-N	59	154	16	39	8	0	5	14	17	34	0	0	.253	.339	.403	.742	86	-3	22	5.02	-3	C-48	5	-0.3
Total	9	598	1739	179	479	87	5	30	241	182	324	1	5	.275	.349	.383	.732	92	-21	229	4.61	-13	C-522	54	0.0

• EUSTACE, Frank

Frank John Eustace b: 11/7/1873, New York, NY d: 10/16/1932, Pottsville, PA, 5'9", 160 lbs. Deb: 4/16/1896

YEAR	TM-L	G	AB	R	H	2B	3B	HR	RBI	BB	SO	SB	CS	AVG	OBP	SLG	OPS	OPS+	BR/A	RC	RC/G	FR	G/POS	WS	TPW
1896	Lou-N	25	100	18	17	2	2	1	11	6	14	4	....	.170	.217	.260	.477	26	-11	7	2.14	-7	S-22/2-3	0	-1.4

• EVANS,

Evans Deb: 6/1/1875

YEAR	TM-L	G	AB	R	H	2B	3B	HR	RBI	BB	SO	SB	CS	AVG	OBP	SLG	OPS	OPS+	BR/A	RC	RC/G	FR	G/POS	WS	TPW
1875	NH-n	1	4	1	2	0	0	0	1	0	0	0	0	.500	.500	.500	1.000	285	1	1	15.12	0	/0-1	....	0.1

• EVANS, Al

Alfred Hubert Evans b: 9/28/1916, Kenly, NC d: 4/6/1979, Wilson, NC BR/TR, 5'11", 190 lbs. Deb: 9/13/1939

YEAR	TM-L	G	AB	R	H	2B	3B	HR	RBI	BB	SO	SB	CS	AVG	OBP	SLG	OPS	OPS+	BR/A	RC	RC/G	FR	G/POS	WS	TPW
1939	Was-A	7	21	2	7	0	0	0	1	5	2	0	0	.333	.462	.333	.795	115	1	4	7.39	0	/C-6	1	0.2
1940	Was-A	14	25	1	8	2	0	0	7	6	7	1	0	.320	.452	.400	.852	131	2	6	8.84	0	/C-9	1	0.2
1941	Was-A	53	159	16	44	8	4	1	19	9	18	0	3	.277	.315	.396	.712	91	-4	19	4.30	-1	C-51	3	-0.2
1942	Was-A	74	223	22	51	4	1	0	10	25	36	3	0	.229	.309	.256	.565	60	-10	19	2.93	1	C-67	4	-0.5
1944	Was-A	14	22	5	2	0	0	0	0	2	6	0	0	.091	.167	.091	.258	-27	-4	0	.41	0	/C-8	0	-0.3
1945	Was-A	51	150	19	39	11	2	2	19	17	22	2	1	.260	.339	.400	.739	125	5	21	4.91	-4	C-41	6	0.3
1946	Was-A	88	272	30	69	10	4	2	30	30	28	1	2	.254	.332	.342	.674	94	-2	32	4.05	-4	C-81	7	-0.2
1947	Was-A	99	319	17	77	8	3	2	23	28	25	2	1	.241	.303	.304	.607	71	-12	29	3.05	2	C-94	7	-0.6
1948	Was-A	93	228	19	59	6	3	2	28	38	20	1	1	.259	.367	.338	.705	91	-2	29	4.32	2	C-85	8	0.4
1949	Was-A	109	321	32	87	12	3	2	42	50	19	4	1	.271	.369	.346	.715	92	-2	45	4.90	-3	*C-107	9	0.0
1950	Was-A	90	289	24	68	8	3	2	30	29	21	0	0	.235	.309	.304	.614	60	-17	28	3.33	-2	C-88	3	-1.4
1951	Bos-A	12	24	1	3	1	0	0	2	4	2	0	0	.125	.250	.167	.417	13	-3	1	1.65	-1	C-10	0	-0.3
Total	12	704	2053	188	514	70	23	13	211	243	206	14	9	.250	.332	.326	.658	82	-48	234	3.91	-10	C-647	49	-2.5

• EVANS, Barry

Barry Steven Evans b: 11/30/1955, Atlanta, GA BR/TR, 6'1", 180 lbs. Deb: 9/4/1978

YEAR	TM-L	G	AB	R	H	2B	3B	HR	RBI	BB	SO	SB	CS	AVG	OBP	SLG	OPS	OPS+	BR/A	RC	RC/G	FR	G/POS	WS	TPW
1978	SD-N	24	90	7	24	1	1	0	4	4	10	0	0	.267	.298	.300	.598	73	-3	8	3.36	0	3-24	2	-0.4
1979	SD-N	56	162	9	35	5	0	1	14	5	16	0	2	.216	.240	.265	.505	40	-15	10	1.94	3	3-53/S-2,2-1	1	-1.3
1980	SD-N	73	125	11	29	3	2	1	14	17	21	1	1	.232	.324	.312	.636	83	-3	14	3.51	-1	3-43,2-19/S-4,1-1	3	-0.3
1981	SD-N	54	93	11	30	5	0	0	7	9	9	2	2	.323	.382	.376	.759	125	3	12	4.60	-5	3-24,1-10/2-6,S-2	3	-0.3
1982	NY-A	17	31	2	8	3	0	0	2	6	6	0	0	.258	.395	.355	.750	109	1	5	5.94	0	/2-8,3-6,S-4	1	0.1
Total	5	224	501	40	126	17	3	2	41	41	62	3	5	.251	.309	.309	.619	78	-17	49	3.29	-3	3-150/2-34,S-12,1-11	10	-2.2

• EVANS, Darrell

Darrell Wayne Evans b: 5/26/1947, Pasadena, CA BL/TR, 6'2", 205 lbs. Deb: 4/20/1969 C Career OF: 84-0-0

YEAR	TM-L	G	AB	R	H	2B	3B	HR	RBI	BB	SO	SB	CS	AVG	OBP	SLG	OPS	OPS+	BR/A	RC	RC/G	FR	G/POS	WS	TPW
1969	Atl-N	12	26	3	6	0	0	0	1	1	8	0	0	.231	.259	.231	.490	38	-2	2	2.18	0	/3-6	0	-0.2
1970	Atl-N	12	44	4	14	1	1	0	9	7	5	0	0	.318	.423	.386	.809	112	1	7	6.19	1	3-12	2	0.2
1971	Atl-N	89	260	42	63	11	1	12	38	39	54	2	3	.242	.343	.431	.774	111	4	39	5.08	3	3-72/0-3(3-0-0)	9	0.7
1972	Atl-N	125	418	67	106	12	0	19	71	90	58	4	2	.254	.391	.419	.809	119	15	76	6.20	13	*3-123	20	3.0
1973	Atl-N★	161	595	114	167	25	8	41	104	**124**	104	6	3	.281	.407	.556	.964	153	47	143	8.54	9	*3-146,1-20	31	5.7
1974	Atl-N	160	571	99	137	21	3	25	79	**126**	88	4	2	.240	.383	.419	.801	119	20	100	5.93	24	*3-160	28	4.5
1975	Atl-N	156	567	82	138	22	2	22	73	105	106	12	3	.243	.364	.406	.769	109	11	91	5.46	18	*3-156/1-3	28	3.0
1976	Atl-N	44	139	11	24	0	0	1	10	30	33	3	0	.173	.320	.194	.514	45	-8	11	2.51	2	1-36/3-7	1	-0.9
	SF-N	92	257	42	57	9	1	10	36	42	38	6	1	.222	.331	.381	.712	99	1	36	4.69	7	1-83/3-5	8	0.3
	Yr.	136	396	53	81	9	1	11	46	72	71	9	1	.205	.327	.316	.643	80	-7	47	3.90	9	*1-119,3-12	9	-0.7
1977	SF-N	144	461	64	117	18	3	17	72	69	50	9	6	.254	.355	.416	.771	106	5	71	5.24	0	0-81(81-0-0),1-41,3-35	13	0.0
1978	SF-N	159	547	82	133	24	2	20	78	105	64	4	5	.243	.365	.404	.769	119	16	87	5.35	16	*3-155	26	3.2
1979	SF-N	160	562	68	142	23	2	17	70	91	80	6	7	.253	.359	.391	.750	112	10	83	5.10	16	*3-159	23	2.5
1980	SF-N	154	556	69	147	23	0	20	78	83	65	17	5	.264	.362	.414	.776	119	17	87	5.39	19	*3-140,1-14	27	3.5
1981	SF-N	102	357	51	92	13	4	12	48	54	33	2	3	.258	.358	.417	.776	122	10	56	5.41	5	3-87,1-12	14	1.4
1982	SF-N	141	465	64	119	20	4	16	61	77	64	5	4	.256	.364	.419	.783	119	13	74	5.47	0	3-84,1-49,S-13	20	1.1

YEAR TM-L	G	AB	R	H	2B	3B	HR	RBI	BB	SO	SB	CS	AVG	OBP	SLG	OPS	OPS+	BR/A	RC	RC/G	FR	G/POS	WS	TPW
1983 SF-N★	142	523	94	145	29	3	30	82	84	81	6	6	.277	.379	.516	.896	151	35	104	7.14	4	*1-113,3-32/S-9	28	3.5
1984*Det-A	131	401	60	93	11	1	16	63	77	70	2	2	.232	.356	.384	.740	105	6	58	4.89	6	D-62,1-47,3-19	12	0.7
1985 Det-A	151	505	81	125	17	0	**40**	94	85	85	0	4	.248	.357	.519	.876	137	25	96	6.62	11	*1-113,D-33/3-7	18	2.8
1986 Det-A	151	507	78	122	15	0	29	85	91	105	3	2	.241	.357	.442	.799	116	14	85	5.84	9	*1-105,D-42/3-2	17	1.5
1987*Det-A	150	499	90	128	20	0	34	99	100	84	6	5	.257	.383	.501	.884	138	29	103	7.22	10	*1-105,D-44/3-7	22	3.0
1988 Det-A	144	437	48	91	9	0	22	64	84	89	1	4	.208	.337	.380	.717	104	3	57	4.21	5	D-72,1-65	11	0.1
1989 Atl-N	107	276	31	57	6	1	11	39	41	46	0	1	.207	.309	.355	.664	87	-5	33	3.90	5	1-50,3-28	5	-0.3
Total 21	2687	8973	1344	2223	329	36	414	1354	1605	1410	98	68	.248	.364	.431	.795	119	270	1499	5.72	182	*3-1442,1-856,D-253/0-84,S	363	39.4

• EVANS, Dwight

Dwight Michael "Dewey" Evans b: 11/3/1951, Santa Monica, CA BR/TR, 6'2", 205 lbs. Deb: 9/16/1972 C Career OF: 35-32-2092

YEAR TM-L	G	AB	R	H	2B	3B	HR	RBI	BB	SO	SB	CS	AVG	OBP	SLG	OPS	OPS+	BR/A	RC	RC/G	FR	G/POS	WS	TPW
1972 Bos-A	18	57	2	15	3	1	1	6	7	13	0	0	.263	.344	.404	.747	115	1	8	4.76	1	0-17(16-0-1)	2	0.2
1973 Bos-A	119	282	46	63	13	1	10	32	40	52	5	0	.223	.322	.383	.705	92	-1	36	4.20	-3	*0-113(17-2-95)/D-2	7	-0.9
1974 Bos-A	133	463	60	130	19	8	10	70	38	77	4	4	.281	.338	.421	.759	110	5	65	4.91	5	*0-122(1-3-120)/D-7	15	0.4
1975*Bos-A	128	412	61	113	24	6	13	56	47	60	3	4	.274	.354	.456	.811	118	9	66	5.54	14	*0-115(0-0-115)/D-7	17	1.7
1976 Bos-A	146	501	61	121	34	5	17	62	57	92	6	7	.242	.326	.431	.757	107	3	69	4.61	7	*0-145(0-8-140)/D-1	15	0.4
1977 Bos-A	73	230	39	66	9	2	14	36	28	58	4	2	.287	.364	.526	.890	125	8	45	6.90	-2	0-63(0-14-54)/D-6	9	0.3
1978 Bos-A★	147	497	75	123	24	2	24	63	65	119	8	5	.247	.337	.449	.786	108	5	74	4.95	0	*0-142(0-3-140)/D-4	17	-0.2
1979 Bos-A	152	489	69	134	24	1	21	58	69	76	6	9	.274	.365	.456	.821	114	8	79	5.56	5	*0-149(0-0-149)	16	0.6
1980 Bos-A	148	463	72	123	37	5	18	60	64	98	3	1	.266	.361	.484	.845	123	16	85	6.43	3	*0-144(0-1-144)/D-2	17	1.1
1981 Bos-A★	108	412	84	122	19	4	**22**	71	**85**	85	3	2	.296	.418	.522	**.940**	159	**36**	95	**8.38**	6	*0-108(1-0-107)	26	3.8
1982 Bos-A	162	609	122	178	37	7	32	98	112	125	3	2	.292	**.403**	.534	.937	146	43	134	7.95	0	*0-161(0-0-161)/D-1	31	3.4
1983 Bos-A	126	470	74	112	19	4	22	58	70	97	3	0	.238	.339	.436	.776	104	4	71	5.16	-2	0-99(0-0-99),D-21	13	-0.3
1984 Bos-A	162	630	**121**	186	37	8	32	104	96	115	3	1	.295	.392	.532	**.924**	146	43	132	7.55	-1	*0-161(0-0-161)/D-1	29	3.4
1985 Bos-A	159	617	110	162	29	1	29	78	**114**	105	7	2	.263	.382	.454	.836	123	24	112	6.30	-1	*0-152(0-0-152)/D-7	21	1.5
1986*Bos-A	152	529	86	137	33	2	26	97	97	117	3	3	.259	.380	.476	.856	131	25	100	6.53	2	*0-149(0-0-149)/D-1	24	2.0
1987 Bos-A★	154	541	109	165	37	2	34	123	**106**	98	4	6	.305	.422	.569	.991	155	46	134	9.05	-8	1-79,0-77(0-0-77)/D-4	25	2.8
1988*Bos-A	149	559	96	164	31	7	21	111	76	99	5	1	.293	.379	.487	.866	135	28	104	6.65	-7	0-85(0-1-84),1-64/D-6	23	1.5
1989 Bos-A	146	520	82	148	27	3	20	100	99	84	3	3	.285	.402	.463	.865	135	28	100	6.77	-0	0-77(0-0-77),D-69	21	2.4
1990*Bos-A	123	445	66	111	18	3	13	63	67	73	3	4	.249	.353	.391	.744	103	3	60	4.48	0	*D-122	9	-0.2
1991 Bal-A	101	270	35	73	9	1	6	38	54	54	2	3	.270	.396	.378	.773	120	10	43	5.52	3	0-67(0-0-67),D-21	10	1.1
Total 20	2606	8996	1470	2446	483	73	385	1384	1391	1697	78	59	.272	.373	.470	.843	126	343	1611	6.24	23	*0-2146,D-282,1-143	347	24.9

• EVANS, Jake

Uriah L. P. "Bloody Jake" Evans b: 9/1856, Baltimore, MD d: 1/16/1907, Baltimore, MD TR, 5'8", 154 lbs. Deb: 5/1/1879 Career OF: 25-17-411

YEAR TM-L	G	AB	R	H	2B	3B	HR	RBI	BB	SO	SB	CS	AVG	OBP	SLG	OPS	OPS+	BR/A	RC	RC/G	FR	G/POS	WS	TPW
1879 Tro-N	72	280	30	65	9	5	0	17	5	18	....	....	.232	.246	.300	.546	84	-4	21	2.75	20	*0-72(2-7-64)	5	1.4
1880 Tro-N	47	180	31	46	8	1	0	22	7	15	....	....	.256	.283	.311	.595	96	-1	16	3.34	-1	0-47(0-6-41)/P-1	4	-0.7
1881 Tro-N	83	315	35	76	11	5	0	28	14	30	....	....	.241	.274	.308	.581	78	-8	27	3.07	12	*0-83(0-0-83)	6	0.3
1882 Wor-N	80	334	33	71	10	4	0	25	7	22	....	....	.213	.229	.266	.495	57	-16	21	2.18	15	*0-68(0-4-64),S-11/2-1,3-1,P	2	-0.3
1883 Cle-N	90	332	36	79	13	2	0	31	8	38	....	....	.238	.256	.289	.545	66	-13	25	2.74	6	*0-86(0-0-86)/3-3,S-3,2-1,P	7	-0.7
1884 Cle-N	80	313	32	81	18	3	1	38	15	49	....	....	.259	.293	.345	.638	96	-2	32	3.84	8	*0-76(23-0-53)/2-4,S-2	6	0.4
1885 Bal-a	20	77	18	17	1	1	0	7	7	....	....	....	.221	.318	.260	.578	85	-1	7	2.94	1	0-20(0-0-20)	2	0.0
Total 7	472	1831	215	435	70	21	1	168	63	172	....	....	.238	.264	.300	.565	78	-44	150	2.94	60	0-452/S-16,2-6,3-4,P-3	32	0.4

• EVANS, Joe

Joseph Patton "Doc" Evans b: 5/15/1895, Meridan, MS d: 8/9/1953, Gulfport, MS BR/TR, 5'9", 160 lbs. Deb: 7/3/1915 Career OF: 172-85-54

YEAR TM-L	G	AB	R	H	2B	3B	HR	RBI	BB	SO	SB	CS	AVG	OBP	SLG	OPS	OPS+	BR/A	RC	RC/G	FR	G/POS	WS	TPW
1915 Cle-A	42	109	17	28	4	2	0	11	22	18	6	1	.257	.382	.330	.712	111	4	17	4.97	-2	3-30/2-2	4	0.3
1916 Cle-A	33	82	4	12	1	0	0	1	7	12	4	....	.146	.213	.159	.372	11	-9	4	1.45	-2	3-28	1	-1.1
1917 Cle-A	132	385	36	73	4	5	2	33	42	44	12	....	.190	.271	.242	.513	53	-22	31	2.32	-5	*3-127	5	-2.5
1918 Cle-A	79	243	38	64	6	7	1	22	30	29	7	....	.263	.344	.358	.702	102	1	32	4.31	-3	3-74	9	0.1
1919 Cle-A	21	14	9	1	0	0	0	0	2	1	1	....	.071	.188	.071	.259	-24	-2	0	.63	0	/S-6	0	-0.2
1920*Cle-A	56	172	32	60	9	9	0	23	15	3	6	2	.349	.404	.506	.910	136	10	36	8.20	0	0-43(43-0-0)/S-6	8	0.9
1921 Cle-A	57	153	36	51	11	0	0	21	19	5	4	1	.333	.410	.405	.816	107	3	27	6.86	0	0-47(47-0-0)	5	0.0
1922 Cle-A	75	145	35	39	6	2	0	22	8	4	11	2	.269	.307	.338	.645	67	-5	16	3.65	-3	0-49(30-17-3)	2	-1.0
1923 Was-A	106	372	42	98	15	3	0	38	27	18	6	4	.263	.313	.320	.633	70	-16	39	3.43	-4	0-72(2-65-5),3-21/1-5	6	-2.1
1924 StL-A	77	209	30	53	3	3	0	19	24	12	4	4	.254	.330	.297	.627	59	-13	22	3.39	0	0-49(38-1-10)	2	-1.6
1925 StL-A	55	159	27	50	12	0	0	20	16	6	6	2	.314	.377	.390	.767	90	-1	25	5.48	1	0-47(12-2-36)	5	-0.4
Total 11	733	2043	306	529	71	31	3	210	212	152	67	16	.259	.329	.328	.658	78	-51	248	3.98	-16	0-307,3-280/S-12,1-5,2-2	47	-7.7

• EVANS, Steve

Louis Richard Evans b: 2/17/1885, Cleveland, OH d: 12/28/1943, Cleveland, OH BL/TL, 5'10", 175 lbs. Deb: 4/16/1908 Career OF: 38-3-862

YEAR TM-L	G	AB	R	H	2B	3B	HR	RBI	BB	SO	SB	CS	AVG	OBP	SLG	OPS	OPS+	BR/A	RC	RC/G	FR	G/POS	WS	TPW
1908 NY-N	2	2	0	1	0	0	0	0	0	....	0	....	.500	.500	.500	1.000	209	0	0	12.79	0	/0-1	0	0.0
1909 StL-N	143	498	67	129	17	6	2	56	66	....	14	....	.259	.362	.329	.691	122	17	65	4.41	-4	*0-141(0-0-141)/1-2	16	0.7
1910 StL-N	151	506	73	122	21	8	2	73	78	63	10	....	.241	.376	.326	.702	109	12	66	4.36	-4	*0-141(0-0-141),1-10	17	0.2
1911 StL-N	154	547	74	161	24	13	5	71	46	52	13	....	.294	.369	.413	.782	122	16	88	5.71	-2	*0-150(0-0-150)	22	0.6
1912 StL-N	135	491	59	139	23	9	6	72	36	51	11	....	.283	.353	.403	.756	109	6	73	5.11	2	*0-134(0-0-134)	14	0.1
1913 StL-N	97	245	18	61	15	6	1	31	20	28	5	....	.249	.321	.371	.692	99	-1	29	4.00	-1	0-74(2-1-71)/1-1	6	-0.5
1914 Bro-F	145	514	93	179	41	**15**	12	96	50	49	18	....	.348	.416	**.556**	.973	**174**	**49**	121	9.04	-4	*0-112(36-1-76),1-27	30	4.1
1915 Bro-F	63	216	44	64	14	4	3	30	35	22	7	....	.296	.411	.440	.851	154	17	40	6.76	-2	0-61(0-0-61)/1-1	10	1.3
Bal-F	88	340	50	107	20	6	1	37	28	34	8	....	.315	.379	.418	.796	125	11	54	5.97	-5	0-88(0-0-88)/1-4	11	0.2
Yr.	151	556	94	171	**34**	10	4	67	63	56	15	....	.308	.392	.426	.818	137	28	94	6.29	-6	*0-149(0-0-149)/1-5	21	1.5
Total 8	978	3359	478	963	175	67	32	466	359	299	86	....	.287	.374	.407	.782	127	127	537	5.63	-19	0-902/1-45	126	6.8

• EVANS, Tom

Thomas John Evans b: 7/9/1974, Kirkland, WA BR/TR, 6'1", 200 lbs. Deb: 9/2/1997

YEAR TM-L	G	AB	R	H	2B	3B	HR	RBI	BB	SO	SB	CS	AVG	OBP	SLG	OPS	OPS+	BR/A	RC	RC/G	FR	G/POS	WS	TPW
1997 Tor-A	12	38	7	11	2	0	1	2	2	10	0	1	.289	.341	.421	.763	97	-1	5	5.13	1	3-12	1	0.0
1998 Tor-A	7	10	0	0	0	0	0	0	1	2	0	0	.000	.091	.000	.091	-73	-3	0	.00	-1	/3-7	0	-0.3
2000 Tex-A	23	54	10	15	4	0	0	5	10	13	0	3	.278	.400	.352	.752	91	-1	8	4.51	2	3-21/1-1,D-1	1	0.1
Total 3	42	102	17	26	6	0	1	7	13	25	0	4	.255	.350	.343	.694	78	-5	13	4.13	2	/3-40,1-1,D-1	2	-0.2

• EVERETT, Adam

Jeffrey Adam Everett b: 2/2/1977, Austell, GA BR/TR, 6', 156 lbs. Deb: 8/30/2001

YEAR TM-L	G	AB	R	H	2B	3B	HR	RBI	BB	SO	SB	CS	AVG	OBP	SLG	OPS	OPS+	BR/A	RC	RC/G	FR	G/POS	WS	TPW
2001 Hou-N	9	3	1	0	0	0	0	0	0	1	1	0	.000	.000	.000	.000	-95	-1	0	.00	0	/S-6	0	-0.1
2002 Hou-N	40	88	11	17	3	0	0	4	12	19	3	0	.193	.297	.227	.524	39	-7	7	2.64	3	S-34	1	-0.2
2003 Hou-N	128	387	51	99	18	3	8	51	28	66	8	1	.256	.321	.380	.701	78	-11	49	4.26	15	*S-128	11	1.3
Total 3	177	478	63	116	21	3	8	55	40	86	12	1	.243	.314	.349	.664	70	-19	56	3.91	18	S-168	12	1.1

• EVERETT, Carl

Carl Edward Everett b: 6/3/1971, Tampa, FL BB/TR, 6', 190 lbs. Deb: 7/1/1993 Career OF: 86-675-281

YEAR TM-L	G	AB	R	H	2B	3B	HR	RBI	BB	SO	SB	CS	AVG	OBP	SLG	OPS	OPS+	BR/A	RC	RC/G	FR	G/POS	WS	TPW
1993 Fla-N	11	19	0	2	0	0	0	0	1	9	1	0	.105	.150	.105	.255	-29	-3	0	.66	-1	/0-8(0-8-0)	0	-0.4
1994 Fla-N	16	51	7	11	1	0	2	6	3	15	4	0	.216	.259	.353	.612	56	-3	5	3.65	1	0-16(1-8-8)	0	-0.2
1995 NY-N	79	289	48	75	13	1	12	54	39	67	2	5	.260	.352	.436	.788	110	2	42	4.86	4	0-77(0-10-68)	8	0.3
1996 NY-N	101	192	29	46	8	1	1	16	21	53	6	0	.240	.327	.307	.634	72	-6	21	3.76	-1	0-55(8-15-37)	2	-0.9
1997 NY-N	142	443	58	110	28	3	14	57	32	102	17	9	.248	.309	.420	.729	92	-7	58	4.49	1	*0-128(9-71-65)	13	-0.9
1998*Hou-N	133	467	72	138	34	4	15	76	44	102	14	12	.296	.360	.482	.842	122	12	77	5.82	9	*0-123(0-121-5)	16	2.2
1999*Hou-N	123	464	86	151	33	3	25	108	50	94	27	7	.325	.404	.571	.975	145	35	112	9.00	1	*0-121(2-118-16)/D-2	25	3.4
2000 Bos-A★	137	496	82	149	32	4	34	108	52	113	11	4	.300	.376	.587	.963	135	26	112	8.43	0	*0-126(0-126-0)/D-5	24	2.4
2001 Bos-A	102	409	61	105	24	4	14	58	27	104	9	2	.257	.323	.438	.761	97	-2	60	5.27	-8	0-93(0-84-9)/D-7	11	-0.9
2002 Tex-A	105	374	47	100	16	0	16	62	33	77	2	3	.267	.337	.439	.775	99	-2	55	5.10	-7	0-83(18-33-39),D-18	9	-1.2
2003 Tex-A★	74	270	53	74	13	3	18	51	31	48	4	1	.274	.359	.544	.904	123	9	55	7.24	2	0-72(40-15-33)/D-1	12	0.8
Chi-A	73	256	40	77	14	0	10	41	22	36	4	3	.301	.378	.473	.851	123	9	46	6.57	-1	0-68(8-66-1)/D-3	9	0.8
Yr.	147	526	93	151	27	3	28	92	53	84	8	4	.287	.369	.510	.878	123	18	101	6.92	1	*0-140(48-81-34)/D-4	21	1.6
Total 11	1096	3730	583	1038	216	23	161	637	355	820	101	46	.278	.352	.478	.830	113	70	644	6.13	0	0-970/D-36	129	5.3

• EVERITT, Bill

William Lee "Wild Bill" Everitt b: 12/13/1868, Fort Wayne, IN d: 1/19/1938, Denver, CO BL/TR, 6'.5", 185 lbs. Deb: 4/18/1895 Career OF: 31-10-2

YEAR TM-L	G	AB	R	H	2B	3B	HR	RBI	BB	SO	SB	CS	AVG	OBP	SLG	OPS	OPS+	BR/A	RC	RC/G	FR	G/POS	WS	TPW
1895 Chi-N	133	550	129	197	16	10	3	88	33	42	47	....	.358	.399	.440	.839	109	6	119	8.87	-8	*3-130/2-3	19	0.1
1896 Chi-N	132	575	130	184	16	13	2	46	41	43	46	....	.320	.367	.403	.771	99	-2	105	7.02	-9	*3-97,0-35(27-6-2)	16	-1.0

YEAR TM-L	G	AB	R	H	2B	3B	HR	RBI	BB	SO	SB	CS	AVG	OBP	SLG	OPS	OPS+	BR/A	RC	RC/G	FR	G/POS	WS	TPW
1897 Chi-N	92	379	63	119	14	7	5	39	36	....	26	....	.314	.373	.427	.801	107	3	73	7.15	-11	3-83/0-8(4-4-0)	11	-0.6
1898 Chi-N	149	596	102	190	15	6	0	69	53	....	28	....	.319	.377	.364	.741	113	11	96	6.13	-5	*1-149	18	0.5
1899 Chi-N	136	536	87	166	17	5	1	74	31	....	30	....	.310	.351	.366	.717	99	-1	83	5.72	9	*1-136	14	0.7
1900 Chi-N	23	91	10	24	4	0	0	17	3	....	2	....	.264	.287	.308	.595	67	-4	9	3.49	0	1-23	1	-0.4
1901 Was-A	33	115	14	22	3	2	0	8	15	....	7	....	.191	.301	.252	.553	55	-6	12	3.18	-4	1-33	1	-1.0
Total 7	698	2842	535	902	85	43	11	341	212	85	186	....	.317	.368	.389	.757	102	8	497	6.63	-28	1-341,3-310/0-43,2-3	80	-1.7

• EVERS, Hoot Walter Arthur Evers b: 2/8/1921, St. Louis, MO d: 1/25/1991, Houston, TX BR/TR, 6'2", 185 lbs. Deb: 9/16/1941 C Career OF: 503-486-97

YEAR TM-L	G	AB	R	H	2B	3B	HR	RBI	BB	SO	SB	CS	AVG	OBP	SLG	OPS	OPS+	BR/A	RC	RC/G	FR	G/POS	WS	TPW
1941 Det-A	1	4	0	0	0	0	0	0	0	2	0	0	.000	.000	.000	.000	-91	-1	0	.00	0	/0-1	0	-0.1
1946 Det-A	81	304	42	81	8	4	4	33	34	43	7	1	.266	.344	.359	.703	91	-2	41	4.79	-1	0-76(1-76-0)	10	-0.5
1947 Det-A	126	460	67	136	24	5	10	67	45	49	8	7	.296	.366	.435	.801	118	10	73	5.51	3	*0-123(0-123-0)	17	1.1
1948 Det-A★	139	538	81	169	33	6	10	103	51	31	3	4	.314	.378	.454	.831	117	11	92	6.17	-5	*0-138(0-138-0)	20	0.2
1949 Det-A	132	432	68	131	21	6	7	72	70	38	6	7	.303	.403	.428	.831	120	13	76	6.23	8	*0-123(81-42-2)	18	1.4
1950 Det-A★	143	526	100	170	35	**11**	21	103	71	40	5	9	.323	.408	.551	.959	139	28	116	8.03	8	*0-139(139-3-0)	26	2.4
1951 Det-A	116	393	47	88	15	2	11	46	40	47	5	3	.224	.297	.356	.653	76	-15	40	3.31	-1	*0-108(66-45-1)	5	-2.1
1952 Det-A	1	1	0	1	0	0	0	0	0	0	0	0	1.000	1.000	1.000	2.000	454	0	1	∞	0	....	0	0.0
Bos-A	106	401	53	105	17	4	14	59	29	55	5	2	.262	.318	.429	.747	99	-2	54	4.63	2	*0-105(90-12-20)	11	-0.7
Yr.	107	402	53	106	17	4	14	59	29	55	5	2	.264	.320	.430	.750	100	-1	55	4.63	2	*0-105(90-12-20)	11	-0.6
1953 Bos-A	99	300	39	72	10	1	11	31	23	41	2	1	.240	.301	.390	.691	81	-9	35	3.86	-3	0-93(78-16-0)	5	-1.6
1954 Bos-A	6	8	1	0	0	0	0	0	0	2	0	0	.000	.000	.000	.000	-90	-2	0	.00	-0	/0-1	0	-0.2
NY-N	12	11	1	1	0	0	1	3	0	6	0	0	.091	.091	.364	.455	12	-2	0	.98	0	/0-4(2-2-0)	0	-0.2
Det-A	30	60	5	11	4	0	0	5	5	8	1	0	.183	.258	.250	.508	40	-5	4	2.06	1	0-24(17-2-6)	0	-0.5
Yr.	36	68	6	11	4	0	0	5	5	10	1	0	.162	.230	.221	.450	26	-7	4	1.78	0	0-25(18-2-6)	0	-0.7
1955 Bal-A	60	185	21	44	10	1	6	30	19	28	2	1	.238	.309	.400	.709	96	-2	21	3.52	-2	0-55(10-16-31)	4	-0.5
Cle-A	39	66	10	19	7	1	2	9	3	12	0	1	.288	.319	.515	.834	117	1	10	5.45	0	0-25(15-9-2)	2	0.0
Yr.	99	251	31	63	17	2	8	39	22	40	2	2	.251	.311	.430	.742	101	-1	31	3.98	-2	0-80(25-25-33)	6	-0.6
1956 Cle-A	3	0	1	0	0	0	0	0	1	0	0	0	....	1.000	....	1.000	180	0	0	∞	0	....	0	0.0
Bal-A	48	112	20	27	3	0	1	4	24	18	1	0	.241	.375	.295	.670	85	-1	15	4.68	0	0-36(3-2-34)	4	-0.1
Yr.	51	112	21	27	3	0	1	4	25	18	1	0	.241	.380	.295	.674	86	-0	15	4.68	0	0-36(3-2-34)	4	-0.1
Total 12	1142	3801	556	1055	187	41	98	565	415	420	45	36	.278	.353	.426	.778	106	26	578	5.25	10	*0-1051	122	-1.5

• EVERS, Joe Joseph Francis Evers b: 9/10/1891, Troy, NY d: 1/4/1949, Albany, NY BR/TR, 5'9", 135 lbs. Deb: 4/24/1913

YEAR TM-L	G	AB	R	H	2B	3B	HR	RBI	BB	SO	SB	CS	AVG	OBP	SLG	OPS	OPS+	BR/A	RC	RC/G	FR	G/POS	WS	TPW
1913 NY-N	1	0	0	0	0	0	0	0	0	0	0	....	....	....	....	....	-99	0	0	....	0	....	0	0.0

• EVERS, Johnny John Joseph "Crab,Trojan" Evers b: 7/21/1881, Troy, NY d: 3/28/1947, Albany, NY BL/TR, 5'9", 125 lbs. Deb: 9/1/1902 M/C HOF: 1946

YEAR TM-L	G	AB	R	H	2B	3B	HR	RBI	BB	SO	SB	CS	AVG	OBP	SLG	OPS	OPS+	BR/A	RC	RC/G	FR	G/POS	WS	TPW
1902 Chi-N	26	90	7	20	0	0	0	2	3	....	1	....	.222	.263	.222	.485	51	-5	6	2.20	-1	2-18/S-8	1	-0.6
1903 Chi-N	124	464	70	136	27	7	0	52	19	....	25	....	.293	.325	.381	.707	104	0	68	5.35	3	*2-110,S-11/3-2	15	0.5
1904 Chi-N	152	532	49	141	14	7	0	47	28	....	26	....	.265	.307	.318	.624	93	-5	64	4.02	36	*2-152	20	3.4
1905 Chi-N	99	340	44	94	11	2	1	37	27	....	19	....	.276	.333	.329	.663	94	-2	47	4.61	12	2-99	11	1.1
1906*Chi-N	154	533	65	136	17	6	1	51	36	....	49	....	.255	.305	.315	.620	88	-8	70	4.34	21	*2-153/3-1	20	1.5
1907*Chi-N	151	508	66	127	18	4	2	51	38	....	46	....	.250	.309	.313	.622	89	-7	66	4.37	31	*2-151	22	2.9
1908*Chi-N	126	416	83	125	19	6	0	37	66	....	36	....	.300	.402	.375	.777	142	24	79	6.53	2	*2-122/0-1	28	3.2
1909 Chi-N	127	463	88	122	19	6	1	24	73	....	28	....	.263	.369	.337	.705	116	12	68	5.00	8	*2-126	27	2.4
1910 Chi-N	125	433	87	114	11	7	0	28	108	18	28	....	.263	.413	.321	.734	115	17	70	5.49	2	*2-125	22	2.2
1911 Chi-N	46	155	29	35	4	3	0	7	34	10	6	....	.226	.372	.290	.662	86	-1	19	4.04	3	2-33,3-11	5	0.3
1912 Chi-N	143	478	73	163	23	11	1	63	74	18	16	....	.341	**.431**	.441	.873	139	30	98	7.61	6	*2-143	27	3.8
1913 Chi-N	136	446	81	127	20	5	3	49	50	14	11	....	.285	.361	.372	.733	109	7	64	4.76	21	*2-136	20	3.1
1914*Bos-N	139	491	81	137	20	3	1	40	87	26	12	....	.279	.390	.338	.728	118	16	72	4.84	3	*2-139	25	2.3
1915 Bos-N	83	278	38	73	4	1	1	22	50	16	7	8	.263	.375	.295	.670	106	3	35	3.95	1	2-82	11	0.6
1916 Bos-N	71	241	33	52	4	1	0	15	40	19	5	....	.216	.330	.241	.570	81	-3	23	2.96	-14	2-71	8	-1.8
1917 Bos-N	24	83	5	16	0	0	0	0	13	8	1	....	.193	.302	.193	.495	56	-3	5	1.95	-1	2-24	1	-0.5
Phi-N	56	183	20	41	5	1	1	12	30	13	8	....	.224	.333	.279	.612	85	-2	19	3.40	0	2-49/3-7	5	0.0
Yr.	80	266	25	57	5	1	1	12	43	21	9	....	.214	.324	.252	.576	76	-5	25	2.94	-1	2-73/3-7	6	-0.5
1922 Chi-A	1	3	0	0	0	0	0	1	2	0	0	0	.000	.400	.000	.400	12	-0	0	1.76	-0	/2-1	0	0.0
1929 Bos-N	1	0	0	0	0	0	0	0	0	0	0	....	....	....	....	....	-104	0	0	....	-1	/2-1	0	-0.1
Total 18	1784	6137	919	1659	216	70	12	538	778	142	324	8	.270	.356	.334	.690	106	74	875	4.79	132	*2-1735/3-21,S-19,0-1	268	24.3

• EVERS, Tom Thomas Francis Evers b: 3/31/1852, Troy, NY d: 3/23/1925, Washington, DC TL, 5'9" Deb: 5/25/1882

YEAR TM-L	G	AB	R	H	2B	3B	HR	RBI	BB	SO	SB	CS	AVG	OBP	SLG	OPS	OPS+	BR/A	RC	RC/G	FR	G/POS	WS	TPW
1882 Bal-a	1	4	0	0	0	0	0	....	0	....	....	....	.000	.000	.000	.000	-108	-1	0	.00	-1	/2-1	0	-0.2
1884 Was-U	109	427	54	99	6	1	0	....	7	....	....	....	.232	.244	.251	.495	70	-12	27	2.29	10	*2-109	9	0.1
Total 2	110	431	54	99	6	1	0	....	7	....	....	....	.230	.242	.248	.490	68	-13	27	2.26	8	2-110	9	-0.1

• EWELL, George George W. Ewell b: 2/1851, Philadelphia, PA d: 10/20/1910, Philadelphia, PA Deb: 6/26/1871

YEAR TM-L	G	AB	R	H	2B	3B	HR	RBI	BB	SO	SB	CS	AVG	OBP	SLG	OPS	OPS+	BR/A	RC	RC/G	FR	G/POS	WS	TPW
1871 Cle-n	1	3	0	0	0	0	0	0	0	0	0	0	.000	.000	.000	.000	-106	-1	0	.00	0	/0-1	....	0.0

• EWING, Buck William Ewing
b: 10/17/1859, Hoagland, OH d: 10/20/1906, Cincinnati, OH BR/TR, 5'10", 188 lbs. Deb: 9/9/1880 M/U HOF: 1939 Career OF: 9-34-193

YEAR TM-L	G	AB	R	H	2B	3B	HR	RBI	BB	SO	SB	CS	AVG	OBP	SLG	OPS	OPS+	BR/A	RC	RC/G	FR	G/POS	WS	TPW
1880 Tro-N	13	45	1	8	1	0	0	5	1	3	....	....	.178	.196	.200	.396	33	-3	2	1.34	-2	C-10/0-4(0-0-4)	0	-0.5
1881 Tro-N	67	272	40	68	14	7	0	25	7	8	....	....	.250	.269	.353	.622	89	-4	26	3.50	25	C-44,S-22/0-2(2-0-0),3-1	10	2.2
1882 Tro-N	74	328	67	89	16	11	2	29	10	15	....	....	.271	.293	.405	.698	127	10	40	4.59	16	3-44,C-25/2-4,1-1,0-1,P-1	13	2.6
1883 NY-N	88	376	90	114	11	13	**10**	41	20	14	....	....	.303	.338	.481	.820	147	21	63	6.59	9	C-63,0-14(0-10-4),2-11/S-4,3	17	3.1
1884 NY-N	94	382	90	106	15	**20**	3	41	28	22	....	....	.277	.327	.445	.772	137	16	57	5.67	15	*C-80,0-12(3-1-8)/S-3,3-1,P	21	3.5
1885 NY-N	81	342	81	104	15	12	6	63	13	17	....	....	.304	.330	.471	.800	159	21	54	6.17	7	C-63,0-14(1-3-10)/3-8,1-1,P,S	19	3.1
1886 NY-N	73	275	59	85	11	7	4	31	16	17	18	....	.309	.347	.444	.791	137	12	50	7.08	9	C-50,0-23(2-18-3)/1-2	17	2.2
1887 NY-N	77	348	83	127	17	13	6	44	30	33	26	....	.365	.370	.497	.867	145	20	70	8.38	-4	3-51,2-19/C-8	11	1.5
1888*NY-N	103	415	83	127	18	15	6	58	24	28	53	....	.306	.348	.465	.813	159	27	88	8.24	9	C-78,3-21/S-4,P-2	27	4.3
1889*NY-N	99	407	91	133	23	13	4	87	37	32	34	....	.327	.383	.477	.860	139	21	89	8.65	8	*C-97/P-3,0-1	23	3.2
1890 NY-P	83	352	98	119	19	15	8	72	39	12	36	....	.338	.406	.545	.951	140	18	95	10.98	7	C-81/2-1,P-1	20	2.7
1891 NY-N	14	49	8	17	2	1	0	18	5	5	5	....	.347	.407	.429	.836	150	3	11	9.16	1	/2-8,C-6	2	0.4
1892 NY-N	105	393	58	122	10	15	8	76	38	26	42	....	.310	.371	.473	.845	157	26	87	8.64	6	1-73,C-30/2-2	20	3.1
1893 Cle-N	116	500	117	172	28	15	6	122	41	18	47	....	.344	.394	.496	.890	128	17	119	9.62	1	*0-112(0-1-112)/2-5,1-1,C	19	1.0
1894 Cle-N	53	211	32	53	12	4	2	39	24	9	18	....	.251	.328	.374	.702	67	-13	33	5.36	-2	0-52(0-0-52)/2-1	4	-1.3
1895 Cin-N	105	434	90	138	24	13	5	94	30	22	34	....	.318	.363	.468	.831	109	3	88	8.01	2	*1-105	11	0.3
1896 Cin-N	69	263	41	73	14	4	1	38	29	13	41	....	.278	.349	.373	.722	85	-6	50	6.85	5	1-69	7	-0.1
1897 Cin-N	1	1	0	0	0	0	0	0	0	....	0	....	.000	.500	.000	.500	36	0	0	.00	0	/1-1	0	0.0
Total 18	1315	5393	1129	1655	250	178	71	883	392	294	354	....	.307	.351	.456	.807	131	187	1022	7.34	112	C-636,1-253,0-235,3-127/2,S,P	241	31.2

• EWING, John John "Long John" Ewing b: 6/1/1863, Cincinnati, OH d: 4/23/1895, Denver, CO TR, 6'1" Deb: 6/18/1883 U Career OF: 0-2-1 ♦

YEAR TM-L	G	AB	R	H	2B	3B	HR	RBI	BB	SO	SB	CS	AVG	OBP	SLG	OPS	OPS+	BR/A	RC	RC/G	FR	G/POS	WS	TPW
1883 StL-a	1	5	0	0	0	0	0	0	0	....	....	....	.000	.000	.000	.000	-95	-1	0	.00	-1	/0-1	0	-0.1
1884 Cin-U	1	4	0	0	0	0	0	....	0	....	....	....	.000	.000	.000	.000	-93	-1	0	.00	-0	/0-1	0	-0.1
Was-U	1	5	1	1	0	1	0	....	0	....	....	....	.200	.200	.600	.800	166	0	1	4.31	0	/0-1	0	0.0
Yr.	2	9	1	1	0	1	0	....	0	....	....	....	.111	.111	.333	.444	51	-0	1	2.15	0	/0-2(0-1-1)	0	0.0
1888 Lou-a	21	79	6	16	1	1	0	5	1	....	7	....	.203	.213	.241	.453	46	-1	6	2.43	0	P-21	6	0.9
1889 Lou-a	41	134	12	23	2	0	0	6	9	30	5	....	.172	.234	.187	.421	21	-6	7	1.72	1	P-40/1-1	7	-3.1
1890 NY-P	35	114	18	24	2	1	2	17	5	35	2	....	.211	.244	.298	.542	41	-2	9	2.70	0	P-35	19	0.3
1891 NY-N	33	113	10	23	1	0	0	8	3	14	4	....	.204	.224	.212	.437	28	-2	6	1.93	0	P-33	21	2.0
Total 6	133	454	47	87	6	3	2	36	18	79	18	....	.192	.226	.231	.457	31	-13	29	2.12	0	P-129/0-3,1-1	53	-0.1

• EWING, Reuben Reuben Ewing b: 11/30/1899, Odessa, Ukraine d: 10/5/1970, West Hartford, CT BR/TR, 5'4.5", 150 lbs. Deb: 6/21/1921

YEAR TM-L	G	AB	R	H	2B	3B	HR	RBI	BB	SO	SB	CS	AVG	OBP	SLG	OPS	OPS+	BR/A	RC	RC/G	FR	G/POS	WS	TPW
1921 StL-N	3	1	0	0	0	0	0	0	0	1	0	0	.000	.000	.000	.000	-102	-0	0	.00	0	/S-1	0	0.0

YEAR TM-L	G	AB	R	H	2B	3B	HR	RBI	BB	SO	SB	CS	AVG	OBP	SLG	OPS	OPS+	BR/A	RC	RC/G	FR	G/POS	WS	TPW
• EWING, Sam	Samuel James Ewing b: 4/9/1949, Lewisburg, TN BL/TL, 6'3", 200 lbs. Deb: 9/11/1973 Career OF: 15-0-34																							
1973 Chi-A	11	20	1	3	1	0	0	2	2	6	0	0	.150	.227	.200	.427	20	-2	1	1.23	1	/1-4	0	-0.2
1976 Chi-A	19	41	3	9	2	1	0	2	2	8	0	0	.220	.256	.317	.573	67	-2	3	2.92	0	D-12/1-1	0	-0.2
1977 Tor-A	97	244	24	70	8	2	4	34	19	42	1	1	.287	.338	.385	.724	95	-1	30	4.36	-1	O-46(15-0-31),D-27/1-2	4	-0.5
1978 Tor-A	40	56	3	10	0	0	2	9	5	9	0	0	.179	.246	.286	.532	48	-4	4	2.40	-0	/D-9,O-3(0-0-3)	0	-0.4
Total 4	167	361	31	92	11	3	6	47	28	65	1	1	.255	.308	.352	.660	81	-9	39	3.68	-1	/O-49,D-48,1-7	4	-1.3
• EWOLDT, Art	Arthur Lee "Sheriff" Ewoldt b: 1/8/1894, Paullina, IA d: 12/8/1977, Des Moines, IA BR/TR, 5'10", 165 lbs. Deb: 9/17/1919																							
1919 Phi-A	9	32	2	7	1	0	0	2	1	5	0	....	.219	.242	.250	.492	38	-3	2	1.86	0	/3-9	0	-0.3
• EZZELL, Homer	Homer Estell Ezzell b: 2/28/1896, Victoria, TX d: 8/3/1976, San Antonio, TX BR/TR, 5'10", 158 lbs. Deb: 4/22/1923																							
1923 StL-A	88	279	31	68	6	0	0	14	15	20	4	3	.244	.287	.265	.552	43	-23	22	2.59	6	3-73/2-8	3	-1.2
1924 Bos-A	90	277	35	75	8	4	0	32	14	21	12	5	.271	.311	.329	.639	65	-14	29	3.56	2	3-64,S-21/C-1	5	-0.6
1925 Bos-A	58	186	40	53	6	4	0	15	19	18	9	7	.285	.351	.360	.711	81	-6	24	4.19	-11	3-47/2-9	3	-1.3
Total 3	236	742	106	196	20	8	0	61	48	59	25	15	.264	.312	.313	.625	61	-43	75	3.35	-3	3-184/S-21,2-17,C-1	11	-3.0
• FAATZ, Jay	Jayson S. Faatz b: 10/24/1860, Weedsport, NY d: 4/10/1923, Syracuse, NY BR/TR, 6'4" Deb: 8/22/1884 M																							
1884 Pit-a	29	112	18	27	2	3	0	0	1	....	....	....	.241	.274	.313	.586	89	-1	10	3.17	-2	1-29	2	-0.5
1888 Cle-a	120	470	73	124	10	2	0	51	12	....	64	....	.264	.312	.294	.606	97	-1	65	5.04	-5	*1-120	12	-1.4
1889 Cle-N	117	442	50	102	12	5	2	38	17	28	27	....	.231	.275	.294	.569	60	-24	44	3.45	4	*1-117	4	-2.7
1890 Buf-P	32	111	18	21	0	2	1	16	9	5	2	....	.189	.297	.252	.549	52	-7	9	2.74	-3	1-32	1	-1.0
Total 4	298	1135	159	274	24	12	3	105	39	33	93	....	.241	.293	.292	.584	77	-33	128	3.99	-5	1-298	19	-5.5
• FABREGAS, Jorge	Jorge Fabregas b: 3/13/1970, Miami, FL BL/TR, 6'3", 205 lbs. Deb: 4/24/1994																							
1994 Cal-A	43	127	12	36	3	0	0	16	7	18	2	1	.283	.321	.307	.628	62	-7	12	3.18	0	C-41	2	-0.4
1995 Cal-A	73	227	24	56	10	0	1	22	17	28	0	2	.247	.299	.304	.603	58	-15	19	2.74	2	C-73	2	-0.8
1996 Cal-A	90	254	18	73	6	0	2	26	17	27	0	1	.287	.332	.335	.667	71	-12	27	3.74	4	C-89/D-1	6	-0.2
1997 Ana-A	21	38	2	3	1	0	0	3	3	3	0	0	.079	.146	.105	.252	-33	-8	1	.37	0	C-21	1	-0.6
Chi-A	100	322	31	90	10	1	7	48	11	43	1	1	.280	.305	.382	.687	81	-10	33	3.52	2	C-92/1-1	8	-0.2
Yr.	121	360	33	93	11	1	7	51	14	46	1	1	.258	.288	.353	.641	69	-18	34	3.11	2	*C-113/1-1	9	-0.8
1998 Ari-N	50	151	8	30	4	0	1	15	13	26	0	0	.199	.267	.245	.512	36	-14	10	2.18	3	C-41	2	-0.8
NY-N	20	32	3	6	0	0	1	5	1	6	0	0	.188	.212	.281	.493	29	-3	2	1.66	0	C-12	0	-0.2
Yr.	70	183	11	36	4	0	2	20	14	32	0	0	.197	.258	.251	.509	35	-17	12	2.09	4	C-53	2	-1.0
1999 Fla-N	82	223	20	46	10	2	3	21	26	27	0	0	.206	.295	.309	.604	56	-15	20	2.86	4	C-78	5	-0.6
*Atl-N	6	8	0	0	0	0	0	0	0	0	0	0	.000	.000	.000	.000	-100	-2	0	.00	0	/C-4,1-1	0	-0.2
Yr.	88	231	20	46	10	2	3	21	26	27	0	0	.199	.286	.299	.584	51	-18	20	2.72	4	C-82/1-1	5	-0.8
2000 KC-A	43	142	13	40	4	0	3	17	8	11	1	0	.282	.320	.373	.693	72	-6	17	4.48	2	C-39/D-1	3	-0.1
2001 Ana-A	53	148	9	33	4	2	2	16	3	15	0	0	.223	.238	.318	.556	44	-13	10	2.15	4	C-53	3	-0.6
2002 Ana-A	35	88	8	17	1	0	0	8	6	6	0	0	.193	.245	.205	.449	21	-10	4	1.51	0	C-32	1	-0.8
Mil-N	30	67	5	11	3	0	3	14	2	7	0	0	.164	.188	.343	.532	37	-7	4	1.68	1	C-20	1	-0.4
Total 9	646	1827	153	441	56	5	23	211	114	217	4	5	.241	.287	.315	.603	56	-122	159	2.87	22	C-595/1-2,D-2	34	-5.9
• FABRIQUE, Bunny	Albert La Verne Fabrique b: 12/23/1887, Clinton, MI d: 1/10/1960, Ann Arbor, MI BB/TR, 5'8.5", 150 lbs. Deb: 10/4/1916																							
1916 Bro-N	2	2	0	0	0	0	0	0	0	1	0	....	.000	.000	.000	.000	-97	-0	0	.00	0	/S-2	0	0.0
1917 Bro-N	25	88	8	18	3	0	1	3	8	9	0	....	.205	.271	.273	.544	65	-4	6	2.27	-1	S-21	1	-0.3
Total 2	27	90	8	18	3	0	1	3	8	10	0	....	.200	.265	.267	.532	62	-4	6	2.21	-1	/S-23	1	-0.4
• FAEDO, Lenny	Leonardo Lago Faedo b: 5/13/1960, Tampa, FL BR/TR, 6', 170 lbs. Deb: 9/6/1980																							
1980 Min-A	5	8	1	2	1	0	0	0	0	0	0	0	.250	.250	.375	.625	64	-0	1	3.02	-1	/S-5	0	-0.1
1981 Min-A	12	41	3	8	0	1	0	6	1	5	0	0	.195	.214	.244	.458	30	-4	2	1.79	1	S-12	0	-0.1
1982 Min-A	90	255	16	62	8	0	3	22	16	22	1	0	.243	.290	.310	.600	63	-13	22	2.86	-4	S-88/D-1	4	-0.8
1983 Min-A	51	173	16	48	7	0	1	18	4	19	0	0	.277	.294	.335	.629	70	-7	16	3.26	-7	S-51	2	-0.9
1984 Min-A	16	52	6	13	1	0	1	6	4	3	0	0	.250	.304	.327	.630	71	-2	5	3.48	-2	S-15/D-1	1	-0.2
Total 5	174	529	42	133	17	1	5	52	25	49	1	0	.251	.286	.316	.602	64	-26	46	2.96	-13	S-171/D-2	7	-2.2
• FAGIN, Fred	Frederick H. Fagin b: Cincinnati, OH Deb: 6/25/1895																							
1895 StL-N	1	3	0	1	0	0	0	2	0	0	0	....	.333	.333	.333	.667	73	-0	0	3.99	0	/C-1	0	0.0
• FAHEY, Bill	William Roger Fahey b: 6/14/1950, Detroit, MI BL/TR, 6', 200 lbs. Deb: 9/26/1971 C																							
1971 Was-A	2	8	0	0	0	0	0	0	0	0	0	0	.000	.000	.000	.000	-106	-2	0	.00	0	/C-2	0	-0.2
1972 Tex-A	39	119	8	20	2	0	1	10	12	23	4	0	.168	.250	.210	.460	39	-8	7	1.83	4	C-39	2	-0.3
1974 Tex-A	6	16	1	4	0	0	0	0	0	1	0	0	.250	.250	.250	.500	45	-1	1	2.21	0	/C-6	0	-0.1
1975 Tex-A	21	37	3	11	1	1	0	3	1	10	0	0	.297	.316	.378	.694	96	-0	4	4.02	0	C-21	1	0.0
1976 Tex-A	38	80	12	20	2	0	1	9	11	6	1	0	.250	.348	.313	.660	92	-0	9	4.00	3	C-38	4	0.4
1977 Tex-A	37	68	3	15	4	0	0	5	1	8	0	0	.221	.232	.279	.511	38	-6	4	2.05	0	C-34	1	-0.5
1979 SD-N	73	209	14	60	8	1	3	19	21	17	1	1	.287	.352	.378	.730	106	2	28	4.72	2	C-68	8	0.6
1980 SD-N	93	241	18	62	4	0	1	22	21	16	2	0	.257	.317	.286	.603	74	-8	23	3.27	-2	C-85	4	-0.7
1981 Det-A	27	67	5	17	2	0	1	9	2	4	0	1	.254	.275	.328	.604	71	-3	6	2.79	0	C-27	1	-0.2
1982 Det-A	28	67	7	10	2	0	0	4	0	5	1	0	.149	.149	.179	.328	-10	-10	2	.89	3	C-28	1	-0.6
1983 Det-A	19	22	4	6	1	0	0	2	5	3	0	0	.273	.407	.318	.726	106	1	3	5.53	0	C-18	1	0.1
Total 11	383	934	75	225	26	2	7	83	74	93	9	2	.241	.298	.296	.594	70	-36	87	3.15	8	C-366	23	-1.5
• FAHEY, Frank	Francis Raymond Fahey b: 1/22/1896, Milford, MA d: 3/19/1954, Boston, MA BB/TR, 6'1", 190 lbs. Deb: 4/25/1918																							
1918 Phi-A	10	17	2	3	1	0	0	1	0	3	0	....	.176	.176	.235	.412	24	-1	1	1.22	-1	/O-5(4-1-0),P-3	0	-0.6
• FAHEY, Howard	Howard Simpson "Cap,Kid" Fahey b: 6/24/1892, Medford, MA d: 10/24/1971, Clearwater, FL BR/TR, 5'7.5", 145 lbs. Deb: 7/23/1912																							
1912 Phi-A	5	8	0	0	0	0	0	0	0	....	0	....	.000	.000	.000	.000	-104	-2	0	.00	-1	/3-2,2-1,S-1	0	-0.3
• FAIN, Ferris	Ferris Roy "Burrhead,Cocky" Fain b: 5/29/1921, San Antonio, TX d: 10/18/2001, Georgetown, CA BL/TL, 5'11", 186 lbs. Deb: 4/15/1947																							
1947 Phi-A	136	461	70	134	28	6	7	71	95	34	4	5	.291	.414	.423	.837	130	23	86	6.54	4	*1-132	19	2.4
1948 Phi-A	145	520	81	146	27	6	7	88	113	37	10	5	.281	.412	.396	.808	115	18	93	6.24	5	*1-145	21	1.8
1949 Phi-A	150	525	81	138	21	5	3	78	136	51	8	1	.263	.415	.339	.754	104	14	87	5.70	-3	*1-150	19	0.6
1950 Phi-A★	151	522	83	147	25	4	10	83	133	26	8	5	.282	.430	.402	.832	116	22	101	6.83	2	*1-151	17	1.7
1951 Phi-A★	117	425	63	146	30	3	6	57	80	20	0	3	**.344**	.451	.471	.921	146	32	96	8.83	8	*1-108,O-11(1-0-10)	19	3.6
1952 Phi-A★	145	538	82	176	**43**	3	2	59	105	26	3	5	**.327**	**.438**	.429	.867	134	31	107	7.39	11	*1-144	28	3.8
1953 Chi-A★	128	446	73	114	18	2	6	52	108	28	3	2	.256	.405	.345	.750	101	8	72	5.57	9	*1-127	16	1.0
1954 Chi-A★	65	235	30	71	10	1	5	51	40	14	5	1	.302	.406	.417	.823	121	10	44	6.90	-2	1-64	10	0.4
1955 Det-A	58	140	23	37	8	0	2	23	52	12	2	1	.264	.464	.364	.828	128	11	28	6.79	1	1-44	7	0.9
Cle-A	56	118	9	30	3	0	0	8	42	13	3	0	.254	.453	.280	.733	97	4	19	5.55	2	1-51	5	0.4
Yr.	114	258	32	67	11	0	2	31	94	25	5	1	.260	.459	.326	.785	114	15	48	6.23	4	1-95	12	1.4
Total 9	1151	3930	595	1139	213	30	48	570	904	261	46	28	.290	.425	.396	.821	120	173	735	6.64	38	*1-1116/O-11	161	16.7
• FAIR, George	George T. Fair b: 1/14/1856, Boston, MA d: 2/12/1939, Roslindale, MA, 5'7.5", 140 lbs. Deb: 7/29/1876																							
1876 NY-N	1	4	0	0	0	0	0	0	0	0	....	....	.000	.000	.000	.000	-115	-1	0	.00	0	/2-1	0	-0.1
• FAIREY, Jim	James Burke Fairey b: 9/22/1944, Orangeburg, SC BL/TL, 5'10", 190 lbs. Deb: 4/14/1968 Career OF: 150-47-46																							
1968 LA-N	99	156	17	31	3	3	1	10	9	32	1	1	.199	.242	.276	.518	60	-8	10	2.16	0	O-63(40-2-23)	1	-1.2
1969 Mon-N	20	49	6	14	1	0	1	6	1	7	0	2	.286	.300	.367	.667	86	-2	4	2.73	-1	O-13(1-12-0)	0	-0.3
1970 Mon-N	92	211	35	51	9	3	3	25	14	38	1	3	.242	.295	.355	.651	74	-10	21	3.24	-2	O-59(33-30-4)	3	-1.3
1971 Mon-N	92	200	19	49	8	1	1	19	12	23	3	3	.245	.288	.310	.598	69	-9	18	2.91	4	O-58(56-2-1)	3	-0.8
1972 Mon-N	86	141	9	33	7	0	1	15	10	21	1	3	.234	.285	.305	.590	66	-7	12	2.82	-1	O-37(20-1-18)	1	-1.1

YEAR TM-L	G	AB	R	H	2B	3B	HR	RBI	BB	SO	SB	CS	AVG	OBP	SLG	OPS	OPS+	BR/A	RC	RC/G	FR	G/POS	WS	TPW
1973 LA-N	10	9	0	2	0	0	0	0	1	1	0	0	.222	.300	.222	.522	49	-0	1	2.62	0	....	0	-0.1
Total 6	399	766	86	180	28	7	7	75	47	122	6	12	.235	.281	.317	.598	69	-36	65	2.82	1	0-230	8	-4.7

• FAIRLY, Ron Ronald Ray Fairly b: 7/12/1938, Macon, GA BL/TL, 5'10", 181 lbs. Deb: 9/9/1958 Career OF: 212-120-727

YEAR TM-L	G	AB	R	H	2B	3B	HR	RBI	BB	SO	SB	CS	AVG	OBP	SLG	OPS	OPS+	BR/A	RC	RC/G	FR	G/POS	WS	TPW
1958 LA-N	15	53	6	15	1	0	2	8	6	7	0	0	.283	.356	.415	.771	100	0	8	5.42	-1	0-15(4-11-1)	2	-0.2
1959*LA-N	118	244	27	58	12	1	4	23	31	29	0	4	.238	.326	.344	.670	73	-10	28	3.77	1	0-88(7-23-62)	5	-1.2
1960 LA-N	14	37	6	4	0	3	1	3	7	12	0	0	.108	.250	.351	.601	59	-2	3	2.63	0	0-13(5-0-8)	0	-0.2
1961 LA-N	111	245	42	79	15	2	10	48	48	22	0	0	.322	.435	.522	.958	140	17	60	9.20	1	0-71(6-15-53),1-23	15	1.4
1962 LA-N	147	460	80	128	15	7	14	71	75	59	1	1	.278	.383	.433	.816	126	20	80	5.98	-13	*1-120,0-48(4-5-42)	21	-0.2
1963*LA-N	152	490	62	133	21	0	12	77	58	69	5	2	.271	.350	.388	.737	120	15	68	4.72	-7	*1-119,0-45(16-22-10)	21	0.0
1964 LA-N	150	454	62	116	19	5	10	74	65	59	4	0	.256	.351	.385	.737	116	13	66	5.00	1	*1-141	17	0.7
1965*LA-N	158	555	73	152	28	1	9	70	76	72	2	0	.274	.364	.377	.741	117	16	82	5.12	-1	*0-148(0-17-133),1-13	26	0.5
1966*LA-N	117	351	53	101	20	0	14	61	52	38	3	2	.288	.383	.464	.847	145	23	63	6.44	-2	0-98(0-6-95),1-25	17	1.6
1967 LA-N	153	486	45	107	19	0	10	55	54	51	1	4	.220	.299	.321	.620	84	-10	46	3.03	4	0-97(1-0-97),1-68	9	-1.7
1968 LA-N	141	441	32	103	15	1	4	43	41	61	0	2	.234	.305	.299	.604	88	-6	40	2.99	3	*0-105(0-0-105),1-36	9	-1.3
1969 LA-N	30	64	3	14	3	2	0	8	9	6	0	0	.219	.315	.328	.643	86	-1	7	3.64	1	1-12,0-10(1-0-10)	1	-0.1
Mon-N	70	253	35	73	13	4	12	39	28	22	1	0	.289	.359	.514	.873	142	14	46	6.67	0	1-52,0-21(3-18-0)	9	1.0
Yr.	100	317	38	87	16	6	12	47	37	28	1	0	.274	.350	.476	.827	130	13	53	6.01	1	1-64,0-31(4-18-10)	10	0.9
1970 Mon-N	119	385	54	111	19	0	15	61	72	64	10	2	.288	.406	.455	.860	130	21	76	6.94	6	*1-118/0-4(2-2-0)	19	1.9
1971 Mon-N	146	447	58	115	23	0	13	71	81	65	1	3	.257	.377	.396	.773	119	14	71	5.47	6	*1-135,0-10(10-1-0)	19	1.0
1972 Mon-N	140	446	51	124	15	1	17	68	46	45	3	4	.278	.349	.430	.780	118	10	66	5.23	5	0-70(0-0-70),1-68	17	0.7
1973 Mon-N★	142	413	70	123	13	1	17	49	86	33	2	2	.298	.422	.458	.880	139	27	85	7.55	8	*0-121(121-0-0)/1-5	20	3.1
1974 Mon-N	101	282	35	69	9	1	12	43	57	28	2	1	.245	.374	.411	.785	113	7	46	5.54	3	1-67,0-20(19-0-1)	10	0.4
1975 StL-N	107	229	32	69	13	2	7	37	45	22	0	1	.301	.422	.467	.890	142	15	46	7.22	2	1-56,0-20(4-0-16)	11	1.4
1976 StL-N	73	110	13	29	4	0	0	21	23	12	0	0	.264	.391	.300	.691	97	1	14	4.17	2	1-27	3	0.1
Oak-A	15	46	9	11	1	0	3	10	9	12	0	0	.239	.364	.457	.820	145	3	8	5.85	1	1-15	2	0.3
1977 Tor-A★	132	458	60	128	24	2	19	64	58	58	0	4	.279	.363	.465	.828	122	14	75	5.71	3	D-58,1-40,0-33(9-0-24)	12	1.1
1978 Cal-A	91	235	23	51	5	0	10	40	25	31	0	1	.217	.295	.366	.661	88	-4	25	3.35	-2	1-78/D-5	4	-1.0
Total 21	2442	7184	931	1913	307	33	215	1044	1052	877	35	33	.266	.363	.408	.771	117	194	1107	5.32	21	*1-1218,0-1037/D-63	269	9.3

• FALCH, Anton Anton C. Falch b: 12/4/1860, Milwaukee, WI d: 3/31/1936, Wauwatosa, WI, 6'6", 220 lbs. Deb: 9/30/1884

YEAR TM-L	G	AB	R	H	2B	3B	HR	RBI	BB	SO	SB	CS	AVG	OBP	SLG	OPS	OPS+	BR/A	RC	RC/G	FR	G/POS	WS	TPW
1884 Mil-U	5	18	0	2	0	0	0	....	0	....	....	....	.111	.111	.111	.222	-25	-2	0	.40	1	/0-3(3-0-0),C-2	0	-0.1

• FALK, Bibb Bibb August "Jockey" Falk b: 1/27/1899, Austin, TX d: 6/8/1989, Austin, TX BL/TL, 6', 175 lbs. Deb: 9/17/1920 M/C Career OF: 1107-3-115

YEAR TM-L	G	AB	R	H	2B	3B	HR	RBI	BB	SO	SB	CS	AVG	OBP	SLG	OPS	OPS+	BR/A	RC	RC/G	FR	G/POS	WS	TPW
1920 Chi-A	7	17	1	5	1	1	0	2	0	5	0	0	.294	.294	.471	.765	100	-0	2	4.31	0	/0-4(0-0-4)	0	0.0
1921 Chi-A	152	585	62	167	31	11	5	82	37	69	4	4	.285	.330	.402	.732	87	-13	78	4.61	-9	*0-149(148-1-0)	11	-3.1
1922 Chi-A	131	483	58	144	27	1	12	79	27	55	2	6	.298	.335	.433	.768	99	-4	68	4.88	-10	*0-129(126-2-1)	13	-2.3
1923 Chi-A	87	274	44	84	18	6	5	38	25	12	5	5	.307	.367	.471	.837	121	7	47	5.87	-1	0-80(80-0-0)	9	0.1
1924 Chi-A	138	526	77	185	37	8	6	99	47	21	6	6	.352	.406	.487	.893	134	25	103	7.46	7	*0-134(134-0-0)	21	2.1
1925 Chi-A	154	602	80	181	35	9	4	99	51	25	4	5	.301	.357	.409	.766	99	-1	89	5.24	-4	*0-153(153-0-0)	15	-1.6
1926 Chi-A	155	566	86	195	43	4	8	108	66	22	9	10	.345	.415	.477	.892	137	30	112	7.37	7	*0-155(155-0-0)	24	2.5
1927 Chi-A	145	535	76	175	35	6	9	83	52	19	5	7	.327	.391	.465	.856	124	18	97	6.63	18	*0-145(145-0-0)	21	2.4
1928 Chi-A	98	286	42	83	18	4	1	37	25	16	5	1	.290	.347	.392	.739	95	-1	40	5.00	-1	0-78(78-0-0)	8	-0.8
1929 Cle-A	125	426	65	133	30	7	13	93	42	14	4	4	.312	.374	.507	.881	120	12	80	6.73	0	*0-120(61-0-61)	15	0.2
1930 Cle-A	82	191	34	62	12	1	4	36	23	8	2	0	.325	.397	.461	.858	112	5	36	7.24	2	0-42(25-0-18)	7	0.3
1931 Cle-A	79	161	30	49	13	1	2	28	17	13	1	1	.304	.371	.435	.806	105	2	26	6.11	-2	0-33(2-0-31)	4	-0.2
Total 12	1353	4652	655	1463	300	59	69	784	412	279	47	49	.314	.372	.449	.821	113	80	780	6.03	7	*0-1222	148	-0.3

• FALLON, Charlie Charles Augustus Fallon b: 3/7/1881, New York, NY d: 6/10/1960, King's Park, NY BR/TR, 5'6" Deb: 6/30/1905

YEAR TM-L	G	AB	R	H	2B	3B	HR	RBI	BB	SO	SB	CS	AVG	OBP	SLG	OPS	OPS+	BR/A	RC	RC/G	FR	G/POS	WS	TPW
1905 NY-A	1	0	0	0	0	0	0	0	0	....	0	....	....	....	....	....	-90	0	0	....	0	....	0	0.0

• FALLON, George George Decatur "Flash" Fallon b: 7/8/1914, Jersey City, NJ d: 10/25/1994, Lake Worth, FL BR/TR, 5'9", 155 lbs. Deb: 9/27/1937

YEAR TM-L	G	AB	R	H	2B	3B	HR	RBI	BB	SO	SB	CS	AVG	OBP	SLG	OPS	OPS+	BR/A	RC	RC/G	FR	G/POS	WS	TPW
1937 Bro-N	4	8	0	2	1	0	0	0	1	0	0	....	.250	.333	.375	.708	91	-0	0	1.25	-1	/2-4	0	-0.1
1943 StL-N	36	78	6	18	1	0	0	5	2	9	0	....	.231	.259	.244	.503	44	-6	5	1.85	3	2-36	1	-0.1
1944*StL-N	69	141	16	28	6	0	1	9	16	11	1	....	.199	.285	.262	.547	54	-8	11	2.37	5	2-38,S-24/3-6	3	-0.1
1945 StL-N	24	55	4	13	2	1	0	7	6	6	1	....	.236	.311	.309	.621	71	-2	6	3.67	0	S-20/2-4	2	-0.1
Total 4	133	282	26	61	10	1	1	21	25	26	2	....	.216	.285	.270	.554	55	-16	22	2.42	7	/2-82,S-44,3-6	6	-0.4

• FALSEY, Pete Peter James Falsey b: 4/24/1891, New Haven, CT d: 5/23/1976, Los Angeles, CA BL/TL, 5'6.5", 132 lbs. Deb: 7/16/1914

YEAR TM-L	G	AB	R	H	2B	3B	HR	RBI	BB	SO	SB	CS	AVG	OBP	SLG	OPS	OPS+	BR/A	RC	RC/G	FR	G/POS	WS	TPW
1914 Pit-N	3	1	0	0	0	0	0	0	0	1	0	....	.000	.000	.000	.000	-105	-0	0	.00	0	....	0	0.0

• FANEYTE, Rikkert Rikkert Faneyte b: 5/31/1969, Amsterdam, Holland BR/TR, 6', 170 lbs. Deb: 8/29/1993 Career OF: 6-33-15

YEAR TM-L	G	AB	R	H	2B	3B	HR	RBI	BB	SO	SB	CS	AVG	OBP	SLG	OPS	OPS+	BR/A	RC	RC/G	FR	G/POS	WS	TPW
1993 SF-N	7	15	2	2	0	0	0	0	2	4	0	0	.133	.235	.133	.369	2	-2	1	1.23	-0	/0-6(1-5-0)	0	-0.2
1994 SF-N	19	26	1	3	3	0	0	4	3	11	0	0	.115	.207	.231	.438	15	-3	1	1.32	0	/0-6(0-2-4)	0	-0.4
1995 SF-N	46	86	7	17	4	1	0	4	11	27	1	0	.198	.289	.267	.556	49	-6	7	2.68	0	0-34(3-22-11)	0	-0.6
1996 Tex-A	8	5	0	1	0	0	0	1	0	0	0	0	.200	.200	.200	.400	1	-1	0	1.31	0	/0-6(2-4-0),D-2	0	-0.1
Total 4	80	132	10	23	7	1	0	9	16	42	1	0	.174	.264	.242	.506	35	-12	9	2.16	0	/0-52,D-2	0	-1.3

• FANNING, Jim William James Fanning b: 9/14/1927, Chicago, IL BR/TR, 5'11", 180 lbs. Deb: 9/11/1954 M/C

YEAR TM-L	G	AB	R	H	2B	3B	HR	RBI	BB	SO	SB	CS	AVG	OBP	SLG	OPS	OPS+	BR/A	RC	RC/G	FR	G/POS	WS	TPW
1954 Chi-N	11	38	2	7	0	0	0	1	1	7	0	0	.184	.205	.184	.389	2	-5	1	.57	0	C-11	0	-0.5
1955 Chi-N	5	10	0	0	0	0	0	0	1	2	0	0	.000	.091	.000	.091	-73	-3	0	.00	0	/C-5	0	-0.2
1956 Chi-N	1	4	0	1	0	0	0	0	0	0	0	0	.250	.250	.250	.500	36	-0	0	.00	1	/C-1	0	0.0
1957 Chi-N	47	89	3	16	2	0	0	4	4	17	0	0	.180	.223	.202	.426	16	-11	4	1.30	1	C-35	1	-0.9
Total 4	64	141	5	24	2	0	0	5	6	26	0	0	.170	.209	.184	.394	6	-19	4	.95	2	/C-52	1	-1.5

• FANZONE, Carmen Carmen Ronald Fanzone b: 8/30/1943, Detroit, MI BR/TR, 6', 200 lbs. Deb: 7/21/1970 Career OF: 13-0-1

YEAR TM-L	G	AB	R	H	2B	3B	HR	RBI	BB	SO	SB	CS	AVG	OBP	SLG	OPS	OPS+	BR/A	RC	RC/G	FR	G/POS	WS	TPW
1970 Bos-A	10	15	0	3	1	0	0	3	2	2	0	0	.200	.333	.267	.600	63	-1	1	2.69	-2	/3-5	0	-0.2
1971 Chi-N	12	43	5	8	2	0	2	5	2	7	0	0	.186	.222	.372	.594	57	-3	3	2.48	0	/0-6(5-0-1),3-3,1-2	0	-0.3
1972 Chi-N	86	222	26	50	11	0	8	42	35	45	2	3	.225	.338	.383	.721	94	-1	28	4.14	-4	3-36,1-21,2-13/0-1,S-1	6	-0.7
1973 Chi-N	64	150	22	41	7	0	6	22	20	38	1	2	.273	.359	.440	.799	112	2	24	5.49	-6	3-25,1-24/0-6(6-0-0)	4	-0.6
1974 Chi-N	65	158	13	30	6	0	4	22	15	27	0	1	.190	.269	.304	.572	57	-10	13	2.66	-9	3-35,2-10/1-7,0-1	1	-1.9
Total 5	237	588	66	132	27	0	20	94	74	119	3	6	.224	.317	.372	.690	86	-12	70	3.88	-20	3-104/1-54,2-23,0-14,S-1	11	-3.8

• FARIES, Paul Paul Tyrrell Faries b: 2/20/1965, Berkeley, CA BR/TR, 5'10", 165 lbs. Deb: 9/6/1990

YEAR TM-L	G	AB	R	H	2B	3B	HR	RBI	BB	SO	SB	CS	AVG	OBP	SLG	OPS	OPS+	BR/A	RC	RC/G	FR	G/POS	WS	TPW
1990 SD-N	14	37	4	7	1	0	0	2	4	7	0	1	.189	.286	.216	.502	40	-3	3	2.11	3	/2-7,S-4,3-1	0	0.0
1991 SD-N	57	130	13	23	3	1	0	7	14	21	3	1	.177	.262	.215	.477	35	-11	8	1.76	0	2-36,3-12/S-8	2	-1.0
1992 SD-N	10	11	3	5	1	0	0	1	1	2	0	0	.455	.500	.545	1.045	193	1	3	14.09	-1	/2-4,3-2,S-1	1	0.0
1993 SF-N	15	36	6	8	2	1	0	4	1	4	2	0	.222	.243	.333	.577	54	-2	3	2.56	1	/2-7,S-4,3-1	1	-0.1
Total 4	96	214	26	43	7	2	0	14	20	34	5	2	.201	.275	.252	.528	46	-15	16	2.35	3	/2-54,S-17,3-16	4	-1.1

• FARISS, Monty Monty Ted Fariss b: 10/13/1967, Cordell, OK BR/TR, 6'4", 180 lbs. Deb: 9/6/1991 Career OF: 37-10-19

YEAR TM-L	G	AB	R	H	2B	3B	HR	RBI	BB	SO	SB	CS	AVG	OBP	SLG	OPS	OPS+	BR/A	RC	RC/G	FR	G/POS	WS	TPW
1991 Tex-A	19	31	6	8	1	0	1	6	7	11	0	0	.258	.395	.387	.782	119	1	5	6.40	1	/0-8(8-0-0),2-4,D-4	1	0.2
1992 Tex-A	67	166	13	36	7	1	3	21	17	51	0	2	.217	.297	.325	.623	77	-6	16	3.16	-2	0-49(28-10-12),2-17/D-4,1	2	-0.9
1993 Fla-N	18	29	3	5	2	1	0	2	5	13	0	0	.172	.294	.310	.604	59	-2	2	2.52	0	/0-8(1-0-7)	0	-0.2
Total 3	104	226	22	49	10	2	4	29	29	75	0	2	.217	.311	.332	.643	81	-6	24	3.47	-1	/0-65,2-21,D-8,1-1	3	-0.9

• FARLEY, Bob Robert Jacob Farley b: 11/15/1937, Watsontown, PA BL/TL, 6'2", 200 lbs. Deb: 4/15/1961 Career OF: 3-0-11

YEAR TM-L	G	AB	R	H	2B	3B	HR	RBI	BB	SO	SB	CS	AVG	OBP	SLG	OPS	OPS+	BR/A	RC	RC/G	FR	G/POS	WS	TPW
1961 SF-N	13	20	3	2	0	0	0	1	3	5	0	0	.100	.217	.100	.317	-13	-3	1	.91	0	/0-3(3-0-0),1-1	0	-0.3
1962 Chi-A	35	53	7	10	1	1	1	4	13	13	0	1	.189	.348	.302	.650	77	-2	6	3.96	-1	1-14	1	-0.3
Det-A	36	50	9	8	2	0	1	4	14	10	0	0	.160	.344	.260	.604	63	-2	6	3.65	-1	0-11(0-0-11)/1-6	1	-0.4

YEAR TM-L	G	AB	R	H	2B	3B	HR	RBI	BB	SO	SB	CS	AVG	OBP	SLG	OPS	OPS+	BR/A	RC	RC/G	FR	G/POS	WS	TPW
Yr.	71	103	16	18	3	1	2	8	27	23	0	1	.175	.346	.282	.628	70	-4	12	3.81	-2	1-20,0-11(0-0-11)	2	-0.7
Total 2	**84**	**123**	**19**	**20**	**3**	**1**	**2**	**9**	**30**	**28**	**0**	**1**	**.163**	**.327**	**.252**	**.579**	**58**	**-7**	**13**	**3.31**	**-2**	**/1-21,0-14**	**2**	**-1.0**
• FARLEY, Tom	Thomas T. Farley b: Chicago, IL Deb: 6/24/1884																							
1884 Was-a	14	52	5	11	4	0	0	0	1	....	....	....	.212	.241	.288	.529	81	-1	4	2.48	1	0-14(14-0-0)	1	0.0
• FARMER, Alex	Alexander Johnson Farmer b: 5/9/1880, New York, NY d: 3/5/1920, New York, NY BR/TR, 6', 175 lbs. Deb: 9/1/1908																							
1908 Bro-N	12	30	1	5	1	0	0	2	1	....	0	....	.167	.194	.200	.394	27	-3	1	1.16	0	C-11	1	-0.2
• FARMER, Bill	William Farmer b: 12/27/1870, Philadelphia, PA BR/TR, 5'11.5", 187 lbs. Deb: 5/1/1888																							
1888 Pit-N	2	4	0	0	0	0	0	0	0	1	0	....	.000	.000	.000	.000	-108	-1	0	.00	-1	/C-1,0-1	0	-0.1
Phi-a	3	12	0	2	0	0	0	1	0	....	0	....	.167	.167	.167	.333	7	-1	0	.92	0	/C-3	0	-0.1
• FARMER, Jack	Floyd Haskell Farmer b: 7/14/1892, Granville, TN d: 5/21/1970, Columbia, LA BR/TR, 6', 180 lbs. Deb: 7/8/1916 Career OF: 10-0-8																							
1916 Pit-N	55	166	10	45	6	4	0	14	7	24	1	....	.271	.309	.355	.664	103	0	19	3.97	-9	2-31,0-15(8-0-7)/S-4,3-1	4	-1.0
1918 Cle-A	7	9	1	2	0	0	0	1	0	3	2	....	.222	.300	.222	.522	52	-0	1	3.80	-2	/0-3(2-0-1)	0	-0.3
Total 2	**62**	**175**	**11**	**47**	**6**	**4**	**0**	**15**	**7**	**27**	**3**	**....**	**.269**	**.308**	**.349**	**.657**	**100**	**-0**	**20**	**3.96**	**-11**	**/2-31,0-18,S-4,3-1**	**4**	**-1.2**
• FARRAR, Sid	Sidney Douglas Farrar b: 8/10/1859, Paris Hill, ME d: 5/7/1935, New York, NY TR, 5'10", 185 lbs. Deb: 5/1/1883																							
1883 Phi-N	99	377	41	88	19	8	0	29	4	37	....	....	.233	.241	.326	.568	77	-9	30	2.90	2	*1-99	3	-1.3
1884 Phi-N	111	428	62	105	16	6	1	45	9	25	....	....	.245	.261	.318	.579	85	-7	36	3.10	7	*1-111	10	-0.9
1885 Phi-N	111	420	49	103	20	3	3	36	28	34	....	....	.245	.292	.329	.621	103	2	41	3.52	3	*1-111	11	-0.5
1886 Phi-N	118	439	55	109	19	7	5	50	16	47	10	....	.248	.275	.358	.632	90	-7	47	3.85	6	*1-118	12	-1.0
1887 Phi-N	116	485	83	167	20	9	4	72	42	29	24	....	.344	.358	.395	.753	103	2	73	6.08	12	*1-116	15	0.3
1888 Phi-N	131	508	53	124	24	7	1	53	31	38	21	....	.244	.304	.325	.629	96	-2	58	4.08	3	*1-131	12	-1.1
1889 Phi-N	130	477	70	128	22	2	3	58	52	36	28	....	.268	.348	.342	.689	86	-10	68	5.17	-4	*1-130	10	-2.2
1890 Phi-P	127	481	84	123	17	11	1	69	51	23	9	....	.256	.333	.343	.676	79	-15	59	4.48	3	*1-127	8	-1.9
Total 8	**943**	**3615**	**497**	**947**	**157**	**53**	**18**	**412**	**233**	**269**	**92**	**....**	**.262**	**.305**	**.342**	**.647**	**90**	**-46**	**414**	**4.17**	**32**	**1-943**	**81**	**-8.4**
• FARRELL, Bill	William Farrell b: Bridgeport, CT Deb: 5/3/1882																							
1882 Phi-a	2	7	2	2	1	0	0	1	1	....	....	....	.286	.375	.429	.804	152	0	1	6.46	-1	/0-2(0-1-1),C-1	0	0.0
1883 Bal-a	2	7	0	0	0	0	0	0	1	....	....	....	.000	.125	.000	.125	-55	-1	0	.00	-1	/S-2	0	-0.2
Total 2	**4**	**14**	**2**	**2**	**1**	**0**	**0**	**1**	**2**	**....**	**....**	**....**	**.143**	**.250**	**.214**	**.464**	**49**	**-1**	**1**	**2.69**	**-2**	**/0-2,S-2,C-1**	**0**	**-0.2**
• FARRELL, Doc	Edward Stephen Farrell b: 12/26/1901, Johnson City, NY d: 12/20/1966, Livingston, NJ BR/TR, 5'8", 160 lbs. Deb: 6/15/1925																							
1925 NY-N	27	56	6	12	1	0	0	4	4	6	0	1	.214	.267	.232	.499	30	-6	3	1.97	1	S-13/3-7,2-1	0	-0.3
1926 NY-N	67	171	19	49	10	1	2	23	12	17	4	....	.287	.341	.392	.732	98	-1	22	4.60	-5	S-53/2-3	5	-0.1
1927 NY-N	42	142	13	55	10	1	3	34	12	11	0	....	.387	.442	.535	.978	161	13	33	9.45	-2	S-36/3-2	9	1.4
Bos-N	110	424	44	124	13	2	1	58	14	21	4	....	.292	.315	.340	.655	82	-12	44	3.58	-5	S-57,2-40,3-18	8	-0.9
Yr.	152	566	57	179	23	3	4	92	26	32	4	....	.316	.348	.389	.737	102	1	77	4.87	-7	S-93,2-40,3-20	17	0.5
1928 Bos-N	134	483	36	104	14	2	3	43	26	26	3	....	.215	.263	.271	.534	42	-42	35	2.27	-22	*S-132/2-1	2	-4.8
1929 Bos-N	5	8	0	1	0	0	0	2	0	1	0	....	.125	.125	.125	.250	-39	-2	0	.43	0	/2-1,S-1	0	-0.2
NY-N	63	178	18	38	6	0	0	16	9	17	2	....	.213	.251	.247	.499	24	-21	11	1.99	-2	3-28,2-25/S-4	2	-1.9
Yr.	68	186	18	39	6	0	0	18	9	18	2	....	.210	.246	.242	.488	22	-23	11	1.91	-2	3-28,2-26/S-5	2	-2.1
1930 StL-N	23	61	3	13	1	1	0	6	4	2	1	....	.213	.262	.262	.524	26	-7	4	2.22	0	S-15/2-6,1-1	1	-0.5
Chi-N	46	113	21	33	6	0	1	16	9	5	0	....	.292	.344	.372	.716	73	-5	14	4.48	-4	S-38/2-1	2	-0.5
Yr.	69	174	24	46	7	1	1	22	13	7	1	....	.264	.316	.333	.649	57	-12	18	3.64	-4	S-53/2-7,1-1	3	-1.0
1932 NY-A	26	63	4	11	1	1	0	4	2	8	0	0	.175	.212	.222	.434	13	-8	3	1.53	1	2-16/S-5,1-2,3-1	1	-0.6
1933 NY-A	44	93	16	25	0	0	0	6	16	6	0	0	.269	.376	.269	.645	78	-2	11	4.03	-4	S-22,2-20	2	-0.3
1935 Bos-A	4	7	1	2	1	0	0	1	1	0	0	0	.286	.375	.429	.804	101	0	1	6.22	-1	/2-4	0	0.0
Total 9	**591**	**1799**	**181**	**467**	**63**	**8**	**10**	**213**	**109**	**120**	**14**	**1**	**.260**	**.306**	**.320**	**.626**	**66**	**-93**	**182**	**3.40**	**-42**	**S-376,2-118/3-56,1-3**	**32**	**-8.7**
• FARRELL, Duke	Charles Andrew Farrell b: 8/31/1866, Oakdale, MA d: 2/15/1925, Boston, MA BB/TR, 6'1", 208 lbs. Deb: 4/21/1888 U Career OF: 48-22-39																							
1888 Chi-N	64	241	34	56	6	3	3	19	4	41	8	....	.232	.245	.320	.564	73	-8	21	3.11	-5	C-33,0-31(10-2-19)/1-1	4	-1.1
1889 Chi-N	101	407	66	101	19	7	11	75	41	21	13	....	.248	.318	.410	.729	98	-4	59	5.09	3	C-76,0-25(7-15-3)	12	0.4
1890 Chi-P	117	451	79	131	21	12	2	84	42	28	8	....	.290	.352	.404	.756	97	-4	69	5.79	15	C-90,1-22,0-10(0-2-8)	17	1.4
1891 Bos-a	122	473	108	143	19	13	**12**	**110**	59	48	21	....	.302	.384	.474	.858	147	28	97	7.75	17	3-66,C-37,0-23(20-0-3)/1-4	24	**4.2**
1892 Pit-N	152	605	96	130	10	13	8	77	46	53	20	....	.215	.276	.314	.590	78	-18	59	3.38	-9	*3-133,0-20(11-3-6)	13	-2.5
1893 Was-N	124	511	84	144	13	13	4	75	47	12	11	....	.282	.348	.382	.730	96	-3	74	5.31	17	C-81,3-41/1-3	14	1.8
1894*NY-N	116	404	50	116	20	12	5	69	38	15	9	....	.287	.353	.433	.786	56	-38	55	3.81	8	*C-104/3-5,1-4	14	-1.5
1895 NY-N	90	312	38	90	16	9	1	58	38	18	11	....	.288	.371	.407	.778	103	2	53	6.33	1	C-62,3-24/1-2	11	0.8
1896 NY-N	58	191	23	54	7	3	1	37	19	7	2	....	.283	.351	.366	.717	92	-2	27	4.94	-2	C-34,S-13/3-7	4	-0.1
Was-N	37	130	18	39	7	3	1	30	7	3	2	....	.300	.345	.423	.768	102	-0	21	5.72	2	C-18,3-14	4	0.3
Yr.	95	321	41	93	14	6	2	67	26	10	4	....	.290	.349	.389	.738	96	-2	48	5.25	0	C-52,3-21,S-13	8	0.3
1897 Was-N	78	261	41	84	9	6	0	53	17	....	8	....	.322	.366	.402	.768	103	1	43	6.25	11	C-63/1-1	9	1.5
1898 Was-N	99	338	47	106	12	6	1	53	34	....	12	....	.314	.383	.393	.776	123	11	57	6.46	7	C-61,1-28	11	2.1
1899 Was-N	5	12	2	4	1	0	0	1	2	....	1	....	.333	.429	.417	.845	134	1	3	8.73	1	/C-4	1	0.2
Bro-N	80	254	40	76	10	7	2	55	35	....	6	....	.299	.399	.417	.816	121	9	46	6.80	6	C-78	15	2.0
Yr.	85	266	42	80	11	7	2	56	37	....	7	....	.301	.400	.417	.817	122	10	49	6.88	6	C-82	16	2.1
1900*Bro-N	76	273	33	75	11	5	0	39	11	....	3	....	.275	.310	.352	.662	78	-9	32	4.19	-5	C-74	6	-0.7
1901 Bro-N	80	284	38	84	10	6	1	31	7	....	7	....	.296	.320	.384	.704	101	-1	38	5.02	2	C-59,1-17	9	0.6
1902 Bro-N	74	264	14	64	5	2	0	24	12	....	6	....	.242	.281	.277	.557	71	-9	24	3.02	6	C-49,1-24	5	0.1
1903*Bos-A	17	52	5	21	5	1	0	8	5	....	1	....	.404	.466	.538	1.004	190	6	14	10.79	1	C-17	4	0.9
1904 Bos-A	68	198	11	42	9	2	0	15	15	....	1	....	.212	.281	.278	.559	73	-6	17	2.77	-6	C-56	5	-0.7
1905 Bos-A	7	21	2	6	1	0	0	2	1	....	0	....	.286	.318	.333	.652	106	0	2	4.03	1	/C-7	1	0.1
Total 18	**1565**	**5682**	**829**	**1566**	**211**	**123**	**52**	**915**	**480**	**246**	**150**	**....**	**.276**	**.337**	**.383**	**.721**	**97**	**-45**	**810**	**5.06**	**70**	***C-1003,3-290,0-109,1-106/S**	**183**	**10.1**
• FARRELL, Jack	John A. "Moose" Farrell b: 7/5/1857, Newark, NJ d: 2/9/1914, Cedar Grove, NJ BR/TR, 5'9", 165 lbs. Deb: 5/1/1879 M																							
1879 Syr-N	54	241	40	73	6	2	1	21	3	13	....	....	.303	.311	.357	.668	135	9	27	4.58	1	2-54	9	1.2
Pro-N	12	51	5	13	2	0	0	5	0	0	....	....	.255	.255	.294	.549	82	-1	4	2.89	6	2-12	1	0.5
Yr.	66	292	45	86	8	2	1	26	3	13	....	....	.295	.302	.346	.648	125	8	31	4.26	7	*2-66	10	1.7
1880 Pro-N	80	339	46	92	12	5	3	36	10	6	....	....	.271	.292	.363	.655	124	9	37	4.10	-5	*2-80	13	0.7
1881 Pro-N	84	345	69	82	16	5	5	36	29	23	....	....	.238	.297	.357	.653	106	3	37	3.84	-4	*2-82/0-3(0-3-0)	13	0.3
1882 Pro-N	84	366	67	93	21	6	2	31	16	23	....	....	.254	.285	.361	.646	106	3	39	3.89	0	*2-84	11	0.5
1883 Pro-N	95	420	92	128	24	11	3	61	15	21	....	....	.305	.329	.436	.764	126	12	62	5.81	22	*2-95	18	3.3
1884*Pro-N	111	469	70	102	13	6	1	37	35	44	....	....	.217	.272	.277	.549	75	-12	36	2.71	15	*2-109/3-3	11	0.7
1885 Pro-N	68	257	27	53	7	1	1	19	10	25	....	....	.206	.236	.253	.489	61	-11	16	2.08	-9	2-68	4	-1.7
1886 Phi-N	17	60	7	11	0	1	0	3	3	11	1	....	.183	.222	.217	.439	33	-5	3	1.76	-4	2-17	0	-0.7
Was-N	47	171	24	41	11	4	2	18	15	12	12	....	.240	.301	.386	.687	114	3	24	5.00	-6	2-47	4	-0.1
Yr.	64	231	31	52	11	5	2	21	18	23	13	....	.225	.281	.342	.623	94	-2	27	4.11	-9	2-64	4	-0.8
1887 Was-N	87	359	40	95	14	9	0	41	20	12	31	....	.265	.267	.316	.582	64	-16	38	3.79	-4	S-48,2-40	6	-1.4
1888 Bal-a	103	398	72	81	19	5	4	36	26	....	29	....	.204	.256	.307	.562	82	-8	40	3.37	6	S-54,2-52	10	0.1
1889 Bal-a	42	157	25	33	3	0	1	26	15	15	14	....	.210	.287	.248	.536	54	-9	16	3.34	-4	S-42	3	-0.9
Total 11	**884**	**3633**	**584**	**897**	**148**	**55**	**23**	**370**	**197**	**205**	**87**	**....**	**.247**	**.283**	**.333**	**.616**	**94**	**-22**	**378**	**3.76**	**15**	**2-740,S-144/3-3,0-3**	**103**	**2.4**
• FARRELL, Jack	John J. Farrell b: 6/17/1889, Chicago, IL d: 12/2/1918, Chicago, IL BB/TR, 5'8", 145 lbs. Deb: 4/16/1914																							
1914 Chi-F	156	524	58	123	23	4	0	35	52	65	12	....	.235	.307	.294	.601	76	-16	50	3.06	14	*2-155/S-3	13	0.2
1915 Chi-F	70	222	27	48	10	1	0	14	25	18	8	....	.216	.298	.270	.569	72	-7	20	2.87	1	2-70/S-1	5	-0.5
Total 2	**226**	**746**	**85**	**171**	**33**	**5**	**0**	**49**	**77**	**83**	**20**	**....**	**.229**	**.305**	**.287**	**.592**	**75**	**-23**	**70**	**3.00**	**15**	**2-225/S-4**	**18**	**-0.3**

YEAR TM-L	G	AB	R	H	2B	3B	HR	RBI	BB	SO	SB	CS	AVG	OBP	SLG	OPS	OPS+	BR/A	RC	RC/G	FR	G/POS	WS	TPW
• FARRELL, Jack	John "Hartford Jack" Farrell b: 1/2/1856, Hartford, CT d: 11/15/1916, Hartford, CT Deb: 10/27/1874																							
1874 Har-n	3	13	3	5	0	0	0	0	1	0	0	0	.385	.429	.385	.813	155	1	2	8.24	0	/0-3(0-3-0)	....	0.1
• FARRELL, Joe	Joseph F. Farrell b: 1857, Brooklyn, NY d: 4/18/1893, Brooklyn, NY BR, 5'6", 160 lbs. Deb: 5/1/1882 Career OF: 1-1-0																							
1882 Det-N	69	283	34	70	12	2	1	24	4	20	....	....	.247	.258	.314	.572	83	-6	24	3.04	-2	3-42,2-18/S-9	6	-0.5
1883 Det-N	101	444	58	108	13	5	0	36	5	29	....	....	.243	.252	.295	.547	69	-16	34	2.77	15	*3-101	9	0.2
1884 Det-N	110	461	59	104	10	5	3	41	14	66	....	....	.226	.248	.289	.537	73	-13	34	2.61	-6	*3-110/0-1	6	-1.5
1886 Bal-a	73	301	36	63	8	3	1	31	12	....	5	....	.209	.240	.266	.505	60	-14	21	2.37	-8	2-45,3-27/0-1	5	-1.8
Total 4	353	1489	187	345	43	15	5	132	35	115	5	....	.232	.249	.291	.540	71	-49	112	2.68	-1	3-280/2-63,S-9,0-2	26	-3.7
• FARRELL, John	John Sebastian Farrell b: 12/4/1876, Covington, KY d: 5/14/1921, Kansas City, MO BR/TR, 5'10", 160 lbs. Deb: 4/26/1901 Career OF: 2-72-0																							
1901 Was-A	135	555	100	151	32	11	3	63	52	....	25	....	.272	.336	.386	.721	101	1	83	5.36	6	2-72,0-62(0-62-0)/3-1	17	0.5
1902 StL-N	138	565	68	141	13	5	0	25	43	....	9	....	.250	.308	.290	.599	88	-7	56	3.42	10	*2-118,S-21	15	0.5
1903 StL-N	130	519	83	141	25	8	1	32	48	....	17	....	.272	.336	.356	.692	100	1	70	4.86	17	*2-118,0-12(2-10-0)	16	1.7
1904 StL-N	131	509	72	130	23	3	0	20	46	....	16	....	.255	.320	.312	.632	100	1	58	3.93	15	*2-130	16	1.8
1905 StL-N	7	24	6	4	0	1	0	1	4	....	1	....	.167	.286	.250	.536	62	-1	2	2.67	-3	/2-7	0	-0.5
Total 5	541	2172	329	567	93	28	4	141	193	....	68	....	.261	.324	.335	.659	97	-5	269	4.36	45	2-445/0-74,S-21,3-1	64	4.0
• FARRELL, Kerby	Major Kerby Farrell b: 9/3/1913, Leapwood, TN d: 12/17/1975, Nashville, TN BL/TL, 5'11", 172 lbs. Deb: 4/24/1943 M/C																							
1943 Bos-N	85	280	11	75	14	1	0	21	16	15	1	....	.268	.307	.325	.632	84	-6	26	3.21	3	1-69/P-5	5	-1.0
1945 Chi-A	103	396	44	102	11	3	0	34	24	18	4	9	.258	.300	.301	.601	76	-15	35	2.98	-3	1-97	6	-2.5
Total 2	188	676	55	177	25	4	0	55	40	33	5	9	.262	.303	.311	.614	80	-21	61	3.08	-1	1-166/P-5	11	-3.5
• FARROW, John	John Jacob Farrow b: 11/8/1853, Verplanck, NY d: 12/31/1914, Perth Amboy, NJ BL/TR Deb: 4/28/1873 NA OF: 0-2-4																							
1873 Res-n	12	48	2	8	1	0	0	3	0	3	0	0	.167	.167	.188	.354	5	-5	2	1.17	-3	/C-9,0-3(0-0-3),1-1,S-1	....	-0.5
1874 Atl-n	27	122	16	26	3	0	0	10	1	1	0	0	.213	.220	.238	.457	52	-5	7	2.04	5	C-16,2-12/0-3(0-2-1)	....	-0.1
1884 Bro-a	16	58	7	11	2	0	0	0	3	....	....	....	.190	.230	.224	.454	48	-3	3	1.79	0	C-16	1	-0.1
Total 2 n	39	170	18	34	4	0	0	13	1	4	0	0	.200	.205	.224	.428	39	-10	8	1.78	2	/C-25,2-12,0-6,1-1,S-1	....	-0.6
• FASANO, Sal	Salvatore Frank Fasano b: 8/10/1971, Chicago, IL BR/TR, 6'2", 220 lbs. Deb: 4/3/1996																							
1996 KC-A	51	143	20	29	2	0	6	19	14	25	1	1	.203	.283	.343	.626	57	-10	14	3.15	-3	C-51	4	-0.8
1997 KC-A	13	38	4	8	2	0	1	1	1	12	0	0	.211	.231	.342	.573	46	-3	3	2.37	0	C-12/D-1	1	-0.3
1998 KC-A	74	216	21	49	10	0	8	31	10	56	1	0	.227	.310	.384	.694	77	-7	27	4.08	-2	C-70/1-5,3-1	7	-0.4
1999 KC-A	23	60	11	14	2	0	5	16	7	17	0	1	.233	.378	.517	.895	123	2	12	6.72	2	C-23	3	0.5
2000*Oak-A	52	126	21	27	6	0	7	19	14	47	0	0	.214	.308	.429	.736	86	-3	17	4.40	-2	C-52	2	-0.2
2001 Oak-A	11	21	2	1	0	0	0	0	1	12	0	0	.048	.130	.048	.178	-50	-5	0	.17	-2	/C-9,D-1	0	-0.6
KC-A	3	1	0	0	0	0	0	0	0	0	0	0	.000	.000	.000	.000	-92	-0	0	.00	0	/C-3	0	-0.1
Yr.	14	22	2	1	0	0	0	0	1	12	0	0	.045	.125	.045	.170	-52	-5	0	.16	-2	C-12/D-1	0	-0.6
Col-N	25	63	10	16	5	0	3	9	4	19	0	0	.254	.329	.476	.805	85	-1	10	5.42	5	C-25	2	0.5
2002 Ana-A	2	1	0	0	0	0	0	0	0	1	0	0	.000	.000	.000	.000	-100	-0	0	.00	2	/C-2	0	0.1
Total 7	254	669	89	144	27	0	30	95	51	189	2	2	.215	.302	.390	.692	74	-28	82	4.03	0	C-247/1-5,D-2,3-1	19	-1.2
• FAUSETT, Buck	Robert Shaw "Leaky" Fausett b: 4/8/1908, Sheridan, AR d: 5/2/1994, College Station, TX BL/TR, 5'10", 170 lbs. Deb: 4/18/1944																							
1944 Cin-N	13	31	2	3	0	1	0	1	1	2	0	....	.097	.125	.161	.286	-21	-4	0	.31	3	/3-6,P-2	0	-0.5
• FAUTSCH, Joe	Joseph Roamon Fautsch b: 2/28/1887, Minneapolis, MN d: 3/16/1971, New Hope, MN BR/TR, 5'10", 162 lbs. Deb: 4/24/1916																							
1916 Chi-A	1	1	0	0	0	0	0	0	0	0	0	....	.000	.000	.000	.000	-99	-0	0	.00	0	....	0	0.0
• FAZIO, Ernie	Ernest Joseph Fazio b: 1/25/1942, Oakland, CA BR/TR, 5'7", 165 lbs. Deb: 7/3/1962																							
1962 Hou-N	12	12	3	1	0	0	0	1	2	5	0	0	.083	.214	.083	.298	-18	-2	0	.80	-2	S-10	0	-0.4
1963 Hou-N	102	228	31	42	10	3	2	5	27	70	4	4	.184	.273	.281	.554	64	-11	18	2.56	-9	2-84/3-1,S-1	3	-1.6
1966 KC-A	27	34	3	7	0	1	0	2	4	10	1	0	.206	.289	.265	.554	62	-1	3	2.91	1	2-10/S-4	1	0.0
Total 3	141	274	37	50	10	4	2	8	33	85	5	4	.182	.273	.270	.543	60	-14	22	2.52	-10	/2-94,S-15,3-1	4	-1.9
• FEBLES, Carlos	Carlos Manuel Febles b: 5/24/1976, El Seibo, Dominican Republic BR/TR, 5'11", 185 lbs. Deb: 9/14/1998																							
1998 KC-A	11	25	5	10	1	2	0	2	4	7	2	1	.400	.483	.600	1.083	175	3	8	12.92	-1	2-11	2	0.2
1999 KC-A	123	453	71	116	22	9	10	53	47	91	20	4	.256	.338	.411	.749	88	-6	63	4.61	-3	*2-122	10	-0.3
2000 KC-A	100	339	59	87	12	1	2	29	36	48	17	6	.257	.345	.316	.661	67	-15	40	3.79	-5	2-99	7	-1.4
2001 KC-A	79	292	45	69	9	2	8	25	22	58	5	2	.236	.292	.363	.655	66	-15	30	3.49	-4	2-78	5	-1.5
2002 KC-A	119	351	44	86	16	4	4	26	41	63	16	5	.245	.336	.348	.683	74	-11	44	4.15	-5	*2-116/S-1	7	-1.1
2003 KC-A	74	196	31	46	5	0	0	11	13	30	8	2	.235	.299	.260	.559	44	-15	15	2.52	-13	2-67/D-3,S-1	1	-2.4
Total 6	506	1656	255	414	65	18	24	146	163	297	68	20	.250	.329	.354	.683	73	-59	200	3.99	-31	2-493/D-3,S-2	32	-6.4
• FEDEROFF, Al	Alfred "Whitey" Federoff b: 7/11/1924, Bairdford, PA BR/TR, 5'10.5", 165 lbs. Deb: 9/27/1951																							
1951 Det-A	2	4	0	0	0	0	0	0	0	0	0	0	.000	.000	.000	.000	-100	-1	0	.00	0	/2-1	0	-0.1
1952 Det-A	74	231	14	56	4	2	0	14	16	13	1	0	.242	.294	.277	.571	59	-12	20	2.91	-9	2-70/S-7	2	-1.8
Total 2	76	235	14	56	4	2	0	14	16	13	1	0	.238	.290	.272	.562	57	-13	20	2.85	-9	/2-71,S-7	2	-1.9
• FEHRING, Dutch	William Paul "Dutch" Fehring b: 5/31/1912, Columbus, IN BB/TR, 6', 195 lbs. Deb: 6/25/1934																							
1934 Chi-A	1	1	0	0	0	0	0	0	0	1	0	0	.000	.000	.000	.000	-97	-0	0	.00	-0	/C-1	0	0.0
• FEINBERG, Eddie	Edward Isadore "Itzzy" Feinberg b: 9/20/1918, Philadelphia, PA d: 4/20/1986, Hollywood, FL BB/TR, 5'9", 165 lbs. Deb: 9/11/1938																							
1938 Phi-N	10	20	0	3	0	0	0	0	0	1	0	....	.150	.150	.150	.300	-17	-3	0	.73	0	/S-4,0-2(1-0-2)	0	-0.3
1939 Phi-N	6	18	2	4	1	0	0	0	2	0	0	....	.222	.300	.278	.578	59	-1	2	3.02	-1	/2-4,S-1	0	-0.2
Total 2	16	38	2	7	1	0	0	0	2	1	0	....	.184	.225	.211	.436	23	-4	2	1.84	0	/S-5,2-4,0-2	0	-0.4
• FELDER, Mike	Michael Otis "Tiny" Felder b: 11/18/1961, Vallejo, CA BB/TR, 5'8", 160 lbs. Deb: 9/11/1985 Career OF: 408-212-169																							
1985 Mil-A	15	56	8	11	1	0	0	0	5	6	4	1	.196	.262	.214	.477	33	-5	3	1.84	-1	0-14(0-14-0)	0	-0.6
1986 Mil-A	44	155	24	37	2	4	1	13	13	16	16	2	.239	.298	.323	.620	67	-5	17	3.60	-1	0-42(30-7-6)/D-1	3	-0.7
1987 Mil-A	108	289	48	77	5	7	2	31	28	23	34	8	.266	.331	.353	.684	79	-5	38	4.39	2	0-99(80-22-0)/D-3,2-1	7	-0.6
1988 Mil-A	50	81	14	14	1	0	0	5	0	11	8	2	.173	.183	.185	.368	3	-10	3	1.10	-1	0-28(12-11-5),D-16/2-1	0	-1.1
1989 Mil-A	117	315	50	76	11	3	3	23	23	38	26	5	.241	.293	.324	.617	74	-8	33	3.44	3	0-93(30-34-38),D-11,2-10	6	-0.7
1990 Mil-A	121	237	38	65	7	2	3	27	22	17	20	9	.274	.336	.359	.695	95	-1	31	4.31	4	*0-109(61-15-44)/2-1,3-1,D	7	0.0
1991 SF-N	132	348	51	92	10	6	0	18	30	31	21	6	.264	.325	.328	.652	87	-4	41	4.12	-2	*0-107(45-38-44)/3-3,2-1	9	-0.9
1992 SF-N	145	322	44	92	13	3	4	23	21	29	14	4	.286	.333	.382	.715	108	4	43	4.76	-3	*0-105(53-58-11)/2-3	10	-0.1
1993 Sea-A	109	342	31	72	7	5	1	20	22	34	15	9	.211	.262	.269	.531	43	-29	25	2.33	2	0-95(89-7-0)/D-6,3-2	2	-2.9
1994 Hou-N	58	117	10	28	2	2	0	13	4	12	3	0	.239	.264	.291	.555	47	-9	9	2.78	0	0-32(8-6-21)	1	-0.9
Total 10	899	2262	318	564	59	32	14	173	168	217	161	46	.249	.303	.322	.625	74	-69	243	3.59	4	0-724/D-38,2-17,3-6	45	-8.4
• FELDERMAN, Marv	Marvin Wilfred "Coonie" Felderman b: 12/20/1915, Bellevue, IA d: 8/6/2000, Riverside, CA BR/TR, 6'1", 187 lbs. Deb: 4/19/1942																							
1942 Chi-N	3	6	0	1	0	0	0	0	1	4	0	....	.167	.286	.167	.452	35	-0	0	1.94	0	/C-2	0	0.0
• FELIX, Gus	August Guenther Felix b: 5/24/1895, Cincinnati, OH d: 5/12/1960, Montgomery, AL BR/TR, 6', 180 lbs. Deb: 4/19/1923 Career OF: 344-196-5																							
1923 Bos-N	139	506	64	138	17	2	6	44	51	65	8	13	.273	.348	.350	.697	88	-10	62	4.18	-4	*0-123(121-6-0)/2-5,3-4	8	-2.2
1924 Bos-N	59	204	25	43	7	1	1	10	18	16	0	3	.211	.275	.270	.544	48	-15	15	2.40	2	0-51(11-38-2)	1	-1.6
1925 Bos-N	121	459	60	141	25	7	2	66	30	34	5	5	.307	.356	.405	.762	103	2	66	5.22	9	*0-114(42-74-3)	13	0.4
1926 Bro-N	134	432	64	121	21	7	3	53	51	32	9	....	.280	.360	.382	.742	101	2	60	4.88	-1	*0-125(53-74-0)	13	-0.5
1927 Bro-N	130	445	43	118	21	8	0	57	39	47	6	....	.265	.327	.348	.675	81	-12	51	3.90	-6	*0-119(117-4-0)	8	-2.7
Total 5	583	2046	256	561	91	25	12	230	189	194	28	21	.274	.341	.361	.701	89	-33	254	4.30	-1	0-532/2-5,3-4	43	-6.6

YEAR TM-L	G	AB	R	H	2B	3B	HR	RBI	BB	SO	SB	CS	AVG	OBP	SLG	OPS	OPS+	BR/A	RC	RC/G	FR	G/POS	WS	TPW
• FELIX, Junior	Junior Francisco (Sanchez) Felix b: 10/3/1967, Laguna Salada, Dominican Republic BB/TR, 6', 165 lbs. Deb: 5/3/1989 Career OF: 5-245-313																							
1989*Tor-A	110	415	62	107	14	8	9	46	33	101	18	12	.258	.317	.395	.712	106	1	51	4.20	-1	*O-107(0-24-86)/D-2	11	-0.3
1990 Tor-A	127	463	73	122	23	7	15	65	45	99	13	8	.263	.331	.441	.772	108	4	69	5.16	-4	*O-125(0-28-99)/D-1	15	-0.4
1991 Cal-A	66	230	32	65	10	2	2	26	11	55	7	5	.283	.324	.370	.693	91	-4	26	3.99	-3	O-65(0-63-2)	4	-0.8
1992 Cal-A	139	509	63	125	22	5	9	72	33	128	8	8	.246	.294	.361	.656	82	-15	52	3.39	2	*O-128(0-125-4)/D-8	12	-1.6
1993 Fla-N	57	214	25	51	11	1	7	22	10	50	2	1	.238	.276	.397	.673	73	-9	22	3.44	-3	O-52(0-3-50)	3	-1.4
1994 Det-A	86	301	54	92	25	1	13	49	26	76	1	6	.306	.376	.525	.901	129	10	57	6.82	-1	O-81(5-2-72)/D-2	10	0.5
Total 6	**585**	**2132**	**309**	**562**	**105**	**24**	**55**	**280**	**158**	**509**	**49**	**40**	**.264**	**.320**	**.413**	**.733**	**99**	**-13**	**277**	**4.46**	**-9**	**O-558/D-13**	**55**	**-4.0**
• FELIZ, Pedro	Pedro Julio Feliz b: 4/27/1975, Azua, Dominican Republic BR/TR, 6'1", 180 lbs. Deb: 9/5/2000 Career OF: 15-0-1																							
2000 SF-N	8	7	1	2	0	0	0	0	0	1	0	0	.286	.286	.286	.571	49	-1	1	3.09	-1	/3-4	0	-0.1
2001 SF-N	94	220	23	50	9	1	7	22	10	50	2	1	.227	.267	.373	.640	68	-11	21	3.10	-13	3-86/D-1	0	-2.3
2002*SF-N	67	146	14	37	4	1	2	13	6	27	0	0	.253	.283	.336	.619	65	-8	14	3.28	1	3-44/O-1,S-1	2	-0.7
2003*SF-N	95	235	31	58	9	3	16	48	10	53	2	2	.247	.280	.515	.795	104	-1	30	4.35	7	3-49,O-15(14-0-1),1-12	8	0.5
Total 4	**264**	**608**	**69**	**147**	**22**	**5**	**25**	**83**	**26**	**131**	**4**	**3**	**.242**	**.276**	**.418**	**.694**	**81**	**-21**	**66**	**3.63**	**-6**	**3-183/O-16,1-12,D-1,S-1**	**10**	**-2.6**
• FELLER, Jack	Jack Leland Feller b: 12/10/1936, Adrian, MI BR/TR, 5'10.5", 185 lbs. Deb: 9/13/1958																							
1958 Det-A	1	0	0	0	0	0	0	0	0	0	0	0	....	....	....	....	-93	0	0	....	0	/C-1	0	0.0
• FELSCH, Happy	Oscar Emil Felsch b: 8/22/1891, Milwaukee, WI d: 8/17/1964, Milwaukee, WI BR/TR, 5'11", 175 lbs. Deb: 4/14/1915 Career OF: 34-696-10																							
1915 Chi-A	121	427	65	106	18	11	3	53	51	59	16	18	.248	.334	.363	.697	105	-2	52	3.91	-8	*O-118(34-73-10)	14	-1.8
1916 Chi-A	146	546	73	164	24	12	7	70	31	67	13	....	.300	.341	.427	.768	129	16	85	5.61	1	*O-141(0-141-0)	24	0.8
1917*Chi-A	152	575	75	177	17	10	6	102	33	52	26	....	.308	.352	.403	.755	128	17	87	5.45	3	*O-152(0-152-0)	30	1.1
1918 Chi-A	53	206	16	52	2	5	1	20	15	13	6	....	.252	.306	.325	.632	90	-3	22	3.45	3	O-53(0-53-0)	4	-0.4
1919*Chi-A	135	502	68	138	34	11	7	86	40	35	19	....	.275	.336	.428	.764	113	7	76	5.15	17	*O-135(0-135-0)	21	1.6
1920 Chi-A	142	556	88	188	40	15	14	115	37	25	8	13	.338	.384	.540	.923	143	29	109	7.29	10	*O-142(0-142-0)	30	2.9
Total 6	**749**	**2812**	**385**	**825**	**135**	**64**	**38**	**446**	**207**	**251**	**88**	**31**	**.293**	**.347**	**.427**	**.774**	**122**	**62**	**431**	**5.36**	**25**	**O-741**	**123**	**4.2**
• FELSKE, John	John Frederick Felske b: 5/30/1942, Chicago, IL BR/TR, 6'3", 195 lbs. Deb: 7/26/1968 M/C																							
1968 Chi-N	4	2	0	0	0	0	0	0	0	1	0	0	.000	.000	.000	.000	-94	-0	0	.00	-1	/C-3	0	-0.1
1972 Mil-A	37	80	6	11	3	0	1	5	8	23	0	0	.138	.216	.213	.428	28	-7	4	1.40	-1	C-23/1-8	1	-0.9
1973 Mil-A	13	22	1	3	0	1	0	4	1	11	0	0	.136	.174	.227	.401	12	-3	1	1.30	0	/C-7,1-6	0	-0.2
Total 3	**54**	**104**	**7**	**14**	**3**	**1**	**1**	**9**	**9**	**35**	**0**	**0**	**.135**	**.204**	**.212**	**.415**	**23**	**-10**	**5**	**1.35**	**-2**	**/C-33,1-14**	**1**	**-1.2**
• FENNELLY, Frank	Francis John Fennelly b: 2/18/1860, Fall River, MA d: 8/4/1920, Fall River, MA BR/TR, 5'8", 168 lbs. Deb: 5/1/1884																							
1884 Was-a	62	257	52	75	17	7	2	0	20	....	....	....	.292	.343	.436	.779	172	22	39	5.95	10	S-60/2-4	12	3.0
Cin-a	28	122	42	43	5	8	2	0	11	....	....	....	.352	.415	.574	.989	209	15	30	10.36	-4	S-28	9	1.1
Yr.	90	379	94	118	22	15	4	0	31	....	....	....	.311	.367	.480	.847	184	36	69	7.28	6	*S-88/2-4	21	4.1
1885 Cin-a	112	454	82	124	14	17	10	**89**	38	....	....	....	.273	.333	.445	.778	141	21	69	5.65	-2	*S-112	23	2.0
1886 Cin-a	132	497	113	124	13	17	6	72	60	....	32	....	.249	.351	.380	.732	125	16	80	5.76	11	*S-132	23	2.8
1887 Cin-a	134	608	133	222	15	16	8	97	82	....	74	....	.365	.369	.401	.770	112	10	108	7.55	2	*S-134	20	1.3
1888 Cin-a	120	448	64	88	8	7	2	56	63	....	43	....	.196	.297	.259	.556	75	-11	48	3.63	19	*S-112/2-4,O-4(2-2-0)	16	1.0
Phi-a	15	47	13	11	2	2	1	12	9	....	5	....	.234	.357	.426	.783	151	3	9	6.86	0	S-15	3	0.3
Yr.	135	495	77	99	10	9	3	68	72	....	48	....	.200	.303	.275	.578	82	-8	58	3.92	18	*S-127/2-4,O-4(2-2-0)	19	1.3
1889 Phi-a	138	513	70	132	20	5	1	64	65	78	15	....	.257	.344	.322	.666	91	-4	64	4.42	-17	*S-138	12	-1.4
1890 Bro-a	45	178	40	44	8	3	2	18	30	....	6	....	.247	.356	.360	.715	115	4	26	5.05	-4	S-38/3-7	5	0.1
Total 7	**786**	**3124**	**609**	**863**	**102**	**82**	**34**	**408**	**378**	**78**	**175**	**....**	**.276**	**.345**	**.378**	**.723**	**119**	**76**	**472**	**5.63**	**14**	**S-769/2-8,3-7,O-4**	**123**	**10.3**
• FENWICK, Bobby	Robert Richard Fenwick b: 12/10/1946, Naha, Okinawa BR/TR, 5'9", 165 lbs. Deb: 4/26/1972																							
1972 Hou-N	36	50	7	9	3	0	0	4	3	13	0	1	.180	.226	.240	.466	33	-5	2	1.48	-2	2-17/S-4,3-2	0	-0.6
1973 StL-N	5	6	0	1	0	0	0	1	0	2	0	0	.167	.167	.167	.333	-7	-1	0	.90	-1	/2-3	0	-0.2
Total 2	**41**	**56**	**7**	**10**	**3**	**0**	**0**	**5**	**3**	**15**	**0**	**1**	**.179**	**.220**	**.232**	**.452**	**29**	**-6**	**3**	**1.42**	**-2**	**/2-20,S-4,3-2**	**0**	**-0.8**
• FERGUSON, Bob	Robert Vavasour "Death to Flying Things" Ferguson b: 1/31/1845, Brooklyn, NY d: 5/3/1894, Brooklyn, NY BB/TR, 5'9.5", 149 lbs. Deb: 5/18/1871 M/U																							
1871 Mut-n	33	158	30	38	6	1	0	25	3	2	4	4	.241	.255	.291	.546	62	-7	13	3.32	6	*3-20,2-11/C-5,P-1	....	-0.3
1872 Atl-n	37	165	33	46	5	0	0	19	3	0	4	2	.279	.292	.309	.601	72	-8	16	4.21	27	*3-37/C-1	....	1.3
1873 Atl-n	51	228	36	59	3	5	0	25	4	9	1	2	.259	.272	.316	.587	83	-2	20	3.62	22	*3-50/P-4	....	0.9
1874 Atl-n	56	245	34	64	4	0	0	18	2	7	4	3	.261	.267	.278	.545	85	-2	20	3.22	1	*3-55/C-2,P-1	....	-0.3
1875 Har-n	85	366	65	88	10	4	0	43	3	5	2	1	.240	.247	.290	.536	81	-8	27	2.89	15	*3-85/P-1	....	0.3
1876 Har-N	69	312	48	82	8	5	0	32	2	11	....	....	.263	.269	.323	.592	89	-5	28	3.39	5	*3-69	9	0.1
1877 Har-N	58	254	40	65	7	2	0	35	3	10	....	....	.256	.265	.299	.564	86	-2	21	3.00	18	*3-56/P-3	7	1.1
1878 Chi-N	61	259	44	91	10	2	0	39	10	12	....	....	.351	**.375**	.405	.781	147	13	40	6.61	16	*S-57/2-4,C-1	11	3.0
1879 Tro-N	30	123	18	31	5	2	0	4	4	3	....	....	.252	.276	.325	.601	104	1	11	3.44	0	3-24/2-6	3	0.2
1880 Tro-N	82	332	55	87	9	0	0	22	**24**	24	....	....	.262	.312	.289	.601	100	0	31	3.44	0	*2-82	9	0.4
1881 Tro-N	85	339	56	96	13	5	1	35	29	12	....	....	.283	.340	.360	.700	114	6	42	4.72	-9	*2-85	12	0.1
1882 Tro-N	81	319	44	82	15	2	0	32	23	21	....	....	.257	.307	.317	.624	106	3	32	3.69	-17	*2-79/S-2	9	-1.0
1883 Phi-N	86	329	39	85	9	2	0	27	18	21	....	....	.258	.297	.298	.595	89	-2	30	3.36	-21	*2-86/P-1	4	-1.8
1884 Pit-a	10	41	2	6	0	0	0	0	0	....	....	....	.146	.146	.146	.293	-4	-5	1	.71	-2	/O-6(0-1-5),1-3,3-1	0	-0.7
Total 5 n	**262**	**1162**	**198**	**295**	**28**	**10**	**0**	**130**	**15**	**23**	**15**	**12**	**.254**	**.263**	**.295**	**.559**	**78**	**-26**	**97**	**3.34**	**70**	**3-247/2-11,C-8,P-7**	**....**	**1.9**
Total 9	**562**	**2308**	**346**	**625**	**76**	**20**	**1**	**226**	**113**	**114**	**....**	**....**	**.271**	**.305**	**.323**	**.628**	**102**	**10**	**236**	**3.85**	**-10**	**2-342,3-150/S-59,O-6,P-4,1,C**	**64**	**1.5**
• FERGUSON, Charlie	Charles J. Ferguson b: 4/17/1863, Charlottesville, VA d: 4/29/1888, Philadelphia, PA BB/TR, 6', 165 lbs. Deb: 5/1/1884 U Career OF: 13-22-18 ♦																							
1884 Phi-N	52	203	26	50	6	3	0	20	19	54	....	....	.246	.311	.305	.616	99	8	20	3.55	-3	P-50/O-5(1-3-1)	16	0.2
1885 Phi-N	61	235	42	72	8	3	1	27	23	18	....	....	.306	.368	.379	.747	145	20	34	5.56	-0	P-48,O-15(2-10-3)	41	3.9
1886 Phi-N	72	261	56	66	9	1	2	25	37	28	9	....	.253	.346	.318	.664	102	12	33	4.51	6	P-48,O-27(8-5-14)	49	7.3
1887 Phi-N	72	298	67	123	14	6	3	85	34	19	13	....	.413	.417	.470	.886	138	21	59	8.86	-2	P-37,2-27/O-6(2-4-0),3-5	36	5.6
Total 4	**257**	**997**	**191**	**311**	**37**	**13**	**6**	**157**	**113**	**119**	**22**	**....**	**.312**	**.364**	**.372**	**.735**	**121**	**61**	**144**	**5.66**	**1**	**P-183/O-53,2-27,3-5**	**142**	**17.0**
• FERGUSON, Joe	Joseph Vance Ferguson b: 9/19/1946, San Francisco, CA BR/TR, 6'2", 200 lbs. Deb: 9/12/1970 C Career OF: 18-1-188																							
1970 LA-N	5	4	0	1	0	0	0	1	2	2	0	0	.250	.500	.250	.750	112	0	1	5.90	0	/C-3	0	0.0
1971 LA-N	36	102	13	22	3	0	2	7	12	15	1	0	.216	.304	.304	.608	77	-3	10	3.14	-1	C-35	2	-0.3
1972 LA-N	8	24	2	7	3	0	1	5	2	4	0	0	.292	.346	.542	.888	152	2	4	4.91	0	/C-7,O-2(0-0-2)	1	0.2
1973 LA-N	136	487	84	128	26	0	25	88	87	81	1	1	.263	.376	.470	.846	139	28	92	6.60	0	*C-122,O-20(5-1-14)	29	3.4
1974*LA-N	111	349	54	88	14	1	16	57	75	73	2	2	.252	.384	.436	.820	134	18	60	5.82	-3	C-82,O-32(0-0-32)	19	1.8
1975 LA-N	66	202	15	42	2	1	5	23	35	47	2	1	.208	.328	.302	.630	79	-5	22	3.49	3	C-35,O-34(2-0-32)	5	-0.2
1976 LA-N	54	185	24	41	7	0	6	18	25	41	2	0	.222	.318	.357	.674	93	-1	22	4.06	0	O-39(0-0-39),C-17	6	-0.2
StL-N	71	189	22	38	8	4	4	21	32	40	4	2	.201	.320	.349	.669	89	-2	22	3.60	1	C-48,O-14(0-0-14)	5	0.1
Yr.	125	374	46	79	15	4	10	39	57	81	6	2	.211	.319	.353	.672	91	-3	44	3.82	1	C-65,O-53(0-0-53)	11	-0.1
1977 Hou-N	132	421	59	108	21	3	16	61	85	79	6	2	.257	.381	.435	.816	130	22	74	6.01	0	*C-122/1-1	20	2.7
1978 Hou-N	51	150	20	31	5	0	7	22	37	30	0	0	.207	.367	.380	.747	118	5	22	4.65	0	C-51	7	0.9
*LA-N	67	198	20	47	11	0	7	28	34	41	1	2	.237	.352	.399	.751	110	3	27	4.40	-2	C-62/O-3(2-0-1)	7	0.4
Yr.	118	348	40	78	16	0	14	50	71	71	1	2	.224	.359	.391	.749	113	8	49	4.51	-1	*C-113/O-3(2-0-1)	14	1.3
1979 LA-N	122	363	54	95	14	0	20	69	70	68	1	0	.262	.384	.466	.849	133	19	68	6.40	1	C-67,O-52(5-0-47)	17	2.2
1980 LA-N	77	172	20	41	3	2	9	29	38	46	2	2	.238	.376	.436	.812	128	8	27	5.11	-2	C-66/O-1	8	0.9
1981 LA-N	17	14	2	2	1	0	0	1	2	5	0	0	.143	.250	.214	.464	34	-1	1	1.98	0	/O-1	0	-0.1
Cal-A	12	30	5	7	1	0	1	5	9	8	0	0	.233	.410	.367	.777	125	2	5	5.46	0	/C-8,O-4(3-0-1)	1	0.2
1982 Cal-A	36	84	10	19	2	0	3	8	12	19	0	0	.226	.323	.357	.680	87	-1	9	3.61	1	C-32/O-2(0-0-2)	3	0.1
1983 Cal-A	12	27	3	2	0	0	0	2	5	8	0	0	.074	.219	.074	.293	-15	-4	0	.43	0	/C-9,O-3(1-0-2)	0	-0.4
Total 14	**1013**	**3001**	**407**	**719**	**121**	**11**	**122**	**445**	**562**	**607**	**22**	**12**	**.240**	**.361**	**.409**	**.770**	**118**	**89**	**465**	**5.17**	**-3**	**C-766,O-207/1-1**	**130**	**11.7**

YEAR TM-L	G	AB	R	H	2B	3B	HR	RBI	BB	SO	SB	CS	AVG	OBP	SLG	OPS	OPS+	BR/A	RC	RC/G	FR	G/POS	WS	TPW
• FERMIN, Felix	Felix Jose (Minaya) Fermin b: 10/9/1963, Mao Valverde, Dominican Republic BR/TR, 5'11", 170 lbs. Deb: 7/8/1987																							
1987 Pit-N	23	68	6	17	0	0	0	4	4	9	0	0	.250	.301	.250	.551	48	-5	5	2.33	0	S-23	1	-0.3
1988 Pit-N	43	87	9	24	0	2	0	2	8	10	3	1	.276	.357	.322	.679	98	0	10	4.03	-5	S-43	2	-0.2
1989 Cle-A	156	484	50	115	9	1	0	21	41	27	6	4	.238	.302	.260	.563	59	-26	40	2.54	22	*S-153/2-2	9	0.8
1990 Cle-A	148	414	47	106	13	2	1	40	26	22	3	3	.256	.300	.304	.604	70	-18	36	2.87	1	*S-147/2-1	9	-0.5
1991 Cle-A	129	424	30	111	13	2	0	31	26	27	5	4	.262	.309	.302	.611	69	-18	37	2.87	-9	*S-129	8	-1.6
1992 Cle-A	79	215	27	58	7	2	0	13	18	10	0	0	.270	.329	.321	.650	84	-4	23	3.50	0	S-55,3-17/2-7,1-2	5	0.0
1993 Cle-A	140	480	48	126	16	2	2	45	24	14	4	5	.263	.303	.317	.620	67	-24	44	3.13	-25	*S-140	8	-3.7
1994 Sea-A	101	379	52	120	21	0	1	35	11	22	4	4	.317	.343	.380	.723	84	-10	47	4.40	-8	S-77,2-25	6	-1.1
1995*Sea-A	73	200	21	39	6	0	0	15	6	6	2	0	.195	.233	.225	.458	20	-24	10	1.56	-1	S-46,2-29	2	-1.8
1996 Chi-N	11	16	4	2	1	0	0	1	2	0	0	0	.125	.222	.188	.410	9	-2	0	.68	-1	/2-6,S-2	0	-0.3
Total 10	903	2767	294	718	86	11	4	207	166	147	27	21	.259	.307	.303	.610	67	-130	253	3.00	-25	S-815/2-70,3-17,1-2	50	-8.8
• FERNANDES, Ed	Edward Paul Fernandes b: 3/11/1918, Oakland, CA d: 11/27/1968, Hayward, CA BB/TR, 5'9", 185 lbs. Deb: 6/9/1940																							
1940 Pit-N	28	33	1	4	1	0	0	2	7	6	0	....	.121	.275	.152	.427	21	-3	2	1.75	0	C-27	0	-0.3
1946 Chi-A	14	32	4	8	2	0	0	4	8	7	0	0	.250	.400	.313	.713	105	1	5	4.99	-1	C-12	1	0.1
Total 2	42	65	5	12	3	0	0	6	15	13	0	0	.185	.338	.231	.568	63	-2	6	3.25	-1	/C-39	1	-0.2
• FERNANDEZ, Chico	Lorenzo Marto (Mosquera) Fernandez b: 4/23/1939, Havana, Cuba BR/TR, 5'10", 160 lbs. Deb: 4/20/1968																							
1968 Bal-A	24	18	0	2	0	0	0	0	1	2	0	0	.111	.158	.111	.269	-17	-3	0	.60	-1	/S-7,2-4	0	-0.4
• FERNANDEZ, Chico	Humberto (Perez) Fernandez b: 3/2/1932, Havana, Cuba BR/TR, 6', 170 lbs. Deb: 7/14/1956																							
1956 Bro-N	34	66	11	15	2	0	1	9	3	10	2	3	.227	.261	.303	.564	47	-6	4	1.89	0	S-25	1	-0.4
1957 Phi-N	149	500	42	131	14	4	5	51	31	64	18	5	.262	.306	.336	.642	75	-16	48	3.19	-2	*S-149	11	-0.6
1958 Phi-N	148	522	38	120	18	5	6	51	37	48	12	6	.230	.283	.318	.601	60	-31	45	2.79	7	*S-148	9	-1.2
1959 Phi-N	45	123	15	26	5	1	0	3	10	11	2	1	.211	.271	.268	.539	43	-10	9	2.22	0	S-40/2-2	1	-0.8
1960 Det-A	133	435	44	105	13	3	4	35	39	50	13	4	.241	.305	.313	.618	64	-21	41	2.99	3	*S-130	8	-0.8
1961 Det-A	133	435	41	108	15	4	3	40	36	45	8	5	.248	.306	.322	.628	65	-22	41	3.13	4	*S-121/3-8	10	-0.8
1962 Det-A	141	503	64	125	17	2	20	59	42	69	10	3	.249	.306	.410	.716	88	-9	62	4.12	-3	*S-138/3-2,1-1	14	-0.1
1963 Det-A	15	49	3	7	1	0	0	2	6	11	0	1	.143	.236	.163	.400	14	-6	1	.81	2	S-14	1	-0.3
NY-N	58	145	12	29	6	0	1	9	9	30	3	0	.200	.247	.262	.509	46	-9	10	2.36	-6	S-45/3-5,2-3	1	-1.4
Total 8	856	2778	270	666	91	19	40	259	213	338	68	28	.240	.295	.329	.624	66	-130	262	3.07	3	S-810/3-15,2-5,1-1	56	-6.4
• FERNANDEZ, Frank	Frank Fernandez b: 4/16/1943, Staten Island, NY BR/TR, 6', 192 lbs. Deb: 9/12/1967 Career OF: 4-1-22																							
1967 NY-A	9	28	1	6	2	0	1	4	2	7	1	1	.214	.290	.393	.683	104	-0	3	3.03	1	/C-7,0-2(0-0-2)	1	0.1
1968 NY-A	51	135	15	23	6	1	7	30	35	50	1	0	.170	.341	.385	.726	124	6	20	4.64	2	C-45/0-4(0-0-4)	8	1.1
1969 NY-A	89	229	34	51	6	1	12	29	65	68	1	3	.223	.401	.415	.816	133	13	42	6.16	-1	C-65,0-14(0-0-14)	12	1.6
1970 Oak-A	94	252	30	54	5	0	15	44	40	76	1	0	.214	.327	.413	.739	106	3	35	4.64	1	C-76/0-1	10	0.7
1971 Oak-A	2	4	0	0	0	0	0	0	1	2	0	0	.000	.200	.000	.200	-40	-1	0	.35	0	/C-2	0	-0.1
Was-A	18	30	0	3	0	0	0	4	4	10	0	0	.100	.206	.100	.306	-12	-4	1	.64	0	/0-6(3-1-2),C-1	0	-0.4
Oak-A	2	5	1	1	1	0	0	1	0	1	0	0	.200	.200	.400	.600	68	-0	0	2.70	0	/C-1	0	0.0
Yr.	22	39	1	4	1	0	0	5	5	13	0	0	.103	.205	.128	.333	-6	-5	1	.82	0	/0-6(3-1-2),C-4	0	-0.5
Chi-N	17	41	11	7	1	0	4	4	17	15	0	0	.171	.414	.488	.902	135	3	10	8.02	-1	C-16	3	0.3
1972 Chi-N	3	3	0	0	0	0	0	0	0	2	0	0	.000	.000	.000	.000	-90	-1	0	.00	0	/C-1	0	-0.1
Total 6	285	727	92	145	21	2	39	116	164	231	4	4	.199	.351	.395	.746	114	18	111	4.95	2	C-214/0-27	34	3.1
• FERNANDEZ, Jose	Jose Mayobanex (Rojas) Fernandez b: 11/2/1974, La Vega, Dominican Republic BR/TR, 6'2", 195 lbs. Deb: 7/3/1999																							
1999 Mon-N	8	24	0	5	2	0	0	1	1	7	0	0	.208	.240	.292	.532	35	-2	1	1.96	-1	/3-6	0	-0.3
2001 Ana-A	13	25	1	2	1	0	0	0	2	10	0	1	.080	.148	.120	.268	-27	-5	0	.44	0	/D-7,1-2,3-1	0	-0.6
Total 2	21	49	1	7	3	0	0	1	3	17	0	1	.143	.192	.204	.396	2	-8	2	1.13	-1	/3-7,D-7,1-2	0	-0.9
• FERNANDEZ, Nanny	Froilan Fernandez b: 10/25/1918, Wilmington, CA d: 9/19/1996, Harbor City, CA BR/TR, 5'9", 170 lbs. Deb: 4/14/1942 Career OF: 56-3-8																							
1942 Bos-N	145	577	63	147	29	3	6	55	38	61	15	....	.255	.303	.347	.650	92	-8	58	3.52	1	3-98,0-44(42-3-0)	13	-0.7
1946 Bos-N	115	372	37	95	15	2	2	42	30	44	1	....	.255	.313	.323	.635	79	-11	37	3.36	2	3-81,S-18,0-14(14-0-0)	9	-1.0
1947 Bos-N	83	209	16	43	4	0	2	21	22	20	2	....	.206	.281	.254	.535	44	-17	16	2.39	-7	S-62/0-8(0-0-8),3-6	2	-2.0
1950 Pit-N	65	198	23	51	11	0	6	27	19	17	2	....	.258	.326	.404	.730	88	-4	24	4.17	-5	3-52	3	-0.9
Total 4	408	1356	139	336	59	5	16	145	109	142	20	....	.248	.306	.334	.640	80	-39	135	3.38	-9	3-237/S-80,0-66	27	-4.5
• FERNANDEZ, Tony	Octavio Antonio (Castro) Fernandez b: 6/30/1962, San Pedro de Macoris, Dominican Republic BB/TR, 6'2", 175 lbs. Deb: 9/2/1983																							
1983 Tor-A	15	34	5	9	1	1	0	2	2	2	0	1	.265	.324	.353	.677	81	-1	4	3.38	1	S-13/D-1	1	0.0
1984 Tor-A	88	233	29	63	5	3	3	19	17	15	5	7	.270	.320	.356	.676	84	-7	25	3.72	3	S-73,3-10/D-1	6	0.3
1985*Tor-A	161	564	71	163	31	10	2	51	43	41	13	6	.289	.342	.390	.732	97	-2	75	4.71	19	*S-160	21	3.4
1986 Tor-A★	163	687	91	213	33	9	10	65	27	52	25	12	.310	.340	.428	.768	105	3	99	5.29	7	*S-163	24	2.7
1987 Tor-A★	146	578	90	186	29	8	5	67	51	48	32	12	.322	.382	.426	.807	112	12	94	5.98	16	*S-146	24	4.1
1988 Tor-A	154	648	76	186	41	4	5	70	45	65	15	5	.287	.337	.386	.723	102	2	86	4.80	11	*S-154	25	2.5
1989*Tor-A★	140	573	64	147	25	9	11	64	29	51	22	6	.257	.296	.389	.685	97	-2	66	3.94	19	*S-140	20	2.8
1990 Tor-A	161	635	84	175	27	**17**	4	66	71	70	26	13	.276	.355	.391	.745	102	4	88	4.78	16	*S-161	25	3.3
1991 SD-N	145	558	81	152	27	5	4	38	55	74	23	9	.272	.338	.360	.698	93	-3	69	4.30	9	*S-145	21	1.8
1992 SD-N★	155	622	84	171	32	4	4	37	56	62	20	20	.275	.339	.359	.697	96	-7	75	4.15	-10	*S-154	18	-0.6
1993 NY-N	48	173	20	39	5	2	1	14	25	19	6	2	.225	.327	.295	.621	69	-7	19	3.50	2	S-48	3	-0.1
*Tor-A	94	353	45	108	18	9	4	50	31	26	15	8	.306	.362	.442	.804	114	7	53	5.23	8	S-94	17	2.2
1994 Cin-N	104	366	50	102	18	6	8	50	44	40	12	7	.279	.364	.426	.790	106	4	58	5.55	7	3-93/S-9,2-5	14	1.3
1995*NY-A	108	384	57	94	20	2	5	45	42	40	6	6	.245	.326	.346	.672	76	-15	41	3.52	-1	*S-103/2-4	9	-0.7
1997*Cle-A	120	409	55	117	21	1	11	44	22	47	6	6	.286	.326	.423	.749	90	-8	52	4.46	3	*2-109,S-10/D-1	11	0.1
1998 Tor-A	138	486	71	156	36	2	9	72	45	53	13	8	.321	.391	.459	.850	120	15	87	6.54	9	2-82,3-54/D-1	19	2.6
1999 Tor-A★	142	485	73	159	41	0	6	75	77	62	6	7	.328	.430	.449	.880	123	20	97	7.52	-10	*3-132,D-11/2-1	20	1.1
2001 Mil-N	28	64	6	18	0	0	1	3	7	9	1	2	.281	.352	.328	.680	80	-2	7	3.94	-1	3-13	1	-0.3
Tor-A	48	59	5	18	4	0	1	12	1	8	0	1	.305	.328	.424	.752	94	-1	7	4.28	0	D-13	1	-0.1
Total 17	2158	7911	1057	2276	414	92	94	844	690	784	246	138	.288	.350	.399	.749	101	11	1102	4.91	109	*S-1573,3-302,2-201/D-28	280	26.5
• FERRARA, Al	Alfred John "The Bull" Ferrara b: 12/22/1939, Brooklyn, NY BR/TR, 6'1", 203 lbs. Deb: 7/30/1963 Career OF: 248-2-121																							
1963 LA-N	21	44	2	7	0	0	1	1	6	9	0	0	.159	.275	.227	.502	49	-3	3	2.36	0	0-11(7-0-4)	0	-0.3
1965 LA-N	41	81	5	17	2	1	1	10	9	20	0	0	.210	.297	.296	.593	72	-3	8	3.16	-2	0-27(10-0-19)	2	-0.7
1966*LA-N	63	115	15	31	4	0	5	23	9	35	0	0	.270	.339	.435	.773	123	4	17	5.09	-2	0-32(4-1-27)	4	0.0
1967 LA-N	122	347	41	96	16	1	16	50	33	73	0	1	.277	.345	.467	.812	142	18	56	5.87	-3	0-94(27-0-71)	15	1.1
1968 LA-N	2	7	0	1	0	0	0	0	0	2	0	0	.143	.143	.143	.286	-15	-1	0	.64	0	/0-2(2-0-0)	0	-0.2
1969 SD-N	138	366	39	95	22	1	14	56	45	69	0	0	.260	.352	.440	.792	125	13	58	5.58	1	0-96(95-1-0)	13	1.0
1970 SD-N	138	372	44	103	15	4	13	51	46	63	0	0	.277	.373	.444	.817	123	13	64	6.17	-3	0-96(96-0-0)	12	0.6
1971 SD-N	17	17	0	2	1	0	0	2	5	5	0	0	.118	.318	.176	.495	46	-1	1	1.46	0	/0-2(2-0-0)	0	-0.1
Cin-N	32	33	2	6	0	0	1	5	3	10	0	0	.182	.270	.273	.543	57	-2	2	2.35	0	/0-5(5-0-0)	0	-0.2
Yr.	49	50	2	8	1	0	1	7	8	15	0	0	.160	.288	.240	.528	53	-3	3	2.02	0	/0-7(7-0-0)	0	-0.3
Total 8	574	1382	148	358	60	7	51	198	156	286	0	1	.259	.346	.423	.769	119	38	209	5.32	-9	0-365	46	1.2
• FERRARO, Mike	Michael Dennis Ferraro b: 8/18/1944, Kingston, NY BR/TR, 5'11", 175 lbs. Deb: 9/6/1966 M/C																							
1966 NY-A	10	28	4	5	0	0	0	0	3	3	0	0	.179	.281	.179	.460	37	-2	2	1.70	1	3-10	0	-0.1
1968 NY-A	23	87	5	14	0	1	0	1	2	17	0	0	.161	.180	.184	.364	11	-9	2	.84	2	3-22	1	-0.8
1969 Sea-A	5	4	0	0	0	0	0	0	1	0	0	0	.000	.200	.000	.200	-41	-1	0	.35	0	....	0	-0.1
1972 Mil-A	124	381	19	97	18	1	2	29	17	41	0	5	.255	.286	.323	.609	83	-11	29	2.52	-6	*3-115/S-1	5	-2.0
Total 4	162	500	28	116	18	2	2	30	23	61	0	5	.232	.267	.288	.555	67	-24	33	2.15	-3	3-147/S-1	6	-3.0

YEAR TM-L	G	AB	R	H	2B	3B	HR	RBI	BB	SO	SB	CS	AVG	OBP	SLG	OPS	OPS+	BR/A	RC	RC/G	FR	G/POS	WS	TPW
• FERRELL, Rick	Richard Benjamin Ferrell b: 10/12/1905, Durham, NC d: 7/27/1995, Bloomfield Hills, MI BR/TR, 5'10", 160 lbs. Deb: 4/19/1929 C HOF: 1984																							
1929 StL-A	64	144	21	33	6	1	0	20	32	10	1	2	.229	.373	.285	.658	69	-5	18	4.01	-3	C-45	4	-0.5
1930 StL-A	101	314	43	84	18	4	1	41	46	10	1	4	.268	.363	.360	.723	81	-9	43	4.66	2	*C-101	9	-0.1
1931 StL-A	117	386	47	118	30	4	3	57	56	12	2	3	.306	.394	.427	.821	112	9	67	6.50	5	*C-108	15	2.0
1932 StL-A	126	438	67	138	30	5	2	65	66	18	5	5	.315	.406	.420	.826	108	8	78	6.58	5	*C-120	17	1.8
1933 StL-A	22	72	8	18	2	0	1	5	12	4	2	0	.250	.357	.319	.677	76	-2	9	4.52	3	C-21	2	0.3
Bos-A★	118	421	50	125	19	4	3	72	58	19	2	2	.297	.385	.382	.767	105	6	66	5.57	5	*C-116	15	1.7
Yr.	140	493	58	143	21	4	4	77	70	23	4	2	.290	.381	.373	.754	100	4	75	5.42	8	*C-137	17	2.0
1934 Bos-A★	132	437	50	130	29	4	1	48	66	20	0	0	.297	.390	.389	.779	95	-1	70	5.98	0	*C-128	18	0.7
1935 Bos-A★	133	458	54	138	34	4	3	61	65	15	5	8	.301	.388	.413	.801	100	0	75	5.84	3	*C-131	17	1.0
1936 Bos-A★	121	410	59	128	27	5	8	55	65	17	0	1	.312	.406	.461	.867	107	6	80	7.37	3	*C-121	16	1.4
1937 Bos-A	18	65	8	20	2	0	1	4	15	4	0	0	.308	.438	.385	.822	105	2	12	7.15	0	C-18	3	0.3
Was-A★	86	279	31	64	6	0	1	32	50	18	1	1	.229	.348	.262	.610	59	-15	29	3.52	0	C-84	6	-1.0
Yr.	104	344	39	84	8	0	2	36	65	22	1	1	.244	.366	.285	.651	68	-14	41	4.14	0	*C-102	9	-0.7
1938 Was-A★	135	411	55	120	24	5	1	58	75	17	1	0	.292	.401	.382	.783	104	7	69	6.07	0	*C-131	16	1.4
1939 Was-A	87	274	32	77	13	1	0	31	41	12	1	1	.281	.377	.336	.712	90	-2	38	4.88	-1	C-83	7	0.2
1940 Was-A	103	326	35	89	18	2	0	28	47	15	1	1	.273	.365	.340	.705	90	-3	44	4.76	2	C-99	9	0.5
1941 Was-A	21	66	8	18	5	0	0	13	15	4	1	0	.273	.407	.348	.756	106	2	10	5.42	0	C-21	2	0.3
StL-A	100	321	30	81	14	3	2	23	52	22	2	1	.252	.357	.333	.690	81	-7	41	4.40	2	C-98	9	0.0
Yr.	121	387	38	99	19	3	2	36	67	26	3	1	.256	.366	.336	.702	85	-5	52	4.58	1	*C-119	11	0.3
1942 StL-A	99	273	20	61	6	1	0	26	33	13	0	1	.223	.307	.253	.560	57	-15	23	2.80	1	C-95	6	-0.8
1943 StL-A	74	209	12	50	7	0	0	20	34	14	0	0	.239	.348	.273	.621	81	-3	23	3.76	3	C-70	7	0.5
1944 Was-A★	99	339	14	94	11	1	0	25	46	13	2	1	.277	.364	.316	.679	99	2	41	4.32	6	C-96	12	1.5
1945 Was-A★	91	286	33	76	12	1	1	38	43	13	2	4	.266	.366	.325	.691	110	5	35	4.17	-3	C-83	11	0.8
1947 Was-A	37	99	10	30	11	0	0	12	14	7	0	0	.303	.389	.414	.804	127	4	16	5.85	2	C-37	5	0.8
Total 18	1884	6028	687	1692	324	45	28	734	931	277	29	35	.281	.378	.363	.741	95	-10	888	5.22	35	*C-1806	206	12.9
• FERRER, Sergio	Sergio (Marrero) Ferrer b: 1/29/1951, Santurce, Puerto Rico BB/TR, 5'7", 145 lbs. Deb: 4/5/1974																							
1974 Min-A	24	57	12	16	0	2	0	0	8	6	3	2	.281	.379	.351	.730	107	1	8	5.06	-4	S-20/2-1	2	-0.2
1975 Min-A	32	81	14	20	3	1	0	2	3	11	3	4	.247	.282	.309	.591	66	-5	7	2.61	-2	S-18,2-10/D-2	0	-0.5
1978 NY-N	37	33	8	7	0	1	0	1	4	7	1	0	.212	.316	.273	.589	68	-1	3	2.67	0	S-29/2-3,3-2	1	0.0
1979 NY-N	32	7	7	0	0	0	0	0	2	3	0	2	.000	.222	.000	.222	-35	-2	0	.00	-3	3-12/S-5,2-4	0	-0.5
Total 4	125	178	41	43	3	4	0	3	17	27	7	8	.242	.318	.303	.622	75	-7	18	3.19	-10	/S-72,2-18,3-14,D-2	3	-1.2
• FERRIS, Hobe	Albert Sayles Ferris b: 12/7/1877, Providence, RI d: 3/18/1938, Detroit, MI BR/TR, 5'8", 162 lbs. Deb: 4/26/1901																							
1901 Bos-A	138	523	68	131	16	15	2	63	23	....	13	....	.250	.290	.350	.640	78	-17	60	3.91	14	*2-138/S-1	11	-0.1
1902 Bos-A	134	499	57	122	16	14	8	63	21	....	11	....	.244	.276	.381	.657	79	-17	58	3.95	27	*2-134	12	1.1
1903*Bos-A	141	525	69	132	19	7	9	66	25	....	11	....	.251	.287	.366	.652	90	-8	61	3.98	18	*2-139/S-2	15	1.2
1904 Bos-A	156	563	50	120	23	10	3	63	23	....	7	....	.213	.245	.306	.551	70	-21	47	2.70	18	*2-156	12	-0.1
1905 Bos-A	142	523	51	115	24	16	6	59	23	....	11	....	.220	.253	.361	.614	93	-7	53	3.34	20	*2-142	15	1.5
1906 Bos-A	130	495	47	121	25	13	2	44	10	....	8	....	.244	.262	.360	.622	94	-6	51	3.52	-1	*2-126/3-4	10	-0.6
1907 Bos-A	150	561	41	135	25	2	4	60	10	....	11	....	.241	.254	.314	.568	82	-15	50	3.02	20	*2-150	10	0.7
1908 StL-A	148	555	54	150	26	7	2	74	14	....	6	....	.270	.291	.353	.644	108	2	59	3.54	18	*3-148	20	2.8
1909 StL-A	148	556	36	120	18	5	4	58	12	....	11	....	.216	.232	.288	.520	69	-23	39	2.23	5	*3-114,2-34	8	-1.6
Total 9	1287	4800	473	1146	192	89	40	550	161	....	89	....	.239	.265	.341	.606	85	-111	477	3.32	139	*2-1019,3-266/S-3	113	4.7
• FETZER, Willy	William McKinnon Fetzer b: 6/24/1884, Concord, NC d: 5/3/1959, Butner, NC BL/TR, 5'10.5", 180 lbs. Deb: 9/4/1906																							
1906 Phi-A	1	1	0	0	0	0	0	0	0	....	0	....	.000	.000	.000	.000	-97	-0	0	.00	0	....	0	0.0
• FEWSTER, Chick	Wilson Lloyd Fewster b: 11/10/1895, Baltimore, MD d: 4/16/1945, Baltimore, MD BR/TR, 5'11", 160 lbs. Deb: 9/19/1917 Career OF: 42-52-30																							
1917 NY-A	11	36	2	8	0	0	0	1	5	5	1	....	.222	.317	.222	.539	64	-1	3	2.46	-1	2-11	1	-0.2
1918 NY-A	5	2	1	1	0	0	0	0	0	0	0	....	.500	.500	.500	1.000	197	0	0	12.24	-1	/2-2	0	-0.1
1919 NY-A	81	244	38	69	9	3	1	15	34	36	8	....	.283	.386	.357	.743	108	5	36	5.13	6	0-41(0-13-28),S-24/2-4,3-2	10	1.1
1920 NY-A	21	21	8	6	1	0	0	1	7	2	0	1	.286	.464	.333	.798	110	1	4	5.78	-3	/S-6,2-3	1	-0.2
1921*NY-A	66	207	44	58	19	0	1	19	28	43	4	4	.280	.382	.386	.768	94	-1	32	5.33	-2	0-43(7-35-1),2-15	6	-0.4
1922 NY-A	44	132	20	32	4	1	1	9	16	23	2	4	.242	.324	.311	.635	65	-8	14	3.17	2	0-38(35-4-0)/2-2	2	-0.8
Bos-A	23	83	8	24	4	1	0	9	6	10	8	3	.289	.344	.361	.706	85	-1	11	4.41	4	3-23	3	0.4
Yr.	67	215	28	56	8	2	1	18	22	33	10	7	.260	.332	.330	.662	72	-9	25	3.62	6	0-38(35-4-0),3-23/2-2	5	-0.4
1923 Bos-A	90	284	32	67	10	1	0	15	39	35	7	14	.236	.334	.278	.613	62	-18	26	2.97	-16	2-49,S-37/3-3	3	-2.8
1924 Cle-A	101	322	36	86	12	2	0	36	24	36	12	12	.267	.324	.317	.641	65	-19	32	3.35	-26	2-94/3-5	3	-4.0
1925 Cle-A	93	294	39	73	16	1	1	38	36	25	6	9	.248	.330	.320	.650	65	-17	32	3.45	-14	2-83,3-10/0-1	3	-2.7
1926 Bro-N	105	337	53	82	16	3	2	24	45	49	9	....	.243	.341	.326	.667	82	-7	39	3.88	-10	*2-103	6	-1.4
1927 Bro-N	4	1	1	0	0	0	0	0	0	0	0	....	.000	.000	.000	.000	-100	-0	0	.00	0	....	0	0.0
Total 11	644	1963	282	506	91	12	6	167	240	264	57	47	.258	.346	.326	.672	77	-67	230	3.85	-60	2-366,0-123/S-67,3-43	38	-11.1
• FIALA, Neil	Neil Stephen Fiala b: 8/24/1956, St. Louis, MO BL/TR, 6'1", 185 lbs. Deb: 9/3/1981																							
1981 StL-N	3	3	0	0	0	0	0	0	0	1	0	0	.000	.000	.000	.000	-97	-1	0	.00	0	....	0	-0.1
Cin-N	2	2	1	1	0	0	0	1	0	1	0	0	.500	.500	.500	1.000	181	0	1	13.50	0	....	0	0.0
Yr.	5	5	1	1	0	0	0	1	0	2	0	0	.200	.200	.200	.400	14	-1	1	3.38	0	....	0	-0.1
• FICK, Robert	Robert Charles John Fick b: 3/15/1974, Torrance, CA BL/TR, 6'1", 189 lbs. Deb: 9/19/1998 Career OF: 0-0-148																							
1998 Det-A	7	22	6	8	1	0	3	7	2	7	1	0	.364	.417	.818	1.235	209	4	7	12.85	-1	/C-3,D-2,1-1	2	0.3
1999 Det-A	15	41	6	9	0	0	3	10	7	6	1	0	.220	.333	.439	.772	94	-0	6	5.07	0	/D-8,C-4	2	-0.1
2000 Det-A	66	163	18	41	7	2	3	22	22	39	2	1	.252	.344	.374	.718	84	-4	22	4.50	-3	1-34,C-16,D-12	4	-0.7
2001 Det-A	124	401	62	109	21	2	19	61	39	62	0	3	.272	.342	.476	.819	118	8	63	5.52	4	C-78,1-26/D-8,0-8(0-0-8)	10	1.4
2002 Det-A★	148	556	66	150	36	2	17	63	46	90	0	1	.270	.333	.433	.767	108	5	77	4.86	9	*0-140(0-0-140)/D-6	12	0.6
2003*Atl-N	126	409	52	110	26	1	11	80	42	47	1	0	.269	.340	.418	.758	96	-2	58	5.01	-7	*1-115	14	-1.9
Total 6	486	1592	210	427	91	7	56	243	158	251	5	5	.268	.340	.440	.779	106	11	234	5.13	2	1-176,0-148,C-101/D-36	44	-0.4
• FIELD, Jim	James C. Field b: 4/24/1863, Philadelphia, PA d: 5/13/1953, Atlantic City, NJ, 6'1", 170 lbs. Deb: 6/2/1883																							
1883 Col-a	76	295	31	75	10	6	1	0	7	....	....	....	.254	.272	.339	.611	103	2	28	3.54	-11	*1-76	6	-1.4
1884 Col-a	105	417	74	97	9	7	4	0	23	....	....	....	.233	.292	.317	.609	107	6	40	3.40	-1	*1-105	11	-0.3
1885 Pit-a	56	209	28	50	9	1	1	15	13	....	....	....	.239	.306	.306	.612	95	-0	20	3.41	3	1-56	5	-0.2
Bal-a	38	144	16	30	3	2	0	10	13	....	....	....	.208	.278	.257	.535	71	-4	11	2.50	-1	1-38	2	-0.8
Yr.	94	353	44	80	12	3	1	25	26	....	....	....	.227	.295	.286	.581	85	-5	31	3.03	2	*1-94	7	-1.0
1890 Roc-a	52	188	30	38	7	5	4	25	21	....	8	....	.202	.309	.356	.665	104	2	24	4.19	-4	1-51/P-2	6	-0.5
1898 Was-N	5	21	1	2	0	0	0	0	0	....	1	....	.095	.095	.095	.190	-46	-4	0	.41	0	/1-5	0	-0.4
Total 5	332	1274	180	292	38	21	10	50	77	....	9	....	.229	.288	.316	.603	97	1	122	3.39	-15	1-331/P-2	30	-3.6
• FIELD, Sam	Samuel Jay Field b: 10/12/1848, Philadelphia, PA d: 10/28/1904, Sinking Spring, PA BR/TR, 5'9.5", 182 lbs. Deb: 5/19/1875																							
1875 Cen-n	3	11	2	1	0	0	0	0	0	0	0	0	.091	.091	.091	.182	-40	-1	0	.27	-2	/C-2,0-1	....	-0.2
Was-n	5	16	0	5	0	0	0	1	0	1	1	0	.313	.313	.313	.625	122	1	2	5.15	-2	/C-4,0-1	....	-0.1
Yr.	8	27	2	6	0	0	0	1	0	1	1	0	.222	.222	.222	.444	56	-1	2	2.83	-3	/C-6,0-2(0-0-2)	....	-0.3
1876 Cin-N	4	15	2	0	0	0	0	0	1	3	....	....	.000	.067	.000	.067	-89	-2	0	.00	-3	/C-3,2-2	0	-0.5
• FIELDER, Cecil	Cecil Grant "Big Daddy" Fielder b: 9/21/1963, Los Angeles, CA BR/TR, 6'3", 240 lbs. Deb: 7/20/1985																							
1985*Tor-A	30	74	6	23	4	0	4	16	6	16	0	0	.311	.363	.527	.890	137	4	14	6.85	1	1-25	3	0.3
1986 Tor-A	34	83	7	13	2	0	4	13	6	27	0	0	.157	.222	.325	.548	46	-7	5	2.01	-1	D-22/1-7,3-2,0-1	0	-0.8
1987 Tor-A	82	175	30	47	7	1	14	32	20	48	0	1	.269	.347	.560	.907	132	7	32	6.36	-1	D-55,1-16/3-2	6	0.4
1988 Tor-A	74	174	24	40	6	1	9	23	14	53	0	1	.230	.291	.431	.722	99	-1	20	3.81	0	D-50,1-17/3-3,2-2	3	-0.4

YEAR TM-L	G	AB	R	H	2B	3B	HR	RBI	BB	SO	SB	CS	AVG	OBP	SLG	OPS	OPS+	BR/A	RC	RC/G	FR	G/POS	WS	TPW
1990 Det-A★	159	573	104	159	25	1	**51**	**132**	90	182	0	1	.277	.380	**.592**	.972	167	51	129	7.98	-3	*1-143,D-15	29	3.8
1991 Det-A★	162	624	102	163	25	0	**44**	**133**	78	151	0	0	.261	.349	.513	.862	133	27	110	6.17	-3	*1-122,D-42	26	1.4
1992 Det-A	155	594	80	145	22	0	35	**124**	73	151	0	0	.244	.329	.458	.787	118	13	89	5.13	4	*1-114,D-43	19	0.8
1993 Det-A★	154	573	80	153	23	0	30	117	90	125	0	1	.267	.370	.464	.835	124	21	96	5.81	-2	*1-119,D-36	17	0.6
1994 Det-A	109	425	67	110	16	2	28	90	50	110	0	0	.259	.340	.504	.843	113	7	69	5.54	14	*1-102/D-7	12	1.1
1995 Det-A	136	494	70	120	18	1	31	82	75	116	0	1	.243	.348	.472	.820	112	8	80	5.45	6	1-77,D-58	13	0.4
1996 Det-A	107	391	55	97	12	0	26	80	63	91	2	0	.248	.357	.478	.835	109	6	68	5.93	3	1-71,D-36	14	0.0
*NY-A	53	200	30	52	8	0	13	37	24	48	0	0	.260	.345	.495	.840	109	2	33	5.66	0	D-43/1-9	3	-0.2
Yr.	160	591	85	149	20	0	39	117	87	139	2	0	.252	.353	.484	.837	109	8	101	5.84	2	1-80,D-79	17	-0.2
1997*NY-A	98	361	40	94	15	0	13	61	51	87	0	0	.260	.363	.410	.773	102	3	54	5.05	1	D-87/1-8	7	-0.3
1998 Ana-A	103	381	48	92	16	1	17	68	52	98	0	1	.241	.337	.423	.760	95	-3	52	4.52	-3	1-72,D-31	8	-1.3
Cle-A	14	35	1	5	1	0	0	0	1	13	0	0	.143	.189	.171	.361	-5	-6	1	.92	0	D-10/1-3	0	-0.6
Yr.	117	416	49	97	17	1	17	68	53	111	0	1	.233	.326	.401	.727	88	-8	53	4.19	-3	1-75,D-41	8	-1.9
Total 13	1470	5157	744	1313	200	7	319	1008	693	1316	2	6	.255	.348	.482	.829	119	132	852	5.66	15	1-905,D-535/3-7,2-2,0-1	160	5.2

• FIELDS, Bruce Bruce Alan Fields b: 10/6/1960, Cleveland, OH BL/TR, 6', 185 lbs. Deb: 9/3/1986 Career OF: 28-1-9

YEAR TM-L	G	AB	R	H	2B	3B	HR	RBI	BB	SO	SB	CS	AVG	OBP	SLG	OPS	OPS+	BR/A	RC	RC/G	FR	G/POS	WS	TPW
1986 Det-A	16	43	4	12	1	1	0	6	1	6	1	1	.279	.295	.349	.644	75	-2	4	3.42	0	0-14(14-0-0)/D-1	1	-0.3
1988 Sea-A	39	67	8	18	5	0	1	5	4	11	0	1	.269	.310	.388	.698	90	-1	7	3.65	0	0-23(14-1-8)/D-6	0	-0.2
1989 Sea-A	3	3	2	1	1	0	0	0	0	1	0	0	.333	.333	.667	1.000	170	0	1	9.00	0	/0-1	0	0.0
Total 3	58	113	14	31	7	1	1	11	5	18	1	2	.274	.305	.381	.686	86	-3	12	3.68	-1	/0-38,D-7	1	-0.5

• FIELDS, George George W. Fields b: 7/1853, Waterbury, CT d: 9/22/1933, Waterbury, CT Deb: 5/2/1872

YEAR TM-L	G	AB	R	H	2B	3B	HR	RBI	BB	SO	SB	CS	AVG	OBP	SLG	OPS	OPS+	BR/A	RC	RC/G	FR	G/POS	WS	TPW
1872 Man-n	18	87	16	21	3	1	0	9	0	2	0	0	.241	.241	.299	.540	69	-3	6	3.02	-12	3-12/0-5(1-0-4),S-1	....	-1.0

• FIELDS, Jocko John Joseph Fields b: 10/20/1864, Cork, Ireland d: 10/14/1950, Jersey City, NJ BR/TR, 5'10", 160 lbs. Deb: 5/31/1887 Career OF: 160-20-27

YEAR TM-L	G	AB	R	H	2B	3B	HR	RBI	BB	SO	SB	CS	AVG	OBP	SLG	OPS	OPS+	BR/A	RC	RC/G	FR	G/POS	WS	TPW
1887 Pit-N	43	171	26	51	9	2	0	17	7	13	7	....	.298	.306	.348	.654	86	-3	20	4.44	0	0-27(7-13-7),C-14/1-3,3-1,P	4	-0.1
1888 Pit-N	45	169	22	33	7	2	1	15	8	19	9	....	.195	.232	.278	.510	67	-6	13	2.64	-3	0-29(23-2-4),C-14/3-3	2	-0.9
1889 Pit-N	75	289	41	90	22	5	2	43	29	30	7	....	.311	.376	.443	.819	142	17	52	6.93	-4	0-60(54-2-4),C-16	12	1.1
1890 Pit-P	126	526	101	148	18	20	9	86	57	52	24	....	.281	.355	.443	.798	122	17	94	6.68	-8	0-80(76-3-1),2-30,C-15/S-4	16	0.7
1891 Pit-N	23	75	10	18	3	0	0	5	10	13	1	....	.240	.337	.280	.617	82	-1	8	3.60	-2	C-15/S-8	1	-0.2
Phi-N	8	30	4	7	2	1	0	5	4	2	0	....	.233	.324	.367	.690	98	-0	4	4.28	-2	/C-8	1	-0.1
Yr.	31	105	14	25	5	1	0	10	14	15	1	....	.238	.333	.305	.638	87	-1	11	3.80	-4	C-23/S-8	2	-0.3
1892 NY-N	21	66	8	18	4	2	0	5	9	10	2	....	.273	.368	.394	.762	133	3	11	5.95	1	0-11(0-0-11),C-10	3	0.4
Total 6	341	1326	212	365	65	32	12	176	124	139	50	....	.275	.338	.397	.734	113	27	201	5.60	-18	0-207/C-92,2-30,S-12,3-4,1,P	39	0.9

• FIGGA, Mike Michael Anthony Figga b: 7/31/1970, Tampa, FL BR/TR, 6', 200 lbs. Deb: 9/16/1997

YEAR TM-L	G	AB	R	H	2B	3B	HR	RBI	BB	SO	SB	CS	AVG	OBP	SLG	OPS	OPS+	BR/A	RC	RC/G	FR	G/POS	WS	TPW
1997 NY-A	2	4	0	0	0	0	0	0	0	3	0	0	.000	.000	.000	.000	-101	-1	0	.00	0	/C-1,D-1	0	-0.1
1998 NY-A	1	4	1	1	0	0	0	0	0	1	0	0	.250	.250	.250	.500	32	-0	0	2.25	0	/C-1	0	0.0
1999 NY-A	2	0	0	0	0	0	0	0	0	0	0	0	....	....	....	....	-101	0	0	....	0	/C-2	0	0.0
Bal-A	41	86	12	19	4	0	1	5	2	27	0	2	.221	.239	.302	.541	38	-9	6	2.05	-2	C-41	1	-0.8
Yr.	43	86	12	19	4	0	1	5	2	27	0	2	.221	.239	.302	.541	38	-9	6	2.05	-2	C-43	1	-0.9
Total 3	46	94	13	20	4	0	1	5	2	31	0	2	.213	.229	.287	.516	32	-11	6	1.96	-2	/C-45,D-1	1	-1.0

• FIGGINS, Chone Desmond DeChone Figgins b: 1/22/1978, Leary, GA BB/TR, 5'8", 155 lbs. Deb: 8/25/2002

YEAR TM-L	G	AB	R	H	2B	3B	HR	RBI	BB	SO	SB	CS	AVG	OBP	SLG	OPS	OPS+	BR/A	RC	RC/G	FR	G/POS	WS	TPW
2002*Ana-A	15	12	6	2	1	0	0	1	0	5	2	1	.167	.167	.250	.417	9	-2	0	.00	0	/2-8	0	-0.1
2003 Ana-A	71	240	34	71	9	4	0	27	20	38	13	7	.296	.350	.367	.717	93	-2	32	4.67	-3	0-47(3-44-0),2-14/S-8,D-3	8	-0.4
Total 2	86	252	40	73	10	4	0	28	20	43	15	8	.290	.342	.361	.703	90	-4	32	4.39	-3	/0-47,2-22,S-8,D-3	8	-0.5

• FIGUEROA, Bien Bienvenido Figueroa b: 2/7/1964, Santo Domingo, Dominican Republic BR/TR, 5'10", 170 lbs. Deb: 5/17/1992

YEAR TM-L	G	AB	R	H	2B	3B	HR	RBI	BB	SO	SB	CS	AVG	OBP	SLG	OPS	OPS+	BR/A	RC	RC/G	FR	G/POS	WS	TPW
1992 StL-N	12	11	1	2	1	0	0	4	1	2	0	0	.182	.250	.273	.523	49	-1	1	2.45	-2	/S-9,2-3	0	-0.2

• FIGUEROA, Jesus Jesus Maria (Figueroa) Figueroa b: 2/20/1957, Santo Domingo, Dominican Republic BL/TL, 5'10", 160 lbs. Deb: 4/22/1980

YEAR TM-L	G	AB	R	H	2B	3B	HR	RBI	BB	SO	SB	CS	AVG	OBP	SLG	OPS	OPS+	BR/A	RC	RC/G	FR	G/POS	WS	TPW
1980 Chi-N	115	198	20	50	5	0	1	11	14	16	2	1	.253	.308	.293	.601	64	-9	18	3.23	2	0-57(22-36-1)	2	-0.9

• FIGUEROA, Luis Luis R. Figueroa b: 2/16/1974, Bayamon, Puerto Rico BB/TR, 5'9", 152 lbs. Deb: 6/27/2001

YEAR TM-L	G	AB	R	H	2B	3B	HR	RBI	BB	SO	SB	CS	AVG	OBP	SLG	OPS	OPS+	BR/A	RC	RC/G	FR	G/POS	WS	TPW
2001 Pit-N	4	2	0	0	0	0	0	0	0	0	0	0	.000	.000	.000	.000	-98	-1	0	.00	1	/2-3	0	0.0

• FILE, Sam Lawrence Samuel File b: 5/18/1922, Chester, PA BR/TR, 5'11", 160 lbs. Deb: 9/10/1940

YEAR TM-L	G	AB	R	H	2B	3B	HR	RBI	BB	SO	SB	CS	AVG	OBP	SLG	OPS	OPS+	BR/A	RC	RC/G	FR	G/POS	WS	TPW
1940 Phi-N	7	13	0	1	0	0	0	1	0	1	0	....	.077	.077	.077	.154	-60	-3	0	.00	-1	/S-6,3-1	0	-0.3

• FILIPOWICZ, Steve Stephen Charles "Flip" Filipowicz b: 6/28/1921, Donora, PA d: 2/21/1975, Wilkes-Barre, PA BR/TR, 5'8", 195 lbs. Deb: 9/3/1944 Career OF: 40-6-2

YEAR TM-L	G	AB	R	H	2B	3B	HR	RBI	BB	SO	SB	CS	AVG	OBP	SLG	OPS	OPS+	BR/A	RC	RC/G	FR	G/POS	WS	TPW
1944 NY-N	15	41	10	8	2	1	0	7	3	7	0	....	.195	.250	.293	.543	53	-3	3	2.00	-1	0-10(6-4-0)/C-1	0	-0.4
1945 NY-N	35	112	14	23	5	0	2	16	4	13	0	....	.205	.239	.304	.543	50	-8	8	2.42	-1	0-31(27-2-2)	0	-1.1
1948 Cin-N	7	26	0	9	0	1	0	3	2	1	0	....	.346	.393	.423	.816	125	1	5	7.19	0	/0-7(7-0-0)	1	0.1
Total 3	57	179	24	40	7	2	2	26	9	21	0	....	.223	.265	.318	.583	61	-10	15	2.87	-2	/0-48,C-1	1	-1.4

• FIMPLE, Jack John Joseph Fimple b: 2/10/1959, Darby, PA BR/TR, 6'2", 185 lbs. Deb: 7/30/1983

YEAR TM-L	G	AB	R	H	2B	3B	HR	RBI	BB	SO	SB	CS	AVG	OBP	SLG	OPS	OPS+	BR/A	RC	RC/G	FR	G/POS	WS	TPW
1983*LA-N	54	148	16	37	8	1	2	22	11	39	1	0	.250	.302	.358	.660	83	-4	16	3.50	-2	C-54	5	-0.3
1984 LA-N	12	26	2	5	1	0	0	3	1	6	0	0	.192	.222	.231	.453	28	-3	1	.78	0	C-12	0	-0.3
1986 LA-N	13	13	2	1	0	0	0	2	6	6	0	0	.077	.368	.077	.445	32	-1	1	2.05	0	/C-7,1-1,2-1	0	-0.1
1987 Cal-A	13	10	1	2	0	0	0	1	1	2	0	0	.200	.273	.200	.473	29	-1	1	2.08	-2	C-13	0	-0.2
Total 4	92	197	21	45	9	1	2	28	19	53	1	0	.228	.296	.315	.611	69	-8	18	2.92	-4	/C-86,1-1,2-1	5	-0.8

• FINIGAN, Jim James Leroy Finigan b: 8/19/1928, Quincy, IL d: 5/16/1981, Quincy, IL BR/TR, 5'11", 175 lbs. Deb: 4/25/1954

YEAR TM-L	G	AB	R	H	2B	3B	HR	RBI	BB	SO	SB	CS	AVG	OBP	SLG	OPS	OPS+	BR/A	RC	RC/G	FR	G/POS	WS	TPW
1954 Phi-A★	136	487	57	147	25	6	7	51	64	66	2	8	.302	.383	.421	.804	120	12	76	5.45	2	*3-136	21	1.4
1955 KC-A★	150	545	72	139	30	7	9	68	61	49	1	3	.255	.333	.385	.719	92	-8	68	4.22	-6	2-90,3-59	14	-0.7
1956 KC-A	91	250	29	54	7	2	2	21	30	28	3	1	.216	.302	.284	.586	55	-16	23	2.91	-1	2-52,3-32	2	-1.3
1957 Det-A	64	174	20	47	4	2	0	17	23	18	1	1	.270	.359	.316	.675	84	-3	21	4.17	-1	3-59/2-3	4	-0.4
1958 SF-N	23	25	3	5	2	0	0	1	3	5	0	0	.200	.310	.280	.590	59	-1	2	2.76	-1	/2-8,3-4	0	-0.3
1959 Bal-A	48	119	14	30	6	0	1	10	9	10	1	0	.252	.305	.328	.632	75	-4	11	3.03	1	3-42/2-6,S-2	2	-0.3
Total 6	512	1600	195	422	74	17	19	168	190	176	8	13	.264	.344	.367	.711	92	-19	200	4.24	-6	3-332,2-159/S-2	43	-1.5

• FINLEY, Bill William James Finley b: 10/4/1863, New York, NY d: 10/6/1912, Asbury Park, NJ, 5'3", 170 lbs. Deb: 7/12/1886

YEAR TM-L	G	AB	R	H	2B	3B	HR	RBI	BB	SO	SB	CS	AVG	OBP	SLG	OPS	OPS+	BR/A	RC	RC/G	FR	G/POS	WS	TPW
1886 NY-N	13	44	2	8	0	0	0	5	1	8	2	....	.182	.200	.182	.382	17	-4	2	1.54	0	/C-8,0-8(0-7-1)	0	-0.4

• FINLEY, Bob Robert Edward Finley b: 11/25/1915, Ennis, TX d: 1/2/1986, West Covina, CA BR/TR, 6'1", 200 lbs. Deb: 7/4/1943

YEAR TM-L	G	AB	R	H	2B	3B	HR	RBI	BB	SO	SB	CS	AVG	OBP	SLG	OPS	OPS+	BR/A	RC	RC/G	FR	G/POS	WS	TPW
1943 Phi-N	28	81	9	21	2	0	1	7	4	10	0	....	.259	.294	.321	.615	81	-2	7	3.00	2	C-24	2	0.2
1944 Phi-N	94	281	18	70	11	1	1	21	12	25	1	....	.249	.292	.306	.598	71	-11	24	2.85	-1	C-74	4	-0.8
Total 2	122	362	27	91	13	1	2	28	16	35	1	....	.251	.292	.309	.602	73	-14	31	2.89	1	/C-98	6	-0.7

• FINLEY, Steve Steven Allen Finley b: 3/12/1965, Paducah, KY BL/TL, 6'2", 180 lbs. Deb: 4/3/1989 Career OF: 36-1896-183

YEAR TM-L	G	AB	R	H	2B	3B	HR	RBI	BB	SO	SB	CS	AVG	OBP	SLG	OPS	OPS+	BR/A	RC	RC/G	FR	G/POS	WS	TPW
1989 Bal-A	81	217	35	54	5	2	2	25	15	30	17	3	.249	.300	.318	.618	77	-4	23	3.48	-2	0-76(14-23-41)/D-3	5	-0.8
1990 Bal-A	142	464	46	119	16	4	3	37	32	53	22	9	.256	.307	.328	.635	80	-12	48	3.40	-2	*0-133(21-44-73)/D-2	8	-1.7
1991 Hou-N	159	596	84	170	28	10	8	54	42	65	34	18	.285	.334	.406	.740	114	9	80	4.60	-1	*0-153(1-124-69)	18	0.5
1992 Hou-N	162	607	84	177	29	13	5	55	58	63	44	9	.292	.356	.407	.763	121	23	94	5.42	-5	*0-160(0-160-0)	28	1.7
1993 Hou-N	142	545	69	145	15	**13**	8	44	28	65	19	6	.266	.306	.385	.691	87	-10	64	4.11	3	*0-140(0-140-0)	14	-0.7
1994 Hou-N	94	373	64	103	16	5	11	33	28	52	13	7	.276	.330	.434	.764	102	0	54	4.98	2	0-92(0-92-0)	9	0.2
1995 SD-N	139	562	104	167	23	8	10	44	59	62	36	12	.297	.367	.420	.787	112	12	90	5.80	-1	*0-138(0-138-0)	19	1.2
1996*SD-N	161	655	126	195	45	9	30	95	56	87	22	8	.298	.357	.531	.888	139	35	119	6.48	2	*0-160(0-160-0)	27	3.7
1997 SD-N★	143	560	101	146	26	5	28	92	43	92	15	3	.261	.317	.475	.792	114	10	84	5.23	9	*0-140(0-140-0)	19	2.0
1998*SD-N	159	619	92	154	40	6	14	67	45	103	12	3	.249	.303	.401	.703	89	-10	76	4.25	5	*0-157(0-157-0)	15	-0.4
1999*Ari-N	156	590	100	156	32	10	34	103	63	94	8	4	.264	.338	.525	.864	113	9	108	6.47	-1	*0-155(0-155-0)/D-1	24	0.9

YEAR TM-L	G	AB	R	H	2B	3B	HR	RBI	BB	SO	SB	CS	AVG	OBP	SLG	OPS	OPS+	BR/A	RC	RC/G	FR	G/POS	WS	TPW
2000 Ari-N★	152	539	100	151	27	5	35	96	65	87	12	6	.280	.366	.544	.910	122	17	108	7.05	-3	*O-148(0-148-0)/D-2	21	1.5
2001*Ari-N	140	495	66	136	27	4	14	73	47	67	11	7	.275	.339	.430	.769	91	-7	71	5.09	1	*O-131(0-131-0)/P-1	15	-0.5
2002*Ari-N	150	505	82	145	24	4	25	89	65	73	16	4	.287	.372	.499	.871	116	14	96	6.85	-2	*O-144(0-144-0)	23	1.3
2003 Ari-N	147	516	82	148	24	**10**	22	70	57	94	15	8	.287	.364	.500	.864	111	9	96	6.71	-3	*O-140(0-140-0)	18	0.6
Total 15	2127	7843	1235	2166	377	108	249	977	703	1087	296	107	.276	.339	.447	.786	108	94	1211	5.41	1	*O-2067/D-8,P-1	263	9.6

• FINN, Neal

Cornelius Francis "Mickey" Finn b: 1/24/1904, Brooklyn, NY d: 7/7/1933, Allentown, PA BR/TR, 5'11", 168 lbs. Deb: 4/21/1930

YEAR TM-L	G	AB	R	H	2B	3B	HR	RBI	BB	SO	SB	CS	AVG	OBP	SLG	OPS	OPS+	BR/A	RC	RC/G	FR	G/POS	WS	TPW
1930 Bro-N	87	273	42	76	13	0	3	30	26	18	3	....	.278	.350	.359	.709	73	-11	35	4.37	0	2-81	5	-0.8
1931 Bro-N	118	413	46	113	22	2	0	45	21	42	2	....	.274	.314	.337	.650	75	-15	45	3.74	-8	*2-112	9	-1.6
1932 Bro-N	65	189	22	45	5	2	0	14	11	15	2	....	.238	.284	.286	.569	55	-12	16	2.84	2	3-50/2-2,S-1	2	-0.8
1933 Phi-N	51	169	15	40	4	1	0	13	10	14	2	....	.237	.287	.272	.559	54	-10	14	2.66	-2	2-51	1	-0.9
Total 4	321	1044	125	274	44	5	3	102	68	89	9	....	.262	.314	.323	.637	67	-48	109	3.55	-8	2-246/3-50,S-1	17	-4.2

• FINNEY, Hal

Harold Wilson Finney b: 7/30/1905, Lafayette, AL d: 12/20/1991, Lafayette, AL BR/TR, 5'11", 170 lbs. Deb: 6/24/1931

YEAR TM-L	G	AB	R	H	2B	3B	HR	RBI	BB	SO	SB	CS	AVG	OBP	SLG	OPS	OPS+	BR/A	RC	RC/G	FR	G/POS	WS	TPW
1931 Pit-N	10	26	2	8	1	0	0	2	0	1	1	....	.308	.333	.346	.679	84	-1	3	4.34	0	/C-6	1	0.0
1932 Pit-N	31	33	14	7	3	0	0	4	3	4	0	....	.212	.297	.303	.600	63	-2	3	3.13	-1	C-11	1	-0.2
1933 Pit-N	56	133	17	31	4	1	1	18	3	19	0	....	.233	.250	.301	.551	57	-8	9	2.20	0	C-47	2	-0.6
1934 Pit-N	5	0	3	0	0	0	0	0	0	0	0	....	....	1.000	....	1.000	188	0	0	∞	0	/C-1	0	0.0
1936 Pit-N	21	35	3	0	0	0	0	3	0	8	0	....	.000	.000	.000	.000	-98	-10	0	.00	0	C-14	0	-0.9
Total 5	123	227	39	46	8	1	1	27	6	32	1	....	.203	.233	.260	.493	39	-19	16	2.13	-2	/C-79	4	-1.8

• FINNEY, Lou

Louis Klopsche Finney b: 8/13/1910, Buffalo, AL d: 4/22/1966, Lafayette, AL BL/TR, 6', 180 lbs. Deb: 9/12/1931 Career OF: 113-104-479

YEAR TM-L	G	AB	R	H	2B	3B	HR	RBI	BB	SO	SB	CS	AVG	OBP	SLG	OPS	OPS+	BR/A	RC	RC/G	FR	G/POS	WS	TPW
1931 Phi-A	9	24	7	9	0	1	0	3	6	1	0	0	.375	.516	.458	.974	149	3	6	10.61	1	/O-8(0-0-8)	2	0.3
1933 Phi-A	74	240	26	64	12	2	3	32	13	17	1	3	.267	.307	.371	.678	78	-9	27	3.86	-2	O-63(17-1-46)	3	-1.4
1934 Phi-A	92	272	32	76	11	4	1	28	14	17	4	3	.279	.315	.360	.675	77	-11	31	3.94	0	O-54(12-4-40),1-15	4	-1.4
1935 Phi-A	109	410	45	112	11	6	0	31	18	18	7	2	.273	.307	.329	.636	65	-21	42	3.66	-2	O-76(5-0-72),1-18	4	-2.8
1936 Phi-A	151	653	100	197	26	10	1	41	47	22	7	9	.302	.351	.377	.728	81	-22	85	4.86	-5	1-78,O-73(22-21-32)	10	-3.4
1937 Phi-A	92	379	53	95	14	9	1	20	20	16	2	5	.251	.288	.343	.631	59	-27	36	3.27	-4	1-50,O-39(2-37-0)/2-1	2	-3.3
1938 Phi-A	122	454	61	125	21	12	10	48	39	25	5	8	.275	.333	.441	.773	95	-8	65	4.97	-4	1-64,O-46(19-21-6)	9	-1.8
1939 Phi-A	9	22	1	3	0	0	0	1	2	0	0	0	.136	.208	.136	.345	-10	-4	1	1.04	0	/O-4(0-3-1)	0	-0.4
Bos-A	95	249	43	81	18	3	1	46	24	11	2	5	.325	.385	.434	.818	105	0	41	6.04	-6	1-32,O-24(3-16-5)	7	-0.8
Yr.	104	271	44	84	18	3	1	47	26	11	2	5	.310	.370	.410	.780	96	-3	41	5.57	-6	1-32,O-28(3-19-6)	7	-1.2
1940 Bos-A★	130	534	73	171	31	15	5	73	33	13	5	2	.320	.360	.463	.822	107	5	87	6.04	-1	O-69(0-0-69),1-51	15	-0.5
1941 Bos-A	127	497	83	143	24	10	4	53	38	17	2	5	.288	.340	.400	.740	93	-7	66	4.69	-3	O-92(1-0-91),1-24	10	-1.8
1942 Bos-A	113	397	58	113	16	7	3	61	29	11	3	3	.285	.335	.383	.718	98	-2	51	4.57	2	O-95(3-1-92)/1-2	11	-0.6
1944 Bos-A	68	251	37	72	11	2	0	32	23	7	1	0	.287	.347	.347	.693	100	1	31	4.34	-3	1-59/O-2(1-0-1)	6	-0.6
1945 Bos-A	2	2	0	0	0	0	0	0	0	1	0	0	.000	.000	.000	.000	-98	-0	0	.00	0	....	0	-0.1
StL-A	57	213	24	59	8	4	2	22	21	6	0	0	.277	.345	.380	.725	105	2	27	4.40	1	O-36(24-0-13),1-22/3-1	6	0.0
Yr.	59	215	24	59	8	4	2	22	21	7	0	0	.274	.342	.377	.719	103	1	27	4.35	1	O-36(24-0-13),1-22/3-1	6	0.0
1946 StL-A	16	30	0	9	0	0	0	3	2	4	0	0	.300	.344	.300	.644	77	-1	3	4.20	0	/O-7(4-0-3)	1	-0.1
1947 Phi-N	4	4	0	0	0	0	0	0	0	0	0	....	.000	.000	.000	.000	-104	-1	0	.00	0	....	0	-0.1
Total 15	1270	4631	643	1329	203	85	31	494	329	186	39	45	.287	.336	.388	.723	88	-102	599	4.62	-26	O-688,1-415/2-1,3-1	90	-18.6

• FIORE, Mike

Michael Gary Joseph Fiore b: 10/11/1944, Brooklyn, NY BL/TL, 6', 185 lbs. Deb: 9/21/1968 Career OF: 5-8-4

YEAR TM-L	G	AB	R	H	2B	3B	HR	RBI	BB	SO	SB	CS	AVG	OBP	SLG	OPS	OPS+	BR/A	RC	RC/G	FR	G/POS	WS	TPW
1968 Bal-A	6	17	2	1	0	0	0	0	4	4	0	0	.059	.273	.059	.332	5	-2	1	1.06	0	/1-5,O-1	0	-0.2
1969 KC-A	107	339	53	93	14	1	12	35	84	63	4	4	.274	.421	.428	.849	137	22	66	6.81	13	1-91,O-13(3-8-2)	16	2.9
1970 KC-A	25	72	6	13	2	0	0	4	13	24	1	1	.181	.306	.208	.514	44	-5	5	2.36	2	1-20	0	-0.4
Bos-A	41	50	5	7	0	0	0	4	8	4	0	0	.140	.259	.140	.399	12	-6	2	1.33	0	1-17/O-2(1-0-1)	0	-0.6
Yr.	66	122	11	20	2	0	0	8	21	28	1	1	.164	.287	.180	.467	31	-11	8	1.92	3	1-37/O-2(1-0-1)	0	-1.1
1971 Bos-A	51	62	9	11	2	0	1	6	12	14	0	3	.177	.311	.258	.569	58	-4	5	2.37	0	1-12	0	-0.5
1972 StL-N	17	10	0	1	0	0	0	1	2	3	0	0	.100	.250	.100	.350	3	-1	0	.77	-1	/1-6,O-1	0	-0.2
SD-N	7	6	0	0	0	0	0	0	1	3	0	0	.000	.143	.000	.143	-61	-1	0	.00	0	....	0	-0.1
Yr.	24	16	0	1	0	0	0	1	3	6	0	0	.063	.211	.063	.273	-19	-2	0	.50	-1	/1-6,O-1	0	-0.3
Total 5	254	556	75	126	18	1	13	50	124	115	5	8	.227	.370	.333	.703	98	2	79	4.69	15	1-151/O-17	16	0.7

• FIROVA, Dan

Daniel Michael Firova b: 10/16/1956, Refugio, TX BR/TR, 6', 185 lbs. Deb: 9/1/1981

YEAR TM-L	G	AB	R	H	2B	3B	HR	RBI	BB	SO	SB	CS	AVG	OBP	SLG	OPS	OPS+	BR/A	RC	RC/G	FR	G/POS	WS	TPW
1981 Sea-A	13	2	0	0	0	0	0	0	0	1	0	0	.000	.000	.000	.000	-96	-0	0	.00	-3	C-13	0	-0.4
1982 Sea-A	3	5	0	0	0	0	0	0	0	0	0	0	.000	.000	.000	.000	-97	-1	0	.00	0	/C-3	0	-0.2
1988 Cle-A	1	0	0	0	0	0	0	0	0	0	0	0	....	....	....	....	-97	0	0	....	0	/C-1	0	0.0
Total 3	17	7	0	0	0	0	0	0	0	1	0	0	.000	.000	.000	.000	-97	-2	0	.00	-4	/C-17	0	-0.6

• FISCHER, William

William Charles Fischer b: 3/2/1891, New York, NY d: 9/4/1945, Richmond, VA BL/TR, 6', 174 lbs. Deb: 6/11/1913

YEAR TM-L	G	AB	R	H	2B	3B	HR	RBI	BB	SO	SB	CS	AVG	OBP	SLG	OPS	OPS+	BR/A	RC	RC/G	FR	G/POS	WS	TPW
1913 Bro-N	62	165	16	44	9	4	1	12	10	5	0	....	.267	.313	.388	.700	97	-1	19	3.96	1	C-51	4	0.3
1914 Bro-N	43	105	12	27	1	2	0	8	8	12	1	....	.257	.310	.305	.614	81	-2	10	3.22	1	C-30	3	0.0
1915 Chi-F	105	292	30	96	15	4	4	50	24	19	5	....	.329	.384	.449	.832	153	19	51	6.41	-6	C-80	16	2.0
1916 Chi-N	65	179	15	35	9	2	1	14	11	8	2	....	.196	.246	.285	.531	57	-9	14	2.38	-2	C-56	2	-0.8
Pit-N	42	113	11	29	7	1	1	6	10	3	1	....	.257	.323	.363	.685	109	1	14	4.18	2	C-35	5	0.7
Yr.	107	292	26	64	16	3	2	20	21	11	3	....	.219	.276	.315	.591	77	-8	28	3.05	0	C-91	7	-0.1
1917 Pit-N	95	245	25	70	9	2	3	25	27	19	11	....	.286	.359	.376	.734	121	7	35	5.11	-1	C-69/1-2	8	1.2
Total 5	412	1099	109	301	50	15	10	115	90	66	20	....	.274	.332	.374	.706	111	14	143	4.49	-6	C-321/1-2	38	3.5

• FISCHLIN, Mike

Michael Thomas Fischlin b: 9/13/1955, Sacramento, CA BR/TR, 6'1", 165 lbs. Deb: 9/3/1977

YEAR TM-L	G	AB	R	H	2B	3B	HR	RBI	BB	SO	SB	CS	AVG	OBP	SLG	OPS	OPS+	BR/A	RC	RC/G	FR	G/POS	WS	TPW
1977 Hou-N	13	15	0	3	0	0	0	0	0	2	0	0	.200	.200	.200	.400	8	-2	1	1.35	0	S-12	0	-0.1
1978 Hou-N	44	86	3	10	1	0	0	0	4	9	1	0	.116	.165	.128	.293	-19	-13	2	.72	-8	S-41	1	-1.9
1980 Hou-N	1	1	0	0	0	0	0	0	0	1	0	0	.000	.000	.000	.000	-109	-0	0	.00	0	/S-1	0	-0.1
1981 Cle-A	22	43	3	10	1	0	0	5	3	6	3	2	.233	.283	.256	.538	57	-3	3	2.40	-2	S-19/2-1	1	-0.4
1982 Cle-A	112	276	34	74	12	1	0	21	34	36	9	5	.268	.353	.319	.671	86	-4	34	4.17	2	*S-101/3-8,2-6,C-1	8	0.7
1983 Cle-A	95	225	31	47	5	2	2	23	26	32	9	2	.209	.296	.276	.572	56	-12	22	2.98	2	2-71,S-15/3-4,D-1	4	-0.5
1984 Cle-A	85	133	17	30	4	2	1	14	12	20	2	2	.226	.290	.308	.598	64	-7	12	2.92	2	2-55,3-17,S-15	2	-0.2
1985 Cle-A	73	60	12	12	4	1	0	2	5	7	0	1	.200	.262	.300	.562	54	-4	5	2.53	-2	2-31,S-22/1-6,D-5,3-3	1	-0.4
1986 NY-A	71	102	9	21	2	0	0	3	8	29	0	1	.206	.264	.225	.489	35	-10	6	1.80	1	S-42,2-27	2	-0.6
1987 Atl-N	1	0	0	0	0	0	0	0	0	0	0	0	....	....	....	....	-95	0	0	....	0	....	0	0.0
Total 10	517	941	109	207	29	6	3	68	92	142	24	13	.220	.293	.273	.566	57	-54	85	2.85	-6	S-268,2-191/3-32,1-6,D-6,C	19	-3.5

• FISHBURN, Sam

Samuel E. Fishburn b: 5/15/1893, Haverhill, MA d: 4/11/1965, Bethlehem, PA BR/TR, 5'9", 157 lbs. Deb: 5/30/1919

YEAR TM-L	G	AB	R	H	2B	3B	HR	RBI	BB	SO	SB	CS	AVG	OBP	SLG	OPS	OPS+	BR/A	RC	RC/G	FR	G/POS	WS	TPW
1919 StL-N	9	6	0	2	1	0	0	2	0	0	0	....	.333	.333	.500	.833	158	0	1	6.11	0	/1-1,2-1	0	0.0

• FISHEL, John

John Alan Fishel b: 11/8/1962, Fullerton, CA BR/TR, 5'11", 185 lbs. Deb: 7/14/1988

YEAR TM-L	G	AB	R	H	2B	3B	HR	RBI	BB	SO	SB	CS	AVG	OBP	SLG	OPS	OPS+	BR/A	RC	RC/G	FR	G/POS	WS	TPW
1988 Hou-N	19	26	1	6	0	0	1	2	3	6	0	0	.231	.310	.346	.656	92	-0	3	3.97	-1	/O-6(5-0-2)	1	-0.1

• FISHER, Bob

Robert Taylor Fisher b: 11/3/1886, Nashville, TN d: 8/4/1963, Jacksonville, FL BR/TR, 5'9.5", 170 lbs. Deb: 6/3/1912

YEAR TM-L	G	AB	R	H	2B	3B	HR	RBI	BB	SO	SB	CS	AVG	OBP	SLG	OPS	OPS+	BR/A	RC	RC/G	FR	G/POS	WS	TPW
1912 Bro-N	82	257	27	60	10	3	0	26	14	32	7	....	.233	.273	.296	.569	58	-16	23	2.79	-10	S-74/2-1,3-1	1	-2.1
1913 Bro-N	132	474	42	124	11	10	4	54	10	43	16	....	.262	.278	.352	.631	77	-16	49	3.39	-12	*S-131	8	-2.0
1914 Chi-N	15	50	5	15	2	2	0	5	3	4	2	....	.300	.340	.420	.760	126	1	8	5.24	0	S-15	2	0.2
1915 Chi-N	147	568	70	163	22	5	5	53	30	51	9	20	.287	.326	.370	.696	110	-2	69	3.94	-20	*S-145	17	-1.3
1916 Cin-N	61	136	9	37	4	3	0	11	8	14	7	....	.272	.313	.346	.658	104	0	17	4.34	-6	S-29/2-6,O-1	3	-0.4
1918 StL-N	63	246	36	78	11	3	2	20	15	11	7	....	.317	.356	.411	.767	138	10	37	5.53	10	2-63	11	2.4
1919 StL-N	3	11	0	3	1	0	0	1	0	2	0	....	.273	.273	.364	.636	96	-0	1	3.25	0	/2-3	0	0.0
Total 7	503	1742	189	480	61	26	11	170	80	157	48	20	.276	.309	.359	.668	98	-22	203	3.88	-39	S-394/2-73,3-1,O-1	42	-3.1

YEAR TM-L	G	AB	R	H	2B	3B	HR	RBI	BB	SO	SB	CS	AVG	OBP	SLG	OPS	OPS+	BR/A	RC	RC/G	FR	G/POS	WS	TPW
• FISHER, Charles	Charles Fisher b: Baltimore, MD Deb: 6/15/1889																							
1889 Lou-a	1	2	0	1	0	0	0	0	0	0	0	....	.500	.500	.500	1.000	188	0	1	13.58	0	/O-1	0	0.0
• FISHER, Charles	Charles G. Fisher b: 3/10/1852, Boxford, MA d: 2/18/1917, Eagle, AK BL/TR, 5'8", 143 lbs. Deb: 6/7/1884																							
1884 KC-U	10	40	3	8	2	0	0	....	0	....	....	....	.200	.200	.250	.450	59	-1	2	1.79	0	/3-9,S-1	0	-0.1
CP-U	1	3	1	2	0	0	0	....	1	....	....	....	.667	.750	.667	1.417	408	1	2	43.05	0	/3-1	1	0.1
Yr.	11	43	4	10	2	0	0	....	1	....	....	....	.233	.250	.279	.529	91	-0	4	3.04	-1	3-10/S-1	1	-0.1
• FISHER, Cherokee	William Charles Fisher b: 12/1845, Philadelphia, PA d: 9/26/1912, New York, NY BR/TR, 5'9", 164 lbs. Deb: 5/6/1871 U NA OF: 5-14-66 ♦																							
1871 Rok-n	25	123	24	28	3	3	1	22	3	1	1	2	.228	.246	.325	.571	65	-4	10	3.36	4	*P-24/1-2,2-1	....	-0.1
1872 Bal-n	46	225	39	52	10	3	1	36	2	5	0	1	.231	.238	.316	.553	66	-9	17	3.08	-2	O-19(0-3-17),P-19,3-18	....	0.3
1873 Ath-n	51	253	50	66	4	3	1	35	4	5	1	2	.261	.272	.312	.585	68	-10	22	3.60	5	*O-45(1-2-43),P-13/2-3,1-1	....	0.8
1874 Har-n	52	241	28	54	7	0	0	28	2	6	0	2	.224	.230	.253	.484	52	-8	14	2.29	-4	P-39,O-12(0-8-6)/3-7,S-2	....	0.6
1875 Phi-n	41	177	26	41	3	1	0	11	1	6	4	3	.232	.236	.260	.496	69	-2	12	2.57	-3	P-41/O-5(4-1-0)	....	1.7
1876 Cin-N	35	129	12	32	1	0	0	4	0	8	....	....	.248	.248	.256	.504	79	-0	8	2.42	-5	P-28,O-11(0-7-4)/1-1,S-1	2	-0.9
1877 Chi-N	1	4	0	0	0	0	0	0	0	2	....	....	.000	.000	.000	.000	-89	-1	0	.00	0	/3-1	0	-0.1
1878 Pro-N	1	3	0	0	0	0	0	0	0	0	....	....	.000	.000	.000	.000	-100	-0	0	.00	0	/P-1	0	-0.2
Total 5 n	**215**	**1019**	**167**	**241**	**27**	**10**	**3**	**132**	**12**	**23**	**6**	**10**	**.237**	**.245**	**.291**	**.537**	**64**	**-33**	**76**	**2.96**	**1**	**P-136/O-81,3-25,2-4,1-3,S**	**....**	**3.3**
Total 3	**37**	**136**	**12**	**32**	**1**	**0**	**0**	**4**	**0**	**10**	**....**	**....**	**.235**	**.235**	**.243**	**.478**	**70**	**-2**	**8**	**2.26**	**-5**	**/P-29,O-11,1-1,3-1,S-1**	**2**	**-1.2**
• FISHER, George	George Cresse Fisher b: 8/20/1855, Wilmington, DE d: 1/29/1937, Oakland, CA BL Deb: 8/9/1884																							
1884 Cle-N	6	24	2	3	0	0	0	0	0	3	....	....	.125	.125	.125	.250	-21	-3	0	.50	-2	/2-6,C-1	0	-0.4
Wil-U	8	29	0	2	0	0	0	....	0	....	....	....	.069	.069	.069	.138	-52	-5	0	.15	-1	/O-6(0-6-1),S-2	0	-0.5
• FISHER, Gus	August Harris Fisher b: 10/21/1885, Pottsboro, TX d: 4/8/1972, Portland, OR BL/TR, 5'10", 175 lbs. Deb: 4/18/1911																							
1911 Cle-A	70	203	20	53	6	3	0	12	7	....	6	....	.261	.302	.320	.623	73	-8	21	3.56	3	C-58/1-1	5	0.0
1912 NY-A	4	10	1	1	0	0	0	0	0	....	0	....	.100	.100	.100	.200	-40	-2	0	.24	0	/C-4	0	-0.1
Total 2	**74**	**213**	**21**	**54**	**6**	**3**	**0**	**12**	**7**	**....**	**6**	**....**	**.254**	**.293**	**.310**	**.603**	**68**	**-10**	**21**	**3.37**	**4**	**/C-62,1-1**	**5**	**-0.1**
• FISHER, Newt	Newton "Ike" Fisher b: 6/28/1871, Nashville, TN d: 2/28/1947, Chicago, IL BR/TR, 5'9.5", 171 lbs. Deb: 5/17/1898																							
1898 Phi-N	9	26	0	3	1	0	0	0	0	....	1	....	.115	.148	.154	.302	-14	-4	1	.87	-2	/C-8,3-1	0	-0.5
• FISHER, Red	John Gus Fisher b: 6/22/1887, Pittsburgh, PA d: 1/31/1940, Louisville, KY BL/TR, 5'9", 176 lbs. Deb: 4/25/1910																							
1910 StL-A	23	72	5	9	2	1	0	3	8	....	5	....	.125	.222	.181	.403	28	-6	4	1.61	-1	O-19(14-0-5)	0	-0.8
• FISHER, Showboat	George Aloys Fisher b: 1/16/1899, Wesley, IA d: 5/15/1994, St. Cloud, MN BL/TR, 5'10", 170 lbs. Deb: 4/24/1923 Career OF: 29-0-58																							
1923 Was-A	13	23	4	6	2	0	0	2	4	3	0	0	.261	.370	.348	.718	94	0	3	5.01	0	/O-5(0-0-5)	0	0.0
1924 Was-A	15	41	7	9	1	0	0	6	6	6	2	0	.220	.319	.244	.563	48	-2	4	3.19	-1	O-11(0-0-11)	0	-0.4
1930*StL-N	92	254	49	95	18	6	8	61	25	21	4	....	.374	.432	.587	1.019	139	16	62	9.83	-2	O-67(24-0-42)	11	0.8
1932 StL-A	18	22	2	4	0	0	0	2	2	5	0	0	.182	.250	.182	.432	13	-3	1	1.60	-0	/O-5(5-0-0)	0	-0.3
Total 4	**138**	**340**	**62**	**114**	**21**	**6**	**8**	**71**	**37**	**35**	**6**	**0**	**.335**	**.402**	**.503**	**.905**	**117**	**11**	**71**	**7.92**	**-3**	**/O-88**	**11**	**0.2**
• FISHER, Wilbur	Wilbur McCullough Fisher b: 7/18/1894, Green Bottom, WV d: 10/24/1960, Welch, WV BL/TR, 6', 174 lbs. Deb: 6/13/1916																							
1916 Pit-N	1	1	0	0	0	0	0	0	0	0	0	....	.000	.000	.000	.000	-99	-0	0	.00	0	....	0	0.0
• FISK, Carlton	Carlton Ernest "Pudge" Fisk b: 12/26/1947, Bellows Falls, VT BR/TR, 6'3", 220 lbs. Deb: 9/18/1969 HOF: 2000 Career OF: 41-0-0																							
1969 Bos-A	2	5	0	0	0	0	0	0	0	2	0	0	.000	.000	.000	.000	-95	-1	0	.00	0	/C-1	0	-0.2
1971 Bos-A	14	48	7	15	2	1	2	6	1	10	0	0	.313	.327	.521	.847	128	1	8	6.14	-1	C-14	2	0.2
1972 Bos-A★	131	457	74	134	28	**9**	22	61	52	83	5	2	.293	.370	.538	.909	159	33	90	7.23	2	*C-131	33	4.8
1973 Bos-A★	135	508	65	125	21	0	26	71	37	99	7	2	.246	.310	.441	.751	103	1	69	4.65	0	*C-131/D-3	17	0.8
1974 Bos-A★	52	187	36	56	12	1	11	26	24	23	5	1	.299	.385	.551	.936	156	14	40	7.70	2	C-50/D-2	11	2.0
1975*Bos-A	79	263	47	87	14	4	10	52	27	32	4	3	.331	.397	.529	.926	147	16	54	7.70	-3	C-71/D-6	15	1.7
1976 Bos-A★	134	487	76	124	17	5	17	58	56	71	12	5	.255	.339	.415	.754	107	5	70	4.85	6	*C-133/D-1	19	1.9
1977 Bos-A★	152	536	106	169	26	3	26	102	75	85	7	6	.315	.408	.521	.929	135	29	117	8.00	-5	*C-151	30	3.2
1978 Bos-A★	157	571	94	162	39	5	20	88	71	83	7	2	.284	.370	.475	.844	123	20	103	6.48	5	*C-154/D-1,O-1	31	3.3
1979 Bos-A	91	320	49	87	23	2	10	42	10	38	3	0	.272	.307	.450	.757	96	-2	42	4.61	-3	D-42,C-39/O-1	6	-0.5
1980 Bos-A★	131	478	73	138	25	3	18	62	36	62	11	5	.289	.355	.467	.821	117	11	77	5.81	1	*C-115/D-5,O-5(5-0-0),1-3,3	18	1.7
1981 Chi-A★	96	338	44	89	12	0	7	45	38	37	3	2	.263	.358	.361	.719	110	6	45	4.58	5	C-92/1-3,O-1	13	1.7
1982 Chi-A★	135	476	66	127	17	3	14	65	46	60	17	2	.267	.339	.403	.742	103	5	67	4.85	3	*C-133/1-2	19	1.4
1983*Chi-A	138	488	85	141	26	4	26	86	46	88	9	6	.289	.357	.518	.876	133	21	90	6.62	-3	*C-133/D-2	26	2.4
1984 Chi-A	102	359	54	83	20	1	21	43	26	60	6	0	.231	.292	.468	.760	102	1	49	4.59	0	C-90/D-5	10	0.4
1985 Chi-A★	153	543	85	129	23	1	37	107	52	81	17	9	.238	.324	.488	.812	114	9	85	5.22	3	*C-130,D-28	24	1.7
1986 Chi-A	125	457	42	101	11	0	14	63	22	92	2	4	.221	.266	.337	.603	61	-27	39	2.77	5	C-71,O-31(31-0-0),D-22	6	-2.1
1987 Chi-A	135	454	68	116	22	1	23	71	39	72	1	4	.256	.325	.460	.786	103	-1	66	4.97	8	*C-122/1-9,D-7,O-2(2-0-0)	16	1.2
1988 Chi-A	76	253	37	70	8	1	19	50	37	40	0	0	.277	.380	.542	.921	155	19	52	7.36	3	C-74	15	2.7
1989 Chi-A	103	375	47	110	25	2	13	68	36	60	1	0	.293	.360	.475	.835	137	18	61	5.73	1	C-90,D-13	18	2.4
1990 Chi-A	137	452	65	129	21	0	18	65	61	73	7	2	.285	.379	.451	.830	134	23	79	6.28	6	*C-116,D-14	22	3.6
1991 Chi-A★	134	460	42	111	25	0	18	74	32	86	1	2	.241	.301	.413	.714	98	-4	52	3.75	4	*C-106,D-13,1-12	13	0.6
1992 Chi-A	62	188	12	43	4	1	3	21	23	38	3	0	.229	.316	.309	.625	77	-5	20	3.61	-0	C-54/D-2	4	-0.2
1993 Chi-A	25	53	2	10	0	0	1	4	2	11	0	1	.189	.232	.245	.477	29	-6	3	1.80	0	C-25	0	-0.5
Total 24	**2499**	**8756**	**1276**	**2356**	**421**	**47**	**376**	**1330**	**849**	**1386**	**128**	**58**	**.269**	**.343**	**.457**	**.800**	**116**	**189**	**1375**	**5.49**	**39**	***C-2226,D-166/O-41,1-27,3-4**	**368**	**34.3**
• FISLER, Wes	Weston Dickson "Icicle" Fisler b: 7/5/1841, Camden, NJ d: 12/25/1922, Philadelphia, PA BR/TR, 5'6", 137 lbs. Deb: 5/20/1871 NA OF: 0-1-10																							
1871 Ath-n	28	147	43	41	8	2	0	16	3	2	6	3	.279	.293	.361	.654	87	-3	18	5.13	-1	*1-26/2-2	....	-0.2
1872 Ath-n	47	243	49	85	13	3	0	48	4	4	3	0	.350	.360	.428	.788	141	12	40	7.75	10	*2-47	....	1.3
1873 Ath-n	44	218	44	75	11	4	1	42	2	2	2	1	.344	.350	.445	.795	125	5	36	7.52	6	*2-36,1-10	....	0.7
1874 Ath-n	37	180	26	59	12	1	0	22	0	1	2	0	.328	.328	.406	.733	123	4	25	6.25	5	1-28/2-9,O-1	....	0.7
1875 Ath-n	58	268	54	74	13	3	0	31	4	4	1	4	.276	.287	.347	.634	107	-1	28	4.12	-3	1-46,O-10(0-1-9)/2-5	....	-0.3
1876 Phi-N	59	280	42	80	15	1	1	30	2	4	....	....	.286	.293	.360	.653	117	5	30	4.24	-2	O-24(0-15-9),2-21,1-14/S-1	5	0.2
Total 5 n	**214**	**1056**	**216**	**334**	**57**	**13**	**1**	**159**	**13**	**13**	**14**	**8**	**.316**	**.325**	**.398**	**.722**	**119**	**17**	**146**	**6.08**	**17**	**1-110/2-99,O-11**	**....**	**2.1**
• FITZ GERALD, Ed	Edward Raymond Fitz Gerald b: 5/21/1924, Santa Ynez, CA BR/TR, 6' Deb: 4/19/1948 C																							
1948 Pit-N	102	262	31	70	9	3	1	35	32	37	3	....	.267	.349	.336	.685	84	-5	33	4.50	-4	C-96	8	-0.5
1949 Pit-N	75	160	16	42	7	0	2	18	8	27	1	....	.263	.302	.344	.646	71	-7	16	3.39	1	C-56	3	-0.4
1950 Pit-N	6	15	1	1	1	0	0	0	0	3	0	....	.067	.067	.133	.200	-47	-3	0	.00	0	/C-5	0	-0.3
1951 Pit-N	55	97	8	22	6	0	0	13	7	10	1	1	.227	.286	.289	.574	53	-7	7	2.26	0	C-38	1	-0.5
1952 Pit-N	51	73	4	17	1	0	1	7	7	15	0	2	.233	.300	.288	.588	62	-4	5	2.29	0	C-18/3-2	0	-0.4
1953 Pit-N	6	17	2	2	1	0	0	1	0	2	0	0	.118	.118	.176	.294	-25	-3	0	.65	0	/C-5	0	-0.2
Was-A	88	288	23	72	13	0	3	39	19	34	2	1	.250	.299	.326	.625	70	-12	27	3.18	-2	C-85	6	-1.0
1954 Was-A	115	360	33	104	13	5	4	40	33	22	0	1	.289	.352	.386	.738	108	3	48	4.67	-8	*C-107	9	0.1
1955 Was-A	74	236	28	56	3	1	4	19	25	23	0	1	.237	.318	.309	.628	73	-9	23	3.21	-2	C-72	4	-0.7
1956 Was-A	64	148	15	45	8	0	2	12	20	16	0	0	.304	.387	.399	.786	108	2	23	5.82	-1	C-50	6	0.3
1957 Was-A	45	125	14	34	8	0	1	13	10	9	2	0	.272	.331	.360	.691	90	-1	13	3.41	-2	C-37	2	-0.1
1958 Was-A	58	114	7	30	3	0	0	11	8	15	0	0	.263	.311	.289	.601	68	-5	9	2.51	-2	C-21/1-5	1	-0.7
1959 Was-A	19	62	5	12	3	0	0	5	4	8	0	0	.194	.242	.242	.484	34	-6	4	1.92	1	C-16	1	-0.4
Cle-A	49	129	12	35	6	1	1	4	12	14	0	0	.271	.343	.357	.699	96	-0	15	4.14	0	C-45	5	0.1
Yr.	68	191	17	47	9	1	1	9	16	22	0	0	.246	.311	.319	.630	76	-6	19	3.37	1	C-61	6	-0.2
Total 12	**807**	**2086**	**199**	**542**	**82**	**10**	**19**	**217**	**185**	**235**	**9**	**6**	**.260**	**.324**	**.336**	**.660**	**81**	**-56**	**223**	**3.64**	**-18**	**C-651/1-5,3-2**	**46**	**-4.7**
• FITZBERGER, Charlie	Charles Caspar Fitzberger b: 2/13/1904, Baltimore, MD d: 1/25/1965, Baltimore, MD BL/TL, 6'1.5", 170 lbs. Deb: 9/11/1928																							
1928 Bos-N	7	7	0	2	0	0	0	0	0	3	0	....	.286	.286	.286	.571	52	-0	1	2.76	0	....	0	0.0

YEAR TM-L	G	AB	R	H	2B	3B	HR	RBI	BB	SO	SB	CS	AVG	OBP	SLG	OPS	OPS+	BR/A	RC	RC/G	FR	G/POS	WS	TPW
• FITZGERALD, Dennis	Dennis S. Fitzgerald b: 3/1865, England d: 10/16/1936, New Haven, CT, 5'10", 160 lbs. Deb: 4/17/1890																							
1890 Phi-a	2	8	0	2	0	0	0	0	0	....	0	....	.250	.250	.250	.500	48	-1	1	2.26	-1	/S-2	0	-0.1
• FITZGERALD, Howie	Howard Chumney "Lefty" Fitzgerald b: 5/16/1902, Eagle Lake, TX d: 2/27/1959, Mathews, TX BL/TL, 5'11.5", 163 lbs. Deb: 9/17/1922 Career OF: 21-1-12																							
1922 Chi-N	10	24	3	8	1	0	0	4	3	2	1	0	.333	.407	.375	.782	101	1	4	6.35	-1	/O-6(0-0-6)	1	-0.1
1924 Chi-N	7	19	1	3	0	0	0	2	0	2	0	0	.158	.158	.158	.316	-15	-3	0	.75	0	/O-5(0-1-4)	0	-0.3
1926 Bos-A	31	97	11	25	2	0	0	8	5	7	1	4	.258	.294	.278	.572	51	-8	7	2.45	-2	O-23(21-0-2)	0	-1.2
Total 3	**48**	**140**	**15**	**36**	**3**	**0**	**0**	**14**	**8**	**11**	**2**	**4**	**.257**	**.297**	**.279**	**.576**	**52**	**-11**	**12**	**2.80**	**-4**	**/O-34**	**1**	**-1.6**
• FITZGERALD, Matty	Matthew William Fitzgerald b: 8/31/1880, Albany, NY d: 9/22/1949, Albany, NY BR/TR, 6', 185 lbs. Deb: 9/15/1906																							
1906 NY-N	4	6	2	4	0	0	0	2	0	....	1	....	.667	.667	.667	1.333	309	1	3	29.10	0	/C-3	1	0.2
1907 NY-N	7	15	1	2	1	0	0	1	0	....	0	....	.133	.133	.200	.333	4	-2	0	.89	0	/C-6	0	-0.2
Total 2	**11**	**21**	**3**	**6**	**1**	**0**	**0**	**3**	**0**	**....**	**1**	**....**	**.286**	**.286**	**.333**	**.619**	**97**	**-0**	**4**	**5.87**	**0**	**/C-9**	**1**	**0.0**
• FITZGERALD, Mike	Michael Roy Fitzgerald b: 7/13/1960, Long Beach, CA BR/TR, 6', 190 lbs. Deb: 9/13/1983 Career OF: 15-0-15																							
1983 NY-N	8	20	1	2	0	0	1	2	3	6	0	0	.100	.217	.250	.467	29	-2	1	1.80	1	/C-8	0	-0.1
1984 NY-N	112	360	20	87	15	1	2	33	24	71	1	0	.242	.291	.306	.596	69	-15	29	2.61	1	*C-107	8	-1.0
1985 Mon-N	108	295	25	61	7	1	5	34	38	55	5	3	.207	.301	.288	.590	70	-12	26	2.78	-3	*C-108	6	-1.0
1986 Mon-N	73	209	20	59	13	1	6	37	27	34	3	2	.282	.367	.440	.807	123	7	34	5.69	1	C-71	9	1.1
1987 Mon-N	107	287	32	69	11	0	3	36	42	54	3	4	.240	.339	.310	.649	71	-12	30	3.42	-8	*C-104/1-1,2-1	3	-1.5
1988 Mon-N	63	155	17	42	6	1	5	23	19	22	2	2	.271	.351	.419	.770	115	3	23	4.89	-1	C-47/O-4(3-0-1)	5	0.5
1989 Mon-N	100	290	33	69	18	2	7	42	35	61	3	4	.238	.324	.386	.710	101	-1	35	4.03	0	C-77/3-8,O-6(6-0-0)	9	0.4
1990 Mon-N	111	313	36	76	18	1	9	41	60	60	8	1	.243	.368	.393	.761	114	9	51	5.45	1	C-98/O-6(1-0-5)	13	1.6
1991 Mon-N	71	198	17	40	5	2	4	28	22	35	4	2	.202	.282	.308	.590	67	-9	17	2.74	3	C-54/1-3,O-3(0-0-3)	5	-0.3
1992 Cal-A	95	189	19	40	2	0	6	17	22	34	2	2	.212	.294	.317	.611	71	-8	18	3.06	-2	C-74,O-11(5-0-6)/3-3,1-2,2,D	4	-0.7
Total 10	**848**	**2316**	**220**	**545**	**95**	**9**	**48**	**293**	**292**	**432**	**31**	**20**	**.235**	**.323**	**.346**	**.670**	**87**	**-39**	**264**	**3.74**	**-8**	**C-748/O-30,3-11,1-6,2-2,D-1**	**62**	**-0.9**
• FITZGERALD, Mike	Michael Patrick Fitzgerald b: 3/28/1964, Savannah, GA BR/TR, 6'1", 196 lbs. Deb: 6/23/1988																							
1988 StL-N	13	46	4	9	1	0	0	1	0	9	0	0	.196	.213	.217	.430	23	-5	2	1.59	-2	1-12	0	-0.8
• FITZGERALD, Mike	Justin Howard Fitzgerald b: 6/22/1890, San Mateo, CA d: 1/18/1945, San Mateo, CA BL/TR, 5'8", 160 lbs. Deb: 6/20/1911 Career OF: 43-2-19																							
1911 NY-A	16	37	6	10	1	0	0	6	4	....	4	....	.270	.341	.297	.639	74	-1	5	4.67	-1	/O-9(9-0-0)	1	-0.3
1918 Phi-N	66	133	21	39	8	0	0	6	13	6	3	....	.293	.361	.353	.714	110	2	18	4.68	-8	O-59(34-2-19)	4	-0.8
Total 2	**82**	**170**	**27**	**49**	**9**	**0**	**0**	**12**	**17**	**6**	**7**	**....**	**.288**	**.356**	**.341**	**.698**	**102**	**1**	**23**	**4.68**	**-9**	**/O-68**	**5**	**-1.1**
• FITZGERALD, Ray	Raymond Francis Fitzgerald b: 12/5/1904, Chicopee, MA d: 9/6/1977, Westfield, MA BR/TR, 5'9", 168 lbs. Deb: 4/18/1931																							
1931 Cin-N	1	1	0	0	0	0	0	0	0	0	0	....	.000	.000	.000	.000	-106	-0	0	.00	0	....	0	0.0
• FITZMAURICE, Shaun	Shaun Earle Fitzmaurice b: 8/25/1942, Worcester, MA BR/TR, 6', 180 lbs. Deb: 9/9/1966																							
1966 NY-N	9	13	2	2	0	0	0	0	2	6	1	0	.154	.267	.154	.421	21	-1	1	1.99	1	/O-5(2-3-0)	0	-0.1
• FITZPATRICK, Ed	Edward Henry Fitzpatrick b: 12/9/1889, Lewiston, PA d: 10/23/1965, Bethlehem, PA BR/TR, 5'8", 165 lbs. Deb: 4/17/1915 Career OF: 6-16-52																							
1915 Bos-N	105	303	54	67	19	3	0	24	43	36	13	8	.221	.344	.304	.648	99	2	36	3.66	0	2-71,O-29(0-7-22)	10	0.2
1916 Bos-N	83	216	17	46	8	0	1	18	15	26	5	....	.213	.280	.264	.544	71	-7	19	2.72	-13	2-46,O-28(2-3-23)	4	-2.3
1917 Bos-N	63	178	20	45	8	4	0	17	12	22	4	....	.253	.318	.343	.661	109	2	20	3.78	-10	2-22,O-19(4-6-7),3-15	5	-0.9
Total 3	**251**	**697**	**91**	**158**	**35**	**7**	**1**	**59**	**70**	**84**	**22**	**8**	**.227**	**.319**	**.301**	**.620**	**93**	**-3**	**75**	**3.39**	**-23**	**2-139/O-76,3-15**	**19**	**-3.1**
• FITZSIMMONS, Tom	Thomas William Fitzsimmons b: 4/6/1890, Oakland, CA d: 12/20/1971, Oakland, CA BR/TR, 6'1", 190 lbs. Deb: 6/12/1919																							
1919 Bro-N	4	4	1	0	0	0	0	0	1	2	0	....	.000	.200	.000	.200	-36	-1	0	.00	-1	/3-4	0	-0.2
• FLACK, Max	Max John Flack b: 2/5/1890, Belleville, IL d: 7/31/1975, Belleville, IL BL/TL, 5'7", 148 lbs. Deb: 4/16/1914 Career OF: 218-8-1122																							
1914 Chi-F	134	502	66	124	15	3	2	39	51	48	37	....	.247	.324	.301	.625	83	-10	57	3.77	0	*O-133(112-0-23)	13	-1.6
1915 Chi-F	141	523	88	164	20	14	3	45	40	21	37	....	.314	.365	.423	.787	139	24	90	6.19	4	*O-138(61-0-81)	26	2.3
1916 Chi-N	141	465	65	120	14	3	3	20	42	43	24	19	.258	.320	.320	.640	87	-9	53	3.42	10	*O-136(0-0-136)	10	-0.6
1917 Chi-N	131	447	65	111	18	7	0	21	51	34	17	....	.248	.325	.320	.645	91	-3	50	3.76	-4	*O-117(40-6-77)	13	-1.5
1918*Chi-N	123	478	74	123	17	10	4	41	56	19	17	....	.257	.343	.360	.702	112	8	63	4.43	1	*O-121(0-0-121)	20	0.3
1919 Chi-N	116	469	71	138	20	4	6	35	34	13	18	....	.294	.346	.392	.738	121	12	67	5.08	3	*O-116(0-0-116)	17	1.0
1920 Chi-N	135	520	85	157	30	6	4	49	52	15	13	19	.302	.373	.406	.779	121	13	77	5.14	-2	*O-132(0-1-131)	20	0.4
1921 Chi-N	133	572	80	172	31	4	6	37	32	15	17	11	.301	.342	.400	.742	96	-3	77	4.89	-1	*O-130(0-0-130)	13	-1.4
1922 Chi-N	17	54	7	12	1	0	0	6	2	4	2	1	.222	.250	.241	.491	27	-6	3	1.98	-2	O-15(0-0-15)	0	-0.8
StL-N	66	267	46	78	12	1	2	21	31	11	3	5	.292	.368	.367	.735	94	-2	37	4.91	-4	O-66(0-1-65)	6	-1.0
Yr.	83	321	53	90	13	1	2	27	33	15	5	6	.280	.349	.346	.695	84	-8	40	4.38	-6	O-81(0-1-80)	6	-1.8
1923 StL-N	128	505	82	147	16	9	3	28	41	16	7	8	.291	.348	.376	.724	93	-5	66	4.63	-5	*O-121(0-0-121)	11	-1.9
1924 StL-N	67	209	31	55	11	3	2	21	21	5	3	5	.263	.330	.373	.704	90	-4	25	4.12	2	O-52(0-0-52)	4	-0.6
1925 StL-N	79	241	23	60	7	8	0	28	21	9	5	3	.249	.309	.344	.654	65	-13	26	3.69	1	O-59(5-0-54)	3	-1.4
Total 12	**1411**	**5252**	**783**	**1461**	**212**	**72**	**35**	**391**	**474**	**253**	**200**	**71**	**.278**	**.342**	**.366**	**.708**	**101**	**3**	**691**	**4.51**	**3**	***O-1336**	**156**	**-6.7**
• FLAGER, Wally	Walter Leonard Flager b: 11/3/1921, Chicago Heights, IL d: 12/16/1990, Keizer, OR BL/TR, 5'11", 160 lbs. Deb: 4/17/1945																							
1945 Cin-N	21	52	5	11	1	0	0	6	8	5	0	....	.212	.317	.231	.547	55	-3	4	2.72	-2	S-15	1	-0.4
Phi-N	49	168	21	42	4	1	2	15	17	15	1	....	.250	.323	.321	.644	82	-4	18	3.84	2	S-48/2-1	4	0.1
Yr.	70	220	26	53	5	1	2	21	25	20	1	....	.241	.321	.300	.621	75	-7	23	3.57	0	S-63/2-1	5	-0.2
• FLAGSTEAD, Ira	Ira James "Pete" Flagstead b: 9/22/1893, Montague, MI d: 3/13/1940, Olympia, WA BR/TR, 5'9", 165 lbs. Deb: 7/20/1917 Career OF: 56-695-288																							
1917 Det-A	4	4	0	0	0	0	0	0	0	1	0	....	.000	.000	.000	.000	-100	-1	0	.00	0	/O-2(0-0-2)	0	-0.1
1919 Det-A	97	287	43	95	22	3	5	41	35	39	6	....	.331	.416	.481	.897	155	22	59	7.50	0	O-83(0-0-83)	16	1.8
1920 Det-A	110	311	40	73	13	5	3	35	37	27	3	4	.235	.318	.338	.656	76	-11	35	3.66	7	O-82(1-6-75)	6	-0.8
1921 Det-A	85	259	40	79	16	2	0	31	21	21	8	4	.305	.371	.382	.753	93	-1	38	5.18	-7	S-55,O-12(6-2-5)/2-8,3-1	6	-0.3
1922 Det-A	44	91	21	28	5	3	3	8	14	16	0	1	.308	.411	.527	.939	148	6	20	7.97	-1	O-32(8-9-15)	4	0.4
1923 Det-A	1	1	0	0	0	0	0	0	0	0	0	0	.000	.000	.000	.000	-102	-0	0	.00	0	....	0	0.0
Bos-A	109	382	55	119	23	4	8	53	37	26	7	10	.312	.380	.455	.835	119	8	65	6.05	17	*O-102(0-3-99)/S-1	14	1.6
Yr.	110	383	55	119	23	4	8	53	37	26	7	10	.311	.379	.454	.833	118	8	65	6.03	17	*O-102(0-3-99)/S-1	14	1.6
1924 Bos-A	149	560	106	172	35	7	5	43	77	41	10	13	.307	.401	.421	.823	112	11	97	6.21	-8	*O-144(0-143-1)	19	-0.2
1925 Bos-A	148	572	84	160	38	2	6	61	63	30	5	6	.280	.356	.385	.741	88	-10	81	4.94	15	*O-144(0-144-0)	14	0.0
1926 Bos-A	98	415	65	124	31	7	3	31	36	22	4	6	.299	.363	.429	.792	110	4	64	5.63	9	O-98(0-98-0)	12	0.9
1927 Bos-A	131	466	63	133	26	8	4	69	57	25	12	2	.285	.374	.401	.775	103	6	76	5.60	5	*O-129(0-128-1)	14	0.6
1928 Bos-A	140	510	84	148	41	4	1	39	60	23	12	9	.290	.366	.392	.758	101	2	75	5.15	5	*O-135(0-135-0)	15	0.1
1929 Bos-A	14	36	9	11	2	0	0	3	5	1	1	3	.306	.390	.361	.751	97	-1	5	4.16	-1	O-13(13-1-0)	1	-0.2
Was-A	18	39	5	7	1	0	0	9	4	5	1	0	.179	.256	.205	.461	20	-4	3	1.91	3	O-11(1-10-0)	1	-0.2
Yr.	32	75	14	18	3	0	0	12	9	6	2	3	.240	.321	.280	.601	56	-5	7	2.90	2	O-24(14-11-0)	2	-0.4
Pit-N	26	50	8	14	2	1	0	6	4	2	1	....	.280	.333	.360	.693	70	-2	6	4.17	0	/O-9(6-1-2)	1	-0.3
1930 Pit-N	44	156	21	39	7	4	2	21	17	9	1	....	.250	.324	.385	.708	70	-8	20	4.13	1	O-40(21-15-5)	2	-0.8
Total 13	**1218**	**4139**	**644**	**1202**	**262**	**50**	**40**	**450**	**467**	**288**	**71**	**58**	**.290**	**.370**	**.407**	**.776**	**103**	**21**	**643**	**5.43**	**45**	***O-1036/S-56,2-8,3-1**	**125**	**2.3**
• FLAHERTY, John	John Timothy Flaherty b: 10/21/1967, New York, NY BR/TR, 6'1", 195 lbs. Deb: 4/12/1992																							
1992 Bos-A	35	66	3	13	2	0	0	2	3	7	0	0	.197	.232	.227	.459	27	-6	4	1.86	-1	C-34	0	-0.6
1993 Bos-A	13	25	3	3	2	0	0	2	2	6	0	0	.120	.214	.200	.414	11	-3	1	1.53	1	C-13	0	-0.1
1994 Det-A	34	40	2	6	1	0	0	4	1	11	0	1	.150	.171	.175	.346	-11	-7	1	.69	1	C-33/D-1	1	-0.5
1995 Det-A	112	354	39	86	22	1	11	40	18	47	0	0	.243	.285	.404	.689	77	-14	40	3.73	-4	*C-112	7	-1.0
1996 Det-A	47	152	18	38	12	0	4	23	8	25	1	0	.250	.292	.408	.700	75	-6	17	3.73	-2	C-46	3	-0.5
*SD-N	72	264	22	80	12	0	9	41	9	36	2	3	.303	.331	.451	.782	110	1	36	4.85	-2	C-72	7	0.4

YEAR	TM-L	G	AB	R	H	2B	3B	HR	RBI	BB	SO	SB	CS	AVG	OBP	SLG	OPS	OPS+	BR/A	RC	RC/G	FR	G/POS	WS	TPW
1997	SD-N	129	439	38	120	21	1	9	46	33	62	4	4	.273	.324	.387	.711	93	-6	52	4.19	2	*C-124	11	0.3
1998	TB-A	91	304	21	63	11	0	3	24	22	46	0	5	.207	.263	.273	.536	39	-30	20	2.06	1	C-91	5	-2.1
1999	TB-A	117	446	53	124	19	0	14	71	19	64	0	2	.278	.316	.415	.731	84	-13	54	4.21	9	*C-115/D-1	12	0.4
2000	TB-A	109	394	36	103	15	0	10	39	20	57	0	0	.261	.297	.376	.673	70	-19	41	3.66	0	*C-108	8	-1.1
2001	TB-A	78	248	20	59	17	1	4	29	10	33	1	0	.238	.270	.363	.633	66	-13	22	2.93	-4	C-78	4	-1.1
2002	TB-A	76	281	27	73	20	0	4	33	15	50	2	2	.260	.300	.374	.673	79	-10	30	3.68	1	C-75	7	-0.3
2003*	NY-A	40	105	16	28	8	0	4	14	4	19	0	0	.267	.300	.457	.757	98	-1	12	3.68	-7	C-40	3	-0.5
Total	**12**	**953**	**3118**	**298**	**796**	**162**	**3**	**72**	**368**	**164**	**463**	**10**	**17**	**.255**	**.296**	**.378**	**.675**	**75**	**-128**	**331**	**3.58**	**-5**	**C-941/D-2**	**68**	**-6.8**

• FLAHERTY, Martin Martin J. Flaherty b: 9/24/1853, Worcester, MA d: 6/10/1920, Providence, RI BL/TL Deb: 8/18/1881

YEAR	TM-L	G	AB	R	H	2B	3B	HR	RBI	BB	SO	SB	CS	AVG	OBP	SLG	OPS	OPS+	BR/A	RC	RC/G	FR	G/POS	WS	TPW
1881	Wor-N	1	2	0	0	0	0	0	0	0	2	....	....	.000	.000	.000	.000	-95	-0	0	.00	-1	/O-1	0	-0.1

• FLAHERTY, Pat Patrick Henry Flaherty b: 1/31/1866, St. Louis, MO d: 1/28/1946, Chicago, IL BR, 5'9", 166 lbs. Deb: 7/11/1894

YEAR	TM-L	G	AB	R	H	2B	3B	HR	RBI	BB	SO	SB	CS	AVG	OBP	SLG	OPS	OPS+	BR/A	RC	RC/G	FR	G/POS	WS	TPW
1894	Lou-N	38	145	15	43	5	3	0	15	9	6	2	....	.297	.342	.372	.714	78	-5	20	5.00	-2	3-38	2	-0.5

• FLAHERTY, Patsy Patrick Joseph Flaherty b: 6/29/1876, Mansfield, PA d: 1/23/1968, Alexandria, LA BL/TL, 5'8", 165 lbs. Deb: 9/8/1899 U Career OF: 7-15-12 ♦

YEAR	TM-L	G	AB	R	H	2B	3B	HR	RBI	BB	SO	SB	CS	AVG	OBP	SLG	OPS	OPS+	BR/A	RC	RC/G	FR	G/POS	WS	TPW
1899	Lou-N	7	24	3	5	1	1	0	6	3	....	0	....	.208	.296	.333	.630	73	0	2	3.39	-1	/P-5,O-2(0-0-2)	3	0.7
1900	Pit-N	4	9	0	1	0	0	0	0	1	....	0	....	.111	.200	.111	.311	-13	-1	0	.68	1	/P-4	0	-0.6
1903	Chi-A	40	102	7	14	4	0	0	5	5	....	4	....	.137	.178	.176	.354	7	-3	4	1.25	2	P-40	7	-2.9
1904	Chi-A	5	12	1	4	1	0	0	0	4	....	0	....	.333	.500	.417	.917	199	2	3	8.49	1	/P-5	3	0.4
	Pit-N	36	104	9	22	3	4	2	19	8	....	0	....	.212	.268	.375	.643	95	6	11	3.36	5	P-29/O-2(0-2-0)	22	2.4
1905	Pit-N	30	76	7	15	4	2	0	4	3	....	0	....	.197	.228	.303	.530	56	2	5	2.30	2	P-27/O-2(0-1-1)	11	-1.3
1907	Bos-N	41	115	9	22	3	2	2	11	2	....	1	....	.191	.212	.304	.516	62	1	8	2.19	3	P-27/O-8(6-0-2)	10	-0.4
1908	Bos-N	32	86	8	12	0	2	0	5	6	....	2	....	.140	.196	.186	.382	22	-0	4	1.23	2	P-31	8	-3.3
1910	Phi-N	2	2	0	1	0	0	0	0	0	0	0	....	.500	.500	.500	1.000	186	0	0	12.79	0	/O-1,P-1	0	0.0
1911	Bos-N	38	94	9	27	3	2	2	20	8	11	2	....	.287	.343	.426	.769	106	1	14	5.39	-1	O-19(1-11-7)/P-4	2	-0.5
Total	**9**	**235**	**624**	**53**	**123**	**19**	**13**	**6**	**70**	**40**	**11**	**9**	**....**	**.197**	**.247**	**.298**	**.545**	**62**	**9**	**52**	**2.64**	**13**	**P-173/O-34**	**66**	**-5.5**

• FLAIR, Al Albert Dell "Broadway" Flair b: 7/24/1916, New Orleans, LA d: 7/25/1988, New Orleans, LA BL/TL, 6'4", 195 lbs. Deb: 9/6/1941

YEAR	TM-L	G	AB	R	H	2B	3B	HR	RBI	BB	SO	SB	CS	AVG	OBP	SLG	OPS	OPS+	BR/A	RC	RC/G	FR	G/POS	WS	TPW
1941	Bos-A	10	30	3	6	2	1	0	2	1	1	1	1	.200	.226	.333	.559	45	-3	2	1.85	0	/1-8	0	-0.4

• FLANAGAN, Charlie Charles James Flanagan b: 12/31/1891, Oakland, CA d: 1/8/1930, San Francisco, CA BR/TR, 6', 175 lbs. Deb: 7/9/1913

YEAR	TM-L	G	AB	R	H	2B	3B	HR	RBI	BB	SO	SB	CS	AVG	OBP	SLG	OPS	OPS+	BR/A	RC	RC/G	FR	G/POS	WS	TPW
1913	StL-A	4	3	0	0	0	0	0	0	1	0	0	....	.000	.250	.000	.250	-26	-0	0	.00	-1	/3-1,O-1	0	-0.2

• FLANAGAN, Ed Edward J. "Sleepy" Flanagan b: 9/15/1861, Lowell, MA d: 11/10/1926, Lowell, MA, 6'1", 190 lbs. Deb: 4/16/1887

YEAR	TM-L	G	AB	R	H	2B	3B	HR	RBI	BB	SO	SB	CS	AVG	OBP	SLG	OPS	OPS+	BR/A	RC	RC/G	FR	G/POS	WS	TPW
1887	Phi-a	19	83	12	23	5	0	1	10	3	....	3	....	.277	.286	.350	.636	77	-3	9	4.09	-1	1-19	1	-0.5
1889	Lou-a	23	88	11	22	7	3	0	8	7	11	1	....	.250	.305	.398	.703	101	-0	11	4.52	-2	1-23	1	-0.4
Total	**2**	**42**	**171**	**23**	**45**	**12**	**3**	**1**	**18**	**10**	**11**	**4**	**....**	**.263**	**.296**	**.375**	**.671**	**90**	**-3**	**20**	**4.31**	**-3**	**/1-42**	**2**	**-0.8**

• FLANAGAN, Steamer James Paul Flanagan b: 4/20/1881, Kingston, PA d: 4/21/1947, Wilkes-Barre, PA BL/TL, 6'1", 185 lbs. Deb: 9/25/1905

YEAR	TM-L	G	AB	R	H	2B	3B	HR	RBI	BB	SO	SB	CS	AVG	OBP	SLG	OPS	OPS+	BR/A	RC	RC/G	FR	G/POS	WS	TPW
1905	Pit-N	7	25	7	7	1	1	0	3	1	....	3	....	.280	.308	.400	.708	108	0	4	5.92	1	/O-5(0-5-0)	1	0.1

• FLANNERY, John John Michael Flannery b: 1/25/1957, Long Beach, CA BR/TR, 6'3", 173 lbs. Deb: 9/2/1977

YEAR	TM-L	G	AB	R	H	2B	3B	HR	RBI	BB	SO	SB	CS	AVG	OBP	SLG	OPS	OPS+	BR/A	RC	RC/G	FR	G/POS	WS	TPW
1977	Chi-A	7	2	1	0	0	0	0	0	1	1	0	0	.000	.333	.000	.333		-0	0	1.17	0	/S-4,3-1,D-1	0	0.0

• FLANNERY, Tim Timothy Earl Flannery b: 9/29/1957, Tulsa, OK BL/TR, 5'11", 175 lbs. Deb: 9/3/1979 C

YEAR	TM-L	G	AB	R	H	2B	3B	HR	RBI	BB	SO	SB	CS	AVG	OBP	SLG	OPS	OPS+	BR/A	RC	RC/G	FR	G/POS	WS	TPW
1979	SD-N	22	65	2	10	0	1	0	4	4	5	0	0	.154	.225	.185	.410	14	-8	3	1.15	-1	2-21	1	-0.7
1980	SD-N	95	292	15	70	12	0	0	25	18	30	2	2	.240	.284	.281	.565	62	-16	23	2.65	-4	2-53,3-41	4	-1.9
1981	SD-N	37	67	4	17	4	1	0	6	2	4	1	0	.254	.275	.343	.619	80	-2	6	3.17	-1	3-15/2-7	1	-0.3
1982	SD-N	122	379	40	100	11	7	0	30	30	32	1	0	.264	.321	.330	.651	87	-6	42	3.81	-10	*2-104/3-5,S-2	11	-1.2
1983	SD-N	92	214	24	50	7	3	3	19	20	23	2	2	.234	.314	.336	.650	83	-5	23	3.48	13	3-52,2-21/S-7	7	0.9
1984*	SD-N	86	128	24	35	3	3	2	10	12	17	4	1	.273	.350	.391	.740	108	2	19	5.19	3	2-22,3-14,S-14	6	0.6
1985	SD-N	126	384	50	108	14	3	1	40	58	39	2	5	.281	.388	.341	.729	107	6	55	5.14	1	*2-121/3-1	15	1.3
1986	SD-N	134	368	48	103	11	2	3	28	54	61	3	6	.280	.379	.345	.725	103	2	50	4.74	14	*2-108,3-23/S-8	13	2.2
1987	SD-N	106	276	23	63	5	1	0	20	42	30	2	4	.228	.334	.254	.588	61	-15	25	2.97	2	2-84/3-8,S-2	4	-1.0
1988	SD-N	79	170	16	45	5	4	0	19	24	32	3	2	.265	.369	.341	.710	107	2	23	4.39	0	3-51/2-2,S-1	6	0.2
1989	SD-N	73	130	9	30	5	0	0	8	13	20	2	0	.231	.301	.269	.570	64	-5	11	2.97	0	3-33/2-1	2	-0.6
Total	**11**	**972**	**2473**	**255**	**631**	**77**	**25**	**9**	**209**	**277**	**293**	**22**	**22**	**.255**	**.338**	**.317**	**.655**	**86**	**-45**	**279**	**3.84**	**15**	**2-544,3-243/S-34**	**70**	**-0.5**

• FLASKAMPER, Roy Raymond Harold "Flash" Flaskamper b: 10/31/1901, St. Louis, MO d: 2/3/1978, San Antonio, TX BB/TR, 5'7", 140 lbs. Deb: 8/16/1927

YEAR	TM-L	G	AB	R	H	2B	3B	HR	RBI	BB	SO	SB	CS	AVG	OBP	SLG	OPS	OPS+	BR/A	RC	RC/G	FR	G/POS	WS	TPW
1927	Chi-A	26	95	12	21	5	0	0	6	3	8	0	0	.221	.260	.274	.534	40	-9	7	2.40	-1	S-25	1	-0.6

• FLEET, Frank Frank H. Fleet b: 1848, New York, NY d: 6/13/1900, New York, NY Deb: 10/18/1871 NA OF: 1-2-1 ♦

YEAR	TM-L	G	AB	R	H	2B	3B	HR	RBI	BB	SO	SB	CS	AVG	OBP	SLG	OPS	OPS+	BR/A	RC	RC/G	FR	G/POS	WS	TPW
1871	Mut-n	1	6	1	2	0	0	0	1	0	0	0	0	.333	.333	.333	.667	101	0	1	5.38	1	/P-1	....	-0.4
1872	Eck-n	13	53	10	13	1	0	0	5	0	1	1	0	.245	.245	.264	.509	67	-1	4	2.92	2	3-10/2-2,O-2(0-1-1)	....	0.1
1873	Res-n	22	90	11	23	2	0	0	10	1	2	0	1	.256	.264	.278	.542	66	-3	7	3.03	1	/2-9,S-9,P-3,3-2,1-1	....	-0.5
1874	Atl-n	22	97	18	22	0	0	0	10	1	1	1	0	.227	.235	.227	.461	55	-3	6	2.21	-5	C-13,2-11/O-1	....	-0.7
1875	StL-n	4	16	1	1	0	0	0	1	0	0	0	0	.063	.063	.063	.125	-62	-2	0	.13	0	/P-3,3-1,O-1	....	-0.3
	Atl-n	26	111	13	25	2	0	0	9	1	1	0	0	.225	.232	.243	.475	75	-1	6	2.20	-7	C-11,2-10/S-9,P-2,3-1	....	-1.1
	Yr.	30	127	14	26	2	0	0	10	1	1	0	0	.205	.211	.220	.431	58	-3	6	1.90	-7	C-11,2-10/S-9,P-5,3-2,O-1	....	-1.3
Total	**5 n**	**88**	**373**	**54**	**86**	**5**	**0**	**0**	**36**	**3**	**5**	**2**	**1**	**.231**	**.237**	**.244**	**.481**	**61**	**-10**	**23**	**2.44**	**-9**	**/2-32,C-24,S-18,3-14,P-9,O,1**	**....**	**-2.8**

• FLEITAS, Angel Angel Felix Husta Fleitas b: 11/10/1914, Los Abreus, Cuba BR/TR, 5'9", 160 lbs. Deb: 7/5/1948

YEAR	TM-L	G	AB	R	H	2B	3B	HR	RBI	BB	SO	SB	CS	AVG	OBP	SLG	OPS	OPS+	BR/A	RC	RC/G	FR	G/POS	WS	TPW
1948	Was-A	15	13	1	1	0	0	0	1	3	5	0	2	.077	.250	.077	.327	-11	-3	0	.44	-1	/S-7	0	-0.3

• FLEMING, Les Leslie Harvey "Moe" Fleming b: 8/7/1915, Singleton, TX d: 3/5/1980, Cleveland, TX BL/TL, 5'10", 185 lbs. Deb: 4/22/1939 Career OF: 1-0-36

YEAR	TM-L	G	AB	R	H	2B	3B	HR	RBI	BB	SO	SB	CS	AVG	OBP	SLG	OPS	OPS+	BR/A	RC	RC/G	FR	G/POS	WS	TPW
1939	Det-A	8	16	0	0	0	0	0	1	0	4	0	0	.000	.000	.000	.000	-93	-5	0	.00	-0	/O-3(1-0-2)	0	-0.5
1941	Cle-A	2	8	0	2	1	0	0	2	0	0	0	0	.250	.250	.375	.625	67	-0	1	3.46	0	/1-2	0	-0.1
1942	Cle-A	156	548	71	160	27	4	14	82	106	57	6	8	.292	.412	.432	.845	146	38	105	6.88	-7	*1-156	29	1.7
1945	Cle-A	42	140	18	46	10	2	3	22	11	5	0	0	.329	.382	.493	.874	160	10	27	7.37	-1	O-33(0-0-33)/1-5	6	0.7
1946	Cle-A	99	306	40	85	17	5	8	42	50	42	1	0	.278	.383	.444	.827	140	18	55	6.52	2	1-80/O-1	14	1.8
1947	Cle-A	103	281	39	68	14	2	4	43	53	42	0	0	.242	.362	.349	.711	101	3	40	4.81	6	1-77	8	0.6
1949	Pit-N	24	31	0	8	0	2	0	7	6	2	0	....	.258	.395	.387	.782	108	1	5	6.40	-1	/1-5	1	0.0
Total	**7**	**434**	**1330**	**168**	**369**	**69**	**15**	**29**	**199**	**226**	**152**	**7**	**8**	**.277**	**.386**	**.417**	**.804**	**133**	**64**	**232**	**6.24**	**-1**	**1-325/O-37**	**58**	**4.3**

• FLEMING, Tom Thomas Vincent "Sleuth" Fleming b: 11/20/1873, Philadelphia, PA d: 12/26/1957, Boston, MA BL/TL, 5'11", 155 lbs. Deb: 9/19/1899 Career OF: 0-22-6

YEAR	TM-L	G	AB	R	H	2B	3B	HR	RBI	BB	SO	SB	CS	AVG	OBP	SLG	OPS	OPS+	BR/A	RC	RC/G	FR	G/POS	WS	TPW
1899	NY-N	22	77	9	16	1	1	0	4	1	....	1	....	.208	.218	.247	.465	28	-8	5	1.98	1	O-22(0-22-0)	0	-0.7
1902	Phi-N	5	16	2	6	0	0	0	2	1	....	0	....	.375	.412	.375	.787	143	1	3	6.46	1	/O-5(0-0-5)	0	0.2
1904	Phi-N	3	6	0	0	0	0	0	0	0	....	0	....	.000	.000	.000	.000	-104	-1	0	.00	1	/O-1	0	-0.1
Total	**3**	**30**	**99**	**11**	**22**	**1**	**1**	**0**	**6**	**2**	**....**	**1**	**....**	**.222**	**.238**	**.253**	**.490**	**40**	**-8**	**7**	**2.44**	**3**	**/O-28**	**0**	**-0.6**

• FLETCHER, Art Arthur Fletcher b: 1/5/1885, Collinsville, IL d: 2/6/1950, Los Angeles, CA BR/TR, 5'10.5", 170 lbs. Deb: 4/15/1909 M/C

YEAR	TM-L	G	AB	R	H	2B	3B	HR	RBI	BB	SO	SB	CS	AVG	OBP	SLG	OPS	OPS+	BR/A	RC	RC/G	FR	G/POS	WS	TPW
1909	NY-N	33	98	7	21	0	1	0	6	1	....	0	....	.214	.238	.235	.472	46	-7	5	1.74	-6	S-22/2-7,3-6	1	-1.2
1910	NY-N	51	125	12	28	2	1	0	13	4	9	9	....	.224	.248	.256	.504	47	-9	10	2.57	-4	S-22,2-11,3-11	1	-1.3
1911*	NY-N	112	326	73	104	17	8	1	37	30	27	20	....	.319	.400	.429	.829	129	14	64	7.21	-2	S-74,3-21,2-13	17	1.8
1912*	NY-N	129	419	64	118	17	9	1	57	16	29	16	....	.282	.330	.372	.702	89	-8	56	4.56	11	*S-126/2-2,3-1	18	1.3
1913*	NY-N	136	538	76	160	20	9	4	71	24	35	32	....	.297	.345	.390	.735	109	5	80	5.15	6	*S-136	24	2.2
1914	NY-N	135	514	62	147	26	8	2	79	22	37	15	....	.286	.332	.379	.711	115	8	68	4.56	6	*S-135	22	2.6
1915	NY-N	149	562	59	143	17	7	3	74	6	36	12	18	.254	.280	.326	.606	88	-16	50	2.93	28	*S-149	18	2.5
1916	NY-N	133	500	53	143	23	8	3	66	13	36	15	....	.286	.323	.382	.705	122	11	68	4.75	17	*S-133	25	4.3
1917*	NY-N	151	557	70	145	24	5	4	56	23	28	12	....	.260	.312	.343	.655	104	2	60	3.73	36	*S-151	27	5.5
1918	NY-N	124	468	51	123	20	2	0	47	18	26	12	....	.263	.311	.314	.625	93	-4	48	3.48	31	*S-124	20	3.9

YEAR TM-L	G	AB	R	H	2B	3B	HR	RBI	BB	SO	SB	CS	AVG	OBP	SLG	OPS	OPS+	BR/A	RC	RC/G	FR	G/POS	WS	TPW
1919 NY-N	127	488	54	135	20	5	3	54	9	28	6	....	.277	.300	.357	.656	98	-3	52	3.69	23	*S-127	20	3.3
1920 NY-N	41	171	21	44	7	2	0	24	1	15	3	2	.257	.282	.322	.604	74	-6	15	3.02	-2	S-41	4	-0.5
Phi-N	102	379	36	112	25	7	4	38	15	28	4	6	.296	.329	.430	.759	112	4	52	4.78	6	*S-102	14	1.8
Yr.	143	550	57	156	32	9	4	62	16	43	7	8	.284	.315	.396	.711	100	-1	67	4.21	4	*S-143	18	1.4
1922 Phi-N	110	396	46	111	20	5	7	53	21	14	3	2	.280	.325	.409	.734	80	-12	53	4.71	-10	*S-106	7	-1.1
Total 13	1533	5541	684	1534	238	77	32	675	203	348	159	28	.277	.319	.365	.684	100	-20	680	4.23	141	*S-1448/3-39,2-33	218	25.1

• FLETCHER, Darrin Darrin Glen Fletcher b: 10/3/1966, Elmhurst, IL BL/TR, 6'2", 199 lbs. Deb: 9/10/1989

YEAR TM-L	G	AB	R	H	2B	3B	HR	RBI	BB	SO	SB	CS	AVG	OBP	SLG	OPS	OPS+	BR/A	RC	RC/G	FR	G/POS	WS	TPW
1989 LA-N	5	8	1	4	0	0	1	2	1	0	0	0	.500	.556	.875	1.431	308	2	4	27.23	0	/C-5	1	0.2
1990 LA-N	2	1	0	0	0	0	0	0	0	1	0	0	.000	.000	.000	.000	-103	-0	0	.00	-1	/C-1	0	-0.1
Phi-N	9	22	3	3	1	0	0	1	1	5	0	0	.136	.174	.182	.356	-2	-3	1	1.05	0	/C-6	0	-0.3
Yr.	11	23	3	3	1	0	0	1	1	6	0	0	.130	.167	.174	.341	-6	-3	1	1.00	0	/C-7	0	-0.4
1991 Phi-N	46	136	5	31	8	0	1	12	5	15	0	1	.228	.255	.309	.564	59	-8	10	2.52	-1	C-45	2	-0.7
1992 Mon-N	83	222	13	54	10	2	2	26	14	28	0	2	.243	.294	.333	.627	78	-8	20	2.90	1	C-69	4	-0.3
1993 Mon-N	133	396	33	101	20	1	9	60	34	40	0	0	.255	.323	.379	.702	84	-9	50	4.30	-5	*C-127	8	-0.7
1994 Mon-N★	94	285	28	74	18	1	10	57	25	23	0	0	.260	.326	.435	.761	95	-3	40	4.75	-4	C-81	7	-0.2
1995 Mon-N	110	350	42	100	21	1	11	45	32	23	0	1	.286	.352	.446	.798	105	2	51	5.16	3	C-98	8	1.1
1996 Mon-N	127	394	41	105	22	0	12	57	27	42	0	0	.266	.323	.414	.737	90	-7	50	4.42	-2	*C-112	8	-0.2
1997 Mon-N	96	310	39	86	20	1	17	55	17	35	1	1	.277	.325	.513	.838	116	5	50	5.80	-6	C-83	10	0.5
1998 Tor-A	124	407	37	115	23	1	9	52	25	39	0	0	.283	.333	.410	.744	92	-5	51	4.28	0	*C-121/D-1	11	0.3
1999 Tor-A	115	412	48	120	26	0	18	80	26	47	0	0	.291	.342	.485	.828	106	3	64	5.53	-5	*C-113	13	0.5
2000 Tor-A	122	416	43	133	19	1	20	58	20	45	1	0	.320	.358	.514	.873	114	8	75	6.86	-6	*C-117/D-2	14	0.9
2001 Tor-A	134	416	36	94	20	0	11	56	24	43	0	1	.226	.278	.353	.631	63	-24	36	2.83	-12	*C-129/D-1	5	-2.6
2002 Tor-A	45	127	8	28	6	0	3	22	4	13	0	0	.220	.244	.339	.583	51	-9	10	2.41	0	C-36/D-3	2	-0.7
Total 14	1245	3902	377	1048	214	8	124	583	255	399	2	6	.269	.321	.423	.744	92	-57	512	4.53	-36	*C-1143/D-7	93	-2.2

• FLETCHER, Elbie Elburt Preston Fletcher b: 3/18/1916, Milton, MA d: 3/9/1994, Milton, MA BL/TL, 6', 180 lbs. Deb: 9/16/1934

YEAR TM-L	G	AB	R	H	2B	3B	HR	RBI	BB	SO	SB	CS	AVG	OBP	SLG	OPS	OPS+	BR/A	RC	RC/G	FR	G/POS	WS	TPW
1934 Bos-N	8	4	4	2	0	0	0	0	0	2	1	....	.500	.500	.500	1.000	182	0	1	13.84	0	/1-1	0	0.0
1935 Bos-N	39	148	12	35	7	1	1	9	7	13	1	....	.236	.271	.318	.589	63	-8	13	2.90	2	1-39	1	-0.9
1937 Bos-N	148	539	56	133	22	4	1	38	56	64	3	....	.247	.321	.308	.629	79	-14	56	3.52	13	*1-148	11	-1.6
1938 Bos-N	147	529	71	144	24	7	6	48	60	40	5	....	.272	.351	.378	.729	112	10	73	4.92	17	*1-146	20	1.3
1939 Bos-N	35	106	14	26	2	0	0	6	19	5	1	....	.245	.365	.264	.629	77	-2	12	3.95	-7	1-31	2	-1.2
Pit-N	102	370	49	112	23	4	12	71	48	28	3	....	.303	.386	.484	.869	134	19	69	6.72	-3	*1-101	14	0.6
Yr.	137	476	63	138	25	4	12	77	67	33	4	....	.290	.381	.435	.816	121	16	81	6.10	-10	*1-132	16	-0.6
1940 Pit-N	147	510	94	139	22	7	16	104	**119**	54	5	....	.273	**.418**	.437	.856	137	34	103	7.17	6	*1-147	26	2.7
1941 Pit-N	151	521	95	150	29	13	11	74	**118**	54	5	....	.288	**.421**	.457	.878	148	40	111	7.97	9	*1-151	28	3.6
1942 Pit-N	145	506	86	146	22	5	7	57	105	60	0	....	.289	**.417**	.393	.810	134	29	94	6.84	13	*1-144	26	3.1
1943 Pit-N★	154	544	91	154	24	5	9	70	95	49	1	....	.283	.395	.395	.791	124	22	91	6.08	6	*1-154	22	2.2
1946 Pit-N	148	532	72	136	25	8	4	66	111	37	4	....	.256	.384	.355	.739	108	11	82	5.38	-4	*1-147	17	0.2
1947 Pit-N	69	157	22	38	9	1	1	22	29	24	2	....	.242	.364	.331	.695	83	-3	20	4.39	-1	1-50	3	-0.4
1949 Bos-N	122	413	57	108	19	3	11	51	84	65	1	....	.262	.396	.402	.798	121	17	72	5.94	-1	*1-121	15	1.2
Total 12	1415	4879	723	1323	228	58	79	616	851	495	32	....	.271	.384	.390	.774	118	155	796	5.80	51	*1-1380	185	10.9

• FLETCHER, Frank Oliver Frank Fletcher b: 3/6/1891, Hildreth, IL d: 10/7/1974, St. Petersburg, FL BR/TR, 5'10", 165 lbs. Deb: 7/14/1914

YEAR TM-L	G	AB	R	H	2B	3B	HR	RBI	BB	SO	SB	CS	AVG	OBP	SLG	OPS	OPS+	BR/A	RC	RC/G	FR	G/POS	WS	TPW
1914 Phi-N	1	1	0	0	0	0	0	0	0	1	0	....	.000	.000	.000	.000	-94	-0	0	.00	0	....	0	0.0

• FLETCHER, George George Horace Elliot Fletcher b: 4/21/1845, Brooklyn, NY d: 6/18/1879, Brooklyn, NY Deb: 6/21/1872

YEAR TM-L	G	AB	R	H	2B	3B	HR	RBI	BB	SO	SB	CS	AVG	OBP	SLG	OPS	OPS+	BR/A	RC	RC/G	FR	G/POS	WS	TPW
1872 Eck-n	2	8	1	3	0	0	0	0	0	0	0	0	.375	.375	.375	.750	155	1	1	7.15	-1	/O-2(0-0-2)	....	0.0

• FLETCHER, Scott Scott Brian Fletcher b: 7/30/1958, Fort Walton Beach, FL BR/TR, 5'11", 173 lbs. Deb: 4/25/1981

YEAR TM-L	G	AB	R	H	2B	3B	HR	RBI	BB	SO	SB	CS	AVG	OBP	SLG	OPS	OPS+	BR/A	RC	RC/G	FR	G/POS	WS	TPW
1981 Chi-N	19	46	6	10	4	0	0	1	2	4	0	0	.217	.250	.304	.554	54	-3	4	2.72	0	2-13/S-4,3-1	1	-0.3
1982 Chi-N	11	24	4	4	0	0	0	1	4	5	1	0	.167	.286	.167	.452	29	-2	2	2.14	-1	S-11	0	-0.3
1983★Chi-A	114	262	42	62	16	5	3	31	29	22	5	1	.237	.317	.370	.688	85	-4	31	3.87	8	*S-100,2-12/3-7,D-1	9	1.2
1984 Chi-A	149	456	46	114	13	3	3	35	46	46	10	4	.250	.329	.311	.641	75	-13	51	3.79	13	*S-134,2-28/3-3	13	1.3
1985 Chi-A	119	301	38	77	8	1	2	31	35	47	5	5	.256	.333	.309	.642	74	-11	31	3.37	2	3-55,S-44,2-37/D-2	7	-0.4
1986 Tex-A	147	530	82	159	34	5	3	50	47	59	12	11	.300	.361	.400	.761	104	2	76	5.05	2	*S-136,3-12,2-11/D-1	20	1.8
1987 Tex-A	156	588	82	169	28	4	5	63	61	66	13	12	.287	.359	.374	.733	95	-5	78	4.61	8	*S-155	17	1.7
1988 Tex-A	140	515	59	142	19	4	0	47	62	34	8	5	.276	.367	.328	.695	94	-1	66	4.33	6	*S-139	17	1.5
1989 Tex-A	83	314	47	75	14	1	0	22	38	41	1	0	.239	.325	.290	.615	73	-10	31	3.34	-11	S-81	4	-1.5
Chi-A	59	232	30	63	11	1	1	21	26	19	1	1	.272	.347	.341	.688	97	-0	29	4.22	3	2-53/S-8,D-1	6	0.4
Yr.	142	546	77	138	25	2	1	43	64	60	2	1	.253	.334	.311	.646	83	-10	60	3.71	-8	S-89,2-53/D-1	10	-1.1
1990 Chi-A	151	509	54	123	18	3	4	56	45	63	1	3	.242	.307	.312	.619	75	-18	50	3.22	4	*2-151	13	-1.0
1991 Chi-A	90	248	14	51	10	1	1	28	17	26	0	2	.206	.265	.266	.531	48	-18	18	2.31	-3	2-86/3-4	3	-1.9
1992 Mil-A	123	386	53	106	18	3	3	51	30	33	17	10	.275	.338	.360	.698	98	-2	48	4.30	19	*2-106,S-22/3-1	17	2.2
1993 Bos-A	121	480	81	137	31	5	5	45	37	35	16	3	.285	.343	.402	.745	94	-2	67	4.92	19	*2-116/S-2,3-1,D-1	14	2.2
1994 Bos-A	63	185	31	42	9	1	3	11	16	14	8	1	.227	.296	.335	.631	59	-10	18	3.19	11	2-53/D-4	3	0.3
1995 Det-A	67	182	19	42	10	1	1	17	19	27	1	0	.231	.314	.313	.627	64	-9	20	3.59	0	2-63/S-3,1-1,D-1	4	-0.6
Total 15	1612	5258	688	1376	243	38	34	510	514	541	99	58	.262	.334	.342	.676	84	-106	619	3.98	80	S-839,2-729/3-84,D-11,1-1	148	6.8

• FLICK, Elmer Elmer Harrison Flick b: 1/11/1876, Bedford, OH d: 1/9/1971, Bedford, OH BL/TR, 5'9", 168 lbs. Deb: 4/26/1898 HOF: 1963 Career OF: 9-127-1320

YEAR TM-L	G	AB	R	H	2B	3B	HR	RBI	BB	SO	SB	CS	AVG	OBP	SLG	OPS	OPS+	BR/A	RC	RC/G	FR	G/POS	WS	TPW
1898 Phi-N	134	453	84	137	16	13	8	81	86	....	23	....	.302	.430	.448	.878	158	41	101	8.19	2	*O-133(0-0-133)	26	3.4
1899 Phi-N	127	485	98	166	22	11	2	98	42	....	31	....	.342	.407	.445	.852	138	27	104	8.42	5	*O-125(0-0-125)	23	2.3
1900 Phi-N	138	545	106	200	32	16	11	**110**	56	....	35	....	.367	.441	.545	.986	172	**55**	151	11.37	1	*O-138(0-0-138)	32	**4.5**
1901 Phi-N	138	540	112	180	32	17	8	88	52	....	30	....	.333	.399	.500	.899	157	39	124	8.80	14	*O-138(1-0-137)	30	4.5
1902 Phi-A	11	37	15	11	2	1	0	3	6	....	4	....	.297	.435	.405	.840	128	2	9	8.27	0	O-11(0-0-11)	2	0.2
Cle-A	110	424	70	126	19	11	2	61	47	....	20	....	.297	.371	.408	.779	121	13	74	6.45	-3	*O-110(0-0-110)	15	0.5
Yr.	121	461	85	137	21	12	2	64	53	....	24	....	.297	.377	.408	.785	121	15	83	6.60	-3	*O-121(0-0-121)	17	0.6
1903 Cle-A	140	523	81	155	23	16	2	51	51	....	24	....	.296	.368	.413	.781	136	25	92	6.42	3	*O-140(6-0-134)	25	2.2
1904 Cle-A	150	579	97	177	31	17	6	56	51	....	**38**	....	.306	.371	.449	.820	160	40	115	7.24	6	*O-145(0-6-139)/2-6	31	4.3
1905 Cle-A	132	500	72	154	29	**18**	4	64	53	....	35	....	**.308**	.383	**.462**	**.845**	**165**	**38**	106	**7.82**	-1	*O-131(0-0-131)/2-1	29	3.4
1906 Cle-A	157	624	**98**	194	34	**22**	1	62	54	....	**39**	....	.311	.372	.441	.813	156	40	121	7.23	-7	*O-150(0-86-65)/2-8	30	2.8
1907 Cle-A	147	549	80	166	15	**18**	3	58	64	....	41	....	.302	.386	.412	.798	153	36	107	7.18	5	*O-147(1-23-122)	37	3.7
1908 Cle-A	9	35	4	8	1	1	0	2	3	....	0	....	.229	.289	.314	.604	96	-0	3	2.95	0	/O-9(0-0-9)	1	-0.1
1909 Cle-A	66	235	28	60	10	2	0	15	22	....	9	....	.255	.322	.315	.637	97	-0	26	3.83	-2	O-61(1-12-48)	7	-0.6
1910 Cle-A	24	68	5	18	2	1	1	7	10	....	1	....	.265	.359	.368	.727	126	2	9	4.73	-3	O-18(0-0-18)	3	-0.2
Total 13	1483	5597	950	1752	268	164	48	756	597	....	330	....	.313	.389	.445	.834	149	357	1142	7.63	19	*O-1456/2-15	291	31.0

• FLICK, Lew Lewis Miller "Noisy" Flick b: 2/18/1915, Bristol, TN d: 12/7/1990, Weber City, VA BL/TL, 5'9", 155 lbs. Deb: 9/28/1943 Career OF: 0-1-6

YEAR TM-L	G	AB	R	H	2B	3B	HR	RBI	BB	SO	SB	CS	AVG	OBP	SLG	OPS	OPS+	BR/A	RC	RC/G	FR	G/POS	WS	TPW
1943 Phi-A	1	5	2	3	0	0	0	0	0	0	0	0	.600	.600	.600	1.200	253	1	2	24.91	0	/O-1	1	0.1
1944 Phi-A	19	35	1	4	0	0	0	2	1	2	1	0	.114	.139	.114	.253	-28	-6	0	.22	0	/O-6(0-1-5)	0	-0.6
Total 2	20	40	3	7	0	0	0	2	1	2	1	0	.175	.195	.175	.370	7	-5	2	1.59	-0	/O-7	1	-0.5

• FLINN, Don Don Raphael Flinn b: 11/17/1892, Bluffdale, TX d: 3/9/1959, Waco, TX BR/TR, 6'1", 185 lbs. Deb: 9/2/1917

YEAR TM-L	G	AB	R	H	2B	3B	HR	RBI	BB	SO	SB	CS	AVG	OBP	SLG	OPS	OPS+	BR/A	RC	RC/G	FR	G/POS	WS	TPW
1917 Pit-N	14	37	1	11	1	1	0	1	1	6	1	....	.297	.316	.378	.694	109	0	4	4.40	0	O-12(7-1-4)	1	-0.1

• FLINT, Silver Frank Sylvester Flint b: 8/3/1855, Philadelphia, PA d: 1/14/1892, Chicago, IL BR/TR, 6', 180 lbs. Deb: 5/4/1875 M Career OF: 5-4-57

YEAR TM-L	G	AB	R	H	2B	3B	HR	RBI	BB	SO	SB	CS	AVG	OBP	SLG	OPS	OPS+	BR/A	RC	RC/G	FR	G/POS	WS	TPW
1875 RS-n	17	61	4	5	0	0	0	1	1	10	2	0	.082	.097	.082	.179	-41	-7	1	.37	0	C-16/O-2(1-0-1),3-1	....	-0.6
1878 Ind-N	63	254	23	57	7	0	0	18	2	15	....	....	.224	.230	.252	.482	67	-7	15	2.11	-1	*C-59/O-9(5-0-4)	5	-0.6
1879 Chi-N	79	324	46	92	22	6	1	41	6	44	....	....	.284	.297	.398	.695	120	6	39	4.74	3	*C-78/O-1	13	1.0
1880 Chi-N	74	284	30	46	10	4	0	17	5	32	....	....	.162	.176	.225	.402	33	-20	12	1.34	1	*C-67,O-13(0-4-10)	5	-1.6
1881 Chi-N	80	306	46	95	18	0	1	34	6	39	....	....	.310	.324	.379	.703	112	3	38	4.93	-10	*C-80/O-8(0-0-8),1-1	11	-0.4

YEAR TM-L	G	AB	R	H	2B	3B	HR	RBI	BB	SO	SB	CS	AVG	OBP	SLG	OPS	OPS+	BR/A	RC	RC/G	FR	G/POS	WS	TPW
1882 Chi-N	81	331	48	83	18	8	4	44	2	50	....	....	.251	.255	.390	.645	102	-0	34	3.74	-5	*C-81,0-10(0-0-10)	10	0.2
1883 Chi-N	85	332	57	88	23	4	0	32	3	69	....	....	.265	.272	.358	.630	83	-8	33	3.73	-1	*C-83,0-23(0-0-23)	9	-0.2
1884 Chi-N	73	279	35	57	5	2	9	45	7	57	....	....	.204	.224	.333	.557	67	-12	21	2.64	1	C-73	4	-0.4
1885*Chi-N	68	249	27	52	8	2	1	17	2	52	....	....	.209	.215	.269	.484	49	-16	15	2.02	5	C-68/0-1	5	-0.5
1886*Chi-N	54	173	30	35	6	2	1	13	12	36	1	....	.202	.254	.277	.532	53	-11	13	2.50	4	C-54/1-3	4	-0.2
1887 Chi-N	49	191	22	54	8	6	3	21	4	28	7	....	.283	.283	.422	.705	82	-6	25	4.82	2	C-47/1-2	5	0.0
1888 Chi-N	22	77	6	14	3	0	0	3	1	21	1	....	.182	.203	.221	.423	32	-6	4	1.60	5	C-22	1	0.1
1889 Chi-N	15	56	6	13	1	0	1	9	3	18	1	....	.232	.271	.304	.575	58	-4	5	3.08	-2	C-15	1	-0.3
Total 12	**743**	**2856**	**376**	**686**	**129**	**34**	**21**	**294**	**53**	**461**	**10**	**....**	**.240**	**.253**	**.330**	**.584**	**78**	**-81**	**254**	**3.20**	**3**	**C-727/0-65,1-6**	**73**	**-3.1**

• FLOOD, Curt Curtis Charles Flood b: 1/18/1938, Houston, TX d: 1/20/1997, Los Angeles, CA BR/TR, 5'9", 165 lbs. Deb: 9/9/1956 Career OF: 3-1693-1

YEAR TM-L	G	AB	R	H	2B	3B	HR	RBI	BB	SO	SB	CS	AVG	OBP	SLG	OPS	OPS+	BR/A	RC	RC/G	FR	G/POS	WS	TPW
1956 Cin-N	5	1	0	0	0	0	0	0	0	1	0	0	.000	.000	.000	.000	-94	-0	0	.00	0	....	0	0.0
1957 Cin-N	3	3	2	1	0	0	1	1	0	0	0	0	.333	.333	1.333	1.667	299	1	1	18.00	-1	/3-2,2-1	0	0.0
1958 StL-N	121	422	50	110	17	2	10	41	31	56	2	12	.261	.317	.382	.699	81	-17	44	3.41	14	*0-120(0-120-0)/3-1	10	-0.9
1959 StL-N	121	208	24	53	7	3	7	26	16	35	2	1	.255	.308	.418	.726	86	-5	26	4.21	-16	*0-106(2-103-1)/2-1	4	-2.5
1960 StL-N	140	396	37	94	20	1	8	38	35	54	0	3	.237	.306	.354	.659	73	-15	41	3.37	1	*0-134(1-133-0)/3-1	8	-2.0
1961 StL-N	132	335	53	108	15	5	2	21	35	33	6	2	.322	.391	.415	.806	104	4	56	6.29	6	*0-119(0-119-0)	13	0.7
1962 StL-N	151	635	99	188	30	5	12	70	42	57	8	6	.296	.349	.416	.765	95	-5	92	5.19	11	*0-151(0-151-0)	22	0.1
1963 StL-N	158	662	112	200	34	9	5	63	42	57	17	12	.302	.346	.403	.749	105	4	92	5.12	2	*0-158(0-158-0)	24	0.1
1964*StL-N★	162	679	97	**211**	25	3	5	46	43	53	8	11	.311	.356	.378	.735	98	-2	90	4.88	7	*0-162(0-162-0)	25	-0.1
1965 StL-N	156	617	90	191	30	3	11	83	51	50	9	3	.310	.368	.421	.789	111	12	97	5.87	-1	*0-151(0-151-0)	24	0.7
1966 StL-N★	160	626	64	167	21	5	10	78	26	50	14	7	.267	.300	.364	.665	84	-14	67	3.69	5	*0-159(0-159-0)	18	-1.4
1967*StL-N	134	514	68	172	24	1	5	50	37	46	2	2	.335	.382	.414	.796	130	20	82	6.11	2	*0-126(0-126-0)	26	2.0
1968*StL-N★	150	618	71	186	17	4	5	60	33	58	11	6	.301	.341	.366	.707	114	10	78	4.60	5	*0-149(0-149-0)	27	1.2
1969 StL-N	153	606	80	173	31	3	4	57	48	57	9	7	.285	.345	.366	.711	99	-1	76	4.44	7	*0-152(0-152-0)	20	0.3
1971 Was-A	13	35	4	7	0	0	0	2	5	2	0	1	.200	.300	.200	.500	47	-3	2	1.87	0	0-10(0-10-0)	0	-0.4
Total 15	**1759**	**6357**	**851**	**1861**	**271**	**44**	**85**	**636**	**444**	**609**	**88**	**73**	**.293**	**.344**	**.389**	**.733**	**100**	**-11**	**844**	**4.76**	**44**	***0-1697/3-4,2-2**	**221**	**-2.1**

• FLOOD, Tim Timothy A. Flood b: 3/13/1877, Montgomery City, MO d: 6/15/1929, St. Louis, MO BR/TR, 5'9", 160 lbs. Deb: 9/24/1899 Career OF: 1-1-0

YEAR TM-L	G	AB	R	H	2B	3B	HR	RBI	BB	SO	SB	CS	AVG	OBP	SLG	OPS	OPS+	BR/A	RC	RC/G	FR	G/POS	WS	TPW
1899 StL-N	10	31	0	9	0	0	0	3	4	....	1	....	.290	.371	.290	.662	81	-1	4	4.56	-2	2-10	1	-0.2
1902 Bro-N	132	476	43	104	11	4	3	51	23	....	8	....	.218	.268	.277	.545	68	-19	41	2.76	1	*2-132/0-1	7	-1.7
1903 Bro-N	89	309	27	77	15	2	0	32	15	....	14	....	.249	.291	.311	.601	73	-11	34	3.70	-39	2-84/S-2,0-1	4	-4.7
Total 3	**231**	**816**	**70**	**190**	**26**	**6**	**3**	**86**	**42**	**....**	**23**	**....**	**.233**	**.280**	**.290**	**.571**	**70**	**-31**	**79**	**3.17**	**-39**	**2-226/0-2,S-2**	**12**	**-6.6**

• FLORA, Kevin Kevin Scot Flora b: 6/10/1969, Fontana, CA BR/TR, 6', 180 lbs. Deb: 9/27/1991

YEAR TM-L	G	AB	R	H	2B	3B	HR	RBI	BB	SO	SB	CS	AVG	OBP	SLG	OPS	OPS+	BR/A	RC	RC/G	FR	G/POS	WS	TPW
1991 Cal-A	3	8	1	1	0	0	0	0	1	5	1	0	.125	.222	.125	.347	-1	-1	0	.69	-2	/2-3	0	-0.3
1995 Cal-A	2	1	1	0	0	0	0	0	0	1	0	0	.000	.000	.000	.000	-101	-0	0	.00	0	/D-1	0	0.0
Phi-N	24	75	12	16	3	0	2	7	4	22	1	0	.213	.253	.333	.586	53	-5	7	3.02	0	0-20(5-15-0)	1	-0.5
Total 2	**29**	**84**	**14**	**17**	**3**	**0**	**2**	**7**	**5**	**28**	**2**	**0**	**.202**	**.247**	**.310**	**.557**	**45**	**-6**	**7**	**2.68**	**-1**	**/0-20,2-3,D-1**	**1**	**-0.8**

• FLORENCE, Paul Paul Robert "Pep" Florence b: 4/22/1900, Chicago, IL d: 5/28/1986, Gainesville, FL BB/TR, 6'1", 185 lbs. Deb: 5/22/1926

YEAR TM-L	G	AB	R	H	2B	3B	HR	RBI	BB	SO	SB	CS	AVG	OBP	SLG	OPS	OPS+	BR/A	RC	RC/G	FR	G/POS	WS	TPW
1926 NY-N	76	188	19	43	4	3	2	14	23	12	2	....	.229	.322	.314	.636	73	-7	20	3.50	-6	C-76	3	-0.8

• FLORES, Gil Gilberto (Garcia) Flores b: 10/27/1952, Ponce, Puerto Rico BR/TR, 6', 185 lbs. Deb: 5/8/1977 Career OF: 42-57-39

YEAR TM-L	G	AB	R	H	2B	3B	HR	RBI	BB	SO	SB	CS	AVG	OBP	SLG	OPS	OPS+	BR/A	RC	RC/G	FR	G/POS	WS	TPW
1977 Cal-A	104	342	41	95	19	4	1	26	23	39	12	10	.278	.325	.365	.691	91	-6	36	3.54	-2	0-85(41-45-9)/D-8	6	-1.1
1978 NY-N	11	29	8	8	0	1	0	1	3	5	1	0	.276	.344	.345	.689	96	0	4	4.84	-1	/0-8(1-6-2)	1	-0.1
1979 NY-N	70	93	9	18	1	1	1	10	8	17	2	0	.194	.265	.258	.523	45	-7	7	2.44	-1	0-32(0-6-28)	0	-0.8
Total 3	**185**	**464**	**58**	**121**	**20**	**6**	**2**	**37**	**34**	**61**	**15**	**10**	**.261**	**.314**	**.343**	**.657**	**82**	**-12**	**47**	**3.38**	**-4**	**0-125/D-8**	**7**	**-2.0**

• FLORES, Jose Jose Carlos Flores b: 6/28/1973, New York, NY BR/TR, 5'11", 180 lbs. Deb: 9/7/2002

YEAR TM-L	G	AB	R	H	2B	3B	HR	RBI	BB	SO	SB	CS	AVG	OBP	SLG	OPS	OPS+	BR/A	RC	RC/G	FR	G/POS	WS	TPW
2002 Oak-A	7	3	2	0	0	0	0	0	1	0	1	1	.000	.400	.000	.400	20	-0	0	1.40	-1	/2-2,S-1	0	-0.1

• FLOWERS, Dickie Charles Richard Flowers b: 1850, Philadelphia, PA d: 10/5/1892, Philadelphia, PA Deb: 6/3/1871

YEAR TM-L	G	AB	R	H	2B	3B	HR	RBI	BB	SO	SB	CS	AVG	OBP	SLG	OPS	OPS+	BR/A	RC	RC/G	FR	G/POS	WS	TPW
1871 Tro-n	21	105	39	33	5	4	0	18	4	0	8	2	.314	.339	.438	.778	120	3	19	8.00	-5	*S-20/2-1,P-1	....	-0.1
1872 Ath-n	3	15	1	4	0	0	0	4	2	2	0	0	.267	.353	.267	.620	93	0	1	4.08	-1	/S-3	....	-0.1
Total 2 n	**24**	**120**	**40**	**37**	**5**	**4**	**0**	**22**	**6**	**2**	**8**	**2**	**.308**	**.341**	**.417**	**.758**	**116**	**3**	**20**	**7.49**	**-6**	**/S-23,2-1,P-1**	**....**	**-0.2**

• FLOWERS, Jake D'Arcy Raymond Flowers b: 3/16/1902, Cambridge, MD d: 12/27/1962, Clearwater, FL BR/TR, 5'11.5", 170 lbs. Deb: 9/7/1923 C Career OF: 0-0-2

YEAR TM-L	G	AB	R	H	2B	3B	HR	RBI	BB	SO	SB	CS	AVG	OBP	SLG	OPS	OPS+	BR/A	RC	RC/G	FR	G/POS	WS	TPW
1923 StL-N	13	32	0	3	1	0	0	2	2	7	1	2	.094	.147	.125	.272	-28	-7	0	.38	0	/S-7,2-2,3-2	1	-0.5
1926*StL-N	40	74	13	20	1	0	3	9	5	9	1	....	.270	.325	.405	.730	92	-1	10	4.52	1	2-11/1-3,S-1	2	0.0
1927 Bro-N	67	231	26	54	5	5	2	20	21	25	3	....	.234	.300	.325	.625	67	-11	23	3.24	-2	S-65/2-1	4	-0.6
1928 Bro-N	103	339	51	93	11	6	2	44	47	30	10	....	.274	.366	.360	.726	92	-2	47	4.58	0	2-94/S-6	9	0.0
1929 Bro-N	46	130	16	26	6	0	1	16	22	6	9	....	.200	.316	.269	.585	47	-10	12	2.89	-8	2-39	1	-1.6
1930 Bro-N	89	253	37	81	18	3	2	50	21	18	5	....	.320	.372	.439	.811	96	-1	40	5.72	-2	2-65/0-1	7	-0.1
1931 Bro-N	22	31	3	7	0	0	0	1	7	4	1	....	.226	.368	.226	.594	64	-1	3	3.41	-1	/2-6,S-1	1	-0.1
*StL-N	45	137	19	34	11	1	2	19	9	6	7	....	.248	.295	.387	.681	79	-5	16	3.97	5	S-24,2-21/3-1	4	0.3
Yr.	67	168	22	41	11	1	2	20	16	10	8	....	.244	.310	.357	.667	76	-6	19	3.87	4	2-27,S-25/3-1	5	0.1
1932 StL-N	67	247	35	63	11	1	2	18	31	18	7	....	.255	.341	.332	.672	79	-6	30	4.19	-1	3-54/S-7,2-2	6	-0.5
1933 Bro-N	78	210	28	49	11	2	2	22	24	15	13	....	.233	.312	.333	.645	88	-3	23	3.57	-5	S-36,2-19/3-8,0-1	5	-0.4
1934 Cin-N	13	9	1	3	0	0	0	0	1	1	1	....	.333	.455	.333	.788	117	1	2	7.35	0	....	1	0.0
Total 10	**583**	**1693**	**229**	**433**	**75**	**18**	**16**	**201**	**190**	**139**	**58**	**2**	**.256**	**.333**	**.350**	**.683**	**80**	**-46**	**206**	**4.06**	**-13**	**2-260,S-147/3-65,1-3,0-2**	**41**	**-3.5**

• FLOYD, Bobby Robert Nathan Floyd b: 10/20/1943, Hawthorne, CA BR/TR, 6'1", 181 lbs. Deb: 9/18/1968

YEAR TM-L	G	AB	R	H	2B	3B	HR	RBI	BB	SO	SB	CS	AVG	OBP	SLG	OPS	OPS+	BR/A	RC	RC/G	FR	G/POS	WS	TPW
1968 Bal-A	5	9	0	1	1	0	0	1	0	3	0	0	.111	.111	.222	.333	-1	-1	0	.76	1	/S-4	0	0.0
1969 Bal-A	39	84	7	17	4	0	0	1	6	17	0	0	.202	.256	.250	.506	41	-7	5	1.77	1	2-15,S-15/3-9	1	-0.3
1970 Bal-A	3	2	0	0	0	0	0	0	0	2	0	0	.000	.000	.000	.000	-99	-1	0	.00	-1	/S-2,2-1	0	-0.2
KC-A	14	43	5	14	4	0	0	9	4	9	0	1	.326	.383	.419	.802	121	1	7	6.03	0	/S-8,3-6	2	0.2
Yr.	17	45	5	14	4	0	0	9	4	11	0	1	.311	.367	.400	.767	108	0	7	5.50	-1	S-10/3-6,2-1	2	0.0
1971 KC-A	31	66	8	10	3	0	0	2	7	21	0	0	.152	.233	.197	.430	23	-7	3	1.66	1	S-15/2-8,3-1	1	-0.4
1972 KC-A	61	134	9	24	3	0	0	5	5	29	1	0	.179	.209	.201	.410	22	-13	5	1.23	-5	3-30,S-29/2-2	1	-1.8
1973 KC-A	51	78	10	26	3	1	0	8	4	14	1	1	.333	.366	.397	.763	107	1	10	4.84	-2	2-25,S-24	3	0.1
1974 KC-A	10	9	1	1	0	0	0	0	2	4	0	0	.111	.273	.111	.384	13	-1	0	1.40	-1	/2-5,3-2,S-1	0	-0.1
Total 7	**214**	**425**	**40**	**93**	**18**	**1**	**0**	**26**	**28**	**99**	**2**	**2**	**.219**	**.267**	**.266**	**.533**	**50**	**-27**	**32**	**2.40**	**-5**	**/S-98,2-56,3-48**	**8**	**-2.4**

• FLOYD, Bubba Leslie Roe Floyd b: 6/23/1917, Dallas, TX d: 12/15/2000, Dallas, TX BR/TR, 5'11", 160 lbs. Deb: 6/16/1944

YEAR TM-L	G	AB	R	H	2B	3B	HR	RBI	BB	SO	SB	CS	AVG	OBP	SLG	OPS	OPS+	BR/A	RC	RC/G	FR	G/POS	WS	TPW
1944 Det-A	3	9	1	4	1	0	0	0	1	0	0	0	.444	.500	.556	1.056	191	1	3	14.54	1	/S-3	1	0.2

• FLOYD, Cliff Cornelius Cliff Floyd b: 12/5/1972, Chicago, IL BL/TR, 6'5", 230 lbs. Deb: 9/18/1993 Career OF: 719-28-89

YEAR TM-L	G	AB	R	H	2B	3B	HR	RBI	BB	SO	SB	CS	AVG	OBP	SLG	OPS	OPS+	BR/A	RC	RC/G	FR	G/POS	WS	TPW
1993 Mon-N	10	31	3	7	0	0	1	2	0	9	0	0	.226	.226	.323	.548	43	-3	2	2.54	0	1-10	1	-0.4
1994 Mon-N	100	334	43	94	19	4	4	41	24	63	10	3	.281	.335	.398	.733	89	-5	46	5.00	-2	1-77,0-26(17-0-9)	9	-1.3
1995 Mon-N	29	69	6	9	1	0	1	8	7	22	3	0	.130	.221	.188	.409	9	-9	3	1.53	0	1-18/0-4(2-1-1)	1	-1.0
1996 Mon-N	117	227	29	55	15	4	6	26	30	52	7	1	.242	.344	.423	.766	98	1	36	5.36	-2	0-85(69-16-7)/1-2	6	-0.4
1997*Fla-N	61	137	23	32	9	1	6	19	24	33	6	2	.234	.356	.445	.801	113	4	23	5.57	-1	0-38(24-9-6)/1-9	5	0.1
1998 Fla-N	153	588	85	166	45	3	22	90	47	112	27	14	.282	.339	.481	.820	117	12	93	5.58	-5	*0-146(146-2-0)/D-3	18	0.1
1999 Fla-N	69	251	37	76	19	1	11	49	30	47	5	6	.303	.382	.518	.900	132	10	46	6.56	1	0-62(62-0-0)/D-3	9	0.9
2000 Fla-N	121	420	75	126	30	0	22	91	50	82	24	3	.300	.385	.529	.914	134	26	92	8.01	-2	*0-108(108-0-0)/D-1	19	1.8
2001 Fla-N★	149	555	123	176	44	4	31	103	59	101	18	3	.317	.393	.578	.971	152	45	128	8.74	4	*0-142(142-0-0)/D-3	26	4.2
2002 Fla-N	84	296	49	85	20	0	18	57	58	68	10	5	.287	.416	.537	.953	155	26	71	8.82	2	0-80(20-0-60)/D-1	17	2.4
Mon-N	15	53	7	11	2	0	3	4	3	10	1	0	.208	.263	.415	.678	73	-2	6	3.94	-1	0-13(13-0-0)	0	-0.4
Yr.	99	349	56	96	22	0	21	61	61	78	11	5	.275	.395	.519	.913	143	24	77	8.03	1	0-93(33-0-60)/D-1	17	2.0
Bos-A	47	171	30	54	21	0	7	18	15	28	4	0	.316	.378	.561	.939	142	11	35	7.65	-1	0-26(21-0-6)/D-19	5	0.8

YEAR TM-L	G	AB	R	H	2B	3B	HR	RBI	BB	SO	SB	CS	AVG	OBP	SLG	OPS	OPS+	BR/A	RC	RC/G	FR	G/POS	WS	TPW
2003 NY-N	108	365	57	106	25	2	18	68	51	66	3	0	.290	.382	.518	.900	136	21	73	7.18	2	0-95(95-0-0)/D-9	15	1.8
Total 11	1063	3497	567	997	250	19	150	576	398	693	118	37	.285	.366	.496	.862	125	137	656	6.73	-4	0-825,1-116/D-39	131	8.6

• FLUHRER, John John Lister Fluhrer b: 1/3/1894, Adrian, MI d: 7/17/1946, Columbus, OH BR/TR, 5'9", 165 lbs. Deb: 9/5/1915

YEAR TM-L	G	AB	R	H	2B	3B	HR	RBI	BB	SO	SB	CS	AVG	OBP	SLG	OPS	OPS+	BR/A	RC	RC/G	FR	G/POS	WS	TPW
1915 Chi-N	6	6	0	2	0	0	0	0	1	0	1	....	.333	.429	.333	.762	132	0	1	8.09	0	/0-2(2-0-0)	0	0.0

• FLYNN, Clipper William Flynn b: 4/29/1849, Lansingburg, NY d: 11/5/1881, Troy, NY TR, 5'7", 140 lbs. Deb: 5/9/1871

YEAR TM-L	G	AB	R	H	2B	3B	HR	RBI	BB	SO	SB	CS	AVG	OBP	SLG	OPS	OPS+	BR/A	RC	RC/G	FR	G/POS	WS	TPW
1871 Tro-n	29	142	43	48	6	1	0	27	4	2	3	3	.338	.356	.394	.751	114	1	22	6.99	4	1-19/0-8(0-0-8),2-1,3-1	....	0.4
1872 Oly-n	9	40	4	9	1	0	0	2	0	0	0	0	.225	.225	.250	.475	48	-2	2	2.31	-1	/1-9	....	-0.2
Total 2 n	38	182	47	57	7	1	0	29	4	2	3	3	.313	.328	.363	.691	100	-1	24	5.86	4	/1-28,0-8,2-1,3-1	....	0.2

• FLYNN, Doug Robert Douglas Flynn b: 4/18/1951, Lexington, KY BR/TR, 5'11", 165 lbs. Deb: 4/9/1975

YEAR TM-L	G	AB	R	H	2B	3B	HR	RBI	BB	SO	SB	CS	AVG	OBP	SLG	OPS	OPS+	BR/A	RC	RC/G	FR	G/POS	WS	TPW
1975 Cin-N	89	127	17	34	7	0	1	20	11	13	3	0	.268	.326	.346	.673	85	-2	14	3.70	3	3-40,2-30,S-17	4	0.4
1976*Cin-N	93	219	20	62	5	2	1	20	10	24	2	0	.283	.314	.338	.652	83	-5	24	3.84	3	2-55,3-23,S-20	5	0.2
1977 Cin-N	36	32	0	8	1	1	0	5	0	6	0	0	.250	.250	.344	.594	56	-2	3	3.02	-1	3-25/2-9,S-4	1	-0.3
NY-N	90	282	14	54	6	1	0	14	11	23	1	3	.191	.222	.220	.442	20	-33	13	1.48	-5	S-65,2-29/3-2	3	-3.1
Yr.	126	314	14	62	7	2	0	19	11	29	1	3	.197	.225	.232	.457	23	-35	16	1.62	-6	S-69,2-38,3-27	4	-3.4
1978 NY-N	156	532	37	126	12	8	0	36	30	50	3	5	.237	.279	.289	.568	61	-30	40	2.49	0	*2-128,S-60	7	-2.1
1979 NY-N	157	555	35	135	19	5	4	61	17	46	0	3	.243	.266	.317	.583	61	-33	42	2.56	1	*2-148,S-20	6	-2.3
1980 NY-N	128	443	46	113	9	8	0	24	22	20	2	2	.255	.290	.312	.602	70	-19	36	2.75	11	*2-128/S-3	8	-0.2
1981 NY-N	105	325	24	72	12	4	1	20	11	19	1	2	.222	.247	.292	.539	53	-22	20	1.98	11	*2-100/S-5	5	-0.6
1982 Tex-A	88	270	13	57	6	2	0	19	4	14	6	2	.211	.223	.248	.471	31	-25	15	1.79	-8	2-55,S-35	3	-2.7
Mon-N	58	193	13	47	6	2	0	20	4	23	0	2	.244	.259	.295	.554	54	-13	13	2.19	4	2-58	2	-0.6
1983 Mon-N	143	452	44	107	18	4	0	26	19	38	2	1	.237	.268	.294	.562	56	-28	33	2.46	6	*2-107,S-37	5	-1.4
1984 Mon-N	124	366	23	89	12	1	0	17	12	41	0	0	.243	.267	.281	.549	57	-22	27	2.53	-3	2-88,S-34	4	-1.9
1985 Mon-N	9	6	0	1	0	0	0	0	0	0	0	0	.167	.167	.167	.333	-7	-1	0	.90	-3	/2-6,S-1	0	-0.4
Det-A	32	51	2	13	2	1	0	2	0	3	0	0	.255	.255	.333	.588	60	-3	4	2.61	-1	2-20/S-8,3-4	1	-0.2
Total 11	1308	3853	288	918	115	39	7	284	151	320	20	20	.238	.267	.294	.561	57	-239	285	2.46	19	2-961,S-309/3-94	54	-15.3

• FLYNN, Ed Edward J. Flynn b: 6/25/1864, Chicago, IL d: 8/28/1929, Chicago, IL BL, 5'9", 165 lbs. Deb: 5/5/1887

YEAR TM-L	G	AB	R	H	2B	3B	HR	RBI	BB	SO	SB	CS	AVG	OBP	SLG	OPS	OPS+	BR/A	RC	RC/G	FR	G/POS	WS	TPW
1887 Cle-a	7	28	0	6	1	0	0	4	1	....	3	....	.214	.214	.222	.437	22	-3	2	2.43	-1	/3-6,0-1	0	-0.3

• FLYNN, George George A. "Dibby" Flynn b: 5/24/1871, Chicago, IL d: 12/28/1901, Chicago, IL, 5'9" Deb: 4/17/1896

YEAR TM-L	G	AB	R	H	2B	3B	HR	RBI	BB	SO	SB	CS	AVG	OBP	SLG	OPS	OPS+	BR/A	RC	RC/G	FR	G/POS	WS	TPW
1896 Chi-N	29	106	15	27	1	2	0	4	11	9	12	....	.255	.336	.302	.638	66	-5	16	5.02	1	0-29(29-0-0)	2	-0.5

• FLYNN, Jocko John A. Flynn b: 6/30/1864, Lawrence, MA d: 12/30/1907, Lawrence, MA BR/TR, 5'6.5", 143 lbs. Deb: 5/1/1886 U Career OF: 5-3-21 ♦

YEAR TM-L	G	AB	R	H	2B	3B	HR	RBI	BB	SO	SB	CS	AVG	OBP	SLG	OPS	OPS+	BR/A	RC	RC/G	FR	G/POS	WS	TPW
1886 Chi-N	57	205	40	41	6	2	4	19	18	45	9	....	.200	.265	.307	.572	64	-1	20	3.21	3	P-32,0-28(5-3-20)	27	2.6
1887 Chi-N	1	0	0	0	0	0	0	0	0	0	0	....	....	....	....	....	-89	0	0	....	0	/0-1	0	0.0
Total 2	58	205	40	41	6	2	4	19	18	45	9	....	.200	.265	.307	.572	64	-1	20	3.21	2	/P-32,0-29	27	2.6

• FLYNN, Joe Joseph Nicholas Flynn b: 1/1862, Providence, RI d: 12/22/1932, Providence, RI Deb: 4/18/1884

YEAR TM-L	G	AB	R	H	2B	3B	HR	RBI	BB	SO	SB	CS	AVG	OBP	SLG	OPS	OPS+	BR/A	RC	RC/G	FR	G/POS	WS	TPW
1884 Phi-U	52	209	38	52	9	4	4	....	11	....	....	....	.249	.286	.388	.674	136	9	24	4.24	-9	0-43(2-0-41),C-10/1-1,S-1	5	0.0
Bos-U	9	31	4	7	2	0	0	....	2	....	....	....	.226	.273	.290	.563	92	-0	3	2.94	3	/C-7,0-4(1-2-2),1-1	1	0.2
Yr.	61	240	42	59	11	4	4	....	13	....	....	....	.246	.285	.375	.660	131	9	26	4.07	-7	0-47(3-2-43),C-17/1-2,S-1	6	0.2

• FLYNN, John John Anthony Flynn b: 9/7/1883, Providence, RI d: 3/23/1935, Providence, RI BR/TR, 6'.5", 175 lbs. Deb: 4/22/1910

YEAR TM-L	G	AB	R	H	2B	3B	HR	RBI	BB	SO	SB	CS	AVG	OBP	SLG	OPS	OPS+	BR/A	RC	RC/G	FR	G/POS	WS	TPW
1910 Pit-N	96	332	32	91	10	2	6	52	30	47	6	....	.274	.336	.370	.707	100	-1	44	4.44	-7	1-93	8	-1.0
1911 Pit-N	33	59	5	12	0	1	0	3	9	8	0	....	.203	.309	.237	.546	52	-4	4	2.38	1	1-13/0-1	0	-0.3
1912 Was-A	20	71	9	12	4	1	0	5	7	....	2	....	.169	.253	.254	.507	45	-5	5	2.14	0	1-20	0	-0.5
Total 3	149	462	46	115	14	4	6	60	46	55	8	....	.249	.320	.335	.655	85	-10	53	3.79	-6	1-126/0-1	8	-1.8

• FLYNN, Mike Michael J. Flynn b: 3/15/1872, County Kildare, Ireland d: 6/16/1941, Los Angeles, CA Deb: 8/31/1891

YEAR TM-L	G	AB	R	H	2B	3B	HR	RBI	BB	SO	SB	CS	AVG	OBP	SLG	OPS	OPS+	BR/A	RC	RC/G	FR	G/POS	WS	TPW
1891 Bos-a	1	2	0	0	0	0	0	0	0	1	0	....	.000	.000	.000	.000	-101	-1	0	.00	0	/C-1	0	0.0

• FOGARTY, Jim James G. Fogarty b: 2/12/1864, San Francisco, CA d: 5/20/1891, Philadelphia, PA BR/TR, 5'10.5", 180 lbs. Deb: 5/1/1884 M Career OF: 0-312-373

YEAR TM-L	G	AB	R	H	2B	3B	HR	RBI	BB	SO	SB	CS	AVG	OBP	SLG	OPS	OPS+	BR/A	RC	RC/G	FR	G/POS	WS	TPW
1884 Phi-N	97	378	42	80	12	6	1	37	20	54	....	....	.212	.251	.283	.534	71	-11	28	2.54	-1	*0-78(0-72-6),3-14/2-4,S-3,P	7	-1.3
1885 Phi-N	111	427	49	99	13	3	0	39	30	37	....	....	.232	.282	.276	.559	83	-7	34	2.81	18	*0-88(0-88-0),2-10/S-8,3-5	15	0.8
1886 Phi-N	77	280	54	82	13	5	3	47	42	16	30	....	.293	.385	.407	.792	139	15	57	7.75	-5	0-60(0-1-59),2-13/3-3,S-3,P	18	1.1
1887 Phi-N	126	577	113	211	26	12	8	50	**82**	44	102	....	.366	.376	.410	.787	112	11	118	8.52	26	*0-123(0-0-123)/3-2,S-2,2,P	25	2.8
1888 Phi-N	121	454	72	107	14	6	1	35	53	66	58	....	.236	.325	.300	.624	95	-0	65	5.03	13	*0-117(0-0-117)/3-5,S-1	19	1.0
1889 Phi-N	128	499	107	129	15	17	3	54	65	60	**99**	....	.259	.352	.375	.727	95	-4	103	7.39	11	*0-128(0-128-0)/P-4	18	0.1
1890 Phi-P	91	347	71	83	17	6	4	58	59	50	36	....	.239	.364	.357	.721	91	-3	60	6.10	5	0-91(0-23-68)/3-1	11	0.0
Total 7	751	2962	508	791	110	55	20	320	351	327	325	....	.267	.335	.343	.678	97	0	464	5.72	68	0-685/3-30,2-28,S-17,P-7	113	4.6

• FOGARTY, Joe John J. Fogarty b: 11/8/1868, San Francisco, CA d: 3/28/1918, San Francisco, CA, 5'9" Deb: 9/18/1885

YEAR TM-L	G	AB	R	H	2B	3B	HR	RBI	BB	SO	SB	CS	AVG	OBP	SLG	OPS	OPS+	BR/A	RC	RC/G	FR	G/POS	WS	TPW
1885 StL-N	2	8	1	1	0	0	0	0	0	1	....	....	.125	.125	.125	.250	-20	-1	0	.49	0	/0-2(2-0-0)	0	-0.1

• FOHL, Lee Leo Alexander Fohl b: 11/28/1870, Pittsburgh, PA d: 10/30/1965, Cleveland, OH BL/TR, 5'10", 175 lbs. Deb: 8/29/1902 M/C

YEAR TM-L	G	AB	R	H	2B	3B	HR	RBI	BB	SO	SB	CS	AVG	OBP	SLG	OPS	OPS+	BR/A	RC	RC/G	FR	G/POS	WS	TPW
1902 Pit-N	1	3	0	0	0	0	0	1	0	....	0	....	.000	.000	.000	.000	-97	-1	0	.00	0	/C-1	0	-0.1
1903 Cin-N	4	14	3	5	1	1	0	2	0	....	0	....	.357	.400	.571	.971	158	1	3	9.66	-1	/C-4	1	0.1
Total 2	5	17	3	5	1	1	0	3	0	....	0	....	.294	.333	.471	.804	116	0	3	7.24	-1	/C-5	1	0.0

• FOILES, Hank Henry Lee Foiles b: 6/10/1929, Richmond, VA BR/TR, 6', 195 lbs. Deb: 4/21/1953

YEAR TM-L	G	AB	R	H	2B	3B	HR	RBI	BB	SO	SB	CS	AVG	OBP	SLG	OPS	OPS+	BR/A	RC	RC/G	FR	G/POS	WS	TPW
1953 Cin-N	5	13	1	2	0	0	0	0	1	2	0	0	.154	.214	.154	.368	-2	-2	0	1.22	0	/C-3	0	-0.2
Cle-A	7	7	2	1	0	0	0	0	1	1	0	0	.143	.250	.143	.393	9	-1	0	1.45	-0	/C-7	0	-0.1
1955 Cle-A	62	111	13	29	9	0	1	7	17	18	0	0	.261	.359	.369	.729	93	-1	15	4.46	2	C-41	5	0.4
1956 Cle-A	1	0	0	0	0	0	0	0	0	0	0	0	....	....	....	....	-98	0	0	....	0	/C-1	0	0.0
Pit-N	79	222	24	47	10	2	7	25	17	56	0	1	.212	.268	.369	.637	71	-10	21	3.03	2	C-73	4	-0.6
1957 Pit-N★	109	281	32	76	10	4	9	36	37	53	1	3	.270	.355	.431	.786	113	5	43	5.35	-2	*C-109	9	0.7
1958 Pit-N	104	264	31	54	10	2	8	30	45	53	0	1	.205	.323	.348	.671	80	-7	31	3.86	2	*C-103	9	0.0
1959 Pit-N	53	80	10	18	3	0	3	4	7	16	0	0	.225	.287	.375	.662	75	-3	8	3.45	-1	C-51	2	-0.3
1960 KC-A	6	7	1	4	0	0	0	1	3	2	0	0	.571	.700	.571	1.271	246	2	3	30.11	-1	/C-2	1	0.2
Cle-A	24	68	9	19	1	0	1	6	7	5	0	0	.279	.347	.338	.685	89	-1	9	4.68	1	C-22	3	0.1
Det-A	26	56	5	14	3	0	0	3	1	8	1	0	.250	.263	.304	.567	50	-4	4	2.35	1	C-22	1	-0.2
Yr.	56	131	15	37	4	0	1	10	11	15	1	0	.282	.338	.336	.674	83	-3	16	4.33	1	C-46	5	0.0
1961 Bal-A	43	124	18	34	6	0	6	19	12	27	0	2	.274	.338	.468	.806	115	1	18	4.94	1	C-38	5	0.4
1962 Cin-N	43	131	17	36	6	1	7	25	13	39	0	0	.275	.340	.496	.836	117	3	22	6.08	-1	C-41	6	0.4
1963 Cin-N	1	3	0	0	0	0	0	0	1	0	1	0	.000	.250	.000	.250	-21	-0	0	1.17	0	/C-1	0	0.0
LA-A	41	84	8	18	1	1	4	10	8	13	0	0	.214	.290	.393	.683	95	-1	9	3.51	1	C-30	2	0.1
1964 LA-A	4	4	0	1	0	0	0	0	0	2	0	0	.250	.250	.250	.500	44	-0	0	2.25	0	....	0	0.0
Total 11	608	1455	171	353	59	10	46	166	170	295	3	7	.243	.323	.392	.714	92	-19	185	4.28	5	C-544	47	0.9

• FOLEY, Curry Charles Joseph Foley b: 1/14/1856, Milltown, Ireland d: 10/20/1898, New York, NY TL, 5'10", 160 lbs. Deb: 5/13/1879 Career OF: 4-28-185 ♦

YEAR TM-L	G	AB	R	H	2B	3B	HR	RBI	BB	SO	SB	CS	AVG	OBP	SLG	OPS	OPS+	BR/A	RC	RC/G	FR	G/POS	WS	TPW
1879 Bos-N	35	146	16	46	3	1	0	17	3	4	....	....	.315	.329	.349	.678	121	6	17	4.81	-6	P-21,0-17(0-2-15)/1-2	12	-0.4
1880 Bos-N	80	332	44	97	13	2	2	31	8	14	....	....	.292	.309	.361	.670	130	13	38	4.45	-2	P-36,0-35(0-0-35),1-25	18	-2.7
1881 Buf-N	83	375	58	96	20	2	1	25	7	27	....	....	.256	.270	.328	.598	88	-5	34	3.29	-3	*0-55(3-4-50),1-27,P-10	7	-1.7
1882 Buf-N	84	341	51	104	16	4	3	49	12	26	....	....	.305	.329	.402	.730	130	11	46	5.35	-1	*0-84(0-1-84)/P-1	12	0.6
1883 Buf-N	23	111	23	30	5	3	0	6	4	12	....	....	.270	.296	.369	.665	98	-0	12	4.22	-2	0-23(1-21-1)/P-1	3	-0.2
Total 5	305	1305	192	373	57	12	6	128	34	83	....	....	.286	.304	.362	.666	114	24	148	4.35	-14	0-214/P-69,1-54	52	-4.5

• FOLEY, Marv Marvis Edwin Foley b: 8/29/1953, Stanford, KY BL/TR, 6', 195 lbs. Deb: 9/11/1978 C

YEAR TM-L	G	AB	R	H	2B	3B	HR	RBI	BB	SO	SB	CS	AVG	OBP	SLG	OPS	OPS+	BR/A	RC	RC/G	FR	G/POS	WS	TPW
1978 Chi-A	11	34	3	12	0	0	0	6	4	6	0	1	.353	.421	.353	.774	119	1	5	5.40	-1	C-10	1	0.0

YEAR TM-L	G	AB	R	H	2B	3B	HR	RBI	BB	SO	SB	CS	AVG	OBP	SLG	OPS	OPS+	BR/A	RC	RC/G	FR	G/POS	WS	TPW
1979 Chi-A	34	97	6	24	3	0	2	10	7	5	0	0	.247	.298	.340	.638	72	-4	9	3.01	1	C-33	1	-0.2
1980 Chi-A	68	137	14	29	5	0	4	15	9	22	0	0	.212	.270	.336	.606	65	-7	13	3.17	-1	C-64/1-3	2	-0.5
1982 Chi-A	27	36	1	4	0	0	0	1	6	4	0	0	.111	.238	.111	.349		-5	1	1.06	-1	C-15/3-2,1-1,D-1	0	-0.5
1984 Tex-A	63	115	13	25	2	0	6	19	15	24	0	0	.217	.313	.391	.704	91	-1	15	4.33	0	C-36/D-4,1-1,3-1	3	0.0
Total 5	203	419	37	94	10	0	12	51	41	61	0	1	.224	.298	.334	.632	72	-16	44	3.40	-2	C-158/1-5,D-5,3-3	7	-1.2

• FOLEY, Ray Raymond Kirwin Foley b: 6/23/1906, Naugatuck, CT d: 3/22/1980, Vero Beach, FL BL/TR, 5'11", 173 lbs. Deb: 7/4/1928

YEAR TM-L	G	AB	R	H	2B	3B	HR	RBI	BB	SO	SB	CS	AVG	OBP	SLG	OPS	OPS+	BR/A	RC	RC/G	FR	G/POS	WS	TPW
1928 NY-N	2	1	1	0	0	0	0	0	1	1	0	....	.000	.500	.000	.500	41	0	0	3.14	0	....	0	0.0

• FOLEY, Tom Thomas J. Foley b: 1847, Chicago, IL d: 1/4/1896, La Grange, IL, 5'9.5", 157 lbs. Deb: 5/8/1871 U

YEAR TM-L	G	AB	R	H	2B	3B	HR	RBI	BB	SO	SB	CS	AVG	OBP	SLG	OPS	OPS+	BR/A	RC	RC/G	FR	G/POS	WS	TPW
1871 Chi-n	18	84	18	22	3	1	0	13	3	2	1	4	.262	.287	.321	.609	67	-6	8	3.94	-5	0-16(2-9-5)/C-4,3-1	....	-0.7

• FOLEY, Tom Thomas Michael Foley b: 9/9/1959, Fort Benning, GA BL/TR, 6'1", 180 lbs. Deb: 4/9/1983 C

YEAR TM-L	G	AB	R	H	2B	3B	HR	RBI	BB	SO	SB	CS	AVG	OBP	SLG	OPS	OPS+	BR/A	RC	RC/G	FR	G/POS	WS	TPW
1983 Cin-N	68	98	7	20	4	1	0	9	13	17	1	0	.204	.297	.265	.563	55	-5	9	2.87	0	S-37/2-5	2	-0.2
1984 Cin-N	106	277	26	70	8	3	5	27	24	36	3	2	.253	.312	.357	.670	84	-6	32	3.98	-4	S-83,2-10/3-1	7	-0.2
1985 Cin-N	43	92	7	18	5	1	0	6	6	16	1	0	.196	.245	.272	.517	42	-7	7	2.40	1	2-18,S-15/3-1	1	-0.4
Phi-N	46	158	17	42	8	0	3	17	13	18	1	3	.266	.322	.373	.695	91	-3	18	3.99	-1	S-45	4	0.1
Yr.	89	250	24	60	13	1	3	23	19	34	2	3	.240	.294	.336	.630	73	-10	24	3.38	0	S-60,2-18/3-1	5	-0.3
1986 Phi-N	39	61	8	18	2	1	0	5	10	11	2	0	.295	.394	.361	.755	106	1	10	5.83	-1	S-24/2-1,3-1	3	0.2
Mon-N	64	202	18	52	13	2	1	18	20	26	8	3	.257	.324	.356	.681	88	-3	24	4.03	0	S-29,2-25,3-15	5	0.0
Yr.	103	263	26	70	15	3	1	23	30	37	10	3	.266	.341	.357	.699	93	-1	34	4.42	-2	S-53,2-26,3-16	8	0.2
1987 Mon-N	106	280	35	82	18	3	5	28	11	40	6	10	.293	.322	.432	.754	95	-6	34	4.27	-6	S-49,2-39/3-9	8	-0.7
1988 Mon-N	127	377	33	100	21	3	5	43	30	49	2	7	.265	.321	.377	.698	95	-5	41	3.74	4	2-89,S-32/3-9	11	0.3
1989 Mon-N	122	375	34	86	19	2	7	39	45	53	2	3	.229	.317	.347	.663	88	-6	44	3.92	5	*2-108,3-16,S-14/P-1	13	0.2
1990 Mon-N	73	164	11	35	2	1	0	12	12	22	0	1	.213	.267	.238	.505	42	-14	10	2.00	-5	S-45,2-20/3-7,1-1	3	-1.6
1991 Mon-N	86	168	12	35	11	1	0	15	14	30	2	0	.208	.273	.286	.559	58	-9	13	2.54	-2	S-43,1-31/3-6,2-2	2	-1.1
1992 Mon-N	72	115	7	20	3	1	0	5	8	21	3	0	.174	.234	.217	.451	29	-10	6	1.41	-3	S-33,2-13,1-12/3-4,0-1	1	-1.2
1993 Pit-N	86	194	18	49	11	1	3	22	11	26	0	0	.253	.293	.366	.659	75	-7	20	3.55	-4	2-35,1-12/3-7,S-6	3	-1.0
1994 Pit-N	59	123	13	29	7	0	3	15	13	18	0	0	.236	.309	.366	.675	74	-5	14	4.07	3	2-17,3-14/S-8,1-3	3	0.0
1995 Mon-N	11	24	2	5	2	0	0	2	2	4	1	0	.208	.269	.292	.561	46	-2	2	1.99	1	/1-4,2-3	0	-0.1
Total 13	1108	2708	248	661	134	20	32	263	232	387	32	29	.244	.305	.344	.649	78	-88	283	3.52	-12	S-463,2-385/3-90,1-63,0-1,P	66	-5.8

• FOLEY, Will William Brown Foley b: 11/15/1855, Chicago, IL d: 11/12/1916, Chicago, IL BR/TR, 5'9.5", 150 lbs. Deb: 8/23/1875

YEAR TM-L	G	AB	R	H	2B	3B	HR	RBI	BB	SO	SB	CS	AVG	OBP	SLG	OPS	OPS+	BR/A	RC	RC/G	FR	G/POS	WS	TPW
1875 Chi-n	3	12	0	3	1	0	0	1	0	2	0	0	.250	.250	.333	.583	100	-0	1	3.36	1	/3-3	....	0.1
1876 Cin-N	58	221	19	50	3	2	0	9	0	14	....	....	.226	.226	.258	.484	71	-4	13	2.16	-3	*3-46,C-20	1	-0.5
1877 Cin-N	56	216	23	41	5	1	0	18	4	13	....	....	.190	.205	.222	.427	39	-13	10	1.58	3	*3-56	1	-0.8
1878 Mil-N	56	229	33	62	8	5	0	22	7	14	....	....	.271	.292	.349	.642	103	0	24	3.95	-6	*3-53/C-7	4	-0.3
1879 Cin-N	56	218	22	46	5	1	0	25	2	16	....	....	.211	.218	.243	.461	55	-10	12	1.93	2	3-29,0-25(0-0-25)/2-3	2	-0.6
1881 Det-N	5	15	0	2	0	0	0	1	2	3	....	....	.133	.235	.133	.369	18	-1	0	1.00	-1	/3-5	0	-0.2
1884 CP-U	19	71	15	20	1	1	0	....	5	....	....	....	.282	.329	.324	.653	129	3	8	4.26	-2	3-19	3	0.1
Total 6	250	970	112	221	22	10	0	75	20	60	....	....	.228	.243	.271	.515	71	-26	67	2.49	-7	3-208/C-27,0-25,2-3	11	-2.4

• FOLI, Tim Timothy John Foli b: 12/6/1950, Culver City, CA BR/TR, 6', 179 lbs. Deb: 9/11/1970 C Career OF: 1-2-0

YEAR TM-L	G	AB	R	H	2B	3B	HR	RBI	BB	SO	SB	CS	AVG	OBP	SLG	OPS	OPS+	BR/A	RC	RC/G	FR	G/POS	WS	TPW
1970 NY-N	5	11	0	4	0	0	0	1	0	2	0	0	.364	.364	.364	.727	95	-0	1	5.61	1	/3-2,S-2	0	0.1
1971 NY-N	97	288	32	65	12	2	0	24	18	50	5	0	.226	.274	.281	.555	58	-15	22	2.55	-2	2-58,3-36,S-12/0-1	4	-1.3
1972 Mon-N	149	540	45	130	12	2	2	35	25	43	11	7	.241	.282	.281	.563	59	-29	44	2.68	3	*S-148/2-1	9	-0.9
1973 Mon-N	126	458	37	110	11	0	2	36	28	40	6	3	.240	.285	.277	.563	55	-28	33	2.36	10	*S-123/2-2,0-1	6	-0.4
1974 Mon-N	121	441	41	112	10	3	0	39	28	27	8	2	.254	.303	.290	.593	63	-21	40	3.00	9	*S-120/3-1	8	0.3
1975 Mon-N	152	572	64	136	25	2	1	29	36	49	13	3	.238	.285	.294	.579	58	-32	49	2.83	6	*S-151/2-1	9	-0.8
1976 Mon-N	149	546	41	144	36	1	6	54	16	33	6	5	.264	.285	.366	.651	80	-17	52	3.25	-3	*S-146/3-1	10	-0.4
1977 Mon-N	13	57	2	10	5	1	0	3	0	4	0	0	.175	.175	.298	.474	25	-6	3	1.50	2	S-13	1	-0.3
SF-N	104	368	30	84	17	3	4	27	11	16	2	4	.228	.251	.323	.574	53	-27	28	2.49	12	*S-102/2-1,3-1,0-1	6	-0.5
Yr.	117	425	32	94	22	4	4	30	11	20	2	4	.221	.241	.320	.561	49	-33	31	2.35	14	*S-115/2-1,3-1,0-1	7	-0.7
1978 NY-N	113	413	37	106	21	1	1	27	14	30	2	5	.257	.284	.320	.604	71	-19	35	2.80	-3	*S-112	7	-1.1
1979 NY-N	3	7	0	0	0	0	0	0	0	0	0	0	.000	.000	.000	.000	-104	-2	0	.00	-0	/S-3	0	-0.2
*Pit-N	133	525	70	153	23	1	1	65	28	14	6	5	.291	.338	.345	.683	83	-13	63	4.14	12	*S-132	17	1.4
Yr.	136	532	70	153	23	1	1	65	28	14	6	5	.288	.334	.340	.674	81	-15	63	4.06	12	*S-135	17	1.2
1980 Pit-N	127	495	61	131	22	0	3	38	19	23	11	7	.265	.300	.327	.627	74	-19	49	3.35	8	*S-125	12	0.2
1981 Pit-N	86	316	32	78	12	2	0	20	17	10	7	7	.247	.287	.297	.585	64	-17	28	2.82	-3	S-81	5	-1.2
1982*Cal-A	150	480	46	121	14	2	3	56	14	22	2	4	.252	.276	.308	.585	60	-28	40	2.72	-2	*S-139/2-8,3-2	6	-1.5
1983 Cal-A	88	330	29	83	10	0	2	29	5	18	2	3	.252	.265	.300	.565	56	-22	25	2.53	4	S-74,3-13	4	-1.0
1984 NY-A	61	163	8	41	11	0	0	16	2	16	0	0	.252	.265	.319	.584	63	-8	13	2.66	-1	S-28,2-21,3-10/1-2	2	-0.6
1985 Pit-N	19	37	1	7	0	0	0	2	4	2	0	0	.189	.268	.189	.457	30	-3	1	1.05	1	S-13	1	-0.1
Total 16	1696	6047	576	1515	241	20	25	501	265	399	81	55	.251	.286	.309	.595	64	-306	527	2.89	56	*S-1524/2-92,3-66,0-3,1-2	107	-8.3

• FONDY, Dee Dee Virgil Fondy b: 10/13/1924, Slaton, TX d: 8/19/1999, Redlands, CA BL/TL, 6'3", 196 lbs. Deb: 4/17/1951

YEAR TM-L	G	AB	R	H	2B	3B	HR	RBI	BB	SO	SB	CS	AVG	OBP	SLG	OPS	OPS+	BR/A	RC	RC/G	FR	G/POS	WS	TPW
1951 Chi-N	49	170	23	46	7	2	3	20	11	20	5	6	.271	.319	.388	.707	88	-5	20	4.07	-3	1-44	3	-0.9
1952 Chi-N	145	554	69	166	21	9	10	67	28	60	13	11	.300	.334	.424	.759	108	2	75	4.82	6	*1-143	15	0.3
1953 Chi-N	150	595	79	184	24	11	18	78	44	106	10	7	.309	.358	.477	.835	113	9	104	6.60	7	*1-149	18	0.8
1954 Chi-N	141	568	77	162	30	4	9	49	35	84	20	5	.285	.328	.400	.727	87	-9	75	4.78	7	*1-138	13	-1.0
1955 Chi-N	150	574	69	152	23	8	17	65	35	87	8	9	.265	.309	.422	.731	92	-10	71	4.31	0	*1-147	13	-1.9
1956 Chi-N	137	543	52	146	22	9	9	46	20	74	9	7	.269	.295	.392	.687	84	-15	62	3.91	-8	*1-133	9	-3.1
1957 Chi-N	11	51	3	16	3	1	0	2	0	9	1	2	.314	.314	.412	.725	94	-1	5	3.51	-1	1-11	1	-0.3
Pit-N	95	323	42	101	13	2	2	35	25	59	11	5	.313	.364	.384	.748	104	3	46	5.19	-3	1-73	7	-0.5
Yr.	106	374	45	117	16	3	2	37	25	68	12	7	.313	.358	.388	.745	103	1	51	4.95	-4	1-84	8	-0.8
1958 Cin-N	89	124	23	27	1	1	1	11	5	27	7	1	.218	.248	.266	.514	34	-11	9	2.39	1	1-36,0-22(7-0-15)	1	-1.1
Total 8	967	3502	437	1000	144	47	69	373	203	526	84	53	.286	.326	.413	.739	95	-36	467	4.75	6	1-874/0-22	80	-7.6

• FONSECA, Lew Lewis Albert Fonseca b: 1/21/1899, Oakland, CA d: 11/26/1989, Ely, IA BR/TR, 5'10.5", 180 lbs. Deb: 4/13/1921 M Career OF: 99-15-5

YEAR TM-L	G	AB	R	H	2B	3B	HR	RBI	BB	SO	SB	CS	AVG	OBP	SLG	OPS	OPS+	BR/A	RC	RC/G	FR	G/POS	WS	TPW
1921 Cin-N	82	297	38	82	10	3	1	41	8	13	2	3	.276	.304	.340	.644	74	-11	30	3.51	-3	2-50,1-16,0-16(14-0-2)	5	-1.5
1922 Cin-N	81	291	55	105	20	3	4	45	14	18	7	8	.361	.390	.491	.882	128	10	53	6.73	7	2-71	13	1.8
1923 Cin-N	65	237	33	66	11	4	3	28	9	16	4	0	.278	.310	.397	.707	87	-4	30	4.42	6	2-45,1-14	7	0.2
1924 Cin-N	20	57	5	13	2	1	0	9	4	4	1	0	.228	.279	.298	.577	55	-3	5	2.92	1	2-10/1-6	1	-0.3
1925 Phi-N	126	467	78	149	30	5	7	60	21	42	6	2	.319	.352	.450	.802	95	-3	74	5.82	-2	2-69,1-55	11	-0.6
1927 Cle-A	112	428	60	133	20	7	2	40	12	17	12	4	.311	.333	.404	.737	90	-7	57	4.80	-6	2-96,1-13	11	-1.0
1928 Cle-A	75	263	38	86	19	4	3	36	13	17	4	2	.327	.361	.464	.825	114	5	44	6.07	-2	1-56,3-15/S-4,2-1	7	0.1
1929 Cle-A	148	566	97	209	44	15	6	103	50	23	19	11	**.369**	.427	.532	.959	140	35	128	8.73	-2	*1-147	25	2.2
1930 Cle-A	40	129	20	36	9	2	0	17	7	7	1	0	.279	.316	.380	.696	73	-5	16	4.30	0	1-28/3-6	2	-0.6
1931 Cle-A	26	108	21	40	9	1	1	14	8	7	3	2	.370	.419	.500	.919	133	6	22	8.12	0	1-26	4	0.3
Chi-A	121	465	65	139	26	5	2	71	32	22	4	4	.299	.348	.389	.737	99	1	63	4.95	-4	0-95(80-15-0),2-21/1-2,3-1	12	-0.6
Yr.	147	573	86	179	35	6	3	85	40	29	7	6	.312	.361	.410	.772	106	6	85	5.51	-4	0-95(80-15-0),1-28,2-21/3-1	16	-0.4
1932 Chi-A	18	37	0	5	1	0	0	6	1	7	0	0	.135	.158	.162	.320	-18	-6	1	.80	1	/0-8(5-0-3),P-1	0	-0.5
1933 Chi-A	23	59	8	12	2	0	2	15	7	6	1	0	.203	.288	.339	.627	68	-2	6	3.48	3	1-12	1	-0.1
Total 12	937	3404	518	1075	203	50	31	485	186	199	64	36	.316	.355	.432	.788	103	14	528	5.65	0	1-375,2-363,0-119/3-22,S-4,P	99	-0.6

• FONVILLE, Chad Chad Everette Fonville b: 3/5/1971, Jacksonville, NC BB/TR, 5'6", 155 lbs. Deb: 4/28/1995 Career OF: 30-22-0

YEAR TM-L	G	AB	R	H	2B	3B	HR	RBI	BB	SO	SB	CS	AVG	OBP	SLG	OPS	OPS+	BR/A	RC	RC/G	FR	G/POS	WS	TPW
1995 Mon-N	14	12	2	4	0	0	0	0	0	3	0	2	.333	.333	.333	.667	74	-1	1	1.80	-1	/2-2	0	-0.2
*LA-N	88	308	41	85	6	1	0	16	23	39	20	5	.276	.328	.302	.630	74	-9	34	3.83	4	S-38,2-36,0-11(10-2-0)	7	-0.1
Yr.	102	320	43	89	6	1	0	16	23	42	20	7	.278	.328	.303	.632	74	-10	34	3.75	2	2-38,S-38,0-11(10-2-0)	7	-0.4
1996 LA-N	103	201	34	41	4	1	0	13	17	31	7	2	.204	.266	.234	.500	36	-18	14	2.28	-1	0-35(19-18-0),2-23,S-20/3-2	3	-1.7
1997 LA-N	9	14	1	2	0	0	0	1	2	3	0	1	.143	.250	.143	.393	7	-2	0	.98	0	/2-3	0	-0.3

YEAR TM-L	G	AB	R	H	2B	3B	HR	RBI	BB	SO	SB	CS	AVG	OBP	SLG	OPS	OPS+	BR/A	RC	RC/G	FR	G/POS	WS	TPW
Chi-A	9	9	1	1	0	0	0	1	1	1	2	0	.111	.200	.111	.311	-17	-1	1	1.54	-1	/0-3(1-2-0),2-2,S-2,D-1	0	-0.2
1999 Bos-A	3	2	1	0	0	0	0	0	2	0	1	0	.000	.500	.000	.500	41	0	1	7.02	-1	/2-2	0	0.0
Total 4	226	546	80	133	10	2	0	31	45	77	30	10	.244	.302	.269	.572	56	-31	50	3.08	-1	/2-68,S-60,0-49,3-2,D-1	10	-2.6

• FOOTE, Barry Barry Clifton Foote b: 2/16/1952, Smithfield, NC BR/TR, 6'3", 210 lbs. Deb: 9/14/1973 C

YEAR TM-L	G	AB	R	H	2B	3B	HR	RBI	BB	SO	SB	CS	AVG	OBP	SLG	OPS	OPS+	BR/A	RC	RC/G	FR	G/POS	WS	TPW
1973 Mon-N	6	6	0	4	0	1	0	1	0	0	0	0	.667	.667	1.000	1.667	343	2	4	54.00	0	....	1	0.2
1974 Mon-N	125	420	44	110	23	4	11	60	35	74	2	1	.262	.323	.414	.737	100	-1	52	4.07	5	*C-122	15	1.0
1975 Mon-N	118	387	25	75	16	1	7	30	17	48	0	1	.194	.230	.295	.524	43	-32	24	2.00	-2	*C-115	6	-3.0
1976 Mon-N	105	350	32	82	12	2	7	27	17	32	2	1	.234	.272	.340	.612	70	-15	31	2.99	7	C-96/3-2,1-1	7	-0.4
1977 Mon-N	15	49	4	12	3	1	2	8	4	10	0	0	.245	.302	.469	.771	106	0	7	4.83	0	C-13	1	0.1
Phi-N	18	32	3	7	1	0	1	3	3	6	0	0	.219	.286	.344	.629	65	-2	1	1.17	0	C-17	0	-0.1
Yr.	33	81	7	19	4	1	3	11	7	16	0	0	.235	.295	.420	.715	90	-1	8	3.19	0	C-30	1	-0.1
1978*Phi-N	39	57	4	9	0	0	1	4	1	11	0	0	.158	.172	.211	.383	6	-7	2	.91	-1	C-31	1	-0.8
1979 Chi-N	132	429	47	109	26	0	16	56	34	49	5	2	.254	.316	.427	.743	92	-5	56	4.48	-4	*C-129	11	-0.3
1980 Chi-N	63	202	16	48	13	1	6	28	13	18	1	1	.238	.284	.401	.685	83	-6	21	3.45	4	C-55	5	0.1
1981 Chi-N	9	22	0	0	0	0	0	1	3	7	0	0	.000	.120	.000	.120	-61	-5	0	.11	1	/C-8	0	-0.4
*NY-A	40	125	12	26	4	0	6	10	8	21	0	0	.208	.256	.384	.640	83	-3	10	2.52	3	C-34/D-4,1-1	3	0.1
1982 NY-A	17	48	4	7	5	0	0	2	1	11	0	0	.146	.163	.250	.413	12	-6	2	.94	-2	C-17	0	-0.7
Total 10	687	2127	191	489	103	10	57	230	136	287	10	6	.230	.279	.368	.647	75	-80	209	3.23	12	C-637/D-4,1-2,3-2	50	-4.1

• FORAN, Jim James H. Foran b: 1848, NY d: 1/30/1928, Los Angeles, CA, 5'6.5", 159 lbs. Deb: 5/4/1871

YEAR TM-L	G	AB	R	H	2B	3B	HR	RBI	BB	SO	SB	CS	AVG	OBP	SLG	OPS	OPS+	BR/A	RC	RC/G	FR	G/POS	WS	TPW
1871 Kek-n	19	89	21	31	1	3	1	18	2	1	1	0	.348	.363	.461	.823	132	3	16	8.48	-1	1-16/0-4(3-1-0)	....	0.2

• FORBES, P.J. Patrick Joseph Forbes b: 9/22/1967, Pittsburg, KS BR/TR, 5'10", 160 lbs. Deb: 7/21/1998

YEAR TM-L	G	AB	R	H	2B	3B	HR	RBI	BB	SO	SB	CS	AVG	OBP	SLG	OPS	OPS+	BR/A	RC	RC/G	FR	G/POS	WS	TPW
1998 Bal-A	9	10	0	1	0	0	0	2	0	0	0	0	.100	.100	.100	.200	-48	-2	0	.30	-1	/2-7,3-1,S-1	0	-0.3
2001 Phi-N	3	7	1	2	0	0	0	1	0	2	0	0	.286	.286	.286	.571	50	-1	1	3.09	0	/2-1	0	-0.1
Total 2	12	17	1	3	0	0	0	3	0	2	0	0	.176	.176	.176	.353	-8	-3	1	1.29	-1	/2-8,3-1,S-1	0	-0.4

• FORCE, Davy David W. "Wee Davy,Tom Thumb" Force b: 7/27/1849, New York, NY d: 6/21/1918, Englewood, NJ BR/TR, 5'4", 130 lbs. Deb: 5/5/1871 U ♦

YEAR TM-L	G	AB	R	H	2B	3B	HR	RBI	BB	SO	SB	CS	AVG	OBP	SLG	OPS	OPS+	BR/A	RC	RC/G	FR	G/POS	WS	TPW
1871 Oly-n	32	162	45	45	9	4	0	29	4	0	8	0	.278	.295	.383	.678	98	2	21	5.70	16	*S-31/3-1	....	1.1
1872 Tro-n	25	130	40	53	11	0	0	16	1	0	2	2	.408	.412	.492	.905	175	10	28	10.94	6	3-16/S-9	....	1.1
Bal-n	19	95	29	41	2	2	0	13	1	0	3	0	.432	.438	.495	.932	178	9	22	12.87	7	3-19	....	1.1
Yr.	44	225	69	94	13	2	0	29	2	0	5	2	.418	.423	.493	.916	176	19	50	11.73	13	*3-35/S-9	....	2.2
1873 Bal-n	49	234	77	86	8	1	0	31	9	0	1	0	.368	.391	.410	.801	139	12	39	8.01	10	3-34,S-17/P-3	....	1.5
1874 Chi-n	59	294	61	92	9	0	0	26	3	1	4	0	.313	.320	.344	.663	112	4	34	5.11	10	*3-42,S-18/P-1	....	-0.3
1875 Ath-n	77	386	78	120	22	5	0	49	7	5	6	3	.311	.323	.394	.717	133	10	52	5.74	12	*S-77/3-2	....	1.7
1876 Phi-N	60	289	48	66	6	0	0	17	5	3	....	....	.228	.246	.254	.499	67	-9	18	2.33	14	*S-60/3-2	2	0.6
NY-N	1	3	0	0	0	0	0	0	0	0	....	....	.000	.000	.000	.000	-115	-1	0	.00	0	/S-1	0	-0.1
Yr.	61	292	48	66	6	0	0	17	5	3	....	....	.226	.243	.251	.494	65	-10	18	2.30	14	*S-61/3-2	2	0.6
1877 StL-N	58	225	24	59	5	3	0	22	11	15	....	....	.262	.297	.311	.608	97	0	21	3.53	8	*S-50/3-8	8	1.0
1879 Buf-N	79	316	36	66	5	2	0	8	13	37	....	....	.209	.240	.237	.477	57	-14	18	2.07	6	*S-78/3-1	5	-0.4
1880 Buf-N	81	290	22	49	10	0	0	17	10	35	....	....	.169	.197	.203	.400	35	-19	12	1.36	19	2-53,S-30	3	0.4
1881 Buf-N	75	278	21	50	9	1	0	15	11	29	....	....	.180	.211	.219	.430	36	-20	13	1.56	18	2-51,S-21/0-3(0-0-3),3-1	5	0.1
1882 Buf-N	73	278	39	67	10	1	1	28	12	17	....	....	.241	.272	.295	.567	81	-6	23	2.98	6	*S-61,3-11/2-1	7	0.2
1883 Buf-N	96	378	40	82	11	3	0	35	12	39	....	....	.217	.241	.262	.503	52	-22	24	2.27	-7	*S-78,3-13/2-7	6	-2.3
1884 Buf-N	106	403	47	83	13	3	0	36	27	41	....	....	.206	.256	.253	.509	59	-19	27	2.30	-5	*S-105/2-1	8	-1.8
1885 Buf-N	71	253	20	57	6	1	0	15	13	19	....	....	.225	.263	.257	.520	66	-10	18	2.42	-3	2-42,S-24/3-6	3	-1.0
1886 Was-N	68	242	26	44	5	1	0	16	17	26	9	....	.182	.236	.211	.446	39	-17	14	1.98	10	S-56/2-8,3-4	3	-0.4
Total 5 n	261	1301	330	437	61	12	0	164	25	6	24	5	.336	.348	.401	.750	132	48	197	6.89	60	S-152,3-114/P-4	....	6.2
Total 10	768	2955	323	623	80	15	1	209	131	261	9	....	.211	.245	.249	.494	58	-136	189	2.23	66	S-564,2-163/3-46,0-3	50	-3.5

• FORD, Curt Curtis Glenn Ford b: 10/11/1960, Jackson, MS BL/TR, 5'10", 150 lbs. Deb: 6/22/1985 Career OF: 90-7-146

YEAR TM-L	G	AB	R	H	2B	3B	HR	RBI	BB	SO	SB	CS	AVG	OBP	SLG	OPS	OPS+	BR/A	RC	RC/G	FR	G/POS	WS	TPW
1985 StL-N	11	12	2	6	2	0	0	3	4	1	1	0	.500	.625	.667	1.292	264	3	6	26.89	0	/0-4(1-0-4)	2	0.3
1986 StL-N	85	214	30	53	15	2	2	29	23	29	13	5	.248	.321	.364	.685	89	-3	27	4.25	3	0-64(24-0-40)	6	-0.2
1987*StL-N	89	228	32	65	9	5	3	26	14	32	11	8	.285	.329	.408	.737	92	-4	28	4.26	2	0-75(15-2-61)	7	-0.6
1988 StL-N	91	128	11	25	6	0	1	18	8	26	6	1	.195	.243	.266	.508	45	-8	8	1.98	0	0-40(24-3-13)/1-7	1	-1.0
1989 Phi-N	108	142	13	31	5	1	1	13	16	33	5	3	.218	.302	.289	.591	70	-6	12	2.81	1	0-52(26-2-25)/1-1,2-1	1	-0.6
1990 Phi-N	22	18	0	2	0	0	0	0	1	5	0	0	.111	.158	.111	.269	-25	-3	0	.38	0	/0-3(0-0-3)	0	-0.3
Total 6	406	742	88	182	37	8	7	89	66	126	36	17	.245	.309	.345	.654	80	-21	82	3.67	5	0-238/1-8,2-1	17	-2.4

• FORD, Dan Darnell Glenn "Disco Dan" Ford b: 5/19/1952, Los Angeles, CA BR/TR, 6'1", 185 lbs. Deb: 4/12/1975 Career OF: 2-295-783

YEAR TM-L	G	AB	R	H	2B	3B	HR	RBI	BB	SO	SB	CS	AVG	OBP	SLG	OPS	OPS+	BR/A	RC	RC/G	FR	G/POS	WS	TPW
1975 Min-A	130	440	72	123	21	1	15	59	30	79	6	7	.280	.333	.434	.767	113	5	60	4.83	-7	*0-120(0-118-2)/D-3	12	-0.5
1976 Min-A	145	514	87	137	24	7	20	86	36	118	17	6	.267	.327	.457	.784	124	15	75	5.02	-6	*0-139(1-0-139)/D-3	18	0.2
1977 Min-A	144	453	66	121	25	7	11	60	41	79	6	4	.267	.341	.426	.767	109	6	65	4.94	-1	*0-137(1-3-135)/D-3	12	0.0
1978 Min-A	151	592	78	162	36	10	11	82	48	88	7	7	.274	.333	.424	.757	109	6	80	4.69	-8	*0-149(0-145-4)/D-1	15	-0.4
1979*Cal-A	142	569	100	165	26	5	21	101	40	86	8	5	.290	.340	.464	.804	118	13	85	5.20	-2	*0-141(0-29-124)	18	0.4
1980 Cal-A	65	226	22	63	11	0	7	26	19	45	0	1	.279	.340	.420	.760	110	2	28	4.12	-2	0-45(0-0-45),D-15	4	-0.1
1981 Cal-A	97	375	53	104	14	1	15	48	23	71	2	2	.277	.328	.440	.768	119	8	49	4.48	-7	0-97(0-0-97)	10	-0.4
1982 Bal-A	123	421	46	99	21	3	10	43	23	71	5	2	.235	.281	.371	.652	77	-14	43	3.41	1	*0-119(0-0-119)/D-1	7	-1.9
1983*Bal-A	103	407	63	114	30	4	9	55	29	55	9	2	.280	.333	.440	.772	113	7	59	5.11	-2	*0-103(0-0-103)	13	0.0
1984 Bal-A	25	91	7	21	4	0	1	5	7	13	1	0	.231	.286	.308	.593	66	-4	8	2.82	1	0-15(0-0-15)/D-8	1	-0.4
1985 Bal-A	28	75	4	14	2	0	1	1	7	17	0	1	.187	.256	.253	.509	41	-7	4	1.79	0	D-28	0	-0.7
Total 11	1153	4163	598	1123	214	38	121	566	303	722	61	37	.270	.326	.427	.753	109	38	556	4.60	-33	*0-1065/D-62	110	-3.9

• FORD, Ed Edward L. Ford b: 1862, Richmond, VA, 5'9.5", 160 lbs. Deb: 10/9/1884

YEAR TM-L	G	AB	R	H	2B	3B	HR	RBI	BB	SO	SB	CS	AVG	OBP	SLG	OPS	OPS+	BR/A	RC	RC/G	FR	G/POS	WS	TPW
1884 Ric-a	2	5	0	0	0	0	0	0	0	....	....	....	.000	.000	.000	.000	-101	-1	0	.00	1	/1-1,S-1	0	0.0

• FORD, Hod Horace Hills Ford b: 7/23/1897, New Haven, CT d: 1/29/1977, Winchester, MA BR/TR, 5'10", 165 lbs. Deb: 9/8/1919

YEAR TM-L	G	AB	R	H	2B	3B	HR	RBI	BB	SO	SB	CS	AVG	OBP	SLG	OPS	OPS+	BR/A	RC	RC/G	FR	G/POS	WS	TPW
1919 Bos-N	10	28	4	6	0	1	0	3	2	6	0	....	.214	.290	.286	.576	77	-1	2	2.64	2	/S-8,3-2	1	0.2
1920 Bos-N	88	257	16	62	12	5	1	30	18	25	3	3	.241	.296	.339	.635	86	-5	26	3.33	3	2-59,S-18/1-4	5	0.1
1921 Bos-N	152	555	50	155	29	5	2	61	36	49	2	11	.279	.328	.360	.688	87	-13	64	3.92	15	*2-119,S-33	14	0.9
1922 Bos-N	143	515	58	140	23	9	2	60	30	36	2	1	.272	.317	.363	.680	78	-16	61	4.01	-1	*S-115,2-28	12	-0.3
1923 Bos-N	111	380	27	103	16	7	2	50	31	30	1	1	.271	.326	.366	.692	86	-7	46	4.22	-10	2-95,S-19	8	-1.2
1924 Phi-N	145	530	58	144	27	5	3	53	27	40	1	9	.272	.308	.358	.667	70	-25	56	3.61	-3	*2-145	8	-2.4
1925 Bro-N	66	216	32	59	11	0	1	15	26	15	0	3	.273	.357	.338	.695	81	-6	27	4.34	-2	S-66	5	-0.2
1926 Cin-N	57	197	14	55	6	1	0	18	14	12	1	....	.279	.336	.320	.656	79	-5	21	3.70	1	S-57	4	0.2
1927 Cin-N	115	409	45	112	16	2	1	46	33	34	0	....	.274	.331	.330	.661	80	-11	45	3.77	-7	*S-104,2-12	11	-0.6
1928 Cin-N	149	506	49	122	17	4	0	54	47	31	1	....	.241	.308	.291	.599	58	-30	47	3.03	16	*S-149	15	0.2
1929 Cin-N	148	529	68	146	14	6	3	50	41	25	8	....	.276	.329	.342	.671	70	-25	59	3.85	1	*S-108,2-42	11	-0.9
1930 Cin-N	132	424	36	98	16	7	1	34	24	28	2	....	.231	.272	.309	.581	42	-40	36	2.65	0	S-74,2-66	6	-2.8
1931 Cin-N	84	175	18	40	8	1	0	13	13	13	0	....	.229	.286	.286	.571	57	-10	15	2.83	-2	S-73/2-3,3-1	3	-0.9
1932 StL-N	1	2	0	0	0	0	0	0	0	0	0	....	.000	.000	.000	.000	-97	-1	0	.00	-1	/S-1	0	-0.1
Bos-N	40	95	9	26	5	2	0	6	6	9	0	....	.274	.324	.368	.692	89	-1	12	4.19	-3	2-20,S-16/3-2	3	-0.3
Yr.	41	97	9	26	5	2	0	6	6	9	0	....	.268	.317	.361	.678	85	-2	12	4.08	-4	2-20,S-17/3-2	3	-0.4
1933 Bos-N	5	15	0	1	0	0	0	1	3	1	0	....	.067	.222	.067	.289	-16	-2	0	.00	4	/S-5	1	0.3
Total 15	1446	4833	484	1269	200	55	16	494	351	354	21	28	.263	.316	.337	.652	72	-197	517	3.60	15	S-846,2-589/3-5,1-4	107	-7.8

• FORD, Lew Jon Lewis Ford b: 8/12/1976, Beaumont, TX BR/TR, 6', 190 lbs. Deb: 5/29/2003

YEAR TM-L	G	AB	R	H	2B	3B	HR	RBI	BB	SO	SB	CS	AVG	OBP	SLG	OPS	OPS+	BR/A	RC	RC/G	FR	G/POS	WS	TPW
2003*Min-A	34	73	16	24	7	1	3	15	8	9	2	0	.329	.402	.575	.978	153	6	18	9.37	-2	0-25(8-13-6)/D-4	4	0.3

YEAR TM-L	G	AB	R	H	2B	3B	HR	RBI	BB	SO	SB	CS	AVG	OBP	SLG	OPS	OPS+	BR/A	RC	RC/G	FR	G/POS	WS	TPW
• FORD, Ted	Theodore Henry Ford b: 2/7/1947, Vineland, NJ BR/TR, 5'10", 180 lbs. Deb: 4/7/1970 Career OF: 30-27-148																							
1970 Cle-A	26	46	5	8	1	0	1	1	3	13	0	0	.174	.224	.261	.485	32	-4	3	2.03	1	O-12(2-1-10)	0	-0.5
1971 Cle-A	74	196	15	38	6	0	2	14	9	34	2	2	.194	.229	.255	.484	34	-18	10	1.70	0	O-55(12-20-29)	1	-2.2
1972 Tex-A	129	429	43	101	19	1	14	50	37	80	4	3	.235	.301	.382	.683	107	2	50	3.87	4	*O-119(16-0-104)	14	0.0
1973 Cle-A	11	40	3	9	0	1	0	3	2	7	1	0	.225	.262	.275	.537	50	-2	3	2.36	-1	O-10(0-6-5)	0	-0.3
Total 4	240	711	66	156	26	2	17	68	51	134	7	5	.219	.275	.333	.608	80	-22	66	3.05	4	O-196	15	-2.9
• FORDYCE, Brook	Brook Alexander Fordyce b: 5/7/1970, New London, CT BR/TR, 6'1", 185 lbs. Deb: 4/26/1995																							
1995 NY-N	4	2	1	1	1	0	0	0	1	0	0	0	.500	.667	1.000	1.667	343	1	2	40.68	0	....	0	0.1
1996 Cin-N	4	7	0	2	1	0	0	1	3	1	0	0	.286	.500	.429	.929	149	1	2	10.21	0	/C-4	1	0.1
1997 Cin-N	47	96	7	20	5	0	1	8	8	15	2	0	.208	.269	.292	.561	46	-7	8	2.93	-1	C-30/D-1	1	-0.7
1998 Cin-N	57	146	8	37	9	0	3	14	11	28	0	1	.253	.306	.377	.682	77	-6	16	3.92	-1	C-54	2	-0.4
1999 Chi-A	105	333	36	99	25	1	9	49	21	48	2	0	.297	.345	.459	.804	102	1	53	5.80	-5	*C-103	12	0.2
2000 Chi-A	40	125	18	34	7	1	5	21	6	23	0	0	.272	.316	.464	.780	93	-2	19	5.28	6	C-40	4	0.6
Bal-A	53	177	23	57	11	0	9	28	11	27	0	0	.322	.368	.537	.905	132	8	35	7.38	-2	C-52	7	0.9
Yr.	93	302	41	91	18	1	14	49	17	50	0	0	.301	.347	.507	.853	116	6	53	6.48	4	C-92	11	1.5
2001 Bal-A	95	292	30	61	18	0	5	19	21	56	1	2	.209	.269	.322	.591	58	-19	24	2.70	-2	C-95	2	-1.4
2002 Bal-A	56	130	7	30	8	0	1	8	9	19	1	0	.231	.301	.315	.616	67	-6	12	3.02	-3	C-55	1	-0.5
2003 Bal-A	108	348	28	95	12	2	6	31	19	44	2	3	.273	.313	.371	.683	82	-10	38	3.72	-1	*C-107	5	-0.4
Total 9	569	1656	158	436	97	4	39	179	110	261	8	6	.263	.315	.397	.712	85	-40	208	4.36	-9	C-540/D-1	35	-1.5
• FORSTER, Tom	Thomas W. Forster b: 5/1/1859, New York, NY d: 7/17/1946, New York, NY BR, 5'9", 153 lbs. Deb: 8/4/1882 Career OF: 5-4-0																							
1882 Det-N	21	76	5	7	0	0	0	2	5	12	....	....	.092	.148	.092	.240	-21	-10	1	.42	-5	2-21	0	-1.3
1884 Pit-a	35	126	10	28	5	0	0	0	7	....	....	....	.222	.263	.262	.525	71	-4	9	2.50	5	S-28/3-6,2-1	3	0.2
1885 NY-a	57	213	28	47	7	2	0	18	17	....	....	....	.221	.281	.272	.554	82	-3	17	2.72	-12	2-52/O-5(3-2-0)	4	-1.2
1886 NY-a	67	251	33	49	3	2	1	20	20	....	9	....	.195	.263	.235	.498	59	-11	18	2.45	-6	2-62/O-4(2-2-0),S-1	3	-1.3
Total 4	180	666	76	131	15	4	1	40	49	12	9	....	.197	.256	.236	.492	59	-28	45	2.28	-18	2-136/S-29,O-9,3-6	10	-3.6
• FORSYTH, Ed	Edward James Forsyth b: 4/30/1887, Kingston, NY d: 6/22/1956, Hoboken, NJ BR/TR, 5'10", 155 lbs. Deb: 10/2/1915																							
1915 Bal-F	1	3	0	0	0	0	0	0	1	0	0	....	.000	.250	.000	.250	-23	-0	0	.00	0	/3-1	0	-0.1
• FOSS, George	George Dueward "Deeby" Foss b: 6/13/1897, Register, GA d: 11/10/1969, Brandon, FL BR/TR, 5'10.5", 170 lbs. Deb: 4/16/1921																							
1921 Was-A	4	7	0	0	0	0	0	0	0	1	0	0	.000	.000	.000	.000	-105	-2	0	.00	0	/3-1	0	-0.2
• FOSSE, Ray	Raymond Earl Fosse b: 4/4/1947, Marion, IL BR/TR, 6'2", 215 lbs. Deb: 9/8/1967																							
1967 Cle-A	7	16	0	1	0	0	0	0	0	5	0	0	.063	.063	.063	.125	-62	-3	0	.11	1	/C-7	0	-0.3
1968 Cle-A	1	0	0	0	0	0	0	0	0	0	0	0	....	....	....	....	-102	0	0	....	0	/C-1	0	0.0
1969 Cle-A	37	116	11	20	3	0	2	9	8	29	1	0	.172	.232	.250	.482	34	-10	7	1.79	-1	C-37	1	-1.0
1970 Cle-A★	120	450	62	138	17	1	18	61	39	55	1	5	.307	.363	.469	.832	122	11	74	6.00	1	*C-120	17	1.9
1971 Cle-A★	133	486	53	134	21	1	12	62	36	62	4	1	.276	.331	.397	.728	97	-2	61	4.47	8	*C-126/1-4	16	1.3
1972 Cle-A	134	457	42	110	20	1	10	41	45	46	5	1	.241	.313	.354	.667	95	-2	48	3.50	2	*C-124/1-3	14	0.7
1973*Oak-A	143	492	37	126	23	2	7	52	25	62	2	2	.256	.293	.354	.647	86	-11	49	3.41	-3	*C-141/D-2	14	-0.7
1974*Oak-A	69	204	20	40	8	3	4	23	11	31	1	1	.196	.244	.324	.568	66	-10	15	2.30	-1	C-68/D-1	3	-0.8
1975*Oak-A	82	136	14	19	3	2	0	12	8	19	0	1	.140	.193	.191	.384	9	-17	4	.95	-3	C-82/1-1,2-1	2	-1.8
1976 Cle-A	90	276	26	83	9	1	2	30	20	20	1	2	.301	.348	.362	.710	109	3	33	4.35	2	C-85/1-3,D-1	12	0.8
1977 Cle-A	78	238	25	63	7	1	6	27	7	26	0	5	.265	.294	.378	.673	84	-8	24	3.30	-1	C-77/1-1,D-1	5	-0.5
Sea-A	11	34	3	12	3	0	0	5	2	2	0	1	.353	.389	.441	.830	127	1	5	5.12	-1	/C-8,D-2	1	0.0
Yr.	89	272	28	75	10	1	6	32	9	28	0	6	.276	.306	.386	.692	90	-7	28	3.51	-2	C-85/D-3,1-1	6	-0.5
1979 Mil-A	19	52	6	12	3	1	0	2	2	6	0	0	.231	.286	.327	.613	65	-3	5	3.18	0	C-13/D-5,1-1	1	-0.2
Total 12	924	2957	299	758	117	13	61	324	203	363	15	19	.256	.308	.367	.675	89	-50	325	3.74	4	C-889/1-13,D-12,2-1	86	-0.5
• FOSTER, Eddie	Edward Cunningham "Kid" Foster b: 2/13/1887, Chicago, IL d: 1/15/1937, Washington, DC BR/TR, 5'6.5", 145 lbs. Deb: 4/14/1910																							
1910 NY-A	30	83	5	11	2	0	0	1	8	....	2	....	.133	.217	.157	.374	16	-8	3	1.11	-1	S-22	1	-0.9
1912 Was-A	154	618	98	176	34	9	2	70	53	....	27	....	.285	.345	.379	.724	106	4	88	5.13	9	*3-154	26	1.8
1913 Was-A	106	409	56	101	11	5	1	41	36	31	22	....	.247	.309	.306	.615	78	-11	42	3.47	4	*3-105	11	-0.5
1914 Was-A	157	616	82	174	16	10	2	50	60	47	31	18	.282	.348	.351	.699	106	3	79	4.48	-13	*3-157	23	-0.5
1915 Was-A	154	618	75	170	25	10	0	52	48	30	20	6	.275	.329	.348	.677	101	0	76	4.34	4	3-79,2-75	22	0.8
1916 Was-A	158	606	75	153	18	9	1	44	68	26	23	16	.252	.332	.317	.649	96	-4	66	3.62	-4	3-84,2-72	17	-0.5
1917 Was-A	143	554	66	130	16	8	0	43	46	23	11	....	.235	.293	.292	.586	80	-14	50	2.93	1	3-86,2-57	13	-1.1
1918 Was-A	129	519	70	147	13	3	0	29	41	20	12	....	.283	.339	.320	.659	101	0	59	3.89	10	*3-127/2-2	18	1.6
1919 Was-A	120	478	57	126	12	5	0	26	33	21	20	....	.264	.314	.310	.623	76	-15	51	3.61	14	*3-115	11	0.2
1920 Bos-A	117	386	48	100	17	6	0	41	42	17	10	4	.259	.336	.334	.671	81	-7	46	4.08	9	3-88,2-21	11	0.4
1921 Bos-A	120	412	51	117	18	6	0	35	57	15	13	7	.284	.371	.357	.728	89	-4	58	4.86	-10	3-94,2-22	13	-0.7
1922 Bos-A	48	109	11	23	3	0	0	3	9	10	1	1	.211	.277	.239	.516	36	-10	8	2.27	-4	3-28/S-3	0	-1.2
StL-A	37	144	29	44	4	0	0	12	20	8	3	1	.306	.394	.333	.727	88	-1	21	5.20	1	3-37	4	0.3
Yr.	85	253	40	67	7	0	0	15	29	18	4	2	.265	.345	.292	.638	66	-11	29	3.85	-3	3-65/S-3	4	-1.0
1923 StL-A	27	100	9	18	2	0	0	4	7	7	0	0	.180	.241	.200	.441	16	-12	6	1.66	-1	2-20/3-7	1	-1.2
Total 13	1500	5652	732	1490	191	71	6	451	528	255	195	53	.264	.329	.326	.655	89	-80	652	3.94	19	*3-1161,2-269/S-25	171	-1.5
• FOSTER, Elmer	Elmer Ellsworth Foster b: 8/15/1861, Minneapolis, MN d: 7/22/1946, Deephaven, MN BR/TL, 5'10", 178 lbs. Deb: 4/17/1886 Career OF: 25-59-0																							
1886 NY-a	35	125	16	23	0	1	0	7	7	....	3	....	.184	.239	.200	.439	40	-8	7	1.81	-3	2-21,O-14(9-5-0)	1	-1.0
1888 NY-N	37	136	15	20	3	2	0	10	9	20	13	....	.147	.216	.199	.415	33	-10	9	2.06	-2	O-37(16-21-0)/3-1	1	-1.3
1889 NY-N	2	4	2	0	0	0	0	0	3	1	2	....	.000	.429	.000	.429	25	-0	1	5.82	0	/O-2(0-2-0)	0	0.0
1890 Chi-N	27	105	20	26	4	2	5	23	9	21	18	....	.248	.325	.467	.791	125	2	22	7.48	2	O-27(0-27-0)	5	0.3
1891 Chi-N	4	16	3	3	0	0	1	1	1	2	1	....	.188	.235	.375	.610	77	-1	2	3.51	0	/O-4(0-4-0)	0	-0.1
Total 5	105	386	56	72	7	5	6	41	29	44	37	....	.187	.258	.277	.535	62	-16	41	3.45	-3	/O-84,2-21,3-1	7	-2.0
• FOSTER, George	George Arthur Foster b: 12/1/1948, Tuscaloosa, AL BR/TR, 6'1.5", 185 lbs. Deb: 9/10/1969 Career OF: 1534-267-178																							
1969 SF-N	9	5	1	2	0	0	0	1	0	1	0	0	.400	.400	.400	.800	127	0	1	7.20	0	/O-8(0-0-8)	0	0.0
1970 SF-N	9	19	2	6	1	1	1	4	2	5	0	0	.316	.381	.632	1.013	168	2	4	7.88	0	/O-7(6-0-1)	1	0.1
1971 SF-N	36	105	11	28	5	0	3	8	6	27	0	1	.267	.306	.400	.706	100	-1	11	3.69	-1	O-30(24-0-7)	2	-0.4
Cin-N	104	368	39	86	18	4	10	50	23	93	7	6	.234	.291	.386	.677	95	-5	36	3.18	5	*O-102(1-101-1)	10	-0.3
Yr.	140	473	50	114	23	4	13	58	29	120	7	7	.241	.295	.389	.684	96	-6	48	3.29	4	*O-132(25-101-8)	12	-0.6
1972*Cin-N	59	145	15	29	4	1	2	12	5	44	2	1	.200	.232	.283	.515	48	-10	8	1.76	-2	O-47(2-1-44)	1	-1.6
1973 Cin-N	17	39	6	11	3	0	4	9	4	7	0	1	.282	.349	.667	1.016	185	4	8	7.36	1	O-13(1-11-5)	2	0.4
1974 Cin-N	106	276	31	73	18	0	7	41	30	52	3	2	.264	.345	.406	.751	111	4	38	4.73	-2	O-98(6-45-69)	9	-0.1
1975*Cin-N	134	463	71	139	24	4	23	78	40	73	2	1	.300	.360	.518	.878	139	22	82	6.46	-3	*O-125(95-30-18)/1-1	21	1.2
1976*Cin-N★	144	562	86	172	21	9	29	**121**	52	89	17	3	.306	.369	.530	.899	149	37	111	7.25	-7	*O-142(116-36-24)/1-1	25	2.4
1977 Cin-N★	158	615	**124**	197	31	2	**52**	**149**	61	107	6	4	.320	.386	**.631**	**1.017**	164	**54**	144	8.69	0	*O-158(136-32-1)	32	4.7
1978 Cin-N★	158	604	97	170	26	7	**40**	**120**	70	138	4	4	.281	.363	.546	.909	151	38	115	6.72	-7	*O-157(154-11-0)	30	2.5
1979*Cin-N★	121	440	68	133	18	3	30	98	59	105	0	2	.302	.388	.561	.950	155	33	95	7.92	-2	*O-116(116-0-0)	22	2.6
1980 Cin-N	144	528	79	144	21	5	25	93	75	99	1	0	.273	.364	.473	.838	132	24	91	6.12	-1	*O-141(141-0-0)	23	1.7
1981 Cin-N★	108	414	64	122	23	2	22	90	51	75	4	0	.295	.376	.519	.895	149	28	81	7.06	0	*O-108(108-0-0)	24	2.4
1982 NY-N	151	550	64	136	23	2	13	70	50	123	1	1	.247	.312	.367	.680	90	-8	62	3.86	5	*O-138(138-0-0)	12	-0.9
1983 NY-N	157	601	74	145	19	2	28	90	38	111	1	1	.241	.291	.419	.710	95	-7	68	3.84	2	*O-153(153-0-0)	14	-1.3
1984 NY-N	146	553	67	149	22	1	24	86	30	122	2	2	.269	.314	.443	.757	112	5	73	4.61	-2	*O-141(141-0-0)	18	-0.3
1985 NY-N	129	452	57	119	24	1	21	77	46	87	0	1	.263	.334	.460	.794	123	12	69	5.41	-5	*O-123(123-0-0)	17	0.1
1986 NY-N	72	233	28	53	6	1	13	38	21	53	1	1	.227	.291	.429	.721	99	-2	28	3.91	2	O-62(62-0-0)	6	-0.2
Chi-A	15	51	2	11	0	2	1	4	3	8	0	0	.216	.259	.353	.612	63	-3	4	2.68	1	O-11(11-0-0)/D-3	0	-0.2
Total 18	1977	7023	986	1925	307	47	348	1239	666	1419	51	31	.274	.341	.480	.821	127	226	1129	5.65	-15	*O-1880/D-3,1-2	269	12.8

YEAR TM-L	G	AB	R	H	2B	3B	HR	RBI	BB	SO	SB	CS	AVG	OBP	SLG	OPS	OPS+	BR/A	RC	RC/G	FR	G/POS	WS	TPW
• FOSTER, Leo	Leonard Norris Foster b: 2/2/1951, Covington, KY BR/TR, 5'11", 165 lbs. Deb: 7/9/1971																							
1971 Atl-N	9	10	1	0	0	0	0	0	0	1	0	0	.000	.000	.000	.000	-94	-3	0	.00	0	/S-3	0	-0.3
1973 Atl-N	3	6	1	1	1	0	0	0	0	2	0	0	.167	.167	.333	.500	33	-1	0	1.62	0	/S-1	0	-0.1
1974 Atl-N	72	112	16	22	2	0	1	5	9	22	1	2	.196	.256	.241	.497	38	-10	7	1.82	-2	S-43,2-10/3-3,0-1	1	-0.9
1976 NY-N	24	59	11	12	2	0	1	15	8	5	3	0	.203	.299	.288	.587	71	-1	6	3.49	1	/3-9,S-7,2-3	2	0.0
1977 NY-N	36	75	6	17	3	0	0	6	5	14	3	1	.227	.284	.267	.551	51	-5	6	2.53	-1	2-20/S-8,3-2	1	-0.5
Total 5	144	262	35	52	8	0	2	26	22	44	7	3	.198	.263	.252	.515	45	-19	19	2.27	-3	/S-62,2-33,3-14,0-1	4	-1.7
• FOSTER, Pop	Clarence Francis Foster b: 4/8/1878, New Haven, CT d: 4/16/1944, Princeton, NJ BR/TR, 5'8.5" Deb: 9/13/1898 U Career OF: 121-0-108																							
1898 NY-N	32	112	10	30	6	1	0	9	0	....	0	....	.268	.268	.339	.607	76	-4	11	3.37	-4	0-21(17-0-4),3-10/S-2	1	-0.9
1899 NY-N	84	301	48	89	9	7	3	57	20	....	7	....	.296	.348	.402	.750	109	3	46	5.67	-5	0-84(1-0-84)/3-1,S-1	7	-0.5
1900 NY-N	31	84	19	22	3	1	0	11	11	....	0	....	.262	.347	.321	.669	89	-1	10	4.11	-1	0-12(1-0-11)/S-7,2-5	2	-0.1
1901 Was-A	103	392	65	109	16	9	6	54	41	....	10	....	.278	.352	.411	.763	113	7	62	5.77	-4	*0-102(102-0-0)/S-2	13	-0.2
Chi-A	12	35	4	10	2	2	1	6	4	....	0	....	.286	.359	.543	.902	151	2	7	7.41	-1	/0-9(0-0-9)	2	0.1
Yr.	115	427	69	119	18	11	7	60	45	....	10	....	.279	.353	.422	.774	116	10	69	5.91	-4	*0-111(102-0-9)/S-2	15	-0.1
Total 4	262	924	146	260	36	20	10	137	76	....	17	....	.281	.341	.396	.737	107	8	135	5.35	-14	0-228/S-12,3-11,2-5	25	-1.7
• FOSTER, Reddy	Oscar E. Foster b: 8/1864, Richmond, VA d: 12/19/1908, Richmond, VA Deb: 6/3/1896																							
1896 NY-N	1	1	0	0	0	0	0	0	0	0	0	....	.000	.000	.000	.000	-103	-0	0	.00	0	....	0	0.0
• FOSTER, Robert	Robert Foster Deb: 6/18/1884																							
1884 Phi-a	4	11	4	2	0	0	0	0	3	....	....	....	.182	.357	.182	.539	76	-0	1	2.24	0	/C-4,0-1	0	0.0
Phi-U	1	3	0	1	0	1	0	....	0	....	....	....	.333	.333	1.000	1.333	363	1	1	14.35	-1	/C-1	0	0.0
• FOSTER, Roy	Roy Foster b: 7/29/1945, Bixby, OK BR/TR, 6', 185 lbs. Deb: 4/7/1970 Career OF: 175-0-112																							
1970 Cle-A	139	477	66	128	26	0	23	60	54	75	3	3	.268	.357	.468	.825	120	13	78	5.71	0	*0-131(114-0-17)	13	0.7
1971 Cle-A	125	396	51	97	21	1	18	45	35	48	6	1	.245	.316	.439	.755	103	2	54	4.61	0	*0-107(46-0-64)	10	-0.4
1972 Cle-A	73	143	19	32	4	0	4	13	21	23	0	2	.224	.331	.336	.667	96	-1	16	3.49	0	0-45(15-0-31)	3	-0.3
Total 3	337	1016	136	257	51	1	45	118	110	146	9	6	.253	.338	.438	.776	110	14	147	4.95	0	0-283	26	0.0
• FOTHERGILL, Bob	Robert Roy "Fats" Fothergill b: 8/16/1897, Massillon, OH d: 3/20/1938, Detroit, MI BR/TR, 5'10.5", 230 lbs. Deb: 4/18/1922 Career OF: 594-65-175																							
1922 Det-A	42	152	20	49	12	4	0	29	8	9	1	5	.322	.356	.454	.810	113	1	22	5.35	-4	0-38(2-10-26)	4	-0.6
1923 Det-A	101	241	34	76	18	2	1	49	12	19	5	4	.315	.358	.419	.777	106	1	36	5.26	-3	0-68(45-20-3)	7	-0.5
1924 Det-A	54	166	28	50	8	3	0	15	5	13	2	3	.301	.326	.386	.711	84	-5	20	4.19	-1	0-45(43-0-2)	3	-0.9
1925 Det-A	71	204	38	72	14	0	2	28	6	3	3	2	.353	.377	.451	.828	111	3	34	6.21	2	0-59(40-16-4)	6	0.2
1926 Det-A	110	387	63	142	31	7	3	73	33	23	4	12	.367	.421	.506	.927	139	18	78	7.65	-5	*0-103(76-19-9)	17	0.6
1927 Det-A	143	527	93	189	38	9	9	114	47	31	9	15	.359	.413	.516	.929	138	25	108	7.71	-7	*0-137(137-0-0)	22	0.7
1928 Det-A	111	347	49	110	28	10	3	63	24	19	8	3	.317	.366	.481	.848	119	10	61	6.51	-4	0-90(70-0-20)	12	-0.1
1929 Det-A	115	277	42	98	24	9	6	62	11	11	3	1	.354	.378	.570	.949	140	15	58	8.36	-4	0-59(39-0-20)	10	0.7
1930 Det-A	55	143	14	37	9	3	2	14	6	10	1	1	.259	.289	.406	.694	72	-7	16	3.91	-2	0-38(32-0-6)	2	-1.0
Chi-A	52	135	10	40	9	0	0	24	4	8	0	0	.296	.326	.363	.689	77	-5	16	4.35	-2	0-31(8-0-22)	2	-0.8
Yr.	107	278	24	77	18	3	2	38	10	18	1	1	.277	.307	.385	.692	75	-11	32	4.11	-4	0-69(40-0-28)	4	-1.8
1931 Chi-A	108	312	25	88	9	4	3	56	17	17	2	2	.282	.323	.365	.689	86	-6	37	4.26	-3	0-74(48-0-26)	6	-1.2
1932 Chi-A	116	346	36	102	24	1	7	50	27	10	4	4	.295	.348	.431	.778	107	3	51	5.44	-4	0-86(53-0-34)	8	-0.5
1933 Bos-A	28	32	1	11	1	0	0	5	2	4	0	0	.344	.382	.375	.757	102	0	5	5.80	-0	/0-4(1-0-3)	1	0.0
Total 12	1106	3269	453	1064	225	52	36	582	202	177	42	52	.325	.368	.459	.828	115	54	542	6.13	-37	0-832	100	-3.5
• FOURNIER, Jack	John Frank Fournier b: 9/28/1889, Au Sable, MI d: 9/5/1973, Tacoma, WA BL/TR, 6', 195 lbs. Deb: 4/13/1912 Career OF: 53-14-20																							
1912 Chi-A	35	73	6	14	5	2	0	2	4	....	1	....	.192	.263	.315	.578	67	-3	6	2.65	3	1-17	1	0.0
1913 Chi-A	68	172	20	40	8	5	1	23	21	23	9	....	.233	.323	.355	.678	99	-0	21	4.05	4	1-29,0-23(11-0-12)	5	0.2
1914 Chi-A	109	379	44	118	14	9	6	44	31	44	10	13	.311	.368	.443	.811	146	16	61	5.64	8	1-97/0-6(3-1-2)	17	2.4
1915 Chi-A	126	422	86	136	20	18	5	77	64	37	21	16	.322	.429	**.491**	.920	170	36	91	7.68	5	1-65,0-57(38-13-6)	28	4.0
1916 Chi-A	105	313	36	75	13	9	3	44	36	40	19	....	.240	.328	.367	.695	107	3	44	4.67	0	1-85/0-1	9	0.1
1917 Chi-A	1	1	0	0	0	0	0	0	0	1	0	....	.000	.000	.000	.000	-98	-0	0	.00	0	....	0	0.0
1918 NY-A	27	100	9	35	6	1	0	12	7	7	7	....	.350	.393	.430	.823	145	5	19	7.02	-5	1-27	5	0.0
1920 StL-N	141	530	77	162	33	14	3	61	42	42	26	20	.306	.370	.438	.808	134	23	84	5.41	-6	*1-138	19	1.5
1921 StL-N	149	574	103	197	27	9	16	86	56	48	20	22	.343	.409	.505	.914	143	34	114	7.16	-5	*1-149	24	1.9
1922 StL-N	128	404	64	119	23	9	10	61	40	21	6	8	.295	.368	.470	.838	120	11	69	6.04	0	*1-109/P-1	13	0.4
1923 Bro-N	133	515	91	181	30	13	22	102	43	28	11	4	.351	.411	.588	.999	165	49	125	9.47	-1	*1-133	27	3.8
1924 Bro-N	154	563	93	188	25	4	**27**	116	83	46	7	5	.334	.428	.536	.965	162	54	133	8.98	4	*1-153	34	4.7
1925 Bro-N	145	545	99	191	21	16	22	130	**86**	39	4	6	.350	.446	.569	1.015	162	54	141	10.10	1	*1-145	29	4.2
1926 Bro-N	87	243	39	69	9	2	11	48	30	16	0	....	.284	.365	.473	.838	126	9	42	6.04	-2	1-64	9	0.3
1927 Bos-N	122	374	55	106	18	2	10	53	44	16	4	....	.283	.368	.422	.790	120	12	59	5.51	-3	*1-102	11	0.2
Total 15	1530	5208	822	1631	252	113	136	859	587	408	145	94	.313	.392	.483	.875	142	302	1010	6.97	3	*1-1313/0-87,P-1	231	23.7
• FOUSER, Bill	William C. Fouser b: 10/1855, Philadelphia, PA d: 3/1/1919, Philadelphia, PA Deb: 4/22/1876 U																							
1876 Phi-N	21	89	11	12	0	1	0	2	0	0	....	....	.135	.135	.157	.292	-3	-9	2	.70	1	2-14/0-7(0-1-6),1-1	0	-0.7
• FOUTZ, Dave	David Luther "Scissors" Foutz b: 9/7/1856, Carroll County, MD d: 3/5/1897, Waverly, MD BR/TR, 6'2", 161 lbs. Deb: 7/29/1884 M Career OF: 92-33-196 ♦																							
1884 StL-a	33	119	17	27	4	0	0	0	8	....	....	....	.227	.276	.261	.536	73	0	9	2.62	0	P-25,0-14(0-3-11)	19	1.6
1885*StL-a	65	238	42	59	6	4	0	34	11	....	....	....	.248	.281	.307	.588	82	2	21	3.17	7	P-47,1-15/0-4(4-0-0)	37	1.8
1886*StL-a	102	414	66	116	18	9	3	59	9	....	17	....	.280	.297	.389	.686	109	8	54	4.91	3	P-59,0-34(0-0-34),1-11	62	7.0
1887*StL-a	102	446	79	174	26	13	4	108	23	....	22	....	.390	.393	.508	.901	136	24	95	9.47	-2	0-50(0-0-50),P-40,1-15	43	3.0
1888 Bro-a	140	563	91	156	20	13	3	99	28	....	35	....	.277	.314	.375	.688	120	14	79	5.25	3	0-78(0-1-77),1-42,P-23	**33**	1.8
1889*Bro-a	138	553	118	152	19	8	6	113	64	23	43	....	.275	.353	.371	.724	106	6	90	5.93	7	*1-134,P-12	24	-0.2
1890*Bro-N	129	509	106	154	25	13	5	98	52	25	42	....	.303	.368	.432	.801	132	20	99	7.38	7	*1-113,0-13(4-9-1)/P-5	27	2.0
1891 Bro-N	130	521	87	134	26	8	2	73	40	25	48	....	.257	.313	.349	.662	93	-4	74	5.14	1	*1-124/P-6,S-1	16	-1.1
1892 Bro-N	61	220	33	41	5	3	1	26	14	14	19	....	.186	.235	.250	.485	48	-8	18	2.69	1	0-29(11-7-11),P-27/1-6	13	-1.6
1893 Bro-N	130	557	91	137	20	10	7	67	32	34	39	....	.246	.287	.355	.642	74	-23	70	4.40	-5	0-77(66-11-0),1-54/P-6	10	-3.4
1894 Bro-N	73	297	40	90	12	9	0	52	14	13	14	....	.303	.337	.404	.741	84	-8	46	5.81	-0	1-72/P-1	6	-0.8
1895 Bro-N	31	115	14	34	4	1	0	21	4	2	1	....	.296	.319	.348	.667	78	-4	14	4.45	-3	0-20(7-2-11)/1-8	2	-0.6
1896 Bro-N	2	8	0	2	1	0	0	0	1	0	0	....	.250	.333	.375	.708	92	-0	1	4.53	1	/1-1,0-1	0	0.1
Total 13	1136	4560	784	1276	186	91	31	750	300	136	280	....	.280	.323	.378	.701	101	28	669	5.45	20	1-595,0-320,P-251/S-1	292	9.5
• FOUTZ, Frank	Frank Hayes Foutz b: 4/8/1877, Baltimore, MD d: 12/25/1961, Lima, OH BR/TR, 5'11", 165 lbs. Deb: 4/26/1901																							
1901 Bal-A	20	72	13	17	4	1	2	14	8	....	0	....	.236	.321	.403	.724	96	-1	10	4.57	0	1-20	1	-0.1
• FOWLER, Boob	Joseph Chester "Gink" Fowler b: 11/11/1900, Waco, TX d: 10/8/1988, Dallas, TX BL/TR, 5'11.5", 180 lbs. Deb: 5/6/1923																							
1923 Cin-N	11	33	9	11	0	1	1	6	1	3	1	0	.333	.353	.485	.838	121	1	6	6.84	-4	S-10	1	-0.1
1924 Cin-N	59	129	20	43	6	1	0	9	5	15	2	2	.333	.358	.395	.754	103	0	18	5.29	-3	S-32/2-4,3-2	3	0.0
1925 Cin-N	6	5	0	2	1	0	0	2	0	1	0	0	.400	.400	.600	1.000	155	0	1	10.18	0	....	0	0.0
1926 Bos-A	2	8	1	1	0	0	0	1	0	0	0	0	.125	.125	.125	.250	-36	-2	0	.45	0	/3-2	0	-0.2
Total 4	78	175	30	57	7	2	1	18	6	19	3	2	.326	.348	.406	.754	102	0	25	5.42	-7	/S-42,2-4,3-4	4	-0.3
• FOX, Andy	Andrew Junipero Fox b: 1/12/1971, Sacramento, CA BL/TR, 6'4", 205 lbs. Deb: 4/7/1996 Career OF: 23-10-46																							
1996*NY-A	113	189	26	37	4	0	3	13	20	28	11	3	.196	.276	.265	.541	38	-17	16	2.59	-8	2-72,3-31/S-9,D-3,0-1	2	-2.0
1997*NY-A	22	31	13	7	1	0	0	1	7	9	2	1	.226	.368	.258	.626	68	-1	4	3.44	1	3-11/2-5,D-2,0-2(0-0-2),S	1	0.0
1998 Ari-N	139	502	67	139	21	6	9	44	43	97	14	7	.277	.355	.396	.752	98	-1	75	5.46	-7	2-60,0-48(10-8-33),3-26,1-12	15	-0.8
1999*Ari-N	99	274	34	70	12	2	6	33	33	61	4	1	.255	.354	.380	.734	85	-5	39	4.95	-5	S-82,3-12	7	-0.4
2000 Ari-N	31	86	10	18	4	0	1	10	4	16	2	1	.209	.244	.291	.535	33	-9	6	2.30	-1	3-20/0-6(1-1-4),1-1	1	-1.0

YEAR TM-L	G	AB	R	H	2B	3B	HR	RBI	BB	SO	SB	CS	AVG	OBP	SLG	OPS	OPS+	BR/A	RC	RC/G	FR	G/POS	WS	TPW
Fla-N	69	164	19	40	4	2	3	10	18	37	8	3	.244	.330	.348	.677	75	-6	20	4.28	0	S-33,0-14(9-0-5),3-12/2-2	3	-0.3
Yr.	100	250	29	58	8	2	4	20	22	53	10	4	.232	.302	.328	.630	61	-15	26	3.58	-1	S-33,3-32,0-20(10-1-9)/2-2,1	4	-1.3
2001 Fla-N	54	81	8	15	0	1	3	7	15	17	1	0	.185	.327	.321	.648	71	-3	9	3.73	-2	S-12/3-9,2-2,0-2(1-1-0)	1	-0.4
2002 Fla-N	133	435	55	109	14	5	4	41	49	94	31	7	.251	.340	.333	.673	81	-7	54	4.18	-1	*S-112/2-7,3-4,0-1	14	0.1
2003 Fla-N	70	108	12	21	5	1	0	8	7	29	1	2	.194	.269	.259	.528	40	-10	7	2.18	-5	2-15/S-9,3-5,1-2,0-2(2-0-0)	1	-1.4
Total 8	730	1870	244	456	65	17	29	167	196	388	74	25	.244	.331	.343	.674	76	-58	231	4.20	-29	S-259,2-163,3-130/0-76,1-15,D	45	-6.1
• FOX, Bill	William Henry Fox b: 1/15/1872, Sturbridge, MA d: 5/7/1946, Minneapolis, MN BB/TR, 5'10", 160 lbs. Deb: 8/20/1897																							
1897 Was-N	4	14	4	4	0	0	0	0	1	....	0	....	.286	.333	.286	.619	65	-1	1	3.62	0	/2-2,S-2	0	-0.1
1901 Cin-N	43	159	9	28	2	1	0	7	4	....	9	....	.176	.201	.201	.402	18	-16	9	1.75	4	2-43	1	-1.1
Total 2	47	173	13	32	2	1	0	7	5	....	9	....	.185	.212	.208	.420	22	-17	10	1.88	4	/2-45,S-2	1	-1.2
• FOX, Charlie	Charles Francis "Irish" Fox b: 10/7/1921, New York, NY d: 2/16/2004, San Francisco, CA BR/TR, 5'11", 180 lbs. Deb: 9/24/1942 M/C																							
1942 NY-N	3	7	1	3	0	0	0	1	1	2	0	....	.429	.500	.429	.929	172	1	2	9.07	0	/C-3	1	0.1
• FOX, Eric	Eric Hollis Fox b: 8/15/1963, Lemoore, CA BB/TL, 5'10", 180 lbs. Deb: 7/7/1992 Career OF: 28-55-30																							
1992*Oak-A	51	143	24	34	5	2	3	13	13	29	3	4	.238	.301	.364	.665	90	-3	16	3.48	0	0-43(20-19-16)/D-4	2	-0.4
1993 Oak-A	29	56	5	8	1	0	1	5	2	7	0	2	.143	.172	.214	.387	3	-9	2	.94	0	0-26(5-18-3)/D-2	0	-0.9
1994 Oak-A	26	44	7	9	2	0	1	1	3	8	2	0	.205	.255	.318	.574	51	-3	4	3.12	0	0-24(0-16-8)	0	-0.3
1995 Tex-A	10	15	2	0	0	0	0	0	3	4	0	0	.000	.167	.000	.167	-51	-3	0	.35	0	/0-8(3-2-3),D-1	0	-0.4
Total 4	116	258	38	51	8	2	5	19	21	48	5	6	.198	.258	.302	.560	56	-18	22	2.60	0	0-101/D-7	2	-1.9
• FOX, Jack	John Paul Fox b: 5/21/1885, Reading, PA d: 6/28/1963, Reading, PA BR/TR, 5'10", 185 lbs. Deb: 6/2/1908																							
1908 Phi-A	9	30	2	6	0	0	0	0	0	....	2	....	.200	.200	.200	.400	28	-2	2	1.62	-1	/0-8(0-1-7)	0	-0.5
• FOX, John	John Joseph Fox b: 2/7/1859, Roxbury, MA d: 4/18/1893, Boston, MA Deb: 6/2/1881 Career OF: 0-0-16 ♦																							
1881 Bos-N	30	118	8	21	0	0	0	4	0	11	....	....	.178	.178	.178	.356	13	-9	4	1.07	-1	P-17,0-12(0-0-12)/1-6	4	-1.8
1883 Bal-a	23	92	12	14	3	0	0	0	4	....	....	....	.152	.188	.185	.372	20	-5	3	1.17	-2	P-20/0-4(0-0-4),1-1	6	-0.6
1884 Pit-a	8	25	4	6	2	0	0	0	0	....	....	....	.240	.240	.320	.560	80	0	2	2.85	0	/P-7,S-1	1	-1.2
1886 Was-N	1	3	0	1	0	0	0	0	0	0	0	....	.333	.333	.333	.667	109	0	0	4.61	0	/P-1	0	-0.4
Total 4	62	238	24	42	5	0	0	4	4	11	0	....	.176	.190	.197	.388	23	-14	9	1.32	-3	/P-45,0-16,1-7,S-1	11	-4.0
• FOX, Nellie	Jacob Nelson Fox b: 12/25/1927, St. Thomas, PA d: 12/1/1975, Baltimore, MD BL/TR, 5'10", 150 lbs. Deb: 6/8/1947 C HOF: 1997																							
1947 Phi-A	7	3	2	0	0	0	0	0	1	0	0	0	.000	.250	.000	.250	-27	-0	0	.59	0	/2-1	0	-0.1
1948 Phi-A	3	13	0	2	0	0	0	0	1	0	1	0	.154	.214	.154	.368	-1	-2	1	1.49	-1	/2-3	0	-0.2
1949 Phi-A	88	247	42	63	6	2	0	21	32	9	2	2	.255	.354	.296	.650	75	-8	28	3.59	3	2-77	6	-0.1
1950 Chi-A	130	457	45	113	12	7	0	30	35	17	4	3	.247	.304	.304	.608	58	-30	45	3.32	-2	*2-121	5	-2.3
1951 Chi-A★	147	604	93	189	32	12	4	55	43	11	9	12	.313	.372	.425	.798	118	11	98	5.81	10	*2-147	22	3.0
1952 Chi-A★	152	648	76	**192**	25	10	0	39	34	14	5	5	.296	.334	.366	.700	94	-7	80	4.44	13	*2-151	22	1.5
1953 Chi-A★	154	624	92	178	31	8	3	72	49	18	4	5	.285	.344	.375	.719	91	-8	81	4.59	3	*2-154	21	0.7
1954 Chi-A★	155	631	111	**201**	24	8	2	47	51	12	16	9	.319	.374	.391	.766	106	6	93	5.34	1	*2-155	26	2.0
1955 Chi-A★	154	636	100	198	28	7	6	59	38	15	7	9	.311	.366	.406	.772	104	2	95	5.42	24	*2-154	25	3.8
1956 Chi-A★	154	649	109	192	20	10	4	52	44	14	8	4	.296	.350	.376	.726	90	-9	84	4.55	12	*2-154	19	1.5
1957 Chi-A★	155	619	110	**196**	27	8	6	61	75	13	5	6	.317	.404	.415	.819	124	24	109	6.66	22	*2-155	32	6.0
1958 Chi-A★	155	623	82	**187**	21	6	0	49	47	11	5	6	.300	.360	.353	.713	99	-0	79	4.54	6	*2-155	22	1.9
1959*Chi-A★	156	624	84	191	34	6	2	70	71	13	5	6	.306	.383	.389	.773	114	14	97	5.72	2	*2-156	**30**	2.9
1960 Chi-A★	150	605	85	175	24	**10**	2	59	50	13	2	4	.289	.353	.372	.725	97	-3	81	4.70	5	*2-149	21	1.4
1961 Chi-A★	159	606	67	152	11	5	2	51	59	12	2	3	.251	.326	.295	.622	69	-26	60	3.26	-11	*2-159	11	-2.3
1962 Chi-A	157	621	79	166	27	7	2	54	38	12	1	2	.267	.317	.343	.660	78	-20	67	3.72	3	*2-154	16	-0.4
1963 Chi-A★	137	539	54	140	19	0	2	42	24	17	0	2	.260	.300	.306	.606	72	-22	49	3.12	-3	*2-134	12	-1.4
1964 Hou-N	133	442	45	117	12	6	0	28	27	13	0	2	.265	.322	.319	.641	86	-8	47	3.51	0	*2-115	13	0.1
1965 Hou-N	21	41	3	11	2	0	0	1	0	2	0	0	.268	.286	.317	.603	75	-1	3	3.02	1	/3-6,1-2,2-1	1	-0.1
Total 19	2367	9232	1279	2663	355	112	35	790	719	216	76	80	.288	.349	.363	.712	94	-88	1197	4.56	90	*2-2295/3-6,1-2	304	17.9
• FOX, Paddy	George B. Fox b: 12/1/1868, Pottstown, PA d: 5/8/1914, Philadelphia, PA Deb: 7/13/1891																							
1891 Lou-a	6	19	1	2	0	1	0	2	2	3	0	....	.105	.261	.211	.471	36	-2	1	1.67	0	/3-6	0	-0.2
1899 Pit-N	13	41	4	10	0	1	1	3	3	....	2	....	.244	.311	.366	.677	86	-1	6	4.58	1	/1-9,C-3	1	0.0
Total 2	19	60	5	12	0	2	1	5	5	3	2	....	.200	.294	.317	.611	69	-2	7	3.57	1	/1-9,3-6,C-3	1	-0.1
• FOX, Pete	Ervin Fox b: 3/8/1909, Evansville, IN d: 7/5/1966, Detroit, MI BR/TR, 5'11", 165 lbs. Deb: 4/12/1933 Career OF: 37-166-1170																							
1933 Det-A	128	535	82	154	26	13	7	57	23	38	9	6	.288	.320	.424	.744	94	-7	71	4.78	-3	*0-124(0-116-8)	14	-1.3
1934*Det-A	128	516	101	147	31	2	2	45	49	53	25	10	.285	.351	.364	.716	85	-10	69	4.72	6	*0-121(0-11-110)	13	-1.0
1935*Det-A	131	517	116	166	38	8	15	73	45	52	14	4	.321	.382	.513	.895	134	26	103	7.41	-2	*0-125(0-6-123)	21	1.5
1936 Det-A	73	220	46	67	12	1	4	26	34	23	1	3	.305	.405	.423	.827	104	2	39	6.28	0	0-55(5-0-50)	6	-0.1
1937 Det-A	148	628	116	208	39	8	12	82	41	43	12	8	.331	.372	.476	.848	110	7	109	6.62	-4	*0-143(11-27-106)	19	-0.5
1938 Det-A	155	634	91	186	35	10	7	96	31	39	16	7	.293	.328	.413	.742	80	-22	85	4.88	-2	*0-155(1-0-154)	13	-3.0
1939 Det-A	141	519	69	153	24	6	7	66	35	41	23	12	.295	.342	.405	.746	84	-14	69	4.70	7	*0-126(0-0-126)	11	-1.4
1940*Det-A	93	350	49	101	17	4	5	48	21	30	7	7	.289	.329	.403	.732	81	-12	46	4.73	0	0-85(2-1-82)	7	-1.6
1941 Bos-A	73	268	38	81	12	7	0	31	21	32	9	2	.302	.357	.399	.757	97	0	41	5.55	1	0-62(8-5-49)	7	-0.2
1942 Bos-A	77	256	42	67	15	5	3	42	20	28	8	7	.262	.323	.395	.717	98	-3	31	3.94	-5	0-71(7-0-64)	5	-1.2
1943 Bos-A	127	489	54	141	24	4	2	44	34	40	22	8	.288	.337	.366	.703	104	3	62	4.36	-1	*0-125(3-0-122)	13	-0.6
1944 Bos-A★	121	496	70	156	37	6	1	64	27	34	10	5	.315	.354	.419	.773	122	13	75	5.57	-3	*0-119(0-0-119)	17	0.2
1945 Bos-A	66	208	21	51	4	1	0	20	11	18	2	2	.245	.296	.274	.570	64	-10	18	3.06	-1	0-57(0-0-57)	3	-1.5
Total 13	1461	5636	895	1678	314	75	65	694	392	471	158	81	.298	.347	.415	.762	98	-26	819	5.21	-7	*0-1368	149	-10.8
• FOXX, Jimmie	James Emory "Beast,Double X" Foxx b: 10/22/1907, Sudlersville, MD d: 7/21/1967, Miami, FL BR/TR, 6', 195 lbs. Deb: 5/1/1925 C HOF: 1951 Career OF: 12-0-9 ♦																							
1925 Phi-A	10	9	2	6	1	0	0	0	0	1	0	0	.667	.667	.778	1.444	249	2	4	39.57	0	/C-1	1	0.2
1926 Phi-A	26	32	8	10	2	1	0	5	1	6	1	0	.313	.333	.438	.771	95	-0	5	5.26	1	C-12/0-3(0-0-3)	1	0.0
1927 Phi-A	61	130	23	42	6	5	3	20	14	11	2	1	.323	.393	.515	.908	127	5	27	7.85	-1	1-32/C-5	6	0.3
1928 Phi-A	118	400	85	131	29	10	13	79	60	43	3	8	.328	.416	.548	.964	147	26	91	8.30	3	3-60,1-30,C-19	22	3.2
1929*Phi-A	149	517	123	183	23	9	33	118	103	70	9	7	.354	**.463**	.625	1.088	171	59	154	11.39	0	*1-142/3-8	**34**	4.7
1930*Phi-A	153	562	127	188	33	13	37	156	93	66	7	7	.335	.429	.637	1.066	159	51	154	10.25	1	*1-153	34	3.8
1931*Phi-A	139	515	93	150	32	10	30	120	73	84	4	3	.291	.380	.567	.947	138	29	113	8.04	1	*1-112,3-26/0-1	24	1.9
1932 Phi-A	154	585	**151**	213	33	9	**58**	**169**	116	96	3	7	.364	.469	**.749**	**1.218**	203	**90**	207	**14.48**	1	*1-141,3-13	**40**	**7.2**
1933 Phi-A★	149	573	125	204	37	9	**48**	**163**	96	93	2	2	**.356**	.449	**.703**	**1.153**	**199**	**82**	184	**13.14**	6	*1-149/S-1	**41**	**7.1**
1934 Phi-A★	150	539	120	180	28	6	44	130	**111**	75	11	2	.334	.449	.653	1.102	188	75	165	12.11	6	*1-140/3-9	32	6.3
1935 Phi-A★	147	535	118	185	33	7	**36**	115	114	99	6	4	.346	.461	**.636**	**1.096**	**182**	70	163	**12.18**	7	*1-121,C-26/3-2	30	**6.3**
1936 Bos-A★	155	585	130	198	32	8	41	143	105	119	13	4	.338	.440	.631	1.071	153	51	168	11.33	2	*1-139,0-16(11-0-5)/3-1	26	3.4
1937 Bos-A★	150	569	111	162	24	6	36	127	99	96	10	8	.285	.392	.538	.929	127	23	123	7.77	8	*1-150/C-1	23	1.6
1938 Bos-A★	149	565	139	197	33	9	50	**175**	**119**	76	5	4	**.349**	**.462**	**.704**	**1.166**	**180**	**72**	189	**13.42**	-3	*1-149	**34**	5.0
1939 Bos-A★	124	467	130	168	31	10	**35**	105	89	72	4	3	.360	**.464**	**.694**	**1.158**	185	**62**	150	**12.46**	-2	*1-123/P-1	30	4.5
1940 Bos-A★	144	515	106	153	30	4	36	119	101	87	4	7	.297	.412	.581	.993	148	37	124	8.64	0	1-95,C-42/3-1	24	3.0
1941 Bos-A★	135	487	87	146	27	8	19	105	93	103	2	5	.300	.412	.505	.917	138	28	102	7.46	4	*1-124/3-5,0-1	20	2.0
1942 Bos-A	30	100	18	27	4	0	5	14	18	15	0	0	.270	.392	.460	.852	134	5	20	7.32	5	1-27	4	0.8
Chi-N	70	205	25	42	8	0	3	19	22	55	1	....	.205	.282	.288	.570	70	-8	16	2.46	-4	1-52/C-1	1	-1.8
1944 Chi-N	15	20	0	1	1	0	0	2	2	5	0	....	.050	.136	.100	.236	-33	-4	0	.49	1	/3-2,C-1	0	-0.3
1945 Phi-N	89	224	30	60	11	1	7	38	23	39	0	....	.268	.336	.420	.756	112	4	32	5.21	-2	1-40,3-14/P-9	8	0.7
Total 20	2317	8134	1751	2646	458	125	534	1922	1452	1311	87	72	.325	.428	.609	1.038	161	761	2191	10.22	34	*1-1919,3-141,C-108/0-21,P,S	435	59.9

YEAR TM-L	G	AB	R	H	2B	3B	HR	RBI	BB	SO	SB	CS	AVG	OBP	SLG	OPS	OPS+	BR/A	RC	RC/G	FR	G/POS	WS	TPW
• FOY, Joe	Joseph Anthony Foy b: 2/21/1943, New York, NY d: 10/12/1989, Bronx, NY BR/TR, 6', 215 lbs. Deb: 4/13/1966 Career OF: 5-13-2																							
1966 Bos-A	151	554	97	145	23	8	15	63	91	80	2	5	.262	.368	.413	.781	112	11	86	5.31	-1	*3-139,S-13	22	1.2
1967*Bos-A	130	446	70	112	22	4	16	49	46	87	8	6	.251	.325	.426	.751	111	6	59	4.45	-8	*3-118/O-1	13	-0.2
1968 Bos-A	150	515	65	116	18	2	10	60	84	91	26	8	.225	.338	.326	.665	96	3	64	4.02	2	*3-147/O-3(3-0-0)	19	0.6
1969 KC-A	145	519	72	136	19	2	11	71	74	75	37	15	.262	.360	.370	.729	104	6	73	4.68	-6	*3-113,1-16,O-16(2-13-1)/S,2	16	-0.2
1970 NY-N	99	322	39	76	12	0	6	37	68	58	22	13	.236	.376	.329	.705	90	-2	45	4.55	8	3-97	10	0.6
1971 Was-A	41	128	12	30	8	0	0	11	27	14	4	1	.234	.368	.297	.665	96	1	16	4.08	-1	3-37/2-3,S-1	4	0.1
Total 6	716	2484	355	615	102	16	58	291	390	405	99	48	.248	.354	.372	.725	103	27	343	4.59	-5	3-651/O-20,S-19,1-16,2-6	84	2.1
• FRANCO, Julio	Julio Cesar Franco b: 8/23/1958, Hato Mayor, Dominican Republic BR/TR, 6', 165 lbs. Deb: 4/23/1982																							
1982 Phi-N	16	29	3	8	1	0	0	3	2	4	0	2	.276	.323	.310	.633	76	-2	2	2.31	-0	S-11/3-2	0	-0.1
1983 Cle-A	149	560	68	153	24	8	8	80	27	50	32	12	.273	.309	.388	.696	87	-9	61	3.68	-16	*S-149	12	-0.9
1984 Cle-A	160	658	82	188	22	5	3	79	43	68	19	10	.286	.335	.348	.683	88	-10	73	3.84	8	*S-159/D-1	17	1.5
1985 Cle-A	160	636	97	183	33	4	6	90	54	74	13	9	.288	.347	.381	.728	100	-0	79	4.27	-5	*S-151/2-8,D-1	16	1.0
1986 Cle-A	149	599	80	183	30	5	10	74	32	66	10	7	.306	.341	.422	.763	108	5	76	4.51	2	*S-134,2-13/D-3	18	2.1
1987 Cle-A	128	495	86	158	24	3	8	52	57	56	32	9	.319	.393	.428	.821	117	17	82	5.91	-8	*S-111/2-9,D-8	14	2.0
1988 Cle-A	152	613	88	186	23	6	10	54	56	72	25	11	.303	.364	.409	.773	113	12	90	5.26	-5	*2-151/D-1	22	1.1
1989 Tex-A★	150	548	80	173	31	5	13	92	66	69	21	3	.316	.390	.462	.852	137	31	95	6.26	-4	*2-140,D-10	30	3.1
1990 Tex-A★	157	582	96	172	27	1	11	69	82	83	31	10	.296	.384	.402	.786	120	21	95	5.91	-2	*2-152/D-3	27	2.4
1991 Tex-A★	146	589	108	201	27	3	15	78	65	78	36	9	**.341**	.409	.474	.883	146	43	118	7.72	-25	*2-146	28	2.2
1992 Tex-A	35	107	19	25	7	0	2	8	15	17	1	1	.234	.328	.355	.683	95	-1	12	3.85	-2	D-15/2-9,O-4(4-0-1)	2	-0.3
1993 Tex-A	144	532	85	154	31	3	14	84	62	95	9	3	.289	.365	.438	.803	119	16	85	5.58	0	*D-140	18	0.6
1994 Chi-A	112	433	72	138	19	2	20	98	62	75	8	1	.319	.410	.510	.920	138	28	92	7.87	-1	D-99,1-14	15	1.8
1996*Cle-A	112	432	72	139	20	1	14	76	61	82	8	8	.322	.409	.470	.879	122	15	82	6.92	6	1-97,D-13	13	1.0
1997 Cle-A	78	289	46	82	13	1	3	25	38	75	8	5	.284	.367	.367	.734	89	-4	37	4.46	2	D-42,2-35/1-1	5	-0.2
Mil-A	42	141	22	34	3	0	4	19	31	41	7	1	.241	.382	.348	.729	91	1	22	5.02	1	D-28,1-13	4	-0.1
Yr.	120	430	68	116	16	1	7	44	69	116	15	6	.270	.372	.360	.732	90	-3	59	4.65	3	D-70,2-35,1-14	9	-0.3
1999 TB-A	1	1	0	0	0	0	0	0	0	1	0	0	.000	.000	.000	.000	-99	-0	0	.00	0	/1-1	0	0.0
2001*Atl-N	25	90	13	27	4	0	3	11	10	20	0	0	.300	.376	.444	.821	109	1	15	6.04	1	1-23	3	0.0
2002*Atl-N	125	338	51	96	13	1	6	30	39	75	5	1	.284	.360	.382	.741	95	-1	46	4.74	-1	1-95/D-2	6	-0.9
2003*Atl-N	103	197	28	58	12	2	5	31	25	43	0	1	.294	.374	.452	.826	114	4	31	5.70	1	1-75	6	0.1
Total 19	2144	7869	1196	2358	364	50	155	1053	827	1144	265	103	.300	.369	.418	.787	113	166	1192	5.38	-46	S-715,2-663,D-366,1-319/O-4,3	256	16.4
• FRANCO, Matt	Matthew Neil Franco b: 8/19/1969, Santa Monica, CA BL/TR, 6'2", 200 lbs. Deb: 9/6/1995 Career OF: 34-0-8																							
1995 Chi-N	16	17	3	5	1	0	0	1	0	4	0	0	.294	.294	.353	.647	71	-1	2	3.97	-1	/2-3,1-1,3-1	0	-0.2
1996 NY-N	14	31	3	6	1	0	1	2	1	5	0	0	.194	.242	.323	.565	50	-2	2	2.27	-1	/3-8,1-2	0	-0.3
1997 NY-N	112	163	21	45	5	0	5	21	13	23	1	0	.276	.330	.399	.728	93	-2	21	4.61	1	3-39,1-13/D-1,O-1	4	-0.1
1998 NY-N	103	161	20	44	7	2	1	13	23	26	0	1	.273	.368	.360	.728	94	-1	20	4.24	0	3-13,O-13(12-0-1),1-11/D-2	3	-0.2
1999*NY-N	122	132	18	31	5	0	4	21	28	21	0	0	.235	.369	.364	.732	89	-1	17	4.16	2	1-19,O-18(15-0-3),3-12/D-4,P	3	-0.2
2000*NY-N	101	134	9	32	4	0	2	14	21	22	0	0	.239	.342	.313	.655	70	-6	15	3.83	-1	1-28,3-22/O-3(3-0-0),D-2,2	3	-0.7
2002*Atl-N	81	205	25	65	15	4	6	30	27	31	1	0	.317	.397	.517	.914	137	12	42	7.84	-2	1-51/O-4(2-0-2)	9	0.6
2003*Atl-N	112	134	11	33	5	0	3	15	11	26	0	1	.246	.303	.351	.654	70	-7	14	3.36	-1	1-15/D-3,O-3(1-0-2)	1	-0.9
Total 8	661	977	110	261	43	6	22	117	124	158	2	2	.267	.351	.391	.742	94	-8	133	4.72	-3	1-140/3-95,O-42,D-12,2-4,P	23	-1.9
• FRANCONA, Terry	Terry Jon Francona b: 4/22/1959, Aberdeen, SD BL/TL, 6'1", 190 lbs. Deb: 8/19/1981 M/C Career OF: 104-6-100																							
1981*Mon-N	34	95	11	26	0	1	1	8	5	6	1	0	.274	.317	.326	.643	82	-2	11	3.97	0	O-26(24-0-2)/1-1	3	-0.3
1982 Mon-N	46	131	14	42	3	0	0	9	8	11	2	3	.321	.360	.344	.703	96	-1	16	4.32	-5	O-33(30-1-3),1-16	3	-0.8
1983 Mon-N	120	230	21	59	11	1	3	22	6	20	0	2	.257	.275	.352	.628	73	-10	20	2.90	-1	O-51(13-3-37),1-47	2	-1.5
1984 Mon-N	58	214	18	74	19	2	1	18	5	12	0	0	.346	.364	.467	.831	138	9	35	6.41	8	1-50/O-6(5-0-2)	8	1.5
1985 Mon-N	107	281	19	75	15	1	2	31	12	12	5	5	.267	.299	.349	.648	86	-8	29	3.63	3	1-57,O-28(5-0-24)/3-1	6	-0.9
1986 Chi-N	86	124	13	31	3	0	2	8	6	8	0	1	.250	.290	.323	.613	64	-7	11	2.99	-1	O-30(20-2-10),1-23	1	-0.9
1987 Cin-N	102	207	16	47	5	0	3	12	10	12	2	0	.227	.266	.295	.561	46	-16	16	2.56	5	1-57/O-8(2-0-6)	1	-1.4
1988 Cle-A	62	212	24	66	8	0	1	12	5	18	0	0	.311	.327	.363	.690	91	-3	24	4.26	1	D-38/1-5,O-5(5-0-0)	5	-0.4
1989 Mil-A	90	233	26	54	10	1	3	23	8	20	2	1	.232	.257	.322	.579	63	-12	18	2.66	0	1-46,D-23,O-16(0-0-16)/P-1	3	-1.6
1990 Mil-A	3	4	1	0	0	0	0	0	0	0	0	0	.000	.000	.000	.000	-101	-1	0	.00	0	/1-2,D-1	0	-0.1
Total 10	708	1731	163	474	74	6	16	143	65	119	12	12	.274	.302	.351	.653	82	-52	179	3.65	10	1-304,O-203/D-62,3-1,P-1	32	-6.5
• FRANCONA, Tito	John Patsy Francona b: 11/4/1933, Aliquippa, PA BL/TL, 5'11", 190 lbs. Deb: 4/17/1956 Career OF: 546-105-299																							
1956 Bal-A	139	445	62	115	16	4	9	57	51	60	11	5	.258	.336	.373	.709	94	-3	58	4.55	1	*O-122(1-41-97),1-21	12	-0.7
1957 Bal-A	97	279	35	65	8	3	7	38	29	48	7	3	.233	.312	.358	.670	88	-4	31	3.68	-2	O-73(28-2-55)/1-4	6	-0.9
1958 Chi-A	41	128	10	33	3	2	1	10	14	24	2	3	.258	.331	.336	.667	86	-3	13	3.54	1	O-35(7-0-32)	3	-0.3
Det-A	45	69	11	17	5	0	0	10	15	16	0	0	.246	.381	.319	.700	88	-0	9	4.49	0	O-18(11-0-9)/1-1	2	-0.1
Yr.	86	197	21	50	8	2	1	20	29	40	2	3	.254	.350	.330	.680	87	-3	22	3.86	0	O-53(18-0-41)/1-1	5	-0.4
1959 Cle-A	122	399	68	145	17	2	20	79	35	42	2	0	.363	.419	.566	.985	174	40	93	9.26	-2	O-64(4-61-0),1-35	27	3.4
1960 Cle-A	147	544	84	159	**36**	2	17	79	67	67	4	1	.292	.375	.460	.835	128	23	96	6.39	-5	*O-138(138-0-1),1-13	24	0.9
1961 Cle-A★	155	592	87	178	30	8	16	85	56	52	2	1	.301	.365	.459	.824	122	18	100	6.13	-4	*O-138(138-0-0),1-14	21	0.6
1962 Cle-A	158	621	82	169	28	5	14	70	47	74	3	2	.272	.330	.401	.731	99	-2	84	4.75	6	*1-158	18	-0.6
1963 Cle-A	142	500	57	114	29	0	10	41	47	77	9	1	.228	.297	.346	.643	80	-12	52	3.53	-7	*O-122(121-0-1),1-11	10	-2.8
1964 Cle-A	111	270	35	67	13	2	8	24	44	46	1	3	.248	.362	.400	.762	112	5	41	5.22	-3	O-69(1-1-68),1-17	9	-0.1
1965 StL-N	81	174	15	45	6	2	5	19	17	30	0	0	.259	.325	.402	.727	95	-1	23	4.54	-2	O-34(1-0-34),1-13	4	-0.5
1966 StL-N	83	156	14	33	4	1	4	17	7	27	0	0	.212	.250	.327	.577	59	-9	13	2.81	1	1-30/O-9(9-0-0)	1	-1.0
1967 Phi-N	27	73	7	15	1	0	0	3	7	10	0	1	.205	.275	.219	.494	43	-6	4	1.85	1	1-24/O-1	0	-0.6
Atl-N	82	254	28	63	5	1	6	25	20	34	1	0	.248	.305	.346	.652	87	-4	27	3.58	2	1-56/O-6(5-0-1)	5	-0.5
Yr.	109	327	35	78	6	1	6	28	27	44	1	1	.239	.299	.318	.617	77	-9	31	3.17	4	1-80/O-7(5-0-2)	5	-1.1
1968 Atl-N	122	346	32	99	13	1	2	47	51	45	3	0	.286	.378	.347	.725	118	11	47	4.80	-3	O-65(65-0-0),1-33	12	0.4
1969 Atl-N	51	88	5	26	1	0	2	22	13	10	0	1	.295	.386	.375	.761	114	2	13	5.31	0	O-15(15-0-0)/1-7	4	0.1
Oak-A	32	85	12	29	6	1	3	20	12	11	0	0	.341	.423	.541	.964	175	9	21	9.57	-1	1-19/O-1	6	0.6
1970 Oak-A	32	33	2	8	0	0	1	6	6	6	0	0	.242	.375	.333	.708	100	0	4	3.16	1	/1-6,O-1	0	0.1
Mil-A	52	65	4	15	3	0	0	4	6	15	1	0	.231	.296	.277	.573	58	-3	6	3.12	1	1-13	1	-0.3
Yr.	84	98	6	23	3	0	1	10	12	21	1	0	.235	.324	.296	.620	73	-3	10	3.13	1	1-19/O-1	1	-0.3
Total 15	1719	5121	650	1395	224	34	125	656	544	694	46	21	.272	.346	.403	.749	108	62	734	5.05	-17	O-911,1-475	165	-2.5
• FRANK, Charlie	Charles Frank b: 5/30/1870, Mobile, AL d: 5/24/1922, Memphis, TN BL/TL, 5'10", 170 lbs. Deb: 8/18/1893 Career OF: 117-0-1																							
1893 StL-N	40	164	29	55	6	3	1	17	18	8	8	....	.335	.408	.427	.834	122	5	33	7.92	1	O-40(40-0-0)	5	0.3
1894 StL-N	80	319	52	89	12	7	4	42	44	13	14	....	.279	.372	.398	.770	86	-7	54	6.07	-3	O-77(77-0-1)/1-3,P-2	6	-1.6
Total 2	120	483	81	144	18	10	5	59	62	21	22	....	.298	.384	.408	.792	98	-1	86	6.67	-2	O-117/1-3,P-2	11	-1.3
• FRANK, Fred	Frederick Frank b: 3/11/1874, Louisa, KY d: 3/27/1950, Ashland, KY Deb: 9/27/1898																							
1898 Cle-N	17	53	3	11	1	1	0	3	4	....	1	....	.208	.276	.264	.540	56	-3	4	2.68	2	O-17(0-6-11)	1	-0.2
• FRANK, Mike	Stephen Michael Frank b: 1/14/1974, Pomona, CA BL/TL, 6'2" Deb: 6/19/1998																							
1998 Cin-N	28	89	14	20	6	0	0	7	7	12	0	0	.225	.281	.292	.573	51	-6	7	2.58	-1	O-28(1-25-2)	2	-0.7
• FRANKLIN,	Franklin Deb: 9/27/1884																							
1884 Was-U	1	3	0	0	0	0	0	....	0	....	....	....	.000	.000	.000	.000	-103	-1	0	.00	0	/O-1	0	0.0
• FRANKLIN, Micah	Micah Ishanti Franklin b: 4/25/1972, San Francisco, CA BB/TR, 6', 205 lbs. Deb: 5/13/1997																							
1997 StL-N	17	34	6	11	0	0	2	2	3	10	0	0	.324	.378	.500	.878	129	1	7	7.90	-1	O-13(4-0-9)	1	0.0
• FRANKLIN, Moe	Murray Asher Franklin b: 4/1/1914, Chicago, IL d: 3/16/1978, Harbor City, CA BR/TR, 6', 175 lbs. Deb: 8/12/1941																							
1941 Det-A	13	10	1	3	1	0	0	0	2	2	0	0	.300	.417	.400	.817	106	0	2	5.20	-2	/S-4,3-1	0	-0.1

YEAR TM-L	G	AB	R	H	2B	3B	HR	RBI	BB	SO	SB	CS	AVG	OBP	SLG	OPS	OPS+	BR/A	RC	RC/G	FR	G/POS	WS	TPW
1942 Det-A	48	154	24	40	7	0	2	16	7	5	0	0	.260	.301	.344	.645	75	-5	16	3.63	-4	S-32/2-7	3	-0.7
Total 2	61	164	25	43	8	0	2	16	9	7	0	0	.262	.309	.348	.656	77	-5	18	3.73	-6	/S-36,2-7,3-1	3	-0.9

• FRANKS, Herman Herman Louis Franks b: 1/4/1914, Price, UT BL/TR, 5'10.5", 187 lbs. Deb: 4/27/1939 M/C

YEAR TM-L	G	AB	R	H	2B	3B	HR	RBI	BB	SO	SB	CS	AVG	OBP	SLG	OPS	OPS+	BR/A	RC	RC/G	FR	G/POS	WS	TPW
1939 StL-N	17	17	1	1	0	0	0	3	3	3	0	....	.059	.200	.059	.259	-26	-3	0	.49	-1	C-13	0	-0.3
1940 Bro-N	65	131	11	24	4	0	1	14	20	6	2	....	.183	.296	.237	.533	46	-9	10	2.39	1	C-43	2	-0.6
1941★Bro-N	57	139	10	28	7	0	1	11	14	13	0	....	.201	.275	.273	.548	52	-9	11	2.67	0	C-54/0-1	3	-0.7
1947 Phi-A	8	15	2	3	0	1	0	1	4	4	0	0	.200	.368	.333	.702	94	0	2	4.04	-0	/C-4	0	0.0
1948 Phi-A	40	98	10	22	7	1	1	14	16	11	0	0	.224	.345	.347	.692	84	-2	12	4.01	2	C-27	3	0.2
1949 NY-N	1	3	1	2	0	0	0	0	0	0	0	....	.667	.667	.667	1.333	259	1	1	36.00	0	/C-1	0	0.1
Total 6	188	403	35	80	18	2	3	43	57	37	2	0	.199	.302	.275	.578	58	-22	37	2.94	3	C-142/0-1	8	-1.3

• FRAZIER, Joe Joseph Filmore Frazier b: 10/6/1922, Liberty, NC BL/TR, 6', 180 lbs. Deb: 8/31/1947 M Career OF: 7-0-48

YEAR TM-L	G	AB	R	H	2B	3B	HR	RBI	BB	SO	SB	CS	AVG	OBP	SLG	OPS	OPS+	BR/A	RC	RC/G	FR	G/POS	WS	TPW
1947 Cle-A	9	14	1	1	1	0	0	0	1	1	0	0	.071	.133	.143	.276	-24	-2	0	.30	0	/O-5(0-0-5)	0	-0.3
1954 StL-N	81	88	8	26	5	2	3	18	13	17	0	0	.295	.392	.500	.892	129	4	18	7.69	-1	O-11(2-0-8)/1-1	3	0.3
1955 StL-N	58	70	12	14	1	0	4	9	6	12	0	0	.200	.273	.386	.658	72	-3	7	3.01	0	O-14(1-0-13)	1	-0.4
1956 StL-N	14	19	1	4	2	0	1	4	3	3	0	1	.211	.318	.474	.792	109	-0	3	4.50	0	/O-3(0-0-3)	1	-0.1
Cin-N	10	17	2	4	0	0	1	2	1	7	0	0	.235	.278	.412	.690	77	-1	2	3.11	-1	/O-4(4-0-0)	0	-0.1
Yr.	24	36	3	8	2	0	2	6	4	10	0	1	.222	.300	.444	.744	95	-1	4	3.85	-1	/O-7(4-0-3)	1	-0.2
Bal-A	45	74	7	19	6	0	1	12	11	6	0	0	.257	.360	.378	.739	103	1	10	4.83	1	O-19(0-0-19)	2	0.1
Total 4	217	282	31	68	15	2	10	45	35	46	0	1	.241	.331	.415	.746	97	-1	40	4.74	-2	/O-56,1-1	7	-0.5

• FRAZIER, Lou Arthur Louis Frazier b: 1/26/1965, St. Louis, MO BB/TR, 6'2", 175 lbs. Deb: 4/8/1993 Career OF: 148-35-7

YEAR TM-L	G	AB	R	H	2B	3B	HR	RBI	BB	SO	SB	CS	AVG	OBP	SLG	OPS	OPS+	BR/A	RC	RC/G	FR	G/POS	WS	TPW
1993 Mon-N	112	189	27	54	7	1	1	16	16	24	17	2	.286	.341	.349	.691	82	-2	25	4.68	1	O-60(52-7-2)/1-8,2-1	6	-0.3
1994 Mon-N	76	140	25	38	3	1	0	14	18	23	20	4	.271	.358	.307	.666	75	-2	19	4.78	-1	O-36(31-5-0)/2-6,1-1	5	-0.4
1995 Mon-N	35	63	6	12	2	0	0	3	8	12	4	0	.190	.301	.222	.524	39	-4	5	2.78	-1	O-25(10-11-5)/2-1	1	-0.6
Tex-A	49	99	19	21	2	0	0	8	7	20	9	1	.212	.278	.232	.510	34	-8	8	2.47	0	O-47(43-6-0)/D-2	1	-0.9
1996 Tex-A	30	50	5	13	2	1	0	5	8	10	4	2	.260	.373	.340	.713	78	-1	7	4.23	0	O-15(12-3-0),D-13/2-1	1	-0.2
1998 Chi-A	7	7	0	0	0	0	0	0	2	6	4	0	.000	.222	.000	.222	-36	-0	1	2.11	-0	/O-3(0-3-0)	0	0.0
Total 5	309	548	82	138	16	3	1	46	59	95	58	9	.252	.331	.297	.629	64	-18	65	3.97	-2	O-186/D-15,1-9,2-9	14	-2.4

• FREDERICK, Johnny John Henry Frederick b: 1/26/1902, Denver, CO d: 6/18/1977, Tigard, OR BL/TL, 5'11", 165 lbs. Deb: 4/18/1929 Career OF: 33-503-196

YEAR TM-L	G	AB	R	H	2B	3B	HR	RBI	BB	SO	SB	CS	AVG	OBP	SLG	OPS	OPS+	BR/A	RC	RC/G	FR	G/POS	WS	TPW
1929 Bro-N	148	628	127	206	**52**	6	24	75	39	34	6	....	.328	.372	.545	.917	126	23	122	7.35	-2	*O-143(0-143-0)	22	1.3
1930 Bro-N	142	616	120	206	44	11	17	76	46	34	1	....	.334	.383	.524	.908	118	17	120	7.44	8	*O-142(0-142-0)	24	1.7
1931 Bro-N	146	611	81	165	34	8	17	71	31	46	2	....	.270	.312	.435	.747	99	-3	84	4.86	0	*O-145(0-145-0)	16	-0.7
1932 Bro-N	118	384	54	115	28	2	16	56	25	35	1	....	.299	.349	.508	.856	129	15	69	6.62	-0	O-88(1-47-39)	15	1.1
1933 Bro-N	147	556	65	171	22	7	7	64	36	14	9	....	.308	.355	.410	.765	123	16	84	5.72	-10	*O-138(10-26-102)	19	-0.1
1934 Bro-N	104	307	51	91	20	1	4	35	33	13	4	....	.296	.370	.407	.777	114	7	49	5.95	4	O-77(22-0-55)/1-1	9	0.7
Total 6	805	3102	498	954	200	35	85	377	210	176	23	....	.308	.357	.477	.833	118	74	527	6.33	-1	O-733/1-1	105	4.0

• FREED, Ed Edwin Charles Freed b: 8/22/1919, Centre Valley, PA d: 11/15/2002, Rock Hill, SC BR/TR, 5'6", 165 lbs. Deb: 9/11/1942

YEAR TM-L	G	AB	R	H	2B	3B	HR	RBI	BB	SO	SB	CS	AVG	OBP	SLG	OPS	OPS+	BR/A	RC	RC/G	FR	G/POS	WS	TPW
1942 Phi-N	13	33	3	10	3	1	0	1	4	3	1	....	.303	.378	.455	.833	151	2	6	6.12	1	O-11(3-7-1)	1	0.3

• FREED, Roger Roger Vernon Freed b: 6/2/1946, Los Angeles, CA d: 1/9/1996, Chino, CA BR/TR, 6', 190 lbs. Deb: 9/18/1970 Career OF: 11-0-155

YEAR TM-L	G	AB	R	H	2B	3B	HR	RBI	BB	SO	SB	CS	AVG	OBP	SLG	OPS	OPS+	BR/A	RC	RC/G	FR	G/POS	WS	TPW
1970 Bal-A	4	13	0	2	0	0	0	1	3	4	0	0	.154	.313	.154	.466	32	-1	1	2.18	0	/1-3,0-1	0	-0.1
1971 Phi-N	118	348	23	77	12	1	6	37	44	86	0	3	.221	.314	.313	.627	78	-10	35	3.30	-1	*O-106(7-0-99)/C-1	6	-1.8
1972 Phi-N	73	129	10	29	4	0	6	18	23	39	0	1	.225	.346	.395	.742	108	2	18	4.62	3	O-46(1-0-45)	4	0.3
1974 Cin-N	6	6	1	2	0	0	1	3	1	1	0	0	.333	.429	.833	1.262	251	1	2	8.12	0	/1-1	1	0.1
1976 Mon-N	8	15	0	3	1	0	0	1	0	3	0	0	.200	.200	.267	.467	30	-1	1	1.80	0	/1-3,0-1	0	-0.2
1977 StL-N	49	83	10	33	2	1	5	21	11	9	0	0	.398	.468	.627	1.095	194	11	24	12.47	0	1-18/O-6(0-0-7)	6	1.0
1978 StL-N	52	92	3	22	6	0	2	20	8	17	1	0	.239	.300	.370	.670	87	-2	10	3.81	1	1-15/O-6(3-0-3)	2	-0.2
1979 StL-N	34	31	2	8	2	0	2	8	5	7	0	0	.258	.361	.516	.877	135	2	6	6.49	-0	/1-1	1	0.1
Total 8	344	717	49	176	27	2	22	109	95	166	1	4	.245	.337	.381	.718	100	1	97	4.58	2	O-166/1-41,C-1	20	-0.6

• FREEHAN, Bill William Ashley Freehan b: 11/29/1941, Detroit, MI BR/TR, 6'3", 205 lbs. Deb: 9/26/1961 Career OF: 1-0-1

YEAR TM-L	G	AB	R	H	2B	3B	HR	RBI	BB	SO	SB	CS	AVG	OBP	SLG	OPS	OPS+	BR/A	RC	RC/G	FR	G/POS	WS	TPW
1961 Det-A	4	10	1	4	0	0	0	4	1	0	0	0	.400	.455	.400	.855	126	0	2	8.71	1	/C-3	1	0.1
1963 Det-A	100	300	37	73	12	2	9	36	39	56	2	0	.243	.334	.387	.721	98	0	40	4.47	0	C-73,1-19	10	0.3
1964 Det-A★	144	520	69	156	14	8	18	80	36	68	5	1	.300	.355	.462	.816	123	16	86	6.09	4	*C-141/1-1	25	2.9
1965 Det-A★	130	431	45	101	15	0	10	43	39	63	4	2	.234	.308	.339	.647	83	-9	45	3.50	-0	*C-129	14	-0.3
1966 Det-A★	136	492	47	115	22	0	12	46	40	72	5	2	.234	.295	.352	.647	83	-10	50	3.41	2	*C-132/1-5	16	-0.2
1967 Det-A★	155	517	66	146	23	1	20	74	73	71	1	2	.282	.392	.447	.839	143	32	94	6.54	-5	*C-147,1-11	30	3.7
1968★Det-A★	155	540	73	142	24	2	25	84	65	64	0	1	.263	.367	.454	.821	143	31	94	6.13	2	*C-138,1-21/O-1	35	4.4
1969 Det-A★	143	489	61	128	16	3	16	49	53	55	1	2	.262	.344	.405	.749	104	3	68	4.83	-1	*C-120,1-20	20	0.6
1970 Det-A★	117	395	44	95	17	3	16	52	52	48	0	3	.241	.335	.420	.755	106	2	55	4.60	-5	*C-114	16	0.3
1971 Det-A★	148	516	57	143	26	4	21	71	54	48	2	7	.277	.356	.465	.821	126	15	82	5.54	-7	*C-144/O-1	25	1.7
1972★Det-A★	111	374	51	98	18	2	10	56	48	51	0	1	.262	.355	.401	.756	121	11	55	5.22	2	*C-105/1-1	20	2.0
1973 Det-A★	110	380	33	89	10	1	6	29	40	30	0	0	.234	.325	.313	.638	75	-11	39	3.42	5	C-98/1-7,D-3	12	-0.1
1974 Det-A	130	445	58	132	17	5	18	60	42	44	2	0	.297	.364	.479	.842	136	21	77	6.19	4	1-65,C-63/D-1	23	2.4
1975 Det-A★	120	427	42	105	17	3	14	47	32	56	2	0	.246	.308	.398	.706	94	-4	51	4.12	-1	*C-113/1-5	13	0.1
1976 Det-A	71	237	22	64	10	1	5	27	12	27	0	0	.270	.308	.384	.692	98	-1	28	4.12	1	C-61/D-3,1-2	7	0.3
Total 15	1774	6073	706	1591	241	35	200	758	626	753	24	21	.262	.342	.412	.754	112	97	867	4.95	2	*C-1581,1-157/D-7,O-2	267	18.1

• FREEL, Ryan Ryan Paul Freel b: 3/8/1976, Jacksonville, FL BR/TR, 5'10", 185 lbs. Deb: 4/4/2001 Career OF: 6-20-0

YEAR TM-L	G	AB	R	H	2B	3B	HR	RBI	BB	SO	SB	CS	AVG	OBP	SLG	OPS	OPS+	BR/A	RC	RC/G	FR	G/POS	WS	TPW
2001 Tor-A	9	22	1	6	1	0	0	3	1	4	2	1	.273	.333	.318	.652	71	-1	2	3.97	1	/2-7,O-1	0	0.0
2003 Cin-N	43	137	23	39	6	1	4	12	9	13	9	4	.285	.347	.431	.777	103	1	21	5.19	-3	O-24(5-20-0),2-11/3-2	3	-0.2
Total 2	52	159	24	45	7	1	4	15	10	17	11	5	.283	.345	.415	.760	99	-0	23	5.02	-2	/O-25,2-18,3-2	3	-0.2

• FREEMAN, Buck John Frank Freeman
b: 10/30/1871, Catasauqua, PA d: 6/25/1949, Wilkes-Barre, PA BL/TL, 5'9", 169 lbs. Deb: 6/27/1891 U Career OF: 16-7-814 ♦

YEAR TM-L	G	AB	R	H	2B	3B	HR	RBI	BB	SO	SB	CS	AVG	OBP	SLG	OPS	OPS+	BR/A	RC	RC/G	FR	G/POS	WS	TPW
1891 Was-a	5	18	1	4	1	0	0	1	2	2	0	....	.222	.300	.278	.578	68	0	2	2.91	0	/P-5	2	0.2
1898 Was-N	29	107	19	39	2	3	3	21	7	....	2	....	.364	.424	.523	.947	171	10	25	9.71	1	O-29(0-0-29)	4	0.9
1899 Was-N	155	588	107	187	19	25	**25**	122	23	....	21	....	.318	.362	.563	.925	154	37	131	8.56	-17	*O-155(0-0-155)/P-2	25	0.9
1900 Bos-N	117	418	58	126	19	13	6	65	25	....	10	....	.301	.355	.452	.808	109	3	73	6.48	-8	O-91(16-3-72),1-19	10	-0.9
1901 Bos-A	129	490	88	166	23	15	12	114	44	....	17	....	.339	.400	.520	.920	157	37	112	8.96	-4	*1-128/2-1,O-1	24	2.7
1902 Bos-A	138	564	75	174	38	19	11	**121**	32	....	17	....	.309	.352	.502	.854	131	21	109	7.28	2	*O-138(0-0-138)	23	1.5
1903★Bos-A	141	567	74	163	39	20	**13**	**104**	30	....	5	....	.287	.328	.496	.823	137	23	97	6.20	-5	*O-141(0-0-141)	24	1.2
1904 Bos-A	157	597	64	167	20	**19**	7	84	32	....	7	....	.280	.329	.412	.741	126	17	87	5.20	-9	*O-157(0-0-157)	25	0.0
1905 Bos-A	130	455	59	109	20	8	3	49	46	....	8	....	.240	.316	.338	.655	106	4	54	4.01	-11	1-66,O-57(0-1-56)/3-2	13	-1.1
1906 Bos-A	121	392	42	98	18	9	1	30	28	....	5	....	.250	.302	.349	.651	104	1	46	3.92	3	O-65(0-3-62),1-43/3-4	9	0.0
1907 Bos-A	4	12	1	2	0	0	1	2	3	....	0	....	.167	.333	.417	.750	140	1	2	4.53	-0	/O-3(0-0-3)	1	0.1
Total 11	1126	4208	588	1235	199	131	82	713	272	2	92	....	.293	.346	.462	.808	131	154	737	6.41	-50	O-837,1-256/P-7,3-6,2-1	160	5.5

• FREEMAN, Jerry Frank Ellsworth "Buck" Freeman b: 12/26/1879, Placerville, CA d: 9/30/1952, Los Angeles, CA BL/TR, 6'2", 220 lbs. Deb: 4/14/1908

YEAR TM-L	G	AB	R	H	2B	3B	HR	RBI	BB	SO	SB	CS	AVG	OBP	SLG	OPS	OPS+	BR/A	RC	RC/G	FR	G/POS	WS	TPW
1908 Was-A	154	531	45	134	15	5	1	45	36	....	6	....	.252	.304	.305	.609	107	4	50	3.21	-17	*1-154	11	-1.8
1909 Was-A	19	48	2	8	0	1	0	3	4	....	3	....	.167	.245	.208	.454	46	-3	3	2.04	-2	1-14/O-1	0	-0.6
Total 2	173	579	47	142	15	6	1	48	40	....	9	....	.245	.299	.297	.596	101	1	54	3.10	-19	1-168/O-1	11	-2.4

• FREEMAN, John John Edward Freeman b: 1/24/1901, Boston, MA d: 4/14/1958, Washington, DC BR/TR, 5'8", 160 lbs. Deb: 6/17/1927

YEAR TM-L	G	AB	R	H	2B	3B	HR	RBI	BB	SO	SB	CS	AVG	OBP	SLG	OPS	OPS+	BR/A	RC	RC/G	FR	G/POS	WS	TPW
1927 Bos-A	4	2	0	0	0	0	0	0	0	0	0	0	.000	.000	.000	.000	-102	-1	0	.00	-1	/O-3(1-2-0)	0	-0.1

YEAR TM-L	G	AB	R	H	2B	3B	HR	RBI	BB	SO	SB	CS	AVG	OBP	SLG	OPS	OPS+	BR/A	RC	RC/G	FR	G/POS	WS	TPW
• FREEMAN, La Vel																								
La Vel Maurice Freeman b: 2/18/1963, Oakland, CA BL/TL, 5'9", 170 lbs. Deb: 4/7/1989																								
1989 Mil-A	2	3	1	0	0	0	0	0	0	2	0	0	.000	.000	.000	.000	-101	-1	0	.00	0	/D-2	0	-0.1
• FREESE, Gene																								
Eugene Lewis "Augie" Freese b: 1/8/1934, Wheeling, WV BR/TR, 5'11", 175 lbs. Deb: 4/13/1955 Career OF: 11-0-1																								
1955 Pit-N	134	455	69	115	21	8	14	44	34	57	5	1	.253	.310	.426	.737	94	-4	60	4.38	-9	3-65,2-57	13	-0.9
1956 Pit-N	65	207	17	43	9	0	3	14	16	45	2	1	.208	.274	.295	.569	54	-13	18	2.89	-2	3-47,2-26	3	-1.4
1957 Pit-N	114	346	44	98	18	2	6	31	17	42	9	4	.283	.321	.399	.719	95	-3	44	4.55	-3	3-74,2-10,0-10(10-0-0)	8	-0.6
1958 Pit-N	17	18	1	3	0	0	1	2	1	2	0	0	.167	.211	.333	.544	42	-2	1	1.67	0	/3-1	0	-0.1
StL-N	62	191	28	49	11	1	6	16	10	32	1	1	.257	.294	.419	.712	83	-6	24	4.39	-11	S-28,2-14/3-3	3	-1.4
Yr.	79	209	29	52	11	1	7	18	11	34	1	1	.249	.286	.411	.698	79	-7	25	4.12	-11	S-28,2-14/3-4	3	-1.6
1959 Phi-N	132	400	60	107	14	5	23	70	43	61	8	4	.268	.346	.500	.846	120	11	69	5.93	-17	*3-109/2-6	15	-0.6
1960 Chi-A	127	455	60	124	32	6	17	79	29	65	10	6	.273	.318	.481	.799	114	6	64	4.67	-3	*3-122	14	0.2
1961*Cin-N	152	575	78	159	27	2	26	87	27	78	8	2	.277	.309	.466	.775	101	-1	77	4.75	-8	*3-151/2-1	17	-0.9
1962 Cin-N	18	42	2	6	1	0	0	1	6	8	0	0	.143	.250	.167	.417	14	-5	2	1.19	0	3-10	0	-0.5
1963 Cin-N	66	217	20	53	9	1	6	26	17	42	4	2	.244	.305	.378	.683	93	-2	26	4.03	0	3-62/0-1	6	-0.2
1964 Pit-N	99	289	33	65	13	2	9	40	19	45	1	2	.225	.273	.377	.650	81	-8	28	3.05	-6	3-72	4	-1.5
1965 Pit-N	43	80	6	21	4	0	0	8	6	18	0	2	.263	.330	.313	.642	82	-3	7	2.72	-2	3-19	1	-0.5
Chi-A	17	32	2	9	0	1	1	4	5	9	0	0	.281	.378	.438	.816	140	2	6	6.56	-1	/3-8	2	0.0
1966 Chi-A	48	106	8	22	2	0	3	10	8	20	2	1	.208	.270	.311	.581	71	-4	9	2.86	0	3-34	2	-0.5
Hou-N	21	33	1	3	0	0	0	0	5	11	1	0	.091	.211	.091	.301	-13	-5	1	.77	-1	/3-4,2-3,0-1	0	-0.5
Total 12	1115	3446	429	877	161	28	115	432	243	535	51	26	.254	.307	.418	.725	94	-36	434	4.27	-63	3-781,2-117/S-28,0-12	88	-9.4
• FREESE, George																								
George Walter "Bud" Freese b: 9/12/1926, Wheeling, WV BR/TR, 6', 190 lbs. Deb: 4/29/1953 C																								
1953 Det-A	1	1	0	0	0	0	0	0	0	0	0	0	.000	.000	.000	.000	-101	-0	0	.00	0	....	0	0.0
1955 Pit-N	51	179	17	46	8	2	3	22	17	18	1	1	.257	.328	.374	.703	87	-3	21	3.89	-9	3-50	4	-1.3
1961 Chi-N	9	7	0	2	0	0	0	1	1	4	0	0	.286	.375	.286	.661	78	-0	1	4.58	0	....	0	0.0
Total 3	61	187	17	48	8	2	3	23	18	22	1	1	.257	.329	.369	.697	86	-4	22	3.89	-9	/3-50	4	-1.3
• FREGOSI, Jim																								
James Louis Fregosi b: 4/4/1942, San Francisco, CA BR/TR, 6'1", 190 lbs. Deb: 9/14/1961 M Career OF: 8-0-0																								
1961 LA-A	11	27	7	6	0	0	0	3	1	4	0	0	.222	.250	.222	.472	24	-3	1	1.32	-1	S-11	0	-0.3
1962 LA-A	58	175	15	51	3	4	3	23	18	27	2	1	.291	.358	.406	.763	108	2	25	5.21	-2	S-52	7	0.5
1963 LA-A	154	592	83	170	29	12	9	50	36	104	2	2	.287	.328	.422	.750	115	10	81	4.86	-7	*S-151	20	1.7
1964 LA-A★	147	505	86	140	22	9	18	72	72	87	8	3	.277	.372	.463	.835	145	33	89	6.14	2	*S-137	28	4.8
1965 Cal-A	161	602	66	167	19	7	15	64	54	107	13	5	.277	.341	.407	.748	114	12	85	4.87	-2	*S-160	24	2.5
1966 Cal-A★	162	611	78	154	32	7	13	67	67	89	17	8	.252	.328	.391	.719	109	8	80	4.37	9	*S-162/1-1	26	3.4
1967 Cal-A★	151	590	75	171	23	6	9	56	49	77	9	6	.290	.349	.395	.744	124	17	82	5.00	-5	*S-151	28	2.8
1968 Cal-A★	159	614	77	150	21	**13**	9	49	60	101	9	4	.244	.317	.365	.681	110	8	72	3.95	-9	*S-159	22	1.4
1969 Cal-A★	161	580	78	151	22	6	12	47	93	86	9	2	.260	.364	.381	.745	114	15	86	5.16	-8	*S-160	26	2.7
1970 Cal-A★	158	601	95	167	33	5	22	82	69	92	0	2	.278	.355	.459	.814	127	21	101	6.05	10	*S-150/1-6	33	5.1
1971 Cal-A	107	347	31	81	15	1	5	33	39	61	2	1	.233	.320	.326	.645	90	-4	39	3.73	-9	S-74,1-18/0-7(7-0-0)	9	-0.6
1972 NY-N	101	340	31	79	15	4	5	32	38	71	0	1	.232	.311	.344	.655	88	-5	37	3.71	3	3-85/S-6,1-3	10	-0.2
1973 NY-N	45	124	7	29	4	1	0	11	20	25	1	2	.234	.340	.282	.623	75	-4	12	3.40	-1	3-17,S-17/1-3,0-1	3	-0.4
Tex-A	45	157	25	42	6	2	6	16	12	31	0	1	.268	.324	.446	.769	120	3	23	5.17	-3	3-34,1-10/S-6	5	-0.1
1974 Tex-A	78	230	31	60	5	0	12	34	22	41	0	1	.261	.325	.439	.765	121	5	29	4.34	-1	1-47,3-32	7	0.1
1975 Tex-A	77	191	25	50	5	0	7	33	20	39	0	1	.262	.335	.398	.733	107	2	24	4.32	0	1-54,D-13/3-4	5	-0.1
1976 Tex-A	58	133	17	31	7	0	2	12	23	33	2	0	.233	.346	.331	.677	97	1	17	4.05	-1	1-26,D-18/3-5	3	-0.2
1977 Tex-A	13	28	4	7	1	0	1	5	3	4	0	0	.250	.323	.393	.715	93	-0	4	4.72	1	/1-5,D-3	1	0.0
Pit-N	36	56	10	16	1	1	3	16	13	10	2	0	.286	.420	.500	.920	142	4	13	8.22	-1	1-15/3-1	3	0.3
1978 Pit-N	20	20	3	4	1	0	0	1	6	8	0	0	.200	.385	.250	.635	77	-0	3	4.26	-1	/3-5,1-2,2-1	1	-0.2
Total 18	1902	6523	844	1726	264	78	151	706	715	1097	76	40	.265	.340	.398	.739	114	124	904	4.79	-26	*S-1396,1-190,3-183/D-34,0,2	261	23.2
• FREIBURGER, Vern																								
Vern Donald Freiburger b: 12/19/1923, Detroit, MI d: 2/27/1990, Palm Springs, CA BR/TL, 6'1", 170 lbs. Deb: 9/6/1941																								
1941 Cle-A	2	8	0	1	0	0	0	1	0	2	0	0	.125	.125	.125	.250	-35	-2	0	.00	0	/1-2	0	-0.1
• FREIGAU, Howard																								
Howard Earl "Ty" Freigau b: 8/1/1902, Dayton, OH d: 7/18/1932, Chattanooga, TN BR/TR, 5'10.5", 160 lbs. Deb: 9/13/1922 Career OF: 1-1-0																								
1922 StL-N	3	1	0	0	0	0	0	0	0	0	0	0	.000	.000	.000	.000	-105	-0	0	.00	0	/S-2,3-1	0	0.0
1923 StL-N	113	358	30	94	18	1	1	35	25	36	5	4	.263	.314	.327	.641	71	-15	37	3.59	1	S-87,2-16/1-9,3-1,0-1	8	-0.4
1924 StL-N	98	376	35	101	17	6	2	39	19	24	10	3	.269	.306	.362	.667	80	-9	42	3.89	4	3-98/S-2	7	0.1
1925 StL-N	9	26	2	4	0	0	0	0	2	1	0	0	.154	.214	.154	.368	-4	-4	1	1.12	2	/S-7,2-1	1	-0.1
Chi-N	117	476	77	146	22	10	8	71	30	31	10	6	.307	.349	.445	.794	100	-1	73	5.51	-6	3-96,S-17/1-7	14	0.1
Yr.	126	502	79	150	22	10	8	71	32	32	10	6	.299	.342	.430	.772	95	-5	74	5.25	-5	3-96,S-24/1-7,2-1	15	-0.1
1926 Chi-N	140	508	51	137	27	7	3	51	43	42	6	....	.270	.327	.368	.695	86	-11	61	4.06	-7	*3-135/S-2,0-1	12	-0.9
1927 Chi-N	30	86	12	20	5	0	0	10	9	10	0	....	.233	.313	.291	.603	62	-4	8	3.16	-3	3-30	1	-0.6
1928 Bro-N	17	34	6	7	2	0	0	3	1	3	0	....	.206	.229	.265	.493	29	-4	2	1.81	-3	3-10/S-1	0	-0.6
Bos-N	52	109	11	28	8	1	1	17	9	14	1	....	.257	.319	.376	.695	86	-2	13	3.99	-6	S-14,2-11	2	-0.7
Yr.	69	143	17	35	10	1	1	20	10	17	1	....	.245	.299	.350	.648	72	-6	15	3.42	-9	S-15,2-11,3-10	2	-1.3
Total 7	579	1974	224	537	99	25	15	226	138	161	32	13	.272	.322	.370	.692	82	-50	238	4.15	-19	3-371,S-132/2-28,1-16,0-2	45	-3.2
• FRENCH, Bill																								
William French b: Baltimore, MD Deb: 4/14/1873																								
1873 Mar-n	5	18	3	4	0	0	0	1	0	0	0	0	.222	.222	.222	.444	42	-0	1	1.98	-1	/1-2,0-2(0-0-2),3-1,P-1	....	-0.5
• FRENCH, Charlie																								
Charles Calvin French b: 10/12/1883, Indianapolis, IN d: 3/30/1962, Indianapolis, IN BL/TR, 5'6", 140 lbs. Deb: 5/23/1909																								
1909 Bos-A	51	167	15	42	3	1	0	13	15	....	8	....	.251	.324	.281	.606	90	-1	18	3.59	-4	2-28,S-23	5	-0.5
1910 Bos-A	9	40	4	8	1	0	0	3	1	....	0	....	.200	.220	.225	.445	38	-3	2	1.50	1	/2-8	0	-0.2
Chi-A	45	170	17	28	1	1	0	4	10	....	5	....	.165	.224	.182	.406	29	-14	8	1.44	-12	2-28,0-16(0-0-16)	1	-2.9
Yr.	54	210	21	36	2	1	0	7	11	....	5	....	.171	.223	.190	.414	31	-17	10	1.45	-11	2-36,0-16(0-0-16)	1	-3.1
Total 2	105	377	36	78	5	2	0	20	26	....	13	....	.207	.269	.231	.500	57	-18	28	2.34	-14	/2-64,S-23,0-16	6	-3.6
• FRENCH, Jim																								
Richard James French b: 8/13/1941, Warren, OH BL/TR, 5'8", 182 lbs. Deb: 9/12/1965																								
1965 Was-A	13	37	4	11	0	0	1	7	9	5	1	0	.297	.435	.378	.813	135	3	7	6.86	0	C-13	2	0.4
1966 Was-A	10	24	0	5	1	0	0	3	4	5	0	1	.208	.321	.250	.571	67	-1	2	2.72	-1	C-10	0	-0.2
1967 Was-A	6	16	0	1	0	0	0	1	3	4	0	0	.063	.211	.063	.273	-17	-2	0	.58	-1	/C-6	0	-0.3
1968 Was-A	59	165	9	32	5	0	1	10	19	19	1	2	.194	.281	.242	.524	62	-8	13	2.38	2	C-53	3	-0.3
1969 Was-A	63	158	14	29	6	3	2	13	41	15	1	0	.184	.352	.297	.649	88	-0	20	4.12	3	C-63	8	0.6
1970 Was-A	69	166	20	35	3	1	1	13	38	23	0	1	.211	.358	.259	.617	76	-3	17	3.37	-4	C-62/0-1	3	-0.5
1971 Was-A	14	41	6	6	2	0	0	4	7	7	0	2	.146	.271	.195	.466	36	-4	2	1.11	0	C-14	1	-0.4
Total 7	234	607	53	119	17	4	5	51	121	78	3	6	.196	.331	.262	.593	74	-16	61	3.19	1	C-221/0-1	17	-0.6
• FRENCH, Pat																								
Frank Alexander French b: 9/22/1893, Dover, NH d: 7/13/1969, Bath, ME BR/TR, 6'1", 180 lbs. Deb: 7/2/1917																								
1917 Phi-A	3	2	0	0	0	0	0	0	0	0	0	....	.000	.000	.000	.000	-101	-0	0	.00	0	/0-1	0	-0.1
• FRENCH, Ray																								
Raymond Edward French b: 1/9/1895, Alameda, CA d: 4/3/1978, Alameda, CA BR/TR, 5'9.5", 158 lbs. Deb: 9/17/1920																								
1920 NY-A	2	2	2	0	0	0	0	1	0	1	0	0	.000	.000	.000	.000	-97	-1	0	.00	-1	/S-1	0	-0.1
1923 Bro-N	43	73	14	16	2	1	0	7	4	7	0	0	.219	.269	.274	.543	45	-6	6	2.49	-6	S-30	1	-0.8
1924 Chi-A	37	112	13	20	4	0	0	11	10	13	3	1	.179	.246	.214	.460	20	-13	7	1.83	-3	S-28/2-3	0	-1.2
Total 3	82	187	29	36	6	1	0	19	14	21	3	1	.193	.252	.235	.488	29	-19	12	2.06	-9	/S-59,2-3	1	-2.1
• FRENCH, Walter																								
Walter Edward "Piggy,Fitz" French b: 7/12/1899, Moorestown, NJ d: 5/13/1984, Mountain Home, AR BL/TR, 5'7.5", 155 lbs. Deb: 9/15/1923 Career OF: 25-17-209																								
1923 Phi-A	16	39	7	9	3	0	0	2	5	7	0	1	.231	.318	.308	.626	64	-2	4	3.22	-1	0-10(0-10-0)	1	-0.4
1925 Phi-A	67	100	20	37	9	0	0	14	1	9	1	1	.370	.376	.460	.836	104	0	16	6.52	0	0-19(3-0-16)	3	-0.1

YEAR TM-L	G	AB	R	H	2B	3B	HR	RBI	BB	SO	SB	CS	AVG	OBP	SLG	OPS	OPS+	BR/A	RC	RC/G	FR	G/POS	WS	TPW
1926 Phi-A	112	397	51	121	18	7	1	36	18	24	2	3	.305	.340	.393	.733	86	-9	53	4.63	4	0-99(0-1-98)	9	-1.3
1927 Phi-A	109	326	48	99	10	5	0	41	16	14	9	1	.304	.338	.365	.703	78	-9	42	4.59	0	0-94(8-5-81)	7	-1.6
1928 Phi-A	48	74	9	19	4	0	0	7	2	5	1	1	.257	.286	.311	.597	55	-5	6	3.01	0	0-19(8-0-11)	1	-0.6
1929*Phi-A	45	45	7	12	1	0	1	9	2	3	0	0	.267	.298	.356	.653	65	-2	5	3.64	0	0-10(6-1-3)	0	-0.3
Total 6	397	981	142	297	45	12	2	109	44	62	13	7	.303	.336	.379	.715	81	-28	126	4.56	3	0-251	21	-4.2

• FREUND, Lawrence Lawrence Lentz Freund Freund b: 7/5/1875, Jeffersonville, IN d: 11/5/1933, Jeffersonville, IN TR, 5'10", 180 lbs. Deb: 8/2/1896

YEAR TM-L	G	AB	R	H	2B	3B	HR	RBI	BB	SO	SB	CS	AVG	OBP	SLG	OPS	OPS+	BR/A	RC	RC/G	FR	G/POS	WS	TPW
1896 Lou-N	2	5	1	1	0	0	0	0	1	1	0	....	.200	.333	.200	.533	44	-0	0	2.26	0	/C-2	0	0.0

• FREY, Lonny Linus Reinhard "Junior" Frey b: 8/23/1910, St. Louis, MO BL/TR, 5'10", 160 lbs. Deb: 8/29/1933 Career OF: 7-15-12

YEAR TM-L	G	AB	R	H	2B	3B	HR	RBI	BB	SO	SB	CS	AVG	OBP	SLG	OPS	OPS+	BR/A	RC	RC/G	FR	G/POS	WS	TPW
1933 Bro-N	34	135	25	43	5	3	0	12	13	13	4	....	.319	.378	.400	.778	128	5	21	5.71	-7	S-34	5	0.0
1934 Bro-N	125	490	77	139	24	5	8	57	52	54	11	....	.284	.358	.402	.760	109	7	75	5.54	1	*S-109,3-13	16	1.6
1935 Bro-N	131	515	88	135	35	11	11	77	66	68	6	....	.262	.352	.437	.788	113	10	82	5.61	-5	*S-127/2-4	19	1.5
1936 Bro-N	148	524	63	146	29	4	4	60	71	56	7	....	.279	.369	.372	.741	99	2	77	5.18	-20	*S-117,2-30/0-1	13	-0.7
1937 Chi-N	78	198	33	55	9	3	1	22	33	15	6	....	.278	.381	.369	.750	100	2	31	5.39	-6	S-30,2-13/3-9,0-5(4-1-0)	7	-0.1
1938 Cin-N	124	501	76	133	26	6	4	36	49	50	4	....	.265	.331	.365	.696	94	-4	66	4.76	3	*2-121/S-3	14	0.7
1939*Cin-N★	125	484	95	141	27	9	11	55	72	46	5	....	.291	.388	.452	.840	124	19	91	6.56	17	*2-124	25	**4.4**
1940*Cin-N	150	563	102	150	23	6	8	54	80	48	**22**	....	.266	.361	.371	.732	101	4	82	5.08	33	*2-150	24	**4.8**
1941 Cin-N★	146	543	78	138	29	5	6	59	72	37	16	....	.254	.345	.359	.704	98	0	72	4.60	1	*2-145	24	1.1
1942 Cin-N	141	523	66	139	23	6	2	39	87	38	9	....	.266	.373	.344	.717	111	11	75	5.11	8	*2-140	23	3.1
1943 Cin-N★	144	586	78	154	20	8	2	43	76	56	7	....	.263	.347	.334	.682	99	1	75	4.59	8	*2-144	25	1.9
1946 Cin-N	111	333	46	82	10	3	3	24	63	31	5	....	.246	.368	.321	.689	100	3	44	4.60	8	2-65,0-28(3-13-12)	11	1.4
1947 Chi-N	24	43	4	9	0	0	0	3	4	6	0	....	.209	.277	.209	.486	32	-4	3	2.21	-1	/2-9	0	-0.4
*NY-A	24	28	10	5	2	0	0	2	10	1	3	0	.179	.410	.250	.660	87	1	5	4.91	0	/2-8	1	0.2
1948 NY-A	1	0	1	0	0	0	0	0	0	0	0	0	....	....	....	....	-101	0	0	....	0		0	0.0
NY-N	29	51	6	13	1	0	1	6	4	6	0	....	.255	.309	.333	.642	73	-2	6	3.96	-2	2-13	1	-0.3
Total 14	1535	5517	848	1482	263	69	61	549	752	525	105	0	.269	.359	.374	.734	104	56	803	5.15	40	2-966,S-420/0-34,3-22	208	19.0

• FRIAS, Hanley Hanley (Acevedo) Frias b: 12/5/1973, Villa Altagracia, Dominican Republic BB/TR, 6', 160 lbs. Deb: 6/21/1997

YEAR TM-L	G	AB	R	H	2B	3B	HR	RBI	BB	SO	SB	CS	AVG	OBP	SLG	OPS	OPS+	BR/A	RC	RC/G	FR	G/POS	WS	TPW
1997 Tex-A	14	26	4	5	1	0	0	1	1	4	0	0	.192	.222	.231	.453	18	-3	1	1.42	0	S-12/2-1	0	-0.3
1998 Ari-N	15	23	4	3	0	1	1	2	0	5	0	0	.130	.130	.348	.478	20	-3	1	.89	-1	/2-3,3-2,S-2	0	-0.3
1999*Ari-N	69	150	27	41	3	2	1	16	29	18	4	3	.273	.391	.340	.731	87	-2	22	5.14	-2	S-53/2-8	4	-0.1
2000 Ari-N	75	112	18	23	5	0	2	6	17	18	2	2	.205	.310	.304	.614	54	-8	11	3.08	-2	S-21,2-15/3-7	1	-0.8
Total 4	173	311	53	72	9	3	4	25	47	45	6	5	.232	.332	.318	.651	66	-16	34	3.69	-5	/S-88,2-27,3-9	5	-1.6

• FRIAS, Pepe Jesus Maria (Andujar) Frias b: 7/14/1948, San Pedro de Macoris, Dominican Republic BR/TR, 5'10", 159 lbs. Deb: 4/6/1973 Career OF: 1-0-3

YEAR TM-L	G	AB	R	H	2B	3B	HR	RBI	BB	SO	SB	CS	AVG	OBP	SLG	OPS	OPS+	BR/A	RC	RC/G	FR	G/POS	WS	TPW
1973 Mon-N	100	225	19	52	10	1	0	22	10	24	1	3	.231	.267	.284	.551	51	-16	16	2.29	1	S-46,2-44/3-6,0-1	3	-0.9
1974 Mon-N	75	112	12	24	4	1	0	7	7	10	1	0	.214	.261	.268	.528	45	-8	8	2.51	-2	S-30,3-27,2-15/0-3(1-0-2)	2	-0.8
1975 Mon-N	51	64	4	8	2	0	0	4	3	13	0	1	.125	.164	.156	.320	-10	-10	2	.70	-7	S-29,3-11/2-7	1	-1.5
1976 Mon-N	76	113	7	28	5	0	0	8	4	14	1	1	.248	.274	.292	.566	58	-7	9	2.52	-6	2-35,S-35/3-4,0-1	1	-1.0
1977 Mon-N	53	70	10	18	1	0	0	5	0	10	1	0	.257	.257	.271	.529	43	-5	5	2.38	1	2-16,S-14/3-1	1	-0.3
1978 Mon-N	73	15	5	4	2	1	0	5	0	3	0	0	.267	.267	.533	.800	120	0	2	4.42	-21	2-61/S-3	1	-2.0
1979 Atl-N	140	475	41	123	18	4	1	44	20	36	3	2	.259	.292	.320	.612	62	-25	42	2.98	-10	*S-137	7	-2.2
1980 Tex-A	116	227	27	55	5	1	0	10	4	23	5	1	.242	.259	.273	.532	47	-16	15	2.10	-11	*S-106/3-7,2-2	2	-2.0
LA-N	14	9	1	2	1	0	0	0	0	0	0	0	.222	.222	.333	.556	54	-1	0	1.13	-1	S-11	0	-0.2
1981 LA-N	25	36	6	9	1	0	0	3	1	3	0	0	.250	.289	.278	.567	64	-2	3	2.93	-3	S-15/2-6,3-1	1	-0.4
Total 9	723	1346	132	323	49	8	1	108	49	136	12	8	.240	.269	.290	.560	52	-90	102	2.48	-60	S-426,2-186/3-57,0-5	19	-11.4

• FRIBERG, Bernie Bernard Albert Friberg b: 8/18/1899, Manchester, NH d: 12/8/1958, Lynn, MA BR/TR, 5'11", 178 lbs. Deb: 8/20/1919 Career OF: 84-52-62

YEAR TM-L	G	AB	R	H	2B	3B	HR	RBI	BB	SO	SB	CS	AVG	OBP	SLG	OPS	OPS+	BR/A	RC	RC/G	FR	G/POS	WS	TPW
1919 Chi-N	8	20	0	4	1	0	0	1	0	2	0	....	.200	.200	.250	.450	35	-2	1	1.46	-1	/0-7(2-5-0)	0	-0.3
1920 Chi-N	50	114	11	24	5	1	0	7	6	20	2	2	.211	.250	.272	.522	49	-8	8	2.13	-3	2-24,0-24(15-8-3)	1	-1.1
1922 Chi-N	97	296	51	92	8	2	0	23	37	37	8	10	.311	.391	.351	.742	91	-4	41	4.94	3	0-74(8-11-55)/1-6,3-5,2-3	8	-0.6
1923 Chi-N	146	547	91	174	27	11	12	88	45	49	13	19	.318	.372	.473	.846	122	12	91	5.81	11	*3-146	23	3.1
1924 Chi-N	142	495	67	138	19	3	5	82	66	53	19	27	.279	.369	.360	.729	95	-6	65	4.22	6	*3-142	18	0.9
1925 Chi-N	44	152	12	39	5	3	1	16	14	22	0	1	.257	.327	.349	.676	72	-6	18	4.03	-3	3-26,0-12(12-0-0)/1-6,S-2	3	-0.8
Phi-N	91	304	41	82	12	1	5	22	39	35	1	1	.270	.353	.365	.718	77	-9	41	4.78	-3	2-77,3-14/C-1,P-1	7	-0.8
Yr.	135	456	53	121	17	4	6	38	53	57	1	2	.265	.344	.360	.704	75	-16	59	4.52	-6	2-77,3-40,0-12(12-0-0)/1-6,S,C,P	10	-1.7
1926 Phi-N	144	478	38	128	21	3	1	51	57	77	2	....	.268	.346	.331	.676	79	-13	56	3.98	1	*2-144	11	-0.8
1927 Phi-N	111	335	31	78	8	2	1	28	41	49	3	....	.233	.322	.278	.600	61	-17	32	3.05	10	*3-103/2-5	6	0.0
1928 Phi-N	52	94	11	19	3	0	1	7	12	16	0	....	.202	.292	.266	.558	45	-7	8	2.54	-5	S-31/3-5,2-3,0-3(2-1-0),1	1	-1.0
1929 Phi-N	128	455	74	137	21	10	7	55	49	54	1	....	.301	.370	.437	.808	93	-5	73	5.75	-20	S-73,0-40(18-19-4)/2-8,1-2	9	-1.8
1930 Phi-N	105	331	62	113	21	1	4	42	47	35	1	....	.341	.425	.447	.872	104	5	64	7.31	-11	2-44,0-35(27-8-0),S-12/3-8	8	-0.6
1931 Phi-N	103	353	33	92	19	5	1	26	33	25	1	....	.261	.324	.351	.675	75	-12	42	4.09	1	2-64,3-25/1-5,S-3	6	-0.6
1932 Phi-N	61	154	17	37	8	2	0	14	19	23	0	....	.240	.324	.318	.642	66	-7	17	3.68	-7	2-56	2	-1.1
1933 Bos-A	17	41	5	13	3	0	0	9	6	1	0	0	.317	.404	.390	.794	112	1	7	6.28	1	/2-6,3-5,S-2	1	0.3
Total 14	1299	4169	544	1170	181	44	38	471	471	498	51	60	.281	.356	.373	.728	87	-78	564	4.63	-19	3-479,2-434,0-195,S-123/1,C,P	104	-5.2

• FRIDLEY, Jim James Riley "Big Jim" Fridley b: 9/6/1924, Phillippi, WV d: 2/28/2003, Port Charlotte, FL BR/TR, 6'2", 205 lbs. Deb: 4/15/1952 Career OF: 103-0-23

YEAR TM-L	G	AB	R	H	2B	3B	HR	RBI	BB	SO	SB	CS	AVG	OBP	SLG	OPS	OPS+	BR/A	RC	RC/G	FR	G/POS	WS	TPW
1952 Cle-A	62	175	23	44	2	0	4	16	14	40	3	3	.251	.311	.331	.642	84	-5	18	3.52	-1	0-54(37-0-20)	4	-0.8
1954 Bal-A	85	240	25	59	8	5	4	36	21	41	0	1	.246	.312	.371	.683	93	-3	25	3.37	-4	0-67(64-0-3)	3	-1.2
1958 Cin-N	5	9	2	2	2	0	0	1	0	2	0	0	.222	.222	.444	.667	67	-0	1	3.43	0	/0-2(2-0-0)	0	-0.1
Total 3	152	424	50	105	12	5	8	53	35	83	3	4	.248	.310	.356	.666	89	-8	44	3.43	-5	0-123	7	-2.0

• FRIEL, Bill William Edward Friel b: 4/1/1876, Renovo, PA d: 12/24/1959, St. Louis, MO BL/TR, 5'10", 165 lbs. Deb: 5/3/1901 C/U Career OF: 6-27-39

YEAR TM-L	G	AB	R	H	2B	3B	HR	RBI	BB	SO	SB	CS	AVG	OBP	SLG	OPS	OPS+	BR/A	RC	RC/G	FR	G/POS	WS	TPW
1901 Mil-A	106	376	51	100	13	7	4	35	23	....	15	....	.266	.310	.370	.680	92	-4	50	4.61	-9	3-61,0-29(5-23-1)/2-9,S-6	7	-1.1
1902 StL-A	80	267	26	64	9	2	2	20	14	....	4	....	.240	.283	.311	.594	65	-13	26	3.29	-2	0-33(1-0-32),2-25,1-10/3-8,S,C,P	3	-1.5
1903 StL-A	97	351	46	80	11	8	0	25	23	....	4	....	.228	.279	.305	.584	77	-10	33	3.11	-15	2-63,3-24/0-9(0-4-6)	7	-2.4
Total 3	283	994	123	244	33	17	6	80	60	....	23	....	.245	.292	.331	.623	80	-26	109	3.72	-26	/2-97,3-93,0-71,1-10,S-9,C,P	17	-5.0

• FRIEL, Pat Patrick Henry Friel b: 6/11/1860, Lewisburg, WV d: 1/15/1924, Providence, RI BB, 5'11", 170 lbs. Deb: 7/13/1890 Career OF: 13-0-51

YEAR TM-L	G	AB	R	H	2B	3B	HR	RBI	BB	SO	SB	CS	AVG	OBP	SLG	OPS	OPS+	BR/A	RC	RC/G	FR	G/POS	WS	TPW
1890 Syr-a	62	261	51	65	8	2	3	21	17	....	34	....	.249	.302	.330	.632	96	-1	37	5.03	-6	0-62(13-0-49)	6	-0.7
1891 Phi-a	2	8	2	2	1	0	0	0	0	0	0	....	.250	.250	.375	.625	76	-0	1	3.40	0	/0-2(0-0-2)	0	0.0
Total 2	64	269	53	67	9	2	3	21	17	0	34	....	.249	.301	.331	.632	96	-2	38	4.98	-6	/0-64	6	-0.8

• FRIEND, Owen Owen Lacey "Red" Friend b: 3/21/1927, Granite City, IL BR/TR, 6'1", 180 lbs. Deb: 10/2/1949 C

YEAR TM-L	G	AB	R	H	2B	3B	HR	RBI	BB	SO	SB	CS	AVG	OBP	SLG	OPS	OPS+	BR/A	RC	RC/G	FR	G/POS	WS	TPW
1949 StL-A	2	8	1	3	0	0	0	1	0	0	0	0	.375	.375	.375	.750	95	-0	1	6.23	0	/2-2	0	0.1
1950 StL-A	119	372	48	88	15	2	8	50	40	68	2	1	.237	.312	.352	.665	67	-19	41	3.53	-6	2-93,3-24/S-3	5	-1.8
1953 Det-A	31	96	10	17	4	0	3	10	6	9	0	1	.177	.233	.313	.546	47	-8	6	1.80	-4	2-26	1	-1.0
Cle-A	34	68	7	16	2	0	2	13	5	16	0	0	.235	.288	.353	.641	74	-3	7	3.37	3	2-19/S-8,3-1	2	0.1
Yr.	65	164	17	33	6	0	5	23	11	25	0	1	.201	.256	.329	.585	58	-11	12	2.40	-1	2-45/S-8,3-1	3	-0.8
1955 Bos-A	14	42	3	11	3	0	0	2	4	11	0	0	.262	.326	.333	.659	71	-2	4	3.48	-1	S-14/2-1	1	-0.2
Chi-N	6	10	0	1	0	0	0	0	0	3	0	0	.100	.100	.100	.200	-47	-2	0	.30	-1	/3-2,S-1	0	-0.3
1956 Chi-N	2	2	0	0	0	0	0	0	0	2	0	0	.000	.000	.000	.000	-102	-1	0	.00	0	....	0	-0.1
Total 5	208	598	69	136	24	2	13	76	55	109	2	2	.227	.295	.339	.634	63	-34	59	3.17	-8	2-141/3-27,S-26	9	-3.1

• FRIERSON, Buck Robert Lawrence Frierson b: 7/29/1917, Chicota, TX d: 6/26/1996, Paris, TX BR/TR, 6'3", 195 lbs. Deb: 9/9/1941

YEAR TM-L	G	AB	R	H	2B	3B	HR	RBI	BB	SO	SB	CS	AVG	OBP	SLG	OPS	OPS+	BR/A	RC	RC/G	FR	G/POS	WS	TPW
1941 Cle-A	5	11	2	3	1	0	0	2	1	1	0	0	.273	.333	.364	.697	89	-0	1	4.91	0	/0-3(2-0-1)	0	0.0

• FRIES, Pete Peter Martin Fries b: 10/30/1857, Scranton, PA d: 7/30/1937, Chicago, IL BL/TL, 5'8", 160 lbs. Deb: 8/10/1883 ♦

YEAR TM-L	G	AB	R	H	2B	3B	HR	RBI	BB	SO	SB	CS	AVG	OBP	SLG	OPS	OPS+	BR/A	RC	RC/G	FR	G/POS	WS	TPW
1883 Col-a	3	10	1	3	1	0	0	0	1	....	....	....	.300	.364	.400	.764	158	1	1	5.96	0	/P-3	0	-0.7

YEAR TM-L	G	AB	R	H	2B	3B	HR	RBI	BB	SO	SB	CS	AVG	OBP	SLG	OPS	OPS+	BR/A	RC	RC/G	FR	G/POS	WS	TPW
1884 Ind-a	1	3	0	1	1	0	0	0	1	....	....	....	.333	.500	.667	1.167	285	1	1	14.09	0	/O-1	0	0.1
Total 2	4	13	1	4	2	0	0	0	2	....	....	....	.308	.400	.462	.862	192	2	3	7.77	0	/P-3,O-1	0	-0.7
• FRINK, Fred	Frederick Ferdinand Frink b: 8/25/1911, Macon, GA d: 5/19/1995, Miami Springs, FL BR/TR, 6'1", 180 lbs. Deb: 7/1/1934																							
1934 Phi-N	2	0	0	0	0	0	0	0	0	0	0	....	....	....	....	....	-88	0	0	....	0	/O-1	0	0.0
• FRISBEE, Charlie	Charles Augustus "Bunt" Frisbee b: 2/2/1874, Dows, IA d: 11/7/1954, Iowa Falls, IA BB/TR, 5'9", 175 lbs. Deb: 6/22/1899 Career OF: 0-36-8																							
1899 Bos-N	42	152	22	50	4	2	0	20	9	....	10	....	.329	.374	.382	.756	98	-1	27	6.57	-2	O-40(0-36-4)	5	-0.4
1900 NY-N	4	13	2	2	1	0	0	3	2	....	0	....	.154	.267	.231	.497	40	-1	1	2.19	-2	/O-4(0-0-4)	0	-0.3
Total 2	46	165	24	52	5	2	0	23	11	....	10	....	.315	.365	.370	.735	93	-2	28	6.10	-3	/O-44	5	-0.7
• FRISCH, Frankie	Frank Francis "The Fordham Flash" Frisch b: 9/9/1898, Bronx, NY d: 3/12/1973, Wilmington, DE BB/TR, 5'11", 165 lbs. Deb: 6/14/1919 M/C HOF: 1947																							
1919 NY-N	54	190	21	43	3	2	2	24	4	14	15	....	.226	.242	.295	.537	62	-9	16	2.71	3	2-29,3-20/S-1	3	-0.7
1920 NY-N	110	440	57	123	10	10	4	77	20	18	34	11	.280	.311	.375	.686	97	2	52	4.04	10	*3-109/S-2	15	1.6
1921*NY-N	153	618	121	211	31	17	8	100	42	28	**49**	13	.341	.384	.485	.870	128	32	118	6.99	12	3-93,2-61	31	5.1
1922*NY-N	132	514	101	168	16	13	5	51	47	13	31	17	.327	.387	.438	.824	111	10	87	6.06	6	2-85,3-53/S-1	20	2.1
1923*NY-N	151	641	116	**223**	32	10	12	111	46	12	29	12	.348	.395	.485	.880	133	32	123	7.39	10	*2-135,3-17	**31**	4.6
1924*NY-N	145	603	**121**	198	33	15	7	69	56	24	22	9	.328	.387	.468	.855	132	30	111	6.86	31	*2-143,S-10/3-2	30	6.5
1925 NY-N	120	502	89	166	26	6	11	48	32	14	21	12	.331	.374	.472	.846	119	14	87	6.52	2	3-46,2-42,S-39	20	2.3
1926 NY-N	135	545	75	171	29	4	5	44	33	16	23	....	.314	.353	.409	.762	106	4	76	5.15	15	*2-127/3-7	20	2.3
1927 StL-N	153	617	112	208	31	11	10	78	43	10	**48**	....	.337	.387	.472	.858	125	22	109	6.54	52	*2-153/S-1	34	**7.7**
1928*StL-N	141	547	107	164	29	9	10	86	64	17	29	....	.300	.374	.441	.815	110	9	90	5.82	25	*2-139	22	3.6
1929 StL-N	138	527	93	176	40	12	5	74	53	12	24	....	.334	.397	.484	.881	116	14	99	7.02	0	*2-121,3-13/S-1	20	1.7
1930*StL-N	133	540	121	187	46	9	10	114	55	16	15	....	.346	.407	.520	.927	118	17	111	7.86	31	*2-123,3-10	25	4.5
1931*StL-N	131	518	96	161	24	4	4	82	45	13	**28**	....	.311	.368	.396	.764	101	2	78	5.60	11	*2-129	21	2.1
1932 StL-N	115	486	59	142	26	2	3	60	25	13	18	....	.292	.327	.372	.699	85	-10	60	4.49	11	2-75,3-37/S-4	14	0.7
1933 StL-N★	147	585	74	177	32	6	4	66	48	16	18	....	.303	.358	.398	.757	110	9	83	5.11	4	*2-132,S-15	22	2.3
1934*StL-N★	140	550	74	168	30	6	3	75	45	10	11	....	.305	.359	.398	.757	96	-2	79	5.19	13	*2-115,3-25	19	1.8
1935 StL-N★	103	354	52	104	16	2	1	55	33	16	2	....	.294	.356	.359	.714	89	-4	48	4.75	10	2-88/3-5	12	1.0
1936 StL-N	93	303	40	83	10	0	1	26	36	10	2	....	.274	.353	.317	.670	82	-6	36	4.08	-5	2-60,3-22/S-1	7	-0.6
1937 StL-N	17	32	3	7	2	0	0	4	1	0	0	....	.219	.242	.281	.524	41	-3	2	1.70	0	/2-5	0	-0.2
Total 19	2311	9112	1532	2880	466	138	105	1244	728	272	419	74	.316	.369	.432	.801	110	161	1464	5.86	240	*2-1762,3-459/S-75	366	48.4
• FRISK, Emil	John Emil Frisk b: 10/15/1874, Kalkaska, MI d: 1/27/1922, Seattle, WA BL/TR, 6'1", 190 lbs. Deb: 9/2/1899 Career OF: 0-1-116 ♦																							
1899 Cin-N	9	25	5	7	1	0	0	2	2	....	0	....	.280	.357	.320	.677	85	1	3	4.31	0	/P-9	4	0.1
1901 Det-A	20	48	10	15	3	0	1	7	3	....	0	....	.313	.365	.438	.803	117	4	8	6.32	2	P-11/O-2(0-1-1)	5	-0.2
1905 StL-A	124	429	58	112	11	6	3	36	42	....	7	....	.261	.342	.336	.678	122	12	55	4.41	-3	*O-115(0-0-115)	13	0.5
1907 StL-A	5	4	0	1	0	0	0	0	1	....	0	....	.250	.400	.250	.650	108	0	0	3.62	0	....	0	0.0
Total 4	158	506	73	135	15	6	4	45	48	....	7	....	.267	.346	.344	.690	119	17	66	4.56	-1	O-117/P-20	22	0.4
• FRITZ, Harry	Harry Koch "Dutchman" Fritz b: 9/30/1890, Philadelphia, PA d: 11/4/1974, Columbus, OH BR/TR, 5'8", 170 lbs. Deb: 9/29/1913																							
1913 Phi-A	5	13	1	0	0	0	0	0	2	4	0	....	.000	.188	.000	.188	-45	-2	0	.25	-1	/3-5	0	-0.3
1914 Chi-F	65	174	16	37	5	1	0	13	18	18	2	....	.213	.297	.253	.550	61	-8	14	2.48	-5	3-46/S-9,2-1	3	-1.2
1915 Chi-F	79	236	27	59	8	4	3	26	13	27	4	....	.250	.298	.356	.654	97	-2	26	3.57	-1	3-70/2-6,S-1	7	-0.1
Total 3	149	423	44	96	13	5	3	39	33	49	6	....	.227	.294	.303	.596	77	-12	40	2.99	-6	3-121/S-10,2-7	10	-1.5
• FRITZ, Larry	Lawrence Joseph Fritz b: 2/14/1949, East Chicago, IN BL/TL, 6'2", 225 lbs. Deb: 5/30/1975																							
1975 Phi-N	1	1	0	0	0	0	0	0	0	0	0	0	.000	.000	.000	.000	-96	-0	0	.00	0	....	0	0.0
• FROBEL, Doug	Douglas Steven Frobel b: 6/6/1959, Ottawa, Canada BL/TR, 6'4", 196 lbs. Deb: 9/5/1982 Career OF: 41-4-156																							
1982 Pit-N	16	34	5	7	2	0	2	3	1	11	1	1	.206	.229	.441	.670	81	-1	3	3.04	0	O-12(0-0-12)	0	-0.2
1983 Pit-N	32	60	10	17	4	1	3	11	4	17	1	1	.283	.328	.533	.861	132	2	9	5.54	-1	O-24(18-0-6)	2	0.0
1984 Pit-N	126	276	33	56	9	3	12	28	24	84	7	5	.203	.272	.388	.659	83	-8	27	3.11	8	*O-112(0-0-112)	5	-0.5
1985 Pit-N	53	109	14	22	5	0	0	7	19	24	4	3	.202	.320	.248	.568	62	-5	9	2.69	0	O-36(20-0-16)	1	-0.8
Mon-N	12	23	3	3	1	0	1	4	2	6	0	0	.130	.200	.304	.504	41	-2	1	1.09	0	/O-6(1-2-3)	0	-0.3
Yr.	65	132	17	25	6	0	1	11	21	30	4	3	.189	.301	.258	.558	58	-7	10	2.37	-1	O-42(21-2-19)	1	-1.0
1987 Cle-A	29	40	5	4	0	0	2	5	5	13	0	0	.100	.200	.250	.450	18	-5	2	1.43	-1	O-12(2-2-7)/D-5	0	-0.6
Total 5	268	542	70	109	21	4	20	58	55	155	13	10	.201	.277	.365	.642	77	-20	52	3.02	5	O-202/D-5	8	-2.3
• FROELICH, Ben	William Palmer Froelich b: 11/12/1887, Pittsburgh, PA d: 9/1/1916, Pittsburgh, PA BR/TR Deb: 7/2/1909																							
1909 Phi-N	1	1	0	0	0	0	0	0	0	....	0	....	.000	.000	.000	.000	-99	-0	0	.00	-1	/C-1	0	-0.1
• FRY, Jerry	Jerry Ray Fry b: 2/29/1956, Salinas, CA BR/TR, 6', 185 lbs. Deb: 9/4/1978																							
1978 Mon-N	4	9	0	0	0	0	0	0	1	5	0	0	.000	.100	.000	.100	-71	-2	0	.08	0	/C-4	0	-0.2
• FRYE, Jeff	Jeffrey Dustin Frye b: 8/31/1966, Oakland, CA BR/TR, 5'9", 165 lbs. Deb: 7/9/1992 Career OF: 9-8-18																							
1992 Tex-A	67	199	24	51	9	1	1	12	16	27	1	3	.256	.321	.327	.648	85	-5	22	3.55	-1	2-67	4	-0.4
1994 Tex-A	57	205	37	67	20	3	0	18	29	23	6	1	.327	.413	.454	.866	124	9	42	7.71	-10	2-54/3-1,D-1	8	0.2
1995 Tex-A	90	313	38	87	15	2	4	29	24	45	3	3	.278	.339	.377	.716	84	-8	40	4.35	-5	2-83	8	-0.9
1996 Bos-A	105	419	74	120	27	2	4	41	54	57	18	4	.286	.374	.389	.763	92	-1	67	5.68	8	*2-100/O-5(2-1-2),S-3,D-1	14	1.0
1997 Bos-A	127	404	56	126	36	2	3	51	27	44	19	8	.312	.358	.433	.791	103	2	60	5.29	5	2-80,3-18,O-13(5-5-3),D-11/S,1	12	1.0
1999 Bos-A	41	114	14	32	3	0	1	12	14	11	2	2	.281	.364	.333	.698	77	-4	14	4.40	-2	2-26/3-7,D-2,S-2	3	-0.4
2000 Bos-A	69	239	35	69	13	0	1	13	28	38	1	3	.289	.366	.356	.721	81	-7	32	4.65	-3	2-52,O-15(1-2-13)/3-3,D-3	6	-0.8
Col-N	37	87	14	31	6	0	0	3	8	16	4	0	.356	.417	.425	.842	91	0	16	7.10	0	2-27/3-1	2	0.1
2001 Tor-A	74	175	24	43	6	1	2	15	12	18	2	1	.246	.305	.326	.631	65	-9	18	3.53	-2	2-47,3-27/S-2,O-1	3	-0.9
Total 8	667	2155	316	626	135	11	16	194	212	279	56	25	.290	.360	.386	.746	91	-22	311	5.07	-11	2-536/3-57,O-34,D-18,S-10,1	60	-1.1
• FRYMAN, Travis	David Travis Fryman b: 3/25/1969, Lexington, KY BR/TR, 6'1", 194 lbs. Deb: 7/7/1990																							
1990 Det-A	66	232	32	69	11	1	9	27	17	51	3	3	.297	.348	.470	.818	126	7	37	5.93	2	3-48,S-17/D-1	8	1.0
1991 Det-A	149	557	65	144	36	3	21	91	40	149	12	5	.259	.312	.447	.759	106	3	75	4.59	-6	3-85,S-71	17	0.2
1992 Det-A★	161	659	87	175	31	4	20	96	45	144	8	4	.266	.318	.416	.734	104	1	86	4.54	1	*S-137,3-26	19	1.3
1993 Det-A★	151	607	98	182	37	5	22	97	77	128	9	4	.300	.382	.486	.868	132	29	117	7.12	-7	S-81,3-69/D-1	28	2.9
1994 Det-A★	114	464	66	122	34	5	18	85	45	128	2	2	.263	.335	.474	.809	105	2	75	5.55	-5	*3-114	15	-0.1
1995 Det-A	144	567	79	156	21	5	15	81	63	100	4	2	.275	.351	.409	.760	97	-2	80	4.94	21	*3-144	19	2.0
1996 Det-A★	157	616	90	165	32	3	22	100	57	118	4	3	.268	.334	.437	.771	93	-9	87	4.87	10	*3-128,S-29	17	0.5
1997 Det-A	154	595	90	163	27	3	22	102	46	113	16	3	.274	.331	.440	.772	100	1	86	5.03	8	*3-153	17	1.1
1998*Cle-A	146	557	74	160	33	2	28	96	44	125	10	8	.287	.343	.504	.847	113	7	92	5.93	-12	*3-144/S-3,D-2	18	-0.2
1999*Cle-A	85	322	45	82	16	2	10	48	25	57	2	1	.255	.310	.410	.720	78	-12	38	3.98	-4	3-85	7	-1.4
2000 Cle-A★	155	574	93	184	38	4	22	106	73	111	1	1	.321	.398	.516	.914	126	24	118	7.65	-11	*3-154/1-1,D-1	22	1.4
2001*Cle-A	98	334	34	88	15	0	3	38	30	63	1	2	.263	.330	.335	.665	75	-12	37	3.83	-14	3-96/D-2,S-1	5	-2.4
2002 Cle-A	118	397	42	86	14	3	11	55	40	82	0	0	.217	.292	.350	.642	71	-17	40	3.31	-12	*3-113	7	-2.6
Total 13	1698	6481	895	1776	345	40	223	1022	602	1369	72	38	.274	.340	.443	.782	104	23	968	5.24	-29	*3-1359,S-339/D-7,1-1	199	3.8
• FUENTES, Mike	Michael Jay Fuentes b: 6/11/1958, Miami, FL BR/TR, 6'3", 190 lbs. Deb: 9/2/1983																							
1983 Mon-N	6	4	1	1	0	0	0	0	0	2	0	0	.250	.250	.250	.500	39	-0	0	2.25	0	....	0	0.0
1984 Mon-N	3	4	0	1	0	0	0	0	1	2	0	0	.250	.400	.250	.650	90	0	1	4.54	0	/O-1	0	0.0
Total 2	9	8	1	2	0	0	0	0	1	4	0	0	.250	.333	.250	.583	67	-0	1	3.39	0	/O-1	0	0.0
• FUENTES, Tito	Rigoberto (Peat) Fuentes b: 1/4/1944, Havana, Cuba BB/TR, 5'11", 175 lbs. Deb: 8/18/1965																							
1965 SF-N	26	72	12	15	1	0	0	1	5	14	0	1	.208	.269	.222	.491	39	-6	4	1.80	-5	S-18/2-7,3-1	1	-1.0

YEAR TM-L	G	AB	R	H	2B	3B	HR	RBI	BB	SO	SB	CS	AVG	OBP	SLG	OPS	OPS+	BR/A	RC	RC/G	FR	G/POS	WS	TPW
1966 SF-N	133	541	63	141	21	3	9	40	9	57	6	3	.261	.277	.360	.637	73	-20	53	3.39	4	S-76,2-60	14	-0.5
1967 SF-N	133	344	27	72	12	1	5	29	27	61	4	3	.209	.267	.294	.560	61	-18	26	2.43	6	*2-130/S-5	7	-0.2
1969 SF-N	67	183	28	54	4	3	1	14	15	25	2	4	.295	.352	.366	.718	103	-0	24	4.74	-1	3-36,S-30	6	0.0
1970 SF-N	123	435	49	116	13	7	2	32	36	52	4	5	.267	.327	.343	.670	81	-13	49	3.83	-8	2-78,S-36,3-24	9	-1.4
1971*SF-N	152	630	63	172	28	6	4	52	18	46	12	2	.273	.300	.356	.655	86	-12	65	3.58	17	*2-152	17	1.7
1972 SF-N	152	572	64	151	33	6	7	53	39	56	16	5	.264	.314	.379	.694	95	-3	69	4.12	-8	*2-152	14	-0.2
1973 SF-N	160	656	78	182	25	5	6	63	45	62	12	6	.277	.331	.358	.689	87	-11	79	4.16	8	*2-160/3-1	19	0.9
1974 SF-N	108	390	33	97	15	2	0	22	22	32	7	3	.249	.294	.297	.591	63	-20	33	2.79	-1	*2-103	5	-1.5
1975 SD-N	146	565	57	158	21	3	4	43	25	51	8	8	.280	.314	.349	.662	89	-12	58	3.48	-2	*2-142	15	-0.5
1976 SD-N	135	520	48	137	18	0	2	36	18	38	5	3	.263	.289	.310	.599	76	-18	45	2.92	-4	*2-127	9	-1.4
1977 Det-A	151	615	83	190	19	10	5	51	38	61	4	4	.309	.351	.397	.748	98	-1	85	5.00	-9	*2-151/D-1	16	-0.2
1978 Oak-A	13	43	5	6	1	0	0	2	1	6	0	0	.140	.159	.163	.322	-10	-6	1	.86	-1	2-13	0	-0.7
Total 13	**1499**	**5566**	**610**	**1491**	**211**	**46**	**45**	**438**	**298**	**561**	**80**	**47**	**.268**	**.309**	**.347**	**.656**	**82**	**-141**	**593**	**3.63**	**-5**	***2-1275,S-165/3-62,D-1**	**132**	**-5.0**

• FUHRMAN, Ollie Alfred George Fuhrman b: 7/20/1896, Jordan, MN d: 1/11/1969, Peoria, IL BB/TR, 5'11", 185 lbs. Deb: 4/13/1922

YEAR TM-L	G	AB	R	H	2B	3B	HR	RBI	BB	SO	SB	CS	AVG	OBP	SLG	OPS	OPS+	BR/A	RC	RC/G	FR	G/POS	WS	TPW
1922 Phi-A	6	6	1	2	1	0	0	0	0	0	0	0	.333	.333	.500	.833	112	0	1	6.36	0	/C-4	0	0.0

• FULGHUM, Dot James Lavoisier Fulghum b: 7/4/1900, Valdosta, GA d: 11/11/1967, Miami, FL BR/TR, 5'8.5", 165 lbs. Deb: 9/15/1921

YEAR TM-L	G	AB	R	H	2B	3B	HR	RBI	BB	SO	SB	CS	AVG	OBP	SLG	OPS	OPS+	BR/A	RC	RC/G	FR	G/POS	WS	TPW
1921 Phi-A	2	2	0	0	0	0	0	0	1	1	0	0	.000	.333	.000	.333	-9	-0	0	1.10	-1	/S-1	0	-0.1

• FULLER, Ed Edward Ashton White Fuller b: 3/22/1869, Washington, DC d: 3/15/1935, Hyattsville, MD BR/TR, 6', 158 lbs. Deb: 7/17/1886

YEAR TM-L	G	AB	R	H	2B	3B	HR	RBI	BB	SO	SB	CS	AVG	OBP	SLG	OPS	OPS+	BR/A	RC	RC/G	FR	G/POS	WS	TPW
1886 Was-N	2	7	0	1	0	0	0	0	0	3	0	....	.143	.143	.143	.286	-14	-1	0	.66	0	/P-2,0-1	0	-0.5

• FULLER, Frank Frank Edward "Rabbit" Fuller b: 1/1/1893, Detroit, MI d: 10/29/1965, Warren, MI BB/TR, 5'7", 150 lbs. Deb: 4/14/1915

YEAR TM-L	G	AB	R	H	2B	3B	HR	RBI	BB	SO	SB	CS	AVG	OBP	SLG	OPS	OPS+	BR/A	RC	RC/G	FR	G/POS	WS	TPW
1915 Det-A	14	32	6	5	0	0	0	2	9	7	2	3	.156	.341	.156	.498	47	-2	2	1.59	-1	/2-9,S-1	0	-0.3
1916 Det-A	20	10	2	1	0	0	0	1	1	4	3	....	.100	.182	.100	.282	-15	-1	1	1.91	-3	/2-8,S-1	0	-0.4
1923 Bos-A	6	21	3	5	0	0	0	0	1	1	1	1	.238	.273	.238	.511	35	-2	1	1.96	1	/2-6	0	-0.1
Total 3	**40**	**63**	**11**	**11**	**0**	**0**	**0**	**3**	**11**	**12**	**6**	**4**	**.175**	**.297**	**.175**	**.472**	**33**	**-6**	**4**	**1.76**	**-3**	**/2-23,S-2**	**0**	**-0.9**

• FULLER, Harry Henry W. Fuller b: 12/5/1862, Cincinnati, OH d: 12/12/1895, Cincinnati, OH, 5'8" Deb: 9/19/1891

YEAR TM-L	G	AB	R	H	2B	3B	HR	RBI	BB	SO	SB	CS	AVG	OBP	SLG	OPS	OPS+	BR/A	RC	RC/G	FR	G/POS	WS	TPW
1891 StL-a	1	2	0	0	0	0	0	0	0	1	0	....	.000	.000	.000	.000	-87	-1	0	.00	-1	/3-1	0	-0.1

• FULLER, Jim James Hardy Fuller b: 11/28/1950, Bethesda, MD BR/TR, 6'3", 215 lbs. Deb: 9/10/1973 Career OF: 30-0-62

YEAR TM-L	G	AB	R	H	2B	3B	HR	RBI	BB	SO	SB	CS	AVG	OBP	SLG	OPS	OPS+	BR/A	RC	RC/G	FR	G/POS	WS	TPW
1973 Bal-A	9	26	2	3	0	0	2	4	1	17	0	0	.115	.148	.346	.494	36	-2	1	1.61	1	/O-5(0-0-5),1-2,D-1	0	-0.2
1974 Bal-A	64	189	17	42	11	0	7	28	8	68	1	0	.222	.265	.392	.657	90	-3	19	3.33	-1	O-59(4-0-56)/1-4,D-2	4	-0.7
1977 Hou-N	34	100	5	16	6	0	2	9	10	45	0	1	.160	.243	.280	.523	44	-9	7	2.27	3	O-27(26-0-1)/1-1	1	-0.7
Total 3	**107**	**315**	**24**	**61**	**17**	**0**	**11**	**41**	**19**	**130**	**1**	**1**	**.194**	**.249**	**.352**	**.601**	**70**	**-14**	**27**	**2.83**	**3**	**/O-91,1-7,D-3**	**5**	**-1.6**

• FULLER, John John Edward Fuller b: 1/29/1950, Lynwood, CA BL/TL, 6'2", 180 lbs. Deb: 5/9/1974

YEAR TM-L	G	AB	R	H	2B	3B	HR	RBI	BB	SO	SB	CS	AVG	OBP	SLG	OPS	OPS+	BR/A	RC	RC/G	FR	G/POS	WS	TPW
1974 Atl-N	3	3	1	1	0	0	0	0	0	0	0	0	.333	.333	.333	.667	83	-0	0	4.50	-0	/O-1	0	0.0

• FULLER, Nig Charles F. Fuller b: 3/30/1879, Toledo, OH d: 11/12/1947, Toledo, OH BR/TR, 5'11", 165 lbs. Deb: 7/1/1902

YEAR TM-L	G	AB	R	H	2B	3B	HR	RBI	BB	SO	SB	CS	AVG	OBP	SLG	OPS	OPS+	BR/A	RC	RC/G	FR	G/POS	WS	TPW
1902 Bro-N	3	9	0	0	0	0	0	1	0	....	0	....	.000	.000	.000	.000	-99	-2	0	.00	0	/C-3	0	-0.2

• FULLER, Shorty William Benjamin Fuller b: 10/10/1867, Cincinnati, OH d: 4/11/1904, Cincinnati, OH BR/TR, 5'6", 157 lbs. Deb: 7/19/1888

YEAR TM-L	G	AB	R	H	2B	3B	HR	RBI	BB	SO	SB	CS	AVG	OBP	SLG	OPS	OPS+	BR/A	RC	RC/G	FR	G/POS	WS	TPW
1888 Was-N	49	170	11	31	5	2	0	12	10	14	6	....	.182	.232	.235	.467	52	-9	11	2.13	-1	S-47/2-2	2	-0.8
1889 StL-a	140	517	91	117	18	6	0	51	52	56	38	....	.226	.303	.284	.587	60	-30	57	3.81	15	*S-140	13	-0.9
1890 StL-a	130	526	118	146	9	9	1	40	73	....	60	....	.278	.377	.335	.712	96	-2	91	6.36	-3	*S-130	17	-0.1
1891 StL-a	135	576	105	122	14	7	2	61	67	28	42	....	.212	.298	.271	.569	55	-38	61	3.53	4	*S-103,2-39	12	-2.6
1892 NY-N	141	508	74	116	11	4	1	48	52	24	37	....	.228	.300	.272	.572	74	-15	54	3.71	-1	*S-141	11	-0.9
1893 NY-N	130	474	78	112	14	8	0	51	60	21	26	....	.236	.325	.300	.624	66	-23	56	4.09	6	*S-130	9	-0.8
1894*NY-N	95	377	82	104	14	4	2	46	52	16	32	....	.276	.367	.350	.717	74	-14	62	5.87	-5	*S-89/3-2,O-2(0-0-2),2-1	10	-1.1
1895 NY-N	126	458	82	103	11	3	0	32	64	34	15	....	.225	.323	.262	.585	53	-29	46	3.41	21	*S-126	11	-0.2
1896 NY-N	18	72	10	12	0	0	0	7	14	5	4	....	.167	.310	.167	.477	28	-7	5	2.25	-1	S-18	1	-0.5
Total 9	**964**	**3678**	**651**	**863**	**96**	**43**	**6**	**348**	**444**	**198**	**260**	**....**	**.235**	**.322**	**.289**	**.611**	**67**	**-167**	**442**	**4.16**	**35**	**S-924/2-42,3-2,O-2**	**86**	**-7.9**

• FULLER, Vern Vernon Gordon Fuller b: 3/1/1944, Menomonie, WI BR/TR, 6'1", 170 lbs. Deb: 9/5/1964

YEAR TM-L	G	AB	R	H	2B	3B	HR	RBI	BB	SO	SB	CS	AVG	OBP	SLG	OPS	OPS+	BR/A	RC	RC/G	FR	G/POS	WS	TPW
1964 Cle-A	2	1	0	0	0	0	0	0	0	0	0	0	.000	.000	.000	.000	-101	-0	0	.00	0	....	0	0.0
1966 Cle-A	16	47	7	11	2	1	2	2	7	6	0	0	.234	.357	.447	.804	129	2	8	6.25	2	2-16	3	0.5
1967 Cle-A	73	206	18	46	10	0	7	21	19	55	2	3	.223	.301	.374	.675	97	-1	24	3.79	2	2-64/S-2	7	0.7
1968 Cle-A	97	244	14	59	8	2	0	18	24	49	2	2	.242	.320	.291	.611	87	-3	24	3.21	-1	2-73,3-23/S-4	7	0.0
1969 Cle-A	108	254	25	60	11	1	4	22	20	53	2	1	.236	.297	.335	.632	74	-9	24	3.11	0	*2-102/3-7	6	-0.4
1970 Cle-A	29	33	3	6	2	0	1	2	3	9	0	0	.182	.250	.333	.583	57	-2	3	2.95	-1	2-16/3-4,1-1	1	-0.2
Total 6	**325**	**785**	**67**	**182**	**33**	**4**	**14**	**65**	**73**	**172**	**6**	**6**	**.232**	**.307**	**.338**	**.644**	**87**	**-14**	**82**	**3.49**	**2**	**2-271/3-34,S-6,1-1**	**24**	**0.6**

• FULLIS, Chick Charles Philip Fullis b: 2/27/1904, Girardville, PA d: 3/28/1946, Ashland, PA BR/TR, 5'9", 170 lbs. Deb: 4/13/1928 Career OF: 105-348-10

YEAR TM-L	G	AB	R	H	2B	3B	HR	RBI	BB	SO	SB	CS	AVG	OBP	SLG	OPS	OPS+	BR/A	RC	RC/G	FR	G/POS	WS	TPW
1928 NY-N	11	1	5	0	0	0	0	0	1	1	0	....	.000	.500	.000	.500	41	0	0	3.14	0	....	0	0.0
1929 NY-N	86	274	67	79	11	1	7	29	30	26	7	....	.288	.365	.412	.777	92	-3	41	5.40	-7	O-78(33-46-1)	6	-1.2
1930 NY-N	13	6	2	0	0	0	0	0	0	1	1	....	.000	.000	.000	.000	-102	-2	0	.00	0	/O-2(1-1-0)	0	-0.2
1931 NY-N	89	302	61	99	15	2	3	28	23	13	13	....	.328	.383	.421	.804	119	8	50	6.31	-2	O-68(1-65-0)/2-9	11	0.6
1932 NY-N	96	235	35	70	14	3	1	21	11	12	1	....	.298	.332	.396	.728	97	-1	31	4.82	-3	O-55(36-19-0)/2-1	5	-0.6
1933 Phi-N	151	647	91	200	31	6	1	45	36	34	18	....	.309	.350	.380	.731	96	-2	87	4.97	1	*O-151(0-151-0)/3-1	15	-0.5
1934 Phi-N	28	102	8	23	6	0	0	12	10	4	2	....	.225	.301	.284	.585	51	-7	10	3.19	-1	O-27(24-3-0)	1	-0.9
*StL-N	69	199	21	52	9	1	0	26	14	11	4	....	.261	.310	.317	.626	64	-10	19	3.35	-3	O-56(8-48-0)	3	-1.4
Yr.	97	301	29	75	15	1	0	38	24	15	6	....	.249	.307	.306	.612	59	-17	29	3.30	-3	O-83(32-51-0)	4	-2.2
1936 StL-N	47	89	15	25	6	1	0	6	7	11	0	....	.281	.333	.371	.704	90	-1	12	5.01	0	O-26(2-15-9)	3	-0.2
Total 8	**590**	**1855**	**305**	**548**	**92**	**14**	**12**	**167**	**132**	**113**	**46**	**....**	**.295**	**.347**	**.380**	**.726**	**92**	**-18**	**250**	**4.91**	**-14**	**O-463/2-10,3-1**	**44**	**-4.4**

• FULLMER, Brad Bradley Ryan Fullmer b: 1/17/1975, Chatsworth, CA BL/TR, 6'1", 185 lbs. Deb: 9/2/1997

YEAR TM-L	G	AB	R	H	2B	3B	HR	RBI	BB	SO	SB	CS	AVG	OBP	SLG	OPS	OPS+	BR/A	RC	RC/G	FR	G/POS	WS	TPW
1997 Mon-N	19	40	4	12	2	0	3	8	2	7	0	0	.300	.349	.575	.924	137	2	8	7.91	0	/1-8,O-2(2-0-0)	2	0.2
1998 Mon-N	140	505	58	138	44	2	13	73	39	70	6	6	.273	.328	.446	.773	102	-1	70	4.91	-3	*1-137	15	-1.5
1999 Mon-N	100	347	38	96	34	2	9	47	22	35	2	3	.277	.323	.464	.787	99	-3	46	4.62	-5	1-94	5	-1.5
2000 Tor-A	133	482	76	142	29	1	32	104	30	68	3	1	.295	.344	.558	.902	119	12	88	6.57	0	*D-129/1-1	15	0.3
2001 Tor-A	146	522	71	143	31	2	18	83	38	88	5	2	.274	.330	.444	.775	99	-1	74	5.00	0	*D-135/1-1	9	-1.0
2002*Ana-A	130	429	75	124	35	6	19	59	32	44	10	3	.289	.359	.531	.891	133	20	82	7.00	-2	D-94,1-29	13	1.0
2003 Ana-A	63	206	32	63	9	2	9	35	26	31	5	4	.306	.389	.500	.889	138	11	40	7.05	0	D-41,1-19	8	0.7
Total 7	**731**	**2531**	**354**	**718**	**184**	**15**	**103**	**409**	**189**	**343**	**31**	**19**	**.284**	**.342**	**.490**	**.832**	**113**	**39**	**409**	**5.76**	**-9**	**D-399,1-289/O-2**	**67**	**-1.8**

• FULMER, Chris Christopher Fulmer b: 7/4/1858, Tamaqua, PA d: 11/9/1931, Tamaqua, PA BR/TR, 5'8", 165 lbs. Deb: 8/4/1884 U Career OF: 16-24-17

YEAR TM-L	G	AB	R	H	2B	3B	HR	RBI	BB	SO	SB	CS	AVG	OBP	SLG	OPS	OPS+	BR/A	RC	RC/G	FR	G/POS	WS	TPW
1884 Was-U	48	181	39	50	9	0	0	....	11	....	....	....	.276	.318	.326	.644	122	5	19	4.11	0	C-34,O-16(0-7-9)/1-5	7	0.6
1886 Bal-a	80	270	54	66	9	3	1	30	48	....	29	....	.244	.363	.311	.674	115	8	42	5.56	10	C-68,O-12(6-5-1)/P-1	14	2.1
1887 Bal-a	56	237	52	90	11	4	0	32	36	....	35	....	.380	.382	.363	.746	115	7	42	7.77	-2	C-48/O-8(8-0-0)	8	0.6
1888 Bal-a	52	166	20	31	5	1	0	10	21	....	10	....	.187	.286	.229	.515	67	-5	14	2.81	-13	C-45/O-7(2-1-4)	3	-1.3
1889 Bal-a	16	58	11	15	3	1	0	13	6	12	2	....	.259	.338	.345	.683	97	-0	8	4.70	-2	O-14(0-11-3)/C-2	1	-0.1
Total 5	**252**	**912**	**176**	**252**	**37**	**9**	**1**	**85**	**122**	**12**	**76**	**....**	**.276**	**.343**	**.313**	**.655**	**106**	**15**	**125**	**5.15**	**-6**	**C-197/O-57,1-5,P-1**	**33**	**1.9**

• FULMER, Washington Washington Fayette Fulmer b: 6/15/1840, Philadelphia, PA d: 12/8/1907, Philadelphia, PA Deb: 7/19/1875

YEAR TM-L	G	AB	R	H	2B	3B	HR	RBI	BB	SO	SB	CS	AVG	OBP	SLG	OPS	OPS+	BR/A	RC	RC/G	FR	G/POS	WS	TPW
1875 Atl-n	1	4	1	2	0	0	0	1	0	0	0	0	.500	.500	.500	1.000	285	1	1	15.12	-0	/O-1	....	0.1

• FULTZ, Dave David Lewis Fultz b: 5/29/1875, Staunton, VA d: 10/29/1959, DeLand, FL BR/TR, 5'11", 170 lbs. Deb: 7/1/1898 Career OF: 34-510-10

YEAR TM-L	G	AB	R	H	2B	3B	HR	RBI	BB	SO	SB	CS	AVG	OBP	SLG	OPS	OPS+	BR/A	RC	RC/G	FR	G/POS	WS	TPW
1898 Phi-N	19	55	7	10	2	2	0	5	6	....	1	....	.182	.262	.291	.553	61	-3	5	2.69	-1	O-14(8-3-3)/2-3,S-1	0	-0.5
1899 Phi-N	2	5	0	2	0	0	0	0	0	....	1	....	.400	.400	.400	.800	124	0	1	10.87	-1	/2-1,S-1	0	0.0

YEAR TM-L	G	AB	R	H	2B	3B	HR	RBI	BB	SO	SB	CS	AVG	OBP	SLG	OPS	OPS+	BR/A	RC	RC/G	FR	G/POS	WS	TPW
Bal-N	57	210	31	62	3	2	0	18	13	....	17	....	.295	.342	.329	.671	80	-6	31	5.31	-5	O-31(14-14-3),3-20/2-2,1-1	5	-1.1
Yr.	59	215	31	64	3	2	0	18	13	....	18	....	.298	.343	.330	.674	81	-6	32	5.42	-5	O-31(14-14-3),3-20/2-3,1-1,S	5	-1.2
1901 Phi-A	132	561	95	164	17	9	0	52	32	....	36	....	.292	.334	.355	.689	87	-10	82	5.28	-3	*O-106(11-95-0),2-18/S-9	14	-1.7
1902 Phi-A	129	506	**109**	153	20	5	1	49	62	....	44	....	.302	.381	.368	.748	104	5	94	6.42	-8	*O-114(0-114-0),2-16	20	-0.7
1903 NY-A	79	295	39	66	12	1	0	25	25	....	29	....	.224	.295	.271	.567	67	-11	34	3.79	-2	O-77(1-73-3)/3-2	8	-1.7
1904 NY-A	97	339	39	93	17	4	2	32	24	....	17	....	.274	.324	.366	.690	113	5	49	4.90	4	O-90(0-90-0)	14	0.5
1905 NY-A	129	422	49	98	13	3	0	42	39	....	44	....	.232	.308	.277	.585	77	-10	52	4.11	-17	*O-122(0-121-1)	12	-3.6
Total 7	**644**	**2393**	**369**	**648**	**84**	**26**	**3**	**223**	**201**	**....**	**189**	**....**	**.271**	**.332**	**.331**	**.664**	**89**	**-30**	**348**	**5.01**	**-32**	**O-554/2-40,3-22,S-11,1-1**	**73**	**-8.9**

• FUNDERBURK, Mark Mark Clifford Funderburk b: 5/16/1957, Charlotte, NC BR/TR, 6'4", 226 lbs. Deb: 9/4/1981 Career OF: 11-0-0

YEAR TM-L	G	AB	R	H	2B	3B	HR	RBI	BB	SO	SB	CS	AVG	OBP	SLG	OPS	OPS+	BR/A	RC	RC/G	FR	G/POS	WS	TPW
1981 Min-A	8	15	2	3	1	0	0	2	2	1	0	0	.200	.294	.267	.561	59	-1	1	2.91	0	/O-6(6-0-0),D-1	0	0.0
1985 Min-A	23	70	7	22	7	1	2	13	5	12	0	1	.314	.360	.529	.889	132	2	11	5.52	0	D-15/O-5(5-0-0),1-1	2	0.2
Total 2	**31**	**85**	**9**	**25**	**8**	**1**	**2**	**15**	**7**	**13**	**0**	**1**	**.294**	**.348**	**.482**	**.830**	**118**	**2**	**13**	**5.02**	**0**	**/D-16,O-11,1-1**	**2**	**0.1**

• FUNK, Liz Elias Calvin Funk b: 10/28/1904, La Cygne, KS d: 1/16/1968, Norman, OK BL/TL, 5'8.5", 160 lbs. Deb: 4/26/1929 Career OF: 5-244-2

YEAR TM-L	G	AB	R	H	2B	3B	HR	RBI	BB	SO	SB	CS	AVG	OBP	SLG	OPS	OPS+	BR/A	RC	RC/G	FR	G/POS	WS	TPW
1929 NY-A	1	0	0	0	0	0	0	0	0	0	0	0	....	....	....	....	-107	0	0	....	0		0	0.0
1930 Det-A	140	527	74	145	26	11	4	65	29	39	12	6	.275	.319	.389	.708	77	-19	66	4.25	-4	*O-129(0-128-1)	11	-2.6
1932 Chi-A	122	440	59	114	21	5	2	40	43	19	17	15	.259	.325	.343	.668	78	-16	49	3.67	8	*O-120(4-115-1)	7	-1.1
1933 Chi-A	10	9	1	2	0	0	0	0	1	0	0	0	.222	.300	.222	.522	42	-1	1	2.46	0	/O-2(1-1-0)	0	-0.1
Total 4	**273**	**976**	**134**	**261**	**47**	**16**	**6**	**105**	**73**	**58**	**29**	**21**	**.267**	**.322**	**.367**	**.688**	**77**	**-36**	**115**	**3.97**	**3**	**O-251**	**18**	**-3.8**

• FURCAL, Rafael Rafael Antoni Furcal b: 8/24/1978, Loma de Cabrera, Dominican Republic BB/TR, 5'10", 165 lbs. Deb: 4/4/2000

YEAR TM-L	G	AB	R	H	2B	3B	HR	RBI	BB	SO	SB	CS	AVG	OBP	SLG	OPS	OPS+	BR/A	RC	RC/G	FR	G/POS	WS	TPW
2000*Atl-N	131	455	87	134	20	4	4	37	73	80	40	14	.295	.395	.382	.778	98	4	79	6.12	-3	*S-110,2-31	17	1.0
2001 Atl-N	79	324	39	89	19	0	4	30	24	56	22	6	.275	.327	.370	.697	78	-8	41	4.32	3	S-79	9	0.1
2002*Atl-N	154	636	95	175	31	8	8	47	43	114	27	15	.275	.324	.387	.711	85	-15	79	4.33	13	*S-150/2-4	20	1.1
2003*Atl-N★	156	664	130	194	35	**10**	15	61	60	76	25	2	.292	.354	.443	.796	106	10	113	6.36	-3	*S-155	25	1.9
Total 4	**520**	**2079**	**351**	**592**	**105**	**22**	**31**	**175**	**200**	**326**	**114**	**37**	**.285**	**.350**	**.401**	**.752**	**94**	**-9**	**312**	**5.34**	**10**	**S-494/2-35**	**71**	**4.1**

• FURILLO, Carl Carl Anthony "Skoonj,The Reading Rifle" Furillo
b: 3/8/1922, Stony Creek Mills, PA d: 1/21/1989, Stony Creek Mills, PA BR/TR, 6', 190 lbs. Deb: 4/16/1946 Career OF: 53-308-1408

YEAR TM-L	G	AB	R	H	2B	3B	HR	RBI	BB	SO	SB	CS	AVG	OBP	SLG	OPS	OPS+	BR/A	RC	RC/G	FR	G/POS	WS	TPW
1946 Bro-N	117	335	29	95	18	6	3	35	31	20	6	....	.284	.346	.400	.746	110	4	46	4.73	6	*O-112(5-103-4)	14	0.7
1947*Bro-N	124	437	61	129	24	7	8	88	34	24	7	....	.295	.347	.437	.785	103	1	62	5.12	0	*O-121(28-93-2)	14	-0.3
1948 Bro-N	108	364	55	108	20	4	4	44	43	32	6	....	.297	.374	.407	.781	107	5	57	5.77	5	*O-104(0-96-12)	15	0.7
1949*Bro-N	142	549	95	177	27	10	18	106	37	29	4	....	.322	.368	.506	.875	127	19	98	6.73	1	*O-142(0-0-142)	23	1.6
1950 Bro-N	153	620	99	189	30	6	18	106	41	40	8	....	.305	.353	.460	.813	110	7	96	5.74	1	*O-153(0-0-153)	18	0.3
1951 Bro-N	158	667	93	197	32	4	16	91	43	33	8	7	.295	.344	.427	.772	104	2	97	5.26	15	*O-157(0-0-157)	21	1.2
1952*Bro-N★	134	425	52	105	18	1	8	59	31	33	1	4	.247	.304	.351	.655	80	-13	42	3.35	0	*O-131(0-0-131)	7	-1.7
1953*Bro-N★	132	479	82	165	38	6	21	92	34	32	1	1	**.344**	.393	.580	.973	146	31	107	8.71	1	*O-131(0-0-131)	23	2.6
1954 Bro-N	150	547	56	161	23	1	19	96	49	35	2	4	.294	.358	.444	.802	104	2	83	5.46	3	*O-149(3-5-145)	17	0.0
1955*Bro-N	140	523	83	164	24	3	26	95	43	43	4	5	.314	.373	.520	.894	130	21	97	6.81	-2	*O-140(6-1-139)	22	1.5
1956*Bro-N	149	523	66	151	30	0	21	83	57	41	1	1	.289	.360	.467	.826	111	9	80	5.31	-3	*O-146(9-3-143)	17	0.1
1957 Bro-N	119	395	61	121	17	4	12	66	29	33	0	2	.306	.361	.461	.822	108	5	62	5.60	-1	*O-107(1-0-106)	12	0.1
1958 LA-N	122	411	54	119	19	3	18	83	35	28	0	2	.290	.348	.482	.830	113	6	64	5.44	-8	*O-119(1-7-116)	13	-0.6
1959*LA-N	50	93	8	27	4	0	0	13	7	11	0	0	.290	.340	.333	.673	75	-3	10	3.48	-2	O-25(0-0-25)	1	-0.5
1960 LA-N	8	10	1	2	0	1	0	1	0	2	0	0	.200	.200	.400	.600	56	-1	1	2.70	-0	/O-2(0-0-2)	0	-0.1
Total 15	**1806**	**6378**	**895**	**1910**	**324**	**56**	**192**	**1058**	**514**	**436**	**48**	**26**	**.299**	**.356**	**.458**	**.814**	**112**	**96**	**1004**	**5.67**	**17**	***O-1739**	**217**	**5.7**

• FUSSELBACK, Eddie Edward L. Fusselback b: 7/4/1858, Philadelphia, PA d: 4/14/1926, Philadelphia, PA BR, 5'6", 156 lbs. Deb: 5/3/1882 Career OF: 5-2-13

YEAR TM-L	G	AB	R	H	2B	3B	HR	RBI	BB	SO	SB	CS	AVG	OBP	SLG	OPS	OPS+	BR/A	RC	RC/G	FR	G/POS	WS	TPW
1882 StL-a	35	136	13	31	2	0	0	....	5	....	....	....	.228	.255	.243	.498	66	-5	9	2.30	1	C-19,O-15(4-0-11)/P-4	3	-0.5
1884 Bal-U	68	303	60	86	16	3	1	....	3	....	....	....	.284	.291	.366	.657	110	1	33	4.27	15	C-54/3-6,S-5,O-4(1-2-1)	13	1.8
1885 Phi-a	5	19	2	6	1	0	0	2	0	....	....	....	.316	.316	.368	.684	109	0	2	4.71	0	/C-5	1	0.1
1888 Lou-a	1	4	0	1	0	0	0	1	0	....	0	....	.250	.250	.250	.500	62	-0	0	2.31	1	/O-1	0	0.0
Total 4	**109**	**462**	**75**	**124**	**19**	**3**	**1**	**3**	**8**	**....**	**0**	**....**	**.268**	**.281**	**.329**	**.610**	**96**	**-4**	**44**	**3.66**	**17**	**/C-78,O-20,3-6,S-5,P-4**	**17**	**1.4**

• FUSSELMAN, Les Lester Leroy Fusselman b: 3/7/1921, Pryor, OK d: 5/21/1970, Cleveland, OH BR/TR, 6'1", 195 lbs. Deb: 4/16/1952

YEAR TM-L	G	AB	R	H	2B	3B	HR	RBI	BB	SO	SB	CS	AVG	OBP	SLG	OPS	OPS+	BR/A	RC	RC/G	FR	G/POS	WS	TPW
1952 StL-N	32	63	5	10	3	0	1	3	0	9	0	0	.159	.159	.254	.413	13	-8	2	1.02	-1	C-32	1	-0.7
1953 StL-N	11	8	1	2	1	0	0	0	0	0	0	0	.250	.250	.375	.625	60	-0	0	1.35	-0	C-11	0	0.0
Total 2	**43**	**71**	**6**	**12**	**4**	**0**	**1**	**3**	**0**	**9**	**0**	**0**	**.169**	**.169**	**.268**	**.437**	**19**	**-8**	**3**	**1.06**	**-1**	**/C-43**	**1**	**-0.8**

• GABLER, Gabe William Louis Gabler b: 8/4/1930, St. Louis, MO BL/TR, 6'1", 190 lbs. Deb: 9/16/1958

YEAR TM-L	G	AB	R	H	2B	3B	HR	RBI	BB	SO	SB	CS	AVG	OBP	SLG	OPS	OPS+	BR/A	RC	RC/G	FR	G/POS	WS	TPW
1958 Chi-N	3	3	0	0	0	0	0	0	0	3	0	0	.000	.000	.000	.000	-102	-1	0	.00	0	....	0	-0.1

• GABRIELSON, Len Leonard Gary Gabrielson b: 2/14/1940, Oakland, CA BL/TR, 6'4", 210 lbs. Deb: 9/9/1960 Career OF: 269-21-183

YEAR TM-L	G	AB	R	H	2B	3B	HR	RBI	BB	SO	SB	CS	AVG	OBP	SLG	OPS	OPS+	BR/A	RC	RC/G	FR	G/POS	WS	TPW
1960 Mil-N	4	3	1	0	0	0	0	0	1	0	0	0	.000	.250	.000	.250	-27	-0	0	.59	0	/O-1	0	-0.1
1963 Mil-N	46	120	14	26	5	0	3	15	8	23	1	1	.217	.266	.333	.599	72	-5	11	3.08	-2	O-22(18-6-1),1-16/3-3	2	-0.9
1964 Mil-N	24	38	0	7	2	0	0	1	1	8	1	0	.184	.205	.237	.442	24	-4	2	1.75	-1	1-12/O-2(0-0-2)	0	-0.5
Chi-N	89	272	22	67	11	2	5	23	19	37	9	4	.246	.298	.357	.655	80	-7	30	3.84	3	O-68(1-12-58)/1-8	5	-0.9
Yr.	113	310	22	74	13	2	5	24	20	45	10	4	.239	.287	.342	.629	74	-10	32	3.57	2	O-70(1-12-60),1-20	5	-1.4
1965 Chi-N	28	48	4	12	0	0	3	5	7	16	0	2	.250	.345	.438	.783	116	0	7	4.90	-1	O-14(0-2-12)/1-1	1	-0.1
SF-N	88	269	36	81	6	5	4	26	26	48	4	0	.301	.367	.405	.772	114	7	42	5.81	1	O-77(70-0-9)/1-5	11	0.4
Yr.	116	317	40	93	6	5	7	31	33	64	4	2	.293	.364	.410	.774	114	7	49	5.66	0	O-91(70-2-21)/1-6	12	0.2
1966 SF-N	94	240	27	52	7	0	4	16	21	51	0	1	.217	.280	.296	.576	58	-13	21	2.83	-2	O-67(61-0-9)/1-6	3	-1.9
1967 Cal-A	11	12	2	1	0	0	0	2	2	4	0	0	.083	.214	.083	.298	-9	-2	0	.80	0	/O-1	0	-0.2
LA-N	90	238	20	62	10	3	7	29	15	41	3	1	.261	.307	.416	.723	114	4	30	4.40	3	O-68(47-1-26)	7	0.3
1968 LA-N	108	304	38	82	16	1	10	35	32	47	1	1	.270	.339	.428	.767	140	14	44	4.98	2	O-86(57-0-30)	13	1.4
1969 LA-N	83	178	13	48	5	1	1	18	12	25	1	2	.270	.316	.326	.642	86	-4	18	3.41	0	O-47(13-0-34)/1-2	3	-0.6
1970 LA-N	43	42	1	8	2	0	0	6	1	15	0	0	.190	.209	.238	.447	20	-5	2	1.70	0	/O-2(0-0-2),1-1	0	-0.5
Total 9	**708**	**1764**	**178**	**446**	**64**	**12**	**37**	**176**	**145**	**315**	**20**	**12**	**.253**	**.311**	**.366**	**.677**	**95**	**-14**	**206**	**4.04**	**3**	**O-455/1-51,3-3**	**45**	**-3.6**

• GABRIELSON, Len Leonard Hilbourne Gabrielson b: 9/8/1915, Oakland, CA d: 11/14/2000, Stanford, CA BL/TL, 6'3", 210 lbs. Deb: 4/21/1939

YEAR TM-L	G	AB	R	H	2B	3B	HR	RBI	BB	SO	SB	CS	AVG	OBP	SLG	OPS	OPS+	BR/A	RC	RC/G	FR	G/POS	WS	TPW
1939 Phi-N	5	18	3	4	0	0	0	1	2	3	0	....	.222	.300	.222	.522	44	-1	1	2.62	2	/1-5	0	0.0

• GAEDEL, Eddie Edward Carl Gaedel b: 6/8/1925, Chicago, IL d: 6/18/1961, Chicago, IL BR/TL, 3'7", 65 lbs. Deb: 8/19/1951

YEAR TM-L	G	AB	R	H	2B	3B	HR	RBI	BB	SO	SB	CS	AVG	OBP	SLG	OPS	OPS+	BR/A	RC	RC/G	FR	G/POS	WS	TPW
1951 StL-A	1	0	0	0	0	0	0	0	1	0	0	0	....	1.000	....	1.000	181	0	0	∞	0	....	0	0.0

• GAETTI, Gary Gary Joseph "The Rat,G-Man" Gaetti b: 8/19/1958, Centralia, IL BR/TR, 6', 200 lbs. Deb: 9/20/1981 Career OF: 13-0-1

YEAR TM-L	G	AB	R	H	2B	3B	HR	RBI	BB	SO	SB	CS	AVG	OBP	SLG	OPS	OPS+	BR/A	RC	RC/G	FR	G/POS	WS	TPW
1981 Min-A	9	26	4	5	0	0	2	3	0	6	0	0	.192	.192	.423	.615	68	-1	2	2.08	1	/3-8,D-1	0	-0.1
1982 Min-A	145	508	59	117	25	4	25	84	37	107	0	4	.230	.286	.443	.729	94	-7	59	3.73	9	*3-142/S-2,D-1	11	0.0
1983 Min-A	157	584	81	143	30	3	21	78	54	121	7	1	.245	.313	.414	.727	95	-4	74	4.27	16	*3-154/S-3,D-1	17	1.1
1984 Min-A	162	588	55	154	29	4	5	65	44	81	11	5	.262	.318	.350	.668	81	-14	67	3.94	23	*3-154/O-8(8-0-0),S-2	16	0.7
1985 Min-A	160	560	71	138	31	0	20	63	37	89	13	5	.246	.301	.409	.710	87	-10	66	4.01	17	*3-156/O-4(4-0-0),1-1,D-1	15	0.5
1986 Min-A	157	596	91	171	34	1	34	108	52	108	14	15	.287	.350	.518	.869	129	19	99	5.75	17	*3-156/S-2,2-1,O-1	23	3.4
1987*Min-A	154	584	95	150	36	2	31	109	37	92	10	7	.257	.304	.485	.789	101	-3	75	4.32	-1	*3-150/D-2	17	-0.5
1988 Min-A★	133	468	66	141	29	2	28	88	36	85	7	4	.301	.358	.551	.909	146	27	89	6.94	3	*3-115/D-5,S-2	22	3.1
1989 Min-A★	130	498	63	125	11	4	19	75	25	87	6	2	.251	.291	.404	.694	88	-10	56	3.80	20	*3-125/D-3,1-2	12	1.2
1990 Min-A	154	577	61	132	27	5	16	85	36	101	6	1	.229	.278	.376	.654	76	-19	56	3.15	14	*3-151/1-2,S-2	13	-0.4
1991 Cal-A	152	586	58	144	22	1	18	66	33	104	5	5	.246	.295	.379	.674	85	-15	63	3.63	15	*3-152	14	0.1
1992 Cal-A	130	456	41	103	13	2	12	48	21	79	3	1	.226	.269	.342	.611	70	-20	41	3.01	8	3-67,1-44,D-17	9	-1.5
1993 Cal-A	20	50	3	9	2	0	0	4	5	12	1	0	.180	.255	.220	.475	28	-5	3	1.57	0	/3-7,1-6,D-5	0	-0.6
KC-A	82	281	37	72	18	1	14	46	16	75	0	3	.256	.315	.477	.792	103	-1	42	5.11	4	3-72,1-18/D-1	9	0.3
Yr.	102	331	40	81	20	1	14	50	21	87	1	3	.245	.306	.438	.744	92	-6	45	4.51	4	3-79,1-24/D-6	9	-0.3

YEAR TM-L	G	AB	R	H	2B	3B	HR	RBI	BB	SO	SB	CS	AVG	OBP	SLG	OPS	OPS+	BR/A	RC	RC/G	FR	G/POS	WS	TPW
1994 KC-A	90	327	53	94	15	3	12	57	19	63	0	2	.287	.330	.462	.792	97	-3	47	5.07	1	3-85/1-9	10	-0.1
1995 KC-A	137	514	76	134	27	0	35	96	47	91	3	3	.261	.332	.518	.850	115	8	88	5.97	-8	*3-123,1-11/D-6	17	0.1
1996*StL-N	141	522	71	143	27	4	23	80	35	97	2	2	.274	.329	.473	.802	109	4	80	5.37	0	*3-133,1-14	16	0.5
1997 StL-N	148	502	63	126	24	1	17	69	36	88	7	3	.251	.309	.404	.713	86	-12	58	3.84	3	*3-132,1-20/P-1	9	-0.7
1998 StL-N	91	306	39	81	23	1	11	43	31	39	1	1	.265	.342	.454	.796	108	3	46	5.21	-2	3-83/1-3,2-1,0-1,P-1	8	0.2
*Chi-N	37	128	21	41	11	0	8	27	12	23	0	0	.320	.400	.594	.994	152	10	31	9.18	1	3-36	8	1.1
Yr.	128	434	60	122	34	1	19	70	43	62	1	1	.281	.359	.495	.855	121	13	77	6.31	-1	*3-119/1-3,2-1,0-1,P-1	16	1.3
1999 Chi-N	113	280	22	57	9	1	9	46	21	51	0	1	.204	.264	.339	.603	52	-22	25	2.87	1	3-81/1-8,P-1,S-1	3	-2.1
2000 Bos-A	5	10	0	0	0	0	0	1	0	3	0	0	.000	.000	.000	.000	-97	-3	0	.00	0	/D-5	0	-0.3
Total 20	**2507**	**8951**	**1130**	**2280**	**443**	**39**	**360**	**1341**	**634**	**1602**	**96**	**65**	**.255**	**.311**	**.434**	**.745**	**97**	**-78**	**1165**	**4.43**	**143**	***3-2282,1-138/D-48,0-14,S,P,2**	**249**	**5.9**

• GAFFKE, Fabian Fabian Sebastian Gaffke b: 8/5/1913, Milwaukee, WI d: 2/8/1992, Milwaukee, WI BR/TR, 5'10", 185 lbs. Deb: 9/9/1936 Career OF: 26-4-55

YEAR TM-L	G	AB	R	H	2B	3B	HR	RBI	BB	SO	SB	CS	AVG	OBP	SLG	OPS	OPS+	BR/A	RC	RC/G	FR	G/POS	WS	TPW
1936 Bos-A	15	55	5	7	2	0	1	3	4	5	0	0	.127	.200	.218	.418	3	-9	3	1.41	0	0-15(5-0-10)	0	-0.9
1937 Bos-A	54	184	32	53	10	4	6	34	15	25	1	2	.288	.342	.484	.825	102	-1	30	5.73	-3	0-50(16-1-33)	5	-0.6
1938 Bos-A	15	10	2	1	0	0	0	1	3	2	0	0	.100	.308	.100	.408	6	-1	1	1.55	0	/0-2(0-0-2),C-1	0	-0.1
1939 Bos-A	1	1	0	0	0	0	0	1	0	0	0	0	.000	.000	.000	.000	-96	-0	0	.00	0	....	0	0.0
1941 Cle-A	4	4	0	1	0	0	0	0	2	2	0	0	.250	.500	.250	.750	109	0	1	6.95	0	/0-2(0-2-0)	0	0.0
1942 Cle-A	40	67	4	11	2	0	0	3	6	13	1	0	.164	.243	.194	.437	25	-6	3	1.33	0	0-16(5-1-10)	0	-0.8
Total 6	**129**	**321**	**43**	**73**	**14**	**4**	**7**	**42**	**30**	**47**	**2**	**2**	**.227**	**.297**	**.361**	**.659**	**65**	**-18**	**37**	**3.75**	**-4**	**/0-85,C-1**	**5**	**-2.4**

• GAGLIANO, Phil Philip Joseph Gagliano b: 12/27/1941, Memphis, TN BR/TR, 6'1", 185 lbs. Deb: 4/16/1963 Career OF: 34-0-31

YEAR TM-L	G	AB	R	H	2B	3B	HR	RBI	BB	SO	SB	CS	AVG	OBP	SLG	OPS	OPS+	BR/A	RC	RC/G	FR	G/POS	WS	TPW
1963 StL-N	10	5	1	2	0	0	0	1	1	1	0	0	.400	.500	.400	.900	149	0	1	10.17	0	/2-3,3-1	0	0.0
1964 StL-N	40	58	5	15	4	0	1	9	3	10	0	1	.259	.295	.379	.674	81	-2	6	3.53	-1	2-12/0-2(1-0-1),1-1,3-1	1	-0.2
1965 StL-N	122	363	46	87	14	2	8	53	40	45	2	1	.240	.317	.355	.672	81	-8	41	3.73	-4	2-57,0-25(4-0-23),3-19	9	-1.0
1966 StL-N	90	213	23	54	8	2	2	15	24	29	2	1	.254	.332	.338	.670	87	-3	24	3.84	1	3-41/1-8,0-5(5-0-0),2-1	5	-0.3
1967*StL-N	73	217	20	48	7	0	2	21	19	26	0	0	.221	.287	.281	.568	64	-10	17	2.61	-5	2-27,3-25/1-4,S-2	3	-1.4
1968*StL-N	53	105	13	24	4	2	0	13	7	12	0	0	.229	.283	.305	.588	77	-3	9	2.91	2	2-17,3-10/0-5(4-0-1)	3	0.0
1969 StL-N	62	128	7	29	2	0	1	10	14	12	0	0	.227	.303	.266	.568	60	-6	10	2.51	-2	2-20/1-9,3-9,0-2(0-0-2)	1	-0.8
1970 StL-N	18	32	0	6	0	0	0	2	1	3	0	1	.188	.212	.188	.400	8	-5	1	1.14	-2	/3-6,1-3,2-2	0	-0.6
Chi-N	26	40	5	6	0	0	0	5	5	5	0	0	.150	.244	.150	.394	7	-5	2	1.28	0	2-16/1-3,3-1	0	-0.5
Yr.	44	72	5	12	0	0	0	7	6	8	0	1	.167	.231	.167	.397	8	-10	3	1.22	-2	2-18/3-7,1-4	0	-1.1
1971 Bos-A	47	68	11	22	5	0	0	13	11	5	0	0	.324	.418	.397	.815	123	3	12	6.73	0	0-11(7-0-4)/2-7,3-4	3	0.3
1972 Bos-A	52	82	9	21	4	1	0	10	10	13	1	0	.256	.337	.329	.666	93	-0	10	4.20	1	0-12(12-0-0)/3-5,2-4,1-2	3	0.0
1973*Cin-N	63	69	8	20	2	0	0	7	13	16	0	0	.290	.402	.319	.721	108	2	10	5.45	-1	/3-7,2-4,1-1,0-1	2	0.0
1974 Cin-N	46	31	2	2	0	0	0	0	15	7	0	0	.065	.370	.065	.434	27	-2	2	1.94	-1	/2-2,1-1,3-1	0	-0.3
Total 12	**702**	**1411**	**150**	**336**	**50**	**7**	**14**	**159**	**163**	**184**	**5**	**4**	**.238**	**.319**	**.313**	**.632**	**77**	**-38**	**146**	**3.45**	**-12**	**2-172,3-130/0-63,1-30,S-2**	**30**	**-4.7**

• GAGLIANO, Ralph Ralph Michael Gagliano b: 10/8/1946, Memphis, TN BL/TR, 5'11", 170 lbs. Deb: 9/21/1965

YEAR TM-L	G	AB	R	H	2B	3B	HR	RBI	BB	SO	SB	CS	AVG	OBP	SLG	OPS	OPS+	BR/A	RC	RC/G	FR	G/POS	WS	TPW
1965 Cle-A	1	0	0	0	0	0	0	0	0	0	0	0	....	....	....	....	-99	0	0	....	0	....	0	0.0

• GAGNE, Greg Gregory Carpenter Gagne b: 11/12/1961, Fall River, MA BR/TR, 5'11", 172 lbs. Deb: 6/5/1983 Career OF: 0-7-1

YEAR TM-L	G	AB	R	H	2B	3B	HR	RBI	BB	SO	SB	CS	AVG	OBP	SLG	OPS	OPS+	BR/A	RC	RC/G	FR	G/POS	WS	TPW
1983 Min-A	10	27	2	3	1	0	0	3	0	6	0	0	.111	.111	.148	.259	-28	-5	1	.54	-2	S-10	0	-0.6
1984 Min-A	2	1	0	0	0	0	0	0	0	0	0	0	.000	.000	.000	.000	-96	-0	0	.00	0	....	0	0.0
1985 Min-A	114	293	37	66	15	3	2	23	20	57	10	4	.225	.282	.317	.599	60	-16	27	2.97	-7	*S-106/D-5	4	-1.3
1986 Min-A	156	472	63	118	22	6	12	54	30	108	12	10	.250	.303	.398	.701	87	-11	57	3.98	-16	*S-155/2-4	10	-1.1
1987*Min-A	137	437	68	116	28	7	10	40	25	84	6	6	.265	.311	.430	.741	91	-9	58	4.60	15	*S-136/0-4(0-3-1),2-1,D-1	18	1.9
1988 Min-A	149	461	70	109	20	6	14	48	27	110	15	7	.236	.289	.397	.686	87	-9	50	3.50	2	*S-146/0-2(0-2-0),2-1,3-1	12	0.4
1989 Min-A	149	460	69	125	29	7	9	48	17	80	11	4	.272	.301	.424	.725	96	-4	56	4.20	4	*S-146/0-1	12	1.0
1990 Min-A	138	388	38	91	22	3	7	38	24	76	8	8	.235	.281	.361	.642	73	-17	38	3.20	-1	*S-135/D-2,0-1	7	-0.8
1991*Min-A	139	408	52	108	23	3	8	42	26	72	11	9	.265	.314	.395	.708	90	-8	45	3.67	2	*S-137/D-1	12	0.4
1992 Min-A	146	439	53	108	23	0	7	39	19	83	6	7	.246	.280	.346	.627	72	-19	39	2.93	22	*S-141	13	1.3
1993 KC-A	159	540	66	151	32	3	10	57	33	93	10	12	.280	.321	.406	.727	89	-13	67	4.36	5	*S-159	18	0.5
1994 KC-A	107	375	39	97	23	3	7	51	27	79	10	17	.259	.315	.392	.707	78	-19	41	3.60	8	*S-106	11	-0.2
1995 KC-A	120	430	58	110	25	4	6	49	38	60	3	5	.256	.319	.374	.694	79	-16	50	3.85	8	*S-118/D-2	10	0.2
1996*LA-N	128	428	48	109	13	2	10	55	50	93	4	2	.255	.335	.364	.700	92	-5	54	4.38	18	*S-127	20	2.3
1997 LA-N	144	514	49	129	20	3	9	57	31	120	2	5	.251	.299	.354	.653	76	-21	51	3.38	-7	*S-143	10	-1.7
Total 15	**1798**	**5673**	**712**	**1440**	**296**	**50**	**111**	**604**	**367**	**1121**	**108**	**96**	**.254**	**.304**	**.382**	**.686**	**82**	**-171**	**633**	**3.74**	**51**	***S-1765/D-11,0-8,2-6,3-1**	**157**	**2.2**

• GAGNIER, Ed Edward James Gagnier b: 4/16/1883, Paris, France d: 9/13/1946, Detroit, MI BR/TR, 5'9", 170 lbs. Deb: 4/14/1914

YEAR TM-L	G	AB	R	H	2B	3B	HR	RBI	BB	SO	SB	CS	AVG	OBP	SLG	OPS	OPS+	BR/A	RC	RC/G	FR	G/POS	WS	TPW
1914 Bro-F	94	337	22	63	12	2	0	25	13	24	8	....	.187	.219	.234	.454	29	-32	18	1.64	2	S-88/3-6	4	-2.4
1915 Bro-F	20	50	8	13	1	0	0	4	10	5	2	....	.260	.393	.280	.673	102	1	6	4.23	1	S-13/2-6	2	0.3
Buf-F	1	2	0	0	0	0	0	0	0	0	0	....	.000	.000	.000	.000	-100	-0	0	.00	-1	/2-1	0	-0.1
Yr.	21	52	8	13	1	0	0	4	10	5	2	....	.250	.381	.269	.650	95	0	6	4.03	0	S-13/2-7	2	0.2
Total 2	**115**	**389**	**30**	**76**	**13**	**2**	**0**	**29**	**23**	**29**	**10**	**....**	**.195**	**.244**	**.239**	**.483**	**39**	**-32**	**25**	**1.95**	**2**	**S-101/2-7,3-6**	**6**	**-2.3**

• GAGNON, Chick Harold Dennis Gagnon b: 9/27/1897, Milbury, MA d: 4/30/1970, Wilmington, DE BR/TR, 5'7.5", 158 lbs. Deb: 6/27/1922

YEAR TM-L	G	AB	R	H	2B	3B	HR	RBI	BB	SO	SB	CS	AVG	OBP	SLG	OPS	OPS+	BR/A	RC	RC/G	FR	G/POS	WS	TPW
1922 Det-A	10	4	2	1	0	0	0	0	0	2	0	0	.250	.250	.250	.500	32	-0	0	2.12	-1	/3-1,S-1	0	-0.1
1924 Was-A	4	5	1	1	0	0	0	1	0	0	0	0	.200	.200	.200	.400	3	-1	0	1.27	0	/S-2	0	0.0
Total 2	**14**	**9**	**3**	**2**	**0**	**0**	**0**	**1**	**0**	**2**	**0**	**0**	**.222**	**.222**	**.222**	**.444**	**16**	**-1**	**0**	**1.64**	**-1**	**/S-3,3-1**	**0**	**-0.2**

• GAINER, Del Dellos Clinton "Sheriff" Gainer b: 11/10/1886, Montrose, WV d: 1/29/1947, Elkins, WV BR/TR, 6', 180 lbs. Deb: 10/2/1909 Career OF: 24-10-1

YEAR TM-L	G	AB	R	H	2B	3B	HR	RBI	BB	SO	SB	CS	AVG	OBP	SLG	OPS	OPS+	BR/A	RC	RC/G	FR	G/POS	WS	TPW
1909 Det-A	2	5	0	1	0	0	0	0	0	....	0	....	.200	.200	.200	.400	25	-0	0	1.20	0	/1-2	0	-0.1
1911 Det-A	70	248	32	75	11	4	2	25	20	....	10	....	.302	.366	.403	.770	109	3	40	5.74	-3	1-69	8	-0.1
1912 Det-A	52	179	28	43	5	6	0	20	18	....	14	....	.240	.320	.335	.655	90	-2	24	4.28	-1	1-50/0-1	4	-0.4
1913 Det-A	105	363	47	97	16	8	2	25	30	45	10	....	.267	.333	.372	.705	108	3	46	4.33	2	*1-103	9	0.3
1914 Det-A	1	0	0	0	0	0	0	0	0	0	0	....	....	....	....	....	-97	0	0	....	0	/1-1	0	0.0
Bos-A	38	84	11	20	9	2	2	13	8	14	2	2	.238	.312	.464	.776	133	2	12	4.67	0	1-18,2-11/0-1	4	0.2
Yr.	39	84	11	20	9	2	2	13	8	14	2	2	.238	.312	.464	.776	133	2	12	4.67	0	1-19,2-11/0-1	4	0.2
1915*Bos-A	82	200	30	59	5	8	1	29	21	31	7	2	.295	.371	.415	.786	139	10	35	5.77	4	1-56/0-6(0-5-1)	10	1.3
1916*Bos-A	56	142	14	36	6	0	3	18	10	24	5	....	.254	.303	.359	.662	98	-1	18	4.08	2	1-48/2-2	4	0.0
1917 Bos-A	52	172	28	53	10	2	2	19	15	21	1	....	.308	.374	.424	.798	145	9	27	5.65	2	1-50	8	1.1
1919 Bos-A	47	118	9	28	6	2	0	13	13	15	5	....	.237	.318	.322	.640	85	-2	13	3.68	0	1-21,0-18(18-0-0)	2	-0.3
1922 StL-N	43	97	19	26	7	4	2	23	14	6	0	2	.268	.360	.485	.845	122	2	17	5.68	0	1-26,0-10(6-4-0)	3	0.0
Total 10	**548**	**1608**	**218**	**438**	**75**	**36**	**14**	**185**	**149**	**156**	**54**	**6**	**.272**	**.342**	**.390**	**.732**	**114**	**24**	**232**	**4.87**	**4**	**1-444/0-36,2-13**	**52**	**2.1**

• GAINER, Jay Johnathan Keith Gainer b: 10/8/1966, Panama City, FL BL/TL, 6', 190 lbs. Deb: 5/14/1993

YEAR TM-L	G	AB	R	H	2B	3B	HR	RBI	BB	SO	SB	CS	AVG	OBP	SLG	OPS	OPS+	BR/A	RC	RC/G	FR	G/POS	WS	TPW
1993 Col-N	23	41	4	7	0	0	3	6	4	12	1	1	.171	.244	.390	.635	57	-3	4	3.01	-1	/1-7	0	-0.4

• GAINES, Joe Arnesta Joe Gaines b: 11/22/1936, Bryan, TX BR/TR, 6'1", 190 lbs. Deb: 6/29/1960 Career OF: 80-7-128

YEAR TM-L	G	AB	R	H	2B	3B	HR	RBI	BB	SO	SB	CS	AVG	OBP	SLG	OPS	OPS+	BR/A	RC	RC/G	FR	G/POS	WS	TPW
1960 Cin-N	11	15	2	3	0	0	0	1	0	1	0	0	.200	.200	.200	.400	10	-2	1	1.35	0	/0-3(1-1-2)	0	-0.2
1961 Cin-N	5	3	2	0	0	0	0	0	2	1	0	0	.000	.400	.000	.400	18	-0	0	1.87	-1	/0-3(1-2-0)	0	-0.1
1962 Cin-N	64	52	12	12	3	0	1	7	8	16	0	0	.231	.333	.346	.679	80	-1	6	4.19	0	0-13(11-0-2)	1	-0.2
1963 Bal-A	66	126	24	36	4	1	6	20	20	39	2	1	.286	.384	.476	.860	142	8	23	6.51	-2	0-39(34-4-2)	6	0.4
1964 Bal-A	16	26	2	4	0	0	1	2	3	7	0	0	.154	.241	.269	.511	42	-2	2	2.30	0	/0-5(5-0-0)	0	-0.3
Hou-N	89	307	37	78	9	7	7	34	27	69	8	2	.254	.318	.397	.716	106	4	39	4.34	-4	0-81(1-0-81)	9	-0.6
1965 Hou-N	100	229	21	52	8	1	6	31	18	59	4	1	.227	.292	.349	.641	86	-4	24	3.46	-6	0-65(26-0-39)	4	-1.5
1966 Hou-N	11	13	4	1	1	0	0	0	3	5	0	0	.077	.250	.154	.404	16	-1	1	1.56	-1	/0-3(1-0-2)	0	-0.2
Total 7	**362**	**771**	**104**	**186**	**25**	**9**	**21**	**95**	**81**	**197**	**14**	**4**	**.241**	**.317**	**.379**	**.696**	**99**	**1**	**96**	**4.20**	**-14**	**0-212**	**20**	**-2.6**

• GAINEY, Ty Telmanch Gainey b: 12/25/1960, Cheraw, SC BL/TR, 6'1", 190 lbs. Deb: 4/24/1985 Career OF: 13-22-4

YEAR TM-L	G	AB	R	H	2B	3B	HR	RBI	BB	SO	SB	CS	AVG	OBP	SLG	OPS	OPS+	BR/A	RC	RC/G	FR	G/POS	WS	TPW
1985 Hou-N	13	37	5	6	0	0	0	0	2	9	0	0	.162	.244	.162	.406	16	-4	2	1.52	-1	/0-9(0-8-1)	0	-0.6

YEAR TM-L	G	AB	R	H	2B	3B	HR	RBI	BB	SO	SB	CS	AVG	OBP	SLG	OPS	OPS+	BR/A	RC	RC/G	FR	G/POS	WS	TPW
1986 Hou-N	26	50	6	15	3	1	1	6	6	19	3	1	.300	.375	.460	.835	133	2	9	7.00	-1	0-19(7-14-3)	3	0.1
1987 Hou-N	18	24	1	3	0	0	0	1	2	9	1	0	.125	.192	.125	.317	-14	-4	1	1.00	0	/0-6(6-0-0)	0	-0.4
Total 3	57	111	12	24	3	1	1	7	10	37	4	1	.216	.293	.288	.581	62	-5	12	3.61	-2	/0-34	3	-0.8

• GALAN, Augie August John Galan b: 5/23/1912, Berkeley, CA d: 12/28/1993, Fairfield, CA BB/TR, 6', 175 lbs. Deb: 4/29/1934 C Career OF: 1000-335-38

YEAR TM-L	G	AB	R	H	2B	3B	HR	RBI	BB	SO	SB	CS	AVG	OBP	SLG	OPS	OPS+	BR/A	RC	RC/G	FR	G/POS	WS	TPW
1934 Chi-N	66	192	31	50	6	2	5	22	16	15	4	....	.260	.317	.391	.708	90	-3	25	4.68	-3	2-43/3-3,S-1	5	-0.4
1935*Chi-N	154	646	**133**	203	41	11	12	79	87	53	**22**	....	.314	.399	.467	.866	131	32	133	7.92	10	*O-154(154-0-0)	32	3.1
1936 Chi-N★	145	575	74	152	26	4	8	81	67	50	16	....	.264	.344	.365	.709	89	-7	77	4.79	0	*O-145(8-139-0)	16	-1.1
1937 Chi-N	147	611	104	154	24	10	18	78	79	48	**23**	....	.252	.339	.412	.751	99	-1	92	5.30	10	*O-140(133-6-1)/2-8,S-2	20	0.2
1938*Chi-N	110	395	52	113	16	9	6	69	49	17	8	....	.286	.368	.418	.785	112	8	64	5.95	9	*O-103(103-0-0)	16	1.2
1939 Chi-N	148	549	104	167	36	8	6	71	75	26	8	....	.304	.392	.432	.823	119	17	97	6.49	-5	*O-145(145-0-0)	22	0.4
1940 Chi-N	68	209	33	48	14	2	3	22	37	23	9	....	.230	.346	.359	.704	96	0	29	4.69	2	O-54(31-24-0)/2-2	6	0.0
1941 Chi-N	65	120	18	25	3	0	1	13	22	10	0	....	.208	.331	.258	.589	70	-4	12	3.33	-1	O-31(17-11-4)	2	-0.6
*Bro-N	17	27	3	7	3	0	0	4	3	1	0	....	.259	.333	.370	.704	94	-0	4	4.69	1	/O-6(0-6-0)	1	0.0
Yr.	82	147	21	32	6	0	1	17	25	11	0	....	.218	.331	.279	.610	74	-4	16	3.58	-1	O-37(17-17-4)	3	-0.6
1942 Bro-N	69	209	24	55	16	0	0	22	24	12	2	....	.263	.339	.340	.679	97	-0	25	4.32	-2	O-55(20-26-10)/1-4,2-3	7	-0.5
1943 Bro-N★	139	495	83	142	26	3	9	67	**103**	39	6	....	.287	.412	.406	.818	136	29	93	6.98	7	*O-124(28-97-0),1-13	29	3.3
1944 Bro-N★	151	547	96	174	43	9	12	93	**101**	23	4	....	.318	.426	.495	.922	162	50	123	8.65	-9	*O-147(126-25-2)/2-2	32	3.4
1945 Bro-N	152	576	114	177	36	7	9	92	114	27	13	....	.307	.423	.441	.864	142	39	116	7.61	-3	1-66,O-49(49-0-0),3-40	30	3.0
1946 Bro-N	99	274	53	85	22	5	3	38	68	21	8	....	.310	.451	.460	.910	157	26	65	9.01	-3	O-60(60-0-0),3-19,1-12	18	1.9
1947 Cin-N	124	392	60	123	18	2	6	61	94	19	0	....	.314	**.449**	.416	.865	132	25	83	8.05	-5	*O-118(118-1-1)	21	1.2
1948 Cin-N	54	77	18	22	3	2	2	16	26	4	0	....	.286	.471	.455	.926	157	9	19	8.74	-1	O-18(1-0-17)	4	0.7
1949 NY-N	22	17	0	1	1	0	0	2	5	3	0	....	.059	.273	.118	.390	8	-2	1	1.19	0	/1-3,O-1	0	-0.2
Phi-A	12	26	4	8	2	0	0	0	9	2	0	0	.308	.486	.385	.870	136	2	6	7.87	0	/O-9(7-0-2)	2	0.2
Total 16	1742	5937	1004	1706	336	74	100	830	979	393	123	0	.287	.390	.419	.810	122	220	1064	6.58	5	*O-1359/1-98,3-62,2-58,S-3	263	16.0

• GALARRAGA, Andres Andres Jose "Big Cat" Galarraga b: 6/18/1961, Caracas, Venezuela BR/TR, 6'3", 235 lbs. Deb: 8/23/1985

YEAR TM-L	G	AB	R	H	2B	3B	HR	RBI	BB	SO	SB	CS	AVG	OBP	SLG	OPS	OPS+	BR/A	RC	RC/G	FR	G/POS	WS	TPW
1985 Mon-N	24	75	9	14	1	0	2	4	3	18	1	2	.187	.228	.280	.508	44	-7	5	1.96	3	1-23	0	-0.5
1986 Mon-N	105	321	39	87	13	0	10	42	30	79	6	5	.271	.339	.405	.744	105	1	43	4.61	-5	*1-102	8	-1.0
1987 Mon-N	147	551	72	168	40	3	13	90	41	127	7	10	.305	.364	.459	.823	113	7	88	5.81	7	*1-146	19	0.5
1988 Mon-N★	157	609	99	**184**	**42**	8	29	92	39	153	13	4	.302	.354	.540	.894	147	35	114	6.94	0	*1-156	25	2.6
1989 Mon-N	152	572	76	147	30	1	23	85	48	158	12	5	.257	.329	.434	.762	115	10	81	4.90	-4	*1-147	16	-0.5
1990 Mon-N	155	579	65	148	29	0	20	87	40	169	10	1	.256	.308	.409	.718	99	-1	72	4.29	5	*1-154	15	-0.7
1991 Mon-N	107	375	34	82	13	2	9	33	23	86	5	6	.219	.268	.336	.604	70	-18	32	2.81	-0	*1-105	2	-2.6
1992 StL-N	95	325	38	79	14	2	10	39	11	69	5	4	.243	.285	.391	.676	92	-6	34	3.49	0	1-90	3	-1.2
1993 Col-N★	120	470	71	174	35	4	22	98	24	73	2	4	**.370**	.408	.602	1.010	143	27	110	9.44	6	*1-119	23	2.3
1994 Col-N	103	417	77	133	21	0	31	85	19	93	8	3	.319	.360	.592	.953	123	13	85	7.57	1	*1-103	13	0.4
1995*Col-N	143	554	89	155	29	3	31	106	32	146	12	2	.280	.334	.511	.845	92	-6	92	5.91	8	*1-142	14	-1.0
1996 Col-N	159	626	119	190	39	3	**47**	**150**	40	157	18	8	.304	.362	.601	.962	120	16	136	8.02	-2	*1-159/3-1	25	0.0
1997 Col-N★	154	600	120	191	31	3	41	**140**	54	141	15	8	.318	.390	.585	.975	123	21	134	8.27	-6	*1-154	20	0.1
1998*Atl-N★	153	555	103	169	27	1	44	121	63	146	7	6	.305	.400	.595	.994	157	46	134	8.91	-7	*1-149/D-2	27	2.5
2000*Atl-N★	141	494	67	149	25	1	28	100	36	126	3	5	.302	.369	.526	.896	122	14	91	6.73	-7	*1-132/D-1	16	-0.4
2001 Tex-A	72	243	33	57	16	0	10	34	18	68	1	0	.235	.311	.424	.735	88	-5	31	4.22	-2	D-38,1-25	4	-1.0
SF-N	49	156	17	45	12	1	7	35	13	49	0	3	.288	.355	.513	.867	130	5	27	6.09	-5	1-41	7	-0.3
2002 Mon-N	104	292	30	76	12	0	9	40	30	81	2	2	.260	.347	.394	.741	92	-3	40	4.68	-1	1-89	5	-1.1
2003*SF-N	110	272	36	82	15	0	12	42	19	61	1	3	.301	.352	.489	.841	119	6	43	5.76	-4	1-69/D-2	9	-0.4
Total 18	2250	8086	1194	2330	444	32	398	1423	583	2000	128	81	.288	.349	.499	.848	116	155	1389	6.17	-12	*1-2105/D-43,3-1	251	-2.4

• GALATZER, Milt Milton Galatzer b: 5/4/1907, Chicago, IL d: 1/29/1976, San Francisco, CA BL/TL, 5'10", 168 lbs. Deb: 6/25/1933 Career OF: 28-31-154

YEAR TM-L	G	AB	R	H	2B	3B	HR	RBI	BB	SO	SB	CS	AVG	OBP	SLG	OPS	OPS+	BR/A	RC	RC/G	FR	G/POS	WS	TPW
1933 Cle-A	57	160	19	38	2	1	1	17	23	21	2	3	.238	.333	.281	.615	61	-9	16	3.32	1	O-40(11-4-25)/1-5	2	-1.0
1934 Cle-A	49	196	29	53	10	2	0	15	21	8	3	2	.270	.344	.342	.686	76	-7	24	4.29	2	O-49(3-0-46)	4	-0.7
1935 Cle-A	93	259	45	78	9	3	0	19	35	8	4	5	.301	.389	.359	.748	93	-2	38	5.20	-4	O-81(8-18-56)	6	-1.0
1936 Cle-A	49	97	12	23	4	1	0	6	13	8	1	2	.237	.333	.299	.632	57	-7	10	3.48	0	O-42(6-9-27)/1-1,P-1	1	-0.7
1939 Cin-N	3	5	0	0	0	0	0	0	0	1	0	....	.000	.000	.000	.000	-99	-1	0	.00	0	/1-2	0	-0.2
Total 5	251	717	105	192	25	7	1	57	92	46	10	12	.268	.354	.326	.681	75	-26	88	4.23	-2	O-212/1-8,P-1	13	-3.6

• GALLAGHER, Al Alan Mitchell Edward George Patrick Henry Gallagher b: 10/19/1945, San Francisco, CA BR/TR, 6', 180 lbs. Deb: 4/7/1970

YEAR TM-L	G	AB	R	H	2B	3B	HR	RBI	BB	SO	SB	CS	AVG	OBP	SLG	OPS	OPS+	BR/A	RC	RC/G	FR	G/POS	WS	TPW
1970 SF-N	109	282	31	75	15	2	4	28	30	37	2	1	.266	.337	.376	.712	92	-3	35	4.23	-8	3-91	6	-1.1
1971*SF-N	136	429	47	119	18	5	5	57	40	57	2	1	.277	.342	.378	.719	105	3	53	4.30	-7	*3-128	13	-0.4
1972 SF-N	82	233	19	52	3	1	2	18	33	39	2	1	.223	.322	.270	.592	69	-8	21	2.85	0	3-69	4	-0.8
1973 SF-N	5	9	1	2	0	0	0	1	0	0	0	0	.222	.300	.222	.522	45	-1	0	1.53	-1	/3-5	0	-0.2
Cal-A	110	311	16	85	6	1	0	26	35	31	1	3	.273	.349	.299	.648	91	-3	32	3.60	4	3-98/2-1,S-1	9	0.0
Total 4	442	1264	114	333	42	9	11	130	138	164	7	6	.263	.338	.337	.675	91	-12	142	3.81	-11	3-391/2-1,S-1	32	-2.5

• GALLAGHER, Bill William John Gallagher b: Philadelphia, PA TL Deb: 5/2/1883 ♦

YEAR TM-L	G	AB	R	H	2B	3B	HR	RBI	BB	SO	SB	CS	AVG	OBP	SLG	OPS	OPS+	BR/A	RC	RC/G	FR	G/POS	WS	TPW
1883 Bal-a	16	61	9	10	3	1	0	0	3	....	....	....	.164	.203	.246	.449	42	-3	3	1.71	-3	/O-9(1-0-8),P-7,S-4	1	-1.1
Phi-N	2	8	1	0	0	0	0	0	0	4	....	....	.000	.000	.000	.000	-110	-2	0	.00	0	/O-2(0-2-0)	0	-0.2
1884 Phi-U	3	11	1	1	0	0	0	....	0	....	....	....	.091	.091	.091	.182	-42	-1	0	.26	0	/P-3	0	-0.1
Total 2	21	80	11	11	3	1	0	0	3	4	....	....	.138	.169	.200	.369	17	-6	3	1.31	-3	/O-11,P-10,S-4	1	-1.4

• GALLAGHER, Bob Robert Collins Gallagher b: 7/7/1948, Newton, MA BL/TL, 6'3", 185 lbs. Deb: 5/17/1972 Career OF: 30-17-74

YEAR TM-L	G	AB	R	H	2B	3B	HR	RBI	BB	SO	SB	CS	AVG	OBP	SLG	OPS	OPS+	BR/A	RC	RC/G	FR	G/POS	WS	TPW
1972 Bos-A	7	5	0	0	0	0	0	0	0	3	0	0	.000	.000	.000	.000	-95	-1	0	.00	0	....	0	-0.1
1973 Hou-N	71	148	16	39	3	1	2	10	3	27	0	1	.264	.278	.338	.616	70	-7	13	3.22	-1	O-42(15-12-16)/1-1	3	-1.0
1974 Hou-N	102	87	13	15	2	0	0	3	12	23	1	0	.172	.280	.195	.475	36	-7	6	2.07	-2	O-62(5-4-53)/1-4	0	-1.1
1975 NY-N	33	15	5	2	1	0	0	0	1	3	0	0	.133	.188	.200	.388	8	-2	0	.79	-1	O-16(10-1-5)	0	-0.3
Total 4	213	255	34	56	6	1	2	13	16	56	1	1	.220	.268	.275	.543	51	-17	20	2.56	-4	O-120/1-5	3	-2.5

• GALLAGHER, Dave David Thomas Gallagher b: 9/20/1960, Trenton, NJ BR/TR, 6', 184 lbs. Deb: 4/12/1987 Career OF: 166-396-173

YEAR TM-L	G	AB	R	H	2B	3B	HR	RBI	BB	SO	SB	CS	AVG	OBP	SLG	OPS	OPS+	BR/A	RC	RC/G	FR	G/POS	WS	TPW
1987 Cle-A	15	36	2	4	1	1	0	1	2	5	2	0	.111	.158	.194	.352	-7	-5	1	.92	0	O-14(0-14-0)	0	-0.5
1988 Chi-A	101	347	59	105	15	3	5	31	29	40	5	4	.303	.356	.406	.763	114	6	49	5.06	2	O-95(5-78-17)/D-2	13	0.6
1989 Chi-A	161	601	74	160	22	2	1	46	46	79	5	6	.266	.320	.314	.635	82	-16	62	3.51	-6	*O-160(1-138-27)/D-1	10	-2.5
1990 Chi-A	45	75	5	21	3	1	0	5	3	9	0	1	.280	.316	.347	.663	87	-2	7	3.18	0	O-37(14-22-1)/D-4	1	-0.2
Bal-A	23	51	7	11	1	0	0	2	4	3	1	1	.216	.273	.235	.508	45	-4	4	2.24	1	O-20(17-2-1)/D-2	1	-0.3
Yr.	68	126	12	32	4	1	0	7	7	12	1	2	.254	.299	.302	.600	70	-6	11	2.79	1	O-57(31-24-2)/D-6	2	-0.6
1991 Cal-A	90	270	32	79	17	0	1	30	24	43	2	4	.293	.355	.367	.721	100	-1	35	4.45	2	O-87(7-61-23)/D-2	9	-0.1
1992 NY-N	98	175	20	42	11	1	1	21	19	16	4	5	.240	.318	.331	.649	85	-5	17	2.99	2	O-76(22-13-48)	2	-0.4
1993 NY-N	99	201	34	55	12	2	6	28	20	18	1	1	.274	.339	.443	.782	109	2	29	4.81	2	O-72(19-39-20)/1-9	6	0.3
1994 Atl-N	89	152	27	34	5	0	2	14	22	17	0	2	.224	.326	.296	.622	62	-9	15	3.09	0	O-77(71-5-7)/1-1	3	-1.1
1995 Phi-N	62	157	12	50	12	0	1	12	16	20	0	0	.318	.382	.414	.796	109	2	25	5.75	-1	O-55(8-21-28)	3	0.0
Cal-A	11	16	1	3	1	0	0	0	2	1	0	0	.188	.278	.250	.528	39	-1	1	2.61	1	/O-6(2-3-1),D-1	0	0.0
Total 9	794	2081	273	564	100	10	17	190	187	251	20	24	.271	.333	.353	.686	90	-33	244	3.97	4	O-699/D-12,1-10	48	-4.3

• GALLAGHER, Gil Lawrence Kirby Gallagher b: 9/5/1896, Washington, DC d: 1/6/1957, Washington, DC BB/TR, 5'8", 155 lbs. Deb: 9/13/1922

YEAR TM-L	G	AB	R	H	2B	3B	HR	RBI	BB	SO	SB	CS	AVG	OBP	SLG	OPS	OPS+	BR/A	RC	RC/G	FR	G/POS	WS	TPW
1922 Bos-N	7	22	1	1	1	0	0	2	1	7	0	0	.045	.087	.091	.178	-57	-5	0	.24	0	/S-6	0	-0.4

• GALLAGHER, Jackie John Laurence Gallagher b: 1/28/1902, Providence, RI d: 9/10/1984, Gladwyn, PA BL/TR, 5'10", 175 lbs. Deb: 8/24/1923

YEAR TM-L	G	AB	R	H	2B	3B	HR	RBI	BB	SO	SB	CS	AVG	OBP	SLG	OPS	OPS+	BR/A	RC	RC/G	FR	G/POS	WS	TPW
1923 Cle-A	1	1	0	1	0	0	0	0	0	0	0	0	1.000	1.000	1.000	2.000	428	0	1	∞	0	/O-1	0	0.0

• GALLAGHER, Jim James E. Gallagher b: Findlay, OH d: 3/29/1894, Scranton, PA Deb: 9/4/1886

YEAR TM-L	G	AB	R	H	2B	3B	HR	RBI	BB	SO	SB	CS	AVG	OBP	SLG	OPS	OPS+	BR/A	RC	RC/G	FR	G/POS	WS	TPW
1886 Was-N	1	5	1	1	0	0	0	0	0	2	0	....	.200	.200	.200	.400	23	-0	0	1.38	1	/S-1	0	0.0

YEAR TM-L	G	AB	R	H	2B	3B	HR	RBI	BB	SO	SB	CS	AVG	OBP	SLG	OPS	OPS+	BR/A	RC	RC/G	FR	G/POS	WS	TPW
• GALLAGHER, Joe	Joseph Emmett "Muscles" Gallagher b: 3/7/1914, Buffalo, NY d: 2/25/1998, Houston, TX BR/TR, 6'2", 210 lbs. Deb: 4/20/1939 Career OF: 74-0-40																							
1939 NY-A	14	41	8	10	0	1	2	9	3	8	1	0	.244	.311	.439	.750	91	-1	6	5.02	1	O-12(0-0-12)	1	0.0
StL-A	71	266	41	75	17	2	9	40	17	42	0	1	.282	.327	.462	.790	98	-3	38	5.05	1	O-67(56-0-11)	5	-0.5
Yr.	85	307	49	85	17	3	11	49	20	50	1	1	.277	.325	.459	.785	97	-3	44	5.05	2	O-79(56-0-23)	6	-0.6
1940 StL-A	23	70	14	19	3	1	2	8	4	12	2	0	.271	.311	.429	.739	88	-1	9	4.37	0	O-15(15-0-0)	1	-0.2
Bro-N	57	110	10	29	6	1	3	16	2	14	1	....	.264	.283	.418	.701	86	-3	13	4.23	-2	O-20(3-0-17)	2	-0.6
Total 2	**165**	**487**	**73**	**133**	**26**	**5**	**16**	**73**	**26**	**76**	**4**	**1**	**.273**	**.314**	**.446**	**.760**	**93**	**-7**	**66**	**4.77**	**0**	**O-114**	**9**	**-1.3**
• GALLAGHER, John	John Carroll Gallagher b: 2/18/1892, Pittsburgh, PA d: 3/30/1952, Norfolk, VA BR/TR, 5'10.5", 156 lbs. Deb: 8/20/1915																							
1915 Bal-F	40	126	11	25	4	0	0	4	5	22	1	....	.198	.229	.230	.459	33	-11	7	1.69	-3	2-37/S-5,3-1	1	-1.4
• GALLAGHER, Shorty	Charles William Gallagher b: 4/30/1872, Detroit, MI d: 6/23/1924, Detroit, MI Deb: 8/13/1901																							
1901 Cle-A	2	4	0	0	0	0	0	0	0	....	0	....	.000	.000	.000	.000	-104	-1	0	.00	0	/O-2(0-0-2)	0	-0.1
• GALLAGHER, William	William Henry Gallagher b: 2/4/1874, Boston, MA d: 3/11/1950, Worcester, MA BR/TR Deb: 8/19/1896																							
1896 Phi-N	14	49	9	15	2	0	0	6	10	0	0	....	.306	.433	.347	.780	108	2	8	5.87	-2	S-14	2	0.0
• GALLE, Stan	Stanley Joseph Galle b: 2/7/1919, Milwaukee, WI BR/TR, 5'7", 165 lbs. Deb: 4/14/1942																							
1942 Was-A	13	18	3	2	0	0	0	1	1	0	0	0	.111	.158	.111	.269	-24	-3	0	.00	-1	/3-3	0	-0.4
• GALLEGO, Mike	Michael Anthony Gallego b: 10/31/1960, Whittier, CA BR/TR, 5'8", 160 lbs. Deb: 4/11/1985																							
1985 Oak-A	76	77	13	16	5	1	1	9	12	14	1	1	.208	.322	.338	.660	87	-1	9	3.54	1	2-42,S-21,3-12	2	0.1
1986 Oak-A	20	37	2	10	2	0	0	4	1	6	0	2	.270	.289	.324	.614	72	-2	3	2.61	2	2-19/3-2,S-1	1	0.0
1987 Oak-A	72	124	18	31	6	0	2	14	12	21	0	1	.250	.321	.347	.668	83	-3	13	3.38	1	2-31,3-24,S-17	3	0.0
1988*Oak-A	129	277	38	58	8	0	2	20	34	53	2	3	.209	.298	.260	.558	60	-15	23	2.59	8	2-83,S-42,3-16	6	-0.4
1989*Oak-A	133	357	45	90	14	2	3	30	35	43	7	5	.252	.329	.328	.657	89	-5	39	3.58	13	S-94,2-41/3-3,D-1	12	1.6
1990*Oak-A	140	389	36	80	13	2	3	34	35	50	5	5	.206	.278	.272	.551	57	-23	29	2.27	18	2-83,S-38,3-27/D-1,O-1	7	-0.1
1991 Oak-A	159	482	67	119	15	4	12	49	67	84	6	9	.247	.345	.369	.714	103	1	63	4.34	22	*2-135,S-55	18	2.9
1992 NY-A	53	173	24	44	7	1	3	14	20	22	0	1	.254	.345	.358	.704	98	-0	22	4.21	0	2-40,S-14	5	0.2
1993 NY-A	119	403	63	114	20	1	10	54	50	65	3	2	.283	.368	.412	.780	113	8	60	5.14	5	S-55,2-52,3-27/D-1	13	2.0
1994 NY-A	89	306	39	73	17	1	6	41	38	46	0	1	.239	.330	.359	.690	81	-9	39	4.22	8	S-72,2-26	7	0.6
1995 Oak-A	43	120	11	28	0	0	0	8	9	24	0	1	.233	.292	.233	.526	41	-11	8	2.25	0	2-18,S-14,3-12	1	-0.8
1996*StL-N	51	143	12	30	2	0	0	4	12	31	0	0	.210	.276	.224	.499	34	-14	10	2.31	6	2-43/3-7,S-1	1	-0.5
1997 StL-N	27	43	6	7	2	0	0	1	1	6	0	0	.163	.182	.209	.391	2	-6	2	1.27	1	2-11,S-10/3-7	1	-0.4
Total 13	**1111**	**2931**	**374**	**700**	**111**	**12**	**42**	**282**	**326**	**465**	**24**	**31**	**.239**	**.322**	**.328**	**.650**	**81**	**-80**	**319**	**3.55**	**86**	**2-624,S-434,3-137/D-3,O-1**	**77**	**5.3**
• GALLIGAN, Jim	James M. Galligan b: 1868, Easton, PA d: 7/17/1906, New York, NY, 5'10", 160 lbs. Deb: 9/2/1889																							
1889 Lou-a	31	120	6	20	0	2	0	7	6	17	1	....	.167	.213	.200	.413	18	-13	5	1.44	2	O-31(31-0-0)	0	-1.0
• GALLOWAY, Chick	Clarence Edward Galloway b: 8/4/1896, Clinton, SC d: 11/7/1969, Clinton, SC BR/TR, 5'8", 160 lbs. Deb: 9/9/1919																							
1919 Phi-A	17	63	2	9	0	0	0	4	1	8	0	....	.143	.156	.143	.299	-16	-10	1	.66	-1	S-17	1	-1.0
1920 Phi-A	98	298	28	60	9	3	0	18	22	22	2	2	.201	.259	.252	.510	35	-27	21	2.16	-12	S-84/2-4,3-3	2	-3.2
1921 Phi-A	131	465	42	123	28	5	3	47	29	43	12	7	.265	.310	.366	.676	71	-21	53	3.88	-19	*S-110,3-20/2-1	6	-2.5
1922 Phi-A	155	571	83	185	26	9	6	69	39	39	10	19	.324	.368	.433	.801	105	-1	85	5.35	0	*S-155	19	1.5
1923 Phi-A	134	504	64	140	18	9	2	62	37	30	12	10	.278	.327	.361	.688	80	-16	59	4.03	3	*S-134	13	0.2
1924 Phi-A	129	464	41	128	16	4	2	48	23	23	11	12	.276	.311	.341	.652	67	-26	48	3.45	-10	*S-129	8	-2.0
1925 Phi-A	149	481	52	116	11	4	3	71	59	28	16	9	.241	.324	.299	.623	55	-32	51	3.38	1	*S-148	9	-1.4
1926 Phi-A	133	408	37	98	13	6	0	49	31	20	8	7	.240	.295	.301	.597	53	-29	37	2.94	-19	*S-133	5	-3.4
1927 Phi-A	77	181	25	48	10	4	0	22	18	9	1	3	.265	.332	.365	.696	76	-7	22	4.09	-5	S-61/3-7	5	-0.6
1928 Det-A	53	148	17	39	5	2	1	17	15	3	7	2	.264	.331	.345	.676	77	-4	18	4.12	-1	S-22,3-21/1-1,O-1	3	-0.2
Total 10	**1076**	**3583**	**391**	**946**	**136**	**46**	**17**	**407**	**274**	**225**	**79**	**71**	**.264**	**.317**	**.342**	**.659**	**69**	**-174**	**395**	**3.69**	**-61**	**S-993/3-51,2-5,1-1,O-1**	**71**	**-12.4**
• GALLOWAY, Jim	James Cato "Bad News" Galloway b: 9/16/1887, Iredell, TX d: 5/3/1950, Fort Worth, TX BB/TR, 6'3", 187 lbs. Deb: 8/24/1912																							
1912 StL-N	21	54	4	10	2	0	0	4	5	8	2	....	.185	.254	.222	.476	32	-5	4	2.02	1	2-16/S-1	0	-0.4
• GALVIN, Jim	James Joseph Galvin b: 8/11/1907, Somerville, MA d: 9/30/1969, Marietta, GA BR/TR, 5'11.5", 180 lbs. Deb: 9/27/1930																							
1930 Bos-A	2	2	0	0	0	0	0	0	0	0	0	0	.000	.000	.000	.000	-104	-1	0	.00	0	....	0	-0.1
• GALVIN, John	John S. Galvin b: 1842, d: 4/20/1904, Brooklyn, NY, 5'7", 178 lbs. Deb: 5/7/1872																							
1872 Atl-n	1	4	0	0	0	0	0	0	0	0	0	0	.000	.000	.000	.000	-85	-1	0	.00	-2	/2-1	....	-0.2
• GAMBLE, John	John Robert Gamble b: 2/10/1948, Reno, NV BR/TR, 5'10", 165 lbs. Deb: 9/7/1972																							
1972 Det-A	6	3	0	0	0	0	0	0	0	0	0	0	.000	.000	.000	.000	-97	-1	0	.00	0	/S-1	0	-0.1
1973 Det-A	7	0	1	0	0	0	0	0	0	0	0	0	....	....	....	....	-94	0	0	....	0	....	0	0.0
Total 2	**13**	**3**	**1**	**0**	**0**	**0**	**0**	**0**	**0**	**0**	**0**	**0**	**.000**	**.000**	**.000**	**.000**	**-97**	**-1**	**0**	**.00**	**0**	**/S-1**	**0**	**-0.1**
• GAMBLE, Lee	Lee Jesse Gamble b: 6/28/1910, Renovo, PA d: 10/5/1994, Punxsutawney, PA BL/TR, 6'1", 170 lbs. Deb: 9/15/1935 Career OF: 68-1-8																							
1935 Cin-N	2	4	2	2	1	0	0	2	1	0	1	....	.500	.600	.750	1.350	269	1	2	17.35	-0	/O-2(2-0-0)	1	0.1
1938 Cin-N	53	75	13	24	3	1	0	5	0	6	0	....	.320	.320	.387	.707	96	-1	9	4.59	0	/O-9(9-0-0)	2	-0.2
1939*Cin-N	72	221	24	59	7	2	0	14	9	14	5	....	.267	.296	.317	.612	64	-11	21	3.42	-2	O-56(55-1-0)	4	-1.7
1940 Cin-N	38	42	12	6	1	0	0	0	0	1	0	....	.143	.143	.167	.310	-15	-7	1	.65	0	O-10(2-0-8)	0	-0.7
Total 4	**165**	**342**	**51**	**91**	**12**	**3**	**0**	**21**	**10**	**21**	**6**	**....**	**.266**	**.287**	**.319**	**.606**	**64**	**-18**	**34**	**3.39**	**-3**	**/O-77**	**7**	**-2.5**
• GAMBLE, Oscar	Oscar Charles Gamble b: 12/20/1949, Ramer, AL BL/TR, 5'11", 165 lbs. Deb: 8/27/1969 Career OF: 274-81-469																							
1969 Chi-N	24	71	6	16	1	1	1	5	10	12	0	2	.225	.321	.310	.631	68	-4	7	3.22	-1	O-24(1-23-0)	1	-0.6
1970 Phi-N	88	275	31	72	12	4	1	19	27	37	5	4	.262	.330	.345	.675	84	-7	30	3.77	-3	O-74(0-47-28)	5	-1.3
1971 Phi-N	92	280	24	62	11	1	6	23	21	35	5	2	.221	.278	.332	.610	72	-10	27	3.24	0	O-80(54-1-26)	4	-1.6
1972 Phi-N	74	135	17	32	5	2	1	13	19	16	0	1	.237	.335	.326	.661	86	-2	15	3.69	2	O-35(0-0-35)/1-1	3	-0.2
1973 Cle-A	113	390	56	104	11	3	20	44	34	37	3	4	.267	.330	.464	.794	120	8	60	5.41	-1	D-70,O-37(2-1-35)	14	0.4
1974 Cle-A	135	454	74	132	16	4	19	59	48	51	5	6	.291	.365	.469	.834	140	22	77	6.17	1	*D-115,O-13(12-0-1)	20	2.0
1975 Cle-A	121	348	60	91	16	3	15	45	53	39	11	5	.261	.362	.454	.816	130	15	58	5.80	3	O-82(81-0-1),D-29	14	1.3
1976*NY-A	110	340	43	79	13	1	17	57	38	38	5	3	.232	.317	.426	.743	117	7	47	4.71	3	*O-104(0-0-104)/D-1	12	0.5
1977 Chi-A	137	408	75	121	22	2	31	83	54	54	1	2	.297	.387	.588	.975	162	35	96	8.83	-3	D-79,O-49(5-7-38)	22	2.8
1978 SD-N	126	375	46	103	15	3	7	47	51	45	1	2	.275	.370	.387	.757	121	12	57	5.49	5	*O-107(39-0-70)	15	1.2
1979 Tex-A	64	161	27	54	6	0	8	32	37	15	2	1	.335	.462	.522	.984	167	18	39	9.16	1	D-37,O-21(0-0-21)	9	1.7
NY-A	36	113	21	44	4	1	11	32	13	13	0	0	.389	.452	.735	1.187	219	19	38	14.76	1	O-27(25-2-0)/D-6	10	1.8
Yr.	100	274	48	98	10	1	19	64	50	28	2	1	.358	.458	.609	1.068	187	37	78	11.27	3	O-48(25-2-21),D-43	19	3.5
1980*NY-A	78	194	40	54	10	2	14	50	28	21	2	0	.278	.381	.567	.948	159	16	44	8.19	1	O-49(36-0-14),D-20	11	1.5
1981*NY-A	80	189	24	45	8	0	10	27	35	23	0	2	.238	.360	.439	.799	131	8	31	5.45	-1	O-43(16-0-27),D-33	7	0.5
1982 NY-A	108	316	49	86	21	2	18	57	58	47	6	3	.272	.392	.522	.914	151	24	69	7.68	4	D-74,O-29(1-0-28)	15	2.4
1983 NY-A	74	180	26	47	10	2	7	26	25	23	0	0	.261	.361	.456	.816	128	7	31	6.12	-1	O-32(2-0-30),D-21	7	0.4
1984 NY-A	54	125	17	23	2	0	10	27	25	18	1	0	.184	.320	.440	.760	112	3	19	5.05	1	D-28,O-12(0-0-11)	4	0.2
1985 Chi-A	70	148	20	30	5	0	4	20	34	22	0	0	.203	.355	.318	.673	83	-2	19	4.37	0	D-48	4	-0.3
Total 17	**1584**	**4502**	**656**	**1195**	**188**	**31**	**200**	**666**	**610**	**546**	**47**	**37**	**.265**	**.358**	**.454**	**.813**	**127**	**168**	**766**	**5.99**	**10**	**O-818,D-561/1-1**	**177**	**12.8**
• GAMMONS, Daff	John Ashley Gammons b: 3/17/1876, New Bedford, MA d: 3/24/1963, East Greenwich, RI BR/TR, 5'11", 170 lbs. Deb: 4/23/1901																							
1901 Bos-N	28	93	10	18	0	1	0	10	3	....	5	....	.194	.242	.215	.457	30	-8	7	2.24	-2	O-23(20-0-3)/2-2,3-1	1	-1.2
• GANDIL, Chick	Arnold Gandil b: 1/19/1887, St. Paul, MN d: 12/13/1970, Calistoga, CA BR/TR, 6'1.5", 190 lbs. Deb: 4/14/1910																							
1910 Chi-A	77	275	21	53	7	3	2	21	24	....	12	....	.193	.267	.262	.529	69	-10	22	2.53	7	1-74/O-2(2-0-0)	5	-0.4
1912 Was-A	117	443	59	135	20	15	2	81	27	....	21	....	.305	.350	.431	.781	122	11	74	5.88	-4	*1-117	18	0.4
1913 Was-A	148	550	61	175	25	8	1	72	36	33	22	....	.318	.363	.398	.762	120	13	84	5.51	3	*1-145	23	1.4

YEAR TM-L	G	AB	R	H	2B	3B	HR	RBI	BB	SO	SB	CS	AVG	OBP	SLG	OPS	OPS+	BR/A	RC	RC/G	FR	G/POS	WS	TPW
1914 Was-A	145	526	48	136	24	10	3	75	44	44	30	19	.259	.324	.359	.683	101	-2	67	4.00	16	*1-145	17	1.2
1915 Was-A	136	485	53	141	20	15	2	64	29	33	20	13	.291	.340	.406	.746	121	8	70	4.92	-3	*1-134	16	0.2
1916 Cle-A	146	533	51	138	26	9	0	72	36	48	13	....	.259	.312	.341	.653	91	-8	64	3.96	3	*1-145	12	-0.8
1917*Chi-A	149	553	53	151	9	7	0	57	30	36	16	....	.273	.316	.315	.631	91	-7	58	3.62	-1	*1-149	16	-1.2
1918 Chi-A	114	439	49	119	18	4	0	55	27	19	9	....	.271	.319	.330	.649	95	-4	47	3.66	-2	*1-114	10	-0.9
1919*Chi-A	115	441	54	128	24	7	1	60	20	20	10	....	.290	.325	.383	.709	98	-3	57	4.47	-1	*1-115	13	-0.6
Total 9	1147	4245	449	1176	173	78	11	557	273	233	153	32	.277	.327	.362	.689	102	-2	544	4.33	19	*1-1138/0-2	130	-0.7

• GANDY, Bob Robert Brinkley "String" Gandy b: 8/25/1893, Jacksonville, FL d: 6/19/1945, Jacksonville, FL BL/TR, 6'3", 180 lbs. Deb: 10/5/1916

YEAR TM-L	G	AB	R	H	2B	3B	HR	RBI	BB	SO	SB	CS	AVG	OBP	SLG	OPS	OPS+	BR/A	RC	RC/G	FR	G/POS	WS	TPW
1916 Phi-N	1	2	0	0	0	0	0	0	0	1	0	....	.000	.000	.000	.000	-97	-0	0	.00	0	/0-1	0	-0.1

• GANLEY, Bob Robert Stephen Ganley b: 4/23/1875, Lowell, MA d: 10/9/1945, Lowell, MA BL/TL, 5'7", 156 lbs. Deb: 9/1/1905 Career OF: 223-113-228

YEAR TM-L	G	AB	R	H	2B	3B	HR	RBI	BB	SO	SB	CS	AVG	OBP	SLG	OPS	OPS+	BR/A	RC	RC/G	FR	G/POS	WS	TPW
1905 Pit-N	32	127	12	40	1	2	0	7	8	....	3	....	.315	.356	.354	.710	109	1	19	5.07	-1	0-32(0-6-27)	4	-0.1
1906 Pit-N	137	511	63	132	7	6	0	31	41	....	19	....	.258	.316	.295	.611	87	-8	60	3.74	-3	*0-134(0-12-122)	12	-1.9
1907 Was-A	154	605	73	167	10	5	1	35	54	....	40	....	.276	.337	.314	.651	117	13	83	4.73	1	*0-154(62-13-78)	16	0.6
1908 Was-A	150	549	61	131	19	9	1	36	45	....	30	....	.239	.299	.311	.610	107	4	63	3.49	4	*0-150(150-0-0)	14	0.0
1909 Was-A	19	63	5	16	3	0	0	5	1	....	4	....	.254	.266	.302	.567	83	-2	6	3.12	-1	0-17(11-5-1)	1	-0.3
Phi-A	80	274	32	54	4	2	0	9	28	....	16	....	.197	.272	.226	.498	56	-13	24	2.46	3	0-77(0-77-0)	6	-1.5
Yr.	99	337	37	70	7	2	0	14	29	....	20	....	.208	.270	.240	.511	61	-15	30	2.57	3	0-94(11-82-1)	7	-1.9
Total 5	572	2129	246	540	44	24	2	123	177	....	112	....	.254	.313	.300	.612	98	-3	255	3.80	4	0-564	53	-3.1

• GANNON, Bill William G. Gannon b: 1876, New Haven, CT d: 4/26/1927, Fort Worth, TX, 5'9", 170 lbs. Deb: 9/9/1901

YEAR TM-L	G	AB	R	H	2B	3B	HR	RBI	BB	SO	SB	CS	AVG	OBP	SLG	OPS	OPS+	BR/A	RC	RC/G	FR	G/POS	WS	TPW
1901 Chi-N	15	61	2	9	0	0	0	0	1	....	5	....	.148	.161	.148	.309	-11	-9	2	1.20	0	0-15(0-0-15)	0	-0.9

• GANT, Ron Ronald Edwin Gant b: 3/2/1965, Victoria, TX BR/TR, 6', 192 lbs. Deb: 9/6/1987 Career OF: 1184-299-9

YEAR TM-L	G	AB	R	H	2B	3B	HR	RBI	BB	SO	SB	CS	AVG	OBP	SLG	OPS	OPS+	BR/A	RC	RC/G	FR	G/POS	WS	TPW
1987 Atl-N	21	83	9	22	4	0	2	9	1	11	4	2	.265	.274	.386	.659	69	-4	7	2.94	0	2-20	1	-0.4
1988 Atl-N	146	563	85	146	28	8	19	60	46	118	19	10	.259	.319	.439	.757	110	5	78	4.80	-4	*2-122,3-22	16	0.5
1989 Atl-N	75	260	26	46	8	3	9	25	20	63	9	6	.177	.238	.335	.573	61	-15	21	2.56	-3	3-53,0-14(2-14-0)	1	-2.0
1990 Atl-N	152	575	107	174	34	3	32	84	50	86	33	16	.303	.359	.539	.899	136	26	109	6.86	-3	*0-146(38-113-3)	21	2.0
1991*Atl-N	154	561	101	141	35	3	32	105	71	104	34	15	.251	.341	.496	.836	125	19	96	5.84	1	*0-148(0-148-0)	25	1.9
1992*Atl-N★	153	544	74	141	22	6	17	80	45	101	32	10	.259	.324	.415	.739	102	3	74	4.67	-3	*0-147(138-23-0)	17	-0.5
1993*Atl-N	157	606	113	166	27	4	36	117	67	117	26	9	.274	.348	.510	.858	125	22	107	6.14	-10	*0-155(155-0-0)	25	0.5
1995*Cin-N★	119	410	79	113	19	4	29	88	74	108	23	8	.276	.390	.554	.944	146	30	90	7.59	3	*0-117(117-0-0)	21	2.8
1996*StL-N	122	419	74	103	14	2	30	82	73	98	13	4	.246	.362	.504	.865	126	17	79	6.41	0	*0-116(116-0-0)	18	1.2
1997 StL-N	139	502	68	115	21	4	17	62	58	162	14	6	.229	.310	.388	.699	82	-13	64	4.38	0	*0-128(128-0-0)/D-1	11	-1.8
1998 StL-N	121	383	60	92	17	1	26	67	51	92	8	0	.240	.333	.493	.826	115	9	66	5.95	-4	*0-104(104-0-0)	11	0.1
1999 Phi-N	138	516	107	134	27	5	17	77	85	112	13	3	.260	.365	.430	.796	97	1	88	6.04	2	*0-133(133-0-0)/D-2	16	-0.3
2000 Phi-N	89	343	54	87	16	2	20	38	36	73	5	4	.254	.326	.487	.813	101	-2	53	5.31	2	0-84(84-0-0)	5	-0.3
Ana-A	34	82	15	19	3	1	6	16	20	18	1	2	.232	.382	.512	.895	121	2	17	7.09	2	0-21(21-0-0),D-12	2	0.3
2001 Col-N	59	171	31	44	8	2	8	22	24	56	3	1	.257	.349	.468	.817	89	-3	30	6.15	-1	0-51(51-0-0)	2	-0.5
*Oak-A	34	81	15	21	5	1	2	13	11	24	2	0	.259	.348	.420	.768	101	1	13	5.85	-3	D-20,0-11(11-0-0)	2	-0.3
2002 SD-N	102	309	58	81	14	1	18	59	36	59	4	6	.262	.343	.489	.832	127	9	49	5.37	3	0-80(78-1-5)/D-4	12	0.9
2003 Oak-A	17	41	4	6	0	0	1	4	2	9	0	0	.146	.186	.220	.406	6	-6	2	1.17	0	/0-9(8-0-1),D-6	0	-0.6
Total 16	1832	6449	1080	1651	302	50	321	1008	770	1411	243	102	.256	.338	.468	.806	112	101	1046	5.58	-17	*0-1464,2-142/3-75,D-45	206	3.6

• GANTENBEIN, Joe Joseph Steven "Sep" Gantenbein b: 8/25/1915, San Francisco, CA d: 8/2/1993, Novato, CA BL/TR, 5'9", 168 lbs. Deb: 4/20/1939

YEAR TM-L	G	AB	R	H	2B	3B	HR	RBI	BB	SO	SB	CS	AVG	OBP	SLG	OPS	OPS+	BR/A	RC	RC/G	FR	G/POS	WS	TPW
1939 Phi-A	111	348	47	101	14	4	4	36	32	22	1	5	.290	.353	.388	.741	91	-6	48	4.95	-19	2-76,3-14/S-5	7	-1.9
1940 Phi-A	75	197	21	47	6	2	4	23	11	21	1	0	.239	.282	.350	.633	64	-11	20	3.59	-1	3-45/1-6,S-3,0-1	2	-1.0
Total 2	186	545	68	148	20	6	8	59	43	43	2	5	.272	.328	.374	.703	82	-17	68	4.45	-21	/2-76,3-59,S-8,1-6,0-1	9	-3.0

• GANTNER, Jim James Elmer Gantner b: 1/5/1953, Fond du Lac, WI BL/TR, 6', 180 lbs. Deb: 9/3/1976 C

YEAR TM-L	G	AB	R	H	2B	3B	HR	RBI	BB	SO	SB	CS	AVG	OBP	SLG	OPS	OPS+	BR/A	RC	RC/G	FR	G/POS	WS	TPW
1976 Mil-A	26	69	6	17	1	0	0	7	6	11	1	0	.246	.316	.261	.577	71	-2	6	3.07	-1	3-24/D-2	1	-0.3
1977 Mil-A	14	47	4	14	1	0	1	2	2	5	2	1	.298	.327	.383	.710	93	-1	6	4.31	-1	3-14	1	-0.2
1978 Mil-A	43	97	14	21	1	0	1	8	5	10	2	0	.216	.269	.258	.527	49	-6	8	2.65	-3	2-21,3-15/1-1,S-1	1	-0.8
1979 Mil-A	70	208	29	59	10	3	2	22	16	17	3	5	.284	.341	.389	.730	96	-2	27	4.40	1	3-42,2-22/S-3,P-1	6	0.0
1980 Mil-A	132	415	47	117	21	3	4	40	30	29	11	10	.282	.332	.376	.708	97	-4	50	4.09	4	3-69,2-66/S-1	10	0.3
1981*Mil-A	107	352	35	94	14	1	2	33	29	29	3	6	.267	.328	.330	.658	95	-4	38	3.60	9	*2-107	13	1.1
1982*Mil-A	132	447	48	132	17	2	4	43	26	36	6	3	.295	.337	.369	.706	100	-0	56	4.53	11	*2-131	15	1.8
1983 Mil-A	161	603	85	170	23	8	11	74	38	46	5	6	.282	.331	.401	.732	109	4	79	4.57	17	*2-158	21	3.0
1984 Mil-A	153	613	61	173	27	1	3	56	30	51	6	5	.282	.319	.344	.663	87	-12	64	3.67	-3	*2-153	16	-0.7
1985 Mil-A	143	523	63	133	15	4	5	44	33	42	11	8	.254	.302	.327	.629	73	-21	49	3.14	15	*2-124,3-24/S-1	11	0.1
1986 Mil-A	139	497	58	136	25	1	7	38	26	50	13	7	.274	.318	.370	.688	84	-12	56	3.84	2	*2-135/3-3,D-1,S-1	13	-0.2
1987 Mil-A	81	265	37	72	14	0	4	30	19	22	6	2	.272	.332	.370	.702	84	-6	32	4.22	1	2-57,3-38/D-1	7	-0.2
1988 Mil-A	155	539	67	149	28	2	0	47	34	50	20	8	.276	.323	.336	.659	84	-11	60	3.79	1	*2-154/3-1	14	-0.6
1989 Mil-A	116	409	51	112	18	3	0	34	21	33	20	6	.274	.325	.333	.658	86	-6	45	3.73	10	*2-114/D-2	12	0.7
1990 Mil-A	88	323	36	85	8	5	0	25	29	19	18	3	.263	.328	.319	.647	82	-4	35	3.73	0	2-80/3-9	7	-0.3
1991 Mil-A	140	526	63	149	27	4	2	47	27	34	4	6	.283	.322	.361	.683	91	-9	58	3.82	-1	3-90,2-59	10	-0.8
1992 Mil-A	101	256	22	63	12	1	1	18	12	17	6	2	.246	.280	.313	.592	67	-11	21	2.67	7	2-68,3-31/1-2,D-2	5	-0.2
Total 17	1801	6189	726	1696	262	38	47	568	383	501	137	78	.274	.322	.351	.673	88	-107	689	3.82	70	*2-1449,3-360/D-8,S-7,1-3,P	163	2.7

• GANZEL, Babe Foster Pirie Ganzel b: 5/22/1901, Malden, MA d: 2/6/1978, Jacksonville, FL BR/TR, 5'10.5", 172 lbs. Deb: 9/19/1927 Career OF: 8-11-2

YEAR TM-L	G	AB	R	H	2B	3B	HR	RBI	BB	SO	SB	CS	AVG	OBP	SLG	OPS	OPS+	BR/A	RC	RC/G	FR	G/POS	WS	TPW
1927 Was-A	13	48	7	21	4	2	1	13	7	3	0	0	.438	.509	.667	1.176	206	8	16	14.47	-1	0-13(4-9-0)	4	0.6
1928 Was-A	10	26	2	2	1	0	0	4	1	4	0	0	.077	.111	.115	.226	-41	-5	0	.41	0	/0-7(4-2-2)	0	-0.5
Total 2	23	74	9	23	5	2	1	17	8	7	0	0	.311	.378	.473	.851	125	2	17	8.08	0	/0-20	4	0.1

• GANZEL, Charlie Charles William Ganzel b: 6/18/1862, Waterford, WI d: 4/7/1914, Quincy, MA BR/TR, 6', 161 lbs. Deb: 9/27/1884 U Career OF: 25-5-71

YEAR TM-L	G	AB	R	H	2B	3B	HR	RBI	BB	SO	SB	CS	AVG	OBP	SLG	OPS	OPS+	BR/A	RC	RC/G	FR	G/POS	WS	TPW
1884 StP-U	7	23	2	5	0	0	0	....	0	....	....	....	.217	.217	.217	.435	47	-1	1	1.73	0	/C-6,0-1	0	-0.1
1885 Phi-N	34	125	15	21	3	1	0	6	4	13	....	....	.168	.194	.208	.402	31	-9	5	1.34	-4	C-33/0-1	1	-1.0
1886 Phi-N	1	3	0	0	0	0	0	0	0	1	0	....	.000	.000	.000	.000	-99	-1	0	.00	-1	/C-1	0	-0.1
Det-N	57	213	28	58	7	2	1	31	7	22	5	....	.272	.295	.338	.633	89	-3	23	4.06	-2	C-45/0-7(7-0-0),1-5	7	-0.2
Yr.	58	216	28	58	7	2	1	31	7	23	5	....	.269	.291	.333	.625	87	-4	23	3.98	-3	C-46/0-7(7-0-0),1-5	7	-0.3
1887*Det-N	57	235	40	67	6	5	0	20	8	2	3	....	.285	.288	.330	.619	69	-10	23	3.63	-1	C-51/0-4(4-0-0),1-2,3-1	6	-0.6
1888 Det-N	95	386	45	96	13	5	1	46	14	15	12	....	.249	.277	.316	.593	89	-6	38	3.54	3	2-49,C-28/3-9,0-5(0-0-5),S,1	9	0.1
1889 Bos-N	73	275	30	73	3	5	1	43	15	11	13	....	.265	.308	.324	.632	72	-11	32	4.23	4	C-39,0-26(0-1-25)/1-7,S-6,3	8	-0.4
1890 Bos-N	38	163	21	44	7	3	0	24	5	6	1	....	.270	.300	.350	.650	83	-5	18	3.97	2	C-22,0-15(1-0-14)/S-3,2-1	4	-0.1
1891 Bos-N	70	263	33	68	18	5	1	29	12	13	7	....	.259	.304	.376	.680	87	-7	33	4.57	1	C-59,0-13(5-1-7)	8	-0.1
1892*Bos-N	54	198	25	53	9	3	0	25	18	12	7	....	.268	.332	.343	.675	95	-2	26	4.75	-2	C-51/0-2(1-1-0),1-1	6	0.1
1893 Bos-N	73	281	50	75	10	2	1	48	22	9	6	....	.267	.325	.327	.652	68	-14	33	4.19	0	C-40,0-23(6-0-18),1-10	7	-1.0
1894 Bos-N	70	266	51	74	7	6	3	56	19	6	1	....	.278	.326	.383	.710	63	-19	34	4.67	-5	C-59/1-7,0-3(1-0-2),S-2,2	5	-1.4
1895 Bos-N	81	280	38	73	2	5	1	52	25	6	1	....	.261	.324	.314	.638	62	-17	30	3.85	-2	C-76/1-2,S-2	7	-0.9
1896 Bos-N	47	179	28	47	2	0	1	18	9	5	2	....	.263	.305	.291	.596	54	-12	18	3.40	3	C-41/1-3,S-2	3	-0.5
1897 Bos-N	30	105	15	28	4	3	0	14	4	....	2	....	.267	.300	.362	.662	70	-5	13	4.18	-1	C-27/1-2	3	-0.3
Total 14	787	2995	421	782	91	45	10	412	162	121	60	....	.261	.301	.330	.631	73	-122	327	3.92	-3	C-578,0-100/2-51,1-40,S-18,3	74	-6.3

• GANZEL, John John Henry Ganzel b: 4/7/1874, Kalamazoo, MI d: 1/14/1959, Orlando, FL BR/TR, 6'.5", 195 lbs. Deb: 4/21/1898 M

YEAR TM-L	G	AB	R	H	2B	3B	HR	RBI	BB	SO	SB	CS	AVG	OBP	SLG	OPS	OPS+	BR/A	RC	RC/G	FR	G/POS	WS	TPW
1898 Pit-N	15	45	5	6	0	0	0	2	4	....	0	....	.133	.220	.133	.353	2	-6	1	.92	0	1-12	0	-0.6
1900 Chi-N	78	284	29	78	14	4	4	32	10	....	5	....	.275	.316	.394	.710	99	-2	39	4.80	0	1-78	7	-0.2
1901 NY-N	138	526	42	113	13	3	2	66	20	....	6	....	.215	.256	.262	.518	52	-32	39	2.44	5	*1-138	3	-2.9
1903 NY-A	129	476	62	132	25	7	3	71	30	....	9	....	.277	.336	.378	.714	107	5	67	4.94	8	*1-129	18	1.1
1904 NY-A	130	465	50	121	16	10	6	48	24	....	13	....	.260	.309	.376	.686	111	5	60	4.57	0	*1-118/2-9,S-1	15	0.4
1907 Cin-N	145	531	61	135	20	**16**	2	64	29	....	9	....	.254	.297	.363	.660	102	-1	63	4.00	5	*1-143	14	0.2

YEAR TM-L	G	AB	R	H	2B	3B	HR	RBI	BB	SO	SB	CS	AVG	OBP	SLG	OPS	OPS+	BR/A	RC	RC/G	FR	G/POS	WS	TPW
1908 Cin-N	112	388	32	97	16	10	1	53	19	....	6	....	.250	.289	.351	.639	107	1	41	3.46	3	*1-108	11	0.3
Total 7	**747**	**2715**	**281**	**682**	**104**	**50**	**18**	**336**	**136**	**....**	**48**	**....**	**.251**	**.298**	**.346**	**.644**	**94**	**-29**	**309**	**3.89**	**21**	**1-726/2-9,S-1**	**68**	**-1.8**

• GARAGIOLA, Joe Joseph Henry Garagiola b: 2/12/1926, St. Louis, MO BL/TR, 6', 190 lbs. Deb: 5/26/1946

YEAR TM-L	G	AB	R	H	2B	3B	HR	RBI	BB	SO	SB	CS	AVG	OBP	SLG	OPS	OPS+	BR/A	RC	RC/G	FR	G/POS	WS	TPW
1946*StL-N	74	211	21	50	4	1	3	22	23	25	0	....	.237	.312	.308	.620	73	-7	21	3.41	-1	C-70	6	-0.5
1947 StL-N	77	183	20	47	10	2	5	25	40	14	0	....	.257	.398	.415	.814	111	5	33	6.21	-2	C-74	9	0.6
1948 StL-N	24	56	9	6	1	0	2	7	12	9	0	....	.107	.275	.232	.508	36	-5	5	2.44	1	C-23	1	-0.3
1949 StL-N	81	241	25	63	14	0	3	26	31	19	0	....	.261	.348	.357	.705	85	-4	31	4.48	-5	C-80	8	-0.5
1950 StL-N	34	88	8	28	6	1	2	20	10	7	0	....	.318	.388	.477	.865	120	3	15	6.24	0	C-30	4	0.4
1951 StL-N	27	72	9	14	3	2	2	9	9	7	0	0	.194	.284	.375	.659	75	-3	7	3.24	0	C-23	1	-0.2
Pit-N	72	212	24	54	8	2	9	35	32	20	4	1	.255	.358	.439	.796	110	4	36	5.84	2	C-61	8	0.9
Yr.	99	284	33	68	11	4	11	44	41	27	4	1	.239	.339	.423	.762	101	1	43	5.14	1	C-84	9	0.7
1952 Pit-N	118	344	35	94	15	4	8	54	50	24	0	1	.273	.369	.410	.779	113	7	55	5.76	8	*C-105	11	2.2
1953 Pit-N	27	73	9	17	5	0	2	14	10	11	1	0	.233	.341	.384	.725	89	-1	10	4.72	1	C-22	2	0.1
Chi-N	74	228	21	62	9	4	1	21	21	23	0	0	.272	.336	.360	.696	80	-6	27	4.22	2	C-68	6	-0.1
Yr.	101	301	30	79	14	4	3	35	31	34	1	0	.262	.337	.365	.703	82	-7	38	4.34	3	C-90	8	0.0
1954 Chi-N	63	153	16	43	5	0	5	21	28	12	0	0	.281	.405	.412	.817	112	5	27	6.39	-1	C-55	6	0.5
NY-N	5	11	1	3	2	0	0	1	1	2	0	0	.273	.333	.455	.788	102	0	2	5.34	0	/C-3	1	0.0
Yr.	68	164	17	46	7	0	5	22	29	14	0	0	.280	.401	.415	.816	112	5	29	6.32	-2	C-58	7	0.5
Total 9	**676**	**1872**	**198**	**481**	**82**	**16**	**42**	**255**	**267**	**173**	**5**	**2**	**.257**	**.355**	**.385**	**.740**	**96**	**-3**	**270**	**5.00**	**5**	**C-614**	**63**	**3.1**

• GARBARK, Bob Robert Michael Garbark b: 11/13/1909, Houston, TX d: 8/15/1990, Meadville, PA BR/TR, 5'11", 178 lbs. Deb: 9/3/1934

YEAR TM-L	G	AB	R	H	2B	3B	HR	RBI	BB	SO	SB	CS	AVG	OBP	SLG	OPS	OPS+	BR/A	RC	RC/G	FR	G/POS	WS	TPW
1934 Cle-A	5	11	1	0	0	0	0	0	1	3	0	0	.000	.083	.000	.083	-76	-3	0	.05	0	/C-5	0	-0.3
1935 Cle-A	6	18	4	6	1	0	0	4	5	1	0	0	.333	.478	.389	.867	124	1	4	8.42	1	/C-6	1	0.3
1937 Chi-N	1	1	0	0	0	0	0	0	0	0	0	....	.000	.000	.000	.000	-96	-0	0	.00	0	....	0	0.0
1938 Chi-N	23	54	2	14	0	0	0	5	1	0	0	....	.259	.273	.259	.532	46	-4	3	1.59	-1	C-20/1-1	1	-0.4
1939 Chi-N	24	21	1	3	0	0	0	0	0	3	0	....	.143	.143	.143	.286	-23	-4	0	.41	-2	C-21	0	-0.6
1944 Phi-A	18	23	2	6	2	0	0	2	1	0	0	0	.261	.292	.348	.639	83	-1	2	3.06	0	C-15	0	-0.1
1945 Bos-A	68	199	21	52	6	0	0	17	18	10	0	1	.261	.329	.291	.620	79	-5	20	3.30	-1	C-67	5	-0.3
Total 7	**145**	**327**	**31**	**81**	**9**	**0**	**0**	**28**	**26**	**17**	**0**	**1**	**.248**	**.307**	**.275**	**.582**	**65**	**-15**	**29**	**2.87**	**-4**	**C-134/1-1**	**7**	**-1.3**

• GARBARK, Mike Nathaniel Michael Garbark b: 2/2/1916, Houston, TX d: 8/31/1994, Charlotte, NC BR/TR, 6', 200 lbs. Deb: 4/18/1944

YEAR TM-L	G	AB	R	H	2B	3B	HR	RBI	BB	SO	SB	CS	AVG	OBP	SLG	OPS	OPS+	BR/A	RC	RC/G	FR	G/POS	WS	TPW
1944 NY-A	89	299	23	78	9	4	1	33	25	27	0	1	.261	.320	.328	.648	82	-7	30	3.45	2	C-85	8	0.1
1945 NY-A	60	176	23	38	5	3	1	26	23	12	0	1	.216	.310	.295	.605	73	-6	16	3.04	0	C-59	4	-0.3
Total 2	**149**	**475**	**46**	**116**	**14**	**7**	**2**	**59**	**48**	**39**	**0**	**2**	**.244**	**.316**	**.316**	**.632**	**79**	**-13**	**47**	**3.29**	**2**	**C-144**	**12**	**-0.2**

• GARBEY, Barbaro Barbaro (Garbey) Garbey b: 12/4/1956, Santiago de Cuba, Cuba BR/TR, 5'10", 170 lbs. Deb: 4/3/1984 Career OF: 25-2-16

YEAR TM-L	G	AB	R	H	2B	3B	HR	RBI	BB	SO	SB	CS	AVG	OBP	SLG	OPS	OPS+	BR/A	RC	RC/G	FR	G/POS	WS	TPW
1984*Det-A	110	327	45	94	17	1	5	52	17	35	6	7	.287	.327	.391	.718	98	-3	38	4.15	-2	1-65,3-20,D-17,O-10(8-1-1)/2	7	-0.8
1985 Det-A	86	237	27	61	9	1	6	29	15	37	3	2	.257	.310	.380	.690	88	-4	27	3.79	0	1-37,O-24(10-1-14),D-21/3-1	3	-0.8
1988 Tex-A	30	62	4	12	2	0	0	5	4	11	0	0	.194	.242	.226	.468	31	-6	3	1.51	1	/O-8(7-0-1),1-7,D-7,3-3	0	-0.5
Total 3	**226**	**626**	**76**	**167**	**28**	**2**	**11**	**86**	**36**	**83**	**9**	**9**	**.267**	**.312**	**.371**	**.682**	**88**	**-13**	**68**	**3.72**	**-1**	**1-109/D-45,O-42,3-24,2-3**	**10**	**-2.1**

• GARBOWSKI, Alex Alexander Garbowski b: 6/25/1925, Yonkers, NY BR/TR, 6'1", 185 lbs. Deb: 4/16/1952

YEAR TM-L	G	AB	R	H	2B	3B	HR	RBI	BB	SO	SB	CS	AVG	OBP	SLG	OPS	OPS+	BR/A	RC	RC/G	FR	G/POS	WS	TPW
1952 Det-A	2	0	0	0	0	0	0	0	0	0	0	0	....	....	....	....	-99	0	0	....	0	....	0	0.0

• GARCIA, Amaury Amaury Miguel (Paula) Garcia b: 5/20/1975, Santo Domingo, Dominican Republic BR/TR, 5'10", 160 lbs. Deb: 7/5/1999

YEAR TM-L	G	AB	R	H	2B	3B	HR	RBI	BB	SO	SB	CS	AVG	OBP	SLG	OPS	OPS+	BR/A	RC	RC/G	FR	G/POS	WS	TPW
1999 Fla-N	10	24	6	6	0	1	2	2	3	11	0	0	.250	.333	.583	.917	133	1	5	7.39	0	/2-8	1	0.1

• GARCIA, Carlos Carlos Jesus (Guerrero) Garcia b: 10/15/1967, Tachira, Venezuela BR/TR, 6'1", 185 lbs. Deb: 9/20/1990

YEAR TM-L	G	AB	R	H	2B	3B	HR	RBI	BB	SO	SB	CS	AVG	OBP	SLG	OPS	OPS+	BR/A	RC	RC/G	FR	G/POS	WS	TPW
1990 Pit-N	4	4	1	2	0	0	0	0	0	2	0	0	.500	.500	.500	1.000	183	0	1	13.50	0	/S-3	0	0.1
1991 Pit-N	12	24	2	6	0	2	0	1	1	8	0	0	.250	.280	.417	.697	95	-0	2	3.50	1	/S-9,3-2,2-1	0	0.1
1992*Pit-N	22	39	4	8	1	0	0	4	0	9	0	0	.205	.205	.231	.436	23	-4	2	1.36	0	2-14/S-8	1	-0.4
1993 Pit-N	141	546	77	147	25	5	12	47	31	67	18	11	.269	.319	.399	.718	91	-9	68	4.27	-27	*2-140/S-3	10	-2.9
1994 Pit-N★	98	412	49	114	15	2	6	28	16	67	18	9	.277	.310	.367	.677	75	-16	46	3.90	-5	2-98	9	-1.6
1995 Pit-N	104	367	41	108	24	2	6	50	25	55	8	4	.294	.343	.420	.762	98	-2	53	5.21	-8	2-92,S-15	10	-0.4
1996 Pit-N	101	390	66	111	18	4	6	44	23	58	16	6	.285	.331	.397	.728	89	-6	53	4.85	-6	2-77,S-19,3-14	11	-0.8
1997 Tor-A	103	350	29	77	18	2	3	23	15	60	11	3	.220	.256	.309	.565	46	-27	28	2.51	0	2-96/S-5,3-4	4	-2.2
1998 Ana-A	19	35	4	5	1	0	0	0	3	11	2	0	.143	.231	.171	.402	7	-4	2	1.69	0	2-11/S-5,D-3	1	-0.3
1999 SD-N	6	11	1	2	0	0	0	0	1	3	0	0	.182	.250	.182	.432	13	-1	0	.46	-1	/3-4,1-1	0	-0.3
Total 10	**610**	**2178**	**274**	**580**	**102**	**17**	**33**	**197**	**115**	**340**	**73**	**33**	**.266**	**.310**	**.374**	**.684**	**79**	**-71**	**254**	**4.02**	**-46**	**2-529/S-67,3-24,D-3,1-1**	**46**	**-8.7**

• GARCIA, Chico Vinicio Uzcanga Garcia b: 12/24/1924, Veracruz, Mexico BR/TR, 5'8", 170 lbs. Deb: 4/24/1954

YEAR TM-L	G	AB	R	H	2B	3B	HR	RBI	BB	SO	SB	CS	AVG	OBP	SLG	OPS	OPS+	BR/A	RC	RC/G	FR	G/POS	WS	TPW
1954 Bal-A	39	62	6	7	0	2	0	5	8	3	0	0	.113	.214	.177	.392	9	-8	3	1.39	-2	2-24	1	-0.9

• GARCIA, Damaso Damaso Domingo (Sanchez) Garcia b: 2/7/1957, Moca, Dominican Republic BR/TR, 6'1", 170 lbs. Deb: 6/24/1978

YEAR TM-L	G	AB	R	H	2B	3B	HR	RBI	BB	SO	SB	CS	AVG	OBP	SLG	OPS	OPS+	BR/A	RC	RC/G	FR	G/POS	WS	TPW
1978 NY-A	18	41	5	8	0	0	0	1	2	6	1	0	.195	.233	.195	.428	22	-4	2	1.51	-2	2-16/S-3	1	-0.5
1979 NY-A	11	38	3	10	1	0	0	4	0	2	2	0	.263	.263	.289	.553	50	-2	3	2.65	-1	S-10/3-1	1	-0.3
1980 Tor-A	140	543	50	151	30	7	4	46	12	55	13	13	.278	.297	.381	.679	81	-19	54	3.44	10	*2-138/D-1	12	-0.2
1981 Tor-A	64	250	24	63	8	1	1	13	9	32	13	3	.252	.278	.304	.582	64	-10	21	2.81	-5	2-62/D-1	3	-1.2
1982 Tor-A	147	597	89	185	32	3	5	42	21	44	54	20	.310	.339	.399	.737	93	-3	81	4.89	15	*2-141/D-4	21	1.9
1983 Tor-A	131	525	84	161	23	6	3	38	24	34	31	17	.307	.339	.390	.730	94	-5	67	4.50	1	*2-130	13	0.3
1984 Tor-A★	152	633	79	180	32	5	5	46	16	46	46	12	.284	.312	.374	.686	86	-9	76	4.30	5	*2-149/D-1	16	0.4
1985*Tor-A★	146	600	70	169	25	4	8	65	15	41	28	15	.282	.304	.377	.680	83	-16	64	3.68	-4	*2-143	13	-1.3
1986 Tor-A	122	424	57	119	22	0	6	46	13	32	9	6	.281	.308	.375	.683	83	-12	44	3.63	-8	*2-106,D-11/1-1	9	-1.4
1988 Atl-N	21	60	3	7	1	0	1	4	3	10	1	0	.117	.159	.183	.342	-2	-8	1	.56	0	2-13	0	-0.8
1989 Mon-N	80	203	26	55	9	1	3	18	15	20	5	4	.271	.321	.369	.691	96	-2	23	3.75	3	2-62/3-1	5	0.3
Total 11	**1032**	**3914**	**490**	**1108**	**183**	**27**	**36**	**323**	**130**	**322**	**203**	**90**	**.283**	**.311**	**.371**	**.682**	**83**	**-90**	**435**	**3.88**	**14**	**2-960/D-18,S-13,3-2,1-1**	**94**	**-2.8**

• GARCIA, Danny Daniel Raphael Garcia b: 4/29/1954, Brooklyn, NY BL/TL, 6'1", 182 lbs. Deb: 4/26/1981

YEAR TM-L	G	AB	R	H	2B	3B	HR	RBI	BB	SO	SB	CS	AVG	OBP	SLG	OPS	OPS+	BR/A	RC	RC/G	FR	G/POS	WS	TPW
1981 KC-A	12	14	4	2	0	0	0	0	0	2	0	0	.143	.143	.143	.286	-18	-2	0	.64	0	/O-6(1-0-5),1-2	0	-0.3

• GARCIA, Danny Daniel Joseph Garcia b: 4/12/1980, Riverside, CA BR/TR, 6', 174 lbs. Deb: 9/2/2003

YEAR TM-L	G	AB	R	H	2B	3B	HR	RBI	BB	SO	SB	CS	AVG	OBP	SLG	OPS	OPS+	BR/A	RC	RC/G	FR	G/POS	WS	TPW
2003 NY-N	19	56	5	12	2	0	2	6	2	11	0	0	.214	.279	.357	.636	66	-3	5	2.99	-1	2-17/O-1	0	-0.4

• GARCIA, Freddy Freddy Adrian (Felix) Garcia b: 8/1/1972, La Romana, Dominican Republic BR/TR, 6'2", 190 lbs. Deb: 5/3/1995 Career OF: 28-0-7

YEAR TM-L	G	AB	R	H	2B	3B	HR	RBI	BB	SO	SB	CS	AVG	OBP	SLG	OPS	OPS+	BR/A	RC	RC/G	FR	G/POS	WS	TPW
1995 Pit-N	42	57	5	8	1	1	0	1	8	17	0	1	.140	.246	.193	.439	17	-7	3	1.64	0	O-10(10-0-0)/3-8	0	-0.7
1997 Pit-N	20	40	4	6	1	0	3	5	2	17	0	0	.150	.190	.400	.590	49	-3	3	2.50	-2	3-10/1-2	0	-0.5
1998 Pit-N	56	172	27	44	11	1	9	26	18	45	0	2	.256	.333	.488	.822	111	1	27	5.48	2	3-47/1-4	5	0.4
1999 Pit-N	55	130	16	30	5	0	6	23	4	41	0	0	.231	.254	.408	.661	64	-8	13	3.25	0	O-24(17-0-7)/3-9,D-2,1-1	1	-0.9
Atl-N	2	2	1	1	0	0	1	1	1	1	0	0	.500	.667	2.000	2.667	540	1	3	76.68	0	/O-1	0	0.1
Yr.	57	132	17	31	5	0	7	24	5	42	0	0	.235	.263	.432	.695	74	-7	15	3.95	0	O-25(18-0-7)/3-9,D-2,1-1	1	-0.7
Total 4	**175**	**401**	**53**	**89**	**18**	**2**	**19**	**56**	**33**	**121**	**0**	**3**	**.222**	**.284**	**.419**	**.703**	**79**	**-16**	**49**	**4.07**	**0**	**/3-74,O-35,1-7,D-2**	**6**	**-1.6**

• GARCIA, Guillermo Guillermo Antonio (Morel) Garcia b: 4/4/1972, Santiago, Dominican Republic BR/TR, 6'3", 215 lbs. Deb: 7/19/1998

YEAR TM-L	G	AB	R	H	2B	3B	HR	RBI	BB	SO	SB	CS	AVG	OBP	SLG	OPS	OPS+	BR/A	RC	RC/G	FR	G/POS	WS	TPW
1998 Cin-N	12	36	3	7	2	0	2	4	2	13	0	0	.194	.237	.417	.654	67	-2	3	2.49	-0	C-11	0	-0.1
1999 Fla-N	4	4	0	1	0	0	0	0	0	2	0	0	.250	.250	.250	.500	29	-0	0	2.25	0	/C-3	0	-0.1
Total 2	**16**	**40**	**3**	**8**	**2**	**0**	**2**	**4**	**2**	**15**	**0**	**0**	**.200**	**.238**	**.400**	**.638**	**63**	**-2**	**3**	**2.47**	**0**	**/C-14**	**0**	**-0.2**

• GARCIA, Jesse Jesus Jesse Garcia b: 9/24/1973, Corpus Christi, TX BR/TR, 5'10", 171 lbs. Deb: 4/5/1999

YEAR TM-L	G	AB	R	H	2B	3B	HR	RBI	BB	SO	SB	CS	AVG	OBP	SLG	OPS	OPS+	BR/A	RC	RC/G	FR	G/POS	WS	TPW
1999 Bal-A	17	29	6	6	0	0	2	2	2	3	0	0	.207	.258	.414	.672	70	-1	3	2.90	1	/S-7,2-6,3-2,D-1	0	0.0
2000 Bal-A	14	17	2	1	0	0	0	0	2	2	0	0	.059	.158	.059	.217	-44	-4	0	.41	2	/2-6,S-5	0	-0.1

YEAR TM-L	G	AB	R	H	2B	3B	HR	RBI	BB	SO	SB	CS	AVG	OBP	SLG	OPS	OPS+	BR/A	RC	RC/G	FR	G/POS	WS	TPW
2001 Atl-N	22	5	3	1	0	0	0	0	0	1	6	2	.200	.200	.200	.400	4	-0	0	.00	0	/2-4,S-2	0	0.0
2002 Atl-N	39	61	6	12	1	0	0	5	0	14	0	1	.197	.197	.213	.410	8	-9	2	1.13	4	2-21/S-5,0-4(2-0-2)	1	-0.3
2003*Atl-N	13	10	6	4	0	1	0	2	0	1	0	1	.400	.400	.600	1.000	156	0	2	6.94	-1	/2-6,S-3,3-2	1	0.0
Total 5	**105**	**122**	**23**	**24**	**1**	**1**	**2**	**9**	**4**	**21**	**6**	**4**	**.197**	**.222**	**.270**	**.493**	**28**	**-14**	**7**	**1.77**	**7**	**/2-43,S-22,3-4,0-4,D-1**	**2**	**-0.5**

• GARCIA, Karim Gustavo Karim Garcia b: 10/29/1975, Ciudad Obregon, Mexico BL/TL, 6', 200 lbs. Deb: 9/2/1995 Career OF: 72-21-283

YEAR TM-L	G	AB	R	H	2B	3B	HR	RBI	BB	SO	SB	CS	AVG	OBP	SLG	OPS	OPS+	BR/A	RC	RC/G	FR	G/POS	WS	TPW
1995 LA-N	13	20	1	4	0	0	0	0	0	4	0	0	.200	.200	.200	.400	6	-3	1	1.35	2	/0-5(2-0-3)	0	-0.1
1996 LA-N	1	1	0	0	0	0	0	0	0	1	0	0	.000	.000	.000	.000	-109	-0	0	.00	0	....	0	0.0
1997 LA-N	15	39	5	5	0	0	1	8	6	14	0	0	.128	.244	.205	.450	21	-5	2	1.81	0	0-12(12-0-2)	1	-0.5
1998 Ari-N	113	333	39	74	10	8	9	43	18	78	5	4	.222	.262	.381	.643	67	-18	31	3.12	-2	*0-103(0-8-100)	4	-2.4
1999 Det-A	96	288	38	69	10	3	14	32	20	67	2	4	.240	.289	.441	.730	82	-11	36	4.28	0	0-81(35-0-55)/D-6	4	-1.4
2000 Det-A	8	17	1	3	0	0	0	0	0	4	0	0	.176	.176	.176	.353	-10	-3	0	.64	-1	/0-7(0-0-7),D-4	0	-0.4
Bal-A	8	16	0	0	0	0	0	0	0	6	0	0	.000	.000	.000	.000	-105	-5	0	.00	0	/0-2(2-0-0),D-1	0	-0.4
Yr.	16	33	1	3	0	0	0	0	0	10	0	0	.091	.091	.091	.182	-56	-8	0	.31	-1	/0-9(2-0-7),D-5	0	-0.8
2001 Cle-A	20	45	8	14	3	0	5	9	3	13	0	0	.311	.367	.711	1.078	173	4	11	9.34	0	0-18(6-0-13)/1-2	3	0.4
2002 NY-A	2	5	1	1	0	0	0	0	0	1	0	0	.200	.200	.200	.400	7	-1	0	1.35	0	/0-2(1-0-1)	0	-0.1
Cle-A	51	197	29	59	8	0	16	52	6	40	0	3	.299	.320	.584	.904	136	7	32	5.82	-1	0-51(1-3-48)	7	0.3
Yr.	53	202	30	60	8	0	16	52	6	41	0	3	.297	.317	.574	.892	132	6	32	5.70	-1	0-53(2-3-49)	7	0.2
2003 Cle-A	24	93	8	18	1	0	5	14	5	20	0	0	.194	.242	.366	.608	59	-6	7	2.40	-2	0-23(0-7-17)/D-1	0	-0.9
*NY-A	52	151	17	46	5	0	6	21	9	32	0	2	.305	.344	.457	.801	111	1	22	5.25	3	0-50(13-3-37)/D-1	5	0.2
Yr.	76	244	25	64	6	0	11	35	14	52	0	2	.262	.305	.422	.727	91	-5	29	4.06	1	0-73(13-10-54)/D-2	5	-0.6
Total 9	**403**	**1205**	**147**	**293**	**37**	**11**	**56**	**179**	**67**	**280**	**7**	**13**	**.243**	**.284**	**.432**	**.716**	**84**	**-38**	**143**	**4.04**	**-1**	**0-354/D-13,1-2**	**24**	**-5.4**

• GARCIA, Kiko Alfonso Rafael Garcia b: 10/14/1953, Martinez, CA BR/TR, 5'11", 180 lbs. Deb: 9/11/1976 Career OF: 3-0-0

YEAR TM-L	G	AB	R	H	2B	3B	HR	RBI	BB	SO	SB	CS	AVG	OBP	SLG	OPS	OPS+	BR/A	RC	RC/G	FR	G/POS	WS	TPW
1976 Bal-A	11	32	2	7	1	1	1	4	0	4	2	1	.219	.219	.406	.625	86	-1	3	2.73	1	S-11	1	0.2
1977 Bal-A	65	131	20	29	6	0	2	10	6	31	2	3	.221	.255	.313	.568	57	-9	9	2.19	11	S-61/2-2	3	0.7
1978 Bal-A	79	186	17	49	6	4	0	13	7	43	7	1	.263	.290	.339	.629	81	-4	18	3.26	3	S-74/2-3	5	0.5
1979*Bal-A	126	417	54	103	15	9	5	24	32	87	11	9	.247	.304	.362	.666	82	-13	42	3.31	-4	*S-113,2-25/3-2,0-2(2-0-0)	9	-0.5
1980 Bal-A	111	311	27	62	8	0	1	27	24	57	8	4	.199	.257	.235	.491	36	-27	18	1.80	2	S-96,2-27/0-1	5	-1.5
1981*Hou-N	48	136	9	37	6	1	0	15	10	16	2	2	.272	.327	.331	.657	91	-2	15	3.71	-1	S-28,3-13/2-9	4	0.0
1982 Hou-N	34	76	5	16	5	0	1	5	3	15	1	0	.211	.241	.316	.556	59	-4	5	2.33	-0	S-21/3-2,2-1	1	-0.2
1983 Phi-N	84	118	22	34	7	1	2	9	9	20	1	2	.288	.344	.415	.759	111	1	15	4.15	-2	2-52,S-22,3-10	4	0.1
1984 Phi-N	57	60	6	14	2	0	0	5	4	11	0	0	.233	.281	.267	.548	54	-4	4	1.98	0	S-30,3-23/2-1	1	-0.3
1985 Phi-N	4	3	0	0	0	0	0	0	0	1	0	0	.000	.000	.000	.000	-97	-1	0	.00	-1	/S-3,3-1	0	-0.2
Total 10	**619**	**1470**	**162**	**351**	**56**	**16**	**12**	**112**	**95**	**285**	**34**	**22**	**.239**	**.287**	**.323**	**.610**	**71**	**-63**	**128**	**2.84**	**10**	**S-459,2-120/3-51,0-3**	**33**	**-1.3**

• GARCIA, Leo Leonardo Antonio (Peralta) Garcia b: 11/6/1962, Santiago, Dominican Republic BL/TL, 5'8", 160 lbs. Deb: 4/6/1987 Career OF: 2-17-4

YEAR TM-L	G	AB	R	H	2B	3B	HR	RBI	BB	SO	SB	CS	AVG	OBP	SLG	OPS	OPS+	BR/A	RC	RC/G	FR	G/POS	WS	TPW
1987 Cin-N	31	30	8	6	0	0	1	2	4	8	3	1	.200	.294	.300	.594	55	-2	3	3.24	0	0-14(0-13-1)	0	-0.2
1988 Cin-N	23	28	2	4	1	0	0	0	4	5	0	1	.143	.250	.179	.429	24	-3	1	1.37	-0	/0-9(2-4-3)	0	-0.4
Total 2	**54**	**58**	**10**	**10**	**1**	**0**	**1**	**2**	**8**	**13**	**3**	**2**	**.172**	**.273**	**.241**	**.514**	**40**	**-5**	**4**	**2.32**	**0**	**/0-23**	**0**	**-0.5**

• GARCIA, Luis Luis Rafael Garcia b: 5/20/1975, San Francisco de Macoris, Dominican Republic BR/TR, 6', 175 lbs. Deb: 4/5/1999

YEAR TM-L	G	AB	R	H	2B	3B	HR	RBI	BB	SO	SB	CS	AVG	OBP	SLG	OPS	OPS+	BR/A	RC	RC/G	FR	G/POS	WS	TPW
1999 Det-A	8	9	0	1	1	0	0	0	0	2	0	0	.111	.111	.222	.333	-18	-2	0	.75	-3	/S-7,2-1	0	-0.4

• GARCIA, Luis Luis Carlos Garcia b: 9/22/1975, Hermosillo, Mexico BR/TR, 6'3", 208 lbs. Deb: 4/10/2002

YEAR TM-L	G	AB	R	H	2B	3B	HR	RBI	BB	SO	SB	CS	AVG	OBP	SLG	OPS	OPS+	BR/A	RC	RC/G	FR	G/POS	WS	TPW
2002 Bal-A	6	3	0	1	0	0	0	0	0	1	0	0	.333	.333	.333	.667	82	-0	0	4.50	0	/0-2(0-1-1)	0	0.0

• GARCIA, Pedro Pedro Modesto (Delfi) Garcia b: 4/17/1950, Guayama, Puerto Rico BR/TR, 5'10", 175 lbs. Deb: 4/6/1973

YEAR TM-L	G	AB	R	H	2B	3B	HR	RBI	BB	SO	SB	CS	AVG	OBP	SLG	OPS	OPS+	BR/A	RC	RC/G	FR	G/POS	WS	TPW
1973 Mil-A	160	580	67	142	**32**	5	15	54	40	119	11	10	.245	.299	.395	.694	96	-7	66	3.77	1	*2-160	12	0.6
1974 Mil-A	141	452	46	90	15	4	12	54	26	67	8	5	.199	.251	.330	.580	66	-21	37	2.63	-4	*2-140	7	-1.7
1975 Mil-A	98	302	40	68	15	2	6	38	18	59	12	6	.225	.273	.348	.621	74	-11	27	2.76	13	2-94/D-1	6	0.9
1976 Mil-A	41	106	12	23	7	1	1	9	4	23	2	2	.217	.259	.330	.589	73	-4	9	2.65	-1	2-39	2	-0.3
Det-A	77	227	21	45	10	2	3	20	9	40	2	3	.198	.242	.300	.541	56	-14	16	2.23	-8	2-77	2	-1.8
Yr.	118	333	33	68	17	3	4	29	13	63	4	5	.204	.247	.309	.556	61	-19	25	2.36	-9	*2-116	4	-2.1
1977 Tor-A	41	130	10	27	10	1	0	9	5	21	0	0	.208	.254	.300	.554	50	-9	10	2.49	-3	2-34/D-4	0	-1.1
Total 5	**558**	**1797**	**196**	**395**	**89**	**15**	**37**	**184**	**102**	**329**	**35**	**26**	**.220**	**.270**	**.348**	**.618**	**75**	**-67**	**164**	**2.95**	**-2**	**2-544/D-5**	**29**	**-3.5**

• GARCIAPARRA, Nomar Anthony Nomar Garciaparra b: 7/23/1973, Whittier, CA BR/TR, 6', 165 lbs. Deb: 8/31/1996

YEAR TM-L	G	AB	R	H	2B	3B	HR	RBI	BB	SO	SB	CS	AVG	OBP	SLG	OPS	OPS+	BR/A	RC	RC/G	FR	G/POS	WS	TPW
1996 Bos-A	24	87	11	21	2	3	4	16	4	14	5	0	.241	.275	.471	.746	82	-2	12	4.88	-1	S-22/2-1,D-1	2	-0.1
1997 Bos-A★	153	684	122	**209**	44	**11**	30	98	35	92	22	9	.306	.345	.534	.878	122	20	124	6.65	-2	*S-153	26	2.9
1998*Bos-A	143	604	111	195	37	8	35	122	33	62	12	6	.323	.366	.584	.950	139	32	120	7.34	-5	*S-143	27	3.6
1999*Bos-A★	135	532	103	190	42	4	27	104	51	39	14	3	**.357**	.421	.603	1.025	153	44	136	10.19	5	*S-134	32	**5.6**
2000 Bos-A★	140	529	104	197	51	3	21	96	61	50	5	2	**.372**	.439	.599	1.038	155	46	140	10.80	0	*S-136/D-1	29	5.2
2001 Bos-A	21	83	13	24	3	0	4	8	7	9	0	1	.289	.352	.470	.822	113	1	14	5.99	1	S-21	3	0.3
2002 Bos-A★	156	635	101	197	**56**	5	24	120	41	63	5	2	.310	.358	.528	.885	129	25	115	6.64	10	*S-154	27	4.5
2003*Bos-A★	156	658	120	198	37	13	28	105	39	61	19	5	.301	.350	.524	.875	124	22	121	6.72	-6	*S-156	25	2.8
Total 8	**928**	**3812**	**685**	**1231**	**272**	**47**	**173**	**669**	**271**	**390**	**82**	**28**	**.323**	**.374**	**.555**	**.929**	**134**	**188**	**781**	**7.71**	**1**	**S-919/D-2,2-1**	**171**	**24.8**

• GARDELLA, Al Alfred Stephan Gardella b: 1/11/1918, New York, NY BL/TL, 5'10", 172 lbs. Deb: 5/17/1945

YEAR TM-L	G	AB	R	H	2B	3B	HR	RBI	BB	SO	SB	CS	AVG	OBP	SLG	OPS	OPS+	BR/A	RC	RC/G	FR	G/POS	WS	TPW
1945 NY-N	16	26	2	2	0	0	0	1	4	3	0	....	.077	.226	.077	.303	-14	-4	1	.96	-1	/1-9,0-1	0	-0.5

• GARDELLA, Danny Daniel Lewis Gardella b: 2/26/1920, New York, NY BL/TL, 5'7.5", 160 lbs. Deb: 5/14/1944 Career OF: 96-4-19

YEAR TM-L	G	AB	R	H	2B	3B	HR	RBI	BB	SO	SB	CS	AVG	OBP	SLG	OPS	OPS+	BR/A	RC	RC/G	FR	G/POS	WS	TPW
1944 NY-N	47	112	20	28	2	2	6	14	11	13	0	....	.250	.323	.464	.787	120	2	17	5.25	1	0-25(11-4-10)	3	0.2
1945 NY-N	121	430	54	117	10	1	18	71	46	55	2	....	.272	.349	.426	.775	113	7	65	5.40	-1	0-94(85-0-9),1-15	12	0.0
1950 StL-N	1	1	0	0	0	0	0	0	0	0	0	....	.000	.000	.000	.000	-95	-0	0	.00	0	....	0	0.0
Total 3	**169**	**543**	**74**	**145**	**12**	**3**	**24**	**85**	**57**	**68**	**2**	**....**	**.267**	**.343**	**.433**	**.776**	**114**	**9**	**82**	**5.35**	**0**	**0-119/1-15**	**15**	**0.1**

• GARDENHIRE, Ron Ronald Clyde Gardenhire b: 10/24/1957, Butzbach, West Germany BR/TR, 6', 175 lbs. Deb: 9/1/1981 M/C

YEAR TM-L	G	AB	R	H	2B	3B	HR	RBI	BB	SO	SB	CS	AVG	OBP	SLG	OPS	OPS+	BR/A	RC	RC/G	FR	G/POS	WS	TPW
1981 NY-N	27	48	2	13	1	0	0	3	5	9	2	2	.271	.340	.292	.631	82	-1	5	3.49	-1	S-18/2-6,3-1	1	-0.1
1982 NY-N	141	384	29	92	17	1	3	33	23	55	5	6	.240	.283	.313	.595	67	-19	32	2.62	2	*S-135/2-1,3-1	7	-0.4
1983 NY-N	17	32	1	2	0	0	0	1	1	4	0	0	.063	.091	.063	.153	-57	-7	0	.12	1	S-15	0	-0.5
1984 NY-N	74	207	20	51	7	1	1	10	9	43	6	1	.246	.278	.304	.582	64	-9	17	2.69	-4	S-49,2-18/3-7	4	-0.9
1985 NY-N	26	39	5	7	2	1	0	2	8	11	0	0	.179	.319	.282	.601	71	-1	4	2.81	-1	S-13/2-5,3-2	1	-0.1
Total 5	**285**	**710**	**57**	**165**	**27**	**3**	**4**	**49**	**46**	**122**	**13**	**9**	**.232**	**.279**	**.296**	**.575**	**62**	**-38**	**57**	**2.57**	**-3**	**S-230/2-30,3-11**	**13**	**-2.1**

• GARDNER, Alex Alexander Gardner b: 4/28/1861, Toronto, Canada d: 6/18/1926, Danvers, MA Deb: 5/10/1884

YEAR TM-L	G	AB	R	H	2B	3B	HR	RBI	BB	SO	SB	CS	AVG	OBP	SLG	OPS	OPS+	BR/A	RC	RC/G	FR	G/POS	WS	TPW
1884 Was-a	1	3	0	0	0	0	0	0	0	....	....	....	.000	.000	.000	.000	-113	-1	0	.00	-1	/C-1	0	-0.1

• GARDNER, Art Arthur Junior Gardner b: 9/21/1952, Madden, MS BL/TL, 5'11", 175 lbs. Deb: 9/2/1975 Career OF: 17-10-8

YEAR TM-L	G	AB	R	H	2B	3B	HR	RBI	BB	SO	SB	CS	AVG	OBP	SLG	OPS	OPS+	BR/A	RC	RC/G	FR	G/POS	WS	TPW
1975 Hou-N	13	31	3	6	0	0	0	2	1	8	1	0	.194	.242	.194	.436	24	-3	1	1.23	0	/0-8(3-1-4)	0	-0.4
1977 Hou-N	66	65	7	10	0	0	0	3	3	15	0	0	.154	.203	.154	.357	-3	-9	2	.81	1	0-26(14-9-4)	0	-0.9
1978 SF-N	7	3	2	0	0	0	0	0	0	2	0	1	.000	.000	.000	.000	-104	-1	0	.00	0	....	0	-0.1
Total 3	**86**	**99**	**12**	**16**	**0**	**0**	**0**	**5**	**4**	**25**	**1**	**1**	**.162**	**.210**	**.162**	**.371**	**2**	**-14**	**3**	**.90**	**1**	**/0-34**	**0**	**-1.4**

• GARDNER, Billy William Frederick "Whitey,Shotgun" Gardner b: 7/19/1927, Waterford, CT BR/TR, 6', 180 lbs. Deb: 4/22/1954 M/C

YEAR TM-L	G	AB	R	H	2B	3B	HR	RBI	BB	SO	SB	CS	AVG	OBP	SLG	OPS	OPS+	BR/A	RC	RC/G	FR	G/POS	WS	TPW
1954 NY-N	62	108	10	23	5	0	1	7	6	19	0	1	.213	.261	.287	.548	42	-10	8	2.48	2	3-30,2-13/S-5	2	-0.7
1955 NY-N	59	187	26	38	10	1	3	17	13	19	0	0	.203	.262	.316	.578	52	-13	16	2.79	-1	S-38,3-10/2-4	2	-1.1
1956 Bal-A	144	515	53	119	16	2	11	50	29	53	5	5	.231	.281	.334	.615	67	-27	45	2.89	-12	*2-132,S-25/3-6	7	-2.8
1957 Bal-A	154	644	79	169	**36**	3	6	55	53	67	10	7	.262	.326	.356	.682	92	-8	75	3.98	17	*2-148/S-9	20	2.3
1958 Bal-A	151	560	32	126	28	2	3	33	34	53	2	3	.225	.273	.298	.571	60	-31	45	2.63	-2	*2-151,S-13	9	-2.3
1959 Bal-A	140	401	34	87	13	2	6	27	38	61	2	1	.217	.286	.304	.591	64	-20	34	2.73	20	*2-139/3-1,S-1	9	1.0

YEAR TM-L	G	AB	R	H	2B	3B	HR	RBI	BB	SO	SB	CS	AVG	OBP	SLG	OPS	OPS+	BR/A	RC	RC/G	FR	G/POS	WS	TPW
1960 Was-A	145	592	71	152	26	5	9	56	43	76	0	4	.257	.314	.363	.677	82	-18	66	3.82	-5	*2-145,S-13	13	-1.1
1961 Min-A	45	154	13	36	9	0	1	11	10	14	0	0	.234	.280	.312	.592	55	-10	12	2.52	-2	2-41/3-2	1	-0.8
*NY-A	41	99	11	21	5	0	1	2	6	18	0	0	.212	.278	.293	.571	55	-6	8	2.47	4	3-33/2-6	1	-0.2
Yr.	86	253	24	57	14	0	2	13	16	32	0	0	.225	.279	.304	.584	55	-16	20	2.50	2	2-47,3-35	2	-1.0
1962 NY-A	4	1	1	0	0	0	0	0	0	1	0	0	.000	.000	.000	.000	-103	-0	0	.00	0	/2-1,3-1	0	0.0
Bos-A	53	199	22	54	9	2	0	12	10	39	0	1	.271	.310	.337	.646	71	-9	20	3.56	-4	2-38/3-7,S-4	3	-0.9
Yr.	57	200	23	54	9	2	0	12	10	40	0	1	.270	.308	.335	.643	71	-9	20	3.54	-4	2-39/3-8,S-4	3	-0.9
1963 Bos-A	36	84	4	16	2	1	0	1	4	19	0	0	.190	.236	.238	.474	32	-8	5	1.85	1	2-21/3-2	1	-0.5
Total 10	1034	3544	356	841	159	18	41	271	246	439	19	22	.237	.293	.327	.620	70	-160	334	3.14	19	2-839,S-108/3-92	68	-7.2

• GARDNER, Earle Earle McClurkin Gardner b: 1/24/1884, Sparta, IL d: 3/2/1943, Sparta, IL BR/TR, 5'11", 160 lbs. Deb: 9/18/1908

YEAR TM-L	G	AB	R	H	2B	3B	HR	RBI	BB	SO	SB	CS	AVG	OBP	SLG	OPS	OPS+	BR/A	RC	RC/G	FR	G/POS	WS	TPW
1908 NY-A	20	75	7	16	2	0	0	4	1	....	0	....	.213	.234	.240	.474	53	-4	4	1.79	2	2-20	0	-0.2
1909 NY-A	22	85	12	28	4	0	0	15	3	....	4	....	.329	.352	.376	.729	129	2	12	5.56	-8	2-22	3	-0.6
1910 NY-A	86	271	36	66	4	2	1	24	21	....	9	....	.244	.303	.284	.587	79	-6	26	3.18	8	2-70	7	0.3
1911 NY-A	102	357	36	94	13	2	0	39	20	....	14	....	.263	.312	.311	.622	69	-15	39	3.68	1	*2-101	6	-1.2
1912 NY-A	43	160	14	45	3	1	0	26	5	....	11	....	.281	.303	.313	.616	72	-6	18	3.95	-7	2-43	2	-1.3
Total 5	273	948	105	249	26	5	1	108	50	....	38	....	.263	.305	.304	.609	77	-30	100	3.57	-4	2-256	18	-3.1

• GARDNER, Gid Franklin Washington Gardner b: 5/6/1859, Boston, MA d: 8/1/1914, Cambridge, MA, 165 lbs. Deb: 8/23/1879 Career OF: 16-36-69 ♦

YEAR TM-L	G	AB	R	H	2B	3B	HR	RBI	BB	SO	SB	CS	AVG	OBP	SLG	OPS	OPS+	BR/A	RC	RC/G	FR	G/POS	WS	TPW
1879 Tro-N	2	6	1	1	0	0	0	0	0	0	....	....	.167	.167	.167	.333	11	-0	0	.96	-1	/P-2	0	-0.5
1880 Cle-N	10	32	0	6	1	1	0	4	2	4	....	....	.188	.235	.281	.517	76	0	2	2.30	0	/P-9,O-1	2	-0.3
1883 Bal-a	42	161	28	44	10	3	1	0	18	....	....	....	.273	.346	.391	.738	133	7	22	5.35	-3	O-35(0-35-0)/2-4,3-3,P-2	5	0.2
1884 Bal-a	41	173	32	37	6	8	2	0	14	....	....	....	.214	.280	.376	.656	108	1	19	3.78	3	O-40(1-0-39)/1-2	7	0.3
CP-U	38	149	22	38	10	2	0	....	10	....	....	....	.255	.302	.349	.651	127	5	16	4.06	-1	O-29(15-0-14)/3-8,2-1,P-1	5	0.1
Bal-U	1	4	0	1	0	0	0	....	0	....	....	....	.250	.250	.250	.500	63	-0	0	2.39	0	/S-1	0	0.0
Yr.	39	153	22	39	10	2	0	....	10	....	....	....	.255	.301	.346	.647	126	5	16	4.02	-2	O-29(15-0-14)/3-8,2-1,P-1,S	5	0.0
1885 Bal-a	44	170	22	37	5	4	0	17	12	....	....	....	.218	.269	.294	.563	79	-4	14	2.80	1	2-39/O-5(0-0-5),1-1,P-1	3	-0.7
1887 Ind-N	18	75	8	23	1	0	1	8	12	11	7	....	.307	.307	.238	.545	55	-3	7	3.52	-1	O-11(0-0-11)/2-7	1	-0.3
1888 Was-N	1	3	0	1	0	0	0	0	1	1	0	....	.333	.500	.333	.833	180	0	1	6.92	0	/S-1	0	0.1
Phi-N	1	3	0	2	0	0	0	1	0	0	0	....	.667	.667	.667	1.333	310	1	1	36.90	0	/2-1	0	0.1
Was-N	1	1	0	0	0	0	0	0	0	0	0	....	.000	.000	.000	.000	-106	-0	0	.00	0	/2-1	0	0.0
Yr.	3	7	0	3	0	0	0	1	1	1	0	....	.429	.500	.429	.929	193	1	2	12.68	0	/2-2,S-1	0	0.1
Total 7	199	777	113	190	33	18	4	30	69	16	7	....	.245	.298	.339	.636	104	7	82	3.87	-2	O-121/2-53,P-15,3-11,1-3,S	23	-1.2

• GARDNER, Jeff Jeffrey Scott Gardner b: 2/4/1964, Newport Beach, CA BL/TR, 5'11", 165 lbs. Deb: 9/10/1991

YEAR TM-L	G	AB	R	H	2B	3B	HR	RBI	BB	SO	SB	CS	AVG	OBP	SLG	OPS	OPS+	BR/A	RC	RC/G	FR	G/POS	WS	TPW
1991 NY-N	13	37	3	6	0	0	0	1	4	6	0	0	.162	.244	.162	.406	16	-4	2	1.52	-2	/S-8,2-3	0	-0.6
1992 SD-N	15	19	0	2	0	0	0	0	1	8	0	0	.105	.150	.105	.255	-26	-3	0	.54	0	2-11	0	-0.3
1993 SD-N	140	404	53	106	21	7	1	24	45	69	2	6	.262	.338	.356	.694	85	-10	50	4.37	1	*2-133/3-1,S-1	10	-0.4
1994 Mon-N	18	32	4	7	0	1	0	1	3	5	0	0	.219	.286	.281	.567	48	-2	3	2.61	-2	/3-9,2-4	0	-0.4
Total 4	186	492	60	121	21	8	1	26	53	88	2	6	.246	.321	.327	.648	73	-20	55	3.84	-3	2-151/3-10,S-9	10	-1.7

• GARDNER, Larry William Lawrence Gardner b: 5/13/1886, Enosburg Falls, VT d: 3/11/1976, St. George, VT BL/TR, 5'8", 165 lbs. Deb: 6/25/1908

YEAR TM-L	G	AB	R	H	2B	3B	HR	RBI	BB	SO	SB	CS	AVG	OBP	SLG	OPS	OPS+	BR/A	RC	RC/G	FR	G/POS	WS	TPW
1908 Bos-A	3	10	0	3	1	0	0	1	0	....	0	....	.300	.300	.400	.700	124	0	1	4.26	-1	/3-3	0	-0.1
1909 Bos-A	19	37	7	11	1	2	0	5	4	....	1	....	.297	.381	.432	.813	153	2	7	5.98	-2	/3-8,S-5	2	0.1
1910 Bos-A	113	413	56	117	12	10	2	36	41	....	8	....	.283	.354	.375	.729	125	12	58	4.83	0	*2-113	15	1.5
1911 Bos-A	138	492	80	140	17	8	4	44	64	....	27	....	.285	.373	.376	.749	110	9	81	5.49	23	3-72,2-62	18	3.4
1912*Bos-A	143	517	88	163	24	18	3	86	56	....	25	....	.315	.383	.449	.832	131	20	98	6.88	5	*3-143	29	3.0
1913 Bos-A	131	473	64	133	17	10	0	63	47	34	18	....	.281	.347	.359	.707	104	2	63	4.55	-13	*3-130	16	-0.7
1914 Bos-A	155	553	50	143	23	19	3	68	35	39	16	23	.259	.303	.385	.688	107	-6	61	3.64	13	*3-153	20	1.2
1915*Bos-A	127	430	51	111	14	6	1	55	39	24	11	12	.258	.327	.326	.653	98	-4	49	3.64	0	*3-127	14	-0.1
1916*Bos-A	148	493	47	152	19	7	2	62	48	27	12	....	.308	.372	.387	.759	128	17	79	5.63	-6	*3-147	27	1.6
1917 Bos-A	146	501	53	133	23	7	1	61	54	37	16	....	.265	.341	.345	.686	110	7	66	4.23	-4	*3-146	18	0.8
1918 Phi-A	127	463	50	132	22	6	1	52	43	22	9	....	.285	.346	.365	.711	113	7	60	4.44	3	*3-127	17	1.5
1919 Cle-A	139	524	67	157	29	7	2	79	39	29	7	....	.300	.352	.393	.745	103	1	75	4.92	-6	*3-139	20	-0.1
1920*Cle-A	154	597	72	185	31	11	3	118	53	25	3	20	.310	.367	.414	.781	103	-3	86	4.90	1	*3-154	23	0.3
1921 Cle-A	153	586	101	187	32	14	3	120	65	16	3	3	.319	.391	.437	.828	109	10	103	6.31	5	*3-152	23	2.3
1922 Cle-A	137	470	74	134	31	3	2	68	49	21	9	8	.285	.355	.377	.732	90	-7	64	4.72	-9	*3-128	14	-0.7
1923 Cle-A	52	79	4	20	5	1	0	12	12	7	0	1	.253	.352	.342	.693	83	-2	10	4.26	3	3-19	2	0.2
1924 Cle-A	38	50	3	10	0	0	0	4	5	1	0	1	.200	.273	.200	.473	23	-6	3	1.78	-2	/3-8,2-6	0	-0.7
Total 17	1923	6688	867	1931	301	129	27	934	654	282	165	68	.289	.355	.384	.739	109	60	965	4.91	10	*3-1656,2-181/S-5	258	13.5

• GARDNER, Ray Raymond Vincent Gardner b: 10/25/1901, Frederick, MD d: 5/3/1968, Frederick, MD BR/TR, 5'8", 145 lbs. Deb: 4/16/1929

YEAR TM-L	G	AB	R	H	2B	3B	HR	RBI	BB	SO	SB	CS	AVG	OBP	SLG	OPS	OPS+	BR/A	RC	RC/G	FR	G/POS	WS	TPW
1929 Cle-A	82	256	28	67	3	2	1	24	29	16	10	13	.262	.337	.301	.638	63	-16	26	3.19	5	S-82	5	-0.4
1930 Cle-A	33	13	7	1	0	0	0	1	0	0	0	1	.077	.077	.077	.154	-59	-4	0	.00	-6	S-22/2-5,3-1	0	-0.8
Total 2	115	269	35	68	3	2	1	25	29	16	10	14	.253	.326	.290	.615	58	-20	26	2.99	-2	S-104/2-5,3-1	5	-1.2

• GARIBALDI, Art Arthur Edward Garibaldi b: 8/21/1907, San Francisco, CA d: 10/19/1967, Sacramento, CA BR/TR, 5'8", 165 lbs. Deb: 6/20/1936

YEAR TM-L	G	AB	R	H	2B	3B	HR	RBI	BB	SO	SB	CS	AVG	OBP	SLG	OPS	OPS+	BR/A	RC	RC/G	FR	G/POS	WS	TPW
1936 StL-N	71	232	30	64	12	0	1	20	16	30	3	....	.276	.323	.341	.663	79	-7	26	4.01	-3	3-46,2-24	5	-0.7

• GARMS, Debs Debs C. "Tex" Garms b: 6/26/1908, Bangs, TX d: 12/16/1984, Glen Rose, TX BL/TR, 5'8.5", 165 lbs. Deb: 8/10/1932 Career OF: 263-73-171

YEAR TM-L	G	AB	R	H	2B	3B	HR	RBI	BB	SO	SB	CS	AVG	OBP	SLG	OPS	OPS+	BR/A	RC	RC/G	FR	G/POS	WS	TPW
1932 StL-A	34	134	20	38	7	1	1	8	17	7	4	3	.284	.364	.373	.737	86	-3	19	4.96	-2	O-33(0-32-1)	3	-0.5
1933 StL-A	78	189	35	60	10	2	4	24	30	21	2	5	.317	.416	.455	.871	123	6	36	7.04	0	O-47(28-17-3)	5	0.4
1934 StL-A	91	232	25	68	14	4	0	31	27	19	0	0	.293	.372	.388	.760	89	-3	35	5.50	-4	O-56(42-1-13)	5	-0.9
1935 StL-A	10	15	1	4	0	0	0	0	2	2	0	0	.267	.353	.267	.620	59	-1	2	3.69	0	/O-2(0-0-2)	0	-0.1
1937 Bos-N	125	478	60	124	15	8	2	37	37	33	2	....	.259	.317	.337	.653	85	-10	54	4.07	-4	O-81(64-15-2),3-36	13	-1.6
1938 Bos-N	117	428	62	135	19	1	0	47	34	22	4	....	.315	.371	.364	.736	114	9	60	5.19	-3	O-63(51-2-12),3-54/2-1	18	0.5
1939 Bos-N	132	513	68	153	24	9	2	37	39	20	2	....	.298	.350	.392	.742	107	4	73	5.25	6	O-96(25-0-73),3-37	17	0.6
1940 Pit-N	103	358	76	127	23	7	5	57	23	6	3	....	**.355**	.395	.500	.895	147	22	72	8.18	1	3-64,O-19(8-4-8)	19	2.5
1941 Pit-N	83	220	25	58	9	3	3	42	22	12	0	....	.264	.331	.373	.703	98	-1	28	4.60	-4	3-29,O-24(23-0-1)	6	-0.5
1943*StL-N	90	249	26	64	10	2	0	22	13	8	1	....	.257	.299	.313	.612	74	-9	24	3.29	-3	O-47(18-0-29),3-23/S-1	4	-1.6
1944*StL-N	73	149	17	30	3	0	0	5	13	8	0	....	.201	.265	.221	.487	37	-12	9	2.05	0	O-23(3-2-18),3-21	1	-1.4
1945 StL-N	74	146	23	49	7	2	0	18	31	3	0	....	.336	.452	.411	.863	137	10	30	7.81	2	3-32,O-10(1-0-9)	8	1.2
Total 12	1010	3111	438	910	141	39	17	328	288	161	18	8	.293	.355	.379	.735	103	13	442	5.19	-10	O-501,3-296/2-1,S-1	99	-1.3

• GARNER, Phil Philip Mason Garner b: 4/30/1949, Jefferson City, TN BR/TR, 5'10", 177 lbs. Deb: 9/10/1973 M/C

YEAR TM-L	G	AB	R	H	2B	3B	HR	RBI	BB	SO	SB	CS	AVG	OBP	SLG	OPS	OPS+	BR/A	RC	RC/G	FR	G/POS	WS	TPW
1973 Oak-A	9	5	0	0	0	0	0	0	0	3	0	0	.000	.000	.000	.000	-106	-1	0	.00	-1	/3-9	0	-0.2
1974 Oak-A	30	28	4	5	1	0	0	1	1	5	1	1	.179	.207	.214	.421	23	-3	1	1.31	-1	3-19/S-8,2-3,D-2	0	-0.4
1975*Oak-A	160	488	46	120	21	5	6	54	30	65	4	6	.246	.296	.346	.643	83	-13	48	3.17	20	*2-160/S-1	12	1.7
1976 Oak-A★	159	555	54	145	29	12	8	74	36	71	35	13	.261	.309	.400	.709	111	7	67	4.09	-4	*2-159	19	1.5
1977 Pit-N	153	585	99	152	35	10	17	77	55	65	32	9	.260	.326	.441	.767	101	3	84	4.90	6	*3-107,2-50,S-12	20	1.0
1978 Pit-N	154	528	66	138	25	9	10	66	66	71	27	14	.261	.349	.400	.749	104	4	71	4.46	5	2-81,3-81/S-4	19	1.3
1979*Pit-N	150	549	76	161	32	8	11	59	55	74	17	8	.293	.361	.441	.802	112	10	89	5.88	9	2-83,3-78,S-14	23	2.4
1980 Pit-N★	151	548	62	142	27	6	5	58	46	53	32	7	.259	.319	.358	.676	87	-6	64	3.95	19	*2-151/S-1	16	2.2
1981 Pit-N★	56	181	22	46	6	2	1	20	21	21	4	6	.254	.332	.326	.658	84	-5	19	3.50	-2	2-50	4	-0.5
*Hou-N	31	113	13	27	3	1	0	6	15	11	6	2	.239	.328	.283	.611	78	-2	12	3.48	2	2-31	3	0.2
Yr.	87	294	35	73	9	3	1	26	36	32	10	8	.248	.330	.310	.640	82	-7	31	3.49	0	2-81	7	-0.2
1982 Hou-N	155	588	65	161	33	8	13	83	40	92	24	13	.274	.323	.423	.747	116	9	78	4.58	-1	*2-136,3-18	22	1.7
1983 Hou-N	154	567	76	135	24	2	14	79	63	84	18	12	.238	.320	.362	.681	94	-6	68	4.03	8	*3-154	16	0.0
1984 Hou-N	128	374	60	104	17	6	4	45	43	63	3	2	.278	.359	.388	.746	118	9	53	4.94	6	3-82,2-35	14	1.7
1985 Hou-N	135	463	65	124	23	10	6	51	34	72	4	4	.268	.321	.400	.720	103	-0	57	4.24	-4	*3-123,2-15	14	-0.5

YEAR TM-L	G	AB	R	H	2B	3B	HR	RBI	BB	SO	SB	CS	AVG	OBP	SLG	OPS	OPS+	BR/A	RC	RC/G	FR	G/POS	WS	TPW
1986*Hou-N	107	313	43	83	14	3	9	41	30	45	12	6	.265	.331	.415	.747	108	3	39	4.20	4	3-84/2-7	9	0.6
1987 Hou-N	43	112	15	25	5	0	3	15	8	20	1	0	.223	.275	.348	.623	66	-6	11	3.15	2	3-36/2-2	2	-0.4
LA-N	70	126	14	24	4	0	2	8	20	24	5	1	.190	.301	.270	.571	54	-7	11	2.74	0	3-46,2-12/S-2	2	-0.7
Yr.	113	238	29	49	9	0	5	23	28	44	6	1	.206	.289	.307	.596	60	-13	22	2.93	1	3-82,2-14/S-2	4	-1.2
1988 SF-N	15	13	0	2	0	0	0	1	1	3	0	1	.154	.214	.154	.368	8	-2	0	.73	-1	/3-2	0	-0.3
Total 16	**1860**	**6136**	**780**	**1594**	**299**	**82**	**109**	**738**	**564**	**842**	**225**	**105**	**.260**	**.326**	**.389**	**.714**	**99**	**-7**	**774**	**4.26**	**66**	**2-975,3-839/S-42,D-2**	**195**	**11.2**

• GARR, Ralph Ralph Allen "Road Runner,Gator" Garr b: 12/12/1945, Monroe, LA BL/TR, 5'11", 197 lbs. Deb: 9/3/1968 Career OF: 844-62-337

YEAR TM-L	G	AB	R	H	2B	3B	HR	RBI	BB	SO	SB	CS	AVG	OBP	SLG	OPS	OPS+	BR/A	RC	RC/G	FR	G/POS	WS	TPW
1968 Atl-N	11	7	3	2	0	0	0	0	1	0	1	0	.286	.375	.286	.661	100	0	1	5.63	0	....	0	0.0
1969 Atl-N	22	27	6	6	1	0	0	2	2	4	1	1	.222	.276	.259	.535	50	-2	2	2.30	0	/0-7(7-0-0)	0	-0.3
1970 Atl-N	37	96	18	27	3	0	0	8	5	12	5	2	.281	.317	.313	.629	65	-5	9	3.26	-1	0-21(1-8-12)	1	-0.6
1971 Atl-N	154	639	101	219	24	6	9	44	30	68	30	14	.343	.374	.441	.815	122	18	105	6.14	7	*0-153(153-0-0)	25	1.8
1972 Atl-N	134	554	87	180	22	0	12	53	25	41	25	9	.325	.361	.430	.790	113	11	86	5.76	1	*0-131(70-13-59)	19	0.6
1973 Atl-N	148	668	94	200	32	6	11	55	22	64	35	11	.299	.324	.415	.738	96	-3	87	4.74	-4	*0-148(21-0-127)	14	-1.5
1974 Atl-N★	143	606	87	**214**	24	**17**	11	54	28	52	26	16	**.353**	.384	.503	.887	141	29	113	7.21	-2	*0-139(107-0-80)	27	2.0
1975 Atl-N	151	625	74	174	26	**11**	6	31	44	50	14	9	.278	.329	.384	.713	94	-7	78	4.43	-2	*0-148(148-0-0)	16	-2.0
1976 Chi-A	136	527	63	158	22	6	4	36	17	41	14	5	.300	.324	.387	.711	107	3	66	4.55	-2	*0-125(35-41-57)/D-6	14	-0.5
1977 Chi-A	134	543	78	163	29	7	10	54	27	44	12	7	.300	.333	.435	.768	108	4	77	5.21	-5	*0-126(125-0-1)/D-2	15	-0.7
1978 Chi-A	118	443	67	122	18	9	3	29	24	41	7	5	.275	.314	.377	.691	93	-6	51	3.96	-1	*0-109(109-0-0)/D-9	10	-1.2
1979 Chi-A	102	307	34	86	10	2	9	39	17	19	2	4	.280	.320	.414	.734	96	-4	39	4.49	0	0-67(67-0-0),D-17	6	-0.6
Cal-A	6	24	0	3	0	0	0	0	0	3	0	0	.125	.125	.125	.250	-33	-4	0	.48	0	/D-6	0	-0.5
Yr.	108	331	34	89	10	2	9	39	17	22	2	4	.269	.307	.393	.699	87	-8	39	4.16	0	0-67(67-0-0),D-23	6	-1.1
1980 Cal-A	21	42	5	8	1	0	0	3	4	6	0	0	.190	.261	.214	.475	33	-4	2	1.97	0	/D-8,0-2(1-0-1)	0	-0.4
Total 13	**1317**	**5108**	**717**	**1562**	**212**	**64**	**75**	**408**	**246**	**445**	**172**	**83**	**.306**	**.340**	**.416**	**.756**	**106**	**31**	**716**	**5.11**	**-10**	***0-1176/D-48**	**147**	**-3.8**

• GARRETT, Adrian Henry Adrian "Pat,Smokey" Garrett b: 1/3/1943, Brooksville, FL BL/TR, 6'3", 185 lbs. Deb: 4/13/1966 C Career OF: 10-0-8

YEAR TM-L	G	AB	R	H	2B	3B	HR	RBI	BB	SO	SB	CS	AVG	OBP	SLG	OPS	OPS+	BR/A	RC	RC/G	FR	G/POS	WS	TPW
1966 Atl-N	4	3	0	0	0	0	0	0	0	2	0	0	.000	.000	.000	.000	-99	-1	0	.00	0	/0-1	0	-0.1
1970 Chi-N	3	3	0	0	0	0	0	0	0	3	0	0	.000	.000	.000	.000	-89	-1	0	.00	0	....	0	-0.1
1971 Oak-A	14	21	1	3	0	0	1	2	5	7	0	0	.143	.308	.286	.593	70	-1	2	3.25	-0	/0-5(4-0-1)	0	-0.1
1972 Oak-A	14	11	0	0	0	0	0	0	1	4	0	0	.000	.083	.000	.083	-78	-2	0	.05	0	/0-2(2-0-0)	0	-0.3
1973 Chi-N	36	54	7	12	0	0	3	8	4	18	1	0	.222	.276	.389	.665	77	-2	6	3.50	0	/0-7(3-0-4),C-6	1	-0.2
1974 Chi-N	10	8	0	0	0	0	0	0	1	1	0	0	.000	.111	.000	.111	-64	-2	0	.00	-1	/C-3,1-1,0-1	0	-0.2
1975 Chi-N	16	21	1	2	0	0	1	6	1	8	0	0	.095	.136	.238	.374	2	-3	1	1.02	1	/1-4	0	-0.2
Cal-A	37	107	17	28	5	0	6	18	14	28	3	0	.262	.347	.477	.824	141	6	20	6.52	0	D-23,1-10/0-2(0-0-2),C-1	5	0.5
1976 Cal-A	29	48	4	6	3	0	0	3	5	16	0	0	.125	.208	.188	.395	17	-5	2	1.08	-1	C-15/D-4,1-1	0	-0.6
Total 8	**163**	**276**	**30**	**51**	**8**	**0**	**11**	**37**	**31**	**87**	**4**	**0**	**.185**	**.267**	**.333**	**.600**	**72**	**-10**	**30**	**3.46**	**-1**	**/D-27,C-25,0-18,1-16**	**6**	**-1.4**

• GARRETT, Wayne Ronald Wayne Garrett b: 12/3/1947, Brooksville, FL BL/TR, 5'11", 183 lbs. Deb: 4/12/1969

YEAR TM-L	G	AB	R	H	2B	3B	HR	RBI	BB	SO	SB	CS	AVG	OBP	SLG	OPS	OPS+	BR/A	RC	RC/G	FR	G/POS	WS	TPW
1969*NY-N	124	400	38	87	11	3	1	39	40	75	4	2	.218	.293	.268	.561	57	-22	34	2.77	3	3-72,2-47/S-9	7	-1.7
1970 NY-N	114	366	74	93	17	4	12	45	81	60	5	1	.254	.392	.421	.813	117	13	68	6.44	4	3-70,2-45/S-1	16	2.0
1971 NY-N	56	202	20	43	2	0	1	11	28	31	1	3	.213	.312	.238	.549	58	-11	15	2.42	3	3-53/2-9	2	-0.9
1972 NY-N	111	298	41	69	13	3	2	29	70	58	3	2	.232	.378	.315	.693	101	5	41	4.54	-1	3-82,2-22	13	0.5
1973*NY-N	140	504	76	129	20	3	16	58	72	74	6	5	.256	.350	.403	.753	110	7	74	4.99	16	*3-130/S-9,2-6	21	2.5
1974 NY-N	151	522	55	117	14	3	13	53	89	96	4	6	.224	.339	.337	.676	91	-5	64	4.10	15	*3-144/S-9	16	1.1
1975 NY-N	107	274	49	73	8	3	6	34	50	45	3	2	.266	.382	.383	.765	118	9	44	5.64	7	3-94/S-3,2-1	13	1.6
1976 NY-N	80	251	36	56	8	1	4	26	52	26	7	5	.223	.359	.311	.669	97	1	31	4.03	8	3-64,2-10/S-1	9	1.0
Mon-N	59	177	15	43	4	1	2	11	30	20	2	2	.243	.353	.311	.663	86	-2	21	4.12	-4	2-54/3-2	5	-0.3
Yr.	139	428	51	99	12	2	6	37	82	46	9	7	.231	.356	.311	.667	92	-1	52	4.06	4	3-66,2-64/S-1	14	0.6
1977 Mon-N	68	159	17	43	6	1	2	22	30	18	2	2	.270	.389	.358	.748	105	3	24	5.24	1	3-49/2-1	5	0.3
1978 Mon-N	49	69	6	12	0	0	1	2	8	10	0	0	.174	.260	.217	.477	35	-6	4	1.80	1	3-13	0	-0.5
StL-N	33	63	11	21	4	0	1	10	11	16	1	0	.333	.432	.444	.877	148	5	12	7.32	-1	3-19	3	0.4
Yr.	82	132	17	33	4	0	2	12	19	26	1	0	.250	.344	.326	.670	90	-1	16	4.19	0	3-32	3	-0.1
Total 10	**1092**	**3285**	**438**	**786**	**107**	**22**	**61**	**340**	**561**	**529**	**38**	**30**	**.239**	**.352**	**.341**	**.693**	**95**	**-4**	**432**	**4.43**	**51**	**3-792,2-195/S-32**	**110**	**5.9**

• GARRIDO, Gil Gil Gonzalo Garrido b: 6/26/1941, Panama City, Panama BR/TR, 5'9", 160 lbs. Deb: 4/24/1964

YEAR TM-L	G	AB	R	H	2B	3B	HR	RBI	BB	SO	SB	CS	AVG	OBP	SLG	OPS	OPS+	BR/A	RC	RC/G	FR	G/POS	WS	TPW
1964 SF-N	14	25	1	2	0	0	0	1	2	7	1	0	.080	.148	.080	.228	-33	-4	0	.41	1	S-14	0	-0.3
1968 Atl-N	18	53	5	11	0	0	0	2	2	2	0	0	.208	.236	.208	.444	34	-4	3	1.55	1	S-17	1	-0.2
1969*Atl-N	82	227	18	50	5	1	0	10	16	11	0	0	.220	.272	.251	.523	47	-16	14	1.99	1	S-81	3	-0.7
1970 Atl-N	101	367	38	97	5	4	1	19	15	16	0	2	.264	.293	.308	.601	58	-23	28	2.57	-5	S-80,2-26	3	-1.7
1971 Atl-N	79	125	8	27	3	0	0	12	15	12	0	1	.216	.300	.240	.540	51	-8	9	2.41	-2	S-32,3-28,2-18	2	-0.7
1972 Atl-N	40	75	11	20	1	0	0	7	11	6	1	1	.267	.368	.280	.648	79	-1	8	3.59	-2	2-21,S-10/3-3	2	-0.2
Total 6	**334**	**872**	**81**	**207**	**14**	**5**	**1**	**51**	**61**	**54**	**2**	**4**	**.237**	**.288**	**.268**	**.556**	**52**	**-57**	**63**	**2.34**	**-5**	**S-234/2-65,3-31**	**11**	**-3.8**

• GARRIOTT, Cecil Virgil Cecil Garriott b: 8/15/1916, Harristown, IL d: 2/20/1990, Lake Elsinore, CA BL/TR, 5'8", 165 lbs. Deb: 9/4/1946

YEAR TM-L	G	AB	R	H	2B	3B	HR	RBI	BB	SO	SB	CS	AVG	OBP	SLG	OPS	OPS+	BR/A	RC	RC/G	FR	G/POS	WS	TPW
1946 Chi-N	6	5	1	0	0	0	0	0	0	2	0	....	.000	.167	.000	.167	-52	-1	0	.23	0	....	0	-0.1

• GARRISON, Ford Robert Ford "Rocky,Snapper" Garrison
b: 8/29/1915, Greenville, SC d: 6/6/2001, Largo, FL BR/TR, 5'10.5", 180 lbs. Deb: 4/22/1943 C Career OF: 134-6-36

YEAR TM-L	G	AB	R	H	2B	3B	HR	RBI	BB	SO	SB	CS	AVG	OBP	SLG	OPS	OPS+	BR/A	RC	RC/G	FR	G/POS	WS	TPW
1943 Bos-A	36	129	13	36	5	1	1	11	5	14	0	1	.279	.306	.357	.663	92	-2	13	3.67	0	0-32(26-6-0)	3	-0.4
1944 Bos-A	13	49	5	12	3	0	0	2	6	4	0	0	.245	.327	.306	.633	83	-1	6	4.04	0	0-12(0-0-12)	1	-0.1
Phi-A	121	449	58	121	13	2	4	37	22	40	10	4	.269	.307	.334	.641	84	-10	47	3.49	4	*0-119(95-0-24)	9	-1.4
Yr.	134	498	63	133	16	2	4	39	28	44	10	4	.267	.309	.331	.640	84	-11	52	3.54	4	*0-131(95-0-36)	10	-1.5
1945 Phi-A	6	23	3	7	1	0	1	6	4	3	1	0	.304	.407	.478	.886	157	2	5	8.82	1	/0-5(5-0-0)	1	0.2
1946 Phi-A	9	37	1	4	0	0	0	0	0	6	0	0	.108	.108	.108	.216	-40	-7	0	.17	0	/0-8(8-0-0)	0	-0.8
Total 4	**185**	**687**	**80**	**180**	**22**	**3**	**6**	**56**	**37**	**67**	**11**	**5**	**.262**	**.302**	**.329**	**.631**	**82**	**-18**	**71**	**3.50**	**5**	**0-176**	**14**	**-2.5**

• GARRISON, Webster Webster Leotis Garrison b: 8/24/1965, Marrero, LA BR/TR, 5'11", 170 lbs. Deb: 8/2/1996

YEAR TM-L	G	AB	R	H	2B	3B	HR	RBI	BB	SO	SB	CS	AVG	OBP	SLG	OPS	OPS+	BR/A	RC	RC/G	FR	G/POS	WS	TPW
1996 Oak-A	5	9	0	0	0	0	0	0	1	0	0	0	.000	.100	.000	.100	-74	-2	0	.08	0	/2-3,1-1	0	-0.2

• GARRITY, Hank Francis Joseph Garrity b: 2/4/1908, Boston, MA d: 9/1/1962, Boston, MA BR/TR, 6'1", 185 lbs. Deb: 7/26/1931

YEAR TM-L	G	AB	R	H	2B	3B	HR	RBI	BB	SO	SB	CS	AVG	OBP	SLG	OPS	OPS+	BR/A	RC	RC/G	FR	G/POS	WS	TPW
1931 Chi-A	8	14	0	3	1	0	0	2	1	2	0	0	.214	.267	.286	.552	48	-1	1	2.63	0	/C-7	0	0.0

• GARVEY, Steve Steven Patrick Garvey b: 12/22/1948, Tampa, FL BR/TR, 5'10", 192 lbs. Deb: 9/1/1969

YEAR TM-L	G	AB	R	H	2B	3B	HR	RBI	BB	SO	SB	CS	AVG	OBP	SLG	OPS	OPS+	BR/A	RC	RC/G	FR	G/POS	WS	TPW
1969 LA-N	3	3	0	1	0	0	0	0	0	1	0	0	.333	.333	.333	.667	94	-0	0	4.50	0	....	0	0.0
1970 LA-N	34	93	8	25	5	0	1	6	6	17	1	1	.269	.313	.355	.668	82	-3	10	3.56	3	3-27/2-1	2	0.0
1971 LA-N	81	225	27	51	12	1	7	26	21	33	1	2	.227	.293	.382	.675	95	-3	24	3.49	8	3-79	6	0.5
1972 LA-N	96	294	36	79	14	2	9	30	19	36	4	2	.269	.315	.422	.737	110	3	37	4.39	5	3-85/1-3	8	0.8
1973 LA-N	114	349	37	106	17	3	8	50	11	42	0	2	.304	.331	.438	.769	116	5	47	4.98	-4	1-76,0-10(8-0-2)	11	-0.6
1974*LA-N★	156	642	95	200	32	3	21	111	31	66	5	4	.312	.346	.469	.815	132	22	102	5.97	2	*1-156	27	1.2
1975 LA-N★	160	659	85	210	38	6	18	95	33	66	11	2	.319	.354	.476	.830	135	28	106	5.98	8	*1-160	25	2.4
1976 LA-N★	162	631	85	200	37	4	13	80	50	69	19	8	.317	.368	.450	.818	134	27	100	5.70	-4	*1-162	26	1.0
1977*LA-N★	162	646	91	192	25	3	33	115	38	90	9	6	.297	.337	.498	.836	121	16	103	5.70	-6	*1-160	21	0.1
1978*LA-N★	162	639	89	**202**	36	9	21	113	40	70	10	5	.316	.357	.499	.857	138	29	108	6.24	-6	*1-161	25	1.4
1979 LA-N★	162	648	92	204	32	1	28	110	37	59	3	6	.315	.354	.497	.851	131	23	102	5.67	6	*1-162	22	2.0
1980 LA-N★	163	658	78	**200**	27	1	26	106	36	67	6	11	.304	.343	.467	.809	126	16	97	5.29	4	*1-162	22	1.0
1981*LA-N★	110	431	63	122	23	1	10	64	25	49	3	5	.283	.324	.411	.735	111	3	54	4.51	-2	*1-110	13	-0.6
1982 LA-N	162	625	66	176	35	1	16	86	20	86	5	3	.282	.305	.418	.723	103	-2	76	4.33	5	*1-158	15	-0.6
1983 SD-N	100	388	76	114	22	0	14	59	29	39	4	1	.294	.348	.459	.806	126	13	57	5.21	-8	*1-100	14	-0.1
1984*SD-N★	161	617	72	175	27	2	8	86	24	64	1	2	.284	.312	.373	.684	92	-10	64	3.61	0	*1-159	15	-2.0
1985 SD-N★	162	654	80	184	34	6	17	81	35	67	0	0	.281	.321	.430	.750	110	5	82	4.44	-2	*1-162	17	-0.6
1986 SD-N	155	557	58	142	22	0	21	81	23	72	1	2	.255	.286	.408	.693	91	-11	59	3.61	-10	*1-148	10	-3.0

YEAR TM-L	G	AB	R	H	2B	3B	HR	RBI	BB	SO	SB	CS	AVG	OBP	SLG	OPS	OPS+	BR/A	RC	RC/G	FR	G/POS	WS	TPW
1987 SD-N	27	76	5	16	2	0	1	9	1	10	0	0	.211	.231	.276	.507	35	-7	4	1.77	0	1-20	0	-0.8
Total 19	**2332**	**8835**	**1143**	**2599**	**440**	**43**	**272**	**1308**	**479**	**1003**	**83**	**62**	**.294**	**.333**	**.446**	**.779**	**118**	**154**	**1233**	**4.99**	**-0**	***1-2059,3-191/0-10,2-1**	**279**	**1.9**
• GASPAR, Rod	Rodney Earl Gaspar b: 4/3/1946, Long Beach, CA BB/TR, 5'11", 165 lbs. Deb: 4/8/1969 Career OF: 26-25-70																							
1969*NY-N	118	215	26	49	6	1	1	14	25	19	7	3	.228	.314	.279	.593	66	-9	21	3.25	7	0-91(22-16-64)	5	-0.4
1970 NY-N	11	14	4	0	0	0	0	0	1	4	1	0	.000	.067	.000	.067	-80	-3	0	.10	0	/0-8(0-4-5)	0	-0.4
1971 SD-N	16	17	1	2	0	0	0	2	3	3	0	1	.118	.250	.118	.368	8	-2	1	.94	-0	/0-2(2-0-0)	0	-0.3
1974 SD-N	33	14	4	3	0	0	0	1	4	3	0	0	.214	.389	.214	.603	75	-0	2	3.86	0	/0-8(2-5-1),1-2	1	-0.1
Total 4	**178**	**260**	**35**	**54**	**6**	**1**	**1**	**17**	**33**	**29**	**8**	**4**	**.208**	**.302**	**.250**	**.552**	**55**	**-15**	**24**	**2.91**	**7**	**0-109/1-2**	**6**	**-1.2**
• GASTALL, Tom	Thomas Everett Gastall b: 6/13/1932, Fall River, MA d: 9/20/1956, Riviera Beach, MD BR/TR, 6'2", 187 lbs. Deb: 6/21/1955																							
1955 Bal-A	20	27	4	4	1	0	0	0	3	5	0	0	.148	.233	.185	.419	15	-3	1	1.30	0	C-15	0	-0.3
1956 Bal-A	32	56	3	11	2	0	0	4	3	8	0	0	.196	.250	.232	.482	30	-6	3	1.74	1	C-20	1	-0.4
Total 2	**52**	**83**	**7**	**15**	**3**	**0**	**0**	**4**	**6**	**13**	**0**	**0**	**.181**	**.244**	**.217**	**.461**	**25**	**-9**	**4**	**1.60**	**0**	**/C-35**	**1**	**-0.7**
• GASTFIELD, Ed	Edward Gastfield b: 8/1/1865, Chicago, IL d: 12/1/1899, Chicago, IL BR, 5'9.5", 155 lbs. Deb: 8/13/1884																							
1884 Det-N	23	82	6	6	1	0	0	2	2	34	....	....	.073	.095	.085	.181	-46	-13	1	.25	6	C-19/1-2,0-2(0-0-2)	1	-0.5
1885 Det-N	1	3	0	0	0	0	0	0	0	2	....	....	.000	.000	.000	.000	-100	-1	0	.00	0	/C-1	0	-0.1
Chi-N	1	3	0	0	0	0	0	0	0	1	....	....	.000	.000	.000	.000	-87	-1	0	.00	0	/C-1	0	-0.1
Yr.	2	6	0	0	0	0	0	0	0	3	....	....	.000	.000	.000	.000	-93	-1	0	.00	-1	/C-2	0	-0.2
Total 2	**25**	**88**	**6**	**6**	**1**	**0**	**0**	**2**	**2**	**37**	**....**	**....**	**.068**	**.089**	**.080**	**.168**	**-49**	**-14**	**1**	**.23**	**5**	**/C-21,1-2,0-2**	**1**	**-0.7**
• GASTON, Alex	Alexander Nathaniel Gaston b: 3/12/1893, New York, NY d: 2/8/1976, Santa Monica, CA BR/TR, 5'9", 170 lbs. Deb: 9/26/1920																							
1920 NY-N	4	10	2	1	0	0	0	1	1	2	0	0	.100	.182	.100	.282	-18	-1	0	.75	-1	/C-3	0	-0.2
1921 NY-N	20	22	1	5	1	1	0	3	1	9	0	0	.227	.261	.364	.625	63	-1	2	3.22	-1	C-11	0	-0.2
1922 NY-N	16	26	1	5	0	0	0	1	0	3	1	0	.192	.192	.192	.385	-1	-4	1	1.28	-1	C-13	0	-0.4
1923 NY-N	22	39	3	8	2	0	1	5	0	6	0	0	.205	.225	.333	.558	46	-3	3	2.45	0	C-21	1	-0.3
1926 Bos-A	98	301	37	67	5	3	0	21	21	28	3	0	.223	.282	.259	.541	43	-24	24	2.60	-2	C-98	2	-1.9
1929 Bos-A	55	116	14	26	5	2	2	9	6	8	1	0	.224	.262	.353	.616	58	-7	11	3.08	2	C-49	2	-0.3
Total 6	**215**	**514**	**58**	**112**	**13**	**6**	**3**	**40**	**29**	**56**	**5**	**0**	**.218**	**.266**	**.284**	**.550**	**44**	**-40**	**41**	**2.61**	**-3**	**C-195**	**5**	**-3.2**
• GASTON, Cito	Clarence Edwin Gaston b: 3/17/1944, San Antonio, TX BR/TR, 6'3", 210 lbs. Deb: 9/14/1967 M/C Career OF: 92-412-282																							
1967 Atl-N	9	25	1	3	0	1	0	1	0	5	1	0	.120	.120	.200	.320	-10	-3	0	.25	0	/0-7(0-6-1)	0	-0.4
1969 SD-N	129	391	20	90	11	7	2	28	24	117	4	4	.230	.276	.309	.586	67	-19	32	2.68	1	*0-113(0-113-0)	4	-2.1
1970 SD-N★	146	584	92	186	26	9	29	93	41	142	4	1	.318	.365	.543	.908	146	35	111	7.22	-3	*0-142(1-142-0)	24	2.8
1971 SD-N	141	518	57	118	13	9	17	61	24	121	1	0	.228	.265	.386	.651	88	-11	51	3.34	-4	*0-133(6-126-1)	9	-2.0
1972 SD-N	111	379	30	102	14	0	7	44	22	76	0	2	.269	.313	.361	.674	98	-3	39	3.63	0	0-94(18-7-73)	8	-0.8
1973 SD-N	133	476	51	119	18	4	16	57	20	88	0	0	.250	.282	.405	.687	96	-6	52	3.78	3	*0-119(1-0-118)	10	-0.8
1974 SD-N	106	267	19	57	11	0	6	33	16	51	0	0	.213	.261	.322	.583	65	-14	22	2.66	1	0-63(18-0-50)	2	-1.6
1975 Atl-N	64	141	17	34	4	0	6	15	17	33	1	0	.241	.323	.397	.720	95	-1	18	4.19	-1	0-35(2-17-17)/1-1	4	-0.3
1976 Atl-N	69	134	15	39	4	0	4	25	13	21	1	0	.291	.354	.410	.764	109	2	18	4.91	-1	0-28(25-0-3)/1-2	4	0.0
1977 Atl-N	56	85	6	23	4	0	3	21	5	19	1	0	.271	.311	.424	.735	85	-2	11	4.20	0	/0-9(7-0-2),1-5	1	-0.2
1978 Atl-N	60	118	5	27	1	0	1	9	3	20	0	0	.229	.248	.263	.511	38	-10	7	1.93	-2	0-29(13-1-17)/1-4	1	-1.3
Pit-N	2	2	1	1	0	0	0	0	0	0	0	0	.500	.500	.500	1.000	172	0	1	13.50	0	/0-1	0	0.0
Yr.	62	120	6	28	1	0	1	9	3	20	0	0	.233	.252	.267	.519	41	-10	7	2.04	-2	0-30(14-1-17)/1-4	1	-1.3
Total 11	**1026**	**3120**	**314**	**799**	**106**	**30**	**91**	**387**	**185**	**693**	**13**	**7**	**.256**	**.300**	**.397**	**.696**	**95**	**-31**	**361**	**4.00**	**-5**	**0-773/1-12**	**67**	**-7.0**
• GATES, Brent	Brent Robert Gates b: 3/14/1970, Grand Rapids, MI BB/TR, 6'1", 180 lbs. Deb: 5/5/1993																							
1993 Oak-A	139	535	64	155	29	2	7	69	56	75	7	3	.290	.361	.391	.752	109	8	75	4.90	12	*2-139	18	2.6
1994 Oak-A	64	233	29	66	11	1	2	24	21	32	3	0	.283	.345	.365	.710	91	-2	29	4.30	-4	2-63/1-1	3	-0.3
1995 Oak-A	136	524	60	133	24	4	5	56	46	84	3	3	.254	.314	.344	.658	76	-20	55	3.52	11	*2-132/D-3,1-1	10	-0.2
1996 Oak-A	64	247	26	65	19	2	2	30	18	35	1	1	.263	.318	.381	.699	78	-9	28	3.84	-3	2-63	3	-0.8
1997*Sea-A	65	151	18	36	8	0	3	20	14	21	0	0	.238	.303	.351	.654	71	-7	15	3.29	1	3-32,2-21/S-5,1-1,D-1,0-1	2	-0.5
1998 Min-A	107	333	31	83	15	0	3	42	36	46	3	3	.249	.326	.321	.647	68	-16	36	3.68	-4	3-77,2-21/D-2,1-1,S-1	8	-1.7
1999 Min-A	110	306	40	78	13	2	3	38	34	56	1	3	.255	.331	.340	.671	69	-15	33	3.63	3	3-61,2-47/1-5,D-1,S-1	4	-0.9
Total 7	**685**	**2329**	**268**	**616**	**119**	**11**	**25**	**279**	**225**	**349**	**18**	**13**	**.264**	**.332**	**.357**	**.689**	**83**	**-60**	**273**	**3.96**	**17**	**2-486,3-170/1-9,D-7,S-7,0-1**	**48**	**-1.8**
• GATES, Joe	Joseph Daniel Gates b: 10/3/1954, Gary, IN BL/TR, 5'7", 175 lbs. Deb: 9/12/1978																							
1978 Chi-A	8	24	6	6	0	0	0	1	4	6	1	0	.250	.379	.250	.629	80	-0	3	3.75	0	/2-8	1	0.1
1979 Chi-A	16	16	5	1	0	1	0	1	2	3	1	1	.063	.167	.188	.354	-5	-3	0	.76	-1	/2-8,3-1,D-1	0	-0.3
Total 2	**24**	**40**	**11**	**7**	**0**	**1**	**0**	**2**	**6**	**9**	**2**	**1**	**.175**	**.298**	**.225**	**.523**	**48**	**-3**	**3**	**2.42**	**-1**	**/2-16,3-1,D-1**	**1**	**-0.3**
• GATES, Mike	Michael Grant Gates b: 9/20/1956, Culver City, CA BL/TR, 6', 165 lbs. Deb: 5/6/1981																							
1981 Mon-N	1	2	1	1	0	1	0	1	0	1	0	0	.500	.500	1.500	2.000	445	1	2	40.50	0	/2-1	0	0.1
1982 Mon-N	36	121	16	28	2	3	0	8	9	19	0	0	.231	.285	.298	.582	62	-6	11	3.02	6	2-36	2	0.1
Total 2	**37**	**123**	**17**	**29**	**2**	**4**	**0**	**9**	**9**	**20**	**0**	**0**	**.236**	**.288**	**.317**	**.605**	**68**	**-5**	**12**	**3.41**	**6**	**/2-37**	**2**	**0.2**
• GATINS, Frank	Frank Anthony Gatins b: 3/6/1871, Johnstown, PA d: 11/8/1911, Johnstown, PA Deb: 9/21/1898																							
1898 Was-N	17	58	6	13	2	0	0	5	3	....	2	....	.224	.274	.259	.533	53	-4	5	2.81	-3	S-17	0	-0.6
1901 Bro-N	50	197	21	45	7	2	1	21	5	....	6	....	.228	.255	.299	.554	59	-11	17	2.96	-8	3-46/S-5	2	-1.7
Total 2	**67**	**255**	**27**	**58**	**9**	**2**	**1**	**26**	**8**	**....**	**8**	**....**	**.227**	**.259**	**.290**	**.550**	**57**	**-15**	**22**	**2.93**	**-12**	**/3-46,S-22**	**2**	**-2.3**
• GAUDET, Jim	James Jennings Gaudet b: 6/3/1955, New Orleans, LA BR/TR, 6', 185 lbs. Deb: 9/10/1978																							
1978 KC-A	3	8	0	0	0	0	0	0	0	3	0	0	.000	.000	.000	.000	-97	-2	0	.00	0	/C-3	0	-0.2
1979 KC-A	3	6	0	1	0	0	0	0	0	0	0	0	.167	.167	.167	.333	-10	-1	0	.90	0	/C-3	0	-0.1
Total 2	**6**	**14**	**0**	**1**	**0**	**0**	**0**	**0**	**0**	**3**	**0**	**0**	**.071**	**.071**	**.071**	**.143**	**-60**	**-3**	**0**	**.35**	**0**	**/C-6**	**0**	**-0.3**
• GAULE, Mike	Michael John Gaule b: 8/4/1869, Baltimore, MD d: 1/24/1918, Baltimore, MD BL/TL, 6'2" Deb: 6/15/1889																							
1889 Lou-a	1	2	0	0	0	0	0	0	0	1	0	....	.000	.000	.000	.000	-102	-1	0	.00	0	/0-1	0	-0.1
• GAUTREAU, Doc	Walter Paul "Punk" Gautreau b: 7/26/1901, Cambridge, MA d: 8/23/1970, Salt Lake City, UT BR/TR, 5'4", 129 lbs. Deb: 6/22/1925																							
1925 Phi-A	4	7	0	0	0	0	0	0	0	3	0	0	.000	.000	.000	.000	-94	-2	0	.00	0	/2-4	0	-0.2
Bos-N	68	279	45	73	13	3	0	23	35	13	11	7	.262	.346	.330	.676	81	-7	33	4.09	0	2-68	5	-0.4
1926 Bos-N	79	266	36	71	9	4	0	8	35	24	17	....	.267	.356	.331	.687	94	-0	33	4.10	-17	2-74	6	-1.5
1927 Bos-N	87	236	38	58	12	2	0	20	25	20	11	....	.246	.321	.314	.634	76	-7	24	3.42	-6	2-57	4	-1.2
1928 Bos-N	23	18	3	5	0	1	0	1	4	3	1	....	.278	.409	.389	.798	115	1	3	6.12	-2	/2-4,S-1	1	-0.1
Total 4	**261**	**806**	**122**	**207**	**34**	**10**	**0**	**52**	**99**	**63**	**40**	**7**	**.257**	**.341**	**.324**	**.665**	**83**	**-16**	**94**	**3.89**	**-26**	**2-207/S-1**	**16**	**-3.5**
• GAUTREAUX, Sid	Sidney Allen "Pudge" Gautreaux b: 5/4/1912, Schriever, LA d: 4/19/1980, Morgan City, LA BB/TR, 5'8", 190 lbs. Deb: 4/15/1936																							
1936 Bro-N	75	71	8	19	3	0	0	16	9	7	0	....	.268	.358	.310	.668	80	-1	9	4.43	0	C-15	1	-0.1
1937 Bro-N	11	10	0	1	1	0	0	2	1	1	0	....	.100	.182	.200	.382	4	-1	0	1.26	0	....	0	-0.1
Total 2	**86**	**81**	**8**	**20**	**4**	**0**	**0**	**18**	**10**	**8**	**0**	**....**	**.247**	**.337**	**.296**	**.633**	**71**	**-3**	**9**	**3.97**	**0**	**/C-15**	**1**	**-0.3**
• GAVERN,	Gavern Deb: 6/15/1874																							
1874 Atl-n	1	4	1	0	0	0	0	0	0	0	0	0	.000	.000	.000	.000	-113	-1	0	.00	1	/2-1	....	0.0
• GAZELLA, Mike	Michael Gazella b: 10/13/1896, Olyphant, PA d: 9/11/1978, Odessa, TX BR/TR, 5'7.5", 165 lbs. Deb: 7/2/1923																							
1923 NY-A	8	13	2	1	0	0	0	1	2	3	0	0	.077	.200	.077	.277	-25	-2	0	.64	-1	/S-4,2-2,3-2	0	-0.3
1926*NY-A	66	168	21	39	6	0	0	20	25	24	2	2	.232	.335	.268	.603	60	-9	17	3.23	-5	3-45,S-11	2	-1.0
1927 NY-A	54	115	17	32	8	4	0	9	23	16	4	1	.278	.403	.417	.820	117	5	22	6.19	-8	3-44/S-6	4	-0.1

YEAR TM-L	G	AB	R	H	2B	3B	HR	RBI	BB	SO	SB	CS	AVG	OBP	SLG	OPS	OPS+	BR/A	RC	RC/G	FR	G/POS	WS	TPW
1928 NY-A	32	56	11	13	0	0	0	2	6	7	2	1	.232	.317	.232	.550	48	-4	5	2.74	-2	3-16/2-4,S-3	1	-0.5
Total 4	**160**	**352**	**51**	**85**	**14**	**4**	**0**	**32**	**56**	**50**	**8**	**4**	**.241**	**.350**	**.304**	**.654**	**74**	**-11**	**44**	**3.99**	**-16**	**3-107/S-24,2-6**	**7**	**-1.8**
• GEAR, Dale	Dale Dudley Gear b: 2/2/1872, Lone Elm, KS d: 9/23/1951, Topeka, KS BR/TR, 5'11", 165 lbs. Deb: 8/15/1896 Career OF: 12-7-22 ♦																							
1896 Cle-N	4	15	5	6	1	1	0	3	1	1	0	....	.400	.438	.600	1.038	163	2	4	11.88	-1	/P-3,1-1	1	-0.1
1897 Cle-N	7	24	3	4	1	0	0	2	3	....	2	....	.167	.286	.208	.494	30	-2	2	2.72	0	/O-6(0-6-0)	0	-0.2
1901 Was-A	58	199	17	47	9	2	0	20	4	....	2	....	.236	.251	.302	.553	54	-8	16	2.78	2	O-35(12-1-22),P-24	9	-1.2
Total 3	**69**	**238**	**25**	**57**	**11**	**3**	**0**	**25**	**8**	**1**	**4**	**....**	**.239**	**.267**	**.311**	**.578**	**58**	**-8**	**22**	**3.22**	**2**	**/O-41,P-27,1-1**	**10**	**-1.5**
• GEARHART, Lloyd	Lloyd William Gearhart b: 8/10/1923, New Lebanon, OH d: 4/23/2001, Dayton, OH BR/TL, 5'11", 180 lbs. Deb: 4/18/1947																							
1947 NY-N	73	179	26	44	9	0	6	17	17	30	1	....	.246	.315	.397	.711	87	-4	22	4.30	0	O-44(17-28-0)	4	-0.5
• GEARY, Huck	Eugene Francis Joseph Geary b: 1/22/1917, Buffalo, NY d: 1/27/1981, Cuba, NY BL/TR, 5'10.5", 170 lbs. Deb: 7/17/1942																							
1942 Pit-N	9	22	3	5	0	0	0	2	2	3	0	....	.227	.292	.227	.519	52	-1	2	2.56	-2	/S-8	0	-0.3
1943 Pit-N	46	166	17	25	4	0	1	13	18	6	3	....	.151	.234	.193	.426	23	-16	8	1.59	-1	S-46	2	-1.5
Total 2	**55**	**188**	**20**	**30**	**4**	**0**	**1**	**15**	**20**	**9**	**3**	**....**	**.160**	**.240**	**.197**	**.437**	**26**	**-18**	**10**	**1.70**	**-3**	**/S-54**	**2**	**-1.8**
• GEDEON, Elmer	Elmer John Gedeon b: 4/15/1917, Cleveland, OH d: 4/20/1944, St. Pol, France BR/TR, 6'4", 196 lbs. Deb: 9/18/1939																							
1939 Was-A	5	15	1	3	0	0	0	1	2	5	0	0	.200	.294	.200	.494	31	-1	1	2.33	0	/O-5(0-4-1)	0	-0.1
• GEDEON, Joe	Elmer Joseph Gedeon b: 12/5/1893, Sacramento, CA d: 5/19/1941, San Francisco, CA BR/TR, 6', 167 lbs. Deb: 5/13/1913 Career OF: 14-1-2																							
1913 Was-A	29	71	3	13	1	3	0	6	1	6	3	....	.183	.205	.282	.487	41	-6	4	1.86	0	O-15(14-0-0)/3-7,2-2,S-2,P	1	-0.7
1914 Was-A	4	2	0	0	0	0	0	1	0	1	0	....	.000	.333	.000	.333	1	-0	0	1.88	-1	/O-4(0-1-2)	0	-0.1
1916 NY-A	122	435	50	92	14	4	0	27	40	61	14	....	.211	.282	.262	.544	62	-20	38	2.75	-7	*2-122	5	-2.8
1917 NY-A	33	117	15	28	7	0	0	8	7	13	4	....	.239	.288	.299	.587	78	-3	11	3.06	1	2-31	2	-0.2
1918 StL-A	123	441	39	94	14	3	1	41	27	29	7	....	.213	.271	.265	.536	64	-20	34	2.37	16	*2-123	6	-0.2
1919 StL-A	120	437	57	111	13	4	0	27	50	35	4	....	.254	.340	.302	.642	79	-10	51	3.59	-2	*2-118	10	-1.0
1920 StL-A	153	606	95	177	33	6	0	61	55	36	1	3	.292	.355	.366	.721	89	-8	82	4.54	-20	*2-153	11	-2.4
Total 7	**584**	**2109**	**259**	**515**	**82**	**20**	**1**	**171**	**180**	**181**	**33**	**3**	**.244**	**.311**	**.303**	**.615**	**74**	**-68**	**220**	**3.33**	**-12**	**2-549/O-19,3-7,S-2,P-1**	**35**	**-7.4**
• GEDMAN, Rich	Richard Leo Gedman b: 9/26/1959, Worcester, MA BL/TR, 6', 215 lbs. Deb: 9/7/1980																							
1980 Bos-A	9	24	2	5	0	0	0	1	0	5	0	0	.208	.208	.208	.417	14	-3	1	1.13	0	/D-4,C-2	0	-0.3
1981 Bos-A	62	205	22	59	15	0	5	26	9	31	0	0	.288	.321	.434	.755	109	2	26	4.35	-1	C-59	6	0.4
1982 Bos-A	92	289	30	72	17	2	4	26	10	37	0	1	.249	.279	.363	.642	71	-13	25	2.89	-4	C-86	4	-1.3
1983 Bos-A	81	204	21	60	16	1	2	18	15	37	0	1	.294	.345	.412	.757	100	-0	28	4.99	1	C-68	7	0.3
1984 Bos-A	133	449	54	121	26	4	24	72	29	72	0	0	.269	.315	.506	.821	118	9	71	5.64	-6	*C-125	15	0.9
1985 Bos-A★	144	498	66	147	30	5	18	80	50	79	2	0	.295	.363	.484	.847	124	17	86	6.34	4	*C-139	20	2.7
1986*Bos-A★	135	462	49	119	29	0	16	65	37	61	1	0	.258	.318	.424	.742	99	-1	59	4.37	1	*C-134	18	0.7
1987 Bos-A	52	151	11	31	8	0	1	13	10	24	0	0	.205	.255	.278	.533	40	-13	11	2.34	-4	C-51	1	-1.4
1988*Bos-A	95	299	33	69	14	0	9	39	18	49	0	0	.231	.281	.368	.649	77	-10	31	3.34	-2	C-93/D-1	8	-0.6
1989 Bos-A	93	260	24	55	9	0	4	16	23	47	0	1	.212	.276	.292	.568	57	-16	20	2.49	-1	C-91	3	-1.2
1990 Bos-A	10	15	3	3	0	0	0	0	5	6	0	0	.200	.429	.200	.629	78	0	2	3.61	1	/C-9	0	0.1
Hou-N	40	104	4	21	7	0	1	10	15	24	0	0	.202	.303	.298	.601	68	-4	10	2.98	3	C-39	4	0.1
1991 StL-N	46	94	7	10	1	0	3	8	4	15	0	1	.106	.143	.213	.356	-1	-13	2	.74	-1	C-43	2	-1.3
1992 StL-N	41	105	5	23	4	0	1	8	11	22	0	0	.219	.293	.286	.579	67	-5	10	3.13	-2	C-40	2	-0.4
Total 13	**1033**	**3159**	**331**	**795**	**176**	**12**	**88**	**382**	**236**	**509**	**3**	**4**	**.252**	**.307**	**.399**	**.705**	**90**	**-50**	**381**	**4.11**	**-11**	**C-979/D-5**	**90**	**-1.3**
• GEDNEY, Count	Alfred W. Gedney b: 5/10/1849, Brooklyn, NY d: 3/26/1922, Hackensack, NJ, 5'9", 140 lbs. Deb: 4/27/1872 NA OF: 189-9-1																							
1872 Tro-n	9	47	14	20	3	0	3	18	0	0	1	0	.426	.426	.681	1.106	232	7	14	16.53	-1	/O-9(0-9-0)	....	0.4
Eck-n	18	71	4	13	1	0	0	7	0	1	2	1	.183	.183	.197	.380	20	-5	3	1.58	0	O-18(18-0-0)	....	-0.3
Yr.	27	118	18	33	4	0	3	25	0	1	3	1	.280	.280	.390	.669	104	2	17	6.27	-1	O-27(18-9-0)	....	0.1
1873 Mut-n	53	224	41	60	5	5	1	25	7	5	1	0	.268	.290	.348	.638	89	-2	23	4.37	11	*O-53(53-0-0)	....	0.7
1874 Ath-n	54	222	49	61	4	1	1	34	7	11	2	2	.275	.297	.315	.612	89	-4	22	4.03	-3	*O-51(51-0-0)/1-4	....	-0.5
1875 Mut-n	68	267	30	55	12	2	0	17	0	8	2	3	.206	.206	.266	.472	59	-12	15	2.11	10	*O-67(67-0-1)/P-2	....	0.0
Total 4 n	**202**	**831**	**138**	**209**	**25**	**8**	**5**	**101**	**14**	**25**	**8**	**6**	**.252**	**.264**	**.319**	**.583**	**82**	**-17**	**78**	**3.77**	**16**	**O-198/1-4,P-2**	**....**	**0.3**
• GEER, Billy	William Henry Harrison Geer TR, 5'8", 160 lbs. Deb: 10/15/1874 U NA OF: 5-12-3																							
1874 Mut-n	2	8	0	2	0	0	0	1	0	0	0	0	.250	.250	.250	.500	59	-0	1	2.56	2	/O-2(1-1-0)	....	0.1
1875 NH-n	37	164	20	40	4	1	0	9	1	4	2	2	.244	.248	.280	.529	95	0	12	2.86	-1	O-17(4-11-3),2-13/S-6,1-1,3	....	-0.1
1878 Cin-N	61	237	31	52	13	2	0	20	10	18	....	....	.219	.251	.291	.542	86	-2	18	2.64	-2	*S-60/2-2	6	-0.2
1880 Wor-N	2	6	0	0	0	0	0	0	0	0	....	....	.000	.000	.000	.000	-92	-1	0	.00	0	/O-1,S-1	0	-0.1
1884 Phi-U	9	36	7	9	2	1	0	....	4	....	....	....	.250	.325	.361	.686	143	2	4	4.49	1	/S-9	1	0.3
Bro-a	107	391	68	82	15	7	0	0	38	....	....	....	.210	.281	.284	.565	84	-5	32	2.85	18	*S-107/2-2,P-2	14	1.0
1885 Lou-a	14	51	2	6	2	0	0	3	2	....	....	....	.118	.167	.157	.324	3	-6	1	.82	2	S-14	1	-0.3
Total 2 n	**39**	**172**	**20**	**42**	**4**	**1**	**0**	**10**	**1**	**4**	**2**	**2**	**.244**	**.249**	**.279**	**.528**	**94**	**0**	**13**	**2.85**	**1**	**/O-19,2-13,S-6,1-1,3-1**	**....**	**0.0**
Total 4	**193**	**721**	**108**	**149**	**32**	**10**	**0**	**23**	**54**	**18**	**....**	**....**	**.207**	**.264**	**.279**	**.543**	**81**	**-12**	**55**	**2.67**	**18**	**S-191/2-4,P-2,O-1**	**22**	**0.7**
• GEHRIG, Lou	Henry Louis "The Iron Horse,Biscuit Pants" Gehrig b: 6/19/1903, New York, NY d: 6/2/1941, Riverdale, NY BL/TL, 6', 200 lbs. Deb: 6/15/1923 HOF: 1939 Career OF: 3-0-6																							
1923 NY-A	13	26	6	11	4	1	1	9	2	5	0	0	.423	.464	.769	1.234	217	4	9	14.99	-1	/1-9	2	0.3
1924 NY-A	10	12	2	6	1	0	0	5	1	3	0	0	.500	.538	.583	1.122	189	2	4	16.58	0	/1-2,O-1	1	0.2
1925 NY-A	126	437	73	129	23	10	20	68	46	49	6	3	.295	.365	.531	.896	127	17	85	6.99	0	*1-114/O-6(2-0-4)	15	0.8
1926*NY-A	155	572	135	179	47	**20**	16	112	105	73	6	5	.313	.420	.549	.969	154	47	137	8.70	2	*1-155	30	3.8
1927*NY-A	155	584	149	218	**52**	18	47	**175**	109	84	10	8	.373	.474	.765	1.240	224	107	212	14.23	-1	*1-155	44	9.1
1928*NY-A	154	562	139	210	**47**	13	27	**142**	95	69	4	11	.374	**.467**	.648	1.115	196	78	169	11.82	2	*1-154	42	6.8
1929 NY-A	154	553	127	166	32	10	35	126	122	68	4	4	.300	.431	.584	1.015	170	63	146	9.60	-3	*1-154	32	4.7
1930 NY-A	154	581	143	220	42	17	41	**174**	101	63	12	14	.379	.473	.721	1.194	207	95	195	13.17	-6	*1-153/O-1	**39**	7.1
1931 NY-A	155	619	**163**	**211**	31	15	**46**	**184**	117	56	17	12	.341	.446	.662	1.108	199	92	185	11.62	-14	*1-154/O-1	36	5.9
1932*NY-A	156	596	138	208	42	9	34	151	108	38	4	11	.349	.451	.621	1.072	184	75	168	11.11	-8	*1-156	38	4.8
1933 NY-A★	152	593	**138**	198	41	12	32	139	92	42	9	13	.334	.424	.605	1.030	181	66	151	9.78	-7	*1-152	36	4.3
1934 NY-A★	154	579	128	210	40	6	**49**	**165**	109	31	9	5	**.363**	**.465**	**.706**	**1.172**	**213**	**99**	195	**13.79**	0	*1-153/S-1	**41**	**7.9**
1935 NY-A★	149	535	**125**	176	26	10	30	119	**132**	38	8	7	.329	**.466**	.583	1.049	180	**70**	154	11.13	9	*1-149	**34**	6.1
1936*NY-A★	155	579	**167**	205	37	7	**49**	152	**130**	46	3	4	.354	**.478**	**.696**	**1.174**	**193**	**89**	199	**13.87**	4	*1-155	**38**	**6.9**
1937*NY-A★	157	569	138	200	37	9	37	159	**127**	49	4	3	.351	**.473**	.643	**1.116**	**177**	**74**	181	**12.89**	-6	*1-157	36	4.9
1938*NY-A★	157	576	115	170	32	6	29	114	107	75	6	1	.295	.410	.523	.932	133	33	131	8.49	-1	*1-157	25	1.5
1939 NY-A★	8	28	2	4	0	0	0	1	5	1	0	0	.143	.273	.143	.416	9	-4	1	1.17	0	/1-8	0	-0.4
Total 17	**2164**	**8001**	**1888**	**2721**	**534**	**163**	**493**	**1995**	**1508**	**790**	**102**	**101**	**.340**	**.447**	**.632**	**1.080**	**182**	**1006**	**2321**	**11.21**	**-29**	***1-2137/O-9,S-1**	**489**	**74.6**
• GEHRINGER, Charlie	Charles Leonard "The Mechanical Man" Gehringer b: 5/11/1903, Fowlerville, MI d: 1/21/1993, Bloomfield Hills, MI BL/TR, 5'11", 180 lbs. Deb: 9/22/1924 C HOF: 1949																							
1924 Det-A	5	13	2	6	0	0	0	1	0	2	1	1	.462	.462	.462	.923	141	1	2	7.96	0	/2-5	1	0.0
1925 Det-A	8	18	3	3	0	0	0	0	2	0	0	1	.167	.250	.167	.417	7	-3	1	1.12	2	/2-6	0	0.0
1926 Det-A	123	459	62	127	19	17	1	48	30	42	9	7	.277	.322	.399	.721	86	-12	59	4.25	0	*2-112/3-6	11	-0.8
1927 Det-A	133	508	110	161	29	11	4	61	52	31	17	8	.317	.383	.441	.824	112	10	87	6.37	16	*2-121	20	2.7
1928 Det-A	154	603	108	193	29	16	6	74	69	22	15	9	.320	.395	.451	.846	120	20	110	6.75	2	*2-154	23	2.5
1929 Det-A	155	634	**131**	**215**	**45**	**19**	13	106	64	19	**27**	9	.339	.405	.532	.936	138	39	139	8.38	-7	*2-154	27	3.5
1930 Det-A	154	610	144	201	47	15	16	98	69	17	19	15	.330	.404	.534	.938	133	30	130	7.90	11	*2-154	29	4.0
1931 Det-A	101	383	67	119	24	5	4	53	29	15	13	4	.311	.359	.431	.790	103	4	60	5.91	-2	2-78/1-9	10	0.6
1932 Det-A	152	618	112	184	44	11	19	107	68	34	9	8	.298	.370	.497	.867	118	14	114	6.77	1	*2-152	25	2.4
1933 Det-A★	155	628	103	204	42	6	12	105	68	27	5	4	.325	.393	.468	.862	125	24	117	7.17	9	*2-155	28	4.1

YEAR TM-L	G	AB	R	H	2B	3B	HR	RBI	BB	SO	SB	CS	AVG	OBP	SLG	OPS	OPS+	BR/A	RC	RC/G	FR	G/POS	WS	TPW
1934*Det-A★	154	601	**134**	**214**	50	7	11	127	99	25	11	8	.356	.450	.517	.967	149	47	144	9.57	5	*2-154	37	5.8
1935*Det-A★	150	610	123	201	32	8	19	108	79	16	11	4	.330	.409	.502	.911	139	38	129	7.96	10	*2-149	31	5.3
1936 Det-A★	154	641	144	227	**60**	12	15	116	83	13	4	1	.354	.431	.555	.987	141	44	157	9.96	14	*2-154	34	5.9
1937 Det-A★	144	564	133	209	40	1	14	96	90	25	11	4	**.371**	.458	.520	.978	143	43	140	10.19	6	*2-142	30	5.3
1938 Det-A★	152	568	133	174	32	5	20	107	113	21	14	1	.306	.425	.486	.911	121	26	128	8.49	-3	*2-152	27	2.9
1939 Det-A	118	406	86	132	29	6	16	86	68	16	4	3	.325	.423	.544	.967	135	23	97	8.88	9	*2-107	19	3.5
1940*Det-A	139	515	108	161	33	3	10	81	101	17	10	0	.313	.428	.447	.875	116	21	111	8.05	-22	*2-138	20	0.7
1941 Det-A	127	436	65	96	19	4	3	46	95	26	1	2	.220	.363	.303	.666	71	-15	55	4.16	-1	*2-116	10	-0.9
1942 Det-A	45	45	6	12	0	0	1	7	7	4	0	0	.267	.365	.333	.699	90	-0	6	5.14	0	/2-3	1	0.0
Total 19	2323	8860	1774	2839	574	146	184	1427	1186	372	181	89	.320	.404	.480	.884	123	352	1787	7.57	49	*2-2206/1-9,3-6	383	47.6
• GEIER, Phil	Philip Louis "Little Phil" Geier b: 11/3/1876, Washington, DC d: 9/25/1967, Spokane, WA BL/TR, 5'7", 145 lbs. Deb: 8/17/1896 Career OF: 14-167-98																							
1896 Phi-N	17	56	12	13	0	1	0	6	6	7	3	....	.232	.317	.268	.585	56	-3	6	3.61	-1	O-12(2-0-10)/2-3,C-2	0	-0.4
1897 Phi-N	92	316	51	88	6	2	1	35	56	....	19	....	.278	.392	.320	.712	91	0	49	5.58	-1	O-45(2-3-40),2-37/S-6,3-2	7	-0.1
1900 Cin-N	30	113	18	29	1	4	0	10	7	....	3	....	.257	.306	.336	.642	79	-3	13	4.03	1	O-27(0-9-18)/3-2	2	-0.4
1901 Phi-A	50	211	42	49	5	2	0	23	24	....	7	....	.232	.314	.275	.588	61	-11	21	3.42	-4	O-50(6-14-30)/S-2,3-1	3	-1.5
Mil-A	11	39	4	7	1	1	0	1	5	....	4	....	.179	.273	.256	.529	50	-2	4	3.24	1	/O-8(0-8-0),3-3	1	-0.2
Yr.	61	250	46	56	6	3	0	24	29	....	11	....	.224	.307	.272	.579	60	-13	25	3.39	-3	O-58(6-22-30)/3-4,S-2	4	-1.7
1904 Bos-N	149	580	70	141	17	2	1	27	56	....	18	....	.243	.314	.284	.599	88	-6	60	3.49	-1	*O-137(4-133-0)/3-7,2-5,S	12	-1.4
Total 5	349	1315	197	327	30	12	2	102	154	7	54	....	.249	.332	.294	.626	81	-26	153	4.01	-5	O-279/2-45,3-15,S-9,C-2	25	-3.9
• GEIGER, Gary	Gary Merle Geiger b: 4/4/1937, Sand Ridge, IL d: 4/24/1996, Murphysboro, IL BL/TR, 6', 168 lbs. Deb: 4/15/1958 Career OF: 117-542-114																							
1958 Cle-A	91	195	28	45	3	1	1	6	27	43	2	2	.231	.333	.272	.605	70	-7	20	3.46	1	O-53(1-44-8)/3-2,P-1	4	-1.0
1959 Bos-A	120	335	45	82	10	4	11	48	21	55	9	3	.245	.289	.397	.686	83	-9	38	3.90	-3	O-95(46-61-1)	7	-1.6
1960 Bos-A	77	245	32	74	13	3	9	33	23	38	2	2	.302	.369	.490	.859	126	8	43	6.37	4	O-66(5-7-59)	9	1.0
1961 Bos-A	140	499	82	116	21	6	18	64	87	91	16	4	.232	.351	.407	.758	99	3	78	5.23	5	*O-137(0-137-0)	18	0.4
1962 Bos-A	131	466	67	116	18	4	16	54	67	66	18	11	.249	.346	.408	.754	99	-1	69	4.96	3	*O-129(0-129-0)	14	-0.2
1963 Bos-A	121	399	67	105	13	5	16	44	36	63	9	4	.263	.329	.441	.770	110	5	59	5.20	5	O-95(2-89-4)/1-6	14	0.7
1964 Bos-A	5	13	3	5	0	1	0	1	2	2	0	0	.385	.467	.538	1.005	170	1	4	11.84	0	/O-4(0-1-3)	1	0.1
1965 Bos-A	24	45	5	9	3	0	1	2	13	10	3	0	.200	.379	.333	.713	98	1	7	5.60	-1	O-16(5-10-1)	1	0.0
1966 Atl-N	78	126	23	33	5	3	4	10	21	29	0	1	.262	.372	.444	.816	124	5	22	6.09	2	O-49(5-33-15)	5	0.6
1967 Atl-N	69	117	17	19	1	1	1	5	20	35	1	1	.162	.285	.214	.498	45	-8	8	2.15	-1	O-38(6-26-7)	1	-1.0
1969 Hou-N	93	125	19	28	4	1	0	16	24	34	2	1	.224	.353	.272	.625	79	-2	14	3.71	0	O-65(47-5-14)	3	-0.4
1970 Hou-N	5	4	0	1	0	0	0	0	0	0	0	0	.250	.250	.250	.500	36	-0	0	2.25	0	/O-2(0-0-2)	0	0.0
Total 12	954	2569	388	633	91	29	77	283	341	466	62	29	.246	.339	.394	.733	97	-3	363	4.80	15	O-749/1-6,3-2,P-1	77	-1.5
• GEISS, Bill	William J. Geiss b: 7/15/1858, Chicago, IL d: 9/18/1924, Chicago, IL, 5'10", 164 lbs. Deb: 5/1/1884																							
1884 Det-N	75	283	22	50	11	4	2	16	6	60	....	....	.177	.194	.265	.459	45	-17	15	1.76	-11	2-73/1-1,O-1,P-1	1	-2.8
• GEISS, Emil	Emil August Geiss b: 3/20/1867, Chicago, IL d: 10/4/1911, Chicago, IL BR/TR, 5'11", 170 lbs. Deb: 5/18/1887 ♦																							
1887 Chi-N	3	12	0	1	0	0	0	0	0	7	0	....	.083	.083	.083	.167	-47	-2	0	.21	-1	/1-1,2-1,P-1	0	-0.6
• GELBERT, Charlie	Charles Magnus Gelbert b: 1/26/1906, Scranton, PA d: 1/13/1967, Easton, PA BR/TR, 5'11", 170 lbs. Deb: 4/16/1929																							
1929 StL-N	146	512	60	134	29	8	3	65	51	46	8	....	.262	.329	.367	.696	71	-23	62	4.10	20	*S-146	15	1.2
1930*StL-N	139	513	92	156	39	11	3	72	43	41	6	....	.304	.360	.441	.801	89	-9	80	5.58	10	*S-139	18	1.4
1931*StL-N	131	447	61	129	29	5	1	62	54	31	7	....	.289	.365	.383	.748	97	0	66	5.32	5	*S-130	20	1.5
1932 StL-N	122	455	60	122	28	9	1	45	39	30	8	....	.268	.330	.376	.706	87	-8	59	4.50	-6	*S-122	14	-0.4
1935 StL-N	62	168	24	49	7	2	2	21	17	18	0	....	.292	.357	.393	.750	97	-0	25	5.49	6	3-37,S-21/2-3	7	0.8
1936 StL-N	93	280	33	64	15	2	3	27	25	26	2	....	.229	.292	.329	.620	67	-13	25	2.95	5	3-60,S-28/2-8	5	-0.5
1937 Cin-N	43	114	12	22	4	0	1	13	15	12	1	....	.193	.287	.254	.541	50	-7	9	2.60	-1	S-37/2-9,3-1	2	-0.6
Det-A	20	47	4	4	2	0	0	1	4	11	0	0	.085	.157	.128	.285	-27	-9	1	.65	0	S-16	0	-0.8
1939 Was-A	68	188	36	48	7	5	3	29	30	11	2	0	.255	.361	.394	.754	100	1	28	5.15	1	S-28,3-20/2-1	5	0.4
1940 Was-A	22	54	7	20	7	1	0	7	4	3	0	0	.370	.424	.537	.961	157	5	13	9.74	-4	S-12/P-2,2-1	3	0.0
Bos-A	30	91	9	18	2	0	0	8	8	16	0	0	.198	.263	.220	.482	25	-10	6	2.08	1	3-29/S-1	1	-0.8
Yr.	52	145	16	38	9	1	0	15	12	19	0	0	.262	.323	.338	.661	75	-5	18	4.54	-3	3-29,S-13/P-2,2-1	4	-0.8
Total 9	876	2869	398	766	169	43	17	350	290	245	34	0	.267	.336	.374	.709	82	-74	373	4.51	37	S-680,3-147/2-22,P-2	90	2.2
• GENINS, Frank	C. Frank "Frenchy" Genins b: 11/2/1866, St. Louis, MO d: 9/30/1922, St. Louis, MO TR Deb: 7/5/1892 Career OF: 21-36-13																							
1892 Cin-N	35	110	12	20	4	0	0	7	12	12	7	....	.182	.262	.218	.480	46	-7	8	2.50	3	S-17,O-14(7-7-0)/3-4	2	-0.4
StL-N	15	51	5	10	1	0	0	4	1	11	3	....	.196	.212	.216	.427	31	-4	3	2.00	-5	S-14/O-1	0	-0.8
Yr.	50	161	17	30	5	0	0	11	13	23	10	....	.186	.247	.217	.465	42	-11	11	2.34	-2	S-31,O-15(7-7-1)/3-4	2	-1.2
1895 Pit-N	73	252	43	63	8	0	2	24	22	14	19	....	.250	.315	.306	.621	64	-13	34	4.29	0	O-29(14-3-12),2-16,3-16/S-8,1	4	-1.1
1901 Cle-A	26	101	15	23	5	0	0	9	8	....	3	....	.228	.284	.277	.562	59	-5	10	3.08	1	O-26(0-26-0)	1	-0.5
Total 3	149	514	75	116	18	0	2	44	43	37	32	....	.226	.288	.272	.560	56	-30	55	3.45	-2	/O-70,S-39,3-20,2-16,1-2	7	-2.9
• GENOVESE, George	George Michael Genovese b: 2/22/1922, Staten Island, NY BL/TR, 5'6.5", 160 lbs. Deb: 4/29/1950																							
1950 Was-A	3	1	1	0	0	0	0	0	1	0	0	0	.000	.500	.000	.500	39	0	0	3.51	0	....	0	0.0
• GENTILE, Jim	James Edward "Diamond Jim" Gentile b: 6/3/1934, San Francisco, CA BL/TL, 6'3.5", 215 lbs. Deb: 9/10/1957																							
1957 Bro-N	4	6	1	1	0	0	1	1	1	1	0	0	.167	.286	.667	.952	133	0	1	6.57	0	/1-2	0	0.0
1958 LA-N	12	30	0	4	1	0	0	4	4	6	0	0	.133	.235	.167	.402	8	-4	1	1.19	-1	/1-8	0	-0.6
1960 Bal-A★	138	384	67	112	17	0	21	98	68	72	0	0	.292	.407	.500	.907	146	27	82	7.78	-6	*1-124	21	1.5
1961 Bal-A★	148	486	96	147	25	2	46	141	96	106	1	1	.302	.428	.646	1.074	186	63	138	10.38	4	*1-144	32	5.8
1962 Bal-A★	152	545	80	137	21	1	33	87	77	100	1	0	.251	.351	.475	.827	126	21	92	5.76	1	*1-150	20	1.3
1963 Bal-A	145	496	65	123	16	1	24	72	76	101	1	0	.248	.355	.429	.784	121	16	77	5.32	5	*1-143	20	1.4
1964 KC-A	136	439	71	110	10	0	28	71	84	122	0	0	.251	.376	.465	.840	128	20	81	6.36	-2	*1-128	15	1.1
1965 KC-A	38	118	14	29	5	0	10	22	9	26	0	0	.246	.305	.542	.847	138	5	19	5.48	0	1-35	4	0.3
Hou-N	81	227	22	55	11	1	7	31	34	72	0	0	.242	.353	.392	.745	118	7	33	4.91	2	1-68	8	0.6
1966 Hou-N	49	144	16	35	6	1	7	18	21	39	0	0	.243	.355	.444	.799	129	7	24	5.63	3	1-43	5	0.7
Cle-A	33	47	2	6	1	0	2	4	5	18	0	0	.128	.212	.277	.488	39	-4	3	1.74	0	/1-9	0	-0.4
Total 9	936	2922	434	759	113	6	179	549	475	663	3	1	.260	.372	.486	.858	136	158	550	6.55	6	1-854	125	11.8
• GENTILE, Sam	Samuel Christopher Gentile b: 10/12/1916, Charlestown, MA d: 5/4/1998, Everett, MA BL/TR, 5'11", 180 lbs. Deb: 4/24/1943																							
1943 Bos-N	8	4	1	1	1	0	0	0	1	0	0	....	.250	.400	.500	.900	162	0	1	8.14	0	....	0	0.0
• GENTRY, Harvey	Harvey William Gentry b: 5/27/1926, Winston-Salem, NC BL/TR, 6', 170 lbs. Deb: 4/14/1954																							
1954 NY-N	5	4	0	1	0	0	0	1	1	0	0	0	.250	.400	.250	.650	73	-0	1	4.54	0	....	0	0.0
• GEORGE, Alex	Alex Thomas M. George b: 9/27/1938, Kansas City, MO BL/TR, 5'11.5", 170 lbs. Deb: 9/16/1955																							
1955 KC-A	5	10	0	1	0	0	0	0	1	7	0	0	.100	.182	.100	.282	-22	-2	0	.69	-1	/S-5	0	-0.3
• GEORGE, Bill	William M. George b: 1/27/1865, Bellaire, OH d: 8/23/1916, Wheeling, WV BR/TL, 5'8", 165 lbs. Deb: 5/11/1887 U Career OF: 0-1-13 ♦																							
1887 NY-N	13	54	6	10	0	0	0	5	1	6	2	....	.185	.185	.170	.355	-1	-4	2	1.26	1	P-13/O-1	2	-2.0
1888*NY-N	9	39	7	9	1	0	1	6	0	2	1	....	.231	.231	.333	.564	79	0	3	2.98	0	/O-6(0-0-6),P-4	4	0.5
1889 NY-N	3	15	1	4	0	0	0	0	0	3	1	....	.267	.267	.267	.533	49	-1	1	3.29	0	/O-3(0-1-2)	0	-0.1
Col-a	5	17	1	4	0	0	0	3	1	1	1	....	.235	.278	.235	.513	49	-1	1	2.90	-1	/O-4(0-0-4),P-2	0	-0.5
Total 3	30	125	15	27	1	0	1	14	2	12	5	....	.216	.222	.242	.464	37	-5	8	2.23	0	/P-19,O-14	6	-2.1
• GEORGE, Greek	Charles Peter George b: 12/25/1912, Waycross, GA d: 8/15/1999, Metairie, LA BR/TR, 6'2", 200 lbs. Deb: 6/30/1935																							
1935 Cle-A	2	0	0	0	0	0	0	0	0	0	0	0	....	....	....	....	-98	0	0	....	0	/C-1	0	0.0
1936 Cle-A	23	77	3	15	3	0	0	5	9	16	0	0	.195	.279	.234	.513	28	-9	5	2.33	12	C-22	2	0.4
1938 Bro-N	7	20	0	4	0	1	0	2	0	4	0	....	.200	.200	.300	.500	35	-2	1	1.47	1	/C-7	0	-0.1

YEAR TM-L	G	AB	R	H	2B	3B	HR	RBI	BB	SO	SB	CS	AVG	OBP	SLG	OPS	OPS+	BR/A	RC	RC/G	FR	G/POS	WS	TPW
1941 Chi-N	35	64	4	10	2	0	0	6	2	10	0	....	.156	.182	.188	.369	4	-8	2	1.03	0	C-18	0	-0.8
1945 Phi-A	51	138	8	24	4	1	0	11	17	29	0	0	.174	.265	.217	.482	41	-10	8	1.79	-3	C-46	1	-1.1
Total 5	118	299	15	53	9	2	0	24	28	59	0	0	.177	.248	.221	.468	30	-29	17	1.73	10	/C-94	3	-1.6

• GERAGHTY, Ben Benjamin Raymond Geraghty b: 7/19/1912, Jersey City, NJ d: 6/18/1963, Jacksonville, FL BR/TR, 5'11", 175 lbs. Deb: 4/17/1936

YEAR TM-L	G	AB	R	H	2B	3B	HR	RBI	BB	SO	SB	CS	AVG	OBP	SLG	OPS	OPS+	BR/A	RC	RC/G	FR	G/POS	WS	TPW
1936 Bro-N	51	129	11	25	4	0	0	9	8	16	4	....	.194	.241	.225	.466	26	-14	7	1.61	-6	S-31/2-9,3-5	1	-1.6
1943 Bos-N	8	1	2	0	0	0	0	0	0	0	0	....	.000	.000	.000	.000	-102	-0	0	.00	-1	/2-1,3-1,S-1	0	-0.1
1944 Bos-N	11	16	3	4	0	0	0	0	1	2	0	....	.250	.294	.250	.544	52	-1	1	2.82	-1	/2-4,3-3	0	-0.2
Total 3	70	146	16	29	4	0	0	9	9	18	4	....	.199	.245	.226	.471	28	-15	8	1.71	-8	/S-32,2-14,3-9	1	-2.0

• GERBER, Craig Craig Stuart Gerber b: 1/8/1959, Chicago, IL BL/TR, 6', 175 lbs. Deb: 4/11/1985

YEAR TM-L	G	AB	R	H	2B	3B	HR	RBI	BB	SO	SB	CS	AVG	OBP	SLG	OPS	OPS+	BR/A	RC	RC/G	FR	G/POS	WS	TPW
1985 Cal-A	65	91	8	24	1	2	0	6	2	3	0	3	.264	.280	.319	.598	64	-6	7	2.43	4	S-53/3-9,2-1,D-1	2	0.1

• GERBER, Wally Walter "Spooks" Gerber b: 8/18/1891, Columbus, OH d: 6/19/1951, Columbus, OH BR/TR, 5'10", 152 lbs. Deb: 9/23/1914

YEAR TM-L	G	AB	R	H	2B	3B	HR	RBI	BB	SO	SB	CS	AVG	OBP	SLG	OPS	OPS+	BR/A	RC	RC/G	FR	G/POS	WS	TPW
1914 Pit-N	17	54	5	13	1	1	0	5	2	8	0	....	.241	.281	.296	.577	75	-2	4	2.68	2	S-17	2	0.2
1915 Pit-N	56	144	8	28	2	0	0	7	9	16	6	1	.194	.252	.208	.460	40	-9	9	2.00	-1	3-23,S-21/2-2	2	-0.9
1917 StL-A	14	39	2	12	1	1	0	2	3	2	1	....	.308	.357	.385	.742	131	1	6	5.13	1	S-12/2-2	2	0.4
1918 StL-A	56	171	10	41	4	0	0	10	19	11	2	....	.240	.316	.263	.579	77	-4	15	2.79	-5	S-56	3	-0.6
1919 StL-A	140	462	43	105	14	6	1	37	49	36	1	....	.227	.308	.290	.598	67	-20	44	2.95	-8	*S-140	9	-1.8
1920 StL-A	154	584	70	163	26	2	2	60	58	32	4	13	.279	.346	.341	.687	80	-18	69	4.03	15	*S-154	14	0.7
1921 StL-A	114	436	55	121	12	9	2	48	34	19	4	7	.278	.337	.360	.697	73	-19	53	4.12	7	*S-113	10	0.0
1922 StL-A	153	604	81	161	22	8	1	51	52	34	6	4	.267	.326	.334	.660	70	-26	69	3.81	12	*S-153	15	0.4
1923 StL-A	154	605	85	170	26	3	1	62	54	50	4	6	.281	.342	.339	.681	75	-21	72	4.09	24	*S-154	17	1.9
1924 StL-A	148	496	61	135	20	4	0	55	43	34	4	5	.272	.341	.329	.670	69	-22	58	4.00	6	*S-147	12	-0.1
1925 StL-A	72	246	29	67	13	1	0	19	26	15	1	2	.272	.344	.333	.678	69	-11	29	4.18	5	S-71	6	0.1
1926 StL-A	131	411	37	111	8	0	0	42	40	29	0	2	.270	.339	.290	.629	62	-21	43	3.56	-4	*S-129	7	-1.2
1927 StL-A	142	438	44	98	13	9	0	45	35	25	3	6	.224	.284	.295	.579	49	-35	38	2.71	-2	*S-141/3-1	6	-2.2
1928 StL-A	6	18	1	5	1	0	0	0	1	3	0	0	.278	.316	.333	.649	68	-1	2	3.87	-1	/S-6	0	-0.2
Bos-A	104	300	21	64	6	1	0	28	32	31	6	1	.213	.289	.240	.529	41	-24	24	2.53	10	*S-103	5	-0.3
Yr.	110	318	22	69	7	1	0	28	33	34	6	1	.217	.291	.245	.536	43	-24	26	2.59	8	*S-109	5	-0.5
1929 Bos-A	61	91	6	15	3	1	0	5	8	12	1	0	.165	.232	.220	.452	17	-11	5	1.74	-5	S-30,2-22	1	-1.3
Total 15	1522	5099	558	1309	172	46	7	476	465	357	43	47	.257	.323	.313	.635	66	-244	540	3.52	55	*S-1447/2-26,3-24	111	-4.9

• GEREN, Bob Robert Peter Geren b: 9/22/1961, San Diego, CA BR/TR, 6'3", 221 lbs. Deb: 5/17/1988

YEAR TM-L	G	AB	R	H	2B	3B	HR	RBI	BB	SO	SB	CS	AVG	OBP	SLG	OPS	OPS+	BR/A	RC	RC/G	FR	G/POS	WS	TPW
1988 NY-A	10	10	0	1	0	0	0	0	2	3	0	0	.100	.250	.100	.350	2	-1	0	1.14	0	C-10	0	-0.1
1989 NY-A	65	205	26	59	5	1	9	27	12	44	0	0	.288	.330	.454	.784	120	5	28	4.57	2	C-60/D-2	8	1.0
1990 NY-A	110	277	21	59	7	0	8	31	13	73	0	0	.213	.261	.325	.586	63	-15	23	2.64	2	*C-107/D-1	7	-0.7
1991 NY-A	64	128	7	28	3	0	2	12	9	31	0	1	.219	.270	.289	.559	55	-8	9	2.24	-1	C-63	2	-0.6
1993 SD-N	58	145	8	31	6	0	3	6	13	28	0	0	.214	.278	.317	.596	58	-9	12	2.76	3	C-49/1-1,3-1	2	-0.3
Total 5	307	765	62	178	21	1	22	76	49	179	0	1	.233	.284	.349	.633	75	-29	72	3.07	7	C-289/D-3,1-1,3-1	19	-0.7

• GERHARDT, Joe John Joseph "Move Up Joe" Gerhardt
b: 2/14/1855, Washington, DC d: 3/11/1922, Middletown, NY BR/TR, 6', 160 lbs. Deb: 9/1/1873 M/U Career OF: 2-1-0

YEAR TM-L	G	AB	R	H	2B	3B	HR	RBI	BB	SO	SB	CS	AVG	OBP	SLG	OPS	OPS+	BR/A	RC	RC/G	FR	G/POS	WS	TPW
1873 Was-n	13	56	6	12	3	0	0	7	0	5	0	0	.214	.214	.268	.482	44	-4	3	2.28	-6	S-13	....	-0.7
1874 Bal-n	14	61	10	19	0	1	0	6	0	0	0	0	.311	.311	.344	.656	111	1	7	4.79	-2	S-14	....	-0.1
1875 Mut-n	58	252	29	54	7	3	0	20	0	2	0	5	.214	.214	.266	.480	62	-12	15	2.14	3	3-47,2-13/0-1,S-1	....	-0.9
1876 Lou-N	65	295	33	76	10	3	2	18	3	5	....	....	.258	.268	.336	.603	85	-7	27	3.49	12	*1-54/2-5,S-3,3-2,0-2(2-0-0)	6	0.2
1877 Lou-N	59	250	41	76	6	5	1	35	5	8	....	....	.304	.318	.380	.698	101	-1	31	4.89	18	*2-57/1-1,0-1,S-1	6	1.7
1878 Cin-N	60	259	46	77	7	2	0	28	7	14	....	....	.297	.316	.340	.656	127	8	28	4.30	8	*2-60	10	1.7
1879 Cin-N	79	313	22	62	12	3	1	39	3	19	....	....	.198	.206	.265	.471	57	-13	17	1.95	7	*2-55,3-16/1-8,S-1	4	-0.3
1881 Det-N	80	297	35	72	13	6	0	36	7	31	....	....	.242	.260	.327	.586	80	-8	26	3.10	6	*2-79/3-1	6	0.2
1883 Lou-a	78	319	56	84	11	9	0	0	14	....	....	....	.263	.294	.354	.649	116	7	34	4.06	19	*2-78	13	2.5
1884 Lou-a	106	404	39	89	7	8	0	40	13	....	....	....	.220	.254	.277	.531	76	-9	29	2.54	28	*2-106	11	2.1
1885 NY-N	112	399	43	62	12	2	0	33	24	47	....	....	.155	.203	.195	.399	30	-30	16	1.30	21	*2-112	5	-0.4
1886 NY-N	123	426	44	81	11	7	0	40	22	63	8	....	.190	.230	.249	.479	45	-28	27	2.10	8	*2-123	7	-1.4
1887 NY-N	1	4	0	0	0	0	0	0	0	0	0	....	.000	.000	.000	.000	-105	-1	0	.00	0	/3-1	0	-0.1
NY-a	85	331	40	92	13	2	0	27	24	....	15	....	.278	.280	.277	.557	58	-16	29	3.24	-6	*2-84/3-1	4	-1.6
1890 Bro-a	99	369	34	75	10	4	2	40	30	....	9	....	.203	.270	.268	.539	61	-18	30	2.70	25	*2-99	6	0.9
StL-a	37	125	15	32	0	0	1	11	9	....	5	....	.256	.321	.280	.601	68	-6	13	3.75	4	2-20,3-17	3	-0.1
Yr.	136	494	49	107	10	4	3	51	39	....	14	....	.217	.283	.271	.555	62	-24	43	2.95	29	*2-119,3-17	9	0.8
1891 Lou-a	2	6	0	0	0	0	0	0	1	0	0	....	.000	.143	.000	.143	-59	-1	0	.00	0	/2-2	0	-0.1
Total 3 n	85	369	45	85	10	4	0	33	0	7	0	5	.230	.230	.279	.509	68	-15	25	2.55	-6	/3-47,S-28,2-13,0-1	....	-1.8
Total 12	986	3797	448	878	112	51	7	347	162	187	37	....	.231	.261	.289	.550	72	-125	308	2.88	150	2-880/1-63,3-38,S-5,0-3	81	5.3

• GERHART, Ken Harold Kenneth Gerhart b: 5/19/1961, Charleston, SC BR/TR, 6', 190 lbs. Deb: 9/14/1986 Career OF: 89-113-10

YEAR TM-L	G	AB	R	H	2B	3B	HR	RBI	BB	SO	SB	CS	AVG	OBP	SLG	OPS	OPS+	BR/A	RC	RC/G	FR	G/POS	WS	TPW
1986 Bal-A	20	69	4	16	2	0	1	7	4	18	0	1	.232	.274	.304	.578	58	-5	6	2.62	-1	0-20(6-14-0)	0	-0.6
1987 Bal-A	92	284	41	69	10	2	14	34	17	53	9	2	.243	.288	.440	.728	92	-4	35	4.06	-4	0-91(53-42-0)	5	-0.9
1988 Bal-A	103	262	27	51	10	1	9	23	21	57	7	3	.195	.260	.344	.603	69	-11	24	2.91	-1	0-93(30-57-10)/D-3	2	-1.5
Total 3	215	615	72	136	22	3	24	64	42	128	16	6	.221	.274	.384	.658	78	-19	64	3.40	-6	0-204/D-3	7	-3.0

• GERKEN, George George Herbert "Pickles" Gerken b: 7/28/1903, Chicago, IL d: 10/23/1977, Arcadia, CA BR/TR, 5'11.5", 175 lbs. Deb: 4/19/1927 Career OF: 16-19-4

YEAR TM-L	G	AB	R	H	2B	3B	HR	RBI	BB	SO	SB	CS	AVG	OBP	SLG	OPS	OPS+	BR/A	RC	RC/G	FR	G/POS	WS	TPW
1927 Cle-A	6	14	1	3	0	0	0	2	1	3	0	0	.214	.267	.214	.481	26	-2	1	2.01	0	/0-5(2-3-0)	0	-0.1
1928 Cle-A	38	115	16	26	7	2	0	9	12	22	3	3	.226	.305	.322	.626	64	-7	12	3.18	-1	0-34(14-16-4)	1	-0.9
Total 2	44	129	17	29	7	2	0	11	13	25	3	3	.225	.301	.310	.611	60	-8	12	3.06	-1	/0-39	1	-1.1

• GERLACH, Johnny John Glenn Gerlach b: 5/11/1917, Shullsburg, WI d: 8/28/1999, Madison, WI BR/TR, 5'9", 165 lbs. Deb: 9/3/1938

YEAR TM-L	G	AB	R	H	2B	3B	HR	RBI	BB	SO	SB	CS	AVG	OBP	SLG	OPS	OPS+	BR/A	RC	RC/G	FR	G/POS	WS	TPW
1938 Chi-A	9	25	2	7	0	0	0	1	4	2	0	0	.280	.379	.280	.659	66	-1	3	4.20	1	/S-8	1	0.0
1939 Chi-A	3	2	0	2	0	0	0	0	0	0	0	0	1.000	1.000	1.000	2.000	402	1	2	∞	0	/3-1	0	0.1
Total 2	12	27	2	9	0	0	0	1	4	2	0	0	.333	.419	.333	.753	87	-0	5	4.20	1	/S-8,3-1	1	0.1

• GERMAN, Esteban Esteban (Guridi) German b: 1/26/1978, Haina, Dominican Republic BR/TR, 5'10", 165 lbs. Deb: 5/21/2002

YEAR TM-L	G	AB	R	H	2B	3B	HR	RBI	BB	SO	SB	CS	AVG	OBP	SLG	OPS	OPS+	BR/A	RC	RC/G	FR	G/POS	WS	TPW
2002 Oak-A	9	35	4	7	0	0	0	0	4	11	1	0	.200	.300	.200	.500	37	-3	3	2.55	-1	/2-8	0	-0.3
2003 Oak-A	5	4	0	1	0	0	0	1	0	1	0	0	.250	.250	.250	.500	32	-0	0	.00	1	/2-5	0	0.1
Total 2	14	39	4	8	0	0	0	1	4	12	1	0	.205	.295	.205	.501	36	-3	3	2.23	0	/2-13	0	-0.2

• GERNERT, Dick Richard Edward Gernert b: 9/28/1928, Reading, PA BR/TR, 6'3", 210 lbs. Deb: 4/16/1952 C Career OF: 98-0-7

YEAR TM-L	G	AB	R	H	2B	3B	HR	RBI	BB	SO	SB	CS	AVG	OBP	SLG	OPS	OPS+	BR/A	RC	RC/G	FR	G/POS	WS	TPW
1952 Bos-A	102	367	58	89	20	2	19	67	35	83	4	1	.243	.317	.463	.780	107	2	56	5.30	-4	1-99	11	-0.5
1953 Bos-A	139	494	73	125	15	1	21	71	88	82	0	7	.253	.371	.415	.786	106	5	81	5.62	-5	*1-136	14	-0.8
1954 Bos-A	14	23	2	6	2	0	0	1	6	4	0	0	.261	.414	.348	.762	99	0	3	4.54	-1	/1-6	0	-0.1
1955 Bos-A	7	20	6	4	2	0	0	1	1	5	0	0	.200	.238	.300	.538	40	-2	1	1.89	0	/1-5	0	-0.2
1956 Bos-A	106	306	53	89	11	0	16	68	56	57	1	0	.291	.404	.484	.888	119	11	63	7.39	7	0-50(50-0-0),1-37	12	1.3
1957 Bos-A	99	316	45	75	13	3	14	58	39	62	1	1	.237	.327	.430	.757	99	-0	44	4.72	0	1-71,0-16(16-0-0)	7	-0.5
1958 Bos-A	122	431	59	102	19	1	20	69	59	78	2	0	.237	.331	.425	.756	100	1	60	4.61	5	*1-114	11	-0.1
1959 Bos-A	117	298	41	78	14	1	11	42	52	49	1	2	.262	.371	.426	.798	113	6	47	5.40	4	1-75,0-25(21-0-7)	9	0.5
1960 Chi-N	52	96	8	24	3	0	0	11	10	19	1	0	.250	.321	.281	.602	67	-4	8	2.87	3	1-18/0-5(5-0-0)	1	-0.2
Det-A	21	50	6	15	4	0	1	5	4	5	0	0	.300	.352	.440	.792	106	0	8	5.76	-1	1-13/0-6(6-0-0)	1	-0.2
1961 Det-A	6	5	1	1	0	0	1	1	1	2	0	0	.200	.333	.800	1.133	186	1	1	3.83	0	....	0	0.1
*Cin-N	40	63	4	19	1	0	0	7	7	9	0	0	.302	.371	.317	.689	84	-1	8	4.79	3	1-21	2	0.1
1962 Hou-N	10	24	1	5	0	0	0	1	5	7	0	0	.208	.345	.208	.553	57	-1	2	3.09	-1	/1-9	0	-0.2
Total 11	835	2493	357	632	104	8	103	402	363	462	10	11	.254	.352	.426	.778	104	18	382	5.26	9	1-604,0-102	68	-0.9

YEAR TM-L	G	AB	R	H	2B	3B	HR	RBI	BB	SO	SB	CS	AVG	OBP	SLG	OPS	OPS+	BR/A	RC	RC/G	FR	G/POS	WS	TPW
• GERONIMO, Cesar	Cesar Francisco (Zorrilla) Geronimo b: 3/11/1948, El Seibo, Dominican Republic BL/TL, 6', 170 lbs. Deb: 4/16/1969 Career OF: 87-1079-225																							
1969 Hou-N	28	8	8	2	1	0	0	0	0	3	0	0	.250	.250	.375	.625	74	-0	1	3.38	-1	/O-9(4-1-4)	0	-0.2
1970 Hou-N	47	37	5	9	0	0	0	2	2	5	0	0	.243	.300	.243	.543	49	-3	3	2.17	-1	O-26(12-5-10)	0	-0.4
1971 Hou-N	94	82	13	18	2	2	1	6	5	31	2	2	.220	.264	.329	.594	69	-4	7	2.87	-1	O-64(47-3-15)	1	-0.7
1972*Cin-N	120	255	32	70	9	7	4	29	24	64	2	7	.275	.344	.412	.756	121	4	34	4.54	1	*O-106(0-21-91)	9	0.1
1973*Cin-N	139	324	35	68	14	3	4	33	23	74	5	5	.210	.269	.309	.577	63	-18	26	2.61	2	*O-130(0-104-26)	4	-2.0
1974 Cin-N	150	474	73	133	17	8	7	54	46	96	9	5	.281	.347	.395	.741	109	5	65	4.86	6	*O-145(0-145-0)	17	0.7
1975*Cin-N	148	501	69	129	25	5	6	53	48	97	13	5	.257	.327	.363	.691	90	-7	61	4.27	9	*O-148(0-148-0)	16	-0.2
1976*Cin-N	149	486	59	149	24	11	2	49	56	95	22	5	.307	.385	.414	.799	124	20	82	6.27	-6	*O-146(0-146-0)	19	1.1
1977 Cin-N	149	492	54	131	22	4	10	52	35	89	10	4	.266	.321	.388	.710	88	-8	60	4.23	3	*O-147(0-147-0)	11	-0.8
1978 Cin-N	122	296	28	67	15	1	5	27	43	67	8	3	.226	.330	.334	.665	86	-4	35	3.85	-2	*O-115(0-116-0)	8	-0.7
1979*Cin-N	123	356	38	85	17	4	4	38	37	56	1	1	.239	.314	.343	.657	79	-10	38	3.61	3	*O-118(0-118-0)	8	-0.9
1980 Cin-N	103	145	16	37	5	0	2	9	14	24	2	1	.255	.321	.331	.652	82	-3	16	3.75	0	O-86(0-86-0)	4	-0.4
1981*KC-A	59	118	14	29	0	2	2	13	11	16	6	1	.246	.310	.331	.641	85	-1	13	3.51	-2	O-57(5-4-50)	2	-0.5
1982 KC-A	53	119	14	32	6	3	4	23	8	16	2	0	.269	.315	.471	.786	112	2	16	4.56	-0	O-44(10-32-3)/D-1	4	0.1
1983 KC-A	38	87	2	18	4	0	0	4	2	13	0	1	.207	.242	.253	.495	36	-8	5	1.93	0	O-35(9-3-26)	1	-0.9
Total 15	**1522**	**3780**	**460**	**977**	**161**	**50**	**51**	**392**	**354**	**746**	**82**	**40**	**.258**	**.327**	**.368**	**.695**	**93**	**-36**	**462**	**4.19**	**10**	***O-1376/D-1**	**104**	**-5.7**
• GERTENRICH, Lou	Louis Wilhelm Gertenrich b: 5/4/1875, Chicago, IL d: 10/20/1933, Chicago, IL BR/TR, 5'8", 175 lbs. Deb: 9/15/1901 Career OF: 0-0-2																							
1901 Mil-A	2	3	1	1	0	0	0	0	0	....	0	....	.333	.333	.333	.667	90	-0	0	4.53	0	/O-1	0	0.0
1903 Pit-N	1	3	0	0	0	0	0	0	0	....	0	....	.000	.000	.000	.000	-97	-1	0	.00	0	/O-1	0	-0.1
Total 2	**3**	**6**	**1**	**1**	**0**	**0**	**0**	**0**	**0**	**....**	**0**	**....**	**.167**	**.167**	**.167**	**.333**	**-17**	**-1**	**0**	**1.51**	**0**	**/O-2**	**0**	**-0.1**
• GERUT, Jody	Joseph Gerut b: 9/18/1977, Elmhurst, IL BL/TL, 6', 190 lbs. Deb: 4/26/2003																							
2003 Cle-A	127	480	66	134	33	2	22	75	35	70	4	5	.279	.337	.494	.831	119	10	75	5.55	5	*O-113(36-14-63),D-11	14	1.0
• GESSLER, Doc	Harry Homer "Brownie" Gessler b: 12/23/1880, Greensburg, PA d: 12/24/1924, Greensburg, PA BL/TR, 5'10", 180 lbs. Deb: 4/23/1903 M Career OF: 17-94-602																							
1903 Det-A	29	105	9	25	5	4	0	12	3	....	1	....	.238	.273	.362	.635	92	-1	11	3.57	-2	O-28(0-0-28)	2	-0.5
Bro-N	49	154	20	38	8	3	0	18	17	....	9	....	.247	.366	.338	.704	104	2	24	5.12	-5	O-43(0-2-41)	4	-0.5
1904 Bro-N	104	341	41	99	18	4	2	28	30	....	13	....	.290	.355	.384	.739	131	13	53	5.57	0	O-88(14-72-2)/1-1,2-1	11	1.0
1905 Bro-N	126	431	44	125	17	4	3	46	38	....	26	....	.290	.366	.369	.735	129	17	70	5.88	0	*1-107,O-12(1-1-10)	16	1.5
1906 Bro-N	9	33	3	8	1	2	0	4	3	....	3	....	.242	.324	.394	.718	134	1	5	5.53	1	/1-9	2	0.2
*Chi-N	34	83	8	21	3	0	0	10	12	....	4	....	.253	.354	.289	.643	95	0	11	4.25	1	O-21(0-19-2)/1-1	4	0.0
Yr.	43	116	11	29	4	2	0	14	15	....	7	....	.250	.346	.319	.665	106	1	16	4.61	1	O-21(0-19-2),1-10	6	0.2
1908 Bos-A	128	435	55	134	13	14	3	63	51	....	19	....	.308	**.394**	.423	.817	161	32	80	6.66	-4	*O-126(0-0-126)	26	2.5
1909 Bos-A	111	396	57	115	24	1	0	46	31	....	16	....	.290	.354	.356	.710	122	10	55	4.97	-1	*O-109(0-0-109)	16	0.5
Was-A	17	54	10	13	2	1	0	8	12	....	4	....	.241	.406	.315	.721	134	3	9	5.30	0	O-16(0-0-16)/1-1	3	0.3
Yr.	128	450	67	128	26	2	0	54	43	....	20	....	.284	.361	.351	.712	123	14	63	5.01	-2	*O-125(0-0-125)/1-1	19	0.8
1910 Was-A	145	487	58	126	17	12	2	50	62	....	18	....	.259	.361	.355	.716	131	20	69	4.81	-2	*O-144(0-0-144)	17	1.4
1911 Was-A	128	450	65	127	19	5	4	78	74	....	29	....	.282	.406	.373	.780	120	18	80	6.26	-7	*O-126(2-0-124)/1-1	18	0.5
Total 8	**880**	**2969**	**370**	**831**	**127**	**50**	**14**	**363**	**333**	**....**	**142**	**....**	**.280**	**.370**	**.370**	**.741**	**128**	**117**	**466**	**5.52**	**-20**	**O-713,1-120/2-1**	**119**	**6.8**
• GETTIG, Charlie	Charles Henry Gettig b: 12/1870, Baltimore, MD d: 4/11/1935, Baltimore, MD BR, 5'10", 172 lbs. Deb: 8/5/1896 Career OF: 3-1-21 ♦																							
1896 NY-N	6	9	3	3	1	0	0	0	0	0	0	....	.333	.333	.444	.778	107	1	1	6.04	0	/P-4	0	-0.7
1897 NY-N	22	75	8	15	6	0	0	12	6	....	3	....	.200	.277	.280	.557	49	-5	7	3.01	-5	/3-7,2-6,O-3(3-0-0),P-3,S-3	0	-1.1
1898 NY-N	64	196	30	49	6	2	0	26	15	....	5	....	.250	.310	.301	.611	78	-2	20	3.66	-2	O-21(0-1-20),P-17,2-12/S-9,3,1,C	8	-0.8
1899 NY-N	34	97	7	24	3	0	0	9	7	....	4	....	.247	.305	.278	.583	62	-1	10	3.52	-4	P-18/3-8,1-3,2-3,O-1	5	-1.3
Total 4	**126**	**377**	**48**	**91**	**16**	**2**	**0**	**47**	**28**	**0**	**12**	**....**	**.241**	**.302**	**.294**	**.597**	**68**	**-7**	**39**	**3.54**	**-11**	**/P-42,O-25,2-21,3-19,S-12,1,C**	**13**	**-3.9**
• GETTINGER, Tom	Lewis Thomas Leyton Gettinger b: 12/11/1868, Frederick, MD d: 7/26/1943, Pensacola, FL BL/TL, 5'10", 180 lbs. Deb: 9/21/1889 Career OF: 59-37-29																							
1889 StL-a	4	16	2	7	0	0	1	2	2	1	0	....	.438	.500	.625	1.125	194	2	5	15.09	-1	/O-4(1-3-0)	1	0.1
1890 StL-a	58	227	31	54	7	5	3	30	20	....	8	....	.238	.302	.352	.655	81	-8	27	4.18	-5	O-58(58-0-0)	4	-1.3
1895 Lou-N	63	260	28	70	11	5	2	32	8	15	6	....	.269	.296	.373	.669	77	-10	32	4.40	-6	O-63(0-34-29)/P-2	2	-1.7
Total 3	**125**	**503**	**61**	**131**	**18**	**10**	**6**	**64**	**30**	**16**	**14**	**....**	**.260**	**.306**	**.372**	**.678**	**83**	**-15**	**64**	**4.56**	**-12**	**O-125/P-2**	**7**	**-2.9**
• GETTMAN, Jake	Jacob John Gettman b: 10/25/1876, Frank, Russia d: 10/4/1956, Denver, CO BB/TL, 5'11", 185 lbs. Deb: 8/20/1897 Career OF: 12-29-150																							
1897 Was-N	36	143	28	45	7	3	3	29	7	....	8	....	.315	.359	.469	.828	118	3	28	7.42	-1	O-36(0-0-36)	4	0.1
1898 Was-N	142	567	75	157	16	5	5	47	29	....	32	....	.277	.319	.349	.668	92	-8	76	4.82	-3	*O-139(6-19-114)/1-3	9	-1.7
1899 Was-N	19	62	5	13	1	0	0	2	4	....	4	....	.210	.258	.226	.483	33	-6	5	2.58	0	O-16(6-10-0)/1-2	0	-0.6
Total 3	**197**	**772**	**108**	**215**	**24**	**8**	**8**	**78**	**40**	**....**	**44**	**....**	**.278**	**.322**	**.361**	**.683**	**92**	**-11**	**109**	**5.07**	**-3**	**O-191/1-5**	**13**	**-2.2**
• GETZ, Gus	Gustave "Gee-Gee" Getz b: 8/3/1889, Pittsburgh, PA d: 5/28/1969, Red Bank, NJ BR/TR, 5'11", 165 lbs. Deb: 8/15/1909																							
1909 Bos-N	40	148	6	33	2	0	0	9	1	....	2	....	.223	.228	.236	.465	42	-11	8	1.81	1	3-36/2-2,S-2	1	-1.0
1910 Bos-N	54	144	14	28	0	1	0	7	6	10	2	....	.194	.232	.208	.440	27	-14	7	1.60	2	3-22,2-13/O-8(4-1-3),S-4	1	-1.2
1914 Bro-N	55	210	13	52	8	1	0	20	2	15	9	....	.248	.255	.295	.550	62	-11	17	2.71	13	3-55	4	0.4
1915 Bro-N	130	477	39	123	10	5	2	46	8	14	19	15	.258	.275	.312	.587	76	-18	41	2.90	12	*3-128/S-2	13	-0.3
1916*Bro-N	40	96	9	21	1	2	0	8	0	5	9	....	.219	.219	.271	.490	49	-6	8	2.56	0	3-20/S-7,1-3	1	-0.7
1917 Cin-N	7	14	2	4	0	0	0	3	3	0	0	....	.286	.412	.286	.697	121	1	2	4.11	-1	/2-4,3-3	1	-0.1
1918 Cle-A	6	15	2	2	1	0	0	0	4	1	0	....	.133	.350	.200	.550	60	-0	1	1.97	-1	/3-5	0	-0.1
Pit-N	7	10	0	2	0	0	0	0	0	1	0	....	.200	.200	.200	.400	21	-1	0	1.17	0	/3-2	0	-0.1
Total 7	**339**	**1114**	**85**	**265**	**22**	**9**	**2**	**93**	**24**	**46**	**41**	**15**	**.238**	**.257**	**.279**	**.536**	**60**	**-60**	**85**	**2.50**	**25**	**3-271/2-19,S-15,O-8,1-3**	**21**	**-3.0**
• GEYGAN, Chappie	James Edward Geygan b: 6/3/1903, Ironton, OH d: 3/15/1966, Columbus, OH BR/TR, 5'11", 170 lbs. Deb: 7/16/1924																							
1924 Bos-A	33	82	7	21	5	2	0	4	4	16	0	2	.256	.307	.366	.673	73	-4	9	3.47	-2	S-32	1	-0.3
1925 Bos-A	3	11	0	2	0	0	0	0	0	2	0	0	.182	.182	.182	.364	-8	-2	0	1.03	-2	/S-3	0	-0.3
1926 Bos-A	4	10	0	3	0	0	0	0	1	1	0	0	.300	.364	.300	.664	77	-0	1	4.31	-1	/3-3	0	-0.1
Total 3	**40**	**103**	**7**	**26**	**5**	**2**	**0**	**4**	**5**	**19**	**0**	**2**	**.252**	**.300**	**.340**	**.640**	**66**	**-6**	**10**	**3.27**	**-5**	**/S-35,3-3**	**1**	**-0.7**
• GHARRITY, Patsy	Edward Patrick Gharrity b: 3/13/1892, Parnell, IA d: 10/10/1966, Beloit, WI BR/TR, 5'10", 170 lbs. Deb: 5/16/1916 C Career OF: 31-2-2																							
1916 Was-A	39	92	8	21	5	1	0	9	8	18	2	....	.228	.297	.304	.601	81	-2	9	3.28	-3	1-16,C-16	2	-0.5
1917 Was-A	76	176	15	50	5	0	0	18	14	18	7	....	.284	.337	.313	.649	99	-0	20	4.01	-3	1-46/C-5,O-1	5	-0.4
1918 Was-A	4	4	0	1	1	0	0	2	0	1	0	....	.250	.250	.500	.750	129	0	0	3.91	0	....	0	0.0
1919 Was-A	111	347	35	94	19	4	2	43	25	39	4	....	.271	.325	.366	.691	95	-3	42	4.10	1	C-60,O-33(30-2-1)/1-7	9	0.1
1920 Was-A	131	428	51	105	18	3	3	44	37	52	6	5	.245	.307	.322	.629	69	-19	44	3.35	11	*C-121/1-7,O-1	10	0.1
1921 Was-A	121	387	62	120	19	8	7	55	45	44	4	3	.310	.386	.455	.841	119	12	70	6.45	5	*C-115	19	2.3
1922 Was-A	96	273	40	70	16	6	5	45	36	30	3	3	.256	.351	.414	.765	104	2	41	5.09	8	C-87	11	1.4
1923 Was-A	93	251	26	52	9	4	3	33	22	27	6	2	.207	.276	.311	.587	57	-15	23	2.92	0	C-35,1-33	4	-1.5
1929 Was-A	3	2	0	0	0	0	0	0	1	2	0	0	.000	.333	.000	.333	-7	-0	0	1.10	0	....	0	0.0
1930 Was-A	2	1	0	0	0	0	0	0	0	0	0	0	.000	.000	.000	.000	-100	-0	0	.00	0	/1-1	0	0.0
Total 10	**676**	**1961**	**237**	**513**	**92**	**26**	**20**	**249**	**188**	**231**	**32**	**13**	**.262**	**.331**	**.366**	**.696**	**90**	**-26**	**250**	**4.30**	**19**	**C-439,1-110/O-35**	**60**	**1.5**
• GIAMBI, Jason	Jason Gilbert Giambi b: 1/8/1971, West Covina, CA BL/TR, 6'2", 200 lbs. Deb: 5/8/1995 Career OF: 112-0-1																							
1995 Oak-A	54	176	27	45	7	0	6	25	28	31	2	1	.256	.367	.398	.765	105	2	27	5.30	-5	3-30,1-26/D-2	5	-0.4
1996 Oak-A	140	536	84	156	40	1	20	79	51	95	0	1	.291	.358	.481	.839	113	9	90	6.05	6	1-45,O-45(44-0-1),3-39,D-12	15	0.9
1997 Oak-A	142	519	66	152	41	2	20	81	55	89	0	1	.293	.367	.495	.862	125	19	94	6.59	1	O-68(68-0-0),1-51,D-25	18	1.1
1998 Oak-A	153	562	92	166	28	0	27	110	81	102	2	2	.295	.389	.489	.878	130	26	107	6.85	-3	*1-146/D-7	23	1.0
1999 Oak-A	158	575	115	181	36	1	33	123	105	106	1	1	.315	.426	.553	.980	154	51	142	9.24	-8	*1-142,D-15/3-1	30	2.8
2000*Oak-A★	152	510	108	170	29	1	43	137	**137**	96	2	0	.333	**.482**	.647	1.129	**187**	**78**	172	12.99	-3	*1-124,D-24	**38**	5.7
2001*Oak-A★	154	520	109	178	**47**	2	38	120	**129**	83	2	0	.342	**.483**	**.660**	**1.143**	**197**	**83**	171	**12.57**	0	*1-136,D-17	**38**	6.7

YEAR TM-L	G	AB	R	H	2B	3B	HR	RBI	BB	SO	SB	CS	AVG	OBP	SLG	OPS	OPS+	BR/A	RC	RC/G	FR	G/POS	WS	TPW
2002*NY-A★	155	560	120	176	34	1	41	122	109	112	2	2	.314	.439	.598	1.037	173	65	150	9.92	-2	1-92,D-63	34	4.9
2003*NY-A★	156	535	97	134	25	0	41	107	**129**	140	2	1	.250	.415	.527	.942	149	45	128	8.31	-9	1-85,D-69	28	2.4
Total 9	**1264**	**4493**	**818**	**1358**	**287**	**8**	**269**	**904**	**824**	**854**	**13**	**9**	**.302**	**.420**	**.549**	**.969**	**153**	**377**	**1082**	**8.81**	**-21**	1-847,D-234,0-113/3-70	**229**	**25.1**
• GIAMBI, Jeremy	Jeremy Dean Giambi b: 9/30/1974, San Jose, CA BL/TL, 6', 200 lbs. Deb: 9/1/1998 Career OF: 82-0-106																							
1998 KC-A	18	58	6	13	4	0	2	8	11	9	0	1	.224	.348	.397	.744	91	-1	8	4.07	0	/0-9(9-0-0),D-7	0	-0.2
1999 KC-A	90	288	34	82	13	1	3	34	40	67	0	0	.285	.378	.368	.746	89	-3	42	5.15	-4	D-52,1-26/0-5(5-0-0)	4	-1.1
2000*Oak-A	104	260	42	66	10	2	10	50	32	61	0	0	.254	.342	.423	.765	95	-2	38	4.94	-1	0-55(6-0-49),D-21,1-15	6	-0.7
2001*Oak-A	124	371	64	105	26	0	12	57	63	83	0	1	.283	.393	.450	.843	121	13	67	6.31	-7	D-61,0-47(11-0-37),1-10	12	0.0
2002 Oak-A	42	157	26	43	7	0	8	17	27	40	0	0	.274	.390	.471	.862	127	7	30	6.91	-3	0-40(40-0-0)/D-2	5	0.3
Phi-N	82	156	32	38	10	0	12	28	52	54	0	1	.244	.435	.538	.974	162	17	41	9.25	-3	1-21,0-20(2-0-18)/D-8	9	1.1
2003 Bos-A	50	127	15	25	5	0	5	15	26	42	1	0	.197	.342	.354	.696	82	-2	17	4.35	0	D-29,0-11(9-0-2)	1	-0.4
Total 6	**510**	**1417**	**219**	**372**	**75**	**3**	**52**	**209**	**251**	**356**	**1**	**3**	**.263**	**.379**	**.430**	**.809**	**111**	**29**	**243**	**5.92**	**-19**	0-187,D-180/1-72	**37**	**-1.0**
• GIANNELLI, Ray	Raymond John Giannelli b: 2/5/1966, Brooklyn, NY BL/TR, 6', 195 lbs. Deb: 5/4/1991																							
1991 Tor-A	9	24	2	4	1	0	0	0	5	9	1	0	.167	.310	.208	.519	45	-1	2	2.86	1	/3-9	0	0.0
1995 StL-N	9	11	0	1	0	0	0	0	3	4	0	0	.091	.286	.091	.377	5	-1	1	1.37	0	/1-2,0-2(1-0-1)	0	-0.2
Total 2	**18**	**35**	**2**	**5**	**1**	**0**	**0**	**0**	**8**	**13**	**1**	**0**	**.143**	**.302**	**.171**	**.474**	**32**	**-3**	**3**	**2.36**	**1**	/3-9,1-2,0-2	**0**	**-0.2**
• GIANNINI, Joe	Joseph Francis Giannini b: 9/8/1888, San Francisco, CA d: 9/26/1942, San Francisco, CA BL/TR, 5'8", 155 lbs. Deb: 8/7/1911																							
1911 Bos-A	1	2	0	1	1	0	0	0	0	....	0	....	.500	.500	1.000	1.500	318	1	1	25.58	-1	/S-1	0	0.0
• GIBBONS, Jay	Jay Jonathan Gibbons b: 3/2/1977, Rochester, MI BL/TL, 6', 200 lbs. Deb: 4/6/2001 Career OF: 28-0-236																							
2001 Bal-A	73	225	27	53	10	0	15	36	17	39	0	1	.236	.301	.480	.781	107	1	30	4.57	2	D-28,0-28(28-0-0)/1-7	4	-0.1
2002 Bal-A	136	490	71	121	29	1	28	69	45	66	1	3	.247	.313	.482	.794	112	6	72	5.06	1	0-92(0-0-92),1-30,D-12	12	-0.2
2003 Bal-A	160	625	80	173	39	2	23	100	49	89	0	1	.277	.332	.456	.788	109	6	93	5.33	-2	*0-144(0-0-144),1-13/D-5	18	-0.5
Total 3	**369**	**1340**	**178**	**347**	**78**	**3**	**66**	**205**	**111**	**194**	**1**	**5**	**.259**	**.320**	**.469**	**.789**	**110**	**13**	**195**	**5.09**	**0**	0-264/1-50,D-45	**34**	**-0.8**
• GIBBONS, John	John Michael Gibbons b: 6/8/1962, Great Falls, MT BR/TR, 5'11", 187 lbs. Deb: 4/11/1984																							
1984 NY-N	10	31	1	2	0	0	0	1	3	11	0	0	.065	.171	.065	.236	-32	-5	0	.44	0	/C-9	0	-0.5
1986 NY-N	8	19	4	9	4	0	1	1	3	5	0	0	.474	.545	.842	1.388	285	5	8	20.27	0	/C-8	3	0.5
Total 2	**18**	**50**	**5**	**11**	**4**	**0**	**1**	**2**	**6**	**16**	**0**	**0**	**.220**	**.316**	**.360**	**.676**	**91**	**-1**	**9**	**5.90**	**0**	/C-17	**3**	**0.0**
• GIBBS, Jake	Jerry Dean Gibbs b: 11/7/1938, Grenada, MS BL/TR, 6', 185 lbs. Deb: 9/11/1962																							
1962 NY-A	2	0	2	0	0	0	0	0	0	0	0	0	....	....	....	....	-103	0	0	....	0	/3-1	0	0.0
1963 NY-A	4	8	1	2	0	0	0	0	0	1	0	0	.250	.250	.250	.500	41	-1	1	2.25	0	/C-1	0	-0.1
1964 NY-A	3	6	1	1	0	0	0	0	0	2	0	0	.167	.167	.167	.333	-7	-1	0	.90	0	/C-2	0	-0.1
1965 NY-A	37	68	6	15	1	0	2	7	4	20	0	0	.221	.274	.324	.598	70	-3	7	3.15	1	C-21	1	-0.2
1966 NY-A	62	182	19	47	6	0	3	20	19	16	5	2	.258	.328	.341	.669	96	-0	20	3.74	1	C-54	5	0.4
1967 NY-A	116	374	33	87	7	1	4	25	28	57	7	6	.233	.293	.289	.582	75	-12	31	2.76	1	C-99	7	-0.7
1968 NY-A	124	423	31	90	12	3	3	29	27	68	9	8	.213	.270	.277	.546	68	-18	30	2.33	1	*C-121	9	-1.3
1969 NY-A	71	219	18	49	9	2	0	18	23	30	3	4	.224	.298	.283	.581	65	-11	18	2.74	0	C-66	5	-0.8
1970 NY-A	49	153	23	46	9	2	8	26	7	14	2	0	.301	.335	.542	.878	146	9	27	6.37	0	C-44	9	1.1
1971 NY-A	70	206	23	45	9	0	5	21	12	23	2	2	.218	.271	.335	.606	76	-8	18	2.95	-3	C-51	4	-0.9
Total 10	**538**	**1639**	**157**	**382**	**53**	**8**	**25**	**146**	**120**	**231**	**28**	**22**	**.233**	**.291**	**.321**	**.612**	**80**	**-45**	**152**	**3.09**	**-1**	C-459/3-1	**40**	**-2.6**
• GIBRALTER, Steve	Stephan Benson Gibralter b: 10/9/1972, Dallas, TX BR/TR, 6', 185 lbs. Deb: 6/1/1995 Career OF: 1-3-0																							
1995 Cin-N	4	3	0	1	0	0	0	0	0	0	0	0	.333	.333	.333	.667	77	-0	0	4.50	0	/0-2(0-2-0)	0	0.0
1996 Cin-N	2	2	0	0	0	0	0	0	0	2	0	0	.000	.000	.000	.000	-101	-1	0	.00	-1	/0-2(1-1-0)	0	-0.1
Total 2	**6**	**5**	**0**	**1**	**0**	**0**	**0**	**0**	**0**	**2**	**0**	**0**	**.200**	**.200**	**.200**	**.400**	**6**	**-1**	**0**	**2.25**	**-1**	/0-4	**0**	**-0.1**
• GIBSON, Charlie	Charles Ellsworth "Gibby" Gibson b: 11/17/1879, Sharon, PA d: 11/22/1954, Sharon, PA BR/TR, 6', 160 lbs. Deb: 9/23/1905																							
1905 StL-A	1	3	0	0	0	0	0	0	0	....	0	....	.000	.000	.000	.000	-106	-1	0	.00	0	/C-1	0	-0.1
• GIBSON, Charlie	Charles Griffin Gibson b: 11/21/1899, LaGrange, GA d: 12/18/1990, LaGrange, GA BR/TR, 5'8", 160 lbs. Deb: 5/30/1924																							
1924 Phi-A	12	15	1	2	0	0	0	1	2	0	0	0	.133	.235	.133	.369	-3	-2	1	1.16	-1	C-12	0	-0.3
• GIBSON, Derrick	Derrick Lamont Gibson b: 2/5/1975, Winter Haven, FL BR/TR, 6'2", 244 lbs. Deb: 9/8/1998 Career OF: 7-0-10																							
1998 Col-N	7	21	4	9	1	0	0	2	1	4	0	0	.429	.478	.476	.954	125	1	5	11.32	1	/0-7(7-0-0)	1	0.2
1999 Col-N	10	28	2	5	1	0	2	6	0	7	0	0	.179	.207	.429	.635	43	-3	2	1.83	1	0-10(0-0-10)	1	-0.2
Total 2	**17**	**49**	**6**	**14**	**2**	**0**	**2**	**8**	**1**	**11**	**0**	**0**	**.286**	**.327**	**.449**	**.776**	**79**	**-2**	**7**	**4.91**	**2**	/0-17	**2**	**-0.1**
• GIBSON, Frank	Frank Gilbert Gibson b: 9/27/1890, Omaha, NE d: 4/27/1961, Austin, TX BB/TR, 6'.5", 172 lbs. Deb: 4/22/1913																							
1913 Det-A	23	57	8	8	1	0	0	2	3	9	2	....	.140	.197	.158	.355	4	-7	2	1.03	-3	C-19/0-2(0-0-1)	0	-1.0
1921 Bos-N	63	125	14	33	5	4	2	13	3	17	0	0	.264	.292	.416	.708	90	-2	15	4.20	1	C-41	4	0.2
1922 Bos-N	66	164	15	49	7	2	3	20	10	27	4	1	.299	.339	.421	.760	99	0	24	5.19	1	C-29,1-20	5	0.2
1923 Bos-N	41	50	13	15	1	0	0	5	7	7	0	2	.300	.386	.320	.706	92	-1	6	4.30	-1	C-20	1	-0.1
1924 Bos-N	90	229	25	71	15	6	1	30	10	23	1	1	.310	.342	.441	.783	113	4	34	5.60	2	C-46,1-10/3-2	9	0.9
1925 Bos-N	104	316	36	88	23	5	2	50	15	28	3	3	.278	.313	.402	.715	89	-6	39	4.31	0	C-86/1-2	7	-0.1
1926 Bos-N	24	47	3	16	4	0	0	7	4	6	0	....	.340	.392	.426	.818	132	2	8	6.25	2	C-13	3	0.4
1927 Bos-N	60	167	7	37	1	2	0	19	3	10	2	....	.222	.235	.251	.487	33	-16	9	1.86	-4	C-47	2	-1.7
Total 8	**471**	**1155**	**121**	**317**	**57**	**19**	**8**	**146**	**55**	**127**	**12**	**7**	**.274**	**.310**	**.377**	**.688**	**85**	**-25**	**137**	**4.17**	**-2**	C-301/1-32,3-2,0-2	**31**	**-1.2**
• GIBSON, George	George C. "Moon" Gibson b: 7/22/1880, London, Canada d: 1/25/1967, London, Canada BR/TR, 5'11.5", 190 lbs. Deb: 7/2/1905 M/C																							
1905 Pit-N	46	135	14	24	2	2	2	14	15	....	2	....	.178	.270	.267	.536	58	-7	11	2.49	-3	C-44	3	-0.6
1906 Pit-N	81	259	8	46	6	1	0	20	16	....	1	....	.178	.225	.208	.434	34	-20	14	1.60	-5	C-81	3	-2.0
1907 Pit-N	113	382	28	84	8	7	3	35	18	....	2	....	.220	.261	.301	.562	75	-13	32	2.73	-7	*C-109/1-1	8	-1.0
1908 Pit-N	143	486	37	111	19	4	2	45	19	....	4	....	.228	.260	.296	.557	78	-14	38	2.54	-13	*C-140	12	-1.5
1909*Pit-N	150	510	42	135	25	9	2	52	44	....	9	....	.265	.326	.361	.686	108	4	63	4.17	-3	*C-150	24	1.7
1910 Pit-N	143	482	53	125	22	6	3	44	47	31	7	....	.259	.333	.349	.681	93	-5	58	4.09	-1	*C-143	18	1.0
1911 Pit-N	100	311	32	65	12	2	0	19	29	16	3	....	.209	.281	.260	.541	50	-21	23	2.41	-2	C-98	6	-1.6
1912 Pit-N	95	300	23	72	14	3	2	35	20	16	0	....	.240	.290	.327	.616	69	-14	28	3.04	-9	C-94	8	-1.4
1913 Pit-N	48	118	6	33	4	2	0	12	10	8	2	....	.280	.341	.347	.689	101	0	15	4.13	0	C-48	5	0.3
1914 Pit-N	102	274	19	78	9	5	0	30	27	27	4	....	.285	.359	.354	.713	117	7	36	4.55	0	*C-101	12	1.4
1915 Pit-N	120	351	28	88	15	6	1	30	31	25	5	2	.251	.313	.336	.649	98	-1	40	3.79	-3	*C-118	11	0.7
1916 Pit-N	33	84	4	17	2	2	0	4	3	7	0	....	.202	.239	.274	.512	57	-4	6	2.19	1	C-29	2	-0.1
1917 NY-N	35	82	1	14	3	0	0	5	7	2	1	....	.171	.236	.207	.443	38	-6	4	1.54	-2	C-35	1	-0.6
1918 NY-N	4	2	0	1	1	0	0	0	0	0	0	....	.500	.500	1.000	1.500	360	1	1	24.96	-1	/C-4	0	0.0
Total 14	**1213**	**3776**	**295**	**893**	**142**	**49**	**15**	**345**	**286**	**132**	**40**	**2**	**.236**	**.295**	**.312**	**.607**	**81**	**-93**	**368**	**3.20**	**-49**	*C-1194/1-1	**113**	**-3.7**
• GIBSON, Kirk	Kirk Harold Gibson b: 5/28/1957, Pontiac, MI BL/TL, 6'3", 215 lbs. Deb: 9/8/1979 Career OF: 477-325-456																							
1979 Det-A	12	38	3	9	3	0	1	4	1	3	3	3	.237	.256	.395	.651	70	-2	3	2.55	0	0-10(7-1-2)	0	-0.3
1980 Det-A	51	175	23	46	2	1	9	16	10	45	4	7	.263	.306	.440	.746	100	-3	22	4.29	-3	0-49(0-49-0)/D-1	4	-0.6
1981 Det-A	83	290	41	95	11	3	9	40	18	64	17	5	.328	.371	.479	.850	138	15	50	6.34	-4	0-67(8-26-37)/D-9	13	0.9
1982 Det-A	69	266	34	74	16	2	8	35	25	41	9	7	.278	.342	.444	.786	114	4	40	5.35	2	0-64(0-64-0)/D-4	9	0.5
1983 Det-A	128	401	60	91	12	9	15	51	53	96	14	3	.227	.323	.414	.737	104	4	59	4.90	-1	D-66,0-54(29-22-4)	11	0.0
1984*Det-A	149	531	92	150	23	10	27	91	63	103	29	9	.282	.367	.516	.883	142	33	106	7.09	-13	*0-139(0-1-140)/D-6	26	1.4
1985 Det-A	154	581	96	167	37	5	29	97	71	137	30	4	.287	.370	.518	.888	141	38	118	7.33	-10	*0-144(0-20-127)/D-8	24	2.1
1986 Det-A	119	441	84	118	11	2	28	86	68	107	34	6	.268	.374	.492	.866	134	27	88	6.94	-6	*0-114(0-1-114)/D-4	20	1.6
1987*Det-A	128	487	95	135	25	3	24	79	71	117	26	7	.277	.375	.489	.863	132	27	95	6.97	1	*0-121(119-2-0)/D-4	20	2.1
1988*LA-N	150	542	106	157	28	1	25	76	73	120	31	4	.290	.381	.483	.864	151	42	107	7.10	4	*0-148(148-1-0)	31	4.4

YEAR TM-L	G	AB	R	H	2B	3B	HR	RBI	BB	SO	SB	CS	AVG	OBP	SLG	OPS	OPS+	BR/A	RC	RC/G	FR	G/POS	WS	TPW
1989 LA-N	71	253	35	54	8	2	9	28	35	55	12	3	.213	.314	.368	.681	96	0	31	3.99	0	O-70(62-15-0)	5	-0.2
1990 LA-N	89	315	59	82	20	0	8	38	39	65	26	2	.260	.347	.400	.747	108	9	50	5.58	2	O-81(11-70-0)	14	1.0
1991 KC-A	132	462	81	109	17	6	16	55	69	103	18	4	.236	.343	.403	.745	105	7	68	5.00	-5	O-94(91-0-3),D-30	12	-0.2
1992 Pit-N	16	56	6	11	0	0	2	5	3	12	3	1	.196	.237	.304	.541	53	-3	4	2.23	0	O-13(0-0-13)	0	-0.4
1993 Det-A	116	403	62	105	18	6	13	62	44	87	15	6	.261	.339	.432	.771	106	4	62	5.44	0	D-76,O-32(2-30-0)	9	-0.1
1994 Det-A	98	330	71	91	17	2	23	72	42	69	4	5	.276	.363	.548	.911	130	13	67	7.12	-1	D-56,O-38(0-23-15)	14	0.7
1995 Det-A	70	227	37	59	12	2	9	35	33	61	9	2	.260	.361	.449	.811	110	5	38	5.79	0	D-63/O-1	6	0.1
Total 17	**1635**	**5798**	**985**	**1553**	**260**	**54**	**255**	**870**	**718**	**1285**	**284**	**78**	**.268**	**.355**	**.463**	**.818**	**124**	**219**	**1008**	**6.08**	**-33**	***O-1239,D-327**	**218**	**12.8**

• GIBSON, Russ John Russell Gibson b: 5/6/1939, Fall River, MA BR/TR, 6'1", 195 lbs. Deb: 4/14/1967

YEAR TM-L	G	AB	R	H	2B	3B	HR	RBI	BB	SO	SB	CS	AVG	OBP	SLG	OPS	OPS+	BR/A	RC	RC/G	FR	G/POS	WS	TPW
1967*Bos-A	49	138	8	28	7	0	1	15	12	31	0	0	.203	.267	.275	.542	56	-7	9	2.03	0	C-48	2	-0.6
1968 Bos-A	76	231	15	52	11	1	3	20	8	38	1	2	.225	.251	.320	.571	68	-10	17	2.41	-4	C-74/1-1	3	-1.2
1969 Bos-A	85	287	21	72	9	1	3	27	15	25	1	1	.251	.290	.321	.611	67	-13	24	2.85	-5	C-83	3	-1.5
1970 SF-N	24	69	3	16	6	0	0	6	7	12	0	0	.232	.303	.319	.621	67	-3	6	2.79	-2	C-23	1	-0.4
1971 SF-N	25	57	2	11	1	1	1	7	2	13	0	0	.193	.220	.298	.519	46	-4	3	1.84	-2	C-22	0	-0.6
1972 SF-N	5	12	0	2	0	1	0	3	0	4	0	0	.167	.167	.333	.500	38	-1	0	.00	0	/C-5	0	-0.1
Total 6	**264**	**794**	**49**	**181**	**34**	**4**	**8**	**78**	**44**	**123**	**2**	**3**	**.228**	**.269**	**.311**	**.580**	**63**	**-39**	**60**	**2.44**	**-13**	**C-255/1-1**	**9**	**-4.4**

• GIBSON, Whitey Leighton P. Gibson b: 10/6/1868, Lancaster, PA d: 10/12/1907, Talmadge, PA TR, 5'9", 178 lbs. Deb: 5/2/1888

YEAR TM-L	G	AB	R	H	2B	3B	HR	RBI	BB	SO	SB	CS	AVG	OBP	SLG	OPS	OPS+	BR/A	RC	RC/G	FR	G/POS	WS	TPW
1888 Phi-a	1	3	0	0	0	0	0	0	0	....	0	....	.000	.000	.000	.000	-101	-1	0	.00	1	/C-1	0	0.1

• GIEBEL, Joe Joseph Henry Giebel b: 11/30/1891, Washington, DC d: 3/17/1981, Silver Spring, MD BR/TR, 5'10.5", 175 lbs. Deb: 9/30/1913

YEAR TM-L	G	AB	R	H	2B	3B	HR	RBI	BB	SO	SB	CS	AVG	OBP	SLG	OPS	OPS+	BR/A	RC	RC/G	FR	G/POS	WS	TPW
1913 Phi-A	1	3	0	1	0	0	0	0	0	1	0	....	.333	.333	.333	.667	97	-0	0	4.00	0	/C-1	0	0.0

• GIGON, Norm Norman Phillip Gigon b: 5/12/1938, Teaneck, NJ BR/TR, 6', 195 lbs. Deb: 4/12/1967

YEAR TM-L	G	AB	R	H	2B	3B	HR	RBI	BB	SO	SB	CS	AVG	OBP	SLG	OPS	OPS+	BR/A	RC	RC/G	FR	G/POS	WS	TPW
1967 Chi-N	34	70	8	12	3	1	1	6	4	14	0	0	.171	.237	.286	.523	47	-5	5	2.03	1	2-12/O-4(0-0-4),3-1	0	-0.3

• GIL, Benji Romar Benjamin (Aguilar) Gil b: 10/6/1972, Tijuana, Mexico BR/TR, 6'2", 180 lbs. Deb: 4/5/1993

YEAR TM-L	G	AB	R	H	2B	3B	HR	RBI	BB	SO	SB	CS	AVG	OBP	SLG	OPS	OPS+	BR/A	RC	RC/G	FR	G/POS	WS	TPW
1993 Tex-A	22	57	3	7	0	0	0	2	5	22	1	2	.123	.194	.123	.316	-14	-10	2	.80	0	S-22	1	-0.8
1995 Tex-A	130	415	36	91	20	3	9	46	26	147	2	4	.219	.267	.347	.614	57	-29	38	2.97	7	*S-130	8	-1.1
1996 Tex-A	5	5	0	2	0	0	0	1	1	1	0	1	.400	.500	.400	.900	125	-0	1	4.29	-1	/S-5	0	-0.1
1997 Tex-A	110	317	35	71	13	2	5	31	17	96	1	2	.224	.266	.325	.591	50	-25	28	2.86	1	*S-106/D-4	4	-1.4
2000 Ana-A	110	301	28	72	14	1	6	23	30	59	10	6	.239	.318	.352	.671	68	-15	34	3.68	5	S-94/2-7,D-6,1-3	4	-0.4
2001 Ana-A	104	260	33	77	15	4	8	39	14	57	3	4	.296	.332	.477	.809	107	1	38	5.24	5	S-44,2-21,1-18,D-14/O-1	6	0.8
2002*Ana-A	61	130	11	37	8	1	3	20	5	33	2	1	.285	.311	.431	.742	95	-1	18	4.91	6	2-26,S-14,1-10/D-8	5	0.6
2003 Ana-A	62	125	12	24	5	1	1	9	4	33	5	1	.192	.217	.272	.489	29	-12	7	1.58	4	2-28,S-20/1-5,3-4,D-2	1	-0.6
Total 8	**604**	**1610**	**158**	**381**	**75**	**12**	**32**	**171**	**102**	**448**	**24**	**21**	**.237**	**.285**	**.358**	**.643**	**64**	**-92**	**165**	**3.36**	**28**	**S-435/2-82,1-36,D-34,3-4,O**	**29**	**-2.9**

• GIL, Geronimo Geronimo Gil b: 8/7/1975, Oaxaca, Mexico BR/TR, 6'2", 195 lbs. Deb: 9/8/2001

YEAR TM-L	G	AB	R	H	2B	3B	HR	RBI	BB	SO	SB	CS	AVG	OBP	SLG	OPS	OPS+	BR/A	RC	RC/G	FR	G/POS	WS	TPW
2001 Bal-A	17	58	3	17	2	0	0	6	5	7	0	0	.293	.369	.328	.697	91	-1	7	4.67	4	C-17	2	0.4
2002 Bal-A	125	422	33	98	19	0	12	45	21	88	2	2	.232	.270	.363	.633	70	-20	36	2.82	3	*C-125	6	-0.8
2003 Bal-A	54	169	22	40	4	0	3	16	12	34	0	0	.237	.299	.314	.613	64	-9	17	3.35	8	C-53	3	0.3
Total 3	**196**	**649**	**58**	**155**	**25**	**0**	**15**	**67**	**38**	**129**	**2**	**2**	**.239**	**.287**	**.347**	**.634**	**70**	**-29**	**60**	**3.11**	**15**	**C-195**	**11**	**-0.1**

• GIL, Gus Tomas Gustavo (Guillen) Gil b: 4/19/1939, Caracas, Venezuela BR/TR, 5'10", 180 lbs. Deb: 4/11/1967

YEAR TM-L	G	AB	R	H	2B	3B	HR	RBI	BB	SO	SB	CS	AVG	OBP	SLG	OPS	OPS+	BR/A	RC	RC/G	FR	G/POS	WS	TPW
1967 Cle-A	51	96	11	11	4	0	0	5	9	18	0	0	.115	.198	.156	.354	6	-11	3	.99	0	2-49/1-1	2	-1.0
1969 Sea-A	92	221	20	49	7	0	0	17	16	28	2	0	.222	.274	.253	.528	49	-15	16	2.35	-1	3-38,2-18,S-12	2	-1.5
1970 Mil-A	64	119	12	22	4	0	1	12	21	12	2	0	.185	.307	.244	.551	53	-6	10	2.62	-2	2-38,3-14	2	-0.7
1971 Mil-A	14	32	3	5	1	0	0	3	10	5	1	0	.156	.357	.188	.545	59	-1	3	3.14	-1	/2-8,3-6	1	-0.1
Total 4	**221**	**468**	**46**	**87**	**16**	**0**	**1**	**37**	**56**	**63**	**5**	**0**	**.186**	**.274**	**.226**	**.501**	**42**	**-33**	**33**	**2.18**	**-4**	**2-113/3-58,S-12,1-1**	**7**	**-3.2**

• GILBERT, Andy Andrew Gilbert b: 7/18/1914, Bradenville, PA d: 8/29/1992, Davis, CA BR/TR, 6', 203 lbs. Deb: 9/14/1942 C Career OF: 0-6-0

YEAR TM-L	G	AB	R	H	2B	3B	HR	RBI	BB	SO	SB	CS	AVG	OBP	SLG	OPS	OPS+	BR/A	RC	RC/G	FR	G/POS	WS	TPW
1942 Bos-A	6	11	0	1	0	0	0	1	1	3	0	0	.091	.167	.091	.258	-26	-2	0	.75	0	/O-5(0-5-0)	0	-0.2
1946 Bos-A	2	1	1	0	0	0	0	0	0	0	0	0	.000	.000	.000	.000	-95	-0	0	.00	0	/O-1	0	0.0
Total 2	**8**	**12**	**1**	**1**	**0**	**0**	**0**	**1**	**1**	**3**	**0**	**0**	**.083**	**.154**	**.083**	**.237**	**-30**	**-2**	**0**	**.69**	**0**	**/O-6**	**0**	**-0.2**

• GILBERT, Billy William Oliver Gilbert b: 6/21/1876, Tullytown, PA d: 8/8/1927, New York, NY BR/TR, 5'4", 153 lbs. Deb: 4/25/1901

YEAR TM-L	G	AB	R	H	2B	3B	HR	RBI	BB	SO	SB	CS	AVG	OBP	SLG	OPS	OPS+	BR/A	RC	RC/G	FR	G/POS	WS	TPW
1901 Mil-A	127	492	77	133	14	7	0	43	31	....	19	....	.270	.320	.327	.647	84	-10	61	4.32	-9	*2-127	9	-1.6
1902 Bal-A	129	445	74	109	12	3	2	38	45	....	38	....	.245	.327	.299	.626	71	-16	60	4.45	-6	*S-129	11	-1.7
1903 NY-N	128	413	62	104	9	0	1	40	41	....	37	....	.252	.348	.281	.629	77	-10	58	4.60	19	*2-128	13	1.0
1904 NY-N	146	478	57	121	13	3	1	54	46	....	33	....	.253	.340	.299	.639	94	-1	64	4.43	-2	*2-146	19	-0.1
1905*NY-N	115	376	45	93	11	3	0	24	41	....	11	....	.247	.331	.293	.624	84	-6	43	3.77	10	*2-115	13	0.6
1906 NY-N	104	307	44	71	6	1	1	27	42	....	22	....	.231	.341	.267	.608	88	-2	38	3.99	6	2-98	12	0.5
1908 StL-N	89	276	12	59	7	0	0	10	20	....	6	....	.214	.274	.239	.513	67	-10	20	2.30	-5	2-89	4	-1.6
1909 StL-N	12	29	4	5	0	0	0	1	4	....	1	....	.172	.333	.172	.506	61	-1	2	2.11	-2	2-12	1	-0.3
Total 8	**850**	**2816**	**375**	**695**	**72**	**17**	**5**	**237**	**270**	**....**	**167**	**....**	**.247**	**.328**	**.290**	**.618**	**81**	**-54**	**346**	**4.06**	**11**	**2-715,S-129**	**82**	**-3.2**

• GILBERT, Buddy Drew Edward Gilbert b: 7/26/1935, Knoxville, TN BL/TR, 6'3", 195 lbs. Deb: 9/9/1959

YEAR TM-L	G	AB	R	H	2B	3B	HR	RBI	BB	SO	SB	CS	AVG	OBP	SLG	OPS	OPS+	BR/A	RC	RC/G	FR	G/POS	WS	TPW
1959 Cin-N	7	20	4	3	0	0	2	2	3	4	0	0	.150	.261	.450	.711	82	-1	3	4.05	0	/O-6(0-0-6)	1	-0.1

• GILBERT, Charlie Charles Mader Gilbert b: 7/8/1919, New Orleans, LA d: 8/13/1983, New Orleans, LA BL/TL, 5'9", 165 lbs. Deb: 4/16/1940 Career OF: 32-136-59

YEAR TM-L	G	AB	R	H	2B	3B	HR	RBI	BB	SO	SB	CS	AVG	OBP	SLG	OPS	OPS+	BR/A	RC	RC/G	FR	G/POS	WS	TPW
1940 Bro-N	57	142	23	35	9	1	2	8	8	13	0	....	.246	.287	.366	.653	74	-5	16	3.89	-2	O-43(0-43-0)	3	-0.8
1941 Chi-N	39	86	11	24	2	1	0	12	11	6	1	....	.279	.361	.326	.686	98	0	11	4.35	-1	O-22(0-21-1)	2	-0.2
1942 Chi-N	74	179	18	33	6	3	0	7	25	24	1	....	.184	.284	.251	.536	60	-9	14	2.57	1	O-47(3-44-0)	1	-0.9
1943 Chi-N	8	20	1	3	0	0	0	0	3	3	1	....	.150	.261	.150	.411	20	-2	1	1.57	0	/O-6(3-3-0)	0	-0.2
1946 Chi-N	15	13	2	1	0	0	0	1	1	4	0	....	.077	.143	.077	.220	-38	-2	0	.19	1	/O-2(0-2-0)	0	-0.2
Phi-N	88	260	34	63	5	2	1	17	25	18	3	....	.242	.314	.288	.602	73	-9	26	3.37	3	O-69(8-16-46)	5	-0.9
Yr.	103	273	36	64	5	2	1	18	26	22	3	....	.234	.306	.278	.584	68	-11	26	3.18	3	O-71(8-18-46)	5	-1.1
1947 Phi-N	83	152	20	36	5	2	2	10	13	14	1	....	.237	.301	.336	.637	71	-6	15	3.31	1	O-37(18-7-12)	2	-0.7
Total 6	**364**	**852**	**109**	**195**	**27**	**9**	**5**	**55**	**86**	**82**	**7**	**....**	**.229**	**.302**	**.299**	**.601**	**70**	**-33**	**82**	**3.25**	**3**	**O-226**	**13**	**-3.9**

• GILBERT, Harry Harry H. Gilbert b: 7/8/1868, Pottstown, PA d: 12/23/1909, Pottstown, PA Deb: 6/23/1890

YEAR TM-L	G	AB	R	H	2B	3B	HR	RBI	BB	SO	SB	CS	AVG	OBP	SLG	OPS	OPS+	BR/A	RC	RC/G	FR	G/POS	WS	TPW
1890 Pit-N	2	8	1	2	0	0	0	0	0	3	0	....	.250	.250	.250	.500	52	-0	1	2.26	1	/2-2	0	0.0

• GILBERT, Jack John Robert "Jackrabbit" Gilbert b: 9/4/1875, Rhinecliff, NY d: 7/7/1941, Albany, NY Deb: 9/11/1898 Career OF: 25-1-2

YEAR TM-L	G	AB	R	H	2B	3B	HR	RBI	BB	SO	SB	CS	AVG	OBP	SLG	OPS	OPS+	BR/A	RC	RC/G	FR	G/POS	WS	TPW
1898 Was-N	2	5	0	1	0	0	0	1	1	....	1	....	.200	.429	.200	.629	82	0	1	5.57	0	/O-2(0-1-1)	0	0.0
NY-N	1	4	0	1	0	0	0	0	0	....	1	....	.250	.250	.250	.500	45	-0	1	4.53	0	/O-1	0	-0.1
Yr.	3	9	0	2	0	0	0	1	1	....	2	....	.222	.364	.222	.586	69	-0	2	5.18	0	/O-3(0-1-2)	0	-0.1
1904 Pit-N	25	87	13	21	0	0	0	3	12	....	3	....	.241	.353	.241	.594	82	-1	9	3.42	-4	O-25(25-0-0)	2	-0.7
Total 2	**28**	**96**	**13**	**23**	**0**	**0**	**0**	**4**	**13**	**....**	**5**	**....**	**.240**	**.354**	**.240**	**.594**	**81**	**-1**	**10**	**3.61**	**-5**	**/O-28**	**2**	**-0.7**

• GILBERT, John John G. Gilbert b: 1/8/1864, Pottstown, PA d: 11/12/1903, Pottstown, PA Deb: 6/23/1890

YEAR TM-L	G	AB	R	H	2B	3B	HR	RBI	BB	SO	SB	CS	AVG	OBP	SLG	OPS	OPS+	BR/A	RC	RC/G	FR	G/POS	WS	TPW
1890 Pit-N	2	8	0	0	0	0	0	0	0	2	0	....	.000	.000	.000	.000	-113	-2	0	.00	0	/S-2	0	-0.2

• GILBERT, Larry Lawrence William Gilbert b: 12/3/1891, New Orleans, LA d: 2/17/1965, New Orleans, LA BL/TL, 5'9", 158 lbs. Deb: 4/14/1914 Career OF: 5-6-77

YEAR TM-L	G	AB	R	H	2B	3B	HR	RBI	BB	SO	SB	CS	AVG	OBP	SLG	OPS	OPS+	BR/A	RC	RC/G	FR	G/POS	WS	TPW
1914*Bos-N	72	224	32	60	6	1	5	25	26	34	3	....	.268	.347	.371	.717	114	4	30	4.44	1	O-60(3-6-51)	9	0.3
1915 Bos-N	45	106	11	16	4	0	0	4	11	13	4	1	.151	.231	.189	.419	28	-9	6	1.59	1	O-27(2-0-26)	0	-1.0
Total 2	**117**	**330**	**43**	**76**	**10**	**1**	**5**	**29**	**37**	**47**	**7**	**1**	**.230**	**.310**	**.312**	**.622**	**87**	**-4**	**35**	**3.44**	**2**	**/O-87**	**9**	**-0.7**

• GILBERT, Mark Mark David Gilbert b: 8/22/1956, Atlanta, GA BB/TR, 6', 175 lbs. Deb: 7/21/1985

YEAR TM-L	G	AB	R	H	2B	3B	HR	RBI	BB	SO	SB	CS	AVG	OBP	SLG	OPS	OPS+	BR/A	RC	RC/G	FR	G/POS	WS	TPW
1985 Chi-A	7	22	3	6	1	0	0	3	4	5	0	0	.273	.385	.318	.703	92	-0	3	4.42	0	/O-7(2-5-1)	1	-0.1

YEAR TM-L	G	AB	R	H	2B	3B	HR	RBI	BB	SO	SB	CS	AVG	OBP	SLG	OPS	OPS+	BR/A	RC	RC/G	FR	G/POS	WS	TPW
• GILBERT, Pete	Peter Gilbert b: 9/6/1867, Baltic, CT d: 1/1/1912, Springfield, MA TR, 5'8", 180 lbs. Deb: 9/6/1890																							
1890 Bal-a	29	100	25	28	2	1	1	18	10	....	12	....	.280	.363	.350	.713	100	-0	17	6.43	-2	3-29	3	-0.1
1891 Bal-a	139	513	81	118	15	7	3	72	37	77	31	....	.230	.317	.304	.621	77	-16	61	4.07	6	*3-139	13	-0.6
1892 Bal-N	4	15	0	3	0	0	0	0	1	3	1	....	.200	.250	.200	.450	35	-1	1	2.31	1	/3-4	0	0.0
1894 Bro-N	6	25	1	2	0	0	0	1	1	3	2	....	.080	.148	.080	.228	-47	-6	1	.69	2	/2-3,3-3	0	-0.3
Lou-N	28	108	13	33	3	1	1	14	5	4	2	....	.306	.353	.380	.733	83	-3	16	5.40	-8	3-28	2	-0.8
Yr.	34	133	14	35	3	1	1	15	6	7	4	....	.263	.315	.323	.638	58	-9	16	4.29	-6	3-31/2-3	2	-1.1
Total 4	206	761	120	184	20	9	5	105	54	87	48	....	.242	.321	.311	.633	76	-26	95	4.37	-1	3-203/2-3	18	-1.8
• GILBERT, Shawn	Albert Shawn Gilbert b: 3/12/1965, Camden, NJ BR/TR, 5'9", 170 lbs. Deb: 6/4/1997 Career OF: 9-4-2																							
1997 NY-N	29	22	3	3	0	0	1	1	1	8	1	0	.136	.174	.273	.447	15	-3	1	1.68	-4	/2-8,S-6,3-3,0-1	0	-0.6
1998 NY-N	3	3	1	0	0	0	0	0	0	1	0	0	.000	.000	.000	.000	-102	-1	0	.00	0	/3-1	0	-0.1
StL-N	4	2	0	1	0	0	0	0	0	1	1	0	.500	.500	.500	1.000	166	0	1	20.52	-1	/2-2	0	-0.1
Yr.	7	5	1	1	0	0	0	0	0	2	1	0	.200	.200	.200	.400	5	-0	1	5.13	-1	/2-2,3-1	0	-0.2
2000 LA-N	15	20	5	3	1	0	1	3	2	7	0	0	.150	.227	.350	.577	46	-2	2	2.62	2	0-14(8-4-2)	0	0.0
Total 3	51	47	9	7	1	0	2	4	3	17	2	0	.149	.200	.298	.498	28	-5	4	2.43	-4	/0-15,2-10,S-6,3-4	0	-0.9
• GILBERT, Tookie	Harold Joseph Gilbert b: 4/4/1929, New Orleans, LA d: 6/23/1967, New Orleans, LA BL/TR, 6'2.5", 185 lbs. Deb: 5/5/1950																							
1950 NY-N	113	322	40	71	12	2	4	32	43	36	3	....	.220	.314	.307	.622	64	-16	33	3.43	-1	*1-111	3	-2.0
1953 NY-N	70	160	12	27	3	0	3	16	22	21	1	0	.169	.269	.244	.513	34	-15	12	2.39	-1	1-44	1	-1.7
Total 2	183	482	52	98	15	2	7	48	65	57	4	0	.203	.299	.286	.586	54	-31	45	3.07	-2	1-155	4	-3.8
• GILBERT, Wally	Walter John Gilbert b: 12/19/1900, Oscoda, MI d: 9/7/1958, Duluth, MN BR/TR, 6', 180 lbs. Deb: 8/18/1928																							
1928 Bro-N	39	153	26	31	4	0	0	3	14	8	2	....	.203	.274	.229	.503	33	-15	10	2.10	1	3-39	2	-1.1
1929 Bro-N	143	569	88	173	31	4	3	58	42	29	7	....	.304	.359	.388	.748	87	-11	79	4.88	8	*3-142	14	0.5
1930 Bro-N	150	623	92	183	34	5	3	67	47	33	7	....	.294	.345	.379	.724	76	-24	80	4.58	15	*3-150	14	0.1
1931 Bro-N	145	552	60	147	25	6	0	46	39	38	3	....	.266	.322	.333	.655	77	-18	62	3.86	3	*3-145	13	-0.9
1932 Cin-N	114	420	35	90	18	2	1	40	20	23	2	....	.214	.252	.274	.526	43	-34	30	2.30	-6	*3-111	4	-3.6
Total 5	591	2317	301	624	112	17	7	214	162	131	21	....	.269	.322	.341	.663	70	-101	261	3.87	21	3-587	47	-4.9
• GILBREATH, Rod	Rodney Joe Gilbreath b: 9/24/1952, Laurel, MS BR/TR, 6'2", 185 lbs. Deb: 6/17/1972																							
1972 Atl-N	18	38	2	9	1	0	0	1	2	10	1	1	.237	.293	.263	.556	54	-2	3	2.40	2	/2-7,3-4	0	0.0
1973 Atl-N	29	74	10	21	2	1	0	2	6	10	2	1	.284	.346	.338	.684	84	-1	9	4.06	1	3-22	1	-0.1
1974 Atl-N	3	6	2	2	0	0	0	0	2	0	0	0	.333	.500	.333	.833	131	0	1	7.30	0	/2-2	0	0.1
1975 Atl-N	90	202	24	49	3	1	2	16	24	26	5	5	.243	.326	.297	.623	71	-8	21	3.34	-5	2-52,3-10/S-1	5	-1.1
1976 Atl-N	116	383	57	96	11	8	1	32	42	36	7	7	.251	.331	.329	.660	82	-9	43	3.54	-3	*2-104/3-7,S-1	9	-0.6
1977 Atl-N	128	407	47	99	15	2	8	43	45	79	3	9	.243	.322	.349	.670	71	-19	44	3.50	0	*2-122/3-1	7	-1.3
1978 Atl-N	116	326	22	80	13	3	3	31	26	51	7	6	.245	.301	.331	.632	69	-15	32	3.26	3	3-62,2-39	6	-1.1
Total 7	500	1436	164	356	45	15	14	125	147	212	25	29	.248	.322	.329	.651	74	-55	152	3.45	-4	2-326,3-106/S-2	28	-4.2
• GILE, Don	Donald Loren "Bear" Gile b: 4/19/1935, Modesto, CA BR/TR, 6'6", 220 lbs. Deb: 9/25/1959																							
1959 Bos-A	3	10	1	2	1	0	0	1	0	2	0	0	.200	.273	.300	.573	55	-1	1	1.70	0	/C-3	0	0.0
1960 Bos-A	29	51	6	9	1	1	1	4	1	13	0	0	.176	.192	.294	.486	29	-5	3	1.62	-3	C-15,1-11	0	-0.8
1961 Bos-A	8	18	2	5	0	0	1	1	1	5	0	0	.278	.316	.444	.760	98	-0	3	5.42	-1	/1-6,C-1	1	-0.2
1962 Bos-A	18	41	3	2	0	0	1	3	3	15	0	0	.049	.133	.122	.255	-30	-8	0	.26	-1	1-14	0	-0.9
Total 4	58	120	12	18	2	1	3	9	5	35	0	0	.150	.197	.258	.455	21	-14	6	1.56	-5	/1-31,C-19	1	-2.0
• GILES, Brian	Brian Stephen Giles b: 1/21/1971, El Cajon, CA BL/TL, 5'11", 195 lbs. Deb: 9/16/1995 Career OF: 645-283-103																							
1995 Cle-A	6	9	6	5	0	0	1	3	0	1	0	0	.556	.556	.889	1.444	265	2	4	30.00	1	/0-3(0-0-3),D-1	1	0.2
1996*Cle-A	51	121	26	43	14	1	5	27	19	13	3	0	.355	.443	.612	1.054	164	13	32	9.85	-0	D-21,0-16(11-0-5)	6	1.1
1997*Cle-A	130	377	62	101	15	3	17	61	63	50	13	3	.268	.374	.459	.833	112	10	68	6.12	-2	*0-115(82-20-25)/D-9	13	0.3
1998*Cle-A	112	350	56	94	19	0	16	66	73	75	10	5	.269	.399	.460	.859	119	13	68	6.78	4	*0-101(95-3-6)/D-6	14	1.1
1999 Pit-N	141	521	109	164	33	3	39	115	95	80	6	2	.315	.423	.614	1.037	159	49	138	9.76	-2	*0-138(8-108-25)/D-3	27	4.4
2000 Pit-N★	156	559	111	176	37	7	35	123	114	69	6	0	.315	.437	.594	1.031	158	56	151	10.01	4	*0-155(46-72-39)	27	5.4
2001 Pit-N★	160	576	116	178	37	7	37	95	90	67	13	6	.309	.406	.590	.996	150	45	140	9.07	-5	*0-160(124-61-0)	29	3.5
2002 Pit-N	153	497	95	148	37	5	38	103	135	74	15	6	.298	.454	.622	1.076	178	65	149	10.87	4	*0-152(151-3-0)	32	6.3
2003 Pit-N	105	388	70	116	30	4	16	70	85	48	0	3	.299	.432	.521	.953	144	29	91	8.64	4	*0-105(99-16-0)	19	2.9
SD-N	29	104	23	31	4	2	4	18	20	10	4	0	.298	.421	.490	.911	150	10	23	7.80	0	0-29(29-0-0)	6	0.9
Yr.	134	492	93	147	34	6	20	88	105	58	4	3	.299	.430	.514	.944	146	39	114	8.46	5	*0-134(128-16-0)	25	3.8
Total 9	1043	3502	674	1056	226	32	208	681	694	487	70	25	.302	.422	.563	.984	150	292	864	8.97	9	0-974/D-40	174	26.0
• GILES, Brian	Brian Jeffrey Giles b: 4/27/1960, Manhattan, KS BR/TR, 6'1", 165 lbs. Deb: 9/12/1981																							
1981 NY-N	9	7	0	0	0	0	0	0	0	3	0	0	.000	.000	.000	.000	-102	-2	0	.00	0	/2-2,S-2	0	-0.2
1982 NY-N	45	138	14	29	5	0	3	10	12	29	6	1	.210	.273	.312	.585	64	-6	13	3.17	2	2-45/S-2	3	-0.2
1983 NY-N	145	400	39	98	15	0	2	27	36	77	17	10	.245	.311	.298	.608	70	-17	37	3.09	11	*2-140,S-12	9	0.1
1985 Mil-A	34	58	6	10	1	0	1	1	7	16	2	1	.172	.262	.241	.503	39	-5	4	2.10	-1	S-20,2-13/D-2	1	-0.4
1986 Chi-A	9	11	0	3	0	0	0	1	0	2	0	0	.273	.273	.273	.545	48	-1	1	1.64	0	/2-7,S-1	0	-0.1
1990 Sea-A	45	95	15	22	6	0	4	11	15	24	2	1	.232	.336	.421	.757	109	1	14	5.15	0	S-37/2-2,3-1,D-1	3	0.3
Total 6	287	709	74	162	27	0	10	50	70	151	27	13	.228	.300	.309	.609	70	-29	69	3.22	10	2-209/S-74,D-3,3-1	16	-0.4
• GILES, Marcus	Marcus William Giles b: 5/18/1978, San Diego, CA BR/TR, 5'8", 180 lbs. Deb: 4/17/2001																							
2001*Atl-N	68	244	36	64	10	2	9	31	28	37	2	5	.262	.338	.430	.769	95	-4	33	4.58	0	2-62	9	-0.1
2002*Atl-N	68	213	27	49	10	1	8	23	25	41	1	1	.230	.317	.399	.716	86	-5	27	4.21	3	2-52/3-8	5	0.1
2003*Atl-N★	145	551	101	174	49	2	21	69	59	80	14	4	.316	.393	.526	.919	137	32	118	7.94	7	*2-139	28	4.5
Total 3	281	1008	164	287	69	5	38	123	112	158	17	10	.285	.364	.476	.840	116	23	178	6.26	10	2-253/3-8	42	4.5
• GILHAM, George	George Louis Gilham b: 9/8/1899, Shamokin, PA d: 4/25/1937, Lansdowne, PA BR/TR, 5'11", 164 lbs. Deb: 9/24/1920																							
1920 StL-N	1	3	0	0	0	0	0	0	0	1	0	0	.000	.000	.000	.000	-102	-1	0	.00	0	/C-1	0	-0.1
1921 StL-N	1	1	0	0	0	0	0	0	0	0	0	0	.000	.000	.000	.000	-102	-0	0	.00	0	....	0	0.0
Total 2	2	4	0	0	0	0	0	0	0	1	0	0	.000	.000	.000	.000	-102	-1	0	.00	0	/C-1	0	-0.1
• GILHOOLEY, Frank	Frank Patrick "Flash" Gilhooley b: 6/10/1892, Toledo, OH d: 7/11/1959, Toledo, OH BL/TR, 5'8", 155 lbs. Deb: 9/18/1911 Career OF: 30-19-236																							
1911 StL-N	1	0	0	0	0	0	0	0	0	0	0	....	....	....	....	....	-103	0	0	....	0	/0-1	0	0.0
1912 StL-N	13	49	5	11	0	0	0	2	3	8	0	....	.224	.269	.224	.494	37	-4	3	1.89	0	0-11(0-11-0)	0	-0.4
1913 NY-A	24	85	10	29	2	1	0	14	4	9	6	....	.341	.378	.388	.766	124	2	14	6.10	-1	0-24(0-0-24)	3	0.0
1914 NY-A	1	3	0	2	0	0	0	0	1	0	0	....	.667	.750	.667	1.417	327	1	2	39.75	0	/0-1	1	0.1
1915 NY-A	1	4	0	0	0	0	0	0	0	1	0	....	.000	.000	.000	.000	-100	-1	0	.00	-0	/0-1	0	-0.1
1916 NY-A	58	223	40	62	5	3	1	10	37	17	16	....	.278	.383	.341	.724	115	6	35	5.54	3	0-57(0-2-55)	9	0.6
1917 NY-A	54	165	14	40	6	1	0	8	30	13	6	....	.242	.362	.291	.653	99	2	19	3.86	-1	0-46(0-0-46)	5	-0.2
1918 NY-A	112	427	59	118	13	5	1	23	53	24	7	....	.276	.358	.337	.695	107	5	53	4.22	3	*0-111(0-4-107)	14	0.3
1919 Bos-A	48	112	14	27	4	0	0	1	12	8	2	....	.241	.315	.277	.591	71	-4	10	3.01	0	0-33(30-2-1)	1	-0.6
Total 9	312	1068	142	289	30	10	2	58	140	80	37	....	.271	.357	.323	.680	102	7	136	4.35	4	0-285	33	-0.2
• GILKEY, Bernard	Otis Bernard Gilkey b: 9/24/1966, St. Louis, MO BR/TR, 6', 190 lbs. Deb: 9/4/1990 Career OF: 997-3-87																							
1990 StL-N	18	64	11	19	5	2	1	3	8	5	6	1	.297	.375	.484	.859	134	4	13	7.22	1	0-18(18-1-0)	3	0.4
1991 StL-N	81	268	28	58	7	2	5	20	39	33	14	8	.216	.318	.313	.632	78	-7	25	2.90	2	0-74(74-0-0)	3	-0.8
1992 StL-N	131	384	56	116	19	4	7	43	39	52	18	12	.302	.368	.427	.795	128	13	60	5.58	2	*0-111(110-0-1)	17	1.3
1993 StL-N	137	557	99	170	40	5	16	70	56	66	15	10	.305	.373	.481	.854	129	22	96	6.22	0	*0-134(133-0-2)/1-3	21	1.6
1994 StL-N	105	380	52	96	22	1	6	45	39	65	15	8	.253	.338	.363	.701	85	-8	48	4.35	-1	*0-102(102-0-0)	9	-1.3
1995 StL-N	121	480	73	143	33	4	17	69	42	70	12	6	.298	.361	.490	.850	122	14	80	5.94	4	*0-118(118-0-0)	16	1.3

YEAR TM-L	G	AB	R	H	2B	3B	HR	RBI	BB	SO	SB	CS	AVG	OBP	SLG	OPS	OPS+	BR/A	RC	RC/G	FR	G/POS	WS	TPW
1996 NY-N	153	571	108	181	44	3	30	117	73	125	17	9	.317	.398	.562	.960	157	46	124	7.88	16	*0-151(151-0-0)	30	5.5
1997 NY-N	145	518	85	129	31	1	18	78	70	111	7	11	.249	.345	.417	.762	102	-1	75	4.80	12	*0-136(136-1-0)/D-2	16	0.5
1998 NY-N	82	264	33	60	15	0	4	28	32	66	5	1	.227	.320	.330	.650	72	-9	30	3.69	4	0-77(76-1-4)	5	-0.8
Ari-N	29	101	8	25	0	0	1	5	11	14	4	2	.248	.327	.277	.605	61	-5	9	2.85	1	0-27(27-0-0)	1	-0.5
Yr.	111	365	41	85	15	0	5	33	43	80	9	3	.233	.322	.315	.637	69	-15	38	3.46	6	*0-104(103-1-4)	6	-1.3
1999*Ari-N	94	204	28	60	16	1	8	39	29	42	2	2	.294	.387	.500	.887	121	7	39	6.57	1	0-53(15-0-40)	8	0.5
2000 Ari-N	38	73	6	8	1	0	2	6	7	16	0	0	.110	.188	.205	.393	-1	-12	2	.98	-0	0-17(2-0-16)	0	-1.2
Bos-A	36	91	11	21	5	1	1	9	10	12	0	0	.231	.327	.341	.668	67	-4	10	3.45	1	0-22(7-0-16)/D-8	1	-0.4
2001*Atl-N	69	106	8	29	6	0	2	14	11	31	0	1	.274	.347	.387	.734	88	-2	14	4.32	-1	0-36(28-0-8)/D-1	1	-0.4
Total 12	**1239**	**4061**	**606**	**1115**	**244**	**24**	**118**	**546**	**466**	**708**	**115**	**71**	**.275**	**.355**	**.434**	**.789**	**111**	**56**	**625**	**5.29**	**43**	***0-1076/D-11,1-3**	**131**	**5.6**

• GILKS, Bob Robert James Gilks b: 7/2/1864, Cincinnati, OH d: 8/21/1944, Brunswick, GA BR/TR, 5'8", 178 lbs. Deb: 8/25/1887 Career OF: 181-56-21 ♦

YEAR TM-L	G	AB	R	H	2B	3B	HR	RBI	BB	SO	SB	CS	AVG	OBP	SLG	OPS	OPS+	BR/A	RC	RC/G	FR	G/POS	WS	TPW
1887 Cle-a	22	86	12	29	2	0	0	13	3	....	5	....	.337	.352	.337	.690	96	2	12	5.64	1	P-13/1-6,0-3(0-2-1),2-1	7	1.7
1888 Cle-a	119	484	59	111	14	4	1	63	7	....	16	....	.229	.245	.281	.526	70	-17	38	2.76	-3	0-87(57-27-3),3-28/P-4,S-4,2	6	-3.1
1889 Cle-N	53	210	17	50	5	2	0	18	7	20	6	....	.238	.273	.281	.554	56	-13	18	3.01	3	0-29(2-26-1),S-13,1-10/2-1	3	-0.9
1890 Cle-N	130	544	65	116	10	3	0	41	32	38	17	....	.213	.265	.243	.507	49	-35	40	2.50	2	*0-123(121-1-1)/P-4,S-3,2	4	-3.4
1893 Bal-N	15	64	10	17	2	0	0	7	0	3	3	....	.266	.277	.297	.574	52	-5	6	3.52	2	0-15(1-0-15)	1	-0.3
Total 5	**339**	**1388**	**163**	**323**	**33**	**9**	**1**	**142**	**49**	**61**	**47**	**....**	**.233**	**.265**	**.270**	**.535**	**60**	**-67**	**115**	**2.88**	**6**	**0-257/3-28,P-21,S-20,1-16,2**	**21**	**-6.0**

• GILL, Jim James C. Gill b: 7/1866, d: 4/10/1923, Beaver Falls, PA Deb: 6/27/1889

YEAR TM-L	G	AB	R	H	2B	3B	HR	RBI	BB	SO	SB	CS	AVG	OBP	SLG	OPS	OPS+	BR/A	RC	RC/G	FR	G/POS	WS	TPW
1889 StL-a	2	8	2	2	1	0	0	1	1	2	1	....	.250	.333	.375	.708	90	-0	1	6.04	-1	/2-1,0-1	0	-0.1

• GILL, Johnny John Wesley "Patcheye" Gill b: 3/27/1905, Nashville, TN d: 12/26/1984, Nashville, TN BL/TR, 6'2", 190 lbs. Deb: 8/28/1927 Career OF: 51-4-24

YEAR TM-L	G	AB	R	H	2B	3B	HR	RBI	BB	SO	SB	CS	AVG	OBP	SLG	OPS	OPS+	BR/A	RC	RC/G	FR	G/POS	WS	TPW
1927 Cle-A	21	60	8	13	3	0	1	4	7	13	1	1	.217	.319	.317	.636	65	-3	6	3.52	1	0-17(14-3-0)	1	-0.2
1928 Cle-A	2	2	0	0	0	0	0	0	0	1	0	0	.000	.000	.000	.000	-99	-1	0	.00	0	....	0	-0.1
1931 Was-A	8	30	2	8	2	1	0	5	1	6	0	1	.267	.313	.400	.713	86	-1	3	3.54	3	/0-8(0-0-8)	1	0.2
1934 Was-A	13	53	7	13	3	0	2	7	2	3	0	0	.245	.286	.415	.701	82	-2	6	4.14	-0	0-13(2-0-11)	1	-0.2
1935 Chi-N	3	3	2	1	1	0	0	1	0	1	0	....	.333	.333	.667	1.000	161	0	1	9.23	0	....	0	0.0
1936 Chi-N	71	174	20	44	8	0	7	28	13	19	0	....	.253	.309	.420	.728	92	-3	23	4.75	-1	0-41(35-1-5)	4	-0.6
Total 6	**118**	**322**	**39**	**79**	**17**	**1**	**10**	**45**	**23**	**43**	**1**	**2**	**.245**	**.306**	**.398**	**.703**	**84**	**-9**	**40**	**4.29**	**3**	**/0-79**	**7**	**-0.9**

• GILL, Warren Warren Darst "Doc" Gill b: 12/21/1878, Ladoga, IN d: 11/26/1952, Laguna Beach, CA BR/TR, 6'1", 175 lbs. Deb: 8/26/1908

YEAR TM-L	G	AB	R	H	2B	3B	HR	RBI	BB	SO	SB	CS	AVG	OBP	SLG	OPS	OPS+	BR/A	RC	RC/G	FR	G/POS	WS	TPW
1908 Pit-N	27	76	10	17	0	1	0	14	11	....	3	....	.224	.366	.250	.616	97	1	9	3.57	-1	1-25	3	-0.1

• GILLEN, Sam Samuel Gillen b: 1/1871, Pittsburgh, PA d: 5/13/1905, Pittsburgh, PA, 5'8" Deb: 8/19/1893

YEAR TM-L	G	AB	R	H	2B	3B	HR	RBI	BB	SO	SB	CS	AVG	OBP	SLG	OPS	OPS+	BR/A	RC	RC/G	FR	G/POS	WS	TPW
1893 Pit-N	3	6	0	0	0	0	0	0	0	1	0	....	.000	.000	.000	.000	-102	-2	0	.00	0	/S-3	0	-0.2
1897 Phi-N	75	270	32	70	10	3	0	27	35	....	2	....	.259	.353	.319	.671	80	-6	33	4.21	-12	S-69/3-6	4	-1.2
Total 2	**78**	**276**	**32**	**70**	**10**	**3**	**0**	**27**	**35**	**1**	**2**	**....**	**.254**	**.346**	**.312**	**.658**	**77**	**-8**	**33**	**4.10**	**-12**	**/S-72,3-6**	**4**	**-1.4**

• GILLEN, Tom Thomas J. Gillen b: 5/18/1862, Philadelphia, PA d: 1/26/1889, Philadelphia, PA, 5'8", 160 lbs. Deb: 4/18/1884

YEAR TM-L	G	AB	R	H	2B	3B	HR	RBI	BB	SO	SB	CS	AVG	OBP	SLG	OPS	OPS+	BR/A	RC	RC/G	FR	G/POS	WS	TPW
1884 Phi-U	29	116	5	18	2	0	0	....	1	....	....	....	.155	.162	.172	.335	14	-9	3	.95	0	C-27/0-3(1-0-0)	1	-0.6
1886 Det-N	2	10	2	4	0	0	0	4	0	1	0	....	.400	.400	.400	.800	140	0	2	7.38	0	/C-2	0	0.1
Total 2	**31**	**126**	**7**	**22**	**2**	**0**	**0**	**4**	**1**	**1**	**0**	**....**	**.175**	**.181**	**.190**	**.372**	**24**	**-9**	**5**	**1.32**	**1**	**/C-29,0-3**	**1**	**-0.5**

• GILLENWATER, Carden Carden Edison Gillenwater b: 5/13/1917, Riceville, TN d: 5/10/2000, Largo, FL BR/TR, 6'1", 178 lbs. Deb: 9/22/1940 Career OF: 19-275-2

YEAR TM-L	G	AB	R	H	2B	3B	HR	RBI	BB	SO	SB	CS	AVG	OBP	SLG	OPS	OPS+	BR/A	RC	RC/G	FR	G/POS	WS	TPW
1940 StL-N	7	25	1	4	1	0	0	5	0	2	0	....	.160	.160	.200	.360	-1	-4	1	1.03	0	/0-7(5-2-0)	0	-0.4
1943 Bro-N	8	17	1	3	0	0	0	2	2	3	0	....	.176	.263	.176	.440	28	-2	1	1.79	0	/0-4(2-1-1)	0	-0.1
1945 Bos-N	144	517	74	149	20	2	7	72	73	70	13	....	.288	.379	.375	.755	110	10	75	5.19	19	*0-140(0-140-0)	17	2.5
1946 Bos-N	99	224	30	51	10	1	1	14	39	27	3	....	.228	.342	.295	.637	80	-4	25	3.73	0	0-78(11-67-0)	6	-0.6
1948 Was-A	77	221	23	54	10	4	3	21	39	36	4	2	.244	.358	.367	.724	95	-0	30	4.54	-6	0-67(1-65-1)	7	-0.8
Total 5	**335**	**1004**	**129**	**261**	**41**	**7**	**11**	**114**	**153**	**138**	**20**	**2**	**.260**	**.359**	**.348**	**.707**	**96**	**0**	**133**	**4.53**	**14**	**0-296**	**30**	**0.6**

• GILLESPIE, Jim James Wheatfield Gillespie BL/TR Deb: 10/1/1890

YEAR TM-L	G	AB	R	H	2B	3B	HR	RBI	BB	SO	SB	CS	AVG	OBP	SLG	OPS	OPS+	BR/A	RC	RC/G	FR	G/POS	WS	TPW
1890 Buf-P	1	3	0	0	0	0	0	0	0	2	0	....	.000	.000	.000	.000	-109	-1	0	.00	0	/0-1	0	-0.1

• GILLESPIE, Paul Paul Allen Gillespie b: 9/18/1920, Cartersville, GA d: 8/11/1970, Anniston, AL BL/TR, 6'3", 195 lbs. Deb: 9/11/1942

YEAR TM-L	G	AB	R	H	2B	3B	HR	RBI	BB	SO	SB	CS	AVG	OBP	SLG	OPS	OPS+	BR/A	RC	RC/G	FR	G/POS	WS	TPW
1942 Chi-N	5	16	3	4	0	0	2	4	1	2	0	....	.250	.294	.625	.919	172	1	3	6.79	0	/C-4	1	0.2
1944 Chi-N	9	26	2	7	1	0	1	2	3	3	0	....	.269	.345	.423	.768	116	1	4	4.94	-1	/C-7	1	0.0
1945*Chi-N	75	163	12	47	6	0	3	25	18	9	2	....	.288	.366	.380	.746	110	3	24	5.59	-2	C-45/0-1	7	0.3
Total 3	**89**	**205**	**17**	**58**	**7**	**0**	**6**	**31**	**22**	**14**	**2**	**....**	**.283**	**.358**	**.405**	**.763**	**115**	**4**	**31**	**5.60**	**-2**	**/C-56,0-1**	**9**	**0.5**

• GILLESPIE, Pete Peter Patrick Gillespie b: 11/30/1851, Carbondale, PA d: 5/5/1910, Carbondale, PA BL/TR, 6'1.5", 178 lbs. Deb: 5/1/1880 Career OF: 710-2-2

YEAR TM-L	G	AB	R	H	2B	3B	HR	RBI	BB	SO	SB	CS	AVG	OBP	SLG	OPS	OPS+	BR/A	RC	RC/G	FR	G/POS	WS	TPW
1880 Tro-N	82	346	50	84	20	5	2	24	17	35	....	....	.243	.278	.347	.625	105	2	34	3.59	4	*0-82(82-0-0)	10	0.1
1881 Tro-N	84	348	43	96	14	3	0	41	9	24	....	....	.276	.294	.333	.627	92	-4	35	3.75	4	*0-84(84-0-0)	9	-0.5
1882 Tro-N	74	298	46	82	5	4	2	33	9	14	....	....	.275	.296	.339	.635	108	3	31	3.91	-6	*0-74(74-0-0)	8	-0.5
1883 NY-N	98	411	64	129	23	12	1	62	9	27	....	....	.314	.329	.436	.764	131	15	60	5.88	2	*0-98(97-1-0)	15	1.2
1884 NY-N	101	413	75	109	7	4	2	44	19	35	....	....	.264	.296	.315	.611	90	-5	39	3.57	-6	*0-101(100-0-1)	11	-1.3
1885 NY-N	102	420	67	123	17	6	0	52	15	32	....	....	.293	.317	.362	.679	121	9	49	4.49	-3	*0-102(102-0-0)	15	0.2
1886 NY-N	97	396	65	108	13	8	0	58	16	30	17	....	.273	.301	.346	.647	95	-3	48	4.45	-11	*0-97(95-1-1)	11	-1.6
1887 NY-N	76	307	40	90	9	3	3	37	12	21	37	....	.293	.304	.346	.650	84	-6	43	5.30	1	0-76(76-0-0)/3-1	6	-0.7
Total 8	**714**	**2939**	**450**	**821**	**108**	**45**	**10**	**351**	**106**	**218**	**54**	**....**	**.279**	**.303**	**.354**	**.657**	**104**	**10**	**340**	**4.36**	**-15**	**0-714/3-1**	**85**	**-3.0**

• GILLIAM, Jim James William "Junior" Gilliam
b: 10/17/1928, Nashville, TN d: 10/8/1978, Inglewood, CA BB/TR, 5'10.5", 175 lbs. Deb: 4/14/1953 C Career OF: 207-5-26

YEAR TM-L	G	AB	R	H	2B	3B	HR	RBI	BB	SO	SB	CS	AVG	OBP	SLG	OPS	OPS+	BR/A	RC	RC/G	FR	G/POS	WS	TPW
1953*Bro-N	151	605	125	168	31	**17**	6	63	100	38	21	14	.278	.383	.415	.798	106	7	104	6.12	11	*2-149	25	2.9
1954 Bro-N	146	607	107	171	28	8	13	52	76	30	8	7	.282	.364	.418	.782	100	0	95	5.52	-7	*2-143/0-4(4-0-2)	20	0.5
1955*Bro-N	147	538	110	134	20	8	7	40	70	37	15	15	.249	.342	.355	.697	83	-14	67	4.10	-2	2-99,0-46(41-4-7)	14	-1.2
1956*Bro-N★	153	594	102	178	23	8	6	43	95	39	21	9	.300	.400	.396	.795	106	12	103	6.34	11	*2-102,0-56(53-0-7)	28	2.8
1957 Bro-N	149	617	89	154	26	4	2	37	64	31	26	10	.250	.324	.314	.639	66	-26	69	3.80	0	*2-148/0-2(2-0-0)	15	-1.5
1958 LA-N	147	555	81	145	25	5	2	43	78	22	18	11	.261	.352	.335	.687	81	-13	71	4.44	9	0-75(71-1-5),3-44,2-32	15	-0.8
1959*LA-N★	145	553	91	156	18	4	3	34	**96**	25	23	10	.282	.388	.345	.734	91	-1	84	5.45	-4	*3-132/2-8,0-3(3-0-1)	20	-0.5
1960 LA-N	151	557	96	138	20	2	5	40	96	28	12	9	.248	.361	.318	.679	82	-10	72	4.32	10	*3-130,2-30	16	0.2
1961 LA-N	144	439	74	107	26	3	4	32	79	34	8	4	.244	.359	.344	.703	81	-9	60	4.55	5	3-74,2-71,0-11(11-0-0)	15	0.1
1962 LA-N	160	588	83	159	24	1	4	43	93	35	17	7	.270	.372	.335	.707	97	3	81	4.71	10	*2-113,3-90/0-1	23	2.1
1963*LA-N	148	525	77	148	27	4	6	49	60	28	19	5	.282	.358	.383	.741	121	19	76	4.97	0	*2-119,3-55	28	3.0
1964 LA-N	116	334	44	76	8	3	2	27	42	21	4	4	.228	.319	.287	.607	78	-9	32	3.13	-5	3-86,2-25/0-2(0-0-2)	6	-1.3
1965*LA-N	111	372	54	104	19	4	4	39	53	31	9	5	.280	.375	.384	.760	122	13	58	5.69	4	3-80,0-22(21-0-1)/2-5	18	1.7
1966*LA-N	88	235	30	51	9	0	1	16	34	17	2	1	.217	.316	.268	.584	70	-8	21	2.99	-4	3-70/1-2,2-2	4	-1.2
Total 14	**1956**	**7119**	**1163**	**1889**	**304**	**71**	**65**	**558**	**1036**	**416**	**203**	**111**	**.265**	**.361**	**.355**	**.717**	**93**	**-36**	**992**	**4.82**	**37**	***2-1046,3-761,0-222/1-2**	**247**	**6.7**

• GILLIGAN, Barney Andrew Bernard Gilligan b: 1/3/1856, Cambridge, MA d: 4/1/1934, Lynn, MA BR/TR, 5'6.5", 130 lbs. Deb: 9/25/1875 Career OF: 23-14-7

YEAR TM-L	G	AB	R	H	2B	3B	HR	RBI	BB	SO	SB	CS	AVG	OBP	SLG	OPS	OPS+	BR/A	RC	RC/G	FR	G/POS	WS	TPW
1875 Atl-n	2	8	2	2	0	0	0	0	0	0	0	0	.250	.250	.250	.500	85	-0	1	2.52	-0	/C-1,0-1	....	0.0
1879 Cle-N	52	205	20	35	6	2	0	11	0	13	....	....	.171	.171	.220	.390	28	-15	8	1.30	-1	C-27,0-23(21-2-0)/S-2	1	-1.5
1880 Cle-N	30	99	9	17	4	3	1	13	6	12	....	....	.172	.219	.303	.522	76	-2	7	2.26	5	C-23/0-4(0-4-0),S-4	3	0.3
1881 Pro-N	46	183	19	40	7	2	0	20	9	24	....	....	.219	.255	.279	.534	69	-6	13	2.52	-2	C-36,S-10/0-1	4	-0.6
1882 Pro-N	56	201	32	45	7	6	0	26	4	26	....	....	.224	.239	.318	.557	77	-5	16	2.76	4	C-54/S-2	5	0.4
1883 Pro-N	74	263	34	52	13	3	0	24	26	32	....	....	.198	.270	.270	.540	63	-11	20	2.56	2	*C-74	7	-0.2
1884*Pro-N	82	294	47	72	13	2	1	38	35	41	....	....	.245	.325	.313	.638	104	3	31	3.80	-4	*C-81/1-1,3-1	13	0.5
1885 Pro-N	71	252	23	54	7	3	0	12	23	33	....	....	.214	.280	.266	.546	80	-4	19	2.62	-5	C-65/S-5,2-1,0-1	8	-0.3
1886 Was-N	81	273	23	52	9	2	0	17	39	35	6	....	.190	.292	.238	.530	66	-8	21	2.59	0	C-71,0-14(1-6-7)/3-1,S-1	4	-0.2
1887 Was-N	28	95	7	23	2	0	1	6	5	18	2	....	.242	.242	.256	.498	40	-7	6	2.28	0	C-26/S-3,0-1	1	-0.5

YEAR TM-L	G	AB	R	H	2B	3B	HR	RBI	BB	SO	SB	CS	AVG	OBP	SLG	OPS	OPS+	BR/A	RC	RC/G	FR	G/POS	WS	TPW
1888 Det-N	1	5	1	1	0	0	0	0	0	1	0	....	.200	.200	.200	.400	28	-0	0	1.38	0	/C-1	0	0.0
Total 10	521	1870	215	391	68	23	3	167	147	235	8	....	.209	.265	.273	.538	71	-56	141	2.60	0	C-458/0-44,S-27,3-2,1-1,2-1	46	-2.1

• GILLIS, Grant Grant Gillis b: 1/24/1901, Grove Hill, AL d: 2/4/1981, Thomasville, AL BR/TR, 5'10", 165 lbs. Deb: 9/19/1927

YEAR TM-L	G	AB	R	H	2B	3B	HR	RBI	BB	SO	SB	CS	AVG	OBP	SLG	OPS	OPS+	BR/A	RC	RC/G	FR	G/POS	WS	TPW
1927 Was-A	10	36	8	8	3	1	0	2	2	0	0	0	.222	.263	.361	.624	61	-2	3	3.23	1	S-10	1	0.0
1928 Was-A	24	87	13	22	5	1	0	10	4	5	0	1	.253	.309	.333	.642	69	-4	9	3.47	-3	S-16/2-5,3-3	1	-0.5
1929 Bos-A	28	73	5	18	4	0	0	11	6	8	0	1	.247	.304	.301	.605	58	-5	7	3.01	-3	2-25	1	-0.7
Total 3	62	196	26	48	12	2	0	23	12	13	0	2	.245	.299	.327	.625	63	-11	19	3.25	-4	/2-30,S-26,3-3	3	-1.2

• GILMAN, Jim James Gilman b: 6/14/1870, Cleveland, OH d: 12/21/1912, Cleveland, OH Deb: 7/10/1893

YEAR TM-L	G	AB	R	H	2B	3B	HR	RBI	BB	SO	SB	CS	AVG	OBP	SLG	OPS	OPS+	BR/A	RC	RC/G	FR	G/POS	WS	TPW
1893 Cle-N	2	7	1	2	0	0	0	1	0	2	0	....	.286	.286	.286	.571	49	-1	1	3.10	-1	/3-2	0	-0.1

• GILMAN, Pit Pitkin Clark Gilman b: 3/14/1864, La Porte, OH d: 8/17/1950, Elyria, OH BL/TL, 170 lbs. Deb: 9/18/1884

YEAR TM-L	G	AB	R	H	2B	3B	HR	RBI	BB	SO	SB	CS	AVG	OBP	SLG	OPS	OPS+	BR/A	RC	RC/G	FR	G/POS	WS	TPW
1884 Cle-N	2	10	0	1	0	0	0	0	0	3	....	....	.100	.100	.100	.200	-36	-2	0	.31	0	/0-2(2-0-0)	0	-0.1

• GILMORE, Grover Ernest Grover Gilmore b: 11/1/1888, Chicago, IL d: 11/25/1919, Sioux City, IA BL/TL, 5'9.5", 170 lbs. Deb: 4/18/1914 Career OF: 0-10-241

YEAR TM-L	G	AB	R	H	2B	3B	HR	RBI	BB	SO	SB	CS	AVG	OBP	SLG	OPS	OPS+	BR/A	RC	RC/G	FR	G/POS	WS	TPW
1914 KC-F	139	530	91	152	25	5	1	32	37	108	23	....	.287	.337	.358	.695	103	1	70	4.46	5	*0-132(0-10-122)	14	-0.1
1915 KC-F	119	411	53	117	22	15	1	47	26	50	19	....	.285	.347	.418	.765	129	14	64	5.35	11	*0-119(0-0-119)	21	2.0
Total 2	258	941	144	269	47	20	2	79	63	158	42	....	.286	.341	.385	.726	114	15	134	4.85	16	0-251	35	1.9

• GILMORE, Jim James Gilmore b: 5/1853, Baltimore, MD d: 11/18/1928, Baltimore, MD Deb: 4/26/1875

YEAR TM-L	G	AB	R	H	2B	3B	HR	RBI	BB	SO	SB	CS	AVG	OBP	SLG	OPS	OPS+	BR/A	RC	RC/G	FR	G/POS	WS	TPW
1875 Was-n	3	12	2	3	0	0	0	0	0	3	0	0	.250	.250	.250	.500	77	-0	1	2.52	0	/C-2,3-1,0-1	....	0.0

• GILROY, Gilroy Deb: 9/7/1874

YEAR TM-L	G	AB	R	H	2B	3B	HR	RBI	BB	SO	SB	CS	AVG	OBP	SLG	OPS	OPS+	BR/A	RC	RC/G	FR	G/POS	WS	TPW
1874 Chi-n	8	38	4	8	1	0	0	7	1	3	0	0	.211	.231	.237	.468	50	-2	2	2.13	0	/C-8	....	-0.1
1875 Ath-n	2	6	0	1	0	0	0	0	0	0	0	0	.167	.167	.167	.333	15	-1	0	1.01	1	/C-1,0-1	....	0.0
Total 2 n	10	44	4	9	1	0	0	7	1	3	0	0	.205	.222	.227	.449	45	-3	2	1.97	1	/C-9,0-1	....	-0.1

• GINN, Tinsley Tinsley Rucker Ginn b: 9/26/1891, Royston, GA d: 8/30/1931, Atlanta, GA BL/TR, 5'9", 180 lbs. Deb: 6/27/1914

YEAR TM-L	G	AB	R	H	2B	3B	HR	RBI	BB	SO	SB	CS	AVG	OBP	SLG	OPS	OPS+	BR/A	RC	RC/G	FR	G/POS	WS	TPW
1914 Cle-A	2	1	0	0	0	0	0	0	0	0	0	....	.000	.000	.000	.000	-96	-0	0	.00	0	/0-2(0-0-0)	0	-0.1

• GINSBERG, Joe Myron Nathan Ginsberg b: 10/11/1926, New York, NY BL/TR, 5'11", 180 lbs. Deb: 9/15/1948

YEAR TM-L	G	AB	R	H	2B	3B	HR	RBI	BB	SO	SB	CS	AVG	OBP	SLG	OPS	OPS+	BR/A	RC	RC/G	FR	G/POS	WS	TPW
1948 Det-A	11	36	7	13	0	0	0	1	3	1	0	0	.361	.410	.361	.771	103	0	5	6.10	-1	C-11	1	0.0
1950 Det-A	36	95	12	22	6	0	0	12	11	6	1	0	.232	.318	.295	.612	56	-6	10	3.44	-2	C-31	2	-0.6
1951 Det-A	102	304	44	79	10	2	8	37	43	21	0	2	.260	.355	.385	.740	100	-0	43	4.91	0	C-95	10	0.5
1952 Det-A	113	307	29	68	13	2	6	36	51	21	1	1	.221	.338	.336	.673	87	-4	37	4.01	-1	*C-101	6	0.0
1953 Det-A	18	53	6	16	2	0	0	3	10	1	0	0	.302	.422	.340	.761	109	2	9	6.44	2	C-15	3	0.4
Cle-A	46	109	10	31	4	0	0	10	14	4	0	0	.284	.371	.321	.692	91	-1	14	4.34	-3	C-39	3	-0.2
Yr.	64	162	16	47	6	0	0	13	24	5	0	0	.290	.388	.327	.715	97	1	23	4.99	-1	C-54	6	0.2
1954 Cle-A	3	2	0	1	0	1	0	1	0	0	0	0	.500	.667	1.500	2.167	472	1	2	58.68	0	/C-1	0	0.1
1956 KC-A	71	195	15	48	8	1	1	12	23	17	1	1	.246	.326	.313	.639	69	-9	19	3.34	4	C-57	3	-0.2
Bal-A	15	28	0	2	0	0	0	2	2	4	0	0	.071	.133	.071	.205	-48	-6	0	.20	0	/C-8	0	-0.5
Yr.	86	223	15	50	8	1	1	14	25	21	1	1	.224	.302	.283	.585	54	-14	20	2.83	4	C-65	3	-0.7
1957 Bal-A	85	175	15	48	8	2	1	18	18	19	2	1	.274	.349	.360	.709	100	1	23	4.42	-2	C-66	5	0.1
1958 Bal-A	61	109	4	23	1	0	3	16	13	14	0	0	.211	.306	.303	.609	72	-4	11	3.49	0	C-39	3	-0.3
1959 Bal-A	65	166	14	30	2	0	1	14	21	13	1	0	.181	.273	.211	.484	35	-14	10	1.84	1	C-62	2	-1.0
1960 Bal-A	14	30	3	8	1	0	0	6	6	1	0	0	.267	.389	.300	.689	90	-0	4	4.28	-3	C-14	1	-0.2
Chi-A	28	75	8	19	4	0	0	9	10	8	1	0	.253	.349	.307	.656	80	-1	9	4.14	0	C-25	3	0.0
Yr.	42	105	11	27	5	0	0	15	16	9	1	0	.257	.361	.305	.665	83	-1	13	4.18	-3	C-39	4	-0.3
1961 Chi-A	6	3	0	0	0	0	0	0	1	2	0	0	.000	.250	.000	.250	-27	-1	0	1.05	0	/C-2	0	-0.1
Bos-A	19	24	1	6	0	0	0	5	0	2	0	0	.250	.250	.250	.500	33	-2	1	1.78	0	/C-6	0	-0.2
Yr.	25	27	1	6	0	0	0	5	1	4	0	0	.222	.250	.222	.472	23	-3	1	1.65	0	/C-8	0	-0.3
1962 NY-N	2	5	0	0	0	0	0	0	0	1	0	0	.000	.000	.000	.000	-98	-1	0	.00	0	/C-2	0	-0.1
Total 13	695	1716	168	414	59	8	20	182	226	135	7	5	.241	.334	.320	.654	79	-45	198	3.87	-4	C-574	42	-2.4

• GINTER, Keith Keith Michael Ginter b: 5/5/1976, Norwalk, CA BR/TR, 5'10", 190 lbs. Deb: 9/20/2000

YEAR TM-L	G	AB	R	H	2B	3B	HR	RBI	BB	SO	SB	CS	AVG	OBP	SLG	OPS	OPS+	BR/A	RC	RC/G	FR	G/POS	WS	TPW
2000 Hou-N	5	8	3	2	0	0	1	3	1	3	0	0	.250	.333	.625	.958	128	0	2	6.69	0	/2-2	0	0.0
2001 Hou-N	1	1	0	0	0	0	0	0	0	0	0	0	.000	.000	.000	.000	-95	-0	0	.00	0	....	0	0.0
2002 Hou-N	7	5	1	1	1	0	0	0	2	1	0	0	.200	.500	.400	.900	135	1	1	9.38	1	/3-4,S-1	0	0.2
Mil-N	21	76	6	18	8	0	1	8	15	14	0	0	.237	.363	.382	.744	98	0	12	5.55	-3	3-21	2	-0.3
Yr.	28	81	7	19	9	0	1	8	17	15	0	0	.235	.374	.383	.756	101	1	13	5.80	-2	3-25/S-1	2	-0.1
2003 Mil-N	127	358	51	92	15	2	14	44	37	87	1	1	.257	.354	.427	.782	105	3	56	5.41	-14	2-53,3-40/0-2(2-0-0),S-2	9	-0.8
Total 4	161	448	61	113	24	2	16	55	55	105	1	1	.252	.357	.422	.779	104	4	71	5.49	-16	/3-65,2-55,S-3,0-2	11	-0.9

• GIONFRIDDO, Al Albert Francis Gionfriddo b: 3/8/1922, Dysart, PA d: 3/14/2003, Solvang, CA BL/TL, 5'6", 165 lbs. Deb: 9/23/1944 Career OF: 32-96-29

YEAR TM-L	G	AB	R	H	2B	3B	HR	RBI	BB	SO	SB	CS	AVG	OBP	SLG	OPS	OPS+	BR/A	RC	RC/G	FR	G/POS	WS	TPW
1944 Pit-N	4	6	0	1	0	0	0	0	1	1	0	....	.167	.286	.167	.452	28	-1	0	1.94	0	/0-1	0	-0.1
1945 Pit-N	122	409	74	116	18	9	2	42	60	22	12	....	.284	.377	.386	.763	108	6	64	5.73	-6	*0-106(13-82-11)	15	-0.3
1946 Pit-N	64	102	11	26	2	2	0	10	14	5	1	....	.255	.345	.314	.659	85	-2	12	4.20	-1	0-33(8-13-12)	2	-0.4
1947 Pit-N	1	1	0	0	0	0	0	0	0	0	0	....	.000	.000	.000	.000	-97	-0	0	.00	0	....	0	0.0
*Bro-N	37	62	10	11	2	1	0	6	16	11	2	....	.177	.346	.242	.588	56	-3	7	3.25	-1	0-17(11-0-6)	1	-0.4
Yr.	38	63	10	11	2	1	0	6	16	11	2	....	.175	.342	.238	.580	55	-3	7	3.19	-1	0-17(11-0-6)	1	-0.5
Total 4	228	580	95	154	22	12	2	58	91	39	15	....	.266	.366	.355	.721	97	1	83	5.09	-8	0-157	18	-1.2

• GIORDANO, Tommy Thomas Arthur "T-Bone" Giordano b: 10/9/1925, Newark, NJ BR/TR, 6', 175 lbs. Deb: 9/11/1953

YEAR TM-L	G	AB	R	H	2B	3B	HR	RBI	BB	SO	SB	CS	AVG	OBP	SLG	OPS	OPS+	BR/A	RC	RC/G	FR	G/POS	WS	TPW
1953 Phi-A	11	40	6	7	2	0	2	5	5	6	0	1	.175	.267	.375	.642	69	-2	4	3.24	1	2-11	1	-0.1

• GIOVANOLA, Ed Edward Thomas Giovanola b: 3/4/1969, Los Gatos, CA BL/TR, 5'10", 170 lbs. Deb: 9/10/1995

YEAR TM-L	G	AB	R	H	2B	3B	HR	RBI	BB	SO	SB	CS	AVG	OBP	SLG	OPS	OPS+	BR/A	RC	RC/G	FR	G/POS	WS	TPW
1995 Atl-N	13	14	2	1	0	0	0	0	3	5	0	0	.071	.235	.071	.307	-14	-2	0	.61	-2	/2-7,3-3,S-1	0	-0.4
1996 Atl-N	43	82	10	19	2	0	0	7	8	13	1	0	.232	.308	.256	.564	48	-6	7	2.65	-1	S-25/3-6,2-5	1	-0.5
1997 Atl-N	14	8	0	2	0	0	0	0	2	1	0	0	.250	.400	.250	.650	73	-0	0	1.53	-1	/3-8,2-1,S-1	0	-0.1
1998 SD-N	92	139	19	32	3	3	1	9	22	22	1	2	.230	.335	.317	.652	78	-4	16	3.70	3	3-37,2-36/S-1	4	0.0
1999 SD-N	56	58	10	11	0	1	0	3	9	8	2	0	.190	.299	.224	.523	38	-5	5	2.59	-2	3-25,2-19/S-7,P-1	1	-0.5
Total 5	218	301	41	65	5	4	1	19	44	49	4	2	.216	.318	.269	.587	58	-17	28	2.97	-2	/3-79,2-68,S-35,P-1	6	-1.5

• GIPSON, Charles Charles Wells Gipson b: 12/16/1972, Orange, CA BR/TR, 6'2", 180 lbs. Deb: 3/31/1998 Career OF: 134-55-81

YEAR TM-L	G	AB	R	H	2B	3B	HR	RBI	BB	SO	SB	CS	AVG	OBP	SLG	OPS	OPS+	BR/A	RC	RC/G	FR	G/POS	WS	TPW
1998 Sea-A	44	51	11	12	1	0	0	2	5	9	2	1	.235	.316	.255	.571	51	-4	4	2.84	-1	0-36(14-11-13)/3-4	1	-0.5
1999 Sea-A	55	80	16	18	5	2	0	9	6	13	3	4	.225	.287	.338	.625	57	-6	7	2.59	4	0-28(8-9-15),3-17/D-4,2-3,S	1	-0.2
2000*Sea-A	59	29	7	9	1	1	0	3	4	9	2	3	.310	.394	.414	.808	111	-0	4	5.01	1	0-48(14-8-29)/3-5,S-5,D-1	1	0.0
2001*Sea-A	94	64	16	14	2	2	0	5	4	20	1	1	.219	.286	.313	.598	61	-4	5	2.68	0	0-65(41-14-11),D-10/3-9,S,2	1	-0.5
2002 Sea-A	79	72	22	17	5	2	0	8	9	14	4	0	.236	.329	.361	.690	87	-0	9	4.08	1	0-73(57-5-13)/3-4,D-2	1	0.0
2003 NY-A	18	10	3	2	0	0	0	2	1	2	2	1	.200	.273	.200	.473	28	-1	1	1.72	0	/0-8(0-8-0),D-3	0	-0.1
Total 6	349	306	75	72	14	7	0	29	29	67	14	10	.235	.312	.327	.639	68	-15	30	3.17	4	0-258/3-39,D-20,S-14,2-4	5	-1.3

• GIRARDI, Joe Joseph Elliott Girardi b: 10/14/1964, Peoria, IL BR/TR, 5'11", 195 lbs. Deb: 4/4/1989

YEAR TM-L	G	AB	R	H	2B	3B	HR	RBI	BB	SO	SB	CS	AVG	OBP	SLG	OPS	OPS+	BR/A	RC	RC/G	FR	G/POS	WS	TPW
1989*Chi-N	59	157	15	39	10	0	1	14	11	26	2	1	.248	.306	.331	.637	76	-5	15	3.31	-2	C-59	4	-0.3
1990 Chi-N	133	419	36	113	24	2	1	38	17	50	8	3	.270	.303	.344	.647	72	-16	40	3.31	-5	*C-133	9	-1.4
1991 Chi-N	21	47	3	9	2	0	0	6	6	6	0	0	.191	.283	.234	.517	45	-3	4	2.47	0	C-21	1	-0.2
1992 Chi-N	91	270	19	73	3	1	1	12	19	38	0	2	.270	.321	.300	.621	75	-9	25	3.18	4	C-86	6	-0.1
1993 Col-N	86	310	35	90	14	5	3	31	24	41	6	6	.290	.347	.397	.744	85	-8	42	4.63	1	C-84	9	0.0
1994 Col-N	93	330	47	91	9	4	4	34	21	48	3	3	.276	.323	.364	.687	67	-16	36	3.66	9	C-93	8	-0.1
1995*Col-N	125	462	63	121	17	2	8	55	29	76	3	3	.262	.308	.359	.668	59	-29	48	3.51	0	*C-122	10	-2.0

YEAR TM-L	G	AB	R	H	2B	3B	HR	RBI	BB	SO	SB	CS	AVG	OBP	SLG	OPS	OPS+	BR/A	RC	RC/G	FR	G/POS	WS	TPW
1996*NY-A	124	422	55	124	22	3	2	45	30	55	13	4	.294	.348	.374	.722	83	-10	55	4.57	2	*C-120/D-2	11	0.0
1997*NY-A	112	398	38	105	23	1	1	50	26	53	2	3	.264	.312	.334	.646	69	-19	38	3.26	3	*C-111/D-1	9	-0.7
1998*NY-A	78	254	31	70	11	4	3	31	14	38	2	4	.276	.319	.386	.704	85	-7	28	3.62	3	C-78	7	0.1
1999*NY-A	65	209	23	50	16	1	2	27	10	26	3	1	.239	.274	.354	.628	59	-13	16	2.27	1	C-65	3	-0.7
2000 Chi-N★	106	363	47	101	15	1	6	40	32	61	1	0	.278	.342	.375	.716	83	-9	46	4.35	-2	*C-103	9	-0.4
2001 Chi-N	78	229	22	58	10	1	3	25	21	50	0	1	.253	.316	.345	.661	75	-9	26	3.89	-4	C-71	8	-0.9
2002 Chi-N	90	234	19	53	10	1	1	13	16	35	1	0	.226	.276	.291	.567	50	-17	17	2.37	-4	C-88	3	-1.6
2003 StL-N	16	23	1	3	0	0	0	1	3	4	0	0	.130	.231	.130	.361	-3	-3	1	.71	-4	C-13	0	-0.7
Total 15	1277	4127	454	1100	186	26	36	422	279	607	44	31	.267	.317	.350	.667	72	-175	436	3.57	2	*C-1247/D-3	97	-9.1

• GIULIANI, Tony Angelo John Giuliani b: 11/24/1912, St. Paul, MN BR/TR, 5'11", 175 lbs. Deb: 4/18/1936

YEAR TM-L	G	AB	R	H	2B	3B	HR	RBI	BB	SO	SB	CS	AVG	OBP	SLG	OPS	OPS+	BR/A	RC	RC/G	FR	G/POS	WS	TPW
1936 StL-A	71	198	17	43	3	0	0	13	11	13	0	0	.217	.258	.232	.491	21	-25	12	2.07	1	C-66	2	-1.7
1937 StL-A	19	53	6	16	1	0	0	3	3	3	0	0	.302	.339	.321	.660	67	-3	6	4.02	0	C-19	1	-0.1
1938 Was-A	46	115	10	25	4	0	0	15	8	3	1	0	.217	.268	.252	.520	33	-12	8	2.36	1	C-46	1	-0.8
1939 Was-A	54	172	20	43	6	2	0	18	4	7	0	1	.250	.267	.308	.575	50	-14	13	2.40	0	C-50	1	-1.0
1940 Bro-N	1	1	0	0	0	0	0	0	0	1	0	....	.000	.000	.000	.000	-94	-0	0	.00	0	/C-1	0	0.0
1941 Bro-N	3	2	0	0	0	0	0	0	0	0	0	....	.000	.000	.000	.000	-96	-1	0	.00	0	/C-3	0	0.0
1943 Was-A	49	133	5	30	4	1	0	20	12	14	0	1	.226	.290	.271	.560	67	-6	11	2.71	-4	C-49	2	-0.8
Total 7	243	674	58	157	18	3	0	69	38	41	1	2	.233	.274	.269	.542	43	-59	50	2.46	-2	C-234	7	-4.5

• GLADD, Jim James Walter Gladd b: 10/2/1922, Fort Gibson, OK d: 11/8/1977, Long Beach, CA BR/TR, 6'2", 190 lbs. Deb: 9/9/1946

YEAR TM-L	G	AB	R	H	2B	3B	HR	RBI	BB	SO	SB	CS	AVG	OBP	SLG	OPS	OPS+	BR/A	RC	RC/G	FR	G/POS	WS	TPW
1946 NY-N	4	11	0	1	0	0	0	0	1	4	0	....	.091	.167	.091	.258	-26	-2	0	.57	2	/C-4	0	0.1

• GLADDEN, Dan Clinton Daniel Gladden b: 7/7/1957, San Jose, CA BR/TR, 5'11", 180 lbs. Deb: 9/5/1983 Career OF: 798-349-4

YEAR TM-L	G	AB	R	H	2B	3B	HR	RBI	BB	SO	SB	CS	AVG	OBP	SLG	OPS	OPS+	BR/A	RC	RC/G	FR	G/POS	WS	TPW
1983 SF-N	18	63	6	14	2	0	1	9	5	11	4	3	.222	.279	.302	.581	63	-4	4	2.02	0	0-18(0-17-1)	1	-0.4
1984 SF-N	86	342	71	120	17	2	4	31	33	37	31	16	.351	.411	.447	.859	146	21	64	6.99	2	0-85(0-85-0)	17	2.3
1985 SF-N	142	502	64	122	15	8	7	41	40	78	32	15	.243	.308	.347	.654	87	-9	54	3.47	-5	*0-124(14-111-1)	10	-1.7
1986 SF-N	102	351	55	97	16	1	4	29	39	59	27	10	.276	.357	.362	.719	104	4	49	4.76	7	0-89(0-90-0)	13	1.1
1987*Min-A	121	438	69	109	21	2	8	38	38	72	25	9	.249	.313	.361	.674	75	-14	50	3.90	3	*0-111(105-8-2)/D-4	9	-1.6
1988 Min-A	141	576	91	155	32	6	11	62	46	74	28	8	.269	.327	.403	.730	100	2	78	4.72	2	*0-140(140-0-0)/2-1,3-1,P	18	-0.1
1989 Min-A	121	461	69	136	23	3	8	46	23	53	23	7	.295	.335	.410	.745	102	2	64	4.97	-2	*0-117(116-2-0)/D-2,P-1	12	-0.4
1990 Min-A	136	534	64	147	27	6	5	40	26	67	25	9	.275	.316	.376	.693	87	-9	60	3.88	5	*0-133(133-1-0)/D-2	11	-0.8
1991*Min-A	126	461	65	114	14	9	6	52	36	60	15	9	.247	.309	.356	.665	80	-14	49	3.47	1	*0-126(126-0-0)	7	-1.7
1992 Det-A	113	417	57	106	20	1	7	42	30	64	4	2	.254	.307	.357	.665	85	-9	45	3.66	2	*0-108(95-17-0)/D-2	8	-1.1
1993 Det-A	91	356	52	95	16	2	13	56	21	50	8	5	.267	.313	.433	.746	99	-2	43	4.10	4	0-86(69-18-0)/D-5	8	-0.2
Total 11	1197	4501	663	1215	203	40	74	446	337	625	222	93	.270	.327	.382	.709	95	-31	561	4.26	20	*0-1137/D-15,P-2,2-1,3-1	114	-4.5

• GLADMON, Buck James Henry Gladmon b: 11/1863, Washington, DC d: 1/13/1890, Washington, DC Deb: 7/7/1883

YEAR TM-L	G	AB	R	H	2B	3B	HR	RBI	BB	SO	SB	CS	AVG	OBP	SLG	OPS	OPS+	BR/A	RC	RC/G	FR	G/POS	WS	TPW
1883 Phi-N	1	4	1	0	0	0	0	0	0	2	....	....	.000	.000	.000	.000	-110	-1	0	.00	0	/3-1	0	-0.1
1884 Was-a	56	224	17	35	5	3	1	0	3	....	....	....	.156	.178	.219	.397	33	-15	9	1.30	-8	3-53/0-2(0-0-2),S-1	0	-1.9
1886 Was-N	44	152	17	21	5	3	1	15	12	30	5	....	.138	.201	.230	.431	33	-12	8	1.70	-4	3-44	1	-1.4
Total 3	101	380	35	56	10	6	2	15	15	32	5	....	.147	.186	.221	.407	31	-27	17	1.45	-12	/3-98,0-2,S-1	1	-3.4

• GLADU, Roland Roland Edouard Gladu b: 5/10/1911, Montreal, Canada d: 7/26/1994, Montreal, Canada BL/TR, 5'8.5", 185 lbs. Deb: 4/18/1944

YEAR TM-L	G	AB	R	H	2B	3B	HR	RBI	BB	SO	SB	CS	AVG	OBP	SLG	OPS	OPS+	BR/A	RC	RC/G	FR	G/POS	WS	TPW
1944 Bos-N	21	66	5	16	2	1	1	7	3	8	0	....	.242	.275	.348	.624	72	-3	6	3.01	-2	3-15/0-3(3-0-0)	1	-0.5

• GLANVILLE, Doug Douglas Metunwa Glanville b: 8/25/1970, Hackensack, NJ BR/TR, 6'2", 170 lbs. Deb: 6/9/1996 Career OF: 142-829-10

YEAR TM-L	G	AB	R	H	2B	3B	HR	RBI	BB	SO	SB	CS	AVG	OBP	SLG	OPS	OPS+	BR/A	RC	RC/G	FR	G/POS	WS	TPW
1996 Chi-N	49	83	10	20	5	1	1	10	3	11	2	0	.241	.267	.361	.629	62	-4	9	3.53	-1	0-35(19-9-8)	2	-0.6
1997 Chi-N	146	474	79	142	22	5	4	35	24	46	19	11	.300	.335	.392	.727	87	-10	60	4.46	5	*0-138(120-30-1)	9	-0.9
1998 Phi-N	158	678	106	189	28	7	8	49	42	89	23	6	.279	.326	.376	.703	83	-15	87	4.57	3	*0-158(0-158-0)	17	-1.0
1999 Phi-N	150	628	101	204	38	6	11	73	48	82	34	2	.325	.378	.457	.835	107	13	116	7.01	5	*0-148(0-148-0)	23	1.8
2000 Phi-N	154	637	89	175	27	6	8	52	31	76	31	8	.275	.310	.374	.684	71	-26	75	4.03	-1	*0-150(0-150-0)	10	-2.5
2001 Phi-N	153	634	74	166	24	3	14	55	19	91	28	6	.262	.288	.375	.663	71	-25	70	3.78	5	*0-150(0-150-0)	11	-1.8
2002 Phi-N	138	422	49	105	16	3	6	29	25	57	19	2	.249	.294	.344	.638	70	-16	45	3.65	-2	*0-117(0-117-0)	5	-1.7
2003 Tex-A	52	195	22	53	5	0	4	14	6	25	4	0	.272	.294	.359	.653	65	-9	21	3.86	-2	0-18(0-52-0)	1	-1.0
*Chi-N	28	51	2	12	0	0	1	2	2	4	0	1	.235	.264	.294	.558	46	-5	4	2.52	3	0-52(3-15-1)	1	-0.2
Total 8	1028	3802	532	1066	165	31	57	319	200	481	160	36	.280	.320	.385	.705	80	-98	485	4.51	15	0-966	79	-7.9

• GLASSCOCK, Jack John Wesley "Pebbly Jack" Glasscock b: 7/22/1859, Wheeling, WV d: 2/24/1947, Wheeling, WV BR/TR, 5'8", 160 lbs. Deb: 5/1/1879 M

YEAR TM-L	G	AB	R	H	2B	3B	HR	RBI	BB	SO	SB	CS	AVG	OBP	SLG	OPS	OPS+	BR/A	RC	RC/G	FR	G/POS	WS	TPW
1879 Cle-N	80	325	31	68	9	3	0	29	6	24	....	....	.209	.224	.255	.479	58	-14	19	2.07	-4	*2-66,3-14	4	-1.4
1880 Cle-N	77	296	37	72	13	3	0	27	2	21	....	....	.243	.248	.307	.556	89	-4	23	2.84	10	*S-77	10	1.0
1881 Cle-N	85	335	49	86	9	5	0	33	15	8	....	....	.257	.289	.313	.602	94	-2	31	3.37	20	*S-79/2-6	10	2.1
1882 Cle-N	84	358	66	104	27	9	4	46	13	9	....	....	.291	.315	.450	.765	147	18	52	5.63	19	*S-83/3-1	19	3.7
1883 Cle-N	96	383	67	110	19	6	0	46	13	23	....	....	.287	.311	.368	.679	107	3	45	4.52	24	*S-93/2-3	14	2.7
1884 Cle-N	72	281	45	70	4	4	1	22	25	16	....	....	.249	.310	.302	.613	91	-2	27	3.53	22	S-69/2-3,P-2	8	1.8
Cin-U	38	172	48	72	9	5	2	....	8	....	....	....	.419	.444	.564	1.008	221	21	44	12.37	7	S-36/2-2	14	2.5
1885 StL-N	111	446	66	125	18	3	1	40	29	10	....	....	.280	.324	.341	.665	123	13	51	4.25	20	*S-110/2-1	17	3.4
1886 StL-N	121	486	96	158	29	7	3	40	38	13	38	....	.325	.374	.432	.806	154	33	95	7.83	15	*S-120/0-1	22	4.7
1887 Ind-N	122	524	91	183	18	7	0	40	41	8	62	....	.349	.361	.360	.722	105	6	87	6.79	21	*S-122/P-1	17	2.6
1888 Ind-N	113	442	63	119	17	3	1	45	14	17	48	....	.269	.302	.328	.630	99	-1	60	5.00	10	*S-110/2-3,P-1	16	1.0
1889 Ind-N	134	582	128	**205**	40	3	7	85	31	10	57	....	.352	.390	.467	.857	136	26	132	9.24	27	*S-132/2-2,P-1	27	**4.9**
1890 NY-N	124	512	91	**172**	32	9	1	66	41	8	54	....	**.336**	.395	.439	.834	143	27	113	8.80	9	*S-124	25	3.6
1891 NY-N	97	369	46	89	12	6	0	55	36	11	29	....	.241	.317	.306	.623	85	-6	46	4.45	-10	*S-97	10	-1.1
1892 StL-N	139	566	83	151	27	5	3	72	44	19	26	....	.267	.327	.348	.675	110	6	75	4.87	4	*S-139	20	1.7
1893 StL-N	48	195	32	56	8	1	1	26	25	3	20	....	.287	.382	.354	.736	96	-0	35	6.65	1	S-48	6	0.3
Pit-N	66	293	49	100	7	11	1	74	17	4	16	....	.341	.385	.451	.836	124	9	58	8.03	9	S-66	12	1.7
Yr.	114	488	81	156	15	12	2	100	42	7	36	....	.320	.384	.412	.796	112	9	93	7.45	9	*S-114	18	2.0
1894 Pit-N	87	335	47	94	10	7	1	65	32	4	18	....	.281	.350	.361	.712	73	-15	50	5.39	-4	*S-85	7	-1.1
1895 Lou-N	18	74	9	25	3	1	1	6	3	1	1	....	.338	.388	.446	.833	122	2	14	7.36	0	S-13/1-5	2	0.3
Was-N	25	100	20	23	2	0	0	10	7	3	3	....	.230	.300	.250	.550	43	-8	9	3.05	1	S-25	1	-0.5
Yr.	43	174	29	48	5	1	1	16	10	4	4	....	.276	.337	.333	.670	76	-6	23	4.71	2	S-38/1-5	3	-0.2
Total 17	1737	7074	1164	2082	313	98	27	827	440	212	372	....	.294	.337	.374	.712	113	113	1066	5.73	202	*S-1628/2-86,3-15,1-5,P-5,0	261	33.9

• GLAUS, Troy Troy Edward Glaus b: 8/3/1976, Newport Beach, CA BR/TR, 6'5", 245 lbs. Deb: 7/31/1998

YEAR TM-L	G	AB	R	H	2B	3B	HR	RBI	BB	SO	SB	CS	AVG	OBP	SLG	OPS	OPS+	BR/A	RC	RC/G	FR	G/POS	WS	TPW
1998 Ana-A	48	165	19	36	9	0	1	23	15	51	1	0	.218	.283	.291	.574	50	-12	14	2.84	-1	3-48	3	-1.1
1999 Ana-A	154	551	85	132	29	0	29	79	71	143	5	1	.240	.333	.450	.783	98	-2	86	5.36	0	*3-153/D-1	16	0.0
2000 Ana-A★	159	563	120	160	37	1	**47**	102	112	163	14	11	.284	.405	.604	1.009	147	40	138	8.69	18	*3-156/S-6,D-4	25	5.5
2001 Ana-A★	161	588	100	147	38	2	41	108	107	158	10	3	.250	.371	.531	.902	131	29	119	6.86	-13	*3-159/D-2,S-2	21	1.7
2002*Ana-A	156	569	99	142	24	1	30	111	88	144	10	3	.250	.356	.453	.809	113	13	96	5.75	7	*3-156/S-2	22	2.2
2003 Ana-A★	91	319	53	79	17	2	16	50	46	73	7	2	.248	.344	.464	.808	115	8	52	5.55	-6	3-87/D-4	10	0.3
Total 6	769	2755	476	696	154	6	164	473	439	732	47	20	.253	.360	.491	.851	118	76	504	6.29	5	3-759/D-11,S-10	97	8.6

• GLAVIANO, Tommy Thomas Giatano "Rabbit" Glaviano b: 10/26/1923, Sacramento, CA BR/TR, 5'9", 175 lbs. Deb: 4/19/1949

YEAR TM-L	G	AB	R	H	2B	3B	HR	RBI	BB	SO	SB	CS	AVG	OBP	SLG	OPS	OPS+	BR/A	RC	RC/G	FR	G/POS	WS	TPW
1949 StL-N	87	258	32	69	16	1	6	36	41	35	0	....	.267	.380	.407	.787	106	4	42	5.70	3	3-73/2-7	9	0.7
1950 StL-N	115	410	92	117	29	2	11	44	90	74	6	....	.285	.421	.446	.867	122	19	85	7.60	0	*3-106/2-5,S-1	18	1.8
1951 StL-N	54	104	20	19	4	0	1	4	26	18	3	0	.183	.356	.250	.606	66	-3	12	3.51	-2	0-17(2-14-1)/2-9	2	-0.5
1952 StL-N	80	162	30	39	5	1	3	19	27	26	0	0	.241	.366	.340	.705	97	1	21	4.43	-4	3-52/2-1	4	-0.3
1953 Phi-N	53	74	17	15	1	2	3	5	24	20	2	0	.203	.410	.392	.802	111	3	14	5.81	-2	3-14,2-12/S-1	3	0.2
Total 5	389	1008	191	259	55	6	24	108	208	173	11	0	.257	.395	.395	.789	107	24	174	5.98	-5	3-245/2-34,0-17,S-2	36	1.9

YEAR TM-L	G	AB	R	H	2B	3B	HR	RBI	BB	SO	SB	CS	AVG	OBP	SLG	OPS	OPS+	BR/A	RC	RC/G	FR	G/POS	WS	TPW
• GLAVINE, Mike	Michael Patrick Glavine b: 1/24/1973, Concord, MA BL/TL, 6'3", 210 lbs. Deb: 9/14/2003																							
2003 NY-N	6	7	0	1	0	0	0	0	0	2	0	0	.143	.143	.143	.286	-26	-1	0	.64	0	/1-3	0	-0.1
• GLEASON, Bill	William G. "Will" Gleason b: 11/12/1858, St. Louis, MO d: 7/21/1932, St. Louis, MO BR/TR, 5'8", 170 lbs. Deb: 5/2/1882 U																							
1882 StL-a	79	347	63	100	11	6	1	....	6	....	....	....	.288	.300	.363	.663	118	5	39	4.40	10	*S-79	16	1.6
1883 StL-a	98	425	81	122	21	9	2	42	15	....	....	....	.287	.311	.393	.704	118	7	53	4.93	1	*S-98	16	1.0
1884 StL-a	110	472	97	127	21	7	1	0	27	....	....	....	.269	.325	.350	.674	116	9	55	4.38	-16	*S-110/3-1	19	-0.3
1885*StL-a	112	472	79	119	9	5	3	53	29	....	....	....	.252	.316	.311	.627	94	-3	48	3.64	-31	*S-112	17	-2.7
1886*StL-a	125	524	97	141	18	5	0	61	43	....	19	....	.269	.333	.323	.655	101	0	64	4.52	-16	*S-125	15	-1.0
1887*StL-a	135	639	135	213	19	1	0	76	41	....	23	....	.333	.342	.323	.664	77	-20	76	4.79	6	*S-135	17	-0.8
1888 Phi-a	123	499	55	112	10	2	0	61	12	....	27	....	.224	.256	.253	.508	63	-21	40	2.80	-13	*S-121/1-1,3-1	9	-2.7
1889 Lou-a	16	58	6	14	2	0	0	5	4	1	1	....	.241	.302	.276	.577	66	-2	5	3.17	-2	S-16	0	-0.3
Total 8	**798**	**3436**	**613**	**948**	**111**	**35**	**7**	**298**	**177**	**1**	**70**	**....**	**.276**	**.313**	**.327**	**.640**	**96**	**-25**	**380**	**4.17**	**-61**	**S-796/3-2,1-1**	**109**	**-5.3**
• GLEASON, Billy	William Patrick Gleason b: 9/6/1894, Chicago, IL d: 1/9/1957, Holyoke, MA BR/TR, 5'6.5", 157 lbs. Deb: 9/25/1916																							
1916 Pit-N	1	2	0	0	0	0	0	0	0	0	0	....	.000	.000	.000	.000	-99	-0	0	.00	0	/2-1	0	-0.1
1917 Pit-N	13	42	3	7	1	0	0	0	5	5	1	....	.167	.255	.190	.446	36	-3	2	1.56	0	2-13	0	-0.3
1921 StL-A	26	74	6	19	0	1	0	8	6	6	0	1	.257	.329	.284	.613	54	-5	7	3.30	-1	2-25	1	-0.5
Total 3	**40**	**118**	**9**	**26**	**1**	**1**	**0**	**8**	**11**	**11**	**1**	**1**	**.220**	**.298**	**.246**	**.543**	**46**	**-9**	**9**	**2.58**	**-1**	**/2-39**	**1**	**-0.9**
• GLEASON, Harry	Harry Gilbert Gleason b: 3/28/1875, Camden, NJ d: 10/21/1961, Camden, NJ BR/TR, 5'6", 160 lbs. Deb: 9/27/1901 Career OF: 8-16-0																							
1901 Bos-A	1	1	0	1	0	0	0	0	0	....	1	....	1.000	1.000	1.000	2.000	464	0	2	∞	0	/3-1	0	0.0
1902 Bos-A	71	240	30	54	5	5	2	25	10	....	6	....	.225	.265	.313	.577	58	-14	23	3.13	-1	3-35,0-23(8-15-0)/2-4	3	-1.5
1903 Bos-A	6	13	3	2	1	0	0	2	0	....	0	....	.154	.154	.231	.385	13	-1	0	1.14	0	/3-2	0	-0.2
1904 StL-A	46	155	10	33	7	1	0	6	4	....	1	....	.213	.247	.271	.518	68	-6	11	2.39	-4	3-20,S-20/2-5,0-1	1	-1.0
1905 StL-A	150	535	45	116	11	5	1	57	34	....	23	....	.217	.269	.262	.530	72	-17	47	2.85	-27	*3-144/2-7	7	-4.3
Total 5	**274**	**944**	**88**	**206**	**24**	**11**	**3**	**90**	**48**	**....**	**31**	**....**	**.218**	**.263**	**.276**	**.540**	**68**	**-38**	**84**	**2.82**	**-32**	**3-202/0-24,S-20,2-16**	**11**	**-6.9**
• GLEASON, Jack	John Day Gleason b: 7/14/1854, St. Louis, MO d: 9/4/1944, St. Louis, MO BR/TR, 170 lbs. Deb: 10/2/1877 Career OF: 9-1-6																							
1877 StL-N	1	4	0	1	0	0	0	0	0	1	....	....	.250	.250	.250	.500	61	-0	0	2.35	0	/0-1	0	0.0
1882 StL-a	78	331	53	84	10	1	2	....	**27**	....	....	....	.254	.310	.308	.618	105	2	32	3.67	2	*3-73/0-6(0-0-6),2-1	12	0.6
1883 StL-a	9	34	2	8	0	0	0	0	4	....	....	....	.235	.316	.235	.551	76	-1	3	2.79	1	/0-9(9-0-0),3-1	1	0.0
Lou-a	84	355	69	106	11	4	2	0	25	....	....	....	.299	.345	.369	.714	140	18	46	5.21	-30	*3-83/S-1	13	-0.9
Yr.	93	389	71	114	11	4	2	0	29	....	....	....	.293	.342	.357	.699	134	17	49	4.98	-29	*3-84/0-9(9-0-0),S-1	14	-0.9
1884 StL-U	92	395	90	128	30	2	4	....	23	....	....	....	.324	.361	.441	.802	164	25	64	6.76	0	*3-92	20	2.4
1885 StL-N	2	7	0	1	0	0	0	0	0	1	....	....	.143	.143	.143	.286	-8	-1	0	.66	0	/3-2	0	-0.1
1886 Phi-a	77	299	39	56	8	7	1	31	16	....	8	....	.187	.255	.271	.526	64	-13	23	2.58	-9	3-77	4	-1.8
Total 6	**343**	**1425**	**253**	**384**	**59**	**14**	**9**	**31**	**95**	**2**	**8**	**....**	**.269**	**.320**	**.349**	**.670**	**120**	**31**	**169**	**4.53**	**-36**	**3-328/0-16,2-1,S-1**	**50**	**0.1**
• GLEASON, Kid	William J. Gleason b: 10/26/1866, Camden, NJ d: 1/2/1933, Philadelphia, PA BB/TR, 5'7", 158 lbs. Deb: 4/20/1888 M/C/U Career OF: 14-15-13 ♦																							
1888 Phi-N	24	83	4	17	2	0	0	5	3	16	3	....	.205	.233	.229	.461	45	0	5	2.15	-3	P-24/0-1	13	0.6
1889 Phi-N	30	99	11	25	5	0	0	8	8	12	4	....	.253	.308	.303	.611	65	2	11	3.85	-1	P-29/0-3(0-1-0),2-2	8	-1.6
1890 Phi-N	63	224	22	47	3	0	0	17	12	21	10	....	.210	.250	.223	.473	37	-6	15	2.30	-1	P-60/2-2	45	4.0
1891 Phi-N	65	214	31	53	5	2	0	17	20	17	6	....	.248	.318	.290	.608	75	5	22	3.71	-6	P-53/0-9(1-8-0),S-4	29	-0.4
1892 StL-N	66	233	35	50	4	2	3	25	34	23	7	....	.215	.315	.288	.602	87	8	24	3.52	4	P-47,0-10(3-2-6)/2-9,1-1	25	1.5
1893 StL-N	59	199	25	51	6	4	0	20	19	8	2	....	.256	.327	.327	.654	74	2	22	4.02	0	P-48,0-11(5-0-6)/S-1	22	0.6
1894 StL-N	9	28	3	7	0	1	0	1	2	1	0	....	.250	.300	.321	.621	50	-1	3	3.43	1	/P-8,1-1	3	-0.3
*Bal-N	26	86	22	30	5	1	0	17	7	2	1	....	.349	.398	.430	.828	96	5	15	7.19	-2	P-21/1-1	16	1.4
Yr.	35	114	25	37	5	2	0	18	9	3	1	....	.325	.374	.404	.777	84	4	18	6.17	-1	P-29/1-2	19	1.1
1895*Bal-N	112	421	90	130	14	12	0	74	33	18	19	....	.309	.366	.399	.765	95	-3	71	6.44	-7	*2-85,3-12/P-9,0-4(4-0-0)	12	-1.7
1896 NY-N	133	541	79	162	17	5	4	89	42	13	46	....	.299	.352	.372	.724	93	-5	90	6.15	9	*2-130/3-3,0-1	15	0.8
1897 NY-N	132	543	86	172	16	4	1	106	27	....	43	....	.317	.353	.366	.719	92	-6	88	6.20	-4	*2-129/S-3	17	-0.3
1898 NY-N	150	570	78	126	8	5	0	62	39	....	21	....	.221	.278	.253	.531	54	-34	48	2.81	-3	*2-144/S-6	8	-2.7
1899 NY-N	147	580	73	154	14	5	0	59	24	....	29	....	.266	.295	.307	.602	67	-27	63	3.87	4	*2-146	10	-1.5
1900 NY-N	111	420	60	104	11	3	1	29	17	....	23	....	.248	.280	.295	.575	62	-22	43	3.52	-7	*2-111/S-1	5	-2.2
1901 Det-A	135	547	82	150	16	12	3	75	41	....	32	....	.274	.327	.364	.691	87	-10	79	5.09	-4	*2-135	15	-1.2
1902 Det-A	118	441	42	109	11	4	1	38	25	....	17	....	.247	.292	.297	.589	62	-23	46	3.53	-0	*2-118	6	-2.1
1903 Phi-N	106	412	65	117	19	6	1	49	23	....	12	....	.284	.326	.367	.693	101	-1	57	4.78	2	*2-102/0-4(0-2-0)	10	0.1
1904 Phi-N	153	587	61	161	23	6	0	42	37	....	17	....	.274	.319	.334	.653	106	3	74	4.17	-2	*2-152/3-1	15	0.2
1905 Phi-N	155	608	95	150	17	7	1	50	45	....	16	....	.247	.302	.303	.604	83	-12	67	3.49	11	*2-155	12	0.0
1906 Phi-N	135	494	47	112	17	2	0	34	36	....	17	....	.227	.281	.269	.550	71	-17	47	2.95	-12	*2-135	7	-3.1
1907 Phi-N	36	126	11	18	3	0	0	6	7	....	3	....	.143	.200	.167	.367	15	-12	6	1.32	0	2-26/1-4,S-4,0-1	1	-1.4
1908 Phi-N	2	1	0	0	0	0	0	0	0	....	0	....	.000	.000	.000	.000	-97	-0	0	.00	-0	/2-1,0-1	0	0.0
1912 Chi-A	1	2	0	1	0	0	0	0	0	....	1	....	.500	.500	.500	1.000	192	0	0	12.79	0	/2-1	0	0.0
Total 22	**1968**	**7459**	**1022**	**1946**	**216**	**81**	**15**	**823**	**501**	**131**	**328**	**....**	**.261**	**.311**	**.318**	**.628**	**78**	**-153**	**898**	**4.15**	**-20**	***2-1583,P-299/0-45,S-19,3,1**	**294**	**-9.2**
• GLEASON, Roy	Roy William Gleason b: 4/9/1943, Melrose Park, IL BB/TR, 6'5.5", 220 lbs. Deb: 9/3/1963																							
1963 LA-N	8	1	3	1	1	0	0	0	0	0	0	0	1.000	1.000	2.000	3.000	795	1	2	∞	0	....	1	0.1
• GLEESON, Jim	James Joseph "Gee Gee" Gleeson b: 3/5/1912, Kansas City, MO d: 5/1/1996, Kansas City, MO BB/TR, 6'1", 191 lbs. Deb: 4/25/1936 C Career OF: 71-109-164																							
1936 Cle-A	41	139	26	36	9	2	4	12	18	17	2	1	.259	.344	.439	.783	91	-2	22	5.46	-2	0-33(4-0-30)	3	-0.5
1939 Chi-N	111	332	43	74	19	6	4	45	39	46	7	....	.223	.308	.352	.661	76	-11	38	3.77	-5	0-91(13-12-66)	6	-2.2
1940 Chi-N	129	485	76	152	39	11	5	61	54	52	4	....	.313	.389	.470	.859	139	27	91	7.11	3	*0-123(32-82-13)	20	2.6
1941 Cin-N	102	301	47	70	10	0	3	34	45	30	7	....	.233	.340	.296	.636	80	-6	33	3.61	-5	0-84(22-15-50)	8	-1.6
1942 Cin-N	9	20	3	4	0	0	0	2	2	2	0	....	.200	.304	.200	.504	49	-1	2	2.46	0	/0-5(0-0-5)	0	-0.2
Total 5	**392**	**1277**	**195**	**336**	**77**	**19**	**16**	**154**	**158**	**147**	**20**	**1**	**.263**	**.350**	**.391**	**.741**	**102**	**5**	**185**	**5.06**	**-8**	**0-336**	**37**	**-1.9**
• GLEICH, Frank	Frank Elmer "Inch" Gleich b: 3/7/1894, Columbus, OH d: 3/27/1949, Columbus, OH BL/TR, 5'11", 175 lbs. Deb: 9/17/1919 Career OF: 12-5-2																							
1919 NY-A	5	4	0	1	0	0	0	1	1	0	0	....	.250	.400	.250	.650	84	-0	0	3.33	-1	/0-4(3-1-0)	0	-0.1
1920 NY-A	24	41	6	5	0	0	0	3	6	10	0	0	.122	.234	.122	.356	-4	-6	2	1.11	-2	0-15(9-4-2)	0	-0.8
Total 2	**29**	**45**	**6**	**6**	**0**	**0**	**0**	**4**	**7**	**10**	**0**	**0**	**.133**	**.250**	**.133**	**.383**	**5**	**-6**	**2**	**1.28**	**-3**	**/0-19**	**0**	**-0.9**
• GLENALVIN, Bob	Robert J. Glenalvin b: 1/17/1867, Indianapolis, IN d: 3/24/1944, Detroit, MI TR, 5'9", 160 lbs. Deb: 7/12/1890																							
1890 Chi-N	66	250	43	67	10	3	4	26	19	31	30	....	.268	.337	.380	.717	105	1	43	6.25	-5	2-66	9	-0.2
1893 Chi-N	16	61	11	21	3	1	0	12	7	3	7	....	.344	.412	.426	.838	125	2	14	9.23	-3	2-16	2	0.0
Total 2	**82**	**311**	**54**	**88**	**13**	**4**	**4**	**38**	**26**	**34**	**37**	**....**	**.283**	**.352**	**.389**	**.741**	**109**	**3**	**57**	**6.79**	**-7**	**/2-82**	**11**	**-0.1**
• GLENN, Ed	Edward C. "Mouse" Glenn b: 9/19/1860, Richmond, VA d: 2/10/1892, Richmond, VA BR/TR, 5'10", 160 lbs. Deb: 8/5/1884 Career OF: 136-0-0																							
1884 Ric-a	43	175	26	43	2	4	1	0	5	....	....	....	.246	.271	.320	.591	93	-1	16	3.24	5	0-43(43-0-0)	3	0.2
1886 Pit-a	71	277	32	53	6	5	0	26	17	....	19	....	.191	.241	.249	.490	54	-15	22	2.62	-1	0-71(71-0-0)	4	-1.7
1888 KC-a	3	8	0	0	0	0	0	0	0	....	1	....	.000	.200	.000	.200	-32	-1	0	.69	0	/0-3(3-0-0)	0	-0.1
Bos-N	20	65	8	10	0	2	0	3	2	8	0	....	.154	.203	.215	.418	32	-5	3	1.43	2	0-19(19-0-0)/3-1	1	-0.4
Total 3	**137**	**525**	**66**	**106**	**8**	**11**	**1**	**29**	**24**	**8**	**20**	**....**	**.202**	**.245**	**.265**	**.510**	**62**	**-23**	**40**	**2.62**	**5**	**0-136/3-1**	**8**	**-2.0**
• GLENN, Ed	Edward D. Glenn b: 10/1875, OH d: 12/6/1911, Ludlow, KY BR/TR Deb: 9/7/1898																							
1898 Was-N	1	4	0	0	0	0	0	0	0	....	0	....	.000	.000	.000	.000	-100	-1	0	.00	0	/S-1	0	-0.1
NY-N	2	4	1	1	0	0	0	0	3	....	1	....	.250	.571	.250	.821	142	1	2	6.95	0	/S-2	0	0.0
Yr.	3	8	1	1	0	0	0	0	3	....	1	....	.125	.364	.125	.489	77	-0	2	4.42	0	/S-3	0	0.0

YEAR TM-L	G	AB	R	H	2B	3B	HR	RBI	BB	SO	SB	CS	AVG	OBP	SLG	OPS	OPS+	BR/A	RC	RC/G	FR	G/POS	WS	TPW
1902 Chi-N	2	7	0	0	0	0	0	0	1	....	0	....	.000	.125	.000	.125	-63	-1	0	.00	0	/S-2	0	-0.1
Total 2	5	15	1	1	0	0	0	0	4	....	1	....	.067	.263	.067	.330	28	-2	2	2.70	0	/S-5	0	-0.1
• GLENN, Harry	Harry Melville "Husky" Glenn b: 6/9/1890, Shelburn, IN d: 10/12/1918, St. Paul, MN BR/TR, 6'1", 200 lbs. Deb: 4/14/1915																							
1915 StL-N	6	16	1	5	0	0	0	1	3	0	0	....	.313	.421	.313	.734	123	1	2	5.07	-1	/C-5	1	0.0
• GLENN, Joe	Joseph Charles "Gabby" Glenn b: 11/19/1908, Dickson City, PA d: 5/6/1985, Tunkhannock, PA BR/TR, 5'11", 175 lbs. Deb: 9/15/1932																							
1932 NY-A	6	16	0	2	0	0	0	0	1	5	0	0	.125	.222	.125	.347	-8	-2	1	1.02	0	/C-5	0	-0.2
1933 NY-A	5	21	1	3	0	0	0	1	0	3	0	0	.143	.143	.143	.286	-26	-4	0	.61	0	/C-5	0	-0.3
1935 NY-A	17	43	7	10	4	0	0	6	4	1	0	0	.233	.298	.326	.623	65	-2	4	3.34	-1	C-16	1	-0.2
1936 NY-A	44	129	21	35	7	0	1	20	20	10	1	1	.271	.373	.349	.722	82	-3	18	5.01	-1	C-44	4	-0.1
1937 NY-A	25	53	6	15	2	2	0	4	10	11	0	0	.283	.397	.396	.793	100	0	9	6.15	0	C-24	2	0.2
1938 NY-A	41	123	10	32	7	2	0	25	10	14	1	0	.260	.316	.350	.665	67	-6	14	4.07	-2	C-40	3	-0.6
1939 StL-A	88	286	29	78	13	1	4	29	31	40	4	4	.273	.344	.367	.711	80	-9	36	4.41	0	C-82	5	-0.5
1940 Bos-A	22	47	3	6	1	0	0	4	5	7	0	0	.128	.212	.149	.360	-5	-7	1	.70	-2	C-19	0	-0.8
Total 8	248	718	77	181	34	5	5	89	81	91	6	5	.252	.330	.334	.664	69	-34	84	4.00	-7	C-235	15	-2.6
• GLENN, John	John Glenn b: 7/10/1928, Moultrie, GA BR/TR, 6'3", 180 lbs. Deb: 6/16/1960																							
1960 StL-N	32	31	4	8	0	1	0	5	0	9	0	0	.258	.258	.323	.581	53	-2	3	2.96	-1	0-28(19-5-4)	0	-0.3
• GLENN, John	John W. Glenn b: 1849, Rochester, NY d: 11/10/1888, Sandy Hill, NY BR/TR, 5'8.5", 169 lbs. Deb: 5/13/1871 U NA OF: 51-9-43 Career OF: 92-0-1																							
1871 Oly-n	26	120	25	37	3	2	0	21	3	1	1	1	.308	.325	.367	.692	104	1	15	5.63	1	*O-26(1-0-25)	....	0.2
1872 Oly-n	9	39	6	6	0	0	0	3	1	0	0	1	.154	.175	.154	.329	2	-4	1	.98	3	/O-9(9-0-0)	....	-0.1
Nat-n	1	4	0	2	0	0	0	0	0	0	0	0	.500	.500	.500	1.000	179	0	1	15.89	0	/O-1	....	0.0
Yr.	10	43	6	8	0	0	0	3	1	0	0	1	.186	.205	.186	.391	18	-4	2	1.81	2	O-10(9-1-0)	....	-0.1
1873 Was-n	39	185	39	49	8	2	1	21	3	0	2	1	.265	.277	.346	.623	87	-2	19	4.17	-4	*1-39	....	-0.4
1874 Chi-n	55	237	33	67	9	0	0	33	5	4	2	2	.283	.298	.321	.618	97	-1	24	4.15	0	1-37,O-19(2-1-17)	....	0.0
1875 Chi-n	69	308	46	75	8	0	0	27	3	6	10	2	.244	.251	.269	.520	80	-5	24	3.00	0	O-44(39-7-1),1-29	....	-0.3
1876 Chi-N	66	288	55	84	9	2	0	32	12	6	....	....	.292	.333	.351	.685	115	3	33	4.83	-3	*O-56(56-0-0),1-15	8	-0.3
1877 Chi-N	50	202	31	46	6	1	0	20	8	16	....	....	.228	.257	.267	.524	58	-10	14	2.51	1	O-36(36-0-1),1-14	3	-1.1
Total 5 n	199	893	149	236	28	4	1	105	15	11	15	7	.264	.276	.308	.584	86	-12	84	3.81	0	1-105/O-99	....	-0.6
Total 2	116	490	86	130	15	3	0	52	20	22	....	....	.265	.301	.316	.617	91	-7	47	3.79	-3	/O-92,1-29	11	-1.4
• GLOAD, Ross	Ross P. Gload b: 4/5/1976, Brooklyn, NY BL/TL, 6'2", 185 lbs. Deb: 8/31/2000 Career OF: 9-0-1																							
2000 Chi-N	18	31	4	6	0	1	1	3	3	10	0	0	.194	.265	.355	.620	56	-2	3	2.81	-1	/O-8(7-0-1),1-2	0	-0.3
2002 Col-N	26	31	4	8	1	0	1	4	3	7	0	0	.258	.324	.387	.711	74	-1	4	4.85	1	/1-4,O-2(2-0-0)	0	0.0
Total 2	44	62	8	14	1	1	2	7	6	17	0	0	.226	.294	.371	.665	65	-3	7	3.75	1	/O-10,1-6	0	-0.3
• GLOCKSON, Norm	Norman Stanley Glockson b: 6/15/1894, Blue Island, IL d: 8/5/1955, Maywood, IL BR/TR, 6'2", 200 lbs. Deb: 9/16/1914																							
1914 Cin-N	7	12	0	0	0	0	0	0	1	6	0	....	.000	.077	.000	.077	-74	-3	0	.00	-1	/C-7	0	-0.3
• GLOSSOP, Al	Alban Glossop b: 7/12/1914, Christopher, IL d: 7/2/1991, Walnut Creek, CA BB/TR, 6', 170 lbs. Deb: 9/23/1939																							
1939 NY-N	10	32	3	6	0	0	1	3	4	2	0	....	.188	.278	.281	.559	50	-2	3	2.48	2	2-10	0	0.0
1940 NY-N	27	91	16	19	3	0	4	8	10	16	1	....	.209	.294	.374	.668	82	-2	10	3.88	0	2-24	2	-0.1
Bos-N	60	148	17	35	2	1	3	14	17	22	1	....	.236	.315	.324	.639	81	-4	16	3.73	1	2-18,3-18/S-1	4	-0.1
Yr.	87	239	33	54	5	1	7	22	27	38	2	....	.226	.307	.343	.650	82	-6	26	3.79	1	2-42,3-18/S-1	6	-0.2
1942 Phi-N	121	454	33	102	15	1	4	40	29	35	3	....	.225	.273	.289	.561	68	-20	36	2.71	5	*2-118/3-1	5	-0.8
1943 Bro-N	87	217	28	37	9	0	3	21	28	27	0	....	.171	.268	.253	.522	51	-13	17	2.45	-8	S-33,2-24,3-17/O-1	2	-1.9
1946 Chi-N	4	10	2	0	0	0	0	0	1	3	0	....	.000	.231	.000	.231	-32	-2	0	.68	-1	/2-2,S-2	0	-0.3
Total 5	309	952	99	199	29	2	15	86	89	105	5	....	.209	.280	.291	.571	65	-43	83	2.87	-1	2-196/3-36,S-36,O-1	13	-3.1
• GLYNN, Bill	William Vincent Glynn b: 7/30/1925, Sussex, NJ BL/TL, 6', 190 lbs. Deb: 9/16/1949 Career OF: 1-0-2																							
1949 Phi-N	8	10	0	2	0	0	0	1	0	3	0	....	.200	.200	.200	.400	8	-1	0	1.35	0	/1-1	0	-0.1
1952 Cle-A	44	92	15	25	5	0	2	7	5	16	1	0	.272	.309	.391	.701	101	-0	11	4.11	1	1-32	2	0.0
1953 Cle-A	147	411	60	100	14	2	3	30	44	65	1	3	.243	.324	.309	.633	73	-15	45	3.64	7	*1-135/O-2(1-0-1)	7	-1.4
1954★Cle-A	111	171	19	43	3	2	5	18	12	21	3	2	.251	.301	.380	.681	84	-5	19	3.72	2	1-96/O-1	4	-0.5
Total 4	310	684	94	170	22	4	10	56	61	105	5	5	.249	.315	.336	.651	79	-21	75	3.68	11	1-264/O-3	13	-2.1
• GOCHNAUR, John	John Peter Gochnaur b: 9/12/1875, Altoona, PA d: 9/27/1929, Altoona, PA BR/TR, 5'9", 160 lbs. Deb: 9/29/1901																							
1901 Bro-N	3	11	1	4	0	0	0	2	1	....	1	....	.364	.417	.364	.780	124	0	2	8.08	1	/S-3	1	0.1
1902 Cle-A	127	459	45	85	16	4	0	37	38	....	7	....	.185	.247	.237	.485	36	-39	31	2.11	-9	*S-127	4	-4.1
1903 Cle-A	134	438	48	81	16	4	0	48	48	....	10	....	.185	.265	.240	.505	53	-23	35	2.39	-27	*S-134	4	-4.7
Total 3	264	908	94	170	32	8	0	87	87	....	18	....	.187	.258	.240	.498	46	-62	67	2.31	-35	S-264	9	-8.8
• GODAR, John	John Michael Godar b: 10/25/1864, Cincinnati, OH d: 6/23/1949, Park Ridge, IL BR/TR, 5'9", 170 lbs. Deb: 7/8/1892																							
1892 Bal-N	5	14	2	3	0	0	0	1	2	1	1	....	.214	.353	.214	.567	70	-0	1	3.55	1	/O-5(0-0-5)	0	0.0
• GODBY, Danny	Danny Ray Godby b: 11/4/1946, Logan, WV BR/TR, 6', 185 lbs. Deb: 8/10/1974																							
1974 StL-N	13	13	2	2	0	0	0	1	3	4	0	0	.154	.313	.154	.466	34	-1	1	2.01	1	/O-4(2-0-2)	0	-0.1
• GODDARD, Joe	Joseph Harold Goddard b: 7/23/1950, Beckley, WV BR/TR, 5'11", 181 lbs. Deb: 7/31/1972																							
1972 SD-N	12	35	0	7	2	0	0	2	5	9	0	0	.200	.300	.257	.557	64	-1	3	2.28	0	C-12	0	-0.2
• GODWIN, John	John Henry "Bunny" Godwin b: 3/10/1877, East Liverpool, OH d: 5/5/1956, East Liverpool, OH BR/TR, 6', 190 lbs. Deb: 8/14/1905 Career OF: 5-3-9																							
1905 Bos-A	15	43	4	14	1	0	0	10	3	....	3	....	.326	.408	.349	.757	139	2	8	6.69	0	/O-7(5-2-0),2-5	3	0.2
1906 Bos-A	66	193	11	36	2	1	0	15	6	....	6	....	.187	.215	.207	.422	32	-15	11	1.77	-2	3-27,S-14,O-10(0-1-9)/2-3,1	1	-1.8
Total 2	81	236	15	50	3	1	0	25	9	....	9	....	.212	.253	.233	.486	53	-13	19	2.54	-2	/3-27,O-17,S-14,2-8,1-1	4	-1.6
• GOEBEL, Ed	Edwin Goebel b: 9/1/1899, Brooklyn, NY d: 8/12/1959, Brooklyn, NY BR/TR, 5'11", 170 lbs. Deb: 5/13/1922																							
1922 Was-A	37	59	13	16	1	0	1	3	8	16	1	1	.271	.358	.339	.697	87	-1	7	4.48	0	O-16(2-1-13)	1	-0.2
• GOECKEL, Billy	William John Goeckel b: 9/3/1871, Wilkes-Barre, PA d: 11/1/1922, Philadelphia, PA BR/TL, 5'11" Deb: 8/10/1899																							
1899 Phi-N	37	141	17	37	3	1	0	16	1	....	6	....	.262	.283	.298	.581	61	-8	15	3.49	-3	1-36	1	-1.0
• GOFF, Jerry	Jerry Leroy Goff b: 4/12/1964, San Rafael, CA BL/TR, 6'3", 207 lbs. Deb: 5/15/1990																							
1990 Mon-N	52	119	14	27	1	0	3	7	21	36	0	2	.227	.343	.311	.654	84	-3	14	3.89	-5	C-38/1-3,3-3	1	-0.6
1992 Mon-N	3	3	0	0	0	0	0	0	0	3	0	0	.000	.000	.000	.000	-101	-1	0	.00	0	....	0	-0.1
1993 Pit-N	14	37	5	11	2	0	2	6	8	9	0	0	.297	.422	.514	.936	149	3	9	8.81	-0	C-14	3	0.4
1994 Pit-N	8	25	0	2	0	0	0	1	0	11	0	0	.080	.080	.080	.160	-57	-6	0	.10	0	/C-7	0	-0.6
1995 Hou-N	12	26	2	4	2	0	1	3	4	13	0	0	.154	.267	.346	.613	65	-1	2	2.75	0	C-11	1	0.0
1996 Hou-N	1	4	1	2	0	0	1	2	0	1	0	0	.500	.500	1.250	1.750	371	1	3	33.75	0	/C-1	1	0.2
Total 6	90	214	22	46	5	0	7	19	33	73	0	2	.215	.320	.336	.656	82	-6	27	4.23	-5	/C-71,1-3,3-3	6	-0.7
• GOGGIN, Chuck	Charles Francis Goggin b: 7/7/1945, Pompano Beach, FL BB/TR, 5'11", 175 lbs. Deb: 9/8/1972																							
1972 Pit-N	5	7	0	2	0	0	0	0	1	1	0	0	.286	.375	.286	.661	92	-0	1	4.58	0	/2-1	0	0.1
1973 Pit-N	1	1	1	1	0	0	0	0	0	0	0	0	1.000	1.000	1.000	2.000	468	0	1	∞	0	/C-1	0	0.0
Atl-N	64	90	18	26	5	0	0	7	9	19	0	1	.289	.354	.344	.698	88	-2	11	4.30	-2	2-19/O-6(5-0-1),S-5,C-1	1	-0.3
Yr.	65	91	19	27	5	0	0	7	9	19	0	1	.297	.360	.352	.712	91	-1	12	4.30	-2	2-19/O-6(5-0-1),S-5,C-2	1	-0.3
1974 Bos-A	2	1	0	0	0	0	0	0	0	1	0	0	.000	.000	.000	.000	-93	-0	0	.00	0	/2-2	0	0.0
Total 3	72	99	19	29	5	0	0	7	10	21	0	1	.293	.358	.343	.701	90	-1	13	4.26	-2	/2-22,O-6,S-5,C-2	1	-0.3

YEAR TM-L	G	AB	R	H	2B	3B	HR	RBI	BB	SO	SB	CS	AVG	OBP	SLG	OPS	OPS+	BR/A	RC	RC/G	FR	G/POS	WS	TPW
• GOLDEN, Mike	Michael Henry Golden b: 9/11/1851, Shirley, MA d: 1/11/1929, Rockford, IL BR/TR, 5'7", 168 lbs. Deb: 5/5/1875 ♦																							
1875 Wes-n	13	46	6	6	0	0	0	1	0	3	0	0	.130	.130	.130	.261	-9	-4	1	.59	-1	P-13	....	-0.4
Chi-n	39	155	16	40	3	0	0	14	2	10	3	2	.258	.268	.277	.545	89	-1	13	3.18	1	O-27(25-0-2),P-14	....	-0.4
Yr.	52	201	22	46	3	0	0	15	2	13	3	2	.229	.236	.244	.480	67	-4	13	2.52	0	O-27(25-0-2),P-27	....	-0.9
1878 Mil-N	55	214	16	44	6	3	0	20	3	35	....	....	.206	.217	.262	.478	53	-8	12	2.01	-5	O-39(0-25-14),P-22/1-1	2	-3.0
• GOLDMAN, Jonah	Jonah John Goldman b: 8/29/1906, New York, NY d: 8/17/1980, Palm Beach, FL BR/TR, 5'7", 170 lbs. Deb: 9/22/1928																							
1928 Cle-A	7	21	1	5	1	0	0	2	3	0	0	0	.238	.333	.286	.619	63	-1	2	3.49	-2	/S-7	0	-0.2
1930 Cle-A	111	306	32	74	18	0	1	44	28	25	3	5	.242	.312	.310	.622	56	-21	31	3.23	1	S-93,3-20	5	-1.0
1931 Cle-A	30	62	0	8	1	0	0	3	4	6	1	1	.129	.182	.145	.327	-12	-10	2	.86	3	S-30	1	-0.6
Total 3	**148**	**389**	**33**	**87**	**20**	**0**	**1**	**49**	**35**	**31**	**4**	**6**	**.224**	**.293**	**.283**	**.576**	**46**	**-33**	**35**	**2.81**	**2**	**S-130/3-20**	**6**	**-1.7**
• GOLDSBERRY, Gordon	Gordon Frederick Goldsberry b: 8/30/1927, Sacramento, CA d: 2/23/1996, Lake Forest, CA BL/TL, 6', 170 lbs. Deb: 4/20/1949 Career OF: 3-0-2																							
1949 Chi-A	39	145	25	36	3	2	1	13	18	9	2	0	.248	.331	.317	.649	74	-5	17	3.99	-1	1-38	2	-0.7
1950 Chi-A	82	127	19	34	8	2	2	25	26	18	0	2	.268	.392	.409	.802	108	2	22	5.85	3	1-40/O-3(1-0-2)	3	0.3
1951 Chi-A	10	11	4	1	0	0	0	1	2	2	0	0	.091	.231	.091	.322	-11	-2	0	.96	1	/1-8	0	-0.1
1952 StL-A	86	227	30	52	9	3	3	17	34	37	0	2	.229	.330	.335	.664	83	-5	27	3.94	-3	1-72/O-2(2-0-0)	4	-1.0
Total 4	**217**	**510**	**78**	**123**	**20**	**7**	**6**	**56**	**80**	**66**	**2**	**4**	**.241**	**.344**	**.343**	**.687**	**85**	**-10**	**66**	**4.35**	**0**	**1-158/O-5**	**9**	**-1.5**
• GOLDSBY, Walt	Walton Hugh Goldsby b: 12/31/1861, LA d: 1/11/1924, Dallas, TX BL Deb: 5/28/1884 U Career OF: 49-18-6																							
1884 StL-a	5	20	2	4	0	0	0	1	0	....	....	....	.200	.200	.200	.400	30	-2	1	1.41	-1	/O-5(1-4-0)	0	-0.2
Was-a	6	24	4	9	0	0	0	3	1	....	....	....	.375	.400	.375	.775	174	2	4	6.77	1	/O-6(1-3-2)	1	0.2
Ric-a	11	40	4	9	1	0	0	4	1	....	....	....	.225	.262	.250	.512	69	-1	3	2.38	0	O-11(2-6-3)	0	-0.2
Yr.	22	84	10	22	1	0	0	8	2	....	....	....	.262	.287	.274	.561	90	-1	7	3.19	0	O-22(4-13-5)	1	-0.1
1886 Was-N	6	18	0	4	1	0	0	1	2	3	0	....	.222	.300	.278	.578	81	-0	2	2.97	-1	/O-6(0-5-1)	0	-0.1
1888 Bal-a	45	165	13	39	1	1	0	14	8	....	17	....	.236	.288	.255	.543	76	-4	17	3.73	-4	O-45(45-0-0)	3	-0.8
Total 3	**73**	**267**	**23**	**65**	**3**	**1**	**0**	**23**	**12**	**3**	**17**	**....**	**.243**	**.289**	**.262**	**.551**	**81**	**-5**	**26**	**3.51**	**-5**	**/O-73**	**4**	**-1.1**
• GOLDSMITH, Fred	Fredrick Ernest Goldsmith b: 5/15/1852, New Haven, CT d: 3/28/1939, Berkley, MI BR/TR, 6'1", 195 lbs. Deb: 10/23/1875 U Career OF: 11-16-6 ♦																							
1875 NH-n	1	4	0	2	0	0	0	1	0	0	0	0	.500	.500	.500	1.000	285	1	1	15.12	0	/2-1	....	0.0
1879 Tro-N	9	38	6	9	1	0	0	2	1	3	....	....	.237	.256	.263	.520	77	0	3	2.54	0	/P-8,O-2(0-2-0),1-1	2	0.8
1880 Chi-N	35	142	24	37	4	2	0	15	2	15	....	....	.261	.271	.317	.588	93	1	12	3.27	2	P-26,O-10(0-10-0)/1-4	24	1.2
1881 Chi-N	42	158	24	38	3	4	0	16	6	17	....	....	.241	.268	.310	.578	76	1	13	3.03	6	P-39/O-3(0-1-2)	25	-0.1
1882 Chi-N	45	183	23	42	11	1	0	19	4	29	....	....	.230	.246	.301	.547	73	-2	14	2.70	-2	P-45/1-1	29	-0.5
1883 Chi-N	60	235	38	52	12	3	1	16	4	35	....	....	.221	.234	.311	.545	59	-5	18	2.63	1	P-46,O-16(10-3-3)/1-2	27	-0.8
1884 Chi-N	22	81	11	11	2	0	2	6	7	26	....	....	.136	.205	.235	.439	35	-3	4	1.56	-3	P-21/O-2(1-0-1)	7	-2.9
Bal-a	4	14	2	2	0	0	0	0	2	....	....	....	.143	.250	.143	.393	30	-0	1	1.17	1	/P-4,1-1	2	0.2
Total 6	**217**	**851**	**128**	**191**	**33**	**10**	**3**	**74**	**26**	**125**	**....**	**....**	**.224**	**.247**	**.297**	**.545**	**69**	**-9**	**64**	**2.68**	**5**	**P-189/O-33,1-9**	**116**	**-2.1**
• GOLDSMITH, Wally	Warren M. Goldsmith b: 10/1848, Baltimore, MD d: 9/16/1915, Washington, DC, 5'7", 146 lbs. Deb: 5/4/1871																							
1871 Kek-n	19	88	8	18	1	0	0	12	4	2	0	0	.205	.239	.216	.455	31	-8	5	2.10	-4	S-14/3-8,C-2	....	-0.8
1872 Oly-n	9	41	4	10	2	0	0	5	0	0	0	0	.244	.244	.293	.537	68	-1	3	3.00	-5	/S-5,2-4	....	-0.4
1873 Mar-n	1	4	0	0	0	0	0	0	0	0	0	0	.000	.000	.000	.000	-130	-1	0	.00	-1	/2-1	....	-0.1
1875 Wes-n	13	51	3	6	0	0	0	1	0	2	0	0	.118	.118	.118	.235	-17	-6	1	.47	-1	3-13	....	-0.6
Total 4 n	**42**	**184**	**15**	**34**	**3**	**0**	**0**	**18**	**4**	**4**	**0**	**0**	**.185**	**.202**	**.201**	**.403**	**23**	**-16**	**8**	**1.74**	**-11**	**/3-21,S-19,2-5,C-2**	**....**	**-2.0**
• GOLDSTEIN, Lonnie	Leslie Elmer Goldstein b: 5/13/1918, Austin, TX BL/TL, 6'2.5", 190 lbs. Deb: 9/11/1943																							
1943 Cin-N	5	5	1	1	0	0	0	0	2	1	0	....	.200	.429	.200	.629	85	0	0	2.35	0	/1-2	0	0.0
1946 Cin-N	6	5	1	0	0	0	0	0	1	1	0	....	.000	.167	.000	.167	-53	-1	0	.23	0	....	0	-0.1
Total 2	**11**	**10**	**2**	**1**	**0**	**0**	**0**	**0**	**3**	**2**	**0**	**....**	**.100**	**.308**	**.100**	**.408**	**22**	**-1**	**0**	**1.29**	**0**	**/1-2**	**0**	**-0.1**
• GOLDY, Purnal	Purnal William Goldy b: 11/28/1937, Camden, NJ BR/TR, 6'5", 200 lbs. Deb: 4/12/1962																							
1962 Det-A	20	70	8	16	1	1	3	12	0	12	0	0	.229	.239	.400	.639	66	-4	6	2.61	-1	O-15(0-0-15)	1	-0.6
1963 Det-A	9	8	1	2	0	0	0	0	0	4	0	0	.250	.250	.250	.500	39	-1	1	2.25	0	....	0	-0.1
Total 2	**29**	**78**	**9**	**18**	**1**	**1**	**3**	**12**	**0**	**16**	**0**	**0**	**.231**	**.241**	**.385**	**.625**	**63**	**-4**	**6**	**2.57**	**-1**	**/O-15**	**1**	**-0.6**
• GOLETZ, Stan	Stanley "Stash" Goletz b: 5/21/1918, Crescent, OH d: 6/7/1997, Temple, TX BL/TL, 6'3", 200 lbs. Deb: 9/9/1941																							
1941 Chi-A	5	5	0	3	0	0	0	0	0	2	0	0	.600	.600	.600	1.200	221	1	2	24.91	0	....	1	0.1
• GOLIAT, Mike	Mike Mitchell Goliat b: 11/5/1925, Yatesboro, PA d: 1/14/2004, Seven Hills, OH BR/TR, 6', 180 lbs. Deb: 8/3/1949																							
1949 Phi-N	55	189	24	40	6	3	3	19	20	32	0	....	.212	.290	.323	.613	66	-9	17	2.88	2	2-50/1-5	3	-0.5
1950*Phi-N	145	483	49	113	13	6	13	64	53	75	3	....	.234	.314	.366	.680	80	-15	53	3.66	0	*2-145	13	-0.6
1951 Phi-N	41	138	14	31	2	1	4	15	9	18	0	1	.225	.277	.341	.618	66	-7	13	3.28	-3	2-37/3-2	2	-0.8
StL-A	5	11	0	2	0	0	0	1	0	1	0	0	.182	.182	.182	.364	-1	-2	0	1.17	1	/2-2	0	-0.1
1952 StL-A	3	4	0	0	0	0	0	0	1	1	0	0	.000	.200	.000	.200	-40	-1	0	.35	0	/2-3	0	0.0
Total 4	**249**	**825**	**87**	**186**	**21**	**10**	**20**	**99**	**83**	**127**	**3**	**1**	**.225**	**.300**	**.348**	**.648**	**72**	**-34**	**84**	**3.35**	**1**	**2-237/1-5,3-2**	**18**	**-2.0**
• GOLVIN, Walt	Walter George Golvin b: 2/1/1894, Hershey, NE d: 6/11/1973, Gardena, CA BL/TL, 6', 165 lbs. Deb: 4/15/1922																							
1922 Chi-N	2	2	0	0	0	0	0	1	0	0	0	0	.000	.000	.000	.000	-98	-1	0	.00	0	/1-2	0	-0.1
• GOMES, Jonny	Jonny Johnson Gomes b: 11/22/1980, Petaluma, CA BR/TR, 6'1", 205 lbs. Deb: 9/12/2003																							
2003 TB-A	8	15	1	2	1	0	0	0	0	6	0	0	.133	.188	.200	.388	2	-2	1	1.27	0	/D-6	0	-0.2
• GOMEZ, Alexis	Alexis DeJesus Gomez b: 8/8/1978, Loma de Cabrera, Dominican Republic BL/TL, 6'2", 180 lbs. Deb: 6/16/2002																							
2002 KC-A	5	10	0	2	0	0	0	0	0	2	0	0	.200	.200	.200	.400	6	-1	0	1.35	1	/O-2(0-0-2)	0	0.0
• GOMEZ, Chile	Jose Luis (Gonzales) Gomez b: 3/23/1909, Villa Union, Mexico d: 12/1/1992, Nuevo Laredo, Mexico BR/TR, 5'10", 165 lbs. Deb: 7/27/1935																							
1935 Phi-N	67	222	24	51	3	0	0	16	17	34	2	....	.230	.285	.243	.528	39	-19	15	2.20	3	S-36,2-32	3	-1.1
1936 Phi-N	108	332	24	77	4	1	0	28	14	32	0	....	.232	.265	.250	.515	36	-30	22	2.19	-1	2-71,S-40	3	-2.4
1942 Was-A	25	73	8	14	2	2	0	6	9	7	1	0	.192	.280	.274	.554	57	-4	6	2.47	-2	2-23/3-1	1	-0.4
Total 3	**200**	**627**	**56**	**142**	**9**	**3**	**0**	**50**	**40**	**73**	**3**	**0**	**.226**	**.274**	**.250**	**.524**	**40**	**-53**	**43**	**2.22**	**1**	**2-126/S-76,3-1**	**7**	**-3.9**
• GOMEZ, Chris	Christopher Cory Gomez b: 6/16/1971, Los Angeles, CA BR/TR, 6'1", 183 lbs. Deb: 7/19/1993																							
1993 Det-A	46	128	11	32	7	1	0	11	9	17	2	2	.250	.304	.320	.625	68	-6	12	3.26	0	S-29,2-17/D-1	2	-0.4
1994 Det-A	84	296	32	76	19	0	8	53	33	64	5	3	.257	.337	.402	.739	89	-5	40	4.59	-16	S-57,2-30	8	-1.4
1995 Det-A	123	431	49	96	20	2	11	50	41	96	4	1	.223	.295	.355	.650	68	-21	44	3.37	-12	S-97,2-31/D-2	6	-2.3
1996 Det-A	48	128	21	31	5	0	1	16	18	20	1	1	.242	.340	.305	.645	65	-7	13	3.44	-5	S-47	2	-0.8
*SD-N	89	328	32	86	16	1	3	29	39	64	2	2	.262	.351	.345	.696	90	-4	40	4.15	-4	S-89	9	-0.1
1997 SD-N	150	522	62	132	19	2	5	54	53	114	5	8	.253	.328	.326	.653	78	-18	54	3.47	-16	*S-150	7	-2.2
1998*SD-N	145	449	55	120	32	3	4	39	51	87	1	3	.267	.349	.379	.727	98	-2	59	4.53	5	*S-143	15	1.4
1999 SD-N	76	234	20	59	8	1	1	15	27	49	1	2	.252	.332	.308	.640	69	-11	24	3.49	4	S-75	6	-0.2
2000 SD-N	33	54	4	12	0	0	0	3	7	5	0	0	.222	.311	.222	.534	41	-5	4	2.55	2	S-17/2-3	1	-0.2
2001 SD-N	40	112	6	21	3	0	0	7	9	14	1	0	.188	.248	.214	.462	23	-12	6	1.56	-11	S-36/2-8	1	-2.0
TB-A	58	189	31	57	16	0	8	36	8	24	3	0	.302	.337	.513	.850	121	6	32	6.05	-9	S-58	7	0.2
2002 TB-A	130	461	51	122	31	3	10	46	21	58	1	3	.265	.307	.410	.717	90	-9	56	4.23	8	*S-130	11	0.9
2003*Min-A	58	175	14	44	9	3	1	15	7	13	2	1	.251	.280	.354	.635	65	-9	14	2.66	-1	2-23,3-18,S-17/D-1	2	-0.8
Total 11	**1080**	**3507**	**388**	**888**	**185**	**16**	**52**	**374**	**323**	**625**	**28**	**26**	**.253**	**.322**	**.360**	**.682**	**81**	**-104**	**400**	**3.85**	**-57**	**S-945,2-112/3-18,D-4**	**77**	**-7.8**
• GOMEZ, Leo	Leonardo (Velez) Gomez b: 3/2/1966, Canovanas, Puerto Rico BR/TR, 6', 208 lbs. Deb: 9/17/1990																							
1990 Bal-A	12	39	3	9	0	0	0	1	8	7	0	0	.231	.362	.231	.592	71	-1	4	2.97	-1	3-12	1	-0.2
1991 Bal-A	118	391	40	91	17	2	16	45	40	82	1	1	.233	.307	.409	.716	100	-1	48	4.03	-13	*3-105,D-10/1-3	7	-1.4

YEAR TM-L	G	AB	R	H	2B	3B	HR	RBI	BB	SO	SB	CS	AVG	OBP	SLG	OPS	OPS+	BR/A	RC	RC/G	FR	G/POS	WS	TPW
1992 Bal-A	137	468	62	124	24	0	17	64	63	78	2	3	.265	.362	.425	.787	117	11	72	5.22	-6	*3-137	15	0.6
1993 Bal-A	71	244	30	48	7	0	10	25	32	60	0	1	.197	.297	.348	.646	70	-11	27	3.60	8	3-70/D-1	4	-0.2
1994 Bal-A	84	285	46	78	20	0	15	56	41	55	0	0	.274	.371	.502	.873	116	7	55	6.87	2	3-78/D-5,1-1	12	0.9
1995 Bal-A	53	127	16	30	5	0	4	12	18	23	0	1	.236	.340	.370	.710	83	-3	17	4.70	2	3-44/D-5,1-3	3	-0.1
1996 Chi-N	136	362	44	86	19	0	17	56	53	94	1	4	.238	.346	.431	.777	101	-1	55	5.05	-5	*3-124/1-8,S-1	10	-0.5
Total 7	611	1916	241	466	92	2	79	259	255	399	4	10	.243	.340	.417	.757	101	2	279	4.87	-14	3-570/D-21,1-15,S-1	52	-0.9

• GOMEZ, Luis Luis (Sanchez) Gomez b: 8/19/1951, Guadalajara, Mexico BR/TR, 5'9", 150 lbs. Deb: 4/28/1974 Career OF: 0-2-0

YEAR TM-L	G	AB	R	H	2B	3B	HR	RBI	BB	SO	SB	CS	AVG	OBP	SLG	OPS	OPS+	BR/A	RC	RC/G	FR	G/POS	WS	TPW
1974 Min-A	82	168	18	35	1	0	0	3	12	16	2	3	.208	.261	.214	.475	37	-14	10	1.83	-3	S-74/2-2,D-1	2	-1.0
1975 Min-A	89	72	7	10	0	0	0	5	4	12	0	2	.139	.184	.139	.323	-7	-11	2	.71	-2	S-70/D-7,2-6	1	-1.0
1976 Min-A	38	57	5	11	1	0	0	3	3	3	1	0	.193	.233	.211	.444	30	-5	3	1.35	0	S-24/2-8,3-4,D-1,0-1	1	-0.3
1977 Min-A	32	65	6	16	4	2	0	11	4	9	0	2	.246	.290	.369	.659	79	-3	7	3.24	0	2-19/S-7,3-4,D-2,0-1	1	-0.2
1978 Tor-A	153	413	39	92	7	3	0	32	34	41	2	10	.223	.282	.254	.536	51	-30	28	2.12	-10	*S-153	5	-2.6
1979 Tor-A	59	163	11	39	7	0	0	11	6	17	1	0	.239	.266	.282	.548	48	-12	11	2.22	2	3-22,2-20,S-15	1	-0.8
1980 Atl-N	121	278	18	53	6	0	0	24	17	27	0	4	.191	.240	.212	.452	26	-29	13	1.41	0	*S-119	4	-2.0
1981 Atl-N	35	35	4	7	0	0	0	1	6	4	0	1	.200	.317	.200	.517	48	-2	3	2.33	-4	S-21/3-9,2-3,P-1	0	-0.9
Total 8	609	1251	108	263	26	5	0	90	86	129	6	22	.210	.262	.239	.501	40	-107	76	1.87	-18	S-483/2-58,3-39,D-11,0-2,P	15	-8.9

• GOMEZ, Preston Preston (Martinez) Gomez b: 4/20/1923, Central Preston, Cuba BR/TR, 5'11", 170 lbs. Deb: 5/5/1944 M/C

YEAR TM-L	G	AB	R	H	2B	3B	HR	RBI	BB	SO	SB	CS	AVG	OBP	SLG	OPS	OPS+	BR/A	RC	RC/G	FR	G/POS	WS	TPW
1944 Was-A	8	7	2	2	1	0	0	2	0	4	0	0	.286	.286	.429	.714	107	-0	1	4.74	-2	/2-2,S-2	0	-0.2

• GOMEZ, Randy Randell Scott Gomez b: 2/4/1957, San Mateo, CA BR/TR, 5'10", 185 lbs. Deb: 8/21/1984

YEAR TM-L	G	AB	R	H	2B	3B	HR	RBI	BB	SO	SB	CS	AVG	OBP	SLG	OPS	OPS+	BR/A	RC	RC/G	FR	G/POS	WS	TPW
1984 SF-N	14	30	0	5	1	0	0	0	8	3	0	0	.167	.342	.200	.542	57	-1	2	2.34	-1	C-14	0	-0.1

• GONDER, Jesse Jesse Lemar Gonder b: 1/20/1936, Monticello, AR BL/TR, 5'10", 190 lbs. Deb: 9/23/1960

YEAR TM-L	G	AB	R	H	2B	3B	HR	RBI	BB	SO	SB	CS	AVG	OBP	SLG	OPS	OPS+	BR/A	RC	RC/G	FR	G/POS	WS	TPW
1960 NY-A	7	7	1	2	0	0	1	3	1	1	0	0	.286	.375	.714	1.089	199	1	2	8.67	0	/C-1	1	0.1
1961 NY-A	15	12	2	4	1	0	0	3	3	1	0	0	.333	.467	.417	.883	146	1	2	6.62	0	....	0	0.1
1962 Cin-N	4	4	0	0	0	0	0	0	0	3	0	0	.000	.000	.000	.000	-97	-1	0	.00	0	....	0	-0.1
1963 Cin-N	31	32	5	10	2	0	3	5	1	12	0	0	.313	.333	.656	.990	172	3	7	8.70	0	/C-7	2	0.3
NY-N	42	126	12	38	4	0	3	15	6	25	1	2	.302	.333	.405	.738	110	1	16	4.48	1	C-31	4	0.3
Yr.	73	158	17	48	6	0	6	20	7	37	1	2	.304	.333	.456	.789	122	3	23	5.27	1	C-38	6	0.6
1964 NY-N	131	341	28	92	11	1	7	35	29	65	0	0	.270	.331	.370	.700	99	0	38	3.87	7	C-97	9	1.2
1965 NY-N	53	105	6	25	4	0	4	9	11	20	0	0	.238	.310	.390	.701	99	-0	11	3.45	3	C-31	2	0.4
Mil-N	31	53	2	8	2	0	1	5	4	9	0	0	.151	.211	.245	.456	28	-5	2	1.42	0	C-13	1	-0.4
Yr.	84	158	8	33	6	0	5	14	15	29	0	0	.209	.277	.342	.619	76	-5	14	2.74	3	C-44	3	0.0
1966 Pit-N	59	160	13	36	3	1	7	16	12	39	0	0	.225	.287	.388	.675	85	-3	16	3.35	-2	C-52	3	-0.3
1967 Pit-N	22	36	4	5	1	0	0	3	5	9	0	0	.139	.279	.167	.446	30	-3	2	1.39	0	C-18	0	-0.2
Total 8	395	876	73	220	28	2	26	94	72	184	1	2	.251	.312	.377	.689	94	-7	97	3.72	9	C-250	22	1.4

• GONZALES, Dan Daniel David Gonzales b: 9/30/1953, Whittier, CA BL/TR, 6'1", 195 lbs. Deb: 4/7/1979 Career OF: 1-0-3

YEAR TM-L	G	AB	R	H	2B	3B	HR	RBI	BB	SO	SB	CS	AVG	OBP	SLG	OPS	OPS+	BR/A	RC	RC/G	FR	G/POS	WS	TPW
1979 Det-A	7	18	1	4	1	0	0	2	0	2	1	0	.222	.222	.278	.500	33	-2	1	1.04	0	/O-3(0-0-3),D-1	0	-0.2
1980 Det-A	2	7	1	1	0	0	0	0	0	1	0	0	.143	.143	.143	.286	-21	-1	0	.64	0	/D-1,0-1	0	-0.1
Total 2	9	25	2	5	1	0	0	2	0	3	1	0	.200	.200	.240	.440	18	-3	1	.93	0	/0-4,D-2	0	-0.3

• GONZALES, Larry Lawrence Chris Gonzales b: 3/28/1967, West Covina, CA BR/TR, 6'3", 200 lbs. Deb: 6/13/1993

YEAR TM-L	G	AB	R	H	2B	3B	HR	RBI	BB	SO	SB	CS	AVG	OBP	SLG	OPS	OPS+	BR/A	RC	RC/G	FR	G/POS	WS	TPW
1993 Cal-A	2	2	0	1	0	0	0	1	1	0	0	0	.500	.667	.500	1.167	212	0	1	22.68	0	/C-2	0	0.0

• GONZALES, Rene Rene Adrian Gonzales b: 9/3/1960, Austin, TX BR/TR, 6'3", 201 lbs. Deb: 7/27/1984 Career OF: 1-0-2

YEAR TM-L	G	AB	R	H	2B	3B	HR	RBI	BB	SO	SB	CS	AVG	OBP	SLG	OPS	OPS+	BR/A	RC	RC/G	FR	G/POS	WS	TPW
1984 Mon-N	29	30	5	7	1	0	0	2	2	5	0	0	.233	.303	.267	.570	64	-1	3	3.12	-1	S-27	0	-0.2
1986 Mon-N	11	26	1	3	0	0	0	0	2	7	0	2	.115	.179	.115	.294	-17	-5	0	.41	1	/S-6,3-5	0	-0.4
1987 Bal-A	37	60	14	16	2	1	1	7	3	11	1	0	.267	.302	.383	.685	82	-1	7	3.73	1	3-29/2-6,S-1	1	-0.1
1988 Bal-A	92	237	13	51	6	0	2	15	13	32	2	0	.215	.265	.266	.531	50	-15	17	2.34	6	3-80,2-14/S-2,1-1,0-1	3	-0.9
1989 Bal-A	71	166	16	36	4	0	1	11	12	30	5	3	.217	.270	.259	.529	51	-11	11	2.04	5	2-54,3-17/S-1	2	-0.5
1990 Bal-A	67	103	13	22	3	1	1	12	12	14	1	2	.214	.296	.291	.587	67	-5	9	2.59	4	2-43,3-16/S-9,0-1	2	0.0
1991*Tor-A	71	118	16	23	3	0	1	6	12	22	0	0	.195	.291	.246	.537	48	-8	9	2.24	0	S-36,3-26,2-11/1-2	2	-0.6
1992 Cal-A	104	329	47	91	17	1	7	38	41	46	7	4	.277	.364	.398	.762	113	6	45	4.60	5	3-53,2-42,1-13/S-8	15	1.3
1993 Cal-A	118	335	34	84	17	0	2	31	49	45	5	5	.251	.348	.319	.667	78	-9	37	3.71	7	3-79,1-31/S-5,2-4,P-1	8	-0.3
1994 Cle-A	22	23	6	8	1	1	1	5	5	3	2	0	.348	.464	.609	1.073	173	3	8	11.96	-1	3-13/1-4,S-4,2-1	1	0.2
1995 Cal-A	30	18	1	6	1	0	1	3	0	4	0	0	.333	.333	.556	.889	127	1	3	5.77	-3	3-18/2-6,D-1,S-1	1	-0.2
1996*Tex-A	51	92	19	20	4	0	2	5	10	11	0	0	.217	.294	.326	.620	54	-7	9	3.06	1	1-23,3-15,S-10/2-5,0-1	1	-0.5
1997 Col-N	2	2	0	1	0	0	0	1	0	0	0	0	.500	.500	.500	1.000	132	0	1	13.50	0	/3-1	0	0.0
Total 13	705	1539	185	368	59	4	19	136	161	230	23	16	.239	.316	.320	.636	75	-53	158	3.31	23	3-352,2-186,S-110/1-74,0,D,P	36	-2.2

• GONZALEZ, Alex Alexander Gonzalez b: 2/15/1977, Cagua, Venezuela BR/TR, 6', 170 lbs. Deb: 8/25/1998

YEAR TM-L	G	AB	R	H	2B	3B	HR	RBI	BB	SO	SB	CS	AVG	OBP	SLG	OPS	OPS+	BR/A	RC	RC/G	FR	G/POS	WS	TPW
1998 Fla-N	25	86	11	13	2	0	3	7	9	30	0	0	.151	.240	.279	.519	37	-8	6	2.08	-1	S-25	1	-0.7
1999 Fla-N★	136	560	81	155	28	8	14	59	15	113	3	5	.277	.310	.430	.740	89	-14	70	4.42	-13	*S-135	11	-1.5
2000 Fla-N	109	385	35	77	17	4	7	42	13	77	7	1	.200	.230	.319	.549	38	-37	28	2.31	-6	*S-104	3	-3.3
2001 Fla-N	145	515	57	129	36	1	9	48	30	107	2	2	.250	.305	.377	.681	77	-19	57	3.77	0	*S-142	10	-0.7
2002 Fla-N	42	151	15	34	7	1	2	18	12	32	3	1	.225	.299	.325	.624	67	-7	16	3.37	4	S-42	3	0.1
2003*Fla-N	150	528	52	135	33	6	18	77	33	106	0	4	.256	.315	.443	.759	99	-5	72	4.68	14	*S-150	20	2.2
Total 6	607	2225	251	543	123	20	53	251	112	465	15	13	.244	.293	.389	.682	77	-89	248	3.77	-1	S-598	48	-4.0

• GONZALEZ, Alex Alexander Scott Gonzalez b: 4/8/1973, Miami, FL BR/TR, 6', 180 lbs. Deb: 4/4/1994

YEAR TM-L	G	AB	R	H	2B	3B	HR	RBI	BB	SO	SB	CS	AVG	OBP	SLG	OPS	OPS+	BR/A	RC	RC/G	FR	G/POS	WS	TPW
1994 Tor-A	15	53	7	8	3	1	0	1	4	17	3	0	.151	.224	.245	.469	21	-6	3	1.72	1	S-15	1	-0.3
1995 Tor-A	111	367	51	89	19	4	10	42	44	114	4	4	.243	.325	.398	.723	88	-8	48	4.30	-16	S-97/3-9,D-3	7	-1.5
1996 Tor-A	147	527	64	124	30	5	14	64	45	127	16	6	.235	.302	.391	.692	74	-22	62	3.87	31	*S-147	14	1.9
1997 Tor-A	126	426	46	102	23	2	12	35	34	94	15	6	.239	.303	.387	.691	78	-14	50	3.83	8	*S-125	10	0.4
1998 Tor-A	158	568	70	136	28	1	13	51	28	121	21	6	.239	.282	.361	.643	66	-29	57	3.29	4	*S-158	9	-1.1
1999 Tor-A	38	154	22	45	13	0	2	12	16	23	4	2	.292	.370	.416	.786	99	0	24	5.59	11	S-37/D-1	6	1.3
2000 Tor-A	141	527	68	133	31	2	15	69	43	113	4	4	.252	.314	.404	.718	77	-20	65	4.07	-10	*S-141	11	-1.7
2001 Tor-A	154	636	79	161	25	5	17	76	43	149	18	11	.253	.308	.388	.696	80	-21	73	3.79	14	*S-154	16	0.6
2002 Chi-N	142	513	58	127	27	5	18	61	46	136	5	3	.248	.313	.425	.738	94	-6	67	4.45	1	*S-142	13	0.6
2003*Chi-N	152	536	71	122	37	0	20	59	47	123	3	3	.228	.297	.409	.706	83	-16	62	3.75	13	*S-150	15	0.8
Total 10	1184	4307	536	1047	236	25	121	470	350	1017	93	45	.243	.306	.394	.700	79	-142	510	3.92	57	*S-1166/3-9,D-4	102	1.1

• GONZALEZ, Denny Denio Mariano (Manzueta) Gonzalez b: 7/22/1963, Sabana Grande de Boya, Dominican Republic BR/TR, 5'11", 185 lbs. Deb: 8/6/1984 Career OF: 16-0-0

YEAR TM-L	G	AB	R	H	2B	3B	HR	RBI	BB	SO	SB	CS	AVG	OBP	SLG	OPS	OPS+	BR/A	RC	RC/G	FR	G/POS	WS	TPW
1984 Pit-N	26	82	9	15	3	1	0	4	7	21	1	1	.183	.247	.244	.491	38	-7	4	1.58	2	3-11,S-10/0-3(3-0-0)	1	-0.5
1985 Pit-N	35	124	11	28	4	0	4	12	13	27	2	4	.226	.299	.355	.654	83	-4	13	3.34	-6	3-21,0-13(13-0-0)/2-6	1	-1.2
1987 Pit-N	5	7	1	0	0	0	0	0	1	2	0	0	.000	.125	.000	.125	-63	-2	0	.13	0	/S-1	0	-0.2
1988 Pit-N	24	32	5	6	1	0	0	1	6	10	0	0	.188	.316	.219	.535	57	-2	3	2.47	-2	S-14/2-4,3-2	0	-0.3
1989 Cle-A	8	17	3	5	1	0	0	1	0	4	0	0	.294	.333	.353	.686	92	-0	2	4.45	-1	/D-6,3-1	0	-0.1
Total 5	98	262	29	54	9	1	4	18	27	64	3	5	.206	.283	.294	.577	62	-15	22	2.61	-8	/3-35,S-25,0-16,2-10,D-6	2	-2.3

• GONZALEZ, Eusebio Eusebio Miguel (Lopez) "Papo" Gonzalez b: 7/13/1892, Havana, Cuba d: 2/14/1976, Havana, Cuba BR/TR, 5'10", 165 lbs. Deb: 7/26/1918

YEAR TM-L	G	AB	R	H	2B	3B	HR	RBI	BB	SO	SB	CS	AVG	OBP	SLG	OPS	OPS+	BR/A	RC	RC/G	FR	G/POS	WS	TPW
1918 Bos-A	3	5	2	2	0	1	0	0	1	1	0	....	.400	.571	.800	1.371	319	2	2	18.94	0	/S-2,3-1	1	0.1

• GONZALEZ, Fernando Jose Fernando (Quinones) Gonzalez b: 6/19/1950, Arecibo, Puerto Rico BR/TR, 5'10", 170 lbs. Deb: 9/15/1972

YEAR TM-L	G	AB	R	H	2B	3B	HR	RBI	BB	SO	SB	CS	AVG	OBP	SLG	OPS	OPS+	BR/A	RC	RC/G	FR	G/POS	WS	TPW
1972 Pit-N	3	2	0	0	0	0	0	0	0	2	0	0	.000	.000	.000	.000	-102	-1	0	.00	-1	/3-1	0	-0.1
1973 Pit-N	37	49	5	11	0	1	1	5	1	11	0	0	.224	.255	.327	.581	62	-3	4	2.69	-1	/3-5	1	-0.4
1974 KC-A	9	21	1	3	1	0	0	2	0	4	1	0	.143	.143	.190	.333	-5	-3	1	.97	-1	/3-8,D-1	0	-0.4
NY-A	51	121	11	26	5	1	1	7	7	7	0	0	.215	.258	.298	.555	61	-6	9	2.42	-3	2-42/3-7,S-3	2	-0.7

YEAR TM-L	G	AB	R	H	2B	3B	HR	RBI	BB	SO	SB	CS	AVG	OBP	SLG	OPS	OPS+	BR/A	RC	RC/G	FR	G/POS	WS	TPW
Yr.	60	142	12	29	6	1	1	9	7	11	1	0	.204	.242	.282	.523	52	-9	10	2.20	-4	2-42,3-15/S-3,D-1	2	-1.1
1977 Pit-N	80	181	17	50	10	0	4	27	13	21	3	3	.276	.325	.398	.723	90	-3	20	3.78	3	3-37,0-16(15-0-1)/2-6,S-2	4	-0.1
1978 Pit-N	9	21	2	4	1	0	0	0	1	3	0	0	.190	.227	.238	.465	29	-2	1	1.90	-2	/2-4,3-3	0	-0.4
SD-N	101	320	27	80	10	2	2	29	18	32	4	4	.250	.290	.313	.602	74	-13	29	3.00	4	2-94	7	-0.5
Yr.	110	341	29	84	11	2	2	29	19	35	4	4	.246	.286	.308	.594	71	-15	30	2.93	2	2-98/3-3	7	-0.9
1979 SD-N	114	323	22	70	13	3	9	34	18	34	0	0	.217	.258	.359	.617	71	-15	28	2.86	-15	*2-103/3-3	4	-2.6
Total 6	404	1038	85	244	40	7	17	104	58	114	8	7	.235	.276	.336	.612	71	-45	92	2.93	-15	2-249/3-64,0-16,S-5,D-1	18	-5.1

• GONZALEZ, Jose Jose Rafael (Gutierrez) Gonzalez b: 11/23/1964, Puerta Plata, Dominican Republic BR/TR, 6'2", 196 lbs. Deb: 9/2/1985 Career OF: 100-164-132

YEAR TM-L	G	AB	R	H	2B	3B	HR	RBI	BB	SO	SB	CS	AVG	OBP	SLG	OPS	OPS+	BR/A	RC	RC/G	FR	G/POS	WS	TPW
1985 LA-N	23	11	6	3	2	0	0	0	1	3	1	1	.273	.333	.455	.788	122	0	1	2.60	-1	0-18(5-6-8)	0	-0.1
1986 LA-N	57	93	15	20	5	1	2	6	7	29	4	3	.215	.270	.355	.625	76	-4	9	3.09	-4	0-57(0-49-8)	1	-0.9
1987 LA-N	19	16	2	3	2	0	0	1	1	2	5	0	.188	.235	.313	.548	45	-0	2	3.59	0	0-16(8-5-3)	1	-0.1
1988*LA-N	37	24	7	2	1	0	0	0	2	10	3	0	.083	.154	.125	.279	-20	-3	1	.96	-1	0-24(9-9-9)	0	-0.5
1989 LA-N	95	261	31	70	11	2	3	18	23	53	9	3	.268	.327	.360	.688	98	-0	32	4.38	1	0-87(4-55-34)	7	-0.1
1990 LA-N	106	99	15	23	5	3	2	8	6	27	3	1	.232	.283	.404	.687	89	-2	11	3.86	-1	0-81(43-18-25)	2	-0.4
1991 LA-N	42	28	3	0	0	0	0	0	2	9	0	0	.000	.067	.000	.067	-82	-7	0	.03	-1	0-27(12-1-15)	0	-0.8
Pit-N	16	20	2	2	0	0	1	3	0	6	0	0	.100	.100	.250	.350	-5	-3	1	.73	0	0-14(3-6-5)	0	-0.3
Yr.	58	48	5	2	0	0	1	3	2	15	0	0	.042	.080	.104	.184	-48	-10	1	.33	-1	0-41(15-7-20)	0	-1.1
Cle-A	33	69	10	11	2	1	1	4	11	27	8	0	.159	.284	.261	.545	51	-3	7	2.95	0	0-32(5-10-17)	1	-0.4
1992 Cal-A	33	55	4	10	2	0	0	2	7	20	0	1	.182	.274	.218	.492	39	-5	3	1.72	1	0-22(11-5-8)/D-1	0	-0.5
Total 8	461	676	95	144	30	7	9	42	60	186	33	9	.213	.279	.318	.597	68	-26	66	3.20	-7	0-378/D-1	12	-4.0

• GONZALEZ, Juan Juan Alberto (Vazquez) "Juan Gone,Igor" Gonzalez b: 10/20/1969, Arecibo, Puerto Rico BR/TR, 6'3", 210 lbs. Deb: 9/1/1989 Career OF: 366-252-730

YEAR TM-L	G	AB	R	H	2B	3B	HR	RBI	BB	SO	SB	CS	AVG	OBP	SLG	OPS	OPS+	BR/A	RC	RC/G	FR	G/POS	WS	TPW
1989 Tex-A	24	60	6	9	3	0	1	7	6	17	0	0	.150	.227	.250	.477	34	-5	3	1.35	-1	0-24(1-24-0)	1	-0.6
1990 Tex-A	25	90	11	26	7	1	4	12	2	18	0	1	.289	.319	.522	.841	131	3	14	5.48	0	0-16(1-12-4)/D-9	2	0.2
1991 Tex-A	142	545	78	144	34	1	27	102	42	118	4	4	.264	.323	.479	.802	121	12	82	5.28	-1	*0-136(92-93-8)/D-4	19	0.7
1992 Tex-A	155	584	77	152	24	2	**43**	109	35	143	0	1	.260	.308	.529	.837	135	22	90	5.29	0	*0-148(31-123-1)/D-4	19	1.9
1993 Tex-A★	140	536	105	166	33	1	**46**	118	37	99	4	1	.310	.369	**.632**	1.001	170	50	122	8.58	2	*0-129(129-0-0),D-10	31	4.4
1994 Tex-A	107	422	57	116	18	4	19	85	30	66	6	4	.275	.333	.472	.805	105	1	60	4.86	4	*0-107(107-0-0)	11	0.1
1995 Tex-A	90	352	57	104	20	2	27	82	17	66	0	0	.295	.328	.594	.922	131	13	61	6.15	1	D-83/0-5(5-0-0)	11	0.7
1996*Tex-A	134	541	89	170	33	2	47	144	45	82	2	0	.314	.370	.643	1.013	142	32	126	8.89	-5	*0-102(0-0-102),D-32	21	1.8
1997 Tex-A	133	533	87	158	24	3	42	131	33	107	0	0	.296	.341	.589	.930	130	20	103	6.99	0	D-69,0-64(0-0-64)	19	1.1
1998*Tex-A★	154	606	110	193	**50**	2	45	**157**	46	126	2	1	.318	.372	.630	1.003	148	40	134	8.12	-5	*0-116(0-0-116),D-38	25	2.5
1999*Tex-A	144	562	114	183	36	1	39	128	51	105	3	3	.326	.386	.601	.987	140	32	128	8.57	-4	*0-131(0-0-131),D-16	24	1.9
2000 Det-A	115	461	69	133	30	2	22	67	32	84	1	2	.289	.337	.505	.843	113	6	74	5.82	-3	0-66(0-0-66),D-48	9	-0.3
2001*Cle-A★	140	532	97	173	34	1	35	140	41	94	1	0	.325	.380	.590	.970	148	36	113	7.78	4	*0-119(0-0-119),D-21	23	3.1
2002 Tex-A	70	277	38	78	21	1	8	35	17	56	2	0	.282	.325	.451	.777	98	-1	38	4.81	5	0-62(0-0-62)/D-8	6	0.1
2003 Tex-A	82	327	49	96	17	1	24	70	14	73	1	1	.294	.330	.572	.902	121	8	57	6.37	5	0-57(0-0-57),D-24	10	0.8
Total 15	1655	6428	1044	1901	384	24	429	1387	448	1254	26	18	.296	.347	.563	.911	133	268	1204	6.77	1	*0-1282,D-366	231	18.1

• GONZALEZ, Julio Julio Cesar (Hernandez) Gonzalez b: 12/25/1952, Caguas, Puerto Rico BR/TR, 5'11", 165 lbs. Deb: 4/8/1977

YEAR TM-L	G	AB	R	H	2B	3B	HR	RBI	BB	SO	SB	CS	AVG	OBP	SLG	OPS	OPS+	BR/A	RC	RC/G	FR	G/POS	WS	TPW
1977 Hou-N	110	383	34	94	18	3	1	27	19	45	3	3	.245	.288	.316	.604	68	-19	34	3.02	-13	S-63,2-45	5	-2.4
1978 Hou-N	78	223	24	52	3	1	1	16	8	31	6	1	.233	.263	.269	.532	53	-14	15	2.22	0	2-54,S-17/3-4	2	-1.1
1979 Hou-N	68	181	16	45	5	2	0	10	5	14	2	1	.249	.280	.298	.579	61	-10	15	2.72	3	2-32,S-21/3-9	4	-0.4
1980 Hou-N	40	52	5	6	1	0	0	1	1	8	1	0	.115	.132	.135	.267	-28	-9	1	.50	0	S-16,3-11/2-2	1	-0.9
1981 StL-N	20	22	2	7	1	0	1	3	1	3	0	0	.318	.348	.500	.848	135	1	3	4.42	0	/S-5,2-4,3-2	1	0.1
1982 StL-N	42	87	9	21	3	2	1	7	1	24	1	1	.241	.258	.356	.615	70	-4	7	2.79	-1	3-21/2-9,S-1	1	-0.6
1983 Det-A	12	21	0	3	1	0	0	2	1	7	0	0	.143	.182	.190	.372	3	-3	1	.84	-1	/S-6,2-5,3-1	0	-0.3
Total 7	370	969	90	228	32	8	4	66	36	132	13	6	.235	.269	.297	.566	58	-57	76	2.58	-13	2-151,S-129/3-48	14	-5.5

• GONZALEZ, Luis Luis Emilio "Gonzo" Gonzalez b: 9/3/1967, Tampa, FL BL/TR, 6'2", 180 lbs. Deb: 9/4/1990 Career OF: 1821-9-0

YEAR TM-L	G	AB	R	H	2B	3B	HR	RBI	BB	SO	SB	CS	AVG	OBP	SLG	OPS	OPS+	BR/A	RC	RC/G	FR	G/POS	WS	TPW
1990 Hou-N	12	21	1	4	2	0	0	0	2	5	0	0	.190	.261	.286	.547	52	-1	2	2.59	1	/3-4,1-2	0	0.0
1991 Hou-N	137	473	51	120	28	9	13	69	40	101	10	7	.254	.322	.433	.756	117	9	65	4.68	2	*0-133(133-0-0)	15	0.6
1992 Hou-N	122	387	40	94	19	3	10	55	24	52	7	7	.243	.291	.385	.676	94	-6	41	3.60	7	*0-111(111-0-0)	11	-0.3
1993 Hou-N	154	540	82	162	34	3	15	72	47	83	20	9	.300	.367	.457	.824	124	18	91	6.03	13	*0-149(149-0-0)	20	2.6
1994 Hou-N	112	392	57	107	29	4	8	67	49	57	15	13	.273	.358	.429	.787	110	4	58	4.96	6	*0-111(111-0-0)	13	0.5
1995 Hou-N	56	209	35	54	10	4	6	35	18	30	1	3	.258	.326	.431	.757	105	-0	27	4.23	0	0-55(55-0-0)	5	-0.2
Chi-N	77	262	34	76	19	4	7	34	39	33	5	5	.290	.388	.473	.861	128	10	47	6.30	4	0-76(74-6-0)	10	1.1
Yr.	133	471	69	130	29	8	13	69	57	63	6	8	.276	.361	.454	.816	118	10	74	5.35	4	*0-131(129-6-0)	15	0.8
1996 Chi-N	146	483	70	131	30	4	15	79	61	49	9	6	.271	.358	.443	.801	107	4	76	5.40	3	*0-139(139-0-0)/1-2	17	0.2
1997*Hou-N	152	550	78	142	31	2	10	68	71	67	10	7	.258	.348	.376	.725	93	-5	73	4.59	6	*0-146(146-0-0)/1-1	12	-0.5
1998 Det-A	154	547	84	146	35	5	23	71	57	62	12	7	.267	.345	.475	.820	110	7	90	5.70	-3	*0-132(132-3-0),D-19	12	-0.3
1999*Ari-N★	153	614	112	**206**	45	4	26	111	66	63	9	5	.336	.406	.549	.955	138	35	136	8.53	0	*0-148(148-0-0)/D-4	26	2.7
2000 Ari-N	162	618	106	192	47	2	31	114	78	85	2	4	.311	.398	.544	.942	131	29	135	7.99	-3	*0-162(162-0-0)	27	1.8
2001*Ari-N★	162	609	128	198	36	7	57	142	100	83	1	1	.325	.432	.688	1.120	172	69	182	11.39	0	*0-161(161-0-0)	37	6.0
2002 Ari-N★	148	524	90	151	19	3	28	103	97	76	9	2	.288	.404	.496	.900	124	24	111	7.57	-4	*0-146(146-0-0)	26	1.4
2003 Ari-N★	156	579	92	176	46	4	26	104	94	67	5	3	.304	.404	.532	.936	129	27	123	7.76	2	*0-154(154-0-0)	24	2.2
Total 14	1903	6808	1060	1959	430	58	275	1124	843	913	115	79	.288	.373	.489	.862	122	223	1256	6.56	36	*0-1823/D-23,1-5,3-4	255	17.6

• GONZALEZ, Mike Miguel Angel (Cordero) Gonzalez
b: 9/24/1890, Havana, Cuba d: 2/19/1977, Havana, Cuba BR/TR, 6'1", 200 lbs. Deb: 9/28/1912 M/C Career OF: 1-1-4

YEAR TM-L	G	AB	R	H	2B	3B	HR	RBI	BB	SO	SB	CS	AVG	OBP	SLG	OPS	OPS+	BR/A	RC	RC/G	FR	G/POS	WS	TPW
1912 Bos-N	1	2	0	0	0	0	0	0	1	1	0	....	.000	.333	.000	.333	-5	-0	0	.00	1	/C-1	0	0.0
1914 Cin-N	95	176	19	41	6	0	0	10	13	16	2	....	.233	.293	.267	.560	65	-8	14	2.63	3	C-83	3	0.0
1915 StL-N	51	97	12	22	2	2	0	10	8	9	4	2	.227	.306	.289	.594	80	-2	9	3.14	3	C-32/1-8	3	0.2
1916 StL-N	118	331	33	79	15	4	0	29	28	18	5	....	.239	.304	.308	.612	89	-4	34	3.36	12	C-93,1-13	11	1.6
1917 StL-N	106	290	28	76	8	1	1	28	22	24	12	....	.262	.316	.307	.623	94	-2	31	3.61	5	C-68,1-18/0-1	10	0.9
1918 StL-N	117	349	33	88	13	4	3	20	39	30	14	....	.252	.327	.338	.665	107	4	41	4.00	2	*C-100/0-5(1-1-3),1-2	12	1.5
1919 NY-N	58	158	18	30	6	0	0	8	20	9	3	....	.190	.293	.228	.521	58	-7	11	2.23	-7	C-52/1-4	3	-1.1
1920 NY-N	11	13	1	3	0	0	0	0	3	1	1	0	.231	.375	.231	.606	77	0	2	4.09	0	/C-8	0	0.1
1921 NY-N	13	24	3	9	1	0	0	0	1	0	0	0	.375	.400	.417	.817	116	1	4	6.25	-1	/1-6,C-2	1	0.0
1924 StL-N	120	402	34	119	27	1	3	53	24	22	1	5	.296	.337	.391	.728	96	-3	52	4.63	0	*C-119	11	0.4
1925 StL-N	22	71	9	22	3	0	0	4	6	2	1	2	.310	.380	.352	.732	86	-2	9	4.81	1	C-22	2	0.1
Chi-N	70	197	26	52	13	1	3	18	13	15	2	1	.264	.316	.386	.702	77	-7	24	4.26	2	C-50/1-9	5	-0.3
Yr.	92	268	35	74	16	1	3	22	19	17	3	3	.276	.333	.377	.710	80	-8	34	4.40	3	C-72/1-9	7	-0.2
1926 Chi-N	80	253	24	63	13	3	1	23	13	17	3	....	.249	.288	.336	624	67	-12	24	3.16	-1	C-78	6	-0.9
1927 Chi-N	39	108	15	26	4	1	1	15	10	8	1	....	.241	.311	.324	.635	70	-5	11	3.36	3	C-36	3	0.1
1928 Chi-N	49	158	12	43	9	2	1	21	12	7	2	....	.272	.324	.373	.697	83	-4	19	4.08	2	C-45	6	0.1
1929*Chi-N	60	167	15	40	3	0	0	18	18	14	1	....	.240	.317	.257	.575	44	-14	14	2.86	1	C-60	4	-0.9
1931 StL-N	15	19	1	2	0	0	0	3	0	3	0	....	.105	.105	.105	.211	-42	-4	0	.31	0	C-12	0	-0.4
1932 StL-N	17	14	0	2	0	0	0	3	0	2	0	....	.143	.143	.143	.286	-22	-2	0	.60	0	/C-7	0	-0.3
Total 17	1042	2829	283	717	123	19	13	263	231	198	52	10	.253	.314	.324	.638	81	-71	300	3.58	25	C-868/1-60,0-6	80	1.3

• GONZALEZ, Orlando Orlando Eugene Gonzalez b: 11/15/1951, Havana, Cuba BL/TL, 6'2", 180 lbs. Deb: 6/7/1976 Career OF: 6-0-14

YEAR TM-L	G	AB	R	H	2B	3B	HR	RBI	BB	SO	SB	CS	AVG	OBP	SLG	OPS	OPS+	BR/A	RC	RC/G	FR	G/POS	WS	TPW
1976 Cle-A	28	68	5	17	2	0	0	4	5	7	1	2	.250	.301	.279	.581	72	-3	5	2.49	-1	1-15/0-7(3-0-4),D-2	0	-0.6
1978*Phi-N	26	26	1	5	0	0	0	0	1	1	0	0	.192	.222	.192	.415	17	-3	1	1.50	-1	0-11(1-0-10)/1-3	0	-0.4
1980 Oak-A	25	70	10	17	0	0	0	1	9	8	0	2	.243	.329	.243	.572	64	-4	6	2.87	1	1-11/D-8,0-2(2-0-0)	1	-0.4
Total 3	79	164	16	39	2	0	0	5	15	16	1	4	.238	.302	.250	.552	60	-10	12	2.49	-1	/1-29,0-20,D-10	1	-1.4

• GONZALEZ, Pedro Pedro (Olivares) Gonzalez b: 12/12/1937, San Pedro de Macoris, Dominican Republic BR/TR, 6', 176 lbs. Deb: 4/11/1963 Career OF: 5-0-19

YEAR TM-L	G	AB	R	H	2B	3B	HR	RBI	BB	SO	SB	CS	AVG	OBP	SLG	OPS	OPS+	BR/A	RC	RC/G	FR	G/POS	WS	TPW
1963 NY-A	14	26	3	5	1	0	0	1	0	5	0	1	.192	.192	.231	.423	18	-3	1	1.13	-2	/2-7	0	-0.5

YEAR TM-L	G	AB	R	H	2B	3B	HR	RBI	BB	SO	SB	CS	AVG	OBP	SLG	OPS	OPS+	BR/A	RC	RC/G	FR	G/POS	WS	TPW
1964*NY-A	80	112	18	31	8	1	0	5	7	22	3	4	.277	.331	.366	.697	92	-2	13	3.85	-3	1-31,0-20(5-0-15)/3-9,2-6	3	-0.7
1965 NY-A	7	5	0	2	1	0	0	0	0	2	0	0	.400	.400	.600	1.000	181	1	1	7.92	0	....	0	0.1
Cle-A	116	400	38	101	14	3	5	39	18	57	7	4	.253	.290	.340	.630	78	-13	38	3.22	6	*2-112/0-3(0-0-3),3-2	9	0.3
Yr.	123	405	38	103	15	3	5	39	18	59	7	4	.254	.291	.343	.634	79	-12	39	3.28	6	*2-112/0-3(0-0-3),3-2	9	0.4
1966 Cle-A	110	352	21	82	9	2	2	17	15	54	8	5	.233	.268	.287	.555	60	-19	27	2.52	6	*2-104/3-1,0-1	7	-0.4
1967 Cle-A	80	189	19	43	6	0	1	8	12	36	4	6	.228	.277	.275	.552	63	-10	13	2.11	-3	2-64/1-4,3-4,S-3	2	-0.9
Total 5	**407**	**1084**	**99**	**264**	**39**	**6**	**8**	**70**	**52**	**176**	**22**	**20**	**.244**	**.283**	**.313**	**.596**	**70**	**-47**	**93**	**2.82**	**4**	**2-293/1-35,0-24,3-16,S-3**	**21**	**-2.2**

• GONZALEZ, Raul Victor Raul Gonzalez b: 12/27/1973, Santurce, Puerto Rico BR/TR, 5'8", 190 lbs. Deb: 5/25/2000 Career OF: 61-43-44

YEAR TM-L	G	AB	R	H	2B	3B	HR	RBI	BB	SO	SB	CS	AVG	OBP	SLG	OPS	OPS+	BR/A	RC	RC/G	FR	G/POS	WS	TPW
2000 Chi-N	3	2	0	0	0	0	0	0	0	2	0	0	.000	.000	.000	.000	-103	-1	0	.00	0	/0-2(2-0-0)	0	-0.1
2001 Cin-N	11	14	0	3	0	0	0	0	1	3	0	0	.214	.267	.214	.481	26	-2	1	2.13	-0	/0-2(2-0-0)	0	-0.2
2002 Cin-N	10	23	4	6	1	0	0	1	2	5	2	0	.261	.320	.304	.624	64	-1	2	3.60	0	/0-6(1-5-0)	0	0.0
NY-N	30	81	9	21	2	0	3	11	4	17	2	2	.259	.294	.395	.689	83	-3	8	3.51	1	0-24(11-13-4)	2	-0.3
Yr.	40	104	13	27	3	0	3	12	6	22	4	2	.260	.300	.375	.675	78	-4	11	3.53	1	0-30(12-18-4)	2	-0.3
2003 NY-N	107	217	28	50	12	2	2	21	27	34	3	0	.230	.318	.332	.650	72	-8	23	3.54	3	0-88(45-25-40)	5	-0.7
Total 4	**161**	**337**	**41**	**80**	**15**	**2**	**5**	**33**	**34**	**61**	**7**	**2**	**.237**	**.309**	**.338**	**.647**	**71**	**-14**	**35**	**3.45**	**4**	**0-122**	**7**	**-1.2**

• GONZALEZ, Tony Andres Antonio (Gonzalez) Gonzalez b: 8/28/1936, Central Cunagua, Cuba BL/TR, 5'9", 170 lbs. Deb: 4/12/1960 Career OF: 462-933-118

YEAR TM-L	G	AB	R	H	2B	3B	HR	RBI	BB	SO	SB	CS	AVG	OBP	SLG	OPS	OPS+	BR/A	RC	RC/G	FR	G/POS	WS	TPW
1960 Cin-N	39	99	10	21	5	1	3	14	4	27	1	0	.212	.250	.374	.624	67	-5	9	3.00	-2	0-31(1-0-30)	1	-0.8
Phi-N	78	241	27	72	17	5	6	33	11	47	2	2	.299	.337	.485	.823	122	6	38	5.89	2	0-67(3-61-5)	8	0.5
Yr.	117	340	37	93	22	6	9	47	15	74	3	2	.274	.312	.453	.765	106	1	47	4.97	0	0-98(4-61-35)	9	-0.2
1961 Phi-N	126	426	58	118	16	8	12	58	49	66	15	5	.277	.360	.437	.796	112	9	68	5.60	0	*0-118(1-86-34)	12	0.5
1962 Phi-N	118	437	76	132	16	4	20	63	40	82	17	8	.302	.372	.494	.867	134	21	80	6.67	-2	*0-114(0-114-1)	20	1.6
1963 Phi-N	155	555	78	170	36	12	4	66	53	68	13	8	.306	.375	.436	.811	134	26	91	5.94	0	*0-151(56-107-9)	26	2.1
1964 Phi-N	131	421	55	117	25	3	4	40	44	74	0	5	.278	.355	.380	.735	108	4	56	4.67	-6	*0-119(6-114-0)	15	-0.6
1965 Phi-N	108	370	48	109	19	1	13	41	31	52	3	4	.295	.354	.457	.811	129	13	54	5.18	-3	*0-104(53-60-2)	13	0.6
1966 Phi-N	132	384	53	110	20	4	6	40	26	60	2	6	.286	.337	.406	.743	105	1	51	4.79	0	*0-121(73-47-4)	12	-0.5
1967 Phi-N	149	508	74	172	23	9	9	59	47	58	10	9	.339	.400	.472	.872	147	31	94	7.01	4	*0-143(105-29-16)	26	2.9
1968 Phi-N	121	416	45	110	13	4	3	38	40	42	6	5	.264	.339	.337	.676	103	3	47	3.77	-3	*0-117(19-98-4)	13	-0.5
1969 SD-N	53	182	17	41	4	0	2	8	19	24	1	0	.225	.309	.280	.589	69	-7	16	2.91	0	0-49(40-11-3)	3	-1.0
*Atl-N	89	320	51	94	15	2	10	50	27	22	3	1	.294	.358	.447	.805	124	10	51	5.80	-4	0-82(35-49-0)	15	0.4
Yr.	142	502	68	135	19	2	12	58	46	46	4	1	.269	.340	.386	.726	104	4	67	4.70	-4	*0-131(75-60-3)	18	-0.6
1970 Atl-N	123	430	57	114	18	2	7	55	46	45	3	5	.265	.347	.365	.712	86	-9	54	4.36	-10	*0-119(3-116-0)	10	-2.2
Cal-A	26	92	9	28	2	0	1	12	2	11	3	2	.304	.326	.359	.685	92	-1	10	3.71	0	0-24(0-23-1)	2	-0.2
1971 Cal-A	111	314	32	77	9	2	3	38	28	28	0	1	.245	.313	.315	.628	84	-7	30	3.20	1	0-88(67-18-9)	7	-1.0
Total 12	**1559**	**5195**	**690**	**1485**	**238**	**57**	**103**	**615**	**467**	**706**	**79**	**61**	**.286**	**.353**	**.413**	**.766**	**114**	**95**	**749**	**5.11**	**-23**	***0-1447**	**183**	**1.8**

• GONZALEZ, Wiki Wiklenman Vicente Gonzalez b: 5/17/1974, Aragua, Venezuela BR/TR, 5'11", 203 lbs. Deb: 8/14/1999

YEAR TM-L	G	AB	R	H	2B	3B	HR	RBI	BB	SO	SB	CS	AVG	OBP	SLG	OPS	OPS+	BR/A	RC	RC/G	FR	G/POS	WS	TPW
1999 SD-N	30	83	7	21	2	1	3	12	1	8	0	0	.253	.271	.410	.680	75	-4	7	2.95	1	C-17	1	-0.1
2000 SD-N	95	284	25	66	15	1	5	30	30	31	1	2	.232	.312	.345	.657	71	-14	31	3.67	5	C-87	6	-0.3
2001 SD-N	64	160	16	44	6	0	8	27	11	28	2	0	.275	.337	.463	.800	114	3	25	5.67	-2	C-47/D-1	7	0.4
2002 SD-N	56	164	16	36	8	1	1	20	27	24	0	0	.220	.333	.299	.632	75	-5	16	3.04	2	C-54	4	0.1
2003 SD-N	24	65	1	13	5	0	0	10	5	13	0	0	.200	.268	.277	.545	47	-5	4	2.11	1	C-23/P-1	1	-0.2
Total 5	**269**	**756**	**65**	**180**	**36**	**3**	**17**	**99**	**74**	**104**	**3**	**2**	**.238**	**.314**	**.361**	**.675**	**79**	**-24**	**84**	**3.69**	**8**	**C-228/D-1,P-1**	**19**	**-0.1**

• GOOCH, Charlie Charles Furman Gooch b: 6/5/1902, Smyrna, TN d: 5/30/1982, Lanham, MD BR/TR, 5'9", 170 lbs. Deb: 4/18/1929

YEAR TM-L	G	AB	R	H	2B	3B	HR	RBI	BB	SO	SB	CS	AVG	OBP	SLG	OPS	OPS+	BR/A	RC	RC/G	FR	G/POS	WS	TPW
1929 Was-A	39	57	6	16	2	1	0	5	7	8	0	1	.281	.359	.351	.710	83	-2	7	4.54	0	/1-7,3-7,S-1	1	-0.1

• GOOCH, Johnny John Beverley Gooch b: 11/9/1897, Smyrna, TN d: 3/15/1975, Nashville, TN BB/TR, 5'11", 175 lbs. Deb: 9/9/1921 C

YEAR TM-L	G	AB	R	H	2B	3B	HR	RBI	BB	SO	SB	CS	AVG	OBP	SLG	OPS	OPS+	BR/A	RC	RC/G	FR	G/POS	WS	TPW
1921 Pit-N	13	38	2	9	0	0	0	3	3	3	1	0	.237	.293	.237	.530	41	-3	3	2.62	0	C-13	1	-0.2
1922 Pit-N	105	353	45	116	15	3	1	42	39	15	1	1	.329	.403	.397	.800	106	6	59	6.42	-3	*C-103	14	0.9
1923 Pit-N	66	202	16	56	10	2	1	20	17	13	2	1	.277	.336	.361	.698	82	-4	25	4.52	-4	C-66	7	-0.4
1924 Pit-N	70	224	26	65	6	5	0	25	16	12	1	3	.290	.343	.362	.705	87	-4	27	4.47	-4	C-69	7	-0.4
1925*Pit-N	79	215	24	64	8	4	0	30	20	16	1	0	.298	.357	.372	.730	81	-5	30	5.11	-1	C-76	7	-0.3
1926 Pit-N	86	218	19	59	15	1	1	42	20	14	1	....	.271	.340	.362	.703	85	-4	27	4.27	-1	C-80	7	-0.1
1927*Pit-N	101	291	22	75	17	2	2	48	19	21	0	....	.258	.305	.351	.656	70	-13	31	3.56	-2	C-91	7	-0.9
1928 Pit-N	31	80	7	19	2	1	0	5	3	6	0	....	.238	.265	.288	.553	43	-7	6	2.39	-1	C-31	1	-0.6
Bro-N	42	101	9	32	1	2	0	12	7	9	0	....	.317	.361	.366	.727	92	-1	13	4.85	-1	C-38	3	0.0
Yr.	73	181	16	51	3	3	0	17	10	15	0	....	.282	.319	.331	.651	70	-8	19	3.66	-2	C-69	4	-0.6
1929 Bro-N	1	1	0	0	0	0	0	0	0	0	0	....	.000	.000	.000	.000	-102	-0	0	.00	0	....	0	0.0
Cin-N	92	287	22	86	13	5	0	34	24	10	4	....	.300	.356	.380	.736	86	-6	38	4.92	1	C-86	9	0.0
Yr.	93	288	22	86	13	5	0	34	24	10	4	....	.299	.355	.378	.733	86	-6	38	4.90	1	C-86	9	0.0
1930 Cin-N	82	276	29	67	10	3	2	30	27	15	0	....	.243	.315	.322	.637	57	-19	28	3.50	-3	C-79	3	-1.5
1933 Bos-A	37	77	6	14	1	1	0	2	11	7	0	0	.182	.284	.221	.505	36	-7	5	2.28	2	C-26	1	-0.3
Total 11	**805**	**2363**	**227**	**662**	**98**	**29**	**7**	**293**	**206**	**141**	**11**	**5**	**.280**	**.342**	**.355**	**.697**	**79**	**-67**	**292**	**4.42**	**-17**	**C-758**	**67**	**-3.8**

• GOOCH, Lee Lee Currin Gooch b: 2/23/1890, Oxford, NC d: 5/18/1966, Raleigh, NC BR/TR, 6', 190 lbs. Deb: 8/17/1915

YEAR TM-L	G	AB	R	H	2B	3B	HR	RBI	BB	SO	SB	CS	AVG	OBP	SLG	OPS	OPS+	BR/A	RC	RC/G	FR	G/POS	WS	TPW
1915 Cle-A	2	2	0	1	0	0	0	0	0	0	0	....	.500	.500	.500	1.000	196	0	1	13.25	0	....	0	0.0
1917 Phi-A	17	59	4	17	2	0	1	8	4	10	0	....	.288	.333	.373	.706	117	1	7	4.28	-2	0-16(0-0-16)	2	-0.2
Total 2	**19**	**61**	**4**	**18**	**2**	**0**	**1**	**8**	**4**	**10**	**0**	**....**	**.295**	**.338**	**.377**	**.716**	**119**	**1**	**8**	**4.48**	**-2**	**/0-16**	**2**	**-0.2**

• GOOD, Gene Eugene J. Good b: 12/13/1882, Roxbury, MA d: 8/6/1947, Boston, MA BL/TL, 5'6", 130 lbs. Deb: 4/12/1906

YEAR TM-L	G	AB	R	H	2B	3B	HR	RBI	BB	SO	SB	CS	AVG	OBP	SLG	OPS	OPS+	BR/A	RC	RC/G	FR	G/POS	WS	TPW
1906 Bos-N	34	119	4	18	0	0	0	0	13	....	2	....	.151	.246	.151	.398	25	-10	5	1.32	-2	0-34(24-10-0)	0	-1.5

• GOOD, Wilbur Wilbur David "Lefty" Good
b: 9/28/1885, Punxsutawney, PA d: 12/30/1963, Brooksville, FL BL/TL, 5'11.5", 180 lbs. Deb: 8/18/1905 Career OF: 23-154-448

YEAR TM-L	G	AB	R	H	2B	3B	HR	RBI	BB	SO	SB	CS	AVG	OBP	SLG	OPS	OPS+	BR/A	RC	RC/G	FR	G/POS	WS	TPW
1905 NY-A	5	8	2	3	0	0	0	0	0	....	0	....	.375	.375	.375	.750	124	1	1	6.11	0	/P-5	0	-0.3
1908 Cle-A	46	154	23	43	1	3	1	14	13	....	7	....	.279	.351	.344	.695	125	5	21	4.74	-7	0-42(2-17-23)	6	-0.4
1909 Cle-A	94	318	33	68	6	5	0	17	28	....	13	....	.214	.296	.264	.560	74	-8	28	2.88	1	0-80(0-0-80)	6	-1.3
1910 Bos-N	23	86	15	29	5	4	0	11	6	13	5	....	.337	.394	.488	.882	150	5	18	7.85	5	0-23(0-22-1)	4	1.0
1911 Bos-N	43	165	21	44	9	3	0	15	12	22	3	....	.267	.316	.358	.674	82	-5	19	4.03	5	0-43(0-41-2)	3	-0.2
Chi-N	58	145	27	39	5	4	2	21	11	17	10	....	.269	.329	.400	.729	103	0	22	5.18	-4	0-40(3-34-3)	4	-0.6
Yr.	101	310	48	83	14	7	2	36	23	39	13	....	.268	.322	.377	.700	92	-5	42	4.57	1	0-83(3-75-5)	7	-0.8
1912 Chi-N	39	35	7	5	0	0	0	1	3	7	3	....	.143	.211	.143	.353	-2	-5	2	1.34	0	0-10(5-4-1)	0	-0.5
1913 Chi-N	49	91	11	23	3	2	1	12	11	16	5	....	.253	.340	.363	.702	100	0	12	4.50	-1	0-26(3-1-22)	3	-0.2
1914 Chi-N	154	580	70	158	24	7	2	43	53	74	31	....	.272	.341	.348	.689	105	4	77	4.51	0	*0-154(0-0-154)	20	-0.4
1915 Chi-N	128	498	66	126	18	9	2	27	34	65	19	17	.253	.307	.337	.645	95	-7	52	3.46	2	*0-125(0-1-125)	12	-1.3
1916 Phi-N	75	136	25	34	4	3	1	15	8	13	7	....	.250	.306	.346	.652	96	-1	17	4.11	-1	0-46(9-1-36)	4	-0.3
1918 Chi-A	35	148	24	37	9	4	0	11	11	16	1	....	.250	.315	.365	.680	104	0	16	3.74	1	0-35(1-33-1)	4	-0.1
Total 11	**749**	**2364**	**324**	**609**	**84**	**44**	**9**	**187**	**190**	**243**	**104**	**17**	**.258**	**.322**	**.342**	**.664**	**98**	**-11**	**286**	**4.07**	**1**	**0-624/P-5**	**66**	**-4.8**

• GOODENOUGH, Bill William B. Goodenough b: 1863, NY d: 5/24/1905, St. Louis, MO BL, 6'1", 170 lbs. Deb: 8/31/1893

YEAR TM-L	G	AB	R	H	2B	3B	HR	RBI	BB	SO	SB	CS	AVG	OBP	SLG	OPS	OPS+	BR/A	RC	RC/G	FR	G/POS	WS	TPW
1893 StL-N	10	31	4	5	1	0	0	2	3	4	2	....	.161	.297	.194	.491	31	-3	2	2.48	-1	0-10(0-10-0)	0	-0.4

• GOODFELLOW, Mike Michael J. Goodfellow b: 10/3/1866, Port Jervis, NY d: 2/12/1920, Newark, NJ BR/TR, 6', 180 lbs. Deb: 6/13/1887

YEAR TM-L	G	AB	R	H	2B	3B	HR	RBI	BB	SO	SB	CS	AVG	OBP	SLG	OPS	OPS+	BR/A	RC	RC/G	FR	G/POS	WS	TPW
1887 StL-a	1	4	0	0	0	0	0	0	0	....	0	....	.000	.000	.000	.000	-90	-1	0	.00	0	/C-1	0	-0.1
1888 Cle-a	68	269	24	66	7	0	0	29	11	....	7	....	.245	.283	.271	.554	80	-6	23	3.08	-4	0-62(11-0-52)/C-4,1-3,S-1	5	-1.0
Total 2	**69**	**273**	**24**	**66**	**7**	**0**	**0**	**29**	**11**	**....**	**7**	**....**	**.242**	**.279**	**.267**	**.546**	**78**	**-7**	**23**	**3.02**	**-4**	**/0-62,C-5,1-3,S-1**	**5**	**-1.1**

• GOODMAN, Billy William Dale Goodman b: 3/22/1926, Concord, NC d: 10/1/1984, Sarasota, FL BL/TR, 5'11", 165 lbs. Deb: 4/19/1947 C Career OF: 68-0-43

YEAR TM-L	G	AB	R	H	2B	3B	HR	RBI	BB	SO	SB	CS	AVG	OBP	SLG	OPS	OPS+	BR/A	RC	RC/G	FR	G/POS	WS	TPW
1947 Bos-A	12	11	1	2	0	0	0	1	1	2	0	0	.182	.250	.182	.432	20	-1	1	1.73	0	/0-1	0	-0.1

YEAR TM-L	G	AB	R	H	2B	3B	HR	RBI	BB	SO	SB	CS	AVG	OBP	SLG	OPS	OPS+	BR/A	RC	RC/G	FR	G/POS	WS	TPW
1948 Bos-A	127	445	65	138	27	2	1	66	74	44	5	3	.310	.414	.387	.801	108	10	75	6.10	-5	*1-117/2-2,3-2	15	0.1
1949 Bos-A★	122	443	54	132	23	3	0	56	58	21	2	0	.298	.382	.363	.745	91	-3	65	5.27	-4	*1-117	11	-1.1
1950 Bos-A	110	424	91	150	25	3	4	68	52	25	2	4	**.354**	.427	.455	.882	115	11	86	7.90	1	0-45(45-0-0),3-27,1-21/2-5,S	16	0.7
1951 Bos-A	141	546	92	162	34	4	0	50	79	37	7	4	.297	.388	.374	.761	97	1	85	5.60	-6	1-62,2-44,0-38(2-0-36)/3-1	17	-0.5
1952 Bos-A	138	513	79	157	27	3	4	56	48	23	8	2	.306	.370	.394	.764	104	5	80	5.71	11	*2-103,1-23/3-5,0-4(4-0-0)	20	2.2
1953 Bos-A★	128	514	73	161	33	5	2	41	57	11	1	4	.313	.384	.409	.793	108	7	87	6.38	4	*2-112,1-20	20	1.8
1954 Bos-A	127	489	71	148	25	4	1	36	51	15	3	3	.303	.371	.376	.747	94	-2	70	5.17	3	2-72,1-27,0-13(13-0-0),3-12	13	0.4
1955 Bos-A	149	599	100	176	31	2	0	52	99	44	5	5	.294	.397	.352	.749	94	0	90	5.33	-17	*2-143/1-5,0-1	15	-0.6
1956 Bos-A	105	399	61	117	22	8	2	38	40	22	0	3	.293	.358	.404	.761	90	-7	59	5.39	4	2-95	11	0.4
1957 Bos-A	18	16	1	1	1	0	0	0	2	1	0	0	.063	.167	.125	.292	-18	-2	0	.76	0	....	0	-0.3
Bal-A	73	263	36	81	10	3	3	33	21	18	0	2	.308	.366	.403	.769	117	6	36	4.76	-5	3-54/0-9(4-0-5),1-8,2-5,S	8	0.1
Yr.	91	279	37	82	11	3	3	33	23	19	0	2	.294	.354	.387	.741	109	3	37	4.49	-5	3-54/0-9(4-0-5),1-8,2-5,S	8	-0.2
1958 Chi-A	116	425	41	127	15	5	0	40	37	21	1	0	.299	.358	.358	.715	99	1	55	4.71	1	*3-111/1-3,2-1,S-1	14	0.2
1959*Chi-A	104	268	21	67	14	1	1	28	19	20	3	0	.250	.304	.321	.625	73	-9	27	3.54	5	3-74/2-3	6	-0.4
1960 Chi-A	30	77	5	18	4	0	0	6	12	8	0	0	.234	.337	.286	.623	71	-3	8	3.46	1	3-20/2-7	2	-0.2
1961 Chi-A	41	51	4	13	4	0	1	10	7	6	0	0	.255	.345	.392	.737	98	-0	7	4.86	-1	/3-7,1-2,2-1	1	-0.1
1962 Hou-N	82	161	12	41	4	1	0	10	12	11	0	0	.255	.306	.292	.598	66	-7	14	2.88	-4	2-31,3-17/1-1	1	-1.0
Total 16	1623	5644	807	1691	299	44	19	591	669	329	37	30	.300	.377	.378	.755	98	6	844	5.42	-12	2-624,1-406,3-330,0-111/S-7	170	1.6

• GOODMAN, Ival

Ival Richard "Goodie,Ol' Mate" Goodman
b: 7/23/1908, Northview, MO d: 11/25/1984, Cincinnati, OH BL/TR, 5'11", 170 lbs. Deb: 4/16/1935 Career OF: 88-26-892

YEAR TM-L	G	AB	R	H	2B	3B	HR	RBI	BB	SO	SB	CS	AVG	OBP	SLG	OPS	OPS+	BR/A	RC	RC/G	FR	G/POS	WS	TPW
1935 Cin-N	148	592	86	159	23	**18**	12	72	35	50	14	....	.269	.314	.429	.743	101	-1	83	5.04	5	*0-146(2-0-144)	16	-0.5
1936 Cin-N	136	489	81	139	15	**14**	17	71	38	53	6	....	.284	.347	.476	.823	128	18	82	5.94	1	*0-120(1-1-118)	18	1.1
1937 Cin-N	147	549	86	150	25	12	12	55	55	58	10	....	.273	.347	.428	.775	115	11	85	5.53	3	*0-141(7-1-133)	16	0.6
1938 Cin-N★	145	568	103	166	27	10	30	92	53	51	3	....	.292	.368	.533	.901	149	37	116	7.36	3	*0-142(0-0-142)	28	3.1
1939*Cin-N★	124	470	85	152	37	16	7	84	54	32	2	....	.323	.401	.515	.916	144	30	101	7.87	12	*0-123(0-0-123)	25	3.4
1940*Cin-N	136	519	78	134	20	6	12	63	60	54	9	....	.258	.335	.389	.724	98	-1	72	4.86	-5	*0-135(0-0-135)	17	-1.5
1941 Cin-N	42	149	14	40	5	2	1	12	16	15	1	....	.268	.343	.349	.692	95	-1	18	4.26	0	0-40(0-0-40)	5	-0.4
1942 Cin-N	87	226	21	55	18	1	0	15	24	32	0	....	.243	.319	.332	.651	91	-3	24	3.53	1	0-57(0-0-57)	5	-0.5
1943 Chi-N	80	225	31	72	10	5	3	45	24	20	4	....	.320	.390	.449	.839	144	13	40	6.90	-6	0-61(55-10-0)	10	0.4
1944 Chi-N	62	141	24	37	8	1	1	16	23	15	0	....	.262	.377	.355	.732	107	3	20	4.98	-2	0-35(23-14-0)	4	0.0
Total 10	1107	3928	609	1104	188	85	95	525	382	380	49	....	.281	.352	.445	.797	120	106	641	5.83	13	*0-1000	144	5.8

• GOODMAN, Jake

Jacob Goodman b: 9/14/1853, Lancaster, PA d: 3/9/1890, Reading, PA, 6'1.5" Deb: 5/2/1878

YEAR TM-L	G	AB	R	H	2B	3B	HR	RBI	BB	SO	SB	CS	AVG	OBP	SLG	OPS	OPS+	BR/A	RC	RC/G	FR	G/POS	WS	TPW
1878 Mil-N	60	252	28	62	4	3	1	27	7	33	....	....	.246	.266	.298	.564	80	-6	20	2.96	1	*1-60	2	-0.8
1882 Pit-a	10	41	5	13	2	2	0	....	2	....	....	....	.317	.349	.463	.812	180	3	7	6.79	1	1-10	2	0.3
Total 2	70	293	33	75	6	5	1	27	9	33	....	....	.256	.278	.321	.599	94	-3	27	3.46	2	/1-70	4	-0.5

• GOODSON, Ed

James Edward Goodson b: 1/25/1948, Pulaski, VA BL/TR, 6'3", 185 lbs. Deb: 9/5/1970

YEAR TM-L	G	AB	R	H	2B	3B	HR	RBI	BB	SO	SB	CS	AVG	OBP	SLG	OPS	OPS+	BR/A	RC	RC/G	FR	G/POS	WS	TPW
1970 SF-N	7	11	1	3	0	0	0	0	0	2	0	0	.273	.273	.273	.545	47	-1	1	2.76	0	/1-2	0	-0.1
1971 SF-N	20	42	4	8	1	0	0	1	2	4	0	0	.190	.227	.214	.442	26	-4	2	1.11	1	1-14	0	-0.4
1972 SF-N	58	150	15	42	1	1	6	30	8	12	0	0	.280	.321	.420	.741	107	1	18	4.28	3	1-42	3	0.1
1973 SF-N	102	384	37	116	20	1	12	53	15	44	0	1	.302	.332	.453	.785	111	4	54	5.19	-2	3-93	11	0.1
1974 SF-N	98	298	25	81	15	0	6	48	18	22	1	0	.272	.320	.383	.702	91	-4	35	4.24	-3	1-73/3-8	6	-1.2
1975 SF-N	39	121	10	25	7	0	1	8	7	14	0	1	.207	.250	.289	.539	47	-9	8	2.04	1	1-16,3-13	1	-1.0
Atl-N	47	76	5	16	2	0	1	8	2	8	0	0	.211	.231	.276	.507	39	-7	4	1.48	0	1-13/3-1	0	-0.7
Yr.	86	197	15	41	9	0	2	16	9	22	0	1	.208	.243	.284	.527	44	-16	11	1.82	1	1-29,3-14	1	-1.7
1976 LA-N	83	118	8	27	4	0	3	17	8	19	0	0	.229	.278	.339	.617	76	-4	9	2.52	-2	3-16/1-3,0-2(2-0-0),2-1	1	-0.7
1977*LA-N	61	66	3	11	1	0	1	5	3	10	0	1	.167	.203	.227	.430	15	-8	2	1.13	0	1-13/3-4	0	-0.9
Total 8	515	1266	108	329	51	2	30	170	63	135	1	3	.260	.298	.374	.673	84	-33	133	3.62	-2	1-176,3-135/0-2,2-1	22	-4.8

• GOODWIN, Curtis

Curtis La Mar Goodwin b: 9/30/1972, Oakland, CA BL/TL, 5'11", 180 lbs. Deb: 6/2/1995 Career OF: 91-271-14

YEAR TM-L	G	AB	R	H	2B	3B	HR	RBI	BB	SO	SB	CS	AVG	OBP	SLG	OPS	OPS+	BR/A	RC	RC/G	FR	G/POS	WS	TPW
1995 Bal-A	87	289	40	76	11	3	1	24	15	53	22	4	.263	.304	.332	.636	64	-13	31	3.62	-2	0-84(0-84-0)/D-3	5	-1.4
1996 Cin-N	49	136	20	31	3	0	0	5	19	34	15	6	.228	.323	.250	.573	54	-8	13	3.11	-1	0-42(9-28-6)	1	-0.9
1997 Cin-N	85	265	27	67	11	0	1	12	24	53	22	13	.253	.317	.306	.623	63	-15	25	3.04	0	0-71(32-41-1)	4	-1.6
1998 Col-N	119	159	27	39	7	0	1	6	16	40	5	1	.245	.314	.308	.622	53	-10	17	3.37	-6	0-91(14-74-7)	2	-1.5
1999 Chi-N	89	157	15	38	6	1	0	9	13	38	2	4	.242	.300	.293	.593	52	-13	12	2.41	1	0-76(36-42-0)	1	-1.2
Tor-A	2	8	0	0	0	0	0	0	0	3	0	0	.000	.000	.000	.000	-99	-2	0	.00	1	/0-2(0-2-0)	0	-0.1
Total 5	431	1014	129	251	38	4	3	56	87	221	66	28	.248	.309	.302	.611	58	-61	98	3.13	-7	0-366/D-3	13	-6.7

• GOODWIN, Danny

Danny Kay Goodwin b: 9/2/1953, St. Louis, MO BL/TR, 6'1", 195 lbs. Deb: 9/3/1975

YEAR TM-L	G	AB	R	H	2B	3B	HR	RBI	BB	SO	SB	CS	AVG	OBP	SLG	OPS	OPS+	BR/A	RC	RC/G	FR	G/POS	WS	TPW
1975 Cal-A	4	10	0	1	0	0	0	0	0	5	0	0	.100	.100	.100	.200	-47	-2	0	.00	0	/D-3	0	-0.2
1977 Cal-A	35	91	5	19	6	1	1	8	5	19	0	0	.209	.250	.330	.580	59	-5	7	2.60	0	D-23	0	-0.6
1978 Cal-A	24	58	9	16	5	0	2	10	10	13	0	0	.276	.382	.466	.848	143	4	11	6.70	0	D-15	3	0.3
1979 Min-A	58	159	22	46	8	5	5	27	11	23	0	0	.289	.335	.497	.832	117	3	25	5.62	-1	D-51/1-8	4	0.1
1980 Min-A	55	115	12	23	5	0	1	11	17	32	0	0	.200	.303	.270	.573	54	-7	10	2.70	-0	D-38,1-13	0	-0.8
1981 Min-A	59	151	18	34	6	1	2	17	16	32	3	1	.225	.299	.318	.617	73	-5	15	3.24	-3	1-40/D-5,0-1	2	-1.0
1982 Oak-A	17	52	6	11	2	1	2	8	2	13	0	0	.212	.241	.404	.645	77	-2	4	2.33	0	D-15	0	-0.2
Total 7	252	636	72	150	32	8	13	81	61	137	3	1	.236	.303	.373	.675	84	-14	72	3.74	-3	D-150/1-61,0-1	9	-2.4

• GOODWIN, Pep

Claire Vernon Goodwin b: 12/19/1891, Pocatello, ID d: 2/15/1972, Oakland, CA BL/TR, 5'10.5", 160 lbs. Deb: 4/16/1914

YEAR TM-L	G	AB	R	H	2B	3B	HR	RBI	BB	SO	SB	CS	AVG	OBP	SLG	OPS	OPS+	BR/A	RC	RC/G	FR	G/POS	WS	TPW
1914 KC-F	112	374	38	88	15	6	1	32	27	23	4	....	.235	.290	.316	.606	76	-12	34	2.97	-14	S-67,3-40/1-1	7	-2.2
1915 KC-F	81	229	22	54	5	1	0	16	15	23	6	....	.236	.291	.266	.558	67	-9	20	2.77	-7	S-42,2-23	4	-1.4
Total 2	193	603	60	142	20	7	1	48	42	46	10	....	.235	.291	.297	.588	72	-22	54	2.89	-21	S-109/3-40,2-23,1-1	11	-3.6

• GOODWIN, Tom

Thomas Jones Goodwin b: 7/27/1968, Fresno, CA BL/TR, 6'1", 170 lbs. Deb: 9/1/1991 Career OF: 223-850-28

YEAR TM-L	G	AB	R	H	2B	3B	HR	RBI	BB	SO	SB	CS	AVG	OBP	SLG	OPS	OPS+	BR/A	RC	RC/G	FR	G/POS	WS	TPW
1991 LA-N	16	7	3	1	0	0	0	0	0	0	1	1	.143	.143	.143	.286	-20	-1	0	.00	-0	/0-5(2-4-0)	0	-0.1
1992 LA-N	57	73	15	17	1	1	0	3	6	10	7	3	.233	.291	.274	.565	62	-3	6	2.92	-1	0-45(35-9-2)	1	-0.6
1993 LA-N	30	17	6	5	1	0	0	1	1	4	1	2	.294	.333	.353	.686	89	-1	1	2.03	0	0-12(6-4-2)	0	-0.1
1994 KC-A	2	2	0	0	0	0	0	0	0	1	0	0	.000	.000	.000	.000	-96	-1	0	.00	-0	/D-1,0-1	0	-0.1
1995 KC-A	133	480	72	138	16	3	4	28	38	72	50	18	.288	.346	.358	.704	83	-9	63	4.46	2	*0-130(37-95-1)/D-2	10	-0.8
1996 KC-A	143	524	80	148	14	4	1	35	39	79	66	22	.282	.335	.330	.665	69	-20	64	4.09	-4	*0-136(75-81-0)/D-5	9	-2.4
1997 KC-A	97	367	51	100	13	4	2	22	19	51	34	10	.272	.312	.346	.658	70	-14	41	3.81	-3	0-96(0-96-0)	5	-1.5
Tex-A	53	207	39	49	13	2	0	17	25	37	16	6	.237	.322	.319	.641	65	-10	23	3.75	1	0-51(5-49-0)	4	-0.8
Yr.	150	574	90	149	26	6	2	39	44	88	50	16	.260	.316	.336	.652	68	-23	65	3.79	-2	*0-147(5-145-0)	9	-2.3
1998*Tex-A	154	520	102	151	13	3	2	33	73	90	38	20	.290	.380	.338	.718	85	-8	74	4.98	0	*0-150(0-150-0)/D-1	13	-0.7
1999*Tex-A	109	405	63	105	12	6	3	33	40	61	39	11	.259	.326	.341	.667	67	-16	49	4.00	-7	*0-107(0-107-0)	5	-2.1
2000 Col-N	91	317	65	86	8	8	5	47	50	76	39	7	.271	.372	.394	.767	75	-7	55	5.92	1	0-89(0-88-0)	11	-0.5
LA-N	56	211	29	53	3	1	1	11	18	41	16	3	.251	.310	.289	.599	56	-12	21	3.38	5	0-55(10-48-0)	3	-0.6
Yr.	147	528	94	139	11	9	6	58	68	117	55	10	.263	.348	.352	.701	68	-18	75	4.91	6	*0-144(10-136-0)	14	-1.1
2001 LA-N	105	286	51	66	8	5	4	22	23	58	22	8	.231	.288	.336	.624	65	-14	29	3.32	-5	0-78(8-70-0)	5	-1.8
2002*SF-N	78	154	23	40	5	2	1	17	14	25	16	2	.260	.321	.338	.659	77	-2	19	4.16	2	0-53(28-22-7)	5	-0.2
2003*Chi-N	87	171	26	49	10	0	1	12	11	33	19	5	.287	.330	.363	.692	82	-3	21	4.38	-1	0-57(17-27-15)	3	-0.5
Total 13	1211	3741	625	1008	117	39	24	281	357	638	364	118	.269	.335	.341	.676	73	-120	467	4.22	-13	*0-1065/D-9	74	-12.8

• GOOLSBY, Ray

Raymond Daniel "Ox" Goolsby b: 9/5/1919, Florala, AL d: 11/13/1999, Apopka, FL BR/TR, 6'1", 185 lbs. Deb: 4/18/1946

YEAR TM-L	G	AB	R	H	2B	3B	HR	RBI	BB	SO	SB	CS	AVG	OBP	SLG	OPS	OPS+	BR/A	RC	RC/G	FR	G/POS	WS	TPW
1946 Was-A	3	4	0	0	0	0	0	0	1	1	0	0	.000	.200	.000	.200	-43	-1	0	.70	-0	/0-1	0	-0.1

• GOOSSEN, Greg

Gregory Bryant Goossen b: 12/14/1945, Los Angeles, CA BR/TR, 6'1.5", 210 lbs. Deb: 9/3/1965 Career OF: 7-0-0

YEAR TM-L	G	AB	R	H	2B	3B	HR	RBI	BB	SO	SB	CS	AVG	OBP	SLG	OPS	OPS+	BR/A	RC	RC/G	FR	G/POS	WS	TPW
1965 NY-N	11	31	2	9	0	0	1	2	1	5	0	0	.290	.313	.387	.700	99	-0	4	4.70	-1	/C-8	1	0.0

YEAR TM-L	G	AB	R	H	2B	3B	HR	RBI	BB	SO	SB	CS	AVG	OBP	SLG	OPS	OPS+	BR/A	RC	RC/G	FR	G/POS	WS	TPW
1966 NY-N	13	32	1	6	2	0	1	5	1	11	0	0	.188	.235	.344	.579	60	-2	2	1.58	0	C-11	0	-0.2
1967 NY-N	37	69	2	11	1	0	0	3	4	26	0	0	.159	.216	.174	.390	13	-8	3	1.23	-1	C-23	0	-0.8
1968 NY-N	38	106	4	22	7	0	0	6	10	21	0	0	.208	.288	.274	.562	69	-4	8	2.50	2	1-31/C-1	1	-0.3
1969 Sea-A	52	139	19	43	8	1	10	24	14	29	1	1	.309	.385	.597	.982	174	13	30	7.98	2	1-31/O-2(2-0-0)	8	1.3
1970 Mil-A	21	47	3	12	3	0	1	3	10	12	0	0	.255	.407	.383	.790	118	2	8	6.17	-1	1-15	2	0.0
Was-A	21	36	2	8	3	0	0	1	2	8	0	0	.222	.263	.306	.569	59	-2	3	2.50	1	/O-5(5-0-0),1-2	0	-0.2
Yr.	42	83	5	20	6	0	1	4	12	20	0	0	.241	.351	.349	.700	95	-0	11	4.50	-0	1-17/O-5(5-0-0)	2	-0.1
Total 6	193	460	33	111	24	1	13	44	42	112	1	1	.241	.317	.383	.700	99	-0	58	4.25	2	/1-79,C-43,O-7	12	-0.2

• GORBOUS, Glen Glen Edward Gorbous b: 7/8/1930, Drumheller, Canada d: 6/12/1990, Calgary, Canada BL/TR, 6'2", 175 lbs. Deb: 4/11/1955 Career OF: 5-4-61

YEAR TM-L	G	AB	R	H	2B	3B	HR	RBI	BB	SO	SB	CS	AVG	OBP	SLG	OPS	OPS+	BR/A	RC	RC/G	FR	G/POS	WS	TPW
1955 Cin-N	8	18	2	6	3	0	0	4	3	1	0	0	.333	.429	.500	.929	137	1	4	9.43	0	/O-5(5-0-0)	1	0.0
Phi-N	91	224	25	53	9	1	4	23	21	17	0	3	.237	.302	.339	.641	71	-10	22	3.18	3	O-57(0-4-53)	3	-0.9
Yr.	99	242	27	59	12	1	4	27	24	18	0	3	.244	.312	.351	.663	76	-9	26	3.56	3	O-62(5-4-53)	4	-0.9
1956 Phi-N	15	33	1	6	0	0	0	1	0	1	0	0	.182	.182	.182	.364	-2	-5	1	1.09	0	/O-8(0-0-8)	0	-0.5
1957 Phi-N	3	2	1	1	1	0	0	1	1	0	0	0	.500	.667	1.000	1.667	351	1	2	40.68	0	....	0	0.1
Total 3	117	277	29	66	13	1	4	29	25	19	0	3	.238	.301	.336	.637	70	-13	28	3.43	2	/O-70	4	-1.3

• GORDON, Joe Joseph Lowell "Flash" Gordon b: 2/18/1915, Los Angeles, CA d: 4/14/1978, Sacramento, CA BR/TR, 5'10", 180 lbs. Deb: 4/18/1938 M/C

YEAR TM-L	G	AB	R	H	2B	3B	HR	RBI	BB	SO	SB	CS	AVG	OBP	SLG	OPS	OPS+	BR/A	RC	RC/G	FR	G/POS	WS	TPW
1938*NY-A	127	458	83	117	24	7	25	97	56	72	11	3	.255	.340	.502	.843	109	5	81	6.16	11	*2-126	19	2.1
1939*NY-A★	151	567	92	161	32	5	28	111	75	57	11	10	.284	.370	.506	.876	124	17	103	6.42	26	*2-151	25	4.9
1940 NY-A★	155	616	112	173	32	10	30	103	52	57	18	8	.281	.340	.511	.851	122	18	107	6.18	24	*2-155	26	**4.9**
1941*NY-A★	156	588	104	162	26	7	24	87	72	80	10	9	.276	.358	.466	.824	118	13	98	5.86	16	*2-131,1-30	24	3.4
1942*NY-A★	147	538	88	173	29	4	18	103	79	95	12	6	.322	.409	.491	.900	156	42	108	7.32	8	*2-147	31	6.1
1943*NY-A★	152	543	82	135	28	5	17	69	98	75	4	7	.249	.365	.413	.778	126	19	84	5.18	33	*2-152	28	6.6
1946 NY-A★	112	376	35	79	15	0	11	47	49	72	2	5	.210	.308	.338	.645	79	-12	38	3.25	10	*2-108	9	0.5
1947 Cle-A★	155	562	89	153	27	6	29	93	62	49	7	3	.272	.346	.496	.842	136	25	96	6.07	1	*2-155	25	3.6
1948*Cle-A★	144	550	96	154	21	4	32	124	77	68	5	2	.280	.371	.507	.879	136	27	106	6.87	-5	*2-144/S-2	24	2.9
1949 Cle-A★	148	541	74	136	18	3	20	84	83	33	5	6	.251	.355	.407	.762	103	1	79	4.89	-10	*2-145	19	-0.1
1950 Cle-A	119	368	59	87	12	1	19	57	56	44	4	1	.236	.340	.429	.770	99	-1	56	5.17	-4	*2-105	12	0.1
Total 11	1566	5707	914	1530	264	52	253	975	759	702	89	60	.268	.357	.466	.822	121	155	959	5.82	109	*2-1519/1-30,S-2	242	35.0

• GORDON, Keith Keith Bradley Gordon b: 1/22/1969, Bethesda, MD BR/TR, 6'1", 205 lbs. Deb: 7/9/1993

YEAR TM-L	G	AB	R	H	2B	3B	HR	RBI	BB	SO	SB	CS	AVG	OBP	SLG	OPS	OPS+	BR/A	RC	RC/G	FR	G/POS	WS	TPW
1993 Cin-N	3	6	0	1	0	0	0	0	0	2	0	0	.167	.167	.167	.333	-10	-1	0	.90	0	/O-2(2-0-0)	0	-0.1

• GORDON, Mike Michael William Gordon b: 9/11/1953, Leominster, MA BB/TR, 6'3", 215 lbs. Deb: 4/7/1977

YEAR TM-L	G	AB	R	H	2B	3B	HR	RBI	BB	SO	SB	CS	AVG	OBP	SLG	OPS	OPS+	BR/A	RC	RC/G	FR	G/POS	WS	TPW
1977 Chi-N	8	23	0	1	0	0	0	2	2	8	0	0	.043	.120	.043	.163	-49	-5	0	.28	-1	/C-8	0	-0.5
1978 Chi-N	4	5	0	1	0	0	0	0	3	2	0	0	.200	.556	.200	.756	106	1	1	6.68	0	/C-4	0	0.1
Total 2	12	28	0	2	0	0	0	2	5	10	0	0	.071	.235	.071	.307	-9	-4	1	1.22	-1	/C-12	0	-0.5

• GORDON, Sid Sidney Gordon b: 8/13/1917, Brooklyn, NY d: 6/17/1975, New York, NY BR/TR, 5'10", 185 lbs. Deb: 9/11/1941 Career OF: 806-6-108

YEAR TM-L	G	AB	R	H	2B	3B	HR	RBI	BB	SO	SB	CS	AVG	OBP	SLG	OPS	OPS+	BR/A	RC	RC/G	FR	G/POS	WS	TPW
1941 NY-N	9	31	4	8	1	1	0	4	6	1	0	....	.258	.378	.355	.733	105	1	5	5.58	0	/O-9(3-6-0)	1	0.0
1942 NY-N	6	19	4	6	0	1	0	2	3	2	0	....	.316	.409	.421	.830	142	1	3	6.16	0	/3-6	1	0.1
1943 NY-N	131	474	50	119	9	11	9	63	43	32	2	....	.251	.315	.373	.688	98	-3	50	3.47	-2	3-53,1-41,O-28(28-0-0)/2-3	10	-0.8
1946 NY-N	135	450	64	132	15	4	5	45	60	27	1	....	.293	.380	.378	.758	115	11	66	5.22	0	*O-101(101-0-0),3-30	13	0.3
1947 NY-N	130	437	57	119	19	8	13	57	50	21	2	....	.272	.347	.442	.789	107	4	67	5.44	-1	*O-124(124-0-0)/3-2	13	-0.6
1948 NY-N★	142	521	100	156	26	4	30	107	74	39	8	....	.299	.390	.537	.927	148	35	108	7.47	-3	*3-115,O-23(18-0-2)	25	3.1
1949 NY-N★	141	489	87	139	26	2	26	90	95	37	1	....	.284	.404	.505	.909	142	33	99	7.12	-11	*3-123,O-15(3-0-12)/1-1	19	2.0
1950 Bos-N	134	481	78	146	33	4	27	103	78	31	2	....	.304	.403	.557	.960	160	43	109	8.42	-1	*O-123(123-0-0),3-10	29	3.2
1951 Bos-N	150	550	96	158	28	1	29	109	80	32	2	0	.287	.383	.500	.883	146	37	103	6.55	-4	*O-122(103-0-23),3-34	22	2.5
1952 Bos-N	144	522	69	151	22	2	25	75	77	49	0	4	.289	.384	.483	.866	144	31	101	6.99	1	*O-142(142-0-0)/3-2	25	2.4
1953 Mil-N	140	464	67	127	22	4	19	75	71	40	1	1	.274	.372	.461	.834	123	17	82	6.25	7	*O-137(137-0-0)	19	1.6
1954 Pit-N	131	363	38	111	12	0	12	49	67	24	0	0	.306	.414	.438	.852	124	16	70	6.74	1	O-73(8-0-66),3-40	16	1.5
1955 Pit-N	16	47	2	8	1	0	0	1	2	6	0	0	.170	.204	.191	.396	6	-6	1	.87	1	/3-8,O-4(4-0-0)	0	-0.6
NY-N	66	144	19	35	6	1	7	25	25	15	0	0	.243	.355	.444	.799	110	3	25	5.88	4	3-31,O-17(12-0-5)	6	0.6
Yr.	82	191	21	43	7	1	7	26	27	21	0	0	.225	.321	.382	.703	87	-4	26	4.54	5	3-39,O-21(16-0-5)	6	0.0
Total 13	1475	4992	735	1415	220	43	202	805	731	356	19	5	.283	.377	.466	.844	130	223	889	6.28	-9	O-918,3-454/1-42,2-3	199	15.3

• GORE, George George F. "Piano Legs" Gore b: 5/3/1857, Saccarappa, ME d: 9/16/1933, Utica, NY BL/TR, 5'11", 195 lbs. Deb: 5/1/1879 M Career OF: 96-1175-31

YEAR TM-L	G	AB	R	H	2B	3B	HR	RBI	BB	SO	SB	CS	AVG	OBP	SLG	OPS	OPS+	BR/A	RC	RC/G	FR	G/POS	WS	TPW
1879 Chi-N	63	266	43	70	17	4	0	32	8	30	....	....	.263	.285	.357	.642	104	1	28	3.96	0	O-54(O-48-6)/1-9	8	-0.2
1880 Chi-N	77	322	70	116	23	2	2	47	21	10	....	....	**.360**	**.399**	**.463**	**.862**	**180**	**27**	61	**8.14**	8	*O-74(0-73-1)/1-7	24	3.0
1881 Chi-N	73	309	**86**	92	18	9	1	44	27	23	....	....	.298	.354	.424	.778	134	12	48	5.92	4	*O-72(0-72-0)/1-1,3-1	15	1.2
1882 Chi-N	84	367	**99**	117	15	7	3	51	**29**	19	....	....	.319	.369	.422	.791	151	22	59	6.44	5	*O-84(0-84-0)	17	2.2
1883 Chi-N	92	392	105	131	30	9	2	52	27	13	....	....	.334	.377	.472	.849	144	20	72	7.53	12	*O-92(0-92-0)	22	2.5
1884 Chi-N	103	422	104	134	18	4	5	34	**61**	26	....	....	.318	.404	.415	.818	146	25	72	6.91	10	*O-103(0-103-1)	16	2.7
1885*Chi-N	109	441	115	138	21	13	5	57	68	25	....	....	.313	.405	.454	.858	154	29	83	7.39	3	*O-109(1-108-0)	**30**	2.6
1886*Chi-N	118	444	150	135	20	12	6	63	**102**	30	23	....	.304	.434	.444	.878	145	29	98	8.55	1	*O-118(0-115-3)	26	2.4
1887 NY-N	111	501	95	175	16	5	1	49	42	18	39	....	.349	.358	.353	.711	103	5	74	6.00	1	*O-111(0-111-0)	14	0.1
1888*NY-N	64	254	37	56	4	4	2	17	30	31	11	....	.220	.308	.291	.599	93	-1	27	3.66	-6	O-64(42-21-1)	7	-0.8
1889*NY-N	120	488	132	149	21	7	7	54	84	28	28	....	.305	.416	.420	.836	134	27	99	7.76	-10	*O-120(0-118-3)	23	1.1
1890 NY-P	93	399	132	127	26	8	10	55	77	23	28	....	.318	.432	.499	.931	136	22	101	9.98	-10	*O-93(52-33-10)	18	0.7
1891 NY-N	130	528	103	150	22	7	2	48	74	34	19	....	.284	.379	.364	.743	122	19	82	5.86	-5	*O-130(1-127-3)	18	0.8
1892 NY-N	53	193	47	49	11	2	0	11	49	16	20	....	.254	.412	.332	.744	127	11	35	6.66	1	O-53(0-50-3)	10	0.8
StL-N	20	73	9	15	0	1	0	4	18	6	2	....	.205	.363	.233	.596	85	0	7	3.29	-2	O-20(0-20-0)	2	-0.3
Yr.	73	266	56	64	11	3	0	15	67	22	22	....	.241	.399	.305	.703	116	11	43	5.69	-1	O-73(0-70-3)	12	0.5
Total 14	1310	5399	1327	1654	262	94	46	618	717	332	170	....	.306	.386	.411	.797	134	247	945	6.83	13	*O-1297/1-17,3-1	250	18.9

• GORINSKI, Bob Robert John Gorinski b: 1/7/1952, Latrobe, PA BR/TR, 6'3", 215 lbs. Deb: 4/10/1977

YEAR TM-L	G	AB	R	H	2B	3B	HR	RBI	BB	SO	SB	CS	AVG	OBP	SLG	OPS	OPS+	BR/A	RC	RC/G	FR	G/POS	WS	TPW
1977 Min-A	54	118	14	23	4	1	3	22	5	29	1	0	.195	.228	.322	.550	49	-8	9	2.42	-2	O-37(30-0-7)/D-9	0	-1.2

• GORMAN, Herb Herbert Allen Gorman b: 12/18/1924, San Francisco, CA d: 4/5/1953, San Diego, CA BL/TL, 5'11", 180 lbs. Deb: 4/19/1952

YEAR TM-L	G	AB	R	H	2B	3B	HR	RBI	BB	SO	SB	CS	AVG	OBP	SLG	OPS	OPS+	BR/A	RC	RC/G	FR	G/POS	WS	TPW
1952 StL-N	1	1	0	0	0	0	0	0	0	0	0	0	.000	.000	.000	.000	-100	-0	0	.00	0	....	0	0.0

• GORMAN, Howie Howard Paul "Lefty" Gorman b: 5/14/1913, Pittsburgh, PA d: 4/29/1984, Harrisburg, PA BL/TL, 6'2", 160 lbs. Deb: 8/7/1937

YEAR TM-L	G	AB	R	H	2B	3B	HR	RBI	BB	SO	SB	CS	AVG	OBP	SLG	OPS	OPS+	BR/A	RC	RC/G	FR	G/POS	WS	TPW
1937 Phi-N	13	19	3	4	1	0	0	1	1	1	1	....	.211	.250	.263	.513	36	-2	1	2.42	-1	/O-7(0-0-7)	0	-0.3
1938 Phi-N	1	1	0	0	0	0	0	0	0	0	0	....	.000	.000	.000	.000	-100	-0	0	.00	0	....	0	0.0
Total 2	14	20	3	4	1	0	0	1	1	1	1	....	.200	.238	.250	.488	30	-2	1	2.27	-1	/O-7	0	-0.3

• GORMAN, Jack John F. "Stooping Jack" Gorman b: 1859, St. Louis, MO d: 9/9/1889, St. Louis, MO Deb: 7/1/1883 Career OF: 5-1-2

YEAR TM-L	G	AB	R	H	2B	3B	HR	RBI	BB	SO	SB	CS	AVG	OBP	SLG	OPS	OPS+	BR/A	RC	RC/G	FR	G/POS	WS	TPW
1883 StL-a	1	4	0	0	0	0	0	0	0	....	....	....	.000	.000	.000	.000	-95	-1	0	.00	0	/O-1	0	0.0
1884 KC-U	8	31	3	4	0	1	0	....	0	....	....	....	.129	.129	.194	.323	9	-2	1	.82	-1	/3-4,O-4(4-0-0)	5	-0.3
Pit-a	8	27	3	4	0	1	0	0	1	....	....	....	.148	.179	.222	.401	29	-1	1	1.31	-1	/O-3(0-1-2),P-3,3-2	1	-0.5
Total 2	17	62	6	8	0	2	0	0	1	....	....	....	.129	.143	.194	.336	11	-5	2	.97	-2	/O-8,3-6,P-3	6	-0.9

• GORMAN, Thomas Thomas "Jumbo" Gorman b: St. Louis, MO BL/TL Deb: 6/10/1884

YEAR TM-L	G	AB	R	H	2B	3B	HR	RBI	BB	SO	SB	CS	AVG	OBP	SLG	OPS	OPS+	BR/A	RC	RC/G	FR	G/POS	WS	TPW
1884 KC-U	25	106	22	34	5	1	0	....	4	....	....	....	.321	.345	.387	.732	169	8	15	5.65	-2	1-24/O-1	0	0.4

• GORYL, Johnny John Albert Goryl b: 10/21/1933, Cumberland, RI BR/TR, 5'10", 175 lbs. Deb: 9/20/1957 M/C

YEAR TM-L	G	AB	R	H	2B	3B	HR	RBI	BB	SO	SB	CS	AVG	OBP	SLG	OPS	OPS+	BR/A	RC	RC/G	FR	G/POS	WS	TPW
1957 Chi-N	9	38	7	8	2	0	0	1	5	9	0	1	.211	.318	.263	.581	59	-2	3	2.97	0	/3-9	0	-0.2
1958 Chi-N	83	219	27	53	9	3	4	14	27	34	0	1	.242	.331	.365	.696	85	-5	24	3.48	0	3-44,2-35	4	-0.3
1959 Chi-N	25	48	1	9	3	1	1	6	5	3	1	1	.188	.264	.354	.618	63	-3	4	2.23	1	2-11/3-4	0	-0.1
1962 Min-A	37	26	6	5	0	1	2	2	2	6	0	0	.192	.250	.500	.750	93	-1	3	3.41	-1	/2-4,S-1	0	-0.1

YEAR TM-L	G	AB	R	H	2B	3B	HR	RBI	BB	SO	SB	CS	AVG	OBP	SLG	OPS	OPS+	BR/A	RC	RC/G	FR	G/POS	WS	TPW
1963 Min-A	64	150	29	43	5	3	9	24	15	29	0	0	.287	.355	.540	.895	144	9	28	6.33	-6	2-34,3-11/S-7	6	0.6
1964 Min-A	58	114	9	16	0	2	0	1	10	25	1	0	.140	.216	.175	.391	10	-14	5	1.19	-3	2-28,3-13	1	-1.5
Total 6	276	595	79	134	19	10	16	48	64	106	2	3	.225	.306	.371	.677	83	-15	66	3.54	-9	2-112/3-81,S-8	11	-1.7
• GOSGER, Jim	James Charles Gosger b: 11/6/1942, Port Huron, MI BL/TL, 5'11", 185 lbs. Deb: 5/4/1963 Career OF: 216-291-83																							
1963 Bos-A	19	16	3	1	0	0	0	0	3	5	0	0	.063	.211	.063	.273	-19	-2	0	.67	-1	/O-4(0-2-2)	0	-0.3
1965 Bos-A	81	324	45	83	15	4	9	35	29	61	3	1	.256	.321	.410	.732	100	0	43	4.55	2	O-81(0-61-22)	8	-0.2
1966 Bos-A	40	126	16	32	4	0	5	17	15	20	0	1	.254	.333	.405	.738	101	0	18	4.85	-3	O-32(0-29-4)	4	-0.5
KC-A	88	272	34	61	14	1	5	27	37	53	5	3	.224	.322	.338	.660	93	-2	32	3.94	-2	O-77(47-33-1)	9	-0.7
Yr.	128	398	50	93	18	1	10	44	52	73	5	4	.234	.325	.359	.685	95	-2	50	4.22	-5	*O-109(47-62-5)	13	-1.2
1967 KC-A	134	356	31	86	14	5	5	36	53	69	5	7	.242	.340	.351	.691	108	3	44	4.17	-1	*O-113(54-30-40)	11	-0.4
1968 Oak-A	88	150	7	27	1	1	0	5	17	21	4	0	.180	.263	.200	.463	44	-9	8	1.70	2	O-64(39-26-4)	1	-1.0
1969 Sea-A	39	55	4	6	2	1	1	1	6	11	2	1	.109	.197	.236	.433	21	-6	3	1.35	0	O-26(1-24-1)	0	-0.7
NY-N	10	15	0	2	2	0	0	1	1	6	0	0	.133	.188	.267	.454	25	-2	1	1.56	0	/O-5(4-1-0)	0	-0.2
1970 Mon-N	91	274	38	72	11	2	5	37	35	35	5	3	.263	.348	.372	.721	93	-2	37	4.73	0	O-71(21-50-4),1-19	8	-0.6
1971 Mon-N	51	102	7	16	2	2	0	8	9	17	1	1	.157	.232	.216	.448	27	-10	5	1.48	0	O-23(20-6-1)/1-6	0	-1.2
1973 NY-N	38	92	9	22	2	0	0	10	9	16	0	1	.239	.307	.261	.568	60	-5	7	2.77	-1	O-35(21-18-0)	1	-0.7
1974 NY-N	26	33	3	3	0	0	0	0	3	2	0	0	.091	.167	.091	.258	-27	-6	0	.36	-1	O-24(9-11-4)	0	-0.7
Total 10	705	1815	197	411	67	16	30	177	217	316	25	18	.226	.311	.331	.642	83	-40	199	3.63	-5	O-555/1-25	42	-7.2
• GOSLIN, Goose	Leon Allen Goslin b: 10/16/1900, Salem, NJ d: 5/15/1971, Bridgeton, NJ BL/TR, 5'11.5", 185 lbs. Deb: 9/16/1921 HOF: 1968 Career OF: 1949-84-170																							
1921 Was-A	14	50	8	13	1	1	1	6	6	5	0	0	.260	.351	.380	.731	91	-0	7	4.92	1	O-14(1-0-14)	1	-0.1
1922 Was-A	101	358	44	116	19	7	3	53	25	26	4	4	.324	.373	.441	.814	117	8	58	6.10	-3	O-93(88-0-5)	12	-0.2
1923 Was-A	150	600	86	180	29	**18**	9	99	40	53	7	2	.300	.347	.453	.800	115	12	95	5.78	8	*O-149(149-0-0)	21	0.9
1924*Was-A	154	579	100	199	30	17	12	**129**	68	29	15	14	.344	.421	.516	.937	145	38	125	8.08	1	*O-154(154-0-0)	29	2.6
1925*Was-A	150	601	116	201	34	**20**	18	113	53	50	27	8	.334	.394	.547	.941	139	37	131	8.31	11	*O-150(140-20-0)	31	3.4
1926 Was-A	147	568	105	201	26	15	17	108	63	38	8	8	.354	.425	.542	.967	155	45	131	8.81	9	*O-147(86-61-0)	33	4.3
1927 Was-A	148	581	96	194	37	15	13	120	50	28	21	6	.334	.392	.516	.908	136	32	119	7.59	-4	*O-148(146-2-0)	28	1.5
1928 Was-A	135	456	80	173	36	10	17	102	48	19	16	3	**.379**	.442	.614	1.056	176	53	125	10.86	10	*O-125(125-0-2)	26	5.2
1929 Was-A	145	553	82	159	28	7	18	91	66	33	10	3	.288	.366	.461	.827	111	10	97	6.17	-6	*O-142(142-0-0)	19	-0.6
1930 Was-A	47	188	34	51	11	5	7	38	19	19	3	2	.271	.344	.495	.839	109	2	32	5.93	-2	O-47(47-0-0)	5	-0.3
StL-A	101	396	81	129	25	7	30	100	48	35	14	9	.326	.400	.652	1.052	156	32	101	9.39	10	*O-101(101-0-0)	20	3.1
Yr.	148	584	115	180	36	12	37	138	67	54	17	11	.308	.382	.601	.983	141	34	133	8.22	8	*O-148(148-0-0)	25	2.8
1931 StL-A	151	591	114	194	42	10	24	105	80	41	9	6	.328	.412	.555	.967	147	43	137	9.02	3	*O-151(151-0-0)	25	3.5
1932 StL-A	150	572	88	171	28	9	17	104	92	35	12	9	.299	.398	.469	.866	117	16	110	7.11	3	*O-149(148-1-0)/3-1	19	1.0
1933*Was-A	132	549	97	163	35	10	10	64	42	32	5	2	.297	.348	.452	.800	112	8	87	5.82	7	*O-128(3-0-125)	20	0.7
1934*Det-A	151	614	106	187	38	7	13	100	65	38	5	4	.305	.373	.453	.826	112	10	105	6.39	3	*O-149(145-0-4)	22	0.4
1935*Det-A	147	590	88	172	34	6	9	109	56	31	5	4	.292	.355	.415	.770	102	1	88	5.49	1	*O-144(128-0-18)	17	-0.5
1936 Det-A★	147	572	122	180	33	8	24	125	85	50	14	4	.315	.403	.526	.930	127	26	126	8.37	-3	*O-144(144-0-0)	23	1.3
1937 Det-A	79	181	30	43	11	1	4	35	35	18	0	1	.238	.367	.376	.743	86	-3	27	5.12	-1	O-40(39-0-1)/1-1	4	-0.6
1938 Was-A	38	57	6	9	3	0	2	8	8	5	0	0	.158	.262	.316	.577	47	-5	5	2.78	0	O-13(12-0-1)	0	-0.5
Total 18	2287	8656	1483	2735	500	173	248	1609	949	585	175	89	.316	.387	.500	.887	128	365	1707	7.33	49	*O-2188/1-1,3-1	355	25.1
• GOSS, Howie	Howard Wayne Goss b: 11/1/1934, Wewoka, OK d: 7/31/1996, Reno, NV BR/TR, 6'4", 204 lbs. Deb: 4/10/1962 Career OF: 47-141-6																							
1962 Pit-N	89	111	19	27	6	0	2	10	9	36	5	2	.243	.306	.351	.657	76	-4	12	3.67	-1	O-66(47-18-6)	2	-0.6
1963 Hou-N	133	411	37	86	18	2	9	44	31	128	4	6	.209	.265	.328	.593	74	-16	36	2.83	0	*O-123(0-123-0)	8	-2.1
Total 2	222	522	56	113	24	2	11	54	40	164	9	8	.216	.274	.333	.607	75	-19	48	3.00	-1	O-189	10	-2.7
• GOSSETT, Dick	John Star Gossett b: 8/21/1891, Dennison, OH d: 10/6/1962, Massillon, OH BR/TR, 5'11", 185 lbs. Deb: 4/30/1913																							
1913 NY-A	39	105	9	17	2	0	0	9	10	22	1	....	.162	.254	.181	.435	28	-9	5	1.47	3	C-38	1	-0.4
1914 NY-A	10	21	3	3	0	0	0	1	5	5	0	....	.143	.333	.143	.476	44	-1	1	1.47	-1	C-10	1	-0.1
Total 2	49	126	12	20	2	0	0	10	15	27	1	....	.159	.269	.175	.444	31	-10	6	1.47	3	/C-48	2	-0.5
• GOTAY, Julio	Julio Enrique (Sanchez) Gotay b: 6/9/1939, Fajardo, Puerto Rico BR/TR, 6', 180 lbs. Deb: 8/6/1960																							
1960 StL-N	3	8	1	3	0	0	0	0	0	2	1	0	.375	.375	.375	.750	98	0	1	7.13	-1	/S-2,3-1	0	0.0
1961 StL-N	10	45	5	11	4	0	0	5	3	5	0	0	.244	.292	.333	.625	59	-3	4	3.24	-4	S-10	0	-0.6
1962 StL-N	127	369	47	94	12	1	2	27	27	47	7	3	.255	.316	.309	.625	62	-19	34	3.13	5	*S-120/2-8,O-2(2-0-0),3-1	7	-0.4
1963 Pit-N	4	2	0	1	0	0	0	0	0	0	0	0	.500	.500	.500	1.000	188	0	1	13.50	-1	/2-1	0	-0.1
1964 Pit-N	3	2	1	1	0	0	0	0	1	0	0	0	.500	.667	.500	1.167	235	1	1	22.68	0	....	0	0.1
1965 Cal-A	40	77	6	19	4	0	1	3	4	9	0	0	.247	.284	.338	.622	78	-2	7	3.07	1	2-23/3-9,S-1	1	0.0
1966 Hou-N	4	5	0	0	0	0	0	0	0	0	0	0	.000	.000	.000	.000	-107	-1	0	.00	-0	/3-1	0	-0.1
1967 Hou-N	77	234	30	66	10	2	2	15	15	30	1	1	.282	.331	.368	.698	103	1	28	4.17	-1	2-30,S-20/3-3	7	0.5
1968 Hou-N	75	165	9	41	3	0	1	11	4	21	1	2	.248	.271	.285	.555	68	-7	11	2.23	-3	2-48/3-1	2	-0.7
1969 Hou-N	46	81	7	21	5	0	0	9	7	13	2	1	.259	.318	.321	.639	81	-2	7	3.11	1	2-16/3-1	2	0.0
Total 10	389	988	106	257	38	3	6	70	61	127	12	7	.260	.309	.323	.632	76	-33	94	3.26	-2	S-153,2-126/3-17,O-2	19	-1.5
• GOULD, Charlie	Charles Harvey Gould b: 8/21/1847, Cincinnati, OH d: 4/10/1917, Flushing, NY BR/TR, 6', 172 lbs. Deb: 5/5/1871 M/U NA OF: 0-0-4																							
1871 Bos-n	31	151	38	43	9	2	2	32	3	1	6	2	.285	.299	.411	.709	98	-1	21	5.96	-3	*1-30/O-1	....	-0.2
1872 Bos-n	45	211	40	54	9	**8**	0	33	2	3	0	0	.256	.263	.374	.637	89	-4	21	4.20	2	*1-44/O-2(0-0-2)	....	-0.1
1874 Bal-n	33	143	20	32	6	0	0	14	2	1	1	0	.224	.234	.266	.500	60	-6	9	2.53	1	1-32/C-1	....	-0.3
1875 NH-n	27	109	9	29	4	1	0	8	1	2	0	1	.266	.273	.321	.594	121	3	10	3.56	0	1-26/C-1,O-1	....	0.3
1876 Cin-N	61	264	27	65	7	0	0	11	6	11	....	....	.246	.269	.279	.548	97	2	20	2.88	-1	*1-61/P-2	3	-0.1
1877 Cin-N	24	91	5	25	2	1	0	13	5	5	....	....	.275	.313	.319	.631	111	2	9	3.87	-1	1-24/O-1	2	-0.1
Total 4 n	136	614	107	158	28	11	2	87	8	7	7	3	.257	.267	.349	.615	90	-9	61	4.11	0	1-132/O-4,C-2	....	-0.4
Total 2	85	355	32	90	9	1	0	24	11	16	....	....	.254	.281	.289	.570	101	4	29	3.13	-2	/1-85,P-2,O-1	5	-0.1
• GOULISH, Nick	Nicholas Edward Goulish b: 11/13/1917, Punxsutawney, PA d: 3/15/1984, Youngstown, OH BL/TL, 6'1", 179 lbs. Deb: 4/19/1944																							
1944 Phi-N	1	1	0	0	0	0	0	0	0	0	0	....	.000	.000	.000	.000	-103	-0	0	.00	0	....	0	0.0
1945 Phi-N	13	11	4	3	0	0	0	2	1	3	0	....	.273	.333	.273	.606	72	-0	1	3.67	0	/O-2(1-0-1)	0	-0.1
Total 2	14	12	4	3	0	0	0	2	1	3	0	....	.250	.308	.250	.558	58	-1	1	3.26	0	/O-2	0	-0.1
• GOUZZIE, Claude	Claude Gouzzie b: 1873, France d: 9/21/1907, Denver, CO BR/TR, 5'9", 170 lbs. Deb: 7/22/1903																							
1903 StL-A	1	1	0	0	0	0	0	0	0	....	0	....	.000	.000	.000	.000	-103	-0	0	.00	0	/2-1	0	0.0
• GOWDY, Hank	Henry Morgan Gowdy b: 8/24/1889, Columbus, OH d: 8/1/1966, Columbus, OH BR/TR, 6'2", 182 lbs. Deb: 9/13/1910 M/C																							
1910 NY-N	7	14	1	3	1	0	0	2	2	3	1	....	.214	.313	.286	.598	75	-0	2	3.57	0	/1-5	0	0.0
1911 NY-N	4	4	1	1	1	0	0	0	2	0	0	....	.250	.500	.500	1.000	176	1	1	8.65	0	/1-2	0	0.0
Bos-N	29	97	9	28	4	2	0	16	4	19	2	....	.289	.324	.371	.695	87	-2	12	4.42	-2	1-26/C-1	2	-0.4
Yr.	33	101	10	29	5	2	0	16	6	19	2	....	.287	.333	.376	.710	92	-2	13	4.60	-2	1-28/C-1	2	-0.4
1912 Bos-N	44	96	16	26	6	1	3	10	16	13	3	....	.271	.386	.448	.834	126	4	18	6.29	0	C-22/1-7	3	0.5
1913 Bos-N	3	5	0	3	1	0	0	2	3	2	0	....	.600	.750	.800	1.550	336	2	3	37.61	0	/C-2	1	0.2
1914*Bos-N	128	366	42	89	17	6	3	46	48	40	14	....	.243	.337	.347	.684	104	3	46	4.17	1	*C-115/1-9	16	1.3
1915 Bos-N	118	316	27	78	15	3	2	30	41	34	10	4	.247	.339	.332	.671	105	4	38	4.08	2	*C-114	15	1.6
1916 Bos-N	118	349	32	88	14	1	1	34	24	33	8	....	.252	.311	.307	.618	95	-2	38	3.57	2	*C-116	17	1.1
1917 Bos-N	49	154	12	33	7	0	0	14	15	13	2	....	.214	.288	.260	.548	73	-5	12	2.50	4	C-49	4	0.3
1919 Bos-N	78	219	18	61	8	1	1	22	19	16	5	....	.279	.339	.338	.677	108	3	26	4.13	6	C-74/1-1	8	1.6
1920 Bos-N	80	214	14	52	11	2	0	18	20	15	6	1	.243	.314	.313	.627	84	-2	23	3.59	13	C-74	8	1.8
1921 Bos-N	64	164	17	49	7	2	2	17	16	11	2	0	.299	.368	.402	.771	110	4	26	5.60	3	C-53	8	0.9
1922 Bos-N	92	221	23	70	11	1	1	27	24	13	2	1	.317	.391	.389	.780	107	4	35	5.91	3	C-72/1-1	9	1.1

YEAR TM-L	G	AB	R	H	2B	3B	HR	RBI	BB	SO	SB	CS	AVG	OBP	SLG	OPS	OPS+	BR/A	RC	RC/G	FR	G/POS	WS	TPW
1923 Bos-N	23	48	5	6	1	1	0	5	15	5	1	1	.125	.354	.188	.541	48	-3	5	2.78	1	C-15	1	-0.1
*NY-N	53	122	13	40	6	3	1	18	21	9	2	0	.328	.427	.451	.877	133	8	25	7.80	-2	C-43	7	0.8
Yr.	76	170	18	46	7	4	1	23	36	14	3	1	.271	.404	.376	.780	107	5	30	6.10	-1	C-58	8	0.7
1924*NY-N	87	191	25	62	9	1	4	37	26	11	1	0	.325	.411	.445	.856	133	11	37	7.52	-4	C-78	11	1.1
1925 NY-N	47	114	14	37	4	3	3	19	12	7	0	0	.325	.389	.491	.880	128	5	22	7.33	2	C-41	7	0.9
1929 Bos-N	10	16	1	7	0	0	0	3	0	2	0	....	.438	.438	.438	.875	122	1	3	8.23	0	/C-9	1	0.1
1930 Bos-N	16	25	0	5	1	0	0	2	3	1	0	....	.200	.310	.240	.550	37	-2	2	2.64	0	C-15	0	-0.2
Total 17	1050	2735	270	738	124	27	21	322	311	247	59	7	.270	.351	.358	.709	104	33	372	4.72	28	C-893/1-51	118	12.4

• GRABARKEWITZ, Billy Billy Cordell Grabarkewitz b: 1/18/1946, Lockhart, TX BR/TR, 5'10", 170 lbs. Deb: 4/22/1969 Career OF: 6-0-1

YEAR TM-L	G	AB	R	H	2B	3B	HR	RBI	BB	SO	SB	CS	AVG	OBP	SLG	OPS	OPS+	BR/A	RC	RC/G	FR	G/POS	WS	TPW
1969 LA-N	34	65	4	6	1	1	0	5	4	19	1	0	.092	.145	.138	.283	-22	-10	1	.46	-2	S-18/3-6,2-3	1	-1.1
1970 LA-N★	156	529	92	153	20	8	17	84	95	149	19	9	.289	.403	.454	.857	135	31	103	6.93	10	3-97,S-50,2-20	29	4.6
1971 LA-N	44	71	9	16	5	0	0	6	19	16	1	2	.225	.389	.296	.685	102	1	9	4.17	1	2-13,3-10/S-1	3	0.3
1972 LA-N	53	144	17	24	4	0	4	16	18	53	3	0	.167	.268	.278	.546	57	-7	12	2.62	-3	3-24,2-19/S-2	2	-1.0
1973 Cal-A	61	129	27	21	6	1	3	9	28	27	2	2	.163	.316	.295	.611	79	-3	13	2.96	-1	2-18,3-12/D-5,0-1,S-1	2	-0.3
Phi-N	25	66	12	19	2	0	2	7	12	18	3	1	.288	.397	.409	.807	121	3	12	6.74	-1	2-20/3-3,0-1	3	0.3
1974 Phi-N	34	30	7	4	0	0	1	2	5	10	3	1	.133	.257	.233	.490	36	-2	2	2.25	0	/0-5(5-0-0),3-1	0	-0.3
Chi-N	53	125	21	31	3	2	1	12	21	28	1	2	.248	.361	.328	.689	90	-1	16	4.50	-7	2-45/S-7,3-6	3	-0.6
Yr.	87	155	28	35	3	2	2	14	26	38	4	3	.226	.341	.310	.650	80	-4	19	4.02	-8	2-45/3-7,S-7,0-5(5-0-0)	3	-0.9
1975 Oak-A	6	2	0	0	0	0	0	0	0	1	0	0	.000	.000	.000	.000	-102	-1	0	.00	-1	/2-4,D-1	0	-0.2
Total 7	466	1161	189	274	41	12	28	141	202	321	33	17	.236	.354	.364	.718	101	10	169	4.85	-5	3-159,2-142/S-79,0-7,D-6	43	1.7

• GRABER, Rod Rodney Blaine Graber b: 6/20/1930, Massillon, OH BL/TL, 5'11", 175 lbs. Deb: 9/9/1958

YEAR TM-L	G	AB	R	H	2B	3B	HR	RBI	BB	SO	SB	CS	AVG	OBP	SLG	OPS	OPS+	BR/A	RC	RC/G	FR	G/POS	WS	TPW
1958 Cle-A	4	8	0	1	0	0	0	0	1	2	0	0	.125	.222	.125	.347	-2	-1	0	1.08	0	/0-2(0-2-0)	0	-0.1

• GRABOWSKI, Jason Jason William Grabowski b: 5/24/1976, New Haven, CT BL/TR, 6'3", 200 lbs. Deb: 9/22/2002 Career OF: 4-0-3

YEAR TM-L	G	AB	R	H	2B	3B	HR	RBI	BB	SO	SB	CS	AVG	OBP	SLG	OPS	OPS+	BR/A	RC	RC/G	FR	G/POS	WS	TPW
2002 Oak-A	4	8	3	3	1	1	0	1	3	1	0	0	.375	.545	.750	1.295	239	2	4	19.97	-0	/0-4(4-0-0)	1	0.2
2003 Oak-A	8	8	0	0	0	0	0	0	1	5	0	0	.000	.111	.000	.111	-66	-2	0	.10	0	/0-3(0-0-3),3-1,D-1	0	-0.2
Total 2	12	16	3	3	1	1	0	1	4	6	0	0	.188	.350	.375	.725	102	-0	4	7.74	0	/0-7,3-1,D-1	1	0.0

• GRABOWSKI, Johnny John Patrick "Nig" Grabowski b: 1/7/1900, Ware, MA d: 5/23/1946, Albany, NY BR/TR, 5'10", 185 lbs. Deb: 7/11/1924

YEAR TM-L	G	AB	R	H	2B	3B	HR	RBI	BB	SO	SB	CS	AVG	OBP	SLG	OPS	OPS+	BR/A	RC	RC/G	FR	G/POS	WS	TPW
1924 Chi-A	20	56	10	14	3	0	0	3	2	4	0	0	.250	.276	.304	.579	51	-4	5	2.79	3	C-19	1	0.0
1925 Chi-A	21	46	5	14	4	1	0	10	2	4	0	1	.304	.333	.435	.768	99	-1	6	4.94	-1	C-21	1	0.0
1926 Chi-A	48	122	6	32	1	1	1	11	4	15	0	1	.262	.286	.311	.597	58	-8	11	2.98	-3	C-38/1-1	1	-0.9
1927*NY-A	70	195	29	54	2	4	0	25	20	15	0	0	.277	.350	.328	.678	79	-5	24	4.29	-1	C-68	7	-0.3
1928 NY-A	75	202	21	48	7	1	1	21	10	21	0	0	.238	.274	.297	.571	51	-14	17	2.80	0	C-75	5	-1.0
1929 NY-A	22	59	4	12	1	0	0	2	3	6	1	0	.203	.242	.220	.462	21	-7	3	1.86	-2	C-22	1	-0.7
1931 Det-A	40	136	9	32	7	1	1	14	6	19	0	0	.235	.268	.324	.591	53	-9	12	2.95	2	C-39	2	-0.5
Total 7	296	816	84	206	25	8	3	86	47	84	1	2	.252	.295	.314	.609	60	-48	77	3.24	-2	C-282/1-1	18	-3.3

• GRACE, Earl Robert Earl Grace b: 2/24/1907, Barlow, KY d: 12/22/1980, Phoenix, AZ BL/TR, 6', 175 lbs. Deb: 4/23/1929

YEAR TM-L	G	AB	R	H	2B	3B	HR	RBI	BB	SO	SB	CS	AVG	OBP	SLG	OPS	OPS+	BR/A	RC	RC/G	FR	G/POS	WS	TPW
1929 Chi-N	27	80	7	20	1	0	2	17	9	7	0	....	.250	.333	.338	.671	67	-4	9	3.79	1	C-27	3	-0.2
1931 Chi-N	7	9	2	1	0	0	0	1	4	1	0	....	.111	.385	.111	.496	39	-0	1	2.53	0	/C-2	0	0.0
Pit-N	47	150	8	42	6	1	1	20	13	5	0	....	.280	.337	.353	.691	87	-3	19	4.34	-3	C-45	4	-0.3
Yr.	54	159	10	43	6	1	1	21	17	6	0	....	.270	.341	.340	.681	83	-3	20	4.21	-3	C-47	4	-0.3
1932 Pit-N	115	390	41	107	17	5	8	55	14	23	0	....	.274	.305	.405	.710	90	-6	48	4.37	-1	*C-114	14	0.0
1933 Pit-N	93	291	22	84	13	1	3	44	26	23	0	....	.289	.349	.371	.720	106	3	40	5.21	-1	C-88	12	0.8
1934 Pit-N	95	289	27	78	17	1	4	24	20	19	0	....	.270	.317	.377	.694	83	-7	35	4.33	-5	C-83/1-1	6	-0.8
1935 Pit-N	77	224	19	59	8	1	3	29	32	17	1	....	.263	.355	.348	.704	87	-3	27	4.14	5	C-69	7	0.5
1936 Phi-N	86	221	24	55	11	0	4	32	34	20	0	....	.249	.352	.353	.705	82	-5	30	4.73	-3	C-65	4	-0.4
1937 Phi-N	80	223	19	47	10	1	6	29	33	15	0	....	.211	.313	.345	.658	73	-8	25	3.66	-1	C-64	4	-0.6
Total 8	627	1877	169	493	83	10	31	251	185	130	1	....	.263	.331	.367	.698	86	-33	235	4.37	-8	C-557/1-1	54	-0.8

• GRACE, Joe Joseph Laverne Grace b: 1/5/1914, Gorham, IL d: 9/18/1969, Murphysboro, IL BL/TR, 6'1", 180 lbs. Deb: 9/24/1938 Career OF: 129-25-234

YEAR TM-L	G	AB	R	H	2B	3B	HR	RBI	BB	SO	SB	CS	AVG	OBP	SLG	OPS	OPS+	BR/A	RC	RC/G	FR	G/POS	WS	TPW
1938 StL-A	12	47	7	16	1	0	0	4	2	3	0	1	.340	.367	.362	.729	83	-2	6	4.83	0	0-12(0-0-12)	1	-0.2
1939 StL-A	74	207	35	63	11	2	3	22	19	24	3	2	.304	.363	.420	.783	98	-1	33	5.90	1	0-53(10-22-21)	4	-0.1
1940 StL-A	80	229	45	59	14	2	5	25	26	23	2	2	.258	.336	.402	.738	88	-4	32	4.80	-1	0-51(3-0-48),C-12	5	-0.7
1941 StL-A	115	362	53	112	17	4	6	60	57	31	1	3	.309	.410	.428	.839	118	12	69	7.14	-1	0-88(0-0-88)/C-9	12	0.6
1946 StL-A	48	161	21	37	7	2	1	13	16	20	1	3	.230	.307	.317	.624	71	-7	16	3.12	2	0-43(0-0-43)	2	-0.7
Was-A	77	321	39	97	17	4	2	31	24	19	1	4	.302	.358	.399	.757	118	6	46	5.23	1	0-74(60-0-14)	11	0.2
Yr.	125	482	60	134	24	6	3	44	40	39	2	7	.278	.341	.371	.712	102	-1	62	4.47	3	*0-117(60-0-57)	13	-0.5
1947 Was-A	78	234	25	58	9	4	3	17	35	15	1	2	.248	.348	.359	.707	99	0	31	4.44	0	0-67(56-3-8)	7	-0.5
Total 6	484	1561	225	442	76	18	20	172	179	135	9	17	.283	.362	.393	.755	102	4	231	5.29	2	0-388/C-21	42	-1.4

• GRACE, Mark Mark Eugene Grace b: 6/28/1964, Winston-Salem, NC BL/TL, 6'2", 190 lbs. Deb: 5/2/1988

YEAR TM-L	G	AB	R	H	2B	3B	HR	RBI	BB	SO	SB	CS	AVG	OBP	SLG	OPS	OPS+	BR/A	RC	RC/G	FR	G/POS	WS	TPW
1988 Chi-N	134	486	65	144	23	4	7	57	60	43	3	3	.296	.374	.403	.777	118	12	74	5.50	-5	*1-133	16	-0.3
1989*Chi-N	142	510	74	160	28	3	13	79	80	42	14	7	.314	.407	.457	.864	136	28	96	6.91	10	*1-142	25	2.9
1990 Chi-N	157	589	72	182	32	1	9	82	59	54	15	6	.309	.377	.413	.789	109	9	94	5.88	24	*1-153	22	2.3
1991 Chi-N	160	619	87	169	28	5	8	58	70	53	3	4	.273	.350	.373	.723	99	-0	84	4.83	21	*1-160	17	1.0
1992 Chi-N	158	603	72	185	37	5	9	79	72	36	6	1	.307	.384	.430	.814	127	25	102	6.20	15	*1-157	25	3.0
1993 Chi-N★	155	594	86	193	39	4	14	98	71	32	8	4	.325	.398	.475	.873	135	31	107	6.56	1	*1-154	23	1.8
1994 Chi-N	106	403	55	120	23	3	6	44	48	41	0	1	.298	.373	.414	.787	106	4	62	5.65	-1	*1-103	12	-0.6
1995 Chi-N★	143	552	97	180	**51**	3	16	92	65	46	6	2	.326	.399	.516	.915	142	34	115	7.93	-2	*1-143	23	1.9
1996 Chi-N	142	547	88	181	39	1	9	75	62	41	2	3	.331	.400	.455	.855	122	18	97	6.65	6	*1-141	20	1.1
1997 Chi-N★	151	555	87	177	32	5	13	78	88	45	2	4	.319	.414	.465	.879	127	24	107	7.08	8	*1-148	20	1.8
1998*Chi-N	158	595	92	184	39	3	17	89	93	56	4	7	.309	.405	.471	.876	125	23	113	6.91	6	*1-156	27	1.5
1999 Chi-N	161	593	107	183	44	5	16	91	83	44	3	4	.309	.395	.481	.876	122	20	114	7.05	-2	*1-160	21	0.4
2000 Chi-N	143	510	75	143	41	1	11	82	95	28	1	2	.280	.399	.429	.829	112	13	94	6.57	2	*1-140	18	0.2
2001*Ari-N	145	476	66	142	31	2	15	78	67	36	1	0	.298	.389	.466	.856	113	12	90	7.03	-4	*1-135	16	-0.4
2002*Ari-N	124	298	43	75	19	0	7	48	46	30	2	0	.252	.354	.386	.740	87	-4	43	5.04	-3	1-98/P-1	8	-1.4
2003 Ari-N	66	135	13	27	5	0	3	16	16	15	0	0	.200	.285	.304	.588	49	-10	11	2.55	1	1-39/D-1	1	-1.2
Total 16	2245	8065	1179	2445	511	45	173	1146	1075	642	70	48	.303	.387	.442	.829	119	239	1404	6.34	77	*1-2162/D-1,P-1	294	14.1

• GRACE, Mike Michael Lee Grace b: 6/14/1956, Pontiac, MI BR/TR, 6', 175 lbs. Deb: 4/18/1978

YEAR TM-L	G	AB	R	H	2B	3B	HR	RBI	BB	SO	SB	CS	AVG	OBP	SLG	OPS	OPS+	BR/A	RC	RC/G	FR	G/POS	WS	TPW
1978 Cin-N	5	3	0	0	0	0	0	0	0	2	0	0	.000	.000	.000	.000	-100	-1	0	.00	0	/3-2	0	-0.1

• GRADY, John John J. Grady b: 6/18/1860, Lowell, MA d: 7/15/1893, Lowell, MA, 5'7", 150 lbs. Deb: 5/10/1884

YEAR TM-L	G	AB	R	H	2B	3B	HR	RBI	BB	SO	SB	CS	AVG	OBP	SLG	OPS	OPS+	BR/A	RC	RC/G	FR	G/POS	WS	TPW
1884 Alt-U	9	36	5	11	3	0	0	....	2	....	....	....	.306	.342	.389	.731	145	2	5	5.50	-1	/1-8,0-1	1	0.0

• GRADY, Mike Michael William Grady
b: 12/23/1869, Kennett Square, PA d: 12/3/1943, Kennett Square, PA BR/TR, 5'11", 190 lbs. Deb: 4/24/1894 U Career OF: 14-7-29

YEAR TM-L	G	AB	R	H	2B	3B	HR	RBI	BB	SO	SB	CS	AVG	OBP	SLG	OPS	OPS+	BR/A	RC	RC/G	FR	G/POS	WS	TPW
1894 Phi-N	61	190	45	69	13	8	0	40	14	13	3	....	.363	.427	.516	.942	130	10	44	9.49	-4	C-44,1-11/0-2(1-0-1)	6	0.6
1895 Phi-N	46	123	21	40	3	1	1	23	14	8	5	....	.325	.407	.390	.797	106	2	23	7.08	-7	C-38/0-5(3-0-2),1-1,3-1	4	-0.3
1896 Phi-N	72	242	49	77	20	7	1	44	16	19	10	....	.318	.382	.471	.853	125	8	49	7.80	-0	C-61/3-7	10	1.2
1897 Phi-N	4	13	1	2	0	0	0	0	1	....	0	....	.154	.214	.154	.368	-2	-2	0	1.06	1	/C-3	0	-0.1
StL-N	84	326	49	91	11	3	8	57	26	....	7	....	.279	.351	.405	.756	101	0	51	5.59	-6	1-83/0-1	6	-0.5
Yr.	88	339	50	93	11	3	8	57	27	....	7	....	.274	.346	.395	.741	97	-2	51	5.39	-5	1-83/C-3,0-1	6	-0.6
1898 NY-N	93	287	64	85	19	5	3	49	38	....	20	....	.296	.399	.429	.827	141	17	59	7.58	-2	C-57,0-30(7-7-16)/1-7,S-3	17	1.7
1899 NY-N	87	315	49	106	18	8	2	54	29	....	20	....	.337	.405	.463	.868	143	19	69	8.64	0	C-43,3-35/1-4,0-4(0-0-4)	14	2.1
1900 NY-N	83	251	36	55	8	4	0	27	34	....	9	....	.219	.331	.283	.614	74	-7	28	3.68	-4	C-41,1-12,S-11/3-7,0-5(0-0-5),2	5	-0.7
1901 Was-A	94	347	57	99	17	10	9	56	27	....	14	....	.285	.351	.470	.821	128	12	64	6.78	6	1-59,C-30/0-3(3-0-0)	14	1.8

YEAR TM-L	G	AB	R	H	2B	3B	HR	RBI	BB	SO	SB	CS	AVG	OBP	SLG	OPS	OPS+	BR/A	RC	RC/G	FR	G/POS	WS	TPW
1904 StL-N	101	323	44	101	15	11	5	43	31	....	6	....	.313	.376	.474	.850	169	26	62	7.05	-16	C-77,1-11/2-3,3-1	17	1.8
1905 StL-N	100	311	41	89	20	7	4	41	33	....	15	....	.286	.360	.434	.794	140	15	56	6.42	-1	C-71,1-20	16	2.2
1906 StL-N	97	280	33	70	11	3	3	27	48	....	5	....	.250	.369	.343	.712	127	12	39	4.72	2	C-60,1-38	11	2.0
Total 11	922	3008	489	884	155	67	36	461	311	40	114	....	.294	.374	.426	.800	127	113	543	6.62	-32	C-525,1-246/3-51,0-50,S-14,2	120	11.9

• GRAFF, Fred Frederick Gottleib Graff b: 8/25/1889, Canton, OH d: 10/4/1979, Chattanooga, TN BR/TR, 5'10.5", 164 lbs. Deb: 5/14/1913

YEAR TM-L	G	AB	R	H	2B	3B	HR	RBI	BB	SO	SB	CS	AVG	OBP	SLG	OPS	OPS+	BR/A	RC	RC/G	FR	G/POS	WS	TPW
1913 StL-A	4	5	1	2	1	0	0	2	3	3	0	....	.400	.625	.600	1.225	266	2	2	13.36	-1	/3-4	1	0.0

• GRAFF, Louis Louis George "Chappie" Graff b: 7/25/1866, Philadelphia, PA d: 4/16/1955, Bryn Mawr, PA TR Deb: 6/23/1890

YEAR TM-L	G	AB	R	H	2B	3B	HR	RBI	BB	SO	SB	CS	AVG	OBP	SLG	OPS	OPS+	BR/A	RC	RC/G	FR	G/POS	WS	TPW
1890 Syr-a	1	5	0	2	1	0	0	3	0	....	0	....	.400	.400	.600	1.000	217	1	1	10.87	-1	/C-1	0	0.0

• GRAFF, Milt Milton Edward Graff b: 12/30/1930, Jefferson Center, PA BL/TR, 5'7.5", 158 lbs. Deb: 4/16/1957 C

YEAR TM-L	G	AB	R	H	2B	3B	HR	RBI	BB	SO	SB	CS	AVG	OBP	SLG	OPS	OPS+	BR/A	RC	RC/G	FR	G/POS	WS	TPW
1957 KC-A	56	155	16	28	4	3	0	10	15	10	2	5	.181	.262	.245	.507	39	-15	10	1.99	-5	2-53	2	-1.7
1958 KC-A	5	1	0	0	0	0	0	0	0	0	0	0	.000	.000	.000	.000	-98	-0	0	.00	0	/2-1	0	-0.1
Total 2	61	156	16	28	4	3	0	10	15	10	2	5	.179	.260	.244	.504	38	-15	10	1.97	-6	/2-54	2	-1.7

• GRAFFANINO, Tony Anthony Joseph Graffanino b: 6/6/1972, Amityville, NY BR/TR, 6'1", 175 lbs. Deb: 4/19/1996

YEAR TM-L	G	AB	R	H	2B	3B	HR	RBI	BB	SO	SB	CS	AVG	OBP	SLG	OPS	OPS+	BR/A	RC	RC/G	FR	G/POS	WS	TPW
1996 Atl-N	22	46	7	8	1	1	0	2	4	13	0	0	.174	.255	.239	.494	30	-5	3	2.22	0	2-18	1	-0.4
1997*Atl-N	104	186	33	48	9	1	8	20	26	46	6	4	.258	.352	.446	.798	105	1	30	5.27	10	2-75/3-2,S-2,1-1	6	1.4
1998*Atl-N	105	289	32	61	14	1	5	22	24	68	1	4	.211	.276	.318	.595	56	-21	24	2.69	0	2-93/S-2,3-1	4	-1.6
1999 TB-A	39	130	20	41	9	4	2	19	9	22	3	2	.315	.364	.492	.857	114	2	23	6.72	2	2-17,S-17/3-1	7	0.6
2000 TB-A	13	20	8	6	1	0	0	1	1	2	0	0	.300	.364	.350	.714	83	-0	2	4.31	2	/2-6,3-3,D-3,S-1	1	0.2
*Chi-A	57	148	25	40	5	1	2	16	21	25	7	4	.270	.365	.358	.723	83	-3	21	4.93	6	S-21,2-19,3-12	5	0.5
Yr.	70	168	33	46	6	1	2	17	22	27	7	4	.274	.365	.357	.722	83	-4	23	4.86	8	2-25,S-22,3-15/D-3	6	0.6
2001 Chi-A	74	145	23	44	9	0	2	15	16	29	4	1	.303	.377	.407	.783	103	2	23	5.47	4	3-38,2-20/S-5,0-3(3-0-0),D,1	3	0.6
2002 Chi-A	70	229	35	60	12	4	6	31	22	38	2	1	.262	.332	.428	.760	97	-1	34	5.13	3	3-35,2-25/S-8	7	0.4
2003 Chi-A	90	250	51	65	15	3	7	23	24	37	8	0	.260	.332	.428	.760	99	1	39	5.52	9	S-36,2-29,3-20/1-2,D-2	9	1.3
Total 8	574	1443	234	373	75	15	32	149	147	280	31	16	.258	.333	.398	.730	89	-24	200	4.73	36	2-302,3-112/S-92,D-7,1-4,0	43	2.8

• GRAHAM, Barney Bernard W. Graham b: Philadelphia, PA d: 12/31/1896, Mobile, AL Deb: 9/4/1889

YEAR TM-L	G	AB	R	H	2B	3B	HR	RBI	BB	SO	SB	CS	AVG	OBP	SLG	OPS	OPS+	BR/A	RC	RC/G	FR	G/POS	WS	TPW
1889 Phi-a	4	18	0	3	0	0	0	0	0	0	0	....	.167	.167	.167	.333	-5	-2	1	.91	2	/3-4	0	-0.1

• GRAHAM, Bernie Bernard Graham b: 1860, Beloit, WI d: 10/30/1886, Mobile, AL BL Deb: 7/11/1884

YEAR TM-L	G	AB	R	H	2B	3B	HR	RBI	BB	SO	SB	CS	AVG	OBP	SLG	OPS	OPS+	BR/A	RC	RC/G	FR	G/POS	WS	TPW
1884 CP-U	1	5	2	1	0	0	0	....	0	....	....	....	.200	.200	.200	.400	38	-0	0	1.44	0	/0-1	0	0.0
Bal-U	41	167	21	45	11	0	0	....	2	....	....	....	.269	.278	.335	.613	97	-2	16	3.66	0	0-40(0-25-15)/1-1	5	-0.2
Yr.	42	172	23	46	11	0	0	....	2	....	....	....	.267	.276	.331	.607	95	-2	16	3.59	0	0-41(1-25-15)/1-1	5	-0.3

• GRAHAM, Bert Bert "B.G." Graham b: 4/3/1886, Tilton, IL d: 6/19/1971, Cottonwood, AZ BB/TR, 5'11.5", 187 lbs. Deb: 9/9/1910

YEAR TM-L	G	AB	R	H	2B	3B	HR	RBI	BB	SO	SB	CS	AVG	OBP	SLG	OPS	OPS+	BR/A	RC	RC/G	FR	G/POS	WS	TPW
1910 StL-A	8	26	1	3	2	1	0	5	1	....	0	....	.115	.148	.269	.417	32	-2	1	1.05	1	/1-5,2-2	0	-0.2

• GRAHAM, Charlie Charles Henry Graham b: 4/25/1878, Santa Clara, CA d: 8/29/1948, San Francisco, CA BR/TR, 5'11", 190 lbs. Deb: 4/16/1906

YEAR TM-L	G	AB	R	H	2B	3B	HR	RBI	BB	SO	SB	CS	AVG	OBP	SLG	OPS	OPS+	BR/A	RC	RC/G	FR	G/POS	WS	TPW
1906 Bos-A	30	90	10	21	1	0	1	12	10	....	1	....	.233	.330	.278	.608	91	-0	9	3.39	8	C-27	3	1.2

• GRAHAM, Dan Daniel Jay Graham b: 7/19/1954, Ray, AZ BL/TR, 6'1", 205 lbs. Deb: 6/8/1979

YEAR TM-L	G	AB	R	H	2B	3B	HR	RBI	BB	SO	SB	CS	AVG	OBP	SLG	OPS	OPS+	BR/A	RC	RC/G	FR	G/POS	WS	TPW
1979 Min-A	2	4	0	0	0	0	0	0	0	0	0	0	.000	.000	.000	.000	-96	-1	0	.00	0	/D-1	0	-0.1
1980 Bal-A	86	266	32	74	7	1	15	54	14	40	0	0	.278	.314	.481	.795	116	4	40	5.31	2	C-73/3-9,D-2,0-1	11	1.0
1981 Bal-A	55	142	7	25	3	0	2	11	13	32	0	0	.176	.245	.239	.485	40	-11	8	1.88	-1	C-40/D-6,3-4	2	-1.1
Total 3	143	412	39	99	10	1	17	65	27	72	0	0	.240	.287	.393	.680	87	-8	48	3.98	1	C-113/3-13,D-9,0-1	13	-0.2

• GRAHAM, Jack John Bernard Graham b: 12/24/1916, Minneapolis, MN d: 12/30/1998, Los Alamitos, CA BL/TL, 6'2", 200 lbs. Deb: 4/16/1946

YEAR TM-L	G	AB	R	H	2B	3B	HR	RBI	BB	SO	SB	CS	AVG	OBP	SLG	OPS	OPS+	BR/A	RC	RC/G	FR	G/POS	WS	TPW
1946 Bro-N	2	5	0	1	0	0	0	0	0	0	0	....	.200	.200	.200	.400	13	-1	0	1.35	0	/1-2	0	-0.1
NY-N	100	270	34	59	6	4	14	47	23	37	1	....	.219	.282	.426	.708	99	-3	32	4.01	-2	0-62(1-0-60)/1-7	5	-0.7
Yr.	102	275	34	60	6	4	14	47	23	37	1	....	.218	.281	.422	.703	97	-3	32	3.96	-2	0-62(1-0-60)/1-9	5	-0.8
1949 StL-A	137	500	71	119	22	1	24	79	61	62	0	1	.238	.326	.430	.756	95	-7	72	4.84	-5	*1-136	10	-1.6
Total 2	239	775	105	179	28	5	38	126	84	99	1	1	.231	.310	.427	.737	96	-10	104	4.53	-7	1-145/0-62	15	-2.3

• GRAHAM, Lee Lee Willard Graham b: 9/22/1959, Summerfield, FL BL/TL, 5'10", 170 lbs. Deb: 9/3/1983

YEAR TM-L	G	AB	R	H	2B	3B	HR	RBI	BB	SO	SB	CS	AVG	OBP	SLG	OPS	OPS+	BR/A	RC	RC/G	FR	G/POS	WS	TPW
1983 Bos-A	5	6	2	0	0	0	0	1	0	0	0	1	.000	.000	.000	.000	-93	-2	0	.00	0	/0-3(0-2-1)	0	-0.2

• GRAHAM, Moonlight Archibald Wright Graham b: 11/9/1876, Fayetteville, NC d: 8/25/1965, Chisholm, MN BL/TR, 5'10.5", 170 lbs. Deb: 6/29/1905

YEAR TM-L	G	AB	R	H	2B	3B	HR	RBI	BB	SO	SB	CS	AVG	OBP	SLG	OPS	OPS+	BR/A	RC	RC/G	FR	G/POS	WS	TPW
1905 NY-N	1	0	0	0	0	0	0	0	0	....	0	....	....	....	....	....	-98	0	0	....	0	/0-1	0	0.0

• GRAHAM, Peaches George Frederick Graham b: 3/23/1877, Aledo, IL d: 7/25/1939, Long Beach, CA BR/TR, 5'9", 180 lbs. Deb: 9/14/1902 Career OF: 1-0-4 ♦

YEAR TM-L	G	AB	R	H	2B	3B	HR	RBI	BB	SO	SB	CS	AVG	OBP	SLG	OPS	OPS+	BR/A	RC	RC/G	FR	G/POS	WS	TPW
1902 Cle-A	2	6	0	2	0	0	0	1	1	....	0	....	.333	.429	.333	.762	118	0	1	5.82	1	/2-1	0	0.1
1903 Chi-N	1	2	0	0	0	0	0	0	0	....	0	....	.000	.000	.000	.000	-103	-0	0	.00	0	/P-1	0	-0.2
1908 Bos-N	75	215	22	59	5	0	0	22	23	....	4	....	.274	.361	.298	.658	112	5	25	3.99	-3	C-62/2-5	8	0.9
1909 Bos-N	92	267	27	64	6	3	0	17	24	....	7	....	.240	.302	.285	.587	79	-7	26	3.10	6	C-76/0-6(1-0-3),3-1,S-1	5	0.8
1910 Bos-N	110	291	31	82	13	2	0	21	33	15	5	....	.282	.359	.340	.699	100	1	38	4.49	-1	C-87/3-2,1-1,0-1	6	0.8
1911 Bos-N	33	88	7	24	6	1	0	12	14	5	2	....	.273	.373	.364	.736	98	0	13	5.01	-1	C-26	2	0.1
Chi-N	36	71	6	17	3	0	0	8	11	8	2	....	.239	.365	.282	.646	82	-1	8	3.81	0	C-28	3	0.1
Yr.	69	159	13	41	9	1	0	20	25	13	4	....	.258	.369	.327	.696	91	-1	21	4.44	0	C-54	5	0.2
1912 Phi-N	24	59	6	17	1	0	1	4	8	5	1	....	.288	.373	.356	.729	94	-0	8	4.87	-1	C-19	2	0.0
Total 7	373	999	99	265	34	6	1	85	114	33	21	....	.265	.347	.314	.661	95	-2	118	4.00	2	C-298/0-7,2-6,3-3,1-1,P-1,S	26	2.6

• GRAHAM, Roy Roy Vincent Graham b: 2/22/1895, San Francisco, CA d: 4/26/1933, Manila, Philippines BR/TR, 5'10.5", 175 lbs. Deb: 5/28/1922

YEAR TM-L	G	AB	R	H	2B	3B	HR	RBI	BB	SO	SB	CS	AVG	OBP	SLG	OPS	OPS+	BR/A	RC	RC/G	FR	G/POS	WS	TPW
1922 Chi-A	5	3	0	0	0	0	0	0	0	0	0	0	.000	.400	.000	.400	12	-0	0	1.76	-1	/C-3	0	-0.1
1923 Chi-A	36	82	3	16	2	0	0	6	9	6	0	0	.195	.290	.220	.510	36	-7	6	2.32	-2	C-33	1	-0.8
Total 2	41	85	3	16	2	0	0	6	9	6	0	0	.188	.296	.212	.508	35	-7	6	2.29	-3	/C-36	1	-0.8

• GRAHAM, Skinny Arthur William Graham b: 8/12/1909, Somerville, MA d: 7/10/1967, Cambridge, MA BL/TR, 5'7", 162 lbs. Deb: 9/14/1934 Career OF: 0-4-11

YEAR TM-L	G	AB	R	H	2B	3B	HR	RBI	BB	SO	SB	CS	AVG	OBP	SLG	OPS	OPS+	BR/A	RC	RC/G	FR	G/POS	WS	TPW
1934 Bos-A	13	47	7	11	2	1	0	3	6	13	2	2	.234	.321	.319	.640	61	-3	5	3.28	0	0-13(0-4-9)	0	-0.3
1935 Bos-A	8	10	1	3	0	0	0	1	1	3	1	0	.300	.364	.300	.664	69	-0	1	5.00	0	/0-2(0-0-2)	0	0.0
Total 2	21	57	8	14	2	1	0	4	7	16	3	2	.246	.328	.316	.644	62	-3	6	3.54	0	/0-15	0	-0.4

• GRAHAM, Tiny Dawson Francis Graham b: 9/9/1892, Nashville, TN d: 12/29/1962, Nashville, TN BR/TR, 6'2", 185 lbs. Deb: 8/30/1914

YEAR TM-L	G	AB	R	H	2B	3B	HR	RBI	BB	SO	SB	CS	AVG	OBP	SLG	OPS	OPS+	BR/A	RC	RC/G	FR	G/POS	WS	TPW
1914 Cin-N	25	61	5	14	1	0	0	3	3	10	1	....	.230	.266	.246	.512	51	-4	4	2.20	-2	1-25	0	-0.6

• GRAHAM, Wayne Wayne Leon Graham b: 4/6/1937, Yoakum, TX BR/TR, 6', 200 lbs. Deb: 4/10/1963

YEAR TM-L	G	AB	R	H	2B	3B	HR	RBI	BB	SO	SB	CS	AVG	OBP	SLG	OPS	OPS+	BR/A	RC	RC/G	FR	G/POS	WS	TPW
1963 Phi-N	10	22	1	4	0	0	0	0	3	1	0	0	.182	.280	.182	.462	36	-2	1	2.01	0	/0-6(6-0-0)	0	-0.2
1964 NY-N	20	33	1	3	1	0	0	0	0	5	0	0	.091	.091	.121	.212	-42	-6	0	.33	0	3-11	0	-0.7
Total 2	30	55	2	7	1	0	0	0	3	6	0	0	.127	.172	.145	.318	-8	-8	2	.96	-1	/3-11,0-6	0	-0.9

• GRAMMAS, Alex Alexander Peter Grammas b: 4/3/1926, Birmingham, AL BR/TR, 6', 178 lbs. Deb: 4/13/1954 M/C

YEAR TM-L	G	AB	R	H	2B	3B	HR	RBI	BB	SO	SB	CS	AVG	OBP	SLG	OPS	OPS+	BR/A	RC	RC/G	FR	G/POS	WS	TPW
1954 StL-N	142	401	57	106	17	4	2	29	40	29	6	1	.264	.339	.342	.680	77	-11	47	4.04	9	*S-142/3-1	11	0.8
1955 StL-N	128	366	32	88	19	2	3	25	33	36	4	1	.240	.308	.328	.636	69	-15	37	3.39	7	*S-126	8	0.1
1956 StL-N	6	12	1	3	0	0	0	1	1	1	0	0	.250	.308	.250	.558	52	-1	1	3.01	0	/S-5	0	0.0
Cin-N	77	140	17	34	11	0	0	16	16	18	0	1	.243	.325	.321	.646	70	-6	16	3.74	-2	3-58,S-12/2-5	3	-0.8
Yr.	83	152	18	37	11	0	0	17	17	19	0	1	.243	.324	.316	.639	69	-7	17	3.69	-2	3-58,S-17/2-5	3	-0.8
1957 Cin-N	73	99	14	30	4	0	0	8	10	6	1	3	.303	.367	.343	.710	86	-2	11	3.93	-3	S-42,2-20/3-9	3	-0.4
1958 Cin-N	105	216	25	47	8	0	0	12	34	24	2	2	.218	.329	.255	.584	54	-13	20	2.92	4	S-61,3-38,2-14	4	-0.6
1959 StL-N	131	368	43	99	14	2	3	30	38	26	3	3	.269	.339	.342	.681	77	-11	43	3.98	-9	*S-130	8	-1.1
1960 StL-N	102	196	20	48	4	1	4	17	12	15	0	1	.245	.292	.337	.629	66	-10	17	2.92	2	S-46,2-38,3-13	4	-0.3

YEAR TM-L	G	AB	R	H	2B	3B	HR	RBI	BB	SO	SB	CS	AVG	OBP	SLG	OPS	OPS+	BR/A	RC	RC/G	FR	G/POS	WS	TPW
1961 StL-N	89	170	23	36	10	1	0	21	19	21	0	1	.212	.295	.282	.577	49	-13	15	2.68	1	S-65,2-18/3-3	2	-0.7
1962 StL-N	21	18	0	2	0	0	0	1	1	6	0	0	.111	.158	.111	.269	-24	-3	0	.33	-2	S-16/2-2	0	-0.4
Chi-N	23	60	3	14	3	0	0	3	2	7	1	1	.233	.270	.283	.553	47	-5	4	2.04	2	S-13/2-3,3-1	1	-0.2
Yr.	44	78	3	16	3	0	0	4	3	13	1	1	.205	.244	.244	.487	30	-8	4	1.61	0	S-29/2-5,3-1	1	-0.7
1963 Chi-N	16	27	1	5	0	0	0	0	0	3	0	0	.185	.185	.185	.370	7	-3	1	1.14	-1	S-13	0	-0.4
Total 10	913	2073	236	512	90	10	12	163	206	192	17	14	.247	.320	.317	.637	67	-94	212	3.40	9	S-671,3-123,2-100	44	-3.9

• GRANEY, Jack John Gladstone Graney b: 6/10/1886, St. Thomas, Canada d: 4/20/1978, Louisiana, MO BL/TL, 5'9", 180 lbs. Deb: 4/30/1908 Career OF: 1176-62-46

YEAR TM-L	G	AB	R	H	2B	3B	HR	RBI	BB	SO	SB	CS	AVG	OBP	SLG	OPS	OPS+	BR/A	RC	RC/G	FR	G/POS	WS	TPW
1908 Cle-A	2	0	0	0	0	0	0	0	0	....	0	....	....	....	....	....	-100	0	0	....	0	/P-2	0	-0.1
1910 Cle-A	116	454	62	107	13	9	1	31	37	....	18	....	.236	.293	.311	.604	88	-7	46	3.35	-1	*O-114(53-43-18)	10	-1.5
1911 Cle-A	146	527	84	142	25	5	1	45	66	....	21	....	.269	.363	.342	.704	96	-0	73	4.75	4	*O-142(139-1-2)	14	-0.2
1912 Cle-A	78	264	44	64	13	2	0	20	50	....	9	....	.242	.367	.307	.674	90	-1	33	4.20	1	O-75(75-0-0)	7	-0.3
1913 Cle-A	148	517	56	138	18	12	3	68	48	55	27	....	.267	.335	.366	.701	102	1	69	4.50	-1	*O-148(144-0-4)	15	-0.8
1914 Cle-A	130	460	63	122	17	10	1	39	67	46	20	18	.265	.362	.352	.714	111	4	60	4.37	0	*O-127(127-0-0)	13	-0.1
1915 Cle-A	116	404	42	105	20	7	1	56	59	29	12	15	.260	.357	.351	.708	110	2	51	4.18	6	*O-115(107-1-8)	10	0.3
1916 Cle-A	155	589	106	142	**41**	14	5	54	102	72	10	....	.241	.355	.384	.739	115	13	85	4.84	3	*O-154(154-0-0)	22	1.1
1917 Cle-A	146	535	87	122	29	7	3	35	**94**	49	16	....	.228	.348	.325	.673	98	2	65	3.93	-4	*O-145(145-0-0)	17	-0.9
1918 Cle-A	70	177	27	42	7	4	0	9	28	13	3	....	.237	.351	.322	.673	94	-0	20	3.78	-4	O-45(44-0-1)	5	-0.7
1919 Cle-A	128	461	79	108	22	8	1	30	**105**	39	7	....	.234	.380	.323	.703	93	2	60	4.20	3	*O-125(125-0-0)	15	0.0
1920*Cle-A	62	152	31	45	11	1	0	13	27	21	4	2	.296	.412	.382	.794	108	4	27	5.97	-1	O-47(44-2-1)	6	0.1
1921 Cle-A	68	107	19	32	3	0	2	18	20	9	1	1	.299	.414	.383	.797	103	2	19	6.08	-2	O-32(17-11-5)	3	-0.1
1922 Cle-A	37	58	6	9	0	0	0	2	9	12	0	0	.155	.279	.155	.435	16	-7	3	1.72	-2	O-13(2-4-7)	0	-0.9
Total 14	1402	4705	706	1178	219	79	18	420	712	345	148	36	.250	.354	.342	.696	100	15	610	4.32	2	*O-1282/P-2	137	-4.1

• GRANT, Eddie Edward Leslie "Harvard Eddie" Grant b: 5/21/1883, Franklin, MA d: 10/5/1918, Argonne, France BL/TR, 5'11.5", 168 lbs. Deb: 8/4/1905

YEAR TM-L	G	AB	R	H	2B	3B	HR	RBI	BB	SO	SB	CS	AVG	OBP	SLG	OPS	OPS+	BR/A	RC	RC/G	FR	G/POS	WS	TPW
1905 Cle-A	2	8	1	3	0	0	0	0	0	....	0	....	.375	.375	.375	.750	136	0	1	6.11	0	/2-2	0	0.0
1907 Phi-N	74	268	26	65	4	3	0	19	10	....	10	....	.243	.272	.280	.552	74	-9	24	3.04	-3	3-74	5	-1.1
1908 Phi-N	147	598	69	146	13	8	0	32	35	....	27	....	.244	.289	.293	.582	83	-12	58	3.21	3	*3-134,S-13	15	-0.6
1909 Phi-N	154	631	75	170	18	4	1	37	35	....	28	....	.269	.311	.315	.626	94	-6	71	3.77	1	*3-154	17	-0.1
1910 Phi-N	152	579	70	155	15	5	1	67	39	54	25	....	.268	.315	.316	.631	81	-15	67	3.81	-9	*3-152	14	-2.0
1911 Cin-N	136	458	49	102	12	7	1	53	51	47	28	....	.223	.301	.286	.587	67	-20	49	3.34	0	*3-122,S-11	8	-1.6
1912 Cin-N	96	255	37	61	6	1	2	20	18	27	11	....	.239	.292	.294	.586	62	-13	25	3.16	2	S-56,3-15	5	-0.7
1913 Cin-N	27	94	12	20	1	0	0	9	11	10	7	....	.213	.295	.223	.519	49	-6	8	2.60	0	3-26	1	-0.5
*NY-N	27	20	8	4	1	0	0	1	2	2	1	....	.200	.273	.250	.523	49	-1	1	2.37	1	/3-5,2-3,S-1	0	0.0
Yr.	54	114	20	24	2	0	0	10	13	12	8	....	.211	.291	.228	.519	49	-7	9	2.56	1	3-31/2-3,S-1	1	-0.5
1914 NY-N	88	282	34	78	7	1	0	29	23	21	11	....	.277	.333	.309	.642	94	-2	32	3.89	2	3-52,S-21,2-16	9	0.3
1915 NY-N	87	192	18	40	2	1	0	10	9	20	5	6	.208	.248	.229	.477	47	-14	11	1.79	-2	3-35/2-9,1-1,S-1	1	-1.7
Total 10	990	3385	399	844	79	30	5	277	233	181	153	6	.249	.300	.295	.595	78	-98	347	3.37	-6	3-769,S-103/2-30,1-1	75	-8.0

• GRANT, Jimmy James Charles Grant b: 10/6/1918, Racine, WI d: 7/8/1970, Rochester, MN BL/TR, 5'8", 166 lbs. Deb: 9/8/1942

YEAR TM-L	G	AB	R	H	2B	3B	HR	RBI	BB	SO	SB	CS	AVG	OBP	SLG	OPS	OPS+	BR/A	RC	RC/G	FR	G/POS	WS	TPW
1942 Chi-A	12	36	0	6	1	1	0	1	5	6	0	0	.167	.268	.250	.518	47	-2	3	2.54	0	3-10	1	-0.2
1943 Chi-A	58	197	23	51	9	2	4	22	18	34	4	3	.259	.321	.386	.707	106	1	23	3.80	-1	3-51	6	0.0
Cle-A	15	22	3	3	2	0	0	1	4	7	0	0	.136	.269	.227	.497	49	-1	2	2.36	0	/3-5	0	-0.1
Yr.	73	219	26	54	11	2	4	23	22	41	4	3	.247	.315	.370	.685	100	-0	24	3.65	-1	3-56	6	0.0
1944 Cle-A	61	99	12	27	4	3	1	12	11	20	1	0	.273	.357	.404	.761	122	3	16	5.95	-5	2-20/3-4	3	-0.1
Total 3	146	354	38	87	16	6	5	36	38	67	5	3	.246	.322	.367	.690	101	0	43	4.12	-5	/3-70,2-20	10	-0.3

• GRANT, Tom Thomas Raymond Grant b: 5/28/1957, Worcester, MA BL/TR, 6'2", 190 lbs. Deb: 6/17/1983

YEAR TM-L	G	AB	R	H	2B	3B	HR	RBI	BB	SO	SB	CS	AVG	OBP	SLG	OPS	OPS+	BR/A	RC	RC/G	FR	G/POS	WS	TPW
1983 Chi-N	16	20	2	3	1	0	0	2	3	4	0	0	.150	.261	.200	.461	28	-2	1	1.98	0	O-10(5-0-5)	0	-0.2

• GRANTHAM, George George Farley "Boots" Grantham b: 5/20/1900, Galena, KS d: 3/16/1954, Kingman, AZ BL/TR, 5'10", 170 lbs. Deb: 9/20/1922

YEAR TM-L	G	AB	R	H	2B	3B	HR	RBI	BB	SO	SB	CS	AVG	OBP	SLG	OPS	OPS+	BR/A	RC	RC/G	FR	G/POS	WS	TPW
1922 Chi-N	7	23	3	4	1	1	0	3	1	3	2	0	.174	.208	.304	.513	30	-2	2	2.31	0	/3-5	0	-0.2
1923 Chi-N	152	570	81	160	36	8	8	70	71	92	43	28	.281	.360	.414	.774	104	3	85	4.85	9	*2-150	17	1.5
1924 Chi-N	127	469	85	148	19	6	12	60	55	63	21	21	.316	.390	.458	.848	125	15	81	6.05	7	*2-118/3-6	21	2.5
1925*Pit-N	114	359	74	117	24	6	8	52	50	29	14	4	.326	.413	.493	.906	122	16	77	7.91	-5	*1-102	15	0.4
1926 Pit-N	141	449	66	143	27	13	8	70	60	42	6	....	.318	.400	.490	.890	131	21	88	7.17	-3	*1-132	19	1.0
1927*Pit-N	151	531	96	162	33	11	8	66	74	39	9	....	.305	.396	.454	.850	119	17	97	6.41	0	*2-124,1-29	21	1.8
1928 Pit-N	124	440	93	142	24	9	10	85	59	37	9	....	.323	.408	.486	.894	128	20	87	7.16	4	*1-119/2-1,3-1	18	1.6
1929 Pit-N	110	349	85	107	23	10	12	90	93	38	10	....	.307	.454	.533	.987	140	27	89	9.01	13	2-76,O-19(19-0-0),1-12	19	3.7
1930 Pit-N	146	552	120	179	34	14	18	99	81	66	5	....	.324	.413	.534	.947	126	26	121	8.08	-8	*2-141/1-4	24	1.9
1931 Pit-N	127	465	91	142	26	6	10	46	71	50	5	....	.305	.400	.452	.851	130	22	89	6.84	-11	1-78,2-51	19	0.7
1932 Cin-N	126	493	81	144	29	6	6	39	56	40	4	....	.292	.364	.412	.776	112	10	77	5.60	-11	*2-115,1-10	13	0.5
1933 Cin-N	87	260	32	53	14	3	4	28	38	21	4	....	.204	.310	.327	.637	83	-5	29	3.58	-5	2-72,1-12	6	-0.7
1934 NY-N	32	29	5	7	2	0	1	4	8	6	0	....	.241	.405	.414	.819	123	1	6	7.15	0	/1-4,3-2	1	0.1
Total 13	1444	4989	912	1508	292	93	105	712	717	526	132	53	.302	.392	.461	.854	120	171	927	6.55	-9	2-848,1-502/O-19,3-14	193	14.9

• GRASSO, Mickey Newton Michael Grasso b: 5/10/1920, Newark, NJ d: 10/15/1975, Miami, FL BR/TR, 6', 195 lbs. Deb: 9/18/1946

YEAR TM-L	G	AB	R	H	2B	3B	HR	RBI	BB	SO	SB	CS	AVG	OBP	SLG	OPS	OPS+	BR/A	RC	RC/G	FR	G/POS	WS	TPW
1946 NY-N	7	22	1	3	0	0	0	1	0	3	0	....	.136	.136	.136	.273	-22	-4	0	.00	0	/C-7	0	-0.3
1950 Was-A	75	195	25	56	4	1	1	22	25	31	1	1	.287	.374	.333	.707	86	-3	26	4.86	-4	C-69	4	-0.3
1951 Was-A	52	175	16	36	3	0	1	14	14	17	0	0	.206	.268	.240	.508	39	-15	10	1.89	-2	C-49	1	-1.4
1952 Was-A	115	361	22	78	9	0	0	27	29	36	1	0	.216	.276	.241	.517	46	-25	24	2.19	-1	*C-114	4	-2.1
1953 Was-A	61	196	13	41	7	0	2	22	9	20	0	0	.209	.251	.276	.527	43	-16	12	2.05	-1	C-59	3	-1.4
1954*Cle-A	4	6	1	2	0	0	1	1	1	1	0	0	.333	.500	.833	1.333	256	1	3	18.63	-1	/C-4	1	0.1
1955 NY-N	8	2	0	0	0	0	0	0	3	0	0	0	.000	.600	.000	.600	77	0	0	2.81	-2	/C-8	0	-0.1
Total 7	322	957	78	216	23	1	5	87	81	108	2	1	.226	.291	.268	.558	53	-61	76	2.62	-11	C-310	13	-5.6

• GRAULICH, Lew Lewis Graulich b: Camden, NJ Deb: 9/17/1891

YEAR TM-L	G	AB	R	H	2B	3B	HR	RBI	BB	SO	SB	CS	AVG	OBP	SLG	OPS	OPS+	BR/A	RC	RC/G	FR	G/POS	WS	TPW
1891 Phi-N	7	26	2	8	0	0	0	3	1	2	0	....	.308	.333	.308	.641	85	-1	3	4.10	-3	/C-4,1-3	0	-0.3

• GRAVES, Frank Frank M. Graves b: 11/2/1860, Cincinnati, OH BR, 6', 163 lbs. Deb: 5/10/1886 U

YEAR TM-L	G	AB	R	H	2B	3B	HR	RBI	BB	SO	SB	CS	AVG	OBP	SLG	OPS	OPS+	BR/A	RC	RC/G	FR	G/POS	WS	TPW
1886 StL-N	43	138	7	21	2	0	0	9	7	48	11	....	.152	.193	.167	.360	11	-14	7	1.55	-3	C-41/O-3(0-3-0),P-1	1	-1.6

• GRAVES, Joe Joseph Ebenezer Graves b: 2/26/1906, Marblehead, MA d: 12/22/1980, Salem, MA BR/TR, 5'10", 160 lbs. Deb: 9/26/1926

YEAR TM-L	G	AB	R	H	2B	3B	HR	RBI	BB	SO	SB	CS	AVG	OBP	SLG	OPS	OPS+	BR/A	RC	RC/G	FR	G/POS	WS	TPW
1926 Chi-N	2	5	0	0	0	0	0	0	0	1	0	....	.000	.000	.000	.000	-99	-1	0	.00	-1	/3-2	0	-0.3

• GRAVES, Sid Samuel Sidney "Whitey" Graves b: 11/30/1901, Marblehead, MA d: 12/26/1983, Biddeford, ME BR/TR, 6', 170 lbs. Deb: 7/23/1927

YEAR TM-L	G	AB	R	H	2B	3B	HR	RBI	BB	SO	SB	CS	AVG	OBP	SLG	OPS	OPS+	BR/A	RC	RC/G	FR	G/POS	WS	TPW
1927 Bos-N	7	20	5	5	1	1	0	2	0	1	1	....	.250	.250	.400	.650	78	-1	2	3.04	0	/O-5(0-5-0)	0	-0.1

• GRAY, Bill William Tobin Gray b: 4/5/1871, Philadelphia, PA d: 12/8/1932, Philadelphia, PA, 5'11", 175 lbs. Deb: 5/14/1890 Career OF: 8-7-9

YEAR TM-L	G	AB	R	H	2B	3B	HR	RBI	BB	SO	SB	CS	AVG	OBP	SLG	OPS	OPS+	BR/A	RC	RC/G	FR	G/POS	WS	TPW
1890 Phi-N	34	128	20	31	8	4	0	21	6	3	5	....	.242	.287	.367	.654	88	-3	15	4.18	-6	O-10(6-3-1)/2-8,3-8,C-7,1	2	-0.7
1891 Phi-N	23	75	11	18	0	0	0	7	3	10	3	....	.240	.296	.240	.536	55	-4	6	3.02	-4	C-11,O-10(0-4-6)/S-3,3-1	1	-0.7
1895 Cin-N	52	181	24	55	17	4	1	29	15	8	4	....	.304	.364	.459	.822	107	1	33	6.92	0	3-27,2-16/C-5,S-5,O-1	5	0.2
1896 Cin-N	46	121	15	25	2	1	0	17	19	11	6	....	.207	.314	.240	.554	44	-10	12	3.16	3	2-12,C-11/S-8,O-3(1-0-2),1,3	2	-0.4
1898 Pit-N	137	528	56	121	17	5	0	67	28	....	5	....	.229	.283	.280	.564	63	-26	47	2.92	-21	*3-137	4	-4.2
Total 5	292	1033	126	250	44	14	1	141	71	32	23	....	.242	.303	.315	.617	71	-42	113	3.74	-28	3-174/2-36,C-34,O-24,S-16,1	14	-5.7

• GRAY, Dick Richard Benjamin Gray b: 7/11/1931, Jefferson, PA BR/TR, 5'11", 165 lbs. Deb: 4/15/1958

YEAR TM-L	G	AB	R	H	2B	3B	HR	RBI	BB	SO	SB	CS	AVG	OBP	SLG	OPS	OPS+	BR/A	RC	RC/G	FR	G/POS	WS	TPW
1958 LA-N	58	197	25	49	5	6	9	30	19	30	1	1	.249	.327	.472	.799	105	1	29	5.09	7	3-55	7	0.8
1959 LA-N	21	52	8	8	1	0	2	4	6	12	0	0	.154	.241	.288	.530	38	-5	4	2.21	1	3-11	0	-0.3
StL-N	36	51	9	16	1	0	1	6	6	8	3	0	.314	.386	.392	.778	101	1	9	6.04	-3	S-13/3-6,2-2,O-1	1	-0.1
Yr.	57	103	17	24	2	0	3	10	12	20	3	0	.233	.313	.340	.653	69	-4	12	3.94	-1	3-17,S-13/2-2,O-1	1	-0.5

YEAR TM-L	G	AB	R	H	2B	3B	HR	RBI	BB	SO	SB	CS	AVG	OBP	SLG	OPS	OPS+	BR/A	RC	RC/G	FR	G/POS	WS	TPW
1960 StL-N	9	5	1	0	0	0	0	1	2	2	0	0	.000	.286	.000	.286	-13	-1	0	1.17	0	/2-4,3-1	0	0.0
Total 3	**124**	**305**	**43**	**73**	**7**	**6**	**12**	**41**	**33**	**52**	**4**	**1**	**.239**	**.322**	**.420**	**.741**	**90**	**-4**	**42**	**4.60**	**6**	**/3-73,S-13,2-6,0-1**	**8**	**0.3**
• GRAY, Gary	Gary George Gray b: 9/21/1952, New Orleans, LA BR/TR, 6', 203 lbs. Deb: 6/23/1977 Career OF: 11-0-0																							
1977 Tex-A	1	2	0	0	0	0	0	0	0	1	0	0	.000	.000	.000	.000	-99	-1	0	.00	0	/0-1	0	-0.1
1978 Tex-A	17	50	4	12	1	0	2	6	1	12	1	0	.240	.255	.380	.635	76	-2	5	3.22	0	D-11	1	-0.2
1979 Tex-A	16	42	4	10	0	0	0	1	2	8	1	1	.238	.273	.238	.511	40	-4	2	1.74	0	D-13	0	-0.4
1980 Cle-A	28	54	4	8	1	0	2	4	3	13	0	0	.148	.193	.278	.471	27	-6	2	1.38	0	/D-9,1-6,0-6(6-0-0)	0	-0.6
1981 Sea-A	69	208	27	51	7	1	13	31	4	44	2	0	.245	.259	.476	.735	104	-0	22	3.52	-2	1-34,D-15/0-4(4-0-0)	3	-0.4
1982 Sea-A	80	269	26	69	14	2	7	29	24	59	1	1	.257	.322	.401	.724	95	-2	35	4.63	-2	1-60,D-14	5	-0.8
Total 6	**211**	**625**	**65**	**150**	**23**	**3**	**24**	**71**	**34**	**137**	**5**	**2**	**.240**	**.281**	**.402**	**.683**	**86**	**-14**	**66**	**3.61**	**-4**	**1-100/D-62,0-11**	**9**	**-2.5**
• GRAY, Jim	James W. Gray b: 8/7/1862, Pittsburgh, PA d: 1/31/1938, Allegheny, PA TR Deb: 10/9/1884																							
1884 Pit-a	1	2	0	1	0	0	0	0	0	....	....	....	.500	.500	.500	1.000	223	0	1	14.09	-1	/3-1	0	0.0
1890 Pit-P	2	9	3	2	0	0	1	3	0	2	0	....	.222	.222	.556	.778	114	0	1	4.39	0	/2-2	0	0.0
Pit-N	1	3	0	0	0	0	0	0	0	1	0	....	.000	.000	.000	.000	-113	-1	0	.00	-1	/S-1	0	-0.2
1893 Pit-N	2	9	0	4	1	0	0	2	0	1	0	....	.444	.444	.556	1.000	168	1	2	12.07	-1	/S-2	0	0.0
Total 3	**6**	**23**	**3**	**7**	**1**	**0**	**1**	**5**	**0**	**4**	**0**	**....**	**.304**	**.304**	**.478**	**.783**	**115**	**0**	**4**	**6.58**	**-3**	**/S-3,2-2,3-1**	**0**	**-0.2**
• GRAY, Lorenzo	Lorenzo Gray b: 3/4/1958, Mound Bayou, MS BR/TR, 6'1", 180 lbs. Deb: 7/8/1982																							
1982 Chi-A	17	28	4	8	1	0	0	0	2	4	1	0	.286	.333	.321	.655	81	-0	3	4.52	-2	3-16	1	-0.3
1983 Chi-A	41	78	18	14	3	0	1	4	8	16	1	0	.179	.256	.256	.512	40	-6	5	2.00	-1	3-31/D-7	1	-0.7
Total 2	**58**	**106**	**22**	**22**	**4**	**0**	**1**	**4**	**10**	**20**	**2**	**0**	**.208**	**.276**	**.274**	**.549**	**50**	**-7**	**8**	**2.58**	**-3**	**/3-47,D-7**	**2**	**-1.0**
• GRAY, Milt	Milton Marshall Gray b: 2/21/1914, Louisville, KY d: 6/30/1969, Quincy, FL BR/TR, 6'1", 170 lbs. Deb: 5/27/1937																							
1937 Was-A	2	6	0	0	0	0	0	0	0	1	0	0	.000	.000	.000	.000	-105	-2	0	.00	0	/C-2	0	-0.2
• GRAY, Pete	Peter J. Gray b: 3/6/1915, Nanticoke, PA d: 6/30/2002, Nanticoke, PA BL/TL, 6'1", 169 lbs. Deb: 4/17/1945																							
1945 StL-A	77	234	26	51	6	2	0	13	13	11	5	6	.218	.259	.261	.520	49	-17	16	2.17	-1	0-61(35-29-0)	2	-2.2
• GRAY, Stan	Stanley Oscar Gray b: 12/10/1888, Ladonia, TX d: 10/11/1964, Snyder, TX BR/TR, 6'.5", 184 lbs. Deb: 9/17/1912																							
1912 Pit-N	6	20	4	5	0	1	0	2	0	3	0	....	.250	.250	.350	.600	64	-1	2	2.77	-1	/1-4	0	-0.2
• GREBECK, Craig	Craig Allen Grebeck b: 12/29/1964, Johnstown, PA BR/TR, 5'8", 148 lbs. Deb: 4/13/1990 Career OF: 4-0-1																							
1990 Chi-A	59	119	7	20	3	1	1	9	8	24	0	0	.168	.233	.235	.468	32	-11	7	1.76	4	3-35,S-16/2-6,D-1	2	-0.6
1991 Chi-A	107	224	37	63	16	3	6	31	38	40	1	3	.281	.388	.460	.848	137	11	42	6.54	4	3-49,2-36,S-26	11	1.7
1992 Chi-A	88	287	24	77	21	2	3	35	30	34	0	3	.268	.344	.387	.731	106	1	39	4.52	1	S-85/3-7,0-2(1-0-1)	10	0.9
1993*Chi-A	72	190	25	43	5	0	1	12	26	26	1	2	.226	.319	.268	.588	61	-10	16	2.64	4	S-46,2-16,3-14	3	-0.2
1994 Chi-A	35	97	17	30	5	0	0	5	12	5	0	0	.309	.391	.361	.752	97	0	15	5.65	2	2-14,S-14/3-7	3	0.3
1995 Chi-A	53	154	19	40	12	0	1	18	21	23	0	0	.260	.360	.357	.717	91	-1	21	4.62	2	S-31,3-18/2-8	5	0.3
1996 Fla-N	50	95	8	20	1	0	1	9	4	14	0	0	.211	.250	.253	.503	34	-9	6	2.00	1	2-29/S-2,3-1	1	-0.7
1997 Ana-A	63	126	12	34	9	0	1	6	18	11	0	1	.270	.361	.365	.726	89	-2	16	4.13	-2	2-26,S-20,3-15/0-3(3-0-0),D	3	-0.2
1998 Tor-A	102	301	33	77	17	2	2	27	29	42	2	2	.256	.329	.346	.675	76	-11	35	3.82	10	2-91/S-6,3-4	7	0.3
1999 Tor-A	34	113	18	41	7	0	0	10	15	13	0	0	.363	.446	.425	.871	122	5	23	7.88	-3	2-17,D-12/S-4,3-2	4	0.2
2000 Tor-A	66	241	38	71	19	0	3	23	25	33	0	0	.295	.366	.411	.776	93	-2	36	5.44	2	2-56/S-8	8	0.3
2001 Bos-A	23	41	1	2	1	0	0	2	2	9	0	0	.049	.093	.073	.166	-55	-9	0	.23	-3	S-23	1	-1.1
Total 12	**752**	**1988**	**239**	**518**	**116**	**8**	**19**	**187**	**228**	**274**	**4**	**11**	**.261**	**.342**	**.356**	**.698**	**87**	**-38**	**255**	**4.32**	**20**	**2-299,S-281,3-152/D-15,0-5**	**58**	**1.3**
• GREEN, Danny	Edward Green b: 11/6/1876, Burlington, NJ d: 11/9/1914, Camden, NJ BL/TR Deb: 8/17/1898 Career OF: 38-204-671																							
1898 Chi-N	47	188	26	59	4	3	4	27	7	....	12	....	.314	.342	.431	.773	121	4	33	6.60	5	0-47(8-2-37)	7	0.6
1899 Chi-N	117	475	90	140	12	11	6	56	35	....	18	....	.295	.352	.404	.756	110	6	77	5.93	6	*0-115(9-0-106)	15	0.5
1900 Chi-N	103	389	63	116	21	5	5	49	17	....	28	....	.298	.339	.416	.755	112	5	67	6.32	-2	*0-102(3-60-39)	14	-0.3
1901 Chi-N	133	537	82	168	16	12	6	61	40	....	31	....	.313	.364	.421	.785	132	22	96	6.82	9	*0-133(0-133-0)	20	2.4
1902 Chi-A	129	481	77	150	16	11	0	62	53	....	35	....	.312	.388	.391	.779	122	17	92	6.84	-3	*0-129(18-2-110)	21	0.8
1903 Chi-A	135	499	75	154	26	7	6	62	47	....	29	....	.309	.375	.425	.800	146	29	94	6.93	3	*0-133(0-0-133)	26	2.7
1904 Chi-A	147	536	83	142	16	10	2	62	63	....	28	....	.265	.352	.343	.695	125	19	78	5.09	5	*0-146(0-0-146)	27	1.9
1905 Chi-A	112	379	56	92	13	6	0	44	53	....	11	....	.243	.345	.309	.653	112	8	48	4.17	-4	*0-107(0-7-100)	14	-0.1
Total 8	**923**	**3484**	**552**	**1021**	**124**	**65**	**29**	**423**	**315**	**....**	**192**	**....**	**.293**	**.359**	**.391**	**.750**	**124**	**110**	**585**	**6.06**	**18**	**0-912**	**144**	**8.4**
• GREEN, David	David Alejandro (Casaya) Green b: 12/4/1960, Managua, Nicaragua BR/TR, 6'3", 170 lbs. Deb: 9/4/1981 Career OF: 29-89-147																							
1981 StL-N	21	34	6	5	1	0	0	2	6	5	0	1	.147	.275	.176	.451	29	-3	2	1.64	0	0-18(0-18-0)	0	-0.4
1982*StL-N	76	166	21	47	7	1	2	23	8	29	11	3	.283	.320	.373	.693	92	-1	20	4.33	1	0-68(7-46-19)	5	-0.1
1983 StL-N	146	422	52	120	14	10	8	69	26	76	34	16	.284	.327	.422	.749	106	2	53	4.26	-3	*0-136(20-19-100)	10	-0.6
1984 StL-N	126	452	49	121	14	4	15	65	20	105	17	9	.268	.300	.416	.716	102	-2	53	4.08	-5	*1-117,0-14(0-6-8)	11	-1.4
1985 SF-N	106	294	36	73	10	2	5	20	22	58	6	5	.248	.303	.347	.650	85	-7	28	3.09	-2	1-78,0-12(1-0-11)	4	-1.5
1987 StL-N	14	30	4	8	2	1	1	1	2	5	0	1	.267	.313	.500	.813	109	-0	4	5.12	0	0-10(1-0-9)/1-3	1	-0.1
Total 6	**489**	**1398**	**168**	**374**	**48**	**18**	**31**	**180**	**84**	**278**	**68**	**35**	**.268**	**.311**	**.394**	**.705**	**97**	**-12**	**161**	**3.90**	**-9**	**0-258,1-198**	**31**	**-4.2**
• GREEN, Dick	Richard Larry Green b: 4/21/1941, Sioux City, IA BR/TR, 5'10", 180 lbs. Deb: 9/9/1963																							
1963 KC-A	13	37	5	10	2	0	1	4	2	10	0	0	.270	.325	.405	.730	99	-0	5	4.44	1	/S-6,2-4	1	0.2
1964 KC-A	130	435	48	115	14	5	11	37	27	87	3	3	.264	.312	.395	.707	92	-6	52	4.17	9	*2-120	12	1.5
1965 KC-A	133	474	64	110	15	1	15	55	50	110	0	2	.232	.309	.363	.672	92	-6	53	3.65	-5	*2-126	11	0.0
1966 KC-A	140	507	58	127	24	3	9	62	27	101	6	1	.250	.298	.363	.661	92	-5	54	3.66	4	*2-137/3-2	16	1.2
1967 KC-A	122	349	26	69	12	4	5	37	30	68	6	3	.198	.261	.298	.559	67	-14	28	2.59	-2	3-59,2-50/1-1,S-1	5	-1.4
1968 Oak-A	76	202	19	47	6	0	6	18	21	41	3	1	.233	.308	.351	.660	105	1	23	3.95	5	2-61/3-1,C-1	8	1.3
1969 Oak-A	136	483	61	133	25	6	12	64	53	94	2	3	.275	.357	.427	.783	123	14	72	5.17	12	*2-131	22	3.7
1970 Oak-A	135	384	34	73	7	0	4	29	38	73	3	0	.190	.268	.240	.508	43	-29	25	2.03	9	*2-127/3-5,C-1	5	-1.2
1971*Oak-A	144	475	58	116	14	1	12	49	51	83	1	1	.244	.321	.354	.675	93	-4	53	3.73	21	*2-143/S-1	20	2.9
1972*Oak-A	26	42	1	12	1	1	0	3	3	5	0	1	.286	.348	.357	.705	116	0	5	3.96	1	2-26	2	0.2
1973*Oak-A	133	332	33	87	17	0	3	42	21	63	0	2	.262	.310	.340	.650	88	-7	33	3.36	15	*2-133/3-1,S-1	10	1.6
1974*Oak-A	100	287	20	61	8	2	2	22	22	50	2	3	.213	.269	.275	.544	61	-15	20	2.26	11	*2-100	5	0.1
Total 12	**1288**	**4007**	**427**	**960**	**145**	**23**	**80**	**422**	**345**	**785**	**26**	**20**	**.240**	**.305**	**.347**	**.652**	**87**	**-70**	**424**	**3.53**	**82**	***2-1158/3-68,S-9,C-2,1-1**	**117**	**10.2**
• GREEN, Gary	Gary Allan Green b: 1/14/1962, Pittsburgh, PA BR/TR, 6'3", 175 lbs. Deb: 9/14/1986																							
1986 SD-N	13	33	2	7	1	0	0	2	1	11	0	0	.212	.235	.242	.478	33	-3	2	2.01	1	S-13	1	0.0
1989 SD-N	15	27	4	7	3	0	0	0	1	1	0	1	.259	.286	.370	.656	86	-1	3	3.30	1	S-11/3-1	1	0.0
1990 Tex-A	62	88	10	19	3	0	0	8	6	18	1	1	.216	.266	.250	.516	45	-7	6	2.08	4	S-58	2	0.0
1991 Tex-A	8	20	0	3	1	0	0	1	1	6	0	0	.150	.190	.200	.390	8	-3	1	1.31	1	/S-8	0	-0.1
1992 Cin-N	8	12	3	4	1	0	0	0	0	2	0	0	.333	.333	.417	.750	108	0	2	5.63	-2	/S-6,3-1	1	-0.1
Total 5	**106**	**180**	**19**	**40**	**9**	**0**	**0**	**11**	**9**	**38**	**1**	**2**	**.222**	**.259**	**.272**	**.531**	**48**	**-13**	**13**	**2.33**	**5**	**/S-96,3-2**	**5**	**-0.3**
• GREEN, Gene	Gene Leroy Green b: 6/26/1933, Los Angeles, CA d: 5/23/1981, St. Louis, MO BR/TR, 6'2.5", 205 lbs. Deb: 9/10/1957 Career OF: 4-1-166																							
1957 StL-N	6	15	0	3	1	0	0	2	0	3	0	0	.200	.200	.267	.467	23	-2	1	1.09	-0	/0-3(0-0-3)	0	-0.2
1958 StL-N	137	442	47	124	18	3	13	55	37	48	2	1	.281	.338	.423	.761	96	-3	56	4.33	6	0-75(0-1-75),C-48	11	0.3
1959 StL-N	30	74	8	14	6	0	1	3	5	18	0	0	.189	.241	.311	.551	43	-6	5	2.42	4	0-19(0-0-19),C-11	1	-0.2
1960 Bal-A	1	4	0	1	0	0	0	0	0	0	0	0	.250	.250	.250	.500	36	-0	0	2.25	1	/0-1	0	0.0
1961 Was-A	110	364	52	102	16	3	18	62	35	65	0	2	.280	.345	.489	.834	126	11	51	4.69	-5	C-79,0-21(0-0-21)	10	0.9
1962 Cle-A	66	143	16	40	4	1	11	28	8	21	0	0	.280	.318	.552	.870	133	5	23	5.53	1	0-33(3-0-30)/1-2	5	0.4
1963 Cle-A	43	78	4	16	3	0	2	7	4	22	0	0	.205	.262	.321	.582	63	-4	6	2.31	0	0-18(1-0-17)	0	-0.5

YEAR TM-L	G	AB	R	H	2B	3B	HR	RBI	BB	SO	SB	CS	AVG	OBP	SLG	OPS	OPS+	BR/A	RC	RC/G	FR	G/POS	WS	TPW
Cin-N	15	31	3	7	1	0	1	3	0	8	0	0	.226	.250	.355	.605	70	-1	2	2.66	-1	/C-8	0	-0.2
Total 7	408	1151	130	307	49	7	46	160	89	185	2	3	.267	.322	.441	.763	103	1	145	4.22	5	0-170,C-146/1-2	27	0.5

• GREEN, Jim James R. Green b: 5/22/1854, Windham County, CT d: 12/12/1912, Cleveland, OH Deb: 7/19/1884

YEAR TM-L	G	AB	R	H	2B	3B	HR	RBI	BB	SO	SB	CS	AVG	OBP	SLG	OPS	OPS+	BR/A	RC	RC/G	FR	G/POS	WS	TPW
1884 Was-U	10	36	4	5	1	0	0	....	0	....	....	....	.139	.139	.167	.306	3	-3	1	.77	1	/3-9,0-1	0	-0.2

• GREEN, Joe Joseph Henry Green b: 9/17/1897, Philadelphia, PA d: 2/4/1972, Bryn Mawr, PA BR/TR, 6'2", 170 lbs. Deb: 7/2/1924

YEAR TM-L	G	AB	R	H	2B	3B	HR	RBI	BB	SO	SB	CS	AVG	OBP	SLG	OPS	OPS+	BR/A	RC	RC/G	FR	G/POS	WS	TPW
1924 Phi-A	1	1	0	0	0	0	0	0	0	0	0	0	.000	.000	.000	.000	-99	-0	0	.00	0	....	0	0.0

• GREEN, Lenny Leonard Charles Green b: 1/6/1933, Detroit, MI BL/TL, 5'11", 170 lbs. Deb: 8/25/1957 Career OF: 331-683-44

YEAR TM-L	G	AB	R	H	2B	3B	HR	RBI	BB	SO	SB	CS	AVG	OBP	SLG	OPS	OPS+	BR/A	RC	RC/G	FR	G/POS	WS	TPW
1957 Bal-A	19	33	2	6	1	1	1	5	1	4	0	1	.182	.206	.364	.570	56	-3	2	2.09	-1	0-15(3-12-2)	0	-0.4
1958 Bal-A	69	91	10	21	4	0	0	4	9	10	0	2	.231	.300	.275	.575	63	-5	8	2.70	-2	0-53(28-30-6)	1	-1.0
1959 Bal-A	27	24	3	7	0	0	1	2	1	3	0	0	.292	.346	.417	.763	111	0	4	5.52	0	0-23(20-0-5)	1	0.0
Was-A	88	190	29	46	6	1	2	15	20	15	9	5	.242	.314	.316	.630	74	-7	20	3.52	0	0-58(21-13-27)	3	-0.9
Yr.	115	214	32	53	6	1	3	17	21	18	9	5	.248	.318	.327	.645	78	-6	24	3.73	0	0-81(41-13-32)	4	-0.9
1960 Was-A	127	330	62	97	16	7	5	33	43	25	21	8	.294	.385	.430	.816	119	11	58	6.17	-5	*0-100(20-92-0)	13	0.1
1961 Min-A	156	600	92	171	28	7	9	50	81	50	17	11	.285	.376	.400	.776	102	3	96	5.74	-11	*0-153(56-141-4)	19	-1.4
1962 Min-A	158	619	97	168	33	3	14	63	88	36	8	4	.271	.369	.402	.771	104	6	98	5.62	-4	*0-156(88-146-0)	23	-0.6
1963 Min-A	145	280	41	67	10	1	4	27	31	21	11	5	.239	.319	.325	.644	80	-7	32	3.82	-7	*0-119(15-118-0)	6	-1.8
1964 Min-A	26	15	3	0	0	0	0	0	4	6	0	1	.000	.211	.000	.211	-35	-3	0	.28	-1	/0-7(6-1-0)	0	-0.4
LA-A	39	92	13	23	2	0	2	4	10	8	2	0	.250	.330	.337	.667	96	0	11	3.90	0	0-23(11-13-0)	2	-0.1
Bal-A	14	21	0	4	0	0	0	1	7	3	1	0	.190	.393	.190	.583	69	-0	2	3.79	0	/0-8(2-6-0)	1	0.0
Yr.	79	128	16	27	2	0	2	5	21	17	3	1	.211	.327	.273	.600	74	-3	13	3.34	-1	0-38(19-20-0)	3	-0.6
1965 Bos-A	119	373	69	103	24	6	7	24	48	43	8	2	.276	.363	.429	.792	117	10	60	5.70	-3	0-95(12-86-0)	11	0.5
1966 Bos-A	85	133	18	32	6	0	1	12	15	19	0	1	.241	.327	.308	.635	76	-4	13	3.01	0	0-27(4-23-0)	1	-0.5
1967 Det-A	58	151	22	42	8	1	1	13	9	17	1	1	.278	.319	.364	.683	99	-1	17	4.16	0	0-44(43-2-0)	4	-0.3
1968 Det-A	6	4	0	1	0	0	0	0	1	0	0	0	.250	.400	.250	.650	97	0	0	1.35	0	/0-2(2-0-0)	0	0.0
Total 12	1136	2956	461	788	138	27	47	253	368	260	78	41	.267	.353	.379	.733	98	2	421	4.94	-36	0-883	85	-6.8

• GREEN, Pumpsie Elijah Jerry Green b: 10/27/1933, Oakland, CA BB/TR, 6', 175 lbs. Deb: 7/21/1959

YEAR TM-L	G	AB	R	H	2B	3B	HR	RBI	BB	SO	SB	CS	AVG	OBP	SLG	OPS	OPS+	BR/A	RC	RC/G	FR	G/POS	WS	TPW
1959 Bos-A	50	172	30	40	6	3	1	10	29	22	4	2	.233	.350	.320	.670	81	-3	22	4.29	1	2-45/S-1	5	0.1
1960 Bos-A	133	260	36	63	10	3	3	21	44	47	3	4	.242	.354	.338	.693	85	-5	32	4.04	-10	2-69,S-41	6	-1.0
1961 Bos-A	88	219	33	57	12	3	6	27	42	32	4	2	.260	.379	.425	.804	112	5	38	5.94	-3	S-57/2-7	9	0.7
1962 Bos-A	56	91	12	21	2	1	2	11	11	18	1	0	.231	.314	.341	.654	74	-3	11	4.09	-2	2-18/S-5	2	-0.4
1963 NY-N	17	54	8	15	1	2	1	5	12	13	0	2	.278	.409	.426	.835	139	3	9	6.11	-2	3-16	3	0.1
Total 5	344	796	119	196	31	12	13	74	138	132	12	10	.246	.360	.364	.724	94	-3	112	4.74	-16	2-139,S-104/3-16	25	-0.5

• GREEN, Scarborough Bertrum Scarborough Green b: 6/9/1974, Creve Coeur, MO BR/TR, 5'10", 170 lbs. Deb: 8/2/1997 Career OF: 13-57-26

YEAR TM-L	G	AB	R	H	2B	3B	HR	RBI	BB	SO	SB	CS	AVG	OBP	SLG	OPS	OPS+	BR/A	RC	RC/G	FR	G/POS	WS	TPW
1997 StL-N	20	31	5	3	0	0	0	1	2	5	0	0	.097	.152	.097	.248	-34	-6	1	.51	0	0-19(7-12-0)	0	-0.6
1999 Tex-A	18	13	4	4	0	0	0	0	1	2	0	1	.308	.357	.308	.665	69	-1	1	3.29	0	/0-9(3-4-3),D-4	0	-0.2
2000 Tex-A	79	124	21	29	1	1	0	9	10	26	10	6	.234	.291	.258	.549	40	-12	9	2.27	6	0-65(3-41-23)/D-6	1	-0.6
Total 3	117	168	30	36	1	1	0	10	13	33	10	7	.214	.271	.232	.503	29	-19	11	2.00	5	/0-93,D-10	1	-1.4

• GREEN, Shawn Shawn David Green b: 11/10/1972, Des Plaines, IL BL/TL, 6'4", 190 lbs. Deb: 9/28/1993 Career OF: 55-38-1201

YEAR TM-L	G	AB	R	H	2B	3B	HR	RBI	BB	SO	SB	CS	AVG	OBP	SLG	OPS	OPS+	BR/A	RC	RC/G	FR	G/POS	WS	TPW
1993 Tor-A	3	6	0	0	0	0	0	0	0	1	0	0	.000	.000	.000	.000	-100	-2	0	.00	0	/0-2(0-0-2),D-1	0	-0.2
1994 Tor-A	14	33	1	3	1	0	0	1	1	8	1	0	.091	.118	.121	.239	-38	-7	0	.37	1	0-14(10-0-5)	0	-0.6
1995 Tor-A	121	379	52	109	31	4	15	54	20	68	1	2	.288	.328	.509	.838	115	5	62	6.03	-1	*0-109(0-0-109)	10	-0.1
1996 Tor-A	132	422	52	118	32	3	11	45	33	75	5	1	.280	.343	.448	.791	98	-1	65	5.54	5	*0-127(0-2-127)/D-1	8	-0.2
1997 Tor-A	135	429	57	123	22	4	16	53	36	99	14	3	.287	.343	.469	.812	109	6	71	6.05	4	0-91(45-0-46),D-35	14	0.5
1998 Tor-A	158	630	106	175	33	4	35	100	50	142	35	12	.278	.336	.510	.845	115	14	109	6.18	-4	*0-157(0-33-127)	21	0.3
1999 Tor-A★	153	614	134	190	**45**	0	42	123	66	117	20	7	.309	.386	.588	.974	142	39	140	8.44	4	*0-152(0-0-152)	24	3.2
2000 LA-N	162	610	98	164	44	4	24	99	90	121	24	5	.269	.370	.472	.842	118	21	109	6.22	-5	*0-161(0-1-161)	22	0.7
2001 LA-N	161	619	121	184	31	4	49	125	72	107	20	4	.297	.375	.598	.973	157	54	141	8.39	-4	*0-159(0-2-159)/1-1	34	4.0
2002 LA-N★	158	582	110	166	31	1	42	114	93	112	8	5	.285	.388	.558	.947	156	47	120	7.14	5	*0-156(0-0-156)/D-1	30	4.4
2003 LA-N	160	611	84	171	49	2	19	85	68	112	6	2	.280	.358	.460	.818	118	16	100	5.77	2	*0-157(0-0-157)/D-2	20	1.0
Total 11	1357	4935	815	1403	319	26	253	799	529	962	134	41	.284	.360	.513	.873	126	194	918	6.66	7	*0-1285/D-40,1-1	183	12.8

• GREENBERG, Hank Henry Benjamin "Hammerin' Hank" Greenberg
b: 1/1/1911, New York, NY d: 9/4/1986, Beverly Hills, CA BR/TR, 6'3.5", 210 lbs. Deb: 9/14/1930 HOF: 1956 Career OF: 239-0-0

YEAR TM-L	G	AB	R	H	2B	3B	HR	RBI	BB	SO	SB	CS	AVG	OBP	SLG	OPS	OPS+	BR/A	RC	RC/G	FR	G/POS	WS	TPW
1930 Det-A	1	1	0	0	0	0	0	0	0	0	0	0	.000	.000	.000	.000	-98	-0	0	.00	0	....	0	0.0
1933 Det-A	117	449	59	135	33	3	12	87	46	78	6	2	.301	.367	.468	.835	118	12	79	6.55	4	*1-117	14	0.5
1934*Det-A	153	593	118	201	**63**	7	26	139	63	93	9	5	.339	.404	.600	1.005	156	46	144	9.37	2	*1-153	31	3.2
1935*Det-A	152	619	121	203	46	16	**36**	**170**	87	91	4	3	.328	.411	.628	1.039	171	63	161	10.11	4	*1-152	**34**	5.0
1936 Det-A	12	46	10	16	6	2	1	16	9	6	1	0	.348	.455	.630	1.085	165	5	14	12.28	1	1-12	3	0.4
1937 Det-A★	154	594	137	200	49	14	40	**183**	102	101	8	3	.337	.436	.668	1.105	170	65	178	11.80	9	*1-154	33	5.5
1938 Det-A★	155	556	**144**	175	23	4	**58**	146	**119**	92	7	5	.315	.438	.683	1.122	167	59	172	11.69	8	*1-155	**34**	4.7
1939 Det-A★	138	500	112	156	42	7	33	112	91	95	8	3	.312	.420	.622	1.042	152	40	136	10.03	1	*1-136	24	2.6
1940*Det-A★	148	573	129	195	**50**	8	**41**	**150**	93	75	6	3	.340	.433	**.670**	**1.103**	165	**57**	171	**11.57**	1	*0-148(148-0-0)	**31**	4.7
1941 Det-A	19	67	12	18	5	1	2	12	16	12	1	0	.269	.410	.463	.872	118	3	14	7.83	-2	0-19(19-0-0)	2	-0.1
1945*Det-A★	78	270	47	84	20	2	13	60	42	40	3	1	.311	.404	.544	.948	164	23	61	8.36	-2	0-72(72-0-0)	16	1.7
1946 Det-A	142	523	91	145	29	5	**44**	**127**	80	88	5	1	.277	.373	.604	.977	160	42	119	8.11	11	*1-140	31	5.0
1947 Pit-N	125	402	71	100	13	2	25	74	**104**	73	0	....	.249	.408	.478	.885	131	22	83	7.03	1	*1-119	14	1.9
Total 13	1394	5193	1051	1628	379	71	331	1276	852	844	58	26	.313	.412	.605	1.017	156	437	1331	9.63	38	*1-1138,0-239	267	35.2

• GREENE, Al Altar Alfonse Greene b: 11/9/1954, Detroit, MI BL/TR, 5'11", 190 lbs. Deb: 7/23/1979

YEAR TM-L	G	AB	R	H	2B	3B	HR	RBI	BB	SO	SB	CS	AVG	OBP	SLG	OPS	OPS+	BR/A	RC	RC/G	FR	G/POS	WS	TPW
1979 Det-A	29	59	9	8	1	0	3	6	10	15	0	1	.136	.261	.305	.566	50	-5	5	2.38	0	D-15/0-6(4-0-2)	0	-0.5

• GREENE, Charlie Charles Patrick Greene b: 1/23/1971, Miami, FL BR/TR, 6'1", 170 lbs. Deb: 9/15/1996

YEAR TM-L	G	AB	R	H	2B	3B	HR	RBI	BB	SO	SB	CS	AVG	OBP	SLG	OPS	OPS+	BR/A	RC	RC/G	FR	G/POS	WS	TPW
1996 NY-N	2	1	0	0	0	0	0	0	0	0	0	0	.000	.000	.000	.000	-105	-0	0	.00	0	/C-1	0	-0.1
1997 Bal-A	5	2	0	0	0	0	0	1	0	1	0	0	.000	.000	.000	.000	-103	-1	0	.00	-1	/C-4	0	-0.2
1998 Bal-A	13	21	1	4	1	0	0	0	0	8	0	0	.190	.190	.238	.429	11	-3	1	1.07	0	C-13	0	-0.2
1999 Mil-N	32	42	4	8	1	0	0	1	5	11	0	0	.190	.277	.214	.491	27	-5	3	2.26	0	C-31	1	-0.3
2000 Tor-A	3	9	0	1	0	0	0	0	0	5	0	0	.111	.111	.111	.222	-42	-2	0	.38	0	/C-3	0	-0.2
Total 5	55	75	5	13	2	0	0	2	5	25	0	0	.173	.225	.200	.425	10	-10	4	1.58	-2	/C-52	1	-1.0

• GREENE, Khalil Khalil Thabit Greene b: 10/21/1979, Butler, PA BR/TR, 5'11", 210 lbs. Deb: 9/3/2003

YEAR TM-L	G	AB	R	H	2B	3B	HR	RBI	BB	SO	SB	CS	AVG	OBP	SLG	OPS	OPS+	BR/A	RC	RC/G	FR	G/POS	WS	TPW
2003 SD-N	20	65	8	14	4	1	2	6	4	19	0	1	.215	.271	.400	.671	79	-3	6	2.87	0	S-20	1	-0.1

• GREENE, Paddy Patrick Joseph "Patsy" Greene b: 3/20/1875, Providence, RI d: 10/20/1934, Providence, RI BR/TR, 5'8", 150 lbs. Deb: 9/10/1902

YEAR TM-L	G	AB	R	H	2B	3B	HR	RBI	BB	SO	SB	CS	AVG	OBP	SLG	OPS	OPS+	BR/A	RC	RC/G	FR	G/POS	WS	TPW
1902 Phi-N	19	65	6	11	1	0	0	1	2	....	2	....	.169	.206	.185	.390	21	-6	3	1.50	-2	3-19	1	-0.8
1903 NY-A	4	13	1	4	1	0	0	0	0	....	0	....	.308	.308	.385	.692	100	-0	2	4.64	2	/3-2,S-1	1	0.2
Det-A	1	3	0	0	0	0	0	0	0	....	0	....	.000	.000	.000	.000	-103	-1	0	.00	-1	/3-1	0	-0.1
Yr.	5	16	1	4	1	0	0	0	0	....	0	....	.250	.250	.313	.563	62	-1	2	3.48	1	/3-3,S-1	1	0.0
Total 2	24	81	7	15	2	0	0	1	2	....	2	....	.185	.214	.210	.424	28	-7	5	1.85	-1	/3-22,S-1	2	-0.7

• GREENE, Todd Todd Anthony Greene b: 5/8/1971, Augusta, GA BR/TR, 5'10", 195 lbs. Deb: 7/30/1996 Career OF: 19-0-25

YEAR TM-L	G	AB	R	H	2B	3B	HR	RBI	BB	SO	SB	CS	AVG	OBP	SLG	OPS	OPS+	BR/A	RC	RC/G	FR	G/POS	WS	TPW
1996 Cal-A	29	79	9	15	1	0	2	9	4	11	2	0	.190	.238	.278	.517	31	-8	5	1.84	3	C-26/D-1	1	-0.3
1997 Ana-A	34	124	24	36	6	0	9	24	7	25	2	0	.290	.328	.556	.885	124	4	23	6.96	-0	C-26/D-8	4	0.5
1998 Ana-A	29	71	3	18	4	0	1	7	2	20	0	0	.254	.274	.352	.626	61	-4	7	3.56	0	0-12(12-0-0)/D-4,1-3	1	-0.5
1999 Ana-A	97	321	36	78	20	0	14	42	12	63	1	4	.243	.277	.436	.713	79	-14	35	3.66	-2	D-44,0-30(5-0-25),C-12	3	-1.7
2000 Tor-A	34	85	11	20	2	0	5	10	5	18	0	0	.235	.278	.435	.713	74	-4	9	3.50	0	D-23/C-2,0-1	0	-0.5

YEAR TM-L	G	AB	R	H	2B	3B	HR	RBI	BB	SO	SB	CS	AVG	OBP	SLG	OPS	OPS+	BR/A	RC	RC/G	FR	G/POS	WS	TPW
2001*NY-A	35	96	9	20	4	0	1	11	3	21	0	0	.208	.240	.281	.521	36	-9	6	2.01	-2	C-34/D-2	0	-0.9
2002 Tex-A	42	112	15	30	5	0	10	19	2	23	0	0	.268	.287	.580	.867	116	2	17	5.02	4	1-15,C-15/D-4,0-1	1	0.5
2003 Tex-A	62	205	25	47	10	1	10	20	2	47	0	0	.229	.244	.434	.678	68	-11	21	3.54	-3	C-51/1-2,D-2	2	-1.0
Total 8	362	1093	132	264	52	1	52	142	37	228	5	4	.242	.272	.434	.705	77	-44	122	3.81	0	C-166/D-88,0-44,1-20	12	-3.9

• GREENE, Willie Willie Louis Greene b: 9/23/1971, Milledgeville, GA BL/TR, 5'11", 184 lbs. Deb: 9/1/1992 Career OF: 26-0-72

YEAR TM-L	G	AB	R	H	2B	3B	HR	RBI	BB	SO	SB	CS	AVG	OBP	SLG	OPS	OPS+	BR/A	RC	RC/G	FR	G/POS	WS	TPW
1992 Cin-N	29	93	10	25	5	2	2	13	10	23	0	2	.269	.340	.430	.770	114	1	13	4.98	0	3-25	4	0.1
1993 Cin-N	15	50	7	8	1	1	2	5	2	19	0	0	.160	.192	.340	.532	39	-5	3	1.88	1	S-10/3-5	1	-0.3
1994 Cin-N	16	37	5	8	2	0	0	3	6	14	0	0	.216	.326	.270	.596	58	-2	3	3.04	1	3-13/0-1	0	-0.1
1995 Cin-N	8	19	1	2	0	0	0	0	3	7	0	0	.105	.227	.105	.333	-9	-3	1	.76	1	/3-7	0	-0.1
1996 Cin-N	115	287	48	70	5	5	19	63	36	88	0	1	.244	.328	.495	.823	114	4	46	5.57	6	3-74,0-10(9-0-1)/1-2,S-1	11	1.1
1997 Cin-N	151	495	62	125	22	1	26	91	78	111	6	0	.253	.355	.459	.814	109	9	84	5.93	-2	*3-103,0-39(6-0-33)/1-7,S	17	0.6
1998 Cin-N	111	356	57	96	18	1	14	49	56	80	6	3	.270	.373	.444	.817	113	8	62	6.11	3	3-76,0-28(9-0-22)/S-2,D-1	13	1.1
Bal-A	24	40	8	6	1	0	1	5	13	10	1	0	.150	.358	.250	.608	63	-1	4	3.34	-0	0-14(1-0-13)/D-1	1	-0.2
1999 Tor-A	81	226	22	46	7	0	12	41	20	56	0	0	.204	.268	.394	.662	65	-13	24	3.46	-1	D-52/3-7,0-3(0-0-3)	2	-1.6
2000 Chi-N	105	299	34	60	15	2	10	37	36	69	4	0	.201	.291	.365	.655	66	-16	33	3.66	8	3-90	7	-0.7
Total 9	655	1902	254	446	76	12	86	307	260	477	17	6	.234	.328	.423	.751	94	-19	274	4.89	18	3-400/0-95,D-54,S-16,1-9	56	0.0

• GREENGRASS, Jim James Raymond Greengrass b: 10/24/1927, Addison, NY BR/TR, 6'1", 200 lbs. Deb: 9/9/1952 Career OF: 310-13-141

YEAR TM-L	G	AB	R	H	2B	3B	HR	RBI	BB	SO	SB	CS	AVG	OBP	SLG	OPS	OPS+	BR/A	RC	RC/G	FR	G/POS	WS	TPW
1952 Cin-N	18	68	10	21	2	1	5	24	7	12	0	0	.309	.373	.588	.962	163	6	15	8.67	0	0-17(4-13-0)	4	0.5
1953 Cin-N	154	606	86	173	22	7	20	100	47	83	6	4	.285	.340	.444	.784	102	0	89	5.31	0	*0-153(153-0-0)	15	-0.9
1954 Cin-N	139	542	79	152	27	4	27	95	41	81	0	3	.280	.331	.494	.826	109	3	82	5.32	-3	*0-137(137-0-0)	15	-0.8
1955 Cin-N	13	39	1	4	2	0	0	1	9	9	0	0	.103	.271	.154	.425	16	-5	2	1.56	1	0-11(11-0-0)	0	-0.4
Phi-N	94	323	43	88	20	2	12	37	33	43	0	2	.272	.342	.458	.800	112	4	48	5.19	-1	0-83(5-0-79)/3-2	9	0.1
Yr.	107	362	44	92	22	2	12	38	42	52	0	2	.254	.333	.425	.759	100	-0	50	4.74	1	0-94(16-0-79)/3-2	9	-0.3
1956 Phi-N	86	215	24	44	9	2	5	25	28	43	0	0	.205	.296	.335	.631	71	-9	20	2.90	-2	0-62(0-0-62)	2	-1.3
Total 5	504	1793	243	482	82	16	69	282	165	271	6	9	.269	.332	.448	.780	102	0	257	4.99	-4	0-463/3-2	45	-2.8

• GREENWELL, Mike Michael Lewis "Gator" Greenwell b: 7/18/1963, Louisville, KY BL/TR, 6', 200 lbs. Deb: 9/5/1985 Career OF: 1124-1-47

YEAR TM-L	G	AB	R	H	2B	3B	HR	RBI	BB	SO	SB	CS	AVG	OBP	SLG	OPS	OPS+	BR/A	RC	RC/G	FR	G/POS	WS	TPW
1985 Bos-A	17	31	7	10	1	0	4	8	3	4	1	0	.323	.382	.742	1.124	191	4	9	11.82	0	0-17(16-0-3)	2	0.3
1986*Bos-A	31	35	4	11	2	0	0	4	5	7	0	0	.314	.400	.371	.771	111	1	5	5.79	1	0-15(8-0-7)/D-3	1	0.1
1987 Bos-A	125	412	71	135	31	6	19	89	35	40	5	4	.328	.389	.570	.959	146	26	90	8.38	0	0-91(64-0-28),D-15/C-1	17	2.0
1988*Bos-A★	158	590	86	192	39	8	22	119	87	38	16	8	.325	.420	.531	.950	158	49	134	8.53	-2	*0-147(143-0-8),D-11	30	4.2
1989 Bos-A★	145	578	87	178	36	0	14	95	56	44	13	5	.308	.372	.443	.815	121	18	91	5.71	-6	*0-139(139-0-0)/D-5	15	0.6
1990*Bos-A	159	610	71	181	30	6	14	73	65	43	8	7	.297	.368	.434	.803	118	15	94	5.53	-1	*0-159(159-0-0)	16	0.8
1991 Bos-A	147	544	76	163	26	6	9	83	43	35	15	5	.300	.354	.419	.773	108	7	81	5.39	4	*0-143(143-0-0)/D-1	17	0.5
1992 Bos-A	49	180	16	42	2	0	2	18	18	19	2	3	.233	.310	.278	.588	62	-10	14	2.57	1	0-41(41-0-0)/D-6	1	-1.1
1993 Bos-A	146	540	77	170	38	6	13	72	54	46	5	4	.315	.381	.480	.861	122	17	95	6.46	2	*0-134(134-0-0),D-10	19	1.2
1994 Bos-A	95	327	60	88	25	1	11	45	38	26	2	2	.269	.352	.453	.805	101	-0	50	5.23	2	0-84(84-0-0)/D-6	8	-0.2
1995*Bos-A	120	481	67	143	25	4	15	76	38	35	9	5	.297	.351	.459	.811	105	3	72	5.35	-3	*0-118(118-0-0)/D-2	13	-0.5
1996 Bos-A	77	295	35	87	20	1	7	44	18	27	4	0	.295	.340	.441	.780	93	-3	42	5.07	2	0-76(75-1-1)	7	-0.4
Total 12	1269	4623	657	1400	275	38	130	726	460	364	80	43	.303	.371	.463	.834	120	126	777	6.09	-2	*0-1164/D-59,C-1	146	7.7

• GREENWOOD, Bill William F. Greenwood b: 1857, Philadelphia, PA d: 5/2/1902, Philadelphia, PA BB/TL, 5'7.5", 180 lbs. Deb: 9/16/1882 U Career OF: 1-0-8

YEAR TM-L	G	AB	R	H	2B	3B	HR	RBI	BB	SO	SB	CS	AVG	OBP	SLG	OPS	OPS+	BR/A	RC	RC/G	FR	G/POS	WS	TPW
1882 Phi-a	7	30	8	9	1	0	0	1	1	....	....	....	.300	.323	.333	.656	109	0	3	4.41	-1	/0-7(0-0-7),2-2	1	-0.1
1884 Bro-a	92	385	52	83	8	3	3	0	10	....	....	....	.216	.237	.275	.513	66	-15	26	2.35	-8	*2-92/S-1	5	-1.8
1887 Bal-a	118	549	114	184	16	6	0	65	54	....	71	....	.335	.336	.319	.656	88	-4	79	5.84	15	*2-117/0-1	15	1.1
1888 Bal-a	115	409	69	78	13	1	0	29	30	....	46	....	.191	.256	.227	.484	57	-18	36	2.98	-13	2-86,S-28/0-1	6	-2.6
1889 Col-a	118	414	62	93	7	10	3	49	58	71	37	....	.225	.327	.312	.639	86	-4	56	4.59	-10	*2-118	10	-0.9
1890 Roc-a	124	437	76	97	11	6	2	41	48	....	40	....	.222	.310	.288	.599	83	-7	53	4.12	3	*2-123/S-1	11	0.0
Total 6	574	2224	381	544	56	26	8	185	201	71	194	....	.245	.298	.287	.584	78	-49	253	4.04	-14	2-538/S-30,0-9	48	-4.2

• GREER, Brian Brian Keith Greer b: 5/14/1959, Lynwood, CA BR/TR, 6'3", 210 lbs. Deb: 9/13/1977

YEAR TM-L	G	AB	R	H	2B	3B	HR	RBI	BB	SO	SB	CS	AVG	OBP	SLG	OPS	OPS+	BR/A	RC	RC/G	FR	G/POS	WS	TPW
1977 SD-N	1	1	0	0	0	0	0	0	0	1	0	0	.000	.000	.000	.000	-112	-0	0	.00	0	....	0	0.0
1979 SD-N	4	3	0	0	0	0	0	0	0	1	0	0	.000	.000	.000	.000	-106	-1	0	.00	-1	/0-4(0-4-0)	0	-0.2
Total 2	5	4	0	0	0	0	0	0	0	2	0	0	.000	.000	.000	.000	-108	-1	0	.00	-1	/0-4	0	-0.2

• GREER, Ed Edward C. Greer b: 1865, Philadelphia, PA d: 2/4/1890, Philadelphia, PA BR Deb: 6/24/1885 Career OF: 87-107-11

YEAR TM-L	G	AB	R	H	2B	3B	HR	RBI	BB	SO	SB	CS	AVG	OBP	SLG	OPS	OPS+	BR/A	RC	RC/G	FR	G/POS	WS	TPW
1885 Bal-a	56	211	32	42	7	0	0	21	8	....	....	....	.199	.235	.232	.468	49	-12	12	1.89	-1	0-47(2-38-7),C-12	1	-1.3
1886 Bal-a	11	38	2	5	1	0	0	4	2	....	4	....	.132	.175	.158	.333	5	-4	2	1.47	1	/0-9(9-0-0),C-2	0	-0.3
Phi-a	71	264	33	51	5	3	1	20	8	....	12	....	.193	.223	.246	.469	46	-17	18	2.23	4	0-70(0-66-4)/C-1	2	-1.3
Yr.	82	302	35	56	6	3	1	24	10	....	16	....	.185	.217	.235	.452	41	-21	19	2.13	5	0-79(9-66-4)/C-3	2	-1.6
1887 Phi-a	3	11	1	2	0	0	0	0	0	....	2	....	.182	.182	.182	.364	2	-1	1	2.24	-0	/0-3(0-3-0)	0	-0.1
Bro-a	91	352	49	108	13	2	2	48	25	....	33	....	.307	.318	.324	.643	78	-10	45	5.02	-1	0-76(76-0-0),C-16	7	-0.9
Yr.	94	363	50	110	13	2	2	48	25	....	35	....	.303	.314	.320	.634	76	-11	46	4.92	-1	0-79(76-3-0),C-16	7	-1.1
Total 3	232	876	117	208	26	5	3	93	43	....	51	....	.237	.261	.268	.529	57	-44	77	3.12	3	0-205/C-31	10	-4.0

• GREER, Rusty Thurman Clyde "The Red Baron" Greer b: 1/21/1969, Fort Rucker, AL BL/TL, 6', 190 lbs. Deb: 5/16/1994 Career OF: 824-49-161

YEAR TM-L	G	AB	R	H	2B	3B	HR	RBI	BB	SO	SB	CS	AVG	OBP	SLG	OPS	OPS+	BR/A	RC	RC/G	FR	G/POS	WS	TPW
1994 Tex-A	80	277	36	87	16	1	10	46	46	46	0	0	.314	.415	.487	.903	132	15	60	8.12	-4	0-73(11-23-53)/1-9	12	0.7
1995 Tex-A	131	417	58	113	21	2	13	61	55	66	3	1	.271	.357	.424	.782	100	1	65	5.50	1	*0-125(51-4-101)/1-3	12	-0.4
1996*Tex-A	139	542	96	180	41	6	18	100	62	86	9	0	.332	.404	.530	.933	127	25	120	8.48	0	*0-137(136-1-0)/1-1,D-1	21	1.7
1997 Tex-A	157	601	112	193	42	3	26	87	83	87	9	5	.321	.406	.531	.937	135	33	132	8.35	-4	*0-153(148-19-1)/D-2	23	2.1
1998*Tex-A	155	598	107	183	31	5	16	108	80	93	2	4	.306	.391	.455	.846	115	14	106	6.42	-8	*0-154(154-2-0)	19	-0.1
1999*Tex-A	147	556	107	167	41	3	20	101	96	67	2	2	.300	.408	.493	.901	123	22	114	7.46	-5	*0-145(145-0-0)/D-1	24	1.0
2000 Tex-A	105	394	65	117	34	3	8	65	51	61	4	1	.297	.382	.459	.841	110	8	69	6.24	-7	0-97(97-0-0)/D-2	12	-0.4
2001 Tex-A	62	245	38	67	23	0	7	29	27	32	1	2	.273	.348	.453	.801	105	1	38	5.42	-2	0-60(60-0-0)/D-1	7	-0.4
2002 Tex-A	51	199	24	59	9	2	1	17	19	17	1	0	.296	.358	.377	.735	91	-2	27	4.99	-4	0-26(22-0-6),D-22/1-1	4	-0.9
Total 9	1027	3829	643	1166	258	25	119	614	519	555	31	15	.305	.391	.478	.869	118	117	731	7.00	-34	0-970/D-29,1-14	134	3.6

• GREGG, Tommy William Thomas Gregg b: 7/29/1963, Boone, NC BL/TL, 6'1", 190 lbs. Deb: 9/14/1987 Career OF: 47-15-96

YEAR TM-L	G	AB	R	H	2B	3B	HR	RBI	BB	SO	SB	CS	AVG	OBP	SLG	OPS	OPS+	BR/A	RC	RC/G	FR	G/POS	WS	TPW
1987 Pit-N	10	8	3	2	1	0	0	0	0	2	0	0	.250	.250	.375	.625	62	-0	0	.00	-1	/0-4(1-2-2)	0	-0.1
1988 Pit-N	14	15	4	3	1	0	1	3	1	4	0	1	.200	.250	.467	.717	103	-1	1	2.65	0	/0-6(5-0-1)	0	-0.1
Atl-N	11	29	1	10	3	0	0	4	2	2	0	0	.345	.387	.448	.835	133	1	5	6.35	1	/0-7(5-3-0)	1	0.3
Yr.	25	44	5	13	4	0	1	7	3	6	0	1	.295	.340	.455	.795	122	1	6	4.83	1	0-13(10-3-1)	1	0.2
1989 Atl-N	102	276	24	67	8	0	6	23	18	45	3	4	.243	.289	.337	.626	76	-10	26	3.18	-3	0-48(7-2-41),1-37	3	-1.8
1990 Atl-N	124	239	18	63	13	1	5	32	20	39	4	3	.264	.323	.389	.712	90	-4	31	4.57	-2	1-50,0-20(7-0-12)	5	-0.9
1991*Atl-N	72	107	13	20	8	1	1	4	12	24	2	2	.187	.275	.308	.583	60	-6	9	2.77	0	0-14(9-0-5),1-13	1	-0.7
1992 Atl-N	18	19	1	5	0	0	1	1	1	7	1	0	.263	.300	.421	.721	96	0	2	3.95	0	/0-9(2-4-4)	0	0.0
1993 Cin-N	10	12	1	2	0	0	0	1	0	0	0	0	.167	.167	.167	.333	-10	-2	0	.95	0	/0-4(3-0-1)	0	-0.2
1995 Fla-N	72	156	20	37	5	0	6	20	16	33	3	1	.237	.316	.385	.701	83	-4	19	4.19	-2	0-38(6-4-30)/1-2	3	-0.7
1997*Atl-N	13	19	1	5	2	0	0	0	1	2	1	1	.263	.300	.368	.668	72	-1	2	3.50	2	/0-6(2-0-0),1-1	0	0.0
Total 9	446	880	86	214	41	2	20	88	71	158	14	12	.243	.303	.363	.665	81	-27	96	3.70	-5	0-156,1-103	13	-4.3

• GREGORIO, Tom Thomas Andrew Gregorio b: 5/5/1977, Brooklyn, NY BR/TR, 6'2", 215 lbs. Deb: 9/5/2003

YEAR TM-L	G	AB	R	H	2B	3B	HR	RBI	BB	SO	SB	CS	AVG	OBP	SLG	OPS	OPS+	BR/A	RC	RC/G	FR	G/POS	WS	TPW
2003 Ana-A	12	19	1	3	0	0	0	2	1	8	0	0	.158	.238	.158	.396	8	-3	1	1.41	-1	C-12	0	-0.2

• GREMMINGER, Ed Lorenzo Edward "Battleship" Gremminger b: 3/30/1874, Canton, OH d: 5/26/1942, Canton, OH BR/TR, 6'1", 200 lbs. Deb: 4/21/1895

YEAR TM-L	G	AB	R	H	2B	3B	HR	RBI	BB	SO	SB	CS	AVG	OBP	SLG	OPS	OPS+	BR/A	RC	RC/G	FR	G/POS	WS	TPW
1895 Cle-N	20	78	10	21	1	0	0	15	5	13	0	....	.269	.313	.282	.595	51	-6	7	3.35	-1	3-20	1	-0.5
1902 Bos-N	140	522	55	134	20	12	1	65	39	....	7	....	.257	.314	.347	.661	103	1	61	4.13	4	*3-140	19	1.0
1903 Bos-N	140	511	57	135	24	9	5	56	31	....	12	....	.264	.313	.376	.688	100	-2	66	4.57	16	*3-140	17	1.7

YEAR TM-L	G	AB	R	H	2B	3B	HR	RBI	BB	SO	SB	CS	AVG	OBP	SLG	OPS	OPS+	BR/A	RC	RC/G	FR	G/POS	WS	TPW
1904 Det-A	83	309	18	66	13	3	1	28	14	....	3	....	.214	.257	.285	.542	73	-10	25	2.63	-12	3-83	4	-2.2
Total 4	383	1420	140	356	58	24	7	164	89	13	22	....	.251	.301	.340	.642	93	-16	160	3.90	7	3-383	41	0.0

• GREMP, Buddy Lewis Edward Gremp b: 8/5/1919, Denver, CO d: 1/30/1995, Manteca, CA BR/TR, 6'1", 175 lbs. Deb: 9/13/1940

YEAR TM-L	G	AB	R	H	2B	3B	HR	RBI	BB	SO	SB	CS	AVG	OBP	SLG	OPS	OPS+	BR/A	RC	RC/G	FR	G/POS	WS	TPW
1940 Bos-N	4	9	0	2	0	0	0	2	0	0	0	....	.222	.222	.222	.444	24	-1	0	.76	0	/1-3	0	-0.1
1941 Bos-N	37	75	7	18	3	0	0	10	5	3	0	....	.240	.288	.280	.568	63	-4	5	2.00	-5	1-21/2-6,C-3	0	-1.0
1942 Bos-N	72	207	12	45	11	0	3	19	13	21	1	....	.217	.267	.314	.581	71	-8	17	2.70	2	1-62/3-1	2	-1.2
Total 3	113	291	19	65	14	0	3	31	18	24	1	....	.223	.271	.302	.573	67	-13	22	2.44	-3	/1-86,2-6,C-3,3-1	2	-2.3

• GREY, Reddy Romer Carl Grey b: 4/8/1875, Zanesville, OH d: 11/8/1934, Altadena, CA BL/TL, 5'11", 175 lbs. Deb: 5/28/1903

YEAR TM-L	G	AB	R	H	2B	3B	HR	RBI	BB	SO	SB	CS	AVG	OBP	SLG	OPS	OPS+	BR/A	RC	RC/G	FR	G/POS	WS	TPW
1903 Pit-N	1	3	1	1	0	0	0	1	1	....	0	....	.333	.500	.333	.833	135	0	1	6.79	0	/0-1	0	0.0

• GRICH, Bobby Robert Anthony Grich b: 1/15/1949, Muskegon, MI BR/TR, 6'2", 190 lbs. Deb: 6/29/1970

YEAR TM-L	G	AB	R	H	2B	3B	HR	RBI	BB	SO	SB	CS	AVG	OBP	SLG	OPS	OPS+	BR/A	RC	RC/G	FR	G/POS	WS	TPW
1970 Bal-A	30	95	11	20	1	3	0	8	9	21	1	1	.211	.279	.284	.563	55	-6	7	2.58	2	S-20/2-9,3-1	2	-0.2
1971 Bal-A	7	30	7	9	0	0	1	6	5	8	1	0	.300	.400	.400	.800	128	2	6	7.11	4	/S-5,2-2	2	0.7
1972 Bal-A★	133	460	66	128	21	3	12	50	53	96	13	6	.278	.362	.415	.777	127	17	71	5.45	9	S-81,2-45,1-16/3-8	23	4.1
1973*Bal-A	162	581	82	146	29	7	12	50	107	91	17	9	.251	.374	.387	.761	116	17	92	5.48	32	*2-162	28	**6.2**
1974*Bal-A★	160	582	92	153	29	6	19	82	90	117	17	11	.263	.380	.431	.811	137	32	99	5.67	10	*2-160	32	5.5
1975 Bal-A	150	524	81	136	26	4	13	57	107	88	14	10	.260	.393	.399	.792	133	28	90	5.73	25	*2-150	29	**6.4**
1976 Bal-A★	144	518	93	138	31	4	13	54	86	99	14	6	.266	.374	.417	.791	140	30	87	5.82	8	*2-140/3-2,D-2	31	5.0
1977 Cal-A	52	181	24	44	6	0	7	23	37	40	6	6	.243	.374	.392	.767	114	4	27	4.76	0	S-52	7	1.0
1978 Cal-A	144	487	68	122	16	2	6	42	75	83	4	3	.251	.359	.329	.687	98	3	64	4.38	14	*2-144	20	2.5
1979*Cal-A★	153	534	78	157	30	5	30	101	59	84	1	0	.294	.366	.537	.904	145	33	103	6.88	22	*2-153	28	6.1
1980 Cal-A★	150	498	60	135	22	2	14	62	84	108	3	7	.271	.381	.408	.788	119	14	78	5.31	21	*2-146/1-3	20	4.3
1981 Cal-A	100	352	56	107	14	2	**22**	61	40	71	2	4	.304	.381	**.543**	.924	**164**	27	73	7.48	12	*2-100	21	**4.7**
1982*Cal-A★	145	506	74	132	28	5	19	65	82	109	3	3	.261	.372	.449	.821	124	19	87	5.90	5	*2-142/D-1	21	3.2
1983 Cal-A	120	387	65	113	17	0	16	62	76	62	2	4	.292	.417	.460	.877	142	26	77	7.05	0	*2-118/S-1	20	3.3
1984 Cal-A	116	363	60	93	15	1	18	58	57	70	2	5	.256	.360	.452	.812	124	12	58	5.31	4	2-91,1-25,3-21	16	1.9
1985 Cal-A	144	479	74	116	17	3	13	53	81	77	3	5	.242	.355	.372	.727	100	1	63	4.35	23	*2-116,1-16,3-15/D-6	18	2.9
1986*Cal-A	98	313	42	84	18	0	9	30	39	54	1	3	.268	.355	.412	.767	109	4	45	4.87	1	2-87,1-11/3-2	11	0.8
Total 17	2008	6890	1033	1833	320	47	224	864	1087	1278	104	83	.266	.373	.424	.796	125	263	1129	5.59	190	*2-1765,S-159/1-71,3-49,D-9	329	58.2

• GRIESENBECK, Tim Carlos Phillipe Timothy Griesenbeck b: 12/10/1897, San Antonio, TX d: 3/25/1953, San Antonio, TX BR/TR, 5'10.5", 190 lbs. Deb: 9/11/1920

YEAR TM-L	G	AB	R	H	2B	3B	HR	RBI	BB	SO	SB	CS	AVG	OBP	SLG	OPS	OPS+	BR/A	RC	RC/G	FR	G/POS	WS	TPW
1920 StL-N	5	3	1	1	0	0	0	0	0	0	0	0	.333	.333	.333	.667	94	-0	0	4.24	-1	/C-3	0	-0.1

• GRIEVE, Ben Benjamin Grieve b: 5/4/1976, Arlington, TX BL/TR, 6'4", 220 lbs. Deb: 9/3/1997 Career OF: 331-0-375

YEAR TM-L	G	AB	R	H	2B	3B	HR	RBI	BB	SO	SB	CS	AVG	OBP	SLG	OPS	OPS+	BR/A	RC	RC/G	FR	G/POS	WS	TPW
1997 Oak-A	24	93	12	29	6	0	3	24	13	25	0	0	.312	.402	.473	.875	130	5	19	7.62	-1	0-24(0-0-24)	4	0.2
1998 Oak-A★	155	583	94	168	41	2	18	89	85	123	2	2	.288	.387	.458	.845	122	21	104	6.46	-10	*0-151(0-0-151)/D-3	22	0.3
1999 Oak-A	148	486	80	129	21	0	28	86	63	108	4	0	.265	.359	.481	.841	117	13	83	6.01	-1	*0-137(131-0-8)/D-4	16	0.7
2000*Oak-A	158	594	92	166	40	1	27	104	73	130	3	0	.279	.361	.487	.848	115	14	97	5.64	-8	*0-144(144-0-0),D-12	17	-0.1
2001 TB-A	154	542	72	143	30	2	11	72	87	159	7	1	.264	.374	.387	.761	103	7	84	5.45	-4	*0-120(56-0-64),D-32	17	-0.5
2002 TB-A	136	482	62	121	30	0	19	64	69	121	8	2	.251	.354	.432	.786	109	9	75	5.32	-3	*0-118(0-0-118),D-16	12	-0.1
2003 TB-A	55	165	28	38	7	0	4	17	32	41	0	0	.230	.374	.345	.720	93	0	24	4.93	0	D-37,0-10(0-0-10)	2	-0.2
Total 7	830	2945	440	794	175	5	110	456	422	707	24	5	.270	.369	.444	.814	112	68	486	5.79	-27	0-704,D-104	90	0.1

• GRIEVE, Tom Thomas Alan Grieve b: 3/4/1948, Pittsfield, MA BR/TR, 6'2", 190 lbs. Deb: 7/5/1970 Career OF: 253-16-135

YEAR TM-L	G	AB	R	H	2B	3B	HR	RBI	BB	SO	SB	CS	AVG	OBP	SLG	OPS	OPS+	BR/A	RC	RC/G	FR	G/POS	WS	TPW
1970 Was-A	47	116	12	23	5	1	3	10	14	38	0	0	.198	.290	.336	.626	76	-4	12	3.48	-2	0-39(15-1-24)	1	-0.7
1972 Tex-A	64	142	12	29	2	1	3	11	11	39	1	3	.204	.271	.296	.567	72	-6	11	2.55	1	0-49(45-3-5)	2	-0.8
1973 Tex-A	66	123	22	38	6	0	7	21	7	25	1	0	.309	.351	.528	.880	151	8	22	6.23	-1	0-59(34-10-19)/D-1	5	0.5
1974 Tex-A	84	259	30	66	10	4	9	32	20	48	0	0	.255	.313	.429	.742	115	4	33	4.26	4	D-40,0-38(31-0-7)/1-1	7	0.5
1975 Tex-A	118	369	46	102	17	1	14	61	22	74	0	2	.276	.317	.442	.759	114	4	48	4.55	0	0-63(46-2-16),D-45	10	0.0
1976 Tex-A	149	546	57	139	23	3	20	81	35	119	4	1	.255	.304	.418	.722	108	3	65	4.00	1	D-96,0-52(45-0-8)	13	-0.2
1977 Tex-A	79	236	24	53	9	0	7	30	13	57	1	0	.225	.274	.352	.626	68	-10	23	3.22	1	0-60(30-0-32),D-13	3	-1.2
1978 NY-N	54	101	5	21	3	0	2	8	9	23	0	1	.208	.273	.297	.570	61	-6	8	2.46	2	0-26(2-0-24)/1-2	1	-0.5
1979 StL-N	9	15	1	3	1	0	0	0	4	1	0	0	.200	.368	.267	.635	75	-0	2	3.96	-1	/0-5(5-0-0)	0	-0.1
Total 9	670	1907	209	474	76	10	65	254	135	424	7	7	.249	.303	.401	.704	100	-7	224	3.95	5	0-391,D-195/1-3	42	-2.5

• GRIFFEY, Ken George Kenneth "Junior,Kid" Griffey, Jr. b: 11/21/1969, Donora, PA BL/TL, 6'3", 205 lbs. Deb: 4/3/1989 Career OF: 3-1813-3

YEAR TM-L	G	AB	R	H	2B	3B	HR	RBI	BB	SO	SB	CS	AVG	OBP	SLG	OPS	OPS+	BR/A	RC	RC/G	FR	G/POS	WS	TPW
1989 Sea-A	127	455	61	120	23	0	16	61	44	83	16	7	.264	.331	.420	.751	107	4	65	4.99	4	*0-127(0-127-0)	14	0.6
1990 Sea-A★	155	597	91	179	28	7	22	80	63	81	16	11	.300	.369	.481	.849	134	26	103	6.27	-3	*0-151(0-151-0)/D-2	24	2.1
1991 Sea-A★	154	548	76	179	42	1	22	100	71	82	18	6	.327	.405	.527	.932	156	44	118	8.02	8	*0-152(0-152-0)/D-1	30	5.0
1992 Sea-A★	142	565	83	174	39	4	27	103	44	67	10	5	.308	.363	.535	.898	148	34	104	6.81	2	*0-137(0-137-0)/D-3	25	3.3
1993 Sea-A★	156	582	113	180	38	3	45	109	96	91	17	9	.309	.412	.617	1.029	170	59	147	9.17	-1	*0-139(0-139-0),D-19/1-1	29	5.6
1994 Sea-A★	111	433	94	140	24	4	**40**	90	56	73	11	3	.323	.403	.674	1.078	168	44	117	10.25	4	*0-103(0-103-1)/D-9	20	4.4
1995*Sea-A★	72	260	52	67	7	0	17	42	52	53	4	2	.258	.381	.481	.862	121	9	50	6.77	2	0-70(0-70-0)/D-2	9	1.1
1996 Sea-A★	140	545	125	165	26	2	49	140	78	104	16	1	.303	.397	.628	1.024	154	47	142	9.65	1	*0-137(0-137-0)/D-5	28	4.5
1997*Sea-A★	157	608	**125**	185	34	3	**56**	**147**	76	121	15	4	.304	.389	**.646**	1.035	165	59	152	9.10	4	*0-153(1-153-0)/D-4	36	**6.0**
1998 Sea-A★	161	633	120	180	33	3	**56**	146	76	121	20	5	.284	.367	.611	.979	148	45	142	8.04	7	*0-158(1-158-1)/D-3,1-1	29	5.0
1999 Sea-A★	160	606	123	173	26	3	**48**	134	91	108	24	7	.285	.385	.576	.961	138	37	139	8.35	-1	*0-158(0-158-0)/D-6	31	3.4
2000 Cin-N★	145	520	100	141	22	3	40	118	94	117	6	4	.271	.392	.556	.947	133	27	118	7.98	2	*0-141(0-141-0)	24	2.9
2001 Cin-N	111	364	57	104	20	2	22	65	44	72	2	0	.286	.369	.533	.902	124	14	72	7.12	-10	0-90(0-90-0)/D-2	14	0.4
2002 Cin-N	70	197	17	52	8	0	8	23	28	39	1	2	.264	.364	.426	.790	105	1	30	5.18	-5	0-55(1-54-1)	5	-0.3
2003 Cin-N	53	166	34	41	12	1	13	26	27	44	1	0	.247	.372	.566	.938	143	11	36	7.54	-3	0-43(0-43-0)/D-3	6	0.7
Total 15	1914	7079	1271	2080	382	36	481	1384	940	1256	177	66	.294	.382	.562	.944	144	460	1535	7.85	11	*0-1814/D-59,1-2	324	44.8

• GRIFFEY, Ken George Kenneth Griffey, Sr. b: 4/10/1950, Donora, PA BL/TL, 5'11", 200 lbs. Deb: 8/25/1973 C Career OF: 532-203-989

YEAR TM-L	G	AB	R	H	2B	3B	HR	RBI	BB	SO	SB	CS	AVG	OBP	SLG	OPS	OPS+	BR/A	RC	RC/G	FR	G/POS	WS	TPW
1973*Cin-N	25	86	19	33	5	1	3	14	6	10	4	2	.384	.424	.570	.994	183	9	21	10.39	0	0-21(0-0-21)	6	0.9
1974 Cin-N	88	227	24	57	9	5	2	19	27	43	9	4	.251	.333	.361	.695	96	-1	29	4.42	1	0-70(2-0-68)	7	-0.4
1975*Cin-N	132	463	95	141	15	9	4	46	67	67	16	7	.305	.394	.402	.795	119	15	77	5.96	-5	*0-119(0-0-119)	18	0.5
1976*Cin-N★	148	562	111	189	28	9	6	74	62	65	34	11	.336	.403	.450	.853	139	33	109	7.57	-8	*0-144(0-0-144)	25	1.9
1977 Cin-N★	154	585	117	186	35	8	12	57	69	84	17	8	.318	.390	.467	.857	126	24	108	6.88	-1	*0-147(0-0-147)	23	1.6
1978 Cin-N	158	614	90	177	33	8	10	63	54	70	23	5	.288	.346	.417	.763	112	12	93	5.47	-5	*0-154(0-13-142)	22	0.0
1979 Cin-N	95	380	62	120	27	4	8	32	36	39	12	5	.316	.376	.471	.848	129	16	68	6.63	-3	0-93(0-8-92)	16	0.9
1980 Cin-N★	146	544	89	160	28	10	13	85	62	77	23	1	.294	.367	.454	.821	128	25	99	6.71	-7	*0-138(0-2-138)	25	1.2
1981 Cin-N	101	396	65	123	21	6	2	34	39	42	12	4	.311	.374	.409	.783	120	12	61	5.65	0	0-99(0-99-0)	19	1.1
1982 NY-A	127	484	70	134	23	2	12	54	39	58	10	4	.277	.331	.407	.738	103	2	65	4.74	1	*0-125(0-26-102)	13	-0.2
1983 NY-A	118	458	60	140	21	3	11	46	34	45	6	1	.306	.356	.437	.793	121	14	74	6.10	-4	*1-101,0-14(2-12-1)/D-2	17	0.3
1984 NY-A	120	399	44	109	20	1	7	56	29	32	2	2	.273	.324	.381	.705	98	-2	49	4.31	-6	0-82(38-35-9),1-27/D-2	9	-1.2
1985 NY-A	127	438	68	120	28	4	10	69	41	51	7	7	.274	.336	.425	.761	109	4	63	5.12	3	*0-110(106-5-1)/D-7,1-1	14	0.1
1986 NY-A	59	198	33	60	7	0	9	26	15	24	2	2	.303	.355	.475	.830	125	6	31	5.53	0	0-51(50-2-1)/D-2	6	0.4
Atl-N	80	292	36	90	15	3	12	32	20	43	12	7	.308	.353	.503	.856	126	9	51	6.49	-2	0-77(77-0-0)/1-1	11	0.3
1987 Atl-N	122	399	65	114	24	1	14	64	46	54	4	7	.286	.361	.456	.817	109	3	62	5.39	-2	*0-107(107-1-0)/1-3	10	-0.4
1988 Atl-N	69	193	21	48	5	0	2	19	17	26	1	3	.249	.310	.306	.615	74	-8	17	3.02	-1	0-42(41-0-2),1-11	2	-1.1
Cin-N	25	50	5	14	1	0	2	4	2	5	0	0	.280	.308	.420	.728	103	-0	7	4.91	0	1-10	1	0.0
Yr.	94	243	26	62	6	0	4	23	19	31	1	3	.255	.309	.329	.638	79	-8	24	3.37	-1	0-42(41-0-2),1-21	3	-1.1
1989 Cin-N	106	236	26	62	8	3	8	30	29	42	4	2	.263	.346	.424	.770	115	5	36	5.47	-2	0-58(58-0-1)/1-9	8	0.2
1990 Cin-N	46	63	6	13	2	0	1	8	2	5	2	1	.206	.242	.286	.528	43	-5	5	2.34	0	/1-9,0-6(5-0-1)	0	-0.6
Sea-A	21	77	13	29	2	0	3	18	10	3	0	0	.377	.448	.519	.968	168	7	19	10.05	-1	0-20(20-0-0)	4	0.6
1991 Sea-A	30	85	10	24	7	0	1	9	13	13	0	0	.282	.384	.400	.784	117	3	14	5.80	0	0-26(26-0-0)/D-1	3	0.2
Total 19	2097	7229	1129	2143	364	77	152	859	719	898	200	83	.296	.361	.431	.792	117	182	1156	5.82	-39	*0-1703,1-172/D-14	259	6.4

YEAR TM-L	G	AB	R	H	2B	3B	HR	RBI	BB	SO	SB	CS	AVG	OBP	SLG	OPS	OPS+	BR/A	RC	RC/G	FR	G/POS	WS	TPW
• GRIFFIN, Alfredo	Alfredo Claudino Griffin b: 10/6/1957, Santo Domingo, Dominican Republic BB/TR, 5'11", 165 lbs. Deb: 9/4/1976 C																							
1976 Cle-A	12	4	0	1	0	0	0	0	0	2	0	1	.250	.250	.250	.500	47	-1	0	.00	-3	/S-6,D-4	0	-0.3
1977 Cle-A	14	41	5	6	1	0	0	3	3	5	2	2	.146	.205	.171	.375	4	-6	1	.85	-2	S-13/D-1	0	-0.7
1978 Cle-A	5	4	1	2	1	0	0	0	2	1	0	0	.500	.667	.750	1.417	301	1	2	31.68	1	/S-2	1	0.3
1979 Tor-A	153	624	81	179	22	10	2	31	40	59	21	16	.287	.335	.364	.699	87	-13	75	4.11	3	*S-153	14	0.5
1980 Tor-A	155	653	63	166	26	**15**	2	41	24	58	18	23	.254	.285	.349	.634	69	-35	59	2.99	-4	*S-155	9	-2.2
1981 Tor-A	101	388	30	81	19	6	0	21	17	38	8	12	.209	.244	.289	.533	50	-29	24	1.98	-6	S-97/3-4,2-1	3	-2.6
1982 Tor-A	162	539	57	130	20	8	1	48	22	48	10	8	.241	.271	.314	.584	55	-35	45	2.75	8	*S-162	10	-1.1
1983 Tor-A	162	528	62	132	22	9	4	47	27	44	8	11	.250	.290	.348	.639	71	-25	52	3.29	6	*S-157/2-5,D-1	11	-0.3
1984 Tor-A★	140	419	53	101	8	2	4	30	4	33	11	3	.241	.250	.298	.548	49	-28	31	2.46	-2	*S-115,2-21/D-5	6	-1.9
1985 Oak-A	162	614	75	166	18	7	2	64	20	50	24	9	.270	.293	.332	.626	77	-20	60	3.43	18	*S-162	16	1.5
1986 Oak-A	162	594	74	169	23	6	4	51	35	52	33	16	.285	.326	.364	.690	95	-5	71	4.16	1	*S-162	17	1.3
1987 Oak-A	144	494	69	130	23	5	3	60	28	41	26	13	.263	.308	.348	.656	79	-16	52	3.52	6	*S-137/2-1	11	0.5
1988*LA-N	95	316	39	63	8	3	1	27	24	30	7	5	.199	.260	.253	.513	49	-22	22	2.15	4	S-93	6	-1.1
1989 LA-N	136	506	49	125	27	2	0	29	29	57	10	7	.247	.288	.308	.596	72	-20	45	3.02	0	*S-131	11	-1.1
1990 LA-N	141	461	38	97	11	3	1	35	29	65	6	3	.210	.260	.254	.514	43	-36	31	2.21	14	*S-139	6	-1.3
1991 LA-N	109	350	27	85	6	2	0	27	22	49	5	4	.243	.290	.271	.561	60	-19	28	2.63	6	*S-109	9	-0.4
1992*Tor-A	63	150	21	35	7	0	0	10	9	19	3	1	.233	.277	.280	.557	54	-9	12	2.58	-3	S-48,2-16	3	-0.9
1993*Tor-A	46	95	15	20	3	0	0	3	3	13	0	0	.211	.235	.242	.477	28	-10	5	1.67	-2	S-20,2-11/3-6	1	-0.9
Total 18	1962	6780	759	1688	245	78	24	527	338	664	192	134	.249	.287	.319	.606	67	-328	616	3.03	45	*S-1861/2-55,D-11,3-10	134	-10.8
• GRIFFIN, Doug	Douglas Lee Griffin b: 6/4/1947, South Gate, CA BR/TR, 6', 170 lbs. Deb: 9/11/1970																							
1970 Cal-A	18	55	2	7	1	0	0	4	6	5	0	0	.127	.213	.145	.359	1	-7	2	.82	2	2-11/3-8	1	-0.5
1971 Bos-A	125	483	51	118	23	2	3	27	31	45	11	5	.244	.293	.319	.611	68	-20	44	3.03	9	*2-124	10	-0.3
1972 Bos-A	129	470	43	122	12	1	2	35	45	48	9	2	.260	.327	.302	.629	83	-7	50	3.59	-2	*2-129	14	0.0
1973 Bos-A	113	396	43	101	14	5	1	33	21	42	7	5	.255	.298	.323	.621	71	-16	36	2.97	-4	*2-113	7	-1.3
1974 Bos-A	93	312	35	83	12	4	0	33	28	21	2	8	.266	.330	.330	.661	84	-8	32	3.46	0	2-91/S-1	7	-0.3
1975*Bos-A	100	287	21	69	6	0	1	29	18	29	2	2	.240	.290	.272	.562	55	-17	22	2.53	-16	2-99/S-1	2	-2.8
1976 Bos-A	49	127	14	24	2	0	0	4	9	14	2	1	.189	.248	.205	.453	30	-11	7	1.57	-5	2-44/D-2	1	-1.5
1977 Bos-A	5	6	0	0	0	0	0	0	0	0	0	0	.000	.000	.000	.000	-89	-2	0	.00	0	/2-3	0	-0.1
Total 8	632	2136	209	524	70	12	7	165	158	204	33	23	.245	.301	.299	.600	68	-88	193	2.96	-16	2-614/3-8,D-2,S-2	42	-6.7
• GRIFFIN, Ivy	Ivy Moore Griffin b: 11/16/1896, Thomasville, AL d: 8/25/1957, Gainesville, FL BL/TR, 5'11", 180 lbs. Deb: 9/9/1919																							
1919 Phi-A	17	68	5	20	2	2	0	6	3	10	0	....	.294	.333	.382	.716	99	-0	8	4.43	4	1-17	1	0.3
1920 Phi-A	129	467	46	111	15	1	0	20	17	49	3	3	.238	.281	.274	.555	47	-35	37	2.63	2	*1-127/2-2	2	-3.4
1921 Phi-A	39	103	14	33	4	2	0	13	5	6	1	2	.320	.369	.398	.767	95	-1	15	5.29	-1	1-27	1	-0.4
Total 3	185	638	65	164	21	5	0	39	25	65	4	5	.257	.301	.306	.607	60	-36	60	3.20	4	1-171/2-2	4	-3.5
• GRIFFIN, Mike	Michael Joseph Griffin b: 3/20/1865, Utica, NY d: 4/10/1908, Utica, NY BL/TR, 5'7", 160 lbs. Deb: 4/16/1887 M Career OF: 7-1459-14																							
1887 Bal-a	136	587	142	215	32	13	3	94	55	....	94	....	.366	.375	.427	.801	131	24	123	8.95	-13	*O-136(1-135-0)	20	0.5
1888 Bal-a	137	542	103	139	21	11	0	46	55	....	46	....	.256	.331	.336	.666	117	12	77	5.18	-2	*O-137(0-137-0)	18	0.5
1889 Bal-a	137	531	**152**	148	21	14	4	48	91	29	39	....	.279	.387	.394	.781	125	22	98	6.81	-17	*O-109(0-109-0),S-25/2-5	23	0.2
1890 Phi-P	115	489	127	140	29	6	6	54	64	19	30	....	.286	.377	.407	.784	107	5	88	6.84	11	*O-115(4-100-13)	17	0.9
1891 Bro-N	134	521	106	139	**36**	9	3	65	57	31	65	....	.267	.340	.388	.728	112	8	93	6.58	12	*O-134(2-132-0)	19	1.3
1892 Bro-N	129	452	103	125	17	11	3	66	68	36	49	....	.277	.376	.383	.759	134	22	86	7.06	9	*O-127(0-126-1)/S-2	23	2.0
1893 Bro-N	95	362	85	103	21	7	6	59	59	23	30	....	.285	.396	.431	.827	125	16	76	7.73	6	*O-93(0-93-0)/2-2	17	1.3
1894 Bro-N	108	406	123	145	29	4	5	76	78	14	39	....	.357	.465	.485	.950	139	33	113	11.21	0	*O-106(0-106-0)	20	2.0
1895 Bro-N	132	524	140	174	38	7	4	65	93	30	27	....	.332	.442	.454	.896	146	44	124	9.40	10	*O-131(0-131-0)/S-1	29	3.7
1896 Bro-N	122	493	101	152	27	9	4	51	48	25	23	....	.308	.380	.424	.804	118	14	91	6.96	2	*O-122(0-122-0)	17	0.7
1897 Bro-N	134	534	136	169	25	11	2	56	81	....	16	....	.316	.416	.416	.832	127	26	103	7.26	1	*O-134(0-134-0)	22	1.6
1898 Bro-N	134	537	88	161	18	6	2	40	60	....	15	....	.300	.379	.367	.745	114	12	83	5.77	9	*O-134(0-134-0)	20	1.1
Total 12	1513	5978	1406	1810	314	108	42	720	809	207	473	....	.303	.388	.407	.795	125	239	1155	7.35	28	*O-1478/S-28,2-7	245	15.9
• GRIFFIN, Pug	Francis Arthur Griffin b: 4/24/1896, Lincoln, NE d: 10/12/1951, Colorado Springs, CO BR/TR, 5'11.5", 187 lbs. Deb: 7/27/1917																							
1917 Phi-A	18	25	4	5	1	0	1	3	1	9	1	....	.200	.231	.360	.591	81	-1	2	2.70	1	/1-3	0	0.0
1920 NY-N	5	4	0	1	0	0	0	0	1	2	0	0	.250	.400	.250	.650	90	0	0	4.27	-1	/O-2(0-1-1)	0	-0.1
Total 2	23	29	4	6	1	0	1	3	2	11	1	0	.207	.258	.345	.603	83	-1	3	2.90	0	/1-3,O-2	0	-0.1
• GRIFFIN, Sandy	Tobias Charles Griffin b: 10/24/1858, Fayetteville, NY d: 6/4/1926, Syracuse, NY BR/TR, 5'10", 160 lbs. Deb: 5/26/1884 M Career OF: 23-132-11																							
1884 NY-N	16	62	7	11	2	0	0	6	1	19	....	....	.177	.190	.210	.400	25	-5	3	1.37	-2	O-16(0-5-11)	0	-0.7
1890 Roc-a	107	407	85	125	28	4	5	53	50	....	21	....	.307	.388	.432	.821	153	28	78	7.37	-20	*O-107(0-107-0)/2-1	18	0.4
1891 Was-a	20	69	15	19	4	2	0	10	10	3	2	....	.275	.398	.391	.789	132	4	12	6.26	-2	O-20(0-20-0)	2	0.1
1893 StL-N	23	92	9	18	1	1	0	9	16	2	2	....	.196	.315	.228	.543	45	-7	7	2.66	-2	O-23(23-0-0)	1	-0.9
Total 4	166	630	116	173	35	7	5	78	77	24	25	....	.275	.361	.376	.737	123	20	100	5.81	-26	O-166/2-1	21	-1.1
• GRIFFIN, Thomas	Thomas William Griffin b: 1/1857, Titusville, PA d: 4/17/1933, Rockford, IL Deb: 9/27/1884																							
1884 Mil-U	11	41	5	9	2	0	0	....	3	....	....	....	.220	.273	.268	.541	83	-1	3	2.69	-1	1-11	1	-0.2
• GRIFFITH, Bert	Bartholomew Joseph "Buck" Griffith b: 3/30/1896, St. Louis, MO d: 5/5/1973, Bishop, CA BR/TR, 5'11", 185 lbs. Deb: 4/13/1922 Career OF: 51-19-72																							
1922 Bro-N	106	325	45	100	22	8	2	35	5	11	5	7	.308	.322	.443	.765	96	-5	43	4.68	1	O-77(0-8-69)/1-6	8	-0.9
1923 Bro-N	79	248	23	73	8	4	2	37	13	16	1	2	.294	.332	.383	.715	91	-4	31	4.51	-3	O-62(51-9-3)	5	-1.1
1924 Was-A	6	8	1	1	0	0	0	0	0	1	0	0	.125	.125	.125	.250	-37	-2	0	.53	0	/O-2(0-2-0)	0	-0.1
Total 3	191	581	69	174	30	12	4	72	18	28	6	9	.299	.324	.413	.737	92	-10	74	4.53	-2	O-141/1-6	13	-2.1
• GRIFFITH, Derrell	Robert Derrell Griffith b: 12/12/1943, Anadarko, OK BL/TR, 6', 168 lbs. Deb: 9/26/1963 Career OF: 21-1-26																							
1963 LA-N	1	2	0	0	0	0	0	0	0	0	0	0	.000	.000	.000	.000	-107	-1	0	.00	-1	/2-1	0	-0.1
1964 LA-N	78	238	27	69	16	2	4	23	5	21	5	1	.290	.307	.424	.732	112	3	29	4.20	-9	3-35,O-29(6-0-23)	7	-0.7
1965 LA-N	22	41	3	7	0	0	1	2	0	9	0	0	.171	.171	.244	.415	16	-5	1	1.13	0	O-11(10-0-1)	0	-0.6
1966 LA-N	23	15	3	1	0	0	0	2	2	3	0	0	.067	.176	.067	.243	-32	-3	0	.46	0	/O-7(5-1-2)	0	-0.3
Total 4	124	296	33	77	16	2	5	27	7	33	5	1	.260	.280	.378	.658	90	-4	31	3.48	-9	/O-47,3-35,2-1	7	-1.7
• GRIFFITH, Tommy	Thomas Herman Griffith b: 10/26/1889, Prospect, OH d: 4/13/1967, Cincinnati, OH BL/TR, 5'10", 175 lbs. Deb: 8/28/1913 Career OF: 7-4-1326																							
1913 Bos-N	37	127	16	32	4	1	1	12	9	8	1	....	.252	.301	.323	.624	77	-4	12	3.20	1	O-35(0-0-35)	3	-0.5
1914 Bos-N	16	48	3	5	0	0	0	1	2	6	0	....	.104	.140	.104	.244	-27	-8	1	.37	3	O-14(1-0-14)	0	-0.5
1915 Cin-N	160	583	59	179	31	16	4	85	41	34	6	24	.307	.355	.436	.790	136	14	85	5.00	-12	*O-160(2-0-160)	20	-0.7
1916 Cin-N	155	595	50	158	28	7	2	61	36	37	16	....	.266	.310	.346	.656	104	1	69	4.04	2	*O-155(0-0-155)	13	-0.5
1917 Cin-N	115	363	45	98	18	7	1	45	19	23	5	....	.270	.308	.366	.674	111	3	41	3.88	4	*O-100(0-0-100)	11	0.3
1918 Cin-N	118	427	47	113	10	4	2	48	39	30	10	....	.265	.326	.321	.647	99	0	47	3.73	-3	*O-118(0-0-118)	11	-1.0
1919 Bro-N	125	484	65	136	18	4	6	57	23	32	8	....	.281	.315	.372	.687	104	1	57	4.11	-3	*O-125(0-0-125)	14	-1.0
1920*Bro-N	93	334	41	87	9	4	2	30	15	18	3	3	.260	.292	.329	.622	76	-10	32	3.22	-6	O-92(0-0-92)	6	-2.2
1921 Bro-N	129	455	66	142	21	6	12	71	36	13	3	3	.312	.364	.464	.828	113	10	77	6.10	13	*O-124(0-0-124)	17	1.3
1922 Bro-N	99	329	44	104	17	8	4	49	23	10	7	1	.316	.361	.453	.814	110	6	55	6.09	2	O-82(0-0-82)	12	0.1
1923 Bro-N	131	481	70	141	21	9	8	66	50	19	8	2	.293	.361	.424	.785	109	9	76	5.68	-4	*O-127(0-0-127)	14	-0.5
1924 Bro-N	140	482	43	121	19	5	3	67	34	19	0	5	.251	.300	.330	.630	71	-21	48	3.31	-7	*O-139(0-0-139)	7	-3.7
1925 Bro-N	7	4	2	0	0	0	0	0	3	2	1	0	.000	.429	.000	.429	20	0	1	3.52	0	/O-2(0-0-2)	0	0.0
Chi-N	76	235	38	67	12	1	7	27	21	11	2	4	.285	.346	.434	.780	97	-2	35	5.19	-2	O-60(4-4-53)	6	-0.9
Yr.	83	239	40	67	12	1	7	27	24	13	3	4	.280	.348	.427	.775	95	-2	35	5.15	-2	O-62(4-4-55)	6	-0.9
Total 13	1401	4947	589	1383	208	72	52	619	351	262	70	42	.280	.328	.382	.711	102	1	634	4.45	-13	*O-1333	134	-9.8

• GRIGGS, Art Arthur Carle Griggs b: 12/10/1883, Topeka, KS d: 12/19/1938, Los Angeles, CA BR/TR, 5'11", 185 lbs. Deb: 5/2/1909 Career OF: 44-2-50

YEAR TM-L	G	AB	R	H	2B	3B	HR	RBI	BB	SO	SB	CS	AVG	OBP	SLG	OPS	OPS+	BR/A	RC	RC/G	FR	G/POS	WS	TPW
1909 StL-A	108	364	38	102	17	5	0	43	24	....	11	....	.280	.330	.354	.684	125	10	46	4.38	-6	1-49,0-41(36-2-3)/2-8,S-1	14	0.0
1910 StL-A	123	416	28	98	22	5	2	30	25	....	11	....	.236	.281	.327	.607	96	-4	40	3.21	-7	0-49(6-0-43),2-41,1-17/3-3,S	9	-1.4
1911 Cle-A	27	68	7	17	3	2	1	7	5	....	1	....	.250	.301	.397	.698	93	-1	8	4.11	-1	2-11/0-4(1-0-3),3-3,1-1	1	-0.2
1912 Cle-A	89	273	29	83	16	7	0	39	33	....	10	....	.304	.381	.414	.795	123	9	47	6.16	-2	1-71	9	0.5
1914 Bro-F	40	112	10	32	6	1	1	15	5	11	1	....	.286	.328	.384	.712	101	-0	14	4.29	-3	1-27/0-1	3	-0.3
1915 Bro-F	27	38	4	11	1	0	1	2	3	7	0	....	.289	.372	.395	.767	128	1	5	5.12	0	/1-5,0-1	1	0.2
1918 Det-A	28	99	11	36	8	0	0	16	10	5	2	....	.364	.422	.444	.866	168	8	19	7.37	-1	1-25	6	0.7
Total 7	**442**	**1370**	**127**	**379**	**73**	**20**	**5**	**152**	**105**	**23**	**36**	**....**	**.277**	**.332**	**.370**	**.702**	**116**	**23**	**179**	**4.54**	**-20**	**1-195/0-96,2-60,3-6,S-4**	**43**	**-0.5**

• GRIGSBY, Denver Denver Clarence Grigsby b: 3/25/1901, Jackson, KY d: 11/10/1973, Sapulpa, OK BL/TR, 5'9", 155 lbs. Deb: 8/29/1923 Career OF: 135-21-27

YEAR TM-L	G	AB	R	H	2B	3B	HR	RBI	BB	SO	SB	CS	AVG	OBP	SLG	OPS	OPS+	BR/A	RC	RC/G	FR	G/POS	WS	TPW
1923 Chi-N	24	72	8	21	5	2	0	5	7	5	1	3	.292	.363	.417	.779	105	-0	10	4.77	0	0-22(6-1-16)	2	-0.2
1924 Chi-N	124	411	58	123	18	2	3	48	31	47	10	19	.299	.357	.375	.732	95	-7	51	4.27	4	*0-121(108-5-8)	12	-1.1
1925 Chi-N	51	137	20	35	5	0	0	20	19	12	1	1	.255	.346	.292	.638	64	-7	16	3.60	1	0-39(21-15-3)	2	-0.8
Total 3	**199**	**620**	**86**	**179**	**28**	**4**	**3**	**73**	**57**	**64**	**12**	**23**	**.289**	**.355**	**.361**	**.717**	**89**	**-14**	**77**	**4.17**	**5**	**0-182**	**16**	**-2.1**

• GRIM, John John Helm Grim b: 8/9/1867, Lebanon, KY d: 7/28/1961, Indianapolis, IN BR/TR, 6'2", 175 lbs. Deb: 9/29/1888 U Career OF: 2-0-12

YEAR TM-L	G	AB	R	H	2B	3B	HR	RBI	BB	SO	SB	CS	AVG	OBP	SLG	OPS	OPS+	BR/A	RC	RC/G	FR	G/POS	WS	TPW
1888 Phi-N	2	7	0	1	0	0	0	0	0	0	0	....	.143	.143	.143	.286	-8	-1	0	.66	0	/2-1,0-1	0	-0.1
1890 Roc-a	50	192	30	51	6	9	2	34	7	....	14	....	.266	.299	.422	.720	121	4	29	5.46	-5	S-21,C-15/3-8,2-4,0-3(0-0-3),1,P	7	0.2
1891 Mil-a	29	119	14	28	5	1	1	14	2	5	1	....	.235	.248	.319	.567	52	-9	10	2.89	-3	C-16,3-10/2-3	2	-0.9
1892 Lou-N	97	370	40	90	16	4	1	36	13	24	18	....	.243	.280	.316	.596	87	-7	39	3.74	1	C-69,1-11,2-10/0-8(1-0-7),3,S	8	0.1
1893 Lou-N	99	415	68	111	19	8	3	54	12	10	15	....	.267	.303	.373	.676	86	-10	53	4.60	5	*C-92/1-3,2-2,0-1,S-1	10	0.3
1894 Lou-N	109	412	66	123	27	7	7	71	17	15	14	....	.299	.342	.449	.791	96	-4	69	6.25	9	C-77,2-24/1-7,3-1	10	1.0
1895 Bro-N	94	333	55	93	17	5	0	44	13	9	10	....	.279	.320	.360	.680	82	-9	43	4.73	7	*C-91/1-1,0-1	11	0.6
1896 Bro-N	81	281	32	75	13	1	2	35	12	14	7	....	.267	.311	.342	.653	76	-10	34	4.18	1	C-77/1-5	6	-0.1
1897 Bro-N	80	290	26	72	10	1	0	25	1	....	3	....	.248	.259	.290	.548	47	-23	24	2.81	7	C-77	3	-0.7
1898 Bro-N	52	178	17	50	5	1	0	11	8	....	1	....	.281	.323	.320	.643	85	-4	20	3.97	2	C-52	4	0.2
1899 Bro-N	15	47	3	13	1	0	0	7	1	....	0	....	.277	.320	.298	.618	68	-2	5	3.58	1	C-12	1	0.0
Total 11	**708**	**2644**	**351**	**707**	**119**	**37**	**16**	**331**	**86**	**77**	**83**	**....**	**.267**	**.303**	**.359**	**.661**	**82**	**-74**	**325**	**4.39**	**25**	**C-578/2-44,1-29,S-23,3-20,0,P**	**62**	**0.5**

• GRIMES, Ed Edward Adelbert Grimes b: 9/8/1905, Chicago, IL d: 10/5/1974, Chicago, IL BR/TR, 5'10", 165 lbs. Deb: 4/19/1931

YEAR TM-L	G	AB	R	H	2B	3B	HR	RBI	BB	SO	SB	CS	AVG	OBP	SLG	OPS	OPS+	BR/A	RC	RC/G	FR	G/POS	WS	TPW
1931 StL-A	43	57	9	15	1	2	0	5	9	3	1	0	.263	.364	.351	.715	86	-0	8	4.95	-4	3-22/2-4,S-3	1	-0.4
1932 StL-A	31	68	7	16	0	1	0	13	6	12	0	1	.235	.297	.265	.562	44	-6	5	2.63	-1	3-18/2-2,S-1	1	-0.5
Total 2	**74**	**125**	**16**	**31**	**1**	**3**	**0**	**18**	**15**	**15**	**1**	**1**	**.248**	**.329**	**.304**	**.633**	**64**	**-6**	**14**	**3.65**	**-5**	**/3-40,2-6,S-4**	**2**	**-0.9**

• GRIMES, Oscar Oscar Ray Grimes, Jr. b: 4/13/1915, Minerva, OH d: 5/19/1993, Westlake, OH BR/TR, 5'11", 178 lbs. Deb: 9/28/1938

YEAR TM-L	G	AB	R	H	2B	3B	HR	RBI	BB	SO	SB	CS	AVG	OBP	SLG	OPS	OPS+	BR/A	RC	RC/G	FR	G/POS	WS	TPW
1938 Cle-A	4	10	2	2	0	1	0	2	2	0	0	0	.200	.333	.400	.733	85	-0	1	4.79	0	/2-2,1-1	0	0.0
1939 Cle-A	119	364	51	98	20	5	4	56	56	61	8	3	.269	.368	.385	.753	96	0	55	5.20	-8	2-48,1-43,S-37/3-3	11	-0.6
1940 Cle-A	11	13	3	0	0	0	0	0	0	5	0	0	.000	.000	.000	.000	-103	-4	0	.00	1	/1-4,3-1	0	-0.3
1941 Cle-A	77	244	28	58	9	3	4	24	39	47	4	0	.238	.345	.348	.693	88	-2	34	4.79	-7	1-62,2-13/3-1	6	-1.3
1942 Cle-A	51	84	10	15	2	0	0	2	13	17	3	2	.179	.289	.202	.491	42	-6	6	2.15	-4	2-24/3-8,1-1,S-1	1	-0.9
1943 NY-A	9	20	4	3	0	0	0	1	3	7	0	0	.150	.261	.150	.411	21	-2	1	1.60	1	/S-3,1-1	0	-0.1
1944 NY-A	116	387	44	108	17	8	5	46	59	57	6	0	.279	.377	.403	.780	119	13	67	6.26	-7	3-97,S-20	16	1.0
1945 NY-A★	142	480	64	127	19	7	4	45	97	73	7	6	.265	.395	.358	.753	114	14	77	5.43	11	*3-141/1-1	21	2.9
1946 NY-A	14	39	1	8	1	0	0	4	1	7	0	1	.205	.225	.231	.456	27	-4	2	1.60	-3	/S-7,2-5	0	-0.6
Phi-A	59	191	28	50	5	0	1	20	27	29	2	0	.262	.356	.304	.660	86	-2	23	3.85	-5	2-43/3-6,S-4	3	-0.4
Yr.	73	230	29	58	6	0	1	24	28	36	2	1	.252	.336	.291	.627	77	-6	25	3.46	-7	2-48,S-11/3-6	3	-1.1
Total 9	**602**	**1832**	**235**	**469**	**73**	**24**	**18**	**200**	**297**	**303**	**30**	**12**	**.256**	**.363**	**.352**	**.715**	**98**	**8**	**266**	**4.94**	**-20**	**3-257,2-135,1-113/S-72**	**58**	**-0.4**

• GRIMES, Ray Oscar Ray Grimes, Sr. b: 9/11/1893, Bergholz, OH d: 5/25/1953, Minerva, OH BR/TR, 5'11", 168 lbs. Deb: 9/24/1920

YEAR TM-L	G	AB	R	H	2B	3B	HR	RBI	BB	SO	SB	CS	AVG	OBP	SLG	OPS	OPS+	BR/A	RC	RC/G	FR	G/POS	WS	TPW
1920 Bos-A	1	4	1	1	0	0	0	0	1	0	0	0	.250	.400	.250	.650	78	-0	0	4.27	0	/1-1	0	0.0
1921 Chi-N	147	530	91	170	38	6	6	79	70	55	5	8	.321	.406	.449	.855	126	23	99	6.81	-3	*1-147	21	1.0
1922 Chi-N	138	509	99	180	45	12	14	99	75	33	7	7	.354	.442	.572	1.014	157	45	130	10.10	3	*1-138	29	3.7
1923 Chi-N	64	216	32	71	7	2	2	36	24	17	5	0	.329	.401	.407	.808	114	7	38	6.73	0	1-62	8	0.3
1924 Chi-N	51	177	33	53	6	5	5	34	28	15	4	2	.299	.401	.475	.876	133	10	35	7.20	-8	1-50	9	-0.1
1926 Phi-N	32	101	13	30	5	0	0	15	6	13	0	....	.297	.343	.347	.689	82	-2	12	4.25	-2	1-28	2	-0.6
Total 6	**433**	**1537**	**269**	**505**	**101**	**25**	**27**	**263**	**204**	**133**	**21**	**17**	**.329**	**.413**	**.480**	**.892**	**132**	**83**	**314**	**7.71**	**-10**	**1-426**	**69**	**4.2**

• GRIMES, Roy Austin Roy "Bummer" Grimes b: 9/11/1893, Bergholz, OH d: 9/13/1954, Hanoverton, OH BR/TR, 6'1", 176 lbs. Deb: 7/5/1920

YEAR TM-L	G	AB	R	H	2B	3B	HR	RBI	BB	SO	SB	CS	AVG	OBP	SLG	OPS	OPS+	BR/A	RC	RC/G	FR	G/POS	WS	TPW
1920 NY-N	26	57	5	9	1	0	0	3	3	8	1	1	.158	.200	.175	.375	8	-7	2	1.07	-3	2-21	0	-1.0

• GRIMM, Charlie Charles John "Jolly Cholly" Grimm
b: 8/28/1898, St. Louis, MO d: 11/15/1983, Scottsdale, AZ BL/TL, 5'11.5", 173 lbs. Deb: 7/30/1916 M/C Career OF: 3-1-5

YEAR TM-L	G	AB	R	H	2B	3B	HR	RBI	BB	SO	SB	CS	AVG	OBP	SLG	OPS	OPS+	BR/A	RC	RC/G	FR	G/POS	WS	TPW
1916 Phi-A	12	22	0	2	0	0	0	0	2	4	0	....	.091	.167	.091	.258	-24	-3	0	.43	-1	/0-7(3-1-3)	0	-0.5
1918 StL-N	50	141	11	31	7	0	0	12	6	15	2	....	.220	.262	.270	.531	64	-6	10	2.34	-3	1-42/0-2(0-0-2),3-1	1	-1.1
1919 Pit-N	14	44	6	14	1	3	0	6	2	4	1	....	.318	.348	.477	.825	141	2	7	6.12	-1	1-13	2	0.0
1920 Pit-N	148	533	38	121	13	7	2	54	30	40	7	8	.227	.273	.289	.562	60	-27	42	2.57	9	*1-148	7	-2.2
1921 Pit-N	151	562	62	154	21	17	7	71	31	38	6	8	.274	.314	.409	.724	88	-11	70	4.31	6	*1-150	14	-1.5
1922 Pit-N	154	593	64	173	28	13	0	76	43	15	6	10	.292	.343	.383	.726	86	-14	76	4.60	4	*1-154	13	-2.0
1923 Pit-N	152	563	78	194	29	13	7	99	41	43	6	9	.345	.389	.480	.869	125	19	102	6.97	0	*1-152	23	0.8
1924 Pit-N	151	542	53	156	25	12	2	63	37	22	3	6	.288	.336	.389	.725	92	-7	70	4.54	-3	*1-151	13	-1.9
1925 Chi-N	141	519	73	159	29	5	10	76	38	25	4	3	.306	.354	.439	.793	100	-0	80	5.72	-3	*1-139	14	-1.2
1926 Chi-N	147	524	58	145	30	6	8	82	49	25	3	....	.277	.342	.403	.745	99	-1	72	4.62	-10	*1-147	11	-2.1
1927 Chi-N	147	543	68	169	29	6	2	74	45	21	3	....	.311	.367	.398	.765	104	4	79	5.11	-3	*1-147	15	-0.9
1928 Chi-N	147	547	67	161	25	5	5	62	39	20	7	....	.294	.342	.386	.728	91	-8	71	4.47	-4	*1-147	13	-2.1
1929*Chi-N	120	463	66	138	28	3	10	91	42	25	3	....	.298	.358	.436	.794	95	-4	71	5.51	0	*1-120	13	-1.1
1930 Chi-N	114	429	58	124	27	2	6	66	41	26	1	....	.289	.359	.403	.763	83	-11	62	5.07	2	*1-113	9	-1.4
1931 Chi-N	146	531	65	176	33	11	4	66	53	29	1	....	.331	.393	.458	.851	126	21	99	7.00	3	*1-144	21	1.0
1932*Chi-N	149	570	66	175	42	2	7	80	35	22	2	....	.307	.349	.425	.774	108	6	86	5.52	1	*1-149	17	-0.7
1933 Chi-N	107	384	38	95	15	2	3	37	23	15	1	....	.247	.290	.320	.610	74	-13	33	2.90	3	*1-104	5	-2.1
1934 Chi-N	75	267	24	79	8	1	5	47	16	12	1	....	.296	.338	.390	.728	96	-2	34	4.63	4	1-74	6	-0.4
1935 Chi-N	2	8	0	0	0	0	0	0	0	1	0	....	.000	.000	.000	.000	-99	-2	0	.00	0	/1-2	0	-0.3
1936 Chi-N	39	132	13	33	4	0	1	16	5	8	0	....	.250	.277	.303	.580	55	-9	10	2.62	4	1-35	1	-0.8
Total 20	**2166**	**7917**	**908**	**2299**	**394**	**108**	**79**	**1078**	**578**	**410**	**57**	**44**	**.290**	**.341**	**.397**	**.738**	**94**	**-66**	**1077**	**4.79**	**6**	***1-2131/0-9,3-1**	**198**	**-20.4**

• GRIMSHAW, Myron Myron Frederick Grimshaw b: 11/30/1875, St. Johnsville, NY d: 12/11/1936, Canajoharie, NY BB/TR, 6'1", 173 lbs. Deb: 4/25/1905

YEAR TM-L	G	AB	R	H	2B	3B	HR	RBI	BB	SO	SB	CS	AVG	OBP	SLG	OPS	OPS+	BR/A	RC	RC/G	FR	G/POS	WS	TPW
1905 Bos-A	85	285	39	68	8	2	4	35	21	....	4	....	.239	.293	.323	.616	94	-2	30	3.52	-4	1-74	6	-0.8
1906 Bos-A	110	428	46	124	16	12	0	48	23	....	5	....	.290	.332	.383	.715	124	11	58	4.96	-3	*1-110	13	0.6
1907 Bos-A	64	181	19	37	7	2	0	33	16	....	6	....	.204	.273	.265	.538	72	-5	16	2.80	-4	1-20,0-18(1-0-22)/S-2	2	-1.1
Total 3	**259**	**894**	**104**	**229**	**31**	**16**	**4**	**116**	**60**	**....**	**15**	**....**	**.256**	**.307**	**.340**	**.647**	**104**	**3**	**104**	**4.02**	**-11**	**1-204/0-18,S-2**	**21**	**-1.3**

• GRISSOM, Marquis Marquis Deon Grissom b: 4/17/1967, Atlanta, GA BR/TR, 5'11", 190 lbs. Deb: 8/22/1989 Career OF: 84-1786-57

YEAR TM-L	G	AB	R	H	2B	3B	HR	RBI	BB	SO	SB	CS	AVG	OBP	SLG	OPS	OPS+	BR/A	RC	RC/G	FR	G/POS	WS	TPW
1989 Mon-N	26	74	16	19	2	0	1	2	12	21	1	0	.257	.360	.324	.685	96	0	10	4.60	-1	0-23(1-22-1)	2	-0.1
1990 Mon-N	98	288	42	74	14	2	3	29	27	40	22	2	.257	.321	.351	.671	88	-1	36	4.39	0	0-87(18-35-40)	8	-0.2
1991 Mon-N	148	558	73	149	23	9	6	39	34	89	**76**	17	.267	.310	.373	.683	93	2	69	4.25	10	*0-138(3-125-11)	19	1.1
1992 Mon-N	159	653	99	180	39	6	14	66	42	81	**78**	13	.276	.324	.418	.742	110	18	94	5.01	0	*0-157(0-157-0)	27	1.7
1993 Mon-N★	157	630	104	188	27	2	19	95	52	76	53	10	.298	.355	.438	.793	106	12	104	5.96	9	*0-157(0-157-0)	30	2.2
1994 Mon-N★	110	475	96	137	25	4	11	45	41	66	36	6	.288	.346	.427	.774	99	4	73	5.51	10	*0-109(0-109-0)	17	1.5
1995*Atl-N	139	551	80	142	23	3	12	42	47	61	29	9	.258	.319	.376	.695	80	-14	68	4.28	8	*0-136(0-136-0)	18	-0.6
1996*Atl-N	158	671	106	207	32	10	23	74	41	73	28	11	.308	.351	.489	.840	112	11	112	6.13	7	*0-158(0-158-0)	24	1.9

YEAR TM-L	G	AB	R	H	2B	3B	HR	RBI	BB	SO	SB	CS	AVG	OBP	SLG	OPS	OPS+	BR/A	RC	RC/G	FR	G/POS	WS	TPW
1997*Cle-A	144	558	74	146	27	6	12	66	43	89	22	13	.262	.321	.396	.717	83	-16	69	4.13	3	*O-144(0-144-0)	14	-1.1
1998 Mil-N	142	542	57	147	28	1	10	60	24	78	13	8	.271	.305	.382	.686	79	-19	59	3.83	-2	*O-137(0-137-0)	11	-1.9
1999 Mil-N	154	603	92	161	27	1	20	83	49	109	24	6	.267	.322	.415	.737	86	-13	81	4.66	-8	*O-149(0-149-0)	13	-1.8
2000 Mil-N	146	595	67	145	18	2	14	62	39	99	20	10	.244	.290	.351	.641	62	-36	60	3.40	-8	*O-142(0-142-0)	8	-4.1
2001 LA-N	135	448	56	99	17	1	21	60	16	107	7	5	.221	.251	.404	.655	71	-23	41	2.98	-3	*O-123(26-95-3)/D-2	6	-2.5
2002 LA-N	111	343	57	95	21	4	17	60	22	68	5	1	.277	.324	.510	.834	124	10	56	5.83	-3	*O-102(36-72-2)	15	0.6
2003*SF-N	149	587	82	176	33	3	20	79	20	82	11	3	.300	.325	.468	.794	107	4	85	5.27	-7	*O-148(0-148-0)	22	-0.2
Total 15	1976	7576	1101	2065	356	54	203	862	509	1139	425	114	.273	.321	.414	.735	93	-60	1017	4.69	16	*O-1910/D-2	234	-3.6

• GROAT, Dick Richard Morrow Groat b: 11/4/1930, Wilkinsburg, PA BR/TR, 5'11.5", 180 lbs. Deb: 6/19/1952

YEAR TM-L	G	AB	R	H	2B	3B	HR	RBI	BB	SO	SB	CS	AVG	OBP	SLG	OPS	OPS+	BR/A	RC	RC/G	FR	G/POS	WS	TPW
1952 Pit-N	95	384	38	109	6	1	1	29	19	27	2	4	.284	.319	.313	.632	74	-15	35	3.05	-1	S-94	5	-1.0
1955 Pit-N	151	521	45	139	28	2	4	51	38	26	0	2	.267	.318	.351	.669	78	-17	54	3.48	1	*S-149	13	-0.3
1956 Pit-N	142	520	40	142	19	3	0	37	35	25	0	3	.273	.319	.321	.640	74	-20	52	3.36	4	*S-141/3-2	12	-0.4
1957 Pit-N	125	501	58	158	30	5	7	54	27	28	0	1	.315	.354	.437	.791	114	9	74	5.22	5	*S-123/3-2	16	2.5
1958 Pit-N	151	584	67	175	36	9	3	66	23	32	2	2	.300	.331	.408	.738	97	-5	72	4.38	4	*S-149	19	1.2
1959 Pit-N★	147	593	74	163	22	7	5	51	32	35	0	2	.275	.314	.361	.675	80	-18	62	3.61	3	*S-145	15	-0.3
1960*Pit-N★	138	573	85	186	26	4	2	50	39	35	0	2	**.325**	.372	.394	.766	109	7	85	5.63	11	*S-136	25	3.0
1961 Pit-N	148	596	71	164	25	6	6	55	40	44	0	4	.275	.322	.367	.689	82	-17	65	3.74	2	*S-144/3-1	15	-0.3
1962 Pit-N★	161	678	76	199	34	3	2	61	31	61	2	1	.294	.327	.361	.689	84	-15	78	4.20	3	*S-161	21	0.2
1963 StL-N★	158	631	85	201	**43**	11	6	73	56	58	3	1	.319	.380	.450	.830	126	24	106	6.24	10	*S-158	31	5.1
1964*StL-N★	161	636	70	186	35	6	1	70	44	42	2	3	.292	.338	.371	.709	92	-6	78	4.35	4	*S-160	20	1.2
1965 StL-N	153	587	55	149	26	5	0	52	56	50	1	1	.254	.320	.315	.635	73	-20	61	3.57	7	*S-148/3-2	16	0.0
1966 Phi-N	155	584	58	152	21	4	2	53	40	38	2	1	.260	.313	.320	.633	76	-17	56	3.26	17	*S-139,3-20/1-1	15	1.2
1967 Phi-N	10	26	3	3	0	0	0	1	4	4	0	0	.115	.233	.115	.349	3	-3	1	1.16	2	/S-6	1	-0.1
SF-N	34	70	4	12	1	1	0	4	6	7	0	0	.171	.237	.214	.451	30	-6	3	1.43	0	S-24/2-1	1	-0.6
Yr.	44	96	7	15	1	1	0	5	10	11	0	0	.156	.236	.188	.423	22	-9	4	1.35	2	S-30/2-1	2	-0.7
Total 14	1929	7484	829	2138	352	67	39	707	490	512	14	27	.286	.332	.366	.698	89	-118	882	4.13	71	*S-1877/3-27,1-1,2-1	225	11.4

• GROH, Heinie Henry Knight Groh b: 9/18/1889, Rochester, NY d: 8/22/1968, Cincinnati, OH BR/TR, 5'8", 158 lbs. Deb: 4/12/1912 M

YEAR TM-L	G	AB	R	H	2B	3B	HR	RBI	BB	SO	SB	CS	AVG	OBP	SLG	OPS	OPS+	BR/A	RC	RC/G	FR	G/POS	WS	TPW
1912 NY-N	27	48	8	13	2	1	0	3	8	7	6	....	.271	.375	.354	.729	97	0	8	6.15	-2	2-12/S-7,3-6	2	-0.2
1913 NY-N	4	2	0	0	0	0	0	0	0	1	0	....	.000	.000	.000	.000	-99	-1	0	.00	-0	/3-2,S-1	0	-0.1
Cin-N	117	397	51	112	19	5	3	48	38	36	24	....	.282	.351	.378	.729	108	5	59	4.99	-1	*2-113/S-4	13	0.7
Yr.	121	399	51	112	19	5	3	48	38	37	24	....	.281	.349	.376	.725	108	4	59	4.96	-1	*2-113/S-5,3-2	13	0.6
1914 Cin-N	139	455	59	131	18	4	2	32	64	28	24	....	.288	.391	.358	.749	120	15	72	5.47	-13	*2-134/S-2	19	0.5
1915 Cin-N	160	587	72	170	32	9	3	50	50	33	12	17	.290	.354	.390	.745	123	12	83	4.74	10	*3-131,2-29	25	2.9
1916 Cin-N	149	553	85	149	24	14	2	28	**84**	34	13	....	.269	.370	.374	.744	132	25	83	5.18	16	*3-110,2-33/S-5	24	**5.1**
1917 Cin-N	156	599	91	**182**	**39**	11	1	53	71	30	15	....	.304	**.385**	.411	.796	150	38	96	5.90	8	*3-154/2-2	37	5.8
1918 Cin-N	126	493	**86**	158	**28**	3	1	37	54	24	11	....	.320	**.395**	.396	.791	144	**28**	79	5.94	5	*3-126	**28**	**4.1**
1919*Cin-N	122	448	79	139	17	11	5	63	56	26	21	....	.310	.392	.431	**.823**	151	30	81	6.52	7	*3-121	30	**4.5**
1920 Cin-N	145	550	86	164	28	12	0	49	60	29	16	19	.298	.375	.393	.768	122	16	81	5.09	6	*3-144/S-1	28	2.8
1921 Cin-N	97	357	54	118	19	6	0	48	36	17	22	14	.331	.398	.417	.815	121	13	60	5.84	5	3-97	15	2.4
1922*NY-N	115	426	63	113	21	3	3	51	53	21	5	6	.265	.353	.350	.703	81	-10	55	4.41	7	*3-110	12	0.3
1923*NY-N	123	465	91	135	22	5	4	48	60	22	3	4	.290	.379	.385	.763	103	5	71	5.47	5	*3-118	18	1.7
1924*NY-N	145	559	82	157	32	3	2	46	52	29	8	6	.281	.354	.360	.713	94	-2	74	4.64	7	*3-145	19	1.5
1925 NY-N	25	65	7	15	4	0	0	4	6	3	0	0	.231	.296	.292	.588	53	-4	6	3.07	-2	3-16/2-2	1	-0.5
1926 NY-N	12	35	2	8	2	0	0	3	2	3	0	....	.229	.270	.286	.556	50	-2	3	2.55	0	/3-7	0	-0.2
1927*Pit-N	14	35	2	10	1	0	0	3	2	2	0	....	.286	.324	.314	.639	67	-2	3	3.61	1	3-12	1	0.0
Total 16	1676	6074	918	1774	308	87	26	566	696	345	180	66	.292	.373	.384	.757	120	166	915	5.27	59	*3-1299,2-325/S-20	272	31.2

• GROH, Lew Lewis Carl "Silver" Groh b: 10/16/1883, Rochester, NY d: 10/20/1960, Rochester, NY BR/TR Deb: 8/2/1919

YEAR TM-L	G	AB	R	H	2B	3B	HR	RBI	BB	SO	SB	CS	AVG	OBP	SLG	OPS	OPS+	BR/A	RC	RC/G	FR	G/POS	WS	TPW
1919 Phi-A	2	4	0	0	0	0	0	0	0	2	0	....	.000	.000	.000	.000	-99	-1	0	.00	0	/3-1	0	-0.1

• GROSKLOSS, Howdy Howard Hoffman Groskloss b: 4/9/1906, Pittsburgh, PA BR/TR, 5'9", 176 lbs. Deb: 6/23/1930

YEAR TM-L	G	AB	R	H	2B	3B	HR	RBI	BB	SO	SB	CS	AVG	OBP	SLG	OPS	OPS+	BR/A	RC	RC/G	FR	G/POS	WS	TPW
1930 Pit-N	2	3	0	1	0	0	0	1	0	0	0	....	.333	.333	.333	.667	62	-0	0	4.03	-1	/S-1	0	-0.1
1931 Pit-N	53	161	13	45	7	2	0	20	11	16	1	....	.280	.326	.348	.673	82	-4	19	4.11	3	2-39/S-3	3	0.1
1932 Pit-N	17	20	1	2	0	0	0	0	0	3	0	....	.100	.100	.100	.200	-47	-4	0	.32	0	/S-1	0	-0.4
Total 3	72	184	14	48	7	2	0	21	11	19	1	....	.261	.303	.321	.623	68	-8	19	3.59	2	/2-39,S-5	3	-0.4

• GROSS, Emil Emil Michael Gross b: 3/4/1858, Chicago, IL d: 8/24/1921, Eagle River, WI BR/TR, 6', 190 lbs. Deb: 8/13/1879 Career OF: 7-1-4

YEAR TM-L	G	AB	R	H	2B	3B	HR	RBI	BB	SO	SB	CS	AVG	OBP	SLG	OPS	OPS+	BR/A	RC	RC/G	FR	G/POS	WS	TPW
1879 Pro-N	30	132	31	46	9	5	0	24	4	8	....	....	.348	.368	.492	.860	183	12	24	7.97	-6	C-30	8	0.6
1880 Pro-N	87	347	43	90	18	3	1	34	16	15	....	....	.259	.292	.337	.629	116	6	35	3.75	-20	*C-87	12	-1.1
1881 Pro-N	51	182	15	50	9	4	1	24	13	11	....	....	.275	.323	.385	.708	123	5	23	4.74	-7	C-50/O-1	9	-0.1
1883 Phi-N	57	231	39	71	25	7	1	25	12	18	....	....	.307	.342	.489	.831	163	18	40	6.80	-10	C-55/O-2(1-1-0)	8	1.1
1884 CP-U	23	95	13	34	6	2	4	....	6	....	....	....	.358	.396	.589	.986	244	14	23	10.43	1	C-15/O-9(6-0-3)	7	1.5
Total 5	248	987	141	291	67	21	7	107	51	52	....	....	.295	.329	.427	.756	150	55	145	5.75	-42	C-237/O-12	44	2.0

• GROSS, Greg Gregory Eugene Gross b: 8/1/1952, York, PA BL/TL, 5'10", 175 lbs. Deb: 9/5/1973 C Career OF: 623-176-524

YEAR TM-L	G	AB	R	H	2B	3B	HR	RBI	BB	SO	SB	CS	AVG	OBP	SLG	OPS	OPS+	BR/A	RC	RC/G	FR	G/POS	WS	TPW
1973 Hou-N	14	39	5	9	2	1	0	1	4	4	2	1	.231	.302	.333	.636	76	-1	4	2.87	1	/O-9(4-2-3)	1	-0.1
1974 Hou-N	156	589	78	185	21	8	0	36	76	39	12	20	.314	.393	.377	.770	121	13	86	5.16	0	*O-151(56-0-143)	20	0.5
1975 Hou-N	132	483	67	142	14	10	0	41	63	37	2	2	.294	.375	.364	.740	114	11	69	5.06	4	*O-121(60-0-61)	14	0.8
1976 Hou-N	128	426	52	122	12	3	0	27	64	39	2	6	.286	.380	.329	.708	112	8	56	4.58	1	*O-115(0-0-115)	16	0.3
1977 Chi-N	115	239	43	77	10	4	5	32	33	19	0	1	.322	.404	.460	.865	118	7	45	6.83	0	O-71(45-25-9)	9	0.5
1978 Chi-N	124	347	34	92	12	7	1	39	33	19	3	1	.265	.329	.349	.678	80	-9	41	4.06	-1	*O-111(40-70-12)	8	-1.2
1979 Phi-N	111	174	21	58	6	3	0	15	29	5	5	2	.333	.429	.402	.831	124	8	32	6.99	1	O-73(49-19-11)	8	0.7
1980*Phi-N	127	154	19	37	7	2	0	12	24	7	1	1	.240	.346	.312	.658	80	-3	18	3.81	1	O-91(58-14-26)/1-1	3	-0.5
1981*Phi-N	83	102	14	23	6	1	0	7	15	5	2	2	.225	.325	.304	.629	76	-3	10	3.00	4	O-55(13-5-38)	1	-0.1
1982 Phi-N	119	134	14	40	4	0	0	10	19	8	4	3	.299	.386	.328	.714	99	1	17	4.25	1	O-71(50-12-19)	4	0.0
1983*Phi-N	136	245	25	74	12	3	0	29	34	16	3	5	.302	.389	.376	.765	114	5	36	5.19	-1	*O-110(77-27-25)/1-1	9	0.1
1984 Phi-N	112	202	19	65	9	1	0	16	24	11	1	0	.322	.396	.376	.773	116	6	31	5.91	1	O-48(30-1-20),1-28	7	0.4
1985 Phi-N	93	169	21	44	5	2	0	14	32	9	1	0	.260	.378	.314	.692	93	0	22	4.44	2	O-52(46-0-9)/1-8	5	0.1
1986 Phi-N	87	101	11	25	5	0	0	8	21	11	1	0	.248	.382	.297	.679	87	-0	12	4.02	1	O-27(21-1-6)/1-5,P-1	2	0.0
1987 Phi-N	114	133	14	38	4	1	1	12	25	12	0	0	.286	.403	.353	.756	99	1	21	5.57	-1	O-50(49-0-1),1-11	4	-0.1
1988 Phi-N	98	133	10	27	1	0	0	5	16	3	0	0	.203	.293	.211	.504	46	-9	9	2.18	-2	O-37(20-0-19),1-14	0	-1.2
1989 Hou-N	60	75	2	15	0	0	0	4	11	6	0	0	.200	.310	.200	.510	51	-4	5	2.08	-1	O-12(5-0-7)/1-6,P-1	2	-0.8
Total 17	1809	3745	449	1073	130	46	7	308	523	250	39	44	.287	.375	.351	.727	103	31	511	4.78	10	*O-1204/1-74,P-2	113	-0.4

• GROSS, Turkey Ewell Gross b: 2/21/1896, Mesquite, TX d: 1/11/1936, Dallas, TX BR/TR, 6', 165 lbs. Deb: 4/14/1925

YEAR TM-L	G	AB	R	H	2B	3B	HR	RBI	BB	SO	SB	CS	AVG	OBP	SLG	OPS	OPS+	BR/A	RC	RC/G	FR	G/POS	WS	TPW
1925 Bos-A	9	32	2	3	0	1	0	2	2	2	0	0	.094	.171	.156	.328	-16	-6	1	.87	2	/S-9	0	-0.3

• GROSS, Wayne Wayne Dale Gross b: 1/14/1952, Riverside, CA BL/TR, 6'2", 210 lbs. Deb: 8/21/1976 Career OF: 2-0-2

YEAR TM-L	G	AB	R	H	2B	3B	HR	RBI	BB	SO	SB	CS	AVG	OBP	SLG	OPS	OPS+	BR/A	RC	RC/G	FR	G/POS	WS	TPW
1976 Oak-A	10	18	0	4	0	0	0	1	2	1	0	0	.222	.300	.222	.522	57	-1	1	2.62	0	/1-3,D-3,O-2(0-0-2)	0	-0.2
1977 Oak-A★	146	485	66	113	21	1	22	63	86	84	5	4	.233	.354	.416	.771	111	10	76	5.29	-21	*3-145/1-1	16	-1.3
1978 Oak-A	118	285	18	57	10	2	7	23	40	63	0	2	.200	.309	.323	.632	82	-6	31	3.47	-6	*3-106,1-15	6	-1.5
1979 Oak-A	138	442	54	99	19	1	14	50	72	62	4	3	.224	.334	.367	.700	94	-2	57	4.26	-10	*3-120,1-18/O-2(2-0-0)	13	-1.4
1980 Oak-A	113	366	45	103	20	3	14	61	44	39	5	3	.281	.360	.467	.827	134	17	64	6.25	-1	3-99,1-10/D-1	16	1.4
1981*Oak-A	82	243	29	50	7	1	10	31	34	28	2	1	.206	.308	.366	.674	98	0	28	3.64	2	3-73/1-2,D-1	8	0.1
1982 Oak-A	129	386	43	97	14	0	9	41	53	50	3	1	.251	.345	.358	.702	98	1	52	4.60	5	*3-108,1-16/D-1	14	0.4
1983 Oak-A	137	339	34	79	18	0	12	44	36	52	3	5	.233	.312	.392	.704	98	-2	41	4.04	-1	1-74,3-67/D-1,P-1	9	-0.6
1984 Bal-A	127	342	53	74	9	1	22	64	68	69	1	2	.216	.348	.442	.789	119	10	55	5.36	0	*3-117/1-3,D-1	13	0.9
1985 Bal-A	103	217	31	51	8	0	11	18	46	48	1	1	.235	.369	.424	.793	120	7	37	5.84	-1	3-67,D-10/1-9	9	0.5

YEAR TM-L	G	AB	R	H	2B	3B	HR	RBI	BB	SO	SB	CS	AVG	OBP	SLG	OPS	OPS+	BR/A	RC	RC/G	FR	G/POS	WS	TPW
1986 Oak-A	3	2	0	0	0	0	0	0	1	0	0	0	.000	.333	.000	.333		-0	0	1.17	-1	/3-1	0	-0.1
Total 11	1106	3125	373	727	126	9	121	396	482	496	24	22	.233	.339	.395	.734	106	33	443	4.75	-34	3-903,1-151/D-18,0-4,P-1	104	-1.6

• GROSSART, George George Albert Grossart b: Meadville, PA d: 4/18/1902, Pittsburgh, PA, 1902' Deb: 1880/6/7

YEAR TM-L	G	AB	R	H	2B	3B	HR	RBI	BB	SO	SB	CS	AVG	OBP	SLG	OPS	OPS+	BR/A	RC	RC/G	FR	G/POS	WS	TPW
1901 Bos-N	7	26	4	3	0	0	0	1	0	....	0	....	.115	.115	.115	.231	-30	-4	0	.41	0	/0-7(7-0-0)	1	-0.5

• GROTE, Jerry Gerald Wayne Grote b: 10/6/1942, San Antonio, TX BR/TR, 5'10", 190 lbs. Deb: 9/21/1963 Career OF: 1-0-2

YEAR TM-L	G	AB	R	H	2B	3B	HR	RBI	BB	SO	SB	CS	AVG	OBP	SLG	OPS	OPS+	BR/A	RC	RC/G	FR	G/POS	WS	TPW
1963 Hou-N	3	5	0	1	0	0	0	1	1	3	0	0	.200	.333	.200	.533	61	-0	1	2.75	0	/C-3	0	0.0
1964 Hou-N	100	298	26	54	9	3	3	24	20	75	0	2	.181	.242	.262	.504	44	-23	18	1.93	3	C-98	4	-1.6
1966 NY-N	120	317	26	75	12	2	3	31	40	81	4	3	.237	.328	.315	.643	82	-7	33	3.45	-1	*C-115/3-2	9	-0.3
1967 NY-N	120	344	25	67	8	0	4	23	14	65	2	2	.195	.228	.253	.481	38	-28	19	1.78	2	*C-119	3	-2.3
1968 NY-N★	124	404	29	114	18	0	3	31	44	81	1	5	.282	.357	.349	.706	112	6	50	4.47	1	*C-115	16	1.5
1969*NY-N	113	365	38	92	12	3	6	40	32	59	2	1	.252	.314	.351	.665	84	-8	39	3.65	3	*C-112	14	0.1
1970 NY-N	126	415	38	106	14	1	2	34	36	39	2	1	.255	.316	.308	.625	68	-18	39	3.17	0	*C-125	10	-1.2
1971 NY-N	125	403	35	109	25	0	2	35	40	47	1	4	.270	.339	.347	.687	96	-3	44	3.65	-4	*C-122	12	-0.1
1972 NY-N	64	205	15	43	5	1	3	21	26	27	1	0	.210	.308	.288	.595	72	-6	19	2.96	2	C-59/3-3,0-1	8	-0.2
1973*NY-N	84	285	17	73	10	2	1	32	13	23	0	0	.256	.291	.316	.607	69	-12	24	2.84	-1	C-81/3-2	7	-0.9
1974 NY-N★	97	319	25	82	8	1	5	36	33	33	0	1	.257	.331	.335	.666	88	-5	35	3.62	-5	C-94	5	-0.6
1975 NY-N	119	386	28	114	14	5	2	39	38	23	0	1	.295	.360	.373	.733	109	4	51	4.76	4	*C-111	18	1.4
1976 NY-N	101	323	30	88	14	2	4	28	38	19	1	2	.272	.351	.365	.716	110	4	39	4.11	0	C-95/0-2(1-0-1)	12	1.0
1977 NY-N	42	115	8	31	3	1	0	7	9	12	0	0	.270	.333	.313	.646	78	-3	11	3.40	1	C-28,3-11	2	-0.1
*LA-N	18	27	3	7	0	0	0	4	2	5	0	1	.259	.310	.259	.570	55	-2	2	1.75	1	C-16/3-2	1	0.0
Yr.	60	142	11	38	3	1	0	11	11	17	0	1	.268	.329	.303	.632	74	-5	13	3.06	3	C-44,3-13	3	-0.1
1978*LA-N	41	70	5	19	5	0	0	9	10	5	0	0	.271	.363	.343	.705	98	0	10	4.87	-1	C-32/3-7	3	0.1
1981 KC-A	22	56	4	17	3	1	1	9	3	2	1	0	.304	.350	.446	.796	129	2	9	5.72	-1	C-22	3	0.3
LA-N	2	2	0	0	0	0	0	0	0	1	0	0	.000	.000	.000	.000	-104	-1	0	.00	0	/C-1	0	-0.1
Total 16	1421	4339	352	1092	160	22	39	404	399	600	15	23	.252	.318	.326	.644	83	-99	443	3.43	5	*C-1348/3-27,0-3	127	-3.1

• GROTEWOLD, Jeff Jeffrey Scott Grotewold b: 12/8/1965, Madera, CA BL/TR, 6', 215 lbs. Deb: 4/12/1992

YEAR TM-L	G	AB	R	H	2B	3B	HR	RBI	BB	SO	SB	CS	AVG	OBP	SLG	OPS	OPS+	BR/A	RC	RC/G	FR	G/POS	WS	TPW
1992 Phi-N	72	65	7	13	2	0	3	5	9	16	0	0	.200	.307	.369	.676	91	-1	7	3.25	-1	/C-2,0-2(2-0-0),1-1	1	-0.1
1995 KC-A	15	36	4	10	1	0	1	6	9	7	0	0	.278	.422	.389	.811	111	1	6	5.95	0	D-11/1-1	1	0.0
Total 2	87	101	11	23	3	0	4	11	18	23	0	0	.228	.350	.376	.726	98	0	13	4.15	-1	/D-11,1-2,C-2,0-2	2	-0.1

• GROTH, Johnny John Thomas Groth b: 7/23/1926, Chicago, IL BR/TR, 6', 182 lbs. Deb: 9/5/1946 Career OF: 121-964-83

YEAR TM-L	G	AB	R	H	2B	3B	HR	RBI	BB	SO	SB	CS	AVG	OBP	SLG	OPS	OPS+	BR/A	RC	RC/G	FR	G/POS	WS	TPW
1946 Det-A	4	9	1	0	0	0	0	0	0	3	0	0	.000	.000	.000	.000	-94	-2	0	.00	0	/0-4(0-4-0)	0	-0.3
1947 Det-A	2	4	1	1	0	0	0	0	2	1	0	0	.250	.500	.250	.750	109	0	0	1.39	1	/0-1	0	0.1
1948 Det-A	6	17	3	8	3	0	1	5	1	1	0	0	.471	.500	.824	1.324	242	3	7	21.92	0	/0-4(0-4-0)	2	0.3
1949 Det-A	103	348	60	102	19	5	11	73	65	27	3	7	.293	.407	.471	.878	132	15	66	6.61	-2	0-99(0-99-0)	15	1.1
1950 Det-A	157	566	95	173	30	8	12	85	95	27	1	5	.306	.407	.451	.858	116	15	106	6.71	-11	*0-157(0-157-0)	22	0.0
1951 Det-A	118	428	41	128	29	1	3	49	31	32	1	1	.299	.349	.393	.742	100	-1	57	4.78	0	*0-112(0-112-0)	12	-0.4
1952 Det-A	141	524	56	149	22	2	4	51	51	39	2	10	.284	.348	.357	.705	96	-6	64	4.33	-5	*0-139(2-137-0)	11	-1.5
1953 StL-A	141	557	65	141	27	4	10	57	42	53	5	6	.253	.308	.370	.678	81	-17	62	3.77	8	*0-141(0-141-0)	10	-1.7
1954 Chi-A	125	422	41	116	20	0	7	60	42	37	3	9	.275	.343	.372	.715	93	-7	49	3.81	-2	*0-125(9-116-2)	11	-1.5
1955 Chi-A	32	77	13	26	7	0	2	11	6	13	1	0	.338	.386	.506	.892	134	4	15	6.89	1	0-26(0-26-0)	4	0.3
Was-A	63	183	22	40	4	5	2	17	18	18	2	0	.219	.289	.328	.616	69	-8	18	3.11	-1	0-48(12-40-1)	2	-1.1
Yr.	95	260	35	66	11	5	4	28	24	31	3	0	.254	.317	.381	.698	89	-4	32	4.16	0	0-74(12-66-1)	6	-0.8
1956 KC-A	95	244	22	63	13	3	5	37	30	31	1	2	.258	.339	.398	.737	94	-3	32	4.31	-2	0-84(13-56-18)	5	-0.8
1957 KC-A	55	59	10	15	0	0	0	2	7	6	0	0	.254	.333	.254	.588	62	-3	5	2.95	-2	0-50(9-3-38)	1	-0.6
Det-A	38	103	11	30	10	0	0	16	6	7	0	0	.291	.336	.388	.725	95	-1	14	4.89	-1	0-36(12-25-0)	3	-0.3
Yr.	93	162	21	45	10	0	0	18	13	13	0	0	.278	.335	.340	.675	82	-3	19	4.14	-3	0-86(21-28-38)	4	-0.9
1958 Det-A	88	146	24	41	5	2	2	11	13	19	0	1	.281	.340	.384	.723	92	-2	18	4.43	-2	0-80(52-19-10)	4	-0.6
1959 Det-A	55	102	12	24	7	1	1	10	7	14	0	0	.235	.284	.353	.637	70	-4	11	3.63	-2	0-41(11-18-13)	2	-0.7
1960 Det-A	25	19	3	7	1	0	0	2	3	1	0	1	.368	.455	.421	.876	130	1	4	7.02	-1	/0-8(0-7-1)	1	0.0
Total 15	1248	3808	480	1064	197	31	60	486	419	329	19	42	.279	.353	.395	.747	99	-16	528	4.80	-21	*0-1155	105	-7.8

• GROVER, Roy Roy Arthur Grover b: 1/17/1892, Snohomish, WA d: 2/7/1978, Milwaukie, OR BR/TR, 5'8", 150 lbs. Deb: 9/13/1916

YEAR TM-L	G	AB	R	H	2B	3B	HR	RBI	BB	SO	SB	CS	AVG	OBP	SLG	OPS	OPS+	BR/A	RC	RC/G	FR	G/POS	WS	TPW
1916 Phi-A	20	77	8	21	1	2	0	7	6	10	5	....	.273	.325	.338	.663	104	0	11	4.51	-5	2-20	2	-0.5
1917 Phi-A	141	482	45	108	15	7	0	34	43	53	12	....	.224	.292	.284	.576	77	-14	46	2.90	-12	*2-139	7	-2.6
1919 Phi-A	22	56	8	13	1	0	0	2	5	6	0	....	.232	.295	.250	.545	53	-3	5	2.58	-6	2-12/3-3	0	-0.9
Was-A	24	75	6	14	0	0	0	7	6	10	2	....	.187	.256	.187	.443	25	-7	4	1.67	-7	2-24	0	-1.4
Yr.	46	131	14	27	1	0	0	9	11	16	2	....	.206	.273	.214	.486	38	-11	9	2.07	-12	2-36/3-3	0	-2.3
Total 3	207	690	67	156	17	9	0	50	60	79	19	....	.226	.292	.277	.569	72	-24	66	2.90	-29	2-195/3-3	9	-5.4

• GRUBB, Harvey Harvey Harrison Grubb b: 9/18/1890, Lexington, NC d: 1/25/1970, Corpus Christi, TX BR/TR, 6', 165 lbs. Deb: 9/27/1912

YEAR TM-L	G	AB	R	H	2B	3B	HR	RBI	BB	SO	SB	CS	AVG	OBP	SLG	OPS	OPS+	BR/A	RC	RC/G	FR	G/POS	WS	TPW
1912 Cle-A	1	0	0	0	0	0	0	0	0	....	0	....	....	1.000	....	1.000	187	0	0	....	0	/3-1	0	0.0

• GRUBB, Johnny John Raymond Grubb b: 8/4/1948, Richmond, VA BL/TR, 6'3", 188 lbs. Deb: 9/10/1972 Career OF: 389-408-280

YEAR TM-L	G	AB	R	H	2B	3B	HR	RBI	BB	SO	SB	CS	AVG	OBP	SLG	OPS	OPS+	BR/A	RC	RC/G	FR	G/POS	WS	TPW
1972 SD-N	7	21	4	7	1	1	0	1	1	3	0	1	.333	.364	.476	.840	147	1	3	4.72	0	/0-6(0-6-0)	1	0.0
1973 SD-N	113	389	52	121	22	3	8	37	37	50	9	3	.311	.374	.445	.819	137	20	66	6.36	1	*0-102(1-102-0)/3-2	18	1.9
1974 SD-N★	140	444	53	127	20	4	8	42	46	47	4	0	.286	.358	.403	.761	118	12	68	5.58	1	*0-122(8-114-0)/3-2	21	0.9
1975 SD-N	144	553	72	149	36	2	4	38	59	59	2	7	.269	.345	.363	.709	103	-0	71	4.48	-9	*0-139(0-139-0)	17	-1.3
1976 SD-N	109	384	54	109	22	1	5	27	65	53	1	2	.284	.393	.385	.778	132	19	62	5.80	-2	0-98(63-15-30)/1-9,3-3	18	1.3
1977 Cle-A	34	93	8	28	3	3	2	14	19	18	0	3	.301	.425	.462	.887	146	6	18	6.74	1	0-28(27-0-1)/D-4	4	0.5
1978 Cle-A	113	378	54	100	16	6	14	61	59	60	5	1	.265	.367	.450	.816	130	17	66	6.10	4	*0-110(108-0-6)	16	1.7
Tex-A	21	33	8	13	3	0	1	6	11	5	1	1	.394	.545	.576	1.121	215	6	12	15.04	1	0-13(8-0-5)/D-3	3	0.7
Yr.	134	411	62	113	19	6	15	67	70	65	6	2	.275	.383	.460	.843	137	24	78	6.69	6	*0-123(116-0-11)/D-3	19	2.5
1979 Tex-A	102	289	42	79	14	0	10	37	34	44	2	4	.273	.352	.426	.777	110	3	43	5.14	4	0-82(38-29-25)	9	0.4
1980 Tex-A	110	274	40	76	12	1	9	32	42	35	2	3	.277	.377	.427	.804	124	10	43	5.34	-3	0-77(19-3-60)/D-8	8	0.3
1981 Tex-A	67	199	26	46	9	1	3	26	23	25	0	3	.231	.317	.332	.649	92	-3	20	3.32	0	0-58(2-0-56)	4	-0.6
1982 Tex-A	103	308	35	86	13	3	3	26	39	37	0	3	.279	.371	.370	.741	110	5	44	5.04	-4	0-77(41-0-40),D-18	9	-0.3
1983 Det-A	57	134	20	34	5	2	4	22	28	17	0	0	.254	.390	.410	.801	124	6	23	5.74	-1	0-26(2-0-24),D-18	5	0.3
1984*Det-A	86	176	25	47	5	0	8	17	36	36	1	0	.267	.397	.432	.829	130	10	33	6.85	-1	0-36(27-0-9),D-33	8	0.7
1985 Det-A	78	155	19	38	7	1	5	25	24	25	0	1	.245	.350	.400	.750	106	1	22	4.65	0	D-33,0-18(14-0-4)	3	0.0
1986 Det-A	81	210	32	70	13	1	13	51	28	28	0	1	.333	.417	.590	1.007	171	21	54	10.19	0	D-52,0-19(10-0-10)	12	1.9
1987*Det-A	59	114	9	23	6	0	2	13	15	16	0	0	.202	.295	.307	.602	63	-6	10	2.89	0	0-31(21-0-10),D-16/3-1	1	-0.7
Total 16	1424	4154	553	1153	207	29	99	475	566	558	27	33	.278	.369	.413	.782	121	127	658	5.60	-9	*0-1042,D-185/1-9,3-8	157	7.8

• GRUBE, Frank Franklin Thomas "Hans" Grube b: 1/7/1905, Easton, PA d: 7/2/1945, New York, NY BR/TR, 5'9", 190 lbs. Deb: 5/12/1931

YEAR TM-L	G	AB	R	H	2B	3B	HR	RBI	BB	SO	SB	CS	AVG	OBP	SLG	OPS	OPS+	BR/A	RC	RC/G	FR	G/POS	WS	TPW
1931 Chi-A	88	265	29	58	13	2	1	24	22	22	2	2	.219	.284	.294	.578	55	-16	23	2.87	3	C-81	4	-0.8
1932 Chi-A	93	277	36	78	16	2	0	31	33	13	6	1	.282	.362	.354	.716	92	-1	38	4.93	0	C-92	7	0.4
1933 Chi-A	85	256	23	59	13	0	0	23	38	20	1	1	.230	.334	.281	.616	67	-10	27	3.50	-6	C-83	3	-1.0
1934 StL-A	65	170	22	49	10	0	0	11	24	11	2	1	.288	.379	.347	.727	82	-4	24	5.19	2	C-55	5	0.1
1935 StL-A	3	6	3	2	1	0	0	0	0	1	0	0	.333	.333	.500	.833	108	0	1	6.36	-0	/C-3	0	0.0
Chi-A	9	19	1	7	2	0	0	6	3	2	0	0	.368	.455	.474	.928	137	1	4	9.42	0	/C-9	1	0.2
Yr.	12	25	4	9	3	0	0	6	3	3	0	0	.360	.429	.480	.909	131	1	5	8.66	0	C-12	1	0.2
1936 Chi-A	33	93	6	15	2	1	0	11	9	15	1	0	.161	.235	.204	.440	9	-14	5	1.68	3	C-32	2	-0.8
1941 StL-A	18	39	1	6	2	0	0	1	2	4	0	0	.154	.195	.205	.400	6	-5	2	1.40	0	C-18	1	-0.4
Total 7	394	1125	121	274	59	5	1	107	131	88	12	5	.244	.326	.308	.634	67	-48	124	3.76	2	C-373	23	-2.4

• GRUBER, Kelly Kelly Wayne Gruber b: 2/26/1962, Houston, TX BR/TR, 6', 185 lbs. Deb: 4/20/1984 Career OF: 8-6-25

YEAR TM-L	G	AB	R	H	2B	3B	HR	RBI	BB	SO	SB	CS	AVG	OBP	SLG	OPS	OPS+	BR/A	RC	RC/G	FR	G/POS	WS	TPW
1984 Tor-A	15	16	1	1	0	0	1	2	0	5	0	0	.063	.063	.250	.313	-18	-3	0	.00	-1	3-12/0-2(0-0-2),S-1	0	-0.3

YEAR TM-L	G	AB	R	H	2B	3B	HR	RBI	BB	SO	SB	CS	AVG	OBP	SLG	OPS	OPS+	BR/A	RC	RC/G	FR	G/POS	WS	TPW
1985 Tor-A	5	13	0	3	0	0	0	1	0	3	0	0	.231	.231	.231	.462	26	-1	1	1.87	-1	/3-5,2-1	0	-0.2
1986 Tor-A	87	143	20	28	4	1	5	15	5	27	2	5	.196	.223	.343	.566	50	-12	8	1.78	-3	3-42,2-14,D-14/0-9(4-2-3),S	1	-1.5
1987 Tor-A	138	341	50	80	14	3	12	36	17	70	12	2	.235	.285	.399	.684	77	-11	37	3.60	-1	*3-119,S-21/2-7,0-2(0-2-0),D	6	-1.1
1988 Tor-A	158	569	75	158	33	5	16	81	38	92	23	5	.278	.331	.438	.768	113	11	79	4.80	24	*3-156/2-7,0-2(0-2-0),D-1,S	23	3.6
1989*Tor-A★	135	545	83	158	24	4	18	73	30	60	10	5	.290	.330	.448	.778	125	15	77	5.09	18	*3-119,0-16(3-0-14)/D-1,S	20	3.4
1990 Tor-A★	150	592	92	162	36	6	31	118	48	94	14	2	.274	.336	.512	.848	127	21	101	5.94	1	*3-145/0-6(0-0-6),D-1	25	2.4
1991*Tor-A	113	429	58	108	18	2	20	65	31	70	12	7	.252	.311	.443	.754	102	-1	58	4.54	12	*3-111/D-2	12	1.2
1992*Tor-A	120	446	42	102	16	3	11	43	26	72	7	7	.229	.277	.352	.629	72	-20	39	2.87	2	*3-120	6	-1.7
1993 Cal-A	18	65	10	18	3	0	3	9	2	11	0	0	.277	.309	.462	.770	101	-0	9	4.57	4	3-17/D-1,0-1	2	0.4
Total 10	939	3159	431	818	148	24	117	443	197	504	80	33	.259	.310	.432	.742	103	-0	409	4.40	57	3-846/0-38,2-29,S-29,D-21	95	6.2

• GRUDZIELANEK, Mark Mark James Grudzielanek b: 6/30/1970, Milwaukee, WI BR/TR, 6'1", 185 lbs. Deb: 4/28/1995

YEAR TM-L	G	AB	R	H	2B	3B	HR	RBI	BB	SO	SB	CS	AVG	OBP	SLG	OPS	OPS+	BR/A	RC	RC/G	FR	G/POS	WS	TPW
1995 Mon-N	78	269	27	66	12	2	1	20	14	47	8	3	.245	.300	.316	.616	61	-15	25	3.13	0	S-34,3-31,2-13	3	-1.1
1996 Mon-N★	153	657	99	201	34	4	6	49	26	83	33	7	.306	.341	.397	.738	92	-5	91	5.14	-10	*S-153	17	-0.3
1997 Mon-N	156	649	76	177	**54**	3	4	51	23	76	25	9	.273	.308	.384	.692	80	-19	75	4.04	2	*S-156	14	-0.5
1998 Mon-N	105	396	51	109	15	1	8	41	21	50	11	5	.275	.326	.379	.705	86	-8	47	4.11	-13	*S-105	9	-1.3
LA-N	51	193	11	51	6	0	2	21	5	23	7	0	.264	.290	.326	.616	66	-8	18	3.08	8	S-51	4	0.4
Yr.	156	589	62	160	21	1	10	62	26	73	18	5	.272	.315	.362	.676	80	-17	65	3.77	-5	*S-156	13	-0.8
1999 LA-N	123	488	72	159	23	5	7	46	31	65	6	6	.326	.378	.436	.815	112	7	78	5.94	-7	*S-119	13	0.9
2000 LA-N	148	617	101	172	35	6	7	49	45	81	12	3	.279	.337	.389	.726	88	-11	80	4.63	-2	*2-148/S-1	15	-0.5
2001 LA-N	133	539	83	146	21	3	13	55	28	83	4	4	.271	.320	.393	.713	90	-10	67	4.37	4	*2-133	17	0.0
2002 LA-N	150	536	56	145	23	0	9	50	22	89	4	1	.271	.303	.364	.667	80	-17	55	3.59	-10	*2-147/D-1	13	-2.0
2003*Chi-N	121	481	73	151	38	1	3	38	30	64	6	2	.314	.368	.416	.784	106	5	73	5.60	8	*2-121	18	1.8
Total 9	1218	4825	649	1377	261	25	60	420	245	661	116	40	.285	.331	.387	.718	88	-82	609	4.49	-20	S-619,2-562/3-31,D-1	123	-2.4

• GRYSKA, Sig Sigmund Stanley Gryska b: 11/4/1914, Chicago, IL d: 8/27/1994, Hines, IL BR/TR, 5'11.5", 173 lbs. Deb: 9/28/1938

YEAR TM-L	G	AB	R	H	2B	3B	HR	RBI	BB	SO	SB	CS	AVG	OBP	SLG	OPS	OPS+	BR/A	RC	RC/G	FR	G/POS	WS	TPW
1938 StL-A	7	21	3	10	2	1	0	4	3	3	0	0	.476	.542	.667	1.208	202	4	8	18.52	-1	/S-7	1	0.3
1939 StL-A	18	49	4	13	2	0	0	8	6	10	3	1	.265	.345	.306	.652	66	-2	6	3.98	-3	S-14	1	-0.4
Total 2	25	70	7	23	4	1	0	12	9	13	3	1	.329	.405	.414	.819	108	1	13	7.24	-4	/S-21	2	-0.2

• GUBANICH, Creighton Creighton Wade Gubanich b: 3/27/1972, Belleville, NJ BR/TR, 6'3", 200 lbs. Deb: 4/16/1999

YEAR TM-L	G	AB	R	H	2B	3B	HR	RBI	BB	SO	SB	CS	AVG	OBP	SLG	OPS	OPS+	BR/A	RC	RC/G	FR	G/POS	WS	TPW
1999 Bos-A	18	47	4	13	2	1	1	11	3	13	0	0	.277	.346	.426	.772	93	-1	6	4.48	1	C-14/D-2,3-1	1	0.1

• GUDAT, Marv Marvin John Gudat b: 8/27/1903, Goliad, TX d: 3/1/1954, Los Angeles, CA BL/TL, 5'11", 162 lbs. Deb: 5/21/1929 ♦

YEAR TM-L	G	AB	R	H	2B	3B	HR	RBI	BB	SO	SB	CS	AVG	OBP	SLG	OPS	OPS+	BR/A	RC	RC/G	FR	G/POS	WS	TPW
1929 Cin-N	9	10	0	2	0	0	0	0	0	0	0	....	.200	.200	.200	.400	-1	-0	0	1.21	-1	/P-7	2	0.3
1932*Chi-N	60	94	15	24	4	1	1	15	16	10	0	....	.255	.369	.351	.720	96	0	13	4.94	-2	0-14(5-1-9)/1-8,P-1	3	-0.2
Total 2	69	104	15	26	4	1	1	15	16	10	0	....	.250	.355	.337	.692	88	0	14	4.56	-2	/0-14,1-8,P-8	5	0.1

• GUERRA, Mike Fermin (Romero) Guerra b: 10/11/1912, Havana, Cuba d: 10/9/1992, Miami Beach, FL BR/TR, 5'10", 162 lbs. Deb: 9/19/1937

YEAR TM-L	G	AB	R	H	2B	3B	HR	RBI	BB	SO	SB	CS	AVG	OBP	SLG	OPS	OPS+	BR/A	RC	RC/G	FR	G/POS	WS	TPW
1937 Was-A	1	3	0	0	0	0	0	0	0	2	0	0	.000	.000	.000	.000	-105	-1	0	.00	0	/C-1	0	-0.1
1944 Was-A	75	210	29	59	7	2	1	29	13	14	8	2	.281	.323	.348	.670	96	-1	25	4.14	-4	C-58/0-1	6	-0.1
1945 Was-A	56	138	11	29	1	1	1	15	10	12	4	1	.210	.268	.254	.522	57	-7	9	2.08	0	C-38	2	-0.5
1946 Was-A	41	83	3	21	2	1	0	4	5	6	1	0	.253	.295	.301	.597	71	-3	7	2.93	0	C-27	1	-0.2
1947 Phi-A	72	209	20	45	2	2	0	18	10	15	1	2	.215	.251	.244	.495	37	-19	13	1.95	2	C-62	3	-1.4
1948 Phi-A	53	142	18	30	4	2	1	23	18	13	2	3	.211	.300	.289	.589	57	-10	12	2.55	-2	C-47	2	-0.9
1949 Phi-A	98	298	41	79	14	1	3	31	37	26	3	0	.265	.346	.349	.695	87	-4	37	4.22	0	C-95	9	0.0
1950 Phi-A	87	252	25	71	10	4	2	26	16	12	1	0	.282	.325	.377	.702	81	-8	31	4.37	1	C-78	5	-0.3
1951 Bos-A	10	32	1	5	0	0	0	2	6	5	1	0	.156	.289	.156	.446	21	-3	2	1.38	0	C-10	1	-0.3
Was-A	72	214	20	43	2	1	1	20	16	18	4	4	.201	.257	.234	.490	34	-21	13	1.87	-3	C-66	1	-2.0
Yr.	82	246	21	48	2	1	1	22	22	23	5	4	.195	.261	.224	.485	32	-24	14	1.80	-3	C-76	2	-2.3
Total 9	565	1581	168	382	42	14	9	168	131	123	25	12	.242	.300	.303	.603	66	-76	148	3.09	-7	C-482/0-1	30	-5.8

• GUERRERO, Juan Juan Antonio Guerrero b: 2/1/1967, Los Llanos, Dominican Republic BR/TR, 5'11", 160 lbs. Deb: 4/9/1992

YEAR TM-L	G	AB	R	H	2B	3B	HR	RBI	BB	SO	SB	CS	AVG	OBP	SLG	OPS	OPS+	BR/A	RC	RC/G	FR	G/POS	WS	TPW
1992 Hou-N	79	125	8	25	4	2	1	14	10	32	1	0	.200	.265	.288	.553	59	-7	10	2.74	1	S-19,3-12/0-3(3-0-0),2-2	1	-0.6

• GUERRERO, Mario Mario Miguel (Abud) Guerrero b: 9/28/1949, Santo Domingo, Dominican Republic BR/TR, 5'10", 155 lbs. Deb: 4/8/1973

YEAR TM-L	G	AB	R	H	2B	3B	HR	RBI	BB	SO	SB	CS	AVG	OBP	SLG	OPS	OPS+	BR/A	RC	RC/G	FR	G/POS	WS	TPW
1973 Bos-A	66	219	19	51	5	2	0	11	10	21	2	2	.233	.273	.274	.547	51	-15	16	2.39	3	S-46,2-24	3	-0.6
1974 Bos-A	93	284	18	70	6	2	0	23	13	22	3	1	.246	.284	.282	.566	59	-15	21	2.43	6	S-93	5	0.2
1975 StL-N	64	184	17	44	9	0	0	11	10	7	0	0	.239	.286	.288	.574	57	-11	14	2.40	5	S-64	3	0.1
1976 Cal-A	83	268	24	76	12	0	1	18	7	12	0	0	.284	.309	.340	.649	96	-2	27	3.54	-7	2-41,S-41/D-7	8	-0.4
1977 Cal-A	86	244	17	69	8	2	1	28	4	16	0	0	.283	.294	.344	.639	76	-8	24	3.51	1	S-31,D-19,2-12	4	-0.4
1978 Oak-A	143	505	27	139	18	4	3	38	15	35	0	5	.275	.304	.345	.649	86	-12	49	3.29	-11	*S-142	11	-0.9
1979 Oak-A	46	166	12	38	5	0	0	18	6	7	0	1	.229	.256	.259	.515	42	-14	10	1.97	-1	S-43	1	-1.0
1980 Oak-A	116	381	32	91	16	2	2	23	19	32	3	3	.239	.277	.307	.584	64	-20	29	2.46	-12	*S-116	3	-2.0
Total 8	697	2251	166	578	79	12	7	170	84	152	8	12	.257	.288	.312	.600	70	-97	190	2.82	-14	S-576/2-77,D-26	38	-5.0

• GUERRERO, Pedro Pedro Guerrero b: 6/29/1956, San Pedro de Macoris, Dominican Republic BR/TR, 5'11", 195 lbs. Deb: 9/22/1978 Career OF: 216-108-239

YEAR TM-L	G	AB	R	H	2B	3B	HR	RBI	BB	SO	SB	CS	AVG	OBP	SLG	OPS	OPS+	BR/A	RC	RC/G	FR	G/POS	WS	TPW
1978 LA-N	5	8	3	5	0	1	0	1	0	0	0	0	.625	.625	.875	1.500	316	2	4	39.38	0	/1-4	1	0.2
1979 LA-N	25	62	7	15	2	0	2	9	1	14	2	0	.242	.254	.371	.625	69	-3	6	3.17	0	0-12(4-1-9)/1-8,3-3	1	-0.4
1980 LA-N	75	183	27	59	9	1	7	31	12	31	2	1	.322	.364	.497	.861	141	9	33	6.79	1	0-40(3-25-15),2-12/3-3,1-2	9	1.0
1981*LA-N★	98	347	46	104	17	2	12	48	34	57	5	9	.300	.366	.464	.830	139	14	54	5.40	0	0-75(0-8-70),3-21/1-1	14	1.1
1982 LA-N	150	575	87	175	27	5	32	100	65	89	22	5	.304	.380	.536	.915	157	**46**	120	7.76	4	*0-137(0-44-105),3-24	30	4.7
1983*LA-N★	160	584	87	174	28	6	32	103	72	110	23	7	.298	.377	.531	.908	150	41	118	7.35	8	*3-157/1-2	32	4.9
1984 LA-N	144	535	85	162	29	4	16	72	49	105	9	8	.303	.362	.462	.824	131	20	89	6.03	-3	3-76,0-58(1-20-38),1-16	23	1.4
1985*LA-N★	137	487	99	156	22	2	33	87	83	68	12	4	.320	**.425**	**.577**	**1.002**	**183**	**58**	121	**9.29**	11	0-81(71-10-1),3-44,1-12	35	**6.8**
1986 LA-N	31	61	7	15	3	0	5	10	2	19	0	0	.246	.281	.541	.822	131	2	9	5.15	-1	0-10(10-0-0)/1-4	2	0.1
1987 LA-N★	152	545	89	184	25	2	27	89	74	85	9	7	.338	.421	.539	.960	156	44	121	8.33	0	*0-109(109-0-0),1-40	28	3.8
1988 LA-N	59	215	24	64	7	1	5	35	25	33	2	1	.298	.379	.409	.788	130	9	35	6.06	-3	3-45,1-15/0-2(1-0-1)	10	0.5
StL-N	44	149	16	40	7	1	5	30	21	26	2	0	.268	.366	.430	.796	126	6	24	5.66	-3	1-37/0-7(7-0-0)	8	0.0
Yr.	103	364	40	104	14	2	10	65	46	59	4	1	.286	.373	.418	.791	129	15	60	5.89	-7	1-52,3-45/0-9(8-0-1)	18	0.6
1989 StL-N★	162	570	60	177	**42**	1	17	117	79	84	2	0	.311	.398	.477	.875	145	36	109	6.95	-9	*1-160	30	1.8
1990 StL-N	136	498	42	140	31	1	13	80	44	70	1	1	.281	.341	.426	.766	109	5	69	4.88	-4	*1-132	10	-0.8
1991 StL-N	115	427	41	116	12	1	8	70	37	46	4	2	.272	.331	.361	.692	94	-3	50	4.08	-3	*1-112	13	-1.4
1992 StL-N	43	146	10	32	6	1	1	16	11	25	2	2	.219	.274	.295	.568	63	-8	11	2.43	-6	1-28,0-10(10-0-0)	0	-1.7
Total 15	1536	5392	730	1618	267	29	215	898	609	862	97	47	.300	.374	.480	.854	139	278	974	6.53	-7	1-573,0-541,3-373/2-12	246	21.9

• GUERRERO, Vladimir Vladimir Alvino Guerrero b: 2/9/1976, Nizao Bani, Dominican Republic BR/TR, 6'2", 218 lbs. Deb: 9/19/1996 Career OF: 0-2-990

YEAR TM-L	G	AB	R	H	2B	3B	HR	RBI	BB	SO	SB	CS	AVG	OBP	SLG	OPS	OPS+	BR/A	RC	RC/G	FR	G/POS	WS	TPW
1996 Mon-N	9	27	2	5	0	0	1	1	0	3	0	0	.185	.185	.296	.481	24	-3	1	1.39	0	/0-8(0-1-7)	0	-0.3
1997 Mon-N	90	325	44	98	22	2	11	40	19	39	3	4	.302	.353	.483	.836	117	6	51	5.65	-1	0-85(0-1-84)	10	0.1
1998 Mon-N	159	623	108	202	37	7	38	109	42	95	11	9	.324	.374	.589	.963	150	41	129	7.74	-1	*0-157(0-0-157)	29	3.1
1999 Mon-N★	160	610	102	193	37	5	42	131	55	62	14	7	.316	.379	.600	.979	147	40	132	8.03	2	*0-160(0-0-160)	28	3.2
2000 Mon-N★	154	571	101	197	28	11	44	123	58	74	9	10	.345	.413	.664	1.077	162	50	147	9.87	1	*0-151(0-0-151)/D-2	29	4.0
2001 Mon-N★	159	599	107	184	45	4	34	108	60	88	37	16	.307	.379	.566	.945	137	34	118	6.95	3	*0-159(0-0-158)	23	2.7
2002 Mon-N★	161	614	106	**206**	37	2	39	111	84	70	40	20	.336	.420	.593	1.013	158	53	145	8.66	3	*0-161(0-0-161)	29	4.7
2003 Mon-N	112	394	71	130	20	3	25	79	63	53	9	5	.330	.430	.586	1.016	137	24	94	8.74	2	*0-112(0-0-112)	16	2.0
Total 8	1004	3763	641	1215	226	34	234	702	381	484	123	71	.323	.392	.588	.980	145	245	818	7.98	10	0-993/D-2	164	19.6

• GUERRERO, Wilton Wilton Alvaro Guerrero b: 10/24/1974, Don Gregorio, Dominican Republic BR/TR, 5'11", 145 lbs. Deb: 9/3/1996 Career OF: 80-19-27

YEAR TM-L	G	AB	R	H	2B	3B	HR	RBI	BB	SO	SB	CS	AVG	OBP	SLG	OPS	OPS+	BR/A	RC	RC/G	FR	G/POS	WS	TPW
1996 LA-N	5	2	1	0	0	0	0	0	0	2	0	0	.000	.000	.000	.000	-109	-1	0	.00	0	....	0	-0.1
1997 LA-N	111	357	39	104	10	9	4	32	8	52	6	5	.291	.307	.403	.710	91	-8	41	3.98	-12	2-90/S-5	8	-1.5
1998 LA-N	64	180	21	51	4	3	0	7	4	33	5	2	.283	.303	.339	.642	73	-7	18	3.52	-3	2-32,S-14/0-7(6-1-0)	1	-0.8

YEAR TM-L	G	AB	R	H	2B	3B	HR	RBI	BB	SO	SB	CS	AVG	OBP	SLG	OPS	OPS+	BR/A	RC	RC/G	FR	G/POS	WS	TPW
Mon-N	52	222	29	63	10	6	2	20	10	30	3	0	.284	.315	.410	.725	90	-3	30	4.88	-11	2-52	6	-1.1
Yr.	116	402	50	114	14	9	2	27	14	63	8	2	.284	.309	.378	.687	82	-11	48	4.26	-14	2-84,S-14/O-7(6-1-0)	7	-2.0
1999 Mon-N	132	315	42	92	15	7	2	31	13	38	7	6	.292	.324	.403	.727	85	-9	40	4.43	-8	2-54,O-22(22-0-0)/D-5	7	-1.6
2000 Mon-N	127	288	30	77	7	2	2	23	19	41	8	1	.267	.313	.326	.639	60	-16	30	3.63	3	O-75(42-13-24)/D-6,2-1	2	-1.4
2001 Cin-N	60	142	16	48	5	1	1	8	3	17	5	2	.338	.352	.408	.760	92	-2	20	5.56	-5	S-16,2-11/O-6(6-0-0),3-4	4	-0.5
2002 Cin-N	59	78	9	19	1	1	0	4	6	13	2	1	.244	.298	.282	.580	52	-5	7	2.88	0	2-10/S-7,3-3	1	-0.5
Mon-N	44	62	3	12	1	0	0	1	1	19	5	0	.194	.206	.210	.416	10	-7	3	1.55	-3	O-12(4-5-3)/2-7,3-2	0	-0.9
Yr.	103	140	12	31	2	1	0	5	7	32	7	1	.221	.259	.250	.509	34	-13	10	2.28	-3	2-17,O-12(4-5-3)/S-7,3-5	1	-1.4
Total 7	654	1646	190	466	53	29	11	126	64	245	41	17	.283	.311	.371	.682	77	-59	190	4.02	-39	2-257,O-122/S-42,D-11,3-9	29	-8.5

• GUEVARA, Giomar Giomar Antonio (Diaz) Guevara b: 10/23/1972, Miranda, Venezuela BB/TR, 5'8", 150 lbs. Deb: 9/19/1997

YEAR TM-L	G	AB	R	H	2B	3B	HR	RBI	BB	SO	SB	CS	AVG	OBP	SLG	OPS	OPS+	BR/A	RC	RC/G	FR	G/POS	WS	TPW
1997 Sea-A	5	4	0	0	0	0	0	0	0	2	1	0	.000	.000	.000	.000	-101	-1	0	.00	-1	/2-2,D-2,S-1	0	-0.1
1998 Sea-A	11	13	4	3	2	0	0	0	4	4	0	0	.231	.444	.385	.829	118	1	2	6.01	-1	/2-5,S-5	0	0.0
1999 Sea-A	10	12	2	3	2	0	0	2	0	2	0	0	.250	.250	.417	.667	65	-1	1	3.75	-1	/S-9	0	-0.1
Total 3	26	29	6	6	4	0	0	2	4	8	1	0	.207	.324	.345	.668	74	-1	4	4.16	-3	/S-15,2-7,D-2	0	-0.3

• GUIEL, Aaron Aaron Colin Guiel b: 10/5/1972, Vancouver, Canada BL/TR, 5'10", 200 lbs. Deb: 6/22/2002 Career OF: 1-2-148

YEAR TM-L	G	AB	R	H	2B	3B	HR	RBI	BB	SO	SB	CS	AVG	OBP	SLG	OPS	OPS+	BR/A	RC	RC/G	FR	G/POS	WS	TPW
2002 KC-A	70	240	30	56	13	0	4	38	19	61	1	5	.233	.300	.338	.638	62	-15	24	3.25	0	O-61(0-1-61)/D-2	4	-1.7
2003 KC-A	99	354	63	98	30	0	15	52	27	63	3	5	.277	.350	.489	.839	104	1	61	6.09	6	O-89(1-1-87)/D-2	12	0.1
Total 2	169	594	93	154	43	0	19	90	46	124	4	10	.259	.330	.428	.758	87	-14	85	4.89	6	O-150/D-4	16	-1.6

• GUILLEN, Carlos Carlos Alfonso Guillen b: 9/30/1975, Maracay, Venezuela BB/TR, 6'1", 180 lbs. Deb: 9/6/1998

YEAR TM-L	G	AB	R	H	2B	3B	HR	RBI	BB	SO	SB	CS	AVG	OBP	SLG	OPS	OPS+	BR/A	RC	RC/G	FR	G/POS	WS	TPW
1998 Sea-A	10	39	9	13	1	1	0	5	3	9	2	0	.333	.381	.410	.791	106	1	7	7.05	-1	2-10	2	0.1
1999 Sea-A	5	19	2	3	0	0	1	3	1	6	0	0	.158	.200	.316	.516	28	-2	1	1.45	1	/S-3,2-2	0	-0.1
2000*Sea-A	90	288	45	74	15	2	7	42	28	53	1	3	.257	.327	.396	.723	87	-7	37	4.28	0	3-68,S-23	8	-0.5
2001*Sea-A	140	456	72	118	21	4	5	53	53	89	4	1	.259	.337	.355	.693	88	-7	57	4.28	2	*S-137/D-1	14	0.5
2002 Sea-A	134	475	73	124	24	6	9	56	46	91	4	5	.261	.328	.394	.721	94	-6	61	4.44	-13	*S-130/D-3	12	-0.8
2003 Sea-A	109	388	63	107	19	3	7	52	52	64	4	4	.276	.363	.394	.757	103	2	55	4.87	3	S-76,3-32/D-1	12	1.1
Total 6	488	1665	264	439	80	16	29	211	183	312	15	13	.264	.338	.383	.722	93	-19	218	4.48	-9	S-369,3-100/2-12,D-5	48	0.3

• GUILLEN, Jose Jose Manuel Guillen b: 5/17/1976, San Cristobal, Dominican Republic BR/TR, 5'11", 165 lbs. Deb: 4/1/1997 Career OF: 38-14-657

YEAR TM-L	G	AB	R	H	2B	3B	HR	RBI	BB	SO	SB	CS	AVG	OBP	SLG	OPS	OPS+	BR/A	RC	RC/G	FR	G/POS	WS	TPW
1997 Pit-N	143	498	58	133	20	5	14	70	17	88	1	2	.267	.302	.412	.714	83	-15	57	3.98	-2	*O-136(0-4-134)	7	-2.3
1998 Pit-N	153	573	60	153	38	2	14	84	21	100	3	5	.267	.300	.414	.714	84	-17	69	4.26	7	*O-151(0-2-149)	11	-1.7
1999 Pit-N	40	120	18	32	6	0	1	18	10	21	1	0	.267	.323	.342	.665	69	-6	12	3.31	0	O-37(0-0-37)	2	-0.7
TB-A	47	168	24	41	10	0	2	13	10	36	0	0	.244	.314	.339	.653	66	-9	17	3.29	1	O-47(0-0-47)	1	-0.9
2000 TB-A	105	316	40	80	16	5	10	41	18	65	3	1	.253	.320	.430	.750	88	-6	44	4.81	4	O-99(0-1-98)	6	-0.6
2001 TB-A	41	135	14	37	5	0	3	11	6	26	2	3	.274	.319	.378	.697	84	-4	15	3.99	7	O-36(0-0-36)/D-3	2	0.0
2002 Ari-N	54	131	13	30	4	0	4	15	7	25	3	4	.229	.279	.351	.630	59	-9	10	2.38	-1	O-37(2-2-34)/D-1	1	-1.2
Cin-N	31	109	12	27	3	0	4	16	7	18	1	1	.248	.299	.385	.684	77	-4	11	3.21	-1	O-27(4-0-26)	1	-0.6
Yr.	85	240	25	57	7	0	8	31	14	43	4	5	.238	.288	.367	.655	67	-13	21	2.75	-2	O-64(6-2-60)/D-1	2	-1.8
2003 Cin-N	91	315	52	106	21	1	23	63	17	63	1	3	.337	.387	.629	1.016	162	26	73	8.59	4	O-78(22-1-63)	17	2.6
*Oak-A	45	170	25	45	7	1	8	23	7	32	0	0	.265	.313	.459	.772	99	-1	22	4.33	-5	O-44(10-4-33)/D-1	4	-0.7
Total 7	750	2535	316	684	130	14	83	354	120	474	15	19	.270	.317	.430	.747	92	-45	328	4.49	16	O-692/D-5	52	-6.1

• GUILLEN, Ozzie Oswaldo Jose (Barrios) Guillen b: 1/20/1964, Oculare del Tuy, Venezuela BL/TR, 5'11", 150 lbs. Deb: 4/9/1985 C

YEAR TM-L	G	AB	R	H	2B	3B	HR	RBI	BB	SO	SB	CS	AVG	OBP	SLG	OPS	OPS+	BR/A	RC	RC/G	FR	G/POS	WS	TPW
1985 Chi-A	150	491	71	134	21	9	1	33	12	36	7	4	.273	.292	.358	.650	74	-19	50	3.63	6	*S-150	15	0.1
1986 Chi-A	159	547	58	137	19	4	2	47	12	52	8	4	.250	.268	.311	.579	55	-35	43	2.58	19	*S-157/D-1	9	0.0
1987 Chi-A	149	560	64	156	22	7	2	51	22	52	25	8	.279	.307	.354	.661	73	-21	61	3.69	23	*S-149	14	1.7
1988 Chi-A★	156	566	58	148	16	7	0	39	25	40	25	13	.261	.295	.314	.610	71	-23	50	2.94	32	*S-156	17	2.1
1989 Chi-A	155	597	63	151	20	8	1	54	15	48	36	17	.253	.271	.318	.590	67	-28	49	2.75	20	*S-155	12	0.5
1990 Chi-A★	160	516	61	144	21	4	1	58	26	37	13	17	.279	.315	.341	.656	85	-16	52	3.39	11	*S-159	18	0.8
1991 Chi-A★	154	524	52	143	20	3	3	49	11	38	21	15	.273	.288	.340	.628	75	-22	48	3.07	11	*S-149	9	0.1
1992 Chi-A	12	40	5	8	4	0	0	7	1	5	1	0	.200	.220	.300	.520	45	-3	3	1.98	1	S-12	1	-0.1
1993*Chi-A	134	457	44	128	23	4	4	50	10	41	5	4	.280	.296	.374	.670	80	-15	49	3.70	-1	*S-133	12	-0.5
1994 Chi-A	100	365	46	105	9	5	1	39	14	35	5	4	.288	.314	.348	.662	72	-17	39	3.77	-3	S-99	8	-1.1
1995 Chi-A	122	415	50	103	20	3	1	41	13	25	6	7	.248	.271	.318	.589	55	-30	32	2.57	9	*S-120/D-1	5	-1.2
1996 Chi-A	150	499	62	131	24	8	4	45	10	27	6	5	.263	.277	.367	.644	64	-30	47	3.18	-4	*S-146/O-2(2-0-0)	7	-2.1
1997 Chi-A	142	490	59	120	21	6	4	52	22	24	5	3	.245	.277	.337	.614	62	-29	45	3.10	-6	*S-139	10	-2.2
1998 Bal-A	12	16	2	1	0	0	0	0	1	2	0	1	.063	.118	.063	.180	-52	-4	0	.00	-1	/S-6,3-1	0	-0.4
*Atl-N	83	264	35	73	15	1	1	22	24	25	1	4	.277	.339	.352	.691	82	-8	32	4.28	-8	S-71/2-2,1-1,3-1	7	-1.0
1999*Atl-N	92	232	21	56	16	0	1	20	15	17	4	2	.241	.287	.323	.611	54	-17	21	2.94	-1	S-53/3-6,2-1	3	-1.3
2000 TB-A	63	107	22	26	4	0	2	12	6	7	1	0	.243	.283	.336	.620	57	-7	10	3.41	-2	S-42,3-11/1-5,2-2	1	-0.7
Total 16	1993	6686	773	1764	275	69	28	619	239	511	169	108	.264	.290	.338	.628	69	-323	632	3.19	107	*S-1896/3-19,1-6,2-5,D-2,O	148	-5.2

• GUINDON, Bobby Robert Joseph Guindon b: 9/4/1943, Brookline, MA BL/TL, 6'2", 185 lbs. Deb: 9/19/1964

YEAR TM-L	G	AB	R	H	2B	3B	HR	RBI	BB	SO	SB	CS	AVG	OBP	SLG	OPS	OPS+	BR/A	RC	RC/G	FR	G/POS	WS	TPW
1964 Bos-A	5	8	0	1	1	0	0	0	1	4	0	0	.125	.222	.250	.472	30	-1	1	1.94	0	/1-1,O-1	0	-0.1

• GUINEY, Ben Benjamin Franklin Guiney b: 11/16/1858, Detroit, MI d: 12/5/1930, Detroit, MI BB/TR, 6', 170 lbs. Deb: 9/4/1883

YEAR TM-L	G	AB	R	H	2B	3B	HR	RBI	BB	SO	SB	CS	AVG	OBP	SLG	OPS	OPS+	BR/A	RC	RC/G	FR	G/POS	WS	TPW
1883 Det-N	1	5	1	1	0	0	0	0	0	1	....	....	.200	.200	.200	.400	23	-0	0	1.41	0	/O-1	0	-0.1
1884 Det-N	2	7	0	0	0	0	0	0	0	3	....	....	.000	.000	.000	.000	-106	-2	0	.00	0	/C-2	0	-0.1
Total 2	3	12	1	1	0	0	0	0	0	4	....	....	.083	.083	.083	.167	-52	-2	0	.51	0	/C-2,O-1	0	-0.2

• GUINTINI, Ben Benjamin John Guintini b: 1/13/1919, Los Banos, CA d: 12/2/1998, Roseville, CA BR/TR, 6'1.5", 190 lbs. Deb: 4/21/1946 Career OF: 1-0-1

YEAR TM-L	G	AB	R	H	2B	3B	HR	RBI	BB	SO	SB	CS	AVG	OBP	SLG	OPS	OPS+	BR/A	RC	RC/G	FR	G/POS	WS	TPW
1946 Pit-N	2	3	0	0	0	0	0	0	0	0	0	....	.000	.000	.000	.000	-98	-1	0	.00	-0	/O-1	0	-0.1
1950 Phi-A	3	4	0	0	0	0	0	0	0	1	0	0	.000	.000	.000	.000	-102	-1	0	.00	1	/O-1	0	-0.1
Total 2	5	7	0	0	0	0	0	0	0	1	0	0	.000	.000	.000	.000	-100	-2	0	.00	1	/O-2	0	-0.2

• GUISTO, Lou Louis Joseph Guisto b: 1/16/1895, Napa, CA d: 10/15/1989, Napa, CA BR/TR, 5'11", 193 lbs. Deb: 9/10/1916

YEAR TM-L	G	AB	R	H	2B	3B	HR	RBI	BB	SO	SB	CS	AVG	OBP	SLG	OPS	OPS+	BR/A	RC	RC/G	FR	G/POS	WS	TPW
1916 Cle-A	6	19	2	3	0	0	0	2	4	3	1	....	.158	.304	.158	.462	37	-1	1	1.90	0	/1-6	0	-0.2
1917 Cle-A	73	200	9	37	4	2	0	29	25	18	3	....	.185	.282	.225	.507	51	-11	14	2.09	-4	1-59	1	-1.8
1921 Cle-A	2	2	0	1	0	0	0	1	0	1	0	0	.500	.500	.500	1.000	153	0	0	12.72	0	/1-1	0	0.0
1922 Cle-A	35	84	7	21	10	1	0	9	2	7	0	0	.250	.276	.393	.669	72	-4	9	3.63	1	1-24	1	-0.4
1923 Cle-A	40	144	17	26	5	0	0	18	15	15	1	1	.181	.263	.215	.478	27	-15	9	1.95	-1	1-40	0	-1.8
Total 5	156	449	35	88	19	3	0	59	46	44	5	1	.196	.277	.252	.528	47	-31	33	2.33	-4	1-130	2	-4.2

• GULAN, Mike Michael Watts Gulan b: 12/18/1970, Steubenville, OH BR/TR, 6'1", 192 lbs. Deb: 5/14/1997

YEAR TM-L	G	AB	R	H	2B	3B	HR	RBI	BB	SO	SB	CS	AVG	OBP	SLG	OPS	OPS+	BR/A	RC	RC/G	FR	G/POS	WS	TPW
1997 StL-N	5	9	2	0	0	0	0	1	1	5	0	0	.000	.100	.000	.100	-72	-2	0	.08	0	/3-3	0	-0.2
2001 Fla-N	6	6	1	0	0	0	0	0	2	2	0	0	.000	.250	.000	.250	-28	-1	0	.59	0	/3-1	0	-0.1
Total 2	11	15	3	0	0	0	0	1	3	7	0	0	.000	.167	.000	.167	-52	-3	0	.28	0	/3-4	0	-0.3

• GULDEN, Brad Bradley Lee Gulden b: 6/10/1956, New Ulm, MN BL/TR, 5'10", 180 lbs. Deb: 9/22/1978

YEAR TM-L	G	AB	R	H	2B	3B	HR	RBI	BB	SO	SB	CS	AVG	OBP	SLG	OPS	OPS+	BR/A	RC	RC/G	FR	G/POS	WS	TPW
1978 LA-N	3	4	0	0	0	0	0	0	0	2	0	0	.000	.000	.000	.000	-100	-1	0	.00	0	/C-3	0	-0.1
1979 NY-A	40	92	10	15	4	0	0	6	9	16	0	1	.163	.238	.207	.444	21	-10	4	1.42	3	C-40	2	-0.6
1980 NY-A	2	3	1	1	0	0	1	2	0	0	0	0	.333	.333	1.333	1.667	339	1	1	18.00	0	/C-2	0	0.1
1981 Sea-A	8	16	0	3	2	0	0	1	0	2	0	0	.188	.188	.313	.500	40	-1	1	1.95	0	/C-6	0	-0.1
1982 Mon-N	5	6	1	0	0	0	0	0	1	1	0	0	.000	.143	.000	.143	-56	-1	0	.17	0	/C-2	0	-0.1
1984 Cin-N	107	292	31	66	8	2	4	33	33	35	2	2	.226	.309	.308	.617	71	-11	28	3.19	2	*C-100	6	-0.6
1986 SF-N	17	22	2	2	0	0	0	1	2	5	0	0	.091	.167	.091	.258	-28	-4	0	.32	0	C-10	0	-0.4
Total 7	182	435	45	87	14	2	5	43	45	61	2	3	.200	.278	.276	.554	53	-28	35	2.57	4	C-163	8	-1.8

YEAR TM-L	G	AB	R	H	2B	3B	HR	RBI	BB	SO	SB	CS	AVG	OBP	SLG	OPS	OPS+	BR/A	RC	RC/G	FR	G/POS	WS	TPW
• GULLEY, Tom	Thomas Jefferson Gulley b: 12/25/1899, Garner, NC d: 11/24/1966, St. Charles, AR BL/TR, 5'11", 178 lbs. Deb: 8/24/1923 Career OF: 0-3-15																							
1923 Cle-A	2	3	1	1	1	0	0	0	0	0	0	0	.333	.333	.667	1.000	159	0	1	8.48	-0	/O-1	0	0.0
1924 Cle-A	8	20	4	3	0	1	0	1	3	2	0	0	.150	.261	.250	.511	32	-2	1	2.26	0	/O-5(0-2-3)	0	-0.2
1926 Chi-A	16	35	5	8	3	1	0	8	5	2	0	0	.229	.325	.371	.696	84	-1	5	4.16	-1	O-12(0-0-12)	1	-0.2
Total 3	**26**	**58**	**10**	**12**	**4**	**2**	**0**	**9**	**8**	**4**	**0**	**0**	**.207**	**.303**	**.345**	**.648**	**70**	**-3**	**7**	**3.67**	**-1**	**/O-18**	**1**	**-0.4**
• GULLIC, Ted	Tedd Jasper Gullic b: 1/2/1907, Koshkonong, MO d: 1/28/2000, West Plains, MO BR/TR, 6'2", 175 lbs. Deb: 4/15/1930 Career OF: 14-16-89																							
1930 StL-A	92	308	39	77	7	5	4	44	27	43	4	0	.250	.310	.344	.655	64	-16	35	3.80	2	O-82(0-0-82)/1-3	4	-1.9
1933 StL-A	104	304	34	74	18	3	5	35	15	38	3	1	.243	.281	.372	.653	67	-15	32	3.61	7	O-36(14-16-7),3-33,1-14	4	-0.9
Total 2	**196**	**612**	**73**	**151**	**25**	**8**	**9**	**79**	**42**	**81**	**7**	**1**	**.247**	**.296**	**.358**	**.654**	**65**	**-31**	**67**	**3.71**	**8**	**O-118/3-33,1-17**	**8**	**-2.9**
• GULLIVER, Glenn	Glenn James Gulliver b: 10/15/1954, Detroit, MI BL/TR, 5'11", 175 lbs. Deb: 7/17/1982																							
1982 Bal-A	50	145	24	29	7	0	1	5	37	18	0	0	.200	.363	.269	.632	77	-2	17	3.87	4	3-50	4	0.1
1983 Bal-A	23	47	5	10	3	0	0	2	9	5	0	1	.213	.339	.277	.616	73	-2	5	3.19	1	3-21	1	-0.1
Total 2	**73**	**192**	**29**	**39**	**10**	**0**	**1**	**7**	**46**	**23**	**0**	**1**	**.203**	**.357**	**.271**	**.628**	**76**	**-4**	**22**	**3.70**	**5**	**/3-71**	**5**	**0.0**
• GUNKLE, Fred	Frederick William Gunkle b: 10/26/1857, Reading, PA d: 12/21/1936, Long Beach, CA Deb: 5/17/1879																							
1879 Cle-N	1	3	1	0	0	0	0	0	0	1	....	....	.000	.000	.000	.000	-101	-1	0	.00	-2	/C-1,O-1	0	-0.2
• GUNNING, Hy	Hyland Gunning b: 8/6/1888, Maplewood, NJ d: 3/28/1975, Togus, ME BL/TR, 6'1.5", 189 lbs. Deb: 8/8/1911																							
1911 Bos-A	4	9	0	1	0	0	0	2	2	....	0	....	.111	.273	.111	.384	9	-1	0	1.21	0	/1-4	0	-0.2
• GUNNING, Tom	Thomas Francis Gunning b: 3/4/1862, Newmarket, NH d: 3/17/1931, Fall River, MA BR/TR, 5'10", 160 lbs. Deb: 7/26/1884 U																							
1884 Bos-N	12	45	4	5	1	1	0	2	1	12	....	....	.111	.130	.178	.308	-4	-5	1	.74	1	C-12	1	-0.3
1885 Bos-N	48	174	17	32	3	0	0	15	5	29	....	....	.184	.207	.201	.408	33	-12	7	1.41	-2	C-48	2	-1.0
1886 Bos-N	27	98	15	22	2	1	0	7	3	19	3	....	.224	.248	.265	.513	58	-5	7	2.61	-8	C-27	1	-1.0
1887 Phi-N	28	109	22	32	6	1	1	16	5	6	18	....	.294	.306	.365	.672	81	-3	18	6.05	5	C-28	4	0.3
1888 Phi-a	23	92	18	18	0	0	0	5	2	....	14	....	.196	.237	.196	.433	39	-6	8	2.84	-2	C-23	2	-0.6
1889 Phi-a	8	24	3	6	0	1	1	1	0	4	3	....	.250	.250	.458	.708	101	-0	4	5.28	-1	/C-8	1	-0.1
Total 6	**146**	**542**	**79**	**115**	**12**	**4**	**2**	**46**	**16**	**70**	**38**	**....**	**.212**	**.235**	**.253**	**.488**	**48**	**-32**	**45**	**2.81**	**-8**	**C-146**	**11**	**-2.6**
• GUNSON, Joe	Joseph Brook Gunson b: 3/23/1863, Philadelphia, PA d: 11/15/1942, Philadelphia, PA BR/TR, 5'6", 160 lbs. Deb: 6/14/1884 U Career OF: 12-13-20																							
1884 Was-U	45	166	15	23	2	0	0	....	3	....	....	....	.139	.154	.151	.304	3	-16	4	.77	2	C-33,O-18(0-10-9)	2	-1.1
1889 KC-a	34	122	15	24	3	1	0	12	3	17	2	....	.197	.228	.238	.466	31	-12	7	1.96	-4	C-32/3-1,O-1	1	-1.1
1892 Bal-N	89	314	35	67	10	5	0	32	16	17	2	....	.213	.267	.277	.544	63	-15	24	2.66	1	C-67,O-20(10-3-7)/1-2,2-1	2	-0.9
1893 StL-N	40	151	20	41	5	0	0	15	6	6	0	....	.272	.321	.305	.626	66	-7	15	3.65	0	C-35/O-5(1-0-4)	3	-0.4
Cle-N	21	73	11	19	1	0	0	9	6	0	0	....	.260	.316	.274	.590	54	-5	6	3.18	1	C-20	1	-0.2
Yr.	61	224	31	60	6	0	0	24	12	6	0	....	.268	.320	.295	.614	62	-12	22	3.49	0	C-55/O-5(1-0-4)	4	-0.6
Total 4	**229**	**826**	**96**	**174**	**21**	**6**	**0**	**68**	**34**	**40**	**4**	**....**	**.211**	**.254**	**.251**	**.505**	**47**	**-55**	**57**	**2.35**	**-1**	**C-187/O-44,1-2,2-1,3-1**	**9**	**-3.6**
• GUST, Ernie	Ernest Herman Frank "Red" Gust b: 1/24/1888, Bay City, MI d: 10/26/1945, Maupin, OR BR/TR, 6', 170 lbs. Deb: 8/17/1911																							
1911 StL-A	3	12	0	0	0	0	0	0	0	....	0	....	.000	.000	.000	.000	-104	-3	0	.00	0	/1-3	0	-0.3
• GUSTINE, Frankie	Frank William Gustine b: 2/20/1920, Hoopeston, IL d: 4/1/1991, Davenport, IA BR/TR, 6', 180 lbs. Deb: 9/13/1939 C																							
1939 Pit-N	22	70	5	13	3	0	0	3	9	4	0	....	.186	.278	.229	.507	38	-6	5	1.97	-0	3-22	1	-0.5
1940 Pit-N	133	524	59	147	32	7	1	55	35	39	7	....	.281	.328	.374	.702	94	-5	63	4.31	-26	*2-130	12	-2.3
1941 Pit-N	121	463	46	125	24	7	1	46	28	38	5	....	.270	.313	.359	.672	89	-8	51	3.94	-4	*2-104,3-15	11	-0.5
1942 Pit-N	115	388	34	89	11	4	2	35	29	27	5	....	.229	.286	.294	.580	68	-16	31	2.65	-15	*2-108/3-2,S-2,C-1	4	-2.6
1943 Pit-N	112	414	40	120	21	3	0	43	32	36	12	....	.290	.341	.355	.696	98	-1	51	4.41	-3	S-68,2-40/1-1	12	0.3
1944 Pit-N	127	405	42	93	18	3	2	42	33	41	8	....	.230	.288	.304	.591	64	-20	34	2.76	-17	*S-116,2-11/3-1	4	-2.9
1945 Pit-N	128	478	67	134	27	5	2	66	37	33	8	....	.280	.335	.370	.705	92	-6	58	4.29	-15	*S-104,2-29/C-1	12	-1.2
1946 Pit-N★	131	495	60	128	23	6	8	52	40	52	2	....	.259	.318	.378	.696	94	-5	59	4.06	2	*2-113,S-13/3-7	11	0.4
1947 Pit-N★	156	616	102	183	30	6	9	67	63	65	5	....	.297	.364	.409	.773	102	2	92	5.45	22	*3-156	19	2.3
1948 Pit-N★	131	449	68	120	19	2	9	42	42	62	5	....	.267	.333	.379	.711	90	-6	56	4.37	10	*3-118	13	0.3
1949 Chi-N	76	261	29	59	13	4	4	27	18	22	3	....	.226	.279	.352	.631	70	-12	24	3.01	-12	3-55,2-16	3	-2.3
1950 StL-A	9	19	1	3	1	0	0	2	3	8	0	1	.158	.273	.211	.483	24	-3	1	1.33	-1	/3-6	0	-0.4
Total 12	**1261**	**4582**	**553**	**1214**	**222**	**47**	**38**	**480**	**369**	**427**	**60**	**1**	**.265**	**.322**	**.359**	**.681**	**87**	**-85**	**525**	**3.98**	**-60**	**2-551,3-382,S-303/C-2,1-1**	**102**	**-9.2**
• GUTH, Bucky	Charles Henry Guth b: 8/18/1947, Baltimore, MD BR/TR, 6'1", 180 lbs. Deb: 9/12/1972																							
1972 Min-A	3	3	1	0	0	0	0	0	0	0	0	0	.000	.000	.000	.000	-95	-1	0	.00	0	/S-1	0	-0.1
• GUTIERREZ, Cesar	Cesar Dario "Cocoa" Gutierrez b: 1/26/1943, Coro, Venezuela BR/TR, 5'9", 155 lbs. Deb: 4/16/1967																							
1967 SF-N	18	21	4	3	0	0	0	0	1	4	1	0	.143	.217	.143	.360	5	-2	1	1.32	-1	S-15/2-1	0	-0.3
1969 SF-N	15	23	4	5	1	0	0	0	6	2	1	0	.217	.379	.261	.640	84	0	3	4.45	-2	/3-7,S-4	1	-0.1
Det-A	17	49	5	12	1	0	0	0	5	3	1	2	.245	.315	.265	.580	61	-3	4	2.27	-1	S-16	1	-0.2
1970 Det-A	135	415	40	101	11	6	0	22	18	39	4	3	.243	.276	.299	.575	58	-25	33	2.64	-14	*S-135	6	-2.5
1971 Det-A	38	37	8	7	0	0	0	4	0	3	0	0	.189	.211	.189	.400	13	-4	2	1.39	-1	S-14/3-5,2-2	0	-0.4
Total 4	**223**	**545**	**61**	**128**	**13**	**6**	**0**	**26**	**30**	**51**	**7**	**5**	**.235**	**.279**	**.281**	**.559**	**55**	**-34**	**43**	**2.54**	**-18**	**S-184/3-12,2-3**	**8**	**-3.6**
• GUTIERREZ, Jackie	Joaquin Fernando Gutierrez b: 6/27/1960, Cartagena, Colombia BR/TR, 5'11", 175 lbs. Deb: 9/6/1983																							
1983 Bos-A	5	10	2	3	0	0	0	0	1	1	0	1	.300	.364	.300	.664	79	-1	1	1.78	-1	/S-4	0	-0.1
1984 Bos-A	151	449	55	118	12	3	2	29	15	49	12	5	.263	.287	.316	.603	64	-22	37	2.68	-37	*S-150	0	-4.4
1985 Bos-A	103	275	33	60	5	2	2	21	12	37	10	2	.218	.251	.273	.524	42	-21	18	2.08	-10	S-99	2	-2.2
1986 Bal-A	61	145	8	27	3	0	0	4	3	27	3	1	.186	.208	.207	.415	14	-17	6	1.31	-3	2-53/3-6,D-1	1	-1.8
1987 Bal-A	3	1	0	0	0	0	0	0	0	0	0	0	.000	.000	.000	.000	-103	-0	0	.00	-1	/2-1,3-1	0	-0.1
1988 Phi-N	33	77	8	19	4	0	0	9	2	9	0	0	.247	.266	.299	.565	61	-4	6	2.49	-2	S-22,3-13	1	-0.6
Total 6	**356**	**957**	**106**	**227**	**24**	**5**	**4**	**63**	**33**	**123**	**25**	**9**	**.237**	**.263**	**.285**	**.549**	**50**	**-65**	**67**	**2.26**	**-54**	**S-275/2-54,3-20,D-1**	**4**	**-9.2**
• GUTIERREZ, Ricky	Ricardo Gutierrez b: 5/23/1970, Miami, FL BR/TR, 6'1", 175 lbs. Deb: 4/13/1993																							
1993 SD-N	133	438	76	110	10	5	5	26	50	97	4	3	.251	.335	.331	.666	78	-13	51	4.03	-4	*S-117/2-6,O-5(3-0-2),3-4	8	-0.8
1994 SD-N	90	275	27	66	11	2	1	28	32	54	2	6	.240	.324	.305	.629	67	-15	26	3.12	-5	S-78/2-7	3	-1.4
1995 Hou-N	52	156	22	43	6	0	0	12	10	33	5	0	.276	.323	.314	.637	74	-5	16	3.67	-5	S-44/3-2	3	-0.7
1996 Hou-N	89	218	28	62	8	1	1	15	23	42	6	1	.284	.361	.344	.705	94	-0	29	4.70	-12	S-74/3-6,2-5	4	-0.7
1997*Hou-N	102	303	33	79	14	4	3	34	21	50	5	2	.261	.315	.363	.678	80	-9	30	3.38	-3	S-64,3-22/2-9	4	-0.8
1998*Hou-N	141	491	55	128	24	3	2	46	54	84	13	7	.261	.341	.334	.675	81	-13	55	3.69	13	*S-141	12	1.1
1999*Hou-N	85	268	33	70	7	5	1	25	37	45	2	5	.261	.355	.336	.691	77	-10	31	3.90	-2	S-80/3-1	6	-0.6
2000 Chi-N	125	449	73	124	19	2	11	56	66	58	8	2	.276	.377	.401	.778	99	2	73	5.51	-7	*S-121	15	0.5
2001 Chi-N	147	528	76	153	23	3	10	66	40	56	4	3	.290	.351	.402	.753	99	-1	75	4.80	-9	*S-144	16	0.2
2002 Cle-A	94	353	38	97	13	0	4	38	20	48	0	1	.275	.326	.346	.672	80	-10	37	3.65	-2	2-93/D-1	8	-0.7
2003 Cle-A	16	50	2	13	3	0	0	3	3	5	0	0	.260	.315	.320	.635	70	-2	5	3.49	-3	/S-9,3-7	0	-0.4
Total 11	**1074**	**3529**	**463**	**945**	**138**	**25**	**38**	**349**	**356**	**572**	**49**	**30**	**.268**	**.343**	**.353**	**.696**	**85**	**-75**	**428**	**4.12**	**-38**	**S-872,2-120/3-42,O-5,D-1**	**79**	**-4.2**
• GUTTERIDGE, Don	Donald Joseph Gutteridge b: 6/19/1912, Pittsburg, KS BR/TR, 5'10.5", 165 lbs. Deb: 9/7/1936 M/C																							
1936 StL-N	23	91	13	29	3	4	3	16	1	14	3	....	.319	.326	.538	.865	130	3	16	6.71	1	3-23	4	0.5
1937 StL-N	119	447	66	121	26	10	7	61	25	66	12	....	.271	.311	.421	.731	95	-5	59	4.84	6	*3-105/S-8	14	0.6
1938 StL-N	142	552	61	141	21	15	9	64	29	49	14	....	.255	.293	.397	.689	83	-15	64	4.11	-2	3-73,S-68	11	-0.9
1939 StL-N	148	524	71	141	27	4	7	54	27	70	5	....	.269	.309	.376	.685	78	-17	61	4.06	-11	*3-143/S-2	9	-2.4
1940 StL-N	69	108	19	29	5	0	3	14	5	15	3	....	.269	.301	.398	.699	86	-2	13	4.14	-5	3-39	2	-0.7
1942 StL-A	147	616	90	157	27	11	1	50	59	54	16	13	.255	.320	.339	.659	84	-15	69	3.79	3	*2-145/3-2	15	-0.2
1943 StL-A	132	538	77	147	35	6	1	36	50	46	10	9	.273	.335	.366	.701	103	0	68	4.46	-26	*2-132	14	-1.9
1944*StL-A	148	603	89	148	27	11	3	36	51	63	20	8	.245	.304	.342	.646	80	-16	67	3.85	-5	*2-146	16	-1.3

YEAR TM-L	G	AB	R	H	2B	3B	HR	RBI	BB	SO	SB	CS	AVG	OBP	SLG	OPS	OPS+	BR/A	RC	RC/G	FR	G/POS	WS	TPW
1945 StL-A	143	543	72	129	24	3	2	49	43	46	9	6	.238	.295	.304	.599	70	-21	51	3.19	-6	*2-128,0-14(14-0-0)	8	-2.2
1946*Bos-A	22	47	8	11	3	0	1	6	2	7	0	0	.234	.265	.362	.627	70	-2	5	3.04	-1	/2-9,3-8	1	-0.3
1947 Bos-A	54	131	20	22	2	0	2	5	17	13	3	1	.168	.264	.229	.493	35	-11	9	2.22	-3	2-20,3-19	1	-1.4
1948 Pit-N	4	2	0	0	0	0	0	0	0	1	0	....	.000	.000	.000	.000	-98	-1	0	.00	0	....	0	-0.1
Total 12	1151	4202	586	1075	200	64	39	391	309	444	95	37	.256	.308	.362	.669	83	-102	484	3.98	-48	2-580,3-412/S-78,0-14	95	-10.4

• GUZMAN, Cristian Cristian Guzman b: 3/21/1978, Santo Domingo, Dominican Republic BB/TR, 6', 195 lbs. Deb: 4/6/1999

YEAR TM-L	G	AB	R	H	2B	3B	HR	RBI	BB	SO	SB	CS	AVG	OBP	SLG	OPS	OPS+	BR/A	RC	RC/G	FR	G/POS	WS	TPW
1999 Min-A	131	420	47	95	12	3	1	26	22	90	9	7	.226	.270	.276	.546	38	-41	32	2.47	-4	*S-131	5	-3.2
2000 Min-A	156	631	89	156	25	**20**	8	54	46	101	28	10	.247	.300	.388	.689	70	-29	76	4.10	-5	*S-151/D-1	12	-2.1
2001 Min-A★	118	493	80	149	28	**14**	10	51	21	78	25	8	.302	.337	.477	.814	109	6	79	5.84	4	*S-118	18	1.9
2002*Min-A	148	623	80	170	31	6	9	59	17	79	12	13	.273	.294	.385	.680	78	-25	64	3.54	8	*S-147	13	-0.5
2003*Min-A	143	534	78	143	15	**14**	3	53	30	79	18	9	.268	.313	.365	.678	77	-18	63	4.02	-7	*S-141	13	-1.3
Total 5	696	2701	374	713	111	57	31	243	136	427	92	47	.264	.303	.382	.685	75	-107	314	3.99	-5	S-688/D-1	61	-5.2

• GUZMAN, Edwards Edwards Guzman b: 9/11/1976, Bayamon, Puerto Rico BL/TR, 5'11", 205 lbs. Deb: 4/6/1999

YEAR TM-L	G	AB	R	H	2B	3B	HR	RBI	BB	SO	SB	CS	AVG	OBP	SLG	OPS	OPS+	BR/A	RC	RC/G	FR	G/POS	WS	TPW
1999 SF-N	14	15	0	0	0	0	0	0	0	4	0	0	.000	.000	.000	.000	-108	-5	0	.00	0	/3-5,C-1	0	-0.5
2001 SF-N	61	115	8	28	6	0	3	7	5	16	0	0	.243	.275	.374	.649	71	-5	11	3.40	-3	C-26/1-7,3-7,2-3,0-2(2-0-0)	1	-0.8
2003 Mon-N	52	146	15	35	5	0	1	14	5	17	0	0	.240	.265	.295	.559	39	-13	10	2.24	-6	3-28,1-13/C-4,D-3	1	-1.9
Total 3	127	276	23	63	11	0	4	21	10	37	0	0	.228	.255	.312	.567	44	-23	21	2.55	-10	/3-40,C-31,1-20,2-3,D-3,0-2	2	-3.2

• GWOSDZ, Doug Doug Wayne "Eyechart" Gwosdz b: 6/20/1960, Houston, TX BR/TR, 5'11", 185 lbs. Deb: 8/17/1981

YEAR TM-L	G	AB	R	H	2B	3B	HR	RBI	BB	SO	SB	CS	AVG	OBP	SLG	OPS	OPS+	BR/A	RC	RC/G	FR	G/POS	WS	TPW
1981 SD-N	16	24	1	4	2	0	0	3	3	6	0	0	.167	.259	.250	.509	48	-2	2	2.14	1	C-13	0	0.0
1982 SD-N	7	17	1	3	0	0	0	0	2	7	0	0	.176	.263	.176	.440	27	-2	1	1.65	0	/C-7	0	-0.2
1983 SD-N	39	55	7	6	1	0	1	4	7	19	0	0	.109	.210	.182	.391	10	-7	2	1.13	-2	C-32	1	-0.8
1984 SD-N	7	8	0	2	0	0	0	1	2	5	0	0	.250	.400	.250	.650	86	0	1	4.54	-1	/C-6	0	-0.1
Total 4	69	104	9	15	3	0	1	8	14	37	0	0	.144	.246	.202	.448	28	-10	6	1.66	-2	/C-58	1	-1.1

• GWYNN, Chris Christopher Karlton Gwynn b: 10/13/1964, Los Angeles, CA BL/TL, 6', 210 lbs. Deb: 8/14/1987 Career OF: 198-12-87

YEAR TM-L	G	AB	R	H	2B	3B	HR	RBI	BB	SO	SB	CS	AVG	OBP	SLG	OPS	OPS+	BR/A	RC	RC/G	FR	G/POS	WS	TPW
1987 LA-N	17	32	2	7	1	0	0	2	1	7	0	0	.219	.242	.250	.492	32	-3	2	2.15	0	0-10(10-0-0)	0	-0.4
1988 LA-N	12	11	1	2	0	0	0	0	1	2	0	0	.182	.250	.182	.432	27	-1	1	1.70	-1	/0-4(4-0-0)	0	-0.2
1989 LA-N	32	68	8	16	4	1	0	7	2	9	1	0	.235	.257	.324	.581	66	-3	6	2.76	1	0-19(14-5-2)	1	-0.3
1990 LA-N	101	141	19	40	2	1	5	22	7	28	0	1	.284	.318	.418	.736	104	-1	18	4.55	-1	0-44(32-5-8)	4	-0.2
1991 LA-N	94	139	18	35	5	1	5	22	10	23	1	0	.252	.307	.410	.717	102	0	17	3.96	0	0-41(31-2-14)	4	0.0
1992 KC-A	34	84	10	24	3	2	1	7	3	10	0	0	.286	.310	.405	.715	96	-1	10	4.43	0	0-19(5-0-14)/D-2	1	-0.2
1993 KC-A	103	287	36	86	14	4	1	25	24	34	0	1	.300	.356	.387	.743	94	-2	39	4.89	1	0-83(66-0-19)/D-5,1-1	6	-0.5
1994 LA-N	58	71	9	19	0	0	3	13	7	7	0	2	.268	.333	.394	.728	95	-2	9	4.32	0	0-20(19-0-1)	2	-0.2
1995*LA-N	67	84	8	18	3	2	1	10	6	23	0	0	.214	.275	.333	.608	65	-4	7	2.45	0	0-17(12-0-5)/1-2	0	-0.5
1996*SD-N	81	90	8	16	4	0	1	10	10	28	0	0	.178	.260	.256	.516	39	-8	6	2.18	0	0-29(5-0-24)/1-1	0	-0.9
Total 10	599	1007	119	263	36	11	17	118	71	171	2	4	.261	.312	.369	.681	85	-25	113	3.87	1	0-286/D-7,1-4	18	-3.2

• GWYNN, Tony Anthony Keith Gwynn b: 5/9/1960, Los Angeles, CA BL/TL, 5'11", 199 lbs. Deb: 7/19/1982 Career OF: 49-158-2144

YEAR TM-L	G	AB	R	H	2B	3B	HR	RBI	BB	SO	SB	CS	AVG	OBP	SLG	OPS	OPS+	BR/A	RC	RC/G	FR	G/POS	WS	TPW
1982 SD-N	54	190	33	55	12	2	1	17	14	16	8	3	.289	.338	.389	.728	109	2	25	4.49	-2	0-52(23-28-13)	7	-0.1
1983 SD-N	86	304	34	94	12	2	1	37	23	21	7	4	.309	.358	.372	.730	106	2	39	4.57	4	0-81(26-6-54)	10	0.2
1984*SD-N★	158	606	88	**213**	21	10	5	71	59	23	33	18	**.351**	.411	.444	.855	140	33	108	6.73	4	*0-156(0-1-156)	35	3.1
1985 SD-N★	154	622	90	197	29	5	6	46	45	33	14	11	.317	.365	.408	.773	118	12	88	5.22	3	*0-152(0-0-152)	20	0.7
1986 SD-N★	160	642	**107**	**211**	33	7	14	59	52	35	37	9	.329	.382	.467	.849	136	34	113	6.55	6	*0-160(0-0-160)	29	3.3
1987 SD-N★	157	589	119	**218**	36	13	7	54	82	35	56	12	**.370**	.450	.511	.961	160	**61**	143	9.57	4	*0-156(0-0-156)	29	**5.8**
1988 SD-N	133	521	64	163	22	5	7	70	51	40	26	11	**.313**	.374	.415	.789	128	20	81	5.64	-4	*0-133(0-32-102)	23	1.4
1989 SD-N★	158	604	82	**203**	27	7	4	62	56	30	40	16	**.336**	.393	.424	.817	133	29	101	6.13	7	*0-157(0-86-73)	30	3.4
1990 SD-N★	141	573	79	177	29	10	4	72	44	23	17	8	.309	.359	.415	.775	111	8	83	5.22	3	*0-141(0-0-141)	17	0.8
1991 SD-N★	134	530	69	168	27	11	4	62	34	19	8	8	.317	.358	.432	.790	118	10	78	5.46	2	*0-134(0-0-134)	22	0.8
1992 SD-N★	128	520	77	165	27	3	6	41	46	16	3	6	.317	.373	.415	.788	121	13	77	5.51	3	*0-127(0-0-127)	18	1.3
1993 SD-N★	122	489	70	175	41	3	7	59	36	19	14	1	.358	.403	.497	.900	137	28	94	7.47	-1	*0-121(0-4-121)	18	2.1
1994 SD-N★	110	419	79	**165**	35	1	12	64	48	19	5	0	**.394**	.458	.568	1.026	171	46	104	10.00	-1	*0-106(0-1-105)	17	3.9
1995 SD-N★	135	535	82	**197**	33	1	9	90	35	15	17	5	**.368**	.408	.484	.892	140	32	100	7.33	3	*0-133(0-0-133)	23	2.7
1996*SD-N★	116	451	67	159	27	2	3	50	39	17	11	4	**.353**	.405	.441	.847	131	21	77	6.50	-9	*0-111(0-0-111)	17	0.6
1997 SD-N★	149	592	97	**220**	49	2	17	119	43	28	12	5	**.372**	.417	.547	.964	164	54	132	8.88	-7	*0-143(0-0-143)/D-3	**39**	3.8
1998*SD-N★	127	461	65	148	35	0	16	69	35	18	3	1	.321	.370	.501	.871	136	23	82	6.58	-4	*0-116(0-0-116)/D-3	19	1.3
1999 SD-N★	111	411	59	139	27	0	10	62	29	14	7	2	.338	.385	.477	.862	126	16	72	6.59	-5	*0-104(0-0-104)/D-2	18	0.6
2000 SD-N	36	127	17	41	12	0	1	17	9	4	0	1	.323	.372	.441	.813	112	2	20	5.63	-4	0-26(0-0-26)/D-6	3	-0.3
2001 SD-N	71	102	5	33	9	1	1	17	10	9	1	0	.324	.384	.461	.845	128	5	19	7.21	-1	0-17(0-0-17)/D-1	4	0.3
Total 20	2440	9288	1383	3141	543	85	135	1138	790	434	319	125	.338	.392	.459	.850	134	451	1634	6.62	1	*0-2326/D-15	398	35.8

• GYSELMAN, Dick Richard Renald Gyselman b: 4/6/1908, San Francisco, CA d: 9/20/1990, Seattle, WA BR/TR, 6'2", 170 lbs. Deb: 4/20/1933

YEAR TM-L	G	AB	R	H	2B	3B	HR	RBI	BB	SO	SB	CS	AVG	OBP	SLG	OPS	OPS+	BR/A	RC	RC/G	FR	G/POS	WS	TPW
1933 Bos-N	58	155	10	37	6	2	0	12	7	21	0	....	.239	.272	.303	.575	70	-6	12	2.51	1	3-42/2-5,S-1	3	-0.4
1934 Bos-N	24	36	7	6	1	1	0	4	2	11	0	....	.167	.211	.250	.461	25	-4	2	1.85	-3	3-15/2-2	0	-0.7
Total 2	82	191	17	43	7	3	0	16	9	32	0	....	.225	.260	.293	.553	61	-10	14	2.39	-2	/3-57,2-7,S-1	3	-1.0

• HAAD, Yamid Yamid Salcedo Haad b: 9/2/1977, Cartagena, Colombia BR/TR, 6'2", 204 lbs. Deb: 7/5/1999

YEAR TM-L	G	AB	R	H	2B	3B	HR	RBI	BB	SO	SB	CS	AVG	OBP	SLG	OPS	OPS+	BR/A	RC	RC/G	FR	G/POS	WS	TPW
1999 Pit-N	1	1	0	0	0	0	0	0	0	0	0	0	.000	.000	.000	.000	-100	-0	0	.00	0	....	0	0.0

• HAAS, Bert Berthold John Haas b: 2/8/1914, Naperville, IL d: 6/23/1999, Tampa, FL BR/TR, 5'11", 180 lbs. Deb: 9/9/1937 Career OF: 11-76-7

YEAR TM-L	G	AB	R	H	2B	3B	HR	RBI	BB	SO	SB	CS	AVG	OBP	SLG	OPS	OPS+	BR/A	RC	RC/G	FR	G/POS	WS	TPW
1937 Bro-N	16	25	2	10	3	0	0	2	1	1	0	....	.400	.423	.520	.943	152	2	5	8.82	-1	/0-4(0-0-4),1-3	1	0.1
1938 Bro-N	1	0	0	0	0	0	0	0	0	0	0	....	....	....	....	....	-98	0	0	....	0	....	0	0.0
1942 Cin-N	154	585	59	140	21	6	6	54	59	54	6	....	.239	.310	.326	.637	87	-10	61	3.58	-7	*3-146/1-6,0-2(2-0-0)	14	-1.3
1943 Cin-N	101	332	39	87	17	6	4	44	22	26	6	....	.262	.308	.386	.693	101	-1	38	4.05	6	1-44,3-23,0-18(0-18-0)	10	0.3
1946 Cin-N	140	535	57	141	24	7	3	50	33	42	22	....	.264	.310	.351	.661	91	-9	58	3.80	3	*1-140/3-6	10	-1.1
1947 Cin-N★	135	482	58	138	17	7	3	67	42	27	9	....	.286	.346	.369	.715	91	-6	63	4.81	-9	0-69(8-58-0),1-53	13	-1.9
1948 Phi-N	95	333	35	94	9	2	4	34	36	25	8	....	.282	.354	.357	.711	95	-2	42	4.62	-3	3-54,1-35	8	-0.6
1949 Phi-N	2	1	0	0	0	0	0	0	1	1	0	....	.000	.500	.000	.500	47	0	0	3.51	0	....	0	0.0
NY-N	54	104	12	27	2	3	1	10	5	8	0	....	.260	.294	.365	.659	76	-4	11	3.67	-2	1-23,3-11	1	-0.6
Yr.	56	105	12	27	2	3	1	10	6	9	0	....	.257	.297	.362	.659	75	-4	11	3.66	-2	1-23,3-11	1	-0.6
1951 Chi-A	23	43	1	7	0	1	1	2	5	4	0	0	.163	.250	.279	.529	44	-3	3	2.27	0	/1-7,0-4(1-0-3),3-1	0	-0.3
Total 9	721	2440	263	644	93	32	22	263	204	188	51	0	.264	.323	.355	.678	91	-34	283	4.09	-12	1-311,3-241/0-97	57	-5.5

• HAAS, Eddie George Edwin Haas b: 5/26/1935, Paducah, KY BL/TR, 5'11", 178 lbs. Deb: 9/8/1957 M/C Career OF: 4-3-2

YEAR TM-L	G	AB	R	H	2B	3B	HR	RBI	BB	SO	SB	CS	AVG	OBP	SLG	OPS	OPS+	BR/A	RC	RC/G	FR	G/POS	WS	TPW
1957 Chi-N	14	24	1	5	1	0	0	4	1	5	0	0	.208	.240	.250	.490	32	-2	2	2.11	0	/0-4(3-1-0)	0	-0.3
1958 Mil-N	9	14	2	5	0	0	0	1	2	1	0	0	.357	.438	.357	.795	124	1	2	7.25	0	/0-3(0-2-1)	0	0.0
1960 Mil-N	32	32	4	7	2	0	1	5	5	14	0	0	.219	.324	.375	.699	98	0	4	4.66	-0	/0-2(1-0-1)	1	0.0
Total 3	55	70	7	17	3	0	1	10	8	20	0	0	.243	.321	.329	.649	82	-2	8	4.15	0	/0-9	1	-0.2

• HAAS, Mule George William Haas b: 10/15/1903, Montclair, NJ d: 6/30/1974, New Orleans, LA BL/TR, 6'1", 175 lbs. Deb: 8/15/1925 C Career OF: 13-809-205

YEAR TM-L	G	AB	R	H	2B	3B	HR	RBI	BB	SO	SB	CS	AVG	OBP	SLG	OPS	OPS+	BR/A	RC	RC/G	FR	G/POS	WS	TPW
1925 Pit-N	4	3	1	0	0	0	0	0	0	1	0	0	.000	.000	.000	.000	-94	-1	0	.00	0	/0-2(0-1-1)	0	-0.1
1928 Phi-A	91	332	41	93	21	4	6	39	23	20	2	3	.280	.331	.422	.752	94	-4	46	4.86	-2	0-82(10-69-4)	9	-1.0
1929*Phi-A	139	578	115	181	41	9	16	82	34	38	0	4	.313	.356	.498	.854	113	8	100	6.02	-11	*0-139(1-139-0)	22	-0.9
1930*Phi-A	132	532	91	159	33	7	2	68	43	33	2	2	.299	.352	.398	.751	86	-11	76	4.97	6	*0-131(0-131-0)	16	-0.9
1931*Phi-A	102	440	82	142	29	7	8	56	30	29	0	0	.323	.366	.475	.841	113	9	77	6.40	-4	*0-102(0-102-0)	17	0.3
1932 Phi-A	143	558	91	170	28	5	6	65	62	49	1	0	.305	.376	.405	.781	99	2	89	5.68	0	*0-137(0-108-29)	17	-0.3
1933 Chi-A	146	585	97	168	33	4	1	51	65	41	0	5	.287	.360	.362	.723	96	-3	79	4.65	-5	*0-146(0-146-0)	14	-1.0
1934 Chi-A	106	351	54	94	16	3	2	22	47	22	1	0	.268	.354	.348	.702	79	-9	47	4.45	-5	0-89(0-85-4)	7	-1.5

YEAR TM-L	G	AB	R	H	2B	3B	HR	RBI	BB	SO	SB	CS	AVG	OBP	SLG	OPS	OPS+	BR/A	RC	RC/G	FR	G/POS	WS	TPW
1935 Chi-A	92	327	44	95	22	1	2	40	37	17	4	1	.291	.363	.382	.745	90	-3	48	5.12	2	0-84(0-22-64)	8	-0.6
1936 Chi-A	119	408	75	116	26	2	0	46	64	29	1	1	.284	.383	.358	.741	81	-10	61	5.12	0	0-96(2-1-94)/1-7	10	-1.5
1937 Chi-A	54	111	8	23	3	3	0	15	16	10	1	0	.207	.313	.288	.601	52	-8	11	3.25	0	1-32/0-2(0-0-2)	1	-0.9
1938 Phi-A	40	78	7	16	2	0	0	12	12	10	0	0	.205	.311	.231	.542	39	-7	7	2.67	0	0-12(0-5-7)/1-6	0	-0.7
Total 12	1168	4303	706	1257	254	45	43	496	433	299	12	16	.292	.359	.402	.761	93	-38	642	5.17	-19	*0-1022/1-45	121	-9.1
• HABERER, Emil	Emil Karl Haberer b: 2/2/1878, Cincinnati, OH d: 10/19/1951, Louisville, KY BR/TR, 6'1", 204 lbs. Deb: 7/9/1901																							
1901 Cin-N	6	18	2	3	0	1	0	1	3	....	0	....	.167	.286	.278	.563	68	-1	1	2.59	-2	/3-3,1-2	0	-0.2
1903 Cin-N	5	13	1	1	0	0	0	0	2	....	0	....	.077	.200	.077	.277	-18	-2	0	.68	0	/C-4	0	-0.2
1909 Cin-N	5	16	1	3	1	0	0	2	0	....	0	....	.188	.188	.250	.438	36	-1	1	1.37	-1	/C-4	0	-0.2
Total 3	16	47	4	7	1	1	0	3	5	....	0	....	.149	.231	.213	.444	32	-4	2	1.60	-3	/C-8,3-3,1-2	0	-0.7
• HACH, Irv	Irvin William "Major" Hach b: 6/6/1873, Louisville, KY d: 8/13/1936, Louisville, KY BR/TR Deb: 7/1/1897																							
1897 Lou-N	16	51	5	11	2	0	0	3	5	....	1	....	.216	.322	.255	.577	55	-3	5	3.14	-3	/2-9,3-7	0	-0.5
• HACK, Stan	Stanley Camfield "Smiling Stan" Hack b: 12/6/1909, Sacramento, CA d: 12/15/1979, Dixon, IL BL/TR, 6', 170 lbs. Deb: 4/12/1932 M/C																							
1932*Chi-N	72	178	32	42	5	6	2	19	17	16	5	....	.236	.306	.365	.671	80	-5	21	3.92	-8	3-51	4	-1.1
1933 Chi-N	20	60	10	21	3	1	1	2	8	3	4	....	.350	.451	.483	.934	167	6	15	10.17	4	3-17	5	1.1
1934 Chi-N	111	402	54	116	16	6	1	21	45	42	11	....	.289	.363	.366	.729	98	0	57	5.05	-1	*3-109	13	0.4
1935*Chi-N	124	427	75	133	23	9	4	64	65	17	14	....	.311	.406	.436	.842	126	19	83	7.26	9	*3-111/1-7	22	3.0
1936 Chi-N	149	561	102	167	27	4	6	78	89	39	17	....	.298	.396	.392	.788	110	13	94	6.01	-9	*3-140,1-11	19	0.8
1937 Chi-N	154	582	106	173	27	6	2	63	83	42	16	....	.297	.388	.375	.762	104	7	94	5.95	-6	*3-150/1-4	23	0.7
1938*Chi-N★	152	609	109	195	34	11	4	67	94	39	**16**	....	.320	.411	.432	.843	128	28	119	7.55	5	*3-152	33	3.9
1939 Chi-N★	156	641	112	191	28	6	8	56	65	35	**17**	....	.298	.364	.398	.762	103	4	97	5.56	-8	*3-156	23	0.1
1940 Chi-N	149	603	101	**191**	38	6	8	40	75	24	21	....	.317	.395	.439	.834	132	29	112	7.18	6	*3-148/1-1	25	4.1
1941 Chi-N★	151	586	111	**186**	33	5	7	45	99	40	10	....	.317	.417	.427	.844	143	39	114	7.51	-16	*3-150/1-1	30	2.9
1942 Chi-N	140	553	91	166	36	3	6	39	94	40	9	....	.300	.402	.409	.811	143	34	100	6.79	-17	*3-139	26	2.4
1943 Chi-N★	144	533	78	154	24	4	3	35	82	27	5	....	.289	.384	.366	.750	119	17	83	5.64	-7	*3-136	21	1.2
1944 Chi-N	98	383	65	108	16	1	3	32	53	21	5	....	.282	.369	.352	.722	104	4	53	4.98	1	3-75,1-18	13	0.5
1945*Chi-N★	150	597	110	193	29	7	2	43	99	30	12	....	.323	.420	.405	.826	133	32	111	7.28	16	*3-146/1-5	**34**	5.0
1946 Chi-N	92	323	55	92	13	4	0	26	83	32	3	....	.285	.431	.350	.781	125	18	56	6.33	-2	3-90	17	1.6
1947 Chi-N	76	240	28	65	11	2	0	12	41	19	0	....	.271	.377	.333	.711	94	-0	33	4.93	3	3-66	8	0.3
Total 16	1938	7278	1239	2193	363	81	57	642	1092	466	165	....	.301	.394	.397	.791	120	246	1241	6.35	-31	*3-1836/1-47	316	27.0
• HACKER, Rich	Richard Warren Hacker b: 10/6/1947, Belleville, IL BB/TR, 6', 160 lbs. Deb: 7/2/1971 C																							
1971 Mon-N	16	33	2	4	1	0	0	2	3	12	0	0	.121	.194	.152	.346	-1	-4	1	1.07	1	S-16	0	-0.2
• HACKETT, Jim	James Joseph "Sunny Jim" Hackett b: 10/1/1877, Jacksonville, IL d: 3/28/1961, Douglas, MI BR/TR, 6'2", 185 lbs. Deb: 9/14/1902 ♦																							
1902 StL-N	6	21	2	6	1	0	0	4	2	....	1	....	.286	.348	.333	.681	115	1	3	5.04	-1	/P-4,0-2(0-0-2)	1	-1.1
1903 StL-N	99	351	24	80	13	8	0	36	19	....	2	....	.228	.272	.311	.582	68	-14	31	3.02	-4	1-89/P-7	5	-2.2
Total 2	105	372	26	86	14	8	0	40	21	....	3	....	.231	.276	.312	.588	71	-13	34	3.13	-5	/1-89,P-11,0-2	6	-3.3
• HACKETT, Mert	Mortimer Martin Hackett b: 11/11/1859, Cambridge, MA d: 2/22/1938, Cambridge, MA BR/TR, 5'10.5", 175 lbs. Deb: 5/2/1883 U Career OF: 1-9-9																							
1883 Bos-N	46	179	20	42	8	6	2	24	1	48	....	....	.235	.239	.380	.619	82	-4	17	3.34	-2	C-44/0-4(0-3-1)	4	-0.3
1884 Bos-N	72	268	28	55	13	2	1	20	2	66	....	....	.205	.211	.280	.491	53	-15	16	2.10	6	C-71/3-1	6	-0.2
1885 Bos-N	34	115	9	21	7	1	0	4	2	28	....	....	.183	.197	.261	.457	49	-6	6	1.74	1	C-34	2	-0.2
1886 KC-N	62	230	18	50	8	3	3	25	4	59	1	....	.217	.231	.317	.548	61	-12	18	2.63	-7	C-53,0-13(0-6-7)	2	-1.4
1887 Ind-N	42	154	12	42	6	3	2	10	7	24	4	....	.273	.282	.361	.643	80	-4	16	3.90	0	C-40/0-2(1-0-1),1-1	2	-0.1
Total 5	256	946	87	210	42	15	8	83	16	225	5	....	.222	.231	.318	.549	64	-41	73	2.69	-2	C-242/0-19,1-1,3-1	16	-2.2
• HACKETT, Walter	Walter Henry Hackett b: 8/15/1857, Cambridge, MA d: 10/2/1920, Cambridge, MA Deb: 4/17/1884																							
1884 Bos-U	103	415	71	101	19	0	1	....	7	....	....	....	.243	.256	.296	.552	87	-5	32	2.88	9	*S-103	12	0.6
1885 Bos-N	35	125	8	23	3	0	0	9	3	22	....	....	.184	.203	.208	.411	34	-9	5	1.43	-10	2-20,S-15	1	-1.7
Total 2	138	540	79	124	22	0	1	9	10	22	....	....	.230	.244	.276	.520	75	-14	38	2.52	-2	S-118/2-20	13	-1.1
• HADLEY, Kent	Kent William Hadley b: 12/17/1934, Pocatello, ID BL/TL, 6'3", 190 lbs. Deb: 9/14/1958																							
1958 KC-A	3	11	1	2	0	0	0	0	0	4	0	0	.182	.182	.182	.364		-1	0	1.09	0	/1-2	0	-0.2
1959 KC-A	113	288	40	73	11	1	10	39	24	74	1	2	.253	.313	.403	.716	93	-4	36	4.21	-4	1-95	6	-1.2
1960 NY-A	55	64	8	13	2	0	4	11	6	19	0	0	.203	.271	.422	.693	90	-1	7	3.81	-1	1-24	1	-0.3
Total 3	171	363	49	88	13	1	14	50	30	97	1	2	.242	.302	.399	.701	90	-7	43	4.04	-5	1-121	7	-1.7
• HAEFFNER, Bill	William Bernhard Haeffner b: 7/8/1894, Philadelphia, PA d: 1/27/1982, Delaware County, PA BR/TR, 5'9", 165 lbs. Deb: 6/29/1915																							
1915 Phi-A	3	4	0	1	0	0	0	0	0	1	0	....	.250	.250	.250	.500	51	-0	0	2.21	-1	/C-3	0	-0.1
1920 Pit-N	54	175	8	34	4	1	0	14	8	14	1	1	.194	.230	.229	.458	31	-15	9	1.71	-6	C-52	2	-1.8
1928 NY-N	2	1	0	0	0	0	0	0	0	0	0	....	.000	.000	.000	.000	-100	-0	0	.00	-1	/C-2	0	-0.1
Total 3	59	180	8	35	4	1	0	14	8	15	1	1	.194	.229	.228	.457	31	-16	10	1.70	-8	/C-57	2	-2.0
• HAFEY, Bud	Daniel Albert Hafey b: 8/6/1912, Berkeley, CA d: 7/27/1986, Sacramento, CA BR/TR, 6', 185 lbs. Deb: 4/21/1935 Career OF: 8-55-29																							
1935 Chi-A	2	0	1	0	0	0	0	0	0	0	0	0	....	....	....	....	-98	0	0	....	0	....	0	0.0
Pit-N	58	184	29	42	11	2	6	16	16	48	0	....	.228	.290	.408	.698	83	-5	22	3.92	2	0-47(1-36-10)	4	-0.4
1936 Pit-N	39	118	19	25	6	1	4	13	10	27	0	....	.212	.273	.381	.655	73	-5	12	3.28	-2	0-29(0-18-10)	2	-0.8
1939 Cin-N	6	13	1	2	1	0	0	1	1	4	1	....	.154	.214	.231	.445	19	-2	1	1.71	0	/0-4(4-0-0)	0	-0.2
Phi-N	18	51	3	9	1	0	0	3	3	12	1	....	.176	.222	.196	.418	14	-6	2	1.23	0	0-13(3-1-9)/P-2	0	-1.1
Yr.	24	64	4	11	2	0	0	4	4	16	2	....	.172	.221	.203	.424	15	-8	3	1.33	0	0-17(7-1-9)/P-2	0	-1.3
Total 3	123	366	53	78	19	3	10	33	30	91	2	0	.213	.273	.363	.636	68	-18	36	3.23	0	/0-93,P-2	6	-2.6
• HAFEY, Chick	Charles James Hafey b: 2/12/1903, Berkeley, CA d: 7/2/1973, Calistoga, CA BR/TR, 6', 185 lbs. Deb: 8/28/1924 HOF: 1971 Career OF: 783-281-133																							
1924 StL-N	24	91	10	23	5	2	2	22	4	8	1	0	.253	.292	.418	.709	90	-1	11	4.14	0	0-24(16-7-1)	2	-0.3
1925 StL-N	93	358	36	108	25	2	5	57	10	29	3	7	.302	.321	.425	.745	87	-10	45	4.56	-2	0-88(25-5-58)	7	-1.7
1926*StL-N	78	225	30	61	19	2	4	38	11	36	2	....	.271	.311	.427	.738	93	-3	29	4.43	-1	0-64(28-0-36)	5	-0.9
1927 StL-N	103	346	62	114	26	5	18	63	36	41	12	....	.329	.401	**.590**	.990	157	27	80	8.67	6	0-94(71-3-22)	21	2.6
1928*StL-N	138	520	101	175	46	6	27	111	40	53	8	....	.337	.386	.604	.990	152	36	116	8.20	-2	*0-133(117-0-16)	25	2.4
1929 StL-N	134	517	101	175	47	9	29	125	45	42	7	....	.338	.394	.632	1.026	148	36	124	9.19	-4	*0-130(130-0-0)	22	1.9
1930*StL-N	120	446	108	150	39	12	26	107	46	51	12	....	.336	.407	.652	1.059	146	32	114	9.54	-2	*0-116(116-0-0)	20	1.9
1931*StL-N	122	450	94	157	35	8	16	95	39	43	11	....	**.349**	**.404**	.569	.973	153	33	105	**9.25**	-3	*0-118(118-0-0)	25	2.3
1932 Cin-N	83	253	34	87	19	3	2	36	22	20	4	....	.344	.403	.466	.869	137	14	49	7.64	-0	0-65(65-0-0)	9	1.1
1933 Cin-N★	144	568	77	172	34	6	7	62	40	44	3	....	.303	.351	.421	.772	121	15	85	5.63	6	*0-144(59-85-0)	23	1.6
1934 Cin-N	140	535	75	157	29	6	18	67	52	63	4	....	.293	.359	.471	.830	123	17	93	6.40	-2	*0-140(18-122-0)	17	1.1
1935 Cin-N	15	59	10	20	6	1	1	9	4	5	1	....	.339	.400	.525	.925	151	4	13	8.44	-3	0-15(0-15-0)	3	0.0
1937 Cin-N	89	257	39	67	11	5	9	41	23	42	2	....	.261	.324	.447	.771	113	4	38	5.10	-2	0-64(20-44-0)	7	0.0
Total 13	1283	4625	777	1466	341	67	164	833	372	477	70	7	.317	.372	.526	.898	133	204	902	7.24	-11	*0-1195	186	12.0
• HAFEY, Tom	Thomas Francis "Heave-O,The Arm" Hafey b: 7/12/1913, Berkeley, CA d: 10/2/1996, El Cerrito, CA BR/TR, 6'1", 180 lbs. Deb: 7/21/1939																							
1939 NY-N	70	256	37	62	10	1	6	26	10	44	1	....	.242	.271	.359	.630	67	-13	24	3.15	-6	3-70	4	-1.6
1944 StL-A	8	14	1	5	2	0	0	2	1	4	0	0	.357	.400	.500	.900	148	1	3	8.92	0	/0-4(3-0-1),1-1	1	0.1
Total 2	78	270	38	67	12	1	6	28	11	48	1	0	.248	.278	.367	.644	72	-12	27	3.39	-5	/3-70,0-4,1-1	5	-1.5
• HAFNER, Travis	Travis Lee Hafner b: 6/3/1977, Jamestown, ND BL/TR, 6'3", 240 lbs. Deb: 8/6/2002																							
2002 Tex-A	23	62	6	15	4	1	1	6	8	15	0	1	.242	.329	.387	.716	85	-2	8	4.56	0	D-13/1-3	1	-0.2

YEAR TM-L	G	AB	R	H	2B	3B	HR	RBI	BB	SO	SB	CS	AVG	OBP	SLG	OPS	OPS+	BR/A	RC	RC/G	FR	G/POS	WS	TPW
2003 Cle-A	91	291	35	74	19	3	14	40	22	81	2	1	.254	.328	.485	.813	114	5	45	5.43	-4	D-43,1-42	7	-0.4
Total 2	**114**	**353**	**41**	**89**	**23**	**4**	**15**	**46**	**30**	**96**	**2**	**2**	**.252**	**.328**	**.467**	**.796**	**109**	**4**	**54**	**5.28**	**-4**	**/D-56,1-45**	**8**	**-0.6**

• HAGUE, Bill William L. Hague b: 1852, Philadelphia, PA BR/TR, 5'9", 164 lbs. Deb: 5/4/1875

YEAR TM-L	G	AB	R	H	2B	3B	HR	RBI	BB	SO	SB	CS	AVG	OBP	SLG	OPS	OPS+	BR/A	RC	RC/G	FR	G/POS	WS	TPW
1875 StL-n	62	260	24	57	2	0	0	22	2	9	3	4	.219	.225	.227	.452	63	-8	14	2.04	-1	*3-62/1-1	....	-0.9
1876 Lou-N	67	296	31	78	8	0	1	22	2	10	....	....	.264	.270	.303	.573	77	-9	25	3.20	-26	*3-67/S-1	3	-2.9
1877 Lou-N	59	263	38	70	7	1	1	24	7	18	....	....	.266	.285	.312	.597	74	-9	24	3.42	-21	*3-59	3	-2.5
1878 Pro-N	62	250	21	51	3	0	0	25	5	34	....	....	.204	.220	.216	.436	44	-15	12	1.68	14	*3-62	3	0.1
1879 Pro-N	51	209	20	47	3	1	0	21	3	19	....	....	.225	.236	.249	.485	61	-8	13	2.17	2	3-51	4	-0.5
Total 4	**239**	**1018**	**110**	**246**	**21**	**2**	**2**	**92**	**17**	**81**	**....**	**....**	**.242**	**.255**	**.273**	**.527**	**65**	**-42**	**73**	**2.64**	**-31**	**3-239/S-1**	**13**	**-5.8**

• HAGUE, Joe Joe Clarence Hague b: 4/25/1944, Huntington, WV d: 11/5/1994, San Antonio, TX BL/TL, 6', 198 lbs. Deb: 9/19/1968 Career OF: 7-0-129

YEAR TM-L	G	AB	R	H	2B	3B	HR	RBI	BB	SO	SB	CS	AVG	OBP	SLG	OPS	OPS+	BR/A	RC	RC/G	FR	G/POS	WS	TPW
1968 StL-N	7	17	2	4	0	0	1	1	2	2	0	0	.235	.316	.412	.728	119	0	2	4.93	-1	/O-3(0-0-3),1-2	1	0.0
1969 StL-N	40	100	8	17	2	1	2	8	12	23	0	2	.170	.259	.270	.529	48	-8	7	2.07	-1	O-17(1-0-16)/1-9	1	-1.1
1970 StL-N	139	451	58	122	16	4	14	68	63	87	2	1	.271	.361	.417	.778	106	5	69	5.32	-3	1-82,O-52(6-0-47)	13	-0.6
1971 StL-N	129	380	46	86	9	3	16	54	58	69	0	3	.226	.332	.392	.724	100	0	51	4.46	0	1-91,O-36(0-0-36)	12	-0.8
1972 StL-N	27	76	8	18	5	1	3	11	17	18	0	1	.237	.376	.447	.824	135	4	13	5.55	0	1-22/O-3(0-0-3)	3	0.2
*Cin-N	69	138	17	34	7	1	4	20	20	18	1	1	.246	.342	.399	.740	116	3	18	4.53	0	1-22,O-19(0-0-19)	5	0.1
Yr.	96	214	25	52	12	2	7	31	37	36	1	2	.243	.355	.416	.770	123	7	32	4.91	0	1-44,O-22(0-0-22)	8	0.3
1973 Cin-N	19	33	2	5	2	0	0	1	5	5	1	0	.152	.263	.212	.475	35	-3	2	2.23	0	/O-5(0-0-5),1-4	0	-0.3
Total 6	**430**	**1195**	**141**	**286**	**41**	**10**	**40**	**163**	**177**	**222**	**4**	**8**	**.239**	**.339**	**.391**	**.730**	**101**	**2**	**163**	**4.58**	**-5**	**1-232,O-135**	**35**	**-2.6**

• HAHN, Dick Richard Frederick Hahn b: 7/24/1916, Canton, OH d: 11/5/1992, Orlando, FL BR/TR, 5'11", 176 lbs. Deb: 9/7/1940

YEAR TM-L	G	AB	R	H	2B	3B	HR	RBI	BB	SO	SB	CS	AVG	OBP	SLG	OPS	OPS+	BR/A	RC	RC/G	FR	G/POS	WS	TPW
1940 Was-A	1	3	0	0	0	0	0	0	0	0	0	0	.000	.000	.000	.000	-107	-1	0	.00	0	/C-1	0	0.0

• HAHN, Don Donald Antone Hahn b: 11/16/1948, San Francisco, CA BR/TR, 6'1", 185 lbs. Deb: 4/8/1969 Career OF: 65-302-25

YEAR TM-L	G	AB	R	H	2B	3B	HR	RBI	BB	SO	SB	CS	AVG	OBP	SLG	OPS	OPS+	BR/A	RC	RC/G	FR	G/POS	WS	TPW
1969 Mon-N	4	9	0	1	0	0	0	2	0	5	0	0	.111	.111	.111	.222	-38	-2	0	.38	1	/O-3(0-3-0)	0	-0.1
1970 Mon-N	82	149	22	38	8	0	0	8	27	27	4	2	.255	.376	.309	.685	86	-1	21	4.51	2	O-61(42-14-9)	5	-0.1
1971 NY-N	98	178	16	42	5	1	1	11	21	32	2	3	.236	.320	.292	.612	75	-6	17	3.12	0	O-80(0-80-0)	3	-0.8
1972 NY-N	17	37	0	6	0	0	0	1	4	12	0	0	.162	.244	.162	.406	18	-4	2	1.30	0	O-10(0-1-9)	0	-0.5
1973*NY-N	93	262	22	60	10	0	2	21	22	43	2	1	.229	.289	.290	.579	62	-13	22	2.71	-3	O-87(4-83-2)	4	-1.9
1974 NY-N	110	323	34	81	14	1	4	28	37	34	2	0	.251	.330	.337	.667	88	-4	36	3.79	-3	*O-106(0-104-2)	7	-1.1
1975 Phi-N	9	5	0	0	0	0	0	0	0	2	0	0	.000	.000	.000	.000	-96	-1	0	.00	0	/O-7(1-4-2)	0	-0.1
StL-N	7	8	3	1	0	0	0	0	1	1	0	0	.125	.222	.125	.347	-2	-1	0	.47	0	/O-4(1-2-1)	0	-0.1
SD-N	34	26	7	6	1	2	0	3	10	2	1	0	.231	.444	.423	.868	151	3	5	6.74	0	O-26(17-11-0)	2	0.3
Yr.	50	39	10	7	1	2	0	3	11	5	1	0	.179	.360	.308	.668	95	0	6	4.22	0	O-37(19-17-3)	2	0.0
Total 7	**454**	**997**	**104**	**235**	**38**	**4**	**7**	**74**	**122**	**158**	**11**	**6**	**.236**	**.321**	**.303**	**.624**	**76**	**-30**	**103**	**3.38**	**-4**	**O-384**	**21**	**-4.5**

• HAHN, Ed William Edgar Hahn b: 8/27/1875, Nevada, OH d: 11/29/1941, Des Moines, IA BL/TR, 160 lbs. Deb: 8/31/1905 Career OF: 96-28-421

YEAR TM-L	G	AB	R	H	2B	3B	HR	RBI	BB	SO	SB	CS	AVG	OBP	SLG	OPS	OPS+	BR/A	RC	RC/G	FR	G/POS	WS	TPW
1905 NY-A	43	160	32	51	5	0	0	11	25	....	1	....	.319	.426	.350	.776	132	8	26	6.01	0	O-43(20-10-13)	8	0.6
1906 NY-A	11	22	2	2	1	0	0	1	3	....	2	....	.091	.259	.136	.396	23	-2	2	1.93	0	/O-7(3-4-0)	0	-0.3
*Chi-A	130	484	80	110	7	5	0	27	69	....	19	....	.227	.335	.262	.597	90	-1	52	3.57	2	*O-130(55-0-75)	18	-0.6
Yr.	141	506	82	112	8	5	0	28	72	....	21	....	.221	.331	.257	.588	87	-3	54	3.48	2	*O-137(58-4-75)	18	-0.8
1907 Chi-A	156	592	87	151	9	7	0	45	84	....	17	....	.255	.359	.294	.653	112	15	72	4.23	8	*O-156(0-0-156)	27	1.7
1908 Chi-A	122	447	58	112	12	8	0	21	39	....	11	....	.251	.329	.313	.642	110	7	50	3.72	-3	*O-118(18-14-86)	19	-0.2
1909 Chi-A	76	287	30	52	6	0	1	16	31	....	9	....	.181	.268	.213	.480	54	-14	19	2.03	-3	O-76(0-0-76)	3	-2.3
1910 Chi-A	15	53	2	6	2	0	0	1	7	....	0	....	.113	.217	.151	.368	16	-5	2	1.15	-1	O-15(0-0-15)	0	-0.7
Total 6	**553**	**2045**	**291**	**484**	**42**	**20**	**1**	**122**	**258**	**....**	**59**	**....**	**.237**	**.335**	**.278**	**.613**	**96**	**9**	**223**	**3.62**	**2**	**O-545**	**75**	**-1.7**

• HAIGH, Ed Edward E. Haigh b: 2/7/1867, Philadelphia, PA d: 2/13/1953, Atlantic City, NJ Deb: 8/14/1892

YEAR TM-L	G	AB	R	H	2B	3B	HR	RBI	BB	SO	SB	CS	AVG	OBP	SLG	OPS	OPS+	BR/A	RC	RC/G	FR	G/POS	WS	TPW
1892 StL-N	1	4	0	1	0	0	0	0	0	2	0	....	.250	.250	.250	.500	54	-0	0	2.31	0	/O-1	0	0.0

• HAINES, Hinkey Henry Luther Haines b: 12/23/1898, Red Lion, PA d: 1/9/1979, Sharon Hills, PA BR/TR, 5'10", 170 lbs. Deb: 4/20/1923

YEAR TM-L	G	AB	R	H	2B	3B	HR	RBI	BB	SO	SB	CS	AVG	OBP	SLG	OPS	OPS+	BR/A	RC	RC/G	FR	G/POS	WS	TPW
1923*NY-A	28	25	9	4	2	0	0	3	4	5	3	1	.160	.276	.240	.516	36	-2	2	2.34	0	O-14(2-8-4)	0	-0.2

• HAIRSTON, Jerry Jerry Wayne Hairston, Jr. b: 5/29/1976, Naperville, IL BR/TR, 5'10", 175 lbs. Deb: 9/11/1998

YEAR TM-L	G	AB	R	H	2B	3B	HR	RBI	BB	SO	SB	CS	AVG	OBP	SLG	OPS	OPS+	BR/A	RC	RC/G	FR	G/POS	WS	TPW
1998 Bal-A	6	7	2	0	0	0	0	0	0	1	0	0	.000	.000	.000	.000	-102	-2	0	.00	-1	/2-4	0	-0.3
1999 Bal-A	50	175	26	47	12	1	4	17	11	24	9	4	.269	.323	.417	.740	90	-3	24	4.65	4	2-50	5	0.3
2000 Bal-A	49	180	27	46	5	0	5	19	21	22	8	5	.256	.353	.367	.719	87	-3	23	4.01	10	2-49	4	0.8
2001 Bal-A	159	532	63	124	25	5	8	47	44	73	29	11	.233	.307	.344	.651	75	-17	58	3.51	19	*2-156	10	0.9
2002 Bal-A	122	426	55	114	25	3	5	32	34	55	21	6	.268	.332	.376	.707	92	-2	56	4.55	4	*2-119	12	0.7
2003 Bal-A	58	218	25	59	12	2	2	21	23	25	14	5	.271	.356	.372	.728	96	0	30	4.34	-1	2-48/D-9	7	0.1
Total 6	**444**	**1538**	**198**	**390**	**79**	**11**	**24**	**136**	**133**	**200**	**81**	**31**	**.254**	**.327**	**.366**	**.693**	**85**	**-28**	**190**	**4.07**	**35**	**2-426/D-9**	**38**	**2.5**

• HAIRSTON, Jerry Jerry Wayne Hairston, Sr. b: 2/16/1952, Birmingham, AL BB/TR, 5'10", 180 lbs. Deb: 7/26/1973 Career OF: 216-39-69

YEAR TM-L	G	AB	R	H	2B	3B	HR	RBI	BB	SO	SB	CS	AVG	OBP	SLG	OPS	OPS+	BR/A	RC	RC/G	FR	G/POS	WS	TPW
1973 Chi-A	60	210	25	57	11	1	0	23	33	30	0	0	.271	.373	.333	.706	97	1	29	4.90	1	O-33(33-0-0),1-19/D-8	6	-0.2
1974 Chi-A	45	109	8	25	7	0	0	8	13	18	0	2	.229	.311	.294	.605	73	-4	10	2.98	-1	O-22(19-0-3),D-10	1	-0.7
1975 Chi-A	69	219	26	62	8	0	0	23	46	23	1	0	.283	.410	.320	.729	107	6	33	5.27	-1	O-59(57-0-3)/D-8	8	0.1
1976 Chi-A	44	119	20	27	2	2	0	10	24	19	1	1	.227	.357	.277	.634	87	-1	14	3.96	-2	O-40(1-0-39)	3	-0.5
1977 Chi-A	13	26	3	8	2	0	0	4	5	7	0	0	.308	.419	.385	.804	121	1	4	5.41	0	O-11(6-6-0)	1	0.1
Pit-N	51	52	5	10	2	0	2	6	6	10	0	0	.192	.276	.346	.622	64	-3	5	3.13	-1	O-14(6-0-8)/2-1	1	-0.4
1981 Chi-A	9	25	5	7	1	0	1	6	2	4	0	0	.280	.357	.440	.797	131	1	4	6.03	-1	/O-7(4-2-1)	1	0.0
1982 Chi-A	85	90	11	21	5	0	5	18	9	15	0	0	.233	.303	.456	.759	105	0	12	4.23	1	O-36(22-7-7)/D-2	2	0.0
1983*Chi-A	101	126	17	37	9	1	5	22	23	16	0	1	.294	.403	.500	.903	142	8	26	7.69	0	O-32(19-11-3)/D-4	7	0.7
1984 Chi-A	115	227	41	59	13	2	5	19	41	29	2	1	.260	.375	.401	.776	110	5	37	5.73	0	O-37(22-13-3),D-20	7	0.3
1985 Chi-A	95	140	9	34	8	0	2	20	29	18	0	0	.243	.380	.343	.723	96	1	20	4.86	0	D-29/O-5(5-0-0)	4	0.0
1986 Chi-A	101	225	32	61	15	0	5	26	26	26	0	0	.271	.349	.404	.754	101	1	31	4.74	0	D-29,1-19,O-11(9-0-2)	5	-0.1
1987 Chi-A	66	126	14	29	8	0	5	20	25	25	0	0	.230	.362	.413	.775	102	1	20	5.11	0	D-13,O-13(13-0-0)/1-7	3	0.0
1988 Chi-A	2	2	0	0	0	0	0	0	0	0	0	0	.000	.000	.000	.000	-100	-1	0	.00	0	....	0	-0.1
1989 Chi-A	3	3	0	1	0	0	0	0	0	0	0	0	.333	.333	.333	.667	91	-0	0	4.50	0	/D-2	0	0.0
Total 14	**859**	**1699**	**216**	**438**	**91**	**6**	**30**	**205**	**282**	**240**	**4**	**5**	**.258**	**.366**	**.371**	**.737**	**102**	**17**	**245**	**4.96**	**-5**	**O-320,D-125/1-45,2-1**	**49**	**-0.5**

• HAIRSTON, Johnny John Louis Hairston b: 8/27/1944, Birmingham, AL BR/TR, 6'2", 200 lbs. Deb: 9/6/1969

YEAR TM-L	G	AB	R	H	2B	3B	HR	RBI	BB	SO	SB	CS	AVG	OBP	SLG	OPS	OPS+	BR/A	RC	RC/G	FR	G/POS	WS	TPW
1969 Chi-N	3	4	0	1	0	0	0	0	0	2	0	0	.250	.250	.250	.500	36	-0	0	2.25	0	/C-1,O-1	0	0.0

• HAIRSTON, Sammy Samuel Harding Hairston b: 1/20/1920, Crawford, MS d: 10/31/1997, Birmingham, AL BR/TR, 5'10.5", 187 lbs. Deb: 7/21/1951 C

YEAR TM-L	G	AB	R	H	2B	3B	HR	RBI	BB	SO	SB	CS	AVG	OBP	SLG	OPS	OPS+	BR/A	RC	RC/G	FR	G/POS	WS	TPW
1951 Chi-A	4	5	1	2	1	0	0	1	2	0	0	0	.400	.571	.600	1.171	222	1	2	18.49	0	/C-2	1	0.1

• HAJDUK, Chet Chester Hajduk b: 7/21/1918, Chicago, IL BR/TR, 6', 195 lbs. Deb: 4/16/1941

YEAR TM-L	G	AB	R	H	2B	3B	HR	RBI	BB	SO	SB	CS	AVG	OBP	SLG	OPS	OPS+	BR/A	RC	RC/G	FR	G/POS	WS	TPW
1941 Chi-A	1	1	0	0	0	0	0	0	0	0	0	0	.000	.000	.000	.000	-101	-0	0	.00	0	....	0	0.0

• HAJEK, Dave David Vincent Hajek b: 10/14/1967, Roseville, CA BR/TR, 5'10", 165 lbs. Deb: 9/15/1995

YEAR TM-L	G	AB	R	H	2B	3B	HR	RBI	BB	SO	SB	CS	AVG	OBP	SLG	OPS	OPS+	BR/A	RC	RC/G	FR	G/POS	WS	TPW
1995 Hou-N	5	2	0	0	0	0	0	0	1	1	1	0	.000	.333	.000	.333	-3	0	0	2.46	0	....	0	0.0
1996 Hou-N	8	10	3	3	1	0	0	0	2	0	0	0	.300	.417	.400	.817	126	0	1	2.03	0	/3-3,2-2	0	0.0
Total 2	**13**	**12**	**3**	**3**	**1**	**0**	**0**	**0**	**3**	**1**	**1**	**0**	**.250**	**.400**	**.333**	**.733**	**88**	**1**	**1**	**2.15**	**0**	**/3-3,2-2**	**0**	**0.1**

• HALAS, George George Stanley Halas b: 2/2/1895, Chicago, IL d: 10/31/1983, Chicago, IL BB/TR, 6', 164 lbs. Deb: 5/6/1919

YEAR TM-L	G	AB	R	H	2B	3B	HR	RBI	BB	SO	SB	CS	AVG	OBP	SLG	OPS	OPS+	BR/A	RC	RC/G	FR	G/POS	WS	TPW
1919 NY-A	12	22	0	2	0	0	0	0	0	8	0	....	.091	.091	.091	.182	-49	-4	0	.18	0	/O-6(0-1-5)	0	-0.5

• HALDEMAN, John John Avery Haldeman b: 12/2/1855, Pewee Valley, KY d: 9/17/1899, Louisville, KY BL/TR, 5'10", 175 lbs. Deb: 7/3/1877

YEAR TM-L	G	AB	R	H	2B	3B	HR	RBI	BB	SO	SB	CS	AVG	OBP	SLG	OPS	OPS+	BR/A	RC	RC/G	FR	G/POS	WS	TPW
1877 Lou-N	1	4	0	0	0	0	0	0	0	0	....	....	.000	.000	.000	.000	-85	-1	0	.00	-1	/2-1	0	-0.2

YEAR TM-L	G	AB	R	H	2B	3B	HR	RBI	BB	SO	SB	CS	AVG	OBP	SLG	OPS	OPS+	BR/A	RC	RC/G	FR	G/POS	WS	TPW
• HALE, Bob	Robert Houston Hale b: 11/7/1933, Sarasota, FL BL/TL, 5'10", 195 lbs. Deb: 7/4/1955																							
1955 Bal-A	67	182	13	65	7	1	0	29	5	19	0	2	.357	.378	.407	.784	119	3	25	5.40	3	1-44	5	0.4
1956 Bal-A	85	207	18	49	10	1	1	24	11	10	0	2	.237	.279	.309	.588	60	-14	16	2.61	0	1-51	1	-1.6
1957 Bal-A	42	44	2	11	0	0	0	7	2	2	0	0	.250	.283	.250	.533	50	-3	2	1.38	0	/1-5	0	-0.3
1958 Bal-A	19	20	2	7	2	0	0	3	2	1	0	0	.350	.409	.450	.859	144	1	3	5.45	1	/1-2	1	0.2
1959 Bal-A	40	54	2	10	3	0	0	7	2	6	0	0	.185	.214	.241	.455	25	-6	3	1.56	0	/1-8	0	-0.6
1960 Cle-A	70	70	2	21	7	0	0	12	3	6	0	0	.300	.329	.400	.729	99	-0	10	4.86	0	/1-5	2	0.0
1961 Cle-A	42	36	0	6	0	0	0	6	1	7	0	0	.167	.211	.167	.377	2	-5	2	1.28	0	....	0	-0.5
NY-A	11	13	2	2	0	0	1	1	0	0	0	0	.154	.154	.385	.538	41	-1	0	.87	0	/1-5	0	-0.1
Yr.	53	49	2	8	0	0	1	7	1	7	0	0	.163	.196	.224	.421	12	-6	2	1.16	0	/1-5	0	-0.6
Total 7	376	626	41	171	29	2	2	89	26	51	0	4	.273	.305	.335	.641	76	-24	61	3.33	4	1-120	9	-2.5
• HALE, Chip	Walter William Hale b: 12/2/1964, San Jose, CA BL/TR, 5'11", 191 lbs. Deb: 8/27/1989 Career OF: 0-0-4																							
1989 Min-A	28	67	6	14	3	0	0	4	1	6	0	0	.209	.221	.254	.474	31	-6	4	1.92	-1	2-16/3-9,D-2	0	-0.7
1990 Min-A	1	2	0	0	0	0	0	2	0	1	0	0	.000	.000	.000	.000	-94	-1	0	.00	1	/2-1	0	0.1
1993 Min-A	69	186	25	62	6	1	3	27	18	17	2	1	.333	.410	.425	.834	124	8	34	6.97	-2	2-21,3-19,D-19/1-1,S-1	7	0.5
1994 Min-A	67	118	13	31	9	0	1	11	16	14	0	2	.263	.356	.364	.720	86	-3	16	4.46	0	3-21,D-10/1-7,2-5,O-1	2	-0.3
1995 Min-A	69	103	10	27	4	0	2	18	11	20	0	0	.262	.333	.359	.693	80	-3	11	3.66	-3	D-27/2-7,3-5,1-3	2	-0.6
1996 Min-A	85	87	8	24	5	0	1	16	10	6	0	0	.276	.351	.368	.718	81	-2	11	4.41	-1	2-14,D-10/1-6,3-3,O-3(0-0-3)	2	-0.3
1997 LA-N	14	12	0	1	0	0	0	0	2	4	0	0	.083	.214	.083	.298	-20	-2	0	.80	0	/3-2	0	-0.2
Total 7	333	575	62	159	27	1	7	78	58	68	2	3	.277	.350	.363	.713	87	-10	76	4.59	-6	/D-68,2-64,3-59,1-17,O-4,S-1	13	-1.5
• HALE, George	George Wagner "Ducky" Hale b: 8/3/1894, Dexter, KS d: 11/1/1945, Wichita, KS BR/TR, 5'10", 160 lbs. Deb: 8/24/1914																							
1914 StL-A	6	11	1	2	0	0	0	0	0	3	0	....	.182	.182	.182	.364	10	-1	0	1.07	0	/C-6	0	-0.1
1916 StL-A	4	1	0	0	0	0	0	0	0	1	0	....	.000	.500	.000	.500	54	0	0	.00	-1	/C-3	0	-0.1
1917 StL-A	38	61	4	12	2	1	0	8	10	12	0	....	.197	.310	.262	.572	77	-1	5	2.57	-1	C-28	1	-0.1
1918 StL-A	12	30	0	4	1	0	0	1	1	5	0	....	.133	.161	.167	.328	-1	-4	1	.70	0	C-11	0	-0.3
Total 4	60	103	5	18	3	1	0	9	11	21	0	....	.175	.261	.223	.484	50	-6	6	1.82	-2	/C-48	1	-0.6
• HALE, John	John Steven Hale b: 8/5/1953, Fresno, CA BL/TR, 6'2", 195 lbs. Deb: 9/8/1974 Career OF: 86-83-165																							
1974 LA-N	4	4	2	4	1	0	0	2	0	0	0	0	1.000	1.000	1.250	2.250	549	2	5	∞	0	/O-3(0-0-3)	1	0.2
1975 LA-N	71	204	20	43	7	0	6	22	26	51	1	2	.211	.306	.333	.639	81	-6	22	3.53	-3	O-68(0-35-42)	5	-1.2
1976 LA-N	44	91	4	14	2	1	0	8	16	14	4	1	.154	.294	.198	.491	42	-6	7	2.40	1	O-37(0-11-27)	1	-0.7
1977 LA-N	79	108	10	26	4	1	2	11	15	28	2	1	.241	.333	.352	.685	84	-2	14	4.48	-2	O-73(25-13-37)	3	-0.6
1978 Sea-A	107	211	24	36	8	0	4	22	34	64	3	4	.171	.286	.265	.551	56	-12	18	2.55	-1	O-98(27-24-47)/D-3	1	-1.7
1979 Sea-A	54	63	6	14	3	0	2	7	12	26	0	0	.222	.347	.365	.712	91	-0	8	4.15	0	O-42(34-0-9)/D-2	1	-0.2
Total 6	359	681	66	137	25	2	14	72	103	183	10	8	.201	.310	.305	.615	72	-24	74	3.25	-7	O-321/D-5	12	-4.2
• HALE, Odell	Arvel Odell "Bad News" Hale b: 8/10/1908, Hosston, LA d: 6/9/1980, El Dorado, AR BR/TR, 5'10", 175 lbs. Deb: 8/1/1931																							
1931 Cle-A	25	92	14	26	2	4	1	5	8	8	2	0	.283	.340	.424	.764	94	-0	14	5.38	-7	3-15,2-10/S-1	2	-0.5
1933 Cle-A	98	351	49	97	19	8	10	64	30	37	2	3	.276	.333	.462	.795	104	0	53	5.41	-1	2-73,3-21	11	0.5
1934 Cle-A	143	563	82	170	44	6	13	101	48	50	8	12	.302	.357	.471	.827	110	3	91	5.90	21	*2-137/3-5	20	3.1
1935 Cle-A	150	589	80	179	37	11	16	101	52	55	15	13	.304	.361	.486	.847	115	9	101	6.23	1	*3-149/2-1	20	1.5
1936 Cle-A	153	620	126	196	50	13	14	87	64	43	8	5	.316	.380	.506	.887	116	14	120	7.26	12	*3-148/2-3	20	2.7
1937 Cle-A	154	561	74	150	32	4	6	82	56	41	9	6	.267	.335	.371	.706	77	-20	71	4.45	2	3-90,2-64	15	-1.0
1938 Cle-A	130	496	69	138	32	2	8	69	44	39	8	1	.278	.338	.399	.737	86	-10	70	4.90	-1	*2-127	13	-0.3
1939 Cle-A	108	253	36	79	16	2	4	48	25	18	4	5	.312	.374	.439	.813	111	3	39	5.36	-5	2-73/3-2	8	0.1
1940 Cle-A	48	50	3	11	3	1	0	6	5	7	0	0	.220	.291	.320	.611	60	-3	5	3.26	-1	/3-3	1	-0.4
1941 Bos-A	12	24	5	5	2	0	1	1	3	4	0	0	.208	.296	.417	.713	85	-1	3	3.71	-3	/3-6,2-1	0	-0.3
NY-N	41	102	13	20	3	0	0	9	18	13	1	....	.196	.317	.225	.542	53	-6	9	2.87	-2	2-29	2	-0.6
Total 10	1062	3701	551	1071	240	51	73	573	353	315	57	45	.289	.352	.441	.793	100	-12	576	5.56	16	2-518,3-439/S-1	112	4.7
• HALE, Sammy	Samuel Douglas Hale b: 9/10/1896, Glen Rose, TX d: 9/6/1974, Wheeler, TX BR/TR, 5'8.5", 160 lbs. Deb: 4/20/1920 Career OF: 4-4-2																							
1920 Det-A	76	116	13	34	3	3	1	14	5	15	2	0	.293	.322	.397	.719	92	-1	15	4.69	0	3-16/O-4(0-4-0),2-1	3	-0.1
1921 Det-A	9	2	2	0	0	0	0	0	0	1	0	1	.000	.000	.000	.000	-101	-1	0	.00	0	....	0	-0.1
1923 Phi-A	115	434	68	125	22	8	3	51	17	31	8	3	.288	.327	.396	.723	88	-8	57	4.60	-14	*3-107	10	-1.5
1924 Phi-A	80	261	41	83	14	2	2	17	17	19	3	2	.318	.367	.410	.777	99	-0	39	5.62	-4	3-55/O-5(4-0-1),S-1	8	-0.1
1925 Phi-A	110	391	62	135	30	11	8	63	17	27	7	4	.345	.376	.540	.915	122	11	77	7.39	-4	3-96/2-1	14	1.2
1926 Phi-A	111	327	49	92	22	9	4	43	13	36	1	4	.281	.311	.440	.751	89	-8	43	4.52	3	3-77/O-1	8	-0.1
1927 Phi-A	131	501	77	157	24	8	5	81	32	32	11	3	.313	.358	.423	.781	97	-2	78	5.48	4	*3-128	18	1.0
1928 Phi-A	88	314	38	97	20	9	4	58	9	21	2	0	.309	.334	.468	.803	106	2	49	5.68	13	3-79	13	1.9
1929 Phi-A	101	379	51	105	14	3	1	40	12	18	6	2	.277	.303	.338	.641	62	-21	40	3.50	4	3-99/2-1	6	-1.0
1930 StL-A	62	190	21	52	8	1	2	25	8	18	1	1	.274	.303	.358	.661	65	-11	20	3.74	0	3-47	3	-0.8
Total 10	883	2915	422	880	157	54	30	392	130	218	41	20	.302	.336	.424	.760	92	-39	417	5.09	1	3-704/O-10,2-3,S-1	83	0.4
• HALEY, Fred	Frederick Haley b: 6/18/1853, Wheeling, WV TR Deb: 6/22/1880																							
1880 Tro-N	2	7	0	0	0	0	0	0	1	2	....	....	.000	.125	.000	.125	-51	-1	0	.00	-1	/C-2	0	-0.2
• HALEY, Ray	Richard Timothy "Pat" Haley b: 1/23/1891, Danbury, IA d: 10/8/1973, Bradenton, FL BR/TR, 5'11", 180 lbs. Deb: 4/21/1915																							
1915 Bos-A	5	7	2	1	1	0	0	0	1	0	0	....	.143	.250	.286	.536	62	-0	1	2.21	0	/C-4	0	0.0
1916 Bos-A	1	1	0	0	0	0	0	0	0	1	0	....	.000	.000	.000	.000	-100	-0	0	.00	0	....	0	0.0
Phi-A	34	108	8	25	5	0	0	4	6	19	0	....	.231	.278	.278	.556	70	-4	8	2.61	8	C-33	1	0.8
Yr.	35	109	8	25	5	0	0	4	6	20	0	....	.229	.276	.275	.551	69	-4	8	2.58	8	C-33	1	0.7
1917 Phi-A	41	98	7	27	2	1	0	11	4	12	2	....	.276	.311	.316	.627	93	-1	10	3.50	-1	C-34	2	0.0
Total 3	81	214	17	53	8	1	0	15	11	32	2	....	.248	.291	.294	.585	79	-6	19	2.98	8	/C-71	3	0.7
• HALL, Al	Archibald W. Hall b: Worcester, MA d: 2/10/1885, Warren, PA Deb: 5/1/1879 Career OF: 5-63-2																							
1879 Tro-N	67	306	30	79	7	3	0	14	3	13	....	....	.258	.265	.301	.566	92	-2	25	3.09	6	*O-67(2-63-2)	5	0.1
1880 Cle-N	3	8	1	1	0	0	0	0	0	0	....	....	.125	.125	.125	.250	-15	-1	0	.50	-1	/O-3(3-0-0)	0	-0.2
Total 2	70	314	31	80	7	3	0	14	3	13	....	....	.255	.262	.296	.558	90	-3	25	3.01	6	/O-70	5	-0.1
• HALL, Albert	Albert Hall b: 3/7/1958, Birmingham, AL BB/TR, 5'11", 155 lbs. Deb: 9/12/1981 Career OF: 65-141-42																							
1981 Atl-N	6	2	1	0	0	0	0	0	1	1	0	0	.000	.333	.000	.333	1	-0	0	1.17	0	/O-2(1-0-1)	0	-0.1
1982 Atl-N	5	0	1	0	0	0	0	0	0	0	0	0	....	....	....	....	-96	0	0	....	0	....	0	0.0
1983 Atl-N	10	8	2	0	0	0	0	0	2	2	1	1	.000	.200	.000	.200	-37	-2	0	.31	0	/O-4(4-1-0)	0	-0.2
1984 Atl-N	87	142	25	37	6	1	1	9	10	18	6	4	.261	.309	.338	.647	76	-5	15	3.50	0	O-66(48-2-17)	3	-0.8
1985 Atl-N	54	47	5	7	0	1	0	3	9	12	1	1	.149	.286	.191	.477	34	-4	3	1.53	0	O-13(6-6-3)	0	-0.4
1986 Atl-N	16	50	6	12	2	0	0	1	5	6	8	3	.240	.309	.280	.589	60	-2	5	3.16	-0	O-14(0-0-14)	1	-0.3
1987 Atl-N	92	292	54	83	20	4	3	24	38	36	33	10	.284	.370	.411	.781	102	4	48	5.64	-1	O-69(0-68-1)	9	0.2
1988 Atl-N	85	231	27	57	7	1	1	15	21	35	15	10	.247	.315	.299	.614	73	-9	22	3.05	2	O-63(1-63-0)	4	-0.9
1989 Pit-N	20	33	4	6	2	1	0	1	3	5	3	0	.182	.250	.303	.553	59	-1	3	3.09	-1	O-12(5-1-6)	0	-0.2
Total 9	375	805	125	202	37	8	5	53	89	115	67	29	.251	.329	.335	.664	79	-19	95	3.89	-1	O-243	17	-2.7
• HALL, Bill	William Lemuel Hall b: 7/30/1928, Moultrie, GA d: 1/1/1986, Moultrie, GA BL/TR, 5'11", 165 lbs. Deb: 4/18/1954																							
1954 Pit-N	5	7	0	0	0	0	0	0	0	0	0	0	.000	.000	.000	.000	-102	-2	0	.00	-0	/C-1	0	-0.2
1956 Pit-N	1	3	0	0	0	0	0	0	0	1	0	0	.000	.000	.000	.000	-102	-1	0	.00	1	/C-1	0	0.0
1958 Pit-N	51	116	15	33	6	0	1	15	15	13	0	0	.284	.366	.362	.728	96	-0	15	4.89	2	C-51	5	0.4
Total 3	57	126	15	33	6	0	1	15	15	14	0	0	.262	.340	.333	.674	82	-3	15	4.37	3	/C-53	5	0.2

YEAR TM-L	G	AB	R	H	2B	3B	HR	RBI	BB	SO	SB	CS	AVG	OBP	SLG	OPS	OPS+	BR/A	RC	RC/G	FR	G/POS	WS	TPW
• HALL, Bill	William Hall b: 12/28/1979, Tupelo, MS BR/TR, 6', 175 lbs. Deb: 9/1/2002																							
2002 Mil-N	19	36	3	7	1	1	1	5	3	13	0	1	.194	.256	.361	.618	61	-3	3	2.46	-3	S-13/3-2	1	-0.5
2003 Mil-N	52	142	23	37	9	2	5	20	7	28	1	2	.261	.300	.458	.758	96	-2	17	3.97	3	2-18,S-18/3-1	3	0.3
Total 2	71	178	26	44	10	3	6	25	10	41	1	3	.247	.291	.438	.729	89	-5	20	3.66	0	/S-31,2-18,3-3	4	-0.2
• HALL, Bob	Robert Prill Hall b: 12/20/1878, Baltimore, MD d: 12/1/1950, Wellesley, MA TR, 5'10", 158 lbs. Deb: 4/18/1904																							
1904 Phi-N	46	163	11	26	4	0	0	17	14	....	5	....	.160	.226	.184	.410	28	-13	8	1.57	-10	3-20,S-15,1-11	0	-2.4
1905 NY-N	1	3	1	1	0	0	0	0	0	....	0	....	.333	.333	.333	.667	97	-0	0	4.44	0	/0-1	0	0.0
Bro-N	56	203	21	48	4	1	2	15	11	....	8	....	.236	.279	.296	.575	77	-6	20	3.25	4	0-42(24-12-7)/2-7,1-3	2	-0.5
Yr.	57	206	22	49	4	1	2	15	11	....	8	....	.238	.280	.296	.576	77	-6	20	3.27	4	0-43(24-12-8)/2-7,1-3	2	-0.5
Total 2	103	369	33	75	8	1	2	32	25	....	13	....	.203	.256	.247	.502	55	-19	29	2.48	-7	/0-43,3-20,S-15,1-14,2-7	2	-2.9
• HALL, Charlie	Charles Walter "Doc" Hall b: 8/24/1863, Toulon, IL d: 6/24/1921, Tacoma, WA, 5'10" Deb: 5/3/1887																							
1887 NY-a	3	14	1	3	0	0	0	0	2	....	1	....	.214	.214	.083	.298	-16	-2	0	1.08	0	/0-3(0-3-0)	0	-0.1
• HALL, Dick	Richard Wallace Hall b: 9/27/1930, St. Louis, MO BR/TR, 6'6", 200 lbs. Deb: 4/15/1952 Career OF: 43-59-20 ♦																							
1952 Pit-N	26	80	6	11	1	0	0	2	2	17	0	1	.138	.159	.150	.309	-14	-13	2	.73	0	0-14(0-12-2)/3-5	0	-1.4
1953 Pit-N	7	24	2	4	0	0	0	1	1	3	1	1	.167	.200	.167	.367	-3	-4	1	1.00	1	/2-7	0	-0.2
1954 Pit-N	112	310	38	74	8	4	2	27	33	46	3	0	.239	.312	.310	.622	64	-15	29	3.05	-3	*0-102(42-44-18)	3	-2.3
1955 Pit-N	21	40	3	7	1	0	1	3	6	5	0	0	.175	.283	.275	.558	49	1	3	2.03	-2	P-15/0-3(1-3-0)	7	0.4
1956 Pit-N	33	29	5	10	0	0	0	1	5	7	0	0	.345	.441	.345	.786	118	4	5	6.28	-1	P-19/1-1	2	-0.2
1957 Pit-N	10	1	0	0	0	0	0	0	0	1	0	0	.000	.000	.000	.000	-103	-0	0	.00	0	/P-8	0	-0.8
1959 Pit-N	2	2	0	0	0	0	0	0	0	0	0	0	.000	.000	.000	.000	-101	-0	0	.00	0	/P-2	0	0.0
1960 KC-A	32	56	5	6	0	0	0	4	4	15	1	0	.107	.167	.107	.274	-24	-2	2	.80	-1	P-29	8	0.0
1961 Bal-A	30	36	4	5	0	0	0	1	3	13	0	0	.139	.205	.139	.344	-6	-1	1	.96	1	P-29	10	0.9
1962 Bal-A	44	24	3	4	1	0	0	1	4	9	0	0	.167	.286	.208	.494	37	1	2	2.32	0	P-43	13	2.0
1963 Bal-A	48	28	7	13	1	0	1	4	0	8	0	0	.464	.464	.607	1.071	202	6	8	12.42	1	P-47	13	1.3
1964 Bal-A	45	16	1	2	0	0	0	3	1	3	0	0	.125	.176	.125	.301	-14	-0	0	.57	0	P-45	13	1.5
1965 Bal-A	49	15	1	5	2	0	0	4	1	4	0	0	.333	.412	.467	.878	146	2	3	7.10	-1	P-48	12	0.5
1966 Bal-A	32	12	0	2	0	0	0	2	0	5	0	0	.167	.231	.167	.397	17	0	1	1.48	0	P-32	5	-0.5
1967 Phi-N	48	14	1	1	0	0	0	0	0	5	0	0	.071	.071	.071	.143	-58	-1	0	.00	1	P-48	10	1.2
1968 Phi-N	32	3	0	1	0	0	0	0	0	1	0	0	.333	.333	.333	.667	100	0	0	4.50	0	P-32	1	-1.0
1969*Bal-A	39	7	1	2	0	0	0	2	1	1	1	0	.286	.375	.286	.661	86	1	1	4.42	-1	P-39	9	1.1
1970*Bal-A	32	12	2	1	0	0	0	1	0	3	0	0	.083	.083	.083	.167	-53	-1	0	.00	-1	P-32	6	0.2
1971*Bal-A	27	5	0	2	1	0	0	0	0	1	0	0	.400	.400	.600	1.000	182	1	1	7.92	-1	P-27	1	-0.8
Total 19	669	714	79	150	15	4	4	56	61	147	6	2	.210	.274	.259	.533	44	-21	59	2.53	-8	P-495,0-119/2-7,3-5,1-1	113	1.7
• HALL, George	George William Hall b: 3/29/1849, Stepney, England d: 6/11/1923, Ridgewood, NY BL, 5'7", 142 lbs. Deb: 5/5/1871 U NA OF: 98-138-10 Career OF: 120-0-1																							
1871 Oly-n	32	136	31	40	3	3	2	17	8	0	2	1	.294	.333	.404	.738	117	3	19	6.32	7	*0-32(1-31-0)	....	0.7
1872 Bal-n	53	250	69	84	17	6	1	37	3	1	6	1	.336	.344	.464	.808	140	11	43	7.98	-5	*0-52(3-51-0)/1-1	....	0.4
1873 Bal-n	35	168	44	58	6	3	0	30	2	0	0	0	.345	.353	.417	.770	128	6	25	7.02	0	*0-35(0-35-0)	....	0.4
1874 Bos-n	47	222	58	64	10	8	1	32	1	0	2	0	.288	.291	.419	.710	118	4	28	5.39	-2	*0-47(20-21-7)	....	0.2
1875 Ath-n	77	358	71	107	10	12	4	62	3	4	8	5	.299	.305	.427	.732	136	10	50	5.79	2	*0-77(74-0-3)/1-1	....	1.2
1876 Phi-N	60	276	51	98	7	13	**5**	45	8	4	....	....	.355	.384	.545	.929	208	30	57	9.47	-3	*0-60(59-0-1)	10	2.1
1877 Lou-N	61	269	53	87	15	8	0	26	12	19	....	....	.323	.352	.439	.791	125	6	43	6.44	-3	*0-61(61-0-0)	8	0.0
Total 5 n	244	1134	273	353	46	32	8	178	17	5	18	7	.311	.321	.429	.751	130	34	166	6.41	2	0-243/1-2	....	2.8
Total 2	121	545	104	185	22	21	5	71	20	23	....	....	.339	.368	.492	.860	166	36	100	7.90	-6	0-121	18	2.0
• HALL, Irv	Irvin Gladstone Hall b: 10/7/1918, Alberton, MD BR/TR, 5'10.5", 160 lbs. Deb: 4/20/1943																							
1943 Phi-A	151	544	37	139	15	4	0	54	22	42	10	7	.256	.292	.298	.590	73	-20	47	2.93	-10	*S-148/2-1,3-1	11	-1.9
1944 Phi-A	143	559	60	150	20	8	0	45	31	46	2	5	.268	.309	.333	.642	85	-14	56	3.46	6	2-97,S-40/1-4	12	0.1
1945 Phi-A	151	616	62	161	17	5	0	50	35	42	3	10	.261	.307	.305	.613	78	-21	58	3.24	13	*2-151	12	0.1
1946 Phi-A	63	185	19	46	6	2	0	19	9	18	1	1	.249	.287	.303	.590	65	-9	16	2.75	-4	2-40/S-7	1	-1.1
Total 4	508	1904	178	496	58	19	0	168	97	148	16	23	.261	.302	.311	.613	77	-64	176	3.16	5	2-289,S-195/1-4,3-1	36	-2.8
• HALL, Jim	James Hall d: 1/30/1886, Brooklyn, NY Deb: 5/20/1872 U NA OF: 1-0-1																							
1872 Atl-n	13	57	9	18	0	1	0	6	1	0	0	0	.316	.328	.351	.678	93	-1	7	5.34	-6	2-13	....	-0.6
1874 Atl-n	2	9	0	1	0	0	0	0	0	0	0	0	.111	.111	.111	.222	-32	-1	0	.43	0	/2-2,0-1	....	-0.1
1875 Wes-n	1	3	0	1	0	1	0	1	0	0	0	0	.333	.333	1.000	1.333	327	1	1	15.12	-1	/0-1	....	0.0
Total 3 n	16	69	9	20	0	2	0	7	1	0	0	0	.290	.300	.348	.648	87	-2	8	4.94	-7	/2-15,0-2	....	-0.6
• HALL, Jimmie	Jimmie Randolph Hall b: 3/7/1938, Mount Holly, NC BL/TR, 6', 175 lbs. Deb: 4/9/1963 Career OF: 221-443-217																							
1963 Min-A	156	497	88	129	21	5	33	80	63	101	3	3	.260	.343	.521	.864	135	22	89	6.18	0	*0-143(87-93-16)	21	1.7
1964 Min-A★	149	510	61	144	20	3	25	75	44	112	5	2	.282	.341	.480	.821	124	16	83	5.79	3	*0-137(0-137-0)	19	1.5
1965*Min-A★	148	522	81	149	25	4	20	86	51	79	14	7	.285	.350	.464	.814	124	16	86	5.90	-1	*0-141(6-140-6)	26	1.1
1966 Min-A	120	356	52	85	7	4	20	47	33	66	1	2	.239	.303	.449	.753	106	2	44	4.11	0	*0-103(69-27-12)	10	-0.3
1967 Cal-A	129	401	54	100	8	3	16	55	42	65	4	1	.249	.321	.404	.725	117	9	52	4.44	0	*0-120(2-6-116)	15	0.1
1968 Cal-A	46	126	15	27	3	0	1	8	16	19	1	0	.214	.303	.262	.565	75	-3	10	2.66	-1	0-39(4-2-33)	2	-0.7
Cle-A	53	111	4	22	4	0	1	8	10	19	1	0	.198	.264	.261	.526	61	-5	8	2.31	0	0-29(20-6-4)	1	-0.7
Yr.	99	237	19	49	7	0	2	16	26	38	2	0	.207	.285	.262	.547	68	-8	18	2.49	-1	0-68(24-8-37)	3	-1.4
1969 Cle-A	4	10	1	0	0	0	0	0	2	3	1	0	.000	.167	.000	.167	-48	-2	0	.16	0	/0-3(2-1-0)	0	-0.2
NY-A	80	212	21	50	8	5	3	26	19	34	8	3	.236	.299	.363	.662	88	-4	24	3.90	-2	0-50(9-19-22)/1-7	5	-0.8
Yr.	84	222	22	50	8	5	3	26	21	37	9	3	.225	.292	.347	.639	81	-5	24	3.67	-2	0-53(11-20-22)/1-7	5	-1.0
Chi-N	11	24	1	5	1	0	0	1	1	5	0	0	.208	.240	.250	.490	33	-2	2	2.13	-0	/0-5(1-4-0)	0	-0.2
1970 Chi-N	28	32	2	3	1	0	0	1	4	12	0	0	.094	.194	.125	.319	-11	-5	1	.87	-0	/0-8(2-7-0)	0	-0.5
Atl-N	39	47	7	10	2	0	2	4	2	14	0	0	.213	.245	.383	.628	62	-3	4	2.91	0	0-28(19-1-8)	1	-0.3
Yr.	67	79	9	13	3	0	2	5	6	26	0	0	.165	.224	.278	.502	31	-8	5	2.03	0	0-36(21-8-8)	1	-0.9
Total 8	963	2848	387	724	100	24	121	391	287	529	38	18	.254	.323	.434	.757	112	41	402	4.87	-1	0-806/1-7	100	0.5
• HALL, Joe	Joseph Geroy Hall b: 3/6/1966, Paducah, KY BR/TR, 6', 180 lbs. Deb: 4/5/1994 Career OF: 12-0-3																							
1994 Chi-A	17	28	6	11	3	0	1	5	2	4	0	0	.393	.452	.607	1.059	173	3	7	9.78	-1	/0-9(7-0-2),D-2	2	0.2
1995 Det-A	7	15	2	2	0	0	0	0	2	3	0	0	.133	.235	.133	.369	-1	-2	0	.86	0	/0-5(5-0-0),D-2	0	-0.2
1997 Det-A	2	4	1	2	1	0	0	3	0	0	0	0	.500	.500	.750	1.250	222	1	2	20.25	-0	/0-1	1	0.1
Total 3	26	47	9	15	4	0	1	8	4	7	0	0	.319	.385	.468	.853	120	2	9	6.81	0	/0-15,D-4	3	0.1
• HALL, Mel	Melvin Hall b: 9/16/1960, Lyons, NY BL/TL, 6', 205 lbs. Deb: 9/3/1981 Career OF: 716-145-214																							
1981 Chi-N	10	11	1	1	0	0	1	2	1	4	0	0	.091	.167	.364	.530	45	-1	1	1.92	-1	/0-3(1-2-0)	0	-0.2
1982 Chi-N	24	80	6	21	3	2	0	4	5	17	0	1	.263	.322	.350	.672	86	-2	9	4.09	0	0-22(0-21-1)	2	-0.3
1983 Chi-N	112	410	60	116	23	5	17	56	42	101	6	6	.283	.354	.488	.842	125	12	71	6.23	-1	*0-112(5-108-0)	15	1.0
1984 Chi-N	48	150	25	42	11	3	4	22	12	23	2	1	.280	.333	.473	.807	114	2	23	5.60	-0	0-46(5-5-40)	5	0.0
Cle-A	83	257	43	66	13	1	7	30	35	55	1	1	.257	.350	.397	.747	104	2	38	5.07	1	0-69(64-1-6)/D-9	8	0.1
1985 Cle-A	23	66	7	21	6	0	0	12	8	12	0	1	.318	.392	.409	.801	121	2	10	5.65	0	0-15(15-0-1)/D-5	2	0.1
1986 Cle-A	140	442	68	131	29	2	18	77	33	65	6	2	.296	.348	.493	.841	128	16	75	6.22	-1	*0-126(123-0-14)/D-7	18	1.0
1987 Cle-A	142	485	57	136	21	1	18	76	20	68	5	4	.280	.310	.439	.749	95	-6	63	4.73	2	*0-122(122-0-0),D-14	10	-1.0
1988 Cle-A	150	515	69	144	32	4	6	71	28	50	7	3	.280	.317	.392	.709	95	-5	63	4.31	-7	*0-141(135-7-3)/D-6	13	-1.7
1989 NY-A	113	361	54	94	9	0	17	58	21	37	0	0	.260	.301	.427	.728	104	0	44	4.19	0	0-75(46-0-31),D-34	8	-0.3
1990 NY-A	113	360	41	93	23	2	12	46	6	46	0	0	.258	.274	.433	.708	95	-5	40	3.93	-1	D-54,0-50(36-0-15)	7	-0.9
1991 NY-A	141	492	67	140	23	2	19	80	26	40	0	1	.285	.324	.455	.780	113	6	72	5.30	2	*0-120(62-1-65),D-10	14	0.4
1992 NY-A	152	583	67	163	36	3	15	81	29	53	4	2	.280	.315	.429	.744	107	3	75	4.59	0	*0-136(99-0-37),D-11	15	-0.2

YEAR TM-L	G	AB	R	H	2B	3B	HR	RBI	BB	SO	SB	CS	AVG	OBP	SLG	OPS	OPS+	BR/A	RC	RC/G	FR	G/POS	WS	TPW
1996 SF-N	25	25	3	3	0	0	0	5	1	4	0	0	.120	.154	.120	.274	-28	-5	1	.66	-1	/O-4(3-0-1)	0	-0.5
Total 13	1276	4237	568	1171	229	25	134	620	267	575	31	22	.276	.322	.437	.759	107	21	585	4.92	-6	*O-1041,D-150	117	-2.5

• HALL, Russ Robert Russell Hall b: 9/29/1871, Shelbyville, KY d: 7/1/1937, Los Angeles, CA BL/TL, 5'10", 170 lbs. Deb: 4/15/1898

YEAR TM-L	G	AB	R	H	2B	3B	HR	RBI	BB	SO	SB	CS	AVG	OBP	SLG	OPS	OPS+	BR/A	RC	RC/G	FR	G/POS	WS	TPW
1898 StL-N	39	143	13	35	2	1	0	10	7	....	1	....	.245	.285	.273	.557	59	-8	12	2.89	-13	S-35/3-3,O-1	0	-1.9
1901 Cle-A	1	4	2	2	0	0	0	0	0	....	0	....	.500	.500	.500	1.000	185	0	1	13.58	-1	/S-1	0	-0.1
Total 2	40	147	15	37	2	1	0	10	7	....	1	....	.252	.290	.279	.569	62	-8	13	3.08	-15	/S-36,3-3,O-1	0	-1.9

• HALL, Toby Toby Jason Hall b: 10/21/1975, Tacoma, WA BR/TR, 6'3", 205 lbs. Deb: 9/15/2000

YEAR TM-L	G	AB	R	H	2B	3B	HR	RBI	BB	SO	SB	CS	AVG	OBP	SLG	OPS	OPS+	BR/A	RC	RC/G	FR	G/POS	WS	TPW
2000 TB-A	4	12	1	2	0	0	1	1	1	0	0	0	.167	.231	.417	.647	60	-1	1	3.28	0	/C-4	0	0.0
2001 TB-A	49	188	28	56	16	0	4	30	4	16	2	2	.298	.323	.447	.770	102	-1	25	4.81	3	C-46	6	0.5
2002 TB-A	85	330	37	85	19	1	6	42	17	27	0	1	.258	.296	.376	.672	78	-11	33	3.31	1	C-83	7	-0.4
2003 TB-A	130	463	50	117	23	0	12	47	23	40	0	1	.253	.298	.380	.678	79	-16	49	3.62	-2	*C-130	10	-0.8
Total 4	268	993	116	260	58	1	23	120	45	83	2	4	.262	.301	.392	.693	82	-29	108	3.73	2	C-263	23	-0.8

• HALLER, Tom Thomas Frank Haller b: 6/23/1937, Lockport, IL BL/TR, 6'4", 195 lbs. Deb: 4/11/1961 C Career OF: 2-0-9

YEAR TM-L	G	AB	R	H	2B	3B	HR	RBI	BB	SO	SB	CS	AVG	OBP	SLG	OPS	OPS+	BR/A	RC	RC/G	FR	G/POS	WS	TPW
1961 SF-N	30	62	5	9	1	0	2	8	9	23	0	1	.145	.264	.258	.522	41	-6	4	2.15	1	C-25	1	-0.3
1962*SF-N	99	272	53	71	13	1	18	55	51	59	1	4	.261	.385	.515	.900	141	16	56	7.17	-2	C-91	16	1.8
1963 SF-N	98	298	32	76	8	1	14	44	34	45	4	6	.255	.335	.430	.765	120	6	41	4.61	0	C-85/O-7(1-0-6)	13	1.1
1964 SF-N	117	388	43	98	14	3	16	48	55	51	4	2	.253	.348	.428	.776	115	9	58	5.18	2	*C-113/O-3(1-0-2)	18	1.8
1965 SF-N	134	422	40	106	4	3	16	49	47	67	0	0	.251	.338	.389	.726	101	2	56	4.57	-5	*C-133	18	0.4
1966 SF-N★	142	471	74	113	19	2	27	67	53	74	1	3	.240	.325	.461	.785	112	7	69	4.95	-7	*C-136/1-4	22	0.6
1967 SF-N★	141	455	54	114	23	5	14	49	62	61	0	4	.251	.345	.415	.761	118	11	68	5.17	-4	*C-136/O-1	21	1.5
1968 LA-N★	144	474	37	135	27	5	4	53	46	76	1	4	.285	.351	.388	.739	131	17	66	4.97	10	*C-139	27	3.9
1969 LA-N	134	445	46	117	18	3	6	39	48	58	0	3	.263	.337	.357	.695	102	1	55	4.32	-3	*C-132	16	0.4
1970 LA-N	112	325	47	93	16	6	10	47	32	35	3	0	.286	.354	.465	.818	123	10	54	5.97	-1	*C-106	15	1.3
1971 LA-N	84	202	23	54	5	0	5	32	25	30	0	2	.267	.354	.366	.720	111	3	26	4.35	1	C-67	8	0.7
1972*Det-A	59	121	7	25	5	2	2	13	15	14	0	1	.207	.294	.331	.625	83	-3	12	3.25	0	C-36	4	-0.1
Total 12	1294	3935	461	1011	153	31	134	504	477	593	14	30	.257	.342	.414	.756	114	73	567	4.96	-9	*C-1199/O-11,1-4	179	12.9

• HALLIDAY, Newt Newton Schurz Halliday b: 6/18/1896, Chicago, IL d: 4/6/1918, Great Lakes, IL BR/TR, 6'1", 175 lbs. Deb: 8/19/1916

YEAR TM-L	G	AB	R	H	2B	3B	HR	RBI	BB	SO	SB	CS	AVG	OBP	SLG	OPS	OPS+	BR/A	RC	RC/G	FR	G/POS	WS	TPW
1916 Pit-N	1	1	0	0	0	0	0	0	0	1	0	....	.000	.000	.000	.000	-99	-0	0	.00	0	/1-1	0	0.0

• HALLIGAN, Jocko William E. Halligan b: 12/8/1868, Avon, NY d: 2/13/1945, Buffalo, NY BL, 5'9", 166 lbs. Deb: 5/13/1890 Career OF: 2-5-145

YEAR TM-L	G	AB	R	H	2B	3B	HR	RBI	BB	SO	SB	CS	AVG	OBP	SLG	OPS	OPS+	BR/A	RC	RC/G	FR	G/POS	WS	TPW
1890 Buf-P	57	211	28	53	9	2	3	33	20	19	7	....	.251	.319	.355	.674	87	-3	27	4.58	-3	O-43(1-5-37),C-16	3	-0.5
1891 Cin-N	61	247	43	77	13	6	3	44	24	25	5	....	.312	.375	.449	.824	139	11	45	7.08	-2	O-61(0-0-61)	8	0.8
1892 Cin-N	26	101	14	29	4	0	2	12	12	9	3	....	.287	.363	.386	.749	128	4	16	5.86	0	O-26(0-0-26)	4	0.2
Bal-N	46	178	38	48	4	7	2	43	30	24	8	....	.270	.381	.404	.785	134	8	31	6.49	-4	O-22(1-0-21),1-19/C-5	6	0.3
Yr.	72	279	52	77	8	7	4	55	42	33	11	....	.276	.375	.398	.772	132	12	47	6.26	-4	O-48(1-0-47),1-19/C-5	10	0.5
Total 3	190	737	123	207	30	15	10	132	86	77	23	....	.281	.359	.403	.762	121	20	118	6.02	-9	O-152/C-21,1-19	21	0.8

• HALLINAN, Ed Edward S. Hallinan b: 8/23/1888, San Francisco, CA d: 8/24/1940, San Francisco, CA BR/TR, 5'9", 168 lbs. Deb: 5/13/1911

YEAR TM-L	G	AB	R	H	2B	3B	HR	RBI	BB	SO	SB	CS	AVG	OBP	SLG	OPS	OPS+	BR/A	RC	RC/G	FR	G/POS	WS	TPW
1911 StL-A	52	169	13	35	3	1	0	14	14	....	4	....	.207	.268	.237	.504	43	-13	11	2.20	-7	S-34,2-15/3-3	1	-1.7
1912 StL-A	29	86	11	19	2	0	0	1	5	....	3	....	.221	.272	.244	.516	50	-6	7	2.45	-3	S-26	1	-0.7
Total 2	81	255	24	54	5	1	0	15	19	....	7	....	.212	.269	.239	.508	45	-18	18	2.28	-11	/S-60,2-15,3-3	2	-2.5

• HALLINAN, Jimmy James H. Hallinan b: 5/27/1849, Ireland d: 10/28/1879, Chicago, IL BL/TL, 5'9", 172 lbs. Deb: 7/26/1871 Career OF: 13-1-21

YEAR TM-L	G	AB	R	H	2B	3B	HR	RBI	BB	SO	SB	CS	AVG	OBP	SLG	OPS	OPS+	BR/A	RC	RC/G	FR	G/POS	WS	TPW
1871 Kek-n	5	25	7	5	0	0	0	2	2	0	1	1	.200	.259	.200	.459	34	-2	2	2.39	-4	/S-5	....	-0.5
1875 Wes-n	13	51	12	14	2	1	0	3	0	1	2	2	.275	.275	.353	.627	110	-0	6	4.26	-4	S-13	....	-0.3
Mut-n	44	203	29	58	6	3	3	21	1	2	2	2	.286	.289	.389	.678	127	4	24	4.82	-6	S-43/3-1,O-1	....	-0.3
Yr.	57	254	41	72	8	4	3	24	1	3	4	4	.283	.286	.382	.668	123	4	30	4.70	-10	*S-56/3-1,O-1	....	-0.6
1876 NY-N	54	242	45	67	7	6	2	36	2	4	....	....	.277	.285	.383	.668	139	11	27	4.35	-13	*S-50/2-4,O-2(0-0-2)	12	0.1
1877 Cin-N	16	73	18	27	1	1	0	7	1	1	....	....	.370	.378	.411	.789	167	6	12	6.96	-6	2-16	3	0.0
Chi-N	19	89	17	25	4	1	0	11	4	2	....	....	.281	.312	.348	.660	96	-1	10	4.26	-2	O-19(0-0-19)	2	-0.2
Yr.	35	162	35	52	5	2	0	18	5	3	....	....	.321	.341	.377	.718	127	5	22	5.39	-7	O-19(0-0-19),2-16	5	-0.2
1878 Chi-N	16	67	14	19	3	0	0	2	5	6	....	....	.284	.333	.328	.662	111	1	8	4.31	-4	O-11(11-0-0)/2-5	2	-0.3
Ind-N	3	12	0	3	2	0	0	1	0	2	....	....	.250	.250	.417	.667	134	0	1	3.91	-1	/O-3(2-1-0)	0	0.0
Yr.	19	79	14	22	5	0	0	3	5	8	....	....	.278	.321	.342	.663	114	1	9	4.24	-5	O-14(13-1-0)/2-5	2	-0.4
Total 2 n	62	279	48	77	8	4	3	26	3	3	5	5	.276	.284	.366	.649	115	2	31	4.47	-14	/S-61,3-1,O-1	....	-1.1
Total 3	108	483	94	141	17	8	2	57	12	15	....	....	.292	.310	.374	.685	131	17	57	4.67	-25	/S-50,O-35,2-25	19	-0.5

• HALLMAN, Bill William Wilson Hallman b: 3/31/1867, Pittsburgh, PA d: 9/11/1920, Philadelphia, PA BR/TR, 5'8", 160 lbs. Deb: 4/23/1888 M/U Career OF: 3-4-32

YEAR TM-L	G	AB	R	H	2B	3B	HR	RBI	BB	SO	SB	CS	AVG	OBP	SLG	OPS	OPS+	BR/A	RC	RC/G	FR	G/POS	WS	TPW
1888 Phi-N	18	63	5	13	4	1	0	6	1	12	1	....	.206	.219	.302	.520	61	-3	4	2.42	-3	C-10/2-4,O-3(3-0-0),3-1,S	0	-0.5
1889 Phi-N	119	462	67	117	21	8	2	60	36	54	20	....	.253	.313	.346	.659	77	-16	58	4.43	5	*S-106,2-13/C-1	13	-0.6
1890 Phi-P	84	356	59	95	16	7	1	37	33	24	6	....	.267	.338	.360	.697	84	-9	46	4.80	-5	O-34(0-3-32),C-26,2-14,3-10/S	8	-0.9
1891 Phi-a	141	587	112	166	21	13	6	69	38	56	18	....	.283	.332	.394	.725	104	-1	85	5.33	1	*2-141	17	0.4
1892 Phi-N	138	586	106	171	27	10	2	84	32	52	19	....	.292	.335	.382	.717	117	10	83	5.43	-16	*2-138	15	0.0
1893 Phi-N	132	596	119	183	28	7	5	76	51	27	22	....	.307	.367	.403	.769	105	3	98	6.32	-9	*2-120,1-12	16	-0.1
1894 Phi-N	122	519	111	162	19	9	0	69	37	15	36	....	.312	.363	.383	.746	82	-14	87	6.36	-13	*2-119	10	-1.7
1895 Phi-N	124	539	94	169	26	5	1	91	34	20	16	....	.314	.359	.386	.745	92	-7	84	5.91	4	*2-122/S-3	13	0.2
1896 Phi-N	120	469	82	150	21	3	2	83	45	23	16	....	.320	.382	.390	.772	105	4	80	6.31	-3	*2-120/P-1	14	0.3
1897 Phi-N	31	126	16	33	3	0	0	15	8	....	1	....	.262	.326	.286	.612	64	-6	13	3.54	-4	2-31	1	-0.8
StL-N	80	302	32	67	7	2	0	26	24	....	12	....	.222	.288	.258	.546	46	-23	28	3.01	-12	2-77/1-3	1	-2.7
Yr.	111	428	48	100	10	2	0	41	32	....	13	....	.234	.299	.266	.566	51	-29	41	3.16	-16	*2-108/1-3	2	-3.5
1898 Bro-N	134	509	57	124	10	7	2	63	29	....	9	....	.244	.291	.303	.594	70	-21	50	3.35	-11	*2-124,3-10	8	-2.4
1901 Cle-A	5	19	2	4	0	0	0	3	2	....	0	....	.211	.286	.211	.496	41	-1	1	2.07	-2	/S-5	0	-0.3
Phi-N	123	445	46	82	13	5	0	38	26	....	13	....	.184	.236	.236	.472	36	-37	32	2.14	2	2-90,3-33	5	-3.2
1902 Phi-N	73	254	14	63	8	4	0	35	14	....	9	....	.248	.287	.311	.598	85	-5	27	3.57	-5	3-72	7	-0.9
1903 Phi-N	63	198	20	42	11	2	0	17	16	....	2	....	.212	.271	.288	.559	61	-10	18	2.81	0	2-22,3-19/1-9,O-4(0-1-0),S	1	-1.0
Total 14	1507	6030	942	1641	235	83	21	772	426	283	200	....	.272	.326	.349	.675	84	-138	795	4.70	-72	*2-1135,3-145,S-120/O,C,1,P	129	-14.3

• HALLMAN, Bill William Harry Hallman b: 3/15/1876, Philadelphia, PA d: 4/23/1950, Philadelphia, PA BL/TL, 5'8" Deb: 4/25/1901 Career OF: 122-58-126

YEAR TM-L	G	AB	R	H	2B	3B	HR	RBI	BB	SO	SB	CS	AVG	OBP	SLG	OPS	OPS+	BR/A	RC	RC/G	FR	G/POS	WS	TPW
1901 Mil-A	139	549	70	135	27	6	2	47	41	....	12	....	.246	.301	.328	.629	78	-16	61	3.77	-1	*O-139(49-15-75)	6	-2.2
1903 Chi-A	63	207	29	43	7	4	0	18	31	....	11	....	.208	.320	.280	.600	85	-2	23	3.65	1	O-57(51-0-6)	6	-0.5
1906 Pit-N	23	89	12	24	3	1	1	6	15	....	3	....	.270	.375	.360	.735	124	3	14	5.36	-1	O-23(8-15-0)	4	0.1
1907 Pit-N	94	302	39	67	6	2	0	15	33	....	21	....	.222	.305	.255	.560	74	-8	32	3.39	-2	O-84(14-28-45)	7	-1.4
Total 4	319	1147	150	269	43	13	3	86	120	....	47	....	.235	.311	.303	.614	82	-22	129	3.76	-3	O-303	23	-4.0

• HALPIN, Jim James Nathaniel Halpin b: 10/4/1863, England d: 1/4/1893, Boston, MA Deb: 6/15/1882

YEAR TM-L	G	AB	R	H	2B	3B	HR	RBI	BB	SO	SB	CS	AVG	OBP	SLG	OPS	OPS+	BR/A	RC	RC/G	FR	G/POS	WS	TPW
1882 Wor-N	2	8	0	0	0	0	0	0	0	2	....	....	.000	.000	.000	.000	-98	-2	0	.00	-1	/3-2	0	-0.3
1884 Was-U	46	168	24	31	3	0	0	....	2	....	....	....	.185	.194	.202	.396	35	-11	7	1.38	-7	S-39/3-7	1	-1.4
1885 Det-N	15	54	3	7	2	0	0	1	1	12	....	....	.130	.145	.167	.312	1	-6	1	.77	0	S-15	0	-0.5
Total 3	63	230	27	38	5	0	0	1	3	14	....	....	.165	.176	.187	.363	23	-18	8	1.18	-8	/S-54,3-9	1	-2.2

• HALT, Al Alva William Halt b: 11/23/1890, Sandusky, OH d: 1/22/1973, Sandusky, OH BR/TR, 6', 180 lbs. Deb: 5/29/1914

YEAR TM-L	G	AB	R	H	2B	3B	HR	RBI	BB	SO	SB	CS	AVG	OBP	SLG	OPS	OPS+	BR/A	RC	RC/G	FR	G/POS	WS	TPW
1914 Bro-F	80	261	26	61	6	2	3	25	13	39	11	....	.234	.270	.307	.577	63	-13	23	2.87	-7	S-71/2-3,O-1	4	-1.6
1915 Bro-F	151	524	41	131	22	7	3	64	39	79	20	....	.250	.307	.336	.643	91	-7	58	3.68	4	*3-111,S-40	13	0.3
1918 Cle-A	26	69	9	12	2	0	0	1	9	12	4	....	.174	.269	.203	.472	39	-5	4	1.96	1	3-14/2-4,S-4,1-2	0	-0.4
Total 3	257	854	76	204	30	9	6	90	61	130	35	....	.239	.293	.316	.609	78	-25	85	3.29	-2	3-125,S-115/2-7,1-2,O-1	17	-1.7

• HALTER, Shane Shane David Halter b: 11/8/1969, La Plata, MD BR/TR, 5'10", 160 lbs. Deb: 4/6/1997 Career OF: 28-15-24 ♦

YEAR TM-L	G	AB	R	H	2B	3B	HR	RBI	BB	SO	SB	CS	AVG	OBP	SLG	OPS	OPS+	BR/A	RC	RC/G	FR	G/POS	WS	TPW
1997 KC-A	74	123	16	34	5	1	2	10	10	28	4	3	.276	.341	.382	.723	86	-3	16	4.57	-2	O-32(10-9-17),2-18,3-12/S-5,D	1	-0.4
1998 KC-A	86	204	17	45	12	0	2	13	12	38	2	5	.221	.267	.309	.576	48	-18	16	2.45	4	S-66/O-9(6-0-3),3-8,2-6,1,P	3	-0.9
1999 NY-N	7	0	0	0	0	0	0	0	0	0	0	0	....	....	....	....	-103	0	0	....	-1	/O-2(0-1-1),S-1	0	-0.1
2000 Det-A	105	238	26	62	12	2	3	27	14	49	5	2	.261	.304	.366	.670	71	-11	26	3.65	5	3-55,1-29,S-17,2-10/O-8(2-5-3),C,P	3	-0.5
2001 Det-A	136	450	53	128	32	7	12	65	37	100	3	3	.284	.348	.467	.815	117	10	70	5.38	4	3-74,S-62/1-8,D-1	16	1.8
2002 Det-A	122	410	46	98	22	6	10	39	39	92	0	4	.239	.311	.395	.706	91	-7	48	3.88	-2	S-81,3-30/O-8(8-0-0),2-4,D,1	8	-0.3
2003 Det-A	114	360	33	78	5	2	12	30	27	77	2	3	.217	.271	.342	.613	65	-20	31	2.78	3	3-50,S-27,2-24,1-12/D-4,O	2	-1.4
Total 7	**644**	**1785**	**191**	**445**	**88**	**18**	**41**	**184**	**139**	**384**	**16**	**20**	**.249**	**.309**	**.388**	**.697**	**85**	**-49**	**208**	**3.86**	**12**	**S-259,3-229/2-62,O-61,1,D,C,P**	**33**	**-1.7**

• HAM, Ralph Ralph A. Ham b: 3/1849, Troy, NY d: 2/13/1905, Troy, NY, 5'8", 158 lbs. Deb: 5/6/1871

YEAR TM-L	G	AB	R	H	2B	3B	HR	RBI	BB	SO	SB	CS	AVG	OBP	SLG	OPS	OPS+	BR/A	RC	RC/G	FR	G/POS	WS	TPW
1871 Rok-n	25	113	25	28	4	0	0	12	1	7	6	2	.248	.254	.283	.538	57	-5	10	3.59	-5	O-19(19-0-0)/3-7,S-2	....	-0.7

• HAMBURG, Charlie Charles M. Hamburg b: 11/22/1863, Louisville, KY d: 5/18/1931, Union, NJ, 6', 175 lbs. Deb: 4/18/1890

YEAR TM-L	G	AB	R	H	2B	3B	HR	RBI	BB	SO	SB	CS	AVG	OBP	SLG	OPS	OPS+	BR/A	RC	RC/G	FR	G/POS	WS	TPW
1890*Lou-a	133	485	93	132	22	2	3	77	69	....	46	....	.272	.370	.344	.714	113	11	81	6.06	-1	*O-133(133-0-0)	17	0.5

• HAMBY, Jim James Sanford "Cracker" Hamby b: 7/29/1897, Wilkesboro, NC d: 10/21/1991, Springfield, IL BR/TR, 6', 170 lbs. Deb: 9/20/1926

YEAR TM-L	G	AB	R	H	2B	3B	HR	RBI	BB	SO	SB	CS	AVG	OBP	SLG	OPS	OPS+	BR/A	RC	RC/G	FR	G/POS	WS	TPW
1926 NY-N	1	3	0	0	0	0	0	0	0	0	0	....	.000	.000	.000	.000	-101	-1	0	.00	-1	/C-1	0	-0.2
1927 NY-N	21	52	6	10	0	1	0	5	7	7	1	....	.192	.288	.231	.519	40	-4	4	2.29	-2	C-19	0	-0.5
Total 2	**22**	**55**	**6**	**10**	**0**	**1**	**0**	**5**	**7**	**7**	**1**	**....**	**.182**	**.274**	**.218**	**.492**	**34**	**-5**	**4**	**2.14**	**-3**	**/C-20**	**0**	**-0.7**

• HAMELIN, Bob Robert James Hamelin b: 11/29/1967, Elizabeth, NJ BL/TL, 6'1", 235 lbs. Deb: 9/12/1993

YEAR TM-L	G	AB	R	H	2B	3B	HR	RBI	BB	SO	SB	CS	AVG	OBP	SLG	OPS	OPS+	BR/A	RC	RC/G	FR	G/POS	WS	TPW
1993 KC-A	16	49	2	11	3	0	2	5	6	15	0	0	.224	.309	.408	.717	86	-1	6	3.97	-1	1-15	1	-0.4
1994 KC-A	101	312	64	88	25	1	24	65	56	62	4	3	.282	.393	.599	.992	145	21	76	8.68	1	D-70,1-24	12	1.5
1995 KC-A	72	208	20	35	7	1	7	25	26	56	0	1	.168	.279	.313	.592	53	-15	18	2.73	1	D-56/1-8	0	-1.6
1996 KC-A	89	239	31	61	14	1	9	40	54	58	5	2	.255	.397	.435	.832	110	6	44	6.27	1	D-47,1-33	7	0.2
1997 Det-A	110	318	47	86	15	0	18	52	48	72	2	1	.270	.368	.487	.855	122	11	58	6.41	0	D-95/1-7	9	0.5
1998 Mil-N	109	146	15	32	6	0	7	22	16	30	0	1	.219	.301	.404	.705	83	-4	16	3.43	-5	1-51/D-1	1	-1.2
Total 6	**497**	**1272**	**179**	**313**	**70**	**3**	**67**	**209**	**206**	**293**	**11**	**8**	**.246**	**.356**	**.464**	**.820**	**109**	**17**	**218**	**5.79**	**-3**	**D-269,1-138**	**30**	**-1.0**

• HAMILTON, Billy William Robert "Sliding Billy" Hamilton
b: 2/16/1866, Newark, NJ d: 12/16/1940, Worcester, MA BL/TR, 5'6", 165 lbs. Deb: 7/31/1888 HOF: 1961 Career OF: 434-986-164

YEAR TM-L	G	AB	R	H	2B	3B	HR	RBI	BB	SO	SB	CS	AVG	OBP	SLG	OPS	OPS+	BR/A	RC	RC/G	FR	G/POS	WS	TPW
1888 KC-a	35	129	21	34	4	4	0	11	4	....	19	....	.264	.307	.357	.663	105	0	20	5.81	1	O-35(3-0-32)	3	0.1
1889 KC-a	137	534	144	161	17	12	3	77	87	41	**111**	....	.301	.413	.395	.808	123	21	136	9.67	-8	*O-137(7-0-130)	24	0.8
1890 Phi-N	123	496	133	161	13	9	2	49	83	37	**102**	....	.325	.430	.399	.829	139	30	132	**10.47**	2	*O-123(123-0-0)	25	2.4
1891 Phi-N	133	527	**141**	**179**	23	7	2	60	**102**	28	**111**	....	**.340**	**.453**	.421	.874	151	42	155	**11.99**	4	*O-133(133-0-0)	**36**	**3.7**
1892 Phi-N	139	554	132	183	21	7	3	53	81	29	57	....	.330	.423	.410	.833	152	40	123	8.96	8	*O-139(138-1-0)	25	3.2
1893 Phi-N	82	355	110	135	22	7	5	44	63	7	43	....	.380	**.490**	.524	**1.014**	**170**	41	115	**13.84**	3	O-82(19-63-0)	20	3.1
1894 Phi-N	132	558	**198**	225	25	15	4	90	**128**	19	**100**	....	.403	**.521**	.523	1.044	157	**66**	208	16.26	-2	*O-129(0-129-0)	29	**4.3**
1895 Phi-N	123	517	**166**	201	22	6	7	74	**96**	30	**97**	....	.389	.490	.495	.985	154	50	178	14.80	-5	*O-123(3-120-0)	30	3.0
1896 Bos-N	131	523	153	192	24	10	3	55	**110**	29	83	....	.367	**.479**	.468	.947	141	39	161	12.59	-9	*O-131(6-125-0)	30	1.9
1897*Bos-N	127	507	**152**	174	17	5	3	61	**105**	....	66	....	.343	.461	.414	.875	124	26	131	10.30	-6	*O-126(0-126-0)	28	1.0
1898 Bos-N	110	417	110	154	16	5	3	50	87	....	54	....	.369	**.480**	.453	**.933**	**159**	40	120	**11.99**	-13	*O-110(0-110-0)	33	1.8
1899 Bos-N	84	297	63	92	7	1	1	33	72	....	19	....	.310	.446	.350	.796	109	9	57	7.21	-3	O-81(2-78-1)	15	0.1
1900 Bos-N	136	520	103	173	20	5	1	47	107	....	32	....	.333	.449	.396	.845	119	22	110	8.31	-3	*O-136(0-136-0)	23	0.9
1901 Bos-N	102	348	71	100	11	2	3	38	64	....	20	....	.287	.404	.356	.760	111	9	61	6.29	0	O-99(0-98-1)	16	0.4
Total 14	**1594**	**6282**	**1697**	**2164**	**242**	**95**	**40**	**742**	**1189**	**220**	**914**	**....**	**.344**	**.455**	**.432**	**.888**	**139**	**435**	**1708**	**10.91**	**-30**	***O-1584**	**337**	**26.8**

• HAMILTON, Darryl Darryl Quinn Hamilton b: 12/3/1964, Baton Rouge, LA BL/TR, 6'1", 180 lbs. Deb: 6/3/1988 Career OF: 176-855-252

YEAR TM-L	G	AB	R	H	2B	3B	HR	RBI	BB	SO	SB	CS	AVG	OBP	SLG	OPS	OPS+	BR/A	RC	RC/G	FR	G/POS	WS	TPW
1988 Mil-A	44	103	14	19	4	0	1	11	12	9	7	3	.184	.276	.252	.528	49	-7	8	2.32	0	O-37(8-6-23)/D-3	1	-0.8
1990 Mil-A	89	156	27	46	5	0	1	18	9	12	10	3	.295	.333	.346	.679	91	-1	19	4.30	-1	O-72(41-6-25)/D-9	5	-0.4
1991 Mil-A	122	405	64	126	15	6	1	57	33	38	16	6	.311	.363	.385	.748	110	7	57	5.02	-1	*O-117(25-55-49)	15	0.3
1992 Mil-A	128	470	67	140	19	7	5	62	45	42	41	14	.298	.360	.400	.760	115	13	70	5.16	-1	*O-124(30-32-74)	18	0.8
1993 Mil-A	135	520	74	161	21	1	9	48	45	62	21	13	.310	.368	.406	.774	109	7	77	5.38	0	*O-129(31-49-70)/D-1	16	0.2
1994 Mil-A	36	141	23	37	10	1	1	13	15	17	3	0	.262	.333	.369	.702	77	-4	18	4.58	1	O-32(0-32-0)/D-4	2	-0.3
1995 Mil-A	112	398	54	108	20	6	5	44	47	35	11	1	.271	.353	.389	.742	88	-5	58	5.00	0	*O-109(0-109-0)/D-2	10	-0.3
1996*Tex-A	148	627	94	184	29	4	6	51	54	66	15	5	.293	.351	.381	.733	81	-17	84	4.79	-5	*O-147(0-147-0)	11	-1.9
1997*SF-N	125	460	78	124	23	3	5	43	61	61	15	10	.270	.355	.365	.720	92	-5	62	4.69	-4	*O-119(0-119-0)	15	-0.8
1998 SF-N	97	367	65	108	19	2	1	26	59	53	9	8	.294	.395	.365	.760	108	6	56	5.42	-3	O-96(0-96-0)	12	0.3
Col-N	51	194	30	65	9	1	5	25	23	20	4	1	.335	.408	.469	.877	107	4	40	7.92	-3	O-48(0-48-0)	7	0.1
Yr.	148	561	95	173	28	3	6	51	82	73	13	9	.308	.399	.401	.800	108	9	97	6.24	-7	*O-144(0-144-0)	19	0.4
1999 Col-N	91	337	63	102	11	3	4	24	38	21	4	5	.303	.375	.389	.764	74	-13	49	5.32	-2	O-82(0-82-0)	5	-1.3
*NY-N	55	168	19	57	8	1	5	21	19	18	2	3	.339	.410	.488	.898	130	7	34	7.80	-3	O-52(0-52-0)	8	0.4
Yr.	146	505	82	159	19	4	9	45	57	39	6	8	.315	.387	.422	.808	92	-6	83	6.11	-5	*O-134(0-134-0)	13	-1.0
2000*NY-N	43	105	20	29	4	1	1	6	14	20	2	0	.276	.361	.362	.723	87	-1	15	5.43	-1	O-33(17-11-8)	3	-0.3
2001 NY-N	52	126	15	27	7	1	1	5	19	20	3	1	.214	.327	.310	.636	69	-5	14	3.59	0	O-37(24-11-3)	2	-0.6
Total 13	**1328**	**4577**	**707**	**1333**	**204**	**37**	**51**	**454**	**493**	**494**	**163**	**73**	**.291**	**.362**	**.385**	**.748**	**96**	**-16**	**662**	**5.13**	**-24**	***O-1234/D-19**	**130**	**-4.6**

• HAMILTON, Jeff Jeffrey Robert Hamilton b: 3/19/1964, Flint, MI BR/TR, 6'3", 207 lbs. Deb: 6/28/1986

YEAR TM-L	G	AB	R	H	2B	3B	HR	RBI	BB	SO	SB	CS	AVG	OBP	SLG	OPS	OPS+	BR/A	RC	RC/G	FR	G/POS	WS	TPW
1986 LA-N	71	147	22	33	5	0	5	19	2	43	0	0	.224	.235	.361	.595	66	-8	12	2.61	3	3-66/S-2	2	-0.6
1987 LA-N	35	83	5	18	3	0	0	1	7	22	0	1	.217	.286	.253	.539	45	-7	6	2.54	1	3-31/S-1	1	-0.7
1988*LA-N	111	309	34	73	14	2	6	33	10	51	0	2	.236	.269	.353	.622	80	-11	27	2.91	-9	*3-105/S-2,1-1	7	-2.1
1989 LA-N	151	548	45	134	35	1	12	56	20	71	0	0	.245	.275	.378	.653	86	-12	55	3.41	-7	*3-147/2-1,P-1,S-1	9	-2.0
1990 LA-N	7	24	1	3	0	0	0	1	0	3	0	0	.125	.125	.125	.250	-32	-4	0	.31	1	/3-7	0	-0.3
1991 LA-N	41	94	4	21	4	0	1	14	4	21	0	0	.223	.255	.298	.553	56	-6	7	2.44	-4	3-33/S-1	2	-1.0
Total 6	**416**	**1205**	**111**	**282**	**61**	**3**	**24**	**124**	**43**	**211**	**0**	**3**	**.234**	**.265**	**.349**	**.615**	**75**	**-48**	**107**	**2.98**	**-16**	**3-389/S-7,1-1,2-1,P-1**	**21**	**-6.7**

• HAMILTON, Tom Thomas Ball "Ham" Hamilton b: 9/29/1925, Altoona, KS d: 11/29/1973, Tyler, TX BL/TR, 6'4", 213 lbs. Deb: 9/4/1952

YEAR TM-L	G	AB	R	H	2B	3B	HR	RBI	BB	SO	SB	CS	AVG	OBP	SLG	OPS	OPS+	BR/A	RC	RC/G	FR	G/POS	WS	TPW
1952 Phi-A	9	10	1	2	1	0	0	1	1	1	0	0	.200	.273	.300	.573	56	-1	1	3.07	-1	/1-5	0	-0.1
1953 Phi-A	58	56	8	11	2	0	0	5	7	11	0	0	.196	.286	.232	.518	40	-5	4	2.21	0	/1-7,O-2(0-0-2)	0	-0.5
Total 2	**67**	**66**	**9**	**13**	**3**	**0**	**0**	**6**	**8**	**12**	**0**	**0**	**.197**	**.284**	**.242**	**.526**	**42**	**-5**	**5**	**2.33**	**-1**	**/1-12,O-2**	**0**	**-0.6**

• HAMLIN, Ken Kenneth Lee Hamlin b: 5/18/1935, Detroit, MI BR/TR, 5'10", 170 lbs. Deb: 6/17/1957

YEAR TM-L	G	AB	R	H	2B	3B	HR	RBI	BB	SO	SB	CS	AVG	OBP	SLG	OPS	OPS+	BR/A	RC	RC/G	FR	G/POS	WS	TPW
1957 Pit-N	2	1	0	0	0	0	0	0	0	0	0	0	.000	.000	.000	.000	-103	-0	0	.00	0	/S-1	0	0.0
1959 Pit-N	3	8	1	1	0	0	0	0	2	1	0	0	.125	.300	.125	.425	19	-1	0	1.76	0	/S-3	0	0.0
1960 KC-A	140	428	51	96	10	2	2	24	44	48	1	1	.224	.298	.271	.569	55	-27	35	2.66	-33	*S-139	3	-5.0
1961 LA-A	42	91	4	19	3	0	1	5	11	9	0	1	.209	.301	.275	.576	49	-7	7	2.18	0	S-39	1	-0.4
1962 Was-A	98	292	29	74	12	0	3	22	22	22	7	7	.253	.306	.325	.631	70	-14	28	3.19	-8	S-87/2-2	3	-1.6
1965 Was-A	117	362	45	99	21	1	4	22	33	45	8	2	.273	.336	.370	.706	102	2	47	4.51	-4	2-77,S-47/3-1	13	0.6
1966 Was-A	66	158	13	34	7	1	1	16	13	21	1	0	.215	.275	.291	.566	63	-7	12	2.33	-1	2-50/3-1	2	-0.4
Total 7	**468**	**1340**	**143**	**323**	**53**	**4**	**11**	**89**	**125**	**146**	**17**	**11**	**.241**	**.307**	**.311**	**.618**	**71**	**-54**	**129**	**3.16**	**-46**	**S-316,2-129/3-2**	**22**	**-6.9**

• HAMMOCK, Robby Robert Wade Hammock b: 5/13/1977, Macon, GA BR/TR, 5'11", 180 lbs. Deb: 4/11/2003

YEAR TM-L	G	AB	R	H	2B	3B	HR	RBI	BB	SO	SB	CS	AVG	OBP	SLG	OPS	OPS+	BR/A	RC	RC/G	FR	G/POS	WS	TPW
2003 Ari-N	65	195	30	55	10	2	8	28	17	44	3	2	.282	.346	.477	.823	102	0	31	5.61	13	C-36,O-17(5-0-12),3-16/D-1	7	1.4

• HAMMOND, Jack Walter Charles "Wobby" Hammond b: 2/26/1891, Amsterdam, NY d: 3/4/1942, Kenosha, WI BR/TR, 5'11", 170 lbs. Deb: 4/15/1915

YEAR TM-L	G	AB	R	H	2B	3B	HR	RBI	BB	SO	SB	CS	AVG	OBP	SLG	OPS	OPS+	BR/A	RC	RC/G	FR	G/POS	WS	TPW
1915 Cle-A	35	84	9	18	2	1	0	4	1	19	0	1	.214	.224	.262	.485	44	-7	5	1.96	-3	2-19	0	-1.0
1922 Cle-A	1	4	1	1	0	0	0	0	0	0	0	0	.250	.250	.250	.500	30	-0	0	2.12	-1	/2-1	0	-0.1
Pit-N	9	11	3	3	0	0	0	0	1	0	0	0	.273	.333	.273	.606	57	-1	1	3.46	-1	/2-4	0	-0.1
Total 2	**45**	**99**	**13**	**22**	**2**	**1**	**0**	**4**	**2**	**19**	**0**	**1**	**.222**	**.238**	**.263**	**.500**	**45**	**-8**	**7**	**2.10**	**-5**	**/2-24**	**0**	**-1.3**

YEAR TM-L	G	AB	R	H	2B	3B	HR	RBI	BB	SO	SB	CS	AVG	OBP	SLG	OPS	OPS+	BR/A	RC	RC/G	FR	G/POS	WS	TPW
• HAMMOND, Steve	Steven Benjamin Hammond b: 5/9/1957, Atlanta, GA BL/TR, 6'2", 190 lbs. Deb: 6/28/1982																							
1982 KC-A	46	126	14	29	5	1	1	11	4	18	0	1	.230	.254	.310	.563	54	-9	8	1.97	2	0-37(0-0-37)/D-1	1	-0.8
• HAMMONDS, Jeffrey	Jeffrey Bryan Hammonds b: 3/5/1971, Plainfield, NJ BR/TR, 6', 195 lbs. Deb: 6/25/1993 Career OF: 223-258-415																							
1993 Bal-A	33	105	10	32	8	0	3	19	2	16	4	0	.305	.318	.467	.784	104	1	15	5.10	0	0-23(14-0-10)/D-8	4	0.0
1994 Bal-A	68	250	45	74	18	2	8	31	17	39	5	0	.296	.346	.480	.826	105	2	43	6.26	-1	0-66(9-0-58)	6	-0.2
1995 Bal-A	57	178	18	43	9	1	4	23	9	30	4	2	.242	.282	.371	.653	67	-9	18	3.43	0	0-46(0-0-46)/D-5	4	-1.1
1996 Bal-A	71	248	38	56	10	1	9	27	23	53	3	3	.226	.302	.383	.685	72	-12	28	3.58	-2	0-70(64-1-11)/D-1	3	-1.6
1997*Bal-A	118	397	71	105	19	3	21	55	32	73	15	1	.264	.324	.486	.810	111	8	65	5.79	-2	*0-114(31-40-54)/D-4	14	0.2
1998 Bal-A	63	171	36	46	12	1	6	28	26	38	7	2	.269	.375	.456	.831	117	6	32	6.47	-1	0-53(7-24-29)/D-7	6	0.3
Cin-N	26	86	14	26	4	1	0	11	13	18	1	1	.302	.394	.372	.766	102	1	14	5.82	1	0-25(0-25-0)	3	0.2
1999 Cin-N	123	262	43	73	13	0	17	41	27	64	3	6	.279	.348	.523	.871	113	2	46	6.12	3	*0-106(46-21-53)	8	0.3
2000 Col-N★	122	454	94	152	24	2	20	106	44	83	14	7	.335	.400	.529	.928	105	5	94	7.76	-4	*0-118(33-9-85)	14	-0.5
2001 Mil-N	49	174	20	43	11	1	6	21	14	42	5	3	.247	.318	.425	.743	92	-3	24	4.63	-1	0-46(0-46-0)	5	-0.4
2002 Mil-N	128	448	47	115	26	5	9	41	52	86	4	5	.257	.337	.397	.734	94	-5	59	4.42	-9	*0-125(2-78-55)	9	-1.7
2003 Mil-N	10	38	2	6	2	0	1	3	3	7	0	0	.158	.220	.289	.509	32	-4	2	1.60	-1	0-10(0-0-10)	0	-0.6
*SF-N	36	94	20	26	10	0	3	10	13	21	1	0	.277	.370	.479	.849	123	4	18	6.95	-1	0-30(17-14-4)	4	0.2
Yr.	46	132	22	32	12	0	4	13	16	28	1	0	.242	.329	.424	.753	98	-0	20	5.18	-2	0-40(17-14-14)	4	-0.4
Total 11	**904**	**2905**	**458**	**797**	**166**	**17**	**107**	**416**	**275**	**570**	**66**	**30**	**.274**	**.342**	**.454**	**.796**	**99**	**-6**	**456**	**5.49**	**-19**	**0-832/D-25**	**80**	**-4.9**
• HAMNER, Garvin	Wesley Garvin Hamner b: 3/18/1924, Richmond, VA BR/TR, 5'11", 172 lbs. Deb: 4/17/1945																							
1945 Phi-N	32	101	12	20	3	0	0	5	7	9	2	....	.198	.250	.228	.478	34	-9	6	1.77	-7	2-21/S-9,3-1	1	-1.4
• HAMNER, Granny	Granville Wilbur Hamner b: 4/26/1927, Richmond, VA d: 9/12/1993, Philadelphia, PA BR/TR, 5'10", 163 lbs. Deb: 9/14/1944																							
1944 Phi-N	21	77	6	19	1	0	0	5	3	7	0	....	.247	.275	.260	.535	53	-5	6	2.49	7	S-21	1	0.4
1945 Phi-N	14	41	3	7	2	0	0	6	1	3	0	....	.171	.190	.220	.410	14	-5	2	1.19	-4	S-13	0	-0.8
1946 Phi-N	2	7	0	1	0	0	0	0	0	3	0	....	.143	.143	.143	.286	-19	-1	0	.64	0	/S-2	0	-0.1
1947 Phi-N	2	7	1	2	0	0	0	0	1	0	0	....	.286	.375	.286	.661	81	-0	1	2.54	0	/S-2	0	0.0
1948 Phi-N	129	446	42	116	21	5	3	48	22	39	2	....	.260	.298	.350	.648	76	-16	45	3.53	-5	2-87,S-37/3-3	8	-1.5
1949 Phi-N	154	662	83	174	32	5	6	53	25	47	6	....	.263	.290	.353	.643	74	-27	63	3.28	17	*S-154	16	0.0
1950*Phi-N	157	637	78	172	27	5	11	82	39	35	2	....	.270	.314	.380	.694	83	-17	74	4.14	9	*S-157	19	0.2
1951 Phi-N	150	589	61	150	23	7	9	72	29	32	10	5	.255	.290	.363	.653	76	-22	58	3.33	14	*S-150	14	0.2
1952 Phi-N★	151	596	74	164	30	5	17	87	27	51	7	3	.275	.307	.428	.734	103	-0	75	4.29	7	*S-151	20	1.7
1953 Phi-N★	154	609	90	168	30	8	21	92	32	28	2	1	.276	.313	.455	.768	98	-5	84	4.88	9	2-93,S-71	19	1.5
1954 Phi-N★	152	596	83	178	39	11	13	89	53	44	1	2	.299	.356	.466	.822	112	10	98	5.93	2	*2-152/S-1	20	2.3
1955 Phi-N	104	405	57	104	12	4	5	43	41	30	0	1	.257	.327	.343	.670	79	-11	46	3.86	-8	2-82,S-32	8	-1.1
1956 Phi-N	122	401	42	90	24	3	4	42	30	42	2	0	.224	.278	.329	.608	64	-20	35	2.85	-2	*S-110,2-11/P-3	8	-1.3
1957 Phi-N	133	502	59	114	19	5	10	62	34	42	3	1	.227	.276	.345	.621	68	-23	43	2.72	-16	*2-125/S-5,P-1	5	-3.0
1958 Phi-N	35	133	18	40	7	3	2	18	8	16	0	0	.301	.340	.444	.784	107	1	17	4.52	2	3-22,2-11/S-3	4	0.4
1959 Phi-N	21	64	10	19	4	0	2	6	5	5	0	1	.297	.348	.453	.801	109	0	9	5.14	1	S-15/3-1	2	0.2
Cle-A	27	67	4	11	1	1	1	3	1	8	0	0	.164	.176	.254	.430	17	-8	3	1.18	-1	S-10/2-7,3-5	0	-0.8
1962 KC-A	3	0	0	0	0	0	0	0	0	0	0	0	....	....	....	....	-97	0	0	....	0	/P-3	0	-0.2
Total 17	**1531**	**5839**	**711**	**1529**	**272**	**62**	**104**	**708**	**351**	**432**	**35**	**14**	**.262**	**.304**	**.383**	**.688**	**83**	**-150**	**657**	**3.86**	**31**	**S-934,2-568/3-31,P-7**	**144**	**-1.9**
• HAMPTON, Ike	Isaac Bernard Hampton b: 8/22/1951, Camden, SC BB/TR, 6'1", 185 lbs. Deb: 9/12/1974																							
1974 NY-N	4	4	0	0	0	0	0	1	0	1	0	0	.000	.000	.000	.000	-102	-1	0	.00	0	/C-1	0	-0.1
1975 Cal-A	31	66	8	10	3	0	0	4	7	19	0	0	.152	.243	.197	.440	28	-6	4	1.65	-3	C-28/S-2,3-1	0	-0.8
1976 Cal-A	3	2	0	0	0	0	0	0	0	0	0	0	.000	.000	.000	.000	-107	-1	0	.00	0	/C-2,S-1	0	-0.1
1977 Cal-A	52	44	5	13	1	0	3	9	2	10	0	0	.295	.340	.523	.863	137	2	7	5.80	-5	C-47/D-2	2	-0.2
1978 Cal-A	19	14	2	3	0	1	1	4	2	7	1	0	.214	.313	.571	.884	149	1	3	6.93	-3	C-13/D-4,1-1	1	-0.1
1979 Cal-A	4	5	0	2	0	0	0	0	0	1	0	0	.400	.400	.400	.800	121	0	1	7.20	0	/1-2	0	0.0
Total 6	**113**	**135**	**15**	**28**	**4**	**1**	**4**	**18**	**11**	**38**	**1**	**0**	**.207**	**.277**	**.341**	**.618**	**71**	**-4**	**14**	**3.41**	**-10**	**/C-91,D-6,1-3,S-3,3-1**	**3**	**-1.3**
• HAMRIC, Bert	Odbert Herman Hamric b: 3/1/1928, Clarksburg, WV d: 8/4/1984, Springboro, OH BL/TR, 6', 165 lbs. Deb: 4/24/1955																							
1955 Bro-N	2	1	0	0	0	0	0	0	0	1	0	0	.000	.000	.000	.000	-97	-0	0	.00	0	....	0	0.0
1958 Bal-A	8	8	0	1	0	0	0	0	0	6	0	0	.125	.125	.125	.250	-33	-1	0	.48	0	....	0	-0.1
• HAMRICK, Ray	Raymond Bernard Hamrick b: 8/1/1921, Nashville, TN BR/TR, 5'11.5", 160 lbs. Deb: 8/14/1943																							
1943 Phi-N	44	160	12	32	3	1	0	9	8	28	0	....	.200	.238	.231	.469	37	-13	9	1.77	-4	2-31,S-12	1	-1.5
1944 Phi-N	74	292	22	60	10	1	1	23	23	34	1	....	.205	.268	.257	.525	50	-19	20	2.26	17	S-74	4	0.4
Total 2	**118**	**452**	**34**	**92**	**13**	**2**	**1**	**32**	**31**	**62**	**1**	**....**	**.204**	**.258**	**.248**	**.506**	**46**	**-32**	**29**	**2.09**	**13**	**/S-86,2-31**	**5**	**-1.2**
• HANCKEN, Buddy	Morris Medlock Hancken b: 8/30/1914, Birmingham, AL BR/TR, 6'1", 175 lbs. Deb: 5/14/1940 C																							
1940 Phi-A	1	0	0	0	0	0	0	0	0	0	0	0	....	....	....	....	-102	0	0	....	0	/C-1	0	0.0
• HANCOCK, Fred	Fred James Hancock b: 3/28/1920, Allenport, PA d: 3/12/1986, Clearwater, FL BR/TR, 5'8", 170 lbs. Deb: 4/26/1949																							
1949 Chi-A	39	52	7	7	2	1	0	9	8	9	0	1	.135	.262	.212	.474	27	-6	3	1.63	-2	S-27/3-3,0-1	0	-0.7
• HANCOCK, Garry	Ronald Garry Hancock b: 1/23/1954, Tampa, FL BL/TL, 6', 175 lbs. Deb: 7/16/1978 Career OF: 45-33-70																							
1978 Bos-A	38	80	10	18	3	0	0	4	1	12	0	0	.225	.235	.263	.497	36	-7	5	1.98	1	0-19(4-5-10),D-13	0	-0.6
1980 Bos-A	46	115	9	33	6	0	4	19	3	11	0	3	.287	.305	.443	.749	97	-2	14	4.32	0	0-27(6-20-1),D-12	2	-0.3
1981 Bos-A	26	45	4	7	3	0	0	3	2	4	0	0	.156	.191	.222	.414	18	-5	2	1.03	1	/0-8(0-5-3),D-4	0	-0.4
1982 Bos-A	11	14	3	0	0	0	0	0	1	1	0	0	.000	.067	.000	.067	-75	-3	0	.03	0	/0-7(0-0-7)	0	-0.4
1983 Oak-A	101	256	29	70	7	3	8	30	5	13	2	0	.273	.290	.418	.708	98	-2	30	4.25	0	0-67(26-1-40),1-27/D-9	6	-0.5
1984 Oak-A	51	60	2	13	2	0	0	8	0	1	0	0	.217	.217	.250	.467	31	-6	2	1.19	-1	0-18(9-2-9)/D-5,1-4,P-1	0	-0.6
Total 6	**273**	**570**	**57**	**141**	**21**	**3**	**12**	**64**	**12**	**42**	**2**	**3**	**.247**	**.264**	**.358**	**.622**	**71**	**-24**	**53**	**3.16**	**1**	**0-146/D-43,1-31,P-1**	**8**	**-2.9**
• HANDIBOE, Mike	Aloysius James "Coalyard Mike" Handiboe b: 7/21/1887, Washington, DC d: 1/31/1953, Savannah, GA BL/TL, 5'10", 155 lbs. Deb: 9/8/1911																							
1911 NY-A	5	15	0	1	0	0	0	0	2	....	0	....	.067	.176	.067	.243	-29	-3	0	.46	0	/0-4(2-0-2)	0	-0.3
• HANDLEY, Gene	Eugene Louis Handley b: 11/25/1914, Kennett, MO BR/TR, 5'10.5", 165 lbs. Deb: 4/16/1946																							
1946 Phi-A	89	251	31	63	8	5	0	21	22	25	8	3	.251	.311	.323	.634	78	-7	26	3.48	-14	2-68/3-4,S-1	3	-1.8
1947 Phi-A	36	90	10	23	2	1	0	8	10	2	1	0	.256	.330	.300	.630	74	-3	9	3.56	-3	2-17,3-10/S-1	2	-0.5
Total 2	**125**	**341**	**41**	**86**	**10**	**6**	**0**	**29**	**32**	**27**	**9**	**3**	**.252**	**.316**	**.317**	**.633**	**77**	**-9**	**35**	**3.50**	**-17**	**/2-85,3-14,S-2**	**5**	**-2.3**
• HANDLEY, Lee	Lee Elmer "Jeep" Handley b: 7/13/1913, Clarion, IA d: 4/8/1970, Pittsburgh, PA BR/TR, 5'7", 160 lbs. Deb: 4/15/1936																							
1936 Cin-N	24	78	10	24	1	0	2	8	7	16	3	....	.308	.365	.397	.762	112	1	12	5.45	-2	2-16/3-7	3	0.0
1937 Pit-N	127	480	59	120	21	12	3	37	37	40	5	....	.250	.305	.363	.668	81	-14	55	4.01	-10	*2-126/3-1	11	-1.5
1938 Pit-N	139	570	91	153	25	8	6	51	53	31	7	....	.268	.332	.372	.704	92	-6	72	4.48	5	*3-136	17	0.5
1939 Pit-N	101	376	43	107	14	5	1	42	32	20	**17**	....	.285	.341	.356	.697	89	-6	45	4.13	-10	*3-100	8	-1.2
1940 Pit-N	98	302	50	85	7	4	1	19	27	16	7	....	.281	.340	.341	.681	89	-4	37	4.46	-7	3-80/2-2	8	-0.8
1941 Pit-N	124	459	59	132	18	4	0	33	35	22	16	....	.288	.338	.344	.682	93	-4	53	4.02	-3	*3-114	11	-0.4
1944 Pit-N	40	86	7	19	2	0	0	5	3	5	1	....	.221	.247	.244	.491	37	-7	4	1.44	-1	2-19,3-11/S-3	1	-0.7
1945 Pit-N	98	312	39	93	16	2	1	32	20	16	7	....	.298	.340	.372	.712	94	-3	40	4.63	10	3-79	10	0.8
1946 Pit-N	116	416	43	99	8	7	1	28	29	20	4	....	.238	.289	.298	.587	65	-20	36	2.86	10	*3-102/2-3	6	-1.0
1947 Phi-N	101	277	17	70	10	3	0	42	24	18	1	....	.253	.312	.310	.623	68	-13	26	3.22	-4	3-83/2-3,S-1	3	-1.6
Total 10	**968**	**3356**	**418**	**902**	**122**	**45**	**15**	**297**	**267**	**204**	**68**	**....**	**.269**	**.323**	**.345**	**.669**	**84**	**-75**	**380**	**3.94**	**-12**	**3-713,2-169/S-4**	**78**	**-6.0**
• HANEBRINK, Harry	Harry Aloysius Hanebrink b: 11/12/1927, St. Louis, MO d: 9/9/1996, Bridgeton, MO BL/TR, 6', 165 lbs. Deb: 5/3/1953 Career OF: 24-0-10																							
1953 Mil-N	51	80	8	19	1	1	1	8	6	8	1	0	.238	.291	.313	.603	61	-4	8	3.53	0	2-21/3-1	2	-0.3
1957 Mil-N	6	7	0	2	0	0	0	0	1	2	0	0	.286	.375	.286	.661	87	-0	1	4.58	0	/3-2	0	-0.1

YEAR TM-L	G	AB	R	H	2B	3B	HR	RBI	BB	SO	SB	CS	AVG	OBP	SLG	OPS	OPS+	BR/A	RC	RC/G	FR	G/POS	WS	TPW
1958*Mil-N	63	133	14	25	3	0	4	10	13	9	0	1	.188	.270	.301	.571	56	-9	10	2.34	1	0-33(24-0-9)/3-7	1	-0.9
1959 Phi-N	57	97	10	25	3	1	1	7	2	12	0	0	.258	.273	.340	.613	61	-6	8	2.90	-2	2-15/3-9,0-1	1	-0.7
Total 4	177	317	32	71	7	2	6	25	22	31	1	1	.224	.279	.315	.594	59	-19	27	2.84	-1	/2-36,0-34,3-19	4	-2.0

• HANEY, Fred — Fred Girard "Pudge" Haney b: 4/25/1898, Albuquerque, NM d: 11/9/1977, Beverly Hills, CA BR/TR, 5'6", 170 lbs. Deb: 4/18/1922 M/C

YEAR TM-L	G	AB	R	H	2B	3B	HR	RBI	BB	SO	SB	CS	AVG	OBP	SLG	OPS	OPS+	BR/A	RC	RC/G	FR	G/POS	WS	TPW
1922 Det-A	81	213	41	75	7	4	0	25	32	14	3	8	.352	.439	.423	.862	129	9	40	6.63	2	3-53,1-11/S-2	9	1.3
1923 Det-A	142	503	85	142	13	4	4	67	45	23	13	5	.282	.347	.348	.695	85	-8	65	4.35	-8	2-69,3-55,S-16	12	-0.9
1924 Det-A	86	256	54	79	11	1	1	30	39	13	7	4	.309	.400	.371	.771	101	3	41	5.64	-1	3-59/S-4,2-3	9	0.5
1925 Det-A	114	398	84	111	15	3	0	40	66	29	11	1	.279	.384	.332	.716	84	-3	58	5.04	0	*3-106	12	0.3
1926 Bos-A	138	462	47	102	15	7	0	52	74	28	13	6	.221	.330	.284	.613	63	-22	50	3.35	-8	*3-137	7	-2.0
1927 Bos-A	47	116	23	32	4	1	3	12	25	14	4	1	.276	.404	.405	.809	113	4	22	6.13	-5	3-34/0-1	4	0.1
Chi-N	4	3	0	0	0	0	0	0	0	0	0	....	.000	.000	.000	.000	-100	-1	0	.00	0	....	0	-0.1
1929 StL-N	10	26	4	3	1	1	0	2	1	2	0	....	.115	.179	.231	.409	1	-4	1	1.22	2	/3-6	0	-0.1
Total 7	622	1977	338	544	66	21	8	228	282	123	51	25	.275	.368	.342	.710	87	-22	275	4.67	-18	3-450/2-72,S-22,1-11,0-1	53	-0.9

• HANEY, Larry — Wallace Larry Haney b: 11/19/1942, Charlottesville, VA BR/TR, 6'2", 195 lbs. Deb: 7/27/1966 C

YEAR TM-L	G	AB	R	H	2B	3B	HR	RBI	BB	SO	SB	CS	AVG	OBP	SLG	OPS	OPS+	BR/A	RC	RC/G	FR	G/POS	WS	TPW
1966 Bal-A	20	56	3	9	1	0	1	3	1	15	0	0	.161	.190	.232	.422	21	-6	3	1.47	-1	C-20	1	-0.7
1967 Bal-A	58	164	13	44	11	0	3	20	6	28	1	0	.268	.294	.390	.684	101	-0	18	3.85	1	C-57	5	0.4
1968 Bal-A	38	89	5	21	3	1	1	5	0	19	0	0	.236	.236	.326	.562	69	-4	6	2.39	1	C-32	2	-0.2
1969 Sea-A	22	59	3	15	3	0	2	7	6	12	1	1	.254	.323	.407	.730	105	0	7	4.01	-1	C-20	2	-0.1
Oak-A	53	86	8	13	4	0	2	12	7	19	0	0	.151	.223	.267	.491	38	-7	4	1.35	0	C-53	1	-0.6
Yr.	75	145	11	28	7	0	4	19	13	31	1	1	.193	.264	.324	.588	66	-7	11	2.36	-2	C-73	3	-0.7
1970 Oak-A	2	2	2	0	0	0	0	0	2	1	0	0	.000	.500	.000	.500	51	0	0	3.51	0	/C-1	0	0.0
1972 Oak-A	5	4	0	0	0	0	0	0	0	1	0	0	.000	.000	.000	.000	-105	-1	0	.00	-2	/C-4,2-1	0	-0.3
1973 Oak-A	2	2	0	1	0	0	0	0	0	0	0	0	.500	.500	.500	1.000	192	0	0	.00	0	/C-2	0	0.0
StL-N	2	1	0	0	0	0	0	0	0	1	0	0	.000	.000	.000	.000	-100	-0	0	.00	0	/C-2	0	-0.1
1974*Oak-A	76	121	12	20	4	0	2	3	3	18	1	0	.165	.185	.248	.433	25	-12	5	1.38	0	C-73/3-3,1-2	2	-1.0
1975 Oak-A	47	26	3	5	0	0	1	2	1	4	0	0	.192	.222	.308	.530	50	-2	2	2.36	-4	C-43/3-4	1	-0.5
1976 Oak-A	88	177	12	40	2	0	0	10	13	26	0	1	.226	.283	.237	.520	56	-10	12	2.16	0	C-87	3	-0.7
1977 Mil-A	63	127	7	29	2	0	0	10	5	30	0	0	.228	.258	.244	.502	38	-11	8	2.10	2	C-63	2	-0.6
1978 Mil-A	4	5	0	1	0	0	0	1	0	1	0	0	.200	.200	.200	.400	13	-1	0	1.35	0	/C-4	0	-0.1
Total 12	480	919	68	198	30	1	12	73	44	175	3	2	.215	.254	.289	.543	57	-53	66	2.32	-6	C-461/3-7,1-2,2-1	19	-4.6

• HANEY, Todd — Todd Michael Haney b: 7/30/1965, Galveston, TX BR/TR, 5'9", 165 lbs. Deb: 9/9/1992

YEAR TM-L	G	AB	R	H	2B	3B	HR	RBI	BB	SO	SB	CS	AVG	OBP	SLG	OPS	OPS+	BR/A	RC	RC/G	FR	G/POS	WS	TPW
1992 Mon-N	7	10	0	3	1	0	0	1	0	0	0	0	.300	.300	.400	.700	97	-0	1	2.47	0	/2-5	0	0.0
1994 Chi-N	17	37	6	6	0	0	1	2	3	3	2	1	.162	.244	.243	.487	28	-4	3	2.01	1	2-11/3-3	0	-0.3
1995 Chi-N	25	73	11	30	8	0	2	6	7	11	0	0	.411	.463	.603	1.065	182	9	21	12.99	2	2-17/3-4	5	1.1
1996 Chi-N	49	82	11	11	1	0	0	3	7	15	1	0	.134	.202	.146	.349	-6	-13	3	1.06	-3	2-23/3-4,S-3	1	-1.4
1998 NY-N	3	3	0	0	0	0	0	0	1	0	0	0	.000	.250	.000	.250	-27	-1	0	.59	-1	/2-1,0-1	0	-0.1
Total 5	101	205	28	50	10	0	3	12	18	29	3	1	.244	.308	.337	.645	71	-9	28	4.50	0	/2-57,3-11,S-3,0-1	6	-0.6

• HANFORD, Charlie — Charles Joseph Hanford b: 6/3/1881, Tunstall, England d: 7/19/1963, Trenton, NJ BR/TR, 5'6.5", 145 lbs. Deb: 4/13/1914 Career OF: 10-156-32

YEAR TM-L	G	AB	R	H	2B	3B	HR	RBI	BB	SO	SB	CS	AVG	OBP	SLG	OPS	OPS+	BR/A	RC	RC/G	FR	G/POS	WS	TPW
1914 Buf-F	155	597	83	174	28	13	12	90	32	81	37	....	.291	.332	.442	.774	114	8	94	5.50	8	*0-155(0-155-0)	29	0.7
1915 Chi-F	77	179	27	43	4	5	0	22	12	28	10	....	.240	.295	.318	.614	85	-4	19	3.47	-2	0-43(10-1-32)	4	-0.8
Total 2	232	776	110	217	32	18	12	112	44	109	47	....	.280	.323	.414	.737	107	4	113	5.01	6	0-198	33	-0.1

• HANKINS, Jay — Jay Nelson Hankins b: 11/7/1935, St. Louis County, MO BL/TR, 5'7", 170 lbs. Deb: 4/15/1961 Career OF: 23-40-14

YEAR TM-L	G	AB	R	H	2B	3B	HR	RBI	BB	SO	SB	CS	AVG	OBP	SLG	OPS	OPS+	BR/A	RC	RC/G	FR	G/POS	WS	TPW
1961 KC-A	76	173	23	32	0	3	3	6	8	17	2	0	.185	.225	.272	.497	32	-17	11	1.94	-2	0-65(23-31-14)	1	-2.1
1963 KC-A	10	34	2	6	0	1	1	4	0	3	0	1	.176	.176	.324	.500	35	-4	2	1.51	0	/0-9(0-9-0)	0	-0.4
Total 2	86	207	25	38	0	4	4	10	8	20	2	1	.184	.218	.280	.498	32	-20	13	1.87	-2	/0-74	1	-2.5

• HANKINSON, Frank — Frank Edward Hankinson b: 4/29/1856, New York, NY d: 4/5/1911, Palisades Park, NJ BR/TR, 5'11", 168 lbs. Deb: 5/1/1878 Career OF: 26-8-1 ♦

YEAR TM-L	G	AB	R	H	2B	3B	HR	RBI	BB	SO	SB	CS	AVG	OBP	SLG	OPS	OPS+	BR/A	RC	RC/G	FR	G/POS	WS	TPW
1878 Chi-N	58	240	38	64	8	3	1	27	5	36	....	....	.267	.282	.338	.619	96	-1	23	3.65	8	*3-57/P-1	5	0.5
1879 Chi-N	44	171	14	31	4	0	0	8	2	14	....	....	.181	.191	.205	.395	29	-9	7	1.37	7	P-26,0-14(10-4-0)/3-5	16	-1.3
1880 Cle-N	69	263	32	55	7	4	1	19	1	23	....	....	.209	.212	.278	.490	66	-9	16	2.10	-10	*3-56,0-12(10-2-0)/P-4	6	-1.5
1881 Tro-N	85	321	34	62	15	0	1	19	10	41	....	....	.193	.218	.249	.467	44	-21	18	1.86	8	*3-84/S-1	5	-1.0
1883 NY-N	94	337	40	74	13	6	2	30	19	38	....	....	.220	.261	.312	.573	74	-10	28	2.94	1	*3-93/0-1	7	-0.6
1884 NY-N	105	389	44	90	16	7	2	43	23	59	....	....	.231	.274	.324	.598	85	-7	35	3.26	0	*3-105/0-1	11	-0.4
1885 NY-a	94	362	43	81	12	2	2	44	12	....	....	....	.224	.251	.285	.535	75	-9	26	2.54	16	*3-94/P-1	7	0.8
1886 NY-a	136	522	66	126	14	5	2	63	49	....	10	....	.241	.306	.299	.605	94	-2	52	3.56	21	*3-136	15	1.9
1887 NY-a	127	550	79	175	29	11	1	71	38	....	19	....	.318	.318	.373	.691	96	-3	68	4.93	-2	*3-127	14	-0.1
1888 KC-a	37	155	20	27	4	1	1	20	11	....	2	....	.174	.229	.232	.461	45	-10	9	1.88	-4	2-13/S-9,3-7,0-7(6-1-0),1	1	-1.2
Total 10	849	3310	410	785	122	39	13	344	170	211	31	....	.237	.267	.301	.568	77	-81	283	3.05	46	3-764/0-35,P-32,2-13,S-10,1	87	-2.9

• HANLON, Bill — William Joseph "Big Bill" Hanlon b: 6/24/1876, Los Angeles, CA d: 11/23/1905, Los Angeles, CA BR, 6', 175 lbs. Deb: 4/16/1903

YEAR TM-L	G	AB	R	H	2B	3B	HR	RBI	BB	SO	SB	CS	AVG	OBP	SLG	OPS	OPS+	BR/A	RC	RC/G	FR	G/POS	WS	TPW
1903 Chi-N	8	21	4	2	0	0	0	2	6	....	1	....	.095	.296	.095	.392	14	-2	1	1.71	0	/1-8	0	-0.2

• HANLON, Ned — Edward Hugh Hanlon
b: 8/22/1857, Montville, CT d: 4/14/1937, Baltimore, MD BL/TR, 5'9.5", 170 lbs. Deb: 5/1/1880 M/U HOF: 1996 Career OF: 119-1130-1

YEAR TM-L	G	AB	R	H	2B	3B	HR	RBI	BB	SO	SB	CS	AVG	OBP	SLG	OPS	OPS+	BR/A	RC	RC/G	FR	G/POS	WS	TPW
1880 Cle-N	73	280	30	69	10	3	0	32	11	30	....	....	.246	.275	.304	.578	98	-0	24	3.12	-3	*0-69(67-2-0)/S-4	8	-0.7
1881 Det-N	76	305	63	85	14	8	2	28	22	11	....	....	.279	.327	.397	.724	121	7	41	4.98	-7	*0-74(2-72-0)/S-2	10	-0.3
1882 Det-N	82	347	68	80	18	6	5	38	26	25	....	....	.231	.284	.360	.644	105	3	36	3.75	9	*0-82(0-82-0)/2-1	11	0.8
1883 Det-N	100	413	65	100	13	2	1	40	34	44	....	....	.242	.300	.291	.590	84	-5	37	3.24	-6	*0-90(2-88-0),2-11	8	-1.3
1884 Det-N	114	450	86	119	18	6	5	39	40	52	....	....	.264	.324	.364	.689	123	14	55	4.53	7	*0-114(0-114-0)	11	1.5
1885 Det-N	105	424	93	128	18	8	1	29	47	18	....	....	.302	.372	.389	.761	146	23	63	5.73	0	*0-105(0-104-0)	14	1.9
1886 Det-N	126	494	105	116	6	6	4	60	57	39	50	....	.235	.314	.296	.610	84	-8	63	4.51	-8	*0-126(0-126-0)/2-1	13	-1.9
1887*Det-N	118	501	79	159	13	7	4	69	30	24	69	....	.317	.320	.357	.677	85	-10	78	6.02	-4	*0-118(1-117-0)	15	-1.5
1888 Det-N	109	459	64	122	6	8	5	39	15	32	38	....	.266	.295	.346	.641	104	1	60	4.77	-9	*0-109(0-109-0)	12	-1.1
1889 Pit-N	116	461	81	110	14	10	2	37	58	25	53	....	.239	.326	.325	.652	91	-2	68	5.13	-3	*0-116(0-116-0)	13	-0.8
1890 Pit-P	118	472	106	131	16	6	1	44	80	24	65	....	.278	.389	.343	.732	105	10	90	7.16	-6	*0-118(0-118-0)	17	0.0
1891 Pit-N	119	455	87	121	12	8	0	60	48	30	54	....	.266	.341	.327	.669	97	-0	71	5.74	-5	*0-119(39-80-0)/S-1	14	-0.8
1892 Bal-N	11	43	3	7	1	1	0	2	3	3	0	....	.163	.217	.233	.450	35	-4	2	1.67	-1	0-11(8-2-1)	0	-0.5
Total 13	1267	5104	930	1347	159	79	30	517	471	357	329	....	.264	.325	.340	.664	102	29	687	4.94	-35	*0-1251/2-13,S-7	146	-4.7

• HANNA, John — John Hanna b: 11/3/1863, Philadelphia, PA d: 11/7/1930, Philadelphia, PA Deb: 5/23/1884

YEAR TM-L	G	AB	R	H	2B	3B	HR	RBI	BB	SO	SB	CS	AVG	OBP	SLG	OPS	OPS+	BR/A	RC	RC/G	FR	G/POS	WS	TPW
1884 Was-a	23	76	8	5	0	0	0	0	6	....	....	....	.066	.134	.066	.200	-37	-10	1	.27	0	C-18/0-6(1-1-4)	0	-0.8
Ric-a	22	67	6	13	2	1	0	0	0	....	....	....	.194	.206	.254	.460	50	-4	4	1.83	4	C-21/S-1	1	0.2
Yr.	45	143	14	18	2	1	0	0	6	....	....	....	.126	.167	.154	.321	2	-14	4	.94	4	C-39/0-6(1-1-4),S-1	1	-0.6

• HANNAH, Truck — James Harrison Hannah b: 6/5/1889, Larimore, ND d: 4/27/1982, Fountain Valley, CA BR/TR, 6'1", 190 lbs. Deb: 4/15/1918

YEAR TM-L	G	AB	R	H	2B	3B	HR	RBI	BB	SO	SB	CS	AVG	OBP	SLG	OPS	OPS+	BR/A	RC	RC/G	FR	G/POS	WS	TPW
1918 NY-A	90	250	24	55	6	0	2	21	51	25	5	....	.220	.361	.268	.629	88	-0	26	3.28	3	C-88	10	1.1
1919 NY-A	75	227	14	54	8	3	1	20	22	19	0	....	.238	.313	.313	.626	75	-7	22	3.20	-6	C-73/1-1	6	-0.8
1920 NY-A	79	259	24	64	11	1	2	25	24	35	2	0	.247	.313	.320	.634	66	-11	28	3.61	-9	C-78	5	-1.4
Total 3	244	736	62	173	25	4	5	66	97	79	7	0	.235	.331	.300	.631	77	-19	76	3.37	-12	C-239/1-1	21	-1.1

• HANNIFAN, Pat — Patrick James Hannifan b: 4/20/1866, Halifax, Canada d: 11/5/1908, Springfield, MA BB/TL Deb: 4/29/1897

YEAR TM-L	G	AB	R	H	2B	3B	HR	RBI	BB	SO	SB	CS	AVG	OBP	SLG	OPS	OPS+	BR/A	RC	RC/G	FR	G/POS	WS	TPW
1897 Bro-N	10	20	4	5	0	0	0	2	1	....	4	....	.250	.375	.250	.625	71	-1	4	5.79	1	/0-3(1-2-0),2-2	1	0.0

• HANNIFIN, Jack — John Joseph Hannifin b: 2/25/1883, Holyoke, MA d: 10/27/1945, Northampton, MA BR/TR, 5'11", 167 lbs. Deb: 4/19/1906 Career OF: 2-2-4

YEAR TM-L	G	AB	R	H	2B	3B	HR	RBI	BB	SO	SB	CS	AVG	OBP	SLG	OPS	OPS+	BR/A	RC	RC/G	FR	G/POS	WS	TPW
1906 Phi-A	1	1	0	1	0	0	0	0	0	....	0	....	1.000	1.000	1.000	2.000	511	0	1	∞	0	....	1	0.1
NY-N	10	30	4	6	0	1	0	3	2	....	1	....	.200	.250	.267	.517	60	-1	2	2.51	-1	/S-6,3-3,2-1	0	-0.2

YEAR TM-L	G	AB	R	H	2B	3B	HR	RBI	BB	SO	SB	CS	AVG	OBP	SLG	OPS	OPS+	BR/A	RC	RC/G	FR	G/POS	WS	TPW
1907 NY-N	56	149	16	34	7	3	1	15	15	....	6	....	.228	.303	.336	.639	97	-1	18	3.91	0	1-29,3-10/S-9,0-2(0-1-1)	4	-0.1
1908 NY-N	1	2	0	0	0	0	0	0	0	....	0	....	.000	.000	.000	.000	-95	-0	0	.00	0	/0-1	0	-0.1
Bos-N	90	257	30	53	6	2	2	22	28	....	7	....	.206	.284	.268	.553	78	-6	22	2.67	-1	3-35,2-22,S-15/0-7(2-1-2)	5	-0.6
Yr.	91	259	30	53	6	2	2	22	28	....	7	....	.205	.282	.266	.549	77	-6	22	2.65	-1	3-35,2-22,S-15/0-8(2-1-3)	5	-0.7
Total 3	**158**	**439**	**50**	**94**	**13**	**6**	**3**	**40**	**45**	**....**	**14**	**....**	**.214**	**.289**	**.292**	**.580**	**83**	**-8**	**43**	**3.05**	**-1**	**/3-48,S-30,1-29,2-23,0-10**	**10**	**-0.9**

• HANSEN, Bob Robert Joseph Hansen b: 5/26/1948, Boston, MA BL/TL, 6', 195 lbs. Deb: 5/10/1974

YEAR TM-L	G	AB	R	H	2B	3B	HR	RBI	BB	SO	SB	CS	AVG	OBP	SLG	OPS	OPS+	BR/A	RC	RC/G	FR	G/POS	WS	TPW
1974 Mil-A	58	88	8	26	4	1	2	9	3	16	2	1	.295	.319	.432	.750	115	1	12	5.25	0	D-18/1-3	3	0.1
1976 Mil-A	24	61	4	10	1	0	0	4	6	8	0	0	.164	.239	.180	.419	24	-6	3	1.46	0	D-14/1-1	0	-0.6
Total 2	**82**	**149**	**12**	**36**	**5**	**1**	**2**	**13**	**9**	**24**	**2**	**1**	**.242**	**.285**	**.329**	**.614**	**77**	**-4**	**15**	**3.54**	**0**	**/D-32,1-4**	**3**	**-0.6**

• HANSEN, Dave David Andrew Hansen b: 11/24/1968, Long Beach, CA BL/TR, 6', 195 lbs. Deb: 9/16/1990 Career OF: 3-0-2

YEAR TM-L	G	AB	R	H	2B	3B	HR	RBI	BB	SO	SB	CS	AVG	OBP	SLG	OPS	OPS+	BR/A	RC	RC/G	FR	G/POS	WS	TPW
1990 LA-N	5	7	0	1	0	0	0	1	0	3	0	0	.143	.143	.143	.286	-22	-1	0	.64	0	/3-2	0	-0.2
1991 LA-N	53	56	3	15	4	0	1	5	2	12	1	0	.268	.293	.393	.686	93	-1	6	3.74	1	3-21/S-1	1	0.0
1992 LA-N	132	341	30	73	11	0	6	22	34	49	0	2	.214	.287	.299	.586	67	-16	29	2.75	-4	*3-108	4	-2.1
1993 LA-N	84	105	13	38	3	0	4	30	21	13	0	1	.362	.468	.505	.973	170	11	27	10.40	-1	3-18	8	1.0
1994 LA-N	40	44	3	15	3	0	0	5	5	5	0	0	.341	.408	.409	.817	122	2	8	7.33	0	/3-7	1	0.1
1995*LA-N	100	181	19	52	10	0	1	14	28	28	0	0	.287	.386	.359	.745	107	3	26	5.30	-4	3-58	5	0.0
1996*LA-N	80	104	7	23	1	0	0	6	11	22	0	0	.221	.296	.231	.526	45	-8	7	2.20	-1	3-19/1-8	0	-0.9
1997 Chi-N	90	151	19	47	8	2	3	21	31	32	1	2	.311	.432	.450	.882	128	8	32	8.01	-1	3-51/1-4,2-1	6	0.7
1999 LA-N	100	107	14	27	8	1	2	17	26	20	0	0	.252	.407	.402	.809	112	4	20	6.44	-1	1-20,3-13/D-2,0-2(0-0-2)	3	0.2
2000 LA-N	102	121	18	35	6	2	8	26	26	32	0	1	.289	.415	.570	.985	155	10	29	8.81	0	1-16,3-16/D-5,0-3(3-0-0)	6	0.9
2001 LA-N	92	140	13	33	10	0	2	20	32	29	0	1	.236	.378	.350	.728	97	1	20	4.75	4	1-25,3-21/D-1	4	0.4
2002 LA-N	96	120	15	35	6	0	2	17	14	22	1	0	.292	.366	.392	.757	107	2	18	5.44	0	1-27,3-11/D-4	4	0.1
2003 SD-N	110	135	13	33	4	1	2	15	23	25	1	0	.244	.358	.333	.692	90	-1	17	4.33	1	1-20,3-11/D-3,2-1	3	-0.1
Total 13	**1084**	**1612**	**167**	**427**	**74**	**6**	**31**	**199**	**253**	**292**	**4**	**7**	**.265**	**.367**	**.376**	**.743**	**103**	**14**	**239**	**5.21**	**-7**	**3-356,1-120/D-15,0-5,2-2,S**	**45**	**0.2**

• HANSEN, Doug Douglas William Hansen b: 12/16/1928, Los Angeles, CA d: 9/16/1999, Orem, UT BR/TR, 6', 180 lbs. Deb: 9/4/1951

YEAR TM-L	G	AB	R	H	2B	3B	HR	RBI	BB	SO	SB	CS	AVG	OBP	SLG	OPS	OPS+	BR/A	RC	RC/G	FR	G/POS	WS	TPW
1951 Cle-A	3	0	2	0	0	0	0	0	0	0	0	0	....	....	....	....	-106	0	0	....	0	....	0	0.0

• HANSEN, Jed Jed Ramon Hansen b: 8/19/1972, Tacoma, WA BR/TR, 6'1", 195 lbs. Deb: 7/29/1997

YEAR TM-L	G	AB	R	H	2B	3B	HR	RBI	BB	SO	SB	CS	AVG	OBP	SLG	OPS	OPS+	BR/A	RC	RC/G	FR	G/POS	WS	TPW
1997 KC-A	34	94	11	29	6	1	1	14	13	29	3	2	.309	.398	.426	.824	112	2	16	6.16	0	2-31	4	0.3
1998 KC-A	4	3	0	0	0	0	0	0	0	3	0	0	.000	.000	.000	.000	-97	-1	0	.00	-1	/2-2	0	-0.2
1999 KC-A	49	79	16	16	1	0	3	5	10	32	0	1	.203	.292	.329	.621	57	-6	8	3.25	0	2-21,S-10/3-4,D-3,0-2(0-2-0),1	1	-0.4
Total 3	**87**	**176**	**27**	**45**	**7**	**1**	**4**	**19**	**23**	**64**	**3**	**3**	**.256**	**.345**	**.375**	**.720**	**84**	**-5**	**25**	**4.64**	**-2**	**/2-54,S-10,3-4,D-3,0-2,1-1**	**5**	**-0.3**

• HANSEN, Ron Ronald Lavern Hansen b: 4/5/1938, Oxford, NE BR/TR, 6'3", 200 lbs. Deb: 4/15/1958 C

YEAR TM-L	G	AB	R	H	2B	3B	HR	RBI	BB	SO	SB	CS	AVG	OBP	SLG	OPS	OPS+	BR/A	RC	RC/G	FR	G/POS	WS	TPW
1958 Bal-A	12	19	1	0	0	0	0	1	0	7	0	0	.000	.050	.000	.050	-90	-5	0	.08	0	S-12	0	-0.5
1959 Bal-A	2	4	0	0	0	0	0	0	1	1	0	0	.000	.200	.000	.200	-41	-1	0	.35	0	/S-2	0	-0.1
1960 Bal-A★	153	530	72	135	22	5	22	86	69	94	3	3	.255	.343	.440	.782	111	8	78	5.00	9	*S-153	24	2.9
1961 Bal-A	155	533	51	132	13	2	12	51	66	96	1	3	.248	.332	.347	.679	83	-13	60	3.77	14	*S-149/2-7	16	1.4
1962 Bal-A	71	196	12	34	7	0	3	17	30	36	0	1	.173	.289	.255	.545	50	-14	14	2.27	0	S-64	2	-0.8
1963 Chi-A	144	482	55	109	17	2	13	67	78	74	1	1	.226	.334	.351	.685	94	-2	57	3.81	24	*S-144	19	**3.6**
1964 Chi-A	158	575	85	150	25	3	20	68	73	73	1	0	.261	.350	.419	.769	116	14	86	5.12	21	*S-158	30	5.1
1965 Chi-A	162	587	61	138	23	4	11	66	60	73	1	1	.235	.308	.344	.652	91	-8	60	3.35	6	*S-161/2-1	18	1.4
1966 Chi-A	23	74	3	13	1	0	0	4	15	10	0	1	.176	.322	.189	.511	55	-4	6	2.37	0	S-23	1	-0.2
1967 Chi-A	157	498	35	116	20	0	8	51	64	51	0	3	.233	.320	.321	.642	93	-3	53	3.53	-1	*S-157	17	1.0
1968 Was-A	86	275	28	51	12	0	8	28	35	49	0	0	.185	.282	.316	.598	84	-5	23	2.55	-4	S-81/3-5	6	-0.2
Chi-A	40	87	7	20	3	0	1	4	11	12	0	0	.230	.316	.299	.615	86	-1	8	3.00	0	3-29/S-7,2-2	2	-0.1
Yr.	126	362	35	71	15	0	9	32	46	61	0	0	.196	.290	.312	.602	84	-6	31	2.65	-4	S-88,3-34/2-2	8	-0.3
1969 Chi-A	85	185	15	48	6	1	2	22	18	25	2	0	.259	.328	.335	.664	82	-4	20	3.62	-5	2-26,1-21/S-8,3-7	3	-0.9
1970 NY-A	59	91	13	27	4	0	4	14	19	9	0	1	.297	.423	.473	.896	155	7	20	7.79	1	S-15,3-11/2-1	6	1.0
1971 NY-A	61	145	6	30	3	0	2	20	9	27	0	0	.207	.253	.269	.522	51	-10	9	2.01	-4	3-30/2-9,S-3	1	-1.3
1972 KC-A	16	30	2	4	0	0	0	2	3	6	0	0	.133	.212	.133	.345	4	-3	1	.82	2	/S-6,3-4,2-1	0	-0.1
Total 15	**1384**	**4311**	**446**	**1007**	**156**	**17**	**106**	**501**	**551**	**643**	**9**	**14**	**.234**	**.323**	**.351**	**.675**	**92**	**-42**	**494**	**3.77**	**62**	***S-1143/3-86,2-47,1-21**	**145**	**12.3**

• HANSKI, Don Donald Thomas Hanski b: 2/27/1916, La Porte, IN d: 9/2/1957, Worth, IL BL/TL, 5'11", 180 lbs. Deb: 5/6/1943 ♦

YEAR TM-L	G	AB	R	H	2B	3B	HR	RBI	BB	SO	SB	CS	AVG	OBP	SLG	OPS	OPS+	BR/A	RC	RC/G	FR	G/POS	WS	TPW
1943 Chi-A	9	21	1	5	1	0	0	2	0	5	0	1	.238	.238	.286	.524	53	-2	1	1.86	0	/1-5,P-1	0	-0.2
1944 Chi-A	2	1	0	0	0	0	0	0	0	0	0	0	.000	.000	.000	.000	-101	-0	0	.00	0	/P-2	0	-0.3
Total 2	**11**	**22**	**1**	**5**	**1**	**0**	**0**	**2**	**0**	**5**	**0**	**1**	**.227**	**.227**	**.273**	**.500**	**46**	**-2**	**1**	**1.76**	**0**	**/1-5,P-3**	**0**	**-0.5**

• HANSON, Harry Harry Francis Hanson b: 1/17/1896, Elgin, IL d: 10/5/1966, Savannah, GA BR/TR, 5'11" Deb: 7/14/1913

YEAR TM-L	G	AB	R	H	2B	3B	HR	RBI	BB	SO	SB	CS	AVG	OBP	SLG	OPS	OPS+	BR/A	RC	RC/G	FR	G/POS	WS	TPW
1913 NY-A	1	2	0	0	0	0	0	0	0	0	0	....	.000	.000	.000	.000	-100	-1	0	.00	0	/C-1	0	0.0

• HAPPENNY, John John Clifford "Cliff" Happenny b: 5/18/1901, Waltham, MA d: 12/29/1988, Coral Springs, FL BR/TR, 5'11", 165 lbs. Deb: 7/2/1923

YEAR TM-L	G	AB	R	H	2B	3B	HR	RBI	BB	SO	SB	CS	AVG	OBP	SLG	OPS	OPS+	BR/A	RC	RC/G	FR	G/POS	WS	TPW
1923 Chi-A	32	86	7	19	5	0	0	10	3	13	0	0	.221	.256	.279	.535	41	-7	6	2.35	-2	2-19/S-9,3-2	1	-0.8

• HARBRIDGE, Bill William Arthur "Yaller Bill" Harbridge
b: 3/29/1855, Philadelphia, PA d: 3/17/1924, Philadelphia, PA BL/TL, 162 lbs. Deb: 5/15/1875 Career OF: 13-112-47

YEAR TM-L	G	AB	R	H	2B	3B	HR	RBI	BB	SO	SB	CS	AVG	OBP	SLG	OPS	OPS+	BR/A	RC	RC/G	FR	G/POS	WS	TPW
1875 Har-n	53	208	32	50	3	3	0	26	9	3	2	4	.240	.272	.284	.556	89	-4	17	3.10	-3	C-31,0-13(0-0-13),2-11/1-3,S	....	-0.5
1876 Har-N	30	109	11	23	2	1	0	6	3	2	....	....	.211	.239	.255	.493	59	-5	7	2.23	-1	C-24/0-6(0-2-4),1-2	2	-0.5
1877 Har-N	41	167	18	37	5	2	0	8	3	6	....	....	.222	.235	.275	.511	67	-5	11	2.35	-5	C-32/0-5(0-3-2),2-4,3-1	3	-0.8
1878 Chi-N	54	240	32	71	12	0	0	37	6	13	....	....	.296	.313	.346	.659	109	2	27	4.33	-7	*C-53/0-8(4-3-1)	6	-0.4
1879 Chi-N	4	18	2	2	0	0	0	1	0	5	....	....	.111	.111	.111	.222	-25	-2	0	.40	-1	/0-4(1-3-0)	0	-0.3
1880 Tro-N	9	27	3	10	0	1	0	2	0	3	....	....	.370	.370	.444	.815	166	2	5	7.37	0	/C-9,0-1	2	0.1
1882 Tro-N	32	123	11	23	1	1	0	13	10	17	....	....	.187	.248	.211	.460	52	-6	7	1.82	-4	0-23(0-23-0)/1-6,C-3	0	-1.0
1883 Phi-N	73	280	32	62	12	3	0	21	24	20	....	....	.221	.283	.286	.569	81	-4	23	2.93	-15	0-44(8-36-0),S-11/2-9,C-7,3	3	-1.7
1884 Cin-U	82	341	59	95	12	5	2	....	25	....	....	....	.279	.328	.361	.689	123	8	41	4.70	2	*0-80(0-41-39)/S-3,1-2	13	0.7
Total 8	**325**	**1305**	**168**	**323**	**44**	**13**	**2**	**88**	**71**	**66**	**....**	**....**	**.248**	**.287**	**.306**	**.593**	**91**	**-11**	**120**	**3.40**	**-31**	**0-171,C-128/S-14,2-13,1-10,3**	**29**	**-3.9**

• HARDESTY, Scott Scott Durbin Hardesty b: 1/26/1870, Bellville, OH d: 10/29/1944, Fostoria, OH Deb: 8/17/1899

YEAR TM-L	G	AB	R	H	2B	3B	HR	RBI	BB	SO	SB	CS	AVG	OBP	SLG	OPS	OPS+	BR/A	RC	RC/G	FR	G/POS	WS	TPW
1899 NY-N	22	72	4	16	0	0	0	4	1	....	2	....	.222	.243	.222	.465	29	-7	5	2.16	2	S-20/1-2	1	-0.4

• HARDGROVE, Pat William Henry Hardgrove b: 5/10/1895, Palmyra, KS d: 1/26/1973, Jackson, MS BR/TR, 5'10", 158 lbs. Deb: 6/8/1918

YEAR TM-L	G	AB	R	H	2B	3B	HR	RBI	BB	SO	SB	CS	AVG	OBP	SLG	OPS	OPS+	BR/A	RC	RC/G	FR	G/POS	WS	TPW
1918 Chi-A	2	2	0	0	0	0	0	0	0	0	0	....	.000	.000	.000	.000	-99	-0	0	.00	0	....	0	-0.1

• HARDIE, Lou Lewis W. Hardie b: 8/24/1864, New York, NY d: 3/5/1929, Oakland, CA BR, 5'11", 180 lbs. Deb: 5/22/1884 U Career OF: 6-7-20

YEAR TM-L	G	AB	R	H	2B	3B	HR	RBI	BB	SO	SB	CS	AVG	OBP	SLG	OPS	OPS+	BR/A	RC	RC/G	FR	G/POS	WS	TPW
1884 Phi-N	3	8	0	3	2	0	0	0	0	2	....	....	.375	.375	.625	1.000	219	1	2	10.57	-1	/C-3	0	0.0
1886 Chi-N	16	51	4	9	0	0	0	3	4	10	1	....	.176	.236	.176	.413	23	-5	2	1.56	0	C-13/0-2(0-0-2),3-1	1	-0.4
1890 Bos-N	47	185	17	42	8	0	3	17	18	36	4	....	.227	.296	.319	.614	73	-7	19	3.54	-2	C-25,0-15(6-4-6)/3-7,1-1,S	4	-0.7
1891 Bal-a	15	56	7	13	0	3	0	1	8	8	3	....	.232	.328	.339	.667	90	-1	7	4.56	1	0-15(0-3-12)	2	0.0
Total 4	**81**	**300**	**28**	**67**	**10**	**3**	**3**	**21**	**30**	**56**	**8**	**....**	**.223**	**.294**	**.307**	**.601**	**72**	**-12**	**31**	**3.52**	**-2**	**/C-41,0-32,3-8,1-1,S-1**	**7**	**-1.1**

• HARDIN, Bud William Edgar Hardin b: 6/14/1922, Shelby, NC d: 7/28/1997, Rancho Santa Fe, CA BR/TR, 5'10", 165 lbs. Deb: 4/15/1952

YEAR TM-L	G	AB	R	H	2B	3B	HR	RBI	BB	SO	SB	CS	AVG	OBP	SLG	OPS	OPS+	BR/A	RC	RC/G	FR	G/POS	WS	TPW
1952 Chi-N	3	7	1	1	0	0	0	0	0	0	0	0	.143	.143	.143	.286	-20	-1	0	.66	0	/S-2,2-1	0	-0.1

• HARDING, Lou Edward H.A. "Jumbo" Harding b: 1862, MO, 5'9.5", 213 lbs. Deb: 10/5/1886

YEAR TM-L	G	AB	R	H	2B	3B	HR	RBI	BB	SO	SB	CS	AVG	OBP	SLG	OPS	OPS+	BR/A	RC	RC/G	FR	G/POS	WS	TPW
1886 StL-a	1	3	0	1	1	0	0	1	0	....	0	....	.333	.333	.667	1.000	201	0	1	9.23	1	/C-1	0	0.1

• HARDTKE, Jason Jason Robert Hardtke b: 9/15/1971, Milwaukee, WI BB/TR, 5'10", 175 lbs. Deb: 9/8/1996

YEAR TM-L	G	AB	R	H	2B	3B	HR	RBI	BB	SO	SB	CS	AVG	OBP	SLG	OPS	OPS+	BR/A	RC	RC/G	FR	G/POS	WS	TPW
1996 NY-N	19	57	3	11	5	0	0	6	2	12	0	0	.193	.233	.281	.514	36	-5	4	2.09	1	2-18	1	-0.4
1997 NY-N	30	56	9	15	2	0	2	8	4	6	1	1	.268	.328	.411	.739	95	-1	6	3.80	-1	2-21/3-1	1	-0.1

YEAR TM-L	G	AB	R	H	2B	3B	HR	RBI	BB	SO	SB	CS	AVG	OBP	SLG	OPS	OPS+	BR/A	RC	RC/G	FR	G/POS	WS	TPW
1998 Chi-N	18	21	2	5	0	0	0	2	2	6	0	0	.238	.304	.238	.542	44	-2	2	2.84	-1	/3-7,D-1,O-1	1	-0.3
Total 3	67	134	14	31	7	0	2	16	8	24	1	1	.231	.285	.328	.613	63	-8	12	2.92	-2	/2-39,3-8,D-1,O-1	3	-0.8

• HARDY, Carroll Carroll William Hardy b: 5/18/1933, Sturgis, SD BR/TR, 6', 185 lbs. Deb: 4/15/1958 Career OF: 88-163-112

YEAR TM-L	G	AB	R	H	2B	3B	HR	RBI	BB	SO	SB	CS	AVG	OBP	SLG	OPS	OPS+	BR/A	RC	RC/G	FR	G/POS	WS	TPW
1958 Cle-A	27	49	10	10	3	0	1	6	6	14	1	2	.204	.304	.327	.630	75	-2	5	3.15	1	O-17(0-16-1)	1	-0.2
1959 Cle-A	32	53	12	11	1	0	0	2	3	7	1	1	.208	.250	.226	.476	33	-5	3	1.93	0	O-15(1-14-0)	1	-0.6
1960 Cle-A	29	18	7	2	1	0	0	1	2	2	0	0	.111	.200	.167	.367		-3	1	.84	0	O-17(4-9-5)	0	-0.3
Bos-A	73	145	26	34	5	2	2	15	17	40	3	2	.234	.315	.338	.653	74	-5	14	3.18	-1	O-59(44-8-14)	2	-0.9
Yr.	102	163	33	36	6	2	2	16	19	42	3	2	.221	.302	.319	.621	66	-8	15	2.89	-1	O-76(48-17-19)	2	-1.2
1961 Bos-A	85	281	46	74	20	2	3	36	26	53	4	2	.263	.330	.381	.711	87	-5	36	4.54	0	O-76(20-38-21)	7	-0.8
1962 Bos-A	115	362	52	78	13	5	8	36	54	68	3	7	.215	.321	.345	.666	77	-14	40	3.53	3	*O-105(3-45-64)	6	-1.7
1963 Hou-N	15	44	5	10	3	0	0	3	3	7	1	0	.227	.277	.295	.572	69	-1	4	2.82	0	O-10(10-0-0)	1	-0.2
1964 Hou-N	46	157	13	29	1	1	2	12	8	30	0	0	.185	.234	.242	.476	36	-13	8	1.68	2	O-41(5-33-4)	1	-1.4
1967 Min-A	11	8	1	3	0	0	1	2	1	1	0	0	.375	.444	.750	1.194	228	1	3	15.02	-1	/O-4(1-0-3)	1	0.1
Total 8	433	1117	172	251	47	10	17	113	120	222	13	14	.225	.304	.330	.634	71	-47	114	3.34	3	O-344	20	-6.0

• HARDY, Jack John Doolittle Hardy b: 6/23/1877, Cleveland, OH d: 10/20/1921, Cleveland, OH BR/TR, 6', 185 lbs. Deb: 8/29/1903 Career OF: 1-0-5

YEAR TM-L	G	AB	R	H	2B	3B	HR	RBI	BB	SO	SB	CS	AVG	OBP	SLG	OPS	OPS+	BR/A	RC	RC/G	FR	G/POS	WS	TPW
1903 Cle-A	5	19	1	3	1	0	0	1	1	....	1	....	.158	.200	.211	.411	24	-2	1	1.70	0	/O-5(0-0-5)	0	-0.2
1907 Chi-N	1	4	0	1	0	0	0	0	0	....	0	....	.250	.250	.250	.500	53	-0	0	2.22	0	/C-1	0	0.0
1909 Was-A	10	24	3	4	0	0	0	4	1	....	0	....	.167	.200	.167	.367	17	-2	1	.96	-1	/C-9,2-1	0	-0.3
1910 Was-A	7	8	1	2	0	0	0	0	0	....	0	....	.250	.250	.250	.500	59	-0	0	2.04	0	/C-4,O-1	0	-0.1
Total 4	23	55	5	10	1	0	0	5	2	....	1	....	.182	.211	.200	.411	28	-5	2	1.45	-1	/C-14,O-6,2-1	0	-0.5

• HARE, Shawn Shawn Robert Hare b: 3/26/1967, St. Louis, MO BL/TL, 6'2", 190 lbs. Deb: 9/6/1991 Career OF: 21-0-18

YEAR TM-L	G	AB	R	H	2B	3B	HR	RBI	BB	SO	SB	CS	AVG	OBP	SLG	OPS	OPS+	BR/A	RC	RC/G	FR	G/POS	WS	TPW
1991 Det-A	9	19	0	1	1	0	0	0	2	1	0	0	.053	.143	.105	.248	-30	-3	0	.00	1	/O-6(0-0-6),D-2	0	-0.3
1992 Det-A	15	26	0	3	1	0	0	5	2	4	0	0	.115	.179	.154	.332	-6	-4	1	.98	0	/O-9(3-0-7),1-4	0	-0.4
1994 NY-N	22	40	7	9	1	1	0	2	4	11	0	0	.225	.295	.300	.595	56	-3	3	2.06	0	O-14(14-0-0)	0	-0.3
1995 Tex-A	18	24	2	6	1	0	0	2	4	6	0	0	.250	.357	.292	.649	70	-1	3	3.67	0	/O-9(4-0-5),D-3,1-1	0	-0.1
Total 4	64	109	9	19	4	1	0	9	12	22	0	0	.174	.256	.229	.486	30	-11	6	1.67	1	/O-38,1-5,D-5	0	-1.1

• HARGIS, Gary Gary Lynn Hargis b: 11/2/1956, Minneapolis, MN BR/TR, 5'11", 165 lbs. Deb: 9/29/1979

YEAR TM-L	G	AB	R	H	2B	3B	HR	RBI	BB	SO	SB	CS	AVG	OBP	SLG	OPS	OPS+	BR/A	RC	RC/G	FR	G/POS	WS	TPW
1979 Pit-N	1	0	0	0	0	0	0	0	0	0	0	0	....	....	....	....	-96	0	0	....	0	....	0	0.0

• HARGRAVE, Bubbles Eugene Franklin Hargrave b: 7/15/1892, New Haven, IN d: 2/23/1969, Cincinnati, OH BR/TR, 5'10.5", 174 lbs. Deb: 9/18/1913

YEAR TM-L	G	AB	R	H	2B	3B	HR	RBI	BB	SO	SB	CS	AVG	OBP	SLG	OPS	OPS+	BR/A	RC	RC/G	FR	G/POS	WS	TPW
1913 Chi-N	3	3	0	1	0	0	0	1	0	0	0	....	.333	.333	.333	.667	90	-0	0	4.00	-0	/C-2	0	0.0
1914 Chi-N	23	36	3	8	2	0	0	2	0	4	2	....	.222	.222	.278	.500	48	-2	2	2.21	-2	C-16	0	-0.4
1915 Chi-N	15	19	2	3	0	1	0	2	1	5	0	....	.158	.200	.263	.463	40	-1	1	1.66	1	/C-9	0	-0.1
1921 Cin-N	93	263	28	76	17	8	1	38	12	15	4	2	.289	.327	.426	.753	102	1	36	4.95	-4	C-73	8	0.2
1922 Cin-N	98	320	49	101	22	10	7	57	26	18	7	4	.316	.371	.513	.883	128	13	60	6.86	-7	C-87	14	1.1
1923 Cin-N	118	378	54	126	23	9	10	78	44	22	4	5	.333	.419	.521	.941	150	28	84	8.31	-2	*C-109	25	3.2
1924 Cin-N	98	312	42	94	19	10	3	33	30	20	2	2	.301	.370	.455	.825	122	10	53	6.19	-4	C-91	14	1.2
1925 Cin-N	87	273	28	82	13	6	2	33	25	23	4	3	.300	.361	.414	.775	100	0	41	5.54	-10	C-84	8	-0.4
1926 Cin-N	105	326	42	115	22	8	6	62	25	17	2	....	**.353**	.406	.525	.930	153	24	67	7.91	-7	C-93	18	2.2
1927 Cin-N	102	305	36	94	18	3	0	35	31	18	0	....	.308	.376	.387	.763	108	4	45	5.22	-1	C-92	13	0.8
1928 Cin-N	65	190	19	56	12	3	0	23	13	14	4	....	.295	.353	.389	.742	95	-1	26	4.75	1	C-57	8	0.3
1930 NY-A	45	108	11	30	7	0	0	12	10	9	0	0	.278	.339	.343	.682	77	-3	13	4.27	0	C-34	2	-0.1
Total 12	852	2533	314	786	155	58	29	376	217	165	29	16	.310	.372	.452	.824	119	73	429	6.17	-36	C-747	110	7.9

• HARGRAVE, Pinky William McKinley Hargrave b: 1/31/1896, New Haven, IN d: 10/3/1942, Fort Wayne, IN BB/TR, 5'8.5", 180 lbs. Deb: 5/18/1923

YEAR TM-L	G	AB	R	H	2B	3B	HR	RBI	BB	SO	SB	CS	AVG	OBP	SLG	OPS	OPS+	BR/A	RC	RC/G	FR	G/POS	WS	TPW
1923 Was-A	33	59	4	17	2	0	0	8	2	6	0	0	.288	.311	.322	.634	70	-3	6	3.63	0	/3-8,C-5,O-1	1	-0.2
1924 Was-A	24	33	3	5	1	1	0	5	1	4	0	0	.152	.176	.242	.419	8	-5	1	1.32	0	/C-8	0	-0.4
1925 Was-A	5	6	0	3	0	0	0	0	1	2	0	0	.500	.571	.500	1.071	177	1	2	15.80	0	/C-1	1	0.1
StL-A	67	225	34	64	15	2	8	43	13	13	2	0	.284	.326	.476	.802	97	-2	35	5.69	0	C-62	8	0.2
Yr.	72	231	34	67	15	2	8	43	14	15	2	0	.290	.333	.476	.810	99	-1	37	5.87	1	C-63	9	0.3
1926 StL-A	92	235	20	66	16	3	7	37	10	38	3	0	.281	.319	.464	.782	98	-2	35	5.23	3	C-58	7	0.5
1928 Det-A	121	320	38	88	13	5	10	63	32	28	4	1	.275	.343	.441	.783	103	2	50	5.50	-4	C-88	10	0.3
1929 Det-A	76	185	26	61	12	0	3	26	20	24	2	2	.330	.401	.443	.844	116	5	33	6.87	1	C-48	7	0.9
1930 Det-A	55	137	18	39	8	0	5	18	20	12	2	0	.285	.380	.453	.832	108	3	25	6.57	-4	C-40	5	0.1
Was-A	10	31	3	6	2	2	1	7	3	1	1	0	.194	.265	.484	.749	85	-1	4	4.23	1	/C-9	1	0.0
Yr.	65	168	21	45	10	2	6	25	23	13	3	0	.268	.359	.458	.818	104	2	29	6.09	-3	C-49	6	0.2
1931 Was-A	40	80	6	26	8	0	1	19	9	12	1	0	.325	.393	.463	.856	124	3	15	7.38	-1	C-25	4	0.3
1932 Bos-N	82	217	20	57	14	3	4	33	24	18	1	....	.263	.336	.410	.746	103	1	31	4.98	1	C-73	9	0.6
1933 Bos-N	45	73	5	13	0	0	0	6	5	7	1	....	.178	.241	.178	.419	23	-7	3	1.40	-2	C-25	1	-0.8
Total 10	650	1601	177	445	91	16	39	265	140	165	17	3	.278	.339	.428	.767	98	-4	241	5.35	-4	C-442/3-8,O-1	54	1.6

• HARGREAVES, Charlie Charles Russell Hargreaves b: 12/14/1896, Trenton, NJ d: 5/9/1979, Neptune, NJ BR/TR, 6', 170 lbs. Deb: 6/27/1923

YEAR TM-L	G	AB	R	H	2B	3B	HR	RBI	BB	SO	SB	CS	AVG	OBP	SLG	OPS	OPS+	BR/A	RC	RC/G	FR	G/POS	WS	TPW
1923 Bro-N	20	57	5	16	0	0	0	4	1	2	0	0	.281	.293	.281	.574	53	-4	5	2.93	-1	C-15	1	-0.4
1924 Bro-N	15	27	4	11	2	0	0	5	1	1	0	1	.407	.429	.481	.910	148	1	5	7.80	-1	/C-9	2	0.1
1925 Bro-N	45	83	9	23	3	1	0	13	6	1	1	1	.277	.326	.337	.663	72	-4	9	3.90	1	C-18/1-2	2	-0.1
1926 Bro-N	85	208	14	52	13	2	2	23	19	10	1	....	.250	.316	.361	.676	83	-5	24	3.85	6	C-70	7	0.4
1927 Bro-N	46	133	9	38	3	1	0	11	14	7	1	....	.286	.362	.323	.686	84	-2	16	4.29	2	C-44	4	0.2
1928 Bro-N	20	61	3	12	2	0	0	5	6	6	1	....	.197	.269	.230	.498	32	-6	4	2.05	0	C-20	1	-0.5
Pit-N	79	260	15	74	8	2	1	32	12	9	1	....	.285	.319	.342	.661	70	-12	28	3.66	-1	C-77	5	-0.8
Yr.	99	321	18	86	10	2	1	37	18	15	2	....	.268	.309	.321	.630	63	-18	32	3.34	-1	C-97	6	-1.3
1929 Pit-N	102	328	33	88	12	5	1	44	16	12	1	....	.268	.306	.345	.651	60	-21	34	3.56	4	*C-101	7	-1.1
1930 Pit-N	11	31	4	7	1	0	0	2	2	1	0	....	.226	.273	.258	.531	29	-4	2	2.30	4	C-11	1	0.1
Total 8	423	1188	96	321	44	11	4	139	77	49	6	2	.270	.318	.336	.654	69	-56	126	3.67	14	C-365/1-2	30	-2.0

• HARGROVE, Mike Dudley Michael "The Human Rain Delay" Hargrove b: 10/26/1949, Perryton, TX BL/TL, 6', 195 lbs. Deb: 4/7/1974 M/C Career OF: 167-0-0

YEAR TM-L	G	AB	R	H	2B	3B	HR	RBI	BB	SO	SB	CS	AVG	OBP	SLG	OPS	OPS+	BR/A	RC	RC/G	FR	G/POS	WS	TPW
1974 Tex-A	131	415	57	134	18	6	4	66	49	42	0	0	.323	.400	.424	.824	141	24	71	6.40	7	1-91,D-32/O-6(6-0-0)	20	2.5
1975 Tex-A★	145	519	82	157	22	2	11	62	79	66	4	3	.303	.399	.416	.815	132	25	88	6.17	3	O-96(96-0-0),1-48,D-12	22	2.0
1976 Tex-A	151	541	80	155	30	1	7	58	**97**	64	2	3	.287	.401	.384	.785	128	24	91	6.07	-1	*1-141/D-5	24	1.3
1977 Tex-A	153	525	98	160	28	4	18	69	103	59	2	5	.305	.424	.476	.900	144	37	110	7.50	1	*1-152	25	2.9
1978 Tex-A	146	494	63	124	24	1	7	40	**107**	47	2	5	.251	.391	.346	.738	109	12	73	5.03	6	*1-140/D-4	16	0.9
1979 SD-N	52	125	15	24	5	0	0	8	25	15	0	2	.192	.327	.232	.559	59	-7	11	2.76	-3	1-37	1	-1.2
Cle-A	100	338	60	110	21	4	10	56	63	40	2	3	.325	.438	.500	.938	152	28	76	8.30	-3	O-65(65-0-0),1-28/D-7	19	1.9
1980 Cle-A	160	589	86	179	22	2	11	85	111	36	4	2	.304	.421	.404	.825	127	30	105	6.33	-7	*1-160	25	1.3
1981 Cle-A	94	322	43	102	21	0	2	49	60	16	5	4	.317	**.432**	.401	.832	143	22	57	6.21	3	1-88/D-4	16	2.1
1982 Cle-A	160	591	67	160	26	1	4	65	101	58	2	2	.271	.380	.338	.718	100	5	79	4.60	6	*1-153/D-5	15	0.2
1983 Cle-A	134	469	57	134	21	4	3	57	78	40	0	6	.286	.393	.367	.760	107	6	71	5.20	5	*1-131/D-1	14	0.3
1984 Cle-A	133	352	44	94	14	2	2	44	53	38	0	2	.267	.363	.335	.698	93	-2	43	4.22	1	*1-124	7	-0.6
1985 Cle-A	107	284	31	81	14	1	1	27	39	29	1	0	.285	.372	.352	.724	100	2	38	4.84	4	1-85	8	0.2
Total 12	1666	5564	783	1614	266	28	80	686	965	550	24	37	.290	.400	.391	.791	121	207	914	5.81	22	*1-1378,O-167/D-70	212	13.7

• HARKNESS, Tim Thomas William Harkness b: 12/23/1937, Lachine, Canada BL/TL, 6'2", 182 lbs. Deb: 9/12/1961

YEAR TM-L	G	AB	R	H	2B	3B	HR	RBI	BB	SO	SB	CS	AVG	OBP	SLG	OPS	OPS+	BR/A	RC	RC/G	FR	G/POS	WS	TPW
1961 LA-N	5	8	4	4	2	0	0	0	3	1	1	0	.500	.636	.750	1.386	245	2	5	31.36	-0	/1-2	1	0.2
1962 LA-N	92	62	9	16	2	0	2	7	10	20	1	0	.258	.370	.387	.757	110	2	10	5.89	-2	1-59	3	-0.2
1963 NY-N	123	375	35	79	12	3	10	41	36	79	4	3	.211	.292	.339	.631	80	-9	38	3.35	12	*1-106	7	-0.3
1964 NY-N	39	117	11	33	2	1	2	13	9	18	1	1	.282	.339	.368	.706	101	0	13	3.98	3	1-32	3	0.1
Total 4	259	562	59	132	18	4	14	61	58	118	7	4	.235	.316	.356	.672	90	-5	66	3.99	13	1-199	14	-0.2

YEAR TM-L	G	AB	R	H	2B	3B	HR	RBI	BB	SO	SB	CS	AVG	OBP	SLG	OPS	OPS+	BR/A	RC	RC/G	FR	G/POS	WS	TPW
• HARLEY, Dick	Richard Joseph Harley b: 9/25/1872, Philadelphia, PA d: 4/3/1952, Philadelphia, PA BL/TR, 5'10.5", 165 lbs. Deb: 6/2/1897 Career OF: 539-93-106																							
1897 StL-N	90	333	43	96	6	4	3	35	36	....	23	....	.288	.376	.357	.734	96	0	56	6.06	0	*O-89(1-88-0)	7	-0.5
1898 StL-N	142	549	74	135	6	5	0	42	34	....	13	....	.246	.316	.275	.591	68	-22	54	3.40	9	*O-141(135-5-1)	5	-2.4
1899 Cle-N	142	567	70	142	15	7	1	50	40	....	15	....	.250	.315	.307	.621	76	-17	61	3.80	-2	*O-142(140-0-2)	2	-2.8
1900 Cin-N	5	21	2	9	1	0	0	5	1	....	4	....	.429	.455	.476	.931	161	2	7	12.50	-1	/O-5(5-0-0)	1	0.0
1901 Cin-N	133	535	69	146	13	2	4	27	31	....	37	....	.273	.323	.327	.651	95	-3	73	4.70	-7	*O-133(133-0-0)	10	-1.8
1902 Det-A	125	491	59	138	9	8	2	44	36	....	20	....	.281	.345	.344	.689	90	-6	68	4.98	1	*O-125(125-0-0)	11	-1.1
1903 Chi-N	104	386	72	89	9	1	0	33	45	....	27	....	.231	.328	.259	.587	70	-12	45	3.81	2	*O-103(0-0-103)	9	-1.4
Total 7	**741**	**2882**	**389**	**755**	**59**	**27**	**10**	**236**	**223**	**....**	**139**	**....**	**.262**	**.332**	**.312**	**.643**	**83**	**-57**	**363**	**4.40**	**1**	**O-738**	**45**	**-10.0**
• HARLOW, Larry	Larry Duane Harlow b: 11/13/1951, Colorado Springs, CO BL/TL, 6'2", 185 lbs. Deb: 9/20/1975 Career OF: 39-258-113																							
1975 Bal-A	4	3	1	1	0	0	0	0	0	1	0	0	.333	.333	.333	.667	95	-0	0	4.50	0	/O-4(2-2-0)	0	0.0
1977 Bal-A	46	48	4	10	0	1	0	0	5	8	6	1	.208	.283	.250	.533	50	-2	4	2.96	-3	O-38(0-37-1)	1	-0.6
1978 Bal-A	147	460	67	112	25	1	8	26	55	72	14	11	.243	.326	.354	.680	97	-2	53	3.84	-3	*O-138(0-135-3)/P-1	12	-1.2
1979 Bal-A	38	41	5	11	1	0	0	1	7	4	1	3	.268	.375	.293	.668	86	-2	4	3.67	-1	O-31(0-12-22)/D-1	1	-0.3
*Cal-A	62	159	22	37	8	2	0	14	25	34	1	3	.233	.344	.308	.652	80	-4	18	3.80	0	O-58(11-33-15)	3	-0.5
Yr.	100	200	27	48	9	2	0	15	32	38	2	6	.240	.350	.305	.655	81	-6	22	3.77	-1	O-89(11-45-37)/D-1	4	-0.8
1980 Cal-A	109	301	47	83	13	4	4	27	48	61	3	2	.276	.377	.385	.763	112	7	45	5.15	2	O-94(5-32-59)/1-1,D-1	10	0.5
1981 Cal-A	43	82	13	17	1	0	0	4	16	25	1	1	.207	.337	.220	.556	63	-3	7	2.62	-1	O-39(21-7-13)	1	-0.6
Total 6	**449**	**1094**	**159**	**271**	**48**	**8**	**12**	**72**	**156**	**205**	**26**	**21**	**.248**	**.344**	**.339**	**.683**	**94**	**-7**	**132**	**4.04**	**-6**	**O-402/D-2,1-1,P-1**	**28**	**-2.7**
• HARMON, Chuck	Charles Byron Harmon b: 4/23/1924, Washington, IN BR/TR, 6'2", 175 lbs. Deb: 4/17/1954 Career OF: 57-10-18																							
1954 Cin-N	94	286	39	68	7	3	2	25	17	27	7	3	.238	.283	.304	.587	51	-20	26	2.96	8	3-67/1-3	3	-1.2
1955 Cin-N	96	198	31	50	6	3	5	28	26	24	9	9	.253	.348	.389	.737	90	-4	27	4.43	-1	3-39,O-32(32-2-0)/1-4	5	-0.7
1956 Cin-N	13	4	2	0	0	0	0	0	0	0	1	0	.000	.000	.000	.000	-94	-1	0	.00	0	/O-6(1-1-4),1-2	0	-0.2
StL-N	20	15	2	0	0	0	0	0	2	2	0	0	.000	.118	.000	.118	-65	-4	0	.11	-1	O-11(3-4-5)/1-2,3-1	0	-0.5
Yr.	33	19	4	0	0	0	0	0	2	2	1	0	.000	.095	.000	.095	-70	-4	0	.09	-2	O-17(4-5-9)/1-4,3-1	0	-0.6
1957 StL-N	9	3	2	1	0	1	0	1	0	0	1	0	.333	.333	1.000	1.333	235	1	1	15.84	0	/O-8(0-1-7)	0	0.0
Phi-N	57	86	14	22	2	1	0	5	1	4	7	2	.256	.264	.302	.567	53	-5	6	2.42	-1	O-25(21-2-2)/3-5,1-2	1	-0.7
Yr.	66	89	16	23	2	2	0	6	1	4	8	2	.258	.267	.326	.593	59	-4	7	2.80	-1	O-33(21-3-9)/3-5,1-2	1	-0.7
Total 4	**289**	**592**	**90**	**141**	**15**	**8**	**7**	**59**	**46**	**57**	**25**	**14**	**.238**	**.298**	**.326**	**.624**	**62**	**-33**	**60**	**3.32**	**5**	**3-112/O-82,1-13**	**9**	**-3.2**
• HARMON, Terry	Terry Walter Harmon b: 4/12/1944, Toledo, OH BR/TR, 6'2", 180 lbs. Deb: 7/23/1967																							
1967 Phi-N	2	0	0	0	0	0	0	0	0	0	0	0	....	....	....	....	-99	0	0	....	0	....	0	0.0
1969 Phi-N	87	201	25	48	8	1	0	16	22	31	1	2	.239	.323	.289	.612	74	-7	20	3.32	4	S-38,2-19/3-2	5	0.3
1970 Phi-N	71	129	16	32	2	4	0	7	12	22	6	3	.248	.317	.326	.642	75	-5	14	3.76	-2	S-35,2-14/3-2	4	-0.4
1971 Phi-N	79	221	27	45	4	2	0	12	20	45	3	2	.204	.282	.240	.521	49	-14	17	2.51	3	2-58/S-9,3-3,1-2	3	-0.8
1972 Phi-N	73	218	35	62	8	2	2	13	29	28	3	2	.284	.373	.367	.740	108	4	32	5.36	-3	2-50,S-15/3-5	8	0.5
1973 Phi-N	72	148	17	31	3	0	0	8	13	14	1	0	.209	.278	.230	.508	41	-11	10	2.18	-2	2-43,S-19/3-1	1	-1.1
1974 Phi-N	27	15	5	2	0	0	0	0	3	3	0	0	.133	.278	.133	.411	17	-2	1	1.72	-3	/S-7,2-5	0	-0.4
1975 Phi-N	48	72	14	13	1	2	0	5	9	13	0	0	.181	.280	.250	.530	46	-5	5	2.17	-3	S-25/2-7,3-1	1	-0.6
1976*Phi-N	42	61	12	18	4	1	0	6	3	10	3	0	.295	.328	.393	.722	101	1	8	4.87	-1	S-19,2-13/3-5	3	0.1
1977 Phi-N	46	60	13	11	1	0	2	5	6	9	0	2	.183	.269	.300	.569	50	-5	4	2.09	-3	2-28,S-16/3-3	1	-0.7
Total 10	**547**	**1125**	**164**	**262**	**31**	**12**	**4**	**72**	**117**	**175**	**17**	**11**	**.233**	**.312**	**.292**	**.605**	**69**	**-45**	**112**	**3.31**	**-10**	**2-237,S-183/3-22,1-2**	**26**	**-3.0**
• HARPER, Brian	Brian David Harper b: 10/16/1959, Los Angeles, CA BR/TR, 6'2", 195 lbs. Deb: 9/29/1979 Career OF: 78-0-38																							
1979 Cal-A	1	2	0	0	0	0	0	0	0	1	0	0	.000	.000	.000	.000	-103	-1	0	.00	0	/D-1	0	-0.1
1981 Cal-A	4	11	1	3	0	0	0	1	0	0	1	0	.273	.273	.273	.545	58	-0	1	3.03	0	/O-2(1-0-1),D-1	0	-0.1
1982 Pit-N	20	29	4	8	1	0	2	4	1	4	0	0	.276	.300	.517	.817	121	1	4	4.70	0	/O-8(0-0-8)	1	0.0
1983 Pit-N	61	131	16	29	4	1	7	20	2	15	0	0	.221	.239	.427	.666	79	-5	12	3.02	-1	O-35(33-0-2)/1-1	1	-0.7
1984 Pit-N	46	112	4	29	4	0	2	11	5	11	0	0	.259	.303	.348	.651	82	-3	11	3.36	1	O-37(34-0-4)/C-2	2	-0.3
1985*StL-N	43	52	5	13	4	0	0	8	2	3	0	0	.250	.278	.327	.605	69	-2	4	2.74	-1	O-13(7-0-6)/3-6,C-2,1-1	1	-0.4
1986 Det-A	19	36	2	5	1	0	0	3	3	3	0	0	.139	.205	.167	.372	3	-5	1	1.06	0	O-11(0-0-11)/D-6,1-2,C-2	0	-0.6
1987 Oak-A	11	17	1	4	1	0	0	3	0	4	0	0	.235	.235	.294	.529	42	-1	1	1.61	0	/D-7,O-1	0	-0.2
1988 Min-A	60	166	15	49	11	1	3	20	10	12	0	3	.295	.346	.428	.774	112	1	20	3.91	-1	C-48/D-5,3-2	3	0.2
1989 Min-A	126	385	43	125	24	0	8	57	13	16	2	4	.325	.356	.449	.806	118	7	57	5.45	-4	*C-101,D-19/O-3(0-0-3),1-2,3	14	0.8
1990 Min-A	134	479	61	141	42	3	6	54	19	27	3	2	.294	.331	.432	.763	105	2	62	4.58	0	*C-120,D-11/3-3,1-2	14	0.9
1991*Min-A	123	441	54	137	28	1	10	69	14	22	1	2	.311	.341	.447	.787	111	4	62	5.10	-10	*C-119/D-2,1-1,O-1	15	0.2
1992 Min-A	140	502	58	154	25	0	9	73	26	22	0	1	.307	.350	.410	.760	109	5	68	4.93	-8	*C-133/D-2	12	0.5
1993 Min-A	147	530	52	161	26	1	12	73	29	29	1	3	.304	.350	.425	.775	107	3	74	5.13	-4	*C-134/D-7	17	0.8
1994 Mil-A	64	251	23	73	15	0	4	32	9	18	0	2	.291	.323	.398	.722	81	-9	29	4.15	2	D-36,C-25/O-3(1-0-3)	3	-0.7
1995 Oak-A	2	7	0	0	0	0	0	0	0	1	0	0	.000	.000	.000	.000	-107	-2	0	.00	0	/C-2	0	-0.2
Total 16	**1001**	**3151**	**339**	**931**	**186**	**7**	**63**	**428**	**133**	**188**	**8**	**17**	**.295**	**.333**	**.419**	**.752**	**102**	**-5**	**408**	**4.58**	**-28**	**C-688,O-114/D-97,3-13,1-9**	**83**	**0.3**
• HARPER, George	George Washington Harper b: 6/24/1892, Arlington, KY d: 8/18/1978, Magnolia, AR BL/TR, 5'8", 167 lbs. Deb: 4/15/1916 Career OF: 223-113-607																							
1916 Det-A	44	56	4	9	1	0	0	3	5	8	0	....	.161	.230	.179	.408	22	-5	2	1.33	-3	O-14(2-4-8)	0	-1.0
1917 Det-A	47	117	6	24	3	0	0	12	11	15	2	....	.205	.290	.231	.521	59	-5	9	2.29	-3	O-31(0-3-28)	1	-1.1
1918 Det-A	69	227	19	55	5	2	0	16	18	14	3	....	.242	.301	.282	.583	79	-6	21	2.86	-5	O-64(0-1-63)	3	-1.6
1922 Cin-N	128	430	67	146	22	8	2	68	35	22	11	10	.340	.397	.442	.839	118	12	75	6.49	2	*O-109(1-5-103)	17	0.5
1923 Cin-N	61	125	14	32	4	2	3	16	11	9	0	2	.256	.316	.392	.708	88	-3	15	4.09	-1	O-29(9-17-3)	3	-0.5
1924 Cin-N	28	74	7	20	3	0	0	3	13	5	1	3	.270	.393	.311	.704	92	-1	10	4.35	1	O-22(12-10-0)	2	-0.1
Phi-N	109	411	68	121	26	6	16	55	38	23	10	11	.294	.361	.504	.865	115	7	72	6.18	2	*O-109(0-3-107)	11	0.1
Yr.	137	485	75	141	29	6	16	58	51	28	11	14	.291	.366	.474	.841	112	7	82	5.89	3	*O-131(12-13-107)	13	0.0
1925 Phi-N	132	495	86	173	35	7	18	97	28	32	10	8	.349	.391	.558	.949	128	19	105	8.08	-5	*O-126(36-61-33)	18	0.6
1926 Phi-N	56	194	32	61	6	5	7	38	16	7	6	....	.314	.367	.505	.872	126	7	35	6.51	-4	O-55(44-8-8)	7	-0.1
1927 NY-N	145	483	85	160	19	6	16	87	84	27	7	....	.331	.435	.495	.930	149	38	106	8.02	2	*O-142(0-0-142)	26	2.9
1928 NY-N	19	57	11	13	1	0	2	7	10	4	1	....	.228	.353	.351	.704	84	-1	8	4.22	2	O-18(0-0-18)	2	0.0
*StL-N	99	272	41	83	8	2	17	58	51	15	2	....	.305	.418	.537	.955	145	20	62	8.02	1	O-84(0-0-84)	14	1.4
Yr.	118	329	52	96	9	2	19	65	61	19	3	....	.292	.407	.505	.912	135	19	70	7.30	3	*O-102(0-0-102)	16	1.4
1929 Bos-N	136	457	65	133	25	5	10	68	69	27	5	....	.291	.389	.433	.822	108	8	79	6.15	2	*O-130(119-1-10)	14	0.0
Total 11	**1073**	**3398**	**505**	**1030**	**158**	**43**	**91**	**528**	**389**	**208**	**58**	**34**	**.303**	**.380**	**.455**	**.836**	**117**	**89**	**597**	**6.24**	**-8**	**O-933**	**118**	**1.1**
• HARPER, Terry	Terry Joe Harper b: 8/19/1955, Douglasville, GA BR/TR, 6'4", 195 lbs. Deb: 9/12/1980 Career OF: 315-4-121																							
1980 Atl-N	21	54	3	10	2	1	0	3	6	5	2	1	.185	.279	.259	.538	49	-4	4	2.43	-1	O-18(15-1-3)	0	-0.6
1981 Atl-N	40	73	9	19	1	0	2	8	11	17	5	1	.260	.357	.356	.713	100	1	10	4.73	0	O-27(9-0-18)	2	0.0
1982*Atl-N	48	150	16	43	3	0	2	16	14	28	7	4	.287	.352	.347	.698	92	-1	19	4.31	1	O-41(29-1-16)	4	-0.3
1983 Atl-N	80	201	19	53	13	1	3	26	20	43	6	5	.264	.333	.383	.716	91	-3	24	4.09	-0	O-60(28-2-32)	4	-0.6
1984 Atl-N	40	102	4	16	3	1	0	8	4	21	4	1	.157	.196	.206	.402	12	-12	3	.93	2	O-29(28-0-1)	1	-1.2
1985 Atl-N	138	492	58	130	15	2	17	72	44	76	9	9	.264	.328	.407	.735	98	-4	62	4.34	0	*O-131(129-0-2)	11	-1.0
1986 Atl-N	106	265	26	68	12	0	8	30	29	39	3	6	.257	.332	.392	.725	94	-4	30	3.74	-1	O-83(66-0-25)	4	-0.9
1987 Det-A	31	64	4	13	3	0	3	10	9	8	1	0	.203	.301	.391	.692	85	-1	8	3.84	-1	D-15,O-14(1-0-13)	1	-0.3
Pit-N	36	66	8	19	3	0	1	7	7	11	0	1	.288	.356	.379	.735	94	-1	7	3.46	0	O-20(10-0-11)	1	-0.2
Total 8	**540**	**1467**	**147**	**371**	**55**	**5**	**36**	**180**	**144**	**248**	**37**	**28**	**.253**	**.323**	**.371**	**.694**	**88**	**-29**	**167**	**3.80**	**0**	**O-423/D-15**	**28**	**-4.9**
• HARPER, Tommy	Tommy Harper b: 10/14/1940, Oak Grove, LA BR/TR, 5'9", 168 lbs. Deb: 4/9/1962 C Career OF: 683-258-348																							
1962 Cin-N	6	23	1	4	0	0	0	1	2	6	1	0	.174	.240	.174	.414	13	-3	1	1.36	0	/3-6	0	-0.3
1963 Cin-N	129	408	67	106	12	3	10	37	44	72	12	1	.260	.336	.377	.714	102	5	54	4.53	-2	*O-118(1-23-94)/3-1	13	-0.6
1964 Cin-N	102	317	42	77	5	2	4	22	39	56	24	3	.243	.328	.309	.637	78	-4	37	3.83	2	O-92(88-4-0)/3-2	8	-0.7
1965 Cin-N	159	646	**126**	166	28	3	18	64	78	127	35	6	.257	.342	.393	.735	99	6	94	4.92	-4	*O-159(156-5-0)/3-2,2-1	18	-0.7
1966 Cin-N	149	553	85	154	22	5	5	31	57	85	29	10	.278	.349	.363	.713	90	-3	74	4.74	-7	*O-147(73-25-95)	15	-2.0

YEAR TM-L	G	AB	R	H	2B	3B	HR	RBI	BB	SO	SB	CS	AVG	OBP	SLG	OPS	OPS+	BR/A	RC	RC/G	FR	G/POS	WS	TPW
1967 Cin-N	103	365	55	82	17	3	7	22	43	51	23	8	.225	.306	.345	.652	77	-9	42	3.81	0	*0-100(2-4-97)	10	-1.7
1968 Cle-A	130	235	26	51	15	2	6	26	26	56	11	7	.217	.298	.374	.672	104	0	26	3.57	-3	*0-115(67-7-46)/2-2	7	-0.7
1969 Sea-A	148	537	78	126	10	2	9	41	95	90	**73**	18	.235	.351	.311	.662	88	4	71	4.34	-14	2-59,3-59,0-26(3-22-1)	17	-0.8
1970 Mil-A★	154	604	104	179	35	4	31	82	77	107	38	16	.296	.380	.522	.901	145	39	122	7.23	4	*3-128,2-22,0-13(8-5-2)	33	4.5
1971 Mil-A	152	585	79	151	26	3	14	52	65	92	25	3	.258	.333	.385	.718	104	8	82	5.04	-13	0-90(77-13-2),3-70/2-1	20	-1.1
1972 Bos-A	144	556	92	141	29	2	14	49	67	104	25	7	.254	.343	.388	.732	111	12	81	5.05	-5	*0-144(0-144-0)	24	0.5
1973 Bos-A	147	566	92	159	23	3	17	71	61	93	**54**	14	.281	.352	.422	.774	111	14	91	5.60	3	*0-143(139-5-0)/D-1	21	1.0
1974 Bos-A	118	443	66	105	15	3	5	24	46	65	28	12	.237	.313	.318	.631	77	-11	47	3.45	-3	0-61(61-0-0),D-51	6	-2.0
1975 Cal-A	89	285	40	68	10	1	3	31	38	51	19	8	.239	.332	.312	.645	89	-2	32	3.59	-1	D-57,1-19/0-9(2-0-7)	6	-0.6
*Oak-A	34	69	11	22	4	0	2	7	5	9	7	0	.319	.373	.464	.837	139	5	12	6.70	-3	1-16/0-9(5-1-4),D-3,3-2	4	0.1
Yr.	123	354	51	90	14	1	5	38	43	60	26	8	.254	.340	.342	.682	98	3	44	4.13	-4	D-60,1-35,0-18(7-1-11)/3-2	10	-0.5
1976 Bal-A	46	77	8	18	5	0	1	7	10	16	4	3	.234	.322	.338	.660	99	-0	9	3.59	0	D-27/1-1,0-1	2	-0.1
Total 15	**1810**	**6269**	**972**	**1609**	**256**	**36**	**146**	**567**	**753**	**1080**	**408**	**116**	**.257**	**.340**	**.379**	**.719**	**100**	**61**	**876**	**4.76**	**-47**	***0-1227,3-270,D-139/2-85,1**	**204**	**-5.3**

• HARRAH, Toby Colbert Dale Harrah b: 10/26/1948, Sissonville, WV BR/TR, 6', 180 lbs. Deb: 9/5/1969 M/C

YEAR TM-L	G	AB	R	H	2B	3B	HR	RBI	BB	SO	SB	CS	AVG	OBP	SLG	OPS	OPS+	BR/A	RC	RC/G	FR	G/POS	WS	TPW
1969 Was-A	8	1	4	0	0	0	0	0	0	0	0	0	.000	.000	.000	.000	-105	-0	0	.00	-1	/S-1	0	-0.1
1971 Was-A	127	383	45	88	11	3	2	22	40	48	10	9	.230	.303	.290	.592	73	-15	33	2.84	-5	*S-116/3-7	7	-0.9
1972 Tex-A★	116	374	47	97	14	3	1	31	34	31	16	7	.259	.321	.321	.642	95	-1	41	3.73	-10	*S-106	13	0.1
1973 Tex-A	118	461	64	120	16	1	10	50	46	49	10	3	.260	.330	.364	.694	100	1	56	4.18	-3	S-76,3-52	13	0.7
1974 Tex-A	161	573	79	149	23	2	21	74	50	65	15	14	.260	.322	.417	.739	114	6	72	4.19	-5	*S-158/3-3	20	2.1
1975 Tex-A★	151	522	81	153	24	1	20	93	98	71	23	9	.293	.406	.458	.864	145	37	105	7.19	0	*S-118,3-28,2-21	32	5.3
1976 Tex-A★	155	584	64	152	21	1	15	67	91	59	8	5	.260	.363	.377	.740	114	14	82	4.78	5	*S-146/3-5,D-4	24	3.8
1977 Tex-A	159	539	90	142	25	5	27	87	**109**	73	27	5	.263	.397	.479	.875	136	36	112	7.05	-27	*3-159/S-1	25	0.7
1978 Tex-A	139	450	56	103	17	3	12	59	83	66	31	8	.229	.351	.360	.711	100	7	65	4.66	-9	3-91,S-49	15	0.2
1979 Cle-A	149	527	99	147	25	1	20	77	89	60	20	9	.279	.391	.444	.835	124	23	98	6.50	-21	*3-127,S-33/D-9	24	0.2
1980 Cle-A	160	561	100	150	22	4	11	72	98	60	17	2	.267	.383	.380	.763	109	15	89	5.48	4	*3-156/D-3,S-2	23	1.8
1981 Cle-A	103	361	64	105	12	4	5	44	57	44	12	1	.291	.389	.388	.777	126	18	60	6.01	-15	*3-101/S-3,D-1	18	0.1
1982 Cle-A★	162	602	100	183	29	4	25	78	84	52	17	3	.304	.400	.490	.890	143	42	123	7.49	-16	*3-159/2-3,S-2	28	2.4
1983 Cle-A	138	526	81	140	23	1	9	53	75	49	16	10	.266	.365	.365	.730	98	1	73	4.73	-15	*3-137/2-1,D-1	16	-1.5
1984 NY-A	88	253	40	55	9	4	1	26	42	28	3	0	.217	.333	.296	.630	79	-5	27	3.44	2	3-74/2-4,D-2,0-1	5	-0.3
1985 Tex-A	126	396	65	107	18	1	9	44	113	60	11	4	.270	.437	.389	.826	127	24	80	7.11	-5	*2-122/S-2,D-1	17	2.5
1986 Tex-A	95	289	36	63	18	2	7	41	44	53	2	5	.218	.325	.367	.692	86	-7	35	3.84	-11	2-93	7	-1.3
Total 17	**2155**	**7402**	**1115**	**1954**	**307**	**40**	**195**	**918**	**1153**	**868**	**238**	**94**	**.264**	**.368**	**.395**	**.763**	**114**	**197**	**1152**	**5.32**	**-132**	***3-1099,S-813,2-244/D-21,0**	**287**	**15.8**

• HARRELL, Billy William Harrell b: 7/18/1928, Norristown, PA BR/TR, 6'1.5", 180 lbs. Deb: 9/2/1955

YEAR TM-L	G	AB	R	H	2B	3B	HR	RBI	BB	SO	SB	CS	AVG	OBP	SLG	OPS	OPS+	BR/A	RC	RC/G	FR	G/POS	WS	TPW
1955 Cle-A	13	19	2	8	0	0	0	1	3	3	1	0	.421	.500	.421	.921	144	2	5	11.41	0	S-11	1	0.2
1957 Cle-A	22	57	6	15	1	1	1	5	4	7	3	1	.263	.311	.368	.680	86	-1	7	4.30	-3	S-14/3-6,2-1	2	-0.3
1958 Cle-A	101	229	36	50	4	0	7	19	15	36	12	2	.218	.272	.328	.600	66	-9	22	3.13	1	3-46,S-45/2-7,0-1	4	-0.5
1961 Bos-A	37	37	10	6	2	0	0	1	1	8	1	0	.162	.184	.216	.400	6	-5	1	1.17	-1	3-10/S-7,1-3	0	-0.5
Total 4	**173**	**342**	**54**	**79**	**7**	**1**	**8**	**26**	**23**	**54**	**17**	**3**	**.231**	**.283**	**.327**	**.611**	**68**	**-13**	**35**	**3.42**	**-2**	**/S-77,3-62,2-8,1-3,0-1**	**7**	**-1.1**

• HARRELL, John John Robert Harrell b: 11/27/1947, Long Beach, CA BR/TR, 6'2", 190 lbs. Deb: 10/1/1969

YEAR TM-L	G	AB	R	H	2B	3B	HR	RBI	BB	SO	SB	CS	AVG	OBP	SLG	OPS	OPS+	BR/A	RC	RC/G	FR	G/POS	WS	TPW
1969 SF-N	2	6	0	3	0	0	0	2	2	1	0	0	.500	.625	.500	1.125	223	1	2	19.80	0	/C-2	1	0.2

• HARRELSON, Bud Derrel McKinley Harrelson b: 6/6/1944, Niles, CA BB/TR, 5'11", 160 lbs. Deb: 9/2/1965 M/C

YEAR TM-L	G	AB	R	H	2B	3B	HR	RBI	BB	SO	SB	CS	AVG	OBP	SLG	OPS	OPS+	BR/A	RC	RC/G	FR	G/POS	WS	TPW
1965 NY-N	19	37	3	4	1	1	0	0	2	11	0	0	.108	.154	.189	.343	-4	-5	1	.95	-2	S-18	0	-0.6
1966 NY-N	33	99	20	22	2	4	0	4	13	23	7	3	.222	.313	.323	.636	79	-2	11	3.55	1	S-29	3	0.1
1967 NY-N	151	540	59	137	16	4	1	28	48	64	12	13	.254	.319	.304	.623	80	-15	54	3.36	4	*S-149	13	0.2
1968 NY-N	111	402	38	88	7	3	0	14	29	68	4	5	.219	.273	.251	.524	58	-21	28	2.35	2	*S-106	6	-1.1
1969*NY-N	123	395	42	98	11	6	0	24	54	54	1	3	.248	.341	.306	.648	81	-9	44	3.81	10	*S-119	14	1.7
1970 NY-N★	157	564	72	137	18	8	1	42	95	74	23	4	.243	.355	.309	.663	79	-9	72	4.22	8	*S-156	17	1.7
1971 NY-N★	142	547	55	138	16	6	0	32	53	59	28	7	.252	.321	.303	.624	79	-11	59	3.65	24	*S-140	19	3.2
1972 NY-N	115	418	54	90	10	4	1	24	58	57	12	4	.215	.315	.266	.581	68	-14	40	3.07	3	*S-115	13	0.2
1973*NY-N	106	356	35	92	12	3	0	20	48	49	5	1	.258	.348	.309	.657	85	-5	42	4.16	1	*S-103	13	0.9
1974 NY-N	106	331	48	75	10	0	1	13	71	39	9	4	.227	.366	.266	.632	80	-4	39	3.86	18	S-97	14	2.7
1975 NY-N	34	73	5	16	2	0	0	3	12	13	0	0	.219	.329	.247	.576	65	-3	7	3.02	0	S-34	1	0.0
1976 NY-N	118	359	34	84	12	4	1	26	63	56	9	3	.234	.351	.298	.649	91	-0	44	4.15	-4	*S-117	13	1.0
1977 NY-N	107	269	25	48	6	2	1	12	27	28	5	4	.178	.256	.227	.483	32	-26	17	1.94	3	S-98	4	-1.4
1978 Phi-N	71	103	16	22	1	0	0	9	18	21	5	2	.214	.331	.223	.554	57	-5	10	3.03	6	2-43,S-15	3	0.3
1979 Phi-N	53	71	7	20	6	0	0	7	13	14	3	3	.282	.400	.366	.766	107	1	11	5.27	-3	2-25,S-17/3-9,0-1	3	-0.1
1980 Tex-A	87	180	26	49	6	0	1	9	29	23	4	4	.272	.373	.322	.695	95	-0	24	4.31	-5	S-87/2-2	5	0.2
Total 16	**1533**	**4744**	**539**	**1120**	**136**	**45**	**7**	**267**	**633**	**653**	**127**	**60**	**.236**	**.329**	**.288**	**.617**	**75**	**-129**	**502**	**3.52**	**66**	***S-1400/2-70,3-9,0-1**	**141**	**9.0**

• HARRELSON, Ken Kenneth Smith "Hawk" Harrelson b: 9/4/1941, Woodruff, SC BR/TR, 6'2", 190 lbs. Deb: 6/9/1963 Career OF: 70-0-296

YEAR TM-L	G	AB	R	H	2B	3B	HR	RBI	BB	SO	SB	CS	AVG	OBP	SLG	OPS	OPS+	BR/A	RC	RC/G	FR	G/POS	WS	TPW
1963 KC-A	79	226	16	52	10	1	6	23	23	58	1	1	.230	.301	.363	.664	82	-6	23	3.25	-2	1-34,0-28(28-0-0)	3	-1.2
1964 KC-A	49	139	15	27	5	0	7	12	13	34	0	1	.194	.263	.381	.644	74	-6	12	2.78	2	0-24(24-0-0),1-15	1	-0.6
1965 KC-A	150	483	61	115	17	3	23	66	66	112	9	7	.238	.331	.429	.759	116	9	65	4.42	0	*1-125/0-4(3-0-1)	13	0.2
1966 KC-A	63	210	24	47	5	0	5	22	27	59	9	2	.224	.312	.319	.631	85	-2	23	3.63	5	1-58/0-3(3-0-1)	5	-0.1
Was-A	71	250	25	62	8	1	7	28	26	53	4	1	.248	.321	.372	.693	100	1	30	3.96	-3	1-70	7	-0.7
Yr.	134	460	49	109	13	1	12	50	53	112	13	3	.237	.317	.348	.665	93	-2	52	3.81	1	*1-128/0-3(3-0-1)	12	-0.9
1967 Was-A	26	79	10	16	0	0	3	10	7	15	1	0	.203	.267	.316	.584	75	-2	6	2.52	-1	1-23	1	-0.5
KC-A	61	174	23	53	11	0	6	30	17	17	8	2	.305	.366	.471	.838	150	12	31	6.44	1	1-45	8	1.1
*Bos-A	23	80	9	16	4	1	3	14	5	12	1	1	.200	.247	.388	.635	78	-3	7	2.76	-1	0-23(0-0-23)/1-1	1	-0.6
Yr.	110	333	42	85	15	1	12	54	29	44	10	3	.255	.315	.414	.729	116	7	44	4.49	-1	1-69,0-23(0-0-23)	10	0.0
1968 Bos-A★	150	535	79	147	17	4	35	**109**	69	90	2	6	.275	.360	.518	.877	153	33	94	6.09	1	*0-132(0-0-132),1-19	28	2.6
1969 Bos-A	10	46	6	10	1	0	3	8	4	6	0	1	.217	.280	.435	.715	92	-1	5	3.51	2	1-10	1	0.0
Cle-A	149	519	83	115	13	4	27	84	95	96	17	8	.222	.344	.418	.762	109	8	76	4.69	0	*0-144(7-0-137),1-16	17	0.0
Yr.	159	565	89	125	14	4	30	92	99	102	17	9	.221	.339	.419	.759	107	7	81	4.59	2	*0-144(7-0-137),1-26	18	0.0
1970 Cle-A	17	39	3	11	1	0	1	1	6	4	0	0	.282	.378	.385	.762	105	1	6	5.48	0	1-13	1	0.0
1971 Cle-A	52	161	20	32	2	0	5	14	24	21	1	0	.199	.303	.304	.607	66	-6	16	3.12	-1	1-40/0-7(5-0-2)	2	-1.2
Total 9	**900**	**2941**	**374**	**703**	**94**	**14**	**131**	**421**	**382**	**577**	**53**	**30**	**.239**	**.328**	**.414**	**.742**	**110**	**37**	**393**	**4.42**	**1**	**1-469,0-365**	**88**	**-1.0**

• HARRINGTON, Andy Andrew Matthew Harrington b: 2/12/1903, Mountain View, CA d: 1/29/1979, Boise, ID BR/TR, 5'11", 170 lbs. Deb: 4/18/1925

YEAR TM-L	G	AB	R	H	2B	3B	HR	RBI	BB	SO	SB	CS	AVG	OBP	SLG	OPS	OPS+	BR/A	RC	RC/G	FR	G/POS	WS	TPW
1925 Det-A	1	1	0	0	0	0	0	0	0	0	0	0	.000	.000	.000	.000	-102	-0	0	.00	0	....	0	0.0

• HARRINGTON, Jerry Jeremiah Peter Harrington b: 8/12/1869, Keokuk, IA d: 4/16/1913, Keokuk, IA BR/TR, 5'11", 220 lbs. Deb: 4/30/1890

YEAR TM-L	G	AB	R	H	2B	3B	HR	RBI	BB	SO	SB	CS	AVG	OBP	SLG	OPS	OPS+	BR/A	RC	RC/G	FR	G/POS	WS	TPW
1890 Cin-N	65	236	25	58	7	1	1	23	15	29	4	....	.246	.299	.297	.596	74	-8	23	3.38	-1	C-65	5	-0.3
1891 Cin-N	92	333	25	76	10	5	2	41	19	34	4	....	.228	.272	.306	.578	68	-15	30	3.10	-3	C-92/3-1	4	-0.9
1892 Cin-N	22	61	6	13	1	0	0	3	6	1	0	....	.213	.284	.230	.513	56	-3	4	2.29	1	C-22/1-1	1	0.0
1893 Lou-N	10	36	4	4	1	0	0	6	3	9	0	....	.111	.179	.139	.318	-16	-6	1	.76	-2	C-10	0	-0.5
Total 4	**189**	**666**	**60**	**151**	**19**	**6**	**3**	**73**	**43**	**73**	**8**	**....**	**.227**	**.278**	**.287**	**.564**	**64**	**-32**	**57**	**2.98**	**-5**	**C-189/1-1,3-1**	**10**	**-1.8**

• HARRINGTON, Joe Joseph C. Harrington b: 12/21/1869, Fall River, MA d: 9/13/1933, Fall River, MA BR/TR, 5'8.5", 162 lbs. Deb: 9/10/1895

YEAR TM-L	G	AB	R	H	2B	3B	HR	RBI	BB	SO	SB	CS	AVG	OBP	SLG	OPS	OPS+	BR/A	RC	RC/G	FR	G/POS	WS	TPW
1895 Bos-N	18	65	21	18	0	2	2	13	7	5	3	....	.277	.356	.431	.787	97	-1	12	6.36	0	2-18	2	0.0
1896 Bos-N	54	199	26	40	5	3	1	25	19	17	2	....	.201	.274	.271	.545	41	-18	16	2.64	-5	3-49/S-4,2-1	1	-1.9
Total 2	**72**	**264**	**47**	**58**	**5**	**5**	**3**	**38**	**26**	**22**	**5**	**....**	**.220**	**.295**	**.311**	**.605**	**56**	**-18**	**28**	**3.50**	**-6**	**/3-49,2-19,S-4**	**3**	**-1.9**

• HARRINGTON, Mickey Charles Michael Harrington b: 10/8/1934, Hattiesburg, MS BR/TR, 6'4", 205 lbs. Deb: 7/10/1963

YEAR TM-L	G	AB	R	H	2B	3B	HR	RBI	BB	SO	SB	CS	AVG	OBP	SLG	OPS	OPS+	BR/A	RC	RC/G	FR	G/POS	WS	TPW
1963 Phi-N	1	0	0	0	0	0	0	0	0	0	0	0	....	....	....	....	-101	0	0	....	0	....	0	0.0

YEAR TM-L	G	AB	R	H	2B	3B	HR	RBI	BB	SO	SB	CS	AVG	OBP	SLG	OPS	OPS+	BR/A	RC	RC/G	FR	G/POS	WS	TPW
• HARRIS, Billy	James William Harris b: 11/24/1943, Hamlet, NC BL/TR, 6', 175 lbs. Deb: 6/16/1968																							
1968 Cle-A	38	94	10	20	5	1	0	3	8	22	2	0	.213	.275	.287	.562	71	-3	7	2.44	2	2-27,3-10/S-1	2	0.1
1969 KC-A	5	7	1	2	1	0	0	0	0	1	0	0	.286	.286	.429	.714	97	-0	1	4.63	-0	/2-1	0	0.0
Total 2	43	101	11	22	6	1	0	3	8	23	2	0	.218	.275	.297	.572	73	-3	8	2.57	2	/2-28,3-10,S-1	2	0.1
• HARRIS, Bucky	Stanley Raymond Harris b: 11/8/1896, Port Jervis, NY d: 11/8/1977, Bethesda, MD BR/TR, 5'9.5", 156 lbs. Deb: 8/28/1919 M HOF: 1975																							
1919 Was-A	8	28	0	6	2	0	0	4	1	3	0	....	.214	.267	.286	.552	56	-2	2	2.40	3	/2-8	0	0.1
1920 Was-A	136	506	76	152	26	6	1	68	41	36	16	17	.300	.377	.381	.758	104	3	73	4.92	-2	*2-134	15	0.3
1921 Was-A	154	584	82	169	22	8	0	54	54	39	29	9	.289	.367	.354	.722	89	-3	83	4.87	18	*2-154	20	1.8
1922 Was-A	154	602	95	162	24	8	2	40	52	38	25	11	.269	.341	.346	.687	83	-11	75	4.25	19	*2-154	17	1.2
1923 Was-A	145	532	60	150	21	13	2	70	50	29	23	16	.282	.358	.382	.740	100	-0	74	4.66	4	*2-144/S-1	18	0.8
1924*Was-A	143	544	88	146	28	9	1	58	56	41	20	10	.268	.344	.358	.703	84	-11	72	4.18	8	*2-143	13	0.1
1925*Was-A	144	551	91	158	30	3	1	66	64	21	14	12	.287	.370	.358	.728	87	-9	77	4.58	15	*2-144	16	0.9
1926 Was-A	141	537	94	152	39	9	1	63	58	41	16	11	.283	.363	.395	.757	100	0	80	4.98	3	*2-141	17	0.7
1927 Was-A	128	475	98	127	20	3	1	55	66	33	18	3	.267	.363	.328	.691	81	-7	65	4.50	14	*2-128	13	1.0
1928 Was-A	99	358	34	73	11	5	0	28	27	26	5	2	.204	.264	.263	.526	39	-31	26	2.36	6	2-96/3-1,0-1	4	-2.1
1929 Det-A	7	11	3	1	0	0	0	0	2	2	1	0	.091	.231	.091	.322	-14	-2	1	1.26	-1	/2-4,S-1	0	-0.3
1931 Det-A	4	8	1	1	1	0	0	0	1	1	0	0	.125	.222	.250	.472	23	-1	0	1.83	0	/2-3	0	-0.1
Total 12	1263	4736	722	1297	224	64	9	506	472	310	167	91	.274	.352	.354	.706	87	-75	628	4.40	87	*2-1253/S-2,3-1,0-1	133	4.3
• HARRIS, Candy	Alonzo Harris b: 9/17/1947, Selma, AL BB/TR, 6', 160 lbs. Deb: 4/13/1967																							
1967 Hou-N	6	1	0	0	0	0	0	0	0	1	0	0	.000	.000	.000	.000	-103	-0	0	.00	0	....	0	0.0
• HARRIS, Charlie	Charles Jenkins Harris b: 10/21/1877, Macon, GA d: 3/14/1963, Gainesville, FL BR/TR, 5'8", 200 lbs. Deb: 5/26/1899																							
1899 Bal-N	30	68	16	19	3	0	0	1	3	....	4	....	.279	.319	.324	.643	73	-3	9	4.58	-1	3-21/0-3(2-0-1),2-2,S-1	1	-0.3
• HARRIS, Dave	David Stanley "Sheriff" Harris b: 7/14/1900, Summerfield, NC d: 9/18/1973, Atlanta, GA BR/TR, 5'11", 170 lbs. Deb: 4/14/1925 Career OF: 164-36-186																							
1925 Bos-N	92	340	49	90	8	7	5	36	27	44	6	4	.265	.321	.374	.694	84	-8	41	4.15	6	0-90(87-4-0)	7	-0.8
1928 Bos-N	7	17	2	2	1	0	0	0	2	6	0	....	.118	.211	.176	.387	2	-2	1	1.19	-1	/0-6(6-0-0)	0	-0.4
1930 Chi-A	33	86	16	21	2	1	5	13	7	22	0	0	.244	.309	.465	.774	96	-1	13	4.88	-1	0-23(23-0-0)/2-1	2	-0.3
Was-A	73	205	40	65	19	8	4	44	28	35	6	3	.317	.399	.546	.945	136	12	45	7.90	5	0-59(19-12-28)	10	1.2
Yr.	106	291	56	86	21	9	9	57	35	57	6	3	.296	.373	.522	.895	125	11	58	6.97	4	0-82(42-12-28)/2-1	12	0.8
1931 Was-A	77	231	49	72	14	8	5	50	49	38	7	6	.312	.434	.506	.941	146	18	53	8.41	-1	0-60(3-0-57)	12	1.3
1932 Was-A	81	156	26	51	7	4	6	29	19	34	4	4	.327	.400	.538	.938	143	9	33	7.87	-1	0-34(7-8-20)	7	0.6
1933*Was-A	82	177	33	46	9	2	5	38	25	26	3	1	.260	.358	.418	.776	106	2	28	5.55	-2	0-45(4-11-32)/1-6,3-2	6	-0.1
1934 Was-A	97	235	28	59	14	3	2	37	39	40	2	3	.251	.358	.362	.719	89	-3	32	4.69	3	0-64(15-1-49)/3-5	4	-0.3
Total 7	542	1447	243	406	74	33	32	247	196	245	28	21	.281	.368	.444	.812	112	26	246	5.97	8	0-381/3-7,1-6,2-1	48	1.1
• HARRIS, Donald	Donald Harris b: 11/12/1967, Waco, TX BR/TR, 6'1", 185 lbs. Deb: 9/4/1991 Career OF: 8-49-21																							
1991 Tex-A	18	8	4	3	0	0	1	2	1	3	1	0	.375	.444	.750	1.194	228	2	3	16.27	-1	0-12(2-7-5)/D-3	1	0.0
1992 Tex-A	24	33	3	6	1	0	0	1	0	15	1	0	.182	.182	.212	.394	10	-4	1	1.37	0	0-24(5-15-5)	0	-0.4
1993 Tex-A	40	76	10	15	2	0	1	8	5	18	0	1	.197	.256	.263	.519	41	-7	5	2.25	0	0-38(1-27-11)/D-3	0	-0.7
Total 3	82	117	17	24	3	0	2	11	6	36	2	1	.205	.250	.282	.532	47	-9	10	2.72	-1	/0-74,D-6	1	-1.1
• HARRIS, Frank	Frank Walter Harris b: 11/2/1858, Pittsburgh, PA d: 11/26/1939, East Moline, IL BR/TR Deb: 4/17/1884																							
1884 Alt-U	24	95	10	25	2	1	0	....	3	....	....	....	.263	.286	.305	.591	99	-0	8	3.40	0	1-17/0-7(4-3-1)	1	-0.2
• HARRIS, Gail	Boyd Gail Harris b: 10/15/1931, Abington, VA BL/TL, 6', 195 lbs. Deb: 6/3/1955																							
1955 NY-N	79	263	27	61	9	0	12	36	20	46	0	0	.232	.291	.403	.694	82	-7	30	3.86	-1	1-75	5	-1.3
1956 NY-N	12	38	2	5	0	1	1	1	3	10	0	0	.132	.233	.263	.496	33	-4	3	2.10	0	1-11	0	-0.4
1957 NY-N	90	225	28	54	7	3	9	31	16	28	1	0	.240	.308	.418	.725	93	-2	29	4.44	0	1-61	5	-0.6
1958 Det-A	134	451	63	123	18	8	20	83	36	60	1	2	.273	.332	.481	.813	113	6	70	5.44	-1	*1-122	13	-0.2
1959 Det-A	114	349	39	77	4	3	9	39	29	49	0	1	.221	.292	.327	.618	66	-17	33	3.18	2	1-93	3	-2.0
1960 Det-A	8	5	0	0	0	0	0	0	2	1	0	0	.000	.286	.000	.286	-15	-1	0	.40	0	/1-5	0	-0.1
Total 6	437	1331	159	320	38	15	51	190	106	194	2	3	.240	.306	.406	.713	88	-25	165	4.22	-1	1-367	26	-4.5
• HARRIS, Joe	Joseph "Moon" Harris b: 5/30/1891, Coulters, PA d: 12/10/1959, Plum Borough, PA BR/TR, 5'9", 170 lbs. Deb: 6/9/1914 Career OF: 235-0-84																							
1914 NY-A	2	1	0	0	0	0	0	0	3	1	0	....	.000	.800	.000	.800	143	1	1	7.51	0	/1-1,0-1	0	0.1
1917 Cle-A	112	369	40	112	22	4	0	65	55	32	11	....	.304	.398	.385	.783	129	16	59	5.80	5	1-95/0-5(0-0-5),3-2	16	2.1
1919 Cle-A	62	184	30	69	16	1	1	46	33	21	2	....	.375	.472	.489	.962	160	17	43	9.11	3	1-46/S-4	12	2.1
1922 Bos-A	119	408	53	129	30	9	6	54	30	15	2	6	.316	.364	.478	.842	119	8	69	6.21	6	0-83(71-0-12),1-21	14	0.7
1923 Bos-A	142	483	82	162	28	11	13	76	52	27	7	3	.335	.406	.520	.925	142	30	104	8.14	0	*0-132(132-0-0)/1-9	23	1.9
1924 Bos-A	133	491	82	148	36	9	3	77	81	25	6	1	.301	.406	.430	.835	115	17	92	6.81	5	*1-128/0-3(3-0-0)	16	1.2
1925 Bos-A	8	19	4	3	0	1	1	2	5	5	0	0	.158	.333	.421	.754	90	-0	3	4.70	-1	/1-6	0	-0.1
*Was-A	100	300	60	97	21	9	12	59	51	28	6	3	.323	.430	.573	1.003	156	27	77	9.53	3	1-58,0-41(16-0-25)	17	2.3
Yr.	108	319	64	100	21	10	13	61	56	33	6	3	.313	.424	.564	.988	151	27	80	9.18	3	1-64,0-41(16-0-25)	17	2.2
1926 Was-A	92	257	43	79	13	9	5	55	37	9	2	3	.307	.405	.486	.891	135	14	52	7.30	-1	1-36,0-35(3-0-32)	12	0.8
1927*Pit-N	129	411	57	134	27	9	5	73	48	19	0	....	.326	.402	.472	.874	124	16	78	6.73	2	*1-116/0-3(3-0-0)	16	1.0
1928 Pit-N	16	23	2	9	2	1	0	2	4	2	0	....	.391	.500	.565	1.065	171	3	7	12.35	1	/1-6	2	0.4
Bro-N	55	89	8	21	6	1	1	8	14	4	0	....	.236	.340	.360	.699	84	-2	11	4.26	1	0-16(6-0-10)	2	-0.2
Yr.	71	112	10	30	8	2	1	10	18	6	0	....	.268	.374	.402	.776	102	1	18	5.62	2	0-16(6-0-10)/1-6	4	0.2
Total 10	970	3035	461	963	201	64	47	517	413	188	36	16	.317	.404	.472	.877	131	146	595	7.18	26	1-522,0-319/S-4,3-2	130	12.3
• HARRIS, John	John Thomas Harris b: 9/13/1954, Portland, OR BL/TL, 6'3", 205 lbs. Deb: 9/26/1979 Career OF: 13-0-0																							
1979 Cal-A	1	2	0	0	0	0	0	0	0	0	0	0	.000	.000	.000	.000	-103	-1	0	.00	0	/1-1	0	-0.1
1980 Cal-A	19	41	8	12	5	0	2	7	7	4	0	1	.293	.396	.561	.957	163	3	8	6.77	0	1-10/0-3(3-0-0)	2	0.3
1981 Cal-A	36	77	5	19	3	0	3	9	3	11	0	0	.247	.275	.403	.678	93	-1	7	3.11	-1	1-11,0-10(10-0-0)/D-1	1	-0.3
Total 3	56	120	13	31	8	0	5	16	10	15	0	1	.258	.315	.450	.765	116	2	15	4.29	-1	/1-22,0-13,D-1	3	-0.1
• HARRIS, Lenny	Leonard Anthony Harris b: 10/28/1964, Miami, FL BL/TR, 5'10", 205 lbs. Deb: 9/7/1988 Career OF: 148-3-154																							
1988 Cin-N	16	43	7	16	1	0	0	8	5	4	4	1	.372	.438	.395	.833	135	3	9	7.49	1	3-10/2-6	3	0.4
1989 Cin-N	61	188	17	42	4	0	2	11	9	20	10	6	.223	.263	.277	.539	52	-12	12	2.12	-4	2-32,S-17,3-16	2	-1.5
LA-N	54	147	19	37	6	1	1	15	11	13	4	3	.252	.308	.327	.635	83	-4	12	2.74	-1	0-21(20-0-1),2-14/3-8,S-1	2	-0.5
Yr.	115	335	36	79	10	1	3	26	20	33	14	9	.236	.283	.299	.581	66	-16	25	2.39	-5	2-46,3-24,0-21(20-0-1),S-18	4	-2.1
1990 LA-N	137	431	61	131	16	4	2	29	29	31	15	10	.304	.349	.374	.723	102	-1	55	4.59	2	3-94,2-44/0-2(0-1-1),S-1	14	0.2
1991 LA-N	145	429	59	123	16	1	3	38	37	32	12	3	.287	.350	.350	.700	100	2	52	4.15	-7	*3-113,2-27,S-20/0-1	13	-0.3
1992 LA-N	135	347	28	94	11	0	0	30	24	24	19	7	.271	.320	.303	.622	78	-9	33	3.25	-1	2-81,3-33,0-15(7-0-8),S-10	9	-0.8
1993 LA-N	107	160	20	38	6	1	2	11	15	15	3	1	.238	.303	.325	.628	72	-6	16	3.28	-2	2-35,3-17/S-3,0-2(0-0-2)	4	-0.6
1994 Cin-N	66	100	13	31	3	1	0	14	5	13	7	2	.310	.343	.360	.703	84	-2	13	4.99	-2	3-15/1-4,0-3(0-0-3),2-2	3	-0.4
1995*Cin-N	101	197	32	41	8	3	2	16	14	20	10	1	.208	.261	.310	.570	50	-13	16	2.60	5	3-24,1-23/0-8(4-0-4),2-1	2	-0.9
1996 Cin-N	125	302	33	86	17	2	5	32	21	31	14	6	.285	.333	.404	.737	94	-3	41	4.78	1	0-37(23-1-18),3-24,1-16/2-8	10	-0.4
1997 Cin-N	120	238	32	65	13	1	3	28	18	18	4	3	.273	.329	.374	.703	82	-7	27	3.82	1	0-42(26-0-17),2-20,3-13,1-11	3	-0.7
1998 Cin-N	57	122	12	36	8	0	0	10	8	9	1	3	.295	.344	.361	.704	84	-4	12	3.30	-1	0-32(13-0-20)/P-1	1	-0.5
NY-N	75	168	18	39	7	0	6	17	9	12	5	2	.232	.275	.381	.656	71	-7	16	3.13	-2	0-65(21-1-53),3-10/2-2,1-1,D	2	-1.1
Yr.	132	290	30	75	15	0	6	27	17	21	6	5	.259	.304	.372	.677	77	-11	29	3.20	-2	0-97(34-1-73),3-10/2-2,1-1,D,P	3	-1.6
1999 Col-N	91	158	15	47	12	0	0	13	6	6	1	1	.297	.323	.373	.697	59	-10	17	3.80	-3	2-24,0-14(3-0-11)/3-2,D-2	2	-1.1
*Ari-N	19	29	2	11	1	0	1	7	0	1	1	0	.379	.379	.517	.897	123	1	6	8.36	1	/3-5,0-2(0-0-2)	2	0.2
Yr.	110	187	17	58	13	0	1	20	6	7	2	1	.310	.332	.396	.727	69	-9	23	4.43	-2	2-24,0-16(3-0-13)/3-7,D-2	4	-1.0
2000 Ari-N	36	85	9	16	1	1	1	13	3	5	5	0	.188	.216	.259	.475	19	-10	5	1.69	-2	3-20/0-3(0-0-3),D-1	0	-1.1
*NY-N	76	138	22	42	6	3	3	13	17	17	8	1	.304	.381	.457	.837	115	5	25	6.52	2	3-16,0-11(6-0-5),1-10/2-3	5	0.6

YEAR TM-L	G	AB	R	H	2B	3B	HR	RBI	BB	SO	SB	CS	AVG	OBP	SLG	OPS	OPS+	BR/A	RC	RC/G	FR	G/POS	WS	TPW
Yr.	112	223	31	58	7	4	4	26	20	22	13	1	.260	.321	.381	.702	80	-5	30	4.49	-0	3-36,0-14(6-0-8),1-10/2-3,D	5	-0.5
2001 NY-N	110	135	12	30	5	1	0	9	8	9	3	2	.222	.266	.274	.540	42	-12	9	2.30	-2	3-11/0-8(5-0-3),1-7,D-2,2	0	-1.4
2002 Mil-N	122	197	23	60	8	2	3	17	14	17	4	1	.305	.357	.411	.768	103	1	29	5.45	0	0-16(16-0-0),3-14,1-12/D-2	4	0.0
2003 Chi-N	75	131	11	24	3	0	1	7	13	20	1	0	.183	.257	.229	.486	29	-14	8	2.07	-3	3-35/1-2,0-2(1-0-1)	1	-1.6
*Fla-N	13	14	3	4	0	0	0	1	3	1	0	0	.286	.412	.286	.697	90	0	2	4.14	0	/0-4(2-0-2)	0	0.0
Yr.	88	145	14	28	3	0	1	8	16	21	1	0	.193	.273	.234	.508	35	-14	10	2.26	-3	3-35/0-6(3-0-3),1-2	1	-1.6
Total 16	**1741**	**3759**	**448**	**1013**	**152**	**21**	**35**	**339**	**269**	**318**	**131**	**53**	**.269**	**.321**	**.349**	**.670**	**81**	**-101**	**416**	**3.78**	**-18**	**3-480,2-300,0-288/1-86,S,D,P**	**82**	**-11.8**

• HARRIS, Ned Robert Ned Harris b: 7/9/1916, Ames, IA d: 12/18/1976, West Palm Beach, FL BL/TL, 5'11", 175 lbs. Deb: 4/20/1941 Career OF: 16-6-190

1941 Det-A	26	61	11	13	3	1	1	4	6	13	1	0	.213	.284	.344	.628	59	-4	7	3.71	-1	0-12(12-0-0)	1	-0.4
1942 Det-A	121	398	53	108	16	10	9	45	49	35	5	4	.271	.351	.430	.781	110	5	63	5.59	-6	*0-104(0-0-104)	11	-0.8
1943 Det-A	114	354	43	90	14	3	6	32	47	29	6	8	.254	.343	.362	.705	99	-1	46	4.30	-1	0-96(4-6-86)	10	-1.0
1946 Det-A	1	1	0	0	0	0	0	0	0	0	0	0	.000	.000	.000	.000	-94	-0	0	.00	0	....	0	0.0
Total 4	**262**	**814**	**107**	**211**	**33**	**14**	**16**	**81**	**102**	**77**	**12**	**12**	**.259**	**.342**	**.393**	**.736**	**101**	**-0**	**115**	**4.86**	**-8**	**0-212**	**22**	**-2.2**

• HARRIS, Spencer Anthony Spencer Harris b: 8/12/1900, Duluth, MN d: 7/3/1982, Minneapolis, MN BL/TL, 5'9", 145 lbs. Deb: 4/14/1925 Career OF: 18-28-67

1925 Chi-A	56	92	12	26	2	0	1	13	14	13	1	3	.283	.383	.337	.720	89	-2	12	4.55	0	0-27(1-12-17)	2	-0.2
1926 Chi-A	80	222	36	56	11	3	2	27	20	15	8	3	.252	.317	.356	.673	78	-7	26	3.83	-1	0-63(7-11-48)	4	-1.2
1929 Was-A	6	14	1	3	1	0	0	1	0	3	1	0	.214	.214	.286	.500	27	-1	1	2.13	-0	/0-4(0-4-0)	0	-0.1
1930 Phi-A	22	49	4	9	1	0	0	5	5	2	0	0	.184	.259	.204	.463	18	-6	3	1.87	1	0-13(10-1-2)	0	-0.5
Total 4	**164**	**377**	**53**	**94**	**15**	**3**	**3**	**46**	**39**	**33**	**10**	**6**	**.249**	**.323**	**.329**	**.652**	**71**	**-16**	**43**	**3.66**	**0**	**0-107**	**6**	**-2.1**

• HARRIS, Vic Victor Lanier Harris b: 3/27/1950, Los Angeles, CA BB/TR, 5'11", 170 lbs. Deb: 7/21/1972 Career OF: 28-147-32

1972 Tex-A	61	186	8	26	5	1	0	10	12	39	7	3	.140	.192	.177	.369	11	-20	7	1.16	-1	2-58/S-1	1	-2.0
1973 Tex-A	152	555	71	138	14	7	8	44	55	81	13	12	.249	.319	.342	.661	90	-9	58	3.47	-17	*0-113(2-111-7),3-25,2-18	10	-3.0
1974 Chi-N	62	200	18	39	6	3	0	11	29	26	9	3	.195	.297	.255	.552	53	-11	18	2.76	-15	2-56	2	-2.4
1975 Chi-N	51	56	6	10	0	0	0	5	6	7	0	0	.179	.258	.179	.437	22	-6	3	1.77	-1	0-11(9-2-0)/3-7,2-5	0	-0.7
1976 StL-N	97	259	21	59	12	3	1	19	16	55	1	2	.228	.275	.309	.584	65	-13	21	2.68	-7	2-37,0-35(9-25-1),3-12/S-1	2	-2.0
1977 SF-N	69	165	28	43	12	0	2	14	19	36	2	1	.261	.337	.370	.707	90	-2	22	4.61	-3	2-27,S-11/3-9,0-3(0-2-1)	4	-0.4
1978 SF-N	53	100	8	15	4	0	1	11	11	24	0	0	.150	.234	.220	.454	29	-10	6	1.83	-1	S-22,2-10/0-6(4-2-1)	1	-1.0
1980 Mil-A	34	89	8	19	4	1	1	7	12	13	4	1	.213	.307	.315	.622	73	-3	10	3.52	-1	0-31(4-5-22)/3-2,2-1	1	-0.5
Total 8	**579**	**1610**	**168**	**349**	**57**	**15**	**13**	**121**	**160**	**281**	**36**	**22**	**.217**	**.289**	**.295**	**.584**	**65**	**-74**	**145**	**2.91**	**-47**	**2-212,0-199/3-55,S-35**	**21**	**-11.9**

• HARRIS, Willie William Charles Harris b: 6/22/1978, Cairo, GA BL/TR, 5'9", 175 lbs. Deb: 9/2/2001 Career OF: 0-75-0

2001 Bal-A	9	24	3	3	1	0	0	0	0	7	0	0	.125	.125	.167	.292	-25	-4	1	.67	1	/0-8(0-8-0)	0	-0.4
2002 Chi-A	49	163	14	38	4	0	2	12	9	21	8	0	.233	.273	.294	.568	50	-10	14	2.88	5	2-38/0-6(0-6-0)	2	-0.3
2003 Chi-A	79	137	19	28	3	1	0	5	10	28	12	2	.204	.259	.241	.499	33	-12	10	2.38	3	0-61(0-61-0),2-12	2	-0.8
Total 3	**137**	**324**	**36**	**69**	**8**	**1**	**2**	**17**	**19**	**56**	**20**	**2**	**.213**	**.257**	**.262**	**.519**	**37**	**-26**	**25**	**2.49**	**9**	**/0-75,2-50**	**4**	**-1.4**

• HARRISON, Ben Leo J. Harrison BR Deb: 9/27/1901

1901 Was-A	1	2	0	0	0	0	0	0	1	....	0	....	.000	.333	.000	.333	-2	-0	0	.00	0	/0-1	0	0.0

• HARRISON, Chuck Charles William Harrison b: 4/25/1941, Abilene, TX BR/TR, 5'10", 190 lbs. Deb: 9/15/1965

1965 Hou-N	15	45	2	9	4	0	1	9	8	9	0	0	.200	.321	.356	.676	97	0	6	4.35	0	1-12	1	-0.1
1966 Hou-N	119	434	52	111	23	2	9	52	37	69	2	0	.256	.317	.380	.697	99	0	51	4.08	4	*1-114	10	-0.2
1967 Hou-N	70	177	13	43	7	3	2	26	13	30	0	0	.243	.295	.350	.645	87	-3	18	3.32	-2	1-59	3	-0.9
1969 KC-A	75	213	18	47	5	1	3	18	16	20	1	2	.221	.278	.296	.574	60	-12	17	2.72	1	1-55	2	-1.6
1971 KC-A	49	143	9	31	4	0	2	21	11	19	0	0	.217	.273	.287	.559	59	-8	12	2.72	1	1-39	1	-1.1
Total 5	**328**	**1012**	**94**	**241**	**43**	**6**	**17**	**126**	**85**	**147**	**3**	**2**	**.238**	**.299**	**.343**	**.642**	**83**	**-23**	**104**	**3.47**	**5**	**1-279**	**17**	**-3.8**

• HARRISON, Rit Washington Ritter Harrison b: 9/16/1849, Haverstraw, NY d: 11/7/1888, Bridgeport, CT Deb: 5/20/1875

1875 NH-n	1	4	0	2	1	0	0	1	0	0	0	1	.500	.500	.750	1.250	376	1	2	15.12	0	/C-1,S-1	....	0.0

• HARSHANEY, Sam Samuel Harshaney b: 4/24/1910, Madison, IL d: 2/1/2001, San Antonio, TX BR/TR, 6', 180 lbs. Deb: 9/28/1937

1937 StL-A	5	11	0	1	1	0	0	0	3	0	0	0	.091	.286	.182	.468	20	-1	1	2.02	0	/C-4	0	-0.1
1938 StL-A	11	24	2	7	0	0	0	0	3	2	0	0	.292	.370	.292	.662	68	-1	3	4.07	0	C-10	0	0.0
1939 StL-A	42	145	15	35	2	0	0	15	9	8	0	1	.241	.290	.255	.545	40	-13	10	2.39	1	C-36	1	-0.9
1940 StL-A	3	1	0	0	0	0	0	0	1	0	0	0	.000	.500	.000	.500	41	0	0	3.51	-1	/C-2	0	-0.1
Total 4	**61**	**181**	**17**	**43**	**3**	**0**	**0**	**15**	**16**	**10**	**0**	**1**	**.238**	**.303**	**.254**	**.557**	**42**	**-16**	**14**	**2.59**	**1**	**/C-52**	**1**	**-1.1**

• HARSHMAN, Jack John Elvin Harshman b: 7/12/1927, San Diego, CA BL/TL, 6'2", 185 lbs. Deb: 9/16/1948 ♦

1948 NY-N	5	8	0	2	0	0	0	1	1	3	0	....	.250	.333	.250	.583	60	-0	1	3.39	0	/1-3	0	-0.1
1950 NY-N	9	32	3	4	0	0	2	4	3	6	0	....	.125	.200	.313	.513	32	-3	2	1.39	0	/1-9	0	-0.4
1952 NY-N	3	2	0	0	0	0	0	0	0	0	0	0	.000	.000	.000	.000	-99	-0	0	.00	0	/P-2	0	-0.8
1954 Chi-A	36	56	6	8	1	0	2	5	12	21	0	0	.143	.294	.268	.562	53	3	5	2.72	-1	P-35/1-1	15	1.7
1955 Chi-A	32	60	6	11	1	0	2	8	9	17	0	0	.183	.290	.300	.590	57	4	6	2.64	0	P-32	13	1.2
1956 Chi-A	36	71	8	12	1	0	6	19	11	21	0	0	.169	.280	.437	.717	86	6	10	4.07	-2	P-34	20	2.9
1957 Chi-A	30	45	5	10	1	0	2	5	10	17	0	0	.222	.364	.378	.741	102	5	7	4.80	-3	P-30	7	-0.4
1958 Bal-A	47	82	11	16	1	0	6	14	17	22	0	0	.195	.333	.427	.760	114	11	12	4.79	0	P-34/0-1	22	3.1
1959 Bal-A	15	10	3	2	0	0	1	1	2	2	0	0	.200	.333	.500	.833	128	1	2	6.21	1	P-14	1	-1.5
Bos-A	9	7	1	1	0	0	0	2	2	2	0	0	.143	.333	.143	.476	34	0	1	2.36	-1	/P-8	0	-0.7
Cle-A	21	34	3	7	1	0	0	5	5	4	0	0	.206	.308	.235	.543	53	2	3	2.84	0	P-13	7	0.9
Yr.	45	51	7	10	1	0	1	8	9	8	0	0	.196	.317	.275	.591	64	3	5	3.37	0	P-35	8	-1.3
1960 Cle-A	15	17	0	3	1	0	0	1	0	4	0	0	.176	.176	.235	.412	11	-0	1	1.34	-1	P-15	1	-0.2
Total 10	**258**	**424**	**46**	**76**	**7**	**0**	**21**	**65**	**72**	**119**	**0**	**0**	**.179**	**.298**	**.344**	**.643**	**74**	**28**	**49**	**3.43**	**-5**	**P-217/1-13,0-1**	**86**	**6.0**

• HART, Bill William Woodrow Hart b: 3/4/1913, Wiconisco, PA d: 7/29/1968, Lykins, PA BR/TR, 6', 175 lbs. Deb: 9/18/1943

1943 Bro-N	8	19	0	3	0	0	0	1	1	2	0	....	.158	.200	.158	.358	4	-2	0	.78	1	/3-6,S-1	0	-0.1
1944 Bro-N	29	90	8	16	4	2	0	4	9	7	1	....	.178	.253	.267	.519	47	-6	7	2.25	-2	S-25/3-2	1	-0.7
1945 Bro-N	58	161	27	37	6	2	3	27	14	21	7	....	.230	.291	.348	.639	78	-5	17	3.53	-3	3-39/S-8	3	-0.8
Total 3	**95**	**270**	**35**	**56**	**10**	**4**	**3**	**32**	**24**	**30**	**8**	**....**	**.207**	**.272**	**.307**	**.580**	**62**	**-14**	**24**	**2.87**	**-4**	**/3-47,S-34**	**4**	**-1.5**

• HART, Bo Bodhi J. Hart Hart b: 9/27/1976, Creswell, OR BR/TR, 5'11", 170 lbs. Deb: 6/19/2003

2003 StL-N	77	296	46	82	13	5	4	28	12	64	3	1	.277	.318	.395	.714	88	-6	38	4.55	2	2-69/S-3	7	0.0

• HART, Burt James Burton Hart b: 6/28/1870, Lone Tree Lake, MN d: 1/29/1921, Sacramento, CA BB, 6'3", 200 lbs. Deb: 6/6/1901

1901 Bal-A	58	206	33	64	3	5	0	23	20	....	7	....	.311	.383	.374	.756	106	2	33	6.10	-7	1-58	5	-0.5

• HART, Hub James Henry Hart b: 2/2/1878, Everett, MA d: 10/10/1960, Fort Wayne, IN BL/TR, 5'11", 170 lbs. Deb: 7/16/1905

1905 Chi-A	11	20	3	2	0	0	0	4	3	....	0	....	.100	.217	.100	.317	2	-2	0	.66	-1	/C-7	0	-0.3
1906 Chi-A	17	37	1	6	0	0	0	0	2	....	0	....	.162	.205	.162	.367	16	-4	1	1.14	-2	C-15	0	-0.5
1907 Chi-A	29	70	6	19	1	0	0	7	5	....	1	....	.271	.329	.286	.615	100	0	8	3.69	-3	C-25	2	-0.1
Total 3	**57**	**127**	**10**	**27**	**1**	**0**	**0**	**11**	**10**	**....**	**1**	**....**	**.213**	**.275**	**.220**	**.496**	**60**	**-5**	**9**	**2.38**	**-6**	**/C-47**	**2**	**-0.9**

• HART, Jason Jason Wyatt Hart b: 9/5/1977, Walnut Creek, CA BR/TR, 6'4", 240 lbs. Deb: 8/18/2002

2002 Tex-A	10	15	2	4	3	0	0	0	2	7	0	0	.267	.353	.467	.820	110	0	3	6.51	0	/0-7(7-0-0),1-2	0	0.0

• HART, Jim Ray James Ray Hart b: 10/30/1941, Hookerton, NC BR/TR, 5'11", 185 lbs. Deb: 7/7/1963 Career OF: 257-0-7

1963 SF-N	7	20	1	4	1	0	0	2	3	6	0	0	.200	.360	.250	.610	80	-0	2	3.07	0	/3-7	0	0.0
1964 SF-N	153	566	71	162	15	6	31	81	47	94	5	2	.286	.345	.498	.843	131	23	95	6.03	13	*3-149/0-6(1-0-5)	25	3.8
1965 SF-N	160	591	91	177	30	6	23	96	47	75	6	4	.299	.353	.487	.840	130	23	98	6.00	-8	*3-144,0-15(14-0-1)	25	1.5

YEAR TM-L	G	AB	R	H	2B	3B	HR	RBI	BB	SO	SB	CS	AVG	OBP	SLG	OPS	OPS+	BR/A	RC	RC/G	FR	G/POS	WS	TPW
1966 SF-N★	156	578	88	165	23	4	33	93	48	75	2	5	.285	.344	.510	.855	130	21	92	5.58	-6	*3-139,O-17(16-0-1)	27	1.5
1967 SF-N	158	578	98	167	26	7	29	99	77	100	1	1	.289	.376	.509	.885	153	41	111	6.92	-10	3-89,O-72(72-0-0)	29	3.0
1968 SF-N	136	480	67	124	14	3	23	78	46	74	3	1	.258	.327	.444	.771	130	17	66	4.73	-8	3-72,O-65(65-0-0)	19	0.6
1969 SF-N	95	236	27	60	9	0	3	26	28	49	0	0	.254	.346	.331	.676	92	-1	27	3.98	-2	O-68(68-0-0)/3-3	5	-0.6
1970 SF-N	76	255	30	72	12	1	8	37	30	29	0	0	.282	.365	.431	.796	114	5	38	5.15	-9	3-56,O-18(18-0-0)	7	-0.5
1971*SF-N	31	39	5	10	0	0	2	5	6	8	0	1	.256	.356	.410	.766	118	1	5	4.76	0	/3-3,O-3(3-0-0)	1	0.0
1972 SF-N	24	79	10	24	5	0	5	8	6	10	0	1	.304	.360	.557	.917	155	5	14	6.58	-3	3-20	4	0.2
1973 SF-N	5	3	0	0	0	0	0	1	3	1	0	0	.000	.500	.000	.500	48	0	1	3.76	0	/3-1	0	0.0
NY-A	114	339	29	86	13	2	13	52	36	45	0	2	.254	.325	.419	.744	112	4	42	4.10	0	*D-106	6	0.1
1974 NY-A	10	19	1	1	0	0	0	0	3	7	0	0	.053	.182	.053	.234	-31	-3	0	.49	0	/D-4	0	-0.3
Total 12	**1125**	**3783**	**518**	**1052**	**148**	**29**	**170**	**578**	**380**	**573**	**17**	**17**	**.278**	**.348**	**.467**	**.816**	**128**	**136**	**593**	**5.49**	**-33**	**3-683,O-264,D-110**	**148**	**9.3**

• HART, Mike Michael Lawrence Hart b: 2/17/1958, Milwaukee, WI BL/TL, 5'11", 185 lbs. Deb: 5/8/1984 Career OF: 12-29-4

YEAR TM-L	G	AB	R	H	2B	3B	HR	RBI	BB	SO	SB	CS	AVG	OBP	SLG	OPS	OPS+	BR/A	RC	RC/G	FR	G/POS	WS	TPW
1984 Min-A	13	29	0	5	0	0	0	5	1	2	0	1	.172	.200	.172	.372	4	-4	1	.97	0	O-11(8-0-3)	0	-0.4
1987 Bal-A	34	76	7	12	2	0	4	12	6	19	1	4	.158	.220	.342	.562	47	-8	5	1.70	-2	O-32(4-29-1)	1	-1.0
Total 2	**47**	**105**	**7**	**17**	**2**	**0**	**4**	**17**	**7**	**21**	**1**	**5**	**.162**	**.214**	**.295**	**.510**	**36**	**-12**	**5**	**1.51**	**-1**	**/O-43**	**1**	**-1.4**

• HART, Mike James Michael Hart b: 12/20/1951, Kalamazoo, MI BB/TR, 6'3", 185 lbs. Deb: 6/12/1980

YEAR TM-L	G	AB	R	H	2B	3B	HR	RBI	BB	SO	SB	CS	AVG	OBP	SLG	OPS	OPS+	BR/A	RC	RC/G	FR	G/POS	WS	TPW
1980 Tex-A	5	4	1	1	0	0	0	0	1	1	0	0	.250	.400	.250	.650	85	0	1	4.54	0	/O-2(0-2-0)	0	0.0

• HART, Tom Thomas Henry "Bushy" Hart b: 6/15/1869, Canaan, NY d: 9/17/1939, Gardner, MA, 5'7", 160 lbs. Deb: 4/15/1891

YEAR TM-L	G	AB	R	H	2B	3B	HR	RBI	BB	SO	SB	CS	AVG	OBP	SLG	OPS	OPS+	BR/A	RC	RC/G	FR	G/POS	WS	TPW
1891 Was-a	8	24	1	3	0	0	0	2	2	1	1	....	.125	.192	.125	.317	-9	-3	1	.99	2	/C-5,O-3(0-3-0)	0	-0.1

• HARTFORD, Bruce Bruce Daniel Hartford b: 5/14/1892, Chicago, IL d: 5/25/1975, Los Angeles, CA BR/TR, 6'.5", 190 lbs. Deb: 6/3/1914

YEAR TM-L	G	AB	R	H	2B	3B	HR	RBI	BB	SO	SB	CS	AVG	OBP	SLG	OPS	OPS+	BR/A	RC	RC/G	FR	G/POS	WS	TPW
1914 Cle-A	8	22	5	4	1	0	0	0	4	9	0	....	.182	.308	.227	.535	59	-1	2	2.26	0	/S-8	0	-0.1

• HARTJE, Chris Christian Henry Hartje b: 3/25/1915, San Francisco, CA d: 6/26/1946, Seattle, WA BR/TR, 5'10.5", 165 lbs. Deb: 9/9/1939

YEAR TM-L	G	AB	R	H	2B	3B	HR	RBI	BB	SO	SB	CS	AVG	OBP	SLG	OPS	OPS+	BR/A	RC	RC/G	FR	G/POS	WS	TPW
1939 Bro-N	9	16	2	5	1	0	0	5	1	0	0	....	.313	.353	.375	.728	92	-0	2	4.14	-1	/C-8	0	-0.1

• HARTLEY, Chick Walter Scott Hartley b: 8/22/1880, Philadelphia, PA d: 7/18/1948, Philadelphia, PA BR/TR, 5'8", 180 lbs. Deb: 6/4/1902

YEAR TM-L	G	AB	R	H	2B	3B	HR	RBI	BB	SO	SB	CS	AVG	OBP	SLG	OPS	OPS+	BR/A	RC	RC/G	FR	G/POS	WS	TPW
1902 NY-N	1	4	0	0	0	0	0	0	0	....	0	....	.000	.000	.000	.000	-101	-1	0	.00	-0	/O-1	0	-0.1

• HARTLEY, Grover Grover Allen "Slick" Hartley b: 7/2/1888, Osgood, IN d: 10/19/1964, Daytona Beach, FL BR/TR, 5'11", 175 lbs. Deb: 5/13/1911 C/U

YEAR TM-L	G	AB	R	H	2B	3B	HR	RBI	BB	SO	SB	CS	AVG	OBP	SLG	OPS	OPS+	BR/A	RC	RC/G	FR	G/POS	WS	TPW
1911 NY-N	11	18	1	4	2	0	0	1	1	1	1	....	.222	.263	.333	.596	65	-1	2	3.19	-1	C-10	1	-0.2
1912 NY-N	25	34	3	8	2	1	0	7	0	4	2	....	.235	.257	.353	.610	64	-2	3	3.35	-2	C-25	1	-0.3
1913 NY-N	23	19	4	6	0	0	0	0	1	2	4	....	.316	.350	.316	.666	90	-0	3	5.89	-2	C-21/1-1	1	-0.1
1914 StL-F	86	212	24	61	13	2	1	25	12	26	4	....	.288	.329	.382	.711	96	-2	27	4.38	-2	C-32,2-13/1-9,3-3,O-2(0-2-0)	6	-0.2
1915 StL-F	120	394	47	108	21	6	1	50	42	21	10	....	.274	.356	.365	.721	107	5	53	4.68	-10	*C-113/1-1	14	0.4
1916 StL-A	89	222	19	50	8	0	0	12	30	24	4	....	.225	.325	.261	.587	80	-4	21	3.06	-4	C-75	5	-0.3
1917 StL-A	19	13	2	3	0	0	0	0	2	1	0	....	.231	.333	.231	.564	75	-0	1	2.70	-1	/C-4,3-1,S-1	0	-0.1
1924 NY-N	4	7	1	2	1	0	0	1	1	0	1	0	.286	.375	.429	.804	118	0	1	7.19	-0	/C-3	0	0.1
1925 NY-N	46	95	9	30	1	1	0	8	8	3	2	0	.316	.375	.347	.722	89	-0	13	5.22	2	C-37/1-8	4	0.3
1926 NY-N	13	21	0	1	0	0	0	0	5	0	0	....	.048	.231	.048	.278	-22	-3	0	.64	-0	C-13	0	-0.3
1927 Bos-A	103	244	23	67	11	0	1	31	22	14	1	0	.275	.337	.332	.669	76	-8	29	4.14	-1	C-86	3	-0.4
1929 Cle-A	24	33	2	9	0	1	0	8	2	1	0	0	.273	.314	.333	.648	64	-2	3	3.84	-1	C-13	0	-0.2
1930 Cle-A	1	4	0	3	0	0	0	1	0	0	0	0	.750	.750	.750	1.500	271	1	2	57.24	0	/C-1	1	0.1
1934 StL-A	5	3	0	1	1	0	0	0	1	0	0	0	.333	.500	.667	1.167	183	0	1	14.37	0	/C-2	0	0.0
Total 14	**569**	**1319**	**135**	**353**	**60**	**11**	**3**	**144**	**127**	**97**	**29**	**0**	**.268**	**.339**	**.337**	**.675**	**89**	**-16**	**161**	**4.20**	**-22**	**C-435/1-19,2-13,3-4,O-2,S-1**	**36**	**-1.2**

• HARTMAN, Fred Frederick Orrin "Dutch" Hartman b: 4/25/1868, Allegheny, PA d: 11/11/1938, McKeesport, PA BR/TR, 5'6", 170 lbs. Deb: 7/26/1894

YEAR TM-L	G	AB	R	H	2B	3B	HR	RBI	BB	SO	SB	CS	AVG	OBP	SLG	OPS	OPS+	BR/A	RC	RC/G	FR	G/POS	WS	TPW
1894 Pit-N	49	182	41	58	4	7	2	20	16	11	12	....	.319	.389	.451	.840	103	1	37	7.86	-4	3-49	6	-0.1
1897 StL-N	125	519	67	158	21	8	2	67	26	....	18	....	.304	.348	.387	.736	96	-4	79	5.71	-15	*3-124	10	-1.4
1898 NY-N	123	475	57	129	16	11	2	88	25	....	11	....	.272	.313	.364	.678	97	-4	59	4.52	-3	*3-123	13	-0.4
1899 NY-N	51	177	25	42	3	5	1	17	12	....	2	....	.237	.318	.328	.646	80	-5	20	3.84	-9	3-50	2	-1.2
1901 Chi-A	120	473	77	146	23	13	3	89	25	....	31	....	.309	.355	.431	.786	120	12	86	6.83	-4	*3-119	19	1.0
1902 StL-N	114	416	30	90	10	3	0	52	14	....	14	....	.216	.251	.255	.505	58	-21	32	2.52	-15	*3-105/S-4,1-3	3	-3.4
Total 6	**582**	**2242**	**297**	**623**	**77**	**47**	**10**	**333**	**118**	**11**	**88**	**....**	**.278**	**.326**	**.368**	**.693**	**94**	**-20**	**313**	**5.04**	**-49**	**3-570/S-4,1-3**	**53**	**-5.5**

• HARTMAN, J.C. J C Hartman b: 4/15/1934, Cottonton, AL BR/TR, 6', 175 lbs. Deb: 7/21/1962

YEAR TM-L	G	AB	R	H	2B	3B	HR	RBI	BB	SO	SB	CS	AVG	OBP	SLG	OPS	OPS+	BR/A	RC	RC/G	FR	G/POS	WS	TPW
1962 Hou-N	51	148	11	33	5	0	0	5	4	16	1	1	.223	.248	.257	.505	39	-13	9	1.93	1	S-48	2	-0.9
1963 Hou-N	39	90	2	11	1	0	0	3	2	13	1	0	.122	.151	.133	.284	-19	-13	2	.52	1	S-32	1	-1.1
Total 2	**90**	**238**	**13**	**44**	**6**	**0**	**0**	**8**	**6**	**29**	**2**	**1**	**.185**	**.211**	**.210**	**.421**	**17**	**-26**	**10**	**1.35**	**1**	**/S-80**	**3**	**-2.0**

• HARTNETT, Gabby Charles Leo Hartnett b: 12/20/1900, Woonsocket, RI d: 12/20/1972, Park Ridge, IL BR/TR, 6'1", 195 lbs. Deb: 4/12/1922 M/C HOF: 1955

YEAR TM-L	G	AB	R	H	2B	3B	HR	RBI	BB	SO	SB	CS	AVG	OBP	SLG	OPS	OPS+	BR/A	RC	RC/G	FR	G/POS	WS	TPW
1922 Chi-N	31	72	4	14	1	1	0	4	6	8	1	0	.194	.256	.236	.493	27	-7	5	2.11	3	C-27	2	-0.3
1923 Chi-N	85	231	28	62	12	2	8	39	25	22	4	0	.268	.347	.442	.789	107	4	37	5.70	0	C-39,1-31	9	0.5
1924 Chi-N	111	354	56	106	17	7	16	67	39	37	10	2	.299	.377	.523	.899	137	21	72	7.36	-4	*C-105	19	2.3
1925 Chi-N	117	398	61	115	28	3	24	67	36	77	1	5	.289	.351	.555	.906	126	12	75	6.77	8	*C-110	19	2.5
1926 Chi-N	93	284	35	78	25	3	8	41	32	37	0	....	.275	.352	.468	.821	118	7	46	5.67	2	C-88	12	1.4
1927 Chi-N	127	449	56	132	32	5	10	80	44	42	2	....	.294	.361	.454	.815	117	10	73	5.73	6	*C-126	21	2.4
1928 Chi-N	120	388	61	117	26	9	14	57	65	32	3	....	.302	.404	.523	.928	143	26	83	7.69	6	*C-118	26	3.9
1929*Chi-N	25	22	2	6	2	1	1	9	5	5	1	....	.273	.407	.591	.998	144	2	5	8.25	0	/C-1	1	0.1
1930 Chi-N	141	508	84	172	31	3	37	122	55	62	0	....	.339	.404	.630	1.034	144	35	125	9.29	-2	*C-136	29	3.7
1931 Chi-N	116	380	53	107	32	1	8	70	52	48	3	....	.282	.370	.434	.804	113	8	64	6.02	6	*C-105	16	2.0
1932*Chi-N	121	406	52	110	25	3	12	52	51	59	0	....	.271	.354	.436	.790	112	8	66	5.69	4	*C-117/1-1	19	1.9
1933 Chi-N★	140	490	55	135	21	4	16	88	37	51	1	....	.276	.326	.433	.759	116	9	67	4.76	3	*C-140	21	2.1
1934 Chi-N★	130	438	58	131	21	1	22	90	37	46	0	....	.299	.358	.502	.860	130	18	77	6.29	6	*C-129	24	3.1
1935*Chi-N★	116	413	67	142	32	6	13	91	41	46	1	....	.344	.404	.545	.949	152	30	91	8.45	4	*C-110	26	4.0
1936 Chi-N★	121	424	49	130	25	6	7	64	30	36	0	....	.307	.361	.443	.804	113	7	68	5.83	0	*C-114	18	1.4
1937 Chi-N★	110	356	47	126	21	6	12	82	43	19	0	....	.354	.424	.548	.971	156	28	85	9.42	-2	*C-103	25	3.2
1938*Chi-N★	88	299	40	82	19	1	10	59	48	17	1	....	.274	.380	.445	.825	123	11	53	6.26	-1	C-83	16	1.5
1939 Chi-N	97	306	36	85	18	2	12	59	37	32	0	....	.278	.358	.467	.825	118	8	50	5.64	0	C-86	15	1.2
1940 Chi-N	37	64	3	17	3	0	1	12	8	7	0	....	.266	.347	.359	.707	97	-0	8	4.08	-2	C-22/1-1	1	-0.1
1941 NY-N	64	150	20	45	5	0	5	26	12	14	0	....	.300	.356	.433	.789	119	4	22	5.38	1	C-34	6	0.6
Total 20	**1990**	**6432**	**867**	**1912**	**396**	**64**	**236**	**1179**	**703**	**697**	**28**	**7**	**.297**	**.370**	**.489**	**.858**	**126**	**239**	**1173**	**6.55**	**38**	***C-1793/1-33**	**325**	**37.7**

• HARTNETT, Pat Patrick J. "Happy" Hartnett b: 10/20/1863, Boston, MA d: 4/10/1935, Boston, MA, 6'1", 175 lbs. Deb: 4/18/1890

YEAR TM-L	G	AB	R	H	2B	3B	HR	RBI	BB	SO	SB	CS	AVG	OBP	SLG	OPS	OPS+	BR/A	RC	RC/G	FR	G/POS	WS	TPW
1890 StL-a	14	53	6	10	2	1	0	4	6	....	1	....	.189	.283	.264	.547	54	-3	4	2.68	-1	1-14	1	-0.5

• HARTS, Greg Gregory Rudolph Harts b: 4/21/1950, Atlanta, GA BL/TL, 6', 168 lbs. Deb: 9/15/1973

YEAR TM-L	G	AB	R	H	2B	3B	HR	RBI	BB	SO	SB	CS	AVG	OBP	SLG	OPS	OPS+	BR/A	RC	RC/G	FR	G/POS	WS	TPW
1973 NY-N	3	2	0	1	0	0	0	0	0	0	0	0	.500	.500	.500	1.000	181	0	1	13.50	0	....	0	0.0

• HARTSEL, Topsy Tully Frederick Hartsel b: 6/26/1874, Polk, OH d: 10/14/1944, Toledo, OH BL/TL, 5'5", 155 lbs. Deb: 9/14/1898 Career OF: 1223-42-47

YEAR TM-L	G	AB	R	H	2B	3B	HR	RBI	BB	SO	SB	CS	AVG	OBP	SLG	OPS	OPS+	BR/A	RC	RC/G	FR	G/POS	WS	TPW
1898 Lou-N	22	71	11	23	0	0	0	9	11	....	2	....	.324	.422	.324	.746	116	3	11	5.92	-1	O-21(0-0-21)	3	0.1
1899 Lou-N	30	75	8	18	1	1	1	7	11	....	1	....	.240	.345	.320	.665	83	-1	9	4.11	-1	O-22(7-0-15)	1	-0.3
1900 Cin-N	18	64	10	21	2	1	2	5	8	....	7	....	.328	.403	.484	.887	148	4	16	8.74	-5	O-18(18-0-0)	3	-0.2
1901 Chi-N	140	558	111	187	25	16	7	54	74	....	41	....	.335	.414	.475	.889	163	48	130	9.22	0	*O-140(131-0-9)	27	3.9
1902 Phi-A	137	545	**109**	154	20	12	5	58	**87**	....	**47**	....	.283	.383	.391	.774	110	11	103	6.90	0	*O-137(137-0-0)	25	0.3
1903 Phi-A	98	373	65	116	19	14	5	26	49	....	13	....	.311	.391	.477	.868	152	25	77	7.78	-5	O-96(94-2-0)	20	1.5
1904 Phi-A	147	534	79	135	17	12	2	25	75	....	19	....	.253	.347	.341	.688	112	11	73	4.72	-5	*O-147(122-25-0)	21	-0.3
1905*Phi-A	150	538	88	148	22	8	0	28	**121**	....	37	....	.275	**.409**	.346	.755	138	33	96	6.28	-11	*O-149(134-15-0)	30	1.4
1906 Phi-A	144	533	96	136	21	9	1	30	**88**	....	31	....	.255	.363	.334	.697	115	14	79	5.16	-1	*O-144(144-0-0)	24	0.5

YEAR TM-L	G	AB	R	H	2B	3B	HR	RBI	BB	SO	SB	CS	AVG	OBP	SLG	OPS	OPS+	BR/A	RC	RC/G	FR	G/POS	WS	TPW
1907 Phi-A	143	507	93	142	23	6	3	29	**106**	....	20	....	.280	**.405**	.367	.771	143	32	87	6.15	-8	*O-143(143-0-0)	29	1.8
1908 Phi-A	129	460	73	112	16	6	4	29	**93**	....	15	....	.243	.371	.330	.701	120	16	62	4.52	-11	*O-129(129-0-0)	19	-0.4
1909 Phi-A	83	267	30	72	4	4	1	18	48	....	3	....	.270	.381	.326	.707	121	10	35	4.47	-3	O-74(72-0-2)	11	0.2
1910*Phi-A	90	285	45	63	10	3	0	22	58	....	11	....	.221	.353	.277	.630	99	3	32	3.65	-5	O-83(83-0-0)	9	-0.7
1911 Phi-A	25	38	8	9	2	0	0	1	8	....	0	....	.237	.396	.289	.685	94	0	5	3.93	1	/O-9(9-0-0)	1	0.1
Total 14	**1356**	**4848**	**826**	**1336**	**182**	**92**	**31**	**341**	**837**	**....**	**247**	**....**	**.276**	**.384**	**.370**	**.754**	**128**	**209**	**815**	**5.97**	**-55**	***O-1312**	**223**	**8.0**

• HARTSFIELD, Roy Roy Thomas "Spec" Hartsfield b: 10/25/1925, Chattahoochee, GA BR/TR, 5'9", 165 lbs. Deb: 4/28/1950 M/C

YEAR TM-L	G	AB	R	H	2B	3B	HR	RBI	BB	SO	SB	CS	AVG	OBP	SLG	OPS	OPS+	BR/A	RC	RC/G	FR	G/POS	WS	TPW
1950 Bos-N	107	419	62	116	15	2	7	24	27	61	7	....	.277	.322	.372	.694	88	-8	52	4.51	-9	2-96	11	-1.2
1951 Bos-N	120	450	63	122	11	2	6	31	41	73	7	2	.271	.333	.344	.678	89	-6	56	4.42	-2	*2-114	11	-0.1
1952 Bos-N	38	107	13	28	4	3	0	4	5	12	0	0	.262	.295	.355	.650	82	-3	11	3.59	-6	2-29	2	-0.7
Total 3	**265**	**976**	**138**	**266**	**30**	**7**	**13**	**59**	**73**	**146**	**14**	**2**	**.273**	**.324**	**.358**	**.682**	**88**	**-17**	**119**	**4.36**	**-16**	**2-239**	**24**	**-2.0**

• HARTUNG, Clint Clinton Clarence "Floppy,The Hondo Hurricane" Hartung b: 8/10/1922, Hondo, TX BR/TR, 6'5", 215 lbs. Deb: 4/15/1947 Career OF: 11-0-35 ♦

YEAR TM-L	G	AB	R	H	2B	3B	HR	RBI	BB	SO	SB	CS	AVG	OBP	SLG	OPS	OPS+	BR/A	RC	RC/G	FR	G/POS	WS	TPW
1947 NY-N	34	94	13	29	4	3	4	13	3	21	0	....	.309	.330	.543	.872	127	10	16	6.45	-2	P-23/O-7(7-0-0)	10	0.1
1948 NY-N	43	56	5	10	1	1	0	3	7	24	0	....	.179	.270	.232	.502	37	2	4	2.35	0	P-36	5	-1.1
1949 NY-N	38	63	7	12	0	0	4	7	4	21	0	....	.190	.239	.381	.620	64	4	6	3.17	2	P-33	5	-1.3
1950 NY-N	32	43	7	13	2	1	3	10	1	13	0	....	.302	.318	.605	.923	136	5	8	7.52	2	P-20/O-2(1-0-1),1-1	2	-1.5
1951*NY-N	21	44	4	9	1	0	0	2	1	9	0	0	.205	.222	.227	.449	21	-5	2	1.36	0	O-12(O-0-12)	0	-0.5
1952 NY-N	28	78	6	17	2	1	3	8	9	24	0	0	.218	.299	.385	.683	88	-1	10	4.14	0	O-24(3-0-22)	2	-0.2
Total 6	**196**	**378**	**42**	**90**	**10**	**6**	**14**	**43**	**25**	**112**	**0**	**0**	**.238**	**.285**	**.407**	**.693**	**83**	**15**	**46**	**4.21**	**3**	**P-112/O-45,1-1**	**24**	**-4.5**

• HARTZELL, Roy Roy Allen Hartzell b: 7/6/1881, Golden, CO d: 11/6/1961, Golden, CO BL/TR, 5'8.5", 155 lbs. Deb: 4/17/1906 Career OF: 213-32-306

YEAR TM-L	G	AB	R	H	2B	3B	HR	RBI	BB	SO	SB	CS	AVG	OBP	SLG	OPS	OPS+	BR/A	RC	RC/G	FR	G/POS	WS	TPW
1906 StL-A	113	404	43	86	7	0	0	24	19	....	21	....	.213	.266	.230	.496	58	-19	32	2.61	2	*3-103/S-6,2-2	5	-1.5
1907 StL-A	60	220	20	52	3	5	0	13	11	....	7	....	.236	.285	.295	.581	85	-4	22	3.31	1	3-38,2-12/O-2(0-0-2),S-2	4	-0.1
1908 StL-A	115	422	41	112	5	6	2	32	19	....	24	....	.265	.302	.320	.622	101	-0	48	3.78	-1	O-82(O-4-78),S-18/3-7,2-4	13	-0.4
1909 StL-A	152	595	64	161	12	5	0	32	29	....	14	....	.271	.312	.308	.620	103	1	61	3.54	5	O-85(O-0-85),S-65/2-1	18	0.5
1910 StL-A	151	542	52	118	13	5	2	30	49	....	18	....	.218	.290	.271	.561	81	-11	48	2.83	-4	3-89,S-38,O-23(O-0-23)	12	-1.4
1911 NY-A	144	527	67	156	17	11	3	91	63	....	22	....	.296	.375	.387	.763	106	6	86	5.66	-10	*3-124,S-12/O-8(2-0-8)	17	0.0
1912 NY-A	125	416	50	113	10	11	1	38	64	....	20	....	.272	.370	.356	.726	102	3	63	5.14	-8	3-56,O-56(O-13-42),S-10/2-2	11	-0.6
1913 NY-A	141	490	60	127	18	1	0	38	67	40	26	....	.259	.353	.300	.653	91	-2	60	4.01	1	2-81,O-31(4-11-16),3-21/S-4	13	-0.1
1914 NY-A	137	481	55	112	15	9	1	32	68	38	22	25	.233	.335	.308	.643	94	-8	52	3.30	0	*O-128(91-3-34)/2-5	12	-1.5
1915 NY-A	119	387	39	97	11	2	3	60	57	37	7	19	.251	.351	.313	.664	99	-6	42	3.42	-4	*O-107(105-0-2)/2-5,3-2	9	-1.5
1916 NY-A	33	64	12	12	1	0	0	7	9	3	1	....	.188	.297	.203	.500	49	-4	5	2.17	-1	O-28(11-1-16)	0	-0.6
Total 11	**1290**	**4548**	**503**	**1146**	**112**	**55**	**12**	**397**	**455**	**118**	**182**	**44**	**.252**	**.327**	**.309**	**.635**	**92**	**-44**	**518**	**3.74**	**-19**	**O-550,3-440,S-155,2-112**	**114**	**-7.3**

• HARVEL, Luther Luther Raymond "Red" Harvel b: 9/30/1905, Cambria, IL d: 4/10/1986, Kansas City, MO BR/TR, 5'11", 180 lbs. Deb: 7/31/1928

YEAR TM-L	G	AB	R	H	2B	3B	HR	RBI	BB	SO	SB	CS	AVG	OBP	SLG	OPS	OPS+	BR/A	RC	RC/G	FR	G/POS	WS	TPW
1928 Cle-A	40	136	12	30	6	1	0	12	4	17	1	1	.221	.264	.279	.543	42	-12	10	2.44	-1	O-39(O-39-0)	1	-1.3

• HARVEY, Ken Kenneth Eugene Harvey b: 3/1/1978, Los Angeles, CA BR/TR, 6'2", 240 lbs. Deb: 9/18/2001

YEAR TM-L	G	AB	R	H	2B	3B	HR	RBI	BB	SO	SB	CS	AVG	OBP	SLG	OPS	OPS+	BR/A	RC	RC/G	FR	G/POS	WS	TPW
2001 KC-A	4	12	1	3	1	0	0	2	0	4	0	1	.250	.250	.333	.583	48	-1	0	.82	0	/1-3,D-1	0	-0.2
2003 KC-A	135	485	50	129	30	0	13	64	29	94	2	3	.266	.314	.408	.722	78	-17	58	4.13	3	1-99,D-32	6	-2.3
Total 2	**139**	**497**	**51**	**132**	**31**	**0**	**13**	**66**	**29**	**98**	**2**	**4**	**.266**	**.313**	**.406**	**.719**	**77**	**-18**	**58**	**4.04**	**3**	**1-102/D-33**	**6**	**-2.5**

• HARVEY, Zaza Ervin King Harvey b: 1/5/1879, Saratoga, CA d: 6/3/1954, Santa Monica, CA BL/TL, 6', 190 lbs. Deb: 5/3/1900 Career OF: 21-0-36 ♦

YEAR TM-L	G	AB	R	H	2B	3B	HR	RBI	BB	SO	SB	CS	AVG	OBP	SLG	OPS	OPS+	BR/A	RC	RC/G	FR	G/POS	WS	TPW
1900 Chi-N	2	3	0	0	0	0	0	0	0	....	0	....	.000	.000	.000	.000	-104	-1	0	.00	0	/P-1	1	0.1
1901 Chi-A	17	40	11	10	3	1	0	3	2	....	1	....	.250	.302	.375	.677	89	2	5	4.28	2	P-16	5	0.1
Cle-A	45	170	21	60	5	5	1	24	9	....	15	....	.353	.392	.459	.851	141	9	37	8.95	0	O-45(21-0-24)	8	0.6
Yr.	62	210	32	70	8	6	1	27	11	....	16	....	.333	.375	.443	.818	131	11	43	7.90	2	O-45(21-0-24),P-16	13	0.7
1902 Cle-A	12	46	5	16	2	0	0	5	3	....	1	....	.348	.388	.391	.779	121	1	8	6.57	1	O-12(O-0-12)	2	0.2
Total 3	**76**	**259**	**37**	**86**	**10**	**6**	**1**	**32**	**14**	**....**	**17**	**....**	**.332**	**.373**	**.429**	**.802**	**127**	**12**	**50**	**7.54**	**3**	**/O-57,P-17**	**16**	**0.9**

• HASBROOK, Ziggy Robert Lyndon "Ziggy" Hasbrook b: 11/21/1893, Grundy Center, IA d: 2/9/1976, Garland, TX BR/TR, 6'1", 180 lbs. Deb: 9/6/1916

YEAR TM-L	G	AB	R	H	2B	3B	HR	RBI	BB	SO	SB	CS	AVG	OBP	SLG	OPS	OPS+	BR/A	RC	RC/G	FR	G/POS	WS	TPW
1916 Chi-A	9	8	1	1	0	0	0	0	1	2	0	....	.125	.222	.125	.347	4	-1	0	.83	1	/1-7	0	0.0
1917 Chi-A	2	1	1	0	0	0	0	0	0	0	0	....	.000	.000	.000	.000	-98	-0	0	.00	0	/2-1	0	-0.1
Total 2	**11**	**9**	**2**	**1**	**0**	**0**	**0**	**0**	**1**	**2**	**0**	**....**	**.111**	**.200**	**.111**	**.311**	**-6**	**-1**	**0**	**.72**	**0**	**/1-7,2-1**	**0**	**-0.1**

• HASELMAN, Bill William Joseph Haselman b: 5/25/1966, Long Branch, NJ BR/TR, 6'3", 220 lbs. Deb: 9/3/1990 Career OF: 2-0-4

YEAR TM-L	G	AB	R	H	2B	3B	HR	RBI	BB	SO	SB	CS	AVG	OBP	SLG	OPS	OPS+	BR/A	RC	RC/G	FR	G/POS	WS	TPW
1990 Tex-A	7	13	0	2	0	0	0	3	1	5	0	0	.154	.214	.154	.368	5	-2	0	1.19	0	/D-3,C-1	0	-0.2
1992 Sea-A	8	19	1	5	0	0	0	0	0	7	0	0	.263	.263	.263	.526	48	-1	1	1.89	0	/C-5,O-2(2-0-0)	0	-0.1
1993 Sea-A	58	137	21	35	8	0	5	16	12	19	2	1	.255	.320	.423	.743	97	-1	18	4.24	0	C-49/D-4,O-2(O-0-2)	2	0.1
1994 Sea-A	38	83	11	16	7	1	1	8	3	11	1	0	.193	.230	.337	.567	43	-7	6	2.37	-1	C-33/D-3,O-2(O-0-2)	1	-0.6
1995*Bos-A	64	152	22	37	6	1	5	23	17	30	0	2	.243	.327	.395	.722	84	-5	19	4.16	-1	C-48,D-11/1-1,3-1	4	-0.3
1996 Bos-A	77	237	33	65	13	1	8	34	19	52	4	2	.274	.331	.439	.770	91	-4	30	4.35	1	C-69/1-2,D-2	4	0.2
1997 Bos-A	67	212	22	50	15	0	6	26	15	44	0	2	.236	.293	.392	.684	75	-9	22	3.35	0	C-66	1	-0.5
1998 Tex-A	40	105	11	33	6	0	6	17	3	17	0	0	.314	.333	.543	.876	118	2	18	6.46	-1	C-36/D-2	5	0.3
1999 Det-A	48	143	13	39	8	0	4	14	10	26	2	0	.273	.320	.413	.733	85	-3	18	4.59	-2	C-39,D-11	3	-0.3
2000 Tex-A	62	193	23	53	18	0	6	26	15	36	0	1	.275	.330	.461	.791	96	-2	30	5.64	2	C-62	7	0.4
2001 Tex-A	47	130	12	37	6	0	3	25	8	27	0	1	.285	.331	.400	.731	88	-3	16	4.23	-1	C-47	5	-0.1
2002 Tex-A	69	179	16	44	7	0	3	18	11	25	0	0	.246	.297	.335	.632	64	-9	17	3.20	-8	C-67/D-2	1	-1.3
2003 Bos-A	4	3	0	0	0	0	0	0	0	1	0	0	.000	.000	.000	.000	-98	-1	0	.00	0	/C-2,D-2	0	-0.1
Total 13	**589**	**1606**	**185**	**416**	**94**	**3**	**47**	**210**	**114**	**300**	**9**	**9**	**.259**	**.313**	**.409**	**.722**	**83**	**-45**	**195**	**4.16**	**-10**	**C-524/D-40,O-6,1-3,3-1**	**33**	**-2.5**

• HASENMAYER, Don Donald Irvin Hasenmayer b: 4/4/1927, Roslyn, PA BR/TR, 5'10.5", 180 lbs. Deb: 5/2/1945

YEAR TM-L	G	AB	R	H	2B	3B	HR	RBI	BB	SO	SB	CS	AVG	OBP	SLG	OPS	OPS+	BR/A	RC	RC/G	FR	G/POS	WS	TPW
1945 Phi-N	5	18	1	2	0	0	0	1	2	1	0	....	.111	.200	.111	.311	-13	-3	1	.85	1	/2-4,3-1	0	-0.2
1946 Phi-N	6	12	0	1	1	0	0	0	0	2	0	....	.083	.083	.167	.250	-31	-2	0	.41	1	/3-3	0	-0.1
Total 2	**11**	**30**	**1**	**3**	**1**	**0**	**0**	**1**	**2**	**3**	**0**	**....**	**.100**	**.156**	**.133**	**.290**	**-19**	**-5**	**1**	**.67**	**2**	**/2-4,3-4**	**0**	**-0.3**

• HASLIN, Mickey Michael Joseph Haslin b: 10/31/1909, Wilkes-Barre, PA d: 3/7/2002, Wilkes-Barre, PA BR/TR, 5'8", 165 lbs. Deb: 9/7/1933

YEAR TM-L	G	AB	R	H	2B	3B	HR	RBI	BB	SO	SB	CS	AVG	OBP	SLG	OPS	OPS+	BR/A	RC	RC/G	FR	G/POS	WS	TPW
1933 Phi-N	26	89	3	21	2	0	0	9	3	5	1	....	.236	.261	.258	.519	43	-7	6	2.35	-2	2-26	1	-0.8
1934 Phi-N	72	166	28	44	8	2	1	11	16	13	1	....	.265	.330	.355	.685	74	-6	19	3.96	-3	3-26,2-21/S-4	2	-0.7
1935 Phi-N	110	407	53	108	17	3	3	52	19	25	5	....	.265	.300	.344	.644	66	-20	42	3.48	-6	S-87,3-11/2-9	6	-1.8
1936 Phi-N	16	64	6	22	1	1	0	6	3	5	0	....	.344	.373	.391	.764	96	-0	9	5.28	-1	2-12/3-5	1	0.0
Bos-N	36	104	14	29	1	2	2	11	5	9	0	....	.279	.312	.385	.697	92	-1	11	3.80	-2	3-17/2-7	2	-0.2
Yr.	52	168	20	51	2	3	2	17	8	14	0	....	.304	.335	.387	.722	94	-2	20	4.35	-3	3-22,2-19	3	-0.3
1937 NY-N	27	42	8	8	1	0	0	5	9	3	1	....	.190	.333	.214	.548	51	-2	3	2.31	2	/S-9,2-4,3-4	1	0.1
1938 NY-N	31	102	13	33	3	0	3	15	4	4	0	....	.324	.361	.441	.802	119	2	16	6.14	-2	3-15,2-13	4	0.2
Total 6	**318**	**974**	**125**	**265**	**33**	**8**	**9**	**109**	**59**	**64**	**8**	**....**	**.272**	**.316**	**.350**	**.666**	**75**	**-34**	**108**	**3.79**	**-15**	**S-100/2-92,3-78**	**17**	**-3.4**

• HASNEY, Pete Peter James Hasney b: 5/26/1865, England d: 5/24/1908, Philadelphia, PA Deb: 9/13/1890

YEAR TM-L	G	AB	R	H	2B	3B	HR	RBI	BB	SO	SB	CS	AVG	OBP	SLG	OPS	OPS+	BR/A	RC	RC/G	FR	G/POS	WS	TPW
1890 Phi-a	2	7	1	1	0	0	0	0	1	....	0	....	.143	.250	.143	.393	16	-1	0	1.13	-1	/O-2(O-0-2)	0	-0.1

• HASSAMAER, Bill William Louis "Roaring Bill" Hassamaer b: 7/26/1864, St. Louis, MO d: 5/29/1910, St. Louis, MO, 6', 180 lbs. Deb: 4/19/1894 Career OF: 3-0-140

YEAR TM-L	G	AB	R	H	2B	3B	HR	RBI	BB	SO	SB	CS	AVG	OBP	SLG	OPS	OPS+	BR/A	RC	RC/G	FR	G/POS	WS	TPW
1894 Was-N	118	494	106	159	33	17	4	90	41	20	16	....	.322	.375	.482	.857	109	6	98	7.58	2	O-68(3-0-65),3-31,2-14/S-4	11	0.4
1895 Was-N	86	363	42	101	18	4	1	60	26	13	8	....	.278	.326	.358	.685	77	-13	47	4.73	-7	O-75(O-0-75)/1-9,3-1,S-1	3	-1.9
Lou-N	23	96	7	20	2	2	0	14	3	4	0	....	.208	.232	.271	.503	31	-10	6	2.22	4	1-21/2-1,S-1	0	-0.5
Yr.	109	459	49	121	20	6	1	74	29	17	8	....	.264	.307	.340	.647	68	-23	53	4.16	-3	O-75(O-0-75),1-30/S-2,2-1,3	3	-2.4
1896 Lou-N	30	106	8	26	5	0	2	14	14	7	1	....	.245	.333	.349	.682	83	-2	13	4.30	6	1-29	2	0.3
Total 3	**257**	**1059**	**163**	**306**	**58**	**23**	**7**	**178**	**84**	**44**	**25**	**....**	**.289**	**.342**	**.407**	**.749**	**89**	**-19**	**164**	**5.68**	**4**	**O-143/1-59,3-32,2-15,S-6**	**16**	**-1.7**

YEAR TM-L	G	AB	R	H	2B	3B	HR	RBI	BB	SO	SB	CS	AVG	OBP	SLG	OPS	OPS+	BR/A	RC	RC/G	FR	G/POS	WS	TPW
• HASSETT, Buddy	John Aloysius Hassett b: 9/5/1911, New York, NY d: 8/23/1997, Westwood, NJ BL/TL, 5'11", 180 lbs. Deb: 4/14/1936 Career OF: 72-6-39																							
1936 Bro-N	156	635	79	197	29	11	3	82	35	17	5	....	.310	.350	.405	.755	102	1	92	5.48	9	*1-156	16	-0.5
1937 Bro-N	137	556	71	169	31	6	1	53	20	19	13	....	.304	.334	.387	.721	94	-6	71	4.65	9	*1-131/0-7(1-6-1)	11	-0.9
1938 Bro-N	115	335	49	98	11	6	0	40	32	19	3	....	.293	.356	.361	.717	95	-1	44	4.72	-4	0-71(71-0-2)/1-8	8	-1.0
1939 Bos-N	147	590	72	182	15	3	2	60	29	14	13	....	.308	.342	.354	.696	94	-6	72	4.43	6	*1-123,0-23(0-0-23)	13	-1.2
1940 Bos-N	124	458	59	107	19	4	0	27	25	16	4	....	.234	.273	.293	.566	59	-26	34	2.53	2	1-98,0-13(0-0-13)	2	-3.4
1941 Bos-N	118	405	59	120	9	4	1	33	36	15	10	....	.296	.354	.346	.699	102	1	51	4.63	6	1-99	11	-0.1
1942*NY-A	132	538	80	153	16	6	5	48	32	16	5	5	.284	.325	.364	.689	95	-5	65	4.32	5	*1-132	13	-1.3
Total 7	**929**	**3517**	**469**	**1026**	**130**	**40**	**12**	**343**	**209**	**116**	**53**	**5**	**.292**	**.333**	**.362**	**.695**	**92**	**-42**	**431**	**4.42**	**32**	**1-747,0-114**	**74**	**-8.5**
• HASSEY, Ron	Ronald William Hassey b: 2/27/1953, Tucson, AZ BL/TR, 6'2", 200 lbs. Deb: 4/23/1978 C																							
1978 Cle-A	25	74	5	15	0	0	2	9	5	7	2	0	.203	.263	.284	.546	54	-4	6	2.60	2	C-24	1	-0.1
1979 Cle-A	75	223	20	64	14	0	4	32	19	19	1	0	.287	.343	.404	.747	100	0	30	4.61	0	C-68/1-2,D-1	7	0.3
1980 Cle-A	130	390	43	124	18	4	8	65	49	51	0	2	.318	.395	.446	.842	130	17	68	6.33	2	*C-113/D-7,1-3	20	2.4
1981 Cle-A	61	190	8	44	4	0	1	25	17	11	0	1	.232	.301	.268	.570	66	-8	16	2.68	5	C-56/1-5,D-1	4	0.0
1982 Cle-A	113	323	33	81	18	0	5	34	53	32	3	2	.251	.358	.353	.711	97	1	42	4.39	-2	*C-105/1-2,D-2	12	0.4
1983 Cle-A	117	341	48	92	21	0	6	42	38	35	2	2	.270	.346	.384	.731	97	-1	45	4.48	1	*C-113/D-1	12	0.5
1984 Cle-A	48	149	11	38	5	1	0	19	15	26	1	0	.255	.323	.302	.625	73	-5	15	3.42	0	C-44/1-1,D-1	3	-0.3
Chi-N	19	33	5	11	0	0	2	5	4	6	0	1	.333	.405	.515	.921	144	2	6	7.03	-1	/C-6,1-4	2	0.1
1985 NY-A	92	267	31	79	16	1	13	42	28	21	0	0	.296	.369	.509	.878	141	15	49	6.84	-5	C-69/1-2,D-2	13	1.3
1986 NY-A	64	191	23	57	14	0	6	29	24	16	1	1	.298	.382	.466	.848	131	9	33	6.11	-3	C-51/D-3	7	0.8
Chi-A	49	150	22	53	11	1	3	20	22	11	0	0	.353	.439	.500	.939	150	12	32	8.26	1	D-34,C-11	7	1.2
Yr.	113	341	45	110	25	1	9	49	46	27	1	1	.323	.408	.481	.889	139	20	65	7.01	-2	C-62,D-37	14	1.9
1987 Chi-A	49	145	15	31	9	0	3	12	17	11	0	0	.214	.305	.338	.643	69	-6	13	2.92	2	C-24,D-18	1	-0.4
1988*Oak-A	107	323	32	83	15	0	7	45	30	42	2	0	.257	.328	.368	.696	98	-0	39	4.13	0	C-91/D-9	12	0.5
1989*Oak-A	97	268	29	61	12	0	5	23	24	45	1	0	.228	.294	.328	.622	78	-8	25	3.07	-3	C-78/D-2,1-1	6	-0.6
1990*Oak-A	94	254	18	54	7	0	5	22	27	29	0	0	.213	.291	.299	.590	68	-11	23	3.05	-2	C-59,D-15/1-3	6	-1.0
1991 Mon-N	52	119	5	27	8	0	1	14	13	16	1	1	.227	.303	.319	.622	76	-4	11	2.91	0	C-34	2	-0.2
Total 14	**1192**	**3440**	**348**	**914**	**172**	**7**	**71**	**438**	**385**	**378**	**14**	**10**	**.266**	**.343**	**.382**	**.725**	**100**	**8**	**453**	**4.52**	**-2**	**C-946/D-96,1-23**	**115**	**4.8**
• HASSLER, Joe	Joseph Frederick Hassler b: 4/7/1905, Fort Smith, AR d: 9/4/1971, Duncan, OK BR/TR, 6', 165 lbs. Deb: 5/26/1928																							
1928 Phi-A	28	34	5	9	2	0	0	3	2	4	0	1	.265	.306	.324	.629	64	-2	3	2.87	-4	S-28	0	-0.4
1929 Phi-A	4	4	1	0	0	0	0	0	0	2	0	0	.000	.000	.000	.000	-97	-1	0	.00	-1	/S-2	0	-0.2
1930 StL-A	5	8	3	2	0	0	0	1	0	1	0	0	.250	.250	.250	.500	26	-1	0	2.12	1	/S-3	0	0.0
Total 3	**37**	**46**	**9**	**11**	**2**	**0**	**0**	**4**	**2**	**7**	**0**	**1**	**.239**	**.271**	**.283**	**.553**	**46**	**-4**	**4**	**2.47**	**-4**	**/S-33**	**0**	**-0.6**
• HASSON, Gene	Charles Eugene Hasson b: 7/20/1915, Connellsville, PA BL/TL, 6', 197 lbs. Deb: 9/9/1937																							
1937 Phi-A	28	98	12	30	6	3	3	14	13	14	0	0	.306	.387	.520	.908	129	4	20	7.88	-3	1-28	3	-0.1
1938 Phi-A	19	69	10	19	6	2	1	12	12	7	0	0	.275	.383	.464	.846	114	2	13	6.72	-2	1-19	2	-0.2
Total 2	**47**	**167**	**22**	**49**	**12**	**5**	**4**	**26**	**25**	**21**	**0**	**0**	**.293**	**.385**	**.497**	**.882**	**122**	**6**	**33**	**7.38**	**-5**	**/1-47**	**5**	**-0.3**
• HASTINGS, Scott	Winfield Scott Hastings b: 8/10/1847, Hillsboro, OH d: 8/14/1907, Sawtelle, CA BR/TR, 5'8", 161 lbs. Deb: 5/6/1871 M/U NA OF: 3-44-34 Career OF: 0-66-0																							
1871 Rok-n	25	118	27	30	6	4	0	20	2	4	11	2	.254	.267	.373	.640	85	-1	15	5.26	1	*C-23/2-2,0-2(2-1-0),1-1	....	0.0
1872 Cle-n	22	115	34	45	4	0	0	16	3	2	5	1	.391	.407	.426	.833	166	10	23	9.83	-6	C-12/0-8(0-3-5),2-6	....	0.3
Bal-n	13	62	16	19	3	1	0	4	1	2	0	1	.306	.317	.387	.705	111	0	8	5.50	2	C-12/2-2,0-1	....	0.1
Yr.	35	177	50	64	7	1	0	20	4	4	5	2	.362	.376	.412	.788	146	10	30	8.17	-4	C-24/0-9(0-4-5),2-8	....	0.4
1873 Bal-n	30	146	41	41	4	0	0	15	4	1	4	2	.281	.300	.308	.608	81	-3	15	4.29	-3	C-19,0-12(0-12-0)/2-1	....	-0.4
1874 Har-n	52	247	60	80	11	2	0	30	4	3	10	4	.324	.335	.385	.719	124	5	35	6.19	-3	C-39,0-26(0-12-14)/2-1,S-1	....	0.2
1875 Chi-n	65	287	43	73	9	0	0	30	9	14	13	11	.254	.277	.286	.563	95	-3	27	3.54	5	C-46,0-29(1-15-15)/2-3	....	0.2
1876 Lou-N	67	288	36	73	6	1	0	21	5	11	....	....	.253	.271	.286	.557	73	-10	22	3.00	-5	*0-65(0-65-0)/C-5	5	-1.6
1877 Cin-N	20	71	7	10	1	0	0	3	3	6	....	....	.141	.176	.155	.331	5	-7	2	.89	-5	C-20/0-1	0	-1.0
Total 5 n	**207**	**975**	**221**	**288**	**37**	**7**	**0**	**115**	**23**	**26**	**43**	**21**	**.295**	**.312**	**.348**	**.659**	**108**	**9**	**123**	**5.26**	**-5**	**C-151/0-78,2-15,1-1,S-1**	**....**	**0.6**
Total 2	**87**	**359**	**43**	**83**	**7**	**1**	**0**	**24**	**8**	**17**	**....**	**....**	**.231**	**.251**	**.260**	**.511**	**59**	**-17**	**24**	**2.52**	**-9**	**/0-66,C-25**	**5**	**-2.5**
• HATCHER, Billy	William Augustus Hatcher b: 10/4/1960, Williams, AZ BR/TR, 5'9", 175 lbs. Deb: 9/10/1984 C Career OF: 583-553-87																							
1984 Chi-N	8	9	1	1	0	0	0	0	1	0	2	0	.111	.200	.111	.311	-10	-1	0	1.38	1	/0-4(4-0-0)	0	0.0
1985 Chi-N	53	163	24	40	12	1	2	10	8	12	2	4	.245	.293	.368	.661	75	-7	14	2.72	0	0-44(16-27-3)	1	-0.9
1986*Hou-N	127	419	55	108	15	4	6	36	22	52	38	14	.258	.303	.356	.658	83	-9	47	3.76	-3	*0-121(39-95-9)	12	-1.5
1987 Hou-N	141	564	96	167	28	3	11	63	42	70	53	9	.296	.354	.415	.769	107	13	89	5.58	4	*0-140(51-94-6)	19	1.4
1988 Hou-N	145	530	79	142	25	4	7	52	37	56	32	13	.268	.325	.370	.695	103	2	66	4.20	-2	*0-142(124-25-0)	17	-0.4
1989 Hou-N	108	395	49	90	15	3	3	44	30	53	22	6	.228	.284	.304	.588	71	-13	37	3.10	-4	*0-104(96-11-0)	9	-2.2
Pit-N	27	86	10	21	4	0	1	7	0	9	2	1	.244	.253	.326	.578	67	-4	7	2.71	0	0-20(2-10-9)	1	-0.5
Yr.	135	481	59	111	19	3	4	51	30	62	24	7	.231	.279	.308	.586	70	-17	44	3.04	-4	*0-124(98-21-9)	10	-2.7
1990*Cin-N	139	504	68	139	28	5	5	25	33	42	30	10	.276	.328	.381	.709	91	-5	65	4.64	5	*0-131(76-69-0)	12	-0.3
1991 Cin-N	138	442	45	116	25	3	4	41	26	55	11	9	.262	.314	.360	.673	86	-10	48	3.68	-4	*0-121(81-54-0)	9	-1.8
1992 Cin-N	43	94	10	27	3	0	2	10	5	11	0	2	.287	.323	.383	.706	97	-1	11	3.89	-1	0-23(23-0-0)	1	-0.3
Bos-A	75	315	37	75	16	2	1	23	17	41	4	6	.238	.284	.311	.595	62	-18	25	2.62	1	0-75(63-13-0)	2	-2.0
1993 Bos-A	136	508	71	146	24	3	9	57	28	46	14	7	.287	.338	.400	.738	92	-6	66	4.50	-10	*0-130(0-129-2)/2-2	13	-1.4
1994 Bos-A	44	164	24	40	9	1	1	18	11	14	4	5	.244	.295	.329	.625	58	-12	15	2.96	0	0-43(0-0-43)/D-1	1	-1.3
Phi-N	43	134	15	33	5	1	2	13	6	14	4	1	.246	.279	.343	.622	60	-8	13	3.19	0	0-40(7-26-11)	1	-0.8
1995 Tex-A	6	12	2	1	1	0	0	0	1	1	0	0	.083	.154	.167	.321	-16	-2	0	.85	1	/0-5(1-0-4),D-1	0	-0.2
Total 12	**1233**	**4339**	**586**	**1146**	**210**	**30**	**54**	**399**	**267**	**476**	**218**	**87**	**.264**	**.315**	**.364**	**.679**	**86**	**-82**	**503**	**3.94**	**-11**	***0-1143/2-2,D-2**	**98**	**-12.4**
• HATCHER, Chris	Christopher Kenneth Hatcher b: 1/7/1969, Anaheim, CA BR/TR, 6'3" Deb: 9/6/1998																							
1998 KC-A	8	15	0	1	0	0	0	1	1	7	0	0	.067	.125	.067	.192	-47	-3	0	.30	0	/0-5(5-0-0)	0	-0.4
• HATCHER, Mickey	Michael Vaughn Hatcher b: 3/15/1955, Cleveland, OH BR/TR, 6'2", 200 lbs. Deb: 8/3/1979 C Career OF: 345-88-146																							
1979 LA-N	33	93	9	25	4	1	1	5	7	12	1	3	.269	.327	.366	.692	90	-2	9	3.19	-2	0-19(1-1-18),3-17	1	-0.5
1980 LA-N	57	84	4	19	2	0	1	5	2	12	0	2	.226	.244	.286	.530	48	-7	4	1.33	0	0-25(4-0-21),3-18	1	-0.8
1981 Min-A	99	377	36	96	23	2	3	37	15	29	3	1	.255	.287	.350	.637	77	-11	36	3.23	-2	0-91(5-86-0)/1-7,3-2,D-1	7	-1.6
1982 Min-A	84	277	23	69	13	2	3	26	8	27	0	2	.249	.270	.343	.613	65	-15	21	2.60	3	0-47(26-1-21),D-29/3-5	1	-1.4
1983 Min-A	106	375	50	119	15	3	9	47	14	19	2	0	.317	.344	.445	.789	111	5	54	5.33	2	0-56(10-0-48),D-39/1-7,3-1	11	0.3
1984 Min-A	152	576	61	174	35	5	5	69	37	34	0	1	.302	.346	.406	.753	103	2	78	4.88	4	*0-100(100-0-0),D-37,1-17/3	16	-0.2
1985 Min-A	116	444	46	125	28	0	3	49	16	23	0	0	.282	.310	.365	.674	79	-13	46	3.69	2	0-97(96-0-1),D-11/1-4	7	-1.7
1986 Min-A	115	317	40	88	13	3	3	32	19	26	2	1	.278	.318	.366	.684	84	-7	36	3.97	1	0-46(45-0-0),D-28,1-22/3-3	5	-1.0
1987 LA-N	101	287	27	81	19	1	7	42	20	19	2	3	.282	.331	.429	.760	102	-1	39	4.76	1	3-49,1-37/0-7(1-0-6)	8	-0.2
1988*LA-N	88	191	22	56	8	0	1	25	7	7	0	0	.293	.325	.351	.676	97	-1	20	3.75	2	0-29(8-0-21),1-25/3-3	6	-0.2
1989 LA-N	94	224	18	66	9	2	2	25	13	16	1	2	.295	.336	.379	.716	106	1	27	4.16	3	0-48(39-0-10),3-16/1-5,P-1	4	0.1
1990 LA-N	85	132	12	28	3	1	0	13	6	22	0	0	.212	.252	.250	.502	40	-11	9	2.17	-1	1-25,3-10,0-10(10-0-0)	0	-1.3
Total 12	**1130**	**3377**	**348**	**946**	**172**	**20**	**38**	**375**	**164**	**246**	**11**	**15**	**.280**	**.316**	**.377**	**.693**	**89**	**-62**	**378**	**3.92**	**11**	**0-575,1-149,D-145,3-125/P-1**	**67**	**-8.6**
• HATFIELD, Fred	Fred James Hatfield b: 3/18/1925, Lanett, AL d: 5/22/1998, Tallahassee, FL BL/TR, 6'1", 171 lbs. Deb: 8/31/1950 C																							
1950 Bos-A	10	12	3	3	0	0	0	2	3	1	0	0	.250	.400	.250	.650	63	-0	2	4.63	1	/3-3	0	0.1
1951 Bos-A	80	163	23	28	4	2	2	14	22	27	1	0	.172	.274	.258	.532	40	-13	13	2.64	9	3-49	2	-0.4
1952 Bos-A	19	25	6	8	1	1	1	3	4	2	0	3	.320	.433	.560	.993	162	1	4	5.12	-0	3-17	1	0.1
Det-A	112	441	42	104	12	2	2	25	35	52	2	2	.236	.301	.286	.587	63	-22	38	2.89	4	*3-107/S-9	5	-1.8
Yr.	131	466	48	112	13	3	3	28	39	54	2	5	.240	.309	.300	.609	69	-21	43	3.02	4	*3-124/S-9	6	-1.7
1953 Det-A	109	311	41	79	11	1	3	19	40	34	3	5	.254	.341	.325	.666	81	-8	36	3.87	1	3-54,2-28/S-1	7	-0.6
1954 Det-A	81	218	31	64	12	0	2	25	28	24	4	2	.294	.386	.376	.763	112	5	33	5.45	-5	2-54,3-15	8	0.3

YEAR TM-L	G	AB	R	H	2B	3B	HR	RBI	BB	SO	SB	CS	AVG	OBP	SLG	OPS	OPS+	BR/A	RC	RC/G	FR	G/POS	WS	TPW
1955 Det-A	122	413	51	96	15	3	8	33	61	49	3	2	.232	.338	.341	.680	85	-7	51	4.08	6	2-92,3-16,S-14	12	0.6
1956 Det-A	8	12	2	3	0	0	0	2	2	1	0	0	.250	.400	.250	.650	75	-0	2	4.54	0	/2-4	1	0.0
Chi-A	106	321	46	84	9	1	7	33	37	36	1	0	.262	.352	.361	.714	88	-4	43	4.61	3	*3-100/S-3	9	-0.2
Yr.	114	333	48	87	9	1	7	35	39	37	1	0	.261	.354	.357	.712	87	-5	44	4.61	3	*3-100/2-4,S-3	10	-0.2
1957 Chi-A	69	114	14	23	3	0	0	8	15	20	1	0	.202	.321	.228	.549	52	-6	10	2.78	5	3-44	2	-0.1
1958 Cle-A	3	8	0	1	0	0	0	1	1	1	0	0	.125	.222	.125	.347	-2	-1	0	1.08	1	/3-2	0	-0.1
Cin-N	3	1	0	0	0	0	0	0	0	0	0	0	.000	.000	.000	.000	-95	-0	0	.00	-1	/2-1,3-1	0	-0.1
Total 9	722	2039	259	493	67	10	25	165	248	247	15	14	.242	.334	.321	.655	78	-57	233	3.82	24	3-408,2-179/S-27	47	-2.1

• HATFIELD, Gil Gilbert "Colonel" Hatfield b: 1/27/1855, Hoboken, NJ d: 5/26/1921, Hoboken, NJ TR, 5'9.5", 168 lbs. Deb: 9/24/1885 U Career OF: 1-2-2 ♦

YEAR TM-L	G	AB	R	H	2B	3B	HR	RBI	BB	SO	SB	CS	AVG	OBP	SLG	OPS	OPS+	BR/A	RC	RC/G	FR	G/POS	WS	TPW
1885 Buf-N	11	30	1	4	0	1	0	0	0	11	....	....	.133	.133	.200	.333	6	-3	1	.85	0	/3-8,2-3	0	-0.3
1887 NY-N	2	7	2	3	1	0	0	3	0	1	0	....	.429	.429	.571	1.000	184	1	2	11.64	0	/3-2	0	0.1
1888*NY-N	28	105	7	19	1	0	0	9	2	18	8	....	.181	.211	.190	.401	29	-8	6	1.90	-1	3-14,S-13/2-1,0-1	1	-0.8
1889 NY-N	32	125	21	23	2	0	1	12	9	15	9	....	.184	.250	.224	.474	33	-9	9	2.46	1	S-24/P-6,3-2	3	-0.7
1890 NY-P	71	287	32	80	13	6	2	37	17	19	12	....	.279	.328	.387	.715	83	-9	41	5.39	-11	3-42,S-27/P-3,0-1	7	-1.4
1891 Was-a	134	500	83	128	11	8	1	48	50	39	43	....	.256	.335	.316	.651	90	-4	69	4.91	-3	*S-105,3-27/P-4,0-3(1-0-2)	14	-1.5
1893 Bro-N	34	120	24	35	3	3	2	19	17	5	9	....	.292	.388	.417	.805	119	4	23	7.32	-5	3-34	4	-0.1
1895 Lou-N	5	16	3	3	0	0	0	1	1	1	0	....	.188	.278	.188	.465	23	-2	1	1.94	-1	/3-3,S-2	0	-0.2
Total 8	317	1190	173	295	31	18	6	129	96	109	81	....	.248	.315	.319	.634	78	-31	153	4.55	-20	S-171,3-132/P-13,0-5,2-4	29	-4.8

• HATFIELD, John John Van Buskirk Hatfield b: 7/20/1847, NJ d: 2/20/1909, Long Island City, NY, 5'10", 165 lbs. Deb: 5/18/1871 M/U NA OF: 83-0-1

YEAR TM-L	G	AB	R	H	2B	3B	HR	RBI	BB	SO	SB	CS	AVG	OBP	SLG	OPS	OPS+	BR/A	RC	RC/G	FR	G/POS	WS	TPW
1871 Mut-n	33	168	41	43	3	2	0	22	4	0	10	3	.256	.273	.298	.571	70	-4	17	4.14	3	*0-24(24-0-0)/2-7,3-2	....	-0.1
1872 Mut-n	56	288	76	92	15	1	1	45	9	6	12	5	.319	.340	.389	.729	132	13	43	6.67	13	*2-56	....	1.6
1873 Mut-n	52	255	54	78	5	6	2	45	3	2	2	0	.306	.314	.396	.710	110	4	33	5.71	3	*3-45,2-11/0-1	....	0.4
1874 Mut-n	63	292	47	66	12	1	0	30	7	12	4	0	.226	.244	.274	.518	64	-11	21	2.79	4	*0-58(58-0-0)/3-7,P-3,1-1,S	....	-0.5
1875 Mut-n	1	4	1	2	1	0	0	1	0	0	0	0	.500	.500	.750	1.250	311	1	2	22.68	0	/0-1	....	0.1
1876 NY-N	1	4	0	1	0	0	0	1	0	0	....	....	.250	.250	.250	.500	77	-0	0	2.39	-0	/2-1	0	0.0
Total 5 n	205	1007	219	281	36	10	3	143	23	20	28	8	.279	.295	.344	.639	97	3	116	4.84	23	/0-84,2-74,3-54,P-3,1-1,S-1	....	1.5

• HATTEBERG, Scott Scott Allen Hatteberg b: 12/14/1969, Salem, OR BL/TR, 6'1", 185 lbs. Deb: 9/8/1995

YEAR TM-L	G	AB	R	H	2B	3B	HR	RBI	BB	SO	SB	CS	AVG	OBP	SLG	OPS	OPS+	BR/A	RC	RC/G	FR	G/POS	WS	TPW
1995 Bos-A	2	2	1	1	0	0	0	0	0	0	0	0	.500	.500	.500	1.000	156	0	0	.00	0	/C-2	0	0.0
1996 Bos-A	10	11	3	2	1	0	0	0	3	2	0	0	.182	.357	.273	.630	61	-1	1	1.99	0	C-10	0	0.0
1997 Bos-A	114	350	46	97	23	1	10	44	40	70	0	1	.277	.355	.434	.789	103	1	53	5.31	-1	*C-106/D-1	6	0.7
1998*Bos-A	112	359	46	99	23	1	12	43	43	58	0	0	.276	.361	.446	.807	106	4	57	5.66	3	*C-108	11	1.3
1999*Bos-A	30	80	12	22	5	0	1	11	18	14	0	0	.275	.414	.375	.789	100	1	14	6.12	1	C-23/D-6	4	0.3
2000 Bos-A	92	230	21	61	15	0	8	36	38	39	0	1	.265	.369	.435	.804	100	0	37	5.48	-3	C-48,D-20/3-1	5	-0.1
2001 Bos-A	94	278	34	68	19	0	3	25	33	26	1	1	.245	.333	.345	.679	79	-8	33	4.04	-8	C-72/D-8	5	-1.1
2002*Oak-A	136	492	58	138	22	4	15	61	68	56	0	0	.280	.375	.433	.807	114	12	84	6.21	6	1-91,D-42	16	0.8
2003*Oak-A	147	541	63	137	34	0	12	61	66	53	0	1	.253	.344	.383	.727	91	-6	73	4.62	-2	*1-128,D-13	14	-2.0
Total 9	737	2343	284	625	142	6	61	281	309	318	1	4	.267	.359	.411	.769	99	3	351	5.25	-3	C-369,1-219/D-90,3-1	61	-0.1

• HATTON, Grady Grady Edgebert Hatton b: 10/7/1922, Beaumont, TX BL/TR, 5'8.5", 175 lbs. Deb: 4/16/1946 M/C Career OF: 5-0-0

YEAR TM-L	G	AB	R	H	2B	3B	HR	RBI	BB	SO	SB	CS	AVG	OBP	SLG	OPS	OPS+	BR/A	RC	RC/G	FR	G/POS	WS	TPW
1946 Cin-N	116	436	56	118	18	3	14	69	66	53	6	....	.271	.369	.422	.791	129	17	73	6.11	-22	*3-116/0-2(2-0-0)	16	-0.5
1947 Cin-N	146	524	91	147	24	8	16	77	81	50	7	....	.281	.377	.448	.825	119	16	92	6.37	-4	*3-136	22	1.1
1948 Cin-N	133	458	58	110	17	2	9	44	72	50	7	....	.240	.343	.345	.688	90	-5	59	4.45	2	*3-123/2-3,S-2,0-1	13	-0.3
1949 Cin-N	137	537	71	141	38	5	11	69	62	48	4	....	.263	.342	.413	.756	100	0	79	5.22	4	*3-136	17	0.4
1950 Cin-N	130	438	67	114	17	1	11	54	70	39	6	....	.260	.366	.379	.745	96	-0	67	5.46	1	*3-126/2-1,S-1	14	0.0
1951 Cin-N	96	331	41	84	9	3	4	37	33	32	4	2	.254	.321	.335	.657	76	-11	38	4.03	7	3-87/0-2(2-0-0)	9	-0.4
1952 Cin-N★	128	433	48	92	14	1	9	57	66	60	5	4	.212	.319	.312	.631	76	-13	48	3.66	-4	*2-120	11	-1.0
1953 Cin-N	83	159	22	37	3	1	7	22	29	24	0	1	.233	.351	.396	.747	94	-1	24	5.01	1	2-35,1-10/3-5	4	0.1
1954 Cin-N	1	1	0	0	0	0	0	0	0	0	0	0	.000	.000	.000	.000	-97	-0	0	.00	0	....	0	0.0
Chi-A	13	30	3	5	1	0	0	3	5	3	1	0	.167	.286	.200	.486	34	-2	2	2.09	0	3-10/1-3	0	-0.3
Bos-A	99	302	40	85	12	3	5	33	58	25	1	1	.281	.401	.391	.791	106	6	51	6.08	0	3-93/1-1,S-1	10	0.5
Yr.	112	332	43	90	13	3	5	36	63	28	2	1	.271	.390	.373	.764	99	3	53	5.66	0	*3-103/1-4,S-1	10	0.3
1955 Bos-A	126	380	48	93	11	4	4	49	76	28	0	1	.245	.371	.326	.697	81	-7	51	4.50	5	*3-111/2-1	10	-0.2
1956 Bos-A	5	5	0	2	0	0	0	2	0	0	0	0	.400	.400	.400	.800	100	0	1	7.20	0	....	0	0.0
StL-N	44	73	10	18	1	2	0	7	13	7	1	0	.247	.360	.315	.676	84	-1	9	3.96	-1	2-13/3-1	2	-0.1
Bal-A	27	61	4	9	1	0	1	3	13	6	0	0	.148	.297	.213	.510	40	-5	5	2.49	-1	2-15,3-12	1	-0.5
Yr.	32	66	4	11	1	0	1	5	13	6	0	0	.167	.304	.227	.531	44	-5	6	2.74	-1	2-15,3-12	1	-0.5
1960 Chi-N	28	38	3	13	0	0	0	7	2	5	0	0	.342	.390	.342	.732	104	0	5	4.41	0	/2-8	1	0.1
Total 12	1312	4206	562	1068	166	33	91	533	646	430	42	9	.254	.355	.374	.729	96	-5	604	5.01	-13	3-956,2-196/1-14,0-5,S-4	130	-1.3

• HAUGER, Arthur John Arthur Hauger b: 11/18/1893, Delhi, OH d: 8/2/1944, Redwood City, CA BL/TR, 5'11", 168 lbs. Deb: 7/17/1912

YEAR TM-L	G	AB	R	H	2B	3B	HR	RBI	BB	SO	SB	CS	AVG	OBP	SLG	OPS	OPS+	BR/A	RC	RC/G	FR	G/POS	WS	TPW
1912 Cle-A	15	18	0	1	0	0	0	0	1	....	0	....	.056	.105	.056	.161	-52	-4	0	.14	0	/0-5(1-2-2)	0	-0.4

• HAUSER, Arnold Arnold George "Peewee,Stub" Hauser b: 9/25/1888, Chicago, IL d: 5/22/1966, Aurora, IL BR/TR, 5'6", 145 lbs. Deb: 4/21/1910

YEAR TM-L	G	AB	R	H	2B	3B	HR	RBI	BB	SO	SB	CS	AVG	OBP	SLG	OPS	OPS+	BR/A	RC	RC/G	FR	G/POS	WS	TPW
1910 StL-N	119	375	37	77	7	2	2	36	49	39	15	....	.205	.312	.251	.562	67	-14	34	2.90	-20	*S-117/3-1	6	-3.1
1911 StL-N	136	515	61	124	11	8	3	46	26	67	24	....	.241	.286	.311	.597	69	-23	53	3.31	-12	*S-134/3-2	8	-2.6
1912 StL-N	133	479	73	124	14	7	1	42	39	69	26	....	.259	.319	.324	.642	78	-15	58	3.94	0	*S-132	10	-0.6
1913 StL-N	22	45	3	13	0	3	0	9	2	2	1	....	.289	.347	.422	.769	121	1	7	5.15	-3	/S-8,2-4	2	-0.1
1915 Chi-F	23	54	6	11	1	0	0	4	5	7	2	....	.204	.283	.222	.506	52	-3	4	2.32	-2	S-16/3-6	1	-0.4
Total 5	433	1468	180	349	33	20	6	137	121	184	68	....	.238	.305	.300	.605	72	-54	157	3.42	-37	S-407/3-9,2-4	27	-6.8

• HAUSER, Joe Joseph John "Unser Choe" Hauser b: 1/12/1899, Milwaukee, WI d: 7/11/1997, Sheboygan, WI BL/TL, 5'10.5", 175 lbs. Deb: 4/18/1922

YEAR TM-L	G	AB	R	H	2B	3B	HR	RBI	BB	SO	SB	CS	AVG	OBP	SLG	OPS	OPS+	BR/A	RC	RC/G	FR	G/POS	WS	TPW
1922 Phi-A	111	368	61	119	21	5	9	43	30	37	1	5	.323	.378	.481	.858	119	8	65	6.60	-1	1-94	12	0.1
1923 Phi-A	146	537	93	165	21	9	17	94	69	52	6	6	.307	.398	.475	.873	127	23	104	7.02	1	*1-146	22	1.3
1924 Phi-A	149	562	97	162	31	8	27	115	56	52	7	5	.288	.358	.516	.874	123	16	104	6.62	3	*1-146	21	0.9
1926 Phi-A	91	229	31	44	10	0	8	36	39	35	1	1	.192	.312	.341	.653	66	-11	27	3.68	-1	1-65	3	-1.6
1928 Phi-A	95	300	61	78	19	5	16	59	52	45	4	2	.260	.369	.517	.886	127	12	60	6.64	-3	1-88	11	0.3
1929 Cle-A	37	48	8	12	1	1	3	9	4	8	0	0	.250	.321	.500	.821	104	0	8	5.73	0	/1-8	1	0.0
Total 6	629	2044	351	580	103	28	80	356	250	229	19	19	.284	.368	.479	.847	117	48	368	6.34	-1	1-547	70	1.0

• HAUSMANN, George George John Hausmann b: 2/11/1916, St. Louis, MO BR/TR, 5'5", 145 lbs. Deb: 4/18/1944

YEAR TM-L	G	AB	R	H	2B	3B	HR	RBI	BB	SO	SB	CS	AVG	OBP	SLG	OPS	OPS+	BR/A	RC	RC/G	FR	G/POS	WS	TPW
1944 NY-N	131	466	70	124	20	4	1	30	40	25	3	....	.266	.324	.333	.657	85	-9	52	3.73	-3	*2-122	9	-0.6
1945 NY-N	154	623	98	174	15	8	2	45	73	46	7	....	.279	.356	.339	.694	92	-4	81	4.61	-4	*2-154	17	0.0
1949 NY-N	16	47	5	6	0	1	0	3	7	6	0	....	.128	.241	.170	.411	12	-6	3	1.58	2	2-13	0	-0.3
Total 3	301	1136	173	304	35	13	3	78	120	77	10	....	.268	.338	.329	.667	86	-19	135	4.09	-5	2-289	26	-0.8

• HAUTZ, Charlie Charles A. Hautz b: 2/5/1852, St. Louis, MO d: 1/24/1929, St. Louis, MO BR, 5'7", 150 lbs. Deb: 5/4/1875 U

YEAR TM-L	G	AB	R	H	2B	3B	HR	RBI	BB	SO	SB	CS	AVG	OBP	SLG	OPS	OPS+	BR/A	RC	RC/G	FR	G/POS	WS	TPW
1875 RS-n	19	83	5	25	3	0	0	4	0	9	5	1	.301	.301	.337	.639	134	4	10	5.09	1	1-19	....	0.5
1884 Pit-a	7	24	0	5	0	0	0	0	3	....	....	....	.208	.296	.208	.505	66	-1	2	2.20	0	/1-5,0-2(0-2-0)	0	-0.1

• HAWES, Bill William Hildreth Hawes b: 11/17/1853, Nashua, NH d: 6/16/1940, Lowell, MA BR/TR, 5'10", 155 lbs. Deb: 5/1/1879 Career OF: 23-16-54

YEAR TM-L	G	AB	R	H	2B	3B	HR	RBI	BB	SO	SB	CS	AVG	OBP	SLG	OPS	OPS+	BR/A	RC	RC/G	FR	G/POS	WS	TPW
1879 Bos-N	38	155	19	31	3	3	0	9	2	13	....	....	.200	.210	.258	.468	52	-8	9	1.95	-2	0-34(1-7-26)/C-5	1	-1.0
1884 Cin-U	79	349	80	97	7	4	4	....	5	....	....	....	.278	.288	.355	.643	108	1	37	4.07	-7	0-58(22-9-28),1-21	10	-0.8
Total 2	117	504	99	128	10	7	4	9	7	13	....	....	.254	.264	.325	.590	91	-7	45	3.37	-9	/0-92,1-21,C-5	11	-1.8

• HAWES, Roy Roy Lee Hawes b: 7/5/1926, Shiloh, IL BL/TL, 6'2", 190 lbs. Deb: 9/23/1951

YEAR TM-L	G	AB	R	H	2B	3B	HR	RBI	BB	SO	SB	CS	AVG	OBP	SLG	OPS	OPS+	BR/A	RC	RC/G	FR	G/POS	WS	TPW
1951 Was-A	3	6	0	1	0	0	0	0	0	1	0	0	.167	.167	.167	.333	-10	-1	0	.92	0	/1-1	0	-0.1

YEAR TM-L	G	AB	R	H	2B	3B	HR	RBI	BB	SO	SB	CS	AVG	OBP	SLG	OPS	OPS+	BR/A	RC	RC/G	FR	G/POS	WS	TPW
• HAWKES, Thorny	Thorndike Proctor Hawkes b: 10/15/1852, Danvers, MA d: 2/3/1929, Danvers, MA BR/TR, 5'8", 135 lbs. Deb: 5/1/1879																							
1879 Tro-N	64	250	24	52	6	1	0	20	4	14	....	....	.208	.220	.240	.460	55	-11	14	1.92	1	*2-64	2	-0.6
1884 Was-a	38	151	16	42	4	2	0	0	4	....	....	....	.278	.297	.331	.628	118	3	15	3.84	-1	2-38/0-2(0-2-0)	4	0.3
Total 2	**102**	**401**	**40**	**94**	**10**	**3**	**0**	**20**	**8**	**14**	**....**	**....**	**.234**	**.249**	**.274**	**.524**	**79**	**-7**	**29**	**2.60**	**0**	**2-102/0-2**	**6**	**-0.3**
• HAWKS, Chicken	Nelson Louis Hawks b: 2/3/1896, San Francisco, CA d: 5/26/1973, San Rafael, CA BL/TL, 5'11", 167 lbs. Deb: 4/14/1921																							
1921 NY-A	41	73	16	21	2	3	2	15	5	12	0	1	.288	.333	.479	.813	103	-0	11	5.49	-1	0-15(5-10-0)	2	-0.2
1925 Phi-N	105	320	52	103	15	5	5	45	32	33	3	6	.322	.387	.447	.834	103	1	55	6.18	2	1-90	8	-0.2
Total 2	**146**	**393**	**68**	**124**	**17**	**8**	**7**	**60**	**37**	**45**	**3**	**7**	**.316**	**.377**	**.453**	**.830**	**103**	**1**	**66**	**6.05**	**1**	**/1-90,0-15**	**10**	**-0.5**
• HAWORTH, Howie	Homer Howard "Cully" Haworth b: 8/27/1893, Newberg, OR d: 1/28/1953, Troutdale, OR BL/TR, 5'10.5", 165 lbs. Deb: 8/14/1915																							
1915 Cle-A	7	7	0	1	0	0	0	1	2	2	0	....	.143	.333	.143	.476	42	-0	0	1.47	0	/C-5	0	-0.1
• HAYDEN, Jack	John Francis Hayden b: 10/21/1880, Bryn Mawr, PA d: 8/3/1942, Haverford, PA BL/TL, 5'9", 170 lbs. Deb: 4/26/1901 Career OF: 30-4-112																							
1901 Phi-A	51	211	35	56	6	4	0	17	18	....	4	....	.265	.323	.332	.655	78	-6	25	4.16	-2	0-50(30-4-16)	3	-1.0
1906 Bos-A	85	322	22	80	6	4	1	14	17	....	6	....	.248	.292	.301	.594	86	-5	32	3.38	-1	0-85(0-0-85)	5	-1.2
1908 Chi-N	11	45	3	9	2	0	0	2	1	....	1	....	.200	.217	.244	.462	45	-3	3	1.79	-1	0-11(0-0-11)	0	-0.5
Total 3	**147**	**578**	**60**	**145**	**14**	**8**	**1**	**33**	**36**	**....**	**11**	**....**	**.251**	**.298**	**.308**	**.606**	**80**	**-15**	**60**	**3.53**	**-4**	**0-146**	**8**	**-2.6**
• HAYES, Bill	William Ernest Hayes b: 10/24/1957, Cheverly, MD BR/TR, 6', 195 lbs. Deb: 9/30/1980 C																							
1980 Chi-N	4	9	0	2	1	0	0	0	0	3	0	0	.222	.222	.333	.556	49	-1	1	2.57	0	/C-3	0	0.0
1981 Chi-N	1	0	0	0	0	0	0	0	0	0	0	0	....	....	....	....	-96	0	0	....	0	/C-1	0	0.0
Total 2	**5**	**9**	**0**	**2**	**1**	**0**	**0**	**0**	**0**	**3**	**0**	**0**	**.222**	**.222**	**.333**	**.556**	**49**	**-1**	**1**	**2.57**	**0**	**/C-4**	**0**	**-0.1**
• HAYES, Charlie	Charles Dewayne Hayes b: 5/29/1965, Hattiesburg, MS BR/TR, 6', 207 lbs. Deb: 9/11/1988 Career OF: 4-0-1																							
1988 SF-N	7	11	0	1	0	0	0	0	0	3	0	0	.091	.091	.091	.182	-50	-2	0	.25	-1	/0-4(3-0-1),3-3	0	-0.3
1989 SF-N	3	5	0	1	0	0	0	0	0	1	0	0	.200	.200	.200	.400	15	-1	0	1.35	0	/3-3	0	-0.1
Phi-N	84	299	26	77	15	1	8	43	11	49	3	1	.258	.284	.395	.679	92	-4	32	3.70	-3	3-82	6	-0.8
Yr.	87	304	26	78	15	1	8	43	11	50	3	1	.257	.283	.391	.674	91	-5	32	3.66	-3	3-85	6	-0.8
1990 Phi-N	152	561	56	145	20	0	10	57	28	91	4	4	.258	.296	.348	.644	77	-21	55	3.40	23	*3-146/1-4,2-1	9	0.3
1991 Phi-N	142	460	34	106	23	1	12	53	16	75	3	3	.230	.258	.363	.621	74	-19	39	2.80	9	*3-138/S-2	8	-0.9
1992 NY-A	142	509	52	131	19	2	18	66	28	100	3	5	.257	.300	.409	.709	97	-6	59	3.92	-14	*3-139/1-4	11	-2.0
1993 Col-N	157	573	89	175	**45**	2	25	98	43	82	11	6	.305	.359	.522	.881	114	10	98	6.02	-4	*3-154/S-1	20	0.8
1994 Col-N	113	423	46	122	23	4	10	50	36	71	3	6	.288	.348	.433	.781	88	-9	60	5.11	-4	*3-110	10	-1.1
1995 Phi-N	141	529	58	146	30	3	11	85	50	88	5	1	.276	.343	.406	.749	96	-3	70	4.61	-2	*3-141	13	-0.2
1996 Pit-N	128	459	51	114	21	2	10	62	36	78	6	0	.248	.303	.368	.671	74	-17	49	3.62	8	*3-124	8	-0.8
*NY-A	20	67	7	19	3	0	2	13	1	12	0	0	.284	.294	.418	.712	77	-3	8	4.28	0	3-19	2	-0.2
1997*NY-A	100	353	39	91	16	0	11	53	40	66	3	2	.258	.335	.397	.732	91	-5	45	4.34	-3	3-98/2-5	6	-0.6
1998 SF-N	111	329	39	94	8	0	12	62	34	61	2	1	.286	.353	.419	.772	108	4	50	5.58	3	3-46,1-45/D-2	11	0.3
1999 SF-N	95	264	33	54	9	1	6	48	33	41	3	1	.205	.295	.314	.610	59	-17	25	3.03	-3	3-55,1-20/D-2,0-1	4	-1.9
2000 Mil-N	121	370	46	93	17	0	9	46	57	84	1	1	.251	.353	.370	.723	85	-8	50	4.53	-7	3-59,1-57/D-1	7	-1.7
2001 Hou-N	31	50	4	10	2	0	0	4	7	16	0	0	.200	.298	.240	.538	40	-4	4	2.50	-1	3-11/1-2,D-1	1	-0.5
Total 14	**1547**	**5262**	**580**	**1379**	**251**	**16**	**144**	**740**	**420**	**918**	**47**	**31**	**.262**	**.319**	**.398**	**.717**	**88**	**-104**	**644**	**4.21**	**0**	***3-1328,1-132/2-6,D-6,0-5,S**	**116**	**-9.7**
• HAYES, Frankie	Frank Witman "Blimp" Hayes b: 10/13/1914, Jamesburg, NJ d: 6/22/1955, Point Pleasant, NJ BR/TR, 6', 185 lbs. Deb: 9/21/1933																							
1933 Phi-A	3	5	0	0	0	0	0	0	0	2	0	0	.000	.000	.000	.000	-99	-1	0	.00	0	/C-3	0	-0.2
1934 Phi-A	92	248	24	56	10	0	6	30	20	44	2	1	.226	.286	.339	.625	63	-14	25	3.35	-4	C-89	2	-1.3
1936 Phi-A	144	505	59	137	25	2	10	67	46	58	3	5	.271	.335	.388	.723	79	-19	66	4.64	-4	*C-143	8	-1.3
1937 Phi-A	60	188	24	49	11	1	10	38	29	34	0	0	.261	.359	.489	.849	114	4	34	6.55	-5	C-56	5	0.2
1938 Phi-A	99	316	56	92	19	3	11	55	54	51	2	3	.291	.396	.475	.871	120	10	62	7.14	-7	C-90	9	0.8
1939 Phi-A★	124	431	66	122	28	5	20	83	40	55	4	1	.283	.348	.510	.859	119	11	76	6.17	1	*C-114	17	1.8
1940 Phi-A★	136	465	73	143	23	4	16	70	61	59	9	3	.308	.389	.477	.866	126	20	89	7.08	2	*C-134/1-2	17	2.8
1941 Phi-A★	126	439	66	123	27	4	12	63	62	56	2	0	.280	.369	.442	.811	117	12	70	5.55	4	*C-123	15	2.2
1942 Phi-A	21	63	8	15	4	0	0	5	9	8	1	1	.238	.333	.302	.635	80	-2	6	3.22	1	C-20	1	0.0
StL-A	56	159	14	40	6	0	2	17	28	39	0	0	.252	.364	.327	.691	94	0	22	4.92	-2	C-51	6	0.1
Yr.	77	222	22	55	10	0	2	22	37	47	1	1	.248	.355	.320	.675	90	-1	28	4.41	-1	C-71	7	0.1
1943 StL-A	88	250	16	47	7	0	5	30	37	36	1	0	.188	.295	.276	.571	66	-9	22	2.77	-2	C-76/1-1	5	-0.8
1944 Phi-A★	155	581	62	144	18	6	13	78	57	59	2	1	.248	.315	.367	.682	96	-4	68	3.99	1	*C-155/1-1	18	0.7
1945 Phi-A	32	110	12	25	2	1	3	14	18	14	1	0	.227	.336	.345	.681	98	1	14	4.36	3	C-32	3	0.5
Cle-A★	119	385	39	91	15	6	6	43	53	52	1	1	.236	.335	.353	.688	104	3	49	4.26	10	*C-119	15	2.2
Yr.	151	495	51	116	17	7	9	57	71	66	2	1	.234	.335	.352	.687	103	4	63	4.28	13	*C-151	18	2.7
1946 Cle-A★	51	156	11	40	12	0	3	18	21	26	1	3	.256	.345	.391	.736	112	2	20	4.13	-3	C-50	5	0.2
Chi-A	53	179	15	38	6	0	2	16	29	33	1	1	.212	.322	.279	.601	72	-6	17	3.02	2	C-52	4	-0.2
Yr.	104	335	26	78	18	0	5	34	50	59	2	4	.233	.332	.331	.664	91	-4	37	3.53	-1	*C-102	9	0.0
1947 Bos-A	5	13	0	2	0	0	0	1	0	1	0	0	.154	.154	.154	.308	-13	-2	0	.77	0	/C-4	0	-0.2
Total 14	**1364**	**4493**	**545**	**1164**	**213**	**32**	**119**	**628**	**564**	**627**	**30**	**20**	**.259**	**.343**	**.400**	**.744**	**100**	**5**	**640**	**4.92**	**-3**	***C-1311/1-4**	**130**	**7.7**
• HAYES, Jackie	Minter Carney Hayes b: 7/19/1906, Clanton, AL d: 2/9/1983, Birmingham, AL BR/TR, 5'10.5", 165 lbs. Deb: 8/5/1927																							
1927 Was-A	10	29	2	7	0	0	0	2	1	2	0	0	.241	.267	.241	.508	33	-3	2	2.22	1	/S-8,3-1	0	-0.1
1928 Was-A	60	210	30	54	7	3	0	22	5	10	3	0	.257	.274	.319	.593	56	-13	19	3.04	6	2-41,S-15/3-2	3	-0.4
1929 Was-A	123	424	52	117	20	3	2	57	24	29	4	5	.276	.316	.351	.668	71	-19	47	3.76	2	3-63,2-57/S-2	8	-1.1
1930 Was-A	51	166	25	47	7	2	1	20	7	8	2	3	.283	.312	.367	.680	71	-8	18	3.81	2	2-29/3-9,1-8	3	-0.5
1931 Was-A	38	108	11	24	2	1	0	8	6	4	2	0	.222	.263	.259	.522	38	-9	8	2.41	-2	2-19/3-8,S-3	1	-0.9
1932 Chi-A	117	475	53	122	20	5	2	54	30	28	7	4	.257	.302	.333	.635	69	-22	48	3.53	-6	2-97,3-10,S-10	7	-1.9
1933 Chi-A	138	535	65	138	23	5	2	47	55	36	2	3	.258	.331	.331	.661	79	-15	61	3.94	6	*2-138	13	0.0
1934 Chi-A	62	226	19	58	9	1	1	31	23	20	3	2	.257	.325	.319	.644	65	-12	25	3.70	-11	2-61	2	-1.7
1935 Chi-A	89	329	45	88	14	0	4	45	29	15	3	1	.267	.327	.347	.673	72	-13	39	4.02	-5	2-85	6	-1.2
1936 Chi-A	108	417	53	130	34	3	5	84	35	25	4	2	.312	.366	.444	.810	96	-4	69	6.11	5	2-89,S-13/3-2	14	0.7
1937 Chi-A	143	573	63	131	27	4	2	79	41	37	1	6	.229	.282	.300	.583	47	-50	49	2.80	20	*2-143	8	-1.9
1938 Chi-A	62	238	40	78	21	2	1	20	24	6	3	2	.328	.389	.445	.835	106	2	42	6.57	-3	2-61	7	0.3
1939 Chi-A	72	269	34	67	12	3	0	23	27	10	0	3	.249	.320	.316	.636	61	-17	28	3.41	2	2-69	5	-0.9
1940 Chi-A	18	41	2	8	0	1	0	1	2	11	0	0	.195	.233	.244	.476	23	-5	3	2.01	1	2-15	0	-0.3
Total 14	**1091**	**4040**	**494**	**1069**	**196**	**33**	**20**	**493**	**309**	**241**	**34**	**31**	**.265**	**.318**	**.344**	**.663**	**70**	**-187**	**456**	**3.88**	**18**	**2-904/3-95,S-51,1-8**	**77**	**-10.1**
• HAYES, Jackie	John J. Hayes b: 6/27/1861, Brooklyn, NY TR, 5'8", 175 lbs. Deb: 5/2/1882 Career OF: 4-75-24																							
1882 Wor-N	78	326	27	88	22	4	4	54	6	26	....	....	.270	.283	.399	.682	113	4	38	4.36	-10	*O-58(0-55-3),C-15/3-5,S-1	7	-0.6
1883 Pit-a	85	351	41	92	23	5	3	0	15	....	....	....	.262	.292	.382	.674	121	9	40	4.34	-4	C-62,O-18(0-15-3)/1-5,S-5,2	9	0.8
1884 Pit-a	33	124	11	28	6	1	0	0	4	....	....	....	.226	.256	.290	.546	76	-3	9	2.70	-2	C-24/1-5,O-3(0-0-3),2-1	2	-0.3
Bro-a	16	51	4	12	3	0	0	0	3	....	....	....	.235	.278	.294	.572	86	-1	4	3.01	2	C-14/O-2(1-1-0)	2	0.2
Yr.	49	175	15	40	9	1	0	0	7	....	....	....	.229	.262	.291	.554	79	-4	14	2.79	0	C-38/1-5,O-5(1-1-3),2-1	4	-0.1
1885 Bro-a	42	137	10	18	3	0	0	10	5	....	....	....	.131	.179	.153	.333	6	-14	4	.88	-4	C-42	1	-1.3
1886 Was-N	26	89	8	17	3	0	3	9	4	23	0	....	.191	.226	.326	.552	70	-3	7	2.52	0	C-14,O-12(1-4-7)/2-1	1	-0.2
1887 Bal-a	8	28	2	4	3	0	0	3	0	....	0	....	.143	.143	.250	.393	9	-3	1	1.15	-2	/O-4(2-0-2),3-3,C-1	0	-0.4
1890 Bro-P	12	42	3	8	0	0	0	5	2	4	0	....	.190	.227	.190	.418	11	-6	2	1.48	-2	/O-6(0-6-0),S-3,C-2,2-1	0	-0.6
Total 7	**300**	**1148**	**106**	**267**	**63**	**10**	**10**	**81**	**39**	**53**	**0**	**....**	**.233**	**.260**	**.331**	**.591**	**88**	**-18**	**105**	**3.29**	**-22**	**C-174,O-103/1-10,S-9,3-8,2**	**22**	**-2.5**
• HAYES, John	John E. Hayes b: 1/1855, Brooklyn, NY, 5'7.5", 170 lbs. Deb: 9/9/1876																							
1876 NY-N	5	21	1	3	0	2	0	2	0	0	....	....	.143	.143	.333	.476	62	-1	1	1.59	0	/O-5(5-0-0)	0	-0.1

YEAR TM-L	G	AB	R	H	2B	3B	HR	RBI	BB	SO	SB	CS	AVG	OBP	SLG	OPS	OPS+	BR/A	RC	RC/G	FR	G/POS	WS	TPW
• HAYES, Von	Von Francis Hayes b: 8/31/1958, Stockton, CA BL/TR, 6'5", 185 lbs. Deb: 4/14/1981 Career OF: 237-398-555																							
1981 Cle-A	43	109	21	28	8	2	1	17	14	10	8	1	.257	.352	.394	.746	116	4	17	5.09	0	D-21,0-13(12-0-1)/3-5	4	0.3
1982 Cle-A	150	527	65	132	25	3	14	82	42	63	32	13	.250	.311	.389	.700	91	-5	63	3.99	2	*0-139(14-7-123)/3-5,1-4	11	-1.1
1983*Phi-N	124	351	45	93	9	5	6	32	36	55	20	12	.265	.338	.370	.709	97	-2	42	3.97	-1	*0-103(33-39-77)	9	-0.7
1984 Phi-N	152	561	85	164	27	6	16	67	59	84	48	13	.292	.360	.447	.807	124	22	94	5.99	-6	*0-148(14-116-36)	21	1.3
1985 Phi-N	152	570	76	150	30	4	13	70	61	99	21	8	.263	.334	.398	.733	101	2	79	4.85	-6	*0-146(66-123-14)	19	-0.9
1986 Phi-N	158	610	**107**	186	**46**	2	19	98	74	77	24	12	.305	.381	.480	.861	131	27	111	6.57	0	*1-134,0-31(24-6-3)	26	1.8
1987 Phi-N	158	556	84	154	36	5	21	84	121	77	16	7	.277	.406	.473	.879	128	28	113	7.21	-7	*1-144,0-32(5-29-3)	23	1.2
1988 Phi-N	104	367	43	100	28	2	6	45	49	59	20	9	.272	.360	.409	.768	118	10	57	5.42	-1	1-85,0-16(4-12-2)/3-3	14	0.2
1989 Phi-N★	154	540	93	140	27	2	26	78	101	103	28	7	.259	.380	.461	.841	139	34	103	6.61	3	*0-128(0-13-124),1-30,3-10	25	3.5
1990 Phi-N	129	467	70	122	14	3	17	73	87	81	16	7	.261	.382	.413	.795	119	16	78	5.66	-4	*0-127(45-4-81)	16	0.8
1991 Phi-N	77	284	43	64	15	1	0	21	31	42	9	2	.225	.308	.285	.593	69	-10	27	3.13	2	0-72(20-49-6)	5	-1.0
1992 Cal-A	94	307	35	69	17	1	4	29	37	54	11	6	.225	.308	.326	.634	77	-9	31	3.18	-1	0-85(0-0-85)/D-5,1-4	4	-1.3
Total 12	1495	5249	767	1402	282	36	143	696	712	804	253	97	.267	.357	.416	.773	113	115	814	5.35	-18	*0-1040,1-401/D-26,3-23	177	4.2
• HAYWORTH, Ray	Raymond Hall Hayworth b: 1/29/1904, High Point, NC d: 9/25/2002, Salisbury, NC BR/TR, 6', 180 lbs. Deb: 6/27/1926 C																							
1926 Det-A	12	11	1	3	0	0	0	5	1	1	0	0	.273	.333	.273	.606	59	-1	1	3.28	-1	/C-8	0	-0.2
1929 Det-A	14	43	5	11	0	0	0	4	3	8	0	0	.256	.304	.256	.560	45	-3	4	2.82	0	C-14	0	-0.2
1930 Det-A	77	227	24	63	15	4	0	22	20	19	0	2	.278	.336	.379	.715	79	-8	29	4.43	-7	C-76	4	-0.9
1931 Det-A	88	273	28	70	10	3	0	25	19	27	0	1	.256	.307	.315	.622	62	-14	27	3.44	1	C-88	4	-0.8
1932 Det-A	109	338	41	99	20	2	2	44	31	22	1	1	.293	.354	.382	.736	87	-6	47	5.07	-1	*C-106	12	0.0
1933 Det-A	134	425	37	104	14	3	1	45	35	28	0	0	.245	.302	.299	.601	59	-25	40	3.24	-2	*C-133	8	-1.8
1934*Det-A	54	167	20	49	5	2	0	27	16	22	0	2	.293	.355	.347	.702	82	-5	21	4.54	-3	C-54	6	-0.4
1935 Det-A	51	175	22	54	14	2	0	22	9	14	0	0	.309	.342	.411	.754	98	-1	25	5.14	2	C-48	7	0.4
1936 Det-A	81	250	31	60	10	0	1	30	39	18	0	0	.240	.347	.292	.639	59	-15	28	3.83	-9	C-81	5	-1.6
1937 Det-A	30	78	9	21	2	0	1	8	14	15	0	0	.269	.394	.333	.727	83	-1	12	5.19	0	C-28	3	0.0
1938 Det-A	8	19	1	4	0	0	0	5	3	4	1	0	.211	.318	.211	.529	33	-2	2	2.86	0	/C-7	0	-0.1
Bro-N	5	4	0	0	0	0	0	0	1	1	0	....	.000	.200	.000	.200	-40	-1	0	.35	0	/C-3	0	-0.1
1939 Bro-N	21	26	0	4	2	0	0	1	4	7	0	....	.154	.267	.231	.497	33	-2	2	1.56	0	C-18	0	-0.2
NY-N	5	13	1	3	0	0	0	0	0	1	0	....	.231	.231	.231	.462	24	-1	1	1.85	0	/C-5	0	-0.1
Yr.	26	39	1	7	2	0	0	1	4	8	0	....	.179	.256	.231	.487	31	-4	2	1.65	1	C-23	0	-0.3
1942 StL-A	1	1	0	1	0	0	0	0	0	0	0	0	1.000	1.000	1.000	2.000	456	0	1	∞	0	....	0	0.0
1944 Bro-N	7	10	0	0	0	0	0	0	2	1	0	....	.000	.167	.000	.167	-51	-2	0	.11	0	/C-6	0	-0.1
1945 Bro-N	2	2	0	0	0	0	0	0	1	0	0	....	.000	.333	.000	.333	-3	-0	0	1.17	0	/C-2	0	0.0
Total 15	699	2062	220	546	92	16	5	238	198	188	2	6	.265	.331	.332	.663	70	-87	237	4.00	-18	C-677	49	-6.2
• HAYWORTH, Red	Myron Claude Hayworth b: 5/14/1916, High Point, NC BR/TR, 6'1.5", 200 lbs. Deb: 4/21/1944																							
1944*StL-A	90	270	20	60	11	1	1	25	10	13	0	0	.222	.253	.281	.534	50	-18	18	2.28	-6	C-87	2	-2.1
1945 StL-A	56	160	7	31	4	0	0	17	7	6	0	2	.194	.228	.219	.446	28	-16	7	1.45	-2	C-55	3	-1.6
Total 2	146	430	27	91	15	1	1	42	17	19	0	2	.212	.243	.258	.501	42	-34	26	1.96	-9	C-142	5	-3.7
• HAZEWOOD, Drungo	Drungo La Rue Hazewood b: 9/2/1959, Mobile, AL BR/TR, 6'3", 210 lbs. Deb: 9/19/1980																							
1980 Bal-A	6	5	1	0	0	0	0	0	0	4	0	0	.000	.000	.000	.000	-101	-1	0	.00	0	/0-3(0-0-3)	0	-0.2
• HAZLE, Bob	Robert Sidney "Hurricane" Hazle b: 12/9/1930, Laurens, SC d: 4/25/1992, Columbia, SC BL/TR, 6', 190 lbs. Deb: 9/8/1955 Career OF: 11-0-64																							
1955 Cin-N	6	13	0	3	0	0	0	0	0	3	0	0	.231	.231	.231	.462	22	-1	1	1.87	2	/0-3(3-0-0)	0	0.0
1957*Mil-N	41	134	26	54	12	0	7	27	18	15	1	3	.403	.477	.649	1.126	214	21	41	12.92	-4	0-40(0-0-40)	10	1.7
1958 Mil-N	20	56	6	10	0	0	0	5	9	4	0	0	.179	.303	.179	.482	34	-5	4	2.24	0	0-20(0-0-20)	1	-0.6
Det-A	43	58	5	14	2	0	2	5	5	13	0	0	.241	.302	.379	.681	80	-2	7	4.31	0	0-12(8-0-4)	1	-0.2
Total 3	110	261	37	81	14	0	9	37	32	35	1	3	.310	.390	.467	.857	137	13	53	7.65	-2	/0-75	12	0.9
• HAZLETON, Doc	Willard Carpenter Hazleton b: 8/28/1876, Strafford, VT d: 3/10/1941, Burlington, VT BR Deb: 4/17/1902																							
1902 StL-N	7	23	0	3	0	0	0	0	2	....	0	....	.130	.231	.130	.361	12	-2	1	.94	-0	/1-7	0	-0.2
• HEALY, Fran	Francis Xavier Healy b: 9/6/1946, Holyoke, MA BR/TR, 6'5", 220 lbs. Deb: 9/3/1969																							
1969 KC-A	6	10	0	4	1	0	0	0	0	5	0	0	.400	.400	.500	.900	149	1	2	9.00	0	/C-5	1	0.1
1971 SF-N	47	93	10	26	3	0	2	11	15	24	1	0	.280	.380	.376	.756	117	3	14	5.57	-2	C-22	3	0.2
1972 SF-N	45	99	12	15	4	0	1	8	13	24	0	1	.152	.257	.222	.479	37	-8	6	1.88	2	C-43	1	-0.6
1973 KC-A	95	279	25	77	15	2	6	34	31	56	3	4	.276	.348	.409	.757	104	1	40	5.03	-1	C-92/D-1	11	0.4
1974 KC-A	139	445	59	112	24	2	9	53	62	73	16	8	.252	.344	.375	.720	101	3	59	4.41	-9	*C-138	12	0.1
1975 KC-A	56	188	16	48	5	2	2	18	14	19	4	3	.255	.307	.335	.642	79	-6	18	3.33	-3	C-51/D-4	4	-0.7
1976 KC-A	8	24	2	3	0	0	0	1	4	10	2	0	.125	.250	.125	.375	12	-2	1	1.34	1	/C-6,D-1	0	-0.1
NY-A	46	120	10	32	3	0	0	9	9	17	3	1	.267	.318	.292	.609	80	-3	11	3.27	0	C-31/D-9	3	-0.2
Yr.	54	144	12	35	3	0	0	10	13	27	5	1	.243	.306	.264	.570	68	-5	12	2.90	1	C-37,D-10	3	-0.3
1977 NY-A	27	67	10	15	5	0	0	7	6	13	1	0	.224	.288	.299	.586	61	-3	6	3.03	-3	C-26	1	-0.5
1978 NY-A	1	1	0	0	0	0	0	0	0	1	0	0	.000	.000	.000	.000	-102	-0	0	.00	0	/C-1	0	-0.1
Total 9	470	1326	144	332	60	6	20	141	154	242	30	17	.250	.329	.350	.679	90	-15	158	4.04	-16	C-415/D-15	36	-1.3
• HEALY, Francis	Francis Xavier Paul Healy b: 7/29/1910, Holyoke, MA d: 2/12/1997, Springfield, MA BR/TR, 5'9.5", 175 lbs. Deb: 4/29/1930																							
1930 NY-N	7	2	2	0	0	0	0	0	0	0	0	....	.000	.000	.000	.000	-102	-1	0	.00	0	/C-1	0	-0.1
1931 NY-N	6	7	1	1	0	0	0	0	0	0	0	....	.143	.143	.143	.286	-24	-1	0	.60	0	/C-4	0	-0.2
1932 NY-N	14	32	5	8	2	0	0	4	2	8	0	....	.250	.294	.313	.607	65	-2	3	3.26	-1	C-11	1	-0.2
1934 StL-N	15	13	1	4	1	0	0	1	0	2	0	....	.308	.308	.385	.692	79	-0	1	3.19	0	/C-2,3-1,0-1	0	0.0
Total 4	42	54	9	13	3	0	0	5	2	10	0	....	.241	.268	.296	.564	51	-4	4	2.71	-2	/C-18,3-1,0-1	1	-0.5
• HEALY, Thomas	Thomas Fitzgerald Healy b: 10/30/1895, Altoona, PA d: 1/10/1977, Cleveland, OH BR/TR, 6', 172 lbs. Deb: 7/13/1915																							
1915 Phi-A	23	77	11	17	1	0	0	5	6	4	0	4	.221	.310	.234	.544	65	-5	5	2.01	4	3-17/S-1	0	0.0
1916 Phi-A	6	23	4	6	1	1	0	2	1	2	1	....	.261	.320	.391	.711	119	0	3	4.82	-0	/3-6	1	0.1
Total 2	29	100	15	23	2	1	0	7	7	6	1	4	.230	.313	.270	.583	77	-4	8	2.59	4	/3-23,S-1	1	0.1
• HEARD, Charlie	Charles Heard b: 1/30/1872, Philadelphia, PA d: 2/20/1945, Philadelphia, PA BR/TR, 6'2", 190 lbs. Deb: 7/14/1890 ♦																							
1890 Pit-N	12	43	2	8	2	0	0	0	1	15	0	....	.186	.205	.233	.437	31	-2	2	1.59	-3	/0-6(1-0-5),P-6	0	-2.4
• HEARN, Ed	Edward John Hearn b: 8/23/1960, Stuart, FL BR/TR, 6'3", 215 lbs. Deb: 5/17/1986																							
1986 NY-N	49	136	16	36	5	0	4	10	12	19	0	1	.265	.324	.390	.714	99	-1	16	4.11	-8	C-45	4	-0.7
1987 KC-A	6	17	2	5	2	0	0	3	4	2	0	0	.294	.429	.412	.840	121	1	3	6.36	0	/C-5	1	0.1
1988 KC-A	7	18	1	4	2	0	0	1	0	1	0	0	.222	.222	.333	.556	53	-1	1	1.80	-0	/C-4,D-2	0	-0.1
Total 3	62	171	19	45	9	0	4	14	16	22	0	1	.263	.326	.386	.712	97	-1	20	4.07	-8	/C-54,D-2	5	-0.8
• HEARNE, Ed	Edmund Hearne b: 9/17/1888, Ventura, CA d: 9/8/1952, Sawtelle, CA BR/TR, 5'9", 160 lbs. Deb: 6/9/1910																							
1910 Bos-A	2	2	0	0	0	0	0	0	0	....	0	....	.000	.000	.000	.000	-98	-0	0	.00	0	/S-2	0	0.0
• HEARNE, Hughie	Hugh Joseph Hearne b: 4/18/1873, Troy, NY d: 9/22/1932, Troy, NY BR/TR, 5'8", 182 lbs. Deb: 8/29/1901																							
1901 Bro-N	2	5	1	2	0	0	0	3	0	....	0	....	.400	.400	.400	.800	129	0	1	7.24	0	/C-2	0	0.0
1902 Bro-N	66	231	22	65	10	0	0	28	16	....	3	....	.281	.336	.325	.661	103	1	28	4.27	-9	C-65	8	-0.1
1903 Bro-N	26	57	8	16	3	2	0	4	3	....	2	....	.281	.328	.404	.731	111	1	9	5.25	-1	C-17/1-2	2	0.1
Total 3	94	293	31	83	13	2	0	35	19	....	5	....	.283	.335	.341	.677	105	2	37	4.50	-10	/C-84,1-2	10	0.0
• HEARRON, Jeff	Jeffrey Vernon Hearron b: 11/19/1961, Long Beach, CA BR/TR, 6'1", 195 lbs. Deb: 8/25/1985																							
1985*Tor-A	4	7	0	1	0	0	0	0	0	2	0	0	.143	.143	.143	.286	-21	-1	0	.64	0	/C-4	0	-0.1

YEAR TM-L	G	AB	R	H	2B	3B	HR	RBI	BB	SO	SB	CS	AVG	OBP	SLG	OPS	OPS+	BR/A	RC	RC/G	FR	G/POS	WS	TPW
1986 Tor-A	12	23	2	5	1	0	0	4	3	7	0	0	.217	.308	.261	.569	55	-1	2	2.59	-1	C-12	0	-0.2
Total 2	16	30	2	6	1	0	0	4	3	9	0	0	.200	.273	.233	.506	39	-3	2	2.13	-1	/C-16	0	-0.3
• HEATH, Bill	William Chris Heath b: 3/10/1939, Yuba City, CA BL/TR, 5'8", 175 lbs. Deb: 10/3/1965																							
1965 Chi-A	1	1	0	0	0	0	0	0	0	0	0	0	.000	.000	.000	.000	-107	-0	0	.00	0	....	0	0.0
1966 Hou-N	55	123	12	37	6	0	0	8	9	11	1	0	.301	.353	.350	.703	103	1	15	4.45	2	C-37	4	0.5
1967 Hou-N	9	11	0	1	0	0	0	0	4	3	0	0	.091	.333	.091	.424	28	-1	1	1.84	1	/C-5	0	0.0
Det-A	20	32	0	4	0	0	0	4	1	4	0	0	.125	.152	.125	.277	-17	-5	1	.62	0	/C-7	0	-0.5
1969 Chi-N	27	32	1	5	0	1	0	1	12	4	0	0	.156	.386	.219	.605	65	-1	4	3.35	0	/C-9	1	-0.1
Total 4	112	199	13	47	6	1	0	13	26	22	1	0	.236	.327	.276	.604	72	-5	20	3.38	3	/C-58	5	-0.1
• HEATH, Jeff	John Geoffrey Heath b: 4/1/1915, Fort William, Canada d: 12/9/1975, Seattle, WA BL/TR, 5'11.5", 200 lbs. Deb: 9/13/1936 Career OF: 1127-17-159																							
1936 Cle-A	12	41	6	14	3	3	1	8	3	4	1	0	.341	.386	.634	1.021	147	3	10	9.94	0	0-12(10-2-0)	1	0.2
1937 Cle-A	20	61	8	14	1	4	0	8	0	9	0	1	.230	.230	.377	.607	50	-6	5	2.60	-1	0-14(2-0-12)	0	-0.6
1938 Cle-A	126	502	104	172	31	**18**	21	112	33	55	3	1	.343	.383	.602	.985	146	32	114	9.06	0	*0-122(113-0-9)	23	2.3
1939 Cle-A	121	431	64	126	31	7	14	69	41	64	8	4	.292	.354	.494	.848	119	10	75	6.43	4	*0-108(108-0-0)	16	0.7
1940 Cle-A	100	356	55	78	16	3	14	50	40	62	5	3	.219	.298	.399	.697	81	-11	45	4.32	0	0-90(90-0-0)	8	-1.6
1941 Cle-A★	151	585	89	199	32	**20**	24	123	50	69	18	12	.340	.396	.586	.982	165	50	138	9.18	-5	*0-151(25-0-126)	28	3.5
1942 Cle-A	147	568	82	158	37	13	10	76	62	66	9	9	.278	.350	.442	.792	130	19	89	5.57	5	*0-146(145-0-2)	24	1.6
1943 Cle-A★	118	424	58	116	22	6	18	79	63	58	5	8	.274	.369	.481	.850	157	28	79	6.63	0	*0-111(107-3-4)	24	2.3
1944 Cle-A	60	151	20	50	5	2	5	33	18	12	0	1	.331	.402	.490	.892	160	12	31	7.97	1	0-37(31-5-1)	7	1.1
1945 Cle-A	102	370	60	113	16	7	15	61	56	39	3	1	.305	.398	.508	.906	170	34	80	8.10	-11	*0-101(101-0-0)	20	1.8
1946 Was-A	48	166	23	47	12	3	4	27	36	36	0	4	.283	.411	.464	.875	153	12	34	7.37	-3	0-47(47-0-0)	9	0.6
StL-A	86	316	46	87	20	4	12	57	37	37	0	2	.275	.353	.478	.831	124	9	56	6.50	-1	0-83(83-0-0)	13	0.3
Yr.	134	482	69	134	32	7	16	84	73	73	0	6	.278	.374	.473	.847	135	21	90	6.80	-4	*0-130(130-0-0)	22	0.9
1947 StL-A	141	491	81	123	20	7	27	85	88	87	2	1	.251	.366	.485	.850	132	23	91	6.39	3	*0-140(140-0-0)	18	1.7
1948 Bos-N	115	364	64	116	26	5	20	76	51	46	2	....	.319	.404	.582	.986	167	34	89	9.41	0	*0-106(99-7-0)	20	2.7
1949 Bos-N	36	111	17	34	7	0	9	23	15	26	0	....	.306	.389	.613	1.002	174	11	27	9.17	1	0-31(26-0-5)	6	1.0
Total 14	1383	4937	777	1447	279	102	194	887	593	670	56	47	.293	.370	.509	.879	141	260	964	7.18	-7	*0-1299	217	17.6
• HEATH, Kelly	Kelly Mark Heath b: 9/4/1957, Plattsburg, NY BR/TR, 5'7", 155 lbs. Deb: 4/20/1982																							
1982 KC-A	1	1	0	0	0	0	0	0	0	0	0	0	.000	.000	.000	.000	-100	-0	0	.00	0	/2-1	0	0.0
• HEATH, Mickey	Minor Wilson Heath b: 10/30/1903, Toledo, OH d: 7/30/1986, Dallas, TX BL/TL, 6', 175 lbs. Deb: 4/18/1931																							
1931 Cin-N	7	26	2	7	0	0	0	3	2	5	0	....	.269	.321	.269	.591	64	-1	2	3.15	0	/1-7	0	-0.2
1932 Cin-N	39	134	14	27	1	3	0	15	20	23	0	....	.201	.310	.254	.563	55	-8	12	2.86	4	1-39	1	-0.7
Total 2	46	160	16	34	1	3	0	18	22	28	0	....	.213	.311	.256	.568	57	-9	15	2.90	4	/1-46	1	-0.9
• HEATH, Mike	Michael Thomas Heath b: 2/5/1955, Tampa, FL BR/TR, 5'11", 190 lbs. Deb: 6/3/1978 Career OF: 79-1-142																							
1978*NY-A	33	92	6	21	3	1	0	8	4	9	0	0	.228	.268	.283	.551	56	-5	7	2.61	-2	C-33	2	-0.6
1979 Oak-A	74	258	19	66	8	0	3	27	17	18	1	0	.256	.309	.322	.631	74	-9	23	2.94	3	0-46(23-0-23),C-22/3-7,D-3	4	-0.7
1980 Oak-A	92	305	27	74	10	2	1	33	16	28	3	3	.243	.280	.298	.579	63	-16	24	2.65	6	C-47,D-31/0-8(4-0-4)	4	-1.0
1981*Oak-A	84	301	26	71	7	1	8	30	13	36	3	3	.236	.270	.346	.615	80	-9	25	2.77	5	C-78/0-6(5-0-1)	8	0.0
1982 Oak-A	101	318	43	77	18	4	3	39	27	36	8	3	.242	.301	.352	.654	82	-7	35	3.74	4	C-90,0-10(9-0-2)/3-5	9	0.1
1983 Oak-A	96	345	45	97	17	0	6	33	18	59	3	4	.281	.319	.383	.701	98	-3	39	4.00	3	C-80,0-24(1-0-23)/3-2,D-2	9	0.2
1984 Oak-A	140	475	49	118	21	5	13	64	26	72	7	4	.248	.289	.396	.685	94	-6	50	3.57	4	*C-108,0-45(13-0-32)/3-2,S	12	0.1
1985 Oak-A	138	436	71	109	18	6	13	55	41	63	7	7	.250	.316	.408	.724	104	0	53	3.98	2	*C-112,0-35(16-0-24),3-13	13	0.6
1986 StL-N	65	190	19	39	8	1	4	25	23	36	2	3	.205	.294	.321	.615	70	-9	17	2.92	-3	C-63/0-2(1-0-1)	3	-0.9
Det-A	30	98	11	26	3	0	4	11	4	17	4	1	.265	.294	.418	.712	91	-1	12	4.37	-1	C-29/3-1	3	-0.1
1987*Det-A	93	270	34	76	16	0	8	33	21	42	1	5	.281	.340	.430	.770	107	0	38	4.93	0	C-67,0-24(4-1-20)/1-4,3-4,S,2	10	0.3
1988 Det-A	86	219	24	54	7	2	5	18	18	32	1	0	.247	.307	.365	.672	91	-3	24	3.75	-2	C-75/0-9(0-0-9)	6	-0.1
1989 Det-A	122	396	38	104	16	2	10	43	24	71	7	1	.263	.311	.389	.700	98	-1	44	3.76	6	*C-117/3-4,0-3(3-0-0),D-1	11	1.2
1990 Det-A	122	370	46	100	18	2	7	38	19	71	7	6	.270	.313	.386	.699	94	-5	41	3.77	-1	*C-117/0-3(0-0-3),D-2,S-1	5	0.1
1991 Atl-N	49	139	4	29	3	1	1	12	7	26	0	0	.209	.252	.266	.518	43	-11	9	2.00	1	C-45	1	-0.8
Total 14	1325	4212	462	1061	173	27	86	469	278	616	54	40	.252	.302	.367	.669	87	-85	443	3.53	24	*C-1083,0-215/D-39,3-38,1,S,2	100	-1.7
• HEATH, Tommy	Thomas George Heath b: 8/18/1913, Akron, CO d: 2/26/1967, Los Gatos, CA BR/TR, 5'10", 185 lbs. Deb: 4/23/1935																							
1935 StL-A	47	93	10	22	3	0	0	9	20	13	0	0	.237	.372	.269	.640	65	-4	11	4.00	1	C-37	2	-0.1
1937 StL-A	17	43	4	10	0	2	1	3	10	3	0	0	.233	.377	.395	.773	94	-0	7	5.70	0	C-14	1	0.1
1938 StL-A	70	194	22	44	13	0	2	22	35	24	0	1	.227	.345	.325	.670	69	-9	24	4.03	5	C-65	4	0.0
Total 3	134	330	36	76	16	2	3	34	65	40	0	1	.230	.357	.318	.675	71	-13	42	4.23	6	C-116	7	0.0
• HEATHCOTE, Cliff	Clifton Earl Heathcote b: 1/24/1898, Glen Rock, PA d: 1/18/1939, York, PA BL/TL, 5'10.5", 160 lbs. Deb: 6/4/1918 Career OF: 31-408-728																							
1918 StL-N	88	348	37	90	12	3	4	32	20	40	12	....	.259	.301	.345	.646	100	-1	38	3.70	-4	0-87(3-84-0)	8	-1.1
1919 StL-N	114	401	53	112	13	4	1	29	20	41	27	....	.279	.315	.339	.654	103	1	49	4.21	2	*0-101(1-85-17)/1-2	11	-0.4
1920 StL-N	133	489	55	139	18	8	3	56	25	31	21	14	.284	.320	.372	.693	101	-0	57	3.95	9	*0-129(0-74-57)	12	0.2
1921 StL-N	62	156	18	38	6	2	0	9	10	9	7	5	.244	.293	.308	.601	60	-9	14	2.83	-3	0-51(1-40-10)	1	-1.3
1922 StL-N	34	98	11	24	5	2	0	14	9	4	0	2	.245	.315	.337	.652	71	-5	10	3.42	-2	0-32(0-32-0)	1	-0.7
Chi-N	76	243	37	68	8	7	1	34	18	15	5	2	.280	.330	.383	.712	82	-6	31	4.48	-2	0-60(0-21-40)	5	-1.2
Yr.	110	341	48	92	13	9	1	48	27	19	5	4	.270	.325	.370	.695	79	-11	42	4.16	-4	0-92(0-53-40)	6	-1.9
1923 Chi-N	117	393	48	98	14	3	1	27	25	22	32	17	.249	.298	.308	.606	60	-22	36	2.96	4	*0-112(1-0-111)	5	-2.7
1924 Chi-N	113	392	66	121	19	7	0	30	28	28	26	24	.309	.356	.393	.749	100	-4	51	4.36	-1	*0-111(1-20-90)	12	-1.2
1925 Chi-N	109	380	57	100	14	5	5	39	39	26	15	11	.263	.343	.366	.709	80	-12	49	4.26	14	0-99(3-8-88)	8	-0.5
1926 Chi-N	139	510	98	141	33	3	10	53	58	30	18	....	.276	.353	.412	.764	104	3	74	4.98	13	*0-133(13-13-110)	16	0.6
1927 Chi-N	83	228	28	67	12	4	2	25	20	16	6	....	.294	.359	.408	.766	105	2	33	5.13	9	0-57(0-9-49)	8	0.6
1928 Chi-N	67	137	26	39	8	0	3	18	17	12	6	....	.285	.364	.409	.772	103	1	21	5.19	1	0-39(7-13-20)	4	0.0
1929*Chi-N	82	224	45	70	17	0	2	31	25	17	9	....	.313	.384	.415	.799	98	-0	36	5.78	3	0-52(1-6-45)	7	-0.1
1930 Chi-N	70	150	30	39	10	1	9	18	18	15	4	....	.260	.343	.520	.863	104	0	26	6.09	1	0-35(0-3-32)	4	-0.1
1931 Cin-N	90	252	24	65	15	6	0	28	32	16	3	....	.258	.342	.365	.707	96	-1	33	4.59	10	0-59(0-0-59)	6	0.6
1932 Cin-N	8	3	3	0	0	0	0	0	0	0	0	....	.000	.000	.000	.000	-103	-1	0	.00	0	....	0	-0.1
Phi-N	30	39	7	11	2	0	1	5	3	3	0	....	.282	.333	.410	.744	88	-1	6	4.77	-1	/1-7	1	-0.2
Yr.	38	42	10	11	2	0	1	5	3	3	0	....	.262	.311	.381	.692	76	-1	6	4.34	-1	/1-7	1	-0.3
Total 15	1415	4443	643	1222	206	55	42	448	367	325	191	75	.275	.333	.375	.708	92	-54	563	4.30	54	*0-1157/1-9	109	-7.6
• HEBNER, Richie	Richard Joseph Hebner b: 11/26/1947, Boston, MA BL/TR, 6'1", 197 lbs. Deb: 9/23/1968 C Career OF: 5-0-27																							
1968 Pit-N	2	1	0	0	0	0	0	0	0	0	0	0	.000	.000	.000	.000	-101	-0	0	.00	0	....	0	0.0
1969 Pit-N	129	459	72	138	23	4	8	47	53	53	4	1	.301	.383	.420	.803	127	19	77	6.10	-6	*3-124/1-1	20	1.3
1970*Pit-N	120	420	60	122	24	8	11	46	42	48	2	3	.290	.365	.464	.829	124	13	71	6.08	-8	*3-117	16	0.5
1971*Pit-N	112	388	50	105	17	8	17	67	32	68	2	2	.271	.331	.487	.818	128	12	62	5.56	-8	*3-108	16	0.4
1972*Pit-N	124	427	63	128	24	4	19	72	52	54	0	0	.300	.384	.508	.892	155	31	85	7.28	-12	*3-121	22	2.0
1973 Pit-N	144	509	73	138	28	1	25	74	56	60	0	1	.271	.348	.477	.825	130	19	85	5.93	-16	*3-139	21	0.3
1974*Pit-N	146	550	97	160	21	6	18	68	60	53	0	3	.291	.367	.449	.816	132	22	90	5.81	0	*3-141	22	2.2
1975*Pit-N	128	472	65	116	16	4	15	57	43	48	0	1	.246	.322	.392	.714	98	-3	61	4.42	-6	*3-126	12	-1.0
1976 Pit-N	132	434	60	108	21	3	8	51	47	39	1	3	.249	.328	.366	.694	96	-3	54	4.27	-12	*3-126	12	-1.6
1977*Phi-N	118	397	67	113	17	4	18	62	61	46	7	8	.285	.384	.484	.868	125	14	74	6.57	0	*1-103,3-13/2-1	16	0.8
1978*Phi-N	137	435	61	123	22	3	17	71	53	58	4	7	.283	.372	.464	.837	131	17	74	5.97	-6	*1-117,3-19/2-1	16	0.4
1979 NY-N	136	473	54	127	25	2	10	79	59	59	3	1	.268	.359	.393	.752	109	8	71	5.24	2	*3-134/1-6	14	0.8
1980 Det-A	104	341	48	99	10	7	12	82	38	45	0	3	.290	.365	.466	.831	123	10	57	5.97	5	1-61,3-32/D-5	12	1.1
1981 Det-A	78	226	19	51	8	2	5	28	27	28	1	2	.226	.314	.345	.659	87	-4	24	3.56	-2	1-61,D-11	4	-1.0
1982 Det-A	68	179	25	49	6	0	8	18	25	21	1	1	.274	.363	.441	.804	119	5	30	6.13	2	1-40,D-20	6	0.5

YEAR TM-L	G	AB	R	H	2B	3B	HR	RBI	BB	SO	SB	CS	AVG	OBP	SLG	OPS	OPS+	BR/A	RC	RC/G	FR	G/POS	WS	TPW
Pit-N	25	70	6	21	2	0	2	12	5	3	4	0	.300	.347	.414	.761	109	2	11	5.73	0	0-21(0-0-21)/1-4,3-1	2	0.1
1983 Pit-N	78	162	23	43	4	1	5	26	17	28	8	3	.265	.339	.395	.734	100	1	22	4.57	-4	3-40/1-7,0-7(2-0-5)	4	-0.5
1984*Chi-N	44	81	12	27	3	0	2	8	10	15	1	0	.333	.407	.444	.851	127	4	15	7.16	-1	3-14/1-3,0-3(2-0-1)	4	0.2
1985 Chi-N	83	120	10	26	2	0	3	22	7	15	0	1	.217	.266	.308	.574	54	-8	9	2.62	-2	1-12/3-7,0-1	0	-1.1
Total 18	1908	6144	865	1694	273	57	203	890	687	741	38	40	.276	.356	.438	.793	120	159	972	5.58	-74	*3-1262,1-415/D-36,0-32,2-2	219	5.6

• HECHINGER, Mike Michael Vincent Hechinger b: 2/14/1890, Chicago, IL d: 8/13/1967, Chicago, IL BR/TR, 6', 175 lbs. Deb: 9/27/1912

YEAR TM-L	G	AB	R	H	2B	3B	HR	RBI	BB	SO	SB	CS	AVG	OBP	SLG	OPS	OPS+	BR/A	RC	RC/G	FR	G/POS	WS	TPW
1912 Chi-N	2	3	0	0	0	0	0	0	2	0	0	....	.000	.400	.000	.400	14	-0	0	.00	0	/C-2	0	0.0
1913 Chi-N	2	2	0	0	0	0	0	0	0	0	0	....	.000	.000	.000	.000	-100	-0	0	.00	0	....	0	-0.1
Bro-N	9	11	1	2	1	0	0	0	0	2	0	....	.182	.182	.273	.455	28	-1	0	1.38	-1	/C-4	0	-0.2
Yr.	11	13	1	2	1	0	0	0	0	2	0	....	.154	.154	.231	.385	8	-2	0	1.13	-1	/C-4	0	-0.2
Total 2	13	16	1	2	1	0	0	0	2	2	0	....	.125	.222	.188	.410	10	-2	0	.88	-1	/C-6	0	-0.2

• HECKER, Guy Guy Jackson Hecker b: 4/3/1856, Youngsville, PA d: 12/3/1938, Wooster, OH BR/TR, 6', 190 lbs. Deb: 5/2/1882 M/U Career OF: 44-18-13 ♦

YEAR TM-L	G	AB	R	H	2B	3B	HR	RBI	BB	SO	SB	CS	AVG	OBP	SLG	OPS	OPS+	BR/A	RC	RC/G	FR	G/POS	WS	TPW
1882 Lou-a	78	340	62	94	14	4	3	....	5	....	....	....	.276	.287	.368	.655	126	11	37	4.18	7	*1-66,P-13/0-2(0-2-0)	17	2.0
1883 Lou-a	81	332	59	90	6	6	1	0	12	....	....	....	.271	.297	.334	.631	111	13	34	3.90	5	P-53,0-23(9-14-0),1-10	36	1.1
1884 Lou-a	78	316	53	94	14	8	4	42	10	....	....	....	.297	.323	.430	.754	150	28	45	5.58	7	*P-75/0-5(4-1-0)	74	9.1
1885 Lou-a	70	297	48	81	9	2	2	35	5	....	....	....	.273	.287	.337	.624	97	9	29	3.68	3	P-53,1-17/0-3(3-0-0)	42	5.8
1886 Lou-a	84	343	76	117	14	5	4	48	32	....	25	....	**.341**	.402	.446	.848	157	28	73	8.76	-1	P-49,1-22,0-17(6-0-11)	39	4.8
1887 Lou-a	91	401	89	149	21	6	4	50	31	....	48	....	.372	.381	.441	.821	126	19	82	8.82	-1	1-43,P-34,0-16(16-0-0)	30	0.9
1888 Lou-a	56	211	32	48	9	2	0	29	11	....	20	....	.227	.285	.289	.574	86	1	24	3.92	-5	1-30,P-26/0-1	9	-0.8
1889 Lou-a	81	327	42	93	17	5	1	36	18	27	17	....	.284	.333	.376	.709	104	5	48	5.42	-4	1-65,P-19/0-1	7	-2.6
1890 Pit-N	86	340	43	77	13	9	0	38	19	17	13	....	.226	.285	.318	.603	86	-2	35	3.57	-2	1-69,P-14/0-7(5-1-1)	5	-2.3
Total 9	705	2907	504	843	117	47	19	278	143	44	123	....	.290	.324	.376	.699	117	111	408	5.36	9	P-336,1-322/0-75	259	18.0

• HEEP, Danny Daniel William Heep b: 7/3/1957, San Antonio, TX BL/TL, 5'11", 185 lbs. Deb: 8/31/1979 Career OF: 181-26-232

YEAR TM-L	G	AB	R	H	2B	3B	HR	RBI	BB	SO	SB	CS	AVG	OBP	SLG	OPS	OPS+	BR/A	RC	RC/G	FR	G/POS	WS	TPW
1979 Hou-N	14	14	0	2	0	0	0	2	1	4	0	0	.143	.200	.143	.343	-5	-2	1	1.03	0	/0-2(2-0-0)	0	-0.2
1980*Hou-N	33	87	6	24	8	0	0	6	8	9	0	0	.276	.344	.368	.712	107	1	12	5.00	-1	1-22	3	-0.2
1981 Hou-N	33	96	6	24	3	0	0	11	10	11	0	0	.250	.321	.281	.602	76	-3	9	3.06	-1	1-22/0-1	1	-0.6
1982 Hou-N	85	198	16	47	14	1	4	22	21	31	0	2	.237	.314	.379	.692	100	-1	23	3.82	-2	0-39(1-0-39),1-16	5	-0.6
1983 NY-N	115	253	30	64	12	0	8	21	29	40	3	3	.253	.332	.395	.727	102	-0	33	4.39	-0	0-61(11-19-31),1-14	7	-0.3
1984 NY-N	99	199	36	46	9	2	1	12	27	22	3	1	.231	.326	.312	.638	81	-4	20	3.21	-1	0-48(25-0-23),1-10	4	-0.9
1985 NY-N	95	271	26	76	17	0	7	42	27	27	2	2	.280	.348	.421	.768	117	5	37	4.64	-5	0-78(45-7-31)/1-4	9	-0.4
1986*NY-N	86	195	24	55	8	2	5	33	30	31	1	4	.282	.381	.421	.801	124	6	31	5.70	1	0-56(44-0-13)	8	0.5
1987 LA-N	60	98	7	16	4	0	0	9	8	10	1	0	.163	.226	.204	.430	16	-12	4	1.18	1	0-22(17-0-6)/1-6	0	-1.2
1988*LA-N	95	149	14	36	2	0	0	11	22	13	2	0	.242	.343	.255	.598	76	-3	14	3.31	1	0-32(17-0-16),1-12/P-1	3	-0.5
1989 Bos-A	113	320	36	96	17	0	5	49	29	26	0	1	.300	.360	.400	.760	107	3	43	4.82	0	0-75(17-0-59),1-19/D-9	9	0.1
1990*Bos-A	41	69	3	12	1	1	0	8	7	14	0	0	.174	.260	.217	.477	33	-6	5	2.10	1	0-14(1-0-13)/D-6,1-5,P-1	0	-0.6
1991 Atl-N	14	12	4	5	1	0	0	3	1	4	0	1	.417	.462	.500	.962	161	1	2	8.13	0	/1-1,0-1	1	0.0
Total 13	883	1961	208	503	96	6	30	229	220	242	12	14	.257	.334	.357	.692	95	-15	233	4.03	-7	0-429,1-131/D-15,P-2	50	-4.7

• HEFFERNAN, Bert Bertram Alexander Heffernan b: 3/3/1965, Centereach, NY BL/TR, 5'10", 185 lbs. Deb: 5/13/1992

YEAR TM-L	G	AB	R	H	2B	3B	HR	RBI	BB	SO	SB	CS	AVG	OBP	SLG	OPS	OPS+	BR/A	RC	RC/G	FR	G/POS	WS	TPW
1992 Sea-A	8	11	0	1	1	0	0	1	0	1	0	0	.091	.091	.182	.273	-25	-2	0	.00	0	/C-5,D-1	0	-0.2

• HEFFNER, Don Donald Henry "Jeep" Heffner b: 2/8/1911, Rouzerville, PA d: 8/1/1989, Pasadena, CA BR/TR, 5'10", 155 lbs. Deb: 4/17/1934 M/C

YEAR TM-L	G	AB	R	H	2B	3B	HR	RBI	BB	SO	SB	CS	AVG	OBP	SLG	OPS	OPS+	BR/A	RC	RC/G	FR	G/POS	WS	TPW
1934 NY-A	72	241	29	63	8	3	0	25	25	18	1	1	.261	.331	.320	.650	73	-9	27	3.86	2	2-68	5	-0.2
1935 NY-A	10	36	3	11	3	1	0	8	4	1	0	0	.306	.375	.444	.819	118	1	6	6.50	0	2-10	1	0.2
1936 NY-A	19	48	7	11	2	1	0	6	6	5	0	0	.229	.315	.313	.627	57	-3	5	3.53	3	/3-8,2-5,S-3	1	0.0
1937 NY-A	60	201	23	50	6	5	0	21	19	19	1	4	.249	.314	.328	.642	62	-13	20	3.45	-1	2-38,S-13/3-3,1-1,0-1	3	-1.1
1938 StL-A	141	473	47	116	23	3	2	69	65	53	1	1	.245	.341	.319	.661	67	-23	56	4.01	-2	*2-141	6	-1.5
1939 StL-A	110	375	45	100	10	2	1	35	48	39	1	7	.267	.350	.312	.662	69	-19	41	3.61	-9	S-73,2-32	4	-1.9
1940 StL-A	126	487	52	115	23	2	3	53	39	37	5	5	.236	.295	.310	.606	56	-33	45	3.15	5	*2-125	6	-1.9
1941 StL-A	110	399	48	93	14	2	0	17	38	27	5	6	.233	.303	.278	.581	53	-28	36	3.04	1	*2-105	4	-2.0
1942 StL-A	19	36	2	6	2	0	0	3	1	4	1	0	.167	.189	.222	.411	15	-4	1	1.02	-1	/2-6,1-4	0	-0.5
1943 StL-A	18	33	2	4	1	0	0	2	2	2	0	0	.121	.171	.152	.323	-5	-4	1	.76	-1	2-13/1-1	0	-0.6
Phi-A	52	178	17	37	6	0	0	8	18	12	3	2	.208	.284	.242	.526	55	-10	13	2.35	-4	2-47/1-1	2	-1.3
Yr.	70	211	19	41	7	0	0	10	20	14	3	2	.194	.267	.227	.495	45	-14	14	2.07	-6	2-60/1-2	2	-1.8
1944 Det-A	6	19	0	4	1	0	0	1	5	1	0	0	.211	.375	.263	.638	80	-0	2	4.34	0	/2-5	1	0.0
Total 11	743	2526	275	610	99	19	6	248	270	218	18	26	.241	.317	.303	.620	61	-146	254	3.38	-7	2-595/S-89,3-11,1-7,0-1	33	-10.7

• HEGAN, Jim James Edward Hegan b: 8/3/1920, Lynn, MA d: 6/17/1984, Swampscott, MA BR/TR, 6'2", 195 lbs. Deb: 9/9/1941 C

YEAR TM-L	G	AB	R	H	2B	3B	HR	RBI	BB	SO	SB	CS	AVG	OBP	SLG	OPS	OPS+	BR/A	RC	RC/G	FR	G/POS	WS	TPW
1941 Cle-A	16	47	4	15	2	0	1	5	4	7	0	0	.319	.373	.426	.798	116	1	8	5.92	0	C-16	2	0.2
1942 Cle-A	68	170	10	33	5	0	0	11	11	31	1	3	.194	.243	.224	.467	34	-16	9	1.68	1	C-66	3	-1.2
1946 Cle-A	88	271	29	64	11	5	0	17	17	44	1	4	.236	.284	.314	.597	71	-12	23	2.74	3	C-87	5	-0.5
1947 Cle-A★	135	378	38	94	14	5	4	42	41	49	3	1	.249	.324	.344	.668	88	-6	44	4.01	2	*C-133	13	0.3
1948*Cle-A	144	472	60	117	21	6	14	61	48	74	6	3	.248	.317	.407	.724	94	-6	62	4.52	6	*C-142	17	0.8
1949 Cle-A★	152	468	54	105	19	5	8	55	49	89	1	0	.224	.298	.338	.635	69	-22	49	3.40	4	*C-152	15	-1.0
1950 Cle-A★	131	415	53	91	16	5	14	58	42	52	1	0	.219	.291	.383	.674	74	-18	47	3.66	9	*C-129	14	-0.2
1951 Cle-A★	133	416	60	99	17	5	6	43	38	72	0	3	.238	.302	.346	.648	79	-14	45	3.66	2	*C-129	14	-0.5
1952 Cle-A★	112	333	39	75	17	2	4	41	29	47	0	2	.225	.287	.324	.612	75	-13	32	3.26	-2	*C-107	9	-1.0
1953 Cle-A	112	299	37	65	10	1	9	37	25	41	1	2	.217	.280	.348	.628	70	-14	29	3.11	-6	*C-106	5	-1.5
1954*Cle-A	139	423	56	99	12	7	11	40	34	48	0	1	.234	.291	.374	.665	80	-14	43	3.32	-2	*C-137	15	-1.0
1955 Cle-A	116	304	30	67	5	2	9	40	34	33	0	1	.220	.299	.339	.638	69	-14	31	3.25	3	*C-111	9	-0.7
1956 Cle-A	122	315	42	70	15	2	6	34	49	54	1	1	.222	.327	.340	.667	75	-11	36	3.78	-6	*C-118	8	-1.2
1957 Cle-A	58	148	14	32	7	0	4	15	16	23	0	1	.216	.293	.345	.637	74	-6	15	3.17	-1	C-58	4	-0.4
1958 Det-A	45	130	14	25	6	0	1	7	10	32	0	0	.192	.250	.262	.512	38	-11	8	1.91	1	C-45	2	-0.8
Phi-N	25	59	5	13	6	0	0	6	4	16	0	0	.220	.270	.322	.592	57	-4	5	3.17	0	C-25	1	-0.3
1959 Phi-N	25	51	1	10	1	0	0	8	3	10	0	1	.196	.241	.216	.456	22	-6	3	1.65	1	C-25	0	-0.4
SF-N	21	30	0	4	1	0	0	0	1	10	0	1	.133	.161	.167	.328	-13	-5	1	.49	0	C-21	1	-0.5
Yr.	46	81	1	14	2	0	0	8	4	20	0	2	.173	.212	.198	.409	10	-11	3	1.21	1	C-46	1	-0.9
1960 Chi-N	24	43	4	9	2	1	1	5	1	10	0	0	.209	.244	.372	.617	67	-2	3	2.48	0	C-22	0	-0.1
Total 17	1666	4772	550	1087	187	46	92	525	456	742	15	24	.228	.296	.344	.640	74	-193	491	3.40	16	*C-1629	137	-9.9

• HEGAN, Mike James Michael Hegan b: 7/21/1942, Cleveland, OH BL/TL, 6'1", 190 lbs. Deb: 9/13/1964 Career OF: 57-1-119

YEAR TM-L	G	AB	R	H	2B	3B	HR	RBI	BB	SO	SB	CS	AVG	OBP	SLG	OPS	OPS+	BR/A	RC	RC/G	FR	G/POS	WS	TPW
1964*NY-A	5	5	0	0	0	0	0	0	1	2	0	0	.000	.167	.000	.167	-48	-1	0	.23	1	/1-2	0	0.0
1966 NY-A	13	39	7	8	0	1	0	2	7	11	1	1	.205	.326	.256	.582	73	-1	3	2.51	0	1-13	0	-0.2
1967 NY-A	68	118	12	16	4	1	1	3	20	40	7	1	.136	.266	.212	.478	44	-6	9	2.21	-2	1-54,0-10(0-0-10)	1	-1.2
1969 Sea-A★	95	267	54	78	9	6	8	37	62	61	6	5	.292	.427	.461	.888	151	21	58	7.95	2	0-64(2-1-61),1-19	15	2.0
1970 Mil-A	148	476	70	116	21	2	11	52	67	116	9	7	.244	.338	.366	.704	93	-4	61	4.24	13	*1-139/0-8(2-0-6)	12	-0.1
1971 Mil-A	46	122	19	27	4	1	4	11	26	19	1	1	.221	.358	.369	.727	107	2	18	4.63	5	1-45	4	0.4
*Oak-A	65	55	5	13	3	0	0	3	5	13	1	0	.236	.300	.291	.591	69	-2	5	3.40	0	1-47/0-2(1-0-1)	1	-0.3
Yr.	111	177	24	40	7	1	4	14	31	32	2	1	.226	.341	.345	.686	97	0	23	4.27	5	1-92/0-2(1-0-1)	5	0.1
1972*Oak-A	98	79	13	26	3	1	1	5	7	20	1	0	.329	.384	.430	.814	150	5	14	6.32	0	1-64/0-3(0-0-3)	4	0.3
1973 Oak-A	75	71	8	13	2	0	1	5	5	17	0	0	.183	.237	.254	.490	40	-6	4	1.94	-3	1-56/D-3,0-3(2-0-1)	0	-1.0
NY-A	37	131	12	36	3	2	6	14	7	34	0	0	.275	.312	.466	.777	121	3	19	4.95	-0	1-37	3	0.0
Yr.	112	202	20	49	5	2	7	19	12	51	0	0	.243	.285	.391	.676	92	-3	23	3.83	-3	1-93/D-3,0-3(2-0-1)	3	-1.0
1974 NY-A	18	53	3	12	2	0	2	9	5	9	1	1	.226	.317	.377	.694	102	-0	6	3.54	-1	1-17	1	-0.2
Mil-A	89	190	21	45	7	1	7	32	33	34	0	4	.237	.350	.395	.745	114	3	27	4.79	-1	D-37,1-17,0-17(4-0-13)	6	0.0
Yr.	107	243	24	57	9	1	9	41	38	43	1	5	.235	.343	.391	.734	112	3	33	4.50	-2	D-37,1-34,0-17(4-0-13)	7	-0.2
1975 Mil-A	93	203	19	51	11	0	5	22	31	42	1	1	.251	.350	.379	.730	106	2	28	4.85	2	0-42(33-0-9),1-27/D-5	6	0.1

YEAR TM-L	G	AB	R	H	2B	3B	HR	RBI	BB	SO	SB	CS	AVG	OBP	SLG	OPS	OPS+	BR/A	RC	RC/G	FR	G/POS	WS	TPW
1976 Mil-A	80	218	30	54	4	3	5	31	25	54	0	0	.248	.328	.362	.690	104	1	27	4.21	0	D-40,0-20(5-0-15),1-10	5	0.0
1977 Mil-A	35	53	8	9	0	0	2	3	10	17	0	0	.170	.313	.283	.596	64	-2	6	3.38	-1	/0-8(8-0-0),D-7,1-6	1	-0.4
Total 12	965	2080	281	504	73	18	53	229	311	489	28	21	.242	.343	.371	.714	104	15	285	4.60	16	1-553,0-177/D-92	59	-0.7

• HEGMAN, Bob Robert Hilmer Hegman b: 2/26/1958, Springfield, MN BR/TR, 6'1", 180 lbs. Deb: 8/8/1985

YEAR TM-L	G	AB	R	H	2B	3B	HR	RBI	BB	SO	SB	CS	AVG	OBP	SLG	OPS	OPS+	BR/A	RC	RC/G	FR	G/POS	WS	TPW
1985 KC-A	1	0	0	0	0	0	0	0	0	0	0	0	....	....	....	....	-100	0	0	....	-1	/2-1	0	-0.1

• HEIDEMANN, Jack Jack Seale Heidemann b: 7/11/1949, Brenham, TX BR/TR, 6', 178 lbs. Deb: 5/2/1969

YEAR TM-L	G	AB	R	H	2B	3B	HR	RBI	BB	SO	SB	CS	AVG	OBP	SLG	OPS	OPS+	BR/A	RC	RC/G	FR	G/POS	WS	TPW
1969 Cle-A	3	3	0	0	0	0	0	0	0	2	0	0	.000	.250	.000	.250	-24	-0	0	.59	0	/S-3	0	0.0
1970 Cle-A	133	445	44	94	14	2	6	37	34	88	2	4	.211	.270	.292	.562	52	-30	35	2.51	-12	*S-132	4	-2.9
1971 Cle-A	81	240	16	50	7	0	0	9	12	46	1	3	.208	.252	.238	.489	36	-21	14	1.83	-8	S-81	2	-2.3
1972 Cle-A	10	20	0	3	0	0	0	0	2	3	0	0	.150	.261	.150	.411	24	-2	1	1.23	-1	S-10	0	-0.2
1974 Cle-A	12	11	2	1	0	0	0	0	0	2	0	0	.091	.091	.091	.182	-48	-2	0	.00	-2	/3-6,S-4,1-1,2-1	0	-0.4
StL-N	47	70	8	19	1	0	0	3	5	10	0	0	.271	.320	.286	.606	71	-3	7	3.34	-1	S-45/3-1	1	-0.2
1975 NY-N	61	145	12	31	4	2	1	16	17	28	1	0	.214	.296	.290	.586	66	-6	13	3.00	-4	S-44/3-4,2-1	2	-0.7
1976 NY-N	5	12	0	1	0	0	0	0	0	0	0	0	.083	.083	.083	.167	-56	-2	0	.20	0	/S-3,2-1	0	-0.2
Mil-A	69	146	11	32	1	0	2	10	7	24	1	3	.219	.255	.267	.522	54	-10	10	2.03	-4	3-40,2-24/D-1	1	-1.3
1977 Mil-A	5	1	1	0	0	0	0	0	1	0	0	0	.000	.500	.000	.500	50	0	0	3.51	0	/D-3,2-1	0	0.0
Total 8	426	1093	94	231	27	4	9	75	78	203	5	10	.211	.268	.268	.536	49	-77	80	2.32	-32	S-322/3-51,2-28,D-4,1-1	10	-8.2

• HEIDRICK, Emmet R. Emmet "Snags" Heidrick b: 7/29/1876, Queenstown, PA d: 1/20/1916, Clarion, PA BL/TR, 6', 185 lbs. Deb: 9/14/1898 Career OF: 3-596-150

YEAR TM-L	G	AB	R	H	2B	3B	HR	RBI	BB	SO	SB	CS	AVG	OBP	SLG	OPS	OPS+	BR/A	RC	RC/G	FR	G/POS	WS	TPW
1898 Cle-N	19	76	10	23	2	2	0	8	3	....	3	....	.303	.329	.382	.711	105	0	11	5.35	0	0-19(1-12-7)	2	-0.1
1899 StL-N	146	591	109	194	21	14	2	82	34	....	55	....	.328	.368	.421	.789	114	9	116	7.40	8	*0-145(0-2-143)	19	0.9
1900 StL-N	85	339	51	102	6	8	2	45	18	....	22	....	.301	.338	.383	.721	99	-1	53	5.81	9	0-83(0-83-0)	9	0.2
1901 StL-N	118	502	94	170	24	12	6	67	21	....	32	....	.339	.366	.470	.837	149	28	102	7.78	2	*0-118(0-118-0)	23	2.4
1902 StL-A	110	447	75	129	19	10	3	56	34	....	17	....	.289	.339	.396	.735	105	2	70	5.45	-1	*0-109(0-109-0)/3-1,P-1,S	16	-0.3
1903 StL-A	120	461	55	129	20	15	1	42	19	....	19	....	.280	.310	.395	.705	113	6	66	4.95	2	*0-119(0-119-0)/C-1	16	0.2
1904 StL-A	133	538	66	147	14	10	1	36	16	....	35	....	.273	.294	.342	.636	107	2	68	4.37	11	*0-130(0-130-0)	17	0.7
1908 StL-A	26	93	8	20	2	2	1	6	1	....	3	....	.215	.223	.312	.535	73	-3	7	2.37	0	0-25(2-23-0)	2	-0.5
Total 8	757	3047	468	914	108	73	16	342	146	....	186	....	.300	.333	.399	.732	114	44	493	5.83	31	0-748/3-1,C-1,P-1,S-1	104	3.6

• HEIFER, Frank Franklin "Heck" Heifer b: 1/18/1854, Reading, PA d: 8/29/1893, Reading, PA, 5'10.5", 175 lbs. Deb: 6/3/1875

YEAR TM-L	G	AB	R	H	2B	3B	HR	RBI	BB	SO	SB	CS	AVG	OBP	SLG	OPS	OPS+	BR/A	RC	RC/G	FR	G/POS	WS	TPW
1875 Bos-n	11	50	11	14	0	3	0	5	0	0	0	0	.280	.280	.400	.680	129	1	6	4.70	-2	/1-9,0-6(4-1-1),P-2	....	-0.1

• HEILEMAN, Chink John George Heileman b: 8/10/1872, Cincinnati, OH d: 7/19/1940, Cincinnati, OH BR/TR, 5'8", 155 lbs. Deb: 7/8/1901

YEAR TM-L	G	AB	R	H	2B	3B	HR	RBI	BB	SO	SB	CS	AVG	OBP	SLG	OPS	OPS+	BR/A	RC	RC/G	FR	G/POS	WS	TPW
1901 Cin-N	5	15	1	2	1	0	0	1	0	....	0	....	.133	.133	.200	.333	-4	-2	0	.84	-2	/3-4,2-1	0	-0.3

• HEILMANN, Harry Harry Edwin "Slug" Heilmann
b: 8/3/1894, San Francisco, CA d: 7/9/1951, Southfield, MI BR/TR, 6'1", 195 lbs. Deb: 5/16/1914 C HOF: 1952 Career OF: 13-62-1518

YEAR TM-L	G	AB	R	H	2B	3B	HR	RBI	BB	SO	SB	CS	AVG	OBP	SLG	OPS	OPS+	BR/A	RC	RC/G	FR	G/POS	WS	TPW
1914 Det-A	68	182	25	41	8	1	2	18	22	29	1	8	.225	.316	.313	.629	86	-6	18	2.93	-1	0-31(2-28-0),1-16/2-6	3	-1.0
1916 Det-A	136	451	57	127	30	11	2	73	42	40	9	....	.282	.349	.410	.760	124	12	70	5.34	-6	0-77(5-6-66),1-30/2-9	17	0.2
1917 Det-A	150	556	57	156	22	11	5	86	41	54	11	....	.281	.333	.387	.720	120	11	73	4.55	-4	*0-123(0-28-95),1-27	18	0.0
1918 Det-A	79	286	34	79	10	6	5	39	35	10	13	....	.276	.359	.406	.765	136	12	45	5.29	-3	0-40(0-0-40),1-37/2-2	12	0.8
1919 Det-A	140	537	74	172	30	15	8	93	37	41	7	....	.320	.366	.477	.843	139	25	93	6.35	-5	*1-140	23	1.8
1920 Det-A	145	543	66	168	28	5	9	89	39	32	3	7	.309	.358	.429	.787	111	6	82	5.43	3	*1-122,0-22(0-0-22)	16	0.6
1921 Det-A	149	602	114	**237**	43	14	19	139	53	37	2	6	**.394**	.444	.606	1.051	167	59	159	10.88	-12	*0-147(0-0-147)/1-3	28	3.4
1922 Det-A	118	455	92	162	27	10	21	92	58	28	8	4	.356	.432	.598	1.030	171	48	119	10.21	-11	*0-115(0-0-115)/1-5	24	2.7
1923 Det-A	144	524	121	211	44	11	18	115	74	40	9	7	**.403**	.481	.632	1.113	195	74	160	12.33	2	*0-130(6-0-124),1-12	35	6.2
1924 Det-A	153	570	107	197	**45**	16	10	114	78	41	13	5	.346	.428	.533	.961	149	45	134	8.78	12	*0-147(0-0-147)/1-4	30	4.2
1925 Det-A	150	573	97	225	40	11	13	134	67	27	6	6	**.393**	.457	.569	1.026	161	**55**	149	10.46	-7	*0-148(0-0-148)	30	3.4
1926 Det-A	141	502	90	184	41	8	9	103	67	19	6	7	.367	.445	.534	.979	152	40	120	9.11	-2	*0-134(0-0-134)	27	2.6
1927 Det-A	141	505	106	201	50	9	14	120	72	16	11	5	**.398**	.475	.616	1.091	179	62	150	12.18	-9	*0-135(0-0-135)	32	4.0
1928 Det-A	151	558	83	183	38	10	14	107	57	45	7	3	.328	.390	.507	.897	132	26	112	7.47	-3	*0-125(0-0-125),1-25	22	1.1
1929 Det-A	125	453	86	156	41	7	15	120	50	39	5	6	.344	.412	.565	.977	148	32	104	8.72	-10	*0-114(0-0-114)/1-2	19	1.2
1930 Cin-N	142	459	79	153	43	6	19	91	64	50	2	....	.333	.416	.577	.993	144	34	109	8.80	7	*0-106(0-0-106),1-19	20	2.7
1932 Cin-N	15	31	3	8	2	0	0	6	0	2	0	....	.258	.258	.323	.581	57	-2	3	2.84	0	/1-6	0	-0.2
Total 17	2147	7787	1291	2660	542	151	183	1539	856	550	113	64	.342	.410	.520	.930	148	533	1698	8.19	-48	*0-1594,1-448/2-17	356	33.8

• HEIM, Val Val Raymond Heim b: 11/4/1920, Plymouth, WI BL/TR, 5'11", 170 lbs. Deb: 8/31/1942

YEAR TM-L	G	AB	R	H	2B	3B	HR	RBI	BB	SO	SB	CS	AVG	OBP	SLG	OPS	OPS+	BR/A	RC	RC/G	FR	G/POS	WS	TPW
1942 Chi-A	13	45	6	9	1	1	0	7	5	3	1	0	.200	.294	.267	.561	60	-2	4	2.88	-1	0-12(9-0-3)	1	-0.4

• HEINE, Bud William Henry Heine b: 9/22/1900, Elmira, NY d: 9/2/1976, Fort Lauderdale, FL BL/TR, 5'8", 145 lbs. Deb: 10/1/1921

YEAR TM-L	G	AB	R	H	2B	3B	HR	RBI	BB	SO	SB	CS	AVG	OBP	SLG	OPS	OPS+	BR/A	RC	RC/G	FR	G/POS	WS	TPW
1921 NY-N	1	2	0	0	0	0	0	0	0	0	0	0	.000	.000	.000	.000	-100	-1	0	.00	0	/2-1	0	0.0

• HEINTZELMAN, Tom Thomas Kenneth Heintzelman b: 11/3/1946, St. Charles, MO BR/TR, 6'1", 180 lbs. Deb: 8/12/1973

YEAR TM-L	G	AB	R	H	2B	3B	HR	RBI	BB	SO	SB	CS	AVG	OBP	SLG	OPS	OPS+	BR/A	RC	RC/G	FR	G/POS	WS	TPW
1973 StL-N	23	29	5	9	0	0	0	0	3	3	0	0	.310	.375	.310	.685	92	-0	3	4.00	1	/2-6	1	0.1
1974 StL-N	38	74	10	17	4	0	1	6	9	14	0	0	.230	.313	.324	.638	79	-2	8	3.91	2	2-28/3-2,S-1	2	0.1
1977 SF-N	2	2	0	0	0	0	0	0	0	0	0	0	.000	.000	.000	.000	-100	-1	0	.00	0	....	0	-0.1
1978 SF-N	27	35	2	8	1	0	2	6	2	5	0	0	.229	.270	.429	.699	96	-0	4	4.19	1	/2-5,3-3,1-2	1	0.1
Total 4	90	140	17	34	5	0	3	12	14	22	0	0	.243	.312	.343	.655	84	-3	16	3.93	4	/2-39,3-5,1-2,S-1	4	0.3

• HEINZMAN, Jack John Peter Heinzman b: 9/27/1863, New Albany, IN d: 11/10/1914, Louisville, KY BR/TR Deb: 10/2/1886

YEAR TM-L	G	AB	R	H	2B	3B	HR	RBI	BB	SO	SB	CS	AVG	OBP	SLG	OPS	OPS+	BR/A	RC	RC/G	FR	G/POS	WS	TPW
1886 Lou-a	1	5	1	0	0	0	0	0	0	....	0	....	.000	.000	.000	.000	-95	-1	0	.00	-0	/1-1	0	-0.1

• HEISE, Bob Robert Lowell Heise b: 5/12/1947, San Antonio, TX BR/TR, 6', 175 lbs. Deb: 9/12/1967

YEAR TM-L	G	AB	R	H	2B	3B	HR	RBI	BB	SO	SB	CS	AVG	OBP	SLG	OPS	OPS+	BR/A	RC	RC/G	FR	G/POS	WS	TPW
1967 NY-N	16	62	7	20	4	0	0	3	3	1	0	1	.323	.354	.387	.741	114	1	8	4.57	0	2-12/S-3,3-2	2	0.2
1968 NY-N	6	23	3	5	0	0	0	1	1	1	0	0	.217	.250	.217	.467	41	-2	1	1.56	0	/S-6,2-1	0	-0.1
1969 NY-N	4	10	1	3	1	0	0	0	3	2	0	0	.300	.462	.400	.862	140	1	2	5.87	-0	/S-3	1	0.1
1970 SF-N	67	154	15	36	5	1	1	22	5	13	0	1	.234	.258	.299	.557	49	-12	11	2.38	-5	S-33,2-28/3-2	1	-1.3
1971 SF-N	13	11	2	0	0	0	0	0	0	1	0	0	.000	.000	.000	.000	-102	-3	0	.00	-1	/S-3,3-2,2-1	0	-0.4
Mil-A	68	189	10	48	7	0	0	7	7	15	1	1	.254	.281	.291	.572	63	-10	14	2.61	1	S-51,3-11/2-3,0-1	3	-0.3
1972 Mil-A	95	271	23	72	10	1	0	12	12	14	1	1	.266	.302	.310	.612	84	-6	25	3.08	-1	2-49,3-24/S-9	6	-0.4
1973 Mil-A	49	98	8	20	2	0	0	4	4	4	1	0	.204	.235	.224	.460	31	-9	5	1.52	-2	S-29/3-9,1-4,2-4,D-2	1	-0.9
1974 StL-N	3	7	0	1	0	0	0	0	0	0	0	0	.143	.143	.143	.286	-20	-1	0	.00	0	/2-3	0	-0.1
Cal-A	29	75	7	20	7	0	0	6	5	10	0	1	.267	.313	.360	.673	99	-1	8	3.72	2	2-17/3-6,S-3	2	0.2
1975 Bos-A	63	126	12	27	3	0	0	21	4	6	0	0	.214	.250	.238	.488	35	-11	8	2.05	-4	3-45,2-14/S-4,1-1	1	-1.4
1976 Bos-A	32	56	5	15	2	0	0	5	1	2	0	1	.268	.293	.304	.597	67	-3	5	2.75	-2	3-22/S-9,2-1	1	-0.4
1977 KC-A	54	62	11	16	2	1	0	5	2	8	0	1	.258	.292	.323	.615	67	-3	6	3.27	0	2-21,S-21,3-12/1-1	2	-0.1
Total 11	499	1144	104	283	43	3	1	86	47	77	3	7	.247	.281	.293	.574	64	-58	92	2.68	-11	S-174,2-154,3-135/1-6,D-2,0	20	-4.9

• HEIST, Al Alfred Michael Heist b: 10/5/1927, Brooklyn, NY BR/TR, 6'2", 185 lbs. Deb: 7/17/1960 C Career OF: 1-154-0

YEAR TM-L	G	AB	R	H	2B	3B	HR	RBI	BB	SO	SB	CS	AVG	OBP	SLG	OPS	OPS+	BR/A	RC	RC/G	FR	G/POS	WS	TPW
1960 Chi-N	41	102	11	28	5	3	1	6	10	12	3	1	.275	.339	.412	.751	106	1	14	5.00	1	0-33(1-32-0)	3	0.0
1961 Chi-N	109	321	48	82	14	3	7	37	39	51	3	3	.255	.338	.383	.721	90	-5	42	4.47	2	0-99(0-99-0)	7	-0.5
1962 Hou-N	27	72	4	16	1	0	0	3	3	9	0	0	.222	.263	.236	.499	38	-6	4	1.58	-1	0-23(0-23-0)	0	-0.7
Total 3	177	495	63	126	20	6	8	46	52	72	6	4	.255	.328	.368	.696	86	-10	60	4.13	2	0-155	10	-1.2

• HEITMULLER, Heinie William Frederick Heitmuller b: 5/25/1883, San Francisco, CA d: 10/8/1912, Los Angeles, CA BR/TR, 6'2", 215 lbs. Deb: 4/26/1909 Career OF: 69-18-2

YEAR TM-L	G	AB	R	H	2B	3B	HR	RBI	BB	SO	SB	CS	AVG	OBP	SLG	OPS	OPS+	BR/A	RC	RC/G	FR	G/POS	WS	TPW
1909 Phi-A	64	210	36	60	9	8	0	15	18	....	7	....	.286	.351	.405	.755	136	8	32	5.30	-2	0-61(54-7-0)	10	0.4
1910 Phi-A	31	111	11	27	2	2	0	7	7	....	6	....	.243	.288	.297	.585	84	-2	11	3.31	-1	0-28(15-11-2)	3	-0.5
Total 2	95	321	47	87	11	10	0	22	25	....	13	....	.271	.330	.368	.697	118	6	43	4.60	-2	/0-89	13	-0.1

YEAR	TM-L	G	AB	R	H	2B	3B	HR	RBI	BB	SO	SB	CS	AVG	OBP	SLG	OPS	OPS+	BR/A	RC	RC/G	FR	G/POS	WS	TPW
• HELD, Woodie	Woodson George Held b: 3/25/1932, Sacramento, CA BR/TR, 5'10.5", 180 lbs. Deb: 9/5/1954 Career OF: 113-276-111																								
1954	NY-A	4	3	2	0	0	0	0	0	2	1	0	0	.000	.400	.000	.400	17	-0	0	1.87	-1	/S-4,3-1	0	-0.1
1957	NY-A	1	1	0	0	0	0	0	0	0	0	0	0	.000	.000	.000	.000	-102	-0	0	.00	0	....	0	0.0
	KC-A	92	326	48	78	14	3	20	50	37	81	4	0	.239	.322	.485	.807	115	7	52	5.44	9	0-92(0-92-0)	13	1.2
	Yr.	93	327	48	78	14	3	20	50	37	81	4	0	.239	.322	.483	.805	115	7	52	5.42	9	0-92(0-92-0)	13	1.2
1958	KC-A	47	131	13	28	2	0	4	16	10	28	0	1	.214	.280	.321	.600	64	-7	11	2.61	-1	0-41(0-41-0)/3-4,S-1	1	-1.0
	Cle-A	67	144	12	28	4	1	3	17	15	36	1	2	.194	.288	.299	.587	63	-8	12	2.67	0	0-43(7-37-0),S-14/3-4	2	-0.9
	Yr.	114	275	25	56	6	1	7	33	25	64	1	3	.204	.284	.309	.593	63	-15	23	2.64	-1	0-84(7-78-0),S-15/3-8	3	-1.9
1959	Cle-A	143	525	82	132	19	3	29	71	46	118	1	2	.251	.314	.465	.779	115	8	74	4.89	1	*S-103,3-40/0-6(0-6-0),2-3	22	1.7
1960	Cle-A	109	376	45	97	15	1	21	67	44	73	0	1	.258	.344	.471	.814	122	10	62	5.79	13	*S-109	19	3.3
1961	Cle-A	146	509	67	136	23	5	23	78	69	111	0	0	.267	.358	.468	.826	122	16	85	5.80	-2	*S-144	21	2.6
1962	Cle-A	139	466	55	116	12	2	19	58	73	107	5	1	.249	.364	.406	.769	110	10	72	5.27	-1	*S-133/3-5,0-1	21	2.0
1963	Cle-A	133	416	61	103	19	4	17	61	61	96	2	2	.248	.355	.435	.790	121	13	66	5.35	9	2-96,0-35(12-12-12)/S-5,3	19	2.9
1964	Cle-A	118	364	50	86	13	0	18	49	43	88	1	0	.236	.329	.420	.749	107	4	51	4.84	-5	2-52,0-41(5-19-18),3-30	13	0.1
1965	Was-A	122	332	46	82	16	2	16	54	49	74	0	0	.247	.349	.452	.801	128	13	53	5.43	-5	*0-106(57-43-50)/3-5,2-4,S	14	0.3
1966	Bal-A	56	82	6	17	3	1	1	7	12	30	0	0	.207	.309	.305	.613	78	-2	9	3.58	-5	0-10(10-0-0)/2-5,3-3,S-3	2	-0.8
1967	Bal-A	26	41	4	6	3	0	1	6	6	12	0	0	.146	.286	.293	.578	72	-1	4	3.07	0	/2-9,3-5,0-2(2-0-0)	1	-0.1
	Cal-A	58	141	15	31	3	0	4	17	18	41	0	2	.220	.317	.326	.643	94	-1	14	3.06	3	3-19,0-17(8-10-1),S-13/2-3	4	0.2
	Yr.	84	182	19	37	6	0	5	23	24	53	0	2	.203	.310	.319	.628	89	-3	18	3.06	2	3-24,0-19(10-10-1),S-13,2-12	5	0.1
1968	Cal-A	33	45	4	5	1	0	0	0	5	15	0	0	.111	.231	.133	.364	13	-4	2	1.24	0	/2-5,3-5,S-5,0-3(0-1-2)	0	-0.5
	Chi-A	40	54	5	9	1	0	0	2	5	14	0	0	.167	.250	.185	.435	33	-4	3	1.60	0	0-33(9-3-23)/3-5,2-1	0	-0.6
	Yr.	73	99	9	14	2	0	0	2	10	29	0	0	.141	.241	.162	.403	24	-9	5	1.44	0	0-36(9-4-25),3-10/2-6,S-5	0	-1.1
1969	Chi-A	56	63	9	9	2	0	3	6	13	19	0	0	.143	.299	.317	.616	69	-2	7	3.15	0	0-18(3-11-5)/3-3,S-3,2-1	1	-0.3
Total	**14**	**1390**	**4019**	**524**	**963**	**150**	**22**	**179**	**559**	**508**	**944**	**14**	**11**	**.240**	**.333**	**.421**	**.755**	**108**	**51**	**578**	**4.84**	**14**	**S-539,0-448,2-179,3-132**	**153**	**10.3**
• HELF, Hank	Henry Hartz Helf b: 8/26/1913, Austin, TX d: 10/27/1984, Austin, TX BR/TR, 6'1", 196 lbs. Deb: 5/5/1938																								
1938	Cle-A	6	13	1	1	0	0	0	1	1	1	0	0	.077	.143	.077	.220	-44	-3	0	.38	0	/C-5	0	-0.2
1940	Cle-A	1	1	0	0	0	0	0	0	0	0	0	0	.000	.000	.000	.000	-103	-0	0	.00	0	/C-1	0	0.0
1946	StL-A	71	182	17	35	11	0	6	21	9	40	0	1	.192	.234	.352	.586	59	-11	14	2.42	0	C-69	2	-0.9
Total	**3**	**78**	**196**	**18**	**36**	**11**	**0**	**6**	**22**	**10**	**41**	**0**	**1**	**.184**	**.227**	**.332**	**.559**	**51**	**-15**	**14**	**2.26**	**0**	**/C-75**	**2**	**-1.1**
• HELFAND, Eric	Eric James Helfand b: 3/25/1969, Erie, PA BL/TR, 6', 195 lbs. Deb: 9/4/1993																								
1993	Oak-A	8	13	1	3	0	0	0	1	0	1	0	0	.231	.231	.231	.462	26	-1	1	1.87	1	/C-5	1	0.0
1994	Oak-A	7	6	1	1	0	0	0	1	0	1	0	0	.167	.167	.167	.333	-15	-1	0	.90	0	/C-6	0	-0.1
1995	Oak-A	38	86	9	14	2	1	0	7	11	25	0	0	.163	.265	.209	.475	27	-9	5	1.89	1	C-36	2	-0.5
Total	**3**	**53**	**105**	**11**	**18**	**2**	**1**	**0**	**9**	**11**	**27**	**0**	**0**	**.171**	**.256**	**.210**	**.466**	**25**	**-11**	**6**	**1.83**	**2**	**/C-47**	**3**	**-0.6**
• HELFRICH, Ty	Emory Wilbur Helfrich b: 10/9/1890, Pleasantville, NJ d: 3/18/1955, Pleasantville, NJ BR/TR, 5'10", 178 lbs. Deb: 6/30/1915																								
1915	Bro-F	43	104	12	25	6	0	0	5	15	21	2	....	.240	.336	.298	.634	89	-1	11	3.49	0	2-34/0-1	2	-0.1
• HELLINGS,	Hellings b: Philadelphia, PA Deb: 7/19/1875																								
1875	Atl-n	1	4	0	1	0	0	0	0	0	0	0	0	.250	.250	.250	.500	85	-0	0	2.52	0	/2-1	....	0.0
• HELLMAN, Tony	Anthony Joseph Hellman b: 5/29/1861, Cincinnati, OH d: 3/29/1898, Cincinnati, OH, 5'9" Deb: 10/10/1886																								
1886	Bal-a	1	3	0	0	0	0	0	0	0	....	0	....	.000	.000	.000	.000	-103	-1	0	.00	0	/C-1	0	-0.1
• HELMS, Tommy	Tommy Vann Helms b: 5/5/1941, Charlotte, NC BR/TR, 5'10", 175 lbs. Deb: 9/23/1964 M/C																								
1964	Cin-N	2	1	0	0	0	0	0	0	0	1	0	0	.000	.000	.000	.000	-97	-0	0	.00	0	....	0	0.0
1965	Cin-N	21	42	4	16	2	2	0	6	3	7	1	0	.381	.435	.524	.959	158	4	10	10.52	1	/S-8,3-2,2-1	3	0.5
1966	Cin-N	138	542	72	154	23	1	9	49	24	31	3	4	.284	.317	.380	.697	85	-12	61	3.92	0	*3-113,2-20	12	-1.0
1967	Cin-N★	137	497	40	136	27	4	2	35	24	41	5	10	.274	.307	.356	.663	80	-16	49	3.41	6	2-88,S-46	12	0.2
1968	Cin-N★	127	507	35	146	28	2	2	47	12	27	5	6	.288	.307	.363	.670	94	-6	53	3.77	10	*2-127/S-2,3-1	13	1.7
1969	Cin-N	126	480	38	129	18	1	1	40	18	33	4	6	.269	.297	.317	.613	68	-22	39	2.73	6	*2-125/S-4	6	-0.8
1970*	Cin-N	150	575	42	136	21	1	1	45	21	33	2	2	.237	.263	.282	.545	44	-47	39	2.25	4	*2-148,S-12	7	-3.3
1971	Cin-N	150	547	40	141	26	1	3	52	26	33	3	4	.258	.293	.325	.618	79	-18	48	2.95	18	*2-149	14	1.1
1972	Hou-N	139	518	45	134	20	5	5	60	24	27	4	3	.259	.297	.346	.642	84	-13	52	3.45	19	*2-139	14	1.7
1973	Hou-N	146	543	44	156	28	2	4	61	32	21	1	1	.287	.327	.368	.695	93	-6	63	4.20	9	*2-145	17	1.3
1974	Hou-N	137	452	32	126	21	1	5	50	23	27	5	4	.279	.315	.363	.678	93	-7	48	3.72	6	*2-133	11	0.8
1975	Hou-N	64	135	7	28	2	0	0	14	10	8	0	0	.207	.267	.222	.489	40	-11	8	1.97	0	2-42/3-3,S-1	1	-0.9
1976	Pit-N	62	87	10	24	5	1	1	13	10	5	0	0	.276	.357	.391	.748	111	2	13	5.38	-1	3-22,2-11/S-1	3	0.1
1977	Pit-N	15	12	0	0	0	0	0	0	0	3	0	0	.000	.000	.000	.000	-97	-3	0	.00	0	....	0	-0.3
	Bos-A	21	59	5	16	2	0	1	5	4	4	0	0	.271	.328	.356	.684	77	-2	7	4.23	0	D-13/3-2,2-1	1	-0.2
Total	**14**	**1435**	**4997**	**414**	**1342**	**223**	**21**	**34**	**477**	**231**	**301**	**33**	**40**	**.269**	**.303**	**.342**	**.645**	**79**	**-156**	**491**	**3.39**	**76**	***2-1129,3-143/S-74,D-13**	**114**	**0.8**
• HELMS, Wes	Wesley Ray Helms b: 5/12/1976, Gastonia, NC BR/TR, 6'4", 230 lbs. Deb: 9/5/1998 Career OF: 6-0-4																								
1998	Atl-N	7	13	2	4	1	0	1	2	0	4	0	0	.308	.308	.615	.923	135	1	2	7.38	-1	/3-4	1	0.0
2000	Atl-N	6	5	0	1	0	0	0	0	0	2	0	0	.200	.200	.200	.400	1	-1	0	1.35	1	/3-5	0	0.0
2001	Atl-N	100	216	28	48	10	3	10	36	21	56	1	1	.222	.294	.435	.729	83	-6	28	4.32	-1	1-77,3-17/0-1	5	-1.2
2002*	Atl-N	85	210	20	51	16	0	6	22	11	57	1	1	.243	.290	.405	.695	80	-7	24	3.70	-4	1-45,3-24/0-9(5-0-4)	1	-1.4
2003	Mil-N	134	476	56	124	21	0	23	67	43	131	0	1	.261	.335	.450	.784	104	2	71	5.21	-6	*3-130	12	-0.2
Total	**5**	**332**	**920**	**106**	**228**	**48**	**3**	**40**	**127**	**75**	**250**	**2**	**3**	**.248**	**.314**	**.437**	**.751**	**94**	**-12**	**125**	**4.65**	**-11**	**3-180,1-122/0-10**	**19**	**-2.9**
• HELTON, Todd	Todd Lynn Helton b: 8/20/1973, Knoxville, TN BL/TL, 6'2", 195 lbs. Deb: 8/2/1997																								
1997	Col-N	35	93	13	26	2	1	5	11	8	11	0	1	.280	.337	.484	.821	91	-2	15	5.84	2	0-15(13-0-2)/1-8	2	-0.1
1998	Col-N	152	530	78	167	37	1	25	97	53	54	3	3	.315	.384	.530	.914	113	10	105	7.31	10	*1-146	17	0.8
1999	Col-N	159	578	114	185	39	5	35	113	68	77	7	6	.320	.397	.587	.984	114	12	132	8.55	-5	*1-156	19	-0.6
2000	Col-N★	160	580	138	**216**	**59**	2	42	**147**	103	61	5	3	**.372**	**.470**	**.698**	**1.168**	152	52	192	**13.34**	12	*1-160	29	4.7
2001	Col-N★	159	587	132	197	54	2	49	146	98	104	7	5	.336	.435	.685	1.120	150	47	174	11.34	2	*1-157	26	3.4
2002	Col-N★	156	553	107	182	39	4	30	109	99	91	5	1	.329	.435	.577	1.012	141	39	144	9.89	5	*1-156	27	3.0
2003	Col-N★	160	583	135	209	49	5	33	117	111	72	0	4	.358	.463	.630	1.092	159	56	168	11.22	15	*1-159	35	5.5
Total	**7**	**981**	**3504**	**717**	**1182**	**279**	**20**	**219**	**740**	**540**	**470**	**27**	**23**	**.337**	**.430**	**.616**	**1.046**	**138**	**214**	**930**	**10.15**	**40**	**1-942/0-15**	**155**	**16.7**
• HELTZEL, Heinie	William Wade Heltzel b: 12/21/1913, York, PA d: 5/1/1998, York, PA BR/TR, 5'10", 150 lbs. Deb: 7/27/1943																								
1943	Bos-N	29	86	6	13	3	0	0	5	7	13	0	....	.151	.215	.186	.401	17	-9	4	1.33	-2	3-29	1	-1.2
1944	Phi-N	11	22	1	4	1	0	0	0	2	3	0	....	.182	.280	.227	.507	45	-2	1	1.97	-3	S-10	0	-0.4
Total	**2**	**40**	**108**	**7**	**17**	**4**	**0**	**0**	**5**	**9**	**16**	**0**	**....**	**.157**	**.229**	**.194**	**.423**	**23**	**-11**	**5**	**1.46**	**-5**	**/3-29,S-10**	**1**	**-1.6**
• HEMINGWAY, Ed	Edson Marshall Hemingway b: 5/8/1893, Sheridan, MI d: 7/5/1969, Grand Rapids, MI BB/TR, 5'11.5", 165 lbs. Deb: 9/17/1914																								
1914	StL-A	3	5	0	0	0	0	0	0	1	1	1	....	.000	.167	.000	.167	-51	-1	0	.75	0	/3-3	0	-0.1
1917	NY-N	7	25	3	8	1	1	0	1	2	1	2	....	.320	.370	.440	.810	153	2	4	6.83	1	/3-7	1	0.3
1918	Phi-N	33	108	7	23	4	1	0	12	7	9	4	....	.213	.267	.269	.536	59	-5	9	2.54	3	2-25/3-3,1-1	1	-0.2
Total	**3**	**43**	**138**	**10**	**31**	**5**	**2**	**0**	**13**	**10**	**11**	**7**	**....**	**.225**	**.282**	**.290**	**.572**	**71**	**-5**	**14**	**3.10**	**4**	**/2-25,3-13,1-1**	**2**	**0.0**
• HEMOND, Scott	Scott Mathew Hemond b: 11/18/1965, Taunton, MA BR/TR, 6', 205 lbs. Deb: 9/9/1989 Career OF: 8-1-3																								
1989	Oak-A	4	0	2	0	0	0	0	0	0	0	0	0	....	....	....	....	-104	0	0	....	0	....	0	0.0
1990	Oak-A	7	13	0	2	0	0	0	1	0	5	0	0	.154	.154	.154	.308	-14	-2	0	.76	0	/3-7,2-1	0	-0.2
1991	Oak-A	23	23	4	5	0	0	0	0	1	7	1	2	.217	.250	.217	.467	32	-3	1	1.30	0	/C-8,2-7,D-4,3-2,S-1	0	-0.2
1992	Oak-A	17	27	7	6	1	0	0	1	3	7	1	0	.222	.300	.259	.559	61	-1	2	2.27	-2	/C-8,S-3,3-2,0-2(1-0-1),D-1	0	-0.2
	Chi-A	8	13	1	3	1	0	0	1	1	6	0	0	.231	.286	.308	.593	67	-1	1	3.13	0	/D-4,0-2(2-0-0),3-1,C-1	0	-0.1
	Yr.	25	40	8	9	2	0	0	2	4	13	1	0	.225	.295	.275	.570	63	-2	3	2.55	-2	/C-9,D-5,0-4(3-0-1),3-3,S-3	0	-0.3
1993	Oak-A	91	215	31	55	16	0	6	26	32	55	14	5	.256	.355	.414	.769	113	6	34	5.35	-1	C-75/0-6(4-1-1),D-3,1-1,2	10	0.9

YEAR TM-L	G	AB	R	H	2B	3B	HR	RBI	BB	SO	SB	CS	AVG	OBP	SLG	OPS	OPS+	BR/A	RC	RC/G	FR	G/POS	WS	TPW
1994 Oak-A	91	198	23	44	11	0	3	20	16	51	7	6	.222	.280	.323	.604	60	-13	17	2.67	0	C-39,2-25,3-12/1-7,D-3,0-2(1-0-1)	3	-0.9
1995 StL-N	57	118	11	17	1	0	3	9	12	31	0	0	.144	.235	.229	.464	23	-13	5	1.32	-1	C-38/2-6	2	-1.2
Total 7	298	607	79	132	30	0	12	58	65	162	23	13	.217	.296	.326	.622	70	-28	61	3.18	-3	C-169/2-40,3-24,D-15,0-12,1,S	15	-1.9

• HEMP, Ducky William H. Hemp b: 12/27/1867, St. Louis, MO d: 3/6/1923, St. Louis, MO Deb: 10/6/1887 Career OF: 4-21-6

YEAR TM-L	G	AB	R	H	2B	3B	HR	RBI	BB	SO	SB	CS	AVG	OBP	SLG	OPS	OPS+	BR/A	RC	RC/G	FR	G/POS	WS	TPW
1887 Lou-a	1	4	1	2	1	0	0	0	1	....	0	....	.500	.500	.667	1.167	219	1	1	13.84	0	/0-1	0	0.0
1890 Pit-N	21	81	9	19	0	2	0	4	8	12	3	....	.235	.311	.284	.595	83	-1	8	3.54	0	0-21(2-14-5)	1	-0.1
Syr-a	9	33	1	5	1	0	0	1	0	....	1	....	.152	.176	.182	.358	6	-4	1	1.20	2	/0-9(2-7-0)	0	-0.2
Total 2	31	118	11	26	2	2	0	5	9	12	4	....	.220	.281	.265	.546	67	-4	11	3.05	2	/0-31	1	-0.3

• HEMPHILL, Bret Bret Ryan Hemphill b: 12/17/1971, Santa Clara, CA BB/TR, 6'3", 215 lbs. Deb: 6/28/1999

YEAR TM-L	G	AB	R	H	2B	3B	HR	RBI	BB	SO	SB	CS	AVG	OBP	SLG	OPS	OPS+	BR/A	RC	RC/G	FR	G/POS	WS	TPW
1999 Ana-A	12	21	3	3	0	0	0	2	4	4	0	0	.143	.280	.143	.423	12	-3	1	1.45	0	C-12	0	-0.2

• HEMPHILL, Charlie Charles Judson "Eagle Eye" Hemphill
b: 4/20/1876, Greenville, MI d: 6/22/1953, Detroit, MI BL/TL, 5'9", 160 lbs. Deb: 6/27/1899 Career OF: 45-607-525

YEAR TM-L	G	AB	R	H	2B	3B	HR	RBI	BB	SO	SB	CS	AVG	OBP	SLG	OPS	OPS+	BR/A	RC	RC/G	FR	G/POS	WS	TPW
1899 StL-N	11	37	4	9	0	0	1	3	6	....	0	....	.243	.364	.324	.688	87	-0	5	4.24	-1	0-10(0-10-0)	1	-0.2
Cle-N	55	202	23	56	3	5	2	23	6	....	3	....	.277	.301	.371	.673	91	-3	24	4.37	-7	0-54(0-0-54)	1	-1.2
Yr.	66	239	27	65	3	5	3	26	12	....	3	....	.272	.312	.364	.676	90	-4	29	4.35	-8	0-64(0-10-54)	2	-1.3
1901 Bos-A	136	545	71	142	10	10	3	62	39	....	11	....	.261	.312	.332	.644	80	-14	63	4.03	0	*0-136(0-2-134)	11	-1.9
1902 Cle-A	25	94	14	25	2	0	0	11	5	....	4	....	.266	.303	.287	.590	67	-4	10	3.68	0	0-19(17-1-1)	1	-0.5
StL-A	103	416	67	132	14	11	6	58	44	....	23	....	.317	.383	.447	.830	131	18	82	7.60	0	*0-101(1-31-71)/2-2	19	1.3
Yr.	128	510	81	157	16	11	6	69	49	....	27	....	.308	.369	.418	.786	120	14	92	6.81	0	*0-120(18-32-72)/2-2	20	0.7
1903 StL-A	105	383	36	94	6	3	3	29	23	....	16	....	.245	.292	.300	.592	80	-9	40	3.58	4	*0-104(4-18-82)	8	-1.1
1904 StL-A	114	438	47	112	13	2	2	45	35	....	23	....	.256	.311	.308	.619	102	2	52	4.07	0	*0-108(6-26-76)/2-1	12	-0.4
1906 StL-A	154	585	90	169	19	12	4	62	43	....	33	....	.289	.338	.383	.720	131	20	91	5.55	-6	*0-154(0-114-40)	24	0.7
1907 StL-A	153	603	66	156	20	9	0	38	51	....	14	....	.259	.319	.322	.640	105	4	70	4.00	-7	*0-153(0-134-19)	16	-1.2
1908 NY-A	142	505	62	150	12	9	0	44	59	....	42	....	.297	.374	.356	.730	136	23	83	5.83	-13	*0-142(4-130-8)	28	0.3
1909 NY-A	73	181	23	44	5	1	0	10	32	....	10	....	.243	.357	.282	.639	101	2	22	4.03	-2	0-45(13-32-0)	7	-0.3
1910 NY-A	102	351	45	84	9	4	0	21	55	....	19	....	.239	.350	.288	.638	95	1	42	3.99	-6	0-94(0-63-31)	12	-1.1
1911 NY-A	69	201	32	57	4	2	1	15	37	....	9	....	.284	.397	.338	.736	99	2	31	5.38	-6	0-55(0-46-9)	6	-0.7
Total 11	1242	4541	580	1230	117	68	22	421	435	....	207	....	.271	.337	.341	.678	106	40	614	4.74	-46	*0-1175/2-3	146	-6.2

• HEMPHILL, Frank Frank Vernon Hemphill b: 5/13/1878, Greenville, MI d: 11/16/1950, Chicago, IL BR/TR, 5'11", 165 lbs. Deb: 4/17/1906 Career OF: 14-0-0

YEAR TM-L	G	AB	R	H	2B	3B	HR	RBI	BB	SO	SB	CS	AVG	OBP	SLG	OPS	OPS+	BR/A	RC	RC/G	FR	G/POS	WS	TPW
1906 Chi-A	13	40	0	3	0	0	0	2	9	....	1	....	.075	.275	.075	.350	11	-3	1	.91	2	0-13(13-0-0)	1	-0.3
1909 Was-A	1	3	0	0	0	0	0	0	0	....	0	....	.000	.000	.000	.000	-105	-1	0	.00	-0	/0-1	0	-0.1
Total 2	14	43	0	3	0	0	0	2	9	....	1	....	.070	.259	.070	.329	5	-4	1	.84	2	/0-14	1	-0.3

• HEMSLEY, Rollie Ralston Burdett Hemsley b: 6/24/1907, Syracuse, OH d: 7/31/1972, Washington, DC BR/TR, 5'10", 170 lbs. Deb: 4/13/1928 C Career OF: 6-1-0

YEAR TM-L	G	AB	R	H	2B	3B	HR	RBI	BB	SO	SB	CS	AVG	OBP	SLG	OPS	OPS+	BR/A	RC	RC/G	FR	G/POS	WS	TPW
1928 Pit-N	50	133	14	36	2	3	0	18	4	10	1	....	.271	.292	.331	.623	60	-8	12	3.21	-1	C-49	2	-0.7
1929 Pit-N	88	235	31	68	13	7	0	37	11	22	1	....	.289	.321	.404	.725	77	-9	29	4.34	1	C-80	7	-0.4
1930 Pit-N	104	324	45	82	19	6	2	45	22	21	3	....	.253	.301	.367	.668	60	-22	35	3.62	6	C-98	8	-0.9
1931 Pit-N	10	35	3	6	3	0	0	1	3	3	0	....	.171	.237	.257	.494	33	-3	2	2.02	1	/C-9	0	-0.2
Chi-N	66	204	28	63	17	4	3	31	17	30	4	....	.309	.362	.475	.837	121	6	36	6.46	2	C-53	9	1.1
Yr.	76	239	31	69	20	4	3	32	20	33	4	....	.289	.344	.444	.787	108	2	38	5.71	3	C-62	9	0.9
1932*Chi-N	60	151	27	36	10	3	4	20	10	16	2	....	.238	.286	.424	.710	89	-3	19	4.07	0	C-47/0-1	4	-0.1
1933 Cin-N	49	116	9	22	8	0	0	7	6	8	0	....	.190	.230	.259	.488	40	-9	6	1.57	-1	C-41	1	-0.8
StL-A	32	95	7	23	2	1	1	15	11	12	0	0	.242	.321	.316	.637	65	-5	10	3.70	-1	C-27	2	-0.3
1934 StL-A	123	431	47	133	31	7	2	52	29	37	6	2	.309	.355	.427	.782	93	-5	66	5.63	15	*C-114/0-6(6-0-0)	15	1.5
1935 StL-A★	144	504	57	146	32	7	0	48	44	41	3	2	.290	.349	.381	.730	85	-11	69	4.92	15	*C-141	15	1.2
1936 StL-A★	116	377	43	99	24	2	2	39	46	30	2	3	.263	.343	.353	.696	70	-18	47	4.40	8	*C-114	7	-0.4
1937 StL-A	100	334	30	74	12	3	3	28	25	29	0	0	.222	.276	.302	.578	45	-29	29	2.87	6	C-94/1-2	3	-1.6
1938 Cle-A	66	203	27	60	11	3	2	28	23	14	1	1	.296	.367	.409	.776	96	-1	31	5.61	7	C-58	8	0.9
1939 Cle-A★	107	395	58	104	17	4	2	36	26	26	2	4	.263	.309	.342	.651	69	-21	41	3.53	1	*C-106	10	-1.2
1940 Cle-A★	119	416	46	111	20	5	4	42	22	25	1	3	.267	.304	.368	.671	75	-17	45	3.79	4	*C-117	14	-0.6
1941 Cle-A	98	288	29	69	10	5	2	24	18	19	2	0	.240	.284	.330	.614	65	-15	27	3.14	-1	C-96	6	-1.0
1942 Cin-N	36	115	7	13	1	2	0	7	4	11	0	....	.113	.143	.157	.299	-12	-17	3	.67	5	C-34	2	-1.0
NY-A	31	85	12	25	3	1	0	15	5	9	1	0	.294	.333	.353	.686	95	-0	10	4.32	1	C-29	3	0.2
1943 NY-A	62	180	12	43	6	3	2	24	13	9	0	1	.239	.290	.339	.629	83	-5	18	3.23	-1	C-52	5	-0.3
1944 NY-A★	81	284	23	76	12	5	2	26	9	13	0	2	.268	.290	.366	.656	84	-8	25	2.98	2	C-76	6	-0.2
1946 Phi-N	49	139	7	31	4	1	0	11	9	10	0	....	.223	.270	.266	.536	54	-9	10	2.45	7	C-45	3	0.1
1947 Phi-N	2	3	0	1	0	0	0	1	0	0	0	....	.333	.333	.333	.667	80	-0	0	4.50	0	/C-2	0	0.0
Total 19	1593	5047	562	1321	257	72	31	555	357	395	29	18	.262	.311	.360	.671	73	-209	571	3.89	73	*C-1482/0-7,1-2	130	-4.8

• HEMUS, Solly Solomon Joseph Hemus b: 4/17/1923, Phoenix, AZ BL/TR, 5'9", 175 lbs. Deb: 4/27/1949 M/C

YEAR TM-L	G	AB	R	H	2B	3B	HR	RBI	BB	SO	SB	CS	AVG	OBP	SLG	OPS	OPS+	BR/A	RC	RC/G	FR	G/POS	WS	TPW
1949 StL-N	20	33	8	11	1	0	0	2	7	3	0	....	.333	.450	.364	.814	115	1	6	6.89	-0	2-16	2	0.2
1950 StL-N	11	15	1	2	1	0	0	0	2	4	0	....	.133	.235	.200	.435	15	-2	1	1.72	1	/3-5	0	-0.1
1951 StL-N	120	420	68	118	18	9	2	32	75	31	7	7	.281	.395	.381	.776	109	8	70	5.84	2	*S-105,2-12	17	1.8
1952 StL-N	151	570	**105**	153	28	8	15	52	96	55	1	5	.268	.392	.425	.817	126	24	103	6.36	-8	*S-148/3-2	27	2.7
1953 StL-N	154	585	110	163	32	11	14	61	86	40	2	1	.279	.382	.443	.825	114	16	107	6.57	0	*S-150/2-3	23	2.7
1954 StL-N	124	214	43	65	15	3	2	27	55	27	5	1	.304	.456	.430	.886	131	16	50	8.75	-3	S-66,3-27,2-12	11	1.6
1955 StL-N	96	206	36	50	10	2	5	21	27	22	1	1	.243	.336	.383	.720	90	-2	28	4.67	-1	3-43,2-10/S-2	6	-0.3
1956 StL-N	8	5	1	1	0	0	0	2	1	1	0	0	.200	.429	.200	.629	77	0	1	4.13	0	....	0	0.0
Phi-N	78	187	24	54	10	4	5	24	28	21	1	1	.289	.401	.465	.866	134	11	36	6.72	-6	2-49/3-1	9	0.8
Yr.	86	192	25	55	10	4	5	26	29	22	1	1	.286	.402	.458	.860	132	11	36	6.63	-6	2-49/3-1	9	0.8
1957 Phi-N	70	108	8	20	6	1	0	5	20	8	1	1	.185	.323	.259	.582	61	-5	8	2.35	-3	2-24	0	-0.7
1958 Phi-N	105	334	53	95	14	3	8	36	51	34	3	1	.284	.392	.416	.808	116	10	59	6.31	-3	2-85/3-1	13	1.4
1959 StL-N	24	17	2	4	2	0	0	1	8	2	0	0	.235	.500	.353	.853	124	2	4	8.66	0	/2-1,3-1	1	0.2
Total 11	961	2694	459	736	137	41	51	263	456	248	21	18	.273	.390	.411	.802	115	78	472	6.18	-20	S-471,2-212/3-80	109	10.2

• HENDERSON, Dave David Lee Henderson b: 7/21/1958, Merced, CA BR/TR, 6'2", 220 lbs. Deb: 4/9/1981 Career OF: 36-1157-229

YEAR TM-L	G	AB	R	H	2B	3B	HR	RBI	BB	SO	SB	CS	AVG	OBP	SLG	OPS	OPS+	BR/A	RC	RC/G	FR	G/POS	WS	TPW
1981 Sea-A	59	126	17	21	3	0	6	13	16	24	2	1	.167	.266	.333	.599	69	-5	11	2.65	0	0-58(2-33-31)	1	-0.7
1982 Sea-A	104	324	47	82	17	1	14	48	36	67	2	5	.253	.328	.441	.769	106	1	46	4.88	3	*0-101(2-99-2)	11	0.2
1983 Sea-A	137	484	50	130	24	5	17	55	28	93	9	3	.269	.310	.444	.754	101	-0	67	4.88	8	*0-133(0-80-56)/D-3	13	0.3
1984 Sea-A	112	350	42	98	23	0	14	43	19	56	5	5	.280	.321	.466	.786	116	5	51	5.19	2	0-97(0-88-11),D-10	11	0.5
1985 Sea-A	139	502	70	121	28	2	14	68	48	104	6	1	.241	.311	.388	.699	90	-7	61	4.17	-3	*0-138(1-126-27)	11	-1.3
1986 Sea-A	103	337	51	93	19	4	14	44	37	95	1	3	.276	.351	.481	.832	123	9	57	6.02	3	0-80(0-51-31),D-22	10	0.9
*Bos-A	36	51	8	10	3	0	1	3	2	15	1	0	.196	.226	.314	.540	45	-4	4	2.25	0	0-32(0-32-0)	1	-0.4
Yr.	139	388	59	103	22	4	15	47	39	110	2	3	.265	.336	.459	.794	113	6	60	5.47	3	*0-112(0-83-31),D-22	11	0.5
1987 Bos-A	75	184	30	43	10	0	8	25	22	48	1	1	.234	.316	.418	.734	90	-3	25	4.52	-3	0-64(5-29-30)/D-1	3	-0.8
SF-N	15	21	2	5	2	0	0	1	8	5	2	0	.238	.448	.333	.782	117	2	5	7.66	0	/0-9(1-8-1)	1	0.2
1988*Oak-A	146	507	100	154	38	1	24	94	47	92	2	4	.304	.367	.525	.892	152	32	94	6.62	-1	*0-143(1-142-0)	26	2.9
1989*Oak-A	152	579	77	145	24	3	15	80	54	131	8	5	.250	.318	.380	.698	99	-2	69	4.08	-3	*0-149(0-149-0)/D-2	19	-0.7
1990*Oak-A	127	450	65	122	28	0	20	63	40	105	3	1	.271	.332	.467	.799	126	14	71	5.69	0	*0-116(1-110-5)/D-6	20	1.3
1991 Oak-A★	150	572	86	158	33	0	25	85	58	113	6	6	.276	.347	.465	.812	130	21	92	5.75	-1	*0-140(4-135-1)/D-7,2-1	25	1.7
1992 Oak-A	20	63	1	9	1	0	0	2	2	16	0	0	.143	.169	.159	.328	-8	-9	2	.89	-1	0-12(0-9-3)/D-4	0	-1.0
1993 Oak-A	107	382	37	84	19	0	20	53	32	113	0	3	.220	.280	.427	.707	93	-7	47	4.06	2	0-76(2-60-14),D-28	4	-0.7
1994 KC-A	56	198	27	49	14	1	5	31	16	28	2	0	.247	.307	.404	.711	78	-7	25	4.37	-1	0-40(17-6-17),D-16	4	-0.9
Total 14	1538	5130	710	1324	286	17	197	708	465	1105	50	38	.258	.322	.436	.758	109	41	725	4.91	5	*0-1388/D-99,2-1	160	1.6

• HENDERSON, Ken Kenneth Joseph Henderson b: 6/15/1946, Carroll, IA BB/TR, 6'2", 180 lbs. Deb: 4/23/1965 Career OF: 434-544-360

YEAR	TM-L	G	AB	R	H	2B	3B	HR	RBI	BB	SO	SB	CS	AVG	OBP	SLG	OPS	OPS+	BR/A	RC	RC/G	FR	G/POS	WS	TPW
1965	SF-N	63	73	10	14	1	1	0	7	9	19	1	1	.192	.280	.233	.513	45	-5	4	1.87	1	O-48(5-31-16)	1	-0.6
1966	SF-N	11	29	4	9	1	1	1	1	2	3	0	0	.310	.375	.517	.892	141	2	6	7.99	-1	O-10(1-7-4)	2	0.1
1967	SF-N	65	179	15	34	3	0	4	14	19	52	0	1	.190	.275	.274	.549	58	-10	14	2.43	0	O-52(8-33-18)	2	-1.3
1968	SF-N	3	3	1	1	0	0	0	0	2	1	0	0	.333	.600	.333	.933	186	1	1	12.31	0	/O-2(1-1-0)	0	0.1
1969	SF-N	113	374	42	84	14	4	6	44	42	64	6	4	.225	.311	.332	.643	82	-9	39	3.41	3	*O-111(64-5-57)/3-3	8	-1.3
1970	SF-N	148	554	104	163	35	3	17	88	87	78	20	3	.294	.395	.460	.855	130	29	106	6.95	1	*O-146(113-25-35)	24	2.2
1971*	SF-N	141	504	80	133	26	6	15	65	84	76	18	3	.264	.372	.429	.801	128	24	86	5.98	-8	*O-138(109-14-26)/1-1	23	0.9
1972	SF-N	130	439	60	113	21	2	18	51	38	66	14	7	.257	.319	.437	.757	111	6	61	4.74	4	*O-123(95-26-2)	14	0.3
1973	Chi-A	73	262	32	68	13	0	6	32	27	49	3	4	.260	.331	.378	.709	96	-2	30	3.93	-2	O-44(8-36-0),D-26	5	-0.7
1974	Chi-A	162	602	76	176	35	5	20	95	66	112	12	7	.292	.364	.467	.831	134	27	100	5.88	-2	*O-162(0-162-0)	26	2.2
1975	Chi-A	140	513	65	129	20	3	9	53	74	65	5	3	.251	.350	.355	.705	98	2	64	4.18	3	*O-137(0-137-0)/D-1	15	0.0
1976	Atl-N	133	435	52	114	19	0	13	61	62	68	5	7	.262	.355	.395	.751	106	3	60	4.69	-12	*O-122(0-20-115)	13	-1.6
1977	Tex-A	75	244	23	63	14	0	5	23	18	37	2	1	.258	.317	.377	.694	87	-4	28	3.89	-3	O-65(0-8-61)/D-3	4	-1.0
1978	NY-N	7	22	2	5	2	0	1	4	4	4	0	1	.227	.346	.455	.801	127	0	3	4.98	-0	/O-7(0-0-7)	1	0.0
	Cin-N	64	144	10	24	6	1	3	19	23	32	0	0	.167	.281	.285	.566	58	-8	11	2.26	-1	O-38(0-30-9)	1	-1.0
	Yr.	71	166	12	29	8	1	4	23	27	36	0	1	.175	.290	.307	.597	68	-7	14	2.59	-1	O-45(0-30-16)	2	-1.0
1979	Cin-N	10	13	1	3	1	0	0	2	0	2	0	0	.231	.231	.308	.538	45	-1	1	2.49	0	/O-2(1-0-1)	0	-0.1
	Chi-N	62	81	11	19	2	0	2	8	15	16	0	0	.235	.361	.333	.694	83	-1	11	4.64	-1	O-23(14-9-0)	2	-0.2
	Yr.	72	94	12	22	3	0	2	10	15	18	0	0	.234	.345	.330	.675	78	-2	12	4.35	-1	O-25(15-9-1)	2	-0.3
1980	Chi-N	44	82	7	16	3	0	2	9	17	19	0	0	.195	.333	.305	.638	74	-2	9	3.40	2	O-22(15-0-9)	1	-0.2
Total	16	1444	4553	595	1168	216	26	122	576	589	763	86	42	.257	.346	.396	.741	106	51	634	4.75	-17	*O-1252/D-30,3-3,1-1	142	-2.2

• HENDERSON, Rickey Rickey Henley "Man of Steal" Henderson b: 12/25/1957, Chicago, IL BR/TL, 5'10", 195 lbs. Deb: 6/24/1979 Career OF: 2421-448-27

YEAR	TM-L	G	AB	R	H	2B	3B	HR	RBI	BB	SO	SB	CS	AVG	OBP	SLG	OPS	OPS+	BR/A	RC	RC/G	FR	G/POS	WS	TPW
1979	Oak-A	89	351	49	96	13	3	1	26	34	39	33	11	.274	.341	.336	.677	88	-2	44	4.24	-5	O-88(62-32-1)	10	-1.0
1980	Oak-A★	158	591	111	179	22	4	9	53	117	54	**100**	26	.303	.422	.399	.821	136	49	120	7.16	8	*O-157(157-1-0)/D-1	34	5.0
1981*	Oak-A	108	423	**89**	**135**	18	7	6	35	64	68	**56**	22	.319	.411	.437	.848	152	34	81	6.82	8	*O-107(107-1-0)	**27**	3.8
1982	Oak-A★	149	536	119	143	24	4	10	51	**116**	94	**130**	42	.267	.399	.382	.782	121	34	99	6.06	-6	*O-144(138-10-0)/D-4	28	2.0
1983	Oak-A★	145	513	105	150	25	7	9	48	**103**	80	**108**	19	.292	.415	.421	.836	139	**50**	109	7.46	-4	*O-142(138-10-0)/D-1	30	4.0
1984	Oak-A★	142	502	113	147	27	4	16	58	86	81	**66**	18	.293	.401	.458	.860	147	43	103	7.27	-9	*O-140(140-6-0)	28	2.8
1985	NY-A★	143	547	**146**	172	28	5	24	72	99	65	**80**	10	.314	.422	.516	.938	159	63	138	9.36	5	*O-141(6-141-0)/D-1	**38**	**6.5**
1986	NY-A★	153	608	**130**	160	31	5	28	74	89	81	**87**	18	.263	.359	.469	.828	125	33	112	6.29	1	*O-146(11-138-0)/D-5	26	3.1
1987	NY-A★	95	358	78	104	17	3	17	37	80	52	41	8	.291	.423	.497	.920	144	33	84	8.35	1	O-69(34-39-0),D-24	20	2.9
1988	NY-A★	140	554	118	169	30	2	6	50	82	54	**93**	13	.305	.397	.399	.796	125	37	107	7.03	3	*O-136(135-3-0)/D-3	28	3.6
1989	NY-A	65	235	41	58	13	1	3	22	56	29	25	8	.247	.394	.349	.743	112	9	40	5.85	0	O-65(65-0-0)	10	0.7
	*Oak-A	85	306	72	90	13	2	9	35	70	39	52	6	.294	.429	.438	.866	150	34	70	8.10	4	O-82(82-0-0)/D-3	20	3.6
	Yr.	150	541	**113**	148	26	3	12	57	**126**	68	**77**	14	.274	.413	.399	.813	134	44	110	7.10	4	*O-147(147-0-0)/D-3	30	4.2
1990*	Oak-A★	136	489	**119**	159	33	3	28	61	97	60	**65**	10	.325	**.441**	.577	**1.017**	**190**	**74**	137	**10.37**	2	*O-118(119-0-0),D-15	**39**	**7.2**
1991	Oak-A★	134	470	105	126	17	1	18	57	98	73	**58**	18	.268	.402	.423	.825	136	34	91	6.63	4	*O-119(119-0-0)/D-10	25	3.3
1992*	Oak-A	117	396	77	112	18	3	15	46	95	56	48	11	.283	.429	.457	.886	156	43	92	8.16	2	*O-108(108-0-0)/D-6	25	4.1
1993	Oak-A	90	318	77	104	19	1	17	47	85	46	31	6	.327	.472	.553	1.025	186	50	93	10.94	1	O-74(74-0-0),D-16	22	4.5
	*Tor-A	44	163	37	35	3	1	4	12	35	19	22	2	.215	.360	.319	.679	84	2	25	5.09	-3	O-44(44-0-0)	3	-0.2
	Yr.	134	481	114	139	22	2	21	59	120	65	53	8	.289	.435	.474	.909	152	52	118	8.79	-1	*O-118(118-0-0),D-16	25	4.3
1994	Oak-A	87	296	66	77	13	0	6	20	72	45	22	7	.260	.413	.365	.778	112	13	55	6.49	3	O-71(66-10-0),D-13	11	1.1
1995	Oak-A	112	407	67	122	31	1	9	54	72	66	32	10	.300	.410	.447	.857	131	25	81	7.15	1	O-90(90-0-0),D-19	19	2.0
1996*	SD-N	148	465	110	112	17	2	9	29	125	90	37	15	.241	.412	.344	.756	108	17	81	5.83	1	*O-134(114-10-17)	16	1.2
1997	SD-N	88	288	63	79	11	0	6	27	71	62	29	4	.274	.424	.375	.799	122	20	56	6.82	0	O-78(55-17-8)/D-2	14	1.6
	Ana-A	32	115	21	21	3	0	2	7	26	23	16	4	.183	.343	.261	.604	60	-4	13	3.56	0	D-19,O-13(11-2-0)	1	-0.5
1998	Oak-A	152	542	101	128	16	1	14	57	**118**	114	**66**	13	.236	.377	.347	.724	92	9	89	5.52	1	*O-151(142-24-0)	20	0.4
1999*	NY-N	121	438	89	138	30	0	12	42	82	82	37	14	.315	.425	.466	.891	129	26	96	8.03	-6	*O-116(116-0-0)/D-1	16	1.5
2000	NY-N	31	96	17	21	1	0	0	2	25	20	5	2	.219	.390	.229	.619	65	-3	11	3.82	-3	O-30(29-0-0)	1	-0.7
	*Sea-A	92	324	58	77	13	2	4	30	63	55	31	9	.238	.365	.327	.692	82	-3	45	4.45	-1	O-88(88-0-0)/D-2	7	-0.7
2001	SD-N	123	379	70	86	17	3	8	42	81	84	25	7	.227	.367	.351	.718	95	4	56	4.90	-4	*O-104(104-0-0)/D-1	12	-0.4
2002	Bos-A	72	179	40	40	6	1	5	16	38	47	8	2	.223	.371	.352	.723	92	1	27	5.08	0	O-54(49-4-1)/D-5	4	-0.2
2003	LA-N	30	72	7	15	1	0	2	5	11	16	3	0	.208	.321	.306	.627	69	-2	9	4.06	0	O-18(18-0-0)	1	-0.3
Total	25	3081	10961	**2295**	3055	510	66	297	1115	**2190**	1694	**1406**	335	.279	.403	.419	.822	128	721	2167	6.88	5	*O-2827,D-151	535	61.0

• HENDERSON, Steve Steven Curtis Henderson b: 11/18/1952, Houston, TX BR/TR, 6'2", 190 lbs. Deb: 6/16/1977 C Career OF: 856-0-43

YEAR	TM-L	G	AB	R	H	2B	3B	HR	RBI	BB	SO	SB	CS	AVG	OBP	SLG	OPS	OPS+	BR/A	RC	RC/G	FR	G/POS	WS	TPW
1977	NY-N	99	350	67	104	16	6	12	65	43	79	6	3	.297	.376	.480	.856	134	17	61	6.20	-2	O-97(97-0-0)	12	1.1
1978	NY-N	157	587	83	156	30	9	10	65	60	109	13	7	.266	.336	.399	.735	108	6	74	4.28	6	*O-155(155-0-0)	16	0.5
1979	NY-N	98	350	42	107	16	8	5	39	38	58	13	5	.306	.380	.440	.820	128	15	59	6.27	3	O-94(94-0-0)	12	1.4
1980	NY-N	143	513	75	149	17	8	8	58	62	90	23	12	.290	.370	.402	.772	119	14	75	5.08	1	*O-136(136-0-0)	17	0.8
1981	Chi-N	82	287	32	84	9	5	5	35	42	61	5	7	.293	.387	.411	.798	121	8	45	5.46	-1	O-77(77-0-0)	9	0.3
1982	Chi-N	92	257	23	60	12	4	2	29	22	64	6	5	.233	.294	.335	.629	73	-10	25	3.19	2	O-70(70-0-0)	3	-1.1
1983	Sea-A	121	436	50	128	32	3	10	54	44	82	10	14	.294	.358	.450	.808	116	6	66	5.31	7	*O-112(112-0-0)/D-6	12	0.8
1984	Sea-A	109	325	42	85	12	3	10	35	38	62	2	4	.262	.341	.409	.750	108	3	45	4.84	-1	O-53(52-0-0),D-51	7	-0.2
1985	Oak-A	85	193	25	58	8	3	3	31	18	34	0	0	.301	.360	.420	.780	122	6	27	4.94	-1	O-58(47-0-11)/D-1	6	0.3
1986	Oak-A	11	26	2	2	1	0	0	3	0	5	0	0	.077	.077	.115	.192	-52	-5	0	.00	-1	/O-7(7-0-0),D-1	0	-0.7
1987	Oak-A	46	114	14	33	7	0	3	9	12	19	0	0	.289	.357	.430	.787	115	3	16	4.80	-2	O-31(5-0-28)/D-9	3	0.0
1988	Hou-N	42	46	4	10	2	0	0	5	7	14	1	1	.217	.321	.261	.582	72	-2	4	2.83	0	/O-8(4-0-4),1-1	0	-0.2
Total	12	1085	3484	459	976	162	49	68	428	386	677	79	58	.280	.354	.413	.767	113	59	497	4.96	12	O-898/D-68,1-1	97	3.0

• HENDRICK, George George Andrew Hendrick b: 10/18/1949, Los Angeles, CA BR/TR, 6'3", 195 lbs. Deb: 6/4/1971 C Career OF: 246-749-897

YEAR	TM-L	G	AB	R	H	2B	3B	HR	RBI	BB	SO	SB	CS	AVG	OBP	SLG	OPS	OPS+	BR/A	RC	RC/G	FR	G/POS	WS	TPW
1971	Oak-A	42	114	8	27	4	1	0	8	3	20	0	1	.237	.256	.289	.546	55	-7	7	1.88	0	O-36(18-16-10)	1	-1.0
1972*	Oak-A	58	121	10	22	1	1	4	15	3	22	3	2	.182	.208	.306	.514	54	-8	7	1.70	-1	O-41(5-28-12)	1	-1.2
1973	Cle-A	113	440	64	118	18	0	21	61	25	71	7	6	.268	.310	.452	.763	111	3	58	4.60	-6	*O-110(0-107-3)	13	-0.6
1974	Cle-A★	139	495	65	138	23	1	19	67	33	73	6	4	.279	.325	.444	.770	121	11	66	4.66	-5	*O-133(2-131-0)/D-1	19	0.2
1975	Cle-A★	145	561	82	145	21	2	24	86	40	78	6	7	.258	.308	.431	.739	107	1	65	3.83	-9	*O-143(1-89-53)	13	-1.3
1976	Cle-A	149	551	72	146	20	3	25	81	51	82	4	4	.265	.327	.448	.776	127	16	77	4.78	3	*O-146(136-13-3)/D-3	20	1.1
1977	SD-N	152	541	75	168	25	2	23	81	61	74	11	6	.311	.382	.492	.874	148	36	102	7.07	-1	*O-142(24-131-9)	28	3.2
1978	SD-N	36	111	9	27	4	0	3	8	12	16	1	1	.243	.317	.360	.677	96	-1	13	3.96	-1	O-33(1-26-6)	3	-0.3
	StL-N	102	382	55	110	27	1	17	67	28	44	1	0	.288	.340	.497	.837	133	15	63	5.95	-1	*O-101(2-87-12)	18	1.2
	Yr.	138	493	64	137	31	1	20	75	40	60	2	1	.278	.335	.467	.801	125	14	76	5.49	-3	*O-134(3-113-18)	21	0.9
1979	StL-N	140	493	67	148	27	1	16	75	49	62	2	3	.300	.363	.456	.820	121	13	78	5.66	8	*O-138(0-14-124)	17	1.5
1980	StL-N★	150	572	73	173	33	2	25	109	32	67	6	1	.302	.344	.498	.842	128	20	94	6.07	2	*O-149(0-54-121)	21	1.7
1981	StL-N	101	394	67	112	19	3	18	61	41	44	4	2	.284	.358	.485	.842	134	17	67	6.12	-2	*O-101(0-51-59)	18	1.3
1982*	StL-N	136	515	65	145	20	5	19	104	37	80	3	2	.282	.331	.450	.781	115	8	74	4.97	-1	*O-134(0-0-134)	17	0.1
1983	StL-N★	144	529	73	168	33	3	18	97	51	76	3	4	.318	.380	.493	.873	140	27	96	6.69	2	1-92,O-51(0-0-51)	21	2.3
1984	StL-N	120	441	57	122	28	1	9	69	32	75	0	2	.277	.327	.406	.733	108	2	55	4.42	-4	*O-116(0-0-116)/1-1	12	-0.8
1985	Pit-N	69	256	23	59	15	0	2	25	18	42	1	0	.230	.281	.313	.594	66	-12	21	2.64	-1	O-65(0-0-65)	2	-1.7
	Cal-A	16	41	5	5	1	0	2	6	4	8	0	0	.122	.200	.293	.493	33	-4	1	.95	0	O-12(0-0-12)/D-1	0	-0.4
1986*	Cal-A	102	283	45	77	13	1	14	47	26	41	1	1	.272	.335	.473	.809	119	6	42	5.01	0	O-93(0-2-92)/1-7,D-4	9	0.2
1987	Cal-A	65	162	14	39	10	0	5	25	14	18	0	0	.241	.301	.395	.696	85	-4	17	3.55	-2	O-45(37-0-11)/1-9,D-5	2	-0.8
1988	Cal-A	69	127	12	31	1	0	3	19	7	20	0	1	.244	.289	.323	.612	73	-5	12	3.05	-1	O-24(20-0-4),1-12/D-3	2	-0.7
Total	18	2048	7129	941	1980	343	27	267	1111	567	1013	59	47	.278	.333	.446	.779	117	136	1015	4.97	-19	*O-1813,1-121/D-17	237	4.2

• HENDRICK, Harvey Harvey "Gink" Hendrick b: 11/9/1897, Mason, TN d: 10/29/1941, Covington, TN BL/TR, 6'2", 190 lbs. Deb: 4/20/1923 Career OF: 128-21-86

YEAR	TM-L	G	AB	R	H	2B	3B	HR	RBI	BB	SO	SB	CS	AVG	OBP	SLG	OPS	OPS+	BR/A	RC	RC/G	FR	G/POS	WS	TPW
1923*	NY-A	37	66	9	18	3	1	3	12	2	8	3	0	.273	.294	.485	.779	101	0	10	5.20	0	O-13(11-2-0)	2	-0.1
1924	NY-A	40	76	7	20	0	0	1	11	2	7	1	0	.263	.291	.303	.594	53	-5	7	3.18	-1	O-17(15-0-2)	1	-0.7
1925	Cle-A	25	28	2	8	1	2	0	9	3	5	0	0	.286	.355	.464	.819	106	0	5	5.70	0	/1-3	1	0.0

YEAR TM-L	G	AB	R	H	2B	3B	HR	RBI	BB	SO	SB	CS	AVG	OBP	SLG	OPS	OPS+	BR/A	RC	RC/G	FR	G/POS	WS	TPW
1927 Bro-N	128	458	55	142	18	11	4	50	24	40	29	....	.310	.350	.424	.773	106	3	66	5.25	-2	0-64(15-0-64),1-53/2-1	12	-0.7
1928 Bro-N	126	425	83	135	15	10	11	59	54	34	16	....	.318	.397	.478	.875	129	19	80	6.92	5	3-91,0-17(6-11-0)	18	2.9
1929 Bro-N	110	384	69	136	25	6	14	82	31	20	14	....	.354	.404	.560	.964	139	22	84	8.50	3	0-42(30-2-10),1-39/3-7,S-4	15	1.9
1930 Bro-N	68	167	29	43	10	1	5	28	20	19	2	....	.257	.344	.419	.763	84	-4	24	4.97	3	0-42(36-6-0)/1-7	3	-0.4
1931 Bro-N	1	1	0	0	0	0	0	0	0	0	0	....	.000	.000	.000	.000	-101	-0	0	.00	0	....	0	0.0
Cin-N	137	530	74	167	32	9	1	75	53	40	3	....	.315	.379	.415	.795	121	17	87	6.08	-2	*1-137	16	0.2
Yr.	138	531	74	167	32	9	1	75	53	40	3	....	.315	.379	.414	.793	120	16	87	6.06	-2	*1-137	16	0.2
1932 StL-N	28	72	8	18	2	0	1	5	5	9	0	....	.250	.299	.319	.618	64	-4	7	3.40	-1	3-12/0-5(0-0-5)	1	-0.5
Cin-N	94	398	56	120	30	3	4	40	23	29	3	....	.302	.341	.422	.763	107	4	58	5.31	3	1-94	9	-0.2
Yr.	122	470	64	138	32	3	5	45	28	38	3	....	.294	.335	.406	.741	101	0	65	5.01	2	1-94,3-12/0-5(0-0-5)	10	-0.7
1933 Chi-N	69	189	30	55	13	3	4	23	13	17	4	....	.291	.346	.455	.801	128	6	31	6.05	-2	1-38/0-8(4-0-4),3-1	8	0.1
1934 Phi-N	59	116	12	34	8	0	0	19	9	15	0	....	.293	.344	.362	.706	79	-3	15	4.54	-2	0-12(11-0-1)/1-7,3-7	2	-0.6
Total 11	922	2910	434	896	157	46	48	413	239	243	75	0	.308	.364	.443	.807	113	55	473	5.95	4	1-378,0-220,3-118/S-4,2-1	88	2.0
• HENDRICKS, Ellie	Elrod Jerome Hendricks b: 12/22/1940, Charlotte Amalie, V.I. BL/TR, 6'1", 175 lbs. Deb: 4/13/1968 C																							
1968 Bal-A	79	183	19	37	8	1	7	23	19	51	0	0	.202	.281	.372	.652	96	-1	19	3.40	-3	C-53	5	-0.2
1969*Bal-A	105	295	36	72	5	0	12	38	39	44	0	1	.244	.336	.383	.719	100	0	40	4.68	-1	C-87/1-4	12	0.3
1970*Bal-A	106	322	32	78	9	0	12	41	33	44	1	0	.242	.320	.382	.702	92	-3	41	4.37	-6	C-95	10	-0.5
1971*Bal-A	101	316	33	79	14	1	9	42	39	38	0	0	.250	.336	.386	.722	105	3	41	4.43	-4	C-90/1-3	10	0.3
1972 Bal-A	33	84	6	13	4	0	0	4	12	19	0	1	.155	.260	.202	.463	38	-6	5	1.74	0	C-28	1	-0.6
Chi-N	17	43	7	5	1	0	2	6	13	8	0	1	.116	.321	.279	.600	65	-2	4	2.67	0	C-16	1	-0.2
1973 Bal-A	41	101	9	18	5	1	3	15	10	22	0	0	.178	.259	.337	.596	67	-5	9	2.71	-2	C-38/D-1	2	-0.5
1974*Bal-A	66	159	18	33	8	2	3	8	17	25	0	0	.208	.288	.340	.628	83	-3	16	3.32	-2	C-54/1-1,D-1	4	-0.3
1975 Bal-A	85	223	32	48	8	2	8	38	34	40	0	1	.215	.322	.377	.698	103	1	28	4.18	-3	C-83	8	0.1
1976 Bal-A	28	79	2	11	1	0	1	4	7	13	0	1	.139	.209	.190	.399	19	-9	3	1.28	-2	C-27	1	-1.0
*NY-A	26	53	6	12	1	0	3	5	3	10	0	0	.226	.268	.415	.683	99	-0	6	3.59	0	C-18	2	0.0
Yr.	54	132	8	23	2	0	4	9	10	23	0	1	.174	.232	.280	.513	51	-9	9	2.17	-2	C-45	3	-1.0
1977 NY-A	10	11	1	3	1	0	1	5	0	2	0	0	.273	.273	.636	.909	141	0	2	6.44	0	/C-6	1	0.0
1978 Bal-A	13	18	4	6	1	0	1	1	3	3	0	0	.333	.429	.556	.984	186	2	4	9.89	0	/C-6,D-1,P-1	2	0.3
1979 Bal-A	1	1	0	0	0	0	0	0	0	0	0	0	.000	.000	.000	.000	-104	-0	0	.00	0	/C-1	0	-0.1
Total 12	711	1888	205	415	66	7	62	230	229	319	1	5	.220	.308	.361	.669	90	-23	218	3.84	-25	C-602/1-8,D-3,P-1	59	-2.4
• HENDRICKS, Jack	John Charles Hendricks b: 4/9/1875, Joliet, IL d: 5/13/1943, Chicago, IL BL/TL, 5'11.5", 160 lbs. Deb: 6/12/1902 M Career OF: 0-0-41																							
1902 NY-N	8	26	1	6	2	0	0	0	2	....	2	....	.231	.286	.308	.593	84	-1	3	3.72	0	/0-7(0-0-7)	0	-0.1
Chi-N	2	7	0	4	0	1	0	0	0	....	0	....	.571	.571	.857	1.429	350	2	3	22.86	0	/0-2(0-0-2)	1	0.2
Yr.	10	33	1	10	2	1	0	0	2	....	2	....	.303	.343	.424	.767	138	1	7	6.55	1	/0-9(0-0-9)	1	0.2
1903 Was-A	32	112	10	20	1	3	0	4	13	....	3	....	.179	.264	.241	.505	51	-6	9	2.42	-2	0-32(0-0-32)	0	-1.0
Total 2	42	145	11	30	3	4	0	4	15	....	5	....	.207	.281	.283	.564	71	-5	16	3.30	-2	/0-41	1	-0.8
• HENDRYX, Tim	Timothy Green Hendryx b: 1/31/1891, Le Roy, IL d: 8/14/1957, Corpus Christi, TX BR/TR, 5'9", 170 lbs. Deb: 9/4/1911 Career OF: 30-184-147																							
1911 Cle-A	4	7	0	2	0	0	0	0	0	....	0	....	.286	.286	.286	.571	59	-0	1	2.82	-1	/3-3	0	-0.1
1912 Cle-A	23	70	9	17	2	4	1	14	8	....	3	....	.243	.329	.429	.758	112	1	11	4.84	-3	0-22(0-22-0)	2	-0.4
1915 NY-A	13	40	4	8	2	0	0	1	4	2	0	3	.200	.289	.250	.539	61	-3	2	1.74	0	0-12(0-12-0)	0	-0.4
1916 NY-A	15	62	10	18	7	1	0	5	8	6	4	....	.290	.380	.435	.816	142	3	12	6.77	-1	0-15(0-0-15)	3	0.1
1917 NY-A	125	393	43	98	14	7	5	44	62	45	6	....	.249	.359	.359	.717	118	11	53	4.41	3	*0-107(0-30-77)	13	0.9
1918 StL-A	88	219	22	61	14	3	0	33	37	35	5	....	.279	.388	.370	.757	133	10	34	5.07	-4	0-65(28-20-18)	9	0.4
1920 Bos-A	99	363	54	119	21	5	0	73	42	27	7	9	.328	.400	.413	.814	121	11	60	6.02	-10	0-98(0-98-0)	13	-0.5
1921 Bos-A	49	137	10	33	8	2	0	22	24	13	1	1	.241	.362	.328	.690	79	-3	18	4.35	-2	0-41(2-2-37)	3	-0.7
Total 8	416	1291	152	356	68	22	6	192	185	128	26	13	.276	.372	.376	.749	116	30	191	4.97	-18	0-360/3-3	43	-0.7
• HENGEL, Dave	David Lee Hengel b: 12/18/1961, Oakland, CA BR/TR, 6', 185 lbs. Deb: 9/3/1986 Career OF: 21-0-17																							
1986 Sea-A	21	63	3	12	1	0	1	6	1	13	0	0	.190	.215	.254	.469	27	-6	3	1.71	0	D-11/0-8(6-0-2)	0	-0.7
1987 Sea-A	10	19	2	6	0	0	1	4	0	4	0	0	.316	.316	.474	.789	100	-0	2	3.41	0	/0-7(2-0-7),D-1	0	-0.1
1988 Sea-A	26	60	3	10	1	0	2	7	1	15	0	0	.167	.180	.283	.464	27	-6	3	1.67	-1	D-12,0-12(4-0-8)	0	-0.8
1989 Cle-A	12	25	2	3	1	0	0	1	2	4	0	0	.120	.185	.160	.345	-2	-3	1	.81	0	/0-9(9-0-0),D-3	0	-0.3
Total 4	69	167	10	31	3	0	4	18	4	36	0	0	.186	.209	.275	.485	30	-16	9	1.72	-1	/0-36,D-27	0	-1.8
• HENGLE, Moxie	Emery J. Hengle b: 10/7/1857, Chicago, IL d: 12/11/1924, River Forest, IL BR, 5'8", 144 lbs. Deb: 4/20/1884 U																							
1884 CP-U	19	74	9	15	2	1	0	....	3	....	....	....	.203	.234	.257	.491	70	-2	5	2.16	-5	2-19	1	-0.6
StP-U	9	33	2	5	1	1	0	....	0	....	....	....	.152	.152	.242	.394	31	-2	1	1.24	1	/2-9	0	-0.1
Yr.	28	107	11	20	3	2	0	....	3	....	....	....	.187	.209	.252	.461	58	-4	6	1.87	-4	2-28	1	-0.7
1885 Buf-N	7	26	2	4	0	0	0	0	1	2	....	....	.154	.185	.154	.339	10	-3	1	.93	-1	/2-5,0-3(0-2-1)	0	-0.3
Total 2	35	133	13	24	3	2	0	0	4	2	....	....	.180	.204	.233	.437	49	-7	7	1.68	-5	/2-33,0-3	1	-1.0
• HENLEY, Bob	Robert Clifton Henley b: 1/30/1973, Mobile, AL BR/TR, 6'2", 205 lbs. Deb: 7/19/1998																							
1998 Mon-N	41	115	16	35	8	1	3	18	11	26	3	0	.304	.380	.470	.849	124	5	21	6.43	0	C-35	5	0.7
• HENLEY, Gail	Gail Curtice Henley b: 10/15/1928, Wichita, KS BL/TR, 5'9", 180 lbs. Deb: 4/13/1954																							
1954 Pit-N	14	30	7	9	1	0	1	2	4	4	0	0	.300	.382	.433	.816	114	1	5	6.64	0	/0-9(1-0-8)	1	0.1
• HENLINE, Butch	Walter John Henline b: 12/20/1894, Fort Wayne, IN d: 10/9/1957, Sarasota, FL BR/TR, 5'10", 175 lbs. Deb: 4/13/1921 U Career OF: 5-1-0																							
1921 NY-N	1	1	0	0	0	0	0	0	0	1	0	0	.000	.000	.000	.000	-100	-0	0	.00	0	....	0	0.0
Phi-N	33	111	8	34	2	0	0	8	2	6	1	0	.306	.319	.324	.643	65	-5	11	3.84	6	C-32	2	0.3
Yr.	34	112	8	34	2	0	0	8	2	7	1	0	.304	.316	.321	.637	64	-5	11	3.79	6	C-32	2	0.3
1922 Phi-N	125	430	57	136	20	4	14	64	36	33	2	2	.316	.380	.479	.859	110	7	79	6.90	2	*C-119	12	1.6
1923 Phi-N	111	330	45	107	14	3	7	46	37	33	7	5	.324	.407	.448	.855	112	8	62	7.04	-1	C-96/0-1	10	1.2
1924 Phi-N	115	289	41	82	18	4	5	35	27	15	1	2	.284	.361	.426	.787	98	0	45	5.62	4	C-83/0-2(1-1-0)	9	0.9
1925 Phi-N	93	263	43	80	12	5	8	48	24	16	3	1	.304	.380	.479	.859	108	4	49	6.86	-3	C-68/0-1	9	0.5
1926 Phi-N	99	283	32	80	14	1	2	30	21	18	1	....	.283	.339	.360	.699	84	-6	35	4.16	2	C-77/1-4,0-2(2-0-0)	6	0.0
1927 Bro-N	67	177	12	47	10	3	1	18	17	10	1	....	.266	.337	.373	.710	89	-2	22	4.26	-1	C-60	6	0.0
1928 Bro-N	55	132	12	28	3	1	2	8	17	8	2	....	.212	.302	.295	.597	57	-8	12	3.00	0	C-45	2	-0.6
1929 Bro-N	27	62	5	15	2	0	1	7	9	9	0	....	.242	.338	.323	.661	66	-3	7	3.77	1	C-21	2	-0.1
1930 Chi-A	3	8	1	1	0	0	0	2	0	3	0	0	.125	.125	.125	.250	-38	-2	0	.53	0	/C-3	0	-0.1
1931 Chi-A	11	15	2	1	1	0	0	2	2	4	0	0	.067	.176	.133	.310	-19	-3	0	.81	-1	/C-4	0	-0.3
Total 11	740	2101	258	611	96	21	40	268	192	156	18	10	.291	.361	.414	.774	95	-10	324	5.51	9	C-608/0-6,1-4	58	3.3
• HENNESSY, Les	Lester Baker Hennessy b: 12/12/1893, Lynn, MA d: 11/20/1976, New York, NY BR/TR, 6', 190 lbs. Deb: 6/4/1913																							
1913 Det-A	14	22	2	3	0	0	0	0	3	6	2	....	.136	.240	.136	.376	11	-2	1	1.51	-2	2-10	0	-0.4
• HENRICH, Bobby	Robert Edward Henrich b: 12/24/1938, Lawrence, KS BR/TR, 6'1", 185 lbs. Deb: 5/3/1957																							
1957 Cin-N	29	10	8	2	0	0	0	1	1	4	0	0	.200	.273	.200	.473	28	-1	1	2.09	-3	/S-7,0-6(4-2-0),3-2,2-1	0	-0.4
1958 Cin-N	5	3	2	0	0	0	0	0	0	2	0	0	.000	.000	.000	.000	-95	-1	0	.00	0	/S-2	0	-0.1
1959 Cin-N	14	3	3	0	0	0	0	0	0	1	0	0	.000	.000	.000	.000	-97	-1	0	.00	-3	/S-5,3-1	0	-0.4
Total 3	48	16	13	2	0	0	0	1	1	7	0	0	.125	.176	.125	.301	-14	-3	1	1.25	-6	/S-14,0-6,3-3,2-1	0	-0.8
• HENRICH, Fritz	Frank Wilde Henrich b: 5/8/1899, Cincinnati, OH d: 5/1/1959, Philadelphia, PA BL/TL, 5'10", 160 lbs. Deb: 4/19/1924																							
1924 Phi-N	36	90	4	19	4	0	0	4	2	12	0	0	.211	.228	.256	.484	26	-9	5	1.91	0	0-32(12-14-10)	0	-1.1
• HENRICH, Tommy	Thomas David "The Clutch,Old Reliable" Henrich b: 2/20/1910, Massillon, OH BL/TL, 6', 180 lbs. Deb: 5/11/1937 C Career OF: 38-92-894																							
1937 NY-A	67	206	39	66	14	5	8	42	35	17	4	0	.320	.419	.553	.972	142	15	50	9.47	0	0-59(30-0-29)	10	1.1
1938*NY-A	131	471	109	127	24	7	22	91	92	32	6	2	.270	.391	.490	.882	120	17	96	7.18	5	*0-130(0-0-130)	19	1.2

YEAR TM-L	G	AB	R	H	2B	3B	HR	RBI	BB	SO	SB	CS	AVG	OBP	SLG	OPS	OPS+	BR/A	RC	RC/G	FR	G/POS	WS	TPW
1939 NY-A	99	347	64	96	18	4	9	57	51	23	7	0	.277	.371	.429	.800	106	5	60	6.21	3	0-88(1-38-50)/1-1	13	0.5
1940 NY-A	90	293	57	90	28	5	10	53	48	30	1	2	.307	.408	.539	.947	149	22	68	8.52	2	0-76(1-24-52)/1-2	14	2.0
1941*NY-A	144	538	106	149	27	5	31	85	81	40	3	1	.277	.377	.519	.895	136	29	113	7.57	0	*0-139(0-19-121)	26	2.1
1942 NY-A★	127	483	77	129	30	5	13	67	58	42	4	4	.267	.352	.431	.782	122	13	79	5.75	2	*0-119(0-0-119)/1-7	19	0.7
1946 NY-A	150	565	92	142	25	4	19	83	87	63	5	2	.251	.358	.411	.769	113	13	92	5.61	2	*0-111(0-0-111),1-41	21	1.0
1947*NY-A★	142	550	109	158	35	**13**	16	98	71	54	3	2	.287	.372	.485	.857	138	28	104	6.91	3	*0-132(0-8-125)/1-6	27	2.7
1948 NY-A★	146	588	**138**	181	42	**14**	25	100	76	42	2	3	.308	.391	.554	.945	151	40	130	8.18	-1	*0-102(6-3-96),1-46	29	3.3
1949*NY-A★	115	411	90	118	20	3	24	85	86	34	2	2	.287	.416	.526	.942	148	30	98	8.77	-4	0-61(0-0-61),1-52	24	2.3
1950 NY-A★	73	151	20	41	6	8	6	34	27	6	0	1	.272	.382	.536	.918	137	8	30	6.95	-4	1-34	6	0.3
Total 11	**1284**	**4603**	**901**	**1297**	**269**	**73**	**183**	**795**	**712**	**383**	**37**	**19**	**.282**	**.382**	**.491**	**.873**	**132**	**220**	**922**	**7.20**	**9**	***0-1017,1-189**	**208**	**17.2**

• HENRIKSEN, Olaf — Olaf "Swede" Henriksen b: 4/26/1888, Kirkerup, Denmark d: 10/17/1962, Norwood, MA BL/TL, 5'7.5", 158 lbs. Deb: 8/11/1911 Career OF: 42-22-61

YEAR TM-L	G	AB	R	H	2B	3B	HR	RBI	BB	SO	SB	CS	AVG	OBP	SLG	OPS	OPS+	BR/A	RC	RC/G	FR	G/POS	WS	TPW
1911 Bos-A	27	93	17	34	2	1	0	8	14	....	4	....	.366	.449	.409	.857	141	6	19	8.11	0	0-25(5-0-20)	4	0.5
1912*Bos-A	44	56	20	18	3	1	0	8	14	....	0	....	.321	.457	.411	.868	142	4	11	6.99	-1	0-11(0-0-10)	3	0.3
1913 Bos-A	31	40	8	15	1	0	0	2	7	5	3	....	.375	.468	.400	.868	151	3	8	8.53	0	/O-7(6-1-0)	2	0.3
1914 Bos-A	63	95	16	25	2	1	1	5	22	12	5	4	.263	.407	.337	.744	124	4	14	4.85	-2	0-29(8-10-10)	5	0.1
1915*Bos-A	73	92	9	18	2	2	0	13	18	7	1	5	.196	.333	.261	.594	80	-3	8	2.51	1	0-25(9-4-12)	1	-0.3
1916*Bos-A	68	99	13	20	2	2	0	11	19	15	2	....	.202	.331	.263	.593	78	-2	10	3.11	0	0-31(14-7-9)	3	-0.3
1917 Bos-A	15	12	1	1	0	0	0	1	3	4	0	....	.083	.267	.083	.350	7	-1	0	.59	0	....	0	-0.1
Total 7	**321**	**487**	**84**	**131**	**12**	**7**	**1**	**48**	**97**	**43**	**15**	**9**	**.269**	**.392**	**.329**	**.721**	**111**	**11**	**70**	**4.82**	**-2**	**0-128**	**18**	**0.4**

• HENRY, George — George Washington Henry b: 8/10/1863, Philadelphia, PA d: 12/30/1934, Lynn, MA BR/TR, 5'9", 180 lbs. Deb: 4/27/1893

YEAR TM-L	G	AB	R	H	2B	3B	HR	RBI	BB	SO	SB	CS	AVG	OBP	SLG	OPS	OPS+	BR/A	RC	RC/G	FR	G/POS	WS	TPW
1893 Cin-N	21	83	11	23	3	0	0	13	11	12	2	....	.277	.375	.313	.688	82	-2	11	4.75	5	0-21(10-0-11)	2	0.1

• HENRY, John — John Michael Henry b: 9/2/1863, Springfield, MA d: 6/11/1939, Hartford, CT TL Deb: 8/13/1884 Career OF: 35-1-7 ♦

YEAR TM-L	G	AB	R	H	2B	3B	HR	RBI	BB	SO	SB	CS	AVG	OBP	SLG	OPS	OPS+	BR/A	RC	RC/G	FR	G/POS	WS	TPW
1884 Cle-N	9	26	2	4	0	0	0	0	0	12	....	....	.154	.154	.154	.308	-3	-2	1	.79	1	/P-5,0-4(0-0-4)	1	-0.4
1885 Bal-a	10	34	4	9	3	0	0	3	1	....	....	....	.265	.286	.353	.639	102	2	4	3.80	2	/P-9,0-1	3	-0.4
1886 Was-N	4	14	3	5	0	0	0	0	0	3	0	....	.357	.357	.357	.714	125	1	2	5.49	-1	/P-4	1	-0.2
1890 NY-N	37	144	19	35	6	0	0	16	7	12	12	....	.243	.283	.285	.568	65	-7	15	3.74	-1	0-37(34-1-3)	2	-0.8
Total 4	**60**	**218**	**28**	**53**	**9**	**0**	**0**	**19**	**8**	**27**	**12**	**....**	**.243**	**.273**	**.284**	**.558**	**67**	**-6**	**21**	**3.45**	**1**	**/O-42,P-18**	**7**	**-1.9**

• HENRY, John — John Park "Bull" Henry b: 12/26/1889, Amherst, MA d: 11/24/1941, Fort Huachuca, AZ BR/TR, 6', 180 lbs. Deb: 7/8/1910

YEAR TM-L	G	AB	R	H	2B	3B	HR	RBI	BB	SO	SB	CS	AVG	OBP	SLG	OPS	OPS+	BR/A	RC	RC/G	FR	G/POS	WS	TPW
1910 Was-A	28	87	2	13	1	1	0	5	2	....	2	....	.149	.169	.184	.352	11	-9	3	.98	4	C-18,1-10	1	-0.5
1911 Was-A	85	261	24	53	5	0	0	21	25	....	8	....	.203	.273	.222	.495	39	-21	18	2.19	8	C-51,1-30	3	-0.9
1912 Was-A	66	191	23	37	4	1	0	9	31	....	10	....	.194	.309	.225	.535	53	-10	16	2.70	6	C-65	7	0.1
1913 Was-A	96	273	26	61	8	4	1	26	30	43	5	....	.223	.309	.293	.602	75	-8	26	3.00	3	C-96	9	0.1
1914 Was-A	92	261	22	44	7	4	0	20	37	47	7	3	.169	.274	.226	.500	49	-16	19	2.16	3	C-92	6	-0.7
1915 Was-A	95	277	20	61	9	2	1	22	36	28	10	2	.220	.323	.278	.601	78	-5	29	3.35	1	C-94	10	0.3
1916 Was-A	117	305	28	76	12	3	0	46	49	40	12	....	.249	.364	.308	.672	103	4	40	4.35	0	*C-116	13	1.3
1917 Was-A	65	163	10	31	6	0	0	18	24	16	1	....	.190	.302	.227	.529	62	-6	12	2.23	5	C-59	4	0.2
1918 Bos-N	43	102	6	21	2	0	0	4	10	15	0	....	.206	.283	.225	.509	58	-5	6	2.02	-2	C-38	1	-0.5
Total 9	**687**	**1920**	**161**	**397**	**54**	**15**	**2**	**171**	**244**	**189**	**55**	**5**	**.207**	**.303**	**.254**	**.557**	**65**	**-76**	**169**	**2.78**	**27**	**C-629/1-40**	**54**	**-0.5**

• HENRY, Ron — Ronald Baxter Henry b: 8/7/1936, Chester, PA BR/TR, 6'1", 180 lbs. Deb: 4/15/1961

YEAR TM-L	G	AB	R	H	2B	3B	HR	RBI	BB	SO	SB	CS	AVG	OBP	SLG	OPS	OPS+	BR/A	RC	RC/G	FR	G/POS	WS	TPW
1961 Min-A	20	28	1	4	0	0	0	3	2	7	0	0	.143	.200	.143	.343	-6	-4	0	.47	0	/C-5,1-1	0	-0.4
1964 Min-A	22	41	4	5	1	1	2	5	2	17	0	0	.122	.163	.341	.504	36	-4	2	1.48	1	C-13	1	-0.3
Total 2	**42**	**69**	**5**	**9**	**1**	**1**	**2**	**8**	**4**	**24**	**0**	**0**	**.130**	**.178**	**.261**	**.439**	**18**	**-8**	**3**	**1.04**	**1**	**/C-18,1-1**	**1**	**-0.7**

• HENRY, Snake — Frederick Marshall Henry b: 7/19/1895, Waynesville, NC d: 10/12/1987, Wendell, NC BL/TL, 6', 170 lbs. Deb: 9/15/1922

YEAR TM-L	G	AB	R	H	2B	3B	HR	RBI	BB	SO	SB	CS	AVG	OBP	SLG	OPS	OPS+	BR/A	RC	RC/G	FR	G/POS	WS	TPW
1922 Bos-N	18	66	5	13	4	1	0	5	2	8	2	2	.197	.221	.288	.508	32	-7	4	1.77	1	1-18	0	-0.7
1923 Bos-N	11	9	1	1	0	0	0	2	1	1	0	0	.111	.200	.111	.311	-17	-1	0	.80	0	....	0	-0.1
Total 2	**29**	**75**	**6**	**14**	**4**	**1**	**0**	**7**	**3**	**9**	**2**	**2**	**.187**	**.218**	**.267**	**.485**	**26**	**-9**	**4**	**1.65**	**1**	**/1-18**	**0**	**-0.8**

• HENSON, Drew — Drew Daniel Henson b: 2/13/1980, San Diego, CA BR/TR, 6'5", 222 lbs. Deb: 9/5/2002

YEAR TM-L	G	AB	R	H	2B	3B	HR	RBI	BB	SO	SB	CS	AVG	OBP	SLG	OPS	OPS+	BR/A	RC	RC/G	FR	G/POS	WS	TPW
2002 NY-A	3	1	1	0	0	0	0	0	0	1	0	0	.000	.000	.000	.000	-101	-0	0	.00	0	/D-2	0	0.0
2003 NY-A	5	8	2	1	0	0	0	0	0	2	0	0	.125	.125	.125	.250	-34	-2	0	.48	0	/3-3	0	-0.1
Total 2	**8**	**9**	**3**	**1**	**0**	**0**	**0**	**0**	**0**	**3**	**0**	**0**	**.111**	**.111**	**.111**	**.222**	**-42**	**-2**	**0**	**.42**	**0**	**/3-3,D-2**	**0**	**-0.1**

• HERMAN, Babe — Floyd Caves Herman b: 6/26/1903, Buffalo, NY d: 11/27/1987, Glendale, CA BL/TL, 6'4", 190 lbs. Deb: 4/14/1926 C Career OF: 191-0-994

YEAR TM-L	G	AB	R	H	2B	3B	HR	RBI	BB	SO	SB	CS	AVG	OBP	SLG	OPS	OPS+	BR/A	RC	RC/G	FR	G/POS	WS	TPW
1926 Bro-N	137	496	64	158	35	11	11	81	44	53	8	....	.319	.375	.500	.875	136	24	91	6.71	0	*1-101,0-35(6-0-29)	20	1.5
1927 Bro-N	130	412	65	112	26	9	14	73	39	41	4	....	.272	.336	.481	.817	116	8	65	5.40	1	*1-105/0-1	12	0.1
1928 Bro-N	134	486	64	165	37	6	12	91	38	36	1	....	.340	.390	.514	.904	136	24	94	7.27	-2	*0-127(0-0-127)	19	1.3
1929 Bro-N	146	569	105	217	42	13	21	113	55	45	21	....	.381	.436	.612	1.047	159	52	146	10.42	-19	*0-141(0-0-141)/1-2	26	2.0
1930 Bro-N	153	614	143	241	48	11	35	130	66	56	18	....	.393	.455	.678	1.132	171	71	183	12.23	-19	*0-153(0-0-153)	32	3.5
1931 Bro-N	151	610	93	191	43	16	18	97	50	65	17	....	.313	.365	.525	.890	137	30	118	7.32	-1	*0-150(0-0-150)	26	1.9
1932 Cin-N	148	577	87	188	38	**19**	16	87	60	45	7	....	.326	.389	.541	.930	152	42	124	8.19	11	*0-146(0-0-146)	24	4.3
1933 Chi-N	137	508	77	147	36	12	16	93	50	57	6	....	.289	.353	.502	.855	142	27	90	6.31	-4	*0-131(0-0-131)	23	1.5
1934 Chi-N	125	467	65	142	34	5	14	84	35	71	1	....	.304	.353	.488	.841	125	15	81	6.48	-9	*0-113(0-0-113)/1-7	17	-0.1
1935 Pit-N	26	81	8	19	8	1	0	7	3	10	0	....	.235	.271	.358	.629	65	-4	7	2.81	-2	0-15(15-0-0)/1-3	1	-0.7
Cin-N	92	349	44	117	23	5	10	58	35	25	5	....	.335	.396	.516	.912	147	23	75	8.56	1	0-76(76-0-0),1-14	17	1.9
Yr.	118	430	52	136	31	6	10	65	38	35	5	....	.316	.373	.486	.859	133	19	82	7.31	-1	0-91(91-0-0),1-17	18	1.2
1936 Cin-N	119	380	59	106	25	2	13	71	39	36	4	....	.279	.348	.458	.806	123	12	61	5.73	-4	0-92(91-0-1)/1-4	13	0.3
1937 Det-A	17	20	2	6	3	0	0	3	1	6	2	0	.300	.364	.450	.814	102	0	4	6.98	-0	/0-2(2-0-0)	1	0.0
1945 Bro-N	37	34	6	9	1	0	1	9	5	7	0	....	.265	.359	.382	.741	107	0	5	4.95	-1	/0-3(0-0-3)	1	0.0
Total 13	**1552**	**5603**	**882**	**1818**	**399**	**110**	**181**	**997**	**520**	**553**	**94**	**0**	**.324**	**.383**	**.532**	**.915**	**141**	**325**	**1143**	**7.66**	**-47**	***0-1185,1-236**	**232**	**17.6**

• HERMAN, Billy — William Jennings Bryan Herman
b: 7/7/1909, New Albany, IN d: 9/5/1992, West Palm Beach, FL BR/TR, 5'11", 180 lbs. Deb: 8/29/1931 M/C HOF: 1975

YEAR TM-L	G	AB	R	H	2B	3B	HR	RBI	BB	SO	SB	CS	AVG	OBP	SLG	OPS	OPS+	BR/A	RC	RC/G	FR	G/POS	WS	TPW
1931 Chi-N	25	98	14	32	7	0	0	16	13	6	2	....	.327	.405	.398	.803	115	3	17	6.27	2	2-25	4	0.6
1932*Chi-N	154	656	102	206	42	7	1	51	40	33	14	....	.314	.358	.404	.762	105	5	97	5.36	9	*2-154	23	2.4
1933 Chi-N	153	619	82	173	35	2	0	44	45	34	5	....	.279	.332	.342	.675	93	-5	70	3.93	25	*2-153	18	3.3
1934 Chi-N★	113	456	79	138	21	6	3	42	34	31	6	....	.303	.355	.395	.750	102	2	66	5.34	7	*2-111	16	1.6
1935*Chi-N★	154	666	113	**227**	**57**	6	7	83	42	29	6	....	.341	.383	.476	.859	129	26	121	6.81	14	*2-154	32	4.9
1936 Chi-N★	153	632	101	211	57	7	5	93	59	30	5	....	.334	.392	.470	.862	128	26	118	7.03	21	*2-153	29	5.6
1937 Chi-N★	138	564	106	189	35	11	8	65	56	22	2	....	.335	.396	.479	.875	131	25	112	7.72	24	*2-137	29	**5.8**
1938*Chi-N★	152	624	86	173	34	7	1	56	59	31	3	....	.277	.342	.359	.701	90	-7	76	4.21	22	*2-151	20	2.5
1939 Chi-N★	156	623	111	191	34	**18**	7	70	66	31	9	....	.307	.378	.453	.830	120	18	104	5.89	-6	*2-156	25	2.2
1940 Chi-N★	135	558	77	163	24	4	5	57	47	30	1	....	.292	.347	.376	.723	101	1	72	4.59	9	*2-135	17	2.0
1941 Chi-N	11	36	4	7	0	1	0	0	9	5	0	....	.194	.356	.250	.606	75	-1	4	3.75	-3	2-11	1	-0.3
*Bro-N★	133	536	77	156	30	4	3	41	58	38	1	....	.291	.361	.379	.740	104	4	75	5.01	-4	*2-133	17	0.9
Yr.	144	572	81	163	30	5	3	41	67	43	1	....	.285	.361	.371	.732	102	3	79	4.93	-7	*2-144	18	0.6
1942 Bro-N★	155	571	76	146	34	2	2	65	72	52	6	....	.256	.339	.333	.672	95	-2	68	4.20	6	*2-153/1-3	20	1.5
1943 Bro-N★	153	585	76	193	41	2	2	100	66	26	4	....	.330	.398	.417	.815	135	28	97	6.18	-1	*2-117,3-37	27	3.6
1946 Bro-N	47	184	24	53	8	4	0	28	26	10	2	....	.288	.376	.375	.751	112	4	26	5.16	1	3-29,2-16	7	0.6
Bos-N	75	252	32	77	23	1	3	22	43	13	1	....	.306	.409	.440	.849	139	15	47	6.74	-5	2-44,1-22/3-5	13	1.2
Yr.	122	436	56	130	31	5	3	50	69	23	3	....	.298	.395	.413	.808	128	19	73	6.07	-4	2-60,3-34,1-22	20	1.8
1947 Pit-N	15	47	3	10	4	0	0	6	2	7	0	....	.213	.245	.298	.543	42	-4	3	1.80	0	2-10/1-2	0	-0.4
Total 15	**1922**	**7707**	**1163**	**2345**	**486**	**82**	**47**	**839**	**737**	**428**	**67**	**....**	**.304**	**.367**	**.407**	**.774**	**112**	**140**	**1173**	**5.51**	**122**	***2-1813/3-71,1-27**	**298**	**37.9**

YEAR TM-L	G	AB	R	H	2B	3B	HR	RBI	BB	SO	SB	CS	AVG	OBP	SLG	OPS	OPS+	BR/A	RC	RC/G	FR	G/POS	WS	TPW
• HERMANN, Al	Albert Bartel Hermann b: 3/28/1899, Milltown, NJ d: 8/20/1980, Lewes, DE BR/TR, 6', 180 lbs. Deb: 7/13/1923																							
1923 Bos-N	31	93	2	22	4	0	0	11	0	7	3	2	.237	.237	.280	.516	37	-9	6	2.03	-3	2-15/3-5,1-4	0	-1.0
1924 Bos-N	1	1	0	0	0	0	0	0	0	1	0	0	.000	.000	.000	.000	-104	-0	0	.00	0	....	0	0.0
Total 2	32	94	2	22	4	0	0	11	0	8	3	2	.234	.234	.277	.511	36	-9	6	2.00	-3	/2-15,3-5,1-4	0	-1.1
• HERMANSEN, Chad	Chad Bruce Hermansen b: 9/10/1977, Salt Lake City, UT BR/TR, 6'2", 185 lbs. Deb: 9/7/1999 Career OF: 15-110-36																							
1999 Pit-N	19	60	5	14	3	0	1	1	7	19	2	2	.233	.324	.333	.657	67	-3	7	3.73	0	0-18(3-9-6)	0	-0.4
2000 Pit-N	33	108	12	20	4	1	2	8	6	37	0	0	.185	.228	.296	.524	31	-12	7	1.98	-4	0-31(0-27-4)	0	-1.5
2001 Pit-N	22	55	5	9	1	0	2	5	1	18	0	1	.164	.179	.291	.469	18	-7	3	1.50	0	0-20(0-6-15)	0	-0.7
2002 Pit-N	65	194	22	40	11	1	7	15	17	68	7	5	.206	.274	.381	.655	70	-10	20	3.35	2	0-60(2-59-2)	3	-0.7
Chi-N	35	43	3	9	3	0	1	3	5	14	0	0	.209	.292	.349	.641	69	-2	5	3.71	-2	0-21(4-9-9)	0	-0.4
Yr.	100	237	25	49	14	1	8	18	22	82	7	5	.207	.277	.376	.652	70	-12	25	3.41	1	0-81(6-68-11)	3	-1.1
2003 LA-N	11	25	2	4	1	0	0	2	2	9	0	0	.160	.222	.200	.422	12	-3	1	1.58	0	/0-6(6-0-0)	0	-0.3
Total 5	185	485	49	96	23	2	13	34	38	165	9	8	.198	.259	.334	.593	52	-38	43	2.81	-4	0-156	3	-4.1
• HERMANSKI, Gene	Eugene Victor Hermanski b: 5/11/1920, Pittsfield, MA BL/TR, 5'11.5", 185 lbs. Deb: 8/15/1943 Career OF: 265-5-311																							
1943 Bro-N	18	60	6	18	2	1	0	12	11	7	1	....	.300	.417	.367	.783	127	3	10	5.99	2	0-17(11-0-6)	3	0.4
1946 Bro-N	64	110	15	22	2	2	0	8	17	10	2	....	.200	.313	.255	.567	61	-5	9	2.59	-3	0-34(12-4-17)	1	-0.9
1947*Bro-N	79	189	36	52	7	1	7	39	28	7	5	....	.275	.377	.434	.811	111	4	33	6.13	2	0-66(64-1-3)	8	0.2
1948 Bro-N	133	400	63	116	22	7	15	60	64	46	15	....	.290	.391	.493	.883	133	20	81	7.37	6	*0-119(6-0-113)	19	2.2
1949*Bro-N	87	224	48	67	12	3	8	42	47	21	12	....	.299	.431	.487	.918	140	16	50	8.04	-4	0-77(64-0-17)	12	0.6
1950 Bro-N	94	289	36	86	17	3	7	34	36	26	2	....	.298	.381	.450	.831	115	7	50	6.21	5	0-78(76-0-3)	10	0.7
1951 Bro-N	31	80	8	20	4	0	1	5	10	12	0	2	.250	.333	.338	.671	79	-3	9	3.69	1	0-19(18-0-1)	2	-0.4
Chi-N	75	231	28	65	12	1	3	20	35	30	3	0	.281	.385	.381	.766	105	4	37	5.78	4	0-63(3-0-60)	8	0.6
Yr.	106	311	36	85	16	1	4	25	45	42	3	2	.273	.372	.370	.742	99	1	46	5.22	5	0-82(21-0-61)	10	0.3
1952 Chi-N	99	275	28	70	6	0	4	34	29	32	2	0	.255	.330	.320	.650	80	-6	32	4.02	4	0-76(3-0-73)	7	-0.4
1953 Chi-N	18	40	1	6	1	0	0	1	4	7	1	0	.150	.227	.175	.402	7	-5	2	1.38	0	0-13(3-0-10)	0	-0.6
Pit-N	41	62	7	11	0	0	1	4	8	14	0	0	.177	.282	.226	.507	35	-6	4	2.16	0	0-13(5-0-8)	0	-0.7
Yr.	59	102	8	17	1	0	1	5	12	21	1	0	.167	.261	.206	.467	24	-11	6	1.85	-1	0-26(8-0-18)	0	-1.2
Total 9	739	1960	276	533	85	18	46	259	289	212	43	2	.272	.372	.404	.776	107	28	316	5.68	16	0-575	70	1.8
• HERMOSO, Remy	Angel Remigio Hermoso b: 10/1/1947, Carabobo, Venezuela BR/TR, 5'8", 155 lbs. Deb: 9/14/1967																							
1967 Atl-N	11	26	3	8	0	0	0	0	2	4	1	0	.308	.357	.308	.665	93	0	3	4.84	-2	/S-9,2-2	1	-0.2
1969 Mon-N	28	74	6	12	0	0	0	3	5	10	3	1	.162	.225	.162	.387	10	-9	3	1.09	0	2-18/S-6	1	-0.7
1970 Mon-N	4	1	1	0	0	0	0	0	0	0	0	0	.000	.000	.000	.000	-100	-0	0	.00	0	/2-1,3-1	0	-0.1
1974 Cle-A	48	122	15	27	3	1	0	5	7	7	2	2	.221	.264	.262	.526	52	-8	9	2.26	3	2-45	2	-0.3
Total 4	91	223	25	47	3	1	0	8	14	21	6	3	.211	.261	.233	.494	42	-17	15	2.08	0	/2-66,S-15,3-1	4	-1.3
• HERNANDEZ, Alex	Alexander (Vargas) Hernandez b: 5/28/1977, San Juan, Puerto Rico BL/TL, 6'4", 190 lbs. Deb: 9/1/2000 Career OF: 3-0-6																							
2000 Pit-N	20	60	4	12	3	0	1	5	0	13	1	1	.200	.200	.300	.500	24	-7	3	1.87	-1	1-12/0-5(3-0-2)	0	-0.9
2001 Pit-N	7	11	0	1	0	0	0	0	0	2	0	0	.091	.091	.091	.182	-52	-2	0	.00	0	/0-4(0-0-4),1-2	0	-0.2
Total 2	27	71	4	13	3	0	1	5	0	15	1	1	.183	.183	.268	.451	12	-10	3	1.53	-1	/1-14,0-9	0	-1.2
• HERNANDEZ, Carlos	Carlos Alberto (Almeida) Hernandez b: 5/24/1967, San Felix, Venezuela BR/TR, 5'11", 218 lbs. Deb: 4/20/1990																							
1990 LA-N	10	20	2	4	1	0	0	1	0	2	0	0	.200	.200	.250	.450	24	-2	1	1.69	0	C-10	0	-0.2
1991 LA-N	15	14	1	3	1	0	0	1	0	5	1	0	.214	.267	.286	.552	57	-1	1	1.28	-1	C-13/3-1	0	-0.1
1992 LA-N	69	173	11	45	4	0	3	17	11	21	0	1	.260	.319	.335	.654	87	-3	17	3.27	3	C-63	4	0.3
1993 LA-N	50	99	6	25	5	0	2	7	2	11	0	0	.253	.267	.364	.631	71	-5	10	3.53	-2	C-43	1	-0.4
1994 LA-N	32	64	6	14	2	0	2	6	1	14	0	0	.219	.231	.344	.575	50	-5	5	2.77	1	C-27	1	-0.2
1995 LA-N	45	94	3	14	1	0	2	8	7	25	0	0	.149	.216	.223	.439	18	-11	4	1.22	2	C-41	2	-0.8
1996 LA-N	13	14	1	4	0	0	0	0	2	2	0	0	.286	.375	.286	.661	84	-0	2	4.58	0	/C-9	0	0.0
1997 SD-N	50	134	15	42	7	1	3	14	3	27	0	2	.313	.328	.448	.776	110	0	17	4.56	2	C-44/1-4	4	0.5
1998*SD-N	129	390	34	102	15	0	9	52	16	54	2	2	.262	.306	.369	.675	82	-11	39	3.36	0	*C-122/1-1	10	-0.4
2000 SD-N	58	191	16	48	11	0	2	25	16	26	1	3	.251	.319	.340	.659	72	-10	20	3.58	3	C-54/1-1	5	-0.2
*StL-N	17	51	7	14	4	0	1	10	5	9	1	0	.275	.351	.412	.763	91	-0	8	5.78	-1	C-16	2	0.0
Yr.	75	242	23	62	15	0	3	35	21	35	2	3	.256	.326	.355	.681	76	-10	28	4.02	3	C-70/1-1	7	-0.3
Total 10	488	1244	102	315	51	1	24	141	63	196	5	8	.253	.299	.354	.653	76	-49	123	3.35	7	C-442/1-6,3-1	29	-1.7
• HERNANDEZ, Carlos	Carlos Eduardo Hernandez b: 12/12/1975, Caracas, Venezuela BR/TR, 5'9", 175 lbs. Deb: 5/26/1999																							
1999 Hou-N	16	14	4	2	0	0	0	1	0	0	3	1	.143	.143	.143	.286	-28	-3	0	.52	-0	/2-7,S-2	0	-0.2
2000 Sea-A	2	1	0	0	0	0	0	0	0	1	0	1	.000	.000	.000	.000	-106	-1	0	.00	0	/3-2	0	-0.1
Total 2	18	15	4	2	0	0	0	1	0	1	3	2	.133	.133	.133	.267	-33	-3	0	.46	0	/2-7,3-2,S-2	0	-0.3
• HERNANDEZ, Cesar	Cesar Dario (Perez) Hernandez b: 9/28/1966, Yamasa, Dominican Republic BR/TR, 6', 160 lbs. Deb: 7/19/1992 Career OF: 29-13-1																							
1992 Cin-N	34	51	6	14	4	0	0	4	0	10	3	1	.275	.275	.353	.627	74	-2	5	3.19	1	0-18(12-6-1)	1	-0.1
1993 Cin-N	27	24	3	2	0	0	0	1	1	8	1	2	.083	.120	.083	.203	-44	-6	0	.14	0	0-23(17-7-0)	0	-0.5
Total 2	61	75	9	16	4	0	0	5	1	18	4	3	.213	.224	.267	.490	34	-7	5	2.00	2	/0-41	1	-0.7
• HERNANDEZ, Chico	Salvador Jose (Ramos) Hernandez b: 1/3/1916, Havana, Cuba d: 1/3/1986, Havana, Cuba BR/TR, 6', 195 lbs. Deb: 4/16/1942																							
1942 Chi-N	47	118	6	27	5	0	0	7	11	13	0	....	.229	.295	.271	.566	69	-5	10	2.92	0	C-43	2	-0.3
1943 Chi-N	43	126	10	34	4	0	0	9	9	9	0	....	.270	.324	.302	.625	82	-3	12	3.34	-3	C-41	3	-0.4
Total 2	90	244	16	61	9	0	0	16	20	22	0	....	.250	.309	.287	.596	76	-7	22	3.14	-4	/C-84	5	-0.7
• HERNANDEZ, Enzo	Enzo Octavio Hernandez b: 2/12/1949, Valle de Guanape, Venezuela BR/TR, 5'8", 155 lbs. Deb: 4/17/1971																							
1971 SD-N	143	549	58	122	9	3	0	12	54	34	21	5	.222	.295	.250	.545	60	-25	46	2.75	-11	*S-143	7	-2.0
1972 SD-N	114	329	33	64	11	2	1	15	22	25	24	3	.195	.245	.249	.494	44	-20	23	2.12	-2	*S-107/0-3(2-0-1)	4	-1.1
1973 SD-N	70	247	26	55	2	1	0	9	17	14	15	4	.223	.273	.239	.512	47	-16	17	2.32	4	S-67	2	-0.5
1974 SD-N	147	512	55	119	19	2	0	34	38	36	37	10	.232	.285	.277	.563	60	-24	45	2.90	-7	*S-145	9	-1.5
1975 SD-N	116	344	37	75	12	2	0	19	26	25	20	4	.218	.277	.265	.541	54	-19	28	2.49	4	*S-111	7	-0.3
1976 SD-N	113	340	31	87	13	3	1	24	32	16	12	7	.256	.320	.321	.640	89	-5	36	3.46	-6	*S-101	9	0.1
1977 SD-N	7	3	1	0	0	0	0	0	0	0	0	0	.000	.000	.000	.000	-112	-1	0	.00	-1	/S-7	0	-0.2
1978 LA-N	4	3	0	0	0	0	0	0	0	1	0	0	.000	.000	.000	.000	-100	-1	0	.00	-1	/S-2	0	-0.2
Total 8	714	2327	241	522	66	13	2	113	189	151	129	33	.224	.284	.266	.550	59	-110	196	2.69	-20	S-683/0-3	38	-5.7
• HERNANDEZ, Jackie	Jacinto (Zulueta) Hernandez b: 9/11/1940, Central Tinguaro, Cuba BR/TR, 5'11", 175 lbs. Deb: 9/14/1965																							
1965 Cal-A	6	6	2	2	1	0	0	1	0	1	1	0	.333	.333	.500	.833	136	0	1	7.92	-1	/S-2,3-1	0	-0.1
1966 Cal-A	58	23	19	1	0	0	0	2	1	4	1	1	.043	.083	.043	.127	-64	-5	0	.12	-3	3-11/2-8,S-8,0-3(0-1-2)	0	-0.8
1967 Min-A	29	28	1	4	0	0	0	3	0	6	0	0	.143	.143	.143	.286	-14	-4	1	.70	-2	S-15,3-13	0	-0.5
1968 Min-A	83	199	13	35	3	0	2	17	9	52	5	2	.176	.219	.221	.440	32	-16	10	1.52	-8	S-79/1-1	1	-2.1
1969 KC-A	145	504	54	112	14	2	4	40	38	111	17	7	.222	.279	.282	.561	57	-29	42	2.81	-5	*S-144	7	-1.7
1970 KC-A	83	238	14	55	4	1	2	10	15	50	1	3	.231	.282	.282	.564	56	-15	18	2.52	-1	S-77	3	-0.8
1971*Pit-N	88	233	30	48	7	3	3	26	17	45	0	2	.206	.260	.300	.560	58	-14	18	2.44	0	S-75/3-9	3	-0.7
1972 Pit-N	72	176	12	33	7	1	1	14	9	43	0	0	.188	.227	.256	.483	38	-15	10	1.77	-3	S-68/3-4	3	-1.2
1973 Pit-N	54	73	8	18	1	2	0	8	4	12	0	0	.247	.286	.315	.601	68	-3	6	2.87	-1	S-49	2	-0.1
Total 9	618	1480	153	308	37	9	12	121	93	324	25	15	.208	.258	.270	.527	49	-101	106	2.32	-24	S-517/3-38,2-8,0-3,1-1	19	-8.1
• HERNANDEZ, Jose	Jose Antonio (Figueroa) Hernandez b: 7/14/1969, Rio Piedras, Puerto Rico BR/TR, 6'1", 180 lbs. Deb: 8/9/1991 Career OF: 47-50-4																							
1991 Tex-A	45	98	8	18	2	1	0	4	3	31	0	1	.184	.208	.224	.432	20	-11	4	1.32	3	S-44/3-1	1	-0.5
1992 Cle-A	3	4	0	0	0	0	0	0	0	2	0	0	.000	.000	.000	.000	-102	-1	0	.00	-1	/S-3	0	-0.2
1994 Chi-N	56	132	18	32	2	3	1	9	8	29	2	2	.242	.291	.326	.617	61	-8	12	2.86	-1	3-28,S-21/2-8,0-1	1	-0.7

YEAR TM-L	G	AB	R	H	2B	3B	HR	RBI	BB	SO	SB	CS	AVG	OBP	SLG	OPS	OPS+	BR/A	RC	RC/G	FR	G/POS	WS	TPW
1995 Chi-N	93	245	37	60	11	4	13	40	13	69	1	0	.245	.283	.482	.765	99	-2	31	4.07	1	S-43,2-29,3-20	6	0.2
1996 Chi-N	131	331	52	80	14	1	10	41	24	97	4	0	.242	.295	.381	.676	75	-12	36	3.62	4	S-87,3-43/2-1,0-1	6	-0.2
1997 Chi-N	121	183	33	50	8	5	7	26	14	42	2	5	.273	.325	.486	.811	106	-1	26	4.76	-4	3-47,S-21,2-20/O-6(6-0-0),1,D	4	-0.3
1998*Chi-N	149	488	76	124	23	7	23	75	40	140	4	6	.254	.312	.471	.783	99	-5	67	4.71	-9	3-72,O-54(31-31-2),S-45/1-3,2	16	-0.9
1999 Chi-N	99	342	57	93	12	2	15	43	40	101	7	2	.272	.357	.450	.807	104	3	57	6.00	9	S-92,O-20(6-14-2)/1-1	13	1.7
*Atl-N	48	166	22	42	8	0	4	19	12	44	4	1	.253	.303	.373	.677	70	-8	18	3.68	0	S-45/1-1,0-1	3	-0.4
Yr.	147	508	79	135	20	2	19	62	52	145	11	3	.266	.340	.425	.765	93	-5	75	5.21	9	*S-137,O-21(7-14-2)/1-2	16	1.3
2000 Mil-N	124	446	51	109	22	1	11	59	41	125	3	7	.244	.316	.372	.689	75	-21	50	3.75	5	3-95,S-37/O-2(2-0-0)	9	-1.1
2001 Mil-N	152	542	67	135	26	2	25	78	39	185	5	4	.249	.302	.443	.745	91	-10	70	4.43	-11	*S-150/O-2(1-1-0)	13	-0.8
2002 Mil-N★	152	525	72	151	24	2	24	73	52	188	3	5	.288	.356	.478	.834	119	12	84	5.67	22	*S-149	19	4.7
2003 Col-N	69	257	33	61	6	1	8	27	27	95	1	1	.237	.310	.362	.672	65	-13	29	3.79	-9	S-69/1-1	3	-1.7
Chi-N	23	69	6	13	3	1	2	9	3	26	0	0	.188	.222	.348	.570	46	-6	5	2.45	0	3-17/S-5,O-2(0-2-0),2-1	1	-0.5
Pit-N	58	193	19	43	9	1	3	21	16	56	1	0	.223	.286	.326	.612	58	-12	17	2.77	9	3-58	2	-0.2
Yr.	150	519	58	117	18	3	13	57	46	177	2	1	.225	.290	.347	.637	60	-31	51	3.22	0	3-75,S-74/O-2(0-2-0),1-1,2	6	-2.4
Total 12	1323	4021	551	1011	170	31	146	524	332	1230	37	34	.251	.312	.418	.730	87	-95	505	4.25	18	S-811,3-381/O-89,2-61,1-7,D	97	-1.1
• HERNANDEZ, Keith	Keith Hernandez b: 10/20/1953, San Francisco, CA BL/TL, 6', 195 lbs. Deb: 8/30/1974 Career OF: 5-0-2																							
1974 StL-N	14	34	3	10	1	2	0	2	7	8	0	0	.294	.415	.441	.856	141	2	7	7.09	-2	/1-9	1	0.0
1975 StL-N	64	188	20	47	8	2	3	20	17	26	0	1	.250	.312	.362	.674	84	-5	20	3.70	2	1-56	3	-0.7
1976 StL-N	129	374	54	108	21	5	7	46	49	53	4	2	.289	.376	.428	.803	126	14	61	5.97	9	*1-110	13	1.6
1977 StL-N	161	560	90	163	41	4	15	91	79	88	7	7	.291	.380	.459	.839	126	21	95	6.05	5	*1-158	24	1.6
1978 StL-N	159	542	90	138	32	4	11	64	82	68	13	5	.255	.355	.389	.744	109	9	78	4.91	3	*1-158	19	0.3
1979 StL-N★	161	610	**116**	210	**48**	11	11	105	80	78	11	6	**.344**	**.421**	.513	.934	152	46	135	**8.66**	11	*1-160	29	4.9
1980 StL-N★	159	595	**111**	191	39	8	16	99	86	73	14	8	.321	**.410**	.494	.904	147	40	122	7.67	4	*1-157	28	3.6
1981 StL-N	103	376	65	115	27	4	8	48	61	45	12	5	.306	.405	.463	.868	142	24	73	7.04	7	1-98/O-3(3-0-0)	20	2.6
1982*StL-N	160	579	79	173	33	6	7	94	100	67	19	11	.299	.404	.413	.817	127	26	101	6.23	4	*1-158/O-4(2-0-2)	24	2.1
1983 StL-N	55	218	34	62	15	4	3	26	24	30	1	1	.284	.355	.431	.787	117	5	34	5.73	4	1-54	7	0.6
NY-N	95	320	43	98	8	3	9	37	64	42	8	4	.306	.425	.434	.859	140	21	64	7.33	7	1-90	16	2.4
Yr.	150	538	77	160	23	7	12	63	88	72	9	5	.297	.398	.433	.831	131	26	98	6.68	11	*1-144	23	3.0
1984 NY-N★	154	550	83	171	31	0	15	94	97	89	2	3	.311	.415	.449	.864	145	37	108	7.26	14	*1-153	33	4.3
1985 NY-N	158	593	87	183	34	4	10	91	77	59	3	3	.309	.390	.430	.820	132	27	100	6.18	18	*1-157	27	3.7
1986*NY-N★	149	551	94	171	34	1	13	83	**94**	69	2	1	.310	.414	.446	.861	142	36	106	7.18	11	*1-149	29	3.9
1987 NY-N★	154	587	87	170	28	2	18	89	81	104	0	2	.290	.379	.436	.816	122	19	98	6.04	13	*1-154	21	2.2
1988*NY-N	95	348	43	96	16	0	11	55	31	57	2	1	.276	.337	.417	.754	121	9	47	4.74	5	1-93	13	0.8
1989 NY-N	75	215	18	50	8	0	4	19	27	39	0	3	.233	.324	.326	.649	90	-3	23	3.56	-2	1-58	3	-1.0
1990 Cle-A	43	130	7	26	2	0	1	8	14	17	0	0	.200	.283	.238	.521	47	-9	9	2.34	-1	1-42	1	-1.3
Total 17	2088	7370	1124	2182	426	60	162	1071	1070	1012	98	63	.296	.388	.436	.824	129	319	1282	6.30	111	*1-2014/O-7	311	31.7
• HERNANDEZ, Leo	Leonardo Jesus Hernandez b: 11/6/1959, Santa Lucia, Venezuela BR/TR, 5'11", 170 lbs. Deb: 9/19/1982																							
1982 Bal-A	2	2	0	0	0	0	0	0	0	2	0	0	.000	.000	.000	.000	-100	-1	0	.00	0	....	0	-0.1
1983 Bal-A	64	203	21	50	6	1	6	26	12	19	1	0	.246	.288	.374	.663	82	-5	21	3.67	-5	3-64	3	-1.1
1985 Bal-A	12	21	0	1	0	0	0	0	0	4	0	0	.048	.048	.048	.095	-76	-5	0	.00	0	/D-8,1-1,0-1	0	-0.5
1986 NY-A	7	22	2	5	2	0	1	4	1	8	0	0	.227	.261	.455	.715	91	-0	3	4.25	0	/3-7,2-1	1	0.0
Total 4	85	248	23	56	8	1	7	30	13	33	1	0	.226	.264	.351	.615	69	-11	24	3.27	-5	/3-71,D-8,1-1,2-1,0-1	4	-1.7
• HERNANDEZ, Michel	Michel Hernandez b: 8/12/1978, Havana, Cuba BR/TR, 6', 208 lbs. Deb: 9/6/2003																							
2003 NY-A	5	4	0	1	0	0	0	0	1	1	0	0	.250	.400	.250	.650	79	-0	1	4.54	0	/C-5	0	0.0
• HERNANDEZ, Pedro	Pedro Julio Hernandez b: 4/4/1959, La Romana, Dominican Republic BR/TR, 6'1", 160 lbs. Deb: 9/8/1979																							
1979 Tor-A	3	0	1	0	0	0	0	0	0	0	0	0	....	....	....	....	-99	0	0	....	0	....	0	0.0
1982 Tor-A	8	9	1	0	0	0	0	0	0	3	0	0	.000	.000	.000	.000	-92	-2	0	.00	-1	/D-3,3-2,0-1	0	-0.3
Total 2	11	9	2	0	0	0	0	0	0	3	0	0	.000	.000	.000	.000	-92	-2	0	.00	-1	/D-3,3-2,0-1	0	-0.3
• HERNANDEZ, Ramon	Ramon Jose (Marin) Hernandez b: 5/20/1976, Caracas, Venezuela BR/TR, 6', 227 lbs. Deb: 6/29/1999																							
1999 Oak-A	40	136	13	38	7	0	3	21	18	11	1	0	.279	.368	.397	.765	99	1	20	5.12	4	C-40	6	0.7
2000*Oak-A	143	419	52	101	19	0	14	62	38	64	1	0	.241	.315	.387	.701	78	-14	50	3.90	0	*C-142	10	-0.5
2001*Oak-A	136	453	55	115	25	0	15	60	37	68	1	1	.254	.319	.408	.727	90	-8	59	4.37	7	*C-135/1-2	13	0.8
2002*Oak-A	136	403	51	94	20	0	7	42	43	64	0	0	.233	.315	.335	.650	73	-15	43	3.57	-1	*C-135	12	-0.7
2003*Oak-A★	140	483	70	132	24	1	21	78	33	79	0	0	.273	.335	.458	.793	105	3	72	5.20	-1	*C-139	17	1.1
Total 5	595	1894	241	480	95	1	60	263	169	286	3	1	.253	.325	.400	.724	88	-34	244	4.35	9	C-591/1-2	58	1.4
• HERNANDEZ, Rudy	Rodolfo (Acosta) Hernandez b: 10/18/1951, Enpalme, Mexico BR/TR, 5'9", 150 lbs. Deb: 9/6/1972																							
1972 Chi-A	8	21	0	4	0	0	0	1	0	3	0	0	.190	.190	.190	.381	13	-2	1	1.21	0	/S-6	0	-0.2
• HERNANDEZ, Toby	Rafael Tobias (Alvarado) Hernandez b: 11/30/1958, Calabozo, Venezuela BR/TR, 6'1", 160 lbs. Deb: 6/22/1984																							
1984 Tor-A	3	2	1	1	0	0	0	0	0	0	0	0	.500	.500	.500	1.000	172	0	1	13.50	-1	/C-3	0	-0.1
• HERNDON, Larry	Larry Darnell Herndon b: 11/3/1953, Sunflower, MS BR/TR, 6'3", 195 lbs. Deb: 9/4/1974 C Career OF: 847-448-76																							
1974 StL-N	12	1	3	1	0	0	0	0	0	0	0	0	1.000	1.000	1.000	2.000	465	0	1	∞	-0	/0-1	0	0.0
1976 SF-N	115	337	42	97	11	3	2	23	23	45	12	10	.288	.337	.356	.693	94	-4	40	4.17	1	*O-110(0-110-0)	9	-0.6
1977 SF-N	49	109	13	26	4	3	1	5	5	20	4	2	.239	.278	.358	.636	69	-5	10	2.86	-1	O-44(0-44-0)	1	-0.7
1978 SF-N	151	471	52	122	15	9	1	32	35	71	13	8	.259	.312	.335	.647	84	-11	48	3.38	-5	*O-149(0-149-0)	10	-1.9
1979 SF-N	132	354	35	91	14	5	7	36	29	70	8	6	.257	.315	.384	.699	96	-3	43	4.19	2	*O-122(40-84-12)	10	-0.5
1980 SF-N	139	493	54	127	17	11	8	49	19	91	8	8	.258	.287	.385	.672	88	-12	50	3.47	-4	*O-122(53-53-28)	10	-2.1
1981 SF-N	96	364	48	105	15	8	5	41	20	55	15	6	.288	.327	.415	.742	111	5	46	4.40	0	O-93(82-7-10)	11	0.0
1982 Det-A	157	614	92	179	21	13	23	88	38	92	12	9	.292	.334	.480	.814	120	14	90	5.17	3	*O-155(155-0-0)/D-3	19	0.9
1983 Det-A	153	603	88	182	28	9	20	92	46	95	9	3	.302	.354	.478	.832	130	24	97	5.82	-5	*O-133(133-0-0),D-19	22	1.1
1984*Det-A	125	407	52	114	18	5	7	43	32	63	6	2	.280	.336	.400	.736	103	2	55	4.82	-1	*O-117(118-0-0)/D-4	12	-0.3
1985 Det-A	137	442	45	108	12	7	12	37	33	79	2	1	.244	.298	.385	.683	86	-9	50	3.89	2	*O-136(136-0-0)	8	-1.4
1986 Det-A	106	283	33	70	13	1	8	37	27	40	2	1	.247	.315	.385	.700	90	-4	36	4.32	1	O-83(83-0-0),D-18	7	-0.7
1987*Det-A	89	225	32	73	13	2	9	47	23	35	1	0	.324	.387	.520	.907	144	14	42	6.65	2	O-57(32-0-26),D-23	9	1.3
1988 Det-A	76	174	16	39	5	0	4	20	23	37	0	1	.224	.318	.322	.640	83	-4	17	3.15	0	D-53,O-15(15-0-0)	2	-0.6
Total 14	1537	4877	605	1334	186	76	107	550	353	793	92	57	.274	.325	.409	.733	103	5	624	4.43	-6	*O-1337,D-120	130	-5.5
• HERNON, Tom	Thomas H. Hernon b: 11/4/1866, East Bridgewater, MA d: 2/4/1902, New Bedford, MA BR/TR, 5'7.5" Deb: 9/13/1897																							
1897 Chi-N	4	16	2	1	0	0	0	2	0	....	1	....	.063	.063	.063	.125	-65	-4	0	.27	0	/O-4(4-0-0)	0	-0.3
• HERR, Joe	Joseph Herr b: 3/1867, MO BR/TR, 5'9.5", 179 lbs. Deb: 4/16/1887 U Career OF: 4-8-3																							
1887 Cle-a	11	50	6	18	2	0	0	6	6	....	2	....	.360	.360	.318	.678	93	-0	6	4.98	-4	3-11	1	-0.3
1888*StL-a	43	172	21	46	7	1	3	43	11	....	9	....	.267	.323	.372	.695	110	1	24	5.17	1	S-28,O-11(4-4-3)/3-4	6	0.2
1890 StL-a	12	41	5	9	2	1	0	1	5	....	2	....	.220	.347	.317	.664	84	-1	5	4.42	-3	/2-7,O-4(0-4-0),3-1	1	-0.3
Total 3	66	263	32	73	11	2	3	50	22	....	13	....	.278	.333	.354	.687	103	0	35	5.01	-6	/S-28,3-16,O-15,2-7	8	-0.4
• HERR, Tom	Thomas Mitchell Herr b: 4/4/1956, Lancaster, PA BB/TR, 6', 185 lbs. Deb: 8/13/1979																							
1979 StL-N	14	10	4	2	0	0	0	1	2	2	1	0	.200	.333	.200	.533	49	-0	1	3.42	0	/2-6	0	0.0
1980 StL-N	76	222	29	55	12	5	0	15	16	21	9	2	.248	.301	.347	.648	78	-6	22	3.32	1	2-58,S-14	4	-0.1
1981 StL-N	103	411	50	110	14	9	0	46	39	30	23	7	.268	.333	.345	.678	90	-3	49	4.04	-1	*2-103	14	0.2
1982*StL-N	135	493	83	131	19	4	0	36	57	56	25	12	.266	.344	.320	.665	86	-7	59	4.09	5	*2-128	15	0.5
1983 StL-N	89	313	43	101	14	4	2	31	43	27	6	8	.323	.406	.412	.818	127	11	53	5.96	-6	2-86	12	1.0
1984 StL-N	145	558	67	154	23	2	4	49	49	56	13	7	.276	.337	.346	.682	94	-4	66	4.09	-2	*2-144	20	0.1
1985*StL-N★	159	596	97	180	38	3	8	110	80	55	31	3	.302	.386	.416	.803	126	28	107	6.50	-20	*2-158	30	1.8

YEAR TM-L	G	AB	R	H	2B	3B	HR	RBI	BB	SO	SB	CS	AVG	OBP	SLG	OPS	OPS+	BR/A	RC	RC/G	FR	G/POS	WS	TPW
1986 StL-N	152	559	48	141	30	4	2	61	73	75	22	8	.252	.344	.331	.675	88	-6	69	4.18	0	*2-152	18	0.3
1987*StL-N	141	510	73	134	29	0	2	83	68	62	19	4	.263	.353	.331	.684	81	-10	65	4.29	-13	*2-137	16	-1.5
1988 StL-N	15	50	4	13	0	0	1	3	11	4	3	0	.260	.393	.320	.713	106	2	8	5.10	-0	2-15	1	0.2
Min-A	86	304	42	80	16	0	1	21	40	47	10	3	.263	.349	.326	.674	88	-3	36	4.10	1	2-73/D-3,S-2	7	0.0
1989 Phi-N	151	561	65	161	25	6	2	37	54	63	10	7	.287	.353	.364	.716	105	4	73	4.68	-4	*2-144	17	0.4
1990 Phi-N	119	447	39	118	21	3	4	50	36	47	7	1	.264	.322	.351	.673	85	-8	51	3.96	-3	*2-114	8	-0.8
NY-N	27	100	9	25	5	0	1	10	14	11	0	0	.250	.342	.330	.672	86	-2	12	4.34	-1	2-26	3	-0.2
Yr.	146	547	48	143	26	3	5	60	50	58	7	1	.261	.326	.347	.673	85	-10	63	4.03	-3	*2-140	11	-1.0
1991 NY-N	70	155	17	30	7	0	1	14	32	21	7	2	.194	.332	.258	.590	68	-4	16	3.35	1	2-57/0-1	3	-0.3
SF-N	32	60	6	15	1	1	0	7	13	7	2	0	.250	.384	.300	.684	98	1	8	4.27	1	2-15/3-3	2	0.3
Yr.	102	215	23	45	8	1	1	21	45	28	9	2	.209	.346	.270	.616	77	-3	24	3.59	2	2-72/3-3,0-1	5	0.0
Total 13	**1514**	**5349**	**676**	**1450**	**254**	**41**	**28**	**574**	**627**	**584**	**188**	**64**	**.271**	**.350**	**.350**	**.700**	**95**	**-7**	**694**	**4.49**	**-40**	***2-1416/S-16,3-3,D-3,0-1**	**170**	**1.9**

• HERRERA, Jose Jose Ramon (Catalino) Herrera b: 8/30/1972, Santo Domingo, Dominican Republic BL/TL, 6', 165 lbs. Deb: 8/12/1995 Career OF: 0-41-97

YEAR TM-L	G	AB	R	H	2B	3B	HR	RBI	BB	SO	SB	CS	AVG	OBP	SLG	OPS	OPS+	BR/A	RC	RC/G	FR	G/POS	WS	TPW
1995 Oak-A	33	70	9	17	1	2	0	2	6	11	1	3	.243	.303	.314	.617	65	-5	6	2.83	0	0-25(0-22-5)/D-5	0	-0.5
1996 Oak-A	108	320	44	86	15	1	6	30	20	59	8	2	.269	.318	.378	.696	77	-11	39	4.32	-5	*0-101(0-19-92)/D-1	5	-1.8
Total 2	**141**	**390**	**53**	**103**	**16**	**3**	**6**	**32**	**26**	**70**	**9**	**5**	**.264**	**.315**	**.367**	**.682**	**75**	**-16**	**45**	**4.03**	**-5**	**0-126/D-6**	**5**	**-2.3**

• HERRERA, Jose Jose Concepcion (Ontiveros) "Loco" Herrera b: 4/8/1942, San Lorenzo, Venezuela BR/TR, 5'8", 165 lbs. Deb: 6/3/1967 Career OF: 25-13-12

YEAR TM-L	G	AB	R	H	2B	3B	HR	RBI	BB	SO	SB	CS	AVG	OBP	SLG	OPS	OPS+	BR/A	RC	RC/G	FR	G/POS	WS	TPW
1967 Hou-N	5	4	0	1	0	0	0	1	0	1	0	0	.250	.250	.250	.500	45	-0	0	2.25	0	....	0	0.0
1968 Hou-N	27	100	9	24	5	0	0	7	4	12	0	2	.240	.269	.290	.559	69	-5	7	2.41	-2	0-17(5-0-12)/2-7	1	-0.8
1969 Mon-N	47	126	7	36	5	0	2	12	3	14	1	2	.286	.302	.373	.675	88	-3	13	3.59	-1	0-31(20-13-0)/2-2,3-1	2	-0.5
1970 Mon-N	1	1	0	0	0	0	0	0	0	1	0	0	.000	.000	.000	.000	-100	-0	0	.00	0	....	0	0.0
Total 4	**80**	**231**	**16**	**61**	**10**	**0**	**2**	**20**	**7**	**28**	**1**	**4**	**.264**	**.286**	**.333**	**.619**	**78**	**-8**	**21**	**3.01**	**-3**	**/0-48,2-9,3-1**	**3**	**-1.4**

• HERRERA, Mike Ramon Herrera b: 12/19/1897, Havana, Cuba d: 2/3/1978, Havana, Cuba BR/TR, 5'6", 147 lbs. Deb: 9/22/1925

YEAR TM-L	G	AB	R	H	2B	3B	HR	RBI	BB	SO	SB	CS	AVG	OBP	SLG	OPS	OPS+	BR/A	RC	RC/G	FR	G/POS	WS	TPW
1925 Bos-A	10	39	2	15	0	0	0	8	2	2	1	0	.385	.415	.385	.799	104	1	6	6.81	2	2-10	1	0.3
1926 Bos-A	74	237	20	61	14	1	0	19	15	13	0	5	.257	.304	.325	.629	66	-14	23	3.12	-3	2-48,3-16/S-4	2	-1.4
Total 2	**84**	**276**	**22**	**76**	**14**	**1**	**0**	**27**	**17**	**15**	**1**	**5**	**.275**	**.320**	**.333**	**.653**	**71**	**-13**	**29**	**3.54**	**-1**	**/2-58,3-16,S-4**	**3**	**-1.1**

• HERRERA, Pancho Juan Francisco (Willavicencio) Herrera b: 6/16/1934, Santiago de Cuba, Cuba BR/TR, 6'3", 220 lbs. Deb: 4/15/1958

YEAR TM-L	G	AB	R	H	2B	3B	HR	RBI	BB	SO	SB	CS	AVG	OBP	SLG	OPS	OPS+	BR/A	RC	RC/G	FR	G/POS	WS	TPW
1958 Phi-N	29	63	5	17	3	0	1	6	7	15	1	2	.270	.352	.365	.717	91	-1	8	4.03	1	3-16,1-11	1	-0.1
1960 Phi-N	145	512	61	144	26	6	17	71	51	136	2	3	.281	.352	.455	.807	119	13	78	5.36	7	*1-134,2-17	15	1.4
1961 Phi-N	126	400	56	103	17	2	13	51	55	120	5	1	.258	.353	.408	.760	102	4	58	5.06	-1	*1-115	9	-0.4
Total 3	**300**	**975**	**122**	**264**	**46**	**8**	**31**	**128**	**113**	**271**	**8**	**6**	**.271**	**.352**	**.430**	**.782**	**110**	**15**	**145**	**5.15**	**6**	**1-260/2-17,3-16**	**25**	**0.8**

• HERRING, Lefty Silas Clarke Herring b: 3/4/1880, Philadelphia, PA d: 2/11/1965, Massapequa, NY BL/TL, 5'11", 160 lbs. Deb: 5/16/1899 ♦

YEAR TM-L	G	AB	R	H	2B	3B	HR	RBI	BB	SO	SB	CS	AVG	OBP	SLG	OPS	OPS+	BR/A	RC	RC/G	FR	G/POS	WS	TPW
1899 Was-N	2	1	1	1	0	0	0	0	1	....	0	....	1.000	1.000	1.000	2.000	454	1	1	∞	0	/P-2	1	0.2
1904 Was-A	15	46	3	8	1	0	0	2	7	....	0	....	.174	.283	.196	.479	54	-2	3	1.94	0	1-10/0-5(0-5-0)	0	-0.2
Total 2	**17**	**47**	**4**	**9**	**1**	**0**	**0**	**2**	**8**	**....**	**0**	**....**	**.191**	**.309**	**.213**	**.522**	**68**	**-1**	**4**	**1.94**	**0**	**/1-10,0-5,P-2**	**1**	**-0.1**

• HERRMANN, Ed Edward Martin Herrmann b: 8/27/1946, San Diego, CA BL/TR, 6'1", 210 lbs. Deb: 9/1/1967

YEAR TM-L	G	AB	R	H	2B	3B	HR	RBI	BB	SO	SB	CS	AVG	OBP	SLG	OPS	OPS+	BR/A	RC	RC/G	FR	G/POS	WS	TPW
1967 Chi-A	2	3	1	2	1	0	0	1	1	0	0	0	.667	.750	1.000	1.750	429	1	2	60.75	0	/C-2	1	0.2
1969 Chi-A	102	290	31	67	8	0	8	31	30	35	0	2	.231	.320	.341	.662	81	-8	32	3.70	-2	C-92	6	-0.6
1970 Chi-A	96	297	42	84	9	0	19	52	31	41	0	1	.283	.356	.505	.862	130	11	54	6.54	4	C-88	12	2.1
1971 Chi-A	101	294	32	63	6	0	11	35	44	48	2	0	.214	.321	.347	.668	86	-4	33	3.72	5	C-97	9	0.5
1972 Chi-A	116	354	23	88	9	0	10	40	43	37	0	0	.249	.337	.359	.695	105	3	41	3.92	7	*C-112	15	1.8
1973 Chi-A	119	379	42	85	17	1	10	39	31	55	2	4	.224	.295	.354	.649	79	-12	37	3.17	8	*C-114/D-2	10	0.2
1974 Chi-A★	107	367	32	95	13	1	10	39	16	49	1	0	.259	.290	.381	.671	90	-6	37	3.43	1	*C-107	10	0.0
1975 NY-A	80	200	16	51	9	2	6	30	16	23	0	0	.255	.310	.410	.720	105	1	24	4.15	3	D-35,C-24	5	0.4
1976 Cal-A	29	46	5	8	3	0	2	8	7	8	0	0	.174	.283	.370	.653	96	-0	5	3.50	-1	C-27	2	-0.1
Hou-N	79	265	14	54	8	0	3	25	22	40	0	0	.204	.275	.268	.543	60	-14	20	2.43	-1	C-79	4	-1.2
1977 Hou-N	56	158	7	46	7	0	1	17	15	18	1	1	.291	.356	.354	.711	100	0	20	4.56	-1	C-49	6	0.2
1978 Hou-N	16	36	1	4	1	0	0	0	3	3	0	0	.111	.179	.139	.318	-11	-5	1	.72	0	C-14	0	-0.5
Mon-N	19	40	1	7	1	0	0	3	1	4	0	0	.175	.195	.200	.395	11	-5	1	.93	0	C-12	0	-0.5
Yr.	35	76	2	11	2	0	0	3	4	7	0	0	.145	.188	.171	.359		-10	2	.83	0	C-26	0	-1.0
Total 11	**922**	**2729**	**247**	**654**	**92**	**4**	**80**	**320**	**260**	**361**	**6**	**8**	**.240**	**.312**	**.364**	**.677**	**90**	**-36**	**308**	**3.79**	**23**	**C-817/D-37**	**80**	**2.5**

• HERRNSTEIN, John John Ellett Herrnstein b: 3/31/1938, Hampton, VA BL/TL, 6'3", 215 lbs. Deb: 9/15/1962 Career OF: 84-6-5

YEAR TM-L	G	AB	R	H	2B	3B	HR	RBI	BB	SO	SB	CS	AVG	OBP	SLG	OPS	OPS+	BR/A	RC	RC/G	FR	G/POS	WS	TPW
1962 Phi-N	6	5	0	1	0	0	0	1	1	3	0	0	.200	.333	.200	.533	48	-0	0	2.84	0	/0-1	0	0.0
1963 Phi-N	15	12	1	2	0	0	1	1	1	5	0	0	.167	.231	.417	.647	83	-0	1	3.28	0	/0-2(2-0-0),1-1	0	-0.1
1964 Phi-N	125	303	38	71	12	4	6	25	22	67	1	2	.234	.291	.360	.650	83	-8	31	3.26	-6	0-69(63-4-3),1-68	6	-1.9
1965 Phi-N	63	85	8	17	2	0	1	5	2	18	0	0	.200	.227	.259	.486	37	-7	4	1.64	-1	1-18,0-14(11-2-1)	0	-0.9
1966 Phi-N	4	10	0	1	0	0	0	1	0	7	0	0	.100	.100	.100	.200	-44	-2	0	.30	0	/0-2(2-0-0)	0	-0.2
Chi-N	9	17	3	3	0	0	0	0	3	8	0	0	.176	.300	.176	.476	36	-1	1	2.19	-1	/1-4,0-1	0	-0.3
Atl-N	17	18	2	4	0	0	0	1	0	7	0	0	.222	.222	.222	.444	24	-2	1	1.71	-0	/0-5(5-0-0)	0	-0.2
Yr.	30	45	5	8	0	0	0	2	3	22	0	0	.178	.229	.178	.407	15	-5	2	1.55	-1	/0-8(8-0-0),1-4	0	-0.7
Total 5	**239**	**450**	**52**	**99**	**14**	**4**	**8**	**34**	**29**	**115**	**1**	**2**	**.220**	**.272**	**.322**	**.594**	**68**	**-20**	**39**	**2.77**	**-8**	**/0-94,1-91**	**6**	**-3.7**

• HERRSCHER, Rick Richard Franklin Herrscher b: 11/3/1936, St. Louis, MO BR/TR, 6'2.5", 187 lbs. Deb: 8/1/1962

YEAR TM-L	G	AB	R	H	2B	3B	HR	RBI	BB	SO	SB	CS	AVG	OBP	SLG	OPS	OPS+	BR/A	RC	RC/G	FR	G/POS	WS	TPW
1962 NY-N	35	50	5	11	3	0	1	6	5	11	0	0	.220	.291	.340	.631	68	-2	5	3.69	-1	1-10/3-6,0-4(3-0-1),S-3	1	-0.3

• HERSH, Earl Earl Walter Hersh b: 5/21/1932, Ebbvale, MD BL/TL, 6', 205 lbs. Deb: 9/4/1956

YEAR TM-L	G	AB	R	H	2B	3B	HR	RBI	BB	SO	SB	CS	AVG	OBP	SLG	OPS	OPS+	BR/A	RC	RC/G	FR	G/POS	WS	TPW
1956 Mil-N	7	13	0	3	3	0	0	0	0	5	0	0	.231	.231	.462	.692	85	-0	1	3.74	0	/0-2(2-0-0)	0	-0.1

• HERSHBERGER, Mike Norman Michael Hershberger b: 10/9/1939, Massillon, OH BR/TR, 5'10", 175 lbs. Deb: 9/5/1961 Career OF: 117-282-708

YEAR TM-L	G	AB	R	H	2B	3B	HR	RBI	BB	SO	SB	CS	AVG	OBP	SLG	OPS	OPS+	BR/A	RC	RC/G	FR	G/POS	WS	TPW
1961 Chi-A	15	55	9	17	3	0	0	5	2	2	1	1	.309	.333	.364	.697	87	-1	6	4.16	1	0-13(1-9-3)	1	-0.1
1962 Chi-A	148	427	54	112	14	2	4	46	37	36	10	6	.262	.325	.333	.658	78	-13	43	3.33	-1	*0-135(1-52-90)	7	-2.1
1963 Chi-A	135	476	64	133	26	2	3	45	39	39	9	3	.279	.339	.361	.700	98	-0	60	4.49	4	*0-119(1-73-67)	15	-0.2
1964 Chi-A	141	452	55	104	15	3	2	31	48	47	8	6	.230	.310	.290	.599	70	-18	42	3.04	2	*0-134(0-64-85)	10	-2.4
1965 KC-A	150	494	43	114	15	5	5	48	37	42	7	3	.231	.291	.312	.603	72	-18	42	2.79	1	*0-144(5-9-134)	6	-2.8
1966 KC-A	146	538	55	136	27	7	2	57	47	37	13	5	.253	.316	.340	.656	92	-5	58	3.62	5	*0-143(12-3-130)	15	-1.1
1967 KC-A	142	480	55	122	25	1	1	49	38	40	10	3	.254	.318	.317	.635	91	-4	49	3.43	5	*0-130(10-0-122)	11	-0.8
1968 Oak-A	99	246	23	67	9	2	5	32	21	22	8	3	.272	.332	.386	.718	123	7	32	4.50	0	0-90(71-6-27)	10	0.3
1969 Oak-A	51	129	11	26	2	0	1	10	10	15	1	2	.202	.259	.240	.499	42	-11	8	1.97	-1	0-35(16-8-13)	0	-1.4
1970 Mil-A	49	98	7	23	5	0	1	6	10	8	1	2	.235	.306	.316	.622	71	-4	9	2.84	-2	0-35(0-0-35)	1	-0.7
1971 Chi-A	74	177	22	46	9	0	2	15	30	23	6	2	.260	.379	.345	.724	103	3	25	4.82	-3	0-59(0-58-2)	5	-0.2
Total 11	**1150**	**3572**	**398**	**900**	**150**	**22**	**26**	**344**	**319**	**311**	**74**	**36**	**.252**	**.319**	**.328**	**.647**	**86**	**-64**	**374**	**3.52**	**11**	***0-1037**	**81**	**-11.3**

• HERSHBERGER, Willard Willard McKee "Bill" Hershberger b: 5/28/1910, Lemoncove, CA d: 8/3/1940, Boston, MA BR/TR, 5'10.5", 167 lbs. Deb: 4/19/1938

YEAR TM-L	G	AB	R	H	2B	3B	HR	RBI	BB	SO	SB	CS	AVG	OBP	SLG	OPS	OPS+	BR/A	RC	RC/G	FR	G/POS	WS	TPW
1938 Cin-N	49	105	12	29	3	1	0	12	5	6	1	....	.276	.315	.324	.639	78	-3	11	3.88	-2	C-39/2-1	2	-0.4
1939*Cin-N	63	174	23	60	9	2	0	32	9	4	1	....	.345	.384	.420	.803	115	4	27	5.61	-2	C-60	7	0.4
1940 Cin-N	48	123	6	38	4	2	0	26	6	6	0	....	.309	.351	.374	.725	99	-0	15	4.44	-3	C-37	4	-0.2
Total 3	**160**	**402**	**41**	**127**	**16**	**5**	**0**	**70**	**20**	**16**	**2**	**....**	**.316**	**.356**	**.381**	**.737**	**101**	**0**	**53**	**4.80**	**-8**	**C-136/2-1**	**13**	**-0.2**

• HERTWECK, Neal Neal Charles Hertweck b: 11/22/1931, St. Louis, MO BL/TL, 6'1.5", 175 lbs. Deb: 9/27/1952

YEAR TM-L	G	AB	R	H	2B	3B	HR	RBI	BB	SO	SB	CS	AVG	OBP	SLG	OPS	OPS+	BR/A	RC	RC/G	FR	G/POS	WS	TPW
1952 StL-N	2	6	0	0	0	0	0	0	1	1	0	0	.000	.143	.000	.143	-57	-1	0	.17	0	/1-2	0	-0.2

• HERTZ, Steve Stephen Allan Hertz b: 2/26/1945, Fairfield, OH BR/TR, 6'1", 195 lbs. Deb: 4/21/1964

YEAR TM-L	G	AB	R	H	2B	3B	HR	RBI	BB	SO	SB	CS	AVG	OBP	SLG	OPS	OPS+	BR/A	RC	RC/G	FR	G/POS	WS	TPW
1964 Hou-N	5	4	2	0	0	0	0	0	0	3	0	0	.000	.000	.000	.000	-106	-1	0	.00	0	/3-2	0	-0.2

YEAR TM-L	G	AB	R	H	2B	3B	HR	RBI	BB	SO	SB	CS	AVG	OBP	SLG	OPS	OPS+	BR/A	RC	RC/G	FR	G/POS	WS	TPW
• HERZOG, Buck	Charles Lincoln Herzog b: 7/9/1885, Baltimore, MD d: 9/4/1953, Baltimore, MD BR/TR, 5'11", 160 lbs. Deb: 4/17/1908 M Career OF: 28-0-4																							
1908 NY-N	64	160	38	48	6	2	0	11	36	....	16	....	.300	.448	.363	.811	152	14	34	7.32	-5	2-42,S-12/3-4,O-1	12	1.1
1909 NY-N	42	130	16	24	2	0	0	8	13	....	2	....	.185	.264	.200	.464	43	-8	7	1.76	-3	O-29(26-0-4)/2-6,3-4,S-1	1	-1.5
1910 Bos-N	106	380	51	95	20	3	3	32	30	34	13	....	.250	.329	.342	.672	92	-4	48	4.10	-1	*3-105	8	-0.2
1911 Bos-N	79	294	53	91	19	5	5	41	33	21	26	....	.310	.398	.459	.857	129	12	65	7.56	-3	S-74/3-4	11	1.5
*NY-N	69	247	37	66	14	4	1	26	14	19	22	....	.267	.325	.368	.693	91	-4	36	4.94	6	3-65/2-3,S-1	9	0.5
Yr.	148	541	90	157	33	9	6	67	47	40	48	....	.290	.365	.418	.783	113	8	101	6.34	3	S-75,3-69/2-3	20	1.9
1912*NY-N	140	482	72	127	20	9	2	47	57	34	37	....	.263	.350	.355	.705	90	-6	73	4.99	19	*3-140	20	1.8
1913*NY-N	96	290	46	83	15	3	3	31	22	12	23	....	.286	.349	.390	.739	110	4	45	5.35	6	3-84/2-2	13	1.3
1914 Cin-N	138	498	54	140	14	8	1	40	42	27	46	....	.281	.348	.347	.695	104	3	72	5.03	25	*S-137/1-2	21	4.0
1915 Cin-N	155	579	61	153	14	10	1	42	34	21	35	16	.264	.314	.328	.642	93	-5	66	3.79	28	*S-153/1-2	20	3.7
1916 Cin-N	79	281	30	75	14	2	1	24	21	12	15	12	.267	.329	.342	.671	109	1	33	3.75	-6	S-65,3-12/O-1	8	0.0
NY-N	77	280	40	73	10	4	0	25	22	24	19	16	.261	.326	.325	.651	106	-1	31	3.42	14	2-44,3-27/S-9	11	1.7
Yr.	156	561	70	148	24	6	1	49	43	36	34	28	.264	.327	.333	.661	107	0	64	3.58	8	S-74,2-44,3-39/O-1	19	1.7
1917*NY-N	114	417	69	98	10	8	2	31	31	36	12	....	.235	.308	.312	.620	93	-3	43	3.34	-2	*2-113	13	-0.2
1918 Bos-N	118	473	57	108	12	6	0	26	29	28	10	....	.228	.280	.279	.559	74	-15	39	2.67	-4	2-99,1-12/S-7	9	-1.9
1919 Bos-N	73	275	27	77	8	5	1	25	13	11	16	....	.280	.327	.356	.683	110	3	36	4.46	-17	2-70/1-1	7	-1.4
Chi-N	52	193	15	53	4	4	0	17	10	7	12	....	.275	.336	.337	.673	102	1	25	4.42	-5	2-52	6	-0.4
Yr.	125	468	42	130	12	9	1	42	23	18	28	....	.278	.331	.348	.679	107	4	61	4.44	-22	*2-122/1-1	13	-1.8
1920 Chi-N	91	305	39	59	9	2	0	19	20	21	8	9	.193	.261	.236	.497	43	-23	20	1.92	-6	2-59,3-28/1-1	2	-2.9
Total 13	**1493**	**5284**	**705**	**1370**	**191**	**75**	**20**	**445**	**427**	**307**	**312**	**53**	**.259**	**.329**	**.335**	**.664**	**96**	**-30**	**674**	**4.19**	**45**	**2-490,3-473,S-459/O-31,1-18**	**171**	**6.9**
• HERZOG, Whitey	Dorrel Norman Elvert Herzog b: 11/9/1931, New Athens, IL BL/TL, 5'11", 182 lbs. Deb: 4/17/1956 M/C Career OF: 117-137-206																							
1956 Was-A	117	421	49	103	13	7	4	35	35	74	8	5	.245	.303	.337	.640	69	-20	44	3.53	-4	*O-103(15-84-7)/1-5	5	-3.0
1957 Was-A	36	78	7	13	3	0	0	4	13	12	1	2	.167	.301	.205	.506	41	-6	6	2.30	-2	O-28(2-26-0)	0	-0.9
1958 Was-A	8	5	0	0	0	0	0	0	1	5	0	0	.000	.167	.000	.167	-51	-1	0	.23	0	/O-7(0-5-2)	0	-0.1
KC-A	88	96	11	23	1	2	0	9	16	21	0	3	.240	.348	.292	.640	77	-4	10	3.62	-1	O-37(29-7-1),1-22	2	-0.7
Yr.	96	101	11	23	1	2	0	9	17	26	0	3	.228	.339	.277	.616	70	-5	10	3.42	-2	O-44(29-12-3),1-22	2	-0.8
1959 KC-A	38	123	25	36	7	1	1	9	34	23	1	0	.293	.446	.390	.836	129	8	25	7.47	0	O-34(1-13-20)/1-1	6	0.7
1960 KC-A	83	252	43	67	10	2	8	38	40	32	0	1	.266	.366	.417	.783	111	4	39	5.47	-2	O-69(29-0-42)/1-2	8	0.0
1961 Bal-A	113	323	39	94	11	6	5	35	50	41	1	4	.291	.388	.409	.796	115	7	53	5.88	0	O-98(27-0-73)	12	0.2
1962 Bal-A	99	263	34	70	13	1	7	35	41	36	2	3	.266	.371	.403	.774	114	6	41	5.30	2	O-70(13-1-59)	9	0.3
1963 Det-A	52	53	5	8	2	1	0	7	11	17	0	0	.151	.308	.226	.534	51	-3	5	2.64	-1	/1-7,O-4(1-1-2)	0	-0.5
Total 8	**634**	**1614**	**213**	**414**	**60**	**20**	**25**	**172**	**241**	**261**	**13**	**18**	**.257**	**.356**	**.365**	**.720**	**95**	**-9**	**222**	**4.74**	**-9**	**O-450/1-37**	**42**	**-4.0**
• HESS, Otto	Otto C. Hess b: 10/10/1878, Berne, Switzerland d: 2/25/1926, Tucson, AZ BL/TL, 6'1", 170 lbs. Deb: 8/3/1902 Career OF: 36-10-5 ♦																							
1902 Cle-A	7	14	2	1	0	0	0	1	2	....	0	....	.071	.188	.071	.259	-27	-1	0	.39	0	/P-7	0	-1.3
1904 Cle-A	34	100	4	12	2	1	0	5	3	....	0	....	.120	.146	.160	.306	-3	-7	2	.74	1	P-21,O-12(7-5-0)	9	0.9
1905 Cle-A	54	173	15	44	8	1	2	13	7	....	2	....	.254	.291	.347	.638	101	4	19	3.78	3	O-28(27-0-1),P-26	14	-0.8
1906 Cle-A	53	154	13	31	5	2	0	11	2	....	1	....	.201	.212	.260	.471	48	-0	9	1.92	-1	P-43/O-5(0-5-0)	24	2.5
1907 Cle-A	19	30	4	4	0	0	0	0	4	....	1	....	.133	.278	.133	.411	32	-0	2	1.56	-1	P-17/O-2(2-0-0)	5	-0.7
1908 Cle-A	9	14	0	0	0	0	0	0	1	....	0	....	.000	.067	.000	.067	-78	-2	0	.00	0	/O-4(0-0-4),P-4	0	-0.6
1912 Bos-N	33	94	10	23	4	4	0	10	0	26	0	....	.245	.245	.372	.617	66	3	9	2.82	-3	P-33	14	0.2
1913 Bos-N	35	83	9	26	0	1	2	11	7	15	0	....	.313	.367	.410	.776	119	9	12	5.21	0	P-29	9	-0.1
1914 Bos-N	31	47	5	11	1	0	1	6	1	11	0	....	.234	.250	.319	.569	69	1	4	2.53	1	P-14/1-5	6	-0.6
1915 Bos-N	5	5	1	2	1	0	0	1	0	2	0	....	.400	.400	.600	1.000	205	1	1	10.60	0	/P-4,1-1	0	-0.1
Total 10	**280**	**714**	**63**	**154**	**21**	**9**	**5**	**58**	**27**	**54**	**4**	**....**	**.216**	**.248**	**.291**	**.540**	**62**	**7**	**58**	**2.62**	**-1**	**P-198/O-51,1-6**	**81**	**-0.7**
• HESS, Tom	Thomas Hess b: 8/15/1875, Brooklyn, NY d: 12/15/1945, Albany, NY TR Deb: 6/6/1892																							
1892 Bal-N	1	2	0	0	0	0	0	0	0	0	0	....	.000	.000	.000	.000	-97	-0	0	.00	0	/C-1	0	-0.1
• HESSMAN, Mike	Michael Steven Hessman b: 3/5/1978, Fountain Valley, CA BR/TR, 6'5", 215 lbs. Deb: 8/22/2003																							
2003 Atl-N	19	21	2	6	2	0	2	3	5	6	0	0	.286	.423	.667	1.090	178	3	5	8.27	0	/O-8(7-0-1),1-4,3-3	1	0.2
• HETLING, Gus	August Julius Hetling b: 11/21/1885, St. Louis, MO d: 10/13/1962, Wichita, KS BR/TR, 5'10", 165 lbs. Deb: 10/6/1906																							
1906 Det-A	2	7	0	1	0	0	0	0	0	....	0	....	.143	.143	.143	.286	-10	-1	0	.65	0	/3-2	0	-0.1
• HEUBEL, George	George A. Heubel b: 1849, Paterson, NJ d: 1/22/1896, Philadelphia, PA, 5'11.5", 178 lbs. Deb: 5/20/1871 U NA OF: 0-5-16																							
1871 Ath-n	17	75	18	23	4	2	0	13	2	0	1	0	.307	.325	.413	.738	111	1	11	6.45	0	O-16(0-0-16)/1-1	....	0.2
1872 Oly-n	5	23	2	3	0	0	0	1	0	0	0	0	.130	.130	.130	.261	-21	-3	0	.62	-1	/O-5(0-5-0)	....	-0.3
1876 NY-N	1	4	0	0	0	0	0	0	0	0	....	....	.000	.000	.000	.000	-115	-1	0	.00	0	/1-1	0	-0.1
Total 2 n	**22**	**98**	**20**	**26**	**4**	**2**	**0**	**14**	**2**	**0**	**1**	**0**	**.265**	**.280**	**.347**	**.627**	**81**	**-2**	**11**	**4.83**	**-1**	**/O-21,1-1**	**....**	**-0.1**
• HEVING, Johnnie	John Aloysius Heving b: 4/29/1896, Covington, KY d: 12/24/1968, Salisbury, NC BR/TR, 6', 175 lbs. Deb: 9/24/1920																							
1920 StL-A	1	1	0	0	0	0	0	0	0	0	0	0	.000	.000	.000	.000	-97	-0	0	.00	0	....	0	0.0
1924 Bos-A	45	109	15	31	5	1	0	11	10	7	0	0	.284	.345	.349	.693	79	-3	14	4.45	2	C-29	2	0.1
1925 Bos-A	45	119	14	20	7	0	0	6	12	7	0	1	.168	.244	.227	.471	20	-15	7	1.81	1	C-34	1	-1.1
1928 Bos-A	82	158	11	41	7	2	0	11	11	10	1	1	.259	.308	.329	.637	69	-7	16	3.51	-3	C-62	2	-0.7
1929 Bos-A	76	188	26	60	4	3	0	23	8	7	1	2	.319	.354	.372	.726	89	-3	24	4.86	2	C-55	6	0.2
1930 Bos-A	75	220	15	61	5	3	0	17	11	14	2	0	.277	.312	.327	.639	65	-11	23	3.75	2	C-71	4	-0.5
1931*Phi-A	42	113	8	27	3	2	1	12	6	8	0	0	.239	.277	.327	.605	55	-7	10	3.12	-2	C-40	2	-0.7
1932 Phi-A	33	77	14	21	6	1	0	10	7	6	0	0	.273	.333	.377	.710	81	-2	10	4.61	0	C-28	2	-0.1
Total 8	**399**	**985**	**103**	**261**	**37**	**12**	**1**	**90**	**65**	**59**	**4**	**4**	**.265**	**.312**	**.330**	**.642**	**66**	**-49**	**104**	**3.71**	**2**	**C-319**	**19**	**-2.8**
• HEYDON, Mike	Michael Edward "Ed" Heydon b: 7/15/1874, MO d: 10/13/1913, Indianapolis, IN BL/TR, 6' Deb: 10/12/1898																							
1898 Bal-N	3	9	2	1	0	0	0	1	2	....	0	....	.111	.333	.111	.444	28	-1	0	1.13	0	/C-3	0	0.0
1899 Was-N	3	3	0	0	0	0	0	0	2	....	0	....	.000	.400	.000	.400	14	-0	0	.00	-0	/C-2	0	0.0
1901 StL-N	16	43	2	9	1	1	1	6	5	....	2	....	.209	.292	.349	.641	90	-1	5	3.93	-2	C-13/O-1	1	-0.1
1904 Chi-A	4	10	0	1	1	0	0	1	1	....	0	....	.100	.250	.200	.450	45	-1	1	1.51	0	/C-4	0	0.0
1905 Was-A	77	245	20	47	7	4	1	26	21	....	5	....	.192	.261	.265	.527	70	-8	19	2.52	13	C-77	7	1.4
1906 Was-A	49	145	14	23	7	1	0	10	14	....	2	....	.159	.238	.221	.458	46	-9	8	1.81	-1	C-49	1	-0.6
1907 Was-A	62	164	14	30	3	0	0	9	25	....	3	....	.183	.302	.201	.503	66	-4	11	2.22	-6	C-57	2	-0.6
Total 7	**214**	**619**	**52**	**111**	**19**	**6**	**2**	**53**	**70**	**....**	**12**	**....**	**.179**	**.271**	**.239**	**.510**	**63**	**-23**	**45**	**2.32**	**4**	**C-205/O-1**	**11**	**0.1**
• HIATT, Jack	Jack E. Hiatt b: 7/27/1942, Bakersfield, CA BR/TR, 6'2", 190 lbs. Deb: 9/7/1964 C																							
1964 LA-A	9	16	2	6	0	0	0	2	2	3	0	0	.375	.444	.375	.819	145	1	3	7.82	0	/C-3,1-2	1	0.1
1965 SF-N	40	67	5	19	4	0	1	7	12	14	0	0	.284	.392	.388	.780	117	2	10	5.29	0	C-21/1-7	3	0.2
1966 SF-N	18	23	2	7	2	0	0	1	4	5	0	0	.304	.407	.391	.799	120	1	4	6.59	1	/1-7	1	0.2
1967 SF-N	73	153	24	42	6	0	6	26	27	37	0	0	.275	.387	.431	.818	136	8	27	6.36	-1	1-36/C-3,O-2(2-0-0)	7	0.6
1968 SF-N	90	224	14	52	10	2	4	34	41	61	0	0	.232	.353	.348	.702	111	5	29	4.38	2	C-58,1-10	9	1.1
1969 SF-N	69	194	18	38	4	0	7	34	48	58	0	0	.196	.355	.325	.680	93	1	25	4.05	0	C-60/1-3	6	0.3
1970 Mon-N	17	43	4	14	2	0	0	7	14	14	0	0	.326	.491	.372	.863	135	4	9	8.37	-2	C-12/1-2	3	0.2
Chi-N	66	178	19	43	12	1	2	22	31	48	0	0	.242	.354	.354	.708	81	-4	23	4.28	-2	C-63/1-2	5	-0.3
Yr.	83	221	23	57	14	1	2	29	45	62	0	0	.258	.383	.357	.741	92	-0	33	4.97	-4	C-75/1-4	8	-0.1
1971 Hou-N	69	174	16	48	8	1	1	16	35	39	0	1	.276	.403	.351	.753	118	6	28	5.73	1	C-65/1-1	10	1.0
1972 Hou-N	10	25	2	5	3	0	0	0	5	5	0	0	.200	.333	.320	.653	88	-0	3	3.39	0	C-10	1	0.0
Cal-A	22	45	4	13	0	1	1	5	5	11	0	0	.289	.360	.400	.760	133	2	7	5.37	0	C-17	2	0.3
Total 9	**483**	**1142**	**110**	**287**	**51**	**5**	**22**	**154**	**224**	**295**	**0**	**1**	**.251**	**.376**	**.363**	**.738**	**110**	**27**	**168**	**5.03**	**-2**	**C-312/1-70,O-2**	**48**	**3.8**
• HIATT, Phil	Phillip Farrell Hiatt b: 5/1/1969, Pensacola, FL BR/TR, 6'3", 200 lbs. Deb: 4/7/1993 Career OF: 2-2-46																							
1993 KC-A	81	238	30	52	12	1	7	36	16	82	6	3	.218	.287	.366	.653	70	-11	24	3.21	-5	3-70/D-9	3	-1.4

YEAR TM-L	G	AB	R	H	2B	3B	HR	RBI	BB	SO	SB	CS	AVG	OBP	SLG	OPS	OPS+	BR/A	RC	RC/G	FR	G/POS	WS	TPW
1995 KC-A	52	113	11	23	6	0	4	12	9	37	1	0	.204	.262	.363	.625	60	-7	11	2.98	1	0-47(1-2-45)/D-2	1	-0.7
1996 Det-A	7	21	3	4	0	1	0	1	2	11	0	0	.190	.261	.286	.547	38	-2	1	2.13	1	/3-3,0-2(1-0-1),D-1	0	-0.1
2001 LA-N	30	50	6	12	3	0	2	6	3	19	0	0	.240	.283	.420	.703	85	-1	6	4.33	-3	3-17/1-6	1	-0.5
Total 4	170	422	50	91	21	2	13	55	30	149	7	3	.216	.279	.367	.646	67	-21	42	3.21	-5	/3-90,0-49,D-12,1-6	5	-2.7

• HIBBS, Jim James Kerr Hibbs b: 9/10/1944, Klamath Falls, OR BR/TR, 6', 190 lbs. Deb: 4/12/1967

YEAR TM-L	G	AB	R	H	2B	3B	HR	RBI	BB	SO	SB	CS	AVG	OBP	SLG	OPS	OPS+	BR/A	RC	RC/G	FR	G/POS	WS	TPW
1967 Cal-A	3	3	0	0	0	0	0	0	0	2	0	0	.000	.000	.000	.000	-104	-1	0	.00	0	....	0	-0.1

• HICKEY, Eddie Edward A. Hickey b: 8/18/1872, Cleveland, OH d: 3/25/1941, Tacoma, WA Deb: 9/3/1901

YEAR TM-L	G	AB	R	H	2B	3B	HR	RBI	BB	SO	SB	CS	AVG	OBP	SLG	OPS	OPS+	BR/A	RC	RC/G	FR	G/POS	WS	TPW
1901 Chi-N	10	37	4	6	0	0	0	3	2	....	1	....	.162	.225	.162	.387	14	-4	2	1.38	-3	3-10	0	-0.6

• HICKEY, Mike Michael Francis Hickey b: 12/25/1871, Chicopee, MA d: 6/11/1918, Springfield, MA BR/TR, 5'10.5", 150 lbs. Deb: 9/14/1899

YEAR TM-L	G	AB	R	H	2B	3B	HR	RBI	BB	SO	SB	CS	AVG	OBP	SLG	OPS	OPS+	BR/A	RC	RC/G	FR	G/POS	WS	TPW
1899 Bos-N	1	3	0	1	0	0	0	0	0	....	0	....	.333	.333	.333	.667	76	-0	0	4.53	1	/2-1	0	0.1

• HICKMAN, Charlie Charles Taylor "Piano Legs,Cheerful Charlie" Hickman
b: 5/4/1876, Taylortown, PA d: 4/19/1934, Morgantown, WV BR/TR, 5'9", 215 lbs. Deb: 9/8/1897 U Career OF: 46-3-242 ♦

YEAR TM-L	G	AB	R	H	2B	3B	HR	RBI	BB	SO	SB	CS	AVG	OBP	SLG	OPS	OPS+	BR/A	RC	RC/G	FR	G/POS	WS	TPW
1897*Bos-N	2	3	1	2	0	0	1	2	0	....	0	....	.667	.667	1.667	2.333	476	2	3	90.54	0	/P-2	1	0.0
1898 Bos-N	19	58	4	15	2	0	0	7	1	....	0	....	.259	.283	.293	.576	62	-2	5	3.05	-1	/0-7(6-1-0),1-6,P-6	5	0.1
1899 Bos-N	19	63	15	25	2	7	0	15	2	....	1	....	.397	.433	.651	1.084	178	8	19	12.69	-2	P-11/0-7(6-1-0),1-1	9	0.1
1900 NY-N	127	473	65	148	19	17	9	91	17	....	10	....	.313	.359	.482	.841	137	22	88	7.08	-16	*3-120/0-7(0-0-7)	16	0.6
1901 NY-N	112	406	44	113	20	6	4	62	15	....	5	....	.278	.315	.387	.702	107	5	52	4.74	-6	0-50(6-1-44),S-23,3-15/P-9,2,1	12	-1.0
1902 Bos-A	28	108	13	32	5	2	3	16	3	....	1	....	.296	.339	.463	.802	118	2	18	6.18	1	0-27(27-0-0)	4	0.1
Cle-A	102	426	61	161	31	11	8	94	12	....	8	....	.378	.399	.559	.958	170	37	101	9.82	-3	1-98/2-3,P-1	19	2.7
Yr.	130	534	74	**193**	36	13	11	110	15	....	9	....	.361	.387	.539	.926	159	39	119	9.03	-2	1-98,0-27(27-0-0)/2-3,P-1	23	2.9
1903 Cle-A	131	522	64	154	31	11	12	97	17	....	14	....	.295	.325	.466	.790	137	21	86	6.09	-9	*1-125/2-7	21	1.0
1904 Cle-A	86	337	34	97	22	10	4	45	13	....	9	....	.288	.318	.448	.766	142	14	53	5.64	1	2-45,1-40/0-1	14	1.6
Det-A	42	144	18	35	6	6	2	22	11	....	3	....	.243	.297	.410	.706	126	4	19	4.52	-4	1-39	5	-0.1
Yr.	128	481	52	132	28	16	6	67	24	....	12	....	.274	.312	.437	.748	137	18	72	5.29	-3	1-79,2-45/0-1	19	1.5
1905 Det-A	59	213	21	47	12	3	2	20	12	....	3	....	.221	.278	.333	.612	93	-2	22	3.36	0	0-47(0-0-47),1-12	5	-0.5
Was-A	88	360	48	112	25	9	2	46	9	....	3	....	.311	.332	.447	.779	152	18	57	5.85	2	2-85/1-3	16	2.3
Yr.	147	573	69	159	37	12	4	66	21	....	6	....	.277	.311	.405	.716	130	16	78	4.85	3	2-85,0-47(0-0-47),1-15	21	1.9
1906 Was-A	120	451	53	128	25	5	9	57	14	....	9	....	.284	.311	.421	.733	135	15	64	5.15	-3	0-95(0-0-95),1-18/3-5,2-1	17	0.8
1907 Was-A	60	198	20	55	9	3	1	23	14	....	4	....	.278	.338	.369	.707	136	8	27	4.93	-2	1-30,0-18(0-0-18)/2-3,P-1	6	0.4
Chi-A	21	23	1	6	2	0	0	1	4	....	0	....	.261	.370	.348	.718	134	1	3	4.73	-1	/0-3(0-0-3)	1	0.1
Yr.	81	221	21	61	11	3	1	24	18	....	4	....	.276	.342	.367	.708	136	9	30	4.91	-3	1-30,0-21(0-0-21)/2-3,P-1	7	0.4
1908 Cle-A	65	197	16	46	6	1	2	16	9	....	2	....	.234	.271	.305	.575	86	-4	16	2.75	0	0-28(0-0-28),1-20/2-1	4	-0.6
Total 12	1081	3982	478	1176	217	91	59	614	153	....	72	....	.295	.331	.440	.771	133	149	633	5.86	-42	1-394,0-290,2-152,3-140/P,S	155	7.9

• HICKMAN, Jim David James Hickman b: 5/19/1892, Union City, TN d: 12/30/1965, Brooklyn, NY BR/TR, 5'7.5", 170 lbs. Deb: 9/17/1915 Career OF: 32-108-67

YEAR TM-L	G	AB	R	H	2B	3B	HR	RBI	BB	SO	SB	CS	AVG	OBP	SLG	OPS	OPS+	BR/A	RC	RC/G	FR	G/POS	WS	TPW
1915 Bal-F	20	81	7	17	4	1	1	7	4	14	5	....	.210	.256	.321	.577	65	-4	7	2.91	3	0-20(0-20-0)	1	-0.2
1916 Bro-N	9	5	3	1	0	0	0	0	2	0	1	....	.200	.429	.200	.629	94	0	1	5.15	-1	/0-3(2-1-0)	0	-0.1
1917 Bro-N	114	370	46	81	15	4	6	36	17	66	14	....	.219	.253	.330	.583	76	-12	33	2.83	3	*0-101(26-71-3)	7	-1.6
1918 Bro-N	53	167	14	39	4	7	1	16	8	31	5	....	.234	.281	.359	.640	95	-2	17	3.41	-3	0-46(0-10-42)	3	-0.8
1919 Bro-N	57	104	14	20	3	1	0	11	6	17	2	....	.192	.236	.240	.477	43	-7	6	1.83	-2	0-29(4-6-22)	0	-1.1
Total 5	253	727	84	158	26	13	8	70	37	128	27	....	.217	.259	.322	.581	75	-25	64	2.84	2	0-199	11	-3.8

• HICKMAN, Jim James Lucius "Gentleman Jim" Hickman b: 5/10/1937, Henning, TN BR/TR, 6'3", 205 lbs. Deb: 4/14/1962 Career OF: 144-365-421

YEAR TM-L	G	AB	R	H	2B	3B	HR	RBI	BB	SO	SB	CS	AVG	OBP	SLG	OPS	OPS+	BR/A	RC	RC/G	FR	G/POS	WS	TPW
1962 NY-N	140	392	54	96	18	2	13	46	47	96	4	4	.245	.330	.401	.731	94	-4	52	4.40	-3	*0-124(7-84-33)	7	-1.2
1963 NY-N	146	494	53	113	21	6	17	51	44	120	0	5	.229	.293	.399	.692	96	-5	56	3.79	-3	0-82(19-42-22),3-59	13	-1.3
1964 NY-N	139	409	48	105	14	1	11	57	36	90	0	1	.257	.320	.377	.696	98	-1	48	4.07	-1	*0-113(39-89-19)/3-1	10	-0.8
1965 NY-N	141	369	32	87	18	0	15	40	27	76	3	1	.236	.291	.407	.698	98	-2	42	3.88	-2	0-91(35-44-16),1-30,3-14	8	-0.9
1966 NY-N	58	160	15	38	7	0	4	16	13	34	2	1	.238	.299	.356	.655	83	-4	17	3.54	4	0-45(16-8-23),1-17	4	-0.2
1967 LA-N	65	98	7	16	6	1	0	10	14	28	1	1	.163	.268	.245	.513	52	-6	6	1.93	1	0-37(13-13-12)/1-2,3-2,P-1	0	-0.7
1968 Chi-N	75	188	22	42	6	3	5	23	18	38	1	1	.223	.295	.367	.662	91	-2	20	3.32	-1	0-66(3-20-49)	5	-0.7
1969 Chi-N	134	338	38	80	11	2	21	54	47	74	2	1	.237	.330	.467	.797	107	3	52	5.22	-2	*0-125(5-9-116)	12	-0.3
1970 Chi-N★	149	514	102	162	33	4	32	115	93	99	0	1	.315	.421	.582	1.003	148	37	129	9.50	7	0-79(2-53-28),1-74	24	3.7
1971 Chi-N	117	383	50	98	13	2	19	60	50	61	0	1	.256	.346	.449	.795	108	5	58	5.16	1	0-69(1-3-66),1-44	12	0.0
1972 Chi-N	115	368	65	100	15	2	17	64	52	64	3	1	.272	.365	.462	.827	121	12	64	6.20	8	1-77,0-27(1-0-26)	13	1.4
1973 Chi-N	92	201	27	49	1	2	3	20	42	42	1	1	.244	.374	.313	.688	86	-2	25	4.10	0	1-51,0-13(3-0-11)	4	-0.6
1974 StL-N	50	60	5	16	0	0	2	4	8	10	0	0	.267	.353	.367	.720	102	0	7	4.27	1	1-14/3-1	1	0.1
Total 13	1421	3974	518	1002	163	25	159	560	491	832	17	19	.252	.337	.426	.763	105	32	578	4.96	12	0-871,1-309/3-77,P-1	113	-1.6

• HICKS, Buddy Clarence Walter Hicks b: 2/15/1927, Belvedere, CA BB/TR, 5'10", 170 lbs. Deb: 4/17/1956

YEAR TM-L	G	AB	R	H	2B	3B	HR	RBI	BB	SO	SB	CS	AVG	OBP	SLG	OPS	OPS+	BR/A	RC	RC/G	FR	G/POS	WS	TPW
1956 Det-A	26	47	5	10	2	0	0	5	3	2	0	1	.213	.260	.255	.515	36	-5	3	1.95	-1	S-16/2-6,3-1	1	-0.4

• HICKS, Jim James Edward Hicks b: 5/18/1940, East Chicago, IN BR/TR, 6'3", 205 lbs. Deb: 10/2/1964 Career OF: 9-3-28

YEAR TM-L	G	AB	R	H	2B	3B	HR	RBI	BB	SO	SB	CS	AVG	OBP	SLG	OPS	OPS+	BR/A	RC	RC/G	FR	G/POS	WS	TPW
1964 Chi-A	2	0	0	0	0	0	0	0	0	0	0	0	....	....	....	....	-103	0	0	....	0	....	0	0.0
1965 Chi-A	13	19	2	5	1	0	1	2	0	9	0	0	.263	.263	.474	.737	112	0	2	3.41	-1	/0-5(3-0-2)	0	-0.1
1966 Chi-A	18	26	3	5	0	1	0	1	1	5	0	0	.192	.222	.269	.491	43	-2	1	1.63	-1	0-10(2-0-8)/1-2	0	-0.3
1969 StL-N	19	44	5	8	0	2	1	3	4	14	0	0	.182	.250	.341	.591	64	-2	4	3.01	1	0-15(0-0-15)	1	-0.2
Cal-A	37	48	6	4	0	0	3	8	13	18	0	1	.083	.279	.271	.550	57	-3	4	2.52	-1	0-10(4-3-3)/1-8	0	-0.5
1970 Cal-A	4	4	0	1	0	0	0	0	0	2	0	0	.250	.250	.250	.500	40	-0	0	2.25	0	....	0	0.0
Total 5	93	141	16	23	1	3	5	14	18	48	0	1	.163	.258	.319	.577	63	-7	12	2.60	-2	/0-40,1-10	1	-1.2

• HICKS, Joe William Joseph Hicks b: 4/7/1933, Ivy, VA BL/TR, 6', 180 lbs. Deb: 9/18/1959 Career OF: 17-68-26

YEAR TM-L	G	AB	R	H	2B	3B	HR	RBI	BB	SO	SB	CS	AVG	OBP	SLG	OPS	OPS+	BR/A	RC	RC/G	FR	G/POS	WS	TPW
1959 Chi-A	6	7	0	3	0	0	0	0	1	1	0	1	.429	.500	.429	.929	160	0	1	6.60	1	/0-4(1-2-1)	0	0.1
1960 Chi-A	36	47	3	9	1	0	0	2	6	3	0	1	.191	.296	.213	.509	40	-4	3	2.06	-0	0-14(3-11-0)	0	-0.4
1961 Was-A	12	29	2	5	0	0	1	1	0	4	0	1	.172	.172	.276	.448	18	-4	1	1.19	0	/0-7(3-0-4)	0	-0.4
1962 Was-A	102	174	20	39	4	2	6	14	15	34	3	1	.224	.286	.374	.659	76	-6	19	3.58	-1	0-42(5-22-16)	2	-0.8
1963 NY-N	56	159	16	36	6	1	5	22	7	31	0	2	.226	.272	.371	.643	82	-5	16	3.36	-3	0-41(5-33-5)	3	-1.0
Total 5	212	416	41	92	11	3	12	39	29	73	3	6	.221	.278	.349	.627	72	-19	40	3.17	-2	0-108	5	-2.6

• HICKS, Nat Nathaniel Woodhull Hicks b: 4/19/1845, Hempstead, NY d: 4/21/1907, Hoboken, NJ BR/TR, 6'1", 186 lbs. Deb: 4/22/1872 M/U NA OF: 0-5-7

YEAR TM-L	G	AB	R	H	2B	3B	HR	RBI	BB	SO	SB	CS	AVG	OBP	SLG	OPS	OPS+	BR/A	RC	RC/G	FR	G/POS	WS	TPW
1872 Mut-n	56	268	55	82	12	2	0	33	5	3	3	0	.306	.319	.366	.684	118	8	33	5.50	-6	*C-54/0-3(0-0-3)	....	0.2
1873 Mut-n	28	121	12	29	1	2	1	14	7	0	2	0	.240	.281	.306	.587	75	-3	11	3.73	-7	C-28	....	-0.6
1874 Phi-n	58	266	51	73	8	1	0	30	5	4	3	2	.274	.288	.312	.600	89	-4	25	3.90	3	*C-57/0-4(0-4-0),2-1	....	0.0
1875 Mut-n	62	269	32	67	10	0	0	22	2	10	1	0	.249	.255	.286	.541	83	-5	20	2.97	0	*C-60/0-5(0-1-4)	....	-0.3
1876 NY-N	45	191	20	44	4	1	0	15	3	4	....	....	.230	.246	.266	.512	81	-2	13	2.45	0	*C-45	5	-0.1
1877 Cin-N	8	32	3	6	0	0	0	3	1	2	....	....	.188	.212	.188	.400	30	-2	1	1.38	2	/C-8	0	0.0
Total 4 n	204	924	150	251	31	5	1	99	19	17	9	2	.272	.286	.319	.606	94	-4	90	4.04	-10	C-199/0-12,2-1	....	-0.8
Total 2	53	223	23	50	4	1	0	18	4	6	....	....	.224	.241	.255	.496	73	-4	14	2.29	2	/C-53	5	-0.1

• HIDALGO, Richard Richard Jose Hidalgo b: 7/2/1975, Caracas, Venezuela BR/TR, 6'3", 190 lbs. Deb: 9/1/1997 Career OF: 165-358-338

YEAR TM-L	G	AB	R	H	2B	3B	HR	RBI	BB	SO	SB	CS	AVG	OBP	SLG	OPS	OPS+	BR/A	RC	RC/G	FR	G/POS	WS	TPW
1997*Hou-N	19	62	8	19	5	0	2	6	4	18	1	0	.306	.358	.484	.842	123	2	11	7.16	0	0-19(0-17-1)	2	0.2
1998*Hou-N	74	211	31	64	15	0	7	35	17	37	3	3	.303	.361	.474	.835	121	5	35	5.91	1	0-72(9-57-13)	6	0.6
1999 Hou-N	108	383	49	87	25	2	15	56	56	73	8	5	.227	.332	.420	.752	90	-7	56	4.85	10	*0-108(97-30-3)	9	0.0
2000 Hou-N	153	558	118	175	42	3	44	122	56	110	13	6	.314	.397	.636	1.033	147	40	140	9.17	6	*0-151(36-125-37)	21	4.2
2001*Hou-N	146	512	70	141	29	3	19	80	54	107	3	5	.275	.363	.455	.818	104	3	83	5.57	9	*0-144(23-128-37)	17	1.1
2002 Hou-N	114	388	54	91	17	4	15	48	43	85	6	2	.235	.320	.415	.735	88	-7	51	4.35	4	*0-110(0-1-110)	7	-0.9

YEAR	TM-L	G	AB	R	H	2B	3B	HR	RBI	BB	SO	SB	CS	AVG	OBP	SLG	OPS	OPS+	BR/A	RC	RC/G	FR	G/POS	WS	TPW
2003	Hou-N	141	514	91	159	43	4	28	88	58	104	9	7	.309	.388	.572	.960	140	29	112	8.06	17	*O-137(0-0-137)/D-1	20	3.7
Total	7	755	2628	421	736	176	16	130	435	288	534	43	28	.280	.364	.508	.871	117	65	488	6.53	46	O-741/D-1	82	8.9
• HIGBEE, Mahlon	Mahlon Jesse Higbee b: 8/16/1901, Louisville, KY d: 4/7/1968, DePauw, IN BR/TR, 5'11", 165 lbs. Deb: 9/27/1922																								
1922	NY-N	3	10	2	4	0	0	1	5	0	2	0	0	.400	.400	.700	1.100	177	1	3	9.92	0	/O-3(2-0-1)	0	0.1
• HIGBY,	Higby Deb: 9/18/1872																								
1872	Atl-n	1	4	0	0	0	0	0	0	0	0	0	0	.000	.000	.000	.000	-85	-1	0	.00	-0	/O-1	....	-0.1
• HIGDON, Bill	William Travis Higdon b: 4/27/1924, Camp Hill, AL d: 4/30/1986, Pascagoula, MS BL/TR, 6'1", 193 lbs. Deb: 9/10/1949																								
1949	Chi-A	11	23	3	7	3	0	0	1	6	3	1	0	.304	.448	.435	.883	139	2	6	9.33	0	/O-6(0-6-0)	1	0.2
• HIGGINS, Bill	William Edward Higgins b: 9/8/1861, Wilmington, DE d: 4/25/1919, Wilmington, DE TR, 5'9", 155 lbs. Deb: 8/9/1888 U																								
1888	Bos-N	14	54	5	10	1	0	0	4	1	3	1	....	.185	.200	.204	.404	28	-4	2	1.51	3	2-14	1	-0.1
1890	StL-a	67	258	39	65	6	2	0	35	24	....	7	....	.252	.316	.291	.606	69	-12	27	3.64	9	2-67	6	0.0
	Syr-a	1	4	1	1	1	0	0	1	0	....	0	....	.250	.250	.500	.750	134	0	1	4.53	1	/2-1	0	0.1
	Yr.	68	262	40	66	7	2	0	36	24	....	7	....	.252	.315	.294	.609	70	-11	27	3.66	10	2-68	6	0.1
Total	2	82	316	45	76	8	2	0	40	25	3	8	....	.241	.296	.278	.575	63	-16	29	3.26	13	/2-82	7	0.0
• HIGGINS, Bob	Robert Stone Higgins b: 9/23/1886, Fayetteville, TN d: 5/25/1941, Chattanooga, TN BR/TR, 5'8", 176 lbs. Deb: 9/13/1909																								
1909	Cle-A	8	23	0	2	0	0	0	0	0	....	0	....	.087	.087	.087	.174	-43	-4	0	.17	1	/C-8	0	-0.3
1911	Bro-N	4	10	1	3	0	0	0	2	1	0	1	....	.300	.364	.300	.664	90	-0	1	5.26	0	/C-2,3-1	0	0.0
1912	Bro-N	1	2	0	0	0	0	0	0	0	1	0	....	.000	.000	.000	.000	-104	-1	0	.00	0	/C-1	0	-0.1
Total	3	13	35	1	5	0	0	0	2	1	1	1	....	.143	.167	.143	.310	-6	-4	2	1.35	0	/C-11,3-1	0	-0.4
• HIGGINS, Kevin	Kevin Wayne Higgins b: 1/22/1967, San Gabriel, CA BL/TR, 5'11", 170 lbs. Deb: 5/29/1993																								
1993	SD-N	71	181	17	40	4	1	0	13	16	17	0	1	.221	.295	.254	.549	48	-14	13	2.35	-1	C-59/3-4,1-3,O-3(1-0-2),2	2	-1.1
• HIGGINS, Mark	Mark Douglas Higgins b: 7/9/1963, Miami, FL BR/TR, 6'2", 210 lbs. Deb: 9/7/1989																								
1989	Cle-A	6	10	1	1	0	0	0	0	1	6	0	0	.100	.182	.100	.282	-18	-2	0	.69	1	/1-5	0	-0.1
• HIGGINS, Pinky	Michael Franklin "Pinky" Higgins b: 5/27/1909, Red Oak, TX d: 3/21/1969, Dallas, TX BR/TR, 6'1", 185 lbs. Deb: 6/25/1930 M																								
1930	Phi-A	14	24	1	6	2	0	0	0	4	5	0	0	.250	.357	.333	.690	73	-1	3	4.56	-1	/3-5,2-2,S-1	0	-0.2
1933	Phi-A	152	567	85	178	34	12	13	99	61	53	2	7	.314	.383	.485	.868	127	20	104	6.90	-5	*3-152	23	2.0
1934	Phi-A★	144	543	89	179	37	6	16	90	56	70	9	2	.330	.392	.508	.901	136	29	110	7.84	-20	*3-144	20	1.3
1935	Phi-A	133	524	69	155	32	4	23	94	42	62	6	2	.296	.350	.504	.854	120	13	93	6.54	-11	*3-131	15	0.6
1936	Phi-A★	146	550	89	159	32	2	12	80	67	61	7	4	.289	.366	.420	.786	96	-4	87	5.80	-12	*3-145	14	-0.9
1937	Bos-A	153	570	88	172	33	5	9	106	76	51	2	6	.302	.385	.425	.809	100	-0	95	6.13	-13	*3-152	16	-0.7
1938	Bos-A	139	524	77	159	29	5	5	106	71	55	10	9	.303	.388	.406	.794	95	-4	85	5.91	-9	*3-138	14	-0.7
1939	Det-A	132	489	57	135	23	2	8	76	56	41	7	4	.276	.353	.380	.733	81	-13	66	4.63	-7	*3-130	10	-1.5
1940*	Det-A	131	480	70	130	24	3	13	76	61	31	4	2	.271	.357	.415	.771	91	-6	73	5.29	-14	*3-129	11	-1.4
1941	Det-A	147	540	79	161	28	3	11	73	67	45	5	4	.298	.378	.422	.800	101	2	86	5.64	-5	*3-145	16	0.2
1942	Det-A	143	499	65	133	34	2	11	79	72	21	3	7	.267	.362	.409	.771	108	5	72	4.90	-19	*3-137	12	-1.0
1943	Det-A	138	523	62	145	20	1	10	84	57	31	2	5	.277	.349	.377	.726	104	2	68	4.49	-7	*3-138	15	-0.2
1944	Det-A★	148	543	79	161	32	4	7	76	81	34	4	4	.297	.392	.409	.801	122	19	91	5.90	-18	*3-146	22	0.2
1946	Det-A	18	60	2	13	3	1	0	8	5	6	0	1	.217	.277	.300	.577	58	-4	5	2.65	-2	3-17	1	-0.6
	*Bos-A	64	200	18	55	11	1	2	28	24	24	0	2	.275	.356	.370	.726	97	-1	26	4.42	-1	3-59	6	-0.2
	Yr.	82	260	20	68	14	2	2	36	29	30	0	3	.262	.338	.354	.692	88	-5	31	4.00	-3	3-76	7	-0.8
Total	14	1802	6636	930	1941	374	51	140	1075	800	590	61	59	.292	.370	.428	.798	106	58	1066	5.74	-146	*3-1768/2-2,S-1	195	-3.1
• HIGGINSON, Bobby	Robert Leigh Higginson b: 8/18/1970, Philadelphia, PA BL/TR, 5'11", 180 lbs. Deb: 4/26/1995 Career OF: 654-22-522																								
1995	Det-A	131	410	61	92	17	5	14	43	62	107	6	4	.224	.333	.393	.726	89	-7	57	4.60	2	*O-123(65-0-67)/D-2	8	-1.0
1996	Det-A	130	440	75	141	35	0	26	81	65	66	6	3	.320	.409	.577	.986	146	32	106	9.00	0	*O-123(63-19-57)/D-4	21	2.5
1997	Det-A	146	546	94	163	30	5	27	101	70	85	12	7	.299	.381	.520	.901	133	27	109	7.30	10	*O-142(105-2-57)/D-2	25	2.9
1998	Det-A	157	612	92	174	37	4	25	85	63	101	3	3	.284	.357	.480	.837	114	12	103	6.03	7	*O-153(17-0-136)/D-2	16	1.0
1999	Det-A	107	377	51	90	18	0	12	46	64	66	4	6	.239	.352	.382	.734	87	-8	54	4.95	-3	O-88(0-0-88),D-17	9	-1.5
2000	Det-A	154	597	104	179	44	4	30	102	74	99	15	3	.300	.379	.538	.917	132	31	127	7.98	13	*O-145(145-0-0),D-10	26	3.4
2001	Det-A	147	541	84	150	28	6	17	71	80	65	20	12	.277	.372	.445	.818	120	16	93	5.95	7	*O-142(142-0-0)/D-5	18	1.6
2002	Det-A	119	444	50	125	24	3	10	63	41	45	12	5	.282	.350	.417	.767	109	7	66	5.23	5	*O-117(117-0-0)/D-1	15	0.7
2003	Det-A	130	469	61	110	13	4	14	52	59	73	8	8	.235	.324	.369	.693	89	-9	55	3.88	-1	*O-118(0-1-117)/D-8	6	-1.5
Total	9	1221	4436	672	1224	246	31	175	644	578	707	86	51	.276	.363	.464	.827	115	100	771	6.14	42	*O-1151/D-51	144	7.9
• HIGH, Andy	Andrew Aird "Handy Andy,Knee" High b: 11/21/1897, Ava, IL d: 2/22/1981, Sylvania, OH BL/TR, 5'6", 155 lbs. Deb: 4/12/1922 C																								
1922	Bro-N	153	579	82	164	27	10	6	65	59	26	3	12	.283	.354	.396	.749	94	-8	80	4.78	-2	*3-130,S-22/2-1	20	0.1
1923	Bro-N	123	426	51	115	23	9	3	37	47	13	4	1	.270	.344	.387	.731	95	-1	60	4.82	-8	3-80,S-45/2-5	13	0.1
1924	Bro-N	144	582	98	191	26	13	6	61	57	16	3	6	.328	.390	.448	.838	128	24	102	6.59	-4	*2-133,S-17/3-1	28	2.5
1925	Bro-N	44	115	11	23	4	1	0	6	14	5	0	1	.200	.287	.252	.539	40	-10	9	2.48	-5	2-11,3-11/S-3	0	-1.4
	Bos-N	60	219	31	63	11	1	4	28	24	2	3	5	.288	.361	.402	.762	104	1	32	4.99	-7	3-60/2-1	6	-0.2
	Yr.	104	334	42	86	15	2	4	34	38	7	3	6	.257	.335	.350	.685	82	-10	40	4.08	-12	3-71,2-12/S-3	6	-1.6
1926	Bos-N	130	476	55	141	17	10	2	66	39	9	4	....	.296	.351	.387	.737	108	5	64	4.72	-11	3-81,2-49	15	0.0
1927	Bos-N	113	384	59	116	15	9	4	46	26	11	4	....	.302	.350	.419	.769	114	7	55	5.13	-20	3-89/2-8,S-2	11	-0.7
1928*	StL-N	111	368	58	105	14	3	6	37	37	10	2	....	.285	.355	.389	.744	93	-3	51	4.79	-13	3-73,2-19	10	-1.1
1929	StL-N	146	603	95	178	32	4	10	63	38	18	7	....	.295	.340	.411	.751	84	-16	82	4.85	-10	*3-123,2-22	14	-1.6
1930*	StL-N	72	215	34	60	12	2	2	29	23	6	1	....	.279	.349	.381	.730	74	-9	29	4.66	-6	3-48/2-3	4	-1.0
1931*	StL-N	63	131	20	35	6	1	0	19	24	4	0	....	.267	.389	.328	.717	91	-0	19	5.05	1	3-23,2-19	5	0.2
1932	Cin-N	84	191	16	36	4	2	0	12	23	6	1	....	.188	.276	.230	.506	39	-16	14	2.23	-2	3-46,2-12	1	-1.6
1933	Cin-N	24	43	4	9	2	0	1	6	5	1	0	....	.209	.292	.326	.617	77	-1	4	2.85	-1	3-11/2-2	1	-0.2
1934	Phi-N	47	68	4	14	2	0	0	7	9	3	1	....	.206	.299	.235	.534	40	-6	4	1.86	-3	3-14/2-2	0	-0.8
Total	13	1314	4400	618	1250	195	65	44	482	425	130	33	25	.284	.350	.388	.738	95	-33	603	4.79	-90	3-790,2-287/S-89	128	-5.6
• HIGH, Charlie	Charles Edwin High b: 12/1/1898, Ava, IL d: 9/11/1960, Oak Grove, OR BL/TR, 5'9", 170 lbs. Deb: 9/5/1919 Career OF: 0-3-23																								
1919	Phi-A	11	29	2	2	0	0	0	1	3	4	2	....	.069	.182	.069	.251	-28	-5	1	.75	0	/O-9(0-1-8)	0	-0.6
1920	Phi-A	17	65	7	20	2	1	1	6	3	6	0	2	.308	.375	.415	.790	108	0	10	5.23	-1	O-17(0-2-15)	1	-0.1
Total	2	28	94	9	22	2	1	1	7	6	10	2	2	.234	.314	.309	.623	64	-5	11	3.57	-1	/O-26	1	-0.7
• HIGH, Hugh	Hugh Jenken "Bunny" High b: 10/24/1887, Pottstown, PA d: 11/16/1962, St. Louis, MO BL/TL, 5'7.5", 155 lbs. Deb: 4/11/1913 Career OF: 268-153-11																								
1913	Det-A	87	183	18	42	6	1	0	16	28	24	6	....	.230	.335	.273	.608	79	-3	18	3.21	1	O-52(3-39-7)	4	-0.6
1914	Det-A	84	184	25	49	5	3	0	17	26	21	7	6	.266	.363	.326	.689	104	1	24	4.18	-4	O-53(13-39-1)	5	-0.7
1915	NY-A	119	427	51	110	19	7	1	43	62	47	22	13	.258	.356	.342	.698	109	5	56	4.36	-6	*O-117(44-71-1)	14	-0.8
1916	NY-A	116	377	44	99	13	4	1	28	47	44	13	....	.263	.349	.326	.675	101	2	51	4.39	-1	*O-110(107-2-1)	12	-0.5
1917	NY-A	103	365	37	86	11	6	1	19	48	31	8	....	.236	.329	.307	.636	93	-2	39	3.50	0	*O-100(99-1-0)	9	-0.6
1918	NY-A	7	10	1	0	0	0	0	0	1	1	0	....	.000	.091	.000	.091	-71	-2	0	.00	1	/O-4(2-1-1)	0	-0.2
Total	6	516	1546	176	386	54	21	3	123	212	168	56	19	.250	.345	.318	.662	98	1	189	3.97	-10	O-436	44	-3.3
• HIGHAM, Dick	Richard Higham b: 7/24/1851, Ipswich, England d: 3/18/1905, Chicago, IL BL/TR, 5'8.5", 171 lbs. Deb: 6/1/1871 M/U NA OF: 0-9-93 Career OF: 0-0-122																								
1871	Mut-n	21	94	21	34	3	1	0	9	2	0	3	2	.362	.375	.415	.790	139	5	16	8.20	-4	2-12/O-8(0-0-8),C-1	....	0.1
1872	Bal-n	50	245	72	84	10	1	2	38	2	3	3	5	.343	.348	.416	.765	128	5	37	7.00	-6	C-25,O-24(0-2-22)/2-5,3-2,1	....	0.0
1873	Mut-n	49	245	57	77	5	4	0	34	2	1	1	3	.314	.320	.367	.687	104	0	30	5.32	-11	O-19(0-1-18),2-18,C-17	....	-0.7
1874	Mut-n	65	333	58	87	14	3	1	37	4	0	5	3	.261	.270	.330	.600	89	-5	32	3.83	-5	*C-48,O-33(0-3-31)/2-1	....	-0.6
1875	Chi-n	42	208	44	49	5	3	0	12	0	0	6	2	.236	.236	.288	.524	80	-4	16	2.92	-6	C-24,O-14(0-3-11),2-13	....	-0.9

YEAR TM-L	G	AB	R	H	2B	3B	HR	RBI	BB	SO	SB	CS	AVG	OBP	SLG	OPS	OPS+	BR/A	RC	RC/G	FR	G/POS	WS	TPW
Mut-n	15	64	12	25	5	0	0	10	0	1	0	0	.391	.391	.469	.859	187	5	12	9.09	-2	/C-8,2-6,0-3(0-0-3),1-2	....	0.3
Yr.	57	272	56	74	10	3	0	22	0	1	6	2	.272	.272	.331	.603	105	1	28	4.12	-8	C-32,2-19,0-17(0-3-14)/1-2	....	-0.6
1876 Har-N	67	314	59	102	**21**	2	0	35	2	7	....	....	.325	.331	.407	.738	133	9	43	5.75	2	*0-59(0-0-59),C-13/2-1,S-1	13	1.0
1878 Pro-N	62	281	**60**	90	**22**	1	1	29	5	16	....	....	.320	.332	.416	.749	145	13	40	5.74	5	*0-62(0-0-62)/C-1	12	1.6
1880 Tro-N	1	5	1	1	0	0	0	0	0	0	....	....	.200	.200	.200	.400	34	-0	0	1.41	-1	/C-1,0-1	0	-0.1
Total 5 n	242	1189	264	356	42	12	3	140	10	5	18	15	.299	.305	.362	.668	108	6	143	5.14	-34	C-123,0-101/2-55,1-3,3-2	....	-1.9
Total 3	130	600	120	193	43	3	1	64	7	23	....	....	.322	.331	.410	.740	138	22	83	5.70	7	0-122/C-15,2-1,S-1	25	2.6
• HILAND, John	John William Hiland b: 9/1860, Baltic, CT d: 4/10/1901, Philadelphia, PA BL/TL, 5'8.5", 165 lbs. Deb: 8/20/1885																							
1885 Phi-N	3	9	0	0	0	0	0	0	0	4	....	....	.000	.000	.000	.000	-102	-2	0	.00	-1	/2-3	0	-0.3
• HILDEBRAND,	R. E. Hildebrand Deb: 8/29/1902																							
1902 Chi-N	1	4	1	0	0	0	0	0	1	....	0	....	.000	.200	.000	.200	-39	-1	0	.00	0	/0-1	0	-0.1
• HILDEBRAND, George	George Albert Hildebrand b: 9/6/1878, San Francisco, CA d: 5/30/1960, Reseda, CA BR/TR, 5'8", 170 lbs. Deb: 4/17/1902 U																							
1902 Bro-N	11	41	3	9	1	0	0	5	3	....	0	....	.220	.289	.244	.533	64	-2	3	2.50	2	0-11(11-0-0)	1	-0.1
• HILDEBRAND, Palmer	Palmer Marion "Pete" Hildebrand b: 12/23/1884, Shauck, OH d: 1/25/1960, North Canton, OH BR/TR, 5'10", 170 lbs. Deb: 5/14/1913																							
1913 StL-N	26	55	3	9	2	0	0	1	1	10	1	....	.164	.207	.200	.407	17	-6	2	1.23	1	C-22/0-1	0	-0.4
• HILL, Belden	Belden L. Hill b: 8/24/1864, Kewanee, IL d: 10/22/1934, Cedar Rapids, IA BR/TR, 6' Deb: 8/27/1890																							
1890 Bal-a	9	30	3	5	2	0	0	2	3	....	6	....	.167	.306	.233	.539	54	-2	4	4.32	1	/3-9	1	-0.1
• HILL, Bobby	William Robert Hill b: 4/3/1978, San Jose, CA BB/TR, 5'10", 190 lbs. Deb: 5/10/2002																							
2002 Chi-N	59	190	26	48	7	2	4	20	17	42	6	1	.253	.327	.374	.701	86	-3	25	4.68	0	2-55/S-1	5	-0.1
2003 Chi-N	5	4	0	1	0	0	0	0	1	2	0	0	.250	.400	.250	.650	76	-0	0	1.70	-1	/2-2	0	-0.1
Pit-N	1	3	1	1	0	0	0	0	1	0	0	0	.333	.500	.333	.833	121	0	1	8.51	0	/2-1	0	0.0
Yr.	6	7	1	2	0	0	0	0	2	2	0	0	.286	.444	.286	.730	96	0	1	3.97	-1	/2-3	0	-0.1
Total 2	65	197	27	50	7	2	4	20	19	44	6	1	.254	.332	.371	.702	86	-3	26	4.66	-1	/2-58,S-1	5	-0.2
• HILL, Donnie	Donald Earl Hill b: 11/12/1960, Pomona, CA BB/TR, 5'10", 160 lbs. Deb: 7/25/1983																							
1983 Oak-A	53	158	20	42	7	0	2	15	4	21	1	1	.266	.284	.348	.632	77	-6	15	3.18	3	S-53	4	0.2
1984 Oak-A	73	174	21	40	6	0	2	16	5	12	1	1	.230	.251	.299	.550	55	-11	13	2.37	0	S-66/2-4,3-2,D-2	2	-0.6
1985 Oak-A	123	393	45	112	13	2	3	48	23	33	9	4	.285	.325	.351	.676	92	-5	45	3.90	-6	*2-122	9	-0.5
1986 Oak-A	108	339	37	96	16	2	4	29	23	38	5	2	.283	.329	.378	.706	99	-1	41	4.27	4	2-68,3-33/D-3,S-2	10	0.5
1987 Chi-A	111	410	57	98	14	6	9	46	30	35	1	0	.239	.293	.368	.661	72	-17	43	3.50	-5	2-84,3-32/D-1	6	-1.7
1988 Chi-A	83	221	17	48	6	1	2	20	26	32	3	1	.217	.300	.281	.580	64	-10	20	2.99	-4	2-59,3-12/D-5	3	-1.3
1990 Cal-A	103	352	36	93	18	2	3	32	29	27	1	2	.264	.322	.352	.674	90	-5	39	3.73	-2	2-60,S-24,3-21/1-3,D-1,P-1	8	-0.4
1991 Cal-A	77	209	36	50	8	1	1	20	30	21	1	0	.239	.335	.301	.636	77	-5	24	3.93	-2	2-39,S-29/1-3	7	-0.5
1992 Min-A	25	51	7	15	3	0	0	2	5	6	0	0	.294	.368	.353	.721	100	0	7	5.21	-1	S-10/2-7,3-5,0-1	2	0.0
Total 9	756	2307	276	594	91	14	26	228	175	225	22	11	.257	.311	.343	.654	82	-59	247	3.62	-13	2-443,S-184,3-105/D-12,,0,P	51	-4.2
• HILL, Glenallen	Glenallen Hill b: 3/22/1965, Santa Cruz, CA BR/TR, 6'3", 210 lbs. Deb: 9/1/1989 Career OF: 336-73-452																							
1989 Tor-A	19	52	4	15	0	0	1	7	3	12	2	1	.288	.327	.346	.673	96	-0	6	4.35	-1	0-16(3-0-13)/D-3	2	-0.2
1990 Tor-A	84	260	47	60	11	3	12	32	18	62	8	3	.231	.281	.435	.715	92	-4	31	3.98	-1	0-60(27-1-34),D-20	5	-0.8
1991 Tor-A	35	99	14	25	5	2	3	11	7	24	2	2	.253	.302	.434	.736	98	-1	12	4.10	0	D-16,0-13(9-0-4)	2	-0.3
Cle-A	37	122	15	32	3	0	5	14	16	30	4	2	.262	.348	.410	.758	108	2	17	4.57	-2	0-33(12-26-1)/D-1	3	-0.1
Yr.	72	221	29	57	8	2	8	25	23	54	6	4	.258	.328	.421	.749	104	0	29	4.36	-2	0-46(21-26-5),D-17	5	-0.4
1992 Cle-A	102	369	38	89	16	1	18	49	20	73	9	6	.241	.288	.436	.724	102	-2	42	3.81	-1	0-59(50-1-8),D-34	6	-0.7
1993 Cle-A	66	174	19	39	7	2	5	25	11	50	7	3	.224	.274	.374	.648	73	-7	17	3.23	-2	0-39(9-0-30),D-18	2	-1.1
Chi-N	31	87	14	30	7	0	10	22	6	21	1	0	.345	.387	.770	1.157	204	12	26	12.10	1	0-21(18-0-4)	6	1.2
1994 Chi-N	89	269	48	80	12	1	10	38	29	57	19	6	.297	.366	.461	.827	115	8	47	6.25	-4	0-78(31-44-7)	8	0.3
1995 SF-N	132	497	71	131	29	4	24	86	39	98	25	5	.264	.318	.483	.801	111	9	76	5.33	-9	*0-125(0-1-124)	15	-0.7
1996 SF-N	98	379	56	106	26	0	19	67	33	95	6	3	.280	.347	.499	.846	125	12	66	6.21	-5	0-98(0-0-98)	13	0.2
1997*SF-N	128	398	47	104	28	4	11	64	19	87	7	4	.261	.302	.435	.736	93	-6	50	4.32	-3	0-97(0-0-97)/D-7	11	-1.4
1998 Sea-A	74	259	37	75	20	2	12	33	14	45	1	1	.290	.333	.521	.855	118	5	39	5.36	-1	0-71(71-0-0)	4	0.2
*Chi-N	48	131	26	46	5	0	8	23	14	34	0	0	.351	.414	.573	.986	151	10	31	9.45	2	0-34(28-0-6)	7	1.1
1999 Chi-N	99	253	43	76	9	1	20	55	22	61	5	1	.300	.356	.581	.937	134	12	51	7.28	-1	0-62(37-0-26)/D-4	7	0.8
2000 Chi-N	64	168	23	44	4	1	11	29	10	43	0	1	.262	.303	.494	.797	99	-2	23	4.77	1	0-29(29-0-0)/D-9	2	-0.2
*NY-A	40	132	22	44	5	0	16	29	9	33	0	0	.333	.380	.735	1.115	175	14	37	11.13	0	D-24,0-12(12-0-0)	6	1.1
2001 Ana-A	16	66	4	9	0	0	1	2	0	20	0	0	.136	.136	.182	.318	-17	-11	1	.49	0	D-16	0	-1.2
Total 13	1162	3715	528	1005	187	21	186	586	270	845	96	38	.271	.323	.482	.806	111	49	571	5.38	-27	0-847,D-152	99	-1.7
• HILL, Herman	Herman Alexander Hill b: 10/12/1945, Tuskegee, AL d: 12/14/1970, Valencia, Venezuela BL/TR, 6'2", 190 lbs. Deb: 9/2/1969 Career OF: 2-12-2																							
1969 Min-A	16	2	4	0	0	0	0	0	0	1	1	2	.000	.000	.000	.000	-98	-1	0	.00	0	/0-2(0-2-0)	0	-0.2
1970 Min-A	27	22	8	2	0	0	0	0	0	6	0	0	.091	.091	.091	.182	-49	-4	0	.28	0	0-14(2-10-2)	0	-0.4
Total 2	43	24	12	2	0	0	0	0	0	7	1	2	.083	.083	.083	.167	-53	-6	0	.24	0	/0-16	0	-0.6
• HILL, Hugh	Hugh Ellis Hill b: 7/21/1879, Ringgold, GA d: 9/6/1958, Cincinnati, OH BL/TR, 5'11.5", 168 lbs. Deb: 5/1/1903																							
1903 Cle-A	1	1	0	0	0	0	0	0	0	....	0	....	.000	.000	.000	.000	-102	-0	0	.00	0	....	0	0.0
1904 StL-N	23	93	13	21	2	1	3	4	2	....	3	....	.226	.242	.366	.608	91	-2	9	3.28	0	0-23(23-0-0)	2	-0.3
Total 2	24	94	13	21	2	1	3	4	2	....	3	....	.223	.240	.362	.601	89	-2	9	3.24	0	/0-23	2	-0.3
• HILL, Hunter	Hunter Benjamin Hill b: 6/21/1879, Austin, TX d: 2/22/1959, Austin, TX BR/TR Deb: 7/1/1903																							
1903 StL-A	86	317	30	77	11	3	0	25	8	....	2	....	.243	.264	.297	.560	70	-12	28	2.87	-2	3-86	5	-1.2
1904 StL-A	58	219	19	47	3	0	0	14	6	....	4	....	.215	.246	.228	.474	54	-12	16	2.19	-17	3-56/0-1	0	-3.0
Was-A	77	290	18	57	6	1	0	17	11	....	10	....	.197	.228	.224	.453	44	-18	18	2.01	-6	3-71/0-5(0-0-5)	1	-2.5
Yr.	135	509	37	104	9	1	0	31	17	....	14	....	.204	.236	.226	.462	48	-30	34	2.09	-23	*3-127/0-6(1-0-5)	1	-5.6
1905 Was-A	104	374	37	78	12	1	1	24	32	....	10	....	.209	.278	.254	.532	72	-11	34	2.75	-4	*3-103	5	-1.3
Total 3	325	1200	104	259	32	5	1	80	57	....	26	....	.216	.257	.253	.510	62	-53	96	2.50	-30	3-316/0-6	11	-8.1
• HILL, Jesse	Jesse Terrill Hill b: 1/20/1907, Yates, MO d: 8/31/1993, Pasadena, CA BR/TR, 5'9", 165 lbs. Deb: 4/17/1935 Career OF: 154-87-2																							
1935 NY-A	107	392	69	115	20	3	4	33	42	32	14	4	.293	.362	.390	.752	100	2	58	5.31	-1	0-94(94-0-0)	12	-0.4
1936 Was-A	85	233	50	71	19	5	0	34	29	23	11	0	.305	.384	.429	.813	106	6	42	6.77	0	0-60(54-4-2)	8	0.3
1937 Was-A	33	92	24	20	2	1	1	4	13	16	2	1	.217	.314	.293	.608	57	-6	9	3.29	1	0-21(3-18-0)	2	-0.5
Phi-A	70	242	32	71	12	3	1	37	31	20	16	3	.293	.374	.380	.754	92	0	38	5.69	-6	0-68(3-65-0)	5	-0.7
Yr.	103	334	56	91	14	4	2	41	44	36	18	4	.272	.357	.356	.713	82	-6	47	4.98	-5	0-89(6-83-0)	7	-1.2
Total 3	295	959	175	277	53	12	6	108	115	91	43	8	.289	.366	.388	.753	95	2	147	5.53	-6	0-243	27	-1.3
• HILL, Koyie	Koyie Dolan Hill b: 3/9/1979, Tulsa, OK BB/TR, 6', 190 lbs. Deb: 9/5/2003																							
2003 LA-N	3	3	0	1	1	0	0	0	0	2	0	0	.333	.333	.667	1.000	161	0	1	9.00	0	....	0	0.0
• HILL, Marc	Marc Kevin Hill b: 2/18/1952, Elsberry, MO BR/TR, 6'3", 210 lbs. Deb: 9/28/1973 C																							
1973 StL-N	1	3	0	0	0	0	0	0	0	1	0	0	.000	.000	.000	.000	-100	-1	0	.00	-0	/C-1	0	-0.1
1974 StL-N	10	21	2	5	1	0	0	2	4	5	0	0	.238	.360	.286	.646	83	-0	2	3.45	0	/C-9	1	0.0
1975 SF-N	72	182	14	39	4	0	5	23	25	27	0	0	.214	.309	.319	.628	71	-7	18	3.09	3	C-60/3-1	4	-0.2
1976 SF-N	54	131	11	24	5	0	3	15	10	19	0	1	.183	.246	.290	.537	50	-9	9	2.11	1	C-49/1-1	2	-0.7
1977 SF-N	108	320	28	80	10	0	9	50	34	34	0	1	.250	.322	.366	.688	84	-7	36	3.69	1	*C-102	8	-0.1
1978 SF-N	117	358	20	87	15	1	3	36	45	39	1	2	.243	.329	.316	.645	84	-7	36	3.43	1	*C-116/1-2	10	-0.1
1979 SF-N	63	169	20	35	3	0	3	15	26	25	0	1	.207	.313	.278	.591	67	-7	15	2.82	2	C-58/1-1	4	-0.3
1980 SF-N	17	41	1	7	2	0	0	0	1	7	0	0	.171	.190	.220	.410	14	-5	2	1.19	0	C-14	1	-0.4

YEAR TM-L	G	AB	R	H	2B	3B	HR	RBI	BB	SO	SB	CS	AVG	OBP	SLG	OPS	OPS+	BR/A	RC	RC/G	FR	G/POS	WS	TPW
Sea-A	29	70	8	16	2	1	2	9	3	10	0	0	.229	.260	.371	.632	70	-3	6	2.75	0	C-29	1	-0.2
1981 Chi-A	16	6	0	0	0	0	0	0	0	1	0	0	.000	.000	.000	.000	-102	-2	0	.00	-4	C-14/1-1,3-1	0	-0.5
1982 Chi-A	53	88	9	23	2	0	3	13	6	13	0	0	.261	.316	.386	.702	92	-1	10	3.72	1	C-49/1-1,3-1	3	0.1
1983 Chi-A	58	133	11	30	6	0	1	11	9	24	0	0	.226	.275	.293	.568	54	-9	10	2.41	-1	C-55/D-2,1-1	2	-0.8
1984 Chi-A	77	193	15	45	10	1	5	20	9	26	0	1	.233	.275	.373	.648	74	-8	16	2.59	-1	C-72/1-2	2	-0.7
1985 Chi-A	40	75	5	10	2	0	0	4	12	9	0	0	.133	.253	.160	.413	16	-9	4	1.46	0	C-37/3-1	1	-0.7
1986 Chi-A	22	19	2	3	0	0	0	0	1	3	0	0	.158	.238	.158	.396	10	-2	1	1.41	1	C-22	1	-0.1
Total 14	737	1809	146	404	62	3	34	198	185	243	1	7	.223	.298	.317	.615	69	-77	165	2.91	3	C-687/1-9,3-4,D-2	40	-4.8

• HILL, Oliver Oliver Clinton Hill b: 10/16/1909, Powder Springs, GA d: 9/20/1970, Decatur, GA BL/TR, 5'11", 178 lbs. Deb: 4/19/1939

YEAR TM-L	G	AB	R	H	2B	3B	HR	RBI	BB	SO	SB	CS	AVG	OBP	SLG	OPS	OPS+	BR/A	RC	RC/G	FR	G/POS	WS	TPW
1939 Bos-N	2	2	1	1	1	0	0	0	0	0	0	....	.500	.500	1.000	1.500	317	1	1	27.00	0	....	0	0.1

• HILLEBRAND, Homer Homer Hiller Henry Hillebrand b: 10/10/1879, Freeport, IL d: 1/20/1974, Elsinore, CA BR/TL, 5'8", 165 lbs. Deb: 4/24/1905 ♦

YEAR TM-L	G	AB	R	H	2B	3B	HR	RBI	BB	SO	SB	CS	AVG	OBP	SLG	OPS	OPS+	BR/A	RC	RC/G	FR	G/POS	WS	TPW
1905 Pit-N	39	110	9	26	3	2	0	7	6	....	1	....	.236	.282	.300	.582	72	-2	10	3.05	-2	1-16,P-10/O-7(1-0-6),C-3	7	-0.4
1906 Pit-N	7	21	1	5	1	0	0	3	1	....	0	....	.238	.273	.286	.558	71	1	2	2.73	1	/P-7	4	0.4
1908 Pit-N	1	0	0	0	0	0	0	0	0	....	0	....	....	....	....	....	-100	0	0	....	0	/P-1	0	0.0
Total 3	47	131	10	31	4	2	0	10	7	....	1	....	.237	.281	.298	.578	71	-1	12	3.00	-1	/P-18,1-16,O-7,C-3	11	0.0

• HILLENBRAND, Shea Shea Matthew Hillenbrand b: 7/27/1975, Mesa, AZ BR/TR, 6'1", 200 lbs. Deb: 4/2/2001

YEAR TM-L	G	AB	R	H	2B	3B	HR	RBI	BB	SO	SB	CS	AVG	OBP	SLG	OPS	OPS+	BR/A	RC	RC/G	FR	G/POS	WS	TPW
2001 Bos-A	139	468	52	123	20	2	12	49	13	61	3	4	.263	.293	.391	.684	77	-18	49	3.64	-7	*3-129/1-6,D-1	5	-2.3
2002 Bos-A★	156	634	94	186	43	4	18	83	25	95	4	2	.293	.332	.459	.791	105	3	91	5.22	-4	*3-156	17	0.2
2003 Bos-A	49	185	20	56	17	0	3	38	7	26	1	0	.303	.342	.443	.785	103	1	25	4.81	-3	3-29,1-28/D-2	5	-0.4
Ari-N	85	330	40	88	18	1	17	59	17	44	0	0	.267	.307	.482	.788	92	-5	44	4.57	-5	1-56,3-34	6	-1.5
Total 3	429	1617	206	453	98	7	50	229	62	226	8	6	.280	.317	.442	.759	94	-19	210	4.57	-19	3-348/1-90,D-3	33	-4.0

• HILLER, Chuck Charles Joseph Hiller b: 10/1/1934, Johnsburg, IL BL/TR, 5'11", 170 lbs. Deb: 4/11/1961 C Career OF: 12-0-1

YEAR TM-L	G	AB	R	H	2B	3B	HR	RBI	BB	SO	SB	CS	AVG	OBP	SLG	OPS	OPS+	BR/A	RC	RC/G	FR	G/POS	WS	TPW
1961 SF-N	70	240	38	57	12	1	2	12	32	30	4	4	.238	.330	.321	.651	76	-8	28	3.84	-3	2-67	5	-0.6
1962*SF-N	161	602	94	166	22	2	3	48	55	49	5	4	.276	.344	.334	.678	84	-12	71	4.14	7	*2-161	17	0.8
1963 SF-N	111	417	44	93	10	2	6	33	20	23	3	2	.223	.262	.300	.562	62	-21	31	2.35	-1	*2-109	4	-1.4
1964 SF-N	80	205	21	37	8	1	1	17	17	23	1	1	.180	.247	.244	.491	38	-17	13	1.97	8	2-60/3-1	3	-0.5
1965 SF-N	7	7	1	1	0	0	1	1	0	1	0	0	.143	.143	.571	.714	88	-0	0	.00	-1	/2-2	0	-0.1
NY-N	100	286	24	68	11	1	5	21	14	24	1	1	.238	.276	.336	.611	74	-11	25	3.01	-7	2-80/O-4(3-0-1),3-2	4	-1.3
Yr.	107	293	25	69	11	1	6	22	14	25	1	1	.235	.273	.341	.614	74	-11	25	2.92	-7	2-82/O-4(3-0-1),3-2	4	-1.4
1966 NY-N	108	254	25	71	8	2	2	14	15	22	0	0	.280	.332	.350	.683	92	-2	31	4.45	2	2-45,3-14/O-9(9-0-0)	9	0.3
1967 NY-N	25	54	0	5	3	0	0	3	2	11	0	0	.093	.125	.148	.273	-23	-9	1	.50	0	2-14	0	-0.8
Phi-N	31	43	4	13	1	0	0	2	2	4	0	2	.302	.333	.326	.659	88	-2	4	3.54	-1	/2-6	1	-0.2
Yr.	56	97	4	18	4	0	0	5	4	15	0	2	.186	.218	.227	.445	26	-10	5	1.67	-1	2-20	1	-1.0
1968 Pit-N	11	13	2	5	1	0	0	1	0	0	0	0	.385	.385	.462	.846	155	1	2	5.54	-1	/2-2	1	0.0
Total 8	704	2121	253	516	76	9	20	152	157	187	14	14	.243	.301	.316	.617	72	-80	206	3.26	4	2-546/3-17,O-13	44	-3.7

• HILLER, Hob Harvey Max Hiller b: 5/12/1893, East Mauch Chuck, PA d: 12/27/1956, Lehighton, PA BR/TR, 5'8", 162 lbs. Deb: 4/22/1920

YEAR TM-L	G	AB	R	H	2B	3B	HR	RBI	BB	SO	SB	CS	AVG	OBP	SLG	OPS	OPS+	BR/A	RC	RC/G	FR	G/POS	WS	TPW
1920 Bos-A	17	29	4	5	1	1	0	2	2	5	0	3	.172	.226	.276	.502	34	-4	1	1.01	-2	/3-6,S-5,2-2,O-1	0	-0.5
1921 Bos-A	1	1	0	0	0	0	0	0	0	0	0	0	.000	.000	.000	.000	-103	-0	0	.00	0	....	0	0.0
Total 2	18	30	4	5	1	1	0	2	2	5	0	3	.167	.219	.267	.485	30	-4	1	.98	-2	/3-6,S-5,2-2,O-1	0	-0.6

• HILLEY, Ed Edward Garfield "Whitey" Hilley b: 6/17/1879, Cleveland, OH d: 11/14/1956, Cleveland, OH BR/TR, 5'10.5", 170 lbs. Deb: 9/29/1903

YEAR TM-L	G	AB	R	H	2B	3B	HR	RBI	BB	SO	SB	CS	AVG	OBP	SLG	OPS	OPS+	BR/A	RC	RC/G	FR	G/POS	WS	TPW
1903 Phi-A	1	3	1	1	0	0	0	0	1	....	0	....	.333	.500	.333	.833	147	0	1	6.27	0	/3-1	0	0.0

• HILLIS, Mack Malcolm David Hillis b: 7/23/1901, Cambridge, MA d: 6/16/1961, Cambridge, MA BR/TR, 5'10", 165 lbs. Deb: 9/13/1924

YEAR TM-L	G	AB	R	H	2B	3B	HR	RBI	BB	SO	SB	CS	AVG	OBP	SLG	OPS	OPS+	BR/A	RC	RC/G	FR	G/POS	WS	TPW
1924 NY-A	1	1	1	0	0	0	0	0	0	0	0	0	.000	.000	.000	.000	-100	-0	0	.00	-1	/2-1	0	-0.1
1928 Pit-N	11	36	6	9	2	3	1	7	0	6	1	....	.250	.250	.556	.806	101	-0	5	4.13	1	/2-8,3-1	1	0.1
Total 2	12	37	7	9	2	3	1	7	0	6	1	0	.243	.243	.541	.784	96	-1	5	3.99	0	/2-9,3-1	1	0.0

• HILLY, Pat William Edward Hilly b: 2/24/1887, Fostoria, OH d: 7/25/1953, Eureka, MO BR/TR, 5'11", 180 lbs. Deb: 5/7/1914

YEAR TM-L	G	AB	R	H	2B	3B	HR	RBI	BB	SO	SB	CS	AVG	OBP	SLG	OPS	OPS+	BR/A	RC	RC/G	FR	G/POS	WS	TPW
1914 Phi-N	8	10	2	3	0	0	0	1	1	5	0	....	.300	.364	.300	.664	92	-0	1	3.85	0	/O-4(0-0-4)	0	-0.1

• HILTON, Dave John David Hilton b: 9/15/1950, Uvalde, TX BR/TR, 5'11", 191 lbs. Deb: 9/10/1972 C

YEAR TM-L	G	AB	R	H	2B	3B	HR	RBI	BB	SO	SB	CS	AVG	OBP	SLG	OPS	OPS+	BR/A	RC	RC/G	FR	G/POS	WS	TPW
1972 SD-N	13	47	2	10	2	1	0	5	3	6	1	0	.213	.260	.298	.558	63	-2	4	2.87	-2	3-13	1	-0.5
1973 SD-N	70	234	21	46	9	0	5	16	19	35	2	1	.197	.260	.299	.559	59	-13	18	2.49	0	3-47,2-23	2	-1.3
1974 SD-N	74	217	17	52	8	2	1	12	13	28	3	5	.240	.283	.309	.591	68	-11	17	2.62	-6	3-55,2-15	2	-1.8
1975 SD-N	4	8	0	0	0	0	0	0	0	0	0	0	.000	.000	.000	.000	-107	-2	0	.00	0	/3-4	0	-0.3
Total 4	161	506	40	108	19	3	6	33	35	69	6	6	.213	.266	.298	.564	61	-29	40	2.52	-9	3-119/2-38	5	-3.8

• HIMES, Jack John Herb Himes b: 9/22/1878, Bryan, OH d: 12/16/1949, Joliet, IL BL/TR, 6'2", 180 lbs. Deb: 9/18/1905 Career OF: 1-32-19

YEAR TM-L	G	AB	R	H	2B	3B	HR	RBI	BB	SO	SB	CS	AVG	OBP	SLG	OPS	OPS+	BR/A	RC	RC/G	FR	G/POS	WS	TPW
1905 StL-N	12	41	3	6	0	0	0	0	1	....	0	....	.146	.167	.146	.313	-7	-5	1	.89	0	O-11(1-0-11)	0	-0.6
1906 StL-N	40	155	10	42	5	2	0	14	7	....	4	....	.271	.307	.329	.636	102	-0	18	3.95	4	O-40(0-32-8)	4	0.2
Total 2	52	196	13	48	5	2	0	14	8	....	4	....	.245	.278	.291	.569	79	-6	19	3.20	4	/O-51	4	-0.4

• HINCH, A.J. Andrew Jay Hinch b: 5/15/1974, Waverly, IA BR/TR, 6'1", 207 lbs. Deb: 4/1/1998

YEAR TM-L	G	AB	R	H	2B	3B	HR	RBI	BB	SO	SB	CS	AVG	OBP	SLG	OPS	OPS+	BR/A	RC	RC/G	FR	G/POS	WS	TPW
1998 Oak-A	120	337	34	78	10	0	9	35	30	89	3	0	.231	.302	.341	.643	69	-15	37	3.49	-1	*C-118	5	-0.8
1999 Oak-A	76	205	26	44	4	1	7	24	11	41	6	2	.215	.261	.346	.608	56	-14	19	2.89	-5	C-73	3	-1.3
2000 Oak-A	6	8	1	2	0	0	0	0	1	1	0	0	.250	.333	.250	.583	52	-1	1	3.39	-1	/C-5,D-1	0	-0.2
2001 KC-A	45	121	10	19	3	0	6	15	8	26	1	1	.157	.227	.331	.558	41	-11	8	1.94	-2	C-43	2	-1.0
2002 KC-A	72	197	25	49	7	1	7	27	18	35	3	3	.249	.321	.401	.722	81	-6	26	4.48	-1	C-68	4	-0.3
2003 Det-A	27	74	7	15	3	1	3	11	3	18	0	0	.203	.253	.392	.645	72	-3	7	2.74	-2	C-27	1	-0.4
Total 6	346	942	103	207	27	3	32	112	71	210	13	6	.220	.284	.357	.641	65	-50	97	3.27	-12	C-334/D-1	15	-4.0

• HINCHMAN, Bill William White Hinchman b: 4/4/1883, Philadelphia, PA d: 2/20/1963, Columbus, OH BR/TR, 5'11", 190 lbs. Deb: 9/24/1905 C Career OF: 330-61-357

YEAR TM-L	G	AB	R	H	2B	3B	HR	RBI	BB	SO	SB	CS	AVG	OBP	SLG	OPS	OPS+	BR/A	RC	RC/G	FR	G/POS	WS	TPW
1905 Cin-N	17	51	10	13	4	1	0	10	13	....	4	....	.255	.415	.373	.788	122	2	10	6.63	-2	O-12(12-0-0)/3-4,1-1	3	0.0
1906 Cin-N	18	54	7	11	1	1	0	1	8	....	2	....	.204	.306	.259	.566	73	-1	5	3.07	1	O-16(8-0-8)	1	-0.1
1907 Cle-A	152	514	62	117	19	9	1	50	47	....	15	....	.228	.311	.305	.616	96	-1	57	3.65	0	*O-148(128-14-8)/1-4,2-1	16	-1.0
1908 Cle-A	137	464	55	107	23	8	6	59	38	....	9	....	.231	.301	.353	.655	112	6	52	3.62	3	O-75(23-1-51),S-51/1-4	17	0.7
1909 Cle-A	139	457	57	118	20	13	2	53	41	....	22	....	.258	.331	.372	.703	117	9	64	4.64	-4	*O-131(87-38-6)/S-6	17	-0.2
1915 Pit-N	156	577	72	177	33	14	5	77	48	75	17	17	.307	.368	.438	.807	146	27	94	5.72	-1	*O-156(6-0-151)	24	1.9
1916 Pit-N	152	555	64	175	18	**16**	4	76	54	61	10	....	.315	.378	.427	.805	145	31	96	6.26	-9	*O-124(23-0-101),1-31	26	1.7
1917 Pit-N	69	244	27	46	5	5	2	29	33	27	5	....	.189	.288	.275	.562	70	-8	20	2.56	-2	O-48(41-8-0),1-20	3	-1.4
1918 Pit-N	50	111	10	26	5	2	0	13	15	8	1	....	.234	.336	.315	.651	96	0	12	3.54	3	O-40(2-0-32)/1-3	3	0.3
1920 Pit-N	18	16	0	3	0	0	0	1	1	3	0	0	.188	.278	.188	.465	34	-1	1	1.91	0	....	0	-0.1
Total 10	908	3043	364	793	128	69	20	369	298	174	85	17	.261	.336	.368	.704	117	64	410	4.54	-12	O-750/1-63,S-57,3-4,2-1	110	1.8

• HINCHMAN, Harry Harry Sibley Hinchman b: 8/4/1878, Philadelphia, PA d: 1/19/1933, Toledo, OH BB/TR, 5'11", 165 lbs. Deb: 7/29/1907

YEAR TM-L	G	AB	R	H	2B	3B	HR	RBI	BB	SO	SB	CS	AVG	OBP	SLG	OPS	OPS+	BR/A	RC	RC/G	FR	G/POS	WS	TPW
1907 Cle-A	15	51	3	11	3	1	0	9	5	....	2	....	.216	.286	.314	.599	90	-1	6	3.47	2	2-15	2	0.2

• HINES, Hunkey Henry Fred Hines b: 9/29/1867, Elgin, IL d: 1/2/1928, Rockford, IL BR/TR, 5'7", 165 lbs. Deb: 5/16/1895

YEAR TM-L	G	AB	R	H	2B	3B	HR	RBI	BB	SO	SB	CS	AVG	OBP	SLG	OPS	OPS+	BR/A	RC	RC/G	FR	G/POS	WS	TPW
1895 Bro-N	2	8	3	2	0	0	0	1	2	0	0	....	.250	.400	.250	.650	76	-0	1	3.69	0	/O-2(0-0-2)	0	0.0

• HINES, Mike Michael P. Hines b: 9/1862, Ireland d: 3/14/1910, New Bedford, MA BR/TL, 5'10", 176 lbs. Deb: 5/1/1883 U Career OF: 2-2-20

YEAR TM-L	G	AB	R	H	2B	3B	HR	RBI	BB	SO	SB	CS	AVG	OBP	SLG	OPS	OPS+	BR/A	RC	RC/G	FR	G/POS	WS	TPW
1883 Bos-N	63	231	38	52	13	1	0	16	7	36	....	....	.225	.248	.290	.538	61	-11	17	2.62	1	C-59/O-7(0-2-5)	5	-0.5
1884 Bos-N	35	132	16	23	3	0	0	3	3	24	....	....	.174	.193	.197	.390	23	-11	5	1.29	5	C-35	3	-0.3
1885 Bos-N	14	56	11	13	4	0	0	4	4	5	....	....	.232	.283	.304	.587	93	-0	5	3.10	-2	O-14(0-0-14)	1	-0.2
Bro-a	3	13	1	1	0	1	0	1	0	....	....	....	.077	.077	.231	.308	-6	-2	0	.53	0	/C-3	0	-0.1

YEAR TM-L	G	AB	R	H	2B	3B	HR	RBI	BB	SO	SB	CS	AVG	OBP	SLG	OPS	OPS+	BR/A	RC	RC/G	FR	G/POS	WS	TPW
Pro-N	1	3	0	0	0	0	0	0	0	2	....	....	.000	.000	.000	.000	-104	-1	0	.00	-1	/C-1	0	-0.1
Yr.	15	59	11	13	4	0	0	4	4	7	....	....	.220	.270	.288	.558	84	-1	5	2.90	-2	0-14(0-0-14)/C-1	1	-0.3
1888 Bos-N	4	16	3	2	0	1	0	2	2	0	0	....	.125	.222	.250	.472	48	-1	1	1.76	0	/0-3(2-0-1),C-1	0	-0.1
Total 4	120	451	69	91	20	3	0	26	16	67	0	....	.202	.229	.259	.489	51	-26	28	2.15	3	/C-99,0-24	9	-1.3

• HINES, Paul Paul A. Hines
b: 3/1/1852, Washington, DC d: 7/10/1935, Hyattsville, MD BR/TR, 5'9.5", 173 lbs. Deb: 4/20/1872 NA OF: 41-85-0 Career OF: 27-1218-7

YEAR TM-L	G	AB	R	H	2B	3B	HR	RBI	BB	SO	SB	CS	AVG	OBP	SLG	OPS	OPS+	BR/A	RC	RC/G	FR	G/POS	WS	TPW
1872 Nat-n	11	49	9	12	1	0	0	5	0	0	0	0	.245	.245	.265	.510	49	-4	3	2.73	-4	/1-9,3-2,C-1	....	-0.5
1873 Was-n	39	181	33	60	6	3	1	29	1	1	0	1	.331	.335	.414	.750	125	5	26	6.44	-2	*0-36(36-0-0)/2-2,C-1	....	0.3
1874 Chi-n	59	271	47	80	10	2	0	34	4	4	4	1	.295	.305	.347	.652	108	2	31	4.79	2	*0-50(1-50-0),2-11/S-2	....	0.3
1875 Chi-n	69	308	45	101	14	4	0	36	1	0	6	9	.328	.330	.399	.729	151	12	44	5.96	10	0-39(4-35-0),2-30/C-1,S-1	....	1.7
1876 Chi-N	64	306	62	101	**21**	3	2	59	1	3	....	....	.330	.333	.439	.773	139	10	46	6.28	4	*0-64(0-64-0)/2-1	12	0.9
1877 Chi-N	60	261	44	73	11	7	0	23	1	8	....	....	.280	.282	.375	.658	94	-3	28	4.15	-10	*0-49(24-18-7),2-11	6	-1.3
1878 Pro-N	62	257	42	92	13	4	**4**	**50**	2	10	....	....	.358	.363	**.486**	**.849**	177	20	47	**7.75**	4	*0-61(0-61-0)/S-1	15	2.0
1879 Pro-N	85	409	81	**146**	25	10	2	52	8	16	....	....	.357	.369	.482	.851	181	**34**	75	7.94	10	*0-85(0-85-0)	22	3.7
1880 Pro-N	85	374	64	115	20	2	3	35	13	17	....	....	.307	.331	.396	.726	150	19	50	5.33	10	*0-75(0-75-0)/2-6,1-4	19	2.4
1881 Pro-N	80	361	65	103	**27**	5	2	31	13	12	....	....	.285	.310	.404	.715	125	10	46	4.86	-2	*0-78(0-78-0)/2-4,1-1	16	0.4
1882 Pro-N	84	379	73	117	28	10	4	34	10	14	....	....	.309	.326	.467	.793	151	21	59	6.22	2	*0-82(0-82-0)/1-2	18	1.8
1883 Pro-N	97	442	94	132	32	4	4	45	18	23	....	....	.299	.326	.416	.742	120	10	62	5.46	9	*0-89(0-89-0)/1-9	17	1.3
1884*Pro-N	114	490	94	148	**36**	10	3	41	44	28	....	....	.302	.360	.435	.794	152	31	78	6.31	-1	*0-108(0-108-0)/1-7,P-1	28	2.3
1885 Pro-N	98	411	63	111	20	4	1	35	19	18	....	....	.270	.302	.345	.648	114	6	44	3.96	1	*0-92(0-92-0)/1-4,2-1,3-1,S	17	0.4
1886 Was-N	121	487	80	152	30	8	9	56	35	21	21	....	.312	.358	.462	.820	157	33	90	7.28	0	*0-92(1-91-0),3-15,1-10/S-5,2	17	2.7
1887 Was-N	123	526	83	195	32	5	10	72	48	24	46	....	.371	.380	.458	.838	139	27	103	8.27	-15	*0-109(0-109-0)/1-7,2-5,S	18	0.7
1888 Ind-N	133	513	84	144	26	3	4	58	41	45	31	....	.281	.343	.366	.710	124	15	77	5.64	-11	*0-125(0-125-0)/1-6,S-2	18	-0.1
1889 Ind-N	121	486	77	148	27	1	6	72	49	22	34	....	.305	.374	.401	.775	114	10	88	6.88	-3	*1-109,0-12(0-12-0)	14	-0.2
1890 Pit-N	31	121	11	22	1	0	0	9	11	7	6	....	.182	.256	.190	.446	34	-9	8	2.03	1	1-17,0-14(0-14-0)	0	-0.9
Bos-N	69	273	41	72	12	3	2	48	32	20	9	....	.264	.350	.352	.701	97	-1	38	4.96	-15	0-69(2-68-0)/1-1	6	-1.7
Yr.	100	394	52	94	13	3	2	57	43	27	15	....	.239	.321	.302	.623	78	-10	45	3.99	-14	0-83(2-82-0),1-18	6	-2.6
1891 Was-a	54	206	25	58	7	5	0	31	21	16	6	....	.282	.376	.364	.740	117	6	31	5.58	-6	0-47(0-47-0)/1-8	6	-0.3
Total 4 n	178	809	134	253	31	9	1	104	6	5	10	11	.313	.318	.377	.695	124	16	103	5.46	6	0-125/2-43,1-9,C-3,S-3,3-2	....	1.8
Total 16	1481	6302	1083	1929	368	84	56	751	366	304	153	....	.306	.343	.413	.756	133	238	970	6.02	-22	*0-1251,1-185/2-31,3-16,S,P	249	14.1

• HINKLE, Gordie Daniel Gordon Hinkle b: 4/3/1905, Toronto, OH d: 3/19/1972, Houston, TX BR/TR, 6', 185 lbs. Deb: 4/19/1934

YEAR TM-L	G	AB	R	H	2B	3B	HR	RBI	BB	SO	SB	CS	AVG	OBP	SLG	OPS	OPS+	BR/A	RC	RC/G	FR	G/POS	WS	TPW
1934 Bos-A	27	75	7	13	6	1	0	9	7	23	0	0	.173	.244	.280	.524	33	-8	5	2.27	0	C-26	1	-0.6

• HINSHAW, George George Addison Hinshaw b: 10/23/1959, Los Angeles, CA BR/TR, 6', 185 lbs. Deb: 9/19/1982

YEAR TM-L	G	AB	R	H	2B	3B	HR	RBI	BB	SO	SB	CS	AVG	OBP	SLG	OPS	OPS+	BR/A	RC	RC/G	FR	G/POS	WS	TPW
1982 SD-N	6	15	1	4	0	0	0	1	3	5	0	0	.267	.389	.267	.656	91	0	2	4.31	1	/0-6(1-0-5)	1	0.0
1983 SD-N	7	16	1	7	1	0	0	4	0	4	1	0	.438	.438	.500	.938	165	2	4	10.05	0	/3-5	1	0.2
Total 2	13	31	2	11	1	0	0	5	3	9	1	0	.355	.412	.387	.799	127	2	5	7.05	1	/0-6,3-5	2	0.2

• HINSKE, Eric Eric Scott Hinske b: 8/5/1977, Menasha, WI BL/TR, 6'2", 225 lbs. Deb: 4/1/2002

YEAR TM-L	G	AB	R	H	2B	3B	HR	RBI	BB	SO	SB	CS	AVG	OBP	SLG	OPS	OPS+	BR/A	RC	RC/G	FR	G/POS	WS	TPW
2002 Tor-A	151	566	99	158	38	2	24	84	77	138	13	1	.279	.367	.481	.848	119	19	104	6.57	-12	*3-148	22	0.9
2003 Tor-A	124	449	74	109	45	3	12	63	59	104	12	2	.243	.332	.437	.769	99	1	67	5.04	-17	*3-124	12	-1.4
Total 2	275	1015	173	267	83	5	36	147	136	242	25	3	.263	.352	.461	.813	110	20	170	5.87	-29	3-272	34	-0.5

• HINSON, Paul James Paul Hinson b: 5/9/1904, Vanleer, TN d: 9/23/1960, Muskogee, OK BR/TR, 5'10", 150 lbs. Deb: 4/19/1928

YEAR TM-L	G	AB	R	H	2B	3B	HR	RBI	BB	SO	SB	CS	AVG	OBP	SLG	OPS	OPS+	BR/A	RC	RC/G	FR	G/POS	WS	TPW
1928 Bos-A	3	0	1	0	0	0	0	0	0	0	0	0	....	....	....	....	-102	0	0	....	0		0	0.0

• HINTON, Chuck Charles Edward Hinton b: 5/3/1934, Rocky Mount, NC BR/TR, 6'1", 197 lbs. Deb: 5/14/1961 Career OF: 525-201-299

YEAR TM-L	G	AB	R	H	2B	3B	HR	RBI	BB	SO	SB	CS	AVG	OBP	SLG	OPS	OPS+	BR/A	RC	RC/G	FR	G/POS	WS	TPW
1961 Was-A	106	339	51	88	13	5	6	34	40	81	22	5	.260	.339	.381	.720	97	2	47	4.84	1	0-92(72-2-20)	9	-0.3
1962 Was-A	151	542	73	168	25	6	17	75	47	66	28	10	.310	.365	.472	.837	124	20	92	6.14	2	*0-136(54-28-67),2-12/S-1	17	1.6
1963 Was-A	150	566	80	152	20	12	15	55	64	79	25	9	.269	.344	.426	.770	115	13	84	4.99	-5	*0-125(86-7-45),3-19/1-6,S	20	-0.1
1964 Was-A★	138	514	71	141	25	7	11	53	57	77	17	6	.274	.348	.414	.762	112	10	71	4.74	1	*0-131(131-1-1)/3-2	16	0.3
1965 Cle-A	133	431	59	110	17	6	18	54	53	65	17	3	.255	.338	.448	.786	120	14	68	5.41	-1	0-72(33-43-4),1-40,2-23/3-1	17	1.0
1966 Cle-A	123	348	46	89	9	3	12	50	35	66	10	6	.256	.326	.402	.728	108	3	45	4.40	-5	*0-104(53-57-11)/1-6,2-2	11	-0.7
1967 Cle-A	147	498	55	122	19	3	10	37	43	100	6	8	.245	.306	.355	.662	94	-6	53	3.60	-6	*0-136(26-53-92)/2-5	11	-2.2
1968 Cal-A	116	267	28	52	10	3	7	23	24	61	3	1	.195	.261	.333	.595	82	-6	22	2.63	3	1-48,0-37(10-6-23),3-13/2-9	4	-0.7
1969 Cle-A	94	121	18	31	3	2	3	19	8	22	2	0	.256	.308	.388	.696	91	-1	15	4.21	-2	0-40(28-4-9),3-14	3	-0.4
1970 Cle-A	107	195	24	62	4	0	9	29	25	34	0	2	.318	.395	.477	.872	133	9	37	7.05	-2	1-40,0-35(17-0-22)/C-4,2-3,3	7	0.4
1971 Cle-A	88	147	13	33	7	0	5	14	20	34	0	0	.224	.317	.374	.692	87	-2	18	4.12	-1	1-20,0-20(15-0-5)/C-5	3	-0.5
Total 11	1353	3968	518	1048	152	47	113	443	416	685	130	50	.264	.335	.412	.747	108	54	553	4.77	-17	0-928,1-160/2-54,3-51,C-9,S	118	-1.7

• HINTON, John John Robert "Red" Hinton b: 6/28/1876, Pittsburgh, PA d: 8/8/1920, Braddock, PA BR/TR, 6', 200 lbs. Deb: 6/3/1901

YEAR TM-L	G	AB	R	H	2B	3B	HR	RBI	BB	SO	SB	CS	AVG	OBP	SLG	OPS	OPS+	BR/A	RC	RC/G	FR	G/POS	WS	TPW
1901 Bos-N	4	13	0	1	0	0	0	0	2	....	0	....	.077	.200	.077	.277	-17	-2	0	.45	-2	/3-4	0	-0.3

• HINZO, Tommy Thomas Lee Hinzo b: 6/18/1964, San Diego, CA BB/TR, 5'10", 170 lbs. Deb: 7/16/1987

YEAR TM-L	G	AB	R	H	2B	3B	HR	RBI	BB	SO	SB	CS	AVG	OBP	SLG	OPS	OPS+	BR/A	RC	RC/G	FR	G/POS	WS	TPW
1987 Cle-A	67	257	31	68	9	3	3	21	10	47	9	4	.265	.297	.358	.655	72	-11	26	3.39	-2	2-67	3	-0.9
1989 Cle-A	18	17	4	0	0	0	0	0	2	6	1	2	.000	.105	.000	.105	-67	-4	0	.00	-3	/2-6,D-1,S-1	0	-0.7
Total 2	85	274	35	68	9	3	3	21	12	53	10	6	.248	.285	.336	.620	63	-15	26	3.08	-5	/2-73,D-1,S-1	3	-1.6

• HISER, Gene Gene Taylor Hiser b: 12/11/1948, Baltimore, MD BL/TL, 5'11", 175 lbs. Deb: 8/20/1971 Career OF: 42-35-38

YEAR TM-L	G	AB	R	H	2B	3B	HR	RBI	BB	SO	SB	CS	AVG	OBP	SLG	OPS	OPS+	BR/A	RC	RC/G	FR	G/POS	WS	TPW
1971 Chi-N	17	29	4	6	0	0	0	1	4	8	1	0	.207	.303	.207	.510	41	-2	2	2.67	-1	/0-9(0-4-5)	0	-0.3
1972 Chi-N	32	46	2	9	0	0	0	4	6	8	1	0	.196	.288	.196	.484	36	-3	3	2.12	1	0-15(4-2-9)	0	-0.3
1973 Chi-N	100	109	15	19	3	0	1	6	11	17	4	5	.174	.256	.229	.486	33	-11	7	1.72	-1	0-64(25-22-18)	1	-1.4
1974 Chi-N	12	17	2	4	1	0	0	1	0	3	0	0	.235	.235	.294	.529	46	-1	1	2.44	0	/0-8(6-1-1)	0	-0.2
1975 Chi-N	45	62	11	15	3	0	0	6	11	7	0	1	.242	.356	.290	.646	77	-2	7	3.63	0	0-18(7-6-5)/1-1	1	-0.3
Total 5	206	263	34	53	7	0	1	18	32	43	6	6	.202	.291	.240	.530	46	-20	20	2.36	-1	0-114/1-1	2	-2.5

• HISLE, Larry Larry Eugene Hisle b: 5/5/1947, Portsmouth, OH BR/TR, 6'2", 195 lbs. Deb: 4/10/1968 C Career OF: 460-502-99

YEAR TM-L	G	AB	R	H	2B	3B	HR	RBI	BB	SO	SB	CS	AVG	OBP	SLG	OPS	OPS+	BR/A	RC	RC/G	FR	G/POS	WS	TPW
1968 Phi-N	7	11	1	4	1	0	0	1	1	4	0	0	.364	.417	.455	.871	161	1	2	8.45	0	/0-6(0-6-0)	1	0.1
1969 Phi-N	145	482	75	128	23	5	20	56	48	152	18	8	.266	.338	.459	.797	125	16	75	5.47	3	*0-140(1-139-0)	18	1.6
1970 Phi-N	126	405	52	83	22	4	10	44	53	139	5	5	.205	.302	.353	.655	77	-15	44	3.43	-5	*0-121(0-86-36)	6	-2.3
1971 Phi-N	36	76	7	15	3	0	0	3	6	22	1	0	.197	.256	.237	.493	40	-6	4	1.84	0	0-27(19-8-0)	0	-0.7
1973 Min-A	143	545	88	148	25	6	15	64	64	128	11	4	.272	.352	.422	.774	113	11	82	5.30	-2	*0-143(49-93-3)	17	0.4
1974 Min-A	143	510	68	146	20	7	19	79	48	112	12	6	.286	.357	.465	.822	130	20	83	5.67	-6	*0-137(74-52-26)	18	0.8
1975 Min-A	80	255	37	80	9	2	11	51	27	39	17	3	.314	.382	.494	.876	143	17	50	7.14	-2	0-58(37-26-9),D-14	11	1.2
1976 Min-A	155	581	81	158	19	5	14	96	56	93	31	18	.272	.340	.394	.734	111	7	77	4.42	9	*0-154(135-5-18)	19	0.8
1977 Min-A★	141	546	95	165	36	3	28	**119**	56	106	21	10	.302	.373	.533	.906	146	35	107	7.00	0	*0-134(68-65-6)/D-6	24	3.0
1978 Mil-A★	142	520	96	151	24	0	34	115	67	90	10	6	.290	.377	.533	.909	153	36	103	7.00	-1	0-87(67-22-1),D-51	23	3.1
1979 Mil-A	26	96	18	27	7	0	3	14	11	19	1	0	.281	.355	.448	.803	115	2	15	5.33	1	D-15,0-10(10-0-0)	3	0.2
1980 Mil-A	17	60	16	17	0	0	6	16	14	7	1	1	.283	.427	.583	1.010	180	7	16	9.13	0	D-17	3	0.7
1981 Mil-A	27	87	11	20	4	0	4	11	6	17	0	0	.230	.295	.414	.709	108	1	11	4.20	0	D-24	3	0.0
1982 Mil-A	9	31	7	4	0	0	2	5	5	13	0	0	.129	.250	.323	.573	60	-2	2	2.05	0	/D-8	0	-0.2
Total 14	1197	4205	652	1146	193	32	166	674	462	941	128	61	.273	.350	.452	.802	123	131	671	5.51	-2	*0-1017,D-135	146	8.6

• HITCHCOCK, Billy William Clyde Hitchcock b: 7/31/1916, Inverness, AL BR/TR, 6'1.5", 185 lbs. Deb: 4/14/1942 M/C

YEAR TM-L	G	AB	R	H	2B	3B	HR	RBI	BB	SO	SB	CS	AVG	OBP	SLG	OPS	OPS+	BR/A	RC	RC/G	FR	G/POS	WS	TPW
1942 Det-A	85	280	27	59	8	1	0	29	26	21	2	2	.211	.280	.246	.527	45	-20	20	2.27	-13	S-80/3-1	2	-2.8
1946 Det-A	3	3	0	0	0	0	0	0	1	0	0	0	.000	.250	.000	.250	-25	-0	0	.59	0	/2-1	0	0.0
Was-A	98	354	27	75	8	3	0	25	26	52	2	4	.212	.268	.251	.519	48	-26	23	2.11	-10	S-53,3-46	3	-3.4
Yr.	101	357	27	75	8	3	0	25	27	52	2	4	.210	.268	.249	.517	48	-26	23	2.09	-10	S-53,3-46/2-1	3	-3.4
1947 StL-A	80	275	25	61	2	2	1	28	21	34	3	0	.222	.277	.255	.532	47	-19	20	2.33	4	2-46,3-17/S-7,1-5	3	-1.3

YEAR TM-L	G	AB	R	H	2B	3B	HR	RBI	BB	SO	SB	CS	AVG	OBP	SLG	OPS	OPS+	BR/A	RC	RC/G	FR	G/POS	WS	TPW
1948 Bos-A	49	124	15	37	3	2	1	20	7	9	0	0	.298	.341	.379	.720	87	-3	16	4.56	3	2-15,3-15	4	0.1
1949 Bos-A	55	147	22	30	6	1	0	9	17	11	2	3	.204	.291	.259	.549	43	-13	11	2.16	-3	1-29/2-8	1	-1.6
1950 Phi-A	115	399	35	109	22	5	1	54	45	32	3	1	.273	.347	.361	.708	83	-10	45	3.72	-9	*2-107/S-1	6	-1.2
1951 Phi-A	77	222	27	68	10	4	1	36	21	23	2	0	.306	.371	.401	.772	106	3	36	6.05	0	3-45,2-23/1-1	7	0.4
1952 Phi-A	119	407	45	100	8	4	1	56	39	45	1	1	.246	.318	.292	.610	66	-17	40	3.35	-1	*3-104,1-13	7	-1.9
1953 Det-A	22	38	8	8	0	0	0	0	3	3	0	0	.211	.268	.211	.479	31	-4	2	1.22	-1	3-12/2-1,S-1	0	-0.5
Total 9	**703**	**2249**	**231**	**547**	**67**	**22**	**5**	**257**	**206**	**230**	**15**	**11**	**.243**	**.310**	**.299**	**.609**	**64**	**-108**	**212**	**3.12**	**-30**	**3-240,2-201,S-142/1-48**	**33**	**-12.2**

• HITCHCOCK, Jim James Franklin Hitchcock b: 6/28/1911, Inverness, AL d: 6/23/1959, Montgomery, AL BR/TR, 5'11", 175 lbs. Deb: 8/24/1938

YEAR TM-L	G	AB	R	H	2B	3B	HR	RBI	BB	SO	SB	CS	AVG	OBP	SLG	OPS	OPS+	BR/A	RC	RC/G	FR	G/POS	WS	TPW
1938 Bos-N	28	76	2	13	0	0	0	7	2	11	1	....	.171	.192	.171	.363	1	-10	2	.97	-4	S-24/3-2	1	-1.3

• HOAG, Myril Myril Oliver Hoag b: 3/9/1908, Davis, CA d: 7/28/1971, High Springs, FL BR/TR, 5'11", 180 lbs. Deb: 4/15/1931 Career OF: 254-334-322

YEAR TM-L	G	AB	R	H	2B	3B	HR	RBI	BB	SO	SB	CS	AVG	OBP	SLG	OPS	OPS+	BR/A	RC	RC/G	FR	G/POS	WS	TPW
1931 NY-A	44	28	6	4	2	0	0	3	1	8	0	0	.143	.172	.214	.387	1	-4	1	1.14	-1	0-23(11-2-10)/3-1	0	-0.5
1932*NY-A	46	54	18	20	5	0	1	7	7	13	1	1	.370	.443	.519	.961	156	5	12	9.40	0	0-35(27-2-9)/1-1	3	0.4
1934 NY-A	97	251	45	67	8	2	3	34	21	21	1	3	.267	.324	.351	.674	79	-9	28	3.95	3	0-86(29-17-50)	4	-0.9
1935 NY-A	48	110	13	28	4	1	1	13	12	19	4	2	.255	.328	.336	.664	76	-4	13	3.92	1	0-37(2-3-32)/3-1	2	-0.4
1936 NY-A	45	156	23	47	9	4	3	34	7	16	3	1	.301	.343	.468	.811	102	-0	25	5.87	-1	0-39(2-26-12)	4	-0.3
1937*NY-A	106	362	48	109	19	8	3	46	33	33	4	7	.301	.364	.423	.787	97	-4	55	5.47	-3	0-99(24-9-70)	10	-1.1
1938*NY-A	85	267	28	74	14	3	0	48	25	31	4	3	.277	.344	.352	.696	75	-11	33	4.40	1	0-70(31-13-28)	5	-1.2
1939 StL-A★	129	482	58	142	23	4	10	75	24	35	9	5	.295	.329	.421	.751	89	-10	62	4.53	-2	*0-117(11-49-60)/P-1	7	-1.5
1940 StL-A	76	191	20	50	11	0	3	26	13	30	2	0	.262	.309	.366	.675	73	-7	22	4.04	0	0-46(1-1-44)	2	-0.9
1941 StL-A	1	1	0	0	0	0	0	0	0	0	0	0	.000	.000	.000	.000	-97	-0	0	.00	0	....	0	0.0
Chi-A	106	380	30	97	13	3	1	44	27	29	6	10	.255	.306	.313	.620	65	-22	34	2.98	-4	0-99(75-25-0)	5	-3.0
Yr.	107	381	30	97	13	3	1	44	27	29	6	10	.255	.306	.312	.618	65	-23	34	2.97	-4	0-99(75-25-0)	5	-3.1
1942 Chi-A	113	412	47	99	18	2	2	37	36	21	17	8	.240	.301	.308	.610	73	-14	38	2.97	1	*0-112(41-81-0)	7	-1.7
1944 Chi-A	17	48	5	11	1	0	0	4	10	1	1	3	.229	.362	.250	.612	77	-2	5	2.95	0	0-14(0-13-1)	1	-0.2
Cle-A	67	277	33	79	9	3	1	27	25	23	6	4	.285	.347	.350	.697	103	1	35	4.44	-1	0-66(0-66-0)	7	-0.2
Yr.	84	325	38	90	10	3	1	31	35	24	7	7	.277	.349	.335	.684	99	-1	39	4.20	-1	0-80(0-79-1)	8	-0.4
1945 Cle-A	40	128	10	27	5	3	0	3	11	18	1	2	.211	.279	.297	.575	70	-5	11	2.80	1	0-33(0-27-6)/P-2	2	-0.5
Total 13	**1020**	**3147**	**384**	**854**	**141**	**33**	**28**	**401**	**252**	**298**	**59**	**49**	**.271**	**.328**	**.364**	**.692**	**83**	**-87**	**374**	**4.10**	**-5**	**0-876/P-3,3-2,1-1**	**59**	**-12.1**

• HOAK, Don Donald Albert "Tiger" Hoak b: 2/5/1928, Roulette, PA d: 10/9/1969, Pittsburgh, PA BR/TR, 6'1", 175 lbs. Deb: 4/18/1954 C

YEAR TM-L	G	AB	R	H	2B	3B	HR	RBI	BB	SO	SB	CS	AVG	OBP	SLG	OPS	OPS+	BR/A	RC	RC/G	FR	G/POS	WS	TPW
1954 Bro-N	88	261	41	64	9	5	7	26	25	39	8	3	.245	.321	.398	.719	83	-6	33	4.22	3	3-75	6	-0.3
1955*Bro-N	94	279	50	67	13	3	5	19	46	50	9	5	.240	.350	.362	.712	87	-4	36	4.24	12	3-78	9	0.8
1956 Chi-N	121	424	51	91	18	4	5	37	41	46	8	3	.215	.285	.311	.597	61	-22	40	3.10	-13	*3-110	5	-3.7
1957 Cin-N★	149	529	78	155	**39**	2	19	89	74	54	8	15	.293	.384	.482	.866	122	14	94	6.18	10	*3-149/2-1	22	2.4
1958 Cin-N	114	417	51	109	30	0	6	50	43	36	6	8	.261	.333	.376	.710	83	-12	50	4.08	8	*3-112/S-1	9	-0.4
1959 Pit-N	155	564	60	166	29	3	8	65	71	75	9	2	.294	.377	.399	.776	108	10	86	5.42	8	*3-155	22	1.8
1960*Pit-N	155	553	97	156	24	9	16	79	74	74	3	2	.282	.368	.445	.813	120	17	90	5.71	1	*3-155	23	1.8
1961 Pit-N	145	503	72	150	27	7	12	61	73	53	4	2	.298	.390	.451	.842	122	19	90	6.44	-7	*3-143	20	1.1
1962 Pit-N	121	411	63	99	14	8	5	48	49	49	4	2	.241	.323	.350	.674	81	-11	44	3.55	-9	*3-116	9	-2.0
1963 Phi-N	115	377	35	87	11	3	6	24	27	52	5	5	.231	.284	.324	.608	75	-13	32	2.81	3	*3-106	7	-1.1
1964 Phi-N	6	4	0	0	0	0	0	0	0	2	0	0	.000	.000	.000	.000	-101	-1	0	.00	0	....	0	-0.1
Total 11	**1263**	**4322**	**598**	**1144**	**214**	**44**	**89**	**498**	**523**	**530**	**64**	**47**	**.265**	**.347**	**.396**	**.743**	**98**	**-8**	**597**	**4.71**	**15**	***3-1199/2-1,S-1**	**132**	**0.4**

• HOBBS, Bill William Lee "Smokey" Hobbs b: 5/7/1893, Grant's Lick, KY d: 1/5/1945, Hamilton, OH BR/TR, 5'9.5", 155 lbs. Deb: 8/9/1913

YEAR TM-L	G	AB	R	H	2B	3B	HR	RBI	BB	SO	SB	CS	AVG	OBP	SLG	OPS	OPS+	BR/A	RC	RC/G	FR	G/POS	WS	TPW
1913 Cin-N	4	4	0	0	0	0	0	0	0	3	0	....	.000	.000	.000	.000	-100	-1	0	.00	0	/2-1,3-1	0	-0.1
1916 Cin-N	6	11	1	2	1	0	0	1	2	0	1	....	.182	.308	.273	.580	81	-0	1	3.50	2	/S-6	0	0.2
Total 2	**10**	**15**	**1**	**2**	**1**	**0**	**0**	**1**	**2**	**3**	**1**	**....**	**.133**	**.235**	**.200**	**.435**	**43**	**-1**	**1**	**2.57**	**2**	**/S-6,2-1,3-1**	**0**	**0.2**

• HOBLITZELL, Dick Richard Carleton "Doc" Hoblitzell b: 10/26/1888, Waverly, WV d: 11/14/1962, Parkersburg, WV BL/TL, 6', 172 lbs. Deb: 9/5/1908

YEAR TM-L	G	AB	R	H	2B	3B	HR	RBI	BB	SO	SB	CS	AVG	OBP	SLG	OPS	OPS+	BR/A	RC	RC/G	FR	G/POS	WS	TPW
1908 Cin-N	32	114	8	29	3	2	0	8	7	....	2	....	.254	.309	.316	.625	102	0	12	3.45	3	1-32	3	0.3
1909 Cin-N	142	517	59	159	23	11	4	67	44	....	17	....	.308	.364	.418	.782	144	25	86	5.76	-4	*1-142	23	2.0
1910 Cin-N	155	611	85	170	24	13	4	70	47	32	28	....	.278	.332	.380	.712	112	7	85	4.84	-6	*1-148/2-7	18	-0.2
1911 Cin-N	158	622	81	180	19	13	11	91	42	44	32	....	.289	.342	.415	.757	116	10	98	5.51	-4	*1-158	18	0.4
1912 Cin-N	148	558	73	164	32	12	2	85	48	28	23	....	.294	.352	.405	.757	110	7	88	5.34	-1	*1-147	19	0.2
1913 Cin-N	137	502	59	143	23	7	3	62	35	26	18	....	.285	.334	.376	.710	103	1	67	4.53	-4	*1-134	12	-0.6
1914 Cin-N	78	248	31	52	8	7	0	26	26	26	7	....	.210	.287	.298	.586	72	-9	24	2.93	-5	1-75	3	-1.6
Bos-A	69	229	31	73	10	3	0	33	19	21	12	12	.319	.386	.389	.774	133	7	35	5.25	-3	1-68	10	0.2
1915*Bos-A	124	399	54	113	15	12	2	61	38	26	9	14	.283	.351	.396	.747	128	8	57	4.60	1	*1-117	16	0.7
1916*Bos-A	130	417	57	108	17	1	0	39	47	28	10	....	.259	.338	.305	.643	93	-2	50	3.91	1	*1-126	13	-0.4
1917 Bos-A	120	420	49	108	19	7	1	47	46	22	12	....	.257	.336	.343	.679	108	4	53	4.09	-2	*1-118	14	0.1
1918 Bos-A	25	69	4	11	1	0	0	4	8	3	3	....	.159	.266	.174	.440	33	-5	4	1.75	2	1-19	0	-0.3
Total 11	**1318**	**4706**	**591**	**1310**	**194**	**88**	**27**	**593**	**407**	**256**	**173**	**26**	**.278**	**.341**	**.374**	**.715**	**111**	**53**	**659**	**4.69**	**-21**	***1-1284/2-7**	**149**	**0.9**

• HOBSON, Butch Clell Lavern Hobson b: 8/17/1951, Tuscaloosa, AL BR/TR, 6'1", 193 lbs. Deb: 9/7/1975 M

YEAR TM-L	G	AB	R	H	2B	3B	HR	RBI	BB	SO	SB	CS	AVG	OBP	SLG	OPS	OPS+	BR/A	RC	RC/G	FR	G/POS	WS	TPW
1975 Bos-A	2	4	0	1	0	0	0	0	0	2	0	0	.250	.250	.250	.500	38	-0	0	2.25	0	/3-1	0	0.0
1976 Bos-A	76	269	34	63	7	5	8	34	15	62	0	1	.234	.275	.387	.661	82	-7	26	3.20	-4	3-76	4	-1.2
1977 Bos-A	159	593	77	157	33	5	30	112	27	162	5	4	.265	.301	.489	.790	99	-3	80	4.61	-29	*3-159	13	-3.4
1978 Bos-A	147	512	65	128	26	2	17	80	50	122	1	0	.250	.317	.408	.725	93	-5	65	4.25	-14	*3-133,D-14	11	-2.1
1979 Bos-A	146	528	74	138	26	7	28	93	30	78	3	2	.261	.301	.496	.797	105	1	70	4.40	-22	*3-142/2-1	11	-2.2
1980 Bos-A	93	324	35	74	6	0	11	39	25	69	1	1	.228	.284	.349	.632	69	-15	30	3.10	-10	3-57,D-36	2	-2.6
1981 Cal-A	85	268	27	63	7	4	4	36	35	60	1	1	.235	.326	.336	.661	91	-2	31	3.90	-12	3-83/D-2	6	-1.6
1982 NY-A	30	58	2	10	2	0	0	3	1	14	0	0	.172	.186	.207	.393	8	-7	2	1.01	-1	D-15,1-11	0	-0.9
Total 8	**738**	**2556**	**314**	**634**	**107**	**23**	**98**	**397**	**183**	**569**	**11**	**9**	**.248**	**.300**	**.423**	**.722**	**90**	**-39**	**305**	**3.98**	**-91**	**3-651/D-67,1-11,2-1**	**47**	**-14.1**

• HOCK, Ed Edward Francis Hock b: 3/27/1899, Franklin Furnace, OH d: 11/21/1963, Portsmouth, OH BL/TL, 5'10.5", 165 lbs. Deb: 7/8/1920 Career OF: 2-2-0

YEAR TM-L	G	AB	R	H	2B	3B	HR	RBI	BB	SO	SB	CS	AVG	OBP	SLG	OPS	OPS+	BR/A	RC	RC/G	FR	G/POS	WS	TPW
1920 StL-N	1	0	0	0	0	0	0	0	0	0	0	0	....	....	....	....	-102	0	0	....	0	/0-1	0	0.0
1923 Cin-N	2	0	0	0	0	0	0	0	0	0	0	0	....	....	....	....	-102	0	0	....	0	....	0	0.0
1924 Cin-N	16	10	7	1	0	0	0	0	0	2	0	0	.100	.182	.100	.282	-23	-2	0	.65	0	/0-2(1-2-0)	0	-0.2
Total 3	**19**	**10**	**7**	**1**	**0**	**0**	**0**	**0**	**0**	**2**	**0**	**0**	**.100**	**.182**	**.100**	**.282**	**-23**	**-2**	**0**	**.65**	**0**	**/0-3**	**0**	**-0.2**

• HOCKETT, Oris Oris Leon "Brown" Hockett b: 9/29/1909, Amboy, IN d: 3/23/1969, Torrance, CA BL/TR, 5'9", 182 lbs. Deb: 9/4/1938 Career OF: 85-269-171

YEAR TM-L	G	AB	R	H	2B	3B	HR	RBI	BB	SO	SB	CS	AVG	OBP	SLG	OPS	OPS+	BR/A	RC	RC/G	FR	G/POS	WS	TPW
1938 Bro-N	21	70	8	23	5	1	1	8	4	9	0	....	.329	.365	.471	.836	125	2	13	7.31	-2	0-17(4-13-0)	3	0.0
1939 Bro-N	9	13	3	3	0	0	0	1	1	1	0	....	.231	.286	.231	.516	39	-1	1	2.51	1	/0-1	0	-0.1
1941 Cle-A	2	6	0	2	0	0	0	1	2	0	0	0	.333	.500	.333	.833	130	1	1	8.67	0	/0-2(0-2-0)	0	0.0
1942 Cle-A	148	601	85	150	22	7	7	48	45	45	12	12	.250	.305	.344	.650	88	-14	63	3.55	-1	*0-145(0-2-144)	13	-2.4
1943 Cle-A	141	601	70	166	33	4	2	51	45	45	13	18	.276	.331	.354	.685	107	-1	69	4.01	4	*0-139(35-81-26)	18	-0.3
1944 Cle-A★	124	457	47	132	29	5	1	50	35	27	8	9	.289	.339	.381	.720	110	3	59	4.60	-3	*0-110(45-65-1)	11	-0.4
1945 Chi-A	106	417	46	122	23	4	2	55	27	30	10	9	.293	.340	.381	.721	112	4	52	4.39	-1	*0-106(0-106-0)	13	0.0
Total 7	**551**	**2165**	**259**	**598**	**112**	**21**	**13**	**214**	**159**	**157**	**43**	**48**	**.276**	**.329**	**.365**	**.694**	**103**	**-6**	**258**	**4.17**	**-2**	**0-520**	**58**	**-3.2**

• HOCKING, Dennis Dennis Lee Hocking b: 4/2/1970, Torrance, CA BB/TR, 5'10", 176 lbs. Deb: 9/10/1993 Career OF: 65-43-97

YEAR TM-L	G	AB	R	H	2B	3B	HR	RBI	BB	SO	SB	CS	AVG	OBP	SLG	OPS	OPS+	BR/A	RC	RC/G	FR	G/POS	WS	TPW
1993 Min-A	15	36	7	5	1	0	0	0	6	8	1	0	.139	.262	.167	.429	18	-4	2	1.62	1	S-12/2-1	0	-0.2
1994 Min-A	11	31	3	10	3	0	0	2	0	4	2	0	.323	.323	.419	.742	89	-0	4	5.00	2	S-10	1	0.2
1995 Min-A	9	25	4	5	0	2	0	3	2	2	1	0	.200	.259	.360	.619	59	-1	2	2.71	1	/S-6	0	0.0
1996 Min-A	49	127	16	25	6	0	1	10	8	24	3	3	.197	.244	.268	.512	29	-15	8	1.87	0	0-33(0-0-33)/S-6,2-2,1-1,D	1	-1.4
1997 Min-A	115	253	28	65	12	4	2	25	18	51	3	5	.257	.309	.360	.669	73	-12	26	3.48	3	S-44,3-39,0-20(7-2-12),2-15/1,D	6	-0.6
1998 Min-A	110	198	32	40	6	1	3	15	16	44	2	1	.202	.262	.288	.550	42	-17	16	2.54	-2	2-47,S-28,0-24(17-1-7),3-11/1,D	2	-1.7
1999 Min-A	136	386	47	103	18	2	7	41	22	54	11	7	.267	.311	.378	.690	72	-18	43	3.75	-2	S-61,2-56,0-38(17-11-13)/3,1	8	-1.5

YEAR TM-L	G	AB	R	H	2B	3B	HR	RBI	BB	SO	SB	CS	AVG	OBP	SLG	OPS	OPS+	BR/A	RC	RC/G	FR	G/POS	WS	TPW
2000 Min-A	134	373	52	111	24	4	4	47	48	77	7	5	.298	.378	.416	.793	97	-1	62	5.97	-3	0-51(16-21-19),2-47,3-16,S,1/D	11	-0.2
2001 Min-A	112	327	34	82	16	2	3	25	29	67	6	1	.251	.316	.339	.655	71	-13	36	3.77	3	S-47,2-17,0-16(6-5-5),1-11/D,3	5	-0.7
2002*Min-A	102	260	28	65	13	0	2	25	24	44	0	2	.250	.316	.323	.639	70	-12	28	3.55	-4	2-56,S-25,3-16/1-6,0-5(0-1-4)	5	-1.1
2003*Min-A	83	188	22	45	10	2	3	22	15	37	0	1	.239	.296	.362	.657	72	-8	20	3.55	6	2-25,3-24,S-17,1-10/0-8(2-2-4),D	4	-0.1
Total 11	876	2204	273	556	109	17	25	215	188	412	36	25	.252	.313	.351	.664	70	-102	247	3.77	7	S-271,2-266,0-195,3-118/1,D	43	-7.3
• HODAPP, Johnny	Urban John Hodapp b: 9/26/1905, Cincinnati, OH d: 6/14/1980, Cincinnati, OH BR/TR, 6', 185 lbs. Deb: 8/19/1925																							
1925 Cle-A	37	130	12	31	5	1	0	14	11	7	2	3	.238	.298	.292	.590	50	-11	11	2.82	2	3-37	1	-0.6
1926 Cle-A	3	5	0	1	0	0	0	0	0	1	0	0	.200	.200	.200	.400	4	-1	0	1.27	0	/3-3	0	-0.1
1927 Cle-A	79	240	25	73	15	3	5	40	14	23	2	2	.304	.343	.454	.797	104	0	37	5.52	0	3-67/1-4	8	0.4
1928 Cle-A	116	449	51	145	31	6	2	73	20	20	2	1	.323	.352	.432	.784	104	2	68	5.65	-7	*3-101,1-13	12	0.0
1929 Cle-A	90	294	30	96	12	7	4	51	15	14	3	3	.327	.361	.456	.817	105	1	47	6.05	1	2-72	10	0.4
1930 Cle-A	154	635	111	**225**	**51**	8	9	121	32	29	6	5	.354	.386	.502	.889	119	17	120	7.35	-5	*2-154	25	1.4
1931 Cle-A	122	468	71	138	19	4	2	56	27	23	1	5	.295	.336	.365	.701	80	-14	56	4.39	-4	*2-121	10	-1.0
1932 Cle-A	7	16	2	2	1	0	0	0	0	2	0	0	.125	.125	.188	.313	-19	-3	0	.71	-0	/2-7	0	-0.3
Chi-A	68	176	21	40	8	0	3	20	11	3	1	0	.227	.273	.324	.597	58	-11	16	3.06	-5	0-31(29-0-2)/2-5,3-4	1	-1.5
Yr.	75	192	23	42	9	0	3	20	11	5	1	0	.219	.261	.313	.574	51	-14	16	2.81	-5	0-31(29-0-2),2-12/3-4	1	-1.8
1933 Bos-A	115	413	55	129	27	5	3	54	33	14	1	1	.312	.365	.424	.788	109	6	64	5.88	-4	*2-101,1-10	12	0.7
Total 9	791	2826	378	880	169	34	28	429	163	136	18	20	.311	.350	.425	.775	98	-13	420	5.49	-21	2-460,3-212/0-31,1-27	79	-0.5
• HODERLEIN, Mel	Melvin Anthony Hoderlein b: 6/26/1923, Mount Carmel, OH d: 5/21/2001, Mount Carmel, OH BB/TR, 5'10", 185 lbs. Deb: 8/16/1951																							
1951 Bos-A	9	14	1	5	1	1	0	1	6	2	0	1	.357	.550	.571	1.121	185	2	4	9.91	-1	/2-3,3-3	1	0.1
1952 Was-A	72	208	16	56	8	2	0	17	18	22	2	0	.269	.333	.327	.660	87	-3	20	3.08	2	2-58	5	0.3
1953 Was-A	23	47	5	9	0	0	0	5	6	9	0	0	.191	.283	.191	.475	31	-4	3	1.79	1	2-11/S-2	1	-0.3
1954 Was-A	14	25	0	4	1	0	0	1	1	4	0	0	.160	.192	.200	.392	8	-3	1	1.30	-2	/S-6,2-5	0	-0.5
Total 4	118	294	22	74	10	3	0	24	31	37	2	1	.252	.327	.306	.633	78	-8	28	3.05	0	/2-77,S-8,3-3	7	-0.4
• HODES, Charlie	Charles Hodes b: 1848, New York, NY d: 2/14/1875, Brooklyn, NY TR, 5'11.5", 175 lbs. Deb: 5/8/1871 U NA OF: 0-20-6																							
1871 Chi-n	28	130	32	36	4	1	2	25	7	0	3	0	.277	.314	.369	.683	86	-4	16	5.50	1	*C-20,3-10/0-4(0-3-1),S-1	....	-0.2
1872 Tro-n	13	61	17	15	3	0	0	12	1	0	0	0	.246	.258	.295	.553	69	-2	5	3.21	2	/S-5,0-4(0-4-0),C-3,3-1	....	-0.1
1874 Atl-n	21	81	8	12	3	0	0	7	0	2	0	0	.148	.148	.185	.333	7	-7	2	.99	-1	0-18(0-13-5)/2-3,C-3,1-1	....	-0.6
Total 3 n	62	272	57	63	10	1	2	44	8	2	3	0	.232	.254	.298	.551	59	-13	23	3.51	1	/C-26,0-26,3-11,S-6,2-3,1-1	....	-0.9
• HODGE, Gomer	Harold Morris Hodge b: 4/3/1944, Rutherfordton, NC BB/TR, 6'2", 185 lbs. Deb: 4/6/1971																							
1971 Cle-A	80	83	3	17	3	0	1	9	4	19	0	0	.205	.258	.277	.536	47	-6	6	2.27	0	/1-3,3-3,2-2	0	-0.7
• HODGES, Bert	Edward Burton Hodges b: 5/25/1917, Knoxville, TN d: 1/8/2001, Knoxville, TN BL/TR, 5'11", 170 lbs. Deb: 4/14/1942																							
1942 Phi-N	8	11	0	2	0	0	0	0	1	0	0	....	.182	.250	.182	.432	29	-1	0	1.02	0	/3-2	0	-0.1
• HODGES, Gil	Gilbert Raymond Hodges b: 4/4/1924, Princeton, IN d: 4/2/1972, West Palm Beach, FL BR/TR, 6'1.5", 200 lbs. Deb: 10/3/1943 M Career OF: 53-1-25																							
1943 Bro-N	1	2	0	0	0	0	0	0	1	2	1	....	.000	.333	.000	.333		-0	0	1.17	0	/3-1	0	0.0
1947*Bro-N	28	77	9	12	3	1	1	7	14	19	0	....	.156	.286	.260	.545	44	-6	6	2.37	0	C-24	1	-0.5
1948 Bro-N	134	481	48	120	18	5	11	70	43	61	7	....	.249	.311	.376	.687	82	-13	56	4.02	-6	1-96,C-38	10	-2.0
1949*Bro-N★	156	596	94	170	23	4	23	115	66	64	10	....	.285	.360	.453	.813	112	10	99	5.92	-3	*1-156	21	0.2
1950 Bro-N★	153	561	98	159	26	2	32	113	73	73	6	....	.283	.367	.508	.875	125	20	105	6.64	-8	*1-153	21	0.6
1951 Bro-N★	158	582	118	156	25	3	40	103	93	99	9	7	.268	.374	.527	.901	137	30	119	7.17	2	*1-158	26	2.7
1952*Bro-N★	153	508	87	129	27	1	32	102	107	90	2	4	.254	.386	.500	.886	142	32	106	7.24	6	*1-153	26	3.3
1953*Bro-N★	141	520	101	157	22	7	31	122	75	84	1	4	.302	.393	.550	.943	139	30	119	8.67	9	*1-127,0-24(18-0-6)	25	2.9
1954 Bro-N★	154	579	106	176	23	5	42	130	74	84	3	3	.304	.384	.579	.962	142	35	128	7.79	10	*1-154	29	3.5
1955*Bro-N★	150	546	75	158	24	5	27	102	80	91	2	1	.289	.383	.500	.883	128	25	105	6.80	6	*1-139,0-16(9-1-6)	23	2.2
1956*Bro-N	153	550	86	146	29	4	32	87	76	91	3	3	.265	.355	.507	.862	119	15	97	6.07	-1	*1-138,0-30(22-0-8)/C-1	21	0.6
1957 Bro-N★	150	579	94	173	28	7	27	98	63	91	5	3	.299	.370	.511	.881	122	19	109	6.86	0	*1-150/3-2,2-1	21	1.0
1958 LA-N	141	475	68	123	15	1	22	64	52	87	8	2	.259	.332	.434	.766	97	-1	67	4.83	-6	*1-122,3-15/0-9(4-0-5),C-1	12	-1.3
1959*LA-N	124	413	57	114	19	2	25	80	58	92	3	2	.276	.369	.513	.883	123	14	77	6.50	-2	*1-113/3-4	17	0.6
1960 LA-N	101	197	22	39	8	1	8	30	26	37	0	1	.198	.295	.371	.665	76	-7	22	3.42	-1	1-92,3-10	3	-1.1
1961 LA-N	109	215	25	52	4	0	8	31	24	43	3	1	.242	.318	.372	.690	76	-7	26	4.00	-2	*1-100	5	-1.3
1962 NY-N	54	127	15	32	1	0	9	17	15	27	0	0	.252	.331	.472	.803	111	2	19	5.26	1	1-47	2	0.1
1963 NY-N	11	22	2	5	0	0	0	3	3	2	0	0	.227	.320	.227	.547	60	-1	2	2.94	1	1-10	0	0.0
Total 18	2071	7030	1105	1921	295	48	370	1274	943	1137	63	31	.273	.361	.487	.848	119	195	1261	6.29	7	*1-1908/0-79,C-64,3-32,2-1	263	11.5
• HODGES, Ron	Ronald Wray Hodges b: 6/22/1949, Rocky Mount, VA BL/TR, 6'1", 185 lbs. Deb: 6/13/1973																							
1973*NY-N	45	127	5	33	2	0	1	18	11	19	0	1	.260	.319	.299	.618	73	-5	11	2.84	0	C-40	4	-0.3
1974 NY-N	59	136	16	30	4	0	4	14	19	11	0	0	.221	.316	.338	.654	84	-3	15	3.74	-6	C-44	2	-0.7
1975 NY-N	9	34	3	7	1	0	2	4	1	6	0	0	.206	.229	.412	.640	78	-1	3	2.61	1	/C-9	1	0.0
1976 NY-N	56	155	21	35	6	0	4	24	27	16	2	0	.226	.341	.342	.683	100	1	19	4.16	-3	C-52	5	0.0
1977 NY-N	66	117	6	31	4	0	1	5	9	17	0	2	.265	.317	.325	.642	76	-5	12	3.71	2	C-27	2	-0.2
1978 NY-N	47	102	4	26	4	1	0	7	10	11	1	2	.255	.327	.314	.641	83	-3	10	3.16	2	C-30	2	0.1
1979 NY-N	59	86	4	14	4	0	0	5	19	16	0	0	.163	.314	.209	.524	47	-5	7	2.61	2	C-22	1	-0.2
1980 NY-N	36	42	4	10	2	0	0	5	10	13	1	1	.238	.385	.286	.670	92	0	5	3.98	1	/C-9	1	0.1
1981 NY-N	35	43	5	13	2	0	1	6	5	8	1	0	.302	.375	.419	.794	127	2	7	6.51	0	/C-7	1	0.2
1982 NY-N	80	228	26	56	12	1	5	27	41	40	4	3	.246	.361	.373	.733	106	3	32	4.65	-1	C-74	9	0.6
1983 NY-N	110	250	20	65	12	0	0	21	49	42	0	3	.260	.385	.308	.693	95	0	31	4.22	-1	C-96	6	0.3
1984 NY-N	64	106	5	22	3	0	1	11	23	18	1	1	.208	.354	.264	.618	77	-2	11	3.42	0	C-35	4	0.0
Total 12	666	1426	119	342	56	2	19	147	224	217	10	13	.240	.345	.322	.666	88	-18	165	3.84	-3	C-445	38	-0.2
• HODGIN, Ralph	Elmer Ralph Hodgin b: 2/10/1916, Greensboro, NC BL/TR, 5'10", 170 lbs. Deb: 4/19/1939 Career OF: 180-2-81																							
1939 Bos-N	32	48	4	10	1	0	0	4	3	4	0	....	.208	.255	.229	.484	33	-4	2	1.52	0	/0-9(2-0-7)	0	-0.5
1943 Chi-A	117	407	52	128	22	8	1	50	20	24	3	5	.314	.356	.415	.771	125	10	59	5.44	-2	3-56,0-42(17-0-25)	18	0.7
1944 Chi-A	121	465	56	137	25	7	1	51	21	14	3	1	.295	.333	.385	.718	106	3	60	4.66	12	3-82,0-33(33-0-0)	17	1.4
1946 Chi-A	87	258	32	65	10	1	0	25	19	6	0	1	.252	.308	.298	.607	73	-10	23	2.98	0	0-57(49-0-8)	3	-1.4
1947 Chi-A	59	180	26	53	10	3	1	24	13	4	1	0	.294	.352	.400	.752	113	3	25	5.06	1	0-41(40-0-1)	6	0.1
1948 Chi-A	114	331	28	88	11	5	1	34	21	11	0	3	.266	.310	.338	.648	75	-14	33	3.45	3	0-79(39-2-40)	4	-1.5
Total 6	530	1689	198	481	79	24	4	188	97	63	7	10	.285	.330	.367	.697	98	-12	203	4.26	13	0-261,3-138	48	-1.3
• HODGSON, Paul	Paul Joseph Denis Hodgson b: 4/14/1960, Montreal, Canada BR/TR, 6'2", 190 lbs. Deb: 8/31/1980																							
1980 Tor-A	20	41	5	9	0	1	1	5	3	12	0	1	.220	.273	.341	.614	64	-3	3	2.26	0	0-11(10-1-0)/D-3	0	-0.3
• HOELSKOETTER, Art	Arthur H. "Holley,Hoss" Hoelskoetter b: 9/30/1882, St. Louis, MO d: 8/3/1954, St. Louis, MO BR/TR, 6'2" Deb: 9/10/1905 Career OF: 1-7-13																							
1905 StL-N	24	83	7	20	2	1	0	5	3	....	1	....	.241	.267	.289	.557	68	-3	7	2.84	1	3-20/2-3,P-1	2	-0.1
1906 StL-N	94	317	21	71	6	3	0	14	4	....	2	....	.224	.238	.262	.500	58	-15	22	2.22	-3	3-53,S-16,0-12(1-1-11),P-12/2	3	-3.2
1907 StL-N	119	397	21	98	6	3	2	28	27	....	5	....	.247	.298	.292	.590	88	-6	38	3.22	-8	2-73,1-27/C-8,0-8(0-6-2),3,P	8	-1.9
1908 StL-N	62	155	10	36	7	1	0	6	6	....	1	....	.232	.265	.290	.556	81	-4	13	2.56	-1	C-41/3-2,1-1,2-1	2	-0.1
Total 4	299	952	59	225	21	8	2	53	40	....	9	....	.236	.271	.282	.552	76	-28	79	2.74	-12	/2-78,3-77,C-49,1-28,0-20,S,P	15	-5.3
• HOEY, Jack	John Bernard Hoey b: 11/10/1881, Watertown, MA d: 11/14/1947, Waterbury, CT BL/TL, 5'9", 185 lbs. Deb: 6/27/1906 Career OF: 111-4-11																							
1906 Bos-A	94	361	27	88	8	4	0	24	14	....	10	....	.244	.274	.288	.562	76	-11	34	3.11	-8	0-94(94-0-0)	3	-2.6
1907 Bos-A	39	96	7	21	2	1	0	8	1	....	2	....	.219	.227	.260	.487	56	-5	6	2.23	-5	0-21(17-4-0)	0	-1.2
1908 Bos-A	13	43	5	7	0	0	0	3	0	....	1	....	.163	.163	.163	.326	6	-5	1	.88	1	0-11(0-0-11)	0	-0.5
Total 3	146	500	39	116	10	5	0	35	15	....	13	....	.232	.256	.272	.528	66	-20	41	2.73	-12	0-126	3	-4.3

YEAR TM-L	G	AB	R	H	2B	3B	HR	RBI	BB	SO	SB	CS	AVG	OBP	SLG	OPS	OPS+	BR/A	RC	RC/G	FR	G/POS	WS	TPW
• HOFFERTH, Stew	Stewart Edward Hofferth b: 1/27/1913, Logansport, IN d: 3/7/1994, Valparaiso, IN BR/TR, 6'2", 195 lbs. Deb: 4/19/1944																							
1944 Bos-N	66	180	14	36	8	0	1	26	11	5	0	....	.200	.246	.261	.507	41	-14	10	1.86	0	C-47	2	-1.2
1945 Bos-N	50	170	13	40	2	0	3	15	14	11	1	....	.235	.297	.300	.597	66	-8	15	3.13	5	C-45	3	0.0
1946 Bos-N	20	58	3	12	1	1	0	10	3	6	0	....	.207	.246	.259	.505	43	-5	4	2.04	-1	C-15	0	-0.6
Total 3	**136**	**408**	**30**	**88**	**11**	**1**	**4**	**51**	**28**	**22**	**1**	**....**	**.216**	**.268**	**.277**	**.545**	**52**	**-27**	**30**	**2.39**	**3**	**C-107**	**5**	**-1.8**
• HOFFMAN, Danny	Daniel John Hoffman b: 3/2/1880, Canton, CT d: 3/14/1922, Manchester, CT BL/TL, 5'9", 175 lbs. Deb: 4/20/1903 Career OF: 77-636-96																							
1903 Phi-A	74	248	29	61	5	7	2	22	6	....	7	....	.246	.267	.347	.613	79	-7	26	3.58	-1	0-62(43-0-19)/P-1	4	-1.2
1904 Phi-A	53	204	31	61	7	5	3	24	5	....	9	....	.299	.329	.426	.755	131	6	33	5.87	-1	0-51(14-14-23)	9	0.4
1905*Phi-A	120	459	66	120	10	10	1	35	33	....	**46**	....	.261	.312	.333	.646	103	1	66	4.87	-6	*0-118(14-102-2)	16	-1.2
1906 Phi-A	7	22	4	5	0	0	0	0	3	....	1	....	.227	.320	.227	.547	70	-1	3	3.19	1	/0-7(0-7-0)	1	0.0
NY-A	100	320	34	82	10	6	0	23	27	....	32	....	.256	.318	.325	.643	92	-3	45	4.85	-6	0-98(0-98-0)	11	-1.4
Yr.	107	342	38	87	10	6	0	23	30	....	33	....	.254	.318	.319	.637	90	-3	48	4.72	-5	*0-105(0-105-0)	12	-1.4
1907 NY-A	136	517	81	131	10	3	5	46	42	....	30	....	.253	.325	.313	.639	96	-1	65	4.37	-2	*0-135(0-135-0)	19	-1.0
1908 StL-A	99	363	41	91	9	7	1	25	23	....	17	....	.251	.304	.322	.627	103	1	40	3.72	11	0-99(6-46-47)	13	0.8
1909 StL-A	110	387	44	104	6	7	2	26	41	....	24	....	.269	.349	.336	.685	125	13	53	4.78	-2	*0-110(0-109-1)	17	0.7
1910 StL-A	106	380	20	90	11	5	0	27	34	....	16	....	.237	.306	.292	.598	93	-2	38	3.36	-2	*0-106(0-102-4)	10	-1.1
1911 StL-A	24	81	11	17	3	2	0	7	12	....	3	....	.210	.326	.296	.623	77	-2	9	3.48	2	0-23(0-23-0)	2	-0.2
Total 9	**829**	**2981**	**361**	**762**	**71**	**52**	**14**	**235**	**226**	**....**	**185**	**....**	**.256**	**.316**	**.328**	**.645**	**101**	**6**	**378**	**4.33**	**-7**	**0-809/P-1**	**102**	**-4.3**
• HOFFMAN, Dutch	Clarence Casper "Red" Hoffman b: 1/28/1904, Freeburg, IL d: 12/6/1962, Belleville, IL BR/TR, 6', 175 lbs. Deb: 4/23/1929																							
1929 Chi-A	107	337	27	87	16	5	3	37	24	28	6	3	.258	.307	.362	.669	72	-14	38	3.87	0	0-88(2-74-12)	7	-1.7
• HOFFMAN, Glenn	Glenn Edward Hoffman b: 7/7/1958, Orange, CA BR/TR, 6'1", 190 lbs. Deb: 4/12/1980 M/C																							
1980 Bos-A	114	312	37	89	15	4	4	42	19	41	2	4	.285	.330	.397	.728	94	-4	39	4.22	-7	*3-110/S-5,2-2	6	-1.2
1981 Bos-A	78	242	28	56	10	0	1	20	12	25	0	1	.231	.271	.285	.556	57	-14	18	2.38	0	S-78/3-1	3	-0.6
1982 Bos-A	150	469	53	98	23	2	7	49	30	69	0	4	.209	.264	.311	.575	54	-32	35	2.38	5	*S-150	9	-1.2
1983 Bos-A	143	473	56	123	24	1	4	41	30	76	1	1	.260	.307	.340	.647	73	-18	51	3.71	3	*S-143	12	0.0
1984 Bos-A	64	74	8	14	4	0	0	4	5	10	0	1	.189	.241	.243	.484	33	-7	4	1.54	-5	S-56/3-4,2-2	0	-0.9
1985 Bos-A	96	279	40	77	17	2	6	34	25	40	2	2	.276	.346	.416	.762	103	1	40	4.92	-5	S-93/2-3,3-3	8	0.5
1986 Bos-A	12	23	1	5	2	0	0	1	2	3	0	0	.217	.280	.304	.584	59	-1	2	2.50	-2	S-11/3-1	0	-0.3
1987 Bos-A	21	55	5	11	3	0	0	6	3	9	0	0	.200	.267	.255	.521	38	-5	4	2.10	-2	S-16/3-3,2-2	1	-0.5
LA-N	40	132	10	29	5	0	0	10	7	23	0	1	.220	.270	.258	.527	42	-12	9	2.09	-2	S-40	1	-1.0
1989 Cal-A	48	104	9	22	3	0	1	3	3	13	0	2	.212	.241	.269	.510	44	-9	6	1.94	-0	S-23,3-18/2-4,1-1,D-1	1	-0.8
Total 9	**766**	**2163**	**247**	**524**	**106**	**9**	**23**	**210**	**136**	**309**	**5**	**16**	**.242**	**.293**	**.331**	**.625**	**68**	**-100**	**207**	**3.16**	**-16**	**S-615,3-140/2-13,1-1,D-1**	**41**	**-6.1**
• HOFFMAN, Hickey	Otto Charles Hoffman b: 10/27/1856, Cleveland, OH d: 10/27/1915, Peoria, IL Deb: 5/10/1879																							
1879 Cle-N	2	6	0	0	0	0	0	0	0	3	....	....	.000	.000	.000	.000	-101	-1	0	.00	0	/C-2,0-1	0	-0.1
• HOFFMAN, Izzy	Harry C. Hoffman b: 1/5/1875, Bridgeport, NJ d: 11/13/1942, Philadelphia, PA BL/TL, 5'9", 160 lbs. Deb: 4/14/1904 Career OF: 3-10-16																							
1904 Was-A	10	30	1	3	1	0	0	1	2	....	0	....	.100	.156	.133	.290	-8	-4	1	.70	0	/0-9(0-9-0)	0	-0.4
1907 Bos-N	19	86	17	24	3	1	0	3	6	....	2	....	.279	.326	.337	.663	108	1	10	4.35	-1	0-19(3-1-16)	3	-0.1
Total 2	**29**	**116**	**18**	**27**	**4**	**1**	**0**	**4**	**8**	**....**	**2**	**....**	**.233**	**.282**	**.284**	**.567**	**78**	**-3**	**11**	**3.21**	**-1**	**/0-28**	**3**	**-0.6**
• HOFFMAN, John	John Edward "Pork Chop" Hoffman b: 10/31/1943, Aberdeen, SD d: 12/27/2001, Seattle, WA BL/TR, 6', 190 lbs. Deb: 7/30/1964																							
1964 Hou-N	6	15	1	1	0	0	0	0	1	7	0	0	.067	.125	.067	.192	-47	-3	0	.14	0	/C-5	0	-0.3
1965 Hou-N	2	6	1	2	0	0	0	1	0	3	0	0	.333	.333	.333	.667	95	-0	1	4.50	0	/C-2	0	0.0
Total 2	**8**	**21**	**2**	**3**	**0**	**0**	**0**	**1**	**1**	**10**	**0**	**0**	**.143**	**.182**	**.143**	**.325**	**-8**	**-3**	**1**	**1.06**	**0**	**/C-7**	**0**	**-0.3**
• HOFFMAN, Larry	Lawrence Charles Hoffman b: 7/18/1882, Chicago, IL d: 12/29/1948, Chicago, IL BR/TR Deb: 7/4/1901																							
1901 Chi-N	6	22	2	7	1	0	0	6	0	....	1	....	.318	.348	.364	.711	111	0	3	5.67	-1	/3-5,2-1	1	-0.1
• HOFFMAN, Ray	Raymond Lamont Hoffman b: 6/14/1917, Detroit, MI BL/TR, 6'.5", 175 lbs. Deb: 8/30/1942																							
1942 Was-A	7	19	2	1	0	0	0	2	1	1	0	0	.053	.100	.053	.153	-57	-4	0	.19	0	/3-6	0	-0.3
• HOFFMAN, Tex	Edward Adolph Hoffman b: 11/30/1893, San Antonio, TX d: 5/19/1947, New Orleans, LA BL/TR, 5'9", 195 lbs. Deb: 7/11/1915																							
1915 Cle-A	9	13	1	2	0	0	0	2	1	5	0	....	.154	.214	.154	.368	10	-1	1	1.26	0	/3-3	0	-0.2
• HOFFMEISTER, Jesse	Jesse H. Hoffmeister b: Toledo, OH TR Deb: 7/24/1897																							
1897 Pit-N	48	188	33	58	6	9	3	36	8	....	6	....	.309	.337	.484	.821	120	4	34	6.79	-10	3-48	5	-0.4
• HOFMAN, Bobby	Robert George Hofman b: 10/5/1925, St. Louis, MO d: 4/5/1994, Chesterfield, MO BR/TR, 5'10", 175 lbs. Deb: 4/19/1949 C																							
1949 NY-N	19	48	4	10	0	0	0	3	5	6	0	....	.208	.296	.208	.505	38	-4	3	2.22	1	2-16	0	-0.3
1952 NY-N	32	63	11	18	2	2	2	4	8	10	0	0	.286	.375	.476	.851	134	3	11	6.60	-4	2-21/3-2,1-1	3	0.0
1953 NY-N	74	169	21	45	7	2	12	34	12	23	1	1	.266	.315	.544	.859	116	3	27	5.38	-1	3-23,2-17	5	0.2
1954 NY-N	71	125	12	28	5	0	8	30	17	15	0	0	.224	.322	.456	.778	99	-0	19	4.80	-4	1-21,2-10/3-8	3	-0.5
1955 NY-N	96	207	32	55	7	2	10	28	22	31	0	2	.266	.339	.464	.803	110	2	30	4.95	-0	1-24,2-19,C-19/3-5	6	0.2
1956 NY-N	47	56	1	10	1	0	0	2	6	8	0	0	.179	.270	.196	.466	28	-5	3	1.72	0	/3-7,C-7,1-3,2-2	0	-0.6
1957 NY-N	2	2	0	0	0	0	0	0	0	1	0	0	.000	.000	.000	.000	-100	-1	0	.00	0	....	0	-0.1
Total 7	**341**	**670**	**81**	**166**	**22**	**6**	**32**	**101**	**70**	**94**	**1**	**3**	**.248**	**.323**	**.442**	**.765**	**99**	**-3**	**93**	**4.66**	**-9**	**/2-85,1-49,3-45,C-26**	**17**	**-0.9**
• HOFMAN, Solly	Arthur Frederick "Circus Solly" Hofman b: 10/29/1882, St. Louis, MO d: 3/10/1956, St. Louis, MO BR/TR, 6', 160 lbs. Deb: 7/28/1903 Career OF: 77-557-79																							
1903 Pit-N	3	2	1	0	0	0	0	0	0	....	0	....	.000	.000	.000	.000	-97	-1	0	.00	0	/O-2(1-1-0)	0	-0.1
1904 Chi-N	7	26	7	7	0	0	1	4	1	....	2	....	.269	.296	.385	.681	109	0	4	4.99	1	/O-6(1-3-2),S-1	1	0.1
1905 Chi-N	86	287	43	68	14	4	1	38	20	....	15	....	.237	.289	.324	.613	79	-8	33	3.76	9	2-59/1-9,S-9,3-3,O-3(O-2-1)	8	0.2
1906*Chi-N	64	195	30	50	2	3	2	20	20	....	13	....	.256	.326	.328	.654	98	-0	26	4.55	2	O-23(1-17-6),1-21/S-9,2-4,3	8	0.0
1907 Chi-N	134	470	67	126	11	3	1	36	41	....	29	....	.268	.328	.311	.639	94	-3	62	4.37	7	O-69(12-23-35),S-42,1-18/3,2	18	0.2
1908*Chi-N	120	411	55	100	15	5	2	42	33	....	15	....	.243	.309	.319	.628	96	-1	47	3.58	-1	O-50(0-50-2),1-37,2-22/3-9	14	-0.6
1909 Chi-N	153	527	60	150	21	4	2	58	53	....	20	....	.285	.351	.351	.702	115	10	74	4.70	6	*O-153(0-143-11)	27	0.9
1910*Chi-N	136	477	83	155	24	16	3	86	65	34	29	....	.325	.406	.461	.867	154	33	102	7.55	2	*O-110(0-110-1),1-24/3-1	31	3.2
1911 Chi-N	143	512	66	129	17	2	2	70	66	40	30	....	.252	.341	.305	.645	81	-11	65	4.14	-8	*O-107(2-107-0),1-36	13	-2.6
1912 Chi-N	36	125	28	34	11	0	0	18	22	13	5	....	.272	.385	.360	.745	105	2	19	5.26	3	O-27(0-27-0)/1-9	5	0.3
Pit-N	17	53	7	15	4	1	0	2	5	6	0	....	.283	.345	.396	.741	104	0	7	4.63	1	O-15(0-15-0)	2	0.0
Yr.	53	178	35	49	15	1	0	20	27	19	5	....	.275	.374	.371	.745	104	2	26	5.07	5	O-42(0-42-0)/1-9	7	0.4
1913 Pit-N	28	83	11	19	5	2	0	7	8	6	3	....	.229	.297	.337	.634	84	-2	9	3.40	-1	O-24(0-23-2)	2	-0.5
1914 Bro-F	147	515	65	148	25	12	5	83	54	41	34	....	.287	.357	.412	.769	118	12	83	5.61	-4	*2-108,1-22,O-21(10-10-1)/S	20	0.9
1915 Buf-F	109	346	29	81	10	6	0	27	30	28	12	....	.234	.295	.298	.593	75	-11	33	3.10	4	O-82(46-20-18),1-11/3-4,2,S	7	-1.2
1916 NY-A	6	27	0	8	1	1	0	2	1	1	1	....	.296	.321	.407	.729	116	0	4	5.12	2	/O-6(0-6-0)	1	0.2
Chi-N	5	16	2	5	2	1	0	2	2	2	0	....	.313	.389	.563	.951	172	1	4	8.27	0	/O-4(4-0-0)	1	0.2
Total 14	**1194**	**4072**	**554**	**1095**	**162**	**60**	**19**	**495**	**421**	**171**	**208**	**....**	**.269**	**.340**	**.352**	**.692**	**104**	**22**	**571**	**4.68**	**23**	**O-702,2-198,1-187/S-63,3-25**	**158**	**1.1**
• HOFMANN, Fred	Fred "Bootnose" Hofmann b: 6/10/1894, St. Louis, MO d: 11/19/1964, St. Helena, CA BR/TR, 5'11.5", 175 lbs. Deb: 9/26/1919 C																							
1919 NY-A	1	1	0	0	0	0	0	0	0	0	0	....	.000	.000	.000	.000	-99	-0	0	.00	0	/C-1	0	0.0
1920 NY-A	15	24	3	7	0	0	0	1	1	2	0	0	.292	.346	.292	.638	68	-1	2	3.90	-2	C-14	0	-0.3
1921 NY-A	23	62	7	11	1	1	1	5	5	13	0	0	.177	.250	.274	.524	33	-6	4	2.31	-3	C-18/1-1	0	-0.8
1922 NY-A	37	91	13	27	5	3	2	10	9	12	0	0	.297	.360	.484	.844	116	2	16	6.54	-4	C-29	3	-0.1
1923*NY-A	72	238	24	69	10	4	3	26	18	27	2	1	.290	.350	.403	.753	96	-1	34	5.25	-9	C-70	8	-0.6
1924 NY-A	62	166	17	29	6	1	1	11	12	15	2	1	.175	.239	.241	.480	24	-19	10	1.91	1	C-54	3	-1.4
1925 NY-A	3	2	0	0	0	0	0	0	0	0	0	0	.000	.000	.000	.000	-102	-1	0	.00	0	/C-1	0	-0.1
1927 Bos-A	87	217	20	59	19	1	0	24	21	26	2	0	.272	.342	.369	.710	86	-4	29	4.59	-4	C-81	4	-0.3

YEAR TM-L	G	AB	R	H	2B	3B	HR	RBI	BB	SO	SB	CS	AVG	OBP	SLG	OPS	OPS+	BR/A	RC	RC/G	FR	G/POS	WS	TPW
1928 Bos-A	78	199	14	45	8	1	0	16	11	25	0	1	.226	.270	.276	.547	45	-16	15	2.52	-1	C-71	2	-1.2
Total 9	378	1000	98	247	49	11	7	93	77	120	6	3	.247	.308	.339	.647	69	-46	111	3.80	-23	C-339/1-1	20	-4.7
• HOGAN, Harry Harry S. Hogan b: 11/1/1875, Syracuse, NY d: 1/24/1934, Syracuse, NY Deb: 8/13/1901																								
1901 Cle-A	1	4	0	0	0	0	0	0	0	....	0	....	.000	.000	.000	.000	-104	-1	0	.00	0	/0-1	0	-0.1
• HOGAN, Kenny Kenneth Sylvester Hogan b: 10/9/1902, Cleveland, OH d: 1/2/1980, Cleveland, OH BL/TR, 5'9", 145 lbs. Deb: 10/2/1921																								
1921 Cin-N	1	2	0	0	0	0	0	0	0	1	0	0	.000	.000	.000	.000	-105	-1	0	.00	0	/0-1	0	-0.1
1923 Cle-A	1	0	0	0	0	0	0	0	0	0	0	0	....	....	....	....	-100	0	0	....	0	....	0	0.0
1924 Cle-A	2	1	0	0	0	0	0	0	0	0	0	0	.000	.000	.000	.000	-99	-0	0	.00	0	....	0	0.0
Total 3	4	3	0	0	0	0	0	0	0	1	0	0	.000	.000	.000	.000	-103	-1	0	.00	0	/0-1	0	-0.1
• HOGAN, Marty Martin F. Hogan b: 10/25/1869, Wensbury, England d: 8/15/1923, Youngstown, OH BR/TR, 5'8", 145 lbs. Deb: 8/6/1894 Career OF: 1-6-34																								
1894 Cin-N	6	23	4	3	0	0	0	3	1	4	2	....	.130	.167	.130	.297	-27	-5	1	1.11	0	/0-6(0-0-6)	0	-0.4
StL-N	29	100	11	28	3	4	0	13	3	13	7	....	.280	.308	.390	.698	67	-6	15	5.24	0	0-29(1-1-28)	1	-0.6
Yr.	35	123	15	31	3	4	0	16	4	17	9	....	.252	.281	.341	.623	50	-11	15	4.34	-1	0-35(1-1-34)	1	-1.0
1895 StL-N	5	18	2	3	1	0	0	2	3	0	2	....	.167	.286	.222	.508	32	-2	2	3.17	0	/0-5(0-5-0)	0	-0.1
Total 2	40	141	17	34	4	4	0	18	7	17	11	....	.241	.282	.326	.608	47	-13	17	4.16	0	/0-40	1	-1.1
• HOGAN, Mortimer Mortimer Edward Hogan b: 1862, IL d: 3/17/1923, Chicago, IL Deb: 9/27/1884 Career OF: 27-2-89																								
1884 Mil-U	11	37	6	3	1	0	0	....	7	....	....	....	.081	.227	.108	.335	17	-3	1	.77	7	0-11(0-0-11)	1	0.4
1887 NY-a	32	150	22	54	6	1	0	5	30	....	12	....	.360	.373	.267	.639	83	0	17	4.73	-6	0-29(26-0-52)/S-4,3-1	3	-0.5
1888 Cle-a	78	269	60	61	16	6	0	24	50	....	30	....	.227	.368	.331	.699	128	13	45	5.82	-3	0-78(1-2-26)	10	0.8
Total 3	121	456	88	118	23	7	0	29	87	....	42	....	.259	.357	.293	.651	106	10	63	5.00	-1	0-118/S-4,3-1	14	0.7
• HOGAN, Shanty James Francis Hogan b: 3/21/1906, Somerville, MA d: 4/7/1967, Boston, MA BR/TR, 6'1", 240 lbs. Deb: 6/23/1925																								
1925 Bos-N	9	21	2	6	1	1	0	3	1	3	0	0	.286	.318	.429	.747	97	-0	3	5.00	0	/0-5(2-0-3)	1	-0.1
1926 Bos-N	4	14	1	4	1	1	0	5	0	0	0	....	.286	.286	.500	.786	119	0	2	4.84	1	/C-4	1	0.1
1927 Bos-N	71	229	24	66	17	1	3	32	9	23	2	....	.288	.324	.410	.734	103	0	29	4.54	4	C-61	8	0.8
1928 NY-N	131	411	48	137	25	2	10	71	42	25	0	....	.333	.406	.477	.883	129	19	79	7.25	-10	*C-124	19	1.6
1929 NY-N	102	317	19	95	13	0	5	45	25	22	1	....	.300	.362	.388	.750	86	-6	44	5.07	-7	C-93	8	-0.7
1930 NY-N	122	389	60	132	26	2	13	75	21	24	2	....	.339	.378	.517	.894	116	9	73	7.05	-3	C-96	15	1.1
1931 NY-N	123	396	42	119	17	1	12	65	29	29	1	....	.301	.354	.439	.794	115	8	63	5.89	-2	*C-113	18	1.2
1932 NY-N	140	502	36	144	18	2	8	77	26	22	0	....	.287	.323	.378	.702	90	-8	62	4.50	-1	*C-136	15	-0.1
1933 Bos-N	96	328	15	83	7	0	3	30	13	9	0	....	.253	.288	.302	.590	75	-11	25	2.58	-1	C-95	9	-0.7
1934 Bos-N	92	279	20	73	5	2	4	34	16	13	0	....	.262	.316	.337	.653	81	-7	27	3.25	3	C-90	7	0.1
1935 Bos-N	59	163	9	49	8	0	2	25	21	8	0	....	.301	.394	.387	.780	120	6	27	6.34	0	C-56	6	0.9
1936 Was-A	19	65	8	21	4	0	1	7	11	2	0	1	.323	.421	.431	.852	117	2	12	7.12	1	C-19	3	0.4
1937 Was-A	21	66	4	10	4	0	0	5	6	8	0	1	.152	.222	.212	.434	10	-10	3	1.45	1	C-21	1	-0.7
Total 13	989	3180	288	939	146	12	61	474	220	188	6	2	.295	.348	.406	.754	100	2	449	5.09	-14	C-908/0-5	111	4.0
• HOGAN, Willie William Henry Hogan b: 9/14/1884, North San Juan, CA d: 9/28/1974, San Jose, CA BR/TR, 5'10", 175 lbs. Deb: 4/12/1911 Career OF: 212-4-6																								
1911 Phi-A	7	19	1	2	1	0	0	2	0	....	0	....	.105	.105	.158	.263	-27	-3	0	.40	0	/0-6(6-0-0)	0	-0.3
StL-A	123	443	53	115	17	8	2	62	43	....	18	....	.260	.328	.348	.675	92	-5	57	4.26	10	*0-117(115-0-2)/1-5	10	0.0
Yr.	130	462	54	117	18	8	2	64	43	....	18	....	.253	.320	.340	.659	88	-8	57	4.08	10	*0-123(121-0-2)/1-5	10	-0.3
1912 StL-A	108	360	32	77	10	2	1	36	34	....	17	....	.214	.284	.261	.545	58	-19	32	2.79	5	*0-100(91-4-4)	3	-1.9
Total 2	238	822	86	194	28	10	3	100	77	....	35	....	.236	.304	.305	.609	75	-27	89	3.50	15	0-223/1-5	13	-2.2
• HOGG, Bert Wilbert George "Sonny" Hogg b: 4/21/1913, Detroit, MI d: 11/5/1973, Detroit, MI BR/TR, 5'11.5", 162 lbs. Deb: 6/1/1934																								
1934 Bro-N	2	1	0	0	0	0	0	0	0	0	0	....	.000	.000	.000	.000	-105	-0	0	.00	0	/3-1	0	-0.1
• HOGRIEVER, George George C. Hogriever b: 3/17/1869, Cincinnati, OH d: 1/26/1961, Appleton, WI BR/TR, 5'8", 160 lbs. Deb: 4/24/1895 U Career OF: 59-53-8																								
1895 Cin-N	69	239	61	65	8	7	2	34	36	17	41	....	.272	.374	.389	.763	93	-2	52	7.85	-1	0-66(10-48-8)/2-3	8	-0.6
1901 Mil-A	54	221	25	52	10	2	0	16	30	....	7	....	.235	.329	.299	.628	79	-5	25	3.87	1	0-54(49-5-0)	4	-0.6
Total 2	123	460	86	117	18	9	2	50	66	17	48	....	.254	.353	.346	.698	86	-7	77	5.90	0	0-120/2-3	12	-1.2
• HOHMAN, Bill William Henry Hohman b: 11/27/1903, Brooklyn, MD d: 10/29/1968, Baltimore, MD BR/TR, 6', 178 lbs. Deb: 8/24/1927																								
1927 Phi-N	7	18	1	5	0	0	0	0	2	3	0	....	.278	.350	.278	.628	69	-1	2	3.59	0	/0-6(6-0-0)	0	-0.1
• HOHNHORST, Eddie Edward Hicks Hohnhorst b: 1/31/1885, Covington, KY d: 3/28/1916, Covington, KY BL/TL, 6'1", 175 lbs. Deb: 9/10/1910																								
1910 Cle-A	18	63	8	20	3	1	0	6	4	....	3	....	.317	.358	.397	.755	135	2	10	5.82	-1	1-18	3	0.1
1912 Cle-A	15	54	5	11	1	0	0	2	2	....	5	....	.204	.232	.222	.454	29	-5	4	2.25	-2	1-15	0	-0.7
Total 2	33	117	13	31	4	1	0	8	6	....	8	....	.265	.301	.316	.617	87	-3	14	4.03	-3	/1-33	3	-0.6
• HOILES, Chris Christopher Allen Hoiles b: 3/20/1965, Bowling Green, OH BR/TR, 6', 213 lbs. Deb: 4/25/1989																								
1989 Bal-A	6	9	0	1	1	0	0	1	1	3	0	0	.111	.200	.222	.422	19	-1	0	1.53	0	/C-3,D-3	0	-0.1
1990 Bal-A	23	63	7	12	3	0	1	6	5	12	0	0	.190	.250	.286	.536	51	-4	5	2.52	0	/C-7,D-7,1-6	0	-0.5
1991 Bal-A	107	341	36	83	15	0	11	31	29	61	0	2	.243	.305	.384	.689	93	-5	37	3.71	2	C-89,D-13/1-2	7	0.2
1992 Bal-A	96	310	49	85	10	1	20	40	55	60	0	2	.274	.387	.506	.893	145	19	62	6.97	-3	C-95/D-1	12	2.2
1993 Bal-A	126	419	80	130	28	0	29	82	69	94	1	1	.310	.419	.585	1.003	160	38	105	9.26	2	*C-124/D-2	26	4.7
1994 Bal-A	99	332	45	82	10	0	19	53	63	73	2	0	.247	.375	.449	.824	106	5	60	6.25	-1	C-98	14	1.0
1995 Bal-A	114	352	53	88	15	1	19	58	67	80	1	0	.250	.376	.460	.836	114	9	63	6.13	-1	*C-107/D-6	14	1.4
1996*Bal-A	127	407	64	105	13	0	25	73	57	97	0	1	.258	.362	.474	.836	110	6	73	6.16	-2	*C-126/1-1	14	1.1
1997*Bal-A	99	320	45	83	15	0	12	49	51	86	1	0	.259	.378	.419	.797	111	8	54	5.90	-1	C-87/D-8,1-4,3-1	14	1.1
1998 Bal-A	97	267	36	70	12	0	15	56	38	50	0	1	.262	.362	.476	.838	117	7	48	6.05	2	C-83/1-6,D-6	12	1.3
Total 10	894	2820	415	739	122	2	151	449	435	616	5	7	.262	.369	.467	.837	119	81	507	6.24	-3	C-819/D-46,1-19,3-1	113	12.5
• HOLBERT, Aaron Aaron Keith Holbert b: 1/9/1973, Torrance, CA BR/TR, 6', 160 lbs. Deb: 4/14/1996																								
1996 StL-N	1	3	0	0	0	0	0	0	0	0	0	0	.000	.000	.000	.000	-101	-1	0	.00	0	/2-1	0	-0.1
• HOLBERT, Bill William Henry Holbert b: 3/14/1855, Baltimore, MD d: 3/20/1935, Laurel, MD BR/TR, 197 lbs. Deb: 9/5/1876 M/U Career OF: 12-19-38																								
1876 Lou-N	12	43	3	11	0	0	0	5	0	3	....	....	.256	.256	.256	.512	60	-2	3	2.52	5	C-12	1	0.3
1878 Mil-N	45	173	10	32	2	0	0	12	3	14	....	....	.185	.199	.197	.395	28	-13	7	1.35	4	0-30(0-0-30),C-21	1	-0.8
1879 Syr-N	59	229	11	46	0	0	0	21	1	20	....	....	.201	.204	.201	.405	38	-13	10	1.47	7	*C-56/0-4(0-3-1)	3	-0.4
Tro-N	4	15	1	4	0	0	0	2	0	1	....	....	.267	.267	.267	.533	82	-0	1	2.78	1	/C-4	0	0.1
Yr.	63	244	12	50	0	0	0	23	1	21	....	....	.205	.208	.205	.413	41	-14	11	1.55	8	*C-60/0-4(0-3-1)	3	-0.4
1880 Tro-N	60	212	18	40	5	1	0	8	9	18	....	....	.189	.222	.222	.443	48	-11	11	1.71	14	*C-58/0-3(0-0-3)	4	0.4
1881 Tro-N	46	180	16	49	3	0	0	14	3	13	....	....	.272	.284	.289	.573	76	-5	15	3.12	8	C-43/0-3(0-0-3)	6	0.4
1882 Tro-N	71	251	24	46	5	0	0	23	11	22	....	....	.183	.218	.203	.421	38	-16	11	1.53	15	*C-58,3-12/0-3(0-3-0)	4	0.4
1883 NY-a	73	299	26	71	9	1	0	0	1	....	....	....	.237	.240	.274	.514	62	-13	20	2.48	21	*C-68/0-5(0-5-0),2-1	8	1.2
1884 NY-a	65	255	28	53	5	0	0	0	7	....	....	....	.208	.235	.227	.462	53	-13	14	1.90	24	C-59/0-5(4-0-1),S-1	6	1.5
1885 NY-a	56	202	13	35	3	0	0	13	8	....	....	....	.173	.205	.188	.393	27	-16	8	1.29	9	C-39,0-13(8-5-0)/3-5	2	-0.3
1886 NY-a	48	171	8	35	4	2	0	13	6	....	4	....	.205	.232	.251	.483	54	-9	11	2.22	12	C-45/0-3(0-3-0),S-1	3	0.6
1887 NY-a	69	262	20	65	4	3	0	32	7	....	12	....	.248	.248	.267	.515	45	-19	20	2.79	5	C-60/1-8,S-2,2-1	3	-0.8
1888 Bro-a	15	50	4	6	1	0	0	1	2	....	0	....	.120	.170	.140	.310		-6	1	.75	1	C-15	1	-0.3
Total 12	623	2342	182	493	41	7	0	144	58	91	16	....	.211	.228	.232	.460	47	-137	133	1.97	127	C-538/0-69,3-17,1-8,S-4,2-2	42	2.2
• HOLBERT, Ray Ray Arthur Holbert b: 9/25/1970, Torrance, CA BR/TR, 6', 170 lbs. Deb: 5/2/1994																								
1994 SD-N	5	5	1	1	0	0	0	0	0	4	0	0	.200	.200	.200	.400	5	-1	0	1.35	-1	/S-1	0	-0.1
1995 SD-N	63	73	11	13	2	1	2	5	8	20	4	0	.178	.277	.315	.592	58	-4	7	2.76	-4	S-30/2-7,0-1	0	-0.6
1998 Atl-N	8	15	2	2	0	0	0	1	2	4	0	0	.133	.235	.133	.369		-2	1	1.30	0	/S-7	0	-0.2

YEAR TM-L	G	AB	R	H	2B	3B	HR	RBI	BB	SO	SB	CS	AVG	OBP	SLG	OPS	OPS+	BR/A	RC	RC/G	FR	G/POS	WS	TPW
Mon-N	2	5	0	0	0	0	0	0	0	1	0	0	.000	.000	.000	.000	-102	-1	0	.00	0	/2-1	0	-0.2
Yr.	10	20	2	2	0	0	0	1	2	5	0	0	.100	.182	.100	.282	-22	-4	1	.96	-1	/S-7,2-1	0	-0.4
1999 KC-A	34	100	14	28	3	0	0	5	8	20	7	4	.280	.333	.310	.643	64	-5	10	3.05	3	S-22,2-11/3-1	1	-0.1
2000 KC-A	3	4	0	1	0	0	0	0	0	2	0	0	.250	.250	.250	.500	26	-0	0	2.25	1	/2-1,3-1,S-1	0	0.0
Total 5	**115**	**202**	**28**	**45**	**5**	**1**	**2**	**11**	**18**	**51**	**11**	**4**	**.223**	**.293**	**.287**	**.580**	**52**	**-14**	**18**	**2.67**	**-2**	**/S-61,2-20,3-2,0-1**	**1**	**-1.1**
• HOLBROOK, Sammy	James Marbury Holbrook b: 7/17/1910, Meridian, MS d: 4/10/1991, Jackson, MS BR/TR, 5'11", 189 lbs. Deb: 4/25/1935																							
1935 Was-A	52	135	20	35	2	2	2	25	30	16	0	0	.259	.408	.348	.756	101	3	22	5.80	-7	C-47	4	-0.2
• HOLDEN, Bill	William Paul Holden b: 9/7/1889, Birmingham, AL d: 9/14/1971, Pensacola, FL BR/TR, 6', 170 lbs. Deb: 9/11/1913 Career OF: 10-56-7																							
1913 NY-A	18	53	6	16	3	1	0	8	8	5	0	....	.302	.393	.396	.790	131	2	9	5.36	2	0-16(0-16-0)	2	0.3
1914 NY-A	50	165	12	30	3	2	0	12	16	26	2	4	.182	.254	.224	.478	44	-13	9	1.76	-1	0-45(3-37-6)	1	-1.8
Cin-N	11	28	2	6	0	0	0	1	3	5	0	....	.214	.290	.214	.505	49	-2	2	1.93	0	0-10(7-3-1)	0	-0.2
Total 2	**79**	**246**	**20**	**52**	**6**	**3**	**0**	**21**	**27**	**36**	**2**	**4**	**.211**	**.289**	**.260**	**.550**	**65**	**-12**	**20**	**2.50**	**1**	**/0-71**	**3**	**-1.6**
• HOLDEN, Joe	Joseph Francis "Socks" Holden b: 6/4/1913, St. Clair, PA d: 5/10/1996, St. Clair, PA BL/TR, 5'8", 175 lbs. Deb: 6/14/1934																							
1934 Phi-N	10	14	1	1	0	0	0	0	0	2	0	....	.071	.071	.071	.143	-54	-3	0	.00	1	/C-6	0	-0.2
1935 Phi-N	6	9	0	1	0	0	0	0	0	3	1	....	.111	.111	.111	.222	-36	-2	0	.00	0	/C-4	0	-0.2
1936 Phi-N	1	1	0	0	0	0	0	0	0	0	0	....	.000	.000	.000	.000	-91	-0	0	.00	0	....	0	0.0
Total 3	**17**	**24**	**1**	**2**	**0**	**0**	**0**	**0**	**0**	**5**	**1**	**....**	**.083**	**.083**	**.083**	**.167**	**-49**	**-5**	**0**	**.00**	**0**	**/C-10**	**0**	**-0.4**
• HOLDSWORTH, Jim	James "Long Jim" Holdsworth b: 7/14/1850, New York, NY d: 3/22/1918, New York, NY BR/TR Deb: 5/14/1872 NA OF: 0-46-5 Career OF: 0-110-0																							
1872 Cle-n	22	110	19	33	5	0	0	11	1	2	3	2	.300	.306	.345	.652	106	1	13	5.05	1	S-22	....	0.1
Eck-n	2	7	1	2	0	0	0	0	0	0	0	0	.286	.286	.286	.571	90	0	1	3.63	1	/S-2	....	0.1
Yr.	24	117	20	35	5	0	0	11	1	2	3	2	.299	.305	.342	.647	105	1	13	4.97	2	S-24	....	0.2
1873 Mut-n	53	233	46	75	4	8	0	28	0	3	1	0	.322	.322	.408	.730	116	5	32	6.11	2	*S-53	....	0.4
1874 Phi-n	57	285	60	97	8	9	0	37	1	0	1	2	.340	.343	.432	.774	141	11	44	6.88	-21	3-31,S-21/0-6(0-3-3),2-2,1	....	-0.8
1875 Mut-n	71	324	45	92	12	1	0	23	1	3	3	3	.284	.286	.327	.613	107	0	32	4.01	-3	0-45(0-43-2),S-26	....	-0.3
1876 NY-N	52	242	23	64	3	2	0	19	1	2	....	....	.264	.269	.295	.563	100	2	20	3.09	-2	*0-49(0-49-0)/2-3	7	-0.2
1877 Har-N	55	260	26	66	5	2	0	20	2	8	....	....	.254	.260	.288	.548	81	-4	20	2.83	-2	*0-55(0-55-0)	5	-0.8
1882 Tro-N	1	3	0	0	0	0	0	0	0	1	....	....	.000	.000	.000	.000	-105	-1	0	.00	0	/0-1	0	0.0
1884 Ind-a	5	18	1	2	0	0	0	0	2	....	....	....	.111	.200	.111	.311	4	-2	0	.70	1	/0-5(0-5-0)	0	-0.1
Total 4 n	**205**	**959**	**171**	**299**	**29**	**18**	**0**	**99**	**3**	**8**	**8**	**7**	**.312**	**.314**	**.380**	**.693**	**119**	**17**	**121**	**5.45**	**-21**	**S-124/0-51,3-31,2-2,1-1**	**....**	**-0.6**
Total 4	**113**	**523**	**50**	**132**	**8**	**4**	**0**	**39**	**5**	**11**	**....**	**....**	**.252**	**.260**	**.284**	**.543**	**86**	**-5**	**40**	**2.84**	**-3**	**0-110/2-3**	**12**	**-1.2**
• HOLKE, Walter	Walter Henry "Union Man" Holke b: 12/25/1892, St. Louis, MO d: 10/12/1954, St. Louis, MO BB/TL, 6'1.5", 185 lbs. Deb: 10/6/1914 C																							
1914 NY-N	2	6	0	2	0	0	0	0	0	0	0	....	.333	.333	.333	.667	102	-0	1	4.07	0	/1-2	0	0.0
1916 NY-N	34	111	16	39	4	2	0	13	6	16	10	....	.351	.390	.423	.813	158	7	22	7.65	-1	1-34	6	0.6
1917*NY-N	153	527	55	146	12	7	2	55	34	54	13	....	.277	.327	.338	.665	107	4	61	3.98	-7	*1-153	17	-0.7
1918 NY-N	88	326	38	82	17	4	1	27	10	26	10	....	.252	.276	.337	.613	88	-6	32	3.24	5	1-88	7	-0.3
1919 Bos-N	137	518	48	151	14	6	0	48	21	25	19	....	.292	.325	.342	.667	105	2	63	4.16	4	*1-136	13	0.4
1920 Bos-N	144	551	53	162	15	11	3	64	28	31	4	11	.294	.329	.377	.707	107	2	66	4.12	-3	*1-143	13	-0.4
1921 Bos-N	150	579	60	151	15	10	3	63	17	41	8	11	.261	.284	.337	.621	67	-29	53	3.04	2	*1-150	6	-3.7
1922 Bos-N	105	395	35	115	9	4	0	46	14	23	6	8	.291	.317	.334	.651	71	-18	40	3.54	-5	*1-105	5	-2.8
1923 Phi-N	147	562	64	175	31	4	7	70	16	37	7	9	.311	.330	.418	.749	86	-14	74	4.72	-3	*1-146/P-1	9	-2.5
1924 Phi-N	148	563	60	169	23	6	6	64	25	33	3	8	.300	.330	.394	.724	83	-15	70	4.46	3	*1-148	9	-2.2
1925 Phi-N	39	86	11	21	5	0	1	17	3	6	0	0	.244	.270	.337	.607	50	-7	8	3.03	2	1-23	0	-0.6
Cin-N	65	232	24	65	8	4	1	20	17	12	1	3	.280	.329	.362	.691	78	-8	28	4.04	1	1-65	4	-1.1
Yr.	104	318	35	86	13	4	2	37	20	18	1	3	.270	.314	.355	.669	71	-15	35	3.76	3	1-88	4	-1.6
Total 11	**1212**	**4456**	**464**	**1278**	**153**	**58**	**24**	**487**	**191**	**304**	**81**	**50**	**.287**	**.318**	**.363**	**.682**	**90**	**-81**	**517**	**4.01**	**-3**	***1-1193/P-1**	**89**	**-13.2**
• HOLLAHAN, Bill	William James "Happy" Hollahan b: 11/22/1896, New York, NY d: 11/27/1965, New York, NY BR/TR, 5'8", 165 lbs. Deb: 9/27/1920																							
1920 Was-A	3	4	0	1	0	0	0	1	1	2	1	0	.250	.400	.250	.650	77	0	1	4.83	0	/3-3	0	0.0
• HOLLAND, Dutch	Robert Clyde Holland b: 10/12/1903, Middlesex, NC d: 6/16/1967, Lumberton, NC BR/TR, 6'1", 190 lbs. Deb: 8/16/1932 Career OF: 61-0-16																							
1932 Bos-N	39	156	15	46	11	1	1	18	12	20	0	....	.295	.345	.397	.743	103	1	22	5.13	2	0-39(39-0-0)	5	0.0
1933 Bos-N	13	31	3	8	3	0	0	3	3	8	1	....	.258	.324	.355	.678	102	0	4	4.58	-1	/0-7(7-0-0)	1	-0.1
1934 Cle-A	50	128	19	32	12	1	2	13	13	11	0	0	.250	.319	.406	.725	85	-3	17	4.65	-2	0-31(15-0-16)	2	-0.6
Total 3	**102**	**315**	**37**	**86**	**26**	**2**	**3**	**34**	**28**	**39**	**1**	**0**	**.273**	**.332**	**.397**	**.729**	**95**	**-3**	**43**	**4.87**	**-1**	**/0-77**	**8**	**-0.7**
• HOLLAND, Will	Willard A. Holland b: 1862, Georgetown, DE d: 7/19/1930, Philadelphia, PA, 5'10", 180 lbs. Deb: 7/10/1889 U																							
1889 Bal-a	40	143	13	27	1	2	0	16	9	28	4	....	.189	.247	.224	.471	35	-12	9	2.08	-7	S-39/0-1	1	-1.5
• HOLLANDSWORTH, Todd	Todd Mathew Hollandsworth b: 4/20/1973, Dayton, OH BL/TL, 6'2", 195 lbs. Deb: 4/25/1995 Career OF: 511-218-77																							
1995*LA-N	41	103	16	24	2	0	5	13	10	29	2	1	.233	.307	.398	.705	92	-1	13	4.24	-3	0-37(9-25-3)	2	-0.5
1996*LA-N	149	478	64	139	26	4	12	59	41	93	21	6	.291	.349	.437	.787	115	11	77	5.92	-2	*0-142(122-18-9)	19	0.4
1997 LA-N	106	296	39	73	20	2	4	31	17	60	5	5	.247	.288	.368	.656	76	-13	29	3.21	0	0-99(80-30-4)	7	-1.5
1998 LA-N	55	175	23	47	6	4	3	20	9	42	4	3	.269	.308	.400	.708	90	-4	21	4.21	-1	0-51(48-10-1)	6	-0.6
1999 LA-N	92	261	39	74	12	2	9	32	24	61	5	2	.284	.346	.448	.794	105	2	42	5.88	0	0-67(27-34-9),1-13	7	-0.1
2000 LA-N	81	261	42	61	12	0	8	24	30	61	11	4	.234	.315	.372	.687	77	-9	32	4.10	3	0-77(9-68-1)	4	-0.5
Col-N	56	167	39	54	8	0	11	23	11	38	7	3	.323	.365	.569	.934	105	1	33	7.42	1	0-48(31-4-18)	4	0.0
Yr.	137	428	81	115	20	0	19	47	41	99	18	7	.269	.334	.449	.783	88	-8	65	5.31	4	*0-125(40-72-19)	8	-0.5
2001 Col-N	33	117	21	43	15	1	6	19	8	20	5	0	.368	.408	.667	1.075	140	8	33	11.83	-1	0-31(25-12-5)	4	0.6
2002 Col-N	95	298	39	88	21	1	11	48	26	71	7	8	.295	.354	.483	.837	102	-1	47	5.52	-2	0-90(74-1-20)	8	-0.7
Tex-A	39	132	16	34	6	0	5	19	14	27	1	0	.258	.329	.417	.745	92	-1	20	5.23	-2	0-38(25-16-4)	4	-0.4
2003*Fla-N	93	228	32	58	23	3	3	20	22	55	2	3	.254	.320	.421	.741	95	-3	31	4.62	2	0-64(61-0-3)/D-1	5	-0.4
Total 9	**840**	**2516**	**370**	**695**	**151**	**17**	**77**	**308**	**212**	**557**	**70**	**35**	**.276**	**.334**	**.442**	**.776**	**99**	**-10**	**376**	**5.31**	**-6**	**0-744/1-13,D-1**	**70**	**-3.6**
• HOLLE, Gary	Gary Charles Holle b: 8/11/1954, Albany, NY BR/TL, 6'6", 210 lbs. Deb: 6/2/1979																							
1979 Tex-A	5	6	0	1	1	0	0	0	1	0	0	0	.167	.286	.333	.619	67	-0	1	3.49	0	/1-1	0	-0.1
• HOLLIDAY, Bug	James Wear Holliday b: 2/8/1867, St. Louis, MO d: 2/15/1910, Cincinnati, OH BR/TR, 5'11", 151 lbs. Deb: 4/17/1889 U Career OF: 209-598-92																							
1889 Cin-a	135	563	107	181	28	7	**19**	104	43	59	46	....	.321	.372	.497	.869	142	27	124	8.62	-9	*0-135(0-135-0)	21	1.1
1890 Cin-N	131	518	93	140	18	14	4	75	49	36	50	....	.270	.341	.382	.724	111	7	87	6.09	-2	*0-131(0-131-0)	18	0.0
1891 Cin-N	111	442	74	141	21	10	9	84	37	28	30	....	.319	.376	.473	.848	145	24	92	8.25	-6	*0-111(49-62-0)	18	1.2
1892 Cin-N	152	602	114	177	23	16	**13**	91	57	39	43	....	.294	.356	.450	.806	145	31	115	7.28	-1	*0-152(1-78-77)/P-1	26	1.6
1893 Cin-N	126	500	108	155	24	10	5	89	73	22	32	....	.310	.401	.428	.829	117	14	101	7.77	-9	*0-125(1-125-0)/1-1	19	-0.3
1894 Cin-N	123	521	126	196	24	8	13	123	41	20	33	....	.376	.424	.528	.952	123	18	133	10.63	3	*0-119(109-5-8)/1-1	18	0.8
1895 Cin-N	32	127	25	38	9	2	0	20	10	3	6	....	.299	.350	.402	.752	90	-2	21	6.17	-1	0-32(5-27-0)	3	-0.4
1896 Cin-N	29	84	17	27	4	0	0	8	9	4	1	....	.321	.394	.369	.763	95	-0	13	5.97	-1	0-16(10-3-3)/1-5,P-1,S-1	2	-0.2
1897 Cin-N	61	195	50	61	9	4	2	20	27	....	6	....	.313	.399	.431	.830	112	4	37	7.23	-3	0-42(32-6-4)/S-4,1-3,2-3	7	-0.2
1898 Cin-N	30	106	21	25	2	1	0	7	14	....	5	....	.236	.325	.274	.599	67	-4	12	3.71	-1	0-28(2-26-0)	2	-0.7
Total 10	**930**	**3658**	**735**	**1141**	**162**	**72**	**65**	**621**	**360**	**211**	**252**	**....**	**.312**	**.377**	**.449**	**.826**	**126**	**117**	**734**	**7.72**	**-30**	**0-891/1-10,S-5,2-3,P-2**	**134**	**3.1**
• HOLLINGSHEAD, Holly	John Samuel Hollingshead b: 1/17/1853, Washington, DC d: 10/6/1926, Washington, DC Deb: 4/20/1872 M NA OF: 4-43-3																							
1872 Nat-n	9	44	12	15	1	1	0	6	1	0	0	0	.341	.356	.409	.765	115	0	7	7.01	-3	/2-9	....	-0.2
1873 Was-n	30	136	25	35	2	2	0	22	0	6	0	0	.257	.257	.301	.559	68	-5	11	3.27	1	0-30(0-30-0)/2-2	....	-0.2
1875 Was-n	19	81	8	20	1	1	0	5	1	2	2	1	.247	.256	.284	.540	91	-1	7	3.12	1	0-19(4-13-3)	....	0.1
Total 3 n	**58**	**261**	**45**	**70**	**4**	**4**	**0**	**33**	**2**	**8**	**2**	**1**	**.268**	**.274**	**.314**	**.588**	**83**	**-5**	**24**	**3.79**	**-1**	**/0-49,2-11**	**....**	**-0.4**

YEAR TM-L	G	AB	R	H	2B	3B	HR	RBI	BB	SO	SB	CS	AVG	OBP	SLG	OPS	OPS+	BR/A	RC	RC/G	FR	G/POS	WS	TPW
• HOLLINS, Damon	Damon Jamall Hollins b: 6/12/1974, Fairfield, CA BR/TR, 5'11" Deb: 4/24/1998																							
1998 Atl-N	3	6	0	1	0	0	0	0	0	1	0	0	.167	.167	.167	.333	-12	-1	0	.90	0	/0-3(2-0-1)	0	-0.1
LA-N	5	9	1	2	0	0	0	2	0	2	0	1	.222	.222	.222	.444	18	-2	0	.75	0	/0-4(1-0-3)	0	-0.2
Yr.	8	15	1	3	0	0	0	2	0	3	0	1	.200	.200	.200	.400	6	-3	0	.81	0	/0-7(3-0-4)	0	-0.3
• HOLLINS, Dave	David Michael Hollins b: 5/25/1966, Buffalo, NY BB/TR, 6'1", 207 lbs. Deb: 4/12/1990 Career OF: 0-0-3																							
1990 Phi-N	72	114	14	21	0	0	5	15	10	28	0	0	.184	.256	.316	.572	56	-7	10	2.69	1	3-30/1-1	2	-0.7
1991 Phi-N	56	151	18	45	10	2	6	21	17	26	1	1	.298	.380	.510	.890	150	10	30	7.34	-1	3-36/1-6	8	1.0
1992 Phi-N	156	586	104	158	28	4	27	93	76	110	9	6	.270	.372	.469	.841	137	30	107	6.45	-10	*3-156/1-1	27	2.3
1993*Phi-N★	143	543	104	148	30	4	18	93	85	109	2	3	.273	.376	.442	.818	120	17	92	5.90	-10	*3-143	20	0.9
1994 Phi-N	44	162	28	36	7	1	4	26	23	32	1	0	.222	.333	.352	.685	77	-5	20	3.92	-7	3-43/0-1	3	-1.1
1995 Phi-N	65	205	46	47	12	2	7	25	53	38	1	1	.229	.399	.410	.809	113	7	38	6.09	-6	1-61	6	-0.4
Bos-A	5	13	2	2	0	0	0	1	4	7	0	0	.154	.353	.154	.507	37	-1	1	2.63	0	/D-3,0-2(0-0-2)	0	-0.1
1996 Min-A	121	422	71	102	26	0	13	53	71	102	6	4	.242	.364	.396	.760	91	-5	64	5.20	6	*3-116/D-3,S-1	11	0.2
Sea-A	28	94	17	33	3	0	3	25	13	15	0	2	.351	.445	.479	.924	134	5	20	7.94	2	3-28/1-1	4	0.7
Yr.	149	516	88	135	29	0	16	78	84	117	6	6	.262	.378	.411	.789	98	0	84	5.67	8	*3-144/D-3,1-1,S-1	15	0.9
1997 Ana-A	149	572	101	165	29	2	16	85	62	124	16	6	.288	.366	.430	.796	106	7	92	5.77	-1	*3-135,1-14	15	0.6
1998 Ana-A	101	363	60	88	16	2	11	39	44	69	11	3	.242	.336	.388	.724	87	-5	51	4.76	-5	3-91/1-7,D-2	9	-0.9
1999 Tor-A	27	99	12	22	5	0	2	6	5	22	0	0	.222	.260	.333	.593	49	-8	8	2.82	0	D-25	0	-0.9
2001 Cle-A	2	5	0	1	0	0	0	0	1	2	0	0	.200	.333	.200	.533	45	-0	1	2.75	0	/D-2	0	0.0
2002 Phi-N	14	17	1	2	0	0	0	0	0	3	0	1	.118	.167	.118	.284	-25	-4	0	.42	0	/1-5	0	-0.4
Total 12	983	3346	578	870	166	17	112	482	464	687	47	27	.260	.361	.420	.781	107	40	532	5.52	-30	3-778/1-96,D-35,0-3,S-1	105	1.1
• HOLLMIG, Stan	Stanley Ernest "Hondo" Hollmig b: 1/2/1926, Fredericksburg, TX d: 12/4/1981, San Antonio, TX BR/TR, 6'2.5", 190 lbs. Deb: 4/19/1949 Career OF: 2-0-67																							
1949 Phi-N	81	251	28	64	11	6	2	26	20	43	1	....	.255	.315	.371	.686	85	-6	28	3.88	-2	0-66(0-0-66)	4	-1.0
1950 Phi-N	11	12	1	3	2	0	0	1	0	3	0	....	.250	.250	.417	.667	73	-1	1	2.25	-0	/0-3(2-0-1)	0	-0.1
1951 Phi-N	2	2	0	0	0	0	0	0	0	0	0	0	.000	.000	.000	.000	-102	-1	0	.00	0	....	0	-0.1
Total 3	94	265	29	67	13	6	2	27	20	46	1	0	.253	.310	.370	.680	84	-7	29	3.76	-3	/0-69	4	-1.1
• HOLLOCHER, Charlie	Charles Jacob Hollocher b: 6/11/1896, St. Louis, MO d: 8/14/1940, Frontenac, MO BL/TR, 5'7", 154 lbs. Deb: 4/16/1918																							
1918*Chi-N	131	509	72	**161**	23	6	2	38	47	30	26	....	.316	.379	.397	.775	133	21	85	5.89	-12	*S-131	**28**	2.1
1919 Chi-N	115	430	51	116	14	5	3	26	44	19	16	....	.270	.347	.347	.694	108	6	57	4.42	2	*S-115	15	1.9
1920 Chi-N	80	301	53	96	17	2	0	22	41	15	20	14	.319	.406	.389	.795	126	12	49	5.39	2	S-80	16	2.1
1921 Chi-N	140	558	71	161	28	8	3	37	43	13	5	16	.289	.342	.384	.725	91	-10	70	4.23	-1	*S-137	14	0.4
1922 Chi-N	152	592	90	201	37	8	3	69	58	5	19	29	.340	.403	.444	.847	116	9	100	5.82	-1	*S-152	24	2.3
1923 Chi-N	66	260	46	89	14	2	1	28	26	5	9	10	.342	.410	.423	.833	120	7	44	6.20	0	S-65	10	1.3
1924 Chi-N	76	286	28	70	12	4	2	21	18	7	4	11	.245	.292	.336	.627	67	-17	26	2.89	2	S-71	6	-0.7
Total 7	760	2936	411	894	145	35	14	241	277	94	99	80	.304	.370	.392	.762	110	29	432	5.00	-9	S-751	113	9.4
• HOLLY, Ed	Edward William Holly b: 7/6/1879, Chicago, IL d: 11/27/1973, Williamsport, PA BR/TR, 5'10", 165 lbs. Deb: 7/18/1906																							
1906 StL-N	10	34	1	2	0	0	0	7	5	....	0	....	.059	.179	.059	.238	-27	-5	0	.39	-3	S-10	0	-0.9
1907 StL-N	150	545	55	125	18	3	1	40	36	....	16	....	.229	.283	.279	.562	79	-14	51	3.03	-6	*S-147/2-3	11	-1.7
1914 Pit-F	100	350	28	86	9	4	0	26	17	52	14	....	.246	.281	.294	.575	67	-16	32	2.93	0	S-94/0-2(1-0-1),2-1	6	-0.9
1915 Pit-F	16	42	8	11	2	0	0	5	5	6	3	....	.262	.354	.310	.664	92	-0	5	4.39	-3	S-11/3-3	1	-0.2
Total 4	276	971	92	224	29	7	1	78	63	58	33	....	.231	.282	.278	.560	71	-35	89	2.94	-12	S-262/2-4,3-3,0-2	18	-3.7
• HOLM, Billy	William Frederick Holm b: 7/21/1912, Chicago, IL d: 7/27/1977, East Chicago, IN BR/TR, 5'10.5", 168 lbs. Deb: 9/24/1943																							
1943 Chi-N	7	15	0	1	0	0	0	0	2	4	0	....	.067	.176	.067	.243	-29	-2	0	.52	0	/C-7	0	-0.2
1944 Chi-N	54	132	10	18	2	0	0	6	16	19	1	....	.136	.235	.152	.386	10	-15	6	1.29	-2	C-50	2	-1.5
1945 Bos-A	58	135	12	25	2	1	0	9	23	17	1	1	.185	.317	.215	.532	54	-7	11	2.54	-1	C-57	2	-0.5
Total 3	119	282	22	44	4	1	0	15	41	40	2	1	.156	.272	.177	.449	30	-24	17	1.84	-3	C-114	4	-2.3
• HOLM, Wattie	Roscoe Albert Holm b: 12/28/1901, Peterson, IA d: 5/19/1950, Everly, IA BR/TR, 5'9.5", 160 lbs. Deb: 4/15/1924 Career OF: 93-92-85																							
1924 StL-N	81	293	40	86	10	4	0	23	8	16	1	4	.294	.317	.355	.672	81	-9	32	3.80	-1	0-64(1-63-0)/C-9,3-4	5	-1.2
1925 StL-N	13	58	10	12	1	1	0	2	3	1	1	0	.207	.246	.259	.505	28	-6	4	2.22	1	0-13(3-0-11)	1	-0.6
1926*StL-N	55	144	18	41	5	1	0	21	18	14	3	....	.285	.364	.333	.698	85	-2	18	4.29	-3	0-39(26-0-13)	3	-0.8
1927 StL-N	110	419	55	120	27	8	3	66	24	29	4	....	.286	.327	.411	.737	93	-5	54	4.50	-6	0-97(55-25-18)/3-9	11	-1.7
1928*StL-N	102	386	61	107	24	6	3	47	32	17	1	....	.277	.334	.394	.728	88	-7	50	4.51	-4	3-83/0-7(0-0-7)	9	-0.6
1929 StL-N	64	176	21	41	5	6	0	14	12	8	1	....	.233	.282	.330	.611	50	-14	16	2.96	0	0-44(6-4-34)/3-1	1	-1.6
1932 StL-N	11	17	2	3	1	0	0	1	3	1	0	....	.176	.333	.235	.569	54	-1	2	3.02	0	/0-4(2-0-2)	0	-0.1
Total 7	436	1493	207	410	73	26	6	174	100	86	11	4	.275	.322	.370	.693	81	-45	176	4.04	-13	0-268/3-97,C-9	30	-6.6
• HOLMAN, Gary	Gary Richard Holman b: 1/25/1944, Long Beach, CA BL/TL, 6'1", 200 lbs. Deb: 6/26/1968 Career OF: 4-0-10																							
1968 Was-A	75	85	10	25	5	1	0	7	13	15	0	0	.294	.388	.376	.764	137	4	13	5.87	0	1-33,0-10(3-0-8)	5	0.3
1969 Was-A	41	31	1	5	1	0	0	2	4	7	0	0	.161	.257	.194	.451	29	-3	2	1.88	-1	1-11/0-3(1-0-2)	0	-0.5
Total 2	116	116	11	30	6	1	0	9	17	22	0	0	.259	.353	.328	.681	108	2	15	4.68	-1	/1-44,0-13	5	-0.1
• HOLMES, Ducky	James William Holmes b: 1/28/1869, Des Moines, IA d: 8/6/1932, Truro, IA BL/TR, 5'6", 170 lbs. Deb: 8/8/1895 Career OF: 563-37-285																							
1895 Lou-N	40	161	33	60	10	2	3	20	12	9	9	....	.373	.426	.516	.942	152	13	40	10.50	-5	0-29(0-3-26)/S-8,3-4,P-2	6	0.4
1896 Lou-N	47	141	22	38	3	2	0	18	13	5	8	....	.270	.360	.319	.679	83	-2	20	4.99	-4	0-33(0-26-7)/P-2,2-1,S-1	2	-1.0
1897 Lou-N	2	4	0	0	0	0	0	0	1	....	0	....	.000	.200	.000	.200	-46	-1	0	.00	0	/S-1	0	0.0
NY-N	80	310	52	82	8	6	1	45	18	....	30	....	.265	.313	.339	.652	74	-12	44	4.98	-6	0-77(77-0-0)/S-1	7	-2.1
Yr.	82	314	52	82	8	6	1	45	19	....	30	....	.261	.312	.334	.646	72	-13	44	4.89	-5	0-77(77-0-0)/S-2	7	-2.2
1898 StL-N	23	101	9	24	1	1	0	0	2	....	4	....	.238	.260	.267	.527	50	-7	8	2.84	2	0-22(11-2-9)	0	-0.6
Bal-N	113	442	54	126	10	9	1	64	23	....	25	....	.285	.333	.355	.689	96	-4	63	5.16	0	*0-113(113-0-0)	13	-1.3
Yr.	136	543	63	150	11	10	1	64	25	....	29	....	.276	.320	.339	.659	87	-11	71	4.71	2	*0-135(124-2-9)	13	-1.9
1899 Bal-N	138	553	80	177	31	7	4	66	39	....	50	....	.320	.381	.423	.804	114	11	112	7.60	1	*0-138(137-0-1)	20	-0.1
1901 Det-A	131	537	90	158	28	10	4	62	37	....	35	....	.294	.347	.406	.753	103	2	91	6.20	3	*0-131(2-0-131)	16	-0.1
1902 Det-A	92	362	50	93	15	4	2	33	28	....	16	....	.257	.319	.337	.656	80	-10	46	4.41	6	0-92(1-0-91)	7	-0.8
1903 Was-A	21	71	13	16	3	1	1	8	5	....	10	....	.225	.286	.338	.624	85	-1	10	4.71	1	0-14(0-3-11)/3-4,2-2	2	-0.1
Chi-A	86	344	53	96	7	5	0	18	25	....	25	....	.279	.335	.328	.664	104	3	49	4.94	3	0-82(82-0-0)/3-3	12	0.1
Yr.	107	415	66	112	10	6	1	26	30	....	35	....	.270	.327	.330	.657	101	1	60	4.90	4	0-96(82-3-11)/3-7,2-2	14	0.0
1904 Chi-A	68	251	42	78	11	9	1	19	14	....	13	....	.311	.354	.438	.793	156	15	46	6.63	4	0-63(53-2-8)	16	1.7
1905 Chi-A	92	328	42	66	15	2	0	22	19	....	11	....	.201	.258	.259	.517	67	-12	29	2.61	3	0-89(87-1-1)	4	-1.6
Total 10	933	3605	540	1014	142	58	17	375	236	14	236	....	.281	.336	.367	.703	99	-6	559	5.49	7	0-883/3-11,S-11,P-4,2-3	105	-5.5
• HOLMES, Ducky	Howard Elbert Holmes b: 7/8/1883, Dayton, OH d: 9/18/1945, Dayton, OH BR/TR, 5'10", 160 lbs. Deb: 4/18/1906 U																							
1906 StL-N	9	27	2	5	0	0	0	2	2	....	0	....	.185	.267	.185	.452	43	-2	1	1.62	0	/C-9	0	-0.1
• HOLMES, Fred	Frederick C. Holmes b: 7/1/1878, Chicago, IL d: 2/13/1956, Norwood Park, IL BR/TR Deb: 8/23/1903																							
1903 NY-A	1	0	0	0	0	0	0	0	1	....	0	....	....	1.000	....	1.000	207	0	0	....	0	/1-1	0	0.0
1904 Chi-N	1	3	1	1	1	0	0	0	0	....	0	....	.333	.333	.667	1.000	206	0	1	8.88	-0	/C-1	0	0.0
Total 2	2	3	1	1	1	0	0	0	1	....	0	....	.333	.500	.667	1.167	206	1	1	8.88	0	/1-1,C-1	0	0.0
• HOLMES, Tommy	Thomas Francis "Kelly" Holmes b: 3/29/1917, Brooklyn, NY BL/TL, 5'10", 180 lbs. Deb: 4/14/1942 M Career OF: 38-442-753																							
1942 Bos-N	141	558	56	155	24	4	4	41	64	10	2	....	.278	.353	.357	.710	110	8	76	4.95	6	*0-140(0-137-3)	21	1.2
1943 Bos-N	152	629	75	170	33	10	5	41	58	20	7	....	.270	.334	.378	.712	107	5	82	4.70	10	*0-152(2-149-1)	23	1.1
1944 Bos-N	155	631	93	195	42	6	13	73	61	11	4	....	.309	.372	.456	.828	127	22	110	6.57	3	*0-155(2-154-0)	27	2.1
1945 Bos-N★	154	636	125	**224**	**47**	6	**28**	117	70	9	15	....	.352	.420	**.577**	**.997**	**175**	**62**	156	**9.89**	-1	*0-154(32-2-121)	29	**5.2**

YEAR TM-L	G	AB	R	H	2B	3B	HR	RBI	BB	SO	SB	CS	AVG	OBP	SLG	OPS	OPS+	BR/A	RC	RC/G	FR	G/POS	WS	TPW
1946 Bos-N	149	568	80	176	35	6	6	79	58	14	7	....	.310	.377	.424	.801	125	19	91	5.86	3	*O-146(0-0-146)	25	1.9
1947 Bos-N	150	618	90	**191**	33	3	9	53	44	16	3	....	.309	.360	.416	.776	108	6	91	5.47	6	*O-147(0-0-147)	21	0.7
1948*Bos-N★	139	585	85	190	35	7	6	61	46	20	1	....	.325	.375	.439	.814	122	17	94	6.01	-1	*O-137(0-0-137)	19	1.1
1949 Bos-N	117	380	47	101	20	4	8	59	39	6	1	....	.266	.337	.403	.740	103	1	51	4.74	7	*O-103(0-0-103)	10	0.6
1950 Bos-N	105	322	44	96	20	1	9	51	33	8	0	....	.298	.370	.450	.821	123	11	53	5.97	0	O-88(0-0-88)	13	0.8
1951 Bos-N	27	29	1	5	2	0	0	5	3	4	0	0	.172	.250	.241	.491	35	-3	2	2.24	0	/O-3(2-0-1)	0	-0.3
1952*Bro-N	31	36	2	4	1	0	0	1	4	4	0	0	.111	.200	.139	.339	-4	-5	1	.88	0	/O-6(0-0-6)	0	-0.5
Total 11	**1320**	**4992**	**698**	**1507**	**292**	**47**	**88**	**581**	**480**	**122**	**40**	**0**	**.302**	**.366**	**.432**	**.798**	**122**	**144**	**809**	**5.98**	**32**	***O-1231**	**188**	**13.9**

• HOLT, Jim — James William Holt b: 5/27/1944, Graham, NC BL/TR, 6', 195 lbs. Deb: 4/17/1968 Career OF: 198-143-63

YEAR TM-L	G	AB	R	H	2B	3B	HR	RBI	BB	SO	SB	CS	AVG	OBP	SLG	OPS	OPS+	BR/A	RC	RC/G	FR	G/POS	WS	TPW
1968 Min-A	70	106	9	22	2	1	0	8	4	20	0	1	.208	.236	.245	.482	44	-8	5	1.63	0	O-38(23-2-14)/1-1	0	-1.0
1969 Min-A	12	14	3	5	0	0	1	2	0	4	0	0	.357	.357	.571	.929	153	1	3	8.57	-1	/O-5(1-0-4),1-1	1	0.0
1970*Min-A	142	319	37	85	9	3	3	40	17	32	3	1	.266	.304	.342	.645	76	-10	32	3.42	-1	*O-130(76-52-4)/1-2	7	-1.7
1971 Min-A	126	340	35	88	11	3	1	29	16	28	5	1	.259	.294	.318	.612	71	-13	30	3.01	-1	*O-106(12-86-12)/1-3	5	-1.7
1972 Min-A	10	27	6	12	1	0	1	6	0	1	0	0	.444	.444	.593	1.037	197	3	6	10.31	0	/O-7(2-0-5),1-1	2	0.4
1973 Min-A	132	441	52	131	25	3	11	58	29	43	0	3	.297	.343	.442	.785	115	7	63	5.19	2	*O-102(80-3-21),1-33	12	0.1
1974 Min-A	79	197	24	50	11	0	0	16	14	16	0	0	.254	.307	.310	.616	75	-6	18	3.13	3	1-67/O-5(2-0-3)	2	-0.8
*Oak-A	30	42	1	6	0	0	0	0	1	9	0	0	.143	.182	.143	.325	-6	-6	1	.91	1	1-17/D-3	0	-0.5
Yr.	109	239	25	56	11	0	0	16	15	25	0	0	.234	.285	.280	.565	61	-12	19	2.71	4	1-84/O-5(2-0-3),D-3	2	-1.4
1975*Oak-A	102	123	7	27	3	0	2	16	11	11	0	0	.220	.294	.293	.587	68	-5	10	2.66	2	1-52/D-4,O-2(2-0-0),C-1	1	-0.5
1976 Oak-A	4	7	0	2	2	0	0	2	1	2	0	0	.286	.375	.571	.946	182	1	2	8.63	0	/D-2	1	0.1
Total 9	**707**	**1616**	**174**	**428**	**64**	**10**	**19**	**177**	**93**	**166**	**8**	**6**	**.265**	**.308**	**.352**	**.660**	**84**	**-36**	**170**	**3.65**	**6**	**O-395,1-177/D-9,C-1**	**31**	**-5.6**

• HOLT, Red — James Emmett Madison Holt b: 7/25/1894, Dayton, TN d: 2/2/1961, Birmingham, AL BL/TL, 5'11", 175 lbs. Deb: 9/5/1925

YEAR TM-L	G	AB	R	H	2B	3B	HR	RBI	BB	SO	SB	CS	AVG	OBP	SLG	OPS	OPS+	BR/A	RC	RC/G	FR	G/POS	WS	TPW
1925 Phi-A	27	88	13	24	7	0	1	8	12	9	0	0	.273	.360	.386	.746	84	-2	13	5.19	0	1-25	2	-0.3

• HOLT, Roger — Roger Boyd Holt b: 4/8/1956, Daytona Beach, FL BB/TR, 5'11", 165 lbs. Deb: 10/4/1980

YEAR TM-L	G	AB	R	H	2B	3B	HR	RBI	BB	SO	SB	CS	AVG	OBP	SLG	OPS	OPS+	BR/A	RC	RC/G	FR	G/POS	WS	TPW
1980 NY-A	2	6	0	1	0	0	0	1	1	2	0	0	.167	.286	.167	.452	28	-1	0	1.94	0	/2-2	0	0.0

• HONAN, Marty — Martin Weldon Honan b: 5/29/1869, Chicago, IL d: 8/20/1908, Chicago, IL Deb: 10/3/1890

YEAR TM-L	G	AB	R	H	2B	3B	HR	RBI	BB	SO	SB	CS	AVG	OBP	SLG	OPS	OPS+	BR/A	RC	RC/G	FR	G/POS	WS	TPW
1890 Chi-N	1	3	0	0	0	0	0	1	0	2	0	....	.000	.000	.000	.000	-96	-1	0	.00	-1	/C-1	0	-0.1
1891 Chi-N	5	12	1	2	0	1	0	3	1	3	0	....	.167	.231	.333	.564	64	-1	1	2.55	0	/C-5	0	0.0
Total 2	**6**	**15**	**1**	**2**	**0**	**1**	**0**	**4**	**1**	**5**	**0**	**....**	**.133**	**.188**	**.267**	**.454**	**34**	**-1**	**1**	**1.97**	**0**	**/C-6**	**0**	**-0.1**

• HOOD, Abie — Albie Larrison Hood b: 1/31/1903, Sanford, NC d: 10/14/1988, Chesapeake, VA BL/TR, 5'7", 152 lbs. Deb: 7/15/1925

YEAR TM-L	G	AB	R	H	2B	3B	HR	RBI	BB	SO	SB	CS	AVG	OBP	SLG	OPS	OPS+	BR/A	RC	RC/G	FR	G/POS	WS	TPW
1925 Bos-N	5	21	2	6	2	0	1	2	1	0	0	0	.286	.318	.524	.842	122	1	3	5.70	-2	/2-5	1	-0.2

• HOOD, Wally — Wallace James Hood, Sr. b: 2/9/1895, Whittier, CA d: 5/2/1965, Hollywood, CA BR/TR, 5'11.5", 160 lbs. Deb: 4/15/1920 Career OF: 3-11-10

YEAR TM-L	G	AB	R	H	2B	3B	HR	RBI	BB	SO	SB	CS	AVG	OBP	SLG	OPS	OPS+	BR/A	RC	RC/G	FR	G/POS	WS	TPW
1920 Bro-N	7	14	4	2	1	0	0	1	4	4	2	0	.143	.333	.214	.548	58	-0	2	3.31	1	/O-5(0-2-3)	1	0.1
Pit-N	2	1	1	0	0	0	0	0	1	0	1	0	.000	.500	.000	.500	50	0	0	9.79	0	....	0	0.0
Yr.	9	15	5	2	1	0	0	1	5	4	3	0	.133	.350	.200	.550	57	0	2	3.75	1	/O-5(0-2-3)	1	0.1
1921 Bro-N	56	65	16	17	1	2	1	4	9	14	2	2	.262	.360	.385	.745	94	-0	9	4.85	-1	O-20(3-9-7)	1	-0.2
1922 Bro-N	2	0	2	0	0	0	0	0	0	0	0	0	....	....	....	....	-101	0	0	....	0	....	0	0.0
Total 3	**67**	**80**	**23**	**19**	**2**	**2**	**1**	**5**	**14**	**18**	**5**	**2**	**.238**	**.358**	**.350**	**.708**	**85**	**-0**	**11**	**4.60**	**0**	**/O-25**	**2**	**-0.1**

• HOOKS, Alex — Alexander Marcus Hooks b: 8/29/1906, Edgewood, TX d: 6/19/1993, Edgewood, TX BL/TL, 6'1", 183 lbs. Deb: 4/17/1935

YEAR TM-L	G	AB	R	H	2B	3B	HR	RBI	BB	SO	SB	CS	AVG	OBP	SLG	OPS	OPS+	BR/A	RC	RC/G	FR	G/POS	WS	TPW
1935 Phi-A	15	44	4	10	3	0	0	4	3	10	0	0	.227	.277	.295	.572	48	-3	4	2.82	0	1-10	0	-0.4

• HOOPER, Harry — Harry Bartholomew Hooper b: 8/24/1887, Bell Station, CA d: 12/18/1974, Santa Cruz, CA BL/TR, 5'10", 168 lbs. Deb: 4/16/1909 HOF: 1971 Career OF: 74-18-2192

YEAR TM-L	G	AB	R	H	2B	3B	HR	RBI	BB	SO	SB	CS	AVG	OBP	SLG	OPS	OPS+	BR/A	RC	RC/G	FR	G/POS	WS	TPW
1909 Bos-A	81	255	29	72	3	4	0	12	16	....	15	....	.282	.337	.325	.662	107	2	33	4.50	4	O-74(62-4-8)	9	0.2
1910 Bos-A	155	584	81	156	9	10	2	27	62	....	40	....	.267	.346	.327	.673	108	7	82	4.60	8	*O-155(9-4-142)	19	0.9
1911 Bos-A	130	524	93	163	20	6	4	45	73	....	38	....	.311	.399	.395	.794	123	20	98	6.78	6	*O-130(0-0-130)	20	1.9
1912*Bos-A	147	590	98	143	20	12	2	53	66	....	29	....	.242	.326	.327	.653	83	-13	73	4.04	-1	*O-147(0-0-147)	15	-2.2
1913 Bos-A	148	586	100	169	29	12	4	40	60	51	26	....	.288	.359	.399	.759	119	14	89	5.30	2	*O-147(1-9-137)/P-1	21	0.9
1914 Bos-A	142	530	85	137	23	15	1	41	58	47	19	14	.258	.336	.364	.700	110	4	66	4.25	6	*O-140(0-1-139)	20	0.4
1915*Bos-A	149	566	90	133	20	13	2	51	89	36	22	20	.235	.342	.327	.669	103	1	66	3.74	10	*O-149(0-0-149)	19	0.3
1916*Bos-A	151	575	75	156	20	11	1	37	80	35	27	11	.271	.361	.350	.711	113	12	80	4.66	6	*O-151(0-0-151)	26	1.2
1917 Bos-A	151	559	89	143	21	11	3	45	80	40	21	....	.256	.355	.349	.704	116	13	76	4.49	-1	*O-151(0-0-151)	22	0.5
1918*Bos-A	126	474	81	137	26	13	1	44	75	25	24	....	.289	.391	.405	.796	142	27	82	5.93	5	*O-126(0-0-126)	**29**	2.8
1919 Bos-A	128	491	76	131	25	6	3	49	79	28	23	....	.267	.374	.360	.734	113	12	72	5.05	6	*O-128(0-0-128)	17	1.2
1920 Bos-A	139	536	91	167	30	17	7	53	88	27	16	18	.312	.411	.470	.881	139	30	104	7.03	8	*O-139(2-0-137)	24	3.0
1921 Chi-A	108	419	74	137	26	5	8	58	55	21	13	7	.327	.406	.470	.876	124	18	82	7.24	1	*O-108(0-0-108)	15	0.9
1922 Chi-A	152	602	111	183	35	8	11	80	68	33	16	12	.304	.379	.444	.823	114	13	102	6.15	6	*O-149(0-0-149)	21	0.7
1923 Chi-A	145	576	87	166	32	4	10	65	68	22	18	18	.288	.370	.410	.780	106	4	88	5.25	-9	*O-143(0-0-143)	15	-1.6
1924 Chi-A	130	476	107	156	27	8	10	62	65	26	16	13	.328	.413	.481	.894	134	24	95	7.29	10	*O-123(0-0-123)	19	2.3
1925 Chi-A	127	442	62	117	23	5	6	55	54	21	12	8	.265	.351	.380	.731	90	-6	62	4.67	3	*O-124(0-0-124)	10	-1.1
Total 17	**2309**	**8785**	**1429**	**2466**	**389**	**160**	**75**	**817**	**1136**	**412**	**375**	**121**	**.281**	**.368**	**.387**	**.755**	**114**	**183**	**1349**	**5.28**	**71**	***O-2284/P-1**	**321**	**12.4**

• HOOPER, Mike — Michael H. Hooper b: 2/7/1850, Baltimore, MD d: 12/2/1917, Baltimore, MD, 5'6", 165 lbs. Deb: 6/27/1873 U

YEAR TM-L	G	AB	R	H	2B	3B	HR	RBI	BB	SO	SB	CS	AVG	OBP	SLG	OPS	OPS+	BR/A	RC	RC/G	FR	G/POS	WS	TPW
1873 Mar-n	3	14	3	3	1	0	0	2	0	0	0	0	.214	.214	.286	.500	62	-0	1	2.44	-1	/O-2(2-0-0),C-1	....	-0.1

• HOOVER, Buster — William James Hoover b: 4/12/1863, Philadelphia, PA d: 4/16/1924, Jersey City, NJ BR/TR, 6'1", 178 lbs. Deb: 4/17/1884 Career OF: 55-45-2

YEAR TM-L	G	AB	R	H	2B	3B	HR	RBI	BB	SO	SB	CS	AVG	OBP	SLG	OPS	OPS+	BR/A	RC	RC/G	FR	G/POS	WS	TPW
1884 Phi-U	63	275	76	100	20	8	0	....	12	....	....	....	.364	.390	.495	.885	214	32	54	8.70	-4	O-37(37-0-0),S-15/1-6,2-6,3-1	13	2.4
Phi-N	10	42	6	8	1	0	1	4	4	9	....	....	.190	.261	.286	.547	75	-1	3	2.60	0	O-10(6-4-0)	1	-0.1
1886 Bal-a	40	157	25	34	2	6	0	10	16	....	15	....	.217	.297	.306	.603	91	-1	19	4.21	-2	O-40(0-40-0)	4	-0.4
1892 Cin-N	14	51	7	9	0	0	0	2	5	4	1	....	.176	.250	.176	.426	30	-4	3	1.65	1	O-14(12-1-2)	1	-0.4
Total 3	**127**	**525**	**114**	**151**	**23**	**14**	**1**	**16**	**37**	**13**	**16**	**....**	**.288**	**.337**	**.390**	**.727**	**146**	**26**	**79**	**5.88**	**-5**	**O-101/S-15,1-6,2-6,3-1**	**19**	**1.5**

• HOOVER, Charlie — Charles E. Hoover b: 9/9/1865, Mound City, IL BL/TR, 5'8" Deb: 10/9/1888

YEAR TM-L	G	AB	R	H	2B	3B	HR	RBI	BB	SO	SB	CS	AVG	OBP	SLG	OPS	OPS+	BR/A	RC	RC/G	FR	G/POS	WS	TPW
1888 KC-a	3	10	0	3	0	0	0	1	0	....	0	....	.300	.300	.300	.600	87	-0	1	3.56	-0	/C-3	0	0.0
1889 KC-a	71	258	44	64	2	5	1	25	29	38	9	....	.248	.329	.306	.635	77	-8	30	4.05	-2	C-66/3-4,O-3(3-0-0)	5	-0.4
Total 2	**74**	**268**	**44**	**67**	**2**	**5**	**1**	**26**	**29**	**38**	**9**	**....**	**.250**	**.328**	**.306**	**.634**	**77**	**-8**	**31**	**4.03**	**-2**	**/C-69,3-4,O-3**	**5**	**-0.4**

• HOOVER, Joe — Robert Joseph Hoover b: 4/15/1915, Brawley, CA d: 9/2/1965, Los Angeles, CA BR/TR, 5'11", 175 lbs. Deb: 4/21/1943

YEAR TM-L	G	AB	R	H	2B	3B	HR	RBI	BB	SO	SB	CS	AVG	OBP	SLG	OPS	OPS+	BR/A	RC	RC/G	FR	G/POS	WS	TPW
1943 Det-A	144	575	78	140	15	8	4	38	36	101	6	5	.243	.289	.318	.607	72	-22	54	3.07	-9	*S-144	9	-2.1
1944 Det-A	120	441	67	104	20	2	0	29	35	66	7	10	.236	.301	.290	.591	66	-22	40	2.99	1	*S-119/2-1	9	-1.2
1945*Det-A	74	222	33	57	10	5	1	17	21	35	6	2	.257	.324	.360	.684	92	-2	28	4.27	-2	S-68	8	0.1
Total 3	**338**	**1238**	**178**	**301**	**45**	**15**	**5**	**84**	**92**	**202**	**19**	**17**	**.243**	**.300**	**.316**	**.616**	**73**	**-45**	**122**	**3.25**	**-10**	**S-331/2-1**	**26**	**-3.2**

• HOOVER, Paul — Paul Hoover b: 4/14/1976, Columbus, OH BR/TR, 6'1", 210 lbs. Deb: 9/8/2001

YEAR TM-L	G	AB	R	H	2B	3B	HR	RBI	BB	SO	SB	CS	AVG	OBP	SLG	OPS	OPS+	BR/A	RC	RC/G	FR	G/POS	WS	TPW
2001 TB-A	3	4	1	1	0	0	0	0	0	1	0	0	.250	.250	.250	.500	33	-0	0	2.25	-1	/C-2	0	-0.1
2002 TB-A	5	17	1	3	0	0	0	2	0	5	0	0	.176	.176	.176	.353	-6	-3	1	1.02	-1	/C-4	0	-0.4
Total 2	**8**	**21**	**2**	**4**	**0**	**0**	**0**	**2**	**0**	**6**	**0**	**0**	**.190**	**.190**	**.190**	**.381**	**2**	**-3**	**1**	**1.24**	**-2**	**/C-6**	**0**	**-0.5**

• HOPKINS, Buck — John Winton "Sis" Hopkins b: 1/3/1883, Grafton, VA d: 10/2/1929, Phoebus, VA BL/TL, 5'10", 165 lbs. Deb: 7/22/1907

YEAR TM-L	G	AB	R	H	2B	3B	HR	RBI	BB	SO	SB	CS	AVG	OBP	SLG	OPS	OPS+	BR/A	RC	RC/G	FR	G/POS	WS	TPW
1907 StL-N	15	44	7	6	3	0	0	3	10	....	2	....	.136	.333	.205	.538	71	-1	4	2.63	-2	O-15(0-15-0)	1	-0.4

• HOPKINS, Don — Donald Hopkins b: 1/9/1952, West Point, MS BL/TR, 6', 175 lbs. Deb: 4/8/1975

YEAR TM-L	G	AB	R	H	2B	3B	HR	RBI	BB	SO	SB	CS	AVG	OBP	SLG	OPS	OPS+	BR/A	RC	RC/G	FR	G/POS	WS	TPW
1975*Oak-A	82	6	25	1	0	0	0	0	2	0	21	9	.167	.375	.167	.542	59	0	0	.00	0	D-20/O-5(1-2-2)	0	0.0

YEAR TM-L	G	AB	R	H	2B	3B	HR	RBI	BB	SO	SB	CS	AVG	OBP	SLG	OPS	OPS+	BR/A	RC	RC/G	FR	G/POS	WS	TPW
1976 Oak-A	3	0	0	0	0	0	0	0	0	0	0	1	....	....	....	....	-104	-0	0	.00	0	....	0	0.0
Total 2	85	6	25	1	0	0	0	0	2	0	21	10	.167	.375	.167	.542	59	0	0	.00	0	/D-20,0-5	0	-0.1

• HOPKINS, Gail Gail Eason Hopkins b: 2/19/1943, Tulsa, OK BL/TR, 5'10", 200 lbs. Deb: 6/29/1968

YEAR TM-L	G	AB	R	H	2B	3B	HR	RBI	BB	SO	SB	CS	AVG	OBP	SLG	OPS	OPS+	BR/A	RC	RC/G	FR	G/POS	WS	TPW
1968 Chi-A	29	37	4	8	2	0	0	2	6	3	0	0	.216	.326	.270	.596	81	-1	4	3.43	-1	/1-7	1	-0.2
1969 Chi-A	124	373	52	99	13	3	8	46	50	28	2	1	.265	.354	.381	.734	100	1	51	4.81	-6	*1-101	9	-1.2
1970 Chi-A	116	287	32	82	8	1	6	29	28	19	0	0	.286	.351	.383	.735	99	0	39	4.93	-4	1-77/C-8	7	-0.9
1971 KC-A	103	295	35	82	16	1	9	47	37	13	3	1	.278	.366	.431	.797	126	11	47	5.59	5	1-83	11	1.1
1972 KC-A	53	71	1	15	2	0	0	5	7	4	0	0	.211	.282	.239	.521	56	-4	5	2.22	-2	1-13/3-1	0	-0.7
1973 KC-A	74	138	17	34	6	1	2	16	29	15	1	2	.246	.385	.348	.732	100	1	18	4.27	0	D-36,1-10	3	0.1
1974 LA-N	15	18	1	4	0	0	0	0	3	1	0	0	.222	.333	.222	.556	60	-1	1	2.74	1	/1-2,C-2	1	0.0
Total 7	514	1219	142	324	47	6	25	145	160	83	6	4	.266	.355	.376	.730	102	9	165	4.72	-6	1-293/D-36,C-10,3-1	32	-1.9

• HOPKINS, Marty Meredith Hilliard Hopkins b: 2/22/1907, Wolfe City, TX d: 11/20/1963, Dallas, TX BR/TR, 5'11", 175 lbs. Deb: 4/17/1934

YEAR TM-L	G	AB	R	H	2B	3B	HR	RBI	BB	SO	SB	CS	AVG	OBP	SLG	OPS	OPS+	BR/A	RC	RC/G	FR	G/POS	WS	TPW
1934 Phi-N	10	25	6	3	2	0	0	3	7	5	0	....	.120	.313	.200	.513	36	-2	2	2.29	0	/3-9	0	-0.2
Chi-A	67	210	22	45	7	0	2	28	42	26	0	3	.214	.348	.276	.624	61	-12	23	3.46	3	3-63	4	-0.7
1935 Chi-A	59	144	20	32	3	0	2	17	36	23	1	0	.222	.378	.285	.663	72	-4	19	4.22	-4	3-49/2-5	3	-0.5
Total 2	136	379	48	80	12	0	4	48	85	54	1	3	.211	.357	.274	.631	63	-18	44	3.66	-1	3-121/2-5	7	-1.4

• HOPKINS, Mike Michael Joseph "Skinner" Hopkins b: 11/1/1872, Glasgow, Scotland d: 2/5/1952, Pittsburgh, PA BR/TR, 5'8", 160 lbs. Deb: 8/24/1902

YEAR TM-L	G	AB	R	H	2B	3B	HR	RBI	BB	SO	SB	CS	AVG	OBP	SLG	OPS	OPS+	BR/A	RC	RC/G	FR	G/POS	WS	TPW
1902 Pit-N	1	2	0	2	1	0	0	0	0	....	0	....	1.000	1.000	1.500	2.500	647	1	3	∞	0	/C-1	1	0.1

• HOPP, Johnny John Leonard "Cotney" Hopp
b: 7/18/1916, Hastings, NE d: 6/1/2003, Scottsbluff, NE BL/TL, 5'10", 175 lbs. Deb: 9/18/1939 C Career OF: 132-471-127

YEAR TM-L	G	AB	R	H	2B	3B	HR	RBI	BB	SO	SB	CS	AVG	OBP	SLG	OPS	OPS+	BR/A	RC	RC/G	FR	G/POS	WS	TPW
1939 StL-N	6	4	1	2	1	0	0	2	1	1	0	....	.500	.600	.750	1.350	245	1	2	26.41	0	/1-2	0	0.1
1940 StL-N	80	152	24	41	7	4	1	14	9	21	3	....	.270	.315	.388	.703	88	-3	18	4.17	-1	0-39(12-27-0),1-10	3	-0.6
1941 StL-N	134	445	83	135	25	11	4	50	50	63	15	....	.303	.378	.436	.813	121	13	77	6.36	0	0-91(58-23-10),1-39	19	0.6
1942*StL-N	95	314	41	81	16	7	3	37	36	40	14	....	.258	.334	.382	.716	102	1	43	4.95	-6	1-88	10	-1.4
1943*StL-N	91	241	33	54	10	2	2	25	24	22	8	....	.224	.297	.307	.604	71	-9	24	3.28	-2	0-52(40-12-0),1-27	4	-1.5
1944*StL-N	139	527	106	177	35	9	11	72	58	47	15	....	.336	.404	.499	.903	150	36	110	8.23	-8	*0-131(1-130-0)/1-6	28	2.5
1945 StL-N	124	446	67	129	22	8	3	44	49	24	14	....	.289	.363	.395	.758	108	5	68	5.57	-3	*0-104(2-26-89),1-15	16	-0.4
1946 Bos-N★	129	445	71	148	23	8	3	48	34	34	21	....	.333	.386	.440	.827	132	19	77	6.66	0	1-68,0-58(1-57-0)	21	1.7
1947 Bos-N	134	430	74	124	20	2	2	32	58	30	13	....	.288	.376	.358	.734	98	1	62	5.11	-7	*0-125(0-123-2)	14	-0.8
1948 Pit-N	120	392	64	109	15	12	1	31	40	25	5	....	.278	.345	.385	.730	95	-2	53	4.90	-2	0-80(1-71-8),1-25	12	-0.7
1949 Pit-N	20	55	5	12	3	1	0	3	7	3	0	0	.218	.306	.309	.616	64	-3	5	3.35	0	/0-7(2-0-5),1-6	0	-0.4
Bro-N	8	14	0	0	0	0	0	0	0	3	0	....	.000	.000	.000	.000	-96	-4	0	.00	1	/0-4(1-0-3),1-2	0	-0.3
Pit-N	85	316	50	106	11	4	5	36	30	26	9	....	.335	.393	.443	.836	121	10	56	6.86	0	1-71/0-9(2-0-7)	12	0.7
Yr.	113	385	55	118	14	5	5	39	37	32	9	0	.306	.367	.408	.775	105	3	61	5.96	1	1-79,0-20(5-0-15)	12	0.1
1950 Pit-N	106	318	51	108	24	5	8	47	43	17	7	....	.340	.420	.522	.942	141	20	71	8.84	-4	1-70/0-7(2-2-3)	12	1.4
*NY-A	19	27	9	9	2	1	1	8	8	1	0	1	.333	.486	.593	1.078	180	3	8	10.69	0	1-12/0-6(6-0-0)	2	0.3
1951*NY-A	46	63	10	13	1	0	2	4	9	11	2	0	.206	.306	.317	.623	71	-2	7	3.89	-2	1-25	2	-0.4
1952 NY-A	15	25	4	4	0	0	0	2	2	3	2	0	.160	.250	.160	.410	17	-2	1	1.56	1	1-12	0	-0.2
Det-A	42	46	5	10	1	0	0	3	6	7	0	0	.217	.308	.239	.547	53	-3	4	2.69	0	/0-4(4-0-0),1-1	0	-0.3
Yr.	57	71	9	14	1	0	0	5	8	10	2	0	.197	.288	.211	.499	41	-5	5	2.27	0	1-13/0-4(4-0-0)	0	-0.5
Total 14	1393	4260	698	1262	216	74	46	458	464	378	128	1	.296	.368	.414	.782	113	81	685	5.93	-32	0-717,1-479	155	0.2

• HORAN, Shags Joseph Patrick Horan b: 9/6/1895, St. Louis, MO d: 2/13/1969, Torrance, CA BR/TR, 5'10", 170 lbs. Deb: 7/14/1924

YEAR TM-L	G	AB	R	H	2B	3B	HR	RBI	BB	SO	SB	CS	AVG	OBP	SLG	OPS	OPS+	BR/A	RC	RC/G	FR	G/POS	WS	TPW
1924 NY-A	22	31	4	9	1	0	0	7	1	5	0	0	.290	.313	.323	.635	64	-2	3	3.61	0	0-14(4-1-9)	0	-0.2

• HORN, Sam Samuel Lee Horn b: 11/2/1963, Dallas, TX BL/TL, 6'5", 250 lbs. Deb: 7/25/1987

YEAR TM-L	G	AB	R	H	2B	3B	HR	RBI	BB	SO	SB	CS	AVG	OBP	SLG	OPS	OPS+	BR/A	RC	RC/G	FR	G/POS	WS	TPW
1987 Bos-A	46	158	31	44	7	0	14	34	17	55	0	1	.278	.356	.589	.945	141	8	32	7.10	0	D-40	5	0.7
1988 Bos-A	24	61	4	9	0	0	2	8	11	20	0	0	.148	.278	.246	.524	46	-4	5	2.29	0	D-16	0	-0.5
1989 Bos-A	33	54	1	8	2	0	0	4	8	16	0	0	.148	.258	.185	.443	25	-5	2	1.24	0	D-14/1-2	0	-0.6
1990 Bal-A	79	246	30	61	13	0	14	45	32	62	0	0	.248	.335	.472	.806	127	9	38	5.26	0	D-63,1-10	8	0.6
1991 Bal-A	121	317	45	74	16	0	23	61	41	99	0	0	.233	.327	.502	.828	131	13	51	5.39	0	*D-102	11	1.0
1992 Bal-A	63	162	13	38	10	1	5	19	21	60	0	0	.235	.326	.401	.727	100	0	20	4.04	0	D-46	1	-0.1
1993 Cle-A	12	33	8	15	1	0	4	8	1	5	0	0	.455	.486	.848	1.334	252	7	13	17.42	0	D-11	2	0.6
1995 Tex-A	11	9	0	1	0	0	0	0	1	6	0	0	.111	.200	.111	.311	-16	-2	0	.85	0	/D-1	0	-0.1
Total 8	389	1040	132	250	49	1	62	179	132	323	0	1	.240	.330	.468	.798	118	25	160	5.18	0	D-293/1-12	27	1.5

• HORNER, Bob James Robert Horner b: 8/6/1957, Junction City, KS BR/TR, 6'1", 210 lbs. Deb: 6/16/1978

YEAR TM-L	G	AB	R	H	2B	3B	HR	RBI	BB	SO	SB	CS	AVG	OBP	SLG	OPS	OPS+	BR/A	RC	RC/G	FR	G/POS	WS	TPW
1978 Atl-N	89	323	50	86	17	1	23	63	24	42	0	0	.266	.321	.539	.860	123	8	54	5.77	6	3-89	14	1.4
1979 Atl-N	121	487	66	153	15	1	33	98	22	74	0	2	.314	.348	.552	.900	132	18	89	6.93	-5	3-82,1-45	19	1.0
1980 Atl-N	124	463	81	124	14	1	35	89	27	50	3	1	.268	.310	.529	.839	126	13	70	5.22	10	*3-121/1-1	19	2.3
1981 Atl-N	79	300	42	83	10	0	15	42	32	39	2	3	.277	.348	.460	.808	124	8	47	5.57	-10	3-79	11	-0.3
1982*Atl-N★	140	499	85	130	24	0	32	97	66	75	3	5	.261	.351	.501	.852	131	19	86	5.96	-18	*3-137	21	-0.1
1983 Atl-N	104	386	75	117	25	1	20	68	50	63	4	2	.303	.384	.528	.913	140	21	76	7.16	-4	*3-104/1-1	17	1.7
1984 Atl-N	32	113	15	31	8	0	3	19	14	17	0	0	.274	.354	.425	.779	110	2	17	5.27	-1	3-32	4	0.0
1985 Atl-N	130	483	61	129	25	3	27	89	50	57	1	1	.267	.337	.499	.836	123	13	77	5.46	-8	1-87,3-40	16	-0.1
1986 Atl-N	141	517	70	141	22	0	27	87	52	72	1	4	.273	.342	.472	.813	116	8	79	5.24	-4	*1-139	15	-0.4
1988 StL-N	60	206	15	53	9	1	3	33	32	23	0	0	.257	.360	.354	.714	105	2	26	4.17	0	1-57	4	-0.2
Total 10	1020	3777	560	1047	169	8	218	685	369	512	14	18	.277	.344	.499	.843	125	113	621	5.76	-35	3-684,1-330	140	5.3

• HORNSBY, Rogers Rogers "Rajah" Hornsby
b: 4/27/1896, Winters, TX d: 1/5/1963, Chicago, IL BR/TR, 5'11", 175 lbs. Deb: 9/10/1915 M/C HOF: 1942 Career OF: 6-1-13

YEAR TM-L	G	AB	R	H	2B	3B	HR	RBI	BB	SO	SB	CS	AVG	OBP	SLG	OPS	OPS+	BR/A	RC	RC/G	FR	G/POS	WS	TPW
1915 StL-N	18	57	5	14	2	0	0	4	2	6	0	2	.246	.271	.281	.552	67	-3	4	2.29	-3	S-18	0	-0.6
1916 StL-N	139	495	63	155	17	15	6	65	40	63	17	....	.313	.369	.444	.814	150	29	88	6.53	-11	3-83,S-45,1-15/2-1	28	2.6
1917 StL-N	145	523	86	171	24	**17**	8	66	45	34	17	....	.327	.385	**.484**	**.868**	**170**	42	100	**7.07**	0	*S-144	**38**	**6.0**
1918 StL-N	115	416	51	117	19	11	5	60	40	43	8	....	.281	.349	.416	.764	138	18	60	5.14	0	*S-109/0-3(0-1-2)	18	2.9
1919 StL-N	138	512	68	163	15	9	8	71	48	41	17	....	.318	.384	.430	.814	**154**	**34**	87	6.34	-2	3-72,S-37,2-25/1-5	26	4.1
1920 StL-N	149	589	96	**218**	**44**	20	9	**94**	60	50	12	15	**.370**	**.431**	**.559**	**.990**	**187**	**64**	138	**9.25**	8	*2-149	**38**	**8.0**
1921 StL-N	154	592	**131**	**235**	**44**	**18**	21	**126**	60	48	13	13	**.397**	**.458**	**.639**	**1.097**	**191**	**77**	169	**11.61**	5	*2-142/0-6(6-0-0),3-3,S-3,1	**41**	**8.5**
1922 StL-N	154	623	**141**	**250**	**46**	14	**42**	**152**	65	50	17	12	**.401**	**.459**	**.722**	**1.181**	**210**	**99**	200	**13.28**	-6	*2-154	**47**	**9.2**
1923 StL-N	107	424	89	163	32	10	17	83	55	29	3	7	**.384**	**.459**	**.627**	**1.086**	**188**	**53**	120	**11.68**	-1	2-96,1-10	26	**5.2**
1924 StL-N	143	536	**121**	**227**	**43**	14	25	94	**89**	32	5	12	**.424**	**.507**	**.696**	**1.203**	**223**	**95**	186	**14.78**	4	*2-143	**38**	**10.2**
1925 StL-N	138	504	133	203	41	10	**39**	**143**	83	39	5	3	**.403**	**.489**	**.756**	**1.245**	**208**	**85**	187	**15.50**	-9	*2-136	**36**	**7.5**
1926*StL-N	134	527	96	167	34	5	11	93	61	39	3	....	.317	.388	.463	.851	123	18	94	6.49	-15	*2-134	21	0.7
1927 NY-N	155	568	**133**	205	32	9	26	125	**86**	38	9	....	.361	**.448**	.586	**1.035**	**175**	**64**	148	**9.88**	-12	*2-155	**40**	5.5
1928 Bos-N	140	486	99	188	42	7	21	94	**107**	41	5	....	**.387**	**.498**	**.632**	**1.130**	**204**	**81**	154	**12.41**	-25	*2-140	33	**5.9**
1929*Chi-N	156	602	**156**	229	47	8	39	149	87	65	2	....	.380	.459	**.679**	**1.139**	**178**	**74**	183	**12.05**	-2	*2-156	**42**	**6.9**
1930 Chi-N	42	104	15	32	5	1	2	18	12	12	0	....	.308	.385	.433	.817	97	-0	17	6.02	-1	2-25	3	0.0
1931 Chi-N	100	357	64	118	37	1	16	90	56	23	1	....	.331	.421	.574	.996	162	33	90	9.58	-5	2-69,3-26	20	3.3
1932 Chi-N	19	58	10	13	2	0	1	7	10	4	0	....	.224	.357	.310	.667	82	-1	7	4.23	-3	0-10(0-0-10)/3-6	1	-0.4
1933 StL-N	46	83	9	27	6	0	2	21	12	6	1	....	.325	.423	.470	.893	147	6	17	7.82	0	2-17	4	0.7
StL-A	11	9	2	3	1	0	1	2	2	1	0	0	.333	.455	.778	1.232	208	2	3	14.49	0	....	0	0.1
1934 StL-A	24	23	2	7	2	0	1	11	7	4	0	0	.304	.484	.522	1.006	147	2	7	10.83	1	/3-1,0-1	1	0.3
1935 StL-A	10	24	1	5	3	0	0	3	3	6	0	0	.208	.296	.333	.630	60	-1	2	3.48	-1	/1-3,2-2,3-1	0	-0.2
1936 StL-A	2	5	1	2	0	0	0	2	1	0	0	0	.400	.500	.400	.900	121	0	1	9.58	0	/1-1	0	0.0
1937 StL-A	20	56	7	18	3	0	1	11	7	5	0	0	.321	.397	.429	.825	107	1	10	6.86	-3	2-17	1	-0.1
Total 23	2259	8173	1579	2930	541	169	301	1584	1038	679	135	64	.358	.434	.577	1.010	175	873	2074	9.86	-82	*2-1561,S-356,3-192/1-35,0	502	86.1

YEAR TM-L	G	AB	R	H	2B	3B	HR	RBI	BB	SO	SB	CS	AVG	OBP	SLG	OPS	OPS+	BR/A	RC	RC/G	FR	G/POS	WS	TPW
• HORNUNG, Joe	Michael Joseph "Ubbo Ubbo" Hornung b: 6/12/1857, Carthage, NY d: 10/30/1931, New York, NY BR/TR, 5'8.5", 164 lbs. Deb: 5/1/1879 U Career OF: 1051-1-5																							
1879 Buf-N	78	319	46	85	18	7	0	38	2	27	....	....	.266	.271	.367	.638	105	1	33	3.89	-1	*0-77(76-0-1)/1-1	9	-0.4
1880 Buf-N	85	342	47	91	8	11	1	42	8	29	....	....	.266	.283	.363	.645	115	5	36	3.94	-1	*0-67(67-0-0),1-18/2-5,P-1	10	-0.2
1881 Bos-N	83	324	40	78	12	8	2	25	5	25	....	....	.241	.252	.346	.598	90	-4	29	3.18	11	*0-83(83-1-0)	8	0.2
1882 Bos-N	85	388	67	117	14	11	1	50	2	25	....	....	.302	.305	.402	.707	124	9	49	4.95	8	*0-84(84-0-0)/1-1	14	1.3
1883 Bos-N	98	446	**107**	124	25	13	8	66	8	54	....	....	.278	.291	.446	.737	117	8	59	5.06	7	*0-98(98-0-0)/3-1	16	0.9
1884 Bos-N	115	518	119	139	27	10	7	51	17	80	....	....	.268	.292	.400	.691	116	8	62	4.49	5	*0-110(110-0-0)/1-6	18	0.8
1885 Bos-N	25	109	14	22	4	1	1	7	1	20	....	....	.202	.209	.284	.493	61	-5	7	2.06	-3	0-25(25-0-0)	1	-0.8
1886 Bos-N	94	424	67	109	12	2	2	40	10	62	16	....	.257	.274	.309	.583	80	-10	41	3.54	1	*0-94(94-0-0)	8	-1.2
1887 Bos-N	98	454	85	135	10	6	5	49	17	28	41	....	.297	.302	.355	.657	84	-10	61	5.04	11	*0-98(98-0-0)	9	-0.2
1888 Bos-N	107	431	61	103	11	7	3	53	16	39	29	....	.239	.269	.318	.587	83	-9	46	3.77	-5	*0-107(106-0-1)	8	-1.8
1889 Bal-a	135	533	73	122	13	9	1	78	22	72	34	....	.229	.269	.293	.561	61	-28	52	3.37	7	*0-134(134-0-1)/3-1	8	-2.2
1890 NY-N	120	513	62	122	18	5	0	65	12	37	39	....	.238	.258	.292	.550	60	-29	50	3.39	1	0-77(76-0-2),1-36/3-5,S-2	6	-3.0
Total 12	1123	4801	788	1247	172	90	31	564	120	498	159	....	.260	.277	.350	.627	91	-64	524	4.00	41	*0-1054/1-62,3-7,2-5,S-2,P	115	-6.4
• HORTON, Tony	Anthony Darrin Horton b: 12/6/1944, Santa Monica, CA BR/TR, 6'3", 210 lbs. Deb: 7/31/1964																							
1964 Bos-A	36	126	9	28	5	0	1	8	3	20	0	0	.222	.240	.286	.526	43	-10	7	1.75	-1	0-24(24-0-0)/1-8	0	-1.3
1965 Bos-A	60	163	23	48	8	1	7	23	18	36	0	2	.294	.365	.485	.849	131	6	29	6.39	-2	1-44	5	0.2
1966 Bos-A	6	22	0	3	0	0	0	2	0	5	0	0	.136	.136	.136	.273	-19	-3	0	.19	1	/1-6	0	-0.3
1967 Bos-A	21	39	2	12	3	0	0	9	0	5	0	0	.308	.308	.385	.692	96	-0	4	3.49	0	/1-6	1	-0.1
Cle-A	106	363	35	102	13	4	10	44	18	52	3	0	.281	.322	.421	.744	117	7	48	4.79	-4	1-94	12	-0.2
Yr.	127	402	37	114	16	4	10	53	18	57	3	0	.284	.321	.418	.739	115	7	52	4.66	-4	*1-100	13	-0.3
1968 Cle-A	133	477	57	119	29	3	14	59	34	56	3	1	.249	.304	.411	.714	117	8	59	4.30	-1	*1-128	16	-0.1
1969 Cle-A	159	625	77	174	25	4	27	93	37	91	3	3	.278	.321	.461	.782	113	7	85	4.79	-7	*1-157	19	-1.4
1970 Cle-A	115	413	48	111	19	3	17	59	30	54	3	2	.269	.324	.453	.777	107	3	55	4.54	-2	*1-112	9	-0.8
Total 7	636	2228	251	597	102	15	76	297	140	319	12	8	.268	.315	.430	.745	109	17	287	4.48	-17	1-555/0-24	62	-4.1
• HORTON, Willie	Willie Watterson Horton b: 10/18/1942, Arno, VA BR/TR, 5'11", 209 lbs. Deb: 9/10/1963 C Career OF: 1117-0-123																							
1963 Det-A	15	43	6	14	2	1	1	4	0	8	2	0	.326	.326	.488	.814	120	1	7	6.68	0	/0-9(8-0-1)	2	0.1
1964 Det-A	25	80	6	13	1	3	1	10	11	20	0	0	.163	.272	.288	.559	55	-5	7	2.80	-1	0-23(20-0-3)	0	-0.7
1965 Det-A★	143	512	69	140	20	2	29	104	48	101	5	9	.273	.343	.490	.833	132	18	81	5.49	-1	*0-141(111-0-34)/3-1	20	0.9
1966 Det-A	146	526	72	138	22	6	27	100	44	103	1	1	.262	.323	.481	.804	125	15	80	5.33	-10	*0-137(129-0-20)	21	-0.4
1967 Det-A	122	401	47	110	20	3	19	67	36	80	0	0	.274	.340	.481	.821	136	18	64	5.60	3	*0-110(109-0-1)	17	1.7
1968*Det-A★	143	512	68	146	20	2	36	85	49	110	0	3	.285	.357	.543	.900	165	38	95	6.55	-6	*0-139(139-0-0)	28	2.7
1969 Det-A	141	508	66	133	17	1	28	91	52	93	3	3	.262	.334	.465	.798	116	9	78	5.42	3	*0-136(135-0-3)	19	0.5
1970 Det-A★	96	371	53	113	18	2	17	69	28	43	0	1	.305	.357	.501	.858	133	15	65	6.50	3	0-96(96-0-2)	15	1.3
1971 Det-A	119	450	64	130	25	1	22	72	37	75	1	5	.289	.352	.496	.848	133	16	73	5.70	-3	*0-118(106-0-29)	17	0.8
1972*Det-A	108	333	44	77	9	5	11	36	27	47	0	0	.231	.295	.387	.682	99	-1	37	3.74	3	0-98(81-0-30)	9	-0.3
1973 Det-A★	111	411	42	130	19	3	17	53	23	57	1	4	.316	.363	.501	.864	132	15	69	6.15	-6	*0-107(107-0-0)/D-1	15	0.4
1974 Det-A	72	238	32	71	8	1	15	47	21	36	0	1	.298	.363	.529	.892	149	14	44	6.81	-3	0-64(64-0-0)/D-1	12	0.8
1975 Det-A	159	615	62	169	13	1	25	92	44	109	1	2	.275	.323	.421	.744	104	2	79	4.49	0	*D-159	13	-0.4
1976 Det-A	114	401	40	105	17	0	14	56	49	63	0	0	.262	.345	.409	.754	116	9	55	4.66	0	*D-105	11	0.6
1977 Det-A	1	4	0	1	0	0	0	0	0	0	0	0	.250	.250	.250	.500	35	-0	0	2.25	0	/0-1	0	0.0
Tex-A	139	519	55	150	23	3	15	75	42	117	2	3	.289	.342	.432	.774	108	5	73	4.99	-1	*D-128,0-10(10-0-0)	12	0.0
Yr.	140	523	55	151	23	3	15	75	42	117	2	3	.289	.342	.430	.772	108	5	73	4.97	-1	*D-128,0-11(11-0-0)	12	-0.1
1978 Cle-A	50	169	15	42	7	0	5	22	15	25	3	0	.249	.314	.379	.692	95	-0	19	3.79	0	D-48	3	-0.2
Oak-A	32	102	11	32	8	0	3	19	9	15	0	1	.314	.369	.480	.850	145	5	18	6.61	-1	D-27/0-1	4	0.4
Tor-A	33	122	12	25	6	0	3	19	4	29	0	0	.205	.230	.328	.558	54	-8	8	1.95	0	D-30	0	-0.9
Yr.	115	393	38	99	21	0	11	60	28	69	3	1	.252	.303	.389	.693	96	-3	44	3.84	-1	*D-105/0-1	7	-0.7
1979 Sea-A	162	646	77	180	19	5	29	106	42	112	1	1	.279	.327	.458	.785	107	5	91	5.01	0	*D-162	12	-0.2
1980 Sea-A	97	335	32	74	10	1	8	36	39	70	0	4	.221	.310	.328	.638	74	-13	35	3.41	0	D-92	3	-1.6
Total 18	2028	7298	873	1993	284	40	325	1163	620	1313	20	38	.273	.335	.457	.791	119	158	1077	5.18	-20	*0-1190,D-753/3-1	233	5.6
• HOSEY, Dwayne	Dwayne Samuel Hosey b: 3/11/1967, Sharon, PA BB/TR, 5'10", 175 lbs. Deb: 9/1/1995 Career OF: 9-39-1																							
1995*Bos-A	24	68	20	23	8	1	3	7	8	16	6	0	.338	.408	.618	1.026	157	7	19	11.28	0	0-21(2-19-1)/D-1	4	0.7
1996 Bos-A	28	78	13	17	2	2	1	3	7	17	6	3	.218	.282	.333	.616	54	-6	8	3.16	0	0-26(7-20-0)/D-2	1	-0.5
Total 2	52	146	33	40	10	3	4	10	15	33	12	3	.274	.342	.466	.807	102	1	27	6.49	1	/0-47,D-3	5	0.1
• HOSEY, Steve	Steven Bernard Hosey b: 4/2/1969, Oakland, CA BR/TR, 6'3", 215 lbs. Deb: 8/29/1992 Career OF: 0-0-19																							
1992 SF-N	21	56	6	14	1	0	1	6	0	15	1	1	.250	.250	.321	.571	64	-3	4	2.38	-1	0-18(0-0-18)	0	-0.5
1993 SF-N	3	2	0	1	1	0	0	1	1	1	0	0	.500	.667	1.000	1.667	350	1	2	40.68	0	/0-1	0	0.1
Total 2	24	58	6	15	2	0	1	7	1	16	1	1	.259	.271	.345	.616	78	-2	6	3.19	-1	/0-19	0	-0.4
• HOSLEY, Tim	Timothy Kenneth Hosley b: 5/10/1947, Spartanburg, SC BR/TR, 5'11", 195 lbs. Deb: 9/8/1970																							
1970 Det-A	7	12	1	2	0	0	1	2	0	6	0	0	.167	.167	.417	.583	55	-1	1	2.08	0	/C-4	0	-0.1
1971 Det-A	7	16	2	3	0	0	2	6	0	1	0	0	.188	.188	.563	.750	102	-0	1	2.17	0	/C-4,1-1	1	-0.1
1973 Oak-A	13	14	3	3	0	0	0	2	2	3	0	0	.214	.313	.214	.527	54	-1	1	2.70	-1	C-13	0	-0.2
1974 Oak-A	11	7	3	2	0	0	0	1	1	2	0	0	.286	.375	.286	.661	99	0	1	3.82	-1	/C-8,1-1	0	-0.1
1975 Chi-N	62	141	22	36	7	0	6	20	27	25	1	1	.255	.382	.433	.815	120	5	24	5.72	-3	C-53	6	0.4
1976 Chi-N	1	1	0	0	0	0	0	0	0	0	0	0	.000	.000	.000	.000	-92	-0	0	.00	0	....	0	0.0
Oak-A	37	55	4	9	2	0	1	4	8	12	0	0	.164	.270	.255	.524	56	-3	4	2.35	0	C-37	1	-0.2
1977 Oak-A	39	78	5	15	0	0	1	10	16	13	0	0	.192	.337	.231	.568	59	-3	7	3.08	0	C-19,D-12/1-3	1	-0.3
1978 Oak-A	13	23	1	7	2	0	0	3	1	6	0	0	.304	.360	.391	.751	117	1	3	5.78	0	/C-6,D-1	1	0.1
1981 Oak-A	18	21	2	2	0	0	1	5	2	5	0	0	.095	.174	.238	.412	19	-2	1	1.36	0	/D-4,1-1	0	-0.3
Total 9	208	368	43	79	11	0	12	53	57	73	1	1	.215	.326	.342	.669	86	-5	44	3.89	-6	C-144/D-17,1-6	10	-0.7
• HOSTETLER, Chuck	Charles Cloyd Hostetler b: 9/22/1903, McClellandtown, PA d: 2/18/1971, Fort Collins, CO BL/TR, 6', 175 lbs. Deb: 4/18/1944 Career OF: 7-5-62																							
1944 Det-A	90	265	42	79	9	2	0	20	21	31	4	4	.298	.350	.347	.697	94	-2	33	4.46	2	0-65(1-4-61)	7	-0.5
1945*Det-A	42	44	3	7	3	0	0	2	7	8	0	0	.159	.275	.227	.502	43	-3	3	2.42	-1	/0-8(6-1-1)	0	-0.4
Total 2	132	309	45	86	12	2	0	22	28	39	4	4	.278	.338	.330	.668	87	-5	36	4.14	1	/0-73	7	-0.9
• HOSTETLER, Dave	David Alan Hostetler b: 3/27/1956, Pasadena, CA BR/TR, 6'4", 215 lbs. Deb: 9/15/1981																							
1981 Mon-N	5	6	1	3	0	0	1	1	0	2	0	0	.500	.500	1.000	1.500	314	2	3	27.00	0	/1-2	1	0.1
1982 Tex-A	113	418	53	97	12	3	22	67	42	113	2	2	.232	.304	.433	.737	105	1	52	4.10	-11	*1-109/D-3	10	-1.7
1983 Tex-A	94	304	31	67	9	2	11	46	42	103	0	2	.220	.325	.372	.696	93	-3	36	3.92	0	D-88/1-2	4	-0.6
1984 Tex-A	37	82	7	18	2	1	3	10	13	27	0	0	.220	.326	.378	.704	91	-1	9	3.68	1	1-14,D-13	1	-0.1
1988 Pit-N	6	8	0	2	0	0	0	0	0	3	0	0	.250	.250	.250	.500	45	-1	1	2.25	0	/1-4,C-1	0	-0.1
Total 5	255	818	92	187	23	6	37	124	97	248	2	4	.229	.315	.407	.722	100	-1	101	4.07	-11	1-131,D-104/C-1	16	-2.3
• HOTALING, Pete	Peter James "Monkey" Hotaling b: 12/16/1856, Mohawk, NY d: 7/3/1928, Cleveland, OH BL/TR, 5'8", 166 lbs. Deb: 5/1/1879 Career OF: 7-816-4																							
1879 Cin-N	81	369	64	103	20	9	1	27	12	17	....	....	.279	.302	.390	.692	133	14	45	4.69	0	*0-69(0-67-2)/C-8,2-6,3-3	14	0.9
1880 Cle-N	78	325	40	78	17	8	0	41	10	30	....	....	.240	.263	.342	.604	105	2	30	3.33	-6	*0-78(2-76-0)/C-2	9	-0.7
1881 Wor-N	77	317	51	98	15	3	1	35	18	12	....	....	.309	.346	.385	.731	122	8	43	5.34	-6	*0-74(2-72-1)/C-3	10	-0.1
1882 Bos-N	84	378	64	98	16	5	0	28	16	21	....	....	.259	.289	.328	.617	97	-1	37	3.61	-2	*0-84(0-84-1)	9	-0.5
1883 Cle-N	100	417	54	108	20	8	0	30	12	31	....	....	.259	.280	.345	.625	90	-5	41	3.67	-1	*0-100(0-100-0)	10	-0.8
1884 Cle-N	102	408	69	99	16	6	3	27	28	50	....	....	.243	.291	.333	.625	93	-4	41	3.61	-1	*0-102(3-99-0)/2-1	7	-0.7
1885 Bro-a	94	370	73	95	9	5	1	34	49	....	....	....	.257	.350	.316	.666	111	7	42	4.12	1	*0-94(0-94-0)	15	0.5
1887 Cle-a	126	558	108	204	28	13	3	94	53	....	43	....	.366	.373	.424	.797	126	19	98	7.50	-3	*0-126(0-126-0)	15	0.9

YEAR TM-L	G	AB	R	H	2B	3B	HR	RBI	BB	SO	SB	CS	AVG	OBP	SLG	OPS	OPS+	BR/A	RC	RC/G	FR	G/POS	WS	TPW
1888 Cle-a	98	403	67	101	7	6	0	55	26	....	35	....	.251	.307	.298	.605	97	-0	49	4.37	-2	*O-98(0-98-0)	9	-0.4
Total 9	840	3545	590	984	148	63	9	371	224	161	78	....	.278	.314	.353	.667	108	40	426	4.53	-19	O-825/C-13,2-7,3-3	98	-1.0
• HOTTMAN, Ken	Kenneth Roger Hottman b: 5/7/1948, Stockton, CA BR/TR, 5'11", 190 lbs. Deb: 9/11/1971																							
1971 Chi-A	6	16	1	2	0	0	0	0	1	2	0	0	.125	.176	.125	.301	-13	-2	0	.48	0	/O-5(5-0-0)	0	-0.3
• HOUCK, Sadie	Sargent Perry Houck b: 3/1856, Washington, DC d: 5/26/1919, Washington, DC BR/TR, 5'7", 151 lbs. Deb: 5/1/1879 Career OF: 39-20-54																							
1879 Bos-N	80	356	69	95	24	9	2	49	4	11	....	....	.267	.275	.402	.677	117	6	40	4.32	-7	O-47(1-5-42),S-33	11	0.0
1880 Bos-N	12	47	2	7	0	0	0	2	0	6	....	....	.149	.149	.149	.298	1	-5	1	.73	-2	O-12(0-2-10)	0	-0.7
Pro-N	49	184	27	37	7	7	1	22	3	6	....	....	.201	.214	.332	.545	84	-3	13	2.50	1	O-49(38-12-2)	4	-0.5
Yr.	61	231	29	44	7	7	1	24	3	12	....	....	.190	.201	.294	.495	68	-7	14	2.12	-1	*O-61(38-14-12)	4	-1.1
1881 Det-N	75	308	43	86	16	6	1	36	6	6	....	....	.279	.293	.380	.673	105	1	35	4.27	1	*S-75	10	0.5
1883 Det-N	101	416	52	105	18	12	0	40	9	18	....	....	.252	.268	.353	.622	91	-4	40	3.57	7	*S-101	12	0.6
1884 Phi-a	108	472	93	140	19	14	0	0	7	....	....	....	.297	.318	.396	.714	124	10	61	5.05	18	*S-108/2-1	18	2.9
1885 Phi-a	93	388	74	99	10	9	0	54	10	....	....	....	.255	.286	.327	.614	88	-7	37	3.48	9	*S-93	9	0.5
1886 Bal-a	61	260	29	50	8	1	0	17	4	....	25	....	.192	.216	.231	.447	41	-18	19	2.42	-9	S-55/2-5,O-1	2	-2.2
Was-N	52	195	14	42	3	0	0	14	2	28	4	....	.215	.223	.231	.454	40	-13	11	1.98	0	S-51/2-1	1	-1.1
1887 NY-a	10	36	3	8	1	0	0	0	3	....	2	....	.222	.243	.182	.425	20	-3	2	1.92	0	S-10/2-1	0	-0.2
Total 8	641	2662	406	669	106	58	4	234	48	75	31	....	.251	.269	.338	.608	90	-36	261	3.58	18	S-526,O-109/2-8	67	-0.1
• HOUK, Ralph	Ralph George "Major" Houk b: 8/9/1919, Lawrence, KS BR/TR, 5'11", 193 lbs. Deb: 4/26/1947 M/C																							
1947*NY-A	41	92	7	25	3	1	0	12	11	5	0	0	.272	.356	.326	.682	91	-1	11	4.46	-2	C-41	3	-0.1
1948 NY-A	14	29	3	8	2	0	0	3	0	0	0	0	.276	.276	.345	.621	65	-2	3	3.64	0	C-14	1	-0.1
1949 NY-A	5	7	0	4	0	0	0	1	0	1	0	0	.571	.571	.571	1.143	203	1	2	21.09	-1	/C-5	1	0.0
1950 NY-A	10	9	0	1	1	0	0	1	0	2	0	0	.111	.111	.222	.333	-17	-2	0	.77	-1	/C-9	0	-0.2
1951 NY-A	3	5	0	1	0	0	0	2	0	1	0	0	.200	.200	.200	.400	9	-1	0	1.38	0	/C-3	0	-0.1
1952*NY-A	9	6	0	2	0	0	0	0	1	0	0	0	.333	.429	.333	.762	121	0	1	6.68	-1	/C-9	0	-0.1
1953 NY-A	8	9	2	2	0	0	0	1	0	1	0	0	.222	.222	.222	.444	21	-1	0	.77	-1	/C-8	0	-0.2
1954 NY-A	1	1	0	0	0	0	0	0	0	0	0	0	.000	.000	.000	.000	-104	-0	0	.00	0	....	0	0.0
Total 8	91	158	12	43	6	1	0	20	12	10	0	0	.272	.327	.323	.650	80	-4	18	4.17	-6	/C-89	5	-0.8
• HOUSE, Frank	Henry Franklin "Pig" House b: 2/18/1930, Bessemer, AL BL/TR, 6'1.5", 190 lbs. Deb: 7/21/1950																							
1950 Det-A	5	5	1	2	1	0	0	0	0	1	0	0	.400	.400	.600	1.000	148	0	1	11.07	-1	/C-5	0	0.0
1951 Det-A	18	41	3	9	2	0	1	4	6	2	1	1	.220	.319	.341	.661	78	-1	4	2.83	-0	C-18	1	-0.1
1954 Det-A	114	352	35	88	12	1	9	38	31	34	2	1	.250	.313	.366	.679	87	-7	41	3.93	3	*C-107	11	0.1
1955 Det-A	102	328	37	85	11	1	15	53	22	25	0	0	.259	.312	.436	.748	102	-1	45	4.78	-3	C-93	11	0.1
1956 Det-A	94	321	44	77	6	2	10	44	21	19	1	1	.240	.293	.364	.657	72	-14	31	3.14	-3	C-88	5	-1.3
1957 Det-A	106	348	31	90	9	0	7	36	35	26	1	1	.259	.328	.345	.673	82	-8	38	3.66	3	C-97	10	0.0
1958 KC-A	76	202	16	51	6	3	4	24	12	13	1	0	.252	.298	.371	.669	81	-5	20	3.34	0	C-55	4	-0.3
1959 KC-A	98	347	32	82	14	3	1	30	20	23	0	3	.236	.282	.303	.584	59	-21	27	2.61	-1	C-95	3	-1.8
1960 Cin-N	23	28	0	5	2	0	0	3	0	2	0	0	.179	.179	.250	.429	15	-3	1	.81	0	/C-8	0	-0.3
1961 Det-A	17	22	3	5	1	1	0	3	4	2	0	0	.227	.346	.364	.710	87	-0	3	3.89	-1	C-14	1	-0.1
Total 10	653	1994	202	494	64	11	47	235	151	147	6	7	.248	.304	.362	.666	80	-61	210	3.53	-1	C-580	46	-3.6
• HOUSE, J.R.	James Rodger House b: 11/11/1979, Charleston, WV BR/TR, 5'10", 202 lbs. Deb: 9/27/2003																							
2003 Pit-N	1	1	0	1	0	0	0	0	0	0	0	0	1.000	1.000	1.000	2.000	417	0	1	∞	0	....	0	0.0
• HOUSEHOLDER, Charlie	Charles F. Householder b: 1856, Harrisburg, PA d: 12/26/1908, Harrisburg, PA BR/TR, 5'7", 150 lbs. Deb: 4/20/1884																							
1884 CP-U	83	310	32	74	12	5	1	....	12	....	....	....	.239	.267	.319	.586	104	2	27	3.22	-7	3-41,O-40(40-0-0)/S-3,P-2	7	-0.5
• HOUSEHOLDER, Charlie	Charles W. Householder b: 2/8/1854, Philadelphia, PA d: 9/3/1913, Philadelphia, PA BL/TL, 5'11", 158 lbs. Deb: 5/2/1882																							
1882 Bal-a	74	307	42	78	10	7	1	....	4	....	....	....	.254	.264	.342	.606	111	4	28	3.47	2	*1-74/C-3	9	0.0
1884 Bro-a	76	273	28	66	15	3	3	0	12	....	....	....	.242	.279	.352	.630	103	1	27	3.64	-1	1-40,C-31/O-6(2-2-1),2-1	8	-0.1
Total 2	150	580	70	144	25	10	4	0	16	....	....	....	.248	.271	.347	.617	107	5	56	3.55	1	1-114/C-34,O-6,2-1	17	-0.1
• HOUSEHOLDER, Ed	Edward H. Householder b: 10/12/1869, Pittsburgh, PA d: 7/3/1924, Los Angeles, CA BL/TL, 5'9.5" Deb: 4/17/1903																							
1903 Bro-N	12	43	5	9	0	0	0	9	2	....	3	....	.209	.244	.209	.454	31	-4	3	2.36	-1	O-12(0-12-0)	0	-0.5
• HOUSEHOLDER, Paul	Paul Wesley Householder b: 9/4/1958, Columbus, OH BB/TR, 6', 180 lbs. Deb: 8/26/1980 Career OF: 33-97-307																							
1980 Cin-N	20	45	3	11	1	1	0	7	1	13	1	0	.244	.261	.311	.572	59	-2	4	3.06	1	O-14(0-1-13)	1	-0.2
1981 Cin-N	23	69	12	19	4	0	2	9	10	16	3	1	.275	.367	.420	.787	121	2	11	5.56	0	O-19(1-6-13)	3	0.2
1982 Cin-N	138	417	40	88	11	5	9	34	30	77	17	11	.211	.267	.326	.593	64	-22	35	2.69	7	*O-131(0-9-123)	4	-2.2
1983 Cin-N	123	380	40	97	24	4	6	43	44	60	12	12	.255	.336	.387	.723	96	-4	48	4.25	1	*O-112(6-36-80)	11	-0.7
1984 Cin-N	14	12	3	1	1	0	0	0	3	3	1	1	.083	.267	.167	.433	23	-1	1	1.37	0	O-10(3-1-6)	0	-0.1
StL-N	13	14	1	2	0	0	0	0	0	3	0	0	.143	.143	.143	.286	-20	-2	0	.30	-1	/O-8(4-1-4)	0	-0.3
Yr.	27	26	4	3	1	0	0	0	3	6	1	1	.115	.207	.154	.361	2	-4	1	.81	0	O-18(7-2-10)	0	-0.5
1985 Mil-A	95	299	41	77	15	0	11	34	27	60	1	2	.258	.321	.418	.739	101	-1	40	4.66	-3	O-91(7-32-59)/D-3	9	-0.7
1986 Mil-A	26	78	4	17	3	1	1	16	7	16	1	2	.218	.291	.321	.611	64	-5	7	2.88	1	O-22(12-5-8)/D-3	1	-0.5
1987 Hou-N	14	12	2	1	1	0	0	1	4	2	0	0	.083	.313	.167	.479	33	-1	1	2.33	-1	/O-7(0-6-1)	0	-0.2
Total 8	466	1326	146	313	60	11	29	144	126	250	36	29	.236	.305	.363	.669	83	-37	146	3.67	5	O-414/D-6	29	-4.8
• HOUSEMAN, John	John Franklin Houseman b: 1/10/1870, Holland d: 11/4/1922, Chicago, IL, 160 lbs. Deb: 9/11/1894																							
1894 Chi-N	4	15	5	6	3	1	0	4	5	3	2	....	.400	.571	.733	1.305	202	3	8	22.00	1	/S-3,2-1	1	0.3
1897 StL-N	80	278	34	68	6	6	0	21	28	....	16	....	.245	.329	.309	.638	70	-11	35	4.33	-11	2-41,O-33(7-7-19)/S-5,3-3	3	-1.9
Total 2	84	293	39	74	9	7	0	25	33	3	18	....	.253	.344	.331	.675	79	-8	43	5.04	-10	/2-42,O-33,S-8,3-3	4	-1.6
• HOUSER, Ben	Benjamin Franklin Houser b: 11/30/1883, Shenandoah, PA d: 1/15/1952, Augusta, ME BL/TL, 6'1", 185 lbs. Deb: 5/2/1910																							
1910 Phi-A	34	69	9	13	3	2	0	7	7	....	0	....	.188	.263	.290	.553	74	-2	5	2.36	-1	1-26	0	-0.4
1911 Bos-N	20	71	11	18	1	0	1	9	8	6	2	....	.254	.329	.310	.639	73	-2	8	3.75	0	1-20	1	-0.3
1912 Bos-N	108	332	38	95	17	3	8	52	22	29	1	....	.286	.332	.428	.760	105	1	47	4.90	-1	1-83	6	-0.2
Total 3	162	472	58	126	21	5	9	68	37	35	3	....	.267	.322	.390	.711	96	-4	60	4.31	-3	1-129	7	-0.9
• HOUSIE, Wayne	Wayne Tyrone Housie b: 5/20/1965, Hampton, VA BB/TR, 5'9", 165 lbs. Deb: 9/17/1991 Career OF: 0-4-2																							
1991 Bos-A	11	8	2	2	1	0	0	0	1	3	1	0	.250	.333	.375	.708	91	0	1	2.90	0	/O-4(0-4-0),D-2	0	0.0
1993 NY-N	18	16	2	3	1	0	0	1	1	1	0	0	.188	.235	.250	.485	30	-2	1	2.08	0	/O-2(0-0-2)	0	-0.2
Total 2	29	24	4	5	2	0	0	1	2	4	1	0	.208	.269	.292	.561	53	-1	2	2.39	0	/O-6,D-2	0	-0.2
• HOUSTON, Tyler	Tyler Sam Houston b: 1/17/1971, Las Vegas, NV BL/TR, 6'2", 210 lbs. Deb: 4/3/1996 Career OF: 1-0-1																							
1996 Atl-N	33	27	3	6	2	1	1	8	1	9	0	0	.222	.250	.481	.731	83	-1	3	3.49	-1	1-11/O-1	1	-0.2
Chi-N	46	115	18	39	7	0	2	19	8	18	3	2	.339	.382	.452	.834	116	2	18	6.08	-1	C-27/3-9,2-2,1-1	5	0.3
Yr.	79	142	21	45	9	1	3	27	9	27	3	2	.317	.358	.458	.815	110	1	21	5.53	-2	C-27,1-12/3-9,2-2,O-1	6	0.1
1997 Chi-N	72	196	15	51	10	0	2	28	9	35	1	0	.260	.293	.342	.635	64	-11	19	3.42	-1	C-41,3-12/1-2,2-1,S-1	4	-0.8
1998*Chi-N	95	255	26	65	7	1	9	33	13	53	2	2	.255	.291	.396	.687	76	-10	28	3.72	-1	C-63,3-12/1-7	7	-0.7
1999 Chi-N	100	249	26	58	9	1	9	27	28	67	1	1	.233	.310	.386	.696	76	-10	29	3.90	-8	3-63,C-18/1-2,O-1	3	-1.6
Cle-A	13	27	2	4	1	0	1	3	3	11	0	0	.148	.233	.296	.530	32	-3	2	2.40	0	3-10/C-1	0	-0.3
2000 Mil-N	101	284	30	71	15	0	18	43	17	72	2	1	.250	.292	.493	.785	95	-4	36	4.16	2	1-35,3-28,C-23	5	-0.3
2001 Mil-N	75	235	36	68	7	0	12	38	18	62	0	0	.289	.343	.472	.815	110	3	38	6.01	-6	3-62/1-3	8	-0.2
2002 Mil-N	76	255	25	77	15	2	7	33	14	41	1	0	.302	.348	.459	.807	112	4	41	5.86	-11	3-72/1-1	7	-0.6
LA-N	35	65	9	13	5	1	0	7	2	21	0	0	.200	.224	.308	.532	41	-6	3	1.45	-1	1-12/3-2	0	-0.8
Yr.	111	320	34	90	20	3	7	40	16	62	1	0	.281	.324	.428	.752	98	-2	44	4.83	-12	3-74,1-13	7	-1.4

YEAR TM-L	G	AB	R	H	2B	3B	HR	RBI	BB	SO	SB	CS	AVG	OBP	SLG	OPS	OPS+	BR/A	RC	RC/G	FR	G/POS	WS	TPW
2003 Phi-N	54	97	7	27	6	0	2	14	6	19	0	0	.278	.320	.402	.722	93	-1	12	4.55	-1	3-21/1-1	2	-0.2
Total 8	**700**	**1805**	**197**	**479**	**84**	**6**	**63**	**253**	**119**	**408**	**10**	**6**	**.265**	**.313**	**.423**	**.736**	**89**	**-37**	**229**	**4.42**	**-28**	**3-291,C-173/1-75,2-3,O-2,S**	**42**	**-5.4**
• HOUTZ, Lefty	Fred Fritz Houtz b: 9/4/1875, Connersville, IN d: 2/15/1959, St. Marys, OH BL/TL, 5'10", 170 lbs. Deb: 7/23/1899																							
1899 Cin-N	5	17	1	4	0	1	0	0	4	....	1	....	.235	.381	.353	.734	100	0	3	5.57	4	/O-5(1-4-0)	1	0.3
• HOVLEY, Steve	Stephen Eugene Hovley b: 12/18/1944, Ventura, CA BL/TL, 5'10", 188 lbs. Deb: 6/26/1969 Career OF: 26-118-190																							
1969 Sea-A	91	329	41	91	14	3	3	20	30	34	10	4	.277	.339	.365	.704	98	-0	43	4.67	2	O-84(3-35-49)	10	-0.2
1970 Mil-A	40	135	17	38	9	0	0	16	17	11	5	1	.281	.366	.348	.714	97	1	18	4.77	-3	O-38(0-4-38)	4	-0.4
Oak-A	72	100	8	19	1	0	0	1	5	11	3	0	.190	.229	.200	.429	20	-10	5	1.54	0	O-42(10-26-7)	1	-1.2
Yr.	112	235	25	57	10	0	0	17	22	22	8	1	.243	.310	.285	.595	66	-9	23	3.32	-3	O-80(10-30-45)	5	-1.6
1971 Oak-A	24	27	3	3	2	0	0	3	7	9	2	0	.111	.314	.185	.499	45	-1	3	2.85	0	O-11(4-3-4)	1	-0.1
1972 KC-A	105	196	24	53	5	1	3	24	24	29	3	3	.270	.353	.352	.705	111	3	26	4.51	1	O-68(5-25-39)	6	0.2
1973 KC-A	104	232	29	59	8	1	2	24	33	34	6	4	.254	.347	.323	.670	83	-4	28	4.11	0	O-79(4-25-53),D-15	6	-0.7
Total 5	**436**	**1019**	**122**	**263**	**39**	**5**	**8**	**88**	**116**	**128**	**29**	**12**	**.258**	**.336**	**.330**	**.666**	**88**	**-12**	**122**	**4.14**	**1**	**O-322/D-15**	**28**	**-2.3**
• HOWARD, Chris	Christopher Hugh Howard b: 2/27/1966, San Diego, CA BR/TR, 6'2", 200 lbs. Deb: 9/15/1991																							
1991 Sea-A	9	6	1	1	1	0	0	0	1	2	0	0	.167	.286	.333	.619	71	-0	1	3.49	-1	/C-9	0	-0.1
1993 Sea-A	4	1	0	0	0	0	0	0	0	0	0	0	.000	.000	.000	.000	-99	-0	0	.00	-1	/C-4	0	-0.1
1994 Sea-A	9	25	2	5	1	0	0	2	1	6	0	0	.200	.259	.240	.499	29	-3	2	2.24	0	/C-9	0	-0.2
Total 3	**22**	**32**	**3**	**6**	**2**	**0**	**0**	**2**	**2**	**8**	**0**	**0**	**.188**	**.257**	**.250**	**.507**	**34**	**-3**	**2**	**2.38**	**-2**	**/C-22**	**0**	**-0.4**
• HOWARD, Dave	David Austin "Del" Howard b: 5/1/1889, Washington, DC d: 1/26/1956, Dallas, TX BR/TR, 5'11", 165 lbs. Deb: 5/8/1912																							
1912 Was-A	1	0	1	0	0	0	0	0	0	....	0	....	....	....	....	....	-99	0	0	....	0	....	0	0.0
1915 Bro-F	24	36	5	8	1	0	0	1	1	8	0	....	.222	.243	.250	.493	46	-3	2	1.92	-1	2-12/O-2(0-1-1),3-1,S-1	0	-0.4
Total 2	**25**	**36**	**6**	**8**	**1**	**0**	**0**	**1**	**1**	**8**	**0**	**....**	**.222**	**.243**	**.250**	**.493**	**46**	**-3**	**2**	**1.92**	**-1**	**/2-12,O-2,3-1,S-1**	**0**	**-0.4**
• HOWARD, David	David Wayne Howard b: 2/26/1967, Sarasota, FL BB/TR, 6', 175 lbs. Deb: 4/14/1991 Career OF: 20-25-28																							
1991 KC-A	94	236	20	51	7	0	1	17	16	45	3	2	.216	.269	.258	.527	46	-17	18	2.43	-4	S-63,2-26/3-1,D-1,O-1	3	-1.5
1992 KC-A	74	219	19	49	6	2	1	18	15	43	3	4	.224	.274	.283	.557	55	-15	17	2.45	-4	S-74/O-2(0-2-0)	4	-1.4
1993 KC-A	15	24	5	8	0	1	0	2	2	5	1	0	.333	.385	.417	.801	109	1	4	6.17	0	/2-7,S-3,3-2,O-1	1	0.1
1994 KC-A	46	83	9	19	4	0	1	13	11	23	3	2	.229	.319	.313	.632	61	-5	9	3.35	2	3-25,S-15/2-3,D-2,O-1,P-1	2	-0.2
1995 KC-A	95	255	23	62	13	4	0	19	24	41	6	1	.243	.311	.325	.636	65	-12	26	3.43	3	2-41,S-33,O-30(11-16-8)/1-1,D	5	-0.6
1996 KC-A	143	420	51	92	14	5	4	48	40	74	5	6	.219	.293	.305	.598	52	-33	39	2.92	13	*S-135/2-3,1-2,O-1	9	-0.8
1997 KC-A	80	162	24	39	8	1	1	13	10	31	2	2	.241	.289	.321	.610	58	-11	15	3.18	1	2-34,O-23(5-2-17)/S-9,3-7,D	2	-0.8
1998 StL-N	46	102	15	25	1	1	2	12	12	22	0	0	.245	.325	.333	.658	74	-4	11	3.76	-1	2-19,S-16,3-14/O-2(0-2-1)	2	-0.3
1999 StL-N	52	82	3	17	4	0	1	6	7	27	0	2	.207	.286	.293	.578	46	-8	7	2.70	0	S-13/1-9,2-9,O-5(3-1-1),3	1	-0.7
Total 9	**645**	**1583**	**169**	**362**	**57**	**14**	**11**	**148**	**137**	**311**	**23**	**19**	**.229**	**.294**	**.303**	**.597**	**57**	**-104**	**147**	**3.00**	**8**	**S-361,2-142/O-66,3-53,1,D,P**	**29**	**-6.3**
• HOWARD, Del	George Elmer Howard b: 12/24/1877, Kenney, IL d: 12/24/1956, Seattle, WA BL/TR, 6', 180 lbs. Deb: 4/15/1905 Career OF: 137-34-85																							
1905 Pit-N	123	435	56	127	18	5	2	63	27	....	19	....	.292	.345	.370	.715	110	5	65	5.27	-4	1-90,O-28(1-0-27)/P-1	15	0.1
1906 Bos-N	147	545	46	142	19	8	1	54	26	....	17	....	.261	.306	.330	.637	101	-1	63	3.97	-18	O-87(87-0-0),2-45,S-14/1-2	11	-2.6
1907 Bos-N	50	187	20	51	4	2	1	13	11	....	11	....	.273	.330	.332	.662	108	2	25	4.72	1	O-45(45-0-0)/2-3	6	0.0
*Chi-N	51	148	10	34	2	2	0	13	6	....	3	....	.230	.269	.270	.540	65	-6	12	2.71	-2	1-33/O-8(0-3-6)	2	-1.0
Yr.	101	335	30	85	6	4	1	26	17	....	14	....	.254	.304	.304	.608	89	-5	37	3.80	-1	O-53(45-3-6),1-33/2-3	8	-1.0
1908*Chi-N	96	315	42	88	7	3	1	26	23	....	11	....	.279	.338	.330	.668	109	4	39	4.27	-3	O-81(4-31-52)/1-5	13	-0.4
1909 Chi-N	69	203	25	40	4	2	1	24	18	....	6	....	.197	.282	.251	.533	64	-8	17	2.52	0	1-57	3	-1.0
Total 5	**536**	**1833**	**199**	**482**	**54**	**22**	**6**	**193**	**111**	**....**	**67**	**....**	**.263**	**.318**	**.326**	**.644**	**98**	**-5**	**221**	**4.11**	**-25**	**O-249,1-187/2-48,S-14,P-1**	**50**	**-4.9**
• HOWARD, Doug	Douglas Lynn Howard b: 2/6/1948, Salt Lake City, UT BR/TR, 6'3", 185 lbs. Deb: 9/6/1972 Career OF: 16-6-2																							
1972 Cal-A	11	38	4	10	1	0	0	2	1	3	0	0	.263	.300	.289	.589	80	-1	3	2.59	0	/O-8(8-0-0),1-1,3-1	1	-0.2
1973 Cal-A	8	21	2	2	0	0	0	1	1	6	0	0	.095	.136	.095	.232	-37	-4	0	.49	0	/O-6(6-0-0),1-1,3-1	0	-0.4
1974 Cal-A	22	39	5	9	0	1	0	5	2	1	1	0	.231	.268	.282	.550	62	-2	2	1.90	0	/O-8(2-6-0),1-5,D-3	0	-0.2
1975 StL-N	17	29	1	6	0	0	1	1	0	7	0	0	.207	.207	.310	.517	41	-3	2	2.19	1	/1-7	0	-0.2
1976 Cle-A	39	90	7	19	4	0	0	13	3	13	1	1	.211	.245	.256	.500	47	-6	5	1.73	0	1-32/D-4,O-2(0-0-2)	0	-0.9
Total 5	**97**	**217**	**19**	**46**	**5**	**1**	**1**	**22**	**7**	**30**	**2**	**1**	**.212**	**.243**	**.258**	**.501**	**46**	**-15**	**13**	**1.82**	**1**	**/1-46,O-24,D-7,3-2**	**1**	**-1.9**
• HOWARD, Elston	Elston Gene Howard b: 2/23/1929, St. Louis, MO d: 12/14/1980, New York, NY BR/TR, 6'2", 200 lbs. Deb: 4/14/1955 C Career OF: 230-0-40																							
1955*NY-A	97	279	33	81	8	7	10	43	20	36	0	0	.290	.340	.477	.817	119	6	45	5.86	6	O-75(62-0-15)/C-9	11	0.9
1956*NY-A	98	290	35	76	8	3	5	34	21	30	0	1	.262	.314	.362	.676	81	-9	30	3.55	1	O-65(62-0-5),C-26	6	-1.0
1957*NY-A★	110	356	33	90	13	4	8	44	16	43	2	5	.253	.285	.379	.664	81	-12	31	2.84	-3	O-71(69-0-2),C-32/1-2	6	-1.7
1958*NY-A★	103	376	45	118	19	5	11	66	22	60	1	1	.314	.352	.479	.830	131	14	60	5.92	0	C-67,O-24(17-0-8)/1-5	18	1.7
1959 NY-A★	125	443	59	121	24	6	18	73	20	57	0	1	.273	.309	.476	.785	116	7	61	4.79	-3	1-50,C-43,O-28(18-0-10)	14	0.1
1960*NY-A★	107	323	29	79	11	3	6	39	28	43	3	0	.245	.305	.353	.658	82	-8	35	3.57	3	C-91/O-1	10	-0.1
1961*NY-A★	129	446	64	155	17	5	21	77	28	65	0	3	.348	.390	.549	.939	156	32	94	8.33	0	*C-111/1-9	29	3.7
1962*NY-A★	136	494	63	138	23	5	21	91	31	76	1	1	.279	.323	.474	.797	115	8	69	4.78	2	*C-129	20	1.6
1963*NY-A★	135	487	75	140	21	6	28	85	35	68	0	0	.287	.343	.528	.871	141	25	83	6.09	-6	*C-132	28	2.6
1964*NY-A★	150	550	63	172	27	3	15	84	48	73	1	1	.313	.373	.455	.828	127	20	93	6.38	3	*C-146	32	3.3
1965 NY-A★	110	391	38	91	15	1	9	45	24	65	0	0	.233	.279	.345	.624	77	-13	34	2.88	-1	C-95/1-5,O-1	8	-1.0
1966 NY-A	126	410	38	105	19	2	6	35	37	65	0	0	.256	.319	.356	.675	97	-1	45	3.80	0	*C-100,1-13	11	0.3
1967 NY-A	66	199	13	39	6	0	3	17	12	36	0	0	.196	.249	.271	.520	56	-11	13	2.03	1	C-48/1-1	2	-0.8
*Bos-A	42	116	9	17	3	0	1	11	9	24	0	0	.147	.214	.198	.413	21	-11	5	1.20	-1	C-41	2	-1.1
Yr.	108	315	22	56	9	0	4	28	21	60	0	0	.178	.236	.244	.480	43	-22	17	1.71	0	C-89/1-1	4	-1.9
1968 Bos-A	71	203	22	49	4	0	5	18	22	45	1	1	.241	.319	.335	.654	92	-2	21	3.54	-1	C-68	6	0.0
Total 14	**1605**	**5363**	**619**	**1471**	**218**	**50**	**167**	**762**	**373**	**786**	**9**	**14**	**.274**	**.325**	**.427**	**.752**	**108**	**44**	**718**	**4.68**	**1**	***C-1138,O-265/1-85**	**203**	**8.5**
• HOWARD, Frank	Frank Oliver "Hondo,Capital Punishment" Howard b: 8/8/1936, Columbus, OH BR/TR, 6'7", 255 lbs. Deb: 9/10/1958 M Career OF: 923-0-530																							
1958 LA-N	8	29	3	7	1	0	1	2	1	11	0	0	.241	.267	.379	.646	66	-1	3	3.08	0	/O-8(3-0-5)	0	-0.2
1959 LA-N	9	21	2	3	0	1	1	6	2	9	0	0	.143	.217	.381	.598	52	-2	2	2.78	0	/O-6(4-0-2)	0	-0.2
1960 LA-N	117	448	54	120	15	2	23	77	32	108	0	1	.268	.321	.464	.785	105	2	66	5.20	1	*O-115(22-0-94)/1-4	13	-0.2
1961 LA-N	92	267	36	79	10	2	15	45	21	50	0	1	.296	.349	.517	.866	116	5	44	5.76	-1	O-65(20-0-46)/1-7	9	0.1
1962 LA-N	141	493	80	146	25	6	31	119	39	108	1	0	.296	.349	.560	.909	148	31	90	6.54	5	*O-131(9-0-128)	25	2.8
1963*LA-N	123	417	58	114	16	1	28	64	33	116	1	2	.273	.333	.518	.851	151	25	70	6.00	-4	*O-111(6-0-107)	23	1.4
1964 LA-N	134	433	60	98	13	2	24	69	51	113	1	0	.226	.308	.432	.740	114	8	56	4.20	-5	*O-122(0-0-122)	13	-0.4
1965 Was-A	149	516	53	149	22	6	21	84	55	112	0	0	.289	.360	.477	.836	137	25	90	6.40	-2	*O-138(138-0-5)	25	1.8
1966 Was-A	146	493	52	137	19	4	18	71	53	104	1	1	.278	.349	.442	.791	127	17	74	5.38	3	*O-135(135-0-0)	21	1.5
1967 Was-A	149	519	71	133	20	2	36	89	60	155	0	1	.256	.339	.511	.850	154	34	88	5.90	2	*O-141(141-0-3)/1-4	28	3.3
1968 Was-A★	158	598	79	164	28	3	**44**	106	54	141	0	1	.274	.340	**.552**	.892	**172**	49	110	6.56	1	*O-107(107-0-0),1-55	38	4.8
1969 Was-A★	161	592	111	175	17	2	48	111	102	96	1	0	.296	.403	.574	.978	180	65	132	7.91	-6	*O-114(108-0-6),1-70	34	5.3
1970 Was-A★	161	566	90	160	15	1	**44**	**126**	**132**	125	1	2	.283	.420	.546	.966	173	62	130	8.00	-2	*O-120(114-0-6),1-48	30	5.2
1971 Was-A★	153	549	60	153	25	2	26	83	77	121	1	0	.279	.369	.474	.843	146	34	89	5.61	11	*O-100(95-0-5),1-68	23	3.9
1972 Tex-A	95	287	28	70	9	0	9	31	42	55	1	0	.244	.342	.369	.712	117	7	34	3.93	-3	1-66,O-21(20-0-1)	9	0.0
Det-A	14	33	1	8	1	0	1	7	4	8	0	0	.242	.324	.364	.688	101	0	4	4.57	0	1-10/O-1	1	-0.1
Yr.	109	320	29	78	10	0	10	38	46	63	1	0	.244	.341	.369	.709	115	8	38	3.99	-3	1-76,O-22(21-0-1)	10	-0.1
1973 Det-A	85	227	26	58	9	1	12	29	24	28	0	1	.256	.327	.463	.789	113	3	30	4.49	-1	D-76/1-2	5	0.1
Total 16	**1895**	**6488**	**864**	**1774**	**245**	**35**	**382**	**1119**	**782**	**1460**	**8**	**9**	**.273**	**.355**	**.499**	**.853**	**144**	**365**	**1110**	**6.00**	**0**	***O-1435,1-334/D-76**	**297**	**29.0**
• HOWARD, Ivan	Ivan Chester Howard b: 10/12/1882, Kenney, IL d: 3/30/1967, Medford, OR BB/TR, 5'10", 170 lbs. Deb: 4/25/1914 Career OF: 6-6-12																							
1914 StL-A	81	209	21	51	6	2	0	20	28	42	14	10	.244	.342	.292	.634	94	-2	23	3.48	-1	3-34,1-28/O-3(1-1-1),S-1	6	-0.2
1915 StL-A	113	324	43	90	10	7	2	43	43	48	29	12	.278	.368	.370	.738	126	12	50	5.17	5	1-48,3-23,O-17(5-1-11)/2-2,S	13	1.7

YEAR TM-L	G	AB	R	H	2B	3B	HR	RBI	BB	SO	SB	CS	AVG	OBP	SLG	OPS	OPS+	BR/A	RC	RC/G	FR	G/POS	WS	TPW
1916 Cle-A	81	246	20	46	11	5	0	23	30	34	9	....	.187	.298	.272	.571	68	-9	24	2.96	0	2-65/1-7	5	-0.9
1917 Cle-A	27	39	7	4	0	0	0	0	3	5	1	....	.103	.167	.103	.269	-17	-5	1	.65	-0	/3-6,2-4,0-4(0-4-0)	0	-0.6
Total 4	**302**	**818**	**91**	**191**	**27**	**14**	**2**	**86**	**104**	**129**	**53**	**22**	**.233**	**.331**	**.308**	**.639**	**93**	**-4**	**98**	**3.81**	**4**	**/1-83,2-71,3-63,0-24,S-3**	**24**	**0.0**

• HOWARD, Larry Lawrence Rayford Howard b: 6/6/1945, Columbus, OH BR/TR, 6'3", 200 lbs. Deb: 8/9/1970 Career OF: 1-0-1

YEAR TM-L	G	AB	R	H	2B	3B	HR	RBI	BB	SO	SB	CS	AVG	OBP	SLG	OPS	OPS+	BR/A	RC	RC/G	FR	G/POS	WS	TPW
1970 Hou-N	31	88	11	27	6	0	2	16	10	23	0	0	.307	.378	.443	.821	124	3	15	6.25	1	C-26/1-2,0-1	4	0.5
1971 Hou-N	24	64	6	15	3	0	2	14	3	17	0	1	.234	.269	.375	.644	83	-2	6	2.84	1	C-22	2	0.0
1972 Hou-N	54	157	16	35	7	0	2	13	17	30	0	0	.223	.299	.306	.605	74	-5	14	2.95	-5	C-53/0-1	3	-0.8
1973 Hou-N	20	48	3	8	3	0	0	4	5	12	0	0	.167	.245	.229	.474	32	-4	3	1.76	0	C-20	0	-0.4
Atl-N	4	8	0	1	0	0	0	0	2	3	0	0	.125	.300	.125	.425	20	-1	0	1.76	0	/C-2	0	-0.1
Yr.	24	56	3	9	3	0	0	4	7	15	0	0	.161	.254	.214	.468	30	-5	3	1.76	-0	C-22	0	-0.5
Total 4	**133**	**365**	**36**	**86**	**19**	**0**	**6**	**47**	**37**	**85**	**0**	**1**	**.236**	**.306**	**.337**	**.643**	**81**	**-9**	**37**	**3.44**	**-3**	**C-123/1-2,0-2**	**9**	**-0.8**

• HOWARD, Matt Matthew Christopher Howard b: 9/22/1967, Fall River, MA BR/TR, 5'10", 170 lbs. Deb: 5/17/1996

YEAR TM-L	G	AB	R	H	2B	3B	HR	RBI	BB	SO	SB	CS	AVG	OBP	SLG	OPS	OPS+	BR/A	RC	RC/G	FR	G/POS	WS	TPW
1996 NY-A	35	54	9	11	1	0	1	9	2	8	1	0	.204	.232	.278	.510	28	-6	3	1.85	-3	2-30/3-6	0	-0.7

• HOWARD, Mike Michael Frederic Howard b: 4/2/1958, Seattle, WA BB/TR, 6'2", 185 lbs. Deb: 9/12/1981 Career OF: 15-8-16

YEAR TM-L	G	AB	R	H	2B	3B	HR	RBI	BB	SO	SB	CS	AVG	OBP	SLG	OPS	OPS+	BR/A	RC	RC/G	FR	G/POS	WS	TPW
1981 NY-N	14	24	4	4	1	0	0	3	4	6	2	0	.167	.286	.208	.494	43	-1	2	2.70	1	0-14(6-1-7)	0	-0.1
1982 NY-N	33	39	5	7	0	0	1	3	6	7	2	0	.179	.304	.256	.561	59	-1	4	3.22	1	0-22(9-7-8)/2-3	1	-0.1
1983 NY-N	1	3	0	1	0	0	0	1	0	1	0	0	.333	.333	.333	.667	86	-0	0	4.50	0	/0-1	0	0.0
Total 3	**48**	**66**	**9**	**12**	**1**	**0**	**1**	**7**	**10**	**14**	**4**	**0**	**.182**	**.299**	**.242**	**.541**	**54**	**-3**	**6**	**3.07**	**1**	**/0-37,2-3**	**1**	**-0.3**

• HOWARD, Paul Paul Joseph "Del" Howard b: 5/20/1884, Boston, MA d: 8/29/1968, Miami, FL BR/TR, 5'8", 170 lbs. Deb: 9/16/1909

YEAR TM-L	G	AB	R	H	2B	3B	HR	RBI	BB	SO	SB	CS	AVG	OBP	SLG	OPS	OPS+	BR/A	RC	RC/G	FR	G/POS	WS	TPW
1909 Bos-A	6	15	2	3	1	0	0	2	3	....	0	....	.200	.368	.267	.635	99	0	2	3.25	-0	/0-6(4-0-2)	0	0.0

• HOWARD, Steve Steven Bernard Howard b: 12/7/1963, Oakland, CA BR/TR, 6'2", 205 lbs. Deb: 6/16/1990

YEAR TM-L	G	AB	R	H	2B	3B	HR	RBI	BB	SO	SB	CS	AVG	OBP	SLG	OPS	OPS+	BR/A	RC	RC/G	FR	G/POS	WS	TPW
1990 Oak-A	21	52	5	12	4	0	0	1	4	17	0	0	.231	.286	.308	.593	69	-2	5	3.24	-1	0-14(4-3-8)/D-7	0	-0.3

• HOWARD, Thomas Thomas Sylvester Howard b: 12/11/1964, Middletown, OH BB/TR, 6'2", 205 lbs. Deb: 7/3/1990 Career OF: 305-228-206

YEAR TM-L	G	AB	R	H	2B	3B	HR	RBI	BB	SO	SB	CS	AVG	OBP	SLG	OPS	OPS+	BR/A	RC	RC/G	FR	G/POS	WS	TPW
1990 SD-N	20	44	4	12	2	0	0	0	0	11	0	1	.273	.273	.318	.591	61	-3	3	2.49	-1	0-13(9-2-2)	0	-0.4
1991 SD-N	106	281	30	70	12	3	4	22	24	57	10	7	.249	.310	.356	.666	84	-7	31	3.66	2	0-86(34-41-14)	7	-0.7
1992 SD-N	5	3	1	1	0	0	0	0	0	0	0	0	.333	.333	.333	.667	88	-0	0	3.42	0	....	0	0.0
Cle-A	117	358	36	99	15	2	2	32	17	60	15	8	.277	.309	.346	.656	85	-8	38	3.65	-3	0-97(68-22-13)/D-2	7	-1.4
1993 Cle-A	74	178	26	42	7	0	3	23	12	42	5	1	.236	.284	.326	.610	64	-9	16	3.01	0	0-47(9-11-28)/D-7	2	-1.0
Cin-N	38	141	22	39	8	3	4	13	12	21	5	6	.277	.333	.461	.794	110	-0	19	4.53	2	0-37(27-12-0)	4	0.1
1994 Cin-N	83	178	24	47	11	0	5	24	10	30	4	2	.264	.303	.410	.713	85	-5	22	4.26	0	0-57(41-7-12)	4	-0.6
1995*Cin-N	113	281	42	85	15	2	3	26	20	37	17	8	.302	.351	.402	.753	98	-1	40	5.18	0	0-82(36-39-14)	8	-0.2
1996 Cin-N	121	360	50	98	19	10	6	42	17	51	6	5	.272	.311	.431	.741	94	-6	46	4.50	-1	*0-103(51-40-32)	9	-1.0
1997*Hou-N	107	255	24	63	16	1	3	22	26	48	1	2	.247	.324	.353	.677	80	-8	30	4.08	3	0-62(10-41-18)	3	-0.5
1998 LA-N	47	76	9	14	4	0	2	4	3	15	1	0	.184	.215	.316	.531	40	-7	5	2.03	0	0-29(11-13-6)/D-1	1	-0.7
1999 StL-N	98	195	16	57	10	0	6	28	17	26	1	1	.292	.355	.436	.791	98	-1	30	5.75	-2	0-48(3-0-45)/D-1	4	-0.5
2000 StL-N	86	133	13	28	4	1	6	28	7	34	1	0	.211	.255	.391	.646	60	-9	13	3.19	-2	0-27(6-0-22)/D-3,1-1	3	-1.1
Total 11	**1015**	**2483**	**297**	**655**	**123**	**22**	**44**	**264**	**165**	**432**	**66**	**41**	**.264**	**.313**	**.384**	**.697**	**85**	**-63**	**294**	**4.08**	**-2**	**0-688/D-14,1-1**	**52**	**-8.0**

• HOWARD, Wilbur Wilbur Leon Howard b: 1/8/1949, Lowell, NC BB/TR, 6'2", 175 lbs. Deb: 9/4/1973 Career OF: 214-69-50

YEAR TM-L	G	AB	R	H	2B	3B	HR	RBI	BB	SO	SB	CS	AVG	OBP	SLG	OPS	OPS+	BR/A	RC	RC/G	FR	G/POS	WS	TPW
1973 Mil-A	16	39	3	8	0	0	0	1	2	10	0	1	.205	.244	.205	.449	28	-4	2	1.54	1	0-12(5-0-7)/D-1	0	-0.4
1974 Hou-N	64	111	19	24	4	0	2	5	5	18	4	5	.216	.250	.306	.556	57	-8	7	1.92	2	0-50(43-4-3)	1	-0.9
1975 Hou-N	121	392	62	111	16	8	0	21	21	67	32	11	.283	.325	.365	.689	98	-0	49	4.41	2	0-95(53-34-12)	10	-0.2
1976 Hou-N	94	191	26	42	7	2	1	18	7	28	7	5	.220	.247	.293	.541	58	-12	12	2.03	-1	0-63(37-11-20)/2-2	1	-1.6
1977 Hou-N	87	187	22	48	6	0	2	13	5	30	11	1	.257	.276	.321	.597	65	-8	17	3.04	0	0-62(46-15-4)/2-4	3	-0.9
1978 Hou-N	84	148	17	34	4	1	1	13	5	22	6	2	.230	.269	.291	.560	61	-8	12	2.57	0	0-38(30-5-4)/C-3,2-1	1	-0.9
Total 6	**466**	**1068**	**149**	**267**	**37**	**11**	**6**	**71**	**45**	**175**	**60**	**25**	**.250**	**.284**	**.322**	**.606**	**73**	**-40**	**98**	**3.08**	**4**	**0-320/2-7,C-3,D-1**	**16**	**-5.0**

• HOWARTH, Jim James Eugene Howarth b: 3/7/1947, Biloxi, MS BL/TL, 5'11", 175 lbs. Deb: 9/5/1971 Career OF: 16-39-10

YEAR TM-L	G	AB	R	H	2B	3B	HR	RBI	BB	SO	SB	CS	AVG	OBP	SLG	OPS	OPS+	BR/A	RC	RC/G	FR	G/POS	WS	TPW
1971 SF-N	7	13	3	3	1	0	0	2	3	3	0	0	.231	.375	.308	.683	97	0	2	4.84	0	/0-6(2-1-3)	1	0.0
1972 SF-N	74	119	16	28	4	0	1	7	16	18	3	2	.235	.326	.294	.620	76	-3	12	3.27	-1	0-25(8-17-0)/1-4	2	-0.6
1973 SF-N	65	90	8	18	1	1	0	7	7	8	0	0	.200	.258	.233	.491	36	-8	6	2.09	0	0-33(5-21-7)/1-1	1	-0.8
1974 SF-N	6	4	0	0	0	0	0	0	0	0	0	0	.000	.000	.000	.000	-95	-1	0	.00	0	/0-1	0	-0.1
Total 4	**152**	**226**	**27**	**49**	**6**	**1**	**1**	**16**	**26**	**29**	**3**	**2**	**.217**	**.298**	**.265**	**.563**	**59**	**-12**	**19**	**2.81**	**-1**	**/0-65,1-5**	**4**	**-1.6**

• HOWE, Art Arthur Henry Howe b: 12/15/1946, Pittsburgh, PA BR/TR, 6'2", 190 lbs. Deb: 7/10/1974 M/C

YEAR TM-L	G	AB	R	H	2B	3B	HR	RBI	BB	SO	SB	CS	AVG	OBP	SLG	OPS	OPS+	BR/A	RC	RC/G	FR	G/POS	WS	TPW
1974*Pit-N	29	74	10	18	4	1	1	5	9	13	0	0	.243	.325	.365	.690	96	-0	9	4.30	1	3-20/S-2	2	0.0
1975 Pit-N	63	146	13	25	9	0	1	10	15	15	1	0	.171	.248	.253	.502	40	-12	9	1.89	-2	3-42/S-3	1	-1.5
1976 Hou-N	21	29	0	4	1	0	0	0	6	6	0	0	.138	.286	.172	.458	35	-2	2	1.68	0	/3-8,2-2	0	-0.2
1977 Hou-N	125	413	44	109	23	7	8	58	41	60	0	1	.264	.338	.412	.749	109	5	57	4.80	3	2-96,3-19,S-11	14	1.4
1978 Hou-N	119	420	46	123	33	3	7	55	34	41	2	3	.293	.347	.436	.783	127	13	60	5.10	-4	*2-107,3-11/1-1	16	1.5
1979 Hou-N	118	355	32	88	15	2	6	33	36	37	3	1	.248	.319	.352	.671	88	-6	41	3.90	6	2-68,3-59/1-3	12	0.3
1980*Hou-N	110	321	34	91	12	5	10	46	34	29	1	0	.283	.354	.445	.799	132	13	50	5.45	5	1-77,3-25/S-5,2-3	12	1.5
1981*Hou-N	103	361	43	107	22	4	3	36	41	23	1	3	.296	.368	.404	.773	125	11	53	5.33	10	3-98/1-2	16	2.2
1982 Hou-N	110	365	29	87	15	1	5	38	41	45	2	0	.238	.317	.326	.643	87	-6	38	3.44	8	3-72,1-35	9	0.0
1984 StL-N	89	139	17	30	5	0	2	12	18	18	0	2	.216	.306	.295	.601	71	-6	12	2.63	-1	3-45,1-11/2-8,S-5	2	-0.7
1985 StL-N	4	3	0	0	0	0	0	0	0	0	0	0	.000	.000	.000	.000	-101	-1	0	.00	0	/1-1,3-1	0	-0.1
Total 11	**891**	**2626**	**268**	**682**	**139**	**23**	**43**	**293**	**275**	**287**	**10**	**10**	**.260**	**.332**	**.379**	**.711**	**104**	**10**	**330**	**4.31**	**26**	**3-400,2-284,1-130/S-26**	**84**	**4.4**

• HOWE, Shorty John Howe b: New York, NY Deb: 6/17/1890 U

YEAR TM-L	G	AB	R	H	2B	3B	HR	RBI	BB	SO	SB	CS	AVG	OBP	SLG	OPS	OPS+	BR/A	RC	RC/G	FR	G/POS	WS	TPW
1890 NY-N	19	64	4	11	0	0	0	4	3	2	3	....	.172	.221	.172	.392	15	-7	3	1.58	-2	2-18/3-1	1	-0.7
1893 NY-N	1	5	1	3	0	0	0	2	0	0	1	....	.600	.600	.600	1.200	218	1	2	32.60	-1	/3-1	0	0.0
Total 2	**20**	**69**	**5**	**14**	**0**	**0**	**0**	**6**	**3**	**2**	**4**	**....**	**.203**	**.247**	**.203**	**.449**	**29**	**-6**	**6**	**2.71**	**-3**	**/2-18,3-2**	**1**	**-0.7**

• HOWELL, Dixie Homer Elliott Howell b: 4/24/1920, Louisville, KY d: 10/5/1990, Binghamton, NY BR/TR, 5'11.5", 195 lbs. Deb: 5/6/1947

YEAR TM-L	G	AB	R	H	2B	3B	HR	RBI	BB	SO	SB	CS	AVG	OBP	SLG	OPS	OPS+	BR/A	RC	RC/G	FR	G/POS	WS	TPW
1947 Pit-N	76	214	23	59	11	0	4	25	27	34	1	....	.276	.357	.383	.740	94	-1	31	5.24	-2	C-74	6	0.0
1949 Cin-N	64	172	17	42	6	1	2	18	8	21	0	....	.244	.286	.326	.611	63	-9	15	3.01	2	C-56	0	-0.5
1950 Cin-N	82	224	30	50	9	1	2	22	32	31	0	....	.223	.326	.299	.625	65	-10	23	3.35	-3	C-81	4	-1.0
1951 Cin-N	77	207	22	52	6	1	2	18	15	34	0	2	.251	.302	.319	.621	66	-11	20	3.37	-3	C-73	3	-1.1
1952 Cin-N	17	37	4	7	1	1	2	4	3	9	0	0	.189	.250	.432	.682	86	-1	3	2.46	1	C-16	1	0.1
1953 Bro-N	1	1	0	0	0	0	0	0	0	1	0	0	.000	.000	.000	.000	-98	-0	0	.00	0	....	0	0.0
1955 Bro-N	16	42	2	11	4	0	0	5	1	7	0	0	.262	.279	.357	.636	65	-2	4	3.56	-1	C-13	1	-0.2
1956 Bro-N	7	13	0	3	2	0	0	1	1	3	0	0	.231	.286	.385	.670	72	-1	2	3.40	0	/C-6	0	0.0
Total 8	**340**	**910**	**98**	**224**	**39**	**4**	**12**	**93**	**87**	**140**	**1**	**2**	**.246**	**.315**	**.337**	**.652**	**73**	**-36**	**98**	**3.68**	**-6**	**C-319**	**15**	**-2.7**

• HOWELL, Harry Henry Harry Howell b: 11/14/1876, NJ d: 5/22/1956, Spokane, WA BR/TR, 5'9" Deb: 10/10/1898 U Career OF: 10-17-6 ♦

YEAR TM-L	G	AB	R	H	2B	3B	HR	RBI	BB	SO	SB	CS	AVG	OBP	SLG	OPS	OPS+	BR/A	RC	RC/G	FR	G/POS	WS	TPW
1898 Bro-N	2	8	1	2	0	0	0	1	1	....	0	....	.250	.333	.250	.583	68	0	1	3.18	0	/P-2	1	-0.2
1899 Bal-N	28	82	4	12	2	2	0	3	3	....	0	....	.146	.195	.220	.415	13	-4	4	1.42	0	P-28	14	-0.3
1900*Bro-N	22	42	6	12	2	0	1	6	6	....	1	....	.286	.388	.405	.793	112	4	7	6.32	1	P-21	9	0.4
1901 Bal-A	53	188	26	41	10	5	2	26	5	....	6	....	.218	.242	.356	.599	62	-2	18	3.24	-3	P-37/0-9(4-2-3),S-6,1-2,2	19	1.2
1902 Bal-A	96	347	42	93	16	11	2	42	18	....	7	....	.268	.312	.395	.706	91	2	47	4.74	-2	2-26,P-26,0-18(5-10-3),3-15,S/1	13	-0.1
1903 NY-A	40	106	14	23	3	2	1	12	5	....	1	....	.217	.259	.311	.570	66	0	9	2.88	1	P-25/3-7,S-5,1-1,2-1	9	-0.9
1904 StL-A	36	113	9	25	5	2	1	6	4	....	0	....	.221	.261	.327	.588	91	5	10	2.97	10	P-34	22	2.2
1905 StL-A	42	135	9	26	6	2	1	10	3	....	0	....	.193	.216	.289	.505	63	2	9	2.10	18	P-38/0-3(1-2-0)	20	3.1
1906 StL-A	35	103	5	13	3	1	0	6	6	....	2	....	.126	.174	.175	.349	10	-3	4	1.10	7	P-35	18	1.2
1907 StL-A	44	114	12	27	5	0	2	7	7	....	2	....	.237	.281	.333	.614	96	5	12	3.45	9	P-42/0-2(0-2-0)	23	2.9

YEAR TM-L	G	AB	R	H	2B	3B	HR	RBI	BB	SO	SB	CS	AVG	OBP	SLG	OPS	OPS+	BR/A	RC	RC/G	FR	G/POS	WS	TPW
1908 StL-A	41	120	10	22	7	0	1	9	4	....	0	....	.183	.210	.267	.476	54	1	6	1.66	1	P-41	23	0.6
1909 StL-A	18	34	5	6	1	0	0	3	2	....	0	....	.176	.222	.206	.428	38	-1	2	1.48	1	P-10/3-7,0-1	1	-0.3
1910 StL-A	1	2	0	0	0	0	0	0	0	....	0	....	.000	.000	.000	.000	-107	-0	0	.00	0	/P-1	0	-0.4
Total 13	**458**	**1394**	**143**	**302**	**60**	**25**	**11**	**131**	**64**	**....**	**19**	**....**	**.217**	**.257**	**.319**	**.576**	**68**	**10**	**130**	**3.04**	**43**	**P-340/0-33,3-29,2-28,S-22,1**	**172**	**9.4**

• HOWELL, Jack Jack Robert Howell b: 8/18/1961, Tucson, AZ BL/TR, 6', 201 lbs. Deb: 5/20/1985 Career OF: 88-1-23

YEAR TM-L	G	AB	R	H	2B	3B	HR	RBI	BB	SO	SB	CS	AVG	OBP	SLG	OPS	OPS+	BR/A	RC	RC/G	FR	G/POS	WS	TPW
1985 Cal-A	43	137	19	27	4	0	5	18	16	33	1	1	.197	.281	.336	.617	68	-6	14	3.16	-4	3-42	2	-1.1
1986*Cal-A	63	151	26	41	14	2	4	21	19	28	2	0	.272	.353	.470	.823	123	5	27	6.24	0	3-39/0-8(7-0-1),D-2	6	0.5
1987 Cal-A	138	449	64	110	18	5	23	64	57	118	4	3	.245	.333	.461	.794	111	6	70	5.37	-5	0-89(78-0-15),3-48,2-13	14	-0.3
1988 Cal-A	154	500	59	127	32	2	16	63	46	130	2	6	.254	.324	.422	.746	110	4	67	4.60	-27	*3-152/0-2(1-1-0)	16	-2.2
1989 Cal-A	144	474	56	108	19	4	20	52	52	125	0	3	.228	.308	.411	.720	103	-1	60	4.22	18	*3-142/0-4(1-0-3)	16	1.8
1990 Cal-A	105	316	35	72	19	1	8	33	46	61	3	0	.228	.328	.370	.698	97	0	42	4.49	-2	*3-102/1-1,S-1	7	-0.1
1991 Cal-A	32	81	11	17	2	0	2	7	11	11	1	1	.210	.304	.309	.613	70	-3	8	3.28	0	2-12/3-8,0-5(1-0-4),1-3,D	2	-0.3
SD-N	58	160	24	33	3	1	6	16	18	33	0	0	.206	.287	.350	.637	76	-5	17	3.56	3	3-54	5	-0.2
1996 Cal-A	66	126	20	34	4	1	8	21	10	30	0	1	.270	.324	.508	.831	108	0	20	5.51	-1	3-43/D-4,1-2,2-1	3	0.0
1997 Ana-A	77	174	25	45	7	0	14	34	13	36	1	0	.259	.310	.540	.850	115	3	28	5.54	2	3-24,D-22,1-12	3	0.3
1998 Hou-N	24	38	4	11	5	0	1	7	4	12	0	0	.289	.357	.500	.857	126	1	7	6.44	0	1-10/3-2	1	0.1
1999 Hou-N	37	33	2	7	2	0	1	1	8	9	0	0	.212	.366	.364	.729	87	-0	5	4.81	0	/1-5,3-3,D-2	0	0.0
Total 11	**941**	**2639**	**345**	**632**	**129**	**16**	**108**	**337**	**300**	**626**	**14**	**15**	**.239**	**.320**	**.423**	**.743**	**103**	**4**	**363**	**4.68**	**-14**	**3-659,0-108/1-33,D-31,2-26,S**	**75**	**-1.4**

• HOWELL, Pat Patrick O'Neal Howell b: 8/31/1968, Mobile, AL BB/TR, 5'11", 155 lbs. Deb: 7/10/1992

YEAR TM-L	G	AB	R	H	2B	3B	HR	RBI	BB	SO	SB	CS	AVG	OBP	SLG	OPS	OPS+	BR/A	RC	RC/G	FR	G/POS	WS	TPW
1992 NY-N	31	75	9	14	1	0	0	1	2	15	4	2	.187	.218	.200	.418	19	-8	3	1.47	-2	0-28(0-28-0)	1	-1.1

• HOWELL, Red Murray Donald "Porky" Howell b: 1/29/1909, Atlanta, GA d: 10/1/1950, Traveler's Rest, SC BR/TR, 6', 215 lbs. Deb: 4/24/1941

YEAR TM-L	G	AB	R	H	2B	3B	HR	RBI	BB	SO	SB	CS	AVG	OBP	SLG	OPS	OPS+	BR/A	RC	RC/G	FR	G/POS	WS	TPW
1941 Cle-A	11	7	0	2	0	0	0	2	4	2	0	0	.286	.545	.286	.831	132	1	2	9.10	0	....	0	0.1

• HOWELL, Roy Roy Lee Howell b: 12/18/1953, Lompoc, CA BL/TR, 6'1", 190 lbs. Deb: 9/9/1974 Career OF: 2-0-8

YEAR TM-L	G	AB	R	H	2B	3B	HR	RBI	BB	SO	SB	CS	AVG	OBP	SLG	OPS	OPS+	BR/A	RC	RC/G	FR	G/POS	WS	TPW
1974 Tex-A	13	44	2	11	1	0	1	3	2	10	0	0	.250	.283	.341	.624	81	-1	4	3.52	-1	3-12	1	-0.2
1975 Tex-A	125	383	43	96	15	2	10	51	39	79	2	2	.251	.325	.379	.703	99	-1	48	4.35	-6	*3-115/D-5	11	-0.8
1976 Tex-A	140	491	55	124	28	2	8	53	30	106	1	0	.253	.297	.367	.664	92	-6	51	3.58	-10	*3-130/D-8	10	-1.8
1977 Tex-A	7	17	0	0	0	0	0	0	2	4	0	0	.000	.105	.000	.105	-68	-4	0	.09	0	/D-2,0-2(2-0-0),1-1,3-1	0	-0.5
Tor-A	96	364	41	115	17	1	10	44	42	76	4	1	.316	.388	.451	.839	126	15	61	6.11	-4	3-87/D-8	12	1.0
Yr.	103	381	41	115	17	1	10	44	44	80	4	1	.302	.376	.430	.806	118	11	61	5.76	-4	3-88,D-10/0-2(2-0-0),1-1	12	0.6
1978 Tor-A★	140	551	67	149	28	3	8	61	44	78	0	1	.270	.326	.376	.701	95	-4	67	4.34	8	*3-131/0-5(0-0-5),D-1	15	0.2
1979 Tor-A	138	511	60	126	28	4	15	72	42	91	1	4	.247	.311	.405	.716	90	-9	62	4.14	-2	*3-133/D-4	10	-1.3
1980 Tor-A	142	528	51	142	28	9	10	57	50	92	0	0	.269	.338	.413	.751	100	0	74	4.95	-18	*3-138/D-2	14	-2.0
1981*Mil-A	76	244	37	58	13	1	6	33	23	39	0	0	.238	.309	.373	.682	101	0	28	3.83	-9	3-53,D-13/1-3,0-1	7	-1.0
1982*Mil-A	98	300	31	78	11	2	4	38	21	39	0	2	.260	.308	.350	.658	86	-7	33	3.83	0	D-84/1-4,0-2(0-0-2)	5	-1.0
1983 Mil-A	69	194	23	54	9	6	4	25	15	29	1	3	.278	.330	.448	.779	121	4	27	4.92	1	D-54/1-2	5	0.3
1984 Mil-A	68	164	12	38	5	1	4	17	8	32	0	1	.232	.284	.348	.632	77	-6	14	2.70	0	3-46/D-8,1-4	1	-0.7
Total 11	**1112**	**3791**	**422**	**991**	**183**	**31**	**80**	**454**	**318**	**675**	**9**	**14**	**.261**	**.322**	**.389**	**.712**	**97**	**-19**	**470**	**4.31**	**-42**	**3-846,D-189/1-14,0-10**	**91**	**-7.6**

• HOWERTON, Bill William Ray "Hopalong" Howerton b: 12/12/1921, Lompoc, CA d: 12/18/2001, Blakely, PA BL/TR, 5'11", 185 lbs. Deb: 9/11/1949 Career OF: 41-98-42

YEAR TM-L	G	AB	R	H	2B	3B	HR	RBI	BB	SO	SB	CS	AVG	OBP	SLG	OPS	OPS+	BR/A	RC	RC/G	FR	G/POS	WS	TPW
1949 StL-N	9	13	1	4	1	0	0	1	0	2	0	....	.308	.308	.385	.692	81	-0	2	4.62	-1	/0-6(2-3-1)	0	-0.1
1950 StL-N	110	313	50	88	20	8	10	59	47	60	0	....	.281	.375	.492	.867	120	10	61	7.10	-4	0-94(32-54-11)	12	0.2
1951 StL-N	24	65	10	17	4	1	1	4	10	12	0	1	.262	.360	.400	.760	103	0	9	4.96	1	0-17(3-0-14)	2	0.1
Pit-N	80	219	29	60	12	2	11	37	26	44	1	0	.274	.351	.498	.849	122	7	37	5.98	-4	0-53(4-38-11)/3-4	7	0.2
Yr.	104	284	39	77	16	3	12	41	36	56	1	1	.271	.353	.475	.828	118	7	47	5.74	-3	0-70(7-38-25)/3-4	9	0.2
1952 Pit-N	13	25	3	8	1	1	0	4	6	5	0	0	.320	.452	.440	.892	144	2	5	8.07	-2	/0-5(0-2-3),3-1	1	0.0
NY-N	11	15	2	1	1	0	0	1	3	2	0	0	.067	.222	.133	.356	1	-2	1	1.21	0	/0-3(0-1-2)	0	-0.2
Yr.	24	40	5	9	2	1	0	5	9	7	0	0	.225	.367	.325	.692	91	0	6	5.07	-2	/0-8(0-3-5),3-1	1	-0.2
Total 4	**247**	**650**	**95**	**178**	**39**	**12**	**22**	**106**	**92**	**125**	**1**	**1**	**.274**	**.364**	**.472**	**.836**	**117**	**16**	**115**	**6.32**	**-9**	**0-178/3-5**	**22**	**0.1**

• HOWITT, Dann Dann Paul John Howitt b: 2/13/1964, Battle Creek, MI BL/TR, 6'5", 205 lbs. Deb: 9/15/1989 Career OF: 36-19-52

YEAR TM-L	G	AB	R	H	2B	3B	HR	RBI	BB	SO	SB	CS	AVG	OBP	SLG	OPS	OPS+	BR/A	RC	RC/G	FR	G/POS	WS	TPW
1989 Oak-A	3	3	0	0	0	0	0	0	0	2	0	0	.000	.000	.000	.000	-104	-1	0	.00	0	/1-1,0-1	0	-0.1
1990 Oak-A	14	22	3	3	0	1	0	1	3	12	0	0	.136	.240	.227	.467	33	-2	1	1.97	-1	0-11(0-0-11)/1-5,3-1	0	-0.3
1991 Oak-A	21	42	5	7	1	0	1	3	1	12	0	0	.167	.186	.262	.448	24	-4	2	1.37	-1	0-20(5-7-10)/1-1	0	-0.6
1992 Oak-A	22	48	1	6	0	0	1	2	5	4	0	0	.125	.208	.188	.395	12	-6	1	.79	1	0-19(4-5-12)/1-4,D-1	0	-0.5
Sea-A	13	37	6	10	4	1	1	8	3	5	1	1	.270	.325	.514	.839	131	1	5	4.16	0	0-11(10-0-1)	1	0.1
Yr.	35	85	7	16	4	1	2	10	8	9	1	1	.188	.258	.329	.587	65	-5	6	2.18	2	0-30(14-5-13)/1-4,D-1	1	-0.4
1993 Sea-A	32	76	6	16	3	1	2	8	4	18	0	0	.211	.250	.355	.605	60	-5	7	3.15	0	0-29(16-6-12)/D-2	1	-0.6
1994 Chi-A	10	14	4	5	3	0	0	0	1	7	0	0	.357	.400	.571	.971	149	1	3	7.43	0	/0-7(1-1-5),1-4	1	0.0
Total 6	**115**	**242**	**25**	**47**	**11**	**3**	**5**	**22**	**17**	**60**	**1**	**1**	**.194**	**.247**	**.326**	**.574**	**56**	**-15**	**19**	**2.52**	**-1**	**/0-98,1-15,D-3,3-1**	**3**	**-1.9**

• HOWLEY, Dan Daniel Philip "Howling Dan,Dapper Dan" Howley b: 10/16/1885, Weymouth, MA d: 3/10/1944, Weymouth, MA BR/TR, 6', 187 lbs. Deb: 5/15/1913 M/C/U

YEAR TM-L	G	AB	R	H	2B	3B	HR	RBI	BB	SO	SB	CS	AVG	OBP	SLG	OPS	OPS+	BR/A	RC	RC/G	FR	G/POS	WS	TPW
1913 Phi-N	26	32	5	4	2	0	0	2	4	4	3	....	.125	.222	.188	.410	17	-3	2	1.59	0	C-22	1	-0.3

• HOWSER, Dick Richard Dalton Howser b: 5/14/1936, Miami, FL d: 6/17/1987, Kansas City, MO BR/TR, 5'8", 155 lbs. Deb: 4/11/1961 M/C

YEAR TM-L	G	AB	R	H	2B	3B	HR	RBI	BB	SO	SB	CS	AVG	OBP	SLG	OPS	OPS+	BR/A	RC	RC/G	FR	G/POS	WS	TPW
1961 KC-A★	158	611	108	171	29	6	3	45	92	38	37	9	.280	.379	.362	.740	99	7	95	5.46	-23	*S-157	20	-0.2
1962 KC-A	83	286	53	68	8	3	6	34	38	8	19	2	.238	.329	.350	.679	80	-4	37	4.27	-5	S-72	7	-0.3
1963 KC-A	15	41	4	8	0	0	0	1	7	3	0	0	.195	.313	.195	.508	44	-3	3	2.45	-1	S-10	0	-0.3
Cle-A	49	162	25	40	5	0	1	10	22	18	9	3	.247	.337	.296	.633	80	-3	17	3.47	-9	S-44	4	-0.9
Yr.	64	203	29	48	5	0	1	11	29	21	9	3	.236	.332	.276	.608	73	-6	21	3.27	-10	S-54	4	-1.2
1964 Cle-A	162	637	101	163	23	4	3	52	76	39	20	7	.256	.337	.319	.656	84	-10	74	3.88	-3	*S-162	20	0.2
1965 Cle-A	107	307	47	72	8	2	1	6	57	25	17	4	.235	.356	.283	.640	83	-2	38	3.97	3	S-73,2-17	11	0.9
1966 Cle-A	67	140	18	32	9	1	2	4	15	23	2	4	.229	.303	.350	.653	87	-4	14	3.06	1	2-26,S-26	3	0.1
1967 NY-A	63	149	18	40	6	0	0	10	25	15	1	4	.268	.381	.309	.689	110	2	19	4.51	-6	2-22,3-12/S-3	6	-0.2
1968 NY-A	85	150	24	23	2	1	0	3	35	17	0	1	.153	.321	.180	.501	57	-6	11	2.21	5	2-29/3-2,S-1	3	0.2
Total 8	**789**	**2483**	**398**	**617**	**90**	**17**	**16**	**165**	**367**	**186**	**105**	**34**	**.248**	**.348**	**.318**	**.666**	**86**	**-21**	**308**	**4.13**	**-38**	**S-548/2-94,3-14**	**74**	**-0.7**

• HOY, Dummy William Ellsworth Hoy b: 5/23/1862, Houcktown, OH d: 12/15/1961, Cincinnati, OH BL/TR, 5'6", 160 lbs. Deb: 4/20/1888 Career OF: 66-1726-5

YEAR TM-L	G	AB	R	H	2B	3B	HR	RBI	BB	SO	SB	CS	AVG	OBP	SLG	OPS	OPS+	BR/A	RC	RC/G	FR	G/POS	WS	TPW
1888 Was-N	136	503	77	138	10	8	2	29	69	48	**82**	....	.274	.374	.338	.712	136	26	97	7.14	1	*0-136(0-136-1)	28	2.2
1889 Was-N	127	507	98	139	11	6	0	39	75	30	35	....	.274	.374	.320	.694	101	6	76	5.44	-7	*0-127(1-126-0)	13	-0.5
1890 Buf-P	122	493	107	147	17	8	1	53	94	36	39	....	.298	.418	.371	.790	122	25	95	7.43	0	*0-122(0-122-0)/2-1	17	1.7
1891 StL-a	139	559	134	163	14	5	5	64	**117**	25	59	....	.292	.424	.361	.786	110	13	115	7.75	-2	*0-141(0-141-0)	28	0.5
1892 Was-N	152	593	108	167	19	8	3	75	86	23	60	....	.282	.376	.356	.732	124	22	104	6.56	-11	*0-152(3-150-0)	20	0.1
1893 Was-N	130	564	106	138	12	6	0	45	66	9	48	....	.245	.337	.287	.625	68	-23	73	4.52	-3	*0-130(0-130-0)	9	-2.8
1894 Cin-N	128	503	118	153	22	13	5	71	90	19	28	....	.304	.421	.429	.851	102	5	105	7.83	8	*0-126(0-126-0)	15	0.4
1895 Cin-N	107	429	93	119	21	12	3	55	52	8	50	....	.277	.363	.403	.767	94	-4	83	7.19	-6	*0-107(62-41-4)	11	-1.5
1896 Cin-N	121	443	120	132	23	7	4	57	65	13	50	....	.298	.403	.409	.812	107	7	99	7.64	1	*0-120(0-120-0)	18	0.0
1897 Cin-N	128	497	87	145	24	6	2	42	54	....	37	....	.292	.375	.376	.751	92	-5	89	6.28	-3	*0-128(0-128-0)	16	-1.4
1898 Lou-N	148	582	104	177	15	16	6	66	49	....	37	....	.304	.367	.416	.783	126	19	107	6.69	-5	*0-148(0-148-0)	24	0.5
1899 Lou-N	155	636	117	194	17	13	5	49	62	....	33	....	.305	.376	.396	.772	113	12	111	6.50	-10	*0-154(0-154-0)	20	-0.7
1901 Chi-A	132	527	112	155	28	11	2	60	**86**	....	27	....	.294	.407	.400	.807	128	26	101	6.95	2	*0-132(0-132-0)	25	2.0
1902 Cin-N	72	279	48	81	15	2	2	20	41	....	11	....	.290	.389	.380	.769	125	11	48	6.10	-6	0-72(0-72-0)	10	0.2
Total 14	**1797**	**7115**	**1429**	**2048**	**248**	**121**	**40**	**725**	**1006**	**211**	**596**	**....**	**.288**	**.386**	**.374**	**.760**	**110**	**140**	**1304**	**6.69**	**-39**	***0-1795/2-1**	**254**	**0.6**

• HRBEK, Kent Kent Allen Hrbek b: 5/21/1960, Minneapolis, MN BL/TR, 6'4", 235 lbs. Deb: 8/24/1981

YEAR TM-L	G	AB	R	H	2B	3B	HR	RBI	BB	SO	SB	CS	AVG	OBP	SLG	OPS	OPS+	BR/A	RC	RC/G	FR	G/POS	WS	TPW
1981 Min-A	24	67	5	16	5	0	1	7	5	9	0	0	.239	.301	.358	.660	84	-1	8	4.04	-2	1-13/D-8	1	-0.5
1982 Min-A★	140	532	82	160	21	4	23	92	54	80	3	1	.301	.365	.485	.850	128	21	91	6.19	4	*1-138/D-2	18	1.6
1983 Min-A	141	515	75	153	41	5	16	84	57	71	4	6	.297	.370	.489	.860	130	20	91	6.36	-2	*1-137/D-2	19	0.9

YEAR TM-L	G	AB	R	H	2B	3B	HR	RBI	BB	SO	SB	CS	AVG	OBP	SLG	OPS	OPS+	BR/A	RC	RC/G	FR	G/POS	WS	TPW
1984 Min-A	149	559	80	174	31	3	27	107	65	87	1	1	.311	.387	.522	.909	142	33	110	7.24	-2	*1-148/D-1	24	2.2
1985 Min-A	158	593	78	165	31	2	21	93	67	87	1	1	.278	.353	.444	.797	110	9	93	5.65	3	*1-156/D-2	19	0.2
1986 Min-A	149	550	85	147	27	1	29	91	71	81	2	2	.267	.357	.478	.835	122	17	93	5.89	-1	*1-147/D-1	17	0.7
1987*Min-A	143	477	85	136	20	1	34	90	84	60	5	2	.285	.392	.545	.937	140	30	103	7.69	-4	*1-137/D-1	25	1.7
1988 Min-A	143	510	75	159	31	0	25	76	67	54	0	3	.312	.392	.520	.911	149	33	104	7.56	0	*1-105,D-37	19	2.5
1989 Min-A	109	375	59	102	17	0	25	84	53	35	3	0	.272	.364	.517	.881	136	19	73	6.94	3	1-89,D-18	18	1.5
1990 Min-A	143	492	61	141	26	0	22	79	69	45	5	2	.287	.382	.474	.856	129	22	89	6.29	1	*1-120,D-20/3-1	19	1.4
1991*Min-A	132	462	72	131	20	1	20	89	67	48	4	4	.284	.374	.461	.835	124	16	78	5.97	4	*1-128	19	1.1
1992 Min-A	112	394	52	96	20	0	15	58	71	56	5	2	.244	.359	.409	.768	111	8	59	5.06	0	*1-104/D-8	10	0.0
1993 Min-A	123	392	60	95	11	1	25	83	71	57	4	2	.242	.360	.467	.827	120	12	67	5.68	1	*1-115/D-2	12	0.3
1994 Min-A	81	274	34	74	11	0	10	53	37	28	0	0	.270	.359	.420	.779	100	0	41	5.24	0	1-72/D-4	10	-0.6
Total 14	1747	6192	903	1749	312	18	293	1086	838	798	37	26	.282	.370	.481	.851	127	238	1100	6.30	4	*1-1609,D-106/3-1	230	13.1

• HRINIAK, Walt Walter John Hriniak b: 5/22/1943, Natick, MA BL/TR, 5'11", 180 lbs. Deb: 9/10/1968 C

YEAR TM-L	G	AB	R	H	2B	3B	HR	RBI	BB	SO	SB	CS	AVG	OBP	SLG	OPS	OPS+	BR/A	RC	RC/G	FR	G/POS	WS	TPW
1968 Atl-N	9	26	0	9	0	0	0	3	0	3	0	0	.346	.346	.346	.692	108	0	3	4.95	-1	/C-9	1	0.0
1969 Atl-N	7	7	0	1	0	0	0	0	2	1	0	0	.143	.333	.143	.476	38	-0	0	1.30	-1	/C-6	0	-0.1
SD-N	31	66	4	15	0	0	0	1	8	11	0	0	.227	.329	.227	.556	61	-3	5	2.67	-1	C-19	1	-0.3
Yr.	38	73	4	16	0	0	0	1	10	12	0	0	.219	.329	.219	.549	58	-3	6	2.51	-2	C-25	1	-0.4
Total 2	47	99	4	25	0	0	0	4	10	15	0	0	.253	.333	.253	.586	70	-3	9	3.05	-3	/C-34	2	-0.5

• HUBBARD, Al Allen Hubbard b: 12/9/1860, Westfield, MA d: 12/14/1930, Newton, MA Deb: 9/13/1883

YEAR TM-L	G	AB	R	H	2B	3B	HR	RBI	BB	SO	SB	CS	AVG	OBP	SLG	OPS	OPS+	BR/A	RC	RC/G	FR	G/POS	WS	TPW
1883 Phi-a	2	6	2	2	0	0	0	2	1	....	....	....	.333	.429	.333	.762	138	0	1	6.15	0	/C-1,S-1	1	0.0

• HUBBARD, Glenn Glenn Dee Hubbard b: 9/25/1957, Hahn, West Germany BR/TR, 5'9", 180 lbs. Deb: 7/14/1978 C

YEAR TM-L	G	AB	R	H	2B	3B	HR	RBI	BB	SO	SB	CS	AVG	OBP	SLG	OPS	OPS+	BR/A	RC	RC/G	FR	G/POS	WS	TPW
1978 Atl-N	44	163	15	42	4	0	2	13	10	20	2	1	.258	.309	.319	.628	68	-7	17	3.48	2	2-44	3	-0.3
1979 Atl-N	97	325	34	75	12	0	3	29	27	43	0	6	.231	.292	.295	.587	56	-22	28	2.83	-2	2-91	4	-2.0
1980 Atl-N	117	431	55	107	21	3	9	43	49	69	7	5	.248	.325	.374	.699	91	-5	53	4.20	10	*2-117	14	1.1
1981 Atl-N	99	361	39	85	13	5	6	33	33	59	4	2	.235	.303	.349	.652	82	-9	39	3.60	-1	2-98	10	-0.5
1982*Atl-N	145	532	75	132	25	1	9	59	59	62	4	3	.248	.327	.350	.676	86	-10	65	4.05	18	*2-144	19	1.7
1983 Atl-N★	148	517	65	136	24	6	12	70	55	71	3	8	.263	.339	.402	.741	97	-4	69	4.45	14	*2-148	19	1.8
1984 Atl-N	120	397	53	93	27	2	9	43	55	61	4	1	.234	.333	.380	.714	93	-2	53	4.46	12	*2-117	15	1.7
1985 Atl-N	142	439	51	102	21	0	5	39	56	54	4	3	.232	.325	.314	.639	75	-14	47	3.47	37	*2-140	14	3.3
1986 Atl-N	143	408	42	94	16	1	4	36	66	74	3	2	.230	.343	.304	.647	76	-11	47	3.81	3	*2-142	12	-0.1
1987 Atl-N	141	443	69	117	33	2	5	38	77	57	1	1	.264	.380	.381	.762	98	2	67	5.25	10	*2-139	15	1.9
1988*Oak-A	105	294	35	75	12	2	3	33	33	50	1	3	.255	.336	.340	.677	93	-3	34	3.73	6	*2-104/D-1	11	0.6
1989 Oak-A	53	131	12	26	6	0	3	12	19	20	2	0	.198	.300	.313	.613	76	-3	13	3.24	7	2-48/D-3	4	0.5
Total 12	1354	4441	545	1084	214	22	70	448	539	640	35	35	.244	.330	.349	.680	85	-89	530	3.99	117	*2-1332/D-4	140	9.8

• HUBBARD, Mike Michael Wayne Hubbard b: 2/16/1971, Lynchburg, VA BR/TR, 6'1", 180 lbs. Deb: 7/13/1995

YEAR TM-L	G	AB	R	H	2B	3B	HR	RBI	BB	SO	SB	CS	AVG	OBP	SLG	OPS	OPS+	BR/A	RC	RC/G	FR	G/POS	WS	TPW
1995 Chi-N	15	23	2	4	0	0	0	1	2	2	0	0	.174	.240	.174	.414	12	-3	1	1.22	-1	/C-9	0	-0.3
1996 Chi-N	21	38	1	4	0	0	1	4	0	15	0	0	.105	.105	.184	.289	-25	-7	1	.43	0	C-14	0	-0.6
1997 Chi-N	29	64	4	13	0	0	1	2	2	21	0	0	.203	.227	.250	.477	24	-7	3	1.79	0	C-20/3-1	1	-0.6
1998 Mon-N	31	55	3	8	1	0	1	3	0	17	0	0	.145	.161	.218	.379	-2	-8	2	.99	-1	C-24/2-1	0	-0.8
2000 Atl-N	2	1	0	0	0	0	0	0	0	1	0	0	.000	.000	.000	.000	-100	-0	0	.00	0	/C-1	0	0.0
2001 Tex-A	5	11	1	3	1	0	1	1	0	4	0	0	.273	.273	.636	.909	125	0	2	6.44	-1	/C-5	0	0.0
Total 6	103	192	11	32	2	0	4	11	4	60	0	0	.167	.188	.240	.427	11	-25	9	1.41	-2	/C-73,2-1,3-1	1	-2.4

• HUBBARD, Trenidad Trenidad Aviel Hubbard b: 5/11/1964, Chicago, IL BR/TR, 5'8", 180 lbs. Deb: 7/7/1994 Career OF: 148-122-59

YEAR TM-L	G	AB	R	H	2B	3B	HR	RBI	BB	SO	SB	CS	AVG	OBP	SLG	OPS	OPS+	BR/A	RC	RC/G	FR	G/POS	WS	TPW
1994 Col-N	18	25	3	7	1	1	1	3	3	4	0	0	.280	.357	.520	.877	107	0	4	6.29	0	/O-5(2-3-0)	1	0.0
1995*Col-N	24	58	13	18	4	0	3	9	8	6	2	1	.310	.394	.534	.928	110	1	12	7.30	0	O-16(4-14-0)	1	0.1
1996 Col-N	45	60	12	13	5	1	1	12	9	22	2	0	.217	.329	.383	.712	70	-2	8	4.71	-1	O-19(3-16-0)	2	-0.3
SF-N	10	29	3	6	0	1	1	2	2	5	0	0	.207	.258	.379	.637	68	-1	2	2.41	1	/O-9(8-1-0)	0	-0.1
Yr.	55	89	15	19	5	2	2	14	11	27	2	0	.213	.307	.382	.689	70	-4	11	3.92	0	O-28(11-17-0)	2	-0.4
1997 Cle-A	7	12	3	3	1	0	0	0	1	3	2	0	.250	.308	.333	.641	65	-0	2	4.89	0	/O-6(5-1-0)	0	-0.1
1998 LA-N	94	208	29	62	9	1	7	18	18	46	9	5	.298	.362	.452	.814	120	6	33	5.55	-1	O-81(34-46-4)/3-1	6	0.4
1999 LA-N	82	105	23	33	5	0	1	13	13	24	4	3	.314	.390	.390	.780	104	1	16	5.52	-2	O-51(29-19-3)/2-1,C-1	4	-0.2
2000 Atl-N	61	81	15	15	2	1	1	6	11	20	2	1	.185	.290	.272	.562	43	-7	7	2.75	0	O-44(36-0-10)	1	-0.8
Bal-A	31	27	3	5	0	1	0	0	0	3	2	1	.185	.185	.259	.444	11	-4	1	.64	-1	O-24(11-0-14)/D-6	0	-0.5
2001 KC-A	5	12	2	3	0	1	0	0	0	2	0	0	.250	.250	.417	.667	66	-1	1	3.75	-1	/O-3(0-2-1)	0	-0.1
2002 SD-N	89	129	16	27	5	0	1	7	14	28	9	6	.209	.287	.271	.558	53	-9	10	2.35	-2	O-57(16-16-26)/3-6,2-4,D-1	0	-1.2
2003 Chi-N	10	16	2	4	1	0	0	2	4	3	1	0	.250	.429	.313	.741	99	1	3	6.58	0	/O-4(0-4-1)	1	0.0
Total 10	476	762	124	196	33	7	16	72	83	166	33	17	.257	.335	.382	.717	85	-17	100	4.38	-8	O-319/3-7,D-7,2-5,C-1	16	-2.8

• HUBBS, Ken Kenneth Douglas Hubbs b: 12/23/1941, Riverside, CA d: 2/15/1964, Provo, UT BR/TR, 6'2", 175 lbs. Deb: 9/10/1961

YEAR TM-L	G	AB	R	H	2B	3B	HR	RBI	BB	SO	SB	CS	AVG	OBP	SLG	OPS	OPS+	BR/A	RC	RC/G	FR	G/POS	WS	TPW
1961 Chi-N	10	28	4	5	1	1	1	2	0	8	0	0	.179	.179	.393	.571	46	-2	2	2.31	0	/2-8	0	-0.2
1962 Chi-N	160	661	90	172	24	9	5	49	35	129	3	7	.260	.300	.346	.647	70	-31	64	3.23	-7	*2-159	9	-2.4
1963 Chi-N	154	566	54	133	19	3	8	47	39	93	8	9	.235	.287	.322	.608	71	-23	48	2.79	13	*2-152	12	0.4
Total 3	324	1255	148	310	44	13	14	98	74	230	11	16	.247	.292	.336	.628	70	-56	114	3.01	6	2-319	21	-2.2

• HUBER, Clarence Clarence Bill "Gilly" Huber b: 10/27/1896, Tyler, TX d: 2/22/1965, Laredo, TX BR/TR, 5'10", 165 lbs. Deb: 9/17/1920

YEAR TM-L	G	AB	R	H	2B	3B	HR	RBI	BB	SO	SB	CS	AVG	OBP	SLG	OPS	OPS+	BR/A	RC	RC/G	FR	G/POS	WS	TPW
1920 Det-A	11	42	4	9	2	1	0	5	0	5	0	0	.214	.214	.310	.524	39	-4	3	2.15	1	3-11	1	-0.3
1921 Det-A	1	0	0	0	0	0	0	0	0	0	0	0	....	....	....	....	-101	0	0	....	0	/3-1	0	0.0
1925 Phi-N	124	436	46	124	28	5	5	54	17	33	3	5	.284	.311	.406	.717	75	-18	53	4.33	-10	*3-120	9	-2.0
1926 Phi-N	118	376	45	92	17	7	1	34	42	29	9	....	.245	.324	.335	.659	74	-13	42	3.69	2	*3-115	8	-0.5
Total 4	254	854	95	225	47	13	6	93	59	67	12	5	.263	.313	.370	.683	73	-36	97	3.93	-8	3-247	18	-2.8

• HUBER, Otto Otto Huber b: 3/12/1914, Garfield, NJ d: 4/9/1989, Passaic, NJ BR/TR, 5'10", 165 lbs. Deb: 6/10/1939

YEAR TM-L	G	AB	R	H	2B	3B	HR	RBI	BB	SO	SB	CS	AVG	OBP	SLG	OPS	OPS+	BR/A	RC	RC/G	FR	G/POS	WS	TPW
1939 Bos-N	11	22	2	6	1	0	0	3	0	1	0	....	.273	.273	.318	.591	63	-1	2	3.12	0	/2-4,3-4	0	-0.1

• HUCKABY, Ken Kenneth Paul Huckaby b: 1/27/1971, San Leandro, CA BR/TR, 6'1", 205 lbs. Deb: 10/6/2001

YEAR TM-L	G	AB	R	H	2B	3B	HR	RBI	BB	SO	SB	CS	AVG	OBP	SLG	OPS	OPS+	BR/A	RC	RC/G	FR	G/POS	WS	TPW
2001 Ari-N	1	1	0	0	0	0	0	0	0	1	0	0	.000	.000	.000	.000	-94	-0	0	.00	0	/C-1	0	0.0
2002 Tor-A	88	273	29	67	6	1	3	22	9	44	0	0	.245	.270	.308	.577	51	-19	20	2.51	-1	C-88	2	-1.4
2003 Tor-A	5	11	1	2	1	0	0	2	0	2	0	0	.182	.182	.273	.455	17	-1	1	1.64	0	/C-4	0	-0.1
Total 3	94	285	30	69	7	1	3	24	9	47	0	0	.242	.265	.305	.571	49	-21	21	2.47	0	/C-93	2	-1.5

• HUDGENS, Dave David Mark Hudgens b: 12/5/1956, Oroville, CA BL/TL, 6'2", 210 lbs. Deb: 9/4/1983 C

YEAR TM-L	G	AB	R	H	2B	3B	HR	RBI	BB	SO	SB	CS	AVG	OBP	SLG	OPS	OPS+	BR/A	RC	RC/G	FR	G/POS	WS	TPW
1983 Oak-A	6	7	0	1	0	0	0	0	0	3	0	0	.143	.143	.143	.286	-22	-1	0	.64	0	/1-3,D-1	0	-0.1

• HUDGENS, Jimmy James Price Hudgens b: 8/24/1902, Newburg, MO d: 8/26/1955, St. Louis, MO BL/TR, 6', 180 lbs. Deb: 9/14/1923

YEAR TM-L	G	AB	R	H	2B	3B	HR	RBI	BB	SO	SB	CS	AVG	OBP	SLG	OPS	OPS+	BR/A	RC	RC/G	FR	G/POS	WS	TPW
1923 StL-N	6	12	2	3	1	0	0	0	3	3	0	0	.250	.400	.333	.733	97	0	2	5.40	0	/1-3,2-1	0	0.0
1925 Cin-N	3	7	0	3	1	1	0	0	1	1	0	0	.429	.500	.857	1.357	245	2	3	19.91	0	/1-3	1	0.1
1926 Cin-N	17	20	2	5	1	0	0	1	1	0	0	....	.250	.286	.300	.586	59	-1	2	2.88	0	/1-6	0	-0.1
Total 3	26	39	4	11	3	1	0	1	5	4	0	0	.282	.364	.410	.774	106	1	7	6.13	1	/1-12,2-1	1	0.0

• HUDLER, Rex Rex Allen "Wonder Dog" Hudler b: 9/2/1960, Tempe, AZ BR/TR, 6'1", 180 lbs. Deb: 9/9/1984 Career OF: 124-65-64

YEAR TM-L	G	AB	R	H	2B	3B	HR	RBI	BB	SO	SB	CS	AVG	OBP	SLG	OPS	OPS+	BR/A	RC	RC/G	FR	G/POS	WS	TPW
1984 NY-A	9	7	2	1	1	0	0	0	1	5	0	0	.143	.333	.286	.619	76	-0	1	3.78	-2	/2-9	0	-0.2
1985 NY-A	20	51	4	8	0	1	0	1	1	9	0	1	.157	.173	.196	.369	1	-7	2	.99	3	2-16/1-1,S-1	1	-0.4
1986 Bal-A	14	1	1	0	0	0	0	0	0	0	1	0	.000	.000	.000	.000	-101	-0	0	.00	-6	2-13/3-1	0	-0.6
1988 Mon-N	77	216	38	59	14	2	4	14	10	34	29	7	.273	.305	.412	.717	100	2	28	4.47	-1	2-41,S-27/O-4(2-0-2)	6	0.4
1989 Mon-N	92	155	21	38	7	0	6	13	6	23	15	4	.245	.278	.406	.684	92	-1	17	3.81	-3	2-38,O-23(14-5-4),S-18	3	-0.3
1990 Mon-N	4	3	1	1	0	0	0	0	0	1	0	0	.333	.333	.333	.667	87	-0	0	4.50	0	....	0	0.0

YEAR TM-L	G	AB	R	H	2B	3B	HR	RBI	BB	SO	SB	CS	AVG	OBP	SLG	OPS	OPS+	BR/A	RC	RC/G	FR	G/POS	WS	TPW
StL-N	89	217	30	61	11	2	7	22	12	31	18	10	.281	.325	.447	.772	110	1	29	4.63	-1	0-45(17-3-27),2-10/1-6,3-6,S	5	-0.1
Yr.	93	220	31	62	11	2	7	22	12	32	18	10	.282	.325	.445	.770	109	1	30	4.63	-1	0-45(17-3-27),2-10/1-6,3-6,S	5	-0.1
1991 StL-N	101	207	21	47	10	2	1	15	10	29	12	8	.227	.263	.309	.572	60	-13	16	2.53	-2	0-58(28-21-10),1-12/2-5	3	-1.7
1992 StL-N	61	98	17	24	4	0	3	5	2	23	2	6	.245	.267	.378	.645	83	-5	8	2.68	-2	2-16,0-12(5-1-7)/1-8	1	-0.7
1994 Cal-A	56	124	17	37	8	0	8	20	6	28	2	2	.298	.331	.556	.887	122	3	19	4.94	-4	2-22,0-18(18-0-0)/3-4,D-4,1	4	-0.1
1995 Cal-A	84	223	30	59	16	0	6	27	10	48	13	0	.265	.311	.417	.728	88	-2	31	5.01	-1	2-52,0-22(18-4-1)/D-3,1-2	7	-0.2
1996 Cal-A	92	302	60	94	20	3	16	40	9	54	14	5	.311	.338	.556	.894	123	9	53	6.46	-10	2-53,0-21(8-14-0)/D-8,1-7	10	0.0
1997 Phi-N	50	122	17	27	4	0	5	10	6	28	1	0	.221	.264	.377	.641	65	-7	12	3.30	-2	0-35(11-16-8)/2-6	1	-0.9
1998 Phi-N	25	41	2	5	1	0	0	2	4	12	0	0	.122	.200	.146	.346	-7	-6	1	.91	0	/0-9(3-1-5),1-1	0	-0.7
Total 13	774	1767	261	461	96	10	56	169	77	325	107	43	.261	.297	.422	.719	91	-26	219	4.20	-31	2-281,0-247/S-47,1-38,D-15,3	41	-5.3

• HUDSON, Johnny John Wilson "Mr. Chips" Hudson b: 6/30/1912, Bryan, TX d: 11/7/1970, Bryan, TX BR/TR, 5'10", 160 lbs. Deb: 6/20/1936

YEAR TM-L	G	AB	R	H	2B	3B	HR	RBI	BB	SO	SB	CS	AVG	OBP	SLG	OPS	OPS+	BR/A	RC	RC/G	FR	G/POS	WS	TPW
1936 Bro-N	6	12	1	2	0	0	0	0	2	1	0	....	.167	.286	.167	.452	24	-1	1	2.02	-2	/S-4,2-1	0	-0.3
1937 Bro-N	13	27	3	5	4	0	0	2	3	9	0	....	.185	.267	.333	.600	61	-2	2	2.74	-1	S-11/2-1	0	-0.3
1938 Bro-N	135	498	59	130	21	5	2	37	39	76	7	....	.261	.315	.335	.650	77	-16	51	3.45	5	*2-132/S-3	9	-0.3
1939 Bro-N	109	343	46	87	17	3	2	32	30	36	5	....	.254	.317	.338	.656	74	-13	36	3.64	-3	S-50,2-45/3-1	7	-1.0
1940 Bro-N	85	179	13	39	4	3	0	19	9	26	2	....	.218	.255	.274	.529	43	-14	12	2.12	2	S-38,2-27/3-1	2	-0.9
1941 Chi-N	50	99	8	20	4	0	0	6	3	15	3	....	.202	.225	.242	.468	33	-9	5	1.59	-2	S-17,2-13,3-10	1	-1.0
1945 NY-N	28	11	8	0	0	0	0	0	1	1	0	....	.000	.083	.000	.083	-75	-3	0	.00	-1	/3-5,2-2	0	-0.4
Total 7	426	1169	138	283	50	11	4	96	87	164	17	....	.242	.296	.314	.610	65	-57	107	3.05	-3	2-221,S-123/3-17	19	-4.1

• HUDSON, Orlando Orlando Thill "O-Dog" Hudson b: 12/12/1977, Darlington, SC BB/TR, 6', 185 lbs. Deb: 7/24/2002

YEAR TM-L	G	AB	R	H	2B	3B	HR	RBI	BB	SO	SB	CS	AVG	OBP	SLG	OPS	OPS+	BR/A	RC	RC/G	FR	G/POS	WS	TPW
2002 Tor-A	54	192	20	53	10	5	4	23	11	27	0	1	.276	.322	.443	.765	97	-2	25	4.65	10	2-52	7	1.1
2003 Tor-A	142	474	54	127	21	6	9	57	39	87	5	4	.268	.330	.395	.725	89	-9	60	4.40	31	*2-139	17	2.7
Total 2	196	666	74	180	31	11	13	80	50	114	5	5	.270	.328	.408	.736	91	-10	85	4.47	41	2-191	24	3.8

• HUELSMAN, Frank Frank Elmer Huelsman b: 6/5/1874, St. Louis, MO d: 6/9/1959, Affton, MO BR/TR, 6'2", 210 lbs. Deb: 10/3/1897 Career OF: 203-3-19

YEAR TM-L	G	AB	R	H	2B	3B	HR	RBI	BB	SO	SB	CS	AVG	OBP	SLG	OPS	OPS+	BR/A	RC	RC/G	FR	G/POS	WS	TPW
1897 StL-N	2	7	0	2	1	0	0	0	0	....	0	....	.286	.286	.429	.714	89	-0	1	4.66	-1	/0-2(2-0-0)	0	-0.1
1904 Chi-A	3	6	0	1	1	0	0	0	0	....	0	....	.167	.167	.333	.500	58	-0	0	1.81	0	/0-1	0	-0.1
Det-A	4	18	1	6	1	0	0	4	1	....	1	....	.333	.368	.389	.757	144	1	3	6.67	0	/0-4(4-0-0)	1	0.1
Chi-A	1	1	0	0	0	0	0	0	0	....	0	....	.000	.000	.000	.000	-104	-0	0	.00	0	....	0	0.0
StL-A	20	68	6	15	2	1	0	1	6	....	0	....	.221	.303	.279	.582	90	-0	6	2.96	-2	0-18(0-0-18)	1	-0.3
Was-A	84	303	21	75	19	4	2	30	24	....	6	....	.248	.313	.356	.670	113	5	37	4.24	-5	0-84(82-2-0)	9	-0.6
Yr.	112	396	28	97	23	5	2	35	31	....	7	....	.245	.311	.343	.654	109	5	46	4.06	-7	*0-107(86-3-18)	11	-0.9
1905 Was-A	121	421	48	114	28	8	3	62	31	....	11	....	.271	.333	.397	.729	136	17	61	5.20	-7	*0-116(115-0-1)	18	0.3
Total 3	235	824	76	213	52	13	5	97	62	....	18	....	.258	.322	.371	.693	123	21	109	4.64	-15	0-225	29	-0.6

• HUFF, Aubrey Aubrey Lewis Huff b: 12/20/1976, Marion, OH BL/TR, 6'4", 221 lbs. Deb: 8/2/2000

YEAR TM-L	G	AB	R	H	2B	3B	HR	RBI	BB	SO	SB	CS	AVG	OBP	SLG	OPS	OPS+	BR/A	RC	RC/G	FR	G/POS	WS	TPW
2000 TB-A	39	122	12	35	7	0	4	14	5	18	0	0	.287	.320	.443	.763	91	-2	15	4.35	-5	3-37	3	-0.6
2001 TB-A	111	411	42	102	25	1	8	45	23	72	1	3	.248	.288	.372	.660	73	-18	38	3.12	-3	3-73,D-20,1-19	5	-2.2
2002 TB-A	113	454	67	142	25	0	23	59	37	55	4	1	.313	.366	.520	.886	134	22	81	6.59	-5	D-53,1-45,3-14	12	0.8
2003 TB-A	162	636	91	198	47	3	34	107	53	80	2	3	.311	.372	.555	.927	142	36	124	7.15	-8	*0-102(0-0-102),D-33,1-22/3	22	1.8
Total 4	425	1623	212	477	104	4	69	225	118	225	7	7	.294	.346	.490	.836	119	38	259	5.70	-21	3-132,D-106,0-102/1-86	42	-0.2

• HUFF, Mike Michael Kale Huff b: 8/11/1963, Honolulu, HI BR/TR, 6'1", 190 lbs. Deb: 8/7/1989 Career OF: 132-121-121

YEAR TM-L	G	AB	R	H	2B	3B	HR	RBI	BB	SO	SB	CS	AVG	OBP	SLG	OPS	OPS+	BR/A	RC	RC/G	FR	G/POS	WS	TPW
1989 LA-N	12	25	4	5	1	0	1	2	3	6	0	1	.200	.310	.360	.670	93	-1	3	3.46	0	/0-9(7-1-2)	0	-0.1
1991 Cle-A	51	146	28	35	6	1	2	10	25	30	11	2	.240	.366	.336	.701	95	2	22	4.89	0	0-48(8-39-5)/2-2	3	0.1
Chi-A	51	97	14	26	4	1	1	15	12	18	3	2	.268	.360	.361	.721	103	1	12	3.95	-1	0-48(9-14-35)/2-2,D-2	4	-0.2
Yr.	102	243	42	61	10	2	3	25	37	48	14	4	.251	.364	.346	.709	98	3	34	4.51	-1	0-96(17-53-40)/2-4,D-2	7	0.0
1992 Chi-A	60	115	13	24	5	0	0	8	10	24	1	2	.209	.278	.252	.530	50	-8	8	2.22	1	0-56(10-3-45)/D-1	1	-0.8
1993 Chi-A	43	44	4	8	2	0	1	6	9	15	1	0	.182	.333	.295	.629	72	-1	6	3.87	-1	0-43(31-8-7)	1	-0.2
1994 Tor-A	80	207	31	63	15	3	3	25	27	27	2	1	.304	.392	.449	.842	116	6	37	6.57	-3	0-76(57-19-8)	6	0.1
1995 Tor-A	61	138	14	32	9	1	1	9	22	21	1	1	.232	.342	.333	.675	77	-4	17	3.82	-1	0-55(9-33-15)	1	-0.5
1996 Tor-A	11	29	5	5	0	1	0	0	1	5	0	0	.172	.200	.241	.441	11	-4	1	1.63	-1	/0-9(1-4-4),3-3	0	-0.4
Total 7	369	801	113	198	42	7	9	75	109	146	19	9	.247	.347	.351	.698	88	-10	105	4.34	-5	0-344/2-4,3-3,D-3	16	-2.1

• HUFFMAN, Ben Bennie F Huffman b: 7/18/1914, Rileyville, VA BL/TR, 5'11.5", 175 lbs. Deb: 4/23/1937

YEAR TM-L	G	AB	R	H	2B	3B	HR	RBI	BB	SO	SB	CS	AVG	OBP	SLG	OPS	OPS+	BR/A	RC	RC/G	FR	G/POS	WS	TPW
1937 StL-A	76	176	18	48	9	0	1	24	10	7	1	0	.273	.323	.341	.664	67	-9	20	4.10	0	C-42	2	-0.6

• HUG, Ed Edward Ambrose Hug b: 7/14/1880, Fayetteville, OH d: 5/11/1953, Cincinnati, OH BR/TR Deb: 7/6/1903

YEAR TM-L	G	AB	R	H	2B	3B	HR	RBI	BB	SO	SB	CS	AVG	OBP	SLG	OPS	OPS+	BR/A	RC	RC/G	FR	G/POS	WS	TPW
1903 Bro-N	1	0	0	0	0	0	0	0	1	....	0	....	....	1.000	....	1.000	199	0	0	....	0	/C-1	0	0.0

• HUGGINS, Miller Miller James "Hug,Mighty Mite" Huggins
b: 3/27/1879, Cincinnati, OH d: 9/25/1929, New York, NY BB/TR, 5'6.5", 140 lbs. Deb: 4/15/1904 M HOF: 1964

YEAR TM-L	G	AB	R	H	2B	3B	HR	RBI	BB	SO	SB	CS	AVG	OBP	SLG	OPS	OPS+	BR/A	RC	RC/G	FR	G/POS	WS	TPW
1904 Cin-N	140	491	96	129	12	7	2	30	88	....	13	....	.263	.377	.328	.705	108	10	70	4.80	9	*2-140	20	2.2
1905 Cin-N	149	564	117	154	11	8	1	38	**103**	....	27	....	.273	.392	.326	.718	103	9	86	5.35	21	*2-149	27	3.3
1906 Cin-N	146	545	81	159	11	7	0	26	71	....	41	....	.292	.376	.338	.714	118	14	90	5.73	22	*2-146	22	4.2
1907 Cin-N	156	561	64	139	12	4	1	31	**83**	....	28	....	.248	.346	.289	.635	95	1	71	4.13	12	*2-156	19	1.6
1908 Cin-N	135	498	65	119	14	5	0	23	58	....	30	....	.239	.321	.287	.608	97	0	57	3.65	12	*2-135	17	1.6
1909 Cin-N	57	159	18	34	3	1	0	6	28	....	11	....	.214	.335	.245	.580	81	-2	17	3.42	7	2-31,3-15	5	0.6
1910 StL-N	151	547	101	145	15	6	1	36	**116**	46	34	....	.265	.399	.320	.719	114	19	85	5.25	-7	*2-151	23	1.4
1911 StL-N	138	509	106	133	19	2	1	24	96	52	37	....	.261	.385	.312	.697	99	5	76	5.07	11	*2-136	18	1.9
1912 StL-N	120	431	82	131	15	4	0	29	87	31	35	....	.304	.422	.357	.779	117	17	80	6.57	-13	*2-114	17	0.6
1913 StL-N	121	382	74	109	12	0	0	27	92	49	23	....	.285	**.432**	.317	.749	117	18	62	5.48	-4	*2-113	18	1.7
1914 StL-N	148	509	85	134	17	4	1	24	**105**	63	32	....	.263	.396	.318	.714	115	17	75	4.99	4	*2-147	22	2.6
1915 StL-N	107	353	57	85	5	2	2	24	74	68	13	12	.241	.377	.283	.660	101	3	40	3.71	6	*2-105	13	1.2
1916 StL-N	18	9	2	3	0	0	0	0	2	3	0	....	.333	.500	.333	.833	159	1	2	6.41	0	/2-7	1	0.1
Total 13	1586	5558	948	1474	146	50	9	318	1003	312	324	12	.265	.382	.314	.696	107	114	812	4.91	80	*2-1530/3-15	222	23.0

• HUGHES, Bill William R. Hughes b: 11/25/1866, Bladinsville, IL d: 8/25/1943, Santa Ana, CA BL/TL Deb: 9/28/1884 Career OF: 0-1-7

YEAR TM-L	G	AB	R	H	2B	3B	HR	RBI	BB	SO	SB	CS	AVG	OBP	SLG	OPS	OPS+	BR/A	RC	RC/G	FR	G/POS	WS	TPW
1884 Was-U	14	49	5	6	0	0	0	....	2	....	....	....	.122	.157	.122	.279	-5	-5	1	.63	-1	/1-9,0-6(0-1-5)	0	-0.6
1885 Phi-a	4	16	3	3	1	1	0	1	1	....	....	....	.188	.278	.375	.653	99	0	2	3.55	0	/0-2(0-0-2),P-2	0	-0.2
Total 2	18	65	8	9	1	1	0	1	3	....	....	....	.138	.188	.185	.373	22	-5	3	1.31	-1	/1-9,0-8,P-2	0	-0.8

• HUGHES, Bobby Robert E. Hughes b: 3/10/1971, Burbank, CA BR/TR, 6'4", 229 lbs. Deb: 4/2/1998

YEAR TM-L	G	AB	R	H	2B	3B	HR	RBI	BB	SO	SB	CS	AVG	OBP	SLG	OPS	OPS+	BR/A	RC	RC/G	FR	G/POS	WS	TPW
1998 Mil-N	85	218	28	50	7	2	9	29	16	54	1	2	.229	.285	.404	.689	78	-8	25	3.78	0	C-72/0-3(0-0-3)	3	-0.4
1999 Mil-N	48	101	10	26	2	0	3	8	5	28	0	0	.257	.292	.366	.659	66	-6	10	3.50	0	C-44/D-1	0	-0.3
Total 2	133	319	38	76	9	2	12	37	21	82	1	2	.238	.287	.392	.679	75	-14	35	3.70	0	C-116/0-3,D-1	3	-0.7

• HUGHES, Ed Edward J. Hughes b: 10/5/1880, Chicago, IL d: 10/14/1927, McHenry, IL BR/TR, 6'1", 180 lbs. Deb: 8/29/1902

YEAR TM-L	G	AB	R	H	2B	3B	HR	RBI	BB	SO	SB	CS	AVG	OBP	SLG	OPS	OPS+	BR/A	RC	RC/G	FR	G/POS	WS	TPW
1902 Chi-A	1	4	0	1	0	0	0	0	0	....	0	....	.250	.250	.250	.500	41	-0	0	2.26	0	/C-1	0	0.0
1905 Bos-A	6	14	2	3	0	0	0	2	0	....	0	....	.214	.214	.214	.429	36	-0	1	1.59	-2	/P-6	0	-0.8
1906 Bos-A	2	3	0	0	0	0	0	0	0	....	0	....	.000	.000	.000	.000	-100	-0	0	.00	0	/P-2	0	-0.4
Total 3	9	21	2	4	0	0	0	2	0	....	0	....	.190	.190	.190	.381	17	-1	1	1.43	-2	/P-8,C-1	0	-1.1

• HUGHES, Joe Joseph Thompson Hughes b: 2/21/1880, Pardo, PA d: 3/13/1951, Cleveland, OH BR/TR, 5'10", 165 lbs. Deb: 8/30/1902

YEAR TM-L	G	AB	R	H	2B	3B	HR	RBI	BB	SO	SB	CS	AVG	OBP	SLG	OPS	OPS+	BR/A	RC	RC/G	FR	G/POS	WS	TPW
1902 Chi-N	1	3	0	0	0	0	0	0	0	....	0	....	.000	.000	.000	.000	-103	-1	0	.00	0	/0-1	0	-0.1

• HUGHES, Keith Keith Wills Hughes b: 9/12/1963, Bryn Mawr, PA BL/TL, 6'3", 210 lbs. Deb: 5/19/1987 Career OF: 19-1-37

YEAR TM-L	G	AB	R	H	2B	3B	HR	RBI	BB	SO	SB	CS	AVG	OBP	SLG	OPS	OPS+	BR/A	RC	RC/G	FR	G/POS	WS	TPW
1987 NY-A	4	4	0	0	0	0	0	0	0	2	0	0	.000	.000	.000	.000	-101	-1	0	.00	0	....	0	-0.1
Phi-N	37	76	8	20	2	0	0	10	7	11	0	0	.263	.333	.289	.623	65	-4	8	3.67	-1	0-19(13-0-6)	1	-0.5

YEAR TM-L	G	AB	R	H	2B	3B	HR	RBI	BB	SO	SB	CS	AVG	OBP	SLG	OPS	OPS+	BR/A	RC	RC/G	FR	G/POS	WS	TPW
1988 Bal-A	41	108	10	21	4	2	2	14	16	27	1	0	.194	.298	.324	.622	76	-3	11	3.20	2	0-31(0-0-31)/D-1	1	-0.2
1990 NY-N	8	9	0	0	0	0	0	0	0	4	0	0	.000	.000	.000	.000	-100	-2	0	.00	0	/0-5(4-1-0)	0	-0.3
1993 Cin-N	3	4	0	0	0	0	0	0	0	0	0	0	.000	.000	.000	.000	-100	-1	0	.00	0	/0-2(2-0-0)	0	-0.1
Total 4	93	201	18	41	6	2	2	24	23	44	1	0	.204	.289	.284	.572	59	-11	19	3.03	1	/0-57,D-1	2	-1.2
• HUGHES, Roy	Roy John "Jeep,Sage" Hughes b: 1/11/1911, Cincinnati, OH d: 3/5/1995, Asheville, NC BR/TR, 5'10.5", 167 lbs. Deb: 4/16/1935																							
1935 Cle-A	82	266	40	78	15	3	0	14	18	17	13	3	.293	.340	.372	.713	83	-5	35	4.71	0	2-40,S-29/3-1	8	-0.1
1936 Cle-A	152	638	112	188	35	9	0	63	57	40	20	9	.295	.356	.378	.734	81	-19	88	5.01	-2	*2-152	13	-1.0
1937 Cle-A	104	346	57	96	12	6	1	40	40	22	11	6	.277	.352	.355	.708	78	-11	45	4.54	1	3-58,2-32	9	-0.5
1938 StL-A	58	96	16	27	3	0	2	13	12	11	3	0	.281	.361	.375	.736	85	-1	14	5.36	0	2-21/3-5,S-2	2	0.0
1939 StL-A	17	23	6	2	0	0	0	1	4	4	0	0	.087	.222	.087	.309	-18	-4	1	.75	0	/2-6,S-1	0	-0.3
Phi-N	65	237	22	54	5	1	1	16	21	18	4	....	.228	.291	.270	.561	54	-15	18	2.47	-2	2-65	1	-1.3
1940 Phi-N	1	0	0	0	0	0	0	0	0	0	0	....	....	....	....	....	-104	0	0	....	0	/2-1	0	0.0
1944 Chi-N	126	478	86	137	16	6	1	28	35	30	16	....	.287	.337	.351	.688	94	-4	58	4.31	4	3-66,S-52	15	0.5
1945*Chi-N	69	222	34	58	8	1	0	8	16	18	6	....	.261	.311	.306	.617	73	-8	22	3.33	0	S-36,2-21/3-9,1-2	5	-0.5
1946 Phi-N	89	276	23	65	11	1	0	22	19	15	7	....	.236	.287	.283	.570	64	-14	23	2.74	-4	S-34,3-31/2-7,1-1	3	-1.6
Total 9	763	2582	396	705	105	27	5	205	222	175	80	18	.273	.332	.340	.673	77	-81	305	4.09	-4	2-345,3-170,S-154/1-3	56	-4.8
• HUGHES, Terry	Terry Wayne Hughes b: 5/13/1949, Spartansburg, SC BR/TR, 6'1", 185 lbs. Deb: 9/2/1970																							
1970 Chi-N	2	3	0	1	0	0	0	0	0	0	0	0	.333	.333	.333	.667	71	-0	0	4.50	0	/3-1,0-1	0	-0.1
1973 StL-N	11	14	1	3	1	0	0	1	1	4	0	0	.214	.267	.286	.552	53	-1	1	1.92	0	/3-5,1-1	0	-0.1
1974 Bos-A	41	69	5	14	2	0	1	6	6	18	0	0	.203	.286	.275	.561	58	-4	6	2.92	-2	3-36/D-1	1	-0.6
Total 3	54	86	6	18	3	0	1	7	7	22	0	0	.209	.284	.279	.563	58	-5	7	2.79	-3	/3-42,1-1,D-1,0-1	1	-0.8
• HUGHES, Tom	Thomas Franklin Hughes b: 8/6/1907, Emmet, AR d: 8/10/1989, Beaumont, TX BL/TR, 6'1", 190 lbs. Deb: 9/9/1930																							
1930 Det-A	17	59	8	22	2	3	0	5	4	8	0	1	.373	.413	.508	.921	130	2	12	8.25	-2	0-16(4-12-0)	2	0.0
• HUHN, Emil	Emil Hugo "Hap" Huhn b: 3/10/1892, North Vernon, IN d: 9/5/1925, Camden, SC BR/TR, 6', 180 lbs. Deb: 4/10/1915																							
1915 New-F	124	415	34	94	18	1	1	41	28	40	13	....	.227	.279	.282	.561	69	-17	35	2.74	-3	*1-101,C-16	5	-2.2
1916 Cin-N	37	94	4	24	3	2	0	3	2	11	0	....	.255	.271	.330	.601	86	-2	8	3.12	1	C-18,1-14/0-1	1	0.0
1917 Cin-N	23	51	2	10	1	2	0	3	2	5	1	....	.196	.226	.294	.521	62	-3	3	2.10	-1	C-15/1-1	0	-0.3
Total 3	184	560	40	128	22	5	1	47	32	56	14	....	.229	.273	.291	.564	71	-21	47	2.74	-3	1-116/C-49,0-1	6	-2.5
• HULEN, Billy	William Franklin Hulen b: 3/12/1870, Dixon, CA d: 10/2/1947, Santa Rosa, CA BL/TL, 5'8", 148 lbs. Deb: 5/2/1896																							
1896 Phi-N	88	339	87	90	18	7	0	38	55	20	23	....	.265	.368	.360	.728	93	-1	56	5.74	-24	S-73,0-12(0-12-0)/2-2	9	-1.9
1899 Was-N	19	68	10	10	1	0	0	3	10	....	5	....	.147	.256	.162	.418	16	-8	4	1.95	2	S-19	1	-0.4
Total 2	107	407	97	100	19	7	0	41	65	20	28	....	.246	.350	.327	.676	81	-9	60	5.04	-22	/S-92,0-12,2-2	10	-2.4
• HULETT, Tim	Timothy Craig Hulett b: 1/12/1960, Springfield, IL BR/TR, 6', 195 lbs. Deb: 9/15/1983																							
1983 Chi-A	6	5	0	1	0	0	0	0	0	0	1	0	.200	.200	.200	.400	10	-0	0	2.05	-2	/2-6	0	-0.2
1984 Chi-A	8	7	1	0	0	0	0	0	1	4	1	0	.000	.125	.000	.125	-59	-1	0	.38	1	/3-4,2-3	0	0.0
1985 Chi-A	141	395	52	106	19	4	5	37	30	81	6	4	.268	.326	.375	.701	88	-7	48	4.20	3	*3-115,2-28/0-1	11	-0.4
1986 Chi-A	150	520	53	120	16	5	17	44	21	91	4	1	.231	.262	.379	.641	70	-23	49	3.16	-2	3-89,2-66	8	-2.2
1987 Chi-A	68	240	20	52	10	0	7	28	10	41	0	2	.217	.248	.346	.594	54	-18	19	2.49	2	3-61/2-8	2	-1.6
1989 Bal-A	33	97	12	27	5	0	3	18	10	17	0	0	.278	.346	.423	.768	119	2	14	5.01	-2	2-23,3-11	5	0.2
1990 Bal-A	53	153	16	39	7	1	3	16	15	41	1	0	.255	.321	.373	.694	97	-1	19	4.40	6	3-24,2-16/D-8	6	0.6
1991 Bal-A	79	206	29	42	9	0	7	18	13	49	0	1	.204	.255	.350	.604	68	-10	18	2.86	-7	3-39,2-26,D-15/S-1	1	-1.7
1992 Bal-A	57	142	11	41	7	2	2	21	10	31	0	1	.289	.340	.408	.748	106	1	17	4.32	6	3-27,D-13,2-10/S-5	6	0.7
1993 Bal-A	85	260	40	78	15	0	2	23	23	56	1	2	.300	.364	.381	.744	96	-1	36	5.08	10	3-75/S-8,2-4,D-2	8	1.0
1994 Bal-A	36	92	11	21	2	1	2	15	12	24	0	0	.228	.317	.337	.654	66	-5	10	3.70	6	2-23/3-9,S-6	3	0.3
1995 StL-N	4	11	0	2	0	0	0	0	0	3	0	0	.182	.182	.182	.364	-4	-2	0	1.09	2	/2-2,S-1	0	0.0
Total 12	720	2128	245	529	90	13	48	220	145	438	14	11	.249	.300	.371	.670	80	-65	232	3.70	24	3-454,2-215/D-38,S-21,0-1	50	-3.4
• HULSE, David	David Lindsey Hulse b: 2/25/1968, San Angelo, TX BL/TL, 5'11", 170 lbs. Deb: 8/11/1992 Career OF: 91-306-30																							
1992 Tex-A	32	92	14	28	4	0	0	2	3	18	3	1	.304	.326	.348	.674	92	-1	11	4.41	-1	0-31(0-29-2)/D-1	1	-0.2
1993 Tex-A	114	407	71	118	9	10	1	29	26	57	29	9	.290	.334	.369	.703	92	-2	51	4.35	-2	*0-112(0-112-0)/D-2	11	-0.3
1994 Tex-A	77	310	58	79	8	4	1	19	21	53	18	2	.255	.306	.316	.622	61	-15	34	3.81	-4	0-76(0-76-0)/D-1	4	-1.7
1995 Mil-A	119	339	46	85	11	6	3	47	18	60	15	3	.251	.289	.345	.634	61	-19	35	3.57	0	*0-115(67-52-17)	5	-2.0
1996 Mil-A	81	117	18	26	3	0	0	6	8	16	4	1	.222	.272	.248	.520	32	-12	8	2.35	0	0-68(24-37-11)/D-4	1	-1.2
Total 5	423	1265	207	336	35	20	5	103	76	204	69	16	.266	.309	.337	.646	70	-49	139	3.81	-7	0-402/D-8	22	-5.4
• HULSWITT, Rudy	Rudolph Edward Hulswitt b: 2/23/1877, Newport, KY d: 1/16/1950, Louisville, KY BR/TR, 5'8.5", 165 lbs. Deb: 6/16/1899 C																							
1899 Lou-N	1	0	0	0	0	0	0	0	0	....	0	....	....	....	....	....	-100	0	0	.00	-2	/S-1	0	-0.2
1902 Phi-N	128	497	59	135	11	7	0	38	30	....	12	....	.272	.316	.322	.638	97	-2	57	4.06	-2	*S-125/3-3	15	0.0
1903 Phi-N	138	519	56	128	22	9	1	58	28	....	10	....	.247	.288	.329	.617	78	-16	55	3.60	7	*S-138	10	-0.5
1904 Phi-N	113	406	36	99	11	4	1	36	16	....	8	....	.244	.276	.298	.574	80	-10	38	3.09	-17	*S-113	6	-2.5
1908 Cin-N	119	386	27	88	5	7	1	28	30	....	7	....	.228	.287	.285	.572	85	-7	34	2.82	0	*S-118/2-1	11	-0.2
1909 StL-N	82	289	21	81	8	3	0	29	19	....	7	....	.280	.329	.329	.658	111	3	33	4.04	-9	S-65,2-12	8	-0.3
1910 StL-N	63	133	9	33	7	2	0	14	13	10	5	....	.248	.320	.331	.651	93	-1	15	3.93	-10	S-30/2-2	3	-1.1
Total 7	644	2230	208	564	64	32	3	203	136	10	49	....	.253	.299	.314	.613	89	-34	231	3.54	-32	S-590/2-15,3-3	53	-4.8
• HUMMEL, John	John Edwin "Silent John" Hummel b: 4/4/1883, Bloomsburg, PA d: 5/18/1959, Springfield, MA BR/TR, 5'11", 160 lbs. Deb: 9/12/1905 Career OF: 145-26-125																							
1905 Bro-N	30	109	19	29	3	4	0	7	9	....	6	....	.266	.322	.367	.689	114	2	16	4.86	0	2-30	4	0.2
1906 Bro-N	97	286	20	57	6	4	1	21	36	....	10	....	.199	.289	.259	.548	77	-7	25	2.84	5	2-50,0-21(15-1-4),1-15	7	-0.3
1907 Bro-N	107	342	41	80	12	3	3	31	26	....	8	....	.234	.294	.313	.607	98	-2	36	3.42	9	2-44,0-33(22-3-9),1-12/S-8	10	0.7
1908 Bro-N	154	594	51	143	11	12	4	41	34	....	20	....	.241	.284	.320	.604	97	-4	58	3.28	12	0-95(92-4-2),2-43/S-9,1-8	14	0.3
1909 Bro-N	146	542	54	152	15	9	4	52	22	....	16	....	.280	.311	.363	.674	113	5	67	4.13	-9	1-54,2-38,S-36,0-17(0-6-11)	14	-0.5
1910 Bro-N	153	578	67	141	21	13	5	74	57	81	21	....	.244	.314	.351	.665	97	-4	69	4.01	-7	*2-153	16	-1.0
1911 Bro-N	137	477	54	129	21	11	5	58	67	66	16	....	.270	.360	.392	.752	115	11	73	5.26	-2	*2-127/1-4,S-2	18	1.1
1912 Bro-N	122	411	55	116	21	7	5	54	49	55	7	....	.282	.359	.404	.763	113	7	62	5.15	-6	2-58,0-44(0-0-44),1-11	12	0.0
1913 Bro-N	67	198	20	48	7	7	2	24	13	23	4	....	.242	.292	.379	.671	88	-4	22	3.65	3	0-28(3-0-25),S-17/1-6,2-3	4	-0.1
1914 Bro-N	73	208	25	55	8	9	0	20	16	25	5	....	.264	.317	.389	.706	107	1	26	4.29	-3	1-36,0-19(5-4-11)/2-1,S-1	5	-0.4
1915 Bro-N	53	100	6	23	2	3	0	8	6	11	1	1	.230	.274	.310	.584	75	-3	9	2.91	-2	0-21(2-1-18),1-11/S-1	2	-0.7
1918 NY-A	22	61	9	18	1	2	0	4	11	8	3	....	.295	.411	.377	.788	135	3	10	5.95	-3	0-15(6-7-1)/1-3,2-1	3	-0.1
Total 12	1161	3906	421	991	128	84	29	394	346	269	117	1	.254	.316	.352	.668	102	5	474	4.05	-4	2-548,0-293,1-160/S-74	109	-0.8
• HUMMEL, Tim	Timothy Robert Hummel b: 11/18/1978, Goshen, NY BR/TR, 6'2", 195 lbs. Deb: 8/26/2003																							
2003 Cin-N	26	84	9	19	5	0	2	10	8	13	0	0	.226	.293	.357	.651	70	-4	9	3.64	-3	3-20/S-2,2-1	1	-0.6
• HUMPHREY, Al	Albert Humphrey b: 2/28/1886, Ashtabula, OH d: 5/13/1961, Ashtabula, OH BL/TR, 5'11", 180 lbs. Deb: 9/1/1911																							
1911 Bro-N	8	27	4	5	0	0	0	0	3	7	0	....	.185	.267	.185	.452	29	-2	2	1.67	-1	/0-8(0-7-1)	0	-0.4
• HUMPHREY, Terry	Terryal Gene Humphrey b: 8/4/1949, Chickasha, OK BR/TR, 6'3", 190 lbs. Deb: 9/5/1971																							
1971 Mon-N	9	26	1	5	1	0	0	1	0	4	0	0	.192	.192	.231	.423	19	-3	1	1.13	0	/C-9	0	-0.3
1972 Mon-N	69	215	13	40	8	0	1	9	16	38	4	1	.186	.249	.237	.486	38	-17	12	1.75	2	C-65	3	-1.3
1973 Mon-N	43	90	5	15	2	0	1	9	5	16	0	1	.167	.211	.222	.433	19	-10	4	1.32	0	C-35	1	-0.9
1974 Mon-N	20	52	3	10	3	0	0	3	4	9	0	0	.192	.250	.250	.500	38	-4	4	2.23	2	C-17	1	-0.1
1975 Det-A	18	41	0	10	0	0	0	1	2	6	0	0	.244	.279	.244	.523	47	-3	3	2.26	1	C-18	1	-0.2
1976 Cal-A	71	196	17	48	10	0	1	19	13	30	0	1	.245	.308	.311	.620	87	-4	18	3.02	-1	C-71	5	-0.1
1977 Cal-A	123	304	17	69	11	0	2	34	21	58	1	1	.227	.286	.283	.569	58	-17	24	2.58	3	*C-123	5	-0.9

YEAR	TM-L	G	AB	R	H	2B	3B	HR	RBI	BB	SO	SB	CS	AVG	OBP	SLG	OPS	OPS+	BR/A	RC	RC/G	FR	G/POS	WS	TPW
1978	Cal-A	53	114	11	25	4	1	1	9	6	12	0	1	.219	.270	.298	.569	62	-6	9	2.54	-1	C-52/2-1,3-1	3	-0.5
1979	Cal-A	9	17	2	1	0	0	0	0	1	2	0	0	.059	.111	.059	.170	-54	-4	0	.30	0	/C-9	0	-0.3
Total	9	415	1055	69	223	39	1	6	85	68	175	5	5	.211	.268	.267	.535	52	-68	75	2.26	7	C-399/2-1,3-1	19	-4.6

• HUMPHREYS, Mike Michael Butler Humphreys b: 4/10/1967, Dallas, TX BR/TR, 6', 185 lbs. Deb: 7/29/1991 Career OF: 21-5-9

YEAR	TM-L	G	AB	R	H	2B	3B	HR	RBI	BB	SO	SB	CS	AVG	OBP	SLG	OPS	OPS+	BR/A	RC	RC/G	FR	G/POS	WS	TPW
1991	NY-A	25	40	9	8	0	0	0	3	9	7	2	0	.200	.347	.200	.547	55	-1	4	3.31	0	/O-9(8-0-2),D-7,3-6	1	-0.2
1992	NY-A	4	10	0	1	0	0	0	0	0	1	0	0	.100	.100	.100	.200	-44	-2	0	.00	1	/O-2(2-0-0),D-1	0	-0.1
1993	NY-A	25	35	6	6	2	1	1	6	4	11	2	1	.171	.256	.371	.628	69	-2	4	3.06	-1	O-21(11-5-7)/D-3	1	-0.3
Total	3	54	85	15	15	2	1	1	9	13	19	4	1	.176	.286	.259	.545	51	-5	8	2.72	0	/O-32,D-11,3-6	2	-0.5

• HUMPHRIES, John John Henry Humphries b: 11/12/1861, North Gower, Canada d: 11/29/1933, Salinas, CA BL/TL, 6', 185 lbs. Deb: 7/7/1883 Career OF: 1-4-19

YEAR	TM-L	G	AB	R	H	2B	3B	HR	RBI	BB	SO	SB	CS	AVG	OBP	SLG	OPS	OPS+	BR/A	RC	RC/G	FR	G/POS	WS	TPW
1883	NY-N	29	107	5	12	1	0	0	4	1	22	....	....	.112	.120	.121	.242	-27	-16	2	.46	-3	C-20,O-12(0-1-11)	1	-1.5
1884	Was-a	49	193	23	34	2	0	0	0	9	....	....	....	.176	.217	.187	.403	37	-11	8	1.38	-5	C-35,O-12(1-3-8)/1-4	0	-1.3
	NY-N	20	64	6	6	0	0	0	2	9	19	....	....	.094	.205	.094	.299	-3	-7	1	.60	1	C-20	2	-0.4
Total	2	98	364	34	52	3	0	0	6	19	41	....	....	.143	.188	.151	.339	12	-34	11	.96	-7	/C-75,O-24,1-4	3	-3.2

• HUNDLEY, Randy Cecil Randolph "Rebel" Hundley b: 6/1/1942, Martinsville, VA BR/TR, 5'11", 175 lbs. Deb: 9/27/1964 C

YEAR	TM-L	G	AB	R	H	2B	3B	HR	RBI	BB	SO	SB	CS	AVG	OBP	SLG	OPS	OPS+	BR/A	RC	RC/G	FR	G/POS	WS	TPW
1964	SF-N	2	1	1	0	0	0	0	0	0	1	0	0	.000	.000	.000	.000	-98	-0	0	.00	-1	/C-2	0	-0.1
1965	SF-N	6	15	0	1	0	0	0	0	0	4	0	0	.067	.067	.067	.133	-61	-3	0	.00	2	/C-6	1	-0.1
1966	Chi-N	149	526	50	124	22	3	19	63	35	113	1	3	.236	.287	.397	.685	87	-11	58	3.63	1	*C-149	11	-0.3
1967	Chi-N	152	539	68	144	25	3	14	60	44	75	2	4	.267	.325	.403	.727	102	1	68	4.37	-11	*C-152	22	-0.3
1968	Chi-N	160	553	41	125	18	4	7	65	39	69	1	0	.226	.282	.311	.593	73	-17	46	2.72	-7	*C-160	13	-1.9
1969	Chi-N★	151	522	67	133	15	1	18	64	61	90	2	3	.255	.336	.391	.727	91	-6	69	4.53	4	*C-151	21	0.6
1970	Chi-N	73	250	13	61	5	0	7	36	16	52	0	1	.244	.289	.348	.637	62	-14	25	3.32	-3	C-73	4	-1.3
1971	Chi-N	9	21	1	7	1	0	0	2	0	2	0	0	.333	.333	.381	.714	89	-0	3	5.14	0	/C-8	1	0.0
1972	Chi-N	114	357	23	78	12	0	5	30	22	62	1	0	.218	.264	.294	.558	53	-22	25	2.22	4	*C-113	6	-1.5
1973	Chi-N	124	368	35	83	11	1	10	43	30	51	5	6	.226	.284	.342	.626	68	-18	33	2.93	4	*C-122	9	-0.9
1974	Min-A	32	88	2	17	2	0	0	3	4	12	0	0	.193	.228	.216	.444	27	-8	4	1.34	-1	C-28	1	-0.8
1975	SD-N	74	180	7	37	5	1	2	14	19	29	0	0	.206	.285	.278	.563	60	-10	14	2.60	-2	C-51	2	-1.0
1976	Chi-N	13	18	3	3	2	0	0	1	1	4	0	0	.167	.211	.278	.488	35	-2	1	1.95	-1	/C-9	0	-0.2
1977	Chi-N	2	4	0	0	0	0	0	0	0	1	0	0	.000	.000	.000	.000	-90	-1	0	.00	0	/C-2	0	-0.1
Total	14	1061	3442	311	813	118	13	82	381	271	565	12	17	.236	.294	.350	.644	76	-112	346	3.33	-13	*C-1026	91	-8.0

• HUNDLEY, Todd Todd Randolph Hundley b: 5/27/1969, Martinsville, VA BB/TR, 5'11", 185 lbs. Deb: 5/18/1990

YEAR	TM-L	G	AB	R	H	2B	3B	HR	RBI	BB	SO	SB	CS	AVG	OBP	SLG	OPS	OPS+	BR/A	RC	RC/G	FR	G/POS	WS	TPW
1990	NY-N	36	67	8	14	6	0	0	2	6	18	0	0	.209	.274	.299	.572	58	-4	6	2.78	0	C-36	1	-0.3
1991	NY-N	21	60	5	8	0	1	1	7	6	14	0	0	.133	.224	.217	.441	25	-6	3	1.31	1	C-20	1	-0.4
1992	NY-N	123	358	32	75	17	0	7	32	19	76	3	0	.209	.257	.316	.573	62	-18	29	2.58	-1	*C-121	6	-1.3
1993	NY-N	130	417	40	95	17	2	11	53	23	62	1	1	.228	.271	.357	.629	68	-21	38	3.05	4	*C-123	7	-0.9
1994	NY-N	91	291	45	69	10	1	16	42	25	73	2	1	.237	.304	.443	.747	93	-4	40	4.68	-6	C-82	8	-0.4
1995	NY-N	90	275	39	77	11	0	15	51	42	64	1	0	.280	.385	.484	.869	132	14	54	7.07	-4	C-89	13	1.5
1996	NY-N★	153	540	85	140	32	1	41	112	79	146	1	3	.259	.357	.550	.907	141	30	106	6.94	-5	*C-150	24	3.5
1997	NY-N★	132	417	78	114	21	2	30	86	83	116	2	3	.273	.398	.549	.947	150	32	92	7.77	-5	*C-122/D-1	22	3.4
1998	NY-N	53	124	8	20	4	0	3	12	16	55	1	1	.161	.262	.266	.529	40	-11	10	2.48	0	O-34(34-0-0)/C-2	1	-1.2
1999	LA-N	114	376	49	78	14	0	24	55	44	113	3	0	.207	.297	.436	.733	87	-9	51	4.46	-3	*C-108	6	-0.4
2000	LA-N	90	299	49	85	16	0	24	70	45	69	0	0	.284	.382	.579	.960	147	21	67	7.95	-7	C-84/D-1	17	1.8
2001	Chi-N	79	246	23	46	10	0	12	31	25	89	0	0	.187	.270	.374	.644	67	-13	24	3.15	-1	C-70	4	-0.9
2002	Chi-N	92	266	32	56	8	0	16	35	32	80	0	0	.211	.302	.421	.723	90	-5	34	4.22	10	C-79/D-1	6	1.1
2003	LA-N	21	33	2	6	1	0	2	11	8	13	0	1	.182	.341	.394	.735	97	-0	5	4.61	-2	C-10	2	-0.2
Total	14	1225	3769	495	883	167	7	202	599	453	988	14	11	.234	.322	.443	.765	103	5	558	5.00	-18	*C-1096/O-34,D-3	118	5.2

• HUNGLING, Bernie Bernard Herman "Bud" Hungling b: 3/5/1896, Dayton, OH d: 3/30/1968, Dayton, OH BR/TR, 6'2", 180 lbs. Deb: 4/14/1922

YEAR	TM-L	G	AB	R	H	2B	3B	HR	RBI	BB	SO	SB	CS	AVG	OBP	SLG	OPS	OPS+	BR/A	RC	RC/G	FR	G/POS	WS	TPW
1922	Bro-N	39	102	9	23	1	2	1	13	6	20	2	0	.225	.269	.304	.572	48	-7	9	2.85	-1	C-36	2	-0.6
1923	Bro-N	2	4	0	0	0	0	0	0	0	2	0	1	.000	.000	.000	.000	-103	-2	0	.00	0	/C-1	0	-0.2
1930	StL-A	10	31	4	10	2	0	0	2	5	3	0	1	.323	.417	.387	.804	102	-0	5	5.98	0	C-10	1	0.0
Total	3	51	137	13	33	3	2	1	15	11	25	2	2	.241	.297	.314	.611	57	-9	14	3.35	-1	/C-47	3	-0.8

• HUNNEFIELD, Bill William Fenton "Wild Bill" Hunnefield b: 1/5/1899, Dedham, MA d: 8/28/1976, Nantucket, MA BB/TR, 5'10", 165 lbs. Deb: 4/17/1926

YEAR	TM-L	G	AB	R	H	2B	3B	HR	RBI	BB	SO	SB	CS	AVG	OBP	SLG	OPS	OPS+	BR/A	RC	RC/G	FR	G/POS	WS	TPW
1926	Chi-A	131	470	81	129	26	4	3	48	37	28	24	9	.274	.329	.366	.695	84	-10	59	4.11	0	S-98,3-17,2-15	12	0.2
1927	Chi-A	112	365	45	104	25	1	2	36	25	24	15	13	.285	.332	.375	.708	85	-11	44	4.03	-8	S-79,2-17/3-1	7	-1.0
1928	Chi-A	94	333	42	98	8	3	2	24	26	24	16	6	.294	.351	.354	.705	87	-4	43	4.63	-2	2-82/S-3,3-1	9	-0.4
1929	Chi-A	47	127	13	23	5	0	0	9	7	3	5	2	.181	.224	.220	.444	15	-16	7	1.62	2	2-29/3-4,S-2	1	-1.2
1930	Chi-A	31	81	11	22	2	0	1	5	4	10	1	1	.272	.314	.333	.647	66	-4	9	3.44	-3	S-22/1-1	1	-0.5
1931	Cle-A	21	71	13	17	4	1	0	4	9	4	3	1	.239	.325	.324	.649	67	-3	8	3.80	-5	S-21/2-1	1	-0.6
	Bos-N	11	21	2	6	0	0	0	1	0	2	0	....	.286	.286	.286	.571	56	-1	2	2.73	-1	/3-5,2-4	0	-0.2
	NY-N	64	196	23	53	5	0	1	17	9	16	3	....	.270	.302	.311	.614	67	-9	19	3.38	-1	2-56/S-5	3	-0.7
	Yr.	75	217	25	59	5	0	1	18	9	18	3	....	.272	.301	.309	.610	66	-11	20	3.31	-1	2-60/3-5,S-5	3	-0.8
Total	6	511	1664	230	452	75	9	9	144	117	111	67	32	.272	.322	.344	.666	76	-58	190	3.84	-17	S-230,2-204/3-28,1-1	34	-4.4

• HUNT, Dick Richard M. Hunt b: 1847, NY d: 11/20/1895, Brooklyn, NY, 5'9", 145 lbs. Deb: 5/7/1872

YEAR	TM-L	G	AB	R	H	2B	3B	HR	RBI	BB	SO	SB	CS	AVG	OBP	SLG	OPS	OPS+	BR/A	RC	RC/G	FR	G/POS	WS	TPW
1872	Eck-n	11	48	11	15	1	1	0	5	1	0	0	1	.313	.327	.375	.702	136	2	6	5.49	-4	/O-8(0-0-8),2-3	....	-0.1

• HUNT, Joel Oliver Joel "Jodie" Hunt b: 10/11/1905, Texico, NM d: 7/24/1978, Teague, TX BR/TR, 5'10", 165 lbs. Deb: 4/27/1931 Career OF: 0-0-6

YEAR	TM-L	G	AB	R	H	2B	3B	HR	RBI	BB	SO	SB	CS	AVG	OBP	SLG	OPS	OPS+	BR/A	RC	RC/G	FR	G/POS	WS	TPW
1931	StL-N	4	1	2	0	0	0	0	0	0	1	0	....	.000	.000	.000	.000	-96	-0	0	.00	0	/O-1	0	0.0
1932	StL-N	12	21	0	4	1	0	0	3	4	3	0	....	.190	.320	.238	.558	51	-1	2	2.87	0	/O-5(0-0-5)	0	-0.2
Total	2	16	22	2	4	1	0	0	3	4	4	0	....	.182	.308	.227	.535	46	-2	2	2.71	0	/O-6	0	-0.2

• HUNT, Ken Kenneth Lawrence Hunt b: 7/13/1934, Grand Forks, ND d: 6/8/1997, Gardena, CA BR/TR, 6'1", 205 lbs. Deb: 9/10/1959 Career OF: 52-151-58

YEAR	TM-L	G	AB	R	H	2B	3B	HR	RBI	BB	SO	SB	CS	AVG	OBP	SLG	OPS	OPS+	BR/A	RC	RC/G	FR	G/POS	WS	TPW
1959	NY-A	6	12	2	4	1	0	0	1	0	3	0	0	.333	.333	.417	.750	108	0	2	5.10	0	/O-5(0-0-5)	0	0.0
1960	NY-A	25	22	4	6	2	0	0	1	4	4	0	0	.273	.407	.364	.771	117	1	4	5.88	0	O-24(17-5-2)	1	0.0
1961	LA-A	149	479	70	122	29	3	25	84	49	120	8	2	.255	.329	.484	.813	103	1	76	5.38	-5	*O-134(8-108-23)/2-1	11	-0.9
1962	LA-A	13	11	4	2	0	0	1	1	1	5	1	0	.182	.250	.455	.705	88	-0	1	2.60	-1	/1-3	0	-0.1
1963	LA-A	59	142	17	26	6	1	5	16	15	49	0	1	.183	.261	.345	.606	72	-6	12	2.75	-1	O-50(22-2-27)	2	-1.0
	Was-A	7	20	1	4	0	0	1	4	2	6	0	0	.200	.273	.350	.623	73	-1	1	1.98	-0	/O-5(1-3-1)	0	-0.1
	Yr.	66	162	18	30	6	1	6	20	17	55	0	1	.185	.263	.346	.608	73	-7	14	2.65	-1	O-55(23-5-28)	2	-1.1
1964	Was-A	51	96	9	13	4	0	1	4	14	35	0	1	.135	.245	.208	.454	28	-10	5	1.54	0	O-37(4-33-0)	1	-1.1
Total	6	310	782	107	177	42	4	33	111	85	222	9	4	.226	.306	.417	.723	87	-14	101	4.22	-8	O-255/1-3,2-1	15	-3.3

• HUNT, Randy James Randall Hunt b: 1/3/1960, Prattville, AL BR/TR, 6', 185 lbs. Deb: 6/4/1985

YEAR	TM-L	G	AB	R	H	2B	3B	HR	RBI	BB	SO	SB	CS	AVG	OBP	SLG	OPS	OPS+	BR/A	RC	RC/G	FR	G/POS	WS	TPW
1985	StL-N	14	19	1	3	0	0	0	1	0	5	0	1	.158	.158	.158	.316	-12	-3	0	.53	-1	C-13	0	-0.4
1986	Mon-N	21	48	4	10	0	0	2	5	5	16	0	0	.208	.283	.333	.616	70	-2	4	2.78	-2	C-21	1	-0.4
Total	2	35	67	5	13	0	0	2	6	5	21	0	1	.194	.250	.284	.534	48	-5	4	2.08	-3	/C-34	1	-0.7

• HUNT, Ron Ronald Kenneth Hunt b: 2/23/1941, St. Louis, MO BR/TR, 6', 186 lbs. Deb: 4/16/1963

YEAR	TM-L	G	AB	R	H	2B	3B	HR	RBI	BB	SO	SB	CS	AVG	OBP	SLG	OPS	OPS+	BR/A	RC	RC/G	FR	G/POS	WS	TPW
1963	NY-N	143	533	64	145	28	4	10	42	40	50	5	4	.272	.338	.396	.734	109	7	71	4.56	-5	*2-142/3-1	19	1.5
1964	NY-N★	127	475	59	144	19	6	6	42	29	30	6	2	.303	.357	.406	.764	117	12	66	5.05	0	*2-109,3-12	17	2.3
1965	NY-N	57	196	21	47	12	1	1	10	14	19	2	7	.240	.310	.327	.637	82	-7	18	2.91	-4	2-46/3-6	3	-0.8
1966	NY-N★	132	479	63	138	19	2	3	33	41	34	8	10	.288	.358	.355	.713	101	0	61	4.38	-6	*2-123/3-1,S-1	18	0.5
1967	LA-N	110	388	44	102	17	3	3	33	39	24	2	1	.263	.346	.345	.691	107	5	48	4.28	-12	2-90/3-8	14	0.1
1968	SF-N	148	529	79	132	19	0	2	28	78	41	6	6	.250	.372	.297	.669	103	8	66	4.16	-12	*2-147	21	1.0
1969	SF-N	128	478	72	125	23	3	3	41	51	47	9	2	.262	.363	.341	.704	100	5	66	4.68	0	*2-125/3-1	19	1.3

YEAR TM-L	G	AB	R	H	2B	3B	HR	RBI	BB	SO	SB	CS	AVG	OBP	SLG	OPS	OPS+	BR/A	RC	RC/G	FR	G/POS	WS	TPW
1970 SF-N	117	367	70	103	17	1	6	41	44	29	1	2	.281	.396	.381	.777	111	8	59	5.69	-14	2-85,3-16	13	-0.1
1971 Mon-N	152	520	89	145	20	3	5	38	58	41	5	7	.279	.403	.358	.761	116	17	85	5.85	-5	*2-133,3-19	26	2.1
1972 Mon-N	129	443	56	112	20	0	0	18	51	29	9	2	.253	.363	.298	.661	88	-1	55	4.24	-4	*2-122/3-5	15	0.3
1973 Mon-N	113	401	61	124	14	0	0	18	52	19	10	7	.309	.419	.344	.763	110	10	63	5.65	-13	*2-102,3-14	15	0.4
1974 Mon-N	115	403	66	108	15	0	0	26	55	17	2	5	.268	.375	.305	.680	87	-5	51	4.35	-13	3-75,2-31/S-1	11	-1.7
StL-N	12	23	1	4	0	0	0	0	3	2	0	0	.174	.321	.174	.495	42	-2	2	2.42	1	/2-5	0	-0.1
Yr.	127	426	67	112	15	0	0	26	58	19	2	5	.263	.372	.298	.670	84	-6	53	4.24	-12	3-75,2-36/S-1	11	-1.7
Total 12	**1483**	**5235**	**745**	**1429**	**223**	**23**	**39**	**370**	**555**	**382**	**65**	**55**	**.273**	**.369**	**.347**	**.716**	**103**	**57**	**711**	**4.70**	**-87**	***2-1260,3-158/S-2**	**191**	**6.8**
• HUNTER, Bill	William Robert Hunter b: 1855, St. Thomas, Canada, 5'7.5", 160 lbs. Deb: 5/2/1884																							
1884 Lou-a	2	7	1	1	0	0	0	0	0	....	....	....	.143	.143	.143	.286	-7	-1	0	.67	-1	/C-2	0	-0.1
• HUNTER, Bill	William Ellsworth Hunter b: 7/8/1887, Buffalo, NY d: 4/10/1934, Buffalo, NY BL/TL, 5'7.5", 155 lbs. Deb: 8/6/1912																							
1912 Cle-A	21	55	6	9	2	0	0	2	10	....	0	....	.164	.303	.200	.503	43	-4	4	1.97	-2	O-16(0-16-0)	1	-0.6
• HUNTER, Billy	Gordon William Hunter b: 6/4/1928, Punxsutawney, PA BR/TR, 6', 180 lbs. Deb: 4/14/1953 M/C																							
1953 StL-A★	154	567	50	124	18	1	1	37	24	45	3	1	.219	.253	.259	.512	38	-49	37	2.16	20	*S-152	11	-1.7
1954 Bal-A	125	411	28	100	9	5	2	27	21	38	5	4	.243	.283	.304	.588	66	-21	33	2.59	-1	*S-124	5	-1.3
1955 NY-A	98	255	14	58	7	1	3	20	15	18	9	2	.227	.270	.298	.568	53	-16	20	2.56	3	S-98	4	-0.6
1956 NY-A	39	75	8	21	3	4	0	11	2	4	0	1	.280	.299	.427	.725	93	-2	8	3.63	4	S-32/3-4	3	0.4
1957 KC-A	116	319	39	61	10	4	8	29	27	43	1	2	.191	.261	.323	.584	57	-20	27	2.66	-9	2-64,S-35,3-17	4	-2.3
1958 KC-A	22	58	6	9	1	1	2	11	5	7	1	1	.155	.222	.310	.533	44	-5	4	1.94	0	S-12/2-8,3-1	1	-0.4
Cle-A	76	190	21	37	10	2	0	9	17	37	4	1	.195	.264	.268	.533	48	-13	14	2.39	-9	S-75/3-2	2	-1.7
Yr.	98	248	27	46	11	3	2	20	22	44	5	2	.185	.255	.278	.533	47	-18	18	2.28	-9	S-87/2-8,3-3	3	-2.1
Total 6	**630**	**1875**	**166**	**410**	**58**	**18**	**16**	**144**	**111**	**192**	**23**	**12**	**.219**	**.265**	**.294**	**.560**	**53**	**-126**	**144**	**2.47**	**8**	**S-528/2-72,3-24**	**30**	**-7.6**
• HUNTER, Brian	Brian Ronald Hunter b: 3/4/1968, Torrance, CA BR/TL, 6', 195 lbs. Deb: 5/31/1991 Career OF: 74-0-30																							
1991*Atl-N	97	271	32	68	16	1	12	50	17	48	0	2	.251	.298	.450	.748	101	-2	34	4.34	-2	1-85/O-6(5-0-1)	8	-0.9
1992*Atl-N	102	238	34	57	13	2	14	41	21	50	1	2	.239	.301	.487	.789	113	2	35	4.84	2	1-92/O-6(1-0-5)	7	-0.1
1993 Atl-N	37	80	4	11	3	1	0	8	2	15	0	0	.138	.159	.200	.359	-5	-12	3	.93	0	1-29/O-2(0-0-2)	0	-1.4
1994 Pit-N	76	233	28	53	15	1	11	47	15	55	0	0	.227	.274	.442	.716	82	-8	28	4.04	-3	1-59/O-5(5-0-0)	6	-1.5
Cin-N	9	23	6	7	1	0	4	10	2	1	0	0	.304	.360	.870	1.230	209	3	7	11.57	0	/O-5(1-0-4),1-1	1	0.3
Yr.	85	256	34	60	16	1	15	57	17	56	0	0	.234	.282	.480	.763	94	-4	35	4.67	-3	1-60,O-10(6-0-4)	7	-1.2
1995 Cin-N	40	79	9	17	6	0	1	9	11	21	2	1	.215	.319	.329	.648	72	-3	9	3.49	-1	1-23/O-4(3-0-1)	0	-0.6
1996 Sea-A	75	198	21	53	10	0	7	28	15	43	0	1	.268	.332	.424	.756	89	-4	27	4.61	-3	1-41,O-29(29-0-2)/D-2	3	-1.0
1998 StL-N	62	112	11	23	9	1	4	13	7	23	1	1	.205	.258	.411	.669	73	-5	11	2.95	-1	O-26(16-0-12),1-10/D-1	0	-0.8
1999*Atl-N	114	181	28	45	12	1	6	30	31	40	0	1	.249	.370	.425	.796	101	0	29	5.27	2	*1-101/O-8(8-0-0)	6	-0.2
2000 Atl-N	2	2	1	1	0	0	1	1	0	0	0	0	.500	.500	2.000	2.500	490	1	2	54.00	0	....	0	0.1
Phi-N	85	138	13	29	5	0	7	22	20	39	0	1	.210	.310	.399	.709	77	-6	17	4.21	1	1-40/O-9(6-0-3),D-1	3	-0.7
Yr.	87	140	14	30	5	0	8	23	20	39	0	1	.214	.313	.421	.734	82	-5	19	4.65	1	1-40/O-9(6-0-3),D-1	3	-0.6
Total 9	**699**	**1555**	**187**	**364**	**90**	**7**	**67**	**259**	**141**	**335**	**4**	**9**	**.234**	**.302**	**.430**	**.733**	**90**	**-32**	**201**	**4.29**	**-6**	**1-481,O-100/D-4**	**34**	**-6.8**
• HUNTER, Brian	Brian Lee Hunter b: 3/5/1971, Portland, OR BR/TR, 6'4", 180 lbs. Deb: 6/27/1994 Career OF: 182-715-33																							
1994 Hou-N	6	24	2	6	1	0	0	0	1	6	2	1	.250	.280	.292	.572	52	-2	2	2.75	1	/O-6(0-6-0)	0	-0.1
1995 Hou-N	78	321	52	97	14	5	2	28	21	52	24	7	.302	.349	.396	.744	103	3	47	5.34	6	O-74(0-74-0)	10	0.9
1996 Hou-N	132	526	74	145	27	2	5	35	17	92	35	9	.276	.301	.363	.664	80	-13	59	3.93	1	*O-127(0-127-0)	7	-1.1
1997 Det-A	162	658	112	177	29	7	4	45	66	121	**74**	18	.269	.337	.353	.689	81	-9	85	4.37	0	*O-162(0-162-0)	17	-0.8
1998 Det-A	142	595	67	151	29	3	4	36	36	94	42	12	.254	.299	.333	.631	64	-29	61	3.55	8	*O-139(0-139-0)	9	-1.8
1999 Det-A	18	55	8	13	2	1	0	0	5	11	0	3	.236	.311	.309	.621	59	-5	5	2.89	0	O-18(0-18-0)	1	-0.4
Sea-A	121	484	71	112	11	5	4	34	32	80	44	5	.231	.280	.300	.580	47	-32	46	3.11	10	*O-121(119-19-0)	3	-2.5
Yr.	139	539	79	125	13	6	4	34	37	91	**44**	8	.232	.284	.301	.584	48	-37	50	3.09	10	*O-139(119-37-0)	4	-2.9
2000 Col-N	72	200	36	55	4	1	1	13	21	31	15	3	.275	.347	.320	.667	56	-11	25	4.45	-1	O-63(27-34-13)	3	-1.2
Cin-N	32	40	11	9	1	0	0	1	6	9	5	0	.225	.326	.250	.576	47	-2	5	3.89	3	O-25(9-16-0)	1	0.1
Yr.	104	240	47	64	5	1	1	14	27	40	20	3	.267	.343	.308	.652	54	-13	30	4.35	2	O-88(36-50-13)	4	-1.1
2001 Phi-N	83	145	22	40	6	0	2	16	16	25	14	3	.276	.348	.359	.706	85	-1	20	4.63	2	O-41(22-18-5)/D-1	5	0.1
2002 Hou-N	98	201	32	54	16	3	3	20	16	39	5	0	.269	.329	.423	.752	92	-2	29	5.20	2	O-88(88-0)	6	0.1
2003 Hou-N	56	98	13	23	6	1	0	13	6	21	0	0	.235	.286	.316	.602	54	-7	9	3.16	-2	O-32(5-14-15)	1	-0.9
Total 10	**1000**	**3347**	**500**	**882**	**146**	**28**	**25**	**241**	**243**	**581**	**260**	**61**	**.264**	**.316**	**.346**	**.662**	**73**	**-109**	**393**	**4.04**	**31**	**O-896/D-1**	**63**	**-7.6**
• HUNTER, Buddy	Harold James Hunter b: 8/9/1947, Omaha, NE BR/TR, 5'10", 170 lbs. Deb: 7/1/1971																							
1971 Bos-A	8	9	2	2	1	0	0	0	2	1	0	0	.222	.364	.333	.697	92	0	1	4.94	0	/2-6	0	0.1
1973 Bos-A	13	7	3	3	1	0	0	2	3	1	0	0	.429	.636	.571	1.208	229	2	3	17.51	1	/3-3,2-2,D-1	1	0.3
1975 Bos-A	1	1	0	0	0	0	0	0	0	0	0	0	.000	.000	.000	.000	-92	-0	0	.00	-1	/2-1	0	-0.1
Total 3	**22**	**17**	**5**	**5**	**2**	**0**	**0**	**2**	**5**	**2**	**0**	**0**	**.294**	**.478**	**.412**	**.890**	**153**	**2**	**5**	**9.39**	**0**	**/2-9,3-3,D-1**	**1**	**0.3**
• HUNTER, Eddie	Edison Franklin Hunter b: 2/6/1905, Bellevue, KY d: 3/14/1967, Colerain, OH BR/TR, 5'7.5", 150 lbs. Deb: 8/5/1933																							
1933 Cin-N	1	0	0	0	0	0	0	0	0	0	0	....	....	....	....	....	-102	0	0	....	0	/3-1	0	0.0
• HUNTER, Herb	Herbert Harrison Hunter b: 12/25/1896, Boston, MA d: 7/25/1970, Orlando, FL BL/TR, 6'.5", 165 lbs. Deb: 4/29/1916																							
1916 NY-N	21	28	3	7	0	0	1	4	0	5	0	....	.250	.250	.357	.607	90	-1	3	3.10	-1	/3-6,1-2	0	-0.1
Chi-N	2	4	0	0	0	0	0	0	0	0	0	....	.000	.000	.000	.000	-90	-1	0	.00	0	/3-1	0	-0.1
Yr.	23	32	3	7	0	0	1	4	0	5	0	....	.219	.219	.313	.531	68	-1	3	2.60	-1	/3-7,1-2	0	-0.3
1917 Chi-N	3	3	0	0	0	0	0	0	0	0	0	....	.000	.000	.000	.000	-93	-1	0	.00	0	/2-1,3-1	0	-0.1
1920 Bos-A	4	12	2	1	0	0	0	0	1	1	0	0	.083	.154	.083	.237	-38	-2	0	.54	0	/O-4(3-1-0)	0	-0.3
1921 StL-N	9	2	3	0	0	0	0	0	1	0	0	3	.000	.333	.000	.333	-4	-2	0	.00	0	/1-1	0	-0.2
Total 4	**39**	**49**	**8**	**8**	**0**	**0**	**1**	**4**	**2**	**6**	**0**	**3**	**.163**	**.196**	**.224**	**.421**	**26**	**-6**	**3**	**1.59**	**-2**	**/3-8,O-4,1-3,2-1**	**0**	**-0.8**
• HUNTER, Lem	Robert Lemuel Hunter b: 1/16/1863, Warren, OH d: 11/9/1956, West Lafayette, OH Deb: 9/1/1883																							
1883 Cle-N	1	4	1	1	0	0	0	0	0	2	....	....	.250	.250	.250	.500	53	-0	0	2.35	0	/O-1,P-1	0	0.1
• HUNTER, Newt	Frederick Creighton Hunter b: 1/5/1880, Chillicothe, OH d: 10/26/1963, Columbus, OH BR/TR, 6', 180 lbs. Deb: 4/12/1911 C																							
1911 Pit-N	65	209	35	53	10	6	2	24	25	43	9	....	.254	.345	.388	.732	101	0	31	4.90	-3	1-61	5	-0.4
• HUNTER, Torii	Torii Kedar Hunter b: 7/18/1975, Pine Bluff, AR BR/TR, 6'2", 205 lbs. Deb: 8/22/1997 Career OF: 17-655-14																							
1997 Min-A	1	0	0	0	0	0	0	0	0	0	0	0	....	....	....	....	-99	0	0	....	0	....	0	0.0
1998 Min-A	6	17	0	4	1	0	0	2	2	6	0	1	.235	.316	.294	.610	59	-1	1	2.09	0	/O-6(0-6-0)	0	-0.2
1999 Min-A	135	384	52	98	17	2	9	35	26	72	10	6	.255	.313	.380	.693	73	-17	44	3.89	4	*O-130(16-107-14)	5	-1.2
2000 Min-A	99	336	44	94	14	7	5	44	18	68	4	3	.280	.320	.408	.728	79	-12	40	4.12	7	O-99(1-98-0)	8	-0.4
2001 Min-A	148	564	82	147	32	5	27	92	29	125	9	6	.261	.306	.479	.785	100	-3	79	4.85	14	*O-147(0-147-0)	19	1.1
2002*Min-A★	148	561	89	162	37	4	29	94	35	118	23	8	.289	.336	.524	.860	123	17	93	5.88	-11	*O-146(0-146-0)/D-1	21	0.7
2003*Min-A	154	581	83	145	31	4	26	102	50	106	6	7	.250	.314	.451	.765	98	-5	78	4.53	-4	*O-151(0-151-0)/D-3	16	-0.8
Total 7	**691**	**2443**	**350**	**650**	**132**	**22**	**96**	**369**	**160**	**495**	**52**	**31**	**.266**	**.318**	**.456**	**.774**	**97**	**-21**	**334**	**4.73**	**9**	**O-679/D-4**	**69**	**-0.7**
• HUNTZ, Steve	Stephen Michael Huntz b: 12/3/1945, Cleveland, OH BB/TR, 6'1", 204 lbs. Deb: 9/19/1967																							
1967 StL-N	3	6	1	1	0	0	0	0	1	2	0	0	.167	.286	.167	.452	33	-0	0	1.94	0	/2-2	0	-0.1
1969 StL-N	71	139	13	27	4	0	3	13	27	34	0	0	.194	.325	.288	.613	73	-4	13	3.08	3	S-52,2-12/3-6	4	0.3
1970 SD-N	106	352	54	77	8	0	11	37	66	69	0	3	.219	.344	.335	.679	86	-6	44	4.12	1	S-57,3-51	9	0.1
1971 Chi-A	35	86	10	18	3	1	2	6	7	9	1	0	.209	.269	.337	.606	69	-4	8	3.08	1	2-14/S-7,3-6	1	-0.2
1975 SD-N	22	53	3	8	4	0	0	4	7	8	0	0	.151	.250	.226	.476	35	-5	3	1.82	-1	3-16/2-2	0	-0.6
Total 5	**237**	**636**	**81**	**131**	**19**	**1**	**16**	**60**	**108**	**122**	**1**	**3**	**.206**	**.322**	**.314**	**.637**	**76**	**-19**	**70**	**3.52**	**4**	**S-116/3-79,2-30**	**14**	**-0.4**

YEAR TM-L	G	AB	R	H	2B	3B	HR	RBI	BB	SO	SB	CS	AVG	OBP	SLG	OPS	OPS+	BR/A	RC	RC/G	FR	G/POS	WS	TPW
• HUPPERT, Dave	David Blain Huppert b: 4/17/1957, South Gate, CA BR/TR, 6'1", 190 lbs. Deb: 9/15/1983																							
1983 Bal-A	2	0	0	0	0	0	0	0	0	0	0	0	....	....	....	....	-102	0	0	....	0	/C-2	0	0.0
1985 Mil-A	15	21	1	1	0	0	0	0	2	7	0	0	.048	.130	.048	.178	-49	-4	0	.24	0	C-15	0	-0.4
Total 2	17	21	1	1	0	0	0	0	2	7	0	0	.048	.130	.048	.178	-49	-4	0	.24	-1	/C-17	0	-0.4
• HURDLE, Clint	Clinton Merrick Hurdle b: 7/30/1957, Big Rapids, MI BL/TR, 6'3", 195 lbs. Deb: 9/18/1977 M/C Career OF: 97-0-238																							
1977 KC-A	9	26	5	8	0	0	2	7	2	7	0	0	.308	.357	.538	.896	139	1	5	7.78	0	/O-9(0-0-9)	1	0.1
1978★KC-A	133	417	48	110	25	5	7	56	56	84	1	3	.264	.352	.398	.750	108	5	61	5.07	-2	O-78(41-0-42),1-52/3-1,D-1	14	-0.3
1979 KC-A	59	171	16	41	10	3	3	30	28	24	0	1	.240	.350	.386	.736	96	-0	24	4.62	-1	O-50(30-0-20)/D-4,3-1	4	-0.4
1980★KC-A	130	395	50	116	31	2	10	60	34	61	0	0	.294	.353	.458	.811	119	10	62	5.64	-6	*O-126(0-0-126)	14	-0.2
1981★KC-A	28	76	12	25	3	1	4	15	13	10	0	0	.329	.427	.553	.980	182	9	18	9.19	-1	O-28(2-0-26)	5	0.7
1982 Cin-N	19	34	2	7	1	0	0	1	2	6	0	1	.206	.270	.235	.506	42	-3	2	1.66	0	O-17(17-0-1)	0	-0.3
1983 NY-N	13	33	3	6	2	0	0	2	2	10	0	0	.182	.229	.242	.471	31	-3	2	1.64	-1	/3-9,O-1	0	-0.4
1985 NY-N	43	82	7	16	4	0	3	7	13	20	0	1	.195	.313	.354	.666	88	-2	9	3.66	0	C-17,O-10(2-0-8)	2	-0.2
1986 StL-N	78	154	18	30	5	1	3	15	26	38	0	0	.195	.315	.299	.614	71	-6	16	3.41	0	1-39,O-10(5-0-5)/C-5,3-4	3	-0.8
1987 NY-N	3	3	1	1	0	0	0	0	0	1	0	0	.333	.333	.333	.667	82	-0	0	4.50	0	/1-1	0	0.0
Total 10	515	1391	162	360	81	12	32	193	176	261	1	6	.259	.345	.403	.748	105	11	199	4.95	-12	O-329/1-92,C-22,3-15,D-5	43	-1.9
• HURLEY, Dick	William H. Hurley b: 1847, Honesdale, PA BL, 5'7", 160 lbs. Deb: 4/18/1872																							
1872 Oly-n	2	7	0	0	0	0	0	0	0	1	0	0	.000	.000	.000	.000	-106	-2	0	.00	0	/O-2(0-0-2)	....	-0.1
• HURLEY, Jerry	Jeremiah Hurley b: 4/1875, New York, NY d: 12/27/1919, New York, NY BR/TR Deb: 9/23/1901																							
1901 Cin-N	9	21	1	1	0	0	0	0	1	....	1	....	.048	.130	.048	.178	-51	-4	0	.44	-1	/C-7	0	-0.4
1907 Bro-N	1	2	0	0	0	0	0	0	1	....	0	....	.000	.333	.000	.333	5	-0	0	.00	0	/C-1	0	0.0
Total 2	10	23	1	1	0	0	0	0	2	....	1	....	.043	.154	.043	.197	-44	-4	0	.40	-1	/C-8	0	-0.4
• HURLEY, Jerry	Jeremiah Joseph Hurley b: 6/15/1863, Boston, MA d: 9/17/1950, Boston, MA BR/TR, 6', 190 lbs. Deb: 5/1/1889 Career OF: 1-0-2																							
1889 Bos-N	1	4	0	0	0	0	0	0	0	0	0	....	.000	.000	.000	.000	-94	-1	0	.00	0	/C-1,O-1	0	-0.1
1890 Pit-P	8	22	5	6	1	0	0	2	2	5	0	....	.273	.333	.318	.652	81	-0	2	4.04	-1	/C-7,O-1	0	-0.1
1891 Cin-a	24	66	10	14	3	2	0	6	12	13	2	....	.212	.333	.318	.652	80	-2	8	4.00	-6	C-24/1-1,O-1	2	-0.5
Total 3	33	92	15	20	4	2	0	8	14	18	2	....	.217	.321	.304	.625	73	-3	10	3.79	-7	/C-32,O-3,1-1	2	-0.7
• HURST, Don	Frank O'Donnell Hurst b: 8/12/1905, Maysville, KY d: 12/6/1952, Los Angeles, CA BL/TL, 6', 215 lbs. Deb: 5/13/1928																							
1928 Phi-N	107	396	73	113	23	4	19	64	68	40	3	....	.285	.391	.508	.899	129	18	80	7.07	-1	*1-104	12	1.0
1929 Phi-N	154	589	100	179	29	4	31	125	80	36	10	....	.304	.390	.525	.914	117	15	120	7.23	2	*1-154	17	0.6
1930 Phi-N	119	391	78	128	19	3	17	78	46	22	6	....	.327	.401	.522	.923	113	9	81	7.62	-8	1-96/O-7(0-7-0)	10	-0.5
1931 Phi-N	137	489	63	149	37	5	11	91	64	28	8	....	.305	.386	.468	.855	119	15	93	6.82	2	*1-135	15	0.5
1932 Phi-N	150	579	109	196	41	4	24	**143**	65	27	10	....	.339	.412	.547	.959	139	34	134	8.80	-3	*1-150	23	1.6
1933 Phi-N	147	550	58	147	27	8	8	76	48	32	3	....	.267	.327	.389	.716	92	-5	72	4.55	0	*1-142	9	-1.9
1934 Phi-N	40	130	16	34	9	0	2	21	12	7	1	....	.262	.324	.377	.701	77	-4	17	4.67	-1	1-34	2	-0.8
Chi-N	51	151	13	30	5	0	3	12	8	18	0	....	.199	.239	.291	.530	42	-13	10	2.26	-1	1-48	1	-1.8
Yr.	91	281	29	64	14	0	5	33	20	25	1	....	.228	.279	.331	.610	58	-17	27	3.32	-3	1-82	3	-2.6
Total 7	905	3275	510	976	190	28	115	610	391	210	41	....	.298	.375	.478	.854	113	69	606	6.62	-11	1-863/O-7	89	-1.3
• HURST, Jimmy	Jimmy O'Neal Hurst b: 3/1/1972, Tuscaloosa, AL BR/TR, 6'6", 225 lbs. Deb: 9/10/1997																							
1997 Det-A	13	17	1	3	1	0	1	1	2	6	0	0	.176	.263	.412	.675	73	-1	2	3.82	0	O-12(1-1-10)/D-1	0	-0.1
• HUSKEY, Butch	Robert Leon Huskey b: 11/10/1971, Anadarko, OK BR/TR, 6'3", 244 lbs. Deb: 9/8/1993 Career OF: 78-0-264																							
1993 NY-N	13	41	2	6	1	0	0	3	1	13	0	0	.146	.167	.171	.337	-10	-6	1	.93	1	3-13	0	-0.5
1995 NY-N	28	90	8	17	1	0	3	11	10	16	1	0	.189	.270	.300	.570	52	-6	7	2.54	0	3-27/O-1	1	-0.6
1996 NY-N	118	414	43	115	16	2	15	60	27	77	1	2	.278	.322	.435	.757	102	-1	55	4.73	-5	1-75,O-40(0-0-40)/3-6	8	-1.3
1997 NY-N	142	471	61	135	26	2	24	81	25	84	8	5	.287	.324	.503	.827	117	8	67	4.89	-4	O-92(30-0-72),1-22,3-15/D-4	12	-0.2
1998 NY-N	113	369	43	93	18	0	13	59	26	66	7	6	.252	.303	.407	.710	86	-10	41	3.67	1	*O-103(0-0-103)/D-1	7	-1.3
1999 Sea-A	74	262	44	76	9	0	15	49	27	45	3	1	.290	.356	.496	.853	112	4	48	6.65	-2	O-53(30-0-24),1-10/D-7,3-1	9	-0.1
*Bos-A	45	124	18	33	6	0	7	28	7	20	0	0	.266	.305	.484	.789	94	-2	16	4.45	0	D-37/O-4(2-0-2),3-2	3	-0.3
Yr.	119	386	62	109	15	0	22	77	34	65	3	1	.282	.340	.492	.833	106	3	63	5.91	-1	O-57(32-0-26),D-44,1-10/3-3	12	-0.4
2000 Min-A	64	215	22	48	13	0	5	27	25	49	0	2	.223	.310	.353	.663	65	-13	23	3.57	2	D-39,O-15(0-0-15)/1-9	1	-1.4
Col-N	45	92	18	32	8	0	4	18	16	14	1	1	.348	.444	.565	1.010	122	4	22	8.58	0	O-23(15-0-8)/1-8	3	0.3
Total 7	642	2078	259	555	98	4	86	336	164	384	21	17	.267	.322	.442	.764	96	-22	281	4.63	-6	O-331,1-124/D-88,3-64	44	-5.5
• HUSON, Jeff	Jeffrey Kent Huson b: 8/15/1964, Scottsdale, AZ BL/TR, 6'3", 180 lbs. Deb: 9/2/1988 Career OF: 10-3-3																							
1988 Mon-N	20	42	7	13	2	0	0	3	4	3	2	1	.310	.370	.357	.727	105	0	5	4.25	-2	S-15/2-2,3-1,O-1	1	0.0
1989 Mon-N	32	74	1	12	5	0	0	2	6	6	3	0	.162	.225	.230	.455	30	-6	3	1.15	-3	S-20/2-9,3-1	1	-0.8
1990 Tex-A	145	396	57	95	12	2	0	28	46	54	12	4	.240	.322	.280	.602	70	-14	39	3.25	7	*S-119,3-36,2-12	9	0.0
1991 Tex-A	119	268	36	57	8	3	2	26	39	32	8	3	.213	.313	.287	.600	68	-10	26	3.11	1	*S-116/2-2,3-1	7	-0.2
1992 Tex-A	123	318	49	83	14	3	4	24	41	43	18	6	.261	.347	.362	.709	102	3	43	4.38	-3	S-82,2-47/O-2(0-2-0),D-1	9	0.7
1993 Tex-A	23	45	3	6	1	1	0	2	0	10	0	0	.133	.133	.200	.333	-12	-7	1	.84	-3	S-12/2-5,3-2,D-2	0	-0.8
1995 Bal-A	66	161	24	40	4	2	1	19	15	20	5	4	.248	.316	.317	.633	64	-9	16	3.22	2	3-33,2-21/D-3,S-1	2	-0.5
1996 Bal-A	17	28	5	9	1	0	0	2	1	3	0	0	.321	.345	.357	.702	78	-1	4	4.85	-1	2-12/3-3,O-1	1	-0.2
1997 Mil-A	84	143	12	29	3	0	0	11	5	15	3	0	.203	.240	.224	.464	22	-16	7	1.52	0	2-32,1-21/O-9(8-0-1),D-4,3	1	-1.5
1998 Sea-A	31	49	8	8	1	0	1	4	5	6	1	1	.163	.241	.245	.486	27	-6	3	1.97	-2	/2-8,3-8,1-7,D-1,O-1,S-1	0	-0.7
1999 Ana-A	97	225	21	59	7	1	0	18	16	27	10	1	.262	.311	.302	.613	58	-12	21	3.16	3	2-41,S-22,D-10/3-9,1-8,O-2(2-0-0)	2	-0.7
2000 Chi-N	70	130	19	28	7	1	0	11	13	9	2	1	.215	.287	.285	.571	46	-11	10	2.42	-2	3-18,2-17,S-17/1-1	1	-1.0
Total 12	827	1879	242	439	65	13	8	150	191	228	64	21	.234	.306	.295	.601	65	-88	178	3.06	-2	S-405,2-208,3-114/1-37,D-21,O	34	-5.9
• HUSTA, Carl	Carl Lawrence "Sox" Husta b: 4/8/1902, Egg Harbor City, NJ d: 11/6/1951, Kingston, NY BR/TR, 5'11", 176 lbs. Deb: 9/24/1925																							
1925 Phi-A	6	22	2	3	0	0	0	2	2	3	0	0	.136	.208	.136	.345	-11	-4	1	1.03	3	/S-6	1	0.0
• HUSTON, Harry	Harry Emanuel Kress Huston b: 10/14/1883, Bellefontaine, OH d: 10/13/1969, Blackwell, OK BR/TR, 5'9", 168 lbs. Deb: 9/3/1906																							
1906 Phi-N	2	4	0	0	0	0	0	0	1	....	0	....	.000	.200	.000	.200	-37	-1	0	.00	0	/C-2	0	0.0
• HUSTON, Warren	Warren Llewellyn Huston b: 10/31/1913, Newtonville, MA d: 8/30/1999, Wareham, MA BR/TR, 6', 170 lbs. Deb: 6/24/1937																							
1937 Phi-A	38	54	5	7	3	0	0	3	2	9	0	1	.130	.161	.185	.346	-13	-10	1	.80	-1	2-16,S-15/3-2	0	-0.9
1944 Bos-N	33	55	7	11	1	0	0	1	8	5	0	....	.200	.313	.218	.531	49	-3	4	2.19	0	3-20/2-5,S-4	1	-0.3
Total 2	71	109	12	18	4	0	0	4	10	14	0	1	.165	.242	.202	.444	20	-13	5	1.48	-2	/3-22,2-21,S-19	1	-1.3
• HUTCHESON, Joe	Joseph Johnson "Slug,Poodles" Hutcheson b: 2/5/1905, Springtown, TX d: 2/23/1993, Tyler, TX BL/TR, 6'2", 200 lbs. Deb: 7/8/1933																							
1933 Bro-N	55	184	19	43	4	1	6	21	15	13	1	....	.234	.295	.364	.659	91	-2	20	3.60	1	O-45(0-0-45)	3	-0.4
• HUTCHINSON, Ed	Edwin Forrest Hutchinson b: 5/19/1867, Pittsburgh, PA d: 7/19/1934, Colfax, CA BL/TR, 5'11", 175 lbs. Deb: 6/17/1890																							
1890 Chi-N	4	17	0	1	1	0	0	0	0	0	0	....	.059	.059	.118	.176	-47	-3	0	.20	1	/2-4	0	-0.2
• HUTSON, Roy	Roy Lee Hutson b: 2/27/1902, Luray, MO d: 5/20/1957, La Mesa, CA BL/TR, 5'9", 165 lbs. Deb: 9/20/1925																							
1925 Bro-N	7	8	1	4	0	0	0	1	1	1	0	0	.500	.556	.500	1.056	177	1	2	12.13	0	/O-4(3-0-1)	1	0.1
• HUTTO, Jim	James Neamon Hutto b: 10/17/1947, Norfolk, VA BR/TR, 5'11", 195 lbs. Deb: 4/17/1970																							
1970 Phi-N	57	92	7	17	2	0	3	12	5	20	0	0	.185	.227	.304	.531	42	-8	6	1.94	0	O-22(16-0-6),1-12/C-5,3-1	0	-0.9
1975 Bal-A	4	5	0	0	0	0	0	0	0	2	0	0	.000	.000	.000	.000	-107	-1	0	.00	0	/C-3	0	-0.1
Total 2	61	97	7	17	2	0	3	12	5	22	0	0	.175	.216	.289	.504	35	-9	6	1.83	-1	/O-22,1-12,C-8,3-1	0	-1.1
• HUTTON, Tom	Thomas George Hutton b: 4/20/1946, Los Angeles, CA BL/TL, 5'11", 180 lbs. Deb: 9/16/1966 Career OF: 82-5-91																							
1966 LA-N	3	2	0	0	0	0	0	0	0	0	0	0	.000	.000	.000	.000	-109	-1	0	.00	0	/1-3	0	-0.1

YEAR TM-L	G	AB	R	H	2B	3B	HR	RBI	BB	SO	SB	CS	AVG	OBP	SLG	OPS	OPS+	BR/A	RC	RC/G	FR	G/POS	WS	TPW
1969 LA-N	16	48	2	13	0	0	0	4	5	7	0	0	.271	.340	.271	.610	78	-1	5	3.33	4	1-16	1	0.2
1972 Phi-N	134	381	40	99	16	2	4	38	56	24	5	8	.260	.355	.344	.699	97	-2	47	4.14	0	1-87,0-48(5-4-39)	9	-0.9
1973 Phi-N	106	247	31	65	11	0	5	29	32	31	3	1	.263	.348	.368	.716	96	-0	31	4.38	1	1-71	6	-0.4
1974 Phi-N	96	208	32	50	6	3	4	33	30	13	2	2	.240	.336	.356	.692	90	-3	25	3.99	-1	1-39,0-33(33-0-0)	5	-0.8
1975 Phi-N	113	165	24	41	6	0	3	24	27	10	2	5	.248	.354	.339	.694	89	-3	19	3.66	3	1-71,0-12(0-0-12)	2	-0.4
1976*Phi-N	95	124	15	25	5	1	1	13	27	11	1	2	.202	.344	.282	.627	77	-3	13	3.31	2	1-72/0-1	2	-0.5
1977*Phi-N	107	81	12	25	3	0	2	11	12	10	1	1	.309	.398	.420	.818	114	2	13	5.73	-1	1-73/0-9(7-0-2)	3	-0.1
1978 Tor-A	64	173	19	44	9	0	2	9	19	11	1	2	.254	.328	.341	.669	87	-3	19	3.65	0	0-55(32-0-23)/1-9	3	-0.6
Mon-N	39	59	4	12	3	0	0	5	10	5	0	0	.203	.319	.254	.573	63	-3	5	2.54	-2	1-17/0-5(3-1-1)	1	-0.5
1979 Mon-N	86	83	14	21	2	1	1	13	10	7	0	0	.253	.333	.337	.671	84	-2	9	3.63	2	1-25/0-9(0-0-9)	2	0.0
1980 Mon-N	62	55	2	12	2	0	0	5	4	10	0	0	.218	.271	.255	.526	47	-4	4	2.31	-1	/1-7,0-4(1-0-3),P-1	0	-0.7
1981 Mon-N	31	29	1	3	0	0	0	2	2	1	0	0	.103	.161	.103	.265	-23	-5	1	.59	0	/1-9,0-2(1-0-1)	0	-0.5
Total 12	**952**	**1655**	**196**	**410**	**63**	**7**	**22**	**186**	**234**	**140**	**15**	**21**	**.248**	**.341**	**.334**	**.675**	**87**	**-26**	**190**	**3.82**	**6**	**1-499,0-178/P-1**	**34**	**-5.5**

• HYATT, Ham Robert Hamilton Hyatt b: 11/1/1884, Buncombe County, NC d: 9/11/1963, Liberty Lake, WA BL/TR, 6'1", 185 lbs. Deb: 4/15/1909 U Career OF: 27-7-49

YEAR TM-L	G	AB	R	H	2B	3B	HR	RBI	BB	SO	SB	CS	AVG	OBP	SLG	OPS	OPS+	BR/A	RC	RC/G	FR	G/POS	WS	TPW
1909*Pit-N	49	67	9	20	3	4	0	7	3	....	1	....	.299	.329	.463	.791	138	2	10	5.54	3	/0-6(5-0-1),1-2	3	0.5
1910 Pit-N	74	175	19	46	5	6	1	30	8	14	3	....	.263	.306	.377	.684	93	-3	20	4.10	-2	1-38/0-4(0-3-1)	4	-0.5
1912 Pit-N	46	97	13	28	3	1	0	22	6	8	2	....	.289	.330	.340	.670	85	-2	11	4.10	-1	0-15(0-1-14)/1-3	2	-0.4
1913 Pit-N	63	81	8	27	6	2	4	16	3	8	0	....	.333	.372	.605	.977	184	8	18	7.97	0	/1-5,0-5(1-0-5)	4	0.8
1914 Pit-N	74	79	2	17	3	1	1	15	7	14	1	....	.215	.295	.316	.612	86	-1	7	3.04	-1	/1-7,C-1	1	-0.3
1915 StL-N	106	295	23	79	8	9	2	46	28	24	3	3	.268	.337	.376	.714	116	5	38	4.51	0	1-64,0-25(0-1-26)	10	0.3
1918 NY-A	53	131	11	30	8	0	2	10	8	8	1	....	.229	.273	.336	.609	82	-4	12	2.90	-1	0-25(21-2-2)/1-5	2	-0.6
Total 7	**465**	**925**	**85**	**247**	**36**	**23**	**10**	**146**	**63**	**76**	**11**	**3**	**.267**	**.321**	**.388**	**.709**	**108**	**6**	**117**	**4.36**	**-1**	**1-124/0-80,C-1**	**26**	**-0.1**

• HYERS, Tim Timothy James Hyers b: 10/3/1971, Atlanta, GA BL/TL, 6'1", 185 lbs. Deb: 4/4/1994 Career OF: 13-0-6

YEAR TM-L	G	AB	R	H	2B	3B	HR	RBI	BB	SO	SB	CS	AVG	OBP	SLG	OPS	OPS+	BR/A	RC	RC/G	FR	G/POS	WS	TPW
1994 SD-N	52	118	13	30	3	0	0	7	9	15	3	0	.254	.307	.280	.587	56	-7	11	3.32	1	1-41/0-2(0-0-2)	1	-0.9
1995 SD-N	6	5	0	0	0	0	0	0	0	1	0	0	.000	.000	.000	.000	-104	-1	0	.00	0	/1-1	0	-0.1
1996 Det-A	17	26	1	2	1	0	0	0	4	5	0	0	.077	.200	.115	.315	-18	-5	1	.63	0	/1-9,D-2,0-1	0	-0.5
1999 Fla-N	58	81	8	18	4	1	2	12	14	11	0	0	.222	.337	.370	.707	83	-2	11	4.58	-1	0-15(12-0-4),1-14/D-1	0	-0.4
Total 4	**133**	**230**	**22**	**50**	**8**	**1**	**2**	**19**	**27**	**32**	**3**	**0**	**.217**	**.300**	**.287**	**.587**	**55**	**-15**	**23**	**3.29**	**-1**	**/1-65,0-18,D-3**	**1**	**-1.9**

• HYNDMAN, Jim James Harvey Hyndman b: 7/9/1866, Hamilton, Canada d: 1/16/1934, Alamosa, CO Deb: 7/23/1886

YEAR TM-L	G	AB	R	H	2B	3B	HR	RBI	BB	SO	SB	CS	AVG	OBP	SLG	OPS	OPS+	BR/A	RC	RC/G	FR	G/POS	WS	TPW
1886 Phi-a	1	4	0	0	0	0	0	0	0	....	0	....	.000	.000	.000	.000	-99	-1	0	.00	0	/0-1,P-1	0	-0.5

• HYNES, Pat Patrick J. Hynes b: 3/12/1884, St. Louis, MO d: 3/12/1907, St. Louis, MO TL Deb: 9/27/1903 ♦

YEAR TM-L	G	AB	R	H	2B	3B	HR	RBI	BB	SO	SB	CS	AVG	OBP	SLG	OPS	OPS+	BR/A	RC	RC/G	FR	G/POS	WS	TPW
1903 StL-N	1	3	0	0	0	0	0	0	0	....	0	....	.000	.000	.000	.000	-103	-0	0	.00	-1	/P-1	0	-0.1
1904 StL-A	66	254	23	60	7	3	0	15	3	....	3	....	.236	.248	.287	.535	74	-8	20	2.65	-11	0-63(0-0-63)/P-5	1	-3.4
Total 2	**67**	**257**	**23**	**60**	**7**	**3**	**0**	**15**	**3**	**....**	**3**	**....**	**.233**	**.245**	**.284**	**.529**	**72**	**-8**	**20**	**2.61**	**-11**	**/0-63,P-6**	**1**	**-3.6**

• HYZDU, Adam Adam Davis Hyzdu b: 12/6/1971, San Jose, CA BR/TR, 6'2", 220 lbs. Deb: 9/8/2000 Career OF: 22-57-46

YEAR TM-L	G	AB	R	H	2B	3B	HR	RBI	BB	SO	SB	CS	AVG	OBP	SLG	OPS	OPS+	BR/A	RC	RC/G	FR	G/POS	WS	TPW
2000 Pit-N	12	18	2	7	2	0	1	4	0	4	0	0	.389	.389	.667	1.056	161	2	5	11.45	0	/0-5(1-0-4)	1	0.1
2001 Pit-N	51	72	7	15	1	0	5	9	4	18	0	1	.208	.260	.431	.690	72	-4	8	3.46	0	0-27(8-1-18)/1-4	1	-0.5
2002 Pit-N	59	155	24	36	6	0	11	34	21	44	0	0	.232	.328	.484	.812	109	2	26	5.76	-1	0-50(10-36-13)/1-1	6	0.1
2003 Pit-N	51	63	16	13	5	0	1	8	10	21	0	0	.206	.324	.333	.658	71	-3	7	3.64	0	0-34(3-20-11)	1	-0.3
Total 4	**173**	**308**	**49**	**71**	**14**	**0**	**18**	**55**	**35**	**87**	**0**	**1**	**.231**	**.315**	**.451**	**.766**	**96**	**-3**	**45**	**5.00**	**-1**	**0-116/1-5**	**9**	**-0.5**

• IBANEZ, Raul Raul Javier Ibanez b: 6/2/1972, New York, NY BL/TR, 6'2", 210 lbs. Deb: 8/1/1996 Career OF: 252-2-146

YEAR TM-L	G	AB	R	H	2B	3B	HR	RBI	BB	SO	SB	CS	AVG	OBP	SLG	OPS	OPS+	BR/A	RC	RC/G	FR	G/POS	WS	TPW
1996 Sea-A	4	5	0	0	0	0	0	0	0	1	0	0	.000	.167	.000	.167	-53	-1	0	.23	0	/D-2	0	-0.1
1997 Sea-A	11	26	3	4	0	1	1	4	0	6	0	0	.154	.154	.346	.500	26	-3	1	1.70	0	/0-8(2-0-6),D-1	0	-0.3
1998 Sea-A	37	98	12	25	7	1	2	12	5	22	0	0	.255	.291	.408	.699	79	-3	10	3.66	-1	0-17(6-0-12),1-16/D-1	1	-0.5
1999 Sea-A	87	209	23	54	7	0	9	27	17	32	5	1	.258	.314	.421	.735	83	-5	28	4.65	-3	0-57(22-0-39),1-21/C-1,D-1	4	-1.1
2000*Sea-A	92	140	21	32	8	0	2	15	14	25	2	0	.229	.303	.329	.632	64	-7	15	3.71	0	0-76(35-0-44)/D-4,1-3	1	-0.8
2001 KC-A	104	279	44	78	11	5	13	54	32	51	0	2	.280	.354	.495	.848	111	3	48	6.15	-1	0-42(17-2-24),D-33,1-10/3-1	9	-0.1
2002 KC-A	137	497	70	146	37	6	24	103	40	76	5	3	.294	.349	.537	.886	117	11	90	6.58	-5	0-55(42-0-16),1-49,D-36	14	-0.3
2003 KC-A	157	608	95	179	33	5	18	90	49	81	8	4	.294	.350	.454	.804	97	-3	96	5.73	0	*0-131(128-0-5),1-22,D-12	15	-1.1
Total 8	**629**	**1862**	**268**	**518**	**103**	**18**	**69**	**305**	**157**	**294**	**20**	**10**	**.278**	**.337**	**.464**	**.801**	**98**	**-8**	**289**	**5.54**	**-10**	**0-386,1-121/D-90,3-1,C-1**	**44**	**-4.4**

• INCAVIGLIA, Pete Peter Joseph Incaviglia b: 4/2/1964, Pebble Beach, CA BR/TR, 6'1", 230 lbs. Deb: 4/8/1986 Career OF: 825-37-189

YEAR TM-L	G	AB	R	H	2B	3B	HR	RBI	BB	SO	SB	CS	AVG	OBP	SLG	OPS	OPS+	BR/A	RC	RC/G	FR	G/POS	WS	TPW
1986 Tex-A	153	540	82	135	21	2	30	88	55	185	3	2	.250	.324	.463	.787	108	5	82	5.20	-4	*0-114(1-0-112),D-36	16	-0.5
1987 Tex-A	139	509	85	138	26	4	27	80	48	168	9	3	.271	.335	.497	.832	116	11	85	5.95	-1	*0-132(132-0-0)/D-6	16	0.4
1988 Tex-A	116	418	59	104	19	3	22	54	39	153	6	4	.249	.323	.467	.790	116	7	63	5.22	6	0-93(93-0-0),D-21	12	0.9
1989 Tex-A	133	453	48	107	27	4	21	81	32	136	5	7	.236	.295	.453	.748	106	-1	56	4.09	-1	*0-125(120-10-0)/D-5	14	-0.6
1990 Tex-A	153	529	59	123	27	0	24	85	45	146	3	4	.233	.304	.420	.723	100	-3	63	3.93	-1	*0-145(135-27-1)/D-2	12	-0.9
1991 Det-A	97	337	38	72	12	1	11	38	36	92	1	3	.214	.291	.353	.645	76	-12	35	3.38	1	0-54(50-0-4),D-41	2	-1.5
1992 Hou-N	113	349	31	93	22	1	11	44	25	99	2	2	.266	.321	.430	.751	116	5	47	4.81	1	0-98(57-0-48)	11	0.4
1993*Phi-N	116	368	60	101	16	3	24	89	21	82	1	1	.274	.324	.530	.854	126	11	60	5.75	-6	0-97(89-0-8)	14	0.1
1994 Phi-N	80	244	28	56	10	1	13	32	16	71	1	0	.230	.280	.439	.718	82	-8	30	4.18	-3	0-63(63-0-0)	3	-1.3
1996 Phi-N	99	269	33	63	7	2	16	42	30	82	2	0	.234	.318	.454	.771	99	-1	39	4.98	-3	0-71(70-0-2)	5	-0.6
*Bal-A	12	33	4	10	2	0	2	8	0	7	0	0	.303	.324	.545	.869	115	0	6	6.64	0	/0-7(7-0-0),D-4	1	0.0
1997 Bal-A	48	138	18	34	4	0	5	12	11	43	0	0	.246	.316	.384	.700	84	-3	17	4.43	-1	D-26,0-18(4-0-14)	1	-0.6
NY-A	5	16	1	4	0	0	0	0	0	3	0	0	.250	.250	.250	.500	31	-2	1	2.25	0	/D-5	0	-0.2
Yr.	53	154	19	38	4	0	5	12	11	46	0	0	.247	.310	.370	.680	79	-5	18	4.21	-1	D-31,0-18(4-0-14)	1	-0.7
1998 Det-A	7	14	0	1	0	0	0	0	1	6	0	0	.071	.133	.071	.205	-44	-3	0	.35	0	/D-4,0-1	0	-0.3
*Hou-N	13	16	0	2	1	0	0	2	1	4	0	0	.125	.176	.188	.364	-4	-2	0	.69	0	/0-3(3-0-0)	0	-0.3
Total 12	**1284**	**4233**	**546**	**1043**	**194**	**21**	**206**	**655**	**360**	**1277**	**33**	**26**	**.246**	**.312**	**.448**	**.760**	**104**	**6**	**585**	**4.73**	**-13**	***0-1021,D-150**	**107**	**-4.9**

• INFANTE, Alexis Fermin Alexis (Carpio) Infante b: 12/4/1961, Barquisimeto, Venezuela BR/TR, 5'10", 175 lbs. Deb: 9/27/1987

YEAR TM-L	G	AB	R	H	2B	3B	HR	RBI	BB	SO	SB	CS	AVG	OBP	SLG	OPS	OPS+	BR/A	RC	RC/G	FR	G/POS	WS	TPW
1987 Tor-A	1	0	0	0	0	0	0	0	0	0	0	0	....	....	....	....	-98	0	0	....	0	....	0	0.0
1988 Tor-A	19	15	7	3	0	0	0	0	2	4	0	0	.200	.294	.200	.494	41	-1	1	1.72	-1	/3-9,D-7,S-2	0	-0.2
1989 Tor-A	20	12	1	2	0	0	0	0	0	1	1	0	.167	.167	.167	.333	-6	-1	0	1.15	-1	/S-9,3-4,D-4,2-1	0	-0.3
1990 Atl-N	20	28	3	1	1	0	0	0	0	7	0	0	.036	.069	.071	.140	-58	-6	0	.00	-1	2-10/3-4,S-3	0	-0.7
Total 4	**60**	**55**	**11**	**6**	**1**	**0**	**0**	**0**	**2**	**12**	**1**	**0**	**.109**	**.155**	**.127**	**.282**	**-20**	**-9**	**1**	**.62**	**-4**	**/3-17,S-14,2-11,D-11**	**0**	**-1.2**

• INFANTE, Omar Omar R. Infante b: 12/26/1981, Puerto la Cruz, Venezuela BR/TR, 6', 150 lbs. Deb: 9/7/2002

YEAR TM-L	G	AB	R	H	2B	3B	HR	RBI	BB	SO	SB	CS	AVG	OBP	SLG	OPS	OPS+	BR/A	RC	RC/G	FR	G/POS	WS	TPW
2002 Det-A	18	72	4	24	3	0	1	6	3	10	0	1	.333	.360	.417	.777	112	1	11	5.88	1	S-16/2-2	3	0.2
2003 Det-A	69	221	24	49	6	1	0	8	18	37	6	3	.222	.280	.258	.538	47	-17	17	2.60	12	S-63/3-4,2-2	3	0.1
Total 2	**87**	**293**	**28**	**73**	**9**	**1**	**1**	**14**	**21**	**47**	**6**	**4**	**.249**	**.299**	**.297**	**.596**	**62**	**-16**	**28**	**3.30**	**13**	**/S-79,2-4,3-4**	**6**	**0.3**

• INGE, Brandon Charles Brandon Inge b: 5/19/1977, Lynchburg, VA BR/TR, 5'11", 185 lbs. Deb: 4/3/2001

YEAR TM-L	G	AB	R	H	2B	3B	HR	RBI	BB	SO	SB	CS	AVG	OBP	SLG	OPS	OPS+	BR/A	RC	RC/G	FR	G/POS	WS	TPW
2001 Det-A	79	189	13	34	11	0	0	15	9	41	1	4	.180	.217	.238	.455	21	-24	9	1.50	2	C-79	3	-1.6
2002 Det-A	95	321	27	65	15	3	7	24	24	101	1	3	.202	.266	.333	.600	62	-19	27	2.76	2	C-94/D-1	5	-1.0
2003 Det-A	104	330	32	67	15	3	8	30	24	79	4	4	.203	.267	.339	.607	63	-19	29	2.75	14	*C-104	4	0.2
Total 3	**278**	**840**	**72**	**166**	**41**	**6**	**15**	**69**	**57**	**221**	**6**	**11**	**.198**	**.256**	**.314**	**.570**	**53**	**-62**	**65**	**2.47**	**18**	**C-277/D-1**	**12**	**-2.4**

• INGERTON, Scotty William John Ingerton b: 4/19/1886, Peninsula, OH d: 6/15/1956, Cleveland, OH BR/TR, 6'1", 172 lbs. Deb: 4/12/1911

YEAR TM-L	G	AB	R	H	2B	3B	HR	RBI	BB	SO	SB	CS	AVG	OBP	SLG	OPS	OPS+	BR/A	RC	RC/G	FR	G/POS	WS	TPW
1911 Bos-N	136	521	63	130	24	4	5	61	39	68	6	....	.250	.304	.340	.644	74	-20	55	3.55	10	3-58,0-43(43-0-2),1-17,2-11/S	7	-1.1

• INGRAHAM, Charlie Charles W. Ingraham b: 4/8/1860, IL d: 2/18/1906, Chicago, IL, 5'11", 170 lbs. Deb: 7/4/1883

YEAR TM-L	G	AB	R	H	2B	3B	HR	RBI	BB	SO	SB	CS	AVG	OBP	SLG	OPS	OPS+	BR/A	RC	RC/G	FR	G/POS	WS	TPW
1883 Bal-a	1	4	0	1	0	0	0	0	0	....	....	....	.250	.250	.250	.500	60	-0	0	2.39	-1	/C-1	0	-0.1

YEAR TM-L	G	AB	R	H	2B	3B	HR	RBI	BB	SO	SB	CS	AVG	OBP	SLG	OPS	OPS+	BR/A	RC	RC/G	FR	G/POS	WS	TPW
• INGRAM, Garey	Garey Lamar Ingram b: 7/25/1970, Columbus, GA BR/TR, 5'11", 180 lbs. Deb: 5/15/1994 Career OF: 10-1-0																							
1994 LA-N	26	78	10	22	1	0	3	8	7	22	0	0	.282	.341	.410	.751	101	0	10	4.57	1	2-23	2	0.2
1995 LA-N	44	55	5	11	2	0	0	3	9	8	3	0	.200	.313	.236	.549	52	-3	5	3.19	-4	3-12/2-7,0-4(4-0-0)	1	-0.7
1997 LA-N	12	9	2	4	1	0	0	1	1	3	1	0	.444	.500	.556	1.056	191	1	3	15.61	0	/0-7(6-1-0)	1	0.1
Total 3	82	142	17	37	4	0	3	12	17	33	4	0	.261	.340	.352	.692	87	-1	18	4.49	-4	/2-30,3-12,0-11	4	-0.4
• INGRAM, Mel	Melvin David Ingram b: 7/4/1904, Asheville, NC d: 10/28/1979, Medford, OR BR/TR, 5'11.5", 175 lbs. Deb: 7/24/1929																							
1929 Pit-N	3	0	1	0	0	0	0	0	0	0	0	....	....	....	....	....	-98	0	0	....	0	....	0	0.0
• INGRAM, Riccardo	Riccardo Benay Ingram b: 9/10/1966, Douglas, GA BR/TR, 6', 205 lbs. Deb: 6/26/1994																							
1994 Det-A	12	23	3	5	0	0	0	2	1	2	0	1	.217	.250	.217	.467	22	-3	1	1.56	1	/0-8(7-1-0),D-1	0	-0.3
1995 Min-A	4	8	0	1	0	0	0	1	2	1	0	0	.125	.300	.125	.425	16	-1	0	1.03	0	/D-3	0	-0.1
Total 2	16	31	3	6	0	0	0	3	3	3	0	1	.194	.265	.194	.458	20	-4	1	1.41	1	/0-8,D-4	0	-0.3
• IORG, Dane	Dane Charles Iorg b: 5/11/1950, Eureka, CA BL/TR, 6', 180 lbs. Deb: 4/9/1977 Career OF: 223-0-124																							
1977 Phi-N	12	30	3	5	1	0	0	2	1	3	0	0	.167	.194	.200	.394	6	-4	1	1.31	0	/1-9	0	-0.5
StL-N	30	32	2	10	1	0	0	4	5	4	0	1	.313	.405	.344	.749	105	0	4	4.74	0	/0-7(4-0-3)	1	0.0
Yr.	42	62	5	15	2	0	0	6	6	7	0	1	.242	.309	.274	.583	60	-4	6	3.02	-1	/1-9,0-7(4-0-3)	1	-0.5
1978 StL-N	35	85	6	23	4	1	0	4	4	10	0	0	.271	.303	.341	.645	81	-2	8	3.50	2	0-25(8-0-18)	2	-0.1
1979 StL-N	79	179	12	52	11	1	1	21	12	28	1	2	.291	.339	.380	.718	95	-2	22	4.29	-1	0-39(22-0-20),1-10	4	-0.5
1980 StL-N	105	251	33	76	23	1	3	36	20	34	1	1	.303	.354	.438	.792	116	5	38	5.60	-2	0-63(49-0-14)/1-5,3-1	8	0.0
1981 StL-N	75	217	23	71	11	2	2	39	7	9	2	0	.327	.348	.424	.772	115	4	30	5.22	-3	0-57(46-0-14)/1-8,3-2	7	-0.1
1982*StL-N	102	238	17	70	14	1	0	34	23	23	0	1	.294	.356	.361	.718	100	0	28	4.20	-1	0-63(47-0-17),1-10/3-2	6	-0.4
1983 StL-N	58	116	6	31	9	1	0	11	10	11	1	0	.267	.331	.362	.693	92	-1	13	3.67	-2	0-22(10-0-13),1-11	2	-0.5
1984 StL-N	15	28	3	4	2	0	0	3	2	6	0	0	.143	.200	.214	.414	17	-3	1	.87	0	/1-6,0-5(3-0-2)	0	-0.4
*KC-A	78	235	27	60	16	2	5	30	13	15	0	1	.255	.294	.404	.699	90	-4	26	3.68	-3	1-43,0-22(18-0-4)/D-5,3-1	4	-1.1
1985*KC-A	64	130	7	29	9	1	1	21	8	16	0	1	.223	.268	.331	.599	63	-7	10	2.42	0	0-32(13-0-19)/1-2,D-2,3-1	1	-0.8
1986 SD-N	90	106	10	24	2	1	2	11	2	21	0	0	.226	.241	.321	.561	55	-7	8	2.45	-2	1-10/3-6,0-3(3-0-0),P-2	0	-1.2
Total 10	743	1647	149	455	103	11	14	216	107	180	5	7	.276	.321	.378	.699	92	-22	190	4.00	-13	0-338,1-114/3-13,D-7,P-2	35	-5.7
• IORG, Garth	Garth Ray Iorg b: 10/12/1954, Arcata, CA BR/TR, 5'11", 170 lbs. Deb: 4/9/1978																							
1978 Tor-A	19	49	3	8	0	0	0	3	3	4	0	0	.163	.226	.163	.390	11	-6	2	.97	-1	2-18	1	-0.5
1980 Tor-A	80	222	24	55	10	1	2	14	12	39	2	1	.248	.286	.329	.615	65	-11	20	3.11	4	2-32,3-20,0-14(13-1-0),1-11/D,S	4	-0.6
1981 Tor-A	70	215	17	52	11	0	0	10	7	31	2	3	.242	.269	.293	.562	58	-13	16	2.54	0	2-46,3-17/S-2,1-1,D-1	2	-1.1
1982 Tor-A	129	417	45	119	20	5	1	36	12	38	3	2	.285	.312	.365	.676	78	-13	47	3.99	-6	*3-100,2-30/D-1	9	-1.8
1983 Tor-A	122	375	40	103	22	5	2	39	13	45	7	0	.275	.301	.376	.677	80	-10	41	3.83	-4	3-85,2-39/S-1	7	-1.3
1984 Tor-A	121	247	24	56	10	3	1	25	5	16	1	3	.227	.245	.304	.549	49	-19	16	2.11	-4	*3-112/2-7,S-2,D-1	2	-2.3
1985*Tor-A	131	288	33	90	22	1	7	37	21	26	3	6	.313	.359	.469	.828	122	6	45	5.74	1	*3-104,2-23	11	0.7
1986 Tor-A	137	327	30	85	19	1	3	44	20	47	3	0	.260	.305	.352	.656	76	-10	35	3.73	-5	3-90,2-52/S-2	6	-1.4
1987 Tor-A	122	310	35	65	11	0	4	30	21	52	2	2	.210	.264	.284	.548	45	-26	23	2.33	-6	2-91,3-28/D-5	3	-2.6
Total 9	931	2450	251	633	125	16	20	238	114	298	23	17	.258	.294	.347	.641	72	-100	244	3.42	-20	3-556,2-338/0-14,1-12,D-10,S	45	-11.0
• IOTT, Happy	Frederick "Happy Jack,Biddo" Iott b: 7/7/1876, Houlton, ME d: 2/17/1941, Island Falls, ME BR/TR, 5'10", 175 lbs. Deb: 9/16/1903																							
1903 Cle-A	3	10	1	2	0	0	0	0	2	....	1	....	.200	.333	.200	.533	64	-0	1	3.40	0	/0-3(0-3-0)	0	-0.1
• IRELAN, Hal	Harold "Grump" Irelan b: 8/5/1890, Burnettsville, IN d: 7/16/1944, Carmel, IN BB/TR, 5'7", 165 lbs. Deb: 4/23/1914																							
1914 Phi-N	67	165	16	39	8	0	1	16	21	22	3	....	.236	.326	.303	.629	82	-3	17	3.37	-4	2-44/S-3,1-2,3-2	4	-0.7
• IRELAND, Tim	Timothy Neal Christopher Ireland b: 3/14/1953, Oakland, CA BR/TR, 6', 180 lbs. Deb: 9/20/1981																							
1981 KC-A	4	0	1	0	0	0	0	0	0	0	0	1	....	....	....	....	-101	-0	0	.00	0	/1-4	0	-0.1
1982 KC-A	7	7	2	1	0	0	0	0	1	1	0	0	.143	.250	.143	.393	11	-1	0	1.42	-1	/2-4,0-2(0-0-2),3-1	0	-0.2
Total 2	11	7	3	1	0	0	0	0	1	1	0	1	.143	.250	.143	.393	11	-1	0	1.22	-1	/1-4,2-4,0-2,3-1	0	-0.2
• IRVIN, Monte	Montford Merrill Irvin b: 2/25/1919, Columbus, AL BR/TR, 6'1", 195 lbs. Deb: 7/8/1949 HOF: 1973 Career OF: 507-1-87																							
1949 NY-N	36	76	7	17	3	2	0	7	17	11	0	....	.224	.366	.316	.681	84	-1	10	4.33	2	0-10(0-0-10)/1-5,3-5	2	0.1
1950 NY-N	110	374	61	112	19	5	15	66	52	41	3	....	.299	.392	.497	.889	131	18	76	7.55	4	1-59,0-49(20-0-30)/3-1	16	1.7
1951*NY-N	151	558	94	174	19	11	24	**121**	89	44	12	2	.312	.415	.514	.929	147	43	127	8.51	7	*0-112(89-0-27),1-39	29	4.1
1952 NY-N★	46	126	10	39	2	1	4	21	10	11	0	1	.310	.365	.437	.801	120	3	20	5.90	1	0-32(30-1-1)	5	0.3
1953 NY-N	124	444	72	146	21	5	21	97	55	34	2	0	.329	.406	.541	.947	142	29	96	8.16	3	*0-113(102-0-13)	18	2.4
1954*NY-N	135	432	62	113	13	3	19	64	70	23	7	4	.262	.367	.438	.805	108	7	69	5.31	2	*0-128(126-0-2)/1-1,3-1	14	0.0
1955 NY-N	51	150	16	38	7	1	1	17	17	15	3	0	.253	.341	.333	.675	80	-3	18	4.02	1	0-45(44-0-4)	3	-0.5
1956 Chi-N	111	339	44	92	13	3	15	50	41	41	1	0	.271	.350	.460	.810	118	9	53	5.44	9	0-96(96-0-0)	11	1.3
Total 8	764	2499	366	731	97	31	99	443	351	220	28	7	.293	.385	.475	.860	126	104	468	6.73	29	0-585,1-104/3-7	98	9.4
• IRWIN, Arthur	Arthur Albert "Doc,Sandy" Irwin b: 2/14/1858, Toronto, Canada d: 7/16/1921, Atlantic Ocean BL/TR, 5'8.5", 158 lbs. Deb: 5/1/1880 M/U																							
1880 Wor-N	85	352	53	91	19	4	1	35	11	27	....	....	.259	.281	.344	.625	102	-0	35	3.67	29	*S-82/3-3,C-1	13	3.1
1881 Wor-N	50	206	27	55	8	2	0	24	7	4	....	....	.267	.291	.325	.616	88	-3	20	3.57	-12	S-50	5	-1.2
1882 Wor-N	84	333	30	73	12	4	0	30	14	34	....	....	.219	.251	.279	.530	68	-12	24	2.53	5	3-51,S-33	4	-0.4
1883 Pro-N	98	406	67	116	22	7	0	44	12	38	....	....	.286	.306	.374	.681	103	1	48	4.52	-10	*S-94/2-4	13	-0.5
1884*Pro-N	102	404	73	97	14	3	2	44	28	52	....	....	.240	.289	.304	.594	89	-4	36	3.27	10	*S-102/P-1	14	0.8
1885 Pro-N	59	218	16	39	2	1	0	14	14	29	....	....	.179	.228	.197	.426	40	-13	10	1.52	3	S-58/2-1,3-1	3	-0.8
1886 Phi-N	101	373	51	87	6	6	0	34	35	39	24	....	.233	.299	.282	.581	76	-10	40	3.73	7	*S-100/3-1	12	0.1
1887 Phi-N	100	422	65	143	14	8	2	56	48	26	19	....	.339	.344	.350	.694	88	-5	53	5.02	-2	*S-100	12	-0.4
1888 Phi-N	125	448	51	98	12	4	0	28	33	56	19	....	.219	.277	.263	.540	69	-15	39	3.00	8	*S-122/2-3	12	-0.3
1889 Phi-N	18	73	9	16	5	0	0	10	6	6	6	....	.219	.278	.288	.566	54	-5	8	3.58	-4	S-18	1	-0.7
Was-N	85	313	49	73	10	5	0	32	42	37	9	....	.233	.326	.297	.623	79	-6	34	3.76	5	S-85/2-1,P-1	7	0.1
Yr.	103	386	58	89	15	5	0	42	48	43	15	....	.231	.317	.295	.613	75	-11	42	3.73	1	*S-103/2-1,P-1	8	-0.6
1890 Bos-P	96	354	60	92	17	1	0	45	57	29	16	....	.260	.364	.314	.678	77	-11	47	4.88	0	*S-96	11	-0.6
1891 Bos-a	6	17	1	2	0	0	0	0	2	1	0	....	.118	.286	.118	.403	16	-2	1	1.03	-1	/S-6	0	-0.3
1894 Phi-N	1	0	0	0	0	0	0	0	0	0	0	....	....	....	....	....	-103	0	0	....	-1	/S-1	0	0.0
Total 13	1010	3919	552	982	141	45	5	396	309	378	93	....	.251	.299	.305	.604	80	-86	394	3.63	36	S-947/3-56,2-9,P-2,C-1	107	-1.1
• IRWIN, Charlie	Charles Edwin Irwin b: 2/15/1869, Clinton, IL d: 9/21/1925, Chicago, IL BL/TR, 5'10", 160 lbs. Deb: 9/3/1893																							
1893 Chi-N	21	82	14	25	6	2	0	13	10	1	4	....	.305	.394	.427	.820	120	3	16	7.32	3	S-21	3	0.5
1894 Chi-N	130	504	85	149	25	9	8	100	64	23	35	....	.296	.385	.429	.813	91	-8	99	7.25	-7	3-67,S-61	11	-0.8
1895 Chi-N	3	10	4	2	0	0	0	0	2	1	0	....	.200	.333	.200	.533	37	-1	1	2.31	0	/S-3	0	0.0
1896 Cin-N	127	476	77	141	16	6	1	67	26	17	31	....	.296	.338	.361	.699	79	-16	71	5.49	11	*3-127	15	-0.2
1897 Cin-N	134	505	89	146	26	6	0	74	47	....	27	....	.289	.360	.364	.724	86	-10	79	5.69	0	*3-134	17	-0.7
1898 Cin-N	136	501	77	120	14	5	3	55	31	....	18	....	.240	.297	.305	.602	68	-22	54	3.61	17	*3-136	13	-0.3
1899 Cin-N	90	314	42	73	4	8	1	52	26	....	26	....	.232	.295	.306	.601	64	-16	38	4.03	-5	3-78/S-6,2-3,1-1	6	-1.8
1900 Cin-N	87	333	59	91	15	6	1	44	14	....	9	....	.273	.314	.363	.678	89	-6	43	4.53	-14	3-61,S-16/0-6(1-0-5),2-3	8	-1.7
1901 Cin-N	67	260	25	62	12	2	0	25	14	....	13	....	.238	.285	.300	.585	75	-8	27	3.55	2	3-67	5	-0.4
Bro-N	65	242	25	52	13	2	0	20	14	....	4	....	.215	.269	.285	.554	59	-13	21	2.82	-3	3-65	3	-1.3
Yr.	132	502	50	114	25	4	0	45	28	....	17	....	.227	.277	.293	.570	67	-21	48	3.19	-1	*3-132	8	-1.8
1902 Bro-N	131	458	59	125	14	0	2	43	39	....	13	....	.273	.346	.317	.662	104	4	58	4.44	0	*3-130/S-1	18	0.8
Total 10	991	3685	556	986	145	46	16	493	287	42	180	....	.268	.331	.345	.676	82	-94	506	4.82	4	3-865,S-108/2-6,0-6,1-1	99	-6.0
• IRWIN, Ed	William Edward Irwin b: 1882, Philadelphia, PA d: 2/5/1916, Philadelphia, PA BR/TR Deb: 5/18/1912																							
1912 Det-A	1	3	0	2	0	2	0	0	0	....	0	....	.667	.667	2.000	2.667	675	2	4	103.40	0	/3-1	1	0.2

• IRWIN, John — John Irwin b: 7/21/1861, Toronto, Canada d: 2/28/1934, Boston, MA BL/TR, 5'10", 168 lbs. Deb: 5/31/1882 U

YEAR TM-L	G	AB	R	H	2B	3B	HR	RBI	BB	SO	SB	CS	AVG	OBP	SLG	OPS	OPS+	BR/A	RC	RC/G	FR	G/POS	WS	TPW
1882 Wor-N	1	4	0	0	0	0	0	0	0	2	....	....	.000	.000	.000	.000	-98	-1	0	.00	-1	/1-1	0	-0.2
1884 Bos-U	105	432	81	101	22	6	1	....	15	....	....	....	.234	.260	.319	.579	96	-1	37	3.11	2	*3-105	13	0.3
1886 Phi-a	3	13	4	3	1	0	0	1	0	....	0	....	.231	.231	.308	.538	68	-1	1	2.55	0	/S-2,3-1	0	0.0
1887 Was-N	8	34	6	14	2	0	2	3	3	6	6	....	.412	.429	.613	1.041	196	4	11	14.55	0	/S-5,3-4	2	0.3
1888 Was-N	37	126	14	28	5	2	0	8	5	18	15	....	.222	.263	.294	.557	82	-2	14	3.86	0	S-27,3-10	4	-0.1
1889 Was-N	58	228	42	66	11	4	0	25	25	14	10	....	.289	.370	.373	.742	115	6	36	5.89	-2	3-58	6	0.4
1890 Buf-P	77	308	62	72	11	4	0	34	43	19	18	....	.234	.335	.295	.631	75	-8	37	4.28	4	3-64,1-12/2-1	5	-0.2
1891 Bos-a	19	72	6	16	2	2	0	15	6	9	6	....	.222	.282	.306	.588	69	-3	8	3.83	1	0-17(9-0-9)/3-2,S-1	1	-0.2
Lou-a	14	55	7	15	1	1	0	7	5	6	1	....	.273	.344	.327	.672	93	-0	7	4.44	-3	3-14	1	-0.3
Yr.	33	127	13	31	3	3	0	22	11	15	7	....	.244	.309	.315	.624	80	-4	15	4.09	-2	0-17(9-0-9),3-16/S-1	2	-0.5
Total 8	322	1272	222	315	55	19	3	93	102	74	56	....	.248	.308	.326	.634	93	-7	151	4.26	1	3-258/S-35,0-17,1-13,2-1	32	0.0

• IRWIN, Tommy — Thomas Andrew Irwin b: 12/20/1912, Altoona, PA d: 4/25/1996, Altoona, PA BR/TR, 5'11", 165 lbs. Deb: 10/1/1938

YEAR TM-L	G	AB	R	H	2B	3B	HR	RBI	BB	SO	SB	CS	AVG	OBP	SLG	OPS	OPS+	BR/A	RC	RC/G	FR	G/POS	WS	TPW
1938 Cle-A	3	9	1	1	0	0	0	0	3	1	0	0	.111	.333	.111	.444	16	-1	1	1.89	1	/S-3	0	0.0

• IRWIN, Walt — Walter Kingsley Irwin b: 9/23/1897, Henrietta, PA d: 8/18/1976, Spring Lake, MI BR/TR, 5'10.5", 170 lbs. Deb: 4/24/1921

YEAR TM-L	G	AB	R	H	2B	3B	HR	RBI	BB	SO	SB	CS	AVG	OBP	SLG	OPS	OPS+	BR/A	RC	RC/G	FR	G/POS	WS	TPW
1921 StL-N	4	1	1	0	0	0	0	0	0	1	0	0	.000	.000	.000	.000	-102	-0	0	.00	0	....	0	0.0

• ISALES, Orlando — Orlando (Pizarro) Isales b: 12/22/1959, Santurce, Puerto Rico BR/TR, 5'9", 175 lbs. Deb: 9/11/1980

YEAR TM-L	G	AB	R	H	2B	3B	HR	RBI	BB	SO	SB	CS	AVG	OBP	SLG	OPS	OPS+	BR/A	RC	RC/G	FR	G/POS	WS	TPW
1980 Phi-N	3	5	1	2	0	1	0	3	1	0	0	0	.400	.500	.800	1.300	244	1	2	19.17	0	/O-2(0-0-2)	1	0.1

• ISBELL, Frank — William Frank "Bald Eagle" Isbell b: 8/21/1875, Delevan, NY d: 7/15/1941, Wichita, KS BL/TR, 5'11", 190 lbs. Deb: 5/1/1898 Career OF: 15-33-54

YEAR TM-L	G	AB	R	H	2B	3B	HR	RBI	BB	SO	SB	CS	AVG	OBP	SLG	OPS	OPS+	BR/A	RC	RC/G	FR	G/POS	WS	TPW
1898 Chi-N	45	159	17	37	4	0	0	8	3	....	3	....	.233	.252	.258	.509	46	-9	12	2.49	-3	0-28(4-12-11),P-13/2-3,3-3,S	4	-1.2
1901 Chi-A	137	556	93	143	15	8	3	70	36	....	**52**	....	.257	.311	.329	.640	79	-15	76	4.74	12	*1-137/2-2,3-1,P-1,S-1	13	-0.5
1902 Chi-A	137	515	62	130	14	4	4	59	14	....	38	....	.252	.276	.318	.595	67	-24	59	3.86	12	*1-133/S-4,C-1,P-1	9	-1.4
1903 Chi-A	138	546	52	132	25	9	2	59	12	....	26	....	.242	.266	.332	.597	82	-13	59	3.56	10	*1-117,3-19/2-2,0-1,S-1	9	-0.5
1904 Chi-A	96	314	27	66	10	3	1	34	16	....	19	....	.210	.255	.271	.526	69	-11	29	2.90	-0	1-57,2-27/0-5(0-0-5),S-4	5	-1.3
1905 Chi-A	94	341	55	101	21	11	2	45	15	....	15	....	.296	.335	.440	.775	151	18	59	5.85	0	2-43,0-41(2-5-34)/1-9,S-2	17	1.8
1906*Chi-A	143	549	71	153	18	11	0	57	30	....	37	....	.279	.324	.352	.676	114	8	80	4.95	-26	*2-132,0-14(4-7-3)/C-1,P-1	26	-1.7
1907 Chi-A	125	486	60	118	19	7	0	41	22	....	22	....	.243	.281	.311	.592	92	-6	52	3.55	-10	*2-119/0-5(5-0-0),P-1,S-1	15	-1.7
1908 Chi-A	84	320	31	79	15	3	1	49	19	....	18	....	.247	.297	.322	.619	103	1	36	3.66	3	1-65,2-18	12	0.3
1909 Chi-A	120	433	33	97	17	6	0	33	23	....	23	....	.224	.265	.291	.556	79	-12	40	2.88	7	*1-101/0-9(0-9-0),2-5	9	-0.8
Total 10	1119	4219	501	1056	158	62	13	455	190	....	253	....	.250	.289	.326	.616	90	-63	502	3.95	7	1-619,2-351,0-103/3-23,P,S,C	119	-7.0

• IVIE, Mike — Michael Wilson Ivie b: 8/8/1952, Atlanta, GA BR/TR, 6'3", 205 lbs. Deb: 9/4/1971 Career OF: 46-0-0

YEAR TM-L	G	AB	R	H	2B	3B	HR	RBI	BB	SO	SB	CS	AVG	OBP	SLG	OPS	OPS+	BR/A	RC	RC/G	FR	G/POS	WS	TPW
1971 SD-N	6	17	0	8	0	0	0	3	1	1	0	0	.471	.526	.471	.997	197	2	3	6.85	0	/C-6	1	0.3
1974 SD-N	12	34	1	3	0	0	1	3	2	8	0	0	.088	.139	.176	.315	-13	-5	1	.79	0	1-11	0	-0.6
1975 SD-N	111	377	36	94	16	2	8	46	20	63	4	4	.249	.294	.366	.660	88	-9	37	3.27	-8	1-78,3-61/C-1	6	-2.3
1976 SD-N	140	405	51	118	19	5	7	70	30	41	6	6	.291	.348	.415	.763	126	11	56	4.87	-1	*1-135/3-2,C-2	15	0.2
1977 SD-N	134	489	66	133	29	2	9	66	39	57	3	2	.272	.328	.395	.723	104	1	64	4.69	-6	*1-105,3-25	15	-1.1
1978 SF-N	117	318	34	98	14	3	11	55	27	45	3	0	.308	.366	.475	.841	139	16	55	6.47	-8	1-76,0-22(22-0-0)	14	0.4
1979 SF-N	133	402	58	115	18	3	27	89	47	80	5	1	.286	.362	.547	.909	155	30	79	7.04	-4	1-98,0-24(24-0-0)/3-4,2-1	22	2.1
1980 SF-N	79	286	21	69	16	1	4	25	19	40	1	2	.241	.289	.346	.635	78	-10	27	3.21	-4	1-72	5	-1.9
1981 SF-N	7	17	1	5	2	0	0	3	0	1	0	0	.294	.294	.412	.706	100	-0	2	4.34	0	/1-5	1	0.0
Hou-N	19	42	2	10	3	0	0	6	2	11	0	1	.238	.273	.310	.582	68	-2	3	2.73	2	1-10	0	0.0
Yr.	26	59	3	15	5	0	0	9	2	12	0	1	.254	.279	.339	.618	77	-2	6	3.17	3	1-15	1	0.0
1982 Hou-N	7	6	0	2	0	0	0	0	1	0	0	0	.333	.429	.333	.762	125	0	1	6.54	0	....	0	0.0
Det-A	80	259	35	60	12	1	14	38	24	51	0	0	.232	.302	.448	.750	102	0	35	4.53	0	D-79	5	-0.2
1983 Det-A	12	42	4	9	4	0	0	7	2	4	0	0	.214	.250	.310	.560	54	-3	3	2.07	0	1-12	0	-0.3
Total 11	857	2694	309	724	133	17	81	411	214	402	22	16	.269	.326	.421	.747	112	32	366	4.75	-27	1-602/3-92,D-79,0-46,C-9,2	84	-3.3

• IZQUIERDO, Hank — Enrique Roberto (Valdes) Izquierdo b: 3/20/1931, Matanzas, Cuba BR/TR, 5'11", 175 lbs. Deb: 8/9/1967

YEAR TM-L	G	AB	R	H	2B	3B	HR	RBI	BB	SO	SB	CS	AVG	OBP	SLG	OPS	OPS+	BR/A	RC	RC/G	FR	G/POS	WS	TPW
1967 Min-A	16	26	4	7	2	0	0	2	1	2	0	0	.269	.296	.346	.642	82	-1	3	3.77	0	C-16	1	0.0

• IZTURIS, Cesar — Cesar D. Izturis b: 2/10/1980, Barquisimeto, Venezuela BB/TR, 5'9", 155 lbs. Deb: 6/23/2001

YEAR TM-L	G	AB	R	H	2B	3B	HR	RBI	BB	SO	SB	CS	AVG	OBP	SLG	OPS	OPS+	BR/A	RC	RC/G	FR	G/POS	WS	TPW
2001 Tor-A	46	134	19	36	6	2	2	9	2	15	8	1	.269	.279	.388	.667	72	-5	16	4.07	-3	2-41/S-6	4	-0.6
2002 LA-N	135	439	43	102	24	2	1	31	14	39	7	7	.232	.256	.303	.559	50	-35	31	2.23	-4	*S-128/2-1,D-1	4	-3.0
2003 LA-N	158	558	47	140	21	6	1	40	25	70	10	5	.251	.283	.315	.598	59	-35	49	2.99	4	*S-158	11	-1.8
Total 3	339	1131	109	278	51	10	4	80	41	124	25	13	.246	.272	.319	.591	57	-74	95	2.81	-4	S-292/2-42,D-1	19	-5.3

• JABLONSKI, Ray — Raymond Leo "Jabbo" Jablonski b: 12/17/1926, Chicago, IL d: 11/25/1985, Chicago, IL BR/TR, 5'10", 183 lbs. Deb: 4/14/1953 Career OF: 29-0-0

YEAR TM-L	G	AB	R	H	2B	3B	HR	RBI	BB	SO	SB	CS	AVG	OBP	SLG	OPS	OPS+	BR/A	RC	RC/G	FR	G/POS	WS	TPW
1953 StL-N	157	604	64	162	23	5	21	112	34	61	2	2	.268	.308	.427	.735	89	-12	77	4.54	-13	*3-157	11	-2.4
1954 StL-N★	152	611	80	181	33	3	12	104	49	42	9	4	.296	.350	.419	.769	99	-1	88	5.11	-19	*3-149/1-1	14	-2.0
1955 Cin-N	74	221	28	53	9	0	9	28	13	35	0	1	.240	.291	.403	.694	77	-8	25	3.88	-2	3-28,0-28(28-0-0)	3	-1.1
1956 Cin-N	130	407	42	104	25	1	15	66	37	57	2	4	.256	.328	.432	.761	96	-3	54	4.45	-9	*3-127/2-1	9	-1.3
1957 NY-N	107	305	37	88	15	1	9	57	31	47	0	2	.289	.354	.433	.787	110	4	46	5.23	4	3-70/1-6,0-1	9	0.7
1958 SF-N	82	230	28	53	15	1	12	46	17	50	2	0	.230	.289	.461	.750	97	-2	27	3.89	-6	3-57	4	-0.8
1959 StL-N	60	87	11	22	4	0	3	14	8	19	1	0	.253	.316	.402	.718	84	-2	11	4.20	-1	3-19/S-1	1	-0.3
KC-A	25	65	4	17	1	0	2	8	3	11	0	0	.262	.294	.369	.663	79	-2	7	4.10	0	3-17	1	-0.2
1960 KC-A	21	32	3	7	1	0	0	3	4	8	0	0	.219	.306	.250	.556	52	-2	3	2.58	0	/3-6	0	-0.2
Total 8	808	2562	297	687	126	11	83	438	196	330	16	13	.268	.324	.423	.747	94	-28	338	4.57	-45	3-630/0-29,1-7,2-1,S-1	52	-7.6

• JACKLITSCH, Fred — Frederick Lawrence Jacklitsch b: 5/24/1876, Brooklyn, NY d: 7/18/1937, Brooklyn, NY BR/TR, 5'9", 180 lbs. Deb: 6/6/1900 U Career OF: 0-2-1

YEAR TM-L	G	AB	R	H	2B	3B	HR	RBI	BB	SO	SB	CS	AVG	OBP	SLG	OPS	OPS+	BR/A	RC	RC/G	FR	G/POS	WS	TPW
1900 Phi-N	5	11	0	2	1	0	0	3	0	....	0	....	.182	.182	.273	.455	25	-1	1	1.65	0	/C-3	0	-0.1
1901 Phi-N	33	120	14	30	4	3	0	24	12	....	2	....	.250	.328	.333	.662	90	-1	14	4.16	0	C-30/3-1	4	0.2
1902 Phi-N	38	114	8	23	4	0	0	8	9	....	2	....	.202	.278	.237	.515	59	-5	8	2.42	-3	C-29/0-1	1	-0.6
1903 Bro-N	60	176	31	47	8	3	1	21	33	....	4	....	.267	.389	.364	.752	118	6	27	5.55	-3	C-53/2-1,0-1	7	0.8
1904 Bro-N	26	77	8	18	3	1	0	8	7	....	7	....	.234	.322	.299	.621	94	-0	10	4.34	-4	1-11/2-8,C-5	2	-0.4
1905 NY-A	1	3	1	0	0	0	0	0	1	....	0	....	.000	.250	.000	.250	-17	-0	0	.00	0	/C-1	0	0.0
1907 Phi-N	73	202	19	43	7	0	0	17	27	....	7	....	.213	.312	.248	.559	76	-4	18	2.98	11	C-58/1-6,0-1	8	1.4
1908 Phi-N	37	86	6	19	3	0	0	7	14	....	3	....	.221	.337	.256	.592	87	-0	9	3.22	2	C-30	4	0.5
1909 Phi-N	20	32	6	10	1	1	0	1	10	....	1	....	.313	.476	.406	.882	173	4	7	7.82	-1	C-11/2-1	2	0.4
1910 Phi-N	25	51	7	10	3	0	0	2	5	9	0	....	.196	.268	.255	.523	51	-3	3	2.14	0	C-13/1-2,2-1,3-1	1	-0.2
1914 Bal-F	122	337	40	93	21	4	2	48	52	66	7	....	.276	.376	.380	.756	116	9	49	5.01	-5	*C-118	16	1.4
1915 Bal-F	49	135	20	32	9	0	2	13	31	25	2	....	.237	.387	.348	.735	109	3	18	4.57	0	C-45/S-1	5	0.7
1917 Bos-N	1	0	0	0	0	0	0	0	0	0	0	....	....	....	....	....	-106	0	0	....	0	/C-1	0	0.0
Total 13	490	1344	160	327	64	12	5	153	201	100	35	....	.243	.349	.320	.669	98	7	165	4.15	-4	C-397/1-19,2-11,0-3,3-2,S-1	50	4.0

• JACKSON, Bill — William Riley Jackson b: 4/4/1881, Pittsburgh, PA d: 9/24/1958, Peoria, IL BL/TL, 5'11.5", 160 lbs. Deb: 4/30/1914 Career OF: 2-3-2

YEAR TM-L	G	AB	R	H	2B	3B	HR	RBI	BB	SO	SB	CS	AVG	OBP	SLG	OPS	OPS+	BR/A	RC	RC/G	FR	G/POS	WS	TPW
1914 Chi-F	26	25	2	1	0	0	0	1	3	5	0	....	.040	.143	.040	.183	-50	-5	0	.13	0	/0-6(2-2-2),1-4	0	-0.5
1915 Chi-F	50	98	15	16	1	0	1	12	14	15	3	....	.163	.268	.204	.472	42	-7	6	1.87	1	1-36/0-1	0	-0.7
Total 2	76	123	17	17	1	0	1	13	17	20	3	....	.138	.243	.171	.414	24	-11	6	1.49	1	/1-40,0-7	0	-1.2

• JACKSON, Bo — Vincent Edward Jackson b: 11/30/1962, Bessemer, AL BR/TR, 6'1", 225 lbs. Deb: 9/2/1986 Career OF: 415-88-63

YEAR TM-L	G	AB	R	H	2B	3B	HR	RBI	BB	SO	SB	CS	AVG	OBP	SLG	OPS	OPS+	BR/A	RC	RC/G	FR	G/POS	WS	TPW
1986 KC-A	25	82	9	17	2	1	2	9	7	34	3	1	.207	.286	.329	.615	65	-4	8	3.28	-2	0-23(0-0-23)/D-1	1	-0.7
1987 KC-A	116	396	46	93	17	2	22	53	30	158	10	4	.235	.297	.455	.752	93	-5	55	4.71	-2	*0-113(95-21-3)/D-1	8	-1.2
1988 KC-A	124	439	63	108	16	4	25	68	25	146	27	6	.246	.288	.472	.760	108	5	59	4.63	2	*0-121(103-5-15)/D-2	12	0.2
1989 KC-A★	135	515	86	132	15	6	32	105	39	172	26	9	.256	.312	.495	.808	125	15	77	5.13	3	*0-110(110-1-0),D-24	19	1.4
1990 KC-A	111	405	74	110	16	1	28	78	44	128	15	9	.272	.346	.523	.869	142	21	70	5.95	-2	0-97(36-61-0),D-10	16	1.6
1991 Chi-A	23	71	8	16	4	0	3	14	12	25	0	1	.225	.337	.408	.746	108	1	9	4.16	0	D-21	2	0.0

YEAR TM-L	G	AB	R	H	2B	3B	HR	RBI	BB	SO	SB	CS	AVG	OBP	SLG	OPS	OPS+	BR/A	RC	RC/G	FR	G/POS	WS	TPW
1993*Chi-A	85	284	32	66	9	0	16	45	23	106	0	2	.232	.290	.433	.723	94	-5	34	4.11	1	0-47(28-0-19),D-36	7	-0.8
1994 Cal-A	75	201	23	56	7	0	13	43	20	72	1	0	.279	.347	.507	.854	115	4	36	6.58	1	0-46(43-0-3)/D-9	7	0.3
Total 8	694	2393	341	598	86	14	141	415	200	841	82	32	.250	.311	.474	.786	112	32	350	5.00	0	0-557,D-104	72	0.9
• JACKSON, Charlie	Charles Herbert "Lefty" Jackson b: 2/7/1894, Granite City, IL d: 5/27/1968, Radford, VA BL/TL, 5'9", 150 lbs. Deb: 8/20/1915																							
1915 Chi-A	1	1	0	0	0	0	0	0	0	1	0	....	.000	.000	.000	.000	-97	-0	0	.00	0	....	0	0.0
1917 Pit-N	41	121	7	29	3	2	0	1	10	22	4	....	.240	.303	.298	.601	82	-2	12	3.19	0	0-36(20-1-15)	2	-0.5
Total 2	42	122	7	29	3	2	0	1	10	23	4	....	.238	.301	.295	.596	80	-3	12	3.15	0	/0-36	2	-0.5
• JACKSON, Chuck	Charles Leo Jackson b: 3/19/1963, Seattle, WA BR/TR, 6', 185 lbs. Deb: 5/26/1987 U Career OF: 1-13-2																							
1987 Hou-N	35	71	3	15	3	0	1	6	7	19	1	1	.211	.282	.296	.578	55	-5	6	2.72	2	3-16,0-13(1-12-0)/S-1	1	-0.3
1988 Hou-N	46	83	7	19	5	1	1	8	7	16	1	1	.229	.289	.349	.638	86	-2	8	3.04	-1	3-32/0-3(0-1-2),S-3	2	-0.3
1994 Tex-A	1	2	0	0	0	0	0	0	0	0	0	0	.000	.000	.000	.000	-100	-1	0	.00	0	/3-1	0	-0.1
Total 3	82	156	10	34	8	1	2	14	14	35	2	2	.218	.282	.321	.603	70	-8	14	2.85	1	/3-49,0-16,S-4	3	-0.7
• JACKSON, Damian	Damian Jacques Jackson b: 8/16/1973, Los Angeles, CA BR/TR, 5'10", 160 lbs. Deb: 9/12/1996 Career OF: 35-21-13																							
1996 Cle-A	5	10	2	3	2	0	0	1	1	4	0	0	.300	.364	.500	.864	116	0	2	7.38	1	/S-5	1	0.1
1997 Cle-A	8	9	2	1	0	0	0	0	0	1	1	0	.111	.200	.111	.311	-15	-1	0	1.20	-1	/S-5,2-1	0	-0.2
Cin-N	12	27	6	6	2	1	1	2	4	7	1	1	.222	.323	.481	.804	105	-0	4	4.89	0	/S-6,2-3	1	0.1
1998 Cin-N	13	38	4	12	5	0	0	7	6	4	2	0	.316	.409	.447	.856	124	2	8	7.33	-1	S-10/0-3(0-3-0)	2	0.2
1999 SD-N	133	388	56	87	20	2	9	39	53	105	34	10	.224	.322	.356	.678	77	-10	50	4.28	1	*S-100,2-21/0-3(2-0-1)	11	-0.1
2000 SD-N	138	470	68	120	27	6	6	37	62	108	28	6	.255	.346	.377	.722	89	-4	67	4.91	18	S-88,2-36,0-17(17-0-0)	15	2.1
2001 SD-N	122	440	67	106	21	6	4	38	44	128	23	6	.241	.318	.343	.662	78	-11	52	3.98	6	*2-118/S-3,0-2(0-2-0)	11	0.1
2002 Det-A	81	245	31	63	20	1	1	25	21	36	12	3	.257	.323	.359	.683	86	-3	30	4.26	-12	2-56/0-6(3-3-0),S-6,D-4,3	7	-1.2
2003*Bos-A	109	161	34	42	7	0	1	13	8	28	16	8	.261	.296	.323	.619	62	-9	14	2.85	-2	2-38,0-38(13-13-12),S-18/D,3,1	2	-0.9
Total 8	621	1788	270	440	104	16	22	162	199	421	117	34	.246	.327	.359	.686	82	-36	228	4.30	10	2-273,S-241/0-69,D-11,3-5,1	50	0.1
• JACKSON, Darrin	Darrin Jay Jackson b: 8/22/1963, Los Angeles, CA BR/TR, 6', 185 lbs. Deb: 6/17/1985 Career OF: 185-510-187																							
1985 Chi-N	5	11	0	1	0	0	0	0	0	3	0	0	.091	.091	.091	.182	-44	-2	0	.25	0	/0-4(0-4-0)	0	-0.2
1987 Chi-N	7	5	2	4	1	0	0	0	0	0	0	0	.800	.800	1.000	1.800	359	2	4	108.00	-1	/0-5(2-3-0)	1	0.1
1988 Chi-N	100	188	29	50	11	3	6	20	5	28	4	1	.266	.289	.452	.741	105	0	24	4.42	-1	0-74(11-46-20)	3	-0.2
1989 Chi-N	45	83	7	19	4	0	1	8	6	17	1	2	.229	.281	.313	.594	65	-5	7	2.77	2	0-39(10-9-20)	2	-0.4
SD-N	25	87	10	18	3	0	3	12	7	17	0	2	.207	.266	.345	.611	73	-4	7	2.66	1	0-24(0-24-0)	1	-0.4
Yr.	70	170	17	37	7	0	4	20	13	34	1	4	.218	.273	.329	.603	69	-9	14	2.71	3	0-63(10-33-20)	3	-0.8
1990 SD-N	58	113	10	29	3	0	3	9	5	24	3	0	.257	.288	.363	.651	77	-3	12	3.81	-1	0-39(4-30-5)	1	-0.5
1991 SD-N	122	359	51	94	12	1	21	49	27	66	5	3	.262	.317	.476	.793	117	6	54	5.19	2	0-98(21-79-0)/P-1	13	0.5
1992 SD-N	155	587	72	146	23	5	17	70	26	106	14	3	.249	.285	.392	.677	88	-10	60	3.43	12	*0-153(5-152-2)	15	0.0
1993 Tor-A	46	176	15	38	8	0	5	19	8	53	0	2	.216	.250	.347	.597	58	-12	12	2.13	-3	0-46(0-10-37)	1	-1.6
NY-N	31	87	4	17	1	0	1	7	2	22	0	0	.195	.213	.241	.455	22	-10	5	1.77	3	0-26(10-16-0)	1	-0.8
1994 Chi-A	104	369	43	115	17	3	10	51	27	56	7	1	.312	.363	.455	.819	111	7	62	6.38	-3	*0-102(0-16-92)	11	0.0
1997 Min-A	49	130	19	33	2	1	3	21	4	21	2	0	.254	.276	.354	.630	62	-7	13	3.31	1	0-44(0-44-0)	2	-0.5
Mil-A	26	81	7	22	7	0	2	15	2	10	2	1	.272	.289	.432	.721	84	-2	9	3.67	2	0-26(21-9-3)	4	-0.1
Yr.	75	211	26	55	9	1	5	36	6	31	4	1	.261	.281	.384	.665	70	-9	22	3.45	3	0-70(21-53-3)	6	-0.6
1998 Mil-N	114	204	20	49	13	1	4	20	9	37	1	1	.240	.276	.373	.648	68	-10	20	3.29	-1	0-94(55-43-5)/D-2	3	-1.2
1999 Chi-A	73	149	22	41	9	1	4	16	3	20	4	1	.275	.289	.430	.719	80	-5	17	4.01	-1	0-64(46-25-3)/D-3	2	-0.6
Total 12	960	2629	311	676	114	15	80	317	131	480	43	17	.257	.295	.403	.698	87	-55	306	3.98	13	0-838/D-5,P-1	60	-5.9
• JACKSON, George	George Christopher "Hickory" Jackson b: 10/14/1882, Springfield, MO d: 11/25/1972, Cleburne, TX BR/TR, 6'.5", 180 lbs. Deb: 8/2/1911 Career OF: 134-15-0																							
1911 Bos-N	39	147	28	51	11	2	0	25	12	21	12	....	.347	.404	.449	.853	128	6	31	8.00	-2	0-39(38-1-0)	5	0.2
1912 Bos-N	110	397	55	104	13	5	4	48	38	72	22	....	.262	.342	.350	.692	88	-6	55	4.59	-1	*0-107(96-11-0)	6	-1.2
1913 Bos-N	3	10	2	3	0	0	0	0	0	2	0	....	.300	.300	.300	.600	70	-0	1	3.12	0	/0-3(0-3-0)	0	0.0
Total 3	152	554	85	158	24	7	4	73	50	95	34	....	.285	.357	.375	.733	98	-1	87	5.40	-4	0-149	11	-1.1
• JACKSON, Henry	Henry Everett Jackson b: 6/23/1861, Union City, IN d: 9/14/1932, Chicago, IL BR/TR, 6'2", 185 lbs. Deb: 9/13/1887																							
1887 Ind-N	10	38	1	10	1	0	0	3	0	12	2	....	.263	.263	.289	.553	55	-2	4	3.32	-2	1-10	0	-0.4
• JACKSON, Jim	James Benner Jackson b: 11/28/1877, Philadelphia, PA d: 10/9/1955, Philadelphia, PA BR/TR, 5'6.5" Deb: 4/26/1901 Career OF: 273-61-6																							
1901 Bal-A	99	364	42	91	17	3	2	50	20	....	11	....	.250	.291	.330	.621	69	-16	41	3.75	-8	0-96(35-59-2)	6	-2.6
1902 NY-N	37	116	14	21	5	1	0	15	16	....	6	....	.181	.280	.241	.522	62	-5	10	2.75	-2	0-34(31-1-2)	1	-0.9
1905 Cle-A	109	426	60	109	12	4	2	31	34	....	15	....	.256	.317	.317	.634	100	0	49	4.06	4	*0-106(104-0-2)/3-3	12	-0.2
1906 Cle-A	105	374	44	80	13	2	0	38	38	....	25	....	.214	.290	.259	.549	73	-10	38	3.27	-4	*0-104(103-1-0)	7	-2.2
Total 4	350	1280	160	301	47	10	4	134	108	....	57	....	.235	.298	.297	.595	80	-31	138	3.61	-9	0-340/3-3	26	-5.9
• JACKSON, Joe	Joseph Jefferson "Shoeless Joe" Jackson b: 7/16/1889, Pickens County, SC d: 12/5/1951, Greenville, SC BL/TR, 6'1", 200 lbs. Deb: 8/25/1908 Career OF: 584-145-559																							
1908 Phi-A	5	23	0	3	0	0	0	3	0	....	0	....	.130	.130	.130	.261	-14	-3	0	.44	-1	/0-5(0-5-0)	0	-0.5
1909 Phi-A	5	17	3	3	0	0	0	3	1	....	0	....	.176	.222	.176	.399	26	-1	1	1.16	0	/0-4(3-1-0)	0	-0.2
1910 Cle-A	20	75	15	29	2	5	1	11	8	....	4	....	.387	.446	.587	1.032	220	10	21	11.27	0	0-20(0-15-5)	6	1.0
1911 Cle-A	147	571	126	233	45	19	7	83	56	....	41	....	.408	**.468**	.590	1.058	192	70	175	13.20	7	*0-147(0-47-100)	39	**6.8**
1912 Cle-A	154	572	121	**226**	44	**26**	3	90	54	....	35	....	.395	.458	.579	1.036	189	66	166	11.96	10	*0-150(0-19-131)	37	6.9
1913 Cle-A	148	528	109	**197**	**39**	17	7	71	80	26	26	....	.373	.460	**.551**	**1.011**	190	**63**	140	10.48	0	*0-148(0-0-148)	36	5.8
1914 Cle-A	122	453	61	153	22	13	3	53	41	34	22	15	.338	.399	.464	.862	153	27	86	6.96	-1	*0-119(0-31-88)	20	2.1
1915 Cle-A	83	303	42	99	16	9	3	45	28	11	10	10	.327	.389	.469	.858	154	17	54	6.66	-1	0-50(5-0-44),1-30	11	1.3
Chi-A	45	158	21	43	4	5	2	36	24	12	6	10	.272	.378	.399	.777	129	3	23	4.64	-3	0-45(19-26-0)	7	-0.2
Yr.	128	461	63	142	20	14	5	81	52	23	16	20	.308	.385	.445	.830	145	20	78	5.89	-4	0-95(24-26-44),1-30	18	1.1
1916 Chi-A	155	592	91	202	40	**21**	3	78	46	25	24	14	.341	.393	.495	.888	165	43	119	7.34	-5	*0-155(131-1-23)	34	3.4
1917*Chi-A	146	538	91	162	20	17	5	75	57	25	13	....	.301	.375	.429	.805	142	27	89	5.89	-3	*0-145(134-0-11)	31	2.0
1918 Chi-A	17	65	9	23	2	2	1	20	8	1	3	....	.354	.425	.492	.917	175	6	15	8.02	-1	0-17(14-0-3)	4	0.5
1919*Chi-A	139	516	79	181	31	14	7	96	60	10	9	....	.351	.422	.506	.928	159	42	111	8.22	-6	*0-139(133-0-6)	32	3.1
1920 Chi-A	146	570	105	218	42	**20**	12	121	56	14	9	12	.382	.444	.589	1.033	172	57	145	10.13	-7	*0-145(145-0-0)	37	4.2
Total 13	1332	4981	873	1772	307	168	54	785	519	158	202	61	.356	.423	.517	.940	168	426	1146	8.79	-12	*0-1289/1-30	294	36.3
• JACKSON, Ken	Kenneth Bernard Jackson b: 8/21/1963, Shreveport, LA BR/TR, 6'1", 170 lbs. Deb: 9/12/1987																							
1987 Phi-N	8	16	1	4	2	0	0	2	1	4	0	0	.250	.333	.375	.708	85	-0	2	4.70	0	/S-8	0	0.0
• JACKSON, Lou	Louis Clarence Jackson b: 7/26/1935, Riverton, LA d: 5/27/1969, Tokyo, Japan BL/TR, 5'10", 168 lbs. Deb: 7/23/1958 Career OF: 5-4-6																							
1958 Chi-N	24	35	5	6	2	1	1	6	1	9	0	1	.171	.194	.371	.566	46	-3	2	1.60	-1	0-12(4-4-6)	0	-0.4
1959 Chi-N	6	4	2	1	0	0	0	1	0	2	0	0	.250	.250	.250	.500	34	-0	0	2.25	0	....	0	0.0
1964 Bal-A	4	8	0	3	0	0	0	0	0	2	0	0	.375	.375	.375	.750	110	0	1	6.08	0	/0-1	0	0.0
Total 3	34	47	7	10	2	1	1	7	1	13	0	1	.213	.229	.362	.591	56	-4	3	2.23	0	/0-13	0	-0.4
• JACKSON, Randy	Ransom Joseph "Handsom Ransom" Jackson b: 2/10/1926, Little Rock, AR BR/TR, 6'1.5", 180 lbs. Deb: 5/2/1950 Career OF: 2-0-0																							
1950 Chi-N	34	111	13	25	4	3	3	6	7	25	4	....	.225	.271	.396	.668	74	-5	11	3.21	-6	3-27	1	-1.0
1951 Chi-N	145	557	78	153	24	6	16	76	47	44	14	3	.275	.332	.425	.758	100	1	77	4.81	1	*3-143	15	0.2
1952 Chi-N	116	379	44	88	8	5	9	34	27	42	6	5	.232	.285	.351	.636	75	-15	36	3.12	0	*3-104/0-1	6	-1.5
1953 Chi-N	139	498	61	142	22	8	19	66	42	61	8	4	.285	.341	.476	.817	108	4	77	5.31	3	*3-133	16	0.7
1954 Chi-N★	126	484	77	132	17	6	19	67	44	55	2	1	.273	.336	.450	.786	102	0	74	5.30	-4	*3-124	13	-0.4
1955 Chi-N★	138	499	73	132	13	7	21	70	58	58	0	2	.265	.342	.445	.787	107	5	75	5.26	-13	*3-134	16	-0.9
1956*Bro-N	101	307	37	84	15	7	8	53	28	38	2	1	.274	.338	.446	.785	101	1	43	4.75	17	3-80	12	1.8
1957 Bro-N	48	131	7	26	1	0	.2	16	9	20	0	0	.198	.250	.252	.502	32	-13	8	1.77	3	3-34	1	-1.0

YEAR TM-L	G	AB	R	H	2B	3B	HR	RBI	BB	SO	SB	CS	AVG	OBP	SLG	OPS	OPS+	BR/A	RC	RC/G	FR	G/POS	WS	TPW
1958 LA-N	35	65	8	12	3	0	1	4	5	10	0	0	.185	.243	.277	.520	36	-6	4	1.84	4	3-17	1	-0.3
Cle-A	29	91	7	22	3	1	4	13	3	18	0	0	.242	.266	.429	.695	90	-2	9	3.49	2	3-24	2	0.1
1959 Cle-A	3	7	0	1	0	0	0	0	0	1	0	0	.143	.143	.143	.286	-22	-1	0	.00	0	/3-2	0	-0.1
Chi-N	41	74	7	18	5	1	1	10	11	10	0	0	.243	.341	.378	.720	92	-1	9	3.58	-2	3-22/0-1	1	-0.2
Total 10	955	3203	412	835	115	44	103	415	281	382	36	16	.261	.322	.421	.742	94	-30	422	4.47	6	3-844/0-2	84	-2.7
• JACKSON, Reggie	Reginald Martinez "Mr. October" Jackson b: 5/18/1946, Wyncote, PA BL/TL, 6', 200 lbs. Deb: 6/9/1967 HOF: 1993 Career OF: 20-186-1939																							
1967 KC-A	35	118	13	21	4	4	1	6	10	46	1	1	.178	.271	.305	.576	72	-4	10	2.79	-2	0-34(19-3-14)	2	-0.9
1968 Oak-A	154	553	82	138	13	6	29	74	50	171	14	4	.250	.317	.452	.770	138	25	83	5.22	4	*0-151(1-9-147)	25	2.1
1969 Oak-A★	152	549	**123**	151	36	3	47	118	114	142	13	5	.275	.410	**.608**	**1.019**	**190**	**70**	144	**9.42**	-2	*0-150(0-10-144)	**41**	6.3
1970 Oak-A	149	426	57	101	21	2	23	66	75	135	26	17	.237	.361	.458	.819	129	17	70	5.31	-5	*0-142(0-49-113)	17	0.7
1971*Oak-A★	150	567	87	157	29	3	32	80	63	161	16	10	.277	.355	.508	.863	145	31	103	6.42	6	*0-145(0-3-145)	32	3.3
1972*Oak-A★	135	499	72	132	25	2	25	75	59	125	9	8	.265	.352	.473	.825	152	30	84	5.90	-4	*0-135(0-92-43)	26	2.4
1973*Oak-A★	151	539	**99**	158	28	2	**32**	**117**	76	111	22	8	.293	.387	**.531**	**.918**	**165**	**49**	112	7.38	0	*0-145(0-1-144)/D-3	**32**	4.3
1974*Oak-A★	148	506	90	146	25	1	29	93	86	105	25	5	.289	.396	.514	.910	**171**	**53**	109	**7.73**	3	*0-127(0-3-126),D-19	30	5.1
1975*Oak-A★	157	593	91	150	39	3	**36**	104	67	133	17	8	.253	.332	.511	.843	138	28	100	5.79	3	*0-147(0-0-147)/D-9	27	2.4
1976 Bal-A	134	498	84	138	27	2	27	91	54	108	28	7	.277	.353	**.502**	.855	**158**	38	86	6.01	0	*0-121(0-16-111),D-11	25	3.3
1977*NY-A★	146	525	93	150	39	2	32	110	74	129	17	3	.286	.377	.550	.928	151	40	116	8.16	-5	*0-127(0-0-127),D-18	27	2.9
1978*NY-A★	139	511	82	140	13	5	27	97	58	133	14	11	.274	.358	.477	.836	136	23	87	6.00	-1	*0-104(0-0-104),D-35	23	1.6
1979 NY-A★	131	465	78	138	24	2	29	89	65	107	9	8	.297	.385	.544	.929	151	32	93	7.02	5	*0-125(0-0-125)/D-3	23	3.0
1980*NY-A★	143	514	94	154	22	4	**41**	111	83	122	1	2	.300	.399	.597	.996	172	51	125	9.10	-2	0-94(0-0-94),D-46	31	4.3
1981*NY-A★	94	334	33	79	17	1	15	54	46	82	0	3	.237	.331	.428	.759	119	7	47	4.73	1	0-61(0-0-61),D-33	10	0.5
1982*Cal-A★	153	530	92	146	17	1	**39**	101	85	156	4	5	.275	.378	.532	.910	147	34	107	7.19	-6	*0-139(0-0-139)/D-5	22	2.2
1983 Cal-A★	116	397	43	77	14	1	14	49	52	140	0	2	.194	.294	.340	.634	74	-14	42	3.38	1	D-62,0-47(0-0-47)	4	-1.7
1984 Cal-A★	143	525	67	117	17	2	25	81	55	141	8	4	.223	.300	.406	.706	94	-5	64	4.06	0	*D-134/0-3(0-0-3)	10	-1.0
1985 Cal-A	143	460	64	116	27	0	27	85	78	138	1	2	.252	.362	.487	.849	130	20	79	5.90	0	0-81(0-0-81),D-52	18	1.6
1986*Cal-A	132	419	65	101	12	2	18	58	92	115	1	1	.241	.381	.408	.789	116	14	68	5.48	0	*D-121/0-4(0-0-4)	13	1.0
1987 Oak-A	115	336	42	74	14	1	15	43	33	97	2	1	.220	.298	.402	.699	89	-6	42	4.23	-1	D-79,0-20(0-0-20)	6	-0.9
Total 21	2820	9864	1551	2584	463	49	563	1702	1375	2597	228	115	.262	.358	.490	.848	140	534	1772	6.25	-6	*0-2102,D-630	444	42.3
• JACKSON, Ron	Ronnie Damien Jackson b: 5/9/1953, Birmingham, AL BR/TR, 6', 205 lbs. Deb: 9/12/1975 C Career OF: 51-1-4																							
1975 Cal-A	13	39	2	9	2	0	0	2	2	10	1	1	.231	.268	.282	.550	60	-2	3	2.49	0	/0-9(9-0-0),3-3,D-1	0	-0.3
1976 Cal-A	127	410	44	93	18	3	8	40	30	58	5	4	.227	.291	.344	.635	91	-6	40	3.20	-4	*3-114/2-7,D-6,0-4(3-0-1)	11	-1.1
1977 Cal-A	106	292	38	71	15	2	8	28	24	42	3	2	.243	.303	.390	.693	91	-4	34	3.91	0	1-43,3-30,D-20/0-3(3-0-0),S	6	-0.7
1978 Cal-A	105	387	49	115	18	6	6	57	16	31	2	3	.297	.340	.421	.761	117	7	53	4.94	-1	1-75,3-31/D-1,0-1	14	0.1
1979 Min-A	159	583	85	158	40	5	14	68	51	59	3	1	.271	.339	.429	.768	102	2	84	5.06	-1	*1-157/3-1,0-1,S-1	14	-0.9
1980 Min-A	131	396	48	105	29	3	5	42	28	41	1	8	.265	.319	.391	.710	87	-11	43	3.63	-1	*1-119,0-15(14-1-0)/3-2,D	7	-1.8
1981 Min-A	54	175	17	46	9	0	4	28	10	15	2	2	.263	.306	.383	.689	91	-3	20	3.89	1	1-36/0-7(6-0-1),D-6,3-3	4	-0.5
Det-A	31	95	12	27	8	1	1	12	8	11	4	1	.284	.340	.421	.761	114	2	15	5.63	1	1-29	4	0.1
Yr.	85	270	29	73	17	1	5	40	18	26	6	3	.270	.318	.396	.715	99	-0	35	4.47	1	1-65/0-7(6-0-1),D-6,3-3	8	-0.3
1982*Cal-A	53	142	15	47	6	0	2	19	10	12	0	1	.331	.383	.415	.799	119	4	22	5.81	0	1-37/3-9	5	0.2
1983 Cal-A	102	348	41	80	16	1	8	39	27	33	2	2	.230	.291	.351	.642	76	-12	34	3.25	-3	3-38,1-35,D-16,0-15(14-0-1)	4	-1.8
1984 Cal-A	33	91	5	15	2	1	0	5	7	13	0	0	.165	.224	.209	.433	21	-10	4	1.37	-2	1-21/3-9,0-1	0	-1.3
Bal-A	12	28	0	8	2	0	0	2	0	4	0	2	.286	.286	.357	.643	78	-2	2	2.63	0	3-10	0	-0.2
Yr.	45	119	5	23	4	1	0	7	7	17	0	2	.193	.238	.244	.482	33	-12	6	1.64	-2	1-21,3-19/0-1	0	-1.5
Total 10	926	2986	356	774	165	22	56	342	213	329	23	27	.259	.316	.385	.701	94	-35	355	4.05	-11	1-552,3-250/0-56,D-51,2-7,S	69	-8.3
• JACKSON, Ron	Ronald Harris Jackson b: 10/22/1933, Kalamazoo, MI BR/TR, 6'7", 225 lbs. Deb: 6/15/1954																							
1954 Chi-A	40	93	10	26	4	0	4	10	6	20	2	1	.280	.337	.452	.788	111	1	14	5.19	-3	1-35	3	-0.3
1955 Chi-A	40	74	10	15	1	1	2	7	8	22	1	0	.203	.280	.324	.605	60	-4	7	3.07	-1	1-29	1	-0.6
1956 Chi-A	22	56	7	12	3	0	1	4	10	13	1	0	.214	.333	.321	.655	73	-2	6	3.71	0	1-19	1	-0.2
1957 Chi-A	13	60	4	19	3	0	2	8	1	12	0	0	.317	.328	.467	.795	114	1	8	5.19	-1	1-13	2	-0.1
1958 Chi-A	61	146	19	34	4	0	7	21	18	46	2	0	.233	.325	.404	.729	101	1	20	4.54	-1	1-38	4	-0.2
1959 Chi-A	10	14	3	3	1	0	1	2	1	0	0	0	.214	.313	.500	.813	121	0	2	4.23	0	/1-5	0	0.0
1960 Bos-A	10	31	1	7	2	0	0	0	1	6	0	0	.226	.250	.290	.540	44	-3	2	1.80	-1	/1-9	0	-0.4
Total 7	196	474	54	116	18	1	17	52	45	119	6	1	.245	.317	.395	.711	92	-5	59	4.20	-7	1-148	11	-1.9
• JACKSON, Ryan	Ryan Dewitte Jackson b: 11/15/1971, Orlando, FL BL/TL, 6'2", 205 lbs. Deb: 3/31/1998 Career OF: 32-1-38																							
1998 Fla-N	111	260	26	65	15	1	5	31	20	73	1	1	.250	.306	.373	.679	81	-8	30	4.03	-7	1-44,0-32(10-0-23)/D-5	4	-1.9
1999 Sea-A	32	68	4	16	3	0	0	10	6	19	3	3	.235	.307	.279	.586	50	-6	5	2.33	-2	1-29/0-1	0	-0.8
2001 Det-A	79	118	19	25	4	2	2	11	5	26	3	1	.212	.250	.331	.581	54	-8	10	2.77	-2	1-35,0-34(19-0-15)/D-4	1	-1.2
2002 Det-A	4	6	0	2	1	1	0	0	1	2	0	0	.333	.429	.833	1.262	238	1	2	15.22	0	/0-3(2-1-0)	1	0.1
Total 4	226	452	49	108	23	4	7	52	32	120	7	5	.239	.294	.354	.648	71	-21	48	3.54	-10	1-108/0-70,D-9	6	-3.8
• JACKSON, Sam	Samuel Jackson b: 3/24/1849, Ripon, England d: 8/4/1930, Clifton Springs, NY BR/TR, 5'5.5", 160 lbs. Deb: 5/16/1871 NA OF: 3-1-0																							
1871 Bos-n	16	76	17	17	5	3	0	11	1	4	0	1	.224	.234	.368	.602	67	-4	7	3.52	-1	2-14/0-1,S-1	....	-0.4
1872 Atl-n	4	12	0	2	0	0	0	0	0	0	0	0	.167	.167	.167	.333	2	-2	0	1.06	-2	/0-3(3-0-0),2-1,3-1	....	-0.2
Total 2 n	20	88	17	19	5	3	0	11	1	4	0	1	.216	.225	.341	.566	59	-6	7	3.17	-3	/2-15,0-4,3-1,S-1	....	-0.7
• JACKSON, Sonny	Roland Thomas Jackson b: 7/9/1944, Washington, DC BL/TR, 5'9", 155 lbs. Deb: 9/27/1963 C Career OF: 48-158-6																							
1963 Hou-N	1	3	0	0	0	0	0	0	0	1	0	0	.000	.000	.000	.000	-107	-1	0	.00	0	/S-1	0	0.0
1964 Hou-N	9	23	3	8	1	0	0	1	2	3	1	0	.348	.400	.391	.791	131	1	4	7.23	-1	/S-7	1	0.0
1965 Hou-N	10	23	1	3	0	0	0	0	1	1	1	1	.130	.167	.130	.297	-16	-4	0	.61	-2	/S-8,3-1	0	-0.5
1966 Hou-N	150	596	80	174	6	5	3	25	42	53	49	14	.292	.342	.334	.676	95	2	74	4.19	0	*S-150	19	1.6
1967 Hou-N	129	520	67	123	18	3	0	25	36	45	22	9	.237	.286	.283	.569	65	-22	42	2.61	-5	*S-128	7	-1.7
1968 Atl-N	105	358	37	81	8	2	1	19	25	35	16	6	.226	.282	.268	.551	66	-13	27	2.42	-5	S-99	6	-1.2
1969*Atl-N	98	318	41	76	3	5	1	27	35	33	12	7	.239	.318	.289	.608	71	-12	32	3.29	-5	S-97	8	-0.5
1970 Atl-N	103	328	60	85	14	3	0	20	45	27	11	4	.259	.350	.320	.670	76	-9	41	4.32	-13	S-87	7	-1.2
1971 Atl-N	149	547	58	141	20	5	2	25	35	45	7	6	.258	.304	.324	.627	73	-20	54	3.36	-8	*0-145(0-145-0)	9	-3.4
1972 Atl-N	60	126	20	30	6	3	0	8	7	9	1	0	.238	.278	.333	.612	67	-5	11	2.97	-2	S-17,0-10(0-9-1)/3-6	1	-0.6
1973 Atl-N	117	206	29	43	5	2	0	12	22	13	6	3	.209	.288	.252	.541	47	-14	17	2.65	-3	0-56(48-4-4),S-36	2	-1.6
1974 Atl-N	5	7	0	3	0	0	0	0	0	0	0	1	.429	.429	.429	.857	134	-0	1	4.63	-0	/0-1	0	0.0
Total 12	936	3055	396	767	81	28	7	162	250	265	126	51	.251	.310	.303	.613	73	-97	301	3.30	-43	S-630,0-212/3-7	60	-9.2
• JACKSON, Travis	Travis Calvin "Stonewall" Jackson b: 11/2/1903, Waldo, AR d: 7/27/1987, Waldo, AR BR/TR, 5'10.5", 160 lbs. Deb: 9/27/1922 C HOF: 1982																							
1922 NY-N	3	8	1	0	0	0	0	0	0	2	0	0	.000	.000	.000	.000	-99	-2	0	.00	0	/S-3	0	-0.2
1923*NY-N	96	327	45	90	12	7	4	37	22	40	3	3	.275	.321	.391	.712	88	-6	41	4.45	-2	S-60,3-31/2-1	10	0.0
1924*NY-N	151	596	81	180	26	8	11	76	21	56	6	7	.302	.326	.428	.754	103	0	80	4.83	1	*S-151	20	1.7
1925 NY-N	112	411	51	117	15	2	9	59	24	43	8	3	.285	.327	.397	.724	87	-7	54	4.68	-5	*S-110	12	0.0
1926 NY-N	111	385	64	126	24	8	8	51	20	26	2	....	.327	.362	.494	.856	130	14	66	6.26	0	*S-108/0-1	18	2.6
1927 NY-N	127	469	67	149	29	4	14	98	32	30	8	....	.318	.363	.486	.849	126	15	80	6.19	15	*S-124/3-2	24	4.4
1928 NY-N	150	537	73	145	35	6	14	77	56	46	8	....	.270	.339	.436	.775	101	-1	79	4.82	23	*S-149	22	3.8
1929 NY-N	149	551	92	162	21	12	21	94	64	56	10	....	.294	.367	.490	.857	111	8	98	6.24	14	*S-149	23	3.5
1930 NY-N	116	431	70	146	27	8	13	82	32	25	6	....	.339	.386	.529	.915	121	14	85	7.28	1	*S-115	17	2.4
1931 NY-N	145	555	65	172	26	10	5	71	36	23	13	....	.310	.353	.420	.773	110	7	83	5.63	16	*S-145	22	3.3
1932 NY-N	52	195	23	50	17	1	4	38	13	16	1	....	.256	.310	.415	.725	95	-2	26	4.56	-7	S-52	5	-0.5
1933*NY-N	53	122	11	30	5	0	0	12	8	11	2	....	.246	.292	.287	.579	67	-5	10	2.85	-2	3-21,S-21	2	-0.6
1934 NY-N★	137	523	75	140	26	7	16	101	37	71	1	....	.268	.316	.436	.752	102	-1	71	4.64	-2	*S-130/3-9	17	0.7
1935 NY-N	128	511	74	154	20	12	9	80	29	64	3	....	.301	.340	.440	.780	110	6	76	5.36	-6	*3-128	16	0.5

YEAR TM-L	G	AB	R	H	2B	3B	HR	RBI	BB	SO	SB	CS	AVG	OBP	SLG	OPS	OPS+	BR/A	RC	RC/G	FR	G/POS	WS	TPW
1936*NY-N	126	465	41	107	8	1	7	53	18	56	0	....	.230	.260	.297	.557	50	-33	36	2.56	-7	*3-116/S-9	3	-3.6
Total 15	1656	6086	833	1768	291	86	135	929	412	565	71	13	.291	.337	.433	.770	102	7	883	5.12	38	*S-1326,3-307/2-1,0-1	211	18.1

• JACOBS, Jake Lamar Gary Jacobs b: 6/9/1937, Youngstown, OH BR/TR, 6', 175 lbs. Deb: 9/13/1960

YEAR TM-L	G	AB	R	H	2B	3B	HR	RBI	BB	SO	SB	CS	AVG	OBP	SLG	OPS	OPS+	BR/A	RC	RC/G	FR	G/POS	WS	TPW
1960 Was-A	6	2	0	0	0	0	0	0	0	0	0	0	.000	.000	.000	.000	-99	-1	0	.00	0	....	0	-0.1
1961 Min-A	4	8	0	2	0	0	0	0	0	2	0	0	.250	.250	.250	.500	32	-1	1	2.25	0	/0-3(0-3-0)	0	-0.1
Total 2	10	10	0	2	0	0	0	0	0	2	0	0	.200	.200	.200	.400	6	-1	1	1.35	0	/0-3	0	-0.1

• JACOBS, Mike Morris Elmore Jacobs b: 12/1877, Louisville, KY d: 3/21/1949, Louisville, KY Deb: 7/16/1902

YEAR TM-L	G	AB	R	H	2B	3B	HR	RBI	BB	SO	SB	CS	AVG	OBP	SLG	OPS	OPS+	BR/A	RC	RC/G	FR	G/POS	WS	TPW
1902 Chi-N	5	19	1	4	0	0	0	2	0	....	0	....	.211	.211	.211	.421	31	-2	1	1.52	-2	/S-5	0	-0.3

• JACOBS, Otto Otto Albert Jacobs b: 4/19/1889, Chicago, IL d: 11/19/1955, Chicago, IL BR/TR, 5'9", 180 lbs. Deb: 6/13/1918

YEAR TM-L	G	AB	R	H	2B	3B	HR	RBI	BB	SO	SB	CS	AVG	OBP	SLG	OPS	OPS+	BR/A	RC	RC/G	FR	G/POS	WS	TPW
1918 Chi-A	29	73	4	15	3	1	0	3	5	8	0	....	.205	.256	.274	.530	59	-4	5	2.09	-2	C-21	1	-0.5

• JACOBS, Ray Raymond Frederick Jacobs b: 1/2/1902, Salt Lake City, UT d: 4/5/1952, Los Angeles, CA BR/TR, 6', 160 lbs. Deb: 4/20/1928

YEAR TM-L	G	AB	R	H	2B	3B	HR	RBI	BB	SO	SB	CS	AVG	OBP	SLG	OPS	OPS+	BR/A	RC	RC/G	FR	G/POS	WS	TPW
1928 Chi-N	2	2	0	0	0	0	0	0	0	1	0	....	.000	.000	.000	.000	-101	-1	0	.00	0	....	0	-0.1

• JACOBS, Spook Robert Forrest Vandergrift Jacobs b: 11/4/1925, Cheswold, DE BR/TR, 5'8.5", 155 lbs. Deb: 4/13/1954

YEAR TM-L	G	AB	R	H	2B	3B	HR	RBI	BB	SO	SB	CS	AVG	OBP	SLG	OPS	OPS+	BR/A	RC	RC/G	FR	G/POS	WS	TPW
1954 Phi-A	132	508	63	131	11	1	0	26	60	22	17	3	.258	.336	.283	.620	71	-15	55	3.77	-15	*2-131	11	-2.1
1955 KC-A	13	23	7	6	0	0	0	1	3	0	1	2	.261	.370	.261	.631	71	-1	2	2.60	0	/2-7	0	-0.1
1956 KC-A	32	97	13	21	3	0	0	5	15	5	4	1	.216	.321	.247	.569	52	-6	8	2.71	-1	2-31	1	-0.4
Pit-N	11	37	4	6	2	0	0	1	2	5	0	2	.162	.225	.216	.441	20	-5	2	1.26	-2	2-11	0	-0.7
Total 3	188	665	87	164	16	1	0	33	80	32	22	8	.247	.329	.274	.603	65	-28	67	3.40	-18	2-180	12	-3.3

• JACOBSON, Baby Doll William Chester Jacobson b: 8/16/1890, Cable, IL d: 1/16/1977, Orion, IL BR/TR, 6'3", 215 lbs. Deb: 4/14/1915 Career OF: 88-1098-194

YEAR TM-L	G	AB	R	H	2B	3B	HR	RBI	BB	SO	SB	CS	AVG	OBP	SLG	OPS	OPS+	BR/A	RC	RC/G	FR	G/POS	WS	TPW
1915 Det-A	37	65	5	14	6	2	0	4	5	14	0	2	.215	.282	.369	.651	90	-2	6	3.05	-1	1-10/0-7(3-5-0)	1	-0.4
StL-A	34	115	13	24	6	1	1	9	10	26	3	3	.209	.295	.304	.599	82	-3	10	2.89	-1	0-32(3-3-26)	1	-0.6
Yr.	71	180	18	38	12	3	1	13	15	40	3	5	.211	.290	.328	.618	85	-5	17	2.95	-2	0-39(6-8-26),1-10	2	-1.0
1917 StL-A	148	529	53	131	23	7	4	55	31	67	10	....	.248	.294	.340	.635	97	-5	53	3.40	4	*0-131(0-54-77),1-11	12	-0.9
1919 StL-A	120	455	70	147	31	8	4	51	24	47	9	....	.323	.362	.453	.815	125	13	75	6.12	-4	*0-106(17-73-16)/1-8	18	0.3
1920 StL-A	154	609	97	216	34	14	9	122	46	37	11	7	.355	.402	.501	.903	134	30	121	7.74	5	*0-154(0-120-34)/1-1	25	2.6
1921 StL-A	151	599	90	211	38	14	5	90	42	30	8	8	.352	.398	.487	.885	118	15	114	7.28	-4	*0-142(0-141-1),1-10	25	0.4
1922 StL-A	145	555	88	176	22	16	9	102	46	36	19	6	.317	.379	.463	.842	114	14	100	6.55	-3	*0-137(11-125-1)/1-7	20	0.4
1923 StL-A	147	592	76	183	29	6	8	81	29	27	6	6	.309	.343	.419	.762	95	-7	84	5.10	-4	*0-146(0-146-0)	15	-1.6
1924 StL-A	152	579	103	184	41	12	19	97	35	45	6	8	.318	.361	.528	.889	120	12	107	6.61	4	*0-152(0-152-0)	23	0.9
1925 StL-A	142	540	103	184	30	9	15	76	45	26	8	11	.341	.392	.513	.905	122	15	105	7.28	-4	*0-139(0-139-0)	23	0.5
1926 StL-A	50	182	18	52	15	1	2	21	9	14	1	2	.286	.319	.412	.731	86	-5	23	4.47	-3	0-50(0-50-0)	4	-0.9
Bos-A	98	394	44	120	36	1	6	69	22	22	4	1	.305	.344	.447	.791	109	4	61	5.48	-4	0-98(6-57-36)	9	-0.6
Yr.	148	576	62	172	51	2	8	90	31	36	5	3	.299	.337	.436	.772	102	-1	84	5.15	-7	*0-148(6-107-36)	13	-1.5
1927 Bos-A	45	155	11	38	9	3	0	24	5	12	1	0	.245	.278	.342	.620	61	-9	15	3.31	0	0-39(39-0-0)	1	-1.1
Cle-A	32	103	13	26	5	0	0	13	6	4	0	0	.252	.300	.301	.601	56	-7	10	3.13	-3	0-31(0-31-0)	1	-1.0
Phi-A	17	35	3	8	3	0	1	5	0	3	0	0	.229	.229	.400	.629	57	-3	3	2.77	-1	0-14(9-2-3)	0	-0.3
Yr.	94	293	27	72	17	3	1	42	11	19	1	0	.246	.280	.334	.615	59	-18	28	3.17	-3	0-84(48-33-3)	2	-2.5
Total 11	1472	5507	787	1714	328	94	83	819	355	410	86	54	.311	.357	.450	.807	110	63	887	5.83	-17	*0-1378/1-47	178	-2.4

• JACOBSON, Merwin Merwin John William Jacobson b: 3/7/1894, New Britian, CT d: 1/13/1978, Baltimore, MD BL/TL, 5'11.5", 165 lbs. Deb: 9/8/1915 Career OF: 2-55-42

YEAR TM-L	G	AB	R	H	2B	3B	HR	RBI	BB	SO	SB	CS	AVG	OBP	SLG	OPS	OPS+	BR/A	RC	RC/G	FR	G/POS	WS	TPW
1915 NY-N	8	24	0	2	0	0	0	0	1	5	0	....	.083	.120	.083	.203	-40	-4	0	.29	0	/0-5(0-2-3)	0	-0.4
1916 Chi-N	4	13	2	3	0	0	0	0	1	4	2	....	.231	.286	.231	.516	54	-1	1	3.49	-0	/0-4(0-0-4)	0	-0.1
1926 Bro-N	110	288	41	71	9	2	0	23	36	24	5	....	.247	.330	.292	.622	69	-11	29	3.37	-3	0-86(2-53-32)	5	-1.8
1927 Bro-N	11	6	4	0	0	0	0	1	0	1	0	....	.000	.000	.000	.000	-100	-2	0	.00	0	/0-3(0-0-3)	0	-0.2
Total 4	133	331	47	76	9	2	0	24	38	34	7	....	.230	.309	.269	.578	58	-17	31	3.03	-3	/0-98	5	-2.6

• JACOBY, Brook Brook Wallace Jacoby b: 11/23/1959, Philadelphia, PA BR/TR, 5'11", 195 lbs. Deb: 9/13/1981

YEAR TM-L	G	AB	R	H	2B	3B	HR	RBI	BB	SO	SB	CS	AVG	OBP	SLG	OPS	OPS+	BR/A	RC	RC/G	FR	G/POS	WS	TPW
1981 Atl-N	11	10	0	2	0	0	0	1	0	3	0	0	.200	.200	.200	.400	13	-1	0	.60	0	/3-3	0	-0.1
1983 Atl-N	4	8	0	0	0	0	0	0	0	1	0	0	.000	.000	.000	.000	-93	-2	0	.00	0	/3-2	0	-0.2
1984 Cle-A	126	439	64	116	19	3	7	40	32	73	3	2	.264	.319	.369	.688	88	-7	50	3.89	-18	*3-126/S-1	8	-2.7
1985 Cle-A	161	606	72	166	26	3	20	87	48	120	2	3	.274	.327	.426	.753	105	2	81	4.65	-5	*3-161/2-1	16	-0.4
1986 Cle-A★	158	583	83	168	30	4	17	80	56	137	2	1	.288	.351	.441	.791	116	13	88	5.51	-9	*3-158	21	0.2
1987 Cle-A	155	540	73	162	26	4	32	69	75	73	2	3	.300	.388	.541	.929	142	33	110	7.41	-1	*3-144/1-7,D-4	22	2.8
1988 Cle-A	152	552	59	133	25	0	9	49	48	101	2	3	.241	.303	.335	.638	76	-18	55	3.40	2	*3-151	10	-1.5
1989 Cle-A	147	519	49	141	26	5	13	64	62	90	2	5	.272	.353	.416	.769	114	9	75	4.96	-4	*3-144/D-3	14	0.5
1990 Cle-A★	155	553	77	162	24	4	14	75	63	58	1	4	.293	.367	.427	.794	122	16	83	5.32	-2	3-99,1-78	19	1.0
1991 Cle-A	66	231	14	54	9	1	4	24	16	32	0	1	.234	.289	.333	.622	71	-10	21	3.04	0	1-55,3-15	3	-1.3
Oak-A	56	188	14	40	12	0	0	20	11	22	2	0	.213	.260	.277	.537	51	-12	13	2.23	0	3-52/1-3	1	-1.2
Yr.	122	419	28	94	21	1	4	44	27	54	2	1	.224	.276	.308	.584	62	-22	34	2.67	0	3-67,1-58	4	-2.5
1992 Cle-A	120	291	30	76	7	0	4	36	28	54	0	3	.261	.328	.326	.655	85	-7	29	3.26	1	*3-111,1-10	6	-0.5
Total 11	1311	4520	535	1220	204	24	120	545	439	764	16	25	.270	.337	.405	.742	103	15	605	4.65	-37	*3-1166,1-153/D-7,2-1,S-1	120	-3.6

• JACOBY, Harry Harry Jacoby b: Philadelphia, PA d: 7/22/1900, Philadelphia, PA Deb: 5/2/1882

YEAR TM-L	G	AB	R	H	2B	3B	HR	RBI	BB	SO	SB	CS	AVG	OBP	SLG	OPS	OPS+	BR/A	RC	RC/G	FR	G/POS	WS	TPW
1882 Bal-a	31	121	17	21	1	1	1	....	7	....	....	....	.174	.219	.223	.442	53	-5	6	1.70	7	3-19,0-13(0-0-13)	1	0.2
1885 Bal-a	11	43	4	6	2	0	0	1	2	....	....	....	.140	.178	.186	.364	15	-4	1	1.06	-2	2-11	0	-0.5
Total 2	42	164	21	27	3	1	1	1	9	....	....	....	.165	.208	.213	.422	43	-9	8	1.52	4	/3-19,0-13,2-11	1	-0.4

• JAHA, John John Emil Jaha b: 5/27/1966, Portland, OR BR/TR, 6'1", 205 lbs. Deb: 7/9/1992

YEAR TM-L	G	AB	R	H	2B	3B	HR	RBI	BB	SO	SB	CS	AVG	OBP	SLG	OPS	OPS+	BR/A	RC	RC/G	FR	G/POS	WS	TPW
1992 Mil-A	47	133	17	30	3	1	2	10	12	30	10	0	.226	.299	.308	.608	72	-3	15	3.66	0	1-38/D-8,0-1	2	-0.5
1993 Mil-A	153	515	78	136	21	0	19	70	51	109	13	9	.264	.340	.416	.755	103	1	74	4.97	9	*1-150/2-1,3-1	15	-0.3
1994 Mil-A	84	291	45	70	14	0	12	39	32	75	3	3	.241	.336	.412	.749	88	-6	40	4.57	-4	1-73,D-11	4	-1.6
1995 Mil-A	88	316	59	99	20	2	20	65	36	66	2	1	.313	.390	.579	.970	140	18	71	8.44	-1	1-81/D-6	13	1.0
1996 Mil-A	148	543	108	163	28	1	34	118	85	118	3	1	.300	.400	.543	.943	130	27	119	8.05	-1	1-85,D-63	19	1.3
1997 Mil-A	46	162	25	40	7	0	11	26	25	40	1	0	.247	.358	.494	.852	118	5	29	5.94	-1	1-27,D-20	3	0.0
1998 Mil-N	73	216	29	45	6	1	7	38	49	66	1	3	.208	.369	.343	.712	89	-2	30	4.48	-7	1-57/D-8	5	-1.4
1999 Oak-A★	142	457	93	126	23	0	35	111	101	129	2	0	.276	.416	.556	.972	151	40	111	8.60	1	*D-130/1-8	22	3.0
2000 Oak-A	33	97	14	17	1	0	1	5	33	38	1	0	.175	.398	.216	.615	63	-3	11	3.66	0	D-30	0	-0.4
2001 Oak-A	12	45	2	4	3	0	0	8	6	15	0	0	.089	.196	.156	.352	-6	-7	1	.73	0	D-12	0	-0.7
Total 10	826	2775	470	730	126	5	141	490	430	686	36	17	.263	.372	.465	.836	114	71	501	6.26	-4	1-519,D-288/2-1,3-1,0-1	83	0.5

• JAHN, Art Arthur Charles Jahn b: 12/2/1895, Struble, IA d: 1/9/1948, Little Rock, AR BR/TR, 6', 180 lbs. Deb: 7/2/1925 Career OF: 67-1-27

YEAR TM-L	G	AB	R	H	2B	3B	HR	RBI	BB	SO	SB	CS	AVG	OBP	SLG	OPS	OPS+	BR/A	RC	RC/G	FR	G/POS	WS	TPW
1925 Chi-N	58	226	30	68	10	8	0	37	11	20	2	2	.301	.336	.416	.752	90	-4	31	4.98	2	0-58(58-0-0)	5	-0.6
1928 NY-N	10	29	7	8	1	0	1	7	2	5	0	....	.276	.323	.414	.736	91	-0	4	4.46	1	/0-8(7-1-0)	1	0.0
Phi-N	36	94	8	21	4	0	0	11	4	11	0	....	.223	.270	.266	.536	39	-8	7	2.38	-1	0-29(2-0-27)	0	-1.1
Yr.	46	123	15	29	5	0	1	18	6	16	0	....	.236	.282	.301	.583	52	-9	10	2.86	0	0-37(9-1-27)	1	-1.1
Total 2	104	349	45	97	15	8	1	55	17	36	2	2	.278	.317	.375	.692	76	-13	41	4.21	2	/0-95	6	-1.8

• JAMES, Art Arthur James b: 8/2/1952, Detroit, MI BL/TL, 6', 170 lbs. Deb: 4/10/1975

YEAR TM-L	G	AB	R	H	2B	3B	HR	RBI	BB	SO	SB	CS	AVG	OBP	SLG	OPS	OPS+	BR/A	RC	RC/G	FR	G/POS	WS	TPW
1975 Det-A	11	40	2	9	2	0	0	1	1	3	1	2	.225	.244	.275	.519	44	-4	2	1.60	1	0-11(0-4-7)	0	-0.3

• JAMES, Bernie Robert Byrne James b: 9/2/1905, Angleton, TX d: 8/1/1994, San Antonio, TX BB/TR, 5'9.5", 150 lbs. Deb: 5/6/1929

YEAR TM-L	G	AB	R	H	2B	3B	HR	RBI	BB	SO	SB	CS	AVG	OBP	SLG	OPS	OPS+	BR/A	RC	RC/G	FR	G/POS	WS	TPW
1929 Bos-N	46	101	12	31	3	2	0	9	9	13	3	....	.307	.369	.376	.746	89	-1	14	5.06	-6	2-32/0-1	2	-0.6
1930 Bos-N	8	11	1	2	1	0	0	1	0	1	0	....	.182	.182	.273	.455	8	-2	1	1.47	0	/2-7	0	-0.1
1933 NY-N	60	125	22	28	2	1	1	10	8	12	5	....	.224	.271	.280	.551	58	-7	10	2.82	-2	2-26/S-6,3-5	3	-0.7
Total 3	114	237	35	61	6	3	1	20	17	26	8	....	.257	.310	.321	.630	69	-10	25	3.65	-8	/2-65,S-6,3-5,0-1	5	-1.5

YEAR TM-L	G	AB	R	H	2B	3B	HR	RBI	BB	SO	SB	CS	AVG	OBP	SLG	OPS	OPS+	BR/A	RC	RC/G	FR	G/POS	WS	TPW
• JAMES, Bert	Berton Hulon "Jesse" James b: 7/7/1886, Coopertown, TN d: 1/2/1959, Adairville, KY BL/TR, 5'11", 175 lbs. Deb: 9/18/1909																							
1909 StL-N	6	21	1	6	0	0	0	0	4	....	1	....	.286	.400	.286	.686	120	1	3	4.77	0	/O-6(0-0-6)	1	0.1
• JAMES, Charlie	Charles Wesley James b: 12/22/1937, St. Louis, MO BR/TR, 6'1", 195 lbs. Deb: 8/2/1960 Career OF: 210-13-212																							
1960 StL-N	43	50	5	9	1	0	2	5	1	12	0	0	.180	.196	.320	.516	35	-5	3	2.10	-1	O-37(23-7-9)	0	-0.7
1961 StL-N	108	349	43	89	19	2	4	44	15	59	2	2	.255	.292	.355	.647	64	-19	34	3.34	-2	O-90(39-4-56)	4	-2.6
1962 StL-N	129	388	50	107	13	4	8	59	10	58	3	4	.276	.301	.392	.693	77	-15	42	3.79	-3	*O-116(17-1-104)	7	-2.4
1963 StL-N	116	347	34	93	14	2	10	45	10	64	2	1	.268	.292	.406	.699	90	-5	37	3.70	0	*O-101(82-1-25)	7	-1.1
1964*StL-N	88	233	24	52	9	1	5	17	11	58	0	0	.223	.261	.335	.596	61	-12	19	2.76	-1	O-60(46-0-14)	2	-1.6
1965 Cin-N	26	39	2	8	0	0	0	2	1	9	0	0	.205	.225	.205	.430	21	-4	1	.99	-1	/O-7(3-0-4)	0	-0.5
Total 6	**510**	**1406**	**158**	**358**	**56**	**9**	**29**	**172**	**48**	**260**	**7**	**7**	**.255**	**.284**	**.369**	**.653**	**71**	**-59**	**137**	**3.33**	**-7**	**O-411**	**20**	**-8.9**
• JAMES, Chris	Donald Chris James b: 10/4/1962, Rusk, TX BR/TR, 6'1", 190 lbs. Deb: 4/23/1986 Career OF: 322-51-229																							
1986 Phi-N	16	46	5	13	3	0	1	5	1	13	0	0	.283	.298	.413	.711	91	-1	5	4.13	0	O-11(4-7-0)	1	-0.1
1987 Phi-N	115	358	48	105	20	6	17	54	27	67	3	1	.293	.346	.525	.871	123	10	66	6.77	-3	*O-108(96-16-5)	14	0.3
1988 Phi-N	150	566	57	137	24	1	19	66	31	73	7	4	.242	.285	.389	.674	90	-10	59	3.51	1	*O-116(8-27-101),3-31	8	-1.3
1989 Phi-N	45	179	14	37	4	0	2	19	4	23	3	1	.207	.224	.263	.487	39	-15	8	1.49	-1	O-37(37-0-0),3-11	1	-1.8
SD-N	87	303	41	80	13	2	11	46	22	45	2	1	.264	.316	.429	.745	111	3	38	4.30	1	O-79(50-0-29)/3-6	7	0.2
Yr.	132	482	55	117	17	2	13	65	26	68	5	2	.243	.283	.367	.650	85	-11	47	3.20	0	*O-116(87-0-29),3-17	8	-1.5
1990 Cle-A	140	528	62	158	32	4	12	70	31	71	4	3	.299	.343	.443	.786	119	11	78	5.39	0	*D-124,O-14(12-1-1)	16	0.6
1991 Cle-A	115	437	31	104	16	2	5	41	18	61	3	4	.238	.275	.318	.593	63	-24	36	2.78	1	D-60,O-39(25-0-18),1-15	2	-2.7
1992 SF-N	111	248	25	60	10	4	5	32	14	45	2	3	.242	.288	.375	.663	91	-5	26	3.64	1	O-62(60-0-2)	5	-0.7
1993 Hou-N	65	129	19	33	10	1	6	19	15	34	2	0	.256	.338	.488	.826	122	4	22	5.88	2	O-34(16-0-18)	5	0.5
Tex-A	8	31	5	11	1	0	3	7	3	6	0	0	.355	.412	.677	1.089	195	4	9	12.11	0	/O-7(4-0-4)	2	0.3
1994 Tex-A	52	133	28	34	8	4	7	19	20	38	0	0	.256	.365	.534	.899	128	6	27	6.86	0	O-48(1-0-47)	3	0.3
1995 KC-A	26	58	6	18	3	0	2	7	6	10	1	0	.310	.385	.466	.850	118	2	11	6.83	0	D-14/O-5(5-0-0)	2	0.1
Bos-A	16	24	2	4	1	0	0	1	1	4	0	0	.167	.200	.208	.408	6	-3	1	1.10	0	/O-8(4-0-4),D-6	0	-0.4
Yr.	42	82	8	22	4	0	2	8	7	14	1	0	.268	.333	.390	.724	86	-2	12	4.83	0	D-20,O-13(9-0-4)	2	-0.3
Total 10	**946**	**3040**	**343**	**794**	**145**	**24**	**90**	**386**	**193**	**490**	**27**	**17**	**.261**	**.310**	**.413**	**.723**	**99**	**-17**	**386**	**4.40**	**1**	**O-568,D-204/3-48,1-15**	**66**	**-4.7**
• JAMES, Cleo	Cleo Joel James b: 8/31/1940, Clarksdale, MS BR/TR, 5'10", 176 lbs. Deb: 4/15/1968 Career OF: 22-126-17																							
1968 LA-N	10	10	2	2	1	0	0	0	0	6	0	0	.200	.200	.300	.500	52	-1	1	2.03	0	/O-2(2-0-0)	0	-0.1
1970 Chi-N	100	176	33	37	7	2	3	14	17	24	5	0	.210	.298	.324	.622	59	-9	18	3.42	3	O-90(5-83-2)	3	-0.8
1971 Chi-N	54	150	25	43	7	0	2	13	10	16	6	2	.287	.355	.373	.729	93	-0	21	4.77	-1	O-48(1-35-14)/3-2	5	-0.3
1973 Chi-N	44	45	9	5	0	0	0	0	1	6	5	0	.111	.130	.111	.242	-30	-7	1	.45	0	O-22(14-8-1)	0	-0.7
Total 4	**208**	**381**	**69**	**87**	**15**	**2**	**5**	**27**	**28**	**52**	**16**	**2**	**.228**	**.300**	**.318**	**.618**	**63**	**-17**	**40**	**3.48**	**3**	**O-162/3-2**	**8**	**-1.9**
• JAMES, Dion	Dion James b: 11/9/1962, Philadelphia, PA BL/TL, 6'1", 170 lbs. Deb: 9/16/1983 Career OF: 322-242-155																							
1983 Mil-A	11	20	1	2	0	0	0	1	2	2	1	0	.100	.182	.100	.282	-22	-3	1	.83	0	/O-9(4-8-1),D-2	0	-0.3
1984 Mil-A	128	387	52	114	19	5	1	30	32	41	10	10	.295	.353	.377	.730	106	2	50	4.56	1	*O-118(2-30-93)	11	-0.2
1985 Mil-A	18	49	5	11	1	0	0	3	6	6	0	0	.224	.309	.245	.554	54	-3	4	2.98	-1	O-11(0-11-0)/D-3	0	-0.4
1987 Atl-N	134	494	80	154	37	6	10	61	70	63	10	8	.312	.399	.472	.871	124	18	95	7.07	-4	*O-126(29-99-0)	19	1.1
1988 Atl-N	132	386	46	99	17	5	3	30	58	59	9	9	.256	.355	.350	.705	98	-1	48	4.11	-4	*O-120(86-49-3)	9	-0.8
1989 Atl-N	63	170	15	44	7	0	1	11	25	23	1	3	.259	.357	.318	.675	92	-2	20	3.90	1	O-46(26-1-23)/1-8	3	-0.3
Cle-A	71	245	26	75	11	0	4	29	24	26	1	4	.306	.368	.400	.768	114	4	35	5.19	-1	O-37(26-10-0),D-27/1-2	6	0.0
1990 Cle-A	87	248	28	68	15	2	1	22	27	23	5	3	.274	.348	.363	.711	99	0	31	4.40	-1	1-35,O-33(24-8-0),D-10	6	-0.4
1992 NY-A	67	145	24	38	8	0	3	17	22	15	1	0	.262	.363	.379	.742	109	3	21	5.14	-1	O-46(8-12-27)/D-5	4	0.1
1993 NY-A	115	343	62	114	21	2	7	36	31	31	0	0	.332	.391	.466	.857	134	17	64	7.28	-1	*O-103(91-14-1)/1-1,D-1	11	1.2
1995*NY-A	85	209	22	60	6	1	2	26	20	16	4	1	.287	.349	.354	.703	85	-4	26	4.51	0	O-29(23-0-6),D-27/1-6	4	-0.6
1996 NY-A	6	12	1	2	0	0	0	0	1	2	1	0	.167	.231	.167	.397	3	-2	0	1.05	0	/O-4(3-0-1),D-1	0	-0.2
Total 11	**917**	**2708**	**362**	**781**	**142**	**21**	**32**	**266**	**318**	**307**	**43**	**38**	**.288**	**.365**	**.392**	**.757**	**107**	**28**	**396**	**5.19**	**-11**	**O-682/D-76,1-52**	**73**	**-0.7**
• JAMES, Skip	Philip Robert James b: 10/21/1949, Elmhurst, IL BL/TL, 6', 185 lbs. Deb: 9/12/1977																							
1977 SF-N	10	15	3	4	1	0	0	3	2	3	0	0	.267	.353	.333	.686	86	-0	2	3.65	0	/1-9	0	0.0
1978 SF-N	41	21	5	2	1	0	0	3	4	5	1	0	.095	.240	.143	.383	10	-2	1	.96	0	1-27	0	-0.2
Total 2	**51**	**36**	**8**	**6**	**2**	**0**	**0**	**6**	**6**	**8**	**1**	**0**	**.167**	**.286**	**.222**	**.508**	**40**	**-2**	**2**	**1.91**	**1**	**/1-36**	**0**	**-0.3**
• JAMIESON, Charlie	Charles Devine "Cuckoo" Jamieson b: 2/7/1893, Paterson, NJ d: 10/27/1969, Paterson, NJ BL/TL, 5'8.5", 165 lbs. Deb: 9/20/1915 Career OF: 1408-34-203 ♦																							
1915 Was-A	17	68	9	19	3	2	0	7	6	9	0	....	.279	.338	.382	.720	113	1	9	4.73	3	O-17(17-0-0)	3	0.4
1916 Was-A	64	145	16	36	4	0	0	13	18	18	5	....	.248	.331	.276	.607	83	-2	16	3.56	-2	O-41(24-2-15)/1-4,P-1	3	-0.8
1917 Was-A	20	35	4	6	2	0	0	2	6	5	0	....	.171	.293	.229	.521	60	-1	2	1.98	-1	/O-9(9-0-0),P-1	0	-1.3
Phi-A	85	345	41	92	6	2	0	27	37	36	8	....	.267	.341	.296	.637	96	-1	36	3.63	-2	O-83(0-0-83)	8	-0.8
Yr.	105	380	45	98	8	2	0	29	43	41	8	....	.258	.336	.289	.626	92	-2	38	3.46	-3	O-92(9-0-83)/P-1	8	-2.1
1918 Phi-A	110	416	50	84	11	2	0	11	54	30	11	....	.202	.297	.238	.535	61	-18	30	2.33	0	*O-102(0-1-101)/P-5	4	-3.0
1919 Cle-A	26	17	3	6	2	1	0	2	0	2	2	....	.353	.353	.588	.941	153	2	4	9.21	0	/P-4,O-3(0-2-1)	1	-0.2
1920*Cle-A	108	370	69	118	17	7	1	40	41	26	2	9	.319	.388	.411	.799	108	3	58	5.63	2	O-98(93-5-0)/1-4	12	0.2
1921 Cle-A	140	536	94	166	33	10	1	46	67	27	8	4	.310	.387	.414	.802	103	5	89	6.26	2	*O-137(125-19-0)	17	-0.2
1922 Cle-A	145	567	87	183	29	11	3	57	54	22	15	9	.323	.388	.429	.816	112	12	96	6.24	2	*O-144(141-2-1)/P-2	19	0.4
1923 Cle-A	152	644	130	**222**	36	12	2	51	80	37	18	14	.345	.422	.447	.869	129	30	124	7.33	7	*O-152(152-0-0)	25	2.4
1924 Cle-A	143	594	98	213	34	8	3	54	47	15	21	12	.359	.407	.458	.865	121	20	111	7.15	0	*O-139(139-0-0)	19	0.8
1925 Cle-A	138	557	109	165	24	5	4	42	72	26	14	18	.296	.380	.379	.759	92	-8	81	5.07	3	*O-135(135-0-0)	12	-1.4
1926 Cle-A	143	555	89	166	33	7	2	45	53	22	9	7	.299	.361	.395	.756	96	-3	81	5.14	2	*O-143(143-0-0)	17	-1.1
1927 Cle-A	127	489	73	151	23	6	0	36	64	14	7	9	.309	.394	.380	.775	101	2	76	5.58	3	*O-127(127-0-0)	15	-0.5
1928 Cle-A	112	433	63	133	18	4	1	37	56	20	3	12	.307	.388	.374	.762	100	-1	63	5.15	18	*O-111(111-0-0)	12	0.8
1929 Cle-A	102	364	56	106	22	1	0	26	50	12	2	13	.291	.378	.357	.735	87	-9	48	4.62	-1	O-93(93-0-0)	7	-1.6
1930 Cle-A	103	366	64	110	22	1	1	52	36	20	5	2	.301	.368	.374	.742	85	-6	53	5.18	0	O-95(93-2-0)	8	-1.1
1931 Cle-A	28	43	7	13	2	1	0	4	5	1	1	1	.302	.375	.395	.770	97	-0	6	5.47	-1	/O-7(6-1-0)	1	-0.1
1932 Cle-A	16	16	0	1	1	0	0	0	2	3	0	0	.063	.211	.125	.336	-10	-3	1	.99	0	/O-2(0-0-2)	0	-0.2
Total 18	**1779**	**6560**	**1062**	**1990**	**322**	**80**	**18**	**552**	**748**	**345**	**131**	**110**	**.303**	**.378**	**.385**	**.763**	**101**	**21**	**983**	**5.38**	**36**	***O-1638/P-13,1-8**	**183**	**-7.3**
• JANOWICZ, Vic	Victor Felix Janowicz b: 2/26/1930, Elyria, OH d: 2/27/1996, Columbus, OH BR/TR, 5'9", 185 lbs. Deb: 5/31/1953																							
1953 Pit-N	42	123	10	31	3	1	2	8	5	31	0	1	.252	.287	.341	.628	63	-7	11	3.17	-1	C-35	1	-0.7
1954 Pit-N	41	73	10	11	3	0	0	2	7	23	0	0	.151	.235	.192	.426	13	-9	4	1.66	-2	3-18/O-1	0	-1.1
Total 2	**83**	**196**	**20**	**42**	**6**	**1**	**2**	**10**	**12**	**54**	**0**	**1**	**.214**	**.267**	**.286**	**.552**	**44**	**-17**	**15**	**2.57**	**-3**	**/C-35,3-18,O-1**	**1**	**-1.8**
• JANSEN, Ray	Raymond William Jansen b: 1/16/1889, St. Louis, MO d: 3/19/1934, St. Louis, MO BR/TR, 5'11", 155 lbs. Deb: 9/30/1910																							
1910 StL-A	1	5	0	4	0	0	0	0	0	....	0	....	.800	.800	.800	1.600	428	2	3	83.15	1	/3-1	1	0.3
• JANTZEN, Heinie	Walter C. Jantzen b: 4/9/1890, Chicago, IL d: 4/1/1948, Hines, IL BR/TR, 5'11.5", 170 lbs. Deb: 6/29/1912																							
1912 StL-A	31	119	10	22	0	1	1	8	4	....	3	....	.185	.218	.227	.445	28	-11	6	1.67	2	O-31(0-0-31)	1	-1.1
• JANVRIN, Hal	Harold Chandler "Childe Harold" Janvrin b: 8/27/1892, Haverhill, MA d: 3/1/1962, Boston, MA BR/TR, 5'11.5", 168 lbs. Deb: 7/9/1911 Career OF: 17-4-1																							
1911 Bos-A	9	27	2	4	1	0	0	1	3	....	0	....	.148	.258	.185	.443	25	-3	1	1.48	-2	/3-5,1-4	0	-0.5
1913 Bos-A	87	276	18	57	5	1	3	25	23	27	17	....	.207	.272	.264	.537	56	-16	24	2.64	-7	S-48,3-19/2-8,1-6	3	-2.0
1914 Bos-A	145	492	65	117	18	6	1	51	38	50	29	20	.238	.296	.305	.601	81	-15	48	3.05	-3	2-59,1-57,S-20/3-6	9	-1.8
1915*Bos-A	99	316	41	85	9	1	0	37	14	27	8	14	.269	.317	.304	.620	88	-10	31	3.11	-6	S-64,3-20/2-8	8	-1.2
1916*Bos-A	117	310	32	69	11	4	0	26	32	32	6	....	.223	.299	.284	.583	75	-9	31	3.10	-4	S-59,2-39/1-4,3-4	9	-1.1
1917 Bos-A	55	127	21	25	3	0	0	8	11	13	2	....	.197	.266	.220	.487	49	-8	9	2.05	-5	2-38,S-10/1-1	1	-1.4

YEAR TM-L	G	AB	R	H	2B	3B	HR	RBI	BB	SO	SB	CS	AVG	OBP	SLG	OPS	OPS+	BR/A	RC	RC/G	FR	G/POS	WS	TPW
1919 Was-A	61	208	17	37	4	1	1	13	19	17	8	....	.178	.253	.221	.474	34	-18	13	1.96	-17	2-56/S-2	0	-3.5
StL-N	7	14	1	3	1	0	0	1	2	2	0	....	.214	.313	.286	.598	86	-0	1	2.92	-1	/2-2,3-1,S-1	0	-0.1
1920 StL-N	87	270	33	74	8	4	1	28	17	19	5	6	.274	.317	.344	.662	92	-3	29	3.63	-4	S-27,1-25,0-20(16-4-0)/2-6	5	-0.8
1921 StL-N	18	32	5	9	1	0	0	5	1	0	1	0	.281	.303	.313	.616	64	-1	3	3.43	0	/1-9,2-1	0	-0.2
Bro-N	44	92	8	18	4	0	0	14	7	6	3	1	.196	.253	.239	.492	30	-9	6	2.06	-6	S-17,2-10/1-8,3-5,0-1	1	-1.4
Yr.	62	124	13	27	5	0	0	19	8	6	4	1	.218	.265	.258	.523	39	-10	9	2.39	-6	1-17,S-17,2-11/3-5,0-1	1	-1.5
1922 Bro-N	30	57	7	17	3	1	0	1	4	4	0	0	.298	.344	.386	.730	89	-1	8	4.95	-3	2-15/S-4,3-2,1-1,0-1	2	-0.3
Total 10	**759**	**2221**	**250**	**515**	**68**	**18**	**6**	**210**	**171**	**197**	**79**	**41**	**.232**	**.292**	**.287**	**.579**	**70**	**-93**	**205**	**2.90**	**-59**	**S-252,2-242,1-115/3-62,0-22**	**38**	**-14.3**

• JARVIS, Roy Leroy Gilbert Jarvis b: 6/27/1926, Shawnee, OK d: 1/13/1990, Oklahoma City, OK BR/TR, 5'9", 160 lbs. Deb: 4/30/1944

YEAR TM-L	G	AB	R	H	2B	3B	HR	RBI	BB	SO	SB	CS	AVG	OBP	SLG	OPS	OPS+	BR/A	RC	RC/G	FR	G/POS	WS	TPW
1944 Bro-N	1	1	0	0	0	0	0	0	0	1	0	....	.000	.000	.000	.000	-102	-0	0	.00	0	/C-1	0	0.0
1946 Pit-N	2	4	0	1	0	0	0	0	1	1	0	....	.250	.400	.250	.650	84	0	1	4.54	0	/C-1	0	0.0
1947 Pit-N	18	45	4	7	1	0	1	4	6	5	0	....	.156	.255	.244	.499	32	-4	3	2.05	0	C-15	0	-0.4
Total 3	**21**	**50**	**4**	**8**	**1**	**0**	**1**	**4**	**7**	**7**	**0**	**....**	**.160**	**.263**	**.240**	**.503**	**34**	**-5**	**3**	**2.17**	**0**	**/C-17**	**0**	**-0.4**

• JATA, Paul Paul Jata b: 9/4/1949, Astoria, NY BR/TR, 6'1", 190 lbs. Deb: 4/19/1972

YEAR TM-L	G	AB	R	H	2B	3B	HR	RBI	BB	SO	SB	CS	AVG	OBP	SLG	OPS	OPS+	BR/A	RC	RC/G	FR	G/POS	WS	TPW
1972 Det-A	32	74	8	17	2	0	0	3	7	14	0	1	.230	.296	.257	.553	63	-4	6	2.58	-1	1-12,0-10(5-0-5)/C-1	1	-0.7

• JAVIER, Al Ignacio Alfredo Javier b: 2/4/1954, San Pedro de Macoris, Dominican Republic BR/TR, 5'11", 170 lbs. Deb: 9/9/1976

YEAR TM-L	G	AB	R	H	2B	3B	HR	RBI	BB	SO	SB	CS	AVG	OBP	SLG	OPS	OPS+	BR/A	RC	RC/G	FR	G/POS	WS	TPW
1976 Hou-N	8	24	1	5	0	0	0	0	2	5	0	0	.208	.269	.208	.478	40	-2	1	1.64	0	/0-7(4-0-4)	0	-0.2

• JAVIER, Julian Manuel Julian (Liranzo) Javier b: 8/9/1936, San Francisco de Macoris, Dominican Republic BR/TR, 6'1", 175 lbs. Deb: 5/28/1960

YEAR TM-L	G	AB	R	H	2B	3B	HR	RBI	BB	SO	SB	CS	AVG	OBP	SLG	OPS	OPS+	BR/A	RC	RC/G	FR	G/POS	WS	TPW
1960 StL-N	119	451	55	107	19	8	4	21	21	72	19	4	.237	.273	.341	.614	61	-22	43	3.13	8	*2-119	9	-0.5
1961 StL-N	113	445	58	124	14	3	2	41	30	51	11	4	.279	.327	.337	.664	70	-18	51	4.07	-1	*2-113	9	-1.0
1962 StL-N	155	598	97	157	25	5	7	39	47	73	26	9	.263	.317	.356	.674	73	-21	70	3.97	2	*2-151/S-4	14	-0.6
1963 StL-N★	161	609	82	160	27	9	9	46	24	86	18	10	.263	.297	.381	.678	86	-12	68	3.78	9	*2-161	15	1.2
1964*StL-N	155	535	66	129	19	5	12	65	30	82	9	7	.241	.283	.363	.645	74	-20	52	3.29	8	*2-154	11	0.0
1965 StL-N	77	229	34	52	6	4	2	23	8	44	5	5	.227	.263	.314	.577	56	-15	17	2.36	4	2-69	3	-0.5
1966 StL-N	147	460	52	105	13	5	7	31	26	63	11	5	.228	.271	.324	.595	65	-22	40	2.88	5	*2-145	10	-0.6
1967*StL-N	140	520	68	146	16	3	14	64	25	92	6	7	.281	.315	.404	.719	106	1	63	4.29	-11	*2-138	17	0.2
1968*StL-N★	139	519	54	135	25	4	4	52	24	61	10	3	.260	.294	.347	.641	93	-4	52	3.46	0	*2-139	16	0.8
1969 StL-N	143	493	59	139	28	2	10	42	40	74	8	4	.282	.337	.408	.745	107	4	67	4.88	-5	*2-141	17	0.9
1970 StL-N	139	513	62	129	16	3	2	42	24	70	6	4	.251	.286	.306	.592	57	-32	42	2.76	9	*2-137	8	-1.4
1971 StL-N	90	259	32	67	6	4	3	28	9	33	5	1	.259	.289	.347	.636	76	-8	25	3.25	-3	2-80/3-1	5	-0.7
1972*Cin-N	44	91	3	19	2	0	2	12	6	11	1	0	.209	.258	.297	.554	61	-5	7	2.47	-1	3-19/2-5,1-1	1	-0.6
Total 13	**1622**	**5722**	**722**	**1469**	**216**	**55**	**78**	**506**	**314**	**812**	**135**	**63**	**.257**	**.298**	**.355**	**.652**	**78**	**-173**	**597**	**3.55**	**23**	***2-1552/3-20,S-4,1-1**	**135**	**-2.9**

• JAVIER, Stan Stanley Julian Antonio (De Javier) Javier
b: 1/9/1964, San Francisco de Macoris, Dominican Republic BB/TR, 6', 185 lbs. Deb: 4/15/1984 Career OF: 463-693-493

YEAR TM-L	G	AB	R	H	2B	3B	HR	RBI	BB	SO	SB	CS	AVG	OBP	SLG	OPS	OPS+	BR/A	RC	RC/G	FR	G/POS	WS	TPW
1984 NY-A	7	7	1	1	0	0	0	0	0	1	0	0	.143	.143	.143	.286	-22	-1	0	.64	0	/O-5(0-3-3)	0	-0.2
1986 Oak-A	59	114	13	23	8	0	0	8	16	27	8	0	.202	.305	.272	.577	63	-3	11	3.33	2	O-51(3-49-0)/D-2	3	-0.2
1987 Oak-A	81	151	22	28	3	1	2	9	19	33	3	2	.185	.276	.258	.535	46	-12	12	2.37	1	O-71(8-52-15)/1-6,D-1	1	-1.2
1988*Oak-A	125	397	49	102	13	3	2	35	32	63	20	1	.257	.316	.320	.635	81	-6	42	3.55	0	*O-115(69-45-29)/1-4,D-2	8	-0.9
1989*Oak-A	112	310	42	77	12	3	1	28	31	45	12	2	.248	.319	.316	.635	82	-5	33	3.66	0	*O-107(23-28-72)/1-1,2-1	9	-0.8
1990 Oak-A	19	33	4	8	0	2	0	3	3	6	0	0	.242	.306	.364	.669	90	-0	4	4.22	0	O-13(4-4-5)/D-2	1	-0.1
LA-N	104	276	56	84	9	4	3	24	37	44	15	7	.304	.387	.399	.785	120	9	44	5.59	0	O-87(9-70-12)	12	0.8
1991 LA-N	121	176	21	36	5	3	1	11	16	36	7	1	.205	.271	.284	.555	57	-9	14	2.59	-1	O-69(49-7-18)/1-2	1	-1.2
1992 LA-N	56	58	6	11	3	0	1	5	6	11	1	2	.190	.277	.293	.570	62	-4	5	2.53	-1	O-27(15-2-11)	1	-0.5
Phi-N	74	276	36	72	14	1	0	24	31	43	17	1	.261	.340	.319	.659	88	-0	34	4.35	2	O-74(27-49-1)	9	0.0
Yr.	130	334	42	83	17	1	1	29	37	54	18	3	.249	.329	.314	.643	83	-4	39	4.01	2	*O-101(42-51-12)	10	-0.4
1993 Cal-A	92	237	33	69	10	4	3	28	27	33	12	2	.291	.366	.405	.771	104	4	36	5.43	-3	O-64(36-16-16),1-12/2-2,D	6	-0.1
1994 Oak-A	109	419	75	114	23	0	10	44	49	76	24	7	.272	.351	.399	.750	101	4	62	5.10	0	*O-108(12-102-1)/1-1,3-1	11	0.4
1995 Oak-A	130	442	81	123	20	2	8	56	49	63	36	5	.278	.356	.387	.742	99	6	67	5.31	-2	*O-124(32-101-1)/3-1	13	0.3
1996 SF-N	71	274	44	74	25	0	2	22	25	51	14	2	.270	.336	.383	.719	93	-1	38	4.84	-1	O-71(0-53-18)	5	-0.3
1997*SF-N	142	440	69	126	16	4	8	50	56	70	25	3	.286	.373	.395	.769	105	9	73	5.93	-3	*O-130(5-46-95)/1-3	17	0.2
1998 SF-N	135	417	63	121	13	5	4	49	65	63	21	5	.290	.387	.374	.761	108	10	64	5.42	-7	*O-121(6-29-95)	12	-0.1
1999 SF-N	112	333	49	92	15	1	3	30	29	55	13	6	.276	.336	.354	.690	81	-10	41	4.27	0	O-94(51-3-42)	6	-1.2
*Hou-N	20	64	12	21	4	1	0	4	9	8	3	1	.328	.411	.422	.833	113	2	11	6.47	0	O-18(6-7-10)/D-1	2	0.1
Yr.	132	397	61	113	19	2	3	34	38	63	16	7	.285	.349	.365	.714	86	-8	52	4.61	0	*O-112(57-10-52)/D-1	8	-1.1
2000*Sea-A	105	342	61	94	18	5	5	40	42	64	4	3	.275	.354	.401	.755	96	-2	49	5.01	-4	O-88(46-14-38)/D-4,1-3	9	-0.9
2001*Sea-A	89	281	44	82	14	1	4	33	36	47	11	1	.292	.376	.391	.768	109	7	44	5.58	-1	O-76(62-13-11)/1-6,D-2	11	0.3
Total 17	**1763**	**5047**	**781**	**1358**	**225**	**40**	**57**	**503**	**578**	**839**	**246**	**51**	**.269**	**.347**	**.363**	**.710**	**93**	**-1**	**686**	**4.69**	**-18**	***O-1513/1-38,D-15,2-3,3-2**	**137**	**-5.4**

• JEANES, Tex Ernest Lee Jeanes b: 12/19/1900, Maypearl, TX d: 4/5/1973, Longview, TX BR/TR, 6', 176 lbs. Deb: 4/20/1921 Career OF: 10-22-6

YEAR TM-L	G	AB	R	H	2B	3B	HR	RBI	BB	SO	SB	CS	AVG	OBP	SLG	OPS	OPS+	BR/A	RC	RC/G	FR	G/POS	WS	TPW
1921 Cle-A	5	3	2	2	1	0	0	4	1	0	0	0	.667	.750	1.000	1.750	338	1	2	28.77	0	/O-5(1-2-1)	0	0.1
1922 Cle-A	1	1	0	0	0	0	0	0	1	0	0	0	.000	.500	.000	.500	39	0	0	3.31	0	/O-1,P-1	0	0.0
1925 Was-A	15	19	2	5	1	0	1	4	3	2	1	0	.263	.364	.474	.837	113	1	4	6.80	-1	O-13(1-10-2)	1	-0.1
1926 Was-A	21	30	6	7	2	0	0	3	0	3	0	0	.233	.233	.300	.533	39	-3	2	2.28	0	O-14(3-10-1)	0	-0.3
1927 NY-N	11	20	5	6	0	0	0	0	2	2	0	....	.300	.364	.300	.664	79	-0	2	4.09	1	/O-6(4-0-2),P-1	0	-0.1
Total 5	**53**	**73**	**15**	**20**	**4**	**0**	**1**	**11**	**7**	**7**	**1**	**0**	**.274**	**.338**	**.370**	**.707**	**88**	**-1**	**10**	**4.87**	**0**	**/O-39,P-2**	**1**	**-0.3**

• JEFFCOAT, Hal Harold Bentley Jeffcoat b: 9/6/1924, West Columbia, SC BR/TR, 5'10.5", 185 lbs. Deb: 4/20/1948 Career OF: 29-435-97 ♦

YEAR TM-L	G	AB	R	H	2B	3B	HR	RBI	BB	SO	SB	CS	AVG	OBP	SLG	OPS	OPS+	BR/A	RC	RC/G	FR	G/POS	WS	TPW
1948 Chi-N	134	473	53	132	16	4	4	42	24	68	8	....	.279	.315	.355	.670	84	-12	54	4.01	9	*O-119(0-119-0)	10	-0.6
1949 Chi-N	108	363	43	89	18	6	2	26	20	48	12	....	.245	.286	.344	.631	70	-16	36	3.42	3	*O-101(1-68-32)	6	-1.6
1950 Chi-N	66	179	21	42	13	1	2	18	6	23	7	....	.235	.259	.352	.611	60	-11	13	2.34	-0	O-53(12-11-31)	1	-1.3
1951 Chi-N	113	278	44	76	20	2	4	27	16	23	8	4	.273	.315	.403	.718	90	-5	35	4.43	4	O-87(14-39-34)	7	-0.3
1952 Chi-N	102	297	29	65	17	2	4	30	15	40	7	2	.219	.259	.330	.589	61	-16	22	2.27	8	O-95(0-95-0)	5	-1.0
1953 Chi-N	106	183	22	43	3	1	4	22	21	26	5	0	.235	.314	.328	.642	66	-8	20	3.70	-3	O-100(2-99-0)	3	-1.3
1954 Chi-N	56	31	13	8	2	1	1	6	1	7	2	0	.258	.281	.484	.765	94	3	4	4.24	0	P-43/O-3(0-3-0)	4	-0.7
1955 Chi-N	52	23	3	4	0	0	1	1	2	9	0	0	.174	.240	.304	.544	43	1	1	1.49	1	P-50	10	1.3
1956 Cin-N	49	54	5	8	2	0	0	5	3	20	0	1	.148	.193	.185	.378	2	-1	2	.98	3	P-38	11	0.3
1957 Cin-N	53	69	13	14	3	1	4	11	5	20	0	0	.203	.267	.449	.716	82	6	8	3.31	-1	P-37	11	-0.4
1958 Cin-N	50	9	2	5	0	0	0	0	1	2	0	0	.556	.600	.556	1.156	198	2	3	21.30	2	P-49/O-1	8	0.5
1959 Cin-N	17	1	1	1	1	0	0	0	0	0	0	0	1.000	1.000	2.000	3.000	655	1	2	∞	0	P-17	2	0.2
StL-N	12	3	0	0	0	0	0	0	0	3	0	0	.000	.000	.000	.000	-94	-0	0	.00	0	P-11	0	-1.0
Yr.	29	4	1	1	1	0	0	0	0	3	0	0	.250	.250	.500	.750	93	0	2	.00	0	P-28	2	-0.7
Total 12	**918**	**1963**	**249**	**487**	**95**	**18**	**26**	**188**	**114**	**289**	**49**	**7**	**.248**	**.291**	**.355**	**.646**	**73**	**-56**	**200**	**3.37**	**26**	**O-559,P-245**	**78**	**-5.8**

• JEFFERIES, Gregg Gregory Scott Jefferies b: 8/1/1967, Burlingame, CA BB/TR, 5'11", 185 lbs. Deb: 9/6/1987 Career OF: 369-0-0

YEAR TM-L	G	AB	R	H	2B	3B	HR	RBI	BB	SO	SB	CS	AVG	OBP	SLG	OPS	OPS+	BR/A	RC	RC/G	FR	G/POS	WS	TPW
1987 NY-N	6	6	0	3	1	0	0	2	0	0	0	0	.500	.500	.667	1.167	217	1	2	18.00	0	....	1	0.1
1988*NY-N	29	109	19	35	8	2	6	17	8	10	5	1	.321	.368	.596	.964	181	11	24	8.55	-1	3-20,2-10	7	1.1
1989 NY-N	141	508	72	131	28	2	12	56	39	46	21	6	.258	.317	.392	.709	107	5	61	4.06	-11	*2-123,3-20	14	-0.3
1990 NY-N	153	604	96	171	**40**	3	15	68	46	40	11	2	.283	.339	.434	.773	111	9	89	5.34	-16	*2-118,3-34	20	-0.4
1991 NY-N	136	486	59	132	19	2	9	62	47	38	26	5	.272	.338	.374	.713	101	5	64	4.60	-14	2-77,3-51	15	-0.8
1992 KC-A	152	604	66	172	36	3	10	75	43	29	19	9	.285	.333	.404	.737	103	1	75	4.27	1	*3-146/2-1,D-1	14	0.4
1993 StL-N★	142	544	89	186	24	3	16	83	62	32	46	9	.342	.411	.485	.896	142	40	113	7.87	-10	*1-140/2-1	28	1.8
1994 StL-N★	103	397	52	129	27	1	12	55	45	26	12	5	.325	.395	.489	.884	131	19	76	7.18	-7	*1-102	17	0.3
1995 Phi-N	114	480	69	147	31	2	11	56	35	26	9	5	.306	.353	.448	.801	109	5	72	5.39	-1	1-59,O-55(55-0-0)	10	-0.4
1996 Phi-N	104	404	59	118	17	3	7	51	36	21	20	6	.292	.351	.401	.752	97	-0	57	5.07	2	1-53,O-51(51-0-0)	10	-0.5
1997 Phi-N	130	476	68	122	25	3	11	48	53	27	12	6	.256	.333	.391	.724	89	-8	63	4.61	0	*O-124(124-0-0)	10	-1.3
1998 Phi-N	125	483	65	142	22	3	8	48	29	27	11	3	.294	.335	.402	.737	91	-6	61	4.51	-3	*O-121(121-0-0)	11	-1.3

YEAR TM-L	G	AB	R	H	2B	3B	HR	RBI	BB	SO	SB	CS	AVG	OBP	SLG	OPS	OPS+	BR/A	RC	RC/G	FR	G/POS	WS	TPW
Ana-A	19	72	7	25	6	0	1	10	0	5	1	0	.347	.347	.472	.819	110	1	11	6.08	-1	O-15(15-0-0)/1-3	3	0.0
1999 Det-A	70	205	22	41	8	0	6	18	13	11	3	4	.200	.261	.327	.588	49	-18	15	2.23	0	D-45/1-3,2-2,O-2(2-0-0)	0	-1.9
2000 Det-A	41	142	18	39	8	0	2	14	16	10	0	2	.275	.348	.373	.721	85	-4	17	3.95	-3	1-20,2-14/3-6,D-2,O-1	2	-0.7
Total 14	1465	5520	761	1593	300	27	126	663	472	348	196	63	.289	.347	.421	.768	107	62	800	5.14	-64	1-380,O-369,2-346,3-277/D-48	162	-3.8
• JEFFERSON, Reggie	Reginald Jirod Jefferson b: 9/25/1968, Tallahassee, FL BL/TL, 6'4", 215 lbs. Deb: 5/18/1991 Career OF: 49-0-0																							
1991 Cin-N	5	7	1	1	0	0	1	1	1	2	0	0	.143	.250	.571	.821	120	0	1	4.79	0	/1-2	0	0.0
Cle-A	26	101	10	20	3	0	2	12	3	22	0	0	.198	.221	.287	.508	39	-9	6	2.07	1	1-26	0	-0.9
1992 Cle-A	24	89	8	30	6	2	1	6	1	17	0	0	.337	.352	.483	.835	134	3	14	6.35	1	1-15/D-7	3	0.3
1993 Cle-A	113	366	35	91	11	2	10	34	28	78	1	3	.249	.311	.372	.682	83	-10	41	3.84	0	D-88,1-15	4	-1.6
1994 Sea-A	63	162	24	53	11	0	8	32	17	32	0	0	.327	.394	.543	.938	136	9	33	7.68	0	D-32,1-13/O-2(2-0-0)	7	0.6
1995*Bos-A	46	121	21	35	8	0	5	26	9	24	0	0	.289	.338	.479	.818	106	1	19	5.63	1	D-32/1-7,O-2(2-0-0)	4	-0.1
1996 Bos-A	122	386	67	134	30	4	19	74	25	89	0	0	.347	.391	.593	.985	141	23	86	8.66	1	D-49,O-45(45-0-0),1-16	14	1.7
1997 Bos-A	136	489	74	156	33	1	13	67	24	93	1	2	.319	.360	.470	.830	112	7	77	5.82	-1	*D-119,1-12	10	-0.2
1998 Bos-A	62	196	24	60	16	1	8	31	21	40	0	0	.306	.376	.520	.897	127	8	37	6.92	0	D-48/1-7	6	0.4
1999 Bos-A	83	206	21	57	13	1	5	17	17	54	0	0	.277	.338	.422	.760	90	-3	27	4.68	0	D-58/1-2	1	-0.6
Total 9	680	2123	285	637	131	11	72	300	146	451	2	5	.300	.351	.474	.825	111	28	342	5.87	3	D-433,1-115/O-49	49	-0.4
• JEFFERSON, Stan	Stanley Jefferson b: 12/4/1962, New York, NY BB/TR, 5'11", 175 lbs. Deb: 9/7/1986 Career OF: 100-142-39																							
1986 NY-N	14	24	6	5	1	0	1	3	2	8	0	0	.208	.296	.375	.671	86	-0	3	3.42	0	/O-7(1-7-0)	0	-0.1
1987 SD-N	116	422	59	97	8	7	8	29	39	92	34	11	.230	.298	.339	.637	71	-16	45	3.48	-2	*O-107(61-83-0)	6	-2.0
1988 SD-N	49	111	16	16	1	2	1	4	9	22	5	1	.144	.215	.216	.431	24	-10	6	1.44	-1	O-38(10-27-0)	1	-1.3
1989 NY-A	10	12	1	1	0	0	0	1	0	4	1	1	.083	.083	.083	.167	-54	-3	0	.00	-1	/O-7(0-2-6),D-1	0	-0.4
Bal-A	35	127	19	33	7	0	4	20	4	22	9	3	.260	.288	.409	.697	97	-1	15	4.04	1	O-32(1-8-26)/D-2	4	-0.1
Yr.	45	139	20	34	7	0	4	21	4	26	10	4	.245	.271	.381	.652	85	-3	15	3.61	-0	O-39(1-10-32)/D-3	4	-0.4
1990 Bal-A	10	19	1	0	0	0	0	0	2	8	1	0	.000	.095	.000	.095	-74	-4	0	.14	0	/O-5(0-3-5),D-1	0	-0.4
Cle-A	49	98	21	27	8	0	2	10	8	18	8	4	.276	.343	.418	.761	112	2	14	4.60	2	O-34(23-11-1)/D-5	3	0.2
Yr.	59	117	22	27	8	0	2	10	10	26	9	4	.231	.302	.350	.653	83	-3	14	3.75	2	O-39(23-14-6)/D-6	3	-0.2
1991 Cin-N	13	19	2	1	0	0	0	0	1	3	2	0	.053	.100	.053	.153	-54	-3	0	.35	0	/O-5(4-1-1)	0	-0.4
Total 6	296	832	125	180	25	9	16	67	65	177	60	20	.216	.279	.326	.604	66	-36	82	3.16	-1	O-235/D-9	14	-4.4
• JEFFRIES, Irv	Irvine Franklin Jeffries b: 9/10/1905, Louisville, KY d: 6/8/1982, Louisville, KY BR/TR, 5'10", 175 lbs. Deb: 4/30/1930																							
1930 Chi-A	40	97	14	23	3	0	2	11	3	2	1	2	.237	.275	.330	.604	54	-7	9	2.75	0	3-20,S-13	1	-0.5
1931 Chi-A	79	223	29	50	10	0	2	16	14	9	3	0	.224	.270	.296	.566	52	-14	19	2.78	0	3-61/2-6,S-5,O-1	2	-1.1
19[illegible] Phi-N	56	175	28	43	6	0	4	19	15	10	2	....	.246	.305	.349	.654	66	-9	18	3.51	4	2-52/3-1	2	-0.1
Total 3	175	495	71	116	19	0	8	46	32	21	6	2	.234	.284	.321	.605	57	-30	46	3.03	3	/3-82,2-58,S-18,O-1	5	-1.8
• JELIC, Chris	Christopher John Jelic b: 12/16/1963, Bethlehem, PA BR/TR, 5'11", 180 lbs. Deb: 9/30/1990																							
1990 NY-N	4	11	2	1	0	0	1	1	0	3	0	0	.091	.091	.364	.455	19	-1	0	.98	0	/O-4(4-0-0)	0	-0.2
• JELINCICH, Frank	Frank Anthony "Jelly" Jelincich b: 9/3/1917, San Jose, CA d: 6/27/1992, Rochester, MN BR/TR, 6'2", 198 lbs. Deb: 9/6/1941																							
1941 Chi-N	4	8	0	1	0	0	0	2	1	2	0	....	.125	.222	.125	.347	-1	-1	0	1.08	0	/O-2(2-0-0)	0	-0.1
• JELKS, Greg	Gregory Dion Jelks b: 8/16/1961, Cherokee, AL BR/TR, 6'2", 190 lbs. Deb: 8/20/1987																							
1987 Phi-N	10	11	2	1	1	0	0	0	3	4	0	0	.091	.286	.182	.468	26	-1	1	2.14	-1	/3-4,1-2,O-1	0	-0.2
• JELTZ, Steve	Larry Steven Jeltz b: 5/28/1959, Paris, France BB/TR, 5'11", 180 lbs. Deb: 7/17/1983 Career OF: 2-2-11																							
1983 Phi-N	13	8	0	1	0	1	0	1	1	2	0	0	.125	.222	.375	.597	63	-0	0	.00	-3	/2-4,3-2,S-2	0	-0.3
1984 Phi-N	28	68	7	14	0	1	1	7	7	11	2	1	.206	.280	.279	.559	57	-4	5	2.25	1	S-27/3-1	1	0.0
1985 Phi-N	89	196	17	37	4	1	0	12	26	55	1	1	.189	.284	.219	.503	41	-15	13	2.02	-3	S-86	2	-1.1
1986 Phi-N	145	439	44	96	11	4	0	36	65	97	6	3	.219	.321	.262	.583	60	-22	40	2.99	0	*S-141	9	-0.7
1987 Phi-N	114	293	37	68	9	6	0	12	39	54	1	2	.232	.324	.304	.628	66	-15	28	3.08	2	*S-114/O-1	6	-0.2
1988 Phi-N	148	379	39	71	11	4	0	27	59	58	3	0	.187	.297	.237	.534	54	-20	29	2.40	6	*S-148	8	-0.5
1989 Phi-N	116	263	28	64	7	3	4	25	45	44	4	2	.243	.356	.338	.694	99	2	34	4.29	0	S-63,3-30,2-23/O-1	9	0.5
1990 KC-A	74	103	11	16	4	0	0	10	6	21	1	1	.155	.202	.194	.396	11	-13	4	1.10	0	2-34,S-23,O-13(1-1-11)/3-3,D	2	-1.1
Total 8	727	1749	183	367	46	20	5	130	248	342	18	10	.210	.309	.268	.577	61	-87	153	2.77	2	S-604/2-61,3-36,O-15,D-3	37	-3.5
• JENKINS, Geoff	Geoffrey Scott Jenkins b: 7/21/1974, Olympia, WA BL/TR, 6'1", 204 lbs. Deb: 4/24/1998 Career OF: 633-0-1																							
1998 Mil-N	84	262	33	60	12	1	9	28	20	61	1	3	.229	.289	.385	.674	75	-11	27	3.42	1	O-81(81-0-1)	1	-1.3
1999 Mil-N	135	447	70	140	43	3	21	82	35	87	5	1	.313	.372	.564	.936	134	22	92	7.73	9	*O-128(128-0-0)	18	2.4
2000 Mil-N	135	512	100	155	36	4	34	94	33	135	11	1	.303	.363	.588	.950	137	28	109	7.96	9	*O-131(131-0-0)	20	3.0
2001 Mil-N	105	397	60	105	21	1	20	63	36	120	4	2	.264	.338	.474	.811	109	5	62	5.37	8	*O-104(104-0-0)	11	0.8
2002 Mil-N	67	243	35	59	17	1	10	29	22	60	1	2	.243	.321	.444	.765	100	-1	33	4.55	3	O-66(66-0-0)	5	-0.2
2003 Mil-N★	124	487	81	144	30	2	28	95	58	120	0	0	.296	.377	.538	.915	138	27	98	7.41	-2	*O-123(123-0-0)/D-1	20	1.9
Total 6	650	2348	379	663	159	12	122	391	204	583	22	9	.282	.351	.516	.867	121	70	421	6.43	27	O-633/D-1	75	6.7
• JENKINS, Joe	Joseph Daniel Jenkins b: 10/12/1890, Shelbyville, TN d: 6/21/1974, Fresno, CA BR/TR, 5'11", 170 lbs. Deb: 4/30/1914																							
1914 StL-A	19	32	0	4	1	1	0	0	1	11	2	....	.125	.152	.219	.370	12	-4	1	1.25	-1	/C-9	0	-0.5
1917 Chi-A	10	9	0	1	0	0	0	2	0	5	0	....	.111	.111	.111	.222	-32	-1	0	.44	0	/C-1	0	-0.2
1919 Chi-A	11	19	0	3	1	0	0	1	1	1	1	....	.158	.200	.211	.411	15	-2	1	1.43	-1	/C-4	0	-0.3
Total 3	40	60	0	8	2	1	0	3	2	17	3	....	.133	.161	.200	.361	6	-7	2	1.16	-3	/C-14	0	-1.0
• JENKINS, John	John Robert Jenkins b: 7/7/1896, Bosworth, MO d: 8/3/1968, Columbia, MO BR/TR, 5'8", 160 lbs. Deb: 8/5/1922																							
1922 Chi-A	5	3	0	0	0	0	0	1	0	2	0	0	.000	.000	.000	.000	-101	-1	0	.00	-1	/2-1,S-1	0	-0.2
• JENKINS, Tom	Thomas Griffith "Tut" Jenkins b: 4/10/1898, Camden, AL d: 5/3/1979, Weymouth, MA BL/TR, 6'1.5", 174 lbs. Deb: 9/15/1925 Career OF: 32-2-75																							
1925 Bos-A	15	64	9	19	2	1	0	5	3	4	0	0	.297	.338	.359	.698	77	-2	8	4.39	-2	O-15(15-0-0)	1	-0.5
1926 Bos-A	21	50	3	9	1	1	0	6	3	7	0	0	.180	.226	.240	.466	22	-6	3	1.77	-1	O-13(12-1-0)	0	-0.7
Phi-A	6	23	3	4	2	0	0	0	0	2	0	0	.174	.174	.261	.435	12	-3	1	1.38	0	/O-6(5-0-1)	0	-0.3
Yr.	27	73	6	13	3	1	0	6	3	9	0	0	.178	.211	.247	.457	19	-9	4	1.65	-1	O-19(17-1-1)	0	-1.1
1929 StL-A	21	22	1	4	0	1	0	0	4	8	0	0	.182	.308	.273	.580	49	-2	2	3.06	0	/O-3(0-1-2)	0	-0.2
1930 StL-A	2	8	1	2	1	1	0	3	0	1	0	0	.250	.250	.625	.875	110	0	1	5.30	0	/O-2(0-0-2)	0	0.0
1931 StL-A	81	230	20	61	7	2	3	25	17	25	1	3	.265	.316	.352	.668	73	-9	25	3.85	-1	O-58(0-0-58)	3	-1.3
1932 StL-A	25	62	5	20	1	0	0	5	1	6	0	0	.323	.333	.339	.672	70	-3	7	4.29	1	O-12(0-0-12)	1	-0.2
Total 6	171	459	42	119	14	6	3	44	28	53	1	3	.259	.303	.336	.639	64	-25	47	3.56	-3	O-109	5	-3.2
• JENNINGS, Alamazoo	Alfred Gorden Jennings b: 11/30/1850, Newport, KY d: 11/2/1894, Cincinnati, OH Deb: 8/15/1878																							
1878 Mil-N	1	2	0	0	0	0	0	0	1	0	....	....	.000	.333	.000	.333	16	-0	0	.00	-2	/C-1	0	-0.2
• JENNINGS, Bill	William Lee Jennings b: 9/28/1925, St. Louis, MO BR/TR, 6'2", 175 lbs. Deb: 7/19/1951																							
1951 StL-A	64	195	20	35	10	2	0	13	26	42	1	0	.179	.276	.251	.527	42	-15	15	2.43	-11	S-64	2	-2.2
• JENNINGS, Doug	James Douglas Jennings b: 9/30/1964, Atlanta, GA BL/TL, 5'10", 170 lbs. Deb: 4/8/1988 Career OF: 58-0-22																							
1988 Oak-A	71	101	9	21	6	0	1	15	21	28	0	1	.208	.355	.297	.652	88	-1	12	3.89	0	O-23(16-0-7),1-14/D-2	3	-0.2
1989 Oak-A	4	4	0	0	0	0	0	0	0	2	0	0	.000	.000	.000	.000	-104	-1	0	.00	0	/O-3(3-0-0)	0	-0.1
1990*Oak-A	64	156	19	30	7	2	2	14	17	48	0	3	.192	.280	.301	.581	65	-9	14	2.73	-1	O-45(33-0-15)/D-8,1-4	1	-1.1
1991 Oak-A	8	9	0	1	0	0	0	0	2	2	0	1	.111	.273	.111	.384	11	-1	0	.37	0	/O-6(6-0-0)	0	-0.2
1993 Chi-N	42	52	8	13	3	1	2	8	3	10	0	0	.250	.316	.462	.777	107	0	8	5.53	-1	1-10	2	-0.2
Total 5	189	322	36	65	16	3	5	37	43	90	0	5	.202	.307	.317	.624	76	-12	34	3.37	-2	/O-77,1-28,D-10	6	-1.7

YEAR TM-L	G	AB	R	H	2B	3B	HR	RBI	BB	SO	SB	CS	AVG	OBP	SLG	OPS	OPS+	BR/A	RC	RC/G	FR	G/POS	WS	TPW

• JENNINGS, Hughie   Hugh Ambrose "Ee-Yah" Jennings   b: 4/2/1869, Pittston, PA   d: 2/1/1928, Scranton, PA   BR/TR, 5'8.5", 165 lbs.   Deb: 6/1/1891   M/C/U   HOF: 1945   Career OF: 1-0-5

YEAR TM-L	G	AB	R	H	2B	3B	HR	RBI	BB	SO	SB	CS	AVG	OBP	SLG	OPS	OPS+	BR/A	RC	RC/G	FR	G/POS	WS	TPW
1891 Lou-a	88	351	51	103	10	8	1	58	17	35	12	....	.293	.342	.376	.718	103	0	50	5.19	6	S-70,1-17/3-3	12	0.6
1892 Lou-N	152	594	65	133	16	4	2	61	30	30	28	....	.224	.272	.274	.546	70	-21	53	3.07	9	*S-152	14	-0.4
1893 Lou-N	23	88	6	12	3	0	0	9	3	3	0	....	.136	.174	.170	.344	-9	-14	3	.93	1	S-23	1	-0.9
Bal-N	16	55	6	14	0	0	1	6	4	3	0	....	.255	.339	.309	.648	71	-2	6	3.81	-4	S-15/0-1	1	-0.4
Yr.	39	143	12	26	3	0	1	15	7	6	0	....	.182	.240	.224	.464	23	-16	9	1.94	-3	S-38/0-1	2	-1.4
1894*Bal-N	128	501	134	168	28	16	4	109	37	17	37	....	.335	.411	.479	.890	109	7	117	9.10	29	*S-128	24	3.3
1895*Bal-N	131	529	159	204	41	7	4	125	24	17	53	....	.386	.444	.512	.957	142	34	150	11.46	47	*S-131	29	7.1
1896*Bal-N	130	521	125	209	27	9	0	121	19	11	70	....	.401	.472	.488	.960	151	43	158	12.94	44	*S-130	36	7.9
1897*Bal-N	117	439	133	156	26	9	2	79	42	....	60	....	.355	.463	.469	.932	146	36	128	11.31	25	*S-116	29	5.7
1898*Bal-N	143	534	135	175	25	11	1	87	78	....	28	....	.328	.454	.421	.876	149	44	119	8.61	14	*S-115,2-27/0-1	32	6.1
1899 Bro-N	16	41	7	7	0	2	0	6	9	....	4	....	.171	.346	.268	.614	68	-0	6	4.13	-3	S-11/1-4	0	-0.3
Bal-N	2	8	2	3	0	2	0	2	0	....	0	....	.375	.375	.875	1.250	227	1	3	14.26	0	/2-2	0	0.1
Bro-N	51	175	35	57	3	8	0	34	13	....	14	....	.326	.424	.434	.859	133	9	40	8.48	1	1-46/2-1,S-1	9	1.0
Yr.	69	224	44	67	3	12	0	42	22	....	18	....	.299	.408	.408	.827	122	10	48	7.69	-1	1-50,S-12/2-3	9	0.8
1900*Bro-N	115	441	61	120	18	6	1	69	31	....	31	....	.272	.348	.347	.695	87	-8	67	5.33	-1	*1-112/2-2	10	-0.8
1901 Phi-N	82	302	38	79	21	2	1	39	25	....	13	....	.262	.342	.354	.696	100	1	43	4.95	1	1-80/2-1,S-1	8	0.0
1902 Phi-N	78	290	32	79	13	4	1	32	14	....	8	....	.272	.330	.355	.685	111	4	38	4.67	1	1-69/S-5,2-4	9	0.4
1903 Bro-N	6	17	2	4	0	0	0	1	1	....	0	....	.235	.316	.235	.551	60	-1	2	3.30	-1	/0-4(1-0-3)	0	-0.1
1907 Det-A	1	4	0	1	1	0	0	0	0	....	0	....	.250	.250	.500	.750	133	0	1	4.53	0	/2-1,S-1	0	-0.1
1909 Det-A	2	4	1	2	0	0	0	2	0	....	0	....	.500	.500	.500	1.000	207	-0	1	12.79	0	/1-2	0	0.1
1912 Det-A	1	1	0	0	0	0	0	0	0	....	0	....	.000	.000	.000	.000	-103	-0	0	.00	0	....	0	0.0
1918 Det-A	1	0	0	0	0	0	0	0	0	....	0	....	....	....	....	....	-104	0	0	....	0	/1-1	0	0.0
Total 17	1283	4895	992	1526	232	88	18	840	347	116	359	....	.312	.391	.406	.797	116	133	982	7.50	170	S-899,1-331/2-38,0-6,3-3	214	29.1

• JENNINGS, Robin   Robin Christopher Jennings   b: 4/11/1972, Singapore, Singapore   BL/TL, 6'2", 205 lbs.   Deb: 4/18/1996   Career OF: 8-2-38

YEAR TM-L	G	AB	R	H	2B	3B	HR	RBI	BB	SO	SB	CS	AVG	OBP	SLG	OPS	OPS+	BR/A	RC	RC/G	FR	G/POS	WS	TPW
1996 Chi-N	31	58	7	13	1	0	0	4	3	9	1	1	.224	.274	.310	.585	52	-4	3	2.96	1	0-11(0-0-11)	1	-0.3
1997 Chi-N	9	18	1	3	1	0	0	2	0	2	0	0	.167	.167	.222	.389	1	-3	1	1.20	0	/0-5(4-2-0)	0	-0.3
1999 Chi-N	5	5	0	1	0	0	0	0	0	2	0	0	.200	.200	.200	.400	2	-1	0	1.35	0	/0-1	0	-0.1
2001 Oak-A	20	52	4	13	3	0	0	4	2	6	0	0	.250	.278	.308	.585	54	-4	5	3.14	0	0-13(3-0-12)/1-6,D-1	0	-0.4
Col-N	1	3	0	0	0	0	0	0	0	1	0	0	.000	.000	.000	.000	-82	-1	0	.00	-1	/0-1	0	-0.1
Cin-N	27	77	10	22	5	2	3	14	5	11	0	0	.286	.329	.519	.849	110	1	14	6.63	1	0-15(0-0-15)/1-8	3	0.1
Yr.	28	80	10	22	5	2	3	14	5	12	0	0	.275	.318	.525	.818	103	-0	14	6.29	1	0-16(1-0-15)/1-8	3	-0.1
Total 4	93	213	22	52	14	2	3	24	10	31	1	0	.244	.281	.371	.652	66	-11	24	3.97	1	/0-45,1-14,D-1	4	-1.2

• JENSEN, Jackie   Jack Eugene Jensen   b: 3/9/1927, San Francisco, CA   d: 7/14/1982, Charlottesville, VA   BR/TR, 5'11", 190 lbs.   Deb: 4/18/1950   Career OF: 54-153-1207

YEAR TM-L	G	AB	R	H	2B	3B	HR	RBI	BB	SO	SB	CS	AVG	OBP	SLG	OPS	OPS+	BR/A	RC	RC/G	FR	G/POS	WS	TPW
1950*NY-A	45	70	13	12	2	2	1	5	7	8	4	0	.171	.247	.300	.547	41	-6	5	2.32	-1	0-23(17-0-7)	0	-0.7
1951 NY-A	56	168	30	50	8	1	8	25	18	18	8	2	.298	.369	.500	.869	138	9	34	7.44	1	0-48(21-27-1)	9	0.8
1952 NY-A	7	19	3	2	1	1	0	2	4	4	1	0	.105	.261	.263	.524	49	-1	1	2.18	0	0-5(0-5-0)	0	-0.1
Was-A	144	570	80	163	29	5	10	80	63	40	17	6	.286	.360	.407	.767	117	15	86	5.39	-4	*0-143(0-7-142)	21	0.7
Yr.	151	589	83	165	30	6	10	82	67	44	18	6	.280	.357	.402	.759	115	14	88	5.26	-4	*0-148(0-12-142)	21	0.6
1953 Was-A	147	552	87	147	32	8	10	84	73	51	18	8	.266	.357	.408	.765	109	9	82	5.10	-11	*0-146(0-1-145)	17	-0.7
1954 Bos-A	152	580	92	160	25	7	25	117	79	52	22	7	.276	.365	.472	.837	115	14	94	5.38	-5	*0-151(8-106-44)	17	0.3
1955 Bos-A	152	574	95	158	27	6	26	116	89	63	16	7	.275	.375	.479	.854	118	16	102	6.04	-2	*0-150(0-0-150)	19	0.8
1956 Bos-A	151	578	80	182	23	11	20	97	89	43	11	3	.315	.407	.492	.904	122	23	116	7.34	-2	*0-151(0-0-151)	23	1.5
1957 Bos-A	145	544	82	153	29	2	23	103	75	66	8	5	.281	.370	.469	.839	121	17	91	5.80	4	*0-144(4-0-143)	18	1.6
1958 Bos-A	154	548	83	157	31	0	35	122	99	65	9	4	.286	.398	.535	.933	144	37	120	7.85	1	*0-153(2-0-153)	27	3.3
1959 Bos-A	148	535	101	148	31	0	28	112	88	67	20	5	.277	.379	.492	.870	131	27	100	6.37	9	*0-146(0-7-142)	22	3.1
1961 Bos-A	137	498	64	131	21	2	13	66	66	69	9	8	.263	.353	.392	.744	96	-3	68	4.60	4	*0-131(2-0-129)	14	-0.8
Total 11	1438	5236	810	1463	259	45	199	929	750	546	143	55	.279	.372	.460	.832	119	157	900	5.95	-6	*0-1391	187	9.8

• JENSEN, Marcus   Marcus Christian Jensen   b: 12/14/1972, Oakland, CA   BB/TR, 6'4", 195 lbs.   Deb: 4/14/1996

YEAR TM-L	G	AB	R	H	2B	3B	HR	RBI	BB	SO	SB	CS	AVG	OBP	SLG	OPS	OPS+	BR/A	RC	RC/G	FR	G/POS	WS	TPW
1996 SF-N	9	19	4	4	1	0	0	4	8	7	0	0	.211	.444	.263	.708	96	1	3	4.87	0	/C-7	1	0.1
1997 SF-N	30	74	5	11	2	0	1	3	7	23	0	0	.149	.222	.216	.438	16	-9	3	1.44	0	C-28	1	-0.8
Det-A	8	11	1	2	0	0	0	1	1	5	0	0	.182	.250	.182	.432	15	-1	1	1.70	-1	/C-8	0	-0.2
1998 Mil-N	2	2	0	0	0	0	0	0	0	2	0	0	.000	.000	.000	.000	-100	-1	0	.00	0	/C-1	0	-0.1
1999 StL-N	16	34	5	8	5	0	1	1	6	12	0	0	.235	.350	.471	.821	104	0	6	5.29	1	C-14	1	0.2
2000 Min-A	52	139	16	29	7	1	3	14	24	36	1	0	.209	.325	.338	.663	66	-8	16	3.77	-1	C-49/D-1	2	-0.5
2001 Bos-A	1	4	0	1	0	0	0	0	0	1	0	0	.250	.250	.250	.500	32	-0	0	2.25	1	/C-1	0	0.1
Tex-A	11	25	0	4	1	0	0	2	0	9	0	0	.160	.160	.200	.360	-6	-4	1	.74	-1	C-11	0	-0.4
Yr.	12	29	0	5	1	0	0	2	0	10	0	0	.172	.172	.207	.379		-4	1	.92	0	C-12	0	-0.4
2002 Mil-N	16	35	2	4	0	0	1	4	4	11	0	0	.114	.205	.200	.405	7	-5	1	.96	1	C-15	1	-0.3
Total 7	145	343	33	63	16	1	6	29	50	106	0	1	.184	.288	.289	.576	49	-27	31	2.81	0	C-134/D-1	6	-1.9

• JENSEN, Woody   Forrest Docenus Jensen   b: 8/11/1907, Bremerton, WA   d: 10/5/2001, Wichita, KS   BL/TL, 5'10.5", 160 lbs.   Deb: 4/20/1931   Career OF: 544-75-10

YEAR TM-L	G	AB	R	H	2B	3B	HR	RBI	BB	SO	SB	CS	AVG	OBP	SLG	OPS	OPS+	BR/A	RC	RC/G	FR	G/POS	WS	TPW
1931 Pit-N	73	267	43	65	5	4	3	17	10	18	4	....	.243	.276	.326	.602	62	-15	25	2.98	3	0-67(64-3-0)	3	-1.6
1932 Pit-N	7	5	2	0	0	0	0	0	0	2	0	....	.000	.000	.000	.000	-102	-1	0	.00	0	/0-1	0	-0.2
1933 Pit-N	70	196	29	58	7	3	0	15	8	2	1	....	.296	.330	.362	.692	98	-1	25	4.67	-2	0-40(40-0-0)	5	-0.6
1934 Pit-N	88	283	34	82	13	4	0	27	4	13	2	....	.290	.304	.364	.668	76	-10	30	3.77	-4	0-66(46-17-4)	4	-1.7
1935 Pit-N	143	627	97	203	28	7	8	62	15	14	9	....	.324	.344	.429	.773	103	1	90	5.41	-9	*0-140(138-0-2)	17	-1.6
1936 Pit-N	153	696	98	197	34	10	10	58	16	19	2	....	.283	.305	.404	.709	87	-15	84	4.33	-7	*0-153(152-1-0)	15	-3.0
1937 Pit-N	124	509	77	142	23	9	5	45	15	29	2	....	.279	.301	.389	.690	86	-12	58	3.98	-3	*0-120(88-32-0)	10	-2.1
1938 Pit-N	68	125	12	25	4	0	0	10	1	3	0	....	.200	.213	.232	.445	22	-14	6	1.50	-3	0-38(15-21-2)	0	-1.7
1939 Pit-N	12	12	0	2	0	0	0	1	0	0	0	....	.167	.167	.167	.333	-10	-2	0	.41	0	/0-3(0-1-2)	0	-0.2
Total 9	738	2720	392	774	114	37	26	235	69	100	20	....	.285	.307	.382	.689	84	-69	318	4.14	-26	0-628	54	-12.7

• JESSEE, Dan   Daniel Edward Jessee   b: 2/22/1901, Olive Hill, KY   d: 4/30/1970, Venice, FL   BL/TR, 5'10", 165 lbs.   Deb: 8/14/1929

YEAR TM-L	G	AB	R	H	2B	3B	HR	RBI	BB	SO	SB	CS	AVG	OBP	SLG	OPS	OPS+	BR/A	RC	RC/G	FR	G/POS	WS	TPW
1929 Cle-A	1	0	0	0	0	0	0	0	0	0	0	....	....	....	....	....	-97	0	0	....	0	....	0	0.0

• JESTADT, Garry   Garry Arthur Jestadt   b: 3/19/1947, Chicago, IL   BR/TR, 6'2", 188 lbs.   Deb: 9/17/1969

YEAR TM-L	G	AB	R	H	2B	3B	HR	RBI	BB	SO	SB	CS	AVG	OBP	SLG	OPS	OPS+	BR/A	RC	RC/G	FR	G/POS	WS	TPW
1969 Mon-N	6	6	1	0	0	0	0	1	0	0	0	0	.000	.000	.000	.000	-100	-2	0	.00	-1	/S-1	0	-0.2
1971 Chi-N	3	3	0	0	0	0	0	0	0	0	0	0	.000	.000	.000	.000	-87	-1	0	.00	0	/3-1	0	-0.1
SD-N	75	189	17	55	13	0	0	13	11	24	1	3	.291	.330	.360	.690	102	-1	19	3.50	-2	3-49,2-23/S-1	4	-0.3
Yr.	78	192	17	55	13	0	0	13	11	24	1	3	.286	.325	.354	.679	99	-2	19	3.43	-2	3-50,2-23/S-1	4	-0.3
1972 SD-N	92	256	15	63	5	1	6	22	13	21	0	0	.246	.283	.344	.626	83	-7	24	3.16	-10	2-48,3-25/S-3	5	-1.5
Total 3	176	454	33	118	18	1	6	36	24	45	1	3	.260	.297	.344	.641	88	-10	44	3.22	-13	/3-75,2-71,S-5	9	-2.1

• JETER, Derek   Derek Sanderson Jeter   b: 6/26/1974, Pequannock, NJ   BR/TR, 6'3", 175 lbs.   Deb: 5/29/1995

YEAR TM-L	G	AB	R	H	2B	3B	HR	RBI	BB	SO	SB	CS	AVG	OBP	SLG	OPS	OPS+	BR/A	RC	RC/G	FR	G/POS	WS	TPW
1995 NY-A	15	48	5	12	4	1	0	7	3	11	0	0	.250	.294	.375	.669	73	-2	6	4.14	-1	S-15	1	-0.2
1996*NY-A	157	582	104	183	25	6	10	78	48	102	14	7	.314	.376	.430	.805	103	3	94	5.85	-5	*S-157	18	1.1
1997*NY-A	159	654	116	190	31	7	10	70	74	125	23	12	.291	.371	.405	.776	103	5	101	5.44	-8	*S-159	19	1.0
1998*NY-A★	149	626	127	203	25	8	19	84	57	119	30	6	.324	.385	.481	.866	128	30	119	7.17	-8	*S-148	27	3.2
1999*NY-A★	158	627	134	219	37	9	24	102	91	116	19	8	.349	.441	.552	.993	153	55	158	9.75	-20	*S-158	35	4.5
2000*NY-A★	148	593	119	201	31	4	15	73	68	99	22	4	.339	.418	.481	.898	128	31	124	8.03	-19	*S-148	23	2.2
2001*NY-A★	150	614	110	191	35	3	21	74	56	99	27	3	.311	.377	.480	.858	122	25	115	7.00	-22	*S-150	28	1.5
2002*NY-A★	157	644	124	191	26	0	18	75	73	114	32	3	.297	.374	.421	.795	112	19	108	6.14	-30	*S-156/D-1	24	0.2
2003*NY-A	119	482	87	156	25	3	10	52	43	88	11	5	.324	.394	.450	.844	124	19	87	6.79	-28	*S-118	18	0.1
Total 9	1212	4870	926	1546	239	41	127	615	513	873	178	48	.317	.391	.462	.853	121	186	911	6.96	-141	*S-1209/D-1	193	13.6

YEAR TM-L	G	AB	R	H	2B	3B	HR	RBI	BB	SO	SB	CS	AVG	OBP	SLG	OPS	OPS+	BR/A	RC	RC/G	FR	G/POS	WS	TPW
• JETER, Johnny	John Jeter b: 10/24/1944, Shreveport, LA BR/TR, 6'1", 180 lbs. Deb: 6/14/1969 Career OF: 75-147-44																							
1969 Pit-N	28	29	7	9	1	1	1	6	3	15	1	1	.310	.375	.517	.892	151	2	6	7.09	0	0-20(16-1-4)	1	0.2
1970*Pit-N	85	126	27	30	3	2	2	12	13	34	9	5	.238	.314	.341	.656	78	-4	13	3.41	-0	0-56(35-10-11)	2	-0.6
1971 SD-N	18	75	8	24	4	0	1	3	2	16	2	0	.320	.338	.413	.751	120	2	11	5.32	3	0-17(0-17-0)	3	0.5
1972 SD-N	110	326	25	72	4	3	7	21	18	92	11	5	.221	.266	.316	.582	70	-14	25	2.56	-2	0-91(0-91-0)	4	-1.9
1973 Chi-A	89	300	38	72	14	4	7	26	9	74	4	3	.240	.262	.383	.645	77	-11	28	3.19	-3	0-72(19-27-29)/D-3	4	-1.8
1974 Cle-A	6	17	3	6	1	0	0	1	1	6	1	2	.353	.389	.412	.801	132	0	2	3.33	0	/0-6(5-1-0)	0	-0.1
Total 6	**336**	**873**	**108**	**213**	**27**	**10**	**18**	**69**	**46**	**237**	**28**	**16**	**.244**	**.284**	**.360**	**.644**	**82**	**-25**	**85**	**3.26**	**-2**	**0-262/D-3**	**14**	**-3.6**
• JETER, Shawn	Shawn Darrell Jeter b: 6/28/1966, Shreveport, LA BL/TR, 6'2", 185 lbs. Deb: 6/13/1992																							
1992 Chi-A	13	18	1	2	0	0	0	0	0	7	0	0	.111	.111	.111	.222	-38	-3	0	.38	0	/0-8(1-1-6),D-3	0	-0.4
• JETHROE, Sam	Samuel "Jet" Jethroe b: 1/20/1918, East St. Louis, IL d: 6/16/2001, Erie, PA BB/TR, 6'1", 178 lbs. Deb: 4/18/1950 Career OF: 14-418-3																							
1950 Bos-N	141	582	100	159	28	8	18	58	52	93	**35**	....	.273	.338	.442	.780	110	7	89	5.51	0	*0-141(0-141-0)	22	0.3
1951 Bos-N	148	572	101	160	29	10	18	65	57	88	**35**	5	.280	.356	.460	.816	127	27	103	6.51	-2	*0-140(13-127-2)	23	2.1
1952 Bos-N	151	608	79	141	23	7	13	58	68	112	28	9	.232	.318	.357	.675	90	-5	76	4.19	-4	*0-151(1-150-0)	16	-1.3
1954 Pit-N	2	1	0	0	0	0	0	0	0	0	0	0	.000	.000	.000	.000	-102	-0	0	.00	-0	/0-1	0	0.0
Total 4	**442**	**1763**	**280**	**460**	**80**	**25**	**49**	**181**	**177**	**293**	**98**	**14**	**.261**	**.337**	**.418**	**.755**	**108**	**29**	**267**	**5.35**	**-6**	**0-433**	**61**	**1.1**
• JEWETT, Nat	Nathan W. Jewett b: 12/25/1842, New York, NY d: 2/23/1914, Bronx, NY, 5'6", 137 lbs. Deb: 7/4/1872																							
1872 Eck-n	2	8	1	1	0	0	0	0	0	0	0	0	.125	.125	.125	.250	-27	-1	0	.57	-1	/C-2	....	-0.1
• JIMENEZ, D'Angelo	D'Angelo Jimenez b: 12/21/1977, Santo Domingo, Dominican Republic BB/TR, 6', 194 lbs. Deb: 9/15/1999																							
1999 NY-A	7	20	3	8	2	0	0	4	3	4	0	0	.400	.478	.500	.978	152	2	5	11.60	1	/3-6,2-1	1	0.2
2001 SD-N	86	308	45	85	19	0	3	33	39	68	2	3	.276	.357	.367	.724	96	-2	40	4.54	4	S-85	8	0.9
2002 SD-N	87	321	39	77	11	4	3	33	34	63	4	2	.240	.313	.327	.640	76	-11	32	3.39	13	2-54,3-32/P-1	7	0.5
Chi-A	27	108	22	31	4	3	1	11	16	10	2	1	.287	.384	.407	.791	108	2	18	6.22	6	2-17,S-10/3-1	4	0.9
2003 Chi-A	73	271	35	69	11	5	7	26	32	46	4	3	.255	.333	.410	.743	95	-2	38	4.84	-5	2-68/3-2	7	-0.4
Cin-N	73	290	34	84	13	2	7	31	34	43	7	4	.290	.368	.421	.789	107	3	47	5.74	3	2-73/3-2	11	1.0
Total 4	**353**	**1318**	**178**	**354**	**60**	**14**	**21**	**138**	**158**	**234**	**19**	**13**	**.269**	**.348**	**.383**	**.731**	**95**	**-8**	**180**	**4.78**	**21**	**2-213/S-95,3-43,P-1**	**38**	**3.1**
• JIMENEZ, Elvio	Felix Elvio (Rivera) Jimenez b: 1/6/1940, San Pedro de Macoris, Dominican Republic BR/TR, 5'9", 170 lbs. Deb: 10/4/1964																							
1964 NY-A	1	6	0	2	0	0	0	0	0	0	0	0	.333	.333	.333	.667	85	-0	1	4.50	0	/0-1	0	0.0
• JIMENEZ, Houston	Alfonso (Gonzales) Jimenez b: 10/30/1957, Navojoa, Mexico BR/TR, 5'8", 144 lbs. Deb: 6/13/1983																							
1983 Min-A	36	86	5	15	5	1	0	9	4	11	0	1	.174	.211	.256	.467	27	-9	5	1.72	-4	S-36	1	-1.0
1984 Min-A	108	298	28	60	11	1	0	19	15	34	0	1	.201	.240	.245	.485	33	-28	17	1.80	-7	*S-107	3	-2.5
1987 Pit-N	5	6	0	0	0	0	0	0	1	2	0	0	.000	.143	.000	.143	-58	-1	0	.17	0	/2-2,S-2	0	-0.1
1988 Cle-A	9	21	1	1	0	0	0	1	0	2	0	0	.048	.048	.048	.095	-71	-5	0	.00	0	/2-7,S-2	0	-0.4
Total 4	**158**	**411**	**34**	**76**	**16**	**2**	**0**	**29**	**20**	**49**	**0**	**2**	**.185**	**.223**	**.234**	**.456**	**25**	**-43**	**21**	**1.64**	**-11**	**S-147/2-9**	**4**	**-4.0**
• JIMENEZ, Manny	Manuel Emilio (Rivera) Jimenez b: 11/19/1938, San Pedro de Macoris, Dominican Republic BL/TR, 6'1", 195 lbs. Deb: 4/11/1962 Career OF: 214-0-22																							
1962 KC-A	139	479	48	144	24	2	11	69	31	34	0	1	.301	.357	.428	.785	107	4	72	5.45	1	*0-122(116-0-6)	13	0.0
1963 KC-A	60	157	12	44	9	0	0	15	16	14	0	1	.280	.365	.338	.703	95	-1	19	4.19	2	0-40(33-0-8)	4	-0.1
1964 KC-A	95	204	19	46	7	0	12	38	15	24	0	0	.225	.295	.436	.731	97	-1	21	3.32	-1	0-49(46-0-4)	2	-0.4
1966 KC-A	13	35	1	4	0	1	0	1	6	4	0	0	.114	.244	.171	.415	22	-3	2	1.40	0	0-12(8-0-4)	0	-0.4
1967 Pit-N	50	56	3	14	2	0	2	10	1	4	0	0	.250	.276	.393	.669	89	-1	5	2.73	-0	/0-6(6-0-0)	1	-0.1
1968 Pit-N	66	66	7	20	1	1	1	11	6	15	0	0	.303	.403	.394	.797	142	4	11	6.46	-1	/0-5(5-0-0)	3	0.4
1969 Chi-N	6	6	0	1	0	0	0	0	0	2	0	0	.167	.167	.167	.333	-6	-1	0	.00	0	....	0	-0.1
Total 7	**429**	**1003**	**90**	**273**	**43**	**4**	**26**	**144**	**75**	**97**	**0**	**2**	**.272**	**.339**	**.401**	**.740**	**101**	**1**	**130**	**4.47**	**2**	**0-234**	**23**	**-0.7**
• JOHNS, Keith	Robert Keith Johns b: 7/19/1971, Jacksonville, FL BR/TR, 6'1" Deb: 5/23/1998																							
1998 Bos-A	2	0	0	0	0	0	0	0	1	0	0	0	....	1.000	....	1.000	188	0	0	∞	0	/2-1,D-1	0	0.0
• JOHNS, Pete	William R. Johns b: 1/17/1889, Cleveland, OH d: 8/9/1964, Cleveland, OH BR/TR, 5'10", 165 lbs. Deb: 8/25/1915																							
1915 Chi-A	28	100	7	21	2	1	0	11	8	11	2	7	.210	.275	.250	.525	56	-8	6	1.77	5	3-28	2	-0.3
1918 StL-A	46	89	5	16	1	1	0	11	4	6	0	....	.180	.215	.213	.429	30	-8	4	1.39	-1	1-10/3-4,0-4(1-3-0),S-4,2	0	-1.0
Total 2	**74**	**189**	**12**	**37**	**3**	**2**	**0**	**22**	**12**	**17**	**2**	**7**	**.196**	**.248**	**.233**	**.480**	**44**	**-16**	**10**	**1.60**	**3**	**/3-32,1-10,0-4,S-4,2-2**	**2**	**-1.3**
• JOHNS, Tommy	Thomas Pearce Johns b: 9/7/1851, Baltimore, MD d: 4/13/1927, Baltimore, MD, 5'11" Deb: 5/14/1873																							
1873 Mar-n	1	4	0	0	0	0	0	0	0	0	0	0	.000	.000	.000	.000	-130	-1	0	.00	-1	/0-1	....	-0.1
• JOHNSON, Abbie	Albert J. Johnson b: 1875, Chicago, IL d: 11/28/1960, Detroit, MI, 5'9.5", 165 lbs. Deb: 9/1/1896																							
1896 Lou-N	25	87	10	20	2	1	0	14	4	6	0	....	.230	.264	.276	.540	44	-7	7	2.59	-3	2-25	0	-0.8
1897 Lou-N	48	165	16	40	6	1	0	23	13	....	2	....	.242	.302	.291	.593	59	-9	15	3.31	-14	2-33,S-12	1	-1.8
Total 2	**73**	**252**	**26**	**60**	**8**	**2**	**0**	**37**	**17**	**6**	**2**	**....**	**.238**	**.289**	**.286**	**.575**	**54**	**-16**	**22**	**3.05**	**-18**	**/2-58,S-12**	**1**	**-2.7**
• JOHNSON, Alex	Alexander Johnson b: 12/7/1942, Helena, AR BR/TR, 6', 205 lbs. Deb: 7/25/1964 Career OF: 937-16-54																							
1964 Phi-N	43	109	18	33	7	1	4	18	6	26	1	2	.303	.345	.495	.840	135	4	18	6.11	-1	0-35(34-0-1)	5	0.2
1965 Phi-N	97	262	27	77	9	3	8	28	15	60	4	4	.294	.337	.443	.780	120	5	37	5.14	-1	0-82(76-9-1)	9	0.1
1966 StL-N	25	86	7	16	0	1	2	6	5	18	1	1	.186	.231	.279	.510	41	-7	4	1.62	1	0-22(22-0-0)	0	-0.7
1967 StL-N	81	175	20	39	9	2	1	12	9	26	6	3	.223	.273	.314	.587	69	-7	15	2.78	3	0-57(5-6-48)	3	-0.8
1968 Cin-N	149	603	79	188	32	6	2	58	26	71	16	6	.312	.343	.395	.738	114	11	77	4.73	0	*0-140(140-0-1)	19	0.3
1969 Cin-N	139	523	86	165	18	4	17	88	25	69	11	8	.315	.357	.463	.820	122	13	82	5.59	-4	*0-132(132-0-0)	19	0.3
1970 Cal-A★	156	614	85	202	26	6	14	86	35	68	17	2	**.329**	.372	.459	.831	133	29	99	6.05	2	*0-156(155-0-1)	28	2.2
1971 Cal-A	65	242	19	63	8	0	2	21	15	34	5	2	.260	.309	.318	.627	84	-5	22	3.07	-2	0-61(61-0-0)	4	-1.1
1972 Cle-A	108	356	31	85	10	1	8	37	22	40	6	8	.239	.285	.340	.625	83	-10	30	2.80	-1	0-95(95-0-0)	4	-1.8
1973 Tex-A	158	624	62	179	26	3	8	68	32	82	10	5	.287	.324	.377	.700	101	-1	72	4.13	1	*D-116,0-41(40-1-0)	12	-0.6
1974 Tex-A	114	453	57	132	14	3	4	41	28	59	20	9	.291	.338	.362	.700	104	3	52	4.01	4	0-81(81-0-0),D-32	11	0.1
NY-A	10	28	3	6	1	0	1	2	0	3	0	0	.214	.214	.357	.571	64	-1	2	2.63	0	/D-4,0-1	0	-0.2
Yr.	124	481	60	138	15	3	5	43	28	62	20	9	.287	.331	.362	.693	102	1	54	3.93	4	0-82(82-0-0),D-36	11	0.0
1975 NY-A	52	119	15	31	5	1	1	15	7	21	2	3	.261	.302	.345	.646	85	-4	11	3.01	0	D-28/0-7(5-0-2)	1	-0.5
1976 Det-A	125	429	41	115	15	2	6	45	19	49	14	10	.268	.302	.354	.657	88	-9	41	3.19	-2	0-90(90-0-0),D-19	7	-1.7
Total 13	**1322**	**4623**	**550**	**1331**	**180**	**33**	**78**	**525**	**244**	**626**	**113**	**63**	**.288**	**.329**	**.392**	**.720**	**105**	**21**	**563**	**4.29**	**1**	***0-1000,D-199**	**122**	**-4.2**
• JOHNSON, Bill	William F. "Sleepy Bill" Johnson b: 9/1862, NJ d: 7/17/1942, Chester, PA BL/TL, 140 lbs. Deb: 6/27/1884 Career OF: 62-24-84																							
1884 Phi-U	1	4	0	0	0	0	0	....	0	....	....	....	.000	.000	.000	.000	-108	-1	0	.00	0	/0-1	0	-0.1
1887 Ind-N	11	42	3	8	0	0	0	3	0	6	5	....	.190	.209	.190	.400	12	-5	3	2.17	-1	0-11(0-0-11)	0	-0.5
1890 Bal-a	24	95	15	28	2	3	0	6	7	....	8	....	.295	.350	.379	.728	105	-0	16	6.23	1	0-24(0-0-24)	3	0.1
1891 Bal-a	129	480	101	130	13	14	2	79	89	55	32	....	.271	.389	.369	.758	116	13	83	6.31	1	*0-129(60-24-46)	18	1.0
1892 Bal-N	4	15	2	2	0	0	0	2	2	0	0	....	.133	.235	.133	.369	12	-2	0	1.00	-1	/0-4(1-0-3)	0	-0.2
Total 5	**169**	**636**	**121**	**168**	**15**	**17**	**2**	**90**	**98**	**61**	**45**	**....**	**.264**	**.368**	**.351**	**.718**	**105**	**6**	**102**	**5.80**	**1**	**0-169**	**21**	**0.2**
• JOHNSON, Bill	William Lawrence Johnson b: 10/18/1892, Chicago, IL d: 11/15/1950, Los Angeles, CA BL/TR, 5'11", 170 lbs. Deb: 9/22/1916 Career OF: 2-5-27																							
1916 Phi-A	4	15	1	4	1	0	0	1	0	4	0	....	.267	.267	.333	.600	84	-0	1	3.15	0	/0-4(0-4-0)	0	-0.1
1917 Phi-A	48	109	7	19	2	2	1	8	8	14	4	....	.174	.237	.257	.494	51	-7	8	2.06	-1	0-30(2-1-27)	0	-1.0
Total 2	**52**	**124**	**8**	**23**	**3**	**2**	**1**	**9**	**8**	**18**	**4**	**....**	**.185**	**.241**	**.266**	**.507**	**55**	**-7**	**9**	**2.17**	**-1**	**/0-34**	**0**	**-1.0**
• JOHNSON, Billy	William Russell "Bull" Johnson b: 8/30/1918, Montclair, NJ BR/TR, 5'10", 180 lbs. Deb: 4/22/1943																							
1943*NY-A	155	592	70	166	24	6	5	94	53	30	3	5	.280	.344	.367	.710	107	4	71	4.11	14	*3-155	22	2.3
1946 NY-A	85	296	51	77	14	5	4	35	31	42	1	0	.260	.334	.382	.716	98	-0	40	4.73	2	3-74	9	0.2

YEAR TM-L	G	AB	R	H	2B	3B	HR	RBI	BB	SO	SB	CS	AVG	OBP	SLG	OPS	OPS+	BR/A	RC	RC/G	FR	G/POS	WS	TPW
1947*NY-A★	132	494	67	141	19	8	10	95	44	43	1	2	.285	.351	.417	.768	114	8	69	4.95	-12	*3-132	16	-0.4
1948 NY-A	127	446	59	131	20	6	12	64	41	30	0	0	.294	.358	.446	.805	114	8	68	5.41	11	*3-118	15	1.7
1949*NY-A	113	329	48	82	11	3	8	56	48	44	1	0	.249	.348	.374	.722	91	-4	43	4.39	0	3-81,1-21/2-1	9	-0.4
1950*NY-A	108	327	44	85	16	2	6	40	42	30	1	0	.260	.346	.376	.722	87	-6	43	4.57	2	*3-100/1-5	9	-0.4
1951 NY-A	15	40	5	12	3	0	0	4	7	0	0	1	.300	.404	.375	.779	116	1	6	4.98	-1	3-13	2	0.0
StL-N	124	442	52	116	23	1	14	64	46	49	5	3	.262	.340	.414	.754	101	1	63	4.90	5	*3-124	14	0.6
1952 StL-N	94	282	23	71	10	2	2	34	34	21	1	0	.252	.339	.323	.661	84	-4	32	3.93	1	3-89	6	-0.4
1953 StL-N	11	5	0	1	1	0	0	1	1	1	0	0	.200	.333	.400	.733	90	-0	1	5.20	0	3-11	0	0.0
Total 9	964	3253	419	882	141	33	61	487	347	290	13	11	.271	.346	.391	.737	102	8	437	4.64	22	3-897/1-26,2-1	102	3.1

• JOHNSON, Bob Robert Lee "Indian Bob" Johnson b: 11/26/1905, Pryor, OK d: 7/6/1982, Tacoma, WA BR/TR, 6', 180 lbs. Deb: 4/12/1933 Career OF: 1592-162-24

YEAR TM-L	G	AB	R	H	2B	3B	HR	RBI	BB	SO	SB	CS	AVG	OBP	SLG	OPS	OPS+	BR/A	RC	RC/G	FR	G/POS	WS	TPW
1933 Phi-A	142	535	103	155	44	4	21	93	85	74	8	3	.290	.387	.505	.892	133	28	109	7.43	-7	*O-142(127-1-15)	21	1.1
1934 Phi-A	141	547	111	168	26	6	34	92	58	60	12	8	.307	.375	.563	.938	145	32	114	7.77	11	*O-139(139-0-0)	22	3.2
1935 Phi-A★	147	582	103	174	29	5	28	109	78	76	2	4	.299	.384	.510	.894	131	25	116	7.40	1	*O-147(147-0-0)	18	1.7
1936 Phi-A	153	566	91	165	29	14	25	121	88	71	6	6	.292	.389	.525	.913	126	22	118	7.66	5	*O-131(131-1-0),2-22/1-1	19	1.8
1937 Phi-A	138	477	91	146	32	6	25	108	98	65	9	7	.306	.425	.556	.981	147	37	117	9.19	5	*O-133(129-6-0)/2-2	19	3.2
1938 Phi-A★	152	563	114	176	27	9	30	113	87	73	9	8	.313	.406	.552	.959	142	35	128	8.60	0	*O-150(29-122-0)/2-3,3-1	23	2.8
1939 Phi-A★	150	544	115	184	30	9	23	114	99	59	15	5	.338	.440	.553	.993	156	51	138	9.66	5	*O-150(138-14-0)/2-1	29	4.4
1940 Phi-A★	138	512	93	137	25	4	31	103	83	64	8	2	.268	.374	.514	.888	130	25	100	6.78	1	*O-136(116-13-8)	19	1.8
1941 Phi-A	149	552	98	152	30	8	22	107	95	75	6	4	.275	.385	.478	.863	130	26	106	6.76	5	*O-122(118-4-0),1-28	21	2.1
1942 Phi-A★	149	550	78	160	35	7	13	80	82	61	3	2	.291	.384	.451	.835	135	27	99	6.51	2	*O-149(148-0-1)	26	2.2
1943 Was-A★	117	438	65	116	22	8	7	63	64	50	11	5	.265	.362	.400	.762	127	17	67	5.35	8	O-88(88-0-0),3-19,1-10	19	2.2
1944 Bos-A★	144	525	106	170	40	8	17	106	95	67	2	7	.324	**.431**	.528	**.959**	**175**	**53**	124	**8.82**	4	*O-142(142-0-0)	31	5.1
1945 Bos-A★	143	529	71	148	27	7	12	74	63	56	5	3	.280	.358	.425	.783	124	16	83	5.62	8	*O-140(140-1-0)	20	1.7
Total 13	1863	6920	1239	2051	396	95	288	1283	1075	851	96	64	.296	.393	.506	.899	139	394	1418	7.49	48	*O-1769/1-39,2-28,3-20	287	33.2

• JOHNSON, Bob Robert Wallace Johnson b: 3/4/1936, Omaha, NE BR/TR, 5'10", 175 lbs. Deb: 4/19/1960 Career OF: 2-0-0

YEAR TM-L	G	AB	R	H	2B	3B	HR	RBI	BB	SO	SB	CS	AVG	OBP	SLG	OPS	OPS+	BR/A	RC	RC/G	FR	G/POS	WS	TPW
1960 KC-A	76	146	12	30	4	0	1	9	19	23	2	0	.205	.301	.253	.555	51	-9	11	2.44	-4	S-30,2-27,3-11	2	-1.0
1961 Was-A	61	224	27	66	13	1	6	28	19	26	4	2	.295	.352	.442	.794	116	5	32	4.99	-3	S-57/2-2,3-2	7	0.7
1962 Was-A	135	466	58	134	20	2	12	43	32	50	9	6	.288	.335	.416	.751	102	-1	59	4.40	-6	3-72,S-50/2-3,O-1	10	-0.2
1963 Bal-A	82	254	34	75	10	0	8	32	18	35	5	1	.295	.347	.429	.776	119	7	39	5.70	2	2-50/1-8,S-7,3-5	12	1.3
1964 Bal-A	93	210	18	52	8	2	3	29	9	37	0	0	.248	.282	.348	.629	74	-8	19	2.93	1	S-18,1-15,2-15/3-1,O-1	3	-0.6
1965 Bal-A	87	273	36	66	13	2	5	27	15	34	1	0	.242	.284	.359	.643	80	-8	26	3.24	-8	1-34,S-23,3-13/2-5	6	-1.7
1966 Bal-A	71	157	13	34	5	0	1	10	12	24	0	1	.217	.276	.268	.544	58	-9	11	2.33	-2	2-20,1-17/3-3	1	-1.0
1967 Bal-A	4	3	1	1	0	0	0	0	1	1	0	0	.333	.500	.333	.833	152	0	1	8.51	0	....	0	0.0
NY-N	90	230	26	80	8	3	5	27	12	29	1	1	.348	.380	.474	.854	145	13	39	6.41	-3	2-39,1-23,S-14/3-1	10	1.3
1968 Cin-N	16	15	2	4	0	0	0	1	1	2	0	0	.267	.313	.267	.579	71	-0	1	3.16	-1	/S-2,1-1	0	-0.2
Atl-N	59	187	15	49	5	1	0	11	10	20	0	0	.262	.299	.299	.599	80	-4	16	2.98	2	3-48/2-4	4	-0.2
Yr.	75	202	17	53	5	1	0	12	11	22	0	0	.262	.300	.297	.597	79	-5	17	3.00	1	3-48/2-4,S-2,1-1	4	-0.4
1969 StL-N	19	29	1	6	0	0	1	2	2	4	0	0	.207	.258	.310	.568	58	-2	2	1.95	-1	/3-4,1-1	0	-0.2
Oak-A	51	67	5	23	1	0	1	9	3	4	0	0	.343	.380	.403	.783	124	2	11	6.37	0	/1-7,2-2	3	0.2
1970 Oak-A	30	46	6	8	1	0	1	2	3	2	2	1	.174	.240	.261	.501	39	-4	3	1.66	1	/3-6,1-1	0	-0.3
Total 11	874	2307	254	628	88	11	44	230	156	291	24	12	.272	.321	.377	.698	95	-18	269	4.04	-23	S-201,2-167,3-166,1-107/O-2	58	-2.1

• JOHNSON, Bob Bobby Earl Johnson b: 7/31/1959, Dallas, TX BR/TR, 6'3", 195 lbs. Deb: 9/1/1981

YEAR TM-L	G	AB	R	H	2B	3B	HR	RBI	BB	SO	SB	CS	AVG	OBP	SLG	OPS	OPS+	BR/A	RC	RC/G	FR	G/POS	WS	TPW
1981 Tex-A	6	18	2	5	0	0	2	4	1	3	0	0	.278	.316	.611	.927	171	1	3	5.71	-1	/C-5,1-1	1	0.1
1982 Tex-A	20	56	4	7	2	0	2	7	3	22	0	1	.125	.183	.268	.451	23	-6	2	.95	0	C-14/1-3	1	-0.6
1983 Tex-A	72	175	18	37	6	1	5	16	16	55	3	0	.211	.281	.343	.624	72	-6	16	2.99	-2	C-62,1-10	4	-0.6
Total 3	98	249	24	49	8	1	9	27	20	80	3	1	.197	.262	.345	.607	68	-11	21	2.65	-3	/C-81,1-14	6	-1.2

• JOHNSON, Brian Brian David Johnson b: 1/8/1968, Oakland, CA BR/TR, 6'2", 210 lbs. Deb: 4/5/1994

YEAR TM-L	G	AB	R	H	2B	3B	HR	RBI	BB	SO	SB	CS	AVG	OBP	SLG	OPS	OPS+	BR/A	RC	RC/G	FR	G/POS	WS	TPW
1994 SD-N	36	93	7	23	4	1	3	16	5	21	0	0	.247	.286	.409	.694	81	-3	10	3.40	1	C-24/1-5	1	-0.1
1995 SD-N	68	207	20	52	9	0	3	29	11	39	0	0	.251	.292	.338	.630	68	-10	21	3.47	-1	C-55/1-2	6	-0.7
1996*SD-N	82	243	18	66	13	1	8	35	4	36	0	0	.272	.295	.432	.727	94	-4	28	3.98	-4	C-66/1-1,3-1	5	-0.3
1997 Det-A	45	139	13	33	6	1	2	18	5	19	1	0	.237	.264	.338	.602	56	-9	12	2.88	-2	C-43/D-2	1	-0.8
*SF-N	56	179	19	50	7	2	11	27	14	26	0	1	.279	.338	.525	.864	126	5	28	5.29	0	C-55/1-2	5	0.9
1998 SF-N	99	308	34	73	8	1	13	34	28	67	0	2	.237	.311	.396	.707	90	-6	36	3.79	-3	C-95/O-1	7	-0.3
1999 Cin-N	45	117	12	27	7	0	5	18	9	31	0	0	.231	.286	.419	.705	73	-5	14	4.03	-1	C-39	2	-0.4
2000 KC-A	37	125	9	26	6	0	4	18	4	28	0	0	.208	.233	.352	.585	44	-11	9	2.34	2	C-37	1	-0.6
2001 LA-N	3	4	0	1	0	0	0	1	0	1	0	0	.250	.250	.250	.500	32	-0	0	2.25	0	/C-2	0	-0.1
Total 8	471	1415	132	351	60	6	49	196	80	268	1	3	.248	.294	.403	.697	83	-44	158	3.73	-9	C-416/1-10,D-2,3-1,O-1	28	-2.4

• JOHNSON, Caleb Caleb Clark Johnson b: 5/23/1844, Fulton, IL d: 3/7/1925, Sterling, IL Deb: 5/20/1871

YEAR TM-L	G	AB	R	H	2B	3B	HR	RBI	BB	SO	SB	CS	AVG	OBP	SLG	OPS	OPS+	BR/A	RC	RC/G	FR	G/POS	WS	TPW
1871 Cle-n	16	67	10	15	1	0	0	7	0	1	1	0	.224	.224	.239	.463	35	-5	4	2.36	-3	2-10/O-6(0-0-6)	....	-0.5

• JOHNSON, Charles Charles Edward Johnson b: 7/20/1971, Fort Pierce, FL BR/TR, 6'2", 215 lbs. Deb: 5/6/1994

YEAR TM-L	G	AB	R	H	2B	3B	HR	RBI	BB	SO	SB	CS	AVG	OBP	SLG	OPS	OPS+	BR/A	RC	RC/G	FR	G/POS	WS	TPW
1994 Fla-N	4	11	5	5	1	0	1	4	1	4	0	0	.455	.500	.818	1.318	229	2	4	12.70	0	/C-4	1	0.3
1995 Fla-N	97	315	40	79	15	1	11	39	46	71	0	2	.251	.353	.410	.763	100	-0	45	4.79	4	C-97	12	1.1
1996 Fla-N	120	386	34	84	13	1	13	37	40	91	1	0	.218	.294	.358	.652	73	-16	37	3.04	6	*C-120	10	-0.2
1997*Fla-N★	124	416	43	104	26	1	19	63	60	109	0	2	.250	.349	.454	.803	113	7	65	5.27	10	*C-123	21	2.5
1998 Fla-N	31	113	13	25	5	0	7	23	16	30	0	1	.221	.318	.451	.769	104	-0	16	4.60	0	C-31	3	0.2
LA-N	102	346	31	75	13	0	12	35	29	99	0	1	.217	.279	.358	.638	70	-16	33	3.19	2	*C-100	12	-0.7
Yr.	133	459	44	100	18	0	19	58	45	129	0	2	.218	.289	.381	.670	79	-17	49	3.54	2	*C-131	15	-0.5
1999 Bal-A	135	426	58	107	19	1	16	54	55	107	0	0	.251	.342	.413	.755	95	-3	60	4.82	3	*C-135	12	0.9
2000 Bal-A	84	286	52	84	16	0	21	55	32	69	2	0	.294	.365	.570	.935	138	16	59	7.45	-5	C-83/D-1	11	1.5
*Chi-A	44	135	24	44	8	0	10	36	20	37	0	0	.326	.417	.607	1.024	153	11	36	10.57	-10	C-43	9	0.4
Yr.	128	421	76	128	24	0	31	91	52	106	2	0	.304	.382	.582	.964	143	27	95	8.40	-15	*C-126/D-1	20	1.9
2001 Fla-N★	128	451	51	117	32	0	18	75	38	133	0	0	.259	.323	.450	.773	100	-1	65	5.12	1	*C-125	17	0.9
2002 Fla-N	83	244	18	53	19	0	6	36	31	61	0	0	.217	.305	.369	.674	80	-7	26	3.42	3	C-82	6	0.1
2003 Col-N	108	356	49	82	20	0	20	61	49	84	1	3	.230	.325	.455	.780	88	-8	52	4.83	-7	*C-107	9	-0.7
Total 10	1060	3485	418	859	187	4	154	518	417	895	4	9	.246	.330	.435	.765	98	-15	499	4.84	8	*C-1050/D-1	123	6.2

• JOHNSON, Charlie Charles Cleveland "Home Run" Johnson b: 3/12/1885, Slatington, PA d: 8/28/1940, Marcus Hook, PA BL/TL, 5'9", 150 lbs. Deb: 9/21/1908

YEAR TM-L	G	AB	R	H	2B	3B	HR	RBI	BB	SO	SB	CS	AVG	OBP	SLG	OPS	OPS+	BR/A	RC	RC/G	FR	G/POS	WS	TPW
1908 Phi-N	6	16	2	4	0	1	0	2	1	....	0	....	.250	.333	.375	.708	122	0	2	4.20	0	/O-4(1-3-0)	1	0.0

• JOHNSON, Cliff Clifford Johnson b: 7/22/1947, San Antonio, TX BR/TR, 6'4", 225 lbs. Deb: 9/13/1972 Career OF: 57-0-4

YEAR TM-L	G	AB	R	H	2B	3B	HR	RBI	BB	SO	SB	CS	AVG	OBP	SLG	OPS	OPS+	BR/A	RC	RC/G	FR	G/POS	WS	TPW
1972 Hou-N	5	4	0	1	0	0	0	0	2	0	0	0	.250	.500	.250	.750	121	0	1	6.84	0	/C-1	0	0.0
1973 Hou-N	7	20	6	6	2	0	2	6	1	7	0	0	.300	.364	.700	1.064	189	2	5	10.18	0	/1-5	1	0.2
1974 Hou-N	83	171	26	39	4	1	10	29	33	45	0	1	.228	.362	.439	.801	129	7	28	5.39	-1	C-28,1-21	7	0.6
1975 Hou-N	122	340	52	94	16	1	20	65	46	64	1	0	.276	.371	.506	.877	152	24	65	6.90	-4	1-47,C-41/O-1	15	1.9
1976 Hou-N	108	318	36	72	21	2	10	49	62	59	0	0	.226	.359	.399	.759	126	13	48	5.07	-5	C-66,O-20(20-0-0),1-16	14	1.0
1977 Hou-N	51	144	22	43	8	0	10	23	23	30	0	1	.299	.409	.563	.972	173	15	35	9.12	2	O-34(33-0-4),1-10	8	1.6
*NY-A	56	142	24	42	8	0	12	31	20	23	0	1	.296	.405	.606	1.010	173	15	36	9.41	0	D-25,C-15,1-11	9	1.4
1978*NY-A	76	174	20	32	9	1	6	19	30	32	0	0	.184	.307	.351	.658	87	-2	19	3.44	0	D-39,C-22/1-1	3	-0.3
1979 NY-A	28	64	11	17	6	0	2	6	10	7	0	0	.266	.365	.453	.818	122	2	11	6.19	-0	D-22/C-4	2	0.2
Cle-A	72	240	37	65	10	0	18	61	24	39	2	0	.271	.343	.538	.887	135	12	45	6.52	0	D-62/C-1	10	0.9
Yr.	100	304	48	82	16	0	20	67	34	46	2	0	.270	.353	.520	.873	132	14	56	6.45	0	D-84/C-5	12	1.1
1980 Cle-A	54	174	25	40	3	1	6	28	25	30	0	1	.230	.327	.362	.689	88	-3	19	3.56	0	D-45	2	-0.4
Chi-N	68	196	28	46	8	0	10	34	29	35	0	0	.235	.336	.429	.765	104	1	29	5.03	-8	1-46/O-3(3-0-0),C-1	5	-1.0
1981*Oak-A	84	273	40	71	8	0	17	59	28	60	5	3	.260	.336	.476	.812	138	13	44	5.60	-1	D-68/1-9	12	1.0
1982 Oak-A	73	214	19	51	10	0	7	31	26	41	1	2	.238	.326	.383	.710	98	-1	27	4.35	1	D-48,1-11	5	-0.2

YEAR TM-L	G	AB	R	H	2B	3B	HR	RBI	BB	SO	SB	CS	AVG	OBP	SLG	OPS	OPS+	BR/A	RC	RC/G	FR	G/POS	WS	TPW
1983 Tor-A	142	407	59	108	23	1	22	76	67	69	0	1	.265	.376	.489	.865	128	17	76	6.53	0	*D-130/1-6	13	1.3
1984 Tor-A	127	359	51	109	23	1	16	61	50	62	0	1	.304	.393	.507	.900	142	22	72	7.38	-1	*D-109/1-2	13	1.8
1985 Tex-A	82	296	31	76	17	1	12	56	31	44	0	0	.257	.333	.443	.776	109	4	45	5.39	0	D-82	5	0.1
*Tor-A	24	73	4	20	0	0	1	10	9	15	0	0	.274	.354	.315	.669	83	-1	9	4.28	0	D-21/1-3	1	-0.2
Yr.	106	369	35	96	17	1	13	66	40	59	0	0	.260	.337	.417	.755	104	2	54	5.17	0	*D-103/1-3	6	-0.2
1986 Tor-A	107	336	48	84	12	1	15	55	52	57	0	1	.250	.357	.426	.783	109	5	52	5.34	0	D-95/1-1	9	0.3
Total 15	1369	3945	539	1016	188	10	196	699	568	719	9	12	.258	.358	.459	.817	126	145	667	5.87	-16	D-746,1-189,C-179/O-58	134	10.2

• JOHNSON, Darrell Darrell Dean Johnson b: 8/25/1928, Horace, NE BR/TR, 6'1", 180 lbs. Deb: 4/20/1952 M/C

YEAR TM-L	G	AB	R	H	2B	3B	HR	RBI	BB	SO	SB	CS	AVG	OBP	SLG	OPS	OPS+	BR/A	RC	RC/G	FR	G/POS	WS	TPW
1952 StL-A	29	78	9	22	2	1	0	9	11	4	0	0	.282	.371	.333	.704	94	-0	10	4.78	1	C-22	3	0.3
Chi-A	22	37	3	4	0	0	0	1	5	9	1	0	.108	.214	.108	.322	-8	-5	1	.92	-1	C-21	0	-0.6
Yr.	51	115	12	26	2	1	0	10	16	13	1	0	.226	.321	.261	.581	61	-5	11	3.33	0	C-43	3	-0.3
1957 NY-A	21	46	4	10	1	0	1	8	3	10	0	0	.217	.280	.304	.584	60	-3	4	2.82	1	C-20	1	-0.1
1958 NY-A	5	16	1	4	0	0	0	0	0	2	0	0	.250	.250	.250	.500	39	-1	1	2.25	0	/C-4	0	-0.1
1960 StL-N	8	2	0	0	0	0	0	0	1	0	0	0	.000	.333	.000	.333		-0	0	1.17	-2	/C-8	0	-0.2
1961 Phi-N	21	61	4	14	1	0	0	3	3	8	0	0	.230	.277	.246	.523	41	-5	4	2.18	1	C-21	1	-0.3
*Cin-N	20	54	3	17	2	0	1	6	1	2	0	0	.315	.327	.407	.735	92	-1	7	4.79	1	C-20	2	0.1
Yr.	41	115	7	31	3	0	1	9	4	10	0	0	.270	.300	.322	.622	65	-6	11	3.33	3	C-41	3	-0.1
1962 Cin-N	2	4	0	0	0	0	0	0	2	0	0	0	.000	.333	.000	.333	-2	-0	0	.59	1	/C-2	0	0.1
Bal-A	6	22	0	4	0	0	0	1	0	4	0	0	.182	.182	.182	.364	-2	-3	1	1.09	0	/C-6	0	-0.3
Total 6	134	320	24	75	6	1	2	28	26	39	1	0	.234	.296	.278	.574	56	-19	28	2.99	4	C-124	7	-1.0

• JOHNSON, Davey David Allen Johnson b: 1/30/1943, Orlando, FL BR/TR, 6'1", 180 lbs. Deb: 4/13/1965 M

YEAR TM-L	G	AB	R	H	2B	3B	HR	RBI	BB	SO	SB	CS	AVG	OBP	SLG	OPS	OPS+	BR/A	RC	RC/G	FR	G/POS	WS	TPW
1965 Bal-A	20	47	5	8	3	0	0	1	5	6	3	0	.170	.250	.234	.484	38	-3	3	1.70	1	/3-9,2-3,S-2	0	-0.2
1966*Bal-A	131	501	47	129	20	3	7	56	31	64	3	4	.257	.302	.351	.653	88	-9	52	3.59	7	*2-126/S-3	13	1.0
1967 Bal-A	148	510	62	126	30	3	10	64	59	82	4	5	.247	.330	.376	.706	109	6	63	4.11	1	*2-144/3-3	16	2.1
1968 Bal-A★	145	504	50	122	24	4	9	56	44	80	7	3	.242	.309	.359	.668	102	1	53	3.53	7	*2-127,S-34	16	2.3
1969*Bal-A★	142	511	52	143	34	1	7	57	57	52	3	4	.280	.356	.391	.747	108	5	70	4.75	14	*2-142/S-2	19	3.0
1970*Bal-A★	149	530	68	149	27	1	10	53	66	68	2	1	.281	.361	.392	.753	106	6	77	5.20	9	*2-149/S-2	23	2.7
1971*Bal-A	142	510	67	144	26	1	18	72	51	55	3	1	.282	.353	.443	.796	125	17	79	5.44	10	*2-140	23	3.9
1972 Bal-A	118	376	31	83	22	3	5	32	52	68	1	1	.221	.322	.335	.657	93	-2	41	3.63	10	*2-116	14	1.8
1973 Atl-N★	157	559	84	151	25	0	43	99	81	93	5	3	.270	.371	.546	.917	140	31	116	7.47	-7	*2-156	21	3.6
1974 Atl-N	136	454	56	114	18	0	15	62	75	59	1	2	.251	.361	.390	.751	105	5	64	4.72	8	1-73,2-71	15	1.2
1975 Atl-N	1	1	0	1	1	0	0	1	0	0	0	0	1.000	1.000	2.000	3.000	691	1	2	∞	0	....	0	0.1
1977*Phi-N	78	156	23	50	9	1	8	36	23	20	1	1	.321	.414	.545	.959	148	11	35	8.08	-2	1-43/2-9,3-6	8	0.8
1978 Phi-N	44	89	14	17	2	0	2	14	10	19	0	0	.191	.287	.281	.568	59	-5	8	2.73	-1	2-15/3-9,1-7	1	-0.5
Chi-N	24	49	5	15	1	1	2	6	5	9	0	0	.306	.393	.490	.883	130	2	10	7.47	-2	3-12	2	0.0
Yr.	68	138	19	32	3	1	4	20	15	28	0	0	.232	.325	.355	.680	84	-3	17	4.24	-2	3-21,2-15/1-7	3	-0.5
Total 13	1435	4797	564	1252	242	18	136	609	559	675	33	25	.261	.343	.404	.747	110	68	673	4.81	55	*2-1198,1-123/S-43,3-39	171	21.9

• JOHNSON, Deron Deron Roger Johnson b: 7/17/1938, San Diego, CA d: 4/23/1992, Poway, CA BR/TR, 6'2", 209 lbs. Deb: 9/20/1960 C Career OF: 216-1-32

YEAR TM-L	G	AB	R	H	2B	3B	HR	RBI	BB	SO	SB	CS	AVG	OBP	SLG	OPS	OPS+	BR/A	RC	RC/G	FR	G/POS	WS	TPW
1960 NY-A	6	4	0	2	1	0	0	0	0	0	0	0	.500	.500	.750	1.250	247	1	2	20.25	-1	/3-5	0	0.0
1961 NY-A	13	19	1	2	0	0	0	2	2	5	0	0	.105	.190	.105	.296	-20	-3	0	.37	2	/3-8	0	-0.1
KC-A	83	283	31	61	11	3	8	42	14	44	0	1	.216	.255	.360	.615	62	-17	24	2.69	1	O-59(28-1-30),3-19/1-3	2	-2.0
Yr.	96	302	32	63	11	3	8	44	16	49	0	1	.209	.251	.344	.595	57	-20	24	2.51	2	O-59(28-1-30),3-27/1-3	2	-2.1
1962 KC-A	17	19	1	2	1	0	0	0	3	8	0	0	.105	.227	.158	.385	6	-3	1	1.03	-1	/1-2,3-2,O-2(0-0-2)	0	-0.3
1964 Cin-N	140	477	63	130	24	4	21	79	37	98	4	3	.273	.328	.472	.799	118	10	71	5.24	4	*1-131,O-10(10-0-0)/3-1	16	0.7
1965 Cin-N	159	616	92	177	30	7	32	**130**	52	97	0	4	.287	.345	.515	.859	129	21	105	6.09	1	*3-159	23	2.3
1966 Cin-N	142	505	75	130	25	3	24	81	39	87	1	2	.257	.313	.461	.775	103	1	70	4.72	-2	*O-106(106-0-0),1-71,3-18	14	-0.7
1967 Cin-N	108	361	39	81	18	1	13	53	22	104	0	1	.224	.273	.388	.661	78	-11	36	3.36	0	1-81,3-24	6	-1.7
1968 Atl-N	127	342	29	71	11	1	8	33	35	79	0	1	.208	.287	.316	.603	80	-8	31	2.92	0	1-97,3-21	5	-1.4
1969 Phi-N	138	475	51	121	19	4	17	80	60	111	4	2	.255	.338	.419	.757	114	9	66	4.71	-5	O-72(72-0-0),3-50,1-18	14	0.0
1970 Phi-N	159	574	66	147	28	3	27	93	72	132	0	0	.256	.339	.456	.795	114	11	89	5.42	-8	*1-154/3-3	19	-1.0
1971 Phi-N	158	582	74	154	29	0	34	95	72	146	0	1	.265	.348	.490	.837	135	26	96	5.77	-8	*1-136,3-22	21	0.7
1972 Phi-N	96	230	19	49	4	1	9	31	26	69	0	1	.213	.301	.357	.658	84	-5	24	3.38	-5	1-62	3	-1.6
1973 Phi-N	12	36	3	6	2	0	1	5	5	10	0	0	.167	.286	.306	.591	62	-2	3	2.78	0	1-10	0	-0.3
*Oak-A	131	464	61	114	14	2	19	81	59	116	0	1	.246	.332	.407	.739	113	8	63	4.62	-1	*D-107,1-23	13	0.2
1974 Oak-A	50	174	16	34	1	2	7	23	11	37	1	0	.195	.243	.345	.588	72	-7	13	2.34	-2	1-28,D-23	1	-1.2
Mil-A	49	152	14	23	3	0	6	18	21	41	1	0	.151	.254	.289	.544	56	-8	11	2.32	0	D-46/1-2	0	-1.0
Bos-A	11	25	0	3	0	0	0	2	0	6	0	0	.120	.120	.120	.240	-29	-4	0	.51	0	/D-8	0	-0.4
Yr.	110	351	30	60	4	2	13	43	32	84	2	0	.171	.240	.305	.545	58	-19	25	2.19	-2	D-77,1-30	1	-2.6
1975 Chi-A	148	555	66	129	25	1	18	72	48	117	0	1	.232	.295	.378	.673	88	-10	58	3.50	-6	D-93,1-55	7	-2.5
Bos-A	3	10	2	6	0	0	1	3	2	0	0	0	.600	.667	.900	1.567	313	3	6	42.84	0	/1-2,D-1	2	0.2
Yr.	151	565	68	135	25	1	19	75	50	117	0	1	.239	.302	.388	.690	92	-7	65	3.85	-7	D-94,1-57	9	-2.2
1976 Bos-A	15	38	3	5	1	1	0	0	5	11	0	0	.132	.233	.211	.443	27	-3	2	1.30	0	/D-9,1-5	0	-0.4
Total 16	1765	5941	706	1447	247	33	245	923	585	1318	11	18	.244	.313	.420	.733	102	9	772	4.39	-33	1-880,3-332,D-287,O-249	146	-10.4

• JOHNSON, Don Donald Spore "Pep" Johnson b: 12/7/1911, Chicago, IL d: 4/6/2000, Laguna Beach, CA BR/TR, 6', 170 lbs. Deb: 9/26/1943

YEAR TM-L	G	AB	R	H	2B	3B	HR	RBI	BB	SO	SB	CS	AVG	OBP	SLG	OPS	OPS+	BR/A	RC	RC/G	FR	G/POS	WS	TPW
1943 Chi-N	10	42	5	8	2	0	0	1	2	4	0	....	.190	.227	.238	.465	35	-4	2	1.89	3	2-10	1	0.0
1944 Chi-N★	154	608	50	169	37	1	2	71	28	48	8	....	.278	.311	.352	.663	87	-12	65	3.86	-14	*2-154	14	-1.9
1945*Chi-N★	138	557	94	168	23	2	2	58	32	34	9	....	.302	.343	.361	.704	98	-3	70	4.47	12	*2-138	18	1.7
1946 Chi-N	83	314	37	76	10	1	1	19	26	39	6	....	.242	.306	.290	.596	71	-12	29	3.05	-7	2-83	6	-1.5
1947 Chi-N	120	402	33	104	17	2	3	26	24	45	2	....	.259	.302	.333	.635	71	-17	41	3.59	-16	*2-108/3-6	8	-2.7
1948 Chi-N	6	12	0	3	0	0	0	0	1	1	1	....	.250	.250	.250	.500	37	-1	1	1.35	-1	/2-2,3-2	0	-0.2
Total 6	511	1935	219	528	89	6	8	175	112	171	26	....	.273	.315	.337	.653	83	-49	208	3.77	-23	2-495/3-8	47	-4.7

• JOHNSON, Ed Edwin Cyril Johnson b: 3/31/1899, Morganfield, KY d: 7/3/1975, Morganfield, KY BL/TR, 5'9", 160 lbs. Deb: 9/26/1920

YEAR TM-L	G	AB	R	H	2B	3B	HR	RBI	BB	SO	SB	CS	AVG	OBP	SLG	OPS	OPS+	BR/A	RC	RC/G	FR	G/POS	WS	TPW
1920 Was-A	4	13	1	3	0	0	0	2	3	2	0	0	.231	.375	.231	.606	65	-0	1	3.50	-2	/O-4(0-0-2)	0	-0.2

• JOHNSON, Elmer Elmer Ellsworth "Hickory" Johnson b: 6/12/1884, Beard, IN d: 10/31/1966, Hollywood, FL BR/TR, 5'9", 185 lbs. Deb: 4/24/1914

YEAR TM-L	G	AB	R	H	2B	3B	HR	RBI	BB	SO	SB	CS	AVG	OBP	SLG	OPS	OPS+	BR/A	RC	RC/G	FR	G/POS	WS	TPW
1914 NY-N	11	12	0	2	1	0	0	0	1	3	0	....	.167	.231	.250	.481	44	-1	1	1.66	-1	C-11	0	-0.2

• JOHNSON, Erik Erik Anthony Johnson b: 10/11/1965, Oakland, CA BR/TR, 5'11", 175 lbs. Deb: 7/8/1993

YEAR TM-L	G	AB	R	H	2B	3B	HR	RBI	BB	SO	SB	CS	AVG	OBP	SLG	OPS	OPS+	BR/A	RC	RC/G	FR	G/POS	WS	TPW
1993 SF-N	4	5	1	2	2	0	0	0	0	1	0	0	.400	.400	.800	1.200	218	1	2	14.40	-1	/2-2,3-1,S-1	0	-0.1
1994 SF-N	5	13	0	2	0	0	0	0	0	4	0	0	.154	.154	.154	.308	-20	-2	0	.76	1	/2-2,S-1	0	-0.1
Total 2	9	18	1	4	2	0	0	0	0	5	0	0	.222	.222	.333	.556	46	-2	2	3.68	0	/2-4,S-2,3-1	0	-0.2

• JOHNSON, Ernie Ernest Rudolph Johnson b: 4/29/1888, Chicago, IL d: 5/1/1952, Monrovia, CA BL/TR, 5'9", 151 lbs. Deb: 8/5/1912

YEAR TM-L	G	AB	R	H	2B	3B	HR	RBI	BB	SO	SB	CS	AVG	OBP	SLG	OPS	OPS+	BR/A	RC	RC/G	FR	G/POS	WS	TPW
1912 Chi-A	21	42	7	11	0	1	0	5	1	....	0	....	.262	.279	.310	.589	70	-2	4	2.90	2	S-16	1	0.1
1915 StL-F	152	512	58	123	18	10	7	67	46	35	32	....	.240	.305	.355	.661	90	-8	63	3.98	21	*S-152	18	2.6
1916 StL-A	74	236	29	54	9	3	0	19	30	23	13	....	.229	.323	.292	.616	89	-2	27	3.74	6	S-60,3-12	7	0.9
1917 StL-A	80	199	28	49	6	2	2	20	12	16	13	....	.246	.296	.327	.622	93	-2	23	3.63	1	S-39,2-18,3-14	6	0.2
1918 StL-A	29	34	7	9	1	0	0	0	0	2	4	....	.265	.286	.294	.580	77	-1	4	3.64	-6	S-11/3-1	0	-0.7
1921 Chi-A	142	613	93	181	28	7	1	51	29	24	22	13	.295	.328	.369	.697	78	-21	73	4.16	4	*S-141	13	-0.1
1922 Chi-A	144	603	85	153	17	3	0	56	40	30	21	18	.254	.304	.292	.596	56	-41	54	2.90	5	*S-141	9	-1.9
1923 Chi-A	12	53	5	10	2	0	0	1	3	5	2	1	.189	.246	.226	.472	25	-6	3	1.85	0	S-12	0	-0.5
*NY-A	19	38	6	17	1	1	1	8	1	1	0	0	.447	.462	.605	1.067	176	4	10	12.37	-1	S-15/3-1	3	0.4
Yr.	31	91	11	27	3	1	1	9	4	6	2	1	.297	.333	.385	.718	87	-2	13	5.30	-1	S-27/3-1	3	0.0
1924 NY-A	64	119	24	42	4	8	3	12	11	7	1	6	.353	.412	.597	1.009	158	7	26	8.07	-1	2-27/S-9,3-2	6	0.7

YEAR TM-L	G	AB	R	H	2B	3B	HR	RBI	BB	SO	SB	CS	AVG	OBP	SLG	OPS	OPS+	BR/A	RC	RC/G	FR	G/POS	WS	TPW
1925 NY-A	76	170	30	48	5	1	5	17	8	10	6	3	.282	.315	.412	.726	85	-5	22	4.43	-5	2-34,S-28/3-2	3	-0.7
Total 10	813	2619	372	697	91	36	19	256	181	153	114	41	.266	.317	.350	.667	82	-76	309	3.93	26	S-624/2-79,3-32	66	1.0

• JOHNSON, Footer

Richard Allan "Treads" Johnson b: 2/15/1932, Dayton, OH BL/TL, 5'11", 175 lbs. Deb: 6/15/1958

YEAR TM-L	G	AB	R	H	2B	3B	HR	RBI	BB	SO	SB	CS	AVG	OBP	SLG	OPS	OPS+	BR/A	RC	RC/G	FR	G/POS	WS	TPW
1958 Chi-N	8	5	1	0	0	0	0	0	0	1	0	0	.000	.000	.000	.000	-102	-1	0	.00	0	....	0	-0.1

• JOHNSON, Frank

Frank Herbert Johnson b: 7/22/1942, El Paso, TX BR/TR, 6'1", 155 lbs. Deb: 9/7/1966 Career OF: 51-10-14

YEAR TM-L	G	AB	R	H	2B	3B	HR	RBI	BB	SO	SB	CS	AVG	OBP	SLG	OPS	OPS+	BR/A	RC	RC/G	FR	G/POS	WS	TPW
1966 SF-N	15	32	2	7	0	0	0	0	2	7	0	1	.219	.265	.219	.483	35	-3	2	1.84	0	0-13(8-2-7)	0	-0.4
1967 SF-N	8	10	3	3	0	0	0	0	1	2	0	0	.300	.364	.300	.664	93	-0	1	3.00	0	/0-3(2-1-1)	0	0.0
1968 SF-N	67	174	11	33	2	0	1	7	12	23	1	0	.190	.246	.218	.464	40	-12	10	1.78	-4	3-36/0-8(4-5-0),S-5,2-3	1	-1.8
1969 SF-N	7	10	2	1	0	0	0	0	0	1	0	0	.100	.100	.100	.200	-45	-2	0	.00	0	/0-7(5-1-1)	0	-0.2
1970 SF-N	67	161	25	44	1	2	3	31	19	18	1	1	.273	.357	.360	.717	94	-1	18	3.71	0	0-33(29-1-4),1-27	3	-0.4
1971 SF-N	32	49	4	4	1	0	0	5	3	9	0	0	.082	.135	.102	.237	-33	-9	1	.41	-1	/1-9,0-4(3-0-1)	0	-1.1
Total 6	196	436	47	92	4	2	4	43	37	60	2	2	.211	.277	.257	.534	52	-27	31	2.28	-6	/0-68,1-36,3-36,S-5,2-3	4	-4.0

• JOHNSON, Gary

Gerald Clyde Johnson b: 10/29/1975, Palo Alto, CA BL/TL, 6'3", 210 lbs. Deb: 4/26/2003

YEAR TM-L	G	AB	R	H	2B	3B	HR	RBI	BB	SO	SB	CS	AVG	OBP	SLG	OPS	OPS+	BR/A	RC	RC/G	FR	G/POS	WS	TPW
2003 Ana-A	5	8	1	3	1	0	0	0	1	1	0	1	.375	.444	.500	.944	155	0	1	6.39	0	/0-4(2-0-2)	0	0.0

• JOHNSON, Howard

Howard Michael "HoJo" Johnson b: 11/29/1960, Clearwater, FL BB/TR, 5'11", 178 lbs. Deb: 4/14/1982 Career OF: 99-86-36

YEAR TM-L	G	AB	R	H	2B	3B	HR	RBI	BB	SO	SB	CS	AVG	OBP	SLG	OPS	OPS+	BR/A	RC	RC/G	FR	G/POS	WS	TPW
1982 Det-A	54	155	23	49	5	0	4	14	16	30	7	4	.316	.384	.426	.810	122	5	25	6.00	-3	3-33,D-10/0-9(3-1-5)	5	0.1
1983 Det-A	27	66	11	14	0	0	3	5	7	10	0	0	.212	.297	.348	.646	79	-2	7	3.63	-3	3-21/D-2	1	-0.5
1984*Det-A	116	355	43	88	14	1	12	50	40	67	10	6	.248	.326	.394	.720	99	-1	46	4.38	-8	*3-108/S-9,D-4,1-1,0-1	10	-0.9
1985 NY-N	126	389	38	94	18	4	11	46	34	78	6	4	.242	.303	.393	.696	96	-4	45	3.96	-7	*3-113/S-7,0-1	11	-1.2
1986*NY-N	88	220	30	54	14	0	10	39	31	64	8	1	.245	.341	.445	.787	119	7	36	5.68	-3	3-45,S-34/0-1	10	0.6
1987 NY-N	157	554	93	147	22	1	36	99	83	113	32	10	.265	.366	.504	.870	135	30	106	6.69	-14	*3-140,S-38/0-2(2-0-0)	24	1.8
1988*NY-N	148	495	85	114	21	1	24	68	86	104	23	7	.230	.348	.422	.770	126	20	78	5.19	-5	*3-131,S-52	21	2.0
1989 NY-N★	153	571	**104**	164	41	3	36	101	77	126	41	8	.287	.373	.559	.932	171	57	127	8.07	-11	*3-143,S-31	38	5.1
1990 NY-N	154	590	89	144	37	3	23	90	69	100	34	8	.244	.323	.434	.757	107	8	87	4.99	4	3-92,S-73	24	1.8
1991 NY-N★	156	564	108	146	34	4	**38**	**117**	78	120	30	16	.259	.350	.535	.885	147	33	107	6.37	-13	*3-104,0-30(0-0-30),S-28	25	2.3
1992 NY-N	100	350	48	78	19	0	7	43	55	79	22	5	.223	.332	.337	.669	91	0	43	4.08	-5	0-98(16-84-1)	10	-0.7
1993 NY-N	72	235	32	56	8	2	7	26	43	43	6	4	.238	.356	.379	.735	98	0	34	4.89	6	3-67	6	0.7
1994 Col-N	93	227	30	48	10	2	10	40	39	73	11	3	.211	.327	.405	.732	77	-7	33	4.79	-1	0-62(62-0-0)/1-1	6	-1.0
1995 Chi-N	87	169	26	33	4	1	7	22	34	46	1	1	.195	.333	.355	.688	83	-4	22	4.27	-2	3-34,0-13(13-0-0)/2-8,1-3,S	3	-0.5
Total 14	1531	4940	760	1229	247	22	228	760	692	1053	231	77	.249	.343	.446	.789	119	144	797	5.50	-64	*3-1031,S-273,0-217/D-16,2,1	194	9.6

• JOHNSON, Keith

Keith Johnson b: 4/17/1971, Hanford, CA BR/TR, 5'11", 200 lbs. Deb: 4/17/2000

YEAR TM-L	G	AB	R	H	2B	3B	HR	RBI	BB	SO	SB	CS	AVG	OBP	SLG	OPS	OPS+	BR/A	RC	RC/G	FR	G/POS	WS	TPW
2000 Ana-A	6	4	2	2	0	0	0	0	2	0	0	0	.500	.667	.500	1.167	196	1	2	15.63	1	/1-3,2-2,S-1	1	0.2

• JOHNSON, Lamar

Lamar Johnson b: 9/2/1950, Bessemer, AL BR/TR, 6'2", 225 lbs. Deb: 5/18/1974 C

YEAR TM-L	G	AB	R	H	2B	3B	HR	RBI	BB	SO	SB	CS	AVG	OBP	SLG	OPS	OPS+	BR/A	RC	RC/G	FR	G/POS	WS	TPW
1974 Chi-A	10	29	1	10	0	0	0	2	0	3	0	0	.345	.345	.345	.690	96	-0	2	2.88	0	/1-7,D-3	0	-0.1
1975 Chi-A	8	30	2	6	3	0	1	1	1	5	0	0	.200	.226	.400	.626	73	-1	3	3.11	-1	/1-6,D-2	0	-0.3
1976 Chi-A	82	222	29	71	11	1	4	33	19	37	2	1	.320	.379	.432	.811	136	10	34	5.44	-1	D-35,1-34/0-1	7	0.7
1977 Chi-A	118	374	52	113	12	5	18	65	24	53	1	1	.302	.344	.505	.850	128	13	59	5.72	2	D-68,1-45	12	1.0
1978 Chi-A	148	498	52	136	23	2	8	72	43	46	6	5	.273	.333	.376	.709	98	-2	59	4.08	6	*1-108,D-36	12	-0.3
1979 Chi-A	133	479	60	148	29	1	12	74	41	56	8	2	.309	.366	.449	.815	118	13	73	5.50	0	1-94,D-37	14	0.7
1980 Chi-A	147	541	51	150	26	3	13	81	47	53	2	3	.277	.335	.409	.744	103	1	71	4.61	3	1-80,D-66	13	-0.2
1981 Chi-A	41	134	10	37	7	0	1	15	5	14	0	2	.276	.302	.351	.653	89	-3	12	3.08	-2	1-36/D-2	2	-0.7
1982 Tex-A	105	324	37	84	11	0	7	38	31	40	3	5	.259	.326	.358	.684	92	-5	35	3.61	-2	D-77,1-12	5	-0.9
Total 9	792	2631	294	755	122	12	64	381	211	307	22	19	.287	.342	.415	.757	109	27	349	4.64	5	1-422,D-326/0-1	65	-0.1

• JOHNSON, Lance

Kenneth Lance "One Dog" Johnson b: 7/6/1963, Cincinnati, OH BL/TL, 5'10", 160 lbs. Deb: 7/10/1987 Career OF: 53-1327-21

YEAR TM-L	G	AB	R	H	2B	3B	HR	RBI	BB	SO	SB	CS	AVG	OBP	SLG	OPS	OPS+	BR/A	RC	RC/G	FR	G/POS	WS	TPW
1987*StL-N	33	59	4	13	2	1	0	7	4	6	6	1	.220	.270	.288	.558	47	-4	5	2.56	-1	0-25(3-6-17)	0	-0.5
1988 Chi-A	33	124	11	23	4	1	0	6	6	11	6	2	.185	.223	.234	.457	28	-12	7	1.74	-1	0-31(0-31-0)/D-1	0	-1.3
1989 Chi-A	50	180	28	54	8	2	0	16	17	24	16	3	.300	.360	.367	.727	108	4	27	5.49	-2	0-45(42-8-0)/D-1	6	0.1
1990 Chi-A	151	541	76	154	18	9	1	51	33	45	36	22	.285	.327	.357	.684	93	-7	59	3.70	-4	*0-148(6-148-0)/D-1	18	-1.4
1991 Chi-A	159	588	72	161	14	**13**	0	49	26	58	26	11	.274	.306	.342	.648	81	-16	59	3.45	11	*0-157(0-157-2)	13	-0.7
1992 Chi-A	157	567	67	158	15	**12**	3	47	34	33	41	14	.279	.321	.363	.684	92	-4	62	3.73	2	*0-157(0-157-0)	15	-0.5
1993*Chi-A	147	540	75	168	18	**14**	0	47	36	33	35	7	.311	.354	.396	.750	104	7	78	5.40	6	*0-146(0-146-0)	21	1.4
1994 Chi-A	106	412	56	114	11	**14**	3	54	26	23	26	6	.277	.323	.393	.716	85	-7	53	4.53	1	*0-103(0-103-0)/D-1	12	-0.4
1995 Chi-A	142	607	98	**186**	18	12	10	57	32	31	40	6	.306	.342	.425	.767	103	7	92	5.69	-4	*0-140(0-140-0)/D-1	18	0.3
1996 NY-N★	160	682	117	**227**	31	**21**	9	69	33	40	50	12	.333	.365	.479	.844	126	28	121	6.77	1	*0-157(0-157-0)	26	3.0
1997 NY-N	72	265	43	82	10	6	1	24	33	21	15	10	.309	.386	.404	.790	111	4	41	5.51	0	0-66(0-66-0)	10	0.5
Chi-N	39	145	17	44	6	2	4	15	9	10	5	2	.303	.344	.455	.799	105	1	23	5.73	-3	0-39(0-39-0)/D-1	4	-0.2
Yr.	111	410	60	126	16	8	5	39	42	31	20	12	.307	.372	.422	.794	109	5	63	5.59	-3	*0-105(0-105-0)/D-1	14	0.3
1998*Chi-N	85	304	51	85	8	4	2	21	26	22	10	6	.280	.336	.352	.688	79	-10	36	4.20	-1	0-78(0-78-0)	6	-1.0
1999 Chi-N	95	335	46	87	11	6	1	21	37	20	13	3	.260	.333	.337	.671	71	-13	40	4.15	2	0-91(0-91-0)	5	-1.0
2000 NY-A	18	30	6	9	1	0	0	2	0	7	2	0	.300	.300	.333	.633	61	-1	3	3.61	-1	/0-4(2-0-2),D-3	1	-0.2
Total 14	1447	5379	767	1565	175	117	34	486	352	384	327	105	.291	.335	.386	.721	95	-21	707	4.67	6	*0-1387/D-9	155	-2.0

• JOHNSON, Larry

Larry Doby Johnson b: 8/17/1950, Cleveland, OH BR/TR, 6', 185 lbs. Deb: 10/3/1972

YEAR TM-L	G	AB	R	H	2B	3B	HR	RBI	BB	SO	SB	CS	AVG	OBP	SLG	OPS	OPS+	BR/A	RC	RC/G	FR	G/POS	WS	TPW
1972 Cle-A	1	2	0	1	0	0	0	0	0	1	0	0	.500	.500	.500	1.000	192	0	1	13.50	0	/C-1	0	0.0
1974 Cle-A	1	0	1	0	0	0	0	0	0	0	0	0	....	....	....	....	-101	0	0	....	0	....	0	0.0
1975 Mon-N	1	3	0	1	1	0	0	1	1	1	0	0	.333	.500	.667	1.167	212	1	1	15.26	0	/C-1	0	0.1
1976 Mon-N	6	13	0	2	1	0	0	0	0	2	0	0	.154	.154	.231	.385	8	-2	1	1.13	0	/C-5	0	-0.1
1978 Chi-A	3	8	0	1	0	0	0	0	1	4	0	0	.125	.222	.125	.347		-1	0	1.08	0	/C-2,D-1	0	-0.1
Total 5	12	26	1	5	2	0	0	1	2	8	0	0	.192	.250	.269	.519	46	-2	2	2.96	0	/C-9,D-1	0	-0.2

• JOHNSON, Lou

Louis Brown "Sweet Lou,Slick" Johnson b: 9/22/1934, Lexington, KY BR/TR, 5'11", 175 lbs. Deb: 4/17/1960 Career OF: 421-38-192

YEAR TM-L	G	AB	R	H	2B	3B	HR	RBI	BB	SO	SB	CS	AVG	OBP	SLG	OPS	OPS+	BR/A	RC	RC/G	FR	G/POS	WS	TPW
1960 Chi-N	34	68	6	14	2	1	0	1	5	19	3	1	.206	.270	.265	.535	48	-5	5	2.26	2	0-25(8-4-13)	1	-0.4
1961 LA-A	1	0	0	0	0	0	0	0	0	0	0	0	....	....	....	....	-90	0	0	....	0	/0-1	0	0.0
1962 Mil-N	61	117	22	33	4	5	2	13	11	27	6	1	.282	.349	.453	.802	116	3	20	6.20	0	0-55(38-20-1)	5	0.2
1965*LA-N	131	468	57	121	24	1	12	58	24	81	15	6	.259	.317	.391	.708	105	3	58	4.26	0	*0-128(124-11-3)	17	-0.4
1966*LA-N	152	526	71	143	20	2	17	73	21	75	8	10	.272	.317	.414	.732	110	3	63	4.03	0	*0-148(104-2-65)	15	-0.6
1967 LA-N	104	330	39	89	14	1	11	41	24	52	4	4	.270	.332	.418	.751	123	9	44	4.54	2	0-91(81-1-11)	11	0.6
1968 Chi-N	62	205	14	50	14	3	1	14	6	23	3	1	.244	.289	.356	.645	87	-3	20	3.29	-4	0-57(1-0-56)	4	-1.2
Cle-A	65	202	25	52	11	1	5	23	9	24	6	1	.257	.302	.396	.698	112	3	24	4.12	2	0-57(41-0-20)	7	0.2
1969 Cal-A	67	133	10	27	8	0	0	9	10	19	5	1	.203	.274	.263	.537	53	-8	10	2.54	-1	0-44(23-0-23)	1	-1.1
Total 8	677	2049	244	529	97	14	48	232	110	320	50	24	.258	.313	.389	.702	104	7	244	4.05	1	0-606	61	-2.7

• JOHNSON, Mark

Mark Patrick Johnson b: 10/17/1967, Worcester, MA BL/TL, 6'4", 230 lbs. Deb: 4/26/1995 Career OF: 15-0-7

YEAR TM-L	G	AB	R	H	2B	3B	HR	RBI	BB	SO	SB	CS	AVG	OBP	SLG	OPS	OPS+	BR/A	RC	RC/G	FR	G/POS	WS	TPW
1995 Pit-N	79	221	32	46	6	1	13	28	37	66	5	2	.208	.327	.421	.748	94	-2	33	4.92	-6	1-70	3	-1.3
1996 Pit-N	127	343	55	94	24	0	13	47	44	64	6	4	.274	.365	.458	.823	112	6	59	6.07	4	*1-100/0-1	12	0.2
1997 Pit-N	78	219	30	47	10	0	4	29	43	78	1	1	.215	.348	.315	.664	74	-7	28	4.24	1	1-63/D-1	4	-1.1
1998 Ana-A	10	14	1	1	0	0	0	0	0	6	0	0	.071	.071	.071	.143	-62	-3	0	.00	0	/1-5,D-2	0	-0.3
2000 NY-N	21	22	2	4	0	0	1	6	5	9	0	0	.182	.333	.318	.652	69	-1	2	3.49	0	/1-4,D-1,0-1	0	-0.1
2001 NY-N	71	118	17	30	6	1	6	23	16	31	0	2	.254	.343	.475	.818	114	2	20	5.79	-3	1-21,0-19(12-0-7)/D-3	4	-0.4
2002 NY-N	42	51	5	7	4	0	1	4	9	18	0	0	.137	.267	.275	.541	45	-4	4	2.65	0	1-15/0-1	0	-0.5
Total 7	428	988	142	229	50	2	38	137	154	272	12	9	.232	.341	.402	.742	93	-10	146	5.00	-5	1-278/0-22,D-7	23	-3.6

• JOHNSON, Mark L.

Mark Landon Johnson b: 9/12/1975, Wheat Ridge, CO BL/TR, 6', 185 lbs. Deb: 9/14/1998

YEAR TM-L	G	AB	R	H	2B	3B	HR	RBI	BB	SO	SB	CS	AVG	OBP	SLG	OPS	OPS+	BR/A	RC	RC/G	FR	G/POS	WS	TPW
1998 Chi-A	7	23	2	2	0	2	0	1	1	8	0	0	.087	.125	.261	.386	-3	-4	1	1.01	0	/C-7	0	-0.3

YEAR TM-L	G	AB	R	H	2B	3B	HR	RBI	BB	SO	SB	CS	AVG	OBP	SLG	OPS	OPS+	BR/A	RC	RC/G	FR	G/POS	WS	TPW
1999 Chi-A	73	207	27	47	11	0	4	16	36	58	3	1	.227	.347	.338	.685	76	-6	27	4.46	-1	C-72/D-2	5	-0.2
2000 Chi-A	75	213	29	48	11	0	3	23	27	40	3	2	.225	.315	.319	.635	60	-13	23	3.48	3	C-74/D-1	5	-0.5
2001 Chi-A	61	173	21	43	6	1	5	18	23	31	2	1	.249	.343	.382	.725	88	-3	24	4.26	1	C-61	5	0.2
2002 Chi-A	86	263	31	55	8	1	4	18	30	52	0	0	.209	.297	.293	.590	56	-16	25	3.05	-4	C-85	3	-1.4
2003 Oak-A	13	27	3	3	1	0	0	3	3	4	0	0	.111	.226	.148	.374	2	-4	1	1.34	1	C-13	1	-0.2
Total 6	**315**	**906**	**113**	**198**	**37**	**4**	**16**	**79**	**120**	**193**	**8**	**4**	**.219**	**.316**	**.321**	**.637**	**65**	**-46**	**101**	**3.58**	**0**	**C-312/D-3**	**19**	**-2.4**
• JOHNSON, Nick	Nicholas Robert Johnson b: 9/19/1978, Sacramento, CA BL/TL, 6'3", 224 lbs. Deb: 8/21/2001																							
2001 NY-A	23	67	6	13	2	0	2	8	7	15	0	0	.194	.308	.313	.621	64	-3	6	3.04	-1	1-15/D-6	0	-0.5
2002*NY-A	129	378	56	92	15	0	15	58	48	98	1	3	.243	.347	.402	.749	99	-0	53	4.70	6	1-78,D-50/O-2(2-0-0)	11	-0.3
2003*NY-A	96	324	60	92	19	0	14	47	70	57	5	2	.284	.423	.472	.895	138	23	69	7.57	2	1-60,D-33	15	1.6
Total 3	**248**	**769**	**122**	**197**	**36**	**0**	**31**	**113**	**125**	**170**	**6**	**5**	**.256**	**.377**	**.424**	**.801**	**113**	**19**	**128**	**5.71**	**7**	**1-153/D-89,O-2**	**26**	**0.8**
• JOHNSON, Otis	Otis L. Johnson b: 11/5/1883, Fowler, IN d: 11/9/1915, Johnson City, NY BB/TR, 5'9", 185 lbs. Deb: 4/12/1911																							
1911 NY-A	71	209	21	49	9	6	3	36	39	....	12	....	.234	.363	.378	.741	100	1	34	5.12	-6	S-47,2-15/3-3	6	-0.2
• JOHNSON, Paul	Paul Oscar Johnson b: 9/2/1896, North Grosvenor Dale, CT d: 2/14/1973, McAllen, TX BR/TR, 5'8", 160 lbs. Deb: 9/13/1920 Career OF: 19-28-3																							
1920 Phi-A	18	72	6	15	0	0	0	5	4	8	1	1	.208	.250	.208	.458	22	-8	4	1.72	-2	O-18(13-4-1)	0	-1.1
1921 Phi-A	48	127	17	40	6	2	1	10	9	17	0	2	.315	.360	.417	.778	97	-1	18	5.32	-3	O-32(6-24-2)	2	-0.6
Total 2	**66**	**199**	**23**	**55**	**6**	**2**	**1**	**15**	**13**	**25**	**1**	**3**	**.276**	**.321**	**.342**	**.662**	**70**	**-9**	**22**	**3.91**	**-6**	**/O-50**	**2**	**-1.6**
• JOHNSON, Randy	Randall Stuart Johnson b: 8/15/1958, Miami, FL BL/TL, 6'2", 195 lbs. Deb: 7/5/1980 Career OF: 1-0-2																							
1980 Chi-A	12	20	0	4	0	0	0	3	2	4	0	0	.200	.304	.200	.504	41	-1	2	2.44	0	/D-4,1-1,O-1	0	-0.2
1982 Min-A	89	234	26	58	10	0	10	33	30	46	0	0	.248	.333	.419	.752	102	1	34	4.96	-0	D-67/O-2(0-0-2)	5	-0.1
Total 2	**101**	**254**	**26**	**62**	**10**	**0**	**10**	**36**	**32**	**50**	**0**	**0**	**.244**	**.331**	**.402**	**.733**	**97**	**-0**	**36**	**4.74**	**0**	**/D-71,O-3,1-1**	**5**	**-0.2**
• JOHNSON, Randy	Randall Glenn Johnson b: 6/10/1956, Escondido, CA BR/TR, 6'1", 190 lbs. Deb: 4/27/1982																							
1982 Atl-N	27	46	5	11	5	0	0	6	6	4	0	1	.239	.352	.348	.700	93	-1	6	3.96	1	2-13/3-4	2	0.1
1983 Atl-N	86	144	22	36	3	0	1	17	20	27	1	3	.250	.345	.292	.637	73	-5	15	3.31	0	3-53/2-4	3	-0.6
1984 Atl-N	91	294	28	82	13	0	5	30	21	21	4	7	.279	.329	.374	.703	91	-6	35	4.19	-5	3-81	7	-1.3
Total 3	**204**	**484**	**55**	**129**	**21**	**0**	**6**	**53**	**47**	**52**	**5**	**11**	**.267**	**.336**	**.347**	**.684**	**85**	**-12**	**56**	**3.89**	**-4**	**3-138/2-17**	**12**	**-1.8**
• JOHNSON, Reed	Reed Cameron Johnson b: 12/8/1976, Riverside, CA BR/TR, 5'10", 180 lbs. Deb: 4/17/2003																							
2003 Tor-A	114	412	79	121	21	2	10	52	20	67	5	3	.294	.356	.427	.783	104	2	62	5.41	-5	*O-111(53-5-71)	11	-0.8
• JOHNSON, Ron	Ronald David Johnson b: 3/23/1956, Long Beach, CA BR/TR, 6'3", 215 lbs. Deb: 9/12/1982																							
1982 KC-A	8	14	2	4	2	0	0	0	4	3	0	0	.286	.444	.429	.873	141	1	3	8.45	-1	/1-7	1	0.0
1983 KC-A	9	27	2	7	0	0	0	1	3	1	0	0	.259	.333	.259	.593	65	-1	3	3.50	-1	/1-7,C-2	1	-0.3
1984 Mon-N	5	5	0	1	0	0	0	1	0	2	0	0	.200	.200	.200	.400	13	-1	0	1.35	0	/1-2,O-1	0	-0.1
Total 3	**22**	**46**	**4**	**12**	**2**	**0**	**0**	**2**	**7**	**6**	**0**	**0**	**.261**	**.358**	**.304**	**.663**	**86**	**-1**	**6**	**4.70**	**-2**	**/1-16,C-2,O-1**	**2**	**-0.3**
• JOHNSON, Rondin	Rondin Allen Johnson b: 12/16/1958, Bremerton, WA BB/TR, 5'10", 160 lbs. Deb: 9/3/1986																							
1986 KC-A	11	31	1	8	0	1	0	2	0	3	0	0	.258	.258	.323	.581	56	-2	3	3.03	1	2-11	1	0.0
• JOHNSON, Rontrez	Rontrez DeMon Johnson b: 12/8/1976, Marshall, TX BR/TR, 5'10", 165 lbs. Deb: 3/31/2003																							
2003 KC-A	8	3	3	1	0	0	0	0	0	2	0	0	.333	.333	.333	.667	68	-0	0	4.50	-1	/O-6(0-6-0),D-2	0	-0.1
• JOHNSON, Roy	Roy Cleveland Johnson b: 2/23/1903, Pryor, OK d: 9/10/1973, Tacoma, WA BL/TR, 5'9", 175 lbs. Deb: 4/18/1929 C Career OF: 527-70-483																							
1929 Det-A	148	640	128	201	**45**	14	10	69	67	60	20	15	.314	.379	.475	.854	118	16	114	6.57	6	*O-146(91-37-23)	19	1.0
1930 Det-A	125	462	84	127	30	13	2	35	40	46	17	10	.275	.333	.409	.742	85	-11	63	4.76	3	*O-118(7-2-110)	9	-1.6
1931 Det-A	151	621	107	173	37	**19**	8	55	72	51	33	21	.279	.355	.438	.793	104	4	96	5.42	13	*O-150(0-5-148)	15	0.8
1932 Det-A	49	195	33	49	14	2	3	22	20	26	7	2	.251	.324	.390	.714	81	-5	26	4.61	0	O-48(0-0-48)	4	-0.8
Bos-A	94	349	70	104	24	4	11	47	44	41	13	4	.298	.378	.484	.862	125	15	66	7.05	-4	O-85(14-16-56)	9	0.5
Yr.	143	544	103	153	38	6	14	69	64	67	20	6	.281	.359	.450	.809	109	10	92	6.14	-5	*O-133(14-16-104)	13	-0.2
1933 Bos-A	133	483	88	151	30	7	10	95	55	36	13	10	.313	.387	.466	.853	126	18	88	6.69	0	*O-125(26-10-95)	16	1.0
1934 Bos-A	143	569	85	182	43	10	7	119	54	36	11	5	.320	.379	.467	.846	110	8	102	6.83	-7	*O-137(137-0-0)	19	-0.6
1935 Bos-A	145	553	70	174	33	9	3	66	74	34	11	12	.315	.398	.423	.822	105	5	95	6.34	1	*O-142(142-0-0)	17	-0.1
1936*NY-A	63	147	21	39	8	2	1	19	21	14	3	1	.265	.361	.367	.728	83	-3	21	5.04	-1	O-33(28-0-3)	3	-0.5
1937 NY-A	12	51	5	15	3	0	0	6	3	2	1	0	.294	.333	.353	.686	73	-2	6	4.55	-2	O-12(12-0-0)	1	-0.4
Bos-N	85	260	24	72	8	3	3	22	38	29	5	....	.277	.369	.365	.735	110	5	37	5.19	0	O-63(63-0-0)/3-1	10	0.1
1938 Bos-N	7	29	2	5	0	0	0	1	1	5	1	....	.172	.200	.172	.372	4	-4	1	1.21	-2	/O-7(7-0-0)	0	-0.6
Total 10	**1155**	**4359**	**717**	**1292**	**275**	**83**	**58**	**556**	**489**	**380**	**135**	**80**	**.296**	**.369**	**.437**	**.806**	**107**	**45**	**715**	**5.96**	**7**	***O-1066/3-1**	**122**	**-1.3**
• JOHNSON, Roy	Roy Edward Johnson b: 6/27/1959, Parkin, AR BL/TL, 6'4", 205 lbs. Deb: 7/3/1982 Career OF: 9-10-6																							
1982 Mon-N	17	32	2	7	2	0	0	2	1	6	0	0	.219	.242	.281	.524	45	-2	2	2.39	-1	O-11(0-9-3)	0	-0.3
1984 Mon-N	16	33	2	5	2	0	1	2	7	10	1	0	.152	.300	.303	.603	73	-1	4	3.57	-1	O-10(9-0-1)	0	-0.2
1985 Mon-N	3	5	0	0	0	0	0	0	0	3	0	0	.000	.000	.000	.000	-106	-1	0	.00	0	/O-3(0-1-2)	0	-0.2
Total 3	**36**	**70**	**4**	**12**	**4**	**0**	**1**	**4**	**8**	**19**	**1**	**0**	**.171**	**.256**	**.271**	**.528**	**50**	**-5**	**6**	**2.75**	**-2**	**/O-24**	**0**	**-0.8**
• JOHNSON, Russ	William Russell Johnson b: 2/22/1973, Baton Rouge, LA BR/TR, 5'10", 185 lbs. Deb: 4/8/1997																							
1997*Hou-N	21	60	7	18	1	0	2	9	6	14	1	1	.300	.364	.417	.780	108	0	9	5.08	0	3-14/2-3	2	0.1
1998 Hou-N	8	13	2	3	1	0	0	0	1	5	1	0	.231	.333	.308	.641	72	-0	1	3.30	0	/3-5,2-1	0	0.0
1999*Hou-N	83	156	24	44	10	0	5	23	20	31	2	3	.282	.364	.442	.806	104	0	25	5.40	2	3-36,2-15/S-2	5	0.3
2000 Hou-N	26	45	4	8	0	0	0	3	2	10	1	1	.178	.213	.178	.391		-7	1	.77	-4	/S-5,3-4,2-3	0	-1.0
TB-A	74	185	28	47	8	0	2	17	25	30	4	1	.254	.346	.330	.676	73	-6	23	4.18	4	3-49,2-18,S-11	4	-0.1
2001 TB-A	85	248	32	73	19	2	4	33	34	57	2	2	.294	.382	.435	.817	116	6	44	6.40	-1	3-36,2-33/S-6,D-2	11	0.7
2002 TB-A	45	111	15	24	5	0	1	12	16	22	5	2	.216	.320	.288	.609	65	-5	11	3.29	-4	3-27/D-5,S-2,2-1	2	-0.8
Total 6	**342**	**818**	**112**	**217**	**44**	**2**	**14**	**97**	**104**	**169**	**16**	**10**	**.265**	**.351**	**.375**	**.726**	**90**	**-12**	**114**	**4.74**	**-2**	**3-171/2-74,S-26,D-7**	**24**	**-0.8**
• JOHNSON, Spud	John Ralph Johnson b: 1860, Canada BL/TL, 5'9", 175 lbs. Deb: 4/18/1889 Career OF: 96-0-187																							
1889 Col-a	116	459	91	130	14	10	2	79	39	47	34	....	.283	.355	.370	.725	112	9	74	5.98	-5	O-69(0-0-69),3-44/1-2,S-1	13	0.3
1890 Col-a	135	538	106	186	23	18	1	**113**	48	....	43	....	.346	.409	.461	.870	168	46	122	9.19	-9	*O-135(96-0-39)	25	2.9
1891 Cle-N	80	327	49	84	8	3	1	46	22	23	16	....	.257	.319	.309	.628	80	-9	38	4.26	-5	O-79(0-0-79)/1-1	6	-1.4
Total 3	**331**	**1324**	**246**	**400**	**45**	**31**	**4**	**238**	**109**	**70**	**93**	**....**	**.302**	**.368**	**.392**	**.760**	**127**	**46**	**235**	**6.75**	**-19**	**O-283/3-44,1-3,S-1**	**44**	**1.9**
• JOHNSON, Stan	Stanley Lucius Johnson b: 2/12/1937, Dallas, TX BL/TL, 5'10", 180 lbs. Deb: 9/18/1960 Career OF: 2-0-2																							
1960 Chi-A	5	6	1	1	0	0	1	1	0	1	0	1	.167	.167	.667	.833	116	-0	0	.00	0	/O-2(2-0-0)	0	-0.1
1961 KC-A	3	3	1	0	0	0	0	0	2	1	0	0	.000	.400	.000	.400	17	-0	0	.70	0	/O-2(0-0-2)	0	-0.1
Total 2	**8**	**9**	**2**	**1**	**0**	**0**	**1**	**1**	**2**	**2**	**0**	**1**	**.111**	**.273**	**.444**	**.717**	**71**	**-1**	**0**	**.28**	**0**	**/O-4**	**0**	**-0.1**
• JOHNSON, Tim	Timothy Evald Johnson b: 7/22/1949, Grand Forks, ND BL/TR, 6'1", 170 lbs. Deb: 4/24/1973 M/C Career OF: 2-0-0																							
1973 Mil-A	136	465	39	99	10	2	0	32	29	93	6	3	.213	.261	.243	.504	43	-34	30	2.04	-6	*S-135	4	-2.6
1974 Mil-A	93	245	25	60	7	7	0	25	11	48	4	3	.245	.280	.331	.611	76	-9	23	3.11	1	S-64,2-26/3-1,D-1,O-1	6	0.0
1975 Mil-A	38	85	6	12	1	0	0	2	6	17	3	0	.141	.198	.153	.351		-10	3	1.04	-1	2-11,3-11,S-10/D-3,1-2	1	-1.0
1976 Mil-A	105	273	25	75	4	3	0	14	19	32	4	1	.275	.327	.311	.638	89	-3	28	3.52	-3	*2-100,3-17/1-1,S-1	7	-0.1
1977 Mil-A	30	33	5	2	1	0	0	2	5	10	1	0	.061	.184	.091	.275	-22	-5	1	.80	-3	2-10/S-6,3-4,D-4,O-1	0	-0.8
1978 Mil-A	3	3	1	0	0	0	0	0	2	0	0	0	.000	.400	.000	.400	22	-0	0	1.87	-1	/S-2	0	-0.1
Tor-A	68	79	9	19	2	0	0	3	8	16	0	1	.241	.318	.266	.584	65	-4	7	3.10	1	S-49,2-13	2	0.0
Yr.	71	82	10	19	2	0	0	3	10	16	0	1	.232	.323	.256	.579	62	-4	8	3.04	0	S-51,2-13	2	-0.1
1979 Tor-A	43	86	6	16	2	1	0	6	8	15	0	1	.186	.255	.233	.488	32	-9	5	1.82	-3	2-25/3-9,1-7	1	-1.0
Total 7	**516**	**1269**	**116**	**283**	**27**	**13**	**0**	**84**	**88**	**231**	**18**	**9**	**.223**	**.276**	**.265**	**.541**	**55**	**-74**	**98**	**2.48**	**-15**	**S-267,2-185/3-42,1-10,D-8,O-8**	**21**	**-5.7**

YEAR TM-L	G	AB	R	H	2B	3B	HR	RBI	BB	SO	SB	CS	AVG	OBP	SLG	OPS	OPS+	BR/A	RC	RC/G	FR	G/POS	WS	TPW
• JOHNSON, Tony	Anthony Clair Johnson b: 6/23/1956, Memphis, TN BR/TR, 6'3", 145 lbs. Deb: 9/28/1981 Career OF: 26-2-2																							
1981 Mon-N	2	1	0	0	0	0	0	0	0	0	0	0	.000	.000	.000	.000	-99	-0	0	.00	0	/0-1	0	0.0
1982 Tor-A	70	98	17	23	2	1	3	14	11	26	3	13	.235	.312	.367	.679	78	-8	7	2.20	0	D-28,0-28(25-2-2)	1	-1.0
Total 2	**72**	**99**	**17**	**23**	**2**	**1**	**3**	**14**	**11**	**26**	**3**	**13**	**.232**	**.309**	**.364**	**.673**	**77**	**-8**	**7**	**2.18**	**-1**	**/0-29,D-28**	**1**	**-1.0**
• JOHNSON, Wallace	Wallace Darnell Johnson b: 12/25/1956, Gary, IN BB/TR, 6', 185 lbs. Deb: 9/8/1981 C																							
1981*Mon-N	11	9	1	2	0	1	0	3	1	1	1	1	.222	.300	.444	.744	108	-0	0	1.36	0	/2-1	0	0.0
1982 Mon-N	36	57	5	11	0	2	0	2	5	5	4	1	.193	.258	.263	.521	45	-4	4	2.55	-1	2-13	0	-0.5
1983 Mon-N	3	2	1	1	0	0	0	0	1	0	1	0	.500	.667	.500	1.167	229	1	1	32.04	0	....	0	0.1
SF-N	7	8	0	1	0	0	0	1	0	0	0	0	.125	.125	.125	.250	-32	-1	0	.48	0	/2-1	0	-0.2
Yr.	10	10	1	2	0	0	0	1	1	0	1	0	.200	.273	.200	.473	39	-1	1	4.43	0	/2-1	0	-0.1
1984 Mon-N	17	24	3	5	0	0	0	4	5	4	0	0	.208	.345	.208	.553	61	-1	2	3.09	0	/1-4	0	-0.1
1986 Mon-N	61	127	13	36	3	1	1	10	7	9	6	3	.283	.321	.346	.667	85	-3	14	3.90	1	1-27	2	-0.3
1987 Mon-N	75	85	7	21	5	0	1	14	7	6	5	0	.247	.304	.341	.646	69	-3	10	4.20	-1	/1-9	2	-0.5
1988 Mon-N	86	94	7	29	5	1	0	3	12	15	0	2	.309	.387	.383	.770	116	2	14	5.25	1	1-13/2-1	1	0.2
1989 Mon-N	85	114	9	31	3	1	2	17	7	12	1	0	.272	.314	.368	.682	93	-1	13	4.06	-2	1-18	1	-0.4
1990 Mon-N	47	49	6	8	1	0	1	5	7	6	1	0	.163	.281	.245	.526	48	-3	4	2.38	-1	/1-7	0	-0.4
Total 9	**428**	**569**	**52**	**145**	**17**	**6**	**5**	**59**	**52**	**58**	**19**	**7**	**.255**	**.318**	**.332**	**.650**	**81**	**-14**	**63**	**3.83**	**-3**	**/1-78,2-16**	**6**	**-2.1**
• JOHNSTON, Dick	Richard Frederick Johnston b: 4/6/1863, Kingston, NY d: 4/4/1934, Detroit, MI BR/TR, 5'8", 155 lbs. Deb: 8/12/1884 U Career OF: 12-729-3																							
1884 Ric-a	39	146	23	41	5	5	2	0	2	....	....	....	.281	.291	.425	.715	132	5	18	4.84	6	0-37(0-37-0)/S-2	5	0.9
1885 Bos-N	26	111	17	26	6	3	1	23	0	15	....	....	.234	.234	.369	.604	96	-1	10	3.13	1	0-26(0-26-0)	2	-0.1
1886 Bos-N	109	413	48	99	18	9	1	57	3	70	11	....	.240	.245	.334	.579	77	-12	37	3.22	7	*0-109(0-109-0)	8	-0.8
1887 Bos-N	127	523	87	147	13	20	5	77	16	35	52	....	.281	.281	.393	.674	87	-10	72	5.10	22	*0-127(0-127-0)	13	0.7
1888 Bos-N	135	585	102	173	31	**18**	12	68	15	33	35	....	.296	.314	.472	.786	142	24	100	6.57	8	*0-135(0-135-0)	24	2.7
1889 Bos-N	132	539	80	123	16	4	5	67	41	60	34	....	.228	.285	.301	.586	60	-31	57	3.65	-6	*0-132(0-132-0)	11	-3.6
1890 Bos-P	2	9	0	1	0	0	0	0	0	1	0	....	.111	.111	.111	.222	-38	-2	0	.38	0	/0-2(0-2-0)	0	-0.1
NY-P	77	306	37	74	9	7	1	43	18	25	7	....	.242	.288	.327	.615	59	-21	32	3.68	0	0-76(12-62-2)/S-2	5	-1.9
Yr.	79	315	37	75	9	7	1	43	18	26	7	....	.238	.284	.321	.604	56	-23	32	3.57	0	0-78(12-64-2)/S-2	5	-2.0
1891 Cin-a	99	376	59	83	11	2	6	51	38	44	12	....	.221	.301	.309	.609	68	-18	39	3.57	-2	*0-99(0-99-1)	6	-2.0
Total 8	**746**	**3008**	**453**	**767**	**109**	**68**	**33**	**386**	**133**	**283**	**151**	**....**	**.255**	**.285**	**.366**	**.651**	**88**	**-66**	**367**	**4.39**	**37**	**0-743/S-4**	**74**	**-4.3**
• JOHNSTON, Doc	Wheeler Roger Johnston b: 9/9/1887, Cleveland, TN d: 2/17/1961, Chattanooga, TN BL/TL, 6', 170 lbs. Deb: 10/3/1909																							
1909 Cin-N	3	10	1	0	0	0	0	1	0	....	0	....	.000	.000	.000	.000	-101	-2	0	.00	0	/1-3	0	-0.2
1912 Cle-A	43	164	22	46	7	4	1	11	11	....	8	....	.280	.326	.390	.716	101	-1	23	4.85	-3	1-41	4	-0.4
1913 Cle-A	133	530	74	135	19	12	2	39	35	65	19	....	.255	.309	.347	.657	89	-9	60	3.76	-4	*1-133	11	-1.6
1914 Cle-A	103	340	43	83	15	1	0	23	28	46	14	9	.244	.311	.294	.605	79	-10	34	3.23	-11	1-90/0-2(0-2-0)	5	-2.5
1915 Pit-N	147	543	71	144	19	12	5	64	38	40	26	17	.265	.328	.372	.700	113	6	72	4.22	-4	*1-147	15	-0.1
1916 Pit-N	114	404	33	86	10	10	0	39	20	42	17	....	.213	.262	.287	.549	68	-16	37	2.84	1	*1-110	4	-1.9
1918 Cle-A	74	273	30	62	12	2	0	25	26	19	12	....	.227	.301	.286	.587	70	-10	27	3.07	-5	1-73	3	-1.8
1919 Cle-A	102	331	42	101	17	3	1	33	25	18	21	....	.305	.359	.384	.743	102	1	53	5.42	-3	1-98	9	-0.4
1920*Cle-A	147	535	68	156	24	10	2	71	28	32	13	7	.292	.333	.385	.718	87	-10	69	4.44	-5	*1-147	11	-1.6
1921 Cle-A	118	384	53	114	20	7	2	46	29	15	2	9	.297	.353	.401	.754	90	-9	53	4.58	0	*1-116	8	-1.4
1922 Phi-A	71	260	41	65	11	7	1	29	24	15	7	6	.250	.316	.358	.673	73	-11	30	3.65	-3	1-65	3	-1.7
Total 11	**1055**	**3774**	**478**	**992**	**154**	**68**	**14**	**381**	**264**	**292**	**139**	**48**	**.263**	**.319**	**.351**	**.670**	**88**	**-69**	**456**	**3.97**	**-35**	***1-1023/0-2**	**73**	**-13.6**
• JOHNSTON, Fred	Wilfred Ivy Johnston b: 7/9/1899, Charlotte, NC d: 7/14/1959, Tyler, TX BR/TR, 5'11.5", 170 lbs. Deb: 6/29/1924																							
1924 Bro-N	4	4	1	1	0	0	0	0	0	1	0	0	.250	.250	.250	.500	35	-0	0	2.12	-1	/2-1,3-1	0	-0.1
• JOHNSTON, Greg	Gregory Bernard Johnston b: 2/12/1955, Los Angeles, CA BL/TL, 6', 175 lbs. Deb: 7/27/1979 Career OF: 13-21-5																							
1979 SF-N	42	74	5	15	2	0	1	7	2	17	0	0	.203	.224	.270	.494	37	-7	4	1.94	-1	0-17(13-1-5)	0	-0.8
1980 Min-A	14	27	3	5	3	0	0	1	2	4	0	0	.185	.241	.296	.538	43	-2	1	1.23	0	0-14(0-14-0)	0	-0.3
1981 Min-A	7	16	2	2	0	0	0	0	2	5	0	0	.125	.222	.125	.347	2	-2	1	1.08	1	/0-6(0-6-0)	0	-0.1
Total 3	**63**	**117**	**10**	**22**	**5**	**0**	**1**	**8**	**6**	**26**	**0**	**0**	**.188**	**.228**	**.256**	**.484**	**33**	**-11**	**6**	**1.63**	**0**	**/0-37**	**0**	**-1.2**
• JOHNSTON, Jimmy	James Harle Johnston b: 12/10/1889, Cleveland, TN d: 2/14/1967, Chattanooga, TN BR/TR, 5'10", 160 lbs. Deb: 5/3/1911 C Career OF: 72-112-177																							
1911 Chi-A	1	2	0	0	0	0	0	2	0	....	0	....	.000	.000	.000	.000	-102	-1	0	.00	0	/0-1	0	-0.1
1914 Chi-N	50	101	9	23	3	2	1	8	4	9	3	....	.228	.264	.327	.591	75	-4	9	2.92	2	0-28(2-22-4)/2-4	2	-0.4
1916*Bro-N	118	425	58	107	13	8	1	26	35	38	22	19	.252	.313	.327	.640	94	-6	44	3.32	1	*0-106(8-45-55)	13	-1.3
1917 Bro-N	103	330	33	89	10	4	0	25	23	28	16	....	.270	.321	.324	.645	95	-2	39	3.93	-3	0-66(37-24-5),1-14/S-4,2-3,3	9	-0.9
1918 Bro-N	123	484	54	136	16	8	0	27	33	31	22	....	.281	.328	.347	.675	106	3	59	4.30	6	0-96(20-5-75),1-21/3-4,2-1	14	0.4
1919 Bro-N	117	405	56	114	11	4	1	23	29	26	11	....	.281	.334	.336	.670	100	0	48	4.10	1	2-87,0-14(1-8-6)/1-2,S-1	13	0.2
1920*Bro-N	155	635	87	185	17	12	1	52	43	23	19	15	.291	.338	.361	.699	98	-1	77	4.15	0	*3-146/0-7(0-0-7),S-3	20	0.3
1921 Bro-N	152	624	104	203	41	14	5	56	45	26	28	16	.325	.372	.460	.832	115	14	105	6.09	-2	*3-150/S-3	24	2.3
1922 Bro-N	138	567	110	181	20	7	4	49	38	17	18	9	.319	.364	.400	.764	98	-0	83	5.43	5	2-62,S-50,3-26	20	1.3
1923 Bro-N	151	625	111	203	29	11	4	60	53	15	16	13	.325	.378	.426	.803	115	13	100	5.86	13	2-84,S-52,3-14	22	3.3
1924 Bro-N	86	315	51	94	11	2	2	29	27	10	5	6	.298	.356	.365	.721	97	-1	41	4.57	-3	S-63,3-10/1-4,0-1	10	0.3
1925 Bro-N	123	431	63	128	13	3	2	43	45	15	7	5	.297	.369	.355	.724	88	-5	59	4.90	-24	3-81,0-20(2-0-18)/1-8,S-2	9	-2.4
1926 Bos-N	23	57	7	14	1	0	1	5	10	3	2	....	.246	.358	.316	.674	91	-0	7	4.15	-2	3-14/2-2,0-1	1	-0.2
NY-N	37	69	11	16	0	0	0	5	6	5	0	....	.232	.293	.232	.525	43	-5	5	2.35	0	0-14(1-7-6)	0	-0.6
Yr.	60	126	18	30	1	0	1	10	16	8	2	....	.238	.324	.270	.594	66	-5	12	3.16	-3	0-15(2-7-6),3-14/2-2	1	-0.7
Total 13	**1377**	**5070**	**754**	**1493**	**185**	**75**	**22**	**410**	**391**	**246**	**169**	**83**	**.294**	**.347**	**.374**	**.721**	**100**	**6**	**676**	**4.68**	**-8**	**3-448,0-354,2-243,S-178/1-49**	**157**	**2.3**
• JOHNSTON, Johnny	John Thomas Johnston b: 3/28/1890, Longview, TX d: 3/7/1940, San Diego, CA BL/TR, 5'11", 172 lbs. Deb: 4/10/1913																							
1913 StL-A	111	380	37	85	14	4	2	27	42	51	11	....	.224	.308	.297	.605	79	-9	38	3.12	10	*0-107(106-0-0)	6	-0.4
• JOHNSTON, Rex	Rex David Johnston b: 11/8/1937, Colton, CA BB/TR, 6'1.5", 202 lbs. Deb: 4/15/1964																							
1964 Pit-N	14	7	1	0	0	0	0	0	3	0	0	0	.000	.300	.000	.300	-7	-1	0	.60	-1	/0-8(6-2-0)	0	-0.2
• JOHNSTONE, Jay	John William Johnstone b: 11/20/1945, Manchester, CT BL/TR, 6'1", 175 lbs. Deb: 7/30/1966 Career OF: 258-521-572																							
1966 Cal-A	61	254	35	67	12	4	3	17	11	36	3	3	.264	.297	.378	.675	95	-3	28	3.83	-1	0-61(41-12-13)	6	-0.8
1967 Cal-A	79	230	18	48	7	1	2	10	5	37	3	2	.209	.226	.274	.499	49	-15	13	1.89	0	0-63(0-62-1)	2	-1.9
1968 Cal-A	41	115	11	30	4	1	0	3	7	15	2	1	.261	.303	.313	.616	90	-2	12	3.55	2	0-29(1-21-7)	3	-0.1
1969 Cal-A	148	540	64	146	20	5	10	59	38	75	3	9	.270	.324	.381	.706	102	-4	65	4.15	4	*0-144(0-144-0)	17	-0.4
1970 Cal-A	119	320	34	76	10	5	11	39	24	53	1	0	.238	.293	.403	.696	93	-4	37	3.87	2	*0-100(2-88-10)	10	-0.5
1971 Chi-A	124	388	53	101	14	1	16	40	38	50	10	5	.260	.331	.425	.756	109	5	56	4.99	-2	*0-119(11-92-23)	12	-0.2
1972 Chi-A	113	261	27	49	9	0	4	17	25	42	2	1	.188	.259	.268	.527	56	-14	19	2.39	-3	0-97(13-85-6)	3	-2.3
1973 Oak-A	23	28	1	3	1	0	0	3	2	4	0	1	.107	.167	.143	.310	-13	-5	1	.63	-1	/0-7(3-1-3),D-4,2-2	0	-0.6
1974 Phi-N	64	200	30	59	10	4	6	30	24	28	5	5	.295	.371	.475	.846	130	7	35	6.36	1	0-59(31-1-40)	9	0.6
1975 Phi-N	122	350	50	115	19	2	7	54	42	39	7	3	.329	.401	.454	.855	131	16	64	6.87	6	*0-101(0-3-100)	14	1.9
1976*Phi-N	129	440	62	140	38	4	5	53	41	39	5	5	.318	.379	.457	.836	132	18	75	6.28	3	*0-122(2-0-120)/1-6	19	1.5
1977*Phi-N	112	363	64	103	18	4	15	59	38	38	3	7	.284	.355	.479	.834	116	6	59	5.56	2	0-91(4-0-87),1-19	13	0.3
1978 Phi-N	35	56	3	10	2	0	0	4	6	9	0	2	.179	.258	.214	.472	33	-6	3	1.42	0	/1-8,0-7(3-0-4)	0	-0.7
*NY-A	36	65	6	17	0	0	1	6	4	10	0	1	.262	.333	.308	.641	83	-2	7	3.80	-1	0-22(8-0-14)/D-5	1	-0.3
1979 NY-A	23	48	7	10	1	0	1	7	2	7	1	0	.208	.240	.292	.532	44	-4	4	2.56	0	0-19(14-4-1)/D-3	1	-0.4
SD-N	75	201	10	59	8	2	0	32	18	21	1	3	.294	.352	.353	.705	99	-1	24	4.08	2	0-45(35-7-4),1-22	5	-0.1
1980 LA-N	109	251	31	77	15	2	2	20	24	29	3	2	.307	.372	.406	.778	119	7	39	5.82	3	0-61(5-0-57)	10	0.7
1981*LA-N	61	83	8	17	3	0	3	6	7	13	0	1	.205	.267	.349	.616	76	-3	7	2.64	1	0-16(8-0-8)/1-2	1	-0.3
1982 LA-N	21	13	1	1	1	0	0	2	5	2	0	0	.077	.333	.154	.487	42	-1	1	2.33	0	....	0	-0.1
Chi-N	98	269	39	67	13	1	10	43	40	41	0	2	.249	.346	.416	.763	109	3	40	5.10	5	0-86(34-0-58)	9	0.4

YEAR	TM-L	G	AB	R	H	2B	3B	HR	RBI	BB	SO	SB	CS	AVG	OBP	SLG	OPS	OPS+	BR/A	RC	RC/G	FR	G/POS	WS	TPW
	Yr.	119	282	40	68	14	1	10	45	45	43	0	2	.241	.346	.404	.750	106	3	41	4.94	5	0-86(34-0-58)	9	0.4
1983	Chi-N	86	140	16	36	7	0	6	22	20	24	1	1	.257	.362	.436	.798	115	3	22	5.33	-1	0-44(36-0-8)	4	0.1
1984	Chi-N	52	73	8	21	2	0	0	3	7	18	0	0	.288	.350	.370	.720	94	-0	9	4.51	0	0-15(7-1-8)	2	-0.1
1985*	LA-N	17	15	0	2	1	0	0	2	1	2	0	0	.133	.188	.200	.388	9	-2	0	.34	0	....	0	-0.2
Total 20		1748	4703	578	1254	215	38	102	531	429	632	50	54	.267	.331	.394	.724	102	-1	618	4.56	20	*0-1308/1-57,D-12,2-2	141	-3.5

• JOK, Stan
Stanley Edward "Tucker" Jok b: 5/3/1926, Buffalo, NY d: 3/6/1972, Buffalo, NY BR/TR, 6', 190 lbs. Deb: 4/13/1954

YEAR	TM-L	G	AB	R	H	2B	3B	HR	RBI	BB	SO	SB	CS	AVG	OBP	SLG	OPS	OPS+	BR/A	RC	RC/G	FR	G/POS	WS	TPW
1954	Phi-N	3	3	0	0	0	0	0	0	0	2	0	0	.000	.000	.000	.000	-100	-1	0	.00	0	....	0	-0.1
	Chi-A	3	12	1	2	0	0	0	2	1	2	0	0	.167	.231	.167	.397	10	-1	0	.85	0	/3-3	0	-0.1
1955	Chi-A	6	4	3	1	0	0	1	2	1	1	0	0	.250	.400	1.000	1.400	259	1	2	10.76	-1	/3-3,0-1	1	0.0
Total 2		12	19	4	3	0	0	1	4	2	5	0	0	.158	.238	.316	.554	63	-1	2	2.91	0	/3-6,0-1	1	-0.2

• JOLLEY, Smead
Smead Powell "Guinea,Smudge" Jolley
b: 1/14/1902, Wesson, AR d: 11/17/1991, Alameda, CA BL/TR, 6'3.5", 210 lbs. Deb: 4/17/1930 Career OF: 290-0-123

YEAR	TM-L	G	AB	R	H	2B	3B	HR	RBI	BB	SO	SB	CS	AVG	OBP	SLG	OPS	OPS+	BR/A	RC	RC/G	FR	G/POS	WS	TPW
1930	Chi-A	152	616	76	193	38	12	16	114	28	52	3	1	.313	.346	.492	.838	114	11	103	6.41	3	*0-151(68-0-83)	18	0.3
1931	Chi-A	54	110	5	33	11	0	3	28	7	4	0	0	.300	.353	.482	.835	125	4	19	6.45	-2	0-23(8-0-15)	4	0.1
1932	Chi-A	12	42	3	15	3	0	0	7	3	0	1	0	.357	.413	.429	.842	127	2	8	7.61	0	0-11(7-0-4)	1	0.1
	Bos-A	137	531	57	164	27	5	18	99	27	29	0	5	.309	.345	.480	.825	115	7	85	6.03	-1	*0-126(120-0-6)/C-5	11	0.0
	Yr.	149	573	60	179	30	5	18	106	30	29	1	5	.312	.350	.476	.826	115	9	92	6.13	-1	*0-137(127-0-10)/C-5	12	0.1
1933	Bos-A	118	411	47	116	32	4	9	65	24	20	1	1	.282	.325	.445	.770	103	0	59	5.28	3	*0-102(87-0-15)	10	-0.1
Total 4		473	1710	188	521	111	21	46	313	89	105	5	7	.305	.343	.475	.818	112	24	274	6.04	3	0-413/C-5	44	0.4

• JONES,
Levin Jones b: Baltimore, MD Deb: 5/14/1873 NA OF: 0-1-1

YEAR	TM-L	G	AB	R	H	2B	3B	HR	RBI	BB	SO	SB	CS	AVG	OBP	SLG	OPS	OPS+	BR/A	RC	RC/G	FR	G/POS	WS	TPW
1873	Mar-n	1	4	0	3	0	0	0	1	0	0	0	0	.750	.750	.750	1.500	452	2	2	70.34	0	/0-1	....	0.1
1874	Bal-n	2	7	0	1	0	0	0	0	0	0	0	0	.143	.143	.143	.286	-8	-1	0	.73	-0	/C-1,0-1	....	-0.1
Total 2 n		3	11	0	4	0	0	0	1	0	0	0	0	.364	.364	.364	.727	159	1	2	10.68	0	/0-2,C-1	....	0.1

• JONES,
Jones b: Johnstown, PA Deb: 7/14/1884

YEAR	TM-L	G	AB	R	H	2B	3B	HR	RBI	BB	SO	SB	CS	AVG	OBP	SLG	OPS	OPS+	BR/A	RC	RC/G	FR	G/POS	WS	TPW
1884	Was-a	4	17	2	5	0	0	0		0				.294	.333	.294	.627	120	0	2	3.91	0	/0-4(4-0-0)	1	0.0

• JONES,
Jones Deb: 4/30/1885

YEAR	TM-L	G	AB	R	H	2B	3B	HR	RBI	BB	SO	SB	CS	AVG	OBP	SLG	OPS	OPS+	BR/A	RC	RC/G	FR	G/POS	WS	TPW
1885	NY-a	1	4	0	1	0	0	0		0				.250	.250	.250	.500	63	-0	0	2.31	1	/3-1	0	0.1

• JONES, Andruw
Andruw Rudolf Jones b: 4/23/1977, Willemstad, Curacao BR/TR, 6'1", 170 lbs. Deb: 8/15/1996 Career OF: 2-1021-115

YEAR	TM-L	G	AB	R	H	2B	3B	HR	RBI	BB	SO	SB	CS	AVG	OBP	SLG	OPS	OPS+	BR/A	RC	RC/G	FR	G/POS	WS	TPW
1996*	Atl-N	31	106	11	23	7	1	5	13	7	29	3	0	.217	.265	.443	.709	78	-3	13	4.16	5	0-29(0-12-20)	3	0.1
1997*	Atl-N	153	399	60	92	18	1	18	70	56	107	20	11	.231	.331	.416	.747	92	-5	54	4.36	10	*0-147(2-57-95)	13	0.1
1998*	Atl-N	159	582	89	158	33	8	31	90	40	129	27	4	.271	.323	.515	.838	116	14	97	5.92	26	*0-159(0-159-0)	26	4.1
1999*	Atl-N	162	592	97	163	35	5	26	84	76	103	24	12	.275	.366	.483	.849	112	11	106	6.28	22	0-162(0-162-0)	28	3.3
2000*	Atl-N★	161	656	122	199	36	6	36	104	59	100	21	6	.303	.369	.541	.910	126	26	132	7.42	11	0-161(0-161-0)	30	3.6
2001*	Atl-N	161	625	104	157	25	2	34	104	56	142	11	4	.251	.316	.461	.777	95	-6	91	5.02	14	0-161(0-161-0)	22	0.9
2002*	Atl-N★	154	560	91	148	34	0	35	94	83	135	8	3	.264	.369	.513	.882	128	24	108	6.70	7	0-154(0-154-0)/D-1	28	3.3
2003*	Atl-N★	156	595	101	165	28	2	36	116	53	125	4	3	.277	.342	.513	.854	119	14	101	5.88	9	0-155(0-155-0)	23	2.4
Total 8		1137	4115	675	1105	216	25	221	675	430	870	118	43	.269	.344	.494	.838	113	75	701	5.95	104	*0-1128/D-1	173	17.7

• JONES, Bill
William Dennis "Midget" Jones b: 4/8/1887, Hartland, Canada d: 10/10/1946, Boston, MA BL/TR, 5'6.5", 157 lbs. Deb: 6/20/1911

YEAR	TM-L	G	AB	R	H	2B	3B	HR	RBI	BB	SO	SB	CS	AVG	OBP	SLG	OPS	OPS+	BR/A	RC	RC/G	FR	G/POS	WS	TPW
1911	Bos-N	24	51	6	11	2	1	0	3	15	7	1	....	.216	.394	.294	.688	87	0	6	4.05	-2	0-18(0-18-0)	1	-0.3
1912	Bos-N	3	2	0	1	0	0	0	2	0	1	0	....	.500	.500	.500	1.000	171	0	0	12.55	0	....	0	0.0
Total 2		27	53	6	12	2	1	0	5	15	8	1		.226	.397	.302	.699	89	0	7	4.26	-2	/0-18	1	-0.3

• JONES, Bill
William Jones b: Syracuse, NY Deb: 5/17/1882 Career OF: 0-1-2

YEAR	TM-L	G	AB	R	H	2B	3B	HR	RBI	BB	SO	SB	CS	AVG	OBP	SLG	OPS	OPS+	BR/A	RC	RC/G	FR	G/POS	WS	TPW
1882	Bal-a	4	15	1	1	0	0	0	....	1	....	....	....	.067	.067	.067	.133	-59	-2	0	.14	1	/C-2,0-2(0-1-1)	0	-0.1
1884	Phi-U	4	14	2	2	0	0	0	....	1	....	....	....	.143	.200	.143	.343	19	-1	0	.96	-2	/C-4,0-1	0	-0.2
Total 2		8	29	3	3	0	0	0		1				.103	.133	.103	.237	-20	-3	0	.52	-1	/C-6,0-3	0	-0.3

• JONES, Binky
John Joseph Jones b: 7/11/1899, St. Louis, MO d: 5/13/1961, St. Louis, MO BR/TR, 5'9", 154 lbs. Deb: 4/15/1924

YEAR	TM-L	G	AB	R	H	2B	3B	HR	RBI	BB	SO	SB	CS	AVG	OBP	SLG	OPS	OPS+	BR/A	RC	RC/G	FR	G/POS	WS	TPW
1924	Bro-N	10	37	0	4	1	0	0	2	0	3	0	0	.108	.108	.135	.243	-36	-7	1	.45	0	S-10	0	-0.7

• JONES, Bob
Robert Oliver Jones b: 10/11/1949, Elkton, MD BL/TL, 6'2", 195 lbs. Deb: 10/1/1974 Career OF: 53-27-73

YEAR	TM-L	G	AB	R	H	2B	3B	HR	RBI	BB	SO	SB	CS	AVG	OBP	SLG	OPS	OPS+	BR/A	RC	RC/G	FR	G/POS	WS	TPW
1974	Tex-A	2	5	0	0	0	0	0	0	0	1	0	0	.000	.000	.000	.000	-103	-1	0	.00	0	/0-2(2-0-0)	0	-0.1
1975	Tex-A	9	11	2	1	0	0	0	0	3	3	0	0	.091	.286	.091	.377	11	-1	1	1.37	0	/0-5(3-1-1),D-1	0	-0.1
1976	Cal-A	78	166	22	35	6	0	6	17	14	30	3	0	.211	.276	.355	.632	90	-2	16	3.06	2	0-62(17-25-21)/D-2	4	-0.2
1977	Cal-A	14	17	3	3	0	0	1	3	4	5	0	0	.176	.333	.353	.686	91	-0	2	3.48	0	/D-6	0	-0.1
1981	Tex-A	10	34	4	9	1	0	3	7	1	7	0	1	.265	.286	.559	.845	146	1	5	5.14	3	0-10(1-0-9)	2	0.4
1983	Tex-A	41	72	5	16	4	0	1	11	5	17	0	2	.222	.291	.319	.611	69	-4	6	2.62	0	D-11,0-11(6-0-5)/1-1	1	-0.5
1984	Tex-A	64	143	14	37	4	0	4	22	10	19	1	1	.259	.312	.371	.682	85	-3	17	4.27	0	0-22(11-0-11),1-15/D-4	3	-0.5
1985	Tex-A	83	134	14	30	2	0	5	23	11	30	1	0	.224	.288	.351	.638	73	-5	14	3.59	-1	0-30(8-1-22),D-10/1-4	1	-0.7
1986	Tex-A	13	21	1	2	0	0	0	3	2	5	0	0	.095	.174	.095	.269	-24	-4	0	.62	-1	/0-9(5-0-4),1-2	0	-0.5
Total 9		314	603	65	133	17	0	20	86	50	117	5	4	.221	.286	.348	.634	78	-19	62	3.35	4	0-151/D-34,1-22	11	-2.2

• JONES, Bob
Robert Walter "Ducky" Jones b: 12/2/1889, Clayton, CA d: 8/30/1964, San Diego, CA BL/TR, 6', 170 lbs. Deb: 4/11/1917

YEAR	TM-L	G	AB	R	H	2B	3B	HR	RBI	BB	SO	SB	CS	AVG	OBP	SLG	OPS	OPS+	BR/A	RC	RC/G	FR	G/POS	WS	TPW
1917	Det-A	46	77	16	12	1	2	0	2	4	8	3	....	.156	.198	.221	.418	28	-7	4	1.44	-3	2-18/3-8	1	-1.1
1918	Det-A	74	287	43	79	14	4	0	21	17	16	7	....	.275	.320	.352	.672	107	1	34	3.94	-6	3-63/1-6,0-1	8	-0.3
1919	Det-A	127	439	37	114	18	6	1	57	34	39	11	....	.260	.314	.335	.649	84	-10	50	3.71	-14	*3-127	11	-2.1
1920	Det-A	81	265	35	66	6	3	1	18	22	13	3	4	.249	.309	.306	.615	65	-13	26	3.18	1	3-67/2-5,S-1	4	-1.0
1921	Det-A	141	554	82	168	23	9	1	72	37	24	8	9	.303	.348	.383	.731	87	-12	73	4.61	13	*3-141	12	0.9
1922	Det-A	124	455	65	117	10	6	3	44	36	18	6	5	.257	.314	.325	.640	69	-20	49	3.47	2	*3-119	9	-0.6
1923	Det-A	100	372	51	93	15	4	1	40	29	13	7	6	.250	.306	.320	.626	66	-19	38	3.19	5	3-97	6	-0.8
1924	Det-A	110	393	52	107	27	4	0	47	20	20	1	5	.272	.308	.361	.669	73	-13	43	3.65	-4	*3-106	7	-1.6
1925	Det-A	50	148	18	35	6	0	0	15	9	5	1	1	.236	.280	.277	.557	42	-13	12	2.61	3	3-46	2	-0.7
Total 9		853	2990	399	791	120	38	7	316	208	156	49	30	.265	.314	.337	.651	76	-112	328	3.61	1	3-774/2-23,1-6,0-1,S-1	60	-7.3

• JONES, Charley
Charles Wesley "Baby" Jones b: 4/30/1850, Alamance County, NC BR/TR, 5'11.5", 202 lbs. Deb: 5/4/1875 Career OF: 624-246-8

YEAR	TM-L	G	AB	R	H	2B	3B	HR	RBI	BB	SO	SB	CS	AVG	OBP	SLG	OPS	OPS+	BR/A	RC	RC/G	FR	G/POS	WS	TPW
1875	Wes-n	12	47	4	13	2	4	0	10	0	5	1	1	.277	.277	.489	.766	152	2	7	5.74	-2	0-12(12-0-0)	....	0.0
	Har-n	1	4	1	0	0	0	0	0	1	0	0	0	.000	.000	.000	.000	-95	-1	0	.00	0	/0-1	....	-0.1
	Yr.	13	51	5	13	2	4	0	10	0	6	1	1	.255	.255	.451	.706	133	1	7	5.15	-2	0-13(12-1-0)	....	-0.1
1876	Cin-N	64	283	40	79	17	4	4	38	7	17	....	....	.279	.304	.420	.724	162	20	36	5.14	-2	*0-64(10-53-1)	9	1.3
1877	Chi-N	17	69	16	21	3	3	1	10	4	8	....	....	.304	.342	.478	.821	175	6	12	6.64	0	1-10/0-8(5-3-0)	0	0.5
	Chi-N	2	8	1	3	1	0	0	2	1	0	....	....	.375	.444	.500	.944	176	1	2	10.02	1	/0-2(0-2-0)	1	0.1
	Cin-N	38	163	36	51	8	7	1	26	10	17	....	....	.313	.353	.466	.819	175	15	27	6.74	9	0-38(38-0-0)	8	1.9
	Yr.	57	240	53	75	12	10	2	38	15	25	....	....	.313	.353	.471	.824	175	22	41	6.81	10	*0-48(43-5-0),1-10	9	2.5
1878	Cin-N	61	261	50	81	11	7	3	39	4	17	....	....	.310	.321	.441	.761	163	18	38	5.78	12	*0-61(51-10-0)	12	1.8
1879	Bos-N	83	355	**85**	112	22	10	**9**	62	29	38			.315	.367	.510	.877	181	32	68	7.85	13	*0-83(83-0-0)	21	3.6
1880	Bos-N	66	270	44	84	15	3	5	31	11	27			.300	.326	.429	.755	158	17	40	5.63	-6	0-66(66-0-0)	12	0.7
1883	Cin-a	90	391	84	115	15	12	10	**80**	20				.294	.328	.471	.799	146	19	62	6.28	2	*0-90(16-75-0)	18	1.2
1884	Cin-a	112	472	117	148	19	17	7	71	37				.314	**.376**	.470	.846	166	35	85	7.26	-4	*0-112(63-51-0)	27	2.5
1885	Cin-a	112	487	100	118	19	17	5	35	21				.242	.362	.462	.824	156	30	83	6.83	8	*0-112(112-0-0)	24	3.0
1886	Cin-a	127	500	87	135	22	10	6	68	61		3		.270	.356	.390	.746	130	18	72	5.35	2	*0-127(127-0-0)	18	1.4
1887	Cin-a	41	172	28	67	7	4	2	40	19		7	....	.390	.400	.451	.851	134	7	31	8.01	1	0-41(41-1-0)	6	0.6
	NY-a	62	259	30	75	11	3	3	29	12		8	....	.290	.306	.360	.666	89	-4	30	4.46	1	0-62(6-50-7)/P-2,1-1	5	-0.3
	Yr.	103	431	58	142	18	7	5	69	31		15	....	.329	.343	.395	.738	107	4	62	5.75	2	*0-103(47-51-7)/P-2,1-1	11	0.3

YEAR TM-L	G	AB	R	H	2B	3B	HR	RBI	BB	SO	SB	CS	AVG	OBP	SLG	OPS	OPS+	BR/A	RC	RC/G	FR	G/POS	WS	TPW
1888 KC-a	6	25	2	4	0	1	0	5	1	....	1	....	.160	.192	.240	.432	36	-2	1	1.77	0	/0-6(6-0-0)	0	-0.2
Total 11	881	3725	728	1132	170	98	56	542	237	124	19	....	.304	.347	.443	.790	151	210	589	6.26	25	0-872/1-11,P-2	161	17.9

• JONES, Charlie Charles F. Jones b: 10/24/1861, New York, NY d: 9/15/1922, New York, NY Deb: 6/28/1884

YEAR TM-L	G	AB	R	H	2B	3B	HR	RBI	BB	SO	SB	CS	AVG	OBP	SLG	OPS	OPS+	BR/A	RC	RC/G	FR	G/POS	WS	TPW
1884 Bro-a	25	90	10	16	1	0	0	0	5	....	....	....	.178	.221	.189	.410	35	-6	4	1.43	-2	2-13,3-11/0-2(1-0-1)	0	-0.7

• JONES, Charlie Charles Claude "Casey" Jones b: 6/2/1876, Butler, PA d: 4/2/1947, Two Harbors, MN BR/TR, 6'1" Deb: 5/2/1901 Career OF: 12-443-12

YEAR TM-L	G	AB	R	H	2B	3B	HR	RBI	BB	SO	SB	CS	AVG	OBP	SLG	OPS	OPS+	BR/A	RC	RC/G	FR	G/POS	WS	TPW
1901 Bos-A	10	41	6	6	2	0	0	6	1	....	2	....	.146	.167	.195	.362		-6	2	1.32	-1	0-10(0-8-2)	0	-0.6
1904 Chi-A	5	17	2	4	0	1	0	1	1	....	0	....	.235	.278	.353	.631	103	0	2	3.44	1	/0-5(0-5-0)	1	0.1
1905 Was-A	142	544	68	113	18	4	2	41	31	....	24	....	.208	.254	.267	.521	68	-20	45	2.71	14	*0-142(0-142-0)	9	-1.5
1906 Was-A	131	497	56	120	11	11	3	42	24	....	34	....	.241	.283	.326	.609	95	-4	59	3.93	-1	*0-128(0-128-0)/2-1	12	-1.3
1907 Was-A	121	437	48	116	14	10	0	37	22	....	26	....	.265	.304	.343	.647	115	6	57	4.44	-11	*0-111(12-90-8)/2-5,1-4,S	11	-1.1
1908 StL-A	74	263	37	61	11	2	0	17	14	....	14	....	.232	.279	.289	.568	84	-5	25	3.08	3	0-72(0-70-2)	7	-0.6
Total 6	483	1799	217	420	56	28	5	144	93	....	100	....	.233	.276	.304	.580	88	-29	189	3.48	5	0-468/2-6,1-4,S-2	40	-4.9

• JONES, Chipper Larry Wayne Jones b: 4/24/1972, Deland, FL BB/TR, 6'3", 185 lbs. Deb: 9/11/1993 Career OF: 327-0-9

YEAR TM-L	G	AB	R	H	2B	3B	HR	RBI	BB	SO	SB	CS	AVG	OBP	SLG	OPS	OPS+	BR/A	RC	RC/G	FR	G/POS	WS	TPW
1993 Atl-N	8	3	2	2	1	0	0	0	1	1	0	0	.667	.750	1.000	1.750	360	1	2	66.02	-1	/S-3	0	0.0
1995*Atl-N	140	524	87	139	22	3	23	86	73	99	8	4	.265	.355	.450	.805	107	6	86	5.75	1	*3-123,0-20(15-0-5)	20	0.8
1996*Atl-N★	157	598	114	185	32	5	30	110	87	88	14	1	.309	.397	.530	.927	134	34	130	8.06	-28	*3-118,S-38/0-1	26	1.1
1997*Atl-N★	157	597	100	176	41	3	21	111	76	88	20	5	.295	.374	.479	.854	119	19	107	6.38	-14	*3-152/0-5(3-0-3)	23	0.7
1998*Atl-N★	160	601	123	188	29	5	34	107	96	93	16	6	.313	.408	.547	.956	148	45	136	8.25	-6	*3-158	29	4.2
1999*Atl-N	157	567	116	181	41	1	45	110	126	94	25	3	.319	.445	.633	1.078	168	**68**	165	10.72	-27	*3-156/S-1	32	4.1
2000*Atl-N★	156	579	118	180	38	1	36	111	95	64	14	7	.311	.410	.566	.976	143	40	136	8.51	-5	*3-152/S-6	27	3.5
2001*Atl-N★	159	572	113	189	33	5	38	102	98	82	9	10	.330	.430	.605	1.035	160	52	147	9.66	-20	*3-149/0-8(8-0-0),D-1	29	3.3
2002*Atl-N	158	548	90	179	35	1	26	100	107	89	8	2	.327	.438	.536	.975	154	49	131	8.96	0	*0-152(152-0-0)	31	4.3
2003*Atl-N	153	555	103	169	33	2	27	106	94	83	2	2	.305	.406	.517	.923	139	34	120	8.02	-9	*0-149(149-0-0)/D-1	26	1.9
Total 10	1405	5144	966	1588	305	26	280	943	853	781	116	40	.309	.408	.541	.949	142	349	1159	8.26	-107	*3-1008,0-335/S-48,D-2	243	23.9

• JONES, Chris Christopher Dale Jones b: 7/13/1957, Los Angeles, CA BL/TL, 6', 183 lbs. Deb: 6/8/1985

YEAR TM-L	G	AB	R	H	2B	3B	HR	RBI	BB	SO	SB	CS	AVG	OBP	SLG	OPS	OPS+	BR/A	RC	RC/G	FR	G/POS	WS	TPW
1985 Hou-N	31	25	0	5	0	0	0	1	3	7	0	0	.200	.286	.200	.486	39	-2	2	2.23	0	0-15(2-9-4)	0	-0.2
1986 SF-N	3	1	0	0	0	0	0	0	0	0	1	0	.000	.000	.000	.000	-105	-0	0	.00	0	....	0	0.0
Total 2	34	26	0	5	0	0	0	1	3	7	1	0	.192	.276	.192	.468	34	-2	2	2.12	0	/0-15	0	-0.2

• JONES, Chris Christopher Carlos Jones b: 12/16/1965, Utica, NY BR/TR, 6'2", 205 lbs. Deb: 4/21/1991 Career OF: 127-100-168

YEAR TM-L	G	AB	R	H	2B	3B	HR	RBI	BB	SO	SB	CS	AVG	OBP	SLG	OPS	OPS+	BR/A	RC	RC/G	FR	G/POS	WS	TPW
1991 Cin-N	52	89	14	26	1	2	2	6	2	31	2	1	.292	.308	.416	.723	98	-1	11	4.28	0	0-26(18-3-9)	1	-0.1
1992 Hou-N	54	63	7	12	2	1	1	4	7	21	3	0	.190	.271	.302	.573	65	-2	6	2.90	-3	0-43(17-5-25)	1	-0.6
1993 Col-N	86	209	29	57	11	4	6	31	10	48	9	4	.273	.306	.450	.756	85	-5	26	4.24	-2	0-70(16-52-4)	5	-0.8
1994 Col-N	21	40	6	12	2	1	0	2	2	14	0	1	.300	.333	.400	.733	77	-2	5	4.18	-1	0-14(4-13-0)	0	-0.3
1995 NY-N	79	182	33	51	6	2	8	31	13	45	2	1	.280	.332	.467	.799	111	2	28	5.51	0	0-52(25-0-28)/1-5	6	0.0
1996 NY-N	89	149	22	36	7	0	4	18	12	42	1	0	.242	.307	.369	.676	81	-4	17	3.95	-2	0-66(17-8-44)/1-5	3	-0.8
1997 SD-N	92	152	24	37	9	0	7	25	16	45	7	2	.243	.324	.441	.764	107	2	22	4.78	0	0-61(24-19-25)	5	0.1
1998 Ari-N	20	31	3	6	1	0	0	3	3	9	0	0	.194	.265	.226	.491	31	-3	2	1.60	0	/0-8(1-0-7)	0	-0.4
SF-N	43	90	14	17	2	1	2	10	8	28	2	1	.189	.255	.300	.555	48	-7	7	2.66	-1	0-29(5-0-24)/D-2	0	-0.9
Yr.	63	121	17	23	3	1	2	13	11	37	2	1	.190	.258	.281	.539	44	-10	9	2.38	-1	0-37(6-0-31)/D-2	0	-1.3
2000 Mil-N	12	16	3	3	2	0	0	1	1	4	0	0	.188	.235	.313	.548	37	-2	1	2.57	0	/0-2(0-0-2)	0	-0.1
Total 9	548	1021	155	257	43	11	30	131	74	287	26	10	.252	.305	.404	.709	86	-22	125	4.15	-9	0-371/1-10,D-2	21	-3.9

• JONES, Clarence Clarence Woodrow Jones b: 11/7/1941, Zanesville, OH BL/TL, 6'2", 185 lbs. Deb: 4/20/1967 C

YEAR TM-L	G	AB	R	H	2B	3B	HR	RBI	BB	SO	SB	CS	AVG	OBP	SLG	OPS	OPS+	BR/A	RC	RC/G	FR	G/POS	WS	TPW
1967 Chi-N	53	135	13	34	7	0	2	16	14	33	0	0	.252	.322	.348	.670	88	-2	16	3.89	-2	0-31(2-0-29),1-13	3	-0.7
1968 Chi-N	5	2	0	0	0	0	0	0	2	1	0	0	.000	.500	.000	.500	56	0	0	3.51	0	/1-1	0	0.0
Total 2	58	137	13	34	7	0	2	16	16	34	0	0	.248	.327	.343	.670	87	-2	16	3.89	-2	/0-31,1-14	3	-0.7

• JONES, Cleon Cleon Joseph Jones b: 8/4/1942, Plateau, AL BR/TL, 6', 200 lbs. Deb: 9/14/1963 Career OF: 802-273-103

YEAR TM-L	G	AB	R	H	2B	3B	HR	RBI	BB	SO	SB	CS	AVG	OBP	SLG	OPS	OPS+	BR/A	RC	RC/G	FR	G/POS	WS	TPW
1963 NY-N	6	15	1	2	0	0	0	1	0	4	0	0	.133	.133	.133	.267	-23	-2	0	.55	0	/0-5(1-5-0)	0	-0.3
1965 NY-N	30	74	2	11	1	0	1	9	2	23	1	0	.149	.171	.203	.374	5	-9	3	1.18	0	0-23(2-18-3)	1	-1.0
1966 NY-N	139	495	74	136	16	4	8	57	30	62	16	8	.275	.320	.372	.692	94	-4	57	3.92	1	*0-129(3-107-35)	15	-0.9
1967 NY-N	129	411	46	101	10	5	5	30	19	57	12	2	.246	.286	.331	.617	77	-11	39	3.18	-2	*0-115(20-86-21)	7	-1.9
1968 NY-N	147	509	63	151	29	4	14	55	31	98	23	12	.297	.343	.452	.795	136	21	77	5.39	1	*0-139(117-28-18)	20	1.8
1969*NY-N★	137	483	92	164	25	4	12	75	64	60	16	8	.340	.424	.482	.907	150	36	100	7.92	5	*0-122(121-1-0),1-15	30	3.4
1970 NY-N	134	506	71	140	25	8	10	63	57	87	12	3	.277	.356	.417	.773	106	6	71	4.79	1	*0-130(125-6-1)	14	-0.1
1971 NY-N	136	505	63	161	24	6	14	69	53	87	6	5	.319	.386	.473	.859	144	29	92	6.80	2	*0-132(132-1-0)	24	2.4
1972 NY-N	106	375	39	92	15	1	5	52	30	83	1	6	.245	.308	.331	.639	84	-10	36	3.18	2	0-84(71-5-14),1-20	7	-1.6
1973*NY-N	92	339	48	88	13	0	11	48	28	51	1	1	.260	.322	.395	.717	99	-1	41	4.08	-3	0-92(73-13-8)	9	-1.0
1974 NY-N	124	461	62	130	23	1	13	60	38	79	3	3	.282	.345	.421	.765	115	8	66	5.05	1	*0-120(117-3-3)	14	0.3
1975 NY-N	21	50	2	12	1	0	0	2	3	6	0	0	.240	.283	.260	.543	54	-3	4	2.77	0	0-12(12-0-0)	0	-0.4
1976 Chi-A	12	40	2	8	1	0	0	3	5	5	0	0	.200	.304	.225	.529	56	-2	3	2.43	0	/0-8(8-0-0),D-3	0	-0.3
Total 13	1213	4263	565	1196	183	33	93	524	360	702	91	48	.281	.342	.404	.747	111	57	589	4.83	7	*0-1111/1-35,D-3	141	0.6

• JONES, Cobe Coburn Dyas Jones b: 8/21/1907, Denver, CO d: 6/3/1969, Denver, CO BB/TR, 5'7", 155 lbs. Deb: 9/27/1928

YEAR TM-L	G	AB	R	H	2B	3B	HR	RBI	BB	SO	SB	CS	AVG	OBP	SLG	OPS	OPS+	BR/A	RC	RC/G	FR	G/POS	WS	TPW
1928 Pit-N	1	2	0	1	0	0	0	0	0	0	0	....	.500	.500	.500	1.000	156	0	0	12.09	0	/S-1	0	0.0
1929 Pit-N	25	63	6	16	5	1	0	4	1	5	1	....	.254	.266	.365	.631	53	-5	6	3.18	-5	S-15	1	-0.7
Total 2	26	65	6	17	5	1	0	4	1	5	1	....	.262	.273	.369	.642	56	-5	6	3.36	-5	/S-16	1	-0.7

• JONES, Dalton James Dalton Jones b: 12/10/1943, McComb, MS BL/TR, 6'1", 180 lbs. Deb: 4/17/1964 Career OF: 12-0-8

YEAR TM-L	G	AB	R	H	2B	3B	HR	RBI	BB	SO	SB	CS	AVG	OBP	SLG	OPS	OPS+	BR/A	RC	RC/G	FR	G/POS	WS	TPW
1964 Bos-A	118	374	37	86	16	4	6	39	22	38	6	3	.230	.275	.342	.617	67	-17	36	3.27	-11	2-85/3-1,S-1	5	-2.2
1965 Bos-A	112	367	41	99	13	5	5	37	28	45	8	1	.270	.325	.373	.698	92	-2	46	4.41	-6	3-81/2-8	8	-0.9
1966 Bos-A	115	252	26	59	11	5	4	23	22	27	1	2	.234	.303	.365	.668	83	-6	27	3.68	-6	2-70/3-3	5	-0.8
1967*Bos-A	89	159	18	46	6	2	3	25	11	23	0	1	.289	.335	.409	.744	110	2	21	4.89	-2	3-30,2-19/1-1	5	0.0
1968 Bos-A	111	354	38	83	13	0	5	29	17	53	1	1	.234	.272	.314	.585	72	-13	28	2.64	-2	1-56,2-26/3-8	4	-1.9
1969 Bos-A	111	336	50	74	18	3	3	33	39	36	1	1	.220	.305	.318	.623	71	-13	34	3.31	2	1-81/3-9,2-1	5	-1.8
1970 Det-A	89	191	29	42	7	0	6	21	33	33	1	1	.220	.338	.351	.689	89	-2	24	4.19	1	2-35,3-18,1-10	5	0.0
1971 Det-A	83	138	15	35	5	0	5	11	9	21	1	3	.254	.304	.399	.703	94	-3	15	3.78	-1	0-16(10-0-8),3-13/1-3,2-1	3	-0.4
1972 Det-A	7	7	0	0	0	0	0	0	0	2	0	0	.000	.000	.000	.000	-97	-2	0	.00	0	....	0	-0.2
Tex-A	72	151	14	24	2	0	4	19	10	31	1	0	.159	.211	.252	.463	39	-11	8	1.69	-1	3-23,2-17/1-7,0-2(2-0-0)	1	-1.4
Yr.	79	158	14	24	2	0	4	19	10	33	1	0	.152	.202	.241	.443	33	-13	8	1.60	-1	3-23,2-17/1-7,0-2(2-0-0)	1	-1.5
Total 9	907	2329	268	548	91	19	41	237	191	309	20	13	.235	.296	.343	.640	78	-67	240	3.48	-26	2-262,3-186,1-158/0-18,S-1	41	-9.6

• JONES, Darryl Darryl Lee Jones b: 6/5/1951, Meadville, PA BR/TR, 5'10", 175 lbs. Deb: 6/6/1979

YEAR TM-L	G	AB	R	H	2B	3B	HR	RBI	BB	SO	SB	CS	AVG	OBP	SLG	OPS	OPS+	BR/A	RC	RC/G	FR	G/POS	WS	TPW
1979 NY-A	18	47	6	12	5	1	0	6	2	7	0	0	.255	.286	.404	.690	86	-1	5	3.72	0	D-15/0-2(1-0-1)	1	-0.2

• JONES, Davy David Jefferson "Kangaroo" Jones
b: 6/30/1880, Cambria, WI d: 3/30/1972, Mankato, MN BL/TR, 5'10", 165 lbs. Deb: 9/15/1901 Career OF: 555-281-171

YEAR TM-L	G	AB	R	H	2B	3B	HR	RBI	BB	SO	SB	CS	AVG	OBP	SLG	OPS	OPS+	BR/A	RC	RC/G	FR	G/POS	WS	TPW
1901 Mil-A	14	52	12	9	0	0	3	5	11	....	4	....	.173	.328	.346	.674	91	-0	7	4.56	1	0-14(14-0-0)	1	0.0
1902 StL-A	15	49	4	11	1	1	0	3	6	....	5	....	.224	.309	.286	.595	67	-2	6	4.17	5	0-15(0-0-15)	2	0.2
Chi-N	64	243	41	74	12	3	0	14	38	....	12	....	.305	.399	.379	.777	144	15	44	6.44	-1	0-64(0-47-17)	12	1.1
1903 Chi-N	130	497	64	140	18	3	1	62	53	....	15	....	.282	.352	.336	.688	99	1	67	4.85	0	*0-130(0-97-33)	17	-0.5
1904 Chi-N	98	336	44	82	11	5	3	39	41	....	14	....	.244	.330	.333	.663	105	3	43	4.35	-8	0-97(0-1-97)	14	-1.0
1906 Det-A	84	323	41	84	12	2	0	24	41	....	21	....	.260	.347	.310	.657	103	3	43	4.76	1	0-83(0-82-1)	13	0.0
1907*Det-A	126	491	101	134	10	6	0	27	60	....	30	....	.273	.357	.318	.674	111	9	70	5.01	7	*0-125(121-4-0)	24	1.0
1908*Det-A	56	121	17	25	2	1	0	10	13	....	11	....	.207	.284	.240	.523	67	-4	11	2.95	1	0-32(4-26-2)	2	-0.5
1909*Det-A	69	204	44	57	2	2	0	10	28	....	12	....	.279	.369	.309	.678	110	4	28	4.74	-1	0-57(42-13-2)	8	0.0

YEAR TM-L	G	AB	R	H	2B	3B	HR	RBI	BB	SO	SB	CS	AVG	OBP	SLG	OPS	OPS+	BR/A	RC	RC/G	FR	G/POS	WS	TPW
1910 Det-A	113	377	77	100	6	6	0	24	51	....	25	....	.265	.362	.313	.675	104	5	52	4.70	0	*O-101(95-6-0)	14	-0.1
1911 Det-A	98	341	78	93	10	0	0	19	41	....	25	....	.273	.354	.302	.656	80	-8	45	4.60	-1	O-92(92-0-0)	8	-1.2
1912 Det-A	99	316	54	93	5	2	0	24	38	....	16	....	.294	.370	.323	.693	102	3	44	4.90	5	O-81(72-5-4)	9	0.4
1913 Chi-A	12	21	2	6	0	0	0	0	9	0	1	....	.286	.500	.286	.786	132	2	4	5.77	0	/O-9(9-0-0)	2	0.1
1914 Pit-F	97	352	58	96	9	8	2	24	42	16	15	....	.273	.355	.361	.716	110	6	50	4.67	4	O-93(93-0-0)	11	0.6
1915 Pit-F	14	49	6	16	0	1	0	4	6	0	1	....	.327	.400	.367	.767	121	2	7	5.68	-1	O-13(13-0-0)	2	0.0
Total 14	**1089**	**3772**	**643**	**1020**	**98**	**40**	**9**	**289**	**478**	**16**	**207**	**....**	**.270**	**.356**	**.325**	**.681**	**104**	**39**	**522**	**4.80**	**12**	***O-1006**	**139**	**0.3**

• JONES, Dax Dax Xenos Jones b: 8/4/1970, Pittsburgh, PA BR/TR, 6', 170 lbs. Deb: 7/11/1996

YEAR TM-L	G	AB	R	H	2B	3B	HR	RBI	BB	SO	SB	CS	AVG	OBP	SLG	OPS	OPS+	BR/A	RC	RC/G	FR	G/POS	WS	TPW
1996 SF-N	34	58	7	10	0	2	1	7	8	12	2	2	.172	.273	.293	.566	51	-5	5	2.61	0	O-33(0-29-4)	1	-0.4

• JONES, Deacon Grover William Jones b: 4/18/1934, White Plains, NY BL/TR, 5'10", 185 lbs. Deb: 9/8/1962 C

YEAR TM-L	G	AB	R	H	2B	3B	HR	RBI	BB	SO	SB	CS	AVG	OBP	SLG	OPS	OPS+	BR/A	RC	RC/G	FR	G/POS	WS	TPW
1962 Chi-A	18	28	3	9	2	0	0	8	4	6	0	0	.321	.406	.393	.799	117	1	5	5.77	0	/1-6	1	0.0
1963 Chi-A	17	16	4	3	0	1	1	2	2	2	0	0	.188	.316	.500	.816	127	1	2	4.32	0	/1-1	0	0.1
1966 Chi-A	5	5	0	2	0	0	0	0	0	0	0	0	.400	.400	.400	.800	140	0	1	7.20	0	....	0	0.0
Total 3	**40**	**49**	**7**	**14**	**2**	**1**	**1**	**10**	**6**	**8**	**0**	**0**	**.286**	**.375**	**.429**	**.804**	**122**	**2**	**8**	**5.37**	**0**	**/1-7**	**1**	**0.1**

• JONES, Fielder Fielder Allison Jones b: 8/13/1871, Shinglehouse, PA d: 3/13/1934, Portland, OR BL/TR, 5'11", 180 lbs. Deb: 4/18/1896 M Career OF: 4-1255-516

YEAR TM-L	G	AB	R	H	2B	3B	HR	RBI	BB	SO	SB	CS	AVG	OBP	SLG	OPS	OPS+	BR/A	RC	RC/G	FR	G/POS	WS	TPW
1896 Bro-N	104	395	82	140	10	8	3	46	48	15	18	....	.354	.427	.443	.870	137	24	85	8.65	-3	*O-103(0-0-103)	16	1.3
1897 Bro-N	135	548	134	172	15	10	1	49	61	....	48	....	.314	.392	.383	.775	111	12	105	7.16	2	*O-135(2-0-133)	18	0.6
1898 Bro-N	146	596	89	181	15	9	1	69	46	....	36	....	.304	.362	.364	.726	108	7	96	5.88	-3	*O-144(0-4-144)/S-2	19	-0.3
1899 Bro-N	102	365	75	104	8	2	2	38	54	....	18	....	.285	.390	.334	.724	97	2	56	5.68	-3	O-96(2-89-6)	14	-0.6
1900*Bro-N	136	552	106	171	26	4	4	54	57	....	33	....	.310	.383	.393	.777	108	7	100	6.74	-5	*O-136(0-136-0)	20	-0.6
1901 Chi-A	133	521	120	162	16	3	2	65	84	....	38	....	.311	.412	.365	.777	120	21	99	6.96	2	*O-133(0-5-128)	23	1.5
1902 Chi-A	135	532	98	171	16	5	0	54	57	....	33	....	.321	.390	.370	.761	117	15	95	6.58	11	*O-135(0-135-0)	25	1.9
1903 Chi-A	136	530	71	152	18	5	0	45	47	....	21	....	.287	.348	.340	.688	112	10	75	4.94	-3	*O-136(0-136-0)	20	0.0
1904 Chi-A	149	547	72	133	14	5	3	42	53	....	25	....	.243	.316	.303	.619	100	2	66	3.91	8	*O-149(0-149-0)	22	0.3
1905 Chi-A	153	568	91	139	17	12	2	38	73	....	20	....	.245	.335	.327	.662	115	13	73	4.34	16	*O-153(0-153-0)	29	2.4
1906*Chi-A	144	496	77	114	22	4	2	34	83	....	26	....	.230	.346	.302	.648	106	9	67	4.29	14	*O-144(0-144-0)	27	1.7
1907 Chi-A	154	559	72	146	18	1	0	47	67	....	17	....	.261	.345	.297	.642	109	9	70	4.14	15	*O-154(0-154-0)	25	1.8
1908 Chi-A	149	529	92	134	11	7	1	50	86	....	26	....	.253	.366	.306	.672	121	18	71	4.39	9	*O-149(0-149-0)	32	2.3
1914 StL-F	5	3	0	1	0	0	0	0	1	0	0	....	.333	.500	.333	.833	132	0	0	6.18	0	....	0	0.0
1915 StL-F	7	6	1	0	0	0	0	0	0	0	0	....	.000	.000	.000	.000	-95	-1	0	.00	0	/O-3(0-1-2)	0	-0.2
Total 15	**1788**	**6747**	**1180**	**1920**	**206**	**75**	**21**	**631**	**817**	**15**	**359**	**....**	**.285**	**.368**	**.347**	**.715**	**112**	**148**	**1058**	**5.51**	**59**	***O-1770/S-2**	**290**	**12.1**

• JONES, Frank Frank M. Jones b: 8/25/1858, Princeton, IL d: 2/4/1936, Marietta, OH BL Deb: 7/2/1884

YEAR TM-L	G	AB	R	H	2B	3B	HR	RBI	BB	SO	SB	CS	AVG	OBP	SLG	OPS	OPS+	BR/A	RC	RC/G	FR	G/POS	WS	TPW
1884 Det-N	2	8	0	1	0	0	0	0	0	1	....	....	.125	.125	.125	.250	-23	-1	0	.50	-1	/O-1,S-1	0	-0.2

• JONES, Hal Harold Marion Jones b: 4/9/1936, Louisiana, MO BR/TR, 6'2", 194 lbs. Deb: 4/25/1961

YEAR TM-L	G	AB	R	H	2B	3B	HR	RBI	BB	SO	SB	CS	AVG	OBP	SLG	OPS	OPS+	BR/A	RC	RC/G	FR	G/POS	WS	TPW
1961 Cle-A	12	35	2	6	0	0	2	4	2	12	0	0	.171	.216	.343	.559	48	-3	2	2.13	-1	1-10	0	-0.5
1962 Cle-A	5	16	2	5	1	0	0	1	0	4	0	0	.313	.353	.375	.728	99	-0	2	5.42	0	/1-4	1	0.0
Total 2	**17**	**51**	**4**	**11**	**1**	**0**	**2**	**5**	**2**	**16**	**0**	**0**	**.216**	**.259**	**.353**	**.612**	**64**	**-3**	**5**	**3.01**	**-1**	**/1-14**	**1**	**-0.5**

• JONES, Henry Henry Monroe "Baldy" Jones b: 5/10/1857, NY d: 5/31/1955, Manistee, MI BB, 5'6", 149 lbs. Deb: 8/20/1884 U

YEAR TM-L	G	AB	R	H	2B	3B	HR	RBI	BB	SO	SB	CS	AVG	OBP	SLG	OPS	OPS+	BR/A	RC	RC/G	FR	G/POS	WS	TPW
1884 Det-N	34	127	24	28	3	1	0	3	16	18	....	....	.220	.308	.260	.568	85	-1	10	2.89	-1	2-16,O-11(0-0-11)/S-7	2	-0.1

• JONES, Howie Howard "Cotton" Jones b: 3/1/1897, Irwin, PA d: 7/15/1972, Jeannette, PA BL/TL, 5'11", 165 lbs. Deb: 9/5/1921

YEAR TM-L	G	AB	R	H	2B	3B	HR	RBI	BB	SO	SB	CS	AVG	OBP	SLG	OPS	OPS+	BR/A	RC	RC/G	FR	G/POS	WS	TPW
1921 StL-N	3	2	0	0	0	0	0	0	0	1	0	0	.000	.000	.000	.000	-102	-1	0	.00	0	/O-1	0	-0.1

• JONES, Jack (RL) Ryerson L. "Ri,Angel Sleeves" Jones b: Cincinnati, OH BR/TR Deb: 8/13/1883

YEAR TM-L	G	AB	R	H	2B	3B	HR	RBI	BB	SO	SB	CS	AVG	OBP	SLG	OPS	OPS+	BR/A	RC	RC/G	FR	G/POS	WS	TPW
1883 Lou-a	2	7	1	0	0	0	0	0	0	....	....	....	.000	.000	.000	.000	-108	-2	0	.00	0	/O-2(0-2-0),S-1	0	-0.2
1884 Cin-U	69	272	36	71	5	1	2	....	12	....	....	....	.261	.292	.309	.601	96	-2	25	3.51	9	S-41,2-19,3-10	9	0.8
Total 2	**71**	**279**	**37**	**71**	**5**	**1**	**2**	**0**	**12**	**....**	**....**	**....**	**.254**	**.285**	**.301**	**.586**	**91**	**-4**	**25**	**3.39**	**8**	**/S-42,2-19,3-10,O-2**	**9**	**0.6**

• JONES, Jacque Jacque Dewayne Jones b: 4/25/1975, San Diego, CA BL/TL, 5'10", 176 lbs. Deb: 6/9/1999 Career OF: 461-147-33

YEAR TM-L	G	AB	R	H	2B	3B	HR	RBI	BB	SO	SB	CS	AVG	OBP	SLG	OPS	OPS+	BR/A	RC	RC/G	FR	G/POS	WS	TPW
1999 Min-A	95	322	54	93	24	2	9	44	17	63	3	4	.289	.332	.460	.792	96	-4	47	5.15	3	O-93(1-82-19)	9	-0.1
2000 Min-A	154	523	66	149	26	5	19	76	26	111	7	5	.285	.319	.463	.781	91	-10	70	4.77	2	*O-147(90-63-1)	11	-1.1
2001 Min-A	149	475	57	131	25	0	14	49	39	92	12	9	.276	.335	.417	.751	94	-6	64	4.73	0	*O-140(137-2-2)/D-4	10	-1.1
2002*Min-A	149	577	96	173	37	2	27	85	37	129	6	7	.300	.344	.511	.855	122	15	98	6.20	7	*O-143(143-0-0)/D-2	25	1.5
2003*Min-A	136	517	76	157	33	1	16	69	21	105	13	1	.304	.336	.464	.800	107	6	80	5.72	-5	*O-101(90-0-11),D-29	14	-0.5
Total 5	**683**	**2414**	**349**	**703**	**145**	**10**	**85**	**323**	**140**	**500**	**41**	**26**	**.291**	**.333**	**.465**	**.799**	**103**	**0**	**359**	**5.35**	**6**	**O-624/D-35**	**69**	**-1.3**

• JONES, Jake James Murrell Jones b: 11/23/1920, Epps, LA d: 12/13/2000, Delhi, LA BR/TR, 6'3", 197 lbs. Deb: 9/20/1941

YEAR TM-L	G	AB	R	H	2B	3B	HR	RBI	BB	SO	SB	CS	AVG	OBP	SLG	OPS	OPS+	BR/A	RC	RC/G	FR	G/POS	WS	TPW
1941 Chi-A	3	11	0	0	0	0	0	0	0	4	0	0	.000	.000	.000	.000	-101	-3	0	.00	-1	/1-3	0	-0.4
1942 Chi-A	7	20	2	3	1	0	0	0	2	2	1	0	.150	.227	.200	.427	21	-2	1	1.86	-1	/1-5	0	-0.3
1946 Chi-A	24	79	10	21	5	1	3	13	2	13	0	0	.266	.284	.468	.752	112	1	10	4.14	-3	1-20	2	-0.4
1947 Chi-A	45	171	15	41	7	1	3	20	13	25	1	0	.240	.297	.345	.642	81	-4	18	3.59	-2	1-43	3	-0.8
Bos-A	109	404	50	95	14	3	16	76	41	60	5	4	.235	.310	.403	.714	91	-7	52	4.33	-3	*1-109	9	-1.4
Yr.	154	575	65	136	21	4	19	96	54	85	6	4	.237	.306	.386	.693	88	-11	70	4.12	-5	*1-152	12	-2.2
1948 Bos-A	36	105	3	21	4	0	1	8	11	26	1	0	.200	.276	.267	.543	42	-9	8	2.38	1	1-31	0	-0.9
Total 5	**224**	**790**	**80**	**181**	**31**	**5**	**23**	**117**	**69**	**130**	**8**	**4**	**.229**	**.294**	**.368**	**.663**	**80**	**-24**	**88**	**3.75**	**-9**	**1-211**	**14**	**-4.1**

• JONES, Jason Jason D. Jones b: 10/17/1976, Marietta, GA BB/TR, 6'3", 210 lbs. Deb: 7/23/2003

YEAR TM-L	G	AB	R	H	2B	3B	HR	RBI	BB	SO	SB	CS	AVG	OBP	SLG	OPS	OPS+	BR/A	RC	RC/G	FR	G/POS	WS	TPW
2003 Tex-A	40	107	11	23	6	0	3	11	10	21	0	1	.215	.300	.355	.655	66	-6	12	3.65	1	O-27(14-0-13)/D-6,1-3	1	-0.6

• JONES, Jeff Jeffrey Raymond Jones b: 10/22/1957, Philadelphia, PA BR/TR, 6'2", 200 lbs. Deb: 4/4/1983 C

YEAR TM-L	G	AB	R	H	2B	3B	HR	RBI	BB	SO	SB	CS	AVG	OBP	SLG	OPS	OPS+	BR/A	RC	RC/G	FR	G/POS	WS	TPW
1983 Cin-N	16	44	6	10	3	0	0	5	11	13	2	0	.227	.393	.295	.688	90	1	7	5.18	-0	O-13(8-0-5)/1-1	2	0.0

• JONES, Jim James Tilford "Sheriff" Jones b: 12/25/1876, London, KY d: 5/6/1953, London, KY BR/TR, 5'10", 162 lbs. Deb: 6/29/1897 Career OF: 49-3-35

YEAR TM-L	G	AB	R	H	2B	3B	HR	RBI	BB	SO	SB	CS	AVG	OBP	SLG	OPS	OPS+	BR/A	RC	RC/G	FR	G/POS	WS	TPW
1897 Lou-N	2	4	2	1	1	0	0	0	1	....	0	....	.250	.400	.500	.900	142	1	1	7.24	0	/P-1	0	-0.9
1901 NY-N	21	91	10	19	4	3	0	5	4	....	2	....	.209	.250	.319	.569	67	-4	8	2.92	1	O-20(0-0-20)/P-1	1	-0.8
1902 NY-N	67	249	16	59	11	1	0	19	13	....	7	....	.237	.275	.289	.564	75	-8	23	3.10	-1	O-67(49-3-15)	3	-1.4
Total 3	**90**	**344**	**28**	**79**	**16**	**4**	**0**	**24**	**18**		**9**	**....**	**.230**	**.270**	**.299**	**.569**	**73**	**-11**	**31**	**3.10**	**-1**	**/O-87,P-2**	**4**	**-3.0**

• JONES, John John William "Skins" Jones b: 5/13/1901, Coatesville, PA d: 11/3/1956, Baltimore, MD BL/TL, 5'11", 185 lbs. Deb: 9/26/1923 Career OF: 0-1-1

YEAR TM-L	G	AB	R	H	2B	3B	HR	RBI	BB	SO	SB	CS	AVG	OBP	SLG	OPS	OPS+	BR/A	RC	RC/G	FR	G/POS	WS	TPW
1923 Phi-A	1	4	0	1	0	0	0	1	0	1	0	0	.250	.250	.250	.500	31	-0	0	2.12	0	/O-1	0	0.0
1932 Phi-A	4	6	0	1	0	0	0	0	0	3	0	0	.167	.167	.167	.333	-13	-1	0	.85	0	/O-1	0	-0.1
Total 2	**5**	**10**	**0**	**2**	**0**	**0**	**0**	**1**	**0**	**4**	**0**	**0**	**.200**	**.200**	**.200**	**.400**	**5**	**-1**	**0**	**1.33**	**0**	**/O-2**	**0**	**-0.1**

• JONES, Lynn Lynn Morris Jones b: 1/1/1953, Meadville, PA BR/TR, 5'9", 175 lbs. Deb: 4/13/1979 C Career OF: 154-85-237

YEAR TM-L	G	AB	R	H	2B	3B	HR	RBI	BB	SO	SB	CS	AVG	OBP	SLG	OPS	OPS+	BR/A	RC	RC/G	FR	G/POS	WS	TPW
1979 Det-A	95	213	33	63	8	0	4	26	17	22	9	6	.296	.351	.390	.740	96	-2	28	4.65	-2	O-84(20-42-25)/D-6	6	-0.6
1980 Det-A	30	55	9	14	2	2	0	6	10	5	1	0	.255	.369	.364	.733	99	1	8	4.51	-1	O-17(4-4-9)/D-6	1	-0.1
1981 Det-A	71	174	19	45	5	0	2	19	18	10	1	2	.259	.332	.322	.653	86	-3	18	3.44	1	O-60(9-0-52)/D-4	4	-0.4
1982 Det-A	58	139	15	31	3	1	0	14	7	14	0	2	.223	.260	.259	.519	43	-12	9	2.11	0	O-56(5-2-49)/D-1	1	-1.3
1983 Det-A	49	64	9	17	1	2	0	6	3	6	1	0	.266	.299	.344	.642	78	-2	7	3.57	0	O-31(9-1-22)/D-6	1	-0.3
1984*KC-A	47	103	11	31	6	0	1	10	4	9	1	3	.301	.333	.388	.722	98	-1	11	3.80	-1	O-45(13-7-29)	2	-0.4
1985*KC-A	110	152	12	32	7	0	0	9	8	15	0	1	.211	.264	.257	.520	43	-12	10	1.95	-1	*O-100(57-21-32)/D-2	1	-1.6
1986 KC-A	67	47	1	6	2	0	0	1	6	5	0	0	.128	.226	.170	.397	10	-6	2	1.15	-4	O-62(37-8-19)/D-3,2-1	0	-1.1
Total 8	**527**	**947**	**109**	**239**	**34**	**5**	**7**	**91**	**73**	**86**	**13**	**14**	**.252**	**.310**	**.321**	**.631**	**73**	**-37**	**92**	**3.22**	**-9**	**O-455/D-28,2-1**	**16**	**-5.8**

• JONES, Mack Mack "Mack The Knife" Jones b: 11/6/1938, Atlanta, GA BL/TR, 6'1", 180 lbs. Deb: 7/13/1961 Career OF: 331-476-91

YEAR TM-L	G	AB	R	H	2B	3B	HR	RBI	BB	SO	SB	CS	AVG	OBP	SLG	OPS	OPS+	BR/A	RC	RC/G	FR	G/POS	WS	TPW
1961 Mil-N	28	104	13	24	3	2	0	12	12	28	4	4	.231	.322	.298	.620	70	-5	10	3.33	-4	O-26(0-26-0)	2	-0.9

YEAR TM-L	G	AB	R	H	2B	3B	HR	RBI	BB	SO	SB	CS	AVG	OBP	SLG	OPS	OPS+	BR/A	RC	RC/G	FR	G/POS	WS	TPW
1962 Mil-N	91	333	51	85	17	4	10	36	44	100	5	1	.255	.354	.420	.775	110	6	52	5.42	-7	0-91(0-9-85)	10	-0.6
1963 Mil-N	93	228	36	50	11	4	3	22	26	59	8	4	.219	.318	.342	.660	91	-2	26	3.85	-1	0-80(12-69-0)	6	-0.5
1965 Mil-N	143	504	78	132	18	7	31	75	29	122	8	2	.262	.314	.510	.824	127	17	81	5.74	-4	*0-133(31-119-0)	19	0.9
1966 Atl-N	118	417	60	110	14	1	23	66	39	85	16	10	.264	.338	.468	.806	119	10	65	5.30	-9	*0-112(1-112-3)/1-1	14	-0.2
1967 Atl-N	140	454	72	115	23	4	17	50	64	108	10	6	.253	.357	.434	.791	127	18	73	5.52	-5	*0-126(26-100-0)	18	0.8
1968 Cin-N	103	234	40	59	9	1	10	34	28	46	2	3	.252	.345	.427	.772	123	7	34	4.79	-4	0-60(24-34-3)	8	0.1
1969 Mon-N	135	455	73	123	23	5	22	79	67	110	6	7	.270	.382	.488	.870	142	26	85	6.48	1	*0-129(125-5-0)	16	2.1
1970 Mon-N	108	271	51	65	11	3	14	32	59	74	5	3	.240	.399	.458	.857	129	14	56	7.10	-1	0-87(85-2-0)	14	1.0
1971 Mon-N	43	91	11	15	3	0	3	9	15	24	1	0	.165	.296	.297	.593	68	-3	9	3.19	0	0-27(27-0-0)	2	-0.5
Total 10	**1002**	**3091**	**485**	**778**	**132**	**31**	**133**	**415**	**383**	**756**	**65**	**40**	**.252**	**.349**	**.444**	**.792**	**120**	**88**	**492**	**5.46**	**-33**	**0-871/1-1**	**109**	**2.2**
• JONES, Nippy	Vernal Leroy Jones b: 6/29/1925, Los Angeles, CA d: 10/3/1995, Sacramento, CA BR/TR, 6'1", 185 lbs. Deb: 6/8/1946 Career OF: 0-0-3																							
1946*StL-N	16	12	3	4	0	0	0	1	2	2	0	....	.333	.429	.333	.762	113	0	1	3.49	-1	/2-3	0	0.0
1947 StL-N	23	73	6	18	4	0	1	5	2	10	0	....	.247	.267	.342	.609	58	-5	6	2.84	-1	2-13/0-2(0-0-2)	1	-0.5
1948 StL-N	132	481	58	122	21	9	10	81	36	45	2	....	.254	.307	.397	.704	84	-12	52	3.61	-7	*1-128	7	-2.3
1949 StL-N	110	380	51	114	20	2	8	62	16	20	1	....	.300	.330	.426	.756	97	-3	50	4.83	-9	1-98	8	-1.5
1950 StL-N	13	26	0	6	1	0	0	6	3	1	0	....	.231	.310	.269	.580	52	-2	2	1.89	0	/1-8	0	-0.2
1951 StL-N	80	300	20	79	12	0	3	41	9	13	1	2	.263	.287	.333	.620	66	-16	25	2.87	-1	1-71	2	-1.9
1952 Phi-N	8	30	3	5	0	0	1	5	0	4	0	0	.167	.167	.267	.433	19	-3	1	.82	0	/1-8	16	-0.4
1957*Mil-N	30	79	5	21	2	1	2	8	3	7	0	0	.266	.293	.392	.685	88	-2	9	4.24	-0	1-20/0-1	2	-0.3
Total 8	**412**	**1381**	**146**	**369**	**60**	**12**	**25**	**209**	**71**	**102**	**4**	**2**	**.267**	**.304**	**.382**	**.687**	**81**	**-42**	**147**	**3.65**	**-18**	**1-333/2-16,0-3**	**36**	**-7.1**
• JONES, Red	Maurice Morris Jones b: 11/2/1911, Timpson, TX d: 6/30/1974, Lincoln, CA BL/TR, 6'3", 190 lbs. Deb: 4/16/1940																							
1940 StL-N	12	11	0	1	0	0	0	1	1	2	0	....	.091	.167	.091	.258	-26	-2	0	.57	-0	/0-1	0	-0.2
• JONES, Ricky	Ricky Miron Jones b: 6/4/1958, Tupelo, MS BR/TR, 6'3", 186 lbs. Deb: 9/3/1986																							
1986 Bal-A	16	33	2	6	2	0	0	4	6	8	0	0	.182	.308	.242	.550	53	-2	3	2.94	2	2-11/3-6	1	0.0
• JONES, Ron	Ronald Glen Jones b: 6/11/1964, Seguin, TX BL/TR, 5'10", 195 lbs. Deb: 8/26/1988 Career OF: 11-0-50																							
1988 Phi-N	33	124	15	36	6	1	8	26	2	14	0	0	.290	.302	.548	.850	136	5	20	5.68	0	0-32(0-0-32)	5	0.4
1989 Phi-N	12	31	7	9	0	0	2	4	9	1	1	0	.290	.450	.484	.934	167	4	7	7.92	1	0-12(3-0-10)	1	0.4
1990 Phi-N	24	58	5	16	2	0	3	7	9	9	0	1	.276	.373	.466	.839	130	2	10	6.18	0	0-16(8-0-8)	2	0.1
1991 Phi-N	28	26	0	4	2	0	0	3	2	9	0	0	.154	.214	.231	.445	25	-2	1	1.37	0	....	0	-0.2
Total 4	**97**	**239**	**27**	**65**	**10**	**1**	**13**	**40**	**22**	**33**	**1**	**1**	**.272**	**.333**	**.485**	**.819**	**128**	**8**	**38**	**5.55**	**1**	**/0-60**	**8**	**0.7**
• JONES, Ross	Ross A. Jones b: 1/14/1960, Miami, FL BR/TR, 6'2", 185 lbs. Deb: 4/2/1984																							
1984 NY-N	17	10	2	1	1	0	0	1	3	4	0	0	.100	.308	.200	.508	46	-1	1	2.57	-1	/S-6,2-1,3-1	0	-0.2
1986 Sea-A	11	21	0	2	0	0	0	0	0	4	0	1	.095	.095	.095	.190	-48	-5	0	.13	-1	/S-4,2-3,3-2,D-1	0	-0.5
1987 KC-A	39	114	10	29	4	2	0	10	5	15	1	0	.254	.292	.325	.616	62	-6	10	2.86	0	S-36/2-3	2	-0.2
Total 3	**67**	**145**	**12**	**32**	**5**	**2**	**0**	**11**	**8**	**23**	**1**	**1**	**.221**	**.266**	**.283**	**.549**	**46**	**-12**	**11**	**2.39**	**-2**	**/S-46,2-7,3-3,D-1**	**2**	**-0.9**
• JONES, Ruppert	Ruppert Sanderson Jones b: 3/12/1955, Dallas, TX BL/TL, 5'10", 175 lbs. Deb: 8/1/1976 Career OF: 174-917-157																							
1976 KC-A	28	51	9	11	1	1	1	7	3	16	0	2	.216	.259	.333	.593	72	-3	4	2.54	0	0-17(2-7-9)/D-3	1	-0.4
1977 Sea-A★	160	597	85	157	26	8	24	76	55	120	13	9	.263	.327	.454	.781	111	8	89	5.14	11	*0-155(0-155-0)/D-4	22	1.6
1978 Sea-A	129	472	48	111	24	3	6	46	55	85	22	6	.235	.315	.337	.652	84	-7	51	3.51	7	*0-128(0-128-0)	9	-0.2
1979 Sea-A	162	622	109	166	29	9	21	78	85	78	33	12	.267	.358	.444	.801	113	15	99	5.43	7	*0-161(0-161-0)	18	1.9
1980 NY-A	83	328	38	73	11	3	9	42	34	50	18	8	.223	.301	.357	.658	81	-8	36	3.55	4	0-82(0-82-0)	8	-0.5
1981 SD-N	105	397	53	99	34	1	4	39	43	66	7	9	.249	.323	.370	.693	104	-1	47	3.88	7	*0-104(0-104-0)	10	0.5
1982 SD-N★	116	424	69	120	20	2	12	61	62	90	18	15	.283	.376	.425	.800	130	16	69	5.62	-2	*0-114(0-114-0)	22	1.3
1983 SD-N	133	335	42	78	12	3	12	49	35	58	11	11	.233	.305	.394	.699	96	-5	37	3.60	-4	*0-111(0-111-0)/1-5	9	-1.1
1984*Det-A	79	215	26	61	12	1	12	37	21	47	2	4	.284	.347	.516	.864	136	9	36	5.98	1	0-73(61-24-0)/D-2	9	0.7
1985 Cal-A	125	389	66	90	17	2	21	67	57	82	7	4	.231	.330	.447	.777	111	6	60	5.07	8	0-73(31-18-31),D-43	14	0.8
1986*Cal-A	126	393	73	90	21	3	17	49	64	87	10	3	.229	.341	.427	.769	109	7	60	5.04	-1	*0-121(28-10-96)	13	0.1
1987 Cal-A	85	192	25	47	8	2	8	28	20	38	2	1	.245	.316	.432	.748	99	-1	26	4.64	-3	0-66(52-3-21)/D-3	4	-0.6
Total 12	**1331**	**4415**	**643**	**1103**	**215**	**38**	**147**	**579**	**534**	**817**	**143**	**84**	**.250**	**.332**	**.416**	**.748**	**106**	**35**	**614**	**4.66**	**34**	***0-1205/D-55,1-5**	**139**	**4.2**
• JONES, Terry	Terry Lee Jones b: 2/15/1971, Birmingham, AL BB/TR, 5'10", 160 lbs. Deb: 9/8/1996 Career OF: 70-115-9																							
1996 Col-N	12	10	6	3	0	0	0	1	0	3	0	0	.300	.300	.300	.600	48	-1	1	3.24	0	/0-4(0-4-0)	0	-0.1
1998 Mon-N	60	212	30	46	7	2	1	15	21	46	16	4	.217	.288	.283	.571	52	-13	20	2.89	5	0-60(0-60-0)	3	-0.7
1999 Mon-N	17	63	4	17	1	1	0	3	3	14	1	2	.270	.303	.317	.620	59	-5	6	3.27	2	0-17(5-12-0)	1	-0.3
2000 Mon-N	108	168	30	42	8	2	0	13	10	32	7	2	.250	.292	.321	.614	53	-12	16	3.22	3	0-78(55-26-7)	3	-0.9
2001 Mon-N	30	77	8	20	5	0	0	2	2	11	3	0	.260	.278	.325	.603	54	-5	7	3.14	1	0-23(10-13-2)	1	-0.3
Total 5	**227**	**530**	**78**	**128**	**21**	**5**	**1**	**34**	**36**	**106**	**27**	**8**	**.242**	**.290**	**.306**	**.595**	**53**	**-35**	**50**	**3.07**	**11**	**0-182**	**8**	**-2.3**
• JONES, Tex	William Roderick Jones b: 8/4/1885, Marion, KS d: 2/26/1938, Wichita, KS BR/TR, 6', 192 lbs. Deb: 4/13/1911																							
1911 Chi-A	9	31	4	6	1	0	0	4	3	....	1	....	.194	.265	.226	.491	38	-3	2	2.14	3	/1-9	0	0.0
• JONES, Tim	William Timothy Jones b: 12/1/1962, Sumter, SC BL/TR, 5'10", 175 lbs. Deb: 7/26/1988 Career OF: 1-1-0																							
1988 StL-N	31	52	2	14	0	0	0	3	4	10	4	1	.269	.321	.269	.591	70	-1	5	3.30	0	/S-9,2-8,3-1	2	-0.1
1989 StL-N	42	75	11	22	6	0	0	7	7	8	1	0	.293	.361	.373	.735	107	1	10	4.83	-1	2-12,S-12/3-5,C-1,0-1	2	0.0
1990 StL-N	67	128	9	28	7	1	1	12	12	20	3	4	.219	.291	.313	.603	66	-7	12	2.88	-3	S-29,2-19/3-6,P-1	2	-0.9
1991 StL-N	16	24	1	4	2	0	0	2	2	6	0	1	.167	.231	.250	.481	35	-3	1	1.54	-2	S-14/2-4	0	-0.4
1992 StL-N	67	145	9	29	4	0	0	3	11	29	5	2	.200	.256	.228	.484	39	-11	9	2.05	3	S-34,2-28/3-2,0-1	2	-0.7
1993 StL-N	29	61	13	16	6	0	0	1	9	8	2	2	.262	.366	.361	.727	97	-0	9	4.83	3	S-21/2-7	2	0.4
Total 6	**252**	**485**	**45**	**113**	**25**	**1**	**1**	**28**	**45**	**81**	**15**	**10**	**.233**	**.302**	**.295**	**.597**	**68**	**-22**	**46**	**3.12**	**0**	**S-119/2-78,3-14,0-2,C-1,P-1**	**10**	**-1.6**
• JONES, Tom	Thomas Jones b: 1/22/1877, Honesdale, PA d: 6/19/1923, Danville, PA BR/TR, 6'1", 195 lbs. Deb: 8/25/1902																							
1902 Bal-A	37	159	22	45	8	4	0	14	2	....	1	....	.283	.292	.384	.676	83	-5	19	4.31	-2	1-37/2-1	2	-0.7
1904 StL-A	156	625	53	152	15	10	2	68	15	....	16	....	.243	.270	.309	.579	88	-10	59	3.23	9	*1-134,2-23/0-4(0-0-4)	10	-0.4
1905 StL-A	135	504	44	122	16	2	0	48	30	....	5	....	.242	.290	.282	.572	86	-8	47	3.06	14	*1-135	7	0.4
1906 StL-A	144	539	51	136	22	6	0	30	24	....	27	....	.252	.290	.315	.606	94	-5	63	3.77	22	*1-143	11	1.6
1907 StL-A	155	549	52	137	17	3	0	34	34	....	24	....	.250	.298	.291	.590	88	-7	60	3.59	4	*1-155	9	-0.7
1908 StL-A	155	549	43	135	14	2	1	50	30	....	18	....	.246	.290	.284	.574	86	-9	52	3.03	-8	*1-155	10	-2.3
1909 StL-A	97	337	30	84	9	3	0	29	18	....	13	....	.249	.299	.294	.593	94	-3	34	3.29	2	1-95/3-2	8	-0.3
*Det-A	44	153	13	43	9	0	0	18	5	....	9	....	.281	.317	.340	.657	103	0	20	4.24	5	1-44	4	0.5
Yr.	141	490	43	127	18	3	0	47	23	....	22	....	.259	.305	.308	.613	97	-2	54	3.58	7	*1-139/3-2	12	0.2
1910 Det-A	135	432	32	110	12	4	1	45	35	....	22	....	.255	.325	.308	.633	92	-3	53	3.86	-5	*1-135	10	-1.2
Total 8	**1058**	**3847**	**340**	**964**	**122**	**34**	**4**	**336**	**193**	**....**	**135**	**....**	**.251**	**.294**	**.303**	**.597**	**90**	**-49**	**407**	**3.46**	**40**	***1-1033/2-24,0-4,3-2**	**71**	**-3.1**
• JONES, Tracy	Tracy Donald Jones b: 3/31/1961, Hawthorne, CA BR/TR, 6'3", 220 lbs. Deb: 4/7/1986 Career OF: 231-52-83																							
1986 Cin-N	46	86	16	30	3	0	2	10	9	5	7	1	.349	.411	.453	.864	132	5	17	7.63	0	0-24(23-3-0)/1-2	4	0.5
1987 Cin-N	117	359	53	104	17	3	10	44	23	40	31	8	.290	.338	.437	.775	99	2	52	5.09	-3	0-95(56-34-17)	10	-0.4
1988 Cin-N	37	83	9	19	1	0	1	9	8	6	9	0	.229	.304	.277	.581	65	-2	8	3.06	-1	0-25(3-0-23)	1	-0.3
Mon-N	53	141	20	47	5	1	2	15	12	12	9	6	.333	.390	.426	.815	128	5	23	6.08	-1	0-43(26-9-15)	6	0.3
Yr.	90	224	29	66	6	1	3	24	20	18	18	6	.295	.358	.371	.728	105	3	31	4.88	-1	0-68(29-9-38)	7	0.0
1989 SF-N	40	97	5	18	4	0	0	12	5	14	2	1	.186	.233	.227	.460	33	-9	4	1.41	-1	0-30(9-5-22)	0	-1.0
Det-A	46	158	17	41	10	0	3	26	16	16	1	1	.259	.331	.380	.711	102	0	21	4.58	-1	0-36(34-0-3)/D-8	5	-0.2
1990 Det-A	50	118	15	27	4	1	4	9	6	13	1	1	.229	.283	.381	.665	84	-3	12	3.40	1	0-27(27-0-0),D-20	0	-0.3
Sea-A	25	86	8	26	4	0	2	15	3	12	0	1	.302	.341	.419	.759	110	0	11	4.37	-1	0-18(18-1-0)/D-5	3	-0.1
Yr.	75	204	23	53	8	1	6	24	9	25	1	2	.260	.307	.397	.704	95	-3	23	3.80	0	0-45(45-1-0),D-25	3	-0.5

YEAR TM-L	G	AB	R	H	2B	3B	HR	RBI	BB	SO	SB	CS	AVG	OBP	SLG	OPS	OPS+	BR/A	RC	RC/G	FR	G/POS	WS	TPW
1991 Sea-A	79	175	30	44	8	1	3	24	18	22	2	0	.251	.325	.360	.685	89	-2	20	3.72	0	D-37,0-36(35-0-3)	2	-0.4
Total 6	**493**	**1303**	**173**	**356**	**56**	**6**	**27**	**164**	**100**	**140**	**62**	**19**	**.273**	**.331**	**.388**	**.719**	**96**	**-3**	**168**	**4.45**	**-5**	**0-334/D-70,1-2**	**31**	**-2.0**
• JONES, Willie	Willie Edward "Puddin' Head" Jones b: 8/16/1925, Dillon, SC d: 10/18/1983, Cincinnati, OH BR/TR, 6'1", 192 lbs. Deb: 9/10/1947																							
1947 Phi-N	18	62	5	14	0	1	0	10	7	0	2	....	.226	.304	.258	.562	53	-4	5	2.46	2	3-17	1	-0.2
1948 Phi-N	17	60	9	20	2	0	2	9	3	5	0	....	.333	.365	.467	.832	126	2	9	5.51	1	3-17	3	0.3
1949 Phi-N	149	532	71	130	35	1	19	77	65	66	3	....	.244	.328	.421	.749	102	1	71	4.49	6	*3-145	15	0.7
1950*Phi-N★	157	610	100	163	28	6	25	88	61	40	5	....	.267	.337	.456	.793	108	5	93	5.38	4	*3-157	22	0.9
1951 Phi-N★	148	564	79	161	28	5	22	81	60	47	6	2	.285	.358	.470	.828	123	18	100	6.21	3	*3-147	22	2.1
1952 Phi-N	147	541	60	135	12	3	18	72	53	36	5	3	.250	.323	.383	.706	96	-3	68	4.25	8	*3-147	0	0.5
1953 Phi-N	149	481	61	108	16	2	19	70	85	45	1	1	.225	.342	.385	.727	90	-6	69	4.79	6	*3-147	15	0.0
1954 Phi-N	142	535	64	145	28	3	12	56	61	54	4	1	.271	.346	.402	.748	94	-3	77	5.00	14	*3-141	16	1.0
1955 Phi-N	146	516	65	133	20	3	16	81	77	51	6	2	.258	.357	.401	.759	103	5	77	5.03	3	*3-146	16	0.7
1956 Phi-N	149	520	88	144	20	4	17	78	92	49	5	4	.277	.387	.429	.815	121	19	89	5.94	10	*3-149	25	3.0
1957 Phi-N	133	440	58	96	19	2	9	47	61	41	1	0	.218	.313	.332	.645	76	-13	47	3.42	5	*3-126	10	-0.9
1958 Phi-N	118	398	52	108	15	1	14	60	49	45	1	2	.271	.354	.420	.774	105	3	60	5.27	-4	*3-110/1-1	12	-0.1
1959 Phi-N	47	160	23	43	9	1	7	24	19	14	0	0	.269	.346	.469	.815	112	3	26	5.62	-4	3-46	6	-0.1
Cle-A	11	18	1	4	1	0	0	1	1	3	0	0	.222	.263	.278	.541	51	-1	1	2.67	1	/3-4	0	0.0
Cin-N	72	233	33	58	12	1	7	31	28	26	0	2	.249	.332	.399	.731	91	-4	30	4.25	-2	3-68	5	-0.6
Yr.	119	393	56	101	21	2	14	55	47	40	0	2	.257	.338	.427	.765	100	-1	55	4.79	-6	*3-114	11	-0.7
1960 Cin-N	79	149	16	40	7	0	3	27	31	16	1	0	.268	.394	.376	.770	110	4	25	5.80	1	3-46/2-1	5	0.5
1961 Cin-N	9	7	1	0	0	0	0	0	2	3	0	0	.000	.222	.000	.222	-34	-1	0	.45	-1	/3-1	0	-0.2
Total 15	**1691**	**5826**	**786**	**1502**	**252**	**33**	**190**	**812**	**755**	**541**	**40**	**17**	**.258**	**.345**	**.410**	**.755**	**102**	**25**	**845**	**4.96**	**54**	***3-1614/1-1,2-1**	**173**	**7.5**
• JONNARD, Bubber	Clarence James Jonnard b: 11/23/1897, Nashville, TN d: 8/23/1977, New York, NY BR/TR, 6'1", 185 lbs. Deb: 10/1/1920 C																							
1920 Chi-A	2	5	0	0	0	0	0	0	0	1	0	0	.000	.000	.000	.000	-100	-1	0	.00	0	/C-1	0	-0.1
1922 Pit-N	10	21	4	5	0	1	0	2	2	4	0	0	.238	.304	.333	.638	64	-1	2	3.64	0	C-10	0	-0.1
1926 Phi-N	19	34	3	4	1	0	0	2	3	4	0	....	.118	.189	.147	.336	-8	-5	1	.90	0	C-15	0	-0.5
1927 Phi-N	53	143	18	42	6	0	0	14	7	7	0	....	.294	.327	.336	.662	77	-5	15	3.79	-1	C-41	2	-0.4
1929 StL-N	18	31	1	3	0	0	0	2	0	6	0	....	.097	.097	.097	.194	-51	-7	0	.29	-1	C-18	1	-0.7
1935 Phi-N	1	1	0	0	0	0	0	0	0	1	0	....	.000	.000	.000	.000	-91	-0	0	.00	0	/C-1	0	0.0
Total 6	**103**	**235**	**26**	**54**	**7**	**1**	**0**	**20**	**12**	**23**	**0**	**0**	**.230**	**.267**	**.268**	**.535**	**42**	**-20**	**19**	**2.62**	**-2**	**/C-86**	**3**	**-1.8**
• JOOST, Eddie	Edwin David Joost b: 6/5/1916, San Francisco, CA BR/TR, 6', 175 lbs. Deb: 9/11/1936 M																							
1936 Cin-N	13	26	1	4	1	0	0	1	2	5	0	....	.154	.214	.192	.407	11	-3	1	1.50	0	/S-7,2-5	0	-0.2
1937 Cin-N	6	12	0	1	0	0	0	0	0	0	0	....	.083	.083	.083	.167	-57	-3	0	.27	-1	/2-6	0	-0.3
1939 Cin-N	42	143	23	36	6	3	0	14	12	15	1	....	.252	.310	.336	.645	73	-6	15	3.35	-1	2-32/S-6	3	-0.4
1940*Cin-N	88	278	24	60	7	2	1	24	32	40	4	....	.216	.301	.266	.567	57	-15	24	2.73	2	S-78/2-7,3-4	6	-0.7
1941 Cin-N	152	537	67	136	25	4	4	40	69	59	9	....	.253	.340	.337	.678	91	-5	66	4.22	-6	*S-147/2-4,1-2,3-1	21	0.0
1942 Cin-N	142	562	65	126	30	3	6	41	62	57	9	....	.224	.307	.320	.627	84	-11	59	3.54	0	*S-130,2-15	15	0.0
1943 Bos-N	124	421	34	78	16	3	2	20	68	80	5	....	.185	.299	.252	.550	61	-19	35	2.67	-1	3-67,2-60/S-2	7	-1.7
1945 Bos-N	35	141	16	35	7	1	0	9	13	7	0	....	.248	.312	.312	.624	73	-5	14	3.37	-3	2-19,3-16	2	-0.7
1947 Phi-A	151	540	76	111	22	3	13	64	114	110	6	6	.206	.348	.330	.678	87	-6	73	4.25	10	*S-151	18	1.4
1948 Phi-A	135	509	99	127	22	2	16	55	119	87	2	4	.250	.393	.395	.788	109	11	91	6.17	10	*S-135	26	2.9
1949 Phi-A★	144	525	128	138	25	3	23	81	149	80	2	1	.263	.429	.453	.883	138	38	119	8.10	16	*S-144	35	6.1
1950 Phi-A	131	476	79	111	12	3	18	58	103	68	5	1	.233	.373	.384	.757	96	1	77	5.39	-5	*S-131	14	0.4
1951 Phi-A	140	553	107	160	28	5	19	78	106	70	10	8	.289	.409	.461	.870	132	28	115	7.58	-3	*S-140	25	3.4
1952 Phi-A★	146	540	94	132	26	3	20	75	122	94	5	8	.244	.388	.415	.803	116	16	98	6.21	-6	*S-146	26	2.0
1953 Phi-A	51	177	39	44	6	0	6	15	45	24	3	2	.249	.401	.384	.785	109	5	32	6.31	-5	S-51	6	0.4
1954 Phi-A	19	47	7	17	3	0	1	9	10	10	0	1	.362	.474	.489	.963	164	4	10	7.62	1	/S-9,3-5,2-1	3	0.6
1955 Bos-A	55	119	15	23	2	0	5	17	17	21	0	0	.193	.299	.336	.635	65	-6	13	3.44	1	S-20,2-17/3-2	2	-0.2
Total 17	**1574**	**5606**	**874**	**1339**	**238**	**35**	**134**	**601**	**1043**	**827**	**61**	**31**	**.239**	**.361**	**.366**	**.727**	**99**	**25**	**842**	**5.07**	**9**	***S-1297,2-166/3-95,1-2**	**209**	**12.8**
• JORDAN, Brian	Brian O'Neal Jordan b: 3/29/1967, Baltimore, MD BR/TR, 6'1", 205 lbs. Deb: 4/8/1992 Career OF: 243-143-884																							
1992 StL-N	55	193	17	40	9	4	5	22	10	48	7	2	.207	.250	.373	.623	77	-6	16	2.77	0	0-53(27-9-21)	2	-0.9
1993 StL-N	67	223	33	69	10	6	10	44	12	35	6	6	.309	.356	.543	.898	139	10	39	6.26	-1	0-65(23-37-12)	10	0.7
1994 StL-N	53	178	14	46	8	2	5	15	16	40	4	3	.258	.323	.410	.733	91	-3	22	4.17	3	0-46(18-9-22)/1-1	1	-0.1
1995 StL-N	131	490	83	145	20	4	22	81	22	79	24	9	.296	.340	.488	.828	116	10	81	6.08	1	*0-126(0-13-116)	18	0.5
1996*StL-N	140	513	82	159	36	1	17	104	29	84	22	5	.310	.355	.483	.839	120	15	90	6.45	4	*0-136(0-13-128)/1-1	27	1.2
1997 StL-N	47	145	17	34	5	0	0	10	10	21	6	1	.234	.311	.269	.580	54	-9	13	2.99	-1	0-44(0-14-30)	1	-1.1
1998 StL-N	150	564	100	178	34	7	25	91	40	66	17	5	.316	.370	.534	.904	135	29	107	7.01	4	*0-141(0-33-124)/D-3,3-1	21	2.7
1999*Atl-N★	153	576	100	163	28	4	23	115	51	81	13	8	.283	.351	.465	.816	104	2	94	5.79	4	*0-150(0-0-150)	22	-0.3
2000*Atl-N	133	489	71	129	26	0	17	77	38	80	10	2	.264	.323	.421	.745	86	-11	66	4.71	8	*0-130(0-0-130)	14	-0.9
2001*Atl-N	148	560	82	165	32	3	25	97	31	88	3	2	.295	.338	.496	.835	109	6	88	5.62	10	*0-145(0-1-144)/D-2	19	0.8
2002 LA-N	128	471	65	134	27	3	18	80	34	86	2	2	.285	.341	.469	.810	118	10	74	5.62	4	*0-125(121-0-4)/D-3	19	0.9
2003 LA-N	66	224	28	67	9	0	6	28	23	30	1	1	.299	.375	.420	.794	113	5	36	6.00	1	0-62(54-14-3)/D-2	7	0.3
Total 12	**1271**	**4626**	**692**	**1329**	**244**	**34**	**173**	**764**	**316**	**738**	**115**	**46**	**.287**	**.342**	**.467**	**.809**	**110**	**58**	**727**	**5.61**	**37**	***0-1223/D-10,1-2,3-1**	**161**	**3.9**
• JORDAN, Buck	Baxter Byerly Jordan b: 1/16/1907, Cooleemee, NC d: 3/18/1993, Salisbury, NC BL/TR, 6', 170 lbs. Deb: 9/15/1927																							
1927 NY-N	5	5	0	1	0	0	0	0	0	3	0	....	.200	.200	.200	.400	7	-1	0	1.21	0	....	0	-0.1
1929 NY-N	2	2	1	1	1	0	0	0	0	0	0	....	.500	.500	1.000	1.500	262	0	1	24.18	0	/1-1	0	0.0
1931 Was-A	9	18	3	4	2	0	0	1	1	3	0	0	.222	.263	.333	.596	56	-1	2	2.99	-1	/1-7	0	-0.2
1932 Bos-N	49	212	27	68	12	3	2	29	4	5	1	....	.321	.333	.434	.767	108	2	30	5.35	-1	1-49	7	-0.4
1933 Bos-N	152	588	77	168	29	9	4	46	34	22	4	....	.286	.327	.386	.713	112	8	74	4.44	6	*1-150	19	0.0
1934 Bos-N	124	489	68	152	26	9	2	58	35	19	3	....	.311	.358	.413	.771	114	10	74	5.58	1	*1-117	18	0.0
1935 Bos-N	130	470	62	131	24	5	5	35	19	17	3	....	.279	.307	.383	.690	91	-7	54	4.18	3	1-95/3-8,0-2(0-0-2)	7	-1.2
1936 Bos-N	138	555	81	179	27	5	3	66	45	22	2	....	.323	.375	.405	.781	118	14	83	5.57	2	*1-136	16	0.4
1937 Bos-N	8	8	1	2	0	0	0	0	0	0	0	....	.250	.250	.250	.500	40	-1	0	.99	0	....	0	-0.1
Cin-N	98	316	45	89	14	3	1	28	25	14	6	....	.282	.334	.354	.689	92	-4	39	4.40	-5	1-76	6	-1.5
Yr.	106	324	46	91	14	3	1	28	25	14	6	....	.281	.332	.352	.684	90	-4	39	4.30	-5	1-76	6	-1.6
1938 Cin-N	9	7	0	2	0	0	0	0	2	0	0	....	.286	.444	.286	.730	107	0	1	6.17	0	....	0	0.0
Phi-N	87	310	31	93	18	1	0	18	17	4	1	....	.300	.336	.365	.701	92	-4	38	4.52	2	3-58,1-17	7	-0.1
Yr.	96	317	31	95	18	1	0	18	19	4	1	....	.300	.339	.363	.702	93	-3	39	4.56	2	3-58,1-17	7	0.0
Total 10	**811**	**2980**	**396**	**890**	**153**	**35**	**17**	**281**	**182**	**109**	**20**	**0**	**.299**	**.340**	**.391**	**.731**	**105**	**18**	**397**	**4.84**	**8**	**1-648/3-66,0-2**	**80**	**-3.1**
• JORDAN, Dutch	Adolf Otto Jordan b: 1/5/1880, Pittsburgh, PA d: 12/23/1972, West Allegheny, PA BR/TR, 5'10", 185 lbs. Deb: 4/25/1903																							
1903 Bro-N	78	267	27	63	11	1	0	21	19	....	9	....	.236	.289	.285	.574	66	-12	26	3.28	-30	2-54,3-18/0-4(1-0-3),1-1	3	-4.0
1904 Bro-N	87	252	21	45	10	2	0	19	13	....	7	....	.179	.225	.234	.459	43	-17	17	1.97	-18	2-70,3-11/1-4	1	-3.6
Total 2	**165**	**519**	**48**	**108**	**21**	**3**	**0**	**40**	**32**	**....**	**16**	**....**	**.208**	**.258**	**.260**	**.518**	**54**	**-29**	**43**	**2.60**	**-48**	**2-124/3-29,1-5,0-4**	**4**	**-7.6**
• JORDAN, Jimmy	James William "Lord" Jordan b: 1/13/1908, Tucapau, SC d: 12/4/1957, Gastonia, NC BR/TR, 5'9", 157 lbs. Deb: 4/20/1933																							
1933 Bro-N	70	211	16	54	12	1	0	17	4	6	3	....	.256	.270	.322	.592	71	-8	18	2.97	3	S-51,2-11	4	-0.1
1934 Bro-N	97	369	34	98	17	2	0	43	9	32	1	....	.266	.285	.322	.607	65	-19	33	3.13	-8	S-51,2-41/3-9	4	-2.0
1935 Bro-N	94	295	26	82	7	0	0	30	9	17	3	....	.278	.302	.302	.603	64	-15	27	3.21	8	2-46,S-28/3-5	5	-0.1
1936 Bro-N	115	398	26	93	15	1	2	28	15	21	1	....	.234	.262	.291	.553	48	-30	31	2.64	-8	2-98/S-9,3-6	2	-3.1
Total 4	**376**	**1273**	**102**	**327**	**51**	**4**	**2**	**118**	**37**	**76**	**8**	**....**	**.257**	**.279**	**.308**	**.587**	**61**	**-72**	**108**	**2.96**	**-4**	**2-196,S-139/3-20**	**15**	**-5.3**
• JORDAN, Kevin	Kevin Wayne Jordan b: 10/9/1969, San Francisco, CA BR/TR, 6'1", 185 lbs. Deb: 8/8/1995																							
1995 Phi-N	24	54	6	10	1	0	2	6	2	9	0	0	.185	.228	.315	.543	41	-5	4	2.45	5	/2-9,3-1	1	0.0
1996 Phi-N	43	131	15	37	10	0	3	12	5	20	2	1	.282	.314	.427	.741	92	-2	17	4.41	-2	1-30/2-7,3-1	2	-0.6

YEAR TM-L	G	AB	R	H	2B	3B	HR	RBI	BB	SO	SB	CS	AVG	OBP	SLG	OPS	OPS+	BR/A	RC	RC/G	FR	G/POS	WS	TPW
1997 Phi-N	84	177	19	47	8	0	6	30	3	26	0	1	.266	.278	.412	.690	78	-7	18	3.52	-3	1-25,3-12/2-6,D-1	2	-1.2
1998 Phi-N	112	250	23	69	13	0	2	27	8	30	0	0	.276	.304	.352	.656	71	-11	26	3.72	1	1-24,2-22/D-8,3-6	3	-1.1
1999 Phi-N	120	347	36	99	17	3	4	51	24	34	0	0	.285	.342	.386	.728	81	-10	44	4.52	9	3-62,2-33,1-13	7	0.0
2000 Phi-N	109	337	30	74	16	2	5	36	17	41	0	1	.220	.259	.323	.583	46	-30	26	2.50	1	2-47,3-39/1-9	3	-2.5
2001 Phi-N	68	113	9	27	5	0	1	13	14	21	0	0	.239	.323	.310	.633	67	-5	12	3.73	-1	1-10,2-10,3-10	3	-0.7
Total 7	560	1409	138	363	70	5	23	175	73	181	2	3	.258	.299	.363	.663	69	-70	146	3.59	9	2-134,3-131,1-111/D-9	21	-6.0
• JORDAN, Mike	Michael Henry "Mitty" Jordan b: 2/7/1863, Lawrence, MA d: 9/25/1940, Lawrence, MA, 5'7.5", 155 lbs. Deb: 8/21/1890																							
1890 Pit-N	37	125	8	12	1	0	0	6	15	19	5	....	.096	.210	.104	.314	-9	-16	4	.91	2	0-37(29-8-0)	0	-1.3
• JORDAN, Ricky	Paul Scott Jordan b: 5/26/1965, Richmond, CA BR/TR, 6'5", 209 lbs. Deb: 7/17/1988																							
1988 Phi-N	69	273	41	84	15	1	11	43	7	39	1	1	.308	.325	.491	.816	129	8	41	5.68	-4	1-69	12	-0.1
1989 Phi-N	144	523	63	149	22	3	12	75	23	62	4	3	.285	.321	.407	.729	107	2	62	4.17	-9	*1-140	12	-1.7
1990 Phi-N	92	324	32	78	21	0	5	44	13	39	2	0	.241	.281	.352	.633	73	-13	30	3.15	-7	1-84	3	-2.6
1991 Phi-N	101	301	38	82	21	3	9	49	14	49	0	2	.272	.309	.452	.761	113	2	38	4.28	-5	1-72	9	-0.8
1992 Phi-N	94	276	33	84	19	0	4	34	5	44	3	0	.304	.317	.417	.733	106	1	34	4.53	-1	1-54,0-11(11-0-0)	6	-0.3
1993*Phi-N	90	159	21	46	4	1	5	18	8	32	0	0	.289	.327	.421	.749	100	-0	22	5.04	-4	1-33	3	-0.7
1994 Phi-N	72	220	29	62	14	2	8	37	6	32	0	0	.282	.304	.473	.777	96	-2	29	4.69	-6	1-49	5	-1.2
1996 Sea-A	15	28	4	7	0	0	1	4	1	6	0	0	.250	.300	.357	.657	65	-2	3	3.93	-1	/1-9,D-2	0	-0.3
Total 8	677	2104	261	592	116	10	55	304	77	303	10	6	.281	.311	.424	.736	103	-3	259	4.37	-35	1-510/0-11,D-2	50	-7.6
• JORDAN, Scott	Scott Allan Jordan b: 5/27/1963, Waco, TX BR/TR, 6', 175 lbs. Deb: 9/2/1988																							
1988 Cle-A	7	9	0	1	0	0	0	1	0	3	0	0	.111	.111	.111	.222	-37	-2	0	.46	-0	/0-6(0-5-1)	0	-0.2
• JORDAN, Slats	Clarence Veasey Jordan b: 9/26/1879, Baltimore, MD d: 12/7/1953, Catonsville, MD BL/TL, 6'1", 190 lbs. Deb: 9/28/1901																							
1901 Bal-A	1	3	0	0	0	0	0	0	0	....	0	....	.000	.000	.000	.000	-96	-1	0	.00	-1	/1-1	0	-0.1
1902 Bal-A	1	4	0	0	0	0	0	0	0	....	0	....	.000	.000	.000	.000	-96	-1	0	.00	0	/0-1	0	-0.1
Total 2	2	7	0	0	0	0	0	0	0	....	0	....	.000	.000	.000	.000	-96	-2	0	.00	-1	/1-1,0-1	0	-0.2
• JORDAN, Tim	Timothy Joseph Jordan b: 2/14/1879, New York, NY d: 9/13/1949, Bronx, NY BL/TL, 6'1", 170 lbs. Deb: 8/10/1901																							
1901 Was-A	6	20	2	4	1	0	0	2	3	....	0	....	.200	.304	.250	.554	56	-1	2	2.58	-1	/1-6	0	-0.2
1903 NY-A	2	8	2	1	0	0	0	0	0	....	0	....	.125	.125	.125	.250	-23	-1	0	.49	-1	/1-2	0	-0.2
1906 Bro-N	129	450	67	118	20	8	**12**	78	59	....	16	....	.262	.352	.422	.774	153	28	75	5.73	-9	*1-126	25	1.8
1907 Bro-N	147	485	43	133	15	8	4	53	74	....	10	....	.274	.371	.363	.734	141	26	73	5.17	-3	*1-143	22	2.3
1908 Bro-N	148	515	58	127	18	5	**12**	60	59	....	9	....	.247	.328	.371	.698	128	17	65	4.22	-14	*1-146	16	0.0
1909 Bro-N	103	330	47	90	20	3	3	36	59	....	13	....	.273	.386	.379	.765	142	20	54	5.56	-4	1-95	14	1.5
1910 Bro-N	5	5	1	1	0	0	1	3	0	2	0	....	.200	.200	.800	1.000	195	0	1	4.80	0	....	0	0.0
Total 7	540	1813	220	474	74	24	32	232	254	2	48	....	.261	.355	.382	.737	139	88	270	5.05	-33	1-518	77	5.2
• JORDAN, Tom	Thomas Jefferson Jordan b: 9/5/1919, Lawton, OK BR/TR, 6'1.5", 195 lbs. Deb: 9/4/1944																							
1944 Chi-A	14	45	2	12	1	1	0	3	1	0	0	0	.267	.283	.333	.616	77	-2	4	3.24	-1	C-14	1	-0.2
1946 Chi-A	10	15	1	4	2	1	0	0	0	1	0	0	.267	.267	.533	.800	124	0	1	1.05	0	/C-2	0	0.1
Cle-A	14	35	2	7	1	0	1	3	3	1	1	1	.200	.263	.314	.577	65	-2	2	1.98	0	C-13	0	-0.2
Yr.	24	50	3	11	3	1	1	3	3	2	1	1	.220	.264	.380	.644	81	-2	3	1.70	1	C-15	0	-0.1
1948 StL-A	1	1	0	0	0	0	0	0	0	0	0	0	.000	.000	.000	.000	-98	-0	0	.00	0	....	0	0.0
Total 3	39	96	5	23	4	2	1	6	4	2	1	1	.240	.270	.354	.624	77	-3	7	2.33	0	/C-29	1	-0.3
• JORGENS, Art	Arndt Ludwig Jorgens b: 5/18/1905, Modum, Norway d: 3/1/1980, Evanston, IL BR/TR, 5'9", 160 lbs. Deb: 4/26/1929																							
1929 NY-A	18	34	6	11	3	0	0	4	6	7	0	2	.324	.425	.412	.837	124	1	6	5.75	0	C-15	1	0.1
1930 NY-A	16	30	7	11	3	0	0	1	2	4	0	0	.367	.406	.467	.873	126	1	6	6.89	-1	C-16	1	0.1
1931 NY-A	46	100	12	27	1	2	0	14	9	3	0	1	.270	.330	.320	.650	76	-3	11	3.73	-3	C-40	2	-0.4
1932 NY-A	56	151	13	33	7	1	2	19	14	11	0	0	.219	.285	.318	.603	59	-9	14	3.16	-4	C-56	3	-1.0
1933 NY-A	21	50	9	11	3	0	2	13	12	3	1	0	.220	.371	.400	.771	111	2	8	5.72	-2	C-19	2	0.1
1934 NY-A	58	183	14	38	6	1	0	20	23	24	2	0	.208	.296	.251	.547	45	-14	15	2.75	-1	C-56	4	-1.1
1935 NY-A	36	84	6	20	2	0	0	8	12	10	0	0	.238	.333	.262	.595	59	-4	8	3.29	0	C-33	3	-0.3
1936 NY-A	31	66	5	18	3	1	0	5	2	3	0	0	.273	.294	.348	.643	60	-4	7	3.62	0	C-30	1	-0.3
1937 NY-A	13	23	3	3	1	0	0	3	2	5	0	0	.130	.200	.174	.374	-5	-4	1	1.15	0	C-11	0	-0.3
1938 NY-A	9	17	3	4	2	0	0	2	3	3	0	0	.235	.350	.353	.703	77	-1	2	4.42	0	/C-8	0	0.0
1939 NY-A	3	0	1	0	0	0	0	0	0	0	0	0	....	....	....	....	-102	0	0	....	0	/C-2	0	0.0
Total 11	307	738	79	176	31	5	4	89	85	73	3	3	.238	.317	.310	.627	66	-36	78	3.58	-12	C-286	17	-3.2
• JORGENSEN, Mike	Michael Jorgensen b: 8/16/1948, Passaic, NJ BL/TL, 6', 195 lbs. Deb: 9/10/1968 M Career OF: 108-76-102																							
1968 NY-N	8	14	0	2	1	0	0	0	0	4	0	0	.143	.143	.214	.357	6	-2	0	.96	0	/1-4	0	-0.3
1970 NY-N	76	87	15	17	3	1	3	4	10	23	2	2	.195	.278	.356	.635	69	-5	9	3.29	1	1-50,0-10(0-9-1)	2	-0.5
1971 NY-N	45	118	16	26	1	1	5	11	11	24	1	2	.220	.303	.373	.676	92	-2	12	3.40	-1	0-31(4-25-4)/1-1	2	-0.4
1972 Mon-N	113	372	48	86	12	3	13	47	53	75	12	13	.231	.333	.384	.718	102	-1	47	4.02	4	1-76,0-28(2-26-0)	10	-0.4
1973 Mon-N	138	413	49	95	16	2	9	47	64	49	16	7	.230	.338	.344	.681	86	-5	52	4.17	6	*1-123,0-11(9-2-0)	10	-0.8
1974 Mon-N	131	287	45	89	16	1	11	59	70	39	3	5	.310	.448	.488	.936	153	24	68	8.52	8	1-91,0-29(28-1-0)	17	2.6
1975 Mon-N	144	445	58	116	18	0	18	67	79	75	3	3	.261	.380	.422	.803	117	13	76	5.94	3	*1-133/0-6(5-1-0)	16	0.6
1976 Mon-N	125	343	36	87	13	0	6	23	52	48	7	1	.254	.352	.344	.696	94	0	45	4.56	2	1-81,0-41(25-0-16)	9	-0.5
1977 Mon-N	19	20	3	4	1	0	0	0	3	4	0	0	.200	.304	.250	.554	52	-1	2	2.36	1	/1-5	0	0.0
Oak-A	66	203	18	50	4	1	8	32	25	44	3	2	.246	.335	.394	.729	99	0	28	4.58	3	1-48,0-20(6-1-13)/D-2	5	0.0
1978 Tex-A	96	97	20	19	3	0	1	9	18	10	3	1	.196	.322	.258	.579	65	-3	9	2.89	3	1-78/0-9(2-4-4),D-1	1	-0.3
1979 Tex-A	90	157	21	35	7	0	6	16	14	29	0	2	.223	.295	.382	.677	82	-5	17	3.53	4	1-60,0-20(4-7-9)/D-2	3	-0.4
1980 NY-N	119	321	43	82	11	0	7	43	46	55	0	3	.255	.349	.355	.704	100	-0	39	4.17	0	1-72,0-31(9-0-22)	8	-0.6
1981 NY-N	86	122	8	25	5	2	3	15	12	24	4	0	.205	.276	.352	.629	79	-3	13	3.30	0	1-40,0-19(4-0-15)	2	-0.5
1982 NY-N	120	114	16	29	6	0	2	14	21	24	2	0	.254	.370	.360	.730	106	2	17	5.12	-5	1-56,0-16(1-0-15)	4	-0.5
1983 NY-N	38	24	5	6	3	0	1	3	2	4	0	1	.250	.333	.500	.833	129	0	3	4.47	-1	1-19	1	-0.1
Atl-N	57	48	5	12	1	0	1	8	8	8	0	0	.250	.357	.333	.690	86	-1	6	4.41	-1	1-19/0-6(6-0-0)	1	-0.2
Yr.	95	72	10	18	4	0	2	11	10	12	0	1	.250	.349	.389	.738	100	-0	10	4.43	-2	1-38/0-6(6-0-0)	2	-0.3
1984 Atl-N	31	26	4	7	1	0	0	5	3	6	0	0	.269	.345	.308	.653	79	-1	3	3.49	-1	/1-8,0-4(1-0-3)	0	-0.2
StL-N	59	98	5	24	4	2	1	12	10	17	0	0	.245	.315	.357	.672	91	-1	11	4.11	2	1-39	2	-0.1
Yr.	90	124	9	31	5	2	1	17	13	23	0	1	.250	.321	.347	.668	88	-2	14	3.97	1	1-47/0-4(1-0-3)	2	-0.3
1985*StL-N	72	112	14	22	6	0	0	11	31	27	2	1	.196	.375	.250	.625	79	-1	13	3.70	-2	1-49/0-2(2-0-0)	3	-0.6
Total 17	1633	3421	429	833	132	13	95	426	532	589	58	44	.243	.349	.373	.722	100	8	470	4.61	24	*1-1052,0-283/D-5	96	-3.2
• JORGENSEN, Pinky	Carl Jorgensen b: 11/21/1914, Laton, CA d: 5/2/1996, Santa Cruz, CA BR/TR, 6'1", 195 lbs. Deb: 9/14/1937																							
1937 Cin-N	6	14	1	4	0	0	0	1	1	2	0	....	.286	.333	.286	.619	73	-0	2	3.74	0	/0-4(4-0-0)	0	-0.1
• JORGENSEN, Spider	John Donald Jorgensen b: 11/3/1919, Folsom, CA d: 11/6/2003, Rancho Cucamonga, CA BL/TR, 5'9", 155 lbs. Deb: 4/15/1947																							
1947*Bro-N	129	441	57	121	29	8	5	67	58	45	4	....	.274	.360	.410	.770	100	1	69	5.63	3	*3-128	16	0.4
1948 Bro-N	31	90	15	27	6	2	1	13	16	13	1	....	.300	.411	.444	.856	127	4	18	7.43	-3	3-24	4	0.1
1949*Bro-N	53	134	15	36	5	1	1	14	23	13	0	....	.269	.376	.343	.719	90	-1	19	5.14	2	3-36	5	0.1
1950 Bro-N	2	2	0	0	0	0	0	1	1	0	0	....	.000	.333	.000	.333	-4	-0	0	1.17	0	/3-1	0	0.0
NY-N	24	37	5	5	0	0	0	4	5	2	0	....	.135	.238	.135	.373	1	-5	2	1.27	1	/3-5	0	-0.4
Yr.	26	39	5	5	0	0	0	5	6	2	0	....	.128	.244	.128	.373	1	-6	2	1.26	1	/3-6	0	-0.4
1951 NY-N	28	51	5	12	0	0	2	8	3	2	0	0	.235	.291	.353	.644	72	-2	6	3.86	0	0-11(0-0-11)/3-1	1	-0.2
Total 5	267	755	97	201	40	11	9	107	106	75	5	0	.266	.359	.384	.743	95	-3	114	5.36	3	3-195/0-11	26	-0.1
• JORGENSEN, Terry	Terry Allen Jorgensen b: 9/2/1966, Kewaunee, WI BR/TR, 6'4", 208 lbs. Deb: 9/10/1989																							
1989 Min-A	10	23	1	4	1	0	0	2	4	5	0	0	.174	.296	.217	.514	44	-2	2	2.11	2	/3-9	0	0.0

YEAR TM-L	G	AB	R	H	2B	3B	HR	RBI	BB	SO	SB	CS	AVG	OBP	SLG	OPS	OPS+	BR/A	RC	RC/G	FR	G/POS	WS	TPW
1992 Min-A	22	58	5	18	1	0	0	5	3	11	1	2	.310	.355	.328	.682	89	-1	5	3.08	1	1-13/3-9,S-2	1	-0.1
1993 Min-A	59	152	15	34	7	0	1	12	10	21	1	0	.224	.272	.289	.561	51	-10	11	2.32	3	3-45/1-9,S-6	2	-0.7
Total 3	91	233	21	56	9	0	1	19	17	37	2	2	.240	.295	.292	.587	60	-13	18	2.48	5	/3-63,1-22,S-8	3	-0.8

• JOSE, Felix Domingo Felix Andujar Jose b: 5/2/1965, Santo Domingo, Dominican Republic BB/TR, 6'1", 190 lbs. Deb: 9/2/1988 Career OF: 39-36-629

YEAR TM-L	G	AB	R	H	2B	3B	HR	RBI	BB	SO	SB	CS	AVG	OBP	SLG	OPS	OPS+	BR/A	RC	RC/G	FR	G/POS	WS	TPW
1988 Oak-A	8	6	2	2	1	0	0	1	0	1	1	0	.333	.333	.500	.833	135	0	1	7.92	0	/0-6(1-0-5)	0	0.0
1989 Oak-A	20	57	3	11	2	0	0	5	4	13	0	1	.193	.246	.228	.474	36	-5	3	1.52	0	0-19(4-0-16)	1	-0.6
1990 Oak-A	101	341	42	90	12	0	8	39	16	65	8	2	.264	.307	.370	.676	92	-4	38	3.88	0	0-92(26-24-53)/D-7	12	-0.7
StL-N	25	85	12	23	4	1	3	13	8	16	4	4	.271	.333	.447	.780	112	0	12	4.75	-1	0-23(1-2-21)	3	-0.1
1991 StL-N★	154	568	69	173	40	6	8	77	50	113	20	12	.305	.363	.438	.801	123	16	88	5.60	-4	*0-153(0-0-153)	25	0.9
1992 StL-N	131	509	62	150	22	3	14	75	40	100	28	12	.295	.347	.432	.779	123	15	75	5.33	0	*0-127(0-0-127)	15	1.2
1993 KC-A	149	499	64	126	24	3	6	43	36	95	31	13	.253	.304	.349	.653	71	-20	54	3.69	-3	*0-144(0-10-136)/D-1	8	-2.8
1994 KC-A	99	366	56	111	28	1	11	55	35	75	10	12	.303	.364	.475	.840	110	2	58	5.66	1	0-98(0-0-98)	11	-0.2
1995 KC-A	9	30	2	4	1	0	0	1	2	9	0	0	.133	.188	.167	.354	-7	-5	1	.86	2	/0-7(0-0-7)	0	-0.3
2000 NY-A	20	29	4	7	0	0	1	5	2	9	0	1	.241	.290	.345	.635	60	-2	2	2.61	-1	0-14(6-0-8)/D-2	0	-0.3
2002 Ari-N	13	19	5	5	0	0	2	4	4	8	0	0	.263	.391	.579	.970	139	1	4	6.65	-1	/0-5(1-0-4)	0	0.0
2003 Ari-N	18	18	1	6	1	0	1	6	6	3	0	0	.333	.500	.556	1.056	159	2	5	10.76	0	/D-1,0-1	1	0.2
Total 11	747	2527	322	708	135	14	54	324	203	507	102	57	.280	.336	.409	.745	103	1	341	4.75	-7	0-689/D-11	76	-2.8

• JOSEPH, Rick Ricardo Emelindo (Harrigan) Joseph b: 8/24/1939, San Pedro de Macoris, Dominican Republic d: 9/8/1979, Santo Domingo, Dominican Republic BR/TR, 6'1", 195 lbs. Deb: 6/18/1964 Career OF: 13-0-0

YEAR TM-L	G	AB	R	H	2B	3B	HR	RBI	BB	SO	SB	CS	AVG	OBP	SLG	OPS	OPS+	BR/A	RC	RC/G	FR	G/POS	WS	TPW
1964 KC-A	17	54	3	12	2	0	0	1	3	11	0	1	.222	.263	.259	.522	45	-4	3	2.07	-2	1-12/3-3	0	-0.7
1967 Phi-N	17	41	4	9	2	0	1	5	4	10	0	0	.220	.289	.341	.630	79	-1	4	3.60	1	1-13	1	-0.1
1968 Phi-N	66	155	20	34	5	0	3	12	16	35	0	1	.219	.297	.310	.606	82	-3	14	3.04	-2	1-30,3-14/0-1	3	-0.8
1969 Phi-N	99	264	35	72	15	0	6	37	22	57	2	1	.273	.331	.398	.729	106	2	34	4.55	-1	3-58,1-17/2-1	7	0.0
1970 Phi-N	71	119	7	27	2	1	3	10	6	28	0	0	.227	.264	.336	.600	61	-7	9	2.58	-2	0-12(12-0-0),1-10/3-9	0	-1.0
Total 5	270	633	69	154	26	1	13	65	51	141	2	3	.243	.302	.349	.651	85	-14	66	3.51	-6	/3-84,1-82,0-13,2-1	11	-2.6

• JOSEPHSON, Duane Duane Charles Josephson b: 6/3/1942, New Hampton, IA d: 1/30/1997, New Hampton, IA BR/TR, 6', 195 lbs. Deb: 9/15/1965

YEAR TM-L	G	AB	R	H	2B	3B	HR	RBI	BB	SO	SB	CS	AVG	OBP	SLG	OPS	OPS+	BR/A	RC	RC/G	FR	G/POS	WS	TPW
1965 Chi-A	4	9	2	1	0	0	0	0	2	4	0	0	.111	.273	.111	.384	14	-1	0	1.40	-0	/C-4	0	-0.1
1966 Chi-A	11	38	3	9	1	0	0	3	3	3	0	0	.237	.293	.263	.556	65	-2	3	2.29	1	C-11	1	0.0
1967 Chi-A	62	189	11	45	5	1	1	9	6	24	0	3	.238	.262	.291	.553	65	-10	13	2.19	1	C-59	4	-0.8
1968 Chi-A★	128	434	35	107	16	6	6	45	18	52	2	4	.247	.286	.353	.639	92	-7	41	3.19	16	*C-122	14	1.8
1969 Chi-A	52	162	19	39	6	2	1	20	13	17	0	0	.241	.301	.321	.622	71	-6	16	3.34	0	C-47	2	-0.5
1970 Chi-A	96	285	28	90	12	1	4	41	24	28	0	1	.316	.375	.407	.782	111	5	42	5.35	2	C-84	9	1.1
1971 Bos-A	91	306	38	75	14	1	10	39	22	35	2	0	.245	.296	.395	.691	88	-5	31	3.28	-3	C-87	7	-0.4
1972 Bos-A	26	82	11	22	4	1	1	7	4	11	0	2	.268	.310	.378	.688	99	-1	7	2.96	-1	1-16/C-6	1	-0.4
Total 8	470	1505	147	388	58	12	23	164	92	174	4	10	.258	.305	.358	.663	88	-27	153	3.43	16	C-420/1-16	38	0.7

• JOSHUA, Von Von Everett Joshua b: 5/1/1948, Oakland, CA BL/TL, 5'10", 170 lbs. Deb: 9/2/1969 C Career OF: 129-419-57

YEAR TM-L	G	AB	R	H	2B	3B	HR	RBI	BB	SO	SB	CS	AVG	OBP	SLG	OPS	OPS+	BR/A	RC	RC/G	FR	G/POS	WS	TPW
1969 LA-N	14	8	2	2	0	0	0	0	0	2	1	0	.250	.250	.250	.500	43	-0	1	2.84	-1	/0-8(7-0-2)	0	-0.1
1970 LA-N	72	109	23	29	1	3	1	8	6	24	2	2	.266	.304	.358	.662	80	-4	12	3.85	0	0-41(21-10-16)	2	-0.5
1971 LA-N	11	7	2	0	0	0	0	0	0	1	0	0	.000	.000	.000	.000	-106	-2	0	.00	0	/0-5(4-1-0)	0	-0.2
1973 LA-N	75	159	19	40	4	1	2	17	8	29	7	2	.252	.292	.327	.619	74	-5	16	3.33	-1	0-46(42-1-4)	3	-0.9
1974*LA-N	81	124	11	29	5	1	1	16	7	17	3	2	.234	.280	.315	.595	69	-6	10	2.68	-1	0-35(12-17-6)	1	-0.8
1975 SF-N	129	507	75	161	25	10	7	43	32	75	20	10	.318	.359	.448	.807	118	11	81	5.97	2	*0-117(0-117-0)	19	1.0
1976 SF-N	42	156	13	41	5	2	0	2	4	20	1	3	.263	.281	.321	.602	68	-8	13	2.75	0	0-35(3-33-0)	1	-1.0
Mil-A	107	423	44	113	13	5	5	28	18	58	8	10	.267	.297	.357	.654	93	-8	42	3.42	1	*0-105(26-82-0)/D-1	9	-1.2
1977 Mil-A	144	536	58	140	25	7	9	49	21	74	12	9	.261	.289	.384	.673	82	-16	53	3.31	-4	*0-140(0-140-0)	8	-2.2
1979 LA-N	94	142	22	40	7	1	3	14	7	23	1	1	.282	.315	.408	.724	97	-1	17	4.13	-1	0-46(11-10-28)	3	-0.3
1980 SD-N	53	63	8	15	2	1	2	7	5	15	0	1	.238	.294	.397	.691	97	-1	7	3.45	0	0-12(3-8-1)/1-2	1	-0.1
Total 10	822	2234	277	610	87	31	30	184	108	338	55	40	.273	.307	.380	.687	91	-41	250	3.88	-6	0-590/1-2,D-1	47	-6.4

• JOURDAN, Ted Theodore Charles Jourdan b: 9/5/1895, New Orleans, LA d: 9/23/1961, New Orleans, LA BL/TL, 6', 175 lbs. Deb: 9/18/1916

YEAR TM-L	G	AB	R	H	2B	3B	HR	RBI	BB	SO	SB	CS	AVG	OBP	SLG	OPS	OPS+	BR/A	RC	RC/G	FR	G/POS	WS	TPW
1916 Chi-A	3	2	0	0	0	0	0	0	1	1	2	....	.000	.333	.000	.333	1	-0	1	7.37	0	....	0	0.0
1917 Chi-A	17	34	2	5	0	1	0	2	1	3	0	....	.147	.171	.206	.377	15	-4	1	.95	0	1-14	0	-0.5
1918 Chi-A	7	10	1	1	0	0	0	1	0	0	0	....	.100	.100	.100	.200	-39	-2	0	.23	0	/1-2	0	-0.2
1920 Chi-A	48	150	16	36	5	2	0	8	17	17	3	2	.240	.337	.300	.637	70	-5	17	3.68	-3	1-40	2	-0.9
Total 4	75	196	19	42	5	3	0	11	19	21	5	2	.214	.300	.270	.570	55	-11	18	3.03	-3	/1-56	2	-1.6

• JOY, Pop Aloysius C. Joy b: 6/11/1860, Washington, DC d: 6/28/1937, Washington, DC Deb: 6/3/1884

YEAR TM-L	G	AB	R	H	2B	3B	HR	RBI	BB	SO	SB	CS	AVG	OBP	SLG	OPS	OPS+	BR/A	RC	RC/G	FR	G/POS	WS	TPW
1884 Was-U	36	130	12	28	0	0	0	....	2	....	....	....	.215	.227	.215	.443	52	-6	7	1.79	-2	1-36	1	-0.9

• JOYCE, George W. Joyce b: 1847, Washington, DC Deb: 8/14/1886

YEAR TM-L	G	AB	R	H	2B	3B	HR	RBI	BB	SO	SB	CS	AVG	OBP	SLG	OPS	OPS+	BR/A	RC	RC/G	FR	G/POS	WS	TPW
1886 Was-N	1	0	0	0	0	0	0	0	0	0	0	....	....	....	....	....	-106	0	0	....	0	/0-1	0	0.0

• JOYCE, Bill William Michael "Scrappy Bill" Joyce b: 9/21/1865, St. Louis, MO d: 5/8/1941, St. Louis, MO BL/TR, 5'11", 185 lbs. Deb: 4/19/1890 M

YEAR TM-L	G	AB	R	H	2B	3B	HR	RBI	BB	SO	SB	CS	AVG	OBP	SLG	OPS	OPS+	BR/A	RC	RC/G	FR	G/POS	WS	TPW
1890 Bro-P	133	489	121	123	18	18	1	78	**123**	77	43	....	.252	.413	.368	.782	103	8	95	6.97	-10	*3-133	18	0.1
1891 Bos-a	65	243	76	75	9	15	3	51	63	27	36	....	.309	.460	.506	.966	179	30	75	11.82	-2	3-64/1-1	17	2.5
1892 Bro-N	97	372	89	91	15	12	6	45	82	55	23	....	.245	.392	.398	.790	144	25	69	6.60	-15	3-94/0-3(3-0-0)	16	1.1
1894 Was-N	99	355	103	126	25	14	17	89	87	33	21	....	.355	.496	.648	1.143	180	52	128	14.48	-4	*3-99	18	3.8
1895 Was-N	127	479	110	149	26	13	17	97	**96**	56	29	....	.311	.440	.526	.966	150	41	127	10.21	-14	*3-126	16	2.3
1896 Was-N	81	310	85	97	16	10	8	51	67	20	32	....	.313	.454	.506	.960	153	29	88	10.94	-10	3-48,2-33	18	1.8
NY-N	49	165	36	61	9	2	5	43	34	14	13	....	.370	.500	.539	1.039	179	23	53	13.13	3	3-49	11	2.3
Yr.	130	475	121	158	25	12	**13**	94	101	34	45	....	.333	.470	.518	.988	162	51	140	11.67	-7	*3-97,2-33	29	4.0
1897 NY-N	109	389	111	118	15	13	3	64	81	....	35	....	.303	.444	.432	.875	135	27	92	8.82	-6	*3-106/1-2	18	1.9
1898 NY-N	145	508	91	131	20	9	10	91	88	....	34	....	.258	.386	.392	.778	127	23	93	6.44	2	*1-130,3-14/2-2	25	2.3
Total 8	905	3310	822	971	153	106	70	609	721	282	266	....	.293	.435	.467	.902	144	258	818	9.23	-56	3-733,1-133/2-35,0-3	157	18.1

• JOYNER, Wally Wallace Keith Joyner b: 6/16/1962, Atlanta, GA BL/TL, 6'2", 203 lbs. Deb: 4/8/1986

YEAR TM-L	G	AB	R	H	2B	3B	HR	RBI	BB	SO	SB	CS	AVG	OBP	SLG	OPS	OPS+	BR/A	RC	RC/G	FR	G/POS	WS	TPW
1986*Cal-A★	154	593	82	172	27	3	22	100	57	58	5	2	.290	.354	.457	.811	120	17	96	5.71	4	*1-152	21	1.2
1987 Cal-A	149	564	100	161	33	1	34	117	72	64	8	2	.285	.371	.528	.900	140	33	111	6.93	1	*1-149	22	2.4
1988 Cal-A	158	597	81	176	31	2	13	85	55	51	8	2	.295	.359	.419	.778	120	17	89	5.37	8	*1-156	22	1.4
1989 Cal-A	159	593	78	167	30	2	16	79	46	58	3	2	.282	.340	.420	.759	115	10	82	4.93	-2	*1-159	19	-0.3
1990 Cal-A	83	310	35	83	15	0	8	41	41	34	2	1	.268	.355	.394	.749	111	6	43	4.79	0	1-83	9	0.0
1991 Cal-A	143	551	79	166	34	3	21	96	52	66	2	0	.301	.363	.488	.851	133	25	98	6.53	-1	*1-141	25	1.4
1992 KC-A	149	572	66	154	36	2	9	66	55	50	11	5	.269	.338	.386	.724	100	0	72	4.40	12	*1-145/D-4	14	0.2
1993 KC-A	141	497	83	145	36	3	15	65	66	67	5	9	.292	.378	.467	.845	119	12	88	6.34	15	*1-140	17	1.4
1994 KC-A	97	363	52	113	20	3	8	57	47	43	3	2	.311	.390	.449	.839	111	7	63	6.27	5	1-86,D-11	11	0.3
1995 KC-A	131	465	69	144	28	0	12	83	69	65	3	2	.310	.401	.447	.848	119	15	86	6.68	10	*1-126/D-2	18	1.3
1996*SD-N	121	433	59	120	29	1	8	65	69	71	5	3	.277	.380	.404	.784	114	11	71	5.84	2	*1-119	16	0.2
1997 SD-N	135	455	59	149	29	2	13	83	51	51	3	5	.327	.398	.486	.883	142	26	85	6.84	-3	*1-131	21	1.3
1998*SD-N	131	439	58	131	30	1	12	80	51	44	1	2	.298	.373	.453	.826	125	15	73	6.09	-2	*1-127	22	0.2
1999 SD-N	110	323	34	80	14	2	5	43	58	54	0	1	.248	.366	.350	.715	89	-4	44	4.62	2	*1-105/D-1	7	-0.9
2000*Atl-N	119	224	24	63	12	0	5	32	31	31	0	0	.281	.371	.402	.773	95	-1	36	5.76	2	1-55/D-7	7	-0.3
2001 Ana-A	53	148	14	36	5	1	3	14	13	18	1	1	.243	.304	.351	.656	71	-7	16	3.64	0	1-39/D-9	2	-1.0
Total 16	2033	7127	973	2060	409	26	204	1106	833	825	60	39	.289	.366	.440	.806	118	183	1151	5.77	52	*1-1913/D-34	253	8.8

YEAR TM-L	G	AB	R	H	2B	3B	HR	RBI	BB	SO	SB	CS	AVG	OBP	SLG	OPS	OPS+	BR/A	RC	RC/G	FR	G/POS	WS	TPW

• JUDE, Frank　　Frank Jude　b: 1884, Libby, MN　d: 5/4/1961, Brownsville, TX　BR/TR, 5'7", 150 lbs.　Deb: 7/9/1906

| 1906 Cin-N | 80 | 308 | 31 | 64 | 6 | 4 | 1 | 31 | 16 | .... | 7 | .... | .208 | .261 | .263 | .524 | 61 | -15 | 24 | 2.52 | -3 | 0-80(0-0-80) | 3 | -2.3 |

• JUDGE, Joe　　Joseph Ignatius Judge　b: 5/25/1894, Brooklyn, NY　d: 3/11/1963, Washington, DC　BL/TL, 5'8.5", 155 lbs.　Deb: 9/20/1915　C

1915 Was-A	12	41	7	17	2	0	0	9	4	6	2	3	.415	.500	.463	.963	185	4	10	8.46	-1	1-10/0-2(0-0-2)	3	0.3
1916 Was-A	103	336	42	74	10	8	0	28	54	44	18	....	.220	.333	.298	.631	90	-2	40	3.83	-1	*1-103	8	-0.5
1917 Was-A	102	393	62	112	15	15	2	30	50	40	17	....	.285	.369	.415	.783	141	19	63	5.73	-4	*1-100	19	1.5
1918 Was-A	130	502	56	131	23	7	1	46	49	32	20	....	.261	.332	.341	.672	105	2	63	4.04	-2	*1-130	13	-0.2
1919 Was-A	135	521	83	150	33	12	2	31	81	35	23	....	.288	.386	.409	.795	124	20	87	5.98	-4	*1-133	17	1.3
1920 Was-A	126	493	103	164	19	15	5	51	65	34	12	12	.333	.416	.462	.878	136	27	96	7.17	-3	*1-124	22	2.1
1921 Was-A	153	622	87	187	26	11	7	72	68	35	21	6	.301	.372	.422	.784	105	9	100	5.74	-11	*1-152	19	-1.1
1922 Was-A	148	591	84	174	32	15	10	81	50	20	5	15	.294	.355	.450	.806	114	6	91	5.39	-13	*1-147	18	-1.6
1923 Was-A	113	405	56	127	24	6	2	63	58	20	11	7	.314	.406	.417	.823	123	17	72	6.33	-2	*1-112	17	0.7
1924*Was-A	140	516	71	167	38	9	3	79	53	21	13	8	.324	.393	.450	.843	121	17	93	6.55	2	*1-140	19	0.9
1925*Was-A	112	376	65	118	31	5	8	66	55	21	7	12	.314	.406	.487	.892	128	14	73	6.94	-1	*1-109	15	0.6
1926 Was-A	134	453	70	132	25	11	7	92	53	25	7	5	.291	.367	.442	.808	113	8	75	5.69	8	*1-128	16	0.7
1927 Was-A	137	522	68	161	29	11	2	71	45	22	10	5	.308	.366	.418	.783	104	4	81	5.54	-8	*1-136	16	-1.2
1928 Was-A	153	542	78	166	31	10	3	93	80	19	16	4	.306	.396	.417	.813	115	17	96	6.34	-4	*1-149	17	0.3
1929 Was-A	143	543	83	171	35	8	6	71	73	33	12	5	.315	.397	.442	.839	115	16	100	6.64	1	*1-142	20	0.8
1930 Was-A	126	442	83	144	29	11	10	80	60	29	13	6	.326	.410	.509	.919	131	23	95	8.00	-0	*1-117	18	1.4
1931 Was-A	35	74	11	21	3	0	0	9	8	8	0	0	.284	.354	.324	.678	79	-2	9	4.33	1	1-15	2	-0.1
1932 Was-A	82	291	45	75	16	3	3	29	37	19	3	3	.258	.354	.364	.708	84	-6	38	4.53	1	1-78	7	-1.1
1933 Bro-N	42	112	7	24	2	1	0	9	7	10	1	....	.214	.261	.250	.511	48	-7	7	2.12	1	1-29	0	-1.0
Bos-N	35	108	20	32	8	1	0	22	13	4	2	1	.296	.372	.389	.761	103	1	16	5.31	0	1-29	3	-0.1
1934 Bos-A	10	15	3	5	2	0	0	2	2	1	0	0	.333	.412	.467	.878	118	0	3	7.23	-0	/1-2	1	0.0
Total 20	2171	7898	1184	2352	433	159	71	1034	965	478	213	92	.298	.378	.420	.798	115	187	1308	5.85	-39	*1-2084/0-2	270	3.6

• JUDNICH, Wally　　Walter Franklin Judnich　b: 1/24/1916, San Francisco, CA　d: 7/10/1971, Glendale, CA　BL/TL, 6'1", 205 lbs.　Deb: 4/16/1940　Career OF: 6-583-16

1940 StL-A	137	519	97	157	27	7	24	89	54	71	8	5	.303	.368	.520	.888	125	18	102	7.32	-2	*0-133(0-133-0)	20	1.2
1941 StL-A	146	546	90	155	40	6	14	83	80	45	5	5	.284	.377	.454	.833	116	13	98	6.42	-2	*0-140(0-140-0)	17	0.7
1942 StL-A	132	457	78	143	22	6	17	82	74	41	3	2	.313	.413	.499	.912	153	35	101	8.25	-7	*0-122(0-122-0)	25	2.6
1946 StL-A	142	511	60	134	23	4	15	72	60	54	0	4	.262	.340	.411	.751	104	1	74	5.09	1	*0-137(6-131-1)	18	-0.2
1947 StL-A	144	500	58	129	24	3	18	64	60	62	2	5	.258	.338	.426	.764	109	4	75	5.23	-11	*1-129,0-15(0-14-1)	13	-1.2
1948*Cle-A	79	218	36	56	13	3	2	29	56	23	1	0	.257	.411	.372	.782	112	6	38	5.85	0	0-49(0-35-14),1-20	8	0.5
1949 Pit-N	10	35	5	8	1	0	1	1	1	2	0	....	.229	.250	.257	.507	35	-3	2	2.32	0	/0-8(0-8-0)	0	-0.3
Total 7	790	2786	424	782	150	29	90	420	385	298	20	24	.281	.369	.452	.822	119	74	491	6.30	-21	0-604,1-149	101	3.2

• JUDY, Lyle　　Lyle Leroy "Punch" Judy　b: 11/15/1913, Lawrenceville, IL　d: 1/15/1991, Ormond Beach, FL　BR/TR, 5'10", 150 lbs.　Deb: 9/17/1935

| 1935 StL-N | 8 | 11 | 2 | 0 | 0 | 0 | 0 | 0 | 2 | 2 | 2 | 1 | .000 | .154 | .000 | .154 | -53 | -2 | 0 | .00 | 0 | /2-5 | 0 | -0.2 |

• JUELICH, Red　　John Samuel Juelich　b: 9/20/1916, St. Louis, MO　d: 12/25/1970, St. Louis, MO　BR/TR, 5'11.5", 170 lbs.　Deb: 5/30/1939

| 1939 Pit-N | 17 | 46 | 5 | 11 | 0 | 2 | 0 | 4 | 2 | 4 | 0 | .... | .239 | .271 | .326 | .597 | 61 | -3 | 3 | 1.96 | -2 | 2-10/3-2 | 0 | -0.4 |

• JUMONVILLE, George　　George Benedict Jumonville　b: 5/16/1917, Mobile, AL　d: 12/12/1996, Mobile, AL　BR/TR, 6', 175 lbs.　Deb: 9/13/1940

1940 Phi-N	11	34	0	3	0	0	0	0	1	6	0	....	.088	.139	.088	.227	-38	-6	0	.43	-1	S-10/3-1	0	-0.7
1941 Phi-N	6	7	1	3	0	0	1	2	0	0	0	....	.429	.429	.857	1.286	266	1	3	17.36	-0	/2-1,S-1	1	0.1
Total 2	17	41	1	6	0	0	1	2	1	6	0	....	.146	.186	.220	.406	12	-5	3	2.36	-1	/S-11,2-1,3-1	1	-0.5

• JURAK, Ed　　Edward James Jurak　b: 10/24/1957, Hollywood, CA　BR/TR, 6'2", 185 lbs.　Deb: 6/30/1982　Career OF: 2-1-1

1982 Bos-A	12	21	3	7	0	0	0	7	2	4	0	0	.333	.391	.333	.725	96	-0	3	5.43	-2	3-11/0-1	1	-0.2
1983 Bos-A	75	159	19	44	8	4	0	18	18	25	1	2	.277	.354	.377	.731	95	-1	21	4.53	4	S-38,1-19,3-12/D-5,2-1	5	0.3
1984 Bos-A	47	66	6	16	3	1	1	7	12	12	0	2	.242	.359	.364	.723	96	-1	4	4.37	-1	1-19,2-14/3-9,S-2	2	-0.2
1985 Bos-A	26	13	4	3	0	0	0	1	3	0	0	0	.231	.286	.231	.516	42	-1	1	1.71	-1	/3-7,S-3,D-2,1-1,0-1	0	-0.2
1988 Oak-A	3	1	1	0	0	0	0	0	0	0	0	0	.000	.000	.000	.000	-104	-0	0	.00	0	/3-1,D-1	0	-0.1
1989 SF-N	30	42	2	10	0	0	0	1	5	5	0	0	.238	.319	.238	.557	63	-2	3	2.74	-2	/S-6,3-5,2-4,0-2(1-0-1),1-1	1	-0.4
Total 6	193	302	35	80	11	5	1	33	38	49	1	4	.265	.349	.344	.693	88	-5	37	4.15	-3	/S-49,3-45,1-40,2-19,D-8,0-4	9	-0.8

• JURGES, Billy　　William Frederick Jurges　b: 5/9/1908, Bronx, NY　d: 3/3/1997, Clearwater, FL　BR/TR, 5'11", 175 lbs.　Deb: 5/4/1931　M/C

1931 Chi-N	88	293	34	59	15	5	0	23	25	41	1	....	.201	.264	.287	.551	47	-22	24	2.50	4	3-54,2-33/S-3	3	-1.4
1932*Chi-N	115	396	40	100	24	4	2	52	19	26	1	....	.253	.288	.348	.637	71	-17	41	3.45	22	*S-108/3-5	12	1.3
1933 Chi-N	143	487	49	131	17	6	5	50	26	39	3	....	.269	.313	.359	.672	92	-6	52	3.67	16	*S-143	18	2.2
1934 Chi-N	100	358	43	88	15	2	8	33	19	34	1	....	.246	.289	.366	.655	76	-13	37	3.51	11	S-98	7	0.5
1935*Chi-N	146	519	69	125	33	1	1	59	42	39	1	....	.241	.304	.314	.618	66	-24	50	3.18	24	*S-146	14	1.0
1936 Chi-N	118	429	51	120	25	1	1	42	23	25	4	....	.280	.321	.350	.671	79	-13	46	3.78	16	*S-116	13	1.1
1937 Chi-N★	129	450	53	134	18	10	1	65	42	41	2	....	.298	.365	.389	.754	101	2	66	5.29	-10	*S-128	16	0.2
1938*Chi-N	137	465	53	114	18	3	1	47	58	53	3	....	.245	.335	.303	.638	75	-14	48	3.36	-7	*S-136	11	-1.1
1939 NY-N★	138	543	84	155	21	11	6	63	47	34	3	....	.285	.349	.398	.747	99	-0	71	4.45	1	*S-137	17	1.1
1940 NY-N★	63	214	23	54	3	3	2	36	25	14	2	....	.252	.347	.322	.669	85	-3	23	3.64	0	S-63	5	0.1
1941 NY-N	134	471	50	138	25	2	5	61	47	36	0	....	.293	.361	.386	.747	108	6	66	5.04	0	*S-134	18	1.7
1942 NY-N	127	464	45	119	7	1	2	30	43	42	1	....	.256	.324	.289	.612	79	-11	42	3.03	2	*S-124	11	0.0
1943 NY-N	136	481	46	110	8	2	4	29	53	38	2	....	.229	.310	.279	.589	70	-17	44	3.03	-9	S-99,3-28	8	-1.9
1944 NY-N	85	246	28	52	2	1	1	23	23	20	1	....	.211	.279	.240	.519	47	-17	17	2.14	7	3-61,S-10/2-1	2	-0.8
1945 NY-N	61	176	22	57	3	1	3	24	24	11	2	....	.324	.405	.403	.808	123	7	30	6.62	-2	3-44/S-8	8	0.6
1946 Chi-N	82	221	26	49	9	2	0	17	43	28	1	....	.222	.351	.281	.631	82	-3	24	3.49	1	S-73/3-7,2-2	6	0.2
1947 Chi-N	14	40	5	8	2	0	1	2	4	1	0	....	.200	.347	.325	.672	83	-1	5	4.49	0	S-14	1	0.0
Total 17	1816	6253	721	1613	245	55	43	656	568	530	36	....	.258	.325	.350	.660	82	-147	686	3.71	79	*S-1540,3-199/2-36	170	4.8

• JUST, Joe　　Joseph Erwin Just　b: 1/8/1916, Milwaukee, WI　BR/TR, 5'11", 185 lbs.　Deb: 5/13/1944

1944 Cin-N	11	11	0	2	0	0	0	0	0	2	0	....	.182	.250	.182	.432	24	-1	0	1.02	-1	C-10	0	-0.2
1945 Cin-N	14	34	2	5	0	0	0	2	4	7	0	....	.147	.237	.147	.384	8	-4	1	1.19	0	C-14	0	-0.4
Total 2	25	45	2	7	0	0	0	2	4	9	0	....	.156	.240	.156	.396	12	-5	2	1.15	-1	/C-24	0	-0.5

• JUSTICE, David　　David Christopher Justice　b: 4/14/1966, Cincinnati, OH　BL/TL, 6'3", 200 lbs.　Deb: 5/24/1989　Career OF: 312-3-842

1989 Atl-N	16	51	7	12	3	0	1	3	3	9	2	1	.235	.291	.353	.644	81	-1	5	3.27	0	0-16(3-0-13)	0	-0.2
1990 Atl-N	127	439	76	124	23	2	28	78	64	92	11	6	.282	.374	.535	.909	139	23	92	7.64	-6	1-69,0-61(0-0-60)	20	1.1
1991*Atl-N	109	396	67	109	25	1	21	87	65	81	8	8	.275	.381	.503	.884	138	20	78	6.91	1	*0-106(0-0-106)	22	1.8
1992*Atl-N	144	484	78	124	19	5	21	72	79	85	2	4	.256	.363	.446	.809	121	14	84	6.10	6	*0-140(0-0-140)	23	1.8
1993*Atl-N★	157	585	90	158	15	4	40	120	78	90	3	5	.270	.359	.515	.873	129	22	108	6.57	4	*0-157(0-0-157)	29	1.8
1994 Atl-N★	104	352	61	110	16	2	19	59	69	45	2	4	.313	.428	.531	.959	145	25	82	8.68	0	*0-102(0-0-102)	19	1.9
1995*Atl-N	120	411	73	104	17	2	24	78	73	68	4	2	.253	.368	.479	.848	118	12	77	6.52	3	*0-120(0-0-120)	19	0.8
1996 Atl-N	40	140	23	45	9	0	6	25	21	22	1	1	.321	.414	.514	.928	135	8	29	7.70	5	0-40(0-0-40)	7	1.0
1997*Cle-A★	139	495	84	163	31	1	33	101	80	79	3	5	.329	.423	.596	1.019	156	42	124	9.37	-2	0-78(74-0-5),D-61	26	3.2
1998*Cle-A	146	540	94	151	39	2	21	88	76	98	9	3	.280	.369	.476	.844	114	12	98	6.44	0	*D-123,0-21(19-0-2)	13	0.4
1999*Cle-A	133	429	75	123	18	0	21	88	94	90	1	1	.287	.417	.476	.893	121	17	87	7.19	0	0-94(79-0-15),D-36	16	1.0
2000 Cle-A	68	249	46	66	14	1	21	58	38	49	1	1	.265	.362	.582	.945	131	11	52	7.28	0	0-47(25-2-23),D-20	9	0.6
*NY-A	78	275	43	84	17	0	20	60	39	42	1	0	.305	.391	.585	.976	145	19	64	8.72	4	0-60(43-1-25),D-18	11	1.7
Yr.	146	524	89	150	31	1	41	118	77	91	2	1	.286	.384	.584	.963	138	30	116	8.02	3	0-107(68-3-48),D-38	20	2.4
2001*NY-A	111	381	58	92	16	1	18	51	54	83	1	1	.241	.336	.430	.766	99	-1	56	5.06	4	D-85,0-25(16-0-11)	8	-0.3
2002 Oak-A	118	398	54	106	18	3	11	49	70	66	4	1	.266	.377	.410	.787	109	8	64	5.63	0	0-75(53-0-23),D-36	11	0.3
Total 14	1610	5625	929	1571	280	24	305	1017	903	999	53	46	.279	.381	.500	.881	127	231	1100	6.98	19	*0-1142,D-379/1-69	233	16.9

YEAR TM-L	G	AB	R	H	2B	3B	HR	RBI	BB	SO	SB	CS	AVG	OBP	SLG	OPS	OPS+	BR/A	RC	RC/G	FR	G/POS	WS	TPW
• JUTZE, Skip	Alfred Henry Jutze b: 5/28/1946, Bayside, NY BR/TR, 5'11", 195 lbs. Deb: 9/1/1972																							
1972 StL-N	21	71	1	17	2	0	0	5	1	16	0	1	.239	.250	.268	.518	48	-5	4	1.89	1	C-17	1	-0.4
1973 Hou-N	90	278	18	62	6	0	0	18	19	37	0	1	.223	.275	.245	.520	45	-21	17	1.88	-4	C-86	2	-2.2
1974 Hou-N	8	13	0	3	0	0	0	1	1	1	0	0	.231	.286	.231	.516	48	-1	1	1.04	0	/C-7	0	-0.1
1975 Hou-N	51	93	9	21	2	0	0	6	2	4	1	0	.226	.242	.247	.489	39	-8	6	2.04	1	C-47	1	-0.6
1976 Hou-N	42	92	7	14	2	3	0	6	4	16	0	0	.152	.188	.239	.427	22	-10	4	1.30	1	C-42	1	-0.7
1977 Sea-A	42	109	10	24	2	0	3	15	7	12	0	4	.220	.267	.321	.588	60	-8	8	2.20	-1	C-40	1	-0.7
Total 6	**254**	**656**	**45**	**141**	**14**	**3**	**3**	**51**	**34**	**86**	**1**	**6**	**.215**	**.255**	**.259**	**.514**	**44**	**-52**	**39**	**1.85**	**-1**	**C-239**	**6**	**-4.6**
• KADING, Jack	John Frederick Kading b: 11/27/1884, Waukesha, WI d: 6/2/1964, Chicago, IL BR/TR, 6'3", 190 lbs. Deb: 9/12/1910																							
1910 Pit-N	8	23	5	7	2	1	0	4	4	5	0	....	.304	.407	.478	.886	149	2	5	6.71	1	/1-8	1	0.3
1914 Chi-F	3	3	0	0	0	0	0	0	0	0	0	....	.000	.000	.000	.000	-106	-1	0	.00	0		0	-0.1
Total 2	**11**	**26**	**5**	**7**	**2**	**1**	**0**	**4**	**4**	**5**	**0**	**....**	**.269**	**.367**	**.423**	**.790**	**125**	**1**	**5**	**5.75**	**1**	**/1-8**	**1**	**0.2**
• KAFORA, Jake	Frank Jacob "Tomatoes" Kafora b: 10/16/1888, Chicago, IL d: 3/23/1928, Chicago, IL BR/TR, 6', 180 lbs. Deb: 10/5/1913																							
1913 Pit-N	1	1	1	0	0	0	0	0	0	1	0	....	.000	.500	.000	.500	52	0	0	.00	0	/C-1	0	0.0
1914 Pit-N	21	23	2	3	0	0	0	0	0	6	0	....	.130	.200	.130	.330	-1	-3	1	.71	-1	C-17	0	-0.3
Total 2	**22**	**24**	**3**	**3**	**0**	**0**	**0**	**0**	**0**	**7**	**0**	**....**	**.125**	**.222**	**.125**	**.347**	**3**	**-3**	**1**	**.67**	**-1**	**/C-18**	**0**	**-0.4**
• KAHDOT, Ike	Isaac Leonard "Chief" Kahdot b: 10/22/1901, Georgetown, OK d: 3/31/1999, Oklahoma City, OK BR/TR, 5'5.5", 145 lbs. Deb: 9/5/1922																							
1922 Cle-A	4	2	0	0	0	0	0	0	0	1	0	0	.000	.000	.000	.000	-99	-1	0	.00	-0	/3-2	0	-0.1
• KAHL, Nick	Nicholas Alexander Kahl b: 4/10/1879, Coulterville, IL d: 7/13/1959, Sparta, IL BR/TR, 5'9", 185 lbs. Deb: 5/2/1905																							
1905 Cle-A	40	135	16	29	4	1	0	21	4	....	1	....	.215	.248	.259	.507	60	-6	9	2.30	-2	2-32/O-1,S-1	1	-0.9
• KAHLE, Bob	Robert Wayne Kahle b: 11/23/1915, New Castle, IN d: 12/16/1988, Inglewood, CA BR/TR, 6', 170 lbs. Deb: 4/21/1938																							
1938 Bos-N	8	3	2	1	0	0	0	0	0	0	0	....	.333	.333	.333	.667	93	-0	0	4.61	0	....	0	0.0
• KAHN, Owen	Owen Earle "Jack" Kahn b: 6/5/1905, Richmond, VA d: 1/17/1981, Richmond, VA BR/TR, 5'11", 160 lbs. Deb: 5/24/1930																							
1930 Bos-N	1	0	1	0	0	0	0	0	0	0	0	....	....	....	....	....	-103	0	0	....	0	....	0	0.0
• KAHOE, Mike	Michael Joseph Kahoe b: 9/3/1873, Yellow Springs, OH d: 5/14/1949, Akron, OH BR/TR, 6', 185 lbs. Deb: 9/22/1895 U																							
1895 Cin-N	3	4	0	0	0	0	0	0	0	0	0	....	.000	.000	.000	.000	-96	-1	0	.00	0	/C-3	0	-0.1
1899 Cin-N	14	42	2	7	1	1	0	4	0	....	1	....	.167	.167	.238	.405	10	-5	2	1.46	0	C-13	1	-0.4
1900 Cin-N	52	175	18	33	3	3	1	9	4	....	3	....	.189	.215	.257	.473	31	-17	11	1.99	2	C-51/S-1	3	-0.9
1901 Cin-N	4	13	0	4	0	0	0	0	1	....	0	....	.308	.357	.308	.665	100	0	1	4.31	0	/C-4	1	0.0
Chi-N	67	237	21	53	12	2	1	21	8	....	5	....	.224	.249	.304	.553	62	-12	20	2.83	3	C-63/1-6	3	-0.3
Yr.	71	250	21	57	12	2	1	21	9	....	5	....	.228	.255	.304	.559	64	-12	22	2.89	3	C-67/1-6	4	-0.3
1902 Chi-N	7	18	0	4	1	0	0	2	0	....	0	....	.222	.222	.278	.500	56	-1	1	2.19	-2	/C-4,3-2,S-1	0	-0.2
StL-A	55	197	21	48	9	2	2	28	6	....	4	....	.244	.270	.340	.610	69	-9	20	3.47	-2	C-53	4	-0.5
1903 StL-A	77	244	26	46	7	5	0	23	11	....	1	....	.189	.227	.258	.485	46	-16	16	2.02	-1	C-71/O-2(0-1-1)	4	-1.1
1904 StL-A	72	236	9	51	6	1	0	12	8	....	4	....	.216	.242	.250	.492	59	-11	17	2.27	1	C-69	4	-0.3
1905 Phi-N	16	51	2	13	2	0	0	4	1	....	1	....	.255	.269	.294	.563	70	-2	5	3.02	2	C-15	1	0.1
1907 Chi-N	5	10	0	4	0	0	0	1	0	....	0	....	.400	.400	.400	.800	142	0	2	7.11	0	/C-3,1-1	0	0.0
Was-A	17	47	3	9	1	0	0	1	0	....	0	....	.191	.191	.213	.404	31	-4	2	1.37	0	C-15	0	-0.3
1908 Was-A	17	27	1	5	1	0	0	0	0	....	0	....	.185	.185	.222	.407	35	-2	1	1.20	-1	C-11	0	-0.2
1909 Was-A	4	8	0	1	0	0	0	0	0	....	2	....	.125	.125	.125	.250	-22	-1	0	1.20	0	/C-3	0	-0.1
Total 11	**410**	**1309**	**103**	**278**	**43**	**14**	**4**	**105**	**39**	**0**	**21**	**....**	**.212**	**.237**	**.276**	**.513**	**53**	**-81**	**98**	**2.43**	**0**	**C-378/1-7,3-2,O-2,S-2**	**21**	**-4.4**
• KAISER, Al	Alfred Edward "Deerfoot" Kaiser b: 8/3/1886, Cincinnati, OH d: 4/11/1969, Cincinnati, OH BR/TR, 5'9", 165 lbs. Deb: 4/18/1911 Career OF: 80-52-2																							
1911 Chi-N	26	84	16	21	0	5	0	7	7	12	6	....	.250	.308	.369	.677	89	-2	11	4.43	-2	O-22(1-21-0)	2	-0.5
Bos-N	66	197	20	40	5	2	2	15	10	26	4	....	.203	.249	.279	.528	44	-16	15	2.32	-3	O-58(35-21-2)	0	-2.1
Yr.	92	281	36	61	5	7	2	22	17	38	10	....	.217	.267	.306	.573	58	-18	26	2.92	-4	O-80(36-42-2)	2	-2.6
1912 Bos-N	4	13	0	0	0	0	0	0	0	3	0	....	.000	.000	.000	.000	-98	-4	0	.00	0	/O-4(4-0-0)	0	-0.4
1914 Ind-F	59	187	22	43	10	0	1	16	17	41	6	....	.230	.301	.299	.600	64	-9	19	3.10	-4	O-50(40-10-0)/1-1	3	-1.6
Total 3	**155**	**481**	**58**	**104**	**15**	**7**	**3**	**38**	**34**	**82**	**16**	**....**	**.216**	**.274**	**.295**	**.569**	**56**	**-30**	**45**	**2.89**	**-8**	**O-134/1-1**	**5**	**-4.5**
• KALAHAN, John	John Joseph Kalahan b: 9/30/1878, Philadelphia, PA d: 6/20/1952, Philadelphia, PA BR/TR, 6', 165 lbs. Deb: 9/29/1903																							
1903 Phi-A	1	5	0	0	0	0	0	0	0	....	0	....	.000	.000	.000	.000	-96	-1	0	.00	0	/C-1	0	-0.1
• KALBFUS, Charlie	Charles Henry "Skinny" Kalbfus b: 12/28/1864, Washington, DC d: 11/18/1941, Washington, DC BR/TR, 5'11", 145 lbs. Deb: 4/18/1884																							
1884 Was-U	1	5	1	1	0	0	0	....	0	....	....	....	.200	.200	.200	.400	37	-0	0	1.44	0	/O-1	0	-0.1
• KALIN, Frank	Frank Bruno "Fats" Kalin b: 10/3/1917, Steubenville, OH d: 1/12/1975, Weirton, WV BR/TR, 6', 200 lbs. Deb: 9/25/1940																							
1940 Pit-N	3	3	0	0	0	0	0	1	2	0	0	....	.000	.400	.000	.400	19	-0	0	.70	0	/O-2(1-0-1)	0	-0.1
1943 Chi-A	4	4	0	0	0	0	0	0	0	0	0	0	.000	.000	.000	.000	-100	-1	0	.00	0	....	0	-0.1
Total 2	**7**	**7**	**0**	**0**	**0**	**0**	**0**	**1**	**2**	**0**	**0**	**0**	**.000**	**.222**	**.000**	**.222**	**-34**	**-1**	**0**	**.31**	**0**	**/O-2**	**0**	**-0.2**
• KALINE, Al	Albert William Kaline b: 12/19/1934, Baltimore, MD BR/TR, 6'1.5", 180 lbs. Deb: 6/25/1953 HOF: 1980 Career OF: 16-484-2040																							
1953 Det-A	30	28	9	7	0	0	1	2	1	5	1	0	.250	.300	.357	.657	78	-1	3	3.69	-1	O-20(5-11-4)	1	-0.2
1954 Det-A	138	504	42	139	18	3	4	43	22	45	9	5	.276	.306	.347	.653	80	-15	48	3.24	8	*O-135(0-0-135)	7	-1.2
1955 Det-A★	152	588	121	**200**	24	8	27	102	82	57	6	8	**.340**	.425	.546	.971	163	52	135	8.81	1	*O-152(0-0-152)	31	4.7
1956 Det-A★	153	617	96	194	32	10	27	128	70	55	7	1	.314	.385	.530	.915	139	35	129	7.90	9	*O-153(1-12-142)	26	3.7
1957 Det-A★	149	577	83	170	29	4	23	90	43	38	11	9	.295	.347	.478	.825	120	13	92	5.69	3	*O-145(5-21-137)	20	1.1
1958 Det-A★	146	543	84	170	34	7	16	85	54	47	7	4	.313	.377	.490	.867	127	21	96	6.46	17	*O-145(0-0-145)	23	3.4
1959 Det-A★	136	511	86	167	19	2	27	94	72	42	10	4	.327	.414	**.530**	**.944**	149	37	114	**8.37**	-3	*O-136(0-122-15)	27	2.8
1960 Det-A★	147	551	77	153	29	4	15	68	65	47	19	4	.278	.357	.426	.784	104	7	84	5.30	-3	*O-142(0-142-0)	17	-0.4
1961 Det-A★	153	586	116	190	**41**	7	19	82	66	42	14	1	.324	.396	.515	.912	137	34	121	7.75	3	*O-147(1-22-141)/3-1	29	2.6
1962 Det-A★	100	398	78	121	16	6	29	94	47	39	4	0	.304	.379	.593	.972	152	29	85	7.65	2	*O-100(0-0-100)	19	2.4
1963 Det-A★	145	551	89	172	24	3	27	101	54	48	6	4	.312	.378	.514	.891	142	31	105	7.04	-5	*O-140(0-2-140)	25	1.8
1964 Det-A★	146	525	77	154	31	5	17	68	75	51	4	1	.293	.385	.469	.853	134	27	97	6.74	5	*O-136(0-0-136)	24	2.3
1965 Det-A★	125	399	72	112	18	2	18	72	72	49	6	0	.281	.391	.471	.862	142	26	77	6.95	-5	*O-112(0-62-51)/3-1	20	1.7
1966 Det-A★	142	479	85	138	29	1	29	88	81	66	5	5	.288	.396	.534	.931	161	40	105	7.86	5	*O-136(0-86-53)	31	4.2
1967 Det-A★	131	458	94	141	28	2	25	78	83	47	8	2	.308	.415	.541	.957	176	48	104	8.16	5	*O-130(0-1-130)	30	4.8
1968*Det-A	102	327	49	94	14	1	10	53	55	39	6	4	.287	.395	.428	.823	145	20	59	6.46	0	O-74(4-0-75),1-22	18	1.7
1969 Det-A	131	456	74	124	17	0	21	69	54	61	1	2	.272	.350	.447	.798	117	9	71	5.44	-2	*O-118(0-0-118)/1-9	17	0.1
1970 Det-A	131	467	64	130	24	4	16	71	77	49	2	2	.278	.382	.450	.831	127	20	79	5.77	-1	O-91(0-0-91),1-52	19	1.1
1971 Det-A★	133	405	69	119	19	2	15	54	82	57	4	6	.294	.421	.462	.883	144	27	81	7.03	-3	*O-129(0-3-128)/1-5	22	2.0
1972*Det-A	106	278	46	87	11	2	10	32	28	33	1	0	.313	.380	.475	.855	148	17	48	6.23	-3	O-84(0-0-84),1-11	14	1.1
1973 Det-A	91	310	40	79	13	0	10	45	29	28	4	1	.255	.325	.394	.718	95	-1	39	4.22	-4	O-63(0-0-63),1-36	8	-1.0
1974 Det-A★	147	558	71	146	28	2	13	64	65	75	2	2	.262	.340	.389	.729	105	5	75	4.67	0	*D-146	15	0.0
Total 22	**2834**	**10116**	**1622**	**3007**	**498**	**75**	**399**	**1583**	**1277**	**1020**	**137**	**65**	**.297**	**.379**	**.480**	**.859**	**134**	**480**	**1846**	**6.56**	**27**	***O-2488,D-146,1-135/3-2**	**443**	**38.8**
• KAMM, Willie	William Edward Kamm b: 2/2/1900, San Francisco, CA d: 12/21/1988, Belmont, CA BR/TR, 5'10.5", 170 lbs. Deb: 4/18/1923																							
1923 Chi-A	149	544	57	159	39	9	6	87	62	82	18	13	.292	.366	.430	.796	110	7	86	5.48	9	*3-149	20	2.5
1924 Chi-A	147	528	58	134	28	6	6	93	64	59	10	9	.254	.337	.364	.700	83	-14	68	4.11	6	*3-146	14	0.1
1925 Chi-A	152	509	82	142	32	4	6	83	**90**	36	11	13	.279	.391	.393	.784	105	6	83	5.29	-1	*3-152	19	1.4
1926 Chi-A	143	480	63	141	24	10	0	62	77	24	12	4	.294	.396	.385	.781	108	11	80	5.89	18	*3-142	22	3.7
1927 Chi-A	148	540	85	146	32	13	0	59	70	18	8	9	.270	.354	.378	.732	92	-7	75	4.63	7	*3-146	15	1.0
1928 Chi-A	155	552	70	170	30	12	1	84	73	22	17	9	.308	.391	.411	.802	112	13	93	5.89	0	*3-155	24	2.2
1929 Chi-A	147	523	72	140	33	6	3	63	75	23	12	5	.268	.363	.371	.734	90	-4	76	4.95	3	*3-145	16	0.8

YEAR TM-L	G	AB	R	H	2B	3B	HR	RBI	BB	SO	SB	CS	AVG	OBP	SLG	OPS	OPS+	BR/A	RC	RC/G	FR	G/POS	WS	TPW
1930 Chi-A	112	331	49	89	21	6	3	47	51	20	5	4	.269	.368	.396	.764	97	-0	51	5.22	7	*3-106	10	1.2
1931 Chi-A	18	59	9	15	4	1	0	9	7	6	1	1	.254	.333	.356	.689	86	-1	7	4.14	0	3-18	1	0.0
Cle-A	114	410	68	121	31	4	0	66	64	13	13	9	.295	.392	.390	.782	100	4	66	5.68	-8	*3-114	13	0.0
Yr.	132	469	77	136	35	5	0	75	71	19	14	10	.290	.384	.386	.770	99	3	73	5.48	-8	*3-132	14	0.0
1932 Cle-A	148	524	76	150	34	9	3	83	75	36	6	3	.286	.379	.403	.781	96	-0	85	5.76	8	*3-148	21	1.2
1933 Cle-A	133	447	59	126	17	2	1	47	54	27	6	3	.282	.359	.336	.695	81	-10	58	4.50	-1	*3-131	13	-0.6
1934 Cle-A	121	386	52	104	23	3	0	42	62	38	7	1	.269	.372	.345	.716	85	-5	55	4.99	4	*3-118	13	0.3
1935 Cle-A	6	18	2	6	0	0	0	1	0	1	0	1	.333	.333	.333	.667	72	-1	2	3.26	-1	/3-4	0	-0.2
Total 13	**1693**	**5851**	**802**	**1643**	**348**	**85**	**29**	**826**	**824**	**405**	**126**	**84**	**.281**	**.372**	**.384**	**.756**	**97**	**0**	**884**	**5.17**	**50**	***3-1674**	**201**	**13.5**

• KAMPOURIS, Alex Alexis William Kampouris b: 11/13/1912, Sacramento, CA d: 5/29/1993, Sacramento, CA BR/TR, 5'8", 155 lbs. Deb: 7/31/1934 Career OF: 1-0-1

YEAR TM-L	G	AB	R	H	2B	3B	HR	RBI	BB	SO	SB	CS	AVG	OBP	SLG	OPS	OPS+	BR/A	RC	RC/G	FR	G/POS	WS	TPW
1934 Cin-N	19	66	6	13	1	0	0	3	3	18	2	....	.197	.254	.212	.466	27	-7	4	1.87	-2	2-16	0	-0.8
1935 Cin-N	148	499	46	123	26	5	7	62	32	84	8	....	.246	.295	.361	.655	77	-17	55	3.72	-13	*2-141/S-6	9	-2.0
1936 Cin-N	122	355	43	85	10	4	5	46	24	46	3	....	.239	.289	.332	.622	72	-15	35	3.31	8	*2-119/O-1	7	0.0
1937 Cin-N	146	458	62	114	21	4	17	71	60	65	2	....	.249	.342	.424	.766	112	8	67	4.96	-2	*2-146	14	1.5
1938 Cin-N	21	74	13	19	1	0	2	7	10	13	0	....	.257	.353	.351	.704	97	0	9	4.09	1	2-21	2	0.3
NY-N	82	268	35	66	9	1	5	37	27	50	0	....	.246	.318	.343	.661	81	-7	30	3.83	0	2-79	7	-0.2
Yr.	103	342	48	85	10	1	7	44	37	63	0	....	.249	.325	.345	.670	85	-7	39	3.89	1	*2-100	9	0.1
1939 NY-N	74	201	23	50	12	2	5	29	30	41	0	....	.249	.349	.403	.752	101	1	29	4.72	0	2-62,3-11	7	0.5
1941 Bro-N	16	51	8	16	4	2	2	9	11	8	0	....	.314	.444	.588	1.033	181	6	15	10.74	1	2-15	4	0.8
1942 Bro-N	10	21	3	5	2	1	0	3	0	4	0	....	.238	.238	.429	.667	92	-0	2	3.62	0	/2-9	1	0.0
1943 Bro-N	19	44	9	10	4	1	0	4	17	6	0	....	.227	.452	.364	.815	136	4	9	6.27	-2	2-18	3	0.3
Was-A	51	145	24	30	4	0	2	13	30	25	7	1	.207	.361	.276	.637	91	2	19	4.24	-4	3-33,2-10/0-1	5	-0.1
Total 9	**708**	**2182**	**272**	**531**	**94**	**20**	**45**	**284**	**244**	**360**	**22**	**1**	**.243**	**.325**	**.367**	**.692**	**91**	**-24**	**272**	**4.21**	**-12**	**2-636/3-44,S-6,0-2**	**59**	**0.3**

• KANE, Frank Francis Thomas "Sugar" Kane b: 3/9/1895, Whitman, MA d: 12/2/1962, Brockton, MA BL/TR, 5'11.5", 175 lbs. Deb: 9/13/1915

YEAR TM-L	G	AB	R	H	2B	3B	HR	RBI	BB	SO	SB	CS	AVG	OBP	SLG	OPS	OPS+	BR/A	RC	RC/G	FR	G/POS	WS	TPW
1915 Bro-F	3	10	2	2	0	1	0	2	0	0	0	....	.200	.200	.400	.600	76	-0	1	2.34	1	/O-2(2-0-0)	0	0.0
1919 NY-A	1	1	0	0	0	0	0	0	0	0	0	....	.000	.000	.000	.000	-99	-0	0	.00	0	....	0	0.0
Total 2	**4**	**11**	**2**	**2**	**0**	**1**	**0**	**2**	**0**	**0**	**0**	**....**	**.182**	**.182**	**.364**	**.545**	**60**	**-1**	**1**	**2.08**	**1**	**/O-2**	**0**	**0.0**

• KANE, Jerry William Jeremiah Kane b: 4/1869, Baltimore, MD d: 6/16/1949, East St. Louis, IL BR/TR, 6', 175 lbs. Deb: 5/2/1890

YEAR TM-L	G	AB	R	H	2B	3B	HR	RBI	BB	SO	SB	CS	AVG	OBP	SLG	OPS	OPS+	BR/A	RC	RC/G	FR	G/POS	WS	TPW
1890 StL-a	8	25	3	5	0	0	0	2	2	....	0	....	.200	.259	.200	.459	31	-2	1	1.76	0	/1-5,C-4	0	-0.2

• KANE, Jim James Joseph "Shamus" Kane b: 11/27/1881, Scranton, PA d: 10/2/1947, Omaha, NE BL/TL, 6'2", 225 lbs. Deb: 4/21/1908

YEAR TM-L	G	AB	R	H	2B	3B	HR	RBI	BB	SO	SB	CS	AVG	OBP	SLG	OPS	OPS+	BR/A	RC	RC/G	FR	G/POS	WS	TPW
1908 Pit-N	55	145	16	35	3	3	0	22	12	....	5	....	.241	.299	.303	.603	93	-1	15	3.31	0	1-40	4	-0.2

• KANE, John John Francis Kane b: 2/19/1900, Chicago, IL d: 7/25/1956, Chicago, IL BB/TR, 5'10.5", 162 lbs. Deb: 9/3/1925

YEAR TM-L	G	AB	R	H	2B	3B	HR	RBI	BB	SO	SB	CS	AVG	OBP	SLG	OPS	OPS+	BR/A	RC	RC/G	FR	G/POS	WS	TPW
1925 Chi-A	14	56	6	10	1	0	0	3	0	3	0	0	.179	.193	.196	.389	-1	-9	2	1.22	2	/S-8,2-6	1	-0.5

• KANE, John John Francis Kane b: 9/24/1882, Chicago, IL d: 1/28/1934, St. Anthony, ID BR/TR, 5'6", 138 lbs. Deb: 4/11/1907 Career OF: 53-130-13

YEAR TM-L	G	AB	R	H	2B	3B	HR	RBI	BB	SO	SB	CS	AVG	OBP	SLG	OPS	OPS+	BR/A	RC	RC/G	FR	G/POS	WS	TPW
1907 Cin-N	79	262	40	65	9	4	3	19	22	....	20	....	.248	.325	.347	.673	106	2	39	4.71	-2	0-42(38-0-4),3-25/S-6,2-2	9	-0.2
1908 Cin-N	130	455	61	97	11	7	3	23	43	....	30	....	.213	.299	.288	.587	90	-4	49	3.35	-7	*0-127(0-120-7)/2-1	14	-1.9
1909 Chi-N	20	45	6	4	1	0	0	5	2	....	1	....	.089	.146	.111	.257	-20	-6	1	.64	3	/0-8(6-1-1),3-3,S-3,2-2	1	-0.4
1910*Chi-N	32	62	11	15	0	0	1	12	9	10	2	....	.242	.338	.290	.628	84	-1	7	3.64	-3	0-18(9-9-1)/2-6,3-4,S-2	2	-0.4
Total 4	**261**	**824**	**118**	**181**	**21**	**11**	**7**	**59**	**76**	**10**	**53**	**....**	**.220**	**.303**	**.297**	**.600**	**89**	**-9**	**97**	**3.61**	**-9**	**0-195/3-32,2-11,S-11**	**26**	**-2.9**

• KANE, Tom Thomas Joseph "Sugar" Kane b: 12/15/1906, Chicago, IL d: 11/26/1973, Chicago, IL BR/TR, 5'10.5", 160 lbs. Deb: 8/3/1938

YEAR TM-L	G	AB	R	H	2B	3B	HR	RBI	BB	SO	SB	CS	AVG	OBP	SLG	OPS	OPS+	BR/A	RC	RC/G	FR	G/POS	WS	TPW
1938 Bos-N	2	2	0	0	0	0	0	0	2	0	0	....	.000	.500	.000	.500	53	0	0	1.17	0	/2-2	0	0.0

• KANEHL, Rod Roderick Edwin "Hot Rod" Kanehl b: 4/1/1934, Wichita, KS BR/TR, 6'1", 180 lbs. Deb: 4/15/1962 Career OF: 42-56-7

YEAR TM-L	G	AB	R	H	2B	3B	HR	RBI	BB	SO	SB	CS	AVG	OBP	SLG	OPS	OPS+	BR/A	RC	RC/G	FR	G/POS	WS	TPW
1962 NY-N	133	351	52	87	10	2	4	27	23	36	8	6	.248	.296	.322	.618	65	-19	32	3.11	-4	2-62,3-30,0-20(10-7-3)/1-3,S	3	-1.7
1963 NY-N	109	191	26	46	6	0	1	9	5	26	6	3	.241	.268	.288	.556	59	-10	13	2.25	-4	0-58(30-26-4),3-13,2-12/1-3	1	-1.7
1964 NY-N	98	254	25	59	7	1	1	11	7	18	3	1	.232	.256	.280	.535	52	-16	19	2.53	2	2-34,0-25(2-23-0),3-19/1-2	3	-1.3
Total 3	**340**	**796**	**103**	**192**	**23**	**3**	**6**	**47**	**35**	**80**	**17**	**10**	**.241**	**.277**	**.300**	**.577**	**59**	**-45**	**64**	**2.71**	**-6**	**2-108,0-103/3-62,1-8,S-2**	**7**	**-4.7**

• KAPLER, Gabe Gabriel Stefan Kapler b: 7/31/1975, Hollywood, CA BR/TR, 6'2", 208 lbs. Deb: 9/20/1998 Career OF: 86-365-162

YEAR TM-L	G	AB	R	H	2B	3B	HR	RBI	BB	SO	SB	CS	AVG	OBP	SLG	OPS	OPS+	BR/A	RC	RC/G	FR	G/POS	WS	TPW
1998 Det-A	7	25	3	5	0	1	0	0	1	4	2	0	.200	.231	.280	.511	32	-2	2	2.59	0	/O-6(0-0-6),D-1	0	-0.2
1999 Det-A	130	416	60	102	22	4	18	49	42	74	11	5	.245	.317	.447	.765	92	-6	59	4.80	-3	*O-128(0-114-32)/D-2	8	-0.9
2000 Tex-A	116	444	59	134	32	1	14	66	42	57	8	4	.302	.362	.473	.835	108	5	74	6.04	-2	*O-116(0-84-40)	10	0.1
2001 Tex-A	134	483	77	129	29	1	17	72	61	70	23	6	.267	.353	.437	.790	103	5	78	5.53	-3	*O-133(0-133-0)/D-1	13	0.3
2002 Tex-A	72	196	25	51	12	1	0	17	8	30	5	2	.260	.289	.332	.621	61	-11	19	3.19	5	0-64(31-23-18)/1-1,D-1	3	-0.7
Col-N	40	119	12	37	4	3	2	17	8	23	6	2	.311	.359	.445	.805	95	-0	19	6.02	1	0-38(15-1-23)	5	-0.1
2003 Col-N	39	67	10	15	2	0	0	4	8	18	2	0	.224	.307	.254	.560	42	-5	5	2.60	1	0-29(15-2-13)	0	-0.4
*Bos-A	68	158	29	46	11	1	4	23	14	23	4	2	.291	.349	.449	.798	106	1	24	5.36	-1	0-61(25-8-30)/1-1,D-1	4	-0.2
Total 6	**606**	**1908**	**275**	**519**	**112**	**12**	**55**	**248**	**184**	**299**	**61**	**21**	**.272**	**.338**	**.430**	**.768**	**94**	**-14**	**280**	**5.09**	**-2**	**0-575/D-6,1-2**	**43**	**-2.2**

• KAPPEL, Heinie Henry Kappel b: 9/1863, Philadelphia, PA d: 8/27/1905, Philadelphia, PA BR/TR, 5'8", 160 lbs. Deb: 5/22/1887

YEAR TM-L	G	AB	R	H	2B	3B	HR	RBI	BB	SO	SB	CS	AVG	OBP	SLG	OPS	OPS+	BR/A	RC	RC/G	FR	G/POS	WS	TPW
1887 Cin-a	23	80	11	24	3	2	0	15	2	....	3	....	.300	.309	.372	.680	87	-2	10	4.88	1	/3-9,0-7(2-0-5),2-6,S-1	2	-0.1
1888 Cin-a	36	143	18	37	4	4	1	15	2	....	20	....	.259	.274	.364	.638	98	-1	20	5.15	-14	S-25,2-10/3-1	4	-1.3
1889 Col-a	46	173	25	47	7	5	3	21	21	28	10	....	.272	.354	.422	.776	127	6	30	6.33	-4	3-23,S-23	6	0.3
Total 3	**105**	**396**	**54**	**108**	**14**	**11**	**4**	**51**	**25**	**28**	**33**	**....**	**.273**	**.318**	**.391**	**.708**	**109**	**3**	**60**	**5.61**	**-17**	**/S-49,3-33,2-16,0-7**	**12**	**-1.0**

• KAPPEL, Joe Joseph Kappel b: 4/27/1857, Philadelphia, PA d: 7/8/1929, Philadelphia, PA BR, 5'10", 175 lbs. Deb: 5/26/1884

YEAR TM-L	G	AB	R	H	2B	3B	HR	RBI	BB	SO	SB	CS	AVG	OBP	SLG	OPS	OPS+	BR/A	RC	RC/G	FR	G/POS	WS	TPW
1884 Phi-N	4	15	1	1	0	0	0	0	0	2	....	....	.067	.067	.067	.133	-61	-3	0	.13	-2	/C-4	0	-0.4
1890 Phi-a	56	208	29	50	8	1	1	22	20	....	12	....	.240	.310	.303	.613	82	-5	24	4.00	-4	0-23(11-8-5),S-18,3-11/C-3,2	5	-0.8
Total 2	**60**	**223**	**30**	**51**	**8**	**1**	**1**	**22**	**20**	**2**	**12**	**....**	**.229**	**.295**	**.287**	**.582**	**74**	**-7**	**24**	**3.68**	**-6**	**/0-23,S-18,3-11,C-7,2-2**	**5**	**-1.2**

• KARKOVICE, Ron Ronald Joseph Karkovice b: 8/8/1963, Union, NJ BR/TR, 6'1", 215 lbs. Deb: 8/17/1986 Career OF: 1-0-1

YEAR TM-L	G	AB	R	H	2B	3B	HR	RBI	BB	SO	SB	CS	AVG	OBP	SLG	OPS	OPS+	BR/A	RC	RC/G	FR	G/POS	WS	TPW
1986 Chi-A	37	97	13	24	7	0	4	13	9	37	1	0	.247	.318	.443	.761	101	0	13	4.64	3	C-37	4	0.5
1987 Chi-A	39	85	7	6	0	0	2	7	7	40	3	0	.071	.160	.141	.301	-19	-14	2	.74	2	C-37/D-1	1	-1.0
1988 Chi-A	46	115	10	20	4	0	3	9	7	30	4	2	.174	.228	.287	.515	43	-9	8	2.05	3	C-46	2	-0.4
1989 Chi-A	71	182	21	48	9	2	3	24	10	56	0	0	.264	.309	.385	.694	97	-1	23	4.34	5	C-68/D-2	7	0.8
1990 Chi-A	68	183	30	45	10	0	6	20	16	52	2	0	.246	.310	.399	.709	99	-0	24	4.44	3	C-64/D-2	8	0.6
1991 Chi-A	75	167	25	41	13	0	5	22	15	42	0	0	.246	.311	.413	.725	101	-0	22	4.35	1	C-69/O-1	7	0.5
1992 Chi-A	123	342	39	81	12	1	13	50	30	89	10	4	.237	.304	.392	.696	95	-3	42	4.17	-0	*C-119/O-1	13	0.4
1993*Chi-A	128	403	60	92	17	1	20	54	29	126	2	2	.228	.290	.424	.714	91	-7	47	3.74	1	*C-127	15	0.3
1994 Chi-A	77	207	33	44	9	1	11	29	36	68	0	3	.213	.329	.425	.754	94	-3	31	4.87	-3	C-76	5	-0.2
1995 Chi-A	113	323	44	70	14	1	13	51	39	84	2	3	.217	.311	.387	.698	84	-9	40	3.94	2	*C-113	10	0.0
1996 Chi-A	111	355	44	78	22	0	10	38	24	93	0	0	.220	.271	.366	.637	62	-22	35	3.20	2	*C-111	6	-1.1
1997 Chi-A	51	138	10	25	3	0	6	18	11	32	0	0	.181	.257	.333	.590	55	-10	12	2.62	0	C-51	2	-0.7
Total 12	**939**	**2597**	**336**	**574**	**120**	**6**	**96**	**335**	**233**	**749**	**24**	**14**	**.221**	**.292**	**.383**	**.674**	**82**	**-78**	**300**	**3.74**	**19**	**C-918/D-5,O-2**	**80**	**-0.3**

• KARLON, Bill William John "Hank" Karlon b: 1/21/1909, Palmer, MA d: 12/7/1964, Ware, MA BR/TR, 6'1", 190 lbs. Deb: 4/28/1930

YEAR TM-L	G	AB	R	H	2B	3B	HR	RBI	BB	SO	SB	CS	AVG	OBP	SLG	OPS	OPS+	BR/A	RC	RC/G	FR	G/POS	WS	TPW
1930 NY-A	2	5	0	0	0	0	0	0	0	1	0	0	.000	.000	.000	.000	-105	-2	0	.00	-0	/O-1	0	-0.1

• KAROW, Marty Martin Gregory Karow b: 7/18/1904, Braddock, PA d: 4/27/1986, Bryan, TX BR/TR, 5'10.5", 170 lbs. Deb: 6/21/1927

YEAR TM-L	G	AB	R	H	2B	3B	HR	RBI	BB	SO	SB	CS	AVG	OBP	SLG	OPS	OPS+	BR/A	RC	RC/G	FR	G/POS	WS	TPW
1927 Bos-A	6	10	0	2	1	0	0	0	0	2	0	0	.200	.200	.300	.500	29	-1	1	1.80	1	/S-3,3-2	0	0.0

• KARROS, Eric Eric Peter Karros b: 11/4/1967, Hackensack, NJ BR/TR, 6'4", 216 lbs. Deb: 9/1/1991

YEAR TM-L	G	AB	R	H	2B	3B	HR	RBI	BB	SO	SB	CS	AVG	OBP	SLG	OPS	OPS+	BR/A	RC	RC/G	FR	G/POS	WS	TPW
1991 LA-N	14	14	0	1	1	0	0	1	1	6	0	0	.071	.133	.143	.276	-23	-2	0	.63	0	1-10	0	-0.3
1992 LA-N	149	545	63	140	30	1	20	88	37	103	2	4	.257	.307	.426	.732	107	1	67	4.19	4	*1-143	13	-0.5
1993 LA-N	158	619	74	153	27	2	23	80	34	82	0	1	.247	.289	.409	.697	89	-13	69	3.80	9	*1-157	10	-1.8

YEAR TM-L	G	AB	R	H	2B	3B	HR	RBI	BB	SO	SB	CS	AVG	OBP	SLG	OPS	OPS+	BR/A	RC	RC/G	FR	G/POS	WS	TPW
1994 LA-N	111	406	51	108	21	1	14	46	29	53	2	0	.266	.318	.426	.744	98	-2	53	4.42	10	*1-109	7	-0.1
1995*LA-N	143	551	83	164	29	3	32	105	61	115	4	4	.298	.372	.535	.907	149	36	107	7.08	7	*1-143	25	2.9
1996*LA-N	154	608	84	158	29	1	34	111	53	121	8	0	.260	.320	.479	.799	116	13	86	4.81	9	*1-154	20	0.8
1997 LA-N	162	628	86	167	28	0	31	104	61	116	15	7	.266	.333	.459	.791	113	10	96	5.34	13	*1-162	18	0.8
1998 LA-N	139	507	59	150	20	1	23	87	47	93	7	2	.296	.359	.475	.834	125	18	88	6.40	6	*1-136/D-2	22	1.2
1999 LA-N	153	578	74	176	40	0	34	112	53	119	8	5	.304	.365	.550	.915	135	28	111	6.92	12	*1-151	20	2.5
2000 LA-N	155	584	84	146	29	0	31	106	63	122	4	3	.250	.327	.459	.786	102	-1	85	4.87	14	*1-153/D-1	14	-0.1
2001 LA-N	121	438	42	103	22	0	15	63	41	101	3	1	.235	.305	.388	.693	84	-11	50	3.79	6	*1-119	8	-1.6
2002 LA-N	142	524	52	142	26	1	13	73	37	74	4	2	.271	.326	.399	.725	96	-4	68	4.55	14	*1-142	18	-0.3
2003*Chi-N	114	336	37	96	16	1	12	40	28	46	1	1	.286	.341	.446	.787	105	1	47	4.98	-3	1-97	8	-0.9
Total 13	1715	6338	789	1704	318	11	282	1016	545	1151	58	30	.269	.330	.456	.786	111	74	926	5.09	101	*1-1676/D-3	183	2.7

• KARST, John

John Gottlieb "Big Jack,King" Karst b: 10/15/1893, Philadelphia, PA d: 5/21/1976, Cape May, NJ BL/TR, 5'11.5", 175 lbs. Deb: 10/6/1915

YEAR TM-L	G	AB	R	H	2B	3B	HR	RBI	BB	SO	SB	CS	AVG	OBP	SLG	OPS	OPS+	BR/A	RC	RC/G	FR	G/POS	WS	TPW
1915 Bro-N	1	0	0	0	0	0	0	0	0	0	0	....	....	....	....	....	-98	0	0	....	0	/3-1	0	0.0

• KASKO, Eddie

Edward Michael Kasko b: 6/27/1932, Linden, NJ BR/TR, 6', 180 lbs. Deb: 4/18/1957 M

YEAR TM-L	G	AB	R	H	2B	3B	HR	RBI	BB	SO	SB	CS	AVG	OBP	SLG	OPS	OPS+	BR/A	RC	RC/G	FR	G/POS	WS	TPW
1957 StL-N	134	479	59	131	16	5	1	35	33	53	6	1	.273	.320	.334	.654	75	-16	52	3.88	-10	*3-120,S-13/2-1	11	-2.5
1958 StL-N	104	259	20	57	8	1	2	22	21	25	1	2	.220	.279	.282	.560	47	-20	19	2.34	-9	S-77,2-12/3-1	1	-2.3
1959 Cin-N	118	329	39	93	14	1	2	31	14	38	2	2	.283	.312	.350	.661	74	-13	35	3.79	12	S-84,3-31/2-2	8	0.6
1960 Cin-N	126	479	56	140	21	1	6	51	46	37	9	9	.292	.362	.378	.739	101	0	66	4.88	9	3-86,2-33,S-15	14	1.3
1961*Cin-N★	126	469	64	127	22	1	2	27	32	36	4	3	.271	.323	.335	.658	74	-17	52	3.98	-4	*S-112,3-12/2-6	11	-1.2
1962 Cin-N	134	533	74	148	26	2	4	41	35	44	3	3	.278	.328	.356	.685	81	-15	59	3.90	2	*3-114,S-21	12	-1.2
1963 Cin-N	76	199	25	48	9	0	3	10	21	29	0	2	.241	.314	.332	.645	83	-4	21	3.50	2	3-48,S-15/2-1	5	-0.2
1964 Hou-N	133	448	45	109	16	1	0	22	37	52	4	6	.243	.302	.283	.586	70	-18	38	2.81	7	*S-128/3-2	11	-0.1
1965 Hou-N	68	215	18	53	7	1	1	10	11	20	1	3	.247	.296	.302	.598	74	-9	17	2.60	-5	S-59/3-2	3	-1.0
1966 Bos-A	58	136	11	29	7	0	1	12	15	19	1	0	.213	.291	.287	.578	61	-6	11	2.69	3	S-20,3-10/2-8	2	-0.2
Total 10	1077	3546	411	935	146	13	22	261	265	353	31	31	.264	.318	.331	.649	76	-119	370	3.61	6	S-544,3-426/2-63	78	-6.9

• KATA, Matt

Matthew John Kata b: 3/14/1978, Avon Lakes, OH BB/TR, 6'1", 185 lbs. Deb: 6/15/2003

YEAR TM-L	G	AB	R	H	2B	3B	HR	RBI	BB	SO	SB	CS	AVG	OBP	SLG	OPS	OPS+	BR/A	RC	RC/G	FR	G/POS	WS	TPW
2003 Ari-N	78	288	42	74	16	5	7	29	25	53	3	2	.257	.318	.420	.739	82	-8	39	4.61	-1	2-52,3-23/S-6	8	-0.6

• KATT, Ray

Raymond Frederick Katt b: 5/9/1927, New Braunfels, TX d: 10/19/1999, New Braunfels, TX BR/TR, 6'2", 200 lbs. Deb: 9/16/1952 C

YEAR TM-L	G	AB	R	H	2B	3B	HR	RBI	BB	SO	SB	CS	AVG	OBP	SLG	OPS	OPS+	BR/A	RC	RC/G	FR	G/POS	WS	TPW
1952 NY-N	9	27	4	6	0	0	0	1	1	5	0	0	.222	.250	.222	.472	32	-2	1	1.34	0	/C-8	0	-0.2
1953 NY-N	8	29	2	5	1	0	0	1	1	3	0	0	.172	.200	.207	.407	6	-4	1	1.45	0	/C-8	0	-0.3
1954 NY-N	86	200	26	51	7	1	9	33	19	29	1	0	.255	.320	.435	.755	94	-2	28	4.71	-5	C-82	6	-0.4
1955 NY-N	124	326	27	70	7	2	7	28	22	38	0	0	.215	.269	.313	.581	53	-22	25	2.47	-3	*C-122	4	-2.0
1956 NY-N	37	101	10	23	4	0	7	14	6	16	0	1	.228	.278	.475	.753	98	-1	13	4.29	1	C-37	3	0.1
StL-N	47	158	11	41	4	0	6	20	6	24	0	1	.259	.291	.399	.690	83	-5	18	3.91	-2	C-47	4	-0.5
Yr.	84	259	21	64	8	0	13	34	12	40	0	2	.247	.286	.429	.714	89	-6	31	4.06	-1	C-84	7	-0.3
1957 NY-N	72	165	11	38	3	1	2	17	15	35	1	0	.230	.302	.297	.599	62	-8	15	2.80	0	C-68	2	-0.6
1958 StL-N	19	41	1	7	1	0	1	4	4	6	0	0	.171	.244	.268	.513	34	-4	2	1.54	0	C-14	1	-0.4
1959 StL-N	15	24	0	7	2	0	0	2	0	8	0	0	.292	.292	.375	.667	71	-1	2	2.57	0	C-14	0	-0.1
Total 8	417	1071	92	248	29	4	32	120	74	164	2	2	.232	.285	.356	.641	69	-50	105	3.20	-10	C-400	20	-4.4

• KAUFF, Benny

Benjamin Michael Kauff b: 1/5/1890, Pomeroy, OH d: 11/17/1961, Columbus, OH BL/TL, 5'8", 157 lbs. Deb: 4/20/1912 Career OF: 36-750-68

YEAR TM-L	G	AB	R	H	2B	3B	HR	RBI	BB	SO	SB	CS	AVG	OBP	SLG	OPS	OPS+	BR/A	RC	RC/G	FR	G/POS	WS	TPW
1912 NY-A	5	11	4	3	0	0	0	2	3	....	1	....	.273	.429	.273	.701	96	0	2	5.50	0	/O-4(O-4-0)	0	0.0
1914 Ind-F	154	571	**120**	**211**	**44**	13	8	95	72	55	**75**	....	**.370**	**.447**	.534	**.981**	161	49	160	**10.87**	12	*O-154(33-54-68)	**38**	**5.5**
1915 Bro-F	136	483	92	165	23	11	12	83	85	50	**55**	....	**.342**	**.446**	**.509**	**.955**	**185**	**56**	127	**10.13**	11	*O-136(O-136-0)	**34**	**6.3**
1916 NY-N	154	552	71	146	22	15	9	74	68	65	40	26	.264	.348	.408	.756	139	24	81	4.75	-2	*O-154(O-154-0)	27	1.3
1917*NY-N	153	559	89	172	22	4	5	68	59	54	30	....	.308	.379	.388	.767	140	28	91	5.79	-10	*O-153(3-150-0)	30	1.0
1918 NY-N	67	270	41	85	19	4	2	39	16	30	9	....	.315	.355	.437	.792	144	13	43	5.86	-5	O-67(O-67-0)	15	0.4
1919 NY-N	135	491	73	136	27	7	10	67	39	45	21	....	.277	.334	.422	.756	128	16	72	5.14	-2	*O-134(O-134-0)	24	0.6
1920 NY-N	55	157	31	43	12	3	3	26	25	14	3	7	.274	.380	.446	.826	138	7	26	5.50	-1	O-51(O-51-0)	7	0.3
Total 8	859	3094	521	961	169	57	49	454	367	313	234	33	.311	.389	.450	.838	149	192	602	6.95	1	O-853	175	15.2

• KAUFFMAN, Dick

Howard Richard Kauffman b: 6/22/1888, East Lewisburg, PA d: 4/16/1948, Mifflinburg, PA BB/TR, 6'3", 190 lbs. Deb: 9/17/1914

YEAR TM-L	G	AB	R	H	2B	3B	HR	RBI	BB	SO	SB	CS	AVG	OBP	SLG	OPS	OPS+	BR/A	RC	RC/G	FR	G/POS	WS	TPW
1914 StL-A	7	15	1	4	1	0	0	2	0	3	0	....	.267	.267	.333	.600	83	-0	1	3.21	-1	/1-7	0	-0.1
1915 StL-A	37	124	9	32	8	2	0	14	5	27	0	3	.258	.298	.355	.653	99	-2	12	3.38	-3	1-32/O-1	2	-0.6
Total 2	44	139	10	36	9	2	0	16	5	30	0	3	.259	.295	.353	.647	97	-3	14	3.36	-3	/1-39,O-1	2	-0.7

• KAUFMANN, Tony

Anthony Charles Kaufmann b: 12/16/1900, Chicago, IL d: 6/4/1982, Elgin, IL BR/TR, 5'11", 165 lbs. Deb: 9/23/1921 C Career OF: 6-8-4 ♦

YEAR TM-L	G	AB	R	H	2B	3B	HR	RBI	BB	SO	SB	CS	AVG	OBP	SLG	OPS	OPS+	BR/A	RC	RC/G	FR	G/POS	WS	TPW
1921 Chi-N	2	5	0	2	1	0	0	0	0	1	0	0	.400	.400	.600	1.000	161	1	1	10.18	0	/P-2	2	0.0
1922 Chi-N	38	45	4	9	2	1	1	4	2	14	0	0	.200	.234	.356	.590	49	1	4	2.50	-1	P-37	10	0.2
1923 Chi-N	33	74	10	16	2	0	2	10	7	17	0	0	.216	.284	.324	.608	60	3	7	3.15	-1	P-33	18	1.8
1924 Chi-N	35	76	6	24	5	0	1	14	3	10	0	0	.316	.342	.421	.763	102	6	11	5.48	-1	P-34	16	0.0
1925 Chi-N	31	78	8	15	7	0	2	13	2	17	0	0	.192	.213	.359	.571	42	1	6	2.42	0	P-31	12	-0.6
1926 Chi-N	30	60	9	15	2	0	1	7	2	10	1	....	.250	.274	.333	.608	62	2	5	2.93	-2	P-26	14	1.4
1927 Chi-N	9	16	2	5	1	0	1	6	4	4	0	....	.313	.450	.500	.950	154	3	4	7.58	1	/P-9	1	-1.3
Phi-N	8	7	1	1	0	0	1	2	0	1	0	....	.143	.143	.571	.714	83	0	1	2.30	-1	/P-5,O-1	0	-1.3
StL-N	1	0	0	0	0	0	0	0	0	0	0	0	....	....	....	....	-97	0	0	....	0	/P-1	0	-0.3
Yr.	18	23	3	6	0	0	2	8	4	5	0	0	.261	.370	.522	.892	137	3	4	5.91	1	P-15/O-1	1	-2.9
1928 StL-N	5	0	0	0	0	0	0	0	0	0	0	0	....	....	....	....	-98	0	0	....	0	/P-4	0	-0.3
1929 NY-N	39	32	18	1	0	0	0	1	6	4	3	....	.031	.184	.031	.215	-43	-7	1	.45	-1	O-16(4-8-4)	0	-0.8
1930 StL-N	2	3	1	1	0	0	0	0	1	1	0	....	.333	.500	.333	.833	103	0	1	7.62	0	/P-2	0	-0.3
1931 StL-N	20	18	1	2	0	0	0	0	1	3	0	....	.111	.158	.111	.269	-26	-1	0	.56	0	P-15/O-1	0	-1.3
1935 StL-N	7	0	2	0	0	0	0	0	0	0	0	0	....	....	....	....	-96	0	0	....	0	/P-3	0	0.1
Total 12	260	414	62	91	19	1	9	57	28	82	4	0	.220	.269	.336	.605	57	10	40	3.12	-6	P-202/O-18	73	-2.6

• KAVANAGH, Charlie

Charles Hugh "Silk" Kavanagh b: 6/9/1893, Chicago, IL d: 9/6/1973, Reedsburg, WI BR/TR, 5'9", 165 lbs. Deb: 6/11/1914

YEAR TM-L	G	AB	R	H	2B	3B	HR	RBI	BB	SO	SB	CS	AVG	OBP	SLG	OPS	OPS+	BR/A	RC	RC/G	FR	G/POS	WS	TPW
1914 Chi-A	6	5	0	1	0	0	0	0	0	2	0	....	.200	.333	.200	.533	62	-0	0	2.21	0	....	0	0.0

• KAVANAGH, Leo

Leo Daniel Kavanagh b: 8/9/1894, Chicago, IL d: 8/10/1950, Chicago, IL BR/TR, 5'9", 180 lbs. Deb: 4/22/1914

YEAR TM-L	G	AB	R	H	2B	3B	HR	RBI	BB	SO	SB	CS	AVG	OBP	SLG	OPS	OPS+	BR/A	RC	RC/G	FR	G/POS	WS	TPW
1914 Chi-F	5	11	0	3	0	0	0	1	1	0	0	....	.273	.333	.273	.606	78	-0	1	3.01	0	/S-5	0	0.0

• KAVANAGH, Marty

Martin Joseph Kavanagh b: 6/13/1891, Harrison, NJ d: 7/28/1960, Eloise, MI BR/TR, 6', 187 lbs. Deb: 4/18/1914 Career OF: 3-2-18

YEAR TM-L	G	AB	R	H	2B	3B	HR	RBI	BB	SO	SB	CS	AVG	OBP	SLG	OPS	OPS+	BR/A	RC	RC/G	FR	G/POS	WS	TPW
1914 Det-A	128	439	60	109	21	6	4	35	41	42	16	14	.248	.318	.351	.669	98	-5	51	3.73	-21	*2-115/1-4	11	-2.6
1915 Det-A	113	332	55	98	14	13	4	49	42	44	8	8	.295	.378	.452	.829	141	15	57	6.03	-6	1-44,2-42/O-2(2-0-0),S-2,3	16	0.9
1916 Det-A	58	78	6	11	4	0	0	5	9	15	0	....	.141	.239	.192	.431	29	-7	4	1.47	-1	O-11(1-0-10)/2-2,3-1	0	-0.9
Cle-A	19	44	4	11	2	1	1	10	2	5	0	....	.250	.283	.409	.692	102	-0	5	4.01	-3	/2-9,1-1,3-1	1	-0.3
Yr.	77	122	10	22	6	1	1	15	11	20	0	....	.180	.254	.270	.524	53	-7	9	2.29	-4	2-11,O-11(1-0-10)/3-2,1-1	1	-1.2
1917 Cle-A	14	14	1	0	0	0	0	0	3	2	0	....	.000	.176	.000	.176	-43	-2	0	.00	0	/O-2(O-2-0)	0	-0.2
1918 Cle-A	13	38	4	8	2	0	0	6	7	7	1	....	.211	.348	.263	.611	77	-1	4	3.18	-2	1-12	1	-0.3
StL-N	12	44	6	8	1	0	1	8	3	1	1	....	.182	.234	.273	.507	56	-2	3	2.08	-2	/O-8(O-0-8),2-4	0	-0.5
Det-A	13	44	2	12	3	0	0	9	11	6	0	....	.273	.418	.341	.759	134	3	6	4.81	-1	1-12	2	0.2
Yr.	26	82	6	20	5	0	0	15	18	13	1	....	.244	.386	.305	.691	108	2	10	3.99	-2	1-24	3	-0.1
Total 5	370	1033	138	257	47	20	10	122	118	122	26	22	.249	.330	.362	.693	104	0	130	4.13	-34	2-172/1-73,O-23,3-3,S-2	31	-3.7

• KAVANAUGH,

Kavanaugh Deb: 9/11/1872

YEAR TM-L	G	AB	R	H	2B	3B	HR	RBI	BB	SO	SB	CS	AVG	OBP	SLG	OPS	OPS+	BR/A	RC	RC/G	FR	G/POS	WS	TPW
1872 Eck-n	5	23	3	6	1	0	0	2	0	1	0	0	.261	.261	.304	.565	86	0	2	3.41	-1	/1-4,O-2(O-0-2)	....	0.0

YEAR TM-L	G	AB	R	H	2B	3B	HR	RBI	BB	SO	SB	CS	AVG	OBP	SLG	OPS	OPS+	BR/A	RC	RC/G	FR	G/POS	WS	TPW
• KAY, Bill	Walter Brocton "King Bill" Kay b: 2/14/1878, New Castle, VA d: 12/3/1945, Roanoke, VA BL/TR, 6'2", 180 lbs. Deb: 8/12/1907																							
1907 Was-A	25	60	8	20	1	1	0	7	0	....	0	....	.333	.333	.383	.717	139	2	8	5.21	0	0-12(0-1-11)	2	0.2
• KAZAK, Eddie	Edward Terrance Kazak b: 7/18/1920, Steubenville, OH d: 12/15/1999, Austin, TX BR/TR, 6', 175 lbs. Deb: 9/29/1948																							
1948 StL-N	6	22	1	6	3	0	0	2	0	2	0	....	.273	.273	.409	.682	78	-1	2	3.25	0	/3-6	0	-0.1
1949 StL-N★	92	326	43	99	15	3	6	42	29	17	0	....	.304	.362	.423	.786	105	2	49	5.47	-0	3-80/2-5	10	0.2
1950 StL-N	93	207	21	53	2	2	5	23	18	19	0	....	.256	.319	.357	.676	74	-8	23	3.87	1	3-48	3	-0.7
1951 StL-N	11	33	2	6	2	0	0	4	5	5	0	0	.182	.289	.242	.532	44	-2	3	2.41	-1	3-10	0	-0.4
1952 StL-N	3	2	1	0	0	0	0	0	0	0	0	0	.000	.000	.000	.000	-100	-1	0	.00	0	/3-1	0	-0.1
Cin-N	13	15	1	1	0	1	0	0	0	2	0	0	.067	.067	.200	.267	-29	-3	0	.40	-1	/3-3,1-1	0	-0.4
Yr.	16	17	2	1	0	1	0	0	0	2	0	0	.059	.059	.176	.235	-37	-3	0	.33	-1	/3-4,1-1	0	-0.4
Total 5	218	605	69	165	22	6	11	71	52	45	0	0	.273	.332	.383	.716	87	-12	77	4.47	-2	3-148/2-5,1-1	13	-1.4
• KAZANSKI, Ted	Theodore Stanley Kazanski b: 1/25/1934, Hamtramck, MI BR/TR, 6'1", 175 lbs. Deb: 6/25/1953																							
1953 Phi-N	95	360	39	78	17	5	2	27	26	53	1	1	.217	.275	.308	.583	52	-26	31	2.87	-11	S-95	5	-2.8
1954 Phi-N	39	104	7	14	2	0	1	8	4	14	0	1	.135	.167	.183	.349	-9	-17	2	.69	0	S-38	1	-1.5
1955 Phi-N	9	12	1	1	0	0	1	1	1	1	0	0	.083	.154	.333	.487	25	-1	1	1.61	0	/3-4,S-4	0	-0.1
1956 Phi-N	117	379	35	80	11	1	4	34	20	41	0	2	.211	.253	.277	.530	43	-32	25	2.15	-10	*2-116/S-1	3	-3.4
1957 Phi-N	62	185	15	49	7	1	3	11	17	20	1	1	.265	.327	.362	.689	88	-3	21	3.82	2	3-36,2-22/S-3	4	0.0
1958 Phi-N	95	289	21	66	12	2	3	35	22	34	2	3	.228	.292	.315	.607	61	-17	25	2.85	0	2-59,S-22,3-16	3	-1.2
Total 6	417	1329	118	288	49	9	14	116	90	163	4	8	.217	.270	.299	.569	52	-96	105	2.58	-19	2-197,S-163/3-56	16	-9.0
• KEARNEY, Bob	Robert Henry Kearney b: 10/3/1956, San Antonio, TX BR/TR, 6', 190 lbs. Deb: 9/25/1979																							
1979 SF-N	2	0	0	0	0	0	0	0	1	0	0	0	....	1.000	....	1.000	211	0	0	∞	0	/C-1	0	0.0
1981 Oak-A	1	0	0	0	0	0	0	0	0	0	0	0	....	....	....	....	-105	0	0	....	0	/C-1	0	0.0
1982 Oak-A	22	71	7	12	3	0	0	5	3	10	0	0	.169	.224	.211	.435	21	-8	4	1.55	3	C-22	1	-0.3
1983 Oak-A	108	298	33	76	11	0	8	32	21	50	1	4	.255	.313	.372	.685	93	-5	32	3.52	2	*C-101/D-3	7	0.2
1984 Sea-A	133	431	39	97	24	1	7	43	18	72	7	5	.225	.259	.334	.594	64	-23	36	2.72	1	*C-133	7	-1.5
1985 Sea-A	108	305	24	74	14	1	6	27	11	59	1	1	.243	.278	.354	.632	71	-13	29	3.16	4	*C-108	7	-0.4
1986 Sea-A	81	204	23	49	10	0	6	25	12	35	0	2	.240	.282	.377	.660	77	-8	20	3.11	2	C-79	5	-0.2
1987 Sea-A	24	47	5	8	4	1	0	1	1	9	0	0	.170	.188	.298	.485	25	-5	3	1.79	-0	C-24	1	-0.4
Total 8	479	1356	131	316	66	3	27	133	67	235	9	12	.233	.275	.346	.621	70	-61	123	2.95	13	C-469/D-3	28	-2.7
• KEARNS, Austin	Austin Ryan Kearns b: 5/20/1980, Lexington, KY BR/TR, 6'3", 220 lbs. Deb: 4/17/2002 Career OF: 13-46-146																							
2002 Cin-N	107	372	66	117	24	3	13	56	54	81	6	3	.315	.410	.500	.910	135	21	77	7.64	6	*O-103(13-6-95)	16	2.1
2003 Cin-N	82	292	39	77	11	0	15	58	41	68	5	2	.264	.364	.455	.819	114	7	50	5.99	2	O-80(0-40-51)	13	0.6
Total 2	189	664	105	194	35	3	28	114	95	149	11	5	.292	.390	.480	.870	126	28	127	6.90	7	O-183	29	2.8
• KEARNS, Teddy	Edward Joseph Kearns b: 1/1/1900, Trenton, NJ d: 12/21/1949, Trenton, NJ BR/TR, 5'11", 180 lbs. Deb: 10/1/1920																							
1920 Phi-A	1	1	0	0	0	0	0	0	0	0	0	0	.000	.000	.000	.000	-99	-0	0	.00	0	....	0	0.0
1924 Chi-N	4	16	0	4	0	1	0	1	1	1	0	0	.250	.294	.375	.669	77	-0	2	3.90	0	/1-4	0	-0.1
1925 Chi-N	3	2	0	1	0	0	0	0	0	0	0	0	.500	.500	.500	1.000	154	0	0	12.72	0	/1-3	0	0.0
Total 3	8	19	0	5	0	1	0	1	1	1	0	0	.263	.300	.368	.668	76	-1	2	4.25	-0	/1-7	0	-0.1
• KEARNS, Tom	Thomas J. "Dasher" Kearns b: 11/9/1860, Rochester, NY d: 12/7/1938, Buffalo, NY BR/TR, 5'7", 160 lbs. Deb: 8/26/1880																							
1880 Buf-N	2	7	0	0	0	0	0	0	0	0	....	....	.000	.000	.000	.000	-98	-1	0	.00	-2	/C-2	0	-0.3
1882 Det-N	4	13	2	4	2	0	0	1	0	4	....	....	.308	.308	.462	.769	143	1	2	5.78	-1	/2-4	0	-0.1
1884 Det-N	21	79	9	16	0	1	0	7	2	10	....	....	.203	.222	.228	.450	44	-5	4	1.79	-6	2-21	0	-0.9
Total 3	27	99	11	20	2	1	0	8	2	14	....	....	.202	.218	.242	.460	47	-6	6	2.09	-9	/2-25,C-2	0	-1.3
• KEARSE, Eddie	Edward Paul "Truck" Kearse b: 2/23/1916, San Francisco, CA d: 7/15/1968, Eureka, CA BR/TR, 6'1", 195 lbs. Deb: 6/13/1942																							
1942 NY-A	11	26	2	5	0	0	0	2	3	1	1	0	.192	.276	.192	.468	34	-2	2	1.90	0	C-11	1	-0.1
• KEATING, Chick	Walter Francis Keating b: 8/8/1891, Philadelphia, PA d: 7/13/1959, Philadelphia, PA BR/TR, 5'9.5", 155 lbs. Deb: 9/26/1913																							
1913 Chi-N	2	5	1	1	1	0	0	0	0	1	0	....	.200	.200	.400	.600	69	-0	0	2.30	-1	/S-2	0	-0.1
1914 Chi-N	20	30	3	3	0	1	0	0	6	9	0	....	.100	.250	.167	.417	25	-3	1	1.12	-1	S-14	0	-0.3
1915 Chi-N	4	8	1	0	0	0	0	0	0	3	1	....	.000	.000	.000	.000	-100	-2	0	.00	-1	/S-2	0	-0.3
1926 Phi-N	4	2	0	0	0	0	0	0	0	0	0	....	.000	.000	.000	.000	-95	-1	0	.00	-2	/2-2,S-2,3-1	0	-0.3
Total 4	30	45	5	4	1	1	0	0	6	13	1	....	.089	.196	.156	.352	5	-5	2	.96	-5	/S-20,2-2,3-1	0	-1.0
• KEATLEY, Greg	Gregory Steven Keatley b: 9/12/1953, Princeton, WV BR/TR, 6'2", 200 lbs. Deb: 9/27/1981																							
1981 KC-A	2	0	0	0	0	0	0	0	0	0	0	0	....	....	....	....	-101	0	0	....	-1	/C-2	0	0.0
• KEEDY, Pat	Charles Patrick Keedy b: 1/10/1958, Birmingham, AL BR/TR, 6'4", 205 lbs. Deb: 9/10/1985 Career OF: 5-0-0																							
1985 Cal-A	3	4	1	2	1	0	1	1	0	0	0	1	.500	.500	1.500	2.000	424	1	2	13.50	-1	/3-2,0-1	1	0.0
1987 Chi-A	17	41	6	7	1	0	2	2	2	14	1	0	.171	.209	.341	.551	42	-3	3	2.46	1	3-11/1-2,2-1,D-1,0-1,S-1	1	-0.2
1989 Cle-A	9	14	3	3	2	0	0	1	2	5	0	0	.214	.313	.357	.670	87	-0	2	4.23	0	/O-3(3-0-0),3-2,1-1,D-1,S-1	0	0.0
Total 3	29	59	10	12	4	0	3	4	4	19	1	1	.203	.254	.424	.678	77	-2	6	3.53	1	/3-15,0-5,1-3,D-2,S-2,2-1	2	-0.2
• KEELER, Willie	William Henry "Wee Willie" Keeler b: 3/3/1872, Brooklyn, NY d: 1/1/1923, Brooklyn, NY BL/TL, 5'4.5", 140 lbs. Deb: 9/30/1892 U HOF: 1939 Career OF: 17-9-2013																							
1892 NY-N	14	53	7	17	3	0	0	6	3	3	5	....	.321	.368	.377	.746	128	2	9	7.08	-1	3-14	2	0.1
1893 NY-N	7	24	5	8	2	1	1	7	5	1	3	....	.333	.448	.625	1.073	183	3	8	13.70	-1	/O-3(3-0-0),2-2,S-2	1	0.2
Bro-N	20	80	14	25	1	1	1	9	4	4	2	....	.313	.353	.388	.740	101	-0	12	5.75	0	3-12/O-8(8-0-0)	2	0.0
Yr.	27	104	19	33	3	2	2	16	9	5	5	....	.317	.377	.442	.820	122	3	20	7.54	0	3-12,O-11(8-3-0)/2-2,S-2	3	0.2
1894*Bal-N	129	590	165	219	27	22	5	94	40	6	32	....	.371	.427	.517	.944	122	20	148	10.35	5	*O-128(0-0-128)/2-1	23	1.4
1895*Bal-N	131	565	162	213	24	15	4	78	37	12	47	....	.377	.429	.494	.922	134	28	145	10.50	10	*O-131(0-0-131)	23	2.6
1896*Bal-N	126	544	153	210	22	13	4	82	37	9	67	....	.386	.432	.496	.928	142	33	150	11.46	2	*O-126(2-0-124)	25	2.4
1897*Bal-N	129	564	145	**239**	27	19	0	74	35	....	64	....	**.424**	.464	.539	**1.003**	164	52	176	**13.81**	1	*O-129(0-0-129)	**32**	4.0
1898 Bal-N	129	561	126	**216**	7	2	1	44	31	....	28	....	**.385**	.420	.410	.830	136	26	112	8.40	0	*O-128(0-0-128)/3-1	23	1.8
1899 Bro-N	141	570	**140**	216	12	13	1	61	37	....	45	....	.379	.425	.451	.876	137	30	133	9.53	2	*O-141(0-0-141)	29	2.3
1900*Bro-N	136	563	106	**204**	13	12	4	68	30	....	41	....	.362	.402	.449	.851	127	20	123	8.61	3	*O-136(0-0-136)/2-1	22	1.4
1901 Bro-N	136	595	123	202	18	12	2	43	21	....	23	....	.339	.369	.420	.789	125	17	106	6.75	-4	*O-125(0-0-125),3-10/2-3	20	0.8
1902 Bro-N	133	559	86	186	20	5	0	38	21	....	19	....	.333	.365	.386	.751	131	19	91	6.04	0	*O-133(0-0-133)	24	1.3
1903 NY-A	132	512	95	160	14	7	0	32	32	....	24	....	.313	.368	.367	.735	114	10	83	5.83	-7	*O-128(0-5-123)/3-4	20	-0.3
1904 NY-A	143	543	78	186	14	8	2	40	35	....	21	....	.343	.390	.409	.799	146	29	100	6.92	2	*O-142(0-0-142)	25	2.7
1905 NY-A	149	560	81	169	14	4	4	38	43	....	19	....	.302	.357	.363	.719	115	10	86	5.29	-4	*O-137(3-0-134),2-12/3-3	19	0.0
1906 NY-A	152	592	96	180	8	3	2	33	40	....	23	....	.304	.353	.338	.691	106	5	85	5.06	-4	*O-152(1-0-151)	19	-0.7
1907 NY-A	107	423	50	99	5	2	0	17	15	....	7	....	.234	.265	.255	.521	61	-19	34	2.61	-6	*O-107(0-0-107)	2	-3.3
1908 NY-A	91	323	38	85	3	1	1	14	31	....	14	....	.263	.337	.288	.625	102	2	38	3.80	-4	O-88(2-0-86)	10	-0.7
1909 NY-A	99	360	44	95	7	5	1	32	24	....	10	....	.264	.327	.319	.647	104	2	44	3.80	-4	O-95(0-0-95)	11	-0.7
1910 NY-N	19	10	5	3	0	0	0	0	3	1	1	....	.300	.462	.300	.762	123	1	2	6.53	0	/O-2(1-1-0)	1	0.0
Total 19	2123	8591	1719	2932	241	145	33	810	524	36	495	....	.341	.388	.415	.802	125	290	1686	7.43	-10	*O-2039/3-44,2-19,S-2	333	15.3
• KEELY, Bob	Robert William Keely b: 8/22/1909, St. Louis, MO d: 5/20/2001, Sarasota, FL BR/TR, 6', 175 lbs. Deb: 7/25/1944 C																							
1944 StL-N	1	0	0	0	0	0	0	0	0	0	0	....	....	....	....	....	-98	0	0	....	0	/C-1	0	0.0
1945 StL-N	1	1	0	0	0	0	0	0	0	0	0	....	.000	.000	.000	.000	-98	-0	0	.00	0	/C-1	0	0.0
Total 2	2	1	0	0	0	0	0	0	0	0	0	....	.000	.000	.000	.000	-98	-0	0	.00	0	/C-2	0	-0.1

YEAR TM-L	G	AB	R	H	2B	3B	HR	RBI	BB	SO	SB	CS	AVG	OBP	SLG	OPS	OPS+	BR/A	RC	RC/G	FR	G/POS	WS	TPW
• KEEN, Bill	William Brown "Buster" Keen b: 8/16/1892, Oglethorpe, GA d: 7/16/1947, South Point, OH BR/TR, 6', 181 lbs. Deb: 8/8/1911																							
1911 Pit-N	6	7	0	0	0	0	0	0	1	4	0	....	.000	.125	.000	.125	-62	-2	0	.00	0	/1-1	0	-0.2
• KEENAN, Jim	James William Keenan b: 2/10/1858, New Haven, CT d: 9/21/1926, Cincinnati, OH BR/TR, 5'10", 186 lbs. Deb: 5/17/1875 U Career OF: 0-1-15																							
1875 NH-n	5	13	1	1	0	0	0	0	0	0	0	0	.077	.077	.077	.154	-53	-2	0	.19	-4	/C-3,3-2,0-1	....	-0.4
1880 Buf-N	2	7	1	1	0	0	0	0	1	1	....	....	.143	.250	.143	.393	36	-0	0	1.17	2	/C-2	0	0.1
1882 Pit-a	25	96	10	21	7	0	1	....	1	....	....	....	.219	.227	.323	.550	87	-1	7	2.69	-1	C-22/0-3(0-1-2),S-1	2	0.0
1884 Ind-a	68	249	36	73	14	4	3	0	16	....	....	....	.293	.343	.418	.761	151	14	37	5.72	-7	C-59/1-6,0-2(0-0-5),S-2,P	10	1.2
1885 Cin-a	36	132	16	35	2	2	1	15	8	....	....	....	.265	.307	.333	.640	100	0	14	3.86	-3	C-33/1-4,P-1	6	0.1
1886 Cin-a	44	148	31	40	4	3	3	24	18	....	0	....	.270	.357	.399	.756	132	6	22	5.40	-3	C-30/0-7(0-0-7),3-5,1-4,P	7	0.5
1887 Cin-a	47	185	19	55	4	1	0	17	11	....	7	....	.297	.301	.287	.588	63	-9	18	3.65	3	C-38,1-11	4	-0.2
1888 Cin-a	85	313	38	73	9	8	1	40	22	....	9	....	.233	.294	.323	.617	93	-3	33	3.73	4	C-69,1-16	10	0.5
1889 Cin-a	87	300	52	86	10	11	6	60	48	35	18	....	.287	.395	.453	.849	137	16	62	7.73	1	C-66,1-21/3-1	14	1.8
1890 Cin-N	54	202	21	28	4	2	3	19	19	36	5	....	.139	.216	.223	.439	28	-19	11	1.69	3	C-50/1-2,3-1,0-1	3	-1.1
1891 Cin-N	75	252	30	51	7	5	4	33	33	39	2	....	.202	.302	.317	.620	80	-6	25	3.41	-2	1-41,C-34/3-1	4	-0.9
Total 10	**523**	**1884**	**254**	**463**	**61**	**36**	**22**	**208**	**177**	**111**	**41**	**....**	**.246**	**.314**	**.348**	**.661**	**100**	**-3**	**229**	**4.35**	**-2**	**C-403,1-105/0-13,3-8,P-4,S**	**60**	**2.0**
• KEERL, George	George Henry Keerl b: 4/10/1847, Baltimore, MD d: 9/9/1923, Menominee, MI BR/TR, 5'7", 145 lbs. Deb: 5/4/1875																							
1875 Chi-n	6	23	2	3	0	0	0	3	0	2	0	0	.130	.130	.130	.261	-9	-2	0	.59	-1	/2-6	....	-0.3
• KEESEY, Jim	James Ward Keesey b: 10/27/1902, Perryville, MO d: 9/5/1951, Boise, ID BR/TR, 6'.5", 170 lbs. Deb: 9/6/1925																							
1925 Phi-A	5	5	1	2	0	0	0	1	0	2	0	0	.400	.400	.400	.800	97	-0	1	6.78	0	/1-2	0	0.0
1930 Phi-A	11	12	2	3	1	0	0	2	1	2	0	0	.250	.308	.333	.641	60	-1	1	3.71	0	/1-3	0	-0.1
Total 2	**16**	**17**	**3**	**5**	**1**	**0**	**0**	**3**	**1**	**4**	**0**	**0**	**.294**	**.333**	**.353**	**.686**	**70**	**-1**	**2**	**4.47**	**-1**	**/1-5**	**0**	**-0.1**
• KEISTER, Bill	William Hoffman "Wagon Tongue" Keister b: 8/17/1874, Baltimore, MD d: 8/19/1924, Baltimore, MD BL/TR, 5'5.5", 168 lbs. Deb: 5/20/1896 Career OF: 1-12-154																							
1896 Bal-N	15	58	8	14	3	0	0	5	3	5	4	....	.241	.302	.293	.595	56	-4	6	3.91	-2	/2-8,3-6	1	-0.4
1898 Bos-N	10	30	5	5	2	0	0	4	0	....	0	....	.167	.167	.233	.400	14	-4	1	1.27	3	/2-4,S-4,0-1	0	-0.1
1899 Bal-N	136	523	96	172	22	16	3	73	16	....	33	....	.329	.368	.449	.817	117	10	102	7.51	1	S-90,2-46/0-1	18	1.5
1900 StL-N	126	497	78	149	26	10	1	72	25	....	32	....	.300	.347	.398	.745	106	3	82	6.17	-23	*2-116/S-7,3-3	13	-1.3
1901 Bal-A	115	442	78	145	20	**21**	2	93	18	....	24	....	.328	.365	.482	.847	128	15	89	7.84	-4	*S-112	18	1.3
1902 Was-A	119	483	82	145	33	9	9	90	14	....	27	....	.300	.329	.462	.791	117	8	85	6.47	-3	0-65(0-12-53),2-40,3-14/S-2	15	0.2
1903 Phi-N	100	400	53	128	27	7	3	63	14	....	11	....	.320	.352	.445	.797	131	14	69	6.52	2	*0-100(0-0-100)	13	1.1
Total 7	**621**	**2433**	**400**	**758**	**133**	**63**	**18**	**400**	**90**	**5**	**131**	**....**	**.312**	**.349**	**.440**	**.789**	**116**	**42**	**435**	**6.74**	**-27**	**S-215,2-214,0-167/3-23**	**78**	**2.3**
• KELIHER, Mickey	Maurice Michael Keliher b: 1/11/1890, Washington, DC d: 9/7/1930, Washington, DC BL/TL, 6', 175 lbs. Deb: 9/10/1911																							
1911 Pit-N	3	7	0	0	0	0	0	0	0	5	0	....	.000	.000	.000	.000	-96	-2	0	.00	-0	/1-3	0	-0.2
1912 Pit-N	2	0	1	0	0	0	0	0	0	0	0	....	....	....	....	....	-102	0	0	....	0	....	0	0.0
Total 2	**5**	**7**	**1**	**0**	**0**	**0**	**0**	**0**	**0**	**5**	**0**	**....**	**.000**	**.000**	**.000**	**.000**	**-96**	**-2**	**0**	**.00**	**-0**	**/1-3**	**0**	**-0.2**
• KELL, George	George Clyde Kell b: 8/23/1922, Swifton, AR BR/TR, 5'9", 175 lbs. Deb: 9/28/1943 HOF: 1983 Career OF: 10-0-1																							
1943 Phi-A	1	5	1	1	0	1	0	1	0	0	0	0	.200	.200	.600	.800	131	0	1	4.15	0	/3-1	0	0.1
1944 Phi-A	139	514	51	138	15	3	0	44	22	23	5	2	.268	.300	.309	.609	75	-17	43	2.72	1	*3-139	8	-1.5
1945 Phi-A	147	567	50	154	30	3	4	56	27	15	2	0	.272	.306	.356	.662	92	-7	61	3.83	14	*3-147	15	1.0
1946 Phi-A	26	87	3	26	6	1	0	11	10	6	0	0	.299	.378	.391	.768	116	2	14	5.89	4	3-26	4	0.6
Det-A	105	434	67	142	19	9	4	41	30	14	3	2	.327	.371	.440	.811	118	11	71	6.00	4	*3-105/1-1	18	1.4
Yr.	131	521	70	168	25	10	4	52	40	20	3	2	.322	.372	.432	.804	118	13	85	5.98	7	*3-131/1-1	22	2.1
1947 Det-A★	152	588	75	188	29	5	5	93	61	16	9	11	.320	.387	.412	.798	118	14	95	5.88	12	*3-152	24	2.7
1948 Det-A★	92	368	47	112	24	3	2	44	33	15	2	2	.304	.369	.402	.772	102	1	56	5.44	-4	3-92	11	-0.3
1949 Det-A★	134	522	97	179	38	9	3	59	71	13	7	5	**.343**	.424	.467	.892	136	28	106	7.52	2	*3-134	24	2.9
1950 Det-A★	157	641	114	**218**	**56**	6	8	101	66	18	3	3	.340	.403	.484	.886	122	21	123	7.17	-9	*3-157	26	1.1
1951 Det-A★	147	598	92	**191**	**36**	3	2	59	61	18	10	3	.319	.386	.400	.786	112	13	97	6.04	2	*3-147	22	1.4
1952 Det-A	39	152	11	45	8	0	1	17	15	13	0	1	.296	.359	.368	.728	102	0	21	5.00	0	3-39	4	0.0
Bos-A★	75	276	41	88	15	2	6	40	31	10	0	1	.319	.390	.453	.843	124	9	48	6.35	-7	3-73	10	0.2
Yr.	114	428	52	133	23	2	7	57	46	23	0	2	.311	.379	.423	.802	116	10	69	5.87	-7	*3-112	14	0.2
1953 Bos-A★	134	460	68	141	41	2	12	73	52	22	5	2	.307	.383	.483	.866	126	18	88	7.13	-8	*3-124/0-7(7-0-0)	18	0.9
1954 Bos-A	26	93	15	24	3	0	0	10	15	3	0	0	.258	.361	.290	.651	72	-3	11	4.00	-4	3-25	2	-0.7
Chi-A★	71	233	25	66	10	0	5	48	18	12	1	1	.283	.335	.391	.725	95	-2	30	4.47	-1	1-32,3-31/0-2(2-0-1)	6	-0.5
Yr.	97	326	40	90	13	0	5	58	33	15	1	1	.276	.343	.362	.705	88	-5	41	4.34	-5	3-56,1-32/0-2(2-0-1)	8	-1.3
1955 Chi-A	128	429	44	134	24	1	8	81	51	36	2	2	.312	.393	.429	.822	117	12	75	6.32	-13	*3-105,1-24/0-1	16	-0.2
1956 Chi-A	21	80	7	25	5	0	1	11	8	6	0	0	.313	.375	.413	.788	106	1	12	5.35	1	3-18/1-4	2	0.1
Bal-A★	102	345	45	90	17	2	8	37	25	31	0	1	.261	.316	.391	.708	93	-5	42	4.05	-4	3-97/1-2,2-1	9	-0.9
Yr.	123	425	52	115	22	2	9	48	33	37	0	1	.271	.328	.395	.723	95	-4	54	4.28	-3	*3-115/1-6,2-1	11	-0.8
1957 Bal-A★	99	310	28	92	9	0	9	44	25	16	2	0	.297	.353	.413	.766	116	7	44	4.98	0	3-80,1-22	10	0.6
Total 15	**1795**	**6702**	**881**	**2054**	**385**	**50**	**78**	**870**	**621**	**287**	**51**	**36**	**.306**	**.368**	**.414**	**.782**	**111**	**103**	**1038**	**5.56**	**-11**	***3-1692/1-85,0-10,2-1**	**229**	**8.9**
• KELL, Skeeter	Everett Lee Kell b: 10/11/1929, Swifton, AR BR/TR, 5'9", 160 lbs. Deb: 4/19/1952																							
1952 Phi-A	75	213	24	47	8	3	0	17	14	18	5	1	.221	.275	.286	.561	53	-13	18	2.72	-10	2-68	2	-2.1
• KELLEHER, Duke	Albert Aloysius Kelleher b: 9/30/1893, New York, NY d: 9/28/1947, Staten Island, NY TR Deb: 8/18/1916																							
1916 NY-N	1	0	0	0	0	0	0	0	0	0	0	....	....	....	....	....	-106	0	0	....	-1	/C-1	0	-0.1
• KELLEHER, Frankie	Francis Eugene Kelleher b: 8/22/1916, San Francisco, CA d: 4/13/1979, Stockton, CA BR/TR, 6'1", 195 lbs. Deb: 7/18/1942 Career OF: 30-0-1																							
1942 Cin-N	38	110	13	20	3	1	3	12	16	20	0	....	.182	.286	.309	.595	74	-4	10	2.99	0	0-30(30-0-0)	2	-0.5
1943 Cin-N	9	10	1	0	0	0	0	0	2	0	0	....	.000	.167	.000	.167	-51	-2	0	.23	-0	/0-1	0	-0.2
Total 2	**47**	**120**	**14**	**20**	**3**	**1**	**3**	**12**	**18**	**20**	**0**	**....**	**.167**	**.275**	**.283**	**.559**	**63**	**-5**	**10**	**2.73**	**0**	**/0-31**	**2**	**-0.8**
• KELLEHER, John	John Patrick Kelleher b: 9/13/1893, Brookline, MA d: 8/21/1960, Brighton, MA BR/TR, 5'11", 150 lbs. Deb: 7/31/1912																							
1912 StL-N	8	12	0	4	1	0	0	1	0	2	0	....	.333	.333	.417	.750	107	0	2	5.12	0	/3-3	0	0.0
1916 Bro-N	2	3	0	0	0	0	0	0	0	0	0	....	.000	.000	.000	.000	-97	-1	0	.00	0	/3-1,S-1	0	-0.1
1921 Chi-N	95	301	31	93	11	7	4	47	16	16	2	5	.309	.346	.432	.778	104	1	44	4.88	-2	3-37,2-27,1-11,S-11/0-1	9	0.2
1922 Chi-N	63	193	23	50	7	1	0	20	15	14	5	7	.259	.316	.306	.621	60	-13	18	3.00	1	3-46/S-7,1-4	3	-0.8
1923 Chi-N	66	193	27	59	10	0	6	21	14	9	2	4	.306	.353	.451	.803	110	2	29	5.42	-4	1-22,S-14,3-11/2-6	6	-0.2
1924 Bos-N	1	1	0	0	0	0	0	0	0	1	0	0	.000	.000	.000	.000	-104	-0	0	.00	0	....	0	0.0
Total 6	**235**	**703**	**81**	**206**	**29**	**8**	**10**	**89**	**45**	**42**	**9**	**16**	**.293**	**.337**	**.400**	**.737**	**93**	**-11**	**93**	**4.44**	**-6**	**/3-98,1-37,2-33,S-33,0-1**	**18**	**-0.9**
• KELLEHER, Mick	Michael Dennis Kelleher b: 7/25/1947, Seattle, WA BR/TR, 5'9", 176 lbs. Deb: 9/1/1972 C																							
1972 StL-N	23	63	5	10	2	1	0	1	6	15	0	0	.159	.232	.222	.454	30	-6	4	1.69	-1	S-23	1	-0.4
1973 StL-N	43	38	4	7	2	0	0	2	4	11	0	0	.184	.279	.237	.516	44	-3	3	2.43	0	S-42	1	0.0
1974 Hou-N	19	57	4	9	0	0	0	2	5	10	1	1	.158	.226	.158	.384	9	-7	2	1.13	-1	S-18	1	-0.6
1975 StL-N	7	4	0	0	0	0	0	0	0	1	0	0	.000	.000	.000	.000	-97	-1	0	.00	-1	/S-7	0	-0.1
1976 Chi-N	124	337	28	77	12	1	0	22	15	32	0	4	.228	.266	.270	.536	48	-25	22	2.16	-6	*S-101,3-22/2-5	5	-2.1
1977 Chi-N	63	122	14	28	5	2	0	11	9	12	0	0	.230	.288	.303	.591	53	-8	10	2.87	2	2-40,S-14/3-1	2	-0.4
1978 Chi-N	68	95	8	24	1	0	0	6	7	11	4	1	.253	.304	.263	.567	53	-5	7	2.44	2	3-37,2-17,S-10	2	-0.3
1979 Chi-N	73	142	14	36	4	1	0	10	7	9	2	0	.254	.298	.296	.594	57	-8	13	2.91	1	3-32,2-29,S-14	3	-0.5
1980 Chi-N	105	96	12	14	1	1	0	4	9	17	1	3	.146	.219	.177	.396	11	-13	3	.85	-8	2-57,3-31,S-17	1	-1.9
1981 Det-A	61	77	10	17	4	0	0	6	7	10	0	0	.221	.286	.273	.558	59	-4	6	2.05	2	3-39,2-11/S-9	1	-0.1
1982 Det-A	2	1	0	0	0	0	0	0	0	0	0	0	.000	.000	.000	.000	-100	-0	0	.00	-1	/2-1,3-1	0	-0.1
Cal-A	34	49	9	8	1	0	0	1	5	5	1	1	.163	.255	.184	.438	23	-5	2	.94	-2	S-28/3-6	1	-0.6

YEAR TM-L	G	AB	R	H	2B	3B	HR	RBI	BB	SO	SB	CS	AVG	OBP	SLG	OPS	OPS+	BR/A	RC	RC/G	FR	G/POS	WS	TPW
Yr.	36	50	9	8	1	0	0	1	5	5	1	1	.160	.250	.180	.430	21	-6	2	.92	-3	S-28/3-7,2-1	1	-0.6
Total 11	622	1081	108	230	32	6	0	65	74	133	9	10	.213	.268	.253	.521	43	-85	72	2.06	-11	S-283,3-169,2-160	18	-7.1

• KELLER, Charlie

Charles Ernest "King Kong" Keller
b: 9/12/1916, Middletown, MD d: 5/23/1990, Frederick, MD BL/TR, 5'10", 190 lbs. Deb: 4/22/1939 C Career OF: 881-0-138

YEAR TM-L	G	AB	R	H	2B	3B	HR	RBI	BB	SO	SB	CS	AVG	OBP	SLG	OPS	OPS+	BR/A	RC	RC/G	FR	G/POS	WS	TPW
1939*NY-A	111	398	87	133	21	6	11	83	81	49	6	3	.334	.447	.500	.947	144	31	97	9.23	-2	*O-105(47-0-58)	22	2.1
1940 NY-A★	138	500	102	143	18	15	21	93	**106**	65	8	2	.286	.411	.508	.919	142	37	114	8.24	-1	*O-136(65-0-71)	24	2.6
1941*NY-A★	140	507	102	151	24	10	33	122	102	65	6	4	.298	.416	.580	.996	163	48	134	9.98	3	*O-137(137-0-0)	32	4.2
1942*NY-A	152	544	106	159	24	9	26	108	114	61	14	2	.292	.417	.513	.930	164	53	131	9.02	0	*O-152(152-0-0)	34	4.6
1943*NY-A★	141	512	97	139	15	11	31	86	**106**	60	7	5	.271	.396	.525	**.922**	**167**	**46**	116	**8.07**	4	*O-141(141-0-0)	36	4.5
1945 NY-A	44	163	26	49	7	4	10	34	31	21	0	2	.301	.412	.577	.989	178	16	41	9.36	2	O-44(44-0-0)	11	1.7
1946 NY-A★	150	538	98	148	29	10	30	101	113	101	1	4	.275	.405	.533	.938	158	45	127	8.60	0	*O-149(149-0-0)	31	3.5
1947 NY-A★	45	151	36	36	6	1	13	36	41	18	0	0	.238	.404	.550	.954	165	15	37	8.54	0	O-43(43-0-0)	10	1.3
1948 NY-A	83	247	41	66	15	2	6	44	41	25	1	1	.267	.372	.417	.789	110	4	40	5.71	-5	O-66(66-0-0)	8	-0.5
1949 NY-A	60	116	17	29	4	1	3	16	25	15	2	0	.250	.392	.379	.771	104	2	20	5.86	-2	O-31(31-0-0)	5	-0.1
1950 Det-A	50	51	7	16	1	3	2	16	13	6	0	0	.314	.453	.569	1.022	155	5	15	11.57	0	/O-6(1-0-5)	3	0.4
1951 Det-A	54	62	6	16	2	0	3	21	11	12	0	0	.258	.370	.435	.805	117	2	11	6.51	1	/O-8(4-0-4)	2	0.2
1952 NY-A	2	1	0	0	0	0	0	0	0	1	0	0	.000	.000	.000	.000	-106	-0	0	.00	0	/O-1	0	0.0
Total 13	1170	3790	725	1085	166	72	189	760	784	499	45	23	.286	.410	.518	.928	153	304	883	8.52	0	*O-1019	218	24.4

• KELLER, Hal

Harold Kefauver Keller b: 7/7/1927, Middletown, MD BL/TR, 6'1", 200 lbs. Deb: 9/13/1949

YEAR TM-L	G	AB	R	H	2B	3B	HR	RBI	BB	SO	SB	CS	AVG	OBP	SLG	OPS	OPS+	BR/A	RC	RC/G	FR	G/POS	WS	TPW
1949 Was-A	3	3	1	1	0	0	0	0	0	0	0	0	.333	.333	.333	.667	78	-0	0	4.61	0	....	0	0.0
1950 Was-A	11	28	1	6	3	0	1	5	2	2	0	0	.214	.267	.429	.695	79	-1	3	3.51	0	/C-8	0	-0.1
1952 Was-A	11	23	2	4	2	0	0	0	1	1	0	0	.174	.208	.261	.469	31	-2	1	1.90	0	C-11	0	-0.2
Total 3	25	54	4	11	5	0	1	5	3	3	0	0	.204	.246	.352	.597	59	-3	5	2.86	0	/C-19	0	-0.3

• KELLERT, Frank

Frank William Kellert b: 7/6/1924, Oklahoma City, OK d: 11/19/1976, Oklahoma City, OK BR/TR, 6'2.5", 185 lbs. Deb: 4/18/1953

YEAR TM-L	G	AB	R	H	2B	3B	HR	RBI	BB	SO	SB	CS	AVG	OBP	SLG	OPS	OPS+	BR/A	RC	RC/G	FR	G/POS	WS	TPW
1953 StL-A	2	4	0	0	0	0	0	0	0	0	0	0	.000	.000	.000	.000	-98	-1	0	.00	0	/1-1	0	-0.1
1954 Bal-A	10	34	3	7	2	0	0	1	5	4	0	0	.206	.308	.265	.572	62	-2	3	3.17	-1	/1-9	0	-0.3
1955*Bro-N	39	80	12	26	4	2	4	19	9	10	0	1	.325	.393	.575	.968	149	5	18	8.34	0	1-22	4	0.4
1956 Chi-N	71	129	10	24	3	1	4	17	12	22	0	0	.186	.255	.318	.573	54	-9	9	2.06	1	1-27	0	-1.0
Total 4	122	247	25	57	9	3	8	37	26	36	0	1	.231	.304	.389	.693	84	-6	30	3.95	-1	/1-59	4	-1.0

• KELLETT, Red

Donald Stafford Kellett b: 7/15/1909, Brooklyn, NY d: 11/3/1970, Fort Lauderdale, FL BR/TR, 6', 185 lbs. Deb: 7/2/1934

YEAR TM-L	G	AB	R	H	2B	3B	HR	RBI	BB	SO	SB	CS	AVG	OBP	SLG	OPS	OPS+	BR/A	RC	RC/G	FR	G/POS	WS	TPW
1934 Bos-A	9	9	0	0	0	0	0	0	1	5	0	0	.000	.100	.000	.100	-68	-2	0	.07	-1	/S-4,2-2,3-1	0	-0.3

• KELLEY, Joe

Joseph James Kelley
b: 12/9/1871, Cambridge, MA d: 8/14/1943, Baltimore, MD BR/TR, 5'11", 190 lbs. Deb: 7/27/1891 M/C HOF: 1971 Career OF: 1131-328-8

YEAR TM-L	G	AB	R	H	2B	3B	HR	RBI	BB	SO	SB	CS	AVG	OBP	SLG	OPS	OPS+	BR/A	RC	RC/G	FR	G/POS	WS	TPW
1891 Bos-N	12	45	7	11	1	1	0	3	2	7	0	....	.244	.277	.311	.588	63	-2	4	3.15	-1	0-12(12-1-0)	1	-0.3
1892 Pit-N	56	205	26	49	7	7	0	28	17	21	8	....	.239	.297	.341	.639	93	-3	24	4.11	1	0-56(0-56-0)	6	-0.5
Bal-N	10	33	3	7	0	0	0	4	4	7	2	....	.212	.316	.212	.528	59	-1	3	3.03	-1	0-10(0-10-0)	0	-0.3
Yr.	66	238	29	56	7	7	0	32	21	28	10	....	.235	.300	.324	.624	88	-4	27	3.96	-0	0-66(0-66-0)	6	-0.8
1893 Bal-N	125	502	120	153	27	16	9	76	77	44	33	....	.305	.401	.476	.877	131	22	112	8.50	0	*O-125(18-107-1)	20	1.1
1894*Bal-N	129	507	165	199	48	20	6	111	107	36	46	....	.393	.502	.602	1.104	158	55	181	15.26	4	*O-129(129-0-0)	30	3.7
1895*Bal-N	131	518	148	189	26	19	10	134	77	29	54	....	.365	.456	.546	1.003	153	44	159	12.55	0	*O-131(130-1-0)	27	2.6
1896*Bal-N	131	519	148	189	31	19	8	100	91	19	**87**	....	.364	.469	.543	1.013	164	54	178	14.07	0	*O-131(129-0-2)	31	3.6
1897*Bal-N	131	505	113	183	31	9	5	118	70	....	44	....	.362	.447	.489	.936	147	38	134	10.74	2	*O-130(130-0-0)/S-3,3-2	26	2.5
1898 Bal-N	124	464	71	149	18	15	2	110	56	....	24	....	.321	.398	.438	.835	137	23	93	7.68	-1	*O-122(39-83-0)/3-2	22	1.2
1899 Bro-N	143	538	108	175	21	14	6	93	70	....	31	....	.325	.410	.450	.860	133	26	116	8.22	10	*O-143(143-0-0)	30	2.1
1900*Bro-N	121	454	90	145	23	17	6	91	53	....	26	....	.319	.398	.485	.882	135	22	100	8.60	-2	0-77(77-0-0),1-32,3-13	22	1.2
1901 Bro-N	120	492	77	151	22	12	4	65	40	....	18	....	.307	.363	.425	.787	124	15	85	6.52	1	*1-115/3-5	18	1.4
1902 Bal-A	60	222	50	69	17	7	1	34	34	....	12	....	.311	.405	.464	.869	134	12	48	8.07	-3	0-48(1-47-0)/3-8,1-5	8	0.7
Cin-N	40	156	24	50	9	2	1	12	15	....	3	....	.321	.380	.423	.803	135	7	27	6.69	5	0-20(18-2-0),2-10/3-9,S-2	7	1.1
1903 Cin-N	105	383	85	121	22	4	3	45	51	....	18	....	.316	.402	.418	.820	120	12	74	7.31	-1	0-67(61-6-0),S-12,2-11/3-8,1	15	0.7
1904 Cin-N	123	449	75	126	21	13	0	63	49	....	15	....	.281	.359	.385	.744	119	11	71	5.47	-4	*1-117/0-6(0-3-3),2-1	16	0.5
1905 Cin-N	90	321	43	89	7	6	1	37	27	....	8	....	.277	.346	.346	.692	96	-1	44	4.68	-1	0-85(84-0-1)/1-2	10	-0.7
1906 Cin-N	129	465	43	106	19	11	1	53	44	....	9	....	.228	.300	.323	.623	90	-6	52	3.52	-5	*O-122(122-0-0)/1-3,3-1,S	8	-2.0
1908 Bos-N	73	228	25	59	8	2	2	17	27	....	5	....	.259	.342	.338	.680	119	6	28	4.17	-1	0-51(38-12-1),1-11	8	0.3
Total 17	1853	7006	1421	2220	358	194	65	1194	911	163	443	....	.317	.402	.451	.853	131	333	1533	8.26	4	*O-1465,1-291/3-48,2-22,S-18	305	18.8

• KELLEY, Mike

Michael Joseph Kelley b: 12/2/1875, Templeton, MA d: 6/6/1955, Minneapolis, MN BR/TR, 6', 210 lbs. Deb: 7/15/1899

YEAR TM-L	G	AB	R	H	2B	3B	HR	RBI	BB	SO	SB	CS	AVG	OBP	SLG	OPS	OPS+	BR/A	RC	RC/G	FR	G/POS	WS	TPW
1899 Lou-N	76	282	48	68	11	2	3	33	21	....	10	....	.241	.307	.326	.634	74	-10	33	3.96	2	1-76	4	-0.8

• KELLIHER, Frank

Francis Mortimer "Yucca" Kelliher b: 5/23/1899, Somerville, MA d: 3/4/1956, Somerville, MA BL/TL, 5'9.5", 175 lbs. Deb: 9/19/1919

YEAR TM-L	G	AB	R	H	2B	3B	HR	RBI	BB	SO	SB	CS	AVG	OBP	SLG	OPS	OPS+	BR/A	RC	RC/G	FR	G/POS	WS	TPW
1919 Was-A	1	1	0	0	0	0	0	0	0	0	0	0	.000	.000	.000	.000	-101	-0	0	.00	0	....	0	0.0

• KELLOGG, Bill

William Dearstyne Kellogg b: 5/25/1884, Albany, NY d: 12/12/1971, Baltimore, MD BR/TR, 5'10", 153 lbs. Deb: 4/14/1914

YEAR TM-L	G	AB	R	H	2B	3B	HR	RBI	BB	SO	SB	CS	AVG	OBP	SLG	OPS	OPS+	BR/A	RC	RC/G	FR	G/POS	WS	TPW
1914 Cin-N	71	126	14	22	0	1	0	7	14	28	7	....	.175	.262	.190	.453	34	-10	8	1.91	-4	1-38,2-11/0-2(0-2-0),3-1	0	-1.5

• KELLOGG, Nate

Nathaniel Monroe Kellogg b: 9/28/1858, Rochester, IA d: 1915, Minneapolis, MN, 5'9", 175 lbs. Deb: 8/27/1885

YEAR TM-L	G	AB	R	H	2B	3B	HR	RBI	BB	SO	SB	CS	AVG	OBP	SLG	OPS	OPS+	BR/A	RC	RC/G	FR	G/POS	WS	TPW
1885 Det-N	5	17	4	2	1	0	0	0	1	5	....	....	.118	.167	.176	.343	11	-2	1	.92	-2	/S-5	0	-0.4

• KELLY, Bill

William Henry "Big Bill" Kelly b: 12/28/1898, Syracuse, NY d: 4/8/1990, Syracuse, NY BR/TR, 6', 190 lbs. Deb: 9/6/1920

YEAR TM-L	G	AB	R	H	2B	3B	HR	RBI	BB	SO	SB	CS	AVG	OBP	SLG	OPS	OPS+	BR/A	RC	RC/G	FR	G/POS	WS	TPW
1920 Phi-A	9	13	0	3	1	0	0	0	0	2	0	0	.231	.231	.308	.538	41	-1	1	2.35	0	/1-2	0	-0.1
1928 Phi-N	23	71	6	12	1	1	0	5	7	20	0	....	.169	.244	.211	.455	19	-8	4	1.67	0	1-23	0	-1.0
Total 2	32	84	6	15	2	1	0	5	7	22	0	0	.179	.242	.226	.468	22	-10	5	1.77	0	/1-25	0	-1.1

• KELLY, Bill

William J. Kelly b: New York, NY Deb: 5/4/1871

YEAR TM-L	G	AB	R	H	2B	3B	HR	RBI	BB	SO	SB	CS	AVG	OBP	SLG	OPS	OPS+	BR/A	RC	RC/G	FR	G/POS	WS	TPW
1871 Kek-n	18	67	16	15	1	1	0	7	6	1	0	0	.224	.288	.269	.556	60	-4	5	3.22	-2	0-18(1-4-14)	....	-0.3

• KELLY, Billy

William Joseph Kelly b: 5/1/1886, Baltimore, MD d: 6/3/1940, Detroit, MI BR/TR, 6'.5", 183 lbs. Deb: 5/2/1910

YEAR TM-L	G	AB	R	H	2B	3B	HR	RBI	BB	SO	SB	CS	AVG	OBP	SLG	OPS	OPS+	BR/A	RC	RC/G	FR	G/POS	WS	TPW
1910 StL-N	2	2	1	0	0	0	0	0	1	0	0	....	.000	.333	.000	.333	-1	-0	0	.00	0	/C-1	0	-0.1
1911 Pit-N	6	8	0	1	0	0	0	0	0	2	0	....	.125	.125	.125	.250	-29	-1	0	.40	1	/C-1	0	-0.1
1912 Pit-N	48	132	20	42	3	2	1	11	2	16	8	....	.318	.328	.394	.722	99	-1	20	5.15	-5	C-39	4	-0.3
1913 Pit-N	48	82	11	22	2	2	0	9	2	12	1	....	.268	.302	.341	.644	87	-2	8	3.48	-2	C-40	3	-0.1
Total 4	104	224	32	65	5	4	1	20	5	30	9	....	.290	.312	.362	.673	89	-4	28	4.27	-6	/C-81	7	-0.5

• KELLY, Charlie

Charles H. Kelly Deb: 6/14/1883

YEAR TM-L	G	AB	R	H	2B	3B	HR	RBI	BB	SO	SB	CS	AVG	OBP	SLG	OPS	OPS+	BR/A	RC	RC/G	FR	G/POS	WS	TPW
1883 Phi-N	2	7	1	1	0	1	0	0	0	3	....	....	.143	.143	.429	.571	71	-0	0	2.01	-1	/3-2	0	-0.1
1886 Phi-a	1	3	0	0	0	0	0	0	0	....	0	....	.000	.000	.000	.000	-99	-1	0	.00	-1	/S-1	0	-0.2
Total 2	3	10	1	1	0	1	0	0	0	3	0	....	.100	.100	.300	.400	20	-1	0	1.34	-2	/3-2,S-1	0	-0.2

• KELLY, George

George Lange "Highpockets" Kelly
b: 9/10/1895, San Francisco, CA d: 10/13/1984, Burlingame, CA BR/TR, 6'4", 190 lbs. Deb: 8/18/1915 C HOF: 1973 Career OF: 27-16-19

YEAR TM-L	G	AB	R	H	2B	3B	HR	RBI	BB	SO	SB	CS	AVG	OBP	SLG	OPS	OPS+	BR/A	RC	RC/G	FR	G/POS	WS	TPW
1915 NY-N	17	38	2	6	0	0	1	4	1	9	0	1	.158	.179	.237	.416	27	-4	1	1.15	0	/1-9,0-4(0-4-0)	0	-0.5
1916 NY-N	49	76	4	12	2	1	0	3	6	24	1	....	.158	.220	.211	.430	34	-6	4	1.57	-2	1-13,0-12(0-2-5)/3-1	0	-1.0
1917 NY-N	11	7	0	0	0	0	0	0	0	3	0	....	.000	.000	.000	.000	-103	-2	0	.00	0	/0-4(3-0-1),1-1,2-1,P-1	1	0.0
Pit-N	8	23	2	2	0	1	0	0	1	9	0	....	.087	.125	.174	.299	-9	-3	0	.52	-1	/1-8	0	-0.5
Yr.	19	30	2	2	0	1	0	0	1	12	0	....	.067	.097	.133	.230	-30	-5	0	.39	-1	/1-9,0-4(3-0-1),2-1,P-1	1	-0.4
1919 NY-N	32	107	12	31	6	2	1	14	3	15	1	....	.290	.315	.411	.727	119	2	14	4.46	-3	1-32	4	-0.2
1920 NY-N	155	590	69	157	22	11	11	**94**	41	92	6	16	.266	.320	.397	.717	106	0	71	4.07	8	*1-155	16	0.6

YEAR TM-L	G	AB	R	H	2B	3B	HR	RBI	BB	SO	SB	CS	AVG	OBP	SLG	OPS	OPS+	BR/A	RC	RC/G	FR	G/POS	WS	TPW
1921*NY-N	149	587	95	181	42	9	**23**	122	40	73	4	12	.308	.356	.528	.884	131	21	104	6.36	5	*1-149	24	1.6
1922*NY-N	151	592	96	194	33	8	17	107	30	65	12	3	.328	.363	.497	.860	119	17	106	6.77	11	*1-151	20	1.7
1923*NY-N	145	560	82	172	23	5	16	103	47	64	14	7	.307	.362	.452	.814	115	13	92	6.03	1	*1-145	20	0.4
1924*NY-N	144	571	91	185	37	9	21	**136**	38	52	7	2	.324	.371	.531	.902	143	35	112	7.42	-1	*1-125,0-14(5-9-0)/2-5,3-1	26	2.5
1925 NY-N	147	586	87	181	29	3	20	99	35	54	5	2	.309	.350	.471	.821	112	10	96	6.11	13	*2-108,1-25,0-17(8-0-9)	22	2.1
1926 NY-N	136	499	70	151	24	4	13	80	36	52	4	....	.303	.352	.445	.797	115	9	76	5.45	11	*1-114,2-18	17	1.3
1927 Cin-N	61	222	27	60	16	4	5	21	11	23	1	....	.270	.308	.446	.754	103	-0	29	4.63	1	1-49,2-13/0-2(2-0-0)	6	-0.2
1928 Cin-N	116	402	46	119	33	7	3	58	28	35	2	....	.296	.345	.435	.780	104	1	59	5.10	10	1-99,0-13(9-0-4)	14	0.4
1929 Cin-N	147	577	73	169	45	9	5	103	33	61	7	....	.293	.332	.428	.760	91	-10	79	4.81	10	*1-147	12	-0.9
1930 Cin-N	51	188	18	54	10	1	5	35	7	20	1	....	.287	.313	.431	.744	81	-6	24	4.34	3	1-50	3	-0.6
Chi-N	39	166	22	55	6	1	3	19	7	16	0	....	.331	.362	.434	.796	91	-3	25	5.65	4	1-39	4	-0.1
Yr.	90	354	40	109	16	2	8	54	14	36	1	....	.308	.336	.432	.768	86	-9	49	4.92	7	1-89	7	-0.7
1932 Bro-N	64	202	23	49	9	1	4	22	22	27	0	....	.243	.317	.356	.673	82	-5	24	4.03	-5	1-62/0-1	4	-1.5
Total 16	**1622**	**5993**	**819**	**1778**	**337**	**76**	**148**	**1020**	**386**	**694**	**65**	**43**	**.297**	**.342**	**.452**	**.794**	**110**	**70**	**918**	**5.47**	**65**	***1-1373,2-145/0-67,3-2,P-1**	**193**	**5.1**

• KELLY, Jim

James Robert Kelly b: 2/1/1884, Bloomfield, NJ d: 4/10/1961, Kingsport, TN BL/TR, 5'10.5", 180 lbs. Deb: 4/26/1914 Career OF: 50-4-139

YEAR TM-L	G	AB	R	H	2B	3B	HR	RBI	BB	SO	SB	CS	AVG	OBP	SLG	OPS	OPS+	BR/A	RC	RC/G	FR	G/POS	WS	TPW
1914 Pit-N	32	44	4	10	2	1	0	3	2	3	0	....	.227	.261	.318	.579	75	-2	4	2.63	0	/0-7(1-0-6)	1	-0.2
1915 Pit-F	148	524	68	154	12	17	4	50	35	46	38	....	.294	.340	.405	.745	114	8	81	5.44	9	*0-148(14-4-133)	20	0.9
1918 Bos-N	35	146	19	48	1	4	0	4	9	9	4	....	.329	.376	.390	.766	139	7	22	5.65	1	0-35(35-0-0)	7	0.7
Total 3	**215**	**714**	**91**	**212**	**15**	**22**	**4**	**57**	**46**	**58**	**42**	**....**	**.297**	**.343**	**.396**	**.739**	**117**	**13**	**107**	**5.29**	**9**	**0-190**	**28**	**1.4**

• KELLY, Joe

Joseph Henry Kelly b: 9/23/1886, Weir City, KS d: 8/16/1977, St. Joseph, MO BR/TR, 5'10", 175 lbs. Deb: 4/14/1914 Career OF: 136-211-6

YEAR TM-L	G	AB	R	H	2B	3B	HR	RBI	BB	SO	SB	CS	AVG	OBP	SLG	OPS	OPS+	BR/A	RC	RC/G	FR	G/POS	WS	TPW
1914 Pit-N	141	508	47	113	19	9	1	48	39	59	21	....	.222	.283	.301	.584	77	-15	48	3.00	-7	*0-139(0-139-0)	9	-3.3
1916 Chi-N	54	169	18	43	7	1	2	15	9	16	10	....	.254	.296	.343	.639	87	-3	20	4.06	-1	0-46(16-25-6)	4	-0.7
1917 Bos-N	116	445	41	99	9	8	3	36	26	45	21	....	.222	.268	.299	.567	78	-12	40	2.85	9	*0-116(82-29-0)	7	-1.0
1918 Bos-N	47	155	20	36	2	4	0	15	6	12	12	....	.232	.265	.297	.562	74	-5	14	3.03	-3	0-45(22-18-0)	2	-1.1
1919 Bos-N	18	64	3	9	1	0	0	3	0	11	2	....	.141	.154	.156	.310	-7	-8	2	.77	0	0-16(16-0-0)	0	-1.0
Total 5	**376**	**1341**	**129**	**300**	**38**	**22**	**6**	**117**	**80**	**143**	**66**	**....**	**.224**	**.272**	**.298**	**.570**	**75**	**-44**	**123**	**2.96**	**-2**	**0-362**	**22**	**-7.2**

• KELLY, Joe

Joseph James Kelly b: 4/23/1900, New York, NY d: 11/24/1967, Lynnbrook, NY BL/TL, 6', 180 lbs. Deb: 4/13/1926

YEAR TM-L	G	AB	R	H	2B	3B	HR	RBI	BB	SO	SB	CS	AVG	OBP	SLG	OPS	OPS+	BR/A	RC	RC/G	FR	G/POS	WS	TPW
1926 Chi-N	65	176	16	59	15	3	0	32	7	11	0	....	.335	.361	.455	.815	117	3	27	5.81	0	0-39(25-0-14)	5	0.1
1928 Chi-N	32	52	3	11	1	0	1	7	1	3	0	....	.212	.255	.288	.543	42	-5	4	2.31	0	1-10	0	-0.5
Total 2	**97**	**228**	**19**	**70**	**16**	**3**	**1**	**39**	**8**	**14**	**0**	**....**	**.307**	**.336**	**.417**	**.753**	**99**	**-1**	**31**	**4.90**	**-1**	**/0-39,1-10**	**5**	**-0.5**

• KELLY, John

John Francis "Honest John,Father" Kelly
b: 3/3/1859, Paterson, NJ d: 4/13/1908, Paterson, NJ BR/TR, 6', 185 lbs. Deb: 6/7/1879 M/U Career OF: 0-3-14

YEAR TM-L	G	AB	R	H	2B	3B	HR	RBI	BB	SO	SB	CS	AVG	OBP	SLG	OPS	OPS+	BR/A	RC	RC/G	FR	G/POS	WS	TPW
1879 Cle-N	1	4	0	1	0	0	0	0	0	0	....	....	.250	.250	.250	.500	66	-0	0	2.39	-1	/1-1,C-1	0	-0.1
1882 Cle-N	30	104	6	14	2	0	0	5	1	24	....	....	.135	.143	.154	.297	-5	-12	2	.72	-14	C-30	1	-2.1
1883 Bal-a	48	202	18	46	9	2	0	0	3	....	....	....	.228	.239	.292	.531	68	-8	14	2.59	-13	C-38,0-13(0-1-12)	1	-1.5
Phi-N	1	3	0	0	0	0	0	0	0	2	....	....	.000	.000	.000	.000	-110	-1	0	.00	1	/0-1	0	0.0
1884 Cin-U	38	142	23	40	5	1	1	....	6	....	....	....	.282	.311	.352	.663	114	2	16	4.37	-7	C-37/0-2(0-1-1)	6	-0.2
Was-U	4	14	1	5	1	0	0	....	0	....	....	....	.357	.357	.429	.786	170	1	2	6.83	1	/C-3,0-1	1	0.2
Yr.	42	156	24	45	6	1	1	....	6	....	....	....	.288	.315	.359	.674	119	3	18	4.57	-6	C-40/0-3(0-1-2)	7	0.0
Total 4	**122**	**469**	**48**	**106**	**17**	**3**	**1**	**5**	**10**	**26**	**....**	**....**	**.226**	**.242**	**.281**	**.524**	**68**	**-18**	**35**	**2.71**	**-33**	**C-109/0-17,1-1**	**9**	**-3.7**

• KELLY, John

John B. Kelly b: 3/13/1879, Clifton Heights, PA d: 3/19/1944, Baltimore, MD, 5'9", 165 lbs. Deb: 4/11/1907

YEAR TM-L	G	AB	R	H	2B	3B	HR	RBI	BB	SO	SB	CS	AVG	OBP	SLG	OPS	OPS+	BR/A	RC	RC/G	FR	G/POS	WS	TPW
1907 StL-N	53	197	12	37	5	0	0	6	13	....	7	....	.188	.245	.213	.458	45	-12	13	2.04	-0	0-52(0-16-36)	1	-1.7

• KELLY, Kenny

Kenneth Alphonso Kelly b: 1/26/1979, Plant City, FL BR/TR, 6'3", 180 lbs. Deb: 9/7/2000

YEAR TM-L	G	AB	R	H	2B	3B	HR	RBI	BB	SO	SB	CS	AVG	OBP	SLG	OPS	OPS+	BR/A	RC	RC/G	FR	G/POS	WS	TPW
2000 TB-A	2	1	0	0	0	0	0	0	0	0	0	0	.000	.000	.000	.000	-101	-0	0	.00	0	/D-1	0	0.0

• KELLY, Kick

John O. "Diamond John" Kelly b: 10/31/1856, New York, NY d: 3/27/1926, Malba, NY, 6'.5", 185 lbs. Deb: 5/1/1879

YEAR TM-L	G	AB	R	H	2B	3B	HR	RBI	BB	SO	SB	CS	AVG	OBP	SLG	OPS	OPS+	BR/A	RC	RC/G	FR	G/POS	WS	TPW
1879 Syr-N	10	36	4	4	1	0	0	2	0	6	....	....	.111	.111	.139	.250	-20	-4	1	.50	-1	/C-8,1-2	0	-0.5
Tro-N	6	22	1	5	0	0	0	0	0	1	....	....	.227	.227	.227	.455	54	-1	1	1.92	-3	/C-3,0-2(0-0-2),3-1	0	-0.3
Yr.	16	58	5	9	1	0	0	2	0	7	....	....	.155	.155	.172	.328	8	-5	2	.99	-4	C-11/1-2,0-2(0-0-2),3-1	0	-0.8

• KELLY, King

Michael Joseph Kelly
b: 12/31/1857, Troy, NY d: 11/8/1894, Boston, MA BR/TR, 5'10", 170 lbs. Deb: 5/1/1878 M/U HOF: 1945 Career OF: 2-8-742 ♦

YEAR TM-L	G	AB	R	H	2B	3B	HR	RBI	BB	SO	SB	CS	AVG	OBP	SLG	OPS	OPS+	BR/A	RC	RC/G	FR	G/POS	WS	TPW
1878 Cin-N	60	237	29	67	7	1	0	27	7	7	....	....	.283	.303	.321	.624	116	5	24	3.82	6	*0-47(0-0-47),C-17/3-2	8	1.0
1879 Cin-N	77	345	78	120	20	12	2	47	8	14	....	....	.348	.363	.493	.855	**188**	32	63	7.86	11	3-33,0-29(0-2-27),C-21/2-1	20	**4.0**
1880 Chi-N	84	344	72	100	17	9	1	60	12	22	....	....	.291	.315	.401	.716	133	11	45	5.02	1	*0-64(0-0-64),C-17,3-14/2-1,P,S	16	1.3
1881 Chi-N	82	353	84	114	**27**	3	2	55	16	14	....	....	.323	.352	.433	.786	136	14	55	6.24	6	*0-72(0-0-72),C-11/3-8	16	1.9
1882 Chi-N	84	377	81	115	**37**	4	1	55	10	27	....	....	.305	.323	.432	.755	138	15	54	5.66	5	S-42,0-38(0-0-38),C-12/3-3,1	16	1.9
1883 Chi-N	98	428	92	109	28	10	3	61	16	35	....	....	.255	.282	.388	.669	93	-5	48	4.13	11	*0-82(0-0-82),C-38/2-3,3-2,P	13	0.6
1884 Chi-N	108	452	**120**	160	28	5	13	95	46	24	....	....	.354	**.414**	.524	.938	178	**41**	100	**9.46**	7	0-63(0-0-63),C-28,S-12,3-10/1,P,2	21	4.2
1885*Chi-N	107	438	**124**	126	24	7	9	75	46	24	....	....	.288	.355	.436	.791	135	16	70	6.02	16	0-69(0-1-69),C-37/2-6,1-2,3	24	3.2
1886*Chi-N	118	451	**155**	175	32	11	4	79	83	33	53	....	**.388**	**.483**	.534	1.018	181	49	146	**14.24**	15	0-56(0-1-55),C-53/1-9,3-8,2,S	35	**6.0**
1887 Bos-N	116	539	120	211	34	11	8	63	55	40	84	....	.391	.393	.488	.880	147	32	129	10.40	-7	0-61(1-0-61),2-30,C-24/P-3,3,S	23	2.3
1888 Bos-N	107	440	85	140	22	11	9	71	31	39	56	....	.318	.368	.480	.848	162	30	101	9.07	3	C-76,0-34(0-0-34)	24	3.9
1889 Bos-N	125	507	120	149	**41**	5	9	78	65	40	68	....	.294	.376	.448	.824	122	14	114	8.42	1	*0-113(0-0-113),C-23	24	1.3
1890 Bos-P	89	340	83	111	18	6	4	66	52	22	51	....	.326	.419	.450	.869	124	12	88	10.32	-3	C-56,S-27/0-6(0-2-4),1-4,3,P	16	1.1
1891 Cin-a	82	283	56	84	15	7	1	53	51	28	22	....	.297	.408	.410	.818	123	12	58	7.68	13	C-66/3-8,0-7(0-2-5),2-6,1,P,S	13	2.2
Bos-a	4	15	2	4	0	0	1	4	0	2	1	....	.267	.267	.467	.733	111	-0	2	5.27	0	/C-4	1	0.0
Yr.	86	298	58	88	15	7	2	57	51	30	23	....	.295	.402	.413	.814	123	10	60	7.55	13	C-70/3-8,0-7(0-2-5),2-6,1,P,S	14	2.2
Bos-N	16	52	7	12	1	0	0	5	6	10	6	....	.231	.322	.250	.572	60	-3	6	4.23	-3	C-11/0-6(0-0-6)	1	-0.4
1892*Bos-N	78	281	40	53	7	0	2	41	39	32	24	....	.189	.288	.235	.522	53	-16	27	3.14	-3	C-72/1-2,3-2,0-2(1-0-1),P	6	-0.9
1893 NY-N	20	67	9	18	1	0	0	15	6	5	3	....	.269	.329	.284	.612	63	-3	7	4.01	-1	C-17/0-1	1	-0.2
Total 16	**1455**	**5949**	**1357**	**1868**	**359**	**102**	**69**	**950**	**549**	**418**	**368**	**....**	**.314**	**.368**	**.438**	**.806**	**137**	**256**	**1135**	**7.52**	**78**	**0-750,C-583/3-96,S-90,2,1,P**	**278**	**33.4**

• KELLY, Mike

Michael Raymond Kelly b: 6/2/1970, Los Angeles, CA BR/TR, 6'4", 195 lbs. Deb: 4/5/1994 Career OF: 143-35-102

YEAR TM-L	G	AB	R	H	2B	3B	HR	RBI	BB	SO	SB	CS	AVG	OBP	SLG	OPS	OPS+	BR/A	RC	RC/G	FR	G/POS	WS	TPW
1994 Atl-N	30	77	14	21	10	1	2	9	2	17	0	1	.273	.300	.506	.806	103	-1	11	5.09	-1	0-25(19-6-1)	1	-0.2
1995 Atl-N	97	137	26	26	6	1	3	17	11	49	7	3	.190	.260	.314	.574	49	-10	11	2.60	-3	0-83(58-8-17)	2	-1.5
1996 Cin-N	19	49	5	9	4	0	1	7	9	11	4	0	.184	.333	.327	.660	76	-1	6	4.04	0	0-17(6-10-1)	1	0.0
1997 Cin-N	73	140	27	41	13	2	6	19	10	30	6	1	.293	.340	.543	.883	124	5	26	6.65	-1	0-59(17-11-31)/D-1	5	0.3
1998 TB-A	106	279	39	67	11	2	10	33	22	80	13	6	.240	.296	.401	.697	78	-10	31	3.67	2	0-93(43-0-51)/D-6	3	-1.1
1999 Col-N	2	2	0	1	1	0	0	1	0	0	0	0	.500	.500	1.000	1.500	210	0	1	27.00	0	/0-1	0	0.0
Total 6	**327**	**684**	**111**	**165**	**45**	**6**	**22**	**86**	**54**	**187**	**30**	**11**	**.241**	**.301**	**.421**	**.723**	**84**	**-16**	**86**	**4.22**	**-3**	**0-278/D-7**	**12**	**-2.6**

• KELLY, Pat

Harold Patrick Kelly b: 7/30/1944, Philadelphia, PA BL/TL, 6'1", 185 lbs. Deb: 9/6/1967 Career OF: 244-60-715

YEAR TM-L	G	AB	R	H	2B	3B	HR	RBI	BB	SO	SB	CS	AVG	OBP	SLG	OPS	OPS+	BR/A	RC	RC/G	FR	G/POS	WS	TPW
1967 Min-A	8	1	1	0	0	0	0	0	0	1	0	0	.000	.000	.000	.000	-93	-0	0	.00	0	....	0	0.0
1968 Min-A	12	35	2	4	2	0	1	2	3	10	0	2	.114	.205	.257	.462	38	-4	1	1.02	0	0-10(2-5-4)	0	-0.5
1969 KC-A	112	417	61	110	20	4	8	32	49	70	40	13	.264	.348	.388	.737	105	7	61	5.02	4	*0-107(2-44-63)	16	0.6
1970 KC-A	136	452	56	106	16	1	6	38	76	105	34	16	.235	.347	.314	.661	84	-6	55	4.01	2	*0-118(1-3-115)	11	-1.0
1971 Chi-A	67	213	32	62	6	3	3	22	36	29	14	9	.291	.396	.390	.786	119	7	34	5.64	3	0-61(0-1-61)	7	0.8
1972 Chi-A	119	402	57	105	14	7	5	24	55	69	32	9	.261	.356	.368	.724	113	12	59	5.04	-2	*0-109(0-0-109)	17	0.6
1973 Chi-A★	144	550	77	154	24	5	1	44	65	91	22	15	.280	.358	.347	.705	96	-2	67	4.16	1	*0-141(0-3-138)/D-1	13	-0.8
1974 Chi-A	122	424	60	119	16	3	4	21	46	58	18	11	.281	.354	.361	.715	103	3	54	4.44	-1	D-67,0-52(0-1-52)	10	-0.3
1975 Chi-A	133	471	73	129	21	7	9	45	58	69	18	10	.274	.356	.406	.761	113	9	67	4.82	-1	*0-115(0-0-115),D-14	14	0.2
1976 Chi-A	107	311	42	79	20	3	5	34	45	45	15	7	.254	.354	.386	.740	116	8	44	4.67	-1	D-63,0-26(14-0-12)	9	0.4
1977 Bal-A	120	360	50	92	13	0	10	49	53	75	25	7	.256	.357	.375	.732	106	8	53	4.88	-3	*0-109(91-1-33)/D-1	13	0.1
1978 Bal-A	100	274	38	75	12	1	11	40	34	58	10	8	.274	.358	.445	.803	133	11	41	5.06	0	0-80(73-1-7)/D-2	10	0.8

YEAR TM-L	G	AB	R	H	2B	3B	HR	RBI	BB	SO	SB	CS	AVG	OBP	SLG	OPS	OPS+	BR/A	RC	RC/G	FR	G/POS	WS	TPW
1979*Bal-A	68	153	25	44	11	0	9	25	20	25	4	5	.288	.374	.536	.910	147	9	30	6.75	0	0-24(23-0-1),D-18	7	0.7
1980 Bal-A	89	200	38	52	10	1	3	26	34	54	16	2	.260	.368	.365	.733	102	5	31	5.32	1	0-36(34-2-0),D-30	7	0.4
1981 Cle-A	48	75	8	16	4	0	1	16	14	9	2	4	.213	.337	.307	.644	88	-2	7	2.69	0	D-18/0-8(3-0-5)	1	-0.3
Total 15	1385	4338	620	1147	189	35	76	418	588	768	250	118	.264	.356	.377	.733	107	64	604	4.71	2	0-997,D-214	135	1.6

• KELLY, Pat   Dale Patrick Kelly   b: 8/27/1955, Santa Maria, CA   BR/TR, 6'3", 210 lbs.   Deb: 5/28/1980

YEAR TM-L	G	AB	R	H	2B	3B	HR	RBI	BB	SO	SB	CS	AVG	OBP	SLG	OPS	OPS+	BR/A	RC	RC/G	FR	G/POS	WS	TPW
1980 Tor-A	3	7	0	2	0	0	0	0	0	4	0	0	.286	.286	.286	.571	55	-0	1	3.09	0	/C-3	0	0.0

• KELLY, Pat   Patrick Franklin Kelly   b: 10/14/1967, Philadelphia, PA   BR/TR, 6', 182 lbs.   Deb: 5/20/1991

YEAR TM-L	G	AB	R	H	2B	3B	HR	RBI	BB	SO	SB	CS	AVG	OBP	SLG	OPS	OPS+	BR/A	RC	RC/G	FR	G/POS	WS	TPW
1991 NY-A	96	298	35	72	12	4	3	23	15	52	12	1	.242	.289	.339	.628	73	-9	31	3.50	-4	3-80,2-19	5	-1.2
1992 NY-A	106	318	38	72	22	2	7	27	25	72	8	5	.226	.303	.374	.677	89	-5	36	3.68	-1	*2-101/D-1	7	-0.4
1993 NY-A	127	406	49	111	24	1	7	51	24	68	14	11	.273	.322	.389	.711	93	-6	48	3.93	-4	*2-125	10	-0.5
1994 NY-A	93	286	35	80	21	2	3	41	19	51	6	5	.280	.335	.399	.734	92	-5	36	4.05	-8	2-93	6	-0.8
1995*NY-A	89	270	32	64	12	1	4	29	23	65	6	3	.237	.309	.333	.642	68	-13	29	3.49	5	2-87/D-1	5	-0.3
1996 NY-A	13	21	4	3	0	0	0	2	2	9	0	1	.143	.217	.143	.360	-6	-4	0	.62	0	2-10/D-3	0	-0.3
1997 NY-A	67	120	25	29	6	1	2	10	14	37	8	1	.242	.326	.358	.684	79	-2	15	4.04	1	2-48,D-16	2	-0.0
1998 StL-N	53	153	18	33	5	0	4	14	13	48	5	1	.216	.286	.327	.613	61	-8	15	3.19	-2	2-41/0-3(3-0-0),S-2	2	-0.9
1999 Tor-A	37	116	17	31	7	0	6	20	10	23	1		.267	.325	.483	.808	101	-1	18	5.40	-1	2-35/D-2	3	-0.1
Total 9	681	1988	253	495	109	11	36	217	145	425	61	29	.249	.311	.369	.680	82	-53	229	3.77	-15	2-559/3-80,D-23,0-3,S-2	40	-4.4

• KELLY, Red   Albert Michael Kelly   b: 11/15/1884, Union, IL   d: 2/4/1961, Zephyrhills, FL   BR/TR, 5'11.5", 165 lbs.   Deb: 6/18/1910

YEAR TM-L	G	AB	R	H	2B	3B	HR	RBI	BB	SO	SB	CS	AVG	OBP	SLG	OPS	OPS+	BR/A	RC	RC/G	FR	G/POS	WS	TPW
1910 Chi-A	14	45	6	7	0	1	0	1	7	....	0	....	.156	.296	.200	.496	59	-2	3	1.83	-1	0-14(0-0-14)	1	-0.3

• KELLY, Roberto   Roberto Conrado (Gray) "Bobby" Kelly   b: 10/1/1964, Panama City, Panama   BR/TR, 6'2", 192 lbs.   Deb: 7/29/1987   Career OF: 246-886-184

YEAR TM-L	G	AB	R	H	2B	3B	HR	RBI	BB	SO	SB	CS	AVG	OBP	SLG	OPS	OPS+	BR/A	RC	RC/G	FR	G/POS	WS	TPW
1987 NY-A	23	52	12	14	3	0	1	7	5	15	9	3	.269	.333	.385	.718	91	-0	7	4.60	-2	0-17(16-1-0)/D-2	2	-0.1
1988 NY-A	38	77	9	19	4	1	1	7	3	15	5	2	.247	.275	.364	.639	78	-2	8	3.36	-1	0-30(1-28-2)/D-3	1	-0.4
1989 NY-A	137	441	65	133	18	3	9	48	41	89	35	12	.302	.369	.417	.786	122	16	70	5.59	3	*0-137(0-137-0)	16	1.7
1990 NY-A	162	641	85	183	32	4	15	61	33	148	42	17	.285	.324	.418	.743	106	4	87	4.78	1	*0-160(11-151-0)/D-1	19	0.3
1991 NY-A	126	486	68	130	22	2	20	69	45	77	32	9	.267	.336	.444	.780	114	11	72	5.03	-2	*0-125(52-73-0)	16	0.7
1992 NY-A★	152	580	81	158	31	2	10	66	41	96	28	5	.272	.325	.384	.709	99	2	71	4.25	-1	0-146(47-99-0)	13	-0.3
1993 Cin-N★	78	320	44	102	17	3	9	35	17	43	21	5	.319	.357	.475	.832	120	11	53	6.01	-4	0-77(0-77-0)	10	0.7
1994 Cin-N	47	179	29	54	8	0	3	21	11	35	9	8	.302	.352	.397	.749	96	-3	23	4.61	0	0-47(0-47-0)	5	-0.3
Atl-N	63	255	44	73	15	3	6	24	24	36	10	3	.286	.348	.439	.787	101	1	39	5.54	-1	0-63(0-63-0)	10	0.1
Yr.	110	434	73	127	23	3	9	45	35	71	19	11	.293	.350	.422	.771	99	-2	63	5.15	-1	*0-110(0-110-0)	15	-0.2
1995 Mon-N	24	95	11	26	4	0	1	9	7	14	4	3	.274	.337	.347	.684	78	-3	10	3.55	0	0-24(0-24-0)	1	-0.3
*LA-N	112	409	47	114	19	2	6	48	15	65	15	7	.279	.311	.379	.690	89	-8	45	3.84	-4	0-110(61-48-2)	8	-1.4
Yr.	136	504	58	140	23	2	7	57	22	79	19	10	.278	.316	.373	.689	87	-12	55	3.78	-4	0-134(61-72-2)	9	-1.7
1996 Min-A	98	322	41	104	17	4	6	47	23	53	10	2	.323	.381	.457	.837	109	6	52	5.84	0	0-93(6-40-54)/D-2	9	0.3
1997 Min-A	75	247	39	71	19	2	5	37	17	50	7	4	.287	.338	.441	.780	100	-1	36	5.24	-2	0-59(1-1-57)/D-12	6	-0.5
*Sea-A	30	121	19	36	7	0	7	22	5	17	2	1	.298	.331	.529	.860	121	3	20	6.13	-1	0-29(28-1-0)/D-1	6	0.1
Yr.	105	368	58	107	26	2	12	59	22	67	9	5	.291	.336	.478	.806	107	2	57	5.53	-2	0-88(29-2-57)/D-13	12	-0.5
1998*Tex-A	75	257	48	83	7	3	16	46	8	46	0	2	.323	.351	.560	.911	127	8	48	7.15	-2	0-71(14-41-31)/D-2	8	0.4
1999*Tex-A	87	290	41	87	17	3	8	37	21	57	6	1	.300	.358	.448	.806	99	0	47	6.07	-3	0-85(18-37-37)	8	0.2
2000 NY-A	10	25	4	3	1	0	1	1	1	6	0	0	.120	.185	.280	.465	16	-3	1	1.71	0	0-10(7-3-0)	0	-0.4
Total 14	1337	4797	687	1390	241	30	124	585	317	862	235	84	.290	.340	.430	.770	106	42	692	5.09	-17	*0-1283/D-23	137	0.2

• KELLY, Speed   Robert Brown Kelly   b: 8/19/1884, Bryan, OH   d: 5/6/1949, Goshen, IN   BR/TR, 6'2", 185 lbs.   Deb: 7/13/1909

YEAR TM-L	G	AB	R	H	2B	3B	HR	RBI	BB	SO	SB	CS	AVG	OBP	SLG	OPS	OPS+	BR/A	RC	RC/G	FR	G/POS	WS	TPW
1909 Was-A	17	42	3	6	2	1	0	1	3	....	1	....	.143	.200	.238	.438	40	-3	2	1.48	-2	3-10/2-3,0-1	0	-0.5

• KELLY, Tom   Jay Thomas Kelly   b: 8/15/1950, Graceville, MN   BL/TL, 5'11", 188 lbs.   Deb: 5/11/1975   M/C

YEAR TM-L	G	AB	R	H	2B	3B	HR	RBI	BB	SO	SB	CS	AVG	OBP	SLG	OPS	OPS+	BR/A	RC	RC/G	FR	G/POS	WS	TPW
1975 Min-A	49	127	11	23	5	0	1	11	5	26	1	....	.181	.268	.244	.512	44	-9	9	2.15	0	1-43/0-2(1-0-1)	1	-1.2

• KELLY, Van   Van Howard Kelly   b: 3/18/1946, Charlotte, NC   BL/TR, 5'11", 180 lbs.   Deb: 6/13/1969

YEAR TM-L	G	AB	R	H	2B	3B	HR	RBI	BB	SO	SB	CS	AVG	OBP	SLG	OPS	OPS+	BR/A	RC	RC/G	FR	G/POS	WS	TPW
1969 SD-N	73	209	16	51	7	1	3	15	12	24	0	1	.244	.285	.330	.615	56	-8	19	3.25	1	3-49,2-10	3	-0.8
1970 SD-N	38	89	9	15	3	0	1	9	15	21	0	1	.169	.288	.236	.524	44	-7	7	2.38	-0	3-27/2-1	1	-0.7
Total 2	111	298	25	66	10	1	4	24	27	45	0	2	.221	.286	.302	.588	65	-15	26	2.97	1	/3-76,2-11	4	-1.5

• KELSEY, Billy   George William Kelsey   b: 8/24/1881, Covington, OH   d: 4/25/1968, Springfield, OH   BR/TR, 5'10", 150 lbs.   Deb: 10/4/1907

YEAR TM-L	G	AB	R	H	2B	3B	HR	RBI	BB	SO	SB	CS	AVG	OBP	SLG	OPS	OPS+	BR/A	RC	RC/G	FR	G/POS	WS	TPW
1907 Pit-N	2	5	1	2	0	0	0	0	0	....	0	....	.400	.400	.400	.800	149	0	1	7.11	0	/C-2	0	0.0

• KELTNER, Ken   Kenneth Frederick "Butch" Keltner   b: 10/31/1916, Milwaukee, WI   d: 12/12/1991, New Berlin, WI   BR/TR, 6', 190 lbs.   Deb: 10/2/1937

YEAR TM-L	G	AB	R	H	2B	3B	HR	RBI	BB	SO	SB	CS	AVG	OBP	SLG	OPS	OPS+	BR/A	RC	RC/G	FR	G/POS	WS	TPW
1937 Cle-A	1	1	0	0	0	0	0	0	0	0	0	0	.000	.000	.000	.000	-99	-0	0	.00	0	/3-1	0	0.0
1938 Cle-A	149	576	86	159	31	9	26	113	33	75	4	3	.276	.319	.497	.815	103	-2	90	5.56	-8	*3-149	18	-0.5
1939 Cle-A	154	587	84	191	35	11	13	97	51	41	6	6	.325	.379	.489	.868	125	19	105	6.65	9	*3-154	26	3.1
1940 Cle-A	149	543	67	138	24	10	15	77	51	56	10	5	.254	.322	.418	.740	93	-7	75	4.66	3	*3-148	16	0.2
1941 Cle-A★	149	581	83	156	31	13	23	84	51	56	2	1	.269	.330	.445	.815	119	12	95	5.75	22	*3-149	23	3.9
1942 Cle-A★	152	624	72	179	34	4	6	78	20	36	4	3	.287	.312	.383	.695	101	-3	72	4.06	19	*3-151	20	2.2
1943 Cle-A	110	427	41	111	31	3	4	39	36	20	2	2	.260	.317	.375	.692	109	3	50	4.00	6	*3-107	15	1.1
1944 Cle-A★	149	573	74	169	41	9	13	91	53	29	4	3	.295	.355	.466	.821	139	26	91	5.62	10	*3-149	22	4.0
1946 Cle-A	116	398	47	96	17	1	13	45	30	38	0	3	.241	.294	.387	.681	95	-5	42	3.51	-5	3-112	9	-1.1
1947 Cle-A	151	541	49	139	29	3	11	76	59	45	5	4	.257	.331	.441	.714	101	-0	72	4.57	-3	*3-150	17	-0.4
1948*Cle-A★	153	558	91	166	24	4	31	119	89	52	2	1	.297	.395	.522	.917	146	37	116	7.36	-2	*3-153	25	3.4
1949 Cle-A	80	246	35	57	9	2	8	30	38	26	0	1	.232	.335	.382	.717	91	-4	32	4.12	-3	3-69	7	-0.7
1950 Bos-A	13	28	2	9	1	0	1	5	2	5	0	0	.321	.387	.500	.780	91	-0	4	4.82	0	/3-8,1-1	1	-0.1
Total 13	1526	5683	737	1570	308	69	163	852	514	480	39	33	.276	.338	.441	.778	113	76	843	5.17	48	*3-1500/1-1	199	15.1

• KELTON, David   David Wayne Kelton   b: 12/17/1979, Dothan, AL   BR/TR, 6'3", 205 lbs.   Deb: 6/8/2003

YEAR TM-L	G	AB	R	H	2B	3B	HR	RBI	BB	SO	SB	CS	AVG	OBP	SLG	OPS	OPS+	BR/A	RC	RC/G	FR	G/POS	WS	TPW
2003 Chi-N	10	12	1	2	1	0	0	0	5	0	0		.167	.167	.250	.417	7	-2	1	1.35	0	/0-2(0-0)	0	-0.1

• KELTY, John   John James "Chief" Kelty   b: 3/10/1871, Jersey City, NJ   d: 4/13/1929, Jersey City, NJ, 5'10", 175 lbs.   Deb: 4/19/1890

YEAR TM-L	G	AB	R	H	2B	3B	HR	RBI	BB	SO	SB	CS	AVG	OBP	SLG	OPS	OPS+	BR/A	RC	RC/G	FR	G/POS	WS	TPW
1890 Pit-N	59	207	24	49	10	2	1	27	22	42	10	....	.237	.322	.319	.641	98	1	25	4.21	-4	0-59(59-0-0)	3	-0.5

• KEMMER, Bill   William Edward Kemmer   b: 11/15/1873, PA   d: 6/8/1945, Washington, DC   BR/TR, 6'2"   Deb: 6/3/1895

YEAR TM-L	G	AB	R	H	2B	3B	HR	RBI	BB	SO	SB	CS	AVG	OBP	SLG	OPS	OPS+	BR/A	RC	RC/G	FR	G/POS	WS	TPW
1895 Lou-N	11	38	5	7	0	0	1	3	2	4	0	....	.184	.225	.263	.488	27	-4	2	2.04	0	/3-9,1-2	0	-0.3

• KEMMLER, Rudy   Rudolph Kemmler   b: 1860, Chicago, IL   d: 6/20/1909, Chicago, IL   BR/TR, 5'11"   Deb: 7/26/1879   Career OF: 1-2-2

YEAR TM-L	G	AB	R	H	2B	3B	HR	RBI	BB	SO	SB	CS	AVG	OBP	SLG	OPS	OPS+	BR/A	RC	RC/G	FR	G/POS	WS	TPW
1879 Pro-N	2	7	0	1	0	0	0	0	0	1	....	....	.143	.143	.143	.286	-6	-1	0	.68	1	/C-2	0	0.0
1881 Cle-N	1	3	0	0	0	0	0	0	0	1	....	....	.000	.000	.000	.000	-106	-1	0	.00	0	/C-1	0	0.0
1882 Cin-a	3	11	0	1	1	0	0	....	0	1	....	....	.091	.091	.182	.273	-10	-1	0	.52	0	/C-3,0-1	0	-0.1
Pit-a	24	99	7	25	4	0	0	....	1	....	....	....	.253	.260	.293	.553	90	-1	8	2.92	2	C-23/0-1	2	0.3
Yr.	27	110	7	26	5	0	0	....	1	....	....	....	.236	.243	.282	.525	80	-2	8	2.64	2	C-26/0-2(0-0-2)	2	0.2
1883 Col-a	84	318	27	66	6	2	0	13	....	....	....	....	.208	.239	.239	.478	59	-12	19	2.07	4	*C-82/0-2(0-2-0)	4	-0.1
1884 Col-a	61	211	28	42	3	3	0	15	....	....	....	....	.199	.252	.242	.494	67	-6	13	2.15	-2	C-58/1-2,0-1	4	-0.3
1885 Pit-a	18	64	2	13	2	0	0	5	2	....	....	....	.203	.239	.266	.504	60	-3	4	2.20	-1	C-18	2	-0.2
1886 StL-a	35	123	13	17	2	0	0	6	8	....	....	....	.138	.197	.154	.351	10	-13	4	.98	4	C-32/1-3	2	-0.5
1889 Col-a	8	26	2	3	0	0	0	0	3	5	....	....	.115	.207	.115	.322	-8	-4	1	.73	2	/C-8	0	-0.1
Total 8	236	862	79	168	18	6	0	11	42	5	0	....	.195	.234	.220	.464	53	-41	48	1.93	11	C-227/1-5,0-5	13	-1.1

• KEMP, Steve   Steven F Kemp   b: 8/7/1954, San Angelo, TX   BL/TL, 6', 195 lbs.   Deb: 4/7/1977   Career OF: 925-0-90

YEAR TM-L	G	AB	R	H	2B	3B	HR	RBI	BB	SO	SB	CS	AVG	OBP	SLG	OPS	OPS+	BR/A	RC	RC/G	FR	G/POS	WS	TPW
1977 Det-A	151	552	75	142	29	4	18	88	71	93	3	5	.257	.347	.422	.769	103	4	83	5.18	-7	*0-148(148-0-0)	14	-1.1
1978 Det-A	159	582	75	161	18	4	15	79	97	87	2	3	.277	.381	.399	.780	116	16	94	5.78	-2	*0-157(157-0-0)	20	0.7
1979 Det-A★	134	490	88	156	26	3	26	105	68	70	5	6	.318	.404	.543	.946	148	33	106	7.87	-1	*0-120(117-0-3),D-11	25	2.5

YEAR TM-L	G	AB	R	H	2B	3B	HR	RBI	BB	SO	SB	CS	AVG	OBP	SLG	OPS	OPS+	BR/A	RC	RC/G	FR	G/POS	WS	TPW
1980 Det-A	135	508	88	149	23	3	21	101	69	64	5	1	.293	.382	.474	.857	130	24	89	6.10	0	O-85(85-0-0),D-46	19	1.8
1981 Det-A	105	372	52	103	18	4	9	49	70	48	9	3	.277	.393	.419	.812	129	19	64	5.94	0	O-92(92-0-0),D-12	17	1.4
1982 Chi-A	160	580	91	166	23	1	19	98	89	83	7	7	.286	.384	.428	.812	122	20	99	6.14	-7	*O-154(154-0-0)/D-2	22	0.6
1983 NY-A	109	373	53	90	17	3	12	49	41	37	1	0	.241	.320	.399	.719	100	0	45	3.98	0	*O-101(25-0-86)/D-2	8	-0.5
1984 NY-A	94	313	37	91	12	1	7	41	40	54	4	1	.291	.373	.403	.775	119	10	47	5.24	-2	O-75(75-0-0),D-12	10	0.4
1985 Pit-N	92	236	19	59	13	2	2	21	25	54	1	0	.250	.322	.347	.669	88	-4	27	3.92	1	O-63(63-0-0)	4	-0.5
1986 Pit-N	13	16	1	3	0	0	1	1	4	6	1	0	.188	.350	.375	.725	98	0	2	4.37	0	/O-4(4-0-0)	0	0.0
1988 Tex-A	16	36	2	8	0	0	0	2	2	9	1	0	.222	.263	.222	.485	37	-3	2	1.99	0	/D-7,O-5(5-0-1),1-1	0	-0.3
Total 11	1168	4058	581	1128	179	25	130	634	576	605	39	24	.278	.370	.431	.801	119	120	658	5.68	-18	*O-1004/D-92,1-1	139	5.0

• KENDALL, Fred Fred Lyn Kendall b: 1/31/1949, Torrance, CA BR/TR, 6'1", 190 lbs. Deb: 9/8/1969 C

YEAR TM-L	G	AB	R	H	2B	3B	HR	RBI	BB	SO	SB	CS	AVG	OBP	SLG	OPS	OPS+	BR/A	RC	RC/G	FR	G/POS	WS	TPW
1969 SD-N	10	26	2	4	0	0	0	0	2	5	0	0	.154	.214	.154	.368	5	-3	1	.73	0	/C-9	0	-0.3
1970 SD-N	4	9	0	0	0	0	0	1	0	0	0	0	.000	.000	.000	.000	-104	-3	0	.00	0	/C-2,1-1,O-1	0	-0.3
1971 SD-N	49	111	2	19	1	0	1	7	7	16	1	0	.171	.220	.207	.428	23	-11	5	1.29	2	C-39/1-1,3-1	2	-0.8
1972 SD-N	91	273	18	59	3	4	6	18	11	42	0	0	.216	.249	.322	.571	66	-13	21	2.56	4	C-82/1-1	6	-0.6
1973 SD-N	145	507	39	143	22	3	10	59	30	35	3	1	.282	.323	.396	.720	107	3	61	4.19	-3	*C-138	14	0.8
1974 SD-N	141	424	32	98	15	2	8	45	49	33	0	1	.231	.311	.333	.643	84	-10	43	3.36	2	*C-133	12	-0.3
1975 SD-N	103	286	16	57	12	1	0	24	26	28	0	1	.199	.266	.248	.514	46	-21	18	1.98	0	C-85	2	-1.9
1976 SD-N	146	456	30	112	17	0	2	39	36	42	1	1	.246	.305	.296	.601	77	-14	39	2.78	-6	*C-146	9	-1.4
1977 Cle-A	103	317	18	79	13	1	3	39	16	27	0	1	.249	.287	.325	.612	69	-14	29	2.97	-3	*C-102/D-1	5	-1.3
1978 Bos-A	20	41	3	8	1	0	0	4	1	2	0	0	.195	.214	.220	.434	20	-4	2	1.63	0	1-13/C-5,D-1	0	-0.5
1979 SD-N	46	102	8	17	2	0	1	6	11	7	0	0	.167	.248	.216	.463	29	-10	5	1.57	0	C-40/1-2	1	-0.9
1980 SD-N	19	24	2	7	0	0	0	2	0	3	0	0	.292	.292	.292	.583	67	-1	2	3.24	-1	C-14/1-1	0	-0.2
Total 12	877	2576	170	603	86	11	31	244	189	240	5	5	.234	.288	.312	.600	72	-101	225	2.87	-5	C-795/1-19,D-2,3-1,O-1	51	-7.6

• KENDALL, Jason Jason Daniel Kendall b: 6/26/1974, San Diego, CA BR/TR, 6', 180 lbs. Deb: 4/1/1996

YEAR TM-L	G	AB	R	H	2B	3B	HR	RBI	BB	SO	SB	CS	AVG	OBP	SLG	OPS	OPS+	BR/A	RC	RC/G	FR	G/POS	WS	TPW
1996 Pit-N★	130	414	54	124	23	5	3	42	35	30	5	2	.300	.375	.401	.776	102	3	64	5.64	1	*C-129	12	1.2
1997 Pit-N	144	486	71	143	36	4	8	49	49	53	18	6	.294	.394	.434	.828	115	15	88	6.48	10	*C-142	22	3.4
1998 Pit-N★	149	535	95	175	36	3	12	75	51	51	26	5	.327	.417	.473	.889	132	32	115	8.13	-2	*C-144	26	4.0
1999 Pit-N	78	280	61	93	20	3	8	41	38	32	22	3	.332	.433	.511	.944	138	22	67	8.91	3	C-75	13	2.8
2000 Pit-N★	152	579	112	185	33	6	14	58	79	79	22	12	.320	.415	.470	.884	124	25	116	7.39	6	*C-147	24	3.9
2001 Pit-N	157	606	84	161	22	2	10	53	44	48	13	14	.266	.336	.358	.694	78	-22	69	3.89	-5	*C-133,O-27(18-0-10)	9	-1.8
2002 Pit-N	145	545	59	154	25	3	3	44	49	29	15	8	.283	.352	.356	.708	86	-10	69	4.55	-4	*C-143	13	-0.4
2003 Pit-N	150	587	84	191	29	3	6	58	49	40	8	7	.325	.401	.416	.817	111	12	101	6.53	-11	*C-146	20	1.1
Total 8	1105	4032	620	1226	224	29	64	420	394	362	129	57	.304	.388	.422	.809	109	75	688	6.22	-2	*C-1059/O-27	139	14.3

• KENDERS, Al Albert Daniel George Kenders b: 4/4/1937, Barrington, NJ BR/TR, 6', 185 lbs. Deb: 8/14/1961

YEAR TM-L	G	AB	R	H	2B	3B	HR	RBI	BB	SO	SB	CS	AVG	OBP	SLG	OPS	OPS+	BR/A	RC	RC/G	FR	G/POS	WS	TPW
1961 Phi-N	10	23	0	4	1	0	0	1	1	0	0	0	.174	.208	.217	.426	13	-3	1	.85	0	C-10	0	-0.2

• KENNA, Eddie Edward Aloysius "Scrap Iron" Kenna b: 9/30/1897, San Francisco, CA d: 8/21/1972, San Francisco, CA BR/TR, 5'7.5", 150 lbs. Deb: 6/2/1928

YEAR TM-L	G	AB	R	H	2B	3B	HR	RBI	BB	SO	SB	CS	AVG	OBP	SLG	OPS	OPS+	BR/A	RC	RC/G	FR	G/POS	WS	TPW
1928 Was-A	41	118	14	35	4	2	1	20	14	8	1	5	.297	.376	.390	.766	102	-1	16	4.89	-1	C-33	3	0.0

• KENNEDY, Adam Adam Thomas Kennedy b: 1/10/1976, Riverside, CA BL/TR, 6'1", 192 lbs. Deb: 8/21/1999

YEAR TM-L	G	AB	R	H	2B	3B	HR	RBI	BB	SO	SB	CS	AVG	OBP	SLG	OPS	OPS+	BR/A	RC	RC/G	FR	G/POS	WS	TPW
1999 StL-N	33	102	12	26	10	1	1	16	3	8	0	1	.255	.290	.402	.692	72	-5	12	3.85	-1	2-29	2	-0.5
2000 Ana-A	156	598	82	159	33	11	9	72	28	73	22	8	.266	.302	.403	.705	74	-24	71	4.10	-6	*2-155	11	-2.1
2001 Ana-A	137	478	48	129	25	3	6	40	27	71	12	7	.270	.324	.372	.696	81	-14	58	4.13	0	*2-131/D-5	8	-0.7
2002*Ana-A	144	474	65	148	32	6	7	52	19	80	17	4	.312	.348	.449	.797	110	8	76	5.93	23	*2-139/D-1,O-1	17	3.5
2003 Ana-A	143	449	71	121	17	1	13	49	45	73	22	9	.269	.348	.399	.747	100	2	65	4.97	12	*2-140	14	2.0
Total 5	613	2101	278	583	117	22	36	229	122	305	73	29	.277	.327	.406	.732	89	-34	281	4.67	29	2-594/D-6,O-1	52	2.2

• KENNEDY, Bob Robert Daniel Kennedy b: 8/18/1920, Chicago, IL BR/TR, 6'2", 193 lbs. Deb: 9/14/1939 M/C Career OF: 203-30-601

YEAR TM-L	G	AB	R	H	2B	3B	HR	RBI	BB	SO	SB	CS	AVG	OBP	SLG	OPS	OPS+	BR/A	RC	RC/G	FR	G/POS	WS	TPW
1939 Chi-A	3	8	0	2	0	0	0	1	0	0	0	0	.250	.250	.250	.500	27	-1	0	.95	0	/3-2	0	-0.1
1940 Chi-A	154	606	74	153	23	3	3	52	42	58	3	7	.252	.301	.315	.616	59	-39	55	3.09	11	*3-154	8	-2.1
1941 Chi-A	76	257	16	53	9	3	1	29	17	23	5	3	.206	.255	.276	.532	41	-22	19	2.31	5	3-71	3	-1.5
1942 Chi-A	113	412	37	95	18	5	0	38	22	41	11	7	.231	.270	.299	.568	61	-23	31	2.43	8	3-96,O-16(13-0-3)	6	-1.3
1946 Chi-A	113	411	43	106	13	5	5	34	24	42	6	8	.258	.300	.350	.651	85	-12	40	3.37	4	O-75(59-12-4),3-29	7	-1.4
1947 Chi-A	115	428	47	112	19	3	6	48	18	38	3	4	.262	.291	.362	.654	84	-12	42	3.42	-1	*O-106(14-1-91)/3-1	7	-1.8
1948 Chi-A	30	113	4	28	8	1	0	14	4	17	0	2	.248	.274	.336	.610	64	-7	9	2.49	0	O-30(25-0-5)	1	-0.9
*Cle-A	66	73	10	22	3	2	0	5	4	6	0	0	.301	.338	.397	.735	97	-1	10	4.96	1	O-50(2-0-48)/2-2,1-1	2	0.0
Yr.	96	186	14	50	11	3	0	19	8	23	0	2	.269	.299	.360	.659	77	-8	19	3.41	2	O-80(27-0-53)/2-2,1-1	3	-0.9
1949 Cle-A	121	424	49	117	23	5	9	57	37	40	5	5	.276	.334	.417	.752	100	-3	57	4.60	4	O-98(1-0-98),3-21	12	-0.2
1950 Cle-A	146	540	79	157	27	5	9	54	53	31	3	4	.291	.355	.409	.764	99	-3	79	5.10	2	*O-144(0-10-138)	15	-0.5
1951 Cle-A	108	321	30	79	15	4	7	29	34	33	4	2	.246	.320	.383	.703	95	-3	38	3.98	2	*O-106(1-0-105)	7	-0.4
1952 Cle-A	22	40	6	12	3	1	0	12	9	5	1	0	.300	.429	.425	.854	148	3	9	8.38	1	O-13(1-5-8)/3-3	3	0.5
1953 Cle-A	100	161	22	38	5	0	3	22	19	11	0	2	.236	.320	.323	.643	76	-6	16	3.24	-1	O-89(42-2-52)	2	-0.9
1954 Cle-A	1	0	0	0	0	0	0	0	0	0	0	0	....	....	....	....	-98	0	0	....	0	/O-1	0	0.0
Bal-A	106	323	37	81	13	2	6	45	28	43	2	1	.251	.311	.359	.670	90	-5	33	3.33	-8	3-71,O-21(12-0-9)	5	-1.4
Yr.	107	323	37	81	13	2	6	45	28	43	2	1	.251	.311	.359	.670	90	-5	33	3.33	-8	3-71,O-22(13-0-9)	5	-1.5
1955 Bal-A	26	70	10	10	1	0	0	5	10	10	0	1	.143	.250	.157	.407	12	-9	3	1.15	-1	O-14(0-0-14)/1-6,3-1	0	-1.0
Chi-A	83	214	28	65	10	2	9	43	16	16	0	2	.304	.352	.495	.848	122	5	35	5.82	-6	3-55,O-20(4-0-16)/1-3	7	-0.1
Yr.	109	284	38	75	11	2	9	48	26	26	0	3	.264	.326	.412	.738	94	-4	37	4.49	-6	3-56,O-34(4-0-30)/1-9	7	-1.2
1956 Chi-A	8	13	0	1	0	0	0	0	2	4	0	0	.077	.200	.077	.277	-24	-2	0	.68	0	/3-6	0	-0.2
Det-A	69	177	17	41	5	0	4	22	24	19	2	2	.232	.330	.328	.658	74	-7	18	3.18	-5	O-29(20-0-9),3-27	2	-1.3
Yr.	77	190	17	42	5	0	4	22	26	23	2	2	.221	.321	.311	.632	67	-9	18	3.00	-5	3-33,O-29(20-0-9)	2	-1.5
1957 Chi-A	4	2	0	0	0	0	0	0	0	1	0	0	.000	.000	.000	.000	-100	-1	0	.00	0	....	0	-0.1
Bro-N	19	31	5	4	1	0	1	4	1	5	0	0	.129	.156	.258	.414	8	-4	1	.99	-1	/O-9(8-0-1),3-3	0	-0.5
Total 16	1483	4624	514	1176	196	41	63	514	364	443	45	50	.254	.310	.355	.665	80	-151	495	3.59	17	O-821,3-540/1-10,2-2	87	-15.1

• KENNEDY, Doc Michael Joseph Kennedy b: 8/11/1853, Brooklyn, NY d: 5/23/1920, Grove, NY BR/TR, 5'9.5", 185 lbs. Deb: 5/1/1879 U Career OF: 4-5-0

YEAR TM-L	G	AB	R	H	2B	3B	HR	RBI	BB	SO	SB	CS	AVG	OBP	SLG	OPS	OPS+	BR/A	RC	RC/G	FR	G/POS	WS	TPW
1879 Cle-N	49	193	19	56	8	2	1	18	2	10	....	....	.290	.297	.368	.665	119	4	22	4.42	2	C-46/1-4	6	0.7
1880 Cle-N	66	250	26	50	10	1	0	18	5	12	....	....	.200	.216	.248	.464	58	-11	14	1.88	-5	*C-65/O-2(1-1-0)	5	-1.3
1881 Cle-N	39	150	19	47	7	1	0	15	5	13	....	....	.313	.335	.373	.709	129	5	19	5.05	2	C-35/O-3(2-1-0),3-1	5	0.7
1882 Cle-N	1	3	0	1	0	0	0	0	1	0	....	....	.333	.500	.333	.833	180	0	1	7.05	3	/C-1	0	0.4
1883 Buf-N	5	19	3	6	0	0	0	2	2	2	....	....	.316	.381	.316	.697	112	0	2	4.96	-2	/O-4(1-3-0),1-1	0	-0.1
Total 5	160	615	67	160	25	4	1	53	15	37	....	....	.260	.278	.319	.596	97	-1	57	3.48	1	C-147/O-9,1-5,3-1	16	0.3

• KENNEDY, Ed Edward Kennedy b: 4/1/1856, Carbondale, PA d: 5/22/1905, New York, NY, 5'6", 150 lbs. Deb: 5/1/1883 Career OF: 291-6-0

YEAR TM-L	G	AB	R	H	2B	3B	HR	RBI	BB	SO	SB	CS	AVG	OBP	SLG	OPS	OPS+	BR/A	RC	RC/G	FR	G/POS	WS	TPW
1883 NY-a	94	356	57	78	6	7	2	0	17	....	....	....	.219	.255	.292	.547	72	-11	27	2.73	-5	*O-94(94-0-0)	6	-1.7
1884*NY-a	103	378	49	72	6	2	1	0	16	....	....	....	.190	.225	.225	.450	48	-20	20	1.76	7	*O-100(99-1-0)/2-1,C-1,S-1	4	-1.5
1885 NY-a	96	349	35	71	8	4	2	21	12	....	....	....	.203	.238	.266	.505	64	-13	23	2.21	1	*O-96(95-1-0)	2	-1.3
1886 Bro-a	6	22	1	4	0	0	0	2	2	....	1	....	.182	.250	.182	.432	36	-2	1	1.92	0	/O-6(3-4-0)	0	-0.2
Total 4	299	1105	142	225	20	13	5	23	47	....	1	....	.204	.239	.259	.498	61	-46	71	2.21	3	O-296/2-1,C-1,S-1	12	-4.8

• KENNEDY, Ed William Edward Kennedy b: 4/5/1861, Bellevue, KY d: 12/22/1912, Cheyenne, WY BR/TR, 5'7", 160 lbs. Deb: 5/17/1884

YEAR TM-L	G	AB	R	H	2B	3B	HR	RBI	BB	SO	SB	CS	AVG	OBP	SLG	OPS	OPS+	BR/A	RC	RC/G	FR	G/POS	WS	TPW
1884 Cin-U	13	48	6	10	1	1	0	....	1	....	....	....	.208	.224	.271	.495	62	-2	3	2.20	2	/3-8,S-4,O-1	1	0.0

• KENNEDY, Jim James Earl Kennedy b: 11/1/1946, Tulsa, OK BL/TR, 5'9", 160 lbs. Deb: 6/14/1970

YEAR TM-L	G	AB	R	H	2B	3B	HR	RBI	BB	SO	SB	CS	AVG	OBP	SLG	OPS	OPS+	BR/A	RC	RC/G	FR	G/POS	WS	TPW
1970 StL-N	12	24	1	3	0	0	0	0	0	0	0	0	.125	.125	.125	.250	-32	-5	0	.48	-1	/S-7,2-5	0	-0.5

• KENNEDY, John John Irvin Kennedy b: 10/12/1926, Jacksonville, FL d: 4/27/1998, Jacksonville, FL BR/TR, 5'10", 175 lbs. Deb: 4/22/1957

YEAR TM-L	G	AB	R	H	2B	3B	HR	RBI	BB	SO	SB	CS	AVG	OBP	SLG	OPS	OPS+	BR/A	RC	RC/G	FR	G/POS	WS	TPW
1957 Phi-N	5	2	1	0	0	0	0	0	0	1	0	0	.000	.000	.000	.000	-103	-1	0	.00	0	/3-2	0	-0.1

YEAR TM-L	G	AB	R	H	2B	3B	HR	RBI	BB	SO	SB	CS	AVG	OBP	SLG	OPS	OPS+	BR/A	RC	RC/G	FR	G/POS	WS	TPW
• KENNEDY, John	John Edward Kennedy b: 5/29/1941, Chicago, IL BR/TR, 6', 185 lbs. Deb: 9/5/1962																							
1962 Was-A	14	42	6	11	0	1	1	2	2	7	0	1	.262	.295	.381	.676	81	-2	5	3.80	-1	/S-9,3-2	1	-0.2
1963 Was-A	36	62	3	11	1	1	0	4	6	22	2	0	.177	.261	.226	.487	38	-5	4	1.99	-1	3-26/S-2	0	-0.6
1964 Was-A	148	482	55	111	16	4	7	35	29	119	3	3	.230	.281	.324	.605	68	-22	41	2.81	3	*3-106,S-49/2-2	6	-1.7
1965*LA-N	104	105	12	18	3	0	1	5	8	33	1	0	.171	.243	.229	.472	36	-9	6	1.74	1	3-95/S-5	1	-0.7
1966*LA-N	125	274	15	55	9	2	3	24	10	64	1	2	.201	.242	.281	.523	49	-20	18	2.10	1	3-87,S-28,2-15	3	-1.7
1967 NY-A	78	179	22	35	4	0	1	17	17	35	2	1	.196	.269	.235	.504	52	-10	12	2.08	-7	S-36,3-34/2-2	2	-1.6
1969 Sea-A	61	128	18	30	3	1	4	14	14	25	4	0	.234	.315	.367	.682	92	-1	16	4.08	-6	S-33,3-23	4	-0.5
1970 Mil-A	25	55	8	14	2	0	2	6	5	9	0	1	.255	.317	.400	.717	96	-1	6	3.69	-3	2-16/3-5,S-4,1-1	1	-0.3
Bos-A	43	129	15	33	7	1	4	17	6	14	0	0	.256	.294	.419	.713	88	-3	16	4.21	1	3-33/2-2	3	-0.2
Yr.	68	184	23	47	9	1	6	23	11	23	0	1	.255	.301	.413	.714	90	-3	22	4.04	-2	3-38,2-18/S-4,1-1	4	-0.4
1971 Bos-A	74	272	41	75	12	5	5	22	14	42	1	1	.276	.321	.412	.732	99	-1	36	4.64	-6	2-37,S-33/3-5	9	-0.2
1972 Bos-A	71	212	22	52	11	1	2	22	18	40	0	1	.245	.313	.335	.648	88	-3	23	3.63	-6	2-32,S-27,3-11	6	-0.5
1973 Bos-A	67	155	17	28	9	1	1	16	12	45	0	0	.181	.249	.271	.519	44	-12	11	2.16	0	2-31,3-24/D-9	2	-1.0
1974 Bos-A	10	15	3	2	0	0	1	1	1	6	0	0	.133	.188	.333	.521	44	-1	0	.59	-2	/2-6,3-4	0	-0.3
Total 12	**856**	**2110**	**237**	**475**	**77**	**17**	**32**	**185**	**142**	**461**	**14**	**10**	**.225**	**.282**	**.323**	**.605**	**69**	**-88**	**193**	**2.99**	**-26**	**3-455,S-226,2-143/D-9,1-1**	**38**	**-9.4**
• KENNEDY, Junior	Junior Raymond Kennedy b: 8/9/1950, Fort Gibson, OK BR/TR, 5'11", 185 lbs. Deb: 8/9/1974																							
1974 Cin-N	22	19	2	3	0	0	0	0	6	4	0	0	.158	.360	.158	.518	49	-1	1	2.19	-4	2-17/3-5	0	-0.5
1978 Cin-N	89	157	22	40	2	2	0	11	31	28	4	1	.255	.381	.293	.674	91	1	20	4.37	0	2-71/3-4	6	0.4
1979 Cin-N	83	220	29	60	7	0	1	17	28	31	4	3	.273	.355	.318	.673	84	-4	26	4.16	0	2-59/S-5,3-4	6	-0.1
1980 Cin-N	104	337	31	88	16	3	1	34	36	34	3	1	.261	.332	.335	.668	87	-5	39	3.99	5	*2-103	11	0.5
1981 Cin-N	27	44	5	11	1	0	0	5	1	5	0	0	.250	.267	.273	.539	52	-3	3	2.62	1	2-16/3-5	1	-0.1
1982 Chi-N	105	242	22	53	3	1	2	25	21	34	1	4	.219	.281	.264	.546	52	-17	17	2.14	-7	2-71,S-28/3-7	2	-2.0
1983 Chi-N	17	22	3	3	0	0	0	3	1	6	0	0	.136	.174	.136	.310	-12	-3	0	.39	-1	/2-7,3-4,S-1	0	-0.5
Total 7	**447**	**1041**	**114**	**258**	**29**	**6**	**4**	**95**	**124**	**142**	**12**	**9**	**.248**	**.328**	**.299**	**.627**	**75**	**-33**	**107**	**3.43**	**-6**	**2-344/S-34,3-29**	**26**	**-2.2**
• KENNEDY, Ray	Raymond Lincoln Kennedy b: 5/19/1895, Pittsburgh, PA d: 1/18/1969, Casselberry, FL BR/TR, 5'9", 165 lbs. Deb: 9/8/1916																							
1916 StL-A	1	1	0	0	0	0	0	0	0	0	0	....	.000	.000	.000	.000	-105	-0	0	.00	0	....	0	0.0
• KENNEDY, Snapper	Sherman Montgomery Kennedy b: 11/1/1878, Conneaut, OH d: 8/15/1945, Pasadena, TX BB/TR, 5'10", 165 lbs. Deb: 5/1/1902																							
1902 Chi-N	1	5	0	0	0	0	0	0	0	....	0	....	.000	.000	.000	.000	-103	-1	0	.00	0	/0-1	0	-0.1
• KENNEDY, Terry	Terrance Edward Kennedy b: 6/4/1956, Euclid, OH BL/TR, 6'3", 220 lbs. Deb: 9/4/1978																							
1978 StL-N	10	29	0	5	0	0	0	2	4	3	0	0	.172	.273	.172	.445	27	-3	1	1.22	0	C-10	0	-0.3
1979 StL-N	33	109	11	31	7	0	2	17	6	20	0	0	.284	.322	.404	.725	96	-1	14	4.58	-2	C-32	3	-0.2
1980 StL-N	84	248	28	63	12	3	4	34	28	34	0	0	.254	.330	.375	.705	93	-2	30	4.04	-3	C-41,0-28(28-0-0)	6	-0.5
1981 SD-N★	101	382	32	115	24	1	2	41	22	53	0	2	.301	.342	.385	.727	114	5	49	4.68	-1	*C-100	10	1.0
1982 SD-N	153	562	75	166	42	1	21	97	26	91	1	0	.295	.332	.486	.818	133	21	90	5.85	-5	*C-139,1-12	28	2.3
1983 SD-N★	149	549	47	156	27	2	17	98	51	89	1	3	.284	.347	.434	.781	119	12	81	5.27	0	*C-143/1-4	24	2.0
1984*SD-N	148	530	54	127	16	1	14	57	33	99	1	2	.240	.287	.353	.640	79	-17	50	3.16	-6	*C-147	12	-1.7
1985 SD-N★	143	532	54	139	27	1	10	74	31	102	0	0	.261	.302	.372	.674	89	-10	55	3.56	2	*C-140/1-5	14	-0.2
1986 SD-N	141	432	46	114	22	1	12	57	37	74	0	3	.264	.325	.403	.728	102	-1	54	4.37	3	*C-123	14	0.8
1987 Bal-A★	143	512	51	128	13	1	18	62	35	112	1	0	.250	.299	.385	.684	82	-14	57	3.84	3	*C-142	11	-0.5
1988 Bal-A	85	265	20	60	10	0	3	16	15	53	0	0	.226	.270	.298	.569	61	-14	19	2.29	-2	C-79	2	-1.2
1989*SF-N	125	355	19	85	15	0	5	34	35	56	1	3	.239	.308	.324	.632	83	-9	35	3.35	-1	*C-121/1-2	12	-0.4
1990 SF-N	107	303	25	84	22	0	2	26	31	38	1	2	.277	.344	.370	.714	100	-1	38	4.40	-2	*C-103	10	0.2
1991 SF-N	69	171	12	40	7	1	3	13	11	31	0	0	.234	.284	.339	.623	77	-6	16	3.14	1	C-58/1-2	4	-0.1
Total 14	**1491**	**4979**	**474**	**1313**	**244**	**12**	**113**	**628**	**365**	**855**	**6**	**15**	**.264**	**.316**	**.386**	**.702**	**97**	**-40**	**588**	**4.10**	**-15**	***C-1378/0-28,1-25**	**150**	**1.2**
• KENNEY, Jerry	Gerald Tennyson Kenney b: 6/30/1945, St. Louis, MO BL/TR, 6'1", 170 lbs. Deb: 9/5/1967																							
1967 NY-A	20	58	4	18	2	0	1	5	10	8	2	1	.310	.412	.397	.808	145	4	11	6.24	-3	S-18	4	0.3
1969 NY-A	130	447	49	115	14	2	2	34	48	36	25	14	.257	.331	.311	.642	83	-10	47	3.41	16	3-83,0-31(0-31-0),S-10	12	0.6
1970 NY-A	140	404	46	78	10	7	4	35	52	44	20	6	.193	.285	.282	.567	60	-19	34	2.66	6	*3-135/2-2	7	-1.5
1971 NY-A	120	325	50	85	10	3	0	20	56	38	9	8	.262	.372	.311	.682	101	2	40	3.96	2	*3-109/S-5,1-1	10	0.4
1972 NY-A	50	119	16	25	2	0	0	7	16	13	3	0	.210	.304	.227	.531	61	-4	8	2.17	5	S-45/3-1	2	0.6
1973 Cle-A	5	16	0	4	0	1	0	2	2	0	0	0	.250	.333	.375	.708	97	-0	2	4.62	0	/2-5	0	0.0
Total 6	**465**	**1369**	**165**	**325**	**38**	**13**	**7**	**103**	**184**	**139**	**59**	**29**	**.237**	**.329**	**.299**	**.628**	**82**	**-27**	**142**	**3.33**	**26**	**3-328/S-78,0-31,2-7,1-1**	**35**	**0.5**
• KENNEY, John	John Kenney Deb: 5/2/1872 U																							
1872 Atl-n	5	19	0	0	0	0	0	1	0	1	0	0	.000	.000	.000	.000	-85	-5	0	.00	-3	/2-3,0-3(2-0-1)	....	-0.5
• KENT, Jeff	Jeffrey Franklin Kent b: 3/7/1968, Bellflower, CA BR/TR, 6'1", 185 lbs. Deb: 4/12/1992																							
1992 Tor-A	65	192	36	46	13	1	8	35	20	47	2	1	.240	.330	.443	.773	110	2	29	5.10	-2	3-49,2-17/1-3	7	0.1
NY-N	37	113	16	27	8	1	3	15	7	29	0	2	.239	.289	.407	.696	96	-2	12	3.70	1	2-34/3-1,S-1	3	0.0
1993 NY-N	140	496	65	134	24	0	21	80	30	88	4	4	.270	.322	.446	.768	104	0	69	4.78	-14	*2-127,3-12/S-2	13	-0.8
1994 NY-N	107	415	53	121	24	5	14	68	23	84	1	4	.292	.344	.475	.818	112	4	66	5.73	3	*2-107	18	1.3
1995 NY-N	125	472	65	131	22	3	20	65	29	89	3	3	.278	.330	.464	.794	110	4	70	5.31	-8	*2-122	11	0.2
1996 NY-N	89	335	45	97	20	1	9	39	21	56	4	3	.290	.333	.436	.769	106	1	47	5.03	3	3-89	8	0.6
*Cle-A	39	102	16	27	7	0	3	16	10	22	2	1	.265	.336	.422	.758	90	-2	15	5.08	1	1-20/2-9,3-6,D-5	3	-0.1
1997*SF-N	155	580	90	145	38	2	29	121	48	133	11	3	.250	.321	.472	.794	108	6	87	5.08	1	*2-148,1-13	22	1.3
1998 SF-N	137	526	94	156	37	3	31	128	48	110	9	4	.297	.365	.555	.920	146	34	103	6.92	2	*2-134/1-1	25	4.2
1999 SF-N★	138	511	86	148	40	2	23	101	61	112	13	6	.290	.371	.511	.882	129	22	97	6.70	-3	*2-133/1-1	23	2.4
2000*SF-N★	159	587	114	196	41	7	33	125	90	107	12	9	.334	.430	.596	1.026	168	62	149	9.45	-2	*2-150,1-16	**37**	6.2
2001 SF-N★	159	607	84	181	49	6	22	106	65	96	7	6	.298	.376	.507	.884	135	31	116	6.88	12	*2-140,1-30	27	4.6
2002*SF-N	152	623	102	195	42	2	37	108	52	101	5	1	.313	.370	.565	.935	149	41	125	7.45	13	*2-149/1-9	29	6.1
2003 Hou-N	130	505	77	150	39	1	22	93	39	85	6	2	.297	.353	.509	.862	116	11	88	6.40	1	*2-128	21	1.8
Total 12	**1632**	**6064**	**943**	**1754**	**404**	**34**	**275**	**1100**	**543**	**1159**	**79**	**49**	**.289**	**.357**	**.503**	**.860**	**126**	**216**	**1073**	**6.31**	**8**	***2-1398,3-157/1-93,D-5,S-3**	**247**	**27.7**
• KENWORTHY, Bill	William Jennings "Iron Duke" Kenworthy b: 7/4/1886, Cambridge, OH d: 9/21/1950, Eureka, CA BR/TR, 5'7", 165 lbs. Deb: 8/28/1912 Career OF: 7-5-7																							
1912 Was-A	12	38	6	9	1	0	0	2	2	....	3	....	.237	.293	.263	.556	59	-2	4	3.28	2	0-12(7-5-0)	1	-0.1
1914 KC-F	146	545	93	173	40	14	15	91	36	44	37	....	.317	.372	.525	.896	161	40	114	7.45	9	*2-145	30	5.4
1915 KC-F	122	396	59	118	30	7	3	52	28	32	20	....	.298	.355	.432	.787	135	16	66	5.76	-10	*2-108/0-7(0-0-7)	22	0.8
1917 StL-A	5	10	1	1	0	0	0	1	1	1	1	....	.100	.182	.100	.282	-14	-1	0	.87	0	/2-4	0	-0.1
Total 4	**285**	**989**	**159**	**301**	**71**	**21**	**18**	**146**	**67**	**77**	**61**	**....**	**.304**	**.360**	**.473**	**.833**	**145**	**53**	**184**	**6.51**	**1**	**2-257/0-19**	**53**	**6.1**
• KENWORTHY, Dick	Richard Lee Kenworthy b: 4/1/1941, Red Oak, IA BR/TR, 5'9", 170 lbs. Deb: 9/8/1962																							
1962 Chi-A	3	4	0	0	0	0	0	0	0	3	0	0	.000	.000	.000	.000	-101	-1	0	.00	1	/2-2	0	0.0
1964 Chi-A	2	2	0	0	0	0	0	0	0	1	0	0	.000	.000	.000	.000	-103	-1	0	.00	0	....	0	-0.1
1965 Chi-A	3	1	0	0	0	0	0	0	1	0	0	0	.000	.667	.000	.667	113	0	0	9.36	0	....	0	0.0
1966 Chi-A	9	25	1	5	0	0	0	0	0	0	0	0	.200	.200	.200	.400	16	-3	1	1.35	-0	/3-6	0	-0.3
1967 Chi-A	50	97	9	22	4	1	4	11	4	17	0	2	.227	.265	.412	.677	101	-1	9	3.15	1	3-35	2	-0.1
1968 Chi-A	58	122	2	27	2	0	0	2	5	21	0	1	.221	.252	.238	.490	49	-8	7	1.91	-1	3-38	1	-1.1
Total 6	**125**	**251**	**12**	**54**	**6**	**1**	**4**	**13**	**10**	**42**	**0**	**3**	**.215**	**.251**	**.295**	**.546**	**63**	**-13**	**18**	**2.32**	**0**	**/3-79,2-2**	**3**	**-1.5**
• KEOUGH, Joe	Joseph William Keough b: 1/7/1946, Pomona, CA BL/TL, 6', 185 lbs. Deb: 8/7/1968 Career OF: 59-36-135																							
1968 Oak-A	34	98	7	21	2	1	2	18	8	11	1	0	.214	.274	.316	.590	82	-2	9	2.85	0	0-29(28-0-1)/1-1	2	-0.5
1969 KC-A	70	166	17	31	2	0	0	7	13	13	5	2	.187	.254	.199	.453	28	-16	10	1.84	1	0-49(3-26-21)/1-1	1	-1.7
1970 KC-A	57	183	28	59	6	2	4	21	23	18	1	1	.322	.398	.443	.841	132	8	32	6.34	1	0-34(18-1-15),1-18	7	0.7
1971 KC-A	110	351	34	87	14	2	3	30	35	26	0	6	.248	.318	.325	.643	83	-10	34	3.22	-2	*0-100(1-7-93)	6	-1.7
1972 KC-A	56	64	8	14	2	0	0	5	8	7	2	0	.219	.324	.250	.574	73	-1	6	3.37	1	0-16(9-2-5)	1	-0.1

YEAR TM-L	G	AB	R	H	2B	3B	HR	RBI	BB	SO	SB	CS	AVG	OBP	SLG	OPS	OPS+	BR/A	RC	RC/G	FR	G/POS	WS	TPW
1973 Chi-A	5	1	1	0	0	0	0	0	0	0	0	0	.000	.000	.000	.000	-97	-0	0	.00	0	....	0	0.0
Total 6	332	863	95	212	26	5	9	81	87	75	9	9	.246	.318	.319	.637	82	-21	90	3.51	0	0-228/1-20	17	-3.3
• KEOUGH, Marty	Richard Martin Keough b: 4/14/1934, Oakland, CA BL/TL, 6', 180 lbs. Deb: 4/21/1956 Career OF: 127-203-148																							
1956 Bos-A	3	2	1	0	0	0	0	1	1	0	0	0	.000	.333	.000	.333	-5	-0	0	1.17	0	....	0	0.0
1957 Bos-A	9	17	1	1	0	0	0	0	4	3	0	0	.059	.238	.059	.297	-14	-3	0	.82	0	/O-7(0-2-5)	0	-0.3
1958 Bos-A	68	118	21	26	3	3	1	9	7	29	1	1	.220	.264	.322	.586	56	-7	10	2.74	-1	O-25(1-21-3)/1-2	1	-1.0
1959 Bos-A	96	251	40	61	13	5	7	27	26	40	3	1	.243	.321	.418	.740	97	-1	35	4.78	-3	O-69(0-69-0)/1-3	7	-0.8
1960 Bos-A	38	105	15	26	6	1	1	9	8	8	2	2	.248	.301	.352	.653	73	-5	11	3.52	0	O-29(1-28-0)	2	-0.6
Cle-A	65	149	19	37	5	0	3	11	9	23	2	3	.248	.296	.342	.638	74	-7	15	3.35	1	O-42(2-25-16)	2	-0.7
Yr.	103	254	34	63	11	1	4	20	17	31	4	5	.248	.298	.346	.644	74	-11	26	3.42	1	O-71(3-53-16)	4	-1.3
1961 Was-A	135	390	57	97	18	9	9	34	32	60	12	5	.249	.309	.410	.719	95	-4	50	4.31	0	*O-100(63-25-18),1-10	9	-0.9
1962 Cin-N	111	230	34	64	8	2	7	27	21	31	3	1	.278	.349	.422	.771	102	1	35	5.47	1	O-71(48-17-10),1-29	8	-0.1
1963 Cin-N	95	172	21	39	8	2	6	21	25	37	1	4	.227	.338	.401	.739	109	1	24	4.46	1	1-46,O-28(4-3-22)	5	0.0
1964 Cin-N	109	276	29	71	9	1	9	28	22	58	1	2	.257	.314	.395	.709	95	-2	35	4.55	-1	O-81(1-11-71)/1-4	8	-0.8
1965 Cin-N	62	43	14	5	0	0	0	3	3	14	0	0	.116	.191	.116	.308	-10	-6	1	.74	-1	1-32/O-4(3-0-1)	0	-0.9
1966 Atl-N	17	17	1	1	0	0	0	1	1	6	0	0	.059	.111	.059	.170	-50	-3	0	.24	-1	/1-4,O-3(2-0-1)	0	-0.5
Chi-N	33	26	3	6	1	0	0	5	5	9	1	0	.231	.375	.269	.644	82	-0	3	4.60	0	/O-5(2-2-1)	1	0.0
Yr.	50	43	4	7	1	0	0	6	6	15	1	0	.163	.280	.186	.466	34	-3	4	2.66	-2	/O-8(4-2-2),1-4	1	-0.6
Total 11	841	1796	256	434	71	23	43	176	164	318	26	19	.242	.311	.379	.690	87	-36	220	4.15	-5	O-464,1-130	43	-6.7
• KERINS, John	John Nelson Kerins b: 7/15/1858, Indianapolis, IN d: 9/8/1919, Louisville, KY BR/TR, 5'10", 177 lbs. Deb: 5/1/1884 M Career OF: 13-9-49																							
1884 Ind-a	94	364	58	78	10	3	6	0	6	....	....	....	.214	.229	.308	.537	75	-10	26	2.53	7	*1-87/C-5,O-5(0-2-3),3-1	3	-0.9
1885 Lou-a	112	456	65	111	9	16	3	51	20	....	....	....	.243	.281	.353	.634	99	-1	46	3.63	1	*1-96,C-19/O-3(0-0-3),3-1	10	-0.6
1886 Lou-a	120	487	113	131	19	9	4	50	66	....	26	....	.269	.360	.370	.729	122	13	76	5.76	21	C-65,1-47/O-7(2-2-3),S-1	17	3.1
1887 Lou-a	112	514	101	178	18	**19**	5	57	38	....	49	....	.346	.349	.443	.792	118	9	93	7.47	8	1-74,C-35/O-5(1-1-3)	15	1.1
1888 Lou-a	83	319	38	75	11	4	2	41	25	....	16	....	.235	.297	.313	.610	98	-0	35	3.91	-8	O-47(10-2-35),C-33/1-4,3-2,2	8	-0.6
1889 Lou-a	2	9	2	3	1	0	0	3	0	1	0	....	.333	.333	.444	.778	123	0	1	6.04	0	/O-2(0-0-2),C-1	0	0.0
Bal-a	16	53	7	15	2	0	0	12	2	4	2	....	.283	.321	.321	.642	85	-1	6	4.37	0	/1-9,C-4,O-2(0-2-0),S-1	1	-0.1
Yr.	18	62	9	18	3	0	0	15	2	5	2	....	.290	.323	.339	.662	90	-1	8	4.59	-1	/1-9,C-5,O-4(0-2-2),S-1	1	-0.1
1890 StL-a	18	63	8	8	2	0	0	3	8	....	2	....	.127	.225	.159	.384	12	-8	3	1.34	1	1-17/C-1	0	-0.7
Total 7	557	2265	392	599	72	51	20	217	165	5	95	....	.264	.308	.357	.665	102	3	287	4.66	29	1-334,C-163/O-71,3-4,S-2,2	54	1.3
• KERLIN, Orie	Orie Milton "Cy" Kerlin b: 1/23/1891, Summerfield, LA d: 10/29/1974, Shreveport, LA BL/TR, 5'7", 149 lbs. Deb: 6/6/1915																							
1915 Pit-F	3	1	0	0	0	0	0	0	0	0	0	....	.000	.000	.000	.000	-96	-0	0	.00	-2	/C-3	0	-0.2
• KERN, Bill	William George Kern b: 2/28/1933, Coplay, PA BR/TR, 6'2", 184 lbs. Deb: 9/19/1962																							
1962 KC-A	8	16	1	4	0	0	1	1	0	3	0	0	.250	.250	.438	.688	78	-1	2	3.94	1	/O-3(3-0-0)	0	0.0
• KERNAN, Joe	Joseph Kernan b: Baltimore, MD Deb: 4/14/1873																							
1873 Mar-n	2	8	1	3	0	0	0	1	0	0	0	0	.375	.375	.375	.750	161	1	1	7.03	0	/2-1,O-1	....	0.0
• KERNEK, George	George Boyd Kernek b: 1/12/1940, Holdenville, OK BL/TL, 6'3", 170 lbs. Deb: 9/5/1965																							
1965 StL-N	10	31	6	9	3	1	0	3	2	4	0	0	.290	.333	.452	.785	109	0	5	5.94	0	/1-7	1	0.0
1966 StL-N	20	50	5	12	0	1	0	3	4	9	1	0	.240	.309	.280	.589	65	-2	5	3.19	0	1-16	0	-0.3
Total 2	30	81	11	21	3	2	0	6	6	13	1	0	.259	.318	.346	.664	81	-2	9	4.18	0	/1-23	1	-0.3
• KERNS, Russ	Russell Eldon Kerns b: 11/10/1920, Fremont, OH d: 8/21/2000, Placerville, CA BL/TR, 6', 188 lbs. Deb: 8/18/1945																							
1945 Det-A	1	1	0	0	0	0	0	0	0	0	0	0	.000	.000	.000	.000	-94	-0	0	.00	0	....	0	0.0
• KERR, Buddy	John Joseph Kerr b: 11/6/1922, Astoria, NY BR/TR, 6'2", 180 lbs. Deb: 9/8/1943 C																							
1943 NY-N	27	98	14	28	3	0	2	12	8	5	1	....	.286	.352	.378	.729	110	1	13	4.85	-2	S-27	3	0.2
1944 NY-N	150	548	68	146	31	4	9	63	37	32	14	....	.266	.316	.387	.703	97	-3	65	4.15	10	*S-149	16	1.9
1945 NY-N	149	546	53	136	20	3	4	40	41	34	5	....	.249	.304	.319	.623	72	-21	54	3.32	19	*S-148	12	1.0
1946 NY-N	145	497	50	124	20	3	6	40	53	31	7	....	.249	.324	.338	.662	87	-8	57	3.82	2	*S-126,3-18	12	0.2
1947 NY-N	138	547	73	157	23	5	7	49	36	49	2	....	.287	.331	.386	.717	89	-10	69	4.49	4	*S-138	16	0.3
1948 NY-N★	144	496	41	119	16	4	0	46	56	36	9	....	.240	.317	.288	.605	64	-24	48	3.36	5	*S-143	12	-0.9
1949 NY-N	90	220	16	46	4	0	0	19	21	23	0	....	.209	.284	.227	.511	39	-19	16	2.41	4	S-89	3	-1.0
1950 Bos-N	155	507	45	115	24	6	2	46	50	50	0	....	.227	.296	.310	.606	64	-27	45	2.83	15	*S-155	10	-0.2
1951 Bos-N	69	172	18	32	4	0	1	18	22	20	0	0	.186	.282	.227	.509	41	-13	13	2.36	4	S-63/2-5	3	-0.5
Total 9	1067	3631	378	903	145	25	31	333	324	280	38	0	.249	.312	.328	.640	76	-124	380	3.54	60	*S-1038/3-18,2-5	87	0.7
• KERR, Doc	John Jonas Kerr b: 1/17/1882, Dellroy, OH d: 1/9/1937, Baltimore, MD BB/TR, 5'10.5", 190 lbs. Deb: 4/22/1914																							
1914 Pit-F	42	71	3	17	4	2	1	7	10	13	0	....	.239	.333	.394	.728	113	1	9	4.17	1	C-18	2	0.4
Bal-F	14	34	4	9	1	1	0	1	1	6	1	....	.265	.286	.353	.639	82	-1	3	3.49	-3	C-13/1-1	1	-0.3
Yr.	56	105	7	26	5	3	1	8	11	19	1	....	.248	.319	.381	.700	104	0	12	3.96	-1	C-31/1-1	3	0.1
1915 Bal-F	3	6	1	2	0	0	0	0	1	0	0	....	.333	.429	.333	.762	117	0	1	5.35	0	/C-2,1-1	0	0.0
Total 2	59	111	8	28	5	3	1	8	12	19	1	....	.252	.325	.378	.704	104	0	13	4.03	-2	/C-33,1-2	3	0.1
• KERR, John	John Francis Kerr b: 11/26/1898, San Francisco, CA d: 10/19/1993, Long Beach, CA BR/TR, 5'8", 158 lbs. Deb: 5/1/1923																							
1923 Det-A	19	42	4	9	1	0	0	1	4	5	0	0	.214	.283	.238	.521	39	-4	3	2.37	-4	S-15	0	-0.5
1924 Det-A	17	11	3	3	0	0	0	1	0	0	0	0	.273	.273	.273	.545	42	-1	1	2.48	-1	/3-3,O-2(0-0-0)	0	-0.2
1929 Chi-A	127	419	50	108	20	4	1	39	31	24	9	8	.258	.310	.332	.642	66	-22	44	3.37	17	*2-122/S-1	7	-0.2
1930 Chi-A	70	266	37	77	11	6	3	27	21	23	4	2	.289	.351	.410	.760	95	-1	39	5.24	-8	2-52,S-20	7	-0.6
1931 Chi-A	128	444	51	119	17	2	2	50	35	22	9	3	.268	.324	.329	.653	77	-12	50	3.88	-2	*2-117/3-7,S-1	9	-0.5
1932 Was-A	51	132	14	36	6	1	0	15	13	3	3	2	.273	.338	.333	.671	75	-5	15	4.04	1	2-17,S-14/3-8	3	-0.2
1933*Was-A	28	40	5	8	0	0	0	0	3	2	0	0	.200	.256	.200	.456	22	-4	2	1.80	0	2-16/3-1	0	-0.4
1934 Was-A	31	103	8	28	4	0	0	12	8	13	1	1	.272	.324	.311	.635	67	-5	11	3.60	1	3-17,2-13	2	-0.3
Total 8	471	1457	172	388	59	13	6	145	115	92	26	16	.266	.323	.337	.660	73	-54	165	3.84	3	2-337/S-51,3-36,O-2	28	-2.8
• KERR, Mel	John Melville Kerr b: 5/22/1903, Souris, Canada d: 8/9/1980, Vero Beach, FL BL/TL, 5'11.5", 155 lbs. Deb: 9/16/1925																							
1925 Chi-N	1	0	1	0	0	0	0	0	0	0	0	0	....	....	....	....	-99	0	0	....	0	....	0	0.0
• KERWIN, Dan	Daniel Patrick Kerwin b: 7/9/1879, Philadelphia, PA d: 7/13/1960, Philadelphia, PA BL/TL, 5'9", 164 lbs. Deb: 9/27/1903																							
1903 Cin-N	2	6	1	4	1	0	0	1	2	....	0	....	.667	.778	.833	1.611	323	2	4	52.82	0	/O-2(2-0-0)	1	0.2
• KESSINGER, Don	Donald Eulon Kessinger b: 7/17/1942, Forrest City, AR BB/TR, 6'1", 175 lbs. Deb: 9/7/1964 M																							
1964 Chi-N	4	12	1	2	0	0	0	0	0	1	0	0	.167	.167	.167	.333	-6	-2	0	.90	0	/S-4	0	-0.1
1965 Chi-N	106	309	19	62	4	3	0	14	20	44	1	2	.201	.254	.233	.487	37	-26	18	1.93	-9	*S-105	2	-2.7
1966 Chi-N	150	533	50	146	8	2	1	43	26	46	13	7	.274	.308	.302	.610	69	-21	49	3.11	-18	*S-148	6	-2.8
1967 Chi-N	145	580	61	134	10	7	0	42	33	80	6	13	.231	.277	.272	.550	55	-37	43	2.48	-4	*S-143	8	-3.1
1968 Chi-N★	160	655	63	157	14	7	1	32	38	86	9	9	.240	.283	.287	.570	67	-27	54	2.75	13	*S-159	14	-0.1
1969 Chi-N★	158	664	109	181	38	6	4	53	61	70	11	8	.273	.335	.366	.701	85	-13	84	4.48	10	*S-157	23	1.8
1970 Chi-N★	154	631	100	168	21	14	1	39	66	59	12	6	.266	.338	.349	.686	75	-21	76	4.17	-1	*S-154	14	-0.4
1971 Chi-N★	155	617	77	159	18	6	2	38	52	54	15	8	.258	.318	.316	.634	70	-23	63	3.48	-7	*S-154	14	-1.3
1972 Chi-N★	149	577	77	158	20	6	1	39	67	44	8	7	.274	.351	.334	.686	86	-8	70	4.18	-6	*S-146	15	0.4
1973 Chi-N	160	577	52	151	22	3	0	43	57	44	6	6	.262	.328	.310	.638	72	-21	57	3.39	-9	*S-158	12	-1.2
1974 Chi-N★	153	599	83	155	20	7	1	42	62	54	7	7	.259	.332	.321	.653	80	-16	64	3.65	-13	*S-150	13	-1.2
1975 Chi-N	154	601	77	146	26	10	0	46	68	47	4	7	.243	.321	.319	.640	75	-22	66	3.63	-14	*S-140,3-13	13	-2.1
1976 StL-N	145	502	55	120	22	6	1	40	61	51	3	0	.239	.323	.313	.635	80	-11	53	3.49	12	*S-113,2-31/3-2	11	1.6
1977 StL-N	59	134	14	32	4	0	0	7	14	26	0	0	.239	.311	.269	.579	58	-7	12	2.93	3	S-26,2-24/3-4	3	-0.2
Chi-A	39	119	12	28	3	2	0	11	13	7	2	1	.235	.311	.294	.605	66	-5	11	3.07	-2	S-21,2-13/3-9	1	-0.5

YEAR TM-L	G	AB	R	H	2B	3B	HR	RBI	BB	SO	SB	CS	AVG	OBP	SLG	OPS	OPS+	BR/A	RC	RC/G	FR	G/POS	WS	TPW
1978 Chi-A	131	431	35	110	18	1	1	31	36	34	2	4	.255	.313	.309	.621	75	-15	41	3.20	-4	*S-123/2-9	9	-0.8
1979 Chi-A	56	110	14	22	6	0	1	7	10	12	1	0	.200	.267	.282	.548	48	-8	8	2.18	1	S-54/1-1,2-1	1	-0.3
Total 16	2078	7651	899	1931	254	80	14	527	684	759	100	85	.252	.316	.312	.628	72	-284	769	3.40	-47	*S-1955/2-78,3-28,1-1	159	-12.9

• KESSINGER, Keith Robert Keith Kessinger b: 2/19/1967, Forrest City, AR BB/TR, 6'2", 185 lbs. Deb: 9/15/1993

YEAR TM-L	G	AB	R	H	2B	3B	HR	RBI	BB	SO	SB	CS	AVG	OBP	SLG	OPS	OPS+	BR/A	RC	RC/G	FR	G/POS	WS	TPW
1993 Cin-N	11	27	4	7	1	0	1	3	4	4	0	0	.259	.355	.407	.762	103	0	4	4.82	1	S-11	1	0.1

• KESSLER, Henry Henry "Lucky" Kessler b: 1847, Brooklyn, NY d: 1/9/1900, Franklin, PA BR/TR, 5'10", 144 lbs. Deb: 8/4/1873 NA OF: 2-6-3

YEAR TM-L	G	AB	R	H	2B	3B	HR	RBI	BB	SO	SB	CS	AVG	OBP	SLG	OPS	OPS+	BR/A	RC	RC/G	FR	G/POS	WS	TPW
1873 Atl-n	1	5	0	1	0	0	0	1	0	0	0	0	.200	.200	.200	.400	21	-0	0	1.56	0	/1-1	....	0.0
1874 Atl-n	14	56	8	17	1	0	0	4	0	2	0	0	.304	.304	.321	.625	113	1	6	4.31	-5	/C-9,2-4,0-4(2-2-0),3-1	....	-0.3
1875 Atl-n	25	105	17	26	2	0	0	7	1	2	0	2	.248	.255	.267	.521	93	-1	7	2.66	-3	S-18/0-7(0-4-3),C-3,1-1,2	....	-0.3
1876 Cin-N	59	255	26	64	5	0	0	11	7	10	....	....	.251	.278	.278	.557	100	3	20	3.00	-10	*S-46,0-16(0-2-14)	3	-0.5
1877 Cin-N	6	20	0	2	0	0	0	0	2	1	....	....	.100	.182	.100	.282	-10	-2	0	.57	-4	/C-5,1-1	0	-0.6
Total 3 n	40	166	25	44	3	0	0	12	1	4	0	2	.265	.269	.283	.553	98	0	13	3.14	-8	/S-18,C-12,0-11,2-5,1-2,3-1	....	-0.6
Total 2	65	275	26	66	5	0	0	11	9	11	....	....	.240	.271	.265	.536	91	0	20	2.78	-14	/S-46,0-16,C-5,1-1	3	-1.1

• KETCHAM, Fred Frederick L. Ketcham b: 7/27/1875, Elmira, NY d: 3/12/1908, Cortland, NY BL/TR, 5'8", 157 lbs. Deb: 9/12/1899 Career OF: 9-1-10

YEAR TM-L	G	AB	R	H	2B	3B	HR	RBI	BB	SO	SB	CS	AVG	OBP	SLG	OPS	OPS+	BR/A	RC	RC/G	FR	G/POS	WS	TPW
1899 Lou-N	15	61	13	18	1	0	0	5	0	....	2	....	.295	.306	.311	.618	70	-3	7	4.05	0	0-15(4-1-10)	1	-0.3
1901 Phi-A	5	22	5	5	0	0	0	2	0	....	0	....	.227	.227	.227	.455	25	-2	1	1.82	-1	/0-5(5-0-0)	0	-0.3
Total 2	20	83	18	23	1	0	0	7	0	....	2	....	.277	.286	.289	.575	58	-5	8	3.42	-1	/0-20	1	-0.6

• KETTER, Phil Philip Ketter b: 4/13/1884, St. Louis, MO d: 4/9/1965, St. Louis, MO TR Deb: 5/23/1912

YEAR TM-L	G	AB	R	H	2B	3B	HR	RBI	BB	SO	SB	CS	AVG	OBP	SLG	OPS	OPS+	BR/A	RC	RC/G	FR	G/POS	WS	TPW
1912 StL-A	2	6	1	2	0	0	0	0	0	....	0	....	.333	.333	.333	.667	94	-0	1	4.18	0	/C-2	0	0.0

• KHALIFA, Sam Sam Khalifa b: 12/5/1963, Fontana, CA BR/TR, 5'11", 170 lbs. Deb: 6/25/1985

YEAR TM-L	G	AB	R	H	2B	3B	HR	RBI	BB	SO	SB	CS	AVG	OBP	SLG	OPS	OPS+	BR/A	RC	RC/G	FR	G/POS	WS	TPW
1985 Pit-N	95	320	30	76	14	3	2	31	34	56	5	2	.238	.311	.319	.629	77	-9	32	3.21	5	S-95	6	0.6
1986 Pit-N	64	151	8	28	6	0	0	4	19	28	0	2	.185	.276	.225	.502	39	-13	9	1.83	-2	S-60/2-6	2	-1.0
1987 Pit-N	5	17	1	3	0	0	0	2	0	2	0	0	.176	.176	.176	.353	-6	-3	1	1.06	-1	/S-5	0	-0.3
Total 3	164	488	39	107	20	3	2	37	53	86	5	4	.219	.296	.285	.581	63	-25	41	2.69	1	S-160/2-6	8	-0.8

• KIBBIE, Hod Horace Kent Kibbie b: 7/18/1903, Fort Worth, TX d: 10/19/1975, Fort Worth, TX BR/TR, 5'10", 150 lbs. Deb: 6/13/1925

YEAR TM-L	G	AB	R	H	2B	3B	HR	RBI	BB	SO	SB	CS	AVG	OBP	SLG	OPS	OPS+	BR/A	RC	RC/G	FR	G/POS	WS	TPW
1925 Bos-N	11	41	5	11	2	0	0	2	5	6	0	0	.268	.348	.317	.665	78	-1	5	4.22	1	/2-8,S-3	1	0.0

• KIBBLE, Jack John Westly "Happy" Kibble b: 1/2/1892, Seatonville, IL d: 12/13/1969, Roundup, MT BB/TR, 5'9.5", 154 lbs. Deb: 9/10/1912

YEAR TM-L	G	AB	R	H	2B	3B	HR	RBI	BB	SO	SB	CS	AVG	OBP	SLG	OPS	OPS+	BR/A	RC	RC/G	FR	G/POS	WS	TPW
1912 Cle-A	5	8	1	0	0	0	0	0	0	....	0	....	.000	.111	.000	.111	-65	-2	0	.00	1	/3-4,2-1	0	0.0

• KIEFER, Steve Steven George Kiefer b: 10/18/1960, Chicago, IL BR/TR, 6'1", 180 lbs. Deb: 9/3/1984

YEAR TM-L	G	AB	R	H	2B	3B	HR	RBI	BB	SO	SB	CS	AVG	OBP	SLG	OPS	OPS+	BR/A	RC	RC/G	FR	G/POS	WS	TPW
1984 Oak-A	23	40	7	7	1	2	0	2	2	10	2	1	.175	.214	.300	.514	43	-3	3	1.96	0	S-17/D-3,3-2	0	-0.2
1985 Oak-A	40	66	8	13	1	1	1	10	1	18	0	0	.197	.209	.288	.497	37	-6	4	1.82	-3	3-34/D-2	0	-0.9
1986 Mil-A	2	6	0	0	0	0	0	0	0	4	0	0	.000	.000	.000	.000	-97	-2	0	.00	2	/S-2	0	0.1
1987 Mil-A	28	99	17	20	4	0	5	17	7	28	0	0	.202	.262	.394	.656	69	-5	10	3.08	0	3-26/2-4	1	-0.5
1988 Mil-A	7	10	2	3	1	0	1	1	2	3	0	0	.300	.462	.700	1.162	219	2	4	13.85	-1	/2-4,3-4	1	0.1
1989 NY-A	5	8	0	1	0	0	0	0	0	5	0	0	.125	.125	.125	.250	-30	-1	0	.48	-1	/3-5	0	-0.2
Total 6	105	229	34	44	7	3	7	30	12	68	2	1	.192	.239	.341	.579	56	-15	20	2.70	-3	/3-71,S-19,2-8,D-5	2	-1.7

• KIELTY, Bobby Robert Michael Kielty b: 8/5/1976, Fontana, CA BB/TR, 6'1", 215 lbs. Deb: 4/10/2001 Career OF: 24-48-156

YEAR TM-L	G	AB	R	H	2B	3B	HR	RBI	BB	SO	SB	CS	AVG	OBP	SLG	OPS	OPS+	BR/A	RC	RC/G	FR	G/POS	WS	TPW
2001 Min-A	37	104	8	26	8	0	2	14	8	25	3	0	.250	.310	.385	.694	80	-3	13	4.08	-2	0-34(11-11-17)/D-1	1	-0.5
2002*Min-A	112	289	49	84	14	3	12	46	52	66	4	1	.291	.408	.484	.892	134	17	61	7.81	-3	0-82(9-34-50)/D-9,1-5	15	1.1
2003 Min-A	75	238	40	60	13	0	9	32	42	56	6	2	.252	.371	.420	.791	107	4	40	5.75	-3	0-36(1-2-33),D-32	8	-0.2
Tor-A	62	189	31	44	13	1	4	25	29	36	2	1	.233	.347	.376	.723	89	-2	25	4.40	-2	0-60(3-1-56)/1-3	4	-0.7
Yr.	137	427	71	104	26	1	13	57	71	92	8	3	.244	.360	.400	.761	99	2	65	5.14	-6	0-96(4-3-89),D-32/1-3	12	-0.9
Total 3	286	820	128	214	48	4	27	117	131	183	15	4	.261	.371	.428	.799	109	17	139	5.88	-10	0-212/D-42,1-8	28	-0.4

• KIENZLE, Bill William H. Kienzle b: Philadelphia, PA BL/TL Deb: 9/15/1882 Career OF: 0-76-0

YEAR TM-L	G	AB	R	H	2B	3B	HR	RBI	BB	SO	SB	CS	AVG	OBP	SLG	OPS	OPS+	BR/A	RC	RC/G	FR	G/POS	WS	TPW
1882 Phi-a	9	33	8	11	3	2	0	9	5	....	....	....	.333	.421	.545	.967	200	4	8	9.89	-1	/0-9(0-9-0)	3	0.2
1884 Phi-U	67	299	76	76	13	8	0	....	21	....	....	....	.254	.303	.351	.654	131	12	33	4.10	-8	0-67(0-67-0)	7	0.1
Total 2	76	332	84	87	16	10	0	9	26	....	....	....	.262	.316	.370	.686	138	15	40	4.62	-9	/0-76	10	0.3

• KIESCHNICK, Brooks Michael Brooks Kieschnick b: 6/6/1972, Robstown, TX BL/TR, 6'4", 225 lbs. Deb: 4/3/1996 Career OF: 41-0-10 ♦

YEAR TM-L	G	AB	R	H	2B	3B	HR	RBI	BB	SO	SB	CS	AVG	OBP	SLG	OPS	OPS+	BR/A	RC	RC/G	FR	G/POS	WS	TPW
1996 Chi-N	25	29	6	10	2	0	1	6	3	8	0	0	.345	.406	.517	.923	138	2	6	9.11	-1	/0-8(4-0-5)	1	0.1
1997 Chi-N	39	90	9	18	2	0	4	12	12	21	1	0	.200	.294	.356	.650	67	-4	10	3.57	0	0-27(26-0-1)	2	-0.5
2000 Cin-N	14	12	0	0	0	0	0	0	1	5	0	0	.000	.077	.000	.077	-77	-3	0	.05	-0	/1-1	0	-0.3
2001 Col-N	35	42	5	10	2	1	3	9	3	13	0	0	.238	.289	.548	.837	89	-1	6	5.19	-1	0-12(8-0-4)/1-1	1	-0.2
2003 Mil-N	69	70	12	21	1	0	7	12	6	13	0	0	.300	.355	.614	.970	150	11	15	7.76	0	P-42/D-4,0-3(3-0-0)	3	0.4
Total 5	182	243	32	59	7	1	15	39	25	60	1	0	.243	.313	.465	.778	96	4	37	5.32	-1	/0-50,P-42,D-4,1-2	7	-0.5

• KILDUFF, Pete Peter John Kilduff b: 4/4/1893, Weir City, KS d: 2/14/1930, Pittsburg, KS BR/TR, 5'7", 155 lbs. Deb: 4/18/1917

YEAR TM-L	G	AB	R	H	2B	3B	HR	RBI	BB	SO	SB	CS	AVG	OBP	SLG	OPS	OPS+	BR/A	RC	RC/G	FR	G/POS	WS	TPW
1917 NY-N	31	78	12	16	3	0	1	12	4	11	2	....	.205	.253	.282	.535	66	-3	6	2.36	0	2-21/S-5,3-1	1	-0.3
Chi-N	56	202	23	56	9	5	0	15	12	19	11	....	.277	.324	.371	.695	105	1	27	4.52	-17	S-51/2-5	6	-1.3
Yr.	87	280	35	72	12	5	1	27	16	30	13	....	.257	.304	.346	.651	94	-2	33	3.89	-17	S-56,2-26/3-1	7	-1.7
1918 Chi-N	30	93	7	19	2	2	0	13	7	7	1	....	.204	.267	.269	.536	62	-4	8	2.39	-3	2-30	2	-0.7
1919 Chi-N	31	88	5	24	4	2	0	8	10	5	1	....	.273	.360	.364	.724	117	2	12	4.57	-4	3-14/2-8,S-7	3	-0.1
Bro-N	32	73	9	22	3	1	0	8	12	11	5	....	.301	.407	.370	.777	132	4	13	6.13	-3	3-26/2-1	3	0.1
Yr.	63	161	14	46	7	3	0	16	22	16	6	....	.286	.382	.366	.748	124	6	25	5.27	-8	3-40/2-9,S-7	6	0.0
1920*Bro-N	141	478	62	130	26	8	0	58	58	43	2	9	.272	.351	.360	.711	101	1	61	4.29	14	*2-134/3-5	18	1.9
1921 Bro-N	107	372	45	107	15	10	3	45	31	36	6	6	.288	.344	.406	.750	94	-3	52	4.79	1	*2-105/3-1	12	0.1
Total 5	428	1384	163	374	62	28	4	159	134	132	28	15	.270	.338	.364	.702	98	-2	178	4.31	-13	2-304/S-63,3-47	45	-0.4

• KILEY, John John Frederick Kiley b: 7/1/1859, South Dedham, MA d: 12/18/1940, Norwood, MA BL/TL, 5'7", 147 lbs. Deb: 5/1/1884

YEAR TM-L	G	AB	R	H	2B	3B	HR	RBI	BB	SO	SB	CS	AVG	OBP	SLG	OPS	OPS+	BR/A	RC	RC/G	FR	G/POS	WS	TPW
1884 Was-a	14	56	9	12	2	2	0	0	3	....	....	....	.214	.267	.321	.588	103	1	5	3.08	-4	0-14(13-1-1)	1	-0.3
1891 Bos-N	1	2	0	0	0	0	0	0	1	1	0	....	.000	.500	.000	.500	45	0	0	.00	0	/P-1	0	-0.2
Total 2	15	58	9	12	2	2	0	0	4	1	0	....	.207	.281	.310	.592	99	1	5	2.94	-4	/0-14,P-1	1	-0.5

• KILHULLEN, Pat Joseph Isadore Kilhullen b: 8/10/1890, Carbondale, PA d: 11/2/1922, Oakland, CA BR/TR, 5'9", 175 lbs. Deb: 6/10/1914

YEAR TM-L	G	AB	R	H	2B	3B	HR	RBI	BB	SO	SB	CS	AVG	OBP	SLG	OPS	OPS+	BR/A	RC	RC/G	FR	G/POS	WS	TPW
1914 Pit-N	1	1	0	0	0	0	0	0	0	0	0	....	.000	.000	.000	.000	-105	-0	0	.00	0	/C-1	0	-0.1

• KILLEBREW, Harmon Harmon Clayton "Killer" Killebrew b: 6/29/1936, Payette, ID BR/TR, 6', 213 lbs. Deb: 6/23/1954 HOF: 1984 Career OF: 470-0-1

YEAR TM-L	G	AB	R	H	2B	3B	HR	RBI	BB	SO	SB	CS	AVG	OBP	SLG	OPS	OPS+	BR/A	RC	RC/G	FR	G/POS	WS	TPW
1954 Was-A	9	13	1	4	1	0	0	3	2	3	0	0	.308	.400	.385	.785	122	1	2	4.97	0	/2-3	0	0.0
1955 Was-A	38	80	12	16	1	0	4	7	9	31	0	0	.200	.281	.363	.643	76	-3	8	3.12	-3	3-23/2-3	1	-0.6
1956 Was-A	44	99	10	22	2	0	5	13	10	39	0	0	.222	.294	.394	.688	80	-3	11	3.88	-1	3-20/2-4	2	-0.4
1957 Was-A	9	31	4	9	2	0	2	5	2	8	0	0	.290	.333	.548	.882	138	1	6	7.17	-1	/3-7,2-1	2	0.1
1958 Was-A	13	31	2	6	0	0	0	2	0	12	0	0	.194	.219	.194	.412	15	-4	1	1.49	-1	/3-9	0	-0.5
1959 Was-A★	153	546	98	132	20	2	**42**	105	90	116	3	2	.242	.356	.516	.873	137	28	103	6.45	-17	*3-150/0-4(4-0-0)	23	1.1
1960 Was-A	124	442	84	122	19	1	31	80	71	106	1	0	.276	.377	.534	.911	142	27	91	7.39	-7	1-71,3-65	20	1.6
1961 Min-A★	150	541	94	156	20	7	46	122	107	109	1	2	.288	.409	.606	1.015	158	47	138	9.25	1	*1-119,3-45/0-2(2-0-0)	27	4.0
1962 Min-A	155	552	85	134	21	1	**48**	**126**	106	142	1	2	.243	.369	.545	.914	137	29	113	6.98	4	*0-151(151-0-0)/1-4	24	2.7
1963 Min-A★	142	515	88	133	18	0	**45**	96	72	105	0	0	.258	.353	**.555**	.908	147	32	99	6.62	5	*0-137(137-0-0)	23	3.3
1964 Min-A★	158	577	95	156	11	1	**49**	111	93	135	0	0	.270	.379	.548	.927	153	43	122	7.47	-6	*0-157(157-0-1)	24	3.0
1965*Min-A★	113	401	78	108	16	1	25	75	72	69	0	0	.269	.386	.501	.887	144	25	79	7.03	-2	1-72,3-44/0-1	22	2.1
1966 Min-A★	162	569	89	160	27	1	39	110	**103**	98	0	2	.281	.393	.538	.931	155	43	122	7.76	-8	*3-107,1-42,0-18(18-0-0)	33	3.5
1967 Min-A★	163	547	105	147	24	1	**44**	113	**131**	111	1	0	.269	.413	.558	.970	170	55	131	8.34	-3	*1-160/3-3	38	4.8

YEAR TM-L	G	AB	R	H	2B	3B	HR	RBI	BB	SO	SB	CS	AVG	OBP	SLG	OPS	OPS+	BR/A	RC	RC/G	FR	G/POS	WS	TPW
1968 Min-A★	100	295	40	62	7	2	17	40	70	70	0	0	.210	.365	.420	.785	131	15	46	5.02	4	1-77,3-11	12	1.6
1969*Min-A★	162	555	106	153	20	2	**49**	**140**	**145**	84	8	2	.276	**.430**	.584	1.014	177	66	146	9.32	-11	*3-105,1-80	34	5.1
1970*Min-A★	157	527	96	143	20	1	41	113	128	84	0	3	.271	.416	.546	.962	161	48	116	7.43	-9	*3-138,1-28	30	3.9
1971 Min-A★	147	500	61	127	19	1	28	**119**	**114**	96	3	2	.254	.393	.464	.857	137	30	92	6.15	-4	1-90,3-64	23	2.0
1972 Min-A	139	433	53	100	13	2	26	74	94	91	0	1	.231	.369	.450	.820	136	23	73	5.58	10	*1-130	18	2.7
1973 Min-A	69	248	29	60	9	1	5	32	41	59	0	0	.242	.352	.347	.698	94	-0	31	4.17	4	1-57/D-9	5	0.0
1974 Min-A	122	333	28	74	7	0	13	54	45	61	0	0	.222	.315	.360	.675	90	-3	37	3.64	1	D-57,1-33	5	-0.6
1975 KC-A	106	312	25	62	13	0	14	44	54	70	1	2	.199	.319	.375	.694	93	-3	39	4.10	-1	D-92/1-6	5	-0.6
Total 22	2435	8147	1283	2086	290	24	573	1584	1559	1699	19	18	.256	.379	.509	.887	142	498	1609	6.79	-46	1-969,3-791,O-470,D-158/2-11	371	38.7

• KILLEFER, Bill William Lavier "Reindeer Bill" Killefer b: 10/10/1887, Bloomingdale, MI d: 7/3/1960, Elsmere, DE BR/TR, 5'10.5", 200 lbs. Deb: 9/13/1909 M/C

YEAR TM-L	G	AB	R	H	2B	3B	HR	RBI	BB	SO	SB	CS	AVG	OBP	SLG	OPS	OPS+	BR/A	RC	RC/G	FR	G/POS	WS	TPW
1909 StL-A	11	29	0	4	0	0	0	1	0	....	2	....	.138	.138	.138	.276	-14	-4	1	.75	1	C-11	0	-0.3
1910 StL-A	74	193	14	24	2	2	0	7	12	....	0	....	.124	.184	.155	.339	7	-21	6	.86	6	C-73	3	-0.8
1911 Phi-N	6	16	3	3	0	0	0	2	0	2	0	....	.188	.188	.188	.375	5	-2	1	1.18	1	/C-6	0	-0.1
1912 Phi-N	85	268	18	60	6	3	1	21	4	14	6	....	.224	.241	.280	.521	40	-24	20	2.26	10	C-85	5	-0.7
1913 Phi-N	120	360	25	88	14	3	0	24	4	17	2	....	.244	.255	.300	.555	56	-22	27	2.45	7	*C-118/1-1	10	-0.6
1914 Phi-N	98	299	27	70	10	1	0	27	8	17	3	....	.234	.261	.274	.536	56	-17	22	2.37	10	C-90	7	0.1
1915*Phi-N	105	320	26	76	9	2	0	24	18	14	5	3	.238	.287	.278	.565	70	-12	26	2.80	-4	*C-104	9	-0.8
1916 Phi-N	97	286	22	62	5	4	3	27	8	14	2	....	.217	.246	.294	.539	63	-13	22	2.49	-10	C-91	6	-1.8
1917 Phi-N	125	409	28	112	12	0	0	31	15	21	4	....	.274	.306	.303	.609	84	-8	38	3.23	0	*C-120/O-1	15	0.1
1918*Chi-N	104	331	30	77	10	3	0	22	17	10	5	....	.233	.276	.281	.557	68	-13	27	2.62	-5	*C-104	10	-1.0
1919 Chi-N	103	315	17	90	10	2	0	22	15	8	5	....	.286	.322	.330	.652	96	-2	35	3.80	1	*C-100	13	0.8
1920 Chi-N	62	191	16	42	7	1	0	16	8	5	2	2	.220	.280	.267	.547	56	-10	15	2.53	9	C-61	5	0.5
1921 Chi-N	45	133	11	43	1	0	0	16	4	4	3	3	.323	.357	.331	.688	83	-3	15	4.23	1	C-42	4	0.0
Total 13	1035	3150	237	751	86	21	4	240	113	126	39	8	.238	.273	.283	.555	63	-150	255	2.64	27	*C-1005/1-1,O-1	87	-4.5

• KILLEFER, Red Wade Hampton Killefer b: 4/13/1885, Bloomingdale, MI d: 9/4/1958, Los Angeles, CA BR/TR, 5'9", 175 lbs. Deb: 9/16/1907 Career OF: 135-135-27

YEAR TM-L	G	AB	R	H	2B	3B	HR	RBI	BB	SO	SB	CS	AVG	OBP	SLG	OPS	OPS+	BR/A	RC	RC/G	FR	G/POS	WS	TPW
1907 Det-A	1	4	0	0	0	0	0	0	0	....	0	....	.000	.000	.000	.000	-96	-1	0	.00	0	/O-1	0	-0.1
1908 Det-A	28	75	9	16	1	0	0	11	3	....	4	....	.213	.253	.227	.480	54	-4	6	2.27	-7	2-16/S-7,3-4	1	-1.1
1909 Det-A	23	61	6	17	2	2	1	4	3	....	2	....	.279	.343	.426	.770	137	2	9	5.45	-1	2-17/O-1	3	0.2
Was-A	40	121	11	21	1	0	0	5	13	....	4	....	.174	.265	.182	.447	43	-7	7	1.81	-3	O-24(6-17-1)/3-6,2-3,C-3,S	0	-1.2
Yr.	63	182	17	38	3	2	1	9	16	....	6	....	.209	.291	.264	.554	74	-5	17	2.89	-4	O-25(6-17-2),2-20/3-6,C-3,S	3	-1.0
1910 Was-A	106	345	35	79	17	1	0	24	29	....	17	....	.229	.318	.284	.602	93	-1	39	3.44	-9	2-88,O-12(6-0-6)	8	-1.1
1914 Cin-N	42	141	16	39	6	1	0	12	20	18	11	....	.277	.386	.333	.719	111	3	22	5.26	-2	O-37(1-18-18)/2-5,3-1	5	0.0
1915 Cin-N	155	555	75	151	25	11	1	41	38	33	12	18	.272	.340	.362	.702	110	2	69	4.11	3	*O-150(79-73-0)/1-2	18	-0.2
1916 Cin-N	70	234	29	57	9	1	1	18	21	8	7	....	.244	.327	.303	.630	96	0	26	3.72	0	O-68(43-27-0)	5	-0.4
NY-N	2	1	0	1	0	0	0	1	1	0	0	....	1.000	1.000	1.000	2.000	544	1	1	∞	0	....	0	0.1
Yr.	72	235	29	58	9	1	1	19	22	8	7	....	.247	.332	.306	.638	100	1	27	3.72	0	O-68(43-27-0)	5	-0.3
Total 7	467	1537	181	381	61	16	3	116	128	59	57	18	.248	.328	.314	.642	97	-4	179	3.74	-18	O-293,2-129/3-11,S-8,C-3,1	40	-4.0

• KIMBALL, Gene Eugene Boynton Kimball b: 8/31/1850, Rochester, NY d: 8/2/1882, Rochester, NY, 5'10", 160 lbs. Deb: 5/4/1871

YEAR TM-L	G	AB	R	H	2B	3B	HR	RBI	BB	SO	SB	CS	AVG	OBP	SLG	OPS	OPS+	BR/A	RC	RC/G	FR	G/POS	WS	TPW
1871 Cle-n	29	131	18	25	1	0	0	9	3	2	5	1	.191	.209	.198	.407	19	-12	7	1.95	-5	2-17/O-9(2-1-7),S-6,3-2	....	-1.2

• KIMBLE, Dick Richard Lewis Kimble b: 7/27/1915, Buchtel, OH d: 5/7/2001, Toledo, OH BL/TR, 5'9", 160 lbs. Deb: 8/20/1945

YEAR TM-L	G	AB	R	H	2B	3B	HR	RBI	BB	SO	SB	CS	AVG	OBP	SLG	OPS	OPS+	BR/A	RC	RC/G	FR	G/POS	WS	TPW
1945 Was-A	20	49	5	12	1	1	0	1	5	2	0	0	.245	.315	.306	.621	88	-1	5	3.08	0	S-15	1	0.0

• KIMM, Bruce Bruce Edward Kimm b: 6/29/1951, Cedar Rapids, IA BR/TR, 5'11", 175 lbs. Deb: 5/4/1976 M/C

YEAR TM-L	G	AB	R	H	2B	3B	HR	RBI	BB	SO	SB	CS	AVG	OBP	SLG	OPS	OPS+	BR/A	RC	RC/G	FR	G/POS	WS	TPW
1976 Det-A	63	152	13	40	8	0	1	6	15	20	4	3	.263	.329	.336	.665	91	-2	17	3.79	0	C-61/D-2	4	0.1
1977 Det-A	14	25	2	2	1	0	0	1	0	4	0	1	.080	.115	.120	.235	-34	-5	0	.14	-1	C-12/D-2	0	-0.6
1979 Chi-N	9	11	0	1	0	0	0	0	0	0	0	1	.091	.091	.091	.182	-46	-3	0	.00	-1	/C-9	0	-0.3
1980 Chi-A	100	251	20	61	10	1	0	19	17	26	1	3	.243	.291	.291	.582	60	-15	19	2.49	-2	C-98	3	-1.3
Total 4	186	439	35	104	19	1	1	26	32	50	5	8	.237	.290	.292	.582	64	-24	37	2.69	-4	C-180/D-4	7	-2.1

• KIMMICK, Wally Walter Lyons Kimmick b: 5/30/1897, Turtle Creek, PA d: 7/24/1989, Boswell, PA BR/TR, 5'11", 174 lbs. Deb: 9/13/1919

YEAR TM-L	G	AB	R	H	2B	3B	HR	RBI	BB	SO	SB	CS	AVG	OBP	SLG	OPS	OPS+	BR/A	RC	RC/G	FR	G/POS	WS	TPW
1919 StL-N	2	1	1	0	0	0	0	0	1	0	1	....	.000	.500	.000	.500	61	0	0	10.83	0	/S-1	0	0.0
1921 Cin-N	3	6	0	1	0	0	0	1	0	1	0	0	.167	.167	.167	.333	-12	-1	0	.91	-1	/3-2	0	-0.1
1922 Cin-N	39	89	11	22	2	1	0	12	3	12	0	0	.247	.272	.292	.564	46	-7	7	2.74	2	S-30/2-3,3-1	1	-0.2
1923 Cin-N	29	80	11	18	2	1	0	6	5	15	3	0	.225	.271	.275	.546	45	-5	7	2.70	3	2-17/3-4,S-1	1	-0.2
1925 Phi-N	70	141	16	43	3	2	1	10	22	26	0	3	.305	.399	.376	.775	91	-2	21	5.58	-2	S-28,3-21,2-13	4	-0.1
1926 Phi-N	20	28	0	6	2	1	0	2	3	7	0	....	.214	.290	.357	.647	70	-1	3	3.44	-4	/1-5,3-4,S-4,2-1	0	-0.5
Total 6	163	345	39	90	9	5	1	31	34	61	4	3	.261	.327	.325	.652	66	-16	39	3.88	-2	/S-64,2-34,3-32,1-5	6	-1.2

• KINDALL, Jerry Gerald Donald "Slim" Kindall b: 5/27/1935, St. Paul, MN BR/TR, 6'2.5", 175 lbs. Deb: 7/1/1956

YEAR TM-L	G	AB	R	H	2B	3B	HR	RBI	BB	SO	SB	CS	AVG	OBP	SLG	OPS	OPS+	BR/A	RC	RC/G	FR	G/POS	WS	TPW
1956 Chi-N	32	55	7	9	1	1	0	0	6	17	1	0	.164	.246	.218	.464	27	-5	3	1.66	0	S-18	1	-0.4
1957 Chi-N	72	181	18	29	3	0	6	12	8	48	1	0	.160	.196	.276	.472	25	-19	9	1.58	-6	2-28,3-19/S-9	1	-2.4
1958 Chi-N	3	6	0	1	1	0	0	0	0	3	0	0	.167	.167	.333	.500	29	-1	0	1.80	0	/2-3	0	0.0
1960 Chi-N	89	246	17	59	16	2	2	23	5	52	4	3	.240	.255	.346	.601	63	-14	19	2.54	7	2-82/S-2	3	-0.1
1961 Chi-N	96	310	37	75	22	3	9	44	18	89	2	2	.242	.288	.419	.707	84	-9	36	4.01	-11	2-50,S-47	6	-1.3
1962 Cle-A	154	530	51	123	21	1	13	55	45	107	4	3	.232	.292	.349	.641	74	-21	53	3.25	27	*2-154	14	1.9
1963 Cle-A	86	234	27	48	4	1	5	20	18	71	3	1	.205	.268	.295	.563	58	-13	19	2.55	-2	S-46,2-37/1-4	3	-1.0
1964 Cle-A	23	25	5	9	1	0	2	2	2	7	0	0	.360	.407	.640	1.047	187	3	6	9.72	2	1-23	2	0.4
Min-A	62	128	8	19	2	0	1	6	7	44	0	0	.148	.199	.188	.386	8	-16	5	1.17	-1	2-51/S-7,1-1	1	-1.5
Yr.	85	153	13	28	3	0	3	8	9	51	0	0	.183	.233	.261	.495	37	-13	11	2.28	0	2-51,1-24/S-7	3	-1.0
1965 Min-A	125	342	41	67	12	1	6	36	36	97	2	2	.196	.278	.289	.568	59	-19	29	2.63	-7	*2-106,3-10/S-7	6	-1.8
Total 9	742	2057	211	439	83	9	44	198	145	535	17	11	.213	.268	.327	.595	61	-113	180	2.81	8	2-511,S-136/3-29,1-28	37	-6.0

• KINER, Ralph Ralph McPherran Kiner b: 10/27/1922, Santa Rita, NM BR/TR, 6'2", 195 lbs. Deb: 4/16/1946 HOF: 1975 Career OF: 1306-76-0

YEAR TM-L	G	AB	R	H	2B	3B	HR	RBI	BB	SO	SB	CS	AVG	OBP	SLG	OPS	OPS+	BR/A	RC	RC/G	FR	G/POS	WS	TPW
1946 Pit-N	144	502	63	124	17	3	**23**	81	74	109	3	....	.247	.345	.430	.775	116	11	75	5.14	-9	*O-140(64-76-0)	15	-0.5
1947 Pit-N	152	565	118	177	23	4	**51**	127	98	81	1	....	.313	.417	**.639**	**1.055**	**172**	**58**	154	**10.38**	1	*O-152(152-0-0)	30	**4.7**
1948 Pit-N★	156	555	104	147	19	5	**40**	123	112	61	1	....	.265	.391	.533	.924	145	37	120	7.67	4	*O-154(154-0-0)	30	2.9
1949 Pit-N★	152	549	116	170	19	5	**54**	**127**	**117**	61	6	....	.310	.432	**.658**	**1.089**	**183**	**68**	163	**11.33**	-3	*O-152(152-0-0)	37	5.2
1950 Pit-N★	150	547	112	149	21	6	**47**	118	122	79	2	....	.272	.408	.590	.998	154	46	133	8.57	-9	*O-150(150-0-0)	23	2.5
1951 Pit-N★	151	531	**124**	164	31	6	**42**	109	**137**	57	2	1	.309	**.452**	**.627**	**1.079**	182	69	165	11.78	-9	O-94(94-0-0),1-58	35	5.1
1952 Pit-N★	149	516	90	126	17	2	**37**	87	**110**	77	3	0	.244	.384	.500	.884	139	33	111	7.57	-8	*O-149(149-0-0)	19	1.4
1953 Pit-N	41	148	27	40	6	1	7	29	25	21	1	0	.270	.383	.466	.849	121	6	30	7.31	2	O-41(41-0-0)	5	0.5
Chi-N★	117	414	73	117	14	2	28	87	75	67	1	1	.283	.394	.529	.923	135	23	91	7.94	-5	*O-116(116-0-0)	18	1.1
Yr.	158	562	100	157	20	3	35	116	100	88	2	1	.279	.391	.512	.903	131	29	120	7.78	-3	*O-157(157-0-0)	23	1.6
1954 Chi-N	147	557	88	159	36	5	22	73	76	90	2	0	.285	.373	.487	.860	121	18	101	6.47	2	*O-147(147-0-0)	19	1.1
1955 Cle-A	113	321	56	78	13	0	18	54	65	46	0	0	.243	.370	.452	.822	116	9	57	6.00	-5	O-87(87-0-0)	11	-0.1
Total 10	1472	5205	971	1451	216	39	369	1015	1011	749	22	2	.279	.398	.548	.946	148	376	1201	8.32	-40	*O-1382/1-58	242	24.0

• KING, Chick Charles Gilbert King b: 11/10/1930, Paris, TN BR/TR, 6'2", 190 lbs. Deb: 8/27/1954 Career OF: 11-18-0

YEAR TM-L	G	AB	R	H	2B	3B	HR	RBI	BB	SO	SB	CS	AVG	OBP	SLG	OPS	OPS+	BR/A	RC	RC/G	FR	G/POS	WS	TPW
1954 Det-A	11	28	4	6	0	1	0	3	3	8	0	0	.214	.290	.286	.576	59	-2	2	2.66	1	/O-7(0-7-0)	0	-0.1
1955 Det-A	7	21	3	5	0	0	0	0	1	2	0	0	.238	.273	.238	.511	39	-2	1	2.42	-1	/O-6(0-6-0)	0	-0.3
1956 Det-A	7	9	0	2	0	0	0	0	1	4	0	0	.222	.300	.222	.522	40	-1	1	2.62	0	/O-4(4-0-0)	0	-0.1
1958 Chi-N	8	8	1	2	0	0	0	1	3	1	0	0	.250	.455	.250	.705	95	0	1	5.15	0	/O-7(0-7-0)	0	0.0
1959 Chi-N	7	3	3	0	0	0	0	0	0	1	0	0	.000	.000	.000	.000	-101	-1	0	.00	-0	/O-1	0	-0.1
StL-N	5	7	0	3	0	0	0	1	0	2	0	0	.429	.429	.429	.857	121	0	1	7.13	0	/O-4(1-3-0)	0	0.0
Yr.	12	10	3	3	0	0	0	1	0	3	0	0	.300	.300	.300	.600	61	-1	1	4.46	0	/O-5(1-4-0)	0	-0.1
Total 5	45	76	11	18	0	1	0	5	8	18	0	0	.237	.310	.263	.573	56	-4	7	3.08	-1	/O-29	0	-0.6

YEAR TM-L	G	AB	R	H	2B	3B	HR	RBI	BB	SO	SB	CS	AVG	OBP	SLG	OPS	OPS+	BR/A	RC	RC/G	FR	G/POS	WS	TPW
• KING, Hal	Harold King b: 2/1/1944, Oviedo, FL BL/TR, 6'1", 200 lbs. Deb: 9/6/1967																							
1967 Hou-N	15	44	2	11	1	2	0	6	2	9	0	0	.250	.283	.364	.646	86	-1	5	3.82	1	C-11	1	0.0
1968 Hou-N	27	55	4	8	2	1	0	2	7	16	0	0	.145	.242	.218	.460	40	-4	3	1.76	-1	C-19	0	-0.5
1970 Atl-N	89	204	29	53	8	0	11	30	32	41	1	0	.260	.366	.461	.826	113	5	35	6.04	-5	C-62	7	0.2
1971 Atl-N	86	198	14	41	9	0	5	19	29	43	0	0	.207	.320	.328	.649	79	-5	20	3.29	-2	C-60	4	-0.4
1972 Tex-A	50	122	12	22	5	0	4	12	25	35	0	0	.180	.333	.320	.653	99	1	14	3.78	0	C-38	5	0.3
1973*Cin-N	35	43	5	8	0	0	4	10	6	10	0	0	.186	.286	.465	.751	111	0	6	4.75	0	/C-9	2	0.1
1974 Cin-N	20	17	1	3	1	0	0	3	3	4	0	0	.176	.300	.235	.535	52	-1	1	2.77	-1	/C-5	0	-0.2
Total 7	**322**	**683**	**67**	**146**	**26**	**3**	**24**	**82**	**104**	**158**	**1**	**0**	**.214**	**.325**	**.366**	**.691**	**92**	**-4**	**85**	**4.13**	**-8**	**C-204**	**19**	**-0.4**
• KING, Jeff	Jeffrey Wayne King b: 12/26/1964, Marion, IN BR/TR, 6'1", 180 lbs. Deb: 6/2/1989																							
1989 Pit-N	75	215	31	42	13	3	5	19	20	34	4	2	.195	.270	.353	.624	80	-6	21	3.09	-1	1-46,3-13/2-7,S-1	3	-1.0
1990*Pit-N	127	371	46	91	17	1	14	53	21	50	3	3	.245	.288	.410	.697	93	-6	40	3.54	4	*3-115/1-1	7	-0.1
1991 Pit-N	33	109	16	26	1	1	4	18	14	15	3	1	.239	.331	.376	.707	100	0	14	4.20	2	3-33	4	0.3
1992*Pit-N	130	480	56	111	21	2	14	65	27	56	4	6	.231	.275	.371	.646	82	-15	47	3.19	3	3-73,1-32,2-32/S-6,0-1	7	-1.4
1993 Pit-N	158	611	82	180	35	3	9	98	59	54	8	6	.295	.361	.406	.766	105	4	88	5.11	19	*3-156/2-2,S-2	20	2.6
1994 Pit-N	94	339	36	89	23	0	5	42	30	38	3	2	.263	.322	.375	.697	80	-10	41	4.13	8	3-91/2-1	8	-0.1
1995 Pit-N	122	445	61	118	27	2	18	87	55	63	7	4	.265	.347	.456	.803	108	4	70	5.45	1	3-84,1-35/2-8,S-2	14	0.3
1996 Pit-N	155	591	91	160	36	4	30	111	70	95	15	1	.271	.350	.497	.847	117	16	103	6.09	-14	1-92,2-71,3-17	22	-0.1
1997 KC-A	155	543	84	129	30	1	28	112	89	96	16	5	.238	.347	.451	.798	104	5	90	5.51	16	*1-150/D-2	17	0.7
1998 KC-A	131	486	83	128	17	1	24	93	42	73	10	2	.263	.325	.451	.775	96	-3	71	5.06	5	*1-112,D-16/3-4	12	-0.8
1999 KC-A	21	72	14	17	2	0	3	11	15	10	2	0	.236	.389	.389	.778	97	1	13	6.01	0	1-20/D-1	1	-0.1
Total 11	**1201**	**4262**	**600**	**1091**	**222**	**18**	**154**	**709**	**442**	**584**	**75**	**32**	**.256**	**.329**	**.425**	**.754**	**99**	**-10**	**598**	**4.76**	**43**	**3-586,1-488,2-121/D-19,S-11,0**	**115**	**0.1**
• KING, Jim	James Hubert King b: 8/27/1932, Elkins, AR BL/TR, 6', 185 lbs. Deb: 4/17/1955 Career OF: 145-3-707																							
1955 Chi-N	113	301	43	77	12	3	11	45	24	39	2	1	.256	.315	.425	.740	94	-3	41	4.76	5	0-93(17-0-76)	10	-0.1
1956 Chi-N	118	317	32	79	13	2	15	54	30	40	1	2	.249	.316	.445	.761	103	0	44	4.80	11	0-82(69-0-14)	9	0.7
1957 StL-N	22	35	1	11	0	0	0	2	4	2	0	0	.314	.385	.314	.699	89	-0	4	4.98	0	/0-8(1-3-4)	1	-0.1
1958 SF-N	34	56	8	12	2	1	2	8	10	8	0	1	.214	.343	.393	.736	96	-0	8	4.85	0	0-15(9-0-6)	2	-0.1
1961 Was-A	110	263	43	71	12	1	11	46	38	45	4	0	.270	.366	.449	.815	122	10	46	6.32	2	0-91(25-0-67)/C-1	10	0.8
1962 Was-A	132	333	39	81	15	0	11	35	55	37	4	2	.243	.355	.387	.743	101	2	49	4.99	3	*0-101(20-0-81)	8	-0.2
1963 Was-A	136	459	61	106	16	5	24	62	45	43	3	0	.231	.301	.444	.745	106	3	60	4.39	4	*0-123(2-0-122)	13	0.0
1964 Was-A	134	415	46	100	15	1	18	56	55	65	3	1	.241	.337	.412	.749	108	5	60	5.00	6	*0-121(0-0-121)	14	0.3
1965 Was-A	120	258	46	55	10	2	14	49	44	50	1	0	.213	.339	.430	.769	119	8	38	4.84	1	0-88(1-0-87)	10	0.4
1966 Was-A	117	310	41	77	14	2	10	30	38	41	4	0	.248	.330	.403	.734	111	6	41	4.55	-1	0-85(0-0-85)	11	-0.1
1967 Was-A	47	100	10	21	2	2	1	12	15	13	1	1	.210	.331	.300	.631	91	-0	11	3.52	-2	0-31(0-0-31)/C-1	3	-0.5
Chi-A	23	50	2	6	1	0	0	2	4	16	0	0	.120	.185	.140	.325	-3	-6	1	.80	0	0-12(1-0-12)	0	-0.8
Cle-A	19	21	2	3	0	0	0	0	1	2	0	0	.143	.182	.143	.325	-3	-3	1	.89	-0	/0-1	0	-0.3
Yr.	89	171	14	30	3	2	1	14	20	31	1	1	.175	.273	.234	.507	54	-9	13	2.36	-2	0-44(1-0-44)/C-1	3	-1.5
Total 11	**1125**	**2918**	**374**	**699**	**112**	**19**	**117**	**401**	**363**	**401**	**23**	**8**	**.240**	**.328**	**.411**	**.740**	**104**	**21**	**406**	**4.74**	**29**	**0-851/C-2**	**91**	**0.0**
• KING, Lee	Lee King b: 12/26/1892, Hundred, WV d: 9/16/1967, Shinnston, WV BR/TR, 5'8", 160 lbs. Deb: 9/20/1916 Career OF: 109-114-125																							
1916 Pit-N	8	18	0	2	0	0	0	1	0	7	0	....	.111	.111	.111	.222	-31	-3	0	.36	-1	/0-8(2-0-4)	0	-0.4
1917 Pit-N	111	381	32	95	14	5	1	35	15	58	8	....	.249	.281	.320	.602	81	-9	35	3.09	4	*0-102(7-0-95)	5	-1.2
1918 Pit-N	36	112	9	26	3	2	1	11	11	15	3	....	.232	.301	.321	.622	87	-2	11	3.32	-4	0-36(32-0-4)	2	-0.8
1919 NY-N	21	20	5	2	1	0	0	1	1	6	0	....	.100	.143	.150	.293	-12	-3	0	.54	-1	/0-7(2-1-3)	0	-0.4
1920 NY-N	93	261	32	72	11	4	7	42	21	38	3	7	.276	.335	.429	.764	120	5	36	4.66	-12	0-84(0-83-1)	9	-1.3
1921 NY-N	39	94	17	21	4	2	0	7	13	6	0	2	.223	.324	.309	.633	68	-4	10	3.34	0	0-35(0-24-12)/1-1	1	-0.6
Phi-N	64	216	25	58	19	4	4	32	8	37	1	4	.269	.298	.449	.747	88	-5	27	4.30	-3	0-57(55-1-2)	3	-1.2
Yr.	103	310	42	79	23	6	4	39	21	43	1	6	.255	.306	.406	.713	82	-10	37	3.99	-3	0-92(55-25-14)/1-1	4	-1.8
1922 Phi-N	19	53	8	12	5	1	2	13	8	6	0	0	.226	.328	.472	.800	95	-0	9	5.39	-0	0-15(11-4-0)	1	-0.1
*NY-N	20	34	6	6	3	0	0	2	5	2	1	0	.176	.282	.265	.547	41	-3	3	2.73	0	/1-5,0-5(0-1-4)	1	-0.3
Yr.	39	87	14	18	8	1	2	15	13	8	1	0	.207	.310	.391	.701	74	-3	12	4.30	0	0-20(11-5-4)/1-5	2	-0.4
Total 7	**411**	**1189**	**134**	**294**	**60**	**18**	**15**	**144**	**82**	**175**	**16**	**13**	**.247**	**.299**	**.366**	**.665**	**87**	**-25**	**131**	**3.68**	**-16**	**0-349/1-6**	**22**	**-6.4**
• KING, Lee (EL)	Edward Lee King b: 3/28/1894, Waltham, MA d: 9/7/1938, Newton Centre, MA BR/TR, 5'10", 160 lbs. Deb: 6/24/1916																							
1916 Phi-A	42	144	13	27	1	2	0	8	7	15	4	....	.188	.230	.222	.452	38	-11	9	1.88	-7	0-22(21-2-1),S-11/3-5,2-2	0	-2.0
1919 Bos-N	2	1	0	0	0	0	0	0	0	0	0	....	.000	.000	.000	.000	-104	-0	0	.00	0	....	0	0.0
Total 2	**44**	**145**	**13**	**27**	**1**	**2**	**0**	**8**	**7**	**15**	**4**	**....**	**.186**	**.229**	**.221**	**.449**	**37**	**-12**	**9**	**1.87**	**-7**	**/0-22,S-11,3-5,2-2**	**0**	**-2.1**
• KING, Lynn	Lynn Paul "Dig" King b: 11/28/1907, Villisca, IA d: 5/11/1972, Atlantic, IA BL/TR, 5'9", 165 lbs. Deb: 9/21/1935 Career OF: 21-47-16																							
1935 StL-N	8	22	6	4	0	0	0	0	4	1	2	....	.182	.308	.182	.490	34	-2	1	1.60	1	/0-6(0-6-0)	1	-0.1
1936 StL-N	78	100	12	19	2	1	0	10	9	14	2	....	.190	.257	.230	.487	32	-9	6	1.90	-1	0-34(7-12-15)	0	-1.2
1939 StL-N	89	85	10	20	2	0	0	11	15	3	2	....	.235	.350	.259	.609	62	-4	9	3.58	0	0-44(14-29-1)	2	-0.5
Total 3	**175**	**207**	**28**	**43**	**4**	**1**	**0**	**21**	**28**	**18**	**6**	**....**	**.208**	**.302**	**.237**	**.539**	**45**	**-15**	**16**	**2.51**	**0**	**/0-84**	**3**	**-1.7**
• KING, Mart	Marshal Ney King b: 12/1849, Troy, NY d: 10/19/1911, Troy, NY TR, 5'9.5", 176 lbs. Deb: 5/8/1871 NA OF: 1-13-0																							
1871 Chi-n	20	101	23	21	1	0	2	16	8	1	5	0	.208	.266	.277	.543	51	-7	9	3.54	-2	0-11(1-10-0)/C-9,S-3,3-1	....	-0.6
1872 Tro-n	3	11	0	0	0	0	0	1	0	1	0	0	.000	.000	.000	.000	-99	-3	0	.00	0	/0-3(0-3-0)	....	-0.2
Total 2 n	**23**	**112**	**23**	**21**	**1**	**0**	**2**	**17**	**8**	**2**	**5**	**0**	**.188**	**.242**	**.250**	**.492**	**37**	**-9**	**9**	**3.12**	**-2**	**/0-14,C-9,S-3,3-1**	**....**	**-0.8**
• KING, Sam	Samuel Warren King b: 5/17/1852, Peabody, MA d: 8/11/1922, Peabody, MA TL, 6' Deb: 5/1/1884																							
1884 Was-a	12	45	3	8	2	0	0	0	1	....	....	....	.178	.213	.222	.435	47	-2	2	1.62	-2	1-12	0	-0.5
• KING, Steve	Stephen F. King b: 1842, Troy, NY d: 7/8/1895, Troy, NY, 5'9", 175 lbs. Deb: 5/9/1871 NA OF: 54-0-0																							
1871 Tro-n	29	144	45	57	10	6	0	34	1	1	3	3	.396	.400	.549	.949	167	10	34	11.77	2	*0-29(29-0-0)	....	0.8
1872 Tro-n	25	128	33	39	8	0	0	21	1	2	1	1	.305	.310	.367	.677	106	0	15	5.25	0	0-25(25-0-0)	....	0.1
Total 2 n	**54**	**272**	**78**	**96**	**18**	**6**	**0**	**55**	**2**	**3**	**4**	**4**	**.353**	**.358**	**.463**	**.821**	**138**	**11**	**49**	**8.51**	**2**	**/0-54**	**....**	**0.9**
• KINGDON, Wes	Westcott William Kingdon b: 7/4/1900, Los Angeles, CA d: 4/19/1975, Capistrano, CA BR/TR, 5'8", 148 lbs. Deb: 6/12/1932																							
1932 Was-A	18	34	10	11	3	1	0	3	5	2	0	0	.324	.410	.471	.881	129	2	7	7.85	1	/3-8,S-4	2	0.2
• KINGERY, Mike	Michael Scott Kingery b: 3/29/1961, St. James, MN BL/TL, 6', 180 lbs. Deb: 7/7/1986 Career OF: 68-329-292																							
1986 KC-A	62	209	25	54	8	5	3	14	12	30	7	3	.258	.299	.388	.686	83	-5	23	3.85	-1	0-59(1-13-51)	4	-0.9
1987 Sea-A	120	354	38	99	25	4	9	52	27	43	7	9	.280	.334	.449	.783	100	-3	51	5.03	9	*0-114(0-6-111)/D-4	9	0.1
1988 Sea-A	57	123	21	25	6	0	1	9	19	23	3	1	.203	.315	.276	.591	64	-5	12	3.26	-0	0-44(9-24-13),1-10	2	-0.6
1989 Sea-A	31	76	14	17	3	0	2	6	7	14	1	1	.224	.289	.342	.631	75	-3	7	3.09	1	0-23(2-20-1)	2	-0.2
1990 SF-N	105	207	24	61	7	1	0	24	12	19	6	1	.295	.336	.338	.675	89	-2	25	4.45	1	0-95(15-9-74)	7	-0.3
1991 SF-N	91	110	13	20	2	2	0	8	15	21	1	0	.182	.280	.236	.516	48	-7	8	2.24	-1	0-38(14-2-22)/1-6	1	-0.9
1992 Oak-A	12	28	3	3	0	0	0	1	1	3	0	0	.107	.138	.107	.245	-32	-5	0	.35	0	0-10(2-6-2)	0	-0.5
1994 Col-N	105	301	56	105	27	8	4	41	30	26	5	7	.349	.411	.532	.943	123	10	62	7.53	-8	0-98(20-77-2)/1-1	12	0.2
1995*Col-N	119	350	66	94	18	4	8	37	45	40	13	5	.269	.352	.411	.763	78	-10	52	5.14	-3	*0-108(0-108-0)/1-5	7	-1.3
1996 Pit-N	117	276	32	68	12	2	3	27	23	29	2	1	.246	.307	.337	.644	68	-13	29	3.57	-2	0-83(5-64-16)	3	-1.5
Total 10	**819**	**2034**	**292**	**546**	**108**	**26**	**30**	**219**	**191**	**248**	**45**	**28**	**.268**	**.333**	**.391**	**.725**	**85**	**-44**	**271**	**4.59**	**-4**	**0-672/1-22,D-4**	**47**	**-6.0**
• KINGMAN, Dave	David Arthur "Kong,Sky King" Kingman b: 12/21/1948, Pendleton, OR BR/TR, 6'6", 210 lbs. Deb: 7/30/1971 Career OF: 508-0-144																							
1971*SF-N	41	115	17	32	10	2	6	24	9	35	5	0	.278	.336	.557	.893	151	8	22	6.78	-2	1-20,0-14(7-0-7)	6	0.5
1972 SF-N	135	472	65	106	17	4	29	83	51	140	16	6	.225	.306	.462	.767	114	8	67	4.67	4	3-59,1-56,0-22(22-0-0)	15	0.8
1973 SF-N	112	305	54	62	10	1	24	55	41	122	8	5	.203	.302	.479	.780	109	2	42	4.43	0	3-60,1-46/P-2	8	-0.3
1974 SF-N	121	350	41	78	18	2	18	55	37	125	8	8	.223	.303	.440	.743	101	-3	44	4.08	0	1-91,3-21/0-2(0-0-2)	7	-0.9

YEAR TM-L	G	AB	R	H	2B	3B	HR	RBI	BB	SO	SB	CS	AVG	OBP	SLG	OPS	OPS+	BR/A	RC	RC/G	FR	G/POS	WS	TPW
1975 NY-N	134	502	65	116	22	1	36	88	34	153	7	5	.231	.285	.494	.779	119	7	66	4.35	2	O-71(68-0-3),1-58,3-12	15	0.1
1976 NY-N★	123	474	70	113	14	1	37	86	28	135	7	4	.238	.288	.506	.794	130	13	65	4.62	2	*O-111(5-0-106),1-16	17	0.9
1977 NY-N	58	211	22	44	7	0	9	28	13	66	3	2	.209	.264	.370	.634	71	-10	20	3.14	-2	O-45(26-0-20),1-17	2	-1.4
SD-N	56	168	16	40	9	0	11	39	12	48	2	3	.238	.297	.488	.785	119	2	23	4.44	2	O-28(28-0-0),1-13/3-2	5	0.3
Yr.	114	379	38	84	16	0	20	67	25	114	5	5	.222	.279	.422	.701	93	-7	43	3.72	0	O-73(54-0-20),1-30/3-2	7	-1.2
Cal-A	10	36	4	7	2	0	2	4	1	16	0	0	.194	.237	.417	.654	77	-1	4	3.33	-1	/1-8,O-2(2-0-0)	1	-0.3
NY-A	8	24	5	6	2	0	4	7	2	13	0	1	.250	.333	.833	1.167	208	3	6	8.75	0	/D-6	2	0.3
Yr.	18	60	9	13	4	0	6	11	3	29	0	1	.217	.277	.583	.860	131	2	10	5.43	-1	/1-8,D-6,O-2(2-0-0)	3	0.0
1978 Chi-N	119	395	65	105	17	4	28	79	39	111	3	4	.266	.341	.542	.883	128	12	73	6.48	3	*O-100(100-0-0)/1-6	17	1.2
1979 Chi-N★	145	532	97	153	19	5	**48**	115	45	131	4	2	.288	.348	**.613**	**.960**	143	29	112	7.67	4	*O-139(139-0-0)	24	2.7
1980 Chi-N★	81	255	31	71	8	0	18	57	21	44	2	2	.278	.333	.522	.855	126	7	40	5.43	3	O-61(63-0-1)/1-2	8	0.8
1981 NY-N	100	353	40	78	11	3	22	59	55	105	6	0	.221	.328	.456	.784	122	11	54	5.09	-4	1-56,O-48(48-0-0)	10	0.2
1982 NY-N	149	535	80	109	9	1	**37**	99	59	156	4	0	.204	.288	.432	.719	99	-2	67	4.04	-13	*1-143	12	-2.4
1983 NY-N	100	248	25	49	7	0	13	29	22	57	2	1	.198	.266	.383	.649	78	-8	26	3.44	-5	1-50/O-5(0-0-5)	4	-1.7
1984 Oak-A	147	549	68	147	23	1	35	118	44	119	2	1	.268	.329	.505	.833	136	25	91	5.82	-1	*D-139/1-9	21	1.9
1985 Oak-A	158	592	66	141	16	0	30	91	62	114	3	2	.238	.313	.417	.730	105	3	75	4.22	-1	*D-149/1-9	13	-0.3
1986 Oak-A	144	561	70	118	19	0	35	94	33	126	3	3	.210	.258	.431	.689	90	-11	57	3.29	-1	*D-140/1-3	8	-1.7
Total 16	1941	6677	901	1575	240	25	442	1210	608	1816	85	49	.236	.305	.478	.783	115	95	955	4.79	-8	O-648,1-603,D-434,3-154/P-2	195	0.4

• KINGMAN, Harry

Henry Lees Kingman b: 4/3/1892, Tientsin, China d: 12/27/1982, Oakland, CA BL/TL, 6'1.5", 165 lbs. Deb: 7/1/1914

YEAR TM-L	G	AB	R	H	2B	3B	HR	RBI	BB	SO	SB	CS	AVG	OBP	SLG	OPS	OPS+	BR/A	RC	RC/G	FR	G/POS	WS	TPW
1914 NY-A	4	3	0	0	0	0	0	0	1	2	0	....	.000	.250	.000	.250	-24	-0	0	.00	0	/1-1	0	-0.1

• KINGSALE, Gene

Eugene Humphrey Kingsale b: 8/20/1976, Solito, Aruba BB/TR, 6'3", 170 lbs. Deb: 9/3/1996 Career OF: 39-97-54

YEAR TM-L	G	AB	R	H	2B	3B	HR	RBI	BB	SO	SB	CS	AVG	OBP	SLG	OPS	OPS+	BR/A	RC	RC/G	FR	G/POS	WS	TPW
1996 Bal-A	3	0	0	0	0	0	0	0	0	0	0	0	....	....	....	....	-101	0	0	....	-0	/O-2(0-2-0)	0	0.0
1998 Bal-A	11	2	1	0	0	0	0	0	0	1	0	0	.000	.000	.000	.000	-102	-1	0	.00	0	/O-4(0-4-0)	0	-0.1
1999 Bal-A	28	85	9	21	2	0	0	7	5	13	1	3	.247	.304	.271	.575	50	-7	6	2.30	-1	O-24(0-24-0)/D-2	1	-0.8
2000 Bal-A	26	88	13	21	2	1	0	9	2	14	1	2	.239	.256	.284	.540	38	-9	5	1.81	0	O-24(0-24-0)/D-1	1	-0.8
2001 Bal-A	3	4	0	0	0	0	0	0	0	2	1	1	.000	.000	.000	.000	-106	-1	0	.00	0	/O-1	0	-0.2
Sea-A	10	15	4	5	0	0	0	1	2	2	2	0	.333	.444	.333	.778	116	1	3	6.51	0	/O-9(5-1-3)	1	0.1
Yr.	13	19	4	5	0	0	0	1	2	4	3	1	.263	.364	.263	.627	76	-0	3	4.48	0	O-10(5-2-3)	1	-0.1
2002 Sea-A	2	3	0	2	0	0	0	0	0	0	0	0	.667	.667	.667	1.333	266	1	1	9.00	0	/O-2(0-1-1)	0	0.1
SD-N	89	216	27	60	10	3	2	28	20	47	9	2	.278	.347	.380	.727	100	1	30	4.79	3	O-82(26-17-50)	8	0.2
2003 Det-A	39	120	11	25	3	1	1	8	10	17	1	3	.208	.269	.275	.544	48	-10	9	2.17	-4	O-30(8-23-0)/D-4	1	-1.4
Total 7	211	533	65	134	17	5	3	53	39	96	15	11	.251	.310	.319	.629	70	-26	53	3.22	-2	O-178/D-7	12	-2.8

• KINKADE, Mike

Michael A. Kinkade b: 5/6/1973, Livonia, MI BR/TR, 6'1", 210 lbs. Deb: 9/8/1998 Career OF: 83-0-14

YEAR TM-L	G	AB	R	H	2B	3B	HR	RBI	BB	SO	SB	CS	AVG	OBP	SLG	OPS	OPS+	BR/A	RC	RC/G	FR	G/POS	WS	TPW
1998 NY-N	3	2	2	0	0	0	0	0	0	0	0	0	.000	.000	.000	.000	-102	-1	0	.00	0	/3-1	0	-0.1
1999 NY-N	28	46	3	9	2	1	2	6	3	9	1	0	.196	.275	.413	.688	73	-2	5	3.77	0	O-17(12-0-8)/3-3,1-1,C-1	0	-0.3
2000 NY-N	2	2	0	0	0	0	0	0	0	1	0	0	.000	.000	.000	.000	-105	-1	0	.00	0	/O-1	0	-0.1
Bal-A	3	7	0	3	1	0	0	1	0	0	0	0	.429	.500	.571	1.071	179	1	2	14.38	-0	/D-2,1-1	1	0.1
2001 Bal-A	61	160	19	44	5	0	4	16	14	31	2	1	.275	.345	.381	.726	96	-1	20	4.22	-2	O-32(29-0-3),3-10,D-10/1-3,C	2	-0.3
2002 LA-N	37	50	7	19	5	0	2	11	4	10	1	0	.380	.483	.600	1.083	196	8	15	12.19	-1	1-11/O-8(8-0-0)	3	0.6
2003 LA-N	88	162	25	35	7	0	5	14	13	38	1	3	.216	.335	.352	.687	84	-4	18	3.50	-3	O-36(34-0-2),1-13/3-2,D-1	2	-0.9
Total 6	222	429	56	110	20	1	13	48	34	89	5	4	.256	.350	.399	.749	101	1	60	4.72	-5	/O-94,1-29,3-16,D-13,C-3	8	-0.9

• KINLOCK, Walt

Walter Kinlock b: 1874, Providence, RI d: 2/15/1931, New York, NY Deb: 8/1/1895

YEAR TM-L	G	AB	R	H	2B	3B	HR	RBI	BB	SO	SB	CS	AVG	OBP	SLG	OPS	OPS+	BR/A	RC	RC/G	FR	G/POS	WS	TPW
1895 StL-N	1	3	0	1	0	0	0	0	0	2	0	....	.333	.333	.333	.667	73	-0	0	4.61	0	/3-1	0	0.0

• KINSELLA, Bob

Robert Francis "Red" Kinsella b: 1/5/1899, Springfield, IL d: 12/30/1951, Los Angeles, CA BL/TR, 5'9.5", 165 lbs. Deb: 9/20/1919 Career OF: 2-0-2

YEAR TM-L	G	AB	R	H	2B	3B	HR	RBI	BB	SO	SB	CS	AVG	OBP	SLG	OPS	OPS+	BR/A	RC	RC/G	FR	G/POS	WS	TPW
1919 NY-N	3	9	1	2	0	0	0	0	0	3	1	....	.222	.222	.222	.444	34	-1	1	2.14	-1	/O-3(2-0-1)	0	-0.2
1920 NY-N	1	3	0	1	0	0	0	1	0	2	0	0	.333	.333	.333	.667	93	-0	0	4.24	0	/O-1	0	-0.1
Total 2	4	12	1	3	0	0	0	1	0	5	1	0	.250	.250	.250	.500	49	-1	1	2.61	-1	/O-4	0	-0.2

• KINSLER, Bill

William H. Kinsler b: 11/9/1867, New York, NY d: 8/10/1963, Miami Beach, FL Deb: 6/8/1893

YEAR TM-L	G	AB	R	H	2B	3B	HR	RBI	BB	SO	SB	CS	AVG	OBP	SLG	OPS	OPS+	BR/A	RC	RC/G	FR	G/POS	WS	TPW
1893 NY-N	1	3	1	0	0	0	0	0	1	1	0	....	.000	.250	.000	.250	-31	-1	0	.00	-0	/O-1	0	0.0

• KINSLOW, Tom

Thomas F. Kinslow b: 1/12/1866, Washington, DC d: 2/22/1901, Washington, DC BR/TR, 5'10", 160 lbs. Deb: 6/4/1886 U

YEAR TM-L	G	AB	R	H	2B	3B	HR	RBI	BB	SO	SB	CS	AVG	OBP	SLG	OPS	OPS+	BR/A	RC	RC/G	FR	G/POS	WS	TPW
1886 Was-N	3	8	1	2	0	0	0	1	0	1	0	....	.250	.250	.250	.500	55	-0	1	2.31	0	/C-3	0	0.0
1887 NY-a	2	6	0	0	0	0	0	0	0	....	0	....	.000	.000	.000	.000	-105	-2	0	.00	0	/C-2	0	-0.1
1890 Bro-P	64	242	30	64	11	6	4	46	10	22	2	....	.264	.299	.409	.708	83	-9	31	4.70	-1	C-64	7	-0.3
1891 Bro-N	61	228	22	54	6	0	0	33	9	22	3	....	.237	.266	.263	.529	55	-14	17	2.66	-4	C-61	2	-1.2
1892 Bro-N	66	246	37	75	6	11	2	40	13	16	4	....	.305	.342	.443	.785	142	11	40	6.26	1	C-66	12	1.7
1893 Bro-N	78	312	38	76	8	4	4	45	11	13	4	....	.244	.272	.333	.605	63	-18	30	3.38	-1	C-76/O-2(0-0-2)	6	-1.0
1894 Bro-N	62	223	39	68	5	6	2	41	20	11	4	....	.305	.362	.408	.770	92	-2	35	5.92	-7	C-61/1-1	6	-0.3
1895 Pit-N	19	62	10	14	2	0	0	5	2	2	1	....	.226	.250	.258	.508	33	-6	5	2.49	-2	C-18	1	-0.6
1896 Lou-N	8	25	4	7	0	1	0	7	1	5	0	....	.280	.308	.360	.668	79	-1	3	4.12	-1	/C-5,1-1	0	-0.1
1898 Was-N	3	9	0	1	0	0	0	0	0	....	0	....	.111	.111	.111	.222	-36	-2	0	.38	0	/C-3,1-1	0	-0.1
StL-N	14	53	5	15	2	1	0	4	1	....	0	....	.283	.309	.358	.668	89	-1	6	4.20	1	C-14	1	0.1
Yr.	17	62	5	16	2	1	0	4	1	....	0	....	.258	.281	.323	.604	71	-3	6	3.53	1	C-17/1-1	1	0.0
Total 10	380	1414	186	376	40	29	12	222	67	92	18	....	.266	.301	.361	.662	82	-44	167	4.29	-15	C-373/1-3,O-2	35	-2.0

• KINZIE, Walt

Walter Harris Kinzie b: 3/16/1857, Chicago, IL d: 11/5/1909, Chicago, IL BR, 5'10.5", 161 lbs. Deb: 7/17/1882

YEAR TM-L	G	AB	R	H	2B	3B	HR	RBI	BB	SO	SB	CS	AVG	OBP	SLG	OPS	OPS+	BR/A	RC	RC/G	FR	G/POS	WS	TPW
1882 Det-N	13	53	5	5	0	1	0	2	0	8	....	....	.094	.094	.132	.226	-28	-7	1	.39	-1	S-13	1	-0.7
1884 Chi-N	19	82	4	13	3	0	2	8	0	13	....	....	.159	.159	.268	.427	29	-7	4	1.42	-3	S-17/3-2	1	-0.8
StL-a	2	9	0	1	0	0	0	0	0	....	....	....	.111	.111	.111	.222	-26	-1	0	.39	-1	/2-2	0	-0.2
Total 2	34	144	9	19	3	1	2	10	0	21	....	....	.132	.132	.208	.340	4	-16	4	.96	-5	/S-30,2-2,3-2	2	-1.8

• KIPPERT, Ed

Edward August "Kickapoo" Kippert b: 1/3/1880, Detroit, MI d: 6/3/1960, Detroit, MI BR/TR, 5'10.5", 180 lbs. Deb: 4/14/1914

YEAR TM-L	G	AB	R	H	2B	3B	HR	RBI	BB	SO	SB	CS	AVG	OBP	SLG	OPS	OPS+	BR/A	RC	RC/G	FR	G/POS	WS	TPW
1914 Cin-N	2	2	0	0	0	0	0	0	0	0	0	....	.000	.000	.000	.000	-97	-0	0	.00	0	/O-2(1-1-0)	0	-0.1

• KIRBY, Jim

James Herschel Kirby b: 5/5/1923, Nashville, TN BR/TR, 5'11", 175 lbs. Deb: 5/1/1949

YEAR TM-L	G	AB	R	H	2B	3B	HR	RBI	BB	SO	SB	CS	AVG	OBP	SLG	OPS	OPS+	BR/A	RC	RC/G	FR	G/POS	WS	TPW
1949 Chi-N	3	2	0	1	0	0	0	0	0	0	0	....	.500	.500	.500	1.000	174	0	1	13.50	0	....	0	0.0

• KIRBY, La Rue

La Rue Kirby b: 12/30/1889, Eureka, MI d: 6/10/1961, Lansing, MI BB/TR, 6', 185 lbs. Deb: 8/7/1912 Career OF: 9-89-5

YEAR TM-L	G	AB	R	H	2B	3B	HR	RBI	BB	SO	SB	CS	AVG	OBP	SLG	OPS	OPS+	BR/A	RC	RC/G	FR	G/POS	WS	TPW
1912 NY-N	3	5	1	1	1	0	0	0	0	0	0	....	.200	.200	.400	.600	60	0	0	2.35	0	/P-3	0	-0.3
1914 StL-F	52	195	21	48	6	3	2	18	14	30	5	....	.246	.303	.338	.642	78	-6	20	3.48	0	O-50(0-49-1)	4	-0.9
1915 StL-F	61	178	15	38	7	2	0	16	17	31	3	....	.213	.282	.275	.557	61	-8	15	2.60	0	O-52(9-40-4)/P-1	2	-1.3
Total 3	116	378	37	87	14	5	2	34	31	61	8	....	.230	.292	.310	.601	70	-14	36	3.03	-0	O-102/P-4	6	-2.6

• KIRBY, Wayne

Wayne Leonard Kirby b: 1/22/1964, Williamsburg, VA BL/TR, 5'11", 185 lbs. Deb: 9/12/1991 Career OF: 39-129-245

YEAR TM-L	G	AB	R	H	2B	3B	HR	RBI	BB	SO	SB	CS	AVG	OBP	SLG	OPS	OPS+	BR/A	RC	RC/G	FR	G/POS	WS	TPW
1991 Cle-A	21	43	4	9	2	0	0	5	2	6	1	2	.209	.244	.256	.500	38	-4	2	1.31	0	O-21(5-1-17)	0	-0.5
1992 Cle-A	21	18	9	3	1	0	1	1	3	2	0	3	.167	.286	.389	.675	89	-2	1	1.05	0	/D-4,O-2(1-0-1)	0	-0.2
1993 Cle-A	131	458	71	123	19	5	6	60	37	58	17	5	.269	.327	.371	.698	88	-6	57	4.29	7	*O-123(2-15-113)/D-5	13	-0.5
1994 Cle-A	78	191	33	56	6	0	5	23	13	30	11	4	.293	.341	.403	.745	91	-2	27	5.22	-2	O-68(8-6-55)/D-2	4	-0.6
1995*Cle-A	101	188	29	39	10	2	1	14	13	32	10	3	.207	.262	.298	.560	45	-15	15	2.53	0	O-68(1-34-35)/D-7	1	-1.6
1996 Cle-A	27	16	3	4	1	0	0	1	2	2	0	1	.250	.333	.313	.646	65	-1	1	2.37	-1	O-18(2-6-10)	0	-0.3
*LA-N	65	188	23	51	10	1	1	11	17	17	4	2	.271	.335	.351	.686	88	-3	23	4.24	-2	O-53(8-47-0)	4	-0.5
1997 LA-N	46	65	6	11	2	0	0	4	10	12	0	0	.169	.280	.200	.480	31	-6	4	2.04	1	O-26(9-16-2)	1	-0.6
1998 NY-N	26	31	5	6	0	1	0	0	1	9	1	1	.194	.219	.258	.477	25	-4	2	1.69	0	O-19(3-4-12)	0	-0.4
Total 8	516	1198	183	302	51	9	14	119	98	168	44	21	.252	.312	.345	.657	75	-44	132	3.71	3	O-398/D-18	23	-5.0

YEAR TM-L	G	AB	R	H	2B	3B	HR	RBI	BB	SO	SB	CS	AVG	OBP	SLG	OPS	OPS+	BR/A	RC	RC/G	FR	G/POS	WS	TPW
• KIRK, Tom	Thomas Daniel Kirk b: 9/27/1927, Philadelphia, PA d: 8/1/1974, Philadelphia, PA BL/TL, 5'10.5", 182 lbs. Deb: 6/24/1947																							
1947 Phi-A	1	1	0	0	0	0	0	0	0	0	0	0	.000	.000	.000	.000	-98	-0	0	.00	0	....	0	0.0
• KIRKE, Jay	Judson Fabian Kirke b: 6/16/1888, Fleischmanns, NY d: 8/31/1968, New Orleans, LA BL/TR, 6', 195 lbs. Deb: 9/28/1910 Career OF: 102-2-38																							
1910 Det-A	8	25	3	5	1	0	0	3	1	....	1	....	.200	.231	.240	.471	44	-2	2	2.02	-2	/2-7,0-1	0	-0.4
1911 Bos-N	20	89	9	32	5	5	0	12	2	6	3	....	.360	.380	.528	.909	142	4	19	8.22	0	0-14(14-0-0)/1-3,2-1,3-1,S	3	0.3
1912 Bos-N	103	359	53	115	11	4	4	62	9	46	7	....	.320	.339	.407	.745	102	-1	51	5.14	0	0-72(62-0-10),3-14/S-2,1-1	6	-0.3
1913 Bos-N	18	38	3	9	2	0	0	3	1	6	0	....	.237	.293	.289	.582	65	-2	3	2.70	2	0-13(3-2-8)	0	-0.1
1914 Cle-A	67	242	18	66	10	2	1	25	7	30	5	10	.273	.296	.343	.639	89	-8	23	3.19	-1	0-42(22-0-20),1-18	3	-1.2
1915 Cle-A	87	339	35	105	19	2	2	40	14	21	5	6	.310	.346	.395	.742	120	5	47	4.98	-3	1-87	8	0.0
1918 NY-N	17	56	1	14	1	0	0	3	1	3	0	....	.250	.263	.268	.531	63	-3	4	2.32	0	1-16	1	-0.3
Total 7	**320**	**1148**	**122**	**346**	**49**	**13**	**7**	**148**	**35**	**112**	**21**	**16**	**.301**	**.328**	**.385**	**.713**	**103**	**-7**	**149**	**4.55**	**-2**	**0-142,1-125/3-15,2-8,S-3**	**21**	**-1.8**
• KIRKLAND, Willie	Willie Charles Kirkland b: 2/17/1934, Siluria, AL BL/TR, 6'1", 206 lbs. Deb: 4/15/1958 Career OF: 122-92-817																							
1958 SF-N	122	418	48	108	25	6	14	56	43	69	3	2	.258	.335	.447	.782	107	4	64	5.37	0	*0-115(5-0-112)	13	0.0
1959 SF-N	126	463	64	126	22	3	22	68	42	84	5	3	.272	.337	.475	.812	116	9	75	5.77	-1	*0-117(13-0-109)	16	0.4
1960 SF-N	146	515	59	130	21	10	21	65	44	86	12	7	.252	.316	.454	.771	115	9	74	5.02	1	*0-143(3-0-143)	19	0.5
1961 Cle-A	146	525	84	136	22	5	27	95	48	77	7	0	.259	.322	.474	.797	113	9	84	5.63	1	*0-138(0-0-138)	18	0.1
1962 Cle-A	137	419	56	84	9	1	21	72	43	62	9	1	.200	.275	.377	.652	76	-14	44	3.34	4	*0-125(0-12-121)	7	-1.8
1963 Cle-A	127	427	51	98	13	2	15	47	45	99	8	2	.230	.304	.375	.679	90	-5	50	3.90	1	*0-112(5-64-45)	11	-1.0
1964 Bal-A	66	150	14	30	5	0	3	22	17	26	3	2	.200	.286	.293	.579	62	-8	14	2.94	4	0-58(2-10-48)	3	-0.8
Was-A	32	102	8	22	6	0	5	13	6	30	0	0	.216	.259	.422	.681	86	-2	11	3.64	-2	0-27(12-1-15)	2	-0.6
Yr.	98	252	22	52	11	0	8	35	23	56	3	2	.206	.275	.345	.621	71	-10	25	3.22	2	0-85(14-11-63)	5	-1.3
1965 Was-A	123	312	38	72	9	1	14	54	19	65	3	2	.231	.275	.401	.676	91	-5	33	3.57	-3	0-92(32-5-67)	7	-1.4
1966 Was-A	124	163	21	31	2	1	6	17	16	50	2	0	.190	.263	.325	.588	69	-6	14	2.79	1	0-68(50-0-19)	2	-0.7
Total 9	**1149**	**3494**	**443**	**837**	**134**	**29**	**148**	**509**	**323**	**648**	**52**	**19**	**.240**	**.307**	**.422**	**.728**	**98**	**-11**	**463**	**4.51**	**7**	**0-995**	**98**	**-5.3**
• KIRKPATRICK, Ed	Edgar Leon Kirkpatrick b: 10/8/1944, Spokane, WA BL/TR, 5'11.5", 195 lbs. Deb: 9/13/1962 Career OF: 236-62-291																							
1962 LA-A	3	6	0	0	0	0	0	0	0	2	0	0	.000	.000	.000	.000	-103	-2	0	.00	1	/C-1	0	-0.1
1963 LA-A	34	77	4	15	5	0	2	7	6	19	1	0	.195	.262	.338	.600	71	-3	7	3.01	0	C-14,0-10(10-0-0)	2	-0.3
1964 LA-A	75	219	20	53	13	3	2	22	23	30	2	2	.242	.320	.356	.676	97	-1	24	3.61	0	0-63(63-0-1)	5	-0.5
1965 Cal-A	19	73	8	19	5	0	3	8	3	9	1	2	.260	.289	.452	.742	110	-0	8	3.41	1	0-19(0-0-19)	2	0.0
1966 Cal-A	117	312	31	60	7	4	9	44	51	67	7	4	.192	.315	.327	.642	87	-4	35	3.53	0	*0-102(17-0-86)/1-3	8	-1.1
1967 Cal-A	3	8	0	0	0	0	0	0	0	2	0	0	.000	.000	.000	.000	-104	-2	0	.00	0	/C-2,0-1	0	-0.3
1968 Cal-A	89	161	23	37	4	0	1	15	25	32	1	3	.230	.337	.273	.610	90	-2	16	3.32	0	0-45(12-1-34)/C-4,1-2	4	-0.5
1969 KC-A	120	315	40	81	11	4	14	49	43	42	3	5	.257	.352	.451	.803	122	8	52	5.65	3	0-82(29-24-32)/C-8,1-2,3-2,2	13	0.7
1970 KC-A	134	424	59	97	17	2	18	62	55	65	4	4	.229	.319	.406	.724	98	-2	54	4.31	7	C-89,0-19(8-3-8),1-16	12	0.7
1971 KC-A	120	365	46	80	12	1	9	46	48	60	3	4	.219	.313	.332	.645	83	-8	37	3.28	-2	0-61(30-16-18),C-59	9	-1.1
1972 KC-A	113	364	43	100	15	1	9	43	51	50	3	5	.275	.368	.396	.764	128	13	55	5.32	-1	*C-108/1-1	16	1.9
1973 KC-A	126	429	61	113	24	3	6	45	46	48	3	7	.263	.336	.375	.711	93	-5	52	4.06	-2	*0-108(27-11-72),C-14/D-8	11	-1.2
1974*Pit-N	116	271	32	67	9	0	6	38	51	30	1	2	.247	.370	.347	.717	105	4	37	4.65	-5	1-59,0-14(0-2-12)/C-6	8	-0.6
1975*Pit-N	89	144	15	34	5	0	5	16	18	22	1	0	.236	.321	.375	.696	93	-1	17	3.95	-1	1-28,0-14(8-0-6)	3	-0.4
1976 Pit-N	83	146	14	34	9	0	0	16	14	15	1	0	.233	.300	.295	.595	69	-6	13	3.04	0	1-25/0-9(3-4-2),3-1	2	-0.8
1977 Pit-N	21	28	5	4	2	0	1	4	8	6	1	0	.143	.333	.321	.655	74	-1	3	3.21	-1	1-10/0-2(1-1-0),3-1	0	-0.2
Tex-A	20	48	2	9	1	0	0	3	4	11	2	0	.188	.250	.208	.458	26	-4	3	1.65	0	/0-6(5-0-1),D-5,1-3,C-1	0	-0.5
Mil-A	29	77	8	21	4	0	0	6	10	8	0	1	.273	.364	.325	.688	89	-1	10	4.61	0	0-22(22-0-0)/D-3,3-1	2	-0.2
Yr.	49	125	10	30	5	0	0	9	14	19	2	1	.240	.321	.280	.601	66	-5	12	3.37	-0	0-28(27-0-1)/D-8,1-3,3-1,C	2	-0.7
Total 16	**1311**	**3467**	**411**	**824**	**143**	**18**	**85**	**424**	**456**	**518**	**34**	**39**	**.238**	**.330**	**.363**	**.693**	**97**	**-17**	**424**	**4.06**	**-1**	**0-577,C-306,1-149/D-16,3-5,2**	**97**	**-4.3**
• KIRKPATRICK, Enos	Enos Claire Kirkpatrick b: 12/9/1884, Pittsburgh, PA d: 4/14/1964, Pittsburgh, PA BR/TR, 5'10", 175 lbs. Deb: 8/24/1912																							
1912 Bro-N	32	94	13	18	1	1	0	6	9	15	5	....	.191	.269	.223	.493	37	-8	7	2.28	4	3-29/S-3	1	-0.3
1913 Bro-N	48	89	13	22	4	1	1	5	3	18	5	....	.247	.287	.348	.636	79	-3	10	3.59	-2	S-10/1-8,2-6,3-4	1	-0.5
1914 Bal-F	55	174	22	44	7	2	2	16	18	30	10	....	.253	.330	.351	.680	94	-1	22	4.24	-3	3-36,S-11/0-3(2-0-1),1-1	6	-0.3
1915 Bal-F	68	171	22	41	8	2	0	19	24	15	12	....	.240	.337	.310	.647	85	-2	21	4.05	-9	3-28,2-21/1-5,S-5	4	-1.1
Total 4	**203**	**528**	**70**	**125**	**20**	**6**	**3**	**46**	**54**	**78**	**32**	**....**	**.237**	**.315**	**.314**	**.629**	**78**	**-14**	**60**	**3.70**	**-11**	**/3-97,S-29,2-27,1-14,0-3**	**12**	**-2.2**
• KIRRENE, Joe	Joseph John Kirrene b: 10/4/1931, San Francisco, CA BR/TR, 6'2", 195 lbs. Deb: 10/1/1950																							
1950 Chi-A	1	4	0	1	0	0	0	0	0	1	0	0	.250	.250	.250	.500	29	-0	0	2.31	-0	/3-1	0	0.0
1954 Chi-A	9	23	4	7	1	0	0	4	5	2	1	0	.304	.448	.348	.796	116	1	4	6.62	0	/3-9	1	0.1
Total 2	**10**	**27**	**4**	**8**	**1**	**0**	**0**	**4**	**5**	**3**	**1**	**0**	**.296**	**.424**	**.333**	**.758**	**106**	**1**	**4**	**5.98**	**0**	**/3-10**	**1**	**0.1**
• KISH, Ernie	Ernest Alexander Kish b: 2/6/1918, Washington, DC d: 12/21/1993, Kirtland, OH BL/TR, 5'9.5", 170 lbs. Deb: 7/29/1945																							
1945 Phi-A	43	110	10	27	5	1	0	10	9	9	0	3	.245	.320	.309	.629	83	-3	11	3.15	-2	0-30(13-8-11)	1	-0.7
• KITSOS, Chris	Christopher Anestos Kitsos b: 2/11/1928, New York, NY BB/TR, 5'9", 165 lbs. Deb: 4/21/1954																							
1954 Chi-N	1	0	0	0	0	0	0	0	0	0	0	0	....	....	....	....	-99	0	0	....	0	/S-1	0	0.0
• KITTLE, Ron	Ronald Dale Kittle b: 1/5/1958, Gary, IN BR/TR, 6'4", 220 lbs. Deb: 9/2/1982 Career OF: 348-0-5																							
1982 Chi-A	20	29	3	7	2	0	1	7	3	12	0	0	.241	.313	.414	.726	97	-0	4	4.90	0	/0-5(0-0-5),D-3	1	0.0
1983*Chi-A★	145	520	75	132	19	3	35	100	39	150	8	3	.254	.316	.504	.820	117	10	81	5.41	-7	*0-139(139-0-0)/D-2	19	-0.4
1984 Chi-A	139	466	67	100	15	0	32	74	49	137	3	6	.215	.298	.453	.750	100	-3	62	4.34	1	*0-124(124-0-0)/D-7	11	-0.8
1985 Chi-A	116	379	51	87	12	0	26	58	31	92	1	4	.230	.296	.467	.763	101	-2	48	4.19	2	D-57,0-57(57-0-0)	9	-0.5
1986 Chi-A	86	296	34	63	11	0	17	48	28	87	2	1	.213	.287	.422	.710	87	-6	34	3.69	2	D-62,0-20(20-0-0)	5	-0.7
NY-A	30	80	8	19	2	0	4	12	7	23	2	0	.238	.299	.413	.711	92	-1	11	4.59	-0	D-24/0-1	1	-0.1
Yr.	116	376	42	82	13	0	21	60	35	110	4	1	.218	.290	.420	.710	88	-7	45	3.87	2	D-86,0-21(21-0-0)	6	-0.8
1987 NY-A	59	159	21	44	5	0	12	28	10	36	0	1	.277	.324	.535	.858	123	4	26	5.66	1	D-49/0-2(2-0-0)	5	0.3
1988 Cle-A	75	225	31	58	8	0	18	43	16	65	0	0	.258	.329	.533	.863	134	9	42	6.52	0	D-63	8	0.7
1989 Chi-A	51	169	26	51	10	0	11	37	22	42	0	1	.302	.385	.556	.942	166	14	37	7.97	-2	1-27,D-17/0-5(5-0-0)	9	1.0
1990 Chi-A	83	277	29	68	14	0	16	43	24	77	0	0	.245	.313	.469	.782	118	6	41	5.24	-3	D-54,1-25	8	0.0
Bal-A	22	61	4	10	2	0	2	3	2	14	0	0	.164	.203	.295	.498	39	-5	3	1.47	0	D-13/1-5	0	-0.6
Yr.	105	338	33	78	16	0	18	46	26	91	0	0	.231	.293	.438	.731	105	0	44	4.48	-3	D-67,1-30	8	-0.6
1991 Chi-A	17	47	7	9	0	0	2	7	5	9	0	0	.191	.296	.319	.615	72	-2	4	2.91	-1	1-15	0	-0.3
Total 10	**843**	**2708**	**356**	**648**	**100**	**3**	**176**	**460**	**236**	**744**	**16**	**16**	**.239**	**.309**	**.473**	**.783**	**110**	**24**	**392**	**4.90**	**-8**	**0-353,D-351/1-72**	**76**	**-1.4**
• KITTRIDGE, Malachi	Malachi Jeddidah "Jedediah" Kittridge b: 10/12/1869, Clinton, MA d: 6/23/1928, Gary, IN BR/TR, 5'7", 170 lbs. Deb: 4/19/1890 M/U																							
1890 Chi-N	96	333	46	67	8	3	3	35	39	53	7	....	.201	.287	.270	.557	60	-17	29	2.84	0	*C-96	6	-0.8
1891 Chi-N	79	296	26	62	8	5	2	27	17	28	4	....	.209	.252	.291	.543	58	-17	23	2.69	0	C-79	5	-0.9
1892 Chi-N	69	229	19	41	5	0	0	10	11	27	2	....	.179	.217	.201	.418	26	-21	11	1.53	1	C-69	4	-1.2
1893 Chi-N	70	255	32	59	9	5	2	30	17	15	3	....	.231	.279	.329	.609	62	-15	25	3.37	4	C-70	4	-0.4
1894 Chi-N	51	168	36	53	8	2	0	23	26	20	2	....	.315	.407	.387	.794	88	-3	28	6.32	-7	C-51	4	-0.4
1895 Chi-N	60	212	30	48	6	3	3	29	16	9	6	....	.226	.284	.325	.609	53	-16	23	3.57	0	C-59	3	-0.9
1896 Chi-N	65	215	17	48	4	1	1	19	14	14	6	....	.223	.274	.265	.539	41	-19	18	2.82	-1	C-64/P-1	4	-1.2
1897 Chi-N	79	262	25	53	5	5	1	30	22	....	9	....	.202	.264	.271	.535	40	-24	22	2.76	-1	C-79	3	-1.5
1898 Lou-N	86	287	27	70	8	5	1	31	15	....	9	....	.244	.281	.317	.599	73	-11	30	3.50	-5	C-86	5	-0.8
1899 Lou-N	46	131	11	26	2	1	0	13	26	....	3	....	.198	.335	.229	.564	56	-6	14	3.03	2	C-43	3	0.0
Was-N	44	133	14	20	3	0	0	11	10	....	2	....	.150	.215	.173	.388	7	-17	6	1.36	2	C-43	2	-1.0
Yr.	90	264	25	46	5	1	0	24	36	....	5	....	.174	.278	.201	.479	33	-23	20	2.20	4	C-86	5	-1.0
1901 Bos-N	114	381	24	96	14	0	2	40	32	....	2	....	.252	.312	.304	.616	72	-13	39	3.51	3	*C-113	10	0.1
1902 Bos-N	80	255	18	60	7	0	2	30	24	....	4	....	.235	.304	.286	.590	81	-5	25	3.27	2	C-72	9	0.5
1903 Bos-N	32	99	10	21	2	0	0	6	11	....	1	....	.212	.291	.232	.523	52	-6	8	2.53	3	C-30	2	0.0

YEAR TM-L	G	AB	R	H	2B	3B	HR	RBI	BB	SO	SB	CS	AVG	OBP	SLG	OPS	OPS+	BR/A	RC	RC/G	FR	G/POS	WS	TPW
Was-A	60	192	8	41	4	1	0	16	10	....	1	....	.214	.252	.245	.497	49	-12	13	2.22	3	C-60	2	-0.4
1904 Was-A	81	265	11	64	7	0	0	24	8	....	2	....	.242	.266	.268	.534	70	-9	21	2.66	8	C-79	3	0.7
1905 Was-A	77	238	16	39	8	0	0	14	15	....	1	....	.164	.213	.197	.411	32	-18	12	1.48	10	C-76	4	-0.1
1906 Was-A	22	68	5	13	0	0	0	3	1	....	0	....	.191	.203	.191	.394	25	-6	3	1.36	-3	C-22	1	-0.7
Cle-A	5	10	0	1	0	0	0	0	0	....	0	....	.100	.100	.100	.200	-38	-2	0	.30	-1	/C-5	0	-0.2
Yr.	27	78	5	14	0	0	0	3	1	....	0	....	.179	.190	.179	.369	17	-8	3	1.21	-4	C-27	1	-1.0
Total 16	1216	4029	375	882	108	31	17	391	314	166	64	....	.219	.277	.274	.550	56	-239	349	2.86	18	*C-1196/P-1	74	-9.4

• KLASSEN, Danny

Daniel Victor Klassen b: 9/22/1975, Leamington, Canada BR/TR, 6', 190 lbs. Deb: 7/4/1998

YEAR TM-L	G	AB	R	H	2B	3B	HR	RBI	BB	SO	SB	CS	AVG	OBP	SLG	OPS	OPS+	BR/A	RC	RC/G	FR	G/POS	WS	TPW
1998 Ari-N	29	108	12	21	2	1	3	8	9	33	1	1	.194	.263	.315	.578	51	-8	8	2.28	-6	2-29	0	-1.3
1999 Ari-N	1	1	0	1	0	0	0	0	0	0	0	0	1.000	1.000	1.000	2.000	406	0	1	∞	0	....	0	0.0
2000 Ari-N	29	76	13	18	3	0	2	8	8	24	1	1	.237	.318	.355	.673	68	-4	9	4.09	0	3-25/S-3	2	-0.4
2002 Ari-N	4	3	0	1	0	0	0	0	0	1	0	0	.333	.333	.333	.667	70	-0	0	4.50	0	/3-2,S-1	0	0.0
2003 Det-A	22	73	9	18	3	1	1	7	4	26	0	1	.247	.286	.356	.642	74	-3	7	3.29	3	3-13/2-4,S-3	2	0.1
Total 5	85	261	34	59	8	2	6	23	21	84	2	3	.226	.289	.341	.630	64	-15	25	3.09	-3	/3-40,2-33,S-7	4	-1.6

• KLAUS, Billy

William Joseph Klaus b: 12/9/1928, Spring Grove, IL BL/TR, 5'9", 165 lbs. Deb: 4/16/1952

YEAR TM-L	G	AB	R	H	2B	3B	HR	RBI	BB	SO	SB	CS	AVG	OBP	SLG	OPS	OPS+	BR/A	RC	RC/G	FR	G/POS	WS	TPW
1952 Bos-N	7	4	3	0	0	0	0	0	1	1	0	0	.000	.200	.000	.200	-42	-1	0	.35	-2	/S-4	0	-0.3
1953 Mil-N	2	2	1	0	0	0	0	1	0	0	0	0	.000	.000	.000	.000	-107	-1	0	.00	0	....	0	-0.1
1955 Bos-A	135	541	83	153	26	2	7	60	60	44	6	0	.283	.354	.377	.731	89	-6	78	5.25	-4	*S-126/3-8	15	0.0
1956 Bos-A	135	520	91	141	29	5	7	59	90	43	1	0	.271	.380	.387	.766	91	-3	83	5.70	-2	*3-106,S-26	16	-0.3
1957 Bos-A	127	477	76	120	18	4	10	42	55	53	2	0	.252	.329	.369	.698	85	-8	59	4.25	-1	*S-118	13	0.1
1958 Bos-A	61	88	5	14	4	0	1	7	5	16	0	0	.159	.204	.239	.443	20	-10	4	1.45	-3	S-27	0	-1.3
1959 Bal-A	104	321	33	80	11	0	3	25	51	38	2	4	.249	.352	.312	.664	86	-5	37	3.95	-2	S-59,3-49/2-1	9	-0.3
1960 Bal-A	46	43	8	9	2	0	1	6	9	9	0	0	.209	.346	.326	.672	84	-1	5	4.06	1	2-30,S-12/3-2	2	0.2
1961 Was-A	91	251	26	57	8	2	7	30	30	34	2	2	.227	.314	.359	.673	83	-6	30	4.05	2	3-51,S-18/2-1,0-1	5	-0.3
1962 Phi-N	102	248	30	51	8	2	4	20	29	43	1	1	.206	.291	.302	.594	61	-14	23	2.98	-1	3-53,S-30,2-11	4	-1.2
1963 Phi-N	11	18	1	1	0	0	0	0	1	4	0	0	.056	.105	.056	.161	-53	-3	0	.27	-1	/S-5,3-3	0	-0.5
Total 11	821	2513	357	626	106	15	40	250	331	285	14	7	.249	.337	.351	.688	81	-57	320	4.39	-14	S-425,3-272/2-43,0-1	64	-4.1

• KLAUS, Bobby

Robert Francis Klaus b: 12/27/1937, Spring Grove, IL BR/TR, 5'10", 170 lbs. Deb: 4/21/1964

YEAR TM-L	G	AB	R	H	2B	3B	HR	RBI	BB	SO	SB	CS	AVG	OBP	SLG	OPS	OPS+	BR/A	RC	RC/G	FR	G/POS	WS	TPW
1964 Cin-N	40	93	10	17	5	1	2	6	4	13	1	0	.183	.216	.323	.539	48	-6	7	2.24	0	2-18,3-11/S-3	1	-0.5
NY-N	56	209	25	51	8	3	2	11	25	30	3	4	.244	.325	.340	.664	90	-3	24	3.86	-2	3-28,2-25/S-5	5	-0.3
Yr.	96	302	35	68	13	4	4	17	29	43	4	4	.225	.293	.334	.627	77	-10	30	3.33	-2	2-43,3-39/S-8	6	-0.9
1965 NY-N	119	288	30	55	12	0	2	12	45	49	1	6	.191	.302	.253	.556	61	-16	24	2.58	-4	2-72,S-28,3-25	4	-1.5
Total 2	215	590	65	123	25	4	6	29	74	92	5	10	.208	.298	.295	.593	69	-26	54	2.96	-6	2-115/3-64,S-36	10	-2.3

• KLEE, Ollie

Ollie Chester "Babe" Klee b: 5/20/1900, Piqua, OH d: 2/9/1977, Toledo, OH BL/TL, 5'9.5", 160 lbs. Deb: 8/10/1925

YEAR TM-L	G	AB	R	H	2B	3B	HR	RBI	BB	SO	SB	CS	AVG	OBP	SLG	OPS	OPS+	BR/A	RC	RC/G	FR	G/POS	WS	TPW
1925 Cin-N	3	1	0	0	0	0	0	0	0	1	0	0	.000	.000	.000	.000	-102	-0	0	.00	0	/0-1	0	0.0

• KLEIN, Chuck

Charles Herbert Klein
b: 10/7/1904, Indianapolis, IN d: 3/28/1958, Indianapolis, IN BL/TR, 6', 185 lbs. Deb: 7/30/1928 C/U HOF: 1980 Career OF: 261-44-1305

YEAR TM-L	G	AB	R	H	2B	3B	HR	RBI	BB	SO	SB	CS	AVG	OBP	SLG	OPS	OPS+	BR/A	RC	RC/G	FR	G/POS	WS	TPW
1928 Phi-N	64	253	41	91	14	4	11	34	14	22	0	....	.360	.396	.577	.973	146	16	55	8.44	-3	0-63(0-0-63)	9	0.8
1929 Phi-N	149	616	126	219	45	6	**43**	145	54	61	5	....	.356	.407	.657	1.065	149	44	158	10.13	-3	*0-149(0-25-123)	26	2.8
1930 Phi-N	156	648	**158**	250	**59**	8	40	170	54	50	4	....	.386	.436	.687	1.123	155	57	186	11.75	20	*0-156(0-0-156)	28	**5.6**
1931 Phi-N	148	594	**121**	200	34	10	**31**	**121**	59	49	7	....	.337	.398	**.584**	**.982**	149	40	140	9.20	-2	*0-148(90-17-43)	25	3.1
1932 Phi-N	154	650	**152**	**226**	50	15	**38**	137	60	49	**20**	....	.348	.404	**.646**	**1.050**	158	53	171	**10.50**	1	*0-154(0-0-154)	31	4.4
1933 Phi-N★	152	606	101	**223**	**44**	7	**28**	**120**	56	36	15	....	**.368**	**.422**	**.602**	**1.025**	168	**55**	162	**11.24**	6	*0-152(0-1-152)	30	5.4
1934 Chi-N★	115	435	78	131	27	2	20	80	47	38	3	....	.301	.372	.510	.882	136	22	86	7.50	1	*0-110(97-1-15)	19	1.7
1935*Chi-N	119	434	71	127	14	4	21	73	41	42	4	....	.293	.355	.488	.844	124	14	76	6.32	3	*0-111(0-0-111)	17	1.0
1936 Chi-N	29	109	19	32	5	0	5	18	16	14	0	....	.294	.384	.477	.861	128	5	21	7.14	0	0-29(0-0-29)	4	0.3
Phi-N	117	492	83	152	30	7	20	86	33	45	6	....	.309	.352	.520	.873	120	12	92	7.11	-5	*0-117(2-0-115)	13	0.0
Yr.	146	601	102	184	35	7	25	104	49	59	6	....	.306	.358	.512	.871	122	16	114	7.11	-5	*0-146(2-0-144)	17	0.3
1937 Phi-N	115	406	74	132	20	2	15	57	39	21	3	....	.325	.386	.495	.881	127	16	81	7.69	-1	*0-102(29-0-75)	13	0.8
1938 Phi-N	129	458	53	113	22	2	8	61	38	30	7	....	.247	.304	.356	.660	81	-13	52	3.91	-4	*0-119(3-0-118)	7	-2.4
1939 Phi-N	25	47	8	9	2	1	1	9	10	4	1	....	.191	.333	.340	.674	85	-1	6	4.27	0	0-11(0-0-11)/1-1	1	-0.1
Pit-N	85	270	37	81	16	4	11	47	26	17	1	....	.300	.361	.511	.873	134	12	50	6.84	-4	0-66(30-0-37)	10	0.4
Yr.	110	317	45	90	18	5	12	56	36	21	2	....	.284	.357	.486	.843	126	11	57	6.41	-4	0-77(30-0-48)/1-1	11	0.3
1940 Phi-N	116	354	39	77	16	2	7	37	44	30	2	....	.218	.304	.333	.637	79	-10	37	3.47	0	0-96(6-0-90)	5	-1.5
1941 Phi-N	50	73	6	9	0	0	1	3	10	6	0	....	.123	.229	.164	.393	12	-8	3	1.23	0	0-14(2-0-12)	0	-1.0
1942 Phi-N	14	14	0	1	0	0	0	0	0	2	0	....	.071	.071	.071	.143	-61	-3	0	.00	0	....	0	-0.3
1943 Phi-N	12	20	0	2	0	0	0	3	0	3	1	....	.100	.100	.100	.200	-44	-4	0	.30	-1	/0-2(2-0-0)	0	-0.5
1944 Phi-N	4	7	1	1	0	0	0	0	0	2	0	....	.143	.143	.143	.286	-20	-1	0	.64	1	/0-1	0	-0.1
Total 17	1753	6486	1168	2076	398	74	300	1201	601	521	79	....	.320	.379	.543	.922	133	305	1378	8.05	10	*0-1600/1-1	238	20.4

• KLEIN, Lou

Louis Frank Klein b: 10/22/1918, New Orleans, LA d: 6/20/1976, Metaire, LA BR/TR, 5'11", 170 lbs. Deb: 4/21/1943 M/C

YEAR TM-L	G	AB	R	H	2B	3B	HR	RBI	BB	SO	SB	CS	AVG	OBP	SLG	OPS	OPS+	BR/A	RC	RC/G	FR	G/POS	WS	TPW
1943*StL-N	154	627	91	180	28	14	7	62	50	70	9	....	.287	.342	.410	.752	112	8	91	5.30	19	*2-126,S-51	25	3.8
1945 StL-N	19	57	12	13	4	1	1	6	14	9	0	....	.228	.389	.386	.775	113	2	10	6.18	1	/0-7(4-0-3),S-7,3-4,2-2	3	0.2
1946 StL-N	23	93	12	18	3	0	1	4	9	7	1	....	.194	.265	.258	.523	47	-7	7	2.48	0	2-23	2	-0.6
1949 StL-N	58	114	25	25	6	0	2	12	22	20	0	....	.219	.355	.325	.680	80	-2	15	4.26	-1	S-21/2-9,3-7	3	-0.2
1951 Cle-A	2	2	0	0	0	0	0	0	0	1	0	0	.000	.000	.000	.000	-106	-1	0	.00	0	....	0	-0.1
Phi-A	49	144	22	33	7	0	5	17	10	12	0	0	.229	.279	.382	.661	76	-6	15	3.46	-2	2-42	2	-0.5
Yr.	51	146	22	33	7	0	5	17	10	13	0	0	.226	.276	.377	.652	74	-6	15	3.40	-2	2-42	2	-0.6
Total 5	305	1037	162	269	48	15	16	101	105	119	10	0	.259	.330	.381	.711	97	-5	139	4.67	17	2-202/S-79,3-11,0-7	35	2.7

• KLEINOW, Red

John Peter Kleinow b: 7/20/1879, Milwaukee, WI d: 10/9/1929, New York, NY BR/TR, 5'10", 165 lbs. Deb: 5/3/1904

YEAR TM-L	G	AB	R	H	2B	3B	HR	RBI	BB	SO	SB	CS	AVG	OBP	SLG	OPS	OPS+	BR/A	RC	RC/G	FR	G/POS	WS	TPW
1904 NY-A	68	209	12	43	8	4	0	16	15	....	4	....	.206	.259	.282	.541	68	-8	17	2.68	0	C-62/3-2,0-1	4	-0.2
1905 NY-A	88	253	23	56	6	3	1	24	20	....	7	....	.221	.284	.281	.564	71	-8	23	3.06	-5	C-83/1-3	6	-0.7
1906 NY-A	96	268	30	59	9	3	0	31	24	....	8	....	.220	.287	.276	.563	69	-9	26	3.07	-1	C-95/1-1	6	-0.3
1907 NY-A	90	269	30	71	6	4	0	26	24	....	5	....	.264	.327	.316	.643	97	-0	31	4.02	3	C-86/1-1	9	1.2
1908 NY-A	96	279	16	47	3	2	1	13	22	....	5	....	.168	.237	.204	.441	43	-17	15	1.60	0	C-89/2-2	2	-0.9
1909 NY-A	78	206	24	47	11	4	0	15	25	....	7	....	.228	.315	.320	.635	100	0	23	3.61	-2	C-77	8	0.6
1910 NY-A	6	12	2	5	0	0	0	2	1	....	2	....	.417	.462	.417	.878	166	1	3	11.81	0	/C-5	1	0.1
Bos-A	50	147	9	22	1	0	1	8	20	....	3	....	.150	.251	.177	.428	34	-11	7	1.48	-4	C-49	1	-1.0
Yr.	56	159	11	27	1	0	1	10	21	....	5	....	.170	.267	.195	.462	43	-10	10	2.02	-4	C-54	2	-0.9
1911 Bos-A	8	14	0	3	0	0	0	0	2	....	1	....	.214	.313	.214	.527	48	-1	1	2.92	1	/C-8	0	0.0
Phi-N	4	8	0	1	1	0	0	0	0	1	0	....	.125	.125	.250	.375	4	-1	0	.80	0	/C-4	0	-0.1
Total 8	584	1665	146	354	45	20	3	135	153	1	42	....	.213	.282	.269	.551	70	-54	147	2.85	-8	C-558/1-5,2-2,3-2,0-1	37	-1.4

• KLESKO, Ryan

Ryan Anthony Klesko b: 6/12/1971, Westminster, CA BL/TL, 6'3", 220 lbs. Deb: 9/12/1992 Career OF: 627-0-33

YEAR TM-L	G	AB	R	H	2B	3B	HR	RBI	BB	SO	SB	CS	AVG	OBP	SLG	OPS	OPS+	BR/A	RC	RC/G	FR	G/POS	WS	TPW
1992 Atl-N	13	14	0	0	0	0	0	1	0	5	0	0	.000	.067	.000	.067	-75	-3	0	.03	-1	/1-5	0	-0.5
1993 Atl-N	22	17	3	6	1	0	2	5	3	4	0	0	.353	.450	.765	1.215	216	3	6	14.93	-1	/1-3,0-2(2-0-0)	2	0.2
1994 Atl-N	92	245	42	68	13	3	17	47	26	48	1	0	.278	.349	.563	.913	130	10	46	6.61	-3	0-74(74-0-0)/1-6	8	0.5
1995*Atl-N	107	329	48	102	25	2	23	70	47	72	5	4	.310	.399	.608	1.007	156	26	78	8.72	-6	*0-102(102-0-0)/1-4	17	1.6
1996*Atl-N	153	528	90	149	21	4	34	93	68	129	6	3	.282	.366	.530	.897	126	19	103	7.02	-2	*0-144(144-0-0)/1-2	20	1.1
1997*Atl-N	143	467	67	122	23	6	24	84	48	130	4	4	.261	.335	.490	.826	110	5	74	5.50	-6	*0-130(130-0-0),1-22	16	-0.6
1998*Atl-N	129	427	69	117	29	1	18	70	56	66	5	3	.274	.362	.473	.835	117	11	74	6.12	0	*0-120(120-0-0)/1-7	13	0.5
1999*Atl-N	133	404	55	120	28	2	21	80	53	69	5	2	.297	.381	.532	.913	128	17	84	7.56	-3	1-75,0-53(53-0-0)/D-1	18	0.7
2000 SD-N	145	494	88	140	33	2	26	92	91	81	23	7	.283	.396	.516	.912	138	33	106	7.63	-2	*1-136/0-4(2-0-2)	23	1.8
2001 SD-N★	146	538	105	154	34	6	30	113	88	89	23	4	.286	.390	.539	.929	150	45	116	7.57	-3	*1-145	29	2.8

YEAR TM-L	G	AB	R	H	2B	3B	HR	RBI	BB	SO	SB	CS	AVG	OBP	SLG	OPS	OPS+	BR/A	RC	RC/G	FR	G/POS	WS	TPW
2002 SD-N	146	540	90	162	39	1	29	95	76	86	6	2	.300	.390	.537	.927	155	44	117	8.05	-8	*1-112,0-31(0-0-31)/D-1	31	2.4
2003 SD-N	121	397	47	100	18	0	21	67	65	83	2	5	.252	.361	.456	.817	123	12	65	5.46	6	*1-111/D-1	13	0.9
Total 12	1350	4400	704	1240	264	27	245	817	621	862	80	34	.282	.374	.521	.895	133	221	869	7.02	-28	0-660,1-628/D-3	190	11.5

• KLEVEN, Jay Jay Allen Kleven b: 12/2/1949, Oakland, CA BR/TR, 6'2", 190 lbs. Deb: 6/20/1976

YEAR TM-L	G	AB	R	H	2B	3B	HR	RBI	BB	SO	SB	CS	AVG	OBP	SLG	OPS	OPS+	BR/A	RC	RC/G	FR	G/POS	WS	TPW
1976 NY-N	2	5	0	1	0	0	0	2	0	1	0	0	.200	.200	.200	.400	15	-1	0	.00	0	/C-2	0	-0.1

• KLIMCHOCK, Lou Louis Stephen Klimchock b: 10/15/1939, Hostetter, PA BL/TR, 5'11", 180 lbs. Deb: 9/27/1958

YEAR TM-L	G	AB	R	H	2B	3B	HR	RBI	BB	SO	SB	CS	AVG	OBP	SLG	OPS	OPS+	BR/A	RC	RC/G	FR	G/POS	WS	TPW
1958 KC-A	2	10	2	2	0	0	1	1	0	1	0	0	.200	.200	.500	.700	84	-0	1	3.38	0	/2-2	0	0.0
1959 KC-A	17	66	10	18	1	0	4	13	1	6	0	0	.273	.284	.470	.753	101	-0	8	4.21	0	2-16	2	0.0
1960 KC-A	10	10	0	3	0	0	0	0	0	0	0	0	.300	.300	.300	.600	62	-1	1	3.47	-1	/2-1	0	-0.1
1961 KC-A	57	121	8	26	4	1	1	16	5	13	0	0	.215	.246	.289	.535	42	-10	9	2.41	-4	1-11/0-7(4-0-3),3-6,2-1	0	-1.5
1962 Mil-N	8	8	0	0	0	0	0	0	0	2	0	0	.000	.000	.000	.000	-103	-2	0	.00	0	....	0	-0.2
1963 Was-A	9	14	1	2	0	0	0	2	0	1	0	0	.143	.143	.143	.286	-20	-2	0	.64	1	/2-3	0	-0.1
Mil-N	24	46	6	9	1	0	0	1	0	12	0	1	.196	.196	.217	.413	19	-5	2	1.24	-0	1-12	0	-0.6
1964 Mil-N	10	21	3	7	2	0	0	2	1	2	0	0	.333	.364	.429	.792	121	1	3	5.30	0	/3-4,2-2	1	0.0
1965 Mil-N	34	39	3	3	0	0	0	3	2	8	0	0	.077	.122	.077	.199	-42	-7	0	.27	1	/1-4	0	-0.7
1966 NY-N	5	5	0	0	0	0	0	0	0	3	0	0	.000	.000	.000	.000	-102	-1	0	.00	0	....	0	-0.1
1968 Cle-A	11	15	0	2	0	0	0	3	1	0	0	0	.133	.188	.133	.321	-2	-2	0	.86	-1	/3-4,1-1,2-1	0	-0.4
1969 Cle-A	90	258	26	74	13	2	6	26	18	14	0	0	.287	.333	.422	.756	107	2	36	5.10	-5	3-56,2-21/C-1	9	-0.3
1970 Cle-A	41	56	5	9	0	0	1	2	3	9	0	0	.161	.217	.214	.431	18	-6	3	1.44	0	/1-5,2-5	0	-0.7
Total 12	318	669	64	155	21	3	13	69	31	71	0	1	.232	.267	.330	.597	63	-36	63	3.18	-10	/3-70,2-52,1-33,0-7,C-1	12	-4.7

• KLINE, Bobby John Robert Kline b: 1/27/1929, St. Petersburg, FL BR/TR, 6', 179 lbs. Deb: 4/11/1955 ♦

YEAR TM-L	G	AB	R	H	2B	3B	HR	RBI	BB	SO	SB	CS	AVG	OBP	SLG	OPS	OPS+	BR/A	RC	RC/G	FR	G/POS	WS	TPW
1955 Was-A	77	140	12	31	5	0	0	9	11	27	0	0	.221	.288	.257	.545	50	-10	11	2.53	1	S-69/2-4,3-3,P-1	2	-0.7

• KLING, Johnny John "Noisy" Kling b: 2/25/1875, Kansas City, MO d: 1/31/1947, Kansas City, MO BR/TR, 5'9.5", 160 lbs. Deb: 9/11/1900 M/U Career OF: 10-1-13

YEAR TM-L	G	AB	R	H	2B	3B	HR	RBI	BB	SO	SB	CS	AVG	OBP	SLG	OPS	OPS+	BR/A	RC	RC/G	FR	G/POS	WS	TPW
1900 Chi-N	15	51	8	15	3	1	0	7	2	....	0	....	.294	.321	.392	.713	100	-0	7	4.79	-2	C-15	1	-0.1
1901 Chi-N	74	256	26	70	6	3	0	21	9	....	8	....	.273	.301	.320	.621	83	-6	28	3.94	-6	C-69/1-1,0-1	5	-0.6
1902 Chi-N	115	436	50	126	19	3	0	59	29	....	25	....	.289	.333	.346	.680	113	6	62	5.07	2	*C-112/S-1	17	2.0
1903 Chi-N	132	491	67	146	29	13	3	68	22	....	23	....	.297	.330	.428	.758	119	9	80	5.96	-3	*C-132	22	1.9
1904 Chi-N	123	452	41	110	18	0	2	46	16	....	7	....	.243	.271	.296	.567	75	-15	41	2.98	-12	*C-104,0-10(9-0-1)/1-6	10	-1.8
1905 Chi-N	111	380	26	83	8	6	1	52	28	....	13	....	.218	.272	.279	.551	62	-18	35	2.91	-9	*C-106/0-4(0-0-4),1-1	8	-1.7
1906*Chi-N	107	343	45	107	15	8	2	46	23	....	14	....	.312	.357	.420	.777	134	12	59	6.25	-4	C-96/0-3(0-0-3)	21	2.0
1907*Chi-N	104	334	44	95	15	8	1	43	27	....	9	....	.284	.342	.386	.728	120	7	49	5.22	-6	C-98/1-2	19	1.3
1908*Chi-N	126	424	51	117	23	5	4	59	21	....	16	....	.276	.315	.382	.697	117	6	55	4.49	1	*C-117/0-6(1-1-4),1-2	22	2.2
1910*Chi-N	91	297	31	80	17	2	2	32	37	27	3	....	.269	.354	.360	.714	109	4	39	4.51	-1	C-86	14	1.2
1911 Chi-N	27	80	8	14	3	2	1	5	8	14	1	....	.175	.250	.300	.550	53	-5	6	2.35	-1	C-25	1	-0.4
Bos-N	75	241	32	54	8	1	2	24	30	29	0	....	.224	.310	.290	.600	63	-12	22	2.94	6	C-71/3-1	3	0.0
Yr.	102	321	40	68	11	3	3	29	38	43	1	....	.212	.295	.293	.588	61	-17	28	2.79	5	C-96/3-1	4	-0.4
1912 Bos-N	81	252	26	80	10	3	2	30	15	30	3	....	.317	.356	.405	.761	106	1	37	5.28	5	C-74	7	1.2
1913 Cin-N	80	209	20	57	7	6	0	23	14	14	2	....	.273	.318	.364	.682	95	-2	24	3.90	0	C-63	5	0.3
Total 13	1261	4246	475	1154	181	61	20	515	281	114	124	....	.272	.319	.357	.676	100	-12	542	4.43	-30	*C-1168/0-24,1-12,3-1,S-1	155	7.6

• KLING, Rudy Rudolph A. Kling b: 3/23/1870, St. Louis, MO d: 3/14/1937, St. Louis, MO BR/TR, 5'10", 178 lbs. Deb: 9/21/1902

YEAR TM-L	G	AB	R	H	2B	3B	HR	RBI	BB	SO	SB	CS	AVG	OBP	SLG	OPS	OPS+	BR/A	RC	RC/G	FR	G/POS	WS	TPW
1902 StL-N	4	10	1	2	0	0	0	0	4	....	1	....	.200	.429	.200	.629	99	0	2	4.51	-1	/S-4	1	-0.1

• KLINGER, Joe Joseph John Klinger b: 8/2/1902, Canonsburg, PA d: 7/31/1960, Little Rock, AR BR/TR, 6', 190 lbs. Deb: 9/13/1927

YEAR TM-L	G	AB	R	H	2B	3B	HR	RBI	BB	SO	SB	CS	AVG	OBP	SLG	OPS	OPS+	BR/A	RC	RC/G	FR	G/POS	WS	TPW
1927 NY-N	3	5	0	2	0	0	0	0	0	2	0	....	.400	.400	.400	.800	115	0	1	6.45	0	/0-1	0	0.0
1930 Chi-A	4	8	0	3	0	0	0	1	0	0	0	0	.375	.375	.375	.750	94	-0	1	5.72	-1	/1-2,C-2	0	-0.1
Total 2	7	13	0	5	0	0	0	1	0	2	0	0	.385	.385	.385	.769	102	0	2	6.00	0	/1-2,C-2,0-1	0	0.0

• KLOZA, Nap John Clarence Kloza b: 9/7/1903, Poland d: 6/11/1962, Milwaukee, WI BR/TR, 5'11", 180 lbs. Deb: 8/16/1931 Career OF: 1-2-3

YEAR TM-L	G	AB	R	H	2B	3B	HR	RBI	BB	SO	SB	CS	AVG	OBP	SLG	OPS	OPS+	BR/A	RC	RC/G	FR	G/POS	WS	TPW
1931 StL-A	3	7	1	1	0	0	0	0	1	4	0	0	.143	.250	.143	.393	5	-1	0	1.34	0	/0-3(0-0-3)	0	0.0
1932 StL-A	19	13	4	2	0	1	0	2	4	4	0	0	.154	.353	.308	.661	69	-0	2	4.11	0	/0-3(1-2-0)	0	-0.1
Total 2	22	20	5	3	0	1	0	2	5	8	0	0	.150	.320	.250	.570	48	-1	2	3.13	0	/0-6	0	-0.1

• KLUGMANN, Joe Josie Klugmann b: 3/26/1895, St. Louis, MO d: 7/18/1951, Moberly, MO BR/TR, 5'11", 175 lbs. Deb: 9/23/1921

YEAR TM-L	G	AB	R	H	2B	3B	HR	RBI	BB	SO	SB	CS	AVG	OBP	SLG	OPS	OPS+	BR/A	RC	RC/G	FR	G/POS	WS	TPW
1921 Chi-N	6	21	3	6	0	0	0	2	1	2	0	1	.286	.348	.286	.634	69	-1	2	3.07	0	/2-5	0	-0.1
1922 Chi-N	2	2	0	0	0	0	0	0	0	0	0	0	.000	.000	.000	.000	-98	-1	0	.00	0	/2-2	0	0.0
1924 Bro-N	31	79	7	13	2	1	0	3	2	9	0	0	.165	.185	.215	.400	7	-10	3	1.25	-3	2-28/S-1	1	-1.3
1925 Cle-A	38	85	12	28	9	2	0	12	8	4	3	1	.329	.387	.482	.869	119	3	16	7.02	-3	2-29/1-4,3-2	3	0.0
Total 4	77	187	22	47	11	3	0	17	11	15	3	2	.251	.296	.342	.639	66	-9	21	3.84	-6	/2-64,1-4,3-2,S-1	4	-1.4

• KLUMPP, Elmer Elmer Edward Klumpp b: 8/26/1906, St. Louis, MO d: 10/18/1996, Menomonee Falls, WI BR/TR, 6', 184 lbs. Deb: 4/17/1934

YEAR TM-L	G	AB	R	H	2B	3B	HR	RBI	BB	SO	SB	CS	AVG	OBP	SLG	OPS	OPS+	BR/A	RC	RC/G	FR	G/POS	WS	TPW
1934 Was-A	12	15	2	2	0	0	0	0	0	1	0	0	.133	.188	.133	.321	-17	-3	0	.83	-2	C-11	0	-0.4
1937 Bro-N	5	11	0	1	0	0	0	2	1	4	0	....	.091	.167	.091	.258	-28	-2	0	.26	-0	/C-3	0	-0.2
Total 2	17	26	2	3	0	0	0	2	1	5	0	0	.115	.179	.115	.294	-21	-5	1	.57	-2	/C-14	0	-0.5

• KLUSMAN, Billy William F. Klusman b: 3/24/1865, Cincinnati, OH d: 6/24/1907, Cincinnati, OH BR/TR, 5'10.5", 185 lbs. Deb: 6/21/1888 U

YEAR TM-L	G	AB	R	H	2B	3B	HR	RBI	BB	SO	SB	CS	AVG	OBP	SLG	OPS	OPS+	BR/A	RC	RC/G	FR	G/POS	WS	TPW
1888 Bos-N	28	107	9	18	4	0	2	11	5	13	3	....	.168	.205	.262	.467	46	-7	7	1.98	-6	2-28	1	-1.1
1890 StL-a	15	65	9	18	4	1	1	11	1	....	1	....	.277	.288	.415	.703	94	-2	8	4.66	1	2-15	1	0.0
Total 2	43	172	18	36	8	1	3	22	6	13	4	....	.209	.236	.320	.556	64	-8	15	2.91	-4	/2-43	2	-1.1

• KLUSZEWSKI, Ted Theodore Bernard "Big Klu" Kluszewski b: 9/10/1924, Argo, IL d: 3/29/1988, Cincinnati, OH BL/TL, 6'2", 225 lbs. Deb: 4/18/1947 C

YEAR TM-L	G	AB	R	H	2B	3B	HR	RBI	BB	SO	SB	CS	AVG	OBP	SLG	OPS	OPS+	BR/A	RC	RC/G	FR	G/POS	WS	TPW
1947 Cin-N	9	10	1	1	0	0	0	2	1	2	0	....	.100	.182	.100	.282	-24	-2	0	.69	0	/1-2	0	-0.2
1948 Cin-N	113	379	49	104	23	4	12	57	18	32	1	....	.274	.307	.451	.758	107	1	48	4.47	1	1-98	9	-0.2
1949 Cin-N	136	531	63	164	26	2	8	68	19	24	3	....	.309	.333	.411	.743	97	-4	70	5.02	0	*1-134	13	-0.8
1950 Cin-N	134	538	76	165	37	0	25	111	33	28	3	....	.307	.348	.515	.863	123	15	89	6.15	-6	*1-131	16	0.5
1951 Cin-N	154	607	74	157	35	2	13	77	35	33	6	2	.259	.301	.387	.688	82	-16	69	4.00	-2	*1-154	13	-2.3
1952 Cin-N	135	497	62	159	24	11	16	86	47	28	3	3	.320	.383	.509	.892	146	30	97	7.38	-11	*1-133	23	1.5
1953 Cin-N★	149	570	97	180	25	0	40	108	55	34	2	0	.316	.380	.570	.950	142	35	126	8.41	-22	*1-147	24	0.4
1954 Cin-N★	149	573	104	187	28	3	**49**	**141**	78	35	0	2	.326	.410	.642	1.052	164	53	151	10.06	-7	*1-149	33	3.7
1955 Cin-N★	153	612	116	**192**	25	0	47	113	66	40	1	1	.314	.384	.585	.969	144	39	136	8.46	-7	*1-153	25	2.3
1956 Cin-N★	138	517	91	156	14	1	35	102	49	31	1	0	.302	.366	.536	.901	130	22	99	7.08	-6	*1-131	20	0.8
1957 Cin-N	69	127	12	34	7	0	6	21	5	5	0	0	.268	.301	.465	.765	95	-1	17	4.85	-1	1-23	3	-0.3
1958 Pit-N	100	301	29	88	13	4	4	37	26	16	0	0	.292	.351	.402	.753	101	1	41	4.99	-4	1-72	8	-0.7
1959 Pit-N	60	122	11	32	10	1	2	17	5	14	0	0	.262	.291	.410	.701	85	-3	14	3.97	-1	1-20	2	-0.5
*Chi-A	31	101	11	30	2	1	2	10	9	10	0	1	.297	.355	.396	.751	107	1	13	4.48	-2	1-29	3	-0.3
1960 Chi-A	81	181	20	53	9	0	5	39	22	10	0	1	.293	.369	.425	.795	115	4	29	5.72	-2	1-39	6	0.0
1961 LA-A	107	263	32	64	12	0	15	39	24	23	0	0	.243	.307	.460	.767	91	-4	37	4.84	-7	1-66	5	-1.5
Total 15	1718	5929	848	1766	290	29	279	1028	492	365	20	10	.298	.354	.498	.852	122	169	1036	6.44	-77	*1-1481	203	2.4

• KLUTTS, Mickey Gene Ellis Klutts b: 9/20/1954, Montebello, CA BR/TR, 5'11", 189 lbs. Deb: 7/7/1976

YEAR TM-L	G	AB	R	H	2B	3B	HR	RBI	BB	SO	SB	CS	AVG	OBP	SLG	OPS	OPS+	BR/A	RC	RC/G	FR	G/POS	WS	TPW
1976 NY-A	2	3	0	0	0	0	0	0	0	1	0	0	.000	.000	.000	.000	-101	-1	0	.00	-1	/S-2	0	-0.2
1977 NY-A	5	15	3	4	1	0	1	4	2	1	0	1	.267	.389	.533	.922	150	1	3	6.59	2	/3-4,S-1	1	0.2
1978 NY-A	1	2	1	2	1	0	0	0	0	0	0	0	1.000	1.000	1.500	2.500	609	2	3	∞	0	/3-1	1	0.2
1979 Oak-A	24	73	3	14	2	1	1	4	7	20	0	1	.192	.263	.288	.550	51	-5	5	2.40	-3	S-10/2-8,3-6,D-2	0	-0.7
1980 Oak-A	75	197	20	53	14	0	4	21	13	41	1	4	.269	.314	.401	.715	102	-2	22	3.92	-4	3-62/S-8,2-7,D-1	5	-0.5
1981*Oak-A	15	46	9	17	0	0	5	11	2	9	0	0	.370	.396	.696	1.091	220	6	13	11.89	1	3-14	4	0.7
1982 Oak-A	55	157	10	28	8	0	0	14	9	18	0	0	.178	.223	.229	.452	26	-16	8	1.55	1	3-49	1	-1.6

YEAR TM-L	G	AB	R	H	2B	3B	HR	RBI	BB	SO	SB	CS	AVG	OBP	SLG	OPS	OPS+	BR/A	RC	RC/G	FR	G/POS	WS	TPW
1983 Tor-A	22	43	3	11	0	0	3	5	1	11	0	1	.256	.289	.465	.754	98	-1	5	4.42	0	3-17/D-2	1	-0.1
Total 8	**199**	**536**	**49**	**129**	**26**	**1**	**14**	**59**	**34**	**101**	**1**	**7**	**.241**	**.290**	**.371**	**.661**	**85**	**-16**	**60**	**3.57**	**-5**	**3-153/S-21,2-15,D-5**	**13**	**-1.9**

• KLUTTZ, Clyde Clyde Franklin Kluttz b: 12/12/1917, Rockwell, NC d: 5/12/1979, Salisbury, NC BR/TR, 6', 198 lbs. Deb: 4/20/1942

YEAR TM-L	G	AB	R	H	2B	3B	HR	RBI	BB	SO	SB	CS	AVG	OBP	SLG	OPS	OPS+	BR/A	RC	RC/G	FR	G/POS	WS	TPW
1942 Bos-N	72	210	21	56	10	1	1	31	7	13	0	....	.267	.294	.338	.632	86	-5	20	3.41	-2	C-57	5	-0.3
1943 Bos-N	66	207	13	51	7	0	0	20	15	9	0	....	.246	.297	.280	.577	68	-8	17	2.82	1	C-55	4	-0.4
1944 Bos-N	81	229	20	64	12	2	2	19	13	14	0	....	.279	.318	.376	.694	91	-3	28	4.30	2	C-58	7	0.2
1945 Bos-N	25	81	9	24	4	1	0	10	2	6	0	....	.296	.313	.370	.684	89	-2	8	3.76	1	C-19	2	0.1
NY-N	73	222	25	62	14	0	4	21	15	10	1	....	.279	.331	.396	.727	100	-1	29	4.62	1	C-57	7	0.3
Yr.	98	303	34	86	18	1	4	31	17	16	1	....	.284	.326	.389	.716	97	-2	37	4.39	2	C-76	9	0.4
1946 NY-N	5	8	0	3	0	0	0	1	0	1	0	....	.375	.375	.375	.750	112	0	1	6.08	-1	/C-2	0	0.0
StL-N	52	136	8	36	7	0	0	14	10	10	0	....	.265	.315	.316	.631	76	-4	14	3.66	0	C-49	4	-0.2
Yr.	57	144	8	39	7	0	0	15	10	11	0	....	.271	.318	.319	.638	78	-4	15	3.77	0	C-51	4	-0.3
1947 Pit-N	73	232	26	70	9	2	6	42	17	18	1	....	.302	.355	.435	.790	106	1	37	5.92	7	C-69	8	1.1
1948 Pit-N	94	271	26	60	12	2	4	20	20	19	3	....	.221	.275	.325	.600	60	-16	25	3.03	5	C-91	5	-0.7
1951 StL-A	4	4	2	2	1	0	0	1	1	0	0	0	.500	.600	.750	1.350	256	1	2	27.01	0	/C-1	1	0.1
Was-A	53	159	15	49	9	0	1	22	20	8	0	0	.308	.389	.384	.773	111	3	26	6.19	-4	C-46	5	0.1
Yr.	57	163	17	51	10	0	1	23	21	8	0	0	.313	.395	.393	.787	115	4	28	6.56	-4	C-47	6	0.3
1952 Was-A	58	144	7	33	5	0	1	11	12	11	0	0	.229	.293	.285	.578	63	-7	11	2.57	2	C-52	2	-0.3
Total 9	**656**	**1903**	**172**	**510**	**90**	**8**	**19**	**212**	**132**	**119**	**5**	**0**	**.268**	**.318**	**.354**	**.671**	**85**	**-40**	**218**	**4.04**	**11**	**C-556**	**50**	**0.0**

• KMAK, Joe Joseph Robert Kmak b: 5/3/1963, Napa, CA BR/TR, 6', 185 lbs. Deb: 4/6/1993

YEAR TM-L	G	AB	R	H	2B	3B	HR	RBI	BB	SO	SB	CS	AVG	OBP	SLG	OPS	OPS+	BR/A	RC	RC/G	FR	G/POS	WS	TPW
1993 Mil-A	51	110	9	24	5	0	0	7	14	13	6	2	.218	.317	.264	.581	59	-5	10	3.10	2	C-50	3	-0.1
1995 Chi-N	19	53	7	13	3	0	1	6	6	12	0	0	.245	.333	.358	.692	84	-1	6	3.95	0	C-18/3-1	1	0.0
Total 2	**70**	**163**	**16**	**37**	**8**	**0**	**1**	**13**	**20**	**25**	**6**	**2**	**.227**	**.323**	**.294**	**.617**	**67**	**-7**	**17**	**3.37**	**2**	**/C-68,3-1**	**4**	**-0.1**

• KNABE, Otto Franz Otto "Dutch" Knabe b: 6/12/1884, Carrick, PA d: 5/17/1961, Philadelphia, PA BR/TR, 5'8", 175 lbs. Deb: 10/3/1905 M Career OF: 2-0-5

YEAR TM-L	G	AB	R	H	2B	3B	HR	RBI	BB	SO	SB	CS	AVG	OBP	SLG	OPS	OPS+	BR/A	RC	RC/G	FR	G/POS	WS	TPW
1905 Pit-N	3	10	0	3	1	0	0	2	3	....	0	....	.300	.462	.400	.862	154	1	2	7.03	1	/3-3	1	0.2
1907 Phi-N	129	444	67	113	16	9	1	34	52	....	18	....	.255	.339	.338	.677	114	8	64	4.45	7	*2-121/O-5(1-0-3)	18	1.8
1908 Phi-N	151	555	63	121	26	8	0	27	49	....	27	....	.218	.290	.294	.583	84	-10	57	3.14	12	*2-151	15	0.4
1909 Phi-N	113	402	40	94	13	3	0	34	35	....	9	....	.234	.308	.281	.589	82	-8	39	3.08	6	*2-110/O-1	9	-0.1
1910 Phi-N	137	510	73	133	18	6	1	44	47	42	15	....	.261	.327	.325	.652	87	-8	62	3.88	18	*2-136	16	1.2
1911 Phi-N	142	528	99	125	15	6	1	42	94	35	23	....	.237	.352	.294	.646	80	-10	64	3.94	4	*2-142	14	-0.4
1912 Phi-N	126	426	56	120	11	4	0	46	55	20	16	....	.282	.366	.326	.693	85	-7	57	4.59	-3	*2-123	12	-0.8
1913 Phi-N	148	571	70	150	25	7	2	53	45	26	14	....	.263	.320	.342	.661	85	-11	68	3.77	5	*2-148	14	-0.3
1914 Bal-F	147	469	45	106	26	2	2	42	53	28	10	....	.226	.307	.303	.610	74	-15	48	3.12	-15	*2-144	10	-2.8
1915 Bal-F	103	320	38	81	16	2	1	25	37	16	7	....	.253	.334	.325	.659	88	-4	37	3.81	-6	2-94/O-1	8	-0.9
1916 Pit-N	28	89	4	17	3	1	0	9	6	6	1	....	.191	.258	.247	.505	55	-5	7	2.26	-2	2-28	0	-0.7
Chi-N	51	145	17	40	8	0	0	7	9	18	3	....	.276	.327	.331	.658	92	-1	17	4.10	-1	2-42/3-1,O-1,S-1	3	-0.2
Yr.	79	234	21	57	11	1	0	16	15	24	4	....	.244	.300	.299	.600	78	-6	24	3.33	-4	2-70/3-1,O-1,S-1	3	-0.9
Total 11	**1278**	**4469**	**572**	**1103**	**178**	**48**	**8**	**365**	**485**	**191**	**143**	**....**	**.247**	**.325**	**.313**	**.639**	**86**	**-69**	**522**	**3.71**	**25**	***2-1239/O-8,3-4,S-1**	**120**	**-2.7**

• KNAUPP, Cotton Henry Antone Knaupp b: 8/13/1889, San Antonio, TX d: 7/6/1967, New Orleans, LA BR/TR, 5'9", 165 lbs. Deb: 8/30/1910

YEAR TM-L	G	AB	R	H	2B	3B	HR	RBI	BB	SO	SB	CS	AVG	OBP	SLG	OPS	OPS+	BR/A	RC	RC/G	FR	G/POS	WS	TPW
1910 Cle-A	18	59	3	14	3	1	0	11	8	....	1	....	.237	.338	.322	.660	106	1	7	3.79	-5	S-18	2	-0.4
1911 Cle-A	13	39	2	4	1	0	0	0	0	....	3	....	.103	.103	.128	.231	-35	-7	1	.52	1	S-13	0	-0.5
Total 2	**31**	**98**	**5**	**18**	**4**	**1**	**0**	**11**	**8**	**....**	**4**	**....**	**.184**	**.252**	**.245**	**.497**	**55**	**-7**	**8**	**2.39**	**-4**	**/S-31**	**2**	**-0.9**

• KNICELY, Alan Alan Lee Knicely b: 5/19/1955, Harrisonburg, VA BR/TR, 6', 194 lbs. Deb: 8/12/1979 Career OF: 5-0-20

YEAR TM-L	G	AB	R	H	2B	3B	HR	RBI	BB	SO	SB	CS	AVG	OBP	SLG	OPS	OPS+	BR/A	RC	RC/G	FR	G/POS	WS	TPW
1979 Hou-N	7	6	0	0	0	0	0	0	2	3	0	0	.000	.250	.000	.250	-27	-1	0	.00	-1	/C-3,3-1	0	-0.2
1980 Hou-N	1	1	0	0	0	0	0	0	0	1	0	0	.000	.000	.000	.000	-109	-0	0	.00	0	....	0	0.0
1981 Hou-N	3	7	2	4	0	0	2	2	0	1	0	0	.571	.571	1.429	2.000	477	3	6	51.43	0	/C-2,O-1	2	0.4
1982 Hou-N	59	133	10	25	2	0	2	12	14	30	0	1	.188	.270	.248	.518	50	-9	9	2.04	-1	C-23,O-16(1-0-15)/3-1	1	-1.0
1983 Cin-N	59	98	11	22	3	0	2	10	16	28	0	2	.224	.333	.316	.650	78	-3	9	3.02	2	C-31/O-8(3-0-5),1-2	2	-0.1
1984 Cin-N	10	29	0	4	0	0	0	5	3	6	0	0	.138	.219	.138	.357	2	-4	1	1.01	0	/1-8,C-1	0	-0.4
1985 Cin-N	48	158	17	40	9	0	5	26	16	34	0	0	.253	.326	.405	.731	98	-1	20	4.23	-3	C-46	5	-0.2
Phi-N	7	7	0	0	0	0	0	0	0	4	0	0	.000	.000	.000	.000	-97	-2	0	.00	0	/1-1	0	-0.2
Yr.	55	165	17	40	9	0	5	26	16	38	0	0	.242	.313	.388	.701	91	-2	20	4.01	-4	C-46/1-1	5	-0.4
1986 StL-N	34	82	8	16	3	0	1	6	17	21	1	1	.195	.333	.268	.602	69	-3	9	3.33	0	1-29/C-2	2	-0.4
Total 8	**228**	**521**	**48**	**111**	**17**	**0**	**12**	**61**	**68**	**128**	**1**	**4**	**.213**	**.306**	**.315**	**.621**	**72**	**-20**	**53**	**3.25**	**-4**	**C-108/1-40,O-25,3-2**	**12**	**-2.3**

• KNICKERBOCKER, Austin Austin Jay Knickerbocker b: 10/15/1918, Bangall, NY d: 2/18/1997, Clinton Corners, NY BR/TR, 5'11", 185 lbs. Deb: 4/19/1947

YEAR TM-L	G	AB	R	H	2B	3B	HR	RBI	BB	SO	SB	CS	AVG	OBP	SLG	OPS	OPS+	BR/A	RC	RC/G	FR	G/POS	WS	TPW
1947 Phi-A	21	48	8	12	3	2	0	2	3	4	0	1	.250	.294	.396	.690	89	-1	5	3.53	0	O-14(2-2-10)	1	-0.2

• KNICKERBOCKER, Bill William Hart Knickerbocker b: 12/29/1911, Los Angeles, CA d: 9/8/1963, Sebastopol, CA BR/TR, 5'11", 170 lbs. Deb: 4/12/1933

YEAR TM-L	G	AB	R	H	2B	3B	HR	RBI	BB	SO	SB	CS	AVG	OBP	SLG	OPS	OPS+	BR/A	RC	RC/G	FR	G/POS	WS	TPW
1933 Cle-A	80	279	20	63	16	3	2	32	11	30	1	4	.226	.255	.326	.581	51	-22	22	2.55	-2	S-80	3	-1.8
1934 Cle-A	146	593	82	188	32	5	4	67	25	40	6	6	.317	.347	.408	.755	93	-9	82	5.14	-13	*S-146	16	-1.0
1935 Cle-A	132	540	77	161	34	5	0	55	27	31	2	12	.298	.332	.380	.711	82	-20	64	4.22	1	*S-128	14	-0.9
1936 Cle-A	155	618	81	182	35	3	8	73	56	30	5	14	.294	.354	.400	.754	85	-20	85	4.89	-11	*S-155	13	-1.7
1937 StL-A	121	491	53	128	29	5	4	61	30	32	3	2	.261	.303	.365	.668	67	-27	55	3.86	-20	*S-115/2-6	5	-3.5
1938 NY-A	46	128	15	32	8	3	1	21	11	10	0	0	.250	.309	.383	.692	73	-6	16	4.13	2	2-34/S-3	3	-0.2
1939 NY-A	6	13	2	2	1	0	0	1	0	0	0	0	.154	.154	.231	.385	-3	-2	0	.52	1	/2-2,S-2	0	-0.1
1940 NY-A	45	124	17	30	8	1	1	10	14	8	1	1	.242	.333	.347	.680	80	-4	15	4.01	3	S-19,3-17	3	0.1
1941 Chi-A	89	343	51	84	23	2	7	29	41	27	6	5	.245	.329	.385	.714	89	-6	46	4.48	-4	2-88	10	-0.5
1942 Phi-A	87	289	25	73	12	0	1	19	29	30	1	2	.253	.323	.304	.627	77	-9	28	3.21	-4	2-81/S-1	5	-0.8
Total 10	**907**	**3418**	**423**	**943**	**198**	**27**	**28**	**368**	**244**	**238**	**25**	**46**	**.276**	**.326**	**.374**	**.700**	**79**	**-124**	**413**	**4.20**	**-48**	**S-649,2-211/3-17**	**72**	**-10.6**

• KNIGHT, Joe Joseph William "Quiet Joe" Knight b: 9/28/1859, Port Stanley, Canada d: 10/16/1938, Lynhurst, Canada BL/TL, 5'11", 185 lbs. Deb: 5/16/1884 ♦

YEAR TM-L	G	AB	R	H	2B	3B	HR	RBI	BB	SO	SB	CS	AVG	OBP	SLG	OPS	OPS+	BR/A	RC	RC/G	FR	G/POS	WS	TPW
1884 Phi-N	6	24	2	6	3	0	0	2	0	2	....	....	.250	.250	.375	.625	98	1	2	3.52	0	/P-6	1	-1.0
1890 Cin-N	127	481	67	150	26	8	4	67	38	31	17	....	.312	.367	.424	.791	131	18	83	6.66	-3	*O-127(127-0-0)	17	0.9
Total 2	**133**	**505**	**69**	**156**	**29**	**8**	**4**	**69**	**38**	**33**	**17**	**....**	**.309**	**.362**	**.422**	**.784**	**130**	**18**	**85**	**6.50**	**-3**	**O-127/P-6**	**18**	**0.0**

• KNIGHT, John John Wesley "Schoolboy" Knight b: 10/6/1885, Philadelphia, PA d: 12/19/1965, Walnut Creek, CA BR/TR, 6'2.5", 180 lbs. Deb: 4/14/1905

YEAR TM-L	G	AB	R	H	2B	3B	HR	RBI	BB	SO	SB	CS	AVG	OBP	SLG	OPS	OPS+	BR/A	RC	RC/G	FR	G/POS	WS	TPW
1905 Phi-A	88	325	28	66	12	1	3	29	9	....	4	....	.203	.227	.274	.501	58	-17	23	2.23	-19	S-79/3-4	2	-3.7
1906 Phi-A	74	253	29	49	7	2	3	20	19	....	6	....	.194	.250	.273	.523	62	-11	20	2.51	3	3-67/2-7	5	-0.7
1907 Phi-A	40	139	6	29	7	1	0	12	10	....	1	....	.209	.272	.273	.545	72	-4	11	2.63	2	3-40	2	-0.1
Bos-A	98	360	31	78	9	3	2	29	19	....	8	....	.217	.256	.275	.531	70	-13	28	2.64	16	3-92/2-4	5	0.7
Yr.	138	499	37	107	16	4	2	41	29	....	9	....	.214	.260	.275	.535	71	-17	40	2.64	18	*3-132/2-4	7	0.6
1909 NY-A	116	360	46	85	8	5	0	40	37	....	15	....	.236	.311	.286	.597	88	-4	38	3.34	-5	S-76,1-19,2-17/3-3	10	-0.8
1910 NY-A	117	414	58	129	25	4	3	45	34	....	23	....	.312	.372	.413	.785	138	18	72	6.19	2	S-79,1-23/2-7,3-4,O-1	23	2.4
1911 NY-A	132	470	69	126	16	7	3	62	42	....	18	....	.268	.342	.351	.693	88	-8	63	4.52	6	S-82,1-27,2-21/3-1	12	0.5
1912 Was-A	32	93	10	15	2	1	0	9	16	....	4	....	.161	.284	.204	.489	40	-7	7	2.21	-5	2-27/1-5	1	-1.2
1913 NY-A	70	250	24	59	10	0	0	24	25	27	7	....	.236	.310	.276	.586	72	-9	23	2.97	7	1-50,2-21	4	-0.2
Total 8	**767**	**2664**	**301**	**636**	**96**	**24**	**14**	**270**	**211**	**27**	**86**	**....**	**.239**	**.300**	**.309**	**.609**	**83**	**-54**	**285**	**3.52**	**7**	**S-316,3-211,1-124,2-104/O-1**	**64**	**-3.1**

• KNIGHT, Lon Alonzo P. Knight b: 6/16/1853, Philadelphia, PA d: 4/23/1932, Philadelphia, PA BR/TR, 5'11.5", 165 lbs. Deb: 9/4/1875 M/U Career OF: 0-7-473 ♦

YEAR TM-L	G	AB	R	H	2B	3B	HR	RBI	BB	SO	SB	CS	AVG	OBP	SLG	OPS	OPS+	BR/A	RC	RC/G	FR	G/POS	WS	TPW
1875 Ath-n	13	47	5	6	2	0	0	2	0	2	2	0	.128	.128	.170	.298	2	-3	1	.94	0	P-13/S-1	....	-0.5
1876 Phi-N	55	242	32	60	9	3	0	24	2	2	....	....	.248	.256	.313	.569	89	-1	20	3.06	-8	P-34,1-13/O-9(0-3-6),2-6	5	0.4
1880 Wor-N	49	201	31	48	11	3	0	21	5	8	....	....	.239	.257	.323	.581	88	-3	17	3.08	4	O-49(0-0-49)	5	0.1
1881 Det-N	83	340	67	92	16	3	1	52	23	21	....	....	.271	.317	.344	.661	103	1	38	4.14	0	*O-82(0-0-82)/1-1,2-1	8	0.1
1882 Det-N	86	347	39	72	12	6	0	24	16	21	....	....	.207	.242	.277	.519	66	-13	24	2.39	-5	*O-84(0-0-84)/1-2	5	-1.7

YEAR TM-L	G	AB	R	H	2B	3B	HR	RBI	BB	SO	SB	CS	AVG	OBP	SLG	OPS	OPS+	BR/A	RC	RC/G	FR	G/POS	WS	TPW
1883 Phi-a	97	429	98	108	23	9	1	53	21	....	....	....	.252	.287	.354	.641	97	-3	45	3.90	-1	*0-93(0-0-93)/3-3,2-2	15	-0.5
1884 Phi-a	108	484	94	131	18	12	1	0	10	....	....	....	.271	.287	.364	.651	104	0	52	4.03	11	*0-108(0-0-108)/P-2,1-1	13	0.1
1885 Phi-a	29	119	17	25	1	1	0	14	9	....	....	....	.210	.271	.235	.507	58	-6	8	2.24	4	0-29(0-0-29)/P-1	2	-0.1
Pro-N	25	81	8	13	1	0	0	8	11	17	....	....	.160	.261	.173	.434	44	-4	4	1.49	3	0-25(0-4-22)/P-1	1	-0.3
Total 7	532	2243	386	549	91	37	3	196	97	69	....	....	.245	.277	.323	.600	89	-27	207	3.36	7	0-479/P-38,1-17,2-9,3-3	54	-2.0

• KNIGHT, Ray Charles Ray Knight b: 12/28/1952, Albany, GA BR/TR, 6'1", 190 lbs. Deb: 9/10/1974 M/C Career OF: 9-0-1

YEAR TM-L	G	AB	R	H	2B	3B	HR	RBI	BB	SO	SB	CS	AVG	OBP	SLG	OPS	OPS+	BR/A	RC	RC/G	FR	G/POS	WS	TPW
1974 Cin-N	14	11	1	2	1	0	0	2	1	2	0	0	.182	.250	.273	.523	47	-1	1	1.47	-1	3-14	0	-0.2
1977 Cin-N	80	92	8	24	5	1	1	13	9	16	1	1	.261	.327	.370	.696	85	-2	12	4.45	-4	3-37,2-17/O-5(5-0-0),S-3	2	-0.5
1978 Cin-N	83	65	7	13	3	0	1	4	3	13	0	0	.200	.235	.292	.528	47	-5	3	1.68	-6	3-60/2-4,O-3(2-0-1),1-1,S	1	-1.1
1979*Cin-N	150	551	64	175	37	4	10	79	38	57	4	4	.318	.365	.454	.819	121	15	85	5.58	-10	*3-149	20	0.3
1980 Cin-N★	162	618	71	163	39	7	14	78	36	62	1	2	.264	.309	.417	.726	101	-3	72	3.97	-5	*3-162	16	-1.0
1981 Cin-N	106	386	43	100	23	1	6	34	33	51	2	4	.259	.324	.370	.694	95	-4	42	3.60	-6	*3-105	10	-1.2
1982 Hou-N★	158	609	72	179	36	6	6	70	48	58	2	5	.294	.350	.402	.753	119	13	83	4.80	2	1-96,3-67	20	0.8
1983 Hou-N	145	507	43	154	36	4	9	70	42	62	0	3	.304	.362	.444	.805	130	18	77	5.36	-5	*1-143	18	0.5
1984 Hou-N	88	278	15	62	10	0	2	29	14	30	0	3	.223	.263	.281	.543	57	-18	20	2.35	-1	3-54,1-24	2	-2.2
NY-N	27	93	13	26	4	0	1	6	7	13	0	0	.280	.337	.355	.691	96	-1	11	4.52	-1	3-27/1-3	3	-0.2
Yr.	115	371	28	88	14	0	3	35	21	43	0	3	.237	.282	.299	.581	67	-19	31	2.85	-2	3-81,1-27	5	-2.4
1985 NY-N	90	271	22	59	12	0	6	36	13	32	1	1	.218	.256	.328	.585	64	-14	18	2.08	-6	3-73/2-2,1-1	2	-2.2
1986*NY-N	137	486	51	145	24	2	11	76	40	63	2	1	.298	.357	.424	.780	118	11	70	5.07	-7	*3-132/1-1	17	0.2
1987 Bal-A	150	563	46	144	24	0	14	65	39	90	0	0	.256	.311	.373	.684	82	-15	63	3.90	12	*3-130,D-14/1-6	11	-0.5
1988 Det-A	105	299	34	65	12	2	3	33	20	30	1	1	.217	.273	.301	.574	63	-15	23	2.44	-3	1-64,D-25,3-11/O-2(2-0-0)	1	-2.3
Total 13	1495	4829	490	1311	266	27	84	595	343	579	14	25	.271	.325	.390	.714	100	-22	579	4.12	-40	*3-1021,1-339/D-39,2-23,O,S	123	-9.6

• KNISELY, Pete Peter Cole Knisely b: 8/11/1887, Waynesburg, PA d: 7/1/1948, Brownsville, PA BR/TR, 5'9", 185 lbs. Deb: 9/4/1912 Career OF: 18-23-22

YEAR TM-L	G	AB	R	H	2B	3B	HR	RBI	BB	SO	SB	CS	AVG	OBP	SLG	OPS	OPS+	BR/A	RC	RC/G	FR	G/POS	WS	TPW
1912 Cin-N	21	67	10	22	7	3	0	7	4	5	3	....	.328	.375	.522	.897	149	4	14	7.74	0	O-13(0-13-0)/2-3,S-1	4	0.3
1913 Chi-N	2	2	0	0	0	0	0	0	0	1	0	....	.000	.000	.000	.000	-100	-0	0	.00	0	....	0	-0.1
1914 Chi-N	37	69	5	9	0	1	0	5	5	6	0	....	.130	.200	.159	.359	7	-8	2	.91	2	O-17(10-1-6)	1	-0.7
1915 Chi-N	64	134	12	33	9	0	0	17	15	18	1	2	.246	.331	.313	.645	95	-1	14	3.55	-1	O-33(8-9-16)/2-9	4	-0.4
Total 4	124	272	27	64	16	4	0	29	24	30	4	2	.235	.307	.324	.630	85	-5	30	3.66	1	/O-63,2-12,S-1	9	-0.8

• KNOBLAUCH, Chuck Edward Charles Knoblauch b: 7/7/1968, Houston, TX BR/TR, 5'9", 181 lbs. Deb: 4/9/1991 Career OF: 182-1-0

YEAR TM-L	G	AB	R	H	2B	3B	HR	RBI	BB	SO	SB	CS	AVG	OBP	SLG	OPS	OPS+	BR/A	RC	RC/G	FR	G/POS	WS	TPW
1991*Min-A	151	565	78	159	24	6	1	50	59	40	25	5	.281	.354	.350	.704	91	-2	76	4.83	5	*2-148/S-2	20	0.7
1992 Min-A★	155	600	104	178	19	6	2	56	88	60	34	13	.297	.391	.358	.749	108	13	93	5.51	-14	*2-154/D-1,S-1	23	0.3
1993 Min-A	153	602	82	167	27	4	2	41	65	44	29	11	.277	.357	.346	.702	89	-5	79	4.57	-11	*2-148/S-6,O-1	16	-0.8
1994 Min-A★	109	445	85	139	**45**	3	5	51	41	56	35	6	.312	.383	.461	.844	116	16	81	6.70	-20	*2-109/S-1	20	0.2
1995 Min-A	136	538	107	179	34	8	11	63	78	95	46	18	.333	.427	.487	.914	137	35	115	7.87	-1	*2-136/S-2	27	3.8
1996 Min-A★	153	578	140	197	35	**14**	13	72	98	74	45	14	.341	.452	.517	.969	142	48	147	9.69	-2	*2-151/D-2	32	4.8
1997 Min-A★	156	611	117	178	26	10	9	58	84	84	62	10	.291	.392	.411	.803	108	21	112	6.59	-14	*2-154/D-1,S-1	23	1.4
1998*NY-A	150	603	117	160	25	4	17	64	76	70	31	12	.265	.364	.405	.769	104	7	94	5.31	8	*2-149/D-1	22	2.1
1999*NY-A	150	603	120	176	36	4	18	68	83	57	28	9	.292	.396	.454	.850	118	22	118	7.07	-8	*2-150	25	2.0
2000*NY-A	102	400	75	113	22	2	5	26	46	45	15	7	.283	.368	.385	.753	92	-3	60	5.33	-5	2-82,D-20	10	-0.6
2001*NY-A	137	521	66	130	20	3	9	44	58	73	38	9	.250	.341	.351	.692	82	-8	69	4.44	-1	*O-108(108-0-0),D-24	11	-1.5
2002 KC-A	80	300	41	63	9	0	6	22	28	32	19	3	.210	.286	.300	.586	50	-19	28	3.09	0	O-74(74-0-0)/D-2	2	-2.1
Total 12	1632	6366	1132	1839	322	64	98	615	804	730	407	117	.289	.381	.406	.786	106	125	1072	5.99	-63	*2-1381,O-183/D-51,S-13	231	10.2

• KNODE, Mike Kenneth Thomson Knode b: 11/8/1895, Westminster, MD d: 12/20/1980, South Bend, IN BR/TR, 5'10", 160 lbs. Deb: 6/28/1920

YEAR TM-L	G	AB	R	H	2B	3B	HR	RBI	BB	SO	SB	CS	AVG	OBP	SLG	OPS	OPS+	BR/A	RC	RC/G	FR	G/POS	WS	TPW
1920 StL-N	42	65	11	15	1	1	0	12	5	6	0	1	.231	.306	.277	.582	70	-2	6	2.77	-5	/O-9(2-0-7),2-4,3-2,S-2	0	-0.9

• KNODE, Ray Robert Troxell "Bob" Knode b: 1/28/1901, Westminster, MD d: 4/13/1982, Battle Creek, MI BL/TL, 5'10", 160 lbs. Deb: 6/30/1923

YEAR TM-L	G	AB	R	H	2B	3B	HR	RBI	BB	SO	SB	CS	AVG	OBP	SLG	OPS	OPS+	BR/A	RC	RC/G	FR	G/POS	WS	TPW
1923 Cle-A	22	38	7	11	0	0	2	4	2	4	1	0	.289	.325	.447	.772	102	0	6	4.73	-1	1-21	1	-0.1
1924 Cle-A	11	37	6	9	1	0	0	4	3	0	2	1	.243	.300	.270	.570	47	-3	3	2.85	0	1-10	0	-0.3
1925 Cle-A	45	108	13	27	5	0	0	11	10	4	3	3	.250	.314	.296	.610	55	-8	10	3.09	0	1-34	1	-0.9
1926 Cle-A	31	24	6	8	1	1	0	4	3	4	0	0	.333	.407	.458	.866	124	1	5	7.63	0	1-11	1	0.1
Total 4	109	207	32	55	7	1	2	23	18	12	6	4	.266	.324	.338	.663	71	-9	24	3.81	-1	/1-76	3	-1.3

• KNOLL, Punch Charles Elmer Knoll b: 10/7/1881, Evansville, IN d: 2/8/1960, Evansville, IN BR/TR, 5'7.5", 170 lbs. Deb: 4/27/1905

YEAR TM-L	G	AB	R	H	2B	3B	HR	RBI	BB	SO	SB	CS	AVG	OBP	SLG	OPS	OPS+	BR/A	RC	RC/G	FR	G/POS	WS	TPW
1905 Was-A	79	244	24	52	10	5	0	29	9	....	3	....	.213	.247	.295	.542	75	-8	20	2.63	-1	O-63(10-0-53)/C-5,1-2	3	-1.3

• KNOOP, Bobby Robert Frank Knoop b: 10/18/1938, Sioux City, IA BR/TR, 6'1", 170 lbs. Deb: 4/13/1964 C

YEAR TM-L	G	AB	R	H	2B	3B	HR	RBI	BB	SO	SB	CS	AVG	OBP	SLG	OPS	OPS+	BR/A	RC	RC/G	FR	G/POS	WS	TPW
1964 LA-A	162	486	42	105	8	1	7	38	46	109	3	2	.216	.291	.280	.570	66	-22	39	2.55	29	*2-161	11	2.2
1965 Cal-A	142	465	47	125	24	4	7	43	31	101	3	2	.269	.315	.383	.697	99	-2	56	4.24	9	*2-142	16	2.1
1966 Cal-A★	161	590	54	137	18	**11**	17	72	43	144	1	5	.232	.285	.386	.672	94	-8	61	3.39	15	*2-161	18	2.3
1967 Cal-A	159	511	51	125	18	5	9	38	44	136	2	2	.245	.306	.352	.658	98	-2	54	3.61	7	*2-159	18	2.1
1968 Cal-A	152	494	48	123	20	4	3	39	35	128	3	2	.249	.303	.324	.627	93	-5	47	3.24	18	*2-151	15	2.9
1969 Cal-A	27	71	5	14	1	0	1	6	13	16	1	3	.197	.321	.254	.575	66	-4	6	2.46	-2	2-27	1	-0.4
Chi-A	104	345	34	79	14	1	6	41	35	68	2	0	.229	.304	.328	.631	73	-12	34	3.25	1	*2-104	8	-0.4
Yr.	131	416	39	93	15	1	7	47	48	84	3	3	.224	.307	.315	.622	72	-16	40	3.11	0	*2-131	9	-0.8
1970 Chi-A	130	402	34	92	13	2	5	36	34	79	0	1	.229	.292	.308	.601	63	-20	37	3.06	-1	*2-126	6	-1.4
1971 KC-A	72	161	14	33	8	1	1	11	15	36	1	0	.205	.273	.286	.558	59	-8	12	2.38	-5	2-52/3-1	2	-1.1
1972 KC-A	44	97	8	23	5	0	0	7	9	16	0	0	.237	.302	.289	.591	77	-3	8	2.61	-3	2-33/3-4	2	-0.4
Total 9	1153	3622	337	856	129	29	56	331	305	833	16	17	.236	.298	.334	.632	83	-86	353	3.25	70	*2-1116/3-5	97	7.8

• KNORR, Randy Randy Duane Knorr b: 11/12/1968, San Gabriel, CA BR/TR, 6'2", 215 lbs. Deb: 9/5/1991

YEAR TM-L	G	AB	R	H	2B	3B	HR	RBI	BB	SO	SB	CS	AVG	OBP	SLG	OPS	OPS+	BR/A	RC	RC/G	FR	G/POS	WS	TPW
1991 Tor-A	3	1	0	0	0	0	0	0	1	1	0	0	.000	.500	.000	.500	49	0	0	3.51	0	/C-3	0	0.0
1992 Tor-A	8	19	1	5	0	0	1	2	1	5	0	0	.263	.300	.421	.721	96	-0	2	4.63	0	/C-8	0	0.0
1993*Tor-A	39	101	11	25	3	2	4	20	9	29	0	0	.248	.309	.436	.745	97	-1	14	4.57	2	C-39	4	0.3
1994 Tor-A	40	124	20	30	2	0	7	19	10	35	0	0	.242	.304	.427	.731	86	-3	14	3.73	1	C-40	2	0.0
1995 Tor-A	45	132	18	28	8	0	3	16	11	28	0	0	.212	.273	.341	.614	59	-8	11	2.80	-1	C-45	1	-0.6
1996 Hou-N	37	87	7	17	5	0	1	7	5	18	0	1	.195	.247	.287	.535	44	-8	6	2.19	1	C-33	2	-0.5
1997 Hou-N	4	8	1	3	0	0	1	1	0	2	0	0	.375	.375	.750	1.125	193	1	2	12.15	1	/C-3,1-2	0	0.1
1998 Fla-N	15	49	4	10	4	1	2	11	1	10	0	0	.204	.220	.449	.669	73	-2	5	3.32	0	C-15	1	-0.1
1999 Hou-N	13	30	2	5	1	0	0	0	1	8	0	0	.167	.194	.200	.394		-5	1	1.05	0	C-11	0	-0.4
2000 Tex-A	15	34	5	10	2	0	2	2	0	3	0	0	.294	.294	.529	.824	101	-0	5	5.29	-1	C-15	1	0.0
2001 Mon-N	34	91	13	20	2	0	3	10	8	22	0	0	.220	.290	.341	.631	61	-5	8	2.93	-4	C-27	1	-0.8
Total 11	253	676	82	153	27	3	24	88	47	161	0	1	.226	.280	.382	.661	71	-32	69	3.37	-1	C-239/1-2	12	-1.9

• KNOTHE, Fritz Wilfred Edgar Knothe b: 5/1/1903, Passaic, NJ d: 3/27/1963, Passaic, NJ BR/TR, 5'10.5", 180 lbs. Deb: 4/12/1932

YEAR TM-L	G	AB	R	H	2B	3B	HR	RBI	BB	SO	SB	CS	AVG	OBP	SLG	OPS	OPS+	BR/A	RC	RC/G	FR	G/POS	WS	TPW
1932 Bos-N	89	344	45	82	19	1	1	36	39	37	5	....	.238	.318	.308	.626	72	-12	36	3.54	-2	3-87	7	-1.1
1933 Bos-N	44	158	15	36	5	2	1	6	13	25	1	....	.228	.291	.304	.594	76	-5	15	3.16	0	3-33/S-9	4	-0.3
Phi-N	41	113	10	17	2	0	0	11	6	19	2	....	.150	.193	.168	.361	3	-14	3	.91	8	3-32/2-4	2	-0.5
Yr.	85	271	25	53	7	2	1	17	19	44	3	....	.196	.251	.247	.498	47	-19	18	2.17	8	3-65/S-9,2-4	6	-0.9
Total 2	174	615	70	135	26	3	2	53	58	81	8	....	.220	.289	.281	.570	61	-31	55	2.90	6	3-152/S-9,2-4	13	-1.9

• KNOTHE, George George Bertram Knothe b: 1/12/1898, Bayonne, NJ d: 7/3/1981, Toms River, NJ BR/TR, 5'10", 165 lbs. Deb: 4/25/1932

YEAR TM-L	G	AB	R	H	2B	3B	HR	RBI	BB	SO	SB	CS	AVG	OBP	SLG	OPS	OPS+	BR/A	RC	RC/G	FR	G/POS	WS	TPW
1932 Phi-N	6	12	2	1	1	0	0	0	0	0	0	....	.083	.083	.167	.250	-31	-2	0	.38	0	/2-5	0	-0.2

• KNOTTS, Joe Joseph Steven Knotts b: 3/3/1884, Greensboro, PA d: 9/15/1950, Philadelphia, PA BR/TR, 5'9" Deb: 9/18/1907

YEAR TM-L	G	AB	R	H	2B	3B	HR	RBI	BB	SO	SB	CS	AVG	OBP	SLG	OPS	OPS+	BR/A	RC	RC/G	FR	G/POS	WS	TPW
1907 Bos-N	3	8	0	0	0	0	0	0	1	....	0	....	.000	.111	.000	.111	-65	-2	0	.22	0	/C-3	0	-0.1

YEAR TM-L	G	AB	R	H	2B	3B	HR	RBI	BB	SO	SB	CS	AVG	OBP	SLG	OPS	OPS+	BR/A	RC	RC/G	FR	G/POS	WS	TPW
• KNOWDELL, Jake	Jacob Augustus Knowdell b: 7/27/1840, Brooklyn, NY, 5'7.5", 148 lbs. Deb: 6/20/1874 NA OF: 4-3-1																							
1874 Atl-n	24	86	8	12	1	1	0	3	1	3	1	0	.140	.149	.174	.324	4	-7	2	.99	0	C-21/0-4(4-0-0)	....	-0.5
1875 Atl-n	43	163	17	32	2	0	0	9	1	3	0	1	.196	.201	.209	.410	49	-7	7	1.57	-8	C-33,S-11/0-4(0-3-1),2-1	....	-1.2
1878 Mil-N	4	14	2	3	1	0	0	2	0	3	....	....	.214	.214	.286	.500	59	-1	1	2.20	-1	/C-2,0-1,S-1	0	-0.2
Total 2 n	67	249	25	44	3	1	0	12	2	6	1	1	.177	.183	.197	.380	33	-14	9	1.36	-8	/C-54,S-11,0-8,2-1	....	-1.7
• KNOWLES, Jimmy	James "Darby" Knowles b: 9/1856, Toronto, Canada d: 2/11/1912, Jersey City, NJ, 5'9", 160 lbs. Deb: 5/2/1884 U																							
1884 Pit-a	46	182	19	42	5	7	0	0	5	....	....	....	.231	.259	.335	.594	91	-2	16	3.18	-1	1-46	3	-0.7
Bro-a	41	153	19	36	5	1	1	0	3	....	....	....	.235	.255	.301	.555	80	-4	12	2.82	1	1-30,3-11	2	-0.4
Yr.	87	335	38	78	10	8	1	0	8	....	....	....	.233	.257	.319	.577	86	-6	28	3.02	0	*1-76,3-11	5	-1.1
1886 Was-N	115	443	43	94	16	11	3	35	15	73	20	....	.212	.238	.318	.556	72	-15	39	3.04	12	2-62,3-53	6	0.1
1887 NY-a	16	61	12	16	1	1	0	6	1	....	6	....	.262	.262	.300	.562	59	-3	6	3.87	-2	2-16/3-1	1	-0.4
1890 Roc-a	123	491	83	138	12	8	5	84	59	....	55	....	.281	.359	.369	.728	124	16	87	6.53	9	*3-123	21	2.5
1892 NY-N	16	59	9	9	1	0	0	7	6	8	2	....	.153	.231	.169	.400	22	-5	3	1.53	-3	3-15/S-1	0	-0.7
Total 5	357	1389	185	335	40	28	9	132	89	81	83	....	.241	.288	.329	.618	92	-13	164	4.17	17	3-203/2-78,1-76,S-1	33	0.4
• KNOX, Andy	Andrew Jackson "Dasher" Knox b: 1/6/1864, Philadelphia, PA d: 9/14/1940, Philadelphia, PA BR/TR Deb: 9/19/1890																							
1890 Phi-a	21	75	6	19	3	0	0	8	9	....	5	....	.253	.333	.293	.627	87	-1	9	4.37	-2	1-21	2	-0.4
• KNOX, Cliff	Clifford Hiram "Bud" Knox b: 1/7/1902, Coalville, IA d: 9/24/1965, Oskaloosa, IA BB/TR, 5'11.5", 178 lbs. Deb: 7/1/1924																							
1924 Pit-N	6	18	1	4	0	0	0	2	2	0	0	0	.222	.300	.222	.522	41	-1	1	2.40	2	/C-6	0	0.1
• KNOX, John	John Clinton Knox b: 7/26/1948, Newark, NJ BL/TR, 6', 170 lbs. Deb: 8/1/1972																							
1972*Det-A	14	13	1	1	1	0	0	0	1	2	0	0	.077	.143	.154	.297	-11	-2	0	.73	1	/2-4	0	-0.1
1973 Det-A	12	32	1	9	1	0	0	3	3	3	1	1	.281	.343	.313	.655	80	-1	4	3.81	-1	/2-9	1	-0.1
1974 Det-A	55	88	11	27	1	1	0	6	6	13	5	4	.307	.351	.341	.692	96	-1	9	3.52	-4	2-33/D-2,3-1	2	-0.3
1975 Det-A	43	86	8	23	1	0	0	2	10	9	1	2	.267	.344	.279	.623	74	-3	8	2.98	-3	2-23/3-3,D-3	1	-0.4
Total 4	124	219	21	60	4	1	0	11	20	27	7	7	.274	.335	.301	.636	79	-7	21	3.16	-6	/2-69,D-5,3-4	4	-0.9
• KOBACK, Nick	Nicholas Nicholie Koback b: 7/19/1935, Hartford, CT BR/TR, 6', 187 lbs. Deb: 7/29/1953																							
1953 Pit-N	7	16	1	2	0	1	0	0	1	4	0	0	.125	.176	.250	.426	10	-2	0	.43	0	/C-6	0	-0.2
1954 Pit-N	4	10	0	0	0	0	0	0	0	8	0	0	.000	.000	.000	.000	-102	-3	0	.00	0	/C-4	0	-0.3
1955 Pit-N	5	7	0	2	0	0	0	0	0	1	0	0	.286	.286	.286	.571	53	-0	1	3.09	0	/C-2	0	0.0
Total 3	16	33	1	4	0	1	0	0	1	13	0	0	.121	.147	.182	.329	-13	-6	1	.71	0	/C-12	0	-0.5
• KOCH, Barney	Barnett Koch b: 3/23/1923, Campbell, NE d: 6/6/1987, Tacoma, WA BR/TR, 5'8", 140 lbs. Deb: 7/23/1944																							
1944 Bro-N	33	96	11	21	2	0	0	1	3	9	0	....	.219	.242	.240	.482	37	-8	6	1.96	-3	2-29/S-1	0	-1.0
• KOCHER, Brad	Bradley Wilson Kocher b: 1/16/1888, White Haven, PA d: 1/13/1965, White Haven, PA BR/TR, 5'11", 188 lbs. Deb: 4/24/1912																							
1912 Det-A	29	63	5	13	3	1	0	9	2	....	0	....	.206	.231	.286	.516	49	-5	4	2.05	-4	C-24	0	-0.7
1915 NY-N	4	11	3	5	0	1	0	2	0	1	0	....	.455	.455	.636	1.091	243	2	3	12.38	0	/C-3	1	0.2
1916 NY-N	34	65	1	7	2	0	0	1	2	10	0	....	.108	.134	.138	.273	-17	-9	1	.54	-2	C-30	1	-1.1
Total 3	67	139	9	25	5	2	0	12	4	11	0	....	.180	.203	.245	.447	35	-12	9	1.92	-6	/C-57	2	-1.6
• KOEGEL, Pete	Peter John Koegel b: 7/31/1947, Mineola, NY BR/TR, 6'6.5", 230 lbs. Deb: 9/1/1970 Career OF: 2-0-2																							
1970 Mil-A	7	8	2	2	0	0	1	1	1	3	0	0	.250	.333	.625	.958	157	1	2	7.89	-0	/0-1	0	0.1
1971 Mil-A	2	3	0	0	0	0	0	0	2	2	0	0	.000	.400	.000	.400	22	-0	0	1.87	0	/1-1	0	0.0
Phi-N	12	26	1	6	1	0	0	3	2	7	0	0	.231	.286	.269	.555	58	-1	2	2.42	1	/C-7,0-1	0	-0.1
1972 Phi-N	41	49	3	7	2	0	0	1	6	16	0	0	.143	.236	.184	.420	20	-5	2	1.45	-1	/1-8,C-5,3-4,0-2(0-0-2)	0	-0.7
Total 3	62	86	6	15	3	0	1	5	11	28	0	0	.174	.268	.244	.512	44	-6	6	2.27	-1	/C-12,1-9,3-4,0-4	0	-0.7
• KOEHLER, Ben	Bernard James Koehler b: 1/26/1877, Schoerndorn, Germany d: 5/21/1961, South Bend, IN BR/TR, 5'10.5", 175 lbs. Deb: 4/23/1905 Career OF: 1-158-17																							
1905 StL-A	142	536	55	127	14	6	2	47	32	....	22	....	.237	.285	.297	.582	89	-7	54	3.42	10	*0-124(0-124-0),1-12/2-6	12	-0.4
1906 StL-A	66	186	27	41	1	1	0	15	24	....	9	....	.220	.322	.237	.559	79	-3	18	3.23	-2	0-52(1-34-17)/2-7,3-1,S-1	4	-0.7
Total 2	208	722	82	168	15	7	2	62	56	....	31	....	.233	.295	.281	.576	86	-10	73	3.37	8	0-176/2-13,1-12,3-1,S-1	16	-1.1
• KOEHLER, Pip	Horace Levering Koehler b: 1/16/1902, Gilbert, PA d: 12/8/1986, Tacoma, WA BR/TR, 5'10", 165 lbs. Deb: 4/22/1925																							
1925 NY-N	12	2	1	0	0	0	0	0	0	1	0	0	.000	.000	.000	.000	-104	-1	0	.00	0	/0-3(1-0-2)	0	-0.1
• KOELLING, Brian	Brian Wayne Koelling b: 6/11/1969, Cincinnati, OH BR/TR, 6'1", 185 lbs. Deb: 8/21/1993																							
1993 Cin-N	7	15	2	1	0	0	0	0	0	2	0	0	.067	.125	.067	.192	-47	-3	0	.30	0	/2-3,S-2	0	-0.3
• KOENECKE, Len	Leonard George Koenecke b: 1/18/1904, Baraboo, WI d: 9/17/1935, Toronto, Canada BL/TR, 5'11", 180 lbs. Deb: 4/12/1932 Career OF: 51-189-7																							
1932 NY-N	42	137	33	35	5	0	4	14	11	13	3	....	.255	.320	.380	.700	89	-2	17	4.27	-4	0-35(35-0-0)	3	-0.8
1934 Bro-N	123	460	79	147	31	7	14	73	70	38	8	....	.320	.411	.509	.919	152	36	103	8.60	2	*0-121(0-121-0)	23	3.4
1935 Bro-N	100	325	43	92	13	2	4	27	43	45	0	....	.283	.369	.372	.741	102	3	49	5.44	-4	0-91(16-68-7)	10	-0.5
Total 3	265	922	155	274	49	9	22	114	124	96	11	....	.297	.383	.441	.824	125	37	169	6.78	-7	0-247	36	2.2
• KOENIG, Mark	Mark Anthony Koenig b: 7/19/1904, San Francisco, CA d: 4/22/1993, Willows, CA BB/TR, 6', 180 lbs. Deb: 9/8/1925 ♦																							
1925 NY-A	28	110	14	23	6	1	0	4	5	4	0	1	.209	.243	.282	.525	34	-12	7	2.17	0	S-28	1	-0.8
1926*NY-A	147	617	93	167	26	8	5	62	43	37	4	3	.271	.319	.363	.682	79	-20	72	4.09	10	*S-141	16	0.5
1927*NY-A	123	526	99	150	20	11	3	62	25	21	3	2	.285	.320	.382	.702	84	-14	64	4.33	16	*S-122	15	1.5
1928*NY-A	132	533	89	170	19	10	4	63	32	19	3	5	.319	.360	.415	.774	106	3	78	5.48	-7	*S-125	20	1.0
1929 NY-A	116	373	44	109	27	5	3	41	23	17	1	1	.292	.335	.416	.751	98	-1	52	5.11	0	S-61,3-37/2-1	11	0.6
1930 NY-A	21	74	9	17	5	0	0	9	6	5	0	0	.230	.296	.297	.594	53	-5	7	3.02	0	S-19	1	-0.2
Det-A	76	267	37	64	9	2	1	16	20	15	2	0	.240	.295	.300	.595	50	-19	25	3.10	-2	S-70/3-2,P-2,0-1	4	-1.8
Yr.	97	341	46	81	14	2	1	25	26	20	2	0	.238	.295	.299	.595	51	-24	32	3.08	-2	S-89/3-2,P-2,0-1	5	-2.0
1931 Det-A	106	364	33	92	24	4	1	39	14	12	8	2	.253	.282	.349	.631	63	-18	36	3.46	-17	2-55,S-35/P-3	4	-2.8
1932*Chi-N	33	102	15	36	5	1	3	11	3	5	0	....	.353	.377	.510	.887	137	5	19	7.67	4	S-31	6	1.1
1933 Chi-N	80	218	32	62	12	1	3	25	15	9	5	....	.284	.330	.390	.720	105	1	28	4.41	1	3-37,S-26/2-2	8	0.5
1934 Cin-N	151	633	60	172	26	6	1	67	15	24	5	....	.272	.289	.336	.625	68	-29	59	3.24	-9	3-64,S-58,2-26/1-4	8	-2.9
1935 NY-N	107	396	40	112	12	0	3	37	13	18	0	....	.283	.306	.336	.641	73	-15	39	3.44	4	2-64,S-21,3-15	7	-0.5
1936*NY-N	42	58	7	16	4	0	1	7	8	4	0	....	.276	.373	.397	.770	108	1	10	6.10	-1	S-10/2-8,3-3	2	0.1
Total 12	1162	4271	572	1190	195	49	28	443	222	190	31	14	.279	.316	.367	.683	81	-123	497	4.10	-1	S-747,3-158,2-156/P-5,1-4,0	103	-3.9
• KOHLER, Henry	Henry C. Kohler b: 5/5/1852, Baltimore, MD d: 8/27/1934, Baltimore, MD Deb: 7/12/1871 U																							
1871 Kek-n	3	12	0	2	1	0	0	1	0	0	0	0	.167	.167	.250	.417	17	-1	1	1.61	0	/1-2,C-2,3-1	....	-0.1
1873 Mar-n	6	25	2	3	0	0	0	1	0	1	0	0	.120	.120	.120	.240	-37	-3	0	.51	-4	/3-6,1-1,C-1,0-1	....	-0.5
1874 Bal-n	2	4	0	0	0	0	0	0	0	0	0	0	.000	.000	.000	.000	-101	-1	0	.00	-1	/1-1	....	-0.1
Total 3 n	11	41	2	5	1	0	0	2	0	1	0	0	.122	.122	.146	.268	-27	-5	1	.76	-5	/3-7,1-4,C-3,0-1	....	-0.7
• KOKOS, Dick	Richard Jerome Kokos b: 2/28/1928, Chicago, IL d: 4/9/1986, Chicago, IL BL/TL, 5'8.5", 170 lbs. Deb: 7/8/1948 Career OF: 143-0-281																							
1948 StL-A	71	258	40	77	15	3	4	40	28	32	4	3	.298	.374	.426	.800	110	3	44	6.39	1	0-71(0-0-71)	7	0.2
1949 StL-A	143	501	80	131	28	1	23	77	66	91	3	5	.261	.351	.459	.810	109	3	86	6.06	-2	*0-138(0-0-138)	15	-0.3
1950 StL-A	143	490	77	128	27	5	18	67	88	73	8	8	.261	.375	.447	.822	106	3	87	6.11	-2	*0-127(81-0-50)	15	-0.6
1953 StL-A	107	299	41	72	12	0	13	38	56	53	0	5	.241	.361	.411	.772	106	2	47	5.36	-3	0-83(61-0-22)	7	-0.6
1954 Bal-A	11	10	1	2	0	0	1	1	4	3	0	0	.200	.429	.500	.929	166	1	2	6.47	0	/0-1	0	0.1
Total 5	475	1558	239	410	82	9	59	223	242	252	15	21	.263	.365	.441	.806	108	13	266	5.99	-6	0-420	44	-1.1

YEAR TM-L	G	AB	R	H	2B	3B	HR	RBI	BB	SO	SB	CS	AVG	OBP	SLG	OPS	OPS+	BR/A	RC	RC/G	FR	G/POS	WS	TPW
• KOLB, Gary	Gary Alan Kolb b: 3/13/1940, Rock Falls, IL BL/TR, 6', 195 lbs. Deb: 9/7/1960 Career OF: 57-18-77																							
1960 StL-N	9	3	1	0	0	0	0	0	0	0	0	0	.000	.000	.000	.000	-92	-1	0	.00	0	/O-2(1-1-1)	0	-0.1
1962 StL-N	6	14	1	5	0	0	0	0	1	3	0	0	.357	.400	.357	.757	96	-0	2	4.73	0	/O-6(1-0-5)	0	-0.1
1963 StL-N	75	96	23	26	1	5	3	10	22	26	2	1	.271	.407	.479	.886	141	6	21	7.62	-1	O-58(25-0-35)/3-1,C-1	5	0.4
1964 Mil-N	36	64	7	12	1	0	0	2	6	10	3	2	.188	.257	.203	.460	31	-6	4	1.81	-2	O-14(5-3-7)/3-7,2-6,C-2	0	-0.8
1965 Mil-N	24	27	3	7	0	0	0	1	1	6	0	0	.259	.286	.259	.545	54	-2	2	1.91	0	O-13(9-3-2)	0	-0.2
NY-N	40	90	8	15	2	0	1	7	3	28	3	0	.167	.194	.222	.416	17	-9	4	1.35	1	O-29(10-10-9)/1-1,3-1	1	-1.0
Yr.	64	117	11	22	2	0	1	8	4	34	3	0	.188	.215	.231	.446	26	-11	5	1.47	1	O-42(19-13-11)/1-1,3-1	1	-1.2
1968 Pit-N	74	119	16	26	4	1	2	6	11	17	2	1	.218	.285	.319	.604	82	-2	11	3.01	0	O-25(6-1-18),C-10/3-4,2-1	2	-0.4
1969 Pit-N	29	37	4	3	1	0	0	3	2	14	0	0	.081	.128	.108	.236	-34	-7	1	.46	0	/C-7	0	-0.7
Total 7	293	450	63	94	9	6	6	29	46	104	10	4	.209	.282	.296	.578	66	-20	43	3.11	-2	O-147/C-20,3-13,2-7,1-1	8	-2.8
• KOLLOWAY, Don	Donald Martin "Butch,Cab" Kolloway b: 8/4/1918, Posen, IL d: 6/30/1994, Blue Island, IL BR/TR, 6'3", 200 lbs. Deb: 9/16/1940																							
1940 Chi-A	10	40	5	9	1	0	0	3	0	3	1	0	.225	.225	.250	.475	23	-4	2	1.82	-1	2-10	0	-0.4
1941 Chi-A	71	280	33	76	8	3	3	24	6	12	11	4	.271	.292	.354	.645	71	-12	27	3.38	-4	2-62/1-4	5	-1.2
1942 Chi-A	147	601	72	164	**40**	4	3	60	30	39	16	14	.273	.311	.368	.678	92	-11	66	3.74	-6	*2-116,1-33	15	-1.3
1943 Chi-A	85	348	29	75	14	4	1	33	9	30	11	7	.216	.235	.287	.523	53	-23	22	2.03	-1	2-85	3	-2.1
1946 Chi-A	123	482	45	135	23	4	3	53	9	29	14	6	.280	.293	.363	.656	86	-11	52	3.79	1	2-90,3-31	12	-0.5
1947 Chi-A	124	485	49	135	25	4	2	35	17	34	11	4	.278	.303	.359	.662	87	-10	48	3.35	-3	2-99,1-11/3-8	10	-0.8
1948 Chi-A	119	417	60	114	14	4	6	38	18	18	2	4	.273	.303	.369	.673	81	-15	44	3.75	-3	2-83,3-18	7	-1.3
1949 Chi-A	4	4	0	0	0	0	0	0	0	1	0	0	.000	.000	.000	.000	-103	-1	0	.00	-1	/3-2	0	-0.2
Det-A	126	483	71	142	19	3	2	47	49	25	7	7	.294	.361	.358	.720	91	-7	62	4.51	-6	2-62,1-57/3-7	11	-1.2
Yr.	130	487	71	142	19	3	2	47	49	26	7	7	.292	.359	.355	.714	89	-9	62	4.46	-7	2-62,1-57/3-9	11	-1.4
1950 Det-A	125	467	55	135	20	4	6	62	29	28	1	3	.289	.331	.388	.718	81	-16	57	4.35	4	*1-118/2-1	8	-1.5
1951 Det-A	78	212	28	54	7	0	1	17	15	12	2	3	.255	.307	.302	.609	65	-11	19	2.96	5	1-59	2	-0.8
1952 Det-A	65	173	19	42	9	0	2	21	7	19	0	2	.243	.280	.329	.610	69	-9	15	2.83	0	1-32/2-8	1	-0.9
1953 Phi-A	2	1	0	0	0	0	0	0	0	1	0	0	.000	.000	.000	.000	-96	-0	0	.00	0	/3-1	0	-0.1
Total 12	1079	3993	466	1081	180	30	29	393	189	251	76	54	.271	.305	.353	.658	80	-131	413	3.57	-16	2-616,1-314/3-67	74	-12.3
• KOLSETH, Karl	Karl Dickey "Koley" Kolseth b: 12/25/1892, Cambridge, MA d: 5/3/1956, Cumberland, MD BL/TR, 6', 182 lbs. Deb: 9/30/1915																							
1915 Bal-F	6	23	1	6	1	1	0	1	1	0	0	....	.261	.292	.391	.683	93	-0	2	3.75	-2	/1-6	1	-0.2
• KOMMERS, Fred	Frederick Raymond "Bugs" Kommers b: 3/31/1886, Chicago, IL d: 6/14/1943, Chicago, IL BL/TR, 6', 175 lbs. Deb: 6/25/1913 Career OF: 14-77-28																							
1913 Pit-N	40	155	14	36	5	4	0	22	10	29	1	....	.232	.279	.316	.595	73	-6	13	2.80	-5	O-40(0-40-0)	2	-1.4
1914 StL-F	76	244	33	75	9	8	3	41	24	36	7	....	.307	.376	.447	.823	126	9	42	6.12	-3	O-67(3-36-28)	9	0.2
Bal-F	16	42	5	9	1	0	1	1	7	7	0	....	.214	.340	.310	.650	86	-0	4	3.29	-1	O-12(11-1-0)	1	-0.2
Yr.	92	286	38	84	10	8	4	42	31	43	7	....	.294	.371	.427	.797	120	8	47	5.66	-4	O-79(14-37-28)	10	0.0
Total 2	132	441	52	120	15	12	4	64	41	72	8	....	.272	.340	.388	.727	104	2	60	4.61	-10	O-119	12	-1.4
• KOMMINSK, Brad	Brad Lynn Komminsk b: 4/4/1961, Lima, OH BR/TR, 6'2", 205 lbs. Deb: 8/14/1983 Career OF: 74-91-171																							
1983 Atl-N	19	36	2	8	2	0	0	4	5	7	0	0	.222	.317	.278	.595	62	-2	3	3.08	-0	O-13(1-0-12)	0	-0.2
1984 Atl-N	90	301	37	61	10	0	8	36	29	77	18	8	.203	.277	.316	.593	62	-15	27	2.84	-2	O-80(28-2-50)	3	-2.3
1985 Atl-N	106	300	52	68	12	3	4	21	38	71	10	8	.227	.316	.327	.642	75	-11	32	3.47	-6	O-92(28-1-63)	5	-2.3
1986 Atl-N	5	5	1	2	0	0	0	1	0	1	0	1	.400	.400	.400	.800	115	-0	0	2.70	-0	/3-2,O-2(0-0-2)	0	0.0
1987 Mil-A	7	15	0	1	0	0	0	0	1	7	1	0	.067	.125	.067	.192	-46	-3	0	.49	0	/O-5(0-0-5),D-1	0	-0.3
1989 Cle-A	71	198	27	47	8	2	8	33	24	55	8	2	.237	.323	.419	.742	106	2	28	4.67	0	O-68(2-66-2)	9	0.1
1990 SF-N	8	5	2	1	0	0	0	0	1	2	0	0	.200	.333	.200	.533	52	-0	0	2.84	-1	/O-7(2-2-3)	0	-0.1
Bal-A	46	101	18	24	4	0	3	8	14	29	1	1	.238	.342	.366	.708	101	0	13	4.35	1	O-40(6-12-26)/D-2	2	0.0
1991 Oak-A	24	25	1	3	1	0	0	2	2	9	1	0	.120	.185	.160	.345	-4	-3	1	1.15	0	O-22(7-8-8)	0	-0.3
Total 8	376	986	140	215	37	5	23	105	114	258	39	20	.218	.303	.336	.639	76	-32	105	3.46	-8	O-329/D-3,3-2	19	-5.4
• KONERKO, Paul	Paul Henry Konerko b: 3/5/1976, Providence, RI BR/TR, 6'3", 205 lbs. Deb: 9/8/1997																							
1997 LA-N	6	7	0	1	0	0	0	0	1	2	0	0	.143	.250	.143	.393	7	-1	0	.61	0	/1-1,3-1	0	-0.1
1998 LA-N	49	144	14	31	1	0	4	16	10	30	0	1	.215	.276	.306	.581	56	-10	11	2.52	0	1-23,3-11,O-11(11-0-0)	1	-1.1
Cin-N	26	73	7	16	3	0	3	13	6	10	0	0	.219	.288	.384	.671	74	-3	7	2.89	3	/3-9,1-7,O-7(7-0-0),D-3	1	-0.1
Yr.	75	217	21	47	4	0	7	29	16	40	0	1	.217	.280	.332	.611	62	-13	18	2.64	3	1-30,3-20,O-18(18-0-0)/D-3	2	-1.3
1999 Chi-A	142	513	71	151	31	4	24	81	45	68	1	0	.294	.354	.511	.864	117	12	88	6.16	0	1-92,D-54/3-1	14	0.0
2000★Chi-A	143	524	84	156	31	1	21	97	47	72	1	0	.298	.367	.481	.848	111	8	88	6.01	-8	*1-122/3-7,D-7	15	-1.0
2001 Chi-A	156	582	92	164	35	0	32	99	54	89	1	0	.282	.352	.507	.859	118	15	101	6.20	-1	*1-144,D-11	17	0.0
2002 Chi-A★	151	570	81	173	30	0	27	104	44	72	0	0	.304	.363	.498	.861	123	18	100	6.40	-5	*1-140/D-7	17	0.1
2003 Chi-A	137	444	49	104	19	0	18	65	43	50	0	0	.234	.308	.399	.706	85	-10	47	3.42	3	*1-119,D-13	4	-1.7
Total 7	810	2857	398	796	150	5	129	475	250	393	3	1	.279	.344	.470	.815	108	29	442	5.42	-8	1-648/D-95,3-29,O-18	69	-4.0
• KONETCHY, Ed	Edward Joseph "Big Ed" Konetchy b: 9/3/1885, La Crosse, WI d: 5/27/1947, Fort Worth, TX BR/TR, 6'2.5", 195 lbs. Deb: 6/29/1907 Career OF: 2-4-1																							
1907 StL-N	91	331	34	83	11	9	2	30	26	....	13	....	.251	.317	.356	.673	115	5	44	4.38	1	1-91	10	0.5
1908 StL-N	154	545	46	135	19	12	5	50	38	....	16	....	.248	.309	.354	.663	117	9	65	3.88	12	*1-154	18	2.1
1909 StL-N	152	576	88	165	23	14	4	80	65	....	25	....	.286	.366	.396	.762	145	31	92	5.63	7	*1-152	24	3.9
1910 StL-N	144	520	87	157	23	16	3	78	78	59	18	....	.302	.397	.425	.822	145	32	94	6.56	13	*1-144/P-1	27	4.4
1911 StL-N	158	571	90	165	**38**	13	6	88	81	63	27	....	.289	.384	.433	.816	132	26	105	6.42	3	*1-158	26	2.6
1912 StL-N	143	538	81	169	26	13	8	82	62	66	25	....	.314	.389	.455	.844	134	25	105	6.91	2	*1-142/O-1	22	2.4
1913 StL-N	140	504	75	139	18	17	8	68	53	41	27	....	.276	.353	.427	.779	124	16	82	5.47	8	*1-140/P-1	19	2.3
1914 Pit-N	154	563	56	140	23	9	4	51	32	48	20	....	.249	.291	.343	.634	92	-8	61	3.51	8	*1-154	13	-0.2
1915 Pit-F	152	576	79	181	31	18	10	93	41	52	27	....	.314	.363	.483	.846	142	28	106	6.68	8	*1-152	27	3.5
1916 Bos-N	158	566	76	147	29	13	3	70	43	46	13	....	.260	.320	.373	.693	119	12	74	4.39	16	*1-158	26	2.8
1917 Bos-N	130	474	56	129	19	13	2	54	36	40	16	....	.272	.330	.380	.710	124	13	62	4.52	5	*1-129	17	1.8
1918 Bos-N	119	437	33	103	15	5	2	56	32	35	5	....	.236	.291	.307	.598	86	-7	40	2.97	-2	*1-112/O-6(1-4-1),P-1	9	-1.6
1919 Bro-N	132	486	46	145	24	9	1	47	29	39	14	....	.298	.342	.391	.733	117	10	68	4.90	0	*1-132	18	0.8
1920★Bro-N	131	497	62	153	22	12	5	63	33	18	3	2	.308	.352	.431	.783	120	14	75	5.53	-1	*1-130	18	1.2
1921 Bro-N	55	197	25	53	6	5	3	23	19	21	3	3	.269	.336	.396	.732	90	-3	26	4.61	-2	1-54	5	-0.8
Phi-N	72	268	38	86	17	4	8	59	21	17	3	0	.321	.379	.504	.883	122	10	52	7.42	4	1-71	8	0.9
Yr.	127	465	63	139	23	9	11	82	40	38	6	3	.299	.361	.458	.819	108	8	78	6.15	2	*1-125	13	0.1
Total 15	2085	7649	972	2150	344	182	74	992	689	545	255	5	.281	.346	.403	.749	122	213	1152	5.20	82	*1-2073/O-7,P-3	287	26.7
• KONNICK, Mike	Michael Aloysius Konnick b: 1/13/1889, Glen Lyon, PA d: 7/9/1971, Wilkes-Barre, PA BR/TR, 5'9", 180 lbs. Deb: 10/3/1909																							
1909 Cin-N	2	5	0	2	1	0	0	1	0	....	0	....	.400	.400	.600	1.000	211	1	1	7.87	0	/C-2	0	0.1
1910 Cin-N	1	3	0	0	0	0	0	0	1	0	0	....	.000	.250	.000	.250	-27	-0	0	.00	0	/S-1	0	0.0
Total 2	3	8	0	2	1	0	0	1	1	0	0	....	.250	.333	.375	.708	116	0	1	4.50	-0	/C-2,S-1	0	0.0
• KONOPKA, Bruce	Bruno Bruce Konopka b: 9/16/1919, Hammond, IN d: 9/27/1996, Denver, CO BL/TL, 6'2", 190 lbs. Deb: 6/7/1942																							
1942 Phi-A	5	10	2	3	0	0	0	1	1	0	0	0	.300	.364	.300	.664	88	-0	1	4.68	0	/1-3	0	0.0
1943 Phi-A	2	2	0	0	0	0	0	0	0	1	0	0	.000	.000	.000	.000	-101	-0	0	.00	0	....	0	-0.1
1946 Phi-A	38	93	7	22	4	1	0	9	4	8	0	0	.237	.268	.301	.569	59	-5	7	2.56	2	1-20/O-1	0	-0.4
Total 3	45	105	9	25	4	1	0	10	5	9	0	0	.238	.273	.295	.568	59	-6	8	2.67	2	/1-23,O-1	0	-0.5
• KOONCE, Graham	Graham CLinton Koonce b: 5/15/1975, El Cajon, CA BL/TL, 6'4", 225 lbs. Deb: 9/20/2003																							
2003 Oak-A	6	8	0	1	1	0	0	0	0	6	0	0	.125	.125	.250	.375	-4	-1	0	.96	1	/1-5	0	-0.1
• KOONS, Harry	Harry M. Koons b: 1863, Philadelphia, PA BR/TR, 5'8", 174 lbs. Deb: 4/17/1884																							
1884 Alt-U	21	78	8	18	2	1	0	....	2	....	....	....	.231	.250	.282	.532	79	-2	6	2.63	4	3-21/C-1	1	0.3
CP-U	1	3	0	0	0	0	0	....	0	....	....	....	.000	.000	.000	.000	-107	-1	0	.00	0	/3-1	0	-0.1

YEAR TM-L	G	AB	R	H	2B	3B	HR	RBI	BB	SO	SB	CS	AVG	OBP	SLG	OPS	OPS+	BR/A	RC	RC/G	FR	G/POS	WS	TPW
Yr.	22	81	8	18	2	1	0	....	2	....	....	....	.222	.241	.272	.513	72	-2	6	2.51	4	3-22/C-1	1	0.2
• KOPACZ, George — George Felix "Sonny" Kopacz b: 2/26/1941, Chicago, IL BL/TL, 6'1", 195 lbs. Deb: 9/18/1966																								
1966 Atl-N	6	9	1	0	0	0	0	0	1	5	0	0	.000	.100	.000	.100	-68	-2	0	.08	0	/1-2	0	-0.3
1970 Pit-N	10	16	1	3	0	0	0	0	0	5	0	0	.188	.188	.188	.375	1	-2	1	1.20	-1	/1-3	0	-0.3
Total 2	**16**	**25**	**2**	**3**	**0**	**0**	**0**	**0**	**1**	**10**	**0**	**0**	**.120**	**.154**	**.120**	**.274**	**-25**	**-4**	**1**	**.76**	**-1**	**/1-5**	**0**	**-0.6**
• KOPF, Larry — William Lorenz Kopf b: 11/3/1890, Bristol, CT d: 10/15/1986, Hamilton County, OH BB/TR, 5'9", 160 lbs. Deb: 9/2/1913 Career OF: 1-1-0																								
1913 Cle-A	6	10	2	3	1	0	0	1	0	0	0	....	.300	.300	.400	.700	101	-0	1	4.08	1	/2-4,3-1	0	0.1
1914 Phi-A	37	69	8	13	2	2	0	12	8	14	6	....	.188	.300	.275	.575	76	-2	8	3.48	-3	S-13/3-8,2-5	3	-0.4
1915 Phi-A	118	386	39	87	10	2	1	33	41	45	5	9	.225	.314	.269	.584	77	-13	33	2.79	-23	S-74,3-42/2-2	6	-3.1
1916 Cin-N	11	40	2	11	2	0	0	5	1	8	1	....	.275	.293	.325	.618	92	-1	4	3.63	0	S-11	1	0.0
1917 Cin-N	148	573	81	146	19	8	2	26	28	48	17	....	.255	.297	.326	.623	95	-5	59	3.42	-10	*S-145	15	-0.5
1919*Cin-N	135	503	51	136	18	5	0	58	28	27	18	....	.270	.313	.326	.639	95	-4	54	3.74	-17	*S-135	16	-1.2
1920 Cin-N	126	458	56	112	15	6	0	59	35	24	14	13	.245	.305	.303	.609	76	-14	43	3.02	-14	*S-123/2-2,3-2,0-1	10	-2.1
1921 Cin-N	107	367	36	80	8	3	1	25	43	20	3	14	.218	.310	.264	.574	56	-25	30	2.57	-11	S-93/2-4,3-3,0-1	4	-2.5
1922 Bos-N	126	466	59	124	6	3	1	37	45	22	8	9	.266	.332	.298	.630	67	-22	48	3.45	-9	2-78,S-33,3-13	7	-2.3
1923 Bos-N	39	138	15	38	3	1	0	10	13	6	0	3	.275	.338	.312	.649	75	-5	15	3.53	-4	S-37/2-4	3	-0.5
Total 10	**853**	**3010**	**349**	**750**	**84**	**30**	**5**	**266**	**242**	**214**	**72**	**48**	**.249**	**.312**	**.302**	**.614**	**79**	**-90**	**295**	**3.23**	**-90**	**S-664/2-99,3-69,0-2**	**65**	**-12.5**
• KOPF, Wally — Walter Henry Kopf b: 7/10/1899, Stonington, CT d: 4/30/1979, Cincinnati, OH BB/TR, 5'11", 168 lbs. Deb: 10/1/1921																								
1921 NY-N	2	3	0	1	0	0	0	0	1	1	0	0	.333	.500	.333	.833	125	0	1	8.01	1	/3-2	0	0.1
• KOPP, Merlin — Merlin Henry "Manny" Kopp b: 1/2/1892, Toledo, OH d: 5/6/1960, Sacramento, CA BB/TR, 5'8", 158 lbs. Deb: 8/2/1915 Career OF: 162-7-1																								
1915 Was-A	16	32	2	8	0	0	0	0	5	7	1	....	.250	.351	.250	.601	78	-1	3	3.43	-1	/O-9(8-0-1)	1	-0.2
1918 Phi-A	96	363	60	85	7	7	0	18	42	55	22	....	.234	.320	.292	.612	84	-6	40	3.49	14	O-96(96-0-0)	8	0.5
1919 Phi-A	75	235	34	53	2	4	1	12	42	43	16	....	.226	.348	.281	.629	76	-5	27	3.79	-3	O-65(58-7-0)	3	-1.1
Total 3	**187**	**630**	**96**	**146**	**9**	**11**	**1**	**30**	**89**	**105**	**39**	**....**	**.232**	**.332**	**.286**	**.618**	**81**	**-12**	**70**	**3.60**	**11**	**O-170**	**12**	**-0.9**
• KOPPE, Joe — Joseph Koppe b: 10/19/1930, Detroit, MI BR/TR, 5'10", 165 lbs. Deb: 8/9/1958																								
1958 Mil-N	16	9	3	4	0	0	0	0	1	1	0	0	.444	.500	.444	.944	167	1	2	11.50	0	/S-3	1	0.1
1959 Phi-N	126	422	68	110	18	7	7	28	41	80	7	7	.261	.329	.386	.715	88	-8	54	4.38	6	*S-113,2-11	13	0.8
1960 Phi-N	58	170	13	29	6	1	1	13	23	47	3	2	.171	.273	.235	.508	41	-14	12	2.21	-8	S-55/3-2	2	-1.8
1961 Phi-N	6	3	1	0	0	0	0	0	0	0	0	0	.000	.000	.000	.000	-101	-1	0	.00	-2	/S-5	0	-0.2
LA-A	91	338	46	85	12	2	5	40	45	77	3	3	.251	.341	.343	.684	75	-12	42	4.26	0	S-88/2-3,3-1	7	-0.5
1962 LA-A	128	375	47	85	16	0	4	40	73	84	2	1	.227	.356	.301	.657	81	-6	45	3.85	2	*S-118/2-5,3-4	12	0.5
1963 LA-A	76	143	11	30	4	1	1	12	9	30	0	0	.210	.261	.273	.534	53	-9	10	2.39	-2	S-19,3-18,2-14/O-3(0-0-3)	1	-0.9
1964 LA-A	54	113	10	29	4	1	0	6	14	16	0	0	.257	.339	.310	.648	91	-1	13	3.84	-4	S-31,2-13/3-3	4	-0.2
1965 Cal-A	23	33	3	7	1	0	1	2	3	10	1	0	.212	.278	.333	.611	74	-1	3	3.01	1	2-10/3-4,S-4	1	0.1
Total 8	**578**	**1606**	**202**	**379**	**61**	**12**	**19**	**141**	**209**	**345**	**16**	**13**	**.236**	**.327**	**.324**	**.651**	**76**	**-51**	**181**	**3.76**	**-7**	**S-436/2-56,3-32,O-3**	**41**	**-2.1**
• KOPSHAW, George — George Karl Kopshaw b: 7/5/1895, Passaic, NJ d: 12/26/1934, Lynchburg, VA BR/TR, 5'11.5", 176 lbs. Deb: 8/4/1923																								
1923 StL-N	2	5	1	1	1	0	0	0	0	1	0	0	.200	.200	.400	.600	56	-0	0	2.54	0	/C-1	0	0.0
• KORCHECK, Steve — Stephen Joseph "Hoss" Korcheck b: 8/11/1932, McClellandtown, PA BR/TR, 6'1", 205 lbs. Deb: 9/6/1954																								
1954 Was-A	2	7	0	1	0	0	0	0	0	2	0	0	.143	.143	.143	.286	-23	-1	0	.64	0	/C-2	0	-0.2
1955 Was-A	13	36	3	10	2	0	0	2	0	5	0	0	.278	.297	.333	.631	73	-1	4	3.70	1	C-12	1	0.0
1958 Was-A	21	51	6	4	2	1	0	1	1	16	0	0	.078	.096	.157	.253	-32	-9	1	.44	0	C-20	1	-0.9
1959 Was-A	22	51	3	8	2	0	0	4	5	13	0	0	.157	.232	.196	.428	19	-6	3	1.66	-2	C-22	1	-0.6
Total 4	**58**	**145**	**12**	**23**	**6**	**1**	**0**	**7**	**6**	**36**	**0**	**0**	**.159**	**.197**	**.214**	**.411**	**13**	**-18**	**7**	**1.59**	**-1**	**/C-56**	**3**	**-1.6**
• KORES, Art — Arthur Emil "Dutch" Kores b: 7/22/1886, Milwaukee, WI d: 3/26/1974, Milwaukee, WI BR/TR, 5'9", 167 lbs. Deb: 7/24/1915																								
1915 StL-F	60	201	18	47	9	2	1	22	21	13	6	....	.234	.306	.313	.620	78	-5	22	3.36	20	3-60	7	1.7
• KOSCO, Andy — Andrew John Kosco b: 10/5/1941, Youngstown, OH BR/TR, 6'3", 207 lbs. Deb: 8/13/1965 Career OF: 136-14-312																								
1965 Min-A	23	55	3	13	4	0	1	6	1	15	0	0	.236	.250	.364	.614	69	-2	5	3.15	2	O-14(0-0-14)/1-2	1	-0.1
1966 Min-A	57	158	11	35	5	0	2	13	7	31	0	1	.222	.255	.291	.546	53	-10	11	2.22	-1	O-40(31-7-5)/1-5	1	-1.5
1967 Min-A	9	28	4	4	1	0	0	4	2	4	0	0	.143	.200	.179	.379	12	-3	1	.99	0	/O-7(0-0-7)	0	-0.4
1968 NY-A	131	466	47	112	19	1	15	59	16	71	2	2	.240	.270	.382	.652	99	-4	45	3.24	2	O-95(1-0-94),1-28	11	-1.2
1969 LA-N	120	424	51	105	13	2	19	74	21	66	0	1	.248	.285	.422	.707	103	-1	46	3.63	2	*O-109(38-0-76)/1-3	9	-0.5
1970 LA-N	74	224	21	51	12	0	8	27	1	40	1	1	.228	.231	.388	.620	66	-13	17	2.53	0	O-58(3-0-55)/1-1	2	-1.5
1971 Mil-A	98	264	27	60	6	2	10	39	24	57	1	3	.227	.292	.379	.670	90	-5	28	3.46	-1	O-45(26-0-19),1-29,3-12	5	-1.1
1972 Cal-A	49	142	15	34	4	2	6	13	5	23	1	0	.239	.270	.423	.693	110	1	15	3.42	-1	O-36(24-0-13)	4	-0.2
Bos-A	17	47	5	10	2	1	3	6	2	9	0	0	.213	.260	.489	.749	113	0	4	2.82	0	O-12(12-0-0)	1	0.0
Yr.	66	189	20	44	6	3	9	19	7	32	1	0	.233	.268	.439	.707	111	1	19	3.26	-1	O-48(36-0-13)	5	-0.2
1973*Cin-N	47	118	17	33	7	0	9	21	13	26	0	0	.280	.351	.568	.919	159	9	22	6.40	-1	O-36(1-7-28)/1-1	6	0.7
1974 Cin-N	33	37	3	7	2	0	0	5	7	8	0	0	.189	.318	.243	.561	59	-2	3	2.70	-1	/3-8,0-1	0	-0.3
Total 10	**658**	**1963**	**204**	**464**	**75**	**8**	**73**	**267**	**99**	**350**	**5**	**8**	**.236**	**.275**	**.394**	**.669**	**93**	**-30**	**197**	**3.32**	**0**	**O-453/1-69,3-20**	**40**	**-6.1**
• KOSHOREK, Clem — Clement John "Scooter" Koshorek b: 6/20/1925, Royal Oak, MI d: 9/8/1991, Royal Oak, MI BR/TR, 5'4.5", 165 lbs. Deb: 4/15/1952																								
1952 Pit-N	98	322	27	84	17	0	0	15	26	39	4	7	.261	.320	.314	.634	74	-13	33	3.53	2	S-33,2-27,3-26	5	-0.7
1953 Pit-N	1	1	0	0	0	0	0	0	0	1	0	0	.000	.000	.000	.000	-101	-0	0	.00	0	....	0	0.0
Total 2	**99**	**323**	**27**	**84**	**17**	**0**	**0**	**15**	**26**	**40**	**4**	**7**	**.260**	**.319**	**.313**	**.632**	**74**	**-13**	**33**	**3.52**	**2**	**/S-33,2-27,3-26**	**5**	**-0.8**
• KOSKIE, Corey — Cordel Leonard Koskie b: 6/28/1973, Anola, Canada BL/TR, 6'3", 217 lbs. Deb: 9/9/1998																								
1998 Min-A	11	29	2	4	0	0	1	2	2	10	0	0	.138	.194	.241	.435	12	-4	1	1.57	-1	3-10	0	-0.4
1999 Min-A	117	342	42	106	21	0	11	58	40	72	4	4	.310	.390	.468	.858	114	7	63	6.78	3	3-79,O-25(0-0-25),D-12	13	0.9
2000 Min-A	146	474	79	142	32	4	9	65	77	104	5	4	.300	.402	.441	.843	109	9	87	6.67	5	*3-139/D-1	17	1.4
2001 Min-A	153	562	100	155	37	2	26	103	68	118	27	6	.276	.366	.488	.854	119	20	102	6.30	13	*3-150/D-2	24	3.4
2002*Min-A	140	490	71	131	37	3	15	69	72	127	10	11	.267	.371	.447	.818	115	10	80	5.56	19	*3-138	19	3.0
2003*Min-A	131	469	76	137	29	2	14	69	77	113	11	5	.292	.400	.452	.852	123	19	91	7.02	8	*3-131	21	2.8
Total 6	**698**	**2366**	**370**	**675**	**156**	**11**	**76**	**366**	**336**	**544**	**57**	**30**	**.285**	**.383**	**.457**	**.840**	**115**	**62**	**424**	**6.35**	**47**	**3-647/O-25,D-15**	**94**	**11.1**
• KOSLOFSKI, Kevin — Kevin Craig Koslofski b: 9/24/1966, Decatur, IL BL/TR, 5'8", 165 lbs. Deb: 6/28/1992 Career OF: 24-37-33																								
1992 KC-A	55	133	20	33	0	2	3	13	12	23	2	1	.248	.315	.346	.661	83	-3	15	3.80	1	O-52(15-18-23)	3	-0.3
1993 KC-A	15	26	4	7	0	0	1	2	4	5	0	1	.269	.387	.385	.772	102	-0	4	4.53	2	O-13(3-4-7)/D-1	1	0.1
1994 KC-A	2	4	2	1	0	0	0	0	2	1	0	0	.250	.500	.250	.750	97	0	1	5.67	0	/O-2(0-1-1)	0	0.0
1996 Mil-A	25	42	5	9	3	2	0	6	4	12	0	0	.214	.298	.381	.679	67	-2	5	3.74	-2	O-22(6-14-2)/D-1	1	-0.4
Total 4	**97**	**205**	**31**	**50**	**3**	**4**	**4**	**21**	**22**	**41**	**2**	**2**	**.244**	**.326**	**.356**	**.682**	**83**	**-5**	**24**	**3.92**	**1**	**/O-89,D-2**	**5**	**-0.5**
• KOSMAN, Mike — Michael Thomas Kosman b: 12/10/1917, Hamtramck, MI d: 12/10/2002, Lafayette, IN BR/TR, 5'9", 160 lbs. Deb: 4/20/1944																								
1944 Cin-N	1	0	0	0	0	0	0	0	0	0	0	....	....	....	....	....	-104	0	0	....	0	....	0	0.0
• KOSTER, Fred — Frederick Charles "Fritz" Koster b: 12/21/1905, Louisville, KY d: 4/24/1979, St. Matthews, KY BL/TL, 5'10.5", 165 lbs. Deb: 4/27/1931																								
1931 Phi-N	76	151	21	34	2	2	0	8	14	21	4	....	.225	.291	.265	.556	47	-11	13	2.70	-2	O-41(6-14-22)	1	-1.5
• KOSTRO, Frank — Frank Jerry Kostro b: 8/4/1937, Windber, PA BR/TR, 6'2", 190 lbs. Deb: 9/2/1962 Career OF: 21-0-16																								
1962 Det-A	16	41	5	11	3	0	0	3	1	6	0	0	.268	.286	.341	.627	66	-2	4	3.52	1	3-11	1	-0.1
1963 Det-A	31	52	4	12	1	0	0	0	9	13	0	0	.231	.344	.250	.594	67	-2	5	3.05	1	/3-6,1-3,O-3(1-0-2)	1	-0.1
LA-A	43	99	6	22	2	1	2	10	6	17	0	0	.222	.267	.323	.590	68	-4	8	2.68	-2	3-19/1-5,O-3(1-0-2)	1	-0.7
Yr.	74	151	10	34	3	1	2	10	15	30	0	0	.225	.295	.298	.593	68	-6	13	2.81	-1	3-25/1-8,O-6(2-0-4)	2	-0.8
1964 Min-A	59	103	10	28	5	0	3	12	4	21	0	0	.272	.306	.408	.713	96	-1	12	4.31	-1	3-12/2-7,O-2(2-0-0),1-1	2	-0.1

YEAR TM-L	G	AB	R	H	2B	3B	HR	RBI	BB	SO	SB	CS	AVG	OBP	SLG	OPS	OPS+	BR/A	RC	RC/G	FR	G/POS	WS	TPW
1965 Min-A	20	31	2	5	2	0	0	1	4	5	0	0	.161	.257	.226	.483	37	-3	2	1.83	-1	/2-7,3-6,0-2(1-0-1)	0	-0.4
1967 Min-A	32	31	4	10	0	0	0	2	3	2	0	0	.323	.382	.323	.705	102	0	3	4.09	-1	/0-3(2-0-1),3-1	1	0.0
1968 Min-A	63	108	9	26	4	1	0	9	6	20	0	0	.241	.281	.296	.577	71	-4	9	2.76	0	0-24(14-0-10)/1-5	1	-0.5
1969 Min-A	2	2	0	0	0	0	0	0	0	1	0	0	.000	.000	.000	.000	-98	-1	0	.00	0	....	0	-0.1
Total 7	266	467	40	114	17	2	5	37	33	85	0	0	.244	.295	.321	.617	74	-16	44	3.16	-2	/3-55,0-37,1-14,2-14	7	-2.1

• KOTSAY, Mark Mark Steven Kotsay b: 12/2/1975, Whittier, CA BL/TL, 6', 180 lbs. Deb: 7/11/1997 Career OF: 1-448-380

YEAR TM-L	G	AB	R	H	2B	3B	HR	RBI	BB	SO	SB	CS	AVG	OBP	SLG	OPS	OPS+	BR/A	RC	RC/G	FR	G/POS	WS	TPW
1997 Fla-N	14	52	5	10	1	1	0	4	4	7	3	0	.192	.250	.250	.500	33	-4	4	2.26	1	0-14(0-14-0)	1	-0.3
1998 Fla-N	154	578	72	161	25	7	11	68	34	61	10	5	.279	.320	.403	.723	92	-8	70	4.23	8	*0-145(0-46-107)/1-3	13	-0.6
1999 Fla-N	148	495	57	134	23	9	8	50	29	50	7	6	.271	.311	.402	.713	83	-16	59	4.06	9	*0-129(0-0-129),1-19	6	-1.4
2000 Fla-N	152	530	87	158	31	5	12	57	42	46	19	9	.298	.350	.443	.793	103	2	78	5.20	12	*0-142(0-9-139)/1-2	12	0.6
2001 SD-N	119	406	67	118	29	1	10	58	48	58	13	5	.291	.368	.441	.809	118	12	66	5.81	2	*0-111(1-106-5)	16	1.5
2002 SD-N	153	578	82	169	27	7	17	61	59	89	11	9	.292	.361	.452	.812	124	17	94	5.84	4	*0-147(0-147-0)	22	2.2
2003 SD-N	128	482	64	128	28	4	7	38	56	82	6	3	.266	.343	.384	.727	98	-1	65	4.81	12	*0-126(0-126-0)	14	1.2
Total 7	868	3121	434	878	164	34	65	336	272	393	69	37	.281	.340	.418	.758	102	2	436	4.91	47	0-814/1-24	84	3.2

• KOWITZ, Brian Brian Mark Kowitz b: 8/7/1969, Baltimore, MD BL/TL, 5'10", 180 lbs. Deb: 6/4/1995

YEAR TM-L	G	AB	R	H	2B	3B	HR	RBI	BB	SO	SB	CS	AVG	OBP	SLG	OPS	OPS+	BR/A	RC	RC/G	FR	G/POS	WS	TPW
1995 Atl-N	10	24	3	4	1	0	0	3	2	5	0	1	.167	.259	.208	.468	24	-3	1	1.66	0	/0-8(2-1-5)	0	-0.3

• KOY, Ernie Ernest Anyz "Chief" Koy b: 9/17/1909, Sealy, TX BR/TR, 6', 200 lbs. Deb: 4/19/1938 Career OF: 348-125-33

YEAR TM-L	G	AB	R	H	2B	3B	HR	RBI	BB	SO	SB	CS	AVG	OBP	SLG	OPS	OPS+	BR/A	RC	RC/G	FR	G/POS	WS	TPW
1938 Bro-N	142	521	78	156	29	13	11	76	38	76	15	....	.299	.352	.468	.820	121	13	87	6.06	-7	*0-135(54-64-18)/3-1	18	0.1
1939 Bro-N	125	425	57	118	37	5	8	67	39	64	11	....	.278	.338	.445	.783	105	2	63	5.29	-1	*0-114(110-3-3)	13	-0.6
1940 Bro-N	24	48	9	11	2	1	1	8	3	3	1	....	.229	.275	.375	.650	73	-2	5	3.69	-1	0-19(11-5-2)	1	-0.3
StL-N	93	348	44	108	19	5	8	52	28	59	12	....	.310	.368	.463	.831	121	10	60	6.58	-9	0-91(91-0-0)	13	-0.4
Yr.	117	396	53	119	21	6	9	60	31	62	13	....	.301	.357	.452	.809	115	8	65	6.20	-10	*0-110(102-5-2)	14	-0.8
1941 StL-N	13	40	5	8	1	0	2	4	1	8	0	....	.200	.220	.375	.595	61	-2	3	2.83	0	0-12(12-0-0)	0	-0.3
Cin-N	67	204	24	51	11	2	2	27	14	22	1	....	.250	.301	.353	.654	84	-5	22	3.75	-2	0-49(42-1-6)	5	-1.0
Yr.	80	244	29	59	12	2	4	31	15	30	1	....	.242	.288	.357	.645	80	-7	25	3.59	-2	0-61(54-1-6)	5	-1.3
1942 Cin-N	3	2	0	0	0	0	0	0	0	2	0	....	.000	.000	.000	.000	-100	-0	0	.00	0	....	0	-0.1
Phi-N	91	258	21	63	9	3	4	26	14	50	0	....	.244	.283	.349	.632	89	-5	25	3.39	-2	0-78(28-52-4)	4	-1.0
Yr.	94	260	21	63	9	3	4	26	14	52	0	....	.242	.281	.346	.627	87	-5	25	3.36	-2	0-78(28-52-4)	4	-1.1
Total 5	558	1846	238	515	108	29	36	260	137	284	40	....	.279	.332	.427	.759	106	10	266	5.18	-21	0-498/3-1	54	-3.5

• KOZAR, Al Albert Kenneth Kozar b: 7/5/1921, McKees Rocks, PA BR/TR, 5'9.5", 173 lbs. Deb: 4/19/1948

YEAR TM-L	G	AB	R	H	2B	3B	HR	RBI	BB	SO	SB	CS	AVG	OBP	SLG	OPS	OPS+	BR/A	RC	RC/G	FR	G/POS	WS	TPW
1948 Was-A	150	577	61	144	25	8	1	58	66	52	4	2	.250	.327	.326	.652	76	-19	63	3.69	-13	*2-149	9	-2.3
1949 Was-A	105	350	46	94	15	2	4	31	25	23	2	1	.269	.321	.357	.678	81	-11	41	4.16	-11	*2-102	6	-1.7
1950 Was-A	20	55	7	11	1	0	0	3	5	8	0	0	.200	.267	.218	.485	26	-6	3	1.86	0	2-15	1	-0.5
Chi-A	10	10	4	3	0	0	1	2	0	3	0	0	.300	.300	.600	.900	129	0	1	4.15	0	/2-4,3-1	0	0.1
Yr.	30	65	11	14	1	0	1	5	5	11	0	0	.215	.271	.277	.548	41	-6	5	2.19	-0	2-19/3-1	1	-0.5
Total 3	285	992	118	252	41	10	6	94	96	86	6	3	.254	.321	.334	.655	75	-36	108	3.75	-24	2-270/3-1	16	-4.4

• KRACHER, Joe Joseph Peter "Jug" Kracher b: 11/4/1915, Philadelphia, PA d: 12/24/1981, San Angelo, TX BR/TR, 5'11", 185 lbs. Deb: 9/17/1939

YEAR TM-L	G	AB	R	H	2B	3B	HR	RBI	BB	SO	SB	CS	AVG	OBP	SLG	OPS	OPS+	BR/A	RC	RC/G	FR	G/POS	WS	TPW
1939 Phi-N	5	5	1	1	0	0	0	0	2	1	0	....	.200	.429	.200	.629	77	0	1	4.40	0	/C-2	0	0.0

• KRAFT, Clarence Clarence Otto "Big Boy" Kraft b: 6/9/1887, Evansville, IN d: 3/26/1958, Fort Worth, TX BR/TR, 6', 190 lbs. Deb: 5/1/1914

YEAR TM-L	G	AB	R	H	2B	3B	HR	RBI	BB	SO	SB	CS	AVG	OBP	SLG	OPS	OPS+	BR/A	RC	RC/G	FR	G/POS	WS	TPW
1914 Bos-N	3	3	0	1	0	0	0	0	0	1	0	....	.333	.333	.333	.667	99	-0	0	4.07	0	/1-1	0	0.0

• KRANEPOOL, Ed Edward Emil Kranepool b: 11/8/1944, New York, NY BL/TL, 6'3", 215 lbs. Deb: 9/22/1962 Career OF: 132-1-118

YEAR TM-L	G	AB	R	H	2B	3B	HR	RBI	BB	SO	SB	CS	AVG	OBP	SLG	OPS	OPS+	BR/A	RC	RC/G	FR	G/POS	WS	TPW
1962 NY-N	3	6	0	1	1	0	0	0	0	1	0	0	.167	.167	.333	.500	30	-1	0	1.80	1	/1-3	0	0.0
1963 NY-N	86	273	22	57	12	2	2	14	18	50	4	2	.209	.258	.289	.547	56	-15	19	2.19	-1	0-55(6-0-50),1-20	1	-2.3
1964 NY-N	119	420	47	108	19	4	10	45	32	50	0	1	.257	.313	.393	.706	100	-1	51	4.16	-2	*1-104/0-6(0-1-5)	10	-0.9
1965 NY-N★	153	525	44	133	24	4	10	53	39	71	1	4	.253	.307	.371	.679	93	-7	57	3.69	1	*1-147	10	-1.5
1966 NY-N	146	464	51	118	15	2	16	57	41	66	1	1	.254	.319	.399	.718	100	0	60	4.55	1	*1-132,0-11(11-0-0)	16	-0.6
1967 NY-N	141	469	37	126	17	1	10	54	37	51	0	4	.269	.323	.373	.697	100	-1	53	3.87	-2	*1-139	9	-1.2
1968 NY-N	127	373	29	86	13	1	3	20	19	39	0	3	.231	.272	.295	.566	70	-15	29	2.55	3	*1-113/0-2(2-0-0)	4	-2.1
1969*NY-N	112	353	36	84	9	2	11	49	37	32	3	2	.238	.310	.368	.679	87	-6	39	3.69	3	*1-106/0-2(2-0-0)	8	-1.1
1970 NY-N	43	47	2	8	0	0	0	3	5	2	0	0	.170	.250	.170	.420	15	-6	2	1.61	0	/1-8	0	-0.6
1971 NY-N	122	421	61	118	20	4	14	58	38	33	0	4	.280	.341	.447	.788	123	10	63	5.27	-1	*1-108,0-11(6-0-5)	15	0.1
1972 NY-N	122	327	28	88	15	1	8	34	34	35	1	0	.269	.340	.394	.734	111	5	42	4.44	1	*1-108/0-1	11	-0.2
1973*NY-N	100	284	28	68	12	2	1	35	30	28	1	0	.239	.312	.306	.618	73	-10	28	3.27	-2	1-51,0-32(31-0-1)	5	-1.7
1974 NY-N	94	217	20	65	11	1	4	24	18	14	1	0	.300	.353	.415	.768	116	4	32	5.38	-3	0-33(32-0-1),1-24	7	-0.1
1975 NY-N	106	325	42	105	16	0	4	43	27	21	1	1	.323	.375	.409	.784	123	10	47	5.35	-2	1-82/0-4(4-0-0)	12	0.1
1976 NY-N	123	415	47	121	17	1	10	49	35	38	1	0	.292	.347	.410	.756	121	11	58	5.08	-3	1-86,0-31(23-0-8)	15	0.0
1977 NY-N	108	281	28	79	17	0	10	40	23	20	1	4	.281	.336	.448	.784	113	3	38	4.64	2	0-42(10-0-32),1-41	7	0.1
1978 NY-N	66	81	7	17	2	0	3	19	8	12	0	0	.210	.289	.346	.635	79	-2	7	2.82	1	0-12(3-0-9)/1-3	1	-0.2
1979 NY-N	82	155	7	36	5	0	2	17	13	18	0	1	.232	.296	.303	.599	66	-8	13	2.69	1	1-29/0-8(2-0-6)	1	-0.9
Total 18	1853	5436	536	1418	225	25	118	614	454	581	15	27	.261	.319	.377	.696	98	-28	638	4.03	-3	*1-1304,0-250	132	-13.2

• KRAUSE, Charlie Charles Krause b: 10/2/1873, Detroit, MI d: 3/30/1948, Eloise, MI TR Deb: 7/27/1901

YEAR TM-L	G	AB	R	H	2B	3B	HR	RBI	BB	SO	SB	CS	AVG	OBP	SLG	OPS	OPS+	BR/A	RC	RC/G	FR	G/POS	WS	TPW
1901 Cin-N	1	4	0	1	0	0	0	0	0	....	0	....	.250	.250	.250	.500	48	-0	0	2.26	-1	/2-1	0	-0.1

• KRAVITZ, Danny Daniel "Dusty,Beak" Kravitz b: 12/21/1930, Lopez, PA BL/TR, 5'11", 195 lbs. Deb: 4/17/1956

YEAR TM-L	G	AB	R	H	2B	3B	HR	RBI	BB	SO	SB	CS	AVG	OBP	SLG	OPS	OPS+	BR/A	RC	RC/G	FR	G/POS	WS	TPW
1956 Pit-N	32	68	6	18	2	2	2	10	5	9	1	1	.265	.315	.441	.756	103	-0	9	4.34	-2	C-26/3-2	2	-0.1
1957 Pit-N	19	41	2	6	1	0	0	4	2	10	0	0	.146	.186	.171	.357	-3	-6	1	1.08	1	C-15	0	-0.4
1958 Pit-N	45	100	9	24	3	2	1	5	11	10	0	0	.240	.315	.340	.655	75	-3	10	3.33	1	C-37	2	-0.2
1959 Pit-N	52	162	18	41	9	1	3	21	5	14	0	1	.253	.275	.377	.652	72	-7	16	3.44	-1	C-45	3	-0.7
1960 Pit-N	8	6	0	0	0	0	0	0	1	2	0	0	.000	.143	.000	.143	-57	-1	0	.17	0	/C-1	0	-0.2
KC-A	59	175	17	41	7	2	4	14	11	19	0	0	.234	.280	.366	.645	73	-7	16	3.18	-3	C-47	2	-0.8
Total 5	215	552	52	130	22	7	10	54	35	64	1	2	.236	.281	.355	.636	70	-26	53	3.21	-4	C-171/3-2	9	-2.3

• KREEVICH, Mike Michael Andreas Kreevich b: 6/10/1908, Mount Olive, IL d: 4/25/1994, Pana, IL BR/TR, 5'7.5", 168 lbs. Deb: 9/7/1931 Career OF: 27-1095-69

YEAR TM-L	G	AB	R	H	2B	3B	HR	RBI	BB	SO	SB	CS	AVG	OBP	SLG	OPS	OPS+	BR/A	RC	RC/G	FR	G/POS	WS	TPW
1931 Chi-N	5	12	0	2	0	0	0	0	0	6	1	....	.167	.167	.167	.333	-10	-2	0	.84	0	/0-4(1-1-2)	0	-0.1
1935 Chi-A	6	23	3	10	2	0	0	2	1	0	1	1	.435	.458	.522	.980	149	1	5	9.68	-1	/3-6	1	0.1
1936 Chi-A	137	550	99	169	32	11	5	69	61	46	10	5	.307	.378	.433	.811	96	-3	93	6.13	6	*0-133(17-65-57)	16	-0.3
1937 Chi-A	144	583	94	176	29	**16**	12	73	43	45	10	1	.302	.350	.468	.818	104	3	97	6.07	10	*0-138(6-138-1)	23	0.9
1938 Chi-A★	129	489	73	145	26	12	6	73	55	23	13	5	.297	.371	.436	.807	99	0	82	6.14	1	*0-127(0-127-1)	16	-0.2
1939 Chi-A	145	541	85	175	30	8	5	77	59	40	23	10	.323	.390	.436	.826	108	8	93	6.08	8	*0-139(0-139-0)/3-4	22	1.2
1940 Chi-A	144	582	86	154	27	10	8	55	34	49	15	7	.265	.305	.387	.692	77	-21	66	3.76	6	*0-144(0-144-0)	15	-1.8
1941 Chi-A	121	436	44	101	16	8	0	37	35	26	17	5	.232	.289	.305	.594	58	-25	40	2.99	0	*0-113(0-113-0)	8	-2.7
1942 Phi-A	116	444	57	113	19	1	1	30	47	31	7	9	.255	.326	.309	.634	79	-13	46	3.51	-3	*0-107(0-107-0)	10	-1.9
1943 StL-A	60	161	24	41	6	0	0	10	26	13	4	1	.255	.358	.292	.650	89	-0	20	4.17	2	0-51(3-47-1)	5	0.0
1944*StL-A	105	402	55	121	15	6	5	44	27	24	3	3	.301	.348	.405	.754	108	3	56	4.90	-5	*0-100(0-93-7)	16	-0.4
1945 StL-A	84	295	34	70	11	1	2	21	37	27	4	1	.237	.322	.302	.624	78	-7	31	3.50	0	0-81(0-81-0)	8	-0.9
Was-A	45	158	22	44	8	2	1	23	21	9	7	5	.278	.363	.373	.737	124	5	22	4.84	-1	0-40(0-40-0)	6	0.3
Yr.	129	453	56	114	19	3	3	44	58	36	11	6	.252	.337	.327	.663	94	-2	53	3.96	-1	*0-121(0-121-0)	14	-0.6
Total 12	1241	4676	676	1321	221	75	45	514	446	339	115	53	.283	.346	.391	.737	92	-49	651	4.84	24	*0-1177/3-10	146	-5.9

• KREHMEYER, Charlie Charles L. Krehmeyer b: 7/5/1863, St. Louis, MO d: 2/10/1926, St. Louis, MO BL/TL, 5'11", 179 lbs. Deb: 7/8/1884 Career OF: 6-9-2

YEAR TM-L	G	AB	R	H	2B	3B	HR	RBI	BB	SO	SB	CS	AVG	OBP	SLG	OPS	OPS+	BR/A	RC	RC/G	FR	G/POS	WS	TPW
1884 StL-a	21	70	3	16	0	1	0	5	2	....	....	....	.229	.250	.257	.507	63	-3	5	2.35	-4	0-15(5-9-1)/C-7,1-1	1	-0.6
1885 Lou-a	7	31	4	7	1	1	0	5	1	....	....	....	.226	.250	.323	.573	80	-1	3	2.88	0	/C-4,0-2(1-0-1),1-1	0	-0.1

YEAR TM-L	G	AB	R	H	2B	3B	HR	RBI	BB	SO	SB	CS	AVG	OBP	SLG	OPS	OPS+	BR/A	RC	RC/G	FR	G/POS	WS	TPW
StL-N	1	3	0	0	0	0	0	0	0	2	....	....	.000	.000	.000	.000	-107	-1	0	.00	-2	/C-1	0	-0.2
Total 2	29	104	7	23	1	2	0	10	3	2	....	....	.221	.243	.269	.512	64	-4	7	2.42	-5	/0-17,C-12,1-2	1	-0.9

• KREITNER, Mickey Albert Joseph Kreitner b: 10/10/1922, Nashville, TN d: 3/6/2003, Nashville, TN BR/TR, 6'3", 190 lbs. Deb: 9/28/1943

YEAR TM-L	G	AB	R	H	2B	3B	HR	RBI	BB	SO	SB	CS	AVG	OBP	SLG	OPS	OPS+	BR/A	RC	RC/G	FR	G/POS	WS	TPW
1943 Chi-N	3	8	0	3	0	0	0	2	1	2	0	....	.375	.444	.375	.819	140	0	1	7.82	0	/C-3	0	0.1
1944 Chi-N	39	85	3	13	2	0	0	1	8	16	0	....	.153	.234	.176	.411	17	-9	4	1.45	1	C-39	1	-0.7
Total 2	42	93	3	16	2	0	0	3	9	18	0	....	.172	.252	.194	.446	27	-9	6	1.85	0	/C-42	1	-0.7

• KREITZ, Ralph Ralph Wesley "Red" Kreitz b: 11/13/1885, Plum Creek, NE d: 7/20/1941, Portland, OR BR/TR, 5'9.5", 175 lbs. Deb: 8/1/1911

YEAR TM-L	G	AB	R	H	2B	3B	HR	RBI	BB	SO	SB	CS	AVG	OBP	SLG	OPS	OPS+	BR/A	RC	RC/G	FR	G/POS	WS	TPW
1911 Chi-A	7	17	0	4	1	0	0	0	2	....	0	....	.235	.316	.294	.610	72	-1	2	3.05	-1	/C-7	0	-0.1

• KREMERS, Jimmy James Edward Kremers b: 10/8/1965, Little Rock, AR BL/TR, 6'3", 205 lbs. Deb: 6/5/1990

YEAR TM-L	G	AB	R	H	2B	3B	HR	RBI	BB	SO	SB	CS	AVG	OBP	SLG	OPS	OPS+	BR/A	RC	RC/G	FR	G/POS	WS	TPW
1990 Atl-N	29	73	7	8	1	1	1	2	6	27	0	0	.110	.177	.192	.369	1	-10	3	1.13	0	C-27	1	-0.9

• KRENCHICKI, Wayne Wayne Richard Krenchicki b: 9/17/1954, Trenton, NJ BL/TR, 6'1", 180 lbs. Deb: 6/15/1979

YEAR TM-L	G	AB	R	H	2B	3B	HR	RBI	BB	SO	SB	CS	AVG	OBP	SLG	OPS	OPS+	BR/A	RC	RC/G	FR	G/POS	WS	TPW
1979 Bal-A	16	21	1	4	1	0	0	0	0	0	0	0	.190	.190	.238	.429	15	-3	1	1.06	-2	/3-7,2-6	0	-0.4
1980 Bal-A	9	14	1	2	0	0	0	0	1	3	0	0	.143	.200	.143	.343	-4	-2	0	1.02	-1	/S-6,2-1,D-1	0	-0.2
1981 Bal-A	33	56	7	12	4	0	0	6	4	9	0	0	.214	.267	.286	.552	59	-3	4	2.56	1	S-16/2-7,3-6,D-1	1	-0.1
1982 Cin-N	94	187	19	53	6	1	2	21	13	23	5	3	.283	.330	.358	.688	91	-3	22	4.10	-1	3-70/2-9	4	-0.5
1983 Cin-N	51	77	6	21	2	0	0	11	8	4	0	0	.273	.349	.299	.648	78	-2	8	3.73	1	3-39/2-1	2	-0.1
Det-A	59	133	18	37	7	0	1	16	11	27	0	0	.278	.338	.353	.691	93	-1	17	4.50	-2	3-48/2-6,S-6,1-3	4	-0.3
1984 Cin-N	97	181	18	54	9	2	6	22	19	23	0	1	.298	.365	.470	.835	127	6	30	6.04	3	3-62/1-3,2-3	7	0.9
1985 Cin-N	90	173	16	47	9	0	4	25	28	20	0	0	.272	.373	.393	.766	109	3	27	5.44	0	3-52/2-3	7	0.3
1986 Mon-N	101	221	21	53	6	2	2	23	22	32	2	4	.240	.309	.312	.621	72	-10	22	3.27	1	1-41,3-24/2-1,0-1	3	-1.1
Total 8	550	1063	107	283	44	5	15	124	106	141	7	8	.266	.334	.359	.693	91	-14	131	4.28	1	3-308/1-47,2-37,S-28,D-2,0	28	-1.5

• KRESS, Chuck Charles Steven Kress b: 12/9/1921, Philadelphia, PA BL/TL, 6', 190 lbs. Deb: 4/16/1947

YEAR TM-L	G	AB	R	H	2B	3B	HR	RBI	BB	SO	SB	CS	AVG	OBP	SLG	OPS	OPS+	BR/A	RC	RC/G	FR	G/POS	WS	TPW
1947 Cin-N	11	27	4	4	0	0	0	0	6	4	0	....	.148	.303	.148	.451	23	-3	2	2.01	1	/1-8	0	-0.2
1949 Cin-N	27	29	3	6	3	0	0	3	3	5	0	....	.207	.281	.310	.592	58	-2	2	2.70	0	1-16	0	-0.2
Chi-A	97	353	45	98	17	6	1	44	39	44	6	7	.278	.349	.368	.718	93	-5	47	4.41	1	1-95	7	-0.8
1950 Chi-A	3	8	0	0	0	0	0	0	0	2	0	0	.000	.000	.000	.000	-103	-2	0	.00	0	/1-2	0	-0.3
1954 Det-A	24	37	4	7	0	1	0	3	1	4	0	1	.189	.211	.243	.454	24	-4	2	1.49	0	/1-7,0-1	0	-0.5
Bro-N	13	12	1	1	0	0	0	2	0	0	0	0	.083	.083	.083	.167	-55	-3	0	.20	0	/1-1	0	-0.3
Total 4	175	466	57	116	20	7	1	52	49	59	6	8	.249	.320	.328	.649	75	-20	53	3.68	0	1-129/0-1	7	-2.3

• KRESS, Red Ralph Kress b: 1/2/1905, Columbia, CA d: 11/29/1962, Los Angeles, CA BR/TR, 5'11.5", 165 lbs. Deb: 9/24/1927 C Career OF: 22-0-103

YEAR TM-L	G	AB	R	H	2B	3B	HR	RBI	BB	SO	SB	CS	AVG	OBP	SLG	OPS	OPS+	BR/A	RC	RC/G	FR	G/POS	WS	TPW
1927 StL-A	7	23	3	7	2	1	1	3	3	3	0	0	.304	.385	.609	.993	150	2	5	8.47	1	/S-7	1	0.3
1928 StL-A	150	560	78	153	26	10	3	81	48	70	5	4	.273	.332	.371	.703	82	-15	71	4.29	-5	*S-150	16	-0.3
1929 StL-A	147	557	82	170	38	4	9	107	52	54	5	8	.305	.366	.436	.802	102	-0	88	5.67	5	*S-146	21	1.9
1930 StL-A	154	614	94	192	43	8	16	112	50	56	3	12	.313	.366	.487	.853	110	5	105	6.24	-15	*S-123,3-31	20	0.5
1931 StL-A	150	605	87	188	46	8	16	114	46	48	3	16	.311	.360	.493	.853	118	10	101	6.11	-6	3-84,0-40(0-0-40),S-38,1-10	17	0.4
1932 StL-A	14	52	2	9	0	1	2	9	4	6	1	1	.173	.232	.327	.559	41	-5	4	2.27	1	3-14	1	-0.3
Chi-A	135	515	83	147	42	4	9	57	47	36	6	3	.285	.346	.435	.781	108	6	79	5.53	6	0-64(16-0-49),S-53,3-19/1-1	15	1.1
Yr.	149	567	85	156	42	5	11	66	51	42	7	4	.275	.336	.425	.761	102	1	82	5.18	8	0-64(16-0-49),S-53,3-33/1-1	16	0.8
1933 Chi-A	129	467	47	116	20	5	10	78	37	40	4	4	.248	.304	.377	.680	83	-13	54	3.92	-1	*1-111/0-8(0-0-8)	7	-2.4
1934 Chi-A	8	14	3	4	0	0	0	1	3	3	0	0	.286	.412	.286	.697	80	-0	2	5.01	-1	/2-3	0	-0.1
Was-A	56	171	18	39	4	3	4	24	17	19	3	0	.228	.298	.357	.655	71	-7	19	3.81	-2	1-30,0-10(6-0-4)/2-6,3-1,S	2	-1.1
Yr.	64	185	21	43	4	3	4	25	20	22	3	0	.232	.307	.351	.659	72	-7	21	3.89	-2	1-30,0-10(6-0-4)/2-9,3-1,S	2	-1.1
1935 Was-A	84	252	32	75	13	4	2	42	25	16	3	3	.298	.361	.405	.766	101	0	37	5.40	12	S-53/1-5,P-3,0-2(0-0-2),2	9	1.0
1936 Was-A	109	391	51	111	20	6	8	51	39	25	6	0	.284	.349	.427	.776	96	-2	60	5.65	3	S-64,2-33/1-5	12	0.7
1938 StL-A	150	566	74	171	33	3	7	79	69	47	5	4	.302	.378	.408	.786	97	-2	90	5.85	-8	*S-150	15	0.1
1939 StL-A	13	43	5	12	1	0	0	8	6	2	1	0	.279	.367	.302	.670	72	-1	4	3.28	-1	S-13	0	-0.2
Det-A	51	157	19	38	7	0	1	22	17	16	2	1	.242	.316	.306	.622	55	-11	15	3.02	0	S-25,2-16/3-4	2	-0.7
Yr.	64	200	24	50	8	0	1	30	23	18	3	1	.250	.327	.305	.632	59	-12	19	3.08	-1	S-38,2-16/3-4	2	-0.8
1940 Det-A	33	99	13	22	3	1	1	11	10	12	0	0	.222	.294	.303	.597	50	-7	8	2.45	1	3-17,S-12	1	-0.4
1946 NY-N	1	1	0	0	0	0	0	0	1	0	0	....	.000	.500	.000	.500	48	0	0	3.51	1	/P-1	0	-0.4
Total 14	1391	5087	691	1454	298	58	89	799	474	453	47	56	.286	.347	.420	.767	96	-41	742	5.17	-8	S-835,3-170,1-162,0-124/2,P	139	0.2

• KREUTER, Chad Chadden Michael Kreuter b: 8/26/1964, Greenbrae, CA BB/TR, 6'2", 195 lbs. Deb: 9/14/1988

YEAR TM-L	G	AB	R	H	2B	3B	HR	RBI	BB	SO	SB	CS	AVG	OBP	SLG	OPS	OPS+	BR/A	RC	RC/G	FR	G/POS	WS	TPW
1988 Tex-A	16	51	3	14	2	1	1	5	7	13	0	0	.275	.362	.412	.774	113	1	8	5.59	-1	C-16	2	0.2
1989 Tex-A	87	158	16	24	3	0	5	9	27	40	0	1	.152	.276	.266	.541	52	-10	13	2.33	-3	C-85	2	-0.9
1990 Tex-A	22	22	2	1	1	0	0	2	8	9	0	0	.045	.300	.091	.391	14	-2	1	1.69	-1	C-20/D-1	0	-0.3
1991 Tex-A	3	4	0	0	0	0	0	0	0	1	0	0	.000	.000	.000	.000	-102	-1	0	.00	-0	/C-1	0	-0.1
1992 Det-A	67	190	22	48	9	0	2	16	20	38	0	1	.253	.324	.332	.655	83	-4	19	3.35	-2	C-62/D-1	5	-0.3
1993 Det-A	119	374	59	107	23	3	15	51	49	92	2	1	.286	.373	.484	.857	129	16	70	6.80	4	*C-112/D-2,1-1	16	2.6
1994 Det-A	65	170	17	38	8	0	1	19	28	36	0	1	.224	.333	.288	.622	62	-9	18	3.43	-1	C-64/1-1,0-1	3	-0.6
1995 Sea-A	26	75	12	17	5	0	1	8	5	22	0	0	.227	.293	.333	.626	62	-4	8	3.62	-0	C-23	2	-0.3
1996 Chi-A	46	114	14	25	8	0	3	18	13	29	0	0	.219	.310	.368	.678	74	-5	14	3.92	1	C-38/1-2	3	-0.2
1997 Chi-A	19	37	6	8	2	1	1	3	8	9	0	1	.216	.356	.405	.761	102	-0	6	5.12	0	C-13/1-2	1	0.0
Ana-A	70	218	19	51	7	1	4	18	21	57	0	2	.234	.301	.330	.632	64	-12	20	3.12	1	C-67/D-2	4	-0.7
Yr.	89	255	25	59	9	2	5	21	29	66	0	3	.231	.310	.341	.651	70	-13	26	3.41	0	C-80/1-2,D-2	5	-0.7
1998 Chi-A	93	245	26	62	9	1	2	33	32	45	1	0	.253	.346	.322	.669	78	-7	28	3.90	0	C-91	7	-0.1
Ana-A	3	7	1	1	1	0	0	0	1	4	0	0	.143	.250	.286	.536	39	-1	1	2.54	-1	/C-3	0	-0.1
Yr.	96	252	27	63	10	1	2	33	33	49	1	0	.250	.344	.321	.665	77	-7	29	3.86	-1	C-94	7	-0.3
1999 KC-A	107	324	31	73	15	0	5	35	34	65	0	0	.225	.310	.318	.628	59	-20	30	3.03	-1	*C-101/D-1	3	-1.3
2000 LA-N	80	212	32	56	13	0	6	28	54	48	1	0	.264	.418	.410	.828	117	9	41	6.63	0	C-78	9	1.3
2001 LA-N	73	191	21	41	11	1	6	17	41	52	0	0	.215	.356	.377	.733	97	1	28	4.78	7	C-70/D-1	8	1.1
2002 LA-N	41	95	8	25	5	0	2	12	10	31	1	0	.263	.340	.379	.719	95	-0	12	4.33	0	C-41	4	0.2
2003 Tex-A	7	18	0	2	1	0	0	0	3	2	0	0	.111	.238	.167	.405	9	-2	1	1.52	-1	/C-7	0	-0.3
Total 16	944	2505	289	593	123	8	54	274	361	593	5	7	.237	.337	.357	.694	84	-51	318	4.22	0	C-892/D-8,1-6,0-1	69	0.2

• KRICHELL, Paul Paul Bernard Krichell b: 12/19/1882, New York, NY d: 6/4/1957, Bronx, NY BR/TR, 5'7", 150 lbs. Deb: 5/12/1911

YEAR TM-L	G	AB	R	H	2B	3B	HR	RBI	BB	SO	SB	CS	AVG	OBP	SLG	OPS	OPS+	BR/A	RC	RC/G	FR	G/POS	WS	TPW
1911 StL-A	28	82	6	19	3	0	0	8	4	....	2	....	.232	.276	.268	.544	54	-5	7	2.63	1	C-25	1	-0.2
1912 StL-A	59	161	19	35	6	0	0	8	19	....	2	....	.217	.304	.255	.559	62	-7	13	2.63	-0	C-59	2	-0.3
Total 2	87	243	25	54	9	0	0	16	23	....	4	....	.222	.295	.259	.554	60	-12	20	2.63	1	/C-84	3	-0.5

• KRIEG, Bill William Frederick Krieg b: 1/29/1859, Petersburg, IL d: 3/25/1930, Chillicothe, IL BR/TR, 5'8", 180 lbs. Deb: 4/20/1884 U Career OF: 20-8-3

YEAR TM-L	G	AB	R	H	2B	3B	HR	RBI	BB	SO	SB	CS	AVG	OBP	SLG	OPS	OPS+	BR/A	RC	RC/G	FR	G/POS	WS	TPW
1884 CP-U	71	279	35	69	15	4	0	....	11	....	....	....	.247	.276	.330	.606	111	4	26	3.47	8	C-53,0-20(13-6-2)/1-1,S-1	9	1.4
1885 Chi-N	1	3	0	0	0	0	0	0	0	2	....	....	.000	.000	.000	.000	-87	-1	0	.00	2	/0-1	0	0.1
Bro-a	17	60	7	9	4	0	1	5	2	....	....	....	.150	.177	.267	.444	39	-4	3	1.54	-1	C-12/1-5	0	-0.4
1886 Was-N	27	98	11	25	6	3	1	15	3	12	2	....	.255	.277	.408	.685	113	1	12	4.41	-1	1-27	2	-0.2
1887 Was-N	25	102	9	31	4	1	2	17	7	5	2	....	.304	.311	.379	.690	95	-0	12	4.52	0	1-16/0-9(7-2-0)	2	-0.1
Total 4	141	542	62	134	29	8	4	37	23	19	4	....	.247	.270	.344	.614	99	-0	53	3.55	8	/C-65,1-49,0-30,S-1	13	0.8

• KRONER, John John Harold Kroner b: 11/13/1908, St. Louis, MO d: 4/26/1968, St. Louis, MO BR/TR, 6', 185 lbs. Deb: 9/29/1935

YEAR TM-L	G	AB	R	H	2B	3B	HR	RBI	BB	SO	SB	CS	AVG	OBP	SLG	OPS	OPS+	BR/A	RC	RC/G	FR	G/POS	WS	TPW
1935 Bos-A	2	4	1	1	0	0	0	0	1	1	0	0	.250	.400	.250	.650	67	-0	1	3.77	0	/3-2	0	0.0
1936 Bos-A	84	298	40	87	17	8	4	62	26	24	2	3	.292	.349	.443	.792	89	-7	46	5.55	-1	2-38,3-28,S-18/0-1	7	-0.3
1937 Cle-A	86	283	29	67	14	1	2	26	22	25	1	1	.237	.292	.314	.606	52	-21	27	3.14	2	2-64,3-11	4	-1.4
1938 Cle-A	51	117	13	29	16	0	1	17	19	6	0	1	.248	.353	.410	.763	92	-2	18	5.18	3	2-31/1-7,3-3,S-1	4	0.2
Total 4	223	702	83	184	47	9	7	105	68	56	3	5	.262	.327	.385	.712	75	-30	91	4.46	4	2-133/3-44,S-19,1-7,0-1	15	-1.5

YEAR TM-L	G	AB	R	H	2B	3B	HR	RBI	BB	SO	SB	CS	AVG	OBP	SLG	OPS	OPS+	BR/A	RC	RC/G	FR	G/POS	WS	TPW
• KRSNICH, Mike	Michael Krsnich b: 9/24/1931, West Allis, WI BR/TR, 6'1", 190 lbs. Deb: 4/23/1960 Career OF: 6-0-0																							
1960 Mil-N	4	9	0	3	1	0	0	2	0	0	0	0	.333	.333	.444	.778	119	0	1	3.43	0	/O-3(3-0-0)	0	0.0
1962 Mil-N	11	12	0	1	1	0	0	2	0	4	0	0	.083	.083	.167	.250	-36	-2	0	.00	0	/O-3(3-0-0),1-1,3-1	0	-0.2
Total 2	**15**	**21**	**0**	**4**	**2**	**0**	**0**	**4**	**0**	**4**	**0**	**0**	**.190**	**.190**	**.286**	**.476**	**31**	**-2**	**1**	**1.26**	**0**	**/O-6,1-1,3-1**	**0**	**-0.2**
• KRSNICH, Rocky	Rocco Peter Krsnich b: 8/5/1927, West Allis, WI BR/TR, 6'1", 174 lbs. Deb: 9/13/1949																							
1949 Chi-A	16	55	7	12	3	1	1	9	6	4	0	1	.218	.295	.364	.659	76	-3	6	3.47	2	3-16	1	-0.1
1952 Chi-A	40	91	11	21	7	2	1	15	12	9	0	0	.231	.327	.385	.712	97	-0	11	4.13	3	3-37	3	0.3
1953 Chi-A	64	129	9	26	8	0	1	14	12	11	0	2	.202	.270	.287	.556	49	-10	10	2.48	-1	3-57	1	-1.2
Total 3	**120**	**275**	**27**	**59**	**18**	**3**	**3**	**38**	**30**	**24**	**0**	**3**	**.215**	**.294**	**.335**	**.629**	**70**	**-13**	**27**	**3.21**	**3**	**3-110**	**5**	**-1.0**
• KRUEGER, Ernie	Ernest George Krueger b: 12/27/1890, Chicago, IL d: 4/22/1976, Waukegan, IL BR/TR, 5'10.5", 185 lbs. Deb: 8/4/1913																							
1913 Cle-A	5	6	0	0	0	0	0	0	0	2	0	....	.000	.000	.000	.000	-97	-1	0	.00	0	/C-4	0	-0.2
1915 NY-A	10	29	3	5	1	0	0	0	0	5	0	1	.172	.200	.207	.407	22	-3	1	1.13	-2	/C-8	0	-0.5
1917 NY-N	8	10	0	0	0	0	0	0	0	4	0	....	.000	.000	.000	.000	-103	-2	0	.00	-1	/C-5	0	-0.4
Bro-N	31	81	10	22	2	2	1	6	5	7	1	....	.272	.330	.383	.712	115	1	10	4.36	-0	C-23	3	0.4
Yr.	39	91	10	22	2	2	1	6	5	11	1	....	.242	.296	.341	.637	93	-1	10	3.74	-1	C-28	3	0.0
1918 Bro-N	30	87	4	25	4	2	0	7	4	9	2	....	.287	.319	.379	.698	113	1	10	4.36	5	C-23	3	0.9
1919 Bro-N	80	226	24	56	7	4	5	36	19	25	4	....	.248	.312	.381	.692	105	1	27	4.01	0	C-66	8	0.7
1920*Bro-N	52	146	21	42	4	2	1	17	16	13	2	0	.288	.358	.363	.721	104	2	20	5.10	-2	C-46	6	0.3
1921 Bro-N	65	163	18	43	11	4	3	20	14	12	2	2	.264	.322	.436	.758	95	-1	23	4.87	-2	C-52	6	0.0
1925 Cin-N	37	88	7	27	4	0	1	7	6	8	1	2	.307	.351	.386	.737	90	-2	11	4.69	-3	C-30	2	-0.3
Total 8	**318**	**836**	**87**	**220**	**33**	**14**	**11**	**93**	**64**	**85**	**12**	**5**	**.263**	**.319**	**.376**	**.695**	**97**	**-4**	**102**	**4.27**	**-6**	**C-257**	**28**	**0.9**
• KRUEGER, Otto	Arthur William "Oom Paul" Krueger b: 9/17/1876, Chicago, IL d: 2/20/1961, St. Louis, MO BR/TR, 5'7", 165 lbs. Deb: 9/16/1899 Career OF: 51-3-13																							
1899 Cle-N	13	44	4	10	1	0	0	2	8	....	1	....	.227	.358	.250	.608	73	-1	4	3.44	-4	/3-9,2-2,S-2	0	-0.4
1900 StL-N	12	35	8	14	3	2	1	3	10	....	0	....	.400	.543	.686	1.229	240	8	14	13.73	-5	2-12	3	0.3
1901 StL-N	142	520	77	143	16	12	2	79	50	....	19	....	.275	.353	.363	.717	114	11	77	5.24	-10	*3-142	18	0.6
1902 StL-N	128	467	55	124	7	8	0	46	29	....	14	....	.266	.313	.315	.627	98	-2	53	3.96	-14	*S-107,3-18	14	-1.2
1903 Pit-N	80	256	42	63	6	8	1	28	21	....	5	....	.246	.323	.344	.667	87	-4	32	4.19	0	S-29,O-28(28-0-0),3-13/2-3	7	-0.5
1904 Pit-N	86	268	34	52	6	2	1	26	29	....	8	....	.194	.282	.243	.525	61	-11	22	2.58	-1	O-33(23-0-10),S-32,3-10	4	-1.4
1905 Phi-N	46	114	10	21	1	1	0	12	13	....	1	....	.184	.273	.211	.484	47	-7	8	2.03	-2	S-23/O-6(0-3-3),3-1	1	-0.9
Total 7	**507**	**1704**	**230**	**427**	**40**	**33**	**5**	**196**	**160**	**....**	**48**	**....**	**.251**	**.326**	**.322**	**.648**	**95**	**-6**	**210**	**4.18**	**-36**	**3-193,S-193/O-67,2-17**	**47**	**-3.5**
• KRUG, Chris	Everett Ben Krug b: 12/25/1939, Los Angeles, CA BR/TR, 6'4", 200 lbs. Deb: 5/30/1965 C																							
1965 Chi-N	60	169	16	34	5	0	5	24	13	52	0	1	.201	.262	.320	.582	61	-9	12	2.26	0	C-58	2	-0.7
1966 Chi-N	11	28	1	6	1	0	0	1	1	8	0	0	.214	.241	.250	.491	36	-2	2	1.76	1	C-10	0	-0.1
1969 SD-N	8	17	0	1	0	0	0	0	1	6	0	0	.059	.111	.059	.170	-53	-3	0	.30	-1	/C-7	0	-0.4
Total 3	**79**	**214**	**17**	**41**	**6**	**0**	**5**	**25**	**15**	**66**	**0**	**1**	**.192**	**.248**	**.290**	**.538**	**49**	**-15**	**14**	**2.02**	**0**	**/C-75**	**2**	**-1.3**
• KRUG, Gene	Gary Eugene Krug b: 2/12/1955, Garden City, KS BL/TL, 6'4", 225 lbs. Deb: 4/29/1981																							
1981 Chi-N	7	5	0	2	0	0	0	0	1	1	0	0	.400	.500	.400	.900	151	0	1	10.17	0	....	0	0.1
• KRUG, Henry	Henry Charles Krug b: 12/4/1876, San Francisco, CA d: 1/14/1908, San Francisco, CA BR/TR Deb: 7/26/1902																							
1902 Phi-N	53	198	20	45	3	3	0	14	7	....	2	....	.227	.261	.273	.534	65	-9	16	2.62	-5	O-28(28-0-0),2-13/S-9,3-6	1	-1.5
• KRUG, Marty	Martin John Krug b: 9/10/1888, Koblenz, Germany d: 6/27/1966, Glendale, CA BR/TR, 5'9", 165 lbs. Deb: 5/29/1912																							
1912 Bos-A	24	39	6	12	2	1	0	7	5	....	2	....	.308	.386	.410	.797	122	1	7	6.19	0	S-11/2-4	2	0.1
1922 Chi-N	127	450	67	124	23	4	4	60	43	43	7	9	.276	.343	.371	.714	82	-12	58	4.24	-6	*3-104,2-23/S-1	11	-1.0
Total 2	**151**	**489**	**73**	**136**	**25**	**5**	**4**	**67**	**48**	**43**	**9**	**9**	**.278**	**.346**	**.374**	**.721**	**86**	**-11**	**65**	**4.39**	**-6**	**3-104/2-27,S-12**	**13**	**-0.9**
• KRUGER, Art	Arthur T. Kruger b: 3/16/1881, San Antonio, TX d: 11/28/1949, Hondo, CA BR/TR, 6', 185 lbs. Deb: 4/11/1907 Career OF: 128-203-31																							
1907 Cin-N	100	317	25	74	10	9	0	28	18	....	10	....	.233	.285	.322	.607	87	-6	34	3.48	-2	O-96(26-70-1)	7	-1.4
1910 Cle-A	47	168	14	26	4	2	0	10	15	....	10	....	.155	.237	.202	.439	37	-12	11	1.87	1	O-47(47-0-0)	0	-1.5
Bos-N	1	1	0	0	0	0	0	0	0	0	0	....	.000	.000	.000	.000	-96	-0	0	.00	0	....	0	0.0
Cle-A	15	55	5	12	2	1	0	4	5	....	2	....	.218	.295	.291	.586	83	-1	5	3.09	2	O-15(15-0-0)	1	0.1
Yr.	62	223	19	38	6	3	0	14	20	....	12	....	.170	.251	.224	.475	48	-13	16	2.14	4	O-62(62-0-0)	1	-1.4
1914 KC-F	122	441	45	114	24	7	4	47	23	59	11	....	.259	.297	.372	.669	94	-6	50	3.74	-1	*O-120(7-130-0)	10	-1.5
1915 KC-F	80	240	24	57	9	2	2	26	12	29	5	....	.238	.277	.317	.593	77	-8	22	2.96	3	O-66(33-3-30)	5	-0.9
Total 4	**365**	**1222**	**113**	**283**	**49**	**21**	**6**	**115**	**73**	**88**	**38**	**....**	**.232**	**.281**	**.321**	**.602**	**80**	**-32**	**122**	**3.20**	**3**	**O-344**	**23**	**-5.2**
• KRUK, John	John Martin Kruk b: 2/9/1961, Charleston, WV BL/TL, 5'10", 204 lbs. Deb: 4/7/1986 Career OF: 303-11-125																							
1986 SD-N	122	278	33	86	16	2	4	38	45	58	2	4	.309	.406	.424	.830	132	13	47	6.03	-1	O-74(70-0-6)/1-9	11	0.9
1987 SD-N	138	447	72	140	14	2	20	91	73	93	18	10	.313	.410	.488	.897	142	28	92	7.53	4	*1-101,O-29(29-0-0)	18	2.6
1988 SD-N	120	378	54	91	17	1	9	44	80	68	5	3	.241	.373	.362	.736	114	10	56	4.94	0	1-63,O-55(29-0-26)	13	0.5
1989 SD-N	31	76	7	14	0	0	3	6	17	14	0	0	.184	.333	.303	.636	83	-1	8	3.07	2	O-27(2-0-25)	1	0.0
Phi-N	81	281	46	93	13	6	5	38	27	39	3	0	.331	.390	.473	.863	145	17	53	7.23	-1	O-72(63-0-12)/1-7	11	1.5
Yr.	112	357	53	107	13	6	8	44	44	53	3	0	.300	.377	.437	.814	131	16	60	6.16	1	O-99(65-0-37)/1-7	12	1.5
1990 Phi-N	142	443	52	129	25	8	7	67	69	70	10	5	.291	.387	.431	.818	125	17	75	6.06	0	O-87(68-0-21),1-61	17	1.1
1991 Phi-N★	152	538	84	158	27	6	21	92	67	100	7	0	.294	.373	.483	.856	141	31	99	6.65	-2	*1-102,O-52(36-11-6)	25	2.2
1992 Phi-N★	144	507	86	164	30	4	10	70	92	88	3	5	.323	.428	.458	.886	151	38	103	7.59	-7	*1-121,O-35(6-0-29)	24	2.4
1993*Phi-N★	150	535	100	169	33	5	14	85	111	87	6	2	.316	.433	.475	.908	145	41	117	8.25	-5	*1-144	25	2.3
1994 Phi-N	75	255	35	77	17	0	5	38	42	51	4	1	.302	.401	.427	.828	113	7	45	6.27	3	1-69	7	0.5
1995 Chi-A	45	159	13	49	7	0	2	23	26	33	0	1	.308	.405	.390	.795	113	4	26	5.86	0	D-42/1-1	4	0.1
Total 10	**1200**	**3897**	**582**	**1170**	**199**	**34**	**100**	**592**	**649**	**701**	**58**	**31**	**.300**	**.400**	**.446**	**.846**	**134**	**207**	**719**	**6.69**	**-8**	**1-678,O-431/D-42**	**156**	**14.1**
• KRYHOSKI, Dick	Richard David Kryhoski b: 3/24/1925, Leonia, NJ BL/TL, 6'2", 200 lbs. Deb: 4/19/1949																							
1949 NY-A	54	177	18	52	10	3	1	27	9	17	2	4	.294	.335	.401	.736	94	-4	22	4.32	0	1-51	4	-0.5
1950 Det-A	53	169	20	37	10	0	4	19	8	11	0	1	.219	.258	.349	.608	53	-14	15	3.02	0	1-47	1	-1.4
1951 Det-A	119	421	58	121	19	4	12	57	28	29	1	2	.287	.335	.437	.772	107	2	60	5.09	1	*1-112	11	-0.1
1952 StL-A	111	342	38	83	13	1	11	42	23	42	2	0	.243	.296	.383	.679	86	-7	39	3.90	-3	1-86	6	-1.4
1953 StL-A	104	338	35	94	18	4	16	50	26	33	0	5	.278	.333	.497	.830	119	5	52	5.41	4	1-88	8	0.4
1954 Bal-A	100	300	32	78	13	2	1	34	19	24	0	0	.260	.308	.327	.635	80	-9	29	3.27	3	1-69	3	-1.0
1955 KC-A	28	47	2	10	2	0	0	2	6	7	0	1	.213	.302	.255	.557	50	-4	4	2.73	0	1-14	0	-0.4
Total 7	**569**	**1794**	**203**	**475**	**85**	**14**	**45**	**231**	**119**	**163**	**5**	**13**	**.265**	**.315**	**.403**	**.718**	**93**	**-30**	**221**	**4.27**	**4**	**1-467**	**33**	**-4.4**
• KUBEK, Tony	Anthony Christopher Kubek b: 10/12/1936, Milwaukee, WI BL/TR, 6'3", 191 lbs. Deb: 4/20/1957 Career OF: 80-46-31																							
1957*NY-A	127	431	56	128	21	3	3	39	24	48	6	6	.297	.338	.381	.719	98	-3	56	4.55	-3	O-50(29-23-0),S-41,3-38/2-1	14	-0.6
1958*NY-A★	138	559	66	148	21	1	2	48	25	57	5	4	.265	.297	.317	.614	72	-23	52	3.26	20	*S-134/O-3(0-1-2),1-1,2-1	13	0.9
1959 NY-A★	132	512	67	143	25	7	6	51	24	46	3	3	.279	.314	.391	.705	96	-5	60	4.09	5	S-67,O-53(22-15-26),3-17/2	14	0.3
1960*NY-A	147	568	77	155	25	3	14	62	31	42	3	0	.273	.314	.401	.715	97	-4	70	4.27	13	*S-136,O-29(22-6-1)	19	2.0
1961*NY-A★	153	617	84	170	38	6	8	46	27	60	1	3	.276	.307	.395	.702	91	-12	74	4.24	18	*S-145	21	1.9
1962*NY-A	45	169	28	53	6	1	4	17	12	17	2	1	.314	.359	.432	.791	115	3	26	5.73	8	S-35/O-6(6-0-0)	7	1.4
1963*NY-A	135	557	72	143	21	3	7	44	28	68	4	2	.257	.295	.343	.638	79	-17	57	3.62	10	*S-132/O-1	18	0.5
1964 NY-A	106	415	46	95	16	3	8	31	26	55	4	1	.229	.276	.340	.616	69	-18	39	3.18	9	S-99	10	0.0
1965 NY-A	109	339	26	74	5	3	5	35	20	48	1	3	.218	.262	.295	.557	58	-20	25	2.39	-3	S-93/O-3(1-0-2),1-1	4	-1.8
Total 9	**1092**	**4167**	**522**	**1109**	**178**	**30**	**57**	**373**	**217**	**441**	**29**	**23**	**.266**	**.305**	**.364**	**.669**	**85**	**-98**	**459**	**3.83**	**76**	**S-882,O-145/3-55,2-3,1-2**	**120**	**4.5**
• KUBIAK, Ted	Theodore Rodger Kubiak b: 5/12/1942, New Brunswick, NJ BB/TR, 6', 175 lbs. Deb: 4/14/1967																							
1967 KC-A	53	102	6	16	2	1	0	5	12	20	0	0	.157	.246	.196	.442	33	-8	5	1.63	0	S-20,2-10/3-5	1	-0.7

YEAR TM-L	G	AB	R	H	2B	3B	HR	RBI	BB	SO	SB	CS	AVG	OBP	SLG	OPS	OPS+	BR/A	RC	RC/G	FR	G/POS	WS	TPW
1968 Oak-A	48	120	10	30	5	2	0	8	8	18	1	1	.250	.308	.325	.633	97	-1	12	3.53	-2	2-24,S-12	3	-0.1
1969 Oak-A	92	305	38	76	9	1	2	27	25	35	2	0	.249	.308	.305	.613	75	-10	29	3.15	1	S-42,2-33	7	-0.2
1970 Mil-A	158	540	63	136	9	6	4	41	72	51	4	9	.252	.340	.313	.653	81	-15	56	3.39	-19	2-91,S-73	10	-2.0
1971 Mil-A	89	260	26	59	6	5	3	17	41	31	0	5	.227	.332	.323	.655	87	-5	28	3.39	0	2-48,S-39	7	0.2
StL-N	32	72	8	18	3	2	1	10	11	12	1	0	.250	.349	.389	.738	105	1	11	5.27	-2	S-17,2-14	3	0.0
1972 Tex-A	46	116	5	26	3	0	0	7	12	12	0	1	.224	.302	.250	.552	68	-5	8	2.36	-2	2-25,S-15/3-1	1	-0.4
*Oak-A	51	94	14	17	4	1	0	8	9	11	0	0	.181	.252	.245	.497	51	-6	6	2.01	2	2-49/3-1	1	-0.1
Yr.	97	210	19	43	7	1	0	15	21	23	0	1	.205	.280	.248	.528	61	-10	14	2.20	0	2-74,S-15/3-2	2	-0.6
1973*Oak-A	106	182	15	40	6	1	3	17	12	19	1	1	.220	.268	.313	.581	67	-9	15	2.80	9	2-83,S-26/3-2	4	0.6
1974 Oak-A	99	220	22	46	3	0	0	18	18	15	1	1	.209	.269	.223	.492	46	-15	12	1.76	7	2-71,S-19,3-14/D-2	3	-0.4
1975 Oak-A	20	28	2	7	1	0	0	4	2	2	0	0	.250	.300	.286	.586	68	-1	2	2.64	1	/3-7,S-7,2-6	1	0.1
SD-N	87	196	13	44	5	0	0	14	24	18	3	1	.224	.309	.250	.559	60	-10	16	2.66	0	3-64,2-11/1-1	2	-1.0
1976 SD-N	96	212	16	50	5	2	0	26	25	28	0	3	.236	.316	.278	.595	76	-7	18	2.64	-4	3-27,2-25/S-6,1-1	3	-1.0
Total 10	977	2447	238	565	61	21	13	202	271	272	13	22	.231	.309	.289	.598	72	-89	219	2.91	-10	2-490,S-276,3-121/1-2,D-2	46	-5.1

• KUBISZYN, Jack John Henry Kubiszyn b: 12/19/1936, Buffalo, NY BR/TR, 5'11", 170 lbs. Deb: 4/23/1961

YEAR TM-L	G	AB	R	H	2B	3B	HR	RBI	BB	SO	SB	CS	AVG	OBP	SLG	OPS	OPS+	BR/A	RC	RC/G	FR	G/POS	WS	TPW
1961 Cle-A	25	42	4	9	0	0	0	0	2	5	0	0	.214	.250	.214	.464	26	-4	2	1.72	1	/3-8,S-7,2-2	0	-0.3
1962 Cle-A	25	59	3	10	2	0	1	2	5	7	0	0	.169	.234	.254	.489	32	-6	4	1.92	0	S-18/3-1	1	-0.5
Total 2	50	101	7	19	2	0	1	2	7	12	0	0	.188	.241	.238	.478	30	-10	6	1.84	0	/S-25,3-9,2-2	1	-0.8

• KUBSKI, Gil Gilbert Thomas Kubski b: 10/12/1954, Longview, TX BL/TR, 6'3", 185 lbs. Deb: 9/2/1980

YEAR TM-L	G	AB	R	H	2B	3B	HR	RBI	BB	SO	SB	CS	AVG	OBP	SLG	OPS	OPS+	BR/A	RC	RC/G	FR	G/POS	WS	TPW
1980 Cal-A	22	63	11	16	3	0	0	6	6	10	1	1	.254	.319	.302	.620	73	-2	6	3.13	1	O-20(1-0-19)	1	-0.3

• KUCZEK, Steve Stanislaw Leo Kuczek b: 12/28/1924, Amsterdam, NY BR/TR, 6', 160 lbs. Deb: 9/29/1949

YEAR TM-L	G	AB	R	H	2B	3B	HR	RBI	BB	SO	SB	CS	AVG	OBP	SLG	OPS	OPS+	BR/A	RC	RC/G	FR	G/POS	WS	TPW
1949 Bos-N	1	1	0	1	1	0	0	0	0	0	0	....	1.000	1.000	2.000	3.000	723	1	2	∞	0	....	0	0.1

• KUEHNE, Bill William J. Kuehne b: 10/24/1858, Leipzig, Germany d: 10/27/1921, Sulphur Springs, OH BR/TR, 5'8", 185 lbs. Deb: 5/1/1883 Career OF: 33-9-30

YEAR TM-L	G	AB	R	H	2B	3B	HR	RBI	BB	SO	SB	CS	AVG	OBP	SLG	OPS	OPS+	BR/A	RC	RC/G	FR	G/POS	WS	TPW
1883 Col-a	95	374	38	85	8	14	1	0	2	....	....	....	.227	.231	.332	.563	86	-5	29	2.85	-11	*3-69,2-18/S-7,O-3(1-2-0)	7	-1.2
1884 Col-a	110	415	48	98	13	16	5	0	9	....	....	....	.236	.254	.381	.635	113	6	41	3.57	11	*3-110	15	1.8
1885 Pit-a	104	411	54	93	9	19	0	43	15	....	....	....	.226	.257	.341	.598	89	-6	37	3.13	3	*3-97/S-7	9	0.0
1886 Pit-a	117	481	73	98	16	17	1	48	19	....	26	....	.204	.237	.314	.551	72	-17	43	3.03	3	O-54(24-5-24),3-47,1-18	10	-1.5
1887 Pit-N	102	416	68	134	18	15	1	41	14	39	17	....	.322	.324	.425	.749	113	6	62	5.86	-1	*S-91/1-4,3-4,O-3(0-1-2)	13	0.7
1888 Pit-N	138	524	60	123	22	11	3	62	9	68	34	....	.235	.250	.336	.586	93	-5	54	3.63	6	3-75,S-63	18	0.5
1889 Pit-N	97	390	43	96	20	5	5	57	9	36	15	....	.246	.263	.362	.625	82	-11	42	3.79	1	3-75,O-13(8-1-4)/2-5,1-2,S	8	-0.8
1890 Pit-P	126	528	66	126	21	12	5	73	28	37	21	....	.239	.277	.352	.629	73	-21	59	3.95	9	*3-126	10	-0.7
1891 Col-a	68	261	32	56	9	0	2	22	10	22	21	....	.215	.244	.272	.516	50	-18	23	2.97	-2	3-68	4	-1.6
Lou-a	39	152	25	41	3	1	1	17	7	13	9	....	.270	.306	.322	.629	81	-4	19	4.42	1	3-41	4	-0.3
Yr.	107	413	57	97	12	1	3	39	17	35	30	....	.235	.267	.291	.557	62	-22	41	3.48	-2	*3-109	8	-1.9
1892 Lou-N	76	287	22	48	4	5	0	36	13	36	6	....	.167	.203	.216	.419	29	-25	14	1.60	-6	3-76	2	-2.7
StL-N	6	24	1	4	1	0	0	0	0	3	1	....	.167	.200	.208	.408	25	-2	1	1.66	0	/3-5,S-1	0	-0.1
Cin-N	6	24	3	5	1	0	1	4	1	5	0	....	.208	.240	.375	.615	86	-1	2	3.15	1	/3-4,2-2	1	0.0
StL-N	1	4	0	0	0	0	0	0	0	1	0	....	.000	.000	.000	.000	-105	-1	0	.00	1	/3-1	0	0.0
Yr.	89	339	26	57	6	5	1	40	14	45	7	....	.168	.203	.224	.428	31	-28	18	1.69	-4	3-86/2-2,S-1	3	-2.8
Total 10	1085	4291	533	1007	145	115	25	403	136	260	150	....	.235	.258	.337	.595	82	-103	427	3.50	15	3-798,S-171/O-73,2-25,1-24	101	-5.9

• KUENN, Harvey Harvey Edward Kuenn b: 12/4/1930, West Allis, WI d: 2/28/1988, Peoria, AZ BR/TR, 6'2", 190 lbs. Deb: 9/6/1952 M/C Career OF: 354-163-343

YEAR TM-L	G	AB	R	H	2B	3B	HR	RBI	BB	SO	SB	CS	AVG	OBP	SLG	OPS	OPS+	BR/A	RC	RC/G	FR	G/POS	WS	TPW
1952 Det-A	19	80	2	26	2	2	0	8	2	1	2	1	.325	.349	.400	.749	107	1	10	4.72	0	S-19	2	0.2
1953 Det-A★	155	679	94	**209**	33	7	2	48	50	31	6	5	.308	.356	.386	.742	101	1	96	5.32	-29	*S-155	19	-1.5
1954 Det-A★	155	656	81	**201**	28	6	5	48	29	13	9	9	.306	.337	.390	.727	101	-4	80	4.37	7	*S-155	19	1.7
1955 Det-A★	145	620	101	190	**38**	5	8	62	40	27	8	3	.306	.349	.423	.772	109	7	92	5.61	-14	*S-141	22	0.4
1956 Det-A★	146	591	96	**196**	32	7	12	88	55	34	9	5	.332	.391	.470	.862	126	22	109	7.03	-3	*S-141/O-1	26	3.0
1957 Det-A★	151	624	74	173	30	6	9	44	47	28	5	8	.277	.328	.388	.716	92	-9	75	4.22	-10	*S-136,3-17/1-1	15	-0.9
1958 Det-A★	139	561	73	179	**39**	3	8	54	51	34	5	10	.319	.376	.442	.818	116	10	89	5.82	2	*O-138(0-138-0)	21	0.5
1959 Det-A★	139	561	99	**198**	**42**	7	9	71	48	37	7	2	**.353**	.405	.501	.906	140	32	117	8.32	-4	*O-137(0-23-116)	25	2.3
1960 Cle-A★	126	474	65	146	24	0	9	54	55	25	3	0	.308	.381	.416	.797	119	15	77	6.02	-2	*O-119(2-2-117)/3-5	18	0.9
1961 SF-N	131	471	60	125	22	4	5	46	47	34	5	4	.265	.333	.361	.694	87	-8	55	3.98	-4	O-93(67-0-31),3-32/S-1	10	-1.7
1962*SF-N	130	487	73	148	23	5	10	68	49	37	3	6	.304	.369	.433	.802	116	10	77	5.69	-3	*O-105(99-0-10),3-30	18	0.2
1963 SF-N	120	417	61	121	13	2	6	31	44	38	2	1	.290	.361	.374	.735	113	9	57	4.92	-6	O-64(45-0-27),3-53	14	0.1
1964 SF-N	111	351	42	92	16	2	4	22	35	32	0	1	.262	.331	.353	.684	91	-4	42	4.22	-3	O-88(65-0-36),1-11/3-2	8	-1.2
1965 SF-N	23	59	4	14	0	0	0	6	10	3	3	1	.237	.357	.237	.594	69	-1	6	3.40	1	O-14(12-0-2)/1-7	1	-0.1
Chi-N	54	120	11	26	5	0	0	6	22	13	1	0	.217	.338	.258	.596	69	-4	12	3.15	1	O-35(31-0-4)/1-1	2	-0.4
Yr.	77	179	15	40	5	0	0	12	32	16	4	1	.223	.344	.251	.596	69	-5	18	3.23	3	O-49(43-0-6)/1-8	3	-0.5
1966 Chi-N	3	3	0	1	0	0	0	0	0	1	0	0	.333	.333	.333	.667	85	-0	0	4.50	0	/O-1	0	0.0
Phi-N	86	159	15	47	9	0	0	15	10	16	0	0	.296	.337	.352	.689	92	-1	18	3.99	-2	O-31(31-0-0),1-13/3-1	3	-0.5
Yr.	89	162	15	48	9	0	0	15	10	17	0	0	.296	.337	.352	.689	92	-2	19	4.00	-2	O-32(32-0-0),1-13/3-1	3	-0.5
Total 15	1833	6913	951	2092	356	56	87	671	594	404	68	56	.303	.359	.408	.767	108	74	1013	5.34	-67	O-826,S-748,3-140/1-33	223	3.0

• KUHEL, Joe Joseph Anthony Kuhel b: 6/25/1906, Cleveland, OH d: 2/26/1984, Kansas City, KS BL/TL, 6', 180 lbs. Deb: 7/31/1930 M

YEAR TM-L	G	AB	R	H	2B	3B	HR	RBI	BB	SO	SB	CS	AVG	OBP	SLG	OPS	OPS+	BR/A	RC	RC/G	FR	G/POS	WS	TPW
1930 Was-A	18	63	9	18	3	3	0	17	5	6	1	0	.286	.348	.429	.776	95	-0	10	5.61	-1	1-16	2	-0.2
1931 Was-A	139	524	70	141	34	8	8	85	47	45	7	5	.269	.335	.410	.745	94	-3	73	4.95	-1	*1-139	14	-1.6
1932 Was-A	101	347	52	101	21	5	4	52	32	19	5	2	.291	.353	.415	.768	99	0	52	5.53	-2	1-85	10	-0.9
1933*Was-A	153	602	89	194	34	10	11	107	59	48	17	8	.322	.385	.467	.851	126	23	110	6.80	-5	*1-153	26	0.4
1934 Was-A	63	263	49	76	12	3	3	25	30	14	2	7	.289	.364	.392	.756	99	-3	37	4.90	-4	1-63	5	-1.2
1935 Was-A	151	633	99	165	25	9	2	74	78	44	5	4	.261	.345	.338	.684	80	-17	78	4.31	-7	*1-151	12	-3.6
1936 Was-A	149	588	107	189	42	8	16	118	64	30	15	7	.321	.392	.502	.893	126	24	117	7.60	3	*1-149	21	1.1
1937 Was-A	136	547	73	155	24	11	6	61	63	39	6	3	.283	.357	.400	.758	95	-4	81	5.37	7	*1-136	14	-0.9
1938 Chi-A	117	412	67	110	27	4	8	51	72	35	9	7	.267	.376	.410	.786	95	-3	67	5.61	0	*1-111	10	-1.2
1939 Chi-A	139	546	107	164	24	9	15	56	64	51	18	5	.300	.376	.460	.836	110	10	99	6.61	0	*1-136	19	-0.3
1940 Chi-A	155	603	111	169	28	8	27	94	87	59	12	5	.280	.374	.488	.861	120	19	116	6.82	-1	*1-155	21	0.3
1941 Chi-A	153	600	99	150	39	5	12	63	70	55	20	5	.250	.331	.392	.723	92	-5	81	4.58	5	*1-151	17	-1.4
1942 Chi-A	115	413	60	103	14	4	4	52	60	22	22	9	.249	.347	.332	.679	93	-0	54	4.39	-1	*1-112	12	-1.2
1943 Chi-A	153	531	55	113	21	1	5	46	76	45	14	8	.213	.319	.284	.604	77	-12	54	3.34	1	*1-153	12	-2.2
1944 Was-A	139	518	90	144	26	7	4	51	68	40	11	6	.278	.364	.378	.742	117	14	75	5.07	0	*1-138	17	0.7
1945 Was-A	142	533	73	152	29	13	2	75	79	31	10	5	.285	.378	.400	.778	137	28	88	6.00	5	*1-141	25	2.8
1946 Was-A	14	20	2	3	0	0	0	2	5	2	0	0	.150	.320	.150	.470	36	-1	1	2.22	0	/1-5	0	-0.1
Chi-A	64	238	24	65	9	3	4	20	21	24	4	4	.273	.335	.387	.721	105	1	30	4.33	0	1-63	6	-0.2
Yr.	78	258	26	68	9	3	4	22	26	26	4	4	.264	.333	.368	.702	99	-1	31	4.15	0	1-68	6	-0.3
1947 Chi-A	3	3	0	0	0	0	0	0	0	3	0	0	.000	.000	.000	.000	-104	-1	0	.00	0	....	0	-0.1
Total 18	2104	7984	1236	2212	412	111	131	1049	980	612	178	90	.277	.359	.406	.765	104	70	1223	5.42	-3	*1-2057	243	-9.8

• KUHN, Kenny Kenneth Harold Kuhn b: 3/20/1937, Louisville, KY BL/TR, 5'10.5", 175 lbs. Deb: 7/7/1955

YEAR TM-L	G	AB	R	H	2B	3B	HR	RBI	BB	SO	SB	CS	AVG	OBP	SLG	OPS	OPS+	BR/A	RC	RC/G	FR	G/POS	WS	TPW
1955 Cle-A	4	6	0	2	0	0	0	0	1	0	1	0	.333	.429	.333	.762	103	0	1	8.04	-1	/S-4	0	0.0
1956 Cle-A	27	22	7	6	1	0	0	2	0	4	0	1	.273	.273	.318	.591	54	-2	2	2.53	-3	S-17/2-5	0	-0.4
1957 Cle-A	40	53	5	9	0	0	0	5	4	9	0	0	.170	.228	.170	.398	10	-6	2	1.29	-2	2-14/3-2,S-1	0	-0.8
Total 3	71	81	12	17	1	0	0	7	5	13	1	1	.210	.256	.222	.478	29	-8	5	2.00	-6	/S-22,2-19,3-2	0	-1.3

• KUHN, Walt Walter Charles "Red" Kuhn b: 2/2/1884, Fresno, CA d: 6/14/1935, Fresno, CA BR/TR, 5'7", 162 lbs. Deb: 4/18/1912

YEAR TM-L	G	AB	R	H	2B	3B	HR	RBI	BB	SO	SB	CS	AVG	OBP	SLG	OPS	OPS+	BR/A	RC	RC/G	FR	G/POS	WS	TPW
1912 Chi-A	76	178	16	36	7	0	0	10	20	....	5	....	.202	.286	.242	.528	53	-10	14	2.47	3	C-75/2-1	5	-0.3
1913 Chi-A	26	50	5	8	1	0	0	5	13	8	1	....	.160	.333	.180	.513	52	-2	3	1.90	0	C-24	1	-0.1

YEAR TM-L	G	AB	R	H	2B	3B	HR	RBI	BB	SO	SB	CS	AVG	OBP	SLG	OPS	OPS+	BR/A	RC	RC/G	FR	G/POS	WS	TPW
1914 Chi-A	17	40	4	11	1	0	0	0	8	11	2	3	.275	.396	.300	.696	111	0	5	3.78	1	C-16	2	0.2
Total 3	119	268	25	55	9	0	0	15	41	19	8	3	.205	.313	.239	.552	61	-12	22	2.55	3	C-115/2-1	8	-0.2
• KUHNS, Charlie	Charles B. Kuhns b: 10/27/1877, Freeport, PA d: 7/15/1922, Pittsburgh, PA, 5'9", 160 lbs. Deb: 6/4/1897																							
1897 Pit-N	1	3	0	0	0	0	0	0	1	....	0	....	.000	.250	.000	.250	-32	-1	0	.00	0	/3-1	0	0.0
1899 Bos-N	7	18	2	5	0	0	0	3	2	....	0	....	.278	.350	.278	.628	67	-1	2	3.66	-1	/3-3,S-3	0	-0.1
Total 2	8	21	2	5	0	0	0	3	3	....	0	....	.238	.333	.238	.571	50	-1	2	2.97	-1	/3-4,S-3	0	-0.2
• KUIPER, Duane	Duane Eugene Kuiper b: 6/19/1950, Racine, WI BL/TR, 6', 175 lbs. Deb: 9/9/1974																							
1974 Cle-A	10	22	7	11	2	0	0	4	2	2	1	1	.500	.542	.591	1.133	228	3	6	13.37	0	/2-8	2	0.5
1975 Cle-A	90	346	42	101	11	1	0	25	30	26	19	18	.292	.362	.329	.691	97	-4	39	3.84	-1	2-87/D-1	9	0.1
1976 Cle-A	135	506	47	133	13	6	0	37	30	42	10	17	.263	.305	.312	.618	82	-17	43	2.79	11	*2-128/1-5,D-2	11	0.2
1977 Cle-A	148	610	62	169	15	8	1	50	37	55	11	11	.277	.326	.333	.658	83	-16	66	3.68	10	*2-148	13	0.2
1978 Cle-A	149	547	52	155	18	6	0	43	19	35	4	9	.283	.312	.338	.650	84	-15	54	3.41	-24	*2-149	10	-3.2
1979 Cle-A	140	479	46	122	9	5	0	39	37	27	4	9	.255	.313	.294	.608	65	-26	41	2.88	5	*2-140	9	-1.3
1980 Cle-A	42	149	10	42	5	0	0	9	13	8	0	1	.282	.340	.315	.655	80	-4	17	3.94	-3	2-42	3	-0.5
1981 Cle-A	72	206	15	53	6	0	0	14	8	13	1	1	.257	.285	.286	.571	66	-9	17	2.90	-13	2-72	4	-2.0
1982 SF-N	107	218	26	61	9	1	0	17	32	24	2	2	.280	.377	.330	.707	100	1	28	4.39	-6	2-51	7	-0.3
1983 SF-N	72	176	14	44	2	2	0	14	27	13	0	1	.250	.356	.284	.640	82	-3	18	3.37	-9	2-64	3	-1.0
1984 SF-N	83	115	8	23	1	0	0	11	12	10	0	1	.200	.276	.209	.484	39	-9	7	1.86	-3	2-31/1-1	1	-1.2
1985 SF-N	9	5	0	3	0	0	0	0	1	0	0	0	.600	.667	.600	1.267	270	1	2	14.51	0	....	1	0.1
Total 12	1057	3379	329	917	91	29	1	263	248	255	52	71	.271	.326	.316	.643	81	-98	340	3.39	-33	2-920/1-6,D-3	73	-8.5
• KUNKEL, Jeff	Jeffrey William Kunkel b: 3/25/1962, West Palm Beach, FL BR/TR, 6'2", 180 lbs. Deb: 7/23/1984 Career OF: 14-30-5																							
1984 Tex-A	50	142	13	29	2	3	3	7	2	35	4	3	.204	.221	.324	.545	47	-11	9	2.03	-7	S-48/D-1	1	-1.3
1985 Tex-A	2	4	1	1	0	0	0	0	0	3	0	0	.250	.250	.250	.500	37	-0	0	2.25	0	/S-2	0	0.0
1986 Tex-A	8	13	3	3	0	0	1	2	0	2	0	0	.231	.231	.462	.692	81	-0	1	3.74	-2	/S-5,D-1	0	-0.2
1987 Tex-A	15	32	1	7	0	0	1	2	0	10	0	1	.219	.242	.313	.555	46	-3	2	2.22	-2	2-10/3-3,O-3(1-2-0),1-1,D,S	0	-0.4
1988 Tex-A	55	154	14	35	8	3	2	15	4	35	0	1	.227	.252	.357	.609	67	-8	12	2.56	-5	2-28,S-19,3-10/O-6(4-2-0),D,P	1	-1.1
1989 Tex-A	108	293	39	79	21	2	8	29	20	75	3	2	.270	.323	.437	.760	110	3	41	4.72	-11	S-59,O-30(5-24-3)/2-8,D-5,3,P	9	-0.8
1990 Tex-A	99	200	17	34	11	1	3	17	11	66	2	1	.170	.221	.280	.501	39	-17	11	1.70	2	S-67,3-15,2-13/O-5(1-2-2),D	3	-1.1
1992 Chi-N	20	29	0	4	2	0	0	1	0	8	0	0	.138	.138	.207	.345	-4	-4	1	.64	-0	/S-6,2-3,O-3(3-0-0)	0	-0.4
Total 8	357	867	88	192	44	9	18	73	37	234	9	8	.221	.260	.355	.615	69	-41	78	2.88	-24	S-207/2-62,O-47,3-32,D-12,P,1	14	-5.3
• KUNTZ, Rusty	Russell Jay Kuntz b: 2/4/1955, Orange, CA BR/TR, 6'3", 190 lbs. Deb: 9/1/1979 C Career OF: 63-117-63																							
1979 Chi-A	5	11	0	1	0	0	0	0	2	6	0	0	.091	.231	.091	.322	-9	-2	0	.57	1	/O-5(1-1-3)	0	-0.1
1980 Chi-A	36	62	5	14	4	0	0	3	5	13	1	0	.226	.284	.290	.574	58	-3	5	2.72	1	O-34(19-9-6)	1	-0.3
1981 Chi-A	67	55	15	14	2	0	0	4	6	8	1	0	.255	.339	.291	.630	85	-1	6	3.76	-1	O-51(28-13-13)/D-5	1	-0.3
1982 Chi-A	21	26	4	5	1	0	0	3	2	8	0	0	.192	.250	.231	.481	33	-2	1	1.71	0	O-21(1-20-1)	0	-0.3
1983 Chi-A	28	42	6	11	1	0	0	1	6	13	1	0	.262	.354	.286	.640	76	-1	5	3.96	-1	O-27(2-25-0)/D-1	1	-0.2
Min-A	31	100	13	19	3	0	3	5	12	28	0	0	.190	.277	.310	.587	59	-6	8	2.60	0	O-30(0-27-3)	1	-0.6
Yr.	59	142	19	30	4	0	3	6	18	41	1	0	.211	.300	.303	.603	64	-6	13	2.97	-1	O-57(2-52-3)/D-1	2	-0.8
1984*Det-A	84	140	32	40	12	0	2	22	25	28	2	2	.286	.398	.414	.812	126	6	25	6.26	-1	O-67(12-22-37),D-10	6	0.4
1985 Det-A	5	5	0	0	0	0	0	0	2	2	0	1	.000	.286	.000	.286	-13	-1	0	.33	0	/D-3,1-1	0	-0.1
Total 7	277	441	75	104	23	0	5	38	60	106	5	3	.236	.330	.322	.652	82	-10	50	3.81	-1	O-235/D-19,1-1	10	-1.5
• KUROWSKI, Whitey	George John Kurowski b: 4/19/1918, Reading, PA d: 12/9/1999, Sinking Spring, PA BR/TR, 5'11", 193 lbs. Deb: 9/23/1941																							
1941 StL-N	5	9	1	3	2	0	0	2	0	2	0	....	.333	.400	.556	.956	157	1	2	9.47	0	/3-4	1	0.1
1942*StL-N	115	366	51	93	17	3	9	42	33	60	7	....	.254	.326	.391	.717	101	0	48	4.46	9	*3-104/O-1,S-1	13	1.4
1943*StL-N★	139	522	69	150	24	8	13	70	31	54	3	....	.287	.330	.439	.768	116	8	74	5.08	5	*3-137/S-2	18	1.6
1944*StL-N★	149	555	95	150	25	7	20	87	58	40	2	....	.270	.341	.449	.790	119	13	85	5.40	12	*3-146/2-9,S-1	22	2.8
1945 StL-N★	133	511	84	165	27	3	21	102	45	45	1	....	.323	.383	.511	.894	144	28	100	7.36	7	*3-131/S-6	27	3.7
1946*StL-N★	142	519	76	156	32	5	14	89	72	47	2	....	.301	.391	.462	.853	136	26	97	6.96	-1	*3-138	26	2.6
1947 StL-N★	146	513	108	159	27	6	27	104	87	56	4	....	.310	.420	.544	.964	147	38	118	8.47	-12	*3-141	26	2.5
1948 StL-N	77	220	34	47	8	0	2	33	42	28	0	....	.214	.352	.277	.629	68	-8	25	3.80	-4	3-65	5	-1.1
1949 StL-N	10	14	0	2	0	0	0	0	1	0	0	....	.143	.200	.143	.343	-6	-2	0	.63	0	/3-2	0	-0.2
Total 9	916	3229	518	925	162	32	106	529	369	332	19	....	.286	.366	.455	.821	124	104	551	6.12	17	3-868/S-10,2-9,O-1	138	13.4
• KUSICK, Craig	Craig Robert Kusick b: 9/30/1948, Milwaukee, WI BR/TR, 6'3", 232 lbs. Deb: 9/8/1973 Career OF: 11-0-0																							
1973 Min-A	15	48	4	12	2	0	0	4	7	9	0	0	.250	.357	.292	.649	81	-1	6	4.31	-1	1-11/D-2,O-2(2-0-0)	1	-0.3
1974 Min-A	76	201	36	48	7	1	8	26	35	36	0	0	.239	.354	.403	.757	113	5	30	5.11	1	1-75	7	0.2
1975 Min-A	57	156	14	37	8	0	6	27	21	23	0	0	.237	.346	.404	.750	109	3	23	5.04	2	1-51	4	0.1
1976 Min-A	109	266	33	69	13	0	11	36	35	44	5	1	.259	.348	.432	.780	124	9	43	5.61	3	D-79,1-23	10	1.0
1977 Min-A	115	268	34	68	12	0	12	45	49	60	3	1	.254	.375	.433	.808	121	10	43	5.25	-2	D-85,1-23	7	0.6
1978 Min-A	77	191	23	33	3	2	4	20	37	38	3	2	.173	.310	.272	.582	64	-8	17	2.67	1	D-35,1-27/O-9(9-0-0)	1	-1.0
1979 Min-A	24	54	8	13	4	0	3	6	3	11	0	0	.241	.281	.481	.762	97	-1	7	4.53	0	D-12/1-8	1	-0.1
Tor-A	24	54	3	11	1	0	2	7	7	7	0	0	.204	.306	.333	.640	72	-2	6	3.26	-0	1-20/D-1,P-1	1	-0.3
Yr.	48	108	11	24	5	0	5	13	10	18	0	0	.222	.294	.407	.702	84	-2	13	3.87	0	1-28,D-13/P-1	2	-0.5
Total 7	497	1238	155	291	50	3	46	171	194	228	11	4	.235	.345	.392	.736	105	16	174	4.68	4	1-238,D-214/O-11,P-1	32	0.2
• KUSNYER, Art	Arthur William Kusnyer b: 12/19/1945, Akron, OH BR/TR, 6'2", 198 lbs. Deb: 9/21/1970 C																							
1970 Chi-A	4	10	0	1	0	0	0	0	0	4	0	0	.100	.100	.100	.200	-43	-2	0	.30	0	/C-3	0	-0.2
1971 Cal-A	6	13	0	2	0	0	0	0	0	3	0	0	.154	.154	.154	.308	-14	-2	0	.76	0	/C-6	0	-0.2
1972 Cal-A	64	179	13	37	2	1	2	13	16	33	0	0	.207	.276	.263	.538	64	-8	14	2.51	-2	C-63	4	-0.8
1973 Cal-A	41	64	5	8	2	0	0	3	2	12	0	1	.125	.152	.156	.308	-14	-10	1	.69	-1	C-41	1	-1.0
1976 Mil-A	15	34	2	4	1	0	0	3	1	5	1	0	.118	.167	.147	.314	-8	-4	1	.89	-1	C-14	0	-0.5
1978 KC-A	9	13	1	3	1	0	1	2	2	4	0	0	.231	.333	.538	.872	138	1	3	6.77	-1	/C-9	1	0.0
Total 6	139	313	21	55	6	1	3	21	21	61	1	1	.176	.232	.230	.462	38	-25	19	1.94	-4	C-136	6	-2.7
• KUSTUS, Jul	Joseph Julius "Joe,Kul" Kustus b: 9/5/1882, Detroit, MI d: 4/27/1916, Eloise, MI BR/TR, 5'10" Deb: 4/17/1909																							
1909 Bro-N	53	173	12	25	5	0	1	11	11	....	9	....	.145	.204	.191	.395	23	-16	9	1.44	-1	O-50(1-18-31)	1	-2.1
• KUTCHER, Randy	Randy Scott Kutcher b: 4/30/1960, Anchorage, AK BR/TR, 5'11", 175 lbs. Deb: 6/19/1986 Career OF: 26-78-52																							
1986 SF-N	71	186	28	44	9	1	7	16	11	41	6	5	.237	.279	.409	.688	92	-4	20	3.41	-1	O-51(7-44-1),S-13/3-4,2-3	4	-0.6
1987 SF-N	14	16	7	3	1	1	0	1	1	5	1	0	.188	.235	.375	.610	61	-1	2	3.31	-1	/O-6(1-4-1),2-2,3-2,S-1	1	-0.1
1988 Bos-A	19	12	2	2	1	0	0	0	0	2	0	1	.167	.167	.250	.417	14	-2	0	.61	0	/D-7,O-7(5-0-2),3-2	0	-0.2
1989 Bos-A	77	160	28	36	10	3	2	18	11	46	3	0	.225	.275	.363	.637	74	-6	15	3.14	-5	O-57(11-21-25)/3-6,D-6,C-1	3	-1.2
1990*Bos-A	63	74	18	17	4	1	1	5	13	18	3	3	.230	.345	.351	.696	91	-1	9	3.75	-1	O-34(2-9-23),3-11/2-5,D-5	1	-0.3
Total 5	244	448	83	102	25	6	10	40	36	112	13	9	.228	.285	.377	.662	82	-13	46	3.29	-8	O-155/3-25,D-18,S-14,2-10,C	9	-2.4
• KUTINA, Joe	Joseph Peter Kutina b: 1/16/1885, Chicago, IL d: 4/13/1945, Chicago, IL BR/TR, 6'2", 205 lbs. Deb: 9/6/1911																							
1911 StL-A	26	101	12	26	6	2	3	15	2	....	2	....	.257	.279	.446	.724	105	-0	13	4.24	-1	1-26	2	-0.2
1912 StL-A	69	205	18	42	9	3	1	18	13	....	0	....	.205	.262	.293	.555	61	-11	16	2.41	-5	1-51/O-1	1	-1.7
Total 2	95	306	30	68	15	5	4	33	15	....	2	....	.222	.268	.343	.611	75	-12	28	2.99	-6	/1-77,O-1	3	-1.9
• KVASNAK, Al	Alexander Kvasnak b: 1/11/1921, Sagamore, PA d: 9/26/2002, Arcadia, CA BR/TR, 6'1", 170 lbs. Deb: 4/15/1942																							
1942 Was-A	5	11	3	2	0	0	0	0	2	1	0	0	.182	.308	.182	.490	40	-1	1	2.37	0	/O-3(1-0-2)	0	-0.1
• KYLE, Andy	Andrew Ewing Kyle b: 10/29/1889, Toronto, Canada d: 9/6/1971, Toronto, Canada BL/TL, 5'8", 160 lbs. Deb: 9/7/1912																							
1912 Cin-N	9	21	3	7	1	0	0	4	4	2	0	....	.333	.440	.381	.821	129	1	4	6.19	0	/O-7(2-5-0)	1	0.1

YEAR TM-L	G	AB	R	H	2B	3B	HR	RBI	BB	SO	SB	CS	AVG	OBP	SLG	OPS	OPS+	BR/A	RC	RC/G	FR	G/POS	WS	TPW
• LAABS, Chet	Chester Peter Laabs b: 4/30/1912, Milwaukee, WI d: 1/26/1983, Warren, MI BR/TR, 5'8", 175 lbs. Deb: 5/5/1937 Career OF: 343-237-253																							
1937 Det-A	72	242	31	58	13	5	8	37	24	66	6	2	.240	.308	.434	.742	83	-7	33	4.68	-5	0-62(22-40-0)	5	-1.3
1938 Det-A	64	211	26	50	7	3	7	37	15	52	3	2	.237	.288	.398	.686	66	-13	24	3.84	-1	0-53(22-32-0)	3	-1.4
1939 Det-A	5	16	1	5	1	1	0	2	2	0	0	0	.313	.389	.500	.889	117	0	3	6.39	1	/0-5(5-0-0)	1	0.1
StL-A	95	317	52	95	20	5	10	62	33	62	4	1	.300	.368	.489	.856	115	7	57	6.58	-4	0-79(3-70-6)	8	0.0
Yr.	100	333	53	100	21	6	10	64	35	62	4	1	.300	.369	.489	.858	115	7	60	6.57	-4	0-84(8-70-6)	9	0.1
1940 StL-A	105	218	32	59	11	5	10	40	34	59	3	3	.271	.372	.505	.876	122	7	43	7.15	-2	0-63(25-29-10)	8	0.2
1941 StL-A	118	392	64	109	23	6	15	59	51	59	5	2	.278	.361	.482	.843	117	10	71	6.35	-5	*0-100(21-15-64)	12	-0.1
1942 StL-A	144	520	90	143	21	7	27	99	88	88	0	3	.275	.380	.498	.878	144	30	103	6.96	-2	*0-139(36-25-80)	23	2.1
1943 StL-A★	151	580	83	145	27	7	17	85	73	105	5	7	.250	.338	.409	.747	115	10	82	4.78	1	*0-150(125-24-6)	17	0.3
1944*StL-A	66	201	28	47	10	2	5	23	29	33	3	1	.234	.330	.378	.709	96	-0	27	4.55	2	0-55(38-0-18)	7	-0.2
1945 StL-A	35	109	15	26	4	3	1	8	16	17	0	0	.239	.352	.358	.709	101	1	15	4.68	0	0-35(34-2-2)	3	-0.1
1946 StL-A	80	264	40	69	13	0	16	52	20	50	3	1	.261	.316	.492	.808	117	5	38	5.01	1	0-72(6-0-66)	9	0.4
1947 Phi-A	15	32	5	7	1	0	1	5	4	4	0	0	.219	.306	.344	.649	79	-1	4	4.06	1	/0-7(6-0-1)	1	-0.1
Total 11	950	3102	467	813	151	44	117	509	389	595	32	22	.262	.346	.452	.798	113	48	501	5.60	-14	0-820	97	0.0
• LABOY, Coco	Jose Alberto Laboy b: 7/3/1940, Ponce, Puerto Rico BR/TR, 5'10", 170 lbs. Deb: 4/8/1969																							
1969 Mon-N	157	562	53	145	29	1	18	83	40	96	0	2	.258	.312	.409	.721	100	-2	70	4.25	-7	*3-156	13	-1.0
1970 Mon-N	137	432	37	86	26	1	5	53	31	81	0	2	.199	.256	.299	.555	48	-34	31	2.28	-12	*3-132/2-3	2	-4.6
1971 Mon-N	76	151	10	38	4	0	1	14	11	19	0	1	.252	.302	.298	.600	70	-6	13	3.07	-7	3-65/2-2	2	-1.4
1972 Mon-N	28	69	6	18	2	0	3	14	10	16	0	0	.261	.354	.420	.775	117	2	11	5.61	-3	3-24/2-3,S-2	3	-0.1
1973 Mon-N	22	33	2	4	1	0	1	2	5	8	0	0	.121	.237	.242	.479	32	-3	2	1.99	-3	3-20/2-1	0	-0.7
Total 5	420	1247	108	291	62	2	28	166	97	220	0	5	.233	.292	.354	.646	78	-43	127	3.39	-31	3-397/2-9,S-2	20	-7.8
• LACHANCE, Candy	George Joseph LaChance b: 2/15/1870, Putnam, CT d: 8/18/1932, Waterville, CT BB/TR, 6'1", 183 lbs. Deb: 8/15/1893 Career OF: 15-2-7																							
1893 Bro-N	11	35	1	6	1	0	0	6	2	12	0	....	.171	.237	.200	.437	17	-4	2	1.55	-3	/C-6,0-5(4-0-1)	0	-0.5
1894 Bro-N	69	261	48	83	13	8	5	52	16	32	20	....	.318	.360	.487	.846	110	3	54	7.92	-4	1-56,C-10/0-3(0-0-3)	8	-0.1
1895 Bro-N	128	541	102	170	23	9	8	108	29	48	37	....	.314	.358	.434	.793	113	10	100	7.26	3	*1-125/0-3(0-0-3)	19	1.0
1896 Bro-N	89	348	60	99	10	13	7	58	23	32	17	....	.284	.331	.448	.779	110	3	59	6.12	3	*1-89	10	0.5
1897 Bro-N	126	520	86	160	28	16	4	90	15	....	26	....	.308	.333	.446	.779	111	5	89	6.40	6	*1-126	14	0.9
1898 Bro-N	136	526	62	130	23	7	5	65	31	....	23	....	.247	.299	.346	.645	85	-12	64	4.17	-14	1-74,S-48,0-13(11-2-0)	11	-2.3
1899 Bal-N	125	472	65	145	23	10	1	75	21	....	31	....	.307	.350	.405	.755	101	-1	80	6.40	-3	*1-125	11	-0.4
1901 Cle-A	133	548	81	166	22	9	1	75	7	....	11	....	.303	.314	.381	.696	96	-5	72	4.88	2	*1-133	12	-0.5
1902 Bos-A	138	541	60	151	13	4	6	56	18	....	8	....	.279	.309	.351	.660	80	-16	64	4.22	-7	*1-138	9	-2.4
1903*Bos-A	141	522	60	134	22	6	1	53	28	....	12	....	.257	.303	.328	.631	85	-10	60	3.85	-9	*1-141	10	-2.2
1904 Bos-A	157	573	55	130	19	5	1	47	23	....	7	....	.227	.265	.283	.548	69	-20	49	2.77	-3	*1-157	7	-2.9
1905 Bos-A	12	41	1	6	1	0	0	5	6	....	0	....	.146	.255	.171	.426	36	-3	2	1.63	0	1-12	0	-0.3
Total 12	1265	4928	681	1380	198	87	39	690	219	124	192	....	.280	.318	.379	.697	93	-49	695	5.05	-27	*1-1176/S-48,0-24,C-16	111	-9.1
• LACHEMANN, Rene	Rene George Lachemann b: 5/4/1945, Los Angeles, CA BR/TR, 6', 198 lbs. Deb: 5/4/1965 M/C																							
1965 KC-A	92	216	20	49	7	1	9	29	12	57	0	0	.227	.268	.394	.661	87	-5	22	3.35	-0	C-75	4	-0.2
1966 KC-A	7	5	0	1	1	0	0	0	0	1	0	0	.200	.200	.400	.600	70	-0	0	.00	0	/C-6	0	0.0
1968 Oak-A	19	60	3	9	1	0	0	4	1	11	0	0	.150	.177	.167	.344	5	-7	2	1.00	-2	C-16	0	-0.9
Total 3	118	281	23	59	9	1	9	33	13	69	0	0	.210	.247	.345	.593	69	-12	24	2.76	-2	/C-97	4	-1.2
• LACOCK, Pete	Ralph Pierre LaCock b: 1/17/1952, Burbank, CA BL/TL, 6'2", 210 lbs. Deb: 9/6/1972 Career OF: 52-1-65																							
1972 Chi-N	5	6	3	3	0	0	0	4	0	1	1	0	.500	.500	.500	1.000	167	1	2	11.69	-0	/0-3(0-0-3)	1	0.1
1973 Chi-N	11	16	1	4	1	0	0	3	1	2	0	0	.250	.294	.313	.607	63	-1	2	3.48	0	/0-5(0-0-5)	0	-0.1
1974 Chi-N	35	110	9	20	4	1	1	8	12	16	0	0	.182	.268	.264	.532	47	-8	8	2.34	2	0-22(0-0-22),1-11	0	-0.8
1975 Chi-N	106	249	30	57	8	1	6	30	37	27	0	2	.229	.329	.341	.670	82	-6	27	3.46	3	1-53,0-26(11-0-15)	4	-0.8
1976 Chi-N	106	244	34	54	9	2	8	28	42	37	1	4	.221	.338	.373	.711	93	-3	31	4.17	-1	1-54,0-19(7-0-12)	6	-0.8
1977*KC-A	88	218	25	66	12	1	3	29	15	25	2	1	.303	.350	.408	.759	105	2	31	5.21	2	1-29,D-26,0-12(8-1-3)	6	0.2
1978*KC-A	118	322	44	95	21	2	5	48	21	27	1	0	.295	.338	.419	.757	109	4	44	5.01	-1	*1-106	10	-0.3
1979 KC-A	132	408	54	113	25	4	3	56	37	26	2	1	.277	.339	.380	.718	92	-4	50	4.20	3	*1-108,D-16	8	-0.8
1980*KC-A	114	156	14	32	6	0	1	18	17	10	1	0	.205	.287	.263	.550	51	-10	11	2.33	0	1-86,0-29(26-0-5)	1	-1.3
Total 9	715	1729	214	444	86	11	27	224	182	171	8	8	.257	.329	.366	.695	89	-25	206	4.05	8	1-447,0-116/D-42	36	-4.6
• LACY, Guy	Osceola Guy Lacy b: 6/12/1897, Cleveland, TN d: 11/19/1953, Cleveland, TN BR/TR, 5'11.5", 170 lbs. Deb: 5/7/1926																							
1926 Cle-A	13	24	2	4	0	0	1	2	2	2	0	0	.167	.259	.292	.551	43	-2	2	2.35	-1	2-11/3-2	0	-0.2
• LACY, Lee	Leondaus Lacy b: 4/10/1948, Longview, TX BR/TR, 6'1", 175 lbs. Deb: 6/30/1972 Career OF: 417-77-594																							
1972 LA-N	60	243	34	63	7	3	0	12	19	37	5	3	.259	.313	.313	.626	80	-6	24	3.41	-3	2-58	6	-0.6
1973 LA-N	57	135	14	28	2	0	0	8	15	34	2	3	.207	.287	.222	.509	45	-11	9	2.12	-4	2-41	1	-1.3
1974*LA-N	48	78	13	22	6	0	0	8	2	14	2	0	.282	.300	.359	.659	87	-1	9	4.12	0	2-34/3-1	2	0.0
1975 LA-N	101	306	44	96	11	5	7	40	22	29	5	9	.314	.360	.451	.811	129	8	44	5.04	-1	2-43,0-43(37-3-8)/S-1	11	0.6
1976 Atl-N	50	180	25	49	4	2	3	20	6	12	2	2	.272	.299	.367	.666	83	-5	18	3.46	-3	2-44/0-5(1-4-1),3-1	3	-0.6
LA-N	53	158	17	42	7	1	0	14	16	13	1	2	.266	.333	.323	.656	88	-3	16	3.31	-1	0-37(5-23-10)/3-3,2-2	3	-0.5
Yr.	103	338	42	91	11	3	3	34	22	25	3	4	.269	.316	.346	.662	86	-8	34	3.39	-4	2-46,0-42(6-27-11)/3-4	6	-1.2
1977*LA-N	75	169	28	45	7	0	6	21	10	21	4	0	.266	.307	.414	.721	92	-2	22	4.58	1	0-32(18-0-18),2-22,3-12	5	0.0
1978*LA-N	103	245	29	64	16	4	13	40	27	30	7	4	.261	.337	.518	.855	136	11	42	5.93	-4	0-44(17-0-27),2-24/3-9,S-1	10	0.7
1979*Pit-N	84	182	17	45	9	3	5	15	22	36	6	1	.247	.332	.412	.744	97	0	27	5.14	-1	0-41(41-0-0)/2-5	5	-0.2
1980 Pit-N	109	278	45	93	20	4	7	33	28	33	18	9	.335	.399	.511	.910	150	19	57	7.59	2	0-88(86-3-0)/3-3	15	1.7
1981 Pit-N	78	213	31	57	11	4	2	10	11	29	24	3	.268	.307	.385	.692	92	1	28	4.71	2	0-63(34-1-29)/3-1	6	0.0
1982 Pit-N	121	359	66	112	16	3	5	31	32	57	40	15	.312	.370	.415	.785	116	10	56	5.53	0	*0-113(40-17-71)/3-2	13	0.6
1983 Pit-N	108	288	40	87	12	3	4	13	22	36	31	13	.302	.352	.406	.758	107	3	42	5.18	-2	0-98(59-24-28)	9	-0.2
1984 Pit-N	138	474	66	152	26	3	12	70	32	61	21	11	.321	.364	.464	.828	131	18	77	5.83	13	*0-127(78-0-88)/2-2	18	2.5
1985 Bal-A	121	492	69	144	22	4	9	48	39	95	10	3	.293	.347	.409	.756	109	7	70	5.15	3	*0-115(0-1-115)/D-5	14	0.4
1986 Bal-A	130	491	77	141	18	0	11	47	37	71	4	6	.287	.337	.391	.728	99	-3	62	4.44	5	*0-120(0-0-120)/D-3	11	-0.4
1987 Bal-A	87	258	35	63	13	3	7	28	32	49	3	2	.244	.328	.399	.727	94	-2	34	4.53	4	0-80(1-1-79)/D-4	6	-0.2
Total 16	1523	4549	650	1303	207	42	91	458	372	657	185	86	.286	.342	.410	.752	108	43	637	4.93	10	*0-1006,2-275/3-32,D-12,S-2	138	2.4
• LADD, Hi	Arthur Clifford Ladd b: 2/9/1870, Willimantic, CT d: 5/7/1948, Cranston, RI BL/TR, 6'4", 180 lbs. Deb: 7/12/1898																							
1898 Pit-N	1	1	0	0	0	0	0	0	0	....	0	....	.000	.000	.000	.000	-102	-0	0	.00	0	....	0	0.0
Bos-N	1	4	1	1	0	0	0	0	0	....	0	....	.250	.250	.250	.500	41	-0	0	2.26	-0	/0-1	0	0.0
Yr.	2	5	1	1	0	0	0	0	0	....	0	....	.200	.200	.200	.400	12	-1	0	1.70	-0	/0-1	0	-0.1
• LADEW, Steve	Stephen Ladew b: St. Louis, MO Deb: 9/27/1889																							
1889 KC-a	2	4	0	0	0	0	0	0	0	3	0	....	.000	.000	.000	.000	-95	-1	0	.00	0	/0-1,P-1	0	-0.1
• LAFATA, Joe	Joseph Joseph Lafata b: 8/3/1921, Detroit, MI BL/TL, 6', 163 lbs. Deb: 4/17/1947																							
1947 NY-N	62	95	13	21	1	0	2	18	15	18	1	....	.221	.333	.295	.628	68	-4	10	3.45	1	0-19(20-1-0)/1-2	1	-0.4
1948 NY-N	1	1	0	0	0	0	0	0	0	1	0	....	.000	.000	.000	.000	-99	-0	0	.00	0	....	0	0.0
1949 NY-N	64	140	18	33	2	2	3	16	9	23	1	....	.236	.282	.343	.625	67	-7	14	3.42	-3	1-47	2	-1.1
Total 3	127	236	31	54	3	2	5	34	24	42	2	....	.229	.303	.322	.625	66	-11	24	3.42	-2	/1-49,0-19	3	-1.6
• LAFFERTY, Flip	Frank Bernard Lafferty b: 5/4/1854, Scranton, PA d: 2/8/1910, Wilmington, DE TR Deb: 9/15/1876 ♦																							
1876 Phi-N	1	3	0	0	0	0	0	0	0	0	....	....	.000	.000	.000	.000	-101	-1	0	.00	0	/P-1	0	0.2
1877 Lou-N	4	17	2	1	1	0	0	0	0	4	....	....	.059	.059	.118	.176	-39	-3	0	.21	-1	/0-4(0-4-0)	0	-0.3
Total 2	5	20	2	1	1	0	0	0	0	4	....	....	.050	.050	.100	.150	-48	-3	0	.17	-1	/0-4,P-1	0	-0.1

YEAR TM-L	G	AB	R	H	2B	3B	HR	RBI	BB	SO	SB	CS	AVG	OBP	SLG	OPS	OPS+	BR/A	RC	RC/G	FR	G/POS	WS	TPW

• LAFOREST, Pete — Pierre-Luc LaForest b: 1/27/1978, Hull, Canada BL/TR, 6'2", 208 lbs. Deb: 9/2/2003

| 2003 TB-A | 19 | 48 | 0 | 8 | 2 | 0 | 0 | 6 | 1 | 14 | 0 | 0 | .167 | .200 | .208 | .408 | 8 | -6 | 2 | 1.25 | -0 | D-12/C-4 | 0 | -0.7 |

• LAFOREST, Ty — Biron Joseph LaForest b: 4/18/1917, Edmundston, Canada d: 5/5/1947, Arlington, MA BR/TR, 5'9", 165 lbs. Deb: 8/4/1945

| 1945 Bos-A | 52 | 204 | 25 | 51 | 7 | 4 | 2 | 16 | 10 | 35 | 4 | 4 | .250 | .285 | .353 | .638 | 83 | | 19 | 2.95 | 1 | 3-45/O-5(3-0-2) | 3 | -0.5 |

• LAFRANCOIS, Roger — Roger Victor LaFrancois b: 8/2/1954, Norwich, CT BL/TR, 6'2", 215 lbs. Deb: 5/27/1982

| 1982 Bos-A | 8 | 10 | 1 | 4 | 1 | 0 | 0 | 1 | 0 | 0 | 0 | 0 | .400 | .400 | .500 | .900 | 137 | | 2 | 9.00 | 0 | /C-8 | 1 | 0.0 |

• LAGA, Mike — Michael Russell Laga b: 6/14/1960, Ridgewood, NJ BL/TL, 6'2", 210 lbs. Deb: 9/1/1982

1982 Det-A	27	88	6	23	9	0	3	11	4	23	0	0	.261	.293	.466	.759	104	0	12	4.92	-2	1-19/D-8	2	-0.3
1983 Det-A	12	21	2	4	0	0	0	2	1	9	0	0	.190	.227	.190	.418	17	-2	1	1.16	0	/D-6,1-5	0	-0.3
1984 Det-A	9	11	1	6	0	0	0	1	1	2	0	0	.545	.583	.545	1.129	216	2	4	19.72	0	/1-4,D-4	1	0.2
1985 Det-A	9	36	3	6	1	0	2	6	0	9	0	0	.167	.167	.361	.528	40	-3	2	1.57	1	/D-5,1-4	0	-0.3
1986 Det-A	15	45	6	9	1	0	3	8	5	13	0	0	.200	.280	.422	.702	88	-1	6	4.21	-1	1-12/D-2	1	-0.3
StL-N	18	46	7	10	4	0	3	8	5	18	0	0	.217	.308	.500	.808	120	1	7	5.12	2	1-16	2	0.3
1987 StL-N	17	29	4	4	1	0	1	4	2	7	0	0	.138	.194	.276	.469	22	-3	1	1.36	0	1-12	0	-0.4
1988 StL-N	41	100	5	13	0	0	1	4	2	21	0	0	.130	.147	.160	.307	-12	-15	2	.75	-3	1-37	0	-2.1
1989 SF-N	17	20	1	4	1	0	1	7	1	6	0	0	.200	.238	.400	.638	82	-1	2	3.32	0	/1-4	1	-0.1
1990 SF-N	23	27	4	5	1	0	2	4	1	7	0	0	.185	.241	.444	.686	88	-1	3	3.04	1	1-10	0	0.0
Total 9	188	423	39	84	18	0	16	55	22	115	1	0	.199	.242	.355	.596	63	-23	39	3.06	-2	1-123/D-25	7	-3.3

• LAHOUD, Joe — Joseph Michael Lahoud b: 4/14/1947, Danbury, CT BL/TL, 6'1", 202 lbs. Deb: 4/10/1968 Career OF: 198-14-296

1968 Bos-A	29	78	5	15	1	0	1	6	16	16	0	2	.192	.330	.244	.573	71	-3	7	2.82	0	0-25(3-1-22)	1	-0.4
1969 Bos-A	101	218	32	41	5	0	9	21	40	43	2	1	.188	.317	.335	.651	78	-6	26	3.95	-4	0-66(24-12-33)/1-1	4	-1.3
1970 Bos-A	17	49	6	12	1	0	2	5	7	6	0	0	.245	.339	.388	.727	93	-0	7	4.70	1	0-13(9-0-5)	2	0.0
1971 Bos-A	107	256	39	55	9	3	14	32	40	45	2	2	.215	.330	.438	.768	108	3	38	4.98	0	0-69(7-0-63)	9	-0.1
1972 Mil-A	111	316	35	75	9	3	12	34	45	54	3	4	.237	.332	.399	.731	119	7	41	4.92	-3	0-97(38-0-63)	11	-0.1
1973 Mil-A	96	225	29	46	9	0	5	26	27	36	5	5	.204	.304	.311	.615	75	-8	20	2.86	2	D-41,0-40(2-0-39)	2	-1.1
1974 Cal-A	127	325	46	88	16	3	13	44	47	57	4	5	.271	.368	.458	.826	145	19	55	5.98	2	*0-106(70-0-39),D-10	14	1.7
1975 Cal-A	76	192	21	41	6	2	6	33	48	33	2	1	.214	.373	.359	.733	116	7	30	5.23	0	D-35,0-29(7-0-22)	8	0.5
1976 Cal-A	42	96	8	17	4	0	0	4	18	16	0	0	.177	.319	.219	.538	63	-3	8	2.48	0	0-26(21-1-6)/D-3	1	-0.5
Tex-A	38	89	10	20	3	1	1	5	10	16	1	0	.225	.303	.315	.618	79	-2	8	3.13	0	D-22/0-5(4-0-1)	1	-0.3
Yr.	80	185	18	37	7	1	1	9	28	32	1	0	.200	.312	.265	.576	71	-5	16	2.79	0	0-31(25-1-7),D-25	2	-0.8
1977*KC-A	34	65	8	17	5	0	2	8	11	16	1	0	.262	.368	.431	.799	116	2	11	5.66	1	0-15(13-0-2)/D-4	2	0.0
1978 KC-A	13	16	0	2	0	0	0	1	0	6	0	0	.125	.125	.125	.250	-29	-3	0	.48	0	/D-1,0-1	0	-0.3
Total 11	791	1925	239	429	68	12	65	218	309	339	20	20	.223	.335	.372	.707	103	13	252	4.35	-4	0-492,D-116/1-1	55	-1.7

• LAIRD, Gerald — Gerald Lee Laird b: 11/13/1979, Westminster, CA BR/TR, 6'2", 195 lbs. Deb: 4/30/2003

| 2003 Tex-A | 19 | 44 | 9 | 12 | 2 | 1 | 1 | 4 | 5 | 11 | 0 | 0 | .273 | .360 | .432 | .792 | 99 | 0 | 7 | 5.22 | -2 | C-16 | 1 | -0.1 |

• LAJESKIE, Dick — Richard Edward Lajeskie b: 1/8/1926, Passaic, NJ d: 8/15/1976, Ramsey, NJ BR/TR, 5'11", 175 lbs. Deb: 9/10/1946

| 1946 NY-N | 6 | 10 | 3 | 2 | 0 | 0 | 0 | 3 | 2 | 0 | 0 | 0 | .200 | .429 | .200 | .629 | 81 | 0 | 1 | 4.40 | 2 | /2-4 | 0 | 0.3 |

• LAJOIE, Nap — Napoleon "Larry,Poli" Lajoie b: 9/5/1874, Woonsocket, RI d: 2/7/1959, Daytona Beach, FL BR/TR, 6'1", 195 lbs. Deb: 8/12/1896 M HOF: 1937 Career OF: 4-5-18

1896 Phi-N	39	175	36	57	12	7	4	42	1	11	7	....	.326	.330	.543	.872	129	5	35	7.63	-2	1-39	5	0.2
1897 Phi-N	127	545	107	197	40	23	9	127	15	....	20	....	.361	.392	.569	.960	156	39	133	9.97	7	*1-108,0-19(2-0-18)/3-2	21	3.8
1898 Phi-N	147	608	113	197	43	11	6	127	21	....	25	....	.324	.354	.461	.814	139	26	111	7.07	3	*2-146/1-1	26	3.3
1899 Phi-N	77	312	70	118	19	9	6	70	12	....	13	....	.378	.419	.554	.974	172	29	80	10.78	21	2-67/0-5(0-5-0)	19	4.8
1900 Phi-N	102	451	95	152	33	12	7	92	10	....	22	....	.337	.362	.510	.872	140	21	94	8.26	22	2-102/3-1	22	4.4
1901 Phi-A	131	544	145	232	48	14	14	125	24	....	27	....	.426	.463	.643	1.106	196	68	179	15.15	13	*2-119,S-12	42	7.4
1902 Phi-A	1	4	0	1	0	0	0	1	0	....	1	....	.250	.250	.250	.500	37	-0	1	4.53	0	/2-1	0	0.0
Cle-A	86	348	81	132	35	5	7	64	19	....	19	....	.379	.421	.569	.990	180	36	94	11.14	25	2-86	22	5.9
Yr.	87	352	81	133	35	5	7	65	19	....	20	....	.378	.419	.565	.984	178	36	95	11.05	25	2-87	22	5.8
1903 Cle-A	125	485	90	167	41	11	7	93	24	....	21	....	.344	.379	.518	.896	170	39	107	8.54	36	*2-122/1-1,3-1	31	7.9
1904 Cle-A	140	553	92	208	49	15	6	102	27	....	29	....	.376	.413	.552	.965	205	63	142	10.71	41	2-95,S-44/1-2	41	7.5
1905 Cle-A	65	249	29	82	12	2	2	41	17	....	11	....	.329	.377	.418	.795	150	14	45	6.98	11	2-59/1-5	14	2.8
1906 Cle-A	152	602	88	214	48	9	0	91	30	....	20	....	.355	.392	.465	.857	170	46	122	8.00	37	*2-130,3-15/S-7	33	9.3
1907 Cle-A	137	509	53	152	30	6	2	63	30	....	24	....	.299	.345	.393	.738	134	18	81	5.78	39	*2-128/1-9	32	6.5
1908 Cle-A	157	581	77	168	32	6	2	74	47	....	15	....	.289	.352	.375	.727	136	23	83	4.88	58	*2-156/1-1	32	9.4
1909 Cle-A	128	469	56	152	33	7	1	47	35	....	13	....	.324	.378	.431	.809	149	26	81	6.39	20	*2-120/1-8	27	5.3
1910 Cle-A	159	591	94	227	51	7	4	76	60	....	26	....	.384	.445	.514	.960	198	67	147	9.89	11	*2-149,1-10	47	8.8
1911 Cle-A	90	315	36	115	20	1	2	60	26	....	13	....	.365	.420	.454	.874	142	18	65	8.15	-6	1-41,2-37	14	1.2
1912 Cle-A	117	448	66	165	34	4	0	90	28	....	18	....	.368	.414	.462	.876	146	26	93	8.06	10	2-97,1-20	22	3.8
1913 Cle-A	137	465	66	156	25	2	1	68	33	17	17	....	.335	.398	.404	.802	131	19	79	6.26	13	*2-126	23	3.6
1914 Cle-A	121	419	37	108	14	3	0	50	32	15	14	15	.258	.313	.305	.619	83	-13	41	3.22	-2	2-80,1-31	7	-1.6
1915 Phi-A	129	490	40	137	24	5	1	61	11	16	10	6	.280	.301	.355	.656	100	-5	55	3.88	5	*2-110,S-10/1-5,3-2	12	0.3
1916 Phi-A	113	426	33	105	14	4	2	35	14	26	15	....	.246	.272	.312	.584	79	-14	42	3.23	4	*2-105/1-5,0-2(2-0-0)	4	-1.0
Total 21	2480	9589	1504	3242	657	163	83	1599	516	85	380	21	.338	.380	.467	.847	150	552	1907	7.62	326	*2-2035,1-286/S-73,0-26,3-21	496	93.6

• LAKE, Eddie — Edward Erving "Sparky" Lake b: 3/18/1916, Antioch, CA d: 6/7/1995, Castro Valley, CA BR/TR, 5'7", 160 lbs. Deb: 9/26/1939 ◆

1939 StL-N	2	4	0	1	0	0	0	1	0	0	0	....	.250	.400	.250	.650	73	-0	1	4.54	0	/S-2	0	0.0
1940 StL-N	32	66	12	14	3	0	2	7	12	17	1	....	.212	.342	.348	.690	86	-1	8	4.13	-1	2-17/S-6	1	-0.1
1941 StL-N	45	76	9	8	2	0	0	0	15	22	3	....	.105	.253	.132	.384	10	-9	3	1.25	0	3-15,S-15/2-5	0	-0.3
1943 Bos-A	75	216	26	43	10	0	3	16	47	35	3	6	.199	.345	.287	.632	84	-4	24	3.47	2	S-63	7	0.4
1944 Bos-A	57	126	21	26	5	0	0	8	23	22	5	2	.206	.329	.246	.575	66	-3	13	3.22	2	S-41/P-6,2-3,3-1	3	-0.1
1945 Bos-A	133	473	81	132	27	1	11	51	106	37	9	7	.279	.412	.410	.822	136	28	89	6.64	9	*S-130/2-1	27	5.1
1946 Det-A	155	587	105	149	24	1	8	31	103	69	15	9	.254	.369	.339	.708	93	-1	83	4.83	-19	*S-155	19	-1.1
1947 Det-A	158	602	96	127	19	6	12	46	120	54	11	10	.211	.343	.322	.665	83	-11	74	3.91	-36	*S-158	11	-3.9
1948 Det-A	64	198	51	52	6	1	3	18	57	20	3	3	.263	.427	.323	.751	98	3	33	5.58	-2	2-45,3-17	8	0.4
1949 Det-A	94	240	38	47	9	1	1	15	61	33	2	8	.196	.359	.254	.613	63	-13	26	3.25	-2	S-38,2-19,3-18	5	-1.2
1950 Det-A	20	7	3	0	0	0	0	0	1	2	0	0	.000	.125	.000	.125	-64	-2	0	.13	-1	/3-1,S-1	0	-0.3
Total 11	835	2595	442	599	105	9	39	193	546	312	52	45	.231	.366	.323	.689	91	-12	354	4.47	-49	S-609/2-90,3-52,P-6	82	-1.5

• LAKE, Fred — Frederick Lovett Lake b: 10/16/1866, Canada d: 11/24/1931, Boston, MA BR/TR, 5'10", 170 lbs. Deb: 5/7/1891 M

1891 Bos-N	5	7	1	1	0	0	0	1	0	0	0	....	.143	.333	.143	.476	36	-0	0	1.54	0	/C-4,0-1	0	0.0
1894 Lou-N	16	42	8	12	2	0	1	10	11	6	2	....	.286	.474	.405	.878	122	3	9	8.00	-3	/2-6,C-5,S-5	2	0.1
1897*Bos-N	19	62	6	15	2	0	0	5	1	....	0	....	.242	.254	.306	.560	45	-5	6	3.07	1	C-18	1	-0.3
1898 Pit-N	5	13	1	1	0	0	0	0	1	....	0	....	.077	.200	.077	.277	-20	-2	0	.68	0	/1-3	0	-0.2
1910 Bos-N	3	1	0	0	0	0	0	0	1	0	0	....	.000	.500	.000	.500	46	-1	0	.00	0	/...	0	0.0
Total 5	48	125	12	29	6	0	1	16	17	10	4	....	.232	.342	.304	.646	67	-5	16	4.12	-1	/C-27,2-6,S-5,1-3,0-1	3	-0.4

• LAKE, Steve — Steven Michael Lake b: 3/14/1957, Inglewood, CA BR/TR, 6'1", 190 lbs. Deb: 4/9/1983

1983 Chi-N	38	85	9	22	4	1	1	7	2	6	0	0	.259	.284	.365	.649	75	-3	7	3.01	2	C-32	1	0.0
1984*Chi-N	25	54	4	12	4	0	1	7	0	7	0	0	.222	.236	.407	.644	71	-2	3	3.26	0	C-24	1	0.0
1985 Chi-N	58	119	5	18	2	0	1	11	3	21	0	0	.151	.179	.193	.372	4	-15	4	.99	3	C-55	1	-1.2
1986 Chi-N	10	19	4	8	1	0	2	6	1	2	0	0	.421	.450	.474	.924	144	0	4	7.53	-1	C-10	1	0.2
StL-N	26	49	4	12	1	0	0	2	10	2	0	0	.245	.275	.388	.662	81	-1	5	3.18	0	C-26	1	0.2
Yr.	36	68	8	20	2	0	2	8	2	14	0	0	.294	.324	.412	.736	100	-0	8	4.27	0	C-36	2	0.0
1987*StL-N	74	179	19	45	7	2	2	19	10	18	0	0	.251	.291	.346	.637	67	-9	18	3.45	-1	C-59	5	-0.8

YEAR TM-L	G	AB	R	H	2B	3B	HR	RBI	BB	SO	SB	CS	AVG	OBP	SLG	OPS	OPS+	BR/A	RC	RC/G	FR	G/POS	WS	TPW
1988 StL-N	36	54	5	15	3	0	1	4	3	15	0	0	.278	.339	.389	.728	107	0	8	5.23	1	C-19	1	0.2
1989 Phi-N	58	155	9	39	5	1	2	14	12	20	0	0	.252	.305	.335	.641	83	-4	15	3.20	3	C-55	3	0.2
1990 Phi-N	29	80	4	20	2	0	0	6	3	12	0	0	.250	.286	.275	.561	55	-5	6	2.76	2	C-28	3	-0.2
1991 Phi-N	58	158	12	36	4	1	1	11	2	26	0	0	.228	.238	.285	.522	47	-12	10	1.96	-2	C-58	2	-1.1
1992 Phi-N	20	53	3	13	2	0	1	2	1	8	0	0	.245	.259	.340	.599	68	-2	4	2.85	0	C-17	0	-0.2
1993 Chi-N	44	120	11	27	6	0	5	13	4	19	0	0	.225	.250	.400	.650	72	-6	9	2.36	2	C-41	2	-0.2
Total 11	**476**	**1125**	**89**	**267**	**41**	**5**	**18**	**108**	**43**	**159**	**1**	**0**	**.237**	**.269**	**.331**	**.600**	**64**	**-58**	**95**	**2.79**	**8**	**C-424**	**22**	**-3.3**

• LAKEMAN, Al

Albert Wesley "Moose" Lakeman b: 12/31/1918, Cincinnati, OH d: 5/25/1976, Spartanburg, SC BR/TR, 6'2", 195 lbs. Deb: 4/19/1942 C

YEAR TM-L	G	AB	R	H	2B	3B	HR	RBI	BB	SO	SB	CS	AVG	OBP	SLG	OPS	OPS+	BR/A	RC	RC/G	FR	G/POS	WS	TPW
1942 Cin-N	20	38	0	6	1	0	0	2	3	10	0	....	.158	.238	.184	.422	24	-4	2	1.23	-1	C-17	1	-0.4
1943 Cin-N	22	55	5	14	2	1	0	6	3	11	0	....	.255	.293	.327	.620	80	-2	5	3.01	2	C-21	2	0.1
1944 Cin-N	1	1	0	0	0	0	0	0	0	1	0	....	.000	.000	.000	.000	-104	-0	0	.00	0	....	0	0.0
1945 Cin-N	76	258	22	66	9	4	8	31	17	45	0	....	.256	.304	.415	.719	101	-1	31	4.21	-3	C-74	6	0.0
1946 Cin-N	23	30	0	4	0	0	0	4	2	7	0	....	.133	.188	.133	.321	-9	-4	1	.88	0	/C-6	0	-0.4
1947 Cin-N	2	2	0	0	0	0	0	0	0	1	0	....	.000	.000	.000	.000	-101	-1	0	.00	0	....	0	-0.1
Phi-N	55	182	11	29	3	0	6	19	5	39	0	....	.159	.186	.275	.461	22	-21	9	1.57	-2	1-29,C-23	1	-2.3
Yr.	57	184	11	29	3	0	6	19	5	40	0	....	.158	.184	.272	.456	20	-22	9	1.55	-2	1-29,C-23	1	-2.3
1948 Phi-N	32	68	2	11	2	0	1	4	5	22	0	....	.162	.219	.235	.454	23	-7	4	1.65	0	C-22/P-1	1	-0.7
1949 Bos-N	3	6	0	1	0	0	0	0	1	0	0	....	.167	.286	.167	.452	26	-1	0	.81	0	/1-2	0	0.0
1954 Det-A	5	6	0	0	0	0	0	0	0	1	0	0	.000	.000	.000	.000	-102	-2	0	.00	0	/C-4	0	-0.2
Total 9	**239**	**646**	**40**	**131**	**17**	**5**	**15**	**66**	**36**	**137**	**0**	**0**	**.203**	**.248**	**.314**	**.562**	**56**	**-43**	**51**	**2.60**	**-3**	**C-167/1-31,P-1**	**11**	**-3.9**

• LAKER, Tim

Timothy John Laker b: 11/27/1969, Encino, CA BR/TR, 6'2", 195 lbs. Deb: 8/18/1992

YEAR TM-L	G	AB	R	H	2B	3B	HR	RBI	BB	SO	SB	CS	AVG	OBP	SLG	OPS	OPS+	BR/A	RC	RC/G	FR	G/POS	WS	TPW
1992 Mon-N	28	46	8	10	3	0	0	4	2	14	1	1	.217	.250	.283	.533	51	-3	3	2.08	0	C-28	1	-0.3
1993 Mon-N	43	86	3	17	2	1	0	7	2	16	2	0	.198	.225	.244	.469	24	-9	5	1.73	-0	C-43	0	-0.7
1995 Mon-N	64	141	17	33	8	1	3	20	14	38	0	1	.234	.308	.369	.676	75	-6	15	3.46	0	C-61	3	-0.3
1997 Bal-A	7	14	0	0	0	0	0	1	2	9	0	0	.000	.125	.000	.125	-66	-3	0	.29	-1	/C-7	0	-0.4
1998 TB-A	3	5	1	1	0	0	0	0	1	1	0	1	.200	.333	.200	.533	43	-1	0	1.13	0	/C-2,D-1	0	-0.1
Pit-N	14	24	2	9	1	0	1	2	1	3	0	0	.375	.400	.542	.942	143	1	5	7.58	-1	/1-4,C-1	1	0.0
1999 Pit-N	6	9	0	3	0	0	0	0	0	2	0	0	.333	.333	.333	.667	70	-0	1	4.50	0	/C-2	0	0.0
2001 Cle-A	16	33	5	6	0	0	1	5	6	8	0	0	.182	.308	.273	.580	54	-2	3	2.84	1	C-14/P-1	1	0.1
2003 Cle-A	52	162	17	39	11	0	3	21	9	38	2	2	.241	.281	.364	.645	71	-8	15	3.11	-1	C-50/D-2	4	-0.6
Total 8	**233**	**520**	**53**	**118**	**25**	**2**	**8**	**60**	**37**	**129**	**5**	**5**	**.227**	**.281**	**.329**	**.610**	**60**	**-31**	**47**	**2.93**	**-3**	**C-208/1-4,D-3,P-1**	**10**	**-2.3**

• LALLY, Dan

Daniel J. Lally b: 8/12/1867, Jersey City, NJ d: 4/14/1936, Milwaukee, WI BR/TR, 5'11.5", 210 lbs. Deb: 8/19/1891 Career OF: 82-5-38

YEAR TM-L	G	AB	R	H	2B	3B	HR	RBI	BB	SO	SB	CS	AVG	OBP	SLG	OPS	OPS+	BR/A	RC	RC/G	FR	G/POS	WS	TPW
1891 Pit-N	41	143	24	32	6	2	1	17	16	20	0	....	.224	.319	.315	.634	87	-2	15	3.58	-4	O-41(0-4-37)	2	-0.6
1897 StL-N	88	359	57	102	16	5	2	42	9	....	12	....	.284	.315	.373	.688	82	-11	47	4.78	1	O-84(82-1-1)/1-3	3	-1.5
Total 2	**129**	**502**	**81**	**134**	**22**	**7**	**3**	**59**	**25**	**20**	**12**	**....**	**.267**	**.316**	**.357**	**.673**	**84**	**-13**	**62**	**4.42**	**-4**	**O-125/1-3**	**5**	**-2.1**

• LAMANNO, Ray

Raymond Simond Lamanno b: 11/17/1919, Oakland, CA d: 2/9/1994, Berkeley, CA BR/TR, 6', 185 lbs. Deb: 9/11/1941

YEAR TM-L	G	AB	R	H	2B	3B	HR	RBI	BB	SO	SB	CS	AVG	OBP	SLG	OPS	OPS+	BR/A	RC	RC/G	FR	G/POS	WS	TPW
1941 Cin-N	1	0	0	0	0	0	0	0	0	0	0	....	....	1.000	....	1.000	197	0	0	∞	0	/C-1	0	0.0
1942 Cin-N	111	371	40	98	12	2	12	43	31	54	0	....	.264	.324	.404	.729	113	5	46	4.32	-6	*C-104	13	0.5
1946 Cin-N★	85	239	18	58	12	0	1	30	11	26	0	....	.243	.285	.305	.590	70	-10	20	2.75	1	C-61	4	-0.6
1947 Cin-N	118	413	33	106	21	3	5	50	28	39	0	....	.257	.307	.358	.665	77	-15	46	3.90	7	*C-109	12	-0.2
1948 Cin-N	127	385	31	93	12	0	0	27	48	32	2	....	.242	.329	.273	.601	67	-16	35	3.04	-3	*C-125	6	-1.3
Total 5	**442**	**1408**	**122**	**355**	**57**	**5**	**18**	**150**	**118**	**151**	**2**	**....**	**.252**	**.314**	**.338**	**.653**	**82**	**-36**	**147**	**3.57**	**-1**	**C-400**	**35**	**-1.5**

• LAMAR, Bill

William Harmong "Good Time Bill" Lamar
b: 3/21/1897, Rockville, MD d: 5/24/1970, Rockport, MA BL/TR, 6'1", 185 lbs. Deb: 9/19/1917 Career OF: 425-58-11

YEAR TM-L	G	AB	R	H	2B	3B	HR	RBI	BB	SO	SB	CS	AVG	OBP	SLG	OPS	OPS+	BR/A	RC	RC/G	FR	G/POS	WS	TPW
1917 NY-A	11	41	2	10	0	0	0	3	0	2	1	....	.244	.244	.244	.488	48	-3	3	2.08	0	O-11(10-1-0)	0	-0.3
1918 NY-A	28	110	12	25	3	0	0	2	6	2	2	....	.227	.267	.255	.522	56	-6	8	2.26	-2	O-27(8-17-2)	1	-1.1
1919 NY-A	11	16	1	3	1	0	0	0	2	1	1	....	.188	.278	.250	.528	48	-1	1	2.52	0	/O-3(0-1-2),1-1	0	-0.1
Bos-A	48	148	18	43	5	1	0	14	5	9	3	....	.291	.314	.338	.652	88	-3	16	3.83	-3	O-36(6-29-1)	3	-0.8
Yr.	59	164	19	46	6	1	0	14	7	10	4	....	.280	.310	.329	.639	84	-4	18	3.69	-3	O-39(6-30-3)/1-1	3	-1.0
1920★Bro-N	24	44	5	12	4	0	0	4	0	1	0	0	.273	.273	.364	.636	79	-1	4	3.47	0	O-12(0-6-6)	1	-0.2
1921 Bro-N	3	3	2	1	0	0	0	0	0	0	0	0	.333	.333	.333	.667	74	-0	0	4.24	0	/O-1	0	0.0
1924 Phi-A	87	367	68	121	22	5	7	48	18	21	8	8	.330	.361	.474	.835	113	4	60	5.98	3	O-87(87-0-0)	12	0.0
1925 Phi-A	138	568	85	202	39	8	3	77	21	17	2	6	.356	.379	.468	.847	107	3	97	6.62	5	*O-131(131-0-0)	17	-0.2
1926 Phi-A	116	419	62	119	17	6	5	50	18	15	4	5	.284	.315	.389	.704	78	-16	50	4.11	-1	O-107(107-0-0)	7	-2.4
1927 Phi-A	84	324	48	97	23	3	4	47	16	10	4	8	.299	.334	.426	.760	91	-8	43	4.62	-5	O-79(76-3-0)	7	-1.8
Total 9	**550**	**2040**	**303**	**633**	**114**	**23**	**19**	**245**	**86**	**78**	**25**	**27**	**.310**	**.339**	**.417**	**.755**	**93**	**-31**	**283**	**4.97**	**-2**	**O-494/1-1**	**48**	**-6.9**

• LAMB, David

David Christian Lamb b: 6/6/1975, West Hills, CA BB/TR, 6'2", 165 lbs. Deb: 4/12/1999

YEAR TM-L	G	AB	R	H	2B	3B	HR	RBI	BB	SO	SB	CS	AVG	OBP	SLG	OPS	OPS+	BR/A	RC	RC/G	FR	G/POS	WS	TPW
1999 TB-A	55	124	18	28	5	1	1	13	10	18	0	1	.226	.284	.306	.590	50	-10	10	2.67	-2	S-35,2-15/D-3	1	-0.9
2000 NY-N	7	5	1	1	0	0	0	0	1	1	0	0	.200	.333	.200	.533	41	-0	0	2.84	-1	/3-3,2-2,S-2	0	-0.1
2002★Min-A	7	10	0	1	0	0	0	0	0	2	0	0	.100	.100	.100	.200	-46	-2	0	.00	0	/S-4,2-2,3-1	0	-0.2
Total 3	**69**	**139**	**19**	**30**	**5**	**1**	**1**	**13**	**11**	**21**	**0**	**1**	**.216**	**.273**	**.288**	**.561**	**43**	**-12**	**10**	**2.45**	**-2**	**/S-41,2-19,3-4,D-3**	**1**	**-1.2**

• LAMB, Lyman

Laymon Raymond Lamb b: 3/17/1895, Lincoln, NE d: 10/5/1955, Fayetteville, AR BR/TR, 5'7", 150 lbs. Deb: 9/14/1920 Career OF: 7-2-4

YEAR TM-L	G	AB	R	H	2B	3B	HR	RBI	BB	SO	SB	CS	AVG	OBP	SLG	OPS	OPS+	BR/A	RC	RC/G	FR	G/POS	WS	TPW
1920 StL-A	9	24	4	9	2	0	0	4	0	7	2	0	.375	.375	.458	.833	116	1	4	6.38	-1	/O-7(5-2-0)	1	-0.1
1921 StL-A	45	134	18	34	9	2	1	17	4	12	0	0	.254	.281	.373	.654	62	-8	14	3.41	-2	3-25/2-7,O-6(2-0-4)	2	-0.8
Total 2	**54**	**158**	**22**	**43**	**11**	**2**	**1**	**21**	**4**	**19**	**2**	**0**	**.272**	**.294**	**.386**	**.681**	**70**	**-7**	**19**	**3.83**	**-3**	**/3-25,O-13,2-7**	**3**	**-0.9**

• LAMB, Mike

Michael Robert Lamb b: 8/9/1975, West Covina, CA BL/TR, 6'1", 195 lbs. Deb: 4/23/2000 Career OF: 14-0-5

YEAR TM-L	G	AB	R	H	2B	3B	HR	RBI	BB	SO	SB	CS	AVG	OBP	SLG	OPS	OPS+	BR/A	RC	RC/G	FR	G/POS	WS	TPW
2000 Tex-A	138	493	65	137	25	2	6	47	34	60	0	2	.278	.330	.373	.703	76	-19	59	4.27	-3	*3-135/D-2	6	-1.9
2001 Tex-A	76	284	42	87	18	0	4	35	14	27	2	1	.306	.350	.412	.762	96	-2	40	5.24	-3	3-74	8	-0.3
2002 Tex-A	115	314	54	89	13	0	9	33	33	48	0	0	.283	.357	.411	.768	98	0	46	5.29	-3	1-52,D-21,O-16(12-0-5),3-14/C,2	7	-0.7
2003 Tex-A	28	38	3	5	0	0	0	2	2	7	1	0	.132	.195	.132	.327	-10	-6	1	.88	0	/1-5,D-5,O-2(2-0-0),3-1	0	-0.6
Total 4	**357**	**1129**	**164**	**318**	**56**	**2**	**19**	**117**	**83**	**142**	**3**	**3**	**.282**	**.338**	**.385**	**.723**	**85**	**-26**	**147**	**4.65**	**-9**	**3-224/1-57,D-28,O-18,C-3,2**	**21**	**-3.5**

• LAMERS, Pete

Pierre Lamers b: 12/1873, New York, NY d: 10/24/1931, Brooklyn, NY TR, 5'10", 170 lbs. Deb: 9/10/1902

YEAR TM-L	G	AB	R	H	2B	3B	HR	RBI	BB	SO	SB	CS	AVG	OBP	SLG	OPS	OPS+	BR/A	RC	RC/G	FR	G/POS	WS	TPW
1902 Chi-N	2	9	2	2	0	0	0	0	0	....	0	....	.222	.222	.222	.444	38	-1	0	1.72	0	/C-2	0	-0.1
1907 Cin-N	1	2	0	0	0	0	0	0	0	....	0	....	.000	.000	.000	.000	-96	-0	0	.00	0	/C-1	0	-0.1
Total 2	**3**	**11**	**2**	**2**	**0**	**0**	**0**	**0**	**0**	**....**	**0**	**....**	**.182**	**.182**	**.182**	**.364**	**14**	**-1**	**0**	**1.34**	**0**	**/C-3**	**0**	**-0.1**

• LAMONT, Gene

Gene William Lamont b: 12/25/1946, Rockford, IL BL/TR, 6'1", 195 lbs. Deb: 9/2/1970 M/C

YEAR TM-L	G	AB	R	H	2B	3B	HR	RBI	BB	SO	SB	CS	AVG	OBP	SLG	OPS	OPS+	BR/A	RC	RC/G	FR	G/POS	WS	TPW
1970 Det-A	15	44	3	13	3	1	1	4	2	9	0	0	.295	.340	.477	.818	122	1	7	6.27	0	C-15	2	0.2
1971 Det-A	7	15	2	1	0	0	0	1	0	5	0	0	.067	.067	.067	.133	-60	-3	0	.13	-1	/C-7	0	-0.4
1972 Det-A	1	0	0	0	0	0	0	0	0	0	0	0	....	....	....	....	-97	0	0	....	0	/C-1	0	0.0
1974 Det-A	60	92	9	20	4	0	3	8	7	19	0	0	.217	.273	.359	.631	78	-3	9	3.35	0	C-60	2	-0.1
1975 Det-A	4	8	1	3	1	0	0	1	0	2	1	0	.375	.375	.500	.875	139	1	2	9.15	0	/C-4	1	0.1
Total 5	**87**	**159**	**15**	**37**	**8**	**1**	**4**	**14**	**9**	**35**	**1**	**0**	**.233**	**.278**	**.371**	**.649**	**81**	**-4**	**18**	**3.97**	**-2**	**/C-87**	**5**	**-0.4**

• LAMOTTE, Bobby

Robert Eugene LaMotte b: 2/15/1898, Savannah, GA d: 11/2/1970, Chatham, GA BR/TR, 5'11", 160 lbs. Deb: 9/1/1920

YEAR TM-L	G	AB	R	H	2B	3B	HR	RBI	BB	SO	SB	CS	AVG	OBP	SLG	OPS	OPS+	BR/A	RC	RC/G	FR	G/POS	WS	TPW
1920 Was-A	4	3	0	0	0	0	0	0	1	1	0	0	.000	.250	.000	.250	-31	-1	0	.55	0	/3-1,S-1	0	-0.1
1921 Was-A	16	41	5	8	0	0	0	2	5	0	0	0	.195	.283	.195	.478	25	-4	3	2.03	0	S-12	1	-0.3
1922 Was-A	68	214	22	54	10	2	1	23	15	21	6	1	.252	.307	.332	.639	70	-8	23	3.61	1	3-62/S-6	4	-0.2
1925 StL-A	97	356	61	97	20	4	2	51	34	22	5	5	.272	.338	.368	.706	75	-14	45	4.33	0	S-93/3-3	8	-0.3
1926 StL-A	36	79	11	16	4	3	0	9	11	6	0	0	.203	.300	.329	.629	61	-5	9	3.37	-3	S-30/3-1	1	-0.5
Total 5	**221**	**693**	**99**	**175**	**34**	**9**	**3**	**85**	**66**	**50**	**11**	**6**	**.253**	**.320**	**.341**	**.661**	**68**	**-32**	**80**	**3.83**	**-1**	**S-142/3-67**	**14**	**-1.4**

YEAR TM-L	G	AB	R	H	2B	3B	HR	RBI	BB	SO	SB	CS	AVG	OBP	SLG	OPS	OPS+	BR/A	RC	RC/G	FR	G/POS	WS	TPW
• LAMPARD, Keith	Christopher Keith Lampard b: 12/20/1945, Warrington, England BL/TR, 6'2", 197 lbs. Deb: 9/15/1969 Career OF: 14-0-4																							
1969 Hou-N	9	12	2	3	0	0	1	2	0	3	0	0	.250	.250	.500	.750	108	-0	2	4.50	1	/0-1	1	0.1
1970 Hou-N	53	72	8	17	8	1	0	5	5	24	0	0	.236	.295	.375	.670	82	-2	7	3.33	1	0-16(13-0-4)/1-2	1	-0.2
Total 2	62	84	10	20	8	1	1	7	5	27	0	0	.238	.289	.393	.682	85	-2	9	3.48	2	/0-17,1-2	2	-0.1
• LAMPKIN, Tom	Thomas Michael Lampkin b: 3/4/1964, Cincinnati, OH BL/TR, 5'11", 185 lbs. Deb: 9/10/1988 Career OF: 15-0-3																							
1988 Cle-A	4	4	0	0	0	0	0	0	1	0	0	0	.000	.200	.000	.200	-38	-1	0	.00	-1	/C-3	0	-0.1
1990 SD-N	26	63	4	14	0	1	1	4	4	9	0	1	.222	.269	.302	.570	56	-4	4	2.30	0	C-20	1	-0.4
1991 SD-N	38	58	4	11	3	1	0	3	3	9	0	0	.190	.230	.276	.505	40	-5	4	2.21	0	C-11	0	-0.4
1992 SD-N	9	17	3	4	0	0	0	0	6	1	2	0	.235	.458	.235	.694	100	1	3	6.53	0	/C-7,0-1	1	0.2
1993 Mil-A	73	162	22	32	8	0	4	25	20	26	7	3	.198	.286	.321	.607	64	-8	16	3.02	-2	C-60/0-3(2-0-1),D-1	4	-0.7
1995 SF-N	65	76	8	21	2	0	1	9	9	8	2	0	.276	.360	.342	.703	89	-0	10	4.94	0	C-17/0-6(6-0-0)	3	0.0
1996 SF-N	66	177	26	41	8	0	6	29	20	22	1	5	.232	.327	.379	.705	89	-5	22	4.01	3	C-53	6	0.2
1997 StL-N	108	229	28	56	8	1	7	22	28	30	2	1	.245	.337	.380	.717	88	-4	29	4.17	2	C-86	5	0.3
1998 StL-N	93	216	25	50	12	1	6	28	24	32	3	2	.231	.328	.380	.708	86	-4	27	4.21	-3	C-62/0-5(4-0-1),1-2	5	-0.3
1999 Sea-A	76	206	29	60	11	2	9	34	13	32	1	3	.291	.348	.495	.843	109	1	35	6.12	0	C-56/D-2,0-2(2-0-0)	7	0.4
2000 Sea-A	36	103	15	26	6	1	7	23	9	17	0	0	.252	.330	.534	.864	121	3	16	4.90	-1	C-28/D-3	3	0.3
2001*Sea-A	79	204	28	46	10	0	5	22	18	41	1	0	.225	.310	.348	.658	78	-6	23	3.76	-2	C-71/D-1,0-1	6	-0.4
2002 SD-N	104	281	32	61	10	1	10	37	38	59	4	2	.217	.317	.367	.683	87	-5	34	4.00	-3	C-94	8	-0.2
Total 13	777	1796	224	422	78	8	56	236	193	286	23	17	.235	.321	.381	.702	86	-37	223	4.13	-7	C-568/0-18,D-7,1-2	49	-1.2
• LANCELLOTTI, Rick	Richard Anthony Lancellotti b: 7/5/1956, Providence, RI BL/TL, 6'3", 195 lbs. Deb: 8/27/1982 Career OF: 2-0-2																							
1982 SD-N	17	39	2	7	2	0	0	4	2	8	0	0	.179	.220	.231	.450	27	-4	2	1.76	-1	/1-7,0-3(2-0-1)	0	-0.5
1986 SF-N	15	18	2	4	0	0	2	6	0	7	0	0	.222	.222	.556	.778	113	0	2	4.29	0	/1-1,0-1	0	0.0
1990 Bos-A	4	8	0	0	0	0	0	1	0	3	0	0	.000	.000	.000	.000	-96	-2	0	.00	0	/1-2	0	-0.2
Total 3	36	65	4	11	2	0	2	11	2	18	0	0	.169	.194	.292	.486	34	-6	4	2.12	0	/1-10,0-4	0	-0.7
• LAND, Doc	William Gilbert Land b: 5/14/1903, Bennsville, MS d: 4/14/1986, Livingston, AL BL/TL, 5'11", 165 lbs. Deb: 10/6/1929																							
1929 Was-A	1	3	0	0	0	0	0	0	1	0	0	0	.000	.250	.000	.250	-30	-1	0	.55	-0	/0-1	0	-0.1
• LAND, Grover	Grover Cleveland Land b: 9/22/1884, Frankfort, KY d: 7/22/1958, Phoenix, AZ BR/TR, 6', 190 lbs. Deb: 9/2/1908 C																							
1908 Cle-A	8	16	1	3	0	0	0	2	0	....	0	....	.188	.188	.188	.375	22	-1	1	1.12	-1	/C-8	0	-0.2
1909 Cle-A	1	4	0	2	0	0	0	1	0	....	0	....	.500	.500	.500	1.000	207	0	1	12.79	0	/C-1	0	0.1
1910 Cle-A	34	111	4	23	0	0	0	7	2	....	1	....	.207	.228	.207	.435	36	-8	6	1.58	0	C-33	1	-0.6
1911 Cle-A	35	107	5	15	1	2	0	10	3	....	2	....	.140	.164	.187	.351	-2	-15	3	.94	2	C-34/1-1	2	-1.0
1913 Cle-A	17	47	3	11	1	0	0	9	4	1	1	....	.234	.321	.255	.576	67	-2	4	2.89	-1	C-17	2	-0.2
1914 Bro-F	102	335	24	92	6	2	0	29	12	23	7	....	.275	.306	.304	.610	73	-12	32	3.26	-7	C-97	7	-1.1
1915 Bro-F	96	290	25	75	13	2	0	22	6	20	3	....	.259	.279	.317	.596	77	-10	25	2.98	-4	C-81	4	-0.8
Total 7	293	910	62	221	21	6	0	80	27	44	14	....	.243	.271	.279	.550	60	-48	72	2.61	-10	C-271/1-1	16	-3.8
• LANDENBERGER, Ken	Kenneth Henry "Red" Landenberger b: 7/29/1928, Lyndhurst, OH d: 7/28/1960, Cleveland, OH BL/TL, 6'3", 200 lbs. Deb: 9/20/1952																							
1952 Chi-A	2	5	0	1	0	0	0	0	0	2	0	0	.200	.200	.200	.400	11	-1	0	1.38	0	/1-1	0	-0.1
• LANDESTOY, Rafael	Rafael Silvaldo (Santana) Landestoy b: 5/28/1953, Bani, Dominican Republic BB/TR, 5'10", 165 lbs. Deb: 8/27/1977 C Career OF: 12-4-7																							
1977*LA-N	15	18	6	5	0	0	0	0	3	2	2	0	.278	.381	.278	.659	80	0	2	4.20	1	/2-8,S-3	1	0.1
1978 Hou-N	59	218	18	58	5	1	0	9	8	23	7	4	.266	.292	.298	.590	70	-9	19	3.02	-4	S-50/0-3(1-2-0),2-2	3	-0.9
1979 Hou-N	129	282	33	76	9	6	0	30	29	24	13	4	.270	.340	.344	.684	92	-1	36	4.47	8	*2-114/S-3	12	1.2
1980*Hou-N	149	393	42	97	13	8	1	27	31	37	23	12	.247	.307	.328	.635	84	-9	41	3.47	5	2-94,S-65/3-3	11	0.4
1981 Hou-N	35	74	6	11	1	1	0	4	16	9	4	1	.149	.300	.189	.489	43	-4	5	1.87	-4	2-31	1	-0.8
Cin-N	12	11	2	2	0	0	0	1	1	0	1	0	.182	.250	.182	.432	24	-1	0	.57	-1	/2-3	0	-0.2
Yr.	47	85	8	13	1	1	0	5	17	9	5	1	.153	.294	.188	.482	41	-5	5	1.70	-5	2-34	1	-0.9
1982 Cin-N	73	111	11	21	3	0	1	9	8	14	2	0	.189	.250	.243	.493	38	-9	6	1.67	0	3-21,2-16/0-3(3-0-0),S-2	1	-0.9
1983 Cin-N	7	5	0	0	0	0	0	0	0	0	0	0	.000	.000	.000	.000	-97	-1	0	.00	-1	/1-2,3-1,0-1	0	-0.2
*LA-N	64	64	6	11	1	1	1	1	3	8	0	2	.172	.209	.266	.475	31	-7	3	1.41	-1	2-14,3-10,0-10(6-1-3)/S-1	0	-0.8
Yr.	71	69	6	11	1	1	1	1	3	8	0	2	.159	.194	.246	.441	22	-8	3	1.29	-2	2-14,3-11,0-11(7-1-3)/1-2,S	0	-1.0
1984 LA-N	53	54	10	10	0	0	1	2	1	6	2	1	.185	.200	.241	.441	24	-6	2	1.36	-3	2-14,3-11/0-5(1-1-4)	0	-0.9
Total 8	596	1230	134	291	32	17	4	83	100	123	54	24	.237	.297	.300	.597	70	-48	115	3.06	1	2-296,S-124/3-46,0-22,1-2	29	-2.9
• LANDIS, Jim	James Henry Landis b: 3/9/1934, Fresno, CA BR/TR, 6'1", 180 lbs. Deb: 4/16/1957 Career OF: 63-1132-87																							
1957 Chi-A	96	274	38	58	11	3	2	16	45	61	14	4	.212	.329	.296	.625	72	-8	31	3.71	2	0-90(11-38-44)	7	-0.9
1958 Chi-A	142	523	72	145	23	7	15	64	52	80	19	7	.277	.352	.434	.786	117	14	82	5.48	0	*0-142(0-142-0)	22	0.7
1959*Chi-A	149	515	78	140	26	7	5	60	78	68	20	9	.272	.376	.379	.755	109	11	81	5.32	11	*0-148(0-148-0)	25	1.5
1960 Chi-A	148	494	89	125	25	6	10	49	80	84	23	6	.253	.367	.389	.756	106	9	78	5.39	9	*0-147(0-147-0)	19	1.1
1961 Chi-A	140	534	87	151	18	8	22	85	65	71	19	5	.283	.365	.470	.835	123	20	95	6.22	11	*0-139(0-139-0)	23	2.7
1962 Chi-A★	149	534	82	122	21	6	15	61	80	105	19	7	.228	.339	.375	.713	92	-3	73	4.50	10	*0-144(0-144-0)	17	0.3
1963 Chi-A	133	396	56	89	6	6	13	45	47	75	8	6	.225	.316	.369	.685	93	-4	48	4.03	3	*0-124(0-124-0)	12	-0.5
1964 Chi-A	106	298	30	62	8	4	1	18	36	64	5	0	.208	.306	.272	.578	64	-12	28	3.04	1	*0-101(0-101-0)	7	-1.5
1965 KC-A	118	364	46	87	15	1	3	36	57	84	8	3	.239	.347	.310	.657	90	-2	42	3.85	-1	*0-108(0-108-1)	9	-0.7
1966 Cle-A	85	158	23	35	5	1	3	14	20	25	2	1	.222	.317	.323	.639	84	-3	17	3.70	-3	0-61(18-37-17)	4	-0.8
1967 Hou-N	50	143	19	36	11	1	1	14	20	35	2	1	.252	.348	.364	.711	107	2	20	4.90	2	0-44(28-3-14)	5	0.2
Det-A	25	48	4	10	0	0	2	4	7	12	0	2	.208	.309	.333	.642	87	-1	5	3.24	1	0-12(6-1-6)	1	-0.1
Bos-A	5	7	1	1	0	0	1	1	1	3	0	0	.143	.250	.571	.821	126	0	1	4.79	0	/0-5(0-0-5)	0	0.0
Yr.	30	55	5	11	0	0	3	5	8	15	0	2	.200	.302	.364	.665	92	-1	6	3.43	1	0-17(6-1-11)	1	-0.2
Total 11	1346	4288	625	1061	169	50	93	467	588	767	139	51	.247	.346	.375	.721	99	23	602	4.73	45	*0-1265	151	2.0
• LANDREAUX, Ken	Kenneth Francis Landreaux b: 12/22/1954, Los Angeles, CA BL/TR, 5'10", 165 lbs. Deb: 9/11/1977 Career OF: 198-859-105																							
1977 Cal-A	23	76	6	19	5	1	0	5	5	15	1	1	.250	.296	.342	.638	76	-3	8	3.64	4	0-22(0-22-0)	2	0.1
1978 Cal-A	93	260	37	58	7	5	5	23	20	20	7	3	.223	.284	.346	.630	79	-7	25	3.22	0	0-83(32-23-35)/D-1	5	-1.0
1979 Min-A	151	564	81	172	27	5	15	83	37	57	10	3	.305	.352	.450	.802	110	9	88	5.58	-3	*0-147(49-98-0)	16	0.2
1980 Min-A★	129	484	56	136	23	11	7	62	39	42	8	6	.281	.337	.417	.754	98	-2	65	4.66	-1	*0-120(54-68-0)/D-6	13	-0.6
1981*LA-N	99	390	48	98	16	4	7	41	25	42	18	4	.251	.298	.367	.665	91	-4	44	3.84	-7	0-95(0-95-0)	10	-1.3
1982 LA-N	129	461	71	131	23	7	7	50	39	54	31	10	.284	.345	.410	.755	113	10	68	5.06	-1	*0-117(1-116-0)	17	0.8
1983*LA-N	141	481	63	135	25	3	17	66	34	52	30	11	.281	.331	.451	.782	115	10	70	5.10	-5	*0-137(7-131-2)	19	0.3
1984 LA-N	134	438	39	110	11	5	11	47	29	35	10	9	.251	.299	.374	.674	89	-10	47	3.60	-5	*0-129(9-105-18)	10	-1.8
1985*LA-N	147	482	70	129	26	2	12	50	33	37	15	5	.268	.316	.405	.720	103	1	61	4.38	-5	*0-140(11-126-4)	15	-0.7
1986 LA-N	103	283	34	74	13	2	4	29	22	39	10	5	.261	.317	.364	.681	94	-3	32	3.92	-4	0-85(20-69-1)	6	-0.8
1987 LA-N	115	182	17	37	4	0	6	23	16	28	5	3	.203	.271	.324	.596	58	-12	16	2.70	0	0-63(15-6-45)	1	-1.4
Total 11	1264	4101	522	1099	180	45	91	479	299	421	145	60	.268	.321	.400	.721	99	-11	524	4.39	-27	*0-1138/D-7	114	-6.3
• LANDRITH, Hobie	Hobert Neal Landrith b: 3/16/1930, Decatur, IL BL/TR, 5'10", 170 lbs. Deb: 7/30/1950 C																							
1950 Cin-N	4	14	1	3	0	0	0	1	2	1	0	....	.214	.313	.214	.527	41	-1	1	2.70	0	/C-4	0	-0.1
1951 Cin-N	4	13	3	5	1	0	0	0	1	1	0	0	.385	.429	.462	.890	137	1	3	9.27	1	/C-4	1	0.2
1952 Cin-N	15	50	1	13	4	0	0	4	0	4	0	1	.260	.260	.340	.600	65	-3	4	2.65	1	C-14	1	-0.2
1953 Cin-N	52	154	15	37	3	1	3	16	12	8	2	0	.240	.299	.331	.631	64	-8	16	3.70	0	C-47	3	-0.6
1954 Cin-N	48	81	12	16	0	0	5	14	18	9	1	0	.198	.343	.383	.726	86	-1	12	4.78	0	C-42	3	0.1
1955 Cin-N	43	87	9	22	3	0	4	7	10	14	0	1	.253	.330	.425	.755	93	-1	12	4.62	1	C-27	2	0.1
1956 Chi-N	111	312	22	69	10	3	4	32	39	38	0	2	.221	.310	.311	.621	69	-14	32	3.31	2	C-99	6	-0.7
1957 StL-N	75	214	18	52	6	0	3	26	25	27	1	2	.243	.322	.313	.635	70	-9	22	3.48	-0	C-67	6	-0.6
1958 StL-N	70	144	9	31	4	0	3	13	26	21	0	1	.215	.335	.306	.641	68	-6	16	3.66	1	C-45	3	-0.3
1959 SF-N	109	283	30	71	14	0	3	29	43	23	0	4	.251	.350	.332	.682	85	-6	34	3.92	2	*C-109	10	0.1

YEAR TM-L	G	AB	R	H	2B	3B	HR	RBI	BB	SO	SB	CS	AVG	OBP	SLG	OPS	OPS+	BR/A	RC	RC/G	FR	G/POS	WS	TPW
1960 SF-N	71	190	18	46	10	0	1	20	23	11	1	1	.242	.324	.311	.634	79	-5	20	3.40	-4	C-70	4	-0.6
1961 SF-N	43	71	11	17	4	0	2	10	12	7	0	0	.239	.349	.380	.730	97	0	9	4.11	0	C-30	3	0.1
1962 NY-N	23	45	6	13	3	0	1	7	8	3	0	0	.289	.396	.422	.818	118	2	8	6.87	-2	C-21	1	0.0
Bal-A	60	167	18	37	4	1	4	17	19	9	0	0	.222	.305	.329	.634	74	-6	17	3.39	1	C-60	4	-0.2
1963 Bal-A	2	1	0	0	0	0	0	0	0	0	0	0	.000	.000	.000	.000	-102	-0	0	.00	0	/C-1	0	-0.1
Was-A	42	103	6	18	3	0	1	7	15	12	0	0	.175	.280	.233	.513	46	-7	7	2.15	0	C-37	1	-0.6
Yr.	44	104	6	18	3	0	1	7	15	12	0	0	.173	.277	.231	.508	44	-7	7	2.13	-1	C-38	1	-0.7
Total 14	**772**	**1929**	**179**	**450**	**69**	**5**	**34**	**203**	**253**	**188**	**5**	**12**	**.233**	**.323**	**.327**	**.650**	**75**	**-65**	**213**	**3.66**	**3**	**C-677**	**48**	**-3.3**

• LANDRUM, Ced Cedric Bernard Landrum b: 9/3/1963, Butler, AL BL/TR, 5'9", 167 lbs. Deb: 5/28/1991 Career OF: 28-18-8

YEAR TM-L	G	AB	R	H	2B	3B	HR	RBI	BB	SO	SB	CS	AVG	OBP	SLG	OPS	OPS+	BR/A	RC	RC/G	FR	G/POS	WS	TPW
1991 Chi-N	56	86	28	20	2	1	0	6	10	18	27	5	.233	.313	.279	.592	65	-0	10	3.48	-2	0-44(25-18-8)	3	-0.3
1993 NY-N	22	19	2	5	1	0	0	1	0	5	0	0	.263	.263	.316	.579	55	-1	2	2.93	0	/0-3(3-0-0)	0	-0.2
Total 2	**78**	**105**	**30**	**25**	**3**	**1**	**0**	**7**	**10**	**23**	**27**	**5**	**.238**	**.304**	**.286**	**.590**	**63**	**-2**	**11**	**3.39**	**-3**	**/0-47**	**3**	**-0.5**

• LANDRUM, Don Donald Leroy Landrum b: 2/16/1936, Santa Rosa, CA d: 1/9/2003, Pittsburg, CA BL/TR, 6', 180 lbs. Deb: 9/28/1957 Career OF: 66-261-39

YEAR TM-L	G	AB	R	H	2B	3B	HR	RBI	BB	SO	SB	CS	AVG	OBP	SLG	OPS	OPS+	BR/A	RC	RC/G	FR	G/POS	WS	TPW
1957 Phi-N	2	7	1	1	1	0	0	0	2	1	0	0	.143	.333	.286	.619	71	-0	1	3.78	0	/0-2(0-2-0)	0	0.0
1960 StL-N	13	49	7	12	0	1	2	3	4	6	3	0	.245	.315	.408	.723	88	-0	7	5.13	0	0-13(2-13-3)	2	-0.1
1961 StL-N	28	66	5	11	2	0	1	3	5	14	1	0	.167	.225	.242	.468	22	-7	4	1.95	1	0-25(6-20-4)/2-1	1	-0.7
1962 StL-N	32	35	11	11	0	0	0	3	4	2	2	0	.314	.385	.314	.699	82	-0	5	4.62	-1	0-26(16-4-7)	1	-0.2
Chi-N	83	238	29	67	5	2	1	15	30	31	9	2	.282	.369	.332	.701	86	-2	33	5.02	0	0-59(1-41-18)	5	-0.4
Yr.	115	273	40	78	5	2	1	18	34	33	11	2	.286	.371	.330	.701	86	-2	38	4.97	-1	0-85(17-45-25)	6	-0.6
1963 Chi-N	84	227	27	55	4	1	1	10	13	42	6	3	.242	.295	.282	.577	64	-10	19	2.90	-3	0-57(0-55-3)	3	-1.6
1964 Chi-N	11	11	2	0	0	0	0	0	1	2	0	0	.000	.083	.000	.083	-71	-3	0	.00	1	/0-1	0	-0.2
1965 Chi-N	131	425	60	96	20	4	6	34	36	84	14	8	.226	.301	.334	.636	77	-13	45	3.54	0	*0-115(3-111-1)	9	-1.8
1966 SF-N	72	102	9	19	4	0	1	7	9	18	1	1	.186	.259	.255	.514	42	-8	7	2.12	2	0-54(38-14-3)	1	-0.8
Total 8	**456**	**1160**	**151**	**272**	**36**	**8**	**12**	**75**	**104**	**200**	**36**	**14**	**.234**	**.308**	**.310**	**.618**	**69**	**-43**	**121**	**3.52**	**1**	**0-352/2-1**	**22**	**-5.7**

• LANDRUM, Jesse Jesse Glenn Landrum b: 7/31/1912, Crockett, TX d: 6/27/1983, Beaumont, TX BR/TR, 5'11.5", 175 lbs. Deb: 4/26/1938

YEAR TM-L	G	AB	R	H	2B	3B	HR	RBI	BB	SO	SB	CS	AVG	OBP	SLG	OPS	OPS+	BR/A	RC	RC/G	FR	G/POS	WS	TPW
1938 Chi-A	4	6	0	0	0	0	0	1	0	2	0	0	.000	.000	.000	.000	-98	-2	0	.00	-1	/2-3	0	-0.2

• LANDRUM, Tito Terry Lee Landrum b: 10/25/1954, Joplin, MO BR/TR, 5'11", 175 lbs. Deb: 7/23/1980 Career OF: 199-55-276

YEAR TM-L	G	AB	R	H	2B	3B	HR	RBI	BB	SO	SB	CS	AVG	OBP	SLG	OPS	OPS+	BR/A	RC	RC/G	FR	G/POS	WS	TPW
1980 StL-N	35	77	6	19	2	2	0	7	6	17	3	2	.247	.310	.325	.634	75	-3	7	3.01	0	0-29(17-8-6)	1	-0.4
1981 StL-N	81	119	13	31	5	4	0	10	6	14	4	2	.261	.302	.370	.671	87	-2	13	3.59	2	0-67(43-6-24)	3	-0.2
1982 StL-N	79	72	12	20	3	0	2	14	8	18	0	1	.278	.358	.403	.761	111	1	11	5.01	1	0-56(24-6-29)	3	0.1
1983 StL-N	6	5	0	1	0	1	0	0	1	2	1	0	.200	.333	.600	.933	154	1	1	8.51	-1	/0-5(4-0-1)	0	0.0
*Bal-A	26	42	8	13	2	0	1	4	1	11	0	2	.310	.326	.429	.754	108	-1	5	3.84	-1	0-26(11-4-15)	1	-0.2
1984 StL-N	105	173	21	47	9	1	3	26	10	27	3	4	.272	.311	.387	.699	98	-2	18	3.34	-2	0-88(55-20-25)	3	-0.7
1985*StL-N	85	161	21	45	8	2	4	21	19	30	1	4	.280	.356	.429	.784	119	3	24	5.12	0	0-73(10-0-67)	6	0.1
1986 StL-N	96	205	24	43	7	1	2	17	20	41	3	1	.210	.283	.283	.566	57	-12	17	2.64	4	0-78(9-4-70)	3	-1.1
1987 StL-N	30	50	5	10	1	0	0	6	7	14	1	1	.200	.298	.220	.518	39	-4	3	2.17	1	0-23(2-7-17)/1-1	1	-0.5
LA-N	51	67	8	16	3	0	1	4	3	16	1	1	.239	.282	.328	.610	63	-4	6	3.24	-1	0-31(19-0-14)	1	-0.6
Yr.	81	117	13	26	4	0	1	10	10	30	2	2	.222	.289	.282	.571	52	-9	10	2.76	0	0-54(21-7-31)/1-1	2	-1.0
1988 Bal-A	13	24	2	3	0	1	0	2	4	6	0	0	.125	.250	.208	.458	31	-2	2	1.94	0	0-12(5-0-8)/D-1	0	-0.3
Total 9	**607**	**995**	**120**	**248**	**40**	**12**	**13**	**111**	**85**	**196**	**17**	**18**	**.249**	**.312**	**.353**	**.664**	**85**	**-27**	**106**	**3.53**	**3**	**0-488/1-1,D-1**	**22**	**-3.8**

• LANE, Chappy George M. Lane b: Pittsburgh, PA BR, 165 lbs. Deb: 5/16/1882 Career OF: 5-12-5

YEAR TM-L	G	AB	R	H	2B	3B	HR	RBI	BB	SO	SB	CS	AVG	OBP	SLG	OPS	OPS+	BR/A	RC	RC/G	FR	G/POS	WS	TPW
1882 Pit-a	57	214	26	38	8	2	3	....	5	....	....	....	.178	.196	.276	.472	60	-8	12	1.89	6	1-43,0-13(0-12-1)/C-2	2	-0.6
1884 Tol-a	57	215	26	49	9	5	1	0	2	....	....	....	.228	.242	.330	.572	82	-5	18	2.92	3	1-46/0-9(5-0-4),3-2,C-1	3	-0.6
Total 2	**114**	**429**	**52**	**87**	**17**	**7**	**4**	**0**	**7**	**....**	**....**	**....**	**.203**	**.219**	**.303**	**.522**	**71**	**-13**	**29**	**2.39**	**9**	**/1-89,0-22,C-3,3-2**	**5**	**-1.2**

• LANE, Dick Richard Harrison Lane b: 6/28/1927, Highland Park, MI BR/TR, 5'11", 178 lbs. Deb: 6/20/1949

YEAR TM-L	G	AB	R	H	2B	3B	HR	RBI	BB	SO	SB	CS	AVG	OBP	SLG	OPS	OPS+	BR/A	RC	RC/G	FR	G/POS	WS	TPW
1949 Chi-A	12	42	4	5	0	0	0	4	5	3	0	1	.119	.213	.119	.332	-11	-7	1	.76	1	0-11(11-0-0)	0	-0.7

• LANE, Hunter James Hunter "Dodo" Lane b: 7/20/1900, Pulaski, TN d: 9/12/1994, Memphis, TN BR/TR, 5'11", 165 lbs. Deb: 5/13/1924

YEAR TM-L	G	AB	R	H	2B	3B	HR	RBI	BB	SO	SB	CS	AVG	OBP	SLG	OPS	OPS+	BR/A	RC	RC/G	FR	G/POS	WS	TPW
1924 Bos-N	7	15	0	1	0	0	0	0	1	1	0	0	.067	.125	.067	.192	-49	-3	0	.29	-2	/3-4,2-1	0	-0.4

• LANE, Jason Jason Dean Lane b: 12/22/1976, Santa Rosa, CA BR/TL, 6'2", 215 lbs. Deb: 5/10/2002 Career OF: 14-7-29

YEAR TM-L	G	AB	R	H	2B	3B	HR	RBI	BB	SO	SB	CS	AVG	OBP	SLG	OPS	OPS+	BR/A	RC	RC/G	FR	G/POS	WS	TPW
2002 Hou-N	44	69	12	20	3	1	4	10	10	12	1	1	.290	.380	.536	.916	132	3	15	7.75	3	0-38(11-1-27)	3	0.5
2003 Hou-N	18	27	5	8	2	0	4	10	0	2	0	0	.296	.296	.815	1.111	168	2	7	9.26	-1	0-10(3-6-2)	1	0.1
Total 2	**62**	**96**	**17**	**28**	**5**	**1**	**8**	**20**	**10**	**14**	**1**	**1**	**.292**	**.358**	**.615**	**.973**	**141**	**5**	**21**	**8.16**	**2**	**/0-48**	**4**	**0.6**

• LANE, Marvin Marvin Lane b: 1/18/1950, Sandersville, GA BR/TR, 5'11", 180 lbs. Deb: 9/4/1971 Career OF: 57-8-13

YEAR TM-L	G	AB	R	H	2B	3B	HR	RBI	BB	SO	SB	CS	AVG	OBP	SLG	OPS	OPS+	BR/A	RC	RC/G	FR	G/POS	WS	TPW
1971 Det-A	8	14	0	2	0	0	0	1	1	3	0	0	.143	.200	.143	.343	-1	-2	0	1.02	0	/0-6(3-0-3)	0	-0.2
1972 Det-A	8	6	2	0	0	0	0	0	0	2	0	0	.000	.000	.000	.000	-97	-1	0	.00	0	/0-3(1-1-1)	0	-0.2
1973 Det-A	6	8	2	2	0	0	1	2	2	2	0	0	.250	.400	.625	1.025	173	1	2	6.39	0	/0-4(3-0-3)	1	0.1
1974 Det-A	50	103	16	24	4	1	2	9	19	24	2	0	.233	.352	.350	.702	99	1	14	4.60	0	0-46(40-2-6)/D-1	4	-0.1
1976 Det-A	18	48	3	9	1	0	0	5	6	11	0	0	.188	.278	.208	.486	42	-3	3	2.02	0	0-15(10-5-0)	0	-0.4
Total 5	**90**	**179**	**23**	**37**	**5**	**1**	**3**	**17**	**28**	**42**	**2**	**0**	**.207**	**.314**	**.296**	**.610**	**75**	**-5**	**19**	**3.50**	**0**	**/0-74,D-1**	**5**	**-0.9**

• LANG, Don Donald Charles Lang b: 3/15/1915, Selma, CA BR/TR, 6', 175 lbs. Deb: 7/4/1938

YEAR TM-L	G	AB	R	H	2B	3B	HR	RBI	BB	SO	SB	CS	AVG	OBP	SLG	OPS	OPS+	BR/A	RC	RC/G	FR	G/POS	WS	TPW
1938 Cin-N	21	50	5	13	3	1	1	11	2	7	0	....	.260	.288	.420	.708	95	-1	5	3.43	0	3-15/2-1,S-1	1	0.0
1948 StL-N	117	323	30	87	14	1	4	31	47	38	2	....	.269	.364	.356	.720	90	-3	46	5.01	0	3-95/2-2	10	-0.3
Total 2	**138**	**373**	**35**	**100**	**17**	**2**	**5**	**42**	**49**	**45**	**2**	**....**	**.268**	**.355**	**.365**	**.719**	**91**	**-3**	**51**	**4.79**	**0**	**3-110/2-3,S-1**	**11**	**-0.3**

• LANGE, Bill William Alexander "Little Eva" Lange
b: 6/6/1871, San Francisco, CA d: 7/23/1950, San Francisco, CA BR/TR, 6'1.5", 190 lbs. Deb: 4/27/1893 Career OF: 15-700-2

YEAR TM-L	G	AB	R	H	2B	3B	HR	RBI	BB	SO	SB	CS	AVG	OBP	SLG	OPS	OPS+	BR/A	RC	RC/G	FR	G/POS	WS	TPW
1893 Chi-N	117	469	92	132	8	7	8	88	52	20	47	....	.281	.358	.380	.738	97	-1	83	6.49	0	2-57,0-40(14-27-0)/3-8,C-7,S	12	0.0
1894 Chi-N	113	449	86	146	17	9	6	91	56	18	65	....	.325	.401	.443	.844	98	-1	109	9.32	-2	*0-109(1-106-2)/S-2,3-1	13	-0.8
1895 Chi-N	123	478	120	186	27	16	10	98	55	24	67	....	.389	.456	.575	1.032	155	39	160	14.38	8	*0-123(0-123-0)	29	3.2
1896 Chi-N	122	469	114	153	21	16	4	92	65	24	84	....	.326	.414	.465	.879	126	19	129	10.58	7	*0-121(0-121-0)/C-1	24	1.6
1897 Chi-N	118	479	119	163	24	14	5	83	48	....	**73**	....	.340	.406	.480	.886	129	20	127	10.33	3	*0-118(0-118-0)	21	1.3
1898 Chi-N	113	442	79	141	16	11	5	69	36	....	22	....	.319	.377	.439	.816	134	19	84	7.24	9	*0-111(0-111-0)/1-2	21	1.9
1899 Chi-N	107	416	81	135	21	7	1	58	38	....	41	....	.325	.382	.416	.798	122	13	85	7.77	12	0-94(0-94-0),1-14	19	1.7
Total 7	**813**	**3202**	**691**	**1056**	**134**	**80**	**39**	**579**	**350**	**86**	**399**	**....**	**.330**	**.400**	**.458**	**.858**	**123**	**107**	**776**	**9.42**	**37**	**0-716/2-57,1-16,3-9,S-9,C-8**	**139**	**8.7**

• LANGERHANS, Ryan Ryan David Langerhans b: 2/20/1980, San Antonio, TX BL/TL, 6'3", 195 lbs. Deb: 4/28/2002 Career OF: 4-4-9

YEAR TM-L	G	AB	R	H	2B	3B	HR	RBI	BB	SO	SB	CS	AVG	OBP	SLG	OPS	OPS+	BR/A	RC	RC/G	FR	G/POS	WS	TPW
2002 Atl-N	1	1	0	0	0	0	0	0	0	0	0	0	.000	.000	.000	.000	-99	-0	0	.00	0	/0-1	0	0.0
2003 Atl-N	16	15	2	4	0	0	0	0	0	6	0	0	.267	.267	.267	.533	40	-1	1	1.80	1	0-14(3-4-9)	0	-0.1
Total 2	**17**	**16**	**2**	**4**	**0**	**0**	**0**	**0**	**0**	**6**	**0**	**0**	**.250**	**.250**	**.250**	**.500**	**31**	**-2**	**1**	**1.66**	**1**	**/0-15**	**0**	**-0.1**

• LANGFORD, Sam Elton Langford b: 5/21/1901, Briggs, TX d: 7/31/1993, Plainview, TX BL/TR, 6', 180 lbs. Deb: 4/13/1926 Career OF: 33-94-1

YEAR TM-L	G	AB	R	H	2B	3B	HR	RBI	BB	SO	SB	CS	AVG	OBP	SLG	OPS	OPS+	BR/A	RC	RC/G	FR	G/POS	WS	TPW
1926 Bos-A	1	1	1	0	0	0	0	0	0	0	0	0	.000	.000	.000	.000	-103	-0	0	.00	0	....	0	0.0
1927 Cle-A	20	67	10	18	5	0	1	7	5	7	0	1	.269	.347	.388	.735	90	-1	9	4.62	0	0-20(1-18-1)	2	-0.2
1928 Cle-A	110	427	50	118	17	8	4	50	21	35	3	7	.276	.312	.382	.694	80	-15	49	3.95	-3	*0-107(32-76-0)	6	-2.3
Total 3	**131**	**495**	**61**	**136**	**22**	**8**	**5**	**57**	**26**	**42**	**3**	**8**	**.275**	**.316**	**.382**	**.698**	**81**	**-17**	**58**	**4.03**	**-3**	**0-127**	**8**	**-2.5**

• LANGSFORD, Bob Robert William Langsford b: 8/5/1865, Louisville, KY d: 1/10/1907, Louisville, KY BR/TR, 5'7" Deb: 6/18/1899

YEAR TM-L	G	AB	R	H	2B	3B	HR	RBI	BB	SO	SB	CS	AVG	OBP	SLG	OPS	OPS+	BR/A	RC	RC/G	FR	G/POS	WS	TPW
1899 Lou-N	1	4	0	0	0	0	0	0	0	....	0	....	.000	.000	.000	.000	-100	-1	0	.00	0	/S-1	0	-0.1

• LANIER, Hal Harold Clifton Lanier b: 7/4/1942, Denton, NC BR/TR, 6'2", 180 lbs. Deb: 6/18/1964 M/C

YEAR TM-L	G	AB	R	H	2B	3B	HR	RBI	BB	SO	SB	CS	AVG	OBP	SLG	OPS	OPS+	BR/A	RC	RC/G	FR	G/POS	WS	TPW
1964 SF-N	98	383	40	105	16	3	2	28	5	44	2	1	.274	.284	.347	.631	75	-13	34	3.05	15	2-98/S-3	9	1.1

YEAR TM-L	G	AB	R	H	2B	3B	HR	RBI	BB	SO	SB	CS	AVG	OBP	SLG	OPS	OPS+	BR/A	RC	RC/G	FR	G/POS	WS	TPW
1965 SF-N	159	522	41	118	15	9	0	39	21	67	2	1	.226	.256	.289	.545	52	-34	34	2.11	7	*2-158/S-1	7	-1.5
1966 SF-N	149	459	37	106	14	2	3	37	16	49	1	0	.231	.257	.290	.547	50	-31	30	2.09	17	*2-112,S-41	7	-0.1
1967 SF-N	151	525	37	112	16	3	0	42	16	61	2	2	.213	.239	.255	.495	42	-40	29	1.77	16	*S-137,2-34	9	-1.2
1968 SF-N	151	486	37	100	14	1	0	27	12	57	2	2	.206	.225	.239	.464	39	-37	23	1.49	16	*S-150	8	-0.9
1969 SF-N	150	495	37	113	9	1	0	35	25	68	0	1	.228	.265	.251	.516	46	-36	31	2.02	18	*S-150	9	0.0
1970 SF-N	134	438	33	101	13	1	2	41	21	41	1	2	.231	.266	.279	.544	47	-35	28	2.07	3	*S-130/2-4,1-2	6	-1.6
1971*SF-N	109	206	21	48	8	0	1	13	15	26	0	0	.233	.285	.286	.571	63	-10	16	2.60	0	3-83,2-13/S-8,1-3	3	-1.0
1972 NY-A	60	103	5	22	3	0	0	6	2	13	1	2	.214	.236	.243	.479	44	-8	5	1.56	2	3-47/S-9,2-3	1	-0.6
1973 NY-A	35	86	9	18	3	0	0	5	3	10	0	0	.209	.244	.244	.489	39	-7	5	1.77	-1	S-26/2-8,3-1	1	-0.5
Total 10	**1196**	**3703**	**297**	**843**	**111**	**20**	**8**	**273**	**136**	**436**	**11**	**11**	**.228**	**.256**	**.275**	**.531**	**50**	**-250**	**236**	**2.05**	**92**	**S-655,2-430,3-131/1-5**	**60**	**-6.5**

• LANIER, Rimp Lorenzo Lanier b: 10/19/1948, Tuskegee, AL BL/TR, 5'8", 150 lbs. Deb: 9/11/1971

YEAR TM-L	G	AB	R	H	2B	3B	HR	RBI	BB	SO	SB	CS	AVG	OBP	SLG	OPS	OPS+	BR/A	RC	RC/G	FR	G/POS	WS	TPW
1971 Pit-N	6	4	0	0	0	0	0	0	0	1	0	0	.000	.200	.000	.200	-39	-1	0	.35	0	....	0	-0.1

• LANKFORD, Ray Raymond Lewis Lankford b: 6/5/1967, Los Angeles, CA BL/TL, 5'11", 198 lbs. Deb: 8/21/1990 Career OF: 386-1135-2

YEAR TM-L	G	AB	R	H	2B	3B	HR	RBI	BB	SO	SB	CS	AVG	OBP	SLG	OPS	OPS+	BR/A	RC	RC/G	FR	G/POS	WS	TPW
1990 StL-N	39	126	12	36	10	1	3	12	13	27	8	2	.286	.353	.452	.805	119	4	21	6.20	1	0-35(0-35-0)	5	0.5
1991 StL-N	151	566	83	142	23	**15**	9	69	41	114	44	20	.251	.303	.392	.695	93	-6	67	4.00	0	*0-149(0-149-0)	18	-0.8
1992 StL-N	153	598	87	175	40	6	20	86	72	147	42	24	.293	.373	.480	.853	144	34	108	6.37	-1	*0-153(0-153-0)	31	3.2
1993 StL-N	127	407	64	97	17	3	7	45	81	111	14	14	.238	.369	.346	.715	95	-3	56	4.52	-2	*0-121(0-121-0)	12	-0.3
1994 StL-N	109	416	89	111	25	5	19	57	58	113	11	10	.267	.362	.488	.850	121	11	76	6.47	-3	*0-104(0-104-0)	16	0.9
1995 StL-N	132	483	81	134	35	2	25	82	63	110	24	8	.277	.363	.513	.877	128	21	91	6.61	3	*0-129(0-129-0)	22	2.5
1996*StL-N	149	545	100	150	36	8	21	86	79	133	35	7	.275	.370	.486	.856	125	25	103	6.57	4	*0-144(0-144-0)	25	2.9
1997 StL-N★	133	465	94	137	36	3	31	98	95	125	21	11	.295	.414	.585	.999	160	43	115	8.83	-3	*0-132(0-132-0)	24	4.0
1998 StL-N	154	533	94	156	37	1	31	105	86	151	26	5	.293	.394	.540	.934	144	39	123	8.49	-5	*0-145(0-145-0)/D-1	27	3.5
1999 StL-N	122	422	77	129	32	1	15	63	49	110	14	4	.306	.382	.493	.875	118	13	82	7.28	0	*0-106(105-2-0)/D-1	13	0.8
2000*StL-N	128	392	73	99	16	3	26	65	70	148	5	6	.253	.371	.508	.879	119	10	76	6.62	-6	*0-117(116-2-0)/D-1	10	0.0
2001 StL-N	91	264	38	62	18	3	15	39	44	105	4	2	.235	.348	.496	.845	116	6	47	6.00	0	0-85(85-0-0)	8	0.3
SD-N	40	125	20	36	10	1	4	19	18	40	6	0	.288	.386	.480	.866	134	8	25	7.52	-2	0-38(21-16-2)	7	0.5
Yr.	131	389	58	98	28	4	19	58	62	145	10	2	.252	.360	.491	.851	121	15	72	6.46	-2	*0-123(106-16-2)	15	0.8
2002 SD-N	81	205	20	46	7	1	6	26	30	61	2	2	.224	.329	.356	.685	88	-3	25	4.09	1	0-59(59-3-0)/D-1	5	-0.5
Total 13	**1609**	**5547**	**932**	**1510**	**342**	**53**	**232**	**852**	**799**	**1495**	**256**	**115**	**.272**	**.367**	**.478**	**.846**	**124**	**203**	**1017**	**6.42**	**-12**	***0-1517/D-4**	**223**	**17.5**

• LANNING, Red Lester Alfred Lanning b: 5/13/1895, Harvard, IL d: 6/13/1962, Bristol, CT BL/TL, 5'9", 165 lbs. Deb: 6/20/1916 ♦

YEAR TM-L	G	AB	R	H	2B	3B	HR	RBI	BB	SO	SB	CS	AVG	OBP	SLG	OPS	OPS+	BR/A	RC	RC/G	FR	G/POS	WS	TPW
1916 Phi-A	19	33	5	6	2	0	0	1	10	9	0	....	.182	.372	.242	.615	89	1	3	2.99	-1	/O-9(7-0-6),P-6	1	-1.6

• LANSFORD, Carney Carney Ray Lansford b: 2/7/1957, San Jose, CA BR/TR, 6'2", 195 lbs. Deb: 4/8/1978 C

YEAR TM-L	G	AB	R	H	2B	3B	HR	RBI	BB	SO	SB	CS	AVG	OBP	SLG	OPS	OPS+	BR/A	RC	RC/G	FR	G/POS	WS	TPW
1978 Cal-A	121	453	63	133	23	2	8	52	31	67	20	9	.294	.344	.406	.750	115	9	65	5.08	-19	*3-117/S-2,D-1	17	-1.2
1979*Cal-A	157	654	114	188	30	5	19	79	39	115	20	8	.287	.330	.436	.766	108	7	91	4.85	-13	*3-157	21	-0.7
1980 Cal-A	151	602	87	157	27	3	15	80	50	93	14	5	.261	.317	.390	.708	95	-4	75	4.21	-10	*3-150	15	-1.5
1981 Bos-A	102	399	61	134	23	3	4	52	34	28	15	10	**.336**	.391	.439	.829	131	16	68	6.45	0	3-86,D-16	18	1.5
1982 Bos-A	128	482	65	145	28	4	11	63	46	48	9	4	.301	.364	.444	.808	114	10	76	5.62	-12	*3-114,D-13	16	-0.3
1983 Oak-A	80	299	43	92	16	2	10	45	22	33	3	8	.308	.361	.475	.836	136	11	47	5.53	5	3-78/S-1	12	1.5
1984 Oak-A	151	597	70	179	31	5	14	74	40	62	9	3	.300	.347	.439	.786	124	19	90	5.45	14	*3-151	25	3.1
1985 Oak-A	98	401	51	111	18	2	13	46	18	27	2	3	.277	.314	.429	.743	109	2	53	4.61	-7	3-97	12	-0.6
1986 Oak-A	151	591	80	168	16	4	19	72	39	51	16	7	.284	.334	.421	.755	112	9	80	4.79	-10	*3-100,1-60/D-3,2-1	19	-0.5
1987 Oak-A	151	554	89	160	27	4	19	76	60	44	27	8	.289	.368	.455	.822	125	23	96	6.18	3	*3-142,1-17/D-4	23	2.3
1988*Oak-A★	150	556	80	155	20	2	7	57	35	35	29	8	.279	.329	.360	.689	96	-0	65	4.04	-7	*3-143/1-9,2-1,D-1	18	-0.7
1989*Oak-A	148	551	81	185	28	2	2	52	51	25	37	15	.336	.401	.405	.806	132	27	88	5.85	-17	*3-136,1-15/D-3	21	1.0
1990*Oak-A	134	507	58	136	15	1	3	50	45	50	16	14	.268	.335	.320	.655	87	-10	54	3.61	1	*3-126/1-5,D-5	12	-0.9
1991 Oak-A	5	16	0	1	0	0	0	1	0	2	0	0	.063	.063	.063	.125	-69	-4	0	.11	-0	/3-4,D-1	0	-0.4
1992*Oak-A	135	496	65	130	30	1	7	75	43	39	7	2	.262	.330	.369	.699	101	1	61	4.12	-9	*3-119,1-18/D-2,S-1	15	-0.8
Total 15	**1862**	**7158**	**1007**	**2074**	**332**	**40**	**151**	**874**	**553**	**719**	**224**	**104**	**.290**	**.346**	**.411**	**.757**	**112**	**117**	**1007**	**4.96**	**-81**	***3-1720,1-124/D-49,S-4,2-2**	**244**	**1.8**

• LANSFORD, Jody Joseph Dale Lansford b: 1/15/1961, Santa Clara, CA BR/TR, 6'5", 225 lbs. Deb: 7/31/1982

YEAR TM-L	G	AB	R	H	2B	3B	HR	RBI	BB	SO	SB	CS	AVG	OBP	SLG	OPS	OPS+	BR/A	RC	RC/G	FR	G/POS	WS	TPW
1982 SD-N	13	22	6	4	0	0	0	3	6	4	0	1	.182	.357	.182	.539	58	-1	2	2.55	0	/1-9	0	-0.2
1983 SD-N	12	8	1	2	0	0	1	2	0	3	0	0	.250	.250	.625	.875	140	0	1	5.63	0	/1-8	0	0.0
Total 2	**25**	**30**	**7**	**6**	**0**	**0**	**1**	**5**	**6**	**7**	**0**	**1**	**.200**	**.333**	**.300**	**.633**	**76**	**-1**	**3**	**3.26**	**-1**	**/1-17**	**0**	**-0.2**

• LANSING, Mike Michael Thomas Lansing b: 4/3/1968, Rawlins, WY BR/TR, 6', 180 lbs. Deb: 4/7/1993

YEAR TM-L	G	AB	R	H	2B	3B	HR	RBI	BB	SO	SB	CS	AVG	OBP	SLG	OPS	OPS+	BR/A	RC	RC/G	FR	G/POS	WS	TPW
1993 Mon-N	141	491	64	141	29	1	3	45	46	56	23	5	.287	.354	.369	.723	90	-3	65	4.60	5	3-81,S-51,2-25	17	0.7
1994 Mon-N	106	394	44	105	21	2	5	35	30	37	12	8	.266	.329	.368	.697	81	-12	46	4.01	4	2-82,3-27,S-12	10	-0.3
1995 Mon-N	127	467	47	119	30	2	10	62	28	65	27	4	.255	.301	.392	.693	78	-12	54	3.97	7	*2-127/S-2	15	0.1
1996 Mon-N	159	641	99	183	40	2	11	53	44	85	23	8	.285	.341	.406	.747	94	-5	87	4.73	-10	*2-159/S-2	19	-0.7
1997 Mon-N	144	572	86	161	45	2	20	70	45	92	11	5	.281	.339	.472	.811	110	7	91	5.69	5	*2-144	21	1.9
1998 Col-N	153	584	73	161	39	2	12	66	39	88	10	3	.276	.326	.411	.737	76	-20	75	4.47	-4	*2-153/3-1	11	-1.6
1999 Col-N	35	145	24	45	9	0	4	15	7	22	2	0	.310	.346	.455	.802	79	-4	23	5.82	1	2-35	3	-0.1
2000 Col-N	90	365	62	94	14	6	11	47	31	49	8	2	.258	.316	.419	.735	67	-19	46	4.28	-14	2-88	5	-2.7
Bos-A	49	139	10	27	4	0	0	13	7	26	0	0	.194	.233	.223	.456	16	-18	6	1.37	-5	2-49/3-1	2	-2.0
2001 Bos-A	106	352	45	88	23	0	8	34	22	50	3	3	.250	.296	.384	.680	77	-14	39	3.71	-5	S-76,2-31	6	-1.1
Total 9	**1110**	**4150**	**554**	**1124**	**254**	**17**	**84**	**440**	**299**	**570**	**119**	**38**	**.271**	**.325**	**.401**	**.726**	**83**	**-101**	**533**	**4.43**	**-16**	**2-893,S-143,3-110**	**109**	**-6.0**

• LAPAN, Pete Peter Nelson Lapan b: 6/25/1891, Easthampton, MA d: 1/5/1953, Norwalk, CA BR/TR, 5'7", 165 lbs. Deb: 9/16/1922

YEAR TM-L	G	AB	R	H	2B	3B	HR	RBI	BB	SO	SB	CS	AVG	OBP	SLG	OPS	OPS+	BR/A	RC	RC/G	FR	G/POS	WS	TPW
1922 Was-A	11	34	7	11	1	0	1	6	3	4	1	0	.324	.378	.441	.820	119	1	6	6.56	0	C-11	2	0.2
1923 Was-A	2	2	0	0	0	0	0	0	0	0	0	0	.000	.000	.000	.000	-105	-1	0	.00	0	....	0	-0.1
Total 2	**13**	**36**	**7**	**11**	**1**	**0**	**1**	**6**	**3**	**4**	**1**	**0**	**.306**	**.359**	**.417**	**.776**	**108**	**1**	**6**	**6.06**	**0**	**/C-11**	**2**	**0.1**

• LAPOINTE, Ralph Ralph Robert LaPointe b: 1/8/1922, Winooski, VT d: 9/13/1967, Burlington, VT BR/TR, 5'11", 185 lbs. Deb: 4/15/1947

YEAR TM-L	G	AB	R	H	2B	3B	HR	RBI	BB	SO	SB	CS	AVG	OBP	SLG	OPS	OPS+	BR/A	RC	RC/G	FR	G/POS	WS	TPW
1947 Phi-N	56	211	33	65	7	0	1	15	17	15	8	....	.308	.362	.355	.718	95	-1	29	5.32	-2	S-54	6	0.0
1948 StL-N	87	222	27	50	3	0	0	15	18	19	1	....	.225	.283	.239	.522	40	-18	16	2.50	-1	2-44,S-25/3-1	3	-1.6
Total 2	**143**	**433**	**60**	**115**	**10**	**0**	**1**	**30**	**35**	**34**	**9**	**....**	**.266**	**.322**	**.296**	**.618**	**67**	**-20**	**45**	**3.77**	**-4**	**/S-79,2-44,3-1**	**9**	**-1.7**

• LAPORTE, Frank Frank Breyfogle "Pot" LaPorte
b: 2/6/1880, Uhrichsville, OH d: 9/25/1939, Newcomerstown, OH BR/TR, 5'8", 175 lbs. Deb: 9/29/1905 Career OF: 39-16-92

YEAR TM-L	G	AB	R	H	2B	3B	HR	RBI	BB	SO	SB	CS	AVG	OBP	SLG	OPS	OPS+	BR/A	RC	RC/G	FR	G/POS	WS	TPW
1905 NY-A	11	40	4	16	1	0	1	12	1	....	1	....	.400	.415	.500	.915	170	3	9	9.85	-2	2-11	3	0.1
1906 NY-A	123	454	60	120	23	9	2	54	22	....	10	....	.264	.300	.368	.668	99	-2	55	4.29	-2	*3-114/2-5,0-1	14	-0.1
1907 NY-A	130	470	56	127	20	11	0	48	27	....	10	....	.270	.317	.360	.676	107	3	59	4.46	-6	3-64,0-63(14-13-36)/1-1	16	-0.5
1908 Bos-A	62	156	14	37	1	3	0	15	12	....	3	....	.237	.296	.282	.578	86	-2	14	2.93	0	2-27,3-12/0-5(0-2-3)	3	-0.2
NY-A	39	145	7	38	3	4	1	15	8	....	3	....	.262	.301	.359	.659	113	1	16	3.81	-4	2-26,0-11(3-0-8)	5	-0.3
Yr.	101	301	21	75	4	7	1	30	20	....	6	....	.249	.298	.319	.617	99	-1	30	3.35	-4	2-53,0-16(3-2-11),3-12	8	-0.5
1909 NY-A	89	309	35	92	19	3	0	31	18	....	5	....	.298	.340	.379	.719	126	8	41	4.76	-18	2-83	11	-1.0
1910 NY-A	124	432	43	114	14	6	2	67	33	....	16	....	.264	.321	.338	.658	100	-0	52	4.04	-9	2-79,0-23(17-1-5),3-15	14	-1.1
1911 StL-A	136	507	71	159	37	12	2	82	34	....	4	....	.314	.361	.446	.807	130	18	83	5.88	-5	*2-133/3-3	17	1.5
1912 StL-A	80	266	32	83	11	4	1	38	20	....	7	....	.312	.367	.395	.762	122	7	41	5.55	3	2-39,0-32(0-0-32)	8	1.0
Was-A	40	136	13	42	9	1	0	17	12	....	3	....	.309	.365	.390	.755	115	3	20	5.41	-1	2-37	5	0.2
Yr.	120	402	45	125	20	5	1	55	32	....	10	....	.311	.366	.393	.759	120	10	62	5.50	2	2-76,0-32(0-0-32)	13	1.2
1913 Was-A	79	242	25	61	5	4	0	18	17	16	10	....	.252	.309	.306	.615	78	-7	25	3.39	4	3-46,2-13,0-12(4-0-8)	7	-0.2
1914 Ind-F	133	505	86	157	27	12	4	**107**	36	36	15	....	.311	.361	.436	.797	114	8	83	5.72	2	*2-132	18	1.3
1915 New-F	148	550	55	139	28	10	2	56	48	33	14	....	.253	.314	.351	.665	101	-0	63	3.83	8	*2-146	17	1.1
Total 11	**1194**	**4212**	**501**	**1185**	**198**	**79**	**15**	**560**	**288**	**85**	**101**	**....**	**.281**	**.331**	**.377**	**.708**	**109**	**40**	**561**	**4.64**	**-30**	**2-731,3-254,0-147/1-1**	**138**	**1.7**

YEAR TM-L	G	AB	R	H	2B	3B	HR	RBI	BB	SO	SB	CS	AVG	OBP	SLG	OPS	OPS+	BR/A	RC	RC/G	FR	G/POS	WS	TPW
• LAPP, Jack	John Walker Lapp b: 9/10/1884, Frazer, PA d: 2/6/1920, Philadelphia, PA BL/TR, 5'8", 160 lbs. Deb: 9/11/1908																							
1908 Phi-A	13	35	4	5	0	1	0	1	5	....	0	....	.143	.268	.200	.468	49	-2	2	1.63	-1	C-13	1	-0.2
1909 Phi-A	21	56	8	19	3	1	0	10	3	....	1	....	.339	.373	.429	.801	150	3	9	6.10	-1	C-19	3	0.4
1910*Phi-A	71	192	18	45	4	3	0	17	20	....	0	....	.234	.310	.286	.596	88	-2	17	2.94	2	C-63	7	0.6
1911*Phi-A	68	167	35	59	10	3	1	26	24	....	4	....	.353	.435	.467	.902	154	13	36	8.21	-3	C-57/1-4	12	1.4
1912 Phi-A	91	281	26	82	15	6	1	35	19	....	3	....	.292	.337	.399	.735	114	4	38	4.87	-5	C-83	10	0.5
1913*Phi-A	82	238	23	54	4	4	1	20	37	26	1	....	.227	.336	.290	.626	85	-3	23	3.10	-3	C-78/1-1	8	-0.1
1914*Phi-A	69	199	22	46	7	2	0	19	31	14	1	4	.231	.338	.286	.624	91	-2	20	3.23	0	C-67	8	0.2
1915 Phi-A	112	312	26	85	16	5	2	31	30	29	5	2	.272	.340	.375	.715	118	6	43	4.67	11	C-89,1-12	12	2.4
1916 Chi-A	40	101	6	21	0	1	0	7	8	10	1	....	.208	.266	.228	.494	48	-6	7	2.09	2	C-34	2	-0.2
Total 9	567	1581	168	416	59	26	5	166	177	79	16	6	.263	.340	.343	.683	104	11	194	4.17	2	C-503/1-17	63	5.1
• LARKER, Norm	Norman Howard John Larker b: 12/27/1930, Beaver Meadows, PA BL/TL, 6', 200 lbs. Deb: 4/15/1958 Career OF: 71-0-11																							
1958 LA-N	99	253	32	70	16	5	4	29	29	21	1	1	.277	.358	.427	.785	103	2	38	5.23	-1	0-43(41-0-2),1-35	7	-0.3
1959*LA-N	108	311	37	90	14	1	8	49	26	25	0	1	.289	.348	.418	.766	96	-2	43	4.70	3	1-55,0-30(22-0-8)	8	-0.3
1960 LA-N★	133	440	56	142	26	3	5	78	36	24	1	0	.323	.375	.430	.805	112	9	71	5.96	1	*1-119/0-2(2-0-0)	14	0.4
1961 LA-N	97	282	29	76	16	1	5	38	24	22	0	0	.270	.329	.387	.716	82	-7	34	4.08	-2	1-86/0-1	6	-1.4
1962 Hou-N	147	506	58	133	19	5	9	63	70	47	1	1	.263	.360	.374	.734	105	6	71	4.92	7	*1-135/0-6(6-0-0)	15	0.5
1963 Mil-N	64	147	15	26	6	0	1	14	24	24	0	2	.177	.301	.238	.539	58	-8	12	2.46	3	1-42	1	-0.7
SF-N	19	14	0	1	0	0	0	0	2	2	0	0	.071	.188	.071	.259	-22	-2	0	.37	0	1-11	0	-0.3
Yr.	83	161	15	27	6	0	1	14	26	26	0	2	.168	.291	.224	.515	51	-10	12	2.26	3	1-53	1	-1.0
Total 6	667	1953	227	538	97	15	32	271	211	165	3	5	.275	.351	.390	.741	97	-2	269	4.78	11	1-483/0-82	51	-2.1
• LARKIN,	Larkin Deb: 5/29/1884																							
1884 Was-U	17	70	11	17	0	0	0	....	4	....	....	....	.243	.284	.243	.527	82	-1	5	2.61	-5	3-17	1	-0.5
• LARKIN, Barry	Barry Louis Larkin b: 4/28/1964, Cincinnati, OH BR/TR, 6', 190 lbs. Deb: 8/13/1986																							
1986 Cin-N	41	159	27	45	4	3	3	19	9	21	8	0	.283	.321	.403	.724	94	0	22	5.02	2	S-36/2-3	6	0.6
1987 Cin-N	125	439	64	107	16	2	12	43	36	52	21	6	.244	.308	.371	.680	76	-14	52	3.94	9	*S-119	11	0.7
1988 Cin-N★	151	588	91	174	32	5	12	56	41	24	40	7	.296	.350	.429	.779	118	18	94	5.72	12	*S-148	28	4.5
1989 Cin-N★	97	325	47	111	14	4	4	36	20	23	10	5	.342	.383	.446	.829	132	13	54	6.20	14	S-82	15	3.6
1990*Cin-N★	158	614	85	185	25	6	7	67	49	49	30	5	.301	.360	.396	.755	103	7	91	5.33	21	*S-156	25	4.2
1991 Cin-N★	123	464	88	140	27	4	20	69	55	64	24	6	.302	.379	.506	.886	141	28	93	7.34	24	*S-119	26	**6.5**
1992 Cin-N	140	533	76	162	32	6	12	78	63	58	15	4	.304	.382	.454	.836	132	26	94	6.39	12	*S-140	32	5.3
1993 Cin-N★	100	384	57	121	20	3	8	51	51	33	14	1	.315	.397	.445	.842	125	18	69	6.68	2	S-99	18	2.8
1994 Cin-N★	110	427	78	119	23	5	9	52	64	58	26	2	.279	.373	.419	.792	107	11	75	6.18	8	*S-110	19	2.8
1995*Cin-N★	131	496	98	158	29	6	15	66	61	49	51	5	.319	.396	.492	.888	133	34	108	8.19	7	*S-130	30	5.0
1996 Cin-N★	152	517	117	154	32	4	33	89	96	52	36	10	.298	.415	.567	.981	157	49	124	8.34	3	*S-151	31	6.3
1997 Cin-N★	73	224	34	71	17	3	4	20	47	24	14	3	.317	.442	.473	.915	137	17	52	8.79	8	S-63/D-2	12	2.9
1998 Cin-N	145	538	93	166	34	10	17	72	79	69	26	3	.309	.399	.504	.903	134	33	114	7.82	-2	*S-145	25	4.2
1999 Cin-N★	161	583	108	171	30	4	12	75	93	57	30	8	.293	.392	.420	.813	103	9	103	6.33	6	*S-161	24	2.6
2000 Cin-N★	102	396	71	124	26	5	11	41	48	31	14	6	.313	.389	.487	.876	117	11	75	7.00	-9	*S-102/D-1	13	0.9
2001 Cin-N	45	156	29	40	12	0	2	17	27	25	3	2	.256	.373	.372	.745	90	-1	23	5.26	-5	S-44	5	-0.3
2002 Cin-N	145	507	72	124	37	2	7	47	44	57	13	4	.245	.309	.367	.676	75	-18	57	3.72	-3	*S-135	9	-1.0
2003 Cin-N	70	241	39	68	16	1	2	18	22	32	2	0	.282	.345	.382	.726	91	-3	32	4.71	-2	S-60	7	0.0
Total 18	2069	7591	1274	2240	426	73	190	916	905	778	377	77	.295	.374	.446	.820	117	238	1332	6.30	108	*S-2000/2-3,D-3	336	51.6
• LARKIN, Ed	Edward Francis Larkin b: 7/1/1885, Wyalusing, PA d: 3/28/1934, Wyalusing, PA BR/TR, 5'8" Deb: 10/2/1909																							
1909 Phi-A	2	6	0	1	0	0	0	1	1	....	0	....	.167	.286	.167	.452	42	-0	0	1.43	-1	/C-2	0	-0.2
• LARKIN, Gene	Eugene Thomas Larkin b: 10/24/1962, Flushing, NY BB/TR, 6'3", 205 lbs. Deb: 5/21/1987 Career OF: 7-0-193																							
1987*Min-A	85	233	23	62	11	2	4	28	25	31	1	4	.266	.342	.382	.724	89	-5	30	4.46	-1	D-40,1-26	5	-0.7
1988 Min-A	149	505	56	135	30	2	8	70	68	55	3	2	.267	.371	.382	.753	108	9	75	5.16	-1	D-86,1-60	14	0.0
1989 Min-A	136	446	61	119	25	1	6	46	54	57	5	2	.267	.358	.368	.725	98	1	60	4.60	-4	1-67,D-41,0-32(1-0-31)	11	-0.9
1990 Min-A	119	401	46	108	26	4	5	42	42	55	5	3	.269	.346	.392	.738	99	0	56	4.88	0	0-47(0-0-46),D-43,1-28	9	-0.4
1991*Min-A	98	255	34	73	14	1	2	19	30	21	2	3	.286	.364	.373	.736	99	0	33	4.54	-2	0-47(2-0-48),1-39/D-4,2-1,3	4	-0.5
1992 Min-A	115	337	38	83	18	1	6	42	28	43	7	2	.246	.312	.359	.671	85	-6	38	3.84	1	1-55,0-43(0-0-43)/D-4	8	-1.0
1993 Min-A	56	144	17	38	7	1	1	19	21	16	0	1	.264	.365	.347	.712	92	-1	19	4.24	-3	0-28(4-0-25),1-18/D-3,3-2	3	-0.6
Total 7	758	2321	275	618	131	12	32	266	268	278	23	17	.266	.352	.374	.726	98	-2	311	4.61	-9	1-293,D-221,0-197/3-3,2-1	54	-4.1
• LARKIN, Henry	Henry E. "Ted" Larkin b: 1/12/1860, Reading, PA d: 1/31/1942, Reading, PA BR/TR, 5'10", 175 lbs. Deb: 5/1/1884 M Career OF: 308-124-20																							
1884 Phi-a	85	326	59	90	21	9	3	37	15	....	....	....	.276	.324	.423	.747	133	11	46	5.34	-7	*0-85(30-55-0)/2-2	12	0.1
1885 Phi-a	108	453	114	149	**37**	14	8	88	26	....	....	....	.329	.372	.525	.897	171	34	91	8.06	11	*0-108(48-61-0)	23	3.7
1886 Phi-a	139	565	133	180	**36**	16	2	74	59	....	32	....	.319	**.390**	.450	.839	161	41	114	8.01	3	*0-139(139-0-0)	**29**	3.4
1887 Phi-a	126	545	105	202	22	12	3	88	48	....	37	....	.371	.380	.421	.800	123	16	96	7.54	-0	*0-93(86-7-0),1-23,2-10	17	0.9
1888 Phi-a	135	546	92	147	28	12	7	101	33	....	20	....	.269	.326	.403	.729	134	20	80	5.43	-6	*1-122,2-14	19	0.3
1889 Phi-a	133	516	105	164	23	12	3	74	83	41	11	....	.318	.428	.426	.854	145	37	101	7.62	-11	*1-131/2-1,3-1	19	1.2
1890 Cle-P	125	506	93	167	32	15	5	112	65	18	5	....	.330	.419	.482	.901	153	41	107	8.51	-10	*1-125/0-1	18	1.7
1891 Phi-a	133	526	94	147	27	14	10	93	66	56	2	....	.279	.376	.441	.817	130	19	90	6.30	-13	*1-111,0-23(5-0-18)	17	-0.3
1892 Was-N	119	464	76	130	13	7	8	96	39	21	21	....	.280	.346	.390	.736	126	14	72	5.80	1	*1-117/0-2(0-0-2)	12	1.4
1893 Was-N	81	319	54	101	20	3	4	73	50	5	1	....	.317	.422	.436	.857	132	17	61	7.36	-14	1-81	11	0.2
Total 10	1184	4766	925	1477	259	114	53	836	484	141	129	....	.310	.380	.440	.819	141	251	857	7.01	-45	1-710,0-451/2-27,3-1	177	12.7
• LARKIN, Stephen	Stephen Karari Larkin b: 7/24/1973, Cincinnati, OH BL/TL, 6' Deb: 9/27/1998																							
1998 Cin-N	1	3	0	1	0	0	0	0	0	1	0	0	.333	.333	.333	.667	75	-0	0	4.50	0	/1-1	0	0.0
• LARKIN, Terry	Frank S. Larkin b: 1856, Brooklyn, NY d: 9/16/1894, Brooklyn, NY BR/TR Deb: 5/20/1876 Career OF: 3-2-1 ♦																							
1876 NY-N	1	4	0	0	0	0	0	0	0	0	....	....	.000	.000	.000	.000	-115	-1	0	.00	0	/P-1	0	-0.1
1877 Har-N	58	228	28	52	6	5	1	18	5	23	....	....	.228	.245	.311	.556	83	5	18	2.78	0	*P-56/3-2,2-1	31	1.1
1878 Chi-N	58	226	33	65	9	4	0	32	**17**	17	....	....	.288	.337	.363	.700	122	14	28	4.84	-3	*P-56/3-1,0-1	34	1.4
1879 Chi-N	60	228	26	50	12	2	0	18	8	24	....	....	.219	.246	.289	.535	71	1	17	2.62	-6	*P-58/0-3(2-1-0)	39	-1.0
1880 Tro-N	6	20	1	3	1	0	0	1	3	4	....	....	.150	.261	.200	.461	56	-0	1	1.73	0	/P-5,0-2(0-1-1),S-1	0	-2.6
1884 Ric-a	40	139	17	28	1	4	0	0	9	....	....	....	.201	.265	.266	.531	75	-3	10	2.49	-3	2-40	2	-0.4
Total 6	223	845	105	198	29	15	1	69	42	68	....	....	.234	.273	.308	.581	87	15	74	3.15	-13	P-176/2-41,0-6,3-3,S-1	106	-1.7
• LARMORE, Bob	Robert McKahan "Red" Larmore b: 12/6/1896, Anderson, IN d: 1/15/1964, St. Louis, MO BR/TR, 5'10.5", 185 lbs. Deb: 5/14/1918																							
1918 StL-N	4	7	0	2	0	0	0	1	0	2	0	....	.286	.286	.286	.571	77	-0	1	2.76	-1	/S-2	0	-0.2
• LAROCCA, Greg	Gregory Mark LaRocca b: 11/10/1972, Oswego, NY BR/TR, 5'11", 185 lbs. Deb: 9/7/2000																							
2000 SD-N	13	27	1	6	2	0	0	2	1	4	0	0	.222	.250	.296	.546	40	-3	2	2.09	-4	/3-8,S-4,2-2	0	-0.6
2002 Cle-A	21	52	12	14	3	1	0	4	6	6	1	0	.269	.367	.365	.732	97	0	8	5.23	-5	3-15/2-3,D-1	1	-0.5
2003 Cle-A	5	9	3	3	1	0	0	0	1	1	0	0	.333	.400	.444	.844	127	0	2	7.67	1	/3-2	0	0.1
Total 3	39	88	16	23	6	1	0	6	8	11	1	0	.261	.337	.352	.689	83	-2	11	4.35	-9	/3-25,2-5,S-4,D-1	1	-1.0
• LAROQUE, Sam	Samuel H.J. LaRoque b: 2/26/1864, St. Mathias, Canada TR, 5'11", 190 lbs. Deb: 7/30/1888																							
1888 Det-N	2	9	1	4	0	0	0	2	1	1	0	....	.444	.500	.444	.944	203	1	2	11.07	0	/2-2	0	0.2
1890 Pit-N	111	434	59	105	20	4	1	40	35	29	27	....	.242	.316	.313	.629	95	-1	53	4.25	-23	2-78,S-31/1-2,0-1	7	-1.8
1891 Pit-N	1	4	0	0	0	0	0	0	0	1	0	....	.000	.000	.000	.000	-103	-1	0	.00	0	/3-1	0	-0.1
Lou-a	10	35	6	11	2	1	1	8	5	8	1	....	.314	.429	.514	.943	172	3	8	9.22	-4	2-10/1-1	2	0.0
Total 3	124	482	66	120	22	5	2	50	41	39	28	....	.249	.326	.328	.654	101	3	63	4.63	-26	/2-90,S-31,1-3,3-1,0-1	9	-1.7

YEAR TM-L	G	AB	R	H	2B	3B	HR	RBI	BB	SO	SB	CS	AVG	OBP	SLG	OPS	OPS+	BR/A	RC	RC/G	FR	G/POS	WS	TPW
• LAROSE, Vic	Victor Raymond LaRose b: 12/23/1944, Los Angeles, CA BR/TR, 5'11", 180 lbs. Deb: 9/13/1968																							
1968 Chi-N	4	2	0	0	0	0	0	0	0	1	0	0	.000	.333	.000	.333	6	-0	0	1.17	-1	/2-2,S-2	0	-0.1
• LAROSS, Harry	Harry Raymond "Spike" LaRoss b: 1/2/1888, Easton, PA d: 3/22/1954, Chicago, IL BR/TR, 5'11.5", 170 lbs. Deb: 6/24/1914																							
1914 Cin-N	22	48	7	11	1	0	0	5	2	10	4	....	.229	.260	.250	.510	50	-3	4	2.61	-2	0-20(10-10-0)	0	-0.6
• LARSEN, Swede	Erling Adeli Larsen b: 11/15/1913, Jersey City, NJ BR/TR, 5'11", 170 lbs. Deb: 6/17/1936																							
1936 Bos-N	3	1	0	0	0	0	0	0	0	0	0	....	.000	.000	.000	.000	-107	-0	0	.00	-1	/2-2	0	-0.1
• LARSON, Brandon	Brandon John Larson b: 5/24/1976, San Angelo, TX BR/TR, 6', 210 lbs. Deb: 5/4/2001 Career OF: 12-0-0																							
2001 Cin-N	14	33	2	4	2	0	0	1	2	10	0	0	.121	.171	.182	.353	-8	-5	1	.84	2	/3-9	0	-0.3
2002 Cin-N	23	51	8	14	2	0	4	13	6	10	1	0	.275	.362	.549	.911	132	3	10	7.37	0	/0-9(9-0-0),3-5,1-2	2	0.2
2003 Cin-N	32	89	6	9	1	0	1	9	13	31	2	2	.101	.216	.146	.362	-3	-14	3	1.00	5	3-24/0-3(3-0-0)	1	-0.9
Total 3	**69**	**173**	**16**	**27**	**5**	**0**	**5**	**23**	**21**	**51**	**3**	**2**	**.156**	**.251**	**.272**	**.523**	**36**	**-17**	**14**	**2.54**	**7**	**/3-38,0-12,1-2**	**3**	**-1.0**
• LARUE, Jason	Michael Jason LaRue b: 3/19/1974, Houston, TX BR/TR, 5'11", 200 lbs. Deb: 6/15/1999 Career OF: 3-0-0																							
1999 Cin-N	36	90	12	19	7	0	3	10	11	32	4	1	.211	.311	.389	.700	73	-3	11	3.74	-1	C-35	2	-0.2
2000 Cin-N	31	98	12	23	3	0	5	12	5	19	0	0	.235	.299	.418	.717	77	-4	12	4.41	4	C-31	3	0.2
2001 Cin-N	121	364	39	86	21	2	12	43	27	106	3	3	.236	.305	.404	.709	78	-13	42	3.89	10	*C-107/3-3,0-2(2-0-0),1-1	9	0.3
2002 Cin-N	113	353	42	88	17	1	12	52	27	117	1	2	.249	.326	.405	.731	89	-7	44	4.18	-2	*C-110	11	-0.2
2003 Cin-N	118	379	52	87	23	1	16	50	33	111	3	3	.230	.324	.422	.746	94	-4	52	4.53	0	*C-114/1-1,0-1	10	0.4
Total 5	**419**	**1284**	**157**	**303**	**71**	**4**	**48**	**167**	**103**	**385**	**11**	**9**	**.236**	**.316**	**.410**	**.726**	**85**	**-32**	**161**	**4.18**	**11**	**C-397/3-3,0-3,1-2**	**35**	**0.6**
• LARUSSA, Tony	Anthony LaRussa b: 10/4/1944, Tampa, FL BR/TR, 6', 190 lbs. Deb: 5/10/1963 M/C																							
1963 KC-A	34	44	4	11	1	1	0	1	7	12	0	0	.250	.353	.318	.671	86	-0	6	4.42	-2	S-14/2-3	1	-0.1
1968 Oak-A	5	3	0	1	0	0	0	0	0	0	0	0	.333	.333	.333	.667	108	0	0	4.50	0	....	0	0.0
1969 Oak-A	8	8	0	0	0	0	0	0	0	1	0	0	.000	.000	.000	.000	-105	-2	0	.00	0	....	0	-0.2
1970 Oak-A	52	106	6	21	4	1	0	6	15	19	0	0	.198	.303	.255	.558	57	-6	9	2.97	3	2-44	2	-0.1
1971 Oak-A	23	8	3	0	0	0	0	0	0	4	0	0	.000	.000	.000	.000	-102	-2	0	.00	-3	/2-7,S-4,3-2	0	-0.5
Atl-N	9	7	1	2	0	0	0	0	1	1	0	0	.286	.375	.286	.661	84	-0	0	1.09	-1	/2-9	0	-0.1
1973 Chi-N	1	0	1	0	0	0	0	0	0	0	0	0	....	....	....	....	-93	0	0	....	0	....	0	0.0
Total 6	**132**	**176**	**15**	**35**	**5**	**2**	**0**	**7**	**23**	**37**	**0**	**0**	**.199**	**.295**	**.250**	**.545**	**54**	**-10**	**16**	**2.92**	**-3**	**/2-63,S-18,3-2**	**3**	**-1.0**
• LARY, Lyn	Lynford Hobart "Broadway" Lary b: 1/28/1906, Armona, CA d: 1/9/1973, Downey, CA BR/TR, 6', 165 lbs. Deb: 5/11/1929 Career OF: 2-0-0																							
1929 NY-A	80	236	48	73	9	2	5	26	24	15	4	1	.309	.380	.428	.808	115	7	40	6.26	1	3-55,S-14/2-2	9	1.2
1930 NY-A	117	464	93	134	20	8	3	52	45	40	14	2	.289	.357	.386	.743	92	-1	68	5.14	4	*S-113	14	1.3
1931 NY-A	155	610	100	171	35	9	10	107	88	54	13	10	.280	.376	.416	.793	115	17	99	5.77	23	*S-155	24	4.8
1932 NY-A	91	280	56	65	14	4	3	39	52	28	9	3	.232	.358	.343	.701	87	-2	39	4.63	3	S-80/1-5,2-2,3-2,0-1	10	0.6
1933 NY-A	52	127	25	28	3	3	0	13	28	17	2	1	.220	.361	.291	.653	79	-2	16	4.03	0	3-28,S-16/1-3,0-1	4	0.0
1934 NY-A	1	0	0	0	0	0	0	0	1	0	0	0	....	1.000	....	1.000	189	0	0	∞	0	/1-1	0	0.0
Bos-A	129	419	58	101	20	4	2	54	66	51	12	5	.241	.344	.322	.667	68	-18	52	4.05	-8	*S-129	9	-1.5
Yr.	130	419	58	101	20	4	2	54	67	51	12	5	.241	.346	.322	.668	68	-18	52	4.05	-8	*S-129/1-1	9	-1.5
1935 Was-A	39	103	8	20	4	0	0	7	12	10	3	0	.194	.278	.233	.511	35	-9	8	2.40	-6	S-30	1	-1.2
StL-A	93	371	78	107	25	7	2	35	64	43	25	4	.288	.396	.410	.806	104	9	68	6.62	8	S-93	14	2.2
Yr.	132	474	86	127	29	7	2	42	76	53	28	4	.268	.371	.371	.743	89	-1	76	5.57	2	*S-123	15	1.0
1936 StL-A	155	619	112	179	30	6	2	52	117	54	**37**	9	.289	.404	.367	.771	89	-1	105	6.08	-6	*S-155	17	0.4
1937 Cle-A	156	644	110	187	46	7	8	77	88	64	18	8	.290	.378	.421	.799	100	3	107	6.04	-13	*S-156	23	0.2
1938 Cle-A	141	568	94	152	36	4	3	51	88	65	23	6	.268	.366	.361	.727	84	-8	82	5.11	2	*S-141	18	0.3
1939 Cle-A	3	2	0	0	0	0	0	0	0	1	0	0	.000	.000	.000	.000	-104	-1	0	.00	-1	/S-2	0	-0.2
Bro-N	29	31	7	5	1	1	0	1	12	6	1	....	.161	.409	.258	.667	80	0	5	4.69	-2	S-12/3-7	1	-0.2
StL-N	34	75	11	14	3	0	0	9	16	15	1	....	.187	.330	.227	.556	49	-5	6	2.35	0	S-30/3-3	1	-0.3
Yr.	63	106	18	19	4	1	0	10	28	21	2	....	.179	.356	.236	.591	59	-5	11	3.01	-2	S-42,3-10	2	-0.4
1940 StL-A	27	54	5	3	1	1	0	3	4	7	0	0	.056	.136	.111	.247	-35	-11	1	.49	-1	S-12/2-1	0	-1.1
Total 12	**1302**	**4603**	**805**	**1239**	**247**	**56**	**38**	**526**	**705**	**470**	**162**	**49**	**.269**	**.369**	**.372**	**.741**	**90**	**-22**	**696**	**5.26**	**5**	***S-1138/3-95,1-9,2-5,0-2**	**145**	**6.6**
• LASSETTER, Don	Donald O'Neal Lassetter b: 3/27/1933, Newman, GA BR/TR, 6'3", 200 lbs. Deb: 9/21/1957																							
1957 StL-N	4	13	2	2	0	1	0	0	1	3	0	0	.154	.214	.308	.522	37	-1	0	.63	1	/0-3(3-0-0)	0	-0.1
• LATHAM, Arlie	Walter Arlington "The Freshest Man On Earth" Latham b: 3/15/1860, West Lebanon, NH d: 11/29/1952, Garden City, NY BR/TR, 5'8", 150 lbs. Deb: 7/5/1880 M/C/U Career OF: 2-0-11																							
1880 Buf-N	22	79	9	10	3	1	0	3	1	8	....	....	.127	.138	.190	.327	9	-7	2	.84	-3	S-12,0-10(0-0-10)/C-1	0	-1.0
1883 StL-a	98	406	86	96	12	7	0	0	18	....	....	....	.236	.269	.300	.569	78	-11	34	3.04	23	*3-98/C-1	12	1.3
1884 StL-a	110	474	115	130	17	12	1	0	18	....	....	....	.274	.309	.367	.676	116	7	55	4.41	39	*3-110/C-1	23	4.5
1885*StL-a	110	485	84	100	15	3	1	35	18	....	....	....	.206	.242	.256	.498	55	-26	31	2.16	6	*3-109/C-2	10	-1.6
1886*StL-a	134	578	**152**	174	23	8	1	47	55	....	60	....	.301	.368	.374	.741	127	18	104	6.95	10	*3-133/2-1	23	2.7
1887*StL-a	136	672	163	243	35	10	2	83	45	....	129	....	.362	.366	.413	.779	106	2	146	9.17	13	*3-132/2-5,C-2	24	1.4
1888*StL-a	133	570	119	151	19	5	2	31	43	....	**109**	....	.265	.325	.326	.652	98	-3	98	6.34	17	*3-133/S-1	21	1.6
1889 StL-a	118	512	110	126	13	3	4	49	42	30	69	....	.246	.317	.307	.623	69	-24	73	5.04	17	*3-116/2-3	15	-0.3
1890 Chi-P	52	214	47	49	7	2	1	20	22	22	32	....	.229	.310	.294	.604	59	-13	30	4.93	3	3-52	4	-0.7
Cin-N	41	164	35	41	6	2	0	15	23	18	20	....	.250	.346	.311	.657	92	-1	25	5.42	4	3-41/0-1	5	0.4
1891 Cin-N	135	533	119	145	20	10	7	53	74	35	87	....	.272	.372	.386	.759	120	16	112	7.78	15	*3-135/C-1	25	3.0
1892 Cin-N	152	622	111	148	20	4	0	44	60	55	66	....	.238	.310	.283	.593	81	-13	77	4.38	-3	*3-142/2-9,0-1	17	-1.3
1893 Cin-N	127	531	101	150	18	6	2	49	62	20	57	....	.282	.368	.350	.718	89	-7	92	6.38	-11	*3-127	16	-1.3
1894 Cin-N	131	534	132	167	23	6	4	60	61	24	62	....	.313	.392	.401	.793	88	-9	111	7.84	-19	*3-127/2-2	14	-2.0
1895 Cin-N	112	460	93	143	14	6	2	69	42	25	48	....	.311	.375	.380	.755	91	-6	86	7.20	-12	*3-108/1-3,2-1	12	-1.3
1896 StL-N	8	35	3	7	0	0	0	5	4	3	2	....	.200	.282	.200	.482	29	-3	3	2.46	-2	/3-8	0	-0.5
1899 Was-N	6	6	1	1	0	0	0	0	1	....	0	....	.167	.286	.167	.452	26	-1	0	1.55	0	/2-1,0-1	0	-0.1
1909 NY-N	4	2	1	0	0	0	0	0	0	....	1	....	.000	.000	.000	.000	-99	-0	0	.00	0	/2-2	0	-0.1
Total 17	**1629**	**6877**	**1481**	**1881**	**245**	**85**	**27**	**563**	**589**	**240**	**742**	**....**	**.274**	**.334**	**.341**	**.676**	**92**	**-82**	**1079**	**5.79**	**95**	***3-1571/2-24,0-13,S-13,C-8,1**	**221**	**4.7**
• LATHAM, Chris	Christopher Joseph Latham b: 5/26/1973, Coeur d'Alene, ID BB/TR, 6', 195 lbs. Deb: 4/12/1997 Career OF: 34-31-27																							
1997 Min-A	15	22	4	4	1	0	0	1	0	8	0	0	.182	.182	.227	.409	6	-3	1	1.36	-1	0-10(0-8-3)	0	-0.4
1998 Min-A	34	94	14	15	1	0	1	5	13	36	4	2	.160	.262	.202	.464	23	-11	6	1.98	-1	0-32(13-15-5)	0	-1.2
1999 Min-A	14	22	1	2	0	0	0	3	0	13	0	0	.091	.091	.091	.182	-52	-5	0	.31	-1	0-14(6-5-4)	0	-0.5
2001 Tor-A	43	73	12	20	3	1	2	10	10	28	4	1	.274	.369	.425	.794	106	1	12	6.05	4	0-31(15-2-14)	3	0.4
2003 NY-A	4	2	3	2	0	0	0	0	0	0	1	0	1.000	1.000	1.000	2.000	439	1	3	∞	0	/0-2(0-1-1),D-1	0	0.1
Total 5	**110**	**213**	**34**	**43**	**5**	**1**	**3**	**19**	**23**	**85**	**9**	**3**	**.202**	**.283**	**.277**	**.560**	**46**	**-16**	**22**	**2.97**	**1**	**/0-89,D-1**	**3**	**-1.6**
• LATHAM, Juice	George Warren "Jumbo" Latham b: 9/6/1852, Utica, NY d: 5/26/1914, Utica, NY BR/TR, 5'8", 164 lbs. Deb: 4/19/1875 M/U																							
1875 Bos-n	16	78	23	21	4	0	0	13	0	2	0	0	.269	.269	.321	.590	100	-0	7	3.57	0	1-16	....	0.0
NH-n	20	76	6	15	1	0	0	5	0	4	6	0	.197	.197	.211	.408	48	-1	4	2.15	2	1-14/S-4,3-3	....	0.0
Yr.	36	154	29	36	5	0	0	18	0	6	6	0	.234	.234	.266	.500	74	-2	11	2.84	1	1-30/S-4,3-3	....	0.0
1877 Lou-N	59	278	42	81	10	6	0	22	5	6	....	....	.291	.304	.371	.674	94	-4	32	4.48	4	*1-59	5	-0.2
1882 Phi-a	74	323	47	92	10	2	0	38	10	....	....	....	.285	.306	.328	.634	102	-1	33	4.03	-2	*1-74	10	-0.8
1883 Lou-a	88	368	60	92	7	6	0	0	12	....	....	....	.250	.274	.302	.575	92	-2	31	3.16	-2	*1-67,2-14/S-9	9	-0.7
1884 Lou-a	77	308	31	52	3	3	0	23	8	....	....	....	.169	.197	.198	.396	31	-22	12	1.33	0	*1-76/3-1	1	-2.6
Total 4	**298**	**1277**	**180**	**317**	**30**	**17**	**0**	**83**	**35**	**6**	**....**	**....**	**.248**	**.270**	**.298**	**.568**	**80**	**-28**	**109**	**3.15**	**1**	**1-276/2-14,S-9,3-1**	**25**	**-4.4**
• LATHERS, Chick	Charles Ten Eyck Lathers b: 10/22/1888, Detroit, MI d: 7/26/1971, Petoskey, MI BL/TR, 6', 180 lbs. Deb: 5/1/1910																							
1910 Det-A	41	82	4	19	2	0	0	3	8	....	0	....	.232	.300	.256	.556	70	-3	6	2.55	0	3-14/2-7,S-4	1	-0.3

YEAR TM-L	G	AB	R	H	2B	3B	HR	RBI	BB	SO	SB	CS	AVG	OBP	SLG	OPS	OPS+	BR/A	RC	RC/G	FR	G/POS	WS	TPW
1911 Det-A	29	45	5	10	1	0	0	4	5	....	0	....	.222	.314	.244	.558	54	-3	4	2.56	-3	/2-9,3-8,S-4,1-3	1	-0.5
Total 2	70	127	9	29	3	0	0	7	13	....	0	....	.228	.305	.252	.557	64	-5	10	2.56	-4	/3-22,2-16,S-8,1-3	2	-0.8
• LATIMER, Tacks	Clifford Wesley Latimer b: 11/30/1877, Loveland, OH d: 4/24/1936, Loveland, OH BR/TR, 6', 160 lbs. Deb: 10/1/1898																							
1898 NY-N	5	17	1	5	1	0	0	1	0	....	0	....	.294	.294	.353	.647	88	-0	2	3.99	0	/C-4,0-2(0-0-2)	0	0.0
1899 Lou-N	9	29	3	8	1	0	0	4	2	....	1	....	.276	.323	.310	.633	74	-1	3	4.14	-1	/C-8,1-1	1	-0.1
1900 Pit-N	4	12	1	4	1	0	0	2	0	....	0	....	.333	.333	.417	.750	106	0	2	5.66	-1	/C-4	0	-0.1
1901 Bal-A	1	4	0	1	0	0	0	0	0	....	0	....	.250	.250	.250	.500	37	-0	0	2.26	0	/C-1	0	0.0
1902 Bro-N	8	24	0	1	0	0	0	0	0	....	0	....	.042	.042	.042	.083	-74	-5	0	.05	-1	/C-8	0	-0.5
Total 5	27	86	5	19	3	0	0	7	2	....	1	....	.221	.239	.256	.494	39	-7	7	2.83	-2	/C-25,0-2,1-1	1	-0.7
• LAU, Charlie	Charles Richard Lau b: 4/12/1933, Romulus, MI d: 3/18/1984, Key Colony Beach, FL BL/TR, 6', 190 lbs. Deb: 9/12/1956 C																							
1956 Det-A	3	9	1	2	0	0	0	0	0	1	0	0	.222	.222	.222	.444	18	-1	0	1.71	0	/C-3	0	-0.1
1958 Det-A	30	68	8	10	1	2	0	6	12	15	0	0	.147	.293	.221	.513	40	-5	5	2.19	0	C-27	1	-0.4
1959 Det-A	2	6	0	1	0	0	0	0	0	2	0	0	.167	.167	.167	.333	-8	-1	0	.90	0	/C-2	0	-0.1
1960 Mil-N	21	53	4	10	2	0	0	2	6	10	0	0	.189	.271	.226	.498	41	-4	4	2.26	2	C-16	1	-0.2
1961 Mil-N	28	82	3	17	5	0	0	5	14	11	1	1	.207	.330	.268	.598	65	-4	8	3.11	-2	C-25	2	-0.4
Bal-A	17	47	3	8	0	0	1	4	1	3	0	0	.170	.188	.234	.422	12	-6	2	1.24	0	C-17	1	-0.5
1962 Bal-A	81	197	21	58	11	2	6	37	7	11	1	0	.294	.322	.462	.784	113	3	29	5.35	-2	C-56	7	0.3
1963 Bal-A	29	48	4	9	2	0	0	6	1	5	0	0	.188	.204	.229	.433	22	-5	2	1.21	0	/C-8	0	-0.5
KC-A	62	187	15	55	11	0	3	26	14	17	1	0	.294	.343	.401	.744	104	1	24	4.55	-2	C-50	5	0.2
Yr.	91	235	19	64	13	0	3	32	15	22	1	0	.272	.316	.366	.682	88	-4	26	3.80	-2	C-58	5	-0.3
1964 KC-A	43	118	11	32	7	1	2	9	10	18	0	0	.271	.328	.398	.726	98	-0	16	4.86	0	C-35	3	0.2
Bal-A	62	158	16	41	15	1	1	14	17	27	0	0	.259	.335	.386	.721	100	0	20	4.30	-1	C-47	5	0.1
Yr.	105	276	27	73	22	2	3	23	27	45	0	0	.264	.332	.391	.724	99	-0	36	4.53	-1	C-82	8	0.3
1965 Bal-A	68	132	15	39	5	2	2	18	17	18	0	0	.295	.376	.409	.785	120	4	20	5.26	-2	C-35	6	0.4
1966 Bal-A	18	12	1	6	2	1	0	5	4	1	0	0	.500	.625	.833	1.458	320	4	7	26.23	0	....	2	0.4
1967 Bal-A	11	8	0	1	1	0	0	3	2	2	0	0	.125	.300	.250	.550	64	-0	1	2.56	0	....	0	0.0
Atl-N	52	45	3	9	1	0	1	5	4	9	0	0	.200	.265	.289	.554	59	-2	3	2.46	0	....	0	-0.2
Total 11	527	1170	105	298	63	9	16	140	109	150	3	1	.255	.321	.365	.686	89	-16	141	4.10	-6	C-321	33	-0.7
• LAUDER, Billy	William Lauder b: 2/23/1874, New York, NY d: 5/20/1933, Norwalk, CT BR/TR, 5'10", 160 lbs. Deb: 6/25/1898 C																							
1898 Phi-N	97	361	42	95	14	7	2	67	19	....	6	....	.263	.300	.357	.657	92	-5	43	4.08	-18	3-97	5	-2.0
1899 Phi-N	151	583	74	156	17	6	3	90	34	....	15	....	.268	.310	.333	.643	79	-18	67	4.11	-6	*3-151	11	-1.9
1901 Phi-A	2	8	1	1	0	0	0	0	0	....	0	....	.125	.125	.125	.250	-29	-1	0	.49	0	/3-2	0	-0.1
1902 NY-N	125	482	41	114	20	1	1	44	10	....	19	....	.237	.252	.288	.540	67	-21	41	2.94	-2	*3-121/0-4(2-0-2)	5	-2.0
1903 NY-N	108	395	52	111	13	0	0	53	14	....	19	....	.281	.307	.314	.621	74	-14	47	4.14	-2	*3-108	9	-1.3
Total 5	483	1829	210	477	64	14	6	254	77	....	59	....	.261	.292	.321	.613	77	-59	199	3.78	-27	3-479/0-4	30	-7.3
• LAUDNER, Tim	Timothy Jon Laudner b: 6/7/1958, Mason City, IA BR/TR, 6'3", 212 lbs. Deb: 8/28/1981																							
1981 Min-A	14	43	4	7	2	0	2	5	3	17	0	0	.163	.234	.349	.583	62	-2	4	2.77	0	C-12/D-2	1	-0.2
1982 Min-A	93	306	37	78	19	1	7	33	34	74	0	2	.255	.329	.392	.722	95	-3	39	4.45	-3	C-93	7	-0.1
1983 Min-A	62	168	20	31	9	0	6	18	15	49	0	0	.185	.251	.345	.597	60	-10	15	2.88	2	C-57/D-4	2	-0.5
1984 Min-A	87	262	31	54	16	1	10	35	18	78	0	0	.206	.260	.389	.649	73	-10	26	3.31	0	C-81/D-2	5	-0.6
1985 Min-A	72	164	16	39	5	0	7	19	12	45	0	1	.238	.294	.396	.690	82	-5	19	3.88	-2	C-68/1-1	4	-0.5
1986 Min-A	76	193	21	47	10	0	10	29	24	56	1	0	.244	.336	.451	.787	109	3	30	5.21	-3	C-68	6	0.2
1987*Min-A	113	288	30	55	7	1	16	43	23	80	1	0	.191	.253	.389	.642	65	-16	29	3.20	-5	*C-101/1-7,D-2	4	-1.6
1988 Min-A★	117	375	38	94	18	1	13	54	36	89	0	0	.251	.318	.408	.726	99	-1	46	4.16	-3	*C-109/D-4,1-3	9	0.3
1989 Min-A	100	239	24	53	11	1	6	27	25	65	1	0	.222	.295	.351	.647	76	-7	25	3.36	-4	C-68,D-19,1-11	3	-0.8
Total 9	734	2038	221	458	97	5	77	263	190	553	3	3	.225	.293	.391	.684	83	-51	233	3.79	-16	C-657/D-33,1-22	41	-3.8
• LAUER, Chuck	John Charles Lauer b: 4/5/1865, Pittsburgh, PA d: 5/4/1915, Buffalo, NY TR Deb: 7/17/1884 Career OF: 1-2-8																							
1884 Pit-a	13	44	5	5	0	0	0	0	0	....	....	....	.114	.114	.114	.227	-25	-6	1	.41	-1	0-10(0-2-8)/P-3,1-1	0	-1.3
1889 Pit-N	4	16	2	3	0	0	0	1	0	5	0	....	.188	.188	.188	.375	5	-2	1	1.18	1	/C-3,0-1	0	-0.1
1890 Chi-N	2	8	1	2	1	0	0	2	0	0	0	....	.250	.250	.375	.625	78	-0	1	3.40	0	/C-2	0	0.0
Total 3	19	68	8	10	1	0	0	3	0	5	0	....	.147	.147	.162	.309	-6	-8	2	.89	-1	/0-11,C-5,P-3,1-1	0	-1.4
• LAUGHLIN, Ben	Benjamin Laughlin Deb: 4/28/1873 U																							
1873 Res-n	12	50	3	12	0	0	0	6	0	0	0	0	.240	.240	.240	.480	47	-3	3	2.37	-3	2-12	....	-0.4
• LAUTERBORN, Bill	William Bernard Lauterborn b: 6/9/1879, Hornell, NY d: 4/19/1965, Andover, NY BR/TR, 5'6" Deb: 9/20/1904																							
1904 Bos-N	20	69	7	19	2	0	0	2	1	....	1	....	.275	.286	.304	.590	85	-1	7	3.35	-3	2-20	1	-0.4
1905 Bos-N	67	200	11	37	1	1	0	9	12	....	1	....	.185	.238	.200	.438	32	-17	11	1.65	-11	3-29,2-23/S-3,0-2(0-2-0)	1	-2.7
Total 2	87	269	18	56	3	1	0	11	13	....	2	....	.208	.250	.227	.477	45	-18	17	2.04	-13	/2-43,3-29,S-3,0-2	2	-3.1
• LAVAGETTO, Cookie	Harry Arthur Lavagetto b: 12/1/1912, Oakland, CA d: 8/10/1990, Orinda, CA BR/TR, 6', 170 lbs. Deb: 4/17/1934 M/C																							
1934 Pit-N	87	304	41	67	16	3	3	46	32	39	6	....	.220	.295	.322	.617	64	-16	31	3.50	-4	2-83	5	-1.4
1935 Pit-N	78	231	27	67	9	4	0	19	18	15	1	....	.290	.341	.364	.705	87	-4	29	4.66	-4	2-42,3-15	5	-0.5
1936 Pit-N	60	197	21	48	15	2	2	26	15	13	0	....	.244	.300	.371	.671	78	-7	22	3.93	0	2-37,3-13/S-1	4	-0.3
1937 Bro-N	149	503	64	142	26	6	8	70	74	41	13	....	.282	.375	.406	.781	110	10	79	5.55	-6	*2-100,3-45	16	1.1
1938 Bro-N★	137	487	68	133	34	6	6	79	68	31	15	....	.273	.364	.405	.769	109	8	76	5.51	-6	*3-132/2-4	18	0.6
1939 Bro-N★	153	587	93	176	28	5	10	87	78	30	14	....	.300	.387	.416	.802	111	13	95	5.89	1	*3-149	23	2.0
1940 Bro-N★	118	448	56	115	21	3	4	43	70	32	4	....	.257	.361	.344	.705	90	-3	59	4.56	1	*3-116	13	0.2
1941*Bro-N★	132	441	75	122	24	7	1	78	80	21	7	....	.277	.388	.370	.757	109	9	69	5.72	-10	*3-120	16	0.4
1946 Bro-N	88	242	36	57	9	1	3	27	38	17	3	....	.236	.339	.318	.657	86	-3	28	3.78	-2	3-67	6	-0.6
1947*Bro-N	41	69	6	18	1	0	3	11	12	5	0	....	.261	.370	.406	.776	102	1	11	5.70	0	3-18/1-3	3	0.1
Total 10	1043	3509	487	945	183	37	40	486	485	244	63	....	.269	.360	.377	.737	99	7	500	5.03	-29	3-675,2-266/1-3,S-1	109	1.6
• LAVALLIERE, Mike	Michael Eugene LaValliere b: 8/18/1960, Charlotte, NC BL/TR, 5'10", 190 lbs. Deb: 9/9/1984																							
1984 Phi-N	6	7	0	0	0	0	0	0	2	2	0	0	.000	.222	.000	.222	-32	-1	0	.45	0	/C-6	0	-0.1
1985 StL-N	12	34	2	5	1	0	0	6	7	3	0	0	.147	.293	.176	.469	34	-3	2	1.69	0	C-12	1	-0.2
1986 StL-N	110	303	18	71	10	2	3	30	36	37	0	1	.234	.318	.310	.628	75	-10	31	3.32	0	*C-108	7	-0.6
1987 Pit-N	121	340	33	102	19	0	1	36	43	32	0	0	.300	.380	.365	.745	98	1	50	5.40	7	*C-112	17	1.3
1988 Pit-N	120	352	24	92	18	0	2	47	50	34	3	2	.261	.356	.330	.686	99	1	43	4.22	-1	*C-114	17	0.8
1989 Pit-N	68	190	15	60	10	0	2	23	29	24	0	2	.316	.406	.400	.806	136	9	31	6.02	-1	C-65	8	1.3
1990*Pit-N	96	279	27	72	15	0	3	31	44	20	0	3	.258	.363	.344	.707	99	0	36	4.38	0	C-95	12	0.6
1991*Pit-N	108	336	25	97	11	2	3	41	33	27	2	1	.289	.356	.360	.716	103	2	43	4.51	-1	*C-105	12	0.8
1992*Pit-N	95	293	22	75	13	1	2	29	44	21	0	3	.256	.355	.328	.683	95	-1	34	3.91	3	C-92/3-1	11	0.7
1993 Pit-N	1	5	0	1	0	0	0	0	0	0	0	0	.200	.200	.200	.400	7	-1	0	1.35	1	/C-1	0	0.0
*Chi-A	37	97	6	25	2	0	0	8	4	14	0	1	.258	.287	.278	.565	54	-7	8	2.61	4	C-37	3	-0.1
1994 Chi-A	59	139	6	39	4	0	1	24	20	15	0	2	.281	.375	.331	.706	86	-3	18	4.14	-1	C-57	4	-0.1
1995 Chi-A	46	98	7	24	6	0	1	19	9	15	0	0	.245	.308	.337	.645	71	-4	10	3.42	2	C-46	3	0.0
Total 12	879	2473	185	663	109	5	18	294	321	244	5	15	.268	.354	.338	.693	94	-16	306	4.23	12	C-850/3-1	95	4.4
• LAVAN, Doc	John Leonard Lavan b: 10/28/1890, Grand Rapids, MI d: 5/29/1952, Detroit, MI BR/TR, 5'8.5", 151 lbs. Deb: 6/22/1913																							
1913 StL-A	46	149	8	21	2	1	0	4	10	46	3	....	.141	.210	.168	.378	11	-17	6	1.12	-6	S-46	1	-2.1
Phi-A	5	14	1	1	0	1	0	1	0	0	0	....	.071	.071	.214	.286	-17	-2	0	.30	0	/S-5	0	-0.2
Yr.	51	163	9	22	2	2	0	5	10	46	3	....	.135	.199	.172	.371	9	-19	6	1.04	-6	S-51	1	-2.3
1914 StL-A	75	239	21	63	7	4	1	21	17	39	6	12	.264	.318	.339	.657	101	-5	24	3.30	-12	S-74	7	-1.3
1915 StL-A	157	514	44	112	17	7	1	48	42	83	13	19	.218	.281	.284	.565	72	-25	42	2.49	6	*S-157	9	-0.8

YEAR TM-L	G	AB	R	H	2B	3B	HR	RBI	BB	SO	SB	CS	AVG	OBP	SLG	OPS	OPS+	BR/A	RC	RC/G	FR	G/POS	WS	TPW
1916 StL-A	110	343	32	81	13	1	0	19	32	38	7	....	.236	.305	.280	.585	80	-8	32	3.11	24	*S-106	11	2.6
1917 StL-A	118	355	19	85	8	5	0	30	19	34	5	....	.239	.284	.290	.574	78	-10	30	2.78	3	*S-110/2-7	8	0.1
1918 Was-A	117	464	44	129	17	2	0	45	14	21	12	....	.278	.302	.323	.625	90	-8	47	3.45	9	*S-117/O-1	13	1.0
1919 StL-N	100	356	25	86	12	2	1	25	11	30	4	....	.242	.264	.295	.559	72	-13	28	2.59	-8	S-99	5	-1.5
1920 StL-N	142	516	52	149	21	10	1	63	19	38	11	14	.289	.318	.374	.692	100	-3	58	3.75	11	*S-138	15	2.0
1921 StL-N	150	560	58	145	23	11	2	82	23	30	7	7	.259	.291	.350	.641	70	-24	56	3.34	25	*S-150	14	1.8
1922 StL-N	89	264	24	60	8	1	0	27	13	10	3	1	.227	.271	.265	.537	41	-22	20	2.46	-3	S-82/3-5	3	-1.6
1923 StL-N	50	111	10	22	6	0	1	12	9	7	0	3	.198	.264	.279	.544	44	-10	8	2.16	1	S-40/3-4,1-3,2-1	2	-0.6
1924 StL-N	4	6	0	0	0	0	0	0	0	0	0	0	.000	.000	.000	.000	-102	-2	0	.00	0	/2-2,S-2	0	-0.2
Total 12	1163	3891	338	954	134	45	7	377	209	376	71	56	.245	.288	.308	.596	75	-149	351	2.94	51	*S-1126/2-10,3-9,1-3,O-1	88	-0.8

• LAVIGNE, Art Arthur David LaVigne b: 1/26/1885, Worcester, MA d: 7/18/1950, Worcester, MA BR/TR, 5'10", 162 lbs. Deb: 4/24/1914

YEAR TM-L	G	AB	R	H	2B	3B	HR	RBI	BB	SO	SB	CS	AVG	OBP	SLG	OPS	OPS+	BR/A	RC	RC/G	FR	G/POS	WS	TPW
1914 Buf-F	51	90	10	14	2	0	0	4	7	25	0	....	.156	.216	.178	.394	12	-10	3	1.12	1	C-34/1-3	2	-0.8

• LAVIN, Johnny John Lavin b: Troy, NY, 5'11", 175 lbs. Deb: 9/10/1884

YEAR TM-L	G	AB	R	H	2B	3B	HR	RBI	BB	SO	SB	CS	AVG	OBP	SLG	OPS	OPS+	BR/A	RC	RC/G	FR	G/POS	WS	TPW
1884 StL-a	16	52	9	11	2	0	0	0	3	....	....	....	.212	.268	.250	.518	67	-2	4	2.39	-3	O-16(0-15-1)	1	-0.4

• LAW, Rudy Rudy Karl Law b: 10/7/1956, Waco, TX BL/TL, 6'1", 165 lbs. Deb: 9/12/1978 Career OF: 180-484-36

YEAR TM-L	G	AB	R	H	2B	3B	HR	RBI	BB	SO	SB	CS	AVG	OBP	SLG	OPS	OPS+	BR/A	RC	RC/G	FR	G/POS	WS	TPW
1978 LA-N	11	12	2	3	0	0	0	1	1	2	3	1	.250	.308	.250	.558	58	-0	1	3.00	0	/O-6(3-3-0)	0	-0.1
1980 LA-N	128	388	55	101	5	4	1	23	23	27	40	13	.260	.307	.302	.608	72	-12	39	3.46	-2	*O-106(5-102-0)	8	-1.6
1982 Chi-A	121	336	55	107	15	8	3	32	23	41	36	10	.318	.362	.438	.800	118	12	55	5.99	-3	O-94(4-90-0)/D-3	13	0.7
1983*Chi-A	141	501	95	142	20	7	3	34	42	36	77	12	.283	.341	.369	.711	92	6	74	5.23	1	*O-132(0-132-0)/D-3	20	0.6
1984 Chi-A	136	487	68	122	14	7	6	37	39	42	29	17	.251	.310	.345	.655	77	-16	50	3.44	-1	*O-130(10-122-0)	9	-1.8
1985 Chi-A	125	390	62	101	21	6	4	36	27	40	29	6	.259	.312	.374	.686	84	-5	49	4.31	2	*O-120(104-32-0)/D-3	11	-0.7
1986 KC-A	87	307	42	80	26	5	1	36	29	22	14	6	.261	.328	.388	.716	92	-3	40	4.46	-2	O-77(54-3-36)/D-2	7	-0.8
Total 7	749	2421	379	656	101	37	18	199	184	210	228	65	.271	.326	.366	.691	88	-18	308	4.41	-5	O-665/D-11	68	-3.8

• LAW, Vance Vance Aaron Law b: 10/1/1956, Boise, ID BR/TR, 6'2", 190 lbs. Deb: 6/1/1980 Career OF: 6-7-2 ♦

YEAR TM-L	G	AB	R	H	2B	3B	HR	RBI	BB	SO	SB	CS	AVG	OBP	SLG	OPS	OPS+	BR/A	RC	RC/G	FR	G/POS	WS	TPW
1980 Pit-N	25	74	11	17	2	2	0	3	3	7	2	0	.230	.260	.311	.571	58	-4	6	2.63	0	2-11/S-8,3-1	1	-0.3
1981 Pit-N	30	67	1	9	0	1	0	3	2	15	1	1	.134	.159	.164	.324	-8	-10	1	.63	0	2-19/S-7,3-2	1	-0.9
1982 Chi-A	114	359	40	101	20	1	5	54	26	46	4	2	.281	.332	.384	.716	96	-2	45	4.27	-4	S-85,3-39,2-10/O-1	10	0.2
1983*Chi-A	145	408	55	99	21	5	4	42	51	56	3	1	.243	.328	.348	.676	83	-8	49	4.06	4	*3-139/2-3,S-2,D-1,O-1	12	-0.5
1984 Chi-A	151	481	60	121	18	2	17	59	41	75	4	1	.252	.312	.403	.715	92	-5	59	4.16	-13	*3-137,2-22/O-5(O-6-0),S-4	10	-1.9
1985 Mon-N	147	519	75	138	30	6	10	52	86	96	6	5	.266	.372	.405	.777	124	19	82	5.40	3	*2-126,1-20,3-11/O-1	24	2.8
1986 Mon-N	112	360	37	81	17	2	5	44	37	66	3	5	.225	.299	.325	.624	73	-15	34	3.09	15	2-94,1-20,3-13/P-3,O-1	8	0.4
1987 Mon-N	133	436	52	119	27	1	12	56	51	62	8	5	.273	.349	.422	.771	100	-0	65	5.21	5	*2-106,3-22,1-17/P-3	16	0.8
1988 Chi-N★	151	556	73	163	29	2	11	78	55	79	1	4	.293	.360	.412	.772	116	10	80	5.18	-17	*3-150/O-1	20	-0.6
1989*Chi-N	130	408	38	96	22	3	7	42	38	73	2	2	.235	.300	.355	.656	81	-11	43	3.46	-18	*3-119/O-1	3	-3.0
1991 Oak-A	74	134	11	28	7	1	0	9	18	27	0	0	.209	.303	.276	.579	65	-6	12	2.78	-4	3-67/O-3(3-0-0),S-3,1-1,P	3	-0.9
Total 11	1212	3802	453	972	193	26	71	442	408	602	34	26	.256	.329	.376	.705	94	-32	476	4.25	-29	3-700,2-391,S-109/1-58,O,P,D	108	-3.8

• LAWING, Garland Garland Frederick "Knobby" Lawing b: 8/29/1919, Gastonia, NC d: 9/27/1996, Murrells Inlet, SC BR/TR, 6'1", 180 lbs. Deb: 5/29/1946

YEAR TM-L	G	AB	R	H	2B	3B	HR	RBI	BB	SO	SB	CS	AVG	OBP	SLG	OPS	OPS+	BR/A	RC	RC/G	FR	G/POS	WS	TPW
1946 Cin-N	2	3	0	0	0	0	0	0	0	2	0	....	.000	.000	.000	.000	-104	-1	0	.00	0	/O-1	0	-0.1
NY-N	8	12	2	2	0	0	0	0	0	3	0	....	.167	.167	.167	.333	-5	-2	0	.90	0	/O-4(3-0-1)	0	-0.2
Yr.	10	15	2	2	0	0	0	0	0	5	0	....	.133	.133	.133	.267	-25	-2	0	.64	0	/O-5(3-1-1)	0	-0.3

• LAWLESS, Tom Thomas James Lawless b: 12/19/1956, Erie, PA BR/TR, 5'11", 170 lbs. Deb: 7/15/1982 Career OF: 14-0-12

YEAR TM-L	G	AB	R	H	2B	3B	HR	RBI	BB	SO	SB	CS	AVG	OBP	SLG	OPS	OPS+	BR/A	RC	RC/G	FR	G/POS	WS	TPW
1982 Cin-N	49	165	19	35	6	0	0	4	9	30	16	5	.212	.253	.248	.501	40	-12	10	1.94	7	2-47	2	-0.3
1984 Cin-N	43	80	10	20	2	0	1	2	8	12	6	3	.250	.318	.313	.631	74	-3	8	3.41	0	2-23/3-6	1	-0.2
Mon-N	11	17	1	3	1	0	0	0	0	4	1	0	.176	.176	.235	.412	15	-2	0	.00	0	/2-9	0	-0.2
Yr.	54	97	11	23	3	0	1	2	8	16	7	3	.237	.295	.299	.594	65	-4	8	2.70	0	2-32/3-6	1	-0.4
1985*StL-N	47	58	8	12	3	1	0	8	5	4	2	1	.207	.270	.293	.563	58	-3	5	2.79	2	3-13,2-11	1	-0.2
1986 StL-N	46	39	5	11	1	0	0	3	2	8	8	1	.282	.317	.308	.625	74	-0	5	4.20	-1	3-12/2-7,O-1	1	-0.1
1987*StL-N	19	25	5	2	1	0	0	0	3	5	2	0	.080	.179	.120	.299	-19	-4	1	.80	0	/2-7,3-3,O-1	0	-0.4
1988 StL-N	54	65	9	10	2	1	1	3	7	9	6	0	.154	.236	.262	.498	42	-4	5	2.22	0	3-24/O-6(4-0-2),2-5,1-1	0	-0.4
1989 Tor-A	59	70	20	16	1	0	0	3	7	12	12	1	.229	.299	.243	.542	58	-1	7	3.44	-2	O-16(7-0-9),3-12,D-12/2-7,C	1	-0.3
1990 Tor-A	15	12	1	1	0	0	0	1	0	1	0	2	.083	.083	.083	.167	-50	-3	0	.00	-1	/D-5,3-4,O-2(2-0-0),2-1	0	-0.4
Total 8	343	531	78	110	17	2	2	24	41	85	53	13	.207	.264	.258	.522	47	-32	42	2.43	5	2-117/3-74,O-26,D-17,1-1,C	6	-2.5

• LAWLOR, Mike Michael H. Lawlor b: 3/11/1854, Troy, NY d: 8/3/1918, Troy, NY TR, 6', 180 lbs. Deb: 5/27/1880

YEAR TM-L	G	AB	R	H	2B	3B	HR	RBI	BB	SO	SB	CS	AVG	OBP	SLG	OPS	OPS+	BR/A	RC	RC/G	FR	G/POS	WS	TPW
1880 Tro-N	4	9	1	1	0	0	0	0	1	1	....	....	.111	.200	.111	.311	8	-1	0	.70	-1	/C-4	0	-0.2
1884 Was-U	2	7	0	0	0	0	0	....	0	....	....	....	.000	.000	.000	.000	-103	-1	0	.00	1	/C-2	0	0.0
Total 2	6	16	1	1	0	0	0	0	1	1	....	....	.063	.118	.063	.180	-38	-2	0	.38	0	/C-6	0	-0.2

• LAWRENCE, Bill William Henry Lawrence b: 3/11/1906, San Mateo, CA d: 6/15/1997, Redwood City, CA BR/TR, 6'4", 194 lbs. Deb: 4/13/1932

YEAR TM-L	G	AB	R	H	2B	3B	HR	RBI	BB	SO	SB	CS	AVG	OBP	SLG	OPS	OPS+	BR/A	RC	RC/G	FR	G/POS	WS	TPW
1932 Det-A	25	46	10	10	1	0	0	3	5	5	0	2	.217	.294	.239	.533	38	-5	3	2.06	2	O-15(0-8-7)	1	-0.4

• LAWRENCE, Jim James Ross Lawrence b: 2/12/1939, Hamilton, Canada BL/TR, 6'1", 185 lbs. Deb: 5/30/1963

YEAR TM-L	G	AB	R	H	2B	3B	HR	RBI	BB	SO	SB	CS	AVG	OBP	SLG	OPS	OPS+	BR/A	RC	RC/G	FR	G/POS	WS	TPW
1963 Cle-A	2	0	0	0	0	0	0	0	0	0	0	0	....	....	....	....	-101	0	0	....	-1	/C-2	0	-0.1

• LAWRENCE, Joe Joseph Dudley Lawrence b: 2/13/1977, Lake Charles, LA BR/TR, 6'2", 200 lbs. Deb: 4/8/2002

YEAR TM-L	G	AB	R	H	2B	3B	HR	RBI	BB	SO	SB	CS	AVG	OBP	SLG	OPS	OPS+	BR/A	RC	RC/G	FR	G/POS	WS	TPW
2002 Tor-A	55	150	16	27	4	0	2	15	16	38	2	1	.180	.268	.247	.515	37	-14	11	2.33	-6	2-49/D-1	1	-1.6

• LAWRY, Otis Otis Carroll "Rabbit" Lawry b: 11/1/1893, Fairfield, ME d: 10/23/1965, China, ME BL/TR, 5'8", 133 lbs. Deb: 6/28/1916 Career OF: 4-2-0

YEAR TM-L	G	AB	R	H	2B	3B	HR	RBI	BB	SO	SB	CS	AVG	OBP	SLG	OPS	OPS+	BR/A	RC	RC/G	FR	G/POS	WS	TPW
1916 Phi-A	41	123	10	25	0	0	0	4	9	21	4	....	.203	.263	.203	.466	42	-9	8	2.07	-7	2-29/O-5(3-2-0)	0	-1.7
1917 Phi-A	30	55	7	9	1	0	0	1	2	9	1	....	.164	.193	.182	.375	15	-6	2	1.14	-3	2-17/O-1	0	-0.9
Total 2	71	178	17	34	1	0	0	5	11	30	5	....	.191	.242	.197	.439	34	-14	10	1.77	-10	/2-46,O-6	0	-2.6

• LAWTON, Marcus Marcus Dwayne Lawton b: 8/18/1965, Gulfport, MS BB/TR, 6'1", 160 lbs. Deb: 8/11/1989

YEAR TM-L	G	AB	R	H	2B	3B	HR	RBI	BB	SO	SB	CS	AVG	OBP	SLG	OPS	OPS+	BR/A	RC	RC/G	FR	G/POS	WS	TPW
1989 NY-A	10	14	1	3	0	0	0	0	0	3	1	0	.214	.214	.214	.429	21	-1	1	1.13	-1	/O-8(7-0-1),D-1	0	-0.2

• LAWTON, Matt Matthew Lawton b: 11/3/1971, Gulfport, MS BL/TR, 5'10", 180 lbs. Deb: 9/5/1995 Career OF: 234-109-661

YEAR TM-L	G	AB	R	H	2B	3B	HR	RBI	BB	SO	SB	CS	AVG	OBP	SLG	OPS	OPS+	BR/A	RC	RC/G	FR	G/POS	WS	TPW
1995 Min-A	21	60	11	19	4	1	1	12	7	11	1	1	.317	.414	.467	.881	128	3	12	7.54	0	O-19(1-12-8)/D-1	4	0.2
1996 Min-A	79	252	34	65	7	1	6	42	28	28	4	4	.258	.342	.365	.707	78	-9	31	4.26	0	O-75(1-18-60)/D-1	7	-1.1
1997 Min-A	142	460	74	114	29	3	14	60	76	81	7	4	.248	.366	.415	.782	102	4	75	5.64	0	*O-138(58-23-67)	14	-0.1
1998 Min-A	152	557	91	155	36	6	21	77	86	64	16	8	.278	.389	.478	.867	122	21	108	6.89	6	*O-151(12-47-100)	21	2.0
1999 Min-A	118	406	58	105	18	0	7	54	57	42	26	4	.259	.358	.355	.713	80	-7	56	4.72	-6	*O-109(10-6-103)/D-6	8	-1.7
2000 Min-A★	156	561	84	171	44	2	13	88	91	63	23	7	.305	.408	.460	.868	115	18	112	7.36	-10	*O-143(67-3-83)/D-9	20	0.1
2001 Min-A	103	376	71	110	25	0	10	51	63	46	19	6	.293	.398	.439	.837	118	14	67	6.31	-5	O-94(0-0-94)/D-7	13	0.4
NY-N	48	183	24	45	11	1	3	13	22	34	10	2	.246	.352	.366	.718	91	-0	27	5.07	-1	O-48(0-0-48)	7	-0.4
2002 Cle-A	114	416	71	98	19	2	15	57	59	34	8	9	.236	.342	.399	.741	98	-2	56	4.40	7	*O-108(23-0-85)/D-3	9	-0.1
2003 Cle-A	99	374	57	93	19	0	15	53	47	47	10	3	.249	.343	.420	.763	103	3	56	5.16	-2	O-74(62-0-13),D-21	10	-0.3
Total 9	1032	3645	575	975	212	16	105	507	536	450	124	48	.267	.372	.421	.793	104	44	601	5.75	-10	O-959/D-48	113	-1.1

• LAYDEN, Gene Eugene Francis Layden b: 3/14/1894, Pittsburgh, PA d: 12/12/1984, Pittsburgh, PA BL/TL, 5'10", 160 lbs. Deb: 7/29/1915

YEAR TM-L	G	AB	R	H	2B	3B	HR	RBI	BB	SO	SB	CS	AVG	OBP	SLG	OPS	OPS+	BR/A	RC	RC/G	FR	G/POS	WS	TPW
1915 NY-A	3	7	2	2	0	0	0	0	0	1	0	1	.286	.286	.286	.571	71	-1	0	1.26	-1	/O-2(0-2-0)	0	-0.2

• LAYDEN, Pete Peter John Layden b: 12/30/1919, Dallas, TX d: 7/18/1982, Edna, TX BR/TR, 5'11", 185 lbs. Deb: 4/20/1948

YEAR TM-L	G	AB	R	H	2B	3B	HR	RBI	BB	SO	SB	CS	AVG	OBP	SLG	OPS	OPS+	BR/A	RC	RC/G	FR	G/POS	WS	TPW
1948 StL-A	41	104	11	26	2	1	0	4	6	10	4	2	.250	.297	.288	.586	55	-7	9	2.98	-1	O-30(1-24-5)	0	-0.8

• LAYNE, Herman Herman Layne b: 2/13/1901, New Haven, WV d: 8/27/1973, Gallipolis, OH BR/TR, 5'11", 165 lbs. Deb: 4/16/1927

YEAR TM-L	G	AB	R	H	2B	3B	HR	RBI	BB	SO	SB	CS	AVG	OBP	SLG	OPS	OPS+	BR/A	RC	RC/G	FR	G/POS	WS	TPW
1927 Pit-N	11	6	3	0	0	0	0	0	1	0	0	....	.000	.143	.000	.143	-55	-1	0	.15	-1	/O-2(1-1-0)	0	-0.2

• LAYNE, Hillis Ivoria Hillis "Tony" Layne b: 2/23/1918, Whitwell, TN BL/TR, 6', 170 lbs. Deb: 9/16/1941

YEAR TM-L	G	AB	R	H	2B	3B	HR	RBI	BB	SO	SB	CS	AVG	OBP	SLG	OPS	OPS+	BR/A	RC	RC/G	FR	G/POS	WS	TPW
1941 Was-A	13	50	8	14	2	0	0	6	4	5	1	1	.280	.333	.320	.653	77	-2	5	3.45	-1	3-13	1	-0.2
1944 Was-A	33	87	6	17	2	0	0	8	6	10	2	0	.195	.263	.218	.482	40	-6	6	2.05	2	3-18/2-3	1	-0.4
1945 Was-A	61	147	23	44	5	4	1	14	10	7	0	1	.299	.352	.408	.760	131	5	20	4.71	0	3-33	6	0.5
Total 3	**107**	**284**	**37**	**75**	**9**	**4**	**1**	**28**	**20**	**22**	**3**	**2**	**.264**	**.321**	**.335**	**.656**	**94**	**-3**	**30**	**3.62**	**1**	**/3-64,2-3**	**8**	**-0.1**

• LAYTON, Les Lester Lee Layton b: 11/18/1921, Nardin, OK BR/TR, 6', 165 lbs. Deb: 4/24/1948

YEAR TM-L	G	AB	R	H	2B	3B	HR	RBI	BB	SO	SB	CS	AVG	OBP	SLG	OPS	OPS+	BR/A	RC	RC/G	FR	G/POS	WS	TPW
1948 NY-N	63	91	14	21	4	4	2	12	6	21	1	....	.231	.286	.429	.714	90	-2	11	4.06	-1	0-20(12-3-3)	2	-0.4

• LAZOR, Johnny John Paul Lazor b: 9/9/1912, Taylor, WA d: 12/9/2002, Renton, WA BL/TR, 5'9.5", 180 lbs. Deb: 4/22/1943 Career OF: 67-7-90

YEAR TM-L	G	AB	R	H	2B	3B	HR	RBI	BB	SO	SB	CS	AVG	OBP	SLG	OPS	OPS+	BR/A	RC	RC/G	FR	G/POS	WS	TPW
1943 Bos-A	84	208	21	47	10	2	0	13	22	25	6	6	.226	.300	.293	.593	73	-8	19	2.93	-0	0-63(51-7-8)	3	-1.3
1944 Bos-A	16	24	0	2	1	0	0	0	1	0	0	0	.083	.120	.125	.245	-30	-4	0	.49	1	/0-6(1-0-5),C-1	0	-0.4
1945 Bos-A	101	335	35	104	19	2	5	45	18	17	3	2	.310	.346	.424	.769	120	7	50	5.64	-5	0-81(12-0-73)	12	-0.3
1946 Bos-A	23	29	1	4	0	0	1	4	2	11	0	0	.138	.194	.241	.435	20	-3	1	.99	0	/0-7(3-0-4)	0	-0.4
Total 4	**224**	**596**	**57**	**157**	**30**	**4**	**6**	**62**	**43**	**53**	**9**	**8**	**.263**	**.313**	**.357**	**.670**	**92**	**-8**	**70**	**4.11**	**-4**	**0-157/C-1**	**15**	**-2.4**

• LAZZERI, Tony Anthony Michael "Poosh 'Em Up Tony" Lazzeri
b: 12/6/1903, San Francisco, CA d: 8/6/1946, San Francisco, CA BR/TR, 5'11.5", 170 lbs. Deb: 4/13/1926 C HOF: 1991 Career OF: 2-0-0

YEAR TM-L	G	AB	R	H	2B	3B	HR	RBI	BB	SO	SB	CS	AVG	OBP	SLG	OPS	OPS+	BR/A	RC	RC/G	FR	G/POS	WS	TPW
1926*NY-A	155	589	79	162	28	14	18	114	54	96	16	7	.275	.338	.462	.800	109	6	93	5.42	-7	*2-149/S-5,3-1	19	0.4
1927*NY-A	153	570	92	176	29	8	18	102	69	82	22	14	.309	.383	.482	.866	127	22	106	6.54	16	*2-113,S-38/3-9	24	4.2
1928*NY-A	116	404	62	134	30	11	10	82	43	50	15	5	.332	.397	.535	.932	147	29	87	7.96	9	*2-110	22	3.9
1929 NY-A	147	545	101	193	37	11	18	106	68	45	9	10	.354	.429	.561	.991	164	51	130	9.10	7	*2-147	30	5.9
1930 NY-A	143	571	109	173	34	15	9	121	60	62	4	4	.303	.372	.462	.835	115	14	100	6.31	4	2-77,3-60/S-8,1-1,0-1	19	2.2
1931 NY-A	135	484	67	129	27	7	8	83	79	80	18	9	.267	.371	.401	.771	109	11	76	5.51	7	2-90,3-39	15	2.4
1932*NY-A	142	510	79	153	28	16	15	113	82	64	11	11	.300	.399	.506	.905	140	30	104	7.38	15	*2-134/3-5	27	5.0
1933 NY-A★	139	523	94	154	22	12	18	104	73	62	15	7	.294	.383	.486	.869	137	30	100	7.00	-10	*2-138	24	2.7
1934 NY-A	123	438	59	117	24	6	14	67	71	64	11	1	.267	.369	.445	.815	117	14	77	6.28	4	2-92,3-30	17	2.4
1935 NY-A	130	477	72	130	18	6	13	83	63	75	11	5	.273	.361	.417	.778	107	6	75	5.63	-3	*2-118/S-9	15	1.0
1936*NY-A	150	537	82	154	29	6	14	109	97	65	8	5	.287	.397	.441	.838	110	12	100	6.76	-19	*2-148/S-2	18	0.2
1937*NY-A	126	446	56	109	21	3	14	70	71	76	7	1	.244	.348	.399	.747	87	-7	67	5.20	0	*2-125	13	0.0
1938*Chi-N	54	120	21	32	5	0	5	23	22	30	0	....	.267	.380	.433	.814	120	4	20	5.86	-3	S-25/3-7,2-4,0-1	5	0.3
1939 Bro-N	14	39	6	11	2	0	3	6	10	7	1	....	.282	.451	.564	1.015	165	4	11	10.09	1	2-11/3-2	3	0.6
NY-N	13	44	7	13	0	0	1	8	7	6	0	....	.295	.392	.364	.756	103	1	6	5.15	-3	3-13	1	-0.2
Yr.	27	83	13	24	2	0	4	14	17	13	1	....	.289	.422	.458	.879	134	5	17	7.46	-2	3-15,2-11	4	0.4
Total 14	**1740**	**6297**	**986**	**1840**	**334**	**115**	**178**	**1191**	**869**	**864**	**148**	**79**	**.292**	**.380**	**.467**	**.846**	**123**	**227**	**1153**	**6.56**	**18**	***2-1456,3-166/S-87,0-2,1-1**	**252**	**31.1**

• LEACH, Freddy Frederick Leach b: 11/23/1897, Springfield, MO d: 12/10/1981, Hagerman, ID BL/TR, 5'11", 183 lbs. Deb: 5/24/1923 Career OF: 534-325-43

YEAR TM-L	G	AB	R	H	2B	3B	HR	RBI	BB	SO	SB	CS	AVG	OBP	SLG	OPS	OPS+	BR/A	RC	RC/G	FR	G/POS	WS	TPW
1923 Phi-N	52	104	5	27	4	0	1	16	3	14	1	2	.260	.280	.327	.607	54	-8	9	2.95	-2	0-26(17-9-1)	0	-1.0
1924 Phi-N	8	28	6	13	2	1	2	7	2	1	0	0	.464	.500	.821	1.321	221	5	11	18.49	0	/0-7(7-0-0)	2	0.5
1925 Phi-N	65	292	47	91	15	4	5	28	5	21	1	2	.312	.323	.442	.765	86	-7	40	5.12	-9	0-65(0-65-0)	5	-1.8
1926 Phi-N	129	492	73	162	29	7	11	71	16	33	6	....	.329	.352	.484	.835	117	9	79	6.00	3	*0-123(48-84-8)	16	0.5
1927 Phi-N	140	536	69	164	30	4	12	83	21	32	2	....	.306	.342	.444	.786	108	4	78	5.25	12	*0-140(18-123-5)	14	0.9
1928 Phi-N	145	588	83	179	36	11	13	96	30	30	4	....	.304	.342	.469	.812	107	3	91	5.56	7	*0-120(93-22-7),1-25	13	-0.1
1929 NY-N	113	411	74	119	22	6	8	47	17	14	10	....	.290	.324	.431	.755	85	-11	55	4.74	-8	0-95(94-0-1)	8	-2.4
1930 NY-N	126	544	90	178	19	13	13	71	22	25	3	....	.327	.361	.482	.843	104	2	91	6.31	3	*0-124(124-0-0)	15	-0.4
1931 NY-N	129	515	75	159	30	5	6	61	29	9	4	....	.309	.348	.421	.769	108	5	76	5.49	1	*0-125(125-0-0)	15	-0.1
1932 Bos-N	84	223	21	55	9	2	1	29	18	10	1	....	.247	.306	.318	.624	71	-9	23	3.47	-2	0-50(8-22-21)	4	-1.3
Total 10	**991**	**3733**	**543**	**1147**	**196**	**53**	**72**	**509**	**163**	**189**	**32**	**4**	**.307**	**.341**	**.446**	**.787**	**101**	**-7**	**553**	**5.41**	**4**	**0-875/1-25**	**92**	**-5.2**

• LEACH, Jalal Jalal Donnell Leach b: 3/14/1969, San Francisco, CA BL/TL, 6'2", 200 lbs. Deb: 9/5/2001

YEAR TM-L	G	AB	R	H	2B	3B	HR	RBI	BB	SO	SB	CS	AVG	OBP	SLG	OPS	OPS+	BR/A	RC	RC/G	FR	G/POS	WS	TPW
2001 SF-N	8	10	0	1	0	0	0	1	2	3	0	0	.100	.250	.100	.350	-5	-2	0	1.14	0	/0-3(1-0-2)	0	-0.2

• LEACH, Rick Richard Max Leach b: 5/4/1957, Ann Arbor, MI BL/TL, 6'1", 195 lbs. Deb: 4/30/1981 Career OF: 116-1-177

YEAR TM-L	G	AB	R	H	2B	3B	HR	RBI	BB	SO	SB	CS	AVG	OBP	SLG	OPS	OPS+	BR/A	RC	RC/G	FR	G/POS	WS	TPW
1981 Det-A	54	83	9	16	3	1	1	11	16	15	0	1	.193	.323	.289	.612	75	-2	7	2.68	2	1-32,0-15(0-0-15)/D-2	1	-0.2
1982 Det-A	82	218	23	52	7	2	3	12	21	29	4	0	.239	.305	.330	.636	74	-7	24	3.69	1	1-56,0-14(4-0-10)/D-4	3	-0.9
1983 Det-A	99	242	22	60	17	0	3	26	19	21	2	2	.248	.305	.355	.661	83	-6	25	3.59	5	1-73,0-13(2-0-11)/D-3	4	-0.4
1984 Tor-A	65	88	11	23	6	2	0	7	8	14	0	0	.261	.323	.375	.698	89	-1	10	4.02	3	0-23(5-1-17),1-15/D-6,P-1	1	-0.2
1985 Tor-A	16	35	2	7	0	1	0	1	3	9	0	0	.200	.263	.257	.520	42	-3	3	2.42	0	1-10/0-4(1-0-3)	0	-0.3
1986 Tor-A	110	246	35	76	14	1	5	39	13	24	0	0	.309	.344	.435	.779	108	2	35	5.21	-2	D-42,0-39(19-0-20)/1-7	6	-0.2
1987 Tor-A	98	195	26	55	13	1	3	25	25	25	0	1	.282	.372	.405	.777	104	2	30	5.67	0	0-43(21-0-22),D-30/1-5	5	-0.1
1988 Tor-A	87	199	21	55	13	1	0	23	18	27	0	1	.276	.336	.352	.688	93	-2	22	3.85	2	0-49(14-0-36),D-25/1-4	5	-0.2
1989 Tex-A	110	239	32	65	14	1	1	23	32	33	2	1	.272	.360	.351	.712	100	1	31	4.41	-2	D-44,0-41(37-0-3)/1-4	4	-0.3
1990 SF-N	78	174	24	51	13	0	2	16	21	20	0	2	.293	.372	.402	.775	117	4	27	5.67	-1	0-52(13-0-40)/1-7	6	0.1
Total 10	**799**	**1719**	**205**	**460**	**100**	**10**	**18**	**183**	**176**	**217**	**8**	**8**	**.268**	**.338**	**.369**	**.707**	**94**	**-13**	**214**	**4.34**	**8**	**0-293,1-213,D-156/P-1**	**35**	**-2.7**

• LEACH, Tommy Thomas William Leach b: 11/4/1877, French Creek, NY d: 9/29/1969, Haines City, FL BR/TR, 5'6.5", 150 lbs. Deb: 9/28/1898 Career OF: 74-996-13

YEAR TM-L	G	AB	R	H	2B	3B	HR	RBI	BB	SO	SB	CS	AVG	OBP	SLG	OPS	OPS+	BR/A	RC	RC/G	FR	G/POS	WS	TPW
1898 Lou-N	3	10	0	1	0	0	0	0	0	....	0	....	.100	.100	.100	.200	-43	-2	0	.30	-1	/3-3,2-1	0	-0.2
1899 Lou-N	106	406	75	117	10	6	5	57	37	....	19	....	.288	.349	.379	.728	100	-0	63	5.59	-1	3-80,S-25/2-2	13	0.2
1900*Pit-N	51	160	20	34	1	2	1	16	21	....	8	....	.213	.304	.263	.566	57	-9	16	3.29	3	3-31/S-8,2-7,0-4(2-0-2)	3	-0.5
1901 Pit-N	98	374	64	114	12	13	2	44	20	....	16	....	.305	.347	.422	.769	119	8	63	6.17	14	3-92/S-4	17	2.4
1902 Pit-N	135	514	97	143	14	**22**	**6**	85	45	....	25	....	.278	.341	.426	.767	132	18	87	5.98	17	*3-134	27	4.1
1903*Pit-N	127	507	97	151	16	17	7	87	40	....	22	....	.298	.352	.438	.789	121	12	89	6.42	8	*3-127	21	2.2
1904 Pit-N	146	579	92	149	15	12	2	56	45	....	23	....	.257	.316	.335	.651	98	-1	71	4.25	33	*3-146	25	3.8
1905 Pit-N	131	499	71	128	10	14	2	53	37	....	17	....	.257	.309	.345	.654	92	-6	62	4.15	11	0-71(16-51-6),3-58/2-2,S-2	17	0.3
1906 Pit-N	133	476	66	136	10	7	1	39	33	....	21	....	.286	.333	.342	.676	106	3	65	4.73	-1	3-65,0-60(15-44-1)/S-1	19	0.0
1907 Pit-N	149	547	102	166	19	12	4	43	40	....	43	....	.303	.352	.404	.756	135	20	98	6.22	2	*0-111(2-109-0),3-33/S-6,2	29	2.0
1908 Pit-N	152	583	93	151	24	16	5	41	54	....	24	....	.259	.324	.381	.705	125	15	80	4.53	9	*3-150/0-2(0-2-0)	31	3.4
1909*Pit-N	151	587	**126**	153	29	8	6	43	66	....	27	....	.261	.337	.368	.705	113	9	83	4.66	-2	*0-138(0-138-0),3-13	26	0.1
1910 Pit-N	135	529	83	143	24	5	4	52	38	62	18	....	.270	.319	.357	.677	92	-8	66	4.22	0	*0-131(0-131-0)/S-2,2-1	16	-1.5
1911 Pit-N	108	386	60	92	12	6	3	43	46	50	19	....	.238	.323	.324	.646	78	-11	46	3.95	5	0-89(1-89-0),S-13/3-1	10	-1.0
1912 Pit-N	28	97	24	29	4	2	0	19	12	9	6	....	.299	.376	.381	.758	109	2	16	5.88	3	0-24(0-24-0)	4	0.3
Chi-N	82	265	50	64	10	3	2	32	55	20	14	....	.242	.378	.325	.702	93	1	38	4.68	4	0-73(0-73-0)/3-4	10	0.0
Yr.	110	362	74	93	14	5	2	51	67	29	20	....	.257	.377	.340	.717	97	2	54	4.98	6	0-97(0-97-0)/3-4	14	0.2
1913 Chi-N	131	456	**99**	131	23	10	6	32	77	44	21	....	.287	.391	.421	.812	132	22	80	6.13	2	*0-121(3-118-0)/3-2	24	1.8
1914 Chi-N	153	577	80	152	24	9	7	46	79	50	16	....	.263	.353	.373	.726	116	13	80	4.67	4	*0-136(0-136-0),3-16	27	1.0
1915 Cin-N	107	335	42	75	7	5	0	17	56	38	20	14	.224	.338	.275	.613	85	-5	34	3.21	1	0-96(17-81-0)	7	-1.0
1918 Pit-N	30	72	14	14	2	3	0	5	19	5	2	....	.194	.363	.306	.668	101	1	9	3.76	-1	0-23(18-0-4)/S-3	2	-0.1
Total 19	**2156**	**7959**	**1355**	**2143**	**266**	**172**	**63**	**810**	**820**	**278**	**361**	**14**	**.269**	**.340**	**.370**	**.710**	**109**	**82**	**1144**	**4.92**	**108**	***0-1079,3-955/S-64,2-14**	**328**	**17.3**

• LEAHY, Dan Daniel C. Leahy b: 8/8/1870, Nashville, TN d: 12/25/1915, Knoxville, TN, 5'9", 155 lbs. Deb: 9/2/1896

YEAR TM-L	G	AB	R	H	2B	3B	HR	RBI	BB	SO	SB	CS	AVG	OBP	SLG	OPS	OPS+	BR/A	RC	RC/G	FR	G/POS	WS	TPW
1896 Phi-N	2	6	0	2	1	0	0	1	1	2	0	....	.333	.429	.500	.929	146	0	1	8.73	0	/S-2	0	0.0

• LEAHY, Tom Thomas Joseph Leahy b: 6/2/1869, New Haven, CT d: 6/11/1951, New Haven, CT BR/TR, 5'7.5", 168 lbs. Deb: 5/18/1897 U Career OF: 11-12-4

YEAR TM-L	G	AB	R	H	2B	3B	HR	RBI	BB	SO	SB	CS	AVG	OBP	SLG	OPS	OPS+	BR/A	RC	RC/G	FR	G/POS	WS	TPW
1897 Pit-N	24	92	10	24	3	3	0	12	7	....	3	....	.261	.320	.359	.679	82	-2	12	4.58	-3	0-13(7-4-2)/3-6,C-6	1	-0.6
Was-N	19	52	12	20	2	1	0	7	9	....	6	....	.385	.529	.462	.991	164	7	16	13.48	0	0-10(2-8-0)/3-5,2-3,C-1	3	0.6
Yr.	43	144	22	44	5	4	0	19	16	....	9	....	.306	.405	.396	.801	115	4	28	7.40	-3	0-23(9-12-2),3-11/C-7,2-3	4	0.1
1898 Was-N	15	55	10	10	2	0	0	5	8	....	6	....	.182	.297	.218	.515	48	-3	5	3.23	0	3-12/2-3	1	-0.3
1901 Mil-A	33	99	18	24	6	2	0	10	11	....	3	....	.242	.348	.343	.691	97	0	13	4.64	1	C-28/0-2(0-0-2),2-1	3	0.4
Phi-A	5	15	1	5	1	0	0	1	1	....	0	....	.333	.375	.400	.775	110	0	2	6.11	0	/0-2(2-0-0),C-1,S-1	1	0.0
Yr.	38	114	19	29	7	2	0	11	12	....	3	....	.254	.351	.351	.702	98	1	16	4.81	2	C-29/0-4(2-0-2),2-1,S-1	4	0.4

YEAR TM-L	G	AB	R	H	2B	3B	HR	RBI	BB	SO	SB	CS	AVG	OBP	SLG	OPS	OPS+	BR/A	RC	RC/G	FR	G/POS	WS	TPW
1905 StL-N	35	97	3	22	1	3	0	7	8	....	0	....	.227	.286	.299	.585	77	-3	9	2.96	-1	C-29	1	-0.2
Total 4	131	410	54	105	15	9	0	42	44	....	18	....	.256	.348	.337	.685	93	-1	58	4.96	-3	/C-65,0-27,3-23,2-7,S-1	10	0.0
• LEAR, Fred	Frederick Francis "King" Lear b: 4/7/1894, New York, NY d: 10/13/1955, East Orange, NJ BR/TR, 6'.5", 180 lbs. Deb: 6/7/1915																							
1915 Phi-A	2	2	0	0	0	0	0	0	0	2	0	....	.000	.000	.000	.000	-104	-0	0	.00	-1	/3-2	0	-0.2
1918 Chi-N	2	1	0	0	0	0	0	0	1	0	0	....	.000	.500	.000	.500	56	0	0	.00	0	....	0	0.0
1919 Chi-N	40	76	8	17	3	1	1	11	8	11	2	....	.224	.306	.329	.635	90	-1	8	3.41	-5	/1-9,2-9,S-3	2	-0.6
1920 NY-N	31	87	12	22	0	1	1	7	8	15	0	2	.253	.323	.310	.633	83	-2	9	3.34	0	3-24/2-1	2	-0.1
Total 4	75	166	20	39	3	2	2	18	17	28	2	2	.235	.314	.313	.627	84	-3	17	3.30	-6	/3-26,2-10,1-9,S-3	4	-0.9
• LEARD, Bill	William Wallace "Wild Bill" Leard b: 10/14/1885, Oneida, NY d: 1/15/1970, San Francisco, CA BR/TR, 5'10", 155 lbs. Deb: 7/21/1917																							
1917 Bro-N	3	3	0	0	0	0	0	0	0	1	0	....	.000	.000	.000	.000	-97	-1	0	.00	-1	/2-1	0	-0.1
• LEARY, Jack	John J. Leary b: 1858, New Haven, CT TL, 5'11", 186 lbs. Deb: 8/21/1880 Career OF: 4-15-21 ♦																							
1880 Bos-N	1	3	1	0	0	0	0	0	1	0	....	....	.000	.250	.000	.250	-7	-0	0	.00	1	/0-1,P-1	0	-0.4
1881 Det-N	3	11	2	3	1	1	0	4	1	1	....	....	.273	.333	.545	.879	165	1	2	6.92	0	/0-2(0-1-1),P-2	1	-0.1
1882 Pit-a	60	257	32	75	7	3	1	....	5	....	....	....	.292	.305	.354	.659	128	8	28	4.38	-10	3-33,0-27(0-8-19)/P-3,1-1,2	7	-0.9
Bal-a	4	18	3	4	1	0	0	....	0	....	....	....	.222	.222	.278	.500	73	0	1	2.28	0	/P-3,0-1	1	0.4
Yr.	64	275	35	79	8	3	1	....	5	....	....	....	.287	.300	.349	.649	124	8	30	4.23	-10	3-33,0-28(0-9-19)/P-6,1-1,2	8	-0.5
1883 Lou-a	40	165	16	31	1	3	3	0	2	....	....	....	.188	.198	.285	.482	58	-7	10	1.99	-1	S-40	4	-0.6
Bal-a	3	11	1	2	0	2	0	0	0	....	....	....	.182	.182	.545	.727	121	0	1	3.48	-2	/2-3	0	-0.1
Yr.	43	176	17	33	1	5	3	0	2	....	....	....	.188	.197	.301	.498	62	-7	11	2.08	-3	S-40/2-3	4	-0.7
1884 Alt-U	8	33	1	3	0	0	0	....	1	....	....	....	.091	.118	.091	.209	-28	-4	0	.34	-3	/0-6(4-2-0),P-3,3-1	0	-0.9
CP-U	10	40	0	7	1	0	0	....	0	....	....	....	.175	.175	.200	.375	28	-3	1	1.22	-2	/2-4,3-3,0-3(0-3-0),P-2	0	-0.6
Yr.	18	73	1	10	1	0	0	....	1	....	....	....	.137	.149	.151	.299	2	-7	2	.80	-4	/0-9(4-5-0),P-5,2-4,3-4	0	-1.4
Total 5	129	538	56	125	11	9	4	4	10	1	....	....	.232	.246	.309	.555	87	-5	44	2.99	-17	/0-40,S-40,3-37,P-14,2-8,1-1	13	-3.1
• LEARY, John	John Louis "Jack" Leary b: 5/2/1891, Waltham, MA d: 8/18/1961, Waltham, MA BR/TR, 5'11.5", 180 lbs. Deb: 4/14/1914																							
1914 StL-A	144	533	35	141	28	7	0	45	10	71	9	15	.265	.282	.343	.625	91	-15	49	3.16	-1	*1-130,C-15	10	-1.9
1915 StL-A	75	227	19	55	10	0	0	15	5	36	2	4	.242	.268	.286	.554	68	-11	17	2.54	-3	1-53,C-11	2	-1.5
Total 2	219	760	54	196	38	7	0	60	15	107	11	19	.258	.278	.326	.604	84	-26	66	2.97	-4	1-183/C-26	12	-3.4
• LEATHERS, Hal	Harold Langford "Chuck" Leathers b: 12/2/1898, Selma, CA d: 4/12/1977, Modesto, CA BL/TR, 5'8", 152 lbs. Deb: 9/13/1920																							
1920 Chi-N	9	23	3	7	1	0	1	1	1	1	1	0	.304	.333	.478	.812	129	1	4	5.88	-3	/S-6,2-3	1	-0.2
• LEBER, Emil	Emil Bohmiel Leber b: 5/15/1881, Cleveland, OH d: 11/6/1924, Cleveland, OH BR/TR, 5'11", 170 lbs. Deb: 9/2/1905																							
1905 Cle-A	2	6	1	0	0	0	0	0	1	....	0	....	.000	.143	.000	.143	-53	-1	0	.00	1	/3-2	0	-0.1
• LEBOURVEAU, Bevo	De Witt Wiley LeBourveau b: 8/24/1894, Dana, CA d: 12/9/1947, Nevada City, CA BL/TR, 5'11", 175 lbs. Deb: 9/9/1919 Career OF: 126-24-60																							
1919 Phi-N	17	63	4	17	0	0	0	0	10	8	2	....	.270	.370	.270	.640	88	-0	7	3.73	2	0-15(15-0-2)	1	0.1
1920 Phi-N	84	261	29	67	7	2	3	12	11	36	9	6	.257	.295	.333	.628	76	-8	26	3.16	3	0-72(51-17-4)	3	-0.9
1921 Phi-N	93	281	42	83	12	5	6	35	29	51	4	5	.295	.361	.438	.799	102	1	44	5.52	-6	0-76(27-1-48)	6	-1.0
1922 Phi-N	74	167	24	45	8	3	2	20	24	29	0	3	.269	.368	.389	.757	87	-3	24	5.02	-2	0-42(33-4-5)	2	-0.7
1929 Phi-A	12	16	1	5	0	1	0	2	5	1	0	1	.313	.476	.438	.914	132	1	3	7.05	0	/0-3(0-2-1)	1	0.0
Total 5	280	788	100	217	27	11	11	69	79	125	15	15	.275	.345	.379	.725	90	-9	104	4.49	-4	0-208	13	-2.6
• LECROY, Matt	Matthew Hanks LeCroy b: 12/13/1975, Belton, SC BR/TR, 6'2", 225 lbs. Deb: 4/3/2000																							
2000 Min-A	56	167	18	29	10	0	5	17	17	38	0	0	.174	.258	.323	.581	44	-15	13	2.44	1	C-49/1-3,D-3	2	-1.0
2001 Min-A	15	40	6	17	5	0	3	12	0	8	0	1	.425	.439	.775	1.214	206	5	13	13.89	0	/D-9,C-3,1-2	3	0.5
2002*Min-A	63	181	19	47	11	1	7	27	13	38	0	2	.260	.309	.448	.757	97	-2	23	4.35	-1	D-40/1-8,C-6	4	-0.5
2003*Min-A	107	345	39	99	19	0	17	64	25	82	0	1	.287	.342	.490	.832	115	6	56	5.94	-7	D-63,C-22,1-17	12	-0.4
Total 4	241	733	82	192	45	1	32	120	55	166	0	4	.262	.319	.457	.777	99	-6	105	4.98	-7	D-115/C-80,1-30	21	-1.5
• LEDEE, Ricky	Ricardo Alberto Ledee b: 11/22/1973, Ponce, Puerto Rico BL/TL, 6'2", 190 lbs. Deb: 6/14/1998 Career OF: 228-108-122																							
1998*NY-A	42	79	13	19	5	2	1	12	7	29	3	1	.241	.302	.392	.695	82	-2	10	4.13	1	0-42(36-3-4)	2	-0.2
1999*NY-A	88	250	45	69	13	5	9	40	28	73	4	3	.276	.349	.476	.825	109	2	42	6.04	-5	0-77(69-6-3)/D-5	9	-0.6
2000 NY-A	62	191	23	46	11	1	7	31	26	39	7	3	.241	.335	.419	.754	90	-3	26	4.49	-3	0-49(46-4-1),D-10	5	-0.7
Cle-A	17	63	13	14	2	1	2	8	8	9	0	0	.222	.310	.381	.691	72	-3	7	3.62	2	0-17(12-0-6)	1	-0.2
Tex-A	58	213	23	50	6	3	4	38	25	50	6	3	.235	.318	.347	.665	67	-11	23	3.58	-4	0-57(20-3-42)	4	-1.5
Yr.	137	467	59	110	19	5	13	77	59	98	13	6	.236	.324	.381	.705	77	-16	56	3.96	-5	*0-123(78-7-49),D-10	10	-2.5
2001 Tex-A	78	242	33	56	21	1	2	36	23	58	3	3	.231	.306	.351	.657	70	-11	27	3.67	-4	0-72(6-10-60)	4	-1.8
2002 Phi-N	96	203	33	46	13	1	8	23	35	50	1	2	.227	.343	.419	.762	104	1	31	5.05	-2	0-51(10-40-5)	5	-0.1
2003 Phi-N	121	255	37	63	15	2	13	46	34	59	0	0	.247	.336	.475	.810	115	5	41	5.65	-3	0-71(29-42-1)/D-2	7	0.1
Total 6	562	1496	220	363	86	16	46	234	186	367	24	15	.243	.329	.414	.743	92	-21	207	4.68	-19	0-436/D-17	37	-5.0
• LEDESMA, Aaron	Aaron David Ledesma b: 6/3/1971, Union City, CA BR/TR, 6'2", 200 lbs. Deb: 7/2/1995																							
1995 NY-N	21	33	4	8	0	0	0	3	6	7	0	0	.242	.359	.242	.601	64	-1	3	2.86	-2	3-10/1-2,S-2	1	-0.3
1997 Bal-A	43	88	24	31	5	1	2	11	13	9	1	0	.352	.441	.500	.941	149	7	21	9.37	-3	2-22,3-11/1-5,S-4	4	0.5
1998 TB-A	95	299	30	97	16	3	0	29	9	51	9	7	.324	.346	.398	.744	91	-5	38	4.57	5	S-58,2-19/3-7,D-6,1-2	7	0.4
1999 TB-A	93	294	32	78	15	0	0	30	14	35	1	1	.265	.305	.316	.622	58	-19	25	2.93	-1	S-50,3-26,2-17/1-4,D-1	3	-1.4
2000 Col-N	32	40	4	9	2	0	0	3	2	9	0	0	.225	.279	.275	.554	32	-4	3	2.54	0	/3-5,1-3	0	-0.4
Total 5	284	754	94	223	38	4	2	76	44	111	11	8	.296	.340	.365	.704	82	-23	90	4.21	-1	S-114/3-59,2-58,1-16,D-7	15	-1.2
• LEDWITH, Mike	Michael Ledwith b: Brooklyn, NY d: 1/2/1929, Bronx, NY Deb: 8/19/1874																							
1874 Atl-n	1	4	1	1	0	0	0	1	0	0	0	0	.250	.250	.250	.500	69	-0	0	2.56	0	/C-1	....	0.0
• LEE, Billy	William Joseph Lee b: 1/9/1892, Bayonne, NJ d: 1/6/1984, West Hazleton, PA BR/TR, 5'9", 165 lbs. Deb: 4/15/1915 Career OF: 7-8-4																							
1915 StL-A	18	59	2	11	1	0	0	4	6	5	1	1	.186	.262	.203	.465	41	-4	3	1.81	2	0-15(7-6-2)/3-1	1	-0.3
1916 StL-A	7	11	1	2	0	0	0	0	1	1	0	....	.182	.250	.182	.432	31	-1	1	1.44	-1	/0-4(0-2-2)	0	-0.2
Total 2	25	70	3	13	1	0	0	4	7	6	1	1	.186	.260	.200	.460	39	-5	4	1.75	2	/0-19,3-1	1	-0.5
• LEE, Carlos	Carlos (Noriel) "El Caballo" Lee b: 6/20/1976, Aguadulce, Panama BR/TR, 6'2", 235 lbs. Deb: 5/7/1999 Career OF: 677-0-0																							
1999 Chi-A	127	492	66	144	32	2	16	84	13	72	4	2	.293	.316	.463	.780	95	-6	68	5.00	-5	*0-105(105-0-0),D-16/1-5	10	-1.5
2000*Chi-A	152	572	107	172	29	2	24	92	38	94	13	4	.301	.347	.484	.832	106	4	92	5.83	-2	*0-149(149-0-0)/D-2	14	-0.4
2001 Chi-A	150	558	75	150	33	3	24	84	38	85	17	7	.269	.322	.468	.790	101	-0	80	5.00	1	*0-130(130-0-0),D-17	15	-0.6
2002 Chi-A	140	492	82	130	26	2	26	80	75	73	1	4	.264	.364	.484	.848	120	13	90	6.41	-3	*0-137(137-0-0)/D-2	17	0.5
2003 Chi-A	158	623	100	181	35	1	31	113	37	91	18	4	.291	.334	.499	.834	116	15	99	5.63	0	*0-156(156-0-0)/D-1	20	0.8
Total 5	727	2737	430	777	155	10	121	453	201	415	53	21	.284	.337	.480	.818	108	26	429	5.57	-9	0-677/D-38,1-5	76	-1.3
• LEE, Cliff	Clifford Walker Lee b: 8/4/1896, Lexington, NE d: 4/25/1980, Denver, CO BR/TR, 6'1", 175 lbs. Deb: 5/15/1919 Career OF: 148-20-136																							
1919 Pit-N	42	112	5	22	2	4	0	2	6	8	2	....	.196	.237	.286	.523	55	-6	8	2.15	-6	C-28/0-6(2-2-2)	1	-1.2
1920 Pit-N	37	76	9	18	2	2	0	8	4	14	0	1	.237	.275	.316	.591	67	-3	6	2.81	0	C-19/0-2(1-1-0)	1	-0.2
1921 Phi-N	88	286	31	88	14	4	4	29	13	34	5	2	.308	.338	.427	.764	94	-2	41	5.27	-5	1-48,0-27(2-1-24)/C-2	5	-1.1
1922 Phi-N	122	422	65	136	29	6	17	77	32	43	2	3	.322	.371	.540	.912	121	12	83	7.45	0	0-89(83-0-6),1-18/3-1	11	0.3
1923 Phi-N	107	355	54	114	20	4	11	47	20	39	3	3	.321	.357	.493	.850	110	4	61	6.44	-3	0-83(54-0-32),1-16	8	-0.5
1924 Phi-N	21	56	4	14	3	2	1	7	2	5	0	1	.250	.276	.429	.704	77	-2	6	3.68	0	0-13(0-0-13)/1-4	1	-0.4
Cin-N	6	6	1	2	1	0	0	2	0	2	0	0	.333	.333	.500	.833	122	0	1	6.36	0	/0-1	0	0.0
Yr.	27	62	5	16	4	2	1	9	2	7	0	1	.258	.281	.435	.717	81	-2	7	3.90	0	0-14(0-0-14)/1-4	1	-0.4
1925 Cle-A	77	230	43	74	15	6	4	42	21	33	2	1	.322	.378	.491	.870	118	6	43	6.95	0	0-70(0-15-56)	7	0.2
1926 Cle-A	21	40	4	7	1	0	1	2	6	8	0	0	.175	.283	.275	.558	45	-3	3	2.74	-1	/0-9(6-1-2),C-3	0	-0.4
Total 8	521	1583	216	475	87	28	38	216	104	186	14	11	.300	.344	.462	.806	102	5	252	5.82	-15	0-300/1-86,C-52,3-1	34	-3.3

YEAR TM-L	G	AB	R	H	2B	3B	HR	RBI	BB	SO	SB	CS	AVG	OBP	SLG	OPS	OPS+	BR/A	RC	RC/G	FR	G/POS	WS	TPW
• LEE, Derek	Derek Gerald Lee b: 7/28/1966, Chicago, IL BL/TR, 6'1", 200 lbs. Deb: 6/27/1993																							
1993 Min-A	15	33	3	5	1	0	0	4	1	4	0	0	.152	.176	.182	.358	-4	-5	1	1.07	0	0-13(9-0-4)	0	-0.5
• LEE, Derrek	Derrek Leon Lee b: 9/6/1975, Sacramento, CA BR/TR, 6'5", 205 lbs. Deb: 4/28/1997																							
1997 SD-N	22	54	9	14	3	0	1	4	9	24	0	0	.259	.365	.370	.735	102	0	8	5.14	0	1-21	2	-0.1
1998 Fla-N	141	454	62	106	29	1	17	74	47	120	5	2	.233	.319	.414	.733	95	-4	60	4.44	4	*1-132	10	-1.1
1999 Fla-N	70	218	21	45	9	1	5	20	17	70	2	1	.206	.264	.326	.590	51	-17	19	2.86	4	1-66	1	-1.8
2000 Fla-N	158	477	70	134	18	3	28	70	63	123	0	3	.281	.369	.507	.877	124	16	87	6.51	4	*1-147	16	0.8
2001 Fla-N	158	561	83	158	37	4	21	75	50	126	4	2	.282	.349	.474	.823	114	11	90	5.65	9	*1-156	16	0.6
2002 Fla-N	162	581	95	157	35	7	27	86	98	164	19	9	.270	.380	.494	.874	133	30	111	6.67	4	*1-162	23	1.9
2003*Fla-N	155	539	91	146	31	2	31	92	88	131	21	8	.271	.383	.508	.891	135	31	110	7.14	1	*1-155	25	1.8
Total 7	866	2884	431	760	162	18	130	421	372	758	51	25	.264	.355	.467	.822	116	67	485	5.84	26	1-839	93	2.2
• LEE, Dud	Ernest Dudley Lee b: 8/22/1899, Denver, CO d: 1/7/1971, Denver, CO BL/TR, 5'9", 150 lbs. Deb: 10/3/1920																							
1920 StL-A	1	2	2	2	0	0	0	1	0	0	1	0	1.000	1.000	1.000	2.000	418	1	2	51.22	-1	/S-1	0	0.0
1921 StL-A	72	180	18	30	4	2	0	11	14	34	1	1	.167	.235	.211	.446	14	-24	10	1.65	-5	S-31,2-30/3-3	2	-2.3
1924 Bos-A	94	288	36	73	9	4	0	29	40	17	8	4	.253	.350	.313	.663	72	-10	35	3.98	-8	S-90	5	-0.8
1925 Bos-A	84	255	22	57	7	3	0	19	34	19	2	3	.224	.315	.275	.589	51	-19	24	3.04	-3	S-84	3	-1.2
1926 Bos-A	2	7	2	1	0	0	0	0	0	0	0	0	.143	.250	.143	.393	4	-1	0	1.34	0	/S-2	0	-0.1
Total 5	253	732	80	163	20	9	0	60	88	70	12	8	.223	.311	.275	.586	51	-53	71	3.11	-17	S-208/2-30,3-3	10	-4.4
• LEE, Hal	Harold Burnham "Sheriff" Lee b: 2/15/1905, Ludlow, MS d: 9/4/1989, Pascagoula, MS BR/TR, 5'11", 180 lbs. Deb: 4/19/1930 Career OF: 678-25-15																							
1930 Bro-N	22	37	5	6	0	0	1	4	4	5	0	....	.162	.244	.243	.487	19	-5	2	1.87	0	0-12(10-0-1)	0	-0.5
1931 Phi-N	44	131	13	29	10	0	2	12	10	18	0	....	.221	.282	.344	.625	62	-7	13	3.30	-2	0-38(26-11-2)	1	-1.1
1932 Phi-N	149	595	76	180	42	10	18	85	36	45	6	....	.303	.343	.497	.841	110	7	102	6.31	5	*0-148(136-12-0)	17	0.4
1933 Phi-N	46	167	25	48	12	2	0	12	18	13	1	....	.287	.360	.383	.743	100	1	24	5.24	0	0-45(45-0-0)	4	-0.2
Bos-N	88	312	32	69	15	9	1	28	18	26	1	....	.221	.266	.337	.602	77	-10	29	3.05	2	0-87(85-2-0)	6	-1.4
Yr.	134	479	57	117	27	11	1	40	36	39	2	....	.244	.300	.353	.653	85	-9	53	3.76	2	*0-132(130-2-0)	10	-1.6
1934 Bos-N	139	521	70	152	23	6	8	79	47	43	3	....	.292	.353	.405	.758	110	8	76	5.34	2	*0-128(128-0-0)/2-4	20	0.3
1935 Bos-N	112	422	49	128	18	6	0	39	18	25	0	....	.303	.333	.374	.708	98	-2	51	4.42	1	*0-110(98-0-12)	7	-0.7
1936 Bos-N	152	565	46	143	24	7	3	64	52	50	4	....	.253	.318	.336	.655	82	-14	59	3.53	-3	*0-150(150-0-0)	9	-2.5
Total 7	752	2750	316	755	144	40	33	323	203	225	15	....	.275	.326	.392	.718	94	-22	357	4.56	6	0-718/2-4	64	-5.6
• LEE, Leonidas	Leonidas Pyrrhus Lee b: 12/13/1860, St. Louis, MO d: 6/11/1912, Hendersonville, NC Deb: 7/17/1877																							
1877 StL-N	4	18	0	5	1	0	0	0	0	1	....	....	.278	.278	.333	.611	97	-0	2	3.61	-2	/0-4(1-2-1),S-1	0	-0.2
• LEE, Leron	Leron Lee b: 3/4/1948, Bakersfield, CA BL/TR, 6', 196 lbs. Deb: 9/5/1969 Career OF: 315-0-110																							
1969 StL-N	7	23	3	5	1	0	0	0	3	8	0	0	.217	.308	.261	.569	60	-1	2	3.13	0	/0-7(4-0-3)	0	-0.1
1970 StL-N	121	264	28	60	13	1	6	23	24	66	5	1	.227	.294	.352	.646	71	-11	28	3.56	-3	0-77(1-0-76)	4	-1.7
1971 StL-N	25	28	3	5	1	0	1	2	4	12	0	1	.179	.281	.321	.603	68	-2	2	1.95	-1	/0-8(5-0-4)	0	-0.3
SD-N	79	256	29	70	20	2	4	21	18	45	4	5	.273	.321	.414	.735	114	2	32	4.44	-1	0-68(68-0-0)	6	-0.2
Yr.	104	284	32	75	21	2	5	23	22	57	4	6	.264	.317	.405	.722	110	1	34	4.15	-1	0-76(73-0-4)	6	-0.4
1972 SD-N	101	370	50	111	23	7	12	47	29	58	2	5	.300	.356	.497	.853	151	21	62	6.04	2	0-96(96-0-1)	18	1.8
1973 SD-N	118	333	36	79	7	2	3	30	33	61	4	0	.237	.308	.297	.605	74	-10	31	3.16	1	0-84(72-0-14)	5	-1.4
1974 Cle-A	79	232	18	54	13	0	5	25	15	42	3	2	.233	.279	.353	.633	82	-6	21	2.97	2	0-62(60-0-2)/D-2	4	-0.8
1975 Cle-A	13	23	3	3	1	0	0	0	2	5	1	0	.130	.231	.174	.405	16	-2	1	1.65	0	/0-5(5-0-0),D-3	0	-0.3
LA-N	48	43	2	11	4	0	0	2	3	9	0	0	.256	.304	.349	.653	84	-1	5	3.91	0	/0-4(4-0-0)	1	-0.2
1976 LA-N	23	45	1	6	0	1	0	2	2	9	0	0	.133	.170	.178	.348	-1	-6	1	.83	-0	0-10(0-0-10)	0	-0.7
Total 8	614	1617	173	404	83	13	31	152	133	315	19	14	.250	.309	.375	.684	96	-16	185	3.92	0	0-421/D-5	38	-3.7
• LEE, Manuel	Manuel Lora "Manny" Lee b: 6/17/1965, San Pedro de Macoris, Dominican Republic BB/TR, 5'10", 161 lbs. Deb: 4/10/1985																							
1985*Tor-A	64	40	9	8	0	0	0	0	2	9	1	4	.200	.238	.200	.438	21	-6	1	.62	0	2-38/D-8,S-8,3-5	1	-0.5
1986 Tor-A	35	78	8	16	0	1	1	7	4	10	0	1	.205	.244	.269	.513	39	-7	4	1.48	-0	2-29/S-5,3-2	1	-0.6
1987 Tor-A	56	121	14	31	2	3	1	11	6	13	2	0	.256	.291	.347	.638	67	-6	13	3.70	-0	2-27,S-26/D-1	3	-0.2
1988 Tor-A	116	381	38	111	16	3	2	38	26	64	3	3	.291	.337	.365	.701	96	-3	44	4.05	-10	2-98,S-23/3-8,D-2	11	-0.9
1989*Tor-A	99	300	27	78	9	2	3	34	20	60	4	2	.260	.306	.333	.640	85	-6	30	3.41	-5	2-40,S-28,3-17,D-13/0-1	8	-0.9
1990 Tor-A	117	391	45	95	12	4	6	41	26	90	3	1	.243	.290	.340	.630	72	-15	38	3.29	-13	*2-112/S-9	7	-2.5
1991*Tor-A	138	445	41	104	18	3	0	29	24	107	7	2	.234	.276	.288	.564	54	-27	35	2.58	-9	*S-138	4	-2.6
1992*Tor-A	128	396	49	104	10	1	3	39	50	73	6	2	.263	.345	.316	.661	83	-7	46	3.99	-4	*S-128	14	-0.2
1993 Tex-A	73	205	31	45	3	1	1	12	22	39	2	4	.220	.301	.259	.560	54	-14	17	2.62	0	S-72/D-1	3	-0.8
1994 Tex-A	95	335	41	93	18	2	2	38	21	66	3	1	.278	.320	.361	.681	76	-12	38	3.99	-1	S-85,2-13	8	-0.5
1995 StL-N	1	1	1	1	0	0	0	0	0	0	0	0	1.000	1.000	1.000	2.000	431	0	1	∞	-1	/2-1	0	0.0
Total 11	922	2693	304	686	88	20	19	249	201	531	31	20	.255	.307	.323	.631	73	-103	266	3.32	-43	S-522,2-358/3-32,D-25,0-1	60	-9.8
• LEE, Terry	Terry James Lee b: 3/13/1962, San Francisco, CA BR/TR, 6'5", 215 lbs. Deb: 9/3/1990																							
1990 Cin-N	12	19	1	4	1	0	0	3	2	2	0	0	.211	.286	.263	.549	50	-1	1	2.18	0	/1-6	0	-0.1
1991 Cin-N	3	6	0	0	0	0	0	0	0	2	0	0	.000	.000	.000	.000	-96	-2	0	.00	1	/1-2	0	0.0
Total 2	15	25	1	4	1	0	0	3	2	4	0	0	.160	.222	.200	.422	19	-3	1	1.61	1	/1-8	0	-0.2
• LEE, Travis	Travis Reynolds Lee b: 5/26/1975, San Diego, CA BL/TL, 6'3", 214 lbs. Deb: 3/31/1998 Career OF: 10-2-56																							
1998 Ari-N	146	562	71	151	20	2	22	72	67	123	8	1	.269	.347	.429	.775	103	4	85	5.37	2	*1-146	13	-0.7
1999 Ari-N	120	375	57	89	16	2	9	50	58	50	17	3	.237	.339	.363	.702	77	-10	49	4.41	3	*1-114/0-2(0-0-2)	8	-1.5
2000 Ari-N	72	224	34	52	13	0	8	40	25	46	5	1	.232	.309	.397	.707	74	-9	28	4.13	4	0-55(0-2-54),1-23	3	-0.8
Phi-N	56	180	19	43	11	1	1	14	40	33	3	0	.239	.383	.328	.711	81	-3	26	4.78	2	1-47,0-10(10-0-0)	3	-0.4
Yr.	128	404	53	95	24	1	9	54	65	79	8	1	.235	.344	.366	.710	78	-11	53	4.42	6	1-70,0-65(10-2-54)	6	-1.3
2001 Phi-N	157	555	75	143	34	2	20	90	71	109	3	4	.258	.346	.434	.780	103	2	83	5.06	-5	*1-156	15	-1.7
2002 Phi-N	153	536	55	142	26	2	13	70	54	104	5	3	.265	.332	.394	.726	95	-5	69	4.54	0	*1-148	13	-1.8
2003 TB-A	145	542	75	149	37	3	19	70	64	97	6	2	.275	.351	.459	.811	113	11	88	5.70	4	*1-142/D-2	13	0.2
Total 6	849	2974	386	769	157	12	92	406	379	562	47	14	.259	.344	.412	.756	96	-10	427	4.97	11	1-776/0-67,D-2	68	-6.7
• LEE, Watty	Wyatt Arnold Lee b: 8/12/1879, Lynch Station, VA d: 3/6/1936, Washington, DC BL/TL, 5'10.5", 171 lbs. Deb: 4/30/1901 Career OF: 24-31-95 ♦																							
1901 Was-A	43	129	15	33	6	3	0	12	7	....	0	....	.256	.304	.349	.653	82	4	14	3.87	0	P-36/0-7(2-1-4)	14	-1.5
1902 Was-A	109	391	61	100	21	5	4	45	33	....	8	....	.256	.319	.366	.684	89	-3	50	4.46	0	0-96(22-20-54),P-13	11	-2.0
1903 Was-A	75	231	17	48	8	4	0	13	18	....	5	....	.208	.265	.277	.542	62	-6	19	2.73	5	0-47(0-10-37),P-22	13	-0.3
1904 Pit-N	8	12	1	4	0	1	0	0	0	....	0	....	.333	.333	.500	.833	152	1	2	6.66	0	/P-5	1	-1.5
Total 4	235	763	94	185	35	13	4	70	58	....	13	....	.242	.300	.338	.638	80	-3	86	3.84	4	0-150/P-76	39	-5.3
• LEEK, Gene	Eugene Harold Leek b: 7/15/1936, San Diego, CA BR/TR, 6', 185 lbs. Deb: 4/22/1959																							
1959 Cle-A	13	36	7	8	3	0	1	5	2	7	0	0	.222	.263	.389	.652	80	-1	4	3.68	0	3-13/S-1	1	-0.1
1961 LA-A	57	199	16	45	9	1	5	20	7	54	0	1	.226	.260	.357	.616	56	-14	16	2.60	8	3-49/S-7,0-1	2	-0.5
1962 LA-A	7	14	0	2	0	0	0	0	0	6	0	0	.143	.143	.143	.286	-24	-2	0	.64	0	/3-4	0	-0.3
Total 3	77	249	23	55	12	1	6	25	9	67	0	1	.221	.254	.349	.603	56	-17	20	2.63	8	/3-66,S-8,0-1	3	-0.8
• LEEPER, Dave	David Dale Leeper b: 10/30/1959, Santa Ana, CA BL/TL, 5'11", 170 lbs. Deb: 9/10/1984 Career OF: 4-0-6																							
1984 KC-A	4	6	1	0	0	0	0	0	0	1	0	0	.000	.000	.000	.000	-99	-2	0	.00	-0	/0-2(2-0-0),D-1	0	-0.2
1985 KC-A	15	34	1	3	0	0	0	4	1	3	0	0	.088	.114	.088	.203	-43	-7	0	.32	-1	/0-8(2-0-6)	0	-0.8
Total 2	19	40	2	3	0	0	0	4	1	4	0	0	.075	.098	.075	.173	-52	-8	0	.27	-1	/0-10,D-1	0	-0.9
• LEES, George	George Edward Lees b: 2/2/1895, Bethlehem, PA d: 1/2/1980, Mechanicsburg, PA BR/TR, 5'9", 150 lbs. Deb: 5/7/1921																							
1921 Chi-A	20	42	3	9	2	0	0	4	0	3	0	1	.214	.214	.262	.476	21	-5	2	1.56	0	C-16	0	-0.5

YEAR TM-L	G	AB	R	H	2B	3B	HR	RBI	BB	SO	SB	CS	AVG	OBP	SLG	OPS	OPS+	BR/A	RC	RC/G	FR	G/POS	WS	TPW
• LEFEBVRE, Jim	James Kenneth Lefebvre b: 1/7/1942, Inglewood, CA BB/TR, 6', 185 lbs. Deb: 4/12/1965 M/C																							
1965*LA-N	157	544	57	136	21	4	12	69	71	92	3	5	.250	.339	.369	.708	106	5	71	4.38	-7	*2-156	23	1.2
1966*LA-N★	152	544	69	149	23	3	24	74	48	72	1	1	.274	.336	.460	.796	129	20	84	5.37	2	*2-119,3-40	25	3.4
1967 LA-N	136	494	51	129	18	5	8	50	44	64	1	5	.261	.325	.366	.692	106	2	57	3.95	-3	3-92,2-34/1-5	16	0.1
1968 LA-N	84	286	23	69	12	1	5	31	26	55	0	0	.241	.307	.343	.649	102	1	31	3.75	-4	2-62,3-16/O-5(5-0-0),1-3	9	0.1
1969 LA-N	95	275	29	65	15	2	4	44	48	37	2	1	.236	.352	.349	.701	104	4	35	4.21	3	3-44,2-37/1-6	10	0.9
1970 LA-N	109	314	33	79	15	1	4	44	29	42	1	1	.252	.317	.344	.661	80	-9	34	3.71	1	2-70,3-21/1-1	8	-0.4
1971 LA-N	119	388	40	95	14	2	12	68	39	55	0	2	.245	.317	.384	.701	104	1	44	3.75	-11	*2-102/3-7	12	-0.4
1972 LA-N	70	169	11	34	8	0	5	24	17	30	0	0	.201	.274	.337	.611	75	-6	16	3.00	1	2-33,3-11	3	-0.4
Total 8	**922**	**3014**	**313**	**756**	**126**	**18**	**74**	**404**	**322**	**447**	**8**	**15**	**.251**	**.326**	**.378**	**.704**	**105**	**17**	**372**	**4.17**	**-19**	**2-613,3-231/1-15,O-5**	**106**	**4.5**
• LEFEBVRE, Joe	Joseph Henry Lefebvre b: 2/22/1956, Concord, NH BL/TR, 5'10", 175 lbs. Deb: 5/22/1980 Career OF: 82-11-265																							
1980*NY-A	74	150	26	34	1	1	8	21	27	30	0	0	.227	.345	.407	.751	107	2	21	4.72	1	O-71(20-3-52)	4	0.1
1981 SD-N	86	246	31	63	13	4	8	31	35	33	6	4	.256	.353	.439	.792	133	11	35	4.73	5	O-84(0-2-83)	7	1.2
1982 SD-N	102	239	25	57	9	0	4	21	18	50	0	0	.238	.295	.326	.621	78	-8	24	3.34	4	3-39,O-36(24-6-29)/C-3	6	-0.5
1983 SD-N	18	20	1	5	0	0	0	1	2	3	0	0	.250	.318	.250	.568	61	-1	2	2.54	0	/O-6(0-0-6),3-4,C-2	1	-0.1
*Phi-N	101	258	34	80	20	8	8	38	31	46	5	3	.310	.390	.543	.933	158	20	53	7.44	-2	O-74(22-0-58)/3-9,C-3	14	1.5
Yr.	119	278	35	85	20	8	8	39	33	49	5	3	.306	.385	.522	.907	151	19	54	7.06	-2	O-80(22-0-64),3-13/C-5	15	1.5
1984 Phi-N	52	160	22	40	9	0	3	18	23	37	0	2	.250	.351	.363	.714	99	-0	20	4.19	1	O-47(16-0-34)/3-1	3	-0.1
1986 Phi-N	14	18	0	2	0	0	0	0	3	5	0	0	.111	.238	.111	.349	-1	-2	0	.38	-0	/O-3(0-0-3)	0	-0.3
Total 6	**447**	**1091**	**139**	**281**	**52**	**13**	**31**	**130**	**139**	**204**	**11**	**9**	**.258**	**.346**	**.414**	**.760**	**115**	**21**	**155**	**4.81**	**9**	**O-321/3-53,C-8**	**35**	**2.0**
• LEFEVRE, Al	Alfred Modesto Lefevre b: 9/16/1898, New York, NY d: 1/21/1982, Glen Cove, NY BR/TR, 5'10.5", 160 lbs. Deb: 6/28/1920																							
1920 NY-N	17	27	5	4	0	1	0	0	0	13	0	0	.148	.148	.222	.370	5	-3	1	.98	1	/S-9,2-6,3-1	0	-0.2
• LEFLER, Wade	Wade Hampton Lefler b: 6/5/1896, Cooleemee, NC d: 3/6/1981, Hickory, NC BL/TR, 5'11", 162 lbs. Deb: 4/16/1924																							
1924 Bos-N	1	1	0	0	0	0	0	0	0	1	0	0	.000	.000	.000	.000	-104	-0	0	.00	0	....	0	0.0
Was-A	5	8	0	5	3	0	0	4	0	0	0	0	.625	.625	1.000	1.625	325	2	5	42.40	0	/O-1	1	0.2
• LEFLORE, Ron	Ronald LeFlore b: 6/16/1948, Detroit, MI BR/TR, 6', 200 lbs. Deb: 8/1/1974 Career OF: 208-833-0																							
1974 Det-A	59	254	37	66	8	1	2	13	13	58	23	9	.260	.304	.323	.627	78	-6	26	3.41	0	O-59(0-59-0)	5	-0.8
1975 Det-A	136	550	66	142	13	6	8	37	33	139	28	20	.258	.303	.347	.650	80	-18	57	3.50	-2	*O-134(0-134-0)	9	-2.4
1976 Det-A★	135	544	93	172	23	8	4	39	51	111	58	20	.316	.377	.410	.787	125	22	86	5.68	9	*O-132(0-132-0)/D-1	26	2.9
1977 Det-A	154	652	100	212	30	10	16	57	37	121	39	19	.325	.365	.475	.841	121	18	110	6.23	-4	*O-152(0-152-0)	23	1.2
1978 Det-A	155	666	**126**	198	30	3	12	62	65	104	**68**	16	.297	.363	.405	.769	113	20	105	5.67	-2	*O-155(0-155-0)	24	1.7
1979 Det-A	148	600	110	180	22	10	9	57	52	95	78	14	.300	.356	.415	.771	104	14	94	5.60	1	*O-113(0-113-0),D-34	21	1.2
1980 Mon-N	139	521	95	134	21	11	4	39	62	99	**97**	19	.257	.337	.363	.700	95	10	76	4.98	-2	*O-130(130-0-0)	18	0.3
1981 Chi-A	82	337	46	83	10	4	0	24	28	70	36	11	.246	.306	.300	.606	77	-6	32	3.13	-1	O-82(76-7-0)	5	-1.1
1982 Chi-A	91	334	58	96	15	4	4	25	22	91	28	14	.287	.331	.392	.724	98	-1	42	4.46	-2	O-83(2-81-0)/D-2	8	-0.4
Total 9	**1099**	**4458**	**731**	**1283**	**172**	**57**	**59**	**353**	**363**	**888**	**455**	**142**	**.288**	**.344**	**.392**	**.735**	**102**	**54**	**628**	**4.95**	**-2**	***O-1040/D-37**	**139**	**2.5**
• LEGETT, Lou	Louis Alfred "Doc" Legett b: 6/1/1901, New Orleans, LA d: 3/6/1988, New Orleans, LA BR/TR, 5'10", 166 lbs. Deb: 5/8/1929																							
1929 Bos-N	39	81	7	13	2	0	0	6	3	18	2	....	.160	.190	.185	.376	-7	-14	3	1.07	-1	C-28	0	-1.2
1933 Bos-A	8	5	1	1	1	0	0	1	0	0	0	0	.200	.200	.400	.600	56	-0	0	2.54	0	/C-2	0	0.0
1934 Bos-A	19	38	4	11	0	0	0	1	2	4	0	0	.289	.325	.289	.614	56	-2	4	3.53	0	C-17	1	-0.2
1935 Bos-A	2	0	1	0	0	0	0	0	0	0	0	0	....	....	....	....	-94	0	0	....	0	....	0	0.0
Total 4	**68**	**124**	**13**	**25**	**3**	**0**	**0**	**8**	**5**	**22**	**2**	**0**	**.202**	**.233**	**.226**	**.458**	**15**	**-16**	**7**	**1.80**	**-1**	**/C-47**	**1**	**-1.4**
• LEGG, Greg	Gregory Lynn Legg b: 4/21/1960, San Jose, CA BR/TR, 6'1", 185 lbs. Deb: 4/18/1986																							
1986 Phi-N	11	20	2	9	1	0	0	1	0	3	0	0	.450	.450	.500	.950	156	1	5	11.05	1	/2-4,S-1	1	0.2
1987 Phi-N	3	2	1	0	0	0	0	0	0	0	0	0	.000	.000	.000	.000	-97	-1	0	.00	-1	/2-1,3-1,S-1	0	-0.1
Total 2	**14**	**22**	**3**	**9**	**1**	**0**	**0**	**1**	**0**	**3**	**0**	**0**	**.409**	**.409**	**.455**	**.864**	**133**	**1**	**5**	**9.35**	**0**	**/2-5,S-2,3-1**	**1**	**0.1**
• LEHANE, Mike	Michael Patrick Lehane b: 4/15/1865, New York, NY BR, 6'1.5", 180 lbs. Deb: 4/26/1884																							
1884 Was-U	3	12	1	4	2	0	0	....	0	....	....	....	.333	.333	.500	.833	184	1	2	7.18	-1	/S-3,3-1,O-1	1	0.0
1890 Col-a	140	512	54	108	19	5	0	56	43	....	13	....	.211	.276	.268	.544	65	-22	42	2.78	10	*1-140	7	-2.1
1891 Col-a	137	511	59	110	12	7	1	52	34	77	16	....	.215	.268	.272	.540	58	-29	43	2.82	1	*1-137	4	-3.4
Total 3	**280**	**1035**	**114**	**222**	**33**	**12**	**1**	**108**	**77**	**77**	**29**	**....**	**.214**	**.273**	**.272**	**.545**	**63**	**-49**	**87**	**2.84**	**10**	**1-277/S-3,3-1,O-1**	**12**	**-5.5**
• LEHNER, Paul	Paul Eugene "Peanuts,Gulliver" Lehner b: 7/1/1920, Dolomite, AL d: 12/27/1967, Birmingham, AL BL/TL, 5'9", 165 lbs. Deb: 9/10/1946 Career OF: 110-297-37																							
1946 StL-A	16	45	6	10	1	2	0	5	1	5	0	0	.222	.239	.333	.572	56	-3	4	2.88	0	O-12(0-11-1)	1	-0.3
1947 StL-A	135	483	59	120	25	9	7	48	28	29	5	5	.248	.294	.381	.675	85	-13	50	3.41	-10	*O-127(2-125-0)	7	-2.8
1948 StL-A	103	333	23	92	15	4	2	46	30	19	0	2	.276	.336	.363	.699	84	-9	40	4.28	-5	O-89(0-89-0)/1-2	5	-1.6
1949 StL-A	104	297	25	68	13	0	3	37	16	20	0	2	.229	.271	.303	.574	50	-24	22	2.39	-5	O-56(12-35-10),1-18	1	-3.0
1950 Phi-A	114	427	48	132	17	5	9	52	32	33	1	1	.309	.357	.436	.793	104	1	66	5.63	1	*O-101(80-7-15)	10	-0.4
1951 Phi-A	9	28	1	4	1	0	0	1	1	1	0	0	.143	.172	.179	.351	-5	-4	0	.38	1	/O-6(6-0-0)	0	-0.4
Chi-A	23	72	9	15	3	1	0	3	10	4	0	0	.208	.305	.278	.583	59	-4	7	3.29	1	O-20(8-13-9)	1	-0.4
StL-A	21	67	2	9	5	0	1	2	6	5	0	1	.134	.205	.254	.459	23	-8	3	1.37	-1	O-18(1-17-0)	0	-0.9
Cle-A	12	13	2	3	0	0	0	1	1	2	0	0	.231	.286	.231	.516	43	-1	1	2.57	-0	/O-1	0	-0.1
Yr.	65	180	14	31	9	1	1	7	18	12	0	1	.172	.247	.250	.497	35	-17	12	1.98	1	O-45(16-30-9)	1	-1.8
1952 Bos-A	3	3	0	2	0	0	0	2	2	0	0	0	.667	.800	.667	1.467	289	1	2	55.51	0	/O-2(0-0-2)	1	0.1
Total 7	**540**	**1768**	**175**	**455**	**80**	**21**	**22**	**197**	**127**	**118**	**6**	**11**	**.257**	**.309**	**.364**	**.672**	**78**	**-63**	**196**	**3.74**	**-18**	**O-432/1-20**	**26**	**-9.8**
• LEHR, Clarence	Clarence Emanuel "King" Lehr b: 5/16/1886, Escanaba, MI d: 1/31/1948, Highland Park, MI BR/TR, 5'11", 165 lbs. Deb: 5/18/1911																							
1911 Phi-N	23	27	2	4	0	0	0	2	0	7	0	....	.148	.148	.148	.296	-17	-4	1	.59	0	/O-5(1-1-3),2-4,S-4	0	-0.5
• LEIBER, Hank	Henry Edward Leiber b: 1/17/1911, Phoenix, AZ d: 11/8/1993, Tucson, AZ BR/TR, 6'1.5", 205 lbs. Deb: 4/16/1933 Career OF: 37-602-65																							
1933 NY-N	6	10	1	2	0	0	0	0	0	2	0	....	.200	.200	.200	.400	15	-1	0	.62	1	/O-1	0	0.0
1934 NY-N	63	187	17	45	5	3	2	25	4	13	1	....	.241	.257	.332	.588	58	-12	15	2.77	0	O-51(2-49-0)	2	-1.3
1935 NY-N	154	613	110	203	37	4	22	107	48	29	0	....	.331	.389	.512	.901	143	36	121	7.45	-15	*O-154(0-154-0)	28	1.7
1936*NY-N	101	337	44	94	19	7	9	67	37	41	1	....	.279	.352	.457	.809	117	8	57	5.99	0	O-86(7-78-1)/1-1	12	0.6
1937*NY-N	51	184	24	54	7	3	4	32	15	27	1	....	.293	.347	.429	.776	108	2	26	4.88	-1	O-46(1-42-3)	5	0.0
1938 NY-N★	98	360	50	97	18	4	12	65	31	45	0	....	.269	.327	.442	.769	109	3	54	5.37	-4	O-89(2-86-4)	10	-0.4
1939 Chi-N	112	365	65	113	16	1	24	88	59	42	1	....	.310	.411	.556	.967	155	30	83	8.34	-3	O-98(0-98-0)	21	2.4
1940 Chi-N★	117	440	68	133	24	2	17	86	45	68	1	....	.302	.371	.482	.853	136	21	80	6.76	-5	*O-103(0-53-52),1-12	17	1.1
1941 Chi-N★	53	162	20	35	5	0	7	25	16	25	0	....	.216	.291	.377	.667	90	-3	18	3.62	-3	O-29(23-2-5),1-15	3	-0.8
1942 NY-N	58	147	11	32	6	0	4	23	19	27	0	....	.218	.315	.340	.656	91	-1	15	3.15	0	O-41(1-40-0)/P-1	3	-0.5
Total 10	**813**	**2805**	**410**	**808**	**137**	**24**	**101**	**518**	**274**	**319**	**5**	**....**	**.288**	**.356**	**.462**	**.818**	**122**	**84**	**469**	**5.98**	**-30**	**O-698/1-28,P-1**	**101**	**2.8**
• LEIBOLD, Nemo	Harry Loran Leibold b: 2/17/1892, Butler, IN d: 2/4/1977, Detroit, MI BL/TR, 5'6.5", 157 lbs. Deb: 4/12/1913 Career OF: 144-593-381																							
1913 Cle-A	93	286	37	74	11	6	0	12	21	43	16	....	.259	.309	.339	.649	87	-6	33	3.86	-3	O-74(4-66-2)	6	-1.3
1914 Cle-A	115	402	46	106	13	3	0	32	54	56	12	14	.264	.354	.311	.665	96	-3	45	3.75	2	*O-107(0-90-17)	9	-0.9
1915 Cle-A	57	207	28	53	5	4	0	4	24	16	5	3	.256	.339	.319	.658	95	-1	24	3.89	7	O-52(0-52-0)	6	0.3
Chi-A	36	74	10	17	1	0	0	11	15	11	1	3	.230	.360	.243	.603	78	-2	8	2.99	4	O-22(10-12-0)	2	0.0
Yr.	93	281	38	70	6	4	0	15	39	27	6	6	.249	.345	.299	.644	90	-3	31	3.62	11	O-74(10-64-0)	8	0.3
1916 Chi-A	45	82	5	20	1	2	0	13	7	7	7	....	.244	.303	.305	.608	82	-2	10	3.92	-2	O-24(2-16-6)	1	-0.6
1917*Chi-A	125	428	59	101	12	6	0	29	74	34	27	....	.236	.350	.292	.642	94	1	50	3.93	-4	*O-122(16-4-102)	15	-1.0
1918 Chi-A	116	440	57	110	14	7	0	31	63	32	13	....	.250	.344	.314	.658	97	1	50	3.78	3	*O-114(95-7-12)	12	-0.2
1919*Chi-A	122	434	81	131	18	2	0	26	72	30	17	....	.302	.404	.353	.756	113	12	67	5.53	8	*O-122(7-1-114)	18	1.5

YEAR TM-L	G	AB	R	H	2B	3B	HR	RBI	BB	SO	SB	CS	AVG	OBP	SLG	OPS	OPS+	BR/A	RC	RC/G	FR	G/POS	WS	TPW
1920 Chi-A	108	413	61	91	16	3	1	28	55	30	7	15	.220	.316	.281	.597	59	-26	37	2.86	3	*0-105(3-4-98)	4	-2.8
1921 Bos-A	123	467	88	143	26	6	0	31	41	27	13	7	.306	.363	.388	.751	94	-3	67	5.14	2	*0-117(0-107-10)	14	-0.6
1922 Bos-A	81	271	42	70	8	1	1	18	41	14	1	6	.258	.360	.306	.666	76	-10	31	3.90	3	0-71(1-66-4)	7	-1.0
1923 Bos-A	12	18	1	2	0	0	0	0	1	2	0	1	.111	.158	.111	.269	-28	-4	0	.36	0	0-10(0-10-0)	0	-0.4
Was-A	95	315	68	96	13	4	1	22	53	16	7	6	.305	.408	.381	.789	114	9	52	5.93	1	0-84(0-84-0)	13	0.6
Yr.	107	333	69	98	13	4	1	22	54	18	7	7	.294	.396	.366	.762	107	6	53	5.55	1	0-94(0-94-0)	13	0.3
1924*Was-A	84	246	41	72	6	4	0	20	42	10	7	5	.293	.398	.350	.748	97	1	37	5.22	1	0-70(4-52-14)	8	0.0
1925*Was-A	56	84	14	23	1	1	0	7	8	7	1	0	.274	.337	.310	.646	66	-4	9	3.98	0	0-26(2-22-2)/3-1	2	-0.4
Total 13	1268	4167	638	1109	145	49	3	284	571	335	134	60	.266	.357	.327	.683	92	-37	522	4.24	24	*0-1120/3-1	117	-6.7

• LEIFER, Elmer Elmer Edwin Leifer b: 5/23/1893, Clarington, OH d: 9/26/1948, Everett, WA BL/TR, 5'9.5", 170 lbs. Deb: 9/7/1921

YEAR TM-L	G	AB	R	H	2B	3B	HR	RBI	BB	SO	SB	CS	AVG	OBP	SLG	OPS	OPS+	BR/A	RC	RC/G	FR	G/POS	WS	TPW
1921 Chi-A	9	10	0	3	0	0	0	1	0	4	0	0	.300	.300	.300	.600	54	-1	1	3.27	0	/3-1,0-1	0	-0.1

• LEIGHTON, John John Atkinson Leighton b: 10/4/1861, Peabody, MA d: 10/31/1956, Lynn, MA, 5'11", 170 lbs. Deb: 7/12/1890

YEAR TM-L	G	AB	R	H	2B	3B	HR	RBI	BB	SO	SB	CS	AVG	OBP	SLG	OPS	OPS+	BR/A	RC	RC/G	FR	G/POS	WS	TPW
1890 Syr-a	7	27	6	8	2	0	0	0	3	....	2	....	.296	.367	.370	.737	131	1	5	6.29	-1	/0-7(0-7-0)	1	0.0

• LEINHAUSER, Bill William Charles Leinhauser b: 11/4/1893, Philadelphia, PA d: 4/14/1978, Elkins Park, PA BR/TR, 5'10", 150 lbs. Deb: 5/18/1912

YEAR TM-L	G	AB	R	H	2B	3B	HR	RBI	BB	SO	SB	CS	AVG	OBP	SLG	OPS	OPS+	BR/A	RC	RC/G	FR	G/POS	WS	TPW
1912 Det-A	1	4	0	0	0	0	0	0	0	....	0	....	.000	.000	.000	.000	-103	-1	0	.00	1	/0-1	0	0.0

• LEIP, Ed Edgar Ellsworth Leip b: 11/29/1910, Trenton, NJ d: 11/24/1983, Zephyrhills, FL BR/TR, 5'9", 160 lbs. Deb: 9/16/1939

YEAR TM-L	G	AB	R	H	2B	3B	HR	RBI	BB	SO	SB	CS	AVG	OBP	SLG	OPS	OPS+	BR/A	RC	RC/G	FR	G/POS	WS	TPW
1939 Was-A	9	32	4	11	1	0	0	2	2	4	0	1	.344	.382	.375	.757	102	-0	4	4.61	1	/2-8	1	0.1
1940 Pit-N	3	5	2	1	0	0	0	0	0	0	0	....	.200	.200	.200	.400	11	-1	0	.00	-0	/2-2	0	-0.1
1941 Pit-N	15	25	1	5	0	2	0	3	1	2	1	....	.200	.231	.360	.591	65	-1	1	1.75	0	/2-7,3-1	0	-0.1
1942 Pit-N	3	0	0	0	0	0	0	0	0	0	0	....	....	....	....	....	-98	0	0	....	0	....	0	0.0
Total 4	30	62	7	17	1	2	0	5	3	6	1	1	.274	.308	.355	.663	80	-2	6	2.92	0	/2-17,3-1	1	-0.1

• LEIUS, Scott Scott Thomas Leius b: 9/24/1965, Yonkers, NY BR/TR, 6'3", 195 lbs. Deb: 9/3/1990

YEAR TM-L	G	AB	R	H	2B	3B	HR	RBI	BB	SO	SB	CS	AVG	OBP	SLG	OPS	OPS+	BR/A	RC	RC/G	FR	G/POS	WS	TPW
1990 Min-A	14	25	4	6	1	0	1	4	2	2	0	0	.240	.296	.400	.696	87	-0	2	2.90	0	S-12/3-1	0	0.0
1991*Min-A	109	199	35	57	7	2	5	20	30	35	5	5	.286	.380	.417	.797	115	4	32	5.49	1	3-79,S-19/0-2(0-2-0)	8	0.7
1992 Min-A	129	409	50	102	18	2	2	35	34	61	6	5	.249	.309	.318	.626	73	-15	39	3.25	2	*3-125,S-10	7	-1.2
1993 Min-A	10	18	4	3	0	0	0	2	2	4	0	0	.167	.250	.167	.417	14	-2	1	1.24	0	/S-9	0	-0.1
1994 Min-A	97	350	57	86	16	1	14	49	37	58	2	4	.246	.320	.417	.737	88	-8	45	4.34	2	3-95/S-2	6	-0.4
1995 Min-A	117	372	51	92	16	5	4	45	49	54	2	1	.247	.338	.349	.688	79	-11	44	3.94	-1	*3-112/S-7,D-3	6	-1.0
1996 Cle-A	27	43	3	6	4	0	1	3	2	8	0	0	.140	.178	.302	.480	18	-6	2	1.48	0	/3-8,1-7,2-6,D-1	0	-0.6
1998 KC-A	17	46	2	8	0	0	0	4	1	6	0	0	.174	.191	.174	.365	-4	-7	1	.83	-4	3-15/S-2,D-1	0	-1.0
1999 KC-A	37	74	8	15	1	0	1	10	4	8	1	0	.203	.253	.257	.510	30	-8	5	2.22	-1	1-13,3-10/D-6,S-2,2-1	0	-0.9
Total 9	557	1536	214	375	63	10	28	172	161	236	16	15	.244	.318	.353	.671	78	-53	172	3.72	0	3-445/S-63,1-20,D-11,2-7,0	27	-4.5

• LEJA, Frank Frank John Leja b: 2/7/1936, Holyoke, MA d: 5/3/1991, Boston, MA BL/TL, 6'4", 205 lbs. Deb: 5/1/1954

YEAR TM-L	G	AB	R	H	2B	3B	HR	RBI	BB	SO	SB	CS	AVG	OBP	SLG	OPS	OPS+	BR/A	RC	RC/G	FR	G/POS	WS	TPW
1954 NY-A	12	5	2	1	0	0	0	0	0	1	0	0	.200	.200	.200	.400	10	-1	0	1.35	-1	/1-6	0	-0.1
1955 NY-A	7	2	1	0	0	0	0	0	0	1	0	0	.000	.000	.000	.000	-102	-1	0	.00	0	/1-2	0	-0.1
1962 LA-A	7	16	0	0	0	0	0	0	1	6	0	0	.000	.059	.000	.059	-85	-4	0	.00	0	/1-4	0	-0.5
Total 3	26	23	3	1	0	0	0	0	1	8	0	0	.043	.083	.043	.127	-68	-5	0	.23	-1	/1-12	0	-0.7

• LEJEUNE, Larry Sheldon Aldenbert LeJeune b: 7/22/1885, Chicago, IL d: 4/21/1952, Eloise, MI BR/TR, 6', 185 lbs. Deb: 5/10/1911 Career OF: 0-24-0

YEAR TM-L	G	AB	R	H	2B	3B	HR	RBI	BB	SO	SB	CS	AVG	OBP	SLG	OPS	OPS+	BR/A	RC	RC/G	FR	G/POS	WS	TPW
1911 Bro-N	6	19	2	3	0	0	0	2	2	8	2	....	.158	.238	.158	.396	12	-2	1	1.83	-1	/0-6(0-6-0)	0	-0.4
1915 Pit-N	18	65	4	11	0	1	0	2	2	7	4	3	.169	.206	.200	.406	23	-7	3	1.26	1	0-18(0-18-0)	1	-0.8
Total 2	24	84	6	14	0	1	0	4	4	15	6	3	.167	.213	.190	.404	21	-9	4	1.38	0	/0-24	1	-1.1

• LEJOHN, Don Donald Everett LeJohn b: 5/13/1934, Daisytown, PA BR/TR, 5'10", 175 lbs. Deb: 6/30/1965

YEAR TM-L	G	AB	R	H	2B	3B	HR	RBI	BB	SO	SB	CS	AVG	OBP	SLG	OPS	OPS+	BR/A	RC	RC/G	FR	G/POS	WS	TPW
1965*LA-N	34	78	2	20	2	0	0	7	5	13	0	1	.256	.301	.282	.583	70	-4	6	2.91	2	3-26	1	-0.2

• LELIVELT, Jack John Frank Lelivelt b: 11/14/1885, Chicago, IL d: 1/20/1941, Seattle, WA BL/TL, 5'11", 175 lbs. Deb: 6/24/1909 Career OF: 157-87-35

YEAR TM-L	G	AB	R	H	2B	3B	HR	RBI	BB	SO	SB	CS	AVG	OBP	SLG	OPS	OPS+	BR/A	RC	RC/G	FR	G/POS	WS	TPW
1909 Was-A	91	318	25	93	8	6	0	24	19	....	8	....	.292	.334	.355	.690	124	8	40	4.48	5	0-91(41-35-15)	11	0.9
1910 Was-A	110	347	40	92	10	3	0	33	40	....	20	....	.265	.343	.311	.654	110	5	45	4.28	7	0-86(80-5-1)/1-7	10	0.8
1911 Was-A	72	225	29	72	12	4	0	22	22	....	7	....	.320	.386	.409	.794	124	8	38	6.22	5	0-49(36-0-13)/1-7	8	1.0
1912 NY-A	36	149	12	54	6	7	2	23	4	....	7	....	.362	.383	.537	.920	153	9	32	8.88	-3	0-36(0-36-0)	7	0.3
1913 NY-A	18	28	2	6	0	1	0	4	2	2	1	....	.214	.267	.286	.552	61	-1	2	2.54	0	/0-5(0-4-0)	0	-0.1
Cle-A	23	23	0	9	2	0	0	7	0	3	1	....	.391	.391	.478	.870	150	1	4	8.01	0	/0-1	1	0.1
Yr.	41	51	2	15	2	1	0	11	2	5	2	....	.294	.321	.373	.693	100	-0	7	4.67	0	/0-6(0-5-0)	1	0.0
1914 Cle-A	34	64	6	21	5	1	0	13	2	10	2	3	.328	.348	.438	.786	131	1	9	5.14	-1	0-13(0-6-6)/1-1	2	-0.1
Total 6	384	1154	114	347	43	22	2	126	89	15	46	3	.301	.353	.381	.735	122	30	171	5.29	12	0-281/1-15	39	2.9

• LEMASTER, Johnnie Johnnie Lee LeMaster b: 6/19/1954, Portsmouth, OH BR/TR, 6'2", 167 lbs. Deb: 9/2/1975

YEAR TM-L	G	AB	R	H	2B	3B	HR	RBI	BB	SO	SB	CS	AVG	OBP	SLG	OPS	OPS+	BR/A	RC	RC/G	FR	G/POS	WS	TPW
1975 SF-N	22	74	4	14	4	0	2	9	4	15	2	1	.189	.241	.324	.565	53	-5	6	2.66	1	S-22	1	-0.2
1976 SF-N	33	100	9	21	3	2	0	9	2	21	2	0	.210	.225	.280	.505	42	-8	6	2.00	-3	S-31	1	-0.7
1977 SF-N	68	134	13	20	5	1	0	8	13	27	2	1	.149	.224	.201	.426	15	-16	7	1.57	0	S-54/3-2	2	-1.2
1978 SF-N	101	272	23	64	18	3	1	14	21	45	6	6	.235	.293	.335	.627	78	-10	26	3.07	-2	S-96/2-2	7	-0.3
1979 SF-N	108	343	42	87	11	2	3	29	23	55	9	5	.254	.304	.324	.628	77	-12	34	3.35	-7	*S-106	7	-0.9
1980 SF-N	135	405	33	87	16	6	3	31	25	57	0	1	.215	.260	.306	.567	59	-24	32	2.55	-20	*S-134	4	-3.2
1981 SF-N	104	324	27	82	9	1	0	28	24	46	3	7	.253	.307	.287	.594	70	-15	26	2.69	-9	*S-103	5	-1.5
1982 SF-N	130	436	34	94	14	1	2	30	31	78	13	4	.216	.268	.266	.534	50	-28	30	2.19	-6	*S-130	4	-2.2
1983 SF-N	141	534	81	128	16	1	6	30	60	96	39	19	.240	.319	.307	.626	77	-16	57	3.49	-10	*S-139	11	-1.2
1984 SF-N	132	451	46	98	13	2	4	32	31	97	17	5	.217	.268	.282	.549	56	-25	36	2.56	4	*S-129	8	-1.0
1985 SF-N	12	16	1	0	0	0	0	0	1	5	0	0	.000	.059	.000	.059	-86	-4	0	.03	-2	S-10	0	-0.5
Cle-A	11	20	0	3	0	0	0	2	0	6	0	1	.150	.150	.150	.300	-18	-4	0	.48	-1	S-10	0	-0.4
Pit-N	22	58	4	9	0	0	1	6	5	12	1	0	.155	.222	.207	.429	21	-6	3	1.49	3	S-21	1	-0.1
Yr.	34	74	5	9	0	0	1	6	6	17	1	0	.122	.188	.162	.350	-1	-10	3	1.14	1	S-31	1	-0.6
1987 Oak-A	20	24	3	2	0	0	0	1	1	4	0	1	.083	.120	.083	.203	-48	-6	0	.21	0	/3-8,S-7,2-5,D-1	0	-0.5
Total 12	1039	3191	320	709	109	19	22	229	241	564	94	51	.222	.278	.289	.567	60	-178	263	2.67	-53	S-992/3-10,2-7,D-1	51	-13.9

• LEMBO, Steve Stephen Neal Lembo b: 11/13/1926, Brooklyn, NY d: 12/4/1989, Flushing, NY BR/TR, 6'1", 185 lbs. Deb: 9/16/1950

YEAR TM-L	G	AB	R	H	2B	3B	HR	RBI	BB	SO	SB	CS	AVG	OBP	SLG	OPS	OPS+	BR/A	RC	RC/G	FR	G/POS	WS	TPW
1950 Bro-N	5	6	0	1	0	0	0	0	1	0	0	....	.167	.286	.167	.452	22	-1	0	.81	0	/C-5	0	0.0
1952 Bro-N	2	5	0	1	0	0	0	1	0	1	0	0	.200	.200	.200	.400	11	-1	0	1.38	0	/C-2	0	-0.1
Total 2	7	11	0	2	0	0	0	1	1	1	0	0	.182	.250	.182	.432	17	-1	0	1.04	0	/C-7	0	-0.1

• LEMKE, Mark Mark Alan Lemke b: 8/13/1965, Utica, NY BB/TR, 5'10", 167 lbs. Deb: 9/17/1988

YEAR TM-L	G	AB	R	H	2B	3B	HR	RBI	BB	SO	SB	CS	AVG	OBP	SLG	OPS	OPS+	BR/A	RC	RC/G	FR	G/POS	WS	TPW
1988 Atl-N	16	58	8	13	4	0	0	2	4	5	0	2	.224	.274	.293	.567	60	-4	4	2.25	2	2-16	0	-0.2
1989 Atl-N	14	55	4	10	2	1	2	10	5	7	0	1	.182	.250	.364	.614	72	-3	5	2.65	1	2-14	1	-0.2
1990 Atl-N	102	239	22	54	13	0	0	21	21	22	0	1	.226	.288	.280	.569	54	-16	19	2.61	7	3-45,2-44/S-1	4	-0.8
1991*Atl-N	136	269	36	63	11	2	2	23	29	27	1	2	.234	.309	.312	.621	71	-11	25	3.03	-2	*2-110,3-15	4	-1.1
1992*Atl-N	155	427	38	97	7	4	6	26	50	39	0	3	.227	.308	.304	.613	70	-17	41	3.07	-10	*2-145,3-13	7	-2.5
1993*Atl-N	151	493	52	124	19	2	7	49	65	50	1	2	.252	.339	.341	.679	82	-12	55	3.67	15	*2-150	15	1.0
1994 Atl-N	104	350	40	103	15	0	3	31	38	37	0	3	.294	.363	.363	.726	88	-6	44	4.46	0	*2-103	12	-0.2
1995*Atl-N	116	399	42	101	16	5	5	38	44	40	2	2	.253	.327	.356	.683	78	-13	44	3.64	-9	*2-115	11	-1.7
1996*Atl-N	135	498	64	127	17	0	5	37	53	48	5	2	.255	.327	.319	.646	67	-23	54	3.74	3	*2-133	12	-1.3
1997 Atl-N	109	351	33	86	17	1	2	26	33	51	2	0	.245	.310	.316	.626	63	-18	35	3.27	17	*2-104	9	0.4
1998 Bos-A	31	91	10	17	4	0	0	7	6	15	0	1	.187	.237	.231	.468	22	-11	5	1.84	3	2-31	1	-0.7
Total 11	1069	3230	349	795	125	15	32	270	348	341	11	19	.246	.319	.324	.643	71	-133	331	3.40	26	2-965/3-73,S-1	76	-7.2

• LEMON, Bob Robert Granville Lemon
b: 9/22/1920, San Bernardino, CA d: 1/11/2000, Long Beach, CA BL/TR, 6', 185 lbs. Deb: 9/9/1941 M/C HOF: 1976 Career OF: 0-13-1 ♦

YEAR TM-L	G	AB	R	H	2B	3B	HR	RBI	BB	SO	SB	CS	AVG	OBP	SLG	OPS	OPS+	BR/A	RC	RC/G	FR	G/POS	WS	TPW
1941 Cle-A	5	4	0	1	0	0	0	0	0	1	0	0	.250	.250	.250	.500	34	-0	0	2.31	0	/3-1	0	0.0
1942 Cle-A	5	5	0	0	0	0	0	0	0	3	0	0	.000	.000	.000	.000	-106	-1	0	.00	0	/3-1	0	-0.2
1946 Cle-A	55	89	9	16	3	0	1	4	7	18	0	1	.180	.240	.247	.487	39	-3	6	2.02	5	P-32,0-12(0-12-0)	6	0.7
1947 Cle-A	47	56	11	18	4	3	2	5	6	9	0	0	.321	.387	.607	.994	179	10	14	9.48	4	P-37/0-2(0-1-1)	13	0.8
1948*Cle-A★	52	119	20	34	9	0	5	21	8	23	0	0	.286	.331	.487	.818	119	13	20	6.32	9	P-43	26	4.5
1949 Cle-A★	46	108	17	29	6	2	7	19	10	20	0	0	.269	.331	.556	.886	135	15	21	6.55	7	P-37	31	4.2
1950 Cle-A★	72	136	21	37	9	1	6	26	13	25	0	0	.272	.340	.485	.825	113	16	24	6.43	5	P-44	25	2.8
1951 Cle-A★	56	102	11	21	4	1	3	13	9	22	0	0	.206	.270	.353	.623	72	4	10	3.35	4	P-42	19	1.2
1952 Cle-A★	54	124	14	28	5	0	2	9	4	21	0	0	.226	.250	.315	.565	60	6	10	2.57	7	P-42	25	3.9
1953 Cle-A★	51	112	12	26	9	1	2	17	7	20	2	0	.232	.277	.384	.661	79	8	13	3.72	8	P-41	22	2.0
1954*Cle-A★	40	98	11	21	4	1	2	10	6	24	0	0	.214	.260	.337	.596	61	5	9	2.80	4	P-36	24	3.0
1955 Cle-A	49	78	11	19	0	0	1	9	13	16	0	0	.244	.352	.282	.634	69	6	9	3.67	2	P-35	15	0.8
1956 Cle-A	43	93	8	18	0	0	5	12	9	21	0	0	.194	.272	.355	.627	63	5	10	3.13	5	P-39	23	3.8
1957 Cle-A	25	46	2	3	1	0	1	1	0	14	0	0	.065	.065	.152	.217	-43	-3	0	.19	3	P-21	3	-1.4
1958 Cle-A	15	13	1	3	0	0	0	1	1	4	0	0	.231	.286	.231	.516	45	0	1	2.51	0	P-11	0	-0.5
Total 15	615	1183	148	274	54	9	37	147	93	241	2	1	.232	.289	.386	.675	82	80	147	4.10	64	P-460/0-14,3-2	232	25.8

• LEMON, Chet Chester Earl "The Jet" Lemon b: 2/12/1955, Jackson, MS BR/TR, 6', 195 lbs. Deb: 9/9/1975 Career OF: 1-1473-454

YEAR TM-L	G	AB	R	H	2B	3B	HR	RBI	BB	SO	SB	CS	AVG	OBP	SLG	OPS	OPS+	BR/A	RC	RC/G	FR	G/POS	WS	TPW
1975 Chi-A	9	35	2	9	2	0	0	1	2	6	1	0	.257	.297	.314	.612	72	-1	4	3.64	-1	/3-6,D-2,0-1	1	-0.2
1976 Chi-A	132	451	46	111	15	5	4	38	28	65	13	7	.246	.300	.328	.629	83	-10	44	3.26	4	*0-131(1-130-0)	8	-1.0
1977 Chi-A	150	553	99	151	38	4	19	67	52	88	8	7	.273	.347	.459	.807	118	13	89	5.65	12	*0-149(0-149-0)	23	2.3
1978 Chi-A★	105	357	51	107	24	6	13	55	39	46	5	9	.300	.381	.510	.891	147	20	65	6.25	3	0-95(0-84-12),D-10	20	2.2
1979 Chi-A★	148	556	79	177	**44**	2	17	86	56	68	7	11	.318	.394	.496	.890	138	28	104	6.84	2	*0-147(0-147-0)/D-1	26	2.7
1980 Chi-A	147	514	76	150	32	6	11	51	71	56	6	6	.292	.390	.442	.832	128	22	90	6.27	-1	*0-139(0-139-0)/D-6,2-1	24	1.9
1981 Chi-A	94	328	50	99	23	6	9	50	33	48	5	8	.302	.388	.491	.879	155	22	60	6.30	-1	0-93(0-93-0)	16	2.1
1982 Det-A	125	436	75	116	20	1	19	52	56	69	1	4	.266	.369	.447	.816	122	14	72	5.66	0	*0-121(0-29-93)/D-1	15	0.9
1983 Det-A	145	491	78	125	21	5	24	69	54	70	0	7	.255	.352	.464	.817	126	15	79	5.46	4	*0-145(0-145-0)	21	1.7
1984*Det-A★	141	509	77	146	34	6	20	76	51	83	5	5	.287	.360	.495	.855	135	23	86	5.98	5	*0-140(0-140-0)/D-1	24	2.6
1985 Det-A	145	517	69	137	28	4	18	68	45	93	0	2	.265	.336	.439	.775	111	7	78	5.39	2	*0-144(0-144-0)	18	0.7
1986 Det-A	126	403	45	101	21	3	12	53	39	53	2	1	.251	.329	.407	.736	99	-0	52	4.32	1	*0-124(0-124-0)	12	-0.1
1987*Det-A	146	470	75	130	30	3	20	75	70	82	0	0	.277	.380	.481	.860	132	23	86	6.40	2	*0-145(0-145-0)	19	2.3
1988 Det-A	144	512	67	135	29	4	17	64	59	65	1	2	.264	.348	.436	.783	122	15	75	5.05	0	*0-144(0-0-144)	19	1.1
1989 Det-A	127	414	45	98	19	2	7	47	46	71	1	5	.237	.325	.343	.668	90	-6	47	3.81	-5	*0-111(0-0-111),D-13	10	-1.5
1990 Det-A	104	322	39	83	16	4	5	32	48	61	3	2	.258	.361	.379	.740	106	4	46	4.88	2	0-96(0-3-94)/D-6	9	0.4
Total 16	1988	6868	973	1875	396	61	215	884	749	1024	58	76	.273	.357	.442	.800	121	188	1078	5.44	30	*0-1925/D-40,3-6,2-1	265	17.9

• LEMON, Jim James Robert Lemon b: 3/23/1928, Covington, VA BR/TR, 6'4", 200 lbs. Deb: 8/20/1950 M/C Career OF: 441-0-464

YEAR TM-L	G	AB	R	H	2B	3B	HR	RBI	BB	SO	SB	CS	AVG	OBP	SLG	OPS	OPS+	BR/A	RC	RC/G	FR	G/POS	WS	TPW
1950 Cle-A	12	34	4	6	1	0	1	1	3	12	0	0	.176	.243	.294	.537	38	-3	2	1.88	-1	0-10(10-0-0)	0	-0.4
1953 Cle-A	16	46	5	8	1	0	1	5	3	15	0	0	.174	.224	.261	.485	31	-5	3	2.09	-1	0-11(11-0-0)/1-2	0	-0.6
1954 Was-A	37	128	12	30	2	3	2	13	9	34	0	0	.234	.285	.344	.628	76	-5	12	3.10	-4	0-33(1-0-32)	1	-1.0
1955 Was-A	10	25	3	5	2	0	1	3	3	4	0	0	.200	.286	.400	.686	87	-1	3	4.16	-1	/0-6(1-0-5)	0	-0.1
1956 Was-A	146	538	77	146	21	**11**	27	96	65	138	2	4	.271	.352	.502	.854	123	15	94	6.09	6	*0-141(12-0-130)	19	1.6
1957 Was-A	137	518	58	147	23	6	17	64	49	94	1	7	.284	.349	.450	.799	118	10	77	5.27	-7	*0-131(0-0-131)/1-3	16	-0.2
1958 Was-A	142	501	65	123	15	9	26	75	50	120	2	4	.246	.315	.467	.782	114	7	71	4.87	-3	*0-137(2-0-135)	15	0.0
1959 Was-A	147	531	73	148	18	3	33	100	46	99	5	2	.279	.337	.510	.848	130	20	91	6.14	1	*0-142(117-0-25)	19	1.3
1960 Was-A★	148	528	81	142	10	1	38	100	67	114	2	0	.269	.359	.508	.866	130	22	99	6.59	1	*0-145(145-0-0)	21	1.6
1961 Min-A	129	423	57	109	26	1	14	52	44	98	1	1	.258	.333	.423	.757	95	-3	59	4.79	2	*0-120(120-0-1)	9	-0.7
1962 Min-A	12	17	1	3	0	0	1	5	3	4	0	0	.176	.300	.353	.653	72	-1	2	2.93	0	/0-3(2-0-1)	0	-0.1
1963 Min-A	7	17	0	2	0	0	0	1	1	5	0	0	.118	.167	.118	.284	-18	-3	0	.68	0	/0-4(4-0-0)	0	-0.3
Phi-N	31	59	6	16	2	0	2	6	8	18	0	0	.271	.358	.407	.765	121	2	9	5.35	0	0-18(16-0-4)	2	0.1
Chi-A	36	80	4	16	0	1	1	8	12	32	0	0	.200	.304	.263	.567	62	-4	7	3.10	-2	1-25	1	-0.7
Yr.	43	97	4	18	0	1	1	9	13	37	0	0	.186	.282	.237	.519	49	-6	8	2.64	-2	1-25/0-4(4-0-0)	1	-1.0
Total 12	1010	3445	446	901	121	35	164	529	363	787	13	18	.262	.335	.460	.795	113	52	530	5.34	-8	0-901/1-30	103	0.5

• LENHARDT, Don Donald Eugene "Footsie" Lenhardt b: 10/4/1922, Alton, IL BR/TR, 6'3", 190 lbs. Deb: 4/18/1950 C Career OF: 291-1-5

YEAR TM-L	G	AB	R	H	2B	3B	HR	RBI	BB	SO	SB	CS	AVG	OBP	SLG	OPS	OPS+	BR/A	RC	RC/G	FR	G/POS	WS	TPW
1950 StL-A	139	480	75	131	22	6	22	81	90	94	3	2	.273	.390	.481	.871	118	14	98	7.27	-6	1-86,0-39(39-0-0),3-10	17	0.3
1951 StL-A	31	103	9	27	3	0	5	18	6	13	1	0	.262	.303	.437	.740	95	-1	14	4.96	-3	0-27(27-0-0)/1-1	3	-0.5
Chi-A	64	199	23	53	9	1	10	45	24	25	1	1	.266	.351	.472	.823	124	6	35	6.14	-1	0-53(53-0-0)/1-2	7	0.1
Yr.	95	302	32	80	12	1	15	63	30	38	2	1	.265	.335	.460	.796	115	5	49	5.75	-4	0-80(80-0-0)/1-3	10	-0.5
1952 Bos-A	30	105	18	31	4	0	7	24	15	18	0	1	.295	.383	.533	.917	142	6	21	7.33	-1	0-27(27-0-0)	5	0.3
Det-A	45	144	18	27	2	1	3	13	28	18	0	1	.188	.320	.278	.598	67	-6	14	3.00	3	0-43(43-0-0)	1	-0.7
StL-A	18	48	5	13	4	1	1	5	4	8	0	0	.271	.327	.458	.785	114	1	7	5.31	0	0-11(10-1-0)/1-2	2	0.0
Yr.	93	297	41	71	10	2	11	42	47	44	0	2	.239	.343	.397	.740	100	0	43	4.78	2	0-81(80-1-0)/1-2	8	-0.4
1953 StL-A	97	303	37	96	15	0	10	35	41	41	1	2	.317	.400	.465	.865	130	14	58	7.14	-2	0-77(72-0-5)/3-6	9	0.7
1954 Bal-A	13	33	2	5	1	0	0	1	3	9	0	0	.152	.222	.182	.404	12	-4	1	1.24	1	/0-7(7-0-0),1-2	0	-0.4
Bos-A	44	66	5	18	4	0	3	17	3	9	0	0	.273	.314	.470	.784	101	-0	9	4.37	0	0-13(13-0-0)/3-1	1	-0.1
Yr.	57	99	7	23	5	0	3	18	6	18	0	0	.232	.283	.374	.657	71	-4	10	3.25	1	0-20(20-0-0)/1-2,3-1	1	-0.4
Total 5	481	1481	192	401	64	9	61	239	214	235	6	7	.271	.365	.450	.815	113	29	258	6.11	-9	0-297/1-93,3-17	45	-0.3

• LENNON, Bill William H. Lennon b: 1848, Brooklyn, NY, 5'7", 145 lbs. Deb: 5/4/1871 M

YEAR TM-L	G	AB	R	H	2B	3B	HR	RBI	BB	SO	SB	CS	AVG	OBP	SLG	OPS	OPS+	BR/A	RC	RC/G	FR	G/POS	WS	TPW
1871 Kek-n	12	48	5	11	3	0	0	5	1	0	1	0	.229	.245	.292	.537	52	-3	4	3.21	-3	C-12/S-2,0-1	....	-0.4
1872 Nat-n	11	54	11	12	1	0	0	6	0	0	0	0	.222	.222	.241	.463	36	-5	3	2.19	-2	C-11/1-1	....	-0.5
1873 Mar-n	5	19	2	4	0	0	0	2	0	0	0	0	.211	.211	.211	.421	33	-1	1	1.76	-1	/1-4,3-1,C-1	....	-0.1
Total 3 n	28	121	18	27	4	0	0	13	1	0	1	0	.223	.230	.256	.486	42	-9	8	2.52	-6	/C-24,1-5,S-2,3-1,0-1	....	-0.9

• LENNON, Bob Robert Albert "Archie" Lennon b: 9/15/1928, Brooklyn, NY BL/TL, 6', 200 lbs. Deb: 9/9/1954 Career OF: 5-5-18

YEAR TM-L	G	AB	R	H	2B	3B	HR	RBI	BB	SO	SB	CS	AVG	OBP	SLG	OPS	OPS+	BR/A	RC	RC/G	FR	G/POS	WS	TPW
1954 NY-N	3	3	0	0	0	0	0	0	0	0	0	0	.000	.000	.000	.000	-99	-1	0	.00	0	....	0	-0.1
1956 NY-N	26	55	3	10	1	0	0	1	4	17	0	0	.182	.237	.200	.437	19	-6	3	1.68	0	0-21(5-1-18)	0	-0.7
1957 Chi-N	9	21	2	3	1	0	1	3	1	9	0	0	.143	.182	.333	.515	35	-2	1	1.98	0	/0-4(0-4-0)	0	-0.2
Total 3	38	79	5	13	2	0	1	4	5	26	0	0	.165	.214	.228	.442	19	-9	4	1.69	0	/0-25	0	-1.0

• LENNON, Patrick Patrick Orlando Lennon b: 4/27/1968, Whiteville, NC BR/TR, 6'2", 200 lbs. Deb: 9/15/1991 Career OF: 40-1-18

YEAR TM-L	G	AB	R	H	2B	3B	HR	RBI	BB	SO	SB	CS	AVG	OBP	SLG	OPS	OPS+	BR/A	RC	RC/G	FR	G/POS	WS	TPW
1991 Sea-A	9	8	2	1	1	0	0	1	3	1	0	0	.125	.364	.250	.614	73	-0	1	3.90	-0	/D-5,0-1	0	0.0
1992 Sea-A	1	2	0	0	0	0	0	0	0	0	0	0	.000	.000	.000	.000	-99	-1	0	.00	0	/1-1	0	-0.1
1996 KC-A	14	30	5	7	3	0	0	1	7	10	0	0	.233	.378	.333	.712	82	-1	4	5.25	-1	0-11(11-0-0)/D-1	0	-0.2
1997 Oak-A	56	116	14	34	6	1	1	14	15	35	0	1	.293	.374	.388	.762	102	0	17	5.27	-2	0-36(23-1-12),D-17	3	-0.4
1998 Tor-A	2	4	1	2	2	0	0	0	0	1	0	0	.500	.500	1.000	1.500	276	1	2	27.00	0	/0-2(0-0-2)	0	0.1
1999 Tor-A	9	29	3	6	2	0	1	6	2	12	0	0	.207	.281	.379	.661	65	-2	3	3.89	2	/0-8(5-0-4)	1	0.0
Total 6	91	189	25	50	14	1	2	22	27	59	0	1	.265	.359	.381	.740	93	-1	28	5.21	-2	/0-58,D-23,1-1	4	-0.6

• LENNOX, Ed James Edgar "Eggie" Lennox b: 11/3/1885, Camden, NJ d: 10/26/1939, Camden, NJ BR/TR, 5'10", 174 lbs. Deb: 8/8/1906

YEAR TM-L	G	AB	R	H	2B	3B	HR	RBI	BB	SO	SB	CS	AVG	OBP	SLG	OPS	OPS+	BR/A	RC	RC/G	FR	G/POS	WS	TPW
1906 Phi-A	6	17	1	1	1	0	0	0	1	....	0	....	.059	.111	.118	.229	-28	-3	0	.46	4	/3-6	1	0.2
1909 Bro-N	126	435	33	114	18	9	2	44	47	....	11	....	.262	.337	.359	.695	120	10	56	4.37	-5	*3-121	15	0.9
1910 Bro-N	110	367	19	95	19	4	3	32	36	39	7	....	.259	.333	.357	.690	104	2	46	4.23	-11	*3-100	11	-0.7
1912 Chi-N	27	81	13	19	4	1	1	16	12	10	1	....	.235	.347	.346	.693	90	-1	11	3.99	-1	3-24	2	-0.1
1914 Pit-F	124	430	71	134	25	10	11	84	71	38	19	....	.312	.414	.493	.907	167	40	93	7.62	-14	*3-123	24	3.1

YEAR TM-L	G	AB	R	H	2B	3B	HR	RBI	BB	SO	SB	CS	AVG	OBP	SLG	OPS	OPS+	BR/A	RC	RC/G	FR	G/POS	WS	TPW
1915 Pit-F	55	53	1	16	3	1	1	9	7	12	0	....	.302	.383	.453	.836	140	3	9	6.12	2	/3-3	2	0.5
Total 6	**448**	**1383**	**138**	**379**	**70**	**25**	**18**	**185**	**174**	**99**	**38**	**....**	**.274**	**.361**	**.400**	**.760**	**128**	**52**	**215**	**5.27**	**-26**	**3-377**	**55**	**3.9**
• LENTINE, Jim	James Matthew Lentine b: 7/16/1954, Los Angeles, CA BR/TR, 6', 175 lbs. Deb: 9/3/1978 Career OF: 50-13-10																							
1978 StL-N	8	11	1	2	0	0	0	1	0	0	1	0	.182	.250	.182	.432	23	-1	1	2.09	0	/0-3(2-0-1)	0	-0.1
1979 StL-N	11	23	2	9	1	0	0	1	3	6	0	1	.391	.462	.435	.896	145	1	5	8.21	1	/0-8(3-2-3)	1	0.2
1980 StL-N	9	10	1	1	0	0	0	1	0	2	0	0	.100	.100	.100	.200	-43	-2	0	.30	0	/0-6(5-1-0)	0	-0.2
Det-A	67	161	19	42	8	1	1	17	28	30	2	1	.261	.377	.342	.719	96	1	23	4.87	-1	0-55(40-10-6)/D-9	5	-0.2
Total 3	**95**	**205**	**23**	**54**	**9**	**1**	**1**	**20**	**31**	**38**	**3**	**2**	**.263**	**.368**	**.332**	**.700**	**92**	**-1**	**28**	**4.77**	**0**	**/0-72,D-9**	**6**	**-0.4**
• LEON, Eddie	Eduardo Antonio Leon b: 8/11/1946, Tucson, AZ BR/TR, 6', 175 lbs. Deb: 9/9/1968																							
1968 Cle-A	6	1	0	0	0	0	0	0	0	1	0	0	.000	.000	.000	.000	-102	-0	0	.00	0	/S-6	0	0.0
1969 Cle-A	64	213	20	51	6	0	3	19	19	37	2	2	.239	.302	.310	.612	69	-9	20	3.19	2	S-64	5	0.0
1970 Cle-A	152	549	58	136	20	4	10	56	47	89	1	2	.248	.309	.353	.663	78	-17	61	3.63	4	*2-141,S-23/3-1	13	-0.1
1971 Cle-A	131	429	35	112	12	2	4	35	34	69	3	5	.261	.317	.326	.643	75	-15	41	3.18	0	*2-107,S-24	7	-0.6
1972 Cle-A	89	225	14	45	2	1	4	16	20	47	0	2	.200	.268	.271	.539	59	-12	15	2.03	2	2-36,S-35	3	-0.5
1973 Chi-A	127	399	37	91	10	3	3	30	34	103	1	5	.228	.294	.291	.584	63	-21	34	2.68	-8	*S-122/2-3	6	-1.5
1974 Chi-A	31	46	1	5	1	0	0	3	2	12	0	0	.109	.146	.130	.276	-20	-7	1	.28	1	S-21/2-7,3-2,D-1	1	-0.5
1975 NY-A	1	0	0	0	0	0	0	0	0	0	0	0	....	....	....	....	-103	0	0	....	-1	/S-1	0	-0.1
Total 8	**601**	**1862**	**165**	**440**	**51**	**10**	**24**	**159**	**156**	**358**	**7**	**16**	**.236**	**.298**	**.313**	**.611**	**68**	**-81**	**171**	**2.96**	**1**	**S-296,2-294/3-3,D-1**	**35**	**-3.2**
• LEON, Jose	Jose Geraldo (Vega) Leon b: 12/8/1976, Cayey, Puerto Rico BR/TR, 6', 175 lbs. Deb: 6/16/2002																							
2002 Bal-A	36	89	8	22	2	0	3	10	3	20	1	0	.247	.280	.371	.650	75	-3	9	3.49	0	1-17,3-12/D-2,0-2(2-0-0)	1	-0.5
2003 Bal-A	21	54	6	13	1	0	0	0	3	18	0	0	.241	.305	.259	.564	53	-4	4	2.83	0	3-10/1-7,D-2	0	-0.4
Total 2	**57**	**143**	**14**	**35**	**3**	**0**	**3**	**10**	**6**	**38**	**1**	**0**	**.245**	**.289**	**.329**	**.618**	**66**	**-7**	**13**	**3.24**	**0**	**/1-24,3-22,D-4,0-2**	**1**	**-0.8**
• LEONARD,	Leonard Deb: 9/12/1892																							
1892 StL-N	1	0	0	0	0	0	0	0	1	0	1	....	....	1.000	....	1.000	219	0	1	∞	0	/0-1	0	0.0
• LEONARD, Andy	Andrew Jackson Leonard b: 6/1/1846, County Cavan, Ireland d: 8/21/1903, Boston, MA BR/TR, 5'7", 168 lbs. Deb: 5/5/1871 U NA OF: 218-0-0 Career OF: 132-0-0																							
1871 Oly-n	31	148	33	43	8	3	0	30	3	1	14	3	.291	.305	.385	.690	102	2	22	6.47	-3	2-19,0-11(11-0-0)/S-1	....	-0.1
1872 Bos-n	46	240	57	84	7	1	2	43	0	2	8	5	.350	.350	.413	.763	127	5	38	7.39	-1	*0-38(38-0-0)/3-6,2-4,S-1	....	0.4
1873 Bos-n	58	302	81	95	12	7	0	61	4	0	5	6	.315	.324	.401	.724	105	-2	42	5.98	0	*0-45(45-0-0),2-12/1-2,S-1	....	-0.1
1874 Bos-n	71	339	68	108	18	4	0	51	2	2	11	3	.319	.323	.395	.718	122	7	48	6.15	-3	*0-51(51-0-0),2-11,S-11	....	0.4
1875 Bos-n	80	396	87	127	14	6	1	74	2	6	14	8	.321	.324	.394	.718	143	15	56	6.01	0	*0-73(73-0-0)/3-3,S-3,2-2	....	1.4
1876 Bos-N	64	307	53	85	10	2	0	27	4	6	....	....	.277	.290	.327	.617	103	1	29	3.78	-1	0-35(35-0-0),2-30	10	-0.1
1877 Bos-N	58	272	46	78	5	0	0	27	5	5	....	....	.287	.300	.305	.605	88	-4	25	3.61	-2	0-37(37-0-0),S-21	8	-0.7
1878 Bos-N	60	262	41	68	8	5	0	16	3	19	....	....	.260	.268	.328	.596	88	-4	24	3.35	-7	*0-60(60-0-0)	7	-1.4
1880 Cin-N	33	133	15	28	3	0	1	17	8	11	....	....	.211	.255	.256	.511	75	-3	9	2.33	-6	S-23,3-10	2	-0.8
Total 5 n	**286**	**1425**	**326**	**457**	**59**	**21**	**3**	**259**	**11**	**11**	**52**	**25**	**.321**	**.326**	**.398**	**.724**	**123**	**28**	**207**	**6.31**	**-6**	**0-218/2-48,S-17,3-9,1-2**	**....**	**1.9**
Total 4	**215**	**974**	**155**	**259**	**26**	**7**	**1**	**87**	**20**	**41**			**.266**	**.282**	**.311**	**.593**	**91**	**-11**	**87**	**3.40**	**-16**	**0-132/S-44,2-30,3-10**	**27**	**-2.9**
• LEONARD, Jeffrey	Jeffrey Leonard b: 9/22/1955, Philadelphia, PA BR/TR, 6'2", 200 lbs. Deb: 9/2/1977 Career OF: 896-103-171																							
1977 LA-N	11	10	1	3	0	1	0	2	1	4	0	0	.300	.364	.500	.864	130	0	1	4.84	0	0-10(6-0-4)	0	0.0
1978 Hou-N	8	26	2	10	2	0	0	4	1	2	0	1	.385	.407	.462	.869	154	1	5	7.21	1	/0-8(4-2-2)	1	0.2
1979 Hou-N	134	411	47	119	15	5	0	47	46	68	23	10	.290	.364	.350	.714	102	3	53	4.49	-8	*0-123(4-22-100)	14	-1.1
1980*Hou-N	88	216	29	46	7	5	3	20	19	46	4	1	.213	.277	.333	.610	75	-7	19	2.79	-1	0-56(3-9-44),1-11	3	-1.2
1981 Hou-N	7	18	1	3	1	1	0	3	0	4	1	0	.167	.167	.333	.500	41	-1	1	1.88	0	/1-2,0-2(0-0-2)	0	-0.2
SF-N	37	127	20	39	11	3	4	26	12	21	4	2	.307	.371	.535	.907	158	9	23	6.57	0	0-28(8-19-4)/1-5	7	0.8
Yr.	44	145	21	42	12	4	4	29	12	25	5	2	.290	.348	.510	.858	144	8	24	5.90	0	0-30(8-19-6)/1-7	7	0.7
1982 SF-N	80	278	32	72	16	1	9	49	19	65	18	5	.259	.311	.421	.732	103	2	34	4.03	-5	0-74(56-17-2)/1-1	7	-0.6
1983 SF-N	139	516	74	144	17	7	21	87	35	116	26	7	.279	.326	.461	.787	120	14	77	5.26	2	*0-136(127-12-2)	19	1.0
1984 SF-N	136	514	76	155	27	2	21	86	47	123	17	7	.302	.360	.484	.845	140	26	87	6.15	0	*0-131(116-18-4)	20	2.1
1985 SF-N	133	507	49	122	20	3	17	62	21	107	11	6	.241	.272	.393	.665	88	-12	47	3.09	-2	*0-126(125-3-0)	8	-2.1
1986 SF-N	89	341	48	95	11	3	6	42	20	62	16	3	.279	.324	.381	.705	99	1	44	4.63	-2	0-87(87-0-0)	10	-0.6
1987*SF-N★	131	503	70	141	29	4	19	63	21	68	16	7	.280	.312	.467	.779	108	3	66	4.56	-1	*0-127(127-1-0)	12	-0.3
1988 SF-N	44	160	12	41	8	1	2	20	9	24	7	5	.256	.296	.356	.652	90	-3	15	3.07	-2	0-43(43-0-0)	4	-0.7
Mil-A	94	374	45	88	19	0	8	44	16	68	10	4	.235	.272	.350	.623	72	-15	34	2.97	0	0-91(91-0-0)/D-2	4	-1.8
1989 Sea-A★	150	566	69	144	20	1	24	93	38	125	6	1	.254	.307	.420	.728	100	-1	72	4.37	1	*D-123,0-26(25-0-1)	10	-0.6
1990 Sea-A	134	478	39	120	20	0	10	75	37	97	4	2	.251	.309	.356	.665	84	-10	49	3.38	-4	0-79(74-0-6),D-48	8	-1.9
Total 14	**1415**	**5045**	**614**	**1342**	**223**	**37**	**144**	**723**	**342**	**1000**	**163**	**61**	**.266**	**.316**	**.411**	**.726**	**103**	**9**	**627**	**4.26**	**-22**	***0-1147,D-173/1-19**	**127**	**-6.9**
• LEONARD, Joe	Joseph Howard Leonard b: 11/15/1894, West Chicago, IL d: 5/1/1920, Washington, DC BL/TR, 5'7.5", 156 lbs. Deb: 5/7/1914 Career OF: 1-0-1																							
1914 Pit-N	53	126	17	25	2	2	0	4	12	21	4	....	.198	.268	.246	.514	56	-7	10	2.31	-2	3-38/S-1	1	-0.9
1916 Cle-A	3	2	1	0	0	0	0	0	0	1	0	....	.000	.000	.000	.000	-94	-0	0	.00	-0	/2-1	0	-0.1
Was-A	42	168	20	46	7	0	0	14	22	23	4	....	.274	.358	.315	.673	103	1	20	4.31	-5	3-42	5	-0.3
Yr.	45	170	21	46	7	0	0	14	22	24	4	....	.271	.354	.312	.666	101	1	20	4.24	-5	3-42/2-1	5	-0.3
1917 Was-A	99	297	30	57	6	7	0	23	45	40	6	....	.192	.302	.259	.562	72	-8	25	2.62	-1	3-68,1-19/0-1,S-1	6	-0.8
1919 Was-A	71	198	26	51	8	3	2	20	20	28	3	....	.258	.329	.359	.687	94	-2	23	4.04	-4	2-28,3-25/1-4,0-1	5	-0.5
1920 Was-A	1	0	0	0	0	0	0	0	0	0	0	0	....	....	....	....	-103	0	0	....	0	....	0	0.0
Total 5	**269**	**791**	**94**	**179**	**23**	**12**	**2**	**61**	**99**	**113**	**17**	**0**	**.226**	**.315**	**.293**	**.608**	**81**	**-16**	**78**	**3.22**	**-13**	**3-173/2-29,1-23,0-2,S-2**	**17**	**-2.6**
• LEONARD, Mark	Mark David Leonard b: 8/14/1964, Mountain View, CA BL/TR, 6'1", 195 lbs. Deb: 7/21/1990 Career OF: 66-0-26																							
1990 SF-N	11	17	3	3	1	0	1	2	3	8	0	0	.176	.300	.412	.712	97	-0	2	4.50	0	/0-7(2-0-5)	0	0.0
1991 SF-N	64	129	14	31	7	1	2	14	12	25	0	1	.240	.310	.357	.666	90	-2	14	3.60	-1	0-34(24-0-12)	3	-0.4
1992 SF-N	55	128	13	30	7	0	4	16	16	31	0	1	.234	.333	.383	.716	108	1	17	4.34	1	0-37(33-0-4)	4	0.2
1993 Bal-A	10	15	1	1	1	0	0	3	3	7	0	0	.067	.222	.133	.356	-2	-2	1	1.31	0	/0-4(4-0-0),D-3	0	-0.3
1994 SF-N	14	11	2	4	1	1	0	2	3	2	0	0	.364	.500	.636	1.136	203	2	4	15.00	0	/0-2(2-0-0)	1	0.2
1995 SF-N	14	21	4	4	1	0	1	4	5	2	0	0	.190	.346	.381	.727	94	-0	3	4.97	0	/0-6(1-0-5)	1	-0.1
Total 6	**168**	**321**	**37**	**73**	**18**	**2**	**8**	**41**	**42**	**75**	**0**	**2**	**.227**	**.324**	**.371**	**.695**	**97**	**-1**	**41**	**4.18**	**-1**	**/0-90,D-3**	**9**	**-0.4**
• LEOVICH, John	John Joseph Leovich b: 5/5/1918, Portland, OR d: 2/3/2000, Lincoln City, OR BR/TR, 6'.5", 200 lbs. Deb: 5/1/1941																							
1941 Phi-A	1	2	0	1	1	0	0	0	0	0	0	0	.500	.500	1.000	1.500	295	1	0	.00	0	/C-1	0	0.0
• LEPCIO, Ted	Thaddeus Stanley Lepcio b: 7/28/1930, Utica, NY BR/TR, 5'10", 177 lbs. Deb: 4/15/1952																							
1952 Bos-A	84	274	34	72	17	2	5	26	24	41	3	3	.263	.329	.394	.723	93	-3	37	4.67	0	2-57,3-25/S-1	8	0.0
1953 Bos-A	66	161	17	38	4	2	4	11	17	24	0	0	.236	.313	.360	.673	77	-5	18	3.81	5	2-34,S-20,3-11	4	0.3
1954 Bos-A	116	398	42	102	19	4	8	45	42	62	3	4	.256	.332	.384	.716	86	-8	51	4.36	-4	2-80,3-24,S-14	10	-0.6
1955 Bos-A	51	134	19	31	9	0	6	15	12	36	1	1	.231	.313	.433	.746	91	-2	18	4.65	-3	3-45	3	-0.5
1956 Bos-A	83	284	34	74	10	0	15	51	30	77	1	3	.261	.338	.454	.792	96	-4	44	5.33	3	2-57,3-22	8	0.3
1957 Bos-A	79	232	24	56	10	2	9	37	29	61	0	0	.241	.328	.418	.746	97	-1	32	4.80	-7	2-68	6	-0.3
1958 Bos-A	50	136	10	27	3	0	6	14	12	47	0	1	.199	.268	.353	.621	65	-7	13	3.06	-5	2-40	2	-1.0
1959 Bos-A	3	3	1	1	1	0	0	1	0	2	0	0	.333	.333	.667	1.000	160	0	1	9.00	0	/2-1	0	0.0
Det-A	76	215	25	60	8	0	7	24	17	49	2	0	.279	.332	.414	.746	98	-0	28	4.68	2	S-35,2-24,3-11	6	0.6
Yr.	79	218	26	61	9	0	7	25	17	51	2	0	.280	.332	.417	.749	99	-0	29	4.73	2	S-35,2-25,3-11	6	0.6
1960 Phi-N	69	141	16	32	7	0	2	8	17	41	0	3	.227	.319	.319	.638	75	-6	14	3.14	-6	3-50,S-14/2-5	2	-1.2
1961 Chi-A	5	2	0	0	0	0	0	0	1	0	0	0	.000	.333	.000	.333	-3	-0	0	.00	-1	/3-1	0	-0.1
Min-A	47	112	11	19	3	1	7	19	8	31	1	0	.170	.231	.402	.633	62	-7	10	2.90	-1	3-35,2-22/S-6	1	-0.6

YEAR TM-L	G	AB	R	H	2B	3B	HR	RBI	BB	SO	SB	CS	AVG	OBP	SLG	OPS	OPS+	BR/A	RC	RC/G	FR	G/POS	WS	TPW
Yr.	52	114	11	19	3	1	7	19	9	31	1	0	.167	.234	.395	.629	61	-7	10	2.81	-2	3-36,2-22/S-6	1	-0.7
Total 10	729	2092	233	512	91	11	69	251	209	471	11	15	.245	.319	.398	.717	87	-43	266	4.32	-18	2-388,3-224/S-90	50	-3.1
• LEPINE, Pete	Louis Joseph LePine b: 9/5/1876, Montreal, Canada d: 12/3/1949, Woonsocket, RI BL/TL, 5'10", 142 lbs. Deb: 7/21/1902																							
1902 Det-A	30	96	8	20	3	2	1	19	8	....	1	....	.208	.276	.313	.589	62	-5	9	3.06	1	0-19(0-0-19)/1-8	1	-0.4
• LEPPERT, Don	Don Eugene "Tiger" Leppert b: 11/20/1930, Memphis, TN BL/TR, 5'8", 175 lbs. Deb: 4/11/1955																							
1955 Bal-A	40	70	6	8	0	1	0	2	9	10	1	1	.114	.215	.143	.358	-2	-10	2	.89	-6	2-35	0	-1.5
• LEPPERT, Don	Donald George Leppert b: 10/19/1931, Indianapolis, IN BR/TR, 6'2", 220 lbs. Deb: 6/18/1961 C/U																							
1961 Pit-N	22	60	6	16	2	1	3	5	1	11	0	0	.267	.279	.483	.762	97	-1	5	2.80	-1	C-21	1	-0.1
1962 Pit-N	45	139	14	37	6	1	3	18	12	21	0	1	.266	.329	.388	.717	92	-2	16	3.93	-2	C-44	5	-0.2
1963 Was-A★	73	211	20	50	11	0	6	24	20	29	0	0	.237	.306	.374	.680	90	-3	23	3.63	-2	C-60	4	-0.2
1964 Was-A	50	122	6	19	3	0	3	12	11	32	0	0	.156	.226	.254	.480	33	-11	7	1.73	0	C-43	1	-1.0
Total 4	190	532	46	122	22	2	15	59	44	93	0	1	.229	.291	.363	.653	78	-17	51	3.14	-6	C-168	11	-1.6
• LERCHEN, Dutch	Bertram Roe Lerchen b: 4/4/1889, Detroit, MI d: 1/7/1962, Detroit, MI BR/TR, 5'8", 160 lbs. Deb: 8/14/1910																							
1910 Bos-A	6	15	1	0	0	0	0	0	1	....	0	....	.000	.063	.000	.063	-78	-3	0	.00	-1	/S-6	0	-0.5
• LERCHEN, George	George Edward Lerchen b: 12/1/1922, Detroit, MI BB/TR, 5'11", 175 lbs. Deb: 4/15/1952 Career OF: 0-4-4																							
1952 Det-A	14	32	1	5	1	0	1	3	7	10	1	0	.156	.308	.281	.589	64	-1	3	3.15	0	/0-7(0-3-4)	0	-0.2
1953 Cin-N	22	17	2	5	1	0	0	2	5	6	0	0	.294	.455	.353	.807	113	1	3	7.62	-0	/0-1	1	0.1
Total 2	36	49	3	10	2	0	1	5	12	16	1	0	.204	.361	.306	.667	82	-0	7	4.49	0	/0-8	1	-0.1
• LERIAN, Walt	Walter Irvin "Peck" Lerian b: 2/10/1903, Baltimore, MD d: 10/22/1929, Baltimore, MD BR/TR, 5'11", 170 lbs. Deb: 4/16/1928																							
1928 Phi-N	96	239	28	65	16	2	2	25	41	29	1	....	.272	.385	.381	.766	97	1	37	5.26	6	C-74	7	1.1
1929 Phi-N	105	273	28	61	13	2	6	25	53	37	0	....	.223	.354	.352	.705	71	-12	36	4.37	5	*C-103	7	-0.1
Total 2	201	512	56	126	29	4	8	50	94	66	1	....	.246	.368	.365	.733	83	-11	73	4.78	11	C-177	14	1.0
• LESHER, Brian	Brian Herbert Lesher b: 3/5/1971, Wilrijk, Belgium BR/TL, 6'5", 205 lbs. Deb: 8/25/1996 Career OF: 52-0-19																							
1996 Oak-A	26	82	11	19	3	0	5	16	5	17	0	0	.232	.284	.451	.735	84	-3	10	4.08	0	0-25(14-0-14)/1-1	1	-0.3
1997 Oak-A	46	131	17	30	4	1	4	16	9	30	4	1	.229	.279	.366	.645	68	-6	13	3.20	0	0-32(31-0-3)/1-3,D-3	1	-0.8
1998 Oak-A	7	7	0	1	1	0	0	1	0	3	0	0	.143	.143	.286	.429	8	-1	0	1.29	1	/0-4(4-0-0),1-1	0	0.0
2000 Sea-A	5	5	1	4	1	1	0	3	1	0	1	0	.800	.833	1.400	2.233	479	3	6	175.05	0	/1-4,D-1	1	0.3
2002 Tor-A	24	38	2	5	1	0	0	2	4	15	0	0	.132	.214	.158	.372	1	-5	1	.92	1	1-12/0-5(3-0-2),D-3	0	-0.5
Total 5	108	263	31	59	10	2	9	38	19	65	5	1	.224	.279	.380	.659	70	-12	31	3.83	2	/0-66,1-21,D-7	3	-1.3
• LESLIE, Roy	Roy Reid Leslie b: 8/23/1894, Bailey, TX d: 4/9/1972, Sherman, TX BR/TR, 6'1", 175 lbs. Deb: 9/6/1917																							
1917 Chi-N	7	19	1	4	0	0	0	1	1	5	1	....	.211	.250	.211	.461	39	-1	1	1.94	-0	/1-6	0	-0.2
1919 StL-N	12	24	2	5	1	0	0	4	4	3	0	....	.208	.321	.250	.571	78	-0	2	2.50	0	/1-9	0	-0.1
1922 Phi-N	141	513	44	139	23	2	6	50	37	49	3	7	.271	.320	.359	.679	68	-26	58	3.88	-7	*1-139	4	-4.0
Total 3	160	556	47	148	24	2	6	55	42	57	4	7	.266	.318	.349	.667	68	-28	61	3.75	-7	1-154	4	-4.2
• LESLIE, Sam	Samuel Andrew "Sambo" Leslie b: 7/26/1905, Moss Point, MS d: 1/21/1979, Pascagola, MS BL/TL, 6', 192 lbs. Deb: 10/6/1929																							
1929 NY-N	1	1	0	0	0	0	0	1	0	0	0	....	.000	.000	.000	.000	-100	-0	0	.00	-0	/0-1	0	0.0
1930 NY-N	2	2	0	1	0	0	0	0	0	1	0	....	.500	.500	.500	1.000	146	0	0	12.09	0	....	0	0.0
1931 NY-N	53	53	11	16	4	0	3	5	1	2	3	....	.302	.315	.547	.862	131	2	9	6.30	-0	/1-6	2	0.2
1932 NY-N	77	75	5	22	4	0	1	15	2	5	0	....	.293	.329	.387	.716	94	-1	10	4.72	0	/1-2	2	-0.1
1933 NY-N	40	137	21	44	12	3	3	27	12	9	0	....	.321	.380	.518	.898	157	10	27	7.49	-1	1-35	8	0.6
Bro-N	96	364	41	104	11	4	5	46	23	14	1	....	.286	.340	.379	.719	110	5	45	4.36	-4	1-95	9	-0.8
Yr.	136	501	62	148	23	7	8	73	35	23	1	....	.295	.351	.417	.768	123	15	72	5.17	-4	*1-130	17	-0.2
1934 Bro-N	146	546	75	181	29	6	9	102	69	34	5	....	.332	.409	.456	.865	138	32	108	7.70	0	*1-138	22	1.9
1935 Bro-N	142	520	72	160	30	7	5	93	55	19	4	....	.308	.379	.421	.800	117	15	87	6.28	-2	*1-138	18	0.0
1936★NY-N	117	417	49	123	19	5	6	54	23	16	0	....	.295	.335	.408	.743	100	-1	55	4.68	-4	1-99	10	-1.4
1937★NY-N	72	191	25	59	7	2	3	30	20	12	1	....	.309	.380	.414	.794	114	4	30	5.73	2	1-44	6	0.2
1938 NY-N	76	154	12	39	7	1	1	16	11	6	0	....	.253	.307	.331	.638	75	-5	16	3.56	-2	1-32	2	-1.0
Total 10	822	2460	311	749	123	28	36	389	216	118	14	....	.304	.366	.421	.787	117	61	385	5.79	-11	1-589/0-1	79	-0.4
• LETCHAS, Charlie	Charlie Letchas b: 10/3/1915, Thomasville, GA d: 3/14/1995, Tampa, FL BR/TR, 5'10", 150 lbs. Deb: 9/16/1939																							
1939 Phi-N	12	44	2	10	2	0	1	3	1	2	0	....	.227	.244	.341	.585	58	-3	3	2.29	0	2-12	0	-0.2
1941 Was-A	2	8	0	1	0	0	0	1	1	1	0	0	.125	.222	.125	.347	-6	-1	0	1.10	0	/2-2	0	-0.1
1944 Phi-N	116	396	29	94	8	0	0	33	32	27	0	....	.237	.298	.258	.555	59	-21	30	2.56	-5	2-47,3-32,S-29	4	-2.1
1946 Phi-N	6	13	1	3	0	0	0	0	1	1	0	....	.231	.286	.231	.516	49	-1	1	2.51	0	/2-4	0	0.0
Total 4	136	461	32	108	10	0	1	37	35	31	0	0	.234	.291	.262	.554	58	-26	35	2.50	-5	/2-65,3-32,S-29	4	-2.5
• LETCHER, Tom	Frederick Thomas Letcher b: 1/1868, Bryan, OH BL, 6' Deb: 9/27/1891																							
1891 Mil-a	6	21	3	4	1	0	0	2	0	1	1	....	.190	.190	.238	.429	19	-3	1	1.83	0	/0-6(1-0-5)	0	-0.2
• LEUTZ,	Leutz Deb: 5/7/1872																							
1872 Eck-n	4	12	2	1	0	0	0	0	0	0	0	0	.083	.083	.083	.167	-57	-2	0	.24	-1	/C-4	....	-0.2
• LEVAN, Jesse	Jesse Roy Levan b: 7/15/1926, Reading, PA d: 11/30/1998, Reading, PA BL/TR, 6', 172 lbs. Deb: 9/27/1947																							
1947 Phi-N	2	9	3	4	0	0	0	1	0	0	0	....	.444	.444	.444	.889	142	1	2	9.60	-0	/0-2(2-0-0)	0	0.0
1954 Was-A	7	10	1	3	0	0	0	0	0	0	0	0	.300	.300	.300	.600	68	-0	1	3.47	-1	/3-4,1-1	0	-0.2
1955 Was-A	16	16	1	3	0	0	1	4	0	2	0	0	.188	.188	.375	.563	51	-1	1	1.45	0	....	0	-0.1
Total 3	25	35	5	10	0	0	1	5	0	2	0	0	.286	.286	.371	.657	79	-1	3	3.56	-1	/3-4,0-2,1-1	0	-0.3
• LEVEY, Jim	James Julius Levey b: 9/13/1906, Pittsburgh, PA d: 3/14/1970, Dallas, TX BB/TR, 5'10.5", 154 lbs. Deb: 9/17/1930																							
1930 StL-A	8	37	7	9	2	0	0	3	3	2	0	0	.243	.300	.297	.597	50	-3	3	3.21	1	/S-8	1	-0.1
1931 StL-A	139	498	53	104	19	2	5	38	35	83	13	8	.209	.264	.285	.549	43	-41	38	2.48	-24	*S-139	3	-5.1
1932 StL-A	152	568	59	159	30	8	4	63	21	48	6	4	.280	.310	.382	.692	74	-23	66	4.15	-23	*S-152	10	-3.2
1933 StL-A	141	529	43	103	10	4	2	36	26	68	4	6	.195	.237	.240	.477	25	-60	30	1.81	-14	*S-138	5	-6.0
Total 4	440	1632	162	375	61	14	11	140	85	201	23	18	.230	.272	.305	.576	48	-127	138	2.81	-60	S-437	19	-14.5
• LEVIS, Charlie	Charles H. Levis b: 6/21/1860, St. Louis, MO d: 10/16/1926, St. Louis, MO BR Deb: 4/17/1884 U																							
1884 Bal-U	87	373	59	85	11	4	6	....	3	....	....	....	.228	.234	.327	.561	80	-10	29	2.85	-1	*1-87	7	-1.7
Was-U	1	3	0	0	0	0	0	....	0	....	....	....	.000	.000	.000	.000	-103	-1	0	.00	0	/1-1	0	-0.1
Yr.	88	376	59	85	11	4	6	....	3	....	....	....	.226	.232	.324	.557	78	-11	29	2.82	-1	*1-88	7	-1.7
Ind-a	3	10	0	2	0	0	0	0	0	....	....	....	.200	.200	.200	.400	32	-1	0	1.41	0	/1-3	0	-0.1
1885 Bal-a	1	4	2	1	0	0	0	0	0	....	....	....	.250	.400	.250	.650	110	0	0	3.69	0	/1-1	0	0.0
Total 2	92	390	61	88	11	4	6	0	3	....	....	....	.226	.234	.321	.554	77	-12	30	2.79	-1	/1-92	7	-1.8
• LEVIS, Jesse	Jesse Levis b: 4/14/1968, Philadelphia, PA BL/TR, 5'9", 180 lbs. Deb: 4/24/1992																							
1992 Cle-A	28	43	2	12	4	0	1	3	0	5	0	0	.279	.279	.442	.721	101	-0	5	4.10	0	C-21/D-1	1	0.0
1993 Cle-A	31	63	7	11	2	0	0	4	2	10	0	0	.175	.200	.206	.406	9	-8	3	1.41	1	C-29	1	-0.6
1994 Cle-A	1	1	0	1	0	0	0	0	0	0	0	0	1.000	1.000	1.000	2.000	417	0	1	∞	0	....	0	0.0
1995 Cle-A	12	18	1	6	2	0	0	3	1	0	0	0	.333	.368	.444	.813	109	0	3	4.52	1	C-12	1	0.1
1996 Mil-A	104	233	27	55	6	1	1	21	38	15	0	0	.236	.348	.283	.631	60	-13	25	3.59	2	C-90/D-6	5	-0.6
1997 Mil-A	99	200	19	57	7	0	1	19	24	17	1	0	.285	.364	.335	.699	84	-4	26	4.58	1	C-78/D-8	7	0.0
1998 Mil-N	22	37	4	13	0	0	0	4	7	6	1	0	.351	.478	.351	.830	123	2	6	6.04	-1	C-14	1	0.2
1999 Cle-A	10	26	0	4	0	0	0	3	1	6	0	0	.154	.214	.154	.368	-4	-4	1	.98	0	/C-9	0	-0.3

YEAR TM-L	G	AB	R	H	2B	3B	HR	RBI	BB	SO	SB	CS	AVG	OBP	SLG	OPS	OPS+	BR/A	RC	RC/G	FR	G/POS	WS	TPW
2001 Mil-N	12	33	6	8	2	0	0	3	3	7	0	0	.242	.306	.303	.609	60	-2	3	3.11	-1	C-11	0	-0.3
Total 9	319	654	66	167	23	1	3	60	76	66	2	0	.255	.338	.307	.646	68	-28	73	3.71	2	C-264/D-15	16	-1.3

• LEVY, Ed Edward Clarence Levy b: 10/28/1916, Birmingham, AL BR/TR, 6'5.5", 190 lbs. Deb: 4/16/1940

YEAR TM-L	G	AB	R	H	2B	3B	HR	RBI	BB	SO	SB	CS	AVG	OBP	SLG	OPS	OPS+	BR/A	RC	RC/G	FR	G/POS	WS	TPW
1940 Phi-N	1	1	0	0	0	0	0	0	0	0	0	....	.000	.000	.000	.000	-104	-0	0	.00	0	....	0	0.0
1942 NY-A	13	41	5	5	0	0	0	3	4	5	1	0	.122	.200	.122	.322	-9	-6	1	.74	0	1-13	0	-0.7
1944 NY-A	40	153	12	37	11	2	4	29	6	19	1	1	.242	.270	.418	.689	92	-3	17	3.76	-3	0-36(36-0-0)	3	-0.8
Total 3	54	195	17	42	11	2	4	32	10	24	2	1	.215	.254	.354	.608	70	-9	18	3.03	-2	/0-36,1-13	3	-1.5

• LEWIS, Lewis b: Brooklyn, NY Deb: 7/12/1890

YEAR TM-L	G	AB	R	H	2B	3B	HR	RBI	BB	SO	SB	CS	AVG	OBP	SLG	OPS	OPS+	BR/A	RC	RC/G	FR	G/POS	WS	TPW
1890 Buf-P	1	5	1	1	0	0	0	0	0	0	0	....	.200	.200	.200	.400	8	-0	0	1.38	0	/0-1,P-1	0	-1.5

• LEWIS, Allan Allan Sydney "The Panamanian Express" Lewis b: 12/12/1941, Colon, Panama BB/TR, 6', 170 lbs. Deb: 4/11/1967 Career OF: 9-0-1

YEAR TM-L	G	AB	R	H	2B	3B	HR	RBI	BB	SO	SB	CS	AVG	OBP	SLG	OPS	OPS+	BR/A	RC	RC/G	FR	G/POS	WS	TPW
1967 KC-A	34	6	7	1	0	0	0	0	0	3	14	5	.167	.167	.167	.333	-1	0	0	.00	0	....	0	0.0
1968 Oak-A	26	4	9	1	0	0	0	0	1	0	8	4	.250	.400	.250	.650	106	0	0	.00	0	/0-1	0	0.0
1969 Oak-A	12	1	2	0	0	0	0	0	0	0	0	0	.000	.000	.000	.000	-105	-0	0	.00	0	....	0	0.0
1970 Oak-A	25	8	8	2	0	0	1	1	0	0	7	1	.250	.250	.625	.875	138	1	1	3.44	-0	/0-2(2-0-0)	0	0.1
1972*Oak-A	24	10	5	2	1	0	0	2	0	1	8	3	.200	.200	.300	.500	50	-0	0	.00	-1	/0-6(5-0-1)	0	-0.1
1973*Oak-A	35	0	16	0	0	0	0	0	0	0	7	4	....	....	....	....	-106	-0	0	.00	-0	/D-6,0-1	0	0.0
Total 6	156	29	47	6	1	0	1	3	1	4	44	17	.207	.233	.345	.578	70	1	1	.67	-1	/0-10,D-6	0	0.0

• LEWIS, Bill William Henry "Buddy" Lewis b: 10/15/1904, Ripley, TN d: 10/24/1977, Memphis, TN BR/TR, 5'9", 165 lbs. Deb: 6/3/1933

YEAR TM-L	G	AB	R	H	2B	3B	HR	RBI	BB	SO	SB	CS	AVG	OBP	SLG	OPS	OPS+	BR/A	RC	RC/G	FR	G/POS	WS	TPW
1933 StL-N	15	35	8	14	1	0	1	8	2	3	0	....	.400	.432	.514	.947	161	3	8	10.07	0	/C-8	2	0.4
1935 Bos-N	6	4	1	0	0	0	0	0	1	1	0	....	.000	.200	.000	.200	-45	-1	0	.35	0	/C-1	0	-0.1
1936 Bos-N	29	62	11	19	2	0	0	3	12	7	0	....	.306	.419	.339	.758	113	2	10	6.48	0	C-21	3	0.3
Total 3	50	101	20	33	3	0	1	11	15	11	0	....	.327	.414	.386	.800	122	4	19	7.27	0	/C-30	5	0.6

• LEWIS, Buddy John Kelly Lewis b: 8/10/1916, Gastonia, NC BL/TR, 6'1", 175 lbs. Deb: 9/16/1935 Career OF: 8-1-611

YEAR TM-L	G	AB	R	H	2B	3B	HR	RBI	BB	SO	SB	CS	AVG	OBP	SLG	OPS	OPS+	BR/A	RC	RC/G	FR	G/POS	WS	TPW
1935 Was-A	8	28	0	3	0	0	0	2	0	5	0	0	.107	.107	.107	.214	-46	-6	0	.33	1	/3-6	0	-0.5
1936 Was-A	143	601	100	175	21	13	6	67	47	46	6	6	.291	.347	.399	.746	89	-13	83	5.05	7	*3-139	16	-0.1
1937 Was-A	156	668	107	210	32	6	10	79	52	44	11	5	.314	.367	.425	.792	103	4	105	5.90	-11	*3-156	20	-0.2
1938 Was-A★	151	656	122	194	35	9	12	91	58	35	17	9	.296	.354	.431	.785	103	2	101	5.57	0	*3-151	20	0.7
1939 Was-A	140	536	87	171	23	**16**	10	75	72	27	10	9	.319	.402	.478	.879	134	27	106	7.13	11	*3-134	22	4.0
1940 Was-A	148	600	101	190	38	10	6	63	74	36	15	10	.317	.393	.443	.836	124	23	109	6.78	1	*0-112(0-0-112),3-36	22	1.8
1941 Was-A	149	569	97	169	29	11	9	72	82	30	10	7	.297	.386	.434	.820	122	19	99	6.31	2	0-96(0-0-96),3-49	22	1.6
1945 Was-A	69	258	42	86	14	7	2	37	37	15	1	2	.333	.423	.465	.888	172	25	54	7.75	3	0-69(0-0-69)	17	2.4
1946 Was-A	150	582	82	170	28	13	7	45	59	26	5	3	.292	.359	.421	.780	125	19	92	5.66	1	*0-145(8-1-137)	24	1.6
1947 Was-A★	140	506	67	132	15	4	6	48	51	27	6	6	.261	.330	.342	.672	89	-8	56	3.75	-2	*0-130(0-0-130)	10	-1.4
1949 Was-A	95	257	25	63	14	4	3	28	41	12	2	2	.245	.355	.366	.721	93	-2	36	4.73	0	0-67(0-0-67)	6	-0.4
Total 11	1349	5261	830	1563	249	93	71	607	573	303	83	59	.297	.368	.420	.789	113	89	841	5.77	12	3-671,0-619	179	9.5

• LEWIS, Darren Darren Joel Lewis b: 8/28/1967, Berkeley, CA BR/TR, 6', 189 lbs. Deb: 8/21/1990 Career OF: 97-1032-187

YEAR TM-L	G	AB	R	H	2B	3B	HR	RBI	BB	SO	SB	CS	AVG	OBP	SLG	OPS	OPS+	BR/A	RC	RC/G	FR	G/POS	WS	TPW
1990 Oak-A	25	35	4	8	0	0	0	1	7	4	2	0	.229	.372	.229	.601	75	-0	4	3.26	0	0-23(3-16-5)/D-2	0	-0.1
1991 SF-N	72	222	41	55	5	3	1	15	36	30	13	7	.248	.358	.311	.669	93	-1	28	4.22	0	0-68(0-68-0)	7	-0.2
1992 SF-N	100	320	38	74	8	1	1	18	29	46	28	8	.231	.297	.272	.569	66	-11	30	2.98	-3	0-94(0-94-0)	7	-1.6
1993 SF-N	136	522	84	132	17	7	2	48	30	40	46	15	.253	.302	.324	.626	70	-19	55	3.51	2	*0-131(0-131-0)	15	-1.6
1994 SF-N	114	451	70	116	15	**9**	4	29	53	50	30	13	.257	.341	.357	.698	86	-7	58	4.38	-1	*0-113(0-113-0)	11	-0.7
1995 SF-N	74	309	47	78	10	3	1	16	17	37	21	7	.252	.304	.314	.618	65	-14	31	3.27	-1	0-73(0-73-0)	4	-1.4
*Cin-N	58	163	19	40	3	0	0	8	17	20	11	11	.245	.324	.264	.588	58	-12	14	2.57	1	0-57(0-57-0)	2	-1.1
Yr.	132	472	66	118	13	3	1	24	34	57	32	18	.250	.311	.297	.608	63	-26	44	3.02	0	*0-130(0-130-0)	6	-2.5
1996 Chi-A	141	337	55	77	12	2	4	53	45	40	21	5	.228	.325	.312	.636	65	-15	38	3.49	-6	*0-138(1-137-0)	7	-1.8
1997 Chi-A	81	77	15	18	1	0	0	5	11	14	11	4	.234	.330	.247	.576	56	-4	7	2.88	1	0-64(0-64-0)/D-6	1	-0.3
LA-N	26	77	7	23	3	1	1	10	6	17	3	2	.299	.349	.403	.752	104	0	11	4.92	0	0-25(23-2-1)	3	0.0
1998*Bos-A	155	585	95	157	25	3	8	63	70	94	29	12	.268	.354	.362	.717	85	-10	79	4.65	-1	*0-152(4-109-55)/D-1	17	-1.2
1999*Bos-A	135	470	63	113	14	6	2	40	45	52	16	10	.240	.313	.309	.622	58	-31	48	3.35	-3	*0-130(0-88-51)/D-2	7	-3.3
2000 Bos-A	97	270	44	65	12	0	2	17	22	34	10	5	.241	.305	.307	.612	54	-19	27	3.32	-2	0-90(18-41-37)/D-5	4	-2.1
2001 Bos-A	81	164	18	46	9	1	1	12	8	25	5	5	.280	.326	.366	.692	81	-6	19	3.93	3	0-69(26-21-29)/D-5	4	-0.4
2002 Chi-N	58	79	7	19	3	1	0	7	7	11	1	3	.241	.326	.304	.630	68	-5	8	3.34	2	0-47(22-18-9)	1	-0.3
Total 13	1353	4081	607	1021	137	37	27	342	403	514	247	107	.250	.325	.322	.647	72	-153	457	3.69	-7	*0-1274/D-21	90	-16.1

• LEWIS, Duffy George Edward Lewis b: 4/18/1888, San Francisco, CA d: 6/17/1979, Salem, NH BL/TL, 5'10.5", 165 lbs. Deb: 4/16/1910 C Career OF: 1415-15-2

YEAR TM-L	G	AB	R	H	2B	3B	HR	RBI	BB	SO	SB	CS	AVG	OBP	SLG	OPS	OPS+	BR/A	RC	RC/G	FR	G/POS	WS	TPW
1910 Bos-A	151	541	64	153	29	7	8	68	32	....	10	....	.283	.328	.407	.734	127	14	76	4.73	9	*0-149(149-0-0)	19	1.5
1911 Bos-A	130	469	64	144	32	4	7	86	25	....	11	....	.307	.355	.437	.792	122	12	77	5.74	4	*0-125(125-0-0)	15	1.0
1912*Bos-A	154	581	85	165	36	9	6	109	52	....	9	....	.284	.346	.408	.754	110	6	86	5.00	2	*0-154(154-0-0)	21	0.2
1913 Bos-A	149	551	54	164	31	12	0	90	30	55	12	....	.298	.336	.397	.734	112	5	77	4.70	3	*0-142(142-0-0)/3-1,P-1	17	0.1
1914 Bos-A	146	510	53	142	37	9	2	79	57	41	22	31	.278	.357	.398	.755	127	7	70	4.40	-9	*0-142(142-0-0)	20	-0.8
1915*Bos-A	152	557	69	162	31	7	2	76	45	63	14	7	.291	.348	.382	.731	122	13	80	4.93	-8	*0-152(152-0-0)	24	-0.1
1916*Bos-A	152	563	56	151	29	5	1	56	33	56	16	....	.268	.313	.343	.656	97	-5	68	4.08	-4	*0-151(136-15-0)	19	-1.7
1917 Bos-A	150	553	55	167	29	9	1	65	29	54	8	....	.302	.342	.392	.735	125	14	77	4.79	9	*0-150(150-0-0)	24	1.8
1919 NY-A	141	559	67	152	23	4	7	89	17	42	8	....	.272	.293	.365	.658	84	-15	61	3.67	1	*0-141(141-0-0)	13	-2.1
1920 NY-A	107	365	34	99	8	1	4	61	24	32	2	8	.271	.320	.332	.651	70	-18	38	3.45	0	0-99(98-0-1)	7	-2.1
1921 Was-A	27	102	11	19	4	1	0	14	8	10	1	1	.186	.252	.245	.497	29	-11	7	2.03	-2	0-27(26-0-1)	1	-1.4
Total 11	1459	5351	612	1518	289	68	38	793	352	353	113	47	.284	.333	.384	.717	109	22	716	4.51	5	*0-1432/3-1,P-1	180	-3.6

• LEWIS, Fred Frederick Miller Lewis b: 10/13/1858, Buffalo, NY d: 6/5/1945, Utica, NY BB/TR, 5'10.5", 194 lbs. Deb: 7/2/1881 Career OF: 9-284-24

YEAR TM-L	G	AB	R	H	2B	3B	HR	RBI	BB	SO	SB	CS	AVG	OBP	SLG	OPS	OPS+	BR/A	RC	RC/G	FR	G/POS	WS	TPW
1881 Bos-N	27	114	17	25	6	0	0	9	7	5	....	....	.219	.264	.272	.536	72	-3	8	2.55	-2	0-27(0-3-24)	2	-0.6
1883 Phi-N	38	160	21	40	7	0	0	18	4	13	....	....	.250	.268	.294	.562	78	-4	13	2.96	-3	0-38(0-38-0)	1	-0.7
StL-a	49	209	37	63	8	4	1	33	1	....	....	....	.301	.305	.392	.697	116	3	26	4.91	0	0-49(0-49-0)	8	0.1
1884 StL-a	73	300	59	97	25	3	0	0	16	....	....	....	.323	.366	.427	.792	152	17	48	6.50	2	0-73(0-73-0)	18	1.5
StL-U	8	30	6	9	1	0	0	....	3	....	....	....	.300	.364	.333	.697	132	1	4	4.97	-1	/0-8(0-8-0)	1	0.0
1885 StL-N	45	181	12	53	9	0	1	27	9	10	....	....	.293	.326	.359	.685	130	6	22	4.59	6	0-45(9-37-0)	6	1.0
1886 Cin-a	77	324	72	103	14	6	2	32	20	....	8	....	.318	.365	.417	.782	140	14	53	6.54	-4	0-76(0-76-0)/3-1	12	0.6
Total 5	317	1318	224	390	70	13	4	119	60	28	8	....	.296	.330	.378	.708	124	34	174	5.12	-3	0-316/3-1	48	1.9

• LEWIS, Jack John David Lewis b: 2/14/1884, Pittsburgh, PA d: 2/25/1956, Steubenville, OH BR/TR, 5'8", 158 lbs. Deb: 9/16/1911

YEAR TM-L	G	AB	R	H	2B	3B	HR	RBI	BB	SO	SB	CS	AVG	OBP	SLG	OPS	OPS+	BR/A	RC	RC/G	FR	G/POS	WS	TPW
1911 Bos-A	18	59	7	16	0	0	0	6	7	....	2	....	.271	.368	.271	.639	80	-1	7	3.92	0	2-18	2	0.0
1914 Pit-F	117	394	32	92	14	5	1	48	17	46	9	....	.234	.276	.302	.578	68	-17	36	2.79	4	*2-115/S-1	5	-1.2
1915 Pit-F	82	231	24	61	6	5	0	26	8	31	7	....	.264	.292	.333	.625	80	-7	24	3.45	4	2-45,S-11/0-6(0-0-6),1-5,3	5	-0.2
Total 3	217	684	63	169	20	10	1	80	32	77	18	....	.247	.290	.310	.600	73	-25	66	3.10	8	2-178/S-12,0-6,1-5,3-1	12	-1.4

• LEWIS, Johnny Johnny Joe Lewis b: 8/10/1939, Greenville, AL BL/TR, 6'1", 189 lbs. Deb: 4/14/1964 C Career OF: 15-56-175

YEAR TM-L	G	AB	R	H	2B	3B	HR	RBI	BB	SO	SB	CS	AVG	OBP	SLG	OPS	OPS+	BR/A	RC	RC/G	FR	G/POS	WS	TPW
1964 StL-N	40	94	10	22	2	2	2	7	13	23	2	2	.234	.327	.362	.689	86	-2	11	4.07	-1	0-36(2-0-34)	2	-0.5
1965 NY-N	148	477	64	117	15	3	15	45	59	117	4	7	.245	.332	.384	.716	105	2	61	4.34	3	*0-142(0-48-101)	13	-0.4
1966 NY-N	65	166	21	32	6	1	5	20	21	43	2	0	.193	.283	.331	.615	72	-6	17	3.41	1	0-49(11-8-31)	4	-0.8
1967 NY-N	13	34	2	4	1	0	0	2	2	11	0	0	.118	.167	.147	.314	-10	-5	1	.83	0	0-10(2-0-9)	0	-0.5
Total 4	266	771	97	175	24	6	22	74	95	194	8	9	.227	.314	.359	.673	91	-10	91	3.94	3	0-237	19	-2.2

• LEWIS, Mark Mark David Lewis b: 11/30/1969, Hamilton, OH BR/TR, 6'1", 190 lbs. Deb: 4/26/1991

YEAR TM-L	G	AB	R	H	2B	3B	HR	RBI	BB	SO	SB	CS	AVG	OBP	SLG	OPS	OPS+	BR/A	RC	RC/G	FR	G/POS	WS	TPW
1991 Cle-A	84	314	29	83	15	1	0	30	15	45	2	2	.264	.298	.318	.616	70	-14	27	2.91	-1	2-50,S-36	5	-1.0
1992 Cle-A	122	413	44	109	21	0	5	30	25	69	4	5	.264	.311	.351	.662	87	-9	42	3.49	-12	*S-121/3-1	7	-1.3

YEAR TM-L	G	AB	R	H	2B	3B	HR	RBI	BB	SO	SB	CS	AVG	OBP	SLG	OPS	OPS+	BR/A	RC	RC/G	FR	G/POS	WS	TPW
1993 Cle-A	14	52	6	13	2	0	1	5	0	7	3	0	.250	.250	.346	.596	59	-3	5	2.99	-2	S-13	0	-0.4
1994 Cle-A	20	73	6	15	5	0	1	8	2	13	1	0	.205	.227	.315	.542	38	-7	5	2.15	-4	S-13/3-6,2-1	0	-0.9
1995*Cin-N	81	171	25	58	13	1	3	30	21	33	0	3	.339	.411	.480	.891	135	8	34	7.72	7	3-72/2-2,S-2	10	1.5
1996 Det-A	145	545	69	147	30	3	11	55	42	109	6	1	.270	.328	.396	.724	82	-15	71	4.59	-20	*2-144/D-1	11	-2.5
1997*SF-N	118	341	50	91	14	6	10	42	23	62	3	2	.267	.321	.431	.752	98	-3	46	4.67	-2	3-69,2-29/D-1	9	-0.3
1998 Phi-N	142	518	52	129	21	2	9	54	48	111	3	3	.249	.316	.349	.666	74	-20	55	3.56	6	*2-140	8	-0.7
1999 Cin-N	88	173	18	44	16	0	6	28	7	24	0	0	.254	.283	.451	.734	80	-7	19	3.65	1	3-52/2-2	4	-0.5
2000 Cin-N	11	19	1	2	1	0	0	3	1	3	0	0	.105	.150	.158	.308	-22	-4	0	.49	1	/3-5	0	-0.3
Bal-A	71	163	19	44	17	0	2	21	12	31	7	2	.270	.324	.411	.735	89	-3	21	4.45	-5	3-29,2-21,S-14/D-4	4	-0.5
2001 Cle-A	6	13	1	1	0	0	0	0	0	4	0	0	.077	.077	.077	.154	-58	-3	0	.17	0	/3-4,2-3	0	-0.3
Total 11	902	2795	320	736	155	13	48	306	196	511	29	18	.263	.315	.380	.695	83	-78	325	3.99	-31	2-392,3-238,S-199/D-6	58	-7.2

• LEWIS, Phil Philip Lewis b: 10/8/1884, Pittsburgh, PA d: 8/8/1959, Port Wentworth, GA BR/TR, 6', 195 lbs. Deb: 4/14/1905

YEAR TM-L	G	AB	R	H	2B	3B	HR	RBI	BB	SO	SB	CS	AVG	OBP	SLG	OPS	OPS+	BR/A	RC	RC/G	FR	G/POS	WS	TPW
1905 Bro-N	118	433	32	110	9	2	3	33	16	....	16	....	.254	.282	.305	.587	81	-11	44	3.43	-12	*S-118	7	-2.1
1906 Bro-N	136	452	40	110	8	4	0	37	43	....	14	....	.243	.309	.279	.588	90	-4	47	3.38	-16	*S-135	12	-1.8
1907 Bro-N	136	475	52	118	11	1	0	30	23	....	16	....	.248	.286	.276	.562	83	-11	45	3.14	-22	*S-136	8	-3.2
1908 Bro-N	118	415	22	91	5	6	1	30	13	....	9	....	.219	.243	.267	.510	66	-18	29	2.23	-8	*S-116	5	-2.6
Total 4	508	1775	146	429	33	13	4	130	95	....	55	....	.242	.281	.282	.563	80	-44	166	3.05	-58	S-505	32	-9.6

• LEYRITZ, Jim James Joseph "The King" Leyritz b: 12/27/1963, Lakewood, OH BR/TR, 6', 195 lbs. Deb: 6/8/1990 Career OF: 25-0-30

YEAR TM-L	G	AB	R	H	2B	3B	HR	RBI	BB	SO	SB	CS	AVG	OBP	SLG	OPS	OPS+	BR/A	RC	RC/G	FR	G/POS	WS	TPW
1990 NY-A	92	303	28	78	13	1	5	25	27	51	2	3	.257	.332	.356	.689	92	-4	34	3.84	-9	3-69,0-14(10-0-4),C-11	4	-1.2
1991 NY-A	32	77	8	14	3	0	0	4	13	15	0	1	.182	.300	.221	.521	46	-6	6	2.48	-2	3-18/C-5,1-3,D-1	0	-0.7
1992 NY-A	63	144	17	37	6	0	7	26	14	22	0	1	.257	.348	.444	.792	121	4	23	5.45	0	D-31,C-18/1-2,3-2,0-2(0-0-2),2	5	0.4
1993 NY-A	95	259	43	80	14	0	14	53	37	59	0	0	.309	.411	.525	.936	155	22	55	7.68	-3	1-29,0-28(6-0-23),D-21,C-12	14	1.4
1994 NY-A	75	249	47	66	12	0	17	58	35	61	0	0	.265	.369	.518	.887	130	11	47	6.53	-2	C-37,D-25,1-10	10	0.9
1995*NY-A	77	264	37	71	12	0	7	37	37	73	1	1	.269	.375	.394	.769	102	2	42	5.65	-3	C-46,1-18,D-15	8	0.0
1996*NY-A	88	265	23	70	10	0	7	40	30	68	2	0	.264	.359	.381	.740	87	-4	36	4.63	-3	C-55,3-13,D-12/1-5,0-3(3-0-0),2	7	-0.4
1997 Ana-A	84	294	47	81	7	0	11	50	37	56	1	1	.276	.362	.412	.774	100	1	43	5.01	4	C-58,1-15,D-13	10	0.7
Tex-A	37	85	11	24	4	0	0	14	23	22	1	0	.282	.450	.329	.780	102	3	15	6.41	-1	C-11/1-9,D-9	5	0.2
Yr.	121	379	58	105	11	0	11	64	60	78	2	1	.277	.384	.393	.777	101	4	59	5.31	3	C-69,1-24,D-22	15	0.8
1998 Bos-A	52	129	17	37	6	0	8	24	21	34	0	0	.287	.395	.519	.914	132	7	27	7.25	0	D-39/1-1,C-1	3	0.5
*SD-N	62	143	17	38	10	0	4	18	21	40	0	0	.266	.386	.420	.806	120	5	25	6.31	-2	C-24,1-20/3-1,0-1	6	0.3
1999 SD-N	50	134	17	32	5	0	8	21	15	37	0	0	.239	.333	.455	.789	105	1	20	5.10	-2	C-24,1-19/3-1	4	-0.1
*NY-A	31	66	8	15	4	1	0	5	13	17	0	0	.227	.354	.318	.673	74	-2	8	3.82	1	D-14/1-9,3-1,C-1	1	-0.2
2000 NY-A	24	55	2	12	0	0	1	4	7	14	0	0	.218	.317	.273	.590	52	-4	5	2.93	0	D-15/C-2,1-1	0	-0.4
LA-N	41	60	3	12	1	0	1	8	7	12	0	0	.200	.294	.267	.561	46	-5	5	2.58	-2	/1-8,0-6(5-0-1),C-3	1	-0.7
Total 11	903	2527	325	667	107	2	90	387	337	581	7	7	.264	.365	.415	.780	106	31	391	5.33	-22	C-308,D-195,1-149,3-105/0,2	78	0.8

• LEZCANO, Carlos Carlos Manuel (Rubio) Lezcano b: 9/30/1955, Arecibo, Puerto Rico BR/TR, 6'2", 185 lbs. Deb: 4/10/1980 Career OF: 1-39-4

YEAR TM-L	G	AB	R	H	2B	3B	HR	RBI	BB	SO	SB	CS	AVG	OBP	SLG	OPS	OPS+	BR/A	RC	RC/G	FR	G/POS	WS	TPW
1980 Chi-N	42	88	15	18	4	1	3	12	11	29	1	2	.205	.300	.375	.675	81	-3	9	3.18	-2	0-39(0-39-0)	1	-0.6
1981 Chi-N	7	14	1	1	0	0	0	2	0	4	0	0	.071	.071	.071	.143	-57	-3	0	.15	0	/0-5(1-0-4)	0	-0.3
Total 2	49	102	16	19	4	1	3	14	11	33	1	2	.186	.272	.333	.605	65	-6	9	2.75	-2	/0-44	1	-1.0

• LEZCANO, Sixto Sixto Joaquin (Curras) Lezcano b: 11/28/1953, Arecibo, Puerto Rico BR/TR, 5'10", 175 lbs. Deb: 9/10/1974 Career OF: 126-21-1058

YEAR TM-L	G	AB	R	H	2B	3B	HR	RBI	BB	SO	SB	CS	AVG	OBP	SLG	OPS	OPS+	BR/A	RC	RC/G	FR	G/POS	WS	TPW
1974 Mil-A	15	54	5	13	2	0	2	9	4	9	1	1	.241	.293	.389	.682	95	-1	6	3.18	1	0-15(0-0-15)	1	0.0
1975 Mil-A	134	429	55	106	19	3	11	43	46	93	5	5	.247	.326	.382	.708	99	-1	51	3.93	-4	*0-129(0-2-128)/D-2	10	-1.1
1976 Mil-A	145	513	53	146	19	5	7	56	51	112	14	10	.285	.352	.382	.734	117	10	70	4.76	-1	*0-142(64-17-66)/D-3	17	0.2
1977 Mil-A	109	400	50	109	21	4	21	49	52	78	6	5	.273	.359	.503	.862	132	17	72	6.27	8	*0-108(0-0-108)	17	2.0
1978 Mil-A	132	442	62	129	21	4	15	61	64	83	3	3	.292	.383	.459	.842	135	22	81	6.57	9	*0-127(0-0-127)/D-3	20	2.6
1979 Mil-A	138	473	84	152	29	3	28	101	77	74	4	3	.321	.420	.573	.992	165	45	115	8.95	-2	*0-135(0-0-135)/D-1	27	3.6
1980 Mil-A	112	411	51	94	19	3	18	55	39	75	1	1	.229	.300	.421	.721	98	-2	53	4.28	0	*0-108(0-0-108)/D-4	9	-0.8
1981 StL-N	72	214	26	57	8	2	5	28	40	40	0	1	.266	.382	.393	.774	117	6	33	5.20	0	0-65(32-0-34)	8	0.3
1982 SD-N	138	470	73	136	26	6	16	84	78	69	2	1	.289	.393	.472	.865	149	33	90	6.83	9	*0-134(0-0-134)	28	3.7
1983 SD-N	97	317	41	74	11	2	8	49	47	66	0	0	.233	.334	.356	.691	95	-1	39	4.11	1	0-91(0-0-91)	9	-0.4
*Phi-N	18	39	8	11	1	0	0	7	5	9	1	0	.282	.364	.308	.671	89	-0	5	4.75	1	0-15(1-2-13)	1	0.0
Yr.	115	356	49	85	12	2	8	56	52	75	1	0	.239	.337	.351	.689	94	-1	44	4.17	2	*0-106(1-2-104)	10	-0.4
1984 Phi-N	109	256	36	71	6	2	14	40	38	43	0	1	.277	.371	.480	.851	135	12	44	6.00	1	0-87(4-0-83)	9	1.0
1985 Pit-N	72	116	16	24	2	0	3	9	35	17	0	0	.207	.395	.302	.696	98	2	16	4.62	0	0-40(25-0-16)	3	0.0
Total 12	1291	4134	560	1122	184	34	148	591	576	768	37	31	.271	.363	.440	.803	124	143	675	5.65	23	*0-1196/D-13	159	11.0

• LIBBY, Steve Stephen Augustus Libby b: 12/8/1853, Scarborough, ME d: 3/31/1935, Milford, CT, 6'1.5", 168 lbs. Deb: 5/10/1879 U

YEAR TM-L	G	AB	R	H	2B	3B	HR	RBI	BB	SO	SB	CS	AVG	OBP	SLG	OPS	OPS+	BR/A	RC	RC/G	FR	G/POS	WS	TPW
1879 Buf-N	1	2	0	0	0	0	0	0	0	1	....	....	.000	.000	.000	.000	-98	-0	0	.00	0	/1-1	0	0.0

• LIBKE, Al Albert Walter Libke b: 9/12/1918, Tacoma, WA d: 3/7/2003, Wenatchee, WA BL/TR, 6'4", 215 lbs. Deb: 4/19/1945 Career OF: 27-0-197

YEAR TM-L	G	AB	R	H	2B	3B	HR	RBI	BB	SO	SB	CS	AVG	OBP	SLG	OPS	OPS+	BR/A	RC	RC/G	FR	G/POS	WS	TPW
1945 Cin-N	130	449	41	127	23	5	4	53	34	62	6	....	.283	.336	.383	.719	102	0	59	4.74	1	*0-108(27-0-82)/P-4,1-2	13	-0.4
1946 Cin-N	124	431	32	109	22	1	5	42	43	50	0	....	.253	.322	.343	.665	92	-5	46	3.65	0	*0-115(0-0-115)/P-1	8	-0.9
Total 2	254	880	73	236	45	6	9	95	77	112	6	....	.268	.329	.364	.693	97	-4	105	4.19	1	0-223/P-5,1-2	21	-1.3

• LIBRAN, Frankie Francisco (Rosas) Libran b: 5/6/1948, Mayaguez, Puerto Rico BR/TR, 6', 168 lbs. Deb: 9/3/1969

YEAR TM-L	G	AB	R	H	2B	3B	HR	RBI	BB	SO	SB	CS	AVG	OBP	SLG	OPS	OPS+	BR/A	RC	RC/G	FR	G/POS	WS	TPW
1969 SD-N	10	10	1	1	1	0	0	1	1	2	0	0	.100	.182	.200	.382	7	-1	0	1.23	0	/S-9	0	-0.1

• LICKERT, John John Wilbur Lickert b: 4/4/1960, Pittsburgh, PA BR/TR, 5'11", 175 lbs. Deb: 9/19/1981

YEAR TM-L	G	AB	R	H	2B	3B	HR	RBI	BB	SO	SB	CS	AVG	OBP	SLG	OPS	OPS+	BR/A	RC	RC/G	FR	G/POS	WS	TPW
1981 Bos-A	1	0	0	0	0	0	0	0	0	0	0	0	....	....	....	....	-94	0	0	....	0	/C-1	0	0.0

• LIDDELL, Dave David Alexander Liddell b: 6/15/1966, Los Angeles, CA BR/TR, 6', 190 lbs. Deb: 6/3/1990

YEAR TM-L	G	AB	R	H	2B	3B	HR	RBI	BB	SO	SB	CS	AVG	OBP	SLG	OPS	OPS+	BR/A	RC	RC/G	FR	G/POS	WS	TPW
1990 NY-N	1	1	1	1	0	0	0	0	0	0	0	0	1.000	1.000	1.000	2.000	453	0	1	∞	0	/C-1	0	0.0

• LIEBERTHAL, Mike Michael Scott Lieberthal b: 1/18/1972, Glendale, CA BR/TR, 6', 170 lbs. Deb: 6/30/1994

YEAR TM-L	G	AB	R	H	2B	3B	HR	RBI	BB	SO	SB	CS	AVG	OBP	SLG	OPS	OPS+	BR/A	RC	RC/G	FR	G/POS	WS	TPW
1994 Phi-N	24	79	6	21	3	1	1	5	3	5	0	0	.266	.301	.367	.668	71	-3	8	3.27	-3	C-22	0	-0.5
1995 Phi-N	16	47	1	12	2	0	0	4	5	5	0	0	.255	.327	.298	.625	66	-2	5	3.44	0	C-14	1	-0.2
1996 Phi-N	50	166	21	42	8	0	7	23	10	30	0	0	.253	.303	.428	.731	89	-3	21	4.28	0	C-43	3	-0.1
1997 Phi-N	134	455	59	112	27	1	20	77	44	76	3	4	.246	.318	.442	.760	96	-5	63	4.64	-6	*C-129/D-1	15	-0.2
1998 Phi-N	86	313	39	80	15	3	8	45	17	44	2	1	.256	.309	.399	.708	83	-8	39	4.33	-3	C-83	8	-0.5
1999 Phi-N★	145	510	84	153	33	1	31	96	44	86	0	0	.300	.368	.551	.919	125	18	100	7.10	-2	*C-143	20	2.4
2000 Phi-N★	108	389	55	108	30	0	15	71	40	53	2	0	.278	.354	.470	.824	105	3	64	5.82	-2	*C-106	14	0.7
2001 Phi-N	34	121	21	28	8	0	2	11	12	21	0	0	.231	.316	.347	.663	73	-5	14	3.89	2	C-33	3	0.0
2002 Phi-N	130	476	46	133	29	2	15	52	38	58	0	1	.279	.350	.443	.794	113	8	71	5.32	-9	*C-129	14	0.8
2003 Phi-N	131	508	68	159	30	1	13	81	38	59	0	0	.313	.375	.453	.827	122	16	85	6.26	-8	*C-131	17	1.8
Total 10	858	3064	400	848	185	9	112	465	251	437	7	6	.277	.343	.453	.796	105	17	469	5.41	-32	C-833/D-1	95	4.3

• LIEFER, Jeff Jeffrey David Liefer b: 8/17/1974, Fontana, CA BL/TR, 6'3", 210 lbs. Deb: 4/7/1999 Career OF: 74-0-24

YEAR TM-L	G	AB	R	H	2B	3B	HR	RBI	BB	SO	SB	CS	AVG	OBP	SLG	OPS	OPS+	BR/A	RC	RC/G	FR	G/POS	WS	TPW
1999 Chi-A	45	113	8	28	7	1	0	14	8	28	2	0	.248	.298	.327	.625	59	-7	11	3.33	2	0-17(14-0-3),1-15/D-9	1	-0.7
2000 Chi-A	5	11	0	2	0	0	0	0	0	4	0	0	.182	.182	.182	.364	-7	-2	0	1.09	0	/0-5(0-0-5),1-1	0	-0.2
2001 Chi-A	83	254	36	65	13	0	18	39	20	69	0	1	.256	.315	.520	.835	111	2	40	5.41	-6	0-38(35-0-4),1-15,3-15,D-10	6	-0.6
2002 Chi-A	76	204	28	47	8	0	7	26	19	60	0	0	.230	.296	.373	.669	74	-8	23	3.82	-3	0-36(24-0-12),1-31/D-5	3	-1.4
2003 Mon-N	35	88	6	17	3	0	3	18	3	26	0	1	.193	.220	.330	.549	34	-9	6	2.02	-2	1-21	1	-1.2
TB-A	9	25	4	3	1	0	1	3	3	13	0	0	.120	.214	.280	.494	29	-3	2	1.98	0	/3-6,D-2,0-1	0	-0.3
Total 5	253	695	82	162	32	1	29	100	53	200	2	2	.233	.289	.407	.697	78	-26	81	3.95	-10	/0-97,1-83,D-26,3-21	11	-4.4

• LIESE, Fred Frederick Richard Liese b: 10/7/1885, WI d: 6/30/1967, Los Angeles, CA BL/TL, 5'8", 150 lbs. Deb: 4/14/1910

YEAR TM-L	G	AB	R	H	2B	3B	HR	RBI	BB	SO	SB	CS	AVG	OBP	SLG	OPS	OPS+	BR/A	RC	RC/G	FR	G/POS	WS	TPW
1910 Bos-N	5	4	0	0	0	0	0	0	1	2	0	....	.000	.200	.000	.200	-39	-1	0	.00	0	....	0	-0.1

YEAR TM-L	G	AB	R	H	2B	3B	HR	RBI	BB	SO	SB	CS	AVG	OBP	SLG	OPS	OPS+	BR/A	RC	RC/G	FR	G/POS	WS	TPW
• LILLARD, Bill	William Beverly Lillard b: 1/10/1918, Goleta, CA BR/TR, 5'10", 170 lbs. Deb: 9/11/1939																							
1939 Phi-A	7	19	4	6	1	0	0	1	3	1	0	0	.316	.409	.368	.778	102	0	3	6.26	1	/S-7	1	0.2
1940 Phi-A	73	206	26	49	8	2	1	21	28	28	0	1	.238	.332	.311	.643	69	-9	23	3.79	-8	S-69/2-1	3	-1.2
Total 2	80	225	30	55	9	2	1	22	31	29	0	1	.244	.339	.316	.654	72	-9	27	3.98	-7	/S-76,2-1	4	-1.0
• LILLARD, Gene	Robert Eugene Lillard b: 11/12/1913, Santa Barbara, CA d: 4/12/1991, Goleta, CA BR/TR, 5'10.5", 178 lbs. Deb: 5/8/1936 ♦																							
1936 Chi-N	19	34	6	7	1	0	0	2	3	8	0	....	.206	.270	.235	.506	36	-3	2	1.53	-1	/S-4,3-3	0	-0.3
1939 Chi-N	23	10	3	1	0	0	0	0	6	3	0	....	.100	.438	.100	.538	51	1	1	3.36	0	P-20	0	-1.3
1940 StL-N	2	0	0	0	0	0	0	0	0	0	0	0	....	....	....	....	-95	0	0	....	-0	/P-2	0	-0.5
Total 3	44	44	9	8	1	0	0	2	9	11	0	0	.182	.321	.205	.525	41	-2	3	1.95	-1	/P-22,S-4,3-3	0	-2.1
• LILLIE, Jim	James J. "Grasshopper" Lillie b: 7/27/1861, New Haven, CT d: 11/9/1890, Kansas City, MO Deb: 5/17/1883 Career OF: 147-38-204 ♦																							
1883 Buf-N	50	201	25	47	7	3	1	29	1	31	....	....	.234	.238	.313	.551	64	-9	15	2.74	-6	0-47(12-34-1)/P-3,C-2,2-1,3,S	3	-1.3
1884 Buf-N	114	471	68	105	12	5	3	53	5	71	....	....	.223	.231	.289	.520	60	-23	32	2.42	14	*0-114(0-0-114)/P-2	6	-1.4
1885 Buf-N	112	430	49	107	13	3	2	30	6	39	....	....	.249	.259	.307	.566	80	-11	35	2.93	-7	*0-112(21-4-89)/S-3,1-1	5	-2.0
1886 KC-N	114	416	37	73	9	0	0	22	11	80	13	....	.175	.197	.197	.394	19	-42	19	1.51	11	*0-114(114-0-0)/P-1	2	-3.2
Total 4	390	1518	179	332	41	11	6	134	23	221	13	....	.219	.230	.272	.502	55	-84	102	2.34	12	0-387/P-6,S-4,C-2,1-1,2-1,3	16	-7.8
• LILLIS, Bob	Robert Perry Lillis b: 6/2/1930, Altadena, CA BR/TR, 5'11", 160 lbs. Deb: 8/30/1958 M/C																							
1958 LA-N	20	69	10	27	3	1	1	5	4	2	1	2	.391	.432	.507	.940	143	4	14	8.13	-1	S-19	4	0.4
1959 LA-N	30	48	7	11	2	0	0	2	3	4	0	0	.229	.275	.271	.545	43	-4	4	2.71	-2	S-20	1	-0.5
1960 LA-N	48	60	6	16	4	0	0	6	2	6	2	0	.267	.290	.333	.624	66	-2	6	3.14	3	S-23,3-14/2-1	2	0.2
1961 LA-N	19	9	0	1	0	0	0	1	1	1	0	0	.111	.200	.111	.311	-13	-1	0	.00	-2	3-12/2-1,S-1	0	-0.4
StL-N	86	230	24	50	4	0	0	21	7	13	3	3	.217	.247	.235	.482	26	-25	12	1.71	-4	S-56,2-24	2	-2.4
Yr.	105	239	24	51	4	0	0	22	8	14	3	3	.213	.245	.230	.475	24	-26	12	1.62	-7	S-57,2-25,3-12	2	-2.8
1962 Hou-N	129	457	38	114	12	4	1	30	28	23	7	3	.249	.293	.300	.593	64	-23	40	2.95	4	S-99,2-33/3-9	8	-0.9
1963 Hou-N	147	469	31	93	13	1	1	19	15	35	3	4	.198	.230	.237	.466	37	-39	24	1.67	2	*S-124,2-19/3-6	7	-2.8
1964 Hou-N	109	332	31	89	11	2	0	17	11	10	4	9	.268	.292	.313	.605	75	-15	27	2.69	-1	2-52,S-43,3-12	7	-1.0
1965 Hou-N	124	408	34	90	12	1	0	20	20	10	2	2	.221	.267	.255	.522	51	-26	27	2.15	-14	*S-104/3-9,2-6	3	-3.4
1966 Hou-N	68	164	14	38	6	0	0	11	7	4	1	1	.232	.263	.268	.531	52	-11	10	1.79	-8	2-35,S-18/3-6	1	-1.6
1967 Hou-N	37	82	3	20	1	0	0	5	1	8	0	1	.244	.253	.256	.509	48	-6	4	1.63	-1	S-23/2-3,3-2	1	-0.6
Total 10	817	2328	198	549	68	9	3	137	99	116	23	25	.236	.271	.277	.548	54	-149	167	2.36	-26	S-530,2-174/3-70	36	-12.8
• LIMMER, Lou	Louis Limmer b: 3/10/1925, New York, NY BL/TL, 6'2", 190 lbs. Deb: 4/22/1951																							
1951 Phi-A	94	214	25	34	9	1	5	30	28	40	1	0	.159	.256	.280	.537	44	-17	17	2.41	-2	1-58	1	-2.0
1954 Phi-A	115	316	41	73	10	3	14	32	35	37	2	3	.231	.308	.415	.722	96	-4	40	4.20	-0	1-79	7	-0.8
Total 2	209	530	66	107	19	4	19	62	63	77	3	3	.202	.287	.360	.647	75	-21	57	3.44	-2	1-137	8	-2.8
• LINARES, Rufino	Rufino Linares b: 2/28/1951, Ingerio Quiqueya, Dominican Republic d: 5/16/1998, San Pedro de Macoris, Dominican Republic BR/TR, 6', 170 lbs. Deb: 4/10/1981 Career OF: 123-0-7																							
1981 Atl-N	78	253	27	67	9	2	5	25	9	28	8	4	.265	.290	.375	.666	85	-6	23	3.06	1	0-60(60-0-0)	4	-0.8
1982 Atl-N	77	191	28	57	7	1	2	17	7	29	5	2	.298	.327	.377	.704	92	-2	20	3.76	2	0-53(51-0-4)	4	-0.3
1984 Atl-N	34	58	4	12	3	0	1	10	6	12	0	0	.207	.281	.310	.592	62	-3	5	2.92	1	0-13(12-0-1)	1	-0.3
1985 Cal-A	18	43	7	11	2	0	3	11	2	5	2	0	.256	.289	.512	.801	114	1	6	4.99	0	D-14/0-2(0-0-2)	1	0.1
Total 4	207	545	66	147	21	3	11	63	24	74	15	6	.270	.302	.380	.682	87	-10	55	3.43	3	0-128/D-14	10	-1.4
• LIND, Carl	Henry Carl "Hooks" Lind b: 9/19/1903, New Orleans, LA d: 8/2/1946, New York, NY BR/TR, 6', 160 lbs. Deb: 9/14/1927																							
1927 Cle-A	12	37	2	5	0	0	0	1	5	7	1	0	.135	.256	.135	.391	4	-5	2	1.46	0	2-11/S-1	0	-0.4
1928 Cle-A	154	650	102	191	42	4	1	54	36	48	8	5	.294	.331	.375	.706	84	-15	81	4.38	-23	*2-154	13	-3.3
1929 Cle-A	66	225	19	54	8	1	0	13	13	17	0	2	.240	.282	.284	.566	44	-19	18	2.63	-5	2-64/3-1	3	-2.1
1930 Cle-A	24	69	8	17	3	0	0	6	3	7	0	1	.246	.278	.290	.568	43	-6	5	2.57	2	S-22/2-2	1	-0.2
Total 4	256	981	131	267	53	5	1	74	57	79	9	8	.272	.313	.339	.652	69	-46	107	3.70	-26	2-231/S-23,3-1	17	-6.0
• LIND, Jack	Jackson Hugh Lind b: 6/8/1946, Denver, CO BB/TR, 6', 170 lbs. Deb: 9/10/1974 C																							
1974 Mil-A	9	17	4	4	2	0	0	1	3	2	0	0	.235	.350	.353	.703	103	0	2	3.92	-1	/S-5,2-4	1	0.0
1975 Mil-A	17	20	1	1	0	0	0	0	2	12	1	0	.050	.136	.050	.186	-45	-4	0	.40	-2	/S-9,3-6,1-1	0	-0.5
Total 2	26	37	5	5	2	0	0	1	5	14	1	0	.135	.238	.189	.427	25	-3	2	1.89	-3	/S-14,3-6,2-4,1-1	1	-0.5
• LIND, Jose	Jose (Salgado) "Chico" Lind b: 5/1/1964, Toabaja, Puerto Rico BR/TR, 5'11", 175 lbs. Deb: 8/28/1987																							
1987 Pit-N	35	143	21	46	8	4	0	11	8	12	2	1	.322	.358	.434	.791	108	1	21	5.15	7	2-35	5	1.0
1988 Pit-N	154	611	82	160	24	4	2	49	42	75	15	4	.262	.309	.324	.633	83	-13	63	3.53	3	*2-153	15	-0.6
1989 Pit-N	153	578	52	134	21	3	2	48	39	64	15	1	.232	.283	.289	.572	66	-23	49	2.77	-2	*2-151	10	-2.2
1990*Pit-N	152	514	46	134	28	5	1	48	35	52	8	0	.261	.309	.340	.650	82	-12	51	3.33	13	*2-152	15	0.5
1991*Pit-N	150	502	53	133	16	6	3	54	30	56	7	4	.265	.309	.339	.648	83	-12	48	3.20	10	*2-149	13	0.2
1992*Pit-N	135	468	38	110	14	1	0	39	26	29	3	1	.235	.277	.269	.546	56	-27	33	2.33	0	*2-134	8	-2.5
1993 KC-A	136	431	33	107	13	2	0	37	13	36	3	2	.248	.274	.288	.561	48	-32	34	2.60	-5	*2-136	7	-3.0
1994 KC-A	85	290	34	78	16	2	1	31	16	34	9	5	.269	.307	.348	.655	66	-16	30	3.45	-3	2-84/D-1	6	-1.3
1995 KC-A	29	97	4	26	3	0	0	6	3	8	0	1	.268	.290	.299	.589	53	-7	8	2.81	-1	2-29	2	-0.7
Cal-A	15	43	5	7	2	0	0	1	3	4	0	0	.163	.217	.209	.427	12	-6	1	1.03	1	2-15	1	-0.4
Yr.	44	140	9	33	5	0	0	7	6	12	0	1	.236	.267	.271	.539	40	-13	9	2.20	0	2-44	3	-1.0
Total 9	1044	3677	368	935	145	27	9	324	215	370	62	19	.254	.297	.316	.613	71	-147	337	3.07	23	*2-1038/D-1	82	-9.0
• LINDBECK, Em	Emerit Desmond Lindbeck b: 8/27/1935, Kewanee, IL BL/TR, 6', 185 lbs. Deb: 4/22/1960																							
1960 Det-A	2	1	0	0	0	0	0	0	1	0	0	0	.000	.500	.000	.500	44	0	0	3.51	0	....	0	0.0
• LINDELL, Johnny	John Harlan Lindell b: 8/30/1916, Greeley, CO d: 8/27/1985, Newport Beach, CA BR/TR, 6'4.5", 217 lbs. Deb: 4/18/1941 Career OF: 282-293-126 ♦																							
1941 NY-A	1	1	0	0	0	0	0	0	0	0	0	0	.000	.000	.000	.000	-101	-0	0	.00	0	....	0	0.0
1942 NY-A	27	24	1	6	1	0	0	4	0	5	0	0	.250	.250	.292	.542	53	1	2	2.69	0	P-23	3	-0.3
1943*NY-A★	122	441	53	108	17	**12**	4	51	51	55	2	5	.245	.329	.365	.694	102	0	53	3.99	-1	*0-122(3-55-66)	13	-0.8
1944 NY-A	149	594	91	178	33	**16**	18	103	44	56	5	4	.300	.351	.500	.851	137	25	102	6.25	1	*0-149(2-148-0)	26	2.3
1945 NY-A	41	159	26	45	6	3	1	20	17	10	2	1	.283	.363	.377	.740	110	3	23	5.09	0	0-41(0-41-0)	5	0.1
1946 NY-A	102	332	41	86	10	5	10	40	32	47	4	1	.259	.328	.410	.738	104	2	44	4.48	1	0-74(5-31-39),1-14	9	0.0
1947*NY-A	127	476	66	131	18	7	11	67	32	70	1	2	.275	.322	.412	.734	104	0	61	4.48	1	*0-118(102-10-11)	15	-0.7
1948 NY-A	88	309	58	98	17	2	13	55	35	50	0	0	.317	.387	.511	.898	139	16	62	7.63	-2	0-79(72-1-7)	14	0.9
1949*NY-A	78	211	33	51	10	0	6	27	35	27	3	0	.242	.350	.374	.724	92	-2	29	4.58	-2	0-65(63-3-1)	6	-0.7
1950 NY-A	7	21	2	4	0	0	0	2	4	2	0	0	.190	.320	.190	.510	34	-2	1	2.16	0	/0-6(6-0-0)	0	-0.2
StL-N	36	113	16	21	5	2	5	16	15	24	0	....	.186	.287	.398	.685	74	-5	12	3.32	-1	0-33(29-4-0)	2	-0.7
1953 Pit-N	58	91	11	26	6	1	4	15	16	15	0	0	.286	.404	.505	.909	136	15	18	6.87	2	P-27/1-2	12	1.0
Phi-N	11	18	3	7	1	0	0	2	6	2	0	0	.389	.542	.444	.986	162	3	5	12.98	-1	/P-5,0-2(0-0-2)	2	0.3
Yr.	69	109	14	33	7	1	4	17	22	17	0	0	.303	.429	.495	.924	141	18	23	7.69	1	P-32/1-2,0-2(0-0-2)	14	1.3
1954 Phi-N	7	5	0	1	0	0	0	2	2	3	0	0	.200	.429	.200	.629	70	0	1	4.40	0	....	0	0.0
Total 12	854	2795	401	762	124	48	72	404	289	366	17	13	.273	.344	.429	.773	113	57	412	5.16	-2	0-689/P-55,1-16	107	1.2
• LINDEMAN, Jim	James William Lindeman b: 1/10/1962, Evanston, IL BR/TR, 6'1", 200 lbs. Deb: 9/3/1986 Career OF: 48-6-90																							
1986 StL-N	19	55	7	14	1	0	1	6	2	10	1	1	.255	.281	.327	.608	68	-3	4	2.63	0	1-17/3-1,0-1	0	-0.4
1987*StL-N	75	207	20	43	13	0	8	28	11	56	3	1	.208	.258	.386	.644	67	-11	20	3.12	4	0-49(1-0-48),1-20	3	-1.0
1988 StL-N	17	43	3	9	1	0	2	7	2	9	0	0	.209	.244	.372	.617	74	-2	4	2.78	-1	0-12(4-0-8)/1-3	0	-0.3
1989 StL-N	73	45	8	5	1	0	0	2	3	18	0	0	.111	.167	.133	.300	-13	-7	1	.58	-2	1-42/0-5(3-0-2)	0	-1.0
1990 Det-A	12	32	5	7	1	0	2	8	2	13	0	0	.219	.265	.438	.702	92	-1	4	4.15	0	D-10/1-1,0-1	1	-0.1

YEAR TM-L	G	AB	R	H	2B	3B	HR	RBI	BB	SO	SB	CS	AVG	OBP	SLG	OPS	OPS+	BR/A	RC	RC/G	FR	G/POS	WS	TPW
1991 Phi-N	65	95	13	32	5	0	0	12	13	14	0	1	.337	.417	.389	.806	129	4	16	6.41	0	0-30(14-6-10)/1-1	4	0.3
1992 Phi-N	29	39	6	10	1	0	1	6	3	11	0	0	.256	.310	.359	.668	89	-1	4	3.80	-1	/0-9(4-0-7)	1	-0.2
1993 Hou-N	9	23	2	8	3	0	0	0	0	7	0	0	.348	.348	.478	.826	123	1	4	6.89	1	/1-9	0	0.1
1994 NY-N	52	137	18	37	8	1	7	20	6	35	0	0	.270	.306	.496	.802	106	0	21	5.66	-2	0-33(21-0-14)/1-4	5	-0.4
Total 9	**351**	**676**	**82**	**165**	**34**	**1**	**21**	**89**	**42**	**173**	**4**	**3**	**.244**	**.292**	**.391**	**.683**	**83**	**-18**	**78**	**3.93**	**-1**	**0-140/1-97,D-10,3-1**	**14**	**-2.8**
• LINDEMANN, Bob	John Frederick Mann Lindemann b: 6/5/1881, Philadelphia, PA d: 12/19/1951, Williamsport, PA BB/TR, 6', 175 lbs. Deb: 8/28/1901																							
1901 Phi-A	3	9	0	1	0	0	0	0	0	....	0	....	.111	.111	.111	.222	-37	-2	0	.52	0	/0-3(0-0-3)	0	-0.2
• LINDEN, Todd	Todd A. Linden b: 6/30/1980, Edmonds, WA BB/TR, 6'3", 210 lbs. Deb: 8/18/2003																							
2003 SF-N	18	38	2	8	1	0	1	6	1	8	0	0	.211	.231	.316	.547	42	-3	2	1.86	-1	0-13(9-0-6)	1	-0.5
• LINDEN, Walt	Walter Charles Linden b: 3/27/1924, Chicago, IL BR/TR, 6'1", 190 lbs. Deb: 4/30/1950																							
1950 Bos-N	3	5	0	2	1	0	0	0	1	0	0	....	.400	.500	.600	1.100	201	1	2	14.67	0	/C-3	1	0.1
• LINDSAY, Bill	William Gibbons Lindsay b: 2/24/1881, Madison, NC d: 7/14/1963, Greensboro, NC BL/TR, 5'10.5", 165 lbs. Deb: 6/21/1911																							
1911 Cle-A	19	66	6	16	2	0	0	5	1	....	2	....	.242	.265	.273	.537	49	-5	5	2.61	2	3-15/2-1	1	-0.3
• LINDSAY, Chris	Christian Haller "Pinky,The Crab" Lindsay b: 7/24/1878, Beaver County, PA d: 1/25/1941, Cleveland, OH BR/TR, 6', 190 lbs. Deb: 7/6/1905																							
1905 Det-A	88	329	38	88	14	1	0	31	18	....	10	....	.267	.315	.316	.631	100	-0	38	4.03	-7	1-88	9	-0.9
1906 Det-A	141	499	59	112	16	2	0	33	45	....	18	....	.224	.293	.265	.557	73	-14	48	3.10	-15	*1-122,2-17/3-1	6	-3.5
Total 2	**229**	**828**	**97**	**200**	**30**	**3**	**0**	**64**	**63**	**....**	**28**	**....**	**.242**	**.301**	**.285**	**.586**	**83**	**-15**	**86**	**3.45**	**-22**	**1-210/2-17,3-1**	**15**	**-4.4**
• LINDSEY, Bill	William Donald Lindsey b: 4/12/1960, Staten Island, NY BR/TR, 6'3", 195 lbs. Deb: 7/18/1987																							
1987 Chi-A	9	16	2	3	0	0	0	1	0	3	0	0	.188	.188	.188	.375		-2	0	.36	1	/C-9	1	-0.1
• LINDSEY, Doug	Michael Douglas Lindsey b: 9/22/1967, Austin, TX BR/TR, 6'2", 200 lbs. Deb: 10/6/1991																							
1991 Phi-N	1	3	0	0	0	0	0	0	0	3	0	0	.000	.000	.000	.000	-101	-1	0	.00	0	/C-1	0	-0.1
1993 Phi-N	2	2	0	1	0	0	0	0	0	1	0	0	.500	.500	.500	1.000	171	0	1	13.50	0	/C-2	0	0.0
Chi-A	2	1	0	0	0	0	0	0	0	0	0	0	.000	.000	.000	.000	-102	-0	0	.00	0	/C-2	0	-0.1
Total 2	**5**	**6**	**0**	**1**	**0**	**0**	**0**	**0**	**0**	**4**	**0**	**0**	**.167**	**.167**	**.167**	**.333**	**-11**	**-1**	**1**	**2.70**	**-1**	**/C-5**	**0**	**-0.2**
• LINDSEY, Rod	Rodney Lee Lindsey b: 1/28/1976, Opelika, AL BR/TR, 5'8", 175 lbs. Deb: 9/2/2000																							
2000 Det-A	11	3	6	1	1	0	0	0	0	1	2	1	.333	.500	.667	1.167	197	1	1	5.16	0	/0-7(2-4-2)	0	0.0
• LINDSTROM, Chuck	Charles William Lindstrom b: 9/7/1936, Chicago, IL BR/TR, 5'11", 175 lbs. Deb: 9/28/1958																							
1958 Chi-A	1	1	1	1	0	1	0	1	1	0	0	0	1.000	1.000	3.000	4.000	975	1	3	∞	0	/C-1	1	0.1
• LINDSTROM, Freddie	Frederick Charles Lindstrom b: 11/21/1905, Chicago, IL d: 10/4/1981, Chicago, IL BR/TR, 5'11", 170 lbs. Deb: 4/15/1924 HOF: 1976 Career OF: 187-291-74																							
1924*NY-N	52	79	19	20	3	1	0	4	6	10	3	1	.253	.314	.316	.630	71	-3	8	3.56	1	2-23,3-11	2	0.0
1925 NY-N	104	356	43	102	15	12	4	33	22	20	5	9	.287	.332	.430	.761	97	-5	48	4.74	-7	3-96/2-1,S-1	10	-0.6
1926 NY-N	140	543	90	164	19	9	9	76	39	21	11	....	.302	.351	.420	.771	108	5	78	5.01	-1	*3-138/0-1	20	1.2
1927 NY-N	138	562	107	172	36	8	7	58	40	40	10	....	.306	.354	.436	.790	111	8	85	5.42	0	3-87,0-51(51-0-0)	20	0.9
1928 NY-N	153	646	99	**231**	39	9	14	107	25	21	15	....	.358	.383	.511	.894	131	26	120	7.27	12	*3-153	32	4.7
1929 NY-N	130	549	99	175	23	6	15	91	30	28	10	....	.319	.354	.464	.819	101	-1	87	5.70	7	*3-128	17	1.3
1930 NY-N	148	609	127	231	39	7	22	106	48	33	15	....	.379	.425	.575	.999	142	41	143	9.46	2	*3-148	28	4.6
1931 NY-N	78	303	38	91	12	6	5	36	26	12	5	....	.300	.356	.429	.785	113	5	47	5.80	-6	0-73(0-0-73)/2-4	10	-0.5
1932 NY-N	144	595	83	161	26	5	15	92	27	28	6	....	.271	.303	.407	.710	91	-9	74	4.38	-2	*0-128(0-128-0),3-15	13	-1.4
1933 Pit-N	138	538	70	167	39	10	5	55	33	22	1	....	.310	.350	.448	.798	127	17	86	5.69	1	*0-130(20-111-0)	23	1.5
1934 Pit-N	97	383	59	111	24	4	4	49	23	21	1	....	.290	.333	.405	.738	94	-3	51	4.81	-4	0-92(92-0-0)	9	-1.2
1935*Chi-N	90	342	49	94	22	4	3	62	10	13	1	....	.275	.297	.389	.686	82	-10	37	3.75	-3	0-50(0-50-0),3-33	8	-1.3
1936 Bro-N	26	106	12	28	4	0	0	10	5	7	1	....	.264	.297	.302	.599	61	-6	9	2.88	1	0-26(24-2-0)	1	-0.6
Total 13	**1438**	**5611**	**895**	**1747**	**301**	**81**	**103**	**779**	**334**	**276**	**84**	**10**	**.311**	**.351**	**.449**	**.800**	**110**	**66**	**873**	**5.65**	**0**	**3-809,0-551/2-28,S-1**	**193**	**8.7**
• LINHART, Carl	Carl James Linhart b: 12/14/1929, Zborov, Czechoslovakia BL/TR, 5'11", 184 lbs. Deb: 8/2/1952																							
1952 Det-A	3	2	0	0	0	0	0	0	0	0	0	0	.000	.000	.000	.000	-99	-1	0	.00	0	....	0	-0.1
• LINIAK, Cole	Cole Edward Liniak b: 8/23/1976, Encinitas, CA BR/TR, 6'1", 190 lbs. Deb: 9/3/1999																							
1999 Chi-N	12	29	3	7	2	0	0	2	1	4	0	1	.241	.267	.310	.577	46	-3	2	1.67	-1	3-10	0	-0.3
2000 Chi-N	3	3	0	0	0	0	0	0	0	2	0	0	.000	.000	.000	.000	-103	-1	0	.00	0	....	0	-0.1
Total 2	**15**	**32**	**3**	**7**	**2**	**0**	**0**	**2**	**1**	**6**	**0**	**1**	**.219**	**.242**	**.281**	**.524**	**33**	**-4**	**2**	**1.49**	**-1**	**/3-10**	**0**	**-0.4**
• LINTON, Bob	Claud Clarence Linton b: 4/18/1903, Emerson, AR d: 4/3/1980, Destin, FL BL/TR, 6', 185 lbs. Deb: 4/26/1929																							
1929 Pit-N	17	18	0	2	0	0	0	1	1	2	0	....	.111	.158	.111	.269	-31	-4	0	.54	0	/C-8	0	-0.3
• LINTZ, Larry	Larry Lintz b: 10/10/1949, Martinez, CA BB/TR, 5'9", 150 lbs. Deb: 7/14/1973																							
1973 Mon-N	52	116	20	29	1	0	0	3	17	18	12	4	.250	.351	.259	.609	69	-3	14	3.74	-3	2-34,S-15	3	-0.4
1974 Mon-N	113	319	60	76	10	1	0	20	44	50	50	7	.238	.334	.276	.610	68	-4	40	3.94	-4	2-67,S-31/3-1	9	-0.2
1975 Mon-N	46	132	18	26	0	0	0	3	23	18	17	9	.197	.316	.197	.513	43	-10	10	2.19	-2	2-39/S-2	2	-0.9
StL-N	27	18	6	5	1	0	0	1	3	2	4	0	.278	.381	.333	.714	96	1	3	7.01	-1	/2-6,S-6	1	0.1
Yr.	73	150	24	31	1	0	0	4	26	20	21	9	.207	.324	.213	.537	49	-9	14	2.65	-3	2-45/S-8	3	-0.8
1976 Oak-A	68	1	21	0	0	0	0	0	2	0	31	11	.000	.667	.000	.667	111	2	0	.00	-2	D-19/2-5,0-3(1-0-2)	0	0.0
1977 Oak-A	41	30	11	4	1	0	0	0	8	13	13	5	.133	.333	.167	.500	42	-1	3	2.42	0	2-28/D-5,S-2,3-1	1	0.0
1978 Cle-A	3	0	1	0	0	0	0	0	0	0	1	2	....	....	....	....	-101	-1	0	.00	0	....	0	-0.1
Total 6	**350**	**616**	**137**	**140**	**13**	**1**	**0**	**27**	**97**	**101**	**128**	**38**	**.227**	**.336**	**.252**	**.588**	**62**	**-16**	**70**	**3.39**	**-12**	**2-179/S-56,D-24,0-3,3-2**	**16**	**-1.5**
• LINZ, Phil	Philip Francis Linz b: 6/4/1939, Baltimore, MD BR/TR, 6'1", 180 lbs. Deb: 4/13/1962 Career OF: 4-7-11																							
1962 NY-A	71	129	28	37	8	0	1	14	6	17	6	2	.287	.319	.372	.691	88	-2	15	4.20	-6	S-21/3-8,2-5,0-2(0-0-2)	3	-0.7
1963*NY-A	72	186	22	50	9	0	2	12	15	18	1	6	.269	.330	.349	.680	91	-4	19	3.37	3	S-22,3-13,0-12(2-5-5)/2-6	5	0.0
1964*NY-A	112	368	63	92	21	3	5	25	43	61	3	4	.250	.332	.364	.696	92	-4	45	4.12	7	S-55,3-41/2-5,0-3(1-2-0)	12	0.8
1965 NY-A	99	285	37	59	12	1	2	16	30	33	2	1	.207	.283	.277	.560	60	-15	24	2.69	-6	S-71/3-4,0-4(0-0-4),2-1	5	-1.6
1966 Phi-N	40	70	4	14	3	0	0	6	2	14	0	0	.200	.222	.243	.465	29	-7	3	1.18	-2	3-14/S-6,2-3	1	-0.8
1967 Phi-N	23	18	4	4	2	0	1	5	2	1	0	0	.222	.300	.500	.800	124	0	2	4.28	-3	/S-7,3-1	0	-0.3
NY-N	24	58	8	12	2	0	0	1	4	10	0	0	.207	.270	.241	.511	48	-4	4	2.04	-2	2-11/S-8,3-1,0-1	1	-0.5
Yr.	47	76	12	16	4	0	1	6	6	11	0	0	.211	.277	.303	.580	66	-3	6	2.55	-5	S-15,2-11/3-2,0-1	1	-0.7
1968 NY-N	78	258	19	54	7	0	0	17	10	41	1	0	.209	.244	.236	.481	45	-17	14	1.80	-5	2-71	2	-1.9
Total 7	**519**	**1372**	**185**	**322**	**64**	**4**	**11**	**96**	**112**	**195**	**13**	**13**	**.235**	**.296**	**.311**	**.607**	**72**	**-52**	**126**	**3.03**	**-15**	**S-190,2-102/3-82,0-22**	**29**	**-5.0**
• LIPON, Johnny	John Joseph "Skids" Lipon b: 11/10/1922, Martins Ferry, OH d: 8/17/1998, Houston, TX BR/TR, 6', 175 lbs. Deb: 8/16/1942 M/C																							
1942 Det-A	34	131	5	25	2	0	0	9	7	7	1	3	.191	.232	.206	.438	22	-15	6	1.50	4	S-34	1	-0.8
1946 Det-A	14	20	4	6	0	0	0	1	5	3	0	0	.300	.440	.300	.740	103	1	3	6.32	-2	/S-8,3-1	1	-0.1
1948 Det-A	121	458	65	133	18	8	5	52	68	22	4	4	.290	.384	.397	.782	105	5	75	5.77	-5	*S-117/2-1,3-1	18	0.7
1949 Det-A	127	439	57	110	14	6	3	59	75	24	2	4	.251	.362	.330	.693	84	-9	55	4.18	4	*S-120	13	0.3
1950 Det-A	147	601	104	176	27	6	2	63	81	26	9	6	.293	.378	.368	.745	89	-8	87	4.99	1	*S-147	19	0.3
1951 Det-A	129	487	56	129	15	1	0	38	49	27	7	6	.265	.335	.300	.634	72	-19	52	3.70	-16	*S-125	8	-2.6
1952 Det-A	39	136	17	30	4	2	0	12	16	6	3	1	.221	.303	.279	.582	62	-6	12	3.01	-5	S-39	2	-0.9
Bos-A	79	234	25	48	8	1	0	18	32	20	1	1	.205	.301	.248	.549	50	-15	20	2.67	3	S-69/3-7	4	-0.8
Yr.	118	370	42	78	12	3	0	30	48	26	4	2	.211	.301	.259	.561	54	-21	33	2.79	-2	*S-108/3-7	6	-1.8
1953 Bos-A	60	145	18	31	7	0	0	13	14	16	1	0	.214	.283	.262	.545	45	-11	11	2.41	0	S-58	3	-0.7
StL-A	7	9	0	2	0	0	0	1	0	1	0	0	.222	.222	.222	.444	20	-1	0	1.76	-1	/3-6,2-1	0	-0.2
Yr.	67	154	18	33	7	0	0	14	14	17	1	0	.214	.280	.260	.540	44	-12	12	2.38	-1	S-58/3-6,2-1	3	-0.9

YEAR TM-L	G	AB	R	H	2B	3B	HR	RBI	BB	SO	SB	CS	AVG	OBP	SLG	OPS	OPS+	BR/A	RC	RC/G	FR	G/POS	WS	TPW
1954 Cin-N	1	1	0	0	0	0	0	0	0	0	0	0	.000	.000	.000	.000	-97	-0	0	.00	0	....	0	0.0
Total 9	758	2661	351	690	95	24	10	266	347	152	28	25	.259	.346	.324	.671	77	-78	323	4.09	-16	S-717/3-15,2-2	69	-4.8

• LIPSCOMB, Nig Gerard Lipscomb b: 2/24/1911, Rutherfordton, NC d: 2/27/1978, Huntersville, NC BR/TR, 6', 175 lbs. Deb: 4/23/1937

YEAR TM-L	G	AB	R	H	2B	3B	HR	RBI	BB	SO	SB	CS	AVG	OBP	SLG	OPS	OPS+	BR/A	RC	RC/G	FR	G/POS	WS	TPW
1937 StL-A	36	96	11	31	9	1	0	8	11	10	0	0	.323	.398	.438	.836	110	2	17	6.94	-6	2-27/P-3,3-1	2	-0.3

• LIPSKI, Bob Robert Peter Lipski b: 7/7/1938, Scranton, PA BL/TR, 6'1", 180 lbs. Deb: 4/28/1963

YEAR TM-L	G	AB	R	H	2B	3B	HR	RBI	BB	SO	SB	CS	AVG	OBP	SLG	OPS	OPS+	BR/A	RC	RC/G	FR	G/POS	WS	TPW
1963 Cle-A	2	1	0	0	0	0	0	0	0	1	0	0	.000	.000	.000	.000	-101	-0	0	.00	0	/C-2	0	-0.1

• LIRIANO, Nelson Nelson Arturo (Bonilla) Liriano b: 6/3/1964, Puerto Plata, Dominican Republic BB/TR, 5'10", 172 lbs. Deb: 8/25/1987

YEAR TM-L	G	AB	R	H	2B	3B	HR	RBI	BB	SO	SB	CS	AVG	OBP	SLG	OPS	OPS+	BR/A	RC	RC/G	FR	G/POS	WS	TPW
1987 Tor-A	37	158	29	38	6	2	2	10	16	22	13	2	.241	.310	.342	.652	71	-5	18	3.87	3	2-37	4	0.0
1988 Tor-A	99	276	36	73	6	2	3	23	11	40	12	5	.264	.298	.333	.631	76	-9	27	3.39	-5	2-80,D-11/3-1	5	-1.2
1989*Tor-A	132	418	51	110	26	3	5	53	43	51	16	7	.263	.335	.376	.710	106	4	53	4.24	-17	*2-122/D-5	15	-1.0
1990 Tor-A	50	170	16	36	7	2	1	15	16	20	3	5	.212	.283	.294	.578	58	-11	13	2.40	-4	2-49	1	-1.4
Min-A	53	185	30	47	5	7	0	13	22	24	5	2	.254	.333	.357	.690	87	-3	23	4.26	-9	2-50/D-2,S-1	5	-1.0
Yr.	103	355	46	83	12	9	1	28	38	44	8	7	.234	.310	.327	.636	74	-13	36	3.33	-13	2-99/D-2,S-1	6	-2.5
1991 KC-A	10	22	5	9	0	0	0	1	0	2	0	1	.409	.409	.409	.818	127	0	3	5.96	1	2-10	1	0.1
1993 Col-N	48	151	28	46	6	3	2	15	18	22	6	4	.305	.379	.424	.803	98	-0	23	5.12	-6	S-35,2-16/3-1	3	-0.3
1994 Col-N	87	255	39	65	17	5	3	31	42	44	0	2	.255	.360	.396	.756	83	-6	38	5.07	-11	2-79/S-3,3-2	6	-1.3
1995 Pit-N	107	259	29	74	12	1	5	38	24	34	2	2	.286	.351	.398	.749	95	-2	37	5.21	-7	2-67/3-5,S-1	9	-0.6
1996 Pit-N	112	217	23	58	14	2	3	30	14	22	2	0	.267	.312	.392	.703	82	-6	28	4.56	-2	2-36/3-9,S-5	4	-0.7
1997 LA-N	76	88	10	20	6	0	1	11	6	12	0	0	.227	.277	.330	.606	63	-5	8	3.08	-2	2-17/1-2,3-1,S-1	1	-0.6
1998 Col-N	12	17	0	0	0	0	0	0	0	7	0	0	.000	.000	.000	.000	-82	-5	0	.00	0	/2-3,S-1	0	-0.5
Total 11	823	2216	296	576	105	27	25	240	212	300	59	30	.260	.326	.366	.692	85	-47	272	4.17	-59	2-566/S-47,3-19,D-18,1-2	54	-8.5

• LIS, Joe Joseph Anthony Lis b: 8/15/1946, Somerville, NJ BR/TR, 6', 195 lbs. Deb: 9/5/1970 Career OF: 53-0-6

YEAR TM-L	G	AB	R	H	2B	3B	HR	RBI	BB	SO	SB	CS	AVG	OBP	SLG	OPS	OPS+	BR/A	RC	RC/G	FR	G/POS	WS	TPW
1970 Phi-N	13	37	1	7	2	0	1	4	5	11	0	0	.189	.286	.324	.610	65	-2	4	3.42	-1	/O-9(9-0-0)	1	-0.3
1971 Phi-N	59	123	16	26	6	0	6	10	16	43	0	1	.211	.312	.407	.719	102	-0	16	4.34	0	O-35(35-0-0)	3	-0.1
1972 Phi-N	62	140	13	34	6	0	6	18	30	34	0	1	.243	.380	.414	.794	122	5	24	5.87	1	1-30,O-14(8-0-6)	5	0.4
1973 Min-A	103	253	37	62	11	1	9	25	28	66	0	1	.245	.327	.403	.731	101	0	31	3.99	-2	1-96/D-1	5	-0.8
1974 Min-A	24	41	5	8	0	0	0	3	5	12	0	0	.195	.298	.195	.493	42	-3	3	1.89	-1	1-18	0	-0.5
Cle-A	57	109	15	22	3	0	6	16	14	30	1	0	.202	.293	.394	.687	97	-0	12	3.47	-1	1-31/3-9,D-9,O-1	2	-0.3
Yr.	81	150	20	30	3	0	6	19	19	42	1	0	.200	.294	.340	.634	82	-3	14	3.02	-3	1-49/3-9,D-9,O-1	2	-0.9
1975 Cle-A	9	13	4	4	2	0	2	8	3	3	0	0	.308	.471	.923	1.394	286	3	6	16.27	0	/1-8,D-1	2	0.3
1976 Cle-A	20	51	4	16	1	0	2	7	8	8	0	0	.314	.407	.451	.858	153	4	10	7.68	0	1-17/D-1	3	0.2
1977 Sea-A	9	13	1	3	0	0	0	1	1	2	0	0	.231	.286	.231	.516	43	-1	0	.48	-1	/1-4,C-1	0	-0.2
Total 8	356	780	96	182	31	1	32	92	110	209	1	3	.233	.334	.399	.733	106	6	106	4.48	-5	1-204/O-59,D-12,3-9,C-1	21	-1.4

• LISI, Rick Riccardo Patrick Emilio Lisi b: 3/17/1956, Halifax, Canada BR/TR, 6', 175 lbs. Deb: 5/9/1981

YEAR TM-L	G	AB	R	H	2B	3B	HR	RBI	BB	SO	SB	CS	AVG	OBP	SLG	OPS	OPS+	BR/A	RC	RC/G	FR	G/POS	WS	TPW
1981 Tex-A	9	16	6	5	0	0	0	1	4	0	0	1	.313	.450	.313	.763	130	1	2	5.44	0	/O-8(0-2-6)	1	0.0

• LISTACH, Pat Patrick Alan Listach b: 9/12/1967, Natchitoches, LA BB/TR, 5'9", 170 lbs. Deb: 4/8/1992 Career OF: 4-87-2

YEAR TM-L	G	AB	R	H	2B	3B	HR	RBI	BB	SO	SB	CS	AVG	OBP	SLG	OPS	OPS+	BR/A	RC	RC/G	FR	G/POS	WS	TPW
1992 Mil-A	149	579	93	168	19	6	1	47	55	124	54	18	.290	.353	.349	.702	99	5	79	4.77	12	*S-148/2-1,O-1	21	2.9
1993 Mil-A	98	356	50	87	15	1	3	30	37	70	18	9	.244	.321	.317	.638	73	-13	38	3.47	4	S-95/O-6(0-6-0)	8	-0.1
1994 Mil-A	16	54	8	16	3	0	0	2	3	8	2	1	.296	.333	.352	.685	74	-2	6	4.19	3	S-16	1	0.2
1995 Mil-A	101	334	35	73	8	2	0	25	25	61	13	3	.219	.277	.254	.531	37	-30	25	2.47	8	2-59,S-36,O-11(1-10-1)/3-2	4	-1.6
1996 Mil-A	87	317	51	76	16	2	1	33	36	51	25	5	.240	.319	.312	.632	58	-17	37	3.88	2	O-68(2-66-0),2-12/S-7	6	-1.3
1997 Hou-N	52	132	13	24	2	2	0	6	11	24	4	2	.182	.250	.227	.477	27	-14	7	1.49	-2	S-31/O-6(1-4-1)	1	-1.4
Total 6	503	1772	250	444	63	13	5	143	167	338	116	38	.251	.318	.309	.627	69	-71	192	3.60	28	S-333/O-92,2-72,3-2	41	-1.2

• LISTER, Pete Morris Elmer Lister b: 7/21/1881, Savanna, IL d: 3/27/1947, St. Petersburg, FL BR/TR, 6', 190 lbs. Deb: 9/14/1907

YEAR TM-L	G	AB	R	H	2B	3B	HR	RBI	BB	SO	SB	CS	AVG	OBP	SLG	OPS	OPS+	BR/A	RC	RC/G	FR	G/POS	WS	TPW
1907 Cle-A	22	65	5	18	2	0	0	4	3	....	2	....	.277	.319	.308	.627	99	-0	7	4.03	-1	1-22	2	-0.1

• LITTLE, Bryan Richard Bryan "Twig" Little b: 10/8/1959, Houston, TX BB/TR, 5'10", 160 lbs. Deb: 7/29/1982 C

YEAR TM-L	G	AB	R	H	2B	3B	HR	RBI	BB	SO	SB	CS	AVG	OBP	SLG	OPS	OPS+	BR/A	RC	RC/G	FR	G/POS	WS	TPW
1982 Mon-N	29	42	6	9	0	0	0	3	4	6	2	1	.214	.283	.214	.497	40	-3	3	2.04	0	2-16,S-10	0	-0.2
1983 Mon-N	106	350	48	91	15	3	1	36	50	22	4	5	.260	.356	.329	.684	91	-3	42	4.01	-3	S-66,2-51	9	0.1
1984 Mon-N	85	266	31	65	11	1	0	9	34	19	2	3	.244	.332	.293	.625	81	-7	28	3.53	-1	2-77/S-2	6	-0.4
1985 Chi-A	73	188	35	47	9	1	2	27	26	21	0	1	.250	.350	.340	.691	87	-3	24	4.22	1	2-68/3-2,S-1	7	0.1
1986 Chi-A	20	35	3	6	1	0	0	2	4	4	0	0	.171	.256	.200	.456	25	-4	2	1.44	0	2-12/S-7,3-1	1	-0.3
NY-A	14	41	3	8	1	0	0	0	2	7	0	0	.195	.233	.220	.452	24	-4	2	1.58	1	2-14	1	-0.3
Yr.	34	76	6	14	2	0	0	2	6	11	0	0	.184	.244	.211	.454	25	-8	4	1.51	1	2-26/S-7,3-1	2	-0.5
Total 5	327	922	126	226	37	5	3	77	120	79	8	10	.245	.336	.306	.642	80	-24	100	3.60	-2	2-238/S-86,3-3	24	-0.9

• LITTLE, Harry Harry A. Little b: St. Louis, MO TR Deb: 7/16/1877

YEAR TM-L	G	AB	R	H	2B	3B	HR	RBI	BB	SO	SB	CS	AVG	OBP	SLG	OPS	OPS+	BR/A	RC	RC/G	FR	G/POS	WS	TPW
1877 StL-N	3	12	2	2	0	0	0	0	1	6	....	....	.167	.231	.167	.397	28	-1	0	1.30	0	/O-3(0-3-0)	0	-0.1
Lou-N	1	3	0	0	0	0	0	0	1	1	....	....	.000	.250	.000	.250	-13	-0	0	.00	0	/2-1	0	0.0
Yr.	4	15	2	2	0	0	0	0	2	7	....	....	.133	.235	.133	.369	19	-1	0	1.00	0	/O-3(0-3-0),2-1	0	-0.1

• LITTLE, Jack William Arthur Little b: 3/12/1891, Mart, TX d: 7/27/1961, Dallas, TX BR/TR, 5'11", 175 lbs. Deb: 7/2/1912

YEAR TM-L	G	AB	R	H	2B	3B	HR	RBI	BB	SO	SB	CS	AVG	OBP	SLG	OPS	OPS+	BR/A	RC	RC/G	FR	G/POS	WS	TPW
1912 NY-A	3	12	2	3	0	0	0	0	1	....	2	....	.250	.357	.250	.607	70	-0	2	5.03	0	/O-3(0-3-0)	0	0.0

• LITTLE, Mark Mark Travis Little b: 7/11/1972, Edwardsville, IL BR/TR, 6', 195 lbs. Deb: 9/12/1998 Career OF: 36-27-34

YEAR TM-L	G	AB	R	H	2B	3B	HR	RBI	BB	SO	SB	CS	AVG	OBP	SLG	OPS	OPS+	BR/A	RC	RC/G	FR	G/POS	WS	TPW
1998 StL-N	7	12	0	1	0	0	0	0	2	5	1	0	.083	.214	.083	.298	-18	-2	1	1.15	0	/O-7(3-0-4)	0	-0.2
2001 Col-N	51	85	18	29	6	0	3	13	1	20	5	2	.341	.378	.518	.895	105	1	17	7.89	3	O-29(13-14-6)	3	0.3
2002 Col-N	61	105	20	21	5	2	0	5	13	28	2	1	.200	.311	.286	.597	51	-7	11	3.27	2	O-36(16-11-16)	2	-0.6
NY-N	3	3	0	0	0	0	0	0	0	1	0	1	.000	.000	.000	.000	-104	-1	0	.00	0	/O-1	0	-0.1
*Ari-N	15	22	8	6	0	1	0	2	2	5	0	0	.273	.429	.364	.792	102	0	4	6.91	0	O-12(4-2-7)	1	0.0
Yr.	79	130	28	27	5	3	0	7	15	34	2	2	.208	.327	.292	.619	57	-8	15	3.69	2	O-49(20-13-24)	3	-0.8
Total 3	137	227	46	57	11	3	3	20	18	59	8	4	.251	.339	.366	.704	69	-9	32	4.89	4	/O-85	6	-0.6

• LITTLE, Scott Dennis Scott Little b: 1/19/1963, East St. Louis, IL BR/TR, 6', 198 lbs. Deb: 7/27/1989

YEAR TM-L	G	AB	R	H	2B	3B	HR	RBI	BB	SO	SB	CS	AVG	OBP	SLG	OPS	OPS+	BR/A	RC	RC/G	FR	G/POS	WS	TPW
1989 Pit-N	3	4	0	1	0	0	0	0	0	1	0	0	.250	.250	.250	.500	45	-0	0	2.25	1	/O-1	0	0.1

• LITTLEJOHN, Dennis Dennis Gerald Littlejohn b: 10/4/1954, Santa Monica, CA BR/TR, 6'2", 200 lbs. Deb: 7/9/1978

YEAR TM-L	G	AB	R	H	2B	3B	HR	RBI	BB	SO	SB	CS	AVG	OBP	SLG	OPS	OPS+	BR/A	RC	RC/G	FR	G/POS	WS	TPW
1978 SF-N	2	0	0	0	0	0	0	0	0	0	0	0	....	....	....	....	-104	0	0	....	-1	/C-2	0	-0.1
1979 SF-N	63	193	15	38	6	1	1	13	21	46	0	0	.197	.276	.254	.530	49	-13	14	2.31	3	C-63	3	-0.8
1980 SF-N	13	29	2	7	1	0	0	2	7	7	0	0	.241	.389	.276	.665	90	0	4	3.92	0	C-10	1	0.1
Total 3	78	222	17	45	7	1	1	15	28	53	0	0	.203	.292	.257	.549	55	-13	18	2.52	2	/C-75	4	-0.8

• LITTLETON, Larry Larry Marvin Littleton b: 4/3/1954, Charlotte, NC BR/TR, 6'1", 185 lbs. Deb: 4/12/1981

YEAR TM-L	G	AB	R	H	2B	3B	HR	RBI	BB	SO	SB	CS	AVG	OBP	SLG	OPS	OPS+	BR/A	RC	RC/G	FR	G/POS	WS	TPW
1981 Cle-A	26	23	2	0	0	0	0	1	3	6	0	0	.000	.115	.000	.115	-65	-5	0	.05	-2	O-24(19-6-1)	0	-0.8

• LITTON, Greg Jon Gregory Litton b: 7/13/1964, New Orleans, LA BR/TR, 6', 190 lbs. Deb: 5/2/1989 Career OF: 42-0-50

YEAR TM-L	G	AB	R	H	2B	3B	HR	RBI	BB	SO	SB	CS	AVG	OBP	SLG	OPS	OPS+	BR/A	RC	RC/G	FR	G/POS	WS	TPW
1989*SF-N	71	143	12	36	5	3	4	17	7	29	0	2	.252	.291	.413	.704	102	-1	16	3.70	-3	3-34,2-15/S-9,O-6(4-0-2),C	4	-0.4
1990 SF-N	93	204	17	50	9	1	1	24	11	45	1	0	.245	.287	.314	.601	68	-9	18	2.99	3	O-56(14-0-42),2-18/S-7,3-5	3	-0.7
1991 SF-N	59	127	13	23	7	1	1	15	11	25	0	2	.181	.252	.276	.527	50	-9	9	2.10	2	1-15,2-15,3-11/S-9,O-6(2-0-4),C,P	1	-0.9
1992 SF-N	68	140	9	32	5	0	4	15	11	33	0	1	.229	.285	.350	.635	83	-4	14	3.29	4	2-31,3-10/1-8,S-3,O-1	3	0.0
1993 Sea-A	72	174	25	52	17	0	3	25	18	30	0	0	.299	.368	.448	.816	117	4	28	5.50	4	O-22(21-0-2),2-17,1-13,D-12/3,S	6	0.6
1994 Bos-A	11	21	2	2	0	0	0	1	0	5	0	0	.095	.095	.095	.190	-48	-5	0	.31	1	/2-4,1-3,3-2,D-1	0	-0.4
Total 6	374	809	78	195	43	5	13	97	58	167	1	6	.241	.295	.355	.650	82	-25	84	3.45	10	2-100/O-91,3-69,1-39,S,D,C,P	17	-1.7

YEAR TM-L	G	AB	R	H	2B	3B	HR	RBI	BB	SO	SB	CS	AVG	OBP	SLG	OPS	OPS+	BR/A	RC	RC/G	FR	G/POS	WS	TPW
• LITTRELL, Jack	Jack Napier Littrell b: 1/22/1929, Louisville, KY BR/TR, 6', 179 lbs. Deb: 4/19/1952																							
1952 Phi-A	4	2	0	0	0	0	0	0	1	2	0	0	.000	.333	.000	.333	-2	-0	0	1.17	-1	/S-2,3-1	0	-0.1
1954 Phi-A	9	30	7	9	2	0	1	3	6	3	1	0	.300	.417	.467	.883	141	2	6	6.82	0	/S-9	2	0.3
1955 KC-A	37	70	7	14	0	1	0	1	4	12	0	0	.200	.243	.229	.472	27	-7	4	1.85	-3	S-22/1-6,2-4	0	-0.9
1957 Chi-N	61	153	8	29	4	2	1	13	9	43	0	0	.190	.235	.261	.496	34	-14	10	2.07	-9	S-47/2-6,3-5	1	-2.0
Total 4	**111**	**255**	**22**	**52**	**6**	**3**	**2**	**17**	**20**	**60**	**1**	**0**	**.204**	**.262**	**.275**	**.536**	**45**	**-20**	**20**	**2.52**	**-13**	**/S-80,2-10,1-6,3-6**	**3**	**-2.7**
• LITWHILER, Danny	Daniel Webster Litwhiler b: 8/31/1916, Ringtown, PA BR/TR, 5'10.5", 198 lbs. Deb: 4/25/1940 C Career OF: 681-5-234																							
1940 Phi-N	36	142	10	49	2	2	5	17	3	13	1	....	.345	.363	.493	.856	139	7	25	7.27	2	O-34(2-3-31)	5	0.7
1941 Phi-N	151	590	72	180	29	6	18	66	39	43	1	....	.305	.350	.466	.816	134	23	93	5.87	9	*O-150(148-0-2)	17	2.4
1942 Phi-N★	151	591	59	160	25	9	9	56	27	42	2	....	.271	.310	.389	.700	110	4	68	4.10	-3	*O-151(130-0-24)	12	-0.9
1943 Phi-N	36	139	23	36	6	0	5	17	11	14	1	....	.259	.313	.410	.723	113	2	18	4.47	3	O-34(34-0-0)	4	0.2
*StL-N	80	258	40	72	14	3	7	31	19	31	1	....	.279	.333	.438	.771	117	4	38	5.36	3	O-70(70-0-0)	9	0.4
Yr.	116	397	63	108	20	3	12	48	30	45	2	....	.272	.326	.428	.755	115	6	56	5.05	6	*O-104(104-0-0)	13	0.6
1944*StL-N	140	492	53	130	25	5	15	82	37	56	2	....	.264	.328	.427	.755	109	5	69	4.83	-5	*O-136(136-0-0)	15	-0.9
1946 StL-N	6	5	0	0	0	0	0	0	1	1	0	....	.000	.167	.000	.167	-49	-1	0	.23	0	....	0	-0.1
Bos-N	79	247	29	72	12	2	8	38	19	23	1	....	.291	.347	.453	.800	124	7	39	5.69	-1	O-65(65-0-0)/3-2	11	0.2
Yr.	85	252	29	72	12	2	8	38	20	24	1	....	.286	.343	.444	.788	121	6	39	5.55	-1	O-65(65-0-0)/3-2	11	0.1
1947 Bos-N	91	226	38	59	5	2	7	31	25	43	1	....	.261	.337	.394	.731	96	-2	30	4.65	-1	O-66(64-0-1)	6	-0.7
1948 Bos-N	13	33	0	9	2	0	0	6	4	2	0	....	.273	.385	.333	.718	97	0	4	3.78	1	/O-8(8-0-0)	1	0.1
Cin-N	106	338	51	93	19	2	14	44	48	41	1	....	.275	.365	.467	.833	128	13	56	5.68	1	O-83(5-1-77),3-15	12	1.2
Yr.	119	371	51	102	21	2	14	50	52	43	1	....	.275	.367	.456	.823	125	14	60	5.50	2	O-91(13-1-77),3-15	13	1.3
1949 Cin-N	102	292	35	85	18	1	11	48	44	42	0	....	.291	.384	.473	.857	127	12	56	7.11	1	O-82(11-1-71)/3-3	12	1.0
1950 Cin-N	54	112	15	29	4	0	6	12	20	21	0	....	.259	.371	.455	.827	116	3	19	5.69	-2	O-29(8-0-21)	3	0.0
1951 Cin-N	12	29	3	8	1	0	2	3	2	5	0	0	.276	.323	.517	.840	120	1	5	6.59	-1	/O-7(0-0-7)	1	0.0
Total 11	**1057**	**3494**	**428**	**982**	**162**	**32**	**107**	**451**	**299**	**377**	**11**	**0**	**.281**	**.342**	**.438**	**.780**	**119**	**78**	**520**	**5.33**	**7**	**O-915/3-20**	**108**	**3.7**
• LIVINGSTON, Mickey	Thompson Orville Livingston b: 11/15/1914, Newberry, SC d: 4/3/1983, Newberry, SC BR/TR, 6'1.5", 185 lbs. Deb: 9/17/1938																							
1938 Was-A	2	4	0	3	2	0	0	1	0	1	0	0	.750	.750	1.250	2.000	422	2	4	95.40	-1	/C-2	1	0.1
1941 Phi-N	95	207	16	42	6	1	0	18	20	38	2	....	.203	.276	.242	.518	49	-14	13	1.99	0	C-71/1-1	1	-1.1
1942 Phi-N	89	239	20	49	6	1	2	22	25	20	0	....	.205	.283	.264	.547	64	-11	19	2.54	0	C-78/1-6	3	-0.7
1943 Phi-N	84	265	25	66	9	2	3	18	19	18	1	....	.249	.304	.332	.636	87	-5	27	3.54	7	C-84/1-2	7	0.7
Chi-N	36	111	11	29	5	1	4	16	12	8	1	....	.261	.333	.432	.766	122	3	14	4.25	-2	C-31/1-4	3	0.3
Yr.	120	376	36	95	14	3	7	34	31	26	2	....	.253	.313	.362	.675	98	-2	41	3.75	5	*C-115/1-6	10	0.9
1945*Chi-N	71	224	19	57	4	2	2	23	19	6	2	....	.254	.324	.317	.641	80	-6	23	3.47	-3	C-68/1-1	7	-0.5
1946 Chi-N	66	176	14	45	14	0	2	20	20	19	0	....	.256	.338	.369	.708	103	1	23	4.43	-4	C-56	7	0.0
1947 Chi-N	19	33	2	7	2	0	0	3	1	5	0	....	.212	.235	.273	.508	36	-3	2	2.24	0	/C-7	0	-0.3
NY-N	5	6	0	1	0	0	0	0	1	2	0	....	.167	.286	.167	.452	23	-1	0	1.94	0	/C-1	0	-0.1
Yr.	24	39	2	8	2	0	0	3	2	7	0	....	.205	.244	.256	.500	34	-4	3	2.19	0	/C-8	0	-0.4
1948 NY-N	45	99	9	21	4	1	2	12	21	11	1	....	.212	.350	.333	.683	85	-1	13	4.11	-1	C-42	3	-0.1
1949 NY-N	19	57	6	17	2	0	4	12	2	8	0	....	.298	.333	.544	.877	132	2	10	6.13	-1	C-19	2	0.2
Bos-N	28	64	6	15	2	1	0	6	3	5	0	....	.234	.290	.297	.587	61	-4	6	3.24	0	C-22	1	-0.2
Yr.	47	121	12	32	4	1	4	18	5	13	0	....	.264	.310	.413	.723	94	-2	15	4.57	0	C-41	3	0.0
1951 Bro-N	2	5	0	2	0	0	0	2	1	0	0	0	.400	.500	.400	.900	142	0	1	8.19	1	/C-2	0	0.1
Total 10	**561**	**1490**	**128**	**354**	**56**	**9**	**19**	**153**	**144**	**141**	**7**	**0**	**.238**	**.310**	**.326**	**.636**	**82**	**-36**	**154**	**3.47**	**-4**	**C-483/1-14**	**35**	**-1.7**
• LIVINGSTON, Paddy	Patrick Joseph Livingston b: 1/14/1880, Cleveland, OH d: 9/19/1977, Cleveland, OH BR/TR, 5'8", 197 lbs. Deb: 9/2/1901 C																							
1901 Cle-A	1	2	0	0	0	0	0	0	0	....	0	....	.000	.333	.000	.333	-2	-0	0	.00	-0	/C-1	0	0.0
1906 Cin-N	50	139	8	22	1	4	0	8	12	....	0	....	.158	.259	.223	.483	48	-8	9	1.90	2	C-47	2	-0.2
1909 Phi-A	64	175	15	41	6	4	0	15	15	....	4	....	.234	.323	.314	.638	99	1	20	3.57	7	C-64	8	1.5
1910 Phi-A	37	120	11	25	4	3	0	9	6	....	2	....	.208	.264	.292	.555	75	-4	10	2.55	2	C-37	4	0.3
1911 Phi-A	27	71	9	17	4	0	0	8	7	....	1	....	.239	.316	.296	.612	72	-2	7	3.25	0	C-26	3	0.0
1912 Cle-A	20	47	5	11	2	1	0	3	1	....	0	....	.234	.280	.319	.599	69	-2	4	2.89	1	C-14	1	0.0
1917 StL-N	7	20	0	4	0	0	0	2	0	1	2	....	.200	.200	.200	.400	23	-2	1	1.67	0	/C-6	0	-0.2
Total 7	**206**	**574**	**48**	**120**	**17**	**12**	**0**	**45**	**41**	**1**	**9**	**....**	**.209**	**.287**	**.280**	**.568**	**73**	**-18**	**51**	**2.76**	**13**	**C-195**	**18**	**1.3**
• LIVINGSTONE, Scott	Scott Louis Livingstone b: 7/15/1965, Dallas, TX BL/TR, 6', 198 lbs. Deb: 7/19/1991																							
1991 Det-A	44	127	19	37	5	0	2	11	10	25	2	1	.291	.343	.378	.721	98	-0	17	5.06	-3	3-43	3	-0.3
1992 Det-A	117	354	43	100	21	0	4	46	21	36	1	3	.282	.323	.376	.698	95	-4	41	4.07	0	*3-112	8	-0.4
1993 Det-A	98	304	39	89	10	2	2	39	19	32	1	3	.293	.334	.359	.693	87	-7	36	4.25	-6	3-62,D-32	4	-1.4
1994 Det-A	15	23	0	5	1	0	0	1	1	4	0	0	.217	.250	.261	.511	32	-2	2	2.35	0	/1-5,D-5,3-1	0	-0.3
SD-N	57	180	11	49	12	1	2	10	6	22	2	2	.272	.296	.383	.679	78	-7	19	3.60	1	3-50	1	-0.6
1995 SD-N	99	196	26	66	15	0	5	32	15	22	2	1	.337	.384	.490	.874	134	9	37	7.30	-3	1-43,3-13/2-4	8	0.3
1996*SD-N	102	172	20	51	4	1	2	20	9	22	0	1	.297	.331	.366	.698	89	-4	19	4.04	1	1-22,3-16	4	-0.4
1997 SD-N	23	26	1	4	1	0	0	3	2	1	0	0	.154	.214	.192	.407	8	-4	1	1.45	-1	/3-3,1-2,2-1	0	-0.4
StL-N	42	41	3	7	1	0	0	3	1	10	1	0	.171	.190	.195	.386	1	-6	2	1.14	0	/3-2,D-1,0-1	0	-0.6
Yr.	65	67	4	11	2	0	0	6	3	11	1	0	.164	.200	.194	.394	4	-9	3	1.26	-1	/3-5,1-2,2-1,D-1,0-1	0	-1.0
1998 Mon-N	76	110	1	23	6	0	0	12	5	15	1	1	.209	.243	.264	.507	34	-11	7	1.96	0	3-17/D-5,1-3	0	-1.0
Total 8	**673**	**1533**	**163**	**431**	**76**	**4**	**17**	**177**	**89**	**189**	**10**	**12**	**.281**	**.321**	**.369**	**.690**	**87**	**-36**	**180**	**4.16**	**-12**	**3-319/1-75,D-43,2-5,0-1**	**28**	**-5.1**
• LIZOTTE, Abel	Abel Lizotte b: 4/13/1870, Lewiston, ME d: 12/4/1926, Wilkes-Barre, PA, 5'8", 174 lbs. Deb: 9/17/1896																							
1896 Pit-N	7	29	3	3	0	0	0	3	2	2	1	....	.103	.161	.103	.265	-31	-5	1	.74	1	/1-7	0	-0.4
• LLENAS, Winston	Winston Enriquillo (Davila) Llenas b: 9/23/1943, Santiago, Dominican Republic BR/TR, 5'10", 165 lbs. Deb: 8/15/1968 C Career OF: 40-0-8																							
1968 Cal-A	16	39	5	5	1	0	0	1	2	5	0	0	.128	.190	.154	.344	6	-4	1	.87	-3	/3-9	0	-0.8
1969 Cal-A	34	47	4	8	2	0	0	0	2	10	0	0	.170	.204	.213	.417	18	-5	2	1.30	0	/3-9	0	-0.5
1972 Cal-A	44	64	3	17	3	0	0	7	3	8	0	0	.266	.299	.313	.611	87	-1	5	2.58	-1	3-10/2-2,O-2(2-0-0)	1	-0.2
1973 Cal-A	78	130	16	35	1	0	1	25	10	16	0	0	.269	.326	.300	.626	84	-3	13	3.30	-1	2-20,3-11/D-4,O-4(4-0-0)	2	-0.4
1974 Cal-A	72	138	16	36	6	0	2	17	11	19	0	0	.261	.315	.348	.663	96	-1	15	3.55	-1	O-32(25-0-7),2-15,D-10/3-2	3	-0.2
1975 Cal-A	56	113	6	21	4	0	0	11	10	11	0	1	.186	.252	.221	.473	37	-10	6	1.47	4	2-12,O-10(9-0-1)/1-6,D-6,3	1	-0.6
Total 6	**300**	**531**	**50**	**122**	**17**	**0**	**3**	**61**	**38**	**69**	**0**	**1**	**.230**	**.284**	**.279**	**.562**	**66**	**-24**	**42**	**2.49**	**-2**	**/2-49,O-48,3-44,D-20,1-6**	**7**	**-2.8**
• LOAN, Mike	William Joseph Loan b: 9/27/1894, Philadelphia, PA d: 11/21/1966, Springfield, PA BR/TR, 5'11", 185 lbs. Deb: 9/18/1912																							
1912 Phi-N	1	2	1	1	0	0	0	0	0	0	0	....	.500	.500	.500	1.000	163	0	0	12.55	0	/C-1	0	0.0
• LOANE, Bob	Robert Kenneth Loane b: 8/5/1914, Berkeley, CA d: 12/11/2002, Monterey, CA BR/TR, 6', 190 lbs. Deb: 7/29/1939 Career OF: 2-11-0																							
1939 Was-A	3	9	2	0	0	0	0	1	4	4	0	0	.000	.308	.000	.308	-16	-1	0	.96	2	/O-3(0-3-0)	0	0.0
1940 Bos-N	13	22	4	5	3	0	0	1	2	5	2	....	.227	.292	.364	.655	84	-1	3	3.80	1	O-10(2-8-0)	1	0.1
Total 2	**16**	**31**	**6**	**5**	**3**	**0**	**0**	**2**	**6**	**9**	**2**	**0**	**.161**	**.297**	**.258**	**.555**	**50**	**-2**	**3**	**2.85**	**3**	**/O-13**	**1**	**0.1**
• LOBERT, Frank	Frank John Lobert b: 11/26/1883, Williamsport, PA d: 5/29/1932, Pittsburgh, PA BR/TR, 6', 180 lbs. Deb: 6/6/1914																							
1914 Bal-F	11	30	3	6	0	1	0	2	0	0	0	....	.200	.200	.267	.467	32	-3	2	1.57	-3	/3-7,2-1	0	-0.6
• LOBERT, Hans	John Bernard "Honus" Lobert b: 10/18/1881, Wilmington, DE d: 9/14/1968, Philadelphia, PA BR/TR, 5'9", 170 lbs. Deb: 9/21/1903 M/C Career OF: 21-2-0																							
1903 Pit-N	5	13	1	1	1	0	0	0	1	....	1	....	.077	.143	.154	.297	-15	-2	1	1.04	-1	/3-3,2-1,S-1	0	-0.2
1905 Chi-N	14	46	7	9	2	0	0	1	3	....	4	....	.196	.260	.239	.499	47	-3	5	2.79	1	3-13/O-1	1	-0.1
1906 Cin-N	79	268	39	83	5	5	0	19	19	....	20	....	.310	.366	.366	.732	123	7	46	6.02	-9	3-35,S-31,2-10/O-1	9	0.1
1907 Cin-N	148	537	61	132	9	12	1	41	37	....	30	....	.246	.299	.313	.612	88	-8	64	3.84	-6	*S-142/3-5	16	-1.1
1908 Cin-N	155	570	71	167	17	18	4	63	46	....	47	....	.293	.348	.407	.755	145	27	97	5.80	-17	3-99,S-35,O-21(21-0-0)	32	1.6

YEAR TM-L	G	AB	R	H	2B	3B	HR	RBI	BB	SO	SB	CS	AVG	OBP	SLG	OPS	OPS+	BR/A	RC	RC/G	FR	G/POS	WS	TPW
1909 Cin-N	122	425	50	90	13	5	4	52	48	....	30	....	.212	.304	.294	.598	86	-6	47	3.51	-9	*3-122	12	-1.3
1910 Cin-N	93	314	43	97	6	6	3	40	30	9	41	....	.309	.369	.395	.764	129	11	61	6.70	0	3-90	14	1.4
1911 Phi-N	147	541	94	154	20	9	9	72	66	31	40	....	.285	.368	.405	.772	115	11	97	5.93	-17	*3-147	18	-0.2
1912 Phi-N	65	257	37	84	12	5	2	33	19	13	13	....	.327	.373	.436	.809	113	4	46	6.47	-5	3-64	9	0.1
1913 Phi-N	150	573	98	172	28	11	7	55	42	34	41	....	.300	.353	.424	.777	116	11	96	5.75	-17	*3-145/S-3,2-1	20	-0.1
1914 Phi-N	135	505	83	139	24	5	1	52	49	32	31	....	.275	.343	.349	.691	99	0	69	4.62	-33	*3-133/S-2	13	-3.1
1915 NY-N	106	386	46	97	18	4	0	38	25	24	14	15	.251	.304	.319	.622	94	-7	38	3.17	-8	*3-103	10	-1.3
1916 NY-N	48	76	6	17	3	2	0	11	5	8	2	....	.224	.272	.316	.587	84	-2	8	3.11	0	3-20	2	-0.1
1917 NY-N	50	52	4	10	1	0	1	5	5	5	2	....	.192	.276	.269	.545	70	-2	4	2.54	0	3-21	1	-0.1
Total 14	**1317**	**4563**	**640**	**1252**	**159**	**82**	**32**	**482**	**395**	**156**	**316**	**15**	**.274**	**.337**	**.366**	**.703**	**109**	**43**	**679**	**4.95**	**-120**	***3-1000,S-214/O-23,2-12**	**157**	**-4.6**

• LOCHHEAD, Harry Robert Henry Lochhead b: 3/29/1876, Stockton, CA d: 8/22/1909, Stockton, CA BR/TR, 5'11", 172 lbs. Deb: 4/16/1899

YEAR TM-L	G	AB	R	H	2B	3B	HR	RBI	BB	SO	SB	CS	AVG	OBP	SLG	OPS	OPS+	BR/A	RC	RC/G	FR	G/POS	WS	TPW
1899 Cle-N	148	541	52	129	7	1	1	43	21	....	23	....	.238	.280	.261	.540	52	-34	48	3.03	-19	*S-146/2-1,P-1	3	-4.0
1901 Det-A	1	4	2	2	0	0	0	0	0	....	0	....	.500	.600	.500	1.100	198	1	1	16.30	-0	/S-1	0	0.1
Phi-A	9	34	3	3	0	0	0	2	3	....	0	....	.088	.162	.088	.250	-28	-6	0	.43	-4	/S-9	0	-0.8
Yr.	10	38	5	5	0	0	0	2	3	....	0	....	.132	.214	.132	.346	-1	-5	2	1.39	-4	S-10	0	-0.8
Total 2	**158**	**579**	**57**	**134**	**7**	**1**	**1**	**45**	**24**	**....**	**23**	**....**	**.231**	**.275**	**.252**	**.527**	**49**	**-40**	**50**	**2.91**	**-22**	**S-156/2-1,P-1**	**3**	**-4.8**

• LOCK, Don Don Wilson Lock b: 7/27/1936, Wichita, KS BR/TR, 6'2", 202 lbs. Deb: 7/17/1962 Career OF: 102-684-70

YEAR TM-L	G	AB	R	H	2B	3B	HR	RBI	BB	SO	SB	CS	AVG	OBP	SLG	OPS	OPS+	BR/A	RC	RC/G	FR	G/POS	WS	TPW
1962 Was-A	71	225	30	57	6	2	12	37	30	63	4	5	.253	.341	.458	.799	114	3	33	4.88	-1	O-67(67-1-0)	5	-0.2
1963 Was-A	149	531	71	134	20	1	27	82	70	151	7	3	.252	.342	.446	.788	119	14	83	5.32	10	*O-146(10-135-9)	21	2.0
1964 Was-A	152	512	73	127	17	4	28	80	79	137	4	2	.248	.350	.461	.811	124	18	84	5.62	4	*O-149(0-135-25)	22	1.7
1965 Was-A	143	418	52	90	15	1	16	39	57	115	1	3	.215	.317	.371	.687	96	-3	48	3.78	-6	*O-136(0-136-0)	11	-1.3
1966 Was-A	138	386	52	90	13	1	16	48	57	126	2	6	.233	.335	.396	.731	110	4	51	4.37	2	*O-129(0-126-4)	14	0.3
1967 Phi-N	112	313	46	79	13	1	14	51	43	98	9	5	.252	.352	.435	.786	122	10	50	5.43	2	O-97(1-96-1)	13	1.1
1968 Phi-N	99	248	27	52	7	2	8	34	26	64	3	4	.210	.285	.351	.635	90	-4	24	3.05	-4	O-78(8-46-27)	5	-1.4
1969 Phi-N	4	4	0	0	0	0	0	0	0	1	0	0	.000	.000	.000	.000	-103	-1	0	.00	0	/O-1	0	-0.1
Bos-A	53	58	8	13	1	0	1	2	11	21	0	1	.224	.348	.293	.641	77	-2	6	3.60	-1	O-28(15-9-4)/1-4	1	-0.3
Total 8	**921**	**2695**	**359**	**642**	**92**	**12**	**122**	**373**	**373**	**776**	**30**	**29**	**.238**	**.334**	**.417**	**.751**	**111**	**40**	**379**	**4.70**	**6**	**O-831/1-4**	**92**	**1.7**

• LOCKE, Marshall Marshall Pinkney Wilder Locke b: 3/12/1857, Ashland, OH d: 3/6/1940, Ashland, OH Deb: 7/5/1884

YEAR TM-L	G	AB	R	H	2B	3B	HR	RBI	BB	SO	SB	CS	AVG	OBP	SLG	OPS	OPS+	BR/A	RC	RC/G	FR	G/POS	WS	TPW
1884 Ind-a	7	29	5	7	0	1	0	5	0	....	....	....	.241	.241	.310	.552	81	-1	2	2.78	-1	/O-7(0-3-4)	0	-0.1

• LOCKHART, Keith Keith Virgil Lockhart b: 11/10/1964, Whittier, CA BL/TR, 5'10", 170 lbs. Deb: 4/5/1994

YEAR TM-L	G	AB	R	H	2B	3B	HR	RBI	BB	SO	SB	CS	AVG	OBP	SLG	OPS	OPS+	BR/A	RC	RC/G	FR	G/POS	WS	TPW
1994 SD-N	27	43	4	9	0	0	2	6	4	10	1	0	.209	.292	.349	.641	68	-2	4	3.05	-1	3-13/2-5,O-1,S-1	0	-0.3
1995 KC-A	94	274	41	88	19	3	6	33	14	21	8	1	.321	.363	.478	.841	115	7	49	6.75	-2	2-61,3-17,D-14	11	0.6
1996 KC-A	138	433	49	118	33	3	7	55	30	40	11	6	.273	.323	.411	.734	84	-12	56	4.56	0	2-84,3-55/D-1	10	-0.7
1997*Atl-N	96	147	25	41	5	3	6	32	14	17	0	0	.279	.346	.476	.822	110	2	24	5.51	1	2-20,3-11/D-4	5	0.4
1998*Atl-N	109	366	50	94	21	0	9	37	29	37	2	2	.257	.313	.388	.701	83	-10	46	4.41	9	2-97/D-2,3-1	10	0.3
1999*Atl-N	108	161	20	42	3	1	1	21	19	21	3	1	.261	.343	.311	.653	67	-7	19	4.04	2	2-25,3-10/D-4	3	-0.5
2000*Atl-N	113	275	32	73	12	3	2	32	29	31	4	1	.265	.336	.353	.688	74	-10	32	3.87	-2	2-74,3-18	7	-0.9
2001*Atl-N	104	178	17	39	6	0	3	12	16	22	1	2	.219	.291	.303	.594	53	-13	16	3.06	-5	2-47/3-4	2	-1.6
2002*Atl-N	128	296	34	64	13	3	5	32	27	50	0	1	.216	.284	.331	.615	61	-18	28	3.10	4	2-89/3-1	7	-1.0
2003 SD-N	62	95	18	23	5	1	3	8	13	19	0	1	.242	.339	.411	.750	104	0	13	4.69	-2	2-27/3-3	2	-0.1
Total 10	**979**	**2268**	**290**	**591**	**117**	**17**	**44**	**268**	**195**	**268**	**30**	**15**	**.261**	**.323**	**.385**	**.708**	**82**	**-64**	**288**	**4.37**	**4**	**2-529,3-133/D-25,O-1,S-1**	**57**	**-3.9**

• LOCKLEAR, Gene Gene Locklear b: 7/19/1949, Lumberton, NC BL/TR, 5'10", 165 lbs. Deb: 4/5/1973 Career OF: 111-0-10

YEAR TM-L	G	AB	R	H	2B	3B	HR	RBI	BB	SO	SB	CS	AVG	OBP	SLG	OPS	OPS+	BR/A	RC	RC/G	FR	G/POS	WS	TPW
1973 Cin-N	29	26	6	5	0	0	0	0	2	5	0	0	.192	.276	.192	.468	34	-2	1	1.12	0	/O-5(1-0-4)	0	-0.3
SD-N	67	154	20	37	6	1	3	25	21	22	9	4	.240	.331	.351	.682	97	0	19	4.12	-1	O-37(37-0-0)	4	-0.3
Yr.	96	180	26	42	6	1	3	25	23	27	9	4	.233	.324	.328	.651	88	-2	20	3.64	-1	O-42(38-0-4)	4	-0.6
1974 SD-N	39	74	7	20	3	2	1	3	4	12	0	1	.270	.308	.405	.713	103	-1	9	4.43	0	O-12(8-0-4)	2	-0.1
1975 SD-N	100	237	31	76	11	1	5	27	22	26	4	2	.321	.381	.439	.820	135	11	40	6.32	0	O-51(50-0-2)	10	0.8
1976 SD-N	43	67	9	15	3	0	0	8	4	15	0	0	.224	.268	.269	.536	57	-4	5	2.56	-1	O-11(11-0-0)	1	-0.5
NY-A	13	32	2	7	1	0	0	1	2	7	0	0	.219	.265	.250	.515	52	-2	2	2.44	-0	/D-6,O-3(3-0-0)	0	-0.2
1977 NY-A	1	5	1	3	0	0	0	2	0	0	0	0	.600	.600	.600	1.200	231	1	2	24.30	0	/O-1	0	0.1
Total 5	**292**	**595**	**76**	**163**	**24**	**4**	**9**	**66**	**55**	**87**	**13**	**7**	**.274**	**.337**	**.373**	**.711**	**104**	**3**	**78**	**4.63**	**-1**	**O-120/D-6**	**17**	**-0.5**

• LOCKLIN, Stu Stuart Carlton Locklin b: 7/22/1928, Appleton, WI BL/TL, 6'1.5", 190 lbs. Deb: 6/23/1955 Career OF: 0-4-4

YEAR TM-L	G	AB	R	H	2B	3B	HR	RBI	BB	SO	SB	CS	AVG	OBP	SLG	OPS	OPS+	BR/A	RC	RC/G	FR	G/POS	WS	TPW
1955 Cle-A	16	18	4	3	1	0	0	0	3	4	0	0	.167	.286	.222	.508	37	-2	1	1.92	-1	/O-7(0-4-3)	0	-0.2
1956 Cle-A	9	6	0	1	0	0	0	0	0	1	0	0	.167	.167	.167	.333	-12	-1	0	.90	-0	/O-1	0	-0.1
Total 2	**25**	**24**	**4**	**4**	**1**	**0**	**0**	**0**	**3**	**5**	**0**	**0**	**.167**	**.259**	**.208**	**.468**	**26**	**-3**	**1**	**1.68**	**-1**	**/O-8**	**0**	**-0.3**

• LOCKMAN, Whitey Carroll Walter Lockman b: 7/25/1926, Lowell, NC BL/TR, 6'1", 175 lbs. Deb: 7/5/1945 M/C Career OF: 556-163-47

YEAR TM-L	G	AB	R	H	2B	3B	HR	RBI	BB	SO	SB	CS	AVG	OBP	SLG	OPS	OPS+	BR/A	RC	RC/G	FR	G/POS	WS	TPW
1945 NY-N	32	129	16	44	9	0	3	18	13	10	1	....	.341	.410	.481	.890	145	8	27	7.99	-2	O-32(0-32-0)	6	0.5
1947 NY-N	2	2	0	1	0	0	0	1	0	0	0	....	.500	.500	.500	1.000	165	0	1	13.50	0	....	0	0.0
1948 NY-N	146	584	117	167	24	10	18	59	68	63	8	....	.286	.361	.454	.815	119	15	101	6.37	-1	*O-144(53-91-0)	23	0.7
1949 NY-N	151	617	97	186	32	7	11	65	62	31	12	....	.301	.368	.429	.798	113	12	101	6.14	0	*O-151(151-0-0)	19	0.0
1950 NY-N	129	532	72	157	28	5	6	52	42	29	1	....	.295	.349	.400	.749	96	-3	76	5.32	7	*O-128(123-6-0)	16	-0.6
1951*NY-N	153	614	85	173	27	7	12	73	50	32	4	5	.282	.339	.407	.746	99	-3	83	4.80	2	*1-119,O-34(34-0-0)	15	-0.8
1952 NY-N★	154	606	99	176	17	4	13	58	67	52	2	4	.290	.363	.396	.759	109	8	92	5.48	9	*1-154	23	1.2
1953 NY-N	150	607	85	179	22	4	9	61	52	36	3	4	.295	.351	.389	.739	91	-8	87	5.30	9	*1-120,O-30(0-3-28)	14	-0.7
1954*NY-N	148	570	73	143	17	3	16	60	59	31	2	2	.251	.321	.375	.697	80	-17	73	4.44	-3	*1-145/O-2(1-1-0)	11	-2.8
1955 NY-N	147	576	76	157	19	0	15	49	39	34	3	3	.273	.322	.384	.706	86	-12	72	4.42	-3	O-81(79-2-1),1-68	13	-2.4
1956 NY-N	48	169	13	46	7	1	1	10	16	17	0	2	.272	.335	.343	.678	83	-4	20	4.13	-1	O-39(38-1-1)/1-7	3	-0.8
StL-N	70	193	14	48	0	2	0	10	18	8	2	2	.249	.313	.269	.582	58	-11	17	3.00	-4	O-57(32-23-8)/1-2	2	-1.8
Yr.	118	362	27	94	7	3	1	20	34	25	2	4	.260	.323	.304	.627	70	-16	37	3.53	-4	O-96(70-24-9)/1-9	5	-2.6
1957 NY-N	133	456	51	113	9	4	7	30	39	19	5	5	.248	.310	.331	.641	72	-18	48	3.66	-2	*1-102,O-27(22-3-4)	7	-2.8
1958 SF-N	92	122	15	29	5	0	2	7	13	8	0	0	.238	.311	.328	.639	71	-5	14	3.69	-3	O-25(23-0-4),2-15/1-7	2	-0.9
1959 Bal-A	38	69	7	15	1	1	0	2	8	4	0	0	.217	.299	.261	.560	56	-4	6	2.80	-2	1-22/2-5,O-1	1	-0.6
Cin-N	52	84	10	22	5	1	0	7	4	6	0	0	.262	.295	.345	.641	68	-4	9	3.62	1	1-20/2-6,3-1,O-1	1	-0.3
1960 Cin-N	21	10	6	2	0	0	1	1	2	3	0	0	.200	.385	.500	.885	137	1	2	5.34	0	/1-5	0	0.0
Total 15	**1666**	**5940**	**836**	**1658**	**222**	**49**	**114**	**563**	**552**	**383**	**43**	**27**	**.279**	**.342**	**.391**	**.733**	**95**	**-46**	**826**	**5.00**	**5**	**1-771,O-752/2-26,3-1**	**156**	**-12.0**

• LOCKWOOD, Milo Milo Hathaway Lockwood b: 4/7/1858, Solon, OH d: 10/9/1897, Economy, PA, 5'10", 160 lbs. Deb: 4/17/1884 ♦

YEAR TM-L	G	AB	R	H	2B	3B	HR	RBI	BB	SO	SB	CS	AVG	OBP	SLG	OPS	OPS+	BR/A	RC	RC/G	FR	G/POS	WS	TPW
1884 Was-U	20	67	9	14	1	0	0	....	8	....	....	....	.209	.293	.224	.517	80	-0	5	2.38	1	O-11(1-7-3),P-11/3-3	1	-2.8

• LOCKWOOD, Skip Claude Edward Lockwood b: 8/17/1946, Roslindale, MA BR/TR, 6'1", 190 lbs. Deb: 4/23/1965 ♦

YEAR TM-L	G	AB	R	H	2B	3B	HR	RBI	BB	SO	SB	CS	AVG	OBP	SLG	OPS	OPS+	BR/A	RC	RC/G	FR	G/POS	WS	TPW
1965 KC-A	42	33	4	4	0	0	0	0	7	11	0	0	.121	.293	.121	.414	23	-3	2	1.66	0	/3-7	0	-0.4
1969 Sea-A	6	7	0	0	0	0	0	0	0	2	0	0	.000	.000	.000	.000	-102	-1	0	.00	0	/P-6	1	0.0
1970 Mil-A	27	53	2	12	1	0	1	2	1	11	0	0	.226	.241	.302	.543	48	2	4	2.23	-1	P-27	6	-0.4
1971 Mil-A	36	62	2	5	1	0	1	4	5	20	0	0	.081	.149	.145	.294	-17	-1	2	.72	-3	P-33	9	0.0
1972 Mil-A	31	53	3	7	0	0	0	0	3	12	0	1	.132	.193	.132	.325	-2	-1	1	.76	-3	P-29	5	-1.3
1973 Mil-A	37	0	0	0	0	0	0	0	0	0	0	0	....	....	....	....	-102	0	0	....	0	P-37	6	-0.2
1974 Cal-A	37	0	0	0	0	0	0	0	0	0	0	0	....	....	....	....	-106	0	0	....	0	P-37	2	-0.8
1975 NY-N	24	6	0	1	0	0	0	1	0	0	0	0	.167	.167	.167	.333	-8	-0	0	.98	-1	P-24	5	1.0
1976 NY-N	56	18	2	6	1	0	0	2	2	3	0	1	.333	.400	.389	.789	132	2	3	4.66	0	P-56	15	0.9
1977 NY-N	63	15	1	3	0	0	0	1	0	1	0	0	.200	.200	.200	.400	8	-0	1	.86	-2	P-63	13	0.4
1978 NY-N	57	11	1	2	1	0	1	1	0	5	0	0	.182	.182	.545	.727	100	1	1	2.66	-2	P-57	8	0.0
1979 NY-N	28	2	0	0	0	0	0	0	0	1	0	0	.000	.000	.000	.000	-104	-0	0	.00	0	P-27	7	1.0

YEAR TM-L	G	AB	R	H	2B	3B	HR	RBI	BB	SO	SB	CS	AVG	OBP	SLG	OPS	OPS+	BR/A	RC	RC/G	FR	G/POS	WS	TPW
1980 Bos-A	24	0	0	0	0	0	0	0	0	0	0	0	....	....	....	....	-95	0	0	....	-1	P-24	2	-0.6
Total 13	468	260	15	40	4	0	3	11	18	66	0	2	.154	.214	.204	.418	20	-1	14	1.46	-14	P-420/3-7	79	-0.3
• LODIGIANI, Dario	Dario Antonio "Lodi" Lodigiani b: 7/16/1916, San Francisco, CA BR/TR, 5'8", 150 lbs. Deb: 4/18/1938 C																							
1938 Phi-A	93	325	36	91	15	1	6	44	34	25	3	0	.280	.361	.388	.748	90	-4	48	5.32	-6	2-80,3-13	7	-0.4
1939 Phi-A	121	393	46	102	22	4	6	44	42	18	2	0	.260	.337	.382	.719	85	-8	52	4.57	-9	3-89,2-28	9	-1.2
1940 Phi-A	1	1	0	0	0	0	0	0	0	0	0	0	.000	.000	.000	.000	-102	-0	0	.00	0	....	0	0.0
1941 Chi-A	87	322	39	77	19	2	4	40	31	19	0	4	.239	.316	.348	.663	76	-13	34	3.42	10	3-86	7	0.1
1942 Chi-A	59	168	9	47	7	0	0	15	18	10	3	4	.280	.353	.321	.674	92	-2	19	3.94	3	3-43/2-7	5	0.3
1946 Chi-A	44	155	12	38	8	0	0	13	16	14	4	0	.245	.324	.297	.620	77	-3	17	3.77	-1	3-44	3	-0.5
Total 6	405	1364	142	355	71	7	16	156	141	86	12	8	.260	.338	.358	.696	84	-30	170	4.28	-3	3-275,2-115	31	-1.6
• LODUCA, Paul	Paul Anthony LoDuca b: 4/12/1972, Brooklyn, NY BR/TR, 5'10", 185 lbs. Deb: 6/21/1998 Career OF: 26-0-3																							
1998 LA-N	6	14	2	4	1	0	0	1	0	1	0	0	.286	.286	.357	.643	72	-1	1	3.86	0	/C-4	0	0.0
1999 LA-N	36	95	11	22	1	0	3	11	10	9	1	2	.232	.318	.337	.655	70	-5	10	3.18	2	C-34	2	-0.1
2000 LA-N	34	65	6	16	2	0	2	8	6	8	0	2	.246	.310	.369	.679	75	-4	7	3.14	3	C-20/O-8(7-0-2),3-1	2	0.1
2001 LA-N	125	460	71	147	28	0	25	90	39	30	2	4	.320	.380	.543	.924	146	29	92	7.26	-4	C-99,1-33/O-5(4-0-1),D-1	28	2.8
2002 LA-N	149	580	74	163	38	1	10	64	34	31	3	1	.281	.332	.402	.733	99	-2	73	4.45	4	*C-137,1-18/O-9(9-0-0)	19	1.1
2003 LA-N★	147	568	64	155	34	2	7	52	44	54	0	2	.273	.336	.377	.713	91	-9	68	4.14	25	*C-123,1-22/O-6(6-0-0)	19	2.2
Total 6	497	1782	228	507	104	3	47	226	133	133	6	11	.285	.344	.425	.769	106	8	251	4.91	31	C-417/1-73,O-28,3-1,D-1	70	6.1
• LOEPP, George	George Herbert Loepp b: 9/11/1901, Detroit, MI d: 9/4/1967, Los Angeles, CA BR/TR, 5'11", 170 lbs. Deb: 8/29/1928 Career OF: 13-44-9																							
1928 Bos-A	15	51	6	9	3	1	0	3	5	12	0	0	.176	.250	.275	.525	38	-5	4	2.26	0	O-14(1-10-6)	0	-0.5
1930 Was-A	50	134	23	37	7	1	0	14	20	9	0	4	.276	.382	.343	.725	85	-3	18	4.58	0	O-48(12-34-3)	3	-0.5
Total 2	65	185	29	46	10	2	0	17	25	21	0	4	.249	.347	.324	.672	73	-8	22	3.88	0	/O-62	3	-1.0
• LOFTON, James	James O'Neal Lofton b: 3/6/1974, Los Angeles, CA BB/TR, 5'10", 170 lbs. Deb: 9/19/2001																							
2001 Bos-A	8	26	1	5	1	0	0	1	1	4	2	1	.192	.222	.231	.453	20	-3	1	1.26	-1	/S-7	0	-0.4
• LOFTON, Kenny	Kenneth Lofton b: 5/31/1967, East Chicago, IN BL/TL, 6', 180 lbs. Deb: 9/14/1991 Career OF: 0-1620-0																							
1991 Hou-N	20	74	9	15	1	0	0	0	5	19	2	1	.203	.253	.216	.469	35	-6	4	1.98	-1	O-20(0-20-0)	0	-0.8
1992 Cle-A	148	576	96	164	15	8	5	42	68	54	**66**	12	.285	.362	.365	.727	106	16	87	5.41	5	*O-143(0-143-0)	24	1.9
1993 Cle-A	148	569	116	185	28	8	1	42	81	83	**70**	14	.325	.410	.408	.818	121	31	109	7.12	1	*O-146(0-146-0)	25	3.2
1994 Cle-A★	112	459	105	**160**	32	9	12	57	52	56	**60**	12	.349	.417	.536	.953	143	38	111	9.21	7	*O-112(0-112-0)	21	4.3
1995*Cle-A★	118	481	93	149	22	**13**	7	53	40	49	**54**	15	.310	.364	.453	.817	110	11	83	6.20	-1	*O-114(0-114-0)/D-2	21	1.1
1996*Cle-A★	154	662	132	210	35	4	14	67	61	82	**75**	17	.317	.375	.446	.820	107	16	119	6.59	2	*O-153(0-153-0)	23	1.7
1997*Atl-N★	122	493	90	164	20	6	5	48	64	83	27	20	.333	.411	.428	.839	118	13	86	6.40	7	*O-122(0-122-0)	21	2.0
1998*Cle-A★	154	600	101	169	31	6	12	64	87	80	54	10	.282	.374	.413	.788	101	11	105	6.19	1	*O-154(0-154-0)	21	1.3
1999*Cle-A★	120	465	110	140	28	6	7	39	79	84	25	6	.301	.409	.432	.841	110	14	92	7.23	5	*O-119(0-119-0)/D-1	16	1.8
2000 Cle-A	137	543	107	151	23	5	15	73	79	72	30	7	.278	.374	.422	.796	99	4	92	5.86	6	*O-135(0-135-0)/D-1	17	1.1
2001*Cle-A	133	517	91	135	21	4	14	66	47	69	16	8	.261	.325	.398	.724	88	-9	68	4.48	-1	*O-131(0-130-0)	13	-0.9
2002 Chi-A	93	352	68	91	20	6	8	42	49	51	22	8	.259	.349	.418	.767	100	2	56	5.57	-1	O-92(0-92-0)	12	0.2
*SF-N	46	180	30	48	10	3	3	9	23	22	7	3	.267	.353	.406	.758	104	1	28	5.45	1	O-44(0-44-0)	7	0.3
2003 Pit-N	84	339	58	94	19	4	9	26	28	29	18	5	.277	.336	.437	.773	98	-0	52	5.51	2	O-81(0-81-0)	9	0.3
*Chi-N	56	208	39	68	13	4	3	20	18	22	12	4	.327	.386	.471	.857	124	8	38	6.63	2	O-55(0-55-0)	9	1.0
Yr.	140	547	97	162	32	8	12	46	46	51	30	9	.296	.355	.450	.805	108	8	91	5.93	4	*O-136(0-136-0)	18	1.3
Total 13	1645	6518	1245	1943	318	86	115	648	781	855	538	142	.298	.376	.426	.802	108	151	1132	6.23	36	*O-1621/D-4	239	18.4
• LOFTUS, Dick	Richard Joseph Loftus b: 3/7/1901, Concord, MA d: 1/21/1972, Concord, MA BL/TR, 6', 155 lbs. Deb: 4/20/1924 Career OF: 9-14-44																							
1924 Bro-N	46	81	18	22	6	0	0	8	7	2	1	0	.272	.330	.346	.675	84	-1	10	4.26	-1	O-29(6-14-9)/1-1	2	-0.3
1925 Bro-N	51	131	16	31	6	0	0	13	5	5	2	0	.237	.275	.282	.558	44	-10	11	2.73	0	O-38(3-0-35)	0	-1.3
Total 2	97	212	34	53	12	0	0	21	12	7	3	0	.250	.296	.307	.603	59	-12	20	3.29	-1	/O-67,1-1	2	-1.6
• LOFTUS, Tom	Thomas Joseph Loftus b: 11/15/1856, St. Louis, MO d: 4/16/1910, Dubuque, IA BR, 168 lbs. Deb: 8/17/1877 M Career OF: 1-6-2																							
1877 StL-N	3	11	2	2	0	0	0	0	0	1	....	....	.182	.182	.182	.364	16	-1	0	1.14	2	/O-3(1-0-2)	0	0.0
1883 StL-a	6	22	1	4	0	0	0	0	2	....	....	....	.182	.250	.182	.432	39	-1	1	1.59	0	/O-6(0-6-0)	0	-0.1
Total 2	9	33	3	6	0	0	0	0	2	1	....	....	.182	.229	.182	.410	32	-2	1	1.44	2	/O-9	0	-0.1
• LOGAN, Johnny	John "Yatcha" Logan b: 3/23/1927, Endicott, NY BR/TR, 5'11", 175 lbs. Deb: 4/17/1951																							
1951 Bos-N	62	169	14	37	7	1	0	16	18	13	0	0	.219	.298	.272	.570	58	-9	14	2.68	3	S-58	3	-0.3
1952 Bos-N	117	456	56	129	21	3	4	42	31	33	1	2	.283	.334	.368	.702	98	-2	57	4.40	16	*S-117	17	2.2
1953 Mil-N	150	611	100	167	27	8	11	73	41	33	2	2	.273	.326	.398	.724	93	-7	80	4.62	25	*S-150	24	2.9
1954 Mil-N	154	560	66	154	17	7	8	66	51	51	2	0	.275	.342	.373	.715	92	-5	73	4.46	14	*S-154	20	2.1
1955 Mil-N★	154	595	95	177	**37**	5	13	83	58	58	3	3	.297	.364	.442	.806	118	16	96	5.70	-1	*S-154	26	2.8
1956 Mil-N	148	545	69	153	27	5	15	46	46	49	3	0	.281	.342	.431	.773	113	10	81	4.97	12	*S-148	24	3.5
1957*Mil-N★	129	494	59	135	19	7	10	49	31	49	5	0	.273	.321	.401	.722	100	0	62	4.36	18	*S-129	18	3.0
1958*Mil-N★	145	530	54	120	20	0	11	53	40	57	1	2	.226	.287	.326	.613	68	-26	51	3.14	7	*S-144	11	-0.7
1959 Mil-N★	138	470	59	137	17	0	13	50	57	45	1	3	.291	.372	.411	.782	118	12	71	5.39	-0	*S-138	19	2.4
1960 Mil-N	136	482	52	118	14	4	7	42	43	40	1	1	.245	.309	.334	.643	82	-12	50	3.51	3	*S-136	14	0.3
1961 Mil-N	18	19	0	2	1	0	0	1	1	3	0	0	.105	.150	.158	.308	-19	-3	0	.49	0	/S-2	0	-0.3
Pit-N	27	52	5	12	4	0	0	5	4	8	0	0	.231	.286	.308	.593	57	-3	4	2.74	0	/3-7,S-6	0	-0.2
Yr.	45	71	5	14	5	0	0	6	5	11	0	0	.197	.250	.268	.518	37	-6	5	2.06	1	/S-8,3-7	0	-0.5
1962 Pit-N	44	80	7	24	3	0	1	12	7	6	0	0	.300	.356	.375	.731	96	-0	10	4.29	0	3-19	2	-0.1
1963 Pit-N	81	181	15	42	2	1	0	9	23	27	0	0	.232	.325	.254	.579	69	-6	15	2.81	-6	S-44/3-4	3	-0.9
Total 13	1503	5244	651	1407	216	41	93	547	451	472	19	13	.268	.331	.378	.710	95	-35	665	4.35	91	*S-1380/3-30	181	16.6
• LOHMAN, Pete	George F. Lohman b: 10/21/1864, Washington County, MN d: 11/21/1928, Los Angeles, CA BR/TR Deb: 5/11/1891																							
1891 Was-a	32	109	18	21	1	4	1	11	16	17	1	....	.193	.302	.303	.604	76	-3	11	3.17	-3	C-21/O-8(1-1-6),3-4,2-1,S	2	-0.4
• LOHR, Howard	Howard Sylvester Lohr b: 6/3/1892, Philadelphia, PA d: 1/9/1977, Philadelphia, PA BR/TR, 6', 165 lbs. Deb: 6/17/1914 Career OF: 0-17-4																							
1914 Cin-N	18	47	6	10	1	1	0	7	0	8	2	....	.213	.213	.277	.489	44	-4	3	2.01	-1	O-17(0-17-1)	0	-0.6
1916 Cle-A	3	7	0	1	0	0	0	1	0	1	1	....	.143	.143	.143	.286	-13	-1	0	1.15	0	/O-3(0-0-3)	0	-0.1
Total 2	21	54	6	11	1	1	0	8	0	9	3	....	.204	.204	.259	.463	36	-5	3	1.89	-1	/O-20	0	-0.7
• LOHRKE, Jack	Jack Wayne "Lucky" Lohrke b: 2/25/1924, Los Angeles, CA BR/TR, 6', 180 lbs. Deb: 4/18/1947																							
1947 NY-N	112	329	44	79	12	4	11	35	46	29	3	....	.240	.337	.401	.738	95	-3	45	4.50	-6	*3-111	8	-0.9
1948 NY-N	97	280	35	70	15	1	5	31	30	30	3	....	.250	.323	.364	.687	85	-6	33	4.11	-5	3-50,2-36	7	-0.9
1949 NY-N	55	180	32	48	11	4	5	22	16	12	3	....	.267	.333	.456	.789	110	2	27	5.13	-1	2-23,3-19,S-15	5	0.3
1950 NY-N	30	43	4	8	0	0	0	4	4	8	0	....	.186	.255	.186	.441	18	-5	2	1.59	1	3-16/2-1	0	-0.4
1951*NY-N	23	40	3	8	0	0	1	3	10	2	0	0	.200	.360	.275	.635	73	-1	4	3.18	-2	3-17/S-1	1	-0.3
1952 Phi-N	25	29	4	6	0	0	0	1	4	3	0	0	.207	.303	.207	.510	44	-2	2	2.56	0	/S-5,3-3,2-1	0	-0.1
1953 Phi-N	12	13	3	2	0	0	0	1	1	2	0	0	.154	.214	.154	.368	-2	-2	0	1.22	0	/2-2,S-2,3-1	0	-0.2
Total 7	354	914	125	221	38	9	22	96	111	86	9	0	.242	.327	.375	.702	87	-17	114	4.19	-13	3-217/2-63,S-23	21	-2.6
• LOIS, Alberto	Alberto (Pie) Lois b: 5/6/1956, Hato Mayor, Dominican Republic BR/TR, 5'9", 175 lbs. Deb: 9/8/1978																							
1978 Pit-N	3	4	0	1	0	1	0	0	0	1	0	0	.250	.250	.750	1.000	162	0	1	6.75	-0	/O-2(2-1-0)	0	0.0
1979 Pit-N	11	0	6	0	0	0	0	0	0	0	1	1	....	....	....	....	-96	-0	0	.00	0	....	0	0.0
Total 2	14	4	6	1	0	1	0	0	0	1	1	1	.250	.250	.750	1.000	162	0	1	5.06	-0	/O-2	0	0.0
• LOLICH, Ron	Ronald John Lolich b: 9/19/1946, Portland, OR BR/TR, 6'1", 185 lbs. Deb: 7/18/1971 Career OF: 9-0-48																							
1971 Chi-A	2	8	0	1	1	0	0	0	0	2	0	0	.125	.125	.250	.375	4	-1	0	.96	0	/O-2(0-0-2)	0	-0.1

YEAR TM-L	G	AB	R	H	2B	3B	HR	RBI	BB	SO	SB	CS	AVG	OBP	SLG	OPS	OPS+	BR/A	RC	RC/G	FR	G/POS	WS	TPW
1972 Cle-A	24	80	4	15	1	0	2	8	4	20	0	0	.188	.226	.275	.501	47	-5	5	2.13	0	0-22(4-0-19)	1	-0.7
1973 Cle-A	61	140	16	32	7	0	2	15	7	27	0	2	.229	.265	.321	.587	63	-8	11	2.58	-1	0-32(5-0-27),D-12	0	-1.0
Total 3	87	228	20	48	9	0	4	23	11	49	0	2	.211	.247	.303	.549	56	-14	16	2.36	-1	/0-56,D-12	1	-1.9

• LOLLAR, Sherm John Sherman Lollar b: 8/23/1924, Durham, AR d: 9/24/1977, Springfield, MO BR/TR, 6'1", 185 lbs. Deb: 4/20/1946 C

YEAR TM-L	G	AB	R	H	2B	3B	HR	RBI	BB	SO	SB	CS	AVG	OBP	SLG	OPS	OPS+	BR/A	RC	RC/G	FR	G/POS	WS	TPW
1946 Cle-A	28	62	7	15	6	0	1	9	5	9	0	1	.242	.299	.387	.686	97	-1	7	3.67	0	C-24	2	0.0
1947*NY-A	11	32	4	7	0	1	1	6	1	5	0	1	.219	.242	.375	.617	71	-2	2	1.42	-1	/C-9	0	-0.2
1948 NY-A	22	38	0	8	0	0	0	4	1	6	0	0	.211	.231	.211	.441	18	-5	1	.86	0	C-10	0	-0.4
1949 StL-A	109	284	28	74	9	1	8	49	32	22	0	1	.261	.340	.384	.723	88	-6	38	4.58	2	C-93	7	0.1
1950 StL-A★	126	396	55	111	22	3	13	65	64	25	2	0	.280	.391	.449	.841	111	8	74	6.60	2	*C-109	14	1.5
1951 StL-A	98	310	44	78	21	0	8	44	43	26	1	0	.252	.350	.397	.747	99	0	41	4.35	4	C-85/3-1	9	0.9
1952 Chi-A	132	375	35	90	15	0	13	50	54	34	1	0	.240	.354	.384	.738	104	4	53	4.69	-3	*C-120	13	0.8
1953 Chi-A	113	334	46	96	19	0	8	54	47	29	1	0	.287	.388	.416	.804	114	9	59	6.27	1	*C-107/1-1	18	1.4
1954 Chi-A★	107	316	31	77	13	0	7	34	37	28	0	1	.244	.336	.351	.687	85	-6	39	4.25	-2	C-93	12	-0.4
1955 Chi-A★	138	426	67	111	13	1	16	61	68	34	2	2	.261	.375	.408	.783	107	7	68	5.50	2	*C-136	21	1.5
1956 Chi-A★	136	450	55	132	28	2	11	75	53	34	2	0	.293	.387	.438	.825	116	13	76	5.92	-6	*C-132	18	1.2
1957 Chi-A	101	351	33	90	11	2	11	70	35	24	2	0	.256	.346	.393	.739	101	2	50	4.94	-3	C-96	14	0.4
1958 Chi-A★	127	421	53	115	16	0	20	84	57	37	2	1	.273	.370	.454	.824	128	18	72	5.97	2	*C-116	21	2.7
1959*Chi-A★	140	505	63	134	22	3	22	84	55	49	4	3	.265	.348	.451	.799	119	13	73	4.80	7	*C-122,1-24	23	2.4
1960 Chi-A★	129	421	43	106	23	0	7	46	42	39	2	0	.252	.331	.356	.688	87	-7	47	3.63	5	*C-123	13	0.4
1961 Chi-A	116	337	38	95	10	1	7	41	37	22	0	0	.282	.363	.380	.743	100	1	48	5.17	3	*C-107	14	0.8
1962 Chi-A	84	220	17	59	12	0	2	26	32	23	1	0	.268	.369	.350	.719	95	0	29	4.77	-1	C-66	8	0.2
1963 Chi-A	35	73	4	17	4	0	0	6	8	7	0	0	.233	.317	.288	.605	72	-2	7	3.16	0	C-23/1-2	2	-0.2
Total 18	1752	5351	623	1415	244	14	155	808	671	453	20	10	.264	.359	.402	.761	104	48	782	5.02	12	*C-1571/1-27,3-1	209	13.2

• LOMAN, Doug Douglas Edward Loman b: 5/9/1958, Bakersfield, CA BL/TL, 5'11", 185 lbs. Deb: 9/3/1984 Career OF: 21-8-19

YEAR TM-L	G	AB	R	H	2B	3B	HR	RBI	BB	SO	SB	CS	AVG	OBP	SLG	OPS	OPS+	BR/A	RC	RC/G	FR	G/POS	WS	TPW
1984 Mil-A	23	76	13	21	4	0	2	12	15	7	0	2	.276	.402	.408	.810	130	3	13	6.16	2	0-23(21-0-4)	4	0.3
1985 Mil-A	24	66	10	14	3	2	0	7	1	12	0	0	.212	.224	.318	.542	47	-5	5	2.40	2	0-20(0-8-15)	1	-0.4
Total 2	47	142	23	35	7	2	2	19	16	19	0	2	.246	.327	.366	.693	94	-2	18	4.33	4	/0-43	5	0.0

• LOMASNEY, Steve Steven James Lomasney b: 8/29/1977, Melrose, MA BR/TR, 6', 195 lbs. Deb: 10/3/1999

YEAR TM-L	G	AB	R	H	2B	3B	HR	RBI	BB	SO	SB	CS	AVG	OBP	SLG	OPS	OPS+	BR/A	RC	RC/G	FR	G/POS	WS	TPW
1999 Bos-A	1	2	0	0	0	0	0	0	0	2	0	0	.000	.000	.000	.000	-97	-1	0	.00	1	/C-1	0	0.0

• LOMBARD, George George Paul Lombard b: 9/14/1975, Atlanta, GA BL/TR, 6', 212 lbs. Deb: 9/4/1998 Career OF: 39-40-27

YEAR TM-L	G	AB	R	H	2B	3B	HR	RBI	BB	SO	SB	CS	AVG	OBP	SLG	OPS	OPS+	BR/A	RC	RC/G	FR	G/POS	WS	TPW
1998 Atl-N	6	6	2	2	0	0	1	1	0	1	1	0	.333	.333	.833	1.167	194	1	2	12.42	0	/0-2(0-0-2)	0	0.1
1999 Atl-N	6	6	1	2	0	0	0	0	1	2	2	0	.333	.429	.333	.762	96	0	1	9.55	0	/0-4(2-0-2)	0	0.0
2000 Atl-N	27	39	8	4	0	0	0	2	1	14	4	0	.103	.146	.103	.249	-36	-7	1	.47	0	0-15(5-0-11)	0	-0.7
2002 Det-A	72	241	34	58	11	3	5	13	20	78	13	2	.241	.302	.373	.675	83	-4	30	4.23	-3	0-69(29-40-1)/D-1	4	-0.7
2003 TB-A	13	37	8	8	1	0	1	4	0	6	1	0	.216	.237	.324	.561	47	-3	3	2.82	1	0-13(3-0-11)	0	-0.2
Total 5	124	329	53	74	12	3	7	20	22	101	21	2	.225	.280	.343	.623	68	-13	37	3.76	-1	0-103/D-1	4	-1.6

• LOMBARDI, Ernie Ernesto Natali "Schnozz,Bocci" Lombardi b: 4/6/1908, Oakland, CA d: 9/26/1977, Santa Cruz, CA BR/TR, 6'3", 230 lbs. Deb: 4/15/1931 HOF: 1986

YEAR TM-L	G	AB	R	H	2B	3B	HR	RBI	BB	SO	SB	CS	AVG	OBP	SLG	OPS	OPS+	BR/A	RC	RC/G	FR	G/POS	WS	TPW
1931 Bro-N	73	182	20	54	7	1	4	23	12	12	1	....	.297	.340	.412	.752	102	0	26	5.18	-2	C-50	6	0.1
1932 Cin-N	118	413	43	125	22	9	11	68	41	19	0	....	.303	.371	.479	.851	131	18	76	6.83	-3	*C-110	14	2.2
1933 Cin-N	107	350	30	99	21	1	4	47	16	17	2	....	.283	.322	.383	.704	102	0	36	3.46	-1	C-95	8	0.4
1934 Cin-N	132	417	42	127	19	4	9	62	16	22	0	....	.305	.335	.434	.769	107	3	53	4.58	2	*C-111	11	1.1
1935 Cin-N	120	332	36	114	23	3	12	64	16	6	0	....	.343	.379	.539	.918	148	21	65	7.72	0	C-82	17	2.6
1936 Cin-N★	121	387	42	129	23	2	12	68	19	16	1	....	.333	.375	.496	.871	142	21	69	6.82	-3	*C-105	17	2.3
1937 Cin-N★	120	368	41	123	22	1	9	59	14	17	1	....	.334	.362	.473	.835	131	14	60	6.34	-4	C-90	12	1.5
1938 Cin-N★	129	489	60	167	30	1	19	95	40	14	0	....	**.342**	.391	.524	.915	154	34	91	7.00	0	*C-123	24	4.2
1939*Cin-N★	130	450	43	129	26	2	20	85	35	19	0	....	.287	.342	.487	.829	120	11	67	5.17	-5	*C-120	17	1.2
1940*Cin-N★	109	376	50	120	22	0	14	74	31	14	0	....	.319	.382	.489	.871	137	19	66	6.46	-8	*C-101	19	1.7
1941 Cin-N	117	398	33	105	12	1	10	60	36	14	1	....	.264	.325	.374	.699	96	-3	45	3.85	-6	*C-116	13	-0.1
1942 Bos-N★	105	309	32	102	14	0	11	46	37	12	1	....	**.330**	.403	.482	.886	162	24	56	6.79	-3	C-85	16	2.8
1943 NY-N★	104	295	19	90	7	0	10	51	16	11	1	....	.305	.347	.431	.778	123	7	38	4.61	-2	C-73	8	1.0
1944 NY-N	117	373	37	95	13	0	10	58	33	25	0	....	.255	.317	.370	.687	93	-4	38	3.42	-1	*C-100	7	0.0
1945 NY-N★	115	368	46	113	7	1	19	70	43	11	0	....	.307	.387	.486	.873	140	20	69	6.91	-1	C-96	18	2.5
1946 NY-N	88	238	19	69	4	1	12	39	18	24	0	....	.290	.347	.466	.814	129	8	37	5.54	1	C-63	8	1.2
1947 NY-N	48	110	8	31	5	0	4	21	7	9	0	....	.282	.325	.436	.761	100	-1	15	4.66	0	C-24	3	0.0
Total 17	1853	5855	601	1792	277	27	190	990	430	262	8	....	.306	.358	.460	.818	126	194	907	5.62	-36	*C-1544	218	24.9

• LOMBARDI, Phil Phillip Arden Lombardi b: 2/20/1963, Abilene, TX BR/TR, 6'2", 200 lbs. Deb: 4/26/1986

YEAR TM-L	G	AB	R	H	2B	3B	HR	RBI	BB	SO	SB	CS	AVG	OBP	SLG	OPS	OPS+	BR/A	RC	RC/G	FR	G/POS	WS	TPW
1986 NY-A	20	36	6	10	3	0	2	6	4	7	0	0	.278	.366	.528	.894	141	2	6	6.21	-1	/0-8(8-0-0),C-3	1	0.1
1987 NY-A	5	8	0	1	0	0	0	0	0	2	0	0	.125	.125	.125	.250	-34	-2	0	.48	0	/C-3	0	-0.1
1989 NY-N	18	48	4	11	1	0	1	3	5	8	0	0	.229	.302	.313	.614	80	-1	4	2.98	-1	C-16/1-1	1	-0.1
Total 3	43	92	10	22	4	0	3	9	9	17	0	0	.239	.314	.380	.694	96	-1	11	3.97	-1	/C-22,0-8,1-1	2	-0.1

• LOMBARDOZZI, Steve Stephen Paul Lombardozzi b: 4/26/1960, Malden, MA BR/TR, 6', 175 lbs. Deb: 7/12/1985

YEAR TM-L	G	AB	R	H	2B	3B	HR	RBI	BB	SO	SB	CS	AVG	OBP	SLG	OPS	OPS+	BR/A	RC	RC/G	FR	G/POS	WS	TPW
1985 Min-A	28	54	10	20	4	1	0	6	6	6	3	2	.370	.433	.481	.915	142	3	12	7.71	0	2-26	3	0.4
1986 Min-A	156	453	53	103	20	5	8	33	52	76	3	1	.227	.308	.347	.655	76	-15	50	3.70	2	*2-155	11	-0.5
1987*Min-A	136	432	51	103	19	3	8	38	33	66	5	1	.238	.299	.352	.650	69	-19	46	3.51	-1	*2-133	10	-1.2
1988 Min-A	103	287	34	60	15	2	3	27	35	48	2	5	.209	.299	.307	.606	68	-14	28	3.07	2	2-90,S-12/3-5	6	-0.9
1989 Hou-N	21	37	5	8	3	1	1	3	4	9	0	0	.216	.293	.432	.725	109	0	5	4.57	-2	2-18/3-1	1	-0.2
1990 Hou-N	2	1	0	0	0	0	0	0	1	1	0	0	.000	.500	.000	.500	52	0	0	3.51	0	....	0	0.0
Total 6	446	1264	153	294	61	12	20	107	131	206	13	9	.233	.308	.347	.655	76	-44	141	3.67	2	2-422/S-12,3-6	31	-2.3

• LONERGAN, Walter Walter E. Lonergan b: 9/22/1885, Boston, MA d: 1/23/1958, Lexington, MA BR/TR, 5'7", 156 lbs. Deb: 8/17/1911

YEAR TM-L	G	AB	R	H	2B	3B	HR	RBI	BB	SO	SB	CS	AVG	OBP	SLG	OPS	OPS+	BR/A	RC	RC/G	FR	G/POS	WS	TPW
1911 Bos-A	10	26	2	7	0	0	0	1	1	....	1	....	.269	.296	.269	.566	59	-1	3	3.10	-1	/2-7,3-1,S-1	0	-0.2

• LONG, Long Deb: 8/29/1888

YEAR TM-L	G	AB	R	H	2B	3B	HR	RBI	BB	SO	SB	CS	AVG	OBP	SLG	OPS	OPS+	BR/A	RC	RC/G	FR	G/POS	WS	TPW
1888 Lou-a	1	2	0	0	0	0	0	0	1	....	0	....	.000	.333	.000	.333	11	-0	0	.00	0	/0-1	0	0.0

• LONG, Dale Richard Dale Long b: 2/6/1926, Springfield, MO d: 1/27/1991, Palm Coast, FL BL/TL, 6'4", 210 lbs. Deb: 4/21/1951 C

YEAR TM-L	G	AB	R	H	2B	3B	HR	RBI	BB	SO	SB	CS	AVG	OBP	SLG	OPS	OPS+	BR/A	RC	RC/G	FR	G/POS	WS	TPW
1951 Pit-N	10	12	1	2	0	0	1	1	0	3	0	0	.167	.167	.417	.583	50	-1	1	2.31	0	/1-1	0	-0.1
StL-A	34	105	11	25	5	1	2	11	10	22	0	0	.238	.310	.362	.672	79	-3	13	4.21	-1	1-28/0-1	2	-0.5
1955 Pit-N	131	419	59	122	19	**13**	16	79	48	72	0	1	.291	.365	.513	.879	132	19	76	6.33	-1	*1-119	17	1.1
1956 Pit-N★	148	517	64	136	20	7	27	91	54	85	1	0	.263	.333	.485	.818	119	13	83	5.58	-5	*1-138	15	0.0
1957 Pit-N	7	22	0	4	1	0	0	5	4	10	0	0	.182	.308	.227	.535	48	-1	2	2.30	0	/1-7	0	-0.2
Chi-N	123	397	55	121	19	0	21	62	52	63	1	1	.305	.387	.511	.898	141	24	79	7.32	2	*1-104	17	2.0
Yr.	130	419	55	125	20	0	21	67	56	73	1	1	.298	.382	.496	.879	136	22	81	7.00	2	*1-111	17	1.8
1958 Chi-N	142	480	68	130	26	4	20	75	66	64	2	0	.271	.361	.467	.828	119	14	80	5.85	-4	*1-137/C-2	15	0.3
1959 Chi-N	110	296	34	70	10	3	14	37	31	53	0	0	.236	.309	.432	.741	96	-2	39	4.53	-4	1-85	7	-1.1
1960 SF-N	37	54	4	9	0	0	3	6	7	7	0	0	.167	.262	.333	.596	66	-3	4	2.34	0	1-10	0	-0.3
*NY-A	26	41	6	15	3	1	3	10	5	6	0	0	.366	.435	.707	1.142	216	6	12	11.34	-1	1-11	3	0.5
1961 Was-A	123	377	52	94	20	4	17	49	39	41	0	0	.249	.321	.459	.780	111	5	56	5.07	-4	1-95	9	-0.4
1962 Was-A	67	191	17	46	8	0	4	24	18	22	5	1	.241	.310	.346	.655	77	-6	20	3.58	-1	1-51	2	-1.0
*NY-A	41	94	12	28	4	0	4	17	18	9	1	0	.298	.411	.468	.879	140	6	19	7.48	-1	1-31	5	0.4
Yr.	108	285	29	74	12	0	8	41	36	31	6	1	.260	.345	.386	.731	99	1	40	4.80	-1	1-82	7	-0.6
1963 NY-A	14	15	1	3	0	0	0	0	1	3	0	0	.200	.250	.200	.450	28	-1	1	1.83	-1	/1-2	0	-0.2
Total 10	1013	3020	384	805	135	33	132	467	353	460	10	3	.267	.345	.464	.809	116	70	485	5.59	-18	1-819/C-2,0-1	92	0.6

YEAR TM-L	G	AB	R	H	2B	3B	HR	RBI	BB	SO	SB	CS	AVG	OBP	SLG	OPS	OPS+	BR/A	RC	RC/G	FR	G/POS	WS	TPW
• LONG, Dan	Daniel W. Long b: 8/27/1867, Boston, MA d: 4/30/1929, Sausalito, CA Deb: 8/27/1890																							
1890 Bal-a	21	77	19	12	0	0	0	2	14	....	16	....	.156	.301	.156	.457	32	-6	9	3.52	0	0-21(0-21-0)	1	-0.6
• LONG, Herman	Herman C. "Germany,Flying Dutchman" Long b: 4/13/1866, Chicago, IL d: 9/17/1909, Denver, CO BL/TR, 5'8.5", 160 lbs. Deb: 4/17/1889 Career OF: 18-1-0																							
1889 KC-a	136	574	137	158	32	6	3	60	64	63	89	....	.275	.358	.368	.726	101	1	110	7.01	24	*S-128/2-8,0-1	22	2.4
1890 Bos-N	101	431	95	108	15	3	8	52	40	34	49	....	.251	.320	.355	.675	89	-8	66	5.44	15	*S-101	14	0.9
1891 Bos-N	139	577	129	163	21	12	9	75	80	51	60	....	.282	.377	.407	.785	115	11	114	7.44	21	*S-139	29	3.3
1892*Bos-N	151	646	115	181	33	6	6	78	44	36	57	....	.280	.334	.378	.712	105	1	103	5.98	19	*S-141,0-12(11-1-0)/3-1	28	2.4
1893 Bos-N	128	552	**149**	159	22	6	6	58	73	32	38	....	.288	.376	.382	.758	94	-5	96	6.47	22	*S-123/2-5	26	2.0
1894 Bos-N	104	475	136	154	28	11	12	79	35	17	24	....	.324	.375	.505	.881	98	-6	102	8.23	5	*S-98/0-5(5-0-0),2-3	16	0.3
1895 Bos-N	125	540	109	170	23	10	9	75	31	13	36	....	.315	.355	.444	.800	100	-3	102	7.05	-3	*S-122/2-2	19	0.0
1896 Bos-N	120	502	106	173	26	8	6	101	26	16	38	....	.345	.383	.464	.847	116	9	107	8.34	14	*S-120	20	2.5
1897*Bos-N	107	450	89	145	32	7	3	69	23	....	22	....	.322	.358	.444	.802	105	0	83	6.83	11	*S-107/0-1	17	1.4
1898 Bos-N	144	589	99	156	21	10	6	99	39	....	20	....	.265	.311	.365	.676	89	-12	77	4.52	16	*S-142/2-2	19	1.1
1899 Bos-N	145	578	91	153	30	8	6	100	45	....	20	....	.265	.321	.375	.697	83	-17	81	4.76	5	*S-143/1-2	16	-0.4
1900 Bos-N	125	486	80	127	19	4	**12**	66	44	....	26	....	.261	.325	.391	.716	86	-11	74	5.19	7	*S-125	13	0.2
1901 Bos-N	138	518	54	112	14	6	3	68	25	....	20	....	.216	.254	.284	.537	51	-34	45	2.83	10	*S-138	8	-1.9
1902 Bos-N	120	437	40	101	11	0	2	44	31	....	24	....	.231	.284	.270	.554	69	-16	43	3.22	23	*S-107,2-13	13	1.2
1903 NY-A	22	80	6	15	3	0	0	8	2	....	3	....	.188	.207	.225	.432	28	-7	5	1.88	-4	S-22	1	-1.1
Det-A	69	239	21	53	12	0	0	23	10	....	11	....	.222	.256	.272	.528	60	-12	21	2.84	-4	S-38,2-31	4	-1.5
Yr.	91	319	27	68	15	0	0	31	12	....	14	....	.213	.244	.260	.504	52	-19	26	2.58	-8	S-60,2-31	5	-2.5
1904 Phi-N	1	4	0	1	0	0	0	0	0	....	0	....	.250	.250	.250	.500	56	-0	0	2.22	0	/2-1	0	0.0
Total 16	**1875**	**7678**	**1456**	**2129**	**342**	**97**	**91**	**1055**	**612**	**262**	**537**	**....**	**.277**	**.335**	**.383**	**.718**	**92**	**-109**	**1228**	**5.73**	**182**	***S-1794/2-65,0-19,1-2,3-1**	**265**	**12.8**
• LONG, Jeoff	Jeoffrey Keith Long b: 10/9/1941, Covington, KY BR/TR, 6'1", 200 lbs. Deb: 7/31/1963																							
1963 StL-N	5	5	0	1	0	0	0	0	0	1	0	0	.200	.200	.200	.400	14	-0	0	1.35	0	....	0	-0.1
1964 StL-N	28	43	5	10	1	0	1	4	6	18	0	0	.233	.340	.326	.666	81	-1	5	4.02	-1	/0-4(0-0-4),1-3	1	-0.3
Chi-A	23	35	0	5	0	0	0	5	4	15	0	0	.143	.231	.143	.374	7	-4	1	1.11	0	/1-5,0-5(5-0-0)	0	-0.5
Total 2	**56**	**83**	**5**	**16**	**1**	**0**	**1**	**9**	**10**	**34**	**0**	**0**	**.193**	**.287**	**.241**	**.528**	**47**	**-6**	**7**	**2.54**	**-1**	**/0-9,1-8**	**1**	**-0.8**
• LONG, Jim	James M. Long b: 11/15/1862, Louisville, KY d: 12/12/1932, Louisville, KY, 5'10" Deb: 8/9/1891 Career OF: 59-2-0																							
1891 Lou-a	6	25	5	6	0	0	0	4	3	6	1	....	.240	.367	.240	.607	75	-0	3	3.67	0	/0-6(4-2-0)	1	0.0
1893 Bal-N	55	226	31	48	8	1	2	25	16	27	23	....	.212	.276	.283	.560	48	-18	25	3.67	-3	0-55(55-0-0)	2	-2.2
Total 2	**61**	**251**	**36**	**54**	**8**	**1**	**2**	**29**	**19**	**33**	**24**	**....**	**.215**	**.286**	**.279**	**.565**	**51**	**-18**	**27**	**3.67**	**-3**	**/0-61**	**3**	**-2.2**
• LONG, Jimmie	James Albert Long b: 6/29/1898, Fort Dodge, IA d: 9/14/1970, Fort Dodge, IA BR/TR, 5'11", 160 lbs. Deb: 9/12/1922																							
1922 Chi-A	3	3	0	0	0	0	0	0	1	0	0	0	.000	.250	.000	.250	-30	-1	0	.55	-1	/C-2	0	-0.1
• LONG, Ryan	Ryan Marcus Long b: 2/3/1973, Houston, TX BR/TR, 6'2", 215 lbs. Deb: 7/16/1997																							
1997 KC-A	6	9	2	2	0	0	0	2	0	3	0	0	.222	.300	.222	.522	38	-1	1	2.62	0	/0-5(1-0-4),D-1	0	-0.1
• LONG, Terrence	Terrence Deon Long b: 2/29/1976, Montgomery, AL BL/TL, 6'1", 190 lbs. Deb: 4/14/1999 Career OF: 137-373-102																							
1999 NY-N	3	3	0	0	0	0	0	0	0	2	0	0	.000	.000	.000	.000	-103	-1	0	.00	0	....	0	-0.1
2000*Oak-A	138	584	104	168	34	4	18	80	43	77	5	0	.288	.338	.452	.790	100	-1	86	5.31	-8	*0-137(0-137-0)	18	-0.7
2001*Oak-A	162	629	90	178	37	4	12	85	52	103	9	3	.283	.338	.412	.750	96	-4	85	4.81	-2	*0-162(62-74-28)	17	-0.9
2002*Oak-A	162	587	71	141	32	4	16	67	48	96	3	6	.240	.300	.390	.690	81	-19	64	3.66	-2	*0-162(0-162-0)	12	-1.9
2003*Oak-A	140	486	64	119	22	2	14	61	31	67	4	1	.245	.294	.385	.679	76	-17	54	3.86	-2	*0-137(75-0-74)/D-1	11	-2.4
Total 5	**605**	**2289**	**329**	**606**	**125**	**14**	**60**	**293**	**174**	**345**	**21**	**10**	**.265**	**.318**	**.410**	**.729**	**89**	**-41**	**289**	**4.41**	**-15**	**0-598/D-1**	**58**	**-6.1**
• LONG, Tom	Thomas Augustus Long b: 6/1/1890, Mitchum, AL d: 6/15/1972, Mobile, AL BR/TR, 5'10.5", 165 lbs. Deb: 9/11/1911 Career OF: 39-63-294																							
1911 Was-A	14	48	1	11	3	0	0	5	1	....	4	....	.229	.245	.292	.537	50	-3	4	2.88	-1	0-13(4-0-9)	0	-0.5
1912 Was-A	1	1	0	0	0	0	0	0	0	....	0	....	.000	.000	.000	.000	-99	-0	0	.00	0	....	0	0.0
1915 StL-N	140	507	61	149	21	**25**	2	61	31	50	19	15	.294	.339	.446	.785	136	17	77	5.29	0	*0-136(2-51-87)	20	1.1
1916 StL-N	119	403	37	118	11	10	1	33	10	43	21	14	.293	.312	.377	.689	111	2	48	4.07	-2	*0-106(3-12-94)	12	-0.6
1917 StL-N	144	530	49	123	12	14	3	41	37	44	21	....	.232	.285	.325	.609	89	-8	52	3.23	-6	*0-137(30-0-104)	10	-2.2
Total 5	**418**	**1489**	**148**	**401**	**47**	**49**	**6**	**140**	**79**	**137**	**65**	**29**	**.269**	**.309**	**.379**	**.688**	**110**	**8**	**182**	**4.13**	**-10**	**0-392**	**42**	**-2.3**
• LONGMIRE, Tony	Anthony Eugene Longmire b: 8/12/1968, Vallejo, CA BL/TR, 6'1", 197 lbs. Deb: 9/3/1993 Career OF: 34-2-23																							
1993*Phi-N	11	13	1	3	0	0	0	1	0	1	0	0	.231	.231	.231	.462	24	-1	1	1.87	0	/0-2(2-0-0)	0	-0.2
1994 Phi-N	69	139	10	33	11	0	0	17	10	27	2	1	.237	.293	.317	.610	58	-9	12	2.87	-1	0-32(13-0-21)	2	-1.0
1995 Phi-N	59	104	21	37	7	0	3	19	11	19	1	1	.356	.422	.510	.932	143	7	23	8.82	1	0-23(19-2-2)	6	0.7
Total 3	**139**	**256**	**32**	**73**	**18**	**0**	**3**	**37**	**21**	**47**	**3**	**2**	**.285**	**.344**	**.391**	**.735**	**92**	**-4**	**36**	**4.95**	**-0**	**/0-57**	**8**	**-0.6**
• LONNETT, Joe	Joseph Paul Lonnett b: 2/7/1927, Beaver Falls, PA BR/TR, 5'10", 180 lbs. Deb: 4/22/1956 C																							
1956 Phi-N	16	22	2	4	0	0	0	0	2	7	0	0	.182	.250	.182	.432	19	-2	1	1.34	0	/C-7	0	-0.2
1957 Phi-N	67	160	12	27	5	0	5	15	22	39	0	0	.169	.273	.294	.567	54	-10	14	2.66	-1	C-65	3	-0.8
1958 Phi-N	17	50	0	7	2	0	0	2	2	11	0	0	.140	.173	.180	.353	-6	-8	2	.92	1	C-15	1	-0.6
1959 Phi-N	43	93	8	16	1	0	1	10	14	17	0	1	.172	.287	.215	.502	36	-9	6	1.95	-2	C-43	0	-0.9
Total 4	**143**	**325**	**22**	**54**	**8**	**0**	**6**	**27**	**40**	**74**	**0**	**1**	**.166**	**.262**	**.246**	**.508**	**38**	**-29**	**22**	**2.09**	**-2**	**C-130**	**4**	**-2.6**
• LOOK, Bruce	Bruce Michael Look b: 6/9/1943, Lansing, MI BL/TR, 5'11", 183 lbs. Deb: 4/17/1968																							
1968 Min-A	59	118	7	29	4	0	0	9	20	24	0	1	.246	.355	.280	.635	90	-1	12	3.30	1	C-41	4	0.3
• LOOK, Dean	Dean Zachary Look b: 7/23/1937, Lansing, MI BR/TR, 5'11", 185 lbs. Deb: 9/22/1961																							
1961 Chi-A	3	6	0	0	0	0	0	0	0	1	0	0	.000	.000	.000	.000	-102	-2	0	.00	-0	/0-1	0	-0.2
• LOPATA, Stan	Stanley Edward "Stash" Lopata b: 9/12/1925, Delray, MI BR/TR, 6'2", 210 lbs. Deb: 9/19/1948																							
1948 Phi-N	6	15	2	2	1	0	0	2	0	4	0	....	.133	.133	.200	.333	-11	-2	0	.83	0	/C-4	0	-0.2
1949 Phi-N	83	240	31	65	9	2	8	27	21	44	1	....	.271	.330	.425	.755	104	1	33	4.83	-1	C-58	7	0.3
1950*Phi-N	58	129	10	27	2	2	1	11	22	25	1	....	.209	.325	.279	.604	61	-7	12	3.17	-2	C-51	2	-0.6
1951 Phi-N	3	5	0	0	0	0	0	0	0	0	0	0	.000	.000	.000	.000	-102	-1	0	.00	0	/C-1	0	-0.1
1952 Phi-N	57	179	25	49	9	1	4	27	36	33	1	1	.274	.395	.402	.798	123	7	31	6.03	1	C-55	9	1.2
1953 Phi-N	81	234	34	56	12	3	8	31	28	39	3	1	.239	.321	.419	.739	91	-3	35	5.13	-5	C-80	9	-0.4
1954 Phi-N	86	259	42	75	14	5	14	42	33	37	1	3	.290	.372	.544	.916	135	12	50	6.72	-1	C-75/1-1	10	1.5
1955 Phi-N★	99	303	49	82	9	3	22	58	58	62	4	1	.271	.391	.538	.929	146	22	64	7.34	9	C-66,1-24	17	3.3
1956 Phi-N★	146	535	96	143	33	7	32	95	75	93	5	2	.267	.358	.535	.893	138	29	100	6.38	-9	*C-102,1-39	26	2.4
1957 Phi-N	116	388	50	92	18	2	18	67	56	81	2	2	.237	.335	.433	.768	108	4	56	4.85	-3	*C-108	15	0.7
1958 Phi-N	86	258	36	64	9	0	9	33	60	63	0	1	.248	.394	.388	.781	109	6	39	5.00	-1	C-80	9	1.0
1959 Mil-N	25	48	0	5	0	0	0	4	3	13	0	0	.104	.157	.104	.261	-31	-9	1	.49	-1	C-11/1-2	0	-0.9
1960 Mil-N	7	8	0	1	0	0	0	0	1	3	0	0	.125	.222	.125	.347	-2	-1	0	1.08	-1	/C-4	0	-0.2
Total 13	**853**	**2601**	**375**	**661**	**116**	**25**	**116**	**397**	**393**	**497**	**18**	**11**	**.254**	**.354**	**.452**	**.805**	**115**	**59**	**422**	**5.52**	**-12**	**C-695/1-66**	**104**	**7.9**
• LOPES, Davey	David Earl Lopes b: 5/3/1945, East Providence, RI BR/TR, 5'9", 170 lbs. Deb: 9/22/1972 M/C Career OF: 86-98-66																							
1972 LA-N	11	42	6	9	4	0	0	1	7	6	4	0	.214	.327	.310	.636	83	0	5	4.11	-2	2-11	1	-0.1
1973 LA-N	142	535	77	147	13	5	6	37	62	77	36	16	.275	.355	.351	.707	101	4	69	4.30	-10	*2-135/0-5(0-2-3),S-2,3-1	19	0.3
1974*LA-N	145	530	95	141	26	3	10	35	66	71	59	18	.266	.352	.383	.735	110	13	77	4.83	-4	*2-143	21	1.9
1975 LA-N	155	618	108	162	24	6	8	41	91	93	**77**	12	.262	.359	.359	.718	104	18	97	5.35	5	*2-137,0-24(0-23-1),S-14	25	3.4
1976 LA-N	117	427	72	103	17	7	4	20	56	49	**63**	10	.241	.335	.342	.677	94	8	58	4.52	-2	*2-100,0-19(0-19-0)	16	1.2
1977*LA-N	134	502	85	142	19	5	11	53	73	69	47	12	.283	.376	.406	.782	110	15	87	6.06	11	*2-130	24	3.3
1978*LA-N★	151	587	93	163	25	4	17	58	71	70	45	4	.278	.356	.421	.776	117	22	97	5.90	6	*2-147/0-2(0-2-0)	26	3.8

YEAR TM-L	G	AB	R	H	2B	3B	HR	RBI	BB	SO	SB	CS	AVG	OBP	SLG	OPS	OPS+	BR/A	RC	RC/G	FR	G/POS	WS	TPW
1979 LA-N★	153	582	109	154	20	6	28	73	97	88	44	4	.265	.373	.464	.837	129	34	113	6.82	-18	*2-152	27	2.5
1980 LA-N★	141	553	79	139	15	3	10	49	58	71	23	7	.251	.324	.344	.667	88	-7	65	4.00	1	*2-140	16	0.2
1981*LA-N★	58	214	35	44	2	0	5	17	22	35	20	2	.206	.289	.285	.574	65	-6	20	2.90	3	2-55	5	0.0
1982 Oak-A	128	450	58	109	19	3	11	42	40	51	28	12	.242	.305	.371	.677	89	-6	49	3.53	3	*2-125/0-6(0-6-0)	10	0.3
1983 Oak-A	147	494	64	137	13	4	17	67	51	61	22	4	.277	.347	.423	.770	118	15	76	5.32	-4	*2-123,D-12/0-7(0-2-5),3-5	18	1.7
1984 Oak-A	72	230	32	59	11	1	9	36	31	36	12	0	.257	.347	.430	.778	122	10	36	5.29	1	0-42(3-8-31),2-17/D-9,3-5	9	1.0
*Chi-N	16	17	5	4	1	0	0	0	6	5	3	0	.235	.435	.294	.729	99	1	4	7.33	-1	/0-9(2-1-6),2-2	1	0.0
1985 Chi-N	99	275	52	78	11	0	11	44	46	37	47	4	.284	.386	.444	.830	119	16	52	6.44	-1	0-79(46-25-17)/3-4,2-1	11	1.3
1986 Chi-N	59	157	38	47	8	2	6	22	31	16	17	6	.299	.421	.490	.911	140	11	34	7.42	-5	3-32,0-22(21-0-2)	7	0.5
*Hou-N	37	98	11	23	2	1	1	13	12	9	8	2	.235	.318	.306	.624	75	-2	10	3.35	3	0-19(9-10-1)/3-5	3	0.0
Yr.	96	255	49	70	10	3	7	35	43	25	25	8	.275	.383	.420	.803	116	9	44	5.78	-2	0-41(30-10-3),3-37	10	0.5
1987 Hou-N	47	43	4	10	2	0	1	6	13	8	2	1	.233	.411	.349	.760	108	1	7	5.90	0	/0-5(5-0-0)	1	0.1
Total 16	**1812**	**6354**	**1023**	**1671**	**232**	**50**	**155**	**614**	**833**	**852**	**557**	**114**	**.263**	**.351**	**.388**	**.740**	**107**	**148**	**955**	**5.11**	**-14**	***2-1418,0-239/3-52,D-21,S-16**	**240**	**21.5**

• LOPEZ, Al Alfonso Ramon Lopez b: 8/20/1908, Tampa, FL BR/TR, 5'11", 165 lbs. Deb: 9/27/1928 M HOF: 1977

YEAR TM-L	G	AB	R	H	2B	3B	HR	RBI	BB	SO	SB	CS	AVG	OBP	SLG	OPS	OPS+	BR/A	RC	RC/G	FR	G/POS	WS	TPW
1928 Bro-N	3	12	0	0	0	0	0	0	0	0	0	....	.000	.000	.000	.000	-101	-4	0	.00	0	/C-3	0	-0.4
1930 Bro-N	128	421	60	130	20	4	6	57	33	35	3	....	.309	.362	.418	.780	89	-7	62	5.40	3	*C-126	13	0.3
1931 Bro-N	111	360	38	97	13	4	0	40	28	33	1	....	.269	.324	.328	.652	76	-12	40	3.88	-1	*C-105	9	-0.7
1932 Bro-N	126	404	44	111	18	6	1	43	34	35	3	....	.275	.331	.356	.687	87	-7	50	4.30	0	*C-125	12	0.1
1933 Bro-N	126	372	39	112	11	4	3	41	21	39	10	....	.301	.338	.376	.715	108	4	47	4.59	15	*C-124/2-1	16	2.8
1934 Bro-N★	140	439	58	120	23	2	7	54	49	44	2	....	.273	.349	.383	.732	101	2	60	4.63	-1	*C-137/2-2,3-2	12	0.8
1935 Bro-N	128	379	50	95	12	4	3	39	35	36	2	....	.251	.316	.327	.643	75	-13	41	3.67	5	*C-126	9	0.0
1936 Bos-N	128	426	46	103	12	5	7	50	41	41	1	....	.242	.311	.343	.654	81	-11	45	3.58	6	*C-127/1-1	12	0.4
1937 Bos-N	105	334	31	68	11	1	3	38	35	57	3	....	.204	.281	.269	.551	55	-20	25	2.33	5	*C-102	7	-0.9
1938 Bos-N	71	236	19	63	6	1	1	14	11	24	5	....	.267	.305	.314	.619	78	-7	22	3.10	3	C-71	7	0.0
1939 Bos-N	131	412	32	104	22	1	8	49	40	45	1	....	.252	.319	.369	.688	91	-6	49	3.99	3	*C-129	12	0.5
1940 Bos-N	36	119	20	35	3	1	2	17	6	8	1	....	.294	.328	.387	.715	102	-0	15	4.45	5	C-36	4	0.7
Pit-N	59	174	15	45	6	2	1	24	13	13	5	....	.259	.310	.333	.643	78	-5	17	3.18	3	C-59	4	0.1
Yr.	95	293	35	80	9	3	3	41	19	21	6	....	.273	.317	.355	.672	88	-5	31	3.67	7	C-95	8	0.7
1941 Pit-N★	114	317	33	84	9	1	5	43	31	23	0	....	.265	.330	.347	.677	91	-4	36	3.90	-2	*C-114	10	0.1
1942 Pit-N	103	289	17	74	8	2	1	26	34	17	0	....	.256	.338	.308	.646	88	-3	31	3.58	8	C-99	10	1.1
1943 Pit-N	118	372	40	98	9	4	1	39	44	25	2	....	.263	.341	.317	.659	88	-4	43	3.99	4	*C-116/3-1	14	0.7
1944 Pit-N	115	331	27	76	12	1	1	34	34	24	4	....	.230	.303	.281	.584	62	-16	29	2.97	4	*C-115	8	-0.6
1945 Pit-N	91	243	22	53	8	0	0	18	35	12	1	....	.218	.317	.251	.568	57	-13	21	2.89	-1	C-91	6	-1.0
1946 Pit-N	56	150	13	46	2	0	1	12	23	14	1	....	.307	.399	.340	.739	108	3	21	4.98	3	C-56	5	0.9
1947 Cle-A	61	126	9	33	1	0	0	14	9	13	1	1	.262	.311	.270	.581	64	-6	11	3.16	4	C-57	3	-0.1
Total 19	**1950**	**5916**	**613**	**1547**	**206**	**43**	**51**	**652**	**556**	**538**	**46**	**1**	**.261**	**.326**	**.337**	**.663**	**83**	**-130**	**664**	**3.84**	**64**	***C-1918/2-3,3-3,1-1**	**173**	**4.6**

• LOPEZ, Art Arturo (Rodriguez) Lopez b: 5/8/1937, Mayaguez, Puerto Rico BL/TL, 5'9", 170 lbs. Deb: 4/12/1965

YEAR TM-L	G	AB	R	H	2B	3B	HR	RBI	BB	SO	SB	CS	AVG	OBP	SLG	OPS	OPS+	BR/A	RC	RC/G	FR	G/POS	WS	TPW
1965 NY-A	38	49	5	7	0	0	0	0	1	6	0	0	.143	.160	.143	.303	-13	-7	1	.77	-1	0-16(3-0-14)	0	-1.0

• LOPEZ, Carlos Carlos Antonio (Morales) Lopez b: 9/27/1950, Mazatlan, Mexico BR/TR, 6', 190 lbs. Deb: 9/17/1976 Career OF: 1-48-182

YEAR TM-L	G	AB	R	H	2B	3B	HR	RBI	BB	SO	SB	CS	AVG	OBP	SLG	OPS	OPS+	BR/A	RC	RC/G	FR	G/POS	WS	TPW
1976 Cal-A	9	10	1	0	0	0	0	0	2	3	2	0	.000	.167	.000	.167	-52	-1	0	.70	-0	/0-4(1-0-4),D-1	0	-0.2
1977 Sea-A	99	297	39	84	18	1	8	34	14	61	16	4	.283	.322	.431	.753	104	3	44	5.29	6	0-90(0-7-87)/D-2	10	0.5
1978 Bal-A	129	193	21	46	6	0	4	20	9	34	5	7	.238	.276	.332	.607	75	-9	15	2.59	4	*0-114(0-41-91)/D-1	2	-0.8
Total 3	**237**	**500**	**61**	**130**	**24**	**1**	**12**	**54**	**25**	**98**	**23**	**11**	**.260**	**.301**	**.384**	**.685**	**89**	**-8**	**59**	**4.07**	**10**	**0-208/D-4**	**12**	**-0.5**

• LOPEZ, Felipe Felipe Lopez b: 5/12/1980, Bayamon, Puerto Rico BB/TR, 6', 175 lbs. Deb: 8/3/2001

YEAR TM-L	G	AB	R	H	2B	3B	HR	RBI	BB	SO	SB	CS	AVG	OBP	SLG	OPS	OPS+	BR/A	RC	RC/G	FR	G/POS	WS	TPW
2001 Tor-A	49	177	21	46	5	4	5	23	12	39	4	3	.260	.307	.418	.725	86	-4	22	4.32	-4	3-47/S-3	5	-0.7
2002 Tor-A	85	282	35	64	15	3	8	34	23	90	5	4	.227	.288	.387	.674	74	-12	31	3.64	-10	S-79/3-2,D-1	6	-1.5
2003 Cin-N	59	197	28	42	7	2	2	13	28	59	8	5	.213	.314	.299	.614	62	-11	20	3.29	-10	S-50/3-8,2-3	3	-1.7
Total 3	**193**	**656**	**84**	**152**	**27**	**9**	**15**	**70**	**63**	**188**	**17**	**12**	**.232**	**.301**	**.369**	**.670**	**74**	**-27**	**73**	**3.71**	**-24**	**S-132/3-57,2-3,D-1**	**14**	**-3.9**

• LOPEZ, Hector Hector Headley (Swainson) Lopez b: 7/9/1929, Colon, Panama BR/TR, 5'11", 182 lbs. Deb: 5/12/1955 Career OF: 477-21-172

YEAR TM-L	G	AB	R	H	2B	3B	HR	RBI	BB	SO	SB	CS	AVG	OBP	SLG	OPS	OPS+	BR/A	RC	RC/G	FR	G/POS	WS	TPW
1955 KC-A	128	483	50	140	15	2	15	68	33	58	1	4	.290	.339	.422	.761	103	-1	65	4.73	7	3-93,2-36	15	0.9
1956 KC-A	151	561	91	153	27	3	18	69	63	73	4	5	.273	.349	.428	.777	104	1	83	5.13	0	*3-121,0-20(0-20-0)/2-8,S	15	0.1
1957 KC-A	121	391	51	115	19	4	11	35	41	66	1	6	.294	.361	.448	.809	118	7	61	5.51	3	*3-111/2-4,0-3(2-0-1)	13	1.0
1958 KC-A	151	564	84	147	28	4	17	73	49	61	2	2	.261	.322	.415	.737	99	-1	70	4.14	-5	2-96,3-55/0-1,S-1	17	0.1
1959 KC-A	35	135	22	38	10	3	6	24	8	23	1	0	.281	.326	.533	.860	129	5	24	6.46	-6	2-33	6	0.1
NY-A	112	406	60	115	16	2	16	69	28	54	3	1	.283	.339	.451	.789	119	10	61	5.36	-2	3-76,0-35(35-0-0)	14	0.5
Yr.	147	541	82	153	26	5	22	93	36	77	4	1	.283	.336	.471	.807	121	14	85	5.63	-8	3-76,0-35(35-0-0),2-33	20	0.6
1960*NY-A	131	408	66	116	14	6	9	42	46	64	1	1	.284	.362	.414	.777	116	9	63	5.51	2	*0-106(93-0-17)/2-5,3-1	16	0.6
1961*NY-A	93	243	27	54	7	2	3	22	24	38	1	0	.222	.295	.305	.599	64	-12	22	2.90	2	0-72(65-0-9)	3	-1.4
1962*NY-A	106	335	45	92	19	1	6	48	33	53	0	1	.275	.340	.391	.731	99	-1	41	4.14	0	0-84(64-0-21)/2-1,3-1	8	-0.6
1963*NY-A	130	433	54	108	13	4	14	52	35	71	1	2	.249	.306	.395	.700	95	-4	50	3.89	-2	*0-124(104-0-21)/2-1	11	-1.3
1964*NY-A	127	285	34	74	9	3	10	34	24	54	1	1	.260	.319	.418	.737	101	-0	37	4.42	-3	*0-103(80-1-31)/3-1	9	-0.9
1965 NY-A	111	283	25	74	12	2	7	39	26	61	0	0	.261	.326	.392	.718	104	1	34	4.09	-2	0-75(20-0-55)/1-2	7	-0.5
1966 NY-A	54	117	14	25	4	1	4	16	8	20	0	0	.214	.270	.368	.637	84	-3	11	2.97	-1	0-29(13-0-17)	2	-0.6
Total 12	**1450**	**4644**	**623**	**1251**	**193**	**37**	**136**	**591**	**418**	**696**	**16**	**23**	**.269**	**.333**	**.415**	**.747**	**104**	**12**	**622**	**4.61**	**-7**	**0-652,3-459,2-184/S-5,1-2**	**136**	**-2.0**

• LOPEZ, Javy Javier (Torres) Lopez b: 11/5/1970, Ponce, Puerto Rico BR/TR, 6'3", 185 lbs. Deb: 9/18/1992

YEAR TM-L	G	AB	R	H	2B	3B	HR	RBI	BB	SO	SB	CS	AVG	OBP	SLG	OPS	OPS+	BR/A	RC	RC/G	FR	G/POS	WS	TPW
1992*Atl-N	9	16	3	6	2	0	0	2	0	1	0	0	.375	.375	.500	.875	137	1	3	8.10	0	/C-9	1	0.1
1993 Atl-N	8	16	1	6	1	1	1	2	0	2	0	0	.375	.412	.750	1.162	201	2	5	13.63	-1	/C-7	1	0.2
1994 Atl-N	80	277	27	68	9	0	13	35	17	61	0	2	.245	.301	.419	.720	83	-9	31	3.69	-4	C-75	5	-0.7
1995*Atl-N	100	333	37	105	11	4	14	51	14	57	0	1	.315	.347	.498	.845	116	6	52	5.75	-2	C-93	12	0.9
1996*Atl-N	138	489	56	138	19	1	23	69	28	84	1	6	.282	.325	.466	.791	100	-4	66	4.70	3	*C-135	15	0.8
1997*Atl-N★	123	414	52	122	28	1	23	68	40	82	1	1	.295	.364	.534	.898	129	16	79	6.94	-2	*C-117	19	2.1
1998*Atl-N★	133	489	73	139	21	1	34	106	30	85	5	3	.284	.333	.540	.873	125	14	79	5.54	2	*C-128/D-1	25	2.5
1999 Atl-N	65	246	34	78	18	1	11	45	20	41	0	3	.317	.375	.533	.908	126	8	47	7.12	0	C-60/D-4	11	1.1
2000*Atl-N	134	481	60	138	21	1	24	89	35	80	0	0	.287	.340	.484	.825	105	2	73	5.37	-6	*C-132	16	0.4
2001*Atl-N	128	438	45	117	16	1	17	66	28	82	1	0	.267	.326	.425	.750	90	-7	59	4.70	-5	*C-127	13	-0.3
2002*Atl-N	109	347	31	81	15	0	11	52	26	63	0	1	.233	.302	.372	.674	76	-13	35	3.35	7	*C-103	10	0.0
2003*Atl-N★	129	457	89	150	29	3	43	109	33	90	0	1	.328	.379	.687	1.066	170	43	115	9.72	4	*C-120/D-3	31	5.5
Total 12	**1156**	**4003**	**508**	**1148**	**190**	**14**	**214**	**694**	**271**	**728**	**8**	**18**	**.287**	**.340**	**.502**	**.842**	**114**	**59**	**644**	**5.70**	**-4**	***C-1106/D-8**	**159**	**12.7**

• LOPEZ, Luis Luis Manuel (Santos) Lopez b: 9/4/1970, Cidra, Puerto Rico BB/TR, 5'11", 175 lbs. Deb: 9/7/1993

YEAR TM-L	G	AB	R	H	2B	3B	HR	RBI	BB	SO	SB	CS	AVG	OBP	SLG	OPS	OPS+	BR/A	RC	RC/G	FR	G/POS	WS	TPW
1993 SD-N	17	43	1	5	1	0	0	1	0	8	0	0	.116	.116	.140	.256	-31	-8	1	.51	0	2-15	0	-0.7
1994 SD-N	77	235	29	65	16	1	2	20	15	39	3	2	.277	.328	.379	.707	86	-5	28	4.11	-7	S-43,2-29/3-5	5	-0.8
1996*SD-N	63	139	10	25	3	0	2	11	9	35	0	0	.180	.235	.245	.480	28	-15	7	1.52	-2	S-35,2-22/3-2	1	-1.4
1997 NY-N	78	178	19	48	12	1	1	19	12	42	2	4	.270	.330	.365	.695	85	-5	21	4.09	2	S-45,2-20/3-4	5	0.0
1998 NY-N	117	266	37	67	13	2	2	22	20	60	2	2	.252	.314	.338	.652	73	-11	27	3.32	-2	2-50,S-39,3-11/0-9(8-0-1)	5	-0.9
1999 NY-N	68	104	11	22	4	0	2	13	12	33	1	1	.212	.311	.308	.619	59	-7	11	3.40	0	S-33,2-16/3-9	3	-0.5
2000 Mil-N	78	201	24	53	14	0	6	27	9	35	1	2	.264	.312	.423	.735	85	-6	26	4.39	0	S-45,2-22/3-6	4	-0.2
2001 Mil-N	92	222	22	60	8	3	4	18	14	44	0	1	.270	.328	.387	.715	86	-5	27	4.21	-4	3-46,S-17,2-15	4	-0.7
2002 Mil-N	6	8	1	0	0	0	0	1	2	1	0	0	.000	.200	.000	.200	-42	-2	0	.35	-2	/S-4	0	-0.3
Bal-A	52	109	10	23	6	0	2	9	3	20	1	0	.211	.232	.321	.553	47	-8	7	2.26	-6	S-22,2-12/1-1,D-1	1	-1.3
Total 9	**648**	**1505**	**164**	**368**	**77**	**7**	**21**	**141**	**96**	**317**	**10**	**12**	**.245**	**.301**	**.347**	**.648**	**70**	**-72**	**155**	**3.43**	**-20**	**S-283,2-201/3-83,0-9,1-1,D**	**28**	**-6.8**

• LOPEZ, Luis Luis Lopez b: 10/5/1973, Brooklyn, NY BR/TR, 6', 205 lbs. Deb: 4/29/2001

YEAR TM-L	G	AB	R	H	2B	3B	HR	RBI	BB	SO	SB	CS	AVG	OBP	SLG	OPS	OPS+	BR/A	RC	RC/G	FR	G/POS	WS	TPW
2001 Tor-A	41	119	10	29	4	0	3	10	8	16	0	0	.244	.291	.353	.644	67	-6	9	2.50	-1	3-28/1-5,D-4	1	-0.7

YEAR TM-L	G	AB	R	H	2B	3B	HR	RBI	BB	SO	SB	CS	AVG	OBP	SLG	OPS	OPS+	BR/A	RC	RC/G	FR	G/POS	WS	TPW
• LOPEZ, Luis	Luis Antonio Lopez b: 9/1/1964, Brooklyn, NY BR/TR, 6'1", 190 lbs. Deb: 9/14/1990																							
1990 LA-N	6	6	0	0	0	0	0	0	0	2	0	0	.000	.000	.000	.000	-103	-2	0	.00	0	/1-1	0	-0.2
1991 Cle-A	35	82	7	18	4	1	0	7	4	7	0	0	.220	.264	.293	.557	54	-5	7	2.76	-1	C-12,1-10/D-6,3-1,0-1	0	-0.7
Total 2	41	88	7	18	4	1	0	7	4	9	0	0	.205	.247	.273	.520	44	-7	7	2.53	-1	/C-12,1-11,D-6,3-1,0-1	0	-0.9
• LOPEZ, Mendy	Mendy (Aude) Lopez b: 10/15/1974, Pimentel, Dominican Republic BR/TR, 6'2", 190 lbs. Deb: 6/3/1998																							
1998 KC-A	74	206	18	50	10	2	1	15	12	40	5	2	.243	.288	.325	.613	57	-13	19	2.95	9	S-72/3-2	5	0.1
1999 KC-A	7	20	2	8	0	1	0	3	0	5	0	0	.400	.429	.500	.929	133	1	4	9.89	0	/2-6,S-1	1	0.1
2000 Fla-N	4	3	0	0	0	0	0	0	1	1	0	0	.000	.250	.000	.250	-31	-1	0	.59	0	....	0	-0.1
2001 Hou-N	10	15	3	4	0	0	1	3	2	4	0	0	.267	.389	.467	.856	114	0	3	7.43	-1	/2-3,3-2	1	-0.1
Pit-N	22	43	5	10	3	1	0	4	4	16	0	0	.233	.298	.349	.647	65	-2	5	3.78	0	/2-9,S-6,3-4	1	-0.1
Yr.	32	58	8	14	3	1	1	7	6	20	0	0	.241	.323	.379	.702	78	-2	8	4.67	-1	2-12/3-6,S-6	2	-0.2
2002 Pit-N	3	3	0	0	0	0	0	0	0	3	0	0	.000	.000	.000	.000	-99	-1	0	.00	0	....	0	-0.1
2003 KC-A	52	94	13	26	5	1	3	11	4	28	2	0	.277	.306	.447	.753	84	-2	12	4.51	-2	1-17,3-13,2-11/S-4,0-3(1-0-2)	2	-0.3
Total 6	172	384	41	98	18	5	5	36	23	97	7	2	.255	.302	.367	.670	69	-17	43	3.80	6	/S-83,2-29,3-21,1-17,0-3	10	-0.5
• LORD, Bris	Bristol Robotham "The Human Eyeball" Lord b: 9/21/1883, Upland, PA d: 11/13/1964, Prince Frederick, MD BR/TR, 5'9", 185 lbs. Deb: 4/21/1905 Career OF: 320-192-202																							
1905*Phi-A	66	238	38	57	14	0	0	13	14	....	3	....	.239	.285	.298	.583	84	-5	23	3.17	0	0-61(4-38-19)	5	-0.9
1906 Phi-A	118	434	50	101	13	7	1	44	27	....	12	....	.233	.281	.302	.583	80	-11	44	3.26	-6	*0-115(5-103-7)	7	-2.4
1907 Phi-A	57	170	12	31	3	0	1	11	14	....	2	....	.182	.249	.218	.466	48	-10	11	1.98	-2	0-53(10-40-4)/P-1	2	-1.6
1909 Cle-A	69	249	26	67	7	3	1	25	8	....	10	....	.269	.295	.333	.628	94	-3	27	3.68	7	0-67(48-3-16)	7	0.1
1910 Cle-A	58	210	23	46	8	7	0	17	12	....	4	....	.219	.268	.324	.592	84	-5	19	2.91	4	0-56(24-0-32)	4	-0.4
*Phi-A	70	279	54	78	13	11	1	20	23	....	6	....	.280	.337	.416	.752	137	11	41	4.99	3	0-70(64-4-2)	12	1.1
Yr.	128	489	77	124	21	18	1	37	35	....	10	....	.254	.307	.376	.684	115	6	60	4.07	7	*0-126(88-4-34)	16	0.7
1911*Phi-A	134	574	92	178	37	11	3	55	35	....	15	....	.310	.355	.429	.784	120	13	92	5.77	3	*0-132(122-1-9)	22	1.1
1912 Phi-A	97	378	63	90	12	9	0	25	34	....	15	....	.238	.309	.317	.627	82	-9	42	3.62	1	0-97(18-0-78)	7	-1.3
1913 Bos-N	73	235	22	59	12	1	6	26	8	22	7	....	.251	.276	.387	.663	86	-6	25	3.59	-5	0-62(25-3-35)	5	-1.4
Total 8	742	2767	380	707	119	49	13	236	175	22	74	....	.256	.304	.348	.652	95	-23	325	3.90	6	0-713/P-1	71	-5.7
• LORD, Carlton	William Carlton Lord b: 1/7/1900, Philadelphia, PA d: 8/15/1947, Chester, PA BR/TR, 5'11", 170 lbs. Deb: 7/12/1923																							
1923 Phi-N	17	47	3	11	2	0	0	2	2	3	0	1	.234	.265	.277	.542	39	-5	3	2.25	-3	3-14	0	-0.7
• LORD, Harry	Harry Donald Lord b: 3/8/1882, Porter, ME d: 8/9/1948, Westbrook, ME BL/TR, 5'10.5", 165 lbs. Deb: 9/25/1907 M Career OF: 33-4-10																							
1907 Bos-A	10	38	4	6	1	0	0	3	1	....	1	....	.158	.179	.184	.364	16	-4	2	1.32	1	3-10	0	-0.3
1908 Bos-A	145	560	61	145	15	6	2	37	22	....	23	....	.259	.297	.318	.614	97	-3	61	3.52	-9	*3-144	14	-1.0
1909 Bos-A	136	534	89	168	12	7	0	31	20	....	36	....	.315	.349	.363	.712	122	12	81	5.31	-8	*3-134	21	0.9
1910 Bos-A	77	288	25	72	5	5	1	32	14	....	17	....	.250	.294	.313	.607	88	-5	32	3.57	-1	3-70/S-1	7	-0.4
Chi-A	44	165	26	49	6	3	0	10	14	....	17	....	.297	.352	.370	.722	133	6	27	5.78	-10	3-44	9	-0.3
Yr.	121	453	51	121	11	8	1	42	28	....	34	....	.267	.315	.333	.649	104	1	59	4.34	-11	*3-114/S-1	16	-0.7
1911 Chi-A	141	561	103	180	18	18	3	61	32	....	43	....	.321	.364	.433	.797	125	16	104	6.55	-20	*3-138	23	0.1
1912 Chi-A	151	570	81	152	19	12	5	54	52	....	28	....	.267	.333	.368	.702	104	2	80	4.66	-22	*3-106,0-45(32-4-9)	17	-1.9
1913 Chi-A	150	547	62	144	18	12	1	42	45	39	24	....	.263	.327	.346	.673	98	-2	68	4.08	-29	*3-150	15	-2.9
1914 Chi-A	21	69	8	13	1	1	1	3	5	3	2	2	.188	.243	.275	.519	57	-4	5	2.11	0	3-19/0-1	0	-0.5
1915 Buf-F	97	359	50	97	12	6	1	21	21	15	15	....	.270	.311	.345	.656	93	-4	41	3.94	-7	3-92/0-1	10	-1.0
Total 9	972	3691	509	1026	107	70	14	294	226	57	206	2	.278	.326	.356	.682	105	14	501	4.55	-106	3-907/0-47,S-1	116	-7.1
• LORETTA, Mark	Mark David Loretta b: 8/14/1971, Santa Monica, CA BR/TR, 6', 175 lbs. Deb: 9/4/1995																							
1995 Mil-A	19	50	13	13	3	0	1	3	4	7	1	1	.260	.327	.380	.707	79	-2	6	4.12	1	S-13/2-4,D-1	1	0.0
1996 Mil-A	73	154	20	43	3	0	1	13	14	15	2	1	.279	.339	.318	.657	65	-8	16	3.52	7	2-28,3-23,S-21	2	0.1
1997 Mil-A	132	418	56	120	17	5	5	47	47	60	5	5	.287	.362	.388	.749	95	-3	57	4.63	6	2-63,S-44,1-19,3-15/D-1	12	0.7
1998 Mil-N	140	434	55	137	29	0	6	54	42	47	9	6	.316	.385	.424	.809	113	9	69	5.77	4	1-70,S-56,3-22,2-13/0-1	16	1.3
1999 Mil-N	153	587	93	170	34	5	5	67	52	59	4	1	.290	.357	.390	.748	90	-8	83	5.03	-8	S-74,1-66,2-17,3-14	14	-1.4
2000 Mil-N	91	352	49	99	21	1	7	40	37	38	0	3	.281	.351	.406	.758	92	-5	49	4.85	-1	S-90/2-1	12	0.1
2001 Mil-N	102	384	40	111	14	2	2	29	28	46	1	2	.289	.348	.352	.700	84	-9	48	4.47	-2	2-52,3-39/S-9,D-4,P-1	9	-0.7
2002 Mil-N	86	217	23	58	14	0	2	19	23	32	0	0	.267	.351	.359	.710	89	-3	28	4.42	-5	3-47,S-12/1-5,2-3,D-1	6	-0.7
Hou-N	21	66	10	28	4	0	2	8	9	5	1	1	.424	.493	.576	1.069	173	7	19	12.24	-2	3-10/S-6,2-3	4	0.7
Yr.	107	283	33	86	18	0	4	27	32	37	1	1	.304	.384	.410	.794	108	5	47	5.95	-7	3-57,S-18/2-6,1-5,D-1	10	0.0
2003 SD-N	154	589	74	185	28	4	13	72	54	62	5	4	.314	.375	.441	.816	123	19	95	5.93	-1	*2-150/S-3	25	2.4
Total 9	971	3251	433	964	167	17	44	352	310	371	28	24	.297	.364	.399	.763	99	-3	471	5.14	0	2-334,S-328,3-170,1-160/D,0,P	101	2.5
• LOUCKS, Scott	Scott Gregory Loucks b: 11/11/1956, Anchorage, AK BR/TR, 6', 178 lbs. Deb: 9/1/1980 Career OF: 4-49-3																							
1980 Hou-N	8	3	4	1	0	0	0	0	0	2	0	0	.333	.333	.333	.667	94	-0	0	4.50	-1	/0-4(0-2-2)	0	-0.1
1981 Hou-N	10	7	2	4	0	0	0	0	1	3	1	0	.571	.625	.571	1.196	254	2	3	26.89	0	/0-5(0-5-0)	1	0.2
1982 Hou-N	44	49	6	11	2	0	0	3	3	17	4	1	.224	.269	.265	.535	54	-3	4	2.47	1	0-37(0-37-0)	1	-0.2
1983 Hou-N	7	14	2	3	0	0	0	0	1	4	2	2	.214	.267	.214	.481	37	-2	1	1.19	1	/0-6(1-5-0)	0	-0.1
1985 Pit-N	4	7	1	2	2	0	0	1	2	2	0	0	.286	.444	.571	1.016	184	1	2	10.85	0	/0-4(3-0-1)	1	0.1
Total 5	73	80	15	21	4	0	0	4	7	28	7	3	.263	.322	.313	.634	84	-2	10	4.10	1	/0-56	3	-0.1
• LOUDEN, Baldy	William P. Louden b: 8/27/1885, Piedmont, WV d: 12/8/1935, Piedmont, WV BR/TR, 5'11", 175 lbs. Deb: 9/13/1907																							
1907 NY-A	4	9	4	1	0	0	0	0	2	....	1	....	.111	.273	.111	.384	21	-1	1	1.85	0	/3-3	0	0.0
1912 Det-A	122	403	57	97	12	4	1	36	58	....	28	....	.241	.352	.298	.649	89	-2	53	4.28	4	2-87,3-26/S-5	11	0.4
1913 Det-A	76	191	28	46	4	5	0	23	24	22	6	....	.241	.344	.314	.658	94	-0	23	3.78	-3	2-30,3-26/S-6,0-5(0-1-4)	5	-0.2
1914 Buf-F	126	431	73	135	11	4	6	63	52	41	35	....	.313	.391	.399	.790	120	13	78	6.34	-13	*S-115	21	0.9
1915 Buf-F	141	469	67	132	18	5	4	48	64	45	30	....	.281	.372	.367	.739	118	13	73	5.35	5	2-88,S-27,3-19	23	2.4
1916 Cin-N	134	439	38	96	16	4	1	32	54	54	12	....	.219	.313	.280	.593	85	-6	42	3.17	10	*2-108,S-23	10	0.9
Total 6	603	1942	267	507	61	22	12	202	254	162	112	....	.261	.355	.334	.689	102	17	271	4.64	4	2-313,S-176/3-74,0-5	70	4.4
• LOUDENSLAGER, Charlie	Charles Edward Loudenslager b: 5/21/1881, Baltimore, MD d: 10/31/1933, Baltimore, MD TR, 5'9", 186 lbs. Deb: 4/15/1904																							
1904 Bro-N	1	2	0	0	0	0	0	0	0	....	0	....	.000	.000	.000	.000	-103	-0	0	.00	0	/2-1	0	-0.1
• LOUGHLIN, Bill	William H. Loughlin b: Baltimore, MD Deb: 5/9/1883																							
1883 Bal-a	1	5	0	2	0	0	0	0	0	....	....	....	.400	.400	.400	.800	154	0	1	7.65	0	/0-1	0	0.0
• LOUGHRAN, Thomas	Thomas Loughran b: New York, NY Deb: 6/6/1884																							
1884 NY-N	9	29	4	3	1	1	0	3	7	11	....	....	.103	.278	.207	.485	53	-1	2	1.81	-3	/C-9,0-1	0	-0.3
• LOVELACE, Tom	Thomas Rivers Lovelace b: 10/19/1897, Wolfe City, TX d: 7/12/1979, Dallas, TX BR/TR, 5'11", 170 lbs. Deb: 9/23/1922																							
1922 Pit-N	1	1	0	0	0	0	0	0	0	0	0	0	.000	.000	.000	.000	-99	-0	0	.00	0	....	0	0.0
• LOVETT, Len	Leonard Walker Lovett b: 7/17/1852, Lancaster County, PA d: 11/18/1922, Newark, DE BR/TR Deb: 8/4/1873																							
1873 Res-n	1	5	1	2	0	0	0	1	0	0	0	0	.400	.400	.400	.800	150	1	1	8.34	0	/P-1	....	-0.1
1875 Cen-n	6	21	2	5	1	0	0	2	1	5	0	0	.238	.273	.286	.558	103	0	2	3.09	0	/0-6(1-0-5)	....	0.0
Total 2 n	7	26	3	7	1	0	0	3	1	5	0	0	.269	.296	.308	.604	111	1	2	3.92	-1	/0-6,P-1	....	-0.1
• LOVETT, Mem	Merritt Marwood Lovett b: 6/15/1912, Chicago, IL d: 9/19/1995, Downers Grove, IL BR/TR, 5'9.5", 165 lbs. Deb: 9/4/1933																							
1933 Chi-A	1	1	0	0	0	0	0	0	0	0	0	0	.000	.000	.000	.000	-104	-0	0	.00	0	....	0	0.0
• LOVIGLIO, Jay	John Paul Loviglio b: 5/30/1956, Freeport, NY BR/TR, 5'9", 160 lbs. Deb: 9/2/1980																							
1980 Phi-N	16	5	7	0	0	0	0	0	1	0	1	2	.000	.167	.000	.167	-47	-2	0	.00	0	/2-1	0	-0.2
1981 Chi-A	14	15	5	4	0	0	0	2	1	1	2	2	.267	.313	.267	.579	70	-1	0	.60	-1	/3-4,2-3,D-2	0	-0.2

YEAR TM-L	G	AB	R	H	2B	3B	HR	RBI	BB	SO	SB	CS	AVG	OBP	SLG	OPS	OPS+	BR/A	RC	RC/G	FR	G/POS	WS	TPW
1982 Chi-A	15	31	5	6	0	0	0	2	1	4	2	1	.194	.219	.194	.412	14	-4	1	1.42	0	2-13/D-2	0	-0.3
1983 Chi-N	1	1	0	0	0	0	0	0	0	1	0	0	.000	.000	.000	.000	-95	-0	0	.00	0	....	0	0.0
Total 4	**46**	**52**	**17**	**10**	**0**	**0**	**0**	**4**	**3**	**6**	**5**	**5**	**.192**	**.236**	**.192**	**.429**	**22**	**-7**	**2**	**.95**	**-2**	**/2-17,3-4,D-4**	**0**	**-0.8**
• LOVITTO, Joe	Joseph Lovitto b: 1/6/1951, San Pedro, CA d: 5/19/2001, Arlington, TX BB/TR, 6', 185 lbs. Deb: 4/15/1972 Career OF: 26-209-26																							
1972 Tex-A	117	330	23	74	9	1	1	19	37	54	13	11	.224	.306	.267	.573	75	-11	27	2.60	-3	*0-103(8-77-23)	6	-2.0
1973 Tex-A	26	44	3	6	1	0	0	0	5	7	1	0	.136	.224	.159	.384	10	-5	2	1.41	-4	3-20/0-3(0-2-1)	0	-1.0
1974 Tex-A	113	283	27	63	9	3	2	26	25	36	6	8	.223	.286	.297	.583	69	-13	21	2.37	-4	*0-107(0-105-2)/1-5	2	-2.1
1975 Tex-A	50	106	17	22	3	0	1	8	13	16	2	2	.208	.294	.264	.558	59	-6	9	2.53	1	0-38(18-25-0)/1-2,D-2,C-1	1	-0.6
Total 4	**306**	**763**	**70**	**165**	**22**	**4**	**4**	**53**	**80**	**113**	**22**	**21**	**.216**	**.292**	**.271**	**.564**	**67**	**-35**	**59**	**2.43**	**-10**	**0-251/3-20,1-7,D-2,C-1**	**9**	**-5.6**
• LOVULLO, Torey	Salvatore Anthony Lovullo b: 7/25/1965, Santa Monica, CA BB/TR, 6'1", 180 lbs. Deb: 9/10/1988 Career OF: 1-0-2																							
1988 Det-A	12	21	2	8	1	1	1	2	1	2	0	0	.381	.409	.667	1.076	203	3	5	9.25	0	/2-9,3-3	2	0.3
1989 Det-A	29	87	8	10	2	0	1	4	14	20	0	0	.115	.238	.172	.410	18	-9	4	1.33	-2	1-18,3-11	0	-1.2
1991 NY-A	22	51	0	9	2	0	0	2	5	7	0	0	.176	.250	.216	.466	30	-5	3	1.94	-1	3-22	0	-0.6
1993 Cal-A	116	367	42	92	20	0	6	30	36	49	7	6	.251	.319	.354	.674	78	-12	41	3.76	-9	2-91,3-14/S-9,0-2(0-0-2),1	7	-1.6
1994 Sea-A	36	72	9	16	5	0	2	7	9	13	1	0	.222	.309	.375	.684	74	-3	8	3.91	2	2-20/3-5,D-2	1	0.0
1996 Oak-A	65	82	15	18	4	0	3	9	11	17	1	2	.220	.326	.378	.704	79	-3	11	4.18	-1	1-42,3-11/D-4,2-2,0-1,S-1	1	-0.5
1998 Cle-A	6	19	1	4	1	0	0	1	1	2	0	0	.211	.250	.263	.513	33	-2	1	1.75	1	/2-5,3-1	0	-0.1
1999 Phi-N	17	38	3	8	0	0	2	5	3	11	0	0	.211	.268	.368	.637	57	-3	4	3.14	0	/1-6,2-6	0	-0.2
Total 8	**303**	**737**	**80**	**165**	**35**	**1**	**15**	**60**	**80**	**121**	**9**	**8**	**.224**	**.302**	**.335**	**.638**	**68**	**-34**	**77**	**3.41**	**-11**	**2-133/1-67,3-67,S-10,D-6,0**	**11**	**-4.1**
• LOW, Fletcher	Fletcher Low b: 4/7/1893, Essex, MA d: 6/6/1973, Hanover, NH BR/TR, 5'10.5", 175 lbs. Deb: 10/7/1915																							
1915 Bos-N	1	4	1	1	0	1	0	1	0	0	0	....	.250	.250	.750	1.000	201	0	1	6.63	0	/3-1	0	0.0
• LOWE, Bobby	Robert Lincoln "Link" Lowe b: 7/10/1865, Pittsburgh, PA d: 12/8/1951, Detroit, MI BR/TR, 5'10", 150 lbs. Deb: 4/19/1890 M/U Career OF: 173-56-11																							
1890 Bos-N	52	207	35	58	13	2	2	21	26	32	15	....	.280	.366	.391	.757	112	3	36	6.40	-1	S-24,0-15(3-11-1),3-12	8	0.2
1891 Bos-N	125	497	92	129	19	5	6	74	53	54	43	....	.260	.342	.354	.696	92	-6	77	5.63	-4	*0-107(64-38-5),2-17/S-2,3,P	15	-1.3
1892*Bos-N	124	475	79	115	16	7	3	57	37	47	36	....	.242	.308	.324	.632	83	-11	60	4.49	15	0-90(87-3-0),3-14,S-13,2-10	16	-0.3
1893 Bos-N	126	526	130	157	19	5	14	89	55	29	22	....	.298	.369	.433	.803	105	1	95	6.79	10	*2-121/S-5	22	1.4
1894 Bos-N	133	613	158	212	34	11	17	115	50	25	23	....	.346	.401	.520	.921	107	2	140	9.11	0	*2-130/S-2,3-1	20	0.6
1895 Bos-N	100	417	102	124	12	7	7	62	40	16	24	....	.297	.370	.410	.780	96	-3	75	6.62	14	*2-99	14	1.3
1896 Bos-N	73	306	59	98	11	4	2	48	20	12	15	....	.320	.370	.402	.772	98	-1	53	6.61	24	2-73	10	2.2
1897*Bos-N	123	499	87	154	24	8	5	106	32	....	16	....	.309	.355	.419	.774	98	-4	83	6.17	4	*2-123	16	0.5
1898 Bos-N	147	559	65	152	11	7	4	94	29	....	12	....	.272	.311	.338	.649	82	-16	67	4.13	29	*2-145/S-2	15	1.9
1899 Bos-N	152	559	81	152	5	9	4	88	35	....	17	....	.272	.316	.335	.650	71	-24	68	4.25	21	*2-148/S-4	13	0.3
1900 Bos-N	127	474	65	132	11	5	3	71	26	....	15	....	.278	.323	.342	.665	74	-18	60	4.51	3	*2-127	8	-0.9
1901 Bos-N	129	491	47	125	11	1	3	47	17	....	22	....	.255	.284	.299	.583	63	-24	50	3.55	3	*3-111,2-18	8	-1.8
1902 Chi-N	121	480	44	119	13	3	0	35	12	....	17	....	.248	.274	.288	.561	75	-15	45	3.19	28	*2-117/3-2	10	1.4
1903 Chi-N	32	105	14	28	5	3	0	15	4	....	5	....	.267	.319	.371	.690	99	-0	15	4.87	5	2-22/1-6,3-1	3	0.5
1904 Pit-N	1	1	0	0	0	0	0	0	0	....	0	....	.000	.000	.000	.000	-97	-0	0	.00	0	....	0	0.0
Det-A	140	506	47	105	14	6	0	40	17	....	15	....	.208	.236	.259	.495	58	-25	37	2.35	-2	*2-140	5	-2.8
1905 Det-A	58	181	17	35	7	2	0	9	13	....	3	....	.193	.255	.254	.509	61	-8	14	2.38	3	0-24(17-3-4),3-22/2-6,S-4,1	2	-0.6
1906 Det-A	41	145	11	30	3	0	1	12	4	....	3	....	.207	.233	.248	.482	49	-9	10	2.17	6	S-19,2-17/3-5	2	-0.2
1907 Det-A	17	37	2	9	2	0	0	5	4	....	0	....	.243	.317	.297	.614	93	-0	4	3.42	-1	3-10/0-4(2-1-1),S-2	1	-0.1
Total 18	**1821**	**7078**	**1135**	**1934**	**230**	**85**	**71**	**988**	**474**	**215**	**303**	**....**	**.273**	**.325**	**.360**	**.685**	**85**	**-160**	**988**	**4.97**	**156**	***2-1313,0-240,3-179/S-77,1,P**	**188**	**2.2**
• LOWE, Charlie	Charles Lowe b: Baltimore, MD Deb: 9/24/1872																							
1872 Atl-n	7	31	1	5	0	0	0	3	0	2	0	0	.161	.161	.161	.323		-4	1	.99	-2	/2-7	....	-0.4
• LOWE, Dick	Richard Alvern Lowe b: 1/28/1854, Evansville, WI d: 6/28/1922, Janesville, WI Deb: 6/26/1884																							
1884 Det-N	1	3	0	1	0	0	0	0	0	1	....	....	.333	.333	.333	.667	117	0	0	4.70	-2	/C-1	0	-0.1
• LOWELL, Mike	Michael Averett Lowell b: 2/24/1974, San Juan, Puerto Rico BR/TR, 6'4", 205 lbs. Deb: 9/13/1998																							
1998 NY-A	8	15	1	4	0	0	0	0	0	1	0	0	.267	.267	.267	.533	41	-1	1	2.62	1	/3-7	0	-0.1
1999 Fla-N	97	308	32	78	15	0	12	47	26	69	0	0	.253	.322	.419	.740	90	-6	41	4.55	-1	3-83	8	-0.5
2000 Fla-N	140	508	73	137	38	0	22	91	54	75	4	0	.270	.350	.474	.825	111	8	89	6.22	-3	*3-136	20	0.7
2001 Fla-N	146	551	65	156	37	0	18	100	43	79	1	2	.283	.346	.448	.794	107	4	86	5.56	4	*3-144	20	1.0
2002 Fla-N★	160	597	88	165	44	0	24	92	65	92	4	3	.276	.351	.471	.822	119	15	97	5.67	4	*3-159	21	2.1
2003*Fla-N★	130	492	76	136	27	1	32	105	56	78	3	1	.276	.354	.530	.884	132	22	90	6.47	5	*3-128/D-2	23	2.8
Total 6	**681**	**2471**	**335**	**676**	**161**	**1**	**108**	**435**	**244**	**394**	**12**	**6**	**.274**	**.346**	**.471**	**.817**	**113**	**43**	**404**	**5.76**	**9**	**3-657/D-2**	**92**	**6.0**
• LOWENSTEIN, John	John Lee Lowenstein b: 1/27/1947, Wolf Point, MT BL/TR, 6', 175 lbs. Deb: 9/2/1970 Career OF: 687-49-201																							
1970 Cle-A	17	43	5	11	3	1	1	6	1	9	1	0	.256	.273	.442	.715	89	-1	5	4.05	2	2-10/3-2,0-2(2-0-0),S-1	1	0.2
1971 Cle-A	58	140	15	26	5	0	4	9	16	28	1	5	.186	.269	.307	.576	58	-10	11	2.52	-4	2-29,0-18(7-5-8)/S-3	1	-1.3
1972 Cle-A	68	151	16	32	8	1	6	21	20	43	2	4	.212	.304	.397	.701	104	-1	18	3.94	4	0-58(27-3-29)/1-2	4	0.2
1973 Cle-A	98	305	42	89	16	1	6	40	23	41	5	3	.292	.341	.410	.751	109	3	41	4.72	3	0-51(12-4-36),2-25/3-8,D-4,1	10	0.6
1974 Cle-A	140	508	65	123	14	2	8	48	53	85	36	17	.242	.316	.325	.641	85	-8	55	3.54	4	*0-100(88-8-7),3-28,1-12/2	13	-1.0
1975 Cle-A	91	265	37	64	5	1	12	33	28	28	15	10	.242	.314	.404	.718	102	-1	32	4.00	0	0-36(19-3-17),D-31/3-8,2-2	6	-0.3
1976 Cle-A	93	229	33	47	8	2	2	14	25	35	11	8	.205	.283	.284	.567	67	-10	18	2.50	-1	0-61(13-19-29),D-11/1-9	2	-1.5
1977 Cle-A	81	149	24	36	6	1	4	12	21	29	1	8	.242	.335	.376	.711	97	-4	16	3.28	-1	0-39(18-5-17),D-19/1-1	2	-0.7
1978 Tex-A	77	176	28	39	8	3	5	21	37	29	16	3	.222	.363	.386	.749	110	6	29	5.49	-7	3-25,D-21,0-16(14-0-2)	6	-0.2
1979*Bal-A	97	197	33	50	8	2	11	34	30	37	16	4	.254	.355	.482	.837	128	10	36	6.26	2	0-72(44-1-41)/D-3,1-1,3-1	9	0.9
1980 Bal-A	104	196	38	61	8	0	4	27	32	29	7	3	.311	.408	.413	.821	127	9	36	6.78	-4	0-91(88-0-3)/D-3	9	0.2
1981 Bal-A	83	189	19	47	7	0	6	20	22	32	7	6	.249	.330	.381	.711	105	0	22	3.70	-1	0-73(67-0-10)/D-4	5	-0.3
1982 Bal-A	122	322	69	103	15	2	24	66	54	59	7	6	.320	.419	.602	1.022	177	35	81	9.19	0	*0-111(110-0-2)	21	3.0
1983*Bal-A	122	310	52	87	13	2	15	60	49	55	2	1	.281	.381	.481	.861	138	17	61	7.07	1	*0-107(106-1-0)/2-1,D-1	15	1.5
1984 Bal-A	105	270	34	64	13	0	8	28	33	54	1	0	.237	.322	.374	.696	94	-1	34	4.25	1	0-67(68-0-0),D-22/1-2	6	-0.3
1985 Bal-A	12	26	0	2	0	0	0	2	2	3	0	0	.077	.143	.077	.220	-39	-5	0	.45	0	/D-6,0-4(4-0-0)	0	-0.5
Total 16	**1368**	**3476**	**510**	**881**	**137**	**18**	**116**	**441**	**446**	**596**	**128**	**78**	**.253**	**.340**	**.403**	**.743**	**108**	**41**	**496**	**4.80**	**0**	**0-906,D-125/3-72,2-71,1-28,S**	**110**	**0.5**
• LOWERY, Terrell	Quenton Terrell Lowery b: 10/25/1970, Oakland, CA BR/TR, 6'3", 180 lbs. Deb: 9/13/1997 Career OF: 49-58-9																							
1997 Chi-N	9	14	2	4	0	0	0	0	3	3	1	0	.286	.412	.286	.697	85	0	2	5.89	1	/0-6(5-2-0)	1	0.1
1998 Chi-N	24	15	2	3	1	0	0	1	3	7	0	0	.200	.333	.267	.600	58	-1	2	3.59	-2	0-22(2-20-0)	0	-0.2
1999 TB-A	66	185	25	48	15	1	2	17	19	53	0	2	.259	.332	.384	.715	81	-6	24	4.64	0	0-60(29-36-1)	3	-0.7
2000 SF-N	24	34	13	15	4	0	1	5	7	8	1	0	.441	.548	.647	1.195	217	7	13	17.40	-1	0-20(13-0-8)/D-1	3	0.5
Total 4	**123**	**248**	**42**	**70**	**20**	**1**	**3**	**23**	**32**	**71**	**2**	**2**	**.282**	**.369**	**.407**	**.776**	**100**	**0**	**41**	**6.03**	**-2**	**0-108/D-1**	**7**	**-0.3**
• LOWREY, Peanuts	Harry Lee Lowrey b: 8/27/1917, Culver City, CA d: 7/2/1986, Inglewood, CA BR/TR, 5'8.5", 170 lbs. Deb: 4/14/1942 C Career OF: 548-387-62																							
1942 Chi-N	27	58	4	11	0	0	1	4	4	4	0	....	.190	.242	.241	.483	43	-4	4	2.08	0	0-19(7-15-0)	0	-0.5
1943 Chi-N	130	480	59	140	25	12	1	63	35	24	13	....	.292	.340	.400	.740	115	8	64	4.72	5	*0-113(0-113-0),S-16/2-3	16	1.1
1945*Chi-N	143	523	72	148	22	7	7	89	48	27	11	....	.283	.343	.392	.735	106	4	73	4.85	6	*0-138(125-14-0)/S-2	17	0.2
1946 Chi-N★	144	540	75	139	24	5	4	54	56	22	10	....	.257	.328	.343	.671	92	-6	63	3.96	0	*0-126(73-60-0),3-20	15	-1.3
1947 Chi-N	115	448	56	126	17	5	5	37	38	26	2	....	.281	.339	.375	.714	93	-5	58	4.68	3	3-91,0-25(18-6-1)/2-6	12	-0.4
1948 Chi-N	129	435	47	128	12	3	2	54	34	31	2	....	.294	.347	.349	.696	93	-4	52	4.36	4	*0-103(63-43-0)/3-9,2-2,S	9	-0.6
1949 Chi-N	38	111	18	30	5	0	2	10	9	8	3	....	.270	.325	.369	.694	88	-2	13	3.95	-1	0-31(28-3-1)/3-1	2	-0.5
Cin-N	89	309	48	85	16	2	2	25	37	11	1	....	.275	.354	.359	.714	91	-3	39	4.34	6	0-78(77-1-0)	7	-0.3
Yr.	127	420	66	115	21	2	4	35	46	19	4	....	.274	.347	.362	.709	90	-5	52	4.24	4	*0-109(105-4-1)/3-1	9	-0.8
1950 Cin-N	91	264	34	60	14	0	1	11	36	7	0	....	.227	.320	.292	.612	62	-14	25	3.04	-0	0-72(66-2-6)/2-1	3	-1.8
StL-N	17	56	10	15	0	0	1	4	6	1	0	....	.268	.349	.321	.671	74	-2	7	4.25	1	/2-6,3-5,0-4(3-1-0)	1	-0.1
Yr.	108	320	44	75	14	0	2	15	42	8	0	....	.234	.325	.297	.622	64	-16	31	3.23	1	0-76(69-3-6)/2-7,3-5	4	-1.9

YEAR TM-L	G	AB	R	H	2B	3B	HR	RBI	BB	SO	SB	CS	AVG	OBP	SLG	OPS	OPS+	BR/A	RC	RC/G	FR	G/POS	WS	TPW
1951 StL-N	114	370	52	112	19	5	5	40	35	12	0	1	.303	.366	.422	.788	111	6	57	5.44	-3	0-85(13-74-0),3-11/2-3	12	-0.1
1952 StL-N	132	374	48	107	18	2	1	48	34	13	3	2	.286	.352	.353	.705	96	-1	48	4.53	-3	*0-106(63-35-6)/3-6	10	-0.9
1953 StL-N	104	182	26	49	9	2	5	27	15	21	1	0	.269	.325	.423	.748	93	-2	24	4.51	-1	0-38(3-10-25),2-10/3-1	4	-0.3
1954 StL-N	74	61	6	7	1	2	0	5	9	9	0	0	.115	.229	.197	.425	12	-8	3	1.39	-1	0-12(3-1-9)	0	-0.9
1955 Phi-N	54	106	9	20	4	0	0	8	7	10	2	0	.189	.239	.226	.465	25	-11	5	1.30	0	0-28(6-9-14)/2-2,1-1	0	-1.2
Total 13	1401	4317	564	1177	186	45	37	479	403	226	48	3	.273	.336	.362	.699	93	-45	533	4.28	14	0-978,3-144/2-33,S-19,1-1	108	-7.6

• LOWRY, Dwight Dwight Lowry b: 10/23/1957, Lumberton, NC d: 7/10/1997, Jamestown, NY BL/TR, 6'3", 210 lbs. Deb: 4/3/1984

YEAR TM-L	G	AB	R	H	2B	3B	HR	RBI	BB	SO	SB	CS	AVG	OBP	SLG	OPS	OPS+	BR/A	RC	RC/G	FR	G/POS	WS	TPW
1984 Det-A	32	45	8	11	2	0	2	7	3	11	0	0	.244	.292	.422	.714	95	-0	5	3.05	1	C-31	2	0.1
1986 Det-A	56	150	21	46	4	0	3	18	17	19	0	0	.307	.392	.393	.785	115	4	24	5.81	0	C-55/1-1,0-1	6	0.6
1987 Det-A	13	25	0	5	2	0	0	1	0	6	0	0	.200	.200	.280	.480	27	-3	1	1.89	0	C-12/1-1	0	-0.2
1988 Min-A	7	7	0	0	0	0	0	0	0	2	0	0	.000	.000	.000	.000	-97	-2	0	.00	0	/C-5	0	-0.2
Total 4	108	227	29	62	8	0	5	26	20	38	0	0	.273	.343	.374	.717	97	-1	30	4.51	1	C-103/1-2,0-1	8	0.3

• LOWRY, John John D. Lowry b: Baltimore, MD Deb: 6/26/1875

YEAR TM-L	G	AB	R	H	2B	3B	HR	RBI	BB	SO	SB	CS	AVG	OBP	SLG	OPS	OPS+	BR/A	RC	RC/G	FR	G/POS	WS	TPW
1875 Was-n	6	22	2	3	0	0	0	0	1	0	0	1	.136	.174	.136	.310	10	-2	1	.79	-1	/0-6(0-6-0)	....	-0.3

• LOZADO, Willie William Lozado b: 5/12/1959, New York, NY BR/TR, 6', 166 lbs. Deb: 7/16/1984

YEAR TM-L	G	AB	R	H	2B	3B	HR	RBI	BB	SO	SB	CS	AVG	OBP	SLG	OPS	OPS+	BR/A	RC	RC/G	FR	G/POS	WS	TPW
1984 Mil-A	43	107	15	29	8	2	1	20	12	23	0	3	.271	.345	.411	.756	113	1	15	4.60	-1	3-36/S-6,2-1,D-1	4	0.0

• LUBRATICH, Steve Steven George Lubratich b: 5/1/1955, Oakland, CA BR/TR, 6', 170 lbs. Deb: 9/27/1981

YEAR TM-L	G	AB	R	H	2B	3B	HR	RBI	BB	SO	SB	CS	AVG	OBP	SLG	OPS	OPS+	BR/A	RC	RC/G	FR	G/POS	WS	TPW
1981 Cal-A	7	21	2	3	1	0	0	1	0	2	1	0	.143	.143	.190	.333	-5	-3	0	.61	1	/3-6	0	-0.1
1983 Cal-A	57	156	12	34	9	0	0	7	4	17	0	1	.218	.238	.276	.513	41	-13	10	1.93	1	S-23,3-22,2-14	2	-1.0
Total 2	64	177	14	37	10	0	0	8	4	19	1	1	.209	.227	.266	.492	36	-16	10	1.78	2	/3-28,S-23,2-14	2	-1.1

• LUBY, Hal Hugh Max Luby b: 6/13/1913, Blackfoot, ID d: 5/4/1986, Eugene, OR BR/TR, 5'10", 185 lbs. Deb: 9/10/1936

YEAR TM-L	G	AB	R	H	2B	3B	HR	RBI	BB	SO	SB	CS	AVG	OBP	SLG	OPS	OPS+	BR/A	RC	RC/G	FR	G/POS	WS	TPW
1936 Phi-A	9	38	3	7	1	0	0	3	0	7	2	0	.184	.205	.211	.416	3	-5	2	1.57	-2	/2-9	0	-0.6
1944 NY-N	111	323	30	82	10	2	2	35	52	15	2	....	.254	.364	.316	.680	93	-0	40	4.22	3	3-65,2-45/1-1	10	0.5
Total 2	120	361	33	89	11	2	2	38	52	22	4	0	.247	.349	.305	.654	85	-6	42	3.93	1	/3-65,2-54,1-1	10	0.0

• LUCADELLO, Johnny John Lucadello b: 2/22/1919, Thurber, TX d: 10/30/2001, San Antonio, TX BB/TR, 5'11", 160 lbs. Deb: 9/24/1938

YEAR TM-L	G	AB	R	H	2B	3B	HR	RBI	BB	SO	SB	CS	AVG	OBP	SLG	OPS	OPS+	BR/A	RC	RC/G	FR	G/POS	WS	TPW
1938 StL-A	7	20	1	3	1	0	0	0	0	0	0	0	.150	.150	.200	.350	-13	-4	1	.90	0	/3-6	0	-0.3
1939 StL-A	9	30	0	7	2	0	0	4	2	4	0	0	.233	.281	.300	.581	48	-2	3	3.08	-2	/2-7	0	-0.4
1940 StL-A	17	63	15	20	4	2	2	10	6	4	1	0	.317	.394	.540	.934	137	4	15	9.27	1	2-16	3	0.5
1941 StL-A	107	351	58	98	22	4	2	31	48	23	5	2	.279	.366	.382	.748	95	-1	54	5.56	-9	2-70,S-12/3-6,0-1	10	-0.5
1946 StL-A	87	210	21	52	7	1	1	15	36	20	0	1	.248	.358	.305	.662	82	-3	26	4.30	-3	3-37,2-19	6	-0.6
1947 NY-A	12	12	0	1	0	0	0	0	1	5	0	0	.083	.154	.083	.237	-33	-2	0	.22	-2	/2-5	0	-0.4
Total 6	239	686	95	181	36	7	5	60	93	56	6	3	.264	.353	.359	.712	88	-9	98	5.08	-16	2-117/3-49,S-12,0-1	19	-1.7

• LUCAS, Fred Frederick Warrington "Fritz" Lucas b: 1/19/1903, Vineland, NJ d: 3/11/1987, Cambridge, MD BR/TR, 5'10", 165 lbs. Deb: 7/15/1935

YEAR TM-L	G	AB	R	H	2B	3B	HR	RBI	BB	SO	SB	CS	AVG	OBP	SLG	OPS	OPS+	BR/A	RC	RC/G	FR	G/POS	WS	TPW
1935 Phi-N	20	34	1	9	0	0	0	2	3	6	0	....	.265	.324	.265	.589	55	-2	3	3.09	-1	0-10(4-3-3)	0	-0.3

• LUCAS, Johnny John Charles "Buster" Lucas b: 2/10/1903, Glen Carbon, IL d: 10/31/1970, Maryville, IL BR/TL, 5'10", 186 lbs. Deb: 4/15/1931

YEAR TM-L	G	AB	R	H	2B	3B	HR	RBI	BB	SO	SB	CS	AVG	OBP	SLG	OPS	OPS+	BR/A	RC	RC/G	FR	G/POS	WS	TPW
1931 Bos-A	3	2	0	0	0	0	0	0	0	1	0	0	.000	.000	.000	.000	-106	-1	0	.00	0	/0-2(1-1-0)	0	-0.1
1932 Bos-A	1	1	0	0	0	0	0	0	0	0	0	0	.000	.000	.000	.000	-103	-0	0	.00	0	....	0	0.0
Total 2	4	3	0	0	0	0	0	0	0	1	0	0	.000	.000	.000	.000	-105	-1	0	.00	0	/0-2	0	-0.1

• LUCAS, Red Charles Fred "The Nashville Narcissus" Lucas b: 4/28/1902, Columbia, TN d: 7/9/1986, Nashville, TN BL/TR, 5'9.5", 170 lbs. Deb: 4/19/1923 ♦

YEAR TM-L	G	AB	R	H	2B	3B	HR	RBI	BB	SO	SB	CS	AVG	OBP	SLG	OPS	OPS+	BR/A	RC	RC/G	FR	G/POS	WS	TPW
1923 NY-N	3	2	0	0	0	0	0	0	0	1	0	0	.000	.000	.000	.000	-101	-0	0	.00	0	/P-3	0	0.2
1924 Bos-N	33	33	5	11	1	0	0	5	1	4	0	0	.333	.353	.364	.717	96	2	4	5.00	0	P-27/3-2	2	-1.0
1925 Bos-N	6	20	1	3	0	0	0	2	2	4	0	0	.150	.227	.150	.377	-2	-3	1	1.24	-1	/2-6	0	-0.3
1926 Cin-N	66	76	15	23	4	4	0	14	10	13	0	....	.303	.384	.461	.844	130	9	13	6.03	-1	P-39/2-1	12	0.8
1927 Cin-N	80	150	14	47	5	2	0	28	12	10	0	....	.313	.368	.373	.741	102	12	21	4.89	-2	P-37/2-5,S-3,0-1	23	2.2
1928 Cin-N	39	73	8	23	2	1	0	7	4	6	0	....	.315	.351	.370	.721	90	6	9	4.68	0	P-27	15	1.6
1929 Cin-N	76	140	15	41	6	0	0	13	13	15	1	....	.293	.353	.336	.689	75	11	17	4.28	1	P-32	26	3.5
1930 Cin-N	80	113	18	38	4	1	2	19	17	4	0	....	.336	.423	.442	.866	115	15	22	6.82	-3	P-33	14	0.3
1931 Cin-N	97	153	15	43	4	0	0	17	12	9	0	....	.281	.333	.307	.641	78	11	17	3.73	0	P-29	17	1.3
1932 Cin-N	76	150	13	43	11	2	0	19	10	9	0	....	.287	.335	.387	.722	97	14	20	4.72	0	P-31	23	4.2
1933 Cin-N	75	122	14	35	6	1	1	15	12	6	0	....	.287	.356	.377	.733	111	13	17	4.97	0	P-29	15	1.6
1934 Pit-N	68	105	11	23	5	1	0	8	6	16	1	....	.219	.261	.286	.547	45	3	8	2.51	-3	P-29	9	-0.1
1935 Pit-N	47	66	6	21	6	0	0	10	7	11	0	....	.318	.392	.409	.801	112	8	11	6.38	-1	P-20	11	1.7
1936 Pit-N	69	108	11	26	4	1	0	14	8	17	0	....	.241	.293	.296	.589	58	4	9	2.66	-1	P-27	15	2.2
1937 Pit-N	59	82	8	22	3	0	0	17	7	6	0	....	.268	.326	.305	.631	72	5	8	3.63	-2	P-20	7	-0.1
1938 Pit-N	33	46	1	5	0	0	0	2	3	2	0	....	.109	.163	.109	.272	-24	-2	1	.58	-1	P-13	5	-0.1
Total 16	907	1439	155	404	61	13	3	190	124	133	2	0	.281	.340	.347	.687	85	108	177	4.28	-11	P-396/2-12,S-3,3-2,0-1	194	18.0

• LUCE, Frank Frank Edward Luce b: 12/6/1896, Spencer, OH d: 2/3/1942, Milwaukee, WI BL/TR, 5'11", 180 lbs. Deb: 9/17/1923

YEAR TM-L	G	AB	R	H	2B	3B	HR	RBI	BB	SO	SB	CS	AVG	OBP	SLG	OPS	OPS+	BR/A	RC	RC/G	FR	G/POS	WS	TPW
1923 Pit-N	9	12	2	6	0	0	0	3	2	2	2	1	.500	.571	.500	1.071	181	2	4	13.70	0	/0-5(3-1-1)	1	0.1

• LUCEY, Joe Joseph Earl "Scootch" Lucey b: 3/27/1897, Holyoke, MA d: 7/30/1980, Holyoke, MA BR/TR, 6', 168 lbs. Deb: 7/6/1920 ♦

YEAR TM-L	G	AB	R	H	2B	3B	HR	RBI	BB	SO	SB	CS	AVG	OBP	SLG	OPS	OPS+	BR/A	RC	RC/G	FR	G/POS	WS	TPW
1920 NY-A	3	3	0	0	0	0	0	0	0	0	0	0	.000	.000	.000	.000	-97	-1	0	.00	-0	/2-1,S-1	0	-0.1
1925 Bos-A	10	15	0	2	0	0	0	0	0	4	0	0	.133	.133	.133	.267	-32	-2	0	.52	-1	/P-7,S-3	0	-0.9
Total 2	13	18	0	2	0	0	0	0	0	4	0	0	.111	.111	.111	.222	-43	-3	0	.42	-1	/P-7,S-4,2-1	0	-0.9

• LUDERUS, Fred Frederick William Luderus b: 9/12/1885, Milwaukee, WI d: 1/5/1961, Three Lakes, WI BL/TR, 5'11.5", 185 lbs. Deb: 9/23/1909

YEAR TM-L	G	AB	R	H	2B	3B	HR	RBI	BB	SO	SB	CS	AVG	OBP	SLG	OPS	OPS+	BR/A	RC	RC/G	FR	G/POS	WS	TPW
1909 Chi-N	11	37	8	11	1	1	1	9	3	....	0	....	.297	.366	.459	.825	152	2	6	5.83	-2	1-11	2	0.0
1910 Chi-N	24	54	5	11	1	1	0	3	4	3	0	....	.204	.259	.259	.518	52	-3	4	2.11	-1	1-17	0	-0.4
Phi-N	21	68	10	20	5	2	0	14	9	5	2	....	.294	.385	.426	.811	132	3	12	6.32	0	1-19	3	0.3
Yr.	45	122	15	31	6	3	0	17	13	8	2	....	.254	.331	.352	.683	97	-1	15	4.30	0	1-36	3	-0.2
1911 Phi-N	146	551	69	166	24	11	16	99	40	76	6	....	.301	.353	.472	.825	128	17	93	6.03	-1	*1-146	20	1.3
1912 Phi-N	148	572	77	147	31	5	10	69	44	65	8	....	.257	.318	.381	.699	85	-14	70	4.15	10	*1-146	13	-0.7
1913 Phi-N	155	588	67	154	32	7	18	86	34	51	5	....	.262	.304	.432	.736	105	-0	75	4.31	-1	*1-155	14	-0.5
1914 Phi-N	121	443	55	110	16	5	12	55	33	31	2	....	.248	.308	.388	.696	100	-2	51	3.92	-5	*1-121	11	-0.9
1915*Phi-N	141	499	55	157	36	7	7	62	42	36	9	7	.315	.376	.457	.833	150	28	87	6.41	8	*1-141	26	3.7
1916 Phi-N	146	508	52	143	26	3	5	53	41	32	8	....	.281	.341	.374	.715	115	10	69	4.77	-3	*1-146	20	0.4
1917 Phi-N	154	522	57	136	24	4	5	72	65	35	5	....	.261	.349	.351	.700	110	9	64	4.19	0	*1-154	18	0.8
1918 Phi-N	125	468	54	135	23	2	5	67	42	33	4	....	.288	.351	.378	.729	114	9	61	4.67	1	*1-125	15	0.8
1919 Phi-N	138	509	60	149	30	6	5	49	54	48	6	....	.293	.365	.405	.770	122	16	75	5.27	-3	*1-138	18	1.1
1920 Phi-N	16	32	1	5	2	0	0	4	3	6	0	1	.156	.229	.219	.447	28	-3	2	1.41	0	/1-7	0	-0.4
Total 12	1346	4851	570	1344	251	54	84	642	414	421	55	8	.277	.340	.403	.743	114	71	669	4.81	3	*1-1326	160	5.6

• LUDWICK, Ryan Ryan Andrew Ludwick b: 7/13/1978, Satellite Beach, FL BR/TL, 6'3", 203 lbs. Deb: 6/5/2002 Career OF: 19-21-26

YEAR TM-L	G	AB	R	H	2B	3B	HR	RBI	BB	SO	SB	CS	AVG	OBP	SLG	OPS	OPS+	BR/A	RC	RC/G	FR	G/POS	WS	TPW
2002 Tex-A	23	81	10	19	6	0	1	9	7	24	2	1	.235	.295	.346	.641	66	-4	7	2.97	-3	0-22(2-21-1)	0	-0.7
2003 Tex-A	8	26	3	4	1	0	0	0	4	9	0	0	.154	.267	.192	.459	22	-3	2	1.98	0	/0-8(4-0-6)	0	-0.4
Cle-A	39	136	14	36	7	1	7	26	8	39	2	0	.265	.306	.485	.791	107	1	21	5.45	2	0-32(13-0-19)/D-3	6	0.2
Yr.	47	162	17	40	8	1	7	26	12	48	2	0	.247	.299	.438	.737	93	-2	22	4.83	2	0-40(17-0-25)/D-3	6	-0.2
Total 2	70	243	27	59	14	1	8	35	19	72	4	1	.243	.298	.407	.705	84	-6	30	4.18	-2	/0-62,D-3	6	-0.9

• LUDWIG, Bill William Lawrence Ludwig b: 5/27/1882, Louisville, KY d: 9/5/1947, Louisville, KY BR/TR Deb: 4/16/1908

YEAR TM-L	G	AB	R	H	2B	3B	HR	RBI	BB	SO	SB	CS	AVG	OBP	SLG	OPS	OPS+	BR/A	RC	RC/G	FR	G/POS	WS	TPW
1908 StL-N	66	187	15	34	2	2	0	8	16	....	3	....	.182	.246	.214	.460	50	-10	11	1.74	1	C-62	2	-0.4

YEAR TM-L	G	AB	R	H	2B	3B	HR	RBI	BB	SO	SB	CS	AVG	OBP	SLG	OPS	OPS+	BR/A	RC	RC/G	FR	G/POS	WS	TPW
• LUEBBE, Roy	Roy John Luebbe b: 9/17/1900, Parkersburg, IA d: 8/21/1985, Papillion, NE BB/TR, 6', 175 lbs. Deb: 8/22/1925																							
1925 NY-A	8	15	1	0	0	0	0	3	2	6	0	0	.000	.118	.000	.118	-69	-4	0	.18	0	/C-8	0	-0.3
• LUFF, Henry	Henry T. Luff b: 9/14/1856, Philadelphia, PA d: 10/11/1916, Philadelphia, PA, 5'11", 175 lbs. Deb: 4/21/1875 Career OF: 14-3-4 ♦																							
1875 NH-n	38	166	15	45	10	3	2	18	0	5	3	3	.271	.271	.404	.675	150	9	19	4.63	-8	3-30,P-10/0-4(0-1-3),S-1	....	-1.2
1882 Det-N	3	11	1	3	2	0	0	1	0	0	....	....	.273	.273	.455	.727	128	0	1	4.80	-2	/2-3,0-1	0	-0.1
Cin-a	28	120	16	28	2	2	0	6	2	....	....	....	.233	.246	.283	.529	74	-4	9	2.61	-4	1-27/0-1	2	-0.9
1883 Lou-a	6	23	1	4	0	0	0	2	0	....	....	....	.174	.174	.174	.348	13	-2	1	1.05	-1	/1-4,0-2(0-1-1)	0	-0.3
1884 Phi-U	26	111	9	30	4	2	0	....	4	....	....	....	.270	.296	.342	.638	125	3	12	3.98	-3	0-12(11-0-1)/1-6,3-5,2-3	3	-0.1
KC-U	5	19	0	1	0	0	0	....	1	....	....	....	.053	.100	.053	.153	-54	-3	0	.16	-4	/3-4,0-4(3-1-1)	0	-0.6
Yr.	31	130	9	31	4	2	0	....	5	....	....	....	.238	.267	.300	.567	98	1	12	3.29	-7	0-16(14-1-2)/3-9,1-6,2-3	3	-0.6
Total 3	68	284	27	66	8	4	0	9	7	0	....	....	.232	.251	.289	.540	82	-5	22	2.86	-14	/1-37,0-20,3-9,2-6	5	-2.0
• LUGO, Julio	Julio Cesar Lugo b: 11/16/1975, Barahona, Dominican Republic BR/TR, 6', 165 lbs. Deb: 4/15/2000 Career OF: 9-1-4																							
2000 Hou-N	116	420	78	119	22	5	10	40	37	93	22	9	.283	.347	.431	.778	90	-6	63	5.24	-6	S-60,2-45/0-6(3-1-2)	9	-0.5
2001*Hou-N	140	513	93	135	20	3	10	37	46	116	12	11	.263	.330	.372	.702	77	-19	64	4.11	10	*S-133/0-8(6-0-2),2-2	9	0.1
2002 Hou-N	88	322	45	84	15	1	8	35	28	74	9	3	.261	.324	.388	.712	83	-8	41	4.38	-16	S-84	9	-1.7
2003 Hou-N	22	65	6	16	3	0	0	2	9	12	2	1	.246	.338	.292	.630	64	-3	7	3.41	-1	S-22	1	-0.2
TB-A	117	433	58	119	13	4	15	53	35	88	10	3	.275	.335	.427	.762	101	1	64	5.20	13	*S-117	13	2.2
Total 4	483	1753	280	473	73	13	43	167	155	383	55	27	.270	.334	.400	.734	86	-35	238	4.66	0	S-416/2-47,0-14	41	-0.1
• LUKACHYK, Rob	Robert James Lukachyk b: 7/24/1968, Jersey City, NJ BL/TR, 6', 185 lbs. Deb: 7/5/1996																							
1996 Mon-N	2	2	0	0	0	0	0	0	0	1	0	0	.000	.000	.000	.000	-98	-1	0	.00	0	....	0	-0.1
• LUKE, Matt	Matthew Clifford Luke b: 2/26/1971, Long Beach, CA BL/TL, 6'5", 220 lbs. Deb: 4/3/1996 Career OF: 52-0-18																							
1996 NY-A	1	0	1	0	0	0	0	0	0	0	0	0	....	....	....	....	-100	0	0	....	0	....	0	0.0
1998 LA-N	33	77	10	22	7	0	3	11	3	18	0	0	.286	.313	.494	.806	115	1	12	5.85	3	0-15(13-0-2),1-12	0	0.3
Cle-A	2	2	0	0	0	0	0	0	0	0	0	0	.000	.000	.000	.000	-97	-1	0	.00	0	....	0	-0.1
LA-N	69	160	24	34	5	1	9	23	14	42	2	1	.213	.280	.425	.705	87	-4	18	3.73	3	0-48(37-0-12)/1-6	0	-0.3
Yr.	102	237	34	56	12	1	12	34	17	60	2	1	.236	.290	.447	.737	96	-3	30	4.36	6	0-63(50-0-14),1-18	0	0.0
1999 Ana-A	18	30	4	9	0	0	3	6	2	10	0	0	.300	.344	.600	.944	135	1	5	6.11	1	/0-6(2-0-4),1-4	1	0.2
Total 3	123	269	39	65	12	1	15	40	19	70	2	1	.242	.294	.461	.755	99	-2	36	4.51	7	/0-69,1-22	1	0.2
• LUKON, Eddie	Edward Paul "Mongoose" Lukon b: 8/5/1920, Burgettstown, PA d: 11/7/1996, Canonsburg, PA BL/TL, 5'10", 168 lbs. Deb: 8/6/1941 Career OF: 105-2-58																							
1941 Cin-N	23	86	6	23	3	0	0	3	6	6	1	....	.267	.315	.302	.618	74	-3	8	3.51	2	0-22(0-0-22)	2	-0.3
1945 Cin-N	2	8	1	1	0	0	0	0	0	1	0	....	.125	.125	.125	.250	-31	-1	0	.48	-0	/0-2(0-2-0)	0	-0.2
1946 Cin-N	102	312	31	78	8	8	12	34	26	29	3	....	.250	.310	.442	.752	116	4	43	4.80	2	0-83(72-0-11)	9	0.0
1947 Cin-N	86	200	26	41	6	1	11	33	28	36	0	....	.205	.306	.410	.716	89	-4	26	4.25	0	0-55(33-0-25)	5	-0.7
Total 4	213	606	64	143	17	9	23	70	60	72	4	....	.236	.307	.408	.714	99	-4	77	4.37	3	0-162	16	-1.0
• LUM, Mike	Michael Ken-Wai Lum b: 10/27/1945, Honolulu, HI BL/TL, 6', 180 lbs. Deb: 9/12/1967 C Career OF: 359-171-315																							
1967 Atl-N	9	26	1	6	0	0	0	1	1	4	0	1	.231	.259	.231	.490	42	-2	1	1.79	1	/0-6(0-6-0)	0	-0.2
1968 Atl-N	122	232	22	52	7	3	3	21	14	35	3	5	.224	.280	.319	.599	79	-7	19	2.62	1	0-95(74-7-21)	3	-1.1
1969*Atl-N	121	168	20	45	8	0	1	22	16	18	0	0	.268	.332	.333	.665	86	-3	18	3.84	0	0-89(56-16-21)	5	-0.6
1970 Atl-N	123	291	25	74	17	2	7	28	17	43	3	2	.254	.307	.399	.705	83	-8	36	4.31	-2	0-98(36-33-35)	6	-1.4
1971 Atl-N	145	454	56	122	14	1	13	55	47	43	0	3	.269	.344	.390	.734	101	0	61	4.74	2	*0-125(10-17-104)/1-1	14	-0.5
1972 Atl-N	123	369	40	84	14	2	9	38	50	52	1	4	.228	.325	.350	.674	84	-8	43	3.86	-2	*0-109(30-20-62)/1-2	8	-1.7
1973 Atl-N	138	513	74	151	26	6	16	82	41	89	2	5	.294	.354	.462	.816	116	9	84	6.04	-3	1-84,0-64(48-2-14)	14	-0.4
1974 Atl-N	106	361	50	84	11	2	11	50	45	49	0	2	.233	.321	.366	.687	88	-7	42	3.86	-3	1-60,0-50(14-9-25)	7	-1.6
1975 Atl-N	124	364	32	83	8	2	8	36	39	38	2	4	.228	.303	.327	.630	72	-15	34	3.09	-3	1-60,0-38(1-32-5)	5	-2.5
1976*Cin-N	84	136	15	31	5	1	3	20	22	24	0	1	.228	.340	.346	.685	92	-1	17	4.11	-2	0-38(33-2-5)	3	-0.5
1977 Cin-N	81	125	14	20	1	0	5	16	9	33	2	0	.160	.222	.288	.510	35	-11	8	2.05	-1	0-24(12-1-11)/1-8	0	-1.4
1978 Cin-N	86	146	15	39	7	1	6	23	22	18	0	0	.267	.363	.452	.815	126	5	24	5.79	3	0-43(10-26-9)/1-7	6	0.7
1979 Atl-N	111	217	27	54	6	0	6	27	18	34	0	2	.249	.306	.359	.666	75	-8	22	3.38	2	1-51/0-3(3-0-0)	2	-0.9
1980 Atl-N	93	83	7	17	3	0	0	5	18	19	0	0	.205	.347	.241	.587	65	-3	8	2.95	0	0-19(19-0-0),1-10	1	-0.3
1981 Atl-N	10	11	1	1	0	0	0	0	2	2	0	0	.091	.231	.091	.322	-6	-1	0	.79	0	/0-1	0	-0.2
Chi-N	41	58	5	14	1	0	2	7	5	5	0	0	.241	.313	.362	.675	87	-1	7	3.87	-1	0-14(12-0-3)/1-1	1	-0.2
Yr.	51	69	6	15	1	0	2	7	7	7	0	0	.217	.299	.319	.618	72	-2	7	3.32	-1	0-15(13-0-3)/1-1	1	-0.4
Total 15	1517	3554	404	877	128	20	90	431	366	506	13	29	.247	.322	.370	.692	88	-62	426	4.06	-8	0-816,1-284	75	-12.8
• LUMLEY, Harry	Harry G. "Judge" Lumley b: 9/29/1880, Forest City, PA d: 5/22/1938, Binghamton, NY BL/TL, 5'10", 183 lbs. Deb: 4/14/1904 M Career OF: 0-0-700																							
1904 Bro-N	150	577	79	161	23	**18**	**9**	78	41	....	30	....	.279	.331	.428	.759	137	23	95	5.79	-2	*0-150(0-0-150)	20	1.6
1905 Bro-N	130	505	50	148	19	10	7	47	36	....	22	....	.293	.340	.412	.752	134	19	82	5.70	-3	*0-129(0-0-129)	17	1.1
1906 Bro-N	133	484	72	157	23	12	9	61	48	....	35	....	.324	.386	**.477**	.864	**184**	**45**	107	8.01	-2	*0-131(0-0-131)	35	4.1
1907 Bro-N	127	454	47	121	23	11	9	66	31	....	18	....	.267	.316	.425	.741	144	19	70	5.18	-3	*0-118(0-0-118)	19	1.2
1908 Bro-N	127	440	36	95	13	12	4	39	29	....	4	....	.216	.266	.327	.593	93	-5	39	2.82	-3	*0-116(0-0-116)	8	-1.5
1909 Bro-N	55	172	13	43	8	3	0	14	16	....	1	....	.250	.314	.331	.645	104	1	19	3.50	1	0-52(0-0-52)	3	-0.1
1910 Bro-N	8	21	3	3	0	0	0	0	3	6	0	....	.143	.280	.143	.423	25	-2	1	1.17	-1	/0-4(0-0-4)	0	-0.3
Total 7	730	2653	300	728	109	66	38	305	204	6	110	....	.274	.328	.408	.737	136	100	414	5.32	-12	0-700	102	6.0
• LUMPE, Jerry	Jerry Dean Lumpe b: 6/2/1933, Lincoln, MO BL/TR, 6'2", 185 lbs. Deb: 4/17/1956 C																							
1956 NY-A	20	62	12	16	3	0	0	4	5	11	1	1	.258	.313	.306	.620	66	-3	6	3.21	0	S-17/3-1	1	-0.1
1957*NY-A	40	103	15	35	6	2	0	11	9	13	2	2	.340	.393	.437	.830	128	4	18	6.65	1	3-30/S-6	5	0.5
1958*NY-A	81	232	34	59	8	4	3	32	23	21	1	2	.254	.324	.362	.686	92	-3	26	3.79	6	3-65/S-5	6	0.3
1959 NY-A	18	45	2	10	0	0	0	2	6	7	0	0	.222	.314	.222	.536	52	-3	3	2.07	3	3-12/S-4,2-1	1	0.0
KC-A	108	403	47	98	11	5	3	28	41	32	2	1	.243	.313	.318	.631	72	-15	41	3.39	3	2-61,S-56/3-4	8	-0.3
Yr.	126	448	49	108	11	5	3	30	47	39	2	1	.241	.313	.308	.621	70	-17	44	3.25	6	2-62,S-60,3-16	9	-0.3
1960 KC-A	146	574	69	156	19	3	8	53	48	49	1	1	.272	.328	.357	.685	85	-13	67	4.08	6	*2-134,S-15	15	0.5
1961 KC-A	148	569	81	167	29	9	3	54	48	39	1	0	.293	.351	.392	.742	98	-1	79	5.11	8	*2-147	18	2.0
1962 KC-A	156	641	89	193	34	10	10	83	44	38	0	2	.301	.346	.432	.778	105	2	94	5.27	-6	*2-156/S-2	19	0.9
1963 KC-A	157	595	75	161	26	7	5	59	58	44	3	2	.271	.335	.363	.698	92	-6	74	4.41	1	*2-155	18	1.0
1964 Det-A★	158	624	75	160	21	6	6	46	50	61	2	1	.256	.314	.338	.652	80	-16	67	3.69	-12	*2-158	13	-1.5
1965 Det-A	145	502	72	129	15	3	4	39	56	34	7	0	.257	.335	.323	.658	87	-5	58	3.93	-4	*2-139	15	0.2
1966 Det-A	113	385	30	89	14	3	1	26	24	44	0	3	.231	.276	.291	.567	62	-20	31	2.73	2	2-95	5	-1.1
1967 Det-A	81	177	19	41	4	0	4	17	16	18	0	0	.232	.295	.322	.617	80	-4	17	3.30	-1	2-54/3-6	3	-0.2
Total 12	1371	4912	620	1314	190	52	47	454	428	411	20	15	.268	.327	.356	.683	87	-83	581	4.12	8	*2-1100,3-118,S-105	127	2.0
• LUNAR, Fernando	Fernando Jose Lunar b: 5/25/1977, Cantaura, Venezuela BR/TR, 6'1", 190 lbs. Deb: 5/8/2000																							
2000 Atl-N	22	54	5	10	1	0	0	5	3	15	0	2	.185	.267	.204	.470	21	-7	2	1.38	4	C-22	1	-0.2
Bal-A	9	16	0	2	0	0	0	1	0	4	0	0	.125	.176	.125	.301	-23	-3	0	.77	3	/C-9	0	0.0
2001 Bal-A	64	167	8	41	7	0	0	16	7	32	0	0	.246	.288	.287	.576	55	-11	12	2.46	-2	C-64	2	-0.9
2002 Bal-A	2	0	0	0	0	0	0	0	0	0	0	0	....	....	....	....	-105	0	0	....	0	/C-2	0	0.0
Total 3	97	237	13	53	8	0	0	22	10	51	0	2	.224	.276	.257	.533	42	-21	15	2.08	5	/C-97	3	-1.1
• LUND, Don	Donald Andrew Lund b: 5/18/1923, Detroit, MI BR/TR, 6', 200 lbs. Deb: 7/3/1945 C Career OF: 99-32-120																							
1945 Bro-N	4	3	0	0	0	0	0	0	1	1	0	....	.000	.250	.000	.250	-27	-0	0	.59	0	....	0	0.0
1947 Bro-N	11	20	5	6	2	0	2	5	3	7	0	....	.300	.391	.700	1.091	177	2	6	11.15	-0	/0-5(5-0-0)	1	0.2
1948 Bro-N	27	69	9	13	4	0	1	5	5	16	1	....	.188	.243	.290	.533	42	-6	5	2.30	0	0-25(17-0-8)	1	-0.7
StL-A	63	161	21	40	7	4	3	25	10	17	0	0	.248	.305	.398	.702	84	-5	21	4.50	-0	0-45(21-0-25)	2	-0.6

YEAR TM-L	G	AB	R	H	2B	3B	HR	RBI	BB	SO	SB	CS	AVG	OBP	SLG	OPS	OPS+	BR/A	RC	RC/G	FR	G/POS	WS	TPW
1949 Det-A	2	2	0	0	0	0	0	0	0	1	0	0	.000	.000	.000	.000	-100	-1	0	.00	0	....	0	-0.1
1952 Det-A	8	23	1	7	0	0	0	1	3	3	0	1	.304	.385	.304	.689	93	-0	3	4.37	1	/O-7(0-0-7)	1	0.0
1953 Det-A	131	421	51	108	21	4	9	47	39	65	3	3	.257	.323	.390	.712	93	-5	53	4.27	0	*O-123(37-29-69)	8	-1.1
1954 Det-A	35	54	4	7	2	0	0	3	4	3	1	0	.130	.190	.167	.356	-2	-7	2	.80	0	O-31(19-3-11)	0	-0.8
Total 7	**281**	**753**	**91**	**181**	**36**	**8**	**15**	**86**	**65**	**113**	**5**	**4**	**.240**	**.305**	**.369**	**.674**	**81**	**-23**	**89**	**3.96**	**0**	**O-236**	**13**	**-3.2**
• LUND, Gordy	Gordon Thomas Lund b: 2/23/1941, Iron Mountain, MI BR/TR, 5'11", 170 lbs. Deb: 8/1/1967																							
1967 Cle-A	3	8	1	2	1	0	0	0	0	2	0	0	.250	.250	.375	.625	82	-0	1	3.38	-1	/S-2	0	-0.1
1969 Sea-A	20	38	4	10	0	0	0	1	5	7	1	1	.263	.349	.263	.612	74	-1	4	3.50	-2	S-17/2-1,3-1	1	-0.2
Total 2	**23**	**46**	**5**	**12**	**1**	**0**	**0**	**1**	**5**	**9**	**1**	**1**	**.261**	**.333**	**.283**	**.616**	**76**	**-1**	**5**	**3.48**	**-3**	**/S-19,2-1,3-1**	**1**	**-0.3**
• LUNDSTEDT, Tom	Thomas Robert Lundstedt b: 4/10/1949, Davenport, IA BB/TR, 6'4", 195 lbs. Deb: 8/31/1973																							
1973 Chi-N	4	5	0	0	0	0	0	0	0	1	0	0	.000	.000	.000	.000	-93	-1	0	.00	0	/C-4	0	-0.1
1974 Chi-N	22	32	1	3	0	0	0	0	5	7	0	0	.094	.216	.094	.310	-11	-5	1	.87	-1	C-22	0	-0.5
1975 Min-A	18	28	2	3	0	0	0	1	4	5	0	0	.107	.219	.107	.326	-5	-4	1	.74	0	C-14/D-2	0	-0.3
Total 3	**44**	**65**	**3**	**6**	**0**	**0**	**0**	**1**	**9**	**13**	**0**	**0**	**.092**	**.203**	**.092**	**.295**	**-14**	**-10**	**2**	**.74**	**0**	**/C-40,D-2**	**0**	**-0.9**
• LUNSFORD, Trey	James Lewis Lunsford b: 5/25/1979, Odessa, TX BR/TR, 6'1", 195 lbs. Deb: 9/12/2002																							
2002 SF-N	3	3	0	2	1	0	0	1	0	1	0	0	.667	.667	1.000	1.667	348	1	2	54.00	-1	/C-3	0	0.1
2003 SF-N	1	1	0	0	0	0	0	0	0	0	0	0	.000	.000	.000	.000	-103	-0	0	.00	0	/C-1	0	0.0
Total 2	**4**	**4**	**0**	**2**	**1**	**0**	**0**	**1**	**0**	**1**	**0**	**0**	**.500**	**.500**	**.750**	**1.250**	**235**	**1**	**2**	**27.00**	**-1**	**/C-4**	**0**	**0.0**
• LUNTE, Harry	Harry August Lunte b: 9/15/1892, St. Louis, MO d: 7/27/1965, St. Louis, MO BR/TR, 5'11.5", 165 lbs. Deb: 5/19/1919																							
1919 Cle-A	26	77	2	15	2	0	0	2	1	7	0	....	.195	.215	.221	.436	21	-8	4	1.50	0	S-24	1	-0.7
1920*Cle-A	23	71	6	14	0	0	0	7	5	6	0	1	.197	.250	.197	.447	19	-8	3	1.59	5	S-21/2-2	1	-0.2
Total 2	**49**	**148**	**8**	**29**	**2**	**0**	**0**	**9**	**6**	**13**	**0**	**1**	**.196**	**.232**	**.209**	**.442**	**20**	**-17**	**7**	**1.54**	**6**	**/S-45,2-2**	**2**	**-0.9**
• LUPIEN, Tony	Ulysses John Lupien b: 4/23/1917, Chelmsford, MA BL/TL, 5'10.5", 185 lbs. Deb: 9/12/1940																							
1940 Bos-A	10	19	5	9	3	2	0	4	1	1	0	0	.474	.500	.842	1.342	232	4	8	22.49	0	/1-8	2	0.3
1942 Bos-A	128	463	63	130	25	7	3	70	50	20	10	12	.281	.351	.384	.735	103	-0	65	4.83	-11	*1-121	12	-2.3
1943 Bos-A	154	608	65	155	21	9	4	47	54	23	16	9	.255	.317	.339	.656	90	-8	70	4.00	2	*1-153	14	-1.5
1944 Phi-N	153	597	82	169	23	9	5	52	56	29	18	....	.283	.347	.377	.723	107	6	82	5.01	-2	*1-151	15	-0.4
1945 Phi-N	15	54	1	17	1	0	0	3	6	0	2	....	.315	.383	.333	.717	103	1	8	5.38	2	1-15	2	0.2
1948 Chi-A	154	617	69	152	19	3	6	54	74	38	11	7	.246	.327	.316	.643	74	-23	71	3.95	-12	*1-154	9	-3.9
Total 6	**614**	**2358**	**285**	**632**	**92**	**30**	**18**	**230**	**241**	**111**	**57**	**28**	**.268**	**.337**	**.355**	**.692**	**94**	**-21**	**304**	**4.53**	**-21**	**1-602**	**54**	**-7.7**
• LUPLOW, Al	Alvin David Luplow b: 3/13/1939, Saginaw, MI BL/TR, 5'10", 180 lbs. Deb: 9/16/1961 Career OF: 124-44-203																							
1961 Cle-A	5	18	0	1	0	0	0	0	2	6	0	0	.056	.150	.056	.206	-44	-4	0	.36	1	/O-5(1-0-4)	0	-0.3
1962 Cle-A	97	318	54	88	15	3	14	45	36	44	1	0	.277	.361	.475	.836	127	12	57	6.59	-3	O-86(70-0-24)	15	0.4
1963 Cle-A	100	295	34	69	6	2	7	27	33	62	4	4	.234	.317	.339	.656	85	-6	32	3.62	-2	O-85(14-0-73)	7	-1.5
1964 Cle-A	19	18	1	2	0	0	0	1	1	8	0	0	.111	.158	.111	.269	-24	-3	0	.00	0	/O-5(0-1-4)	0	-0.4
1965 Cle-A	53	45	3	6	2	0	1	4	3	14	0	1	.133	.188	.244	.432	22	-5	2	1.13	0	/O-6(2-1-3)	0	-0.6
1966 NY-N	111	334	31	84	9	1	7	31	38	46	2	6	.251	.332	.347	.679	91	-5	37	3.69	1	*O-101(16-24-71)	8	-1.0
1967 NY-N	41	112	11	23	1	0	3	9	8	19	0	0	.205	.264	.295	.559	61	-6	9	2.45	-1	O-33(6-16-16)	1	-0.9
Pit-N	55	103	13	19	1	0	1	8	6	14	1	0	.184	.236	.223	.460	32	-9	6	1.73	2	O-25(15-2-8)	1	-0.9
Yr.	96	215	24	42	2	0	4	17	14	33	1	0	.195	.251	.260	.512	47	-14	14	2.09	1	O-58(21-18-24)	2	-1.8
Total 7	**481**	**1243**	**147**	**292**	**34**	**6**	**33**	**125**	**127**	**213**	**8**	**11**	**.235**	**.312**	**.352**	**.664**	**85**	**-25**	**142**	**3.83**	**-2**	**O-346**	**32**	**-5.0**
• LUSADER, Scott	Scott Edward Lusader b: 9/30/1964, Chicago, IL BL/TR, 5'10", 165 lbs. Deb: 9/1/1987 Career OF: 25-21-69																							
1987 Det-A	23	47	8	15	3	1	1	8	5	7	1	0	.319	.385	.489	.874	135	3	9	7.53	-1	O-22(6-3-16)/D-1	2	0.1
1988 Det-A	16	16	3	1	0	0	1	3	1	4	0	0	.063	.118	.250	.368		-2	0	.42	-0	/D-6,O-4(2-2-2)	0	-0.2
1989 Det-A	40	103	15	26	4	0	1	8	9	21	3	0	.252	.313	.320	.633	80	-2	11	3.69	-3	O-33(4-8-24)/D-1	2	-0.6
1990 Det-A	45	87	13	21	2	0	2	16	12	8	0	0	.241	.333	.333	.667	86	-1	10	3.89	0	O-42(12-5-27)/D-2	3	-0.2
1991 NY-A	11	7	2	1	0	0	0	1	1	3	0	1	.143	.250	.143	.393	12	-1	0	.61	0	/O-4(1-3-0),D-1	0	-0.2
Total 5	**135**	**260**	**41**	**64**	**9**	**1**	**5**	**36**	**28**	**43**	**4**	**1**	**.246**	**.319**	**.346**	**.666**	**86**	**-4**	**31**	**4.01**	**-4**	**O-105/D-11**	**7**	**-1.1**
• LUSH, Billy	William Lucas Lush b: 11/10/1873, Bridgeport, CT d: 8/28/1951, Hawthorne, NY BB/TR, 5'8", 165 lbs. Deb: 9/3/1895 Career OF: 238-138-86																							
1895 Was-N	5	18	2	6	0	0	0	2	2	1	0	....	.333	.400	.333	.733	91	-0	2	5.54	-1	/O-5(4-0-1)	0	-0.1
1896 Was-N	97	352	74	87	9	11	4	45	66	49	28	....	.247	.369	.369	.738	95	-0	60	5.93	-2	*O-91(10-14-68)/2-3	9	-0.6
1897 Was-N	3	12	1	0	0	0	0	0	2	....	0	....	.000	.143	.000	.143	-61	-3	0	.00	1	/O-3(0-0-3)	0	-0.2
1901 Bos-N	7	27	2	5	1	1	0	3	3	....	0	....	.185	.267	.296	.563	58	-2	2	2.63	3	/O-7(0-7-0)	1	0.1
1902 Bos-N	120	413	68	92	8	1	2	19	76	....	30	....	.223	.346	.262	.608	87	-1	51	4.05	7	*O-116(10-104-2)/3-1	14	0.1
1903 Det-A	119	423	71	116	18	14	1	33	70	....	14	....	.274	.379	.390	.769	135	22	74	5.75	11	*O-101(89-0-12),3-12/2-3,S	19	2.9
1904 Cle-A	138	477	76	123	13	8	1	50	72	....	12	....	.258	.359	.325	.684	118	14	65	4.56	0	*O-138(125-13-0)	17	0.6
Total 7	**489**	**1722**	**294**	**429**	**49**	**35**	**8**	**152**	**291**	**50**	**84**	**....**	**.249**	**.360**	**.332**	**.692**	**108**	**30**	**255**	**4.94**	**19**	**O-461/3-13,2-6,S-3**	**60**	**2.7**
• LUSH, Ernie	Ernest Benjamin Lush b: 10/31/1884, Bridgeport, CT d: 2/26/1937, Detroit, MI BR/TL Deb: 7/20/1910																							
1910 StL-N	1	4	0	0	0	0	0	0	1	1	0	....	.000	.200	.000	.200	-42	-1	0	.00	-0	/O-1	0	-0.1
• LUSH, Johnny	John Charles Lush b: 10/8/1885, Williamsport, PA d: 11/18/1946, Beverly Hills, CA BL/TL, 5'9.5", 165 lbs. Deb: 4/22/1904 Career OF: 0-14-58 ♦																							
1904 Phi-N	106	369	39	102	22	3	2	42	27	....	12	....	.276	.336	.369	.704	122	11	52	4.92	-11	1-62,O-33(0-0-33)/P-7	12	-0.7
1905 Phi-N	6	16	3	5	0	0	0	1	1	....	0	....	.313	.389	.313	.701	114	1	2	4.69	-1	/O-3(0-2-1),P-2	2	0.2
1906 Phi-N	76	212	28	56	7	1	0	15	14	....	6	....	.264	.310	.307	.616	92	7	23	3.76	2	P-37,O-22(0-6-16)/1-2	19	1.9
1907 Phi-N	17	40	5	8	1	1	0	5	1	....	1	....	.200	.220	.275	.495	56	-0	3	2.19	0	/P-8,O-4(0-3-1)	3	-0.7
StL-N	27	82	6	23	2	3	0	5	5	....	4	....	.280	.322	.378	.700	123	7	12	5.09	-1	P-20/O-7(0-3-4)	10	0.8
Yr.	44	122	11	31	3	4	0	10	6	....	5	....	.254	.289	.344	.633	102	7	14	4.07	-2	P-28,O-11(0-6-5)	13	0.1
1908 StL-N	45	89	7	15	2	0	0	2	7	....	1	....	.169	.229	.191	.420	36	1	4	1.45	0	P-38	13	1.6
1909 StL-N	45	92	11	22	5	0	0	14	6	....	2	....	.239	.293	.293	.586	87	5	8	3.03	-1	P-34/O-3(0-0-3)	7	-0.5
1910 StL-N	47	93	8	21	1	3	0	10	8	11	2	....	.226	.287	.301	.588	74	4	8	2.98	-2	P-36	10	0.6
Total 7	**369**	**993**	**107**	**252**	**40**	**11**	**2**	**94**	**69**	**11**	**28**	**....**	**.254**	**.307**	**.322**	**.630**	**98**	**36**	**112**	**3.85**	**-15**	**P-182/O-72,1-64**	**76**	**3.2**
• LUSKEY, Charlie	Charles Melton Luskey b: 4/6/1876, Washington, DC d: 12/20/1962, Bethesda, MD BR/TR, 5'7", 165 lbs. Deb: 9/12/1901																							
1901 Was-A	11	41	8	8	3	1	0	3	2	....	0	....	.195	.233	.317	.550	52	-3	3	2.49	-2	/O-8(8-0-0),C-3	0	-0.5
• LUTENBERG, Luke	Charles William Lutenberg b: 10/4/1864, Quincy, IL d: 12/24/1938, Quincy, IL BR/TR, 6'2", 225 lbs. Deb: 7/7/1894																							
1894 Lou-N	69	250	42	48	10	4	0	23	23	21	4	....	.192	.284	.264	.548	35	-26	20	2.62	-1	1-67/2-2	1	-2.1
• LUTTRELL, Lyle	Lyle Kenneth Luttrell b: 2/22/1930, Bloomington, IL d: 7/11/1984, Chattanooga, TN BR/TR, 6', 180 lbs. Deb: 5/15/1956																							
1956 Was-A	38	122	17	23	5	3	2	9	8	19	5	1	.189	.256	.328		.584	53	-8	9	2.18	-6	S-37	1	-1.2
1957 Was-A	19	45	4	9	4	0	0	5	3	8	0	0	.200	.250	.289		.539	47	-3	3	2.04	-2	S-17	0	-0.4
Total 2	**57**	**167**	**21**	**32**	**9**	**3**	**2**	**14**	**11**	**27**	**5**	**1**	**.192**	**.254**	**.317**	**.572**	**52**	**-12**	**12**	**2.15**	**-8**	**/S-54**	**1**	**-1.6**
• LUTZ, Joe	Rollin Joseph Lutz b: 2/18/1925, Keokuk, IA BL/TL, 6', 195 lbs. Deb: 4/17/1951 C																							
1951 StL-A	14	36	7	6	0	1	0	2	6	9	0	0	.167	.286	.222		.508	37	-3	3	2.51	-1	1-11	0	-0.4
• LUTZ, Red	Louis William Lutz b: 12/17/1898, Cincinnati, OH d: 2/22/1984, Cincinnati, OH BR/TR, 5'10", 170 lbs. Deb: 5/31/1922																							
1922 Cin-N	1	1	0	1	1	0	0	0	0	0	0	0	1.000	1.000	2.000	3.000	669	1	2	∞	0	/C-1	0	0.0
• LUTZKE, Rube	Walter John Lutzke b: 11/17/1897, Milwaukee, WI d: 3/6/1938, Granville, WI BR/TR, 5'11", 175 lbs. Deb: 4/18/1923																							
1923 Cle-A	143	511	71	131	20	6	3	65	59	57	9	6	.256	.338	.337		.675	78	-15	62	4.02	10	*3-141/S-2	12	0.4
1924 Cle-A	106	341	37	83	18	3	0	42	38	46	4	0	.243	.328	.314		.642	65	-15	39	3.79	12	*3-103/2-3	7	0.3
1925 Cle-A	81	238	31	52	9	0	1	16	26	29	2	4	.218	.295	.269		.564	44	-21	20	2.59	2	3-69,2-10	2	-1.5

YEAR TM-L	G	AB	R	H	2B	3B	HR	RBI	BB	SO	SB	CS	AVG	OBP	SLG	OPS	OPS+	BR/A	RC	RC/G	FR	G/POS	WS	TPW
1926 Cle-A	142	475	42	124	28	6	0	59	34	35	6	3	.261	.313	.345	.658	71	-20	53	3.72	5	*3-142	11	-0.6
1927 Cle-A	100	311	35	78	12	3	0	41	22	29	2	1	.251	.307	.309	.615	60	-18	31	3.24	1	3-98	5	-1.1
Total 5	572	1876	216	468	87	18	4	223	179	196	23	14	.249	.319	.321	.641	66	-90	206	3.58	30	3-553/2-13,S-2	37	-2.4

• LUULOA, Keith Keith H. M. Luuloa b: 12/24/1974, Honolulu, HI BR/TR, 6', 175 lbs. Deb: 5/17/2000

YEAR TM-L	G	AB	R	H	2B	3B	HR	RBI	BB	SO	SB	CS	AVG	OBP	SLG	OPS	OPS+	BR/A	RC	RC/G	FR	G/POS	WS	TPW
2000 Ana-A	6	18	3	6	0	0	0	0	1	1	0	0	.333	.368	.333	.702	78	-1	2	5.19	-1	/S-4,2-3	0	-0.1

• LUZINSKI, Greg Gregory Michael Luzinski b: 11/22/1950, Chicago, IL BR/TR, 6'1", 225 lbs. Deb: 9/9/1970 C Career OF: 1221-0-1

YEAR TM-L	G	AB	R	H	2B	3B	HR	RBI	BB	SO	SB	CS	AVG	OBP	SLG	OPS	OPS+	BR/A	RC	RC/G	FR	G/POS	WS	TPW
1970 Phi-N	8	12	0	2	0	0	0	0	3	5	0	1	.167	.333	.167	.500	39	-1	1	1.25	1	/1-3	0	-0.1
1971 Phi-N	28	100	13	30	8	0	3	15	12	32	2	0	.300	.386	.470	.856	141	6	19	6.79	5	1-28	4	0.9
1972 Phi-N	150	563	66	158	33	5	18	68	42	114	0	4	.281	.334	.453	.787	119	11	81	5.13	1	*O-145(145-0-1)/1-2	16	0.3
1973 Phi-N	161	610	76	174	26	4	29	97	51	135	3	3	.285	.347	.484	.831	125	18	101	6.02	-7	*O-159(159-0-0)	21	0.2
1974 Phi-N	85	302	29	82	14	1	7	48	29	76	3	0	.272	.335	.394	.729	99	0	40	4.62	5	O-82(82-0-0)	9	0.0
1975 Phi-N★	161	596	85	179	35	3	34	**120**	89	151	3	6	.300	.398	.540	.939	152	41	128	7.82	-6	*O-159(159-0-0)	28	2.8
1976*Phi-N★	149	533	74	162	28	1	21	95	50	107	1	2	.304	.375	.478	.854	137	25	96	6.56	-9	*O-144(144-0-0)	23	1.0
1977*Phi-N★	149	554	99	171	35	3	39	130	80	140	3	2	.309	.399	.594	.993	155	44	132	8.81	-1	*O-148(148-0-0)	30	3.8
1978*Phi-N★	155	540	85	143	32	2	35	101	100	135	8	7	.265	.390	.526	.916	152	40	114	7.37	-2	*O-154(154-0-0)	27	3.3
1979 Phi-N	137	452	47	114	23	1	18	81	56	103	3	3	.252	.347	.427	.774	107	4	68	5.14	-8	*O-125(125-0-0)	13	-0.9
1980*Phi-N	106	368	44	84	19	1	19	56	60	100	3	0	.228	.346	.440	.786	112	7	60	5.48	-6	*O-105(105-0-0)	13	-0.2
1981 Chi-A	104	378	55	100	15	1	21	62	58	80	0	0	.265	.367	.476	.843	144	23	67	6.27	0	*D-103	15	2.0
1982 Chi-A	159	583	87	170	37	1	18	102	89	120	1	1	.292	.391	.451	.842	130	28	103	6.33	0	*D-156	22	2.3
1983*Chi-A	144	502	73	128	26	1	32	95	70	117	2	1	.255	.358	.502	.860	129	21	93	6.34	0	*D-139/1-2	20	1.7
1984 Chi-A	125	412	47	98	13	0	13	58	56	80	5	1	.238	.333	.364	.697	89	-4	52	4.21	0	*D-114	6	-0.8
Total 15	1821	6505	880	1795	344	24	307	1128	845	1495	37	31	.276	.366	.478	.844	129	265	1154	6.27	-28	*O-1221,D-512/1-35	247	16.4

• LYDEN, Mitch Mitchell Scott Lyden b: 12/14/1964, Portland, OR BR/TR, 6'3", 225 lbs. Deb: 6/16/1993

YEAR TM-L	G	AB	R	H	2B	3B	HR	RBI	BB	SO	SB	CS	AVG	OBP	SLG	OPS	OPS+	BR/A	RC	RC/G	FR	G/POS	WS	TPW
1993 Fla-N	6	10	2	3	0	0	1	1	0	3	0	0	.300	.300	.600	.900	127	0	2	6.94	0	/C-2	0	0.0

• LYDY, Scott Donald Scott Lydy b: 10/26/1968, Mesa, AZ BR/TR, 6'5", 195 lbs. Deb: 5/18/1993

YEAR TM-L	G	AB	R	H	2B	3B	HR	RBI	BB	SO	SB	CS	AVG	OBP	SLG	OPS	OPS+	BR/A	RC	RC/G	FR	G/POS	WS	TPW
1993 Oak-A	41	102	11	23	5	0	2	7	8	39	2	0	.225	.288	.333	.622	71	-4	10	3.52	-1	O-38(17-5-16)/D-2	1	-0.6

• LYNCH, Danny Matthew Daniel "Dummy" Lynch b: 2/7/1926, Dallas, TX d: 6/30/1978, Plano, TX BR/TR, 5'11", 174 lbs. Deb: 9/14/1948

YEAR TM-L	G	AB	R	H	2B	3B	HR	RBI	BB	SO	SB	CS	AVG	OBP	SLG	OPS	OPS+	BR/A	RC	RC/G	FR	G/POS	WS	TPW
1948 Chi-N	7	7	3	2	0	0	1	1	1	1	0	....	.286	.375	.714	1.089	197	1	2	10.65	0	/2-1	1	0.1

• LYNCH, Henry Henry W. Lynch b: 4/8/1866, Worcester, MA d: 11/23/1925, Worcester, MA BB, 5'7", 143 lbs. Deb: 9/21/1893

YEAR TM-L	G	AB	R	H	2B	3B	HR	RBI	BB	SO	SB	CS	AVG	OBP	SLG	OPS	OPS+	BR/A	RC	RC/G	FR	G/POS	WS	TPW
1893 Chi-N	4	14	0	3	2	0	0	2	1	1	0	....	.214	.267	.357	.624	66	-1	1	3.29	-1	/O-4(0-0-4)	0	-0.1

• LYNCH, Jerry Gerald Thomas Lynch b: 7/17/1930, Bay City, MI BL/TR, 6'1", 189 lbs. Deb: 4/15/1954 Career OF: 501-4-205

YEAR TM-L	G	AB	R	H	2B	3B	HR	RBI	BB	SO	SB	CS	AVG	OBP	SLG	OPS	OPS+	BR/A	RC	RC/G	FR	G/POS	WS	TPW
1954 Pit-N	98	284	27	68	4	5	8	36	20	43	2	2	.239	.292	.373	.665	73	-12	29	3.39	4	O-83(46-4-36)	4	-1.2
1955 Pit-N	88	282	43	80	18	6	5	28	22	33	2	2	.284	.336	.443	.779	106	2	40	5.04	4	O-71(40-0-32)/C-2	8	0.3
1956 Pit-N	19	19	1	3	0	1	0	0	1	4	0	0	.158	.200	.263	.463	24	-2	1	1.78	0	/O-1	0	-0.2
1957 Cin-N	67	124	11	32	4	1	4	13	6	18	0	0	.258	.292	.403	.696	79	-4	15	4.20	-1	O-24(1-0-22)/C-2	2	-0.5
1958 Cin-N	122	420	58	131	20	5	16	68	18	54	1	4	.312	.340	.498	.838	112	5	67	5.97	-2	*O-101(1-0-101)	12	0.0
1959 Cin-N	117	379	49	102	16	3	17	58	29	50	2	0	.269	.323	.462	.784	103	1	56	5.24	-2	O-98(97-0-1)	10	-0.6
1960 Cin-N	102	159	23	46	8	2	6	27	16	25	0	0	.289	.358	.478	.836	124	5	28	6.38	-1	O-32(31-0-1)	5	0.3
1961*Cin-N	96	181	33	57	13	2	13	50	27	25	2	2	.315	.407	.624	1.031	166	17	46	9.71	-1	O-44(42-0-2)	10	1.4
1962 Cin-N	114	288	41	81	15	4	12	57	24	38	3	3	.281	.339	.486	.825	115	4	46	5.62	1	O-73(70-0-3)	10	0.2
1963 Cin-N	22	32	5	8	3	0	2	9	1	5	0	0	.250	.294	.531	.825	128	1	5	5.80	0	/O-7(4-0-3)	1	0.1
Pit-N	88	237	26	63	6	3	10	36	22	28	0	1	.266	.331	.443	.774	120	6	34	5.05	-3	O-64(64-0-0)	7	0.0
Yr.	110	269	31	71	9	3	12	45	23	33	0	1	.264	.327	.454	.780	121	7	39	5.14	-3	O-71(68-0-3)	8	0.1
1964 Pit-N	114	297	35	81	14	2	16	66	26	57	0	1	.273	.333	.495	.828	130	11	48	5.75	-2	O-78(77-0-1)	10	0.7
1965 Pit-N	73	121	7	34	1	0	5	16	8	26	0	2	.281	.331	.413	.744	108	0	14	3.91	-1	O-26(23-0-3)	2	-0.1
1966 Pit-N	64	56	5	12	1	0	1	6	4	10	0	0	.214	.267	.286	.552	53	-3	4	2.52	0	/O-4(4-0-0)	0	-0.4
Total 13	1184	2879	364	798	123	34	115	470	224	416	12	17	.277	.331	.463	.795	110	30	434	5.35	-5	O-706/C-4	81	-0.2

• LYNCH, Mike Michael Joseph Lynch b: 9/10/1875, St. Paul, MN d: 4/1/1947, Jennings Lodge, OR TR, 5'10", 155 lbs. Deb: 4/24/1902

YEAR TM-L	G	AB	R	H	2B	3B	HR	RBI	BB	SO	SB	CS	AVG	OBP	SLG	OPS	OPS+	BR/A	RC	RC/G	FR	G/POS	WS	TPW
1902 Chi-N	7	28	4	4	0	0	0	0	2	....	0	....	.143	.200	.143	.343	6	-3	1	1.00	0	/O-7(0-7-0)	0	-0.4

• LYNCH, Tom Thomas James Lynch b: 4/3/1860, Bennington, VT d: 3/28/1955, Cohoes, NY BL/TR, 5'10.5", 170 lbs. Deb: 8/18/1884 U Career OF: 18-10-0

YEAR TM-L	G	AB	R	H	2B	3B	HR	RBI	BB	SO	SB	CS	AVG	OBP	SLG	OPS	OPS+	BR/A	RC	RC/G	FR	G/POS	WS	TPW
1884 Wil-U	16	58	6	16	3	1	0	....	5	....	....	....	.276	.333	.362	.695	131	2	7	4.78	1	/C-8,O-8(8-0-0),1-1	1	0.3
Phi-N	13	48	7	15	4	2	0	3	4	5	....	....	.313	.365	.479	.845	171	4	9	7.18	1	/C-7,O-7(1-6-0)	3	0.4
1885 Phi-N	13	53	7	10	3	0	0	1	10	3	....	....	.189	.317	.245	.563	86	-0	4	2.66	2	O-13(9-4-0)	2	0.1
Total 2	42	159	20	41	10	3	0	4	19	8	....	....	.258	.337	.358	.696	127	6	20	4.68	4	/O-28,C-15,1-1	6	0.9

• LYNCH, Walt Walter Edward "Jabber" Lynch b: 4/15/1897, Buffalo, NY d: 12/21/1976, Daytona Beach, FL BR/TR, 6', 176 lbs. Deb: 7/8/1922

YEAR TM-L	G	AB	R	H	2B	3B	HR	RBI	BB	SO	SB	CS	AVG	OBP	SLG	OPS	OPS+	BR/A	RC	RC/G	FR	G/POS	WS	TPW
1922 Bos-A	3	2	1	1	0	0	0	0	0	0	0	0	.500	.500	.500	1.000	163	0	0	12.72	0	/C-3	0	0.0

• LYNN, Byrd Byrd "Birdie" Lynn b: 3/13/1889, Unionville, IL d: 2/5/1940, Napa, CA BR/TR, 5'11", 165 lbs. Deb: 4/16/1916

YEAR TM-L	G	AB	R	H	2B	3B	HR	RBI	BB	SO	SB	CS	AVG	OBP	SLG	OPS	OPS+	BR/A	RC	RC/G	FR	G/POS	WS	TPW
1916 Chi-A	31	40	4	9	1	0	0	3	4	7	2	....	.225	.311	.250	.561	68	-1	4	3.10	0	C-13	1	0.0
1917*Chi-A	35	72	7	16	2	0	0	5	7	11	1	....	.222	.300	.250	.550	66	-3	6	2.59	-3	C-29	2	-0.4
1918 Chi-A	5	8	0	2	0	0	0	0	2	1	0	....	.250	.400	.250	.650	95	0	1	3.26	0	/C-4	0	0.0
1919*Chi-A	29	66	4	15	4	0	0	4	4	9	0	....	.227	.271	.288	.559	57	-4	5	2.51	0	C-28	1	-0.2
1920 Chi-A	16	25	0	8	2	1	0	3	1	3	0	0	.320	.346	.480	.826	117	1	4	5.44	0	C-14	1	0.1
Total 5	116	211	15	50	9	1	0	15	18	31	3	0	.237	.303	.289	.592	71	-7	20	3.02	-3	/C-88	5	-0.6

• LYNN, Fred Frederic Michael Lynn b: 2/3/1952, Chicago, IL BL/TL, 6'1", 190 lbs. Deb: 9/5/1974 Career OF: 135-1584-144

YEAR TM-L	G	AB	R	H	2B	3B	HR	RBI	BB	SO	SB	CS	AVG	OBP	SLG	OPS	OPS+	BR/A	RC	RC/G	FR	G/POS	WS	TPW
1974 Bos-A	15	43	5	18	2	2	2	10	6	6	0	0	.419	.500	.698	1.198	226	7	16	16.20	1	O-12(6-4-2)/D-1	4	0.8
1975*Bos-A★	145	528	**103**	175	**47**	7	21	105	62	90	10	5	.331	.405	**.566**	**.971**	158	41	120	8.52	-1	*O-144(0-144-0)	**33**	3.7
1976 Bos-A★	132	507	76	159	32	8	10	65	48	67	14	9	.314	.374	.467	.842	130	18	88	6.31	1	*O-128(0-127-1)/D-5	22	1.7
1977 Bos-A★	129	497	81	129	29	5	18	76	51	63	2	3	.260	.332	.447	.779	98	-1	72	4.86	-6	*O-125(0-125-0)/D-1	15	-0.9
1978 Bos-A★	150	541	75	161	33	3	22	82	75	50	3	6	.298	.384	.492	.876	131	23	103	6.84	-5	*O-149(0-149-0)	27	1.5
1979 Bos-A★	147	531	116	177	42	1	39	122	82	79	2	2	**.333**	.426	**.637**	**1.063**	**173**	**56**	147	**10.73**	1	*O-143(0-143-0)/D-1	**34**	5.4
1980 Bos-A★	110	415	67	125	32	3	12	61	58	39	12	0	.301	.387	.480	.866	129	21	80	7.12	4	*O-110(0-110-0)	19	2.4
1981 Cal-A★	76	256	28	56	8	1	5	31	38	42	1	2	.219	.327	.316	.643	86	-4	27	3.45	-3	O-69(0-69-0)	5	-0.8
1982*Cal-A★	138	472	89	141	38	1	21	86	58	72	7	8	.299	.379	.517	.896	143	27	91	6.84	-6	*O-133(0-133-0)	21	1.9
1983 Cal-A★	117	437	56	119	20	3	22	74	55	83	2	2	.272	.356	.483	.839	130	17	76	6.16	-4	*O-113(0-113-0)/D-2	16	1.2
1984 Cal-A	142	517	84	140	28	4	23	79	77	97	2	2	.271	.367	.474	.841	132	24	90	6.13	2	*O-140(0-62-112)	22	2.1
1985 Bal-A	124	448	59	118	12	1	23	68	53	100	7	3	.263	.343	.449	.791	118	11	70	5.48	-3	*O-123(0-123-0)	16	0.6
1986 Bal-A	112	397	67	114	13	1	23	67	53	59	2	2	.287	.374	.499	.873	137	21	69	6.06	-10	*O-107(0-107-0)/D-1	14	0.9
1987 Bal-A	111	396	49	100	24	0	23	60	39	72	3	7	.253	.321	.487	.808	113	4	58	5.03	-5	*O-101(0-102-0)/D-8	11	-0.3
1988 Bal-A	87	301	37	76	13	1	18	37	28	66	2	2	.252	.316	.482	.798	123	8	44	5.00	-2	O-83(0-64-21)/D-2	6	0.4
Det-A	27	90	9	20	1	0	7	19	5	16	0	0	.222	.271	.467	.738	106	0	11	3.99	1	O-22(19-3-0)/D-3	2	0.0
Yr.	114	391	46	96	14	1	25	56	33	82	2	2	.246	.306	.478	.784	120	8	55	4.76	-1	*O-105(19-67-21)/D-5	8	0.5
1989 Det-A	117	353	44	85	11	1	11	46	47	71	1	1	.241	.332	.371	.703	100	0	46	4.43	2	O-68(68-0-0),D-46	9	-0.1
1990 SD-N	90	196	18	47	3	1	6	23	22	44	2	0	.240	.320	.357	.677	85	-4	24	4.26	0	O-55(42-6-8)	4	-0.5
Total 17	1969	6925	1063	1960	388	43	306	1111	857	1116	72	54	.283	.364	.484	.848	129	270	1233	6.31	-32	*O-1825/D-70	280	20.0

• LYNN, Jerry Jerome Edward Lynn b: 4/14/1916, Scranton, PA d: 9/25/1972, Scranton, PA BR/TR, 5'10", 164 lbs. Deb: 9/19/1937

YEAR TM-L	G	AB	R	H	2B	3B	HR	RBI	BB	SO	SB	CS	AVG	OBP	SLG	OPS	OPS+	BR/A	RC	RC/G	FR	G/POS	WS	TPW
1937 Was-A	1	3	0	2	1	0	0	0	0	0	0	0	.667	.667	1.000	1.667	329	1	2	50.88	1	/2-1	0	0.1

• LYON, Russ Russell Mayo Lyon b: 6/26/1913, Ball Ground, GA d: 12/24/1975, Charleston, SC BR/TR, 6'1", 230 lbs. Deb: 4/21/1944

YEAR TM-L	G	AB	R	H	2B	3B	HR	RBI	BB	SO	SB	CS	AVG	OBP	SLG	OPS	OPS+	BR/A	RC	RC/G	FR	G/POS	WS	TPW
1944 Cle-A	7	11	1	2	0	0	0	0	1	1	0	0	.182	.250	.182	.432	25	-1	0	1.04	0	/C-3	0	-0.1

• LYONS, Barry Barry Stephen Lyons b: 6/3/1960, Biloxi, MS BR/TR, 6'1", 202 lbs. Deb: 4/19/1986

YEAR TM-L	G	AB	R	H	2B	3B	HR	RBI	BB	SO	SB	CS	AVG	OBP	SLG	OPS	OPS+	BR/A	RC	RC/G	FR	G/POS	WS	TPW
1986 NY-N	6	9	1	0	0	0	0	2	1	2	0	0	.000	.100	.000	.100	-72	-2	0	.00	-1	/C-3	0	-0.3
1987 NY-N	53	130	15	33	4	1	4	24	8	24	0	0	.254	.307	.392	.699	88	-3	16	4.31	-1	C-49	3	-0.2
1988 NY-N	50	91	5	21	7	1	0	11	3	12	0	0	.231	.255	.330	.585	70	-4	7	2.47	-1	C-32/1-1	2	-0.4
1989 NY-N	79	235	15	58	13	0	3	27	11	28	0	1	.247	.286	.340	.627	82	-7	21	3.04	-3	C-76	5	-0.6
1990 NY-N	24	80	8	19	0	0	2	7	2	9	0	0	.238	.265	.313	.578	58	-5	6	2.66	0	C-23	2	-0.4
LA-N	3	5	1	1	0	0	1	2	0	1	0	0	.200	.200	.800	1.000	166	0	1	5.40	0	/C-2	1	0.0
Yr.	27	85	9	20	0	0	3	9	2	10	0	0	.235	.261	.341	.603	65	-4	7	2.83	-1	C-25	3	-0.4
1991 LA-N	9	9	0	0	0	0	0	0	0	2	0	0	.000	.000	.000	.000	-102	-2	0	.00	0	/C-6	0	-0.2
Cal-A	2	5	0	1	0	0	0	0	0	0	0	0	.200	.200	.200	.400	11	-1	0	1.35	0	/1-2	0	-0.1
1995 Chi-A	27	64	8	17	2	0	5	16	4	14	0	0	.266	.309	.531	.840	119	1	11	5.96	2	C-16/D-6,1-4	3	0.3
Total 7	253	628	53	150	26	2	15	89	29	92	0	1	.239	.278	.358	.636	78	-22	63	3.34	-6	C-207/1-7,D-6	16	-1.9

• LYONS, Bill William Allen Lyons b: 4/26/1958, Alton, IL BR/TR, 6'1", 175 lbs. Deb: 7/20/1983

YEAR TM-L	G	AB	R	H	2B	3B	HR	RBI	BB	SO	SB	CS	AVG	OBP	SLG	OPS	OPS+	BR/A	RC	RC/G	FR	G/POS	WS	TPW
1983 StL-N	42	60	3	10	1	1	0	3	1	11	3	2	.167	.180	.217	.397	9	-8	2	.99	-3	2-23/3-8,S-2	0	-1.0
1984 StL-N	46	73	13	16	3	0	0	3	9	13	3	1	.219	.305	.260	.565	62	-3	7	3.06	-1	2-25,S-11/3-3	2	-0.3
Total 2	88	133	16	26	4	1	0	6	10	24	6	3	.195	.252	.241	.492	40	-11	9	2.08	-4	/2-48,S-13,3-11	2	-1.4

• LYONS, Denny Dennis Patrick Aloysius Lyons b: 3/12/1866, Cincinnati, OH d: 1/3/1929, West Covington, KY BR/TR, 5'10", 185 lbs. Deb: 9/18/1885

YEAR TM-L	G	AB	R	H	2B	3B	HR	RBI	BB	SO	SB	CS	AVG	OBP	SLG	OPS	OPS+	BR/A	RC	RC/G	FR	G/POS	WS	TPW
1885 Pro-N	4	16	3	2	1	0	0	1	0	3	....	....	.125	.125	.188	.313		-2	0	.74	0	/3-4	0	-0.2
1886 Phi-a	32	123	22	26	3	1	0	11	8	....	7	....	.211	.281	.252	.534	67	-5	11	3.05	-4	3-32	2	-0.6
1887 Phi-a	137	617	128	256	43	14	6	102	47	....	73	....	.415	.421	.523	.943	162	47	160	11.96	0	*3-137	27	4.0
1888 Phi-a	111	456	93	135	22	5	6	83	41	....	39	....	.296	.363	.406	.769	147	25	83	7.01	-10	*3-111	20	1.6
1889 Phi-a	131	510	135	168	36	4	9	82	79	44	10	....	.329	.426	.469	.895	156	42	109	8.43	9	*3-130/1-1	25	4.5
1890 Phi-a	88	339	79	120	29	5	7	73	57	....	21	....	.354	**.461**	**.531**	.992	196	44	95	11.48	1	3-88	27	4.2
1891 StL-a	120	451	124	142	24	3	11	84	88	58	9	....	.315	.445	.455	.900	137	25	98	8.38	-1	*3-120	23	2.3
1892 NY-N	108	389	71	100	16	7	8	51	59	37	11	....	.257	.359	.396	.755	130	16	61	5.68	-11	*3-108	14	0.6
1893 Pit-N	131	490	103	150	19	16	3	105	97	29	19	....	.306	.430	.429	.858	131	28	101	7.86	5	*3-131	21	2.9
1894 Pit-N	72	257	52	82	14	4	4	51	43	13	14	....	.319	.424	.451	.876	113	7	57	8.40	4	3-71	10	1.0
1895 StL-N	34	132	24	39	6	0	2	25	14	5	3	....	.295	.376	.386	.762	98	0	21	6.02	-4	3-33	2	-0.3
1896 Pit-N	118	436	77	134	25	6	4	71	67	25	13	....	.307	.406	.420	.825	123	18	83	7.03	-12	*3-116	16	0.7
1897 Pit-N	37	131	22	27	6	4	2	17	22	....	5	....	.206	.346	.359	.705	90	-1	19	4.69	0	1-35/3-2	3	-0.1
Total 13	1123	4347	933	1381	244	69	62	756	622	214	224	....	.318	.407	.442	.850	139	244	897	8.02	-23	*3-1083/1-36	190	20.5

• LYONS, Ed Edward Hoyte "Mouse" Lyons b: 5/12/1923, Winston-Salem, NC BR/TR, 5'9", 165 lbs. Deb: 9/15/1947 C

YEAR TM-L	G	AB	R	H	2B	3B	HR	RBI	BB	SO	SB	CS	AVG	OBP	SLG	OPS	OPS+	BR/A	RC	RC/G	FR	G/POS	WS	TPW
1947 Was-A	7	26	2	4	0	0	0	0	2	2	0	0	.154	.214	.154	.368	3	-3	1	1.22	4	/2-7	1	0.1

• LYONS, Harry Harry Pratt Lyons b: 3/25/1866, Chester, PA d: 6/29/1912, Mauricetown, NJ BR/TR, 5'10.5", 157 lbs. Deb: 8/29/1887 Career OF: 142-245-17

YEAR TM-L	G	AB	R	H	2B	3B	HR	RBI	BB	SO	SB	CS	AVG	OBP	SLG	OPS	OPS+	BR/A	RC	RC/G	FR	G/POS	WS	TPW
1887 Phi-N	1	5	0	1	0	0	0	0	1	0	0	....	.200	.200	.000	.200	-38	-1	0	.00	0	/O-1	0	-0.1
*StL-a	2	8	2	1	0	0	0	1	0	....	2	....	.125	.125	.125	.250	-27	-1	0	1.48	1	/2-1,O-1	0	-0.1
1888*StL-a	123	499	66	97	10	5	4	63	20	....	36	....	.194	.230	.259	.488	51	-31	39	2.61	-2	*O-122(O-112-10)/3-2,2-1,S	8	-3.4
1889 NY-N	5	20	1	2	0	1	0	2	2	0	0	....	.100	.182	.200	.382	7	-3	1	1.10	0	/O-5(0-1-4)	0	-0.2
1890 Roc-a	133	584	83	152	11	11	3	58	27	....	47	....	.260	.294	.332	.626	91	-8	73	4.46	11	*O-132(130-0-2)/3-2,C-1,P	15	-0.5
1892 NY-N	96	411	67	98	5	2	0	53	33	29	25	....	.238	.297	.260	.557	70	-15	40	3.46	2	O-96(10-86-0)	8	-1.8
1893 NY-N	47	187	27	51	5	2	0	21	14	6	10	....	.273	.323	.321	.644	71	-8	23	4.52	3	O-47(1-46-0)	3	-0.7
Total 6	407	1714	246	402	31	21	7	198	97	35	120	....	.235	.277	.289	.566	70	-66	176	3.59	14	O-404/3-4,2-2,C-1,P-1,S-1	34	-6.8

• LYONS, Pat Patrick Jerry Lyons b: 3/1860, Canada d: 1/20/1914, Springfield, OH TR Deb: 7/21/1890

YEAR TM-L	G	AB	R	H	2B	3B	HR	RBI	BB	SO	SB	CS	AVG	OBP	SLG	OPS	OPS+	BR/A	RC	RC/G	FR	G/POS	WS	TPW
1890 Cle-N	11	38	2	2	1	0	0	1	4	4	0	....	.053	.143	.079	.222	-36	-7	0	.32	-5	2-11	0	-1.0

• LYONS, Steve Stephen John "Psycho" Lyons b: 6/3/1960, Tacoma, WA BL/TR, 6'3", 195 lbs. Deb: 4/15/1985 Career OF: 59-237-43

YEAR TM-L	G	AB	R	H	2B	3B	HR	RBI	BB	SO	SB	CS	AVG	OBP	SLG	OPS	OPS+	BR/A	RC	RC/G	FR	G/POS	WS	TPW
1985 Bos-A	133	371	52	98	14	3	5	30	32	64	12	9	.264	.324	.358	.683	83	-10	44	4.12	-6	*O-114(2-111-2)/D-5,3-1,S	7	-1.7
1986 Bos-A	59	124	20	31	7	2	1	14	12	23	2	3	.250	.316	.363	.679	84	-4	13	3.54	-1	O-55(0-55-0)	2	-0.5
Chi-A	42	123	10	25	2	1	0	6	7	24	2	3	.203	.252	.236	.488	33	-12	7	1.87	1	O-35(22-6-7)/3-3,1-1,D-1	1	-1.3
Yr.	101	247	30	56	9	3	1	20	19	47	4	6	.227	.285	.300	.584	59	-16	21	2.68	0	O-90(22-61-7)/3-3,1-1,D-1	3	-1.8
1987 Chi-A	76	193	26	54	11	1	1	19	12	37	3	1	.280	.322	.363	.685	79	-6	22	4.07	4	3-51,O-15(6-8-2)/D-6,2-1	5	-0.3
1988 Chi-A	146	472	59	127	28	3	5	45	32	59	1	2	.269	.317	.373	.690	93	-6	57	4.08	7	*3-128,O-14(0-8-6)/2-4,C-2,1	13	0.2
1989 Chi-A	140	443	51	117	21	3	2	50	35	68	9	6	.264	.319	.339	.658	88	-8	50	3.85	-3	2-70,1-40,3-28,O-20(10-1-9)/S,C	11	-1.2
1990 Chi-A	94	146	22	28	6	1	1	11	10	41	1	0	.192	.248	.267	.516	45	-11	11	2.28	-1	1-61,2-15/O-7(2-3-3),D-6,3,P,S	1	-1.4
1991 Bos-A	87	212	15	51	10	1	4	17	11	35	10	3	.241	.278	.354	.632	70	-8	22	3.45	-4	O-45(8-36-3),2-16,3-12/1-2,D,P,S	3	-1.2
1992 Atl-N	11	14	0	1	0	1	0	1	0	4	0	0	.071	.071	.214	.286	-21	-2	0	.00	-1	/O-6(2-0-4),2-2	0	-0.3
Mon-N	16	13	2	3	0	0	0	1	1	3	1	2	.231	.286	.231	.516	48	-2	0	.55	0	/O-8(7-1-0),1-1	0	-0.2
Yr.	27	27	2	4	0	1	0	2	1	7	1	2	.148	.179	.222	.401	15	-4	0	.28	-1	O-14(9-1-4)/2-2,1-1	0	-0.5
Bos-A	21	28	3	7	0	1	0	2	2	1	0	1	.250	.300	.321	.621	69	-2	3	3.12	0	/1-8,O-5(0-2-3),D-2,2-1	0	-0.2
1993 Bos-A	28	23	4	3	1	0	0	0	2	5	1	2	.130	.200	.174	.374	1	-4	1	.74	0	O-10(0-6-4)/2-9,1-1,3-1,C,D	0	-0.4
Total 9	853	2162	264	545	100	17	19	196	156	364	42	32	.252	.304	.340	.644	77	-74	229	3.57	-4	O-334,3-229,2-118,1/D,S,C,P	43	-8.5

• LYONS, Terry Terence Hilbert Lyons b: 12/14/1908, New Holland, OH d: 9/9/1959, Dayton, OH BR/TR, 6'.5", 165 lbs. Deb: 4/19/1929

YEAR TM-L	G	AB	R	H	2B	3B	HR	RBI	BB	SO	SB	CS	AVG	OBP	SLG	OPS	OPS+	BR/A	RC	RC/G	FR	G/POS	WS	TPW
1929 Phi-N	1	0	0	0	0	0	0	0	0	0	0	....	....	....	....	....	-94	0	0	....	0	/1-1	0	0.0

• LYTLE, Dad Edward Benson "Pop" Lytle b: 3/10/1862, Racine, WI d: 12/21/1950, Long Beach, CA BR/TR, 5'11", 160 lbs. Deb: 8/11/1890

YEAR TM-L	G	AB	R	H	2B	3B	HR	RBI	BB	SO	SB	CS	AVG	OBP	SLG	OPS	OPS+	BR/A	RC	RC/G	FR	G/POS	WS	TPW
1890 Chi-N	1	4	1	0	0	0	0	0	0	1	0	....	.000	.000	.000	.000	-96	-1	0	.00	1	/O-1	0	0.0
Pit-N	15	55	2	8	1	0	0	0	8	9	0	....	.145	.254	.164	.418	25	-5	2	1.32	-3	/2-8,O-7(0-4-3)	0	-0.7
Yr.	16	59	3	8	1	0	0	0	8	10	0	....	.136	.239	.153	.391	18	-6	2	1.22	-2	/2-8,O-8(0-4-4)	0	-0.7

• LYTTLE, Jim James Lawrence Lyttle b: 5/20/1946, Hamilton, OH BL/TR, 6', 186 lbs. Deb: 5/17/1969 Career OF: 66-91-113

YEAR TM-L	G	AB	R	H	2B	3B	HR	RBI	BB	SO	SB	CS	AVG	OBP	SLG	OPS	OPS+	BR/A	RC	RC/G	FR	G/POS	WS	TPW
1969 NY-A	28	83	7	15	4	0	0	4	4	19	1	2	.181	.218	.229	.447	26	-9	4	1.55	2	O-28(0-28-0)	1	-0.9
1970 NY-A	87	126	20	39	7	1	3	14	10	26	3	6	.310	.360	.452	.813	129	3	18	5.03	-1	O-70(2-4-64)	5	-0.1
1971 NY-A	49	86	7	17	5	0	1	7	8	18	0	2	.198	.274	.291	.564	64	-5	6	2.14	-1	O-29(3-6-20)	0	-0.7
1972 Chi-A	44	82	8	19	5	2	0	5	1	28	0	1	.232	.241	.341	.582	70	-4	7	2.70	0	O-21(0-16-5)	1	-0.5
1973 Mon-N	49	116	12	30	5	1	4	19	9	14	0	2	.259	.312	.422	.734	98	-1	14	3.93	4	O-36(29-7-0)	3	0.1
1974 Mon-N	25	9	1	3	0	0	0	2	1	3	0	0	.333	.400	.333	.733	101	0	1	4.94	-1	O-18(14-5-0)	0	-0.1
1975 Mon-N	44	55	7	15	4	0	0	6	13	6	0	1	.273	.412	.345	.757	107	1	9	5.48	0	O-16(5-8-3)	2	0.1
1976 Mon-N	42	85	6	23	4	1	1	8	7	13	0	0	.271	.326	.376	.703	95	-1	10	4.26	2	O-29(12-0-20)	2	0.0
LA-N	23	68	3	15	3	0	0	5	8	12	0	1	.221	.303	.265	.567	63	-4	6	2.76	3	O-18(1-17-1)	1	-0.1
Yr.	65	153	9	38	7	1	1	13	15	25	0	1	.248	.315	.327	.642	81	-4	16	3.58	5	O-47(13-17-21)	3	0.0
Total 8	391	710	71	176	37	5	9	70	61	139	4	15	.248	.308	.352	.660	86	-20	75	3.51	8	O-265	15	-2.2

• MAAS, Kevin Kevin Christian Maas b: 1/20/1965, Castro Valley, CA BL/TL, 6'3", 209 lbs. Deb: 6/29/1990

YEAR TM-L	G	AB	R	H	2B	3B	HR	RBI	BB	SO	SB	CS	AVG	OBP	SLG	OPS	OPS+	BR/A	RC	RC/G	FR	G/POS	WS	TPW
1990 NY-A	79	254	42	64	9	0	21	41	43	76	1	2	.252	.367	.535	.902	149	16	52	7.17	-2	1-57,D-18	11	1.0
1991 NY-A	148	500	69	110	14	1	23	63	83	128	5	1	.220	.336	.390	.726	100	2	72	4.86	-2	*D-109,1-36	10	-0.6
1992 NY-A	98	286	35	71	12	0	11	35	25	63	3	1	.248	.309	.406	.714	99	-1	37	4.56	-3	D-62,1-22	5	-0.7
1993 NY-A	59	151	20	31	4	0	9	25	24	32	1	1	.205	.318	.411	.729	97	-1	21	4.50	-1	D-31,1-17	5	-0.4
1995 Min-A	22	57	5	11	4	0	1	5	7	11	0	0	.193	.281	.316	.597	55	-4	4	2.28	-2	D-12/1-8	0	-0.6
Total 5	406	1248	171	287	43	1	65	169	182	310	10	5	.230	.332	.422	.754	108	13	186	5.07	-10	D-232,1-140	31	-1.3

• MABRY, John John Steven Mabry b: 10/17/1970, Wilmington, DE BL/TR, 6'4", 195 lbs. Deb: 4/23/1994 Career OF: 122-10-305

YEAR TM-L	G	AB	R	H	2B	3B	HR	RBI	BB	SO	SB	CS	AVG	OBP	SLG	OPS	OPS+	BR/A	RC	RC/G	FR	G/POS	WS	TPW
1994 StL-N	6	23	2	7	3	0	0	3	2	4	0	0	.304	.360	.435	.795	108	0	4	6.39	0	/O-6(0-0-6)	1	0.0
1995 StL-N	129	388	35	119	21	1	5	41	24	45	0	3	.307	.350	.405	.755	99	-3	54	5.13	4	1-73,O-39(11-0-29)	9	-0.6
1996*StL-N	151	543	63	161	30	2	13	74	37	84	3	2	.297	.345	.431	.776	104	2	74	4.87	-6	*1-146,O-14(1-0-13)	13	-1.7
1997 StL-N	116	388	40	110	19	0	5	36	39	77	0	1	.284	.353	.371	.725	91	-5	50	4.58	0	O-78(4-6-71),1-49/3-1	8	-1.1

YEAR TM-L	G	AB	R	H	2B	3B	HR	RBI	BB	SO	SB	CS	AVG	OBP	SLG	OPS	OPS+	BR/A	RC	RC/G	FR	G/POS	WS	TPW
1998 StL-N	142	377	41	94	22	0	9	46	30	76	0	2	.249	.306	.379	.686	80	-13	43	3.93	0	0-80(46-0-37),3-38,1-16	5	-1.6
1999 Sea-A	87	262	34	64	14	0	9	33	20	60	2	1	.244	.298	.401	.699	74	-11	30	3.95	-3	0-43(7-2-35),3-24,1-20/D-1	3	-1.6
2000 Sea-A	47	103	18	25	5	0	1	7	10	31	0	1	.243	.322	.320	.642	67	-5	11	3.71	-4	3-22,0-19(7-0-12)/D-5,1-3,P	0	-1.1
SD-N	48	123	17	28	8	0	7	25	5	38	0	0	.228	.258	.463	.721	83	-4	14	3.73	-1	0-32(2-0-30)/1-2	3	-0.7
2001 StL-N	5	7	0	0	0	0	0	0	0	2	0	0	.000	.000	.000	.000	-101	-2	0	.00	0	/1-2,0-2(0-0-2)	0	-0.3
Fla-N	82	147	14	32	7	0	6	20	13	44	1	0	.218	.303	.388	.691	80	-4	17	3.64	-2	0-39(3-2-34)/1-1,D-1,P-1	1	-1.2
Yr.	87	154	14	32	7	0	6	20	13	46	1	0	.208	.291	.370	.661	72	-6	17	3.45	-2	0-41(3-2-36)/1-3,D-1,P-1	1	-1.5
2002 Phi-N	21	21	1	6	0	0	0	3	1	5	0	0	.286	.318	.286	.604	64	-1	2	3.35	0	/1-1,0-1	1	-0.1
*Oak-A	89	193	27	53	13	1	11	40	14	37	1	1	.275	.327	.523	.850	121	5	30	5.43	3	0-53(33-0-21),1-50	7	0.4
2003 Sea-A	64	104	12	22	6	0	3	16	15	21	0	0	.212	.328	.356	.684	83	-2	12	3.97	1	0-22(8-0-14),D-11/1-9	2	-0.3
Total 10	987	2679	304	721	148	4	69	344	210	524	7	11	.269	.327	.405	.732	91	-44	341	4.45	-9	0-428,1-372/3-85,D-18,P-2	53	-9.7
• MACDONALD, Harvey	Harvey Forsyth MacDonald b: 5/18/1898, New York, NY d: 10/4/1965, Manoa, PA BL/TL, 5'11", 170 lbs. Deb: 6/12/1928																							
1928 Phi-N	13	16	0	4	0	0	0	2	2	3	0	....	.250	.333	.250	.583	53	-1	1	3.04	0	/0-2(0-0-2)	0	-0.1
• MACEY,	Macey b: Columbus, OH Deb: 10/2/1890																							
1890 Phi-a	1	1	0	0	0	0	0	0	0	....	0	....	.000	.000	.000	.000	-102	-0	0	.00	-1	/C-1	0	-0.1
• MACFARLANE, Mike	Michael Andrew Macfarlane b: 4/12/1964, Stockton, CA BR/TR, 6'1", 205 lbs. Deb: 7/23/1987																							
1987 KC-A	8	19	0	4	1	0	0	3	2	2	0	0	.211	.286	.263	.549	46	-1	1	2.22	0	/C-8	1	-0.1
1988 KC-A	70	211	25	56	15	0	4	26	21	37	0	0	.265	.335	.393	.728	102	1	28	4.60	-1	C-68	7	0.3
1989 KC-A	69	157	13	35	6	0	2	19	7	27	0	0	.223	.265	.299	.564	59	-9	11	2.22	0	C-59/D-4	4	-0.6
1990 KC-A	124	400	37	102	24	4	6	58	25	69	1	0	.255	.310	.380	.690	94	-4	47	4.01	-8	*C-112/D-5	8	-0.6
1991 KC-A	84	267	34	74	18	2	13	41	17	52	1	0	.277	.334	.506	.840	128	9	45	6.07	0	C-69/D-4	11	1.3
1992 KC-A	129	402	51	94	28	3	17	48	30	89	1	5	.234	.311	.445	.756	107	0	54	4.49	-2	*C-104,D-13	10	0.4
1993 KC-A	117	388	55	106	27	0	20	67	40	83	2	5	.273	.365	.497	.862	122	11	70	6.25	2	*C-114	18	1.9
1994 KC-A	92	314	53	80	17	3	14	47	35	71	1	0	.255	.362	.462	.824	106	4	54	5.91	1	C-81/D-8	11	0.9
1995*Bos-A	115	364	45	82	18	1	15	51	38	78	2	1	.225	.322	.404	.726	85	-9	48	4.41	0	*C-111/D-3	8	-0.1
1996 KC-A	112	379	58	104	24	2	19	54	31	57	3	3	.274	.341	.499	.839	109	3	64	6.13	-1	C-99/D-9	13	0.7
1997 KC-A	82	257	34	61	14	2	8	35	24	47	0	2	.237	.317	.401	.718	84	-7	33	4.29	-4	C-81	7	-0.6
1998 KC-A	3	11	1	1	0	0	0	0	0	2	0	0	.091	.091	.091	.182	-51	-2	0	.25	1	/C-3	0	-0.2
Oak-A	78	207	28	52	12	0	7	34	12	34	1	0	.251	.305	.411	.716	86	-5	26	4.38	-1	C-70	5	-0.2
Yr.	81	218	29	53	12	0	7	34	12	36	1	0	.243	.295	.394	.689	80	-7	26	4.14	-1	C-73	5	-0.3
1999 Oak-A	81	226	24	55	17	0	4	31	13	52	0	0	.243	.288	.372	.659	69	-11	23	3.36	1	C-79/D-1	3	-0.5
Total 13	1164	3602	458	906	221	17	129	514	295	700	12	16	.252	.325	.430	.755	98	-21	504	4.79	-13	*C-1058/D-47	106	2.8
• MACGAMWELL, Ed	Edward M. MacGamwell b: 1/10/1879, Buffalo, NY d: 5/26/1924, Albany, NY BL/TL Deb: 4/14/1905																							
1905 Bro-N	4	16	0	4	0	0	0	0	1	....	0	....	.250	.294	.250	.544	68	-1	1	2.61	-1	/1-4	0	-0.1
• MACHA, Ken	Kenneth Edward Macha b: 9/29/1950, Monroeville, PA BR/TR, 6'2", 217 lbs. Deb: 9/14/1974 M/C Career OF: 3-0-4																							
1974 Pit-N	5	5	1	3	1	0	0	1	0	0	0	0	.600	.600	.800	1.400	300	1	2	32.40	0	/C-1	1	0.1
1977 Pit-N	35	95	2	26	4	0	0	11	6	17	1	1	.274	.317	.316	.633	68	-4	8	2.82	0	3-17,1-11/0-4(3-0-1)	1	-0.5
1978 Pit-N	29	52	5	11	1	1	0	5	12	10	2	0	.212	.359	.269	.629	75	-1	6	3.40	1	3-21	1	0.0
1979 Mon-N	25	36	8	10	3	1	0	4	2	9	0	0	.278	.333	.417	.750	104	0	4	3.61	-1	3-13/1-2,0-2(0-0-2),C-1	1	-0.1
1980 Mon-N	49	107	10	31	5	1	1	8	11	17	0	2	.290	.361	.383	.745	108	0	13	4.28	-3	3-33/1-2,C-1,0-1	3	-0.3
1981 Tor-A	37	85	4	17	2	0	0	6	8	15	1	1	.200	.269	.224	.492	41	-6	5	1.94	1	3-19,1-16/D-2,C-1	0	-0.7
Total 6	180	380	30	98	16	3	1	35	39	68	4	4	.258	.330	.324	.654	80	-10	39	3.36	-2	3-103/1-31,0-7,C-4,D-2	7	-1.4
• MACHA, Mike	Michael William Macha b: 2/17/1954, Victoria, TX BR/TR, 5'11", 180 lbs. Deb: 4/20/1979																							
1979 Atl-N	6	13	2	2	0	0	0	1	1	5	0	0	.154	.214	.154	.368	2	-2	0	1.19	0	/3-3	0	-0.2
1980 Tor-A	5	8	0	0	0	0	0	0	0	1	0	0	.000	.000	.000	.000	-96	-2	0	.00	0	/3-2,C-1	0	-0.3
Total 2	11	21	2	2	0	0	0	1	1	6	0	0	.095	.136	.095	.232	-33	-4	0	.69	0	/3-5,C-1	0	-0.4
• MACHADO, Andy	Anderson Javier Machado b: 1/25/1981, Caracas, Venezuela BB/TR, 5'11", 165 lbs. Deb: 9/27/2003																							
2003 Phi-N	1	0	0	0	0	0	0	0	0	0	1	0	....	....	....	....	-107	0	0	....	0	....	0	0.0
• MACHADO, Robert	Robert Alexis Machado b: 6/3/1973, Caracas, Venezuela BR/TR, 6'1", 205 lbs. Deb: 7/24/1996																							
1996 Chi-A	4	6	1	4	1	0	0	2	0	0	0	0	.667	.667	.833	1.500	290	2	3	22.50	-1	/C-4	1	0.1
1997 Chi-A	10	15	1	3	0	1	0	2	1	6	0	0	.200	.250	.333	.583	53	-1	1	2.82	0	C-10	0	0.0
1998 Chi-A	34	111	14	23	6	0	3	15	7	22	0	0	.207	.254	.342	.597	55	-8	9	2.65	-1	C-34	1	-0.6
1999 Mon-N	17	22	3	4	1	0	0	0	2	6	0	0	.182	.250	.227	.477	23	-3	1	2.07	-1	C-17	0	-0.3
2000 Sea-A	8	14	2	3	0	0	1	1	1	4	0	0	.214	.267	.429	.695	76	-1	2	4.10	2	/C-8	0	0.1
2001 Chi-N	52	135	13	30	10	0	2	13	7	26	0	0	.222	.266	.341	.606	58	-9	11	2.74	2	C-47	3	-0.4
2002 Chi-N	22	58	5	16	4	0	1	5	5	11	0	0	.276	.333	.397	.730	93	-1	7	4.42	2	C-21/1-1	1	0.3
Mil-N	51	153	14	39	10	1	2	17	12	30	0	0	.255	.313	.373	.686	81	-5	17	3.75	2	C-48/1-2	3	0.1
Yr.	73	211	19	55	14	1	3	22	17	41	0	0	.261	.319	.379	.698	84	-5	24	3.93	5	C-69/1-3	4	0.4
2003 Bal-A	18	49	8	13	1	0	1	3	6	12	0	0	.265	.345	.347	.692	87	-1	6	4.81	1	C-18	1	0.2
Total 8	216	563	61	135	33	2	10	58	41	117	0	0	.240	.294	.359	.653	71	-25	58	3.46	8	C-207/1-3	10	-0.6
• MACHEMER, Dave	David Ritchie Machemer b: 5/24/1951, St. Joseph, MI BR/TR, 5'11.5", 180 lbs. Deb: 6/21/1978																							
1978 Cal-A	10	22	6	6	1	0	1	2	2	1	0	1	.273	.333	.455	.788	124	0	3	4.64	-1	/2-5,3-3,S-1	1	-0.1
1979 Det-A	19	26	8	5	1	0	0	2	3	2	0	3	.192	.276	.231	.507	37	-4	1	1.31	1	2-11/D-1,0-1	0	-0.2
Total 2	29	48	14	11	2	0	1	4	5	3	0	4	.229	.302	.333	.635	77	-3	4	2.70	0	/2-16,3-3,D-1,0-1,S-1	1	-0.3
• MACIAS, Jose	Jose Prado (Salazar) Macias b: 1/25/1972, Panama City, Panama BB/TR, 5'10", 173 lbs. Deb: 5/12/1999 Career OF: 44-96-15																							
1999 Det-A	5	4	2	1	0	0	1	2	0	1	0	0	.250	.250	1.000	1.250	198	0	1	9.00	1	/2-1	0	0.1
2000 Det-A	73	173	25	44	3	5	2	24	18	24	2	0	.254	.328	.364	.692	77	-6	22	4.32	-4	2-39,3-26/0-3(0-1-2),D-1,S	5	-0.7
2001 Det-A	137	488	62	131	24	6	8	51	32	54	21	6	.268	.317	.391	.709	89	-6	62	4.40	5	3-89,0-29(3-22-4),2-18/D-1	12	0.0
2002 Det-A	33	107	10	25	4	0	0	6	8	13	3	2	.234	.293	.271	.564	55	-7	8	2.38	-3	2-17,0-10(0-9-1)/3-8	1	-0.9
Mon-N	90	231	33	59	17	1	7	33	13	44	5	6	.255	.298	.429	.727	86	-7	28	4.05	6	0-49(0-49-0),3-22/2-6,S-4	7	-0.1
2003 Mon-N	111	272	31	65	15	2	4	22	11	45	4	3	.239	.274	.353	.627	52	-20	25	3.09	-1	0-62(41-15-8),3-25/2-4,D-1	2	-2.1
Total 5	449	1275	163	325	63	14	22	138	82	181	35	17	.255	.304	.378	.682	77	-46	146	3.88	4	3-170,0-153/2-85,S-5,D-3	27	-3.7
• MACK, Connie	Cornelius Alexander "The Tall Tactician" Mack b: 12/22/1862, East Brookfield, MA d: 2/8/1956, Philadelphia, PA BR/TR, 6'1", 150 lbs. Deb: 9/11/1886 M HOF: 1937 Career OF: 6-3-46																							
1886 Was-N	10	36	4	13	2	1	0	5	0	2	0	....	.361	.361	.472	.833	161	2	6	7.39	3	C-10	2	0.5
1887 Was-N	82	322	35	71	6	1	0	20	8	17	26	....	.220	.228	.226	.454	28	-30	23	2.39	-2	C-76/0-5(2-2-1),2-2	3	-2.2
1888 Was-N	85	300	49	56	5	6	3	29	17	18	31	....	.187	.249	.273	.523	70	-9	29	3.19	14	C-79/0-4(2-0-2),1-1,S-1	8	1.2
1889 Was-N	98	386	51	113	16	1	0	42	15	12	26	....	.293	.333	.339	.672	94	-3	54	5.19	6	C-45,0-34(1-0-33),1-22	9	0.4
1890 Buf-P	123	503	95	134	15	12	0	53	47	13	16	....	.266	.353	.344	.697	94	-0	68	5.00	8	*C-112/0-9(0-1-8),1-5	11	1.4
1891 Pit-N	75	280	43	60	10	0	0	29	19	11	4	....	.214	.286	.250	.536	58	-14	22	2.66	-3	C-72/1-3	4	-1.0
1892 Pit-N	97	346	39	84	9	4	1	31	21	22	11	....	.243	.298	.301	.598	81	-9	35	3.61	13	C-92/0-3(1-0-2),1-1	13	1.2
1893 Pit-N	37	133	22	38	3	1	0	15	10	9	4	....	.286	.358	.323	.681	83	-3	17	4.81	3	C-37	4	0.3
1894 Pit-N	70	231	33	57	7	1	1	21	21	14	8	....	.247	.320	.299	.619	51	-18	25	3.78	-1	C-69	5	-1.0
1895 Pit-N	14	49	12	15	2	0	0	4	7	1	1	....	.306	.404	.347	.750	100	1	8	5.83	0	C-12/1-1	1	0.1
1896 Pit-N	33	120	9	26	4	1	0	16	5	8	0	....	.217	.248	.267	.515	37	-11	8	2.30	1	1-28/C-5	1	-0.8
Total 11	724	2706	392	667	79	28	5	265	170	127	127	....	.246	.305	.300	.604	73	-95	295	3.86	42	C-609/1-61,0-55,2-2,S-1	61	0.1
• MACK, Denny	Dennis Joseph Mack b: 1851, Easton, PA d: 4/10/1888, Wilkes-Barre, PA BR/TR, 5'7", 164 lbs. Deb: 5/6/1871 M/U NA OF: 2-1-3 Career OF: 2-4-1																							
1871 Rok-n	25	122	34	30	7	1	0	17	8	7	12	0	.246	.292	.320	.612	79	0	15	5.23	3	*1-24/P-3,0-1,S-1	....	0.3
1872 Ath-n	47	205	68	59	9	1	0	34	**23**	9	9	5	.288	.360	.341	.701	116	5	29	5.98	0	1-26,S-21	....	0.3

YEAR TM-L	G	AB	R	H	2B	3B	HR	RBI	BB	SO	SB	CS	AVG	OBP	SLG	OPS	OPS+	BR/A	RC	RC/G	FR	G/POS	WS	TPW
1873 Phi-n	48	205	55	60	5	0	0	20	15	9	6	2	.293	.341	.317	.658	93	-1	25	5.15	2	*1-42/0-4(1-1-3),S-3,2-1	....	0.1
1874 Phi-n	56	246	48	51	8	4	0	22	2	3	4	0	.207	.214	.272	.486	53	-13	16	2.39	-8	*1-56	....	-1.5
1876 StL-N	48	191	32	39	5	0	1	7	11	5	....	....	.204	.262	.261	.523	79	-3	13	2.50	-4	S-41/2-5,0-2(1-1-0)	5	-0.4
1880 Buf-N	17	59	5	12	0	0	0	3	5	7	....	....	.203	.266	.203	.469	60	-2	3	1.91	-2	S-16/2-1	1	-0.3
1882 Lou-a	72	264	41	48	3	1	0	....	16	....	....	....	.182	.229	.201	.429	49	-12	12	1.61	-3	S-49,2-24/0-5(1-3-1)	3	-1.2
1883 Pit-a	60	224	26	44	5	3	0	0	13	....	....	....	.196	.241	.246	.486	59	-9	14	2.11	0	S-38,1-25/2-1	2	-0.9
Total 4 n	176	778	205	200	29	6	0	93	48	28	31	7	.257	.300	.310	.610	85	-8	85	4.46	-4	1-148/S-25,0-5,P-3,2-1	....	-0.8
Total 4	197	738	104	143	13	4	1	10	45	12	....	....	.194	.244	.230	.473	60	-26	42	2.00	-9	S-144/2-31,1-25,0-7	11	-2.8

• MACK, Earle Earle Thaddeus Mack b: 2/1/1890, Spencer, MA d: 2/4/1967, Upper Darby, PA BL/TR, 5'8", 140 lbs. Deb: 10/5/1910 M/C

YEAR TM-L	G	AB	R	H	2B	3B	HR	RBI	BB	SO	SB	CS	AVG	OBP	SLG	OPS	OPS+	BR/A	RC	RC/G	FR	G/POS	WS	TPW
1910 Phi-A	1	4	0	2	0	1	0	0	0	....	0	....	.500	.500	1.000	1.500	372	1	2	25.58	0	/C-1	1	0.2
1911 Phi-A	2	4	0	0	0	0	0	0	0	....	0	....	.000	.000	.000	.000	-102	-1	0	.00	-2	/3-2	0	-0.3
1914 Phi-A	2	8	0	0	0	0	0	1	0	0	1	....	.000	.000	.000	.000	-104	-2	0	.00	0	/1-2	0	-0.2
Total 3	5	16	0	2	0	1	0	1	0	0	1	....	.125	.125	.250	.375	15	-2	2	3.65	-2	/1-2,3-2,C-1	1	-0.4

• MACK, Joe Joseph John Mack b: 1/4/1912, Chicago, IL d: 12/19/1998, Atlanta, GA BB/TL, 5'11.5", 185 lbs. Deb: 4/17/1945

YEAR TM-L	G	AB	R	H	2B	3B	HR	RBI	BB	SO	SB	CS	AVG	OBP	SLG	OPS	OPS+	BR/A	RC	RC/G	FR	G/POS	WS	TPW
1945 Bos-N	66	260	30	60	13	1	3	44	34	39	1	....	.231	.320	.323	.643	79	-7	29	3.67	2	1-65	3	-0.9

• MACK, Quinn Quinn David Mack b: 9/11/1965, Los Angeles, CA BL/TL, 5'10", 185 lbs. Deb: 6/16/1994

YEAR TM-L	G	AB	R	H	2B	3B	HR	RBI	BB	SO	SB	CS	AVG	OBP	SLG	OPS	OPS+	BR/A	RC	RC/G	FR	G/POS	WS	TPW
1994 Sea-A	5	21	1	5	3	0	0	2	1	3	2	0	.238	.273	.381	.654	65	-1	3	4.28	0	/0-4(3-1-0),D-1	0	-0.1

• MACK, Ray Raymond James Mack b: 8/31/1916, Cleveland, OH d: 5/7/1969, Bucyrus, OH BR/TR, 6', 200 lbs. Deb: 9/9/1938

YEAR TM-L	G	AB	R	H	2B	3B	HR	RBI	BB	SO	SB	CS	AVG	OBP	SLG	OPS	OPS+	BR/A	RC	RC/G	FR	G/POS	WS	TPW
1938 Cle-A	2	6	2	2	0	1	0	2	0	1	0	0	.333	.333	.667	1.000	148	0	1	8.48	1	/2-2	0	0.1
1939 Cle-A	36	112	12	17	4	1	1	6	12	19	0	2	.152	.240	.232	.472	22	-14	6	1.75	0	2-34/3-1	1	-1.1
1940 Cle-A★	146	530	60	150	21	5	12	69	51	77	4	2	.283	.346	.409	.755	98	-2	76	5.14	5	*2-146	18	1.2
1941 Cle-A	145	500	54	114	22	4	9	44	54	69	8	4	.228	.303	.342	.645	74	-19	55	3.66	-8	*2-145	9	-1.8
1942 Cle-A	143	481	43	108	14	6	2	45	41	51	9	3	.225	.288	.291	.579	67	-20	42	2.91	0	*2-143	8	-1.1
1943 Cle-A	153	545	56	120	25	2	7	62	47	61	8	3	.220	.285	.312	.596	79	-14	49	2.91	-3	*2-153	11	-1.0
1944 Cle-A	83	284	24	66	15	3	0	29	28	45	4	1	.232	.301	.306	.608	77	-8	28	3.19	-5	2-83	4	-0.9
1946 Cle-A	61	171	13	35	6	2	1	9	23	27	2	2	.205	.299	.281	.580	67	-7	16	3.10	-3	2-61	3	-0.8
1947 NY-A	1	0	0	0	0	0	0	0	0	0	0	0	....	....	....	....	-101	0	0	....	0		0	0.0
Chi-N	21	78	9	17	6	0	2	12	5	15	0	....	.218	.274	.372	.646	73	-3	7	3.07	4	2-21	2	0.1
Total 9	791	2707	273	629	113	24	34	278	261	365	35	17	.232	.301	.330	.631	76	-88	281	3.46	-10	2-788/3-1	56	-5.1

• MACK, Reddy Joseph Mack b: 5/2/1866, Ireland d: 12/30/1916, Newport, KY, 5'8", 182 lbs. Deb: 9/16/1885

YEAR TM-L	G	AB	R	H	2B	3B	HR	RBI	BB	SO	SB	CS	AVG	OBP	SLG	OPS	OPS+	BR/A	RC	RC/G	FR	G/POS	WS	TPW
1885 Lou-a	11	41	7	10	1	0	0	5	2	....	....	....	.244	.295	.268	.564	79	-1	3	2.90	1	2-11	1	0.0
1886 Lou-a	137	483	82	118	23	11	1	56	68	....	13	....	.244	.342	.344	.686	109	6	63	4.65	-4	*2-137	14	0.6
1887 Lou-a	128	561	117	230	23	8	1	69	83	....	22	....	.410	.415	.395	.811	124	20	90	7.32	1	*2-128	19	2.1
1888 Lou-a	112	446	77	97	13	5	3	34	52	....	18	....	.217	.320	.289	.609	98	2	48	3.73	-1	*2-112	12	0.5
1889 Bal-a	136	519	84	125	24	7	1	87	60	69	23	....	.241	.329	.320	.649	87	-7	64	4.28	-2	*2-135/0-1	13	-0.4
1890 Bal-a	26	95	14	27	3	5	0	11	10	....	7	....	.284	.370	.421	.791	121	2	18	6.95	2	2-26	3	0.5
Total 6	550	2145	381	607	87	36	6	262	275	69	83	....	.283	.352	.340	.692	105	23	286	4.99	-3	2-549/0-1	62	3.3

• MACK, Shane Shane Lee Mack b: 12/7/1963, Los Angeles, CA BR/TR, 6', 190 lbs. Deb: 5/25/1987 Career OF: 393-358-149

YEAR TM-L	G	AB	R	H	2B	3B	HR	RBI	BB	SO	SB	CS	AVG	OBP	SLG	OPS	OPS+	BR/A	RC	RC/G	FR	G/POS	WS	TPW
1987 SD-N	105	238	28	57	11	3	4	25	18	47	4	6	.239	.301	.361	.663	77	-10	22	2.93	-4	0-91(0-90-2)	3	-1.5
1988 SD-N	56	119	13	29	3	0	0	12	14	21	5	1	.244	.338	.269	.607	78	-2	13	3.51	-1	0-55(9-46-6)	4	-0.4
1990 Min-A	125	313	50	102	10	4	8	44	29	69	13	4	.326	.392	.460	.852	129	14	58	6.81	1	*0-109(23-43-51)/D-4	14	1.3
1991*Min-A	143	442	79	137	27	8	18	74	34	79	13	9	.310	.367	.529	.897	138	21	82	6.65	0	*0-140(48-36-81)/D-1	20	1.7
1992 Min-A	156	600	101	189	31	6	16	75	64	106	26	14	.315	.395	.467	.861	136	30	114	6.90	-1	*0-155(150-9-4)	27	2.4
1993 Min-A	128	503	66	139	30	4	10	61	41	76	15	5	.276	.336	.412	.747	99	0	69	4.79	4	*0-128(64-67-2)	16	0.1
1994 Min-A	81	303	55	101	21	2	15	61	32	51	4	1	.333	.408	.564	.972	147	22	68	8.35	-1	0-75(66-24-0)/D-4	15	1.7
1997 Bos-A	60	130	13	41	7	0	3	17	9	24	2	1	.315	.373	.438	.812	109	2	21	5.88	-1	0-45(3-43-0)/D-5	2	0.0
1998 Oak-A	3	2	1	0	0	0	0	0	0	0	0	0	.000	.000	.000	.000	-102	-1	0	.00	0	....	0	-0.1
KC-A	66	207	30	58	15	1	6	29	15	36	8	2	.280	.346	.449	.796	102	1	32	5.46	-2	0-32(30-0-3),D-21	6	-0.3
Yr.	69	209	31	58	15	1	6	29	15	36	8	2	.278	.343	.445	.788	100	1	32	5.40	-2	0-32(30-0-3),D-21	6	-0.4
Total 9	923	2857	436	853	155	28	80	398	256	509	90	43	.299	.367	.456	.823	119	78	478	5.94	-6	0-830/D-35	107	5.0

• MACKANIN, Pete Peter Mackanin b: 8/1/1951, Chicago, IL BR/TR, 6'2", 190 lbs. Deb: 7/3/1973 C Career OF: 4-0-1

YEAR TM-L	G	AB	R	H	2B	3B	HR	RBI	BB	SO	SB	CS	AVG	OBP	SLG	OPS	OPS+	BR/A	RC	RC/G	FR	G/POS	WS	TPW
1973 Tex-A	44	90	3	9	2	0	0	2	4	26	0	0	.100	.147	.122	.270	-24	-15	2	.58	-2	S-33,3-10	1	-1.4
1974 Tex-A	2	6	0	1	0	1	0	0	0	2	0	0	.167	.167	.500	.667	88	-0	1	2.70	1	/S-2	0	0.1
1975 Mon-N	130	448	59	101	19	6	12	44	31	99	11	5	.225	.279	.375	.654	77	-16	46	3.33	2	*2-127/3-1,S-1	9	-0.6
1976 Mon-N	114	380	36	85	15	2	8	33	15	66	6	2	.224	.257	.337	.594	65	-19	31	2.68	-10	*2-100/3-8,S-3,0-1	4	-2.4
1977 Mon-N	55	85	9	19	2	2	1	6	4	17	3	1	.224	.258	.329	.588	58	-5	7	2.84	0	/2-9,S-8,3-5,0-4(3-0-1)	1	-0.4
1978 Phi-N	5	8	0	2	0	0	0	1	0	4	0	0	.250	.250	.250	.500	40	-1	1	2.25	0	/1-1,3-1	0	0.0
1979 Phi-N	13	9	2	1	0	0	1	2	1	2	0	0	.111	.200	.444	.644	68	-0	1	2.88	0	/2-2,3-2,S-2	0	0.0
1980 Min-A	108	319	31	85	18	0	4	35	14	34	6	2	.266	.297	.361	.658	74	-12	33	3.55	-6	2-71,S-30/D-5,1-4,3-3	7	-1.2
1981 Min-A	77	225	21	52	7	1	4	18	7	40	1	2	.231	.258	.324	.582	63	-12	18	2.59	-7	2-31,S-28,1-10/D-6,3-4	2	-1.7
Total 9	548	1570	161	355	63	12	30	141	76	290	27	12	.226	.265	.339	.603	64	-80	138	2.89	-21	2-340,S-107/3-34,1-15,D-11,0	24	-7.6

• MACKENZIE, Eric Eric Hugh MacKenzie b: 8/29/1932, Glendon, Canada BL/TR, 6', 185 lbs. Deb: 4/23/1955

YEAR TM-L	G	AB	R	H	2B	3B	HR	RBI	BB	SO	SB	CS	AVG	OBP	SLG	OPS	OPS+	BR/A	RC	RC/G	FR	G/POS	WS	TPW
1955 KC-A	1	1	0	0	0	0	0	0	0	0	0	0	.000	.000	.000	.000	-99	-0	0	.00	0	/C-1	0	-0.1

• MACKENZIE, Gordon Henry Gordon MacKenzie b: 7/9/1937, St. Petersburg, FL BR/TR, 5'11", 175 lbs. Deb: 8/13/1961 C

YEAR TM-L	G	AB	R	H	2B	3B	HR	RBI	BB	SO	SB	CS	AVG	OBP	SLG	OPS	OPS+	BR/A	RC	RC/G	FR	G/POS	WS	TPW
1961 KC-A	11	24	1	3	0	0	0	1	1	6	0	0	.125	.160	.125	.285	-23	-4	0	.48	1	/C-7	0	-0.3

• MACKIEWICZ, Felix Felix Thaddeus Mackiewicz b: 11/20/1917, Chicago, IL d: 12/20/1993, Olivette, MO BR/TR, 6'2", 195 lbs. Deb: 9/7/1941 Career OF: 0-193-5

YEAR TM-L	G	AB	R	H	2B	3B	HR	RBI	BB	SO	SB	CS	AVG	OBP	SLG	OPS	OPS+	BR/A	RC	RC/G	FR	G/POS	WS	TPW
1941 Phi-A	5	14	3	4	0	1	0	0	1	0	0	0	.286	.333	.429	.762	103	0	2	5.32	0	/0-3(0-1-2)	0	0.0
1942 Phi-A	6	14	3	3	2	0	0	2	0	4	0	0	.214	.214	.357	.571	59	-1	1	2.70	0	/0-3(0-2-1)	0	-0.1
1943 Phi-A	9	16	1	1	0	0	0	0	2	8	0	0	.063	.167	.063	.229	-32	-3	0	.46	0	/0-3(0-2-1)	0	-0.3
1945 Cle-A	120	359	42	98	14	7	2	37	44	41	5	5	.273	.356	.368	.723	115	7	47	4.44	-1	*0-112(0-112-0)	11	0.4
1946 Cle-A	78	258	35	67	15	4	0	16	16	32	5	1	.260	.305	.349	.654	88	-4	28	3.73	-4	0-72(0-71-1)	6	-1.0
1947 Cle-A	2	5	0	0	0	0	0	0	0	2	0	0	.000	.000	.000	.000	-103	-1	0	.00	-0	/0-2(0-2-0)	0	-0.1
Was-A	3	6	1	1	1	0	0	0	0	1	0	0	.167	.167	.333	.500	38	-1	0	1.85	0	/0-3(0-3-0)	0	-0.1
Yr.	5	11	1	1	1	0	0	0	0	3	0	0	.091	.091	.182	.273	-32	-2	0	.71	0	/0-5(0-5-0)	0	-0.2
Total 6	223	672	85	174	32	12	2	55	63	88	10	6	.259	.325	.351	.676	98	-2	79	3.95	-5	0-198	17	-1.2

• MACKO, Steve Steven Joseph Macko b: 9/6/1954, Burlington, IA d: 11/15/1981, Arlington, TX BL/TR, 5'10", 160 lbs. Deb: 8/18/1979

YEAR TM-L	G	AB	R	H	2B	3B	HR	RBI	BB	SO	SB	CS	AVG	OBP	SLG	OPS	OPS+	BR/A	RC	RC/G	FR	G/POS	WS	TPW
1979 Chi-N	19	40	2	9	1	0	0	3	4	8	0	0	.225	.295	.250	.545	46	-3	3	2.84	2	2-10/3-4	1	-0.1
1980 Chi-N	6	20	2	6	2	0	0	2	0	3	0	0	.300	.300	.400	.700	87	-0	2	4.63	1	/S-3,3-2,2-1	0	0.1
Total 2	25	60	4	15	3	0	0	5	4	11	0	0	.250	.297	.300	.597	59	-3	6	3.40	3	/2-11,3-6,S-3	1	0.0

• MACKOWIAK, Rob Robert William Mackowiak b: 6/20/1976, Oak Lawn, IL BL/TR, 5'10", 168 lbs. Deb: 5/19/2001 Career OF: 20-50-130

YEAR TM-L	G	AB	R	H	2B	3B	HR	RBI	BB	SO	SB	CS	AVG	OBP	SLG	OPS	OPS+	BR/A	RC	RC/G	FR	G/POS	WS	TPW
2001 Pit-N	83	214	30	57	15	2	4	21	15	52	4	3	.266	.323	.411	.734	86	-5	28	4.49	1	0-46(10-0-40),2-21/3-2,1-1	4	-0.5
2002 Pit-N	136	385	57	94	22	0	16	48	42	120	9	3	.244	.329	.426	.755	96	-2	58	5.26	2	*0-106(2-42-76),3-26/2-3	12	-0.2
2003 Pit-N	77	174	20	47	4	4	6	19	15	53	6	0	.270	.342	.443	.784	101	1	28	6.01	-5	0-30(8-8-14),3-19,2-15	6	-0.4
Total 3	296	773	107	198	41	6	26	88	72	225	19	6	.256	.331	.426	.756	95	-5	115	5.21	-3	0-182/3-47,2-39,1-1	22	-1.1

• MACLIN, Lonnie Lonnie Lee Maclin b: 2/17/1967, St. Louis, MO BL/TL, 6', 185 lbs. Deb: 9/7/1993

YEAR TM-L	G	AB	R	H	2B	3B	HR	RBI	BB	SO	SB	CS	AVG	OBP	SLG	OPS	OPS+	BR/A	RC	RC/G	FR	G/POS	WS	TPW
1993 StL-N	12	13	2	1	0	0	0	1	0	5	1	0	.077	.077	.077	.154	-60	-3	0	.30	0	/0-5(5-0-0)	0	-0.3

• MACON, Max — Max Cullen Macon b: 10/14/1915, Pensacola, FL d: 8/5/1989, Jupiter, FL BL/TL, 6'3", 175 lbs. Deb: 4/21/1938 Career OF: 21-2-1 ♦

YEAR TM-L	G	AB	R	H	2B	3B	HR	RBI	BB	SO	SB	CS	AVG	OBP	SLG	OPS	OPS+	BR/A	RC	RC/G	FR	G/POS	WS	TPW
1938 StL-N	46	36	5	11	0	0	0	3	2	4	0	....	.306	.342	.306	.648	75	2	4	4.26	1	P-38/O-1	5	0.0
1940 Bro-N	2	1	0	1	0	0	0	0	0	0	0	....	1.000	1.000	1.000	2.000	427	0	1	∞	0	/P-2	0	-0.4
1942 Bro-N	26	43	4	12	2	1	0	1	2	4	1	....	.279	.311	.372	.683	98	3	5	4.19	0	P-14	9	1.6
1943 Bro-N	45	55	7	9	0	0	0	6	0	1	1	....	.164	.164	.164	.327	-5	-3	1	.75	0	P-25/1-3	0	-2.6
1944 Bos-N	106	366	38	100	15	3	3	36	12	23	7	....	.273	.296	.355	.651	79	-11	38	3.74	-1	1-72,O-22(21-2-0)/P-1	6	-2.3
1947 Bos-N	1	1	0	0	0	0	0	0	0	0	0	....	.000	.000	.000	.000	-102	-0	0	.00	0	/P-1	0	0.1
Total 6	226	502	54	133	17	4	3	46	16	32	9	....	.265	.288	.333	.620	72	-8	49	3.43	0	/P-81,1-75,O-23	20	-3.6

• MACPHEE, Waddy — Walter Scott MacPhee b: 12/23/1899, Brooklyn, NY d: 1/20/1980, Charlotte, NC BR/TR, 5'8", 140 lbs. Deb: 9/27/1922

YEAR TM-L	G	AB	R	H	2B	3B	HR	RBI	BB	SO	SB	CS	AVG	OBP	SLG	OPS	OPS+	BR/A	RC	RC/G	FR	G/POS	WS	TPW
1922 NY-N	2	7	2	2	0	1	0	0	1	0	0	0	.286	.375	.571	.946	140	0	2	8.13	0	/3-2	0	0.1

• MACULLAR, Jimmy — James F. "Little Mac" Macullar b: 1/16/1855, Boston, MA d: 4/8/1924, Baltimore, MD BR/TL, 5'6", 155 lbs. Deb: 5/5/1879 M/U Career OF: 2-113-9

YEAR TM-L	G	AB	R	H	2B	3B	HR	RBI	BB	SO	SB	CS	AVG	OBP	SLG	OPS	OPS+	BR/A	RC	RC/G	FR	G/POS	WS	TPW
1879 Syr-N	64	246	24	52	9	0	0	13	3	27	....	....	.211	.221	.248	.469	61	-9	14	1.99	-1	S-37,O-26(0-26-0)/2-4,3-1	4	-0.9
1882 Cin-a	79	299	44	70	6	6	0	22	14	....	....	....	.234	.268	.294	.563	85	-5	24	2.96	-4	*O-79(0-79-0)	8	-1.1
1883 Cin-a	14	48	4	8	2	0	0	4	4	....	....	....	.167	.231	.208	.439	40	-3	2	1.66	-1	O-14(2-6-7)/S-1	1	-0.4
1884 Bal-a	107	360	73	73	16	6	4	0	36	....	....	....	.203	.290	.314	.603	93	-2	34	3.21	-0	*S-107	15	0.2
1885 Bal-a	100	320	52	61	7	6	3	26	49	....	....	....	.191	.306	.278	.584	87	-2	28	2.91	-2	*S-98/O-2(0-0-2),P-1	11	0.0
1886 Bal-a	85	268	49	55	7	1	0	26	49	....	23	....	.205	.332	.239	.571	82	-2	30	3.76	-14	S-82/O-2(0-2-0),2-1,P-1	8	-1.3
Total 6	449	1541	246	319	47	19	7	91	155	27	23	....	.207	.285	.276	.561	82	-22	131	2.95	-24	S-325,O-123/2-5,P-2,3-1	47	-3.6

• MADDEN, Bunny — Thomas Francis Madden b: 9/14/1882, Boston, MA d: 1/20/1954, Cambridge, MA BR/TR, 5'10", 190 lbs. Deb: 6/3/1909

YEAR TM-L	G	AB	R	H	2B	3B	HR	RBI	BB	SO	SB	CS	AVG	OBP	SLG	OPS	OPS+	BR/A	RC	RC/G	FR	G/POS	WS	TPW
1909 Bos-A	10	17	0	4	0	0	0	1	0	....	0	....	.235	.235	.235	.471	48	-1	1	1.77	-1	/C-7	0	-0.2
1910 Bos-A	14	35	4	13	3	0	0	4	3	....	0	....	.371	.436	.457	.893	175	3	7	7.90	-3	C-12	2	0.2
1911 Bos-A	4	15	2	3	0	0	0	2	2	....	0	....	.200	.294	.200	.494	39	-1	1	1.84	0	/C-4	0	-0.1
Phi-N	28	76	4	21	1	1	0	4	0	13	0	....	.276	.276	.316	.592	65	-4	6	2.98	-2	C-22	1	-0.5
Total 3	56	143	10	41	4	1	0	11	5	13	0	....	.287	.315	.329	.644	89	-3	15	3.79	-6	/C-45	3	-0.5

• MADDEN, Frank — Francis A. "Red" Madden b: 10/17/1892, Pittsburgh, PA d: 4/30/1952, Pittsburgh, PA Deb: 7/4/1914

YEAR TM-L	G	AB	R	H	2B	3B	HR	RBI	BB	SO	SB	CS	AVG	OBP	SLG	OPS	OPS+	BR/A	RC	RC/G	FR	G/POS	WS	TPW
1914 Pit-F	2	2	0	1	0	0	0	1	0	0	0	....	.500	.500	.500	1.000	196	0	0	12.24	-1	/C-1	0	0.0

• MADDEN, Gene — Eugene Madden b: 1/5/1890, Elm Grove, WV d: 4/6/1949, Utica, NY BL/TR, 5'10", 155 lbs. Deb: 4/20/1916

YEAR TM-L	G	AB	R	H	2B	3B	HR	RBI	BB	SO	SB	CS	AVG	OBP	SLG	OPS	OPS+	BR/A	RC	RC/G	FR	G/POS	WS	TPW
1916 Pit-N	1	1	0	0	0	0	0	0	0	0	0	....	.000	.000	.000	.000	-99	-0	0	.00	0	....	0	0.0

• MADDEN, Tommy — Thomas Joseph Madden b: 7/31/1883, Philadelphia, PA d: 7/26/1930, Philadelphia, PA BL/TL, 5'11", 160 lbs. Deb: 9/10/1906

YEAR TM-L	G	AB	R	H	2B	3B	HR	RBI	BB	SO	SB	CS	AVG	OBP	SLG	OPS	OPS+	BR/A	RC	RC/G	FR	G/POS	WS	TPW
1906 Bos-N	4	15	1	4	0	0	0	0	1	....	0	....	.267	.313	.267	.579	83	-0	1	3.03	0	/O-4(4-0-0)	0	0.0
1910 NY-A	1	1	0	0	0	0	0	0	0	....	0	....	.000	.000	.000	.000	-95	-0	0	.00	0	....	0	0.0
Total 2	5	16	1	4	0	0	0	0	1	....	0	....	.250	.294	.250	.544	72	-1	1	2.78	0	/O-4	0	0.0

• MADDERN, Clarence — Clarence James Maddern b: 9/26/1921, Bisbee, AZ d: 8/9/1986, Tucson, AZ BR/TR, 6'1", 185 lbs. Deb: 9/19/1946 Career OF: 51-0-10

YEAR TM-L	G	AB	R	H	2B	3B	HR	RBI	BB	SO	SB	CS	AVG	OBP	SLG	OPS	OPS+	BR/A	RC	RC/G	FR	G/POS	WS	TPW
1946 Chi-N	3	3	0	0	0	0	0	0	0	0	0	....	.000	.250	.000	.250	-27	-0	0	.59	-0	/O-2(2-0-0)	0	-0.1
1948 Chi-N	80	214	16	54	12	1	4	27	10	25	0	....	.252	.301	.374	.675	85	-5	25	4.06	2	O-55(48-0-10)	4	-0.7
1949 Chi-N	10	9	1	3	0	0	1	2	2	0	0	....	.333	.455	.667	1.121	202	1	3	13.34	0	/1-1	1	0.2
1951 Cle-A	11	12	0	2	0	0	0	0	0	1	0	0	.167	.167	.167	.333	-10	-2	0	.92	0	/O-1	0	-0.2
Total 4	104	238	17	59	12	1	5	29	12	26	0	0	.248	.301	.370	.671	84	-6	28	4.13	2	/O-58,1-1	5	-0.8

• MADDOX, Elliott — Elliott Maddox b: 12/21/1947, East Orange, NJ BR/TR, 5'11", 181 lbs. Deb: 4/7/1970 Career OF: 77-472-189

YEAR TM-L	G	AB	R	H	2B	3B	HR	RBI	BB	SO	SB	CS	AVG	OBP	SLG	OPS	OPS+	BR/A	RC	RC/G	FR	G/POS	WS	TPW
1970 Det-A	109	258	30	64	13	4	3	24	30	42	2	3	.248	.333	.364	.698	92	-3	31	4.13	-3	3-40,O-37(28-1-9),S-19/2-1	7	-0.8
1971 Was-A	128	258	38	56	8	2	1	18	51	42	10	4	.217	.346	.275	.621	83	-3	28	3.52	3	*O-103(12-84-10),3-12	7	-0.3
1972 Tex-A	98	294	40	74	7	2	0	10	49	53	20	10	.252	.362	.289	.651	100	3	34	3.80	0	O-94(11-70-14)	10	0.0
1973 Tex-A	100	172	24	41	1	0	1	17	29	28	5	4	.238	.358	.262	.619	80	-3	18	3.45	-1	O-89(22-58-11)/3-7,D-1	3	-0.6
1974 NY-A	137	466	75	141	26	2	3	45	69	48	6	5	.303	.397	.386	.783	130	21	74	5.71	1	*O-135(1-112-25)/2-2,3-1	23	1.9
1975 NY-A	55	218	36	67	10	3	1	23	21	24	9	3	.307	.386	.394	.781	124	9	33	5.34	3	O-55(0-55-0)/2-1	8	1.1
1976*NY-A	18	46	4	10	2	0	0	3	4	3	0	1	.217	.280	.261	.541	60	-3	3	1.94	1	O-13(0-6-7)/D-2	0	-0.2
1977 Bal-A	49	107	14	28	7	0	2	9	13	9	2	2	.262	.363	.383	.746	110	2	14	4.32	-3	O-45(1-44-0)/3-1	4	-0.1
1978 NY-N	119	389	43	100	18	2	2	39	71	38	2	11	.257	.374	.329	.704	102	0	50	4.26	1	O-79(0-13-72),3-43/1-1	11	-0.2
1979 NY-N	86	224	21	60	13	0	1	12	20	27	3	2	.268	.336	.339	.675	88	-4	26	4.18	0	O-65(2-26-40),3-11	5	-0.6
1980 NY-N	130	411	35	101	16	1	4	34	52	44	1	9	.246	.339	.319	.658	87	-9	44	3.54	6	*3-115/O-4(0-3-1),1-2	10	-0.5
Total 11	1029	2843	360	742	121	16	18	234	409	358	60	54	.261	.361	.334	.694	100	10	357	4.23	10	O-719,3-230/S-19,2-4,1-3,D	88	-0.3

• MADDOX, Garry — Garry Lee Maddox b: 9/1/1949, Cincinnati, OH BR/TR, 6'3", 184 lbs. Deb: 4/25/1972 Career OF: 20-1660-6

YEAR TM-L	G	AB	R	H	2B	3B	HR	RBI	BB	SO	SB	CS	AVG	OBP	SLG	OPS	OPS+	BR/A	RC	RC/G	FR	G/POS	WS	TPW
1972 SF-N	125	458	62	122	26	7	12	58	14	97	13	6	.266	.294	.432	.726	103	-1	57	4.34	-3	*O-121(20-96-6)	13	-0.8
1973 SF-N	144	587	81	187	30	10	11	76	24	73	24	10	.319	.352	.460	.812	118	14	94	6.06	-5	*O-140(0-140-0)	23	0.5
1974 SF-N	135	538	74	153	31	3	8	50	29	64	21	9	.284	.325	.398	.722	97	-4	68	4.53	-2	*O-131(0-131-0)	16	-1.0
1975 SF-N	17	52	4	7	1	0	1	4	6	3	1	1	.135	.237	.212	.449	24	-6	3	1.69	2	O-13(0-13-0)	1	-0.4
Phi-N	99	374	50	109	25	8	4	46	36	54	24	3	.291	.361	.433	.795	115	11	64	6.29	13	O-97(0-97-0)	17	2.3
Yr.	116	426	54	116	26	8	5	50	42	57	25	4	.272	.346	.406	.752	104	6	67	5.62	16	*O-110(0-110-0)	18	1.9
1976*Phi-N	146	531	75	175	37	6	6	68	42	59	29	12	.330	.383	.456	.839	133	24	92	6.44	9	*O-144(0-144-0)	26	3.0
1977*Phi-N	139	571	85	167	27	10	14	74	24	58	22	6	.292	.326	.448	.774	101	1	84	5.40	9	*O-138(0-138-0)	20	0.8
1978*Phi-N	155	598	62	172	34	3	11	68	39	89	33	7	.288	.333	.410	.743	106	7	83	5.03	10	*O-154(0-154-0)	21	1.5
1979 Phi-N	148	548	70	154	28	6	13	61	17	71	26	13	.281	.308	.425	.733	95	-6	68	4.34	14	*O-140(0-140-0)	16	0.5
1980*Phi-N	143	549	59	142	31	3	11	73	18	52	25	5	.259	.282	.386	.668	80	-14	58	3.60	5	*O-143(0-143-0)	14	-1.2
1981*Phi-N	94	323	37	85	7	1	5	40	17	42	9	4	.263	.302	.337	.640	78	-10	33	3.43	10	O-94(0-93-0)	7	-0.1
1982 Phi-N	119	412	39	117	27	2	8	61	12	32	7	5	.284	.304	.417	.722	98	-4	47	4.04	6	*O-111(0-111-0)	12	0.1
1983*Phi-N	97	324	27	89	14	2	4	32	17	31	7	6	.275	.313	.367	.680	89	-7	34	3.63	-1	O-95(0-95-0)	7	-1.0
1984 Phi-N	77	241	29	68	11	0	5	19	13	29	3	2	.282	.319	.390	.709	97	-2	30	4.50	-1	O-69(0-69-0)	6	-0.4
1985 Phi-N	105	218	22	52	8	1	4	23	13	26	4	2	.239	.284	.339	.624	72	-9	21	3.17	-3	O-94(0-93-0)	3	-1.3
1986 Phi-N	6	7	1	3	0	0	0	1	2	1	0	1	.429	.556	.429	.984	169	0	2	8.45	0	/O-3(0-3-0)	1	0.0
Total 15	1749	6331	777	1802	337	62	117	754	323	781	248	92	.285	.323	.413	.736	100	-4	838	4.71	61	*O-1687	203	2.5

• MADDOX, Jerry — Jerry Glenn Maddox b: 7/28/1953, Whittier, CA BR/TR, 6'2", 200 lbs. Deb: 6/3/1978

YEAR TM-L	G	AB	R	H	2B	3B	HR	RBI	BB	SO	SB	CS	AVG	OBP	SLG	OPS	OPS+	BR/A	RC	RC/G	FR	G/POS	WS	TPW
1978 Atl-N	7	14	1	3	0	0	0	1	1	2	0	0	.214	.267	.214	.481	32	-1	1	1.47	0	/3-5	0	-0.2

• MADISON, Art — Arthur Madison b: 1/14/1871, Clarksburg, MA d: 1/27/1933, North Adams, MA BR/TR, 5'9", 165 lbs. Deb: 9/9/1895

YEAR TM-L	G	AB	R	H	2B	3B	HR	RBI	BB	SO	SB	CS	AVG	OBP	SLG	OPS	OPS+	BR/A	RC	RC/G	FR	G/POS	WS	TPW
1895 Phi-N	11	34	6	12	3	0	0	8	1	1	4	....	.353	.371	.441	.813	109	0	7	8.57	-1	/S-6,2-3,3-2	1	0.0
1899 Pit-N	42	118	20	32	2	4	0	19	11	....	1	....	.271	.338	.356	.694	91	-1	15	4.57	-1	2-19,S-15/3-2	3	-0.1
Total 2	53	152	26	44	5	4	0	27	12	1	5	....	.289	.345	.375	.720	95	-1	22	5.40	-2	/2-22,S-21,3-4	4	-0.2

• MADISON, Scotti — Charles Scott Madison b: 9/12/1959, Pensacola, FL BB/TR, 5'11", 195 lbs. Deb: 7/6/1985

YEAR TM-L	G	AB	R	H	2B	3B	HR	RBI	BB	SO	SB	CS	AVG	OBP	SLG	OPS	OPS+	BR/A	RC	RC/G	FR	G/POS	WS	TPW
1985 Det-A	6	11	0	0	0	0	0	1	2	0	0	0	.000	.154	.000	.154	-54	-2	0	.33	0	/D-3,C-1	0	-0.3
1986 Det-A	2	7	0	0	0	0	0	1	0	3	0	0	.000	.000	.000	.000	-100	-2	0	.00	0	/3-1,D-1	0	-0.2
1987 KC-A	7	15	4	4	3	0	0	0	1	5	0	0	.267	.313	.467	.779	100	-0	2	5.15	-1	/1-4,C-3	0	-0.1
1988 KC-A	16	35	4	6	2	0	0	2	4	5	1	0	.171	.256	.229	.485	37	-3	2	2.28	0	/C-4,D-4,O-3(2-0-1),1-2	0	-0.3
1989 Cin-N	40	98	13	17	7	0	1	7	8	9	0	1	.173	.243	.276	.519	46	-7	6	1.77	1	3-26	1	-0.6
Total 5	71	166	21	27	12	0	1	11	15	22	1	1	.163	.236	.253	.489	35	-14	11	1.93	0	/3-27,C-8,D-8,1-6,O-3	1	-1.5

• MADJESKI, Ed — Edward William Madjeski b: 7/20/1908, Far Rockaway, NY d: 11/11/1994, Montgomery, OH BR/TR, 5'11", 178 lbs. Deb: 5/2/1932

YEAR TM-L	G	AB	R	H	2B	3B	HR	RBI	BB	SO	SB	CS	AVG	OBP	SLG	OPS	OPS+	BR/A	RC	RC/G	FR	G/POS	WS	TPW
1932 Phi-A	17	35	4	8	0	0	0	3	3	6	0	0	.229	.289	.229	.518	35	-3	2	2.39	1	/C-8	1	-0.1
1933 Phi-A	51	142	17	40	4	0	0	17	4	21	0	0	.282	.301	.310	.611	62	-8	13	3.33	-2	C-41	2	-0.7
1934 Phi-A	8	8	1	3	1	0	0	2	0	1	0	0	.375	.375	.500	.875	129	0	1	7.63	-1	/C-1	0	0.0
Chi-A	85	281	36	62	14	2	5	32	14	31	2	0	.221	.260	.338	.598	52	-21	25	3.00	6	C-79	3	-0.9

YEAR TM-L	G	AB	R	H	2B	3B	HR	RBI	BB	SO	SB	CS	AVG	OBP	SLG	OPS	OPS+	BR/A	RC	RC/G	FR	G/POS	WS	TPW
Yr.	93	289	37	65	15	2	5	34	14	32	2	0	.225	.263	.343	.606	54	-21	26	3.11	6	C-80	3	-1.0
1937 NY-N	5	15	0	3	0	0	0	2	0	2	0	....	.200	.200	.200	.400	9	-2	1	1.38	0	/C-5	0	-0.1
Total 4	166	481	58	116	19	2	5	56	21	61	2	0	.241	.274	.320	.595	53	-34	43	3.06	5	C-134	6	-2.0

• MADLOCK, Bill Bill Madlock b: 1/2/1951, Memphis, TN BR/TR, 5'11", 185 lbs. Deb: 9/7/1973 C

YEAR TM-L	G	AB	R	H	2B	3B	HR	RBI	BB	SO	SB	CS	AVG	OBP	SLG	OPS	OPS+	BR/A	RC	RC/G	FR	G/POS	WS	TPW
1973 Tex-A	21	77	16	27	5	3	1	5	7	9	3	2	.351	.412	.532	.944	171	7	17	9.00	-2	3-21	4	0.5
1974 Chi-N	128	453	65	142	21	5	9	54	42	39	11	7	.313	.378	.442	.820	124	14	72	5.71	-16	*3-121	16	-0.3
1975 Chi-N★	130	514	77	182	29	7	7	64	42	34	9	7	**.354**	.406	.479	.885	139	26	98	7.41	-17	*3-128	26	0.8
1976 Chi-N	142	514	68	174	36	1	15	84	56	27	15	11	**.339**	.415	.500	.915	146	31	100	7.14	-24	*3-136	25	0.7
1977 SF-N	140	533	70	161	28	1	12	46	43	33	13	10	.302	.361	.426	.787	110	7	73	4.82	-13	*3-126/2-6	14	-0.8
1978 SF-N	122	447	76	138	26	3	15	44	48	39	16	5	.309	.380	.481	.861	145	28	84	6.83	-1	*2-114/1-3	25	3.5
1979 SF-N	69	249	37	65	9	2	7	41	18	19	11	3	.261	.311	.398	.708	99	-0	31	4.40	-8	2-63/1-5	8	-0.5
*Pit-N	85	311	48	102	17	3	7	44	34	22	21	8	.328	.396	.469	.865	129	14	55	6.19	3	3-85	13	1.7
Yr.	154	560	85	167	26	5	14	85	52	41	32	11	.298	.359	.438	.796	116	14	86	5.39	-5	3-85,2-63/1-5	21	1.2
1980 Pit-N	137	494	62	137	22	4	10	53	45	33	16	10	.277	.343	.399	.741	105	2	64	4.48	-11	*3-127,1-12	13	-1.1
1981 Pit-N★	82	279	35	95	23	1	6	45	34	17	18	6	**.341**	.418	.495	.912	153	22	59	8.07	0	3-78	15	2.3
1982 Pit-N	154	568	92	181	33	3	19	95	48	39	18	6	.319	.376	.488	.863	136	28	103	6.62	-5	*3-146/1-3	25	2.2
1983 Pit-N★	130	473	68	153	21	0	12	68	49	24	3	4	**.323**	.389	.444	.833	127	17	78	6.10	-13	*3-126	17	0.3
1984 Pit-N	103	403	38	102	16	0	4	44	26	29	3	1	.253	.300	.323	.623	75	-14	38	3.19	-4	3-98/1-1	6	-2.0
1985 Pit-N	110	399	49	100	23	1	10	41	39	42	3	3	.251	.325	.388	.714	100	-1	49	4.14	-14	3-98,1-12	7	-1.7
*LA-N	34	114	20	41	4	0	2	15	10	11	7	1	.360	.425	.447	.873	149	9	23	7.92	3	3-32	7	1.2
Yr.	144	513	69	141	27	1	12	56	49	53	10	4	.275	.347	.402	.749	111	8	72	4.88	-11	*3-130,1-12	14	-0.5
1986 LA-N	111	379	38	106	17	0	10	60	30	43	3	3	.280	.341	.404	.744	112	5	52	4.82	-4	*3-101/1-2	12	0.0
1987 LA-N	21	61	5	11	1	0	3	7	6	5	0	0	.180	.265	.344	.609	61	-4	5	2.32	0	3-16/1-1	0	-0.4
*Det-A	87	326	56	91	17	0	14	50	28	45	4	3	.279	.354	.460	.815	119	8	52	5.38	-2	D-64,1-22/3-1	9	0.3
Total 15	1806	6594	920	2008	348	34	163	860	605	510	174	90	.305	.369	.442	.811	123	199	1053	5.72	-126	*3-1440,2-183/D-64,1-61	242	6.8

• MADRID, Sal Salvador Madrid b: 6/9/1920, El Paso, TX d: 2/24/1977, Fort Wayne, IN BR/TR, 5'9", 165 lbs. Deb: 9/17/1947

YEAR TM-L	G	AB	R	H	2B	3B	HR	RBI	BB	SO	SB	CS	AVG	OBP	SLG	OPS	OPS+	BR/A	RC	RC/G	FR	G/POS	WS	TPW
1947 Chi-N	8	24	0	3	1	0	0	1	1	6	0	....	.125	.160	.167	.327	-14	-4	1	.88	0	/S-8	0	-0.4

• MAGADAN, Dave David Joseph Magadan b: 9/30/1962, Tampa, FL BL/TR, 6'3", 200 lbs. Deb: 9/7/1986 C

YEAR TM-L	G	AB	R	H	2B	3B	HR	RBI	BB	SO	SB	CS	AVG	OBP	SLG	OPS	OPS+	BR/A	RC	RC/G	FR	G/POS	WS	TPW
1986 NY-N	10	18	3	8	0	0	0	3	3	1	0	0	.444	.524	.444	.968	175	2	4	10.26	0	/1-9	1	0.2
1987 NY-N	85	192	21	61	13	1	3	24	22	22	0	0	.318	.388	.443	.831	126	7	33	6.45	0	3-50,1-13	8	0.7
1988*NY-N	112	314	39	87	15	0	1	35	60	39	0	1	.277	.396	.334	.731	118	10	45	5.01	-2	1-71,3-48	14	0.5
1989 NY-N	127	374	47	107	22	3	4	41	49	37	1	0	.286	.370	.393	.763	124	13	58	5.75	2	1-87,3-28	16	1.1
1990 NY-N	144	451	74	148	28	6	6	72	74	55	2	1	.328	**.425**	.457	.882	143	30	91	7.49	1	*1-113,3-19	25	2.4
1991 NY-N	124	418	58	108	23	0	4	51	83	50	1	1	.258	.384	.342	.726	106	8	62	5.09	0	*1-122	14	0.0
1992 NY-N	99	321	33	91	9	1	3	28	56	44	1	0	.283	.390	.346	.736	111	8	47	5.33	-8	3-93/1-2	13	0.1
1993 Fla-N	66	227	22	65	12	0	4	29	44	30	0	1	.286	.404	.392	.796	108	5	39	6.23	2	3-63/1-2	8	0.7
Sea-A	71	228	27	59	11	0	1	21	36	33	2	0	.259	.360	.320	.680	83	-3	27	4.02	-0	1-41,3-27/D-2	4	-0.6
1994 Fla-N	74	211	30	58	7	0	1	17	39	25	0	0	.275	.390	.322	.713	86	-2	28	4.66	-1	3-48,1-16	3	-0.3
1995 Hou-N	127	348	44	109	24	0	2	51	71	56	2	1	.313	.430	.399	.829	129	19	64	6.81	-13	*3-100,1-11	15	0.7
1996 Chi-N	78	169	23	43	10	0	3	17	29	23	0	2	.254	.364	.367	.731	91	-2	23	4.72	-1	3-51,1-10	3	-0.4
1997 Oak-A	128	271	38	82	10	1	4	30	50	40	1	0	.303	.415	.391	.806	115	9	47	6.37	1	3-49,1-30,D-25	9	0.8
1998 Oak-A	35	109	12	35	8	0	1	13	13	12	0	1	.321	.393	.422	.815	115	2	17	5.65	1	3-30/1-7	5	0.4
1999 SD-N	116	248	20	68	12	1	2	30	45	36	1	3	.274	.386	.355	.741	97	-0	34	4.65	2	3-52,1-42	4	0.0
2000 SD-N	95	132	13	36	7	0	2	21	32	23	0	0	.273	.415	.371	.786	108	4	22	5.93	1	3-29/1-8,D-2,S-2	4	0.5
2001 SD-N	91	128	12	32	7	0	1	12	12	20	0	0	.250	.319	.328	.647	74	-5	14	3.92	-2	3-22/1-9,D-2,2-1,S-1	1	-0.7
Total 16	1582	4159	516	1197	218	13	42	495	718	546	11	11	.288	.394	.377	.771	113	107	658	5.65	-16	3-709,1-593/D-31,S-3,2-1	147	6.1

• MAGALLANES, Ever Everardo (Espinoza) Magallanes b: 11/6/1965, Chihuahua, Mexico BL/TR, 5'10", 165 lbs. Deb: 5/17/1991

YEAR TM-L	G	AB	R	H	2B	3B	HR	RBI	BB	SO	SB	CS	AVG	OBP	SLG	OPS	OPS+	BR/A	RC	RC/G	FR	G/POS	WS	TPW
1991 Cle-A	3	2	0	0	0	0	0	0	1	1	0	0	.000	.333	.000	.333	1	-0	0	1.17	-1	/S-2	0	-0.1

• MAGEE, Lee Leo Christopher Magee b: 6/4/1889, Cincinnati, OH d: 3/14/1966, Columbus, OH BB/TR, 5'11", 165 lbs. Deb: 7/4/1911 M Career OF: 230-285-8

YEAR TM-L	G	AB	R	H	2B	3B	HR	RBI	BB	SO	SB	CS	AVG	OBP	SLG	OPS	OPS+	BR/A	RC	RC/G	FR	G/POS	WS	TPW
1911 StL-N	26	69	9	18	1	1	0	8	8	8	4	....	.261	.338	.304	.642	82	-1	8	4.18	-2	2-18/S-3	2	-0.3
1912 StL-N	128	458	60	133	13	8	0	40	39	29	16	....	.290	.347	.354	.701	94	-4	63	4.59	6	0-85(85-0-0),2-23/1-6,S-1	11	-0.1
1913 StL-N	137	531	54	142	13	7	2	31	34	30	23	....	.267	.314	.330	.644	85	-11	61	3.76	9	*0-108(108-3-1),2-22/1-6,S	11	-0.7
1914 StL-N	142	529	59	150	23	4	2	40	42	24	36	....	.284	.337	.353	.691	107	4	74	4.67	5	*0-102(2-100-0),1-39/2-6	16	0.2
1915 Bro-F	121	452	87	146	19	10	4	49	22	19	34	....	.323	.356	.436	.792	135	17	78	6.27	0	*2-115/1-2	17	2.1
1916 NY-A	131	510	57	131	18	4	3	45	50	31	29	25	.257	.324	.325	.650	93	-9	56	3.44	3	*0-128(21-107-0)/2-2	15	-1.5
1917 NY-A	51	173	17	38	4	1	0	8	13	18	3	....	.220	.278	.254	.532	62	-8	14	2.46	-3	0-50(2-48-0)	1	-1.5
StL-A	36	112	11	19	1	0	0	4	6	6	3	....	.170	.212	.179	.390	20	-11	5	1.35	5	3-20/2-6,1-5,0-1	1	-0.6
Yr.	87	285	28	57	5	1	0	12	19	24	6	....	.200	.252	.225	.477	46	-19	19	2.01	2	0-51(2-48-1),3-20/2-6,1-5	2	-2.1
1918 Cin-N	119	459	61	133	22	13	0	28	28	19	19	....	.290	.331	.394	.725	123	11	65	4.79	10	*2-114/3-3	18	2.6
1919 Bro-N	45	181	16	43	7	2	0	7	5	8	5	....	.238	.262	.298	.560	67	-8	16	2.71	1	2-36/3-9	3	-0.7
Chi-N	79	267	36	78	12	4	1	17	18	16	14	....	.292	.339	.378	.717	115	5	38	4.89	-5	0-45(12-27-6),S-13,3-10/2-7	9	-0.1
Yr.	124	448	52	121	19	6	1	24	23	24	19	....	.270	.309	.346	.655	96	-3	54	3.96	-4	0-45(12-27-6),2-43,3-19,S-13	12	-0.8
Total 9	1015	3741	467	1031	133	54	12	277	265	208	186	25	.276	.325	.350	.675	99	-15	479	4.23	30	0-519,2-349/1-58,3-42,S-19	104	-0.4

• MAGEE, Sherry Sherwood Robert Magee
b: 8/6/1884, Clarendon, PA d: 3/13/1929, Philadelphia, PA BR/TR, 5'11", 179 lbs. Deb: 6/29/1904 U Career OF: 1601-140-125

YEAR TM-L	G	AB	R	H	2B	3B	HR	RBI	BB	SO	SB	CS	AVG	OBP	SLG	OPS	OPS+	BR/A	RC	RC/G	FR	G/POS	WS	TPW
1904 Phi-N	95	364	51	101	15	12	3	57	14	....	11	....	.277	.308	.409	.717	125	9	51	4.93	2	0-94(19-1-74)/1-1	11	0.6
1905 Phi-N	155	603	100	180	24	17	5	98	44	....	48	....	.299	.354	.420	.774	135	25	111	6.58	3	*0-155(155-0-0)	28	1.9
1906 Phi-N	154	563	77	159	36	8	6	67	52	....	55	....	.282	.348	.407	.755	135	22	102	6.43	3	*0-154(154-0-0)	31	1.7
1907 Phi-N	140	503	75	165	28	12	4	**85**	53	....	46	....	.328	.396	.455	.852	169	40	113	8.45	6	*0-139(139-0-0)	38	4.3
1908 Phi-N	143	508	79	144	30	16	2	57	49	....	40	....	.283	.359	.417	.776	143	25	90	6.11	3	*0-142(142-0-0)	26	2.3
1909 Phi-N	143	522	60	141	33	14	2	66	43	....	38	....	.270	.339	.398	.737	128	16	83	5.31	-7	*0-143(143-0-0)	20	0.0
1910 Phi-N	154	519	**110**	172	39	17	6	**123**	94	36	49	....	**.331**	**.445**	**.507**	**.952**	**172**	**52**	139	**9.80**	-14	*0-154(126-23-5)	**36**	3.1
1911 Phi-N	121	445	79	128	32	5	15	94	49	33	22	....	.288	.366	.483	.849	135	19	86	6.74	2	*0-120(120-0-1)	19	1.6
1912 Phi-N	132	464	79	142	25	9	6	66	55	54	30	....	.306	.388	.438	.825	118	12	91	6.64	-10	*0-124(124-0-0)/1-6	17	-0.3
1913 Phi-N	138	470	92	144	36	6	11	70	38	36	23	....	.306	.369	.479	.848	135	21	89	6.51	-9	*0-123(106-8-9)/1-4	19	0.7
1914 Phi-N	146	544	96	**171**	**39**	11	15	**103**	55	42	25	....	.314	.380	**.509**	.890	154	35	110	**7.38**	1	0-67(67-0-0),S-39,1-32/2-8	29	3.9
1915 Bos-N	156	571	72	160	34	12	2	87	54	39	15	12	.280	.350	.392	.742	127	17	82	4.86	7	*0-135(34-102-0),1-21	26	1.7
1916 Bos-N	122	419	44	101	17	5	3	54	44	52	10	....	.241	.322	.327	.649	105	4	50	3.86	-6	*0-120(102-3-19)/1-2,S-1	16	-0.9
1917 Bos-N	72	246	24	63	8	4	1	29	13	23	7	....	.256	.302	.333	.635	100	-0	27	3.54	1	0-65(63-0-2)/1-2	6	-0.2
Cin-N	45	137	17	44	8	4	0	23	16	7	4	....	.321	.400	.438	.838	164	11	25	6.70	3	0-41(29-0-12)/1-2	9	1.4
Yr.	117	383	41	107	16	8	1	52	29	30	11	....	.279	.338	.371	.709	123	10	52	4.57	4	*0-106(92-0-14)/1-4	15	1.2
1918 Cin-N	115	400	46	119	15	13	2	**76**	37	18	14	....	.298	.370	.415	.785	142	21	64	5.73	-9	1-66,0-38(34-2-1)/2-6	18	1.0
1919*Cin-N	56	163	11	35	6	1	0	21	26	19	4	....	.215	.337	.264	.601	84	-1	16	3.12	-3	0-47(44-1-2)/2-1,3-1	5	-0.7
Total 16	2087	7441	1112	2169	425	166	83	1176	736	359	441	12	.291	.364	.427	.790	136	325	1328	6.22	-28	*0-1861,1-136/S-40,2-15,3-1	354	22.0

• MAGEE, Wendell Wendell Errol Magee b: 8/3/1972, Hattiesburg, MS BR/TR, 6', 225 lbs. Deb: 8/16/1996 Career OF: 70-177-103

YEAR TM-L	G	AB	R	H	2B	3B	HR	RBI	BB	SO	SB	CS	AVG	OBP	SLG	OPS	OPS+	BR/A	RC	RC/G	FR	G/POS	WS	TPW
1996 Phi-N	38	142	9	29	7	0	2	14	9	33	0	0	.204	.252	.296	.547	43	-12	11	2.48	1	0-37(6-18-18)	1	-1.2
1997 Phi-N	38	115	7	23	4	0	1	9	9	20	1	4	.200	.258	.261	.519	36	-12	5	1.36	0	0-38(0-38-0)	1	-1.2
1998 Phi-N	20	75	9	22	6	1	1	11	7	11	0	0	.293	.354	.440	.794	106	1	11	5.03	-1	0-19(19-0-0)	2	-0.1
1999 Phi-N	12	14	4	5	1	0	2	5	1	4	0	0	.357	.400	.857	1.257	201	2	4	11.03	0	/0-4(1-2-1)	1	0.2
2000 Det-A	91	186	31	51	4	2	7	31	10	28	1	0	.274	.311	.430	.741	87	-4	23	4.33	-2	0-76(18-5-56)/D-6	4	-0.8
2001 Det-A	90	207	26	44	11	4	5	17	23	44	3	0	.213	.294	.377	.671	79	-6	22	3.48	2	0-74(21-36-19),D-11	2	-0.5
2002 Det-A	97	347	34	94	19	1	6	35	10	64	2	4	.271	.293	.383	.677	83	-11	35	3.51	6	0-91(5-78-9)/D-4	5	-0.5
Total 7	386	1086	120	268	52	8	24	122	69	204	7	8	.247	.293	.376	.669	76	-43	111	3.43	7	0-339/D-21	16	-4.1

• MAGGERT, Harl Harl Warren Maggert b: 5/4/1914, Los Angeles, CA d: 7/10/1986, Citrus Heights, CA BR/TR, 6', 190 lbs. Deb: 4/19/1938

YEAR TM-L	G	AB	R	H	2B	3B	HR	RBI	BB	SO	SB	CS	AVG	OBP	SLG	OPS	OPS+	BR/A	RC	RC/G	FR	G/POS	WS	TPW
1938 Bos-N	66	89	12	25	3	0	3	19	10	20	0	....	.281	.354	.416	.769	123	3	13	5.28	-1	0-10(8-0-2)/3-8	4	0.2

• MAGGERT, Harl Harl Vestin Maggert b: 2/13/1883, Cromwell, IN d: 1/7/1963, Fresno, CA BL/TR, 5'8", 155 lbs. Deb: 9/4/1907 Career OF: 41-17-5

YEAR TM-L	G	AB	R	H	2B	3B	HR	RBI	BB	SO	SB	CS	AVG	OBP	SLG	OPS	OPS+	BR/A	RC	RC/G	FR	G/POS	WS	TPW
1907 Pit-N	3	6	1	0	0	0	0	0	2	....	1	....	.000	.250	.000	.250	-21	-1	0	1.11	0	/0-2(2-0-0)	0	-0.1
1912 Phi-A	74	242	39	62	8	6	1	13	36	....	10	....	.256	.357	.351	.708	107	3	34	4.75	-3	0-61(39-17-5)	8	-0.2
Total 2	77	248	40	62	8	6	1	13	38	....	11	....	.250	.354	.343	.697	103	3	34	4.64	-2	/0-63	8	-0.2

• MAGNER, John John T. Magner b: 1855, , 5'7.5" Deb: 7/14/1879 U

YEAR TM-L	G	AB	R	H	2B	3B	HR	RBI	BB	SO	SB	CS	AVG	OBP	SLG	OPS	OPS+	BR/A	RC	RC/G	FR	G/POS	WS	TPW
1879 Cin-N	1	4	0	0	0	0	0	1	0	1	....	....	.000	.000	.000	.000	-105	-1	0	.00	0	/0-1	0	-0.1

• MAGNER, Stubby Edmund Burke Magner b: 2/20/1888, Kalamazoo, MI d: 9/6/1956, Chillicothe, OH BR/TR, 5'3", 135 lbs. Deb: 7/12/1911

YEAR TM-L	G	AB	R	H	2B	3B	HR	RBI	BB	SO	SB	CS	AVG	OBP	SLG	OPS	OPS+	BR/A	RC	RC/G	FR	G/POS	WS	TPW
1911 NY-A	13	33	3	7	0	0	0	4	4	....	1	....	.212	.297	.212	.509	40	-3	3	2.45	1	/S-6,2-5	0	-0.1

• MAGOON, George George Henry "Maggie,Topsy" Magoon b: 3/27/1875, St. Albans, ME d: 12/6/1943, Rochester, NH BR/TR, 5'10", 160 lbs. Deb: 6/29/1898

YEAR TM-L	G	AB	R	H	2B	3B	HR	RBI	BB	SO	SB	CS	AVG	OBP	SLG	OPS	OPS+	BR/A	RC	RC/G	FR	G/POS	WS	TPW
1898 Bro-N	93	343	35	77	7	0	1	39	30	....	7	....	.224	.293	.254	.546	57	-19	28	2.81	1	S-93	6	-1.2
1899 Bal-N	62	207	26	53	8	3	0	31	26	....	7	....	.256	.353	.324	.677	82	-4	28	4.59	5	S-62	7	0.3
Chi-N	59	189	24	43	5	1	0	21	24	....	5	....	.228	.333	.265	.598	67	-7	21	3.47	0	S-59	4	-0.4
Yr.	121	396	50	96	13	4	0	52	50	....	12	....	.242	.344	.295	.639	74	-12	48	4.03	4	*S-121	11	-0.1
1901 Cin-N	127	460	47	116	16	7	1	53	52	....	15	....	.252	.331	.324	.655	96	0	57	4.27	-25	*S-112,2-15	12	-2.0
1902 Cin-N	45	162	29	44	9	2	0	23	13	....	7	....	.272	.344	.352	.696	105	1	24	4.95	2	2-41/S-3	4	0.4
1903 Cin-N	42	139	6	30	6	0	0	9	19	....	2	....	.216	.314	.259	.573	58	-7	13	3.03	3	2-32/3-9	2	-0.4
Chi-A	94	334	32	76	11	3	0	25	30	....	4	....	.228	.303	.278	.581	79	-7	31	3.11	-19	2-94	6	-2.6
Total 5	522	1834	199	439	62	16	2	201	194	....	47	....	.239	.321	.294	.615	79	-43	201	3.69	-34	S-329,2-182/3-9	41	-5.9

• MAGRANN, Tom Thomas Joseph Magrann b: 12/9/1963, Hollywood, FL BR/TR, 6'3", 177 lbs. Deb: 9/7/1989

YEAR TM-L	G	AB	R	H	2B	3B	HR	RBI	BB	SO	SB	CS	AVG	OBP	SLG	OPS	OPS+	BR/A	RC	RC/G	FR	G/POS	WS	TPW
1989 Cle-A	9	10	0	0	0	0	0	0	0	4	0	0	.000	.000	.000	.000	-98	-3	0	.00	0	/C-9	0	-0.2

• MAGRUDER, Chris Christopher James Magruder b: 4/26/1977, Tacoma, WA BB/TR, 5'11", 200 lbs. Deb: 9/4/2001 Career OF: 58-21-33

YEAR TM-L	G	AB	R	H	2B	3B	HR	RBI	BB	SO	SB	CS	AVG	OBP	SLG	OPS	OPS+	BR/A	RC	RC/G	FR	G/POS	WS	TPW
2001 Tex-A	17	29	3	5	0	0	0	1	1	5	0	0	.172	.226	.172	.398	7	-4	1	1.15	2	0-12(8-1-3)	0	-0.2
2002 Cle-A	87	258	34	56	15	1	6	29	15	55	2	0	.217	.263	.353	.615	63	-14	23	2.90	-1	0-83(45-20-27)	1	-1.7
2003 Cle-A	9	26	3	9	2	1	1	3	3	6	0	1	.346	.433	.615	1.049	178	3	7	10.22	-1	/0-8(5-0-3)	1	0.1
Total 3	113	313	40	70	17	2	7	33	19	66	2	1	.224	.275	.358	.632	68	-15	31	3.24	0	0-103	2	-1.8

• MAGUIRE, Freddie Frederick Edward Maguire b: 5/10/1899, Roxbury, MA d: 11/3/1961, Boston, MA BR/TR, 5'11", 155 lbs. Deb: 9/22/1922

YEAR TM-L	G	AB	R	H	2B	3B	HR	RBI	BB	SO	SB	CS	AVG	OBP	SLG	OPS	OPS+	BR/A	RC	RC/G	FR	G/POS	WS	TPW
1922 NY-N	5	12	4	4	0	0	0	1	0	1	1	0	.333	.333	.333	.667	72	-0	1	4.78	0	/2-3	0	0.0
1923*NY-N	41	30	11	6	1	0	0	2	2	4	1	0	.200	.250	.233	.483	28	-3	2	2.08	-2	2-16/3-1	0	-0.5
1928 Chi-N	140	574	67	160	24	7	1	41	25	38	6	....	.279	.312	.350	.662	74	-23	62	3.55	40	*2-138	14	2.1
1929 Bos-N	138	496	54	125	26	8	0	41	19	40	8	....	.252	.284	.337	.620	55	-36	46	3.04	3	*2-138/S-1	5	-2.7
1930 Bos-N	146	516	54	138	21	5	0	52	20	22	4	....	.267	.297	.328	.625	53	-40	49	3.21	13	*2-146	9	-2.0
1931 Bos-N	148	492	36	112	18	2	0	26	16	26	3	....	.228	.259	.272	.532	45	-39	37	2.34	9	*2-148	7	-2.1
Total 6	618	2120	226	545	90	22	1	163	82	131	23	0	.257	.289	.322	.611	57	-141	197	3.04	63	2-589/3-1,S-1	35	-5.2

• MAGUIRE, Jack Jack Maguire b: 2/5/1925, St. Louis, MO d: 9/28/2001, Kerrville, TX BR/TR, 5'11", 165 lbs. Deb: 4/18/1950 Career OF: 30-0-13

YEAR TM-L	G	AB	R	H	2B	3B	HR	RBI	BB	SO	SB	CS	AVG	OBP	SLG	OPS	OPS+	BR/A	RC	RC/G	FR	G/POS	WS	TPW
1950 NY-N	29	40	3	7	2	0	0	3	3	13	0	....	.175	.233	.225	.458	21	-5	2	1.40	2	/0-9(4-0-5),1-2	0	-0.3
1951 NY-N	16	20	6	8	1	1	1	4	2	2	0	0	.400	.455	.700	1.155	204	3	7	15.21	0	/0-8(0-0-8)	2	0.3
Pit-N	8	5	1	0	0	0	0	0	1	0	0	0	.000	.167	.000	.167	-50	-1	0	.23	0	/2-1,3-1	0	-0.1
Yr.	24	25	7	8	1	1	1	4	3	2	0	0	.320	.393	.560	.953	150	2	7	10.80	1	/0-8(0-0-8),2-1,3-1	2	0.2
StL-A	41	127	15	31	2	1	1	14	12	21	1	0	.244	.309	.299	.609	63	-6	12	3.10	-1	0-26(26-0-0)/3-5,2-2	1	-0.9
Total 2	94	192	25	46	5	2	2	21	18	36	1	0	.240	.305	.318	.622	66	-9	20	3.54	1	/0-43,3-6,2-3,1-2	3	-1.0

• MAHADY, Jim James Bernard Mahady b: 4/22/1901, Cortland, NY d: 8/9/1936, Cortland, NY BR/TR, 5'11", 170 lbs. Deb: 10/2/1921

YEAR TM-L	G	AB	R	H	2B	3B	HR	RBI	BB	SO	SB	CS	AVG	OBP	SLG	OPS	OPS+	BR/A	RC	RC/G	FR	G/POS	WS	TPW
1921 NY-N	1	0	0	0	0	0	0	0	0	0	0	0	....	....	....	....	-100	0	0	....	0	/2-1	0	0.0

• MAHAN, Art Arthur Leo Mahan b: 6/8/1913, Somerville, MA BL/TL, 5'11", 178 lbs. Deb: 4/30/1940

YEAR TM-L	G	AB	R	H	2B	3B	HR	RBI	BB	SO	SB	CS	AVG	OBP	SLG	OPS	OPS+	BR/A	RC	RC/G	FR	G/POS	WS	TPW
1940 Phi-N	146	544	55	133	24	5	2	39	40	37	4	....	.244	.297	.318	.615	73	-21	52	3.28	0	*1-145/P-1	5	-3.4

• MAHAR, Frank Frank Edward Mahar b: 12/4/1878, Natick, MA d: 12/5/1961, Somerville, MA TR, 5'10.5" Deb: 8/29/1902

YEAR TM-L	G	AB	R	H	2B	3B	HR	RBI	BB	SO	SB	CS	AVG	OBP	SLG	OPS	OPS+	BR/A	RC	RC/G	FR	G/POS	WS	TPW
1902 Phi-N	1	1	0	0	0	0	0	0	0	....	0	....	.000	.000	.000	.000	-100	-0	0	.00	0	....	0	0.0

• MAHARG, Billy William Joseph Maharg b: 3/19/1881, Philadelphia, PA d: 11/20/1953, Philadelphia, PA BR/TR, 5'4.5", 155 lbs. Deb: 5/18/1912

YEAR TM-L	G	AB	R	H	2B	3B	HR	RBI	BB	SO	SB	CS	AVG	OBP	SLG	OPS	OPS+	BR/A	RC	RC/G	FR	G/POS	WS	TPW
1912 Det-A	1	1	0	0	0	0	0	0	0	....	0	....	.000	.000	.000	.000	-103	-0	0	.00	0	/3-1	0	0.0
1916 Phi-N	1	1	0	0	0	0	0	0	0	0	0	....	.000	.000	.000	.000	-97	-0	0	.00	0	/0-1	0	0.0
Total 2	2	2	0	0	0	0	0	0	0	0	0	....	.000	.000	.000	.000	-100	-0	0	.00	-0	/3-1,0-1	0	-0.1

• MAHAY, Ron Ronald Matthew Mahay b: 6/28/1971, Crestwood, IL BL/TL, 6'2", 185 lbs. Deb: 5/21/1995 ♦

YEAR TM-L	G	AB	R	H	2B	3B	HR	RBI	BB	SO	SB	CS	AVG	OBP	SLG	OPS	OPS+	BR/A	RC	RC/G	FR	G/POS	WS	TPW
1995 Bos-A	5	20	3	4	2	0	1	3	1	6	0	0	.200	.273	.450	.723	81	-1	3	4.38	0	/0-5(0-5-0)	0	-0.1
1997 Bos-A	28	0	0	0	0	0	0	0	0	0	0	0	....	....	....	....	-98	0	0	....	0	P-28	3	0.6
1998 Bos-A	29	0	0	0	0	0	0	0	0	0	0	0	....	....	....	....	-98	0	0	....	-1	P-29	2	0.3
1999 Oak-A	6	0	0	0	0	0	0	0	0	0	0	0	....	....	....	....	-104	0	0	....	0	/P-6	3	0.6
2000 Oak-A	1	0	0	0	0	0	0	0	0	0	0	0	....	....	....	....	-102	0	0	....	0	/P-5,D-1	0	-0.7
Fla-N	15	4	0	2	1	0	0	0	0	1	0	0	.500	.500	.750	1.250	220	1	2	20.25	0	P-18	1	-0.3
2001 Chi-N	17	2	0	0	0	0	0	0	0	1	0	0	.000	.000	.000	.000	-105	-0	0	.00	0	P-17	2	0.4
2002 Chi-N	11	0	0	0	0	0	0	0	0	0	0	0	....	....	....	....	-102	0	0	....	0	P-11	0	-0.7
2003 Tex-A	1	0	0	0	0	0	0	0	0	0	0	0	....	....	....	....	-92	0	0	....	0	P-35	4	0.9
Total 8	113	26	3	6	3	0	1	3	1	8	0	0	.231	.286	.462	.747	88	0	4	5.53	-1	P-149/0-5,D-1	15	0.9

• MAHER, Tom Thomas Francis Maher d: 8/25/1929, Philadelphia, PA Deb: 4/24/1902

YEAR TM-L	G	AB	R	H	2B	3B	HR	RBI	BB	SO	SB	CS	AVG	OBP	SLG	OPS	OPS+	BR/A	RC	RC/G	FR	G/POS	WS	TPW
1902 Phi-N	1	0	0	0	0	0	0	0	0	....	0	....	....	....	....	....	-100	0	0	....	0	....	0	0.0

• MAHLBERG, Greg Gregory John Mahlberg b: 8/8/1952, Milwaukee, WI BR/TR, 5'10", 180 lbs. Deb: 9/24/1978

YEAR TM-L	G	AB	R	H	2B	3B	HR	RBI	BB	SO	SB	CS	AVG	OBP	SLG	OPS	OPS+	BR/A	RC	RC/G	FR	G/POS	WS	TPW
1978 Tex-A	1	1	0	0	0	0	0	0	0	0	0	0	.000	.000	.000	.000	-100	-0	0	.00	-0	/C-1	0	0.0
1979 Tex-A	7	17	2	2	0	0	1	1	2	4	0	0	.118	.211	.294	.505	35	-2	1	.89	0	/C-7	0	-0.2
Total 2	8	18	2	2	0	0	1	1	2	4	0	0	.111	.200	.278	.478	29	-2	1	.84	0	/C-8	0	-0.2

• MAHONEY, Dan Daniel J. Mahoney b: 3/20/1864, Springfield, MA d: 2/1/1904, Springfield, MA BR/TR, 5'9.5", 165 lbs. Deb: 8/20/1892

YEAR TM-L	G	AB	R	H	2B	3B	HR	RBI	BB	SO	SB	CS	AVG	OBP	SLG	OPS	OPS+	BR/A	RC	RC/G	FR	G/POS	WS	TPW
1892 Cin-N	5	21	1	4	0	1	0	1	1	4	0	....	.190	.227	.286	.513	56	-1	1	2.22	1	/C-5	0	0.1
1895 Was-N	6	12	2	2	0	0	0	1	0	0	0	....	.167	.167	.167	.333	-14	-2	0	.92	0	/C-2,1-1	0	-0.2
Total 2	11	33	3	6	0	1	0	2	1	4	0	....	.182	.206	.242	.448	31	-3	2	1.74	1	/C-7,1-1	0	-0.1

• MAHONEY, Danny Daniel Joseph Mahoney b: 9/6/1888, Haverhill, MA d: 9/28/1960, Utica, NY BR/TR, 5'6.5", 145 lbs. Deb: 5/15/1911

YEAR TM-L	G	AB	R	H	2B	3B	HR	RBI	BB	SO	SB	CS	AVG	OBP	SLG	OPS	OPS+	BR/A	RC	RC/G	FR	G/POS	WS	TPW
1911 Cin-N	1	0	0	0	0	0	0	0	0	0	0	....	....	....	....	....	-104	0	0	....	0	....	0	0.0

• MAHONEY, Jim James Thomas "Moe" Mahoney b: 5/26/1934, Englewood, NJ BR/TR, 6', 175 lbs. Deb: 7/28/1959 C

YEAR TM-L	G	AB	R	H	2B	3B	HR	RBI	BB	SO	SB	CS	AVG	OBP	SLG	OPS	OPS+	BR/A	RC	RC/G	FR	G/POS	WS	TPW
1959 Bos-A	31	23	10	3	0	0	1	4	3	7	0	0	.130	.231	.261	.492	33	-2	2	2.11	-2	S-30	0	-0.3
1961 Was-A	43	108	10	26	0	1	0	6	5	23	1	2	.241	.274	.259	.534	46	-9	7	2.23	2	S-31/2-2	1	-0.5
1962 Cle-A	41	74	12	18	4	0	3	5	3	14	0	0	.243	.273	.419	.692	86	-2	8	3.45	1	S-23/2-8,3-1	2	0.1
1965 Hou-N	5	5	0	1	0	0	0	0	0	3	0	0	.200	.200	.200	.400	14	-1	0	1.35	0	/S-5	0	-0.1
Total 4	120	210	32	48	4	1	4	15	11	47	1	2	.229	.267	.314	.581	58	-14	17	2.63	0	/S-89,2-10,3-1	3	-0.8

• MAHONEY, Mike Michael John Mahoney b: 12/5/1972, Des Moines, IA BR/TR, 6'1", 200 lbs. Deb: 9/8/2000

YEAR TM-L	G	AB	R	H	2B	3B	HR	RBI	BB	SO	SB	CS	AVG	OBP	SLG	OPS	OPS+	BR/A	RC	RC/G	FR	G/POS	WS	TPW
2000 Chi-N	4	7	1	2	1	0	0	1	1	0	0	0	.286	.444	.429	.873	125	0	2	8.45	-1	/C-4	0	0.0

YEAR TM-L	G	AB	R	H	2B	3B	HR	RBI	BB	SO	SB	CS	AVG	OBP	SLG	OPS	OPS+	BR/A	RC	RC/G	FR	G/POS	WS	TPW
2002 Chi-N	16	29	2	6	3	0	0	3	1	10	0	0	.207	.233	.310	.544	42	-3	2	1.99	0	C-16	0	-0.2
Total 2	**20**	**36**	**3**	**8**	**4**	**0**	**0**	**4**	**2**	**10**	**0**	**0**	**.222**	**.282**	**.333**	**.615**	**61**	**-2**	**3**	**3.07**	**-1**	**/C-20**	**0**	**-0.2**

• MAHONEY, Mike — George W. "Big Mike" Mahoney b: 12/5/1873, Boston, MA d: 1/3/1940, Boston, MA BR, 6'4", 220 lbs. Deb: 5/18/1897

YEAR TM-L	G	AB	R	H	2B	3B	HR	RBI	BB	SO	SB	CS	AVG	OBP	SLG	OPS	OPS+	BR/A	RC	RC/G	FR	G/POS	WS	TPW
1897 Bos-N	2	2	1	1	0	0	0	1	0	....	0	....	.500	.500	.500	1.000	155	0	1	13.58	0	/C-1,P-1	0	-0.1
1898 StL-N	2	7	0	0	0	0	0	0	0	....	0	....	.000	.000	.000	.000	-98	-2	0	.00	0	/1-2	0	-0.2
Total 2	**4**	**9**	**1**	**1**	**0**	**0**	**0**	**1**	**0**	**....**	**0**	**....**	**.111**	**.111**	**.111**	**.222**	**-42**	**-2**	**1**	**1.70**	**0**	**/1-2,C-1,P-1**	**0**	**-0.3**

• MAIER, Bob — Robert Phillip Maier b: 9/5/1915, Dunellen, NJ d: 8/4/1993, South Plainfield, NJ BR/TR, 5'8", 180 lbs. Deb: 4/17/1945

YEAR TM-L	G	AB	R	H	2B	3B	HR	RBI	BB	SO	SB	CS	AVG	OBP	SLG	OPS	OPS+	BR/A	RC	RC/G	FR	G/POS	WS	TPW
1945*Det-A	132	486	58	128	25	7	1	34	38	32	7	11	.263	.317	.350	.667	88	-11	52	3.67	-16	*3-124/O-5(5-0-0)	9	-2.7

• MAILHO, Emil — Emil Pierre "Lefty" Mailho b: 12/16/1909, Berkeley, CA BL/TL, 5'10", 165 lbs. Deb: 4/14/1936

YEAR TM-L	G	AB	R	H	2B	3B	HR	RBI	BB	SO	SB	CS	AVG	OBP	SLG	OPS	OPS+	BR/A	RC	RC/G	FR	G/POS	WS	TPW
1936 Phi-A	21	18	5	1	0	0	0	0	5	3	0	0	.056	.261	.056	.316	-18	-3	1	.90	0	/O-1	0	-0.3

• MAISEL, Charlie — Charles Louis Maisel b: 4/21/1894, Catonsville, MD d: 8/25/1953, Baltimore, MD BR/TR, 6' Deb: 10/2/1915

YEAR TM-L	G	AB	R	H	2B	3B	HR	RBI	BB	SO	SB	CS	AVG	OBP	SLG	OPS	OPS+	BR/A	RC	RC/G	FR	G/POS	WS	TPW
1915 Bal-F	1	4	0	0	0	0	0	0	0	0	0	....	.000	.000	.000	.000	-93	-1	0	.00	0	/C-1	0	-0.1

• MAISEL, Fritz — Frederick Charles "Flash" Maisel b: 12/23/1889, Catonsville, MD d: 4/22/1967, Baltimore, MD BR/TR, 5'7.5", 170 lbs. Deb: 8/11/1913 Career OF: 0-26-1

YEAR TM-L	G	AB	R	H	2B	3B	HR	RBI	BB	SO	SB	CS	AVG	OBP	SLG	OPS	OPS+	BR/A	RC	RC/G	FR	G/POS	WS	TPW
1913 NY-A	51	187	33	48	4	3	0	12	34	20	25	....	.257	.371	.310	.681	99	2	29	5.13	-5	3-51	7	-0.2
1914 NY-A	150	548	78	131	23	9	2	47	76	69	**74**	17	.239	.334	.325	.659	98	9	74	4.50	-16	*3-148	20	-0.3
1915 NY-A	135	530	77	149	16	6	4	46	48	35	51	12	.281	.342	.357	.699	109	11	76	4.99	-7	*3-134	20	0.8
1916 NY-A	53	158	18	36	5	0	0	7	20	18	4	....	.228	.318	.259	.578	72	-5	15	3.07	-4	O-26(0-26-0),3-11/2-4	3	-1.1
1917 NY-A	113	404	46	80	4	4	0	20	36	18	29	....	.198	.267	.228	.495	51	-24	32	2.42	-6	*2-100/3-7	4	-3.1
1918 StL-A	90	284	43	66	4	2	0	16	46	17	11	....	.232	.341	.261	.602	84	-3	31	3.30	-3	3-79/O-1	6	-0.5
Total 6	**592**	**2111**	**295**	**510**	**56**	**24**	**6**	**148**	**260**	**177**	**194**	**29**	**.242**	**.327**	**.299**	**.626**	**88**	**-10**	**258**	**3.97**	**-42**	**3-430,2-104/O-27**	**60**	**-4.3**

• MAISEL, George — George John Maisel b: 3/12/1892, Catonsville, MD d: 11/20/1968, Baltimore, MD BR/TR, 5'10.5", 180 lbs. Deb: 5/1/1913 Career OF: 4-123-12

YEAR TM-L	G	AB	R	H	2B	3B	HR	RBI	BB	SO	SB	CS	AVG	OBP	SLG	OPS	OPS+	BR/A	RC	RC/G	FR	G/POS	WS	TPW
1913 StL-A	11	18	2	3	2	0	0	1	1	7	0	....	.167	.211	.278	.488	44	-1	1	1.63	-1	/O-5(2-3-0)	0	-0.3
1916 Det-A	8	5	2	0	0	0	0	0	0	2	0	....	.000	.000	.000	.000	-97	-1	0	.00	0	/3-3	0	-0.2
1921 Chi-N	111	393	54	122	7	2	0	43	11	13	17	7	.310	.334	.338	.673	78	-10	45	4.01	-1	*O-108(0-107-1)	7	-1.5
1922 Chi-N	38	84	9	16	1	1	0	6	8	2	1	3	.190	.261	.226	.487	26	-10	5	1.75	-1	O-26(2-13-11)	1	-1.1
Total 4	**168**	**500**	**67**	**141**	**10**	**3**	**0**	**50**	**20**	**24**	**18**	**10**	**.282**	**.314**	**.314**	**.628**	**66**	**-22**	**51**	**3.43**	**-3**	**O-139/3-3**	**8**	**-3.1**

• MAJESKI, Hank — Henry "Heeney" Majeski b: 12/13/1916, Staten Island, NY d: 8/9/1991, Staten Island, NY BR/TR, 5'9", 180 lbs. Deb: 5/17/1939

YEAR TM-L	G	AB	R	H	2B	3B	HR	RBI	BB	SO	SB	CS	AVG	OBP	SLG	OPS	OPS+	BR/A	RC	RC/G	FR	G/POS	WS	TPW
1939 Bos-N	106	367	35	100	16	1	7	54	18	30	2	....	.272	.310	.379	.689	91	-6	41	3.92	8	3-99	10	0.5
1940 Bos-N	3	3	0	0	0	0	0	0	0	0	0	....	.000	.000	.000	.000	-106	-1	0	.00	0	....	0	-0.1
1941 Bos-N	19	55	5	8	5	0	0	3	1	13	0	....	.145	.161	.236	.397	11	-7	2	1.22	0	3-11	0	-0.6
1946 NY-A	8	12	1	1	0	1	0	0	0	3	0	0	.083	.083	.250	.333	-9	-2	0	.63	-1	/3-2	0	-0.3
Phi-A	78	264	25	66	14	3	1	25	26	13	3	2	.250	.320	.337	.657	84	-5	29	3.73	8	3-72	5	0.3
Yr.	86	276	26	67	14	4	1	25	26	16	3	2	.243	.310	.333	.644	80	-7	29	3.58	8	3-74	5	0.0
1947 Phi-A	141	479	54	134	26	5	8	72	53	31	1	0	.280	.358	.405	.763	109	7	70	5.08	12	*3-134/S-4,2-1	18	2.0
1948 Phi-A	148	590	88	183	41	4	12	120	48	43	2	1	.310	.368	.454	.822	118	13	98	6.15	3	*3-142/S-8	25	1.6
1949 Phi-A	114	448	62	124	26	5	9	67	29	23	0	1	.277	.326	.417	.744	99	-4	58	4.46	1	*3-113	13	-0.3
1950 Chi-A	122	414	47	128	18	2	6	46	42	34	1	4	.309	.377	.406	.783	103	1	62	5.36	9	*3-112	11	0.9
1951 Chi-A	12	35	4	9	4	0	0	6	1	0	0	0	.257	.278	.371	.649	76	-1	3	3.40	1	/3-9	0	0.0
Phi-A	89	323	41	92	19	4	5	42	35	24	1	2	.285	.358	.415	.773	106	2	48	5.32	12	3-88	10	1.4
Yr.	101	358	45	101	23	4	5	48	36	24	1	2	.282	.351	.411	.762	104	1	52	5.13	13	3-97	10	1.3
1952 Phi-A	34	117	14	30	2	2	2	20	19	10	0	1	.256	.365	.359	.724	96	-0	15	4.15	4	3-34	4	0.4
Cle-A	36	54	7	16	2	0	0	9	7	7	0	0	.296	.377	.333	.710	106	1	6	4.00	-1	3-11/2-3	1	0.0
Yr.	70	171	21	46	4	2	2	29	26	17	0	1	.269	.369	.351	.720	99	1	21	4.10	3	3-45/2-3	5	0.4
1953 Cle-A	50	50	6	15	1	0	2	12	3	8	0	0	.300	.352	.440	.792	116	1	8	5.76	-3	2-10/3-7,O-1	2	-0.1
1954*Cle-A	57	121	10	34	4	0	3	17	7	14	0	0	.281	.320	.388	.709	92	-2	14	4.00	2	2-25,3-10	4	0.2
1955 Cle-A	36	48	3	9	2	0	2	6	8	3	0	0	.188	.328	.354	.682	80	-1	6	3.73	0	/3-9,2-4	1	-0.1
Bal-A	16	41	2	7	1	0	0	2	2	4	0	0	.171	.209	.195	.404	10	-5	2	1.19	0	/3-8,2-5	0	-0.6
Yr.	52	89	5	16	3	0	2	8	10	7	0	0	.180	.277	.281	.558	51	-6	7	2.57	0	3-17/2-9	1	-0.6
Total 13	**1069**	**3421**	**404**	**956**	**181**	**27**	**57**	**501**	**299**	**260**	**10**	**11**	**.279**	**.342**	**.398**	**.740**	**100**	**-9**	**462**	**4.73**	**57**	**3-861/2-48,S-12,O-1**	**104**	**5.2**

• MAKSUDIAN, Mike — Michael Bryant Maksudian b: 5/28/1966, Belleville, IL BL/TR, 5'11", 220 lbs. Deb: 9/2/1992

YEAR TM-L	G	AB	R	H	2B	3B	HR	RBI	BB	SO	SB	CS	AVG	OBP	SLG	OPS	OPS+	BR/A	RC	RC/G	FR	G/POS	WS	TPW
1992 Tor-A	3	3	0	0	0	0	0	0	0	0	0	0	.000	.000	.000	.000	-96	-1	0	.00	0	/1-1	0	-0.1
1993 Min-A	5	12	2	2	1	0	0	2	4	2	0	0	.167	.375	.250	.625	71	-0	1	2.23	1	/1-4,3-1	0	0.1
1994 Chi-N	26	26	6	7	2	0	0	4	10	4	0	1	.269	.472	.346	.818	120	1	5	6.96	0	/1-3,3-2,C-2	1	0.1
Total 3	**34**	**41**	**8**	**9**	**3**	**0**	**0**	**6**	**14**	**6**	**0**	**1**	**.220**	**.418**	**.293**	**.711**	**93**	**0**	**6**	**4.67**	**1**	**/1-8,3-3,C-2**	**1**	**0.1**

• MALAVE, Jose — Jose Francisco Malave b: 5/31/1971, Cumana, Venezuela BR/TR, 6'2", 212 lbs. Deb: 5/23/1996 Career OF: 12-0-30

YEAR TM-L	G	AB	R	H	2B	3B	HR	RBI	BB	SO	SB	CS	AVG	OBP	SLG	OPS	OPS+	BR/A	RC	RC/G	FR	G/POS	WS	TPW
1996 Bos-A	41	102	12	24	3	0	4	17	2	25	0	0	.235	.257	.382	.639	58	-7	10	3.54	-1	O-38(8-0-30)	1	-0.9
1997 Bos-A	4	4	0	0	0	0	0	0	0	2	0	0	.000	.000	.000	.000	-98	-1	0	.00	0	/O-4(4-0-0)	0	-0.1
Total 2	**45**	**106**	**12**	**24**	**3**	**0**	**4**	**17**	**2**	**27**	**0**	**0**	**.226**	**.248**	**.368**	**.616**	**52**	**-8**	**10**	**3.33**	**-1**	**/O-42**	**1**	**-1.0**

• MALAY, Charlie — Charles Francis Malay b: 6/13/1879, Brooklyn, NY d: 9/18/1949, Brooklyn, NY BB/TR, 5'11.5", 175 lbs. Deb: 4/24/1905

YEAR TM-L	G	AB	R	H	2B	3B	HR	RBI	BB	SO	SB	CS	AVG	OBP	SLG	OPS	OPS+	BR/A	RC	RC/G	FR	G/POS	WS	TPW
1905 Bro-N	102	349	33	88	7	2	1	31	22	....	13	....	.252	.300	.292	.593	83	-7	37	3.51	-11	2-75,O-25(1-23-1)/S-1	5	-2.0

• MALAY, Joe — Joseph Charles Malay b: 10/25/1905, Brooklyn, NY d: 3/19/1989, Bridgeport, CT BL/TL, 6', 175 lbs. Deb: 9/7/1933

YEAR TM-L	G	AB	R	H	2B	3B	HR	RBI	BB	SO	SB	CS	AVG	OBP	SLG	OPS	OPS+	BR/A	RC	RC/G	FR	G/POS	WS	TPW
1933 NY-N	8	24	0	3	0	0	0	2	0	0	0	....	.125	.125	.125	.250	-29	-4	0	.31	1	/1-8	0	-0.3
1935 NY-N	1	1	0	1	0	0	0	0	0	0	0	....	1.000	1.000	1.000	2.000	447	0	1	∞	0	....	0	0.0
Total 2	**9**	**25**	**0**	**4**	**0**	**0**	**0**	**2**	**0**	**0**	**0**	**....**	**.160**	**.160**	**.160**	**.320**	**-10**	**-4**	**1**	**.31**	**1**	**/1-8**	**0**	**-0.3**

• MALDONADO, Candy — Candido (Guadarrama) Maldonado b: 9/5/1960, Humacao, Puerto Rico BR/TR, 6', 190 lbs. Deb: 9/7/1981 Career OF: 489-97-688

YEAR TM-L	G	AB	R	H	2B	3B	HR	RBI	BB	SO	SB	CS	AVG	OBP	SLG	OPS	OPS+	BR/A	RC	RC/G	FR	G/POS	WS	TPW
1981 LA-N	11	12	0	1	0	0	0	0	0	5	0	0	.083	.083	.083	.167	-55	-2	0	.20	0	/O-9(4-0-5)	0	-0.3
1982 LA-N	6	4	0	0	0	0	0	0	1	2	0	0	.000	.200	.000	.200	-41	-1	0	.00	0	/O-3(3-0-1)	0	-0.1
1983*LA-N	42	62	5	12	1	1	1	6	5	14	0	0	.194	.254	.290	.544	51	-4	5	2.42	0	O-33(12-3-19)	0	-0.5
1984 LA-N	116	254	25	68	14	0	5	28	19	29	0	3	.268	.321	.382	.703	98	-3	30	4.02	-3	*O-102(7-31-67)/3-4	6	-0.9
1985*LA-N	121	213	20	48	7	1	5	19	19	40	1	1	.225	.289	.338	.627	77	-7	21	3.28	2	*O-113(44-57-24)	5	-0.8
1986 SF-N	133	405	49	102	31	3	18	85	20	77	4	4	.252	.292	.477	.769	114	3	51	4.26	2	*O-101(47-6-62)/3-1	12	0.2
1987*SF-N	118	442	69	129	28	4	20	85	34	78	8	8	.292	.351	.509	.860	131	15	75	6.03	-2	*O-116(4-0-115)	16	0.8
1988 SF-N	142	499	53	127	23	1	12	68	37	89	6	5	.255	.315	.377	.692	102	-1	57	3.88	-2	*O-139(0-0-139)	12	-0.7
1989*SF-N	129	345	39	75	23	0	9	41	37	69	4	1	.217	.299	.362	.661	91	-4	38	3.60	-2	*O-116(0-0-116)	7	-0.9
1990 Cle-A	155	590	76	161	32	2	22	95	49	134	3	5	.273	.334	.446	.780	117	10	85	5.06	0	*O-134(104-0-41),D-20	18	0.4
1991 Mil-A	34	111	11	23	6	0	5	20	13	23	1	0	.207	.290	.396	.687	90	-1	12	3.60	-1	O-24(12-0-13)	3	-0.3
*Tor-A	52	177	26	49	9	0	7	28	23	53	3	0	.277	.379	.446	.825	123	7	31	6.32	-2	O-52(52-0-1)/D-9	8	0.3
Yr.	86	288	37	72	15	0	12	48	36	76	4	0	.250	.345	.427	.773	111	6	44	5.20	-2	O-76(64-0-14)/D-9	11	0.0
1992*Tor-A	137	489	64	133	25	4	20	66	59	112	2	2	.272	.359	.462	.821	123	15	81	5.80	-5	*O-132(129-0-4)/D-4	19	0.5
1993 Chi-N	70	140	8	26	5	0	3	15	13	40	0	0	.186	.260	.286	.545	47	-11	10	2.42	1	O-41(29-0-14)	0	-1.1
Cle-A	28	81	11	20	2	0	5	20	11	18	0	1	.247	.337	.457	.794	112	1	12	4.92	0	O-26(2-0-25)/D-2	4	-0.1
1994 Cle-A	42	92	14	18	5	1	5	12	19	31	1	0	.196	.333	.435	.768	96	-1	14	5.06	0	D-25/O-5(5-0-0)	2	-0.2
1995 Tor-A	61	160	22	43	13	0	7	25	25	45	1	1	.269	.374	.481	.856	121	5	29	6.21	-1	O-58(26-0-38)/D-1	5	0.2
Tex-A	13	30	6	7	3	0	2	5	7	5	0	1	.233	.378	.533	.912	131	1	6	6.24	0	O-11(9-0-4)	1	0.1
Yr.	74	190	28	50	16	0	9	30	32	50	1	2	.263	.375	.489	.864	123	6	35	6.22	-1	O-69(35-0-42)/D-1	6	0.3
Total 15	**1410**	**4106**	**498**	**1042**	**227**	**17**	**146**	**618**	**391**	**864**	**34**	**33**	**.254**	**.325**	**.424**	**.749**	**107**	**23**	**558**	**4.64**	**-14**	***O-1215/D-61,3-5**	**118**	**-3.5**

YEAR TM-L	G	AB	R	H	2B	3B	HR	RBI	BB	SO	SB	CS	AVG	OBP	SLG	OPS	OPS+	BR/A	RC	RC/G	FR	G/POS	WS	TPW
• MALER, Jim																								
James Michael Maler b: 8/16/1958, New York, NY BR/TR, 6'4", 230 lbs. Deb: 9/3/1981																								
1981 Sea-A	12	23	1	8	1	0	0	2	2	1	1	0	.348	.423	.391	.814	131	1	4	7.84	0	/1-5,D-2	1	0.1
1982 Sea-A	64	221	18	50	8	3	4	26	12	35	0	0	.226	.275	.344	.619	67	-10	21	3.12	2	1-57/D-5	2	-1.2
1983 Sea-A	26	66	5	12	1	0	1	3	5	11	0	3	.182	.260	.242	.503	38	-7	3	1.43	-1	1-19/D-5	0	-0.9
Total 3	**102**	**310**	**24**	**70**	**10**	**3**	**5**	**31**	**19**	**47**	**1**	**3**	**.226**	**.284**	**.326**	**.609**	**66**	**-16**	**28**	**3.00**	**2**	**/1-81,D-12**	**3**	**-1.9**
• MALINOSKY, Tony																								
Anthony Francis Malinosky b: 10/5/1909, Collinsville, IL BR/TR, 5'10.5", 165 lbs. Deb: 4/26/1937																								
1937 Bro-N	35	79	7	18	2	0	0	3	9	11	0	....	.228	.307	.253	.560	53	-5	7	2.92	-3	3-13,S-11	0	-0.8
• MALKMUS, Bobby																								
Robert Edward Malkmus b: 7/4/1931, Newark, NJ BR/TR, 5'9", 180 lbs. Deb: 6/1/1957																								
1957 Mil-N	13	22	6	2	0	1	0	0	3	3	0	0	.091	.200	.182	.382	4	-3	1	1.29	0	/2-7	0	-0.2
1958 Was-A	41	70	5	13	2	1	0	3	4	15	0	0	.186	.230	.243	.473	31	-7	3	1.54	-4	2-26/3-2,S-1	1	-0.9
1959 Was-A	6	0	0	0	0	0	0	0	0	0	0	0	....	....	....	....	-100	0	0	....	0	....	0	0.0
1960 Phi-N	79	133	16	28	4	1	1	12	11	28	2	2	.211	.271	.278	.549	50	-9	10	2.44	3	S-29,2-23,3-12	2	-0.4
1961 Phi-N	121	342	39	79	8	2	7	31	20	43	1	3	.231	.277	.327	.605	61	-21	30	2.86	3	2-58,S-34,3-25	4	-1.1
1962 Phi-N	8	5	3	1	1	0	0	0	0	1	0	0	.200	.200	.400	.600	58	-0	0	2.70	0	/S-1	0	0.0
Total 6	**268**	**572**	**69**	**123**	**15**	**5**	**8**	**46**	**38**	**90**	**3**	**5**	**.215**	**.266**	**.301**	**.567**	**52**	**-40**	**45**	**2.53**	**2**	**2-114/S-65,3-39**	**7**	**-2.7**
• MALLETT, Jerry																								
Gerald Gordon Mallett b: 9/18/1935, Bonne Terre, MO BR/TR, 6'5", 208 lbs. Deb: 9/19/1959																								
1959 Bos-A	4	15	1	4	0	0	0	1	1	3	0	0	.267	.313	.267	.579	58	-1	1	2.40	3	/O-4(0-4-0)	0	0.2
• MALLON, Les																								
Leslie Clyde Mallon b: 11/21/1905, Sweetwater, TX d: 4/17/1991, Granbury, TX BR/TR, 5'8", 160 lbs. Deb: 4/14/1931																								
1931 Phi-N	122	375	41	116	19	2	1	45	29	40	0	....	.309	.359	.379	.738	91	-4	53	5.09	0	2-97/1-5,3-3,S-3	8	0.2
1932 Phi-N	103	347	44	90	16	0	5	31	28	28	1	....	.259	.318	.349	.667	71	-14	40	3.94	-15	2-88/3-5	4	-2.4
1934 Bos-N	42	166	23	49	6	1	0	18	15	12	0	....	.295	.354	.343	.697	94	-1	20	4.23	-4	2-42	5	-0.2
1935 Bos-N	116	412	48	113	24	2	2	25	28	37	3	....	.274	.322	.357	.679	89	-6	47	4.03	-13	2-73,3-36/O-1	7	-1.3
Total 4	**383**	**1300**	**156**	**368**	**65**	**5**	**8**	**119**	**100**	**117**	**4**	**....**	**.283**	**.336**	**.359**	**.695**	**86**	**-25**	**161**	**4.32**	**-31**	**2-300/3-44,1-5,S-3,O-1**	**24**	**-3.6**
• MALLONEE, Ben																								
Howard Bennett "Lefty" Mallonee b: 3/31/1894, Baltimore, MD d: 2/19/1978, Baltimore, MD BL/TL, 5'6", 150 lbs. Deb: 9/14/1921																								
1921 Phi-A	7	25	2	6	1	0	0	4	1	2	1	0	.240	.269	.280	.549	40	-2	2	2.73	0	/O-6(0-6-0)	0	-0.2
• MALLONEE, Jule																								
Julius Norris Mallonee b: 4/4/1900, Charlotte, NC d: 10/26/1934, Charlotte, NC BL/TR, 6'2", 180 lbs. Deb: 8/4/1925																								
1925 Chi-A	2	3	1	0	0	0	0	0	1	0	0	0	.000	.250	.000	.250	-34	-1	0	.55	-0	/O-1	0	-0.1
• MALLORY, Jim																								
James Baugh "Sunny Jim" Mallory b: 9/1/1918, Lawrenceville, VA d: 8/6/2001, Greenville, NC BR/TR, 6'1", 170 lbs. Deb: 9/8/1940 Career OF: 17-13-7																								
1940 Was-A	4	12	2	2	0	0	0	0	1	1	0	0	.167	.231	.167	.397	5	-2	1	1.44	0	/O-3(1-1-1)	0	-0.1
1945 StL-N	13	43	3	10	2	0	0	5	0	2	0	....	.233	.233	.279	.512	41	-4	3	2.26	-1	O-11(8-3-2)	0	-0.6
NY-N	37	94	10	28	1	0	0	9	6	7	1	....	.298	.340	.309	.649	80	-2	10	4.03	0	O-21(8-9-4)	2	-0.3
Yr.	50	137	13	38	3	0	0	14	6	9	1	....	.277	.308	.299	.607	68	-6	13	3.44	-1	O-32(16-12-6)	2	-0.9
Total 2	**54**	**149**	**15**	**40**	**3**	**0**	**0**	**14**	**7**	**10**	**1**	**0**	**.268**	**.301**	**.289**	**.590**	**63**	**-8**	**14**	**3.26**	**-1**	**/O-35**	**2**	**-1.0**
• MALLORY, Sheldon																								
Sheldon Mallory b: 7/16/1953, Argo, IL BL/TL, 6'2", 175 lbs. Deb: 4/10/1977																								
1977 Oak-A	64	126	19	27	4	1	0	5	11	18	12	5	.214	.293	.262	.555	53	-7	11	2.62	0	O-45(9-17-21)/D-7,1-4	1	-0.8
• MALLOY, Marty																								
Marty Thomas Malloy b: 4/6/1972, Gainesville, FL BL/TR, 5'10" Deb: 9/6/1998																								
1998*Atl-N	11	28	3	5	1	0	1	1	2	2	0	0	.179	.233	.321	.555	44	-2	2	2.61	0	2-10	1	-0.2
2002 Fla-N	24	25	1	3	0	0	0	1	2	8	0	0	.120	.185	.120	.305	-18	-4	1	.65	0	/2-3,3-2	0	-0.4
Total 2	**35**	**53**	**4**	**8**	**1**	**0**	**1**	**2**	**4**	**10**	**0**	**0**	**.151**	**.211**	**.226**	**.437**	**14**	**-7**	**3**	**1.61**	**0**	**/2-13,3-2**	**1**	**-0.6**
• MALMBERG, Harry																								
Harry William "Swede" Malmberg b: 7/31/1925, Fairfield, AL d: 10/29/1976, San Francisco, CA BR/TR, 6'1", 170 lbs. Deb: 4/12/1955 C																								
1955 Det-A	67	208	25	45	5	2	0	19	29	19	0	1	.216	.312	.260	.572	56	-12	17	2.66	6	2-65	4	-0.2
• MALONE, Eddie																								
Edward Russell Malone b: 6/16/1920, Chicago, IL BR/TR, 5'10", 175 lbs. Deb: 7/17/1949																								
1949 Chi-A	55	170	17	46	7	2	1	16	29	19	2	1	.271	.377	.353	.730	97	0	25	5.13	1	C-51	5	0.3
1950 Chi-A	31	71	2	16	2	0	0	10	10	8	0	0	.225	.321	.254	.575	50	-5	5	2.15	2	C-21	1	-0.2
Total 2	**86**	**241**	**19**	**62**	**9**	**2**	**1**	**26**	**39**	**27**	**2**	**1**	**.257**	**.361**	**.324**	**.684**	**83**	**-5**	**30**	**4.17**	**2**	**/C-72**	**6**	**0.1**
• MALONE, Fergy																								
Ferguson G. Malone b: 1842, Ireland d: 1/1/1905, Seattle, WA BR/TL, 5'8", 156 lbs. Deb: 6/3/1871 M/U																								
1871 Ath-n	27	134	33	46	7	1	1	33	9	4	9	3	.343	.385	.433	.817	136	7	26	9.14	4	*C-27	....	0.7
1872 Ath-n	41	213	46	60	5	3	0	39	4	5	3	0	.282	.295	.333	.628	92	-1	22	4.53	4	C-24,1-17	....	0.2
1873 Phi-n	53	259	59	75	11	2	0	43	14	7	2	1	.290	.326	.347	.673	97	-1	31	5.07	2	*C-53/S-1	....	0.2
1874 Chi-n	47	223	33	56	5	0	0	29	4	0	2	1	.251	.264	.274	.538	72	-7	17	3.05	7	*C-47	....	0.1
1875 Phi-n	29	123	15	28	2	1	0	10	1	2	1	0	.228	.234	.260	.494	69	-4	8	2.46	-4	1-22/C-6,O-2(0-2-0)	....	-0.6
1876 Phi-N	22	96	14	22	2	0	0	6	0	1	....	....	.229	.229	.250	.479	60	-4	6	2.13	1	C-20/O-3(0-0-3),S-1	1	-0.2
1884 Phi-U	1	4	0	1	0	0	0	....	0	....	....	....	.250	.250	.250	.500	75	-0	0	2.39	-1	/C-1	0	-0.1
Total 5 n	**197**	**952**	**186**	**265**	**30**	**7**	**1**	**154**	**32**	**18**	**17**	**5**	**.278**	**.302**	**.328**	**.630**	**92**	**-6**	**105**	**4.64**	**14**	**C-157/1-39,O-2,S-1**	**....**	**0.6**
Total 2	**23**	**100**	**14**	**23**	**2**	**0**	**0**	**6**	**0**	**1**	**....**	**....**	**.230**	**.230**	**.250**	**.480**	**61**	**-4**	**6**	**2.14**	**0**	**/C-21,O-3,S-1**	**1**	**-0.3**
• MALONE, Lew																								
Lewis Aloysius Malone b: 3/13/1897, Baltimore, MD d: 2/17/1972, Brooklyn, NY BR/TR, 5'11", 175 lbs. Deb: 5/31/1915																								
1915 Phi-A	76	201	17	41	4	4	1	17	21	40	7	1	.204	.283	.279	.561	70	-6	18	2.87	-14	2-43,3-12/O-4(0-0-4),S-2	3	-2.1
1916 Phi-A	5	4	1	0	0	0	0	0	1	2	0	....	.000	.200	.000	.200	-42	-1	0	.00	0	/S-1	0	-0.1
1917 Bro-N	1	0	1	0	0	0	0	0	0	0	0	....	....	....	....	....	-97	0	0	....	0	....	0	0.0
1919 Bro-N	51	162	9	33	7	3	0	11	6	18	1	....	.204	.232	.284	.516	54	-10	11	2.09	-7	3-47/2-2,S-2	1	-1.7
Total 4	**133**	**367**	**28**	**74**	**11**	**7**	**1**	**28**	**28**	**60**	**8**	**1**	**.202**	**.260**	**.278**	**.538**	**62**	**-17**	**29**	**2.48**	**-22**	**/3-59,2-45,S-5,O-4**	**4**	**-3.9**
• MALONEY, Billy																								
William Alphonse Maloney b: 6/5/1878, Lewiston, ME d: 9/2/1960, Breckinridge, TX BL/TR, 5'10", 177 lbs. Deb: 5/2/1901 U Career OF: 16-414-163																								
1901 Mil-A	86	290	42	85	3	4	0	22	7	....	11	....	.293	.328	.331	.659	87	-5	37	4.59	5	C-72/O-8(0-8-0)	7	0.7
1902 StL-A	30	112	8	23	3	0	0	11	6	....	0	....	.205	.258	.232	.490	37	-9	7	2.07	-2	O-23(1-0-22)/C-7	1	-1.2
Cin-N	27	89	13	22	4	0	1	7	2	....	8	....	.247	.272	.326	.598	77	-3	11	4.00	-1	O-18(10-6-2)/C-7	1	-0.5
1905 Chi-N	145	558	78	145	17	14	2	56	43	....	**59**	....	.260	.325	.351	.676	98	-2	87	5.26	3	*O-145(0-12-134)	21	-0.6
1906 Bro-N	151	566	71	125	15	7	0	32	49	....	38	....	.221	.286	.272	.558	80	-13	58	3.32	4	*O-151(0-149-2)	14	-1.7
1907 Bro-N	144	502	51	115	7	10	0	32	31	....	25	....	.229	.287	.283	.570	86	-9	52	3.29	0	*O-144(0-144-0)	12	-1.7
1908 Bro-N	113	359	31	70	5	7	3	17	24	....	14	....	.195	.255	.273	.528	71	-12	29	2.46	1	*O-107(5-95-3)/C-4	6	-1.8
Total 6	**696**	**2476**	**294**	**585**	**54**	**42**	**6**	**177**	**162**	**....**	**155**	**....**	**.236**	**.294**	**.299**	**.593**	**83**	**-52**	**280**	**3.71**	**11**	**O-596/C-90**	**62**	**-6.7**
• MALONEY, John																								
John Maloney Deb: 9/15/1876 Career OF: 0-3-0																								
1876 NY-N	2	7	1	2	0	1	0	2	0	1	....	....	.286	.286	.571	.857	206	1	1	6.56	-1	/O-2(0-2-0)	1	0.0
1877 Har-N	1	4	0	1	0	0	0	0	0	0	....	....	.250	.250	.250	.500	65	-0	0	2.35	-1	/O-1	0	-0.1
Total 2	**3**	**11**	**1**	**3**	**0**	**1**	**0**	**2**	**0**	**1**	**....**	**....**	**.273**	**.273**	**.455**	**.727**	**155**	**1**	**1**	**4.98**	**-1**	**/O-3**	**1**	**-0.1**
• MALONEY, Pat																								
Patrick William Maloney b: 1/19/1888, Grosvenor Dale, CT d: 6/27/1979, Pawtucket, RI BR/TR, 6', 150 lbs. Deb: 6/19/1912																								
1912 NY-A	25	79	9	17	1	0	0	4	6	....	3	....	.215	.279	.228	.507	43	-6	6	2.41	1	O-20(0-20-0)	1	-0.6
• MALZONE, Frank																								
Frank James Malzone b: 2/28/1930, Bronx, NY BR/TR, 5'10", 180 lbs. Deb: 9/17/1955																								
1955 Bos-A	6	20	2	7	1	0	0	1	1	3	0	0	.350	.381	.400	.781	101	0	3	6.54	2	/3-4	1	0.2
1956 Bos-A	27	103	15	17	3	1	2	11	9	8	1	0	.165	.232	.272	.504	29	-11	6	1.70	1	3-26	1	-1.0
1957 Bos-A★	153	634	82	185	31	5	15	103	31	41	2	1	.292	.326	.427	.753	98	-3	85	4.86	-1	*3-153	18	-0.4
1958 Bos-A★	155	627	76	185	30	2	15	87	33	53	1	3	.295	.334	.421	.755	100	-2	82	4.66	5	*3-155	18	0.3
1959 Bos-A★	154	604	90	169	34	2	19	92	42	58	6	0	.280	.328	.437	.765	103	2	85	4.93	4	*3-154	19	0.6
1960 Bos-A★	152	595	60	161	30	2	14	79	36	42	2	3	.271	.317	.398	.715	89	-12	70	4.02	1	*3-151	13	-1.1
1961 Bos-A	151	590	74	157	21	4	14	87	44	49	1	3	.266	.318	.386	.705	85	-15	68	3.97	-5	*3-149	14	-2.0

YEAR TM-L	G	AB	R	H	2B	3B	HR	RBI	BB	SO	SB	CS	AVG	OBP	SLG	OPS	OPS+	BR/A	RC	RC/G	FR	G/POS	WS	TPW
1962 Bos-A	156	619	74	175	20	3	21	95	35	43	0	1	.283	.321	.426	.748	96	-6	80	4.60	0	*3-156	17	-0.6
1963 Bos-A★	151	580	66	169	25	2	15	71	31	45	0	2	.291	.331	.419	.750	105	2	73	4.39	3	*3-148	16	0.5
1964 Bos-A★	148	537	62	142	19	0	13	56	37	43	0	0	.264	.314	.372	.687	86	-10	64	4.19	-1	*3-143	14	-1.2
1965 Bos-A	106	364	40	87	20	0	3	34	28	38	1	1	.239	.295	.319	.614	70	-14	31	2.76	-2	3-96	3	-1.7
1966 Cal-A	82	155	6	32	5	0	2	12	10	11	0	0	.206	.255	.277	.532	54	-9	10	2.21	-5	3-35	1	-1.5
Total 12	1441	5428	647	1486	239	21	133	728	337	434	14	14	.274	.318	.399	.717	91	-77	656	4.21	2	*3-1370	135	-8.0

• MANCUSO, Frank Frank Octavius Mancuso b: 5/23/1918, Houston, TX BR/TR, 6', 195 lbs. Deb: 4/18/1944

YEAR TM-L	G	AB	R	H	2B	3B	HR	RBI	BB	SO	SB	CS	AVG	OBP	SLG	OPS	OPS+	BR/A	RC	RC/G	FR	G/POS	WS	TPW
1944*StL-A	88	244	19	50	11	0	1	24	20	32	1	0	.205	.271	.262	.533	50	-16	17	2.16	-7	C-87	1	-1.9
1945 StL-A	119	365	39	98	13	3	1	38	46	44	0	2	.268	.354	.329	.682	94	-2	43	4.03	-5	*C-115	12	0.0
1946 StL-A	87	262	22	63	8	3	3	23	30	31	1	0	.240	.323	.328	.651	78	-7	29	3.81	-5	C-85	6	-0.9
1947 Was-A	43	131	5	30	5	1	0	13	5	11	0	0	.229	.257	.282	.540	51	-9	8	1.92	-3	C-35	1	-1.0
Total 4	337	1002	85	241	37	7	5	98	101	118	2	2	.241	.314	.306	.620	74	-33	96	3.21	-20	C-322	20	-3.8

• MANCUSO, Gus August Rodney "Blackie" Mancuso b: 12/5/1905, Galveston, TX d: 10/26/1984, Houston, TX BR/TR, 5'10", 185 lbs. Deb: 4/30/1928 C

YEAR TM-L	G	AB	R	H	2B	3B	HR	RBI	BB	SO	SB	CS	AVG	OBP	SLG	OPS	OPS+	BR/A	RC	RC/G	FR	G/POS	WS	TPW
1928 StL-N	11	38	2	7	0	1	0	3	0	5	0	....	.184	.184	.237	.421	9	-5	2	1.27	2	C-11	1	-0.2
1930*StL-N	76	227	39	83	17	2	7	59	18	16	1	....	.366	.415	.551	.965	126	10	50	8.54	-3	C-61	11	1.0
1931*StL-N	67	187	13	49	16	1	1	23	18	13	2	....	.262	.327	.374	.701	85	-4	24	4.40	2	C-56	7	0.1
1932 StL-N	103	310	25	88	23	1	5	43	30	15	0	....	.284	.347	.413	.760	100	1	46	5.29	4	C-82	11	1.0
1933*NY-N	144	481	39	127	17	2	6	56	48	21	0	....	.264	.331	.345	.676	95	-2	56	3.97	-8	*C-142	16	-0.1
1934 NY-N	122	383	32	94	14	0	7	46	27	19	0	....	.245	.295	.337	.632	70	-16	39	3.36	-3	*C-122	10	-1.2
1935 NY-N★	128	447	33	133	18	2	5	56	30	16	1	....	.298	.342	.380	.722	95	-3	57	4.47	-3	*C-126	14	0.1
1936*NY-N	139	519	55	156	21	3	9	63	39	28	0	....	.301	.351	.405	.755	104	3	73	5.12	2	*C-138	20	1.3
1937*NY-N★	86	287	30	80	17	1	4	39	17	20	1	....	.279	.319	.387	.706	90	-5	36	4.58	2	C-81	11	0.2
1938 NY-N	52	158	19	55	8	0	2	15	17	13	0	....	.348	.411	.437	.848	132	8	29	7.19	-1	C-44	8	0.9
1939 Chi-N	80	251	17	58	10	0	2	17	24	19	0	....	.231	.298	.295	.593	59	-14	23	3.08	-3	C-76	6	-1.3
1940 Bro-N	60	144	16	33	8	0	0	16	13	7	0	....	.229	.293	.285	.578	56	-8	12	2.79	1	C-56	3	-0.5
1941 StL-N	106	328	25	75	13	1	2	37	37	19	0	....	.229	.309	.293	.601	66	-14	31	3.05	1	*C-105	7	-0.7
1942 StL-N	5	13	0	1	0	0	0	1	0	0	0	....	.077	.077	.077	.154	-51	-2	0	.17	-1	/C-3	0	-0.3
NY-N	39	109	4	21	1	1	0	8	14	7	1	....	.193	.285	.220	.505	48	-7	7	1.96	-1	C-38	1	-0.5
Yr.	44	122	4	22	1	1	0	9	14	7	1	....	.180	.265	.205	.470	39	-9	7	1.76	-1	C-41	1	-0.9
1943 NY-N	94	252	11	50	5	0	2	20	28	16	0	....	.198	.284	.242	.526	52	-15	17	2.04	-2	C-77	2	-1.3
1944 NY-N	78	195	15	49	4	1	1	25	30	20	0	....	.251	.351	.297	.649	84	-3	22	3.87	0	C-72	5	0.2
1945 Phi-N	70	176	11	35	5	0	0	16	28	10	2	....	.199	.309	.227	.536	52	-10	13	2.31	4	C-70	2	-0.3
Total 17	1460	4505	386	1194	197	16	53	543	418	264	8	....	.265	.328	.351	.679	84	-89	536	4.08	-5	*C-1360	135	-1.6

• MANDA, Carl Carl Alan Manda b: 11/16/1888, Little River, KS d: 3/9/1983, Artesia, NM BR/TR, 5'10", 170 lbs. Deb: 9/11/1914

YEAR TM-L	G	AB	R	H	2B	3B	HR	RBI	BB	SO	SB	CS	AVG	OBP	SLG	OPS	OPS+	BR/A	RC	RC/G	FR	G/POS	WS	TPW
1914 Chi-A	9	15	2	4	0	0	0	1	3	3	1	....	.267	.389	.267	.656	99	0	2	4.67	-0	/2-7	1	0.0

• MANEY, Vincent S. Vincent Maney b: 10/14/1887, Batavia, NY d: 3/13/1952, Batavia, NY BR/TR, 6' Deb: 5/18/1912

YEAR TM-L	G	AB	R	H	2B	3B	HR	RBI	BB	SO	SB	CS	AVG	OBP	SLG	OPS	OPS+	BR/A	RC	RC/G	FR	G/POS	WS	TPW
1912 Det-A	1	2	0	0	0	0	0	0	1	....	0	....	.000	.500	.000	.500	48	0	0	.00	0	/S-1	0	0.0

• MANGAN, Jim James Daniel Mangan b: 9/24/1929, San Francisco, CA BR/TR, 5'10", 190 lbs. Deb: 4/16/1952

YEAR TM-L	G	AB	R	H	2B	3B	HR	RBI	BB	SO	SB	CS	AVG	OBP	SLG	OPS	OPS+	BR/A	RC	RC/G	FR	G/POS	WS	TPW
1952 Pit-N	11	13	1	2	0	0	0	2	1	3	0	0	.154	.214	.154	.368	4	-2	0	1.22	0	/C-4	0	-0.2
1954 Pit-N	14	26	2	5	0	0	0	2	4	9	0	0	.192	.300	.192	.492	32	-2	2	2.33	1	/C-7	0	-0.1
1956 NY-N	20	20	2	2	0	0	0	1	4	6	0	0	.100	.250	.100	.350	-1	-3	1	.96	0	C-15	0	-0.2
Total 3	45	59	5	9	0	0	0	5	9	18	0	0	.153	.265	.153	.417	14	-7	3	1.57	1	/C-26	0	-0.6

• MANGUAL, Angel Angel Luis (Guilbe) Mangual b: 3/19/1947, Juana Diaz, Puerto Rico BR/TR, 5'10", 180 lbs. Deb: 9/15/1969 Career OF: 82-130-133

YEAR TM-L	G	AB	R	H	2B	3B	HR	RBI	BB	SO	SB	CS	AVG	OBP	SLG	OPS	OPS+	BR/A	RC	RC/G	FR	G/POS	WS	TPW
1969 Pit-N	6	4	1	1	1	0	0	0	0	0	0	0	.250	.250	.500	.750	108	-0	1	4.50	-1	/0-3(2-0-1)	0	-0.1
1971*Oak-A	94	287	32	82	8	1	4	30	17	27	1	4	.286	.326	.362	.688	97	-3	31	3.83	-1	0-81(17-57-9)	8	-0.8
1972*Oak-A	91	272	19	67	13	2	5	32	14	48	0	1	.246	.286	.364	.650	97	-3	26	3.24	-1	0-74(2-22-52)	6	-0.7
1973*Oak-A	74	192	20	43	4	1	3	13	8	34	1	1	.224	.259	.302	.561	61	-11	15	2.60	-2	0-50(14-17-21),D-14/1-2,2	2	-1.5
1974*Oak-A	115	365	37	85	14	4	9	43	17	59	3	0	.233	.267	.367	.634	87	-7	36	3.36	-1	0-74(26-28-29),D-37/3-1	6	-1.2
1975 Oak-A	62	109	13	24	3	0	1	6	3	18	0	1	.220	.241	.275	.516	47	-8	7	2.02	-1	0-39(21-6-14),D-15	0	-1.1
1976 Oak-A	8	12	0	2	1	0	0	1	0	1	0	1	.167	.167	.250	.417	22	-2	0	.61	0	/0-7(0-0-7)	0	-0.1
Total 7	450	1241	122	304	44	8	22	125	59	187	5	8	.245	.280	.346	.627	83	-34	116	3.17	-5	0-328/D-66,1-2,2-1,3-1	22	-5.5

• MANGUAL, Pepe Jose Manuel (Guilbe) Mangual b: 5/23/1952, Ponce, Puerto Rico BR/TR, 5'10", 165 lbs. Deb: 9/6/1972 Career OF: 89-198-18

YEAR TM-L	G	AB	R	H	2B	3B	HR	RBI	BB	SO	SB	CS	AVG	OBP	SLG	OPS	OPS+	BR/A	RC	RC/G	FR	G/POS	WS	TPW
1972 Mon-N	8	11	2	3	0	0	0	0	1	5	0	1	.273	.333	.273	.606	73	-1	1	2.45	0	/0-3(2-0-1)	0	-0.1
1973 Mon-N	33	62	9	11	2	1	3	7	6	18	2	4	.177	.250	.387	.637	71	-4	5	2.43	0	0-22(20-1-1)	0	-0.4
1974 Mon-N	23	61	10	19	3	0	0	4	5	15	5	0	.311	.364	.361	.724	98	-1	10	5.73	0	0-22(18-2-8)	2	0.0
1975 Mon-N	140	514	84	126	16	2	9	45	74	115	33	11	.245	.345	.337	.681	86	-5	65	4.14	-3	*0-138(1-135-2)	13	-1.2
1976 Mon-N	66	215	34	56	9	1	3	16	50	49	17	7	.260	.404	.353	.758	112	7	37	5.94	-2	0-62(34-36-1)	9	0.3
NY-N	41	102	15	19	5	2	1	9	10	32	7	3	.186	.259	.304	.563	63	-5	9	2.66	-1	0-38(12-22-5)	2	-0.8
Yr.	107	317	49	75	14	3	4	25	60	81	24	10	.237	.361	.338	.699	97	2	46	4.81	-3	*0-100(46-58-6)	11	-0.5
1977 NY-N	8	7	1	1	0	0	0	2	1	4	0	0	.143	.250	.143	.393	9	-1	0	1.42	-1	/0-4(2-2-0)	0	-0.1
Total 6	319	972	155	235	35	6	16	83	147	238	64	26	.242	.345	.340	.684	89	-8	127	4.28	-6	0-289	26	-2.4

• MANGUS, George George Graham Mangus b: 5/22/1890, Red Creek, NY d: 8/10/1933, Rutland, MA BL/TR, 5'11.5", 165 lbs. Deb: 8/20/1912

YEAR TM-L	G	AB	R	H	2B	3B	HR	RBI	BB	SO	SB	CS	AVG	OBP	SLG	OPS	OPS+	BR/A	RC	RC/G	FR	G/POS	WS	TPW
1912 Phi-N	10	25	2	5	3	0	0	3	1	6	0	....	.200	.231	.320	.551	47	-2	2	2.21	-1	/0-5(5-0-0)	0	-0.4

• MANION, Clyde Clyde Jennings "Pete" Manion b: 10/30/1896, Big River, MO d: 9/4/1967, Detroit, MI BR/TR, 5'11", 175 lbs. Deb: 5/5/1920

YEAR TM-L	G	AB	R	H	2B	3B	HR	RBI	BB	SO	SB	CS	AVG	OBP	SLG	OPS	OPS+	BR/A	RC	RC/G	FR	G/POS	WS	TPW
1920 Det-A	32	80	4	22	4	1	0	8	4	7	0	0	.275	.318	.350	.668	79	-2	9	3.99	-1	C-30	1	-0.2
1921 Det-A	12	10	0	2	0	0	0	2	2	2	0	0	.200	.385	.200	.585	53	-0	1	3.32	0	/C-3	0	0.0
1922 Det-A	42	69	9	19	4	1	0	12	4	6	0	1	.275	.315	.362	.677	79	-3	8	3.76	-3	C-22/1-1	1	-0.5
1923 Det-A	23	22	0	3	0	0	0	2	2	2	0	0	.136	.208	.136	.345	-8	-3	1	.98	-1	/C-3,1-1	0	-0.4
1924 Det-A	14	13	1	3	0	0	0	2	1	1	0	0	.231	.286	.231	.516	35	-1	1	2.37	-1	/C-3,1-1	0	-0.2
1926 Det-A	75	176	15	35	4	0	0	14	24	16	1	1	.199	.295	.222	.517	36	-16	13	2.35	-2	C-74	3	-1.4
1927 Det-A	1	0	0	0	0	0	0	0	1	0	0	0	....	1.000	....	1.000	175	0	0	∞	0	....	0	0.0
1928 StL-A	76	243	25	55	5	1	2	31	15	18	3	0	.226	.274	.280	.554	44	-19	20	2.69	4	C-71	5	-1.0
1929 StL-A	35	111	16	27	2	0	0	11	15	3	1	0	.243	.333	.261	.595	53	-7	11	3.34	1	C-34	3	-0.3
1930 StL-A	57	148	12	32	1	0	1	11	24	17	0	1	.216	.326	.243	.569	45	-12	13	2.90	2	C-56	3	-0.6
1932 Cin-N	49	135	7	28	4	0	0	12	14	16	0	....	.207	.282	.237	.519	43	-10	10	2.36	-2	C-47	1	-1.0
1933 Cin-N	36	84	3	14	1	0	0	3	8	7	0	....	.167	.239	.179	.418	21	-8	4	1.44	0	C-34	1	-0.7
1934 Cin-N	25	54	4	10	0	0	0	4	4	7	0	....	.185	.241	.185	.427	16	-6	3	1.52	1	C-24	1	-0.4
Total 13	477	1145	96	250	25	3	3	112	118	102	5	3	.218	.293	.253	.546	44	-88	94	2.64	-1	C-401/1-3	19	-6.4

• MANKOWSKI, Phil Philip Anthony Mankowski b: 1/9/1953, Buffalo, NY BL/TR, 6', 180 lbs. Deb: 8/30/1976

YEAR TM-L	G	AB	R	H	2B	3B	HR	RBI	BB	SO	SB	CS	AVG	OBP	SLG	OPS	OPS+	BR/A	RC	RC/G	FR	G/POS	WS	TPW
1976 Det-A	24	85	9	23	2	1	1	4	4	8	0	0	.271	.303	.353	.656	88	-1	8	3.44	1	3-23	2	-0.1
1977 Det-A	94	286	21	79	7	3	3	27	16	41	1	2	.276	.319	.353	.672	79	-9	32	3.91	8	3-85/2-1	7	-0.2
1978 Det-A	88	222	28	61	8	0	4	20	22	28	2	3	.275	.346	.365	.710	97	-1	26	3.91	1	3-80/D-1	6	-0.1
1979 Det-A	42	99	11	22	4	0	0	8	10	16	0	0	.222	.294	.263	.556	50	-7	8	2.45	2	3-36/D-1	1	-0.5
1980 NY-N	8	12	1	2	1	0	0	1	2	4	0	0	.167	.286	.250	.536	52	-1	1	2.72	-1	/3-3	0	-0.2
1982 NY-N	13	35	2	8	1	0	0	4	1	6	0	1	.229	.250	.257	.507	42	-3	2	1.37	1	3-13	0	-0.3
Total 6	269	739	72	195	23	4	8	64	55	103	3	6	.264	.318	.338	.657	79	-22	76	3.49	11	3-240/D-2,2-1	16	-1.3

• MANLOVE, Charlie Charles Henry Weeks "Chick" Manlove b: 10/8/1862, Philadelphia, PA d: 2/12/1952, Altoona, PA BR/TR, 5'9", 165 lbs. Deb: 5/31/1884

YEAR TM-L	G	AB	R	H	2B	3B	HR	RBI	BB	SO	SB	CS	AVG	OBP	SLG	OPS	OPS+	BR/A	RC	RC/G	FR	G/POS	WS	TPW
1884 Alt-U	2	7	1	3	0	0	0	....	0	....	....	....	.429	.429	.429	.857	188	1	1	9.23	-1	/C-1,0-1	0	0.0
NY-N	3	10	0	0	0	0	0	0	0	4	....	....	.000	.000	.000	.000	-98	-2	0	.00	0	/C-3,0-1	0	-0.2

YEAR TM-L	G	AB	R	H	2B	3B	HR	RBI	BB	SO	SB	CS	AVG	OBP	SLG	OPS	OPS+	BR/A	RC	RC/G	FR	G/POS	WS	TPW
• MANN, Fred	Fred J. Mann b: 4/1/1858, Sutton, VT d: 4/16/1916, Springfield, MA BL, 5'10.5", 178 lbs. Deb: 5/1/1882 Career OF: 39-444-28																							
1882 Wor-N	19	77	12	18	5	0	0	7	2	15	....	....	.234	.253	.299	.552	74	-2	6	2.78	-8	3-18/1-1	1	-0.9
Phi-a	29	121	13	28	7	4	0	....	4	....	....	....	.231	.256	.355	.611	93	-2	11	3.40	-10	3-29	3	-1.0
1883 Col-a	96	394	61	98	18	13	1	0	18	....	....	....	.249	.282	.368	.650	117	9	42	3.96	-5	*O-82(2-80-0)/1-9,3-6,S-1	10	0.0
1884 Col-a	99	366	70	101	12	18	7	0	25	....	....	....	.276	.341	.464	.805	174	31	59	6.16	-6	*O-97(0-97-0)/2-2	20	2.0
1885 Pit-a	99	391	60	99	17	6	0	41	31	....	....	....	.253	.318	.327	.645	106	4	42	3.85	-9	*O-97(0-97-0)/3-3	11	-0.8
1886 Pit-a	116	440	85	110	16	14	2	60	45	....	26	....	.250	.335	.364	.698	119	11	64	5.22	-6	*O-116(0-115-1)	16	0.1
1887 Cle-a	64	282	45	103	15	7	2	41	23	....	25	....	.365	.385	.444	.829	135	13	55	8.33	-1	O-64(37-0-27)	9	0.8
Phi-a	55	244	42	78	14	6	0	32	15	....	16	....	.320	.336	.389	.725	102	0	36	5.88	-4	O-55(0-55-0)	6	-0.4
Yr.	119	526	87	181	29	13	2	73	38	....	41	....	.344	.362	.418	.780	119	13	91	7.15	-5	*O-119(37-55-27)	15	0.4
Total 6	**577**	**2315**	**388**	**635**	**104**	**68**	**12**	**181**	**163**	**15**	**67**	**....**	**.274**	**.323**	**.383**	**.707**	**123**	**64**	**315**	**5.12**	**-48**	**O-511/3-56,1-10,2-2,S-1**	**76**	**-0.1**
• MANN, Garth	Ben Garth "Red" Mann b: 11/16/1915, Brandon, TX d: 9/11/1980, Italy, TX BR/TR, 6', 155 lbs. Deb: 5/14/1944																							
1944 Chi-N	1	0	1	0	0	0	0	0	0	0	0	....	....	....	....	....	-101	0	0	....	0	....	0	0.0
• MANN, Johnny	John Leo Mann b: 2/4/1898, Fontanet, IN d: 3/31/1977, Terre Haute, IN BR/TR, 5'11", 160 lbs. Deb: 4/18/1928																							
1928 Chi-A	6	6	0	2	0	0	0	1	1	0	0	0	.333	.429	.333	.762	104	0	1	6.16	0	/3-2	0	0.0
• MANN, Kelly	Kelly John Mann b: 8/17/1967, Santa Monica, CA BR/TR, 6'3", 215 lbs. Deb: 9/4/1989																							
1989 Atl-N	7	24	1	5	2	0	0	1	0	6	0	0	.208	.240	.292	.532	50	-2	1	1.96	1	/C-7	0	0.0
1990 Atl-N	11	28	2	4	1	0	1	2	0	6	0	0	.143	.143	.286	.429	14	-3	1	.59	0	C-10	0	-0.3
Total 2	**18**	**52**	**3**	**9**	**3**	**0**	**1**	**3**	**0**	**12**	**0**	**0**	**.173**	**.189**	**.288**	**.477**	**31**	**-5**	**2**	**1.19**	**1**	**/C-17**	**0**	**-0.3**
• MANN, Les	Leslie "Major" Mann b: 11/18/1893, Lincoln, NE d: 1/14/1962, Pasadena, CA BR/TR, 5'9", 172 lbs. Deb: 4/30/1913 Career OF: 708-414-277																							
1913 Bos-N	120	407	54	103	24	7	3	51	18	73	7	....	.253	.291	.369	.660	86	-9	43	3.56	2	*O-120(12-103-6)	10	-1.5
1914*Bos-N	126	389	44	96	16	11	4	40	24	50	9	....	.247	.292	.375	.668	98	-3	43	3.71	15	*O-123(5-104-14)	13	0.5
1915 Chi-F	135	470	74	144	12	**19**	4	58	36	40	18	....	.306	.357	.438	.795	142	22	76	5.91	0	*O-130(94-7-33)/S-1	23	1.8
1916 Chi-N	127	415	46	113	13	9	2	29	19	31	11	7	.272	.307	.361	.669	95	-4	48	3.90	-1	*O-115(74-20-26)	9	-1.1
1917 Chi-N	117	444	63	121	19	10	1	44	27	46	14	....	.273	.316	.367	.683	101	-0	54	4.16	-2	*O-116(106-11-2)	14	-0.8
1918*Chi-N	129	489	69	141	27	7	2	55	38	45	21	....	.288	.342	.384	.727	119	11	70	4.89	-4	*O-129(129-0-0)	20	0.1
1919 Chi-N	80	299	31	68	8	8	1	22	11	29	12	....	.227	.257	.318	.575	72	-11	26	2.83	4	O-78(78-0-0)	5	-1.2
Bos-N	40	145	15	41	6	4	3	20	9	14	7	....	.283	.329	.441	.770	136	6	22	5.32	3	O-40(40-0-0)	5	0.8
Yr.	120	444	46	109	14	12	4	42	20	43	19	....	.245	.281	.358	.639	93	-5	49	3.60	7	*O-118(118-0-0)	10	-0.4
1920 Bos-N	115	424	48	117	7	8	3	32	38	42	7	7	.276	.341	.351	.693	104	3	52	4.22	3	*O-110(102-0-8)	12	0.2
1921 StL-N	97	256	57	84	12	7	7	30	23	28	5	5	.328	.390	.512	.902	139	14	50	7.23	-1	O-79(1-66-12)	12	1.0
1922 StL-N	84	147	42	51	14	1	2	20	16	12	0	1	.347	.415	.497	.911	141	9	30	8.06	0	O-57(10-47-0)	7	0.7
1923 StL-N	38	89	20	33	5	2	5	11	9	5	0	0	.371	.434	.640	1.075	184	11	25	11.76	1	O-26(5-6-16)	6	1.0
Cin-N	8	1	1	0	0	0	0	0	0	0	0	0	.000	.000	.000	.000	-102	-0	0	.00	0	....	0	0.0
Yr.	46	90	21	33	5	2	5	11	9	5	0	0	.367	.430	.633	1.063	181	11	25	11.55	1	O-26(5-6-16)	6	0.9
1924 Bos-N	32	102	13	28	7	4	0	10	8	10	1	0	.275	.333	.422	.755	106	1	15	5.19	1	O-28(7-0-21)	3	0.0
1925 Bos-N	60	184	27	63	11	4	2	20	5	11	6	1	.342	.373	.478	.851	127	8	33	6.84	1	O-57(5-11-41)	7	0.5
1926 Bos-N	50	129	23	39	8	2	1	20	9	9	5	....	.302	.348	.419	.766	116	3	18	5.11	1	O-46(17-17-16)	4	0.2
1927 Bos-N	29	66	8	17	3	1	0	6	8	3	2	....	.258	.338	.333	.671	87	-1	8	3.96	1	O-24(5-3-17)	1	-0.1
NY-N	29	67	13	22	4	1	2	10	8	7	2	....	.328	.400	.507	.907	142	4	13	7.75	1	O-22(15-5-2)	3	0.4
Yr.	58	133	21	39	7	2	2	16	16	10	4	....	.293	.369	.421	.790	114	3	21	5.76	2	O-46(20-8-19)	4	0.2
1928 NY-N	82	193	29	51	7	1	2	25	18	9	2	....	.264	.330	.342	.672	76	-7	22	3.75	-2	O-68(3-14-63)	3	-1.1
Total 16	**1498**	**4716**	**677**	**1332**	**203**	**106**	**44**	**503**	**324**	**464**	**129**	**21**	**.282**	**.332**	**.398**	**.731**	**110**	**57**	**649**	**4.80**	**21**	***O-1368/S-1**	**157**	**1.1**
• MANNING, Jack	John E. Manning b: 12/20/1853, Braintree, MA d: 8/15/1929, Boston, MA BR/TR, 5'8.5", 158 lbs. Deb: 4/23/1873 M NA OF: 2-2-67 Career OF: 2-16-605 ♦																							
1873 Bos-n	32	159	29	43	6	1	0	22	1	11	1	0	.270	.275	.321	.596	71	-7	15	3.85	2	1-29/O-5(2-0-3)	....	-0.3
1874 Bal-n	42	174	32	61	8	2	0	18	2	2	0	0	.351	.358	.420	.777	149	11	27	7.11	-12	2-22,P-22/S-4,1-1,3-1	....	-0.6
Har-n	1	5	1	1	0	0	0	0	0	0	0	0	.200	.200	.200	.400	27	-0	0	1.54	-2	/3-1	....	-0.2
Yr.	43	179	33	62	8	2	0	18	2	2	0	0	.346	.354	.413	.767	146	11	27	6.92	-13	2-22,P-22/S-4,3-2,1-1	....	-0.8
1875 Bos-n	77	348	71	94	11	3	1	46	2	9	5	5	.270	.274	.328	.602	104	1	33	3.81	0	*O-65(0-2-64),P-27/1-3,3-1	....	0.3
1876 Bos-N	70	295	52	76	13	0	2	25	7	5	....	....	.258	.281	.330	.611	101	1	27	3.62	-5	*O-56(0-1-55),P-34/2-1,S-1	19	0.0
1877 Cin-N	57	252	47	80	16	7	0	36	5	6	....	....	.317	.331	.437	.767	157	17	37	5.96	-12	S-26,1-17,O-12(1-10-1),P-10/2	8	-1.2
1878 Bos-N	60	248	41	63	10	1	0	23	10	16	....	....	.254	.283	.302	.585	86	-4	22	3.23	-15	*O-59(0-3-56)/P-3	7	-3.2
1880 Cin-N	48	190	20	41	6	3	2	17	7	15	....	....	.216	.244	.311	.554	87	-2	15	2.72	-7	O-47(0-2-47)/1-1	2	-0.9
1881 Buf-N	1	1	0	0	0	0	0	0	0	0	....	....	.000	.000	.000	.000	-101	-0	0	.00	1	/O-1	0	0.0
1883 Phi-N	98	420	60	112	31	5	0	37	20	37	....	....	.267	.300	.364	.664	110	7	47	4.20	2	*O-98(0-0-98)	7	0.7
1884 Phi-N	104	424	71	115	29	4	5	52	40	67	....	....	.271	.334	.394	.728	134	18	57	5.09	-7	*O-104(0-0-104)	19	0.9
1885 Phi-N	107	445	61	114	24	4	3	40	37	27	....	....	.256	.313	.348	.662	116	9	50	4.06	-8	*O-107(0-0-107)	15	-0.1
1886 Bal-a	137	556	78	124	18	7	1	45	50	....	24	....	.223	.291	.286	.577	83	-10	55	3.41	-8	*O-137(0-0-137)	14	-1.8
Total 3 n	**152**	**686**	**133**	**199**	**25**	**6**	**1**	**86**	**5**	**22**	**6**	**5**	**.290**	**.295**	**.348**	**.644**	**107**	**5**	**75**	**4.56**	**-11**	**/O-70,P-49,1-33,2-22,S-4,3**	**....**	**-0.7**
Total 9	**682**	**2831**	**430**	**725**	**147**	**31**	**13**	**275**	**176**	**173**	**24**	**....**	**.256**	**.301**	**.345**	**.646**	**109**	**37**	**310**	**4.04**	**-59**	**O-621/P-47,S-27,1-18,2-3**	**91**	**-5.6**
• MANNING, Jim	James H. Manning b: 1/31/1862, Fall River, MA d: 10/22/1929, Edinburg, TX BB/TR, 5'7", 157 lbs. Deb: 5/16/1884 M/U Career OF: 118-135-8																							
1884 Bos-N	89	345	52	83	8	6	2	35	19	47	....	....	.241	.280	.316	.596	87	-5	31	3.29	0	O-73(1-72-0)/2-9,S-9,3-3	9	-0.6
1885 Bos-N	84	306	34	63	8	9	2	27	19	36	....	....	.206	.252	.310	.563	84	-5	25	2.73	6	*O-83(12-63-8)/S-1	6	-0.1
Det-N	20	78	15	21	4	0	1	9	4	10	....	....	.269	.305	.359	.664	114	1	9	4.14	-8	S-20	2	-0.6
Yr.	104	384	49	84	12	9	3	36	23	46	....	....	.219	.263	.320	.583	90	-4	33	3.00	-2	*O-83(12-63-8),S-21	8	-0.7
1886 Det-N	26	97	14	18	2	3	0	7	6	10	7	....	.186	.233	.268	.501	50	-6	8	2.69	-1	O-26(26-0-0)/S-1	1	-0.7
1887 Det-N	13	57	5	15	1	0	0	3	5	4	3	....	.263	.276	.212	.487	36	-4	4	2.50	-4	O-10(10-0-0)/S-3	0	-0.7
1889 KC-a	132	506	68	103	16	7	3	68	54	61	58	....	.204	.297	.281	.577	61	-27	61	4.00	-13	O-69(69-0-0),2-63/3-1,S-1	7	-3.4
Total 5	**364**	**1389**	**188**	**303**	**39**	**25**	**8**	**149**	**107**	**168**	**68**	**....**	**.218**	**.278**	**.297**	**.575**	**74**	**-46**	**137**	**3.40**	**-19**	**O-261/2-72,S-35,3-4**	**25**	**-6.1**
• MANNING, Rick	Richard Eugene Manning b: 9/2/1954, Niagara Falls, NY BL/TR, 6'1", 180 lbs. Deb: 5/23/1975 Career OF: 90-1317-118																							
1975 Cle-A	120	480	69	137	16	5	3	35	44	62	19	11	.285	.348	.358	.706	100	0	60	4.38	4	*O-118(28-69-32)/D-1	15	-0.1
1976 Cle-A	138	552	73	161	24	7	6	43	41	75	16	10	.292	.341	.393	.734	116	9	72	4.60	-3	*O-136(0-136-0)	19	0.3
1977 Cle-A	68	252	33	57	7	3	5	18	21	35	9	5	.226	.286	.337	.623	71	-10	24	3.09	0	O-68(0-68-0)	4	-1.1
1978 Cle-A	148	566	65	149	27	3	3	50	38	62	12	12	.263	.311	.337	.648	83	-15	57	3.44	-1	*O-144(0-144-0)	11	-1.9
1979 Cle-A	144	560	67	145	12	2	3	51	55	48	30	8	.259	.326	.304	.630	71	-18	59	3.53	-2	*O-141(0-141-0)/D-1	11	-2.2
1980 Cle-A	140	471	55	110	17	4	3	52	63	66	12	6	.234	.326	.306	.632	74	-15	49	3.34	0	*O-139(0-139-0)	8	-1.7
1981 Cle-A	103	360	47	88	15	3	4	33	40	57	25	3	.244	.320	.336	.656	91	1	44	4.17	9	*O-103(0-103-0)	11	0.9
1982 Cle-A	152	562	71	152	18	2	8	44	54	60	12	8	.270	.334	.352	.687	89	-8	66	4.13	-2	*O-152(0-152-0)	12	-1.2
1983 Cle-A	50	194	20	54	6	0	1	10	12	22	7	3	.278	.320	.325	.645	75	-6	20	3.53	0	O-50(0-50-0)	3	-0.7
Mil-A	108	375	40	86	14	4	3	33	26	40	11	2	.229	.281	.312	.593	68	-15	33	2.96	-6	*O-108(0-108-0)	5	-2.2
Yr.	158	569	60	140	20	4	4	43	38	62	18	5	.246	.294	.316	.611	71	-21	53	3.15	-6	*O-158(0-158-0)	8	-2.9
1984 Mil-A	119	341	53	85	10	5	7	31	34	32	5	7	.249	.319	.370	.689	94	-5	39	3.84	-10	*O-114(0-113-0)/D-1	7	-1.6
1985 Mil-A	79	216	19	47	9	1	2	18	14	19	1	0	.218	.265	.296	.562	54	-14	18	2.75	-6	O-74(1-57-17)/D-2	2	-2.1
1986 Mil-A	89	205	31	52	7	3	8	27	17	20	5	3	.254	.314	.434	.748	98	-1	27	4.37	-1	O-83(40-29-18)/D-5	5	-0.5
1987 Mil-A	97	114	21	26	7	1	0	13	12	18	4	0	.228	.302	.307	.609	60	-6	11	3.25	0	O-78(21-8-51)/D-2	1	-0.7
Total 13	**1555**	**5248**	**664**	**1349**	**189**	**43**	**56**	**458**	**471**	**616**	**168**	**78**	**.257**	**.319**	**.341**	**.661**	**85**	**-103**	**580**	**3.74**	**-18**	***O-1508/D-12**	**114**	**-14.8**
• MANNING, Tim	Timothy Edward Manning b: 12/3/1853, Henley-on-Thames, England d: 6/11/1934, Oak Park, IL BR/TR, 5'10", 170 lbs. Deb: 5/1/1882																							
1882 Pro-N	21	76	7	8	0	0	0	8	5	13	....	....	.105	.160	.105	.266	-13	-9	1	.53	-9	S-17/C-4	0	-1.6
1883 Bal-a	35	121	23	26	5	0	0	0	14	....	....	....	.215	.296	.256	.552	77	-3	9	2.77	1	2-35	2	-0.1
1884 Bal-a	91	341	49	70	14	5	2	0	26	....	....	....	.205	.275	.293	.569	82	-6	28	2.86	0	*2-91	10	-0.3
1885 Bal-a	43	157	17	32	8	1	0	16	10	....	....	....	.204	.265	.268	.532	69	-5	11	2.46	0	2-41/3-3	3	-0.3

YEAR TM-L	G	AB	R	H	2B	3B	HR	RBI	BB	SO	SB	CS	AVG	OBP	SLG	OPS	OPS+	BR/A	RC	RC/G	FR	G/POS	WS	TPW
Pro-N	10	35	3	2	1	0	0	0	1	11	....	....	.057	.083	.086	.169	-47	-5	0	.21	-2	S-10	0	-0.7
Total 4	200	730	99	138	28	6	2	24	56	24	....	....	.189	.256	.252	.508	63	-28	51	2.35	-9	2-167/S-27,C-4,3-3	15	-2.8

• MANNO, Don Donald D. Manno b: 5/4/1915, Williamsport, PA d: 3/11/1995, Williamsport, PA BR/TR, 6'1", 190 lbs. Deb: 9/22/1940 Career OF: 5-0-2

YEAR TM-L	G	AB	R	H	2B	3B	HR	RBI	BB	SO	SB	CS	AVG	OBP	SLG	OPS	OPS+	BR/A	RC	RC/G	FR	G/POS	WS	TPW
1940 Bos-N	3	7	1	2	0	0	1	4	0	2	0	....	.286	.286	.714	1.000	177	1	1	7.71	0	/O-2(0-0-2)	1	0.1
1941 Bos-N	22	30	2	5	1	0	0	4	3	7	0	....	.167	.242	.200	.442	27	-3	1	1.23	-1	/O-5(5-0-0),3-3,1-1	0	-0.4
Total 2	25	37	3	7	1	0	1	8	3	9	0	....	.189	.250	.297	.547	53	-2	3	2.25	-1	/O-7,3-3,1-1	1	-0.4

• MANRIQUE, Fred Fred Eloy (Reyes) Manrique b: 11/5/1961, Edo Bolivar, Venezuela BR/TR, 6'1", 175 lbs. Deb: 8/23/1981

YEAR TM-L	G	AB	R	H	2B	3B	HR	RBI	BB	SO	SB	CS	AVG	OBP	SLG	OPS	OPS+	BR/A	RC	RC/G	FR	G/POS	WS	TPW
1981 Tor-A	14	28	1	4	0	0	0	1	0	12	0	1	.143	.172	.143	.315	-8	-4	1	.63	0	S-11/3-2,D-1	0	-0.3
1984 Tor-A	10	9	0	3	0	0	0	1	0	1	0	0	.333	.333	.333	.667	82	-0	1	2.57	0	/2-9,D-1	0	0.0
1985 Mon-N	9	13	5	4	1	1	1	1	1	3	0	0	.308	.357	.769	1.126	219	2	4	10.99	0	/2-2,S-2,3-1	1	0.2
1986 StL-N	13	17	2	3	0	0	1	1	1	1	1	0	.176	.222	.353	.575	57	-1	1	2.03	0	/3-4,2-1	0	-0.1
1987 Chi-A	115	298	30	77	13	3	4	29	19	69	5	3	.258	.305	.362	.667	74	-12	33	3.74	2	2-92,S-23/D-5	7	-0.4
1988 Chi-A	140	345	43	81	10	6	5	37	21	54	6	5	.235	.285	.342	.627	75	-13	33	3.01	-5	*2-129,S-12/D-1	8	-1.5
1989 Chi-A	65	187	23	56	13	1	2	30	8	30	0	4	.299	.335	.412	.747	112	0	23	4.20	-3	2-57/S-2,3-1	7	-0.1
Tex-A	54	191	23	55	12	0	2	22	9	33	4	1	.288	.320	.382	.702	96	-1	24	4.25	-6	S-37,2-17/3-6,D-1	6	-0.5
Yr.	119	378	46	111	25	1	4	52	17	63	4	5	.294	.327	.397	.724	104	-1	46	4.23	-9	2-74,S-39/3-7,D-1	13	-0.6
1990 Min-A	69	228	22	54	10	0	5	29	4	35	2	0	.237	.256	.346	.603	63	-12	18	2.66	-8	2-67/D-1	2	-1.9
1991 Oak-A	9	21	2	3	0	0	0	0	2	1	0	0	.143	.217	.143	.360	2	-3	1	.87	0	/S-7,2-2	0	-0.2
Total 9	498	1337	151	340	59	11	20	151	65	239	18	14	.254	.293	.360	.653	79	-44	137	3.40	-21	2-376/S-94,3-14,D-10	31	-4.9

• MANSELL, John John Mansell b: 1861, Auburn, NY d: 2/20/1925, Romulus, NY BL, 5'10", 168 lbs. Deb: 5/9/1882

YEAR TM-L	G	AB	R	H	2B	3B	HR	RBI	BB	SO	SB	CS	AVG	OBP	SLG	OPS	OPS+	BR/A	RC	RC/G	FR	G/POS	WS	TPW
1882 Phi-a	31	126	17	30	3	1	0	17	4	....	....	....	.238	.262	.278	.539	73	-4	9	2.74	-4	O-31(0-31-0)	2	-0.9

• MANSELL, Mike Michael R. Mansell b: 1/15/1858, Auburn, NY d: 12/4/1902, Auburn, NY BL, 5'11", 175 lbs. Deb: 5/1/1879 Career OF: 335-6-30

YEAR TM-L	G	AB	R	H	2B	3B	HR	RBI	BB	SO	SB	CS	AVG	OBP	SLG	OPS	OPS+	BR/A	RC	RC/G	FR	G/POS	WS	TPW
1879 Syr-N	67	242	24	52	4	2	1	13	5	45	....	....	.215	.231	.260	.491	69	-6	15	2.20	8	*O-67(67-0-0)	3	-0.2
1880 Cin-N	53	187	22	36	6	2	2	12	4	37	....	....	.193	.209	.278	.487	64	-7	11	2.03	8	O-53(53-0-0)	2	-0.1
1882 Pit-a	79	347	59	96	**18**	**16**	2	....	7	....	....	....	.277	.291	.438	.729	150	17	45	5.06	4	*O-79(79-0-0)	12	1.7
1883 Pit-a	96	412	90	106	12	13	3	0	25	....	....	....	.257	.300	.371	.671	120	11	47	4.30	3	*O-96(96-0-0)	11	0.9
1884 Pit-a	27	100	15	14	0	3	1	0	7	....	....	....	.140	.204	.230	.434	40	-6	5	1.54	-2	O-27(24-0-3)	0	-0.9
Phi-a	20	70	6	14	1	1	0	0	5	....	....	....	.200	.253	.243	.496	59	-3	4	2.17	-1	O-20(16-4-0)	1	-0.4
Ric-a	29	113	21	34	2	5	0	0	8	....	....	....	.301	.363	.407	.770	153	7	17	5.96	-4	O-29(0-2-27)	5	0.2
Yr.	76	283	42	62	3	9	1	0	20	....	....	....	.219	.280	.304	.584	90	-3	26	3.28	-8	*O-76(40-6-30)	6	-1.1
Total 5	371	1471	237	352	43	42	9	25	61	82	....	....	.239	.271	.344	.615	106	12	145	3.60	16	O-371	34	1.2

• MANSELL, Tom Thomas E. "Brick" Mansell b: 1/1/1855, Auburn, NY d: 10/6/1934, Auburn, NY BL/TR, 5'8", 160 lbs. Deb: 5/1/1879 Career OF: 127-29-37 ♦

YEAR TM-L	G	AB	R	H	2B	3B	HR	RBI	BB	SO	SB	CS	AVG	OBP	SLG	OPS	OPS+	BR/A	RC	RC/G	FR	G/POS	WS	TPW
1879 Tro-N	40	177	29	43	6	0	0	11	3	9	....	....	.243	.256	.277	.532	81	-3	13	2.68	-4	O-40(38-2-0)	2	-0.9
Syr-N	1	4	0	1	0	0	0	0	0	0	....	....	.250	.250	.250	.500	74	-0	0	2.39	0	/O-1	0	0.0
Yr.	41	181	29	44	6	0	0	11	3	9	....	....	.243	.255	.276	.532	81	-3	13	2.68	-5	O-41(38-2-1)	2	-0.9
1883 Det-N	34	131	22	29	4	1	0	10	8	13	....	....	.221	.266	.267	.533	66	-5	10	2.57	-4	O-34(0-0-34)/P-1	1	-1.8
StL-a	28	112	23	45	8	1	0	24	7	....	....	....	.402	.437	.491	.928	187	11	25	10.30	-4	O-28(25-2-1)	7	0.5
1884 Cin-a	65	266	49	66	4	6	0	23	15	....	....	....	.248	.301	.308	.609	94	-2	25	3.48	-13	O-65(41-25-1)	6	-1.5
Col-a	23	77	9	15	1	3	0	6	6	....	....	....	.195	.262	.286	.548	85	-1	6	2.62	-1	O-23(23-0-0)	1	-0.2
Yr.	88	343	58	81	5	9	0	29	21	....	....	....	.236	.292	.303	.595	92	-2	31	3.27	-14	*O-88(64-25-1)	7	-1.8
Total 3	191	767	132	199	23	11	0	74	39	22	....	....	.259	.300	.318	.619	99	1	78	3.83	-27	O-191/P-1	17	-4.0

• MANTILLA, Felix Felix (Lamela) Mantilla b: 7/29/1934, Isabella, Puerto Rico BR/TR, 6', 160 lbs. Deb: 6/21/1956 Career OF: 74-76-10

YEAR TM-L	G	AB	R	H	2B	3B	HR	RBI	BB	SO	SB	CS	AVG	OBP	SLG	OPS	OPS+	BR/A	RC	RC/G	FR	G/POS	WS	TPW
1956 Mil-N	35	53	9	15	1	1	0	3	1	8	0	1	.283	.309	.340	.649	79	-2	5	3.36	2	S-15/3-3	1	0.1
1957★Mil-N	71	182	28	43	9	1	4	21	14	34	2	0	.236	.298	.363	.661	82	-4	20	3.77	3	S-35,2-13/3-7,O-1	5	0.2
1958★Mil-N	85	226	37	50	5	1	7	19	20	20	2	0	.221	.285	.345	.630	72	-9	22	3.17	-2	O-43(12-33-0),2-21/S-5,3-2	4	-1.1
1959 Mil-N	103	251	26	54	5	0	3	19	16	31	6	1	.215	.268	.271	.539	48	-18	18	2.30	-5	2-60,S-23/3-9,O-7(0-7-0)	2	-1.8
1960 Mil-N	63	148	21	38	7	0	3	11	7	16	3	1	.257	.295	.365	.660	86	-3	16	3.83	-4	2-26,S-25/O-8(3-5-0)	4	-0.5
1961 Mil-N	45	93	13	20	3	0	1	5	10	16	1	1	.215	.298	.280	.578	58	-6	8	2.80	-8	S-19,2-10,O-10(2-6-2)/3-6	1	-1.3
1962 NY-N	141	466	54	128	17	4	11	59	37	51	3	1	.275	.335	.399	.734	94	-4	62	4.66	-8	3-95,S-25,2-14	8	-0.9
1963 Bos-A	66	178	27	56	8	0	6	15	20	14	2	1	.315	.384	.461	.845	131	8	31	6.56	-1	S-27,O-11(0-11-0)/2-5	7	0.9
1964 Bos-A	133	425	69	123	20	1	30	64	41	46	0	1	.289	.357	.553	.910	142	23	81	6.97	-2	O-48(36-5-8),2-45/3-7,S-6	19	2.4
1965 Bos-A★	150	534	60	147	17	2	18	92	79	84	7	3	.275	.377	.416	.793	118	16	83	5.29	-14	*2-123,O-27(20-8-0)/1-2	15	1.2
1966 Hou-N	77	151	16	33	5	0	6	22	11	32	1	0	.219	.280	.371	.651	85	-3	15	3.15	-1	1-14,3-14/2-9,O-1	2	-0.4
Total 11	969	2707	360	707	97	10	89	330	256	352	27	10	.261	.331	.403	.734	100	-1	361	4.59	-41	2-326,S-180,O-156,3-143/1-16	68	-1.2

• MANTLE, Mickey Mickey Charles "The Mick,The Commerce Comet,Muscles" Mantle
b: 10/20/1931, Spavinaw, OK d: 8/13/1995, Dallas, TX BB/TR, 5'11.5", 198 lbs. Deb: 4/17/1951 C HOF: 1974 Career OF: 129-1745-146

YEAR TM-L	G	AB	R	H	2B	3B	HR	RBI	BB	SO	SB	CS	AVG	OBP	SLG	OPS	OPS+	BR/A	RC	RC/G	FR	G/POS	WS	TPW
1951★NY-A	96	341	61	91	11	5	13	65	43	74	8	7	.267	.349	.443	.792	117	6	55	5.67	-3	O-86(0-3-85)	13	0.2
1952★NY-A★	142	549	94	171	37	7	23	87	75	111	4	1	.311	.394	.530	**.924**	165	**49**	123	**8.61**	0	*O-141(0-121-20)/3-1	32	4.7
1953★NY-A★	127	461	105	136	24	3	21	92	79	90	8	4	.295	.398	.497	.895	145	32	100	8.19	1	*O-121(0-116-4)/S-1	26	2.7
1954 NY-A★	146	543	**129**	163	17	12	27	102	102	107	5	2	.300	.411	.525	.936	160	48	127	8.75	1	*O-144(0-143-1)/S-4,2-1	**36**	4.4
1955★NY-A★	147	517	121	158	25	**11**	**37**	99	**113**	97	8	1	.306	**.433**	**.611**	**1.044**	**181**	**64**	148	**10.84**	2	*O-145(0-145-0)/S-2	**41**	**5.9**
1956★NY-A★	150	533	**132**	188	22	5	**52**	**130**	112	99	10	1	**.353**	.467	**.705**	**1.172**	**213**	**92**	188	**14.27**	5	*O-144(0-144-0)	**49**	**8.8**
1957★NY-A★	144	474	**121**	173	28	6	34	94	**146**	75	16	3	.365	.515	.665	1.179	223	**96**	178	15.42	-1	*O-139(0-139-0)	**51**	**9.1**
1958★NY-A★	150	519	**127**	158	21	1	**42**	97	**129**	120	18	3	.304	.445	.592	1.036	**189**	**74**	147	**10.46**	-3	*O-150(0-150-0)	**39**	**6.6**
1959 NY-A★	144	541	104	154	23	4	31	75	93	126	21	3	.285	.392	.514	.905	**152**	**44**	117	7.92	3	*O-143(0-143-0)	**30**	**4.1**
1960★NY-A★	153	527	**119**	145	17	6	**40**	94	111	125	14	3	.275	.402	.558	**.960**	**166**	**54**	125	**8.42**	-1	*O-150(0-150-0)	**36**	**4.6**
1961★NY-A★	153	514	**132**	163	16	6	54	128	**126**	112	12	1	.317	.452	**.687**	1.138	**210**	**88**	174	13.04	0	*O-150(0-150-0)	**48**	8.2
1962★NY-A★	123	377	96	121	15	1	30	89	**122**	78	9	0	.321	**.488**	**.605**	**1.093**	**198**	**64**	126	**12.98**	-6	*O-117(0-94-23)	**33**	**5.5**
1963★NY-A★	65	172	40	54	8	0	15	35	40	32	2	1	.314	.443	.622	1.065	197	24	49	10.52	-0	O-52(0-52-0)	14	2.4
1964★NY-A★	143	465	92	141	25	2	35	111	99	102	6	3	.303	**.426**	.591	**1.017**	**177**	**52**	121	**9.63**	-4	*O-132(17-102-13)	**34**	4.7
1965 NY-A★	122	361	44	92	12	1	19	46	73	76	4	1	.255	.380	.452	.832	136	21	64	6.15	2	*O-108(108-0-0)	16	1.9
1966 NY-A	108	333	40	96	12	1	23	56	57	76	1	1	.288	.392	.538	.930	171	32	71	7.65	0	O-97(4-93-0)	18	3.1
1967 NY-A★	144	440	63	108	17	0	22	55	107	113	1	1	.245	.394	.434	.828	150	34	82	6.39	-1	*1-131	25	2.8
1968 NY-A★	144	435	57	103	14	1	18	54	106	97	6	2	.237	.387	.398	.785	143	30	74	5.78	-4	*1-131	24	2.1
Total 18	2401	8102	1677	2415	344	72	536	1509	1733	1710	153	38	.298	.423	.557	.979	173	903	2069	9.47	-9	*O-2019,1-262/S-7,2-1,3-1	565	81.7

• MANTO, Jeff Jeffrey Paul Manto b: 8/23/1964, Bristol, PA BR/TR, 6'3", 210 lbs. Deb: 6/7/1990 Career OF: 4-0-0

YEAR TM-L	G	AB	R	H	2B	3B	HR	RBI	BB	SO	SB	CS	AVG	OBP	SLG	OPS	OPS+	BR/A	RC	RC/G	FR	G/POS	WS	TPW
1990 Cle-A	30	76	12	17	5	1	2	14	21	18	0	1	.224	.392	.395	.786	121	3	13	6.04	1	1-25/3-5	5	0.3
1991 Cle-A	47	128	15	27	7	0	2	13	14	22	2	0	.211	.308	.313	.621	72	-4	13	3.38	0	3-32,1-14/C-5,O-1	2	-0.5
1993 Phi-N	8	18	0	1	0	0	0	0	0	3	0	0	.056	.105	.056	.161	-56	-4	0	.21	0	/3-6,S-1	0	-0.4
1995 Bal-A	89	254	31	65	9	0	17	38	24	69	0	3	.256	.325	.492	.817	107	0	39	5.26	2	3-69,D-13/1-4	6	0.2
1996 Bos-A	10	30	5	8	3	1	2	4	3	6	0	0	.267	.353	.633	.986	140	2	7	8.68	2	/2-4,S-4	0	0.4
Sea-A	21	54	7	10	3	0	1	4	9	12	0	1	.185	.302	.296	.598	52	-4	5	2.68	0	3-16/D-2,O-1	0	-0.3
Bos-A	12	18	3	2	0	0	0	2	5	6	0	0	.111	.304	.111	.415	11	-2	1	1.69	0	3-10/1-1	0	-0.2
Yr.	43	102	15	20	6	1	3	10	17	24	0	1	.196	.317	.363	.679	69	-5	13	4.05	3	3-26/2-4,S-4,D-2,1-1,O-1	0	-0.2
1997 Cle-A	16	30	3	8	3	0	2	7	1	10	0	0	.267	.290	.567	.857	113	0	4	4.38	-1	/3-7,1-6,O-1	1	-0.1
1998 Cle-A	7	14	3	1	0	0	0	1	1	5	0	0	.071	.133	.071	.205	-43	-3	0	.16	-1	/1-4,3-2,2-1	0	-0.4
Det-A	16	30	6	8	2	0	1	3	3	11	1	0	.267	.353	.433	.786	102	0	5	5.53	-2	1-10/D-6,O-1	0	-0.2
Cle-A	8	23	5	7	1	0	2	5	1	5	0	1	.304	.333	.609	.942	133	1	2	3.21	0	/3-6,1-3	0	0.0
Yr.	31	67	14	16	3	0	3	9	5	21	1	1	.239	.301	.418	.719	83	-2	7	3.40	-3	1-17/3-8,D-6,2-1,O-1	0	-0.5
1999 Cle-A	12	25	5	5	0	0	1	2	11	11	0	0	.200	.444	.320	.764	95	1	5	6.33	-1	3-10/1-1	1	0.0
NY-A	6	8	0	1	0	0	0	0	2	4	0	0	.125	.300	.125	.425	14	-1	0	1.76	0	/1-3,3-1	0	-0.1
Yr.	18	33	5	6	0	0	1	2	13	15	0	0	.182	.413	.273	.686	78	-0	5	5.19	-1	3-11/1-4	1	-0.1

YEAR TM-L	G	AB	R	H	2B	3B	HR	RBI	BB	SO	SB	CS	AVG	OBP	SLG	OPS	OPS+	BR/A	RC	RC/G	FR	G/POS	WS	TPW
2000 Col-N	7	5	2	4	2	0	1	4	2	0	0	0	.800	.857	1.800	2.657	437	3	8	220.32	0	/1-1,3-1	1	0.3
Total 9	289	713	97	164	35	2	31	97	97	182	3	6	.230	.330	.415	.745	92	-9	103	4.82	1	3-165/1-72,D-21,2-5,C-5,S-5,0	16	-1.0

• MANUEL, Charlie Charles Fuqua Manuel b: 1/4/1944, Northfork, WV BL/TR, 6'4", 200 lbs. Deb: 4/8/1969 M/C Career OF: 70-1-16

YEAR TM-L	G	AB	R	H	2B	3B	HR	RBI	BB	SO	SB	CS	AVG	OBP	SLG	OPS	OPS+	BR/A	RC	RC/G	FR	G/POS	WS	TPW
1969*Min-A	83	164	14	34	6	0	2	24	28	33	1	0	.207	.323	.280	.603	68	-6	16	3.27	0	0-46(41-1-4)	2	-0.8
1970*Min-A	59	64	4	12	0	0	1	7	6	17	0	0	.188	.268	.234	.502	39	-5	4	2.10	0	0-11(9-0-2)	0	-0.6
1971 Min-A	18	16	1	2	1	0	0	1	1	8	0	0	.125	.176	.188	.364	3	-2	1	1.11	0	/0-1	0	-0.2
1972 Min-A	63	122	6	25	5	0	1	8	4	16	0	0	.205	.236	.270	.507	48	-8	8	2.15	2	0-28(20-0-9)	1	-0.8
1974 LA-N	4	3	0	1	0	0	0	1	1	0	0	0	.333	.500	.333	.833	142	0	1	8.51	0	....	0	0.0
1975 LA-N	15	15	0	2	0	0	0	2	0	3	0	0	.133	.133	.133	.267	-27	-2	0	.00	0	....	0	-0.3
Total 6	242	384	25	76	12	0	4	43	40	77	1	0	.198	.277	.260	.537	52	-23	30	2.51	2	/0-86	3	-2.6

• MANUEL, Jerry Jerry Manuel b: 12/23/1953, Hahira, GA BB/TR, 6', 165 lbs. Deb: 9/18/1975 M/C

YEAR TM-L	G	AB	R	H	2B	3B	HR	RBI	BB	SO	SB	CS	AVG	OBP	SLG	OPS	OPS+	BR/A	RC	RC/G	FR	G/POS	WS	TPW
1975 Det-A	6	18	0	1	0	0	0	0	0	4	0	0	.056	.056	.056	.111	-66	-4	0	.00	1	/2-6	0	-0.3
1976 Det-A	54	43	4	6	1	0	0	2	3	9	1	0	.140	.213	.163	.376	11	-5	2	1.19	-4	2-47/S-4,D-1	1	-0.8
1980 Mon-N	7	6	0	0	0	0	0	0	0	2	0	0	.000	.000	.000	.000	-100	-2	0	.00	0	/S-7	0	-0.2
1981*Mon-N	27	55	10	11	5	0	3	10	6	11	0	0	.200	.279	.455	.733	104	-0	7	3.99	0	2-23/S-2	2	0.1
1982 SD-N	2	5	0	1	0	1	0	1	1	0	0	0	.200	.333	.600	.933	165	0	1	7.34	-1	/2-1,3-1,S-1	0	0.0
Total 5	96	127	14	19	6	1	3	13	10	26	1	0	.150	.217	.283	.501	44	-10	10	2.30	-5	/2-77,S-14,3-1,D-1	3	-1.2

• MANUSH, Frank Frank Benjamin Manush b: 9/18/1883, Tuscumbia, AL d: 1/5/1965, Laguna Beach, CA BR/TR, 5'10.5", 175 lbs. Deb: 8/31/1908

YEAR TM-L	G	AB	R	H	2B	3B	HR	RBI	BB	SO	SB	CS	AVG	OBP	SLG	OPS	OPS+	BR/A	RC	RC/G	FR	G/POS	WS	TPW
1908 Phi-A	23	77	6	12	2	1	0	0	2	....	2	....	.156	.188	.208	.395	27	-6	3	1.27	-4	3-20/2-2	1	-1.1

• MANUSH, Heinie Henry Emmett Manush
b: 7/20/1901, Tuscumbia, AL d: 5/12/1971, Sarasota, FL BL/TL, 6'1", 200 lbs. Deb: 4/20/1923 C HOF: 1964 Career OF: 1379-309-159

YEAR TM-L	G	AB	R	H	2B	3B	HR	RBI	BB	SO	SB	CS	AVG	OBP	SLG	OPS	OPS+	BR/A	RC	RC/G	FR	G/POS	WS	TPW
1923 Det-A	109	308	59	103	20	5	4	54	20	21	3	5	.334	.406	.471	.877	133	14	59	7.00	-6	0-79(72-0-7)	12	0.2
1924 Det-A	120	422	83	122	24	8	9	68	27	30	14	5	.289	.355	.448	.803	108	5	69	5.62	-3	*0-106(99-1-6)/1-1	13	-0.6
1925 Det-A	99	278	46	84	14	3	5	47	24	21	8	3	.302	.362	.428	.790	101	1	44	5.70	0	0-73(13-56-5)	8	-0.1
1926 Det-A	136	498	95	188	35	8	14	86	31	28	11	5	**.378**	.421	.564	.985	153	38	116	9.00	-10	*0-120(11-104-5)	26	2.2
1927 Det-A	151	593	102	177	31	18	6	90	47	29	12	8	.298	.354	.442	.796	104	2	93	5.59	-9	*0-149(3-147-0)	18	-1.3
1928 StL-A	154	638	104	**241**	**47**	20	13	108	39	14	17	5	.378	.414	.575	.989	153	48	150	9.42	-6	*0-154(154-0-0)	35	2.9
1929 StL-A	142	574	85	204	**45**	10	6	81	43	24	9	8	.355	.401	.500	.901	126	21	113	7.59	-4	*0-141(141-0-0)	23	0.6
1930 StL-A	49	198	26	65	16	4	2	29	5	7	3	1	.328	.345	.480	.825	103	0	32	6.05	3	0-48(48-0-0)	6	0.1
Was-A	88	356	74	129	33	8	7	65	26	17	4	3	.362	.406	.559	.965	141	21	79	8.71	-2	0-86(86-0-0)	17	1.2
Yr.	137	554	100	194	49	12	9	94	31	24	7	4	.350	.385	.531	.915	128	22	111	7.74	2	*0-134(134-0-0)	23	1.2
1931 Was-A	146	616	110	189	41	11	6	70	36	27	3	3	.307	.351	.438	.789	106	6	94	5.70	-15	*0-143(143-0-0)	19	-1.7
1932 Was-A	149	625	121	214	41	14	14	116	36	29	7	2	.342	.383	.520	.903	133	30	124	7.74	-4	*0-146(146-0-0)	28	1.6
1933*Was-A	153	658	115	**221**	32	**17**	5	95	36	18	6	4	.336	.372	.459	.831	120	18	111	6.55	-5	*0-150(150-0-0)	27	0.4
1934 Was-A★	137	556	88	194	42	11	11	89	36	23	7	3	.349	.392	.523	.915	140	30	113	7.99	-1	*0-131(130-1-0)	20	2.0
1935 Was-A	119	479	68	131	26	9	4	56	35	17	2	0	.273	.328	.390	.719	88	-9	62	4.74	1	*0-111(111-0-0)	11	-1.4
1936 Bos-A	82	313	43	91	15	5	0	45	17	11	1	3	.291	.329	.371	.700	69	-17	37	4.35	-5	0-72(72-0-0)	4	-2.3
1937 Bro-N	132	466	57	155	25	7	4	73	40	24	6	....	.333	.389	.442	.831	123	16	84	6.95	-8	*0-123(0-0-123)	17	0.2
1938 Bro-N	17	51	9	12	3	1	0	6	5	4	1	....	.235	.304	.333	.637	73	-2	5	3.30	1	0-12(0-0-12)	1	-0.2
Pit-N	15	13	2	4	1	1	0	4	2	0	0	....	.308	.400	.538	.938	155	1	3	6.93	0	....	0	0.1
Yr.	32	64	11	16	4	2	0	10	7	4	1	....	.250	.324	.375	.699	90	-1	8	4.01	1	0-12(0-0-12)	1	-0.1
1939 Pit-N	10	12	0	0	0	0	0	1	1	1	0	....	.000	.077	.000	.077	-79	-3	0	.00	-0	/0-1	0	-0.3
Total 17	2008	7654	1287	2524	491	160	110	1183	506	345	114	58	.330	.377	.479	.856	121	221	1389	6.84	-74	*0-1845/1-1	285	3.6

• MANWARING, Kirt Kirt Dean Manwaring b: 7/15/1965, Elmira, NY BR/TR, 5'11", 190 lbs. Deb: 9/15/1987

YEAR TM-L	G	AB	R	H	2B	3B	HR	RBI	BB	SO	SB	CS	AVG	OBP	SLG	OPS	OPS+	BR/A	RC	RC/G	FR	G/POS	WS	TPW
1987 SF-N	6	7	0	1	0	0	0	0	0	1	0	0	.143	.250	.143	.393	8	-1	0	.61	-1	/C-6	0	-0.2
1988 SF-N	40	116	12	29	7	0	1	15	2	21	0	1	.250	.281	.336	.617	80	-4	11	3.19	0	C-40	3	-0.3
1989*SF-N	85	200	14	42	4	2	0	18	11	28	2	1	.210	.265	.250	.515	49	-13	13	2.11	-1	C-81	4	-1.1
1990 SF-N	8	13	0	2	0	1	0	1	0	3	0	0	.154	.154	.308	.462	25	-1	1	1.51	0	/C-8	0	-0.1
1991 SF-N	67	178	16	40	9	0	0	19	9	22	1	1	.225	.274	.275	.549	57	-11	14	2.54	1	C-67	4	-0.6
1992 SF-N	109	349	24	85	10	5	4	26	29	42	2	1	.244	.311	.335	.646	88	-6	35	3.38	3	*C-108	10	0.4
1993 SF-N	130	432	48	119	15	1	5	49	41	76	1	3	.275	.347	.350	.696	90	-6	50	4.03	0	*C-130	18	0.3
1994 SF-N	97	316	30	79	17	1	1	29	25	50	1	1	.250	.311	.320	.631	68	-15	31	3.23	2	C-97	8	-0.6
1995 SF-N	118	379	21	95	15	2	4	36	27	72	1	0	.251	.317	.332	.650	74	-14	41	3.65	2	*C-118	8	-0.5
1996 SF-N	49	145	9	34	6	0	1	14	16	24	0	1	.234	.323	.297	.620	68	-7	15	3.40	3	C-49	3	-0.1
Hou-N	37	82	5	18	3	0	0	4	3	16	0	0	.220	.264	.256	.520	41	-7	5	2.19	2	C-37	2	-0.3
Yr.	86	227	14	52	9	0	1	18	19	40	0	1	.229	.303	.282	.585	59	-14	20	2.96	6	C-86	5	-0.3
1997 Col-N	104	337	22	76	6	4	1	27	30	78	1	5	.226	.293	.276	.569	41	-31	26	2.49	-1	*C-100	4	-2.6
1998 Col-N	110	291	30	72	12	3	2	26	38	49	1	5	.247	.340	.330	.670	64	-16	31	3.55	1	*C-108	4	-0.8
1999 Col-N	48	137	17	41	7	1	2	14	12	23	0	0	.299	.377	.409	.785	78	-4	21	5.65	1	C-44/D-1	3	-0.1
Total 13	1008	2982	248	733	111	20	21	278	243	505	10	19	.246	.313	.318	.631	69	-137	295	3.30	13	C-993/D-1	71	-6.5

• MAPES, Cliff Clifford Franklin "Tiger" Mapes b: 3/13/1922, Sutherland, NE d: 12/5/1996, Pryor, OK BL/TR, 6'3", 205 lbs. Deb: 4/20/1948 Career OF: 39-118-238

YEAR TM-L	G	AB	R	H	2B	3B	HR	RBI	BB	SO	SB	CS	AVG	OBP	SLG	OPS	OPS+	BR/A	RC	RC/G	FR	G/POS	WS	TPW
1948 NY-A	53	88	19	22	11	1	1	12	6	13	1	1	.250	.298	.432	.730	93	-2	11	4.51	1	0-21(9-6-6)	2	-0.2
1949*NY-A	111	304	56	75	13	3	7	38	58	50	6	0	.247	.369	.378	.747	98	2	49	5.55	3	*0-108(4-58-49)	12	0.2
1950*NY-A	108	356	60	88	14	6	12	61	47	61	1	6	.247	.338	.421	.760	96	-5	49	4.41	-2	*0-102(4-21-80)	8	-1.0
1951 NY-A	45	51	6	11	3	1	2	8	4	14	0	0	.216	.273	.431	.704	92	-1	6	3.95	-1	0-34(2-3-29)	1	-0.2
StL-A	56	201	32	55	7	2	7	30	26	33	0	1	.274	.360	.433	.792	110	3	32	5.55	0	0-53(15-12-31)	6	0.0
Yr.	101	252	38	66	10	3	9	38	30	47	0	1	.262	.343	.433	.775	107	2	38	5.22	-1	0-87(17-15-60)	7	-0.2
1952 Det-A	86	193	26	38	7	0	9	23	27	42	0	1	.197	.295	.373	.669	85	-5	23	3.87	0	0-63(5-18-43)	3	-0.7
Total 5	459	1193	199	289	55	13	38	172	168	213	8	9	.242	.338	.406	.743	97	-8	170	4.78	0	0-381	32	-1.8

• MAPLE, Howard Howard Albert "Mape" Maple b: 7/20/1903, Adrian, MO d: 11/9/1970, Portland, OR BL/TR, 5'7", 175 lbs. Deb: 5/19/1932

YEAR TM-L	G	AB	R	H	2B	3B	HR	RBI	BB	SO	SB	CS	AVG	OBP	SLG	OPS	OPS+	BR/A	RC	RC/G	FR	G/POS	WS	TPW
1932 Was-A	44	41	6	10	0	1	0	7	7	7	0	0	.244	.367	.293	.660	74	-1	5	4.24	-5	C-41	1	-0.5

• MAPPES, George George Richard "Dick" Mappes b: 12/25/1865, St. Louis, MO d: 2/20/1934, St. Louis, MO Deb: 9/23/1885

YEAR TM-L	G	AB	R	H	2B	3B	HR	RBI	BB	SO	SB	CS	AVG	OBP	SLG	OPS	OPS+	BR/A	RC	RC/G	FR	G/POS	WS	TPW
1885 Bal-a	6	19	2	4	0	1	0	0	1	....	....	....	.211	.250	.316	.566	79	-0	2	2.77	-2	/2-6	0	-0.2
1886 StL-N	6	14	1	2	0	0	0	0	1	5	0	....	.143	.200	.143	.343	6	-1	0	.92	-2	/C-3,3-2,2-1	0	-0.3
Total 2	12	33	3	6	0	1	0	0	2	5	0	....	.182	.229	.242	.471	48	-2	2	1.95	-4	/2-7,C-3,3-2	0	-0.5

• MARANVILLE, Rabbit Walter James Vincent Maranville b: 11/11/1891, Springfield, MA d: 1/5/1954, New York, NY BR/TR, 5'5", 155 lbs. Deb: 9/10/1912 M HOF: 1954

YEAR TM-L	G	AB	R	H	2B	3B	HR	RBI	BB	SO	SB	CS	AVG	OBP	SLG	OPS	OPS+	BR/A	RC	RC/G	FR	G/POS	WS	TPW
1912 Bos-N	26	86	8	18	2	0	0	8	9	14	1	....	.209	.292	.233	.524	44	-7	7	2.30	3	S-26	1	-0.2
1913 Bos-N	143	571	68	141	13	8	2	48	68	62	25	....	.247	.330	.308	.638	81	-12	64	3.68	10	*S-143	17	0.9
1914*Bos-N	156	586	74	144	23	6	4	78	45	56	28	....	.246	.306	.326	.632	88	-9	66	3.64	44	*S-156	24	**5.0**
1915 Bos-N	149	509	51	124	23	6	2	43	45	65	18	12	.244	.308	.324	.632	93	-6	55	3.46	23	*S-149	20	3.1
1916 Bos-N	155	604	79	142	16	13	4	38	50	69	32	15	.235	.296	.325	.620	96	-3	64	3.33	24	*S-155	27	3.6
1917 Bos-N	142	561	69	146	19	13	3	43	40	47	27	....	.260	.312	.357	.668	111	6	67	4.08	17	*S-142	22	3.8
1918 Bos-N	11	38	3	12	0	1	0	3	4	0	0	....	.316	.381	.368	.749	134	2	5	5.08	-2	S-11	2	0.1
1919 Bos-N	131	480	44	128	18	10	5	43	36	23	12	....	.267	.319	.377	.696	113	7	59	4.23	17	*S-131	18	3.8
1920 Bos-N	134	493	48	131	19	15	1	43	28	24	14	11	.266	.305	.371	.676	98	-3	54	3.73	6	*S-133	14	1.3
1921 Pit-N	153	612	90	180	25	12	1	70	47	38	25	12	.294	.347	.379	.727	90	-5	82	4.67	21	*S-153	23	3.2
1922 Pit-N	155	672	115	198	26	15	0	63	61	43	24	13	.295	.355	.378	.733	88	-9	92	4.89	23	*S-138,2-18	22	2.8
1923 Pit-N	141	581	78	161	19	9	1	41	42	34	14	11	.277	.327	.346	.673	76	-20	66	3.95	14	*S-141	16	0.9
1924 Pit-N	152	594	62	158	33	20	2	71	35	53	18	14	.266	.307	.399	.706	86	-14	70	4.03	14	*2-152	15	0.5
1925 Chi-N	75	266	37	62	10	3	0	23	29	20	6	5	.233	.308	.293	.602	54	-18	25	3.07	-3	S-74	4	-1.2
1926 Bro-N	78	234	32	55	8	5	0	24	26	24	7	....	.235	.312	.312	.624	69	-10	23	3.28	3	S-60,2-18	5	0.0

YEAR TM-L	G	AB	R	H	2B	3B	HR	RBI	BB	SO	SB	CS	AVG	OBP	SLG	OPS	OPS+	BR/A	RC	RC/G	FR	G/POS	WS	TPW
1927 StL-N	9	29	0	7	1	0	0	0	2	2	0	....	.241	.290	.276	.566	51	-2	2	2.72	1	/S-9	1	0.0
1928*StL-N	112	366	40	88	14	10	1	34	36	27	3	....	.240	.310	.342	.652	69	-17	39	3.55	11	*S-112/2-2	11	0.6
1929 Bos-N	146	560	87	159	26	10	0	55	47	33	13	....	.284	.344	.366	.710	79	-18	70	4.32	18	*S-145/2-1	17	1.4
1930 Bos-N	142	558	85	157	26	8	2	43	48	23	9	....	.281	.344	.367	.711	75	-22	70	4.38	-2	*S-138/3-4	17	-0.7
1931 Bos-N	145	562	69	146	22	5	0	33	56	34	9	....	.260	.329	.317	.646	77	-17	63	3.78	-24	*S-137,2-11	9	-2.9
1932 Bos-N	149	571	67	134	20	4	0	37	46	28	4	....	.235	.295	.284	.579	59	-32	51	2.94	8	*2-149	11	-1.4
1933 Bos-N	143	478	46	104	15	4	0	38	36	34	2	....	.218	.274	.266	.539	59	-25	35	2.29	-21	*2-142	6	-3.9
1935 Bos-N	23	67	3	10	2	0	0	5	3	3	0	....	.149	.186	.179	.365	-2	-9	2	.75	-2	2-20	0	-1.0
Total 23	2670	10078	1255	2605	380	177	28	884	839	756	291	93	.258	.318	.340	.658	83	-242	1132	3.76	204	*S-2153,2-513/3-4	302	19.6

• MARION, Marty Martin Whiteford "Slats,The Octopus" Marion b: 12/1/1917, Richburg, SC BR/TR, 6'2", 170 lbs. Deb: 4/16/1940 M/C

YEAR TM-L	G	AB	R	H	2B	3B	HR	RBI	BB	SO	SB	CS	AVG	OBP	SLG	OPS	OPS+	BR/A	RC	RC/G	FR	G/POS	WS	TPW
1940 StL-N	125	435	44	121	18	1	3	46	21	34	9	....	.278	.311	.345	.656	76	-15	45	3.59	4	*S-125	11	-0.2
1941 StL-N	155	547	50	138	22	3	3	58	42	48	8	....	.252	.308	.320	.628	72	-20	56	3.37	10	*S-155	14	0.1
1942*StL-N	147	485	66	134	**38**	5	0	54	48	50	8	....	.276	.343	.375	.718	102	2	64	4.58	21	*S-147	22	3.6
1943*StL-N★	129	418	38	117	15	3	1	52	32	37	1	....	.280	.334	.337	.671	90	-5	49	4.22	23	*S-128	17	3.0
1944*StL-N★	144	506	50	135	26	2	6	63	43	50	1	....	.267	.324	.362	.686	91	-6	61	4.13	26	*S-144	20	3.2
1945 StL-N★	123	430	63	119	27	5	1	59	39	39	2	....	.277	.340	.370	.709	95	-3	56	4.71	17	*S-122	17	2.4
1946*StL-N★	146	498	51	116	29	4	3	46	59	53	1	....	.233	.318	.325	.643	79	-13	55	3.63	21	*S-145	19	1.8
1947 StL-N★	149	540	57	147	19	6	4	74	49	58	3	....	.272	.334	.352	.686	79	-16	63	4.05	18	*S-141	18	1.1
1948 StL-N★	144	567	70	143	26	4	4	43	37	54	1	....	.252	.298	.333	.631	67	-27	55	3.35	8	*S-142	13	-1.1
1949 StL-N★	134	515	61	140	31	2	5	70	37	42	0	....	.272	.323	.369	.692	81	-14	59	3.91	7	*S-134	13	0.1
1950 StL-N★	106	372	36	92	10	2	4	40	44	55	1	....	.247	.327	.317	.644	67	-17	39	3.62	-1	*S-101	9	-1.1
1952 StL-A	67	186	16	46	11	0	2	19	19	17	0	2	.247	.320	.339	.659	81	-5	20	3.53	0	S-63	4	-0.2
1953 StL-A	3	7	0	0	0	0	0	0	0	0	0	0	.000	.000	.000	.000	-98	-2	0	.00	-1	/3-2	0	-0.2
Total 13	1572	5506	602	1448	272	37	36	624	470	537	35	2	.263	.323	.345	.668	81	-143	623	3.88	154	*S-1547/3-2	177	12.5

• MARION, Red John Wyeth Marion b: 3/14/1914, Richburg, SC d: 3/13/1975, San Jose, CA BR/TR, 6'2", 175 lbs. Deb: 9/16/1935 Career OF: 5-1-1

YEAR TM-L	G	AB	R	H	2B	3B	HR	RBI	BB	SO	SB	CS	AVG	OBP	SLG	OPS	OPS+	BR/A	RC	RC/G	FR	G/POS	WS	TPW
1935 Was-A	4	11	1	2	1	0	1	1	0	2	0	0	.182	.182	.545	.727	85	-0	1	3.08	0	/O-3(1-1-1)	0	0.0
1943 Was-A	14	17	2	3	0	0	0	1	3	1	0	0	.176	.300	.176	.476	42	-1	1	2.23	0	/O-4(4-0-0)	0	-0.1
Total 2	18	28	3	5	1	0	1	2	3	3	0	0	.179	.258	.321	.579	57	-1	2	2.56	0	/O-7	0	-0.2

• MARIS, Roger Roger Eugene Maris b: 9/10/1934, Hibbing, MN d: 12/14/1985, Houston, TX BL/TR, 6', 204 lbs. Deb: 4/16/1957 Career OF: 26-259-1151

YEAR TM-L	G	AB	R	H	2B	3B	HR	RBI	BB	SO	SB	CS	AVG	OBP	SLG	OPS	OPS+	BR/A	RC	RC/G	FR	G/POS	WS	TPW
1957 Cle-A	116	358	61	84	9	5	14	51	60	79	8	4	.235	.346	.405	.751	105	4	53	4.95	-4	*O-112(26-87-8)	13	-0.6
1958 Cle-A	51	182	26	41	5	1	9	27	17	33	4	2	.225	.291	.412	.704	94	-2	23	4.23	2	O-47(0-27-23)	5	-0.3
KC-A	99	401	61	99	14	3	19	53	28	52	0	0	.247	.299	.439	.738	99	-2	54	4.75	-1	O-99(0-21-90)	12	-0.7
Yr.	150	583	87	140	19	4	28	80	45	85	4	2	.240	.297	.431	.727	97	-4	77	4.58	1	*O-146(0-48-113)	17	-0.9
1959 KC-A★	122	433	69	118	21	7	16	72	58	53	2	1	.273	.362	.464	.827	123	14	76	6.37	2	*O-117(0-6-113)	17	1.2
1960*NY-A★	136	499	98	141	18	7	39	**112**	70	65	2	2	.283	.374	**.581**	.955	163	42	111	8.07	4	*O-131(0-7-128)	31	4.2
1961*NY-A★	161	590	**132**	159	16	4	**61**	**142**	94	67	0	0	.269	.376	.620	.997	170	58	138	8.23	-8	*O-160(0-11-156)	36	3.9
1962*NY-A★	157	590	92	151	34	1	33	100	87	78	1	0	.256	.357	.485	.842	128	24	107	6.41	-4	*O-154(0-64-103)	25	1.2
1963*NY-A	90	312	53	84	14	1	23	53	35	40	1	0	.269	.347	.542	.888	146	19	61	7.08	1	O-86(0-1-86)	17	1.4
1964*NY-A	141	513	86	144	12	2	26	71	62	78	3	0	.281	.365	.464	.829	127	20	91	6.47	-1	*O-137(0-32-105)	25	1.1
1965 NY-A	46	155	22	37	7	0	8	27	29	29	0	0	.239	.359	.439	.797	126	6	25	5.54	-2	O-43(0-0-43)	6	0.2
1966 NY-A	119	348	37	81	9	2	13	43	36	60	0	0	.233	.310	.382	.692	101	1	41	4.00	-3	O-95(0-1-94)	8	-0.8
1967*StL-N	125	410	64	107	18	7	9	55	52	61	0	0	.261	.350	.405	.755	117	11	59	5.02	0	*O-118(0-2-118)	17	0.4
1968*StL-N	100	310	25	79	18	2	5	45	24	38	0	0	.255	.310	.374	.685	106	2	37	4.17	-3	O-84(0-0-84)	11	-0.8
Total 12	1463	5101	826	1325	195	42	275	851	652	733	21	9	.260	.348	.476	.824	128	198	878	6.05	-16	*O-1383	223	10.5

• MARKLAND, Gene Cleneth Eugene "Mousey" Markland b: 12/26/1919, Detroit, MI d: 6/15/1999, Barefoot Bay, FL BR/TR, 5'10", 160 lbs. Deb: 4/25/1950

YEAR TM-L	G	AB	R	H	2B	3B	HR	RBI	BB	SO	SB	CS	AVG	OBP	SLG	OPS	OPS+	BR/A	RC	RC/G	FR	G/POS	WS	TPW
1950 Phi-A	5	8	2	1	0	0	0	0	3	0	0	0	.125	.364	.125	.489	30	-1	1	2.63	-1	/2-5	0	-0.1

• MARNIE, Harry Harry Sylvester Marnie b: 7/6/1918, Philadelphia, PA d: 1/7/2002, Philadelphia, PA BR/TR, 6'1", 178 lbs. Deb: 9/15/1940

YEAR TM-L	G	AB	R	H	2B	3B	HR	RBI	BB	SO	SB	CS	AVG	OBP	SLG	OPS	OPS+	BR/A	RC	RC/G	FR	G/POS	WS	TPW
1940 Phi-N	11	34	4	6	0	0	0	4	4	2	0	....	.176	.263	.176	.440	24	-3	2	1.80	1	2-11	0	-0.1
1941 Phi-N	61	158	12	38	3	3	0	11	13	25	0	....	.241	.298	.297	.596	71	-6	13	2.81	-2	2-39,S-16/3-3	2	-0.6
1942 Phi-N	24	30	3	5	0	0	0	0	1	2	1	....	.167	.194	.167	.360	6	-4	1	.88	-1	2-11/S-7,3-1	0	-0.4
Total 3	96	222	19	49	3	3	0	15	18	29	1	....	.221	.279	.261	.540	55	-13	16	2.38	-2	/2-61,S-23,3-4	2	-1.1

• MAROLEWSKI, Fred Fred Daniel "Fritz" Marolewski b: 10/6/1928, Chicago, IL BR/TR, 6'2.5", 205 lbs. Deb: 9/19/1953

YEAR TM-L	G	AB	R	H	2B	3B	HR	RBI	BB	SO	SB	CS	AVG	OBP	SLG	OPS	OPS+	BR/A	RC	RC/G	FR	G/POS	WS	TPW
1953 StL-N	1	0	0	0	0	0	0	0	0	0	0	0	....	....	....	....	-100	0	0	....	0	/1-1	0	0.0

• MARQUARDT, Ollie Albert Ludwig Marquardt b: 9/22/1902, Toledo, OH d: 2/7/1968, Port Clinton, OH BR/TR, 5'9", 156 lbs. Deb: 4/14/1931

YEAR TM-L	G	AB	R	H	2B	3B	HR	RBI	BB	SO	SB	CS	AVG	OBP	SLG	OPS	OPS+	BR/A	RC	RC/G	FR	G/POS	WS	TPW
1931 Bos-A	17	39	4	7	1	0	0	2	3	4	0	1	.179	.238	.205	.443	18	-5	2	1.46	-2	2-13/3-1,S-1	0	-0.6

• MARQUEZ, Gonzalo Gonzalo Enrique (Moya) Marquez b: 3/31/1946, Caupano, Venezuela d: 12/20/1984, Valencia, Venezuela BL/TL, 5'11", 180 lbs. Deb: 8/11/1972

YEAR TM-L	G	AB	R	H	2B	3B	HR	RBI	BB	SO	SB	CS	AVG	OBP	SLG	OPS	OPS+	BR/A	RC	RC/G	FR	G/POS	WS	TPW
1972*Oak-A	23	21	2	8	0	0	0	4	3	4	1	1	.381	.480	.381	.861	167	2	4	7.68	0	/1-2	1	0.2
1973 Oak-A	23	25	1	6	1	0	0	2	0	4	0	0	.240	.240	.280	.520	49	-2	1	1.89	-1	/2-2,1-1,D-1,O-1	0	-0.3
Chi-N	19	58	5	13	2	0	1	4	3	4	0	0	.224	.274	.310	.585	57	-3	5	2.76	1	1-18	0	-0.3
1974 Chi-N	11	11	1	0	0	0	0	0	1	2	0	0	.000	.083	.000	.083	-72	-3	0	.00	0	/1-1	0	-0.3
Total 3	76	115	9	27	3	0	1	10	7	14	1	1	.235	.290	.287	.577	66	-6	11	3.03	0	/1-22,2-2,D-1,O-1	1	-0.8

• MARQUEZ, Luis Luis Angel (Sanchez) "Canena" Marquez
b: 10/28/1925, Aguadilla, Puerto Rico d: 3/1/1988, Aguadilla, Puerto Rico BR/TR, 5'10.5", 174 lbs. Deb: 4/18/1951 Career OF: 26-34-5

YEAR TM-L	G	AB	R	H	2B	3B	HR	RBI	BB	SO	SB	CS	AVG	OBP	SLG	OPS	OPS+	BR/A	RC	RC/G	FR	G/POS	WS	TPW
1951 Bos-N	68	122	19	24	5	1	0	11	10	20	4	4	.197	.274	.254	.528	46	-10	9	2.20	-2	O-43(21-23-3)	1	-1.4
1954 Chi-N	17	12	2	1	0	0	0	0	2	4	3	0	.083	.214	.083	.298	-19	-1	1	1.62	0	O-14(4-10-0)	0	-0.2
Pit-N	14	9	3	1	0	0	0	0	4	0	0	0	.111	.385	.111	.496	37	-1	1	2.74	-0	/O-4(1-1-2)	0	-0.1
Yr.	31	21	5	2	0	0	0	0	6	4	3	0	.095	.296	.095	.392	8	-2	2	2.10	0	O-18(5-11-2)	0	-0.3
Total 2	99	143	24	26	5	1	0	11	16	24	7	4	.182	.278	.231	.509	40	-12	10	2.18	-2	/O-61	1	-1.6

• MARQUIS, Bob Robert Rudolph Marquis b: 12/23/1924, Oklahoma City, OK BL/TL, 6'1", 170 lbs. Deb: 4/17/1953

YEAR TM-L	G	AB	R	H	2B	3B	HR	RBI	BB	SO	SB	CS	AVG	OBP	SLG	OPS	OPS+	BR/A	RC	RC/G	FR	G/POS	WS	TPW
1953 Cin-N	40	44	9	12	1	1	2	3	4	11	0	0	.273	.333	.477	.811	107	0	8	6.00	-1	O-10(2-8-0)	1	-0.1

• MARQUIS, Roger Roger Julian "Noonie" Marquis b: 4/5/1937, Holyoke, MA BL/TL, 6', 190 lbs. Deb: 9/25/1955

YEAR TM-L	G	AB	R	H	2B	3B	HR	RBI	BB	SO	SB	CS	AVG	OBP	SLG	OPS	OPS+	BR/A	RC	RC/G	FR	G/POS	WS	TPW
1955 Bal-A	1	1	0	0	0	0	0	0	0	0	0	0	.000	.000	.000	.000	-108	-0	0	.00	0	/O-1	0	0.0

• MARR, Lefty Charles W. Marr b: 9/19/1862, Cincinnati, OH d: 1/11/1912, New Britian, CT BL/TL, 5'9" Deb: 10/3/1886 Career OF: 0-9-197

YEAR TM-L	G	AB	R	H	2B	3B	HR	RBI	BB	SO	SB	CS	AVG	OBP	SLG	OPS	OPS+	BR/A	RC	RC/G	FR	G/POS	WS	TPW
1886 Cin-a	8	29	2	8	1	1	0	2	1	....	1	....	.276	.323	.379	.702	116	0	4	5.10	-1	/O-8(0-8-0)	1	-0.1
1889 Col-a	139	546	110	167	26	**15**	1	75	87	32	29	....	.306	.407	.414	.821	141	35	106	7.44	3	3-66,O-47(0-1-47),S-26/1-2,C	24	3.3
1890 Cin-N	130	527	91	157	17	12	1	73	46	29	44	....	.298	.361	.381	.742	117	11	91	6.49	-7	O-64(0-0-64),3-63/S-3	16	0.4
1891 Cin-N	72	286	32	74	9	7	0	32	25	15	16	....	.259	.323	.339	.662	92	-3	37	4.76	-8	O-72(0-0-72)	6	-1.1
Cin-a	14	57	9	11	1	0	0	4	7	4	2	....	.193	.281	.211	.492	38	-5	4	2.33	-0	O-14(0-0-14)	0	-0.4
Total 4	363	1445	244	417	54	35	2	186	166	80	92	....	.289	.368	.379	.746	118	38	242	6.27	-12	O-205,3-129/S-29,1-2,C-1	47	2.1

• MARRERO, Eli Elieser Marrero b: 11/17/1973, Havana, Cuba BR/TR, 6'1", 180 lbs. Deb: 9/3/1997 Career OF: 57-42-74

YEAR TM-L	G	AB	R	H	2B	3B	HR	RBI	BB	SO	SB	CS	AVG	OBP	SLG	OPS	OPS+	BR/A	RC	RC/G	FR	G/POS	WS	TPW
1997 StL-N	17	45	4	11	2	0	2	7	2	13	4	0	.244	.277	.422	.699	81	-1	5	4.10	1	C-17	1	0.1
1998 StL-N	83	254	28	62	18	1	4	20	28	42	6	2	.244	.319	.370	.689	81	-6	30	4.09	-1	C-73/1-2	6	-0.2
1999 StL-N	114	317	32	61	13	1	6	34	18	56	11	2	.192	.238	.297	.535	34	-32	20	1.94	4	C-96,1-20	5	-2.2
2000*StL-N	53	102	21	23	3	1	5	17	9	16	5	0	.225	.307	.422	.729	81	-2	14	4.41	2	C-38/1-7	5	0.1
2001*StL-N	86	203	37	54	11	3	6	23	15	36	6	3	.266	.317	.438	.755	93	-3	27	4.55	2	C-65,O-15(8-0-7)/1-6	7	0.2
2002*StL-N	131	397	63	104	19	1	18	66	40	72	14	2	.262	.330	.451	.780	106	4	61	5.33	7	*O-106(39-36-46),C-44/1-4	14	1.0
2003 StL-N	41	107	10	24	4	2	2	20	7	18	0	1	.224	.272	.355	.627	64	-6	11	3.32	2	O-31(10-6-21)/C-6,1-2	3	-0.5
Total 7	525	1425	195	339	70	9	43	187	119	253	46	10	.238	.298	.390	.689	78	-46	168	3.93	17	C-339,O-152/1-41	41	-1.4

YEAR TM-L	G	AB	R	H	2B	3B	HR	RBI	BB	SO	SB	CS	AVG	OBP	SLG	OPS	OPS+	BR/A	RC	RC/G	FR	G/POS	WS	TPW
• MARRERO, Oreste	Oreste Vilato (Vazquez) Marrero b: 10/31/1969, Bayamon, Puerto Rico BL/TL, 6', 195 lbs. Deb: 8/12/1993																							
1993 Mon-N	32	81	10	17	5	1	1	4	14	16	1	3	.210	.326	.333	.660	74	-4	9	3.70	0	1-32	1	-0.5
1996 LA-N	10	8	2	3	1	0	0	1	1	3	0	0	.375	.444	.500	.944	161	1	2	10.22	0	/1-1	1	0.1
Total 2	42	89	12	20	6	1	1	5	15	19	1	3	.225	.337	.348	.685	81	-3	11	4.15	0	/1-33	2	-0.5
• MARRIOTT, William	William Earl Marriott b: 8/18/1893, Pratt, KS d: 8/11/1969, Berkeley, CA BL/TR, 6', 170 lbs. Deb: 9/6/1917 Career OF: 3-0-0																							
1917 Chi-N	3	6	0	0	0	0	0	0	0	1	0	....	.000	.000	.000	.000	-93	-1	0	.00	0	/O-1	0	-0.2
1920 Chi-N	14	43	7	12	4	2	0	5	6	5	1	1	.279	.367	.465	.832	135	2	7	5.92	-4	2-14	2	-0.2
1921 Chi-N	30	38	3	12	1	1	0	7	4	1	0	1	.316	.381	.395	.776	105	0	6	5.10	-2	/2-6,3-1,O-1,S-1	1	-0.2
1925 Bos-N	103	370	37	99	9	1	1	40	28	26	3	8	.268	.323	.305	.628	67	-20	36	3.30	6	3-89/O-1	5	-0.7
1926 Bro-N	109	360	39	96	13	9	3	42	17	20	12	....	.267	.303	.378	.681	84	-10	40	3.80	-7	*3-104	7	-1.1
1927 Bro-N	6	9	0	1	0	1	0	1	2	2	0	....	.111	.273	.333	.606	61	-1	1	2.90	1	/3-2	0	0.0
Total 6	265	826	86	220	27	14	4	95	57	55	16	10	.266	.317	.347	.664	79	-29	90	3.70	-7	3-196/2-20,O-3,S-1	15	-2.3
• MARSANS, Armando	Armando Marsans b: 10/3/1887, Matanzas, Cuba d: 9/3/1960, Havana, Cuba BR/TR, 5'10", 157 lbs. Deb: 7/4/1911 Career OF: 51-459-71																							
1911 Cin-N	58	138	17	36	2	2	0	11	15	11	11	....	.261	.346	.304	.651	86	-2	18	4.49	-3	O-34(5-16-13)/1-1,3-1	3	-0.6
1912 Cin-N	110	416	59	132	19	7	1	38	20	17	35	....	.317	.353	.404	.757	110	4	70	6.12	-4	O-98(7-82-13)/1-6	15	-0.5
1913 Cin-N	118	435	49	129	7	6	0	38	17	25	37	....	.297	.327	.340	.668	91	-6	57	4.56	-2	O-94(3-56-37),1-22/3-2,S-1	9	-1.3
1914 Cin-N	36	124	16	37	3	0	0	22	14	6	13	....	.298	.374	.323	.697	105	1	19	5.36	1	O-36(36-0-0)	4	0.0
StL-F	9	40	5	14	0	2	0	2	3	0	4	....	.350	.395	.450	.845	133	2	8	7.91	1	/2-7,S-2	2	0.3
1915 StL-F	36	124	16	22	3	0	0	6	14	5	5	....	.177	.261	.202	.462	35	-10	8	1.94	2	O-35(0-35-0)	1	-1.1
1916 StL-A	151	528	51	134	12	1	1	60	57	41	46	26	.254	.333	.286	.619	91	-6	58	3.43	3	*O-150(0-150-0)	14	-1.4
1917 StL-A	75	257	31	59	12	0	0	20	20	6	11	....	.230	.285	.276	.561	74	-8	23	2.85	-7	O-67(0-67-0)/3-5,2-1	4	-2.2
NY-A	25	88	10	20	4	0	0	15	8	3	6	....	.227	.292	.273	.564	72	-3	9	3.08	3	O-25(0-25-0)	2	-0.1
Yr.	100	345	41	79	16	0	0	35	28	9	17	....	.229	.287	.275	.562	73	-11	31	2.91	-4	O-92(0-92-0)/3-5,2-1	6	-2.3
1918 NY-A	37	123	13	29	5	1	0	9	5	3	3	....	.236	.266	.293	.558	67	-6	10	2.61	-6	O-36(0-28-8)	1	-1.5
Total 8	655	2273	267	612	67	19	2	221	173	117	171	26	.269	.325	.318	.643	88	-33	281	4.09	-12	O-575/1-29,2-8,3-8,S-3	55	-8.4
• MARSH, Fred	Fred Francis Marsh b: 1/5/1924, Valley Falls, KS BR/TR, 5'10", 180 lbs. Deb: 4/19/1949 Career OF: 2-0-1																							
1949 Cle-A	1	0	0	0	0	0	0	0	0	0	0	0	....	....	....	....	-102	0	0	....	0	....	0	0.0
1951 StL-A	130	445	44	108	21	4	4	43	36	56	4	4	.243	.299	.335	.634	69	-21	45	3.44	-2	*3-117/S-3,2-2	7	-2.2
1952 StL-A	11	24	3	5	1	0	0	1	5	4	0	1	.208	.345	.250	.595	65	-1	2	3.12	1	/2-9,S-3	0	0.0
Was-A	9	24	1	1	0	0	0	1	1	4	0	0	.042	.080	.042	.122	-68	-5	0	.00	-1	/2-5,O-2(2-0-0)	0	-0.6
StL-A	76	223	25	64	8	1	2	26	22	29	3	2	.287	.351	.359	.710	95	-1	29	4.69	0	S-57,3-21	7	0.2
Yr.	96	271	29	70	9	1	2	28	28	37	3	3	.258	.328	.321	.649	79	-8	32	4.00	1	S-60,3-21,2-14/O-2(2-0-0)	7	-0.4
1953 Chi-A	67	95	22	19	1	0	2	2	13	26	0	3	.200	.303	.274	.576	55	-7	8	2.57	0	3-32,S-17/1-5,2-2	1	-0.7
1954 Chi-A	62	98	21	30	5	2	0	4	9	16	4	2	.306	.364	.398	.762	105	1	14	5.21	3	3-36/S-3,1-2,O-1	4	0.4
1955 Bal-A	89	303	30	66	7	1	2	19	35	33	1	2	.218	.301	.267	.568	58	-18	25	2.67	-16	2-76,3-18,S-16	4	-2.8
1956 Bal-A	20	24	2	3	0	0	0	0	4	3	1	0	.125	.250	.125	.375	2	-3	1	1.47	-2	/3-8,S-8,2-5	0	-0.4
Total 7	465	1236	148	296	43	8	10	96	125	171	13	14	.239	.310	.311	.622	69	-56	125	3.38	-16	3-232,S-107/2-99,1-7,O-3	23	-6.2
• MARSH, Tom	Thomas Owen Marsh b: 12/27/1965, Toledo, OH BR/TR, 6'2", 180 lbs. Deb: 6/5/1992 Career OF: 52-4-17																							
1992 Phi-N	42	125	7	25	3	2	2	16	2	23	0	1	.200	.219	.304	.523	47	-10	8	1.95	-3	O-35(25-0-12)	0	-1.4
1994 Phi-N	8	18	3	5	1	1	0	3	1	1	0	0	.278	.316	.444	.760	93	-0	3	5.08	-1	/O-7(3-0-4)	1	-0.1
1995 Phi-N	43	109	13	32	3	1	3	15	4	25	0	1	.294	.319	.422	.741	93	-2	14	4.79	-1	O-29(24-4-1)	2	-0.4
Total 3	93	252	23	62	7	4	5	34	7	49	0	2	.246	.269	.365	.634	70	-12	25	3.30	-4	/O-71	3	-1.9
• MARSHALL, Bill	William Henry Marshall b: 2/14/1911, Dorchester, MA d: 5/5/1977, Sacramento, CA BR/TR, 5'8.5", 156 lbs. Deb: 6/20/1931																							
1931 Bos-A	1	0	1	0	0	0	0	0	0	0	0	0	....	....	....	....	-106	0	0	....	0	....	0	0.0
1934 Cin-N	6	8	0	1	0	0	0	0	0	2	0	....	.125	.125	.125	.250	-34	-1	0	.49	0	/2-2	0	-0.2
Total 2	7	8	1	1	0	0	0	0	0	2	0	0	.125	.125	.125	.250	-34	-1	0	.49	0	/2-2	0	-0.2
• MARSHALL, Charlie	Charles Anthony Marshall b: 8/28/1919, Wilmington, DE BR/TR, 5'10.5", 178 lbs. Deb: 6/14/1941																							
1941 StL-N	1	0	0	0	0	0	0	0	0	0	0	....	....	....	....	....	-94	0	0	....	0	/C-1	0	0.0
• MARSHALL, Dave	David Lewis Marshall b: 1/14/1943, Artesia, CA BL/TR, 6'1", 190 lbs. Deb: 9/7/1967 Career OF: 141-4-163																							
1967 SF-N	1	0	0	0	0	0	0	0	0	0	0	0	....	....	....	....	-101	0	0	....	0	....	0	0.0
1968 SF-N	76	174	17	46	5	1	1	16	20	37	2	1	.264	.344	.322	.665	101	1	21	4.29	-1	O-50(24-0-28)	6	-0.3
1969 SF-N	110	267	32	62	7	1	2	33	40	68	1	8	.232	.343	.288	.631	80	-8	28	3.54	-1	O-87(79-0-17)	5	-1.4
1970 NY-N	92	189	21	46	10	1	6	29	17	43	4	1	.243	.306	.402	.708	88	-3	23	4.22	-1	O-43(12-0-33)	4	-0.7
1971 NY-N	100	214	28	51	9	1	3	21	26	54	3	1	.238	.326	.332	.658	88	-2	24	3.64	-1	O-64(25-0-39)	5	-0.6
1972 NY-N	72	156	21	39	5	0	4	11	22	28	3	3	.250	.346	.359	.705	103	1	19	4.21	-4	O-42(1-4-38)	5	-0.5
1973 SD-N	39	49	4	14	5	0	0	4	8	9	0	1	.286	.397	.388	.784	128	2	7	4.39	0	/O-8(0-0-8)	1	0.1
Total 7	490	1049	123	258	41	4	16	114	133	239	13	15	.246	.336	.338	.675	92	-10	123	3.94	-8	O-294	26	-3.3
• MARSHALL, Doc	Edward Harbert "Eddie" Marshall b: 6/4/1906, New Albany, MS d: 9/1/1999, Lake San Marcos, CA BR/TR, 5'11", 150 lbs. Deb: 9/28/1929																							
1929 NY-N	5	15	6	6	2	0	0	2	1	0	0	....	.400	.438	.533	.971	140	1	3	8.68	0	/2-5	1	0.1
1930 NY-N	78	223	33	69	5	3	0	21	13	9	0	....	.309	.350	.359	.709	73	-9	27	4.44	-2	S-45,2-17/3-5	5	-0.6
1931 NY-N	68	194	15	39	6	2	0	10	8	8	1	....	.201	.233	.253	.485	31	-19	12	1.92	0	2-47,S-11/3-3	2	-1.5
1932 NY-N	68	226	18	56	8	1	0	28	6	11	1	....	.248	.270	.292	.562	52	-15	18	2.73	-8	S-63	2	-1.9
Total 4	219	658	72	170	21	6	0	61	28	28	2	....	.258	.291	.309	.599	55	-43	61	3.13	-10	S-119/2-69,3-8	10	-3.9
• MARSHALL, Doc	William Riddle Marshall b: 9/22/1875, Butler, PA d: 12/11/1959, Clinton, IL BR/TR, 6', 185 lbs. Deb: 4/15/1904 Career OF: 3-4-17																							
1904 Phi-N	8	20	1	2	0	0	0	1	0	....	0	....	.100	.100	.100	.200	-40	-3	0	.30	1	/C-7	0	-0.1
NY-N	1	0	0	0	0	0	0	0	0	....	0	....	....	....	....	....	-96	0	0	....	-1	/C-1	0	-0.1
Bos-N	13	43	3	9	0	1	0	2	2	....	2	....	.209	.244	.256	.500	56	-2	3	2.49	1	C-10/O-1	1	0.0
NY-N	10	17	3	6	1	0	0	2	1	....	0	....	.353	.389	.412	.801	141	1	3	6.60	2	/C-2,O-2(1-0-1),2-1	1	0.3
Yr.	32	80	7	17	1	1	0	5	3	....	2	....	.213	.241	.250	.491	52	-5	6	2.58	4	C-20/O-3(2-0-1),2-1	2	0.1
1906 NY-N	38	102	8	17	3	2	0	7	7	....	7	....	.167	.234	.235	.470	45	-7	8	2.29	2	O-16(1-3-13),C-13/1-2	1	-0.5
StL-N	39	123	6	34	4	1	0	10	6	....	1	....	.276	.315	.325	.641	104	0	13	3.87	2	C-38	3	0.6
Yr.	77	225	14	51	7	3	0	17	13	....	8	....	.227	.278	.284	.562	77	-6	21	3.09	3	C-51,O-16(1-3-13)/1-2	4	0.1
1907 StL-N	84	268	19	54	8	2	2	18	12	....	2	....	.201	.246	.269	.515	64	-12	19	2.29	7	C-83	3	0.3
1908 StL-N	6	14	0	1	0	0	0	1	0	....	0	....	.071	.071	.071	.143	-57	-2	0	.16	0	/C-6	0	-0.2
Chi-N	12	20	4	6	0	1	0	3	0	....	0	....	.300	.300	.400	.700	118	0	2	4.26	3	/C-4,O-3(0-1-2)	1	0.4
Yr.	18	34	4	7	0	1	0	4	0	....	0	....	.206	.206	.265	.471	43	-2	2	2.21	3	C-10/O-3(0-1-2)	1	0.2
1909 Bro-N	50	149	7	30	7	1	0	10	6	....	3	....	.201	.232	.262	.494	55	-8	9	2.01	2	C-49/O-1	3	-0.2
Total 5	261	756	51	159	23	8	2	54	34	....	15	....	.210	.251	.270	.521	64	-34	58	2.49	20	C-213/O-23,1-2,2-1	13	0.5
• MARSHALL, Jim	Rufus James Marshall b: 5/25/1931, Danville, IL BL/TL, 6'1", 190 lbs. Deb: 4/15/1958 M/C Career OF: 17-0-21																							
1958 Bal-A	85	191	17	41	4	3	5	19	18	30	3	2	.215	.282	.346	.628	76	-7	18	3.13	-1	1-52/O-8(3-0-5)	3	-1.1
Chi-N	26	81	12	22	2	0	5	11	12	13	1	0	.272	.372	.481	.854	126	4	16	7.31	-1	1-15,O-11(0-0-11)	3	0.2
1959 Chi-N	108	294	39	74	10	1	11	40	33	39	0	1	.252	.327	.405	.732	94	-3	39	4.64	4	1-72/O-8(7-0-3)	7	-0.2
1960 SF-N	75	118	19	28	2	2	2	13	17	24	0	1	.237	.333	.339	.672	90	-2	13	3.70	-2	1-28/O-6(6-0-0)	2	-0.5
1961 SF-N	44	36	5	8	0	0	1	7	3	8	0	0	.222	.282	.306	.588	58	-2	3	2.77	0	/1-4,O-2(1-0-1)	0	-0.2
1962 NY-N	17	32	6	11	1	0	3	4	3	6	0	0	.344	.400	.656	1.056	175	3	9	11.20	0	/1-5,O-1	1	0.3
Pit-N	55	100	13	22	5	1	2	12	15	19	1	0	.220	.322	.350	.672	80	-2	12	4.18	0	1-26	2	-0.4
Yr.	72	132	19	33	6	1	5	16	18	25	1	0	.250	.340	.424	.764	102	1	21	5.64	0	1-31/O-1	3	-0.1
Total 5	410	852	111	206	24	7	29	106	101	139	5	4	.242	.323	.388	.711	92	-9	111	4.45	0	1-202/O-36	18	-2.0

YEAR TM-L	G	AB	R	H	2B	3B	HR	RBI	BB	SO	SB	CS	AVG	OBP	SLG	OPS	OPS+	BR/A	RC	RC/G	FR	G/POS	WS	TPW
• MARSHALL, Joe	Joseph Hanley "Home Run Joe" Marshall b: 2/19/1876, Audubon, MN d: 9/11/1931, Santa Monica, CA BR/TR, 5'8", 170 lbs. Deb: 9/7/1903 Career OF: 2-1-23																							
1903 Pit-N	10	23	2	6	1	2	0	2	0	....	0	....	.261	.261	.478	.739	106	-0	3	4.58	-1	/O-3(2-1-0),S-3,2-1	0	-0.1
1906 StL-N	33	95	2	15	1	2	0	7	6	....	0	....	.158	.216	.211	.426	34	-7	4	1.44	0	O-23(0-0-23)/1-4	0	-0.9
Total 2	43	118	4	21	2	4	0	9	6	....	0	....	.178	.224	.263	.487	47	-8	7	1.99	-1	/O-26,1-4,S-3,2-1	0	-1.0
• MARSHALL, Keith	Keith Alan Marshall b: 7/2/1951, San Francisco, CA BR/TR, 6'2", 175 lbs. Deb: 4/7/1973																							
1973 KC-A	8	9	0	2	1	0	0	3	1	4	0	0	.222	.300	.333	.633	73	-0	1	2.20	0	/O-8(5-2-2)	0	-0.1
• MARSHALL, Max	Milo May Marshall b: 9/18/1913, Shenandoah, IA d: 9/16/1993, Salem, OR BL/TR, 6'1", 180 lbs. Deb: 5/10/1942 Career OF: 44-11-266																							
1942 Cin-N	131	530	49	135	17	6	7	43	34	38	4	....	.255	.301	.349	.650	90	-8	56	3.66	-6	*O-129(43-11-79)	12	-2.4
1943 Cin-N	132	508	55	120	11	8	4	39	34	52	8	....	.236	.287	.313	.600	74	-18	47	3.14	0	*O-129(0-0-129)	10	-2.8
1944 Cin-N	66	229	36	56	13	2	4	23	21	10	3	....	.245	.308	.371	.679	94	-2	27	4.15	3	O-59(1-0-58)	7	-0.4
Total 3	329	1267	140	311	41	16	15	105	89	100	15	....	.245	.297	.339	.635	84	-29	131	3.53	-3	O-317	29	-5.5
• MARSHALL, Mike	Michael Allen Marshall b: 1/12/1960, Libertyville, IL BR/TR, 6'5", 220 lbs. Deb: 9/7/1981 Career OF: 123-0-657																							
1981*LA-N	14	25	2	5	3	0	0	1	1	4	0	0	.200	.259	.320	.579	66	-1	2	2.43	0	/1-3,3-3,O-2(1-0-1)	0	-0.2
1982 LA-N	49	95	10	23	3	0	5	9	13	23	2	0	.242	.339	.432	.771	117	3	15	5.49	-1	O-19(3-0-16),1-13	3	0.0
1983*LA-N	140	465	47	132	17	1	17	65	43	127	7	3	.284	.351	.434	.785	117	11	72	5.54	-2	*O-109(0-0-109),1-33	17	0.3
1984 LA-N★	134	495	68	127	27	0	21	65	40	93	4	3	.257	.316	.438	.754	111	5	66	4.61	3	*O-118(116-0-4),1-15	15	0.1
1985*LA-N	135	518	72	152	27	2	28	95	37	137	3	10	.293	.344	.515	.860	141	22	87	5.99	1	*O-125(1-0-124)/1-7	23	1.7
1986 LA-N	103	330	47	77	11	0	19	53	27	90	4	4	.233	.299	.439	.739	109	1	42	4.35	0	O-97(1-0-97)	9	-0.3
1987 LA-N	104	402	45	118	19	0	16	72	18	79	0	5	.294	.330	.460	.790	110	1	55	4.84	-5	*O-102(0-0-102)	11	-0.8
1988*LA-N	144	542	63	150	27	2	20	82	24	93	4	1	.277	.316	.445	.761	120	11	71	4.63	0	O-90(0-0-90),1-53	19	0.5
1989 LA-N	105	377	41	98	21	1	11	42	33	78	2	5	.260	.328	.408	.736	111	3	49	4.44	-3	*O-102(0-0-102)	11	-0.2
1990 NY-N	53	163	24	39	8	1	6	27	7	40	0	2	.239	.283	.411	.694	89	-4	18	3.75	-1	1-42/O-1	2	-0.8
*Bos-A	30	112	10	32	6	1	4	12	4	26	0	0	.286	.316	.464	.781	110	1	16	5.25	1	D-14/1-8,O-8(0-0-8)	3	0.1
1991 Bos-A	22	62	4	18	4	0	1	7	0	19	0	0	.290	.290	.403	.694	85	-2	6	3.79	-2	/D-7,1-5,O-4(1-0-3)	0	-0.4
Cal-A	2	7	0	0	0	0	0	0	0	1	0	0	.000	.000	.000	.000	-100	-2	0	.00	0	/1-1,D-1	0	-0.2
Yr.	24	69	4	18	4	0	1	7	0	20	0	0	.261	.261	.362	.623	67	-3	6	3.29	-2	/D-8,1-6,O-4(1-0-3)	0	-0.6
Total 11	1035	3593	433	971	173	8	148	530	247	810	26	33	.270	.324	.446	.770	115	48	499	4.87	-8	O-777,1-180/D-22,3-3	113	-0.2
• MARSHALL, Willard	Willard Warren Marshall b: 2/8/1921, Richmond, VA d: 11/5/2000, Norwood, NJ BL/TR, 6'1", 205 lbs. Deb: 4/14/1942 Career OF: 145-114-895																							
1942 NY-N★	116	401	41	103	9	2	11	59	26	20	1	....	.257	.307	.372	.679	98	-3	46	3.99	1	*O-107(67-46-1)	11	-0.6
1946 NY-N	131	510	63	144	18	3	13	48	33	29	3	....	.282	.327	.406	.733	107	2	65	4.53	-2	*O-125(51-59-15)	12	-0.6
1947 NY-N★	155	587	102	171	19	6	36	107	67	30	3	....	.291	.366	.528	.894	134	26	113	7.09	12	*O-155(0-0-155)	24	3.3
1948 NY-N	143	537	72	146	21	8	14	86	64	34	2	....	.272	.350	.419	.769	107	5	80	5.38	-1	*O-142(0-0-142)	16	0.0
1949 NY-N★	141	499	81	153	19	3	12	70	78	20	4	....	.307	.401	.429	.830	123	19	90	6.78	0	*O-138(2-0-136)	18	1.5
1950 Bos-N	105	298	38	70	10	2	5	40	36	5	1	....	.235	.319	.332	.652	77	-10	32	3.56	1	O-85(14-9-64)	5	-1.1
1951 Bos-N	136	469	65	132	24	7	11	62	48	18	0	3	.281	.351	.433	.784	118	10	69	5.12	-5	*O-136(0-0-136)	13	0.1
1952 Bos-N	21	66	5	15	4	1	2	11	4	4	0	0	.227	.271	.409	.681	89	-1	7	3.28	1	O-16(0-0-16)	1	-0.1
Cin-N	107	397	52	106	23	1	8	46	37	21	0	1	.267	.333	.390	.723	100	-0	53	4.61	0	*O-105(0-0-105)	11	-0.3
Yr.	128	463	57	121	27	2	10	57	41	25	0	1	.261	.324	.393	.717	99	-1	59	4.41	1	*O-121(0-0-121)	12	-0.4
1953 Cin-N	122	357	51	95	14	6	17	62	41	28	0	0	.266	.342	.482	.824	111	5	59	5.84	2	O-95(0-0-95)	11	0.4
1954 Chi-A	47	71	7	18	2	0	1	7	11	9	0	0	.254	.354	.324	.678	84	-1	9	4.14	-1	O-29(7-0-22)	2	-0.2
1955 Chi-A	22	41	6	7	0	0	0	6	13	1	0	0	.171	.370	.171	.541	48	-2	4	2.98	0	O-12(4-0-8)	1	-0.3
Total 11	1246	4233	583	1160	163	39	130	604	458	219	14	4	.274	.347	.423	.770	109	51	625	5.25	9	*O-1145	125	2.1
• MARTEL, Doc	Leon Alphonse "Marty" Martel b: 1/29/1883, Weymouth, MA d: 10/11/1947, Washington, DC BR/TR, 6', 185 lbs. Deb: 7/6/1909																							
1909 Phi-N	24	41	1	11	3	1	0	7	4	....	0	....	.268	.333	.390	.724	123	1	5	4.48	1	C-12	2	0.3
1910 Bos-N	10	31	0	4	0	0	0	1	2	3	0	....	.129	.182	.129	.311	-9	-4	1	.71	-1	1-10	0	-0.5
Total 2	34	72	1	15	3	1	0	8	6	3	0	....	.208	.269	.278	.547	67	-3	6	2.66	0	/C-12,1-10	2	-0.2
• MARTIN, Al	Albert Lee Martin b: 11/24/1967, West Covina, CA BL/TL, 6'2", 210 lbs. Deb: 7/28/1992 Career OF: 939-152-21																							
1992 Pit-N	12	12	1	2	0	1	0	2	0	5	0	0	.167	.167	.333	.500	39	-1	1	1.71	0	/O-7(7-0-0)	0	-0.1
1993 Pit-N	143	480	85	135	26	8	18	64	42	122	16	9	.281	.340	.481	.822	117	10	78	5.80	-5	*O-136(81-63-6)	16	0.2
1994 Pit-N	82	276	48	79	12	4	9	33	34	56	15	6	.286	.369	.457	.825	112	6	48	6.31	2	O-77(67-13-0)	11	0.5
1995 Pit-N	124	439	70	124	25	3	13	41	44	92	20	11	.282	.351	.442	.792	105	2	68	5.55	2	*O-121(95-42-0)	11	0.2
1996 Pit-N	155	630	101	189	40	1	18	72	54	116	38	12	.300	.357	.452	.810	109	10	104	5.99	-8	*O-152(142-26-0)	17	-0.3
1997 Pit-N	113	423	64	123	24	7	13	59	45	83	23	7	.291	.363	.473	.836	115	11	74	6.27	-6	*O-110(110-0-0)	13	0.0
1998 Pit-N	125	440	57	105	15	2	12	47	32	91	20	3	.239	.298	.364	.661	72	-16	47	3.63	1	*O-114(114-0-0)/D-2	5	-2.0
1999 Pit-N	143	541	97	150	36	8	24	63	49	119	20	3	.277	.338	.506	.845	110	9	95	6.33	-7	*O-134(134-0-0)	14	-0.3
2000 SD-N	93	346	62	106	13	6	11	27	28	54	6	8	.306	.362	.474	.836	117	6	58	6.24	-6	O-89(89-0-0)	9	-0.3
*Sea-A	42	134	19	31	2	4	4	9	8	31	4	1	.231	.285	.396	.680	74	-5	16	3.99	3	O-35(20-7-9)/D-2	1	-0.4
2001*Sea-A	100	283	41	68	15	2	7	42	37	59	9	3	.240	.332	.382	.714	93	-2	39	4.70	2	O-73(72-1-1),D-16	8	-0.3
2003 TB-A	100	238	19	60	12	2	3	26	17	51	2	2	.252	.307	.357	.665	76	-9	24	3.46	0	D-57,O-13(8-0-5)/1-1	2	-1.2
Total 11	1232	4242	664	1172	220	48	132	485	390	879	173	65	.276	.341	.444	.785	103	21	653	5.46	-23	*O-1061/D-77,1-1	107	-3.9
• MARTIN, Al	Albert Martin Deb: 5/7/1872 NA OF: 1-6-0																							
1872 Eck-n	4	18	2	5	0	0	0	2	0	0	0	0	.278	.278	.278	.556	84	0	1	3.39	-3	/2-4	....	-0.2
1874 Atl-n	7	29	1	4	0	0	0	1	0	1	0	0	.138	.138	.138	.276	-13	-3	1	.68	-3	/2-6,O-1	....	-0.5
1875 Atl-n	6	26	1	3	0	0	0	1	0	0	0	0	.115	.115	.115	.231	-22	-3	0	.46	0	/O-6(0-6-0)	....	-0.2
Total 3 n	17	73	4	12	0	0	0	4	0	1	0	0	.164	.164	.164	.329	8	-6	2	1.17	-6	/2-10,O-7	....	-1.0
• MARTIN, Babe	Boris Michael Martin b: 3/28/1920, Seattle, WA BR/TR, 5'11.5", 194 lbs. Deb: 9/25/1944 Career OF: 44-0-6																							
1944 StL-A	2	4	0	3	1	0	0	1	0	0	0	0	.750	.750	1.000	1.750	376	1	3	83.03	-0	/O-1	1	0.1
1945 StL-A	54	185	13	37	5	2	2	16	11	24	0	1	.200	.245	.281	.526	50	-13	12	2.07	4	O-48(43-0-6)/1-6	2	-1.2
1946 StL-A	3	9	0	2	0	0	0	1	1	2	0	0	.222	.300	.222	.522	45	-1	1	2.67	1	/C-2	0	0.1
1948 Bos-A	4	4	0	2	0	0	0	0	0	1	0	0	.500	.500	.500	1.000	158	0	1	13.84	0	/C-1	0	0.0
1949 Bos-A	2	2	0	0	0	0	0	0	0	0	0	0	.000	.000	.000	.000	-93	-1	0	.00	0	/C-1	0	-0.1
1953 StL-A	4	2	0	0	0	0	0	0	1	0	0	0	.000	.333	.000	.333	-4	-0	0	1.17	0	/C-1	0	-0.1
Total 6	69	206	13	44	6	2	2	18	13	27	0	1	.214	.260	.291	.552	55	-12	17	2.66	4	/O-49,1-6,C-5	3	-1.2
• MARTIN, Billy	William Lloyd Martin b: 2/13/1894, Washington, DC d: 9/14/1949, Arlington, VA BR/TR, 5'8.5", 170 lbs. Deb: 10/6/1914																							
1914 Bos-N	1	3	0	0	0	0	0	0	0	0	0	....	.000	.000	.000	.000	-101	-1	0	.00	0	/S-1	0	-0.1
• MARTIN, Billy	Alfred Manuel Martin b: 5/16/1928, Berkeley, CA d: 12/25/1989, Johnson City, NY BR/TR, 5'11.5", 165 lbs. Deb: 4/18/1950 M/C																							
1950 NY-A	34	36	10	9	1	0	1	8	3	3	0	0	.250	.308	.361	.669	73	-2	4	4.34	-2	2-22/3-1	1	-0.3
1951*NY-A	51	58	10	15	1	2	0	2	4	9	0	1	.259	.328	.345	.673	85	-2	5	2.81	2	2-23/S-6,3-2,O-1	1	0.1
1952*NY-A	109	363	32	97	13	3	3	33	22	31	3	6	.267	.323	.344	.668	91	-7	40	3.74	11	*2-107	11	1.1
1953*NY-A	149	587	72	151	24	6	15	75	43	56	6	7	.257	.314	.395	.710	94	-8	70	4.00	1	*2-146,S-18	17	0.5
1955*NY-A	20	70	8	21	2	0	1	9	7	9	1	2	.300	.364	.371	.735	99	-1	9	4.29	3	2-17/S-3	2	0.4
1956*NY-A★	121	458	76	121	24	5	9	49	30	56	7	3	.264	.314	.397	.711	89	-9	57	4.26	2	*2-105,3-16	14	0.1
1957 NY-A	43	145	12	35	5	2	1	12	3	14	2	1	.241	.262	.324	.586	60	-8	11	2.38	-1	2-26,3-13	2	-0.8
KC-A	73	265	33	68	9	3	9	27	12	20	7	1	.257	.296	.415	.712	91	-3	32	4.10	-10	2-52,3-20/S-2	6	-0.9
Yr.	116	410	45	103	14	5	10	39	15	34	9	2	.251	.284	.383	.667	80	-12	42	3.46	-11	2-78,3-33/S-2	8	-1.7
1958 Det-A	131	498	56	127	19	1	7	42	16	62	5	3	.255	.282	.339	.622	65	-24	44	2.92	-10	S-88,3-41	6	-2.8
1959 Cle-A	73	242	37	63	7	0	9	24	8	18	0	2	.260	.292	.401	.693	92	-5	27	3.73	-2	2-67/3-4	7	-0.2
1960 Cin-N	103	317	34	78	17	1	3	16	27	34	0	1	.246	.305	.334	.640	74	-12	30	3.23	-6	2-97	5	-1.2
1961 Mil-N	6	6	1	0	0	0	0	0	0	1	0	0	.000	.000	.000	.000	-106	-2	0	.00	0	....	0	-0.2

YEAR TM-L	G	AB	R	H	2B	3B	HR	RBI	BB	SO	SB	CS	AVG	OBP	SLG	OPS	OPS+	BR/A	RC	RC/G	FR	G/POS	WS	TPW
Min-A	108	374	44	92	15	5	6	36	13	42	3	2	.246	.277	.361	.638	65	-20	35	3.17	-10	*2-105/S-1	4	-2.2
Total 11	1021	3419	425	877	137	28	64	333	188	355	34	29	.257	.301	.369	.671	82	-101	364	3.58	-21	2-767,S-118/3-97,0-1	76	-6.4
• MARTIN, Frank	Frank Martin b: 2/28/1879, Chicago, IL d: 9/30/1924, Chicago, IL Deb: 6/30/1897																							
1897 Lou-N	2	8	1	2	0	0	0	0	0	....	0	....	.250	.250	.250	.500	33	-1	1	2.26	0	/2-2	0	-0.1
1898 Chi-N	1	4	0	0	0	0	0	0	0	....	0	....	.000	.000	.000	.000	-100	-1	0	.00	0	/2-1	0	-0.1
1899 NY-N	17	54	5	14	2	0	0	1	2	....	0	....	.259	.298	.296	.595	65	-3	5	3.24	-4	3-17	0	-0.5
Total 3	20	66	6	16	2	0	0	1	2	....	0	....	.242	.275	.273	.548	52	-4	5	2.86	-3	/3-17,2-3	0	-0.7
• MARTIN, Gene	Thomas Eugene Martin b: 1/12/1947, Americus, GA BL/TR, 6'.5", 190 lbs. Deb: 7/28/1968																							
1968 Was-A	9	11	1	4	1	0	1	1	0	1	0	0	.364	.364	.727	1.091	232	2	2	7.36	0	/0-2(2-0-0)	1	0.1
• MARTIN, Hersh	Hershel Ray Martin b: 9/19/1909, Birmingham, AL d: 11/17/1980, Cuba, MO BB/TR, 6'2", 190 lbs. Deb: 4/23/1937 Career OF: 187-348-21																							
1937 Phi-N	141	579	102	164	35	7	8	49	69	66	11	....	.283	.362	.409	.771	101	2	92	5.86	-7	*0-139(3-136-0)	15	-0.8
1938 Phi-N★	120	466	58	139	36	6	3	39	34	48	8	....	.298	.347	.421	.768	110	6	67	5.22	-7	*0-116(0-115-2)	13	-0.4
1939 Phi-N	111	393	59	111	28	5	1	22	42	27	4	....	.282	.355	.387	.741	104	3	56	5.21	-1	0-95(9-73-13)	11	-0.2
1940 Phi-N	33	83	10	21	6	1	0	5	9	9	1	....	.253	.326	.349	.675	90	-1	10	4.27	2	0-23(0-19-4)	2	0.0
1944 NY-A	85	328	49	99	12	4	9	47	34	26	5	2	.302	.371	.445	.816	128	13	57	6.48	0	0-80(78-2-0)	13	0.8
1945 NY-A	117	408	53	109	18	6	7	53	65	31	4	1	.267	.368	.392	.760	115	11	66	5.77	1	*0-102(97-3-2)	16	0.6
Total 6	607	2257	331	643	135	29	28	215	253	207	33	3	.285	.359	.408	.766	109	33	350	5.62	-11	0-555	70	0.1
• MARTIN, J.C.	Joseph Clifton Martin b: 12/13/1936, Axton, VA BL/TR, 6'2", 200 lbs. Deb: 9/10/1959 C																							
1959 Chi-A	3	4	0	1	0	0	0	1	0	1	0	0	.250	.250	.250	.500	38	-0	0	2.25	0	/3-2	0	-0.1
1960 Chi-A	7	20	0	2	1	0	0	2	0	6	0	0	.100	.100	.150	.250	-34	-4	0	.21	0	/3-5,1-1	0	-0.4
1961 Chi-A	110	274	26	63	8	3	5	32	21	31	1	2	.230	.290	.336	.625	68	-14	27	3.37	4	1-60,3-36	4	-1.2
1962 Chi-A	18	26	0	2	0	0	0	2	0	3	0	0	.077	.077	.077	.154	-59	-6	0	.08	0	/C-6,1-1,3-1	0	-0.6
1963 Chi-A	105	259	25	53	11	1	5	28	26	35	0	0	.205	.280	.313	.592	67	-11	24	3.03	2	C-98/1-3,3-1	6	-0.6
1964 Chi-A	122	294	23	58	10	1	4	22	16	30	0	0	.197	.244	.279	.523	46	-22	20	2.19	-1	*C-120	4	-1.9
1965 Chi-A	119	230	21	60	12	0	2	21	24	29	2	1	.261	.336	.339	.675	98	-0	28	4.21	-1	*C-112/1-4,3-2	9	0.1
1966 Chi-A	67	157	13	40	5	3	2	20	14	24	0	0	.255	.320	.363	.683	103	1	18	3.86	-0	C-63	5	0.3
1967 Chi-A	101	252	22	59	12	1	4	22	30	41	4	4	.234	.318	.337	.655	97	-1	27	3.63	-3	C-96/1-1	10	0.0
1968 NY-N	78	244	20	55	9	2	3	31	21	31	0	0	.225	.300	.316	.616	84	-4	24	3.27	-2	C-53,1-14	6	-0.5
1969*NY-N	66	177	12	37	5	1	4	21	12	32	0	0	.209	.259	.316	.576	59	-10	14	2.45	-2	C-48/1-2	3	-1.0
1970 Chi-N	40	77	11	12	1	0	1	4	20	11	0	0	.156	.337	.208	.545	44	-5	6	2.51	-1	C-36/1-3	1	-0.5
1971 Chi-N	47	125	13	33	5	0	2	17	12	16	1	1	.264	.338	.352	.690	83	-2	15	4.11	1	C-43/0-1	4	0.0
1972 Chi-N	25	50	3	12	3	0	0	7	5	9	1	0	.240	.309	.300	.609	67	-2	4	2.71	-1	C-17	1	-0.2
Total 14	908	2189	189	487	82	12	32	230	201	299	9	8	.222	.293	.315	.608	73	-81	207	3.14	-6	C-692/1-89,3-47,0-1	53	-6.6
• MARTIN, Jack	John Christopher Martin b: 4/19/1887, Plainfield, NJ d: 7/4/1980, Bronx, NY BR/TR, 5'9", 159 lbs. Deb: 4/25/1912																							
1912 NY-A	71	231	30	52	6	1	0	17	37	....	14	....	.225	.347	.260	.606	70	-7	26	3.65	-1	S-65/3-4,2-1	5	-0.3
1914 Bos-N	33	85	10	18	2	0	0	5	6	7	0	....	.212	.264	.235	.499	49	-5	5	1.99	-3	3-26/1-1,2-1	1	-0.8
Phi-N	83	292	26	74	5	3	0	21	27	29	6	....	.253	.319	.291	.610	77	-8	29	3.29	-11	S-83	6	-1.4
Yr.	116	377	36	92	7	3	0	26	33	36	6	....	.244	.307	.279	.585	71	-13	35	2.99	-14	S-83,3-26/1-1,2-1	7	-2.2
Total 2	187	608	66	144	13	4	0	43	70	36	20	....	.237	.323	.271	.594	70	-20	61	3.24	-15	S-148/3-30,2-2,1-1	12	-2.5
• MARTIN, Jerry	Jerry Lindsey Martin b: 5/11/1949, Columbia, SC BR/TR, 6'1", 195 lbs. Deb: 9/7/1974 Career OF: 215-411-337																							
1974 Phi-N	13	14	2	3	1	0	0	1	1	5	0	0	.214	.267	.286	.552	52	-1	1	1.18	-1	0-11(6-3-2)	0	-0.2
1975 Phi-N	57	113	15	24	7	1	2	11	11	16	2	2	.212	.288	.345	.633	72	-5	11	3.20	0	0-49(8-41-0)	2	-0.6
1976*Phi-N	130	121	30	30	7	0	2	15	7	28	3	2	.248	.289	.355	.644	80	-4	11	2.97	-5	*0-110(73-23-15)/1-1	2	-1.2
1977*Phi-N	116	215	34	56	16	3	6	28	18	42	6	4	.260	.329	.447	.776	101	-0	31	5.06	0	*0-106(45-18-51)/1-1	6	-0.3
1978*Phi-N	128	266	40	72	13	4	9	36	28	65	9	5	.271	.342	.451	.794	119	6	42	5.47	2	*0-112(48-22-55)	9	0.5
1979 Chi-N	150	534	74	145	34	3	19	73	38	85	2	4	.272	.323	.453	.777	100	-2	74	4.90	0	*0-144(0-140-4)	15	-0.5
1980 Chi-N	141	494	57	112	22	2	23	73	38	107	8	3	.227	.285	.419	.704	88	-10	57	3.83	-4	*0-129(5-103-42)	9	-1.9
1981 SF-N	72	241	23	58	5	3	4	25	21	52	6	2	.241	.309	.336	.646	85	-4	24	3.33	-1	0-64(10-58-0)	5	-0.8
1982 KC-A	147	519	52	138	22	1	15	65	38	138	1	1	.266	.318	.399	.717	95	-4	66	4.51	0	*0-142(11-3-134)/D-3	14	-1.1
1983 KC-A	13	44	4	14	2	0	2	13	1	7	1	0	.318	.333	.500	.833	125	1	8	6.22	-1	0-13(0-0-13)	2	0.1
1984 NY-N	51	91	6	14	1	0	3	5	6	29	0	0	.154	.206	.264	.470	32	-9	4	1.30	1	0-30(9-0-21)/1-3	0	-1.0
Total 11	1018	2652	337	666	130	17	85	345	207	574	38	23	.251	.309	.409	.718	93	-32	329	4.23	-9	0-910/1-5,D-3	64	-6.9
• MARTIN, Joe	William Joseph "Smokey Joe" Martin b: 8/28/1911, Seymour, MO d: 9/28/1960, Buffalo, NY BR/TR, 5'11.5", 181 lbs. Deb: 4/21/1936																							
1936 NY-N	7	15	0	4	1	0	0	2	0	4	0	....	.267	.313	.333	.646	75	-1	1	2.89	-0	/3-7	0	0.0
1938 Chi-A	1	0	0	0	0	0	0	0	0	0	0	0	....	....	....	....	-98	0	0	....	0	....	0	0.0
Total 2	8	15	0	4	1	0	0	2	0	4	0	0	.267	.313	.333	.646	75	-1	1	2.89	-0	/3-7	0	0.0
• MARTIN, Joe	Joseph Samuel "Silent Joe" Martin b: 1/1/1876, Hollidaysburg, PA d: 5/25/1964, Altoona, PA BL/TR, 5'9.5", 155 lbs. Deb: 4/28/1903																							
1903 Was-A	35	119	11	27	4	5	0	7	5	....	2	....	.227	.258	.345	.603	78	-4	12	3.26	-3	2-15,3-13/0-7(1-0-6)	1	-0.7
StL-A	44	173	18	37	6	4	0	7	6	....	0	....	.214	.249	.295	.543	64	-8	14	2.55	0	0-38(4-0-34)/2-6,3-1	1	-1.0
Yr.	79	292	29	64	10	9	0	14	11	....	2	....	.219	.252	.315	.568	70	-11	26	2.83	-3	0-45(5-0-40),2-21,3-14	2	-1.7
• MARTIN, Mike	Joseph Michael Martin b: 12/3/1958, Portland, OR BL/TR, 6'2", 193 lbs. Deb: 8/15/1986																							
1986 Chi-N	8	13	1	1	1	0	0	2	4	0	0	0	.077	.200	.154	.354	-1	-2	0	1.02	1	/C-8	0	-0.1
• MARTIN, Norberto	Norberto Edonal (McDonald) Martin b: 12/10/1966, San Pedro de Macoris, Dominican Republic BR/TR, 5'10", 164 lbs. Deb: 9/20/1993 Career OF: 12-0-7																							
1993 Chi-A	8	14	3	5	0	0	0	2	1	1	0	0	.357	.400	.357	.757	108	0	2	6.31	-1	/2-5,D-1	1	0.0
1994 Chi-A	45	131	19	36	7	1	1	16	9	16	4	2	.275	.321	.366	.688	78	-4	16	4.04	2	2-28/S-6,3-5,0-2(2-0-0),D	4	-0.1
1995 Chi-A	72	160	17	43	7	4	2	17	3	25	5	0	.269	.287	.400	.687	80	-4	17	3.71	-2	2-17,0-12(5-0-7),D-10/3-9,S	2	-0.5
1996 Chi-A	70	140	30	49	7	0	1	14	6	17	10	2	.350	.377	.421	.798	107	3	22	5.87	-0	S-24,D-22,2-10/3-3	4	0.4
1997 Chi-A	71	213	24	64	7	1	2	27	6	31	1	4	.300	.320	.371	.691	83	-7	24	4.13	-1	S-28,3-17/2-9,D-6	6	-0.6
1998 Ana-A	79	195	20	42	2	0	1	13	6	29	3	1	.215	.239	.241	.480	25	-21	10	1.56	3	2-54,D-10/3-5,0-5(5-0-0),S	3	-1.6
1999 Tor-A	9	27	3	6	2	0	0	0	4	4	0	0	.222	.364	.296	.660	70	-1	3	3.40	1	/2-8,S-1	0	0.1
Total 7	354	880	116	245	32	6	7	89	35	123	23	9	.278	.308	.352	.661	73	-36	94	3.67	3	2-131/S-68,D-50,3-39,0-19	20	-2.4
• MARTIN, Pepper	Johnny Leonard Roosevelt "The Wild Horse Of The Osage" Martin b: 2/29/1904, Temple, OK d: 3/5/1965, McAlester, OK BR/TR, 5'8", 170 lbs. Deb: 4/16/1928 C Career OF: 31-314-273																							
1928*StL-N	39	13	11	4	0	0	0	0	1	2	2	....	.308	.400	.308	.708	86	-0	2	4.52	0	/0-4(0-0-4)	0	-0.1
1930 StL-N	6	1	5	0	0	0	0	0	0	0	0	....	.000	.000	.000	.000	-97	-0	0	.00	0	....	0	0.0
1931*StL-N	123	413	68	124	32	8	7	75	30	40	16	....	.300	.351	.467	.818	114	7	69	6.10	1	*0-110(0-110-0)	16	0.6
1932 StL-N	85	323	47	77	19	6	4	34	30	31	9	....	.238	.305	.372	.677	78	-10	38	4.00	-5	0-69(5-64-0),3-15	6	-1.6
1933 StL-N★	145	599	**122**	189	36	12	8	57	67	46	**26**	....	.316	.387	.456	.843	133	28	111	7.18	2	*3-145	29	3.7
1934*StL-N★	110	454	76	131	25	11	5	49	32	41	**23**	....	.289	.337	.425	.762	96	-3	69	5.74	2	*3-107/P-1	15	0.3
1935 StL-N★	135	539	121	161	41	6	9	54	33	58	20	....	.299	.341	.447	.789	106	3	84	5.90	-4	*3-114,0-16(1-5-10)	19	0.3
1936 StL-N	143	572	121	177	36	11	11	76	58	66	**23**	....	.309	.373	.469	.842	126	21	103	6.79	-7	*0-127(0-3-124),3-15/P-1	24	0.7
1937 StL-N★	98	339	60	103	27	8	5	38	33	50	9	....	.304	.366	.475	.841	124	11	62	6.98	4	0-82(0-40-42)/3-5	14	1.1
1938 StL-N	91	269	34	79	18	2	2	38	18	34	4	....	.294	.340	.398	.738	97	-1	38	5.33	-2	0-62(1-38-23)/3-4	7	-0.6
1939 StL-N	88	281	48	86	17	7	3	37	30	35	6	....	.306	.375	.448	.823	113	6	47	6.21	-1	0-51(8-37-8),3-22	9	0.3
1940 StL-N	86	228	28	72	15	4	3	39	22	24	6	....	.316	.378	.456	.835	122	7	41	7.00	2	0-63(16-10-40)/3-2	9	0.7
1944 StL-N	40	86	15	24	4	0	2	4	15	11	2	....	.279	.386	.395	.781	118	3	14	5.55	-1	0-29(0-7-22)	3	0.1
Total 13	1189	4117	756	1227	270	75	59	501	369	438	146	....	.298	.358	.443	.801	113	71	679	6.17	-10	0-613,3-429/P-2	151	5.5
• MARTIN, Phonney	Alphonse Case Martin b: 8/4/1845, New York, NY d: 5/24/1933, Hollis, NY, 5'7", 148 lbs. Deb: 4/26/1872 U NA OF: 0-0-64 ♦																							
1872 Tro-n	25	117	27	36	2	1	0	14	0	1	0	0	.308	.308	.342	.650	98	-0	13	4.83	-2	0-25(0-0-25)/P-8	....	-0.7

YEAR	TM-L	G	AB	R	H	2B	3B	HR	RBI	BB	SO	SB	CS	AVG	OBP	SLG	OPS	OPS+	BR/A	RC	RC/G	FR	G/POS	WS	TPW
	Eck-n	18	78	13	12	0	0	0	9	1	2	3	1	.154	.165	.154	.318	-2	-6	3	1.17	1	P-10/0-9(0-0-9)	....	-0.3
	Yr.	43	195	40	48	2	1	0	23	1	3	3	1	.246	.250	.267	.517	58	-6	15	3.17	-1	*0-34(0-0-34),P-18	....	-1.0
1873	Mut-n	31	140	12	31	1	0	0	14	0	4	0	1	.221	.221	.229	.450	34	-10	7	2.01	-7	0-30(0-0-30)/P-6	....	-1.0
Total	2 n	74	335	52	79	3	1	0	37	1	7	3	2	.236	.238	.251	.489	48	-16	22	2.68	-8	/0-64,P-24	....	-2.0

• MARTIN, Stu

Stuart McGuire Martin b: 11/17/1913, Rich Square, NC d: 1/11/1997, Severn, NC BL/TR, 6', 155 lbs. Deb: 4/14/1936

YEAR	TM-L	G	AB	R	H	2B	3B	HR	RBI	BB	SO	SB	CS	AVG	OBP	SLG	OPS	OPS+	BR/A	RC	RC/G	FR	G/POS	WS	TPW
1936	StL-N★	92	332	63	99	21	4	6	41	29	27	17	....	.298	.356	.440	.796	114	6	53	5.81	-4	2-83/S-3	13	0.7
1937	StL-N	90	223	34	58	6	1	1	17	32	18	3	....	.260	.353	.309	.662	80	-5	26	3.98	-1	2-48/1-9,S-1	5	-0.4
1938	StL-N	114	417	54	116	26	2	1	27	30	28	4	....	.278	.328	.357	.685	84	-9	52	4.42	-2	2-99	9	-0.5
1939	StL-N	120	425	60	114	26	7	3	30	33	40	4	....	.268	.325	.384	.709	85	-10	54	4.43	7	*2-107/1-1	10	0.3
1940	StL-N	112	369	45	88	12	6	4	32	33	35	4	....	.238	.301	.336	.637	71	-15	39	3.57	-1	3-73,2-33	6	-1.3
1941	Pit-N	88	233	37	71	13	2	0	19	10	17	2	....	.305	.341	.378	.719	103	0	29	4.47	1	2-53/3-2,1-1	7	0.5
1942	Pit-N	42	120	16	27	4	2	1	12	8	10	1	....	.225	.273	.317	.590	71	-5	11	3.02	-4	2-30/1-1,S-1	2	-0.8
1943	Chi-N	64	118	13	26	4	0	0	5	15	10	1	....	.220	.308	.254	.563	64	-5	10	2.84	4	2-22/3-8,1-2	2	0.0
Total	8	722	2237	322	599	112	24	16	183	190	185	36	....	.268	.327	.361	.688	86	-42	273	4.27	-1	2-475/3-83,1-14,S-5	54	-1.4

• MARTINEZ, Buck

John Albert Martinez b: 11/7/1948, Redding, CA BR/TR, 5'10", 190 lbs. Deb: 6/18/1969 M

YEAR	TM-L	G	AB	R	H	2B	3B	HR	RBI	BB	SO	SB	CS	AVG	OBP	SLG	OPS	OPS+	BR/A	RC	RC/G	FR	G/POS	WS	TPW
1969	KC-A	72	205	14	47	6	1	4	23	8	25	0	0	.229	.258	.327	.585	62	-11	16	2.73	-1	C-55/0-1	3	-1.0
1970	KC-A	6	9	1	1	0	0	0	0	2	1	0	0	.111	.273	.111	.384	10	-1	0	.83	0	/C-5	0	-0.1
1971	KC-A	22	46	3	7	2	0	0	1	5	9	0	1	.152	.235	.196	.431	23	-5	2	1.34	-2	C-21	1	-0.6
1973	KC-A	14	32	2	8	1	0	1	6	4	5	0	0	.250	.333	.375	.708	92	-0	4	3.66	0	C-14	1	0.0
1974	KC-A	43	107	10	23	3	1	1	8	14	19	0	1	.215	.317	.290	.607	71	-4	11	3.32	-2	C-38	2	-0.5
1975	KC-A	80	226	15	51	9	2	3	23	21	28	1	0	.226	.294	.323	.617	72	-8	22	3.26	-3	C-79	5	-0.8
1976*	KC-A	95	267	24	61	13	3	5	34	16	45	0	0	.228	.272	.356	.628	82	-7	27	3.28	-3	C-94	8	-0.6
1977	KC-A	29	80	3	18	4	0	1	9	3	12	0	1	.225	.253	.313	.566	53	-6	6	2.45	-1	C-28	1	-0.6
1978	Mil-A	89	256	26	56	10	1	1	20	14	42	1	1	.219	.259	.277	.537	51	-17	19	2.31	-2	C-89	3	-1.6
1979	Mil-A	69	196	17	53	8	0	4	26	8	25	0	1	.270	.299	.372	.671	80	-6	21	3.68	2	C-68/P-1	5	-0.2
1980	Mil-A	76	219	16	49	9	0	3	17	12	33	1	0	.224	.267	.306	.573	58	-13	18	2.77	-1	C-76	4	-0.9
1981	Tor-A	45	128	13	29	8	1	4	21	11	16	1	0	.227	.293	.398	.691	92	-1	14	3.37	3	C-45	4	0.4
1982	Tor-A	96	260	26	63	17	0	10	37	24	34	1	1	.242	.306	.423	.729	90	-4	31	3.94	1	C-93	7	0.0
1983	Tor-A	88	221	27	56	14	0	10	33	29	39	0	1	.253	.340	.452	.792	109	3	33	5.09	0	C-85	9	0.5
1984	Tor-A	102	232	24	51	13	1	5	37	29	49	0	3	.220	.312	.349	.661	80	-7	27	3.66	3	C-98/D-1	7	-0.1
1985	Tor-A	42	99	11	16	3	0	4	14	10	12	0	0	.162	.245	.313	.559	50	-7	8	2.28	1	C-42	2	-0.5
1986	Tor-A	81	160	13	29	8	0	2	12	20	25	0	0	.181	.272	.269	.541	47	-12	12	2.31	-1	C-78/D-1	2	-1.0
Total	17	1049	2743	245	618	128	10	58	321	230	419	5	10	.225	.287	.343	.630	73	-107	272	3.21	-6	*C-1008/D-2,0-1,P-1	64	-7.4

• MARTINEZ, Carlos

Carlos Alberto Escobar Martinez b: 8/11/1964, La Guaira, Venezuela BR/TR, 6'5", 175 lbs. Deb: 9/2/1988 Career OF: 11-0-0

YEAR	TM-L	G	AB	R	H	2B	3B	HR	RBI	BB	SO	SB	CS	AVG	OBP	SLG	OPS	OPS+	BR/A	RC	RC/G	FR	G/POS	WS	TPW
1988	Chi-A	17	55	5	9	1	0	0	0	0	12	1	0	.164	.164	.182	.345	-3	-7	2	.88	0	3-15/D-2	0	-0.7
1989	Chi-A	109	350	44	105	22	0	5	32	21	57	4	1	.300	.341	.406	.747	112	5	45	4.57	-4	3-68,1-34,0-10(10-0-0)/D-1	6	0.0
1990	Chi-A	92	272	18	61	6	5	4	24	10	40	0	4	.224	.252	.327	.579	62	-17	19	2.30	-5	1-82/D-3,0-1	1	-2.7
1991	Cle-A	72	257	22	73	14	0	5	30	10	43	3	2	.284	.316	.397	.713	95	-3	29	3.88	-5	D-41,1-31	4	-1.1
1992	Cle-A	69	228	23	60	9	1	5	35	7	21	1	2	.263	.288	.377	.665	87	-6	23	3.46	0	1-37,3-28/D-4	3	-0.8
1993	Cle-A	80	262	26	64	10	0	5	31	20	29	1	1	.244	.298	.340	.638	71	-11	26	3.41	-5	3-35,1-22,D-19	3	-1.7
1995	Cal-A	26	61	7	11	1	0	1	9	6	7	0	0	.180	.265	.246	.511	34	-6	4	1.99	3	3-16/1-4,D-2	0	-0.3
Total	7	465	1485	145	383	63	6	25	161	74	209	10	10	.258	.295	.359	.654	82	-44	148	3.39	-15	1-210,3-162/D-72,0-11	17	-7.4

• MARTINEZ, Carmelo

Carmelo (Salgado) Martinez b: 7/28/1960, Dorado, Puerto Rico BR/TR, 6'2", 220 lbs. Deb: 8/22/1983 Career OF: 588-0-12

YEAR	TM-L	G	AB	R	H	2B	3B	HR	RBI	BB	SO	SB	CS	AVG	OBP	SLG	OPS	OPS+	BR/A	RC	RC/G	FR	G/POS	WS	TPW
1983	Chi-N	29	89	8	23	3	0	6	16	4	19	0	0	.258	.290	.494	.785	108	0	12	4.49	-1	1-26/3-1,0-1	2	-0.3
1984*	SD-N	149	488	64	122	28	2	13	66	68	82	1	3	.250	.346	.395	.742	108	5	70	4.89	3	*0-142(142-0-0)/1-2	21	0.2
1985	SD-N	150	514	64	130	28	1	21	72	87	82	0	4	.253	.364	.434	.798	124	17	84	5.61	-1	*0-150(150-0-0)/1-3	19	0.8
1986	SD-N	113	244	28	58	10	0	9	25	35	46	1	1	.238	.336	.389	.725	101	1	31	4.27	1	0-60(59-0-0),1-26/3-1	6	-0.1
1987	SD-N	139	447	59	122	21	2	15	70	70	82	5	5	.273	.375	.430	.805	117	11	73	5.72	1	0-78(78-0-0),1-65	13	0.7
1988	SD-N	121	365	48	86	12	0	18	65	35	57	1	1	.236	.303	.416	.719	106	1	44	4.06	8	0-64(55-0-11),1-41	11	0.6
1989	SD-N	111	267	23	59	12	2	6	39	32	54	0	0	.221	.304	.348	.653	86	-5	27	3.24	4	0-65(65-0-0),1-32	4	-0.4
1990	Phi-N	71	198	23	48	8	0	8	31	29	37	2	1	.242	.339	.404	.743	104	1	28	4.99	-1	1-43,0-20(20-0-1)	6	-0.3
	*Pit-N	12	19	3	4	1	0	2	4	1	5	0	0	.211	.250	.579	.829	126	0	3	5.07	1	/1-5,0-2(2-0-0)	1	0.1
	Yr.	83	217	26	52	9	0	10	35	30	42	2	1	.240	.332	.419	.751	106	2	31	5.00	0	1-48,0-22(22-0-1)	7	-0.2
1991	Pit-N	11	16	1	4	0	0	0	0	1	2	0	0	.250	.294	.250	.544	55	-1	1	1.45	-2	/1-8	0	-0.3
	KC-A	44	121	17	25	6	0	4	17	27	25	0	1	.207	.351	.355	.707	96	-0	16	4.18	4	1-43/D-1	3	0.2
	Cin-N	53	138	12	32	5	0	6	19	15	37	0	0	.232	.307	.399	.706	93	-1	18	4.36	-3	1-25,0-16(16-0-0)	2	-0.7
	Yr.	64	154	13	36	5	0	6	19	16	39	0	0	.234	.306	.383	.689	90	-2	19	4.03	-5	1-33,0-16(16-0-0)	2	-1.0
Total	9	1003	2906	350	713	134	7	108	424	404	528	10	16	.245	.340	.408	.747	108	30	407	4.74	15	0-598,1-319/3-2,D-1	88	0.4

• MARTINEZ, Chito

Reyenaldo Ignacio Martinez b: 12/19/1965, Belize City, British Honduras BL/TL, 5'10", 180 lbs. Deb: 7/5/1991 Career OF: 1-0-110

YEAR	TM-L	G	AB	R	H	2B	3B	HR	RBI	BB	SO	SB	CS	AVG	OBP	SLG	OPS	OPS+	BR/A	RC	RC/G	FR	G/POS	WS	TPW
1991	Bal-A	67	216	32	58	12	1	13	33	11	51	1	1	.269	.304	.514	.818	127	6	33	5.54	2	0-54(1-0-53)/D-4,1-1	7	0.6
1992	Bal-A	83	198	26	53	10	1	5	25	31	47	0	1	.268	.372	.404	.776	115	5	29	4.92	0	0-52(0-0-52)/D-4	6	0.3
1993	Bal-A	8	15	0	0	0	0	0	0	4	4	0	0	.000	.211	.000	.211	-37	-3	0	.20	0	/0-5(0-0-5),D-2	0	-0.3
Total	3	158	429	58	111	22	2	18	58	46	102	1	2	.259	.333	.445	.779	115	8	62	5.01	2	0-111/D-10,1-1	13	0.6

• MARTINEZ, Dave

David Martinez b: 9/26/1964, New York, NY BL/TL, 5'10", 175 lbs. Deb: 6/15/1986 Career OF: 144-857-731

YEAR	TM-L	G	AB	R	H	2B	3B	HR	RBI	BB	SO	SB	CS	AVG	OBP	SLG	OPS	OPS+	BR/A	RC	RC/G	FR	G/POS	WS	TPW
1986	Chi-N	53	108	13	15	1	1	1	7	6	22	4	2	.139	.191	.194	.386	6	-14	4	1.16	0	0-46(9-39-1)	0	-1.5
1987	Chi-N	142	459	70	134	18	8	8	36	57	96	16	8	.292	.373	.418	.791	105	4	75	5.98	-3	*0-139(14-134-3)	14	-0.1
1988	Chi-N	75	256	27	65	10	1	4	34	21	46	7	3	.254	.315	.348	.663	86	-4	29	3.94	-2	0-72(0-70-2)	7	-0.8
	Mon-N	63	191	24	49	3	5	2	12	17	48	16	6	.257	.317	.356	.673	89	-2	23	4.05	-1	0-60(1-44-22)	5	-0.4
	Yr.	138	447	51	114	13	6	6	46	38	94	23	9	.255	.316	.351	.667	87	-7	52	3.98	-3	*0-132(1-114-24)	12	-1.3
1989	Mon-N	126	361	41	99	16	7	3	27	27	57	23	4	.274	.325	.382	.707	100	3	49	4.82	-3	*0-118(0-104-38)	12	-0.2
1990	Mon-N	118	391	60	109	13	5	11	39	24	48	13	11	.279	.322	.422	.744	107	-0	49	4.35	-1	*0-108(0-103-22)/P-1	11	-0.5
1991	Mon-N	124	396	47	117	18	5	7	42	20	54	16	7	.295	.334	.419	.753	112	5	56	5.08	6	*0-112(36-34-54)	13	0.9
1992	Cin-N	135	393	47	100	20	5	3	31	42	54	12	8	.254	.326	.354	.680	90	-6	46	3.93	1	*0-111(3-105-6),1-21	9	-0.8
1993	SF-N	91	241	28	58	12	1	5	27	27	39	6	3	.241	.317	.361	.678	84	-6	28	3.91	2	0-73(3-43-34)	6	-0.5
1994	SF-N	97	235	23	58	9	3	4	27	21	22	3	4	.247	.314	.362	.676	79	-8	25	3.64	1	0-58(3-3-53),1-25	3	-1.1
1995	Chi-A	119	303	49	93	16	4	5	37	32	41	8	2	.307	.375	.436	.811	115	8	51	5.97	-1	0-59(30-5-32),1-47/D-5,P-1	10	0.2
1996	Chi-A	146	440	85	140	20	8	10	53	52	52	15	7	.318	.394	.468	.862	123	17	85	7.29	-2	*0-121(3-73-73),1-23	16	1.0
1997	Chi-A	145	504	78	144	16	6	12	55	55	69	12	6	.286	.359	.413	.772	105	5	78	5.54	3	*0-105(4-45-75),1-52/D-1	15	0.2
1998	TB-A	90	309	31	79	11	0	3	20	35	52	8	7	.256	.335	.320	.656	70	-14	34	3.74	3	0-86(0-2-85)/1-1,D-1	3	-1.4
1999	TB-A	143	514	79	146	25	5	6	66	60	76	13	6	.284	.364	.387	.752	91	-5	77	5.26	-1	*0-140(2-52-93)	13	-1.0
2000	TB-A	29	104	12	27	4	2	1	12	10	17	1	4	.260	.325	.365	.690	75	-6	12	3.69	2	0-28(0-0-28)	1	-0.4
	Chi-N	18	54	5	10	1	1	0	1	2	8	1	0	.185	.214	.241	.455	15	-7	3	1.85	0	0-10(9-1-0)/1-9	0	-0.8
	Tex-A	38	119	14	32	4	1	2	12	14	20	2	1	.269	.351	.370	.720	82	-3	14	3.86	2	0-35(0-0-35)/1-4	1	-0.2
	Tor-A	47	180	29	56	10	1	2	22	24	28	4	2	.311	.395	.411	.806	101	1	31	6.37	5	0-47(0-0-47)	5	0.4
	Yr.	114	403	55	115	18	4	5	46	48	65	7	7	.285	.364	.387	.751	89	-7	56	4.86	10	*0-110(0-0-110)/1-4	7	-0.3
2001*	Atl-N	120	237	33	68	11	3	2	20	21	44	3	3	.287	.347	.384	.731	87	-5	29	4.33	0	0-52(27-0-28),1-10/D-1	3	-0.7
Total	16	1919	5795	795	1599	238	72	91	580	567	893	183	94	.276	.343	.389	.732	95	-37	797	4.82	12	*0-1580,1-192/D-8,P-2	147	-7.9

• MARTINEZ, Domingo

Domingo Emilio (La Fontaine) Martinez b: 8/4/1967, Santo Domingo, Dominican Republic BR/TR, 6'2", 215 lbs. Deb: 9/11/1992

YEAR	TM-L	G	AB	R	H	2B	3B	HR	RBI	BB	SO	SB	CS	AVG	OBP	SLG	OPS	OPS+	BR/A	RC	RC/G	FR	G/POS	WS	TPW
1992	Tor-A	7	8	2	5	0	0	1	3	0	1	0	0	.625	.625	1.000	1.625	333	2	5	45.00	0	/1-7	1	0.2
1993	Tor-A	8	14	2	4	0	0	1	3	1	7	0	0	.286	.333	.500	.833	120	0	2	6.53	1	/1-7,3-1	0	0.1
Total	2	15	22	4	9	0	0	2	6	1	8	0	0	.409	.435	.682	1.117	194	3	7	15.41	0	/1-14,3-1	1	0.2

YEAR TM-L	G	AB	R	H	2B	3B	HR	RBI	BB	SO	SB	CS	AVG	OBP	SLG	OPS	OPS+	BR/A	RC	RC/G	FR	G/POS	WS	TPW
• MARTINEZ, Edgar	Edgar Martinez b: 1/2/1963, New York, NY BR/TR, 6', 210 lbs. Deb: 9/12/1987																							
1987 Sea-A	13	43	6	16	5	2	0	5	2	5	0	0	.372	.413	.581	.994	152	3	11	10.65	0	3-12/D-1	2	0.3
1988 Sea-A	14	32	0	9	4	0	0	5	4	7	0	0	.281	.361	.406	.767	110	1	5	5.57	-1	3-13	1	0.0
1989 Sea-A	65	171	20	41	5	0	2	20	17	26	2	1	.240	.319	.304	.623	74	-5	18	3.42	-5	3-61	4	-1.1
1990 Sea-A	144	487	71	147	27	2	11	49	74	62	1	4	.302	.399	.433	.833	131	22	86	6.40	1	*3-143/D-2	17	2.5
1991 Sea-A	150	544	98	167	35	1	14	52	84	72	0	3	.307	.407	.452	.859	137	30	100	6.66	1	*3-144/D-2	20	3.2
1992 Sea-A★	135	528	100	181	**46**	3	18	73	54	61	14	4	**.343**	.408	.544	.951	163	46	116	8.41	5	*3-103,D-28/1-2	24	5.1
1993 Sea-A	42	135	20	32	7	0	4	13	28	19	0	0	.237	.368	.378	.746	100	1	20	4.97	-1	D-24,3-16	4	-0.1
1994 Sea-A	89	326	47	93	23	1	13	51	53	42	6	2	.285	.390	.482	.872	121	12	66	7.38	5	3-64,D-23	11	1.5
1995*Sea-A★	145	511	**121**	182	**52**	0	29	113	116	87	4	3	**.356**	**.482**	.628	**1.110**	**184**	**71**	161	**12.53**	-1	*D-138/3-4,1-3	**32**	**5.7**
1996 Sea-A★	139	499	121	163	52	2	26	103	123	84	3	3	.327	.467	.595	1.062	166	58	144	10.89	-1	*D-134/1-4,3-2	23	4.4
1997*Sea-A★	155	542	104	179	35	1	28	108	119	86	2	4	.330	.460	.554	1.013	164	58	140	9.62	-1	*D-144/1-7,3-1	27	4.6
1998 Sea-A	154	556	86	179	46	1	29	102	106	96	1	1	.322	**.433**	.565	.998	157	51	141	9.56	2	*D-147/1-4	24	4.0
1999 Sea-A	142	502	86	169	35	1	24	86	97	99	7	2	.337	**.450**	.554	1.003	151	45	131	10.10	0	*D-143/1-5	22	3.3
2000*Sea-A★	153	556	100	180	31	0	37	**145**	96	95	3	0	.324	.428	.579	1.007	161	55	142	9.65	0	*D-146/1-2	28	4.2
2001*Sea-A★	132	470	80	144	40	1	23	116	93	90	4	1	.306	.430	.543	.973	163	49	115	8.96	0	*D-127/1-1	25	3.9
2002 Sea-A	97	328	42	91	23	0	15	59	67	69	1	1	.277	.409	.485	.894	141	23	69	7.48	0	D-91	13	1.7
2003 Sea-A★	145	497	72	146	25	0	24	98	92	95	0	1	.294	.411	.489	.900	141	34	102	7.31	0	*D-140	20	2.4
Total 17	1914	6727	1174	2119	491	15	297	1198	1225	1095	48	30	.315	.427	.525	.952	151	554	1567	8.64	3	*D-1290,3-563/1-28	297	45.4
• MARTINEZ, Felix	Felix (Mata) Martinez b: 5/18/1974, Nagua, Dominican Republic BB/TR, 6', 168 lbs. Deb: 9/3/1997																							
1997 KC-A	16	31	3	7	1	1	0	3	6	8	0	0	.226	.351	.323	.674	76	-1	4	3.96	0	S-12/D-2	1	0.0
1998 KC-A	34	85	7	11	1	1	0	5	5	21	3	1	.129	.187	.165	.352	-7	-13	3	1.02	1	S-32/2-2	2	-1.0
1999 KC-A	6	7	1	1	0	0	0	0	0	0	0	0	.143	.143	.143	.286	-26	-1	0	.00	-1	/S-2,2-1	0	-0.2
2000 TB-A	106	299	42	64	11	4	2	17	32	68	9	3	.214	.307	.298	.604	55	-20	31	3.23	22	*S-106	5	0.9
2001 TB-A	77	219	24	54	13	1	1	14	10	46	6	5	.247	.295	.329	.624	65	-12	19	2.83	-3	S-67,2-10	2	-1.0
Total 5	239	641	77	137	26	7	3	39	53	143	18	9	.214	.288	.290	.578	50	-48	57	2.77	18	S-219/2-13,D-2	10	-1.3
• MARTINEZ, Greg	Gregory Alfred Martinez b: 1/27/1972, Las Vegas, NV BB/TR, 5'10" Deb: 3/31/1998																							
1998 Mil-N	13	3	2	0	0	0	0	0	1	2	2	0	.000	.250	.000	.250	-27	-0	0	2.93	-1	/0-6(6-0-0)	0	-0.1
• MARTINEZ, Hector	Rodolfo Hector Martinez b: 5/11/1939, Las Villas, Cuba d: 12/1999, Cuba BR/TR, 5'10", 160 lbs. Deb: 9/30/1962																							
1962 KC-A	1	1	0	0	0	0	0	0	0	1	0	0	.000	.000	.000	.000	-97	-0	0	.00	0	....	0	0.0
1963 KC-A	6	14	2	4	0	0	1	3	1	3	0	1	.286	.375	.500	.875	137	0	2	5.77	0	/0-3(0-3-0)	0	0.0
Total 2	7	15	2	4	0	0	1	3	1	4	0	1	.267	.353	.467	.820	123	0	2	5.29	0	/0-3	0	0.0
• MARTINEZ, Jose	Jose (Azcuiz) Martinez b: 7/26/1942, Cardenas, Cuba BR/TR, 6', 190 lbs. Deb: 4/12/1969 C																							
1969 Pit-N	77	168	20	45	6	0	1	16	9	32	1	3	.268	.309	.321	.630	78	-6	15	3.19	-2	2-42,S-20/3-5,0-2(2-0-0)	4	-0.5
1970 Pit-N	19	20	1	1	0	0	0	0	1	5	0	0	.050	.095	.050	.145	-62	-5	0	.10	-1	/3-7,2-4,S-1	0	-0.6
Total 2	96	188	21	46	6	0	1	16	10	37	1	3	.245	.286	.293	.579	63	-11	16	2.76	-3	/2-46,S-21,3-12,0-2	4	-1.0
• MARTINEZ, Manny	Manuel (DeJesus) Martinez b: 10/3/1970, San Pedro de Macoris, Dominican Republic BR/TR, 6'2", 169 lbs. Deb: 6/14/1996 Career OF: 29-168-17																							
1996 Sea-A	9	17	3	4	2	1	0	3	3	5	2	0	.235	.350	.471	.821	105	1	3	5.68	1	/0-8(2-4-3)	1	0.2
Phi-N	13	36	2	8	0	2	0	0	1	11	2	1	.222	.263	.333	.596	55	-2	3	2.52	0	0-11(1-1-10)	0	-0.3
1998 Pit-N	73	180	21	45	11	2	6	24	9	44	0	3	.250	.293	.433	.727	87	-6	21	3.94	-2	0-62(26-37-3)	3	-0.8
1999 Mon-N	137	331	48	81	12	7	2	26	17	51	19	6	.245	.282	.341	.623	58	-21	32	3.22	2	*0-126(0-126-1)	5	-1.7
Total 3	232	564	74	138	25	12	8	53	30	111	23	10	.245	.286	.374	.661	69	-28	59	3.47	2	0-207	9	-2.6
• MARTINEZ, Marty	Orlando (Oliva) Martinez b: 8/23/1941, Havana, Cuba BB/TR, 6', 175 lbs. Deb: 5/2/1962 M/C																							
1962 Min-A	37	18	13	3	0	1	0	3	3	4	0	0	.167	.286	.278	.563	50	-1	2	2.75	0	S-11/3-1	0	0.0
1967 Atl-N	44	73	14	21	2	1	0	5	11	11	0	1	.288	.388	.342	.731	112	2	10	4.72	-7	S-25/2-9,C-3,3-2,1-1	3	-0.4
1968 Atl-N	113	356	34	82	5	3	0	12	29	28	6	6	.230	.292	.261	.553	67	-15	27	2.45	0	S-54,3-37,2-16,C-14	6	-1.0
1969 Hou-N	78	198	14	61	5	4	0	15	10	21	0	0	.308	.341	.374	.715	102	0	24	4.49	-5	0-21(21-0-0),S-17,3-15/C-7,2,P	6	-0.4
1970 Hou-N	75	150	12	33	3	0	0	12	9	22	0	0	.220	.264	.240	.504	38	-13	9	2.12	-4	S-29,3-10/C-6,2-4	1	-1.4
1971 Hou-N	32	62	4	16	3	1	0	4	3	6	1	0	.258	.292	.339	.631	80	-2	5	3.02	1	/2-9,S-7,1-4,3-3	1	0.0
1972 StL-N	9	7	0	3	0	0	0	2	0	1	0	0	.429	.429	.429	.857	146	0	1	8.68	-2	/S-3,2-2,3-1	0	-0.1
Oak-A	22	40	3	5	0	0	0	1	3	6	0	0	.125	.186	.125	.311	-7	-5	1	.61	1	2-17/S-6,3-1	1	-0.4
Tex-A	26	41	3	6	1	1	0	3	2	8	0	1	.146	.186	.220	.406	21	-5	1	.97	-3	/S-5,3-4,2-1	0	-0.8
Yr.	48	81	6	11	1	1	0	4	5	14	0	1	.136	.186	.173	.359	7	-10	2	.79	-2	2-18,S-11/3-5	1	-1.2
Total 7	436	945	97	230	19	11	0	57	70	107	7	8	.243	.298	.287	.584	69	-38	82	2.87	-19	S-157/3-74,2-59,C-30,0-21,1,P	18	-4.6
• MARTINEZ, Pablo	Pablo Made (Valera) Martinez b: 6/29/1969, Sabana Grande, Dominican Republic BB/TR, 5'10", 155 lbs. Deb: 7/20/1996																							
1996 Atl-N	4	2	1	1	0	0	0	0	0	0	0	1	.500	.500	.500	1.000	156	-0	0	.00	0	/S-1	0	0.0
• MARTINEZ, Ramon	Ramon E. Martinez b: 10/10/1972, Philadelphia, PA BR/TR, 6'1", 187 lbs. Deb: 6/20/1998																							
1998 SF-N	19	19	4	6	1	0	0	0	4	2	0	0	.316	.435	.368	.803	121	1	4	6.88	1	2-14	0	0.2
1999 SF-N	61	144	21	38	6	0	5	19	14	17	1	2	.264	.329	.410	.739	92	-3	19	4.48	-1	2-27,S-12,3-11/D-1	5	-0.2
2000*SF-N	88	189	30	57	13	2	6	25	15	22	3	2	.302	.356	.487	.843	119	5	31	5.77	-6	S-44,2-32/1-2,3-2	7	0.1
2001 SF-N	128	391	48	99	18	3	5	37	38	52	1	2	.253	.327	.353	.680	82	-11	45	3.80	7	3-70,2-42,S-24	9	0.0
2002*SF-N	72	181	26	49	10	2	4	25	14	26	2	0	.271	.337	.414	.751	101	0	27	5.37	-1	S-40,2-17/1-4,0-3(3-0-0),3	9	0.2
2003*Chi-N	108	293	30	83	16	1	3	34	24	50	0	1	.283	.342	.375	.717	88	-5	37	4.31	-7	2-42,3-37,S-32/1-2	7	-0.8
Total 6	476	1217	159	332	64	8	23	140	109	169	7	7	.273	.339	.395	.734	94	-13	162	4.57	-7	2-174,S-152,3-122/1-8,0-3,D	37	-0.4
• MARTINEZ, Sandy	Angel Sandy (Martinez) Martinez b: 10/8/1970, Villa Mella, Dominican Republic BL/TR, 6'2", 200 lbs. Deb: 6/24/1995																							
1995 Tor-A	62	191	12	46	12	0	2	25	7	45	0	0	.241	.271	.335	.606	57	-13	18	3.24	1	C-61	5	-0.7
1996 Tor-A	76	229	17	52	9	3	3	18	16	58	0	0	.227	.289	.332	.621	57	-16	22	3.29	2	C-75	4	-0.8
1997 Tor-A	3	2	1	0	0	0	0	0	1	1	0	0	.000	.333	.000	.333	-3	-0	0	1.17	0	/C-3	0	0.0
1998*Chi-N	45	87	7	23	9	1	0	7	13	21	1	0	.264	.366	.391	.757	96	0	13	5.12	-1	C-33	2	0.0
1999 Chi-N	17	30	1	5	0	0	1	1	0	11	0	0	.167	.167	.267	.433	7	-4	1	1.44	-1	C-12	0	-0.5
2000 Fla-N	10	18	1	4	2	0	0	0	0	8	0	0	.222	.222	.333	.556	39	-2	1	2.57	1	/C-9	1	0.0
2001 Mon-N	1	1	0	0	0	0	0	0	0	0	0	0	.000	.000	.000	.000	-98	-0	0	.00	0	/C-1	0	0.0
Total 7	214	558	39	130	32	4	6	51	37	144	1	0	.233	.288	.337	.625	60	-35	56	3.40	2	C-194	12	-2.0
• MARTINEZ, Ted	Teodoro Noel (Encarnacion) Martinez b: 12/10/1947, Barahona, Dominican Republic BR/TR, 6', 165 lbs. Deb: 7/18/1970 Career OF: 15-31-9																							
1970 NY-N	4	16	0	1	0	0	0	0	0	3	0	0	.063	.063	.063	.125	-66	-4	0	.11	1	/2-4,S-1	0	-0.3
1971 NY-N	38	125	16	36	5	2	1	10	4	22	6	0	.288	.326	.384	.710	102	1	17	4.88	3	S-23,2-13/3-3,0-1	5	0.7
1972 NY-N	103	330	22	74	5	5	1	19	12	49	7	4	.224	.254	.279	.532	52	-21	21	2.09	-4	2-47,S-42,0-15(6-4-5)/3-2	4	-2.1
1973*NY-N	92	263	34	67	11	0	1	14	13	38	3	5	.255	.295	.308	.603	68	-13	22	2.85	-5	S-44,0-21(4-18-0),3-14/2-5	5	-1.4
1974 NY-N	116	334	32	73	15	7	2	43	14	40	3	2	.219	.250	.323	.573	60	-20	23	2.24	8	S-75,3-12,2-11,0-10(1-9-0)	5	-0.4
1975 StL-N	16	21	1	4	2	0	0	2	0	2	0	0	.190	.190	.286	.476	30	-2	1	.79	-1	/0-7(3-0-4),2-2,3-1,S-1	0	-0.4
*Oak-A	86	87	7	15	0	0	0	3	2	9	1	1	.172	.200	.172	.372	6	-11	3	1.18	-4	S-45,2-31,3-14	1	-1.2
1977 LA-N	67	137	21	41	6	1	1	10	2	20	3	4	.299	.309	.380	.689	84	-5	15	3.84	3	2-27,S-13,3-12	4	0.1
1978 LA-N	54	55	13	14	1	0	1	5	4	14	3	2	.255	.317	.327	.644	80	-2	6	3.61	-2	S-17,3-16,2-10	2	-0.2
1979 LA-N	81	112	19	30	5	1	0	2	4	16	3	2	.268	.293	.330	.623	71	-5	10	3.03	-7	3-23,S-21,2-18	2	-1.1
Total 9	657	1480	165	355	50	16	7	108	55	213	29	20	.240	.271	.309	.580	62	-81	118	2.64	-9	S-282,2-168/3-97,0-54	28	-6.3
• MARTINEZ, Tino	Constantino Martinez b: 12/7/1967, Tampa, FL BL/TR, 6'2", 210 lbs. Deb: 8/20/1990																							
1990 Sea-A	24	68	4	15	4	0	0	5	9	9	0	0	.221	.312	.279	.591	66	-3	7	3.36	0	1-23	0	-0.4
1991 Sea-A	36	112	11	23	2	0	4	9	11	24	0	0	.205	.276	.330	.607	67	-5	10	3.04	1	1-29/D-5	1	-0.7
1992 Sea-A	136	460	53	118	19	2	16	66	42	77	2	1	.257	.321	.411	.732	103	1	54	3.91	0	1-78,D-47	7	-0.6

YEAR TM-L	G	AB	R	H	2B	3B	HR	RBI	BB	SO	SB	CS	AVG	OBP	SLG	OPS	OPS+	BR/A	RC	RC/G	FR	G/POS	WS	TPW
1993 Sea-A	109	408	48	108	25	1	17	60	45	56	0	3	.265	.345	.456	.801	112	5	64	5.44	-3	*1-103/D-6	12	-0.8
1994 Sea-A	97	329	42	86	21	0	20	61	29	52	1	2	.261	.323	.508	.831	108	1	51	5.30	-5	1-82/D-8	7	-1.0
1995*Sea-A★	141	519	92	152	35	3	31	111	62	91	0	0	.293	.373	.551	.924	135	26	106	7.46	4	*1-139/D-1	20	1.6
1996*NY-A	155	595	82	174	28	0	25	117	68	85	2	1	.292	.367	.466	.832	109	8	100	6.06	2	*1-151/D-3	21	-0.4
1997*NY-A★	158	594	96	176	31	2	44	141	75	75	3	1	.296	.378	.577	.955	146	39	128	7.72	6	*1-150/D-9	27	2.9
1998*NY-A	142	531	92	149	33	1	28	123	61	83	2	1	.281	.361	.505	.866	127	20	94	6.19	5	*1-142	21	1.2
1999*NY-A	159	589	95	155	27	2	28	105	69	86	3	4	.263	.343	.458	.802	103	1	91	5.41	15	*1-158	19	0.2
2000*NY-A	155	569	69	147	37	4	16	91	52	74	4	1	.258	.329	.422	.751	89	-10	77	4.72	4	*1-154	12	-1.8
2001*NY-A	154	589	89	165	24	2	34	113	42	89	1	2	.280	.330	.501	.831	113	8	94	5.79	4	*1-149/D-2	21	-0.1
2002*StL-N	150	511	63	134	25	1	21	75	58	71	3	2	.262	.340	.438	.778	106	3	75	5.14	6	*1-149	15	-0.3
2003 StL-N	138	476	66	130	25	2	15	69	53	71	1	1	.273	.357	.429	.785	108	6	72	5.28	5	*1-126/D-5	11	-0.1
Total 14	1754	6350	902	1732	336	20	299	1146	676	943	22	19	.273	.347	.473	.820	112	102	1026	5.66	42	*1-1633/D-86	194	-0.1

• MARTINEZ, Tony Gabriel Antonio (Diaz) Martinez b: 3/18/1940, Perico, Cuba d: 8/24/1991, Miami, FL BR/TR, 5'10", 165 lbs. Deb: 4/9/1963

YEAR TM-L	G	AB	R	H	2B	3B	HR	RBI	BB	SO	SB	CS	AVG	OBP	SLG	OPS	OPS+	BR/A	RC	RC/G	FR	G/POS	WS	TPW
1963 Cle-A	43	141	10	22	4	0	0	8	5	18	1	1	.156	.185	.184	.369	4	-18	4	.93	-4	S-41	1	-2.0
1964 Cle-A	9	14	1	3	1	0	0	2	0	2	0	1	.214	.214	.286	.500	38	-2	0	.59	0	/2-4,S-1	0	-0.1
1965 Cle-A	4	3	0	0	0	0	0	0	0	0	0	0	.000	.000	.000	.000	-99	-1	0	.00	0	....	0	-0.1
1966 Cle-A	17	17	2	5	0	0	0	0	1	6	1	1	.294	.333	.294	.627	82	-1	2	3.33	-1	/S-5,2-4	0	-0.2
Total 4	73	175	13	30	5	0	0	10	6	26	2	3	.171	.199	.200	.399	12	-21	6	1.08	-5	/S-47,2-8	1	-2.4

• MARTINEZ, Victor Victor Jesus Martinez b: 12/23/1978, Ciudad Bolivar, Venezuela BB/TR, 6'2", 170 lbs. Deb: 9/10/2002

YEAR TM-L	G	AB	R	H	2B	3B	HR	RBI	BB	SO	SB	CS	AVG	OBP	SLG	OPS	OPS+	BR/A	RC	RC/G	FR	G/POS	WS	TPW
2002 Cle-A	12	32	2	9	1	0	1	5	3	2	0	0	.281	.343	.406	.749	100	0	4	4.72	0	/C-9,D-1	1	0.0
2003 Cle-A	49	159	15	46	4	0	1	16	13	21	1	1	.289	.347	.333	.680	84	-4	17	3.71	3	C-40/D-5	3	0.1
Total 2	61	191	17	55	5	0	2	21	16	23	1	1	.288	.346	.346	.692	86	-4	21	3.88	2	/C-49,D-6	4	0.1

• MARTY, Joe Joseph Anton Marty b: 9/1/1913, Sacramento, CA d: 10/4/1984, Sacramento, CA BR/TR, 6', 182 lbs. Deb: 4/22/1937 Career OF: 8-450-47

YEAR TM-L	G	AB	R	H	2B	3B	HR	RBI	BB	SO	SB	CS	AVG	OBP	SLG	OPS	OPS+	BR/A	RC	RC/G	FR	G/POS	WS	TPW
1937 Chi-N	88	290	41	84	17	2	5	44	28	30	3	....	.290	.356	.414	.770	104	2	41	4.87	-5	0-84(1-83-0)	9	-0.5
1938*Chi-N	76	235	32	57	8	3	7	35	18	26	0	....	.243	.305	.391	.696	88	-5	27	3.81	-6	0-68(0-64-6)	6	-1.2
1939 Chi-N	23	76	6	10	1	0	2	10	4	13	2	....	.132	.175	.224	.399	6	-10	2	.87	1	0-21(1-1-19)	0	-1.1
Phi-N	91	299	32	76	12	6	9	44	24	27	1	....	.254	.310	.425	.734	100	-1	38	4.29	-3	0-79(6-56-18)/P-1	6	-0.6
Yr.	114	375	38	86	13	6	11	54	28	40	3	....	.229	.283	.384	.667	82	-12	40	3.51	-2	*0-100(7-57-37)/P-1	6	-1.7
1940 Phi-N	123	455	52	123	21	8	13	50	17	50	2	....	.270	.298	.437	.735	105	-0	54	4.13	-2	*0-118(0-115-3)	10	-0.5
1941 Phi-N	137	477	60	128	19	3	8	39	51	41	6	....	.268	.344	.371	.715	105	4	63	4.58	-11	*0-132(0-131-1)	10	-1.1
Total 5	538	1832	223	478	78	22	44	222	142	187	14	....	.261	.318	.400	.717	98	-10	225	4.19	-25	0-502/P-1	41	-5.0

• MARTYN, Bob Robert Gordon Martyn b: 8/15/1930, Weiser, ID BL/TR, 6', 176 lbs. Deb: 6/18/1957 Career OF: 40-10-73

YEAR TM-L	G	AB	R	H	2B	3B	HR	RBI	BB	SO	SB	CS	AVG	OBP	SLG	OPS	OPS+	BR/A	RC	RC/G	FR	G/POS	WS	TPW
1957 KC-A	58	131	10	35	2	4	1	12	11	20	1	3	.267	.324	.366	.690	87	-3	15	3.85	-1	0-49(13-9-28)	2	-0.7
1958 KC-A	95	226	25	59	10	7	2	23	26	36	1	4	.261	.337	.394	.731	99	-1	30	4.61	1	0-63(27-1-45)	7	-0.3
1959 KC-A	1	1	0	0	0	0	0	0	0	0	0	0	.000	.000	.000	.000	-98	-0	0	.00	0	....	0	0.0
Total 3	154	358	35	94	12	11	3	35	37	56	2	7	.263	.332	.383	.714	94	-5	45	4.31	0	0-112	9	-1.0

• MARTZ, Gary Gary Arthur Martz b: 1/10/1951, Spokane, WA BR/TR, 6'4", 210 lbs. Deb: 7/8/1975

YEAR TM-L	G	AB	R	H	2B	3B	HR	RBI	BB	SO	SB	CS	AVG	OBP	SLG	OPS	OPS+	BR/A	RC	RC/G	FR	G/POS	WS	TPW
1975 KC-A	1	1	0	0	0	0	0	0	0	0	0	0	.000	.000	.000	.000	-97	-0	0	.00	-0	/0-1	0	0.0

• MARZANO, John John Robert Marzano b: 2/14/1963, Philadelphia, PA BR/TR, 5'11", 197 lbs. Deb: 7/31/1987

YEAR TM-L	G	AB	R	H	2B	3B	HR	RBI	BB	SO	SB	CS	AVG	OBP	SLG	OPS	OPS+	BR/A	RC	RC/G	FR	G/POS	WS	TPW
1987 Bos-A	52	168	20	41	11	0	5	24	7	41	0	1	.244	.287	.399	.685	77	-7	19	3.70	0	C-52	4	-0.4
1988 Bos-A	10	29	3	4	1	0	0	1	1	3	0	0	.138	.167	.172	.339	-5	-4	1	.73	1	C-10	1	-0.3
1989 Bos-A	7	18	5	8	3	0	1	3	0	2	0	0	.444	.444	.778	1.222	224	3	5	10.93	0	/C-7	1	0.3
1990 Bos-A	32	83	8	20	4	0	0	6	5	10	0	1	.241	.284	.289	.573	58	-5	7	2.85	2	C-32	2	-0.2
1991 Bos-A	49	114	10	30	8	0	0	9	1	16	0	0	.263	.276	.333	.609	64	-6	9	2.67	0	C-48	2	-0.4
1992 Bos-A	19	50	4	4	2	1	0	1	2	12	0	0	.080	.132	.160	.292	-17	-8	1	.69	-1	C-18/D-1	0	-0.8
1995 Tex-A	2	6	1	2	0	0	0	0	0	0	0	0	.333	.333	.333	.667	72	-0	1	4.50	0	/C-2	0	0.0
1996 Sea-A	41	106	8	26	6	0	0	6	7	15	0	0	.245	.316	.302	.618	57	-7	11	3.37	-1	C-39	2	-0.5
1997 Sea-A	39	87	7	25	3	0	1	10	7	15	0	0	.287	.340	.356	.697	83	-2	11	4.33	0	C-37/D-1	2	-0.1
1998 Sea-A	50	133	13	31	7	1	4	12	9	24	0	0	.233	.325	.391	.715	85	-3	17	4.36	1	C-48/D-1	3	0.1
Total 10	301	794	79	191	45	2	11	72	39	138	0	2	.241	.291	.344	.635	67	-39	81	3.41	2	C-293/D-3	17	-2.1

• MASHORE, Clyde Clyde Wayne Mashore b: 5/29/1945, Concord, CA BR/TR, 6', 184 lbs. Deb: 7/11/1969 Career OF: 87-48-52

YEAR TM-L	G	AB	R	H	2B	3B	HR	RBI	BB	SO	SB	CS	AVG	OBP	SLG	OPS	OPS+	BR/A	RC	RC/G	FR	G/POS	WS	TPW
1969 Cin-N	2	1	1	0	0	0	0	0	0	0	0	0	.000	.000	.000	.000	-95	-0	0	.00	0	....	0	0.0
1970 Mon-N	13	25	2	4	0	0	1	3	4	11	0	0	.160	.276	.280	.556	49	-2	2	2.67	0	0-10(2-8-0)	0	-0.2
1971 Mon-N	66	114	20	22	5	0	1	7	10	22	1	0	.193	.258	.263	.521	48	-8	8	2.27	-1	0-47(19-29-5)/3-1	1	-1.0
1972 Mon-N	93	176	23	40	7	1	3	23	14	41	6	1	.227	.284	.330	.614	73	-6	18	3.11	-0	0-74(23-8-46)	3	-0.8
1973 Mon-N	67	103	12	21	3	0	3	14	15	28	4	3	.204	.305	.320	.625	71	-4	11	3.02	3	0-44(43-3-1)/2-1	2	-0.3
Total 5	241	419	58	87	15	1	8	47	43	102	11	4	.208	.281	.305	.587	64	-20	38	2.83	1	0-175/2-1,3-1	6	-2.5

• MASHORE, Damon Damon Wayne Mashore b: 10/31/1969, Ponce, Puerto Rico BR/TR, 5'11", 195 lbs. Deb: 6/5/1996 Career OF: 64-85-49

YEAR TM-L	G	AB	R	H	2B	3B	HR	RBI	BB	SO	SB	CS	AVG	OBP	SLG	OPS	OPS+	BR/A	RC	RC/G	FR	G/POS	WS	TPW
1996 Oak-A	50	105	20	28	7	1	3	12	16	31	4	0	.267	.369	.438	.807	106	2	19	6.19	0	0-48(35-7-15)	2	0.1
1997 Oak-A	92	279	55	69	10	2	3	18	50	82	5	4	.247	.371	.330	.701	87	-3	38	4.51	6	0-89(28-71-6)	6	0.2
1998 Ana-A	43	98	13	23	6	0	2	11	9	22	1	0	.235	.318	.357	.675	75	-3	11	3.86	1	0-35(1-7-28)/D-7	2	-0.4
Total 3	185	482	88	120	23	3	8	41	75	135	10	4	.249	.360	.359	.719	89	-5	68	4.73	6	0-172/D-7	10	-0.1

• MASI, Phil Philip Samuel Masi b: 1/6/1916, Chicago, IL d: 3/29/1990, Mount Prospect, IL BR/TR, 5'10", 180 lbs. Deb: 4/23/1939

YEAR TM-L	G	AB	R	H	2B	3B	HR	RBI	BB	SO	SB	CS	AVG	OBP	SLG	OPS	OPS+	BR/A	RC	RC/G	FR	G/POS	WS	TPW
1939 Bos-N	46	114	14	29	7	2	1	14	9	15	0	....	.254	.315	.377	.692	92	-2	13	4.06	-1	C-42	3	-0.1
1940 Bos-N	63	138	11	27	4	1	1	14	14	14	0	....	.196	.270	.261	.531	50	-9	9	2.19	2	C-52	2	-0.5
1941 Bos-N	87	180	17	40	8	2	3	18	16	13	4	....	.222	.286	.339	.625	79	-6	18	3.30	0	C-83	4	-0.2
1942 Bos-N	57	87	14	19	3	1	0	9	12	4	2	....	.218	.313	.276	.589	74	-2	8	3.22	-1	C-39/0-4(1-0-4)	2	-0.2
1943 Bos-N	80	238	27	65	9	1	2	28	27	20	7	....	.273	.347	.345	.692	102	1	28	4.02	-3	C-73	8	0.2
1944 Bos-N	89	251	33	69	13	5	3	23	31	20	4	....	.275	.355	.402	.757	108	3	37	5.30	1	C-63,1-12/3-2	10	0.7
1945 Bos-N★	114	371	55	101	25	4	7	46	42	32	9	....	.272	.348	.418	.766	112	5	54	5.10	3	C-95/1-7	11	1.4
1946 Bos-N★	133	397	52	106	17	5	3	62	55	41	5	....	.267	.358	.358	.715	102	2	53	4.62	-10	*C-124	15	-0.1
1947 Bos-N★	126	411	54	125	22	4	9	50	47	27	7	....	.304	.377	.443	.820	120	12	69	5.99	-0	*C-123	19	1.7
1948*Bos-N★	113	376	43	95	19	0	5	44	35	26	2	....	.253	.318	.343	.661	80	-11	40	3.47	-1	*C-109	10	-0.6
1949 Bos-N	37	105	13	22	2	0	0	6	14	10	1	....	.210	.303	.229	.531	47	-7	7	2.21	1	C-37	1	-0.5
Pit-N	48	135	16	37	6	1	2	13	17	16	1	....	.274	.355	.378	.733	94	-1	18	4.59	4	C-44/1-2	5	0.5
Yr.	85	240	29	59	8	1	2	19	31	26	2	....	.246	.332	.313	.645	74	-8	25	3.50	5	C-81/1-2	6	0.0
1950 Chi-A	122	377	38	105	17	2	7	55	49	36	2	1	.279	.366	.390	.756	96	-1	54	4.97	7	*C-114	11	1.0
1951 Chi-A	84	225	24	61	11	2	4	28	32	27	1	0	.271	.367	.391	.758	107	3	34	5.27	-1	C-78	8	0.5
1952 Chi-A	30	63	9	16	1	1	0	7	10	10	0	0	.254	.356	.302	.658	84	-1	8	4.25	-2	C-25	2	-0.2
Total 14	1229	3468	420	917	164	31	47	417	410	311	45	1	.264	.344	.370	.714	96	-12	450	4.47	-1	*C-1101/1-21,0-4,3-2	111	3.8

• MASKREY, Harry Harry H. Maskrey b: 12/21/1861, Mercer, PA d: 8/17/1930, Mercer, PA Deb: 9/21/1882

YEAR TM-L	G	AB	R	H	2B	3B	HR	RBI	BB	SO	SB	CS	AVG	OBP	SLG	OPS	OPS+	BR/A	RC	RC/G	FR	G/POS	WS	TPW
1882 Lou-a	1	4	0	0	0	0	0	....	0	....	....	....	.000	.000	.000	.000	-106	-1	0	.00	0	/0-1	0	0.0

• MASKREY, Leech Samuel Leech Maskrey b: 2/11/1854, Mercer, PA d: 4/1/1922, Mercer, PA BR/TR, 5'8", 150 lbs. Deb: 5/2/1882 Career OF: 328-48-43

YEAR TM-L	G	AB	R	H	2B	3B	HR	RBI	BB	SO	SB	CS	AVG	OBP	SLG	OPS	OPS+	BR/A	RC	RC/G	FR	G/POS	WS	TPW
1882 Lou-a	76	288	30	65	14	2	0	....	9	....	....	....	.226	.249	.288	.537	85	-4	21	2.66	2	*0-76(75-0-1)/2-1	6	-0.4
1883 Lou-a	96	361	50	73	13	8	1	0	10	....	....	....	.202	.224	.291	.515	69	-11	24	2.34	4	*0-96(45-41-14)/S-1	6	-0.8
1884 Lou-a	105	412	48	103	13	4	0	36	17	....	....	....	.250	.281	.301	.582	94	-2	36	3.18	7	*0-103(97-0-7)/3-3,S-1	11	0.1
1885 Lou-a	109	423	54	97	8	11	1	46	19	....	....	....	.229	.269	.307	.576	82	-9	36	2.97	-2	*0-108(108-0-0)/3-3	8	-1.4
1886 Lou-a	5	19	1	3	1	0	0	2	1	....	0	....	.158	.200	.211	.411	27	-2	1	1.38	0	/0-5(3-0-2)	0	-0.2
Cin-a	27	98	7	19	3	1	0	10	5	....	4	....	.194	.240	.245	.485	51	-6	7	2.36	0	0-26(0-7-19)/3-2	1	-0.5

YEAR TM-L	G	AB	R	H	2B	3B	HR	RBI	BB	SO	SB	CS	AVG	OBP	SLG	OPS	OPS+	BR/A	RC	RC/G	FR	G/POS	WS	TPW
Yr.	32	117	8	22	4	1	0	12	6	....	4	....	.188	.234	.239	.473	47	-8	8	2.19	-0	0-31(3-7-21)/3-2	1	-0.7
Total 5	418	1601	190	360	52	26	2	94	61	....	4	....	.225	.256	.294	.550	80	-32	125	2.76	10	0-414/3-8,S-2,2-1	32	-3.2

• MASON, Charlie Charles E. Mason b: 6/25/1853, New Orleans, LA d: 10/21/1936, Philadelphia, PA BR/TR, 175 lbs. Deb: 4/26/1875 M/U

YEAR TM-L	G	AB	R	H	2B	3B	HR	RBI	BB	SO	SB	CS	AVG	OBP	SLG	OPS	OPS+	BR/A	RC	RC/G	FR	G/POS	WS	TPW
1875 Cen-n	12	47	5	11	0	0	0	3	0	1	0	0	.234	.234	.234	.468	69	-1	3	2.16	0	0-10(3-0-7)/1-2,C-1	....	0.0
Was-n	8	33	2	3	0	0	0	1	0	3	0	0	.091	.091	.091	.182	-38	-4	0	.27	2	/0-8(8-0-0),P-1	....	-0.2
Yr.	20	80	7	14	0	0	0	4	0	4	0	0	.175	.175	.175	.350	25	-5	3	1.30	2	0-18(11-0-7)/1-2,C-1,P-1	....	-0.3
1883 Phi-a	1	2	0	1	0	0	0	1	0	....	....	....	.500	.500	.500	1.000	206	0	1	14.35	0	/0-1	0	0.0

• MASON, Don Donald Stetson Mason b: 12/20/1944, Boston, MA BL/TR, 5'11", 160 lbs. Deb: 4/14/1966

YEAR TM-L	G	AB	R	H	2B	3B	HR	RBI	BB	SO	SB	CS	AVG	OBP	SLG	OPS	OPS+	BR/A	RC	RC/G	FR	G/POS	WS	TPW
1966 SF-N	42	25	8	3	0	0	1	1	0	2	0	1	.120	.120	.240	.360	-3	-4	1	.56	-1	/2-9	0	-0.5
1967 SF-N	4	3	0	0	0	0	0	0	0	0	0	0	.000	.000	.000	.000	-101	-1	0	.00	0	/2-2	0	-0.1
1968 SF-N	10	19	3	3	0	0	0	1	1	4	1	1	.158	.200	.158	.358	8	-2	1	.90	-2	/2-5,S-4,3-2	0	-0.5
1969 SF-N	104	250	43	57	4	2	0	13	36	29	1	5	.228	.325	.260	.585	67	-11	24	3.11	-9	2-51,3-21/S-7	5	-1.7
1970 SF-N	46	36	4	5	0	0	0	1	5	7	0	0	.139	.244	.139	.383	5	-5	1	.85	-3	2-14	0	-0.7
1971 SD-N	113	344	43	73	12	1	2	11	27	35	6	4	.212	.270	.270	.540	57	-20	24	2.22	-9	2-90/3-3	2	-2.5
1972 SD-N	9	11	1	2	0	0	0	0	1	1	0	0	.182	.250	.182	.432	26	-1	1	1.70	-2	/2-3	0	-0.3
1973 SD-N	8	8	0	0	0	0	0	0	0	2	0	0	.000	.000	.000	.000	-109	-2	0	.00	0	/2-1	0	-0.3
Total 8	336	696	102	143	16	3	3	27	70	80	8	11	.205	.278	.250	.528	52	-46	50	2.29	-26	2-175/3-26,S-11	7	-6.6

• MASON, Jim James Percy Mason b: 8/14/1950, Mobile, AL BL/TR, 6'2", 190 lbs. Deb: 9/26/1971

YEAR TM-L	G	AB	R	H	2B	3B	HR	RBI	BB	SO	SB	CS	AVG	OBP	SLG	OPS	OPS+	BR/A	RC	RC/G	FR	G/POS	WS	TPW
1971 Was-A	3	9	0	3	0	0	0	0	1	3	0	0	.333	.400	.333	.733	116	0	1	5.87	2	/S-3	0	0.2
1972 Tex-A	46	147	10	29	3	0	0	10	9	39	0	0	.197	.248	.218	.466	41	-11	8	1.77	-7	S-32,3-10	1	-1.5
1973 Tex-A	92	238	23	49	7	2	3	19	23	48	0	1	.206	.276	.290	.566	62	-12	20	2.70	-2	S-74,2-19/3-1	3	-0.6
1974 NY-A	152	440	41	110	18	6	5	37	35	87	1	2	.250	.305	.352	.658	91	-6	48	3.70	-1	*S-152	13	1.0
1975 NY-A	94	223	17	34	3	2	2	16	22	49	0	2	.152	.229	.211	.439	25	-23	10	1.28	-4	S-93/2-1	3	-1.8
1976*NY-A	93	217	17	39	7	1	1	14	9	37	0	0	.180	.212	.235	.447	31	-19	11	1.53	0	S-93	3	-1.1
1977 Tor-A	22	79	10	13	3	0	0	2	7	10	1	1	.165	.233	.203	.435	20	-9	4	1.53	-5	S-22	0	-1.2
Tex-A	36	55	9	12	3	0	1	7	6	10	0	0	.218	.295	.327	.622	69	-2	6	3.18	3	S-32/3-1,D-1	1	0.3
Yr.	58	134	19	25	6	0	1	9	13	20	1	1	.187	.259	.254	.512	40	-11	10	2.20	-2	S-54/3-1,D-1	1	-0.9
1978 Tex-A	55	105	10	20	4	0	0	3	5	17	0	0	.190	.227	.229	.456	28	-10	6	1.64	-5	S-42,3-11/2-1,D-1	1	-1.3
1979 Mon-N	40	71	3	13	5	1	0	6	7	16	0	2	.183	.256	.282	.538	47	-6	4	1.78	1	S-33/3-6	1	-0.4
Total 9	633	1584	140	322	53	12	12	114	124	316	2	8	.203	.262	.275	.536	54	-98	117	2.35	-19	S-576/3-29,2-21,D-2	26	-6.4

• MASSA, Gordon Gordon Richard "Moose,Duke" Massa b: 9/2/1935, Cincinnati, OH BL/TR, 6'3", 210 lbs. Deb: 9/24/1957

YEAR TM-L	G	AB	R	H	2B	3B	HR	RBI	BB	SO	SB	CS	AVG	OBP	SLG	OPS	OPS+	BR/A	RC	RC/G	FR	G/POS	WS	TPW
1957 Chi-N	6	15	2	7	1	0	0	3	4	3	0	0	.467	.579	.533	1.112	205	3	5	17.66	0	/C-6	1	0.3
1958 Chi-N	2	2	0	0	0	0	0	0	0	2	0	0	.000	.000	.000	.000	-102	-1	0	.00	0	....	0	-0.1
Total 2	8	17	2	7	1	0	0	3	4	5	0	0	.412	.524	.471	.994	175	2	5	14.13	0	/C-6	1	0.2

• MASSEY, Bill William Henry "Big Bill" Massey b: 1/1871, Philadelphia, PA d: 10/9/1940, Manila, Philippines BR/TR, 5'11", 168 lbs. Deb: 9/18/1894

YEAR TM-L	G	AB	R	H	2B	3B	HR	RBI	BB	SO	SB	CS	AVG	OBP	SLG	OPS	OPS+	BR/A	RC	RC/G	FR	G/POS	WS	TPW
1894 Cin-N	13	53	7	15	3	0	0	5	3	2	0	....	.283	.321	.340	.661	57	-4	6	4.06	-1	1-10/2-2,3-1	1	-0.4

• MASSEY, Mike William Herbert Massey b: 9/28/1893, Galveston, TX d: 10/17/1971, Shreveport, LA BB/TR, 6', 195 lbs. Deb: 4/12/1917

YEAR TM-L	G	AB	R	H	2B	3B	HR	RBI	BB	SO	SB	CS	AVG	OBP	SLG	OPS	OPS+	BR/A	RC	RC/G	FR	G/POS	WS	TPW
1917 Bos-N	31	91	12	18	0	0	0	2	15	15	2	....	.198	.318	.198	.516	63	-3	7	2.35	-7	2-25	1	-1.0

• MASSEY, Roy Roy Hardee "Red" Massey b: 10/9/1890, Sevierville, TN d: 6/23/1954, Atlanta, GA BL/TR, 5'11", 170 lbs. Deb: 4/16/1918

YEAR TM-L	G	AB	R	H	2B	3B	HR	RBI	BB	SO	SB	CS	AVG	OBP	SLG	OPS	OPS+	BR/A	RC	RC/G	FR	G/POS	WS	TPW
1918 Bos-N	66	203	20	59	6	2	0	18	23	20	1	....	.291	.363	.340	.703	120	6	25	4.36	-2	0-45(21-29-0)/3-2,1-1,S-1	7	0.1

• MASTELLER, Dan Dan Patrick Masteller b: 3/17/1968, Toledo, OH BL/TL, 6', 185 lbs. Deb: 6/23/1995

YEAR TM-L	G	AB	R	H	2B	3B	HR	RBI	BB	SO	SB	CS	AVG	OBP	SLG	OPS	OPS+	BR/A	RC	RC/G	FR	G/POS	WS	TPW
1995 Min-A	71	198	21	47	12	0	3	21	18	19	1	2	.237	.304	.343	.648	68	-10	19	3.23	-3	1-48,0-22(6-0-16)/D-8	1	-1.7

• MATA, Victor Victor Jose (Abreu) Mata b: 6/17/1961, Santiago, Dominican Republic BR/TR, 6'1", 165 lbs. Deb: 7/22/1984 Career OF: 3-22-10

YEAR TM-L	G	AB	R	H	2B	3B	HR	RBI	BB	SO	SB	CS	AVG	OBP	SLG	OPS	OPS+	BR/A	RC	RC/G	FR	G/POS	WS	TPW
1984 NY-A	30	70	8	23	5	0	1	6	0	12	1	1	.329	.338	.443	.781	119	1	10	4.98	-2	0-28(2-21-8)	2	-0.1
1985 NY-A	6	7	1	1	0	0	0	0	0	0	0	0	.143	.143	.143	.286	-22	-1	0	.64	-1	/0-3(1-1-2)	0	-0.2
Total 2	36	77	9	24	5	0	1	6	0	12	1	1	.312	.321	.416	.736	107	0	10	4.54	-2	/0-31	2	-0.3

• MATCHICK, Tom John Thomas Matchick b: 9/7/1943, Hazleton, PA BL/TR, 6'1", 175 lbs. Deb: 9/2/1967

YEAR TM-L	G	AB	R	H	2B	3B	HR	RBI	BB	SO	SB	CS	AVG	OBP	SLG	OPS	OPS+	BR/A	RC	RC/G	FR	G/POS	WS	TPW
1967 Det-A	8	6	1	1	0	0	0	0	0	2	0	0	.167	.167	.167	.333	-1	-1	0	.90	0	/S-1	0	-0.1
1968*Det-A	80	227	18	46	6	2	3	14	10	46	0	2	.203	.249	.286	.535	60	-12	16	2.24	1	S-59,2-13/1-6	3	-0.8
1969 Det-A	94	298	25	72	11	2	0	32	15	51	3	0	.242	.278	.292	.570	57	-17	23	2.66	7	2-47,3-27/S-6,1-2	4	-0.7
1970 Bos-A	10	14	2	1	0	0	0	0	2	2	0	1	.071	.188	.071	.259	-24	-3	0	.37	0	/3-2,2-1,S-1	0	-0.3
KC-A	55	158	11	31	3	2	0	11	5	23	0	0	.196	.226	.241	.466	29	-16	7	1.38	9	S-43,2-10/3-1	2	-0.2
Yr.	65	172	13	32	3	2	0	11	7	25	0	1	.186	.222	.227	.449	24	-18	7	1.29	8	S-44,2-11/3-3	2	-0.5
1971 Mil-A	42	114	6	25	1	0	1	7	7	23	3	2	.219	.264	.254	.519	48	-8	8	2.27	-2	3-41/2-1	1	-1.1
1972 Bal-A	3	9	0	2	0	0	0	0	0	1	0	1	.222	.222	.222	.444	32	-1	0	.75	0	/3-3	0	-0.2
Total 6	292	826	63	178	21	6	4	64	39	148	6	6	.215	.255	.270	.525	49	-57	54	2.15	14	S-110/3-74,2-72,1-8	10	-3.3

• MATEO, Henry Henry Antonio (Valera) Mateo b: 10/14/1976, Santo Domingo, Dominican Republic BB/TR, 5'11", 180 lbs. Deb: 7/28/2001

YEAR TM-L	G	AB	R	H	2B	3B	HR	RBI	BB	SO	SB	CS	AVG	OBP	SLG	OPS	OPS+	BR/A	RC	RC/G	FR	G/POS	WS	TPW
2001 Mon-N	5	9	1	3	1	0	0	0	0	1	0	0	.333	.333	.444	.778	97	-0	1	6.00	-1	/2-2	0	-0.1
2002 Mon-N	22	23	1	4	0	1	0	0	2	6	2	0	.174	.240	.261	.501	31	-2	2	2.49	1	/2-3,S-2	0	0.0
2003 Mon-N	100	154	29	37	3	1	0	7	11	38	11	1	.240	.304	.273	.576	44	-11	15	3.48	3	2-43,0-10(2-2-6)/D-3,S-2	2	-0.6
Total 3	127	186	31	44	4	2	0	7	13	45	13	1	.237	.297	.280	.577	45	-13	18	3.46	4	/2-48,0-10,S-4,D-3	2	-0.7

• MATEO, Ruben Ruben Amaury Mateo b: 2/10/1978, San Cristobal, Dominican Republic BR/TR, 6', 185 lbs. Deb: 6/12/1999 Career OF: 4-99-101

YEAR TM-L	G	AB	R	H	2B	3B	HR	RBI	BB	SO	SB	CS	AVG	OBP	SLG	OPS	OPS+	BR/A	RC	RC/G	FR	G/POS	WS	TPW
1999 Tex-A	32	122	16	29	9	1	5	18	4	28	3	0	.238	.268	.451	.719	75	-5	15	4.14	0	0-31(0-31-0)	3	-0.4
2000 Tex-A	52	206	32	60	11	0	7	19	10	34	6	0	.291	.339	.447	.786	95	-1	31	5.56	-2	0-52(0-52-0)	3	-0.2
2001 Tex-A	40	129	18	32	5	2	1	13	9	28	1	0	.248	.326	.341	.667	74	-5	15	3.80	-4	0-39(0-0-39)	1	-1.1
2002 Cin-N	46	86	11	22	6	0	2	7	6	20	0	0	.256	.319	.395	.714	85	-2	11	4.62	-1	0-24(0-2-23)	1	-0.4
2003 Cin-N	74	207	16	50	9	0	3	18	12	53	0	0	.242	.293	.329	.621	63	-12	20	3.28	-1	0-54(4-14-39)	3	-1.5
Total 5	244	750	93	193	40	3	18	75	41	163	10	0	.257	.311	.391	.701	78	-23	91	4.26	-9	0-200	11	-3.5

• MATHENY, Mike Michael Scott Matheny b: 9/22/1970, Columbus, OH BR/TR, 6'3", 205 lbs. Deb: 4/7/1994

YEAR TM-L	G	AB	R	H	2B	3B	HR	RBI	BB	SO	SB	CS	AVG	OBP	SLG	OPS	OPS+	BR/A	RC	RC/G	FR	G/POS	WS	TPW
1994 Mil-A	28	53	3	12	3	0	1	2	3	13	0	1	.226	.293	.340	.633	60	-4	5	3.09	-1	C-27	0	-0.3
1995 Mil-A	80	166	13	41	9	1	0	21	12	28	2	1	.247	.306	.313	.619	58	-10	16	3.35	-2	C-80	3	-0.8
1996 Mil-A	106	313	31	64	15	2	8	46	14	80	3	2	.204	.245	.342	.587	45	-28	24	2.43	1	*C-104/D-1	4	-1.9
1997 Mil-A	123	320	29	78	16	1	4	32	17	68	0	1	.244	.297	.338	.634	64	-17	31	3.18	6	*C-121/1-2	8	-0.4
1998 Mil-N	108	320	24	76	13	0	6	27	11	63	1	0	.238	.278	.334	.612	60	-19	29	3.13	0	*C-107	4	-1.3
1999 Tor-A	57	163	16	35	6	0	3	17	12	37	0	0	.215	.273	.307	.579	47	-13	14	2.78	0	C-57	3	-0.8
2000 StL-N	128	417	43	109	22	1	6	47	32	96	0	0	.261	.320	.362	.682	72	-19	47	3.83	5	*C-124/1-8	14	-0.4
2001*StL-N	121	381	40	83	12	0	7	42	28	76	0	1	.218	.278	.304	.583	51	-28	31	2.63	4	*C-121/1-2	8	-1.6
2002*StL-N	110	315	31	77	12	1	3	35	32	49	1	3	.244	.318	.317	.636	70	-15	33	3.48	-2	*C-106/1-1	9	-0.9
2003 StL-N	141	441	43	111	18	2	8	47	44	81	1	1	.252	.322	.356	.678	80	-13	50	3.81	3	*C-138/1-4	13	-0.2
Total 10	1002	2889	273	686	126	8	46	316	205	591	8	10	.237	.296	.334	.630	63	-167	281	3.22	14	C-985/1-17,D-1	66	-8.7

• MATHES, Joe Joseph John Mathes b: 7/28/1891, Milwaukee, WI d: 12/21/1978, St. Louis, MO BB/TR, 6'.5", 180 lbs. Deb: 9/19/1912

YEAR TM-L	G	AB	R	H	2B	3B	HR	RBI	BB	SO	SB	CS	AVG	OBP	SLG	OPS	OPS+	BR/A	RC	RC/G	FR	G/POS	WS	TPW
1912 Phi-A	4	14	0	2	0	0	0	0	0	....	0	....	.143	.200	.143	.343	-2	-2	0	.81	0	/3-4	0	-0.1
1914 StL-F	26	85	10	25	3	0	0	6	9	11	1	....	.294	.362	.329	.691	92	-1	10	4.22	-4	2-23	2	-0.4
1916 Bos-N	2	0	0	0	0	0	0	0	0	0	0	....	....	....	....	....	-106	0	0	....	-1	/2-2	0	-0.2
Total 3	32	99	10	27	3	0	0	6	9	11	1	....	.273	.339	.303	.642	79	-2	10	3.66	-5	/2-25,3-4	2	-0.7

YEAR	TM-L	G	AB	R	H	2B	3B	HR	RBI	BB	SO	SB	CS	AVG	OBP	SLG	OPS	OPS+	BR/A	RC	RC/G	FR	G/POS	WS	TPW

● MATHEWS, Bobby   Robert T. Mathews
b: 11/21/1851, Baltimore, MD   d: 4/17/1898, Baltimore, MD   BR/TR, 5'5.5", 140 lbs.   Deb: 5/4/1871   U   NA OF: 2-0-13   Career OF: 3-10-53   ◆

1871	Kek-n	19	89	15	24	3	1	0	10	2	0	2	1	.270	.286	.326	.612	74	-2	9	4.33	-1	P-19	....	0.2
1872	Bal-n	50	223	36	50	1	0	0	21	3	2	1	1	.224	.235	.229	.463	41	-10	12	2.23	-5	*P-49/0-8(0-0-8),3-3	....	1.3
1873	Mut-n	52	223	40	43	3	3	0	13	10	3	1	1	.193	.227	.233	.461	37	-5	12	2.08	-2	*P-52/0-5(0-0-5)	....	2.6
1874	Mut-n	65	298	46	72	6	1	0	30	3	3	2	0	.242	.249	.268	.518	64	-2	21	2.78	-1	*P-65/3-1,0-1	....	3.6
1875	Mut-n	70	264	23	48	6	2	0	15	2	5	1	2	.182	.188	.220	.408	39	-10	11	1.54	-6	*P-70/0-1	....	0.3
1876	NY-N	56	221	19	40	4	1	0	9	3	2	....	....	.181	.195	.211	.406	40	-8	9	1.44	-3	*P-56/0-1	18	-1.1
1877	Cin-N	15	59	5	10	0	0	0	0	1	2	....	....	.169	.183	.169	.353	13	-3	2	1.05	-4	P-15/0-1,S-1	1	-1.5
1879	Pro-N	43	173	25	35	2	0	1	10	7	12	....	....	.202	.233	.231	.465	55	-5	10	1.94	-3	P-27,0-21(0-0-21)/3-5	14	-0.7
1881	Pro-N	16	57	6	11	1	0	0	4	5	6	....	....	.193	.258	.211	.469	49	-1	3	1.86	-2	P-14/0-5(0-0-5)	3	-0.4
	Bos-N	19	71	2	12	2	0	0	4	0	5	....	....	.169	.169	.197	.366	15	-6	2	1.11	-3	0-18(1-9-9)/P-5	2	-0.8
	Yr.	35	128	8	23	3	0	0	8	5	11	....	....	.180	.211	.203	.414	31	-7	6	1.44	-5	0-23(1-9-14),P-19	5	-1.2
1882	Bos-N	45	169	17	38	6	0	0	13	8	18	....	....	.225	.260	.260	.520	67	-3	12	2.46	-9	P-34,0-13(0-0-13)/S-1	21	-0.3
1883	Phi-a	45	167	15	31	2	0	0	11	5	....	....	....	.186	.209	.198	.407	29	-7	7	1.46	-1	P-44/0-3(1-1-1)	30	4.2
1884	Phi-a	49	184	26	34	5	1	0	0	7	....	....	....	.185	.215	.223	.437	40	-5	9	1.65	-3	P-49/0-1	31	-0.1
1885	Phi-a	48	179	22	30	3	0	0	12	10	....	....	....	.168	.212	.184	.396	24	-6	7	1.30	0	P-48/0-1	26	4.0
1886	Phi-a	24	88	16	21	3	0	0	10	3	....	1	....	.239	.264	.273	.536	68	-1	7	2.72	-1	P-24/0-1	11	-0.5
1887	Phi-a	7	29	5	9	0	0	0	0	4	....	0	....	.310	.310	.200	.510	44	-0	2	2.15	0	/P-7	1	-1.3
Total 5 n		256	1097	160	237	19	7	0	89	20	13	7	5	.216	.230	.246	.476	49	-29	66	2.33	-15	P-255/0-15,3-4	....	8.1
Total 10		367	1397	158	271	28	2	1	73	53	45	1	....	.194	.222	.217	.439	42	-46	70	1.71	-29	P-323/0-65,3-5,S-2	158	1.4

● MATHEWS, Eddie   Edwin Lee Mathews
b: 10/13/1931, Texarkana, TX   d: 2/18/2001, La Jolla, CA   BL/TR, 6'1", 200 lbs.   Deb: 4/15/1952   M/C   HOF: 1978   Career OF: 52-0-0

1952	Bos-N	145	528	80	128	23	5	25	58	59	115	6	4	.242	.320	.447	.767	115	9	78	5.02	-11	*3-142	19	-0.3
1953	Mil-N★	157	579	110	175	31	8	**47**	135	99	83	1	3	.302	.406	.627	1.033	**175**	**64**	157	10.21	5	*3-157	**39**	**6.6**
1954	Mil-N	138	476	96	138	21	4	40	103	113	61	10	3	.290	.428	.603	1.031	**177**	59	131	9.84	0	*3-127,0-10(10-0-0)	33	5.7
1955	Mil-N★	141	499	108	144	23	5	41	101	**109**	98	3	4	.289	.417	.601	1.018	175	57	131	9.51	-9	*3-137	34	4.7
1956	Mil-N	151	552	103	150	21	2	37	95	91	86	6	0	.272	.376	.518	.894	146	39	114	7.46	-10	*3-150	29	2.9
1957	*Mil-N	148	572	109	167	28	9	32	94	90	79	3	1	.292	.388	.540	.928	157	48	126	8.16	-5	*3-147	33	4.3
1958	*Mil-N★	149	546	97	137	18	1	31	77	85	85	5	0	.251	.354	.458	.812	123	21	94	5.82	0	*3-149	24	2.0
1959	Mil-N★	148	594	118	182	16	8	**46**	114	80	71	2	1	.306	.391	.593	.984	172	60	143	9.07	2	*3-148	37	6.3
1960	Mil-N★	153	548	108	152	19	7	39	124	111	113	7	3	.277	.401	.551	.952	**170**	**57**	128	8.32	-11	*3-153	**38**	4.7
1961	Mil-N★	152	572	103	175	23	6	32	91	**93**	95	12	7	.306	.405	.535	.940	156	48	128	8.22	-4	*3-151	33	4.4
1962	Mil-N	152	536	106	142	25	6	29	90	**101**	90	4	2	.265	.383	.496	.880	138	31	106	7.00	6	*3-140/1-7	26	3.7
1963	Mil-N	158	547	82	144	27	4	23	84	**124**	119	3	4	.263	**.400**	.453	.854	147	40	106	6.84	18	*3-121,0-42(42-0-0)	31	6.0
1964	Mil-N	141	502	83	117	19	1	23	74	85	100	2	2	.233	.345	.412	.758	112	10	75	5.12	3	*3-128/1-7	20	1.4
1965	Mil-N	156	546	77	137	23	0	32	95	73	110	1	0	.251	.342	.469	.811	125	19	89	5.68	11	*3-153	22	3.2
1966	Atl-N	134	452	72	113	21	4	16	53	63	82	1	1	.250	.342	.420	.762	109	7	67	5.23	6	*3-127	16	1.4
1967	Hou-N	101	328	39	78	13	2	10	38	48	65	2	4	.238	.337	.381	.718	109	4	43	4.36	-3	1-79,3-24	10	-0.3
	Det-A	36	108	14	25	3	0	6	19	15	23	0	0	.231	.336	.426	.762	120	3	17	5.17	-1	3-21,1-13	4	0.1
1968	*Det-A	31	52	4	11	0	0	3	8	5	12	0	0	.212	.281	.385	.665	97	0	6	3.89	0	/1-6,3-6	2	0.0
Total 17		2391	8537	1509	2315	354	72	512	1453	1444	1487	68	39	.271	.378	.509	.888	145	576	1738	7.24	-2	*3-2181,1-112/0-52	450	56.7

● MATHEWS, Nelson   Nelson Elmer Mathews   b: 7/21/1941, Columbia, IL   BR/TR, 6'4", 195 lbs.   Deb: 9/9/1960   Career OF: 25-242-10

1960	Chi-N	3	8	1	2	0	0	0	0	0	0	0	0	.250	.250	.250	.500	38	-1	1	2.25	0	/0-2(0-0-2)	0	-0.1
1961	Chi-N	3	9	0	1	0	0	0	0	0	2	0	0	.111	.111	.111	.222	-40	-2	0	.38	-0	/0-2(0-2-0)	0	-0.2
1962	Chi-N	15	49	5	15	2	0	2	13	5	4	3	3	.306	.393	.469	.862	126	1	8	5.88	-1	0-14(0-14-0)	1	0.0
1963	Chi-N	61	155	12	24	3	2	4	10	16	48	3	4	.155	.234	.277	.511	44	-12	9	1.69	-3	0-46(0-46-0)	1	-1.8
1964	KC-A	157	573	58	137	27	5	14	60	43	143	2	3	.239	.293	.377	.670	82	-15	59	3.46	-7	*0-154(0-154-0)	8	-2.9
1965	KC-A	67	184	17	39	7	7	2	15	24	49	0	2	.212	.303	.359	.662	88	-4	20	3.45	-1	0-57(25-26-8)	3	-0.7
Total 6		306	978	93	218	39	14	22	98	88	248	8	12	.223	.289	.359	.648	78	-32	96	3.23	-11	0-275	13	-5.6

● MATHISON, Jimmy   James Michael Ignatius Mathison   b: 11/11/1878, Baltimore, MD   d: 7/4/1911, Baltimore, MD   TR   Deb: 8/29/1902

| 1902 | Bal-A | 29 | 91 | 12 | 24 | 2 | 1 | 0 | 7 | 9 | .... | 2 | .... | .264 | .368 | .308 | .676 | 85 | -1 | 12 | 4.46 | -5 | 3-28/S-1 | 1 | -0.5 |

● MATIAS, John   John Roy Matias   b: 8/15/1944, Honolulu, HI   BL/TL, 5'11", 170 lbs.   Deb: 4/7/1970

| 1970 | Chi-A | 58 | 117 | 7 | 22 | 2 | 0 | 2 | 6 | 3 | 22 | 1 | 0 | .188 | .215 | .256 | .471 | 28 | -11 | 6 | 1.73 | 1 | 0-22(5-0-17),1-18 | 0 | -1.2 |

● MATOS, Francisco   Francisco Aguirre (Mancebo) Matos   b: 7/23/1969, Santo Domingo, Dominican Republic   BR/TR, 6'1", 160 lbs.   Deb: 7/17/1994

| 1994 | Oak-A | 14 | 28 | 1 | 7 | 1 | 0 | 0 | 2 | 1 | 2 | 1 | 0 | .250 | .276 | .286 | .562 | 49 | -2 | 2 | 2.55 | -1 | 2-12/D-2 | 0 | -0.3 |

● MATOS, Julius   Julius Matos   b: 12/12/1974, New York, NY   BR/TR, 5'11", 175 lbs.   Deb: 5/31/2002   Career OF: 0-0-4

2002	SD-N	76	185	19	44	3	0	2	19	9	33	1	1	.238	.281	.286	.567	54	-13	14	2.56	0	2-49,3-17/S-4,0-3(0-0-3),1,D	2	-1.0
2003	KC-A	28	57	7	15	1	0	2	7	1	12	1	0	.263	.276	.386	.662	64	-3	6	3.32	-4	3-13,2-11/S-2,D-1,0-1	0	-0.6
Total 2		104	242	26	59	4	0	4	26	10	45	2	1	.244	.280	.310	.589	57	-16	20	2.73	-4	/2-60,3-30,S-6,0-4,1-2,D-2	2	-1.7

● MATOS, Luis   Luis David Matos   b: 10/30/1978, Bayamon, Puerto Rico   BR/TR, 6', 210 lbs.   Deb: 6/19/2000   Career OF: 4-179-46

2000	Bal-A	72	182	21	41	6	3	1	17	12	30	13	4	.225	.284	.308	.592	52	-12	15	2.66	3	0-69(1-44-25)/D-3	2	-0.9
2001	Bal-A	31	98	16	21	7	0	4	12	11	30	7	0	.214	.300	.408	.708	89	-0	14	4.61	0	0-31(1-23-10)	3	-0.1
2002	Bal-A	17	31	0	4	1	0	0	1	1	6	1	0	.129	.156	.161	.318	-16	-5	1	.71	-1	0-14(2-6-7)/D-1	0	-0.6
2003	Bal-A	109	439	70	133	23	3	13	45	28	90	15	7	.303	.354	.458	.812	116	10	70	5.67	4	*0-107(0-106-4)/D-2	13	1.4
Total 4		229	750	107	199	37	6	18	75	52	156	36	11	.265	.322	.403	.725	92	-7	100	4.50	6	0-221/D-6	18	-0.1

● MATOS, Pascual   Pascual (Cuevas) Matos   b: 12/23/1974, Barahona, Dominican Republic   BR/TR, 6'2", 160 lbs.   Deb: 5/11/1999

| 1999 | Atl-N | 6 | 8 | 0 | 1 | 0 | 0 | 0 | 0 | 0 | 2 | 0 | 0 | .125 | .125 | .125 | .250 | -37 | -2 | 0 | .00 | 0 | /C-5 | 0 | -0.1 |

● MATRANGA, Dave   David Michael Matranga   b: 1/8/1977, Orange, CA   BR/TR, 6', 170 lbs.   Deb: 6/27/2003

| 2003 | Hou-N | 6 | 5 | 1 | 1 | 0 | 0 | 1 | 1 | 0 | 2 | 0 | 0 | .200 | .200 | .800 | 1.000 | 138 | 0 | 1 | 5.40 | 0 | /2-2 | 0 | 0.0 |

● MATSUI, Hideki   Hideki "Godzilla" Matsui   b: 6/12/1974, Ishikawa, Japan   BL/TR, 6'2", 210 lbs.   Deb: 3/31/2003

| 2003 | *NY-A★ | 163 | 623 | 82 | 179 | 42 | 1 | 16 | 106 | 63 | 86 | 2 | 2 | .287 | .356 | .435 | .791 | 109 | 8 | 91 | 5.17 | -3 | *0-159(118-46-0)/D-4 | 19 | 0.0 |

● MATTESON, C.V.   Clifford Virgil Matteson   b: 11/24/1861, Seville, OH   d: 12/18/1931, Seville, OH   Deb: 6/13/1884   ◆

| 1884 | StL-U | 1 | 4 | 0 | 0 | 0 | 0 | 0 | .... | 0 | .... | .... | .... | .000 | .000 | .000 | .000 | -96 | -1 | 0 | .00 | 0 | /0-1,P-1 | 0 | -0.5 |

● MATTHEWS, Bob   Robert Matthews   b: Camden, NJ   Deb: 9/25/1891

| 1891 | Phi-a | 1 | 3 | 1 | 1 | 0 | 0 | 0 | 0 | 1 | 0 | .... | .... | .333 | .600 | .333 | .933 | 163 | 1 | 1 | 8.15 | 0 | /0-1 | 0 | 0.0 |

● MATTHEWS, Gary   Gary Nathaniel "Sarge" Matthews, Sr.   b: 7/5/1950, San Fernando, CA   BR/TR, 6'2", 190 lbs.   Deb: 9/6/1972   C   Career OF: 1446-0-431

1972	SF-N	20	62	11	18	1	4	1	14	7	13	0	1	.290	.362	.532	.895	156	3	11	6.44	-1	0-19(10-0-9)	3	0.2
1973	SF-N	148	540	74	162	22	10	12	58	58	83	17	5	.300	.369	.444	.813	119	17	90	6.03	-6	*0-145(144-0-1)	21	0.2
1974	SF-N	154	561	87	161	27	6	16	82	70	69	11	9	.287	.369	.442	.811	120	15	90	5.68	-4	*0-151(150-0-1)	20	0.2
1975	SF-N	116	425	67	119	22	3	12	58	65	53	13	4	.280	.378	.431	.809	119	14	71	5.88	1	*0-113(113-0-0)	16	0.8
1976	SF-N	156	587	79	164	28	4	20	84	75	94	12	5	.279	.362	.443	.805	124	19	98	5.95	-10	*0-156(156-0-0)	24	0.1
1977	Atl-N	148	555	89	157	25	5	17	64	67	90	22	8	.283	.362	.438	.800	101	4	89	5.71	-7	*0-145(145-0-0)	16	-1.0
1978	Atl-N	129	474	73	135	24	5	18	62	61	82	8	7	.285	.369	.462	.831	125	11	78	5.74	-2	*0-127(1-0-127)	17	0.3
1979	Atl-N★	156	631	97	192	34	3	27	90	60	75	18	8	.304	.365	.502	.867	125	22	118	7.02	-5	*0-156(0-0-156)	25	1.0
1980	Atl-N	155	571	79	159	17	3	19	75	42	93	11	3	.278	.328	.419	.746	104	2	76	4.69	-6	*0-143(6-0-137)	17	-1.1
1981	*Phi-N	101	359	62	108	21	3	9	67	59	42	15	2	.301	.404	.451	.855	136	22	71	7.12	3	*0-100(100-0-0)	19	2.2
1982	Phi-N	162	616	89	173	31	1	19	83	66	87	21	4	.281	.352	.427	.779	114	15	91	5.18	4	*0-162(162-0-0)	23	1.2

YEAR TM-L	G	AB	R	H	2B	3B	HR	RBI	BB	SO	SB	CS	AVG	OBP	SLG	OPS	OPS+	BR/A	RC	RC/G	FR	G/POS	WS	TPW
1983*Phi-N	132	446	66	115	18	2	10	50	69	81	13	9	.258	.357	.374	.732	104	3	62	4.70	4	*O-122(122-0-0)	14	0.2
1984*Chi-N	147	491	101	143	21	2	14	82	**103**	97	17	8	.291	**.417**	.428	.845	126	24	96	6.85	1	*O-145(145-0-0)	23	2.1
1985 Chi-N	97	298	45	70	12	0	13	40	59	64	2	0	.235	.365	.406	.771	104	4	47	5.33	2	O-85(85-0-0)	8	0.2
1986 Chi-N	123	370	49	96	16	1	21	46	60	59	3	2	.259	.363	.478	.841	121	11	63	5.78	-4	*O-105(105-0-0)	11	0.3
1987 Chi-N	44	42	3	11	3	0	0	8	4	11	0	0	.262	.326	.333	.659	72	-2	4	3.80	0	/O-2(2-0-0)	0	-0.2
Sea-A	45	119	10	28	1	0	3	15	15	22	0	1	.235	.321	.319	.640	67	-6	11	3.09	0	D-39	0	-0.6
Total 16	2033	7147	1083	2011	319	51	234	978	940	1125	183	74	.281	.367	.439	.805	116	179	1167	5.76	-29	*O-1876/D-39	257	6.2

• MATTHEWS, Gary

Gary Nathaniel "Little Sarge" Matthews, Jr. b: 8/25/1974, San Francisco, CA BB/TR, 6'3", 210 lbs. Deb: 6/4/1999 Career OF: 121-246-123

YEAR TM-L	G	AB	R	H	2B	3B	HR	RBI	BB	SO	SB	CS	AVG	OBP	SLG	OPS	OPS+	BR/A	RC	RC/G	FR	G/POS	WS	TPW
1999 SD-N	23	36	4	8	0	0	0	7	9	9	2	0	.222	.378	.222	.600	62	-1	4	3.77	-1	O-17(6-2-10)	1	-0.2
2000 Chi-N	80	158	24	30	1	2	4	14	15	28	3	0	.190	.264	.297	.562	42	-14	13	2.75	2	O-61(46-21-1)	1	-1.2
2001 Chi-N	106	258	41	56	9	1	9	30	38	55	5	3	.217	.320	.364	.684	80	-7	32	4.00	-4	*O-100(20-88-1)	6	-1.1
Pit-N	46	147	22	36	6	1	5	14	22	45	3	2	.245	.343	.401	.745	90	-2	20	4.68	-2	O-44(0-44-0)	4	-0.3
Yr.	152	405	63	92	15	2	14	44	60	100	8	5	.227	.328	.378	.706	84	-9	52	4.24	-6	*O-144(20-132-1)	10	-1.4
2002 NY-N	2	1	0	0	0	0	0	0	0	0	0	0	.000	.000	.000	.000	-104	-0	0	.00	0	....	0	0.0
Bal-A	109	344	54	95	25	3	7	38	43	69	15	5	.276	.358	.427	.786	113	8	56	5.65	-2	*O-100(16-16-76)/D-2	10	0.3
2003 Bal-A	41	162	21	33	12	1	2	20	9	29	0	3	.204	.250	.327	.577	52	-13	12	2.31	-1	O-40(0-40-0)/D-1	2	-1.3
SD-N	103	306	50	83	19	1	4	22	34	66	12	5	.271	.346	.379	.725	98	-0	42	4.89	-4	O-92(33-35-35)	3	-0.6
Total 5	510	1412	216	341	72	9	31	145	170	301	40	18	.242	.325	.371	.696	86	-29	179	4.28	-11	O-454/D-3	27	-4.5

• MATTHEWS, Wid

Wid Curry "Matty" Matthews b: 10/20/1896, Raleigh, IL d: 10/5/1965, Hollywood, CA BL/TL, 5'8.5", 155 lbs. Deb: 4/18/1923 Career OF: 3-169-0

YEAR TM-L	G	AB	R	H	2B	3B	HR	RBI	BB	SO	SB	CS	AVG	OBP	SLG	OPS	OPS+	BR/A	RC	RC/G	FR	G/POS	WS	TPW
1923 Phi-A	129	485	52	133	11	6	1	25	50	27	16	16	.274	.343	.328	.671	76	-18	55	3.87	-17	*O-127(2-125-0)	9	-3.9
1924 Was-A	53	169	25	51	10	4	0	13	11	4	3	8	.302	.355	.408	.763	100	-3	23	4.33	2	O-44(1-43-0)	5	-0.2
1925 Was-A	10	9	2	4	0	0	0	1	0	1	0	0	.444	.444	.444	.889	128	0	2	9.05	-0	/O-1	0	0.0
Total 3	192	663	79	188	21	10	1	39	61	32	19	24	.284	.348	.350	.697	83	-21	79	4.04	-14	O-172	14	-4.1

• MATTHIAS, Steve

Stephen J. Matthias b: 1860, Mitchellville, MD BR/TR, 5'8", 160 lbs. Deb: 4/20/1884

YEAR TM-L	G	AB	R	H	2B	3B	HR	RBI	BB	SO	SB	CS	AVG	OBP	SLG	OPS	OPS+	BR/A	RC	RC/G	FR	G/POS	WS	TPW
1884 CP-U	37	142	24	39	7	1	0	....	5	....	....	....	.275	.299	.338	.637	123	4	15	4.00	1	S-36/O-2(0-2-0)	6	0.5

• MATTICK, Bobby

Robert James Mattick b: 12/5/1915, Sioux City, IA BR/TR, 5'11", 178 lbs. Deb: 5/5/1938 M

YEAR TM-L	G	AB	R	H	2B	3B	HR	RBI	BB	SO	SB	CS	AVG	OBP	SLG	OPS	OPS+	BR/A	RC	RC/G	FR	G/POS	WS	TPW
1938 Chi-N	1	1	0	1	0	0	0	1	0	0	0	....	1.000	1.000	1.000	2.000	439	0	1	∞	-1	/S-1	0	0.0
1939 Chi-N	51	178	16	51	12	1	0	23	6	19	1	....	.287	.314	.365	.679	80	-5	20	3.94	4	S-48	5	0.2
1940 Chi-N	128	441	30	96	15	0	0	33	19	33	5	....	.218	.250	.252	.502	39	-37	27	2.06	1	*S-126/3-1	5	-2.7
1941 Cin-N	20	60	8	11	3	0	0	7	8	7	1	....	.183	.279	.233	.513	45	-4	4	2.29	-0	S-12/3-5,2-1	1	-0.3
1942 Cin-N	6	10	0	2	1	0	0	0	0	1	0	....	.200	.200	.300	.500	45	-1	1	2.03	0	/S-3	0	-0.1
Total 5	206	690	54	161	31	1	0	64	33	60	7	....	.233	.269	.281	.550	51	-47	53	2.54	4	S-190/3-6,2-1	11	-3.0

• MATTICK, Wally

Walter Joseph "Chink" Mattick b: 3/12/1887, St. Louis, MO d: 11/5/1968, Los Altos, CA BR/TR, 5'10", 180 lbs. Deb: 4/11/1912 Career OF: 9-122-13

YEAR TM-L	G	AB	R	H	2B	3B	HR	RBI	BB	SO	SB	CS	AVG	OBP	SLG	OPS	OPS+	BR/A	RC	RC/G	FR	G/POS	WS	TPW
1912 Chi-A	90	285	45	74	7	9	1	35	27	....	15	....	.260	.334	.358	.692	101	0	40	4.54	-5	O-79(2-66-10)	9	-1.0
1913 Chi-A	71	207	15	39	8	1	0	11	18	16	3	....	.188	.253	.237	.490	44	-15	14	1.96	3	O-64(7-56-0)	3	-1.6
1918 StL-N	8	14	0	2	0	0	0	1	2	3	0	....	.143	.333	.143	.476	49	-1	1	1.38	0	/O-3(0-0-3)	0	0.0
Total 3	169	506	60	115	15	10	1	47	47	19	18	....	.227	.302	.302	.604	76	-15	54	3.34	-2	O-146	12	-2.6

• MATTIMORE, Mike

Michael Joseph Mattimore b: 1859, Renovo, PA d: 4/28/1931, Butte, MT BL/TL, 5'8.5", 160 lbs. Deb: 5/3/1887 U Career OF: 23-10-32 ♦

YEAR TM-L	G	AB	R	H	2B	3B	HR	RBI	BB	SO	SB	CS	AVG	OBP	SLG	OPS	OPS+	BR/A	RC	RC/G	FR	G/POS	WS	TPW
1887 NY-N	8	32	5	8	1	0	0	4	0	6	1	....	.250	.250	.281	.531	49	-1	3	2.83	-1	/P-7,O-2(0-2-0)	4	0.6
1888 Phi-a	41	142	22	38	6	5	0	12	12	....	16	....	.268	.333	.380	.714	129	8	24	6.21	4	P-26,O-16(1-1-15)	15	-0.1
1889 Phi-a	23	73	10	17	1	2	1	8	9	7	6	....	.233	.333	.342	.676	94	0	11	5.01	-2	O-12(3-5-4)/1-7,P-5	3	-0.8
KC-a	19	75	6	12	1	1	0	5	3	16	0	....	.160	.192	.200	.392	11	-9	3	1.24	-2	O-19(19-1-0)/P-1	0	-0.9
Yr.	42	148	16	29	2	3	1	13	12	23	6	....	.196	.265	.270	.536	54	-9	14	3.02	-3	O-31(22-6-4)/1-7,P-6	3	-1.7
1890 Bro-a	33	129	14	17	1	1	0	7	16	....	11	....	.132	.238	.155	.393	16	-7	8	1.79	-4	P-19,O-14(0-1-13)	4	-2.0
Total 4	124	451	57	92	10	9	1	36	40	29	34	....	.204	.278	.273	.550	66	-8	48	3.55	-4	/O-63,P-58,1-7	26	-3.1

• MATTINGLY, Don

Donald Arthur "Donnie Baseball" Mattingly b: 4/20/1961, Evansville, IN BL/TL, 6', 175 lbs. Deb: 9/8/1982 Career OF: 33-2-47

YEAR TM-L	G	AB	R	H	2B	3B	HR	RBI	BB	SO	SB	CS	AVG	OBP	SLG	OPS	OPS+	BR/A	RC	RC/G	FR	G/POS	WS	TPW
1982 NY-A	7	12	0	2	0	0	0	1	0	1	0	0	.167	.167	.167	.333	-8	-2	0	.00	0	/O-6(5-0-1),1-1	0	-0.2
1983 NY-A	91	279	34	79	15	4	4	32	21	31	0	0	.283	.336	.409	.744	108	3	37	4.68	-4	O-48(13-1-39),1-42/2-1	7	-0.5
1984 NY-A★	153	603	91	**207**	**44**	2	23	110	41	33	1	1	**.343**	.386	.537	.923	**159**	46	120	7.58	6	*1-133,O-19(13-1-6)	29	4.3
1985 NY-A★	159	652	107	211	**48**	3	35	**145**	56	41	2	2	.324	.379	.567	.946	159	50	136	7.72	-6	*1-159	32	3.4
1986 NY-A★	162	677	117	**238**	**53**	2	31	113	53	35	0	0	.352	.399	**.573**	**.973**	**163**	57	150	8.68	-6	*1-160/3-3,D-1	34	4.0
1987 NY-A★	141	569	93	186	38	2	30	115	51	38	1	4	.327	.383	.559	.942	147	36	115	7.58	0	*1-140/D-1	27	2.6
1988 NY-A★	144	599	94	186	37	0	18	88	41	29	1	0	.311	.358	.462	.820	129	22	96	6.00	-2	*1-143/D-1,O-1	24	0.9
1989 NY-A★	158	631	79	191	37	2	23	113	51	30	3	0	.303	.356	.477	.833	134	27	104	6.05	-3	*1-145,D-17/O-1	26	1.4
1990 NY-A	102	394	40	101	16	0	5	42	28	20	1	0	.256	.311	.335	.646	80	-10	39	3.37	7	1-89,D-13/O-1	7	-1.1
1991 NY-A	152	587	64	169	35	0	9	68	46	42	2	0	.288	.344	.394	.737	103	3	76	4.56	-4	*1-127,D-22	14	-1.1
1992 NY-A	157	640	89	184	40	0	14	86	39	43	3	0	.288	.329	.416	.745	108	6	87	4.95	8	*1-143,D-15	20	0.3
1993 NY-A	134	530	78	154	27	2	17	86	61	42	0	0	.291	.366	.445	.811	121	16	83	5.63	1	*1-130/D-5	20	0.5
1994 NY-A	97	372	62	113	20	1	6	51	60	24	0	0	.304	.400	.411	.812	114	11	64	6.37	2	1-97	15	0.4
1995*NY-A	128	458	59	132	32	2	7	49	40	35	0	2	.288	.347	.413	.759	98	-3	61	4.69	1	*1-125/D-1	8	-1.2
Total 14	1785	7003	1007	2153	442	20	222	1099	588	444	14	9	.307	.363	.471	.834	128	261	1168	6.11	0	*1-1634/D-76,O-76,3-3,2-1	263	13.8

• MATTIS, Ralph

Ralph "Matty" Mattis b: 8/24/1890, Philadelphia, PA d: 9/13/1960, Williamsport, PA BR/TR, 5'11", 172 lbs. Deb: 4/22/1914

YEAR TM-L	G	AB	R	H	2B	3B	HR	RBI	BB	SO	SB	CS	AVG	OBP	SLG	OPS	OPS+	BR/A	RC	RC/G	FR	G/POS	WS	TPW
1914 Pit-F	36	85	14	21	4	1	0	8	9	11	2	....	.247	.326	.318	.644	89	-1	10	3.56	1	O-24(12-0-12)	1	-0.2

• MATTOX, Cloy

Cloy Mitchell "Monk" Mattox b: 11/24/1902, Leesville, VA d: 8/3/1985, Danville, VA BL/TR, 5'8", 168 lbs. Deb: 9/1/1929

YEAR TM-L	G	AB	R	H	2B	3B	HR	RBI	BB	SO	SB	CS	AVG	OBP	SLG	OPS	OPS+	BR/A	RC	RC/G	FR	G/POS	WS	TPW
1929 Phi-A	3	6	0	1	0	0	0	0	1	1	0	0	.167	.286	.167	.452	19	-1	0	1.83	0	/C-3	0	-0.1

• MATTOX, Jim

James Powell Mattox b: 12/17/1896, Leesville, VA d: 10/12/1973, Myrtle Beach, SC BL/TR, 5'9.5", 168 lbs. Deb: 4/30/1922

YEAR TM-L	G	AB	R	H	2B	3B	HR	RBI	BB	SO	SB	CS	AVG	OBP	SLG	OPS	OPS+	BR/A	RC	RC/G	FR	G/POS	WS	TPW
1922 Pit-N	29	51	11	15	1	1	0	3	1	3	0	0	.294	.308	.353	.661	69	-2	5	3.82	0	C-21	1	-0.2
1923 Pit-N	22	32	4	6	1	1	0	1	0	5	0	0	.188	.235	.281	.517	35	-3	2	2.19	0	/C-8	0	-0.3
Total 2	51	83	15	21	2	2	0	4	1	8	0	0	.253	.279	.325	.604	56	-5	8	3.16	0	/C-29	1	-0.4

• MATUSZEK, Len

Leonard James Matuszek b: 9/27/1954, Toledo, OH BL/TR, 6'2", 195 lbs. Deb: 9/3/1981 Career OF: 53-0-2

YEAR TM-L	G	AB	R	H	2B	3B	HR	RBI	BB	SO	SB	CS	AVG	OBP	SLG	OPS	OPS+	BR/A	RC	RC/G	FR	G/POS	WS	TPW
1981 Phi-N	13	11	1	3	1	0	0	1	3	1	0	1	.273	.429	.364	.792	121	0	2	4.84	1	/1-1,3-1	1	0.1
1982 Phi-N	25	39	1	3	1	0	0	3	1	10	0	1	.077	.122	.103	.225	-36	-8	0	.08	-1	/3-8,1-3	0	-0.9
1983 Phi-N	28	80	12	22	6	1	4	16	4	14	0	1	.275	.310	.525	.835	129	2	12	5.24	-1	1-21	3	0.0
1984 Phi-N	101	262	40	65	17	1	12	43	39	54	4	3	.248	.354	.458	.812	125	9	43	5.45	2	1-81/O-1	9	0.7
1985 Tor-A	62	151	23	32	6	2	2	15	11	24	2	1	.212	.265	.318	.583	57	-9	12	2.52	0	D-54/1-5	0	-1.0
*LA-N	43	63	10	14	2	1	3	13	8	14	0	1	.222	.319	.429	.748	111	0	9	4.47	0	O-17(17-0-0),1-10/3-1	2	-0.1
1986 LA-N	91	199	26	52	7	0	9	28	21	47	2	2	.261	.335	.432	.767	118	4	29	5.10	0	O-37(35-0-2),1-31	6	0.2
1987 LA-N	16	15	0	1	0	0	0	0	1	4	0	0	.067	.125	.067	.192	-49	-3	0	.30	0	/1-3	0	-0.3
Total 7	379	820	113	192	40	5	30	119	88	168	8	10	.234	.314	.405	.719	100	-5	107	4.27	1	1-155/O-55,D-54,3-10	21	-1.4

• MAUCH, Gene

Gene William "Skip" Mauch b: 11/18/1925, Salina, KS BR/TR, 5'10", 165 lbs. Deb: 4/18/1944 M/C

YEAR TM-L	G	AB	R	H	2B	3B	HR	RBI	BB	SO	SB	CS	AVG	OBP	SLG	OPS	OPS+	BR/A	RC	RC/G	FR	G/POS	WS	TPW
1944 Bro-N	5	15	2	2	1	0	0	2	2	3	0	....	.133	.235	.200	.435	24	-2	1	1.72	0	/S-5	0	-0.1
1947 Pit-N	16	30	8	9	0	0	0	1	7	6	0	....	.300	.432	.300	.732	95	0	5	6.02	-3	/2-6,S-4	1	-0.2
1948 Bro-N	12	13	1	2	0	0	0	0	1	4	0	....	.154	.214	.154	.368	1	-2	1	1.25	-1	/2-7,S-1	0	-0.2
Chi-N	53	138	18	28	3	2	1	7	26	10	1	....	.203	.329	.275	.605	68	-5	15	3.59	-5	2-26,S-19	2	-0.8
Yr.	65	151	19	30	3	2	1	7	27	14	1	....	.199	.320	.265	.585	62	-7	15	3.37	-6	2-33,S-20	2	-1.0
1949 Chi-N	72	150	15	37	6	2	1	7	21	15	3	....	.247	.339	.333	.673	83	-3	17	3.72	-4	2-25,S-19/3-7	3	-0.5
1950 Bos-N	48	121	17	28	5	0	1	15	14	9	1	....	.231	.316	.298	.614	67	-6	11	3.06	-2	2-28/3-7,S-5	2	-0.6
1951 Bos-N	19	20	5	2	0	0	0	1	7	4	0	0	.100	.333	.100	.433	24	-2	1	2.01	-2	S-10/3-3,2-2	0	-0.3
1952 StL-N	7	3	0	0	0	0	0	0	1	2	0	0	.000	.250	.000	.250	-25	-0	0	.59	-1	/S-2	0	-0.2

YEAR TM-L	G	AB	R	H	2B	3B	HR	RBI	BB	SO	SB	CS	AVG	OBP	SLG	OPS	OPS+	BR/A	RC	RC/G	FR	G/POS	WS	TPW
1956 Bos-A	7	25	4	8	0	0	0	1	3	3	0	0	.320	.393	.320	.713	80	-0	3	4.70	0	/2-6	1	0.0
1957 Bos-A	65	222	23	60	10	3	2	28	22	26	1	0	.270	.339	.369	.708	88	-3	27	4.14	-12	2-58	5	-1.1
Total 9	304	737	93	176	25	7	5	62	104	82	6	0	.239	.335	.312	.647	74	-22	80	3.66	-30	2-158/S-65,3-17	14	-4.0

• MAUL, Al

Albert Joseph "Smiling Al" Maul
b: 10/9/1865, Philadelphia, PA d: 5/3/1958, Philadelphia, PA BR/TR, 6', 175 lbs. Deb: 6/20/1884 Career OF: 85-20-80 ♦

YEAR TM-L	G	AB	R	H	2B	3B	HR	RBI	BB	SO	SB	CS	AVG	OBP	SLG	OPS	OPS+	BR/A	RC	RC/G	FR	G/POS	WS	TPW
1884 Phi-U	1	4	0	0	0	0	0	....	0	....	....	....	.000	.000	.000	.000	-108	-1	0	.00	0	/P-1	0	-0.2
1887 Phi-N	16	71	15	32	2	2	1	4	15	10	5	....	.451	.451	.464	.915	146	6	14	9.73	-2	/0-8(7-1-0),P-7,1-2	4	-0.2
1888 Pit-N	74	259	21	54	9	4	0	31	21	45	9	....	.208	.276	.274	.550	82	-3	23	2.98	-1	1-38,0-34(0-3-31)/P-3	5	-1.5
1889 Pit-N	68	257	37	71	6	6	4	44	29	41	18	....	.276	.356	.393	.749	121	10	43	6.19	9	0-64(39-0-25)/P-6	9	-1.1
1890 Pit-P	45	162	31	42	6	2	0	21	22	12	5	....	.259	.348	.321	.669	86	6	20	4.57	5	P-30,0-15(11-3-1)/S-1	18	1.3
1891 Pit-N	47	149	15	28	2	4	0	14	20	28	4	....	.188	.284	.255	.539	59	-6	12	2.73	-2	0-40(20-12-8)/P-8	4	-0.4
1893 Was-N	44	134	10	34	8	4	0	12	33	14	1	....	.254	.405	.373	.778	110	11	21	5.61	0	P-37/0-7(5-0-2)	11	-0.3
1894 Was-N	41	124	23	30	3	3	2	20	14	11	1	....	.242	.352	.363	.715	75	2	17	4.59	2	P-28,0-12(1-0-11)	8	-0.8
1895 Was-N	22	72	9	18	5	2	0	16	6	7	0	....	.250	.308	.375	.683	76	1	9	4.22	1	P-16/0-4(2-0-2)	10	3.1
1896 Was-N	8	28	6	8	1	1	0	5	3	2	0	....	.286	.355	.393	.748	97	2	4	5.30	-1	/P-8	3	0.7
1897 Was-N	1	1	0	0	0	0	0	0	0	....	0	....	.000	.000	.000	.000	-101	-0	0	.00	0	/P-1	0	-0.1
Bal-N	2	3	0	1	0	0	0	0	0	....	0	....	.333	.333	.333	.667	76	0	0	4.53	0	/P-2	0	-0.2
Yr.	3	4	0	1	0	0	0	0	0	....	0	....	.250	.250	.250	.500	32	-0	0	3.02	0	/P-3	0	-0.3
1898 Bal-N	29	93	21	19	3	2	0	10	16	....	1	....	.204	.333	.280	.613	75	4	9	3.32	-4	P-28/0-1	24	3.4
1899 Bro-N	4	11	2	3	0	0	0	0	1	....	0	....	.273	.333	.273	.606	65	0	1	3.40	0	/P-4	1	-0.2
1900 Phi-N	5	15	2	3	0	0	0	1	2	....	0	....	.200	.294	.200	.494	38	0	1	2.00	0	/P-5	1	-1.0
1901 NY-N	3	8	1	3	0	0	0	1	0	....	0	....	.375	.375	.375	.750	122	1	1	6.11	0	/P-3	0	-1.6
Total 15	410	1391	193	346	45	30	7	179	182	170	44	....	.249	.336	.332	.668	91	31	176	4.48	6	P-187,0-185/1-40,S-1	98	1.2

• MAULDIN, Mark

Marshall Reese Mauldin b: 11/5/1914, Atlanta, GA d: 9/2/1990, Union City, GA BR/TR, 5'11", 170 lbs. Deb: 9/10/1934

YEAR TM-L	G	AB	R	H	2B	3B	HR	RBI	BB	SO	SB	CS	AVG	OBP	SLG	OPS	OPS+	BR/A	RC	RC/G	FR	G/POS	WS	TPW
1934 Chi-A	10	38	3	10	2	0	1	3	0	3	0	0	.263	.263	.395	.658	66	-2	4	3.49	-1	3-10	1	-0.2

• MAURER, Rob

Robert John Maurer b: 1/7/1967, Evansville, IN BL/TL, 6'3", 210 lbs. Deb: 9/8/1991

YEAR TM-L	G	AB	R	H	2B	3B	HR	RBI	BB	SO	SB	CS	AVG	OBP	SLG	OPS	OPS+	BR/A	RC	RC/G	FR	G/POS	WS	TPW
1991 Tex-A	13	16	0	1	1	0	0	2	2	6	0	0	.063	.211	.125	.336	-5	-2	1	1.05	1	/1-4,D-2	0	-0.2
1992 Tex-A	8	9	1	2	0	0	0	1	1	2	0	0	.222	.300	.222	.522	50	-1	1	2.62	0	/1-3,D-1	0	-0.1
Total 2	21	25	1	3	1	0	0	3	3	8	0	0	.120	.241	.160	.401	14	-3	1	1.55	1	/1-7,D-3	0	-0.2

• MAURO, Carmen

Carmen Louis Mauro b: 11/10/1926, St. Paul, MN BL/TR, 6', 167 lbs. Deb: 10/1/1948 Career OF: 25-48-40

YEAR TM-L	G	AB	R	H	2B	3B	HR	RBI	BB	SO	SB	CS	AVG	OBP	SLG	OPS	OPS+	BR/A	RC	RC/G	FR	G/POS	WS	TPW
1948 Chi-N	3	5	2	1	0	0	1	1	2	0	0	....	.200	.429	.800	1.229	235	1	2	13.08	0	/0-2(0-1-1)	1	0.1
1950 Chi-N	62	185	19	42	4	3	1	10	13	31	3	....	.227	.285	.297	.582	54	-13	16	2.87	-2	0-49(18-1-30)	1	-1.6
1951 Chi-N	13	29	3	5	1	0	0	3	2	6	0	0	.172	.250	.207	.457	24	-3	2	1.95	0	/0-6(0-5-1)	0	-0.3
1953 Bro-N	8	9	1	0	0	0	0	0	0	4	0	0	.000	.000	.000	.000	-98	-3	0	.00	-0	/0-1	0	-0.3
Was-A	17	23	1	4	0	1	0	2	1	3	0	0	.174	.208	.261	.469	27	-2	1	1.90	1	/0-6(3-3-0)	0	-0.2
Phi-A	64	165	14	44	4	4	0	17	19	21	3	4	.267	.342	.339	.682	81	-5	18	3.79	-3	0-49(4-38-7)/3-1	2	-1.0
Yr.	81	188	15	48	4	5	0	19	20	24	3	4	.255	.327	.330	.657	75	-7	20	3.55	-2	0-55(7-41-7)/3-1	2	-1.2
Total 4	167	416	40	96	9	8	2	33	37	65	6	4	.231	.298	.305	.604	61	-24	39	3.15	-4	0-113/3-1	4	-3.2

• MAVIS, Bob

Robert Henry Mavis b: 4/8/1918, Milwaukee, WI BL/TR, 5'7", 160 lbs. Deb: 9/17/1949

YEAR TM-L	G	AB	R	H	2B	3B	HR	RBI	BB	SO	SB	CS	AVG	OBP	SLG	OPS	OPS+	BR/A	RC	RC/G	FR	G/POS	WS	TPW
1949 Det-A	1	0	0	0	0	0	0	0	0	0	0	0	....	....	....	....	-100	0	0	....	0	....	0	0.0

• MAXVILL, Dal

Charles Dallan Maxvill b: 2/18/1939, Granite City, IL BR/TR, 5'11", 160 lbs. Deb: 6/10/1962 C Career OF: 1-0-1

YEAR TM-L	G	AB	R	H	2B	3B	HR	RBI	BB	SO	SB	CS	AVG	OBP	SLG	OPS	OPS+	BR/A	RC	RC/G	FR	G/POS	WS	TPW
1962 StL-N	79	189	20	42	3	1	1	18	17	39	1	2	.222	.290	.265	.554	46	-15	15	2.61	2	S-76/3-1	3	-0.9
1963 StL-N	53	51	12	12	2	0	0	3	6	11	0	0	.235	.316	.275	.590	65	-2	5	3.13	1	S-24/2-9,3-3	1	0.0
1964★StL-N	37	26	4	6	0	0	0	4	0	7	1	0	.231	.231	.231	.462	28	-2	2	2.01	-5	2-15,S-13/3-1,0-1	0	-0.7
1965 StL-N	68	89	10	12	2	2	0	10	7	15	0	0	.135	.206	.202	.408	14	-10	4	1.23	2	2-49,S-12	1	-0.6
1966 StL-N	134	394	25	96	14	3	0	24	37	61	3	0	.244	.312	.294	.606	70	-14	36	3.11	18	*S-128/2-5,0-1	12	1.6
1967★StL-N	152	476	37	108	14	4	1	41	48	66	0	2	.227	.299	.279	.578	68	-19	39	2.76	15	*S-148/2-7	12	1.0
1968★StL-N	151	459	51	116	8	5	1	24	52	71	0	2	.253	.330	.298	.629	91	-4	46	3.51	15	*S-151	20	2.7
1969 StL-N	132	372	27	65	10	2	2	32	44	52	1	1	.175	.264	.228	.492	39	-30	23	1.89	26	*S-131	10	1.2
1970 StL-N	152	399	35	80	5	2	0	28	51	56	0	0	.201	.291	.223	.514	39	-33	29	2.28	29	*S-136,2-22	9	1.0
1971 StL-N	142	356	31	80	10	1	0	24	43	45	1	2	.225	.310	.258	.568	60	-18	28	2.46	18	*S-140	9	1.5
1972 StL-N	105	276	22	61	6	1	1	23	31	47	0	1	.221	.300	.261	.561	61	-14	21	2.39	5	S-95,2-11	4	0.1
★Oak-A	27	36	2	9	1	0	0	1	1	11	0	1	.250	.270	.278	.548	67	-2	3	2.35	1	2-24/S-4	1	0.0
1973 Oak-A	29	19	0	4	0	0	0	1	1	3	0	0	.211	.250	.211	.461	33	-2	1	1.92	-4	S-18,2-11/3-1	0	-0.5
Pit-N	74	217	19	41	4	3	0	17	22	40	0	0	.189	.264	.235	.499	40	-17	14	1.94	6	S-74	3	-0.3
1974 Pit-N	8	22	3	4	0	0	0	0	2	4	0	0	.182	.250	.182	.432	23	-2	1	1.34	0	/S-8	0	-0.1
★Oak-A	60	52	3	10	0	0	0	2	8	10	0	0	.192	.300	.192	.492	47	-3	4	2.16	-4	2-30,S-29/3-1	2	-0.4
1975 Oak-A	20	10	1	2	0	0	0	0	0	0	0	0	.200	.200	.200	.400	14	-1	0	.60	-4	S-20/2-2	0	-0.5
Total 14	1423	3443	302	748	79	24	6	252	370	538	7	11	.217	.295	.259	.554	58	-188	270	2.53	121	*S-1207,2-185/3-7,0-2	87	5.2

• MAXWELL, Charlie

Charles Richard "Smokey,Paw Paw" Maxwell b: 4/8/1927, Lawton, MI BL/TL, 5'11", 185 lbs. Deb: 9/20/1950 Career OF: 783-4-55

YEAR TM-L	G	AB	R	H	2B	3B	HR	RBI	BB	SO	SB	CS	AVG	OBP	SLG	OPS	OPS+	BR/A	RC	RC/G	FR	G/POS	WS	TPW
1950 Bos-A	3	8	1	0	0	0	0	0	1	3	0	0	.000	.111	.000	.111	-63	-2	0	.10	0	/0-2(0-0-1)	0	-0.2
1951 Bos-A	49	80	8	15	1	0	3	12	9	18	0	1	.188	.270	.313	.582	52	-6	7	2.79	-1	0-13(5-0-8)	0	-0.7
1952 Bos-A	8	15	0	1	1	0	0	0	3	11	0	0	.067	.222	.133	.356		-2	1	1.21	1	/1-3,0-3(0-1-2)	0	-0.1
1954 Bos-A	74	104	9	26	4	1	0	5	12	21	3	0	.250	.328	.308	.635	67	-4	11	3.52	0	0-27(21-3-6)	1	-0.4
1955 Bal-A	4	4	0	0	0	0	0	0	0	1	0	0	.000	.000	.000	.000	-108	-1	0	.00	0	....	0	-0.1
Det-A	55	109	19	29	7	1	7	18	8	20	0	0	.266	.328	.541	.869	133	4	19	6.08	0	0-26(22-0-4)/1-2	4	0.2
Yr.	59	113	19	29	7	1	7	18	8	21	0	0	.257	.317	.522	.839	126	3	19	5.81	0	0-26(22-0-4)/1-2	4	0.1
1956 Det-A★	141	500	96	163	14	3	28	87	79	74	1	1	.326	.420	.534	.954	150	38	118	9.02	2	*0-136(134-0-2)	25	3.1
1957 Det-A★	138	492	75	136	23	3	24	82	76	84	3	2	.276	.379	.482	.860	130	22	94	6.86	3	*0-137(137-0-3)	22	1.8
1958 Det-A	131	397	56	108	14	4	13	65	64	54	6	1	.272	.373	.426	.799	111	9	68	6.10	-4	*0-114(113-0-3),1-14	15	-0.2
1959 Det-A	145	518	81	130	12	2	31	95	81	91	0	2	.251	.359	.461	.820	117	13	89	5.92	-3	*0-136(136-0-0)	18	0.1
1960 Det-A	134	482	70	114	16	5	24	81	58	75	5	0	.237	.326	.440	.766	99	-0	73	5.28	-5	*0-120(120-0-0)	13	-1.3
1961 Det-A	79	131	11	30	4	2	5	18	20	24	0	0	.229	.336	.405	.740	93	-1	19	5.01	0	0-25(22-0-4)	4	-0.3
1962 Det-A	30	67	5	13	2	0	1	9	8	10	0	0	.194	.280	.269	.549	47	-5	5	2.57	-1	0-15(0-0-15)/1-1	0	-0.8
Chi-A	69	206	30	61	8	3	9	43	34	32	0	0	.296	.396	.495	.891	139	12	42	7.47	-2	0-56(49-0-7)/1-6	10	0.7
Yr.	99	273	35	74	10	3	10	52	42	42	0	0	.271	.368	.440	.808	117	7	47	6.13	-3	0-71(49-0-22)/1-7	10	0.0
1963 Chi-A	71	130	17	30	4	2	3	17	31	27	0	0	.231	.379	.362	.740	111	4	20	5.02	0	0-24(24-0-0),1-17	5	0.2
1964 Chi-A	2	2	0	0	0	0	0	0	0	0	0	0	.000	.000	.000	.000	-103	-1	0	.00	0	....	0	-0.1
Total 14	1133	3245	478	856	110	26	148	532	484	545	18	7	.264	.363	.451	.814	116	81	566	6.15	-9	0-834/1-43	117	2.1

• MAXWELL, Jason

Jason Ramond Maxwell b: 3/26/1972, Lewisburg, TN BR/TR, 6', 180 lbs. Deb: 9/1/1998

YEAR TM-L	G	AB	R	H	2B	3B	HR	RBI	BB	SO	SB	CS	AVG	OBP	SLG	OPS	OPS+	BR/A	RC	RC/G	FR	G/POS	WS	TPW
1998 Chi-N	7	3	2	1	0	0	1	2	0	2	0	0	.333	.333	1.333	1.667	301	1	1	10.17	0	/2-1	1	0.1
2000 Min-A	64	111	14	27	6	0	1	11	9	32	2	1	.243	.306	.324	.630	57	-7	11	3.39	6	2-30,3-19/D-7,S-5,0-2(0-1-1)	2	-0.1
2001 Min-A	39	68	4	13	4	0	1	10	9	23	2	0	.191	.286	.294	.580	52	-4	6	2.98	-2	S-12,3-11/2-9,D-6	1	-0.5
Total 3	110	182	20	41	10	0	3	23	18	57	4	1	.225	.299	.330	.628	60	-11	19	3.37	4	/2-40,3-30,S-17,D-13,0-2	4	-0.5

• MAY, Carlos

Carlos May b: 5/17/1948, Birmingham, AL BL/TR, 5'11", 215 lbs. Deb: 9/6/1968 Career OF: 653-0-26

YEAR TM-L	G	AB	R	H	2B	3B	HR	RBI	BB	SO	SB	CS	AVG	OBP	SLG	OPS	OPS+	BR/A	RC	RC/G	FR	G/POS	WS	TPW
1968 Chi-A	17	67	4	12	1	0	0	1	3	15	0	0	.179	.214	.194	.408	24	-6	3	1.31	-1	0-17(15-0-2)	0	-0.9
1969 Chi-A★	100	367	62	103	18	2	18	62	58	66	1	4	.281	.387	.488	.875	137	18	69	6.57	0	*0-100(80-0-22)	14	1.3
1970 Chi-A	150	555	83	158	28	4	12	68	79	96	12	5	.285	.377	.414	.791	114	14	84	5.26	6	*0-141(141-0-0)/1-7	15	1.2
1971 Chi-A	141	500	64	147	21	7	7	70	62	61	16	7	.294	.379	.406	.785	119	15	77	5.46	-5	*1-130/0-9(9-0-0)	15	0.0
1972 Chi-A★	148	523	83	161	26	3	12	68	79	70	23	14	.308	.408	.438	.845	148	35	96	6.64	-1	*0-145(145-0-0)/1-5	29	2.9
1973 Chi-A	149	553	62	148	20	0	20	96	53	73	8	6	.268	.337	.412	.749	106	4	75	4.70	2	D-75,0-70(70-0-0)/1-2	15	0.0
1974 Chi-A	149	551	66	137	19	2	8	58	46	76	8	9	.249	.308	.334	.642	82	-14	56	3.43	-2	*0-129(129-0-0),D-13	8	-2.6

YEAR TM-L	G	AB	R	H	2B	3B	HR	RBI	BB	SO	SB	CS	AVG	OBP	SLG	OPS	OPS+	BR/A	RC	RC/G	FR	G/POS	WS	TPW
1975 Chi-A	128	454	55	123	19	2	8	53	67	46	12	7	.271	.375	.374	.750	111	10	66	5.01	1	1-63,0-46(46-0-0),D-19	14	0.3
1976 Chi-A	20	63	7	11	2	0	0	3	9	5	4	0	.175	.278	.206	.484	43	-3	5	2.51	0	D-10/0-9(9-0-0)	0	-0.5
*NY-A	87	288	38	80	11	2	3	40	34	32	1	1	.278	.364	.361	.725	114	6	39	4.82	0	D-71/0-7(7-0-0),1-1	8	0.4
Yr.	107	351	45	91	13	2	3	43	43	37	5	1	.259	.348	.333	.682	101	3	44	4.38	0	D-81/0-16(16-0-0)/1-1	8	-0.1
1977 NY-A	65	181	21	41	7	1	2	16	17	24	0	0	.227	.296	.309	.606	66	-8	16	2.83	0	D-53/0-4(2-0-0)	1	-1.0
Cal-A	11	18	0	6	0	0	0	1	5	1	0	0	.333	.478	.333	.812	131	1	3	6.59	0	/1-3,D-1	1	0.1
Yr.	76	199	21	47	7	1	2	17	22	25	0	0	.236	.315	.312	.627	73	-7	19	3.13	0	D-54/0-4(2-0-2),1-3	2	-0.8
Total 10	1165	4120	545	1127	172	23	90	536	512	565	85	53	.274	.360	.392	.752	111	72	589	4.96	-1	0-677,D-242,1-211	120	1.2

• MAY, Dave
David La France May   b: 12/23/1943, New Castle, DE   BL/TR, 5'10.5", 186 lbs.   Deb: 7/28/1967   Career OF: 88-542-411

YEAR TM-L	G	AB	R	H	2B	3B	HR	RBI	BB	SO	SB	CS	AVG	OBP	SLG	OPS	OPS+	BR/A	RC	RC/G	FR	G/POS	WS	TPW
1967 Bal-A	36	85	12	20	1	1	1	7	6	13	0	0	.235	.286	.306	.592	75	-3	8	3.21	-1	0-19(1-0-18)	1	-0.5
1968 Bal-A	84	152	15	29	6	3	0	7	19	27	3	3	.191	.285	.270	.555	69	-6	11	2.38	-1	0-61(1-16-47)	2	-1.1
1969*Bal-A	78	120	8	29	6	0	3	10	9	23	2	1	.242	.305	.367	.672	86	-2	12	3.46	0	0-40(0-0-40)	2	-0.4
1970 Bal-A	25	31	6	6	0	1	1	6	4	4	0	0	.194	.286	.355	.641	75	-1	2	2.32	0	/0-9(0-0-9)	0	-0.1
Mil-A	100	342	36	82	8	1	7	31	44	56	8	6	.240	.330	.330	.660	82	-8	37	3.61	-1	0-99(0-99-1)	8	-1.2
Yr.	125	373	42	88	8	2	8	37	48	60	8	6	.236	.326	.332	.659	81	-9	40	3.49	-1	*0-108(0-99-10)	8	-1.4
1971 Mil-A	144	501	74	139	20	3	16	65	50	59	15	9	.277	.347	.425	.772	119	12	70	4.75	2	*0-142(2-94-48)	18	0.9
1972 Mil-A	143	500	49	119	20	2	9	45	47	56	11	13	.238	.307	.340	.647	94	-7	49	3.22	2	*0-138(0-138-0)	13	-1.0
1973 Mil-A★	156	624	96	189	23	4	25	93	44	78	6	7	.303	.354	.473	.826	134	24	100	5.86	-9	*0-152(0-152-0)/D-2	24	1.1
1974 Mil-A	135	477	56	108	15	1	10	42	28	73	4	3	.226	.274	.325	.599	72	-18	41	2.85	-1	*0-121(5-17-108)/D-8	6	-2.2
1975 Atl-N	82	203	28	56	8	0	12	40	25	27	1	1	.276	.361	.493	.853	130	8	36	6.43	-1	0-53(13-17-24)	9	0.5
1976 Atl-N	105	214	27	46	5	3	3	23	26	31	5	1	.215	.303	.308	.611	69	-8	21	3.28	-1	0-60(41-0-19)	3	-1.2
1977 Tex-A	120	340	46	82	14	1	7	42	32	43	4	3	.241	.314	.350	.664	80	-9	38	3.77	-1	0-111(21-2-92)/D-5	6	-1.6
1978 Mil-A	39	77	9	15	4	0	2	11	9	10	0	0	.195	.295	.325	.620	74	-2	7	2.93	0	0-16(4-7-5)/D-8	1	-0.3
Pit-N	5	4	0	0	0	0	0	0	1	1	0	0	.000	.000	.000	.200	-38	-0	0	1.05	0	....	0	-0.1
Total 12	1252	3670	462	920	130	20	96	422	344	501	60	47	.251	.320	.375	.695	97	-21	435	4.00	-8	*0-1021/D-23	93	-7.1

• MAY, Derrick
Derrick Brant May   b: 7/14/1968, Rochester, NY   BL/TR, 6'4", 225 lbs.   Deb: 9/6/1990   Career OF: 537-0-83

YEAR TM-L	G	AB	R	H	2B	3B	HR	RBI	BB	SO	SB	CS	AVG	OBP	SLG	OPS	OPS+	BR/A	RC	RC/G	FR	G/POS	WS	TPW
1990 Chi-N	17	61	8	15	3	0	1	11	2	7	1	0	.246	.270	.344	.614	63	-3	6	3.22	1	0-17(17-0-0)	1	-0.4
1991 Chi-N	15	22	4	5	2	0	1	3	2	1	0	0	.227	.292	.455	.746	102	-0	3	3.77	1	/0-7(7-0-0)	1	0.0
1992 Chi-N	124	351	33	96	11	0	8	45	14	40	5	3	.274	.307	.373	.680	89	-6	37	3.72	-1	*0-108(98-0-14)	7	-1.1
1993 Chi-N	128	465	62	137	25	2	10	77	31	41	10	3	.295	.340	.422	.762	104	3	63	4.86	3	0-122(121-0-2)	13	-0.1
1994 Chi-N	100	345	43	98	19	2	8	51	30	34	3	2	.284	.341	.420	.762	99	-1	47	4.84	2	0-92(92-0-0)	9	-0.2
1995 Mil-A	32	113	15	28	3	1	1	9	5	18	0	1	.248	.286	.319	.604	54	-8	10	3.13	0	0-32(32-0-0)	1	-0.9
Hou-N	78	206	29	62	15	1	8	41	19	24	5	0	.301	.363	.500	.863	134	11	38	6.84	-1	0-55(43-0-12)/1-1	9	0.7
1996 Hou-N	109	259	24	65	12	3	5	33	30	33	2	2	.251	.333	.378	.712	95	-2	33	4.47	2	0-71(70-0-3)	6	-0.3
1997 Phi-N	83	149	8	34	5	1	1	13	8	26	4	1	.228	.268	.295	.563	67	-11	11	2.50	1	0-56(7-0-49)	1	-1.2
1998 Mon-N	85	180	13	43	8	0	5	15	11	24	0	0	.239	.283	.367	.649	70	-8	18	3.33	1	0-48(48-0-0)/D-2	1	-1.0
1999 Bal-A	26	49	5	13	0	0	4	12	4	6	0	0	.265	.321	.510	.831	112	1	7	5.11	1	/D-9,0-5(2-0-3)	1	0.1
Total 10	797	2200	244	596	103	10	52	310	156	254	30	12	.271	.321	.398	.719	93	-27	274	4.37	8	0-613/D-11,1-1	50	-4.1

• MAY, Jerry
Jerry Lee May   b: 12/14/1943, Staunton, VA   d: 6/30/1996, Swoope, VA   BR/TR, 6'2", 195 lbs.   Deb: 9/19/1964

YEAR TM-L	G	AB	R	H	2B	3B	HR	RBI	BB	SO	SB	CS	AVG	OBP	SLG	OPS	OPS+	BR/A	RC	RC/G	FR	G/POS	WS	TPW
1964 Pit-N	11	31	1	8	0	0	0	3	3	9	0	0	.258	.324	.258	.582	66	-1	3	2.87	1	C-11	1	0.0
1965 Pit-N	4	2	0	1	0	0	0	0	1	0	0	0	.500	.500	.500	1.000	182	-1	1	13.50	-1	/C-4	0	-0.1
1966 Pit-N	42	52	6	13	4	0	1	2	2	15	0	1	.250	.291	.385	.676	86	-2	6	3.71	-1	C-41	2	-0.1
1967 Pit-N	110	325	23	88	13	2	3	22	36	55	0	0	.271	.349	.351	.700	100	2	37	3.97	2	*C-110	11	1.0
1968 Pit-N	137	416	26	91	15	2	1	33	41	80	0	0	.219	.293	.272	.565	71	-13	33	2.64	-2	*C-135	8	-0.9
1969 Pit-N	62	190	21	44	8	0	7	23	9	53	1	1	.232	.274	.384	.658	84	-5	20	3.51	0	C-52	4	-0.3
1970 Pit-N	51	139	13	29	4	2	1	16	21	25	0	0	.209	.317	.288	.605	65	-6	13	3.13	4	C-45	4	0.0
1971 KC-A	71	218	16	55	13	2	1	24	27	37	0	0	.252	.335	.344	.679	93	-1	25	3.83	3	C-71	7	0.5
1972 KC-A	53	116	10	22	5	1	1	4	14	13	0	0	.190	.277	.276	.553	65	-5	9	2.37	-2	C-41	2	-0.5
1973 KC-A	11	30	4	4	1	1	0	2	3	5	0	0	.133	.235	.233	.469	30	-3	2	1.66	-1	C-11	0	-0.3
NY-A	4	8	0	2	0	0	0	0	1	1	0	0	.250	.333	.250	.583	65	-0	1	3.39	1	/C-4	0	0.0
Total 10	556	1527	120	357	63	10	15	130	157	293	1	2	.234	.310	.318	.627	81	-34	148	3.24	3	C-525	39	-0.9

• MAY, Lee
Lee Andrew May   b: 5/23/1943, Birmingham, AL   BR/TR, 6'3", 205 lbs.   Deb: 9/1/1965   C Career OF: 48-0-40

YEAR TM-L	G	AB	R	H	2B	3B	HR	RBI	BB	SO	SB	CS	AVG	OBP	SLG	OPS	OPS+	BR/A	RC	RC/G	FR	G/POS	WS	TPW
1965 Cin-N	5	4	1	0	0	0	0	0	0	1	0	0	.000	.000	.000	.000	-94	-1	0	.00	0	....	0	-0.1
1966 Cin-N	25	75	14	25	5	1	2	10	0	14	0	1	.333	.333	.507	.840	119	1	12	6.05	0	1-16	2	0.0
1967 Cin-N	127	438	54	116	29	2	12	57	19	80	4	8	.265	.310	.422	.733	97	-5	53	4.14	2	1-81,0-48(32-0-16)	12	-1.1
1968 Cin-N	146	559	78	162	32	1	22	80	34	100	4	7	.290	.337	.469	.806	131	19	79	5.02	2	*1-122,0-33(11-0-22)	20	1.3
1969 Cin-N	158	607	85	169	32	3	38	110	45	142	5	4	.278	.334	.529	.863	132	22	104	6.08	1	*1-156/0-7(5-0-2)	26	1.1
1970*Cin-N	153	605	78	153	34	2	34	94	38	125	1	1	.253	.299	.484	.784	102	-3	81	4.61	3	*1-153	14	-1.2
1971 Cin-N★	147	553	85	154	17	3	39	98	42	135	3	0	.278	.334	.532	.866	149	33	96	6.24	-3	*1-143	24	2.1
1972 Hou-N★	148	592	87	168	31	2	29	98	52	145	3	1	.284	.344	.490	.834	137	27	97	5.99	-8	*1-146	24	0.8
1973 Hou-N	148	545	65	147	24	3	28	105	34	122	1	1	.270	.315	.479	.794	117	10	78	5.01	0	*1-144	19	-0.2
1974 Hou-N	152	556	59	149	26	0	24	85	17	97	1	0	.268	.298	.444	.743	110	3	71	4.44	0	*1-145	14	-0.7
1975 Bal-A	146	580	67	152	28	3	20	99	36	91	1	2	.262	.311	.424	.735	113	7	68	3.98	1	*1-144/D-2	13	-0.5
1976 Bal-A	148	530	61	137	17	4	25	**109**	41	104	4	1	.258	.315	.447	.763	130	17	73	4.79	-1	1-94,D-52	19	0.9
1977 Bal-A	150	585	75	148	16	2	27	99	38	119	2	2	.253	.299	.426	.724	101	-1	68	3.96	-9	*1-110,D-39	14	-1.8
1978 Bal-A	145	556	56	137	16	1	25	80	31	110	5	2	.246	.287	.414	.701	101	-1	61	3.72	0	*D-140/1-4	10	-0.7
1979*Bal-A	124	456	59	116	15	0	19	69	28	100	3	4	.254	.299	.412	.711	93	-7	50	3.66	-1	*D-117/1-2	6	-1.2
1980 Bal-A	78	222	20	54	10	2	7	31	15	53	2	0	.243	.291	.401	.692	88	-4	23	3.43	-1	D-58/1-7	3	-0.6
1981*KC-A	26	55	3	16	3	0	0	8	3	14	0	1	.291	.328	.345	.673	95	-1	5	3.51	1	1-8,D-4	1	-0.2
1982 KC-A	42	91	12	28	5	2	3	12	14	18	0	0	.308	.400	.505	.905	147	6	20	8.22	-1	1-32/D-2	4	0.4
Total 18	2071	7609	959	2031	340	31	354	1244	487	1570	39	35	.267	.315	.459	.774	117	123	1039	4.75	-19	*1-1507,D-414/0-88	225	-1.9

• MAY, Milt
Milton Scott May   b: 8/1/1950, Gary, IN   BL/TR, 6', 190 lbs.   Deb: 9/8/1970   C

YEAR TM-L	G	AB	R	H	2B	3B	HR	RBI	BB	SO	SB	CS	AVG	OBP	SLG	OPS	OPS+	BR/A	RC	RC/G	FR	G/POS	WS	TPW
1970 Pit-N	5	4	1	2	1	0	0	2	0	0	0	0	.500	.600	.750	1.350	268	1	2	26.41	0	....	1	0.1
1971*Pit-N	49	126	15	35	1	0	6	25	9	16	0	0	.278	.326	.429	.754	111	1	16	4.28	1	C-31	5	0.4
1972*Pit-N	57	139	12	39	10	0	0	14	10	13	0	0	.281	.329	.353	.681	96	-1	16	4.08	0	C-33	5	0.1
1973 Pit-N	101	283	29	76	8	1	7	31	34	26	0	1	.269	.351	.378	.729	105	2	36	4.46	-2	C-79	9	0.4
1974 Hou-N	127	405	47	117	17	4	7	54	39	33	0	1	.289	.353	.402	.755	116	8	57	5.02	4	*C-116	17	1.8
1975 Hou-N	111	386	29	93	15	1	4	52	26	41	1	2	.241	.289	.316	.605	73	-16	35	3.03	5	*C-102	7	-0.6
1976 Det-A	6	25	2	7	1	0	0	1	0	1	0	0	.280	.280	.320	.600	72	-1	2	3.36	1	/C-6	0	0.1
1977 Det-A	115	397	32	99	9	3	12	46	26	31	0	0	.249	.296	.378	.673	78	-12	42	3.43	5	*C-111	9	-0.2
1978 Det-A	105	352	24	88	9	0	10	37	27	26	0	0	.250	.307	.361	.668	85	-7	37	3.51	4	C-94	8	-0.1
1979 Det-A	6	11	1	3	2	0	0	3	1	1	0	0	.273	.333	.455	.788	107	0	1	3.75	0	/C-5	0	0.1
Chi-A	65	202	23	51	13	0	7	28	14	27	0	0	.252	.300	.421	.728	94	-2	26	4.51	0	C-65	5	0.1
Yr.	71	213	24	54	15	0	7	31	15	28	0	0	.254	.309	.423	.731	95	-2	27	4.46	0	C-70	5	0.1
1980 SF-N	111	358	27	93	16	2	6	50	25	40	0	0	.260	.310	.366	.676	90	-6	38	3.54	3	*C-103	11	0.1
1981 SF-N	97	316	20	98	17	0	2	33	34	29	1	4	.310	.377	.383	.760	118	7	44	5.14	3	C-93	14	1.5
1982 SF-N	114	395	29	104	19	0	9	39	28	38	0	1	.263	.312	.380	.692	93	-5	47	4.19	3	*C-110	14	0.3
1983 SF-N	66	186	18	46	6	0	2	20	21	23	2	1	.247	.324	.376	.700	96	-1	21	3.88	2	C-56	6	0.3
Pit-N	7	12	0	3	0	0	0	0	1	1	0	0	.250	.308	.250	.558	55	-1	1	2.77	0	/C-4	0	0.0
Yr.	73	198	18	49	6	0	2	20	22	24	2	1	.247	.323	.369	.691	94	-2	22	3.82	2	C-60	6	0.3
1984 Pit-N	50	96	4	17	3	0	0	8	10	15	0	1	.177	.255	.240	.494	40	-8	6	1.79	1	C-26	0	-0.6
Total 15	1192	3693	313	971	147	11	77	443	305	361	4	13	.263	.321	.371	.692	93	-42	426	3.97	28	*C-1034	112	3.7

• MAY, Pinky
Merrill Glend May   b: 1/18/1911, Laconia, IN   d: 9/4/2000, Corydon, IN   BR/TR, 5'11.5", 165 lbs.   Deb: 4/21/1939

YEAR TM-L	G	AB	R	H	2B	3B	HR	RBI	BB	SO	SB	CS	AVG	OBP	SLG	OPS	OPS+	BR/A	RC	RC/G	FR	G/POS	WS	TPW
1939 Phi-N	135	464	49	133	27	3	2	62	41	20	4	....	.287	.346	.371	.717	97	-2	59	4.26	13	*3-132	12	1.6

YEAR TM-L	G	AB	R	H	2B	3B	HR	RBI	BB	SO	SB	CS	AVG	OBP	SLG	OPS	OPS+	BR/A	RC	RC/G	FR	G/POS	WS	TPW
1940 Phi-N★	136	501	59	147	24	2	1	48	58	33	2	....	.293	.371	.355	.727	105	6	69	5.05	10	*3-135/S-1	16	2.2
1941 Phi-N	142	490	46	131	17	4	0	39	55	30	2	....	.267	.344	.318	.662	91	-4	54	3.76	17	*3-140	12	1.9
1942 Phi-N	115	345	25	82	15	0	0	18	51	17	3	....	.238	.338	.281	.619	86	-4	36	3.44	14	*3-107	9	1.5
1943 Phi-N	137	415	31	117	19	2	1	48	56	21	2	....	.282	.369	.345	.713	111	8	53	4.38	12	*3-132	15	2.3
Total 5	665	2215	210	610	102	11	4	215	261	121	13	....	.275	.354	.337	.691	98	4	270	4.21	67	3-646/S-1	64	9.5

• MAYBERRY, John John Claiborn Mayberry b: 2/18/1949, Detroit, MI BL/TL, 6'3", 220 lbs. Deb: 9/10/1968 C

YEAR TM-L	G	AB	R	H	2B	3B	HR	RBI	BB	SO	SB	CS	AVG	OBP	SLG	OPS	OPS+	BR/A	RC	RC/G	FR	G/POS	WS	TPW
1968 Hou-N	4	9	0	0	0	0	0	0	0	2	0	0	.000	.100	.000	.100	-69	-2	0	.08	0	/1-2	0	-0.3
1969 Hou-N	5	4	0	0	0	0	0	0	1	1	0	0	.000	.200	.000	.200	-41	-1	0	.35	0	....	0	-0.1
1970 Hou-N	50	148	23	32	3	2	5	14	21	33	1	1	.216	.322	.365	.687	87	-3	17	3.58	2	1-45	3	-0.5
1971 Hou-N	46	137	16	25	0	1	7	14	13	32	0	0	.182	.263	.350	.614	74	-5	13	3.01	-1	1-37	2	-1.0
1972 KC-A	149	503	65	150	24	3	25	100	78	74	0	2	.298	.396	.507	.903	168	44	101	7.38	0	*1-146	27	3.7
1973 KC-A★	152	510	87	142	20	2	26	100	**122**	79	3	0	.278	**.420**	.478	.898	141	36	113	**8.07**	-4	*1-149/D-1	31	2.0
1974 KC-A★	126	427	63	100	13	1	22	69	77	72	4	2	.234	.359	.424	.783	118	13	70	5.65	1	*1-106,D-16	14	0.5
1975 KC-A	156	554	95	161	38	1	34	106	**119**	73	5	3	.291	.419	.547	.966	**167**	**54**	135	**8.86**	5	*1-131,D-27	**33**	4.9
1976*KC-A	161	594	76	138	22	2	13	95	82	73	3	2	.232	.327	.342	.669	95	-2	70	3.90	-1	*1-160/D-2	15	-1.7
1977*KC-A	153	543	73	125	22	1	23	82	83	86	1	3	.230	.340	.401	.741	100	2	76	4.62	-4	*1-145/D-8	14	-1.2
1978 Tor-A	152	515	51	129	15	2	22	70	60	57	1	2	.250	.333	.416	.749	107	5	71	4.70	-16	*1-139/D-7	14	-2.0
1979 Tor-A	137	464	61	127	22	1	21	74	69	60	1	1	.274	.374	.461	.835	122	16	82	6.31	-7	*1-135	14	0.1
1980 Tor-A	149	501	62	124	19	2	30	82	77	80	0	0	.248	.351	.473	.824	118	13	86	5.90	-4	*1-136/D-8	17	0.1
1981 Tor-A	94	290	34	72	6	1	17	43	44	45	1	1	.248	.363	.452	.814	125	11	49	5.79	-2	1-80,D-10	9	0.5
1982 Tor-A	17	33	7	9	0	0	2	3	7	5	0	0	.273	.415	.455	.869	127	2	7	7.58	0	D-13/1-4	2	0.1
NY-A	69	215	20	45	7	0	8	27	28	38	0	0	.209	.315	.353	.668	84	-4	24	3.66	-4	1-63/D-4	4	-1.2
Yr.	86	248	27	54	7	0	10	30	35	43	0	0	.218	.329	.367	.696	90	-2	31	4.14	-5	1-67,D-17	6	-1.1
Total 15	1620	5447	733	1379	211	19	255	879	881	810	20	17	.253	.363	.439	.802	122	180	913	5.79	-38	*1-1478/D-96	199	4.1

• MAYE, Lee Arthur Lee Maye b: 12/11/1934, Tuscaloosa, AL d: 7/17/2002, Riverside, CA BL/TR, 6'2", 190 lbs. Deb: 7/17/1959 Career OF: 554-259-298

YEAR TM-L	G	AB	R	H	2B	3B	HR	RBI	BB	SO	SB	CS	AVG	OBP	SLG	OPS	OPS+	BR/A	RC	RC/G	FR	G/POS	WS	TPW
1959 Mil-N	51	140	17	42	5	1	4	16	7	26	2	2	.300	.338	.436	.774	113	2	20	5.15	-1	O-44(24-0-21)	4	-0.1
1960 Mil-N	41	83	14	25	6	0	0	2	7	21	5	0	.301	.363	.373	.736	110	3	12	5.58	0	O-19(15-0-4)	3	0.1
1961 Mil-N	110	373	68	101	11	5	14	41	36	50	10	1	.271	.340	.440	.779	112	8	60	5.81	2	O-96(26-0-72)	14	0.4
1962 Mil-N	99	349	40	85	10	0	10	41	25	58	9	3	.244	.296	.358	.654	77	-12	39	3.83	-4	O-94(38-60-2)	7	-2.0
1963 Mil-N	124	442	67	120	22	7	11	34	36	52	14	2	.271	.331	.428	.758	118	12	65	5.21	0	*O-111(70-73-3)	17	0.8
1964 Mil-N	153	588	96	179	**44**	5	10	74	34	54	5	10	.304	.347	.447	.794	121	12	86	5.43	-3	*O-135(54-92-0)/3-5	23	0.4
1965 Mil-N	15	53	8	16	2	0	2	7	2	6	0	0	.302	.339	.453	.792	120	1	8	6.14	0	O-13(4-9-0)	2	0.1
Hou-N	108	415	38	104	17	7	3	36	20	37	1	5	.251	.287	.347	.634	83	-12	40	3.28	-4	*O-103(92-11-3)	7	-2.3
Yr.	123	468	46	120	19	7	5	43	22	43	1	5	.256	.293	.359	.652	87	-11	48	3.57	-4	*O-116(96-20-3)	9	-2.2
1966 Hou-N	115	358	38	103	12	4	9	36	20	26	4	3	.288	.325	.419	.744	113	5	47	4.74	-4	O-97(97-0-0)	10	-0.4
1967 Cle-A	115	297	43	77	20	4	9	27	26	47	3	3	.259	.321	.444	.765	123	7	43	5.08	-3	O-77(23-10-54)/2-1	10	0.0
1968 Cle-A	109	299	20	84	13	2	4	26	15	24	0	0	.281	.317	.378	.695	112	3	36	4.39	0	O-80(71-0-10)/1-1	10	-0.1
1969 Cle-A	43	108	9	27	5	0	1	15	8	15	1	0	.250	.308	.324	.632	74	-4	11	3.51	-2	O-28(26-0-2)	2	-0.8
Was-A	71	238	41	69	9	3	9	26	20	25	1	3	.290	.345	.466	.811	132	8	35	5.29	-4	O-65(6-4-56)	8	0.1
Yr.	114	346	50	96	14	3	10	41	28	40	2	3	.277	.333	.422	.755	114	4	46	4.72	-6	O-93(32-4-58)	10	-0.7
1970 Was-A	96	255	28	67	12	1	7	30	21	32	4	2	.263	.321	.400	.721	103	0	33	4.65	1	O-68(6-0-63)/3-1	6	-0.1
Chi-A	6	6	0	1	0	0	0	1	0	1	0	0	.167	.167	.167	.333	-8	-1	0	.90	0	....	0	-0.1
Yr.	102	261	28	68	12	1	7	31	21	33	4	2	.261	.318	.395	.713	100	-0	33	4.55	1	O-68(6-0-63)/3-1	6	-0.2
1971 Chi-A	32	44	6	9	2	0	1	7	5	7	0	0	.205	.286	.318	.604	69	-2	4	2.65	1	O-10(2-0-8)	0	-0.2
Total 13	1288	4048	533	1109	190	39	94	419	282	481	59	34	.274	.324	.410	.734	108	32	539	4.76	-22	*O-1040/3-6,1-1,2-1	123	-4.1

• MAYER, Ed Edward H. Mayer b: 8/16/1866, Marshall, IL d: 5/18/1913, Chicago, IL, 5'8.5", 155 lbs. Deb: 4/19/1890 U Career OF: 4-28-1

YEAR TM-L	G	AB	R	H	2B	3B	HR	RBI	BB	SO	SB	CS	AVG	OBP	SLG	OPS	OPS+	BR/A	RC	RC/G	FR	G/POS	WS	TPW
1890 Phi-N	117	484	49	117	25	5	1	70	22	36	20	....	.242	.286	.320	.606	75	-18	51	3.70	-3	*3-114/O-4(0-4-0)	8	-1.6
1891 Phi-N	68	268	24	50	2	4	0	31	14	29	7	....	.187	.238	.224	.462	34	-23	16	2.02	-2	3-31,O-29(4-24-1)/S-7,2-1	2	-2.3
Total 2	185	752	73	167	27	9	1	101	36	65	27	....	.222	.269	.286	.555	60	-41	68	3.08	-5	3-145/O-33,S-7,2-1	10	-3.9

• MAYER, Sam Samuel Frankel Mayer b: 2/28/1893, Atlanta, GA d: 7/1/1962, Atlanta, GA BR/TL, 5'10", 164 lbs. Deb: 9/14/1915

YEAR TM-L	G	AB	R	H	2B	3B	HR	RBI	BB	SO	SB	CS	AVG	OBP	SLG	OPS	OPS+	BR/A	RC	RC/G	FR	G/POS	WS	TPW
1915 Was-A	11	29	5	7	0	0	1	4	4	2	1	2	.241	.333	.345	.678	101	-1	3	3.28	0	/O-9(1-0-8),1-1,P-1	0	-0.1

• MAYER, Wally Walter A. Mayer b: 7/8/1890, Cincinnati, OH d: 11/18/1951, Minnetonka, MN BR/TR, 5'11", 168 lbs. Deb: 9/28/1911

YEAR TM-L	G	AB	R	H	2B	3B	HR	RBI	BB	SO	SB	CS	AVG	OBP	SLG	OPS	OPS+	BR/A	RC	RC/G	FR	G/POS	WS	TPW
1911 Chi-A	1	3	0	0	0	0	0	0	2	....	0	....	.000	.400	.000	.400	15	-0	0	.00	0	/C-1	0	0.0
1912 Chi-A	9	9	1	0	0	0	0	0	1	....	0	....	.000	.100	.000	.100	-73	-2	0	.00	-1	/C-6	0	-0.2
1914 Chi-A	40	85	7	14	3	1	0	5	14	23	1	1	.165	.290	.224	.514	55	-4	6	2.12	0	C-33/3-1	2	-0.2
1915 Chi-A	22	54	3	12	3	1	0	5	5	8	0	2	.222	.288	.315	.603	78	-3	5	2.68	-3	C-20	1	-0.4
1917 Bos-A	4	12	2	2	0	0	0	0	5	2	0	....	.167	.412	.167	.578	78	0	1	2.07	2	/C-4	1	0.2
1918 Bos-A	26	49	7	11	4	0	0	5	7	7	0	....	.224	.321	.306	.628	91	-0	5	3.06	-1	C-23	2	-0.1
1919 StL-A	30	62	2	14	4	1	0	5	8	11	0	....	.226	.314	.323	.637	77	-2	7	3.28	0	C-25	2	0.0
Total 7	132	274	22	53	14	3	0	20	42	51	1	3	.193	.303	.266	.569	67	-11	23	2.53	-2	C-112/3-1	8	-0.6

• MAYES, Paddy Adair Bushyhead Mayes b: 3/17/1885, Locust Grove, OK d: 5/28/1962, Fayetteville, AR BL/TR, 5'11", 160 lbs. Deb: 6/11/1911

YEAR TM-L	G	AB	R	H	2B	3B	HR	RBI	BB	SO	SB	CS	AVG	OBP	SLG	OPS	OPS+	BR/A	RC	RC/G	FR	G/POS	WS	TPW
1911 Phi-N	5	5	1	0	0	0	0	0	1	2	0	....	.000	.286	.000	.286	-17	-1	0	.77	-0	/O-2(0-0-0)	0	-0.1

• MAYNARD, Buster James Walter Maynard b: 3/25/1913, Henderson, SC d: 9/7/1977, Durham, NC BR/TR, 5'11", 170 lbs. Deb: 9/17/1940 Career OF: 32-91-23

YEAR TM-L	G	AB	R	H	2B	3B	HR	RBI	BB	SO	SB	CS	AVG	OBP	SLG	OPS	OPS+	BR/A	RC	RC/G	FR	G/POS	WS	TPW
1940 NY-N	7	29	6	8	2	2	1	2	2	6	0	....	.276	.323	.586	.909	145	1	6	7.27	-1	/O-7(0-3-4)	1	0.1
1942 NY-N	89	190	17	47	4	1	4	32	19	19	3	....	.247	.319	.342	.661	93	-2	20	3.57	3	O-58(7-48-4),3-10/2-1	4	0.0
1943 NY-N	121	393	43	81	8	2	9	32	24	27	3	....	.206	.252	.305	.557	60	-22	30	2.45	-4	O-74(25-39-13),3-22	2	-3.0
1946 NY-N	7	4	2	0	0	0	0	0	1	1	0	....	.000	.200	.000	.200	-41	-1	0	.70	-1	/O-3(0-1-2)	0	-0.1
Total 4	224	616	68	136	14	5	14	66	46	53	6	....	.221	.276	.328	.604	74	-23	56	2.97	-2	O-142/3-32,2-1	7	-3.1

• MAYNARD, Chick Le Roy Evans Maynard b: 11/2/1896, Turners Falls, MA d: 1/31/1957, Bangor, ME BL/TR, 5'9", 150 lbs. Deb: 6/27/1922

YEAR TM-L	G	AB	R	H	2B	3B	HR	RBI	BB	SO	SB	CS	AVG	OBP	SLG	OPS	OPS+	BR/A	RC	RC/G	FR	G/POS	WS	TPW
1922 Bos-A	12	24	1	3	0	0	0	0	3	2	0	1	.125	.222	.125	.347	-8	-4	1	.88	-3	S-12	0	-0.6

• MAYNE, Brent Brent Danem Mayne b: 4/19/1968, Loma Linda, CA BL/TR, 6'1", 190 lbs. Deb: 9/18/1990

YEAR TM-L	G	AB	R	H	2B	3B	HR	RBI	BB	SO	SB	CS	AVG	OBP	SLG	OPS	OPS+	BR/A	RC	RC/G	FR	G/POS	WS	TPW
1990 KC-A	5	13	2	3	0	0	0	1	3	3	0	1	.231	.375	.231	.606	74	-1	1	2.90	0	/C-5	0	-0.1
1991 KC-A	85	231	22	58	8	0	3	31	23	42	2	4	.251	.319	.325	.644	78	-8	23	3.29	0	C-80/D-1	8	-0.3
1992 KC-A	82	213	16	48	10	0	0	18	11	26	0	4	.225	.263	.272	.536	49	-17	14	2.09	-1	C-62/3-8,D-1	4	-1.5
1993 KC-A	71	205	22	52	9	1	2	22	18	31	3	2	.254	.317	.337	.654	72	-8	21	3.44	-1	C-68/D-1	5	-0.5
1994 KC-A	46	144	19	37	5	1	2	20	14	27	1	0	.257	.323	.347	.670	70	-6	16	4.02	0	C-42/D-3	4	-0.4
1995 KC-A	110	307	23	77	18	1	1	27	25	41	0	1	.251	.313	.326	.639	66	-16	29	2.99	1	*C-103	7	-0.7
1996 NY-N	70	99	9	26	6	0	1	6	12	22	0	1	.263	.342	.354	.696	88	-2	11	3.83	0	C-21	1	-0.1
1997 Oak-A	85	256	29	74	12	0	6	22	18	33	1	0	.289	.345	.406	.752	97	-1	36	5.03	0	C-83	6	0.4
1998 SF-N	94	275	26	75	15	0	3	32	37	47	2	1	.273	.361	.360	.721	96	-0	36	4.63	-1	C-88	9	0.4
1999 SF-N	117	322	39	97	32	0	2	39	43	65	2	2	.301	.392	.419	.811	113	8	51	5.54	2	*C-105	13	1.6
2000 Col-N	117	335	36	101	21	0	6	64	47	48	1	3	.301	.389	.418	.807	83	-8	53	5.47	-5	*C-105/P-1	8	-0.6
2001 Col-N	49	160	15	53	7	0	0	20	16	24	0	0	.331	.392	.375	.767	82	-3	24	5.59	7	C-44/1-1	4	0.6
KC-A	51	166	13	40	4	1	2	20	10	17	1	2	.241	.288	.313	.601	54	-12	13	2.50	-3	C-49	2	-1.1
2002 KC-A	101	326	35	77	8	2	4	30	34	54	4	4	.236	.312	.310	.622	59	-19	32	3.19	-1	C-99	5	-1.3
2003 KC-A	113	372	39	91	17	1	6	36	32	59	0	2	.245	.310	.344	.654	64	-20	38	3.46	-2	*C-112	10	-1.4
Total 14	1196	3424	345	909	172	7	38	388	343	539	17	27	.265	.336	.353	.689	77	-114	398	3.94	-5	*C-1066/3-8,D-6,1-1,P-1	86	-4.9

• MAYO, Eddie Edward Joseph "Hotshot" Mayo b: 4/15/1910, Holyoke, MA BL/TR, 5'11", 178 lbs. Deb: 5/22/1936 C

YEAR TM-L	G	AB	R	H	2B	3B	HR	RBI	BB	SO	SB	CS	AVG	OBP	SLG	OPS	OPS+	BR/A	RC	RC/G	FR	G/POS	WS	TPW
1936*NY-N	46	141	11	28	4	1	1	8	11	12	0	....	.199	.257	.262	.519	40	-12	10	2.25	0	3-40	1	-1.0
1937 Bos-N	65	172	19	39	6	1	1	18	15	20	1	....	.227	.293	.291	.583	65	-8	15	2.64	-6	3-50	2	-1.2
1938 Bos-N	8	14	2	3	0	0	1	4	1	0	0	....	.214	.267	.429	.695	98	-0	1	2.88	0	/3-6,S-2	0	0.0

YEAR TM-L	G	AB	R	H	2B	3B	HR	RBI	BB	SO	SB	CS	AVG	OBP	SLG	OPS	OPS+	BR/A	RC	RC/G	FR	G/POS	WS	TPW
1943 Phi-A	128	471	49	103	10	1	0	28	34	32	2	0	.219	.278	.244	.523	54	-26	36	2.42	-2	*3-123	6	-2.8
1944 Det-A	154	607	76	151	18	3	5	63	57	23	9	13	.249	.317	.313	.630	76	-21	62	3.28	12	*2-143,S-11	16	-0.1
1945*Det-A★	134	501	71	143	24	3	10	54	47	29	7	7	.285	.347	.405	.752	111	5	72	5.08	15	*2-124	22	2.9
1946 Det-A	51	202	21	51	9	2	0	22	14	12	6	2	.252	.301	.317	.618	68	-8	19	3.12	-1	2-49	4	-0.7
1947 Det-A	142	535	66	149	28	4	6	48	48	28	3	7	.279	.338	.379	.717	96	-5	67	4.28	-18	*2-142	16	-1.7
1948 Det-A	106	370	35	92	20	1	2	42	30	19	1	9	.249	.310	.324	.634	67	-22	35	2.98	-6	2-86,3-10	5	-2.3
Total 9	834	3013	350	759	119	16	26	287	257	175	29	38	.252	.313	.328	.641	78	-97	316	3.45	-7	2-544,3-229/S-13	72	-6.9

• MAYO, Jackie John Lewis Mayo b: 7/26/1925, Litchfield, IL BL/TR, 6'1", 190 lbs. Deb: 9/19/1948 Career OF: 55-2-27

YEAR TM-L	G	AB	R	H	2B	3B	HR	RBI	BB	SO	SB	CS	AVG	OBP	SLG	OPS	OPS+	BR/A	RC	RC/G	FR	G/POS	WS	TPW
1948 Phi-N	12	35	7	8	2	1	0	3	7	7	1	....	.229	.386	.343	.729	101	1	6	5.54	0	0-11(11-0-0)	1	0.0
1949 Phi-N	45	39	3	5	0	0	0	2	4	5	0	....	.128	.209	.128	.338	-8	-6	1	.87	-1	0-25(0-1-24)	0	-0.8
1950*Phi-N	18	36	1	8	3	0	0	3	2	5	0	....	.222	.263	.306	.569	50	-3	3	2.92	-1	0-15(15-0-0)	0	-0.4
1951 Phi-N	9	7	1	1	0	0	0	0	0	0	0	0	.143	.143	.143	.286	-23	-1	0	.66	0	/0-5(5-0-0)	0	-0.1
1952 Phi-N	50	119	13	29	5	0	1	4	12	17	1	3	.244	.313	.311	.624	74	-5	11	2.99	2	0-27(24-1-2)/1-6	2	-0.5
1953 Phi-N	5	4	0	0	0	0	0	0	0	1	0	0	.000	.000	.000	.000	-101	-1	0	.00	0	/0-1	0	-0.1
Total 6	139	240	25	51	10	1	1	12	25	35	2	3	.213	.292	.275	.567	57	-15	21	2.82	0	/0-84,1-6	3	-2.0

• MAYS, Willie Willie Howard "Say Hey" Mays b: 5/6/1931, Westfield, AL BR/TR, 5'10.5", 180 lbs. Deb: 5/25/1951 C HOF: 1979 Career OF: 10-2827-21

YEAR TM-L	G	AB	R	H	2B	3B	HR	RBI	BB	SO	SB	CS	AVG	OBP	SLG	OPS	OPS+	BR/A	RC	RC/G	FR	G/POS	WS	TPW
1951*NY-N	121	464	59	127	22	5	20	68	57	60	7	4	.274	.356	.472	.828	120	13	80	6.09	6	*O-121(0-121-0)	19	1.5
1952 NY-N	34	127	17	30	2	4	4	23	16	17	4	1	.236	.326	.409	.736	102	1	18	4.93	7	O-34(0-34-0)	5	0.7
1954*NY-N★	151	565	119	195	33	**13**	41	110	66	57	8	5	**.345**	.415	**.667**	**1.083**	176	**61**	155	10.60	15	*O-151(0-151-0)	**40**	**6.8**
1955 NY-N★	152	580	123	185	18	**13**	**51**	127	79	60	24	4	.319	.404	**.659**	**1.063**	**175**	**66**	157	**10.11**	17	*O-152(0-152-0)	**40**	**7.5**
1956 NY-N★	152	578	101	171	27	8	36	84	68	65	**40**	10	.296	.371	.557	.928	146	42	118	7.28	9	*O-152(0-152-0)	27	4.4
1957 NY-N★	152	585	112	195	26	**20**	35	97	76	62	**38**	19	.333	.411	**.626**	1.037	**174**	**61**	145	9.12	9	*O-150(0-150-0)	34	**6.4**
1958 SF-N★	152	600	**121**	208	33	11	29	96	78	56	**31**	6	.347	.423	.583	**1.006**	**167**	**63**	152	**9.92**	10	*O-151(0-151-0)	**40**	**6.6**
1959 SF-N★	151	575	125	180	43	5	34	104	65	58	**27**	4	.313	.385	.583	.967	157	50	131	8.53	0	*O-147(2-146-0)	32	4.3
1960 SF-N★	153	595	107	**190**	29	12	29	103	61	70	25	10	.319	.386	.555	.941	164	53	124	7.65	3	*O-152(0-152-0)	**38**	4.9
1961 SF-N★	154	572	**129**	176	32	3	40	123	81	77	18	9	.308	.395	.584	.979	161	51	130	8.30	-5	*O-153(0-153-0)	34	4.1
1962*SF-N★	162	621	130	189	36	5	**49**	141	78	85	18	2	.304	.385	.615	1.001	166	60	146	8.63	1	*O-161(0-161-0)	**41**	**5.6**
1963 SF-N★	157	596	115	187	32	7	38	103	66	83	8	3	.314	.384	.582	.966	176	59	131	8.16	-3	*O-157(0-157-0)/S-1	38	5.5
1964 SF-N★	157	578	121	171	21	9	**47**	111	82	72	19	5	.296	.384	**.607**	**.992**	**171**	**57**	136	**8.63**	8	*O-155(0-155-0)/1-1,3-1,S	38	6.3
1965 SF-N★	157	558	118	177	21	3	**52**	112	76	71	9	4	.317	**.399**	**.645**	**1.044**	**184**	**62**	143	**9.63**	7	*O-151(1-147-5)	**43**	**6.8**
1966 SF-N★	152	552	99	159	29	4	37	103	70	81	5	1	.288	.370	.556	.926	149	38	113	7.42	7	*O-150(1-145-5)	**37**	4.2
1967 SF-N★	141	486	83	128	22	2	22	70	51	92	6	0	.263	.336	.453	.788	125	17	74	5.32	2	*O-134(0-134-0)	21	1.7
1968 SF-N★	148	498	84	144	20	5	23	79	67	81	12	6	.289	.376	.488	.864	158	37	91	6.48	4	*O-142(0-142-0)/1-1	30	4.2
1969 SF-N★	117	403	64	114	17	3	13	58	49	71	6	2	.283	.365	.437	.802	126	15	66	5.84	0	*O-108(0-106-2)/1-1	17	1.3
1970 SF-N★	139	478	94	139	15	2	28	83	79	90	5	0	.291	.395	.506	.901	141	31	101	7.78	2	*O-129(0-129-0)/1-5	24	2.9
1971*SF-N★	136	417	82	113	24	5	18	61	**112**	123	23	3	.271	**.429**	.482	.911	160	44	98	8.27	-3	O-84(0-84-0),1-48	27	3.9
1972 SF-N	19	49	8	9	2	0	0	3	17	5	3	0	.184	.394	.224	.618	79	1	6	3.40	-1	O-14(0-14-0)	1	0.0
NY-N★	69	195	27	52	9	1	8	19	43	43	1	5	.267	.402	.446	.848	144	12	35	6.10	-1	O-49(1-48-0),1-11	11	0.9
Yr.	88	244	35	61	11	1	8	22	60	48	4	5	.250	.400	.402	.802	130	12	41	5.50	-2	O-63(1-62-0),1-11	12	0.9
1973*NY-N★	66	209	24	44	10	0	6	25	27	47	1	0	.211	.304	.344	.648	81	-5	22	3.41	-4	O-45(5-43-9),1-17	5	-1.2
Total 22	2992	10881	2062	3283	523	140	660	1903	1464	1526	338	103	.302	.387	.557	.944	156	889	2372	7.95	91	*O-2842/1-84,S-2,3-1	642	89.6

• MAZEROSKI, Bill William Stanley "Maz" Mazeroski b: 9/5/1936, Wheeling, WV BR/TR, 5'11.5", 183 lbs. Deb: 7/7/1956 C HOF: 2001

YEAR TM-L	G	AB	R	H	2B	3B	HR	RBI	BB	SO	SB	CS	AVG	OBP	SLG	OPS	OPS+	BR/A	RC	RC/G	FR	G/POS	WS	TPW
1956 Pit-N	81	255	30	62	8	1	3	14	18	24	0	0	.243	.293	.318	.611	66	-12	24	3.22	6	2-81	5	0.0
1957 Pit-N	148	526	59	149	27	7	8	54	27	49	3	3	.283	.319	.407	.726	96	-4	68	4.58	5	*2-144	14	1.2
1958 Pit-N★	152	567	69	156	24	6	19	68	25	71	1	1	.275	.309	.439	.748	98	-4	73	4.46	19	*2-152	20	2.7
1959 Pit-N★	135	493	50	119	15	6	7	59	29	54	1	3	.241	.285	.339	.624	66	-26	44	2.93	1	*2-133	9	-1.5
1960*Pit-N★	151	538	58	147	21	5	11	64	40	50	4	0	.273	.325	.392	.717	94	-3	68	4.49	20	*2-151	21	2.9
1961 Pit-N	152	558	71	148	21	2	13	59	26	55	2	1	.265	.302	.380	.681	79	-18	62	3.93	19	*2-152	16	1.5
1962 Pit-N★	159	572	55	155	24	9	14	81	37	47	0	3	.271	.318	.418	.735	95	-7	71	4.33	30	*2-159	23	3.7
1963 Pit-N★	142	534	43	131	22	3	8	52	32	46	2	0	.245	.288	.343	.631	80	-13	50	3.18	36	*2-138	15	3.8
1964 Pit-N★	162	601	66	161	22	8	10	64	29	52	1	1	.268	.302	.381	.683	91	-8	63	3.57	11	*2-162	17	1.8
1965 Pit-N	130	494	52	134	17	1	6	54	18	34	2	1	.271	.300	.346	.646	81	-13	47	3.29	25	*2-127	13	2.4
1966 Pit-N	162	621	56	163	22	7	16	82	31	62	4	3	.262	.299	.398	.696	91	-9	69	3.85	31	*2-162	20	3.8
1967 Pit-N★	163	639	62	167	25	3	9	77	30	55	1	2	.261	.294	.352	.647	84	-15	62	3.34	1	*2-163	14	0.0
1968 Pit-N	143	506	36	127	18	2	3	42	38	38	3	4	.251	.306	.312	.618	87	-8	45	2.96	15	*2-142	13	2.1
1969 Pit-N	67	227	13	52	7	1	3	25	22	16	1	1	.229	.303	.308	.611	73	-8	21	3.06	9	2-65	6	0.5
1970*Pit-N	112	367	29	84	14	0	7	39	27	40	2	0	.229	.285	.324	.610	65	-18	34	3.12	10	*2-102	8	-0.1
1971*Pit-N	70	193	17	49	3	1	1	16	15	8	0	0	.254	.308	.295	.603	71	-7	18	3.22	2	2-46/3-7	4	-0.3
1972*Pit-N	34	64	3	12	4	0	0	3	3	5	0	0	.188	.224	.250	.474	35	-6	3	1.58	3	2-15/3-3	1	-0.2
Total 17	2163	7755	769	2016	294	62	138	853	447	706	27	23	.260	.302	.367	.669	84	-180	824	3.64	242	*2-2094/3-10	219	24.4

• MAZZERA, Mel Melvin Leonard "Mike" Mazzera b: 1/31/1914, Stockton, CA d: 12/17/1997, Stockton, CA BL/TL, 5'11", 180 lbs. Deb: 9/9/1935 Career OF: 73-13-40

YEAR TM-L	G	AB	R	H	2B	3B	HR	RBI	BB	SO	SB	CS	AVG	OBP	SLG	OPS	OPS+	BR/A	RC	RC/G	FR	G/POS	WS	TPW
1935 StL-A	12	30	4	7	2	0	1	2	4	9	0	0	.233	.324	.400	.724	82	-1	4	4.67	0	O-10(4-3-3)	1	-0.2
1937 StL-A	7	7	1	2	2	0	0	0	0	2	0	0	.286	.286	.571	.857	110	0	1	5.81	0	....	0	0.0
1938 StL-A	86	204	33	57	8	2	6	29	12	25	1	1	.279	.329	.426	.755	88	-5	29	5.01	2	O-47(25-8-14)	3	-0.5
1939 StL-A	33	110	21	33	5	2	3	22	10	20	0	0	.300	.364	.464	.827	108	1	19	6.48	0	O-25(18-0-7)	3	0.0
1940 Phi-N	69	156	16	37	5	4	0	13	19	15	1	....	.237	.320	.321	.641	80	-4	16	3.41	2	O-42(26-2-16),1-11	2	-0.4
Total 5	207	507	75	136	22	8	10	66	45	71	2	1	.268	.333	.402	.735	90	-8	69	4.77	3	O-124/1-11	9	-1.1

• MAZZILLI, Lee Lee Louis Mazzilli b: 3/25/1955, New York, NY BB/TR, 6'1", 185 lbs. Deb: 9/7/1976 C Career OF: 201-647-30

YEAR TM-L	G	AB	R	H	2B	3B	HR	RBI	BB	SO	SB	CS	AVG	OBP	SLG	OPS	OPS+	BR/A	RC	RC/G	FR	G/POS	WS	TPW
1976 NY-N	24	77	9	15	2	0	2	7	14	10	5	4	.195	.326	.299	.625	83	-2	8	3.38	1	O-23(2-21-0)	2	-0.2
1977 NY-N	159	537	66	134	24	3	6	46	72	72	22	15	.250	.342	.339	.680	87	-9	66	4.16	-3	*O-156(0-156-0)	13	-1.4
1978 NY-N	148	542	78	148	28	5	16	61	69	82	20	13	.273	.356	.432	.788	124	16	85	5.43	1	*O-144(0-144-0)	21	1.5
1979 NY-N★	158	597	78	181	34	4	15	79	93	74	34	12	.303	.397	.449	.846	135	35	115	7.08	-4	*O-143(0-143-0),1-15	25	2.9
1980 NY-N	152	578	82	162	31	4	16	76	82	92	41	15	.280	.373	.431	.803	127	25	98	5.96	-5	1-92,O-66(0-66-0)	24	1.5
1981 NY-N	95	324	36	74	14	5	6	34	46	53	17	7	.228	.328	.358	.686	96	-0	41	4.12	1	O-89(51-40-0)	8	-0.2
1982 Tex-A	58	195	23	47	8	0	4	17	28	26	11	6	.241	.339	.344	.683	93	-1	24	4.04	-1	O-26(11-15-2),D-24	4	-0.3
NY-A	37	128	20	34	2	0	6	17	15	15	2	3	.266	.347	.422	.769	112	1	19	5.05	-3	1-23/D-9,O-2(2-0-0)	4	-0.3
Yr.	95	323	43	81	10	0	10	34	43	41	13	9	.251	.342	.375	.717	100	0	42	4.43	-3	D-33,O-28(13-15-2),1-23	8	-0.6
1983 Pit-N	109	246	37	59	9	0	5	24	49	43	15	5	.240	.370	.337	.708	95	2	34	4.46	-3	O-57(5-53-0)/1-7	7	-0.3
1984 Pit-N	111	266	37	63	11	1	4	21	40	42	8	1	.237	.339	.331	.670	89	-1	33	4.19	0	O-74(74-0-0)/1-5	6	-0.3
1985 Pit-N	92	117	20	33	8	0	1	9	29	17	4	1	.282	.425	.376	.801	127	7	21	6.45	-2	1-19/O-5(3-3-0)	4	0.3
1986 Pit-N	61	93	18	21	2	1	1	8	26	25	3	3	.226	.395	.301	.696	93	0	13	4.43	-1	O-18(16-3-0)/1-7	2	-0.2
*NY-N	39	58	10	16	3	0	2	7	12	11	1	1	.276	.417	.431	.848	138	4	11	6.90	-1	O-10(8-0-2)/1-8	3	0.2
Yr.	100	151	28	37	5	1	3	15	38	36	4	4	.245	.403	.351	.754	110	4	24	5.32	-2	O-28(24-3-2),1-15	5	0.0
1987 NY-N	88	124	26	38	8	1	3	24	21	14	5	3	.306	.407	.460	.867	136	7	24	6.70	-1	O-25(12-2-13),1-13	5	0.5
1988*NY-N	68	116	9	17	2	0	0	12	12	16	4	1	.147	.233	.164	.396	16	-12	5	1.31	-2	O-18(13-0-6),1-16	0	-1.6
1989 NY-N	48	60	10	11	2	0	2	7	17	19	3	0	.183	.364	.317	.680	101	2	9	4.73	-1	O-10(4-1-5)/1-8	3	0.0
*Tor-A	28	66	12	15	3	0	4	11	17	16	2	0	.227	.400	.455	.855	149	6	14	7.08	0	D-19/1-2,O-2(0-0-2)	3	0.5
Total 14	1475	4124	571	1068	191	24	93	460	642	627	197	90	.259	.361	.385	.746	109	79	618	5.13	-25	O-868,1-215/D-52	134	2.5

• MCALEER, Jimmy James Robert "Loafer" McAleer
b: 7/10/1864, Youngstown, OH d: 4/29/1931, Youngstown, OH BR/TR, 6', 175 lbs. Deb: 4/24/1889 M/U Career OF: 128-886-2

YEAR TM-L	G	AB	R	H	2B	3B	HR	RBI	BB	SO	SB	CS	AVG	OBP	SLG	OPS	OPS+	BR/A	RC	RC/G	FR	G/POS	WS	TPW
1889 Cle-N	110	447	66	105	6	6	0	35	30	49	37	....	.235	.289	.275	.564	59	-24	47	3.67	8	*O-110(0-110-0)	9	-1.8
1890 Cle-P	86	341	58	91	8	7	1	42	37	33	21	....	.267	.340	.340	.681	89	-3	48	5.16	6	O-86(0-86-0)	7	0.0
1891 Cle-N	136	565	97	135	16	11	1	61	49	47	51	....	.239	.305	.312	.617	77	-18	71	4.46	5	*O-136(124-13-0)	12	-1.6
1892*Cle-N	149	571	92	136	26	7	4	70	63	54	40	....	.238	.318	.329	.647	92	-6	74	4.62	5	*O-149(0-149-0)	21	-1.1

YEAR TM-L	G	AB	R	H	2B	3B	HR	RBI	BB	SO	SB	CS	AVG	OBP	SLG	OPS	OPS+	BR/A	RC	RC/G	FR	G/POS	WS	TPW
1893 Cle-N	91	350	63	83	5	1	2	41	35	21	32	....	.237	.314	.274	.588	53	-24	41	4.08	3	*O-91(2-89-0)	6	-2.2
1894 Cle-N	64	253	36	73	15	1	2	40	13	17	14	....	.289	.331	.379	.710	68	-14	37	5.39	1	O-64(0-64-0)	6	-1.3
1895*Cle-N	132	532	85	144	17	3	0	68	38	37	32	....	.271	.326	.314	.640	61	-32	67	4.56	3	*O-131(0-131-0)	14	-3.0
1896*Cle-N	116	455	70	131	16	4	1	54	47	32	24	....	.288	.361	.347	.708	82	-11	70	5.40	8	*O-116(0-116-0)	13	-1.0
1897 Cle-N	24	91	6	20	2	0	0	10	7	....	4	....	.220	.283	.242	.525	37	-8	8	2.82	0	O-24(1-23-0)	1	-0.8
1898 Cle-N	106	366	47	87	3	0	0	48	46	....	7	....	.238	.331	.246	.577	67	-13	34	3.16	-1	*O-104(1-102-1)/2-2	8	-1.9
1901 Cle-A	3	7	0	1	0	0	0	0	0	....	0	....	.143	.143	.143	.286	-22	-1	0	.65	0	/O-2(0-2-0),3-1,P-1	0	-0.1
1902 StL-A	2	3	0	2	0	0	0	0	0	....	0	....	.667	.667	.667	1.333	274	1	1	36.22	0	/O-2(0-1-1)	0	0.0
1907 StL-A	2	0	0	0	0	0	0	0	0	....	0	....	....	....	....	....	-100	0	0	....	0	....	0	0.0
Total 13	**1021**	**3981**	**620**	**1008**	**114**	**40**	**11**	**469**	**365**	**290**	**262**	**....**	**.253**	**.322**	**.310**	**.632**	**72**	**-155**	**499**	**4.43**	**37**	***O-1015/2-2,3-1,P-1**	**97**	**-14.9**

• MCALEESE, Jack John James McAleese b: 8/22/1878, Sharon, PA d: 11/14/1950, New York, NY BR/TR, 5'8" Deb: 8/10/1901

YEAR TM-L	G	AB	R	H	2B	3B	HR	RBI	BB	SO	SB	CS	AVG	OBP	SLG	OPS	OPS+	BR/A	RC	RC/G	FR	G/POS	WS	TPW
1901 Chi-A	1	1	0	0	0	0	0	0	0	....	0	....	.000	.000	.000	.000	-103	-0	0	.00	-0	/P-1	0	-0.2
1909 StL-A	85	267	33	57	7	0	0	12	32	....	18	....	.213	.318	.240	.558	82	-3	26	3.14	-4	O-79(27-32-20)/3-2	6	-1.2
Total 2	**86**	**268**	**33**	**57**	**7**	**0**	**0**	**12**	**32**	**....**	**18**	**....**	**.213**	**.317**	**.239**	**.556**	**82**	**-3**	**26**	**3.13**	**-4**	**/O-79,3-2,P-1**	**6**	**-1.4**

• MCALLESTER, Bill William Lusk McAllester b: 12/29/1888, Chattanooga, TN d: 3/3/1970, Chattanooga, TN BR/TR, 5'11.5", 175 lbs. Deb: 5/2/1913

YEAR TM-L	G	AB	R	H	2B	3B	HR	RBI	BB	SO	SB	CS	AVG	OBP	SLG	OPS	OPS+	BR/A	RC	RC/G	FR	G/POS	WS	TPW
1913 StL-A	49	85	3	13	4	0	0	6	11	12	2	....	.153	.250	.200	.450	33	-7	5	1.63	-3	C-39	1	-0.8

• MCALLISTER, Sport Lewis William McAllister b: 7/23/1874, Austin, MS d: 7/17/1962, Wyandotte, MI BB/TR, 5'11", 180 lbs. Deb: 8/7/1896 U Career OF: 17-13-128 ♦

YEAR TM-L	G	AB	R	H	2B	3B	HR	RBI	BB	SO	SB	CS	AVG	OBP	SLG	OPS	OPS+	BR/A	RC	RC/G	FR	G/POS	WS	TPW
1896 Cle-N	8	27	2	6	2	0	0	1	0	2	1	....	.222	.250	.296	.546	41	-2	2	2.90	-2	/O-4(0-3-9),C-2,P-1	0	-0.5
1897 Cle-N	43	137	23	30	5	1	0	11	12	....	3	....	.219	.287	.270	.557	45	-10	12	2.93	-2	O-28(1-3-24)/P-4,S-4,1-3,C,2	2	-1.3
1898 Cle-N	17	57	8	13	3	1	0	9	5	....	0	....	.228	.290	.316	.606	75	-0	5	3.23	1	/P-9,O-8(0-4-4)	3	-0.6
1899 Cle-N	113	418	29	99	6	8	1	31	19	....	5	....	.237	.273	.297	.570	61	-22	38	3.01	-9	O-79(9-3-70),C-17/3-7,1-6,P,S,2	1	-3.8
1901 Det-A	90	306	45	92	9	4	3	57	15	....	17	....	.301	.344	.386	.729	98	-2	49	5.75	-12	C-35,1-28,O-11(5-0-6),3-10/S	8	-1.0
1902 Det-A	21	67	8	14	1	0	1	8	2	....	0	....	.209	.243	.269	.512	41	-6	5	2.26	1	/1-5,S-5,2-3,3-2,C-2,O-1	0	-0.4
Bal-A	3	11	0	1	0	0	0	1	1	....	0	....	.091	.167	.091	.258	-26	-2	0	.45	0	/2-2,1-1	0	-0.2
Det-A	45	162	11	34	4	2	0	24	3	....	1	....	.210	.229	.259	.488	34	-15	10	2.11	-1	1-21,O-11(1-0-10)/C-7,3-4,S	1	-1.5
Yr.	69	240	19	49	5	2	1	33	6	....	1	....	.204	.230	.254	.484	33	-22	15	2.06	0	1-27,O-12(2-0-10)/C-9,3-6,S,2	1	-2.1
1903 Det-A	78	265	31	69	8	2	0	22	10	....	5	....	.260	.297	.306	.603	84	-5	27	3.54	-5	S-46,C-18/O-5(0-0-5),3-4,1	5	-0.7
Total 7	**418**	**1450**	**157**	**358**	**38**	**18**	**5**	**164**	**67**	**2**	**32**	**....**	**.247**	**.287**	**.308**	**.595**	**67**	**-64**	**148**	**3.48**	**-30**	**O-147/C-83,1-65,S-62,3-27,P,2**	**20**	**-10.2**

• MCANANY, Jim James McAnany b: 9/4/1936, Los Angeles, CA BR/TR, 5'10", 196 lbs. Deb: 9/19/1958 Career OF: 4-2-67

YEAR TM-L	G	AB	R	H	2B	3B	HR	RBI	BB	SO	SB	CS	AVG	OBP	SLG	OPS	OPS+	BR/A	RC	RC/G	FR	G/POS	WS	TPW
1958 Chi-A	5	13	0	0	0	0	0	0	0	5	0	0	.000	.000	.000	.000	-102	-4	0	.00	0	/O-3(0-0-3)	0	-0.3
1959*Chi-A	67	210	22	58	9	3	0	27	19	26	2	1	.276	.339	.348	.687	90	-2	26	4.42	0	O-67(4-2-63)	6	-0.5
1960 Chi-A	3	2	0	0	0	0	0	0	0	2	0	0	.000	.000	.000	.000	-101	-1	0	.00	0	....	0	-0.1
1961 Chi-N	11	10	1	3	1	0	0	0	1	3	0	0	.300	.364	.400	.764	101	0	2	5.98	0	/O-1	0	0.0
1962 Chi-N	7	6	0	0	0	0	0	0	1	2	0	0	.000	.143	.000	.143	-56	-1	0	.17	0	....	0	-0.1
Total 5	**93**	**241**	**23**	**61**	**10**	**3**	**0**	**27**	**21**	**38**	**2**	**1**	**.253**	**.316**	**.320**	**.635**	**76**	**-8**	**27**	**3.98**	**1**	**/O-71**	**6**	**-1.0**

• MCATEE, Bub Michael James "Bub,Butch" McAtee b: 3/1845, Troy, NY d: 10/18/1876, Troy, NY TR, 6'1", 160 lbs. Deb: 5/8/1871

YEAR TM-L	G	AB	R	H	2B	3B	HR	RBI	BB	SO	SB	CS	AVG	OBP	SLG	OPS	OPS+	BR/A	RC	RC/G	FR	G/POS	WS	TPW
1871 Chi-n	26	135	34	37	8	2	0	10	5	2	5	3	.274	.300	.363	.663	81	-6	17	5.18	-1	*1-26	....	-0.4
1872 Tro-n	25	129	30	28	3	1	0	15	1	2	0	2	.217	.223	.256	.479	46	-9	8	2.27	2	1-25	....	-0.4
Total 2 n	**51**	**264**	**64**	**65**	**11**	**3**	**0**	**25**	**6**	**4**	**5**	**5**	**.246**	**.263**	**.311**	**.574**	**64**	**-15**	**24**	**3.71**	**2**	**/1-51**	**....**	**-0.8**

• MCAULEY, Ike James Earl McAuley b: 8/19/1891, Wichita, KS d: 4/6/1928, Des Moines, IA BR/TR, 5'9.5", 150 lbs. Deb: 9/10/1914

YEAR TM-L	G	AB	R	H	2B	3B	HR	RBI	BB	SO	SB	CS	AVG	OBP	SLG	OPS	OPS+	BR/A	RC	RC/G	FR	G/POS	WS	TPW
1914 Pit-N	15	24	3	3	0	0	0	0	0	8	0	....	.125	.125	.125	.250	-27	-4	0	.51	0	/S-5,3-3,2-2	0	-0.4
1915 Pit-N	5	15	0	2	1	0	0	0	0	6	0	....	.133	.133	.200	.333		-2	0	.82	0	/S-5	0	-0.2
1916 Pit-N	4	8	1	2	0	0	0	1	0	1	0	....	.250	.250	.250	.500	53	-0	1	2.35	0	/S-4	0	0.0
1917 StL-N	3	7	0	2	0	0	0	1	0	1	0	....	.286	.286	.286	.571	78	-0	1	2.84	0	/S-3	0	-0.1
1925 Chi-N	37	125	10	35	7	2	0	11	11	12	1	0	.280	.343	.368	.711	80	-3	17	4.52	-8	S-37	3	-0.7
Total 5	**64**	**179**	**14**	**44**	**8**	**2**	**0**	**13**	**11**	**28**	**1**	**0**	**.246**	**.293**	**.313**	**.606**	**60**	**-9**	**19**	**3.39**	**-8**	**/S-54,3-3,2-2**	**3**	**-1.3**

• MCAULIFFE, Dick Richard John McAuliffe b: 11/29/1939, Hartford, CT BL/TR, 5'11", 176 lbs. Deb: 9/17/1960

YEAR TM-L	G	AB	R	H	2B	3B	HR	RBI	BB	SO	SB	CS	AVG	OBP	SLG	OPS	OPS+	BR/A	RC	RC/G	FR	G/POS	WS	TPW
1960 Det-A	8	27	2	7	0	1	0	1	2	6	0	0	.259	.310	.333	.644	70	-1	3	3.38	2	/S-7	0	0.1
1961 Det-A	80	285	36	73	12	4	6	33	24	39	2	3	.256	.323	.389	.712	86	-7	36	4.32	-1	S-55,3-22	8	-0.4
1962 Det-A	139	471	50	124	20	5	12	63	64	76	4	2	.263	.351	.403	.755	99	0	68	5.06	-11	2-70,3-49,S-16	13	-0.3
1963 Det-A	150	568	77	149	18	6	13	61	64	75	11	5	.262	.337	.384	.721	98	-0	75	4.52	-8	*S-133,2-15	17	0.5
1964 Det-A	162	557	85	134	18	7	24	66	77	96	8	5	.241	.336	.427	.763	109	7	81	4.84	1	*S-160	21	2.3
1965 Det-A★	113	404	61	105	13	6	15	54	49	62	6	9	.260	.343	.433	.776	118	7	60	5.22	0	*S-112	17	1.7
1966 Det-A★	124	430	83	118	16	8	23	56	66	80	5	7	.274	.375	.509	.884	148	26	83	6.73	5	*S-105,3-15	26	4.3
1967 Det-A★	153	557	92	133	16	7	22	65	105	118	6	5	.239	.366	.411	.777	126	22	93	5.74	4	*2-145,S-43	27	4.2
1968*Det-A	151	570	**95**	142	24	10	16	56	82	99	8	7	.249	.346	.411	.756	125	18	87	5.32	-4	*2-148/S-5	28	3.1
1969 Det-A	74	271	49	71	10	5	11	33	47	41	2	5	.262	.371	.458	.829	125	8	48	6.16	6	2-72	13	2.0
1970 Det-A	146	530	73	124	21	1	12	50	101	62	5	6	.234	.360	.345	.705	95	-1	74	4.77	-5	*2-127,S-15,3-12	19	0.4
1971 Det-A	128	477	67	99	16	6	18	57	53	67	4	1	.208	.293	.379	.673	86	-9	55	3.79	2	*2-123/S-7	14	0.1
1972*Det-A	122	408	47	98	16	3	8	30	59	59	0	0	.240	.339	.353	.692	103	4	53	4.57	-6	*2-116/S-3,3-1	16	0.5
1973 Det-A	106	343	39	94	18	1	12	47	49	52	0	4	.274	.366	.437	.804	118	8	57	5.97	-5	*2-102/S-2,D-1	16	1.0
1974 Bos-A	100	272	32	57	13	1	5	24	39	40	2	0	.210	.311	.320	.631	76	-7	28	3.38	-8	2-53,3-40/D-3,S-3	6	-1.2
1975 Bos-A	7	15	0	2	0	0	0	1	1	2	0	0	.133	.188	.133	.321	-7	-2	0	.59	-1	/3-7	0	-0.3
Total 16	**1763**	**6185**	**888**	**1530**	**231**	**71**	**197**	**697**	**882**	**974**	**63**	**59**	**.247**	**.344**	**.403**	**.748**	**108**	**74**	**899**	**5.00**	**-31**	**2-971,S-666,3-146/D-4**	**241**	**18.0**

• MCAULIFFE, Gene Eugene Leo McAuliffe b: 2/28/1872, Randolph, MA d: 4/29/1953, Randolph, MA BR/TR, 6'1", 180 lbs. Deb: 8/17/1904

YEAR TM-L	G	AB	R	H	2B	3B	HR	RBI	BB	SO	SB	CS	AVG	OBP	SLG	OPS	OPS+	BR/A	RC	RC/G	FR	G/POS	WS	TPW
1904 Bos-N	1	2	0	1	0	0	0	0	0	....	0	....	.500	.500	.500	1.000	217	0	1	13.33	0	/C-1	0	0.0

• MCAVOY, George George Robert McAvoy b: 3/12/1884, East Liverpool, OH BL/TR Deb: 7/17/1914

YEAR TM-L	G	AB	R	H	2B	3B	HR	RBI	BB	SO	SB	CS	AVG	OBP	SLG	OPS	OPS+	BR/A	RC	RC/G	FR	G/POS	WS	TPW
1914 Phi-N	1	1	0	0	0	0	0	0	0	0	0	....	.000	.000	.000	.000	-94	-0	0	.00	0	....	0	0.0

• MCAVOY, Wickey James Eugene McAvoy b: 10/22/1894, Rochester, NY d: 7/6/1973, Rochester, NY BR/TR, 5'11", 172 lbs. Deb: 9/29/1913 ♦

YEAR TM-L	G	AB	R	H	2B	3B	HR	RBI	BB	SO	SB	CS	AVG	OBP	SLG	OPS	OPS+	BR/A	RC	RC/G	FR	G/POS	WS	TPW
1913 Phi-A	4	9	0	1	0	0	0	0	0	4	0	....	.111	.200	.111	.311	-9	-1	0	.58	0	/C-4	0	-0.1
1914 Phi-A	8	16	1	2	0	1	0	0	0	4	0	....	.125	.125	.250	.375	13	-2	1	.95	0	/C-8	0	-0.2
1915 Phi-A	68	184	12	35	7	2	0	6	11	32	0	2	.190	.236	.250	.486	47	-14	11	1.83	6	C-64	1	-0.4
1917 Phi-A	10	24	1	6	1	0	1	4	0	3	0	....	.250	.250	.417	.667	105	-0	2	3.32	1	/C-8	1	0.2
1918 Phi-A	83	271	14	66	5	3	0	32	13	23	5	....	.244	.283	.284	.567	70	-11	23	2.71	11	C-74/1-1,O-1,P-1	6	0.6
1919 Phi-A	62	170	10	24	5	2	0	11	14	21	1	....	.141	.207	.194	.401	13	-20	7	1.20	6	C-57	3	-1.1
Total 6	**235**	**674**	**38**	**134**	**18**	**8**	**1**	**53**	**38**	**87**	**6**	**2**	**.199**	**.245**	**.254**	**.498**	**48**	**-48**	**43**	**2.01**	**24**	**C-215/1-1,O-1,P-1**	**11**	**-1.0**

• MCBRIDE, Algie Algernon Griggs McBride b: 5/23/1869, Washington, DC d: 1/10/1956, Georgetown, OH BL/TL, 5'9", 152 lbs. Deb: 5/12/1896 Career OF: 43-189-166

YEAR TM-L	G	AB	R	H	2B	3B	HR	RBI	BB	SO	SB	CS	AVG	OBP	SLG	OPS	OPS+	BR/A	RC	RC/G	FR	G/POS	WS	TPW
1896 Chi-N	9	29	2	7	1	1	1	7	7	3	0	....	.241	.389	.448	.837	116	1	5	6.24	0	/O-9(9-0-0)	1	0.0
1898 Cin-N	120	486	94	147	14	12	2	43	51	....	16	....	.302	.383	.393	.776	114	10	82	6.28	1	*O-120(4-115-1)	21	0.2
1899 Cin-N	64	251	57	87	12	5	1	23	30	....	5	....	.347	.431	.446	.877	138	15	52	8.23	-4	O-64(5-45-14)	11	0.6
1900 Cin-N	112	436	59	120	15	8	4	59	25	....	12	....	.275	.320	.374	.694	94	-5	58	4.79	-4	*O-110(14-10-86)	9	-1.3
1901 Cin-N	30	123	19	29	7	0	2	18	7	....	0	....	.236	.282	.341	.624	86	-2	12	3.42	-3	O-28(11-19-0)	1	-0.6
NY-N	68	264	27	74	11	0	2	29	12	....	3	....	.280	.317	.345	.661	95	-2	31	4.23	-3	O-65(0-0-65)	5	-0.8
Yr.	98	387	46	103	18	0	4	47	19	....	3	....	.266	.306	.344	.649	92	-4	43	3.97	-5	O-93(11-19-65)	6	-1.4
Total 5	**403**	**1589**	**258**	**464**	**60**	**26**	**12**	**179**	**132**	**3**	**36**	**....**	**.292**	**.356**	**.385**	**.741**	**108**	**17**	**241**	**5.57**	**-12**	**O-396**	**48**	**-1.9**

• MCBRIDE, Bake Arnold Ray McBride b: 2/3/1949, Fulton, MO BL/TR, 6'2", 190 lbs. Deb: 7/26/1973 Career OF: 1-389-576

YEAR TM-L	G	AB	R	H	2B	3B	HR	RBI	BB	SO	SB	CS	AVG	OBP	SLG	OPS	OPS+	BR/A	RC	RC/G	FR	G/POS	WS	TPW
1973 StL-N	40	63	8	19	3	0	0	5	4	10	0	1	.302	.362	.349	.712	98	-0	8	4.78	0	O-17(1-16-0)	2	-0.1
1974 StL-N	150	559	81	173	19	5	6	56	43	57	30	11	.309	.372	.394	.766	115	14	85	5.57	-0	*O-144(0-144-0)	22	1.0
1975 StL-N	116	413	70	124	10	9	5	36	34	52	26	8	.300	.355	.404	.759	106	5	62	5.36	-4	*O-107(0-107-0)	16	-0.1

YEAR TM-L	G	AB	R	H	2B	3B	HR	RBI	BB	SO	SB	CS	AVG	OBP	SLG	OPS	OPS+	BR/A	RC	RC/G	FR	G/POS	WS	TPW
1976 StL-N★	72	272	40	91	13	4	3	24	18	28	10	5	.335	.389	.445	.833	135	12	48	6.84	4	O-66(0-66-0)	13	1.5
1977 StL-N	43	122	21	32	5	1	4	20	7	19	9	3	.262	.302	.418	.720	93	-1	16	4.32	0	O-33(0-33-0)	4	-0.1
*Phi-N	85	280	55	95	20	5	11	41	25	25	27	4	.339	.399	.564	.964	149	23	67	9.04	3	O-73(0-21-54)	16	2.3
Yr.	128	402	76	127	25	6	15	61	32	44	36	7	.316	.371	.520	.891	132	22	82	7.49	3	*O-106(0-54-54)	20	2.2
1978*Phi-N	122	472	68	127	20	4	10	49	28	68	28	3	.269	.317	.392	.709	96	1	63	4.76	1	*O-119(0-1-118)	13	-0.5
1979 Phi-N	151	582	82	163	16	12	12	60	41	77	25	14	.280	.332	.411	.742	98	-3	79	4.76	10	*O-147(0-0-147)	17	-0.1
1980*Phi-N	137	554	68	171	33	10	9	87	26	58	13	10	.309	.345	.453	.798	115	8	79	5.13	4	*O-133(0-1-133)	18	0.5
1981*Phi-N	58	221	26	60	17	1	2	21	11	25	5	0	.271	.306	.385	.691	91	-2	25	4.03	-1	O-56(0-0-56)	5	-0.5
1982 Cle-A	27	85	8	31	3	3	0	13	2	12	2	2	.365	.379	.471	.850	132	3	14	6.31	0	O-22(0-0-22)	3	0.2
1983 Cle-A	70	230	21	67	8	1	1	18	9	26	8	2	.291	.321	.348	.669	81	-5	24	3.64	1	O-46(0-0-46),D-15	3	-0.7
Total 11	**1071**	**3853**	**548**	**1153**	**167**	**55**	**63**	**430**	**248**	**457**	**183**	**63**	**.299**	**.348**	**.420**	**.768**	**109**	**55**	**570**	**5.33**	**18**	**O-963/D-15**	**132**	**3.6**

• MCBRIDE, George George Florian McBride b: 11/20/1880, Milwaukee, WI d: 7/2/1973, Milwaukee, WI BR/TR, 5'11", 170 lbs. Deb: 9/12/1901 M/C

YEAR TM-L	G	AB	R	H	2B	3B	HR	RBI	BB	SO	SB	CS	AVG	OBP	SLG	OPS	OPS+	BR/A	RC	RC/G	FR	G/POS	WS	TPW
1901 Mil-A	3	12	0	2	0	0	0	0	1	....	0	....	.167	.231	.167	.397	12	-1	0	1.25	1	/S-3	0	0.0
1905 Pit-N	27	87	9	19	4	0	0	7	6	....	2	....	.218	.277	.264	.541	60	-4	8	2.74	0	3-17/S-8	1	-0.3
StL-N	81	281	22	61	1	2	2	34	14	....	10	....	.217	.264	.256	.520	57	-15	23	2.64	-6	S-80/1-1	3	-1.9
Yr.	108	368	31	80	5	2	2	41	20	....	12	....	.217	.267	.258	.525	58	-19	31	2.66	-5	S-88,3-17/1-1	4	-2.2
1906 StL-N	90	313	24	53	8	2	0	13	17	....	5	....	.169	.215	.208	.422	33	-25	16	1.58	1	S-90	3	-2.3
1908 Was-A	155	518	47	120	10	6	0	34	41	....	12	....	.232	.292	.274	.566	92	-4	45	2.84	26	*S-155	17	3.1
1909 Was-A	156	504	38	118	16	0	0	34	36	....	17	....	.234	.294	.266	.560	81	-10	46	2.90	3	*S-156	11	-0.3
1910 Was-A	154	514	54	118	19	4	1	55	61	....	11	....	.230	.321	.288	.609	95	-0	53	3.26	23	*S-154	16	3.0
1911 Was-A	154	557	58	131	11	4	0	59	52	....	15	....	.235	.312	.269	.581	64	-25	52	3.05	6	*S-154	11	-0.8
1912 Was-A	152	521	56	118	13	7	1	52	38	....	17	....	.226	.288	.284	.572	63	-25	48	2.95	27	*S-152	13	1.2
1913 Was-A	150	499	52	107	18	7	1	52	43	46	12	....	.214	.286	.285	.571	66	-22	43	2.70	12	*S-150	14	0.1
1914 Was-A	156	503	49	102	12	4	0	24	43	70	12	14	.203	.274	.243	.516	53	-32	36	2.18	20	*S-156	12	-0.1
1915 Was-A	146	476	54	97	8	6	1	30	29	60	10	5	.204	.251	.252	.503	50	-31	34	2.23	16	*S-146	9	-0.6
1916 Was-A	139	466	36	106	15	4	1	36	23	58	8	....	.227	.271	.283	.555	67	-20	41	2.79	22	*S-139	13	1.3
1917 Was-A	50	141	6	27	3	0	0	9	10	17	1	....	.191	.265	.213	.477	46	-9	9	1.89	2	S-41/3-6,2-2	2	-0.5
1918 Was-A	18	53	2	7	0	0	0	1	0	11	1	....	.132	.132	.132	.264	-21	-8	1	.57	-1	S-14/2-2	1	-0.9
1919 Was-A	15	40	3	8	1	1	0	4	3	6	0	....	.200	.256	.275	.531	49	-3	3	2.26	-1	S-15	1	-0.3
1920 Was-A	13	41	6	9	1	0	0	3	2	3	0	0	.220	.256	.244	.500	34	-4	3	2.04	-2	S-13	0	-0.5
Total 16	**1659**	**5526**	**516**	**1203**	**140**	**47**	**7**	**447**	**419**	**271**	**133**	**19**	**.218**	**.281**	**.264**	**.544**	**65**	**-241**	**461**	**2.63**	**150**	***S-1626/3-23,2-4,1-1**	**127**	**0.4**

• MCBRIDE, John John F. McBride Deb: 10/12/1890

YEAR TM-L	G	AB	R	H	2B	3B	HR	RBI	BB	SO	SB	CS	AVG	OBP	SLG	OPS	OPS+	BR/A	RC	RC/G	FR	G/POS	WS	TPW
1890 Phi-a	1	2	0	0	0	0	0	0	0	....	0	....	.000	.000	.000	.000	-102	-1	0	.00	1	/O-1	0	0.0

• MCBRIDE, Tom Thomas Raymond McBride b: 11/2/1914, Bonham, TX d: 12/26/2001, Wichita Falls, TX BR/TR, 6'.5", 190 lbs. Deb: 4/23/1943 Career OF: 116-91-115

YEAR TM-L	G	AB	R	H	2B	3B	HR	RBI	BB	SO	SB	CS	AVG	OBP	SLG	OPS	OPS+	BR/A	RC	RC/G	FR	G/POS	WS	TPW
1943 Bos-A	26	96	11	23	3	1	0	7	7	3	2	0	.240	.291	.292	.583	69	-3	7	2.48	0	O-24(0-21-3)	1	-0.4
1944 Bos-A	71	216	29	53	7	3	0	24	8	13	4	0	.245	.276	.306	.581	67	-9	18	2.75	2	O-57(23-14-22)/1-5	2	-1.1
1945 Bos-A	100	344	38	105	11	7	1	47	26	17	2	2	.305	.354	.387	.741	112	5	47	5.05	4	O-81(15-50-22),1-11	11	0.5
1946*Bos-A	61	153	21	46	5	2	0	19	9	6	0	1	.301	.340	.359	.699	90	-2	18	4.17	-1	O-43(10-2-32)	4	-0.5
1947 Bos-A	2	5	0	1	0	0	0	0	0	0	0	0	.200	.200	.200	.400	11	-1	0	.00	1	/O-1	0	0.0
Was-A	56	166	19	45	4	2	0	15	15	9	3	1	.271	.331	.319	.651	83	-3	17	3.50	-1	O-51(43-4-5)/3-1	3	-0.8
Yr.	58	171	19	46	4	2	0	15	15	9	3	1	.269	.328	.316	.644	82	-4	17	3.37	-1	O-52(43-4-6)/3-1	3	-0.7
1948 Was-A	92	206	22	53	9	1	1	29	28	15	2	2	.257	.346	.325	.671	81	-5	23	3.59	5	O-55(25-0-30)	4	-0.2
Total 6	**408**	**1186**	**140**	**326**	**39**	**16**	**2**	**141**	**93**	**63**	**13**	**6**	**.275**	**.328**	**.340**	**.668**	**88**	**-19**	**130**	**3.77**	**8**	**O-312/1-16,3-1**	**25**	**-2.5**

• MCCABE, Bill William Francis McCabe b: 10/28/1892, Chicago, IL d: 9/2/1966, Chicago, IL BB/TR, 5'9.5", 180 lbs. Deb: 4/16/1918 Career OF: 7-1-21

YEAR TM-L	G	AB	R	H	2B	3B	HR	RBI	BB	SO	SB	CS	AVG	OBP	SLG	OPS	OPS+	BR/A	RC	RC/G	FR	G/POS	WS	TPW
1918*Chi-N	29	45	9	8	0	1	0	5	4	7	2	....	.178	.245	.222	.467	42	-3	3	1.91	0	2-13/O-4(1-0-2)	1	-0.4
1919 Chi-N	33	84	8	13	3	1	0	5	9	15	3	....	.155	.253	.214	.467	41	-6	5	1.80	-2	O-20(0-1-19)/S-4,3-1	1	-1.0
1920 Chi-N	3	2	1	1	0	0	0	0	0	0	0	0	.500	.500	.500	1.000	184	0	0	12.72	0	....	0	0.0
*Bro-N	41	68	10	10	0	0	0	3	2	6	1	2	.147	.171	.147	.318	-8	-10	2	.68	-8	S-13/O-6(6-0-0),2-4,3-3	1	-1.8
Yr.	44	70	11	11	0	0	0	3	2	6	1	2	.157	.181	.157	.338	-3	-10	2	.87	-8	S-13/O-6(6-0-0),2-4,3-3	1	-1.7
Total 3	**106**	**199**	**28**	**32**	**3**	**2**	**0**	**13**	**15**	**28**	**6**	**2**	**.161**	**.227**	**.196**	**.423**	**27**	**-18**	**10**	**1.49**	**-10**	**/O-30,2-17,S-17,3-4**	**3**	**-3.1**

• MCCABE, Joe Joseph Robert McCabe b: 8/27/1938, Indianapolis, IN BR/TR, 6', 190 lbs. Deb: 4/18/1964

YEAR TM-L	G	AB	R	H	2B	3B	HR	RBI	BB	SO	SB	CS	AVG	OBP	SLG	OPS	OPS+	BR/A	RC	RC/G	FR	G/POS	WS	TPW
1964 Min-A	14	19	1	3	0	0	0	2	0	8	0	0	.158	.158	.158	.316	-12	-3	1	.87	0	C-12	0	-0.3
1965 Was-A	14	27	1	5	0	0	1	5	4	13	1	0	.185	.290	.296	.587	68	-1	3	3.33	0	C-11	1	0.0
Total 2	**28**	**46**	**2**	**8**	**0**	**0**	**1**	**7**	**4**	**21**	**1**	**0**	**.174**	**.240**	**.239**	**.479**	**36**	**-4**	**3**	**2.25**	**1**	**/C-23**	**1**	**-0.3**

• MCCABE, Swat James Arthur McCabe b: 11/20/1881, Towanda, PA d: 12/9/1944, Bristol, CT BL/TR, 5'10", 187 lbs. Deb: 9/23/1909 Career OF: 0-3-9

YEAR TM-L	G	AB	R	H	2B	3B	HR	RBI	BB	SO	SB	CS	AVG	OBP	SLG	OPS	OPS+	BR/A	RC	RC/G	FR	G/POS	WS	TPW
1909 Cin-N	3	11	2	6	1	0	0	0	0	....	1	....	.545	.545	.636	1.182	269	2	4	22.41	-1	/O-3(0-3-0)	1	0.1
1910 Cin-N	13	35	3	9	1	0	0	5	1	2	0	....	.257	.297	.286	.583	73	-1	3	2.85	1	/O-9(0-0-9)	1	-0.1
Total 2	**16**	**46**	**5**	**15**	**2**	**0**	**0**	**5**	**1**	**2**	**1**	**....**	**.326**	**.354**	**.370**	**.724**	**118**	**1**	**7**	**6.01**	**0**	**/O-12**	**2**	**0.0**

• MCCAFFERY, Harry Harry Charles McCaffery b: 11/25/1858, St. Louis, MO d: 4/29/1928, St. Louis, MO BR/TR, 5'10.5", 185 lbs. Deb: 6/15/1882 U Career OF: 5-5-18

YEAR TM-L	G	AB	R	H	2B	3B	HR	RBI	BB	SO	SB	CS	AVG	OBP	SLG	OPS	OPS+	BR/A	RC	RC/G	FR	G/POS	WS	TPW
1882 Lou-a	1	4	1	1	0	0	0	....	0	....	....	....	.250	.250	.250	.500	73	-0	0	2.39	0	/2-1	0	0.0
StL-a	38	153	23	42	8	6	0	....	3	....	....	....	.275	.288	.405	.694	126	4	18	4.62	4	O-23(5-0-18)/2-8,3-7,1-1	7	0.6
Yr.	39	157	24	43	8	6	0	....	3	....	....	....	.274	.288	.401	.689	125	3	19	4.57	4	O-23(5-0-18)/2-9,3-7,1-1	7	0.6
1883 StL-a	5	18	0	1	0	0	0	1	1	....	....	....	.056	.105	.056	.161	-44	-3	0	.18	1	/O-5(0-5-0)	0	-0.2
1885 Cin-a	1	5	0	0	0	0	0	0	0	....	....	....	.000	.000	.000	.000	-98	-1	0	.00	0	/P-1	0	-0.3
Total 3	**45**	**180**	**24**	**44**	**8**	**6**	**0**	**1**	**4**	**....**	**....**	**....**	**.244**	**.261**	**.356**	**.616**	**102**	**-0**	**19**	**3.85**	**4**	**/O-28,2-9,3-7,1-1,P-1**	**7**	**0.1**

• MCCAFFREY, Sparrow Charles P. McCaffrey b: 1868, Philadelphia, PA d: 4/29/1894, Philadelphia, PA, 120 lbs. Deb: 8/13/1889

YEAR TM-L	G	AB	R	H	2B	3B	HR	RBI	BB	SO	SB	CS	AVG	OBP	SLG	OPS	OPS+	BR/A	RC	RC/G	FR	G/POS	WS	TPW
1889 Col-a	2	1	1	1	0	0	0	0	1	0	0	....	1.000	1.000	1.000	2.000	495	1	1	∞	0	/C-2	0	0.1

• MCCALL, Brian Brian Allen "Bam" McCall b: 1/25/1943, Kentfield, CA BL/TL, 5'10", 170 lbs. Deb: 9/18/1962 Career OF: 0-1-2

YEAR TM-L	G	AB	R	H	2B	3B	HR	RBI	BB	SO	SB	CS	AVG	OBP	SLG	OPS	OPS+	BR/A	RC	RC/G	FR	G/POS	WS	TPW
1962 Chi-A	4	8	2	3	0	0	2	3	0	2	0	0	.375	.375	1.125	1.500	287	2	3	18.23	0	/O-1	1	0.2
1963 Chi-A	3	7	1	0	0	0	0	0	1	2	0	0	.000	.125	.000	.125	-62	-2	0	.13	0	/O-2(0-0-2)	0	-0.2
Total 2	**7**	**15**	**3**	**3**	**0**	**0**	**2**	**3**	**1**	**4**	**0**	**0**	**.200**	**.250**	**.600**	**.850**	**112**	**0**	**3**	**7.67**	**0**	**/O-3**	**1**	**0.0**

• MCCANDLESS, Jack Scott Cook McCandless b: 5/5/1891, Pittsburgh, PA d: 8/17/1961, Pittsburgh, PA BL/TR, 6', 170 lbs. Deb: 9/10/1914 Career OF: 23-59-32

YEAR TM-L	G	AB	R	H	2B	3B	HR	RBI	BB	SO	SB	CS	AVG	OBP	SLG	OPS	OPS+	BR/A	RC	RC/G	FR	G/POS	WS	TPW
1914 Bal-F	11	31	5	8	0	1	0	1	3	0	0	....	.258	.343	.323	.665	91	-0	3	3.60	0	/O-8(0-1-7)	1	0.0
1915 Bal-F	117	406	47	87	6	7	5	34	41	99	9	....	.214	.296	.300	.596	70	-15	37	2.96	1	*O-105(23-58-25)	4	-2.1
Total 2	**128**	**437**	**52**	**95**	**6**	**8**	**5**	**35**	**44**	**99**	**9**	**....**	**.217**	**.299**	**.302**	**.601**	**72**	**-15**	**40**	**3.00**	**2**	**O-113**	**5**	**-2.1**

• MCCANN, Emmett Robert Emmett McCann b: 3/4/1902, Philadelphia, PA d: 4/15/1937, Philadelphia, PA BR/TR, 5'11", 150 lbs. Deb: 4/19/1920

YEAR TM-L	G	AB	R	H	2B	3B	HR	RBI	BB	SO	SB	CS	AVG	OBP	SLG	OPS	OPS+	BR/A	RC	RC/G	FR	G/POS	WS	TPW
1920 Phi-A	13	34	4	9	1	1	0	3	3	1	0	1	.265	.342	.353	.695	83	-1	4	4.03	-2	S-11	1	-0.2
1921 Phi-A	52	157	15	35	5	0	0	15	4	6	2	1	.223	.242	.255	.497	27	-17	10	2.03	-3	S-32/3-9,2-2,1-1	1	-1.5
1926 Bos-A	6	3	0	0	0	0	0	0	1	1	0	0	.000	.250	.000	.250	-32	-1	0	.55	-1	/3-1,S-1	0	-0.1
Total 3	**71**	**194**	**19**	**44**	**6**	**1**	**0**	**18**	**8**	**8**	**2**	**2**	**.227**	**.261**	**.268**	**.529**	**36**	**-19**	**14**	**2.34**	**-5**	**/S-44,3-10,2-2,1-1**	**2**	**-1.8**

• MCCARDELL, Roger Roger Morton McCardell b: 8/29/1932, Gorsuch Mills, MD d: 11/13/1996, Perry Point, MD BR/TR, 6', 200 lbs. Deb: 5/8/1959

YEAR TM-L	G	AB	R	H	2B	3B	HR	RBI	BB	SO	SB	CS	AVG	OBP	SLG	OPS	OPS+	BR/A	RC	RC/G	FR	G/POS	WS	TPW
1959 SF-N	4	4	0	0	0	0	0	0	0	0	0	0	.000	.000	.000	.000	-102	-1	0	.00	-0	/C-3	0	-0.1

• MCCARREN, Bill William Joseph McCarren b: 11/4/1895, Fortenia, PA d: 9/11/1983, Denver, CO BR/TR, 5'11.5", 170 lbs. Deb: 5/4/1923

YEAR TM-L	G	AB	R	H	2B	3B	HR	RBI	BB	SO	SB	CS	AVG	OBP	SLG	OPS	OPS+	BR/A	RC	RC/G	FR	G/POS	WS	TPW
1923 Bro-N	69	216	28	53	10	1	3	27	22	39	0	1	.245	.326	.343	.669	79	-6	25	3.95	-5	3-66/O-1	4	-0.7

• MCCARTHY, Alex Alexander George McCarthy b: 5/12/1888, Chicago, IL d: 3/12/1978, Salisbury, MD BR/TR, 5'9", 150 lbs. Deb: 10/7/1910

YEAR TM-L	G	AB	R	H	2B	3B	HR	RBI	BB	SO	SB	CS	AVG	OBP	SLG	OPS	OPS+	BR/A	RC	RC/G	FR	G/POS	WS	TPW
1910 Pit-N	3	12	1	1	0	1	0	0	0	2	0	....	.083	.083	.250	.333	-3	-2	0	.46	0	/S-3	0	-0.1
1911 Pit-N	50	150	18	36	5	1	2	31	14	24	4	....	.240	.305	.327	.632	74	-6	16	3.51	4	S-33,2-11/3-1,O-1	5	0.1

YEAR TM-L	G	AB	R	H	2B	3B	HR	RBI	BB	SO	SB	CS	AVG	OBP	SLG	OPS	OPS+	BR/A	RC	RC/G	FR	G/POS	WS	TPW
1912 Pit-N	111	401	53	111	12	4	1	41	30	26	8	....	.277	.332	.334	.666	84	-9	48	3.97	16	*2-105/3-4	11	0.8
1913 Pit-N	31	74	7	15	5	0	0	10	7	7	1	....	.203	.298	.270	.568	66	-3	7	2.66	-2	3-12,S-12/2-6	2	-0.4
1914 Pit-N	57	173	14	26	0	1	1	14	6	17	2	....	.150	.192	.179	.371	11	-19	6	1.09	7	3-36,2-10/S-6	3	-1.1
1915 Pit-N	21	49	3	10	0	1	0	3	5	10	1	2	.204	.291	.245	.536	64	-3	4	2.20	0	/2-9,S-5,3-4,1-1	1	-0.2
Chi-N	23	72	4	19	3	0	1	6	5	7	2	3	.264	.329	.347	.676	105	-0	8	3.68	6	2-12,3-12/S-1	3	0.7
Yr.	44	121	7	29	3	1	1	9	10	17	3	5	.240	.313	.306	.619	88	-3	12	3.07	6	2-21,3-16/S-6,1-1	4	0.5
1916 Chi-N	37	107	10	26	2	3	0	6	11	7	1	....	.243	.341	.318	.659	93	-0	12	3.86	-3	2-34/S-3	3	-0.3
Pit-N	50	146	11	29	3	0	0	3	15	10	3	....	.199	.282	.219	.501	54	-7	11	2.33	2	S-39/2-7,3-5	2	-0.3
Yr.	87	253	21	55	5	3	0	9	26	17	4	....	.217	.308	.261	.569	71	-7	24	2.94	-1	S-42,2-41/3-5	5	-0.6
1917 Pit-N	49	151	15	33	4	0	0	8	11	13	1	....	.219	.276	.245	.521	58	-7	11	2.22	5	3-26,2-13/S-9	2	-0.1
Total 8	432	1335	136	306	34	11	5	122	104	123	23	5	.229	.295	.282	.577	67	-56	124	2.92	36	2-207,S-111,3-100/1-1,0-1	32	-0.9

• MCCARTHY, Bill William John McCarthy b: 2/14/1886, Boston, MA d: 2/4/1928, Washington, DC TR Deb: 6/5/1905

YEAR TM-L	G	AB	R	H	2B	3B	HR	RBI	BB	SO	SB	CS	AVG	OBP	SLG	OPS	OPS+	BR/A	RC	RC/G	FR	G/POS	WS	TPW
1905 Bos-N	1	3	0	0	0	0	0	0	0	....	0	....	.000	.000	.000	.000	-102	-1	0	.00	-1	/C-1	0	-0.1
1907 Cin-N	3	8	1	1	0	0	0	0	0	....	0	....	.125	.125	.125	.250	-21	-1	0	.48	0	/C-3	0	-0.1
Total 2	4	11	1	1	0	0	0	0	0	....	0	....	.091	.091	.091	.182	-43	-2	0	.33	-1	/C-4	0	-0.2

• MCCARTHY, Jack John Arthur McCarthy b: 3/26/1869, Gilbertville, MA d: 9/11/1931, Chicago, IL BL/TL, 5'9", 155 lbs. Deb: 8/3/1893 U Career OF: 843-121-83

YEAR TM-L	G	AB	R	H	2B	3B	HR	RBI	BB	SO	SB	CS	AVG	OBP	SLG	OPS	OPS+	BR/A	RC	RC/G	FR	G/POS	WS	TPW
1893 Cin-N	49	195	28	55	8	3	0	22	22	7	6	....	.282	.355	.354	.709	86	-4	27	5.16	0	0-47(10-1-37)/1-2	5	-0.6
1894 Cin-N	40	167	29	45	9	1	0	21	17	6	3	....	.269	.348	.335	.683	63	-10	21	4.48	2	0-25(5-0-20),1-15	2	-0.8
1898 Pit-N	137	537	75	155	13	12	4	78	34	....	7	....	.289	.336	.380	.716	107	3	75	4.94	3	*0-137(137-0-0)	16	-0.6
1899 Pit-N	139	565	109	173	22	17	4	69	39	....	28	....	.306	.355	.427	.782	114	9	101	6.37	-4	*0-138(132-6-0)	17	-0.6
1900 Chi-N	124	503	68	148	16	7	0	48	24	....	22	....	.294	.329	.354	.683	92	-6	69	4.98	-0	*0-123(96-1-26)	12	-1.5
1901 Cle-A	86	343	60	110	14	7	0	32	30	....	9	....	.321	.382	.402	.784	123	12	60	6.31	-2	0-86(85-1-0)	11	0.4
1902 Cle-A	95	359	45	102	31	5	0	41	24	....	12	....	.284	.329	.398	.727	105	2	54	5.22	-2	0-95(95-0-0)	9	-0.6
1903 Cle-A	108	415	47	110	20	8	0	43	19	....	15	....	.265	.299	.352	.651	96	-3	52	4.19	1	*0-108(108-0-0)	10	-0.9
Chi-N	24	101	11	28	5	0	0	14	4	....	8	....	.277	.305	.327	.631	82	-3	13	4.60	-2	0-24(24-0-0)	2	-0.6
1904 Chi-N	115	432	36	114	14	2	0	51	23	....	14	....	.264	.307	.306	.613	89	-6	48	3.73	-6	*0-115(25-90-0)	13	-1.9
1905 Chi-N	59	170	16	47	4	3	0	14	10	....	8	....	.276	.320	.335	.656	92	-2	22	4.46	3	0-37(18-19-0)/1-6	5	-0.1
1906 Bro-N	91	322	23	98	13	1	0	35	20	....	9	....	.304	.347	.351	.698	128	9	45	4.96	-1	0-86(83-3-0)	13	0.4
1907 Bro-N	25	91	4	20	2	0	0	8	2	....	4	....	.220	.237	.242	.478	54	-5	7	2.32	-2	0-25(25-0-0)	0	-0.9
Total 12	1092	4200	551	1205	171	66	8	476	268	13	145	....	.287	.333	.365	.698	101	-3	593	4.97	-11	*0-1046/1-23	115	-8.2

• MCCARTHY, Jerry Jerome Francis McCarthy b: 5/23/1923, Brooklyn, NY d: 10/3/1965, Oceanside, NY BL/TL, 6'1", 205 lbs. Deb: 6/19/1948

YEAR TM-L	G	AB	R	H	2B	3B	HR	RBI	BB	SO	SB	CS	AVG	OBP	SLG	OPS	OPS+	BR/A	RC	RC/G	FR	G/POS	WS	TPW
1948 StL-A	2	3	0	1	0	0	0	0	0	0	0	0	.333	.333	.333	.667	76	-0	0	4.61	-1	/1-2	0	-0.1

• MCCARTHY, Joe Joseph N. McCarthy b: 12/25/1881, Syracuse, NY d: 1/12/1937, Syracuse, NY BR/TR Deb: 9/27/1905

YEAR TM-L	G	AB	R	H	2B	3B	HR	RBI	BB	SO	SB	CS	AVG	OBP	SLG	OPS	OPS+	BR/A	RC	RC/G	FR	G/POS	WS	TPW
1905 NY-A	1	2	0	0	0	0	0	0	0	....	0	....	.000	.000	.000	.000	-90	-0	0	.00	0	/C-1	0	0.0
1906 StL-N	15	37	3	9	2	0	0	2	2	....	0	....	.243	.282	.297	.579	84	-1	3	2.95	0	C-15	1	0.0
Total 2	16	39	3	9	2	0	0	2	2	....	0	....	.231	.268	.282	.550	76	-1	3	2.76	0	/C-16	1	0.0

• MCCARTHY, Johnny John Joseph McCarthy b: 1/7/1910, Chicago, IL d: 9/13/1973, Mundelein, IL BL/TL, 6'1.5", 185 lbs. Deb: 9/2/1934 Career OF: 1-1-3

YEAR TM-L	G	AB	R	H	2B	3B	HR	RBI	BB	SO	SB	CS	AVG	OBP	SLG	OPS	OPS+	BR/A	RC	RC/G	FR	G/POS	WS	TPW
1934 Bro-N	17	39	7	7	2	0	1	5	2	2	0	....	.179	.220	.308	.527	42	-3	3	2.02	0	1-13	0	-0.4
1935 Bro-N	22	48	9	12	1	1	0	4	2	9	1	....	.250	.280	.313	.593	60	-3	4	3.34	-3	1-19	0	-0.7
1936 NY-N	4	16	1	7	0	0	1	2	0	1	1	....	.438	.438	.625	1.063	185	2	4	10.38	1	/1-4	1	0.2
1937*NY-N	114	420	53	117	19	3	10	65	24	37	2	....	.279	.322	.410	.732	96	-3	56	4.69	-1	*1-110	11	-1.5
1938 NY-N	134	470	55	128	13	4	8	59	39	28	3	....	.272	.329	.368	.697	91	-6	60	4.56	-1	*1-125	11	-1.9
1939 NY-N	50	80	12	21	6	1	1	11	3	8	0	....	.263	.298	.400	.698	85	-2	9	4.00	-2	1-12/0-4(0-1-3),P-1	1	-0.7
1940 NY-N	51	67	6	16	4	0	0	5	2	8	0	....	.239	.261	.299	.559	53	-4	4	2.23	1	/1-6	0	-0.4
1941 NY-N	14	40	1	13	3	0	0	12	3	0	0	....	.325	.372	.400	.772	115	1	6	5.64	1	/1-8,0-1	1	0.1
1943 Bos-N	78	313	32	95	24	6	2	33	10	19	1	....	.304	.327	.438	.765	122	6	41	4.78	2	1-78	9	0.4
1946 Bos-N	2	7	0	1	0	0	0	1	2	0	0	....	.143	.333	.143	.476	37	-0	1	2.28	0	/1-2	0	-0.1
1948 NY-N	56	57	6	15	0	1	2	12	3	2	0	....	.263	.300	.404	.704	88	-1	7	4.23	-1	/1-6	1	-0.2
Total 11	542	1557	182	432	72	16	25	209	90	114	8	....	.277	.319	.392	.712	96	-14	194	4.45	-4	1-383/0-5,P-1	35	-5.1

• MCCARTHY, Tommy Thomas Francis Michael McCarthy
b: 7/24/1863, Boston, MA d: 8/5/1922, Boston, MA BR/TR, 5'7", 170 lbs. Deb: 7/10/1884 M/U HOF: 1946 Career OF: 514-32-658 ♦

YEAR TM-L	G	AB	R	H	2B	3B	HR	RBI	BB	SO	SB	CS	AVG	OBP	SLG	OPS	OPS+	BR/A	RC	RC/G	FR	G/POS	WS	TPW
1884 Bos-U	53	209	37	45	2	2	0	....	6	....	....	....	.215	.237	.244	.481	64	-7	12	2.12	0	0-48(41-2-7)/P-7	4	-1.9
1885 Bos-N	40	148	16	27	2	0	0	11	5	25	....	....	.182	.209	.196	.405	33	-11	6	1.39	2	0-40(39-0-1)	0	-0.9
1886 Phi-N	8	27	6	5	2	1	0	3	2	3	1	....	.185	.241	.333	.575	72	-1	2	3.04	0	/0-8(0-0-8),P-1	1	-0.1
1887 Phi-N	18	72	7	15	4	0	0	6	2	5	15	....	.208	.219	.243	.462	27	-7	7	3.34	-5	/0-8(6-2-0),2-5,S-3,3-2	1	-1.1
1888*StL-a	131	511	107	140	20	3	1	68	38	....	93	....	.274	.328	.331	.659	100	-1	88	6.41	24	*0-131(0-12-119)/P-2	19	1.8
1889 StL-a	140	604	136	176	24	7	2	63	46	26	57	....	.291	.348	.364	.712	91	-10	99	6.11	10	*0-140(1-3-137)/2-2,P-1	19	-0.4
1890 StL-a	133	548	137	192	28	9	6	69	66	....	**83**	....	.350	.430	.467	.898	144	30	150	**11.13**	5	*0-102(2-0-100),3-32/2-1	24	3.0
1891 StL-a	134	570	124	176	20	6	8	92	49	19	37	....	.309	.374	.407	.781	107	2	103	6.93	5	*0-113(7-0-117),2-14,S-12/3,P	22	0.4
1892*Bos-N	152	603	119	146	19	5	4	63	93	29	53	....	.242	.347	.310	.657	91	-5	85	5.05	4	*0-152(0-1-151)	21	-0.9
1893 Bos-N	116	462	107	160	28	6	5	111	64	10	46	....	.346	.429	.465	.894	128	19	115	10.07	0	*0-108(88-3-17)/2-7,S-3	24	0.9
1894 Bos-N	127	539	118	188	21	8	13	126	59	17	43	....	.349	.419	.490	.909	105	3	132	9.76	9	*0-127(119-9-0)/S-2,2-1,P	19	0.1
1895 Bos-N	117	452	90	131	13	2	2	73	72	12	18	....	.290	.391	.341	.732	85	-7	71	5.73	-9	*0-109(109-0-0)/2-9	11	-2.1
1896 Bro-N	104	377	62	94	8	4	3	47	34	17	22	....	.249	.316	.316	.632	71	-15	47	4.25	-2	*0-103(102-0-1)	5	-2.2
Total 13	1273	5122	1066	1495	191	53	44	732	536	163	468	....	.292	.364	.375	.740	99	-10	918	6.68	42	*0-1189/2-39,3-37,S-20,P-13	170	-3.2

• MCCARTON, Frank Francis McCarton b: 10/6/1854, NY d: 6/17/1907, New York, NY Deb: 4/26/1872

YEAR TM-L	G	AB	R	H	2B	3B	HR	RBI	BB	SO	SB	CS	AVG	OBP	SLG	OPS	OPS+	BR/A	RC	RC/G	FR	G/POS	WS	TPW
1872 Man-n	19	85	17	28	4	1	0	10	1	3	0	0	.329	.337	.400	.737	134	4	12	6.39	-2	0-19(0-18-1)	....	0.1

• MCCARTY, David David Andrew McCarty b: 11/23/1969, Houston, TX BR/TL, 6'5", 215 lbs. Deb: 5/17/1993 Career OF: 92-2-73

YEAR TM-L	G	AB	R	H	2B	3B	HR	RBI	BB	SO	SB	CS	AVG	OBP	SLG	OPS	OPS+	BR/A	RC	RC/G	FR	G/POS	WS	TPW
1993 Min-A	98	350	36	75	15	2	2	21	19	80	2	6	.214	.257	.286	.542	45	-30	22	2.00	2	0-67(38-2-34),1-36/D-2	2	-3.3
1994 Min-A	44	131	21	34	8	2	1	12	7	32	2	1	.260	.322	.374	.696	79	-4	16	4.15	3	1-32,0-14(9-0-5)	2	-0.4
1995 Min-A	25	55	10	12	3	1	0	4	4	18	0	1	.218	.283	.309	.592	54	-4	5	2.72	-1	1-18/0-5(2-0-4)	0	-0.6
SF-N	12	20	1	5	1	0	0	2	2	4	1	0	.250	.318	.300	.618	66	-1	2	4.03	-1	/0-4(0-0-4),1-2	1	-0.2
1996 SF-N	91	175	16	38	3	0	6	24	18	43	2	1	.217	.297	.337	.635	70	-8	17	3.26	-3	1-51,0-20(5-0-15)	2	-1.4
1998 Sea-A	8	18	1	5	0	0	1	2	5	4	1	0	.278	.435	.444	.879	130	1	4	8.87	-1	/0-5(0-0-5),1-2	1	0.0
2000 KC-A	103	270	34	75	14	2	12	53	22	68	0	0	.278	.332	.478	.810	98	-2	42	5.55	10	1-63,0-11(7-0-4)/D-7	7	0.2
2001 KC-A	98	200	26	50	10	0	7	26	24	45	0	0	.250	.333	.405	.738	86	-4	26	4.34	-1	1-68/0-9(8-0-1),D-5	2	-0.9
2002 KC-A	13	32	3	3	1	0	1	2	2	10	0	0	.094	.147	.219	.366	-4	-5	1	.80	0	/1-9,D-2	0	-0.6
TB-A	12	34	2	6	0	0	1	2	4	9	0	0	.176	.300	.265	.565	53	-2	3	3.05	0	0-11(11-0-0)	0	-0.2
Yr.	25	66	5	9	1	0	2	4	6	19	0	0	.136	.230	.242	.472	27	-7	4	1.89	0	0-11(11-0-0)/1-9,D-2	0	-0.8
2003 Oak-A	8	26	2	7	2	0	0	2	1	7	0	0	.269	.296	.346	.642	68	-1	3	3.77	-1	/0-5(5-0-0),1-3	0	-0.3
*Bos-A	16	27	4	11	3	0	1	6	2	7	0	0	.407	.448	.630	1.078	176	3	8	13.25	-1	/0-8(7-0-1),1-5,D-1	2	0.2
Yr.	24	53	6	18	5	0	1	8	3	14	0	0	.340	.375	.491	.866	123	2	11	7.99	-2	0-13(12-0-1)/1-8,D-1	2	-0.1
Total 9	528	1338	156	321	60	7	32	156	110	327	8	9	.240	.303	.367	.670	73	-57	149	3.74	7	1-289,0-159/D-17	19	-7.4

• MCCARTY, Lew George Lewis McCarty b: 11/17/1888, Milton, PA d: 6/9/1930, Reading, PA BR/TR, 5'11.5", 192 lbs. Deb: 8/30/1913

YEAR TM-L	G	AB	R	H	2B	3B	HR	RBI	BB	SO	SB	CS	AVG	OBP	SLG	OPS	OPS+	BR/A	RC	RC/G	FR	G/POS	WS	TPW
1913 Bro-N	9	26	1	6	0	0	0	2	2	2	0	....	.231	.286	.231	.516	47	-2	2	2.04	1	/C-9	0	-0.1
1914 Bro-N	90	284	20	72	14	2	1	30	14	22	1	....	.254	.293	.327	.621	83	-7	27	3.18	1	C-84	7	0.0
1915 Bro-N	84	276	19	66	9	4	0	19	7	23	7	4	.239	.261	.301	.561	68	-12	23	2.74	1	C-81	7	-0.5
1916 Bro-N	55	150	17	47	6	1	0	13	14	16	4	....	.313	.383	.367	.750	127	6	24	5.59	1	C-27,1-17	7	0.9
NY-N	25	68	6	27	3	4	0	9	7	9	0	....	.397	.453	.559	1.012	222	10	18	10.60	-1	C-24	6	1.3
Yr.	80	218	23	74	9	5	0	22	21	25	4	....	.339	.405	.427	.832	156	15	41	6.99	0	C-51,1-17	13	2.1
1917*NY-N	56	162	15	40	3	2	2	19	14	6	1	....	.247	.311	.327	.638	99	-0	16	3.38	-8	C-54	6	-0.4
1918 NY-N	86	257	16	69	7	3	0	24	17	13	3	....	.268	.321	.319	.640	97	-1	27	3.57	-9	C-75	9	-0.4

YEAR TM-L	G	AB	R	H	2B	3B	HR	RBI	BB	SO	SB	CS	AVG	OBP	SLG	OPS	OPS+	BR/A	RC	RC/G	FR	G/POS	WS	TPW
1919 NY-N	85	210	17	59	5	4	2	21	18	15	2	....	.281	.341	.371	.712	115	4	27	4.41	-8	C-59	9	0.1
1920 NY-N	36	38	2	5	0	0	0	0	4	2	2	0	.132	.214	.132	.346	1	-4	1	1.17	0	/C-5	0	-0.4
StL-N	5	7	0	2	0	0	0	0	5	0	0	0	.286	.583	.286	.869	158	1	2	9.79	1	/C-3	1	0.2
Yr.	41	45	2	7	0	0	0	0	9	2	2	0	.156	.296	.156	.452	36	-3	3	2.30	1	/C-8	1	-0.2
1921 StL-N	1	1	0	0	0	0	0	0	0	1	0	0	.000	.000	.000	.000	-102	-0	0	.00	0	....	0	0.0
Total 9	532	1479	113	393	47	20	5	137	102	109	20	4	.266	.318	.335	.653	98	-5	167	3.82	-22	C-421/1-17	52	0.7

• MCCARVER, Tim James Timothy McCarver b: 10/16/1941, Memphis, TN BL/TR, 6', 195 lbs. Deb: 9/10/1959 Career OF: 15-0-1

YEAR TM-L	G	AB	R	H	2B	3B	HR	RBI	BB	SO	SB	CS	AVG	OBP	SLG	OPS	OPS+	BR/A	RC	RC/G	FR	G/POS	WS	TPW
1959 StL-N	8	24	3	4	1	0	0	0	2	1	0	0	.167	.231	.208	.439	17	-3	1	1.72	-1	/C-6	0	-0.3
1960 StL-N	10	10	3	2	0	0	0	0	0	2	0	0	.200	.200	.200	.400	9	-1	0	.60	-1	/C-5	0	-0.2
1961 StL-N	22	67	5	16	2	1	1	6	0	5	0	0	.239	.239	.343	.582	47	-5	5	2.64	-1	C-20	1	-0.5
1963 StL-N	127	405	39	117	12	7	4	51	27	43	5	2	.289	.336	.383	.719	97	-0	53	4.75	-4	*C-126	15	0.2
1964*StL-N	143	465	53	134	19	3	9	52	40	44	2	0	.288	.346	.400	.746	101	2	64	4.99	-9	*C-137	17	0.0
1965 StL-N	113	409	48	113	17	2	11	48	31	26	5	1	.276	.329	.408	.737	97	-1	55	4.84	-6	*C-111	15	0.0
1966 StL-N★	150	543	50	149	19	**13**	12	68	36	38	9	6	.274	.322	.424	.745	105	3	71	4.64	-2	*C-148	21	0.8
1967*StL-N★	138	471	68	139	26	3	14	69	54	32	8	8	.295	.374	.452	.826	138	23	78	5.87	1	*C-130	30	3.3
1968*StL-N	128	434	35	110	15	6	5	48	26	31	4	3	.253	.297	.350	.647	95	-4	44	3.54	-1	*C-109	14	0.1
1969 StL-N	138	515	46	134	27	3	7	51	49	26	4	9	.260	.327	.365	.692	93	-7	60	3.95	0	*C-136	14	0.0
1970 Phi-N	44	164	16	47	11	1	4	14	14	10	2	2	.287	.346	.439	.785	112	2	24	5.31	1	C-44	7	0.5
1971 Phi-N	134	474	51	132	20	5	8	46	43	26	5	3	.278	.340	.392	.732	107	4	62	4.63	2	*C-125	16	1.3
1972 Phi-N	45	152	14	36	8	0	2	14	17	15	1	2	.237	.322	.329	.651	83	-4	17	3.65	0	C-40	3	-0.2
Mon-N	77	239	19	60	5	1	5	20	19	14	4	4	.251	.309	.343	.652	84	-6	24	3.35	0	C-45,0-14(14-0-1)/3-6	6	-0.5
Yr.	122	391	33	96	13	1	7	34	36	29	5	6	.246	.314	.338	.652	83	-10	40	3.47	0	C-85,0-14(14-0-1)/3-6	9	-0.7
1973 StL-N	130	331	30	88	16	4	3	49	38	31	2	0	.266	.345	.366	.711	97	0	44	4.64	-4	1-77,C-11	10	-0.8
1974 StL-N	74	106	13	23	0	1	0	11	22	6	0	1	.217	.366	.236	.602	72	-3	11	3.35	-2	C-21/1-6	2	-0.4
Bos-A	11	28	3	7	1	0	0	1	4	1	1	0	.250	.344	.286	.629	77	-0	3	3.83	0	/C-8,D-2	1	0.0
1975 Bos-A	12	21	1	8	2	1	0	3	1	3	0	0	.381	.409	.571	.981	161	2	5	10.20	0	/C-7,1-1	2	0.2
Phi-N	47	59	6	15	2	0	1	7	14	7	0	0	.254	.397	.339	.736	102	1	9	5.57	-0	C-10/1-1	2	0.1
1976*Phi-N	90	155	26	43	11	2	3	29	35	14	2	1	.277	.414	.432	.846	136	9	31	7.18	-4	C-41/1-2	10	0.8
1977*Phi-N	93	169	28	54	13	2	6	30	28	11	3	5	.320	.422	.527	.949	146	11	37	7.69	-2	C-42/1-3	10	1.1
1978*Phi-N	90	146	18	36	9	1	1	14	28	24	2	2	.247	.375	.342	.717	101	1	20	4.56	-2	C-34,1-11	5	0.0
1979 Phi-N	79	137	13	33	5	1	1	12	19	12	2	0	.241	.338	.314	.651	76	-3	14	3.36	-1	C-31/0-1	3	-0.3
1980 Phi-N	6	5	2	1	1	0	0	2	1	0	0	0	.200	.333	.400	.733	98	0	0	1.79	0	/1-2	0	0.0
Total 21	1909	5529	590	1501	242	57	97	645	548	422	61	49	.271	.340	.388	.729	102	21	735	4.64	-35	*C-1387,1-103/0-15,3-6,D-2	204	5.1

• MCCAULEY, Al Allen A. McCauley b: 3/4/1863, Indianapolis, IN d: 8/24/1917, Indianapolis, IN BL/TL, 6', 180 lbs. Deb: 6/21/1884 U ♦

YEAR TM-L	G	AB	R	H	2B	3B	HR	RBI	BB	SO	SB	CS	AVG	OBP	SLG	OPS	OPS+	BR/A	RC	RC/G	FR	G/POS	WS	TPW
1884 Ind-a	17	53	7	10	0	1	0	5	12	....	....	....	.189	.358	.226	.585	97	3	4	2.82	1	P-10/1-5,0-3(0-0-3)	3	-0.9
1890 Phi-N	116	418	63	102	25	7	1	42	57	38	8	....	.244	.346	.344	.690	99	0	54	4.52	-18	*1-116	8	-2.5
1891 Was-a	59	206	36	58	5	8	1	31	30	13	9	....	.282	.378	.398	.776	128	8	35	6.32	-3	1-59	7	0.1
Total 3	192	677	106	170	30	16	2	78	99	51	17	....	.251	.357	.352	.708	107	11	94	4.90	-20	1-180/P-10,0-3	18	-3.3

• MCCAULEY, Bill William H. McCauley b: 12/20/1869, Washington, DC d: 1/27/1926, Washington, DC Deb: 8/31/1895

YEAR TM-L	G	AB	R	H	2B	3B	HR	RBI	BB	SO	SB	CS	AVG	OBP	SLG	OPS	OPS+	BR/A	RC	RC/G	FR	G/POS	WS	TPW
1895 Was-N	1	2	0	0	0	0	0	0	0	0	0	....	.000	.000	.000	.000	-101	-1	0	.00	0	/S-1	0	-0.1

• MCCAULEY, Jim James Adelbert McCauley b: 3/24/1863, Stanley, NY d: 9/14/1930, Canandaigua, NY BL/TR, 6', 180 lbs. Deb: 9/17/1884

YEAR TM-L	G	AB	R	H	2B	3B	HR	RBI	BB	SO	SB	CS	AVG	OBP	SLG	OPS	OPS+	BR/A	RC	RC/G	FR	G/POS	WS	TPW
1884 StL-a	1	2	0	0	0	0	0	0	0	....	....	....	.000	.000	.000	.000	-97	-0	0	.00	0	/C-1	0	0.0
1885 Buf-N	24	84	4	15	2	1	0	7	11	12	....	....	.179	.274	.226	.500	61	-3	5	2.09	4	C-21/0-4(0-4-0)	1	0.2
Chi-N	3	6	1	1	0	0	0	0	2	3	....	....	.167	.375	.167	.542	70	-0	0	2.08	-1	/C-2,0-2(0-0-2)	0	-0.1
Yr.	27	90	5	16	2	1	0	7	13	15	....	....	.178	.282	.222	.504	62	-3	6	2.08	3	C-23/0-6(0-4-2)	1	0.1
1886 Bro-a	11	30	5	7	1	0	0	3	11	....	2	....	.233	.439	.267	.706	122	2	5	5.28	-3	C-11	2	0.0
Total 3	39	122	10	23	3	1	0	10	24	15	2	....	.189	.322	.230	.551	76	-2	10	2.79	-1	/C-35,0-6	3	0.0

• MCCAULEY, Pat Patrick F. McCauley b: 6/10/1870, Ware, MA d: 1/17/1917, Hoboken, NJ TR, 5'10.5", 156 lbs. Deb: 9/5/1893 U

YEAR TM-L	G	AB	R	H	2B	3B	HR	RBI	BB	SO	SB	CS	AVG	OBP	SLG	OPS	OPS+	BR/A	RC	RC/G	FR	G/POS	WS	TPW
1893 StL-N	5	16	0	1	0	0	0	0	0	1	0	....	.063	.063	.063	.125	-67	-4	0	.11	0	/C-5	0	-0.3
1896 Was-N	26	84	14	21	3	0	3	11	7	8	3	....	.250	.315	.393	.708	86	-2	12	4.80	1	C-24/0-1	2	0.0
1903 NY-A	6	19	0	1	0	0	0	1	0	....	0	....	.053	.053	.053	.105	-64	-4	0	.08	-2	/C-6	0	-0.5
Total 3	37	119	14	23	3	0	3	12	7	9	3	....	.193	.244	.294	.538	45	-10	12	3.23	-1	/C-35,0-1	2	-0.8

• MCCHESNEY, Harry Harry Vincent "Pud" McChesney b: 6/1/1880, Pittsburgh, PA d: 8/11/1960, Pittsburgh, PA BR/TR, 5'9", 165 lbs. Deb: 9/17/1904

YEAR TM-L	G	AB	R	H	2B	3B	HR	RBI	BB	SO	SB	CS	AVG	OBP	SLG	OPS	OPS+	BR/A	RC	RC/G	FR	G/POS	WS	TPW
1904 Chi-N	22	88	9	23	6	2	0	11	4	....	2	....	.261	.293	.375	.668	106	0	11	4.21	-1	0-22(0-1-21)	3	-0.1

• MCCLAIN, Scott Scott Michael McClain b: 5/19/1972, Simi Valley, CA BR/TR, 6'3" Deb: 5/14/1998

YEAR TM-L	G	AB	R	H	2B	3B	HR	RBI	BB	SO	SB	CS	AVG	OBP	SLG	OPS	OPS+	BR/A	RC	RC/G	FR	G/POS	WS	TPW
1998 TB-A	9	20	2	2	0	0	0	0	2	6	0	0	.100	.217	.100	.317	-13	-3	1	.91	0	/1-5,3-3	0	-0.3

• MCCLANAHAN, Pete Robert Hugh McClanahan b: 10/24/1906, Cold Springs, TX d: 10/28/1987, Mont Belvieu, TX BR/TR, 5'9", 170 lbs. Deb: 4/24/1931

YEAR TM-L	G	AB	R	H	2B	3B	HR	RBI	BB	SO	SB	CS	AVG	OBP	SLG	OPS	OPS+	BR/A	RC	RC/G	FR	G/POS	WS	TPW
1931 Pit-N	7	4	2	2	0	0	0	0	2	0	0	....	.500	.667	.500	1.167	220	1	2	21.16	0	....	0	0.1

• MCCLELLAN, Bill William Henry McClellan b: 3/22/1856, Chicago, IL d: 7/3/1929, Chicago, IL BB/TL, 5'5.5", 156 lbs. Deb: 5/20/1878 Career OF: 0-5-49

YEAR TM-L	G	AB	R	H	2B	3B	HR	RBI	BB	SO	SB	CS	AVG	OBP	SLG	OPS	OPS+	BR/A	RC	RC/G	FR	G/POS	WS	TPW
1878 Chi-N	48	205	26	46	6	1	0	29	2	13	....	....	.224	.232	.263	.495	59	-10	13	2.22	-9	2-42/S-5,0-1	2	-1.5
1881 Pro-N	68	259	30	43	3	1	0	16	15	21	....	....	.166	.212	.185	.397	26	-21	10	1.30	-7	S-50,0-17(0-1-16)/2-1	2	-2.4
1883 Phi-N	80	326	42	75	21	4	1	33	19	18	....	....	.230	.272	.328	.601	89	-2	30	3.27	-2	*S-78/0-2(0-2-0),3-1	5	-0.1
1884 Phi-N	111	450	71	116	13	2	3	33	28	43	....	....	.258	.301	.316	.617	99	1	44	3.61	-6	*S-111/0-1	15	-0.1
1885 Bro-a	112	464	85	124	22	7	0	46	28	....	....	....	.267	.317	.345	.662	108	5	52	4.13	-9	3-57,2-55	14	-0.1
1886 Bro-a	141	595	131	152	33	9	1	68	56	....	43	....	.255	.322	.346	.668	108	6	82	5.00	-6	*2-141	19	0.4
1887 Bro-a	136	628	109	224	24	6	1	53	80	....	70	....	.357	.363	.334	.697	94	-1	94	6.29	-28	*2-136	14	-2.0
1888 Bro-a	74	278	33	57	7	3	0	21	40	....	13	....	.205	.307	.252	.559	80	-4	26	3.19	-1	2-56,0-18(0-1-17)	7	-0.3
Cle-a	22	72	6	16	0	0	0	5	6	....	6	....	.222	.282	.222	.504	64	-3	6	3.07	-3	0-15(0-0-15)/2-5,S-2	1	-0.5
Yr.	96	350	39	73	7	3	0	26	46	....	19	....	.209	.302	.246	.548	77	-7	32	3.17	-4	2-61,0-33(0-1-32)/S-2	8	-0.9
Total 8	792	3277	533	853	129	33	6	304	274	95	132	....	.260	.305	.308	.613	89	-29	358	4.00	-71	2-436,S-246/3-58,0-54	79	-6.7

• MCCLELLAN, Harvey Harvey McDowell "Little Mac" McClellan
b: 12/22/1894, Cynthiana, KY d: 11/6/1925, Cynthiana, KY BR/TR, 5'9.5", 143 lbs. Deb: 5/31/1919 Career OF: 0-1-16

YEAR TM-L	G	AB	R	H	2B	3B	HR	RBI	BB	SO	SB	CS	AVG	OBP	SLG	OPS	OPS+	BR/A	RC	RC/G	FR	G/POS	WS	TPW
1919 Chi-A	7	12	2	4	0	0	0	1	1	1	0	....	.333	.385	.333	.718	102	0	1	4.76	0	/3-3,S-2	1	0.0
1920 Chi-A	10	18	4	6	1	1	0	5	4	1	2	0	.333	.455	.500	.955	153	2	5	10.66	-4	/S-4,3-2	1	-0.1
1921 Chi-A	63	196	20	35	4	1	1	14	14	18	2	3	.179	.237	.224	.461	18	-25	11	1.69	7	2-21,0-15(0-0-15),S-15/3-5	2	-1.6
1922 Chi-A	91	301	28	68	17	3	2	28	16	32	3	2	.226	.272	.322	.594	55	-21	27	2.85	-3	3-71/S-8,2-2,0-1	4	-1.8
1923 Chi-A	141	550	67	129	29	3	1	41	27	44	14	11	.235	.270	.304	.574	51	-41	45	2.57	-14	*S-139/2-2	5	-3.8
1924 Chi-A	32	85	9	15	3	0	0	9	6	7	2	0	.176	.239	.212	.451	17	-10	5	1.79	0	S-21/2-7,3-1,0-1	1	-0.8
Total 6	344	1162	130	257	54	8	4	98	68	103	23	16	.221	.267	.292	.559	46	-94	95	2.54	-15	S-189/3-82,2-32,0-17	14	-8.1

• MCCLENDON, Lloyd Lloyd Glenn McClendon b: 1/11/1959, Gary, IN BR/TR, 5'10", 195 lbs. Deb: 4/6/1987 M/C Career OF: 138-0-130

YEAR TM-L	G	AB	R	H	2B	3B	HR	RBI	BB	SO	SB	CS	AVG	OBP	SLG	OPS	OPS+	BR/A	RC	RC/G	FR	G/POS	WS	TPW
1987 Cin-N	45	72	8	15	5	0	2	13	4	15	1	0	.208	.250	.361	.611	57	-5	7	3.00	-1	C-12/1-5,3-1,0-1	0	-0.6
1988 Cin-N	72	137	9	30	4	0	3	14	15	22	4	0	.219	.305	.314	.619	75	-3	13	3.09	-1	C-23,0-17(11-0-6),1-12/3-2	2	-0.5
1989*Chi-N	92	259	47	74	12	1	12	40	37	31	6	4	.286	.377	.479	.856	133	12	48	6.52	-5	0-45(45-0-0),1-28/3-6,C-5	11	0.4
1990 Chi-N	49	107	5	17	3	0	1	10	14	21	1	0	.159	.256	.215	.471	29	-10	6	1.87	0	0-23(23-0-0)/1-8,C-8	1	-1.2
Pit-N	4	3	1	1	0	0	1	2	0	1	0	0	.333	.333	1.333	1.667	349	1	1	18.00	0	/0-1	0	0.1
Yr.	53	110	6	18	3	0	2	12	14	22	1	0	.164	.258	.245	.504	37	-9	8	2.21	0	0-24(24-0-0)/1-8,C-8	1	-1.1
1991*Pit-N	85	163	24	47	7	0	7	24	18	23	2	1	.288	.366	.460	.826	133	7	28	6.45	0	0-32(14-0-18),1-22/C-2	6	0.6
1992*Pit-N	84	190	26	48	8	1	3	20	28	24	1	3	.253	.355	.353	.707	102	0	24	4.24	-1	0-60(10-0-50),1-18	5	-0.3
1993 Pit-N	88	181	21	40	11	1	2	19	23	17	0	3	.221	.309	.326	.635	70	-9	18	3.21	1	0-61(21-0-47)/1-6	1	-1.0

YEAR TM-L	G	AB	R	H	2B	3B	HR	RBI	BB	SO	SB	CS	AVG	OBP	SLG	OPS	OPS+	BR/A	RC	RC/G	FR	G/POS	WS	TPW
1994 Pit-N	51	92	9	22	4	0	4	12	4	11	0	1	.239	.278	.413	.691	76	-4	10	3.80	-1	0-20(12-0-9)/1-2	1	-0.6
Total 8	570	1204	150	294	54	3	35	154	143	165	15	12	.244	.328	.381	.710	95	-11	157	4.38	-9	0-260,1-101/C-50,3-9	27	-3.0
• MCCLESKEY, Jeff	Jefferson Lamar McCleskey b: 11/6/1891, Americus, GA d: 5/11/1971, Americus, GA BL/TR, 5'11", 160 lbs. Deb: 9/8/1913																							
1913 Bos-N	2	3	0	0	0	0	0	0	1	0	0	....	.000	.250	.000	.250	-25	-0	0	.00	-1	/3-2	0	-0.1
• MCCLOSKEY,	McCloskey b: Brooklyn, NY Deb: 5/25/1875																							
1875 Was-n	11	40	1	7	0	0	0	4	1	2	0	1	.175	.195	.175	.370	31	-3	1	1.21	-4	C-11	....	-0.6
• MCCLOSKEY, Bill	William George McCloskey b: 5/1854, Philadelphia, PA, 5'8", 155 lbs. Deb: 8/18/1884																							
1884 Wil-U	9	30	0	3	0	0	0	....	0	....	....	....	.100	.100	.100	.200	-31	-4	0	.32	-2	/C-5,0-5(3-3-0)	0	-0.5
• MCCLURE, Hal	Harold Murray "Mac" McClure b: 8/8/1859, Lewisburg, PA d: 3/1/1919, Lewisburg, PA BR/TR, 6', 165 lbs. Deb: 5/10/1882																							
1882 Bos-N	2	6	1	2	0	0	0	0	0	1	....	....	.333	.333	.333	.667	114	0	1	4.70	-1	/0-2(0-0-2)	0	0.0
• MCCLURE, Larry	Lawrence Ledwith McClure b: 10/3/1885, Wayne, WV d: 8/31/1949, Huntington, WV BR/TR, 5'6.5", 130 lbs. Deb: 7/26/1910																							
1910 NY-A	1	1	0	0	0	0	0	0	0	....	0	....	.000	.000	.000	.000	-95	-0	0	.00	0	/0-1	0	0.0
• MCCONNELL, Amby	Ambrose Moses McConnell b: 4/29/1883, North Powell, VT d: 5/20/1942, Utica, NY BL/TR, 5'7", 150 lbs. Deb: 4/17/1908																							
1908 Bos-A	140	502	77	140	10	6	2	43	38	....	31	....	.279	.343	.335	.678	117	11	68	4.71	-15	*2-126/S-3	20	-0.3
1909 Bos-A	121	453	61	108	7	8	0	36	34	....	26	....	.238	.300	.289	.589	84	-8	47	3.40	14	*2-121	12	0.9
1910 Bos-A	11	35	6	6	0	0	0	1	5	....	4	....	.171	.310	.171	.481	50	-2	3	2.73	0	2-10	1	-0.2
Chi-A	33	120	13	33	2	3	0	5	7	....	4	....	.275	.320	.342	.662	113	1	14	4.12	-6	2-32	5	-0.4
Yr.	44	155	19	39	2	3	0	6	12	....	8	....	.252	.318	.303	.621	97	-0	17	3.77	-6	2-42	6	-0.6
1911 Chi-A	104	396	45	111	11	5	1	34	23	....	7	....	.280	.331	.341	.672	90	-6	47	4.10	-2	*2-103	11	-0.7
Total 4	409	1506	202	398	30	22	3	119	107	....	72	....	.264	.324	.319	.644	98	-3	179	4.05	-9	2-392/S-3	49	-0.7
• MCCONNELL, George	George Neely "Slats" McConnell b: 9/16/1877, Shelbyville, TN d: 5/10/1964, Chattanooga, TN BR/TR, 6'3", 190 lbs. Deb: 4/13/1909 ♦																							
1909 NY-A	13	43	4	9	0	1	0	5	1	....	1	....	.209	.227	.256	.483	52	-2	3	1.97	2	1-11/P-2	0	-0.1
1912 NY-A	42	91	11	27	4	2	0	8	4	....	0	....	.297	.333	.385	.718	99	5	11	4.56	5	P-23/1-2	12	3.1
1913 NY-A	39	67	4	12	2	0	0	2	0	11	0	....	.179	.179	.209	.388	13	-2	3	1.11	4	P-35/1-1	7	-0.6
1914 Chi-N	1	2	0	0	0	0	0	0	0	1	0	....	.000	.000	.000	.000	-100	-0	0	.00	0	/P-1	1	0.1
1915 Chi-F	53	125	14	31	6	2	1	18	0	16	2	....	.248	.254	.352	.606	82	6	11	2.96	3	P-44	25	2.8
1916 Chi-N	28	57	2	9	0	0	0	0	2	4	0	....	.158	.200	.158	.358	10	-1	2	1.08	2	P-28	10	0.8
Total 6	176	385	35	88	12	5	1	33	7	32	3	....	.229	.248	.294	.542	59	5	30	2.51	16	P-133/1-14	55	6.2
• MCCONNELL, Sam	Samuel Faulkner McConnell b: 6/8/1895, Philadelphia, PA d: 6/27/1981, Phoenixville, PA BL/TR, 5'6.5", 150 lbs. Deb: 4/19/1915																							
1915 Phi-A	6	11	1	2	1	0	0	0	1	3	0	....	.182	.250	.273	.523	58	-1	1	2.21	-1	/3-5	0	-0.1
• MCCORMACK, Don	Donald Ross McCormack b: 9/18/1955, Omak, WA BR/TR, 6'3", 205 lbs. Deb: 9/30/1980																							
1980 Phi-N	2	1	0	1	0	0	0	0	0	0	0	0	1.000	1.000	1.000	2.000	436	0	1	∞	0	/C-2	0	0.0
1981 Phi-N	3	4	0	1	0	0	0	0	0	1	0	0	.250	.250	.250	.500	40	-0	0	.00	0	/C-3	0	0.0
Total 2	5	5	0	2	0	0	0	0	0	1	0	0	.400	.400	.400	.800	119	0	1	.00	0	/C-5	0	0.0
• MCCORMICK, Barry	William J. McCormick b: 12/25/1874, Maysville, KY d: 1/28/1956, Cincinnati, OH TR, 5'9" Deb: 9/25/1895 U Career OF: 0-1-1																							
1895 Lou-N	3	12	2	3	0	1	0	0	0	0	1	....	.250	.250	.417	.667	75	-1	2	4.30	0	/S-2,2-1	0	-0.1
1896 Chi-N	45	168	22	37	3	1	1	23	14	30	9	....	.220	.280	.268	.548	43	-14	16	3.14	-4	3-35/S-6,2-3,0-1	1	-1.5
1897 Chi-N	101	419	87	112	8	10	2	55	33	....	44	....	.267	.324	.348	.672	75	-17	63	5.41	-7	3-56,S-46/2-1	9	-1.7
1898 Chi-N	137	530	76	131	15	9	2	78	47	....	15	....	.247	.314	.321	.635	82	-12	61	3.95	4	*3-136/2-1,S-1	13	-0.6
1899 Chi-N	102	376	48	97	15	2	2	52	25	....	14	....	.258	.311	.324	.636	76	-12	45	4.09	-7	2-99/S-3	9	-1.3
1900 Chi-N	110	379	35	83	13	5	3	48	38	....	8	....	.219	.292	.303	.595	67	-17	39	3.30	-12	S-84,3-21/2-5	6	-2.2
1901 Chi-N	115	427	45	100	15	6	1	32	31	....	12	....	.234	.288	.304	.592	74	-14	42	3.39	-12	*S-112/3-3	7	-2.1
1902 StL-A	139	504	55	124	14	4	3	51	37	....	10	....	.246	.304	.308	.612	71	-19	53	3.58	-10	*3-132/S-7,0-1	9	-2.4
1903 StL-A	61	207	13	45	6	1	1	16	18	....	5	....	.217	.283	.271	.554	69	-7	18	2.90	-2	2-28,3-28/S-4	5	-0.9
Was-A	63	219	14	47	10	2	0	23	10	....	3	....	.215	.255	.279	.534	59	-11	17	2.58	6	2-63	2	-0.4
Yr.	124	426	27	92	16	3	1	39	28	....	8	....	.216	.269	.275	.544	64	-18	35	2.74	4	2-91,3-28/S-4	7	-1.3
1904 Was-A	113	404	36	88	11	1	0	39	27	....	9	....	.218	.274	.250	.524	67	-14	32	2.61	-7	*2-113	4	-2.3
Total 10	989	3645	433	867	110	42	15	417	280	30	130	....	.238	.297	.303	.600	71	-139	388	3.60	-51	3-411,2-314,S-265/0-2	65	-15.5
• MCCORMICK, Frank	Frank Andrew "Buck" McCormick b: 6/9/1911, New York, NY d: 11/21/1982, Manhasset, NY BR/TR, 6'4", 205 lbs. Deb: 9/11/1934 C																							
1934 Cin-N	12	16	1	5	2	1	0	5	0	1	0	....	.313	.313	.563	.875	132	1	2	5.19	-1	/1-2	0	0.0
1937 Cin-N	24	83	5	27	5	0	0	9	2	4	1	....	.325	.341	.386	.727	102	-0	9	4.06	-1	1-20/2-4,0-1	1	-0.3
1938 Cin-N★	151	640	89	**209**	40	4	5	106	18	17	1	....	.327	.348	.425	.773	115	10	93	5.49	-5	*1-151	19	-1.0
1939*Cin-N★	156	630	99	**209**	41	4	18	**128**	40	16	1	....	.332	.374	.495	.869	131	25	110	6.44	1	*1-156	25	1.2
1940*Cin-N★	155	618	93	**191**	**44**	3	19	127	52	26	2	....	.309	.367	.482	.850	131	25	104	6.24	5	*1-155	27	1.6
1941 Cin-N★	154	603	77	162	31	5	17	97	40	13	2	....	.269	.318	.421	.740	107	3	76	4.36	4	*1-154	20	-0.8
1942 Cin-N★	145	564	58	156	24	0	13	89	45	18	1	....	.277	.332	.388	.721	111	6	72	4.54	8	*1-144	17	0.1
1943 Cin-N★	126	472	56	143	28	0	8	59	29	15	2	....	.303	.345	.413	.758	120	10	67	5.29	-2	*1-120	19	0.1
1944 Cin-N★	153	581	85	177	37	3	20	102	57	17	7	....	.305	.371	.482	.853	144	33	101	6.40	9	*1-153	29	3.5
1945 Cin-N★	152	580	68	160	33	0	10	81	56	22	6	....	.276	.345	.384	.729	105	4	75	4.57	6	*1-151	17	0.1
1946 Phi-N★	135	504	46	143	20	2	11	66	36	21	2	....	.284	.333	.397	.730	110	4	66	4.73	4	*1-134	17	0.4
1947 Phi-N	15	40	7	9	2	0	1	8	3	2	0	....	.225	.279	.350	.629	68	-2	3	2.81	-1	1-12	0	-0.3
Bos-N	81	212	24	75	18	2	2	43	11	8	2	....	.354	.386	.486	.871	133	9	37	6.81	1	1-46	8	0.9
Yr.	96	252	31	84	20	2	3	51	14	10	2	....	.333	.368	.464	.833	123	7	40	6.07	1	1-58	8	0.6
1948*Bos-N	75	180	14	45	9	2	4	34	10	9	0	....	.250	.289	.389	.678	83	-5	19	3.61	3	1-50	3	-0.3
Total 13	1534	5723	722	1711	334	26	128	954	399	189	27	....	.299	.348	.434	.781	118	122	834	5.30	33	*1-1448/2-4,0-1	202	5.2
• MCCORMICK, Jerry	John McCormick b: Philadelphia, PA d: 9/19/1905, Philadelphia, PA Deb: 5/1/1883																							
1883 Bal-a	93	389	40	102	16	6	0	0	2	....	....	....	.262	.266	.334	.600	89	-6	35	3.46	-2	*3-93	6	-0.5
1884 Phi-U	67	295	41	84	12	2	0	....	4	....	....	....	.285	.294	.339	.633	123	8	30	4.00	10	3-54/2-5,0-5(5-0-1),S-3,P	8	1.5
Was-U	42	157	23	34	8	2	0	....	1	....	....	....	.217	.222	.293	.515	75	-4	10	2.38	-4	3-38/S-4	3	-0.6
Yr.	109	452	64	118	20	4	0	....	5	....	....	....	.261	.269	.323	.592	106	4	41	3.40	5	*3-92/S-7,2-5,0-5(5-0-1),P	11	0.9
Total 2	202	841	104	220	36	10	0	0	7	....	....	....	.262	.268	.328	.596	98	-2	76	3.43	4	3-185/S-7,2-5,0-5,P-1	17	0.4
• MCCORMICK, Jim	James Ambrose McCormick b: 11/2/1868, Spencer, MA d: 2/1/1948, Saco, ME BR/TR, 6'1", 160 lbs. Deb: 9/10/1892																							
1892 StL-N	3	11	0	0	0	0	0	0	1	5	0	....	.000	.083	.000	.083	-78	-2	0	.00	1	/2-2,3-1	0	-0.1
• MCCORMICK, Mike	Michael J. "Kid,Dude" McCormick b: 5/1883, Scotland d: 11/18/1953, Jersey City, NJ BR/TR, 5'3", 155 lbs. Deb: 4/14/1904																							
1904 Bro-N	105	347	28	64	5	4	0	27	43	....	22	....	.184	.278	.222	.500	56	-16	29	2.61	1	*3-104/2-1	6	-1.3
• MCCORMICK, Mike	Myron Winthrop McCormick b: 5/6/1917, Angel's Camp, CA d: 4/14/1976, Ventura, CA BR/TR, 6', 200 lbs. Deb: 4/16/1940 Career OF: 302-310-65																							
1940*Cin-N	110	417	48	125	20	0	1	30	13	36	8	....	.300	.326	.355	.681	87	-8	48	4.07	5	*0-107(51-50-6)	12	-0.8
1941 Cin-N	110	369	52	106	17	3	4	31	30	24	4	....	.287	.341	.382	.723	103	1	48	4.53	4	*0-101(82-19-0)	15	0.0
1942 Cin-N	40	135	18	32	2	3	1	11	13	7	0	....	.237	.304	.319	.623	82	-3	13	3.30	0	0-38(13-26-0)	3	-0.5
1943 Cin-N	4	15	0	2	0	0	0	0	2	0	0	....	.133	.235	.133	.369	8	-2	1	.95	0	/0-4(0-4-0)	0	-0.2
1946 Cin-N	23	74	10	16	2	0	0	5	8	4	0	....	.216	.293	.243	.536	55	-4	6	2.38	0	0-21(0-21-0)	1	-0.5
Bos-N	59	164	23	43	6	2	1	16	11	7	0	....	.262	.309	.341	.650	83	-4	18	3.80	-2	0-48(10-33-5)	4	-0.8
Yr.	82	238	33	59	8	2	1	21	19	11	0	....	.248	.304	.311	.614	74	-8	23	3.32	-2	0-69(10-54-5)	5	-1.4
1947 Bos-N	92	284	42	81	13	7	3	36	20	21	1	....	.285	.332	.412	.744	99	-1	37	4.45	-1	0-79(26-62-1)	7	-0.5
1948*Bos-N	115	343	45	104	22	7	1	39	32	34	1	....	.303	.363	.417	.780	112	6	52	5.57	0	*0-100(56-34-20)	11	0.1
1949*Bro-N	55	139	17	29	5	1	2	14	14	12	1	....	.209	.281	.302	.583	54	-9	12	2.70	-2	0-49(38-7-5)	1	-1.3
1950 NY-N	4	4	0	0	0	0	0	0	0	2	0	....	.000	.000	.000	.000	-99	-1	0	.00	0	....	0	-0.1

YEAR TM-L	G	AB	R	H	2B	3B	HR	RBI	BB	SO	SB	CS	AVG	OBP	SLG	OPS	OPS+	BR/A	RC	RC/G	FR	G/POS	WS	TPW
Chi-A	55	138	16	32	4	3	0	10	16	6	0	1	.232	.312	.304	.616	60	-9	12	2.88	1	0-44(2-42-0)	1	-0.8
1951 Was-A	81	243	31	70	9	3	1	23	29	20	1	2	.288	.364	.362	.726	98	-0	30	4.21	0	0-62(24-12-28)	5	-0.3
Total 10	748	2325	302	640	100	29	14	215	188	173	16	3	.275	.330	.361	.692	90	-35	277	4.09	4	0-653	60	-5.8

• MCCORMICK, Moose Harry Elwood McCormick b: 2/28/1881, Philadelphia, PA d: 7/9/1962, Lewisburg, PA BL/TL, 5'11", 180 lbs. Deb: 4/14/1904 Career OF: 172-55-101

YEAR TM-L	G	AB	R	H	2B	3B	HR	RBI	BB	SO	SB	CS	AVG	OBP	SLG	OPS	OPS+	BR/A	RC	RC/G	FR	G/POS	WS	TPW
1904 NY-N	59	203	28	54	9	5	1	26	13	....	13	....	.266	.323	.374	.697	110	2	29	5.14	-2	0-55(2-52-1)	8	-0.2
Pit-N	66	238	25	69	10	6	2	23	13	....	6	....	.290	.332	.408	.740	125	6	36	5.29	-5	0-66(18-0-48)	9	-0.2
Yr.	125	441	53	123	19	11	3	49	26	....	19	....	.279	.328	.392	.720	118	8	65	5.22	-7	*0-121(20-52-49)	17	-0.4
1908 Phi-N	11	22	0	2	0	0	0	2	2	....	0	....	.091	.167	.091	.258	-17	-3	0	.49	0	/0-5(5-0-0)	0	-0.4
NY-N	73	252	31	76	16	3	0	32	4	....	6	....	.302	.315	.389	.704	119	4	32	4.58	-7	0-65(59-0-12)	8	-0.8
Yr.	84	274	31	78	16	3	0	34	6	....	6	....	.285	.302	.365	.667	107	1	32	4.16	-7	0-70(64-0-12)	8	-1.2
1909 NY-N	110	413	68	120	21	8	3	27	49	....	4	....	.291	.373	.402	.775	138	19	63	5.43	-5	*0-110(87-0-23)	17	1.0
1912*NY-N	42	39	4	13	4	1	0	8	6	9	1	....	.333	.422	.487	.909	144	3	8	8.14	-1	/0-6(1-1-4),1-1	2	0.2
1913*NY-N	57	80	9	22	2	3	0	15	5	13	0	....	.275	.318	.375	.693	97	-1	9	3.94	-0	0-15(0-2-13)	2	-0.1
Total 5	418	1247	165	356	62	26	6	133	92	22	30	....	.285	.340	.391	.732	122	30	178	5.05	-19	0-322/1-1	46	-0.6

• MCCOSKY, Barney William Barney McCosky b: 4/11/1917, Coal Run, PA d: 9/6/1996, Venice, FL BL/TR, 6'1", 184 lbs. Deb: 4/18/1939 Career OF: 477-535-27

YEAR TM-L	G	AB	R	H	2B	3B	HR	RBI	BB	SO	SB	CS	AVG	OBP	SLG	OPS	OPS+	BR/A	RC	RC/G	FR	G/POS	WS	TPW
1939 Det-A	147	611	120	190	33	14	4	58	70	45	20	4	.311	.384	.430	.814	100	4	108	6.59	3	*0-145(0-145-0)	23	0.3
1940*Det-A	143	589	123	**200**	39	**19**	4	57	67	41	13	9	.340	.408	.491	.899	120	19	123	8.09	-3	*0-141(0-141-0)	24	1.2
1941 Det-A	127	494	80	160	25	8	3	55	61	33	8	3	.324	.401	.425	.827	108	9	92	7.09	3	*0-122(21-101-0)	19	0.8
1942 Det-A	154	600	75	176	28	11	7	50	68	37	11	5	.293	.365	.412	.777	109	9	94	5.63	5	*0-154(145-7-2)	19	0.5
1946 Det-A	25	91	11	18	5	0	1	11	17	9	0	0	.198	.324	.286	.610	67	-3	10	3.40	-1	0-24(0-24-0)	2	-0.5
Phi-A	92	308	33	109	17	4	1	34	43	13	2	2	.354	.433	.445	.878	146	21	63	7.89	-4	0-85(0-85-0)	12	1.6
Yr.	117	399	44	127	22	4	2	45	60	22	2	2	.318	.407	.409	.816	128	18	73	6.73	-5	*0-109(0-109-0)	14	1.1
1947 Phi-A	137	546	77	179	22	7	1	52	57	29	1	4	.328	.395	.399	.795	119	15	92	6.43	0	*0-136(114-23-0)	22	0.5
1948 Phi-A	135	515	95	168	21	5	0	46	68	22	1	3	.326	.405	.386	.791	111	10	86	6.09	-2	*0-134(134-0-0)	19	-0.1
1950 Phi-A	66	179	19	43	10	1	0	11	22	12	0	0	.240	.323	.307	.631	63	-10	19	3.55	-2	0-42(42-0-0)	1	-1.3
1951 Phi-A	12	27	4	8	2	0	1	1	3	4	0	0	.296	.367	.481	.848	125	1	5	7.35	-0	/0-7(5-0-2)	1	0.1
Cin-N	25	50	2	16	2	1	1	11	4	2	0	0	.320	.370	.460	.830	120	1	9	7.05	0	0-11(4-7-1)	2	0.1
Cle-A	31	61	8	13	3	0	0	2	8	5	1	0	.213	.304	.262	.567	57	-3	5	2.83	0	0-16(1-2-13)	1	-0.4
Yr.	43	88	12	21	5	0	1	3	11	9	1	0	.239	.323	.330	.653	78	-2	10	4.07	0	0-23(6-2-15)	2	-0.3
1952 Cle-A	54	80	14	17	4	1	1	6	8	5	1	1	.213	.284	.325	.609	74	-3	7	2.99	-1	0-19(11-0-9)	1	-0.4
1953 Cle-A	22	21	3	4	3	0	0	3	1	4	0	0	.190	.227	.333	.561	51	-1	2	2.68	0	....	0	-0.1
Total 11	1170	4172	664	1301	214	71	24	397	497	261	58	31	.312	.386	.414	.801	109	69	715	6.34	-3	*0-1036	146	2.1

• MCCOVEY, Willie Willie Lee "Stretch,Mac,Big Mac" McCovey b: 1/10/1938, Mobile, AL BL/TL, 6'4", 210 lbs. Deb: 7/30/1959 HOF: 1986 Career OF: 257-0-19

YEAR TM-L	G	AB	R	H	2B	3B	HR	RBI	BB	SO	SB	CS	AVG	OBP	SLG	OPS	OPS+	BR/A	RC	RC/G	FR	G/POS	WS	TPW
1959 SF-N	52	192	32	68	9	5	13	38	22	35	2	0	.354	.431	.656	1.087	189	25	53	10.89	0	1-51	12	2.2
1960 SF-N	101	260	37	62	15	3	13	51	45	53	1	1	.238	.351	.469	.820	130	11	45	5.96	-1	1-71	12	0.7
1961 SF-N	106	328	59	89	12	3	18	50	37	60	1	2	.271	.354	.491	.845	126	12	56	6.00	4	1-84	13	1.1
1962*SF-N	91	229	41	67	6	1	20	54	29	35	3	3	.293	.372	.590	.962	156	17	48	7.52	-1	0-57(45-0-12),1-17	12	1.2
1963 SF-N★	152	564	103	158	19	5	**44**	102	50	119	1	1	.280	.350	.566	.916	161	43	111	7.16	-5	*0-135(134-0-2),1-23	29	3.2
1964 SF-N	130	364	55	80	14	1	18	54	61	73	2	1	.220	.340	.412	.752	108	6	53	4.80	-4	0-83(78-0-5),1-26	11	-0.4
1965 SF-N	160	540	93	149	17	4	39	92	88	118	0	4	.276	.383	.539	.922	152	38	115	7.58	3	*1-156	29	3.5
1966 SF-N★	150	502	85	148	26	6	36	96	76	100	2	1	.295	.394	.586	.979	163	45	119	8.73	-0	*1-145	34	3.8
1967 SF-N	135	456	73	126	17	4	31	91	71	110	3	3	.276	.381	.535	.916	161	38	94	7.33	1	*1-127	24	3.3
1968 SF-N★	148	523	81	153	16	4	**36**	**105**	72	71	4	2	.293	.383	**.545**	**.928**	**176**	**50**	110	**7.60**	5	*1-146	**34**	**5.4**
1969 SF-N★	149	491	101	157	26	2	**45**	**126**	121	66	0	0	.320	**.458**	**.656**	**1.114**	**212**	**81**	151	**11.56**	-1	*1-148	**39**	**7.1**
1970 SF-N★	152	495	98	143	39	2	39	126	**137**	75	0	0	.289	.446	**.612**	**1.058**	**183**	**65**	140	10.26	14	*1-146	33	**6.7**
1971*SF-N★	105	329	45	91	13	0	18	70	64	57	0	2	.277	.401	.480	.881	151	24	65	6.98	1	1-95	16	1.9
1972 SF-N	81	263	30	56	8	0	14	35	38	45	0	0	.213	.317	.403	.720	102	1	35	4.53	-4	1-74	7	-0.9
1973 SF-N	130	383	52	102	14	3	29	75	105	78	1	0	.266	.425	.546	.971	161	37	95	8.79	2	*1-117	22	3.2
1974 SD-N	128	344	53	87	19	1	22	63	96	76	1	0	.253	.417	.506	.923	164	35	79	8.00	-7	*1-104	25	2.1
1975 SD-N	122	413	43	104	17	0	23	68	57	80	1	0	.252	.347	.460	.807	130	16	66	5.59	-1	*1-115	16	0.8
1976 SD-N	71	202	20	41	9	0	7	36	21	39	0	0	.203	.281	.351	.633	86	-4	20	3.23	5	1-51	4	-0.3
Oak-A	11	24	0	5	0	0	0	0	3	4	0	0	.208	.296	.208	.505	52	-1	2	2.32	0	/D-9	0	-0.2
1977 SF-N	141	478	54	134	21	0	28	86	67	106	3	0	.280	.369	.500	.869	131	22	86	6.41	-7	*1-136	16	0.8
1978 SF-N	108	351	32	80	19	2	12	64	36	57	1	0	.228	.300	.396	.696	97	-3	40	3.74	-1	1-97	8	-0.9
1979 SF-N	117	353	34	88	9	0	15	57	36	70	0	2	.249	.321	.402	.723	103	-0	45	4.39	-3	1-89	10	-0.8
1980 SF-N	48	113	8	23	8	0	1	16	13	23	0	0	.204	.291	.301	.592	67	-5	10	2.85	-1	1-27	2	-0.8
Total 22	2588	8197	1229	2211	353	46	521	1555	1345	1550	26	22	.270	.377	.515	.892	148	554	1638	7.07	-2	*1-2045,0-275/D-9	408	42.7

• MCCOY, Art Arthur Gray McCoy b: 7/1864, Danville, PA d: 3/22/1904, Danville, PA, 168 lbs. Deb: 7/8/1889

YEAR TM-L	G	AB	R	H	2B	3B	HR	RBI	BB	SO	SB	CS	AVG	OBP	SLG	OPS	OPS+	BR/A	RC	RC/G	FR	G/POS	WS	TPW
1889 Was-N	2	6	0	0	0	0	0	0	2	1	0	....	.000	.250	.000	.250	-29	-1	0	.00	-1	/2-2	0	-0.2

• MCCOY, Benny Benjamin Jenison McCoy b: 11/9/1915, Jenison, MI BL/TR, 5'9", 170 lbs. Deb: 9/14/1938

YEAR TM-L	G	AB	R	H	2B	3B	HR	RBI	BB	SO	SB	CS	AVG	OBP	SLG	OPS	OPS+	BR/A	RC	RC/G	FR	G/POS	WS	TPW
1938 Det-A	7	15	2	3	1	0	0	0	1	2	0	0	.200	.250	.267	.517	28	-2	1	2.26	-1	/2-6,3-1	0	-0.2
1939 Det-A	55	192	38	58	13	6	1	33	29	26	3	1	.302	.394	.448	.842	107	3	35	6.61	0	2-34,S-16	7	0.6
1940 Phi-A	134	490	56	126	26	5	7	62	65	44	2	2	.257	.345	.373	.719	88	-7	65	4.59	-4	*2-130/3-1	10	-0.3
1941 Phi-A	141	517	86	140	12	7	8	61	95	50	3	3	.271	.384	.368	.751	102	6	80	5.39	-3	*2-135	15	1.1
Total 4	337	1214	182	327	52	18	16	156	190	122	8	6	.269	.369	.381	.750	96	-1	182	5.21	-7	2-305/S-16,3-2	32	1.2

• MCCRACKEN, Quinton Quinton Antoine McCracken b: 3/16/1970, Wilmington, NC BB/TR, 5'7", 170 lbs. Deb: 9/17/1995 Career OF: 124-394-109

YEAR TM-L	G	AB	R	H	2B	3B	HR	RBI	BB	SO	SB	CS	AVG	OBP	SLG	OPS	OPS+	BR/A	RC	RC/G	FR	G/POS	WS	TPW
1995 Col-N	3	1	0	0	0	0	0	0	0	1	0	0	.000	.000	.000	.000	-78	-0	0	.00	0	/0-1	0	0.0
1996 Col-N	124	283	50	82	13	6	3	40	32	62	17	6	.290	.364	.410	.774	84	-5	44	5.28	-3	0-93(8-85-4)	7	-0.8
1997 Col-N	147	325	69	95	11	1	3	36	42	62	28	11	.292	.375	.360	.735	76	-9	47	5.02	-3	*0-133(0-133-0)	8	-1.0
1998 TB-A	155	614	77	179	38	7	7	59	41	107	19	10	.292	.339	.410	.749	92	-8	84	4.78	10	*0-153(58-103-0)	12	0.0
1999 TB-A	40	148	20	37	6	1	1	18	14	23	6	5	.250	.319	.324	.643	64	-9	14	2.94	-1	0-40(26-20-0)	2	-1.0
2000 TB-A	15	31	5	4	0	0	0	2	6	4	0	1	.129	.270	.129	.399	6	-5	1	.79	0	0-11(9-3-0)	0	-0.4
2001 Min-A	24	64	7	14	2	2	0	3	5	13	0	1	.219	.275	.313	.588	53	-5	5	2.49	-1	0-10(6-2-3)/D-9	0	-0.6
2002*Ari-N	123	349	60	108	27	8	3	40	32	68	5	4	.309	.371	.458	.829	107	3	61	6.20	2	0-97(7-31-68)	15	0.2
2003 Ari-N	115	203	17	46	5	2	0	18	15	34	5	1	.227	.280	.271	.551	41	-17	16	2.56	-4	0-55(10-16-34)/D-1	1	-2.2
Total 9	746	2018	305	565	102	27	17	216	187	374	80	39	.280	.343	.383	.726	81	-55	272	4.59	0	0-593/D-10	45	-5.9

• MCCRAW, Tommy Tommy Lee McCraw b: 11/21/1940, Malvern, AR BL/TL, 6', 183 lbs. Deb: 6/4/1963 C Career OF: 241-90-125

YEAR TM-L	G	AB	R	H	2B	3B	HR	RBI	BB	SO	SB	CS	AVG	OBP	SLG	OPS	OPS+	BR/A	RC	RC/G	FR	G/POS	WS	TPW
1963 Chi-A	102	280	38	71	11	3	6	33	21	46	15	4	.254	.313	.379	.691	94	-1	34	4.12	-2	1-97	7	-0.8
1964 Chi-A	125	368	47	96	11	5	6	36	32	65	15	7	.261	.327	.367	.694	95	-2	46	4.22	0	1-84,0-36(32-2-3)	11	-0.8
1965 Chi-A	133	273	38	65	12	1	5	21	25	48	12	7	.238	.309	.344	.653	91	-4	28	3.29	2	1-72,0-64(37-31-3)	6	-0.7
1966 Chi-A	151	389	49	89	16	4	5	48	29	40	20	11	.229	.291	.329	.620	83	-9	37	3.06	1	*1-121,0-41(29-0-16)	8	-1.6
1967 Chi-A	125	453	55	107	18	3	11	45	33	55	24	10	.236	.290	.362	.652	95	-3	46	3.40	11	*1-123/0-6(1-4-1)	12	0.0
1968 Chi-A	136	477	51	112	16	12	9	44	36	58	20	5	.235	.295	.375	.671	101	2	53	3.69	4	*1-135	12	-0.3
1969 Chi-A	93	240	21	62	12	2	2	25	21	24	1	3	.258	.326	.350	.676	85	-6	26	3.81	-2	1-44,0-41(11-16-17)	4	-1.2
1970 Chi-A	129	332	39	73	11	2	6	31	21	50	12	3	.220	.275	.319	.594	61	-17	31	3.16	0	1-59,0-49(21-12-18)	3	-2.2
1971 Was-A	122	207	33	44	6	4	7	25	19	38	3	3	.213	.294	.382	.676	96	-2	23	3.57	-5	0-60(26-1-37),1-30	4	-1.1
1972 Cle-A	129	391	43	101	13	5	7	33	41	47	12	10	.258	.335	.371	.706	106	2	47	3.97	2	0-84(42-22-24),1-38	11	-0.3
1973 Cal-A	99	264	25	70	7	0	3	24	30	42	3	2	.265	.345	.326	.670	97	-0	32	4.30	4	0-34(32-1-1),1-25/D-8	8	0.0
1974 Cal-A	56	119	21	34	8	0	3	17	12	13	2	1	.286	.351	.429	.780	131	5	18	5.27	3	1-29,0-12(7-0-5)/D-3	4	0.6
Cle-A	45	112	17	34	8	0	3	17	5	11	0	1	.304	.339	.455	.794	128	3	16	4.97	4	1-38/0-1	4	0.4
Yr.	101	231	38	68	16	0	6	34	17	24	2	2	.294	.345	.442	.787	129	8	33	5.12	6	1-67,0-13(7-1-5)/D-3	8	1.0
1975 Cle-A	23	51	7	14	1	1	2	5	7	7	4	1	.275	.362	.451	.813	129	2	9	6.31	-1	1-16/0-3(3-0-0)	2	0.0
Total 13	1468	3956	484	972	150	42	75	404	332	544	143	68	.246	.311	.362	.672	95	-29	446	3.78	20	1-911,0-431/D-11	96	-7.8

YEAR TM-L	G	AB	R	H	2B	3B	HR	RBI	BB	SO	SB	CS	AVG	OBP	SLG	OPS	OPS+	BR/A	RC	RC/G	FR	G/POS	WS	TPW
• MCCRAY, Rodney	Rodney Duncan McCray b: 9/13/1963, Detroit, MI BR/TR, 5'10", 175 lbs. Deb: 4/30/1990 Career OF: 8-10-17																							
1990 Chi-A	32	6	8	0	0	0	0	0	1	4	6	0	.000	.143	.000	.143	-58	0	0	2.17	-1	0-13(3-7-4)/D-7	0	-0.1
1991 Chi-A	17	7	2	2	0	0	0	0	0	2	1	1	.286	.286	.286	.571	60	-1	0	1.62	0	/0-8(4-2-2),D-6	0	-0.1
1992 NY-N	18	1	3	1	0	0	0	1	0	0	2	0	1.000	1.000	1.000	2.000	474	1	2	∞	-1	0-13(1-1-11)	0	0.0
Total 3	**67**	**14**	**13**	**3**	**0**	**0**	**0**	**1**	**1**	**6**	**9**	**1**	**.214**	**.267**	**.214**	**.481**	**33**	**0**	**3**	**1.90**	**-2**	**/0-34,D-13**	**0**	**-0.2**
• MCCREA, Frank	Francis William McCrea b: 9/6/1896, Jersey City, NJ d: 2/25/1981, Dover, NJ BR/TR, 5'9", 155 lbs. Deb: 9/26/1925																							
1925 Cle-A	1	5	1	1	0	0	0	0	0	0	0	0	.200	.200	.200	.400	2	-1	0	1.27	0	/C-1	0	-0.1
• MCCREDIE, Walt	Walter Henry McCredie b: 11/29/1876, Manchester, IA d: 7/29/1934, Portland, OR BL/TR, 6'2", 195 lbs. Deb: 4/20/1903																							
1903 Bro-N	56	213	40	69	5	0	0	20	24	....	10	....	.324	.397	.347	.745	116	6	35	6.25	-8	0-56(0-0-56)	7	-0.4
• MCCREERY, Tom	Thomas Livingston McCreery b: 10/19/1874, Beaver, PA d: 7/3/1941, Beaver, PA BB/TR, 5'11", 180 lbs. Deb: 6/8/1895 Career OF: 39-202-388 ♦																							
1895 Lou-N	31	108	18	35	3	1	0	10	8	15	3	....	.324	.376	.370	.746	99	2	17	6.07	-4	0-18(0-0-18)/P-8,S-4,1-1,3	4	-0.4
1896 Lou-N	115	441	87	155	23	**21**	7	65	42	58	26	....	.351	.409	.546	.956	157	35	113	10.12	2	*0-111(0-2-109)/2-1,P-1	16	2.3
1897 Lou-N	91	344	55	96	5	6	4	40	40	....	13	....	.279	.354	.363	.718	93	-3	53	5.18	-3	*0-89(1-1-87)	8	-0.9
NY-N	49	177	36	53	8	5	1	27	22	....	15	....	.299	.380	.418	.798	114	4	35	7.20	1	0-45(0-0-45)/2-3	6	0.2
Yr.	140	521	91	149	13	11	5	67	62	....	28	....	.286	.363	.382	.745	100	1	88	5.83	-2	*0-134(1-1-132)/2-3	14	-0.7
1898 NY-N	35	121	15	24	4	3	1	17	19	....	3	....	.198	.307	.306	.613	78	-3	13	3.44	-3	0-35(1-0-35)	2	-0.8
Pit-N	53	190	33	59	5	7	2	20	26	....	3	....	.311	.394	.442	.836	142	11	36	6.96	0	0-51(0-46-5)	9	0.7
Yr.	88	311	48	83	9	10	3	37	45	....	6	....	.267	.360	.389	.749	117	8	49	5.48	-3	0-86(1-46-40)	11	-0.1
1899 Pit-N	119	460	77	149	21	9	3	65	47	....	11	....	.324	.390	.428	.818	125	16	84	7.01	-6	0-97(15-49-33)/S-9,2-7	16	0.4
1900 Pit-N	43	132	20	29	4	3	1	13	16	....	2	....	.220	.304	.318	.622	71	-5	14	3.52	3	0-35(17-1-17)/P-1	2	-0.6
1901 Bro-N	91	335	47	97	11	14	3	53	32	....	13	....	.290	.355	.433	.788	124	10	58	6.39	0	0-82(4-78-0)/1-4,S-2	14	0.6
1902 Bro-N	112	430	49	105	8	4	4	57	29	....	16	....	.244	.295	.309	.604	86	-8	46	3.66	2	*1-108/0-4(1-0-3)	10	-0.9
1903 Bro-N	40	141	13	37	5	2	0	10	20	....	5	....	.262	.354	.326	.680	97	0	19	4.69	-5	0-38(0-2-36)	3	-0.6
Bos-N	23	83	15	18	2	1	1	10	9	....	6	....	.217	.293	.301	.595	72	-3	9	3.79	0	0-23(0-23-0)	2	-0.4
Yr.	63	224	28	55	7	3	1	20	29	....	11	....	.246	.332	.317	.649	88	-3	28	4.35	-5	0-61(0-25-36)	5	-1.0
Total 9	**802**	**2962**	**465**	**857**	**99**	**76**	**27**	**387**	**310**	**73**	**116**	**....**	**.289**	**.359**	**.401**	**.760**	**112**	**57**	**497**	**6.05**	**-13**	**0-628,1-113/S-15,2-11,P-10,3**	**92**	**-0.3**
• MCCUE, Frank	Frank Aloysius McCue b: 10/4/1898, Chicago, IL d: 7/5/1953, Evergreen Park, IL BB/TR, 5'9", 150 lbs. Deb: 9/15/1922																							
1922 Phi-A	2	5	0	0	0	0	0	0	0	0	0	0	.000	.000	.000	.000	-97	-1	0	.00	-1	/3-2	0	-0.2
• MCCULLOUGH, Clyde	Clyde Edward McCullough b: 3/4/1917, Nashville, TN d: 9/18/1982, San Francisco, CA BR/TR, 5'11.5", 180 lbs. Deb: 4/28/1940 C																							
1940 Chi-N	9	26	4	4	1	0	0	1	5	5	0	....	.154	.290	.192	.483	36	-2	2	1.91	3	/C-7	0	0.1
1941 Chi-N	125	418	41	95	9	2	9	53	34	67	5	....	.227	.289	.323	.612	75	-15	39	3.05	-3	*C-119	7	-1.2
1942 Chi-N	109	337	39	95	22	1	5	31	25	47	7	....	.282	.331	.398	.729	117	6	43	4.50	5	C-97	13	1.8
1943 Chi-N	87	266	20	63	5	2	2	23	24	33	6	....	.237	.302	.293	.596	73	-9	24	3.06	-9	C-81	4	-1.5
1946 Chi-N	95	307	38	88	18	5	4	34	22	39	2	....	.287	.338	.417	.755	116	5	42	4.86	-4	C-89	14	0.6
1947 Chi-N	86	234	25	59	12	4	3	30	20	20	1	....	.252	.314	.376	.690	86	-5	27	3.94	1	C-64	6	-0.1
1948 Chi-N★	69	172	10	36	4	2	1	7	15	25	0	....	.209	.273	.273	.546	50	-12	12	2.19	-2	C-51	2	-1.1
1949 Pit-N	91	241	30	57	9	3	4	21	24	30	1	....	.237	.316	.349	.665	76	-8	28	3.99	3	C-90	8	-0.1
1950 Pit-N	103	279	28	71	16	4	6	34	31	35	3	....	.254	.340	.405	.745	92	-3	40	4.95	2	*C-100	8	0.3
1951 Pit-N	92	259	26	77	9	2	8	39	27	31	2	0	.297	.366	.440	.806	112	5	40	5.48	6	C-87	10	1.6
1952 Pit-N	66	172	10	40	5	1	1	15	10	18	0	1	.233	.283	.291	.573	58	-10	14	2.77	5	C-61/1-1	2	-0.2
1953 Chi-N★	77	229	21	59	3	2	6	23	15	23	0	0	.258	.303	.367	.670	72	-10	24	3.57	3	C-73	5	-0.4
1954 Chi-N	31	81	9	21	7	0	3	17	5	5	0	0	.259	.310	.457	.767	96	-1	12	5.10	-2	C-26/3-3	2	-0.2
1955 Chi-N	44	81	7	16	0	0	0	10	8	15	0	0	.198	.278	.198	.475	29	-8	5	1.93	-1	C-37	1	-0.7
1956 Chi-N	14	19	0	4	1	0	0	1	0	5	0	0	.211	.211	.263	.474	27	-2	1	1.27	0	/C-7	0	-0.1
Total 15	**1098**	**3121**	**308**	**785**	**121**	**28**	**52**	**339**	**265**	**398**	**27**	**1**	**.252**	**.314**	**.358**	**.672**	**85**	**-69**	**352**	**3.84**	**6**	**C-989/3-3,1-1**	**82**	**-1.2**
• MCCURDY, Harry	Harry Henry "Hank" McCurdy b: 9/15/1899, Stevens Point, WI d: 7/21/1972, Houston, TX BL/TR, 5'11", 187 lbs. Deb: 7/4/1922																							
1922 StL-N	13	27	3	8	2	2	0	5	1	1	0	0	.296	.321	.519	.840	119	1	4	6.14	-0	/C-9,1-2	1	0.1
1923 StL-N	67	185	17	49	11	2	0	15	11	11	3	1	.265	.306	.346	.652	73	-7	20	3.75	-4	C-58	4	-0.7
1926 Chi-A	44	86	16	28	7	2	1	11	6	10	0	1	.326	.370	.488	.858	127	3	15	6.53	-1	C-25/1-8	3	0.2
1927 Chi-A	86	262	34	75	19	3	1	27	32	24	6	4	.286	.366	.393	.759	99	0	39	5.27	-2	C-82	9	0.3
1928 Chi-A	49	103	12	27	10	0	2	13	8	15	1	3	.262	.315	.417	.733	92	-3	13	4.10	-2	C-34	3	-0.3
1930 Phi-N	80	148	23	49	6	2	1	25	15	12	0	....	.331	.393	.419	.812	90	-2	24	6.15	0	C-41	3	0.0
1931 Phi-N	66	150	21	43	9	0	1	25	23	16	2	....	.287	.382	.367	.748	95	-0	23	5.31	0	C-45	5	0.2
1932 Phi-N	62	136	13	32	6	1	1	14	17	13	0	....	.235	.325	.316	.641	65	-6	15	3.70	-2	C-42	2	-0.6
1933 Phi-N	73	54	9	15	1	0	2	12	16	6	0	....	.278	.451	.407	.858	130	4	12	8.42	-1	/C-2	2	0.3
1934 Cin-N	3	6	0	0	0	0	0	1	0	0	0	....	.000	.000	.000	.000	-103	-2	0	.00	1	/1-1	0	-0.1
Total 10	**543**	**1157**	**148**	**326**	**71**	**12**	**9**	**148**	**129**	**108**	**12**	**9**	**.282**	**.355**	**.387**	**.743**	**92**	**-12**	**165**	**5.04**	**-12**	**C-338/1-11**	**32**	**-0.6**
• MCDANIEL, Terry	Terrance Keith McDaniel b: 12/6/1966, Kansas City, MO BR/TR, 5'9", 205 lbs. Deb: 8/30/1991																							
1991 NY-N	23	29	3	6	1	0	0	2	1	11	2	0	.207	.233	.241	.475	34	-2	2	2.27	0	0-14(7-5-4)	0	-0.3
• MCDAVID, Ray	Ray Darnell McDavid b: 7/20/1971, San Diego, CA BL/TR, 6'3", 190 lbs. Deb: 7/15/1994 Career OF: 4-9-1																							
1994 SD-N	9	28	2	7	1	0	0	2	1	8	1	0	.250	.276	.286	.562	48	-2	2	3.11	0	/0-7(4-2-1)	0	-0.2
1995 SD-N	11	17	2	3	0	0	0	0	2	6	1	1	.176	.263	.176	.440	20	-2	1	1.08	0	/0-7(0-7-0)	0	-0.2
Total 2	**20**	**45**	**4**	**10**	**1**	**0**	**0**	**2**	**3**	**14**	**2**	**1**	**.222**	**.271**	**.244**	**.515**	**37**	**-4**	**3**	**2.23**	**0**	**/0-14**	**0**	**-0.4**
• MCDERMOTT, Joe	Joseph McDermott Deb: 5/4/1871 ♦																							
1871 Kek-n	2	8	3	2	0	0	0	1	1	1	1	0	.250	.333	.250	.583	69	-0	1	5.38	0	/0-2(0-2-0)	....	0.0
1872 Eck-n	7	32	3	9	3	0	0	3	1	2	0	0	.281	.303	.375	.678	127	2	4	5.02	-1	/P-7	....	-1.7
Total 2 n	**9**	**40**	**6**	**11**	**3**	**0**	**0**	**4**	**2**	**3**	**1**	**0**	**.275**	**.310**	**.350**	**.660**	**114**	**2**	**5**	**5.10**	**-2**	**/P-7,0-2**	**....**	**-1.8**
• MCDERMOTT, Red	Frank A. McDermott b: 11/12/1889, Philadelphia, PA d: 9/11/1964, Philadelphia, PA BR/TR, 5'6", 150 lbs. Deb: 8/6/1912																							
1912 Det-A	5	15	2	4	1	0	0	0	0	....	1	....	.267	.313	.333	.646	87	-0	2	4.00	0	/0-5(5-0-0)	1	0.0
• MCDERMOTT, Sandy	Thomas Nathaniel McDermott b: 3/15/1856, Zanesville, OH d: 11/23/1922, Mansfield, OH Deb: 6/18/1885																							
1885 Bal-a	1	0	0	0	0	0	0	0	0	....	....	....	....	....	....	....	-102	0	0	....	-1	/2-1	0	-0.1
• MCDERMOTT, Terry	Terrance Michael McDermott b: 3/20/1951, Rockville Centre, NY BR/TR, 6'3", 205 lbs. Deb: 9/12/1972																							
1972 LA-N	9	23	2	3	0	0	0	0	2	8	0	0	.130	.200	.130	.330	-5	-3	1	.76	0	/1-7	0	-0.4
• MCDONALD, Dave	David Bruce McDonald b: 5/20/1943, New Albany, IN BL/TR, 6'3", 215 lbs. Deb: 9/15/1969																							
1969 NY-A	9	23	0	5	1	0	0	2	2	5	0	1	.217	.280	.261	.541	54	-2	2	2.22	0	/1-7	0	-0.3
1971 Mon-N	24	39	3	4	2	0	1	4	4	14	0	0	.103	.186	.231	.417	17	-4	1	1.02	0	/1-8,0-1	0	-0.6
Total 2	**33**	**62**	**3**	**9**	**3**	**0**	**1**	**6**	**6**	**19**	**0**	**1**	**.145**	**.221**	**.242**	**.463**	**30**	**-6**	**3**	**1.42**	**-1**	**/1-15,0-1**	**0**	**-0.8**
• MCDONALD, Donzell	Donzell McDonald b: 2/20/1975, Long Beach, CA BB/TR, 5'11", 180 lbs. Deb: 4/19/2001 Career OF: 8-2-0																							
2001 NY-A	5	3	0	1	0	0	0	0	0	2	0	0	.333	.333	.333	.667	76	-0	0	3.42	0	/0-3(1-2-0)	0	0.0
2002 KC-A	10	22	3	4	2	0	0	1	4	5	1	0	.182	.308	.273	.580	50	-1	2	3.40	-2	/0-7(7-0-0)	0	-0.3
Total 2	**15**	**25**	**3**	**5**	**2**	**0**	**0**	**1**	**4**	**7**	**1**	**0**	**.200**	**.310**	**.280**	**.590**	**54**	**-1**	**3**	**3.40**	**-2**	**/0-10**	**0**	**-0.4**
• MCDONALD, Ed	Edward C. McDonald b: 10/28/1886, Albany, NY d: 3/11/1946, Albany, NY BR/TR, 6', 180 lbs. Deb: 8/5/1911																							
1911 Bos-N	54	175	28	36	7	3	1	21	40	39	11	....	.206	.359	.297	.657	78	-3	23	4.14	-5	3-53/S-1	3	-0.7
1912 Bos-N	121	459	70	119	23	6	2	34	70	91	22	....	.259	.363	.349	.712	94	-2	65	4.82	-3	*3-118	10	-0.1
1913 Chi-N	1	0	0	0	0	0	0	0	0	0	0	....	....	....	....	....	-100	0	0	....	0	....	0	0.0
Total 3	**176**	**634**	**98**	**155**	**30**	**9**	**3**	**55**	**110**	**130**	**33**	**....**	**.244**	**.362**	**.334**	**.697**	**89**	**-5**	**88**	**4.62**	**-8**	**3-171/S-1**	**13**	**-0.8**

YEAR TM-L	G	AB	R	H	2B	3B	HR	RBI	BB	SO	SB	CS	AVG	OBP	SLG	OPS	OPS+	BR/A	RC	RC/G	FR	G/POS	WS	TPW
• MCDONALD, Jack	Daniel McDonald b: 1847, Brooklyn, NY d: 11/23/1880, Brooklyn, NY, 5'11", 154 lbs. Deb: 5/2/1872																							
1872 Atl-n	15	62	9	16	3	1	0	4	0	1	0	0	.258	.258	.339	.597	70	-3	6	3.74	-1	0-15(1-0-14)	....	-0.3
Eck-n	1	4	0	0	0	0	0	0	0	0	0	0	.000	.000	.000	.000	-118	-1	0	.00	-1	/S-1	....	-0.2
Yr.	16	66	9	16	3	1	0	4	0	1	0	0	.242	.242	.318	.561	59	-4	6	3.44	-3	0-15(1-0-14)/S-1	....	-0.4
• MCDONALD, Jason	Jason Adam McDonald b: 3/20/1972, Modesto, CA BB/TR, 5'8", 175 lbs. Deb: 6/5/1997 Career OF: 71-155-64																							
1997 Oak-A	78	236	47	62	11	4	4	14	36	49	13	8	.263	.363	.394	.757	100	0	37	5.34	-1	0-74(18-66-0)	6	0.0
1998 Oak-A	70	175	25	44	9	0	1	16	27	33	10	4	.251	.361	.320	.681	81	-3	23	4.37	-0	0-60(11-33-25)	4	-0.4
1999 Oak-A	100	187	26	39	2	1	3	8	25	48	6	3	.209	.312	.278	.590	54	-12	18	3.13	-1	0-89(31-53-13)/D-5,2-1	2	-1.3
2000 Tex-A	38	94	15	22	5	0	3	13	17	25	4	4	.234	.357	.383	.740	86	-2	13	4.41	6	0-32(11-3-26)/D-1	3	0.2
Total 4	**286**	**692**	**113**	**167**	**27**	**5**	**11**	**51**	**105**	**155**	**33**	**19**	**.241**	**.348**	**.342**	**.690**	**81**	**-18**	**91**	**4.35**	**4**	**0-255/D-6,2-1**	**15**	**-1.5**
• MCDONALD, Jim	James A. McDonald b: 8/6/1860, San Francisco, CA d: 9/14/1914, San Francisco, CA BR, 5'9.5", 180 lbs. Deb: 6/20/1884 Career OF: 1-13-3																							
1884 Was-U	2	6	0	1	0	0	0	....	0	....	....	....	.167	.167	.167	.333	13	-1	0	.96	-1	/C-1,0-1	0	-0.1
Pit-a	38	145	11	23	3	0	0	0	2	....	....	....	.159	.170	.179	.349	14	-14	5	1.02	-4	3-22,0-15(1-12-2)/2-1	1	-1.6
1885 Buf-N	5	14	0	0	0	0	0	0	0	4	....	....	.000	.000	.000	.000	-97	-3	0	.00	0	/S-4,0-1	0	-0.3
Total 2	**45**	**165**	**11**	**24**	**3**	**0**	**0**	**0**	**2**	**4**	**....**	**....**	**.145**	**.156**	**.164**	**.319**	**4**	**-17**	**5**	**.92**	**-5**	**/3-22,0-17,S-4,2-1,C-1**	**1**	**-2.0**
• MCDONALD, Jim	James McDonald b: Philadelphia, PA BR/TR, 6', 180 lbs. Deb: 6/2/1902																							
1902 NY-N	2	9	0	3	0	0	0	1	0	....	0	....	.333	.333	.333	.667	107	0	1	4.53	0	/O-2(0-0-2)	0	0.0
• MCDONALD, Joe	Malcolm Joseph McDonald b: 4/9/1888, Galveston, TX d: 5/30/1963, Baytown, TX BR/TR, 5'11", 175 lbs. Deb: 9/6/1910																							
1910 StL-A	10	32	4	5	0	0	0	1	1	....	0	....	.156	.182	.156	.338	6	-3	1	.80	-4	3-10	0	-0.8
• MCDONALD, John	John Joseph McDonald b: 9/24/1974, New London, CT BR/TR, 5'11", 175 lbs. Deb: 7/4/1999																							
1999 Cle-A	18	21	2	7	0	0	0	0	0	3	0	1	.333	.333	.333	.667	68	-1	1	2.12	0	/2-7,S-6	0	-0.1
2000 Cle-A	9	9	0	4	0	0	0	0	0	1	0	0	.444	.444	.444	.889	124	0	2	9.60	0	/S-7,2-2	0	0.0
2001 Cle-A	17	22	1	2	1	0	0	0	1	7	0	0	.091	.167	.136	.303	-18	-4	1	.83	-1	/S-9,2-3,3-3	0	-0.4
2002 Cle-A	93	264	35	66	11	3	1	12	10	50	3	0	.250	.290	.326	.616	65	-13	26	3.29	2	2-64,S-21,3-10	5	-0.6
2003 Cle-A	82	214	21	46	9	1	1	14	11	31	3	3	.215	.260	.280	.540	44	-18	15	2.27	-9	2-37,S-27,3-23	2	-2.3
Total 5	**219**	**530**	**59**	**125**	**21**	**4**	**2**	**26**	**22**	**92**	**6**	**4**	**.236**	**.277**	**.302**	**.579**	**54**	**-36**	**45**	**2.77**	**-8**	**2-113/S-70,3-36**	**7**	**-3.4**
• MCDONALD, Keith	William Keith McDonald b: 2/8/1973, Yokosuka, Japan BR/TR, 6'2", 215 lbs. Deb: 7/4/2000																							
2000 StL-N	6	7	3	3	0	0	3	5	2	1	0	0	.429	.556	1.714	2.270	441	4	7	46.95	1	/C-4	1	0.4
2001 StL-N	2	2	0	0	0	0	0	0	0	1	0	0	.000	.000	.000	.000	-101	-1	0	.00	0	/C-2	0	0.0
Total 2	**8**	**9**	**3**	**3**	**0**	**0**	**3**	**5**	**2**	**2**	**0**	**0**	**.333**	**.455**	**1.333**	**1.788**	**342**	**3**	**7**	**26.83**	**1**	**/C-6**	**1**	**0.4**
• MCDONALD, Tex	Charles E. McDonald b: 1/31/1891, Farmersville, TX d: 3/31/1943, Houston, TX BL/TR, 5'10", 160 lbs. Deb: 4/11/1912 Career OF: 14-1-141																							
1912 Cin-N	61	140	16	36	3	4	1	15	13	24	5	....	.257	.329	.357	.686	90	-2	18	4.27	-7	S-42	4	-0.6
1913 Cin-N	11	10	1	3	0	0	0	2	0	1	0	....	.300	.300	.300	.600	72	-0	1	3.12	-1	/S-1	0	-0.1
Bos-N	62	145	24	52	4	4	0	18	15	17	4	....	.359	.422	.441	.864	144	9	28	7.28	-4	3-31/2-6,0-1	8	0.6
Yr.	73	155	25	55	4	4	0	20	15	18	4	....	.355	.415	.432	.847	139	8	29	6.97	-4	3-31/2-6,0-1,S-1	8	0.5
1914 Pit-F	67	223	27	71	16	7	3	29	13	23	9	....	.318	.361	.493	.855	150	13	41	6.71	7	0-29(0-0-29),2-27/S-5	10	2.0
Buf-F	69	250	32	74	13	6	3	32	20	26	11	....	.296	.353	.432	.785	117	5	40	5.58	-2	0-61(2-1-58),2-10	11	0.1
Yr.	136	473	59	145	29	13	6	61	33	49	20	....	.307	.357	.461	.818	133	18	81	6.10	5	0-90(2-1-87),2-37/S-5	21	2.1
1915 Buf-F	87	251	31	68	9	6	6	39	27	34	5	....	.271	.346	.426	.773	127	8	37	5.18	-3	0-65(12-0-53)	10	0.2
Total 4	**357**	**1019**	**131**	**304**	**45**	**27**	**13**	**135**	**88**	**125**	**34**	**....**	**.298**	**.359**	**.434**	**.793**	**126**	**33**	**165**	**5.73**	**-9**	**0-156/S-48,2-43,3-31**	**43**	**2.2**
• MCDONNELL, Jim	James William "Mack" McDonnell b: 8/15/1922, Gagetown, MI d: 4/24/1993, Detroit, MI BL/TR, 5'11", 165 lbs. Deb: 9/23/1943																							
1943 Cle-A	2	1	1	0	0	0	0	0	2	1	0	0	.000	.667	.000	.667	108	0	0	9.36	0	/C-1	0	0.0
1944 Cle-A	20	43	5	10	0	0	0	4	4	3	0	0	.233	.298	.233	.530	55	-2	3	2.22	-2	C-13	0	-0.4
1945 Cle-A	28	51	3	10	2	0	0	8	2	4	0	0	.196	.226	.235	.462	36	-4	3	1.51	2	C-23	1	-0.1
Total 3	**50**	**95**	**9**	**20**	**2**	**0**	**0**	**12**	**8**	**8**	**0**	**0**	**.211**	**.272**	**.232**	**.503**	**46**	**-6**	**6**	**1.92**	**0**	**/C-37**	**1**	**-0.5**
• MCDONOUGH, Ed	Edward Sebastian McDonough b: 9/11/1886, Elgin, IL d: 9/2/1926, Elgin, IL BR/TR, 6', 160 lbs. Deb: 8/3/1909																							
1909 Phi-N	1	1	0	0	0	0	0	0	0	....	0	....	.000	.000	.000	.000	-99	-0	0	.00	0	/C-1	0	0.0
1910 Phi-N	5	9	1	1	0	0	0	0	0	1	0	....	.111	.111	.111	.222	-34	-2	0	.30	0	/C-4	0	-0.2
Total 2	**6**	**10**	**1**	**1**	**0**	**0**	**0**	**0**	**0**	**1**	**0**	**....**	**.100**	**.100**	**.100**	**.200**	**-41**	**-2**	**0**	**.27**	**0**	**/C-5**	**0**	**-0.2**
• MCDOUGALD, Gil	Gilbert James McDougald b: 5/19/1928, San Francisco, CA BR/TR, 6', 180 lbs. Deb: 4/20/1951																							
1951*NY-A	131	402	72	123	23	4	14	63	56	54	14	5	.306	.396	.488	.884	143	26	81	7.08	1	3-82,2-55	23	2.9
1952*NY-A★	152	555	65	146	16	5	11	78	57	73	6	5	.263	.336	.369	.705	102	1	71	4.29	13	*3-117,2-38	18	1.6
1953*NY-A	141	541	82	154	27	7	10	83	60	65	3	4	.285	.361	.416	.777	113	10	85	5.62	12	*3-136,2-26	21	2.2
1954 NY-A	126	394	66	102	22	2	12	48	62	64	3	4	.259	.367	.416	.783	118	10	64	5.52	13	2-92,3-35	20	3.1
1955*NY-A	141	533	79	152	10	8	13	53	65	77	6	4	.285	.365	.407	.772	109	7	83	5.53	27	*2-126,3-17	24	4.4
1956*NY-A★	120	438	79	136	13	3	13	56	68	59	3	8	.311	.407	.443	.850	128	18	82	6.82	17	S-92,2-31/3-5	24	4.3
1957*NY-A★	141	539	87	156	25	**9**	13	62	59	71	2	5	.289	.364	.442	.805	121	15	86	5.52	18	*S-121,2-21/3-7	27	4.5
1958*NY-A★	138	503	69	126	19	1	14	65	59	75	6	2	.250	.333	.376	.708	98	0	64	4.21	3	*2-115,S-19	15	1.4
1959 NY-A★	127	434	44	109	16	8	4	34	35	40	0	3	.251	.311	.353	.664	85	-11	46	3.58	9	2-53,S-52,3-25	10	0.6
1960*NY-A	119	337	54	87	16	4	8	34	38	45	2	4	.258	.339	.401	.739	105	1	47	4.75	9	3-84,2-42	12	1.2
Total 10	**1336**	**4676**	**697**	**1291**	**187**	**51**	**112**	**576**	**559**	**623**	**45**	**44**	**.276**	**.358**	**.410**	**.768**	**112**	**78**	**708**	**5.24**	**121**	**2-599,3-508,S-284**	**194**	**26.3**
• MCDOWELL, Oddibe	Oddibe McDowell b: 8/25/1962, Hollywood, FL BL/TL, 5'9", 165 lbs. Deb: 5/19/1985 Career OF: 75-649-28																							
1985 Tex-A	111	406	63	97	14	5	18	42	36	85	25	7	.239	.306	.431	.737	98	0	55	4.49	5	*O-103(0-103-0)/D-4	10	0.3
1986 Tex-A	154	572	105	152	24	7	18	49	65	112	33	15	.266	.342	.427	.768	105	5	83	4.96	1	*O-148(0-147-0)/D-1	20	0.3
1987 Tex-A	128	407	65	98	26	4	14	52	51	99	24	2	.241	.325	.428	.753	97	3	61	5.06	0	*O-125(0-126-0)	14	0.1
1988 Tex-A	120	437	55	108	19	5	6	37	41	89	33	10	.247	.315	.355	.669	85	-6	53	4.09	0	*O-113(0-113-0)/D-3	12	-0.8
1989 Cle-A	69	239	33	53	5	2	3	22	25	36	12	5	.222	.298	.297	.595	67	-10	23	3.09	2	O-64(63-1-0)/D-2	3	-1.0
Atl-N	76	280	56	85	18	4	7	24	27	37	15	10	.304	.365	.471	.836	134	11	49	6.36	-1	O-68(0-68-0)	11	0.9
1990 Atl-N	113	305	47	74	14	0	7	25	21	53	13	2	.243	.296	.357	.653	74	-10	34	3.89	-2	O-72(12-60-1)	7	-1.3
1994 Tex-A	59	183	34	48	5	1	1	15	28	39	14	2	.262	.360	.317	.677	77	-3	25	4.52	-2	O-53(0-31-27)/D-2	5	-0.5
Total 7	**830**	**2829**	**458**	**715**	**125**	**28**	**74**	**266**	**294**	**550**	**169**	**53**	**.253**	**.325**	**.395**	**.720**	**94**	**-10**	**382**	**4.59**	**3**	**O-746/D-12**	**82**	**-2.0**
• MCELVEEN, Pryor	Pryor Mynatt "Humpty" McElveen b: 11/5/1881, Atlanta, GA d: 10/27/1951, Pleasant Hill, TN BR/TR, 5'10", 168 lbs. Deb: 4/26/1909																							
1909 Bro-N	81	258	22	51	8	1	3	25	14	....	6	....	.198	.242	.271	.513	61	-13	18	2.19	-5	3-37,O-13(1-3-7),S-10/1-5,2	2	-1.8
1910 Bro-N	74	213	19	48	8	3	1	26	22	47	6	....	.225	.307	.305	.612	81	-5	22	3.31	-6	3-54/S-6,2-3,C-1	4	-1.0
1911 Bro-N	16	31	1	6	0	0	0	5	0	3	0	....	.194	.194	.194	.387	9	-4	1	1.11	-1	/2-5,S-1	0	-0.5
Total 3	**171**	**502**	**42**	**105**	**16**	**4**	**4**	**56**	**36**	**50**	**12**	**....**	**.209**	**.268**	**.281**	**.548**	**67**	**-22**	**41**	**2.60**	**-12**	**/3-91,S-17,2-13,O-13,1-5,C-1**	**6**	**-3.3**
• MCELWEE, Lee	Leland Stanford McElwee b: 5/23/1894, La Mesa, CA d: 2/8/1957, Union, ME BR/TR, 5'10.5", 160 lbs. Deb: 7/3/1916																							
1916 Phi-A	54	155	9	41	3	0	0	10	8	17	0	....	.265	.301	.284	.584	79	-4	14	3.07	-4	3-30/O-9(0-0-9),2-3,1-1,S	2	-0.9
• MCELYEA, Frank	Frank McElyea b: 8/4/1918, Hawthorne Township, IL d: 4/19/1987, Evansville, IN BR/TR, 6'6", 221 lbs. Deb: 9/10/1942																							
1942 Bos-N	7	4	2	0	0	0	0	0	0	0	0	....	.000	.000	.000	.000	-102	-1	0	.00	-0	/O-1	0	-0.1
• MCEWING, Joe	Joseph Earl "Super Joe" McEwing b: 10/19/1972, Bristol, PA BR/TR, 5'10", 170 lbs. Deb: 9/2/1998 Career OF: 150-39-77																							
1998 StL-N	10	20	5	4	1	0	0	1	1	3	0	1	.200	.273	.250	.523	39	-2	1	1.97	-0	/2-6,O-3(1-1-1)	0	-0.2
1999 StL-N	152	513	65	141	28	4	9	44	41	87	7	4	.275	.336	.398	.733	84	-13	71	4.88	3	2-96,O-66(32-23-19)/3-6,1,S	11	-0.7
2000*NY-N	87	153	20	34	14	1	2	19	5	29	3	1	.222	.252	.366	.618	56	-11	14	2.88	-2	O-52(43-11-6),3-19,2-16/S-4	2	-1.2
2001 NY-N	116	283	41	80	17	3	8	30	17	57	8	5	.283	.345	.449	.794	108	3	45	5.52	1	O-62(48-2-25),3-25,S-12/2-5,1,D	8	0.2
2002 NY-N	105	196	22	39	8	1	3	26	9	50	4	4	.199	.245	.296	.541	43	-18	15	2.35	2	O-35(10-1-24),S-21,1-20,2-13,3	2	-1.6

YEAR TM-L	G	AB	R	H	2B	3B	HR	RBI	BB	SO	SB	CS	AVG	OBP	SLG	OPS	OPS+	BR/A	RC	RC/G	FR	G/POS	WS	TPW
2003 NY-N	119	278	31	67	11	0	1	16	25	57	3	0	.241	.310	.291	.602	60	-15	26	3.17	5	2-55,S-42,O-18(16-1-2)/1-5,3	5	-0.6
Total 6	589	1443	184	365	79	9	23	136	98	283	25	15	.253	.311	.368	.679	75	-57	172	4.03	9	O-236,2-191/S-80,3-62,1-30,D	28	-4.1

• MCFADDEN, Guy Guy G. McFadden b: 9/3/1872, Topeka, KS d: 3/10/1911, Topeka, KS Deb: 8/24/1895

YEAR TM-L	G	AB	R	H	2B	3B	HR	RBI	BB	SO	SB	CS	AVG	OBP	SLG	OPS	OPS+	BR/A	RC	RC/G	FR	G/POS	WS	TPW
1895 StL-N	4	14	1	3	0	0	0	2	0	2	0	....	.214	.214	.214	.429	11	-2	1	1.72	-1	/1-4	0	-0.2

• MCFADDEN, Leon Leon McFadden b: 4/26/1944, Little Rock, AR BR/TR, 6'2", 195 lbs. Deb: 9/6/1968

YEAR TM-L	G	AB	R	H	2B	3B	HR	RBI	BB	SO	SB	CS	AVG	OBP	SLG	OPS	OPS+	BR/A	RC	RC/G	FR	G/POS	WS	TPW
1968 Hou-N	16	47	2	13	1	0	0	1	6	10	1	0	.277	.358	.298	.656	101	1	6	4.36	-1	S-16	2	0.1
1969 Hou-N	44	74	3	13	2	0	0	3	4	9	1	2	.176	.218	.203	.421	19	-9	3	1.15	-2	O-17(4-0-13)/S-8	0	-1.1
1970 Hou-N	2	0	0	0	0	0	0	0	0	0	0	0	....	....	....	....	-104	0	0	....	0	....	0	0.0
Total 3	62	121	5	26	3	0	0	4	10	19	2	2	.215	.275	.240	.514	52	-8	9	2.25	-3	/S-24,O-17	2	-1.0

• MCFARLAN, Alex Alexander Shepherd McFarlan b: 10/11/1869, St. Louis, MO d: 3/2/1939, Pewee Valley, KY, 5'9" Deb: 6/19/1892

YEAR TM-L	G	AB	R	H	2B	3B	HR	RBI	BB	SO	SB	CS	AVG	OBP	SLG	OPS	OPS+	BR/A	RC	RC/G	FR	G/POS	WS	TPW
1892 Lou-N	14	42	2	7	0	0	0	1	8	11	1	....	.167	.300	.167	.467	45	-2	2	1.90	-3	O-12(0-0-12)/2-2	0	-0.5

• MCFARLAND, Chris Christopher McFarland b: 8/17/1861, Fall River, MA d: 5/24/1918, New Bedford, MA, 5'9", 170 lbs. Deb: 4/19/1884

YEAR TM-L	G	AB	R	H	2B	3B	HR	RBI	BB	SO	SB	CS	AVG	OBP	SLG	OPS	OPS+	BR/A	RC	RC/G	FR	G/POS	WS	TPW
1884 Bal-U	3	14	2	3	1	0	0	....	0	....	....	....	.214	.214	.286	.500	61	-1	1	2.24	-1	/O-3(0-3-0),P-1	0	-0.5

• MCFARLAND, Ed Edward William McFarland b: 8/3/1874, Cleveland, OH d: 11/28/1959, Cleveland, OH BR/TR, 5'10", 180 lbs. Deb: 7/7/1893 U Career OF: 3-5-2

YEAR TM-L	G	AB	R	H	2B	3B	HR	RBI	BB	SO	SB	CS	AVG	OBP	SLG	OPS	OPS+	BR/A	RC	RC/G	FR	G/POS	WS	TPW
1893 Cle-N	8	22	5	9	2	1	0	6	1	2	0	....	.409	.458	.591	1.049	168	2	6	12.45	0	/O-5(0-5-0),3-2,C-1	1	0.1
1896 StL-N	83	290	48	70	13	4	3	36	15	17	7	....	.241	.281	.345	.626	67	-15	32	3.67	15	C-80/O-2(0-0-2)	7	0.7
1897 StL-N	31	107	14	35	5	2	1	17	8	....	2	....	.327	.374	.439	.813	117	2	19	6.66	3	C-23/1-3,O-3(3-0-0),2-1	3	0.6
Phi-N	38	130	18	29	3	5	1	16	14	....	2	....	.223	.308	.346	.654	75	-5	16	3.84	0	C-37	2	-0.1
Yr.	69	237	32	64	8	7	2	33	22	....	4	....	.270	.337	.388	.725	93	-3	35	5.00	2	C-60/1-3,O-3(3-0-0),2-1	5	0.5
1898 Phi-N	121	429	65	121	21	5	3	71	44	....	4	....	.282	.352	.375	.727	113	8	61	5.07	4	*C-121	17	2.1
1899 Phi-N	96	324	59	108	22	9	2	57	36	....	9	....	.333	.403	.475	.879	146	21	68	8.06	1	C-94	20	2.8
1900 Phi-N	94	344	50	105	14	8	0	38	29	....	9	....	.305	.364	.392	.757	110	5	55	5.85	5	C-93/3-1	14	1.7
1901 Phi-N	74	295	33	84	14	2	1	32	18	....	11	....	.285	.326	.356	.682	96	-2	39	4.84	1	C-74	10	0.6
1902 Chi-A	75	246	29	56	9	2	1	25	19	....	8	....	.228	.291	.293	.584	65	-11	25	3.33	-1	C-69/1-1	6	-0.5
1903 Chi-A	61	201	15	42	7	2	1	19	14	....	3	....	.209	.264	.279	.542	66	-8	17	2.68	3	C-56/1-1	4	0.0
1904 Chi-A	50	160	22	44	11	3	0	20	17	....	2	....	.275	.348	.381	.730	136	7	23	5.07	-4	C-49	8	0.9
1905 Chi-A	80	250	24	70	13	4	0	31	23	....	5	....	.280	.345	.364	.709	130	9	35	4.96	1	C-70	13	1.9
1906*Chi-A	12	23	0	4	1	0	0	3	3	....	0	....	.174	.269	.217	.487	54	-1	2	2.14	-2	/C-7	1	-0.2
1907 Chi-A	52	138	11	39	9	1	0	8	12	....	3	....	.283	.340	.362	.702	128	4	19	4.91	-4	C-43	8	0.5
1908 Bos-A	19	48	5	10	2	1	0	4	1	....	0	....	.208	.224	.292	.516	66	-2	3	2.02	3	C-13	1	0.3
Total 14	894	3007	398	826	146	49	13	383	254	19	65	....	.275	.335	.369	.704	104	13	419	4.90	24	C-830/O-10,1-5,3-3,2-1	115	11.3

• MCFARLAND, Herm Hermas Walter McFarland b: 3/11/1870, Des Moines, IA d: 9/21/1935, Richmond, VA BL/TR, 5'6", 150 lbs. Deb: 4/21/1896 Career OF: 189-140-22

YEAR TM-L	G	AB	R	H	2B	3B	HR	RBI	BB	SO	SB	CS	AVG	OBP	SLG	OPS	OPS+	BR/A	RC	RC/G	FR	G/POS	WS	TPW
1896 Lou-N	30	110	11	21	4	1	1	12	9	14	4	....	.191	.252	.273	.525	40	-10	9	2.62	-3	O-28(3-18-9)/C-1	0	-1.2
1898 Cin-N	19	64	10	18	1	3	0	11	7	....	3	....	.281	.361	.391	.752	108	1	10	5.91	0	O-17(13-3-1)	3	-0.1
1901 Chi-A	132	473	83	130	21	9	4	59	75	....	33	....	.275	.384	.383	.767	116	15	86	6.42	7	*O-132(132-0-0)	21	1.3
1902 Chi-A	7	27	5	5	0	0	0	4	2	....	1	....	.185	.241	.185	.427	20	-3	2	1.86	0	/O-7(2-0-5)	0	-0.3
Bal-A	61	242	54	78	19	6	3	36	36	....	10	....	.322	.418	.488	.906	144	16	55	8.87	-2	O-61(0-61-0)	10	1.1
Yr.	68	269	59	83	19	6	3	40	38	....	11	....	.309	.402	.457	.859	132	13	57	8.01	-2	O-68(2-61-5)	10	0.8
1903 NY-A	103	362	41	88	16	9	5	45	46	....	13	....	.243	.333	.378	.712	106	4	53	4.88	-4	*O-103(39-58-7)	16	-0.6
Total 5	352	1278	204	340	61	28	13	167	175	14	64	....	.266	.362	.388	.750	110	23	214	5.89	-3	O-348/C-1	50	0.1

• MCFARLAND, Howie Howard Alexander McFarland b: 3/7/1910, El Reno, OK d: 4/7/1993, Wichita, KS BR/TR, 6', 175 lbs. Deb: 7/16/1945

YEAR TM-L	G	AB	R	H	2B	3B	HR	RBI	BB	SO	SB	CS	AVG	OBP	SLG	OPS	OPS+	BR/A	RC	RC/G	FR	G/POS	WS	TPW
1945 Was-A	6	11	0	1	0	0	0	2	0	3	0	0	.091	.091	.091	.182	-52	-2	0	.00	1	/O-3(1-0-2)	0	-0.2

• MCFARLANE, Orlando Orlando Dejesus (Quesada) McFarlane b: 6/28/1938, Oriente, Cuba BR/TR, 6', 180 lbs. Deb: 4/23/1962

YEAR TM-L	G	AB	R	H	2B	3B	HR	RBI	BB	SO	SB	CS	AVG	OBP	SLG	OPS	OPS+	BR/A	RC	RC/G	FR	G/POS	WS	TPW
1962 Pit-N	8	23	0	2	0	0	0	1	1	4	0	0	.087	.125	.087	.212	-42	-5	0	.26	0	/C-8	0	-0.4
1964 Pit-N	37	78	5	19	5	0	0	1	4	27	0	0	.244	.280	.308	.588	66	-4	7	3.12	-1	C-35/O-1	1	-0.4
1966 Det-A	49	138	16	35	7	0	5	13	9	46	0	0	.254	.304	.413	.717	101	0	17	4.43	1	C-33	5	0.3
1967 Cal-A	12	22	0	5	0	0	0	3	1	7	0	0	.227	.261	.227	.488	47	-1	1	.93	-1	/C-6	0	-0.3
1968 Cal-A	18	31	1	9	0	0	0	2	5	9	0	0	.290	.389	.290	.679	112	1	4	4.26	0	/C-9	1	0.2
Total 5	124	292	22	70	12	0	5	20	20	93	0	0	.240	.291	.332	.623	78	-9	29	3.35	-1	/C-91,O-1	7	-0.6

• MCGAFFIGAN, Patsy Mark Andrew McGaffigan b: 9/12/1888, Carlyle, IL d: 12/22/1940, Carlyle, IL BR/TR, 5'8", 140 lbs. Deb: 4/16/1917

YEAR TM-L	G	AB	R	H	2B	3B	HR	RBI	BB	SO	SB	CS	AVG	OBP	SLG	OPS	OPS+	BR/A	RC	RC/G	FR	G/POS	WS	TPW
1917 Phi-N	19	60	5	10	1	0	0	6	0	7	1	....	.167	.167	.183	.350	7	-7	2	1.05	1	S-17/O-1	1	-0.5
1918 Phi-N	54	192	17	39	3	2	1	8	16	23	3	....	.203	.268	.255	.523	56	-10	14	2.28	-8	2-53/S-1	1	-1.9
Total 2	73	252	22	49	4	2	1	14	16	30	4	....	.194	.245	.238	.483	45	-17	17	1.97	-7	/2-53,S-18,O-1	2	-2.4

• MCGAH, Eddie Edward Joseph McGah b: 9/30/1921, Oakland, CA d: 9/30/2002, Oakland, CA BR/TR, 6', 183 lbs. Deb: 4/26/1946

YEAR TM-L	G	AB	R	H	2B	3B	HR	RBI	BB	SO	SB	CS	AVG	OBP	SLG	OPS	OPS+	BR/A	RC	RC/G	FR	G/POS	WS	TPW
1946 Bos-A	15	37	2	8	1	1	0	1	7	7	0	0	.216	.341	.297	.638	75	-1	5	4.08	-1	C-14	1	-0.2
1947 Bos-A	9	14	1	0	0	0	0	2	3	0	0	0	.000	.176	.000	.176	-45	-3	0	.27	0	/C-7	0	-0.3
Total 2	24	51	3	8	1	1	0	3	10	7	0	0	.157	.295	.216	.511	42	-4	5	2.87	-1	/C-21	1	-0.4

• MCGANN, Ambrose Ambrose McGann b: 1875, Baltimore, MD, 5'7", 170 lbs. Deb: 5/2/1895

YEAR TM-L	G	AB	R	H	2B	3B	HR	RBI	BB	SO	SB	CS	AVG	OBP	SLG	OPS	OPS+	BR/A	RC	RC/G	FR	G/POS	WS	TPW
1895 Lou-N	20	73	9	21	5	2	0	9	8	6	6	....	.288	.358	.411	.769	104	1	13	6.78	-2	/S-8,3-6,O-5(0-0-5)	2	-0.1

• MCGANN, Dan Dennis Lawrence "Cap" McGann b: 7/15/1871, Shelbyville, KY d: 12/13/1910, Louisville, KY BB/TR, 6', 190 lbs. Deb: 8/8/1896

YEAR TM-L	G	AB	R	H	2B	3B	HR	RBI	BB	SO	SB	CS	AVG	OBP	SLG	OPS	OPS+	BR/A	RC	RC/G	FR	G/POS	WS	TPW
1896 Bos-N	43	171	25	55	6	7	2	30	12	10	2	....	.322	.383	.474	.857	118	4	33	7.44	-10	2-43	6	-0.3
1898 Bal-N	145	535	99	161	18	8	5	106	53	....	33	....	.301	.404	.393	.796	126	23	102	7.05	5	*1-145	21	2.5
1899 Bro-N	63	214	49	52	11	4	2	32	21	....	16	....	.243	.362	.360	.722	96	0	35	5.58	2	1-61	7	0.2
Was-N	76	280	65	96	9	8	5	58	14	....	11	....	.343	.410	.486	.896	147	18	62	8.74	2	1-76	13	1.8
Yr.	139	494	114	148	20	12	7	90	35	....	27	....	.300	.389	.431	.820	124	18	98	7.26	4	*1-137	20	2.0
1900 StL-N	121	444	79	132	10	9	4	58	32	....	26	....	.297	.376	.387	.763	112	9	77	6.41	6	*1-121/2-1	13	1.3
1901 StL-N	103	423	73	115	15	9	6	56	16	....	17	....	.272	.333	.392	.726	116	8	63	5.33	-5	*1-103	13	0.2
1902 Bal-A	68	250	40	79	10	8	0	42	19	....	17	....	.316	.378	.420	.798	116	6	48	7.08	2	1-68	7	0.6
NY-N	61	227	25	68	5	7	0	21	12	....	12	....	.300	.356	.383	.740	129	8	37	5.95	4	1-61	7	1.1
1903 NY-N	129	482	75	130	21	6	3	50	32	....	36	....	.270	.331	.357	.688	92	-5	74	5.12	-3	*1-129	12	-1.0
1904 NY-N	141	517	81	148	22	6	6	71	36	....	42	....	.286	.354	.387	.741	123	15	90	5.99	2	*1-141	22	1.5
1905*NY-N	136	491	88	147	23	14	5	75	55	....	22	....	.299	.391	.434	.825	143	28	97	6.92	5	*1-136	24	3.2
1906 NY-N	134	451	62	107	14	8	0	37	60	....	30	....	.237	.344	.304	.647	100	3	62	4.40	-3	*1-133	16	-0.2
1907 NY-N	81	262	29	78	9	1	2	36	29	....	9	....	.298	.383	.363	.745	129	10	42	5.68	7	1-81	11	1.8
1908 Bos-N	135	475	52	114	8	5	2	55	38	....	9	....	.240	.321	.291	.612	97	0	48	3.31	-7	*1-121/2-9	11	-1.0
Total 12	1436	5222	842	1482	181	100	42	727	429	10	282	....	.284	.364	.381	.745	117	126	870	5.86	9	*1-1376/2-53	183	11.7

• MCGARR, Chippy James B. McGarr b: 5/10/1863, Worcester, MA d: 6/6/1904, Worcester, MA BR/TR, 5'9", 168 lbs. Deb: 7/11/1884 U Career OF: 7-0-6

YEAR TM-L	G	AB	R	H	2B	3B	HR	RBI	BB	SO	SB	CS	AVG	OBP	SLG	OPS	OPS+	BR/A	RC	RC/G	FR	G/POS	WS	TPW
1884 CP-U	19	70	10	11	2	0	0	....	0	....	....	....	.157	.157	.186	.343	16	-6	2	.99	-3	2-13/O-6(5-0-1)	0	-0.7
1886 Phi-a	71	267	41	71	9	3	2	31	9	....	17	....	.266	.295	.345	.640	99	-1	33	4.54	-2	S-71	9	-0.1
1887 Phi-a	137	559	93	181	23	6	1	63	23	....	84	....	.324	.326	.366	.692	93	-7	94	6.69	8	*S-137	16	0.4
1888 StL-a	34	132	17	31	1	0	0	13	6	....	25	....	.235	.268	.242	.511	58	-7	16	4.19	0	2-33/S-1	2	-0.5
1889 KC-a	25	108	22	31	3	0	0	16	6	11	12	....	.287	.330	.315	.645	79	-3	16	5.36	-2	3-11/O-6(2-0-4),2-5,S-3	2	-0.4
Bal-a	3	7	1	1	0	0	0	0	1	1	0	....	.143	.250	.143	.393	13	-1	0	1.13	-2	/S-3	0	-0.3
Yr.	28	115	23	32	3	0	0	16	7	12	12	....	.278	.325	.304	.630	75	-4	16	5.06	-4	3-11/O-6(2-0-4),S-6,2-5	2	-0.7
1890 Bos-N	121	487	68	115	12	7	1	51	34	38	39	....	.236	.291	.296	.587	66	-24	55	3.89	4	*3-115/S-5,O-1	11	-1.5
1893 Cle-N	63	249	38	77	12	0	0	28	20	15	24	....	.309	.363	.357	.720	86	-5	42	6.48	-3	3-63	7	-0.6
1894 Cle-N	128	523	94	144	24	6	2	74	28	29	31	....	.275	.316	.356	.672	60	-37	70	4.82	-2	*3-128	8	-2.9
1895*Cle-N	113	422	86	114	14	2	2	59	35	33	19	....	.270	.328	.327	.655	65	-23	54	4.57	-4	*3-108/2-4	10	-2.0

YEAR TM-L	G	AB	R	H	2B	3B	HR	RBI	BB	SO	SB	CS	AVG	OBP	SLG	OPS	OPS+	BR/A	RC	RC/G	FR	G/POS	WS	TPW
1896*Cle-N	113	455	68	122	16	4	1	53	22	30	16	....	.268	.302	.327	.629	62	-27	52	4.04	-9	*3-113/C-1	7	-2.9
Total 10	827	3279	538	898	116	28	9	388	184	157	267	....	.274	.311	.330	.641	72	-141	434	4.81	-15	3-538,S-220/2-55,0-13,C-1	72	-11.4
• MCGARR, Jim	James Vincent "Reds" McGarr b: 11/9/1888, Philadelphia, PA d: 7/21/1981, Miami, FL BR/TR, 5'9.5", 170 lbs. Deb: 5/18/1912																							
1912 Det-A	1	4	0	0	0	0	0	0	0	....	0	....	.000	.000	.000	.000	-103	-1	0	.00	0	/2-1	0	-0.1
• MCGARVEY, Dan	Daniel Francis McGarvey b: 12/2/1887, Philadelphia, PA d: 3/7/1947, Philadelphia, PA BR Deb: 5/18/1912																							
1912 Det-A	1	3	0	0	0	0	0	0	1	....	0	....	.000	.400	.000	.400	18	-0	0	.00	0	/0-1	0	0.0
• MCGEACHEY, Jack	John Charles McGeachey b: 5/13/1864, Clinton, MA d: 4/5/1930, Cambridge, MA BR/TR, 5'8", 165 lbs. Deb: 6/17/1886 Career OF: 72-201-331 ♦																							
1886 Det-N	6	27	3	9	0	1	0	4	0	3	2	....	.333	.333	.407	.741	121	1	4	6.66	0	/0-6(6-0-0)	1	0.0
StL-N	59	226	31	46	12	3	2	24	1	37	8	....	.204	.207	.310	.517	59	-11	17	2.48	1	0-55(0-55-0)/2-2,3-2	2	-1.1
Yr.	65	253	34	55	12	4	2	28	1	40	10	....	.217	.220	.320	.541	66	-11	21	2.86	1	0-61(6-55-0)/2-2,3-2	3	-1.1
1887 Ind-N	99	410	49	114	17	3	1	56	5	16	27	....	.278	.280	.333	.613	72	-16	46	4.16	4	*0-98(0-97-2)/3-1,P-1	6	-1.7
1888 Ind-N	118	452	45	99	15	2	0	30	5	21	49	....	.219	.231	.261	.492	55	-23	40	3.02	1	*0-117(2-6-109)/P-1,S-1	5	-2.7
1889 Ind-N	131	532	83	142	32	1	2	63	9	39	37	....	.267	.282	.342	.624	72	-23	63	4.30	6	*0-131(0-0-131)/P-3	7	-1.9
1890 Bro-P	104	443	84	108	24	4	1	65	19	12	21	....	.244	.278	.323	.601	57	-31	47	3.77	-2	*0-104(22-31-52)	6	-2.9
1891 Phi-a	50	201	24	46	4	3	2	13	6	12	9	....	.229	.255	.308	.563	59	-12	19	3.17	0	0-50(4-12-34)	2	-1.1
Bos-a	41	178	26	45	2	1	1	21	12	8	11	....	.253	.304	.292	.596	72	-7	20	3.91	-1	0-41(38-0-3)	3	-0.8
Yr.	91	379	50	91	6	4	3	34	18	20	20	....	.240	.278	.301	.579	65	-19	38	3.51	-1	0-91(42-12-37)	5	-1.9
Total 6	608	2469	345	609	106	18	9	276	57	148	164	....	.247	.265	.314	.579	65	-123	255	3.66	9	0-602/P-5,3-3,2-2,S-1	32	-12.2
• MCGEARY, Mike	Michael Henry McGeary b: 1851, Philadelphia, PA BR/TR, 5'7", 138 lbs. Deb: 5/9/1871 M/U NA OF: 0-1-7 Career OF: 0-1-2																							
1871 Tro-n	29	148	42	39	4	0	0	12	6	0	**20**	4	.264	.292	.291	.583	67	-4	19	5.26	3	*C-26/S-3	....	-0.1
1872 Ath-n	47	225	68	81	9	2	0	35	2	1	13	8	.360	.366	.418	.783	140	9	40	8.18	5	C-23,S-23/0-1	....	1.0
1873 Ath-n	52	275	63	83	8	1	0	31	1	1	3	6	.302	.304	.338	.643	84	-9	30	4.61	3	*S-44,C-13/3-1	....	-0.5
1874 Ath-n	54	271	61	87	10	2	0	22	1	2	10	2	.321	.324	.373	.696	113	3	37	5.94	7	C-28,S-26/0-4(0-0-4)	....	0.8
1875 Phi-n	68	310	71	90	6	2	0	37	1	1	19	4	.290	.293	.323	.615	109	4	36	4.70	10	3-27,2-23,S-18/0-3(0-1-2)	....	1.1
1876 StL-N	61	278	48	72	3	0	0	30	2	1	....	....	.259	.266	.272	.538	84	-4	20	2.81	11	*2-56/C-5,3-1,0-1	8	0.9
1877 StL-N	57	258	35	65	3	2	0	20	2	6	....	....	.252	.258	.279	.537	73	-7	19	2.71	12	2-39,3-19	6	0.6
1879 Pro-N	85	374	62	103	7	2	0	35	5	13	....	....	.275	.285	.305	.590	96	-2	33	3.44	-3	*2-73,3-12	10	-0.1
1880 Pro-N	18	59	5	8	0	0	0	1	0	6	....	....	.136	.136	.136	.271	-8	-6	1	.60	5	3-17/2-2,S-1	1	-0.1
Cle-N	31	111	14	28	2	1	0	6	4	3	....	....	.252	.278	.288	.567	94	-1	9	3.02	-4	3-29/0-2(0-0-2)	3	-0.3
Yr.	49	170	19	36	2	1	0	7	4	9	....	....	.212	.230	.235	.465	59	-7	10	2.10	1	3-46/2-2,0-2(0-0-2),S-1	4	-0.4
1881 Cle-N	11	41	1	9	0	0	0	5	0	6	....	....	.220	.220	.220	.439	40	-3	2	1.71	-5	3-11	0	-0.7
1882 Det-N	34	133	14	19	4	1	0	2	2	20	....	....	.143	.156	.188	.344	10	-13	4	.96	11	S-33/2-3	3	0.0
Total 5 n	250	1229	305	380	37	7	0	137	11	5	65	24	.309	.315	.351	.666	105	3	161	5.62	28	S-114/C-90,3-28,2-23,0-8	....	2.3
Total 6	297	1254	179	304	19	6	0	99	15	55	....	....	.242	.252	.268	.519	73	-35	89	2.61	27	2-173/3-89,S-34,C-5,0-3	31	0.3
• MCGEE, Dan	Daniel Aloysius McGee b: 9/29/1911, New York, NY d: 12/4/1991, Lakehurst, NJ BR/TR, 5'8.5", 152 lbs. Deb: 7/14/1934																							
1934 Bos-N	7	22	2	3	0	0	0	1	3	6	0	....	.136	.240	.136	.376	4	-3	1	1.36	0	/S-7	0	-0.2
• MCGEE, Frank	Francis De Sales McGee b: 4/29/1899, Columbus, OH d: 1/30/1934, Columbus, OH BR/TR, 5'11.5", 175 lbs. Deb: 9/19/1925																							
1925 Was-A	2	3	0	0	0	0	0	0	0	1	0	0	.000	.000	.000	.000	-102	-1	0	.00	0	/1-2	0	-0.1
• MCGEE, Pat	Patrick McGee d: 6/21/1889, New York, NY Deb: 9/24/1874 NA OF: 6-47-0																							
1874 Atl-n	16	65	4	11	1	0	0	6	0	3	0	0	.169	.169	.185	.354	15	-5	2	1.16	-1	0-15(6-9-0)/S-2,2-1	....	-0.5
1875 Mut-n	25	95	4	17	2	0	0	9	0	10	0	0	.179	.179	.200	.379	30	-7	3	1.32	-3	0-25(0-25-0)	....	-0.9
Atl-n	18	65	3	10	3	1	0	5	1	4	0	0	.154	.167	.231	.397	42	-3	3	1.37	4	0-13(0-13-0)/2-6,3-1	....	0.1
Yr.	43	160	7	27	5	1	0	14	1	14	0	0	.169	.174	.213	.386	35	-10	6	1.34	1	0-38(0-38-0)/2-6,3-1	....	-0.8
Total 2 n	59	225	11	38	6	1	0	20	1	17	0	0	.169	.173	.204	.377	29	-15	8	1.29	0	/0-53,2-7,S-2,3-1	....	-1.2
• MCGEE, Willie	Willie Dean McGee b: 11/2/1958, San Francisco, CA BB/TR, 6'1", 175 lbs. Deb: 5/10/1982 Career OF: 146-1352-535																							
1982*StL-N	123	422	43	125	12	8	4	56	12	58	24	12	.296	.319	.391	.710	97	-4	49	4.12	-5	*0-117(1-116-0)	11	-1.1
1983 StL-N★	147	601	75	172	22	8	5	75	26	98	39	8	.286	.316	.374	.690	90	-5	73	4.40	-4	*0-145(0-145-0)	15	-1.1
1984 StL-N	145	571	82	166	19	11	6	50	29	80	43	10	.291	.326	.394	.720	104	6	74	4.63	8	*0-141(0-141-0)	20	1.2
1985*StL-N★	152	612	114	**216**	26	**18**	10	82	34	86	56	16	**.353**	.387	.503	.890	148	42	123	7.92	4	*0-149(3-146-0)	**36**	4.6
1986 StL-N	124	497	65	127	22	7	7	48	37	82	19	16	.256	.308	.370	.679	87	-13	53	3.62	2	*0-121(0-122-0)	12	-1.3
1987*StL-N★	153	620	76	177	37	11	11	105	24	90	16	4	.285	.314	.434	.748	94	-7	77	4.34	-3	*0-152(0-152-0)/S-1	17	-1.2
1988 StL-N★	137	562	73	164	24	6	3	50	32	84	41	6	.292	.331	.372	.703	100	5	72	4.67	3	*0-135(0-135-0)	16	0.6
1989 StL-N	58	199	23	47	10	2	3	17	10	34	8	6	.236	.276	.352	.628	76	-8	18	3.08	0	0-47(0-47-0)	4	-0.9
1990 StL-N	125	501	76	168	32	5	3	62	38	86	28	9	**.335**	.383	.437	.820	125	19	85	6.49	7	*0-124(0-118-6)	18	2.4
*Oak-A	29	113	23	31	3	2	0	15	10	18	3	0	.274	.333	.336	.670	91	-0	13	3.98	0	0-28(0-28-0)/D-1	3	-0.1
1991 SF-N	131	497	67	155	30	3	4	43	34	74	17	9	.312	.358	.408	.767	119	12	71	5.16	-1	*0-128(0-89-48)	18	0.8
1992 SF-N	138	474	56	141	20	2	1	36	29	88	13	4	.297	.339	.354	.694	102	2	58	4.47	1	*0-119(0-31-90)	15	0.0
1993 SF-N	130	475	53	143	28	1	4	46	38	67	10	9	.301	.354	.389	.744	102	-0	62	4.71	-3	*0-126(0-0-126)	13	-1.0
1994 SF-N	45	156	19	44	3	0	5	23	15	24	3	0	.282	.345	.397	.742	97	0	20	4.35	1	0-42(0-0-42)	3	-0.1
1995*Bos-A	67	200	32	57	11	3	2	15	9	41	5	2	.285	.316	.400	.716	82	-6	24	4.14	3	0-64(3-27-47)	3	-0.4
1996*StL-N	123	309	52	95	15	2	5	41	18	60	5	2	.307	.350	.417	.767	102	1	44	5.20	3	0-83(35-11-42)/1-6	9	0.1
1997 StL-N	122	300	29	90	19	4	3	38	22	59	8	2	.300	.348	.420	.768	101	1	44	5.39	2	0-81(18-18-53)/D-3	7	0.0
1998 StL-N	120	269	27	68	10	1	3	34	14	49	7	2	.253	.290	.331	.621	63	-14	25	3.18	0	0-88(56-7-38)/D-3,1-1	3	-1.6
1999 StL-N	132	271	25	68	7	0	0	20	17	60	7	4	.251	.295	.277	.572	46	-23	22	2.75	-2	0-90(30-19-43)/1-3	1	-2.5
Total 18	2201	7649	1010	2254	350	94	79	856	448	1238	352	121	.295	.335	.396	.731	101	7	1008	4.73	15	*0-1980/1-10,D-7,S-1	224	-1.5
• MCGEEHAN, Dan	Daniel De Sales McGeehan b: 6/7/1885, Jeddo, PA d: 7/12/1955, Hazleton, PA BR/TR, 5'6", 135 lbs. Deb: 4/22/1911																							
1911 StL-N	3	9	0	2	0	0	0	1	0	1	0	....	.222	.222	.222	.444	25	-1	0	1.54	-1	/2-3	0	-0.2
• MCGHEE, Bill	William Mac "Fibber" McGhee b: 9/5/1905, Shawmut, AL d: 3/10/1984, Decatur, GA BL/TL, 5'10.5", 185 lbs. Deb: 7/5/1944																							
1944 Phi-A	77	287	27	83	12	0	1	19	21	20	2	1	.289	.338	.341	.679	96	-1	32	4.06	1	1-75	6	-0.5
1945 Phi-A	93	250	24	63	6	1	0	19	24	16	3	2	.252	.320	.284	.604	76	-7	24	3.43	-1	0-48(40-0-9)/1-8	3	-1.2
Total 2	170	537	51	146	18	1	1	38	45	36	5	3	.272	.329	.315	.644	86	-8	57	3.76	0	/1-83,0-48	9	-1.7
• MCGHEE, Ed	Warren Edward McGhee b: 9/29/1924, Perry, AR d: 2/13/1986, Memphis, TN BR/TR, 5'11", 170 lbs. Deb: 9/20/1950 Career OF: 13-138-13																							
1950 Chi-A	3	6	0	1	0	1	0	0	0	1	0	0	.167	.167	.500	.667	67	-0	1	2.77	0	/0-1	0	0.0
1953 Phi-A	104	358	36	94	11	4	1	29	32	43	4	3	.263	.328	.324	.652	74	-13	38	3.61	-2	0-99(1-97-1)	6	-1.9
1954 Phi-A	21	53	5	11	2	0	2	9	4	8	0	1	.208	.263	.358	.622	69	-3	5	3.05	-1	0-13(2-11-0)	1	-0.5
Chi-A	42	75	12	17	1	0	0	5	12	8	5	0	.227	.333	.240	.573	57	-3	7	2.95	1	0-34(5-18-11)	1	-0.3
Yr.	63	128	17	28	3	0	2	14	16	16	5	1	.219	.306	.289	.595	62	-6	12	2.99	1	0-47(7-29-11)	2	-0.7
1955 Chi-A	26	13	6	1	0	0	0	0	6	1	2	1	.077	.368	.077	.445	24	-1	1	1.36	-1	0-17(5-12-0)	0	-0.2
Total 4	196	505	59	124	14	5	3	43	54	61	11	5	.246	.322	.311	.633	69	-20	51	3.35	-2	0-164	8	-2.9
• MCGILVRAY, Bill	William Alexander "Big Bill" McGilvray b: 4/29/1883, Portland, OR d: 5/23/1952, Denver, CO BL/TL, 6', 160 lbs. Deb: 4/17/1908																							
1908 Cin-N	2	2	0	0	0	0	0	0	0	....	0	....	.000	.000	.000	.000	-103	-0	0	.00	0	....	0	0.0
• MCGINLEY, Tim	Timothy S. McGinley b: 1854, Philadelphia, PA d: 11/2/1899, Oakland, CA, 5'9.5", 155 lbs. Deb: 4/30/1875																							
1875 Cen-n	13	52	5	12	0	1	0	5	0	4	0	0	.231	.231	.269	.500	80	-1	3	2.44	-3	C-12/0-2(0-0-2)	....	-0.3
NH-n	32	131	13	36	3	1	0	10	0	7	1	1	.275	.275	.313	.588	119	3	12	3.64	-3	C-32/3-2	....	0.1
Yr.	45	183	18	48	3	2	0	15	0	11	1	1	.262	.262	.301	.563	108	2	15	3.28	-6	C-44/3-2,0-2(0-0-2)	....	-0.2
1876 Bos-N	9	40	5	6	0	0	0	2	0	1	....	....	.150	.150	.150	.300		-4	1	.76	-3	/0-6(0-6-0),C-3	0	-0.6

YEAR TM-L	G	AB	R	H	2B	3B	HR	RBI	BB	SO	SB	CS	AVG	OBP	SLG	OPS	OPS+	BR/A	RC	RC/G	FR	G/POS	WS	TPW
• MCGINN, Frank	Frank J. McGinn b: 1869, Cincinnati, OH d: 11/19/1897, Cincinnati, OH Deb: 6/9/1890																							
1890 Pit-N	1	4	0	0	0	0	0	0	0	2	0	....	.000	.000	.000	.000	-113	-1	0	.00	0	/0-1	0	-0.1
• MCGINNIS, Russ	Russell Brent McGinnis b: 6/18/1963, Coffeyville, KS BR/TR, 6'3", 225 lbs. Deb: 6/3/1992																							
1992 Tex-A	14	33	2	8	4	0	0	4	3	7	0	0	.242	.306	.364	.669	90	-0	4	3.69	-0	C-10/1-2,3-2	0	0.0
1995 KC-A	3	5	1	0	0	0	0	0	1	1	0	0	.000	.167	.000	.167	-51	-1	0	.23	-1	/1-1,3-1,0-1	0	-0.2
Total 2	**17**	**38**	**3**	**8**	**4**	**0**	**0**	**4**	**4**	**8**	**0**	**0**	**.211**	**.286**	**.316**	**.602**	**70**	**-2**	**4**	**3.13**	**-1**	**/C-10,1-3,3-3,0-1**	**0**	**-0.2**
• MCGLONE, John	John T. McGlone b: 1864, Brooklyn, NY d: 11/24/1927, Brooklyn, NY, 5'10", 165 lbs. Deb: 10/7/1886																							
1886 Was-N	4	15	2	1	0	0	0	1	0	3	0	....	.067	.067	.067	.133	-63	-3	0	.13	-1	/3-4	0	-0.3
1887 Cle-a	21	86	14	27	2	1	0	10	7	....	15	....	.314	.337	.304	.641	82	-1	13	6.17	-1	3-21	2	-0.2
1888 Cle-a	55	203	22	37	1	3	1	22	16	....	26	....	.182	.249	.232	.480	56	-9	19	3.03	-9	3-48/0-7(0-7-0)	2	-1.6
Total 3	**80**	**304**	**38**	**65**	**3**	**4**	**1**	**33**	**23**	**3**	**41**	**....**	**.214**	**.265**	**.242**	**.507**	**57**	**-14**	**32**	**3.63**	**-11**	**/3-73,0-7**	**4**	**-2.1**
• MCGOVERN, Art	Arthur John McGovern b: 2/27/1882, St. John, Canada d: 11/14/1915, Thornton, RI BR/TR, 5'10", 160 lbs. Deb: 4/21/1905																							
1905 Bos-A	15	44	1	5	1	0	0	1	4	....	0	....	.114	.204	.136	.340	9	-4	1	.91	-1	C-15	0	-0.5
• MCGOWAN, Beauty	Frank Bernard McGowan b: 11/8/1901, Branford, CT d: 5/6/1982, Hamden, CT BL/TR, 5'11", 190 lbs. Deb: 4/12/1922 Career OF: 26-118-187																							
1922 Phi-A	99	300	36	69	10	5	1	20	40	46	6	5	.230	.323	.307	.629	63	-16	32	3.37	4	0-82(0-56-28)	4	-1.6
1923 Phi-A	95	287	41	73	9	1	1	19	36	25	4	3	.254	.340	.303	.643	69	-12	32	3.76	2	0-79(26-17-36)	6	-1.4
1928 StL-A	47	168	35	61	13	4	2	18	16	15	2	1	.363	.425	.524	.949	143	11	38	8.20	-2	0-47(0-11-37)	9	0.6
1929 StL-A	125	441	62	112	26	6	2	51	61	34	5	2	.254	.346	.354	.700	77	-13	58	4.40	3	*0-117(0-34-84)	10	-1.7
1937 Bos-N	9	12	0	1	0	0	0	0	1	2	0	....	.083	.154	.083	.237	-37	-2	0	.49	0	/0-2(0-0-2)	0	-0.2
Total 5	**375**	**1208**	**174**	**316**	**58**	**16**	**6**	**108**	**154**	**122**	**17**	**11**	**.262**	**.347**	**.351**	**.698**	**80**	**-31**	**160**	**4.42**	**7**	**0-327**	**29**	**-4.3**
• MCGRAW, John	John Joseph "Mugsy,Little Napoleon" McGraw b: 4/7/1873, Truxton, NY d: 2/25/1934, New Rochelle, NY BL/TR, 5'7", 155 lbs. Deb: 8/26/1891 M HOF: 1937 Career OF: 21-9-30																							
1891 Bal-a	33	115	17	31	3	5	0	14	12	17	4	....	.270	.359	.383	.741	111	2	18	5.57	-9	S-21/0-9(0-0-9),2-3	3	-0.6
1892 Bal-N	79	286	41	77	13	2	1	26	32	21	15	....	.269	.355	.339	.694	107	3	41	5.26	-3	2-34,0-34(8-6-20)/S-8,3-3	7	0.0
1893 Bal-N	127	480	123	154	9	10	5	64	101	11	38	....	.321	.454	.413	.866	129	28	110	8.93	-17	*S-117,0-11(10-0-1)	20	1.4
1894*Bal-N	124	512	156	174	18	14	1	92	91	12	78	....	.340	.451	.436	.887	110	14	139	10.71	1	*3-118/2-6	24	1.3
1895*Bal-N	96	388	110	143	13	6	2	48	60	9	61	....	.369	.459	.448	.908	131	22	111	11.96	11	*3-95/2-1	20	2.8
1896*Bal-N	23	77	20	25	2	2	0	14	11	4	13	....	.325	.422	.403	.825	116	3	19	9.70	-1	3-18/1-1	3	0.2
1897*Bal-N	106	391	90	127	15	3	0	48	99	....	44	....	.325	**.471**	.379	.849	126	25	94	9.16	-8	*3-105	20	1.6
1898 Bal-N	143	515	**143**	176	8	10	0	53	**112**	....	43	....	.342	.475	.396	.871	148	45	121	9.32	2	*3-137/0-3(0-3-0)	31	4.6
1899 Bal-N	117	399	**140**	156	13	3	1	33	**124**	....	73	....	.391	**.547**	.446	.994	165	53	141	**15.27**	9	*3-117	34	**5.8**
1900 StL-N	99	334	84	115	10	4	2	33	85	....	29	....	.344	**.505**	.416	.921	156	38	88	10.38	-5	3-99	21	3.2
1901 Bal-A	73	232	71	81	14	9	0	28	61	....	24	....	.349	.508	.487	.995	169	29	72	12.47	-6	3-69	16	2.3
1902 Bal-A	20	63	14	18	3	2	1	3	17	....	5	....	.286	.451	.444	.896	143	5	16	8.77	-4	3-19	3	0.1
NY-N	35	107	13	25	0	0	0	5	26	....	7	....	.234	.401	.234	.635	97	3	14	4.28	-2	S-34	4	0.2
1903 NY-N	12	11	2	3	0	0	0	1	1	....	1	....	.273	.467	.273	.739	108	1	2	6.34	-2	/2-2,0-2(2-0-0),3-1,S-1	0	-0.1
1904 NY-N	5	12	0	4	0	0	0	0	3	....	0	....	.333	.467	.333	.800	142	1	2	6.22	3	/2-2,S-2	1	0.4
1905 NY-N	3	0	0	0	0	0	0	0	0	....	1	....	....	....	....	....	-98	0	0	....	0	/0-1	0	0.0
1906 NY-N	4	2	0	0	0	0	0	0	1	....	0	....	.000	.333	.000	.333	4	-0	0	.00	0	/3-1	0	-0.1
Total 16	**1099**	**3924**	**1024**	**1309**	**121**	**70**	**13**	**462**	**836**	**74**	**436**	**....**	**.334**	**.466**	**.410**	**.876**	**135**	**273**	**986**	**9.88**	**-32**	**3-782,S-183/0-60,2-48,1-1**	**207**	**23.1**
• MCGRIFF, Fred	Frederick Stanley "Crime Dog" McGriff b: 10/31/1963, Tampa, FL BL/TL, 6'3", 215 lbs. Deb: 5/17/1986																							
1986 Tor-A	3	5	1	1	0	0	0	0	0	2	0	0	.200	.200	.200	.400	9	-1	0	1.35	0	/D-2,1-1	0	-0.1
1987 Tor-A	107	295	58	73	16	0	20	43	60	104	3	2	.247	.376	.505	.881	128	13	60	7.13	-1	D-90,1-14	11	0.9
1988 Tor-A	154	536	100	151	35	4	34	82	79	149	6	1	.282	.378	.552	.930	156	42	113	7.51	-6	*1-153	24	2.6
1989*Tor-A	161	551	98	148	27	3	**36**	92	119	132	7	4	.269	.402	.525	**.927**	**169**	**55**	121	7.64	-2	*1-159/D-2	30	4.2
1990 Tor-A	153	557	91	167	21	1	35	88	94	108	5	3	.300	.403	.530	.932	150	40	124	8.25	8	*1-147/D-6	26	3.8
1991 SD-N	153	528	84	147	19	1	31	106	105	135	4	1	.278	.400	.494	.894	146	37	107	7.18	-8	*1-153	25	1.9
1992 SD-N★	152	531	79	152	30	4	**35**	104	96	108	8	6	.286	.396	.556	.952	164	46	116	7.78	-6	*1-151	27	3.2
1993 SD-N	83	302	52	83	11	1	18	46	42	55	4	3	.275	.365	.497	.862	126	11	54	6.17	-5	1-83	7	-0.1
*Atl-N	68	255	59	79	18	1	19	55	34	51	1	0	.310	.393	.612	1.005	163	23	62	9.20	-2	1-66	16	1.5
Yr.	151	557	111	162	29	2	37	101	76	106	5	3	.291	.378	.549	.927	143	33	116	7.49	-7	*1-149	23	1.4
1994 Atl-N★	113	424	81	135	25	1	34	94	50	76	7	3	.318	.392	.623	1.014	155	34	103	9.15	-4	*1-112	22	1.9
1995*Atl-N★	144	528	85	148	27	1	27	93	65	99	3	6	.280	.365	.489	.853	119	12	89	5.86	5	*1-144	20	0.4
1996*Atl-N★	159	617	81	182	37	1	28	107	68	116	7	3	.295	.367	.494	.861	118	16	108	6.31	7	*1-158	19	0.8
1997*Atl-N	152	564	77	156	25	1	22	97	68	112	5	0	.277	.358	.441	.800	106	6	87	5.42	-3	*1-149	14	-1.0
1998 TB-A	151	564	73	160	33	0	19	81	79	118	7	2	.284	.374	.443	.817	109	10	95	6.06	-11	*1-135,D-14	13	-1.3
1999 TB-A	144	529	75	164	30	1	32	104	86	107	1	0	.310	.407	.552	.959	140	34	121	8.59	-3	*1-125,D-18	24	1.7
2000 TB-A★	158	566	82	157	18	0	27	106	91	120	2	0	.277	.377	.452	.830	110	11	98	6.15	-11	*1-144,D-10	16	-1.2
2001 TB-A	97	343	40	109	18	0	19	61	40	69	1	1	.318	.389	.536	.925	143	21	71	7.85	2	1-74,D-17	13	1.5
Chi-N	49	170	27	48	7	2	12	41	26	37	0	1	.282	.387	.559	.946	148	12	36	7.36	-2	1-49	9	0.5
2002 Chi-N	146	523	67	143	27	2	30	103	63	99	1	2	.273	.356	.505	.861	126	18	93	6.26	-5	*1-137/D-2	17	0.1
2003 LA-N	86	297	32	74	14	0	13	40	31	66	0	0	.249	.322	.428	.750	99	-1	40	4.74	-6	1-79	8	-1.4
Total 18	**2433**	**8685**	**1342**	**2477**	**438**	**24**	**491**	**1543**	**1296**	**1863**	**72**	**38**	**.285**	**.380**	**.511**	**.891**	**135**	**440**	**1698**	**7.01**	**-54**	***1-2233,D-161**	**341**	**19.9**
• MCGRIFF, Terry	Terence Roy McGriff b: 9/23/1963, Fort Pierce, FL BR/TR, 6'2", 195 lbs. Deb: 7/11/1987																							
1987 Cin-N	34	89	6	20	3	0	2	11	8	17	0	0	.225	.289	.326	.615	60	-5	8	3.00	-1	C-33	2	-0.5
1988 Cin-N	35	96	9	19	3	0	1	4	12	31	1	0	.198	.287	.260	.547	56	-5	7	2.50	0	C-32	1	-0.4
1989 Cin-N	6	11	1	3	0	0	0	2	2	3	0	0	.273	.385	.273	.657	88	-0	1	4.23	-1	/C-6	1	0.0
1990 Cin-N	2	4	0	0	0	0	0	0	0	1	0	0	.000	.000	.000	.000	-96	-1	0	.00	0	/C-1	0	-0.1
Hou-N	4	5	0	0	0	0	0	0	0	0	0	0	.000	.000	.000	.000	-103	-1	0	.00	0	/C-4	0	-0.2
Yr.	6	9	0	0	0	0	0	0	0	1	0	0	.000	.000	.000	.000	-100	-2	0	.00	0	/C-5	0	-0.2
1993 Fla-N	3	7	0	0	0	0	0	0	1	2	0	0	.000	.125	.000	.125	-60	-2	0	.13	0	/C-3	0	-0.2
1994 StL-N	42	114	10	25	6	0	0	13	13	11	0	0	.219	.310	.272	.582	55	-7	9	2.38	1	C-39	2	-0.4
Total 6	**126**	**326**	**26**	**67**	**12**	**0**	**3**	**30**	**36**	**65**	**1**	**0**	**.206**	**.288**	**.270**	**.558**	**51**	**-22**	**26**	**2.49**	**0**	**C-118**	**6**	**-1.6**
• MCGRILLIS, Mark	Mark A. McGrillis b: 10/22/1872, Philadelphia, PA d: 5/16/1935, Philadelphia, PA, 6' Deb: 9/17/1892																							
1892 StL-N	1	3	0	0	0	0	0	0	0	1	0	....	.000	.000	.000	.000	-105	-1	0	.00	0	/3-1	0	0.0
• MCGUCKIN, Joe	Joseph W. McGuckin b: 3/13/1862, Paterson, NJ d: 12/31/1903, Yonkers, NY, 5'8.5", 160 lbs. Deb: 8/27/1890																							
1890 Bal-a	11	37	2	4	0	0	0	2	6	....	3	....	.108	.250	.108	.358	5	-4	2	1.44	2	0-11(0-0-11)	1	-0.2
• MCGUINNESS, John	John James McGuinness b: 1857, Ireland d: 12/19/1916, Binghamton, NY, 5'10.5", 150 lbs. Deb: 5/6/1876																							
1876 NY-N	1	4	0	0	0	0	0	0	0	0	....	....	.000	.000	.000	.000	-115	-1	0	.00	-3	/2-1,C-1	0	-0.3
1879 Syr-N	12	51	7	15	1	1	0	4	0	6	....	....	.294	.294	.353	.647	126	2	5	4.22	-1	1-12	2	0.0
1884 Phi-U	53	220	25	52	8	1	0	....	5	....	....	....	.236	.253	.282	.535	87	-2	16	2.68	-1	1-48/2-5,S-1	3	-0.6
Total 3	**66**	**275**	**32**	**67**	**9**	**2**	**0**	**4**	**5**	**6**	**....**	**....**	**.244**	**.257**	**.291**	**.548**	**92**	**-1**	**22**	**2.90**	**-5**	**/1-60,2-6,C-1,S-1**	**5**	**-0.9**
• MCGUIRE, Bill	William Patrick McGuire b: 2/14/1964, Omaha, NE BR/TR, 6'3", 205 lbs. Deb: 8/2/1988																							
1988 Sea-A	9	16	1	3	0	0	0	2	3	2	0	0	.188	.316	.188	.503	43	-1	1	2.49	0	/C-9	0	-0.1
1989 Sea-A	14	28	2	5	0	0	1	4	2	6	0	0	.179	.233	.286	.519	44	-2	1	1.53	0	C-14	1	-0.1
Total 2	**23**	**44**	**3**	**8**	**0**	**0**	**1**	**6**	**5**	**8**	**0**	**0**	**.182**	**.265**	**.250**	**.515**	**44**	**-3**	**3**	**1.88**	**1**	**/C-23**	**1**	**-0.2**
• MCGUIRE, Deacon	James Thomas McGuire b: 11/18/1863, Youngstown, OH d: 10/31/1936, Duck Lake, MI BR/TR, 6'1", 185 lbs. Deb: 6/21/1884 M/C/U Career OF: 4-4-25																							
1884 Tol-a	45	151	12	28	7	0	1	0	5	....	....	....	.185	.217	.252	.468	50	-8	8	1.89	-5	C-41/0-4(1-3-0),S-3	1	-0.9

YEAR TM-L	G	AB	R	H	2B	3B	HR	RBI	BB	SO	SB	CS	AVG	OBP	SLG	OPS	OPS+	BR/A	RC	RC/G	FR	G/POS	WS	TPW
1885 Det-N	34	121	11	23	4	2	0	9	5	23	....	....	.190	.222	.256	.478	54	-6	7	1.95	2	C-31/0-3(3-0-0)	2	-0.1
1886 Phi-N	50	167	25	33	7	1	2	18	19	25	2	....	.198	.280	.287	.567	72	-5	14	2.89	-11	C-49/0-1	4	-1.1
1887 Phi-N	41	161	22	57	6	6	2	23	11	8	3	....	.354	.362	.467	.829	121	4	27	6.90	-6	C-41	7	0.1
1888 Phi-N	12	51	7	17	4	2	0	11	4	9	0	....	.333	.382	.490	.872	167	4	10	7.77	-4	C-10/3-2	3	0.1
Det-N	3	13	0	0	0	0	0	0	0	4	0	....	.000	.000	.000	.000	-100	-3	0	.00	-1	/C-3	0	-0.3
Yr.	15	64	7	17	4	2	0	11	4	13	0	....	.266	.309	.391	.699	116	1	10	5.62	-5	C-13/3-2	3	-0.3
Cle-a	26	94	15	24	1	3	1	13	7	....	2	....	.255	.333	.362	.695	126	3	12	4.74	-3	C-17/1-6,0-3(0-0-3)	4	0.1
1890 Roc-a	87	331	46	99	16	4	4	53	21	....	8	....	.299	.356	.408	.763	135	14	52	5.95	-5	C-71,1-15/0-3(0-1-2),P-1	15	1.1
1891 Was-a	114	413	55	125	22	10	3	66	43	34	10	....	.303	.382	.426	.808	137	20	73	6.70	1	*C-98,0-18(0-0-18)/3-3,1-1	17	2.5
1892 Was-N	97	315	46	73	14	4	4	43	61	49	7	....	.232	.360	.340	.699	115	9	42	4.69	-2	C-89/1-8,0-1	10	1.4
1893 Was-N	63	237	29	61	14	3	1	26	26	12	3	....	.257	.338	.354	.693	86	-4	30	4.54	-3	C-50,1-12	5	-0.3
1894 Was-N	104	425	67	130	18	6	6	78	33	19	11	....	.306	.366	.419	.784	92	-6	71	6.24	4	*C-104	9	0.6
1895 Was-N	133	538	89	181	30	8	10	97	40	18	17	....	.336	.388	.478	.865	126	19	110	8.34	21	*C-132/S-1	17	4.2
1896 Was-N	108	389	60	125	25	3	2	70	30	14	12	....	.321	.379	.416	.795	109	5	68	6.70	-3	*C-98/1-1	14	0.9
1897 Was-N	93	327	51	112	17	7	4	53	21	....	9	....	.343	.386	.474	.860	127	12	65	7.97	3	C-73/1-6	13	1.8
1898 Was-N	131	489	59	131	18	3	1	57	24	....	10	....	.268	.310	.323	.633	82	-13	55	3.94	0	C-93,1-37	8	-0.4
1899 Was-N	59	199	25	54	3	1	1	12	16	....	3	....	.271	.335	.312	.646	78	-5	22	4.08	3	C-56/1-1	5	0.3
Bro-N	46	157	22	50	12	4	0	23	12	....	4	....	.318	.385	.446	.831	125	5	29	7.20	2	C-46	8	1.1
Yr.	105	356	47	104	15	5	1	35	28	....	7	....	.292	.357	.371	.728	99	-0	52	5.40	6	*C-102/1-1	13	1.3
1900*Bro-N	71	241	20	69	15	2	0	34	19	....	2	....	.286	.348	.365	.714	91	-3	32	4.95	-4	C-69	7	0.0
1901 Bro-N	85	301	28	89	16	4	0	40	18	....	4	....	.296	.342	.375	.717	105	2	41	5.09	-6	C-81/1-3	10	0.4
1902 Det-A	73	229	27	52	14	1	2	23	24	....	0	....	.227	.300	.323	.624	71	-9	23	3.41	-2	C-70	4	-0.4
1903 Det-A	72	248	15	62	12	1	0	21	19	....	3	....	.250	.306	.306	.612	87	-4	25	3.53	-5	C-69/1-1	6	-0.1
1904 NY-A	101	322	17	67	12	2	0	20	27	....	2	....	.208	.276	.258	.533	66	-12	25	2.52	3	C-97/1-1	8	0.1
1905 NY-A	72	228	9	50	7	2	0	33	18	....	3	....	.219	.291	.268	.558	69	-8	20	2.86	-8	C-71	5	-0.9
1906 NY-A	51	144	11	43	5	0	0	14	12	....	3	....	.299	.365	.333	.698	108	2	19	5.00	-5	C-49/1-1	6	0.1
1907 NY-A	1	1	0	0	0	0	0	0	0	....	0	....	.000	.000	.000	.000	-93	-0	0	.00	0	/C-1	0	0.0
Bos-A	6	4	1	3	0	0	1	1	0	....	0	....	.750	.750	1.500	2.250	620	2	5	122.23	0	....	1	0.2
Yr.	7	5	1	3	0	0	1	1	0	....	0	....	.600	.600	1.200	1.800	478	2	5	61.12	0	/C-1	1	0.2
1908 Bos-A	1	1	0	0	0	0	0	0	0	....	0	....	.000	.000	.000	.000	-97	-0	0	.00	0	....	0	0.0
Cle-A	1	4	0	1	1	0	0	2	0	....	0	....	.250	.250	.500	.750	142	0	0	4.09	0	/1-1	0	0.0
Yr.	2	5	0	1	1	0	0	2	0	....	0	....	.200	.200	.400	.600	94	-0	0	3.06	0	/1-1	0	0.0
1910 Cle-A	1	3	0	1	0	0	0	0	0	....	0	....	.333	.500	.333	.833	160	0	0	6.46	-0	/C-1	0	0.0
1912 Det-A	1	2	1	1	0	0	0	0	0	....	0	....	.500	.500	.500	1.000	192	0	0	12.79	0	/C-1	0	0.0
Total 26	**1782**	**6306**	**770**	**1761**	**300**	**79**	**45**	**840**	**515**	**215**	**118**	**....**	**.279**	**.341**	**.372**	**.713**	**101**	**16**	**888**	**5.15**	**-33**	***C-1611/1-94,0-33,3-5,S-4,P**	**189**	**10.3**

• MCGUIRE, Jim James A. McGuire b: 2/4/1875, Dunkirk, NY d: 1/26/1917, Buffalo, NY TR Deb: 9/10/1901

YEAR TM-L	G	AB	R	H	2B	3B	HR	RBI	BB	SO	SB	CS	AVG	OBP	SLG	OPS	OPS+	BR/A	RC	RC/G	FR	G/POS	WS	TPW
1901 Cle-A	18	69	4	16	2	0	0	3	0	....	0	....	.232	.232	.261	.493	38	-6	4	2.14	-1	S-18	1	-0.6

• MCGUIRE, Mickey M C Adolphus McGuire b: 1/18/1941, Dayton, OH BR/TR, 5'10", 170 lbs. Deb: 9/7/1962

YEAR TM-L	G	AB	R	H	2B	3B	HR	RBI	BB	SO	SB	CS	AVG	OBP	SLG	OPS	OPS+	BR/A	RC	RC/G	FR	G/POS	WS	TPW
1962 Bal-A	6	4	0	0	0	0	0	0	0	0	0	0	.000	.000	.000	.000	-105	-1	0	.00	-2	/S-5	0	-0.3
1967 Bal-A	10	17	2	4	0	0	0	2	0	2	0	0	.235	.235	.235	.471	40	-1	1	1.36	0	/2-4	0	-0.2
Total 2	**16**	**21**	**2**	**4**	**0**	**0**	**0**	**2**	**0**	**2**	**0**	**0**	**.190**	**.190**	**.190**	**.381**	**12**	**-2**	**1**	**1.06**	**-2**	**/S-5,2-4**	**0**	**-0.4**

• MCGUIRE, Ryan Ryan Byron McGuire b: 11/23/1971, Bellflower, CA BL/TL, 6'2", 210 lbs. Deb: 6/5/1997 Career OF: 70-10-47

YEAR TM-L	G	AB	R	H	2B	3B	HR	RBI	BB	SO	SB	CS	AVG	OBP	SLG	OPS	OPS+	BR/A	RC	RC/G	FR	G/POS	WS	TPW
1997 Mon-N	84	199	22	51	15	2	3	17	19	34	1	4	.256	.321	.397	.718	87	-6	24	4.16	1	0-44(21-2-22),1-30/D-3	4	-0.8
1998 Mon-N	130	210	17	39	9	0	1	10	32	55	0	0	.186	.293	.243	.536	44	-17	15	2.28	0	1-78,0-46(33-7-8)	1	-2.0
1999 Mon-N	88	140	17	31	7	2	2	18	27	33	1	1	.221	.347	.343	.690	78	-4	16	3.57	7	1-58,0-23(16-1-7)	2	-0.1
2000 NY-N	1	2	0	0	0	0	0	0	1	0	0	0	.000	.333	.000	.333	-6	-0	0	.00	0	/0-1	0	0.0
2001 Fla-N	48	54	8	10	2	0	1	8	7	15	1	0	.185	.279	.278	.556	46	-4	5	2.91	0	/0-9(0-0-9),1-4	1	-0.4
2002 Bal-A	17	26	0	2	1	0	0	2	2	7	0	0	.077	.143	.115	.258	-32	-5	0	.26	0	/1-7,D-1	0	-0.5
Total 6	**368**	**631**	**64**	**133**	**34**	**4**	**7**	**55**	**88**	**144**	**3**	**5**	**.211**	**.307**	**.311**	**.618**	**62**	**-36**	**61**	**3.07**	**8**	**1-177,0-123/D-4**	**8**	**-3.9**

• MCGUNNIGLE, Bill William Henry "Gunner" McGunnigle
b: 1/1/1855, Boston, MA d: 3/9/1899, Brockton, MA BR/TR, 5'9", 155 lbs. Deb: 5/2/1879 M/U Career OF: 2-2-36 ♦

YEAR TM-L	G	AB	R	H	2B	3B	HR	RBI	BB	SO	SB	CS	AVG	OBP	SLG	OPS	OPS+	BR/A	RC	RC/G	FR	G/POS	WS	TPW
1879 Buf-N	47	171	22	30	0	1	0	5	5	24	....	....	.175	.199	.187	.386	27	-11	7	1.30	2	0-34(0-0-34),P-14	12	-1.2
1880 Buf-N	7	22	0	4	0	0	0	1	0	4	....	....	.182	.182	.182	.364	23	-1	1	1.14	-2	/P-5,0-3(1-1-1)	1	-0.4
Wor-N	1	4	0	0	0	0	0	0	0	2	....	....	.000	.000	.000	.000	-92	-1	0	.00	0	/0-1	0	-0.1
Yr.	8	26	0	4	0	0	0	1	0	6	....	....	.154	.154	.154	.308	5	-2	1	.93	-2	/P-5,0-4(2-1-2)	1	-0.5
1882 Cle-N	1	5	2	1	0	0	0	0	0	1	....	....	.200	.200	.200	.400	30	-0	0	1.41	0	/0-1	0	-0.1
Total 3	**56**	**202**	**24**	**35**	**0**	**1**	**0**	**6**	**5**	**31**	**....**	**....**	**.173**	**.193**	**.183**	**.376**	**25**	**-14**	**7**	**1.25**	**0**	**/0-39,P-19**	**13**	**-1.8**

• MCGWIRE, Mark Mark David "Big Mac" McGwire b: 10/1/1963, Pomona, CA BR/TR, 6'5", 225 lbs. Deb: 8/22/1986 Career OF: 0-0-4

YEAR TM-L	G	AB	R	H	2B	3B	HR	RBI	BB	SO	SB	CS	AVG	OBP	SLG	OPS	OPS+	BR/A	RC	RC/G	FR	G/POS	WS	TPW
1986 Oak-A	18	53	10	10	1	0	3	9	4	18	0	1	.189	.259	.377	.636	76	-2	5	3.15	-4	3-16	1	-0.7
1987 Oak-A★	151	557	97	161	28	4	**49**	118	71	131	1	1	.289	.374	**.618**	.992	168	53	131	8.64	-7	*1-145/3-8,0-3(0-0-3)	30	3.5
1988*Oak-A★	155	550	87	143	22	1	32	99	76	117	0	0	.260	.354	.478	.832	135	26	93	5.91	-5	*1-154/0-1	28	1.1
1989*Oak-A★	143	490	74	113	17	0	33	95	83	94	1	1	.231	.345	.467	.813	132	21	76	5.01	5	*1-141/D-2	21	1.7
1990*Oak-A★	156	523	87	123	16	0	39	108	**110**	116	2	1	.235	.375	.489	.864	146	36	101	6.43	6	*1-154/D-2	27	3.2
1991 Oak-A★	154	483	62	97	22	0	22	75	93	116	2	1	.201	.333	.383	.716	103	5	65	4.34	6	*1-152	18	0.1
1992*Oak-A★	139	467	87	125	22	0	42	104	90	105	0	1	.268	.391	**.585**	.976	**179**	51	110	8.17	-3	*1-139	29	3.9
1993 Oak-A	27	84	16	28	6	0	9	24	21	19	0	1	.333	.472	.726	1.198	231	16	30	14.06	-1	1-25	6	1.3
1994 Oak-A	47	135	26	34	3	0	9	25	37	40	0	0	.252	.413	.474	.887	140	10	29	7.48	-2	1-40/D-5	6	0.4
1995 Oak-A★	104	317	75	87	13	0	39	90	88	77	1	1	.274	.447	.685	1.132	202	52	102	11.22	-1	1-91,D-10	23	4.0
1996 Oak-A★	130	423	104	132	21	0	**52**	113	116	112	0	0	.312	**.468**	**.730**	**1.199**	**202**	**72**	149	**13.15**	-7	*1-109,D-18	29	5.0
1997 Oak-A★	105	366	48	104	24	0	34	81	58	98	1	0	.284	.388	.628	1.016	163	34	90	8.77	-5	*1-101	15	1.9
StL-N	51	174	38	44	3	0	24	42	43	61	2	0	.253	.414	.684	1.098	183	23	54	11.05	1	1-50	10	1.9
1998 StL-N★	155	509	130	152	21	0	**70**	147	**162**	155	1	0	.299	**.473**	**.752**	**1.225**	**218**	**97**	193	**14.15**	-6	*1-151	**41**	**7.7**
1999 StL-N★	153	521	118	145	21	1	**65**	**147**	133	141	0	0	.278	.427	.697	1.124	**177**	64	160	11.01	-6	*1-151	30	4.3
2000*StL-N★	89	236	60	72	8	0	32	73	76	78	1	0	.305	.486	.746	1.232	204	43	92	14.46	-5	1-70	20	3.0
2001*StL-N	97	299	48	56	4	0	29	64	56	118	0	0	.187	.321	.492	.813	107	3	49	5.15	-7	1-90	8	-1.2
Total 16	**1874**	**6187**	**1167**	**1626**	**252**	**6**	**583**	**1414**	**1317**	**1596**	**12**	**8**	**.263**	**.398**	**.588**	**.986**	**164**	**604**	**1530**	**8.61**	**-41**	***1-1763/D-37,3-24,0-4**	**342**	**41.0**

• MCHALE, Bob Robert Emmet "Rabbit" McHale b: 2/7/1870, Sacramento, CA d: 6/9/1952, Sacramento, CA TR, 5'11", 152 lbs. Deb: 5/9/1898

YEAR TM-L	G	AB	R	H	2B	3B	HR	RBI	BB	SO	SB	CS	AVG	OBP	SLG	OPS	OPS+	BR/A	RC	RC/G	FR	G/POS	WS	TPW
1898 Was-N	11	33	5	6	2	0	0	7	1	....	1	....	.182	.270	.242	.513	47	-2	3	2.48	-2	/0-9(0-9-0),1-1,S-1	0	-0.4

• MCHALE, Jim James Bernard "J.B." McHale b: 12/17/1875, Miners Mills, PA d: 6/17/1959, Los Angeles, CA BR/TR, 5'11", 165 lbs. Deb: 4/14/1908

YEAR TM-L	G	AB	R	H	2B	3B	HR	RBI	BB	SO	SB	CS	AVG	OBP	SLG	OPS	OPS+	BR/A	RC	RC/G	FR	G/POS	WS	TPW
1908 Bos-A	21	67	9	15	2	2	0	7	4	....	4	....	.224	.278	.313	.591	89	-1	7	3.26	-2	0-19(1-18-0)	2	-0.4

• MCHALE, John John Joseph McHale b: 9/21/1921, Detroit, MI BL/TR, 6', 200 lbs. Deb: 5/28/1943

YEAR TM-L	G	AB	R	H	2B	3B	HR	RBI	BB	SO	SB	CS	AVG	OBP	SLG	OPS	OPS+	BR/A	RC	RC/G	FR	G/POS	WS	TPW
1943 Det-A	4	3	0	0	0	0	0	0	1	1	0	0	.000	.250	.000	.250	-23	-0	0	.59	0	....	0	0.0
1944 Det-A	1	1	0	0	0	0	0	0	0	0	0	0	.000	.000	.000	.000	-95	-0	0	.00	0	....	0	0.0
1945*Det-A	19	14	0	2	0	0	0	1	1	4	0	0	.143	.250	.143	.393	14	-1	1	1.45	0	/1-3	0	-0.1
1947 Det-A	39	95	10	20	1	0	3	11	7	24	1	1	.211	.265	.316	.580	59	-6	8	2.97	-2	1-25	1	-0.8
1948 Det-A	1	1	0	0	0	0	0	0	0	0	0	0	.000	.000	.000	.000	-97	-0	0	.00	0	....	0	0.0
Total 5	**64**	**114**	**10**	**22**	**1**	**0**	**3**	**12**	**9**	**29**	**1**	**1**	**.193**	**.258**	**.281**	**.539**	**48**	**-8**	**9**	**2.64**	**-2**	**/1-28**	**1**	**-1.1**

• MCHENRY, Austin Austin Bush "Mac" McHenry
b: 9/22/1895, Wrightsville, OH d: 11/27/1922, Adams County, OH BR/TR, 5'11", 152 lbs. Deb: 6/22/1918 Career OF: 449-78-13

YEAR TM-L	G	AB	R	H	2B	3B	HR	RBI	BB	SO	SB	CS	AVG	OBP	SLG	OPS	OPS+	BR/A	RC	RC/G	FR	G/POS	WS	TPW
1918 StL-N	80	272	32	71	12	6	1	29	21	24	8	....	.261	.319	.360	.679	111	3	33	4.05	4	0-80(80-0-0)	7	0.4
1919 StL-N	110	371	41	106	19	11	1	47	19	57	7	....	.286	.322	.404	.727	125	10	49	4.59	7	*0-103(73-26-7)	13	1.4
1920 StL-N	137	504	66	142	19	11	10	65	25	73	8	11	.282	.316	.423	.738	113	5	64	4.37	1	*0-133(89-52-0)	14	-0.1

YEAR TM-L	G	AB	R	H	2B	3B	HR	RBI	BB	SO	SB	CS	AVG	OBP	SLG	OPS	OPS+	BR/A	RC	RC/G	FR	G/POS	WS	TPW
1921 StL-N	152	574	92	201	37	8	17	102	38	48	10	20	.350	.393	.531	.924	145	31	111	7.21	3	*0-152(146-0-6)	25	2.2
1922 StL-N	64	238	31	72	18	3	5	43	14	27	2	2	.303	.344	.466	.810	112	4	37	5.77	4	0-61(61-0-0)	7	0.3
Total 5	**543**	**1959**	**262**	**592**	**105**	**39**	**34**	**286**	**117**	**229**	**35**	**33**	**.302**	**.343**	**.448**	**.791**	**124**	**53**	**294**	**5.32**	**19**	**0-529**	**66**	**4.2**

• MCHENRY, Vance Vance Loren McHenry b: 7/10/1956, Chico, CA BR/TR, 5'9", 165 lbs. Deb: 8/13/1981

YEAR TM-L	G	AB	R	H	2B	3B	HR	RBI	BB	SO	SB	CS	AVG	OBP	SLG	OPS	OPS+	BR/A	RC	RC/G	FR	G/POS	WS	TPW
1981 Sea-A	15	18	3	4	0	0	0	2	1	1	0	0	.222	.263	.222	.485	39	-1	1	1.60	-1	S-13/D-1	0	-0.1
1982 Sea-A	3	1	0	0	0	0	0	0	0	0	0	0	.000	.000	.000	.000	-97	-0	0	.00	-1	/D-1,S-1	0	-0.1
Total 2	**18**	**19**	**3**	**4**	**0**	**0**	**0**	**2**	**1**	**1**	**0**	**0**	**.211**	**.250**	**.211**	**.461**	**33**	**-2**	**1**	**1.51**	**-1**	**/S-14,D-2**	**0**	**-0.2**

• MCILVEEN, Irish Henry Cooke McIlveen b: 7/27/1880, Belfast, Ireland d: 10/18/1960, Lorain, OH BL/TL, 5'11.5", 180 lbs. Deb: 7/10/1906

YEAR TM-L	G	AB	R	H	2B	3B	HR	RBI	BB	SO	SB	CS	AVG	OBP	SLG	OPS	OPS+	BR/A	RC	RC/G	FR	G/POS	WS	TPW
1906 Pit-N	5	5	1	2	0	0	0	0	0	....	0	....	.400	.400	.400	.800	143	1	1	7.11	0	/P-2	0	-0.4
1908 NY-A	44	169	17	36	3	3	0	8	14	....	6	....	.213	.277	.266	.543	76	-4	14	2.66	-2	0-44(13-1-30)	3	-1.0
1909 NY-A	4	3	0	0	0	0	0	0	1	....	0	....	.000	.250	.000	.250	-20	-0	0	.00	0	....	0	0.0
Total 3	**53**	**177**	**18**	**38**	**3**	**3**	**0**	**8**	**15**	**....**	**6**	**....**	**.215**	**.280**	**.266**	**.545**	**76**	**-4**	**15**	**2.69**	**-2**	**/0-44,P-2**	**3**	**-1.4**

• MCINNIS, Stuffy John Phalen "Jack" McInnis b: 9/19/1890, Gloucester, MA d: 2/16/1960, Ipswich, MA BR/TR, 5'9.5", 162 lbs. Deb: 4/12/1909 M

YEAR TM-L	G	AB	R	H	2B	3B	HR	RBI	BB	SO	SB	CS	AVG	OBP	SLG	OPS	OPS+	BR/A	RC	RC/G	FR	G/POS	WS	TPW
1909 Phi-A	19	46	4	11	0	0	1	4	2	....	0	....	.239	.286	.304	.590	85	-1	4	2.85	1	S-14	1	0.1
1910 Phi-A	38	73	10	22	2	4	0	12	7	....	3	....	.301	.363	.438	.801	152	4	12	6.23	-6	S-17/2-5,3-4,0-1	4	-0.2
1911*Phi-A	126	468	76	150	20	10	3	77	25	....	23	....	.321	.361	.425	.787	121	12	80	6.15	-11	1-97,S-24	18	0.0
1912 Phi-A	153	568	83	186	25	13	3	101	49	....	27	....	.327	.384	.433	.817	138	28	105	6.66	3	*1-153	24	2.8
1913*Phi-A	148	543	79	176	30	4	4	90	45	31	16	....	.324	.382	.416	.798	137	24	91	5.93	2	*1-148	26	2.6
1914*Phi-A	149	576	74	181	12	8	1	95	19	27	25	19	.314	.341	.368	.709	118	6	76	4.54	-2	*1-149	21	0.1
1915 Phi-A	119	456	44	143	14	4	0	49	14	17	8	8	.314	.337	.362	.699	113	2	57	4.52	-1	*1-119	13	-0.1
1916 Phi-A	140	512	42	151	25	3	1	60	25	19	7	....	.295	.331	.361	.693	113	6	67	4.53	2	*1-140	12	0.5
1917 Phi-A	150	567	50	172	19	4	0	44	33	19	18	....	.303	.342	.351	.693	113	7	72	4.52	5	*1-150	17	1.0
1918*Bos-A	117	423	40	115	11	5	0	56	19	10	10	....	.272	.306	.322	.628	91	-7	46	3.45	10	1-94,3-23	12	0.2
1919 Bos-A	120	440	32	134	12	5	1	58	23	11	8	....	.305	.341	.361	.702	103	1	57	4.48	3	*1-118	12	0.1
1920 Bos-A	148	559	50	166	21	3	2	71	18	19	6	11	.297	.321	.356	.677	83	-17	62	3.66	-1	*1-148	10	-2.0
1921 Bos-A	152	584	72	179	31	10	0	76	21	9	2	4	.307	.335	.394	.729	88	-13	76	4.54	5	*1-152	14	-1.6
1922 Cle-A	142	537	58	164	28	7	1	78	15	5	1	5	.305	.325	.389	.715	85	-15	66	4.31	-2	*1-140	11	-2.5
1923 Bos-N	154	607	70	191	23	9	2	95	26	12	7	8	.315	.343	.392	.735	97	-4	80	4.60	3	*1-154	12	-1.1
1924 Bos-N	146	581	57	169	23	7	1	59	15	6	9	3	.291	.311	.360	.671	83	-13	65	4.00	6	*1-146	12	-1.6
1925*Pit-N	59	155	19	57	10	4	0	24	17	1	1	1	.368	.437	.484	.921	126	7	33	8.83	1	1-46	6	0.5
1926 Pit-N	47	127	12	38	6	1	0	13	7	3	1	....	.299	.336	.362	.698	83	-3	15	4.21	-1	1-40	2	-0.6
1927 Phi-N	1	0	0	0	0	0	0	0	0	0	0	....	....	....	....	....	-99	0	0	....	0	/1-1	0	0.0
Total 19	**2128**	**7822**	**872**	**2405**	**312**	**101**	**20**	**1062**	**380**	**189**	**172**	**59**	**.307**	**.343**	**.381**	**.723**	**106**	**24**	**1065**	**4.76**	**17**	***1-1995/S-55,3-27,2-5,0-1**	**227**	**-1.8**

• MCINTOSH, Tim Timothy Allen McIntosh b: 3/21/1965, Minneapolis, MN BR/TR, 5'11", 195 lbs. Deb: 9/3/1990 Career OF: 15-0-7

YEAR TM-L	G	AB	R	H	2B	3B	HR	RBI	BB	SO	SB	CS	AVG	OBP	SLG	OPS	OPS+	BR/A	RC	RC/G	FR	G/POS	WS	TPW
1990 Mil-A	5	5	1	1	0	0	1	1	0	2	0	0	.200	.200	.800	1.000	168	0	1	5.40	-1	/C-4	0	0.0
1991 Mil-A	7	11	2	4	1	0	1	1	0	4	0	0	.364	.364	.727	1.091	199	1	3	11.22	-1	/0-4(4-0-0),D-2,1-1	0	0.0
1992 Mil-A	35	77	7	14	3	0	0	6	3	9	1	3	.182	.232	.221	.452	28	-9	4	1.39	0	C-14,0-10(9-0-1)/1-7,D-3	1	-0.9
1993 Mil-A	1	0	0	0	0	0	0	0	0	0	0	0	....	....	....	....	-102	0	0	....	0	/C-1	0	0.0
Mon-N	20	21	2	2	1	0	0	2	0	7	0	0	.095	.095	.143	.238	-36	-4	0	.41	-2	/0-7(2-0-6),C-5	0	-0.6
1996 NY-A	3	3	0	0	0	0	0	0	0	0	0	0	.000	.000	.000	.000	-100	-1	0	.00	-1	/1-1,3-1,C-1	0	-0.1
Total 5	**71**	**117**	**12**	**21**	**5**	**0**	**2**	**10**	**3**	**22**	**1**	**3**	**.179**	**.213**	**.274**	**.487**	**35**	**-12**	**8**	**2.00**	**-4**	**/C-25,0-21,1-9,D-5,3-1**	**1**	**-1.6**

• MCINTYRE, Matty Matthew W. McIntyre b: 6/12/1880, Stonington, CT d: 4/2/1920, Detroit, MI BL/TL, 5'11", 175 lbs. Deb: 7/3/1901 Career OF: 856-53-128

YEAR TM-L	G	AB	R	H	2B	3B	HR	RBI	BB	SO	SB	CS	AVG	OBP	SLG	OPS	OPS+	BR/A	RC	RC/G	FR	G/POS	WS	TPW
1901 Phi-A	82	308	38	85	12	4	0	46	30	....	11	....	.276	.346	.341	.687	87	-5	42	4.84	-2	0-82(82-0-0)	8	-1.1
1904 Det-A	152	578	74	146	11	10	2	46	44	....	11	....	.253	.310	.317	.627	101	2	65	3.76	12	*0-152(151-0-1)	17	0.5
1905 Det-A	131	495	59	130	21	5	0	30	48	....	9	....	.263	.330	.325	.656	107	5	58	4.17	12	*0-131(131-0-0)	20	1.1
1906 Det-A	133	493	63	128	19	11	0	39	56	....	29	....	.260	.338	.343	.680	110	7	70	4.94	10	*0-133(132-1-0)	19	1.0
1907 Det-A	20	81	6	23	1	1	0	9	7	....	3	....	.284	.341	.321	.662	107	1	10	4.61	2	0-20(20-0-0)	4	0.2
1908*Det-A	151	569	**105**	168	24	13	0	28	83	....	20	....	.295	.392	.383	.775	146	33	93	5.85	14	*0-151(151-0-0)	33	4.4
1909*Det-A	125	476	65	116	18	9	1	34	54	....	13	....	.244	.325	.326	.650	101	2	54	3.80	1	*0-122(119-3-0)	15	-0.5
1910 Det-A	83	305	40	72	15	5	0	25	39	....	4	....	.236	.323	.318	.641	94	-1	32	3.52	2	0-77(58-17-2)	9	-0.4
1911 Chi-A	146	569	102	184	19	11	1	52	64	....	17	....	.323	.397	.401	.797	125	22	96	6.35	2	*0-146(0-31-115)	23	1.6
1912 Chi-A	49	84	10	14	0	0	0	10	14	....	3	....	.167	.300	.167	.467	36	-6	5	1.87	-1	0-25(12-1-10)	0	-0.8
Total 10	**1072**	**3958**	**562**	**1066**	**140**	**69**	**4**	**319**	**439**	**....**	**120**	**....**	**.269**	**.346**	**.343**	**.689**	**110**	**60**	**526**	**4.63**	**52**	***0-1039**	**148**	**6.0**

• MCIVOR, Otto Edward Otto McIvor b: 7/26/1884, Greenville, TX d: 5/4/1954, Dallas, TX BB/TL, 5'11.5", 175 lbs. Deb: 4/18/1911

YEAR TM-L	G	AB	R	H	2B	3B	HR	RBI	BB	SO	SB	CS	AVG	OBP	SLG	OPS	OPS+	BR/A	RC	RC/G	FR	G/POS	WS	TPW
1911 StL-N	30	62	11	14	2	1	1	9	9	14	0	....	.226	.333	.339	.672	91	-1	7	3.69	-1	0-17(3-6-8)	2	-0.2

• MCKAY, Cody Cody Dean McKay b: 1/11/1974, Vancouver, Canada BL/TR, 6', 208 lbs. Deb: 9/22/2002

YEAR TM-L	G	AB	R	H	2B	3B	HR	RBI	BB	SO	SB	CS	AVG	OBP	SLG	OPS	OPS+	BR/A	RC	RC/G	FR	G/POS	WS	TPW
2002 Oak-A	2	3	0	2	0	0	0	2	0	1	0	0	.667	.667	.667	1.333	256	1	1	17.01	0	/C-1	0	0.1

• MCKAY, Dave David Lawrence McKay b: 3/14/1950, Vancouver, Canada BB/TR, 6'1", 195 lbs. Deb: 8/22/1975 C

YEAR TM-L	G	AB	R	H	2B	3B	HR	RBI	BB	SO	SB	CS	AVG	OBP	SLG	OPS	OPS+	BR/A	RC	RC/G	FR	G/POS	WS	TPW
1975 Min-A	33	125	8	32	4	1	2	16	6	14	1	1	.256	.295	.352	.647	81	-4	12	3.22	-1	3-33	2	-0.5
1976 Min-A	45	138	8	28	2	0	0	8	9	27	1	2	.203	.272	.217	.489	43	-10	8	1.70	-1	3-41/S-2,D-1	1	-1.2
1977 Tor-A	95	274	18	54	4	3	3	22	7	51	2	1	.197	.223	.266	.489	32	-26	15	1.66	-9	2-40,3-32,S-20/D-2	2	-3.2
1978 Tor-A	145	504	59	120	20	8	7	45	20	91	4	4	.238	.269	.351	.620	71	-21	43	2.75	-7	*2-140/S-3,3-2,D-1	8	-2.1
1979 Tor-A	47	156	19	34	9	0	0	12	7	19	1	1	.218	.256	.276	.532	43	-13	10	2.08	0	2-46/3-2	2	-1.0
1980 Oak-A	123	295	29	72	16	1	1	29	10	57	1	1	.244	.283	.315	.598	68	-13	27	3.01	-1	2-62,3-54,S-10	5	-1.1
1981*Oak-A	79	224	25	59	11	1	4	21	16	43	4	1	.263	.318	.375	.693	104	1	27	4.16	2	3-43,2-38/S-7	8	0.6
1982 Oak-A	78	212	25	42	4	1	4	17	11	35	6	1	.198	.238	.283	.521	44	-16	16	2.41	0	2-59,3-16/S-3	1	-1.3
Total 8	**645**	**1928**	**191**	**441**	**70**	**15**	**21**	**170**	**86**	**337**	**20**	**12**	**.229**	**.268**	**.313**	**.581**	**63**	**-101**	**157**	**2.64**	**-17**	**2-385,3-223/S-45,D-4**	**29**	**-9.9**

• MCKEAN, Ed Edwin John "Mack" McKean b: 6/6/1864, Grafton, OH d: 8/16/1919, Cleveland, OH BR/TR, 5'9", 160 lbs. Deb: 4/16/1887 Career OF: 47-4-1

YEAR TM-L	G	AB	R	H	2B	3B	HR	RBI	BB	SO	SB	CS	AVG	OBP	SLG	OPS	OPS+	BR/A	RC	RC/G	FR	G/POS	WS	TPW
1887 Cle-a	132	599	97	214	16	13	2	54	60	....	76	....	.357	.358	.375	.733	108	8	102	7.16	-21	*S-123/2-8,0-4(4-0-0)	15	-0.8
1888 Cle-a	131	548	94	164	21	15	6	68	28	....	52	....	.299	.340	.425	.765	149	28	99	6.99	-1	S-78,0-48(43-4-1)/2-9,3-1	25	2.6
1889 Cle-N	123	500	88	159	22	8	5	75	42	25	35	....	.318	.375	.424	.799	124	16	94	7.30	6	*S-122/2-1	20	2.3
1890 Cle-N	136	530	95	157	15	14	7	61	87	25	23	....	.296	.401	.417	.818	141	32	100	7.13	-20	*S-134/2-3	21	1.5
1891 Cle-N	141	603	115	170	13	12	6	69	64	19	14	....	.282	.352	.373	.725	107	5	86	5.37	-18	*S-141	18	-0.8
1892*Cle-N	129	531	76	139	14	10	0	93	49	29	19	....	.262	.325	.326	.651	93	-5	64	4.41	-28	*S-129	12	-2.5
1893 Cle-N	125	545	103	169	29	24	4	133	50	14	16	....	.310	.372	.473	.846	117	9	105	7.37	-11	*S-125	19	0.4
1894 Cle-N	130	554	116	198	30	15	8	128	49	12	33	....	.357	.412	.509	.921	117	14	133	9.71	-11	*S-130	19	0.7
1895*Cle-N	132	569	131	194	32	17	8	119	46	26	13	....	.341	.397	.499	.896	123	17	122	8.53	-15	*S-131	25	0.7
1896*Cle-N	133	571	100	193	29	12	7	112	45	9	13	....	.338	.388	.468	.856	118	13	113	7.66	-40	*S-133	17	-1.7
1897 Cle-N	125	523	83	143	21	14	2	78	40	....	15	....	.273	.330	.379	.708	82	-16	73	4.99	-6	*S-125	9	-1.3
1898 Cle-N	151	604	89	172	23	1	9	94	56	....	11	....	.285	.346	.371	.717	107	5	85	5.07	-33	*S-151	17	-1.9
1899 StL-N	67	277	40	72	7	3	3	40	20	....	4	....	.260	.310	.339	.649	76	-10	32	4.01	-8	S-42,1-15,2-10	4	-1.4
Total 13	**1655**	**6954**	**1227**	**2144**	**272**	**158**	**67**	**1124**	**636**	**159**	**324**	**....**	**.308**	**.365**	**.417**	**.781**	**114**	**116**	**1208**	**6.63**	**-205**	***S-1564/0-52,2-31,1-15,3-1**	**221**	**-2.1**

• MCKECHNIE, Bill William Boyd "Deacon" McKechnie
b: 8/7/1886, Wilkinsburg, PA d: 10/29/1965, Bradenton, FL BB/TR, 5'10", 160 lbs. Deb: 9/8/1907 M/C HOF: 1962 Career OF: 0-1-1

YEAR TM-L	G	AB	R	H	2B	3B	HR	RBI	BB	SO	SB	CS	AVG	OBP	SLG	OPS	OPS+	BR/A	RC	RC/G	FR	G/POS	WS	TPW
1907 Pit-N	3	8	0	1	0	0	0	0	0	....	0	....	.125	.125	.125	.250	-21	-1	0	.48	0	/3-2,2-1	0	-0.1
1910 Pit-N	71	212	23	46	1	2	0	12	11	23	4	....	.217	.256	.241	.496	42	-16	14	2.13	9	2-36,S-14/3-8,1-4	3	-0.7
1911 Pit-N	104	321	40	73	8	7	2	37	28	18	9	....	.227	.293	.315	.608	68	-15	34	3.22	1	1-57,2-17,S-12/3-6	5	-1.4
1912 Pit-N	24	73	8	18	0	1	0	4	4	5	2	....	.247	.286	.274	.560	54	-5	6	2.80	-1	3-13/S-4,2-3,1-2	1	-0.5
1913 Bos-N	1	4	1	0	0	0	0	0	0	1	0	....	.000	.200	.000	.200	-39	-1	0	.00	0	/0-1	0	-0.1
NY-A	45	112	7	15	0	0	0	8	8	17	2	....	.134	.198	.134	.332	-2	-14	3	.86	0	2-28/S-7,3-2	1	-1.4
1914 Ind-F	149	570	107	173	24	6	2	38	53	36	47	....	.304	.368	.377	.745	101	2	94	5.56	22	*3-149	23	2.9

YEAR TM-L	G	AB	R	H	2B	3B	HR	RBI	BB	SO	SB	CS	AVG	OBP	SLG	OPS	OPS+	BR/A	RC	RC/G	FR	G/POS	WS	TPW
1915 New-F	127	451	49	113	22	5	1	43	41	31	28	....	.251	.316	.328	.644	95	-3	54	3.92	2	*3-117/O-1	14	0.3
1916 NY-N	71	260	22	64	9	1	0	17	7	20	7	....	.246	.269	.288	.557	75	-9	22	2.91	-3	3-71	5	-1.1
Cin-N	37	130	4	36	3	0	0	10	3	12	4	....	.277	.293	.300	.593	84	-3	13	3.47	-5	3-35	2	-0.8
Yr.	108	390	26	100	12	1	0	27	10	32	11	....	.256	.277	.292	.569	78	-11	36	3.09	-8	*3-106	7	-1.9
1917 Cin-N	48	134	11	34	3	1	0	15	7	7	5	....	.254	.296	.291	.587	84	-3	12	3.14	-3	2-26,S-13/3-4	3	-0.4
1918 Pit-N	126	435	34	111	13	9	2	43	24	22	12	....	.255	.297	.340	.637	91	-6	47	3.53	4	*3-126	13	0.2
1920 Pit-N	40	133	13	29	3	1	1	13	4	7	7	4	.218	.241	.278	.519	47	-9	9	2.05	1	3-20,S-10/2-6,1-1	2	-0.8
Total 11	**846**	**2843**	**319**	**713**	**86**	**33**	**8**	**240**	**190**	**199**	**127**	**4**	**.251**	**.301**	**.313**	**.614**	**78**	**-81**	**310**	**3.53**	**27**	**3-553,2-117/1-64,S-60,O-2**	**72**	**-3.8**

• MCKEE, Frank Frank McKee b: Philadelphia, PA Deb: 6/11/1884

YEAR TM-L	G	AB	R	H	2B	3B	HR	RBI	BB	SO	SB	CS	AVG	OBP	SLG	OPS	OPS+	BR/A	RC	RC/G	FR	G/POS	WS	TPW
1884 Was-U	4	17	2	3	0	0	0	....	1	....	....	....	.176	.222	.176	.399	38	-1	1	1.37	-2	/O-3(0-0-3),3-2,C-1	0	-0.3

• MCKEE, Red Raymond Ellis McKee b: 7/20/1890, Shawnee, OH d: 8/5/1972, Saginaw, MI BL/TR, 5'11", 180 lbs. Deb: 4/19/1913

YEAR TM-L	G	AB	R	H	2B	3B	HR	RBI	BB	SO	SB	CS	AVG	OBP	SLG	OPS	OPS+	BR/A	RC	RC/G	FR	G/POS	WS	TPW
1913 Det-A	68	187	18	53	3	4	1	20	21	21	7	....	.283	.359	.358	.717	112	3	27	4.69	-5	C-62	6	0.3
1914 Det-A	34	64	7	12	1	1	0	8	14	16	1	2	.188	.342	.234	.576	71	-2	5	2.56	-3	C-27	1	-0.3
1915 Det-A	55	106	10	29	5	0	1	17	13	16	1	....	.274	.353	.349	.702	105	1	14	4.61	-3	C-35	4	-0.1
1916 Det-A	32	76	3	16	1	2	0	4	6	11	0	....	.211	.268	.276	.545	61	-4	6	2.49	-1	C-26	1	-0.4
Total 4	**189**	**433**	**38**	**110**	**10**	**7**	**2**	**49**	**54**	**64**	**9**	**2**	**.254**	**.339**	**.323**	**.663**	**95**	**-2**	**52**	**3.93**	**-12**	**C-150**	**12**	**-0.5**

• MCKEEL, Walt Walt Thomas McKeel b: 1/17/1972, Wilson, NC BR/TR, 6'2", 200 lbs. Deb: 9/14/1996

YEAR TM-L	G	AB	R	H	2B	3B	HR	RBI	BB	SO	SB	CS	AVG	OBP	SLG	OPS	OPS+	BR/A	RC	RC/G	FR	G/POS	WS	TPW
1996 Bos-A	1	0	0	0	0	0	0	0	0	0	0	0	....	....	....	....	-98	0	0	....	-1	/C-1	0	0.0
1997 Bos-A	5	3	0	0	0	0	0	0	0	1	0	0	.000	.000	.000	.000	-98	-1	0	.00	-1	/C-4,1-1	0	-0.2
2002 Col-N	5	13	1	4	0	0	0	0	0	3	0	0	.308	.308	.308	.615	54	-1	1	3.69	0	/C-5	0	-0.1
Total 3	**11**	**16**	**1**	**4**	**0**	**0**	**0**	**0**	**0**	**4**	**0**	**0**	**.250**	**.250**	**.250**	**.500**	**26**	**-2**	**1**	**2.77**	**-2**	**/C-10,1-1**	**0**	**-0.3**

• MCKEEVER, Jim James McKeever b: 4/19/1861, St. John, Canada d: 8/19/1897, Boston, MA, 5'10", 170 lbs. Deb: 4/17/1884

YEAR TM-L	G	AB	R	H	2B	3B	HR	RBI	BB	SO	SB	CS	AVG	OBP	SLG	OPS	OPS+	BR/A	RC	RC/G	FR	G/POS	WS	TPW
1884 Bos-U	16	66	13	9	0	0	0	....	0	....	....	....	.136	.136	.136	.273	-8	-7	1	.62	-6	C-12/O-4(0-0-4)	0	-1.0

• MCKELVEY, John John Wellington McKelvey b: 8/27/1847, Rochester, NY d: 5/31/1944, Rochester, NY BR/TR, 5'7.5", 175 lbs. Deb: 4/19/1875

YEAR TM-L	G	AB	R	H	2B	3B	HR	RBI	BB	SO	SB	CS	AVG	OBP	SLG	OPS	OPS+	BR/A	RC	RC/G	FR	G/POS	WS	TPW
1875 NH-n	43	188	26	43	3	1	0	10	5	8	3	1	.229	.249	.255	.504	86	0	13	2.63	-7	O-39(0-4-35)/3-5	....	-0.4

• MCKELVY, Russ Russell Errett McKelvy b: 9/8/1854, Swissvale, PA d: 10/19/1915, Omaha, NE BR/TR Deb: 5/1/1878 U Career OF: 0-62-1

YEAR TM-L	G	AB	R	H	2B	3B	HR	RBI	BB	SO	SB	CS	AVG	OBP	SLG	OPS	OPS+	BR/A	RC	RC/G	FR	G/POS	WS	TPW
1878 Ind-N	63	253	33	57	4	3	2	36	5	38	....	....	.225	.240	.289	.529	84	-2	18	2.52	4	*O-62(0-62-0)/P-4	4	-0.2
1882 Pit-a	1	4	0	0	0	0	0	....	0	....	....	....	.000	.000	.000	.000	-105	-1	0	.00	0	/O-1	0	-0.1
Total 2	**64**	**257**	**33**	**57**	**4**	**3**	**2**	**36**	**5**	**38**	**....**	**....**	**.222**	**.237**	**.284**	**.521**	**82**	**-3**	**18**	**2.47**	**3**	**/O-63,P-4**	**4**	**-0.3**

• MCKENNA, Ed Edward J. McKenna b: St. Louis, MO Deb: 7/29/1874 Career OF: 0-3-8

YEAR TM-L	G	AB	R	H	2B	3B	HR	RBI	BB	SO	SB	CS	AVG	OBP	SLG	OPS	OPS+	BR/A	RC	RC/G	FR	G/POS	WS	TPW
1874 Phi-n	1	4	0	0	0	0	0	0	0	1	0	0	.000	.000	.000	.000	-97	-1	0	.00	-0	/1-1	....	-0.1
1877 StL-N	1	5	0	1	0	0	0	0	0	1	....	....	.200	.200	.200	.400	28	-0	0	1.41	0	/O-1	0	0.0
1884 Was-U	32	117	19	22	1	0	0	....	4	....	....	....	.188	.215	.197	.411	41	-7	5	1.49	-7	C-23,O-10(0-2-8)/3-7	1	-1.1
Total 2	**33**	**122**	**19**	**23**	**1**	**0**	**0**	**0**	**4**	**1**	**....**	**....**	**.189**	**.214**	**.197**	**.411**	**41**	**-7**	**5**	**1.49**	**-7**	**/C-23,O-11,3-7**	**1**	**-1.1**

• MCKEOUGH, Dave David J. McKeough b: 12/1/1863, Utica, NY d: 7/11/1901, Utica, NY, 5'7", 158 lbs. Deb: 4/22/1890

YEAR TM-L	G	AB	R	H	2B	3B	HR	RBI	BB	SO	SB	CS	AVG	OBP	SLG	OPS	OPS+	BR/A	RC	RC/G	FR	G/POS	WS	TPW
1890 Roc-a	62	218	38	49	5	0	0	20	29	....	14	....	.225	.316	.248	.563	72	-6	22	3.45	4	C-47,S-13/2-2,3-1	6	0.2
1891 Phi-a	15	54	4	14	1	1	0	3	8	6	0	....	.259	.355	.315	.670	89	-1	6	4.10	-2	C-14/S-1	1	-0.1
Total 2	**77**	**272**	**42**	**63**	**6**	**1**	**0**	**23**	**37**	**6**	**14**	**....**	**.232**	**.324**	**.261**	**.585**	**75**	**-7**	**28**	**3.57**	**3**	**/C-61,S-14,2-2,3-1**	**7**	**0.1**

• MCKINNEY, Bob Robert Francis McKinney b: 10/4/1875, McSherrystown, PA d: 8/19/1946, Chicago, IL BR/TR, 5'7", 165 lbs. Deb: 7/23/1901

YEAR TM-L	G	AB	R	H	2B	3B	HR	RBI	BB	SO	SB	CS	AVG	OBP	SLG	OPS	OPS+	BR/A	RC	RC/G	FR	G/POS	WS	TPW
1901 Phi-A	2	2	0	0	0	0	0	0	0	....	0	....	.000	.000	.000	.000	-96	-1	0	.00	-1	/2-1,3-1	0	-0.2

• MCKINNEY, Rich Charles Richard McKinney b: 11/22/1946, Piqua, OH BR/TR, 5'11", 185 lbs. Deb: 6/26/1970 Career OF: 6-0-27

YEAR TM-L	G	AB	R	H	2B	3B	HR	RBI	BB	SO	SB	CS	AVG	OBP	SLG	OPS	OPS+	BR/A	RC	RC/G	FR	G/POS	WS	TPW
1970 Chi-A	43	119	12	20	5	0	4	17	11	25	3	2	.168	.244	.311	.555	50	-9	8	2.12	-4	3-23,S-11	1	-1.2
1971 Chi-A	114	369	35	100	11	2	8	46	35	37	0	0	.271	.337	.377	.714	99	-0	46	4.25	-10	2-67,O-25(0-0-25)/3-5	8	-0.8
1972 NY-A	37	121	10	26	2	0	1	7	7	13	1	0	.215	.258	.256	.514	55	-7	7	1.88	-2	3-33	1	-1.0
1973 Oak-A	48	65	9	16	3	0	1	7	7	4	0	0	.246	.319	.338	.658	90	-1	6	3.20	-1	3-17/2-7,D-6,O-3(3-0-0)	1	-0.2
1974 Oak-A	5	7	0	1	0	0	0	0	0	0	0	0	.143	.143	.143	.286	-19	-1	0	.64	-1	/2-3	0	-0.3
1975 Oak-A	8	7	0	1	0	0	0	2	1	2	0	0	.143	.250	.143	.393	14	-1	0	1.55	0	/D-2,1-1	0	-0.1
1977 Oak-A	86	198	13	35	7	0	6	21	16	43	0	1	.177	.238	.303	.541	47	-15	12	1.80	-3	1-32,D-18/3-7,O-5(3-0-2),2	0	-2.0
Total 7	**341**	**886**	**79**	**199**	**28**	**2**	**20**	**100**	**77**	**124**	**4**	**3**	**.225**	**.289**	**.328**	**.617**	**73**	**-33**	**80**	**2.90**	**-22**	**/3-85,2-80,1-33,O-33,D-26,S**	**11**	**-5.5**

• MCKINNON, Alex Alexander J. McKinnon b: 8/14/1856, Boston, MA d: 7/24/1887, Charlestown, MA BR, 5'11.5", 170 lbs. Deb: 5/1/1884 M/U

YEAR TM-L	G	AB	R	H	2B	3B	HR	RBI	BB	SO	SB	CS	AVG	OBP	SLG	OPS	OPS+	BR/A	RC	RC/G	FR	G/POS	WS	TPW
1884 NY-N	116	470	66	128	21	12	4	73	8	62	....	....	.272	.285	.394	.678	108	3	54	4.34	-7	*1-116	14	-1.3
1885 StL-N	100	411	42	121	21	6	1	44	8	31	....	....	.294	.308	.382	.690	130	13	50	4.61	-2	*1-100	11	0.2
1886 StL-N	122	491	75	148	24	7	8	72	21	23	10	....	.301	.330	.428	.758	138	21	74	5.86	-10	*1-119/O-3(0-3-0)	14	0.1
1887 Pit-N	48	208	26	76	16	4	1	30	8	9	6	....	.365	.365	.475	.840	140	10	38	7.59	3	1-48	7	0.8
Total 4	**386**	**1580**	**209**	**473**	**82**	**29**	**14**	**219**	**45**	**125**	**16**	**....**	**.299**	**.315**	**.412**	**.727**	**127**	**47**	**216**	**5.27**	**-16**	**1-383/O-3**	**46**	**-0.2**

• MCKNIGHT, Jeff Jefferson Alan McKnight b: 2/18/1963, Conway, AR BB/TR, 6', 188 lbs. Deb: 6/6/1989 Career OF: 10-0-6

YEAR TM-L	G	AB	R	H	2B	3B	HR	RBI	BB	SO	SB	CS	AVG	OBP	SLG	OPS	OPS+	BR/A	RC	RC/G	FR	G/POS	WS	TPW
1989 NY-N	6	12	2	3	0	0	0	0	2	1	0	0	.250	.357	.250	.607	80	-0	1	2.72	-1	/2-4,1-1,3-1,S-1	0	-0.1
1990 Bal-A	29	75	11	15	2	0	1	4	5	17	0	0	.200	.259	.267	.526	49	-5	6	2.48	1	1-15/O-8(4-0-4),2-5,D-1,S	0	-0.5
1991 Bal-A	16	41	2	7	1	0	0	2	2	7	1	0	.171	.209	.195	.404	13	-5	1	1.10	0	/O-7(6-0-1),D-4,1-2	0	-0.5
1992 NY-N	31	85	10	23	3	1	2	13	2	8	0	1	.271	.287	.400	.687	94	-2	9	3.63	-2	2-14/1-9,3-3,S-3,O-1	2	-0.4
1993 NY-N	105	164	19	42	3	1	2	13	13	31	0	0	.256	.315	.323	.638	72	-6	17	3.56	-3	S-29,2-15,1-10/3-9,C-1	2	-0.8
1994 NY-N	31	27	1	4	1	0	0	2	4	12	0	0	.148	.258	.185	.443	18	-3	2	1.85	0	/1-2	0	-0.3
Total 6	**218**	**404**	**45**	**94**	**10**	**2**	**5**	**34**	**28**	**76**	**1**	**1**	**.233**	**.286**	**.304**	**.590**	**63**	**-21**	**36**	**2.95**	**-4**	**/1-39,2-38,S-34,O-16,3-13,D,C**	**4**	**-2.6**

• MCKNIGHT, Jim James Arthur McKnight b: 6/1/1936, Bee Branch, AR d: 2/24/1994, Van Buren County, AR BR/TR, 6'1", 185 lbs. Deb: 9/22/1960 Career OF: 0-0-6

YEAR TM-L	G	AB	R	H	2B	3B	HR	RBI	BB	SO	SB	CS	AVG	OBP	SLG	OPS	OPS+	BR/A	RC	RC/G	FR	G/POS	WS	TPW
1960 Chi-N	3	6	0	2	0	0	0	1	0	1	0	0	.333	.333	.333	.667	84	-0	1	4.50	0	/2-1,O-1	0	0.0
1962 Chi-N	60	85	6	19	0	1	0	5	2	13	0	0	.224	.241	.247	.488	30	-8	4	1.51	1	/3-9,O-5(0-0-5),2-2	0	-0.8
Total 2	**63**	**91**	**6**	**21**	**0**	**1**	**0**	**6**	**2**	**14**	**0**	**0**	**.231**	**.247**	**.253**	**.500**	**34**	**-9**	**5**	**1.66**	**1**	**/3-9,O-6,2-3**	**0**	**-0.8**

• MCLANE, Ed Edward Cameron McLane b: 8/20/1881, Weston, MA d: 8/21/1975, Baltimore, MD BR, 5'10", 179 lbs. Deb: 10/5/1907

YEAR TM-L	G	AB	R	H	2B	3B	HR	RBI	BB	SO	SB	CS	AVG	OBP	SLG	OPS	OPS+	BR/A	RC	RC/G	FR	G/POS	WS	TPW
1907 Bro-N	1	2	0	0	0	0	0	0	0	....	0	....	.000	.333	.000	.333	5	-0	0	.00	-1	/O-1	0	-0.1

• MCLARNEY, Art Arthur James McLarney b: 12/20/1908, Fort Worden, WA d: 12/20/1984, Seattle, WA BB/TR, 6', 168 lbs. Deb: 8/23/1932

YEAR TM-L	G	AB	R	H	2B	3B	HR	RBI	BB	SO	SB	CS	AVG	OBP	SLG	OPS	OPS+	BR/A	RC	RC/G	FR	G/POS	WS	TPW
1932 NY-N	9	23	2	3	1	0	0	3	1	3	0	....	.130	.167	.174	.341	-8	-4	1	.93	0	/S-7	0	-0.3

• MCLARRY, Polly Howard Zell McLarry b: 3/25/1891, Leonard, TX d: 11/4/1971, Bonham, TX BL/TR, 6', 185 lbs. Deb: 9/2/1912

YEAR TM-L	G	AB	R	H	2B	3B	HR	RBI	BB	SO	SB	CS	AVG	OBP	SLG	OPS	OPS+	BR/A	RC	RC/G	FR	G/POS	WS	TPW
1912 Chi-A	2	2	0	0	0	0	0	0	0	....	0	....	.000	.000	.000	.000	-103	-1	0	.00	0	....	0	-0.1
1915 Chi-N	68	127	16	25	3	0	1	12	14	20	2	2	.197	.277	.244	.521	58	-7	9	2.28	-2	2-21,1-18	1	-1.0
Total 2	**70**	**129**	**16**	**25**	**3**	**0**	**1**	**12**	**14**	**20**	**2**	**2**	**.194**	**.273**	**.240**	**.513**	**56**	**-7**	**9**	**2.24**	**-2**	**/2-21,1-18**	**1**	**-1.0**

• MCLAUGHLIN, Barney Bernard McLaughlin b: 1857, Ireland d: 2/13/1921, Lowell, MA BR/TR, 5'8" Deb: 8/9/1882 ♦

YEAR TM-L	G	AB	R	H	2B	3B	HR	RBI	BB	SO	SB	CS	AVG	OBP	SLG	OPS	OPS+	BR/A	RC	RC/G	FR	G/POS	WS	TPW
1884 KC-U	42	162	15	37	7	3	0	....	9	....	....	....	.228	.269	.309	.578	109	4	14	3.09	-1	O-24(4-3-17),2-12/P-7,S-2	4	-1.0
1887 Phi-N	50	216	26	56	8	3	1	26	11	27	2	....	.259	.263	.302	.565	53	-14	17	2.85	-5	2-50	2	-1.5
1890 Syr-a	86	329	43	87	8	1	2	40	47	....	13	....	.264	.360	.313	.673	110	8	43	4.68	-6	S-86	12	0.4
Total 3	**178**	**707**	**84**	**180**	**23**	**7**	**3**	**66**	**67**	**27**	**15**	**....**	**.255**	**.312**	**.309**	**.621**	**94**	**-3**	**74**	**3.75**	**-13**	**/S-88,2-62,O-24,P-7**	**18**	**-2.1**

• MCLAUGHLIN, Frank Francis Edward McLaughlin b: 6/19/1856, Lowell, MA d: 4/5/1917, Lowell, MA BR/TR, 5'9", 160 lbs. Deb: 5/1/1883 Career OF: 2-10-4

YEAR TM-L	G	AB	R	H	2B	3B	HR	RBI	BB	SO	SB	CS	AVG	OBP	SLG	OPS	OPS+	BR/A	RC	RC/G	FR	G/POS	WS	TPW
1882 Wor-N	15	55	7	12	0	2	1	4	0	11	....	....	.218	.218	.345	.564	76	-2	4	2.72	-8	S-14/O-1	0	-0.8
1883 Pit-a	29	114	15	25	2	0	1	0	6	....	....	....	.219	.258	.263	.521	71	-3	8	2.50	-5	S-25/O-4(0-3-1),2-2,P-2	1	-1.4
1884 Cin-U	16	67	10	16	4	1	2	....	2	....	....	....	.239	.261	.418	.679	117	1	7	4.11	-4	S-16	2	-0.2

YEAR TM-L	G	AB	R	H	2B	3B	HR	RBI	BB	SO	SB	CS	AVG	OBP	SLG	OPS	OPS+	BR/A	RC	RC/G	FR	G/POS	WS	TPW
CP-U	15	67	11	16	4	1	0	....	1	....	....	....	.239	.250	.328	.578	100	0	6	3.10	4	2-14/0-1,S-1	2	0.4
KC-U	32	123	17	28	11	0	1	....	9	....	....	....	.228	.280	.341	.622	126	5	12	3.56	-8	2-10,0-10(2-6-2)/3-9,S-5,P	4	-0.4
Yr.	63	257	38	60	19	2	3	....	12	....	....	....	.233	.268	.358	.626	117	6	25	3.58	-7	2-24,S-22,0-11(2-6-3)/3-9,P	8	-0.2
Total 3	**107**	**426**	**60**	**97**	**21**	**4**	**5**	**4**	**18**	**11**	**....**	**....**	**.228**	**.259**	**.331**	**.590**	**99**	**1**	**37**	**3.18**	**-20**	**/S-61,2-26,0-16,3-9,P-4**	**9**	**-2.4**
• MCLAUGHLIN, Jim	James Robert McLaughlin b: 1/3/1902, St. Louis, MO d: 12/18/1968, Mount Vernon, IL BR/TR, 5'8.5", 168 lbs. Deb: 4/18/1932																							
1932 StL-A	1	1	0	0	0	0	0	1	0	0	0	0	.000	.000	.000	.000	-95	-0	0	.00	0	/3-1	0	-0.1
• MCLAUGHLIN, Kid	James Anson "Sunshine" McLaughlin b: 4/12/1888, Randolph, NY d: 11/13/1934, Allegheny, NY BL/TR, 5'8.5", 158 lbs. Deb: 6/30/1914																							
1914 Cin-N	3	2	1	0	0	0	0	0	0	0	0	....	.000	.000	.000	.000	-97	-0	0	.00	0	/0-2(0-2-0)	0	-0.1
• MCLAUGHLIN, Tom	Thomas McLaughlin b: 3/28/1860, Louisville, KY d: 7/21/1921, Louisville, KY TR Deb: 7/17/1883 Career OF: 9-9-1																							
1883 Lou-a	42	146	16	28	1	2	0	0	5	....	....	....	.192	.219	.226	.445	47	-8	7	1.75	0	S-19,0-17(8-9-1)/1-5,2-2,3	3	-0.7
1884 Lou-a	98	335	41	67	11	6	0	21	22	....	....	....	.200	.262	.269	.530	77	-7	24	2.48	17	*S-94/3-4,2-1	13	1.2
1885 Lou-a	112	411	49	87	13	9	2	41	15	....	....	....	.212	.245	.302	.546	72	-14	31	2.59	0	*2-93,S-19	7	-0.9
1886 NY-a	74	250	27	34	3	1	0	16	26	....	13	....	.136	.220	.156	.376	19	-22	12	1.47	1	S-63,2-10/0-1	3	-1.6
1891 Was-a	14	41	9	11	0	1	0	3	7	6	3	....	.268	.400	.317	.717	110	1	7	5.79	-1	S-14	2	0.1
Total 5	**340**	**1183**	**142**	**227**	**28**	**19**	**2**	**81**	**75**	**6**	**16**	**....**	**.192**	**.247**	**.253**	**.500**	**60**	**-48**	**81**	**2.30**	**17**	**S-209,2-106/0-18,3-6,1-5**	**28**	**-1.9**
• MCLAUGHLIN, William	William McLaughlin b: San Francisco, CA Deb: 5/3/1884 U																							
1884 Was-U	10	37	3	7	3	0	0	....	0	....	....	....	.189	.189	.270	.459	55	-2	2	1.81	-4	/S-9,3-1	0	-0.5
• MCLAURIN, Ralph	Ralph Edgar McLaurin b: 5/23/1885, Kissimmee, FL d: 2/11/1943, McColl, SC Deb: 9/5/1908																							
1908 StL-N	8	22	2	5	0	0	0	0	0	....	0	....	.227	.227	.227	.455	47	-1	1	1.62	0	/0-6(6-0-0)	0	-0.2
• MCLEAN, Larry	John Bannerman McLean b: 7/18/1881, Fredericton, Canada d: 3/24/1921, Boston, MA BR/TR, 6'5", 228 lbs. Deb: 4/26/1901																							
1901 Bos-A	9	19	4	4	1	0	0	2	0	....	1	....	.211	.211	.263	.474	31	-2	1	2.29	0	/1-5	0	-0.1
1903 Chi-N	1	4	0	0	0	0	0	1	1	....	0	....	.000	.200	.000	.200	-42	-1	0	.00	0	/C-1	0	0.0
1904 StL-N	27	84	5	14	2	1	0	4	4	....	1	....	.167	.205	.214	.419	31	-7	4	1.48	-4	C-24	0	-0.8
1906 Cin-N	12	35	3	7	2	0	0	2	4	....	0	....	.200	.282	.257	.539	65	-1	3	2.42	0	C-12	1	-0.1
1907 Cin-N	113	374	35	108	9	9	0	54	13	....	4	....	.289	.313	.361	.674	107	1	45	4.34	-1	C-89,1-13	13	0.9
1908 Cin-N	99	309	24	67	9	4	1	28	15	....	2	....	.217	.258	.282	.539	74	-10	23	2.36	-4	C-69,1-19	5	-0.8
1909 Cin-N	95	324	26	83	12	2	2	36	21	....	1	....	.256	.307	.324	.632	97	-2	33	3.38	-2	C-95	9	0.6
1910 Cin-N	127	423	27	126	14	7	2	71	26	23	4	....	.298	.340	.378	.718	114	6	55	4.70	4	*C-119	17	2.2
1911 Cin-N	107	328	24	94	7	2	0	34	20	18	1	....	.287	.330	.320	.650	85	-7	34	3.75	8	C-98	10	0.9
1912 Cin-N	102	333	17	81	15	1	1	27	18	15	1	....	.243	.284	.303	.587	63	-18	28	2.81	2	C-98	8	-0.8
1913 StL-N	48	152	7	41	9	0	0	12	6	9	0	....	.270	.297	.329	.626	80	-4	14	3.20	6	C-42	3	0.4
*NY-N	30	75	3	24	4	0	0	9	4	4	1	....	.320	.354	.373	.728	107	1	10	4.84	-2	C-28	3	0.0
Yr.	78	227	10	65	13	0	0	21	10	13	1	....	.286	.316	.344	.660	89	-4	24	3.71	3	C-70	6	0.4
1914 NY-N	79	154	8	40	6	0	0	14	4	9	4	....	.260	.283	.299	.582	75	-5	13	2.98	-4	C-74	4	-0.7
1915 NY-N	13	33	0	5	0	0	0	4	0	1	0	....	.152	.152	.152	.303	-9	-4	1	.79	1	C-12	0	-0.3
Total 13	**862**	**2647**	**183**	**694**	**90**	**26**	**6**	**298**	**136**	**79**	**20**	**....**	**.262**	**.301**	**.323**	**.623**	**86**	**-54**	**263**	**3.42**	**4**	**C-761/1-37**	**73**	**1.3**
• MCLEMORE, Mark	Mark Tremell McLemore b: 10/4/1964, San Diego, CA BB/TR, 5'11", 195 lbs. Deb: 9/13/1986 Career OF: 249-21-147																							
1986 Cal-A	5	4	0	0	0	0	0	0	1	2	0	1	.000	.200	.000	.200	-40	-1	0	.00	1	/2-2	0	0.0
1987 Cal-A	138	433	61	102	13	3	3	41	48	72	25	8	.236	.312	.300	.612	66	-19	45	3.31	5	*2-132/S-6,D-3	8	-0.6
1988 Cal-A	77	233	38	56	11	2	2	16	25	28	13	7	.240	.314	.330	.644	83	-5	24	3.30	1	2-63/3-5,D-1	4	-0.3
1989 Cal-A	32	103	12	25	3	1	0	14	7	19	6	1	.243	.297	.291	.589	68	-4	10	3.09	0	2-27/D-1	3	-0.3
1990 Cal-A	20	48	4	7	2	0	0	2	4	9	1	0	.146	.212	.188	.399	13	-5	2	1.31	-3	/2-8,S-8,D-1	0	-0.8
Cle-A	8	12	2	2	0	0	0	0	0	6	0	0	.167	.167	.167	.333	-7	-2	0	.90	0	/3-4,2-3,D-1	0	-0.2
Yr.	28	60	6	9	2	0	0	2	4	15	1	0	.150	.203	.183	.386	9	-7	2	1.23	-3	2-11/S-8,3-4,D-2	0	-1.0
1991 Hou-N	21	61	6	9	1	0	0	2	6	13	0	1	.148	.224	.164	.388	11	-8	2	1.13	2	2-19	1	-0.6
1992 Bal-A	101	228	40	56	7	2	0	27	21	26	11	5	.246	.309	.294	.603	68	-9	21	2.99	6	2-70,D-17	6	-0.2
1993 Bal-A	148	581	81	165	27	5	4	72	64	92	21	15	.284	.356	.368	.724	91	-7	73	4.20	11	*0-124(0-0-124),2-25/3-4,D	14	-0.2
1994 Bal-A	104	343	44	88	11	1	3	29	51	50	20	5	.257	.354	.321	.675	72	-11	43	4.31	12	2-96/0-7(0-0-7),D-1	9	0.5
1995 Tex-A	129	467	73	122	20	5	5	41	59	71	21	11	.261	.348	.358	.705	82	-11	60	4.27	0	0-73(69-0-5),2-66/D-2	11	-1.1
1996*Tex-A	147	517	84	150	23	4	5	46	87	69	27	10	.290	.392	.379	.771	92	-2	81	5.48	18	*2-147/0-1	16	2.2
1997 Tex-A	89	349	47	91	17	2	1	25	40	54	7	5	.261	.340	.330	.670	72	-14	41	4.02	1	2-89/0-1	5	-0.8
1998*Tex-A	126	461	79	114	15	1	5	53	89	64	12	4	.247	.371	.317	.688	78	-10	60	4.26	1	*2-122/D-2	12	-0.3
1999*Tex-A	144	566	105	155	20	7	6	45	83	79	16	8	.274	.367	.366	.732	84	-11	82	4.99	0	*2-135,0-11(4-0-7)	15	-0.5
2000*Sea-A	138	481	72	118	23	1	3	46	81	78	30	14	.245	.355	.316	.671	76	-14	59	3.95	4	*2-129,0-14(14-1-0)	13	-0.4
2001*Sea-A	125	409	78	117	16	9	5	57	69	84	39	7	.286	.389	.406	.795	117	19	74	6.38	5	0-68(63-8-2),3-36,S-35/2-9,D	18	2.4
2002 Sea-A	104	337	54	91	17	2	7	41	61	63	18	10	.270	.383	.395	.778	111	8	56	5.65	-3	0-89(82-12-1),3-14/D-4,2-2,S	13	0.2
2003 Sea-A	99	309	34	72	15	2	2	37	38	71	5	5	.233	.321	.314	.635	71	-13	33	3.54	8	S-38,3-29,0-16(16-0-0),D-10/2	8	-0.3
Total 18	**1755**	**5942**	**914**	**1540**	**241**	**47**	**51**	**594**	**834**	**950**	**272**	**117**	**.259**	**.352**	**.341**	**.693**	**82**	**-119**	**766**	**4.31**	**69**	***2-1150,0-404/3-92,S-88,D-46**	**156**	**-1.2**
• MCLEOD, Jim	Soule James McLeod b: 9/12/1908, Jones, LA d: 8/3/1981, Little Rock, AR BR/TR, 6', 187 lbs. Deb: 5/22/1930																							
1930 Was-A	18	34	3	9	1	0	0	1	1	5	1	1	.265	.306	.294	.600	53	-3	3	2.94	-1	3-10/S-7	0	-0.2
1932 Was-A	7	0	1	0	0	0	0	0	1	0	0	0	....	1.000	....	1.000	183	0	0	∞	0	/S-1	0	0.0
1933 Phi-N	67	232	20	45	6	1	0	15	12	25	1	....	.194	.237	.228	.465	30	-21	13	1.79	-5	3-67/S-1	2	-2.5
Total 3	**92**	**266**	**24**	**54**	**7**	**1**	**0**	**16**	**14**	**30**	**2**	**1**	**.203**	**.248**	**.237**	**.485**	**33**	**-24**	**16**	**1.93**	**-6**	**/3-77,S-9**	**2**	**-2.8**
• MCLEOD, Ralph	Ralph Alton McLeod b: 10/19/1916, West Quincy, MA BL/TL, 6', 170 lbs. Deb: 9/14/1938																							
1938 Bos-N	6	7	1	2	1	0	0	0	0	2	0	....	.286	.286	.429	.714	105	-0	0	1.98	-0	/0-1	0	0.0
• MCMAHON, Jack	John Henry McMahon b: 10/15/1869, Waterbury, CT d: 12/30/1894, Bridgeport, CT BR/TL, 5'10", 165 lbs. Deb: 8/8/1892																							
1892 NY-N	40	147	21	33	5	7	1	24	10	9	3	....	.224	.278	.374	.653	98	-1	17	3.92	-2	1-36/C-5	3	-0.3
1893 NY-N	11	30	5	10	2	1	0	4	2	0	0	....	.333	.375	.467	.842	123	1	5	7.13	-1	C-11	1	0.0
Total 2	**51**	**177**	**26**	**43**	**7**	**8**	**1**	**28**	**12**	**9**	**3**	**....**	**.243**	**.295**	**.390**	**.685**	**103**	**-0**	**22**	**4.40**	**-3**	**/1-36,C-16**	**4**	**-0.3**
• MCMANUS, Frank	Francis E. McManus b: 9/21/1875, Lawrence, MA d: 9/1/1923, Syracuse, NY TR, 5'7", 150 lbs. Deb: 9/14/1899																							
1899 Was-N	7	21	3	8	1	0	0	2	2	....	3	....	.381	.435	.429	.863	139	1	5	10.90	2	/C-7	1	0.3
1903 Bro-N	2	7	0	0	0	0	0	0	0	....	0	....	.000	.000	.000	.000	-103	-2	0	.00	0	/C-2	0	-0.1
1904 Det-A	1	0	0	0	0	0	0	0	0	....	0	....	....	....	....	....	-103	0	0	....	0	/C-1	0	0.0
NY-A	4	7	0	0	0	0	0	0	0	....	0	....	.000	.000	.000	.000	-95	-2	0	.00	-1	/C-4	0	-0.2
Yr.	5	7	0	0	0	0	0	0	0	....	0	....	.000	.000	.000	.000	-95	-2	0	.00	-1	/C-5	0	-0.3
Total 3	**14**	**35**	**3**	**8**	**1**	**0**	**0**	**2**	**2**	**....**	**3**	**....**	**.229**	**.270**	**.257**	**.527**	**49**	**-2**	**5**	**5.25**	**1**	**/C-14**	**1**	**-0.1**
• MCMANUS, Jim	James Michael McManus b: 7/20/1936, Brookline, MA BL/TL, 6'4", 215 lbs. Deb: 9/21/1960																							
1960 KC-A	5	13	3	4	0	0	1	2	1	2	0	0	.308	.357	.538	.896	138	1	2	5.60	0	/1-3	0	0.0
• MCMANUS, Marty	Martin Joseph McManus b: 3/14/1900, Chicago, IL d: 2/18/1966, St. Louis, MO BR/TR, 5'10.5", 160 lbs. Deb: 9/26/1920 M																							
1920 StL-A	1	3	0	1	0	1	0	1	0	0	0	0	.333	.333	1.000	1.333	236	0	1	7.44	0	/3-1	0	0.0
1921 StL-A	121	412	49	107	19	8	3	64	27	30	5	3	.260	.308	.367	.675	67	-21	48	3.79	-8	2-96,3-13/1-9,S-2	6	-2.4
1922 StL-A	154	606	88	189	34	11	11	109	38	41	9	6	.312	.358	.459	.817	108	6	99	5.98	16	*2-153/1-1	20	2.5
1923 StL-A	154	582	86	180	35	10	15	94	49	50	14	10	.309	.367	.481	.848	115	11	102	6.20	11	*2-133,1-20	19	2.4
1924 StL-A	123	442	71	147	23	5	5	80	55	40	13	9	.333	.409	.441	.850	112	10	82	6.72	17	*2-119	17	2.8
1925 StL-A	154	587	108	169	**44**	8	13	90	73	69	5	11	.288	.371	.457	.828	104	1	99	5.96	3	*2-154/0-1	20	0.7
1926 StL-A	149	549	102	156	30	10	9	68	55	62	5	7	.284	.350	.424	.775	97	-5	82	5.15	5	3-84,2-61/1-4	16	0.7
1927 Det-A	108	369	60	99	19	7	9	69	34	38	8	7	.268	.332	.431	.763	95	-5	52	4.71	3	S-39,2-35,3-22/1-6	11	0.4
1928 Det-A	139	500	78	144	37	5	8	73	51	32	11	13	.288	.355	.430	.785	104	-0	75	5.19	2	3-92,1-45/S-2	15	0.5
1929 Det-A	154	599	99	168	32	8	18	90	60	52	16	11	.280	.347	.451	.798	103	1	93	5.46	8	*3-150/S-8	18	1.8

YEAR TM-L	G	AB	R	H	2B	3B	HR	RBI	BB	SO	SB	CS	AVG	OBP	SLG	OPS	OPS+	BR/A	RC	RC/G	FR	G/POS	WS	TPW
1930 Det-A	132	484	74	155	40	4	9	89	59	28	**23**	8	.320	.396	.475	.872	118	16	95	7.10	12	*3-130/S-3,1-1	21	3.3
1931 Det-A	107	362	39	98	17	3	3	53	49	22	7	3	.271	.361	.359	.720	87	-3	50	4.92	7	3-79,2-21/1-1	9	0.7
Bos-A	17	62	8	18	4	0	1	9	8	1	1	1	.290	.371	.403	.775	109	1	9	5.57	4	3-11/2-7	2	0.6
Yr.	124	424	47	116	21	3	4	62	57	23	8	4	.274	.362	.366	.728	90	-2	59	5.02	11	3-90,2-28/1-1	11	1.3
1932 Bos-A	93	302	39	71	19	4	5	24	36	30	1	2	.235	.317	.374	.691	80	-9	37	4.11	-10	2-49,3-30/S-2,1-1	4	-1.4
1933 Bos-A	106	366	51	104	30	4	3	36	49	21	3	0	.284	.369	.413	.781	108	6	59	5.69	0	3-76,2-26/1-4	11	1.0
1934 Bos-N	119	435	56	120	18	0	8	47	32	42	5	....	.276	.330	.372	.702	95	-3	53	4.34	-4	2-73,3-37	13	-0.2
Total 15	1831	6660	1008	1926	401	88	120	996	675	558	126	91	.289	.357	.430	.787	101	6	1036	5.46	65	2-927,3-725/1-92,S-56,0-1	202	13.4

• MCMATH, Jimmy Jimmy Lee McMath b: 8/10/1949, Tuscaloosa, AL BL/TL, 6'1.5", 195 lbs. Deb: 9/7/1968

YEAR TM-L	G	AB	R	H	2B	3B	HR	RBI	BB	SO	SB	CS	AVG	OBP	SLG	OPS	OPS+	BR/A	RC	RC/G	FR	G/POS	WS	TPW
1968 Chi-N	6	14	0	2	0	0	0	2	0	6	0	0	.143	.143	.143	.286	-13	-2	0	.64	0	/0-3(3-0-0)	0	-0.2

• MCMILLAN, George George A. "Reddy" McMillan b: 9/1/1863, Canada d: 4/18/1920, Cleveland, OH, 5'8", 175 lbs. Deb: 8/11/1890

YEAR TM-L	G	AB	R	H	2B	3B	HR	RBI	BB	SO	SB	CS	AVG	OBP	SLG	OPS	OPS+	BR/A	RC	RC/G	FR	G/POS	WS	TPW
1890 NY-N	10	35	4	5	0	0	0	1	7	4	1	....	.143	.286	.143	.429	26	-3	2	1.55	-1	0-10(1-0-9)	0	-0.4

• MCMILLAN, Norm Norman Alexis "Bub" McMillan b: 10/5/1895, Latta, SC d: 9/28/1969, Marion, SC BR/TR, 6', 175 lbs. Deb: 4/12/1922

YEAR TM-L	G	AB	R	H	2B	3B	HR	RBI	BB	SO	SB	CS	AVG	OBP	SLG	OPS	OPS+	BR/A	RC	RC/G	FR	G/POS	WS	TPW
1922*NY-A	33	78	7	20	1	2	0	11	6	10	4	1	.256	.310	.321	.630	63	-4	8	3.48	-3	0-26(0-15-12)/3-5	1	-0.7
1923 Bos-A	131	459	37	116	24	5	0	42	28	44	13	5	.253	.299	.327	.625	64	-23	46	3.40	-4	3-67,2-34,S-28	9	-1.8
1924 StL-A	76	201	25	56	12	2	0	27	12	17	6	4	.279	.332	.358	.690	73	-8	24	4.06	1	2-37,3-19/S-7,1-2	4	-0.5
1928 Chi-N	49	123	11	27	2	2	1	12	13	19	0	....	.220	.299	.293	.592	56	-8	11	2.88	0	2-19,3-18	2	-0.6
1929*Chi-N	124	495	77	134	35	5	5	55	36	43	13	....	.271	.324	.392	.716	76	-20	62	4.36	2	*3-120	12	-0.9
Total 5	413	1356	157	353	74	16	6	147	95	133	36	10	.260	.313	.352	.665	69	-63	152	3.79	-4	3-229/2-90,S-35,0-26,1-2	28	-4.5

• MCMILLAN, Roy Roy David McMillan b: 7/17/1929, Bonham, TX d: 11/2/1997, Bonham, TX BR/TR, 5'11", 170 lbs. Deb: 4/17/1951 M/C

YEAR TM-L	G	AB	R	H	2B	3B	HR	RBI	BB	SO	SB	CS	AVG	OBP	SLG	OPS	OPS+	BR/A	RC	RC/G	FR	G/POS	WS	TPW
1951 Cin-N	85	199	21	42	4	0	1	8	17	26	0	0	.211	.273	.246	.519	40	-17	15	2.43	2	S-54,3-12/2-1	3	-1.2
1952 Cin-N	154	540	60	132	32	2	7	57	45	81	4	5	.244	.306	.350	.656	82	-15	57	3.63	16	*S-154	16	1.2
1953 Cin-N	155	557	51	130	15	4	5	43	43	52	2	4	.233	.290	.302	.591	54	-39	49	2.95	22	*S-155	11	-0.4
1954 Cin-N	154	588	86	147	21	2	4	42	47	54	4	2	.250	.311	.313	.624	61	-33	61	3.36	20	*S-154	14	0.0
1955 Cin-N	151	470	50	126	21	2	1	37	66	33	4	4	.268	.366	.328	.694	81	-10	60	4.32	26	*S-150	16	2.8
1956 Cin-N★	150	479	51	126	16	7	3	62	76	54	4	3	.263	.370	.344	.714	88	-5	64	4.49	28	*S-150	20	3.7
1957 Cin-N★	151	448	50	122	25	5	1	55	66	44	5	1	.272	.373	.357	.730	91	-1	64	4.88	14	*S-151	17	2.5
1958 Cin-N	145	393	48	90	18	3	1	25	47	33	5	2	.229	.313	.298	.611	60	-22	38	3.25	11	*S-145	10	0.0
1959 Cin-N	79	246	38	65	14	2	9	24	27	27	0	2	.264	.347	.447	.794	106	2	35	4.83	7	S-73	9	1.4
1960 Cin-N	124	399	42	94	12	2	10	42	35	40	2	0	.236	.304	.351	.655	77	-12	43	3.54	1	*S-116,2-10	9	-0.2
1961 Mil-N	154	505	42	111	16	0	7	48	61	86	2	4	.220	.309	.293	.602	65	-25	46	2.90	8	*S-154	10	-0.4
1962 Mil-N	137	468	66	115	13	0	12	41	60	53	2	2	.246	.338	.350	.688	87	-7	57	4.02	5	*S-135	14	1.0
1963 Mil-N	100	320	35	80	10	1	4	29	17	25	1	5	.250	.292	.325	.617	78	-11	29	3.09	10	S-94	9	0.7
1964 Mil-N	8	13	1	4	0	0	0	2	0	2	1	0	.308	.308	.308	.615	73	-0	1	4.17	0	/S-8	0	0.0
NY-N	113	379	30	80	8	2	1	25	14	16	3	1	.211	.247	.251	.498	41	-29	20	1.69	-7	*S-111	3	-2.8
Yr.	121	392	31	84	8	2	1	27	14	18	4	1	.214	.249	.253	.501	42	-29	22	1.76	-7	*S-119	3	-2.8
1965 NY-N	157	528	44	128	19	2	1	42	24	60	1	0	.242	.281	.292	.572	64	-25	44	2.82	-2	*S-153	8	-1.6
1966 NY-N	76	220	24	47	9	1	1	12	20	25	1	1	.214	.285	.277	.562	58	-12	18	2.65	-5	S-71	3	-1.2
Total 16	2093	6752	739	1639	253	35	68	594	665	711	41	36	.243	.316	.321	.637	72	-260	702	3.45	155	*S-2028/3-12,2-11	172	5.3

• MCMILLAN, Tom Thomas Erwin McMillan b: 9/13/1951, Richmond, VA BR/TR, 5'9", 165 lbs. Deb: 9/17/1977

YEAR TM-L	G	AB	R	H	2B	3B	HR	RBI	BB	SO	SB	CS	AVG	OBP	SLG	OPS	OPS+	BR/A	RC	RC/G	FR	G/POS	WS	TPW
1977 Sea-A	2	5	0	0	0	0	0	0	0	0	0	0	.000	.000	.000	.000	-101	-1	0	.00	0	/S-2	0	-0.1

• MCMILLAN, Tommy Thomas Law "Rebel" McMillan b: 4/18/1888, Pittston, PA d: 7/15/1966, Orlando, FL BR/TR, 5'5", 130 lbs. Deb: 8/19/1908

YEAR TM-L	G	AB	R	H	2B	3B	HR	RBI	BB	SO	SB	CS	AVG	OBP	SLG	OPS	OPS+	BR/A	RC	RC/G	FR	G/POS	WS	TPW
1908 Bro-N	43	147	9	35	3	0	0	3	9	....	5	....	.238	.296	.259	.554	80	-3	13	2.86	-8	S-29,0-14(0-14-0)	2	-1.3
1909 Bro-N	108	373	18	79	15	1	0	24	20	....	11	....	.212	.254	.257	.511	61	-18	26	2.29	-17	*S-105/2-2,3-1	3	-3.5
1910 Bro-N	23	74	2	13	1	0	0	2	6	10	4	....	.176	.238	.189	.427	25	-7	4	1.78	0	S-23	1	-0.7
Cin-N	82	248	20	46	0	3	0	13	31	23	7	....	.185	.281	.210	.491	46	-16	18	2.13	6	S-82	3	-0.8
Yr.	105	322	22	59	1	3	0	15	37	33	11	....	.183	.271	.205	.476	41	-23	22	2.05	6	*S-105	4	-1.5
1912 NY-A	41	149	24	34	2	0	0	12	15	....	18	....	.228	.303	.242	.545	53	-9	17	3.52	-3	S-41	3	-0.9
Total 4	297	991	73	207	21	4	0	54	81	33	45	....	.209	.273	.238	.512	56	-53	78	2.48	-23	S-280/0-14,2-2,3-1	12	-7.1

• MCMILLON, Billy William Edward McMillon b: 11/17/1971, Otero, NM BL/TL, 5'11", 172 lbs. Deb: 7/26/1996 Career OF: 92-0-24

YEAR TM-L	G	AB	R	H	2B	3B	HR	RBI	BB	SO	SB	CS	AVG	OBP	SLG	OPS	OPS+	BR/A	RC	RC/G	FR	G/POS	WS	TPW
1996 Fla-N	28	51	4	11	0	0	0	4	5	14	0	0	.216	.286	.216	.501	36	-5	3	2.12	0	0-15(15-0-0)	0	-0.5
1997 Fla-N	13	18	0	2	1	0	0	1	0	7	0	0	.111	.111	.167	.278	-30	-3	0	.56	-0	/0-2(2-0-0)	0	-0.3
Phi-N	24	72	10	21	4	1	2	13	6	17	2	1	.292	.346	.458	.804	109	1	11	5.53	0	0-21(21-0-2)	2	0.0
Yr.	37	90	10	23	5	1	2	14	6	24	2	1	.256	.302	.400	.702	83	-3	12	4.43	0	0-23(23-0-2)	2	-0.3
2000 Det-A	46	123	20	37	7	1	4	24	19	19	1	0	.301	.399	.472	.870	123	5	25	7.09	1	D-24,0-15(3-0-13)	5	0.4
2001 Det-A	20	34	1	3	1	0	1	4	2	12	0	0	.088	.162	.206	.368	-4	-5	1	.89	0	/0-7(1-0-6),D-3	0	-0.5
Oak-A	20	58	6	17	7	1	0	10	5	13	1	0	.293	.359	.448	.808	111	1	10	6.51	-2	0-16(15-0-2)/D-1	2	-0.1
Yr.	40	92	7	20	8	1	1	14	7	25	1	0	.217	.287	.359	.646	69	-4	11	4.08	-2	0-23(16-0-8)/D-4	2	-0.7
2003*Oak-A	66	153	15	41	11	0	6	26	19	36	0	0	.268	.356	.458	.814	111	3	26	5.94	-1	0-36(35-0-1)/D-9,1-3	5	0.0
Total 5	217	509	56	132	31	3	13	82	56	118	4	1	.259	.339	.409	.747	95	-4	76	5.20	-2	0-112/D-37,1-3	14	-1.1

• MCMULLEN, Hugh Hugh Raphael McMullen b: 12/16/1901, La Cygne, KS d: 5/23/1986, Whittier, CA BB/TR, 6'1", 180 lbs. Deb: 9/19/1925

YEAR TM-L	G	AB	R	H	2B	3B	HR	RBI	BB	SO	SB	CS	AVG	OBP	SLG	OPS	OPS+	BR/A	RC	RC/G	FR	G/POS	WS	TPW
1925 NY-N	5	15	1	2	1	0	0	0	0	3	0	0	.133	.133	.200	.333	-17	-3	0	.78	0	/C-5	0	-0.3
1926 NY-N	57	91	5	17	2	0	0	6	2	18	1	....	.187	.204	.209	.413	11	-11	4	1.30	-3	C-56	1	-1.2
1928 Was-A	1	1	0	0	0	0	0	0	0	1	0	0	.000	.000	.000	.000	-101	-0	0	.00	0	....	0	0.0
1929 Cin-N	1	1	0	0	0	0	0	0	0	0	0	....	.000	.000	.000	.000	-105	-0	0	.00	0	/C-1	0	0.0
Total 4	64	108	6	19	3	0	0	6	2	22	1	0	.176	.191	.204	.395	6	-15	4	1.20	-3	/C-62	1	-1.5

• MCMULLEN, Ken Kenneth Lee McMullen b: 6/1/1942, Oxnard, CA BR/TR, 6'3", 195 lbs. Deb: 9/17/1962 Career OF: 12-0-8

YEAR TM-L	G	AB	R	H	2B	3B	HR	RBI	BB	SO	SB	CS	AVG	OBP	SLG	OPS	OPS+	BR/A	RC	RC/G	FR	G/POS	WS	TPW
1962 LA-N	6	11	0	3	0	0	0	0	0	3	0	0	.273	.273	.273	.545	50	-1	1	2.76	0	/0-2(2-0-0)	0	-0.1
1963 LA-N	79	233	16	55	9	0	5	28	20	46	1	2	.236	.299	.339	.638	89	-4	22	3.04	1	3-71/2-1,0-1	6	-0.3
1964 LA-N	24	67	3	14	0	0	1	2	3	7	0	1	.209	.243	.254	.497	43	-5	3	1.53	-2	1-13/3-4,0-3(1-0-2)	0	-0.8
1965 Was-A	150	555	75	146	18	6	18	54	47	90	2	0	.263	.325	.414	.739	110	7	74	4.62	10	*3-142/0-8(3-0-5),1-1	21	1.8
1966 Was-A	147	524	48	122	19	4	13	54	44	89	3	1	.233	.292	.359	.651	87	-9	53	3.33	0	*3-141/1-8,0-1	12	-1.0
1967 Was-A	146	563	73	138	22	2	16	67	46	84	5	3	.245	.303	.377	.680	104	2	62	3.72	8	*3-145	20	1.1
1968 Was-A	151	557	66	138	11	2	20	62	63	66	1	3	.248	.327	.382	.710	118	12	70	4.31	-1	*3-145,S-11	24	1.3
1969 Was-A	158	562	83	153	25	2	19	87	70	103	4	5	.272	.354	.425	.779	123	16	86	5.33	11	*3-154	24	2.8
1970 Was-A	15	59	5	12	2	0	0	3	5	10	0	0	.203	.266	.237	.503	42	-5	4	1.98	5	3-15	1	0.0
Cal-A	124	422	50	98	9	3	14	61	59	81	1	0	.232	.331	.367	.698	96	-1	52	4.08	10	*3-122	15	0.9
Yr.	139	481	55	110	11	3	14	64	64	91	1	0	.229	.323	.351	.674	89	-6	55	3.82	15	*3-137	16	0.9
1971 Cal-A	160	593	63	148	19	2	21	68	53	74	1	1	.250	.314	.395	.709	107	4	71	4.04	-4	*3-158	18	0.0
1972 Cal-A	137	472	36	127	18	1	9	34	48	59	1	2	.269	.337	.369	.705	116	9	58	4.32	1	*3-137	21	1.1
1973 LA-N	42	85	6	21	5	0	5	18	6	13	0	0	.247	.297	.482	.779	118	1	12	5.02	3	3-24	3	0.4
1974*LA-N	44	60	5	15	1	0	3	12	2	12	0	0	.250	.274	.417	.691	95	-1	7	3.80	1	/3-7,2-3	2	0.0
1975 LA-N	39	46	4	11	1	1	2	14	7	12	0	0	.239	.340	.435	.774	119	1	7	5.25	1	3-11/1-3	2	0.2
1976 Oak-A	98	186	20	41	6	2	5	23	22	33	1	1	.220	.306	.355	.661	97	-1	20	3.61	-2	3-35,1-26,D-23/0-5(5-0-0),2	4	-0.5
1977 Mil-A	63	136	15	31	7	1	5	19	15	33	0	0	.228	.305	.404	.709	91	-2	16	4.06	1	D-29,1-11/3-7	2	-0.2
Total 16	1583	5131	568	1273	172	26	156	606	510	815	20	19	.248	.318	.383	.701	105	24	617	4.08	46	*3-1318/1-62,D-52,0-20,S-11,2	175	6.7

• MCMULLIN, Fred Frederick William McMullin b: 10/13/1891, Scammon, KS d: 11/20/1952, Los Angeles, CA BR/TR, 5'11", 170 lbs. Deb: 8/27/1914

YEAR TM-L	G	AB	R	H	2B	3B	HR	RBI	BB	SO	SB	CS	AVG	OBP	SLG	OPS	OPS+	BR/A	RC	RC/G	FR	G/POS	WS	TPW
1914 Det-A	1	1	0	0	0	0	0	0	0	1	0	....	.000	.000	.000	.000	-97	-0	0	.00	0	/S-1	0	-0.1
1916 Chi-A	68	187	8	48	3	0	0	10	19	30	9	....	.257	.332	.273	.604	81	-4	22	3.72	-6	3-63/S-2,2-1	5	-0.8
1917*Chi-A	59	194	35	46	2	1	0	12	27	17	9	....	.237	.339	.258	.597	81	-3	22	3.42	-5	3-52/S-2	6	-0.7
1918 Chi-A	70	235	32	65	7	0	1	16	25	26	7	....	.277	.356	.319	.675	103	2	30	4.13	1	3-69/2-1	8	0.5

YEAR TM-L	G	AB	R	H	2B	3B	HR	RBI	BB	SO	SB	CS	AVG	OBP	SLG	OPS	OPS+	BR/A	RC	RC/G	FR	G/POS	WS	TPW
1919*Chi-A	60	170	31	50	8	4	0	19	11	18	4	....	.294	.355	.388	.743	108	2	25	4.95	-1	3-46/2-5	7	0.3
1920 Chi-A	46	127	14	25	1	4	0	13	9	13	1	1	.197	.255	.268	.523	39	-11	9	2.27	-2	3-29/2-3,S-1	1	-1.2
Total 6	304	914	120	234	21	9	1	70	91	105	30	1	.256	.333	.302	.635	86	-15	108	3.76	-13	3-259/2-10,S-6	27	-2.0

• MCMULLIN, John John F. "Lefty" McMullin b: 1849, Philadelphia, PA d: 4/11/1881, Philadelphia, PA BR/TL, 5'9", 160 lbs. Deb: 5/9/1871 NA OF: 119-84-12 ♦

YEAR TM-L	G	AB	R	H	2B	3B	HR	RBI	BB	SO	SB	CS	AVG	OBP	SLG	OPS	OPS+	BR/A	RC	RC/G	FR	G/POS	WS	TPW
1871 Tro-n	29	136	38	38	0	5	0	32	8	6	11	1	.279	.319	.353	.672	92	2	19	6.15	-1	*P-29/S-1	....	-2.3
1872 Mut-n	54	237	48	61	6	1	0	25	11	6	8	2	.257	.290	.291	.581	85	-1	23	3.99	5	*O-53(41-1-11)/P-3	....	0.4
1873 Ath-n	52	227	54	62	7	1	0	29	8	4	9	1	.273	.298	.313	.611	76	-6	24	4.49	-3	*O-51(51-0-0)/P-1	....	-0.6
1874 Ath-n	55	260	61	90	10	2	2	32	8	12	4	3	.346	.366	.423	.789	140	10	43	7.41	-5	*O-55(5-51-1)	....	0.3
1875 Phi-n	54	222	33	57	9	4	2	19	5	12	6	10	.257	.273	.360	.633	114	-0	24	4.06	-3	*O-54(22-32-0)/P-4	....	-0.7
Total 5 n	244	1082	234	308	32	13	4	137	40	40	38	17	.285	.310	.349	.660	103	5	133	5.13	-8	O-213/P-37,S-1	....	-2.9

• MCNABB, Carl Carl Mac "Skinny" McNabb b: 1/25/1917, Stevenson, AL BR/TR, 5'9", 155 lbs. Deb: 4/20/1945

YEAR TM-L	G	AB	R	H	2B	3B	HR	RBI	BB	SO	SB	CS	AVG	OBP	SLG	OPS	OPS+	BR/A	RC	RC/G	FR	G/POS	WS	TPW
1945 Det-A	1	1	0	0	0	0	0	0	0	1	0	0	.000	.000	.000	.000	-94	-0	0	.00	0	....	0	0.0

• MCNAIR, Eric Donald Eric "Boob" McNair b: 4/12/1909, Meridian, MS d: 3/11/1949, Meridian, MS BR/TR, 5'8", 160 lbs. Deb: 9/20/1929

YEAR TM-L	G	AB	R	H	2B	3B	HR	RBI	BB	SO	SB	CS	AVG	OBP	SLG	OPS	OPS+	BR/A	RC	RC/G	FR	G/POS	WS	TPW
1929 Phi-A	4	8	2	4	1	0	0	3	0	0	1	0	.500	.500	.625	1.125	181	1	3	17.52	0	/S-4	1	0.1
1930*Phi-A	78	237	27	63	12	2	0	34	9	19	5	2	.266	.296	.333	.629	57	-16	23	3.46	-9	S-31,3-29/2-5,O-1	3	-1.8
1931*Phi-A	79	280	41	76	10	1	5	33	11	19	1	4	.271	.306	.368	.674	72	-12	30	3.77	5	3-47,2-16,S-13	6	-0.4
1932 Phi-A	135	554	87	158	**47**	3	18	95	28	29	8	4	.285	.323	.478	.801	101	-2	84	5.50	-2	*S-133	17	0.5
1933 Phi-A	89	310	57	81	15	4	7	48	15	32	2	1	.261	.302	.403	.705	85	-8	38	4.29	-2	S-46,2-27	6	-0.5
1934 Phi-A	151	599	80	168	20	4	17	82	35	42	7	8	.280	.321	.412	.734	92	-12	77	4.58	1	*S-151	14	-0.1
1935 Phi-A	137	526	55	142	22	2	4	57	35	33	3	7	.270	.319	.342	.661	72	-25	57	3.77	-13	*S-121,3-11/1-2	7	-2.7
1936 Bos-A	128	494	68	141	36	2	4	74	27	34	3	3	.285	.329	.391	.720	73	-24	63	4.59	4	S-84,2-35,3-11	11	-1.0
1937 Bos-A	126	455	60	133	29	4	12	76	30	33	10	7	.292	.340	.453	.793	94	-7	69	5.46	-1	*2-106/S-9,3-4,1-1	13	-0.1
1938 Bos-A	46	96	9	15	1	1	0	7	3	6	0	1	.156	.182	.188	.369	-7	-17	3	1.01	-1	S-15,2-14/3-3	1	-1.5
1939 Chi-A	129	479	62	155	18	5	7	82	38	41	17	9	.324	.375	.426	.800	101	1	74	5.64	7	*3-103,2-19/S-9	16	1.2
1940 Chi-A	66	251	26	57	13	1	7	31	12	26	1	7	.227	.265	.371	.636	62	-18	21	2.63	-6	2-65/3-1	2	-1.9
1941 Det-A	23	59	5	11	1	0	0	3	4	4	0	0	.186	.250	.203	.453	19	-7	2	1.19	-1	3-11/S-3	0	-0.7
1942 Det-A	26	68	5	11	2	0	1	4	3	5	0	1	.162	.197	.235	.432	20	-8	2	.83	-5	S-21	0	-1.2
Phi-A	34	103	8	25	2	0	0	4	11	5	1	0	.243	.316	.262	.578	64	-4	9	3.13	-2	S-29/2-1	2	-0.5
Yr.	60	171	13	36	4	0	1	8	14	10	1	1	.211	.270	.251	.522	47	-12	11	2.11	-7	S-50/2-1	2	-1.7
Total 14	1251	4519	592	1240	229	29	82	633	261	328	59	54	.274	.318	.392	.710	80	-157	556	4.31	-26	S-669,2-288,3-220/1-3,O-1	99	-10.3

• MCNALLY, Mike Michael Joseph "Minooka Mike" McNally b: 9/9/1892, Minooka, PA d: 5/29/1965, Bethlehem, PA BR/TR, 5'11", 150 lbs. Deb: 4/21/1915

YEAR TM-L	G	AB	R	H	2B	3B	HR	RBI	BB	SO	SB	CS	AVG	OBP	SLG	OPS	OPS+	BR/A	RC	RC/G	FR	G/POS	WS	TPW
1915 Bos-A	23	53	7	8	0	1	0	0	3	7	0	2	.151	.196	.189	.385	16	-7	2	.91	-1	3-18/2-5	0	-0.8
1916*Bos-A	87	135	28	23	0	0	0	9	10	19	9	....	.170	.228	.170	.398	20	-13	8	1.72	-4	2-35,3-14/S-7,O-1	2	-1.8
1917 Bos-A	42	50	9	15	1	0	0	2	6	3	3	....	.300	.375	.320	.695	113	1	8	4.81	-2	3-14/S-9,2-6	2	0.0
1919 Bos-A	33	42	10	11	4	0	0	6	1	2	4	....	.262	.279	.357	.636	83	-1	5	3.85	1	3-11,S-11/2-3	1	0.0
1920 Bos-A	93	312	42	80	5	1	0	23	31	24	13	10	.256	.326	.279	.604	64	-15	30	3.05	-5	2-76/S-8,1-6	4	-1.9
1921*NY-A	71	215	36	56	4	2	1	24	14	15	5	6	.260	.306	.312	.617	56	-15	20	3.04	8	3-49,2-16	5	-0.4
1922*NY-A	52	143	20	36	2	2	0	18	16	14	3	0	.252	.331	.294	.625	63	-6	16	3.48	-2	3-34/2-9,S-4,1-1	4	-0.5
1923 NY-A	30	38	5	8	0	0	0	1	3	4	2	0	.211	.268	.211	.479	27	-3	3	2.18	-4	S-13/3-7,2-5	0	-0.6
1924 NY-A	49	69	11	17	0	0	0	2	7	5	1	1	.246	.316	.246	.562	46	-5	6	2.76	1	2-25,3-13/S-6	1	-0.3
1925 Was-A	12	21	1	3	0	0	0	0	1	4	0	0	.143	.182	.143	.325	-17	-4	1	.84	-2	/3-7,S-2,2-1	0	-0.5
Total 10	492	1078	169	257	16	6	1	85	92	97	40	19	.238	.299	.267	.567	54	-70	98	2.84	-9	2-181,3-167/S-60,1-7,O-1	19	-6.7

• MCNAMARA, Bob Robert Maxey McNamara b: 9/19/1916, Denver, CO BR/TR, 5'10", 170 lbs. Deb: 5/27/1939

YEAR TM-L	G	AB	R	H	2B	3B	HR	RBI	BB	SO	SB	CS	AVG	OBP	SLG	OPS	OPS+	BR/A	RC	RC/G	FR	G/POS	WS	TPW
1939 Phi-A	9	9	0	2	1	0	0	3	1	1	0	0	.222	.300	.333	.633	63	-1	1	3.77	-1	/3-5,S-2,1-1,2-1	0	-0.1

• MCNAMARA, Dinny John Raymond McNamara b: 9/16/1905, Lexington, MA d: 12/20/1963, Arlington, MA BL/TR, 5'9", 165 lbs. Deb: 7/2/1927 Career OF: 0-4-2

YEAR TM-L	G	AB	R	H	2B	3B	HR	RBI	BB	SO	SB	CS	AVG	OBP	SLG	OPS	OPS+	BR/A	RC	RC/G	FR	G/POS	WS	TPW
1927 Bos-N	11	9	3	0	0	0	0	0	0	3	0	....	.000	.000	.000	.000	-108	-3	0	.00	0	/O-3(0-3-0)	0	-0.3
1928 Bos-N	9	4	2	1	0	0	0	0	0	1	0	....	.250	.250	.250	.500	33	-0	0	1.77	0	/O-3(0-1-2)	0	-0.1
Total 2	20	13	5	1	0	0	0	0	0	4	0		.077	.077	.077	.154	-64	-3	0	.47	0	/O-6	0	-0.3

• MCNAMARA, George George Francis McNamara b: 1/11/1901, Chicago, IL d: 6/12/1990, Hinsdale, IL BL/TR, 6', 175 lbs. Deb: 9/28/1922

YEAR TM-L	G	AB	R	H	2B	3B	HR	RBI	BB	SO	SB	CS	AVG	OBP	SLG	OPS	OPS+	BR/A	RC	RC/G	FR	G/POS	WS	TPW
1922 Was-A	3	11	3	3	0	0	0	1	1	2	0	0	.273	.333	.273	.606	62	-1	1	3.46	0	/O-3(0-0-3)	0	-0.1

• MCNAMARA, Jim James Patrick McNamara b: 6/10/1965, Nashua, NH BL/TR, 6'4", 210 lbs. Deb: 4/9/1992

YEAR TM-L	G	AB	R	H	2B	3B	HR	RBI	BB	SO	SB	CS	AVG	OBP	SLG	OPS	OPS+	BR/A	RC	RC/G	FR	G/POS	WS	TPW
1992 SF-N	30	74	6	16	1	0	1	9	6	25	0	0	.216	.275	.270	.545	58	-4	6	2.50	-1	C-30	3	-0.4
1993 SF-N	4	7	0	1	0	0	0	1	0	1	0	0	.143	.143	.143	.286	-24	-1	0	.64	0	/C-4	0	-0.1
Total 2	34	81	6	17	1	0	1	10	6	26	0	0	.210	.264	.259	.524	52	-5	6	2.34	-1	/C-34	3	-0.5

• MCNAMARA, Tom Thomas Henry McNamara b: 11/5/1895, Roxbury, MA d: 5/5/1974, Danvers, MA BR/TR, 6'2", 200 lbs. Deb: 6/25/1922

YEAR TM-L	G	AB	R	H	2B	3B	HR	RBI	BB	SO	SB	CS	AVG	OBP	SLG	OPS	OPS+	BR/A	RC	RC/G	FR	G/POS	WS	TPW
1922 Pit-N	1	1	0	0	0	0	0	0	0	0	0	0	.000	.000	.000	.000	-99	-0	0	.00	0	....	0	0.0

• MCNEALY, Rusty Robert Lee McNealy b: 8/12/1958, Sacramento, CA BL/TL, 5'8", 160 lbs. Deb: 9/4/1983

YEAR TM-L	G	AB	R	H	2B	3B	HR	RBI	BB	SO	SB	CS	AVG	OBP	SLG	OPS	OPS+	BR/A	RC	RC/G	FR	G/POS	WS	TPW
1983 Oak-A	15	4	5	0	0	0	0	0	0	0	0	1	.000	.000	.000	.000	-106	-2	0	.00	0	/D-7,O-5(1-4-1)	0	-0.2

• MCNEELY, Earl George Earl McNeely b: 5/12/1898, Sacramento, CA d: 7/16/1971, Sacramento, CA BR/TR, 5'9", 155 lbs. Deb: 8/9/1924 C Career OF: 105-281-196

YEAR TM-L	G	AB	R	H	2B	3B	HR	RBI	BB	SO	SB	CS	AVG	OBP	SLG	OPS	OPS+	BR/A	RC	RC/G	FR	G/POS	WS	TPW
1924*Was-A	43	179	31	59	5	6	0	15	5	21	3	1	.330	.355	.425	.779	104	1	27	5.55	-1	O-42(0-42-2)	6	-0.1
1925*Was-A	122	385	76	110	14	2	3	37	48	54	15	16	.286	.378	.356	.734	89	-7	53	4.65	-1	*O-112(7-103-2)/1-1	11	-1.2
1926 Was-A	124	442	84	134	20	12	0	48	44	28	18	6	.303	.373	.403	.775	105	6	70	5.64	-1	*O-118(65-52-2)	15	-0.2
1927 Was-A	73	185	40	51	10	4	0	16	11	13	11	4	.276	.320	.373	.693	80	-5	23	4.13	-2	O-47(3-32-14)/1-4	4	-0.9
1928 StL-A	127	496	66	117	27	7	0	44	37	39	8	6	.236	.299	.319	.618	60	-29	49	3.26	4	*O-120(2-1-118)	6	-3.3
1929 StL-A	69	230	27	56	8	1	1	18	7	13	2	1	.243	.272	.300	.572	45	-19	19	2.70	-3	O-62(18-2-42)	1	-2.4
1930 StL-A	76	235	33	64	19	1	0	20	22	14	8	3	.272	.340	.362	.701	75	-8	30	4.44	-2	O-38(8-26-4),1-27	4	-1.1
1931 StL-A	49	102	12	23	4	0	0	15	9	5	4	4	.225	.288	.265	.553	45	-9	8	2.41	0	O-37(2-23-12)/1-1	0	-0.9
Total 8	683	2254	369	614	107	33	4	213	183	187	69	41	.272	.335	.354	.689	78	-70	278	4.20	-6	O-576/1-33	47	-10.3

• MCNEELY, Jeff Jeffrey Lavern McNeely b: 10/18/1969, Monroe, NC BR/TR, 6'2", 190 lbs. Deb: 9/5/1993

YEAR TM-L	G	AB	R	H	2B	3B	HR	RBI	BB	SO	SB	CS	AVG	OBP	SLG	OPS	OPS+	BR/A	RC	RC/G	FR	G/POS	WS	TPW
1993 Bos-A	21	37	10	11	1	1	0	1	7	9	6	0	.297	.409	.378	.787	106	2	8	8.05	-2	O-13(0-13-0)/D-3	1	0.0

• MCNEIL, Norm Norman Francis McNeil b: 10/22/1892, Chicago, IL d: 4/11/1942, Buffalo, NY BR/TR, 5'11", 180 lbs. Deb: 6/21/1919

YEAR TM-L	G	AB	R	H	2B	3B	HR	RBI	BB	SO	SB	CS	AVG	OBP	SLG	OPS	OPS+	BR/A	RC	RC/G	FR	G/POS	WS	TPW
1919 Bos-A	5	9	0	3	0	0	0	1	1	0	0	....	.333	.400	.333	.733	113	0	1	4.97	-1	/C-5	0	-0.1

• MCNERTNEY, Jerry Gerald Edward McNertney b: 8/7/1936, Boone, IA BR/TR, 6', 195 lbs. Deb: 4/16/1964 C

YEAR TM-L	G	AB	R	H	2B	3B	HR	RBI	BB	SO	SB	CS	AVG	OBP	SLG	OPS	OPS+	BR/A	RC	RC/G	FR	G/POS	WS	TPW
1964 Chi-A	73	186	16	40	5	0	3	23	19	24	0	0	.215	.298	.290	.588	66	-8	16	2.74	1	C-69	5	-0.4
1966 Chi-A	44	59	3	13	0	0	0	1	7	6	1	1	.220	.303	.220	.523	57	-3	4	1.98	0	C-37	1	-0.3
1967 Chi-A	56	123	8	28	6	0	3	13	6	14	0	0	.228	.275	.350	.624	86	-2	11	2.88	5	C-52	5	0.5
1968 Chi-A	74	169	18	37	4	1	3	18	18	29	0	0	.219	.302	.308	.609	84	-3	17	3.22	6	C-64/1-1	6	0.7
1969 Sea-A	128	410	39	99	18	1	8	55	29	63	1	0	.241	.292	.349	.640	80	-12	40	3.22	3	*C-122	9	-0.4
1970 Mil-A	111	296	27	72	11	1	6	22	22	33	1	4	.243	.304	.348	.652	79	-10	27	2.98	4	C-94,1-13	5	-0.4
1971 StL-N	56	128	15	37	4	2	4	22	12	14	0	0	.289	.350	.445	.795	119	3	19	5.02	-3	C-36	5	0.2
1972 StL-N	39	48	3	10	3	1	0	9	6	16	0	0	.208	.296	.313	.609	74	-2	5	3.02	0	C-10	1	-0.1
1973 Pit-N	9	4	0	1	0	0	0	0	0	0	0	0	.250	.250	.250	.500	40	-0	0	2.25	-2	/C-9	0	-0.2
Total 9	590	1423	129	337	51	6	27	163	119	199	3	5	.237	.301	.338	.639	81	-37	140	3.16	13	C-493/1-14	37	-0.4

• MCNULTY, Bill William Francis McNulty b: 8/29/1946, Sacramento, CA BR/TR, 6'4", 205 lbs. Deb: 7/9/1969

YEAR TM-L	G	AB	R	H	2B	3B	HR	RBI	BB	SO	SB	CS	AVG	OBP	SLG	OPS	OPS+	BR/A	RC	RC/G	FR	G/POS	WS	TPW
1969 Oak-A	5	17	0	0	0	0	0	0	0	10	0	0	.000	.000	.000	.000	-105	-5	0	.00	1	/O-5(5-0-0)	0	-0.4

YEAR TM-L	G	AB	R	H	2B	3B	HR	RBI	BB	SO	SB	CS	AVG	OBP	SLG	OPS	OPS+	BR/A	RC	RC/G	FR	G/POS	WS	TPW
1972 Oak-A	4	10	0	1	0	0	0	0	2	1	0	0	.100	.250	.100	.350	7	-1	0	1.14	-1	/3-3	0	-0.2
Total 2	9	27	0	1	0	0	0	0	2	11	0	0	.037	.103	.037	.140	-58	-6	0	.39	1	/0-5,3-3	0	-0.6

• MCNULTY, Pat Patrick Howard McNulty b: 2/27/1899, Cleveland, OH d: 5/4/1963, Hollywood, CA BL/TR, 5'11", 160 lbs. Deb: 9/5/1922 Career OF: 18-84-129

YEAR TM-L	G	AB	R	H	2B	3B	HR	RBI	BB	SO	SB	CS	AVG	OBP	SLG	OPS	OPS+	BR/A	RC	RC/G	FR	G/POS	WS	TPW
1922 Cle-A	22	59	10	16	2	1	0	5	9	5	4	1	.271	.368	.339	.707	84	-0	8	4.74	-2	0-22(1-19-2)	1	-0.3
1924 Cle-A	101	291	46	78	13	5	0	26	33	22	10	7	.268	.347	.347	.694	78	-9	36	4.18	-1	0-75(11-20-44)	4	-1.4
1925 Cle-A	118	373	70	117	18	2	6	43	47	23	7	7	.314	.392	.421	.813	105	4	63	6.07	4	*0-111(3-29-81)	10	0.1
1926 Cle-A	48	56	3	14	2	1	0	6	5	9	0	1	.250	.311	.321	.633	65	-3	6	3.28	1	/0-9(2-5-2)	0	-0.3
1927 Cle-A	19	41	3	13	1	0	0	4	4	3	1	2	.317	.378	.341	.719	87	-1	5	4.30	-1	0-12(1-11-0)	1	-0.2
Total 5	308	820	132	238	36	9	6	84	98	62	22	18	.290	.368	.378	.746	91	-11	118	4.99	1	0-229	16	-2.1

• MCPHEE, Bid John Alexander McPhee b: 11/1/1859, Massena, NY d: 1/3/1943, San Diego, CA BR/TR, 5'8", 152 lbs. Deb: 5/2/1882 M HOF: 2000 Career OF: 0-1-3

YEAR TM-L	G	AB	R	H	2B	3B	HR	RBI	BB	SO	SB	CS	AVG	OBP	SLG	OPS	OPS+	BR/A	RC	RC/G	FR	G/POS	WS	TPW
1882 Cin-a	78	311	43	71	8	7	1	31	11	....	....	....	.228	.255	.309	.563	84	-6	25	2.92	11	*2-78	8	0.7
1883 Cin-a	96	367	61	90	10	10	2	42	18	....	....	....	.245	.281	.343	.624	94	-3	36	3.66	20	*2-96	11	1.8
1884 Cin-a	112	450	107	125	8	7	5	64	27	....	....	....	.278	.327	.360	.687	118	9	54	4.60	28	*2-112	18	3.7
1885 Cin-a	110	431	78	114	12	4	0	46	19	....	....	....	.265	.306	.311	.617	94	-3	42	3.58	15	*2-110	13	1.4
1886 Cin-a	140	560	139	150	23	12	**8**	70	59	....	40	....	.268	.343	.395	.738	127	17	92	6.04	26	*2-140	23	**4.2**
1887 Cin-a	129	595	137	211	20	**19**	2	87	55	....	95	....	.355	.360	.407	.767	111	8	116	8.17	31	*2-129	19	3.5
1888 Cin-a	111	458	88	110	12	10	4	51	43	....	54	....	.240	.312	.336	.648	102	1	67	5.17	30	*2-111	17	3.2
1889 Cin-a	135	540	109	145	25	7	5	57	60	29	63	....	.269	.346	.369	.715	100	-0	93	6.23	39	*2-135/3-1	20	3.7
1890 Cin-N	132	528	125	135	16	22	3	39	82	26	55	....	.256	.362	.386	.748	119	15	96	6.48	28	*2-132	21	**4.2**
1891 Cin-N	138	562	107	144	14	16	6	38	74	35	33	....	.256	.345	.370	.715	107	6	85	5.50	13	*2-138	19	2.1
1892 Cin-N	144	573	111	157	19	12	4	60	84	48	44	....	.274	.373	.370	.743	127	22	98	6.36	21	*2-144	27	4.5
1893 Cin-N	127	491	101	138	17	11	3	68	94	20	25	....	.281	.401	.379	.779	105	7	87	6.51	27	*2-127	21	3.3
1894 Cin-N	128	483	113	151	21	10	5	93	91	23	33	....	.313	.427	.429	.855	103	6	105	8.22	13	*2-126	17	1.9
1895 Cin-N	115	432	107	129	24	12	1	75	73	30	30	....	.299	.409	.417	.826	109	9	89	7.76	12	*2-115	16	2.1
1896 Cin-N	117	433	81	132	18	7	1	87	51	18	48	....	.305	.391	.386	.776	98	0	87	7.46	14	*2-117	17	1.7
1897 Cin-N	81	282	45	85	13	7	1	39	35	....	9	....	.301	.386	.408	.794	103	2	51	6.37	17	2-81	11	1.9
1898 Cin-N	133	486	72	121	26	9	1	60	66	....	21	....	.249	.341	.346	.687	91	-5	68	4.76	-6	*2-130/0-3(0-0-3)	15	-0.5
1899 Cin-N	112	376	60	105	17	7	1	65	41	....	18	....	.279	.361	.370	.731	99	0	59	5.62	3	*2-105/0-1	12	0.7
Total 18	2138	8358	1684	2313	303	189	53	1072	983	229	568	....	.277	.355	.373	.728	106	83	1350	5.93	341	*2-2126/0-4,3-1	305	44.0

• MCQUAID, Mart Mortimer Martin McQuaid b: 6/28/1861, Chicago, IL d: 3/5/1928, Chicago, IL, 5'9" Deb: 8/15/1891 Career OF: 2-0-0

YEAR TM-L	G	AB	R	H	2B	3B	HR	RBI	BB	SO	SB	CS	AVG	OBP	SLG	OPS	OPS+	BR/A	RC	RC/G	FR	G/POS	WS	TPW
1891 StL-a	4	11	1	4	2	0	0	1	0	1	1	....	.364	.364	.545	.909	139	0	3	9.88	1	/2-3,0-1	1	0.1
1898 Was-N	1	4	0	0	0	0	0	0	0	....	0	....	.000	.000	.000	.000	-100	-1	0	.00	-1	/0-1	0	-0.2
Total 2	5	15	1	4	2	0	0	1	0	1	1	....	.267	.267	.400	.667	75	-1	3	6.29	0	/2-3,0-2	1	-0.1

• MCQUAIG, Jerry Gerald Joseph McQuaig b: 1/31/1912, Douglas, GA d: 2/5/2001, Buford, GA BR/TR, 5'11", 183 lbs. Deb: 8/25/1934

YEAR TM-L	G	AB	R	H	2B	3B	HR	RBI	BB	SO	SB	CS	AVG	OBP	SLG	OPS	OPS+	BR/A	RC	RC/G	FR	G/POS	WS	TPW
1934 Phi-A	7	16	2	1	0	0	0	1	2	4	0	0	.063	.167	.063	.229	-40	-3	0	.43	0	/0-6(5-0-1)	0	-0.4

• MCQUERY, Mox William Thomas McQuery b: 6/28/1861, Garrard County, KY d: 6/12/1900, Cincinnati, OH, 6'4" Deb: 8/20/1884

YEAR TM-L	G	AB	R	H	2B	3B	HR	RBI	BB	SO	SB	CS	AVG	OBP	SLG	OPS	OPS+	BR/A	RC	RC/G	FR	G/POS	WS	TPW
1884 Cin-U	35	132	31	37	5	0	2	....	8	....	....	....	.280	.321	.364	.685	121	3	16	4.66	1	1-35	4	0.1
1885 Det-N	70	278	34	76	15	4	3	30	8	29	....	....	.273	.294	.388	.682	119	5	33	4.35	4	1-70/0-1	7	0.2
1886 KC-N	122	449	62	111	27	4	4	38	36	44	4	....	.247	.303	.352	.655	93	-5	50	4.02	-1	*1-122	6	-1.5
1890 Syr-a	122	461	64	142	17	6	2	55	53	....	26	....	.308	.383	.384	.767	140	26	80	6.62	-4	*1-122	19	1.0
1891 Was-a	68	261	40	63	9	4	2	37	18	19	3	....	.241	.305	.330	.635	85	-5	28	3.73	-1	1-68	4	-1.1
Total 5	417	1581	231	429	73	18	13	160	123	92	33	....	.271	.327	.365	.692	113	23	206	4.80	-1	1-417/0-1	40	-1.2

• MCQUILLEN, Glenn Glenn Richard "Red" McQuillen b: 4/19/1915, Strasburg, VA d: 6/8/1989, Gardenville, MD BR/TR, 6', 198 lbs. Deb: 6/16/1938 Career OF: 145-0-17

YEAR TM-L	G	AB	R	H	2B	3B	HR	RBI	BB	SO	SB	CS	AVG	OBP	SLG	OPS	OPS+	BR/A	RC	RC/G	FR	G/POS	WS	TPW
1938 StL-A	43	116	14	33	4	0	0	13	4	12	0	1	.284	.308	.319	.627	58	-8	11	3.41	-2	0-30(30-0-0)	1	-1.1
1941 StL-A	7	21	4	7	2	1	0	3	1	2	0	1	.333	.364	.524	.887	128	0	3	5.31	-1	/0-6(3-0-3)	0	-0.1
1942 StL-A	100	339	40	96	15	12	3	47	10	17	1	1	.283	.306	.425	.730	103	-1	37	3.71	-6	0-77(68-0-9)	6	-1.2
1946 StL-A	59	166	24	40	3	3	1	12	19	18	0	2	.241	.319	.313	.632	73	-6	16	3.18	3	0-48(44-0-5)	2	-0.6
1947 StL-A	1	1	0	0	0	0	0	0	0	0	0	0	.000	.000	.000	.000	-98	-0	0	.00	0	....	0	0.0
Total 5	210	643	82	176	24	16	4	75	34	49	1	5	.274	.311	.379	.691	87	-16	67	3.56	-6	0-161	9	-3.0

• MCQUINN, George George Hartley McQuinn b: 5/29/1910, Arlington, VA d: 12/24/1978, Alexandria, VA BL/TL, 5'11", 165 lbs. Deb: 4/14/1936

YEAR TM-L	G	AB	R	H	2B	3B	HR	RBI	BB	SO	SB	CS	AVG	OBP	SLG	OPS	OPS+	BR/A	RC	RC/G	FR	G/POS	WS	TPW
1936 Cin-N	38	134	5	27	3	4	0	13	10	22	0	....	.201	.262	.284	.546	50	-9	11	2.66	-1	1-38	1	-1.3
1938 StL-A	148	602	100	195	42	7	12	82	58	49	4	5	.324	.384	.477	.861	115	12	110	6.88	-2	*1-148	16	-0.3
1939 StL-A★	154	617	101	195	37	13	20	94	65	42	6	5	.316	.383	.515	.898	125	21	122	7.22	2	*1-154	18	0.8
1940 StL-A★	151	594	78	166	39	10	16	84	57	58	3	3	.279	.343	.460	.802	104	2	95	5.68	5	*1-150	16	-0.7
1941 StL-A	130	495	93	147	28	4	18	80	74	30	5	4	.297	.388	.479	.867	124	18	96	7.09	12	*1-125	17	1.8
1942 StL-A★	145	554	86	145	32	5	12	78	60	77	1	1	.262	.335	.403	.737	105	3	78	4.85	6	*1-144	16	-0.4
1943 StL-A	125	449	53	109	19	2	12	74	56	65	4	3	.243	.327	.374	.701	103	3	58	4.33	5	*1-122	13	0.1
1944*StL-A★	146	516	83	129	26	3	11	72	85	74	4	3	.250	.357	.376	.733	103	5	79	5.20	-2	*1-146	20	-0.5
1945 StL-A★	139	483	69	134	31	3	7	61	65	51	1	1	.277	.364	.398	.762	115	11	75	5.48	4	*1-136	17	0.9
1946 Phi-A	136	484	47	109	23	6	3	35	64	62	4	2	.225	.317	.316	.633	78	-13	54	3.71	4	*1-134	7	-1.4
1947*NY-A★	144	517	84	157	24	3	13	80	78	66	0	2	.304	.395	.437	.832	132	24	97	6.83	7	*1-142	24	2.7
1948 NY-A★	94	302	33	75	11	4	11	41	40	38	0	2	.248	.336	.421	.757	101	-1	45	5.05	2	1-90	8	-0.1
Total 12	1550	5747	832	1588	315	64	135	794	712	634	32	31	.276	.357	.424	.781	109	75	920	5.63	43	*1-1529	173	1.5

• MCRAE, Brian Brian Wesley McRae b: 8/27/1967, Bradenton, FL BB/TR, 6', 185 lbs. Deb: 8/7/1990 Career OF: 0-1307-4

YEAR TM-L	G	AB	R	H	2B	3B	HR	RBI	BB	SO	SB	CS	AVG	OBP	SLG	OPS	OPS+	BR/A	RC	RC/G	FR	G/POS	WS	TPW
1990 KC-A	46	168	21	48	8	3	2	23	9	29	4	3	.286	.322	.405	.727	104	-0	20	4.10	-1	0-45(0-45-0)	5	-0.2
1991 KC-A	152	629	86	164	28	9	8	64	24	99	20	11	.261	.290	.372	.662	81	-19	64	3.50	-4	*0-150(0-150-0)	11	-2.5
1992 KC-A	149	533	63	119	23	5	4	52	42	88	18	5	.223	.287	.308	.595	65	-23	49	3.01	1	*0-148(0-148-0)	11	-2.5
1993 KC-A	153	627	78	177	28	9	12	69	37	105	23	14	.282	.326	.413	.739	92	-9	83	4.58	-3	*0-153(0-153-0)	18	-1.1
1994 KC-A	114	436	71	119	22	6	4	40	54	67	28	8	.273	.361	.378	.739	87	-4	66	5.31	-9	*0-110(0-110-4)/D-4	11	-1.2
1995 Chi-N	137	580	92	167	38	7	12	48	47	92	27	8	.288	.349	.440	.788	108	8	90	5.55	0	*0-137(0-137-0)	18	0.9
1996 Chi-N	157	624	111	172	32	5	17	66	73	84	37	9	.276	.362	.425	.787	104	9	102	5.75	-11	*0-155(0-155-0)	21	-0.1
1997 Chi-N	108	417	63	100	27	5	6	28	52	62	14	6	.240	.330	.372	.702	81	-11	52	4.15	-3	*0-107(0-107-0)	8	-1.3
NY-N	45	145	23	36	5	2	5	15	13	22	3	4	.248	.319	.414	.733	93	-3	18	4.26	-2	0-41(0-41-0)	4	-0.4
Yr.	153	562	86	136	32	7	11	43	65	84	17	10	.242	.327	.383	.710	84	-14	70	4.18	-5	*0-148(0-148-0)	12	-1.7
1998 NY-N	159	552	79	146	36	5	21	79	80	90	20	11	.264	.363	.462	.825	117	14	97	6.09	-14	*0-154(0-154-0)	20	0.1
1999 NY-N	96	298	35	66	12	1	8	36	39	57	2	6	.221	.322	.349	.671	72	-15	33	3.67	-7	0-87(0-87-0)	3	-2.0
Col-N	7	23	1	6	2	0	1	1	2	7	0	0	.261	.370	.478	.849	89	-0	4	7.08	0	/0-7(0-7-0)	0	0.0
Yr.	103	321	36	72	14	1	9	37	41	64	2	6	.224	.325	.358	.683	73	-15	38	3.89	-7	0-94(0-94-0)	3	-2.0
Tor-A	31	82	11	16	3	1	3	11	16	22	0	1	.195	.340	.366	.706	79	-3	11	4.14	1	D-15,0-13(0-13-0)	2	-0.2
Total 10	1354	5114	734	1336	264	58	103	532	488	824	196	86	.261	.332	.396	.728	92	-57	691	4.63	-52	*0-1307/D-19	132	-10.5

• MCRAE, Hal Harold Abraham McRae b: 7/10/1945, Avon Park, FL BR/TR, 5'11", 180 lbs. Deb: 7/11/1968 M/C Career OF: 360-33-94

YEAR TM-L	G	AB	R	H	2B	3B	HR	RBI	BB	SO	SB	CS	AVG	OBP	SLG	OPS	OPS+	BR/A	RC	RC/G	FR	G/POS	WS	TPW
1968 Cin-N	17	51	1	10	1	0	0	2	4	14	1	1	.196	.255	.216	.470	40	-4	2	1.48	-1	2-16	0	-0.5
1970*Cin-N	70	165	18	41	6	1	8	23	15	23	0	2	.248	.315	.442	.757	97	-2	21	4.22	-1	0-46(46-0-1)/3-6,2-1	4	-0.5
1971 Cin-N	99	337	39	89	24	2	9	34	11	35	3	2	.264	.291	.427	.719	107	1	39	4.04	1	0-91(66-28-0)	9	-0.3
1972*Cin-N	61	97	9	27	4	0	5	26	2	10	0	0	.278	.307	.474	.781	126	3	12	4.16	-2	0-12(0-3-9),3-11	3	0.0
1973 KC-A	106	338	36	79	18	3	9	50	34	38	2	2	.234	.315	.385	.699	89	-5	41	4.09	1	0-64(3-0-63),D-37/3-2	8	-0.9
1974 KC-A	148	539	71	167	36	4	15	88	54	68	11	8	.310	.378	.475	.853	136	25	95	6.40	-1	D-90,0-56(40-0-19)/3-1	20	1.8
1975 KC-A★	126	480	58	147	38	6	5	71	47	47	11	8	.306	.373	.442	.815	126	16	75	5.38	2	*0-114(112-2-0),D-12/3-1	17	1.2
1976*KC-A★	149	527	75	175	34	5	8	73	64	43	22	12	.332	**.412**	.461	**.873**	154	38	101	**7.03**	1	*D-117,0-31(31-0-0)	26	3.6
1977*KC-A	162	641	104	191	**54**	11	21	92	59	43	18	14	.298	.369	.515	.884	137	31	119	6.63	2	*D-115,0-47(47-0-0)	26	2.6

YEAR TM-L	G	AB	R	H	2B	3B	HR	RBI	BB	SO	SB	CS	AVG	OBP	SLG	OPS	OPS+	BR/A	RC	RC/G	FR	G/POS	WS	TPW
1978*KC-A	156	623	90	170	39	5	16	72	51	62	17	8	.273	.334	.429	.762	110	8	87	4.82	1	*D-153/0-3(3-0-0)	16	0.3
1979 KC-A	101	393	55	113	32	4	10	74	38	46	5	4	.288	.356	.466	.822	117	9	66	5.95	0	*D-100	12	0.5
1980*KC-A	124	489	73	145	39	5	14	83	29	56	10	2	.297	.346	.483	.829	123	16	79	5.87	-1	*D-110/0-9(9-0-0)	16	1.1
1981*KC-A	101	389	38	106	23	2	7	36	34	33	3	4	.272	.334	.396	.730	111	4	49	4.36	0	D-97/0-4(2-0-2)	8	0.0
1982 KC-A★	159	613	91	189	**46**	8	27	**133**	55	61	4	4	.308	.370	.542	.912	146	37	123	7.53	0	*D-158/0-1	26	3.1
1983 KC-A	157	589	84	183	41	6	12	82	50	68	2	3	.311	.374	.462	.836	128	22	98	6.14	0	*D-156	20	1.7
1984*KC-A	106	317	30	96	13	4	3	42	34	47	0	3	.303	.372	.397	.770	112	5	45	5.05	0	D-94	8	0.2
1985*KC-A	112	320	41	83	19	0	14	70	44	45	0	1	.259	.351	.450	.801	117	8	49	5.20	0	*D-106	8	0.5
1986 KC-A	112	278	22	70	14	0	7	37	18	39	0	0	.252	.300	.378	.677	81	-8	29	3.63	0	D-75	2	-0.9
1987 KC-A	18	32	5	10	3	0	1	9	5	1	0	0	.313	.405	.500	.905	135	2	6	7.57	0	/D-7	1	0.2
Total 19	2084	7218	940	2091	484	66	191	1097	648	779	109	78	.290	.355	.454	.809	122	206	1138	5.58	0	*D-1427,0-478/3-21,2-17	230	13.7

• MCREMER, McRemer Deb: 6/20/1884

1884 Was-U	1	3	0	0	0	0	0	....	0	....	....	....	.000	.000	.000	.000	-103	-1	0	.00	0	/0-1	0	-0.1

• MCREYNOLDS, Kevin Walter Kevin McReynolds b: 10/16/1959, Little Rock, AR BR/TR, 6', 210 lbs. Deb: 6/2/1983 Career OF: 1067-468-27

1983 SD-N	39	140	15	31	3	1	4	14	12	29	2	1	.221	.283	.343	.626	75	-5	14	3.35	1	0-38(3-32-10)	3	-0.5
1984*SD-N	147	525	68	146	26	6	20	75	34	69	3	6	.278	.322	.465	.787	119	8	72	4.76	3	*0-143(0-143-0)	25	0.9
1985 SD-N	152	564	61	132	24	4	15	75	43	81	4	0	.234	.292	.371	.662	85	-12	59	3.48	5	*0-150(0-150-0)	12	-1.0
1986 SD-N	158	560	89	161	31	6	26	96	66	83	8	6	.288	.364	.504	.867	140	28	103	6.48	-7	*0-154(108-109-3)	26	1.7
1987 NY-N	151	590	86	163	32	5	29	95	39	70	14	1	.276	.322	.495	.817	119	15	93	5.56	2	*0-150(150-0-0)	19	1.0
1988*NY-N	147	552	82	159	30	2	27	99	38	56	21	0	.288	.338	.496	.835	144	33	97	6.46	5	*0-147(147-1-0)	31	3.5
1989 NY-N	148	545	74	148	25	3	22	85	46	74	15	7	.272	.329	.450	.779	127	17	80	5.15	1	*0-145(145-0-0)	21	1.4
1990 NY-N	147	521	75	140	23	1	24	82	71	61	9	2	.269	.358	.455	.812	122	17	88	5.95	-1	*0-144(144-0-0)	21	1.1
1991 NY-N	143	522	65	135	32	1	16	74	49	46	6	6	.259	.325	.416	.740	108	3	70	4.63	-3	*0-141(125-33-2)	17	-0.5
1992 KC-A	109	373	45	92	25	0	13	49	67	48	7	1	.247	.361	.418	.780	115	10	61	5.63	-3	*0-106(94-0-12)/D-1	13	0.4
1993 KC-A	110	351	44	86	22	4	11	42	37	56	2	2	.245	.319	.425	.743	92	-5	47	4.50	0	*0-104(104-0-0)/D-1	9	-0.8
1994 NY-N	51	180	23	46	11	2	4	21	20	34	2	0	.256	.330	.406	.736	91	-2	25	4.99	1	0-47(47-0-0)	5	-0.3
Total 12	1502	5423	727	1439	284	35	211	807	522	707	93	32	.265	.331	.447	.779	116	107	808	5.20	4	*0-1469/D-2	202	6.8

• MCSHANNIC, Pete Peter Robert McShannic b: 3/20/1864, Pittsburgh, PA d: 11/30/1946, Toledo, OH BB/TR, 5'7", 190 lbs. Deb: 9/15/1888

1888 Pit-N	26	98	5	19	1	0	0	5	1	9	3	....	.194	.218	.204	.422	38	-7	5	1.76	1	3-26	2	-0.5

• MCSORLEY, Trick John Bernard McSorley b: 12/16/1852, St. Louis, MO d: 2/9/1936, St. Louis, MO BR/TR, 5'4", 142 lbs. Deb: 5/6/1875 U

1875 RS-n	15	52	4	11	0	0	0	2	0	3	3	0	.212	.212	.212	.423	52	-1	3	2.18	0	/3-9,0-7(6-1-0)	....	-0.1
1884 Tol-a	21	68	12	17	1	0	0	0	3	....	....	....	.250	.282	.265	.546	76	-2	5	2.80	2	1-16/0-5(5-0-0),3-1,P-1	1	-0.1
1885 StL-N	2	6	2	3	1	0	0	1	2	1	....	....	.500	.625	.667	1.292	340	2	3	23.06	-1	/3-2	1	0.1
1886 StL-a	5	20	1	3	3	0	0	0	0	....	0	....	.150	.150	.300	.450	38	-2	1	1.47	-1	/S-5	0	-0.3
Total 3	28	94	15	23	5	0	0	1	5	1	0	....	.245	.283	.298	.581	90	-2	9	3.34	-1	/1-16,0-5,S-5,3-3,P-1	2	-0.3

• MCSWEENEY, Paul Paul A. McSweeney b: 4/3/1867, St. Louis, MO d: 8/12/1951, St. Louis, MO Deb: 9/20/1891

1891 StL-a	3	12	2	3	1	0	0	2	0	0	1	....	.250	.308	.333	.641	72	-1	2	4.64	-2	/2-3,3-1	0	-0.2

• MCTAMANY, Jim James Edward McTamany b: 7/1/1863, Philadelphia, PA d: 4/16/1916, Lenni, PA BR/TR, 5'8", 190 lbs. Deb: 8/15/1885 Career OF: 35-723-55

1885 Bro-a	35	131	21	36	7	2	1	13	9	....	....	....	.275	.321	.382	.703	121	3	16	4.68	-4	0-35(35-0-0)	4	-0.2
1886 Bro-a	111	418	86	106	23	10	2	56	54	....	18	....	.254	.353	.371	.724	126	14	63	5.41	12	*0-111(0-107-4)	18	2.0
1887 Bro-a	134	596	123	210	22	10	1	68	76	....	66	....	.352	.365	.344	.709	97	1	92	6.41	7	*0-134(0-134-0)	15	0.3
1888 KC-a	130	516	94	127	12	10	4	41	67	....	55	....	.246	.345	.331	.677	110	8	80	5.55	8	*0-130(0-80-50)	16	1.1
1889 Col-a	139	529	113	146	21	7	4	52	116	66	40	....	.276	.407	.365	.772	127	28	97	6.73	-4	*0-139(0-139-0)	20	1.6
1890 Col-a	125	466	**140**	120	27	7	1	48	**112**	....	43	....	.258	.405	.352	.757	132	29	86	6.59	4	*0-125(0-125-0)	22	2.5
1891 Col-a	81	304	59	76	17	9	3	35	58	48	20	....	.250	.374	.395	.768	127	13	54	6.23	-1	0-81(0-81-0)	13	0.8
Phi-a	58	218	57	49	6	3	3	21	43	44	13	....	.225	.365	.321	.686	94	-0	31	4.86	-2	0-58(0-57-1)	6	-0.4
Yr.	139	522	116	125	23	12	6	56	101	92	33	....	.239	.370	.364	.734	113	13	85	5.65	-4	*0-139(0-138-1)	19	0.4
Total 7	813	3178	693	870	135	58	19	334	535	158	255	....	.274	.373	.355	.728	117	96	519	6.01	19	0-813	114	7.7

• MCVEY, Cal Calvin Alexander McVey
b: 8/30/1850, Montrose, IA d: 8/20/1926, San Francisco, CA BR/TR, 5'9", 170 lbs. Deb: 5/5/1871 M NA OF: 4-32-66 Career OF: 1-1-6 ♦

1871 Bos-n	29	153	43	**66**	9	5	0	43	1	2	6	0	.431	.435	.556	.991	176	15	41	14.69	-3	*C-29/0-5(0-0-5),3-1	....	0.8
1872 Bos-n	46	237	56	76	10	2	0	41	1	1	6	1	.321	.324	.380	.703	110	2	32	6.09	1	*C-40,0-11(2-0-9)/3-1	....	0.3
1873 Bal-n	38	192	49	73	4	5	2	34	3	2	1	0	.380	.390	.484	.874	159	14	38	9.62	-2	C-25/0-6(1-4-1),S-5,2-4,1,3	....	0.9
1874 Bos-n	70	343	**91**	**123**	21	6	3	**71**	1	3	5	0	.359	.360	.481	.842	158	21	63	8.57	-3	*0-57(0-8-49),C-23	....	1.6
1875 Bos-n	82	389	89	138	**36**	9	3	**87**	1	5	7	0	.355	.356	**.517**	**.873**	192	35	76	8.93	5	*1-55,0-23(1-20-2),C-16/P-3	....	3.4
1876 Chi-N	63	310	62	107	15	0	1	53	2	4	....	....	.345	.352	.406	.757	136	10	45	6.28	-2	*1-55,P-11/C-6,3-1,0-1	16	0.8
1877 Chi-N	60	266	58	98	9	7	0	36	8	11	....	....	.368	.387	.455	.842	147	15	48	7.85	-6	C-40,3-17,P-17/1-1,2-1	14	-0.4
1878 Cin-N	61	271	43	83	10	4	2	28	5	10	....	....	.306	.319	.395	.714	147	14	35	5.12	-9	*3-61/C-3	11	0.6
1879 Cin-N	81	354	64	105	18	6	0	55	8	13	....	....	.297	.312	.381	.694	134	13	43	4.86	-9	*1-72/0-7(0-1-6),P-3,3-1,C	13	-0.8
Total 5 n	265	1314	328	476	80	27	8	**276**	7	13	25	1	.362	.366	.482	.848	162	87	249	8.98	-2	C-133,0-102/1-58,S-5,2-4,3,P	....	6.9
Total 4	265	1201	227	393	52	17	3	172	23	38	....	....	.327	.340	.407	.747	140	52	171	5.90	-27	1-128/3-80,C-50,P-31,0-8,2	54	0.2

• MCVEY, George George W. McVey b: 9/16/1865, Port Jervis, NY d: 5/3/1896, Quincy, IL BR/TR, 6'1", 185 lbs. Deb: 9/19/1885

1885 Bro-a	6	21	2	3	0	0	0	1	2	....	....	....	.143	.217	.143	.360	15	-2	1	1.00	0	/1-3,C-3	0	-0.2

• MCWILLIAMS, Bill William Henry McWilliams b: 11/28/1910, Dubuque, IA d: 1/21/1997, Garland, TX BR/TR, 6'1", 185 lbs. Deb: 7/8/1931

1931 Bos-A	2	2	0	0	0	0	0	0	0	1	0	0	.000	.000	.000	.000	-106	-1	0	.00	0	....	0	-0.1

• MEACHAM, Bob Robert Andrew Meacham b: 8/25/1960, Los Angeles, CA BB/TR, 6'1", 180 lbs. Deb: 6/30/1983

1983 NY-A	22	51	5	12	2	0	0	4	4	10	8	0	.235	.304	.275	.578	63	-1	6	4.09	2	S-18/3-4	2	0.3
1984 NY-A	99	360	62	91	13	4	2	25	32	70	9	5	.253	.319	.328	.647	83	-8	41	3.70	-7	S-96/2-2	9	-0.6
1985 NY-A	156	481	70	105	16	2	1	47	54	102	25	7	.218	.304	.266	.570	59	-23	45	2.92	2	*S-155	11	-0.5
1986 NY-A	56	161	19	36	7	1	0	10	17	39	3	6	.224	.309	.280	.589	62	-10	13	2.45	3	S-56	3	-0.2
1987 NY-A	77	203	28	55	11	1	5	21	19	33	6	5	.271	.351	.409	.760	102	-0	30	5.06	-1	S-56,2-25/D-1	7	0.5
1988 NY-A	47	115	18	25	9	0	0	7	14	22	7	1	.217	.313	.296	.609	72	-3	13	3.59	-1	S-24,2-21/3-5	2	-0.2
Total 6	457	1371	202	324	58	8	8	114	140	276	58	24	.236	.316	.308	.624	73	-45	147	3.45	-1	S-405/2-48,3-9,D-1	34	-0.6

• MEAD, Charlie Charles Richard Mead b: 4/9/1921, Vermillion, Canada BL/TR, 6'1.5", 185 lbs. Deb: 8/28/1943 Career OF: 13-7-52

1943 NY-N	37	146	9	40	6	1	1	13	10	15	3	....	.274	.321	.349	.670	93	-2	16	3.95	0	0-37(0-3-34)	3	-0.4
1944 NY-N	39	78	5	14	1	0	1	8	5	7	0	....	.179	.229	.231	.460	30	-7	4	1.61	2	0-23(13-3-7)	0	-0.6
1945 NY-N	11	37	4	10	1	0	1	6	5	2	0	....	.270	.357	.378	.736	103	0	5	5.46	1	0-11(0-1-11)	1	0.1
Total 3	87	261	18	64	8	1	3	27	20	24	3	....	.245	.299	.318	.617	75	-9	26	3.37	4	/0-71	4	-0.9

• MEADOWS, Louie Michael Ray Meadows b: 4/29/1961, Maysville, NC BL/TL, 5'11", 190 lbs. Deb: 7/3/1986 Career OF: 29-3-10

1986 Hou-N	6	6	1	2	0	0	0	0	0	0	1	0	.333	.333	.333	.667	87	0	1	5.67	0	/0-1	0	0.0
1988 Hou-N	35	42	5	8	0	1	2	3	6	8	4	2	.190	.292	.381	.673	95	-0	5	3.28	0	0-10(7-1-3)	1	0.0
1989 Hou-N	31	51	5	9	0	0	3	10	1	14	1	2	.176	.192	.353	.545	55	-4	3	1.75	0	0-14(12-0-4)/1-1	0	-0.5
1990 Hou-N	15	14	3	2	0	0	0	0	2	4	0	0	.143	.250	.143	.393	11	-2	1	1.42	0	/0-9(7-0-2)	0	-0.2
Phi-N	15	14	1	1	0	0	0	0	1	2	0	0	.071	.133	.071	.205	-42	-3	0	.35	-1	/0-4(3-2-0)	0	-0.4
Yr.	30	28	4	3	0	0	0	0	3	6	0	0	.107	.194	.107	.301	-15	-4	1	.86	-1	0-13(10-2-2)	0	-0.6
Total 4	102	127	15	22	0	1	5	13	10	28	6	4	.173	.234	.307	.541	55	-9	9	2.20	-1	/0-38,1-1	1	-1.1

• MEARA, Charlie Charles Edward "Goggy" Meara b: 4/16/1891, New York, NY d: 2/8/1962, Bronx, NY BL/TR, 5'10", 160 lbs. Deb: 6/1/1914

1914 NY-A	4	7	2	2	0	0	0	1	2	2	0	1	.286	.444	.286	.730	120	-0	1	2.94	0	/0-3(0-2-2)	0	0.0

YEAR TM-L	G	AB	R	H	2B	3B	HR	RBI	BB	SO	SB	CS	AVG	OBP	SLG	OPS	OPS+	BR/A	RC	RC/G	FR	G/POS	WS	TPW
• MEARES, Pat	Patrick James Meares b: 9/6/1968, Salina, KS BR/TR, 6', 188 lbs. Deb: 5/5/1993 Career OF: 0-3-1																							
1993 Min-A	111	346	33	87	14	3	0	33	7	52	4	5	.251	.268	.309	.578	55	-24	25	2.41	-3	*S-111	4	-1.9
1994 Min-A	80	229	29	61	12	1	2	24	14	50	5	1	.266	.314	.354	.668	72	-9	27	3.96	-3	S-79	6	-0.5
1995 Min-A	116	390	57	105	19	4	12	49	15	68	10	4	.269	.315	.431	.746	91	-6	48	4.10	-1	*S-114/O-3(0-2-1)	7	0.1
1996 Min-A	152	517	66	138	26	7	8	67	17	90	9	4	.267	.302	.391	.693	72	-24	56	3.64	-12	*S-150/O-1	8	-2.2
1997 Min-A	134	439	63	121	23	3	10	60	18	86	7	7	.276	.328	.410	.738	90	-9	57	4.47	11	*S-134	13	1.2
1998 Min-A	149	543	56	141	26	3	9	70	24	86	7	4	.260	.298	.368	.667	71	-25	57	3.64	-2	*S-149	11	-1.4
1999 Pit-N	21	91	15	28	4	0	0	7	9	20	0	0	.308	.382	.352	.734	88	-1	13	5.37	2	S-21	3	0.2
2000 Pit-N	132	462	55	111	22	2	13	47	36	91	1	0	.240	.306	.381	.687	73	-20	53	3.82	4	*S-126	9	-0.6
2001 Pit-N	87	270	27	57	11	1	4	25	10	45	0	2	.211	.245	.304	.548	40	-26	17	2.08	-7	2-85	2	-2.8
Total 9	982	3287	401	849	157	24	58	382	150	588	43	27	.258	.302	.374	.676	73	-144	353	3.63	-11	S-884/2-85,O-4	63	-7.7
• MEDEIROS, Ray	Ray Antone "Pep" Medeiros b: 5/9/1926, Oakland, CA BR/TR, 5'10", 163 lbs. Deb: 4/25/1945																							
1945 Cin-N	1	0	0	0	0	0	0	0	0	0	0	....	....	....	....	....	-102	0	0	....	0	....	0	0.0
• MEDINA, Luis	Luis Main Medina b: 3/26/1963, Santa Monica, CA BR/TL, 6'4", 200 lbs. Deb: 9/2/1988																							
1988 Cle-A	16	51	10	13	0	0	6	8	2	18	0	0	.255	.309	.608	.917	146	3	10	6.84	0	1-16	2	0.1
1989 Cle-A	30	83	8	17	1	0	4	8	6	35	0	1	.205	.258	.361	.620	72	-4	7	2.60	-1	D-25/O-3(1-0-2),1-1	0	-0.6
1991 Cle-A	5	16	0	1	0	0	0	0	1	7	0	0	.063	.118	.063	.180	-48	-3	0	.33	0	/D-5	0	-0.3
Total 3	51	150	18	31	1	0	10	16	9	60	0	1	.207	.261	.413	.674	84	-4	17	3.63	-1	/D-30,1-17,O-3	2	-0.8
• MEDWICK, Joe	Joseph Michael "Ducky,Muscles" Medwick b: 11/24/1911, Carteret, NJ d: 3/21/1975, St. Petersburg, FL BR/TR, 5'10", 187 lbs. Deb: 9/2/1932 HOF: 1968 Career OF: 1790-19-43																							
1932 StL-N	26	106	13	37	12	1	2	12	2	10	3	....	.349	.367	.538	.905	136	5	21	7.78	-1	O-26(7-19-0)	4	0.3
1933 StL-N	148	595	92	182	40	10	18	98	26	56	5	....	.306	.337	.497	.835	129	20	97	6.09	3	*O-147(147-0-0)	24	1.5
1934*StL-N★	149	620	110	198	40	**18**	18	106	21	83	3	....	.319	.343	.529	.872	122	16	109	6.68	-1	*O-149(144-0-5)	24	0.6
1935 StL-N★	154	634	132	224	46	13	23	126	30	59	4	....	.353	.386	.576	.962	149	41	139	8.81	-3	*O-154(154-0-0)	33	2.8
1936 StL-N★	155	636	115	**223**	**64**	13	18	**138**	34	33	3	....	.351	.387	.577	.964	157	47	141	8.88	8	*O-155(155-0-0)	**36**	4.5
1937 StL-N★	156	633	**111**	**237**	**56**	10	**31**	**154**	41	50	4	....	**.374**	.414	**.641**	**1.056**	**179**	**66**	170	11.25	-4	*O-156(156-0-0)	**40**	5.2
1938 StL-N★	146	590	100	190	**47**	8	21	**122**	42	41	0	....	.322	.369	.536	.905	138	29	113	7.23	2	*O-144(144-0-0)	22	2.2
1939 StL-N★	150	606	98	201	48	8	14	117	45	44	6	....	.332	.380	.507	.886	128	23	114	7.10	2	*O-149(149-0-0)	24	1.7
1940 StL-N	37	158	21	48	12	0	3	20	6	8	0	....	.304	.329	.437	.766	104	0	20	4.53	-3	O-37(37-0-0)	3	-0.5
Bro-N★	106	423	62	127	18	12	14	66	26	28	2	....	.300	.345	.499	.844	123	11	70	6.17	-1	*O-103(103-0-0)	16	0.4
Yr.	143	581	83	175	30	12	17	86	32	36	2	....	.301	.341	.482	.823	118	11	90	5.71	-4	*O-140(140-0-0)	19	-0.1
1941*Bro-N★	133	538	100	171	33	10	18	88	38	35	2	....	.318	.364	.517	.881	140	26	95	6.59	-2	*O-131(130-0-1)	24	1.6
1942 Bro-N★	142	553	69	166	37	4	4	96	32	25	2	....	.300	.338	.403	.742	115	8	72	4.84	-5	*O-140(140-0-0)	21	-0.5
1943 Bro-N	48	173	13	47	10	0	0	25	10	8	1	....	.272	.315	.329	.645	86	-3	18	3.65	-3	O-42(42-0-0)	3	-0.9
NY-N	78	324	41	91	20	3	5	45	9	14	0	....	.281	.300	.407	.708	103	-1	35	3.82	4	O-74(74-0-0)/1-3	6	-0.3
Yr.	126	497	54	138	30	3	5	70	19	22	1	....	.278	.306	.380	.686	97	-5	53	3.76	1	*O-116(116-0-0)/1-3	9	-1.1
1944 NY-N★	128	490	64	165	24	3	7	85	38	24	2	....	.337	.386	.441	.826	133	21	82	6.48	9	*O-122(122-0-0)	19	2.3
1945 NY-N	26	92	14	28	4	0	3	11	2	2	2	....	.304	.319	.446	.765	110	0	12	4.63	-1	O-23(23-0-0)	2	-0.2
Bos-N	66	218	17	62	13	0	0	26	12	12	3	....	.284	.325	.344	.669	85	-5	23	3.90	2	O-38(38-0-0),1-15	3	-0.6
Yr.	92	310	31	90	17	0	3	37	14	14	5	....	.290	.323	.374	.697	93	-4	35	4.12	1	O-61(61-0-0),1-15	5	-0.7
1946 Bro-N	41	77	7	24	4	0	2	18	6	5	0	....	.312	.369	.442	.811	128	3	13	6.30	-1	O-18(18-0-0)/1-1	3	0.1
1947 StL-N	75	150	19	46	12	0	4	28	16	12	0	....	.307	.373	.467	.840	117	3	26	6.65	2	O-43(7-0-36)	5	0.4
1948 StL-N	20	19	0	4	0	0	0	2	1	2	0	....	.211	.250	.211	.461	24	-2	1	1.44	0	/O-1	0	-0.2
Total 17	1984	7635	1198	2471	540	113	205	1383	437	551	42	....	.324	.362	.505	.867	132	307	1372	6.84	6	*O-1852/1-19	312	20.6
• MEE, Tommy	Thomas William "Judge" Mee b: 3/18/1890, Chicago, IL d: 5/16/1981, Chicago, IL BR/TR, 5'8", 165 lbs. Deb: 6/14/1910																							
1910 StL-A	8	19	1	3	2	0	0	1	0	....	0	....	.158	.158	.263	.421	34	-2	1	1.18	-2	/S-6,2-1,3-1	0	-0.4
• MEEK, Dad	Frank J. Meek b: 3/14/1867, St. Louis, MO d: 12/22/1922, St. Louis, MO, 6' Deb: 5/10/1889																							
1889 StL-a	2	2	2	1	0	0	0	1	0	0	1	....	.500	.500	.500	1.000	163	0	1	27.16	0	/C-2	0	0.0
1890 StL-a	4	16	3	5	0	0	0	1	0	....	1	....	.313	.313	.313	.625	74	-1	2	4.63	1	/C-4	0	0.0
Total 2	6	18	5	6	0	0	0	2	0	0	2	....	.333	.333	.333	.667	84	-1	3	6.51	1	/C-6	0	0.1
• MEEKS, Sammy	Samuel Mack Meeks b: 4/23/1923, Anderson, SC BR/TR, 5'9", 160 lbs. Deb: 4/29/1948																							
1948 Was-A	24	33	4	4	1	0	0	2	1	12	0	0	.121	.147	.152	.299	-21	-6	1	.59	-1	S-10/2-1	0	-0.7
1949 Cin-N	16	36	10	11	2	0	2	6	2	6	1	....	.306	.342	.528	.870	128	1	6	6.40	2	/2-8,S-3	2	0.4
1950 Cin-N	39	95	7	27	5	0	1	8	6	14	1	....	.284	.327	.368	.695	82	-3	11	4.33	0	S-29/3-2	2	-0.1
1951 Cin-N	23	35	4	8	0	0	0	2	0	4	1	0	.229	.229	.229	.457	23	-4	1	1.39	-1	/3-4,S-1	0	-0.5
Total 4	102	199	25	50	8	0	3	18	9	36	3	0	.251	.284	.337	.620	63	-11	20	3.38	0	/S-43,2-9,3-6	4	-0.8
• MEIER, Dave	David Keith Meier b: 8/8/1959, Helena, MT BR/TR, 6', 185 lbs. Deb: 4/3/1984 Career OF: 102-3-16																							
1984 Min-A	59	147	18	35	8	1	0	13	6	9	0	1	.238	.273	.306	.579	57	-9	11	2.47	0	O-50(41-0-10)/D-4,3-1	1	-1.1
1985 Min-A	71	104	15	27	6	0	1	8	18	12	0	6	.260	.374	.346	.720	93	-3	13	4.24	0	O-63(55-3-4)/D-3	2	-0.4
1987 Tex-A	13	21	4	6	1	0	0	0	0	4	0	0	.286	.286	.333	.619	63	-1	1	2.12	0	/O-8(6-0-2)	0	-0.2
1988 Chi-N	2	5	0	2	0	0	0	1	0	1	0	0	.400	.400	.400	.800	125	0	1	7.20	0	/3-1	0	0.0
Total 4	145	277	37	70	15	1	1	22	24	26	0	7	.253	.317	.325	.642	73	-13	27	3.17	-1	O-121/D-7,3-2	3	-1.7
• MEIER, Dutch	Arthur Ernst Meier b: 3/30/1879, St. Louis, MO d: 3/23/1948, Chicago, IL BR/TR, 5'10", 175 lbs. Deb: 5/12/1906																							
1906 Pit-N	82	273	32	70	11	4	0	16	13	....	4	....	.256	.298	.326	.624	90	-4	29	3.62	-1	O-52(29-6-18),S-17	7	-0.8
• MEINERT, Walt	Walter Henry Meinert b: 12/11/1890, New York, NY d: 11/9/1958, Decatur, IL BL/TL, 5'7.5", 150 lbs. Deb: 9/6/1913																							
1913 StL-A	4	8	1	3	0	0	0	0	1	3	1	....	.375	.444	.375	.819	144	1	2	8.38	0	/O-2(0-0-2)	0	0.0
• MEINKE, Bob	Robert Bernard Meinke b: 6/25/1887, Chicago, IL d: 12/29/1952, Chicago, IL BR/TR, 5'10", 135 lbs. Deb: 8/22/1910																							
1910 Cin-N	2	1	0	0	0	0	0	0	1	0	0	....	.000	.500	.000	.500	50	0	0	.00	0	/S-2	0	0.0
• MEINKE, Frank	Frank Louis Meinke b: 10/18/1863, Chicago, IL d: 11/8/1931, Chicago, IL BR, 5'10.5", 172 lbs. Deb: 5/1/1884 Career OF: 2-0-4 ♦																							
1884 Det-N	92	341	28	56	5	7	6	24	6	89	....	....	.164	.179	.273	.451	42	-16	17	1.64	-5	S-51,P-35/O-4(1-0-4),2-3,3	11	-1.3
1885 Det-N	1	3	0	0	0	0	0	0	0	1	....	....	.000	.000	.000	.000	-100	-1	0	.00	0	/O-1,P-1	0	-0.1
Total 2	93	344	28	56	5	7	6	24	6	90	....	....	.163	.177	.270	.447	41	-16	17	1.63	-5	/S-51,P-36,O-5,2-3,3-3	11	-1.4
• MEISTER, George	John B. Meister b: 6/5/1864, Dorzbach, Germany d: 8/24/1908, Glenwood, PA Deb: 8/15/1884																							
1884 Tol-a	34	119	9	23	6	0	0	0	3	....	....	....	.193	.244	.244	.488	58	-5	7	2.08	-8	3-34	1	-1.2
• MEISTER, John	John F. Meister b: 5/10/1863, Altoona, PA d: 1/28/1923, Philadelphia, PA, 5'8", 175 lbs. Deb: 8/24/1886																							
1886 NY-a	45	186	35	44	7	3	2	21	4	....	1	....	.237	.253	.339	.591	88	-3	17	3.15	-7	2-45	3	-0.8
1887 NY-a	39	173	24	51	6	2	1	21	16	....	9	....	.295	.303	.306	.609	73	-5	18	3.92	-4	O-22(0-22-0),2-14/3-3,S-1	3	-0.7
Total 2	84	359	59	95	13	5	3	42	20	....	10	....	.265	.277	.324	.600	81	-8	34	3.50	-11	/2-59,O-22,3-3,S-1	6	-1.5
• MEISTER, Karl	Karl Daniel "Dutch" Meister b: 5/15/1891, Marietta, OH d: 8/15/1967, Marietta, OH BR/TR, 6', 178 lbs. Deb: 8/10/1913																							
1913 Cin-N	4	7	1	2	1	0	0	2	0	4	0	....	.286	.286	.429	.714	103	-0	1	4.07	-1	/O-4(1-3-0)	0	-0.1
• MEIXELL, Moxie	Merton Merrill Meixell b: 10/18/1887, Lake Crystal, MN d: 8/17/1982, Los Angeles, CA BL/TR, 5'10", 168 lbs. Deb: 7/7/1912																							
1912 Cle-A	3	2	0	1	0	0	0	0	0	....	0	....	.500	.500	.500	1.000	180	0	0	12.79	0	/O-1	0	0.0
• MEJIA, Miguel	Miguel Mejia b: 3/25/1975, San Pedro de Macoris, Dominican Republic BR/TR, 6'1", 155 lbs. Deb: 4/4/1996																							
1996*StL-N	45	23	10	2	0	0	0	0	0	10	6	3	.087	.087	.087	.174	-55	-5	0	.00	-1	O-21(5-11-6)	0	-0.6

• MEJIA, Roberto Roberto Antonio (Diaz) Mejia b: 4/14/1972, Hato Mayor, Dominican Republic BR/TR, 5'11", 160 lbs. Deb: 7/15/1993

YEAR TM-L	G	AB	R	H	2B	3B	HR	RBI	BB	SO	SB	CS	AVG	OBP	SLG	OPS	OPS+	BR/A	RC	RC/G	FR	G/POS	WS	TPW
1993 Col-N	65	229	31	53	14	5	5	20	13	63	4	1	.231	.276	.402	.677	68	-11	26	3.79	-6	2-65	1	-1.4
1994 Col-N	38	116	11	28	8	1	4	14	15	33	3	1	.241	.328	.431	.759	82	-3	17	5.11	-7	2-34	2	-0.8
1995 Col-N	23	52	5	8	1	0	1	4	0	17	0	1	.154	.170	.231	.401	3	-8	2	.95	-4	2-16	0	-1.1
1997 StL-N	7	14	0	1	1	0	0	2	0	5	0	0	.071	.071	.143	.214	-46	-3	0	.34	0	/2-3,0-1	0	-0.3
Total 4	133	411	47	90	24	6	10	40	28	118	7	3	.219	.272	.380	.652	60	-25	45	3.60	-17	2-118/0-1	3	-3.7

• MEJIAS, Roman Roman (Gomez) Mejias b: 8/9/1930, Abreus, Cuba BR/TR, 6', 175 lbs. Deb: 4/13/1955 Career OF: 117-118-270

YEAR TM-L	G	AB	R	H	2B	3B	HR	RBI	BB	SO	SB	CS	AVG	OBP	SLG	OPS	OPS+	BR/A	RC	RC/G	FR	G/POS	WS	TPW
1955 Pit-N	71	167	14	36	8	1	3	21	9	13	1	3	.216	.256	.329	.585	55	-12	13	2.53	2	0-44(30-1-14)	1	-1.3
1957 Pit-N	58	142	12	39	7	4	2	15	6	13	2	2	.275	.309	.423	.731	97	-2	17	4.18	3	0-42(7-7-29)	3	0.0
1958 Pit-N	76	157	17	42	3	2	5	19	2	27	2	0	.268	.281	.408	.689	82	-4	17	3.66	0	0-57(41-10-8)	4	-0.7
1959 Pit-N	96	276	28	65	6	1	7	28	21	48	1	2	.236	.301	.341	.642	71	-12	28	3.43	3	0-85(15-21-52)	5	-1.3
1960 Pit-N	3	1	1	0	0	0	0	0	0	1	0	0	.000	.000	.000	.000	-99	-0	0	.00	0	....	0	0.0
1961 Pit-N	4	1	1	0	0	0	0	0	0	1	0	0	.000	.000	.000	.000	-100	-0	0	.00	0	/0-2(2-0-0)	0	0.0
1962 Hou-N	146	566	82	162	12	3	24	76	30	83	12	4	.286	.329	.445	.774	114	10	81	5.07	-3	*0-142(1-1-141)	15	-0.3
1963 Bos-A	111	357	43	81	18	0	11	39	14	36	4	1	.227	.262	.370	.632	72	-14	32	2.93	-1	0-86(7-65-15)	4	-1.9
1964 Bos-A	62	101	14	24	3	1	2	4	7	16	0	0	.238	.294	.347	.640	74	-4	9	3.15	0	0-37(14-13-11)	1	-0.6
Total 9	627	1768	212	449	57	12	54	202	89	238	22	12	.254	.296	.391	.688	87	-39	197	3.80	3	0-495	33	-6.0

• MEJIAS, Sam Samuel Elias Mejias b: 5/9/1952, Santiago, Dominican Republic BR/TR, 6', 170 lbs. Deb: 9/6/1976 C Career OF: 54-102-131

YEAR TM-L	G	AB	R	H	2B	3B	HR	RBI	BB	SO	SB	CS	AVG	OBP	SLG	OPS	OPS+	BR/A	RC	RC/G	FR	G/POS	WS	TPW
1976 StL-N	18	21	1	3	1	0	0	0	2	2	2	0	.143	.217	.190	.408	16	-2	1	.93	0	0-17(3-1-13)	0	-0.2
1977 Mon-N	74	101	14	23	4	1	3	8	2	17	1	0	.228	.243	.376	.619	65	-5	9	3.08	-1	0-56(4-21-31)	1	-0.7
1978 Mon-N	67	56	9	13	1	0	0	6	2	5	0	0	.232	.259	.250	.509	43	-4	3	1.73	0	0-52(24-4-25)/P-1	0	-0.6
1979 Chi-N	31	11	4	2	0	0	0	0	2	5	0	0	.182	.308	.182	.490	34	-1	1	2.35	-2	0-23(15-5-3)	0	-0.4
Cin-N	7	2	1	1	0	0	0	0	0	0	0	0	.500	.500	.500	1.000	173	0	1	13.50	-1	/0-5(0-5-0)	0	-0.1
Yr.	38	13	5	3	0	0	0	0	2	5	0	0	.231	.333	.231	.564	51	-1	1	3.36	-3	0-28(15-10-3)	0	-0.4
1980 Cin-N	71	108	16	30	5	1	1	10	6	13	4	2	.278	.322	.370	.692	93	-1	13	4.25	1	0-67(8-50-17)	3	-0.2
1981 Cin-N	66	49	6	14	2	0	0	7	2	9	1	0	.286	.314	.327	.640	80	-1	5	3.42	-3	0-58(0-16-42)	1	-0.5
Total 6	334	348	51	86	13	2	4	31	16	51	8	2	.247	.282	.330	.613	69	-15	32	3.11	-5	0-278/P-1	5	-2.5

• MELE, Dutch Albert Ernest Mele b: 1/11/1915, New York, NY d: 2/12/1975, Hollywood, FL BL/TL, 6'.5", 195 lbs. Deb: 9/14/1937

YEAR TM-L	G	AB	R	H	2B	3B	HR	RBI	BB	SO	SB	CS	AVG	OBP	SLG	OPS	OPS+	BR/A	RC	RC/G	FR	G/POS	WS	TPW
1937 Cin-N	6	14	1	2	1	0	0	1	1	1	0	....	.143	.200	.214	.414	13	-2	1	1.50	-1	/0-5(2-0-3)	0	-0.2

• MELE, Sam Sabath Anthony Mele b: 1/23/1923, Astoria, NY BR/TR, 6'1", 187 lbs. Deb: 4/15/1947 M/C Career OF: 90-101-674

YEAR TM-L	G	AB	R	H	2B	3B	HR	RBI	BB	SO	SB	CS	AVG	OBP	SLG	OPS	OPS+	BR/A	RC	RC/G	FR	G/POS	WS	TPW
1947 Bos-A	123	453	71	137	14	8	12	73	37	35	0	3	.302	.356	.448	.805	114	7	72	5.75	1	*0-116(3-29-87)/1-1	15	0.4
1948 Bos-A	66	180	25	42	12	1	2	25	13	21	1	1	.233	.292	.344	.637	66	-10	18	3.29	0	0-55(3-0-52)	2	-1.1
1949 Bos-A	18	46	1	9	1	1	0	7	7	14	2	0	.196	.302	.261	.563	46	-3	4	2.46	-1	0-11(0-0-11)	0	-0.4
Was-A	78	264	21	64	12	2	3	25	17	34	2	1	.242	.288	.337	.625	67	-14	24	3.08	2	0-63(1-24-44),1-11	2	-1.3
Yr.	96	310	22	73	13	3	3	32	24	48	4	1	.235	.290	.326	.616	63	-17	28	2.98	1	0-74(1-24-55),1-11	2	-1.7
1950 Was-A	126	435	57	119	21	6	12	86	51	40	2	0	.274	.351	.432	.783	105	3	64	5.08	0	0-99(6-26-72),1-16	11	0.0
1951 Was-A	143	558	58	153	**36**	7	5	94	32	31	2	3	.274	.315	.391	.705	92	-10	64	3.97	-3	*0-124(2-17-107),1-15	12	-1.7
1952 Was-A	9	28	2	12	3	0	2	10	1	2	0	0	.429	.448	.750	1.198	237	5	10	16.48	-1	/0-7(0-1-6)	3	0.4
Chi-A	123	423	46	105	18	2	14	59	48	40	1	2	.248	.328	.400	.727	101	-0	53	4.25	-6	*0-112(0-0-112)/1-3	10	-1.0
Yr.	132	451	48	117	21	2	16	69	49	42	1	2	.259	.335	.421	.756	109	4	63	4.80	-7	*0-119(0-1-118)/1-3	13	-0.6
1953 Chi-A	140	481	64	132	26	8	12	82	58	47	3	1	.274	.353	.437	.789	109	6	75	5.52	-4	*0-138(0-4-138)/1-2	18	-0.2
1954 Bal-A	72	230	17	55	9	4	5	32	18	26	1	0	.239	.294	.378	.673	90	-4	23	3.18	0	0-62(40-0-24)	3	-0.7
Bos-A	42	132	22	42	6	0	7	23	12	12	0	1	.318	.384	.523	.906	132	5	25	6.93	-1	1-22,0-13(3-0-13)	5	0.3
Yr.	114	362	39	97	15	4	12	55	30	38	1	1	.268	.327	.431	.758	105	1	48	4.44	-1	0-75(43-0-37),1-22	8	-0.4
1955 Bos-A	14	31	1	4	2	0	0	1	0	7	1	0	.129	.129	.194	.323	-13	-5	1	.61	2	/0-7(6-0-1)	0	-0.4
Cin-N	35	62	4	13	1	0	2	7	5	13	0	1	.210	.279	.323	.602	56	-4	4	2.02	0	0-13(12-0-1)/1-1	0	-0.5
1956 Cle-A	57	114	17	29	7	0	4	20	12	20	0	1	.254	.325	.421	.746	94	-2	15	4.31	1	0-20(14-0-6)/1-8	3	-0.3
Total 10	1046	3437	406	916	168	39	80	544	311	342	15	14	.267	.329	.408	.737	97	-26	451	4.51	-11	0-840/1-79	84	-6.5

• MELENDEZ, Francisco Francisco Javier (Villegas) Melendez b: 1/25/1964, Rio Piedras, Puerto Rico BL/TL, 6', 190 lbs. Deb: 8/26/1984

YEAR TM-L	G	AB	R	H	2B	3B	HR	RBI	BB	SO	SB	CS	AVG	OBP	SLG	OPS	OPS+	BR/A	RC	RC/G	FR	G/POS	WS	TPW
1984 Phi-N	21	23	0	3	0	0	0	2	1	5	0	0	.130	.167	.130	.297	-15	-4	0	.52	1	1-10	0	-0.3
1986 Phi-N	9	8	0	2	0	0	0	0	0	2	0	0	.250	.250	.250	.500	37	-1	1	2.25	0	/1-2	0	-0.1
1987 SF-N	12	16	2	5	0	0	1	1	0	3	0	0	.313	.313	.500	.813	117	0	3	6.14	-1	/1-5	0	0.0
1988 SF-N	23	26	1	5	0	0	0	3	3	2	0	0	.192	.276	.192	.468	38	-2	1	1.71	-1	/1-6,0-1	0	-0.3
1989 Bal-A	9	11	1	3	0	0	0	3	1	2	0	0	.273	.333	.273	.606	75	-0	1	2.36	0	/1-5	0	-0.1
Total 5	74	84	4	18	0	0	1	9	5	14	0	0	.214	.258	.250	.508	43	-6	6	2.19	-1	/1-28,0-1	0	-0.9

• MELENDEZ, Luis Luis Antonio (Santana) Melendez b: 8/11/1949, Aibonito, Puerto Rico BR/TR, 6', 165 lbs. Deb: 9/7/1970 Career OF: 97-265-155

YEAR TM-L	G	AB	R	H	2B	3B	HR	RBI	BB	SO	SB	CS	AVG	OBP	SLG	OPS	OPS+	BR/A	RC	RC/G	FR	G/POS	WS	TPW
1970 StL-N	21	70	11	21	1	0	0	8	2	12	3	0	.300	.319	.314	.634	69	-2	7	3.43	0	0-18(0-5-13)	1	-0.3
1971 StL-N	88	173	25	39	3	1	0	11	24	29	2	0	.225	.320	.254	.574	62	-7	15	2.76	-2	0-66(4-20-45)	2	-1.2
1972 StL-N	118	332	32	79	11	3	5	28	25	34	5	4	.238	.293	.334	.628	79	-10	31	3.17	-3	*0-105(4-69-40)	5	-1.8
1973 StL-N	121	341	35	91	18	1	2	35	27	50	2	7	.267	.321	.343	.664	84	-10	34	3.35	4	0-95(2-65-30)	7	-0.9
1974 StL-N	83	124	15	27	4	3	0	8	11	9	2	2	.218	.287	.298	.585	64	-6	11	2.89	-2	0-46(23-22-10)/S-1	2	-1.0
1975 StL-N	110	291	33	77	8	5	2	27	16	25	3	2	.265	.303	.347	.650	77	-10	28	3.26	-2	0-89(36-49-7)	5	-1.5
1976 StL-N	20	24	0	3	0	0	0	0	0	3	0	0	.125	.125	.125	.250	-29	-4	0	.00	0	/0-8(4-4-0)	0	-0.5
SD-N	72	119	15	29	5	0	0	5	3	12	1	1	.244	.262	.286	.548	60	-7	8	2.30	-1	0-60(24-29-10)	1	-1.0
Yr.	92	143	15	32	5	0	0	5	3	15	1	1	.224	.240	.259	.498	46	-11	8	1.84	-1	0-68(28-33-10)	1	-1.4
1977 SD-N	8	3	1	0	0	0	0	0	1	1	0	0	.000	.250	.000	.250	-29	-1	0	.59	0	/0-2(0-2-0)	0	-0.1
Total 8	641	1477	167	366	50	13	9	122	109	175	18	16	.248	.300	.318	.618	73	-58	135	3.03	-5	0-489/S-1	23	-8.2

• MELHUSE, Adam Adam Michael Melhuse b: 3/27/1972, Santa Clara, CA BB/TR, 6'2", 185 lbs. Deb: 6/16/2000

YEAR TM-L	G	AB	R	H	2B	3B	HR	RBI	BB	SO	SB	CS	AVG	OBP	SLG	OPS	OPS+	BR/A	RC	RC/G	FR	G/POS	WS	TPW
2000 LA-N	1	1	0	0	0	0	0	0	0	1	0	0	.000	.000	.000	.000	-107	-0	0	.00	0	....	0	0.0
Col-N	23	23	3	4	0	1	0	4	3	5	0	0	.174	.269	.261	.530	28	-3	2	2.11	0	/1-3,C-1,0-1	0	-0.3
Yr.	24	24	3	4	0	1	0	4	3	6	0	0	.167	.259	.250	.509	23	-3	2	2.01	0	/1-3,C-1,0-1	0	-0.3
2001 Col-N	40	71	5	13	2	0	1	8	6	18	1	0	.183	.247	.254	.500	24	-8	4	1.83	-3	C-23/1-1	0	-1.0
2003*Oak-A	40	77	13	23	7	0	5	14	9	19	0	0	.299	.372	.584	.957	145	5	17	7.96	-1	C-33/3-2,1-1	4	0.5
Total 3	104	172	21	40	9	1	6	26	18	43	1	0	.233	.305	.401	.706	78	-6	22	4.31	-4	/C-57,1-5,3-2,0-1	4	-0.8

• MELILLO, Ski Oscar Donald "Spinach" Melillo b: 8/4/1899, Chicago, IL d: 11/14/1963, Chicago, IL BR/TR, 5'8", 150 lbs. Deb: 4/18/1926 M/C

YEAR TM-L	G	AB	R	H	2B	3B	HR	RBI	BB	SO	SB	CS	AVG	OBP	SLG	OPS	OPS+	BR/A	RC	RC/G	FR	G/POS	WS	TPW
1926 StL-A	99	385	54	98	18	5	1	30	32	31	6	7	.255	.315	.335	.650	66	-21	41	3.46	6	2-88,3-11	6	-1.1
1927 StL-A	107	356	45	80	18	2	0	26	25	28	3	6	.225	.276	.287	.562	44	-32	28	2.50	-4	*2-101	2	-3.1
1928 StL-A	51	132	9	25	2	0	0	9	9	11	2	1	.189	.241	.205	.446	18	-16	7	1.67	0	2-28,3-19	1	-1.4
1929 StL-A	141	494	57	146	17	10	5	67	29	30	11	6	.296	.337	.401	.738	86	-11	67	4.75	26	*2-141	15	1.8
1930 StL-A	149	574	62	147	30	10	5	59	23	44	15	9	.256	.287	.369	.656	63	-35	60	3.48	18	*2-148	11	-1.1
1931 StL-A	151	617	88	189	34	11	2	75	37	29	7	11	.306	.346	.407	.752	94	-7	84	4.97	21	*2-151	17	2.2
1932 StL-A	154	612	71	148	19	11	3	66	36	42	6	6	.242	.286	.324	.610	54	-43	57	3.13	6	*2-153	7	-2.5
1933 StL-A	132	496	50	145	23	6	3	79	29	18	12	10	.292	.333	.381	.714	83	-14	61	4.43	12	*2-130	11	0.6
1934 StL-A	144	552	54	133	19	3	2	55	28	27	4	6	.241	.279	.297	.576	45	-49	45	2.77	17	*2-141	7	-2.1
1935 StL-A	19	62	8	13	3	0	0	5	8	4	0	0	.210	.300	.258	.558	43	-5	5	2.82	-1	2-18	0	-0.4
Bos-A	106	400	45	104	13	2	1	39	38	22	3	2	.260	.327	.310	.637	61	-22	42	3.72	10	*2-105	8	-0.5
Yr.	125	462	53	117	16	2	1	44	46	26	3	2	.253	.324	.303	.627	59	-27	48	3.59	9	*2-123	8	-1.0
1936 Bos-A	98	327	39	74	12	4	0	32	28	16	0	0	.226	.287	.287	.575	40	-32	29	2.87	-2	2-93	3	-2.5
1937 Bos-A	26	56	8	14	2	0	0	6	5	4	0	1	.250	.311	.286	.597	50	-5	5	2.99	-2	2-19/3-2,S-2	0	-0.5
Total 12	1377	5063	590	1316	210	64	22	548	327	306	69	65	.260	.306	.340	.646	64	-290	532	3.57	108	*2-1316/3-32,S-2	88	-10.7

YEAR TM-L	G	AB	R	H	2B	3B	HR	RBI	BB	SO	SB	CS	AVG	OBP	SLG	OPS	OPS+	BR/A	RC	RC/G	FR	G/POS	WS	TPW
• MELLANA, Joe	Joseph Peter Mellana b: 3/11/1905, Oakland, CA d: 11/1/1969, Larkspur, CA BR/TR, 5'10", 180 lbs. Deb: 9/21/1927																							
1927 Phi-A	4	7	1	2	0	0	0	2	0	1	0	0	.286	.286	.286	.571	46	-1	1	2.91	1	/3-2	0	0.1
• MELLOR, Bill	William Harpin Mellor b: 6/6/1874, Camden, NJ d: 11/5/1940, Bridgeton, RI BR/TR, 6', 190 lbs. Deb: 7/28/1902																							
1902 Bal-A	10	36	4	13	3	0	0	5	3	....	1	....	.361	.410	.444	.855	131	2	7	8.03	-1	1-10	1	0.0
• MELO, Juan	Juan Esteban Melo b: 11/11/1976, Bani, Dominican Republic BB/TR, 6'3", 180 lbs. Deb: 9/2/2000																							
2000 SF-N	11	13	0	1	0	0	0	1	0	5	0	0	.077	.077	.077	.154	-66	-3	0	.17	-2	/2-6	0	-0.5
• MELOAN, Paul	Paul B. "Molly" Meloan b: 8/23/1888, Paynesville, MO d: 2/11/1950, Taft, CA BR/TL, 5'10.5", 175 lbs. Deb: 8/2/1910 Career OF: 1-0-119																							
1910 Chi-A	65	222	23	54	6	6	0	23	17	....	4	....	.243	.314	.324	.639	105	1	24	3.56	6	0-65(0-0-65)	8	0.4
1911 Chi-A	1	3	0	1	0	0	0	1	0	....	0	....	.333	.333	.333	.667	88	-0	0	3.62	0	/0-1	0	0.0
StL-A	64	206	30	54	11	2	3	14	15	....	7	....	.262	.318	.379	.697	98	-1	27	4.37	-3	0-54(1-0-53)	4	-0.7
Yr.	65	209	30	55	11	2	3	15	15	....	7	....	.263	.319	.378	.697	98	-1	27	4.36	-4	0-55(1-0-54)	4	-0.7
Total 2	**130**	**431**	**53**	**109**	**17**	**8**	**3**	**38**	**32**	**....**	**11**	**....**	**.253**	**.316**	**.350**	**.667**	**102**	**0**	**51**	**3.95**	**2**	**0-120**	**12**	**-0.3**
• MELTON, Bill	William Edwin "Beltin' Bill" Melton b: 7/7/1945, Gulfport, MS BR/TR, 6'2", 200 lbs. Deb: 5/4/1968 Career OF: 3-0-79																							
1968 Chi-A	34	109	5	29	8	0	2	16	10	32	1	1	.266	.328	.394	.722	117	2	14	4.42	1	3-33	4	0.4
1969 Chi-A	157	556	67	142	26	2	23	87	56	106	1	2	.255	.329	.433	.762	106	3	79	4.84	-12	*3-148,0-11(3-0-8)	14	-1.0
1970 Chi-A	141	514	74	135	15	1	33	96	56	107	2	4	.263	.345	.488	.834	123	14	88	5.93	-4	0-71(0-0-71),3-70	17	0.7
1971 Chi-A★	150	543	72	146	18	2	**33**	86	61	87	3	3	.269	.354	.492	.846	133	23	96	6.28	15	*3-148	23	4.0
1972 Chi-A	57	208	22	51	5	0	7	30	23	31	1	1	.245	.320	.370	.691	103	1	26	4.29	2	3-56	8	0.3
1973 Chi-A	152	560	83	155	29	1	20	87	75	66	4	4	.277	.364	.439	.803	121	17	87	5.42	11	*3-151/D-1	22	2.7
1974 Chi-A	136	495	63	120	17	0	21	63	59	60	3	2	.242	.329	.404	.733	107	5	65	4.34	-1	*3-123,D-11	13	0.4
1975 Chi-A	149	512	62	123	16	0	15	70	78	106	5	4	.240	.349	.359	.709	99	2	67	4.39	-5	*3-138,D-11	12	-0.4
1976 Cal-A	118	341	31	71	17	3	6	42	44	53	2	0	.208	.302	.328	.631	90	-3	36	3.50	-1	D-51,1-30,3-21	8	-0.8
1977 Cle-A	50	133	17	32	11	0	0	14	17	21	1	3	.241	.336	.323	.659	83	-3	13	2.94	0	1-15,D-14,3-13	1	-0.5
Total 10	**1144**	**3971**	**496**	**1004**	**162**	**9**	**160**	**591**	**479**	**669**	**23**	**24**	**.253**	**.340**	**.419**	**.759**	**111**	**61**	**571**	**4.90**	**6**	**3-901/D-88,0-82,1-45**	**122**	**5.8**
• MELTON, Dave	David Olin Melton b: 10/3/1928, Pampa, TX BR/TR, 6', 185 lbs. Deb: 4/17/1956 Career OF: 5-0-0																							
1956 KC-A	3	3	0	1	0	0	0	0	0	0	0	0	.333	.333	.333	.667	76	-0	0	4.50	0	/0-3(3-0-0)	0	0.0
1958 KC-A	9	6	0	0	0	0	0	0	0	5	0	0	.000	.000	.000	.000	-98	-2	0	.00	0	/0-2(2-0-0)	0	-0.2
Total 2	**12**	**9**	**0**	**1**	**0**	**0**	**0**	**0**	**0**	**5**	**0**	**0**	**.111**	**.111**	**.111**	**.222**	**-40**	**-2**	**0**	**1.13**	**0**	**/0-5**	**0**	**-0.2**
• MELUSKEY, Mitch	Mitchell Wade Meluskey b: 9/18/1973, Yakima, WA BB/TR, 6', 185 lbs. Deb: 8/30/1998																							
1998 Hou-N	8	8	1	2	1	0	0	0	1	4	0	0	.250	.333	.375	.708	88	-0	1	2.79	0	/C-3	0	0.0
1999 Hou-N	10	33	4	7	1	0	1	3	5	6	1	0	.212	.316	.333	.649	65	-2	4	3.64	1	C-10	0	0.0
2000 Hou-N	117	337	47	101	21	0	14	69	55	74	1	0	.300	.404	.487	.891	117	11	69	7.50	0	*C-103/3-1	13	1.6
2002 Det-A	8	27	3	6	0	0	0	1	5	3	0	0	.222	.364	.222	.586	65	-1	3	3.50	-2	/C-8	0	-0.2
2003 Hou-N	12	9	1	1	1	0	0	2	2	2	0	0	.111	.273	.222	.495	30	-1	1	2.28	0	....	0	-0.1
Total 5	**155**	**414**	**56**	**117**	**24**	**0**	**15**	**75**	**68**	**89**	**2**	**0**	**.283**	**.390**	**.449**	**.839**	**107**	**8**	**77**	**6.63**	**-2**	**C-124/3-1**	**13**	**1.2**
• MELVIN, Bob	Robert Paul Melvin b: 10/28/1961, Palo Alto, CA BR/TR, 6'4", 205 lbs. Deb: 5/25/1985 M/C																							
1985 Det-A	41	82	10	18	4	1	0	4	3	21	0	0	.220	.247	.293	.540	47	-6	6	2.39	0	C-41	2	-0.5
1986 SF-N	89	268	24	60	14	2	5	25	15	69	3	2	.224	.265	.347	.612	71	-12	23	2.80	4	C-84/3-1	6	-0.5
1987*SF-N	84	246	31	49	8	0	11	31	17	44	0	4	.199	.251	.366	.617	64	-16	20	2.53	5	C-78/1-1	5	-0.8
1988 SF-N	92	273	23	64	13	1	8	27	13	46	0	2	.234	.269	.377	.647	87	-7	26	3.23	-5	C-89/1-1	5	-0.7
1989 Bal-A	85	278	22	67	10	1	1	32	15	53	1	4	.241	.280	.295	.575	64	-15	20	2.35	-4	C-75/D-9	5	-1.6
1990 Bal-A	93	301	30	73	14	1	5	37	11	53	0	1	.243	.269	.346	.615	73	-12	26	2.88	-3	C-76,D-10/1-1	7	-1.1
1991 Bal-A	79	228	11	57	10	0	1	23	11	46	0	0	.250	.285	.307	.592	66	-11	19	2.88	1	C-72/D-4	5	-0.5
1992 KC-A	32	70	5	22	5	0	0	6	5	13	0	0	.314	.360	.386	.746	106	1	9	4.66	0	C-21/1-3	1	0.1
1993 Bos-A	77	176	13	39	7	0	3	23	7	44	0	0	.222	.255	.313	.568	49	-13	14	2.65	-1	C-76/1-1	2	-1.1
1994 NY-A	9	14	2	4	0	0	1	3	0	3	0	0	.286	.286	.500	.786	101	-0	2	3.68	-1	/1-4,C-4,D-1	1	-0.1
Chi-A	11	19	3	3	0	0	0	1	1	4	0	0	.158	.200	.158	.358	-6	-3	1	.81	-1	C-11	0	-0.3
Yr.	20	33	5	7	0	0	1	4	1	7	0	0	.212	.235	.303	.538	37	-3	2	1.90	-1	C-15/1-4,D-1	1	-0.4
Total 10	**692**	**1955**	**174**	**456**	**85**	**6**	**35**	**212**	**98**	**396**	**4**	**13**	**.233**	**.270**	**.337**	**.607**	**69**	**-95**	**166**	**2.79**	**-5**	**C-627/D-24,1-11,3-1**	**39**	**-7.0**
• MENCH, Kevin	Kevin Ford Mench b: 1/7/1978, Wilmington, DE BR/TR, 6', 215 lbs. Deb: 4/9/2002 Career OF: 91-4-64																							
2002 Tex-A	110	366	52	95	20	2	15	60	31	83	1	1	.260	.331	.448	.779	99	-1	56	5.33	1	*0-106(57-1-62)/D-2	10	-0.4
2003 Tex-A	38	125	15	40	12	0	2	11	10	17	1	1	.320	.384	.464	.848	112	2	22	6.81	-2	0-35(34-3-2)	4	-0.1
Total 2	**148**	**491**	**67**	**135**	**32**	**2**	**17**	**71**	**41**	**100**	**2**	**2**	**.275**	**.344**	**.452**	**.797**	**103**	**1**	**78**	**5.68**	**-1**	**0-141/D-2**	**14**	**-0.6**
• MENDEZ, Carlos	Carlos Alberto Casti Mendez b: 6/18/1974, Caracas, Venezuela BR/TR, 6', 228 lbs. Deb: 5/22/2003																							
2003 Bal-A	26	45	3	10	2	0	0	5	0	12	0	0	.222	.222	.267	.489	29	-5	3	2.04	0	/1-9,D-7	0	-0.5
• MENDEZ, Donaldo	Donaldo Alfonso Mendez b: 6/7/1978, Barquisimeto, Venezuela BR/TR, 6'1", 155 lbs. Deb: 4/5/2001																							
2001 SD-N	46	118	11	18	2	1	1	5	5	37	1	2	.153	.206	.212	.418	9	-17	5	1.23	-6	S-46	0	-1.9
2003 SD-N	26	84	10	19	6	0	2	9	7	32	1	0	.226	.301	.369	.670	81	-2	10	4.16	-4	S-26	2	-0.4
Total 2	**72**	**202**	**21**	**37**	**8**	**1**	**3**	**14**	**12**	**69**	**2**	**2**	**.183**	**.247**	**.277**	**.524**	**40**	**-19**	**15**	**2.36**	**-10**	**/S-72**	**2**	**-2.4**
• MENDOZA, Carlos	Carlos Ramon Mendoza b: 11/4/1974, Bolivar, Venezuela BL/TL, 5'11", 160 lbs. Deb: 9/3/1997 Career OF: 5-3-0																							
1997 NY-N	15	12	6	3	0	0	0	1	4	2	0	0	.250	.500	.250	.750	108	1	2	6.84	-0	/0-3(2-3-0)	1	0.1
2000 Col-N	13	10	0	1	0	0	0	0	1	4	0	1	.100	.182	.100	.282	-21	-2	0	.31	0	/0-3(3-0-0)	0	-0.3
Total 2	**28**	**22**	**6**	**4**	**0**	**0**	**0**	**1**	**5**	**6**	**0**	**1**	**.182**	**.379**	**.182**	**.561**	**59**	**-1**	**2**	**3.40**	**-1**	**/0-6**	**1**	**-0.2**
• MENDOZA, Mario	Mario (Aizpuru) Mendoza b: 12/26/1950, Chihuahua, Mexico BR/TR, 5'11", 187 lbs. Deb: 4/26/1974																							
1974*Pit-N	91	163	10	36	1	2	0	15	8	35	1	1	.221	.262	.252	.513	46	-12	10	1.92	1	S-87	2	-0.5
1975 Pit-N	56	50	8	9	1	0	0	2	3	17	0	0	.180	.226	.200	.426	19	-6	2	1.45	1	S-53/3-1	1	-0.2
1976 Pit-N	50	92	6	17	5	0	0	12	4	15	0	1	.185	.219	.239	.458	30	-9	4	1.38	3	S-45/3-2,2-1	2	-0.3
1977 Pit-N	70	81	5	16	3	0	0	4	3	10	0	0	.198	.226	.235	.461	23	-9	4	1.73	-5	S-45,3-19/P-1	1	-1.3
1978 Pit-N	57	55	5	12	1	0	1	3	2	9	3	1	.218	.283	.291	.574	58	-3	5	2.97	0	2-21,3-18,S-14	1	-0.2
1979 Sea-A	148	373	26	74	10	3	1	29	9	62	3	0	.198	.219	.249	.469	26	-39	19	1.57	1	*S-148	5	-2.4
1980 Sea-A	114	277	27	68	6	3	2	14	16	42	3	4	.245	.287	.310	.597	63	-15	24	2.83	0	*S-114	5	-0.6
1981 Tex-A	88	229	18	53	6	1	0	22	7	25	2	1	.231	.257	.266	.524	54	-14	15	1.95	-6	S-88	2	-1.2
1982 Tex-A	12	17	1	2	0	0	0	0	0	4	0	0	.118	.118	.118	.235	-37	-3	0	.22	-3	S-12	0	-0.5
Total 9	**686**	**1337**	**106**	**287**	**33**	**9**	**4**	**101**	**52**	**219**	**12**	**8**	**.215**	**.247**	**.262**	**.509**	**41**	**-110**	**84**	**1.96**	**-8**	**S-606/3-40,2-22,P-1**	**19**	**-7.4**
• MENDOZA, Minnie	Cristobal Rigoberto (Carreras) Mendoza b: 11/16/1933, Ceiba del Agua, Cuba BR/TR, 6', 180 lbs. Deb: 4/9/1970 C																							
1970 Min-A	16	16	2	3	0	0	0	2	0	1	0	0	.188	.188	.188	.375	4	-2	1	1.17	-1	/3-5,2-4	0	-0.3
• MENECHINO, Frank	Frank Menechino b: 1/7/1971, Staten Island, NY BR/TR, 5'9", 175 lbs. Deb: 9/6/1999																							
1999 Oak-A	9	9	0	2	0	0	0	0	0	4	0	0	.222	.222	.222	.444	14	-1	0	1.71	0	/S-5,3-1	0	-0.1
2000*Oak-A	66	145	31	37	9	1	6	26	20	45	1	4	.255	.349	.455	.805	104	-1	23	5.37	8	2-51/S-5,3-4,D-4,P-1	6	0.6
2001*Oak-A	139	471	82	114	22	2	12	60	79	97	2	3	.242	.373	.374	.746	97	1	70	4.97	9	*2-136/S-3,3-1	18	1.6
2002 Oak-A	38	132	22	27	7	0	3	15	20	32	0	0	.205	.314	.326	.639	70	-5	14	3.43	-10	2-32/3-4,S-2,D-1	3	-1.3
2003*Oak-A	43	83	10	16	0	0	2	9	19	16	0	0	.193	.368	.265	.633	70	-2	10	3.73	-2	2-22,3-19/S-3	2	-0.4
Total 5	**295**	**840**	**145**	**196**	**38**	**3**	**23**	**110**	**138**	**194**	**3**	**7**	**.233**	**.358**	**.368**	**.726**	**91**	**-8**	**118**	**4.63**	**6**	**2-241/3-29,S-18,D-5,P-1**	**29**	**0.5**
• MENEFEE, Jock	John Menefee b: 1/15/1868, Rowlesburg, WV d: 3/11/1953, Belle Vernon, PA BR/TR, 6', 165 lbs. Deb: 8/17/1892 U Career OF: 7-3-44 ♦																							
1892 Pit-N	2	3	0	0	0	0	0	0	0	0	0	....	.000	.000	.000	.000	-100	-1	0	.00	0	/0-1,P-1	0	-0.4
1893 Lou-N	22	73	10	20	2	1	0	12	13	5	2	....	.274	.391	.329	.720	100	4	10	5.21	2	P-15/0-7(1-2-4)	10	0.7

YEAR TM-L	G	AB	R	H	2B	3B	HR	RBI	BB	SO	SB	CS	AVG	OBP	SLG	OPS	OPS+	BR/A	RC	RC/G	FR	G/POS	WS	TPW
1894 Lou-N	29	79	7	13	1	0	0	4	8	7	2	....	.165	.250	.177	.427	5	-6	4	1.62	2	P-28/2-1	10	1.1
Pit-N	13	47	6	12	1	2	0	7	3	3	2	....	.255	.300	.362	.662	60	0	6	4.34	2	P-13	6	-0.1
Yr.	42	126	13	25	2	2	0	11	11	10	4	....	.198	.268	.246	.514	25	-5	10	2.56	4	P-41/2-1	16	1.0
1895 Pit-N	2	0	0	0	0	0	0	0	0	0	0	....	....	....	....	....	-106	0	0	....	0	/P-2	0	-0.2
1898 NY-N	1	5	0	0	0	0	0	0	0	....	0	....	.000	.000	.000	.000	-103	-1	0	.00	0	/P-1	0	-0.2
1900 Chi-N	17	46	5	5	0	0	0	4	2	....	0	....	.109	.180	.109	.289	-20	-3	1	.71	-2	P-16	6	-0.4
1901 Chi-N	48	152	19	39	5	3	0	13	8	....	4	....	.257	.327	.329	.656	94	4	19	4.21	-2	O-24(5-1-18),P-21/1-2,2-1	11	-0.8
1902 Chi-N	65	216	24	50	4	1	0	15	15	....	4	....	.231	.303	.259	.562	76	-1	21	3.03	-4	O-23(1-0-21),P-22,1-18/3-2,2	14	0.0
1903 Chi-N	22	64	3	13	3	0	0	2	3	....	0	....	.203	.239	.250	.489	40	-0	4	2.08	3	P-20/1-2	7	0.0
Total 9	221	685	74	152	16	7	0	57	52	15	14	....	.222	.295	.266	.561	62	-2	65	3.09	1	P-139/O-55,1-22,2-3,3-2	64	-0.2

• MENKE, Denis Denis John Menke b: 7/21/1940, Bancroft, IA BR/TR, 6', 190 lbs. Deb: 4/14/1962 C Career OF: 3-0-2

YEAR TM-L	G	AB	R	H	2B	3B	HR	RBI	BB	SO	SB	CS	AVG	OBP	SLG	OPS	OPS+	BR/A	RC	RC/G	FR	G/POS	WS	TPW
1962 Mil-N	50	146	12	28	3	1	2	16	16	38	0	1	.192	.280	.267	.548	49	-11	11	2.46	-2	2-20,3-15/S-9,1-2,O-1	2	-1.0
1963 Mil-N	146	518	58	121	16	4	11	50	37	106	6	7	.234	.292	.344	.636	83	-13	51	3.28	8	S-82,3-51,2-22/1-1,O-1	13	0.4
1964 Mil-N	151	505	79	143	29	5	20	65	68	77	4	2	.283	.373	.479	.852	137	27	91	6.37	13	*S-141,2-15/3-6	29	5.5
1965 Mil-N	71	181	16	44	13	1	4	18	18	28	1	3	.243	.315	.392	.707	97	-2	22	4.03	0	S-54/1-8,3-4	5	0.2
1966 Atl-N	138	454	55	114	20	4	15	60	71	87	0	7	.251	.360	.412	.772	112	8	68	4.97	-7	*S-106,3-39/1-7	16	1.0
1967 Atl-N	129	418	37	95	14	3	7	39	65	62	5	7	.227	.335	.325	.661	91	-4	48	3.78	-5	*S-124/3-3	12	0.1
1968 Hou-N	150	542	56	135	23	6	6	56	64	81	5	8	.249	.335	.347	.682	107	5	65	4.09	-8	*2-119,S-35/1-5,3-4	21	1.0
1969 Hou-N★	154	553	72	149	25	5	10	90	87	87	2	7	.269	.373	.387	.760	115	13	81	5.01	-14	*S-131,2-23/1-9,3-1	21	1.5
1970 Hou-N★	154	562	82	171	26	6	13	92	82	80	6	5	.304	.398	.441	.839	130	26	103	6.62	-23	*S-133,2-21/1-5,3-5,O-3(1-0-2)	24	1.9
1971 Hou-N	146	475	57	117	26	3	1	43	59	68	4	5	.246	.332	.320	.652	88	-7	51	3.53	2	*1-101,3-32,S-17/2-5	11	-1.2
1972*Cin-N	140	447	41	104	19	2	9	50	58	76	0	1	.233	.327	.345	.672	97	-1	53	3.94	5	*3-130,1-11	14	0.4
1973*Cin-N	139	241	38	46	10	0	3	26	69	53	1	1	.191	.375	.270	.645	86	0	29	3.71	6	*3-123/S-7,2-5,1-1	8	0.7
1974 Hou-N	30	29	2	3	1	0	0	1	4	10	0	0	.103	.212	.138	.350	-1	-4	1	.95	0	1-12/3-7,2-3,S-2	0	-0.4
Total 13	1598	5071	605	1270	225	40	101	606	698	853	34	54	.250	.346	.370	.717	104	37	675	4.48	-24	S-841,3-420,2-233,1-162/O-5	176	9.9

• MENOSKY, Mike Michael William "Leaping Mike" Menosky
b: 10/16/1894, Glen Campbell, PA d: 4/11/1983, Detroit, MI BL/TR, 5'10", 163 lbs. Deb: 4/18/1914 Career OF: 569-49-65

YEAR TM-L	G	AB	R	H	2B	3B	HR	RBI	BB	SO	SB	CS	AVG	OBP	SLG	OPS	OPS+	BR/A	RC	RC/G	FR	G/POS	WS	TPW
1914 Pit-F	68	140	26	37	4	1	2	9	16	30	5	....	.264	.352	.350	.702	106	2	19	4.40	-2	O-41(6-3-32)	4	-0.2
1915 Pit-F	17	21	3	2	0	0	0	1	2	0	2	....	.095	.208	.095	.304	-9	-3	1	.97	-1	/O-9(6-1-2)	0	-0.4
1916 Was-A	11	37	5	6	1	1	0	3	1	10	1	....	.162	.184	.243	.427	29	-3	2	1.59	2	/O-9(1-8-0)	0	-0.2
1917 Was-A	114	322	46	83	12	10	1	34	45	55	22	....	.258	.359	.366	.726	123	10	48	5.05	7	O-94(93-0-1)	14	1.5
1919 Was-A	116	342	62	98	15	3	6	39	44	46	13	....	.287	.379	.401	.780	120	11	54	5.68	-5	*O-103(87-15-1)	11	0.1
1920 Bos-A	141	532	80	158	24	9	3	64	65	52	23	19	.297	.383	.393	.776	110	9	82	5.23	-1	*O-141(141-0-0)	17	0.2
1921 Bos-A	133	477	77	143	18	5	3	45	60	45	12	6	.300	.388	.377	.766	99	3	75	5.52	-2	*O-133(133-0-0)	16	-0.9
1922 Bos-A	126	406	61	115	16	5	3	32	40	33	9	5	.283	.355	.369	.724	90	-5	55	4.78	6	*O-103(74-4-26)	11	-0.7
1923 Bos-A	84	188	22	43	8	4	0	25	22	19	3	6	.229	.310	.314	.623	64	-11	18	3.06	2	O-49(28-18-3)	2	-1.2
Total 9	810	2465	382	685	98	38	18	252	295	290	90	36	.278	.364	.370	.735	102	13	354	4.91	5	O-682	75	-1.8

• MENSOR, Ed Edward "The Midget" Mensor b: 11/7/1886, Woodville, OR d: 4/20/1970, Salem, OR BB/TR, 5'6", 145 lbs. Deb: 7/15/1912 Career OF: 5-46-24

YEAR TM-L	G	AB	R	H	2B	3B	HR	RBI	BB	SO	SB	CS	AVG	OBP	SLG	OPS	OPS+	BR/A	RC	RC/G	FR	G/POS	WS	TPW
1912 Pit-N	39	99	19	26	3	2	0	1	23	12	10	....	.263	.402	.333	.735	104	2	17	5.93	-2	O-32(0-20-12)	4	-0.1
1913 Pit-N	44	56	9	10	1	0	0	1	8	13	2	....	.179	.292	.196	.489	43	-4	4	2.04	-1	O-18(1-16-1)/2-1,S-1	0	-0.5
1914 Pit-N	44	89	15	18	2	1	1	6	22	13	2	....	.202	.372	.281	.653	99	2	11	3.61	0	O-25(4-10-11)	3	0.0
Total 3	127	244	43	54	6	3	1	8	53	38	14	....	.221	.367	.283	.649	89	0	31	4.09	-2	/O-75,2-1,S-1	7	-0.6

• MENZE, Ted Theodore Charles Menze b: 11/4/1897, St. Louis, MO d: 12/23/1969, St. Louis, MO BR/TR, 5'9", 172 lbs. Deb: 4/23/1918

YEAR TM-L	G	AB	R	H	2B	3B	HR	RBI	BB	SO	SB	CS	AVG	OBP	SLG	OPS	OPS+	BR/A	RC	RC/G	FR	G/POS	WS	TPW
1918 StL-N	1	3	0	0	0	0	0	0	0	2	0	....	.000	.000	.000	.000	-104	-1	0	.00	-0	/O-1	0	-0.1

• MEOLI, Rudy Rudolph Bartholomew Meoli b: 5/1/1951, Troy, NY BL/TR, 5'9", 165 lbs. Deb: 9/9/1971

YEAR TM-L	G	AB	R	H	2B	3B	HR	RBI	BB	SO	SB	CS	AVG	OBP	SLG	OPS	OPS+	BR/A	RC	RC/G	FR	G/POS	WS	TPW
1971 Cal-A	7	3	0	0	0	0	0	0	0	1	0	0	.000	.000	.000	.000	-108	-1	0	.00	0	....	0	-0.1
1973 Cal-A	120	305	36	68	12	1	2	23	31	38	2	4	.223	.295	.289	.583	70	-13	26	2.81	-4	S-95,3-13/2-8	6	-0.7
1974 Cal-A	36	90	9	22	2	0	0	3	8	10	2	4	.244	.306	.267	.573	70	-5	6	2.27	-2	3-20/S-8,1-1,2-1	1	-0.6
1975 Cal-A	70	126	12	27	2	1	0	6	15	20	3	0	.214	.298	.246	.544	59	-5	10	2.75	-1	S-28,3-15,2-11/D-3	2	-0.4
1978 Chi-N	47	29	10	3	0	1	0	2	6	4	1	0	.103	.257	.172	.430	20	-3	2	1.89	-1	/2-6,3-5	0	-0.4
1979 Phi-N	30	73	2	13	4	1	0	6	9	15	2	0	.178	.268	.260	.529	43	-5	6	2.33	0	S-16,2-15/3-1	1	-0.3
Total 6	310	626	69	133	20	4	2	40	69	88	10	8	.212	.291	.267	.557	62	-32	51	2.60	-9	S-147/3-54,2-41,D-3,1-1	10	-2.6

• MERCADO, Orlando Orlando (Rodriguez) Mercado b: 11/7/1961, Arecibo, Puerto Rico BR/TR, 6', 195 lbs. Deb: 9/13/1982

YEAR TM-L	G	AB	R	H	2B	3B	HR	RBI	BB	SO	SB	CS	AVG	OBP	SLG	OPS	OPS+	BR/A	RC	RC/G	FR	G/POS	WS	TPW
1982 Sea-A	9	17	1	2	0	0	1	6	0	5	0	0	.118	.118	.294	.412	8	-2	1	1.06	0	/C-8,D-1	0	-0.2
1983 Sea-A	66	178	10	35	11	2	1	16	14	27	2	2	.197	.259	.298	.557	51	-13	14	2.44	2	C-65	3	-0.8
1984 Sea-A	30	78	5	17	3	1	0	5	4	12	1	0	.218	.265	.282	.547	52	-5	6	2.61	0	C-29	1	-0.4
1986 Tex-A	46	102	7	24	1	1	1	7	6	13	0	1	.235	.284	.294	.579	56	-7	7	2.31	2	C-45	3	-0.2
1987 Det-A	10	22	2	3	0	0	0	1	2	0	0	0	.136	.208	.136	.345	-6	-3	1	1.04	1	C-10	0	-0.2
LA-N	7	5	1	3	1	0	0	1	1	1	0	0	.600	.667	.800	1.467	294	2	3	38.34	-1	/C-7	1	0.0
1988 Oak-A	16	24	3	3	0	0	1	1	3	8	0	0	.125	.222	.250	.472	33	-2	2	1.94	-1	C-16	0	-0.3
1989 Min-A	19	38	1	4	0	0	0	1	4	4	1	0	.105	.190	.105	.296	-14	-6	1	.84	1	C-19	1	-0.4
1990 NY-N	42	90	10	19	1	0	3	7	8	11	0	0	.211	.290	.322	.612	68	-4	8	2.77	-1	C-40	1	-0.3
Mon-N	8	8	0	2	0	0	0	0	0	1	0	0	.250	.250	.250	.500	39	-1	1	2.25	0	/C-8	0	-0.1
Yr.	50	98	10	21	1	0	3	7	8	12	0	0	.214	.287	.316	.603	66	-5	8	2.74	-1	C-48	1	-0.3
Total 8	253	562	40	112	17	4	7	45	42	82	4	3	.199	.261	.281	.542	49	-40	42	2.40	3	C-247/D-1	10	-2.8

• MERCED, Orlando Orlando Luis (Villanueva) Merced b: 11/2/1966, Hato Rey, Puerto Rico BB/TR, 6', 170 lbs. Deb: 6/27/1990 Career OF: 93-0-617

YEAR TM-L	G	AB	R	H	2B	3B	HR	RBI	BB	SO	SB	CS	AVG	OBP	SLG	OPS	OPS+	BR/A	RC	RC/G	FR	G/POS	WS	TPW
1990 Pit-N	25	24	3	5	1	0	0	0	1	9	0	0	.208	.240	.250	.490	36	-2	1	1.69	-1	/C-1,O-1	0	-0.3
1991*Pit-N	120	411	83	113	17	2	10	50	64	81	8	4	.275	.374	.399	.773	119	13	65	5.66	-9	*1-105/O-7(0-0-7)	17	-0.4
1992*Pit-N	134	405	50	100	28	5	6	60	52	63	5	4	.247	.336	.385	.721	105	2	54	4.52	-1	*1-114,O-17(0-0-17)	14	-0.6
1993 Pit-N	137	447	68	140	26	4	8	70	77	64	3	3	.313	.415	.443	.858	130	22	85	7.18	4	*O-109(0-0-109),1-42	20	1.8
1994 Pit-N	108	386	48	105	21	3	9	51	42	58	4	1	.272	.345	.412	.757	95	-2	52	4.65	-4	O-68(0-0-68),1-55	10	-1.2
1995 Pit-N	132	487	75	146	29	4	15	83	52	74	7	2	.300	.369	.468	.837	117	12	85	6.41	0	*O-107(4-0-104),1-35	18	0.5
1996 Pit-N	120	453	69	130	24	1	17	80	51	74	8	4	.287	.359	.457	.816	110	7	74	5.93	11	*O-115(0-0-115)/1-1	16	1.1
1997 Tor-A	98	368	45	98	23	2	9	40	47	62	7	3	.266	.354	.413	.767	99	0	56	5.39	3	O-96(0-0-96)/1-1,D-1	8	-0.2
1998 Min-A	63	204	22	59	12	0	5	33	17	29	1	4	.289	.347	.422	.768	97	-3	28	4.93	0	1-38,O-13(0-0-13)/D-8	4	-0.7
Bos-A	9	9	0	0	0	0	0	2	2	3	0	0	.000	.182	.000	.182	-46	-2	0	.47	0	/D-1,O-1	0	-0.2
Yr.	72	213	22	59	12	0	5	35	19	32	1	4	.277	.339	.404	.743	90	-4	28	4.66	0	1-38,O-14(0-0-14)/D-9	4	-0.9
Chi-N	12	10	2	3	0	0	1	5	1	2	0	0	.300	.364	.600	.964	143	1	1	3.05	0	/O-4(4-0-0)	0	0.1
1999 Mon-N	93	194	25	52	12	1	8	26	26	27	2	1	.268	.355	.464	.818	108	2	32	5.80	0	O-44(44-0-0)/1-7,D-2	5	0.0
2001*Hou-N	94	137	19	36	6	1	6	29	14	32	5	1	.263	.336	.453	.788	96	-0	21	5.38	0	O-31(11-0-21)/3-2,1-1	4	-0.2
2002 Hou-N	123	251	35	72	13	3	6	30	26	50	4	0	.287	.354	.434	.788	102	2	38	5.28	5	O-56(20-0-44)/1-7,3-1,D-1	7	0.4
2003 Hou-N	123	212	20	49	17	2	3	26	15	33	3	2	.231	.285	.373	.658	67	-11	22	3.53	2	O-31(10-0-21),1-12/D-7,3-2	2	-1.1
Total 13	1391	3998	564	1108	229	28	103	585	487	661	57	29	.277	.357	.426	.783	106	41	615	5.46	10	O-700,1-418/D-20,3-5,C-1	125	-0.9

• MERCEDES, Henry Henry Felipe (Perez) Mercedes b: 7/23/1969, Santo Domingo, Dominican Republic BR/TR, 5'11", 210 lbs. Deb: 4/22/1992

YEAR TM-L	G	AB	R	H	2B	3B	HR	RBI	BB	SO	SB	CS	AVG	OBP	SLG	OPS	OPS+	BR/A	RC	RC/G	FR	G/POS	WS	TPW
1992 Oak-A	9	5	1	4	0	1	0	1	0	1	0	0	.800	.800	1.200	2.000	478	2	5	129.60	-3	/C-9	1	0.0
1993 Oak-A	20	47	5	10	2	0	0	3	2	15	1	1	.213	.260	.255	.515	42	-4	3	2.27	1	C-18/D-1	1	-0.2
1995 KC-A	23	43	7	11	2	0	0	9	8	13	0	0	.256	.385	.302	.687	81	-1	6	4.74	0	C-22	1	0.0
1996 KC-A	4	4	1	1	0	0	0	0	0	1	0	0	.250	.250	.250	.500	27	-0	0	2.25	-1	/C-4	0	-0.2
1997 Tex-A	23	47	4	10	4	0	0	4	6	25	0	0	.213	.302	.298	.600	54	-3	5	3.30	0	C-23	1	-0.2
Total 5	79	146	18	36	8	1	0	17	16	55	1	1	.247	.329	.315	.644	71	-6	19	4.45	-3	/C-76,D-1	4	-0.6

YEAR TM-L	G	AB	R	H	2B	3B	HR	RBI	BB	SO	SB	CS	AVG	OBP	SLG	OPS	OPS+	BR/A	RC	RC/G	FR	G/POS	WS	TPW
• MERCEDES, Luis	Luis Roberto (Santana) Mercedes b: 2/15/1968, San Pedro de Macoris, Dominican Republic BR/TR, 6', 180 lbs. Deb: 9/8/1991 Career OF: 15-5-25																							
1991 Bal-A	19	54	10	11	2	0	0	2	4	9	0	0	.204	.259	.241	.499	41	-4	3	2.07	0	O-15(13-0-3)/D-1	0	-0.5
1992 Bal-A	23	50	7	7	2	0	0	4	8	9	0	1	.140	.271	.180	.451	28	-5	3	1.49	1	O-16(1-2-13)/D-7	1	-0.5
1993 Bal-A	10	24	1	7	2	0	0	0	5	4	1	1	.292	.414	.375	.789	109	0	4	5.10	1	/O-8(0-0-8),D-2	0	0.1
SF-N	18	25	1	4	0	1	0	3	1	3	0	1	.160	.250	.240	.490	33	-3	2	1.77	0	/O-5(1-3-1)	0	-0.3
Total 3	70	153	19	29	6	1	0	9	18	25	1	3	.190	.287	.242	.529	46	-12	11	2.26	2	/O-44,D-10	1	-1.1
• MERCER, John	John Locke Mercer b: 1/22/1892, Taylortown, LA d: 12/22/1982, Shreveport, LA BL/TL, 5'10.5", 155 lbs. Deb: 6/25/1912																							
1912 StL-N	1	1	0	0	0	0	0	0	0	0	0	....	.000	.000	.000	.000	-102	-0	0	.00	0	/1-1	0	-0.1
• MERCER, Win	George Barclay Mercer b: 6/20/1874, Chester, WV d: 1/12/1903, San Francisco, CA BR/TR, 5'7", 140 lbs. Deb: 4/21/1894 U Career OF: 21-25-29 ♦																							
1894 Was-N	53	165	29	48	5	2	2	29	9	20	9	....	.291	.328	.382	.709	73	3	24	5.37	1	P-50/O-4(0-0-4)	19	5.0
1895 Was-N	64	201	26	51	9	1	1	26	12	33	7	....	.254	.306	.323	.629	63	-2	23	4.03	-8	P-43/S-7,O-5(1-0-4),3-3,2	13	1.0
1896 Was-N	49	156	23	38	1	1	1	14	9	18	9	....	.244	.302	.282	.584	54	0	17	3.68	0	P-46/O-1	18	1.7
1897 Was-N	50	139	23	44	2	5	0	19	6	....	7	....	.317	.354	.403	.757	100	8	23	6.23	-2	P-47	27	4.2
1898 Was-N	80	249	38	80	3	5	2	25	18	....	14	....	.321	.369	.398	.767	120	12	44	6.52	-6	P-33,S-23,O-19(2-17-0)/3-5,2	13	-1.5
1899 Was-N	108	375	73	112	6	7	1	35	32	....	16	....	.299	.360	.360	.720	99	6	57	5.57	-11	3-62,P-23,O-16(15-0-1)/1-1,S	15	-1.3
1900 NY-N	76	248	32	73	4	0	0	27	26	....	15	....	.294	.366	.310	.676	92	6	35	5.20	-4	P-33,3-19,O-14(0-0-14)/S-7,2	20	-0.5
1901 Was-A	51	140	26	42	7	2	0	16	23	....	10	....	.300	.402	.379	.781	119	10	26	6.93	-2	P-24,O-16(3-7-6)/1-7,3-1,S	13	-0.9
1902 Det-A	35	100	8	18	2	0	0	6	6	....	1	....	.180	.226	.200	.426	18	-2	5	1.63	3	P-35	19	1.3
Total 9	566	1773	278	506	39	23	7	197	141	71	88	....	.285	.344	.345	.689	88	42	254	5.17	-29	P-334/3-90,O-75,S-39,1-8,2	157	8.9
• MERCHANT, Andy	James Anderson Merchant b: 8/30/1950, Mobile, AL BL/TR, 5'11", 185 lbs. Deb: 9/28/1975																							
1975 Bos-A	1	4	1	2	0	0	0	0	1	0	0	0	.500	.600	.500	1.100	197	1	1	18.31	0	/C-1	0	0.1
1976 Bos-A	2	2	0	0	0	0	0	0	0	2	0	0	.000	.000	.000	.000	-89	-0	0	.00	0	/C-1	0	-0.1
Total 2	3	6	1	2	0	0	0	0	1	2	0	0	.333	.429	.333	.762	115	0	1	9.15	0	/C-2	0	0.0
• MEREWETHER, Art	Arthur Francis "Merry" Merewether b: 7/7/1902, East Providence, RI d: 2/2/1997, Bayside, NY BR/TR, 5'9.5", 155 lbs. Deb: 7/10/1922																							
1922 Pit-N	1	1	0	0	0	0	0	0	0	0	0	0	.000	.000	.000	.000	-99	-0	0	.00	0	....	0	0.0
• MERKLE, Fred	Frederick Charles Merkle b: 12/20/1888, Watertown, WI d: 3/2/1956, Daytona Beach, FL BR/TR, 6'1", 190 lbs. Deb: 9/21/1907 C Career OF: 11-29-8																							
1907 NY-N	15	47	0	12	1	0	0	5	1	....	0	....	.255	.271	.277	.547	69	-2	4	2.70	-1	1-15	0	-0.3
1908 NY-N	38	41	6	11	2	1	1	7	4	....	0	....	.268	.333	.439	.772	139	2	6	4.89	-1	1-11/O-5(2-0-3),2-1,3-1	2	0.1
1909 NY-N	79	236	15	45	9	1	0	20	16	....	8	....	.191	.245	.237	.482	49	-14	15	2.04	-2	1-70/2-1	1	-2.0
1910 NY-N	144	506	75	148	35	14	4	70	44	59	23	....	.292	.353	.441	.793	131	17	86	5.94	2	*1-144	20	1.8
1911*NY-N	149	541	80	153	24	10	12	84	43	60	49	....	.283	.342	.431	.773	113	7	95	6.13	13	*1-148	18	1.7
1912*NY-N	129	479	82	148	22	6	11	84	42	70	37	....	.309	.374	.449	.823	121	13	93	6.98	-4	*1-129	19	0.6
1913*NY-N	153	563	78	147	30	13	2	69	41	60	35	....	.261	.315	.371	.686	95	-5	72	4.31	-3	*1-153	14	-1.1
1914 NY-N	146	512	71	132	25	7	7	63	52	80	23	....	.258	.327	.375	.702	112	7	66	4.46	3	*1-146	17	0.8
1915 NY-N	140	505	52	151	25	3	4	62	36	39	20	15	.299	.348	.384	.732	129	14	70	4.82	-4	*1-110,O-30(0-27-5)	22	0.7
1916 NY-N	112	401	45	95	19	3	7	44	33	46	17	....	.237	.308	.352	.659	108	4	49	4.06	-3	*1-112	12	-0.1
*Bro-N	23	69	6	16	1	0	0	2	7	4	2	....	.232	.312	.246	.558	70	-2	6	2.90	-1	1-15/O-4(3-1-0)	1	-0.4
Yr.	135	470	51	111	20	3	7	46	40	50	19	....	.236	.308	.336	.644	102	2	55	3.89	-4	*1-127/O-4(3-1-0)	13	-0.6
1917 Bro-N	2	8	1	1	1	0	0	0	0	1	0	....	.125	.125	.250	.375	13	-1	0	.78	0	/1-2	0	-0.1
Chi-N	146	549	65	146	30	9	3	57	42	60	13	....	.266	.323	.370	.692	104	3	67	4.19	4	*1-140/O-6(5-1-0)	19	0.4
Yr.	148	557	66	147	31	9	3	57	42	61	13	....	.264	.320	.368	.688	103	2	67	4.13	4	*1-142/O-6(5-1-0)	19	0.3
1918*Chi-N	129	482	55	143	25	5	3	65	35	36	21	....	.297	.349	.388	.737	122	12	71	5.12	11	*1-129	22	2.3
1919 Chi-N	133	498	52	133	20	6	3	62	33	35	20	....	.267	.315	.349	.665	99	-1	58	4.02	-1	*1-132/2-1	12	-0.4
1920 Chi-N	92	330	33	94	20	4	3	38	24	32	3	5	.285	.335	.397	.732	108	3	43	4.53	0	1-85/O-1	11	0.1
1925 NY-A	7	13	4	5	1	0	0	1	1	1	1	0	.385	.429	.462	.890	128	1	3	7.43	-0	/1-5	1	0.1
1926 NY-A	1	2	0	0	0	0	0	0	0	0	0	0	.000	.000	.000	.000	-102	-1	0	.00	0	/1-1	0	-0.1
Total 16	1638	5782	720	1580	290	82	60	733	454	583	272	20	.273	.331	.383	.714	109	56	804	4.78	13	*1-1547/O-46,2-3,3-1	191	3.9
• MERLONI, Lou	Louis William Merloni b: 4/6/1971, Framingham, MA BR/TR, 5'10", 194 lbs. Deb: 5/10/1998 Career OF: 5-0-1																							
1998 Bos-A	39	96	10	27	6	0	1	15	7	20	1	0	.281	.343	.375	.718	85	-2	13	4.91	-3	2-32/3-5,S-1	4	-0.3
1999*Bos-A	43	126	18	32	7	0	1	13	8	16	0	0	.254	.309	.333	.642	62	-7	12	3.12	-1	S-24/3-9,2-8,D-5,1-1,O-1	2	-0.6
2000 Bos-A	40	128	10	41	11	2	0	18	4	22	1	0	.320	.346	.438	.783	94	-1	17	4.43	0	3-40	3	0.0
2001 Bos-A	52	146	21	39	10	0	3	13	6	31	2	1	.267	.310	.397	.707	84	-4	16	3.74	0	S-45/2-5,3-1	2	-0.1
2002 Bos-A	84	194	28	48	12	2	4	18	20	35	1	2	.247	.333	.392	.725	90	-3	26	4.45	2	2-66/3-8,S-5,1-3,O-2(1-0-1)	6	0.2
2003 SD-N	65	151	20	41	7	2	1	17	22	33	2	3	.272	.368	.364	.732	101	0	21	4.63	1	3-25,S-23,2-10/1-2,O-2(2-0-0)	4	0.3
Bos-A	15	30	4	7	1	0	0	1	4	8	0	0	.233	.324	.267	.590	57	-2	3	3.43	1	/2-7,3-7,O-1	1	-0.1
Total 6	338	871	111	235	54	6	10	95	71	165	7	6	.270	.335	.380	.715	86	-19	107	4.17	1	2-128/S-98,3-95,1-6,O-6,D-5	22	-0.6
• MERRILL, Ed	Edward Mason Merrill b: 5/22/1860, Maysville, KY d: 1/29/1946, Elmwood Park, IL, 5'11", 176 lbs. Deb: 5/5/1882 U																							
1882 Lou-a	1	0	0	0	0	0	0	....	0	....	....	....	....	....	....	....	-106	0	0	....	0	/O-1	0	0.0
Wor-N	2	8	0	1	0	0	0	4	0	1	....	....	.125	.125	.125	.250	-19	-1	0	.50	-1	/3-2	0	-0.1
1884 Ind-a	55	196	14	35	3	1	0	0	6	....	....	....	.179	.207	.204	.411	35	-13	8	1.45	-8	2-55	1	-1.7
Total 2	58	204	14	36	3	1	0	4	6	1	....	....	.176	.204	.201	.405	33	-14	9	1.41	-8	/2-55,3-2,O-1	1	-1.9
• MERRIMAN, Lloyd	Lloyd Archer "Citation" Merriman b: 8/2/1924, Clovis, CA BL/TL, 6', 195 lbs. Deb: 4/24/1949 Career OF: 50-279-20																							
1949 Cin-N	103	287	35	66	12	5	4	26	21	36	2	....	.230	.285	.348	.633	68	-14	28	3.38	-3	O-86(0-86-0)	4	-1.9
1950 Cin-N	92	298	44	77	15	3	2	31	30	23	6	....	.258	.330	.349	.679	79	-9	36	4.29	-7	O-84(2-81-1)	6	-1.8
1951 Cin-N	114	359	34	87	23	2	5	36	31	34	8	4	.242	.303	.359	.662	76	-12	41	3.91	1	*O-102(31-76-0)	10	-1.6
1954 Cin-N	73	112	12	30	8	1	0	16	23	10	3	0	.268	.406	.357	.763	98	2	19	6.11	-1	O-25(9-0-16)	4	0.0
1955 Chi-A	1	1	0	0	0	0	0	0	0	0	0	0	.000	.000	.000	.000	-97	-0	0	.00	0	....	0	0.0
Chi-N	72	145	15	31	6	1	1	8	21	21	1	0	.214	.313	.290	.603	62	-7	15	3.55	0	O-47(8-36-3)	3	-0.9
Total 5	455	1202	140	291	64	12	12	117	126	124	20	4	.242	.317	.345	.662	75	-41	140	4.03	-10	O-344	27	-6.2
• MERRITT, Bill	William Henry Merritt b: 7/30/1870, Lowell, MA d: 11/17/1937, Lowell, MA BR/TR, 5'7", 160 lbs. Deb: 8/8/1891 Career OF: 4-1-1																							
1891 Chi-N	11	42	4	9	1	0	0	4	2	2	0	....	.214	.250	.238	.488	42	-3	3	2.10	0	C-11/1-1	0	-0.2
1892 Lou-N	46	168	22	33	4	2	1	13	11	15	3	....	.196	.246	.262	.508	58	-8	12	2.37	1	C-46	2	-0.3
1893 Bos-N	39	141	30	49	6	3	3	26	13	13	3	....	.348	.403	.496	.899	128	5	30	8.68	-6	C-37/O-2(2-0-0)	7	0.2
1894 Bos-N	10	26	3	6	1	0	0	6	8	0	0	....	.231	.412	.269	.681	59	-1	3	3.84	-1	/C-8,O-1	1	-0.1
Pit-N	36	109	18	30	1	2	1	18	15	7	2	....	.275	.363	.349	.712	73	-4	15	4.90	4	C-28/1-4,O-2(2-0-0)	3	0.1
Cin-N	30	117	17	38	6	1	1	22	10	3	4	....	.325	.388	.419	.806	91	-2	21	6.93	3	C-24/3-3,1-1,O-1	3	0.3
Yr.	76	252	38	74	8	3	2	46	33	10	6	....	.294	.380	.373	.753	80	-8	39	5.68	6	C-60/1-5,O-4(2-1-1),3-3	7	0.3
1895 Cin-N	22	79	9	14	2	0	0	12	6	5	2	....	.177	.235	.203	.438	13	-11	5	1.87	0	C-20/2-1	1	-0.7
Pit-N	67	239	32	68	5	1	0	27	18	16	2	....	.285	.340	.314	.654	73	-9	27	4.23	-3	C-63/1-2	5	-0.4
Yr.	89	318	41	82	7	1	0	39	24	21	4	....	.258	.314	.286	.600	58	-19	32	3.57	-3	C-83/1-2,2-1	6	-1.2
1896 Pit-N	77	282	26	82	8	2	1	42	18	10	3	....	.291	.336	.344	.680	83	-7	36	4.51	3	C-62/3-5,1-3,2-3,S-2	7	0.2
1897 Pit-N	62	209	21	55	6	1	1	26	9	....	2	....	.263	.297	.316	.613	64	-11	21	3.55	-3	C-53/1-7	3	-0.8
1899 Bos-N	1	2	0	0	0	0	0	0	1	....	0	....	.000	.333	.000	.333	-5	-0	0	.00	0	/C-1	0	0.0
Total 8	401	1414	182	384	40	12	8	196	110	71	21	....	.272	.327	.334	.661	74	-52	173	4.35	-1	C-353/1-18,3-8,O-6,2-4,S-2	32	-1.8
• MERRITT, George	George Washington Merritt b: 4/14/1880, Paterson, NJ d: 2/21/1938, Memphis, TN TR, 6', 160 lbs. Deb: 9/6/1901 Career OF: 3-0-6																							
1901 Pit-N	4	11	2	3	0	1	0	0	0	....	0	....	.273	.385	.455	.839	139	1	2	6.53	0	/P-3	1	-0.3
1902 Pit-N	2	9	2	3	1	0	0	2	0	....	0	....	.333	.333	.444	.778	135	0	1	6.04	1	/O-2(2-0-0)	0	0.1
1903 Pit-N	9	27	4	4	0	1	0	3	2	....	1	....	.148	.233	.222	.456	29	-2	2	1.98	-1	/O-7(1-0-6),P-1	0	-0.3
Total 3	15	47	8	10	1	2	0	5	2	....	1	....	.213	.288	.319	.608	74	-1	5	3.58	0	/O-9,P-4	1	-0.5

YEAR TM-L	G	AB	R	H	2B	3B	HR	RBI	BB	SO	SB	CS	AVG	OBP	SLG	OPS	OPS+	BR/A	RC	RC/G	FR	G/POS	WS	TPW
• MERRITT, Herm	Herman G. Merritt b: 11/12/1900, Independence, KS d: 5/26/1927, Kansas City, MO BR/TR Deb: 8/24/1921																							
1921 Det-A	20	46	3	17	1	2	0	6	1	5	1	0	.370	.396	.478	.874	123	2	9	7.74	-4	S-17	1	-0.1
• MERRITT, John	John Howard Merritt b: 10/12/1894, Tupelo, MS d: 11/3/1955, Tupelo, MS BR/TL, 5'11", 170 lbs. Deb: 9/27/1913																							
1913 NY-N	1	0	0	0	0	0	0	0	0	0	0	....	....	....	....	....	-99	0	0	....	0	/0-1	0	0.0
• MERSON, Jack	John Warren Merson b: 1/17/1922, Elkridge, MD d: 4/28/2000, Elkridge, MD BR/TR, 5'11", 175 lbs. Deb: 9/14/1951																							
1951 Pit-N	13	50	6	18	2	2	1	14	1	7	0	0	.360	.373	.540	.913	138	2	10	8.51	0	2-13	2	0.4
1952 Pit-N	111	398	41	98	20	2	5	38	22	38	1	1	.246	.287	.344	.632	72	-16	38	3.27	-3	2-81,3-27	5	-1.5
1953 Bos-A	1	4	0	0	0	0	0	0	0	0	0	0	.000	.000	.000	.000	-95	-1	0	.00	0	/2-1	0	-0.1
Total 3	125	452	47	116	22	4	6	52	23	45	1	1	.257	.294	.363	.657	78	-14	49	3.73	-2	/2-95,3-27	7	-1.2
• MERTES, Sam	Samuel Blair "Sandow" Mertes b: 8/6/1872, San Francisco, CA d: 3/11/1945, San Francisco, CA BR/TR, 5'10", 225 lbs. Deb: 6/30/1896 U Career OF: 687-182-110																							
1896 Phi-N	37	143	20	34	4	4	0	14	8	10	19	....	.238	.288	.322	.609	61	-8	20	4.58	-3	0-35(1-33-1)/2-1,S-1	2	-1.2
1898 Chi-N	83	269	45	80	4	8	1	47	34	....	27	....	.297	.388	.383	.771	121	9	53	7.11	1	0-60(4-5-53),S-14/2-4,1-2	12	0.7
1899 Chi-N	117	426	83	127	13	16	9	81	33	....	45	....	.298	.349	.467	.816	126	13	88	7.45	4	*0-108(16-47-46)/1-3,S-1	18	0.9
1900 Chi-N	127	481	72	142	25	4	7	60	42	....	38	....	.295	.356	.407	.763	114	9	87	6.42	-1	0-88(10-78-0),1-33/S-7	18	0.2
1901 Chi-A	137	545	94	151	16	17	5	98	52	....	46	....	.277	.347	.396	.743	108	7	95	6.09	-3	*2-132/0-5(5-0-0)	21	0.4
1902 Chi-A	129	497	60	140	23	7	1	79	37	....	46	....	.282	.334	.362	.696	97	-1	78	5.68	8	*0-120(111-0-9)/S-5,C-2,1,2,3,P	19	0.2
1903 NY-N	138	517	100	145	**32**	14	7	**104**	61	....	45	....	.280	.360	.437	.797	122	14	101	6.99	9	*0-137(137-0-0)/1-1,C-1	26	1.4
1904 NY-N	148	532	83	147	28	11	4	78	54	....	47	....	.276	.346	.393	.739	123	14	93	5.95	6	*0-147(130-17-0)/S-1	27	1.2
1905★NY-N	150	551	81	154	27	17	5	108	56	....	52	....	.279	.351	.417	.769	126	17	103	6.50	-4	*0-150(149-2-0)	25	0.4
1906 NY-N	71	253	37	60	9	6	1	33	29	....	21	....	.237	.323	.332	.655	102	1	35	4.63	4	0-71(71-0-1)	9	0.1
StL-N	53	191	20	47	7	4	0	19	16	....	10	....	.246	.304	.325	.629	100	-0	23	3.99	-5	0-53(53-0-0)	3	-1.0
Yr.	124	444	57	107	16	10	1	52	45	....	31	....	.241	.315	.329	.644	101	1	59	4.35	-1	*0-124(124-0-1)	12	-0.9
Total 10	1190	4405	695	1227	188	108	40	721	422	10	396	....	.279	.346	.398	.744	114	75	777	6.17	15	0-974,2-138/1-40,S-29,C-3,3,P	180	3.5
• MERULLO, Lennie	Leonard Richard Merullo b: 5/5/1917, Boston, MA BR/TR, 5'11.5", 168 lbs. Deb: 9/12/1941																							
1941 Chi-N	7	17	3	6	1	0	0	1	2	0	1	....	.353	.421	.412	.833	140	1	3	7.77	0	/S-7	1	0.2
1942 Chi-N	143	515	53	132	23	3	2	37	35	45	14	....	.256	.310	.324	.634	89	-8	52	3.33	-8	*S-143	11	-0.6
1943 Chi-N	129	453	37	115	18	3	1	25	26	42	7	....	.254	.297	.313	.611	78	-14	42	3.17	-11	*S-125	9	-1.6
1944 Chi-N	66	193	20	41	8	1	1	16	16	18	3	....	.212	.276	.280	.556	57	-11	16	2.69	-6	S-56/1-1	3	-1.3
1945★Chi-N	121	394	40	94	18	0	2	37	31	30	7	....	.239	.297	.299	.597	68	-17	34	2.82	-1	*S-118	6	-1.0
1946 Chi-N	65	126	14	19	8	0	0	7	11	13	2	....	.151	.219	.214	.433	24	-13	6	1.38	-1	S-44	1	-1.2
1947 Chi-N	108	373	24	90	16	1	0	29	15	26	4	....	.241	.274	.290	.564	52	-27	28	2.53	-8	*S-108	4	-2.8
Total 7	639	2071	191	497	92	8	6	152	136	174	38	....	.240	.291	.301	.591	69	-89	180	2.90	-35	S-601/1-1	35	-8.3
• MERULLO, Matt	Matthew Bates Merullo b: 8/4/1965, Winchester, MA BL/TR, 6'2", 200 lbs. Deb: 4/12/1989																							
1989 Chi-A	31	81	5	18	1	0	1	8	6	14	0	1	.222	.276	.272	.547	56	-5	6	2.29	-1	C-27/D-1	1	-0.5
1991 Chi-A	80	140	8	32	1	0	5	21	9	18	0	0	.229	.275	.343	.618	72	-6	14	3.24	0	C-27,1-16/D-6	1	-0.6
1992 Chi-A	24	50	3	9	1	1	0	3	1	8	0	0	.180	.212	.240	.452	27	-5	3	1.74	-2	C-16/D-1	0	-0.6
1993 Chi-A	8	20	1	1	0	0	0	0	0	1	0	0	.050	.050	.050	.100	-75	-5	0	.00	0	/D-6	0	-0.5
1994 Cle-A	4	10	1	1	0	0	0	0	2	1	0	0	.100	.250	.100	.350	-5	-2	0	1.27	-1	/C-4	0	-0.2
1995 Min-A	76	195	19	55	14	1	1	27	14	27	0	1	.282	.340	.379	.719	87	-4	25	4.43	-2	C-46,D-13/1-2	2	-0.4
Total 6	223	496	37	116	17	2	7	59	32	69	0	2	.234	.286	.319	.604	63	-27	47	3.15	-5	C-120/D-27,1-18	4	-2.7
• MESNER, Steve	Stephan Mathias Mesner b: 1/13/1918, Los Angeles, CA d: 4/6/1981, San Diego, CA BR/TR, 5'9", 178 lbs. Deb: 9/23/1938																							
1938 Chi-N	2	4	2	1	0	0	0	0	1	1	0	....	.250	.400	.250	.650	80	-0	1	4.63	0	/S-1	0	0.0
1939 Chi-N	17	43	7	12	4	0	0	6	3	4	0	....	.279	.340	.372	.713	90	-1	5	4.49	2	S-12/2-1,3-1	2	0.2
1941 StL-N	24	69	8	10	1	0	0	10	5	6	0	....	.145	.203	.159	.362	3	-9	2	1.07	2	3-22	1	-0.6
1943 Cin-N	137	504	53	137	26	1	0	52	26	20	6	....	.272	.309	.327	.636	85	-11	50	3.36	-2	*3-130	12	-1.2
1944 Cin-N	121	414	31	100	17	4	1	47	34	20	1	....	.242	.301	.309	.610	75	-14	38	3.16	-7	*3-120	8	-2.0
1945 Cin-N	150	540	52	137	19	1	1	52	52	18	4	....	.254	.322	.298	.620	74	-18	52	3.24	10	*3-148/2-3	14	-0.5
Total 6	451	1574	153	397	67	6	2	167	121	69	11	....	.252	.308	.306	.614	75	-52	149	3.18	5	3-421/S-13,2-4	37	-4.2
• MESSENGER, Bobby	Charles Walter Messenger b: 3/19/1884, Bangor, ME d: 7/10/1951, Bath, ME BB/TR, 5'10.5", 165 lbs. Deb: 8/30/1909 Career OF: 12-0-32																							
1909 Chi-A	31	112	18	19	1	1	0	0	13	....	7	....	.170	.268	.196	.464	49	-6	8	2.12	0	0-31(0-0-31)	1	-0.8
1910 Chi-A	9	26	7	6	0	1	0	4	4	....	3	....	.231	.375	.308	.683	120	1	4	5.18	0	/0-8(8-0-0)	1	0.1
1911 Chi-A	13	17	4	2	0	1	0	0	3	....	0	....	.118	.250	.235	.485	36	-1	1	1.81	-1	/0-4(4-0-0)	0	-0.2
1914 StL-A	1	2	0	0	0	0	0	0	0	0	0	....	.000	.000	.000	.000	-104	-0	0	.00	0	/0-1	0	-0.1
Total 4	54	157	29	27	1	3	0	4	20	0	10	....	.172	.282	.217	.498	58	-7	13	2.52	-1	/0-44	2	-1.0
• MESSITT, Tom	Thomas John Messitt b: 7/27/1874, Philadelphia, PA d: 9/22/1934, Chicago, IL, 5'9", 177 lbs. Deb: 9/14/1899																							
1899 Lou-N	3	11	0	1	0	0	0	0	0	....	0	....	.091	.091	.091	.182	-50	-2	0	.25	2	/C-3	0	0.0
• METCALFE, Al	Alfred Tristram Metcalfe b: 12/31/1852, Brooklyn, NY d: 9/2/1914, Brooklyn, NY Deb: 5/27/1875																							
1875 Mut-n	8	32	2	7	0	0	0	1	0	3	2	0	.219	.219	.219	.438	50	-1	2	2.38	-1	/3-5,0-2(0-0-2),S-1	....	-0.2
• METCALFE, Mike	Michael Henry Metcalfe b: 1/2/1973, Quantico, VA BR/TR, 5'10", 175 lbs. Deb: 9/18/1998																							
1998 LA-N	4	1	0	0	0	0	0	0	0	1	2	0	.000	.000	.000	.000	-106	0	0	.00	-1	/2-1	0	0.0
2000 LA-N	4	12	0	1	0	0	0	0	1	2	0	0	.083	.154	.083	.237	-40	-3	0	.48	-1	/0-4(3-1-0),2-1	0	-0.3
Total 2	8	13	0	1	0	0	0	0	1	3	2	0	.077	.143	.077	.220	-45	-2	0	.44	-1	/0-4,2-2	0	-0.4
• METHA, Scat	Frank Joseph Metha b: 12/13/1913, Los Angeles, CA d: 3/2/1975, Fountain Valley, CA BR/TR, 5'11", 165 lbs. Deb: 4/22/1940																							
1940 Det-A	26	37	6	9	0	1	0	3	2	8	0	1	.243	.282	.297	.579	46	-3	3	2.77	-1	2-10/3-6	0	-0.3
• METHENY, Bud	Arthur Beauregard Metheny b: 6/1/1915, St. Louis, MO d: 1/2/2003, Virginia Beach, VA BL/TL, 5'11", 190 lbs. Deb: 4/27/1943 Career OF: 11-0-340																							
1943★NY-A	103	360	51	94	18	2	9	36	39	34	2	3	.261	.333	.397	.731	112	5	49	4.69	-9	0-91(0-0-91)	12	-1.1
1944 NY-A	137	518	72	124	16	1	14	67	56	57	5	5	.239	.316	.355	.671	89	-8	59	3.76	-9	*0-132(11-0-121)	9	-2.7
1945 NY-A	133	509	64	126	18	2	8	53	54	31	5	2	.248	.325	.338	.662	88	-6	60	3.98	-8	*0-128(0-0-128)	11	-2.5
1946 NY-A	3	3	0	0	0	0	0	0	0	0	0	0	.000	.000	.000	.000	-99	-1	0	.00	0	....	0	-0.1
Total 4	376	1390	187	344	52	5	31	156	149	122	12	10	.247	.323	.359	.682	94	-11	169	4.07	-26	0-351	32	-6.4
• METKOVICH, Catfish	George Michael Metkovich b: 10/8/1920, Angel's Camp, CA d: 5/17/1995, Costa Mesa, CA BL/TL, 6'1", 185 lbs. Deb: 7/16/1943 Career OF: 33-465-158																							
1943 Bos-A	78	321	34	79	14	4	5	27	19	38	1	3	.246	.294	.361	.656	90	-6	34	3.52	-2	0-76(0-54-25)/1-2	6	-1.2
1944 Bos-A	134	549	94	152	28	8	9	59	31	57	13	4	.277	.319	.406	.725	108	4	73	4.81	-1	0-82(0-81-3),1-50	17	-0.1
1945 Bos-A	138	539	65	140	26	3	5	62	51	70	19	6	.260	.331	.347	.677	94	-1	67	4.40	-3	1-97,0-42(0-29-14)	14	-1.2
1946★Bos-A	86	281	42	69	15	2	4	25	36	39	8	3	.246	.333	.356	.689	88	-3	37	4.57	-7	0-81(6-2-73)	8	-1.3
1947 Cle-A	126	473	68	120	22	7	5	40	32	51	5	3	.254	.302	.362	.664	86	-10	52	3.78	0	*0-119(0-119-2)/1-1	12	-1.4
1949 Chi-A	93	338	50	80	9	4	5	45	41	24	5	4	.237	.321	.331	.652	75	-13	34	3.25	-5	0-87(9-79-1)	4	-2.0
1951 Pit-N	120	423	51	124	21	3	3	40	28	23	3	2	.293	.338	.378	.717	90	-6	54	4.61	-2	0-69(3-66-0),1-37	9	-1.2
1952 Pit-N	125	373	41	101	18	3	7	41	32	29	5	2	.271	.335	.391	.726	98	-0	50	4.69	-5	1-72,0-33(5-21-8)	7	-0.9
1953 Pit-N	26	41	5	6	0	1	1	7	6	3	0	0	.146	.255	.268	.524	37	-4	3	2.53	-1	/1-5,0-4(0-3-1)	0	-0.5
Chi-N	61	124	19	29	9	0	2	12	16	10	2	1	.234	.326	.355	.681	76	-4	14	3.63	-2	0-38(10-11-18)/1-7	2	-0.8
Yr.	87	165	24	35	9	1	3	19	22	13	2	1	.212	.309	.333	.642	66	-8	17	3.35	-3	0-42(10-14-19),1-12	2	-1.3
1954 Mil-N	68	123	7	34	5	1	1	15	15	15	0	0	.276	.360	.358	.717	94	-1	15	4.24	3	1-18,0-13(0-0-13)	3	0.1
Total 10	1055	3585	476	934	167	36	47	373	307	359	61	28	.261	.323	.367	.689	91	-45	434	4.19	-25	0-644,1-289	82	-10.4

YEAR TM-L	G	AB	R	H	2B	3B	HR	RBI	BB	SO	SB	CS	AVG	OBP	SLG	OPS	OPS+	BR/A	RC	RC/G	FR	G/POS	WS	TPW
• METRO, Charlie	Charles Metro b: 4/28/1919, Nanty Glo, PA BR/TR, 5'11.5", 178 lbs. Deb: 5/4/1943 M/C Career OF: 72-22-10																							
1943 Det-A	44	40	12	8	0	0	0	2	3	6	1	1	.200	.256	.200	.456	32	-4	2	1.58	-1	O-14(1-11-2)	0	-0.6
1944 Det-A	38	78	8	15	0	1	0	5	3	10	1	0	.192	.222	.218	.440	25	-8	4	1.54	0	O-20(9-10-2)	1	-0.9
Phi-A	24	40	4	4	0	0	0	1	7	6	0	0	.100	.234	.100	.334	-3	-5	1	.81	0	O-11(9-0-2)/3-5,2-2	0	-0.5
Yr.	62	118	12	19	0	1	0	6	10	16	1	0	.161	.227	.178	.405	15	-13	5	1.27	0	O-31(18-10-4)/3-5,2-2	1	-1.5
1945 Phi-A	65	200	18	42	10	1	3	15	23	33	1	1	.210	.291	.315	.606	76	-6	20	3.27	-1	O-57(53-1-4)	2	-1.1
Total 3	171	358	42	69	10	2	3	23	36	55	3	2	.193	.266	.257	.523	51	-22	27	2.39	-3	O-102/3-5,2-2	3	-3.2
• METZ, Lenny	Leonard Raymond Metz b: 7/6/1899, Superior, CO d: 2/24/1953, Denver, CO BR/TR, 5'10.5", 170 lbs. Deb: 9/11/1923																							
1923 Phi-N	12	37	4	8	0	0	0	3	4	3	0	0	.216	.310	.216	.526	37	-3	3	2.52	-1	/2-6,S-6	0	-0.3
1924 Phi-N	7	7	1	2	0	0	0	1	1	0	0	0	.286	.375	.286	.661	71	-0	1	3.91	-1	/S-6	0	-0.1
1925 Phi-N	11	14	1	0	0	0	0	0	0	2	0	0	.000	.000	.000	.000	-92	-4	0	.00	0	/S-9,2-2	0	-0.4
Total 3	30	58	6	10	0	0	0	4	5	5	0	0	.172	.250	.172	.422	14	-7	4	1.98	-2	/S-21,2-8	0	-0.7
• METZGER, Roger	Roger Henry Metzger b: 10/10/1947, Fredericksburg, TX BB/TR, 6', 165 lbs. Deb: 6/16/1970																							
1970 Chi-N	1	2	0	0	0	0	0	0	0	0	0	0	.000	.000	.000	.000	-89	-1	0	.00	0	/S-1	0	0.0
1971 Hou-N	150	562	64	132	14	**11**	0	26	44	50	15	6	.235	.295	.299	.594	70	-21	52	3.15	2	*S-148	14	-0.1
1972 Hou-N	153	641	84	142	12	3	2	38	60	71	23	9	.222	.289	.259	.548	58	-33	52	2.68	-4	*S-153	11	-2.0
1973 Hou-N	154	580	67	145	11	**14**	1	35	39	70	10	4	.250	.301	.322	.623	73	-21	57	3.33	0	*S-149	15	-0.3
1974 Hou-N	143	572	66	145	18	10	0	30	37	73	9	7	.253	.299	.320	.619	76	-21	54	3.07	-4	*S-143	10	-0.8
1975 Hou-N	127	450	54	102	7	9	2	26	41	39	4	5	.227	.291	.296	.587	68	-21	40	2.83	8	*S-126	8	0.1
1976 Hou-N	152	481	37	101	13	8	0	29	52	63	1	1	.210	.287	.270	.557	65	-22	38	2.56	-1	*S-150/2-2	9	-0.5
1977 Hou-N	97	269	24	50	9	6	0	16	32	24	2	0	.186	.272	.264	.536	49	-19	20	2.35	-15	S-96/2-1	1	-2.4
1978 Hou-N	45	123	11	27	4	1	0	6	12	9	0	0	.220	.289	.268	.557	61	-6	8	2.09	-4	S-42/2-1	1	-0.6
SF-N	75	235	17	61	6	1	0	17	12	17	8	1	.260	.296	.294	.589	68	-9	21	3.10	-2	S-74	5	-0.5
Yr.	120	358	28	88	10	2	0	23	24	26	8	1	.246	.293	.285	.578	65	-15	30	2.73	-6	*S-116/2-1	6	-1.1
1979 SF-N	94	259	24	65	7	8	0	31	23	31	11	3	.251	.312	.340	.652	83	-5	28	3.63	-5	S-78,2-10/3-1	6	-0.3
1980 SF-N	28	27	5	2	0	0	0	0	3	2	0	0	.074	.167	.074	.241	-31	-5	0	.31	-2	S-13/2-1	0	-0.6
Total 11	1219	4201	453	972	101	71	5	254	355	449	83	36	.231	.293	.293	.585	67	-183	372	2.90	-27	*S-1173/2-15,3-1	80	-8.1
• METZIG, William	William Andrew Metzig b: 12/4/1918, Fort Dodge, IA BR/TR, 6'1", 180 lbs. Deb: 9/19/1944																							
1944 Chi-A	5	16	1	2	0	0	0	1	1	4	0	0	.125	.176	.125	.301	-13	-2	0	.49	0	/2-5	0	-0.2
• METZLER, Alex	Alexander Metzler b: 1/4/1903, Fresno, CA d: 11/30/1973, Fresno, CA BL/TR, 5'9", 167 lbs. Deb: 9/16/1925 Career OF: 219-233-75																							
1925 Chi-N	9	38	2	7	2	0	0	2	3	7	0	0	.184	.244	.237	.481	23	-4	2	1.95	2	/O-9(0-9-0)	0	-0.3
1926 Phi-A	20	67	8	16	3	0	0	12	7	5	1	0	.239	.311	.284	.594	53	-4	6	3.28	2	O-17(15-1-1)	1	-0.4
1927 Chi-A	134	543	87	173	29	11	3	61	61	39	15	11	.319	.396	.429	.826	117	15	94	6.38	6	*O-134(0-133-4)	21	1.4
1928 Chi-A	139	464	71	141	18	14	3	55	77	30	16	8	.304	.410	.422	.832	120	19	86	6.51	0	*O-134(50-43-46)	19	1.0
1929 Chi-A	146	568	80	156	23	13	2	49	80	45	9	5	.275	.367	.371	.739	92	-3	82	5.14	0	*O-142(132-10-0)	15	-1.3
1930 Chi-A	56	79	12	14	4	0	0	5	11	6	0	2	.177	.278	.228	.506	31	-9	5	2.01	0	O-27(21-1-5)	0	-0.9
StL-A	56	209	30	54	6	3	1	23	21	12	5	1	.258	.326	.330	.656	65	-10	24	3.90	-3	O-56(1-36-19)	3	-1.5
Yr.	112	288	42	68	10	3	1	28	32	18	5	3	.236	.313	.302	.615	55	-19	30	3.33	-4	O-83(22-37-24)	3	-2.4
Total 6	560	1968	290	561	85	41	9	207	260	144	46	27	.285	.374	.384	.757	98	2	301	5.37	6	O-519	59	-2.0
• MEULENS, Hensley	Hensley Filemon Acasio "Bam-Bam" Meulens b: 6/23/1967, Willemstad, Curacao BR/TR, 6'4", 212 lbs. Deb: 8/23/1989 Career OF: 114-0-18																							
1989 NY-A	8	28	2	5	0	0	0	1	2	8	0	1	.179	.233	.179	.412	18	-3	1	.76	2	/3-8	0	-0.2
1990 NY-A	23	83	12	20	7	0	3	10	9	25	1	0	.241	.337	.434	.771	113	2	12	4.95	2	O-23(23-0-0)	3	0.3
1991 NY-A	96	288	37	64	8	1	6	29	18	97	3	0	.222	.277	.319	.597	64	-14	25	2.93	-1	O-73(61-0-13),D-13/1-7	3	-1.8
1992 NY-A	2	5	1	3	0	0	1	1	1	0	0	0	.600	.667	1.200	1.867	416	2	3	28.17	0	/3-2	1	0.3
1993 NY-A	30	53	8	9	1	1	2	5	8	19	0	1	.170	.279	.340	.618	67	-3	5	2.65	-1	O-24(22-0-1)/1-3,3-1	0	-0.4
1997 Mon-N	16	24	6	7	1	0	2	6	4	10	0	1	.292	.393	.583	.976	152	1	5	7.62	0	/O-8(8-0-0),1-3	1	0.1
1998 Ari-N	7	15	1	1	0	0	1	1	0	6	0	0	.067	.067	.267	.333	-18	-3	0	.51	0	/O-4(0-0-4)	0	-0.2
Total 7	182	496	67	109	17	2	15	53	42	165	4	3	.220	.290	.353	.643	77	-17	52	3.41	2	O-132/1-13,D-13,3-11	8	-2.1
• MEUSEL, Bob	Robert William "Long Bob" Meusel b: 7/19/1896, San Jose, CA d: 11/28/1977, Downey, CA BR/TR, 6'3", 190 lbs. Deb: 4/14/1920 Career OF: 694-43-571																							
1920 NY-A	119	460	75	151	40	7	11	83	20	72	4	4	.328	.359	.517	.876	126	14	83	6.75	-8	O-64(16-0-48),3-45/1-2	19	0.5
1921*NY-A	149	598	104	190	40	16	24	135	34	88	17	6	.318	.356	.559	.915	127	22	117	7.28	7	*O-147(10-0-137)	24	1.7
1922*NY-A	121	473	61	151	26	11	16	84	40	58	13	8	.319	.376	.522	.898	129	19	92	7.12	4	*O-121(47-1-74)	21	1.3
1923*NY-A	132	460	59	144	29	10	9	91	31	52	13	15	.313	.359	.478	.837	117	6	74	5.77	-4	*O-121(78-0-43)	16	-0.7
1924 NY-A	143	579	93	188	40	11	12	120	32	43	26	14	.325	.365	.494	.859	120	15	102	6.43	-4	*O-143(93-2-49)/3-2	19	0.1
1925 NY-A	156	624	101	181	34	12	**33**	**138**	54	55	13	14	.290	.348	.542	.889	125	16	113	6.29	-7	*O-131(86-0-46),3-27	18	0.1
1926*NY-A	108	413	73	130	22	3	12	81	37	32	16	17	.315	.373	.470	.842	121	8	68	5.61	-7	*O-107(68-1-38)	13	-0.7
1927*NY-A	135	516	75	174	47	9	8	103	45	58	24	10	.337	.393	.510	.902	137	28	103	7.35	-2	*O-131(83-0-48)	21	1.5
1928*NY-A	131	518	77	154	45	5	11	113	39	56	6	9	.297	.349	.467	.816	116	8	82	5.56	-1	*O-131(87-0-44)	18	-0.3
1929 NY-A	100	391	46	102	15	3	10	57	17	42	1	5	.261	.292	.391	.683	79	-15	43	3.77	1	O-96(56-0-40)	6	-2.1
1930 Cin-N	113	443	62	128	30	8	10	62	26	63	9	....	.289	.330	.460	.790	93	-7	65	5.12	0	*O-112(70-39-4)	9	-1.1
Total 11	1407	5475	826	1693	368	95	156	1067	375	619	142	102	.309	.356	.497	.852	119	114	941	6.16	-21	*O-1304/3-74,1-2	184	0.2
• MEUSEL, Irish	Emil Frederick Meusel b: 6/9/1893, Oakland, CA d: 3/1/1963, Long Beach, CA BR/TR, 5'11.5", 178 lbs. Deb: 10/1/1914 C Career OF: 1008-61-158																							
1914 Was-A	1	2	0	0	0	0	0	0	0	0	0	....	.000	.000	.000	.000	-96	-0	0	.00	-0	/O-1	0	-0.1
1918 Phi-N	124	473	48	132	25	6	4	62	30	21	18	....	.279	.323	.383	.706	108	3	61	4.54	2	*O-120(71-45-0)/2-4	15	0.0
1919 Phi-N	135	521	65	159	26	7	5	59	15	13	24	....	.305	.327	.411	.738	113	6	74	5.12	-3	*O-128(59-15-54)	14	-0.4
1920 Phi-N	138	518	75	160	27	8	14	69	32	27	17	11	.309	.349	.473	.822	129	18	83	5.75	-6	*O-129(99-0-43)/1-3	17	0.6
1921 Phi-N	84	343	59	121	21	7	12	51	18	17	8	4	.353	.385	.560	.945	136	18	72	8.30	3	O-84(38-1-46)	12	1.4
*NY-N	62	243	37	80	12	6	2	36	15	12	5	9	.329	.373	.453	.826	117	4	38	5.73	1	O-62(62-0-1)	9	0.0
Yr.	146	586	96	201	33	13	14	87	33	29	13	13	.343	.380	.515	.895	128	22	110	7.19	3	*O-146(100-1-47)	21	1.4
1922*NY-N	154	617	100	204	28	17	16	132	35	33	12	10	.331	.369	.509	.877	123	18	112	6.66	-5	*O-154(154-0-0)	23	0.1
1923*NY-N	146	595	102	177	22	14	19	**125**	38	16	8	8	.297	.341	.477	.818	115	10	94	5.66	-6	*O-145(145-0-0)	20	-0.6
1924*NY-N	139	549	75	170	26	9	6	102	33	18	11	7	.310	.351	.423	.774	109	8	81	5.29	-7	*O-138(138-0-0)	17	-1.0
1925 NY-N	135	516	82	169	35	8	21	111	26	19	5	4	.328	.363	.548	.912	135	24	100	7.30	0	*O-126(118-0-8)	20	1.3
1926 NY-N	129	449	51	131	25	10	6	65	16	18	5	....	.292	.322	.432	.754	103	-1	60	4.68	-2	*O-112(112-0-0)	12	-1.0
1927 Bro-N	42	74	7	18	3	1	1	7	11	5	0	....	.243	.341	.351	.693	85	-1	9	4.14	0	O-17(11-0-6)	2	-0.3
Total 11	1289	4900	701	1521	250	93	106	819	269	199	113	53	.310	.348	.464	.813	118	107	783	5.81	-24	*O-1216/2-4,1-3	161	0.0
• MEYER, Benny	Bernhard "Earache" Meyer b: 1/21/1885, Hematite, MO d: 2/6/1974, Festus, MO BR/TR, 5'9", 170 lbs. Deb: 4/9/1913 C Career OF: 87-19-174																							
1913 Bro-N	38	87	12	17	0	1	1	10	10	14	8	....	.195	.278	.253	.531	51	-5	8	2.78	-2	O-26(2-17-7)/C-1	1	-0.9
1914 Bal-F	143	500	76	152	18	10	5	40	71	53	23	....	.304	.395	.410	.805	130	23	88	6.12	-5	*O-132(12-2-118)/S-4	21	1.2
1915 Bal-F	35	120	20	29	2	0	0	5	37	13	6	....	.242	.424	.258	.682	96	3	16	4.31	-4	O-34(0-0-34)	4	-0.4
Buf-F	93	333	37	77	8	6	1	29	40	37	9	....	.231	.316	.300	.616	81	-7	33	3.27	-4	O-88(73-0-15)	7	-1.5
Yr.	128	453	57	106	10	6	1	34	77	50	15	....	.234	.348	.289	.637	86	-4	48	3.55	-8	*O-122(73-0-49)	11	-1.9
1925 Phi-N	1	1	1	1	1	0	0	0	0	0	0	0	1.000	1.000	2.000	3.000	593	1	2	∞	-1	/2-1	0	0.0
Total 4	310	1041	146	276	29	17	7	84	158	117	46	0	.265	.365	.346	.711	105	14	146	4.66	-16	O-280/S-4,2-1,C-1	33	-1.6
• MEYER, Billy	William Adam Meyer b: 1/14/1892, Knoxville, TN d: 3/31/1957, Knoxville, TN BR/TR, 5'9.5", 170 lbs. Deb: 9/6/1913 M																							
1913 Chi-A	1	1	0	1	0	0	0	0	0	0	0	....	1.000	1.000	1.000	2.000	490	0	1	∞	0	/C-1	1	0.0
1916 Phi-A	50	138	6	32	2	2	1	12	8	11	3	....	.232	.274	.297	.571	75	-5	13	2.96	6	C-48	2	0.6
1917 Phi-A	62	162	9	38	5	1	0	9	7	14	0	....	.235	.271	.278	.548	68	-7	12	2.42	0	C-55	2	-0.3
Total 3	113	301	15	71	7	3	1	21	15	25	3	....	.236	.274	.289	.563	73	-11	25	2.67	6	C-104	5	0.3

YEAR TM-L	G	AB	R	H	2B	3B	HR	RBI	BB	SO	SB	CS	AVG	OBP	SLG	OPS	OPS+	BR/A	RC	RC/G	FR	G/POS	WS	TPW
• MEYER, Dan	Daniel Thomas Meyer b: 8/3/1952, Hamilton, OH BL/TR, 5'11", 180 lbs. Deb: 9/14/1974 Career OF: 315-1-11																							
1974 Det-A	13	50	5	10	1	1	3	7	1	1	1	0	.200	.231	.440	.671	86	-1	4	2.82	0	0-12(12-0-0)	1	-0.2
1975 Det-A	122	470	56	111	17	3	8	47	26	25	8	3	.236	.279	.336	.615	70	-19	41	2.89	-2	0-74(74-0-0),1-46	4	-3.0
1976 Det-A	105	294	37	74	8	4	2	16	17	22	10	0	.252	.293	.327	.619	78	-6	28	3.20	-1	0-47(47-0-0),1-19/D-1	4	-1.2
1977 Sea-A	159	582	75	159	24	4	22	90	43	51	11	8	.273	.324	.442	.766	107	4	77	4.50	-3	*1-159	16	-0.8
1978 Sea-A	123	444	38	101	18	1	8	56	24	39	7	3	.227	.267	.327	.594	67	-20	38	2.84	-6	*1-121/0-2(2-0-0),D-1	3	-3.4
1979 Sea-A	144	525	72	146	21	7	20	74	29	35	11	7	.278	.321	.459	.780	106	2	72	4.75	-10	*3-101,0-31(31-0-0),1-15	12	-1.1
1980 Sea-A	146	531	56	146	25	6	11	71	31	42	8	4	.275	.316	.407	.723	96	-4	66	4.38	-4	*0-123(123-0-0)/D-7,3-5,1	11	-1.4
1981 Sea-A	83	252	26	66	10	1	3	22	10	16	4	3	.262	.293	.345	.638	80	-7	24	3.25	-1	3-49,0-14(13-1-0)/1-3,D-3	4	-1.0
1982 Oak-A	120	383	28	92	17	3	8	59	18	33	1	1	.240	.274	.363	.637	77	-13	37	3.28	-1	1-58,D-38,0-11(4-0-8)	5	-1.8
1983 Oak-A	69	169	15	32	9	0	1	13	19	11	0	0	.189	.271	.260	.532	50	-11	11	2.05	-2	1-41,D-12,0-11(9-0-2)/3-1	1	-1.6
1984 Oak-A	20	22	1	7	3	1	0	4	0	2	0	0	.318	.318	.545	.864	143	1	3	4.33	0	/1-3,D-1	1	0.1
1985 Oak-A	14	12	2	0	0	0	0	0	1	0	0	0	.000	.077	.000	.077	-83	-3	0	.00	0	/3-1,D-1,0-1	0	-0.3
Total 12	1118	3734	411	944	153	31	86	459	219	277	61	29	.253	.296	.379	.675	85	-79	402	3.63	-30	1-469,0-326,3-157/D-64	62	-15.8
• MEYER, Dutch	Lambert Dalton Meyer b: 10/6/1915, Waco, TX d: 1/19/2003, Fort Worth, TX BR/TR, 5'10.5", 181 lbs. Deb: 6/23/1937																							
1937 Chi-N	1	0	0	0	0	0	0	0	0	0	0	....	....	....	....	....	-96	0	0	....	0	....	0	0.0
1940 Det-A	23	58	12	15	3	0	0	6	4	10	2	0	.259	.317	.310	.628	58	-3	7	4.03	-3	2-21	1	-0.5
1941 Det-A	46	153	12	29	9	1	1	14	8	13	1	1	.190	.230	.281	.511	31	-16	10	2.02	-4	2-40	2	-1.7
1942 Det-A	14	52	5	17	3	0	2	9	4	4	0	1	.327	.386	.500	.886	137	2	9	6.62	5	2-14	3	0.9
1945 Cle-A	130	524	71	153	29	8	7	48	40	32	2	4	.292	.342	.418	.760	126	14	74	5.13	-13	*2-130	19	0.8
1946 Cle-A	72	207	13	48	5	3	0	16	26	16	0	1	.232	.321	.285	.606	75	-6	20	3.18	-3	2-64	4	-0.6
Total 6	286	994	113	262	49	12	10	93	82	75	5	7	.264	.322	.367	.689	97	-10	119	4.20	-17	2-269	29	-1.1
• MEYER, George	George Francis Meyer b: 8/3/1909, Chicago, IL d: 1/3/1992, Hoffman Estates, IL BR/TR, 5'9", 160 lbs. Deb: 9/3/1938																							
1938 Chi-A	24	81	10	24	2	2	0	9	11	17	3	1	.296	.387	.370	.757	89	-1	13	5.58	2	2-24	2	0.3
• MEYER, Joey	Tanner Joe Meyer b: 5/10/1962, Honolulu, HI BR/TR, 6'3", 260 lbs. Deb: 4/4/1988																							
1988 Mil-A	103	327	22	86	18	0	11	45	23	88	0	1	.263	.313	.419	.732	102	-0	41	4.36	0	D-66,1-33	7	-0.4
1989 Mil-A	53	147	13	33	6	0	7	29	12	36	1	0	.224	.283	.408	.691	93	-2	17	3.86	-1	D-31,1-18	3	-0.4
Total 2	156	474	35	119	24	0	18	74	35	124	1	1	.251	.304	.416	.720	99	-2	58	4.20	-1	/D-97,1-51	10	-0.9
• MEYER, Leo	Leo Meyer b: 3/29/1888, IA d: 9/2/1968, Smyrna, DE TR Deb: 9/27/1909																							
1909 Bro-N	7	23	1	3	0	0	0	0	2	....	0	....	.130	.200	.130	.330	3	-3	1	.83	1	/S-7	0	-0.1
• MEYER, Scott	Scott William Meyer b: 8/19/1957, Evergreen Park, IL BR/TR, 6'1", 195 lbs. Deb: 9/10/1978																							
1978 Oak-A	8	9	1	1	1	0	0	0	0	4	0	0	.111	.111	.222	.333	-9	-1	0	.75	-1	/C-7	0	-0.2
• MEYERLE, Levi	Levi Samuel "Long Levi" Meyerle b: 7/1845, Philadelphia, PA d: 11/4/1921, Philadelphia, PA BR/TR, 6'1", 177 lbs. Deb: 5/20/1871 NA OF: 2-0-29 Career OF: 0-1-4																							
1871 Ath-n	26	130	45	64	9	3	**4**	40	2	1	4	0	**.492**	**.500**	**.700**	**1.200**	**243**	**24**	49	**23.24**	-7	*3-26/P-1	....	1.0
1872 Ath-n	27	146	31	48	10	5	1	31	0	1	0	0	.329	.329	.486	.815	147	7	24	7.57	4	0-26(0-0-26)/3-1	....	0.9
1873 Phi-n	48	238	53	83	14	4	3	58	2	0	5	0	.349	.354	.479	.833	140	11	43	8.50	-7	*3-48/S-1	....	0.3
1874 Chi-n	53	254	65	100	19	1	1	47	3	4	3	1	**.394**	**.401**	.488	**.889**	**182**	**22**	52	**10.10**	-12	2-31,3-14/0-5(2-0-3),S-5	....	0.6
1875 Phi-n	68	301	55	95	14	8	1	54	0	2	7	2	.316	.316	.425	.741	149	14	44	6.19	-3	2-36,3-20,1-16	....	0.8
1876 Phi-N	55	259	46	87	12	8	0	34	3	2	....	....	.336	.347	.449	.797	165	17	41	6.79	-6	*3-49/2-3,0-3(0-0-3),P-2	7	0.8
1877 Cin-N	27	107	11	35	7	2	0	15	0	4	....	....	.327	.327	.430	.757	153	6	15	5.89	-5	S-18,2-12/0-1	4	0.2
1884 Phi-U	3	11	0	1	1	0	0	....	0	....	....	....	.091	.091	.182	.273	-11	-1	0	.52	-1	/1-2,0-1	0	-0.2
Total 5 n	222	1069	249	390	66	21	10	230	7	8	19	3	.365	.369	.494	.863	166	79	212	9.45	-26	3-109/2-67,0-31,1-16,S-6,P	....	3.5
Total 3	85	377	57	123	20	10	0	49	3	6	....	....	.326	.334	.436	.770	157	22	57	6.28	-12	/3-49,S-18,2-15,0-5,1-2,P-2	11	0.8
• MEYERS, Chad	Chad William Meyers b: 8/8/1975, Omaha, NE BR/TR, 6', 185 lbs. Deb: 8/6/1999 Career OF: 9-12-0																							
1999 Chi-N	43	142	17	33	9	0	0	4	9	27	4	2	.232	.292	.296	.588	50	-11	12	2.67	-2	2-32,0-14(4-10-0)	1	-1.1
2000 Chi-N	36	52	8	9	2	0	0	5	3	11	1	0	.173	.232	.212	.444	13	-7	3	1.83	-1	/2-8,3-8	0	-0.7
2001 Chi-N	18	17	1	2	0	0	0	0	2	5	0	1	.118	.348	.118	.465	30	-2	1	1.83	2	/2-4,0-4(2-2-0),3-1	0	0.0
2003 Sea-A	9	1	1	0	0	0	0	0	0	0	1	0	.000	.000	.000	.000	-103	-0	0	.00	0	/D-5,0-3(3-0-0)	0	0.0
Total 4	106	212	27	44	11	0	0	9	14	43	6	3	.208	.282	.259	.541	39	-20	16	2.38	-1	/2-44,0-21,3-9,D-5	1	-1.8
• MEYERS, Chief	John Tortes Meyers b: 7/29/1880, Riverside, CA d: 7/25/1971, San Bernardino, CA BR/TR, 5'11", 194 lbs. Deb: 4/16/1909																							
1909 NY-N	90	220	15	61	10	5	1	30	22	....	3	....	.277	.359	.382	.741	128	8	31	4.94	-7	C-64	10	0.8
1910 NY-N	127	365	25	104	18	0	1	62	40	18	5	....	.285	.362	.342	.704	106	4	48	4.52	-5	*C-117	16	1.0
1911★NY-N	133	391	48	130	18	9	1	61	25	33	7	....	.332	.392	.432	.824	127	14	69	6.58	-15	*C-128	19	0.9
1912★NY-N	126	371	60	133	16	5	6	54	47	20	8	....	.358	.441	.477	.918	146	26	82	8.42	-11	*C-122	23	2.3
1913★NY-N	120	378	37	118	18	5	3	47	37	22	7	....	.312	.387	.410	.797	127	14	60	5.80	-4	*C-116	20	2.0
1914 NY-N	134	381	33	109	13	5	1	55	34	25	4	....	.286	.357	.354	.711	116	8	48	4.49	-4	*C-126	16	1.4
1915 NY-N	110	289	24	67	10	5	1	26	26	18	4	4	.232	.311	.311	.622	94	-3	28	3.27	-2	C-96	10	0.3
1916★Bro-N	80	239	21	59	10	3	0	21	26	15	2	....	.247	.336	.314	.650	97	1	26	3.74	1	C-74	10	0.9
1917 Bro-N	47	132	8	28	3	0	0	3	13	7	4	....	.212	.283	.235	.518	58	-6	10	2.33	-2	C-44	2	-0.5
Bos-N	25	68	5	17	4	4	0	4	4	4	0	....	.250	.311	.426	.737	133	2	9	4.27	3	C-24	3	0.9
Yr.	72	200	13	45	7	4	0	7	17	11	4	....	.225	.292	.300	.592	83	-4	18	2.98	2	C-68	5	0.3
Total 9	992	2834	276	826	120	41	14	363	274	162	44	4	.291	.367	.378	.744	116	68	409	5.12	-45	C-911	129	10.0
• MEYERS, Henry	Henry L. Meyers b: 1860, Philadelphia, PA d: 6/28/1898, Harrisburg, PA Deb: 8/30/1890																							
1890 Phi-a	5	19	2	3	0	0	0	1	1	....	2	....	.158	.238	.158	.396	17	-2	1	2.02	-2	/3-5	0	-0.4
• MEYERS, Lou	Lewis Henry "Crazy Horse" Meyers b: 12/9/1859, Cincinnati, OH d: 11/30/1920, Cincinnati, OH BR/TR, 5'11", 165 lbs. Deb: 5/10/1884																							
1884 Cin-U	2	3	1	0	0	0	0	....	1	....	....	....	.000	.250	.000	.250	-8	-0	0	.00	-1	/C-2,0-1	0	-0.1
• MICELOTTA, Mickey	Robert Peter Micelotta b: 10/20/1928, Corona, NY BR/TR, 5'11", 185 lbs. Deb: 4/20/1954																							
1954 Phi-N	13	3	2	0	0	0	0	0	1	1	0	0	.000	.250	.000	.250	-28	-1	0	.59	0	/S-1	0	-0.1
1955 Phi-N	4	4	0	0	0	0	0	0	0	0	0	0	.000	.000	.000	.000	-102	-1	0	.00	0	/S-2	0	-0.1
Total 2	17	7	2	0	0	0	0	0	1	1	0	0	.000	.125	.000	.125	-69	-2	0	.22	0	/S-3	0	-0.2
• MICHAEL, Gene	Eugene Richard "Stick" Michael b: 6/2/1938, Kent, OH BB/TR, 6'2", 183 lbs. Deb: 7/15/1966 M/C																							
1966 Pit-N	30	33	9	5	2	1	0	2	0	7	0	0	.152	.152	.273	.424	15	-4	1	1.02	-1	/S-8,2-2,3-1	0	-0.5
1967 LA-N	98	223	20	45	3	1	0	7	11	30	1	3	.202	.246	.224	.470	38	-19	12	1.70	-8	S-83	2	-2.3
1968 NY-A	61	116	8	23	3	0	1	8	2	23	3	2	.198	.218	.250	.468	43	-8	6	1.61	-7	S-43/P-1	1	-1.3
1969 NY-A	119	412	41	112	24	4	2	31	43	56	7	4	.272	.342	.364	.706	101	1	52	4.38	-3	*S-118	14	1.2
1970 NY-A	134	435	42	93	10	1	2	38	50	93	3	1	.214	.295	.255	.550	56	-25	35	2.63	-4	*S-123/3-4,2-3	7	-1.5
1971 NY-A	139	456	36	102	15	0	3	35	48	64	3	3	.224	.302	.276	.578	69	-18	37	2.61	11	*S-136	9	0.9
1972 NY-A	126	391	29	91	7	4	1	32	32	45	4	2	.233	.292	.279	.571	73	-13	31	2.66	11	*S-121	9	1.4
1973 NY-A	129	418	30	94	11	1	3	47	26	51	1	3	.225	.270	.278	.548	56	-25	29	2.32	-3	*S-129	5	-1.4
1974 NY-A	81	177	19	46	9	0	0	13	14	24	0	0	.260	.314	.311	.625	83	-4	17	3.24	-1	2-45,S-39/3-2	4	0.0
1975 Det-A	56	145	15	31	2	0	3	13	8	28	0	0	.214	.255	.290	.545	51	-10	11	2.35	-3	S-44/2-7,3-4	1	-0.8
Total 10	973	2806	249	642	86	12	15	226	234	421	22	18	.229	.290	.284	.574	66	-124	231	2.71	-9	S-844/2-57,3-11,P-1	52	-4.2
• MICHAELS, Cass	Casimir Eugene Michaels b: 3/4/1926, Detroit, MI d: 11/12/1982, Grosse Pointe, MI BR/TR, 5'11", 175 lbs. Deb: 8/19/1943																							
1943 Chi-A	2	7	0	0	0	0	0	0	0	0	0	0	.000	.000	.000	.000	-100	-2	0	.00	0	/3-2	0	-0.2
1944 Chi-A	27	68	4	12	4	1	0	5	2	5	0	0	.176	.200	.265	.465	33	-6	4	1.67	-3	S-21/3-3	1	-0.7
1945 Chi-A	129	445	47	109	8	5	2	54	37	28	8	7	.245	.307	.299	.606	78	-13	41	2.98	-2	*S-126/2-1	10	-0.5
1946 Chi-A	91	291	37	75	8	0	1	22	29	36	9	3	.258	.333	.296	.629	80	-6	32	3.72	-6	2-66,3-13/S-6	8	-0.8

YEAR	TM-L	G	AB	R	H	2B	3B	HR	RBI	BB	SO	SB	CS	AVG	OBP	SLG	OPS	OPS+	BR/A	RC	RC/G	FR	G/POS	WS	TPW
1947	Chi-A	110	355	31	97	15	4	3	34	39	28	10	5	.273	.350	.363	.714	102	2	45	4.29	3	2-60,3-44/S-2	11	0.8
1948	Chi-A	145	484	47	120	12	6	5	56	69	42	8	2	.248	.344	.329	.673	82	-10	60	4.24	-1	S-85,2-55/0-1	11	-0.3
1949	Chi-A★	154	561	73	173	27	9	6	83	101	50	5	7	.308	.417	.421	.837	126	24	102	6.55	2	*2-154	22	3.4
1950	Chi-A	36	138	21	43	6	3	4	19	13	8	0	0	.312	.375	.486	.861	122	4	25	6.32	-3	2-35	4	0.3
	Was-A★	106	388	48	97	8	4	4	47	55	39	2	3	.250	.345	.322	.667	75	-14	45	3.95	2	*2-104	9	-0.5
	Yr.	142	526	69	140	14	7	8	66	68	47	2	3	.266	.352	.365	.717	87	-10	70	4.56	-1	*2-139	13	-0.3
1951	Was-A	138	485	59	125	20	4	4	45	61	41	1	1	.258	.342	.340	.682	86	-8	58	4.16	-6	*2-128	10	-0.7
1952	Was-A	22	86	10	20	4	1	1	7	7	15	0	0	.233	.290	.337	.628	77	-3	7	2.84	4	2-22	2	0.2
	StL-A	55	166	21	44	8	2	3	25	23	16	1	0	.265	.354	.392	.746	105	2	25	5.32	3	3-42/2-8	6	0.5
	Phi-A	55	200	22	50	4	5	1	18	23	11	3	0	.250	.330	.335	.665	80	-4	24	4.04	-9	2-55	5	-1.1
	Yr.	132	452	53	114	16	8	5	50	53	42	4	0	.252	.332	.356	.688	89	-5	56	4.25	-2	2-85,3-42	13	-0.3
1953	Phi-A	117	411	53	103	10	0	12	42	51	56	7	0	.251	.335	.363	.697	85	-6	55	4.64	-7	*2-110	9	-0.4
1954	Chi-A	101	282	35	74	13	2	7	44	56	31	10	4	.262	.392	.397	.789	113	8	50	6.23	2	3-91/2-2	13	1.0
Total	**12**	**1288**	**4367**	**508**	**1142**	**147**	**46**	**53**	**501**	**566**	**406**	**64**	**32**	**.262**	**.349**	**.353**	**.702**	**92**	**-31**	**572**	**4.50**	**-20**	**2-800,S-240,3-195/0-1**	**121**	**1.1**

• MICHAELS, Jason Jason Drew Michaels b: 5/4/1976, Tampa, FL BR/TR, 6', 204 lbs. Deb: 4/6/2001 Career OF: 30-19-20

YEAR	TM-L	G	AB	R	H	2B	3B	HR	RBI	BB	SO	SB	CS	AVG	OBP	SLG	OPS	OPS+	BR/A	RC	RC/G	FR	G/POS	WS	TPW
2001	Phi-N	6	6	0	1	0	0	0	1	0	2	0	0	.167	.167	.167	.333	-14	-1	0	.90	0	/0-1	0	-0.1
2002	Phi-N	81	105	16	28	10	3	2	11	13	33	1	1	.267	.353	.476	.829	122	3	18	6.05	-1	0-26(6-14-7)/D-2,3-1	3	0.2
2003	Phi-N	76	109	20	36	11	0	5	17	15	22	0	0	.330	.416	.569	.985	164	10	26	9.18	1	0-38(23-5-13)	4	1.0
Total	**3**	**163**	**220**	**36**	**65**	**21**	**3**	**7**	**29**	**28**	**57**	**1**	**1**	**.295**	**.380**	**.514**	**.894**	**139**	**12**	**44**	**7.36**	**0**	**/0-65,D-2,3-1**	**7**	**1.1**

• MICHAELS, Ralph Ralph Joseph Michaels b: 5/3/1902, Etna, PA d: 8/5/1988, Monroeville, PA BR/TR, 5'10.5", 178 lbs. Deb: 4/16/1924

YEAR	TM-L	G	AB	R	H	2B	3B	HR	RBI	BB	SO	SB	CS	AVG	OBP	SLG	OPS	OPS+	BR/A	RC	RC/G	FR	G/POS	WS	TPW
1924	Chi-N	8	11	0	4	0	0	0	2	0	1	0	0	.364	.364	.364	.727	95	-0	1	4.78	0	/S-4	1	0.0
1925	Chi-N	22	50	10	14	1	0	0	6	6	9	1	0	.280	.357	.300	.657	69	-2	6	4.31	0	3-15/1-1,2-1,S-1	1	-0.1
1926	Chi-N	2	0	1	0	0	0	0	0	0	0	0	....	....	....	....	....	-99	0	0	....	0		0	0.0
Total	**3**	**32**	**61**	**11**	**18**	**1**	**0**	**0**	**8**	**6**	**10**	**1**	**0**	**.295**	**.358**	**.311**	**.670**	**73**	**-2**	**7**	**4.39**	**0**	**/3-15,S-5,1-1,2-1**	**2**	**-0.1**

• MICKELSON, Ed Edward Allen Mickelson b: 9/9/1926, Ottawa, IL BR/TR, 6'3", 205 lbs. Deb: 9/18/1950

YEAR	TM-L	G	AB	R	H	2B	3B	HR	RBI	BB	SO	SB	CS	AVG	OBP	SLG	OPS	OPS+	BR/A	RC	RC/G	FR	G/POS	WS	TPW
1950	StL-N	5	10	1	1	0	0	0	0	2	3	0	....	.100	.250	.100	.350	-4	-1	0	.68	1	/1-4	0	-0.1
1953	StL-A	7	15	1	2	1	0	0	2	2	6	0	0	.133	.235	.200	.435	18	-2	1	1.22	0	/1-3	0	-0.2
1957	Chi-N	6	12	0	0	0	0	0	1	0	4	0	0	.000	.000	.000	.000	-102	-3	0	.00	1	/1-2	0	-0.3
Total	**3**	**18**	**37**	**2**	**3**	**1**	**0**	**0**	**3**	**4**	**13**	**0**	**0**	**.081**	**.171**	**.108**	**.279**	**-23**	**-7**	**1**	**.67**	**1**	**/1-9**	**0**	**-0.6**

• MIDKIFF, Ezra Ezra Millington "Salt Rock" Midkiff b: 11/13/1882, Salt Rock, WV d: 3/20/1957, Huntington, WV BL/TR, 5'10", 180 lbs. Deb: 10/5/1909

YEAR	TM-L	G	AB	R	H	2B	3B	HR	RBI	BB	SO	SB	CS	AVG	OBP	SLG	OPS	OPS+	BR/A	RC	RC/G	FR	G/POS	WS	TPW
1909	Cin-N	1	2	0	0	0	0	0	0	0	....	0	....	.000	.000	.000	.000	-101	-0	0	.00	-1	/3-1	0	-0.1
1912	NY-A	21	86	9	21	1	0	0	9	7	....	4	....	.244	.301	.256	.557	56	-5	8	3.03	1	3-21	1	-0.3
1913	NY-A	83	284	22	56	9	1	0	14	12	33	9	....	.197	.232	.236	.468	37	-24	17	1.83	15	3-76/S-4,2-2	4	-0.6
Total	**3**	**105**	**372**	**31**	**77**	**10**	**1**	**0**	**23**	**19**	**33**	**13**	**....**	**.207**	**.247**	**.239**	**.487**	**41**	**-29**	**25**	**2.08**	**16**	**/3-98,S-4,2-2**	**5**	**-1.1**

• MIENTKIEWICZ, Doug Douglas Andrew Mientkiewicz b: 6/19/1974, Toledo, OH BL/TR, 6'2", 200 lbs. Deb: 9/18/1998

YEAR	TM-L	G	AB	R	H	2B	3B	HR	RBI	BB	SO	SB	CS	AVG	OBP	SLG	OPS	OPS+	BR/A	RC	RC/G	FR	G/POS	WS	TPW
1998	Min-A	8	25	1	5	1	0	0	2	4	3	1	1	.200	.310	.240	.550	45	-2	2	2.68	-1	/1-8	0	-0.3
1999	Min-A	118	327	34	75	21	3	2	32	43	51	1	1	.229	.326	.330	.656	66	-17	35	3.48	-0	*1-110	3	-2.4
2000	Min-A	3	14	0	6	0	0	0	4	0	0	0	0	.429	.429	.429	.857	114	0	2	5.87	-1	/1-3	0	0.0
2001	Min-A	151	543	77	166	39	1	15	74	67	92	2	6	.306	.391	.464	.855	121	17	99	6.70	3	*1-148/D-2	18	0.7
2002	*Min-A	143	467	60	122	29	1	10	64	74	69	1	2	.261	.369	.392	.761	102	3	72	5.36	2	*1-143	16	-0.6
2003	*Min-A	142	487	67	146	38	1	11	65	74	55	4	1	.300	.398	.450	.847	122	19	92	6.89	2	*1-139/0-3(0-0-3),2-1,3-1,D	20	0.8
Total	**6**	**565**	**1863**	**239**	**520**	**128**	**6**	**38**	**241**	**262**	**270**	**9**	**11**	**.279**	**.375**	**.415**	**.791**	**106**	**21**	**302**	**5.73**	**6**	**1-551/D-3,0-3,2-1,3-1**	**57**	**-1.9**

• MIERKOWICZ, Ed Edward Frank "Butch,Mouse" Mierkowicz b: 3/6/1924, Wyandotte, MI BR/TR, 6'4", 205 lbs. Deb: 8/31/1945 Career OF: 17-0-0

YEAR	TM-L	G	AB	R	H	2B	3B	HR	RBI	BB	SO	SB	CS	AVG	OBP	SLG	OPS	OPS+	BR/A	RC	RC/G	FR	G/POS	WS	TPW
1945	*Det-A	10	15	0	2	2	0	0	2	1	3	0	0	.133	.188	.267	.454	29	-1	1	1.70	0	/0-6(6-0-0)	0	-0.2
1947	Det-A	21	42	6	8	1	0	1	1	1	12	1	0	.190	.209	.286	.495	36	-4	2	1.60	-1	0-10(10-0-0)	0	-0.5
1948	Det-A	3	5	0	1	0	0	0	1	2	2	0	0	.200	.429	.200	.629	68	-0	0	2.38	0	/0-1	0	0.0
1950	StL-N	1	1	0	0	0	0	0	0	0	1	0	....	.000	.000	.000	.000	-95	-0	0	.00	0	....	0	0.0
Total	**4**	**35**	**63**	**6**	**11**	**3**	**0**	**1**	**4**	**4**	**18**	**1**	**0**	**.175**	**.224**	**.270**	**.494**	**36**	**-5**	**3**	**1.66**	**-1**	**/0-17**	**0**	**-0.7**

• MIESKE, Matt Mattew Todd Mieske b: 2/13/1968, Midland, MI BR/TR, 6', 192 lbs. Deb: 5/3/1993 Career OF: 142-25-397

YEAR	TM-L	G	AB	R	H	2B	3B	HR	RBI	BB	SO	SB	CS	AVG	OBP	SLG	OPS	OPS+	BR/A	RC	RC/G	FR	G/POS	WS	TPW
1993	Mil-A	23	58	9	14	0	0	3	7	4	14	0	2	.241	.290	.397	.687	84	-2	5	3.01	-1	0-22(1-9-12)	1	-0.4
1994	Mil-A	84	259	39	67	13	1	10	38	21	62	3	5	.259	.322	.432	.754	88	-7	34	4.45	2	0-80(6-0-80)/D-1	6	-0.8
1995	Mil-A	117	267	42	67	13	1	12	48	27	45	2	4	.251	.329	.442	.771	93	-5	37	4.58	5	*0-108(0-0-108)/D-2	6	-0.4
1996	Mil-A	127	374	46	104	24	3	14	64	26	76	1	5	.278	.328	.471	.799	95	-6	54	5.00	3	*0-122(9-10-108)	9	-0.8
1997	Mil-A	84	253	39	63	15	3	5	21	19	50	1	0	.249	.301	.391	.693	78	-8	27	3.56	-1	0-74(26-0-52)/D-5	2	-1.2
1998	Chi-N	77	97	16	29	7	0	1	12	11	17	0	0	.299	.376	.402	.778	101	1	16	6.11	-3	0-62(50-3-12)	3	-0.3
1999	Sea-A	24	41	11	15	0	0	4	7	2	9	0	0	.366	.395	.659	1.054	159	3	11	11.19	0	0-20(6-3-13)/D-1	2	0.3
	*Hou-N	54	109	13	31	5	0	5	22	6	22	0	0	.284	.322	.468	.790	98	-1	15	4.78	0	0-36(30-0-7)	3	-0.2
2000	Hou-N	62	81	7	14	1	2	1	5	7	17	0	0	.173	.247	.272	.519	29	-9	5	2.12	-2	0-18(14-0-4)	0	-1.1
	Ari-N	11	8	3	2	0	0	1	2	1	1	0	0	.250	.333	.625	.958	131	0	2	6.69	0	/0-1	0	0.1
	Yr.	73	89	10	16	1	2	2	7	8	18	0	0	.180	.255	.303	.558	40	-9	7	2.54	-1	0-19(14-0-5)	0	-1.0
Total	**8**	**663**	**1547**	**225**	**406**	**78**	**10**	**56**	**226**	**124**	**313**	**7**	**16**	**.262**	**.322**	**.434**	**.756**	**89**	**-35**	**206**	**4.54**	**4**	**0-543/D-9**	**32**	**-4.9**

• MIGGINS, Larry Lawrence Edward "Irish" Miggins b: 8/20/1925, Bronx, NY BR/TR, 6'4", 198 lbs. Deb: 10/3/1948

YEAR	TM-L	G	AB	R	H	2B	3B	HR	RBI	BB	SO	SB	CS	AVG	OBP	SLG	OPS	OPS+	BR/A	RC	RC/G	FR	G/POS	WS	TPW
1948	StL-N	1	1	1	0	0	0	0	0	0	0	0	....	.000	.000	.000	.000	-95	-0	0	.00	0	....	0	0.0
1952	StL-N	42	96	7	22	5	1	2	10	3	19	0	1	.229	.253	.365	.617	69	-5	9	3.20	-1	0-25(23-0-2)/1-1	1	-0.7
Total	**2**	**43**	**97**	**8**	**22**	**5**	**1**	**2**	**10**	**3**	**19**	**0**	**1**	**.227**	**.250**	**.361**	**.611**	**67**	**-5**	**9**	**3.16**	**-1**	**/0-25,1-1**	**1**	**-0.7**

• MIHALIC, John John Michael Mihalic b: 11/13/1911, Cleveland, OH d: 4/24/1987, Fort Oglethorpe, GA BR/TR, 5'11", 172 lbs. Deb: 9/18/1935

YEAR	TM-L	G	AB	R	H	2B	3B	HR	RBI	BB	SO	SB	CS	AVG	OBP	SLG	OPS	OPS+	BR/A	RC	RC/G	FR	G/POS	WS	TPW
1935	Was-A	6	22	4	5	3	0	0	6	2	3	1	0	.227	.292	.364	.655	71	-1	3	3.95	0	/S-6	1	0.0
1936	Was-A	25	88	15	21	2	1	0	8	14	14	2	1	.239	.343	.284	.627	60	-5	10	3.65	1	2-25	2	-0.2
1937	Was-A	38	107	13	27	5	2	0	8	17	9	2	1	.252	.355	.336	.691	79	-3	14	4.52	2	2-28/S-3	3	0.1
Total	**3**	**69**	**217**	**32**	**53**	**10**	**3**	**0**	**22**	**33**	**26**	**5**	**2**	**.244**	**.344**	**.318**	**.662**	**70**	**-9**	**26**	**4.10**	**3**	**/2-53,S-9**	**6**	**-0.1**

• MIKSIS, Eddie Edward Thomas Miksis b: 9/11/1926, Burlington, NJ BR/TR, 6'.5", 185 lbs. Deb: 6/17/1944 Career OF: 34-106-88

YEAR	TM-L	G	AB	R	H	2B	3B	HR	RBI	BB	SO	SB	CS	AVG	OBP	SLG	OPS	OPS+	BR/A	RC	RC/G	FR	G/POS	WS	TPW
1944	Bro-N	26	91	12	20	2	0	0	11	6	11	4	....	.220	.268	.242	.510	45	-7	6	2.27	-3	3-15,S-10	0	-0.9
1946	Bro-N	23	48	3	7	0	0	0	5	3	3	0	....	.146	.212	.146	.357	2	-6	1	.89	0	3-13/2-1	0	-0.7
1947	*Bro-N	45	86	18	23	1	0	4	10	9	8	0	....	.267	.337	.419	.755	96	-1	12	5.03	0	2-13,0-11(11-0-0)/3-5,S-2	3	-0.1
1948	Bro-N	86	221	28	47	7	1	2	16	19	27	5	....	.213	.278	.281	.559	50	-16	19	2.82	1	2-54,3-22/S-5	4	-1.2
1949	*Bro-N	50	113	17	25	5	0	1	6	7	8	3	....	.221	.267	.292	.559	48	-9	8	2.31	2	3-29/S-4,2-3,1-1	1	-0.6
1950	Bro-N	51	76	13	19	2	1	2	10	5	10	3	....	.250	.296	.382	.678	75	-3	8	3.51	-3	2-15,S-15/3-7	2	-0.5
1951	Bro-N	19	10	6	2	1	0	0	0	1	2	0	0	.200	.333	.300	.633	70	-0	1	4.04	0	/3-6,2-1	0	-0.1
	Chi-N	102	421	48	112	13	3	4	35	33	36	11	5	.266	.319	.340	.659	76	-14	46	3.78	-5	*2-102	9	-1.3
	Yr.	121	431	54	114	14	3	4	35	34	38	11	5	.265	.320	.339	.658	76	-14	48	3.79	-6	*2-103/3-6	9	-1.4
1952	Chi-N	93	383	44	89	20	1	2	19	20	32	4	4	.232	.272	.305	.578	59	-22	31	2.75	-8	2-54,S-40	4	-2.5
1953	Chi-N	142	577	61	145	17	6	8	39	33	59	13	4	.251	.293	.343	.636	64	-30	57	3.28	-11	2-92,S-53	5	-2.9
1954	Chi-N	38	99	9	20	3	0	2	3	3	9	1	0	.202	.225	.293	.518	33	-10	6	2.06	-1	2-21/3-2,0-1	1	-0.9
1955	Chi-N	131	481	52	113	14	2	9	41	32	55	3	6	.235	.283	.328	.611	62	-29	42	2.88	4	*0-111(0-76-41),3-18	7	-3.0
1956	Chi-N	114	356	54	85	10	3	9	27	32	40	4	2	.239	.303	.360	.663	79	-11	38	3.54	7	3-48,0-33(6-25-2),2-19/S-2	6	-0.4
1957	StL-N	49	38	3	8	0	0	1	2	7	7	0	0	.211	.333	.289	.623	68	-1	4	3.06	-2	0-31(11-3-18)	1	-0.4
	Bal-A	1	1	0	0	0	0	0	0	0	0	0	0	.000	.000	.000	.000	-107	-0	0	.00	0	....	0	0.0
1958	Bal-A	3	2	0	0	0	0	0	0	0	1	0	0	.000	.000	.000	.000	-106	-1	0	.00	-1	/S-1	0	-0.1
	Cin-N	69	50	15	7	0	0	0	4	5	5	1	1	.140	.218	.140	.358	-2	-8	2	.90	-2	0-32(5-2-27),3-14/2-7,S-5,1	1	-1.0
Total	**14**	**1042**	**3053**	**383**	**722**	**95**	**17**	**44**	**228**	**215**	**313**	**52**	**22**	**.236**	**.288**	**.322**	**.610**	**62**	**-167**	**283**	**3.06**	**-23**	**2-382,0-219,3-179,S-137/1-2**	**44**	**-16.6**

YEAR TM-L	G	AB	R	H	2B	3B	HR	RBI	BB	SO	SB	CS	AVG	OBP	SLG	OPS	OPS+	BR/A	RC	RC/G	FR	G/POS	WS	TPW
• MILAN, Clyde	Jesse Clyde "Deerfoot" Milan b: 3/25/1887, Linden, TN d: 3/3/1953, Orlando, FL BL/TR, 5'9", 168 lbs. Deb: 8/19/1907 M/C Career OF: 182-1635-88																							
1907 Was-A	48	183	22	51	3	3	0	9	8	....	8	....	.279	.323	.328	.651	117	3	23	4.49	1	O-47(0-30-17)	5	0.2
1908 Was-A	130	485	55	116	10	12	1	32	38	....	29	....	.239	.304	.315	.619	110	6	54	3.73	6	*O-122(0-122-0)	15	0.7
1909 Was-A	130	400	36	80	12	4	1	15	31	....	10	....	.200	.268	.258	.525	69	-14	32	2.39	3	*O-120(29-89-2)	3	-1.9
1910 Was-A	142	531	89	148	17	6	0	16	71	....	44	....	.279	.379	.333	.713	129	23	83	5.53	9	*O-142(0-142-0)	23	2.8
1911 Was-A	154	616	109	194	24	8	3	35	74	....	58	....	.315	.395	.394	.789	123	22	117	7.09	11	*O-154(0-154-0)	27	2.3
1912 Was-A	154	601	105	184	19	11	1	79	63	....	**88**	....	.306	.377	.379	.756	116	14	117	7.19	16	*O-154(0-154-0)	33	2.0
1913 Was-A	154	579	92	174	18	9	3	54	58	25	**75**	....	.301	.367	.378	.745	116	12	102	6.08	-5	*O-154(0-154-0)	28	-0.2
1914 Was-A	115	437	63	129	19	11	1	39	32	26	38	21	.295	.346	.396	.742	118	7	63	4.93	-8	*O-113(1-112-0)	19	-0.9
1915 Was-A	153	573	83	165	13	7	2	66	53	32	40	19	.288	.353	.346	.699	107	5	77	4.63	-9	*O-151(0-151-0)	22	-1.4
1916 Was-A	150	565	58	154	14	3	1	45	56	31	34	21	.273	.343	.313	.657	98	-2	66	3.85	5	*O-149(0-149-0)	18	-0.7
1917 Was-A	155	579	60	170	15	4	0	48	58	26	20	....	.294	.364	.333	.697	114	11	76	4.62	-13	*O-153(0-153-0)	22	-1.2
1918 Was-A	128	503	56	146	18	5	0	56	36	14	26	....	.290	.344	.346	.690	110	5	65	4.55	0	*O-124(0-124-0)	18	-0.3
1919 Was-A	88	321	43	92	12	6	0	37	40	16	11	....	.287	.371	.361	.732	107	4	46	5.00	-3	O-86(0-86-0)	9	-0.3
1920 Was-A	126	506	70	163	22	5	3	41	28	12	10	12	.322	.364	.403	.767	106	2	72	5.03	0	*O-123(115-0-8)	14	-0.3
1921 Was-A	113	406	55	117	19	11	1	40	37	13	4	5	.288	.351	.397	.747	95	-4	57	4.95	2	O-99(34-15-52)	10	-0.9
1922 Was-A	42	74	8	17	5	0	0	5	2	2	0	0	.230	.250	.297	.547	44	-6	5	2.51	2	O-12(3-0-9)	0	-0.5
Total 16	1982	7359	1004	2100	240	105	17	617	685	197	495	78	.285	.353	.353	.706	109	89	1055	4.98	17	*O-1903	266	-0.6
• MILAN, Horace	Horace Robert Milan b: 4/7/1894, Linden, TN d: 6/29/1955, Texarkana, AR BR/TR, 5'9", 175 lbs. Deb: 8/29/1915 Career OF: 25-4-4																							
1915 Was-A	11	27	6	11	1	1	0	7	8	7	2	....	.407	.543	.519	1.061	213	5	9	14.12	0	O-10(2-4-4)	3	0.4
1917 Was-A	31	73	8	21	3	1	0	9	4	9	4	....	.288	.342	.356	.698	114	1	10	4.72	-1	O-23(23-0-0)	2	-0.1
Total 2	42	100	14	32	4	2	0	16	12	16	6	....	.320	.404	.400	.804	144	6	18	6.87	-2	/O-33	5	0.3
• MILBOURNE, Larry	Lawrence William Milbourne b: 2/14/1951, Port Norris, NJ BB/TR, 6', 165 lbs. Deb: 4/6/1974																							
1974 Hou-N	112	136	31	38	2	1	0	9	10	14	6	2	.279	.329	.309	.638	83	-3	15	3.89	0	2-87/S-8,O-4(4-0-0)	4	0.0
1975 Hou-N	73	151	17	32	1	2	1	9	6	14	1	2	.212	.247	.265	.512	45	-12	9	1.88	-3	2-43,S-22	1	-1.2
1976 Hou-N	59	145	22	36	4	0	0	7	14	10	6	1	.248	.319	.276	.595	77	-3	14	3.29	3	2-32	4	0.2
1977 Sea-A	86	242	24	53	10	0	2	21	6	20	3	1	.219	.244	.285	.529	44	-19	17	2.21	4	2-41,S-40/3-1,D-1	3	-1.0
1978 Sea-A	93	234	31	53	6	2	2	20	9	6	5	7	.226	.255	.295	.550	55	-16	15	2.00	-1	3-32,S-23,2-15,D-10	2	-1.6
1979 Sea-A	123	356	40	99	13	4	2	26	19	20	5	3	.278	.315	.354	.669	79	-11	38	3.84	1	S-65,2-49,3-11	7	-0.4
1980 Sea-A	106	258	31	68	6	6	0	26	19	13	7	6	.264	.317	.333	.650	77	-9	26	3.14	3	2-38,S-34/D-8,3-6	4	-0.2
1981*NY-A	61	163	24	51	7	2	1	12	9	14	2	0	.313	.353	.399	.751	118	4	23	5.22	-3	S-39,2-14/3-3,D-3	6	0.5
1982 NY-A	14	27	2	4	1	0	0	0	1	4	0	1	.148	.179	.185	.364		-4	1	.85	-1	/S-9,2-3,3-3	0	-0.4
Min-A	29	98	9	23	1	1	0	1	7	8	1	1	.235	.286	.265	.551	51	-7	7	2.15	-1	2-26	1	-0.7
Cle-A	82	291	29	80	11	4	2	25	12	20	2	5	.275	.308	.361	.669	83	-9	29	3.26	0	2-63,S-21/3-9,D-1	4	-0.4
Yr.	125	416	40	107	13	5	2	26	20	32	3	7	.257	.295	.327	.621	71	-20	36	2.83	-2	2-92,S-30,3-12/D-1	5	-1.5
1983 Phi-N	41	66	3	16	0	1	0	4	4	7	2	1	.242	.286	.273	.558	56	-4	5	2.25	-3	2-27/S-8,3-3	1	-0.6
NY-A	31	70	5	14	4	0	0	2	5	10	1	1	.200	.263	.257	.520	46	-5	5	2.38	1	2-19/S-6,3-4	1	-0.3
1984 Sea-A	79	211	22	56	5	1	1	22	12	16	0	2	.265	.305	.313	.618	72	-9	19	2.90	-8	3-40,2-14/D-6,S-5	2	-1.7
Total 11	989	2448	290	623	71	24	11	184	133	176	41	33	.254	.295	.317	.612	70	-107	222	2.99	-9	2-471,S-280,3-112/D-29,O-4	40	-7.8
• MILES, Aaron	Aaron Wade Miles b: 12/15/1976, Pittsburg, CA BB/TR, 5'8", 170 lbs. Deb: 9/11/2003																							
2003 Chi-A	8	12	3	4	3	0	0	2	0	0	0	0	.333	.333	.583	.917	136	1	2	7.88	0	/2-3,D-2	1	0.1
• MILES, Dee	Wilson Daniel Miles b: 2/15/1909, Kellerman, AL d: 11/2/1976, Birmingham, AL BL/TR, 6', 175 lbs. Deb: 7/7/1935 Career OF: 52-110-165																							
1935 Was-A	60	215	28	57	5	2	0	29	7	13	6	4	.265	.291	.307	.598	57	-14	19	3.04	1	O-45(0-0-45)	1	-1.5
1936 Was-A	25	59	8	14	1	2	0	7	1	5	0	1	.237	.250	.322	.572	43	-6	4	2.49	0	O-10(1-0-9)	0	-0.6
1939 Phi-A	106	320	49	96	17	6	1	37	15	17	3	4	.300	.331	.400	.731	88	-8	42	4.71	-3	O-77(1-20-57)	6	-1.3
1940 Phi-A	88	236	26	71	9	6	1	23	8	18	1	1	.301	.327	.403	.729	90	-4	32	5.04	-2	O-50(15-18-18)	5	-0.8
1941 Phi-A	80	170	14	53	7	1	0	15	4	8	0	1	.312	.331	.365	.696	86	-4	20	4.32	1	O-35(25-2-8)	3	-0.5
1942 Phi-A	99	346	41	94	12	5	0	22	12	10	5	3	.272	.300	.335	.635	79	-11	36	3.69	-3	O-81(9-46-28)	7	-1.7
1943 Bos-A	45	121	9	26	2	2	0	10	3	3	0	2	.215	.234	.264	.498	45	-10	7	1.91	0	O-25(1-24-0)	1	-1.1
Total 7	503	1467	175	411	53	24	2	143	50	74	15	16	.280	.306	.353	.659	76	-57	159	3.88	-6	O-323	23	-7.5
• MILES, Don	Donald Ray Miles b: 3/13/1936, Indianapolis, IN BL/TR, 6'1", 210 lbs. Deb: 9/9/1958																							
1958 LA-N	8	22	2	4	0	0	0	0	0	6	0	0	.182	.217	.182	.399	7	-3	1	1.39	1	/O-5(5-0-0)	0	-0.2
• MILEY, Mike	Michael Wilfred Miley b: 3/30/1953, Yazoo City, MS d: 1/6/1977, Baton Rouge, LA BB/TR, 6'1", 185 lbs. Deb: 7/6/1975																							
1975 Cal-A	70	224	17	39	3	2	4	26	16	54	0	1	.174	.232	.259	.491	42	-18	13	1.77	-3	S-70	2	-1.3
1976 Cal-A	14	38	4	7	2	0	0	4	4	8	1	0	.184	.262	.237	.499	50	-2	3	2.05	-1	S-14	0	-0.2
Total 2	84	262	21	46	5	2	4	30	20	62	1	1	.176	.237	.256	.492	43	-20	16	1.81	-4	/S-84	2	-1.5
• MILLAN, Felix	Felix Bernardo (Martinez) Millan b: 8/21/1943, Yabucoa, Puerto Rico BR/TR, 5'11", 172 lbs. Deb: 6/2/1966																							
1966 Atl-N	37	91	20	25	6	0	0	5	2	6	3	1	.275	.290	.341	.631	73	-3	8	3.11	-2	2-25/3-1,S-1	1	-0.3
1967 Atl-N	41	136	13	32	3	3	2	6	4	10	0	3	.235	.268	.346	.613	75	-6	11	2.64	4	2-41	3	0.2
1968 Atl-N	149	570	49	165	22	2	1	33	22	26	6	6	.289	.323	.340	.663	99	-2	58	3.55	11	*2-145	17	2.5
1969*Atl-N★	162	652	98	174	23	5	6	57	34	35	14	3	.267	.311	.345	.656	83	-13	69	3.64	9	*2-162	19	0.7
1970 Atl-N★	142	590	100	183	25	5	2	37	35	23	16	5	.310	.354	.380	.734	91	-6	79	4.83	-13	*2-142	15	-1.0
1971 Atl-N★	143	577	65	167	20	8	2	45	37	22	11	7	.289	.335	.362	.698	92	-7	69	4.16	10	*2-141	18	1.4
1972 Atl-N	125	498	46	128	19	3	1	38	23	28	6	4	.257	.294	.313	.607	66	-22	46	3.16	-1	*2-120	9	-1.7
1973*NY-N	153	638	82	185	23	4	3	37	35	22	2	2	.290	.333	.353	.686	92	-8	72	3.92	4	*2-153	20	0.7
1974 NY-N	136	518	50	139	15	2	1	33	31	14	5	1	.268	.320	.311	.630	78	-15	53	3.40	-16	*2-134	13	-2.2
1975 NY-N	162	676	81	191	37	2	1	56	36	28	1	6	.283	.330	.348	.678	92	-11	75	3.83	-22	*2-162	17	-2.2
1976 NY-N	139	531	55	150	25	2	1	35	41	19	2	4	.282	.342	.343	.685	100	-1	60	4.00	-16	*2-136	16	-0.8
1977 NY-N	91	314	40	78	11	2	2	21	18	9	1	1	.248	.296	.315	.611	67	-15	28	3.05	-4	2-89	4	-1.5
Total 12	1480	5791	699	1617	229	38	22	403	318	242	67	43	.279	.324	.343	.667	87	-108	628	3.75	-37	*2-1450/3-1,S-1	152	-4.3
• MILLAR, Kevin	Kevin Charles Millar b: 9/24/1971, Los Angeles, CA BR/TR, 6'1", 210 lbs. Deb: 4/11/1998 Career OF: 153-0-101																							
1998 Fla-N	2	2	1	1	0	0	0	0	1	0	0	0	.500	.667	.500	1.167	222	1	1	22.68	0	/3-2	0	0.0
1999 Fla-N	105	351	48	100	17	4	9	67	40	64	1	0	.285	.369	.433	.802	108	5	58	5.88	-2	1-94/3-1,O-1	12	-0.4
2000 Fla-N	123	259	36	67	14	3	14	42	36	47	0	0	.259	.366	.498	.864	121	9	49	6.67	5	1-34,O-18(17-0-1),3-13/D-6	10	1.0
2001 Fla-N	144	449	62	141	39	5	20	85	39	70	0	0	.314	.375	.557	.932	141	27	94	7.95	-7	O-86(27-0-66),1-15,3-10/D-6	20	1.3
2002 Fla-N	126	438	58	134	41	0	16	57	40	74	0	2	.306	.371	.509	.880	134	20	79	6.51	-1	*O-108(89-0-22)/D-6,1-2,3	14	1.3
2003*Bos-A	148	544	83	150	30	1	25	96	60	108	3	2	.276	.353	.472	.825	113	10	90	5.79	8	*1-101,O-31(19-0-12),D-19	16	0.6
Total 6	648	2043	288	593	141	13	84	347	216	363	4	4	.290	.367	.495	.862	124	70	370	6.53	2	1-246,O-244/D-37,3-28	72	3.9
• MILLARD, Frank	Frank E. Millard b: 7/4/1865, East St. Louis, IL d: 7/4/1892, Dallas, TX Deb: 5/4/1890																							
1890 StL-a	1	1	0	0	0	0	0	0	1	....	0	....	.000	.500	.000	.500	42	0	0	.00	0	/2-1	0	0.0
• MILLER, Bill	William Alexander Miller b: 5/23/1879, Bad Schwalbach, Germany d: 9/9/1957, Ashtabula, OH BL/TL, 6'2", 170 lbs. Deb: 8/23/1902																							
1902 Pit-N	1	5	0	1	0	0	0	2	0	....	0	....	.200	.200	.200	.400	23	-0	0	1.36	0	/O-1	0	-0.1
• MILLER, Bing	Edmund John Miller b: 8/30/1894, Vinton, IA d: 5/7/1966, Philadelphia, PA BR/TR, 6', 185 lbs. Deb: 4/16/1921 C Career OF: 380-242-997																							
1921 Was-A	114	420	57	121	28	8	9	71	25	50	3	4	.288	.334	.457	.791	105	1	63	5.22	-2	*O-109(92-3-14)	12	-0.9
1922 Phi-A	143	535	90	179	29	12	21	90	24	42	10	10	.335	.371	.551	.922	134	22	104	7.24	5	*O-139(15-90-36)	22	1.9
1923 Phi-A	123	458	68	137	25	4	12	64	27	34	9	3	.299	.344	.450	.793	106	4	71	5.54	-4	*O-119(104-0-15)	15	-0.9
1924 Phi-A	113	398	62	136	22	4	6	62	12	24	11	5	.342	.376	.462	.839	114	8	69	6.31	-2	O-94(10-9-75)/1-7	13	-0.1
1925 Phi-A	124	474	78	151	29	10	10	81	19	14	11	6	.319	.355	.485	.841	105	1	80	6.05	-6	*O-115(22-0-96),1-12	13	-1.3
1926 Phi-A	38	110	13	32	6	2	2	13	11	6	4	1	.291	.355	.436	.792	100	0	18	5.42	-1	O-34(10-0-26)/1-1	3	-0.2
StL-A	94	353	60	117	27	5	4	50	22	12	7	9	.331	.382	.470	.852	116	6	61	6.15	2	O-94(26-16-54)	11	0.1

YEAR TM-L	G	AB	R	H	2B	3B	HR	RBI	BB	SO	SB	CS	AVG	OBP	SLG	OPS	OPS+	BR/A	RC	RC/G	FR	G/POS	WS	TPW
Yr.	132	463	73	149	33	7	6	63	33	18	11	10	.322	.376	.462	.838	112	6	79	5.97	2	*O-128(36-16-80)/1-1	14	-0.1
1927 StL-A	143	492	83	160	32	7	5	75	30	26	8	7	.325	.375	.449	.824	109	5	82	6.03	1	*O-126(37-61-29)	15	-0.1
1928 Phi-A	139	510	76	168	34	7	8	85	27	24	10	6	.329	.372	.471	.843	117	12	88	6.39	-4	*O-133(28-43-66)	20	-0.1
1929*Phi-A	147	556	84	184	32	16	8	93	40	25	24	9	.331	.380	.489	.869	118	16	104	6.97	-1	*O-145(9-4-133)	23	0.3
1930*Phi-A	154	585	89	177	38	7	9	100	47	22	13	13	.303	.357	.438	.795	96	-6	90	5.40	3	*O-154(0-13-142)	17	-1.3
1931*Phi-A	137	534	75	150	43	5	8	77	36	16	5	3	.281	.338	.425	.763	94	-4	77	5.23	2	*O-137(0-0-137)	15	-0.9
1932 Phi-A	95	305	40	90	17	4	7	58	20	11	7	3	.295	.343	.446	.788	99	-1	47	5.59	2	O-84(5-0-79)	8	-0.3
1933 Phi-A	67	120	22	33	7	1	2	17	12	7	4	2	.275	.346	.400	.746	96	-1	17	5.06	0	O-30(10-3-18)/1-6	3	-0.2
1934 Phi-A	81	177	22	43	10	2	1	22	16	14	1	0	.243	.309	.339	.648	70	-8	19	3.76	0	O-46(4-0-42)	2	-0.9
1935 Bos-A	78	138	18	42	8	1	3	26	10	8	0	1	.304	.356	.442	.798	99	-1	22	5.60	1	O-29(1-0-28)	3	-0.2
1936 Bos-A	30	47	9	14	2	1	1	6	5	5	0	0	.298	.377	.447	.824	97	-0	8	6.24	0	O-13(7-0-7)	1	0.0
Total 16	**1820**	**6212**	**946**	**1934**	**389**	**96**	**116**	**990**	**383**	**340**	**127**	**82**	**.311**	**.359**	**.461**	**.820**	**108**	**54**	**1020**	**5.92**	**-2**	***O-1601/1-26**	**196**	**-5.3**

• MILLER, Bruce Charles Bruce Miller b: 3/4/1947, Fort Wayne, IN BR/TR, 6'1", 185 lbs. Deb: 8/4/1973

YEAR TM-L	G	AB	R	H	2B	3B	HR	RBI	BB	SO	SB	CS	AVG	OBP	SLG	OPS	OPS+	BR/A	RC	RC/G	FR	G/POS	WS	TPW
1973 SF-N	12	21	1	3	0	0	0	2	2	3	0	0	.143	.217	.143	.360	2	-3	1	1.06	-1	/3-4,2-3,S-1	0	-0.3
1974 SF-N	73	198	19	55	7	1	0	16	11	15	1	1	.278	.319	.323	.642	76	-7	19	3.31	3	3-41,S-13/2-9	4	-0.2
1975 SF-N	99	309	22	74	6	3	1	31	15	26	0	1	.239	.277	.288	.565	55	-20	21	2.27	2	3-68,2-21/S-6	3	-1.7
1976 SF-N	12	25	1	4	1	0	0	2	2	5	0	0	.160	.222	.200	.422	20	-3	1	1.50	0	/2-8,3-2	0	-0.3
Total 4	**196**	**553**	**43**	**136**	**14**	**4**	**1**	**51**	**30**	**49**	**1**	**2**	**.246**	**.287**	**.291**	**.578**	**59**	**-32**	**42**	**2.55**	**3**	**3-115/2-41,S-20**	**7**	**-2.6**

• MILLER, Charlie Charles Hess Miller b: 12/30/1877, Conestoga, PA d: 1/13/1951, Millersville, PA BR/TR, 6', 190 lbs. Deb: 10/2/1915

YEAR TM-L	G	AB	R	H	2B	3B	HR	RBI	BB	SO	SB	CS	AVG	OBP	SLG	OPS	OPS+	BR/A	RC	RC/G	FR	G/POS	WS	TPW
1915 Bal-F	1	1	0	0	0	0	0	0	0	0	0	....	.000	.000	.000	.000	-93	-0	0	.00	0	....	0	0.0

• MILLER, Charlie Charles Elmer Miller b: 1/4/1892, Warrensburg, MO d: 4/23/1972, Warrensburg, MO TR Deb: 9/18/1912

YEAR TM-L	G	AB	R	H	2B	3B	HR	RBI	BB	SO	SB	CS	AVG	OBP	SLG	OPS	OPS+	BR/A	RC	RC/G	FR	G/POS	WS	TPW
1912 StL-A	1	2	0	0	0	0	0	0	0	....	0	....	.000	.000	.000	.000	-104	-1	0	.00	0	/S-1	0	0.0

• MILLER, Chuck Charles Marion Miller b: 9/18/1889, Woodville, OH d: 6/16/1961, Houston, TX BL/TL, 5'8.5", 155 lbs. Deb: 9/19/1913 Career OF: 8-5-3

YEAR TM-L	G	AB	R	H	2B	3B	HR	RBI	BB	SO	SB	CS	AVG	OBP	SLG	OPS	OPS+	BR/A	RC	RC/G	FR	G/POS	WS	TPW
1913 StL-N	4	12	0	2	0	0	0	1	0	2	0	....	.167	.167	.167	.333	-5	-2	0	.75	0	/O-3(2-0-1)	0	-0.2
1914 StL-N	36	36	4	7	1	0	0	2	3	9	2	....	.194	.256	.222	.479	43	-3	2	2.07	-0	O-14(6-5-2)	0	-0.3
Total 2	**40**	**48**	**4**	**9**	**1**	**0**	**0**	**3**	**3**	**11**	**2**	**....**	**.188**	**.235**	**.208**	**.444**	**32**	**-4**	**3**	**1.73**	**0**	**/O-17**	**0**	**-0.5**

• MILLER, Corky Abraham Philip Miller b: 3/18/1976, Yucaipa, CA BR/TR, 6'1", 220 lbs. Deb: 9/4/2001

YEAR TM-L	G	AB	R	H	2B	3B	HR	RBI	BB	SO	SB	CS	AVG	OBP	SLG	OPS	OPS+	BR/A	RC	RC/G	FR	G/POS	WS	TPW
2001 Cin-N	17	49	5	9	2	0	3	7	4	16	1	0	.184	.273	.408	.681	70	-2	6	3.57	4	C-17	2	0.2
2002 Cin-N	39	114	9	29	10	0	3	15	9	20	0	0	.254	.331	.421	.752	94	-1	14	4.04	4	C-38	5	0.6
2003 Cin-N	14	30	4	8	0	0	0	1	5	7	0	0	.267	.405	.267	.672	82	-0	4	4.29	2	C-11	1	0.2
Total 3	**70**	**193**	**18**	**46**	**12**	**0**	**6**	**23**	**18**	**43**	**1**	**0**	**.238**	**.329**	**.394**	**.723**	**86**	**-4**	**24**	**3.95**	**10**	**/C-66**	**8**	**1.0**

• MILLER, Damian Damian Donald Miller b: 10/13/1969, La Crosse, WI BR/TR, 6'3", 202 lbs. Deb: 8/10/1997

YEAR TM-L	G	AB	R	H	2B	3B	HR	RBI	BB	SO	SB	CS	AVG	OBP	SLG	OPS	OPS+	BR/A	RC	RC/G	FR	G/POS	WS	TPW
1997 Min-A	25	66	5	18	1	0	2	13	2	12	0	0	.273	.294	.379	.673	73	-3	7	3.50	-1	C-20/D-3	2	-0.3
1998 Ari-N	57	168	17	48	14	2	3	14	11	43	1	0	.286	.337	.446	.783	104	1	26	5.58	1	C-46/D-2,O-2(0-0-2),1-1	6	0.5
1999 Ari-N	86	296	35	80	19	0	11	47	19	78	0	0	.270	.319	.446	.765	90	-6	41	4.85	2	C-86	10	0.2
2000 Ari-N	100	324	43	89	24	0	10	44	36	74	2	2	.275	.349	.441	.790	95	-3	50	5.49	-3	C-97/1-2	11	0.0
2001*Ari-N	123	380	45	103	19	0	13	47	35	80	0	1	.271	.339	.424	.763	90	-6	53	4.92	24	*C-121	10	2.5
2002*Ari-N★	101	297	40	74	22	0	11	42	38	88	0	0	.249	.340	.434	.775	94	-2	41	4.68	4	*C-100	10	0.8
2003*Chi-N	114	352	34	82	19	1	9	36	39	91	1	0	.233	.311	.369	.681	78	-12	38	3.54	15	*C-114	11	1.1
Total 7	**606**	**1883**	**219**	**494**	**118**	**3**	**59**	**243**	**180**	**466**	**4**	**3**	**.262**	**.331**	**.422**	**.753**	**90**	**-31**	**256**	**4.69**	**41**	**C-584/D-5,1-3,O-2**	**60**	**4.8**

• MILLER, Darrell Darrell Keith Miller b: 2/26/1958, Washington, DC BR/TR, 6'2", 200 lbs. Deb: 8/14/1984 Career OF: 34-8-54

YEAR TM-L	G	AB	R	H	2B	3B	HR	RBI	BB	SO	SB	CS	AVG	OBP	SLG	OPS	OPS+	BR/A	RC	RC/G	FR	G/POS	WS	TPW
1984 Cal-A	17	41	5	7	0	0	0	1	4	9	0	0	.171	.244	.171	.415	17	-4	2	1.56	0	1-16/O-1	0	-0.6
1985 Cal-A	51	48	8	18	2	1	2	7	1	10	0	1	.375	.400	.583	.983	166	4	11	9.44	0	O-45(1-3-41)/D-4,3-1,C-1	3	0.3
1986 Cal-A	33	57	6	13	2	1	0	4	4	8	0	0	.228	.279	.298	.577	58	-3	4	2.36	-1	O-23(11-3-9),C-10/D-2	0	-0.5
1987 Cal-A	53	108	14	26	5	0	4	16	9	13	1	0	.241	.311	.398	.709	89	-2	13	3.71	0	C-33,O-18(14-0-4)/3-1,D-1	2	-0.1
1988 Cal-A	70	140	21	31	4	1	2	7	9	29	2	1	.221	.292	.307	.599	70	-6	13	3.19	-1	C-53/O-8(7-2-0),D-1	3	-0.4
Total 5	**224**	**394**	**54**	**95**	**13**	**3**	**8**	**35**	**27**	**69**	**3**	**2**	**.241**	**.303**	**.350**	**.653**	**79**	**-11**	**43**	**3.65**	**-2**	**/C-97,O-95,1-16,D-8,3-2**	**8**	**-1.3**

• MILLER, Doc Roy Oscar Miller b: 2/4/1883, Chatham, Canada d: 7/31/1938, Jersey City, NJ BL/TL, 5'10.5", 170 lbs. Deb: 5/4/1910 Career OF: 29-6-395

YEAR TM-L	G	AB	R	H	2B	3B	HR	RBI	BB	SO	SB	CS	AVG	OBP	SLG	OPS	OPS+	BR/A	RC	RC/G	FR	G/POS	WS	TPW
1910 Chi-N	1	1	0	0	0	0	0	0	0	0	0	....	.000	.000	.000	.000	-101	-0	0	.00	0	....	0	0.0
Bos-N	130	482	48	138	27	4	3	55	33	52	17	....	.286	.333	.378	.711	103	-0	66	4.75	-5	*O-130(6-0-127)	10	-1.2
Yr.	131	483	48	138	27	4	3	55	33	52	17	....	.286	.333	.377	.710	102	-0	66	4.74	-5	*O-130(6-0-127)	10	-1.2
1911 Bos-N	146	577	69	**192**	36	3	7	91	43	43	32	....	.333	.379	.442	.821	120	14	107	7.02	1	*O-146(0-3-143)	18	0.7
1912 Bos-N	51	201	26	47	8	1	2	24	14	17	6	....	.234	.287	.313	.600	63	-11	20	3.13	2	O-50(0-0-50)	1	-1.1
Phi-N	67	177	24	51	12	5	0	21	9	13	3	....	.288	.323	.412	.735	94	-2	24	4.70	2	O-40(0-0-40)	4	-0.3
Yr.	118	378	50	98	20	6	2	45	23	30	9	....	.259	.303	.360	.663	77	-13	44	3.83	4	O-90(0-0-90)	5	-1.4
1913 Phi-N	69	87	9	30	6	0	0	11	6	6	2	....	.345	.400	.414	.814	127	3	14	6.44	-3	O-12(0-0-12)	3	-0.1
1914 Cin-N	93	192	8	49	7	2	0	33	16	18	4	....	.255	.313	.313	.625	83	-4	19	3.41	-2	O-47(23-3-23)	4	-0.8
Total 5	**557**	**1717**	**184**	**507**	**96**	**15**	**12**	**235**	**121**	**149**	**64**	**....**	**.295**	**.343**	**.390**	**.733**	**102**	**-1**	**251**	**5.17**	**-5**	**O-425**	**40**	**-2.8**

• MILLER, Doggie George Frederick "Foghorn,Calliope" Miller
b: 8/15/1864, Brooklyn, NY d: 4/6/1909, Brooklyn, NY BR/TR, 5'6", 145 lbs. Deb: 5/1/1884 U Career OF: 146-68-96

YEAR TM-L	G	AB	R	H	2B	3B	HR	RBI	BB	SO	SB	CS	AVG	OBP	SLG	OPS	OPS+	BR/A	RC	RC/G	FR	G/POS	WS	TPW
1884 Pit-a	89	347	46	78	10	2	0	0	13	....	....	....	.225	.257	.265	.522	69	-12	24	2.48	0	O-49(48-0-1),C-36/3-3,2-1	4	-1.0
1885 Pit-a	42	166	19	27	3	1	0	13	4	....	....	....	.163	.182	.193	.375	19	-15	6	1.16	-4	C-33/O-6(3-3-0),3-2,S-2	2	-1.5
1886 Pit-a	83	317	70	80	15	1	2	36	43	....	35	....	.252	.343	.325	.668	110	6	49	5.54	-13	C-61,O-23(12-10-1)/2-1	11	-0.3
1887 Pit-N	87	377	58	118	17	4	1	34	35	13	33	....	.313	.317	.325	.641	83	-6	47	4.78	-16	C-73,O-14(2-11-1)/3-1	8	-1.4
1888 Pit-N	103	404	50	112	17	5	0	36	18	16	27	....	.277	.319	.344	.663	121	10	54	5.02	-7	C-68,O-32(25-5-2)/3-4	15	0.7
1889 Pit-N	104	422	77	113	25	3	6	56	31	11	16	....	.268	.321	.384	.705	107	4	59	5.02	-4	C-76,O-27(6-5-16)/3-3	13	0.5
1890 Pit-N	138	549	85	150	24	3	4	66	68	11	32	....	.273	.357	.350	.707	120	18	82	5.45	-0	3-88,O-25(1-2-22),S-13,C-10/2	13	1.9
1891 Pit-N	135	548	80	156	19	6	4	57	59	26	35	....	.285	.357	.363	.721	113	10	86	5.90	-9	C-41,S-37,3-34,O-24(22-0-2)/1	17	0.5
1892 Pit-N	149	623	103	158	15	12	2	59	69	14	28	....	.254	.335	.326	.661	99	1	79	4.60	-1	O-76(24-30-23),C-63,S-19/3	24	0.2
1893 Pit-N	41	154	23	28	6	1	0	17	17	8	3	....	.182	.284	.234	.518	39	-13	11	2.39	-1	C-40	2	-0.8
1894 StL-N	127	481	93	163	9	11	8	86	58	9	17	....	.339	.414	.453	.868	109	9	100	8.16	-6	3-52,C-41,2-18,1-12/O-4(2-0-2),S	13	0.6
1895 StL-N	122	494	81	144	15	4	5	74	25	12	18	....	.291	.333	.368	.702	82	-14	68	5.27	-10	3-46,C-46,O-21(0-0-21)/S-9,1	7	-1.6
1896 Lou-N	98	324	54	89	17	4	1	33	27	9	16	....	.275	.334	.361	.695	87	-6	46	5.11	3	C-48,2-25/3-8,O-8(1-2-5),1,S	6	0.1
Total 13	**1318**	**5206**	**839**	**1416**	**192**	**57**	**33**	**567**	**467**	**129**	**260**	**....**	**.272**	**.333**	**.345**	**.678**	**97**	**-9**	**711**	**5.00**	**-67**	**C-636,O-309,3-243/S-83,2-51,1**	**135**	**-2.1**

• MILLER, Dots John Barney Miller b: 9/9/1886, Kearny, NJ d: 9/5/1923, Saranac Lake, NY BR/TR, 5'11.5", 170 lbs. Deb: 4/16/1909

YEAR TM-L	G	AB	R	H	2B	3B	HR	RBI	BB	SO	SB	CS	AVG	OBP	SLG	OPS	OPS+	BR/A	RC	RC/G	FR	G/POS	WS	TPW
1909*Pit-N	151	560	71	156	31	13	3	87	39	....	14	....	.279	.329	.396	.725	119	10	78	4.69	4	*2-150	24	1.7
1910 Pit-N	120	444	45	101	13	10	1	48	33	41	11	....	.227	.284	.309	.592	68	-19	43	3.04	-5	*2-119/1-1,S-1	7	-2.4
1911 Pit-N	137	470	82	126	17	8	6	78	51	48	17	....	.268	.348	.377	.725	99	-1	69	4.83	7	*2-129	16	0.9
1912 Pit-N	148	567	74	156	33	12	4	87	37	45	18	....	.275	.324	.397	.721	98	-4	78	4.62	5	*1-147	14	-0.1
1913 Pit-N	154	580	75	158	24	20	7	90	37	52	20	....	.272	.317	.419	.736	114	8	81	4.60	1	*1-150/S-3	18	0.6
1914 StL-N	155	573	67	166	27	10	4	88	34	52	16	....	.290	.339	.393	.732	119	12	79	4.84	11	1-91,S-60/2-5	21	2.7
1915 StL-N	150	553	73	146	17	10	2	72	43	48	27	19	.264	.324	.342	.666	101	-2	65	3.85	4	1-94,2-55/3-9,S-3	16	0.2
1916 StL-N	143	505	47	120	22	7	1	46	40	49	18	....	.238	.300	.315	.615	89	-6	54	3.55	4	1-93,2-38,S-21/3-1	12	-0.2
1917 StL-N	148	544	61	135	15	9	2	45	33	52	14	....	.248	.295	.320	.615	91	-7	54	3.28	12	2-92,1-46,S-11	15	0.7
1919 StL-N	101	346	38	80	10	4	1	24	13	23	6	....	.231	.265	.292	.557	72	-13	28	2.60	0	1-68,2-28	4	-1.5
1920 Phi-N	98	343	41	87	12	2	1	27	16	17	13	6	.254	.289	.309	.598	68	-13	31	2.99	-14	2-59,3-17,S-12/1-9,O-1	4	-2.6
1921 Phi-N	84	320	37	95	11	3	0	23	15	27	3	5	.297	.330	.350	.680	74	-12	36	4.02	-1	3-41,1-38/2-6	4	-1.3
Total 12	**1589**	**5805**	**711**	**1526**	**232**	**108**	**32**	**715**	**391**	**454**	**177**	**30**	**.263**	**.314**	**.357**	**.671**	**96**	**-46**	**696**	**3.98**	**29**	**1-737,2-681,S-111/3-68,O-1**	**155**	**-1.2**

YEAR TM-L	G	AB	R	H	2B	3B	HR	RBI	BB	SO	SB	CS	AVG	OBP	SLG	OPS	OPS+	BR/A	RC	RC/G	FR	G/POS	WS	TPW
• MILLER, Dusty	Dakin Evans Miller b: 9/3/1876, Malvern, IA d: 4/19/1950, Stockton, CA BL/TR, 5'10", 175 lbs. Deb: 4/17/1902																							
1902 Chi-N	51	187	17	46	4	1	0	13	7	....	10	....	.246	.299	.278	.577	80	-4	20	3.56	2	0-51(46-1-4)	4	-0.5
• MILLER, Dusty	Charles Bradley Miller b: 9/10/1868, Oil City, PA d: 9/3/1945, Memphis, TN BL/TR, 5'11.5", 170 lbs. Deb: 9/23/1889 Career OF: 13-39-594																							
1889 Bal-a	11	40	4	6	1	1	0	6	2	11	3	....	.150	.209	.225	.434	24	-4	3	2.01	-6	/S-8,0-3(2-1-0)	0	-0.8
1890 StL-a	26	96	17	21	5	3	1	10	8	....	4	....	.219	.279	.365	.643	78	-4	11	3.94	2	0-24(9-15-0)/S-3	2	-0.3
1895 Cin-N	132	529	103	177	31	16	10	112	33	34	43	....	.335	.378	.510	.888	123	14	122	9.16	9	*0-132(0-11-121)	18	1.3
1896 Cin-N	125	504	91	162	38	12	4	93	33	30	76	....	.321	.368	.468	.836	112	6	119	8.73	-3	*0-125(1-0-124)	19	-0.3
1897 Cin-N	119	440	83	139	27	1	4	70	48	....	29	....	.316	.393	.409	.802	105	4	87	7.14	-3	*0-119(0-0-119)	15	-0.4
1898 Cin-N	152	586	99	175	24	12	3	90	38	....	32	....	.299	.351	.396	.747	106	3	97	5.97	5	*0-152(0-0-152)	21	0.0
1899 Cin-N	81	327	45	83	12	6	0	37	9	....	18	....	.254	.280	.327	.607	64	-18	36	3.81	2	0-80(1-2-78)	5	-1.8
StL-N	10	39	3	8	1	0	0	3	3	....	1	....	.205	.279	.231	.510	39	-3	3	2.52	-1	0-10(0-10-0)	0	-0.4
Yr.	91	366	48	91	13	6	0	40	12	....	19	....	.249	.280	.317	.597	61	-21	39	3.66	2	0-90(1-12-78)	5	-2.2
Total 7	**656**	**2561**	**445**	**771**	**139**	**51**	**22**	**421**	**174**	**75**	**206**	....	**.301**	**.353**	**.421**	**.774**	**102**	**-2**	**477**	**6.81**	**6**	**0-645/S-11**	**80**	**-2.8**
• MILLER, Ed	L. Edward Miller b: Tecumseh, MI Deb: 7/18/1884																							
1884 Tol-a	8	24	2	6	0	0	0	1	1	....	....	....	.250	.280	.250	.530	72	-1	2	2.63	0	/0-8(6-1-2)	0	-0.1
• MILLER, Ed	Edwin Collins "Big Ed" Miller b: 11/24/1888, Annville, PA d: 4/17/1980, Lebanon, PA BR/TR, 6', 180 lbs. Deb: 6/29/1912 Career OF: 1-0-8																							
1912 StL-A	13	46	4	9	1	0	0	5	2	....	1	....	.196	.245	.217	.462	34	-4	3	1.85	-4	/1-8,S-5	0	-0.8
1914 StL-A	41	58	8	8	0	1	0	4	4	13	1	3	.138	.219	.172	.391	18	-7	2	1.07	-2	/1-8,2-5,0-5(0-0-5),3-2	0	-1.0
1918 Cle-A	32	96	9	22	4	3	0	3	12	10	2	....	.229	.321	.333	.654	89	-1	11	3.54	1	1-22/0-4(1-0-3)	2	-0.1
Total 3	**86**	**200**	**21**	**39**	**5**	**4**	**0**	**12**	**18**	**23**	**4**	**3**	**.195**	**.275**	**.260**	**.535**	**56**	**-12**	**16**	**2.34**	**-5**	**/1-38,0-9,2-5,S-5,3-2**	**2**	**-1.9**
• MILLER, Eddie	Edward Lee Miller b: 6/29/1957, San Pablo, CA BB/TR, 5'9", 175 lbs. Deb: 9/5/1977 Career OF: 32-49-16																							
1977 Tex-A	17	6	7	2	0	0	0	1	1	1	3	1	.333	.429	.333	.762	110	0	1	5.89	-0	/D-3,0-2(0-2-0)	0	0.0
1978 Atl-N	6	21	5	3	1	0	0	2	2	4	3	0	.143	.250	.190	.440	22	-2	2	2.38	0	/0-5(2-3-0)	0	-0.2
1979 Atl-N	27	113	12	35	1	0	0	5	5	24	15	2	.310	.350	.319	.669	78	-1	15	4.78	0	0-27(1-27-0)	3	-0.1
1980 Atl-N	11	19	3	3	0	0	0	0	0	5	1	2	.158	.158	.158	.316	-11	-4	0	.28	-1	/0-9(1-8-0)	0	-0.5
1981 Atl-N	50	134	29	31	3	1	0	7	7	29	23	5	.231	.285	.269	.553	56	-5	12	2.99	0	0-36(28-2-7)	2	-0.7
1982 Det-A	14	25	3	1	0	0	0	0	4	4	0	3	.040	.250	.040	.290	-14	-5	1	.49	0	/0-8(0-3-5),D-1	0	-0.5
1984 SD-N	13	14	4	4	0	1	1	2	0	4	4	0	.286	.286	.643	.929	155	2	3	8.55	1	/0-8(0-4-4)	1	0.3
Total 7	**138**	**332**	**63**	**79**	**5**	**2**	**1**	**17**	**19**	**71**	**49**	**13**	**.238**	**.297**	**.274**	**.571**	**56**	**-14**	**34**	**3.32**	**1**	**/0-95,D-4**	**6**	**-1.6**
• MILLER, Eddie	Edward Robert "Eppie" Miller b: 11/26/1916, Pittsburgh, PA d: 7/31/1997, Lake Worth, FL BR/TR, 5'9", 180 lbs. Deb: 9/9/1936																							
1936 Cin-N	5	10	0	1	0	0	0	0	1	1	0	....	.100	.182	.100	.282	-24	-2	0	.70	-1	/S-4,2-1	0	-0.2
1937 Cin-N	36	60	3	9	3	1	0	5	3	8	0	....	.150	.190	.233	.424	15	-7	2	.81	-2	S-30/3-4	1	-0.8
1939 Bos-N	77	296	32	79	12	2	4	31	16	21	4	....	.267	.315	.361	.677	88	-6	33	3.84	8	S-77	8	0.8
1940 Bos-N★	151	569	78	157	33	3	14	79	41	43	8	....	.276	.330	.418	.748	111	7	76	4.78	8	*S-151	21	2.6
1941 Bos-N★	154	585	54	140	27	3	6	68	35	72	8	....	.239	.288	.326	.614	76	-20	54	3.18	7	*S-154	13	-0.3
1942 Bos-N★	142	534	47	130	28	2	6	47	22	42	11	....	.243	.279	.337	.616	81	-15	47	2.96	2	*S-142	11	-0.3
1943 Cin-N★	154	576	49	129	26	4	2	71	33	43	8	....	.224	.271	.293	.564	64	-28	47	2.64	20	*S-154	14	0.5
1944 Cin-N★	155	536	48	112	21	5	4	55	41	41	9	....	.209	.269	.289	.558	59	-30	43	2.57	17	*S-155	12	0.0
1945 Cin-N	115	421	46	100	27	2	13	49	18	38	4	....	.238	.275	.404	.679	89	-9	44	3.47	2	*S-115	12	0.2
1946 Cin-N★	91	299	30	58	10	0	6	36	25	34	5	....	.194	.258	.288	.546	57	-18	22	2.43	8	S-88	5	-0.5
1947 Cin-N★	151	545	69	146	**38**	4	19	87	49	40	5	....	.268	.333	.457	.790	108	4	81	5.23	-3	*S-151	22	1.1
1948 Phi-N	130	468	45	115	20	1	14	61	19	40	1	....	.246	.281	.382	.664	79	-16	47	3.45	-5	*S-122	10	-1.3
1949 Phi-N	85	266	21	55	10	1	6	29	29	21	1	....	.207	.294	.320	.614	66	-13	26	3.17	-1	2-82/S-1	5	-0.9
1950 StL-N	64	172	17	39	8	0	3	22	19	21	0	....	.227	.307	.326	.633	64	-9	18	3.41	2	S-51/2-1	4	-0.4
Total 14	**1510**	**5337**	**539**	**1270**	**263**	**28**	**97**	**640**	**351**	**465**	**64**	....	**.238**	**.290**	**.352**	**.643**	**80**	**-162**	**540**	**3.40**	**61**	***S-1395/2-84,3-4**	**138**	**0.6**
• MILLER, Elmer	Elmer Miller b: 7/28/1890, Sandusky, OH d: 11/28/1944, Beloit, WI BR/TR, 6', 175 lbs. Deb: 4/26/1912 Career OF: 67-268-60																							
1912 StL-N	12	37	5	7	1	0	0	3	4	9	1	....	.189	.268	.216	.485	34	-3	2	1.96	1	0-11(4-3-4)	0	-0.3
1915 NY-A	26	83	4	12	1	0	0	3	4	14	0	....	.145	.193	.157	.350	5	-10	3	1.01	-3	0-26(0-20-6)	0	-1.5
1916 NY-A	43	152	12	34	3	2	1	18	11	18	8	....	.224	.280	.289	.570	70	-6	15	3.17	5	0-42(18-9-15)	3	-0.3
1917 NY-A	114	379	43	95	11	3	3	35	40	44	11	....	.251	.336	.319	.656	99	1	45	3.84	-4	*0-112(33-53-26)	10	-1.0
1918 NY-A	67	202	18	49	9	2	1	22	19	17	2	....	.243	.317	.322	.639	91	-2	22	3.38	2	0-62(3-53-6)	5	-0.4
1921*NY-A	56	242	41	72	9	8	4	36	19	16	2	2	.298	.356	.450	.806	102	0	39	5.79	2	0-56(0-56-0)	8	0.0
1922 NY-A	51	172	31	46	7	2	3	18	11	12	2	3	.267	.311	.384	.695	79	-7	20	3.95	1	0-51(7-41-3)	4	-0.8
Bos-A	44	147	16	28	2	3	4	16	5	10	3	1	.190	.222	.327	.549	42	-13	11	2.30	-2	0-35(2-33-0)	1	-1.6
Yr.	95	319	47	74	9	5	7	34	16	22	5	4	.232	.271	.357	.628	62	-20	31	3.16	-1	0-86(9-74-3)	5	-2.4
Total 7	**413**	**1414**	**170**	**343**	**43**	**20**	**16**	**151**	**113**	**140**	**29**	**6**	**.243**	**.307**	**.335**	**.642**	**80**	**-40**	**157**	**3.62**	**2**	**0-395**	**31**	**-5.9**
• MILLER, George	George C. Miller b: 2/19/1853, Newport, KY d: 7/24/1929, Norwood, OH BR/TR, 5'5", 160 lbs. Deb: 9/6/1877 M																							
1877 Cin-N	11	37	4	6	1	0	0	3	5	2	....	....	.162	.262	.189	.451	50	-1	2	1.67	1	C-11	0	0.0
1884 Cin-a	6	20	6	5	1	1	0	3	1	....	....	....	.250	.318	.400	.718	127	1	3	4.78	1	/C-6	1	0.2
Total 2	**17**	**57**	**10**	**11**	**2**	**1**	**0**	**6**	**6**	**2**	....	....	**.193**	**.281**	**.263**	**.544**	**76**	**-1**	**4**	**2.68**	**2**	**/C-17**	**1**	**0.2**
• MILLER, Hack	Laurence H. Miller b: 1/1/1894, New York, NY d: 9/16/1971, Oakland, CA BR/TR, 5'9", 195 lbs. Deb: 9/22/1916 Career OF: 306-3-3																							
1916 Bro-N	3	3	0	1	0	1	0	1	1	1	0	....	.333	.500	1.000	1.500	345	1	2	19.50	-1	/0-3(0-2-1)	0	0.0
1918*Bos-A	12	29	2	8	2	0	0	4	0	4	0	....	.276	.276	.345	.621	89	-1	3	3.11	-1	0-10(9-1-0)	1	-0.2
1922 Chi-N	122	466	61	164	28	5	12	78	26	39	3	3	.352	.389	.511	.899	128	18	91	7.73	-3	*0-116(115-0-2)	19	0.6
1923 Chi-N	135	485	74	146	24	2	20	88	27	39	6	5	.301	.343	.482	.825	116	9	79	5.91	4	*0-129(129-0-0)	17	0.3
1924 Chi-N	53	131	17	44	8	1	4	25	8	11	1	0	.336	.379	.504	.882	133	6	25	7.37	-2	0-32(32-0-0)	6	0.3
1925 Chi-N	24	86	10	24	3	2	2	9	2	9	0	1	.279	.303	.430	.734	84	-3	11	4.46	-2	0-21(21-0-0)	1	-0.6
Total 6	**349**	**1200**	**164**	**387**	**65**	**11**	**38**	**205**	**64**	**103**	**10**	**9**	**.323**	**.361**	**.490**	**.851**	**120**	**31**	**209**	**6.59**	**-4**	**0-311**	**44**	**0.4**
• MILLER, Hack	James Eldridge Miller b: 2/13/1913, Celeste, TX d: 11/21/1966, Dallas, TX BR/TR, 5'11.5", 215 lbs. Deb: 4/18/1944																							
1944 Det-A	5	5	1	1	0	0	1	3	1	1	0	0	.200	.333	.800	1.133	207	1	1	9.81	0	/C-5	0	0.1
1945 Det-A	2	4	0	3	0	0	0	1	0	0	0	0	.750	.750	.750	1.500	315	1	1	12.94	0	/C-2	0	0.1
Total 2	**7**	**9**	**1**	**4**	**0**	**0**	**1**	**4**	**1**	**1**	**0**	**0**	**.444**	**.500**	**.778**	**1.278**	**256**	**2**	**3**	**11.15**	**0**	**/C-7**	**0**	**0.2**
• MILLER, Hughie	Hugh Stanley "Cotton" Miller b: 12/28/1887, St. Louis, MO d: 12/24/1945, Jefferson Barracks, MO BR/TR, 6'1.5", 175 lbs. Deb: 6/18/1911																							
1911 Phi-N	1	0	0	0	0	0	0	0	0	0	0	....	....	....	....	....	-99	0	0	....	0	....	0	0.0
1914 StL-F	132	490	51	109	20	5	0	46	27	57	4	....	.222	.264	.284	.548	53	-31	37	2.38	-1	*1-130	2	-3.6
1915 StL-F	7	6	0	3	1	0	0	3	0	0	0	....	.500	.500	.667	1.167	231	1	2	12.97	0	/1-6	0	0.0
Total 3	**140**	**496**	**51**	**112**	**21**	**5**	**0**	**49**	**27**	**57**	**4**	....	**.226**	**.267**	**.288**	**.555**	**55**	**-31**	**39**	**2.49**	**-1**	**1-136**	**2**	**-3.6**
• MILLER, Jake	Jacob George Miller b: 12/1/1895, Baltimore, MD d: 8/24/1974, Towson, MD BR/TR, 5'10", 170 lbs. Deb: 7/15/1922																							
1922 Pit-N	3	11	0	1	0	0	0	0	2	0	1	0	.091	.231	.091	.322	-14	-2	0	1.19	0	/0-3(0-0-3)	0	-0.2
• MILLER, Jim	James McCurdy "Rabbit" Miller b: 10/2/1880, Pittsburgh, PA d: 2/7/1937, Pittsburgh, PA BR/TR, 5'4", 143 lbs. Deb: 9/9/1901																							
1901 NY-N	18	58	3	8	0	0	0	3	6	....	1	....	.138	.219	.138	.357	5	-7	2	1.12	-5	2-18	0	-1.1
• MILLER, Joe	Joseph A. Miller b: 2/17/1861, Baltimore, MD d: 4/23/1928, Wheeling, WV BR, 5'9.5", 165 lbs. Deb: 5/1/1884																							
1884 Tol-a	105	423	46	101	12	8	1	0	26	....	....	....	.239	.284	.312	.597	91	-4	38	3.29	-7	*S-105	11	-0.7
1885 Lou-a	98	339	44	62	9	5	0	24	28	....	....	....	.183	.249	.239	.488	55	-17	21	2.02	4	*S-79,3-11/2-8	6	-0.9
Total 2	**203**	**762**	**90**	**163**	**21**	**13**	**1**	**24**	**54**	....	....	....	**.214**	**.269**	**.280**	**.548**	**75**	**-21**	**59**	**2.70**	**-3**	**S-184/3-11,2-8**	**17**	**-1.6**
• MILLER, Joe	Joseph Wick Miller b: 7/24/1850, Germany d: 8/30/1891, White Bear Lake, MN, 5'10.5", 169 lbs. Deb: 6/26/1872 M/U																							
1872 Nat-n	1	4	0	1	0	0	0	0	0	0	0	0	.250	.250	.250	.500	46	-0	0	2.65	0	/1-1	....	0.0

YEAR TM-L	G	AB	R	H	2B	3B	HR	RBI	BB	SO	SB	CS	AVG	OBP	SLG	OPS	OPS+	BR/A	RC	RC/G	FR	G/POS	WS	TPW
1875 Wes-n	13	50	4	6	1	0	0	0	0	3	0	0	.120	.120	.140	.260	-10	-5	1	.58	5	2-13	....	-0.1
Chi-n	15	54	1	8	0	0	0	1	0	7	0	0	.148	.148	.148	.296	3	-5	1	.78	-5	2-14/0-1	....	-0.9
Yr.	28	104	5	14	1	0	0	1	0	10	0	0	.135	.135	.144	.279	-3	-11	2	.68	-0	2-27/0-1	....	-1.0
Total 2 n	29	108	5	15	1	0	0	1	0	10	0	0	.139	.139	.148	.287	-1	-11	2	.74	0	/2-27,1-1,0-1	....	-1.1

• MILLER, John John Allen Miller b: 3/14/1944, Alhambra, CA BR/TR, 5'11", 195 lbs. Deb: 9/11/1966 Career OF: 9-0-0

YEAR TM-L	G	AB	R	H	2B	3B	HR	RBI	BB	SO	SB	CS	AVG	OBP	SLG	OPS	OPS+	BR/A	RC	RC/G	FR	G/POS	WS	TPW
1966 NY-A	6	23	1	2	0	0	1	2	0	9	0	0	.087	.087	.217	.304	-16	-3	0	.56	0	/1-3,0-3(3-0-0)	0	-0.4
1969 LA-N	26	38	3	8	1	0	1	1	2	9	0	0	.211	.250	.316	.566	62	-2	3	2.82	-1	/0-6(6-0-0),1-5,3-2,2-1	0	-0.3
Total 2	32	61	4	10	1	0	2	3	2	18	0	0	.164	.190	.279	.469	33	-6	4	1.89	-1	/0-9,1-8,3-2,2-1	0	-0.8

• MILLER, Keith Keith Alan Miller b: 6/12/1963, Midland, MI BR/TR, 5'11", 185 lbs. Deb: 6/16/1987 Career OF: 49-65-28

YEAR TM-L	G	AB	R	H	2B	3B	HR	RBI	BB	SO	SB	CS	AVG	OBP	SLG	OPS	OPS+	BR/A	RC	RC/G	FR	G/POS	WS	TPW
1987 NY-N	25	51	14	19	2	2	0	1	2	6	8	1	.373	.407	.490	.898	144	4	11	8.07	-2	2-16	2	0.3
1988 NY-N	40	70	9	15	1	1	1	5	6	10	0	5	.214	.276	.300	.576	69	-5	5	1.93	-5	2-16/S-8,3-6,0-1	0	-1.1
1989 NY-N	57	143	15	33	7	0	1	7	5	27	6	0	.231	.262	.301	.562	63	-6	12	2.71	-5	2-23,0-14(0-10-4)/S-8,3-2	1	-1.0
1990 NY-N	88	233	42	60	8	0	1	12	23	46	16	3	.258	.329	.305	.634	76	-5	27	3.97	-3	0-61(7-53-5),2-11/S-4	6	-0.9
1991 NY-N	98	275	41	77	22	1	4	23	23	44	14	4	.280	.347	.411	.757	113	6	42	5.49	-5	2-60,0-28(14-2-17)/3-2,S-2	11	0.2
1992 KC-A	106	416	57	118	24	4	4	38	31	46	16	6	.284	.354	.389	.743	105	4	62	5.41	-12	2-93,0-16(16-0-0)/D-1	15	-0.6
1993 KC-A	37	108	9	18	3	0	0	3	8	19	3	1	.167	.231	.194	.425	15	-13	5	1.41	-2	3-21/D-6,0-4(4-0-0),2-3	0	-1.5
1994 KC-A	5	15	1	2	0	0	0	0	0	3	0	0	.133	.133	.133	.267	-30	-3	0	.55	0	/0-4(4-0-0),3-2	0	-0.3
1995 KC-A	9	15	2	5	0	0	1	3	2	4	0	0	.333	.412	.533	.945	142	1	3	7.38	1	/D-4,0-4(4-0-1)	1	0.1
Total 9	465	1326	190	347	67	8	12	92	100	205	63	20	.262	.325	.351	.676	89	-16	166	4.34	-33	2-222,0-132/3-33,S-22,D-11	36	-4.7

• MILLER, Keith Neal Keith Miller b: 3/7/1963, Dallas, TX BB/TR, 5'11", 175 lbs. Deb: 4/23/1988 Career OF: 2-3-1

YEAR TM-L	G	AB	R	H	2B	3B	HR	RBI	BB	SO	SB	CS	AVG	OBP	SLG	OPS	OPS+	BR/A	RC	RC/G	FR	G/POS	WS	TPW
1988 Phi-N	47	48	4	8	3	0	0	6	5	13	0	0	.167	.245	.229	.474	36	-4	3	2.04	-1	/0-4(2-1-1),3-3,S-1	1	-0.6
1989 Phi-N	8	10	0	3	1	0	0	0	0	3	0	0	.300	.300	.400	.700	98	-0	1	4.63	-0	/0-2(0-2-0)	0	0.0
Total 2	55	58	4	11	4	0	0	6	5	16	0	0	.190	.254	.259	.513	46	-4	4	2.42	-1	/0-6,3-3,S-1	1	-0.6

• MILLER, Kohly Frank A. Miller b: 1/1874, Cumru Township, PA d: 3/29/1951, Reading, PA Deb: 9/16/1892

YEAR TM-L	G	AB	R	H	2B	3B	HR	RBI	BB	SO	SB	CS	AVG	OBP	SLG	OPS	OPS+	BR/A	RC	RC/G	FR	G/POS	WS	TPW
1892 Was-N	1	3	0	0	0	0	0	0	0	1	0	....	.000	.000	.000	.000	-103	-1	0	.00	-1	/S-1	0	-0.2
StL-N	1	4	0	0	0	0	0	0	0	0	0	....	.000	.000	.000	.000	-105	-1	0	.00	-1	/3-1	0	-0.1
Yr.	2	7	0	0	0	0	0	0	0	1	0	....	.000	.000	.000	.000	-104	-2	0	.00	-2	/3-1,S-1	0	-0.3
1897 Phi-N	3	11	2	2	0	0	0	1	2	....	0	....	.182	.308	.182	.490	32	-1	1	1.86	-1	/2-3	0	-0.2
Total 2	5	18	2	2	0	0	0	1	2	1	0	....	.111	.200	.111	.311	-16	-3	1	1.04	-3	/2-3,3-1,S-1	0	-0.5

• MILLER, Lemmie Lemmie Earl Miller b: 6/2/1960, Dallas, TX BR/TR, 6'1", 190 lbs. Deb: 5/22/1984

YEAR TM-L	G	AB	R	H	2B	3B	HR	RBI	BB	SO	SB	CS	AVG	OBP	SLG	OPS	OPS+	BR/A	RC	RC/G	FR	G/POS	WS	TPW
1984 LA-N	8	12	1	2	0	0	0	0	1	2	0	0	.167	.231	.167	.397	13	-1	1	1.41	0	/0-5(4-0-1)	0	-0.2

• MILLER, Norm Norman Calvin Miller b: 2/5/1946, Los Angeles, CA BL/TR, 5'10", 195 lbs. Deb: 9/11/1965 Career OF: 82-40-266

YEAR TM-L	G	AB	R	H	2B	3B	HR	RBI	BB	SO	SB	CS	AVG	OBP	SLG	OPS	OPS+	BR/A	RC	RC/G	FR	G/POS	WS	TPW
1965 Hou-N	11	15	2	3	0	1	0	1	1	7	0	0	.200	.250	.333	.583	67	-1	1	2.05	-0	/0-2(2-0-0)	0	-0.1
1966 Hou-N	11	34	1	5	0	0	1	3	2	8	0	0	.147	.194	.235	.430	20	-4	2	1.50	0	/0-8(5-0-3),3-2	0	-0.4
1967 Hou-N	64	190	15	39	9	3	1	14	19	42	2	0	.205	.278	.300	.578	67	-7	14	2.40	-2	0-53(53-0-0)	1	-1.4
1968 Hou-N	79	257	35	61	18	2	6	28	22	48	6	5	.237	.310	.393	.703	112	3	31	3.92	-7	0-74(2-7-65)	8	-1.0
1969 Hou-N	119	409	58	108	21	4	4	50	47	77	4	4	.264	.350	.364	.714	102	2	54	4.64	-1	*0-114(8-14-97)	13	-0.5
1970 Hou-N	90	226	29	54	9	0	4	29	41	33	3	1	.239	.358	.332	.690	90	-1	29	4.35	-2	0-72(4-3-68)/C-1	6	-0.6
1971 Hou-N	45	74	5	19	5	0	2	10	5	13	0	0	.257	.313	.405	.718	105	0	9	3.99	-1	0-20(0-6-15)/C-1	2	-0.1
1972 Hou-N	67	107	18	26	4	0	4	13	13	23	1	0	.243	.331	.393	.723	107	1	14	4.21	0	0-29(6-10-13)	3	0.0
1973 Hou-N	3	3	0	0	0	0	0	0	0	2	0	0	.000	.000	.000	.000	-100	-1	0	.00	0	/0-1	0	-0.1
Atl-N	9	8	2	3	1	0	1	6	3	3	0	0	.375	.545	.875	1.420	267	2	4	18.68	0	/0-1	1	0.2
Yr.	12	11	2	3	1	0	1	6	3	5	0	0	.273	.429	.636	1.065	194	1	4	12.45	0	/0-2(1-0-1)	1	0.1
1974 Atl-N	42	41	1	7	1	0	1	5	7	9	0	0	.171	.292	.268	.560	55	-2	4	2.91	1	/0-4(1-0-4)	1	-0.2
Total 10	540	1364	166	325	68	10	24	159	160	265	16	10	.238	.325	.356	.680	95	-7	162	3.95	-13	0-378/3-2,C-2	35	-4.1

• MILLER, Orlando Orlando (Salmon) Miller b: 1/13/1969, Changuinola, Panama BR/TR, 6'1", 180 lbs. Deb: 7/8/1994

YEAR TM-L	G	AB	R	H	2B	3B	HR	RBI	BB	SO	SB	CS	AVG	OBP	SLG	OPS	OPS+	BR/A	RC	RC/G	FR	G/POS	WS	TPW
1994 Hou-N	16	40	3	13	0	1	2	9	2	12	1	0	.325	.386	.525	.911	142	3	9	8.52	-1	S-11/2-3	3	0.3
1995 Hou-N	92	324	36	85	20	1	5	36	22	71	3	4	.262	.319	.377	.696	89	-7	37	3.95	-2	S-89	8	-0.2
1996 Hou-N	139	468	43	120	26	2	15	58	14	116	3	7	.256	.293	.417	.709	91	-11	51	3.66	-17	*S-117,3-29	8	-1.8
1997 Det-A	50	111	13	26	7	1	2	10	5	24	1	0	.234	.292	.369	.661	72	-5	13	3.84	1	S-31,D-11/3-4,1-3	1	-0.2
Total 4	297	943	95	244	53	5	24	113	43	223	8	11	.259	.306	.402	.708	90	-20	109	3.96	-19	S-248/3-33,D-11,1-3,2-3	20	-2.0

• MILLER, Otto Lowell Otto "Moonie" Miller b: 6/1/1889, Minden, NE d: 3/29/1962, Brooklyn, NY BR/TR, 6', 196 lbs. Deb: 7/16/1910 C/U

YEAR TM-L	G	AB	R	H	2B	3B	HR	RBI	BB	SO	SB	CS	AVG	OBP	SLG	OPS	OPS+	BR/A	RC	RC/G	FR	G/POS	WS	TPW
1910 Bro-N	31	66	5	11	3	0	0	2	2	19	1	....	.167	.203	.212	.415	22	-7	3	1.36	3	C-28	2	-0.1
1911 Bro-N	25	62	7	13	2	2	0	8	0	4	2	....	.210	.210	.306	.516	46	-5	4	2.16	0	C-22	1	-0.4
1912 Bro-N	98	316	35	88	18	1	1	31	18	50	11	....	.278	.325	.351	.677	88	-6	39	4.25	10	C-94	8	1.2
1913 Bro-N	104	320	26	87	11	7	0	26	10	31	7	....	.272	.294	.350	.644	81	-9	34	3.54	4	*C-103/1-1	7	0.3
1914 Bro-N	54	169	17	39	6	1	0	9	7	20	0	....	.231	.261	.278	.539	59	-9	12	2.31	-1	C-50/1-1	3	-0.7
1915 Bro-N	84	254	20	57	4	6	0	25	6	28	3	....	.224	.245	.287	.533	60	-13	20	2.54	0	C-83	7	-0.8
1916*Bro-N	73	216	16	55	9	2	1	17	7	29	6	....	.255	.281	.329	.610	85	-5	22	3.46	-3	C-69	7	-0.3
1917 Bro-N	92	274	19	63	5	4	1	17	14	29	5	....	.230	.272	.288	.561	70	-10	23	2.65	0	C-91	6	-0.4
1918 Bro-N	75	228	8	44	6	1	0	8	9	20	1	....	.193	.230	.228	.458	40	-17	11	1.60	1	C-62/1-1	4	-1.1
1919 Bro-N	51	164	18	37	5	0	0	5	7	14	2	....	.226	.257	.256	.513	53	-9	11	2.16	0	C-51	2	-0.6
1920*Bro-N	90	301	16	87	9	2	0	33	9	18	0	5	.289	.312	.332	.644	82	-8	30	3.40	-9	C-89	9	-1.0
1921 Bro-N	91	286	22	67	8	6	1	27	9	26	2	1	.234	.260	.315	.575	50	-20	24	2.65	3	C-91	5	-1.2
1922 Bro-N	59	180	20	47	11	1	1	23	6	13	0	0	.261	.285	.350	.635	63	-10	18	3.30	1	C-57	4	-0.5
Total 13	927	2836	229	695	97	33	5	231	104	301	40	6	.245	.275	.308	.583	67	-127	250	2.90	9	C-890/1-3	65	-5.5

• MILLER, Otto Otis Louis Miller b: 2/2/1901, Belleville, IL d: 7/26/1959, Belleville, IL BR/TR, 5'10.5", 168 lbs. Deb: 4/17/1927

YEAR TM-L	G	AB	R	H	2B	3B	HR	RBI	BB	SO	SB	CS	AVG	OBP	SLG	OPS	OPS+	BR/A	RC	RC/G	FR	G/POS	WS	TPW
1927 StL-A	51	76	8	17	5	0	0	8	8	5	0	1	.224	.306	.289	.595	53	-6	7	2.99	0	S-35,3-11	1	-0.4
1930 Bos-A	112	370	49	106	22	5	0	40	26	21	2	4	.286	.333	.373	.706	82	-11	46	4.36	2	3-83,2-15	8	-0.3
1931 Bos-A	107	389	38	106	12	1	0	43	15	20	1	1	.272	.301	.308	.610	64	-19	36	3.29	-6	3-75,2-25	5	-1.9
1932 Bos-A	2	2	0	0	0	0	0	0	0	0	0	0	.000	.000	.000	.000	-103	-1	0	.00	0	....	0	-0.1
Total 4	272	837	95	229	39	6	0	91	49	46	3	6	.274	.315	.335	.650	71	-36	89	3.72	-4	3-169/2-40,S-35	14	-2.6

• MILLER, Ralph Ralph Joseph Miller b: 2/29/1896, Fort Wayne, IN d: 3/18/1939, Fort Wayne, IN BR/TR, 6', 190 lbs. Deb: 4/14/1920

YEAR TM-L	G	AB	R	H	2B	3B	HR	RBI	BB	SO	SB	CS	AVG	OBP	SLG	OPS	OPS+	BR/A	RC	RC/G	FR	G/POS	WS	TPW
1920 Phi-N	97	338	28	74	14	1	0	28	11	32	3	4	.219	.246	.266	.512	45	-24	22	2.08	3	3-91/1-3,S-2,0-1	3	-1.9
1921 Phi-N	57	204	19	62	10	0	3	26	6	10	3	5	.304	.327	.397	.724	84	-6	25	4.40	-8	S-46,3-10	3	-0.8
1924*Was-A	9	15	1	2	0	0	0	0	1	1	0	0	.133	.188	.133	.321	-17	-3	0	.83	0	/2-3	0	-0.2
Total 3	163	557	48	138	24	1	3	54	18	43	6	9	.248	.274	.311	.584	57	-32	47	2.83	-4	3-101/S-48,1-3,2-3,0-1	6	-3.0

• MILLER, Ray Raymond Peter Miller b: 2/12/1888, Pittsburgh, PA d: 4/7/1927, Pittsburgh, PA BL/TL, 5'10", 168 lbs. Deb: 4/14/1917 C

YEAR TM-L	G	AB	R	H	2B	3B	HR	RBI	BB	SO	SB	CS	AVG	OBP	SLG	OPS	OPS+	BR/A	RC	RC/G	FR	G/POS	WS	TPW
1917 Cle-A	19	21	1	4	1	0	0	2	8	3	0	....	.190	.414	.238	.652	92	1	2	3.05	1	/1-4	1	0.2
Pit-N	6	27	1	4	1	0	0	0	2	3	0	....	.148	.207	.185	.392	20	-3	1	1.15	0	/1-6	0	-0.2

• MILLER, Rick Richard Alan Miller b: 4/19/1948, Grand Rapids, MI BL/TL, 6', 185 lbs. Deb: 9/4/1971 Career OF: 118-854-297

YEAR TM-L	G	AB	R	H	2B	3B	HR	RBI	BB	SO	SB	CS	AVG	OBP	SLG	OPS	OPS+	BR/A	RC	RC/G	FR	G/POS	WS	TPW
1971 Bos-A	15	33	9	11	5	0	1	7	8	8	0	2	.333	.463	.576	1.039	180	3	9	9.44	0	0-14(4-4-6)	2	0.2
1972 Bos-A	89	98	13	21	4	1	3	15	11	27	0	2	.214	.294	.367	.661	91	-2	10	3.43	1	0-75(24-47-4)	3	-0.3
1973 Bos-A	143	441	65	115	17	7	6	43	51	59	12	7	.261	.341	.372	.713	95	-2	58	4.53	-5	*0-137(15-71-61)	12	-1.3
1974 Bos-A	114	280	41	73	8	1	5	22	37	47	13	2	.261	.347	.350	.697	94	1	38	4.64	-2	*0-105(21-77-7)	10	-0.5
1975*Bos-A	77	108	21	21	2	1	0	15	21	20	3	2	.194	.326	.231	.557	55	-6	9	2.56	0	0-65(25-15-26)	1	-0.8
1976 Bos-A	105	269	40	76	15	3	0	27	34	47	11	10	.283	.363	.361	.724	100	-0	36	4.44	-1	0-82(17-37-32)/D-4	8	-0.6
1977 Bos-A	86	189	34	48	9	3	0	24	22	30	11	5	.254	.341	.333	.674	76	-5	23	4.11	0	0-79(2-29-48)/D-1	4	-0.7
1978 Cal-A	132	475	66	125	25	4	1	37	54	70	3	13	.263	.343	.339	.682	96	-6	53	3.64	2	*0-129(0-93-36)	13	-0.7

YEAR TM-L	G	AB	R	H	2B	3B	HR	RBI	BB	SO	SB	CS	AVG	OBP	SLG	OPS	OPS+	BR/A	RC	RC/G	FR	G/POS	WS	TPW
1979*Cal-A	120	427	60	125	15	5	2	28	50	69	5	4	.293	.368	.365	.734	102	3	60	5.00	-1	*O-117(0-117-0)/D-2	14	0.0
1980 Cal-A	129	412	52	113	14	3	2	38	48	71	7	3	.274	.351	.337	.689	92	-2	53	4.54	1	*O-118(0-98-24)	11	-0.4
1981 Bos-A	97	316	38	92	17	2	2	33	28	36	3	5	.291	.351	.377	.727	103	1	41	4.54	-8	O-95(0-95-0)	10	-0.9
1982 Bos-A	135	409	50	104	13	2	4	38	40	41	5	6	.254	.324	.325	.649	74	-15	43	3.62	-6	*O-127(0-127-0)	7	-2.3
1983 Bos-A	104	262	41	75	10	2	2	21	28	30	3	3	.286	.357	.363	.720	92	-2	34	4.64	0	O-66(6-22-40)/1-2,D-2	6	-0.5
1984 Bos-A	95	123	17	32	5	1	0	12	17	22	1	1	.260	.350	.317	.667	82	-2	14	3.99	-2	O-31(0-21-10)/1-8	2	-0.5
1985 Bos-A	41	45	5	15	2	0	0	9	5	6	1	0	.333	.400	.378	.778	110	1	7	6.08	0	/O-8(4-1-3),D-4	1	0.1
Total 15	**1482**	**3887**	**552**	**1046**	**161**	**35**	**28**	**369**	**454**	**583**	**78**	**65**	**.269**	**.348**	**.350**	**.698**	**93**	**-34**	**488**	**4.31**	**-22**	***O-1248/D-13,1-10**	**104**	**-9.1**
• MILLER, Rod	Rodney Carter Miller b: 1/16/1940, Portland, OR BL/TR, 5'10", 160 lbs. Deb: 9/28/1957																							
1957 Bro-N	1	1	0	0	0	0	0	0	0	1	0	0	.000	.000	.000	.000	-91	-0	0	.00	0	....	0	0.0
• MILLER, Rudy	Rudel Charles Miller b: 7/12/1900, Kalamazoo, MI d: 1/22/1994, Kalamazoo, MI BR/TR, 6'1", 180 lbs. Deb: 9/19/1929																							
1929 Phi-A	2	4	1	1	0	0	0	1	3	0	0	0	.250	.571	.250	.821	115	1	1	8.63	0	/3-2	0	0.0
• MILLER, Tom	Thomas P. "Reddy" Miller b: 1850, Philadelphia, PA d: 5/29/1876, Philadelphia, PA, 5'10.5" Deb: 10/24/1874																							
1874 Ath-n	4	16	1	8	0	0	0	5	0	0	0	0	.500	.500	.500	1.000	204	2	4	15.38	-1	/C-4,0-1	....	0.1
1875 StL-n	56	214	18	35	2	0	0	12	1	8	2	0	.164	.167	.173	.340	20	-14	7	1.10	5	*C-53/3-2	....	-0.7
Total 2 n	**60**	**230**	**19**	**43**	**2**	**0**	**0**	**17**	**1**	**8**	**2**	**0**	**.187**	**.190**	**.196**	**.386**	**33**	**-12**	**11**	**1.71**	**3**	**/C-57,3-2,0-1**	**....**	**-0.7**
• MILLER, Tom	Thomas Royall Miller b: 7/5/1897, Powhatan Court House, VA d: 8/13/1980, Richmond, VA BL/TR, 5'11", 180 lbs. Deb: 7/29/1918																							
1918 Bos-N	2	2	0	0	0	0	0	0	0	0	1	....	.000	.000	.000	.000	-104	-0	0	.00	0	....	0	-0.1
1919 Bos-N	7	6	2	2	0	0	0	0	0	1	0	....	.333	.333	.333	.667	105	0	1	4.07	0	....	0	0.0
• MILLER, Ward	Ward Taylor "Windy,Grump" Miller b: 7/5/1884, Mount Carroll, IL d: 9/4/1958, Dixon, IL BL/TR, 5'11", 177 lbs. Deb: 4/14/1909 Career OF: 320-125-185																							
1909 Pit-N	15	56	2	8	0	1	0	4	4	....	2	....	.143	.213	.179	.392	21	-5	3	1.33	-2	O-14(0-14-0)	0	-0.9
Cin-N	43	113	17	35	3	1	0	4	6	....	9	....	.310	.345	.354	.699	118	2	17	5.38	-2	O-26(17-16-3)	4	-0.1
Yr.	58	169	19	43	3	2	0	8	10	....	11	....	.254	.300	.296	.596	85	-3	19	3.84	-3	O-40(17-30-3)	4	-1.0
1910 Cin-N	81	126	21	30	6	0	0	10	22	13	10	....	.238	.356	.286	.641	92	-0	17	4.28	2	O-26(0-11-15)	3	0.0
1912 Chi-N	86	241	45	74	11	4	0	22	26	18	11	....	.307	.377	.386	.763	109	4	39	5.72	-4	O-64(13-38-14)	8	-0.4
1913 Chi-N	80	203	23	48	5	7	1	16	34	33	13	....	.236	.349	.345	.694	98	1	27	4.42	3	O-63(47-11-5)	7	0.1
1914 StL-F	121	402	49	118	17	7	4	50	59	36	18	....	.294	.397	.400	.798	120	14	69	5.96	5	*O-111(74-31-6)	17	1.4
1915 StL-F	154	536	80	164	19	9	1	63	79	39	33	....	.306	.400	.381	.781	124	21	93	6.10	3	*O-154(154-0-0)	22	1.9
1916 StL-A	146	485	72	129	17	5	1	50	72	76	25	21	.266	.371	.328	.699	116	9	65	4.17	-7	*O-136(3-0-133)	16	-0.6
1917 StL-A	43	82	13	17	1	1	1	2	16	15	7	....	.207	.350	.280	.630	96	1	10	3.89	0	O-25(12-4-9)	2	0.0
Total 8	**769**	**2244**	**322**	**623**	**79**	**35**	**8**	**221**	**318**	**230**	**128**	**21**	**.278**	**.375**	**.355**	**.729**	**112**	**45**	**340**	**5.07**	**-1**	**O-619**	**79**	**1.6**
• MILLER, Warren	Warren Lemuel "Gitz" Miller b: 7/14/1885, Philadelphia, PA d: 8/12/1956, Philadelphia, PA BL/TL, 5'10", 160 lbs. Deb: 7/29/1909 Career OF: 2-10-12																							
1909 Was-A	26	51	5	11	0	0	0	1	4	....	0	....	.216	.273	.216	.488	57	-2	3	1.86	0	O-15(1-10-4)	0	-0.3
1911 Was-A	21	34	3	5	0	0	0	0	0	....	0	....	.147	.147	.147	.294	-18	-5	1	.63	-1	/O-9(1-0-8)	0	-0.6
Total 2	**47**	**85**	**8**	**16**	**0**	**0**	**0**	**1**	**4**	**....**	**0**	**....**	**.188**	**.225**	**.188**	**.413**	**28**	**-8**	**4**	**1.33**	**0**	**/O-24**	**0**	**-0.9**
• MILLETTE, Joe	Joseph Anthony Millette b: 8/12/1966, Walnut Creek, CA BR/TR, 6'1", 180 lbs. Deb: 7/16/1992																							
1992 Phi-N	33	78	5	16	0	0	0	2	5	10	1	0	.205	.271	.205	.476	37	-6	3	1.22	5	S-26/3-3,2-1	1	0.1
1993 Phi-N	10	10	3	2	0	0	0	2	1	2	0	0	.200	.273	.200	.473	29	-1	1	1.23	1	/S-7,3-3	0	0.1
Total 2	**43**	**88**	**8**	**18**	**0**	**0**	**0**	**4**	**6**	**12**	**1**	**0**	**.205**	**.271**	**.205**	**.475**	**36**	**-7**	**4**	**1.22**	**7**	**/S-33,3-6,2-1**	**1**	**0.2**
• MILLIARD, Ralph	Ralph Gregory Milliard b: 12/30/1973, Willemstad, Curacao BR/TR, 5'11", 170 lbs. Deb: 5/12/1996																							
1996 Fla-N	24	62	7	10	2	0	0	1	14	16	2	0	.161	.316	.194	.509	40	-4	5	2.53	1	2-24	1	-0.2
1997 Fla-N	8	30	2	6	0	0	0	2	3	3	1	1	.200	.314	.200	.514	40	-3	2	1.79	4	/2-8	1	0.2
1998 NY-N	10	1	3	0	0	0	0	0	0	1	0	0	.000	.000	.000	.000	-102	-0	0	.00	-2	/2-5,S-1	0	-0.2
Total 3	**42**	**93**	**12**	**16**	**2**	**0**	**0**	**3**	**17**	**20**	**3**	**1**	**.172**	**.313**	**.194**	**.506**	**38**	**-7**	**7**	**2.25**	**4**	**/2-37,S-1**	**2**	**-0.2**
• MILLIES, Wally	Walter Louis Millies b: 10/18/1906, Chicago, IL d: 2/28/1995, Oak Lawn, IL BR/TR, 5'10.5", 170 lbs. Deb: 9/23/1934																							
1934 Bro-N	2	7	0	0	0	0	0	0	0	0	0	....	.000	.000	.000	.000	-105	-2	0	.00	0	/C-2	0	-0.1
1936 Was-A	74	215	26	67	10	2	0	25	11	8	1	0	.312	.345	.377	.722	83	-6	28	4.93	0	C-72	6	-0.2
1937 Was-A	59	179	21	40	7	1	0	28	9	15	1	0	.223	.261	.274	.534	36	-17	13	2.46	0	C-56	2	-1.3
1939 Phi-N	84	205	12	48	3	0	0	12	9	5	0	....	.234	.270	.249	.519	42	-17	13	2.08	0	C-84	1	-1.3
1940 Phi-N	26	43	1	3	0	0	0	0	4	4	0	....	.070	.149	.070	.219	-39	-8	0	.28	0	C-24	0	-0.8
1941 Phi-N	1	2	0	0	0	0	0	0	0	0	0	....	.000	.000	.000	.000	-104	-1	0	.00	0	/C-1	0	-0.1
Total 6	**246**	**651**	**60**	**158**	**20**	**3**	**0**	**65**	**33**	**32**	**2**	**0**	**.243**	**.280**	**.283**	**.563**	**46**	**-51**	**55**	**2.83**	**0**	**C-239**	**9**	**-3.7**
• MILLIGAN, Jocko	John Milligan b: 8/8/1861, Philadelphia, PA d: 8/29/1923, Philadelphia, PA BR/TR, 6', 192 lbs. Deb: 5/1/1884 U Career OF: 0-6-3																							
1884 Phi-a	66	268	39	77	20	3	3	0	8	....	....	....	.287	.308	.418	.726	126	6	35	5.09	3	C-65/0-1	11	1.4
1885 Phi-a	67	265	35	71	15	4	2	39	7	....	....	....	.268	.289	.377	.667	103	-1	30	4.13	-2	C-61/1-6,0-2(0-0-2)	7	0.2
1886 Phi-a	75	301	52	76	17	3	5	45	21	....	18	....	.252	.301	.379	.680	111	3	41	4.89	-4	C-40,1-29/0-5(0-4-1),3-2	10	0.0
1887 Phi-a	95	398	54	135	27	4	2	50	21	....	8	....	.339	.344	.411	.755	110	4	57	5.90	-5	1-50,C-47/0-1	11	-0.1
1888*StL-a	63	219	19	55	6	2	5	37	17	....	3	....	.251	.311	.365	.676	105	0	26	4.35	-1	C-58/1-5	9	0.3
1889 StL-a	72	273	53	100	30	2	12	76	16	19	2	....	.366	.408	.623	1.030	169	21	72	11.01	-1	C-66/1-9	17	2.2
1890 Phi-P	62	234	38	69	9	3	3	57	19	19	2	....	.295	.363	.397	.760	101	-0	35	5.78	-4	C-59/1-3	8	0.1
1891 Phi-a	118	455	75	138	**35**	12	11	106	56	51	2	....	.303	.397	.505	.903	153	30	94	7.90	-8	C-87,1-32	21	2.3
1892 Was-N	88	323	40	89	20	9	4	43	26	24	2	....	.276	.335	.430	.766	135	12	48	5.59	8	C-59,1-28	10	2.3
1893 Bal-N	24	102	19	25	5	2	1	19	5	7	2	....	.245	.294	.363	.656	73	-5	12	4.04	2	1-22/C-1	1	-0.2
NY-N	42	147	16	34	5	6	1	25	14	14	2	....	.231	.302	.367	.670	77	-6	17	4.07	6	C-42	3	0.4
Yr.	66	249	35	59	10	8	2	44	19	21	4	....	.237	.299	.365	.664	75	-10	29	4.06	8	C-43,1-22	4	0.2
Total 10	**772**	**2985**	**440**	**869**	**189**	**50**	**49**	**497**	**210**	**134**	**41**	**....**	**.291**	**.341**	**.433**	**.774**	**122**	**66**	**469**	**5.95**	**-6**	**C-585,1-184/0-9,3-2**	**108**	**8.9**
• MILLIGAN, Randy	Randy Andre Milligan b: 11/27/1961, San Diego, CA BR/TR, 6'2", 228 lbs. Deb: 9/12/1987 Career OF: 19-0-0																							
1987 NY-N	3	1	0	0	0	0	0	0	1	1	0	0	.000	.500	.000	.500	49	0	0	3.51	0	....	0	0.0
1988 Pit-N	40	82	10	18	5	0	3	8	20	24	1	2	.220	.379	.390	.769	123	3	13	5.12	-2	1-25/0-2(1-0-0)	3	0.0
1989 Bal-A	124	365	56	98	23	5	12	45	74	75	9	5	.268	.396	.458	.853	144	25	68	6.46	-0	*1-117/D-1	19	1.8
1990 Bal-A	109	362	64	96	20	1	20	60	88	68	6	3	.265	.412	.492	.903	157	32	78	7.38	5	1-98/D-9	17	3.0
1991 Bal-A	141	483	57	127	17	2	16	70	84	108	0	5	.263	.374	.406	.780	121	15	71	4.95	-1	*1-106,D-25/0-9(9-0-0)	13	0.5
1992 Bal-A	137	462	71	111	21	1	11	53	106	81	0	1	.240	.386	.361	.748	108	11	70	5.11	-4	*1-129/D-6	13	-0.2
1993 Cin-N	83	234	30	64	11	1	6	29	46	49	0	2	.274	.395	.406	.801	115	6	40	6.21	3	1-61/0-9(9-0-0)	9	0.4
Cle-A	19	47	7	20	7	0	0	7	14	4	0	0	.426	.557	.574	1.132	206	9	17	17.08	0	1-18/D-1	4	0.7
1994 Mon-N	47	82	10	19	2	0	2	12	14	21	0	0	.232	.344	.329	.673	76	-2	10	4.20	2	1-33	1	-0.3
Total 8	**703**	**2118**	**305**	**553**	**106**	**10**	**70**	**284**	**447**	**431**	**16**	**18**	**.261**	**.393**	**.420**	**.813**	**128**	**98**	**368**	**5.97**	**3**	**1-587/D-42,0-20**	**79**	**5.8**
• MILLS, Bill	William Henry Mills b: 11/2/1920, Boston, MA BR/TR, 5'10", 175 lbs. Deb: 5/19/1944																							
1944 Phi-A	5	4	0	1	0	0	0	0	1	1	0	0	.250	.400	.250	.650	89	0	0	1.73	0	/C-1	0	0.0
• MILLS, Brad	James Bradley Mills b: 1/19/1957, Exeter, CA BL/TR, 6', 195 lbs. Deb: 6/8/1980 C																							
1980 Mon-N	21	60	1	18	1	0	0	8	5	6	0	1	.300	.354	.317	.671	88	-1	7	4.21	-1	3-18	2	-0.3
1981*Mon-N	17	21	3	5	1	0	0	1	2	1	0	0	.238	.304	.286	.590	67	-1	2	2.59	-1	/3-7,2-2	0	-0.2
1982 Mon-N	54	67	6	15	3	0	1	2	5	11	0	0	.224	.278	.313	.591	64	-3	5	2.56	-1	3-13	0	-0.5
1983 Mon-N	14	20	1	5	0	0	0	1	2	3	0	0	.250	.318	.250	.568	60	-1	2	3.16	0	/3-3,1-1	0	-0.1
Total 4	**106**	**168**	**11**	**43**	**5**	**0**	**1**	**12**	**14**	**21**	**0**	**1**	**.256**	**.313**	**.304**	**.617**	**73**	**-6**	**16**	**3.18**	**-3**	**/3-41,2-2,1-1**	**2**	**-1.0**
• MILLS, Buster	Colonel Buster "Bus" Mills b: 9/16/1908, Ranger, TX d: 12/1/1991, Arlington, TX BR/TR, 5'11.5", 195 lbs. Deb: 4/18/1934 M/C Career OF: 255-76-12																							
1934 StL-N	29	72	7	17	4	1	1	8	4	11	0	....	.236	.295	.361	.656	70	-3	8	3.51	-1	O-18(0-17-1)	1	-0.5

YEAR TM-L	G	AB	R	H	2B	3B	HR	RBI	BB	SO	SB	CS	AVG	OBP	SLG	OPS	OPS+	BR/A	RC	RC/G	FR	G/POS	WS	TPW
1935 Bro-N	17	56	12	12	2	1	1	7	5	11	0	....	.214	.323	.339	.662	80	-1	6	3.21	-1	0-17(11-6-0)	1	-0.3
1937 Bos-A	123	505	85	149	25	8	7	58	46	41	11	8	.295	.361	.418	.779	92	-7	77	5.46	-9	*0-120(107-10-5)	12	-2.1
1938 StL-A	123	466	66	133	24	4	3	46	43	46	7	8	.285	.350	.373	.723	81	-15	61	4.64	-2	*0-113(106-6-1)	6	-2.1
1940 NY-A	34	63	10	25	3	3	1	15	7	5	0	0	.397	.457	.587	1.044	176	7	15	9.06	-1	0-14(12-0-2)	3	0.6
1942 Cle-A	80	195	19	54	4	2	1	26	23	18	5	4	.277	.353	.333	.687	99	0	23	4.01	1	0-53(13-37-3)	6	0.0
1946 Cle-A	9	22	1	6	0	0	0	3	3	5	0	1	.273	.360	.273	.633	84	-1	2	2.91	0	/0-6(6-0-0)	0	-0.1
Total 7	415	1379	200	396	62	19	14	163	131	137	23	21	.287	.355	.390	.746	92	-20	191	4.87	-12	0-341	29	-4.5
• MILLS, Charlie	Charles F. Mills b: 9/1844, Brooklyn, NY d: 4/10/1874, Brooklyn, NY, 6', 165 lbs. Deb: 5/18/1871 U NA OF: 0-0-8																							
1871 Mut-n	32	146	27	36	4	3	0	22	1	0	2	0	.247	.252	.315	.567	68	-4	12	3.55	-1	*C-29/0-4(0-0-4),3-1	....	-0.3
1872 Mut-n	6	31	6	4	0	0	0	2	0	0	0	0	.129	.129	.129	.258	-22	-4	1	.61	-1	/0-4(0-0-4),C-3	....	-0.3
Total 2 n	38	177	33	40	4	3	0	24	1	0	2	0	.226	.230	.282	.513	52	-8	13	2.97	-2	/C-32,0-8,3-1	....	-0.6
• MILLS, Everett	Everett Mills b: 1/20/1845, Newark, NJ d: 6/22/1908, Newark, NJ, 6'1", 174 lbs. Deb: 5/5/1871 M																							
1871 Oly-n	32	157	38	43	6	4	1	24	3	1	2	3	.274	.288	.382	.670	95	-2	18	4.92	1	*1-32	....	0.0
1872 Bal-n	55	266	55	79	14	2	0	34	3	2	0	2	.297	.305	.365	.669	100	-2	30	4.97	-3	*1-55	....	-0.3
1873 Bal-n	54	263	64	87	19	**9**	0	57	2	1	1	0	.331	.336	.471	.807	138	12	43	7.46	-2	*1-53/0-1	....	0.8
1874 Har-n	53	243	39	69	6	1	0	17	4	2	0	1	.284	.296	.317	.612	92	-4	23	4.00	-4	*1-53	....	-0.5
1875 Har-n	80	342	59	89	8	4	1	48	0	3	6	4	.260	.260	.316	.576	94	-4	30	3.49	-1	*1-80	....	-0.3
1876 Har-N	63	255	28	66	8	1	0	23	1	3	....	....	.259	.263	.299	.562	80	-6	20	3.05	-2	*1-63	5	-1.0
Total 5 n	274	1271	255	367	53	20	2	180	12	9	9	10	.289	.295	.367	.662	104	1	145	4.84	-8	1-273/0-1	....	-0.3
• MILLS, Frank	Frank Le Moyne Mills b: 5/13/1895, Knoxville, OH d: 8/31/1983, Youngstown, OH BL/TR, 6', 180 lbs. Deb: 9/22/1914																							
1914 Cle-A	4	8	0	1	0	0	0	0	1	2	0	....	.125	.222	.125	.347	4	-1	0	.84	0	/C-2	0	-0.1
• MILLS, Jack	Abbott Paige Mills b: 10/23/1889, South Williamstown, MA d: 6/3/1973, Washington, DC BL/TR, 6', 165 lbs. Deb: 7/1/1911																							
1911 Cle-A	13	17	5	5	0	0	0	1	1	....	1	....	.294	.368	.294	.663	85	-0	2	4.67	0	/3-7	1	0.0
• MILLS, Rupert	Rupert Frank Mills b: 10/12/1892, Newark, NJ d: 7/20/1929, Lake Hopatcong, NJ BR/TR, 6'2", 185 lbs. Deb: 6/23/1915																							
1915 New-F	41	134	12	27	5	1	0	16	6	21	6	....	.201	.241	.254	.495	48	-9	9	2.16	-1	1-37	0	-1.1
• MILNE, Pete	William James Milne b: 4/10/1925, Mobile, AL d: 4/11/1999, Mobile, AL BL/TR, 6'1", 180 lbs. Deb: 9/15/1948 Career OF: 3-5-2																							
1948 NY-N	12	27	0	6	0	1	0	2	1	6	0	....	.222	.250	.296	.546	47	-2	2	2.66	-1	/0-9(2-5-2)	0	-0.3
1949 NY-N	31	29	5	7	1	0	1	6	3	6	0	....	.241	.313	.379	.692	85	-1	3	3.89	-0	/0-1	0	-0.1
1950 NY-N	4	4	1	1	0	1	0	1	0	1	0	....	.250	.250	.750	1.000	151	0	1	6.75	0	....	0	0.0
Total 3	47	60	6	14	1	2	1	9	4	13	0	....	.233	.281	.367	.648	72	-3	6	3.52	-1	/0-10	0	-0.4
• MILNER, Brian	Brian Tate Milner b: 11/17/1959, Fort Worth, TX BR/TR, 6'2", 200 lbs. Deb: 6/23/1978																							
1978 Tor-A	2	9	3	4	0	1	0	2	0	1	0	0	.444	.444	.667	1.111	204	1	3	14.40	-1	/C-2	1	0.1
• MILNER, Eddie	Edward James Milner b: 5/21/1955, Columbus, OH BL/TL, 5'11", 173 lbs. Deb: 9/2/1980 Career OF: 69-633-42																							
1980 Cin-N	6	3	1	0	0	0	0	0	0	0	0	0	.000	.000	.000	.000	-100	-1	0	.00	0	....	0	-0.1
1981 Cin-N	8	5	0	1	1	0	0	1	1	1	0	0	.200	.333	.400	.733	105	0	1	5.09	0	/0-4(2-0-2)	0	0.0
1982 Cin-N	113	407	61	109	23	5	4	31	41	40	18	12	.268	.338	.378	.716	98	-2	52	4.37	-1	*0-107(65-30-37)	9	-0.8
1983 Cin-N	146	502	77	131	23	6	9	33	68	60	41	12	.261	.350	.384	.735	100	5	72	4.80	5	*0-139(0-138-1)	20	0.8
1984 Cin-N	117	336	44	78	8	4	7	29	51	50	21	13	.232	.337	.342	.679	87	-6	42	4.02	5	*0-108(0-108-0)	10	-0.2
1985 Cin-N	145	453	82	115	19	7	3	33	61	31	35	13	.254	.344	.347	.690	89	-3	60	4.50	9	*0-135(0-135-0)	17	0.4
1986 Cin-N	145	424	70	110	22	6	15	47	36	56	18	11	.259	.317	.446	.763	104	-0	59	4.87	3	*0-127(0-127-0)	14	0.1
1987*SF-N	101	214	38	54	14	0	4	19	24	33	10	9	.252	.328	.374	.702	90	-5	26	4.01	-2	0-84(0-84-0)	5	-0.8
1988 Cin-N	23	51	3	9	1	0	0	2	4	9	2	2	.176	.236	.196	.432	24	-5	2	1.48	0	0-15(2-11-2)	0	-0.6
Total 9	804	2395	376	607	111	28	42	195	286	280	145	72	.253	.335	.376	.710	94	-18	314	4.41	19	0-719	75	-1.2
• MILNER, John	John David "The Hammer" Milner b: 12/28/1949, Atlanta, GA d: 1/4/2000, East Point, GA BL/TL, 6', 185 lbs. Deb: 9/15/1971 Career OF: 432-2-6																							
1971 NY-N	9	18	1	3	1	0	0	1	0	3	0	0	.167	.167	.222	.389	9	-2	1	1.20	1	/0-3(3-0-0)	0	-0.1
1972 NY-N	117	362	52	86	12	2	17	38	51	74	2	1	.238	.340	.423	.762	118	10	54	5.00	0	0-91(88-0-3),1-10	15	0.4
1973*NY-N	129	451	69	108	12	3	23	72	62	84	1	1	.239	.333	.432	.765	112	7	64	4.72	-4	1-95,0-29(29-0-0)	15	-0.5
1974 NY-N	137	507	70	128	19	0	20	63	66	77	10	2	.252	.339	.408	.747	110	8	69	4.64	-6	*1-133	15	-0.9
1975 NY-N	91	220	24	42	11	0	7	29	33	22	1	1	.191	.302	.336	.638	81	-6	23	3.37	4	0-31(29-2-0),1-29	4	-0.6
1976 NY-N	127	443	56	120	25	4	15	78	65	53	0	7	.271	.364	.447	.811	137	19	70	5.50	7	*0-112(112-0-0),1-12	19	2.1
1977 NY-N	131	388	43	99	20	3	12	57	61	55	6	2	.255	.356	.415	.771	111	8	59	5.27	1	1-87,0-22(21-0-1)	11	0.4
1978 Pit-N	108	295	39	80	17	0	6	38	34	25	5	0	.271	.347	.390	.736	101	2	41	4.94	-1	0-69(68-0-1),1-28	10	-0.3
1979*Pit-N	128	326	52	90	9	4	16	60	53	37	3	5	.276	.379	.475	.854	126	11	60	6.40	-2	0-64(64-0-0),1-48	13	0.5
1980 Pit-N	114	238	31	58	6	0	8	34	52	29	2	2	.244	.379	.370	.749	108	5	36	5.19	-3	1-70,0-11(10-0-1)	7	-0.2
1981 Pit-N	34	59	6	14	1	0	2	9	5	3	0	0	.237	.297	.356	.653	82	-2	6	3.31	-1	/1-8,0-8(8-0-0)	1	-0.4
*Mon-N	31	76	6	18	5	0	3	9	12	6	0	1	.237	.341	.421	.762	114	1	11	4.95	1	1-21	3	0.1
Yr.	65	135	12	32	6	0	5	18	17	9	0	1	.237	.322	.393	.715	100	-0	17	4.22	0	1-29/0-8(8-0-0)	4	-0.2
1982 Mon-N	26	28	1	3	0	0	0	2	4	2	0	0	.107	.219	.107	.326	-6	-4	1	.83	0	/1-5	0	-0.4
Pit-N	33	25	5	6	2	0	2	8	6	3	1	0	.240	.406	.560	.966	163	3	7	9.28	0	/1-1	2	0.3
Yr.	59	53	6	9	2	0	2	10	10	5	1	0	.170	.313	.321	.633	77	-1	7	4.32	0	/1-6	2	-0.2
Total 12	1215	3436	455	855	140	16	131	498	504	473	31	22	.249	.347	.413	.760	112	60	501	4.97	-3	1-547,0-440	115	0.3
• MILOSEVICH, Mike	Michael "Mollie" Milosevich b: 1/13/1915, Zeigler, IL d: 2/3/1966, East Chicago, IN BR/TR, 5'10.5", 172 lbs. Deb: 4/30/1944																							
1944 NY-A	94	312	27	77	11	4	0	32	30	37	1	2	.247	.313	.308	.621	75	-10	29	3.13	9	S-91	8	0.6
1945 NY-A	30	69	5	15	2	0	0	7	6	6	0	0	.217	.289	.246	.536	54	-4	5	2.26	1	S-22/2-1	1	-0.2
Total 2	124	381	32	92	13	4	0	39	36	43	1	2	.241	.309	.297	.605	71	-14	34	2.96	10	S-113/2-1	9	0.5
• MINCHER, Don	Donald Ray Mincher b: 6/24/1938, Huntsville, AL BL/TR, 6'3", 213 lbs. Deb: 4/18/1960 Career OF: 1-0-1																							
1960 Was-A	27	79	10	19	4	1	2	5	11	11	0	1	.241	.333	.392	.726	95	-1	9	3.61	-4	1-20	1	-0.6
1961 Min-A	35	101	18	19	5	1	5	11	22	11	0	1	.188	.333	.406	.739	91	-1	13	4.08	0	1-29	2	-0.3
1962 Min-A	86	121	20	29	1	1	9	29	34	24	0	0	.240	.406	.488	.894	134	7	26	7.05	-3	1-25	6	0.3
1963 Min-A	82	225	41	58	8	0	17	42	30	51	0	0	.258	.353	.520	.873	138	12	44	7.00	-2	1-60	10	0.7
1964 Min-A	120	287	45	68	12	4	23	56	27	51	0	0	.237	.303	.547	.850	129	10	45	5.25	0	1-76	8	0.6
1965*Min-A	128	346	43	87	17	3	22	65	49	73	1	3	.251	.348	.509	.856	134	15	62	6.17	-2	1-99/0-1	17	0.7
1966 Min-A	139	431	53	108	30	0	14	62	58	68	3	2	.251	.342	.418	.760	110	7	61	4.78	5	*1-130	14	0.5
1967 Cal-A★	147	487	81	133	23	3	25	76	69	69	0	3	.273	.368	.487	.855	156	34	87	6.33	1	*1-142/0-1	28	3.1
1968 Cal-A	120	399	35	94	12	1	13	48	43	65	0	2	.236	.316	.368	.685	111	5	47	3.87	-3	*1-113	13	-0.5
1969 Sea-A★	140	427	53	105	14	0	25	78	78	69	10	11	.246	.369	.454	.823	131	17	72	5.66	8	*1-122	18	1.6
1970 Oak-A	140	463	62	114	18	0	27	74	56	71	5	4	.246	.331	.460	.791	120	11	70	5.08	5	*1-137	15	0.6
1971 Oak-A	28	92	9	22	6	1	2	8	20	14	1	1	.239	.375	.391	.766	120	3	14	5.22	2	1-27	4	0.3
Was-A	100	323	35	94	15	1	10	45	53	52	2	1	.291	.394	.437	.831	143	21	58	6.46	0	1-88	15	1.6
Yr.	128	415	44	116	21	2	12	53	73	66	3	2	.280	.390	.427	.816	138	24	72	6.17	3	*1-115	19	1.9
1972 Tex-A	61	191	23	45	10	0	6	39	46	23	2	1	.236	.389	.382	.771	136	12	33	5.77	5	1-59	11	1.4
*Oak-A	47	54	2	8	1	0	0	5	10	16	0	2	.148	.281	.167	.448	37	-5	2	1.13	-1	1-11	0	-0.7
Yr.	108	245	25	53	11	0	6	44	56	39	2	3	.216	.366	.335	.701	115	7	35	4.60	5	1-70	11	0.7
Total 13	1400	4026	530	1003	176	16	200	643	606	668	24	32	.249	.351	.450	.801	127	146	644	5.42	13	*1-1138/0-2	162	9.4
• MINCHER, Ed	Edward John Mincher b: 6/17/1850, Baltimore, MD d: 12/8/1918, Brooklyn, NY Deb: 5/4/1871 U NA OF: 20-0-0																							
1871 Kek-n	9	36	4	8	0	0	0	5	0	0	1	0	.222	.222	.222	.444	28	-3	2	2.31	-1	/0-9(9-0-0)	....	-0.3
1872 Nat-n	11	53	5	6	0	0	0	4	0	1	0	0	.113	.113	.113	.226	-26	-9	1	.46	1	0-11(11-0-0)	....	-0.5
Total 2 n	20	89	9	14	0	0	0	9	0	1	1	0	.157	.157	.157	.315	-4	-12	3	1.15	0	/0-20	....	-0.8

YEAR TM-L	G	AB	R	H	2B	3B	HR	RBI	BB	SO	SB	CS	AVG	OBP	SLG	OPS	OPS+	BR/A	RC	RC/G	FR	G/POS	WS	TPW
• MINNEHAN, Dan	Daniel Joseph Minnehan b: 11/28/1865, Troy, NY d: 8/8/1929, Troy, NY BR/TR, 5'10", 145 lbs. Deb: 9/20/1895																							
1895 Lou-N	8	34	6	13	0	0	0	6	1	1	0	....	.382	.400	.382	.782	109	1	5	6.85	0	/3-7,0-2(0-2-0)	1	0.0
• MINOR, Damon	Damon Reed Minor b: 1/5/1974, Canton, OH BL/TL, 6'7", 230 lbs. Deb: 9/2/2000																							
2000 SF-N	10	9	3	4	0	0	3	6	2	1	0	0	.444	.545	1.444	1.990	410	4	7	39.82	0	/1-4	2	0.4
2001 SF-N	19	45	3	7	1	0	0	3	3	8	0	0	.156	.208	.178	.386	1	-7	2	1.11	-1	1-11	0	-0.8
2002 SF-N	83	173	21	41	6	0	10	24	24	34	0	0	.237	.337	.445	.782	109	2	24	4.65	0	1-44/D-3	3	-0.1
Total 3	112	227	27	52	7	0	13	33	29	43	0	0	.229	.322	.432	.753	102	-0	33	4.85	-2	/1-59,D-3	5	-0.6
• MINOR, Ryan	Ryan Dale Minor b: 1/5/1974, Canton, OH BR/TR, 6'7", 240 lbs. Deb: 9/13/1998																							
1998 Bal-A	9	14	3	6	1	0	0	1	0	3	0	0	.429	.429	.500	.929	143	1	3	10.13	0	/3-6,1-3,D-1	0	0.0
1999 Bal-A	46	124	13	24	7	0	3	10	8	43	1	0	.194	.242	.323	.565	44	-11	10	2.66	0	3-45/1-1	1	-0.9
2000 Bal-A	32	84	4	11	1	0	0	3	3	20	0	0	.131	.170	.143	.313	-20	-15	2	.82	-1	3-26/1-5	1	-1.5
2001 Mon-N	55	95	10	15	2	0	2	13	9	31	0	1	.158	.238	.242	.480	24	-11	5	1.64	-6	3-24/D-2,0-2(2-0-0),1-1	0	-1.7
Total 4	142	317	30	56	11	0	5	27	20	97	1	1	.177	.230	.259	.489	25	-37	21	2.06	-7	3-101/1-10,D-3,0-2	2	-4.1
• MINOSO, Minnie	Saturnino Orestes Armas (Arrieta) Minoso b: 11/29/1922, Havana, Cuba BR/TR, 5'10", 175 lbs. Deb: 4/19/1949 C Career OF: 1512-83-87																							
1949 Cle-A	9	16	2	3	0	0	1	1	2	2	0	1	.188	.350	.375	.725	94	-1	1	2.43	0	/0-7(0-0-7)	0	-0.1
1951 Cle-A	8	14	3	6	2	0	0	2	1	1	0	0	.429	.529	.571	1.101	209	2	5	16.05	0	/1-7	1	0.2
Chi-A★	138	516	109	167	32	14	10	74	71	41	31	10	.324	.419	.498	.917	150	42	115	8.31	-6	0-82(44-2-41),3-68/S-1	24	3.1
Yr.	146	530	112	173	34	**14**	10	76	72	42	**31**	10	.326	.422	.500	.922	152	44	120	8.48	-6	0-82(44-2-41),3-68/1-7,S-1	25	3.3
1952 Chi-A★	147	569	96	160	24	9	13	61	71	46	**22**	16	.281	.375	.424	.798	121	16	92	5.48	1	*0-143(70-63-10)/3-9,S-1	21	1.0
1953 Chi-A★	151	556	104	174	24	8	15	104	74	43	**25**	16	.313	.410	.466	.875	132	27	106	6.65	6	*0-147(145-0-2),3-10	26	2.4
1954 Chi-A★	153	568	119	182	29	**18**	19	116	77	46	18	11	.320	.416	.535	.951	154	44	125	7.81	9	*0-146(120-16-13)/3-9	32	4.5
1955 Chi-A	139	517	79	149	26	7	10	70	76	43	19	8	.288	.390	.424	.813	115	15	87	5.80	8	*0-138(135-2-7)/3-2	21	1.4
1956 Chi-A	151	545	106	172	29	**11**	21	88	86	40	12	6	.316	.430	.525	.954	149	43	130	8.75	-3	*0-148(147-0-1)/3-8,1-1	29	3.0
1957 Chi-A★	153	568	96	176	**36**	5	12	103	79	54	18	15	.310	.413	.454	.867	136	31	106	6.57	1	*0-152(152-0-0)/3-1	26	2.3
1958 Cle-A	149	556	94	168	25	2	24	80	59	53	14	14	.302	.384	.484	.868	141	29	101	6.43	3	*0-147(147-0-0)/3-1	25	2.4
1959 Cle-A★	148	570	92	172	32	0	21	92	54	46	8	10	.302	.379	.468	.848	136	27	100	6.33	5	*0-148(148-0-0)	29	2.2
1960 Chi-A★	154	591	89	**184**	32	4	20	105	52	63	17	13	.311	.380	.481	.860	132	25	104	6.24	-1	*0-154(152-0-5)	24	1.4
1961 Chi-A	152	540	91	151	28	3	14	82	67	46	9	4	.280	.376	.420	.796	114	13	89	5.80	-3	*0-147(147-0-0)	19	0.2
1962 StL-N	39	97	14	19	5	0	1	10	7	17	4	0	.196	.271	.278	.549	44	-7	8	2.82	0	0-27(27-0-0)	1	-0.8
1963 Was-A	109	315	38	72	12	2	4	30	33	38	8	6	.229	.317	.317	.635	79	-9	30	3.03	-1	0-74(74-0-0)/3-8	4	-1.4
1964 Chi-A	30	31	4	7	0	0	1	5	5	3	0	0	.226	.351	.323	.674	91	-0	4	4.37	0	/0-5(4-0-1)	1	0.0
1976 Chi-A	3	8	0	1	0	0	0	0	0	2	0	0	.125	.125	.125	.250	-26	-1	0	.48	0	/D-3	0	-0.1
1980 Chi-A	2	2	0	0	0	0	0	0	0	0	0	0	.000	.000	.000	.000	-100	-1	0	.00	0	....	0	-0.1
Total 17	1835	6579	1136	1963	336	83	186	1023	814	584	205	130	.298	.391	.459	.851	130	295	1204	6.43	16	*0-1665,3-116/1-8,D-3,S-2	283	21.7
• MIRABELLI, Doug	Douglas Anthony Mirabelli b: 10/18/1970, Kingman, AZ BR/TR, 6'1", 205 lbs. Deb: 8/27/1996																							
1996 SF-N	9	18	2	4	1	0	0	1	3	4	0	0	.222	.333	.278	.611	66	-1	2	3.72	0	/C-8	1	0.0
1997 SF-N	6	7	0	1	0	0	0	0	1	3	0	0	.143	.250	.143	.393	6	-1	0	1.42	0	/C-6	0	-0.1
1998 SF-N	10	17	2	4	2	0	1	4	2	6	0	0	.235	.316	.529	.845	124	1	3	6.24	0	C-10	1	0.1
1999 SF-N	33	87	10	22	6	0	1	10	9	25	0	0	.253	.330	.356	.686	79	-3	11	4.32	1	C-30	3	0.0
2000*SF-N	82	230	23	53	10	2	6	28	36	57	1	0	.230	.340	.370	.709	85	-4	30	4.36	-11	C-80	6	-0.9
2001 Tex-A	23	49	4	5	2	0	2	3	10	21	0	0	.102	.254	.265	.520	36	-5	4	2.22	0	C-23/D-1	1	-0.4
Bos-A	54	141	16	38	8	0	9	26	17	36	0	0	.270	.364	.518	.882	128	6	27	6.87	2	C-52/D-1	6	1.0
Yr.	77	190	20	43	10	0	11	29	27	57	0	0	.226	.335	.453	.787	103	1	31	5.50	2	C-75/D-2	7	0.7
2002 Bos-A	57	151	17	34	7	0	7	25	17	33	0	0	.225	.316	.411	.726	89	-2	19	4.09	-1	C-50/D-4	4	-0.1
2003*Bos-A	62	163	23	42	13	0	6	18	11	36	0	0	.258	.309	.448	.756	94	-2	22	4.80	1	C-55/D-3,1-2	2	0.2
Total 8	336	863	97	203	49	2	32	115	106	221	1	0	.235	.327	.408	.734	91	-12	119	4.63	-9	C-314/D-9,1-2	24	-0.2
• MIRANDA, Willy	Guillermo (Perez) Miranda b: 5/24/1926, Velasco, Cuba d: 9/7/1996, Baltimore, MD BB/TR, 5'9.5", 150 lbs. Deb: 5/6/1951																							
1951 Was-A	7	9	2	4	0	0	0	0	0	0	0	0	.444	.444	.444	.889	143	1	2	9.84	-2	/S-2,1-1	0	-0.1
1952 Chi-A	12	8	1	2	1	0	0	0	3	0	0	0	.250	.455	.375	.830	131	1	2	6.35	1	/3-4,S-4,2-1	0	0.2
StL-A	7	11	2	1	0	1	0	1	3	1	0	0	.091	.286	.273	.558	54	-1	1	2.86	-1	/S-7	0	-0.1
Chi-A	58	142	13	31	3	1	0	7	10	14	1	0	.218	.275	.254	.528	47	-10	11	2.48	3	S-50/2-1,3-1	3	-0.4
Yr.	77	161	16	34	4	2	0	8	16	15	1	0	.211	.287	.261	.547	54	-10	14	2.73	4	S-61/3-5,2-2	3	-0.3
1953 StL-A	17	6	2	1	0	0	0	0	1	1	1	1	.167	.286	.167	.452	24	-1	0	1.16	-2	/S-8,3-6	0	-0.3
NY-A	48	58	12	13	0	0	1	5	5	10	1	1	.224	.286	.276	.562	54	-4	4	2.03	2	S-45	1	0.0
Yr.	65	64	14	14	0	0	1	5	6	11	2	2	.219	.286	.266	.551	51	-5	4	1.94	-0	S-53/3-6	1	-0.3
1954 NY-A	92	116	12	29	4	2	1	12	10	10	0	3	.250	.310	.345	.654	82	-4	12	3.27	-2	S-88/2-4,3-1	4	-0.3
1955 Bal-A	153	487	42	124	12	6	1	38	42	58	4	3	.255	.315	.310	.625	74	-18	48	3.41	19	*S-153/2-1	14	1.3
1956 Bal-A	148	461	38	100	16	4	2	34	46	73	3	6	.217	.288	.282	.570	55	-32	38	2.66	-1	*S-147	7	-2.1
1957 Bal-A	115	314	29	61	3	0	0	20	24	42	2	1	.194	.251	.204	.455	27	-31	17	1.73	6	*S-115	5	-1.7
1958 Bal-A	102	214	15	43	6	0	1	8	14	25	1	1	.201	.250	.243	.493	38	-18	13	2.04	-1	*S-102	4	-1.3
1959 Bal-A	65	88	8	14	5	0	0	7	7	16	0	0	.159	.221	.216	.437	21	-10	4	1.48	-1	S-47,3-11/2-5	2	-0.8
Total 9	824	1914	176	423	50	14	6	132	165	250	13	16	.221	.284	.271	.555	54	-127	152	2.60	23	S-768/3-23,2-12,1-1	40	-5.4
• MISSE, John	John Beverly Misse b: 5/30/1885, Highland, KS d: 3/18/1970, St. Joseph, MO BR/TR, 5'8", 150 lbs. Deb: 5/26/1914																							
1914 StL-F	99	306	28	60	8	1	0	22	36	52	3	....	.196	.281	.229	.509	43	-22	22	2.13	-8	2-50,S-48/3-2	3	-2.6
• MITCHELL, Bobby	Robert Vance Mitchell b: 10/22/1943, Norristown, PA BR/TR, 6'3", 190 lbs. Deb: 7/5/1970 Career OF: 94-11-39																							
1970 NY-A	10	22	1	5	2	0	0	4	2	3	0	2	.227	.320	.318	.638	81	-1	2	2.65	1	/0-7(0-2-5)	1	-0.1
1971 Mil-A	35	55	7	10	1	1	2	6	6	18	0	2	.182	.262	.345	.608	72	-3	5	2.68	1	0-19(2-7-10)	1	-0.3
1973 Mil-A	47	130	12	29	6	0	5	20	5	32	4	1	.223	.252	.385	.636	79	-4	13	3.41	-1	0-20(10-0-10),D-19	2	-0.6
1974 Mil-A	88	173	27	42	6	2	5	20	18	46	7	6	.243	.318	.387	.705	103	-1	20	3.89	0	D-53,0-26(10-2-14)	4	-0.2
1975 Mil-A	93	229	39	57	14	3	9	41	25	69	3	4	.249	.323	.454	.777	117	3	32	4.68	2	0-72(72-0-0),D-11	7	0.2
Total 5	273	609	86	143	29	6	21	91	56	168	14	15	.235	.301	.406	.707	100	-5	72	3.93	3	0-144/D-83	15	-1.0
• MITCHELL, Bobby	Robert Van Mitchell b: 4/7/1955, Salt Lake City, UT BL/TL, 5'10", 170 lbs. Deb: 9/1/1980 Career OF: 7-171-8																							
1980 LA-N	9	3	1	1	0	0	0	0	1	0	0	0	.333	.500	.333	.833	139	0	1	8.51	-1	/0-8(0-7-1)	0	0.0
1981 LA-N	10	8	0	1	0	0	0	0	1	4	0	0	.125	.222	.125	.347		-1	0	1.08	0	/0-7(1-6-1)	0	-0.2
1982 Min-A	124	454	48	113	11	6	2	28	54	53	8	9	.249	.331	.313	.644	76	-15	48	3.64	7	*0-121(5-115-6)	9	-1.1
1983 Min-A	59	152	26	35	4	2	1	15	28	21	1	1	.230	.354	.303	.656	80	-3	18	3.96	-2	0-44(1-43-0)	3	-0.5
Total 4	202	617	75	150	15	8	3	43	84	78	9	10	.243	.337	.308	.645	76	-19	67	3.70	4	0-180	12	-1.8
• MITCHELL, Clarence	Clarence Elmer Mitchell b: 2/22/1891, Franklin, NE d: 11/6/1963, Grand Island, NE BL/TL, 5'11.5", 190 lbs. Deb: 6/2/1911 C Career OF: 12-0-8 ♦																							
1911 Det-A	5	4	2	2	0	0	0	0	1	....	0	....	.500	.600	.500	1.100	198	1	1	15.56	-1	/P-5	0	-0.6
1916 Cin-N	56	117	11	28	2	1	0	11	4	6	1	....	.239	.264	.274	.538	67	2	9	2.55	-1	P-29/1-9,0-3(5-0-0)	9	-1.5
1917 Cin-N	47	90	13	25	3	0	0	5	5	5	0	....	.278	.316	.311	.627	97	4	9	3.35	-1	P-32/1-6,0-5(5-0-0)	7	-0.8
1918 Bro-N	10	24	2	6	1	1	0	2	0	3	0	....	.250	.250	.375	.625	90	-0	2	2.98	-1	/0-6(0-0-6),1-2,P-1	0	-0.6
1919 Bro-N	34	49	7	18	1	0	1	2	4	4	0	....	.367	.415	.449	.864	156	6	9	7.32	1	P-23	8	0.8
1920*Bro-N	55	107	9	25	2	2	0	11	8	9	1	0	.234	.287	.290	.577	64	-1	9	2.97	2	P-19,1-11/0-4(2-0-2)	6	0.1
1921 Bro-N	46	91	11	24	5	0	0	12	5	7	3	1	.264	.316	.319	.635	66	4	10	3.70	3	P-37/1-4	17	2.5
1922 Bro-N	56	155	21	45	6	3	3	28	19	6	0	0	.290	.371	.426	.797	106	3	25	5.98	2	1-42/P-5	6	-1.2
1923 Phi-N	53	78	10	21	3	2	1	9	4	11	0	0	.269	.305	.397	.702	75	4	9	4.36	-3	P-29	8	0.6
1924 Phi-N	69	102	7	26	3	0	0	13	2	7	1	0	.255	.276	.284	.561	45	0	8	2.77	2	P-30	5	-1.7
1925 Phi-N	52	92	7	18	2	0	0	13	5	9	2	0	.196	.237	.217	.455	16	-2	5	1.81	4	P-32/1-2	10	-0.5
1926 Phi-N	39	78	8	19	4	0	0	6	5	5	0	....	.244	.289	.295	.584	55	1	7	2.85	3	P-28/1-4	9	-0.2
1927 Phi-N	18	42	5	10	2	0	1	6	2	1	0	....	.238	.273	.357	.630	67	2	4	3.05	0	P-13	7	0.4

YEAR TM-L	G	AB	R	H	2B	3B	HR	RBI	BB	SO	SB	CS	AVG	OBP	SLG	OPS	OPS+	BR/A	RC	RC/G	FR	G/POS	WS	TPW
1928 Phi-N	5	4	0	1	0	0	0	0	0	0	0	....	.250	.250	.250	.500	30	0	0	2.02	0	/P-3	0	-0.3
*StL-N	19	56	0	7	1	0	0	1	0	3	0	....	.125	.125	.143	.268	-30	-4	1	.53	3	P-19	10	0.7
Yr.	24	60	0	8	1	0	0	1	0	3	0	....	.133	.133	.150	.283	-26	-4	1	.61	3	P-22	10	0.4
1929 StL-N	26	66	9	18	3	1	0	9	4	6	1	....	.273	.314	.348	.663	63	4	7	3.47	-1	P-25	12	1.1
1930 StL-N	1	2	0	1	0	0	0	0	0	0	0	....	.500	.500	.500	1.000	138	0	0	12.09	0	/P-1	0	0.0
NY-N	24	47	9	12	1	0	0	1	1	5	0	....	.255	.271	.277	.547	33	0	3	2.41	2	P-24	10	0.9
Yr.	25	49	9	13	1	0	0	1	1	5	0	....	.265	.280	.286	.566	38	0	4	2.66	2	P-25	10	0.9
1931 NY-N	27	73	5	16	2	0	1	4	2	4	0	....	.219	.240	.288	.528	42	2	5	2.29	-2	P-27	8	-0.8
1932 NY-N	8	10	2	2	0	0	0	0	1	1	0	....	.200	.273	.200	.473	30	0	1	1.95	-1	/P-8	1	-0.1
Total 18	650	1287	138	324	41	10	7	133	72	92	9	1	.252	.293	.315	.609	65	26	125	3.31	12	P-390/1-80,0-18	133	-1.3

• MITCHELL, Dale

Loren Dale Mitchell b: 8/23/1921, Colony, OK d: 1/5/1987, Tulsa, OK BL/TL, 6'1", 195 lbs. Deb: 9/15/1946 Career OF: 888-54-1

YEAR TM-L	G	AB	R	H	2B	3B	HR	RBI	BB	SO	SB	CS	AVG	OBP	SLG	OPS	OPS+	BR/A	RC	RC/G	FR	G/POS	WS	TPW
1946 Cle-A	11	44	7	19	3	0	0	5	1	2	1	0	.432	.444	.500	.944	175	4	10	10.23	-1	0-11(0-11-0)	3	0.3
1947 Cle-A	123	493	69	156	16	10	1	34	23	14	2	5	.316	.347	.396	.742	109	3	69	5.39	-2	*0-115(83-42-1)	16	-0.7
1948*Cle-A	141	608	82	204	30	8	4	56	45	17	13	18	.336	.383	.431	.814	119	11	98	6.15	7	*0-140(140-1-0)	20	0.7
1949 Cle-A★	149	640	81	**203**	16	**23**	3	56	43	11	10	3	.317	.360	.428	.788	110	8	102	6.14	4	*0-149(149-0-0)	23	0.0
1950 Cle-A	130	506	81	156	27	5	3	49	67	21	3	7	.308	.390	.399	.789	106	4	83	6.10	-9	*0-127(127-0-0)	16	-1.3
1951 Cle-A	134	510	83	148	21	7	11	62	53	16	7	7	.290	.358	.424	.782	117	10	79	5.60	-9	*0-124(124-0-0)	19	-0.8
1952 Cle-A★	134	511	61	165	26	3	5	58	52	9	6	6	.323	.387	.415	.801	132	21	82	5.97	-3	*0-128(128-0-0)	21	0.9
1953 Cle-A	134	500	76	150	26	4	13	60	42	20	3	1	.300	.354	.446	.800	118	12	80	5.97	1	*0-125(125-0-0)	18	0.6
1954*Cle-A	53	60	6	17	1	0	1	6	9	1	0	0	.283	.377	.350	.727	98	0	8	5.19	-0	/0-6(6-0-0),1-1	2	0.0
1955 Cle-A	61	58	4	15	2	1	0	10	4	3	0	0	.259	.306	.328	.634	68	-3	5	3.17	0	/1-8,0-3(3-0-0)	0	-0.3
1956 Cle-A	38	30	2	4	0	0	0	6	7	2	0	0	.133	.297	.133	.431	17	-3	2	1.72	0	/0-1	0	-0.3
*Bro-N	19	24	3	7	1	0	0	1	0	3	0	0	.292	.292	.333	.625	63	-1	2	2.37	-0	/0-2(2-0-0)	0	-0.1
Total 11	1127	3984	555	1244	169	61	41	403	346	119	45	47	.312	.368	.416	.784	114	66	622	5.84	-13	0-931/1-9	138	-1.0

• MITCHELL, Fred

Frederick Francis Mitchell
b: 6/5/1878, Cambridge, MA d: 10/13/1970, Newton, MA BR/TR, 5'9.5", 185 lbs. Deb: 4/27/1901 M/C Career OF: 1-2-0 ♦

YEAR TM-L	G	AB	R	H	2B	3B	HR	RBI	BB	SO	SB	CS	AVG	OBP	SLG	OPS	OPS+	BR/A	RC	RC/G	FR	G/POS	WS	TPW
1901 Bos-A	20	44	5	7	0	2	0	4	2	....	0	....	.159	.196	.250	.446	23	-2	2	1.58	-1	P-17/2-2,S-1	5	-1.0
1902 Bos-A	1	1	0	0	0	0	0	0	0	....	0	....	.000	.000	.000	.000	-97	-0	0	.00	0	/P-1	0	-0.3
Phi-A	20	48	7	9	1	1	0	3	1	....	1	....	.188	.204	.250	.454	24	-1	3	1.89	2	P-18/0-1	5	0.0
Yr.	21	49	7	9	1	1	0	3	1	....	1	....	.184	.200	.245	.445	22	-1	3	1.85	2	P-19/0-1	5	-0.3
1903 Phi-N	29	95	11	19	4	0	0	10	0	....	0	....	.200	.200	.242	.442	27	-1	5	1.67	-3	P-28	5	-3.4
1904 Phi-N	25	82	9	17	3	1	0	3	5	....	1	....	.207	.253	.268	.521	63	-0	6	2.41	2	P-13/1-9,3-2,0-1	3	-0.8
Bro-N	8	24	3	7	1	1	0	6	1	....	0	....	.292	.346	.417	.763	139	3	4	5.30	1	/P-8	2	-0.5
Yr.	33	106	12	24	4	2	0	9	6	....	1	....	.226	.274	.302	.576	81	2	10	3.02	3	P-21/1-9,3-2,0-1	5	-1.3
1905 Bro-N	27	79	4	15	0	0	0	8	4	....	0	....	.190	.238	.190	.428	30	-3	4	1.52	-2	P-12/1-7,3-4,0-1,S-1	1	-2.5
1910 NY-A	68	196	16	45	7	2	0	18	9	....	6	....	.230	.274	.286	.560	71	-7	16	2.79	-6	C-62	4	-0.9
1913 Bos-N	4	3	0	1	0	0	0	0	0	2	0	....	.333	.333	.333	.667	89	-0	0	3.70	0	....	0	0.0
Total 7	202	572	55	120	16	7	0	52	22	2	8	....	.210	.245	.262	.508	52	-12	41	2.29	-8	/P-97,C-62,1-16,3-6,0-3,2-2,S	25	-9.4

• MITCHELL, Johnny

John Franklin Mitchell b: 8/9/1894, Detroit, MI d: 11/4/1965, Birmingham, MI BB/TR, 5'8", 155 lbs. Deb: 5/21/1921

YEAR TM-L	G	AB	R	H	2B	3B	HR	RBI	BB	SO	SB	CS	AVG	OBP	SLG	OPS	OPS+	BR/A	RC	RC/G	FR	G/POS	WS	TPW
1921 NY-A	13	42	4	11	1	0	0	2	4	4	1	0	.262	.326	.286	.612	56	-2	4	3.57	-2	/S-7,2-5	1	-0.4
1922 NY-A	4	4	1	0	0	0	0	0	0	1	0	0	.000	.000	.000	.000	-98	-1	0	.00	-1	/S-4	0	-0.2
Bos-A	59	203	20	51	4	1	1	8	16	17	1	2	.251	.318	.296	.614	61	-11	20	3.20	0	S-58	3	-0.5
Yr.	63	207	21	51	4	1	1	8	16	18	1	2	.246	.313	.290	.603	59	-13	20	3.13	-1	S-62	3	-0.7
1923 Bos-A	92	347	40	78	15	4	0	19	34	18	7	11	.225	.296	.291	.587	55	-26	29	2.74	3	S-87/2-5	5	-1.3
1924 Bro-N	64	243	42	64	10	0	1	16	37	22	3	1	.263	.361	.317	.678	86	-2	31	4.22	1	S-64	8	0.6
1925 Bro-N	97	336	45	84	8	3	0	18	28	19	2	0	.250	.308	.292	.599	55	-21	32	3.28	-7	S-90	5	-1.8
Total 5	329	1175	152	288	38	8	2	63	119	81	14	14	.245	.317	.296	.613	62	-63	117	3.30	-6	S-310/2-10	22	-3.5

• MITCHELL, Keith

Keith Alexander Mitchell b: 8/6/1969, San Diego, CA BR/TR, 5'10", 180 lbs. Deb: 7/23/1991 Career OF: 57-5-29

YEAR TM-L	G	AB	R	H	2B	3B	HR	RBI	BB	SO	SB	CS	AVG	OBP	SLG	OPS	OPS+	BR/A	RC	RC/G	FR	G/POS	WS	TPW
1991*Atl-N	48	66	11	21	0	0	2	5	8	12	3	1	.318	.392	.409	.801	118	2	11	6.42	0	0-34(24-1-10)	3	0.1
1994 Sea-A	46	128	21	29	2	0	5	15	18	22	0	0	.227	.327	.359	.686	75	-5	16	4.21	-2	0-38(27-3-11)/D-6	1	-0.7
1996 Cin-N	11	15	2	4	1	0	1	3	1	3	0	0	.267	.313	.533	.846	119	0	3	6.34	0	/0-5(2-1-2)	0	0.0
1998 Bos-A	23	33	4	9	2	0	0	6	7	5	1	0	.273	.400	.333	.733	92	0	5	5.89	0	D-12,0-10(4-0-6)	1	-0.1
Total 4	128	242	38	63	5	0	8	29	34	42	4	1	.260	.354	.380	.734	92	-2	35	5.11	-3	/0-87,D-18	5	-0.6

• MITCHELL, Kevin

Kevin Darnell Mitchell b: 1/13/1962, San Diego, CA BR/TR, 5'10", 210 lbs. Deb: 9/4/1984 Career OF: 756-6-53

YEAR TM-L	G	AB	R	H	2B	3B	HR	RBI	BB	SO	SB	CS	AVG	OBP	SLG	OPS	OPS+	BR/A	RC	RC/G	FR	G/POS	WS	TPW
1984 NY-N	7	14	0	3	0	0	0	1	0	3	0	1	.214	.214	.214	.429	21	-2	0	.96	0	/3-5	0	-0.2
1986*NY-N	108	328	51	91	22	2	12	43	33	61	3	3	.277	.345	.466	.812	125	10	52	5.71	0	0-68(40-6-29),S-24/3-7,1-2	14	0.9
1987 SD-N	62	196	19	48	7	1	7	26	20	38	0	0	.245	.315	.398	.713	91	-3	24	4.22	1	3-51/0-3(3-0-0)	4	-0.3
*SF-N	69	268	49	82	13	1	15	44	28	50	9	6	.306	.376	.530	.906	143	15	52	7.16	-1	3-68/0-3(2-0-1),S-1	12	1.4
Yr.	131	464	68	130	20	2	22	70	48	88	9	6	.280	.350	.474	.824	121	12	76	5.87	0	*3-119/0-6(5-0-1),S-1	16	1.1
1988 SF-N	148	505	60	127	25	7	19	80	48	85	5	5	.251	.323	.442	.764	123	12	71	4.79	8	*3-102,0-40(40-0-0)	20	2.0
1989*SF-N★	154	543	100	158	34	6	**47**	**125**	87	115	3	4	.291	.392	**.635**	**1.027**	**195**	**65**	136	**9.12**	-4	*0-147(147-0-0)/3-2	38	**6.0**
1990 SF-N★	140	524	90	152	24	2	35	93	58	87	4	7	.290	.363	.544	.907	151	32	101	6.98	2	*0-138(138-0-0)	20	3.0
1991 SF-N	113	371	52	95	13	1	27	69	43	57	2	3	.256	.341	.515	.856	142	19	65	6.05	-2	*0-100(100-0-0)/1-1	16	1.4
1992 Sea-A	99	360	48	103	24	0	9	67	35	46	0	2	.286	.354	.428	.782	117	8	55	5.60	0	0-69(69-0-0),D-26	11	0.4
1993 Cin-N	93	323	56	110	21	3	19	64	25	48	1	0	.341	.390	.601	.990	160	26	70	8.17	3	0-87(85-0-2)	15	2.6
1994 Cin-N	95	310	57	101	18	1	30	77	59	62	2	0	.326	.438	.681	1.119	188	42	91	10.70	4	0-89(89-0-0)/1-1	18	4.2
1996 Bos-A	27	92	9	28	4	0	2	13	11	14	0	0	.304	.385	.413	.798	100	0	15	5.90	-2	0-21(1-0-21)/D-4	2	-0.2
Cin-N	37	114	18	37	11	0	6	26	26	16	0	0	.325	.450	.579	1.029	170	13	30	9.74	-2	0-31(31-0-0)/1-3	6	1.0
1997 Cle-A	20	59	7	9	1	0	4	11	9	11	1	0	.153	.275	.373	.648	65	-3	6	3.15	0	D-16/0-1	0	-0.4
1998 Oak-A	51	127	14	29	7	1	2	21	9	26	0	0	.228	.279	.346	.626	63	-7	12	3.07	0	D-23,0-10(10-0-0)/1-2	2	-0.8
Total 13	1223	4134	630	1173	224	25	234	760	491	719	30	31	.284	.364	.520	.883	144	227	780	6.74	5	0-807,3-235/D-69,S-25,1-9	178	20.8

• MITCHELL, Mike

Michael Francis Mitchell b: 12/12/1879, Springfield, OH d: 7/16/1961, Phoenix, AZ BR/TR, 6'1", 185 lbs. Deb: 4/11/1907 Career OF: 126-76-905

YEAR TM-L	G	AB	R	H	2B	3B	HR	RBI	BB	SO	SB	CS	AVG	OBP	SLG	OPS	OPS+	BR/A	RC	RC/G	FR	G/POS	WS	TPW
1907 Cin-N	148	558	64	163	17	12	3	47	37	....	17	....	.292	.339	.382	.721	121	12	82	5.19	21	*0-146(3-0-144)/1-2	21	2.9
1908 Cin-N	119	406	41	90	9	6	1	37	46	....	18	....	.222	.304	.281	.585	89	-4	40	3.19	-4	*0-118(3-0-115)/1-1	10	-1.5
1909 Cin-N	145	523	83	162	17	**17**	4	86	57	....	37	....	.310	.378	.430	.808	152	31	98	6.78	1	*0-145(0-0-144)/1-1	28	2.8
1910 Cin-N	156	583	79	167	16	**18**	5	88	59	56	35	....	.286	.356	.401	.757	126	18	96	5.67	-4	*0-149(0-22-127)/1-7	22	0.8
1911 Cin-N	142	529	74	154	22	22	2	84	44	34	35	....	.291	.348	.427	.775	121	12	90	5.93	8	*0-140(1-0-139)	17	1.3
1912 Cin-N	147	552	60	156	14	13	4	78	41	43	23	....	.283	.333	.377	.710	97	-4	76	4.71	-3	*0-144(0-0-144)	16	-1.4
1913 Chi-N	82	279	37	73	11	6	4	35	32	33	15	....	.262	.340	.387	.727	107	3	41	4.75	3	0-82(72-0-10)	11	0.2
Pit-N	54	199	25	54	8	2	1	16	14	15	8	....	.271	.319	.347	.666	94	-2	23	4.00	1	0-54(0-54-0)	6	-0.4
Yr.	136	478	62	127	19	8	5	51	46	48	23	....	.266	.331	.370	.702	102	1	64	4.45	4	*0-136(72-54-10)	17	-0.3
1914 Pit-N	76	273	31	64	11	5	2	23	16	16	5	....	.234	.279	.333	.613	85	-6	26	3.10	7	0-76(0-0-76)	6	-0.4
Was-A	55	193	20	55	5	3	1	20	22	19	9	7	.285	.361	.358	.719	112	2	27	4.57	3	0-53(47-0-6)	8	0.3
Total 8	1124	4095	514	1138	130	104	27	514	368	216	202	7	.278	.340	.380	.720	114	63	598	5.00	32	*0-1107/1-11	145	4.6

• MITTERLING, Ralph

Ralph "Sarge" Mitterling b: 4/19/1890, Freeburg, PA d: 1/22/1956, Pittsburgh, PA BR/TR, 5'10", 165 lbs. Deb: 7/7/1916

YEAR TM-L	G	AB	R	H	2B	3B	HR	RBI	BB	SO	SB	CS	AVG	OBP	SLG	OPS	OPS+	BR/A	RC	RC/G	FR	G/POS	WS	TPW
1916 Phi-A	13	39	1	6	0	0	0	2	3	6	0	....	.154	.214	.154	.368	11	-4	1	1.01	0	0-12(1-11-0)	0	-0.5

• MITTERWALD, George

George Eugene "Baron von Mitterwald" Mitterwald b: 6/7/1945, Berkeley, CA BR/TR, 6'2", 206 lbs. Deb: 9/15/1966 C

YEAR TM-L	G	AB	R	H	2B	3B	HR	RBI	BB	SO	SB	CS	AVG	OBP	SLG	OPS	OPS+	BR/A	RC	RC/G	FR	G/POS	WS	TPW
1966 Min-A	3	5	1	1	0	0	0	0	0	0	0	0	.200	.200	.200	.400	14	-1	0	1.35	0	/C-3	0	-0.1
1968 Min-A	11	34	1	7	1	0	0	1	3	8	0	0	.206	.270	.235	.506	52	-2	2	2.05	-1	C-10	0	-0.3
1969*Min-A	69	187	18	48	8	0	5	13	17	47	0	1	.257	.329	.380	.708	95	-2	23	4.08	2	C-63/0-1	6	0.3
1970*Min-A	117	369	36	82	12	2	15	46	34	84	3	5	.222	.291	.388	.679	84	-10	39	3.39	3	*C-117	13	-0.1
1971 Min-A	125	388	38	97	13	1	13	44	39	104	3	3	.250	.319	.389	.708	96	-3	47	4.08	4	*C-120	13	0.8

YEAR TM-L	G	AB	R	H	2B	3B	HR	RBI	BB	SO	SB	CS	AVG	OBP	SLG	OPS	OPS+	BR/A	RC	RC/G	FR	G/POS	WS	TPW
1972 Min-A	64	163	12	30	4	1	1	8	9	37	0	1	.184	.227	.239	.466	37	-13	8	1.52	2	C-61	2	-1.0
1973 Min-A	125	432	50	112	15	0	16	64	39	111	3	1	.259	.328	.405	.733	101	1	57	4.62	-1	*C-122/D-3	15	0.6
1974 Chi-N	78	215	17	54	7	0	7	28	18	42	1	3	.251	.315	.381	.696	90	-4	25	3.89	-1	C-68	5	-0.2
1975 Chi-N	84	200	19	44	4	3	5	26	19	42	0	0	.220	.288	.345	.633	72	-8	20	3.32	2	C-59,1-10	4	-0.5
1976 Chi-N	101	303	19	65	7	0	5	28	16	63	1	2	.215	.254	.287	.541	49	-22	20	2.15	0	C-64,1-25	3	-2.1
1977 Chi-N	110	349	40	83	22	0	9	43	28	69	3	1	.238	.296	.378	.675	71	-14	34	3.22	2	*C-109/1-1	7	-0.7
Total 11	887	2645	251	623	93	7	76	301	222	607	14	17	.236	.298	.362	.660	80	-78	275	3.45	13	C-796/1-36,D-3,0-1	68	-3.3

• MIZE, Johnny John Robert "The Big Cat" Mize b: 1/7/1913, Demorest, GA d: 6/2/1993, Demorest, GA BL/TR, 6'2", 215 lbs. Deb: 4/16/1936 C HOF: 1981

YEAR TM-L	G	AB	R	H	2B	3B	HR	RBI	BB	SO	SB	CS	AVG	OBP	SLG	OPS	OPS+	BR/A	RC	RC/G	FR	G/POS	WS	TPW
1936 StL-N	126	414	76	136	30	8	19	93	50	32	1	....	.329	.402	.577	.979	161	35	102	9.59	2	1-97/0-8(0-0-8)	26	2.7
1937 StL-N★	145	560	103	204	40	7	25	113	56	57	2	....	.364	.427	.595	1.021	171	55	150	11.18	-9	*1-144	34	3.3
1938 StL-N	149	531	85	179	34	**16**	27	102	74	47	0	....	.337	.422	**.614**	**1.036**	172	53	141	10.43	-3	*1-140	28	3.7
1939 StL-N★	153	564	104	197	44	14	**28**	108	92	49	0	....	**.349**	.444	**.626**	**1.070**	**174**	**62**	162	**11.36**	-4	*1-152	**33**	4.3
1940 StL-N★	155	579	111	182	31	13	**43**	**137**	82	49	7	....	.314	.404	**.636**	**1.039**	**173**	**57**	152	**10.08**	-1	*1-153	**33**	4.3
1941 StL-N★	126	473	67	150	**39**	8	16	100	70	45	4	....	.317	.406	.535	.941	153	35	106	8.59	2	*1-122	26	2.6
1942 NY-N★	142	541	97	165	25	7	26	**110**	60	39	3	....	.305	.380	**.521**	.901	161	40	110	7.68	-1	*1-138	32	2.8
1946 NY-N★	101	377	70	127	18	3	22	70	62	26	3	....	.337	.437	.576	1.013	185	44	100	10.52	7	*1-101	22	5.0
1947 NY-N★	154	586	**137**	177	26	2	**51**	**138**	74	42	2	....	.302	.384	.614	.998	160	48	143	9.28	2	*1-154	**32**	4.4
1948 NY-N★	152	560	110	162	26	4	**40**	125	94	37	4	....	.289	.395	.564	.959	156	45	131	8.75	3	*1-152	30	4.3
1949 NY-N★	106	388	59	102	15	0	18	62	50	19	1	....	.263	.351	.441	.792	111	6	63	5.81	7	*1-101	11	0.9
*NY-A	13	23	4	6	1	0	1	2	4	2	0	0	.261	.393	.435	.828	119	1	5	7.21	0	/1-6	1	0.0
1950*NY-A	90	274	43	76	12	0	25	72	29	24	0	1	.277	.351	.595	.946	143	14	59	7.79	-1	1-72	12	1.1
1951*NY-A	113	332	37	86	14	1	10	49	36	24	1	0	.259	.339	.398	.736	102	1	47	4.99	-2	1-93	11	-0.3
1952*NY-A	78	137	9	36	9	0	4	29	11	15	0	0	.263	.327	.416	.743	112	2	18	4.47	0	1-27	4	0.2
1953*NY-A★	81	104	6	26	3	0	4	27	12	17	0	0	.250	.339	.394	.733	101	0	15	5.16	-1	1-15	3	-0.1
Total 15	1884	6443	1118	2011	367	83	359	1337	856	524	28	1	.312	.397	.562	.959	157	498	1502	8.91	1	*1-1667/0-8	338	39.0

• MIZEROCK, John John Joseph Mizerock b: 12/8/1960, Punxsutawney, PA BL/TR, 5'11", 190 lbs. Deb: 4/12/1983 M/C

YEAR TM-L	G	AB	R	H	2B	3B	HR	RBI	BB	SO	SB	CS	AVG	OBP	SLG	OPS	OPS+	BR/A	RC	RC/G	FR	G/POS	WS	TPW
1983 Hou-N	33	85	8	13	4	1	1	10	12	15	0	0	.153	.265	.259	.524	49	-6	6	2.21	-1	C-33	1	-0.6
1985 Hou-N	15	38	6	9	4	0	0	6	2	8	0	0	.237	.293	.342	.635	79	-1	3	2.20	-1	C-15	0	-0.1
1986 Hou-N	44	81	9	15	1	1	1	6	24	16	0	0	.185	.377	.259	.637	81	-0	9	3.52	-2	C-42	3	-0.1
1989 Atl-N	11	27	1	6	0	0	0	2	0	3	0	0	.222	.222	.222	.444	27	-3	1	1.71	0	C-11	0	-0.2
Total 4	103	231	24	43	9	2	2	24	38	42	0	0	.186	.309	.268	.577	64	-10	19	2.62	-4	C-101	4	-1.0

• MIZEUR, Bill William Francis "Bad Bill" Mizeur b: 6/22/1897, Nokomis, IL d: 8/27/1976, Decatur, IL BL/TR, 6', 180 lbs. Deb: 9/30/1923

YEAR TM-L	G	AB	R	H	2B	3B	HR	RBI	BB	SO	SB	CS	AVG	OBP	SLG	OPS	OPS+	BR/A	RC	RC/G	FR	G/POS	WS	TPW
1923 StL-A	1	1	0	0	0	0	0	0	0	0	0	0	.000	.000	.000	.000	-95	-0	0	.00	0	....	0	0.0
1924 StL-A	1	1	0	0	0	0	0	0	0	0	0	0	.000	.000	.000	.000	-94	-0	0	.00	0	....	0	0.0

• MOATES, Dave David Allen Moates b: 1/30/1948, Great Lakes, IL BL/TL, 5'9", 163 lbs. Deb: 9/21/1974 Career OF: 9-86-26

YEAR TM-L	G	AB	R	H	2B	3B	HR	RBI	BB	SO	SB	CS	AVG	OBP	SLG	OPS	OPS+	BR/A	RC	RC/G	FR	G/POS	WS	TPW
1974 Tex-A	1	0	0	0	0	0	0	0	0	0	0	0	....	....	....	....	-103	0	0	....	0	....	0	0.0
1975 Tex-A	54	175	21	48	9	0	3	14	13	15	9	2	.274	.324	.377	.702	99	1	20	3.75	2	0-51(1-49-1)/D-1	4	0.2
1976 Tex-A	85	137	21	33	7	1	0	13	11	18	6	3	.241	.297	.307	.604	75	-4	13	3.23	2	0-66(8-37-25)/D-7	3	-0.5
Total 3	140	312	42	81	16	1	3	27	24	33	15	5	.260	.313	.346	.659	88	-4	33	3.52	4	0-117/D-8	7	-0.3

• MOELLER, Chad Chad Edward Moeller b: 2/18/1975, Upland, CA BR/TR, 6'3", 210 lbs. Deb: 6/20/2000

YEAR TM-L	G	AB	R	H	2B	3B	HR	RBI	BB	SO	SB	CS	AVG	OBP	SLG	OPS	OPS+	BR/A	RC	RC/G	FR	G/POS	WS	TPW
2000 Min-A	48	128	13	27	3	1	1	9	9	33	1	0	.211	.263	.273	.536	35	-13	9	2.26	-1	C-48	2	-1.0
2001 Ari-N	25	56	8	13	0	1	1	2	6	12	0	0	.232	.306	.321	.628	59	-3	5	3.14	-4	C-25	0	-0.6
2002*Ari-N	37	105	10	30	11	1	2	16	17	23	0	1	.286	.385	.467	.852	113	2	17	5.62	7	C-35	6	1.1
2003 Ari-N	78	239	29	64	17	1	7	29	23	59	1	2	.268	.337	.435	.772	90	-4	33	4.71	-9	C-76	6	-0.8
Total 4	188	528	60	134	31	4	11	56	55	127	2	3	.254	.326	.390	.717	79	-18	65	4.10	-7	C-184	14	-1.3

• MOELLER, Danny Daniel Edward Moeller b: 3/23/1885, DeWitt, IA d: 4/14/1951, Florence, AL BB/TR, 5'11", 165 lbs. Deb: 9/24/1907 Career OF: 98-4-559

YEAR TM-L	G	AB	R	H	2B	3B	HR	RBI	BB	SO	SB	CS	AVG	OBP	SLG	OPS	OPS+	BR/A	RC	RC/G	FR	G/POS	WS	TPW
1907 Pit-N	11	42	4	12	1	1	0	3	4	....	2	....	.286	.348	.357	.705	119	1	6	5.25	-1	0-11(0-0-11)	1	0.0
1908 Pit-N	36	109	14	21	3	1	0	9	9	....	4	....	.193	.254	.239	.493	57	-5	7	2.14	-5	0-27(3-1-23)	1	-1.3
1912 Was-A	132	519	90	143	26	10	6	46	52	....	30	....	.276	.346	.399	.745	112	7	81	5.43	14	*0-132(31-0-101)	22	1.5
1913 Was-A	153	589	88	139	15	10	5	42	72	103	62	....	.236	.322	.321	.643	86	-9	75	4.16	9	*0-153(16-0-137)	17	-0.9
1914 Was-A	151	571	83	143	19	10	1	45	71	89	26	25	.250	.341	.324	.665	96	-6	65	3.67	0	*0-150(1-1-149)	17	-1.5
1915 Was-A	118	438	65	99	11	10	2	23	59	63	32	10	.226	.319	.311	.630	87	-4	51	3.72	-2	*0-116(21-0-95)	11	-1.2
1916 Was-A	78	240	30	59	8	1	1	23	30	35	13	....	.246	.335	.300	.635	92	-2	29	4.01	2	0-63(23-0-40)	6	-0.3
Cle-A	25	30	5	2	0	0	0	1	5	6	2	....	.067	.200	.067	.267	-19	-4	1	.79	0	/0-8(3-2-3),2-1	0	-0.5
Yr.	103	270	35	61	8	1	1	24	35	41	15	....	.226	.319	.274	.593	79	-6	30	3.58	1	0-71(26-2-43)/2-1	6	-0.8
Total 7	704	2538	379	618	83	43	15	192	302	296	171	35	.243	.328	.328	.656	92	-23	314	4.08	18	0-660/2-1	75	-4.3

• MOFFETT, Joe Joseph W. Moffett b: 6/1859, Wheeling, WV, 6', 179 lbs. Deb: 5/6/1884

YEAR TM-L	G	AB	R	H	2B	3B	HR	RBI	BB	SO	SB	CS	AVG	OBP	SLG	OPS	OPS+	BR/A	RC	RC/G	FR	G/POS	WS	TPW
1884 Tol-a	56	204	17	41	5	3	0	0	2	....	....	....	.201	.209	.255	.464	49	-12	11	1.88	-4	1-38,3-11/2-4,0-3(1-3-0)	1	-1.8

• MOFFETT, Sam Samuel R. Moffett b: 3/14/1857, Wheeling, WV d: 5/5/1907, Butte, MT BR/TR, 6', 175 lbs. Deb: 5/15/1884 Career OF: 14-6-31 ♦

YEAR TM-L	G	AB	R	H	2B	3B	HR	RBI	BB	SO	SB	CS	AVG	OBP	SLG	OPS	OPS+	BR/A	RC	RC/G	FR	G/POS	WS	TPW
1884 Cle-N	67	256	26	47	12	2	0	15	8	56	....	....	.184	.208	.246	.454	41	-14	13	1.77	6	0-42(13-1-28),P-24/1-2,2-1,3	7	-2.4
1887 Ind-N	11	42	6	6	1	0	0	1	1	6	2	....	.143	.143	.146	.289	-20	-5	1	.86	-1	/P-6,0-5(1-2-3)	1	-0.3
1888 Ind-N	10	35	6	4	0	0	0	0	5	4	0	....	.114	.225	.114	.339	11	-1	1	.80	-2	/P-7,0-3(0-3-0)	1	-1.1
Total 3	88	333	38	57	13	2	0	16	14	66	2	....	.171	.202	.220	.422	30	-20	16	1.54	3	/0-50,P-37,1-2,2-1,3-1	9	-3.9

• MOHARDT, John John Henry Mohardt b: 1/21/1898, Pittsburgh, PA d: 11/24/1961, La Jolla, CA BR/TR, 5'10", 165 lbs. Deb: 4/15/1922

YEAR TM-L	G	AB	R	H	2B	3B	HR	RBI	BB	SO	SB	CS	AVG	OBP	SLG	OPS	OPS+	BR/A	RC	RC/G	FR	G/POS	WS	TPW
1922 Det-A	5	1	2	1	0	0	0	0	1	0	0	1	1.000	1.000	1.000	2.000	436	0	1	16.03	-1	/0-3(1-1-1)	0	0.0

• MOHLER, Kid Ernest Follette Mohler b: 12/13/1870, Oneida, IL d: 11/4/1961, San Francisco, CA BR/TL, 5'4.5", 145 lbs. Deb: 9/29/1894

YEAR TM-L	G	AB	R	H	2B	3B	HR	RBI	BB	SO	SB	CS	AVG	OBP	SLG	OPS	OPS+	BR/A	RC	RC/G	FR	G/POS	WS	TPW
1894 Was-N	3	9	0	1	0	0	0	0	2	4	0	....	.111	.273	.111	.384	-5	-1	0	.91	0	/2-3	0	-0.1

• MOHR, Dustan Dustan Kyle Mohr b: 6/19/1976, Hattiesburg, MS BR/TR, 6', 210 lbs. Deb: 8/29/2001 Career OF: 64-12-186

YEAR TM-L	G	AB	R	H	2B	3B	HR	RBI	BB	SO	SB	CS	AVG	OBP	SLG	OPS	OPS+	BR/A	RC	RC/G	FR	G/POS	WS	TPW
2001 Min-A	20	51	6	12	2	0	0	4	5	17	1	1	.235	.304	.275	.578	53	-4	5	3.02	1	0-19(6-0-15)/D-1	1	-0.3
2002*Min-A	120	383	55	103	23	2	12	45	31	86	6	3	.269	.325	.433	.759	98	-2	54	5.04	0	*0-113(28-1-94)/D-3	11	-0.6
2003 Min-A	121	348	50	87	22	0	10	36	33	106	5	2	.250	.317	.399	.716	87	-7	43	4.19	-1	*0-110(30-11-77)/D-6	6	-1.2
Total 3	261	782	111	202	47	2	22	85	69	209	12	6	.258	.320	.408	.728	90	-12	102	4.51	1	0-242/D-10	18	-2.2

• MOKAN, Johnny John Leo Mokan b: 9/23/1895, Buffalo, NY d: 2/10/1985, Buffalo, NY BR/TR, 5'7", 165 lbs. Deb: 4/15/1921 Career OF: 352-66-129

YEAR TM-L	G	AB	R	H	2B	3B	HR	RBI	BB	SO	SB	CS	AVG	OBP	SLG	OPS	OPS+	BR/A	RC	RC/G	FR	G/POS	WS	TPW
1921 Pit-N	19	52	7	14	3	2	0	9	5	3	0	0	.269	.333	.404	.737	92	-0	7	4.78	-2	0-15(6-0-7)	1	-0.3
1922 Pit-N	31	89	9	23	3	1	0	8	9	3	0	1	.258	.327	.315	.641	65	-5	9	3.58	-1	0-23(3-0-20)	1	-0.6
Phi-N	47	151	20	38	7	1	3	27	16	25	1	0	.252	.327	.371	.698	73	-6	19	4.30	-1	0-37(36-2-3)/3-2	2	-0.9
Yr.	78	240	29	61	10	2	3	35	25	28	1	1	.254	.327	.350	.677	70	-10	29	4.04	-2	0-60(39-2-23)/3-2	3	-1.5
1923 Phi-N	113	400	76	125	23	3	10	48	53	31	6	11	.313	.401	.460	.861	113	7	73	6.64	-1	*0-105(84-21-2)/3-1	10	-0.1
1924 Phi-N	96	366	50	95	15	1	7	44	30	27	7	5	.260	.321	.363	.684	74	-13	43	4.03	-2	0-94(93-2-0)	5	-2.3
1925 Phi-N	75	209	30	69	11	2	6	42	27	9	3	5	.330	.417	.488	.905	120	6	43	7.41	-5	0-68(36-32-2)	7	-0.1
1926 Phi-N	127	456	68	138	23	5	6	62	41	31	4	....	.303	.365	.414	.780	104	3	69	5.27	-2	*0-123(67-0-67)	12	-0.8
1927 Phi-N	74	213	22	61	13	2	0	33	25	21	5	....	.286	.361	.366	.728	94	-1	29	4.73	-3	0-63(27-9-28)	4	-0.7
Total 7	582	1936	282	563	98	17	32	273	206	150	26	22	.291	.364	.409	.773	97	-8	292	5.30	-17	0-528/3-3	42	-5.8

• MOLE, Fenton Fenton Le Roy "Muscles" Mole b: 6/14/1925, San Leandro, CA BL/TL, 6'1.5", 200 lbs. Deb: 9/1/1949

YEAR TM-L	G	AB	R	H	2B	3B	HR	RBI	BB	SO	SB	CS	AVG	OBP	SLG	OPS	OPS+	BR/A	RC	RC/G	FR	G/POS	WS	TPW
1949 NY-A	10	27	2	5	2	1	0	2	3	5	0	0	.185	.267	.333	.600	58	-2	2	2.25	1	/1-8	0	-0.1

• MOLINA, Ben Benjamin Jose Molina b: 7/20/1974, Rio Piedras, Puerto Rico BR/TR, 5'11", 210 lbs. Deb: 9/21/1998

YEAR TM-L	G	AB	R	H	2B	3B	HR	RBI	BB	SO	SB	CS	AVG	OBP	SLG	OPS	OPS+	BR/A	RC	RC/G	FR	G/POS	WS	TPW
1998 Ana-A	2	1	0	0	0	0	0	0	0	0	0	0	.000	.000	.000	.000	-99	-0	0	.00	-1	/C-2	0	-0.1

YEAR TM-L	G	AB	R	H	2B	3B	HR	RBI	BB	SO	SB	CS	AVG	OBP	SLG	OPS	OPS+	BR/A	RC	RC/G	FR	G/POS	WS	TPW
1999 Ana-A	31	101	8	26	5	0	1	10	6	6	0	1	.257	.312	.337	.649	66	-6	9	3.09	5	C-30	3	0.2
2000 Ana-A	130	473	59	133	20	2	14	71	23	33	1	0	.281	.323	.421	.743	84	-13	60	4.41	7	*C-127/D-2	13	0.3
2001 Ana-A	96	325	31	85	11	0	6	40	16	51	0	1	.262	.312	.351	.663	73	-14	35	3.66	-4	C-94/D-1	7	-1.1
2002*Ana-A	122	428	34	105	18	0	5	47	15	34	0	0	.245	.277	.322	.600	59	-26	35	2.72	1	*C-121	9	-1.6
2003 Ana-A	119	409	37	115	24	0	14	71	13	31	1	1	.281	.307	.443	.749	98	-3	49	4.16	6	*C-117	16	1.1
Total 6	500	1737	169	464	78	2	40	239	73	155	2	3	.267	.305	.383	.689	78	-61	188	3.70	15	C-491/D-3	48	-1.2

• MOLINA, Izzy Islay Molina b: 6/3/1971, New York, NY BR/TR, 6'1", 200 lbs. Deb: 8/15/1996

YEAR TM-L	G	AB	R	H	2B	3B	HR	RBI	BB	SO	SB	CS	AVG	OBP	SLG	OPS	OPS+	BR/A	RC	RC/G	FR	G/POS	WS	TPW
1996 Oak-A	14	25	0	5	2	0	0	1	1	3	0	0	.200	.231	.280	.511	29	-3	2	2.26	0	C-12/D-1	0	-0.2
1997 Oak-A	48	111	6	22	3	1	3	7	3	17	0	0	.198	.219	.324	.544	40	-10	8	2.31	-1	C-48	1	-0.8
1998 Oak-A	6	2	1	1	0	0	0	0	0	0	0	0	.500	.500	.500	1.000	165	0	1	13.50	0	/C-5	0	0.0
2002 Bal-A	1	3	1	1	0	0	0	0	0	0	0	0	.333	.333	.333	.667	82	-0	0	4.50	0	/C-1	0	0.0
Total 4	69	141	8	29	5	1	3	8	4	20	0	0	.206	.228	.319	.547	41	-13	10	2.44	-1	/C-66,D-1	1	-1.0

• MOLINA, Jose Jose Benjamin (Matta) Molina b: 6/3/1975, Bayamon, Puerto Rico BR/TR, 6'1", 215 lbs. Deb: 9/6/1999

YEAR TM-L	G	AB	R	H	2B	3B	HR	RBI	BB	SO	SB	CS	AVG	OBP	SLG	OPS	OPS+	BR/A	RC	RC/G	FR	G/POS	WS	TPW
1999 Chi-N	10	19	3	5	1	0	0	1	2	4	0	0	.263	.333	.316	.649	66	-1	2	4.02	0	C-10	0	0.0
2001 Ana-A	15	37	8	10	3	0	2	4	3	8	0	0	.270	.325	.514	.839	113	1	5	4.75	2	C-15	1	0.3
2002*Ana-A	29	70	5	19	3	0	0	5	5	15	0	2	.271	.320	.314	.634	70	-4	7	2.89	3	C-29	2	0.1
2003 Ana-A	53	114	12	21	4	0	0	6	1	26	0	0	.184	.212	.219	.431	15	-14	6	1.52	-3	C-53	2	-1.4
Total 4	107	240	28	55	11	0	2	16	11	53	0	2	.229	.272	.300	.572	51	-18	20	2.59	2	C-107	5	-1.0

• MOLINARO, Bob Robert Joseph Molinaro b: 5/21/1950, Newark, NJ BL/TR, 6', 190 lbs. Deb: 9/18/1975 Career OF: 71-1-58

YEAR TM-L	G	AB	R	H	2B	3B	HR	RBI	BB	SO	SB	CS	AVG	OBP	SLG	OPS	OPS+	BR/A	RC	RC/G	FR	G/POS	WS	TPW
1975 Det-A	6	19	2	5	0	1	0	1	1	0	0	0	.263	.300	.368	.668	84	-0	2	4.00	1	/O-6(0-0-6)	0	0.0
1977 Det-A	4	4	0	1	1	0	0	0	0	2	0	0	.250	.250	.500	.750	94	-0	1	4.50	0	....	0	0.0
Chi-A	1	2	0	1	0	0	0	0	0	1	1	0	.500	.500	.500	1.000	174	0	1	20.52	0	/O-1	0	0.0
Yr.	5	6	0	2	1	0	0	0	0	3	1	0	.333	.333	.500	.833	120	0	1	8.51	0	/O-1	0	0.0
1978 Chi-A	105	286	39	75	5	5	6	27	19	12	22	6	.262	.315	.378	.693	93	-1	35	4.19	-1	O-62(12-1-50),D-32	7	-0.5
1979 Bal-A	8	6	0	0	0	0	0	0	1	3	1	0	.000	.143	.000	.143	-60	-1	0	.00	0	/O-5(5-0-0)	0	-0.1
1980 Chi-A	119	344	48	100	16	4	5	36	26	29	18	7	.291	.353	.404	.757	107	5	50	5.20	0	O-49(49-0-0),D-47	10	0.1
1981 Chi-A	47	42	7	11	1	1	1	9	8	1	1	0	.262	.392	.405	.797	133	3	7	5.88	0	/D-4,O-2(1-0-1)	1	0.2
1982 Chi-N	65	66	6	13	1	0	1	12	6	5	1	1	.197	.264	.258	.521	45	-5	5	2.35	0	/O-4(4-0-0)	0	-0.6
Phi-N	19	14	0	4	0	0	0	2	3	1	1	0	.286	.412	.286	.697	96	1	2	5.60	0	....	0	0.1
Yr.	84	80	6	17	1	0	1	14	9	6	2	1	.213	.292	.263	.555	55	-5	7	2.86	0	/O-4(4-0-0)	0	-0.5
1983 Phi-N	19	18	1	2	1	0	1	3	0	2	0	0	.111	.111	.333	.444	19	-2	1	1.09	0	....	0	-0.2
Det-A	8	2	3	0	0	0	0	0	1	1	1	1	.000	.333	.000	.333	1	-0	0	.00	0	/D-1	0	0.0
Total 8	401	803	106	212	25	11	14	90	65	57	46	15	.264	.328	.375	.702	95	-2	104	4.44	-1	O-129/D-84	18	-1.0

• MOLITOR, Paul Paul Leo Molitor b: 8/22/1956, St. Paul, MN BR/TR, 6', 185 lbs. Deb: 4/7/1978 C HOF: 2004 Career OF: 4-43-4

YEAR TM-L	G	AB	R	H	2B	3B	HR	RBI	BB	SO	SB	CS	AVG	OBP	SLG	OPS	OPS+	BR/A	RC	RC/G	FR	G/POS	WS	TPW
1978 Mil-A	125	521	73	142	26	4	6	45	19	54	30	12	.273	.303	.372	.676	89	-8	59	3.86	-9	2-91,S-31/D-2,3-1	12	-0.9
1979 Mil-A	140	584	88	188	27	16	9	62	48	48	33	13	.322	.375	.469	.845	126	23	103	6.50	2	*2-122,S-10/D-8	26	3.1
1980 Mil-A★	111	450	81	137	29	2	9	37	48	48	34	7	.304	.375	.438	.813	126	22	78	6.21	3	2-91,S-12/D-7,3-1	19	3.0
1981*Mil-A	64	251	45	67	11	0	2	19	25	29	10	6	.267	.341	.335	.675	100	1	30	4.08	0	O-46(0-43-4),D-16	8	-0.1
1982*Mil-A	160	666	**136**	201	26	8	19	71	69	93	41	9	.302	.368	.450	.819	132	35	117	6.34	3	*3-150/D-6,S-4	30	3.6
1983 Mil-A	152	608	95	164	28	6	15	47	59	74	41	8	.270	.336	.410	.746	113	16	88	4.97	8	*3-146/D-2	23	2.3
1984 Mil-A	13	46	3	10	1	0	0	6	2	8	1	0	.217	.250	.239	.489	38	-4	3	2.24	3	/3-7,D-4	0	-0.1
1985 Mil-A★	140	576	93	171	28	3	10	48	54	80	21	7	.297	.358	.408	.766	110	10	85	5.29	0	*3-135/D-4	21	0.8
1986 Mil-A	105	437	62	123	24	6	9	55	40	81	20	5	.281	.342	.426	.767	104	4	65	5.25	8	3-91,D-10/O-4(4-0-0)	14	1.1
1987 Mil-A	118	465	**114**	164	**41**	5	16	75	69	67	45	10	.353	.438	.566	1.004	159	48	125	10.54	0	D-58,3-41,2-19	29	4.4
1988 Mil-A★	154	609	115	190	34	6	13	60	71	54	41	10	.312	.386	.452	.837	133	33	112	6.75	-3	*3-105,D-49/2-1	27	2.9
1989 Mil-A	155	615	84	194	35	4	11	56	64	67	27	11	.315	.384	.439	.823	133	29	106	6.28	10	*3-112,D-28,2-16	27	3.9
1990 Mil-A	103	418	64	119	27	6	12	45	37	51	18	3	.285	.344	.464	.808	125	16	68	5.94	-2	2-60,1-37/D-4,3-2	19	1.3
1991 Mil-A★	158	665	**133**	**216**	32	**13**	17	75	77	62	19	8	.325	.400	.489	.888	148	46	132	7.59	-1	*D-112,1-46	30	3.7
1992 Mil-A★	158	609	89	195	36	7	12	89	73	66	31	6	.320	.396	.461	.857	142	40	116	6.98	-3	*D-108,1-48	28	3.0
1993*Tor-A★	160	636	121	**211**	37	5	22	111	77	71	22	4	.332	.406	.509	.916	144	44	136	8.15	-0	*D-137,1-23	29	3.2
1994 Tor-A★	115	454	86	155	30	4	14	75	55	48	20	0	.341	.414	.518	.931	138	31	101	8.56	0	*D-110/1-5	19	2.1
1995 Tor-A	130	525	63	142	31	2	15	60	61	57	12	0	.270	.352	.423	.775	101	4	82	5.56	0	*D-129	12	-0.5
1996 Min-A	161	660	99	**225**	41	8	9	113	56	72	18	6	.341	.395	.468	.863	115	18	119	6.80	1	*D-143,1-17	18	0.5
1997 Min-A	135	538	63	164	32	4	10	89	45	73	11	4	.305	.358	.435	.793	104	4	85	5.72	0	*D-122,1-12	13	-0.6
1998 Min-A	126	502	75	141	29	5	4	69	45	41	9	2	.281	.341	.382	.724	87	-9	63	4.35	1	*D-115/1-9	10	-1.6
Total 21	2683	10835	1782	3319	605	114	234	1307	1094	1244	504	131	.306	.372	.448	.820	123	402	1872	6.29	21	*D-1174,3-791,2-400,1-197/S,O	414	35.2

• MOLLENKAMP, Fred Frederick Henry Mollenkamp b: 3/15/1890, Cincinnati, OH d: 11/1/1948, Cincinnati, OH, 6'2", 195 lbs. Deb: 8/29/1914

YEAR TM-L	G	AB	R	H	2B	3B	HR	RBI	BB	SO	SB	CS	AVG	OBP	SLG	OPS	OPS+	BR/A	RC	RC/G	FR	G/POS	WS	TPW
1914 Phi-N	3	8	0	1	0	0	0	0	2	0	0	....	.125	.300	.125	.425	26	-1	0	1.55	1	/1-3	0	0.1

• MOLLWITZ, Fritz Frederick August Mollwitz b: 6/16/1890, Koburg, Germany d: 10/3/1967, Bradenton, FL BR/TR, 6'2", 170 lbs. Deb: 9/26/1913 Career OF: 4-0-4

YEAR TM-L	G	AB	R	H	2B	3B	HR	RBI	BB	SO	SB	CS	AVG	OBP	SLG	OPS	OPS+	BR/A	RC	RC/G	FR	G/POS	WS	TPW
1913 Chi-N	2	7	1	3	0	0	0	0	0	0	0	....	.429	.429	.429	.857	145	0	1	7.02	0	/1-2	0	0.0
1914 Chi-N	13	20	0	3	0	0	0	1	0	3	1	....	.150	.150	.150	.300	-11	-3	1	.77	0	/1-4,O-1	0	-0.3
Cin-N	32	111	12	18	2	0	0	5	3	9	2	....	.162	.198	.180	.378	12	-12	4	1.13	1	1-32	0	-1.2
Yr.	45	131	12	21	2	0	0	6	3	12	3	....	.160	.191	.176	.367	9	-15	5	1.07	1	1-36/O-1	0	-1.6
1915 Cin-N	153	525	36	136	21	3	1	51	15	49	19	11	.259	.281	.316	.597	79	-16	50	3.16	-7	*1-153	7	-2.8
1916 Cin-N	65	183	12	41	4	4	0	16	5	12	6	....	.224	.245	.290	.534	65	-8	15	2.64	-3	1-54	0	-1.4
Chi-N	33	71	1	19	2	0	0	11	7	6	4	....	.268	.333	.296	.629	85	-1	8	4.08	0	1-19/O-6(4-0-2)	1	-0.1
Yr.	98	254	13	60	6	4	0	27	12	18	10	....	.236	.271	.291	.562	71	-9	24	3.02	-3	1-73/O-6(4-0-2)	1	-1.5
1917 Pit-N	36	140	15	36	4	1	0	12	8	8	4	....	.257	.297	.300	.597	81	-3	14	3.20	-1	1-36/2-1	2	-0.5
1918 Pit-N	119	432	43	116	12	7	0	45	23	24	23	....	.269	.305	.329	.634	90	-6	50	3.78	4	*1-119	9	-0.5
1919 Pit-N	56	168	11	29	2	4	0	12	15	18	9	....	.173	.249	.232	.481	43	-11	11	2.04	1	1-53/O-1	1	-1.3
StL-N	25	83	7	19	3	0	0	5	7	3	2	....	.229	.289	.265	.554	71	-3	7	2.67	1	1-25	1	-0.3
Yr.	81	251	18	48	5	4	0	17	22	21	11	....	.191	.262	.243	.505	53	-14	18	2.24	2	1-78/O-1	2	-1.5
Total 7	534	1740	138	420	50	19	1	158	83	132	70	11	.241	.278	.294	.572	72	-63	162	3.01	-5	1-497/O-8,2-1	21	-8.5

• MONACO, Blas Blas Monaco b: 11/16/1915, San Antonio, TX d: 2/10/2000, San Antonio, TX BB/TR, 5'11", 170 lbs. Deb: 8/18/1937

YEAR TM-L	G	AB	R	H	2B	3B	HR	RBI	BB	SO	SB	CS	AVG	OBP	SLG	OPS	OPS+	BR/A	RC	RC/G	FR	G/POS	WS	TPW
1937 Cle-A	5	7	0	2	0	1	0	2	0	2	0	0	.286	.375	.571	.946	134	0	2	8.13	-0	/2-3	0	0.0
1946 Cle-A	12	6	2	0	0	0	0	0	1	1	0	0	.000	.143	.000	.143	-62	-1	0	.17	0	....	0	-0.1
Total 2	17	13	2	2	0	1	0	2	1	3	0	0	.154	.267	.308	.574	43	-1	2	3.79	-0	/2-3	0	-0.1

• MONAHAN, Shane Shane Hartland Monahan b: 8/12/1974, Syosset, NY BL/TR, 6', 195 lbs. Deb: 7/9/1998 Career OF: 68-3-5

YEAR TM-L	G	AB	R	H	2B	3B	HR	RBI	BB	SO	SB	CS	AVG	OBP	SLG	OPS	OPS+	BR/A	RC	RC/G	FR	G/POS	WS	TPW
1998 Sea-A	62	211	17	51	8	1	4	28	8	53	1	2	.242	.269	.346	.615	59	-14	20	3.23	0	O-62(61-3-2)	2	-1.5
1999 Sea-A	16	15	3	2	0	0	0	0	0	6	0	0	.133	.133	.133	.267	-31	-3	0	.55	0	/O-9(7-0-3),D-3	0	-0.3
Total 2	78	226	20	53	8	1	4	28	8	59	1	2	.235	.261	.332	.593	53	-17	20	3.04	0	/O-71,D-3	2	-1.9

• MONCEWICZ, Freddie Frederick Alfred Moncewicz b: 9/1/1903, Brockton, MA d: 4/23/1969, Brockton, MA BR/TR, 5'8.5", 175 lbs. Deb: 6/19/1928

YEAR TM-L	G	AB	R	H	2B	3B	HR	RBI	BB	SO	SB	CS	AVG	OBP	SLG	OPS	OPS+	BR/A	RC	RC/G	FR	G/POS	WS	TPW
1928 Bos-A	3	1	0	0	0	0	0	0	0	1	0	0	.000	.000	.000	.000	-102	-0	0	.00	-1	/S-2	0	-0.1

• MONCHAK, Alex Alex Monchak b: 3/5/1917, Bayonne, NJ BR/TR, 6', 180 lbs. Deb: 6/22/1940 C

YEAR TM-L	G	AB	R	H	2B	3B	HR	RBI	BB	SO	SB	CS	AVG	OBP	SLG	OPS	OPS+	BR/A	RC	RC/G	FR	G/POS	WS	TPW
1940 Phi-N	19	14	1	2	0	0	0	0	0	6	1	....	.143	.143	.143	.286	-22	-2	0	.64	-4	/S-9,2-1	0	-0.6

• MONDAY, Rick Robert James Monday b: 11/20/1945, Batesville, AR BL/TL, 6'3", 200 lbs. Deb: 9/3/1966 Career OF: 60-1490-170

YEAR TM-L	G	AB	R	H	2B	3B	HR	RBI	BB	SO	SB	CS	AVG	OBP	SLG	OPS	OPS+	BR/A	RC	RC/G	FR	G/POS	WS	TPW
1966 KC-A	17	41	4	4	1	1	0	2	6	16	1	1	.098	.213	.171	.383	12	-5	2	1.24	0	O-15(0-15-0)	0	-0.6
1967 KC-A	124	406	52	102	14	6	14	58	42	107	3	6	.251	.324	.419	.743	122	9	55	4.59	5	*O-113(3-110-0)	16	1.1
1968 Oak-A★	148	482	56	132	24	7	8	49	72	143	14	6	.274	.373	.402	.775	142	27	78	5.73	-4	*O-144(0-144-0)	26	2.2
1969 Oak-A	122	399	57	108	17	4	12	54	72	100	12	3	.271	.389	.424	.812	133	22	71	6.32	-7	*O-119(0-119-0)	20	1.3

YEAR TM-L	G	AB	R	H	2B	3B	HR	RBI	BB	SO	SB	CS	AVG	OBP	SLG	OPS	OPS+	BR/A	RC	RC/G	FR	G/POS	WS	TPW
1970 Oak-A	112	376	63	109	19	7	10	37	58	99	17	11	.290	.388	.457	.845	137	20	68	6.26	-6	*0-109(0-109-0)	19	1.1
1971*Oak-A	116	355	53	87	9	3	18	56	49	93	6	9	.245	.337	.439	.776	121	7	52	4.86	-3	*0-111(0-111-0)	15	0.1
1972 Chi-N	138	434	68	108	22	5	11	42	78	102	12	9	.249	.365	.399	.763	105	5	67	5.26	-3	*0-134(0-132-2)	16	-0.1
1973 Chi-N	149	554	93	148	24	5	26	56	92	124	5	12	.267	.372	.469	.842	123	15	100	6.33	-1	*0-148(0-148-0)	22	1.0
1974 Chi-N	142	538	84	158	19	7	20	58	70	94	7	9	.294	.377	.467	.844	130	20	97	6.54	-4	*0-139(0-139-0)	22	1.3
1975 Chi-N	136	491	89	131	29	4	17	60	83	95	8	3	.267	.374	.446	.820	121	16	86	6.13	-3	*0-131(0-131-0)	22	1.0
1976 Chi-N	137	534	107	145	20	5	32	77	60	125	5	9	.272	.347	.507	.855	129	16	92	6.07	-1	*0-103(5-99-0),1-32	23	1.0
1977*LA-N	118	392	47	90	13	1	15	48	60	109	1	4	.230	.332	.383	.715	91	-5	52	4.46	-9	*0-115(0-114-1)/1-3	10	-1.6
1978*LA-N★	119	342	54	87	14	1	19	57	49	100	2	4	.254	.349	.468	.817	127	11	56	5.69	-4	*0-103(11-80-30)/1-1	13	0.5
1979 LA-N	12	33	2	10	0	0	0	2	5	6	0	0	.303	.395	.303	.698	94	0	4	4.68	-1	0-10(0-8-3)	1	-0.1
1980 LA-N	96	194	35	52	7	1	10	25	28	49	2	2	.268	.363	.469	.832	133	8	35	6.43	-2	0-50(1-31-25)	8	0.5
1981*LA-N	66	130	24	41	1	2	11	25	24	42	1	2	.315	.426	.608	1.033	198	17	35	10.33	-1	0-41(6-0-37)	9	1.5
1982 LA-N	104	210	37	54	6	4	11	42	39	51	2	1	.257	.376	.481	.857	142	13	40	6.59	-0	0-57(18-0-40)/1-4	9	1.1
1983*LA-N	99	178	21	44	7	1	6	20	29	42	0	0	.247	.353	.399	.752	108	3	26	5.05	-1	0-44(14-0-31)/1-4	6	0.0
1984 LA-N	31	47	4	9	2	0	1	7	8	16	0	0	.191	.309	.298	.607	72	-2	5	3.29	-1	1-10/0-2(2-0-1)	1	-0.3
Total 19	1986	6136	950	1619	248	64	241	775	924	1513	98	91	.264	.362	.443	.805	124	198	1020	5.79	-47	*0-1688/1-54	258	11.0

• MONDESI, Raul Raul Ramon (Avelino) Mondesi b: 3/12/1971, San Cristobal, Dominican Republic BR/TR, 5'11", 202 lbs. Deb: 7/19/1993 Career OF: 20-153-1273

YEAR TM-L	G	AB	R	H	2B	3B	HR	RBI	BB	SO	SB	CS	AVG	OBP	SLG	OPS	OPS+	BR/A	RC	RC/G	FR	G/POS	WS	TPW
1993 LA-N	42	86	13	25	3	1	4	10	4	16	4	1	.291	.322	.488	.811	120	2	14	5.71	-0	0-40(20-6-17)	3	0.1
1994 LA-N	112	434	63	133	27	8	16	56	16	78	11	8	.306	.334	.516	.850	126	12	69	5.83	1	*0-112(0-15-109)	15	0.8
1995*LA-N★	139	536	91	153	23	6	26	88	33	96	27	4	.285	.332	.496	.828	126	21	90	6.07	8	*0-138(0-24-114)	22	2.2
1996*LA-N	157	634	98	188	40	7	24	88	32	122	14	7	.297	.335	.495	.831	125	19	104	6.08	6	*0-157(0-0-157)	25	1.6
1997 LA-N	159	616	95	191	42	5	30	87	44	105	32	15	.310	.362	.541	.902	143	36	116	6.91	4	*0-159(0-0-159)	24	3.1
1998 LA-N	148	580	85	162	26	5	30	90	30	112	16	10	.279	.318	.497	.815	117	10	88	5.39	-6	*0-148(0-94-54)	20	0.1
1999 LA-N	159	601	98	152	29	5	33	99	71	134	36	9	.253	.335	.483	.817	110	11	104	6.00	1	*0-158(0-1-158)	21	0.4
2000 Tor-A	96	388	78	105	22	2	24	67	32	73	22	6	.271	.331	.523	.854	108	5	67	5.99	0	0-96(0-0-96)	11	-0.1
2001 Tor-A	149	572	88	144	26	4	27	84	73	128	30	11	.252	.343	.453	.795	105	6	90	5.35	5	*0-149(0-0-149)	15	0.2
2002 Tor-A	75	299	51	67	16	1	15	45	31	57	9	2	.224	.303	.435	.738	90	-4	39	4.34	-2	0-62(0-0-62),D-13	6	-1.0
*NY-A	71	270	39	65	18	0	11	43	28	46	6	4	.241	.317	.430	.746	97	-2	37	4.69	-7	0-70(0-11-59)/D-1	6	-1.2
Yr.	146	569	90	132	34	1	26	88	59	103	15	6	.232	.310	.432	.742	93	-6	76	4.50	-10	*0-132(0-11-121),D-14	12	-2.3
2003 NY-A	98	361	56	93	23	3	16	49	38	66	17	7	.258	.332	.471	.803	111	5	56	5.36	2	0-97(0-0-97)/D-1	7	0.2
Ari-N	45	162	27	49	8	1	8	22	18	31	5	4	.302	.376	.512	.888	117	4	31	6.76	1	0-43(0-2-42)	4	0.2
Total 11	1450	5539	882	1527	303	48	264	828	450	1064	229	88	.276	.335	.491	.825	117	124	904	5.78	12	*0-1429/D-15	179	6.5

• MONEY, Don Donald Wayne "Brooks" Money b: 6/7/1947, Washington, DC BR/TR, 6'1", 190 lbs. Deb: 4/10/1968 Career OF: 63-0-0

YEAR TM-L	G	AB	R	H	2B	3B	HR	RBI	BB	SO	SB	CS	AVG	OBP	SLG	OPS	OPS+	BR/A	RC	RC/G	FR	G/POS	WS	TPW
1968 Phi-N	4	13	1	3	2	0	0	2	2	4	0	1	.231	.333	.385	.718	115	-0	1	3.44	0	/S-4	0	0.0
1969 Phi-N	127	450	41	103	22	2	6	42	43	83	1	3	.229	.298	.327	.624	77	-15	41	2.97	11	*S-126	10	1.2
1970 Phi-N	120	447	66	132	25	4	14	66	43	68	4	7	.295	.366	.463	.829	124	13	75	5.96	16	*3-119/S-2	21	2.9
1971 Phi-N	121	439	40	98	22	8	7	38	31	80	4	1	.223	.279	.358	.637	79	-13	44	3.33	4	3-68,0-40(40-0-0),2-20	8	-1.0
1972 Phi-N	152	536	54	119	16	2	15	52	41	92	5	7	.222	.280	.343	.623	74	-21	50	3.07	17	*3-151/S-2	10	-0.5
1973 Mil-A	145	556	75	158	28	2	11	61	53	53	22	5	.284	.350	.401	.751	113	13	80	5.05	-9	*3-124,S-21	18	0.5
1974 Mil-A★	159	629	85	178	32	3	15	65	62	80	19	6	.283	.349	.415	.764	120	18	93	5.21	-1	*3-157/2-1,D-1	26	1.7
1975 Mil-A	109	405	58	112	16	1	15	43	31	51	7	9	.277	.333	.432	.765	114	4	58	5.08	-10	3-99/S-7	14	-0.5
1976 Mil-A★	117	439	51	117	18	4	12	62	47	50	6	5	.267	.337	.408	.745	120	10	59	4.59	0	*3-103,D-10/S-1	14	1.0
1977 Mil-A★	152	570	86	159	28	3	25	83	57	70	8	5	.279	.352	.470	.822	122	17	92	5.58	5	*2-116,0-23(23-0-0),3-15/D	22	2.7
1978 Mil-A★	137	518	88	152	30	2	14	54	48	70	3	0	.293	.361	.440	.801	124	18	84	5.81	0	1-61,2-36,3-25,D-15/S-2	19	1.6
1979 Mil-A	92	350	52	83	20	1	6	38	40	47	1	0	.237	.319	.351	.670	81	-9	40	3.76	2	D-33,3-26,1-19,2-16	6	-0.9
1980 Mil-A	86	289	39	74	17	1	17	46	40	36	0	0	.256	.348	.498	.847	133	13	52	6.25	1	3-55,1-14,D-14/2-2	11	1.2
1981*Mil-A	60	185	17	40	7	0	2	14	19	27	0	0	.216	.293	.286	.579	71	-6	17	3.05	-5	3-56/D-2,1-1	4	-1.3
1982*Mil-A	96	275	40	78	14	3	16	55	32	38	0	2	.284	.360	.531	.891	150	18	53	6.82	2	D-66,3-16,1-11/2-1	13	1.7
1983 Mil-A	43	114	5	17	5	0	1	8	11	17	0	0	.149	.224	.219	.443	24	-12	6	1.49	4	D-28,3-11/1-2	1	-0.9
Total 16	1720	6215	798	1623	302	36	176	729	600	866	80	51	.261	.330	.406	.736	106	48	847	4.66	37	*3-1025,2-192,D-176,S-165,1/0	197	9.4

• MONROE, Craig Craig Keystone Monroe b: 2/27/1977, Texarkana, TX BR/TR, 6'1", 195 lbs. Deb: 7/28/2001 Career OF: 85-2-64

YEAR TM-L	G	AB	R	H	2B	3B	HR	RBI	BB	SO	SB	CS	AVG	OBP	SLG	OPS	OPS+	BR/A	RC	RC/G	FR	G/POS	WS	TPW
2001 Tex-A	27	52	8	11	1	0	2	5	6	18	2	0	.212	.293	.346	.639	65	-2	6	3.65	4	0-24(6-0-21)	1	0.1
2002 Det-A	13	25	3	3	1	0	1	1	0	5	0	2	.120	.154	.280	.434	13	-4	0	.30	1	/0-9(4-0-5),D-3	0	-0.3
2003 Det-A	128	425	51	102	18	1	23	70	27	89	4	2	.240	.289	.449	.738	98	-3	53	4.18	1	*0-108(75-2-38),D-12	10	-0.7
Total 3	168	502	62	116	20	1	26	76	33	112	6	4	.231	.283	.430	.713	90	-10	58	3.89	6	0-141/D-15	11	-1.0

• MONROE, Frank Frank W. Monroe b: Hamilton, OH Deb: 7/18/1884

YEAR TM-L	G	AB	R	H	2B	3B	HR	RBI	BB	SO	SB	CS	AVG	OBP	SLG	OPS	OPS+	BR/A	RC	RC/G	FR	G/POS	WS	TPW
1884 Ind-a	2	8	1	0	0	0	0	0	0	....	....	....	.000	.000	.000	.000	-103	-2	0	.00	-1	/C-1,0-1	0	-0.2

• MONROE, John John Allen Monroe b: 8/24/1898, Farmersville, TX d: 6/19/1956, Conroe, TX BL/TR, 5'10", 160 lbs. Deb: 4/16/1921

YEAR TM-L	G	AB	R	H	2B	3B	HR	RBI	BB	SO	SB	CS	AVG	OBP	SLG	OPS	OPS+	BR/A	RC	RC/G	FR	G/POS	WS	TPW
1921 NY-N	19	21	4	3	0	0	1	3	3	6	0	0	.143	.280	.286	.566	50	-1	2	2.79	-3	/2-8,S-1	0	-0.5
Phi-N	41	133	13	38	4	2	1	8	11	9	2	2	.286	.345	.368	.713	82	-3	17	4.51	-2	2-28/3-9	3	-0.4
Yr.	60	154	17	41	4	2	2	11	14	15	2	2	.266	.335	.357	.692	78	-4	19	4.25	-6	2-36/3-9,S-1	3	-0.8

• MONTAGUE, Ed Edward Francis Montague b: 7/24/1905, San Francisco, CA d: 6/17/1988, Daly City, CA BR/TR, 5'10", 165 lbs. Deb: 5/14/1928

YEAR TM-L	G	AB	R	H	2B	3B	HR	RBI	BB	SO	SB	CS	AVG	OBP	SLG	OPS	OPS+	BR/A	RC	RC/G	FR	G/POS	WS	TPW
1928 Cle-A	32	51	12	12	0	1	0	3	6	7	0	0	.235	.339	.275	.613	62	-2	5	3.52	-4	S-15/3-9	1	-0.5
1930 Cle-A	58	179	37	47	5	2	1	16	37	38	1	5	.263	.392	.330	.721	82	-5	25	4.62	-3	S-46,3-13	5	-0.3
1931 Cle-A	64	193	27	55	8	3	1	26	21	22	3	4	.285	.358	.373	.731	87	-3	26	4.59	-1	S-64	5	0.0
1932 Cle-A	66	192	29	47	5	1	0	24	21	24	3	3	.245	.326	.281	.607	55	-13	19	3.20	-15	S-57,3-11	2	-2.2
Total 4	220	615	105	161	18	7	2	69	85	91	7	12	.262	.357	.324	.681	74	-23	76	4.07	-23	S-182/3-33	13	-2.9

• MONTANEZ, Willie Guillermo (Naranjo) Montanez b: 4/1/1948, Catano, Puerto Rico BL/TL, 6', 193 lbs. Deb: 4/12/1966 Career OF: 3-267-85

YEAR TM-L	G	AB	R	H	2B	3B	HR	RBI	BB	SO	SB	CS	AVG	OBP	SLG	OPS	OPS+	BR/A	RC	RC/G	FR	G/POS	WS	TPW
1966 Cal-A	8	2	2	0	0	0	0	0	0	2	1	0	.000	.000	.000	.000	-103	-0	0	.00	0	/1-2	0	-0.1
1970 Phi-N	18	25	3	6	0	0	0	3	1	4	0	0	.240	.269	.240	.509	39	-2	2	2.30	1	0-10(1-0-9)/1-5	0	-0.2
1971 Phi-N	158	599	78	153	27	6	30	99	67	105	4	7	.255	.333	.471	.804	126	17	89	4.94	4	*0-158(0-137-24)/1-9	20	1.7
1972 Phi-N	147	531	60	131	**39**	3	13	64	58	108	1	3	.247	.322	.405	.727	103	1	70	4.59	8	*0-130(0-130-0),1-14	16	0.4
1973 Phi-N	146	552	69	145	16	5	11	65	46	80	2	6	.263	.326	.370	.696	90	-9	65	4.08	-1	1-99,0-51(0-0-51)	11	-2.1
1974 Phi-N	143	527	55	160	33	1	7	79	32	57	3	6	.304	.347	.410	.757	107	2	72	5.00	-5	*1-137/0-1	16	-1.5
1975 Phi-N	21	84	9	24	8	0	2	16	4	12	1	0	.286	.318	.452	.771	108	1	11	4.68	0	1-21	2	-0.1
SF-N	135	518	52	158	26	2	8	85	45	50	5	3	.305	.365	.409	.774	110	7	72	4.93	-3	*1-134	13	-0.7
Yr.	156	602	61	182	34	2	10	101	49	62	6	3	.302	.359	.415	.774	110	8	84	4.89	-3	*1-155	15	-0.8
1976 SF-N	60	230	22	71	15	2	2	20	15	15	2	1	.309	.354	.417	.771	115	4	31	4.83	4	1-58	7	0.3
Atl-N	103	420	52	135	14	0	9	64	21	32	0	4	.321	.354	.419	.773	112	4	56	4.90	-5	*1-103	11	-1.0
Yr.	163	650	74	206	29	2	11	84	36	47	2	5	.317	.354	.418	.772	113	8	86	4.87	-1	*1-161	18	-0.7
1977 Atl-N★	136	544	70	156	31	1	20	68	35	60	1	1	.287	.330	.458	.788	97	-3	77	5.05	-3	*1-134	13	-1.5
1978 NY-N	159	609	66	156	32	0	17	96	60	92	9	4	.256	.324	.392	.716	103	2	76	4.30	-4	*1-158	15	-1.3
1979 NY-N	109	410	36	96	19	0	5	47	25	48	0	1	.234	.280	.317	.597	65	-21	33	2.66	-1	*1-108	2	-3.0
Tex-A	38	144	19	46	6	0	8	24	8	14	0	1	.319	.359	.528	.887	138	7	26	6.63	2	1-19,D-17	5	0.6
1980 SD-N	128	481	39	132	12	4	6	63	36	52	3	4	.274	.329	.353	.682	96	-4	55	4.02	-4	*1-124	10	-1.7
Mon-N	14	19	1	4	0	0	0	1	3	3	0	1	.211	.318	.211	.529	50	-2	1	2.08	0	/1-4	0	-0.2
Yr.	142	500	40	136	12	4	6	64	39	55	3	5	.272	.328	.348	.676	94	-6	56	3.94	-4	*1-128	10	-1.9
1981 Mon-N	26	62	6	11	0	1	0	5	4	9	0	0	.177	.227	.210	.437	24	-6	2	1.03	2	1-16	0	-0.6
Pit-N	29	38	2	10	0	0	1	1	1	2	0	0	.263	.282	.342	.624	74	-1	3	3.17	-1	1-11	0	-0.3
Yr.	55	100	8	21	0	1	1	6	5	11	0	0	.210	.248	.260	.508	43	-8	6	1.76	0	1-27	0	-0.9
1982 Pit-N	36	32	4	9	1	0	0	1	3	3	0	0	.281	.343	.313	.655	82	-1	3	3.09	0	/1-2,0-2(2-0-0)	0	-0.1
Phi-N	18	16	0	1	0	0	0	1	1	3	0	0	.063	.118	.063	.180	-47	-3	0	.27	0	/1-6	0	-0.3

YEAR TM-L	G	AB	R	H	2B	3B	HR	RBI	BB	SO	SB	CS	AVG	OBP	SLG	OPS	OPS+	BR/A	RC	RC/G	FR	G/POS	WS	TPW
Yr.	54	48	4	10	1	0	0	2	4	6	0	0	.208	.269	.229	.498	40	-4	3	2.03	0	/1-8,0-2(2-0-0)	0	-0.4
Total 14	**1632**	**5843**	**645**	**1604**	**279**	**25**	**139**	**802**	**465**	**751**	**32**	**42**	**.275**	**.331**	**.402**	**.733**	**101**	**-11**	**744**	**4.45**	**-8**	***1-1164,0-352/D-17**	**141**	**-11.5**
• MONTEAGUDO, Rene	Rene (Miranda) Monteagudo b: 3/12/1916, Havana, Cuba d: 9/14/1973, Hialeah, FL BL/TL, 5'7", 165 lbs. Deb: 9/6/1938 Career OF: 12-0-32 ♦																							
1938 Was-A	5	6	0	3	0	0	0	1	0	0	0	0	.500	.500	.500	1.000	162	1	1	9.59	-1	/P-5	1	-0.2
1940 Was-A	27	33	4	6	1	1	0	1	1	4	0	0	.182	.206	.273	.479	24	0	2	1.95	-1	P-27	1	-1.9
1944 Was-A	10	38	2	11	2	0	0	4	0	1	0	0	.289	.289	.342	.632	84	-1	4	3.86	0	/0-9(0-0-9)	1	-0.1
1945 Phi-N	114	193	26	58	6	0	0	15	28	7	2	....	.301	.389	.332	.721	104	5	26	4.86	-1	0-35(12-0-23),P-14	5	-1.4
Total 4	**156**	**270**	**32**	**78**	**9**	**1**	**0**	**21**	**29**	**12**	**2**	**0**	**.289**	**.358**	**.330**	**.687**	**94**	**6**	**33**	**4.43**	**-3**	**/P-46,0-44**	**8**	**-3.6**
• MONTEMAYOR, Felipe	Felipe Angel "Monty" Montemayor b: 2/7/1930, Monterrey, Mexico BL/TL, 6'2", 185 lbs. Deb: 4/14/1953 Career OF: 7-25-9																							
1953 Pit-N	28	55	5	6	4	0	0	2	4	13	0	0	.109	.210	.182	.391	3	-8	2	1.26	1	0-12(1-11-0)	0	-0.7
1955 Pit-N	36	95	10	20	1	3	2	8	18	24	1	0	.211	.342	.347	.689	85	-1	12	4.32	-1	0-28(6-14-9)	2	-0.3
Total 2	**64**	**150**	**15**	**26**	**5**	**3**	**2**	**10**	**22**	**37**	**1**	**0**	**.173**	**.295**	**.287**	**.582**	**56**	**-9**	**15**	**3.11**	**0**	**/0-40**	**2**	**-1.0**
• MONTGOMERY, Al	Alvin Atlas Montgomery b: 7/3/1920, Loving, NM d: 4/26/1942, Waverly, VA BR/TR, 5'10.5", 185 lbs. Deb: 6/20/1941																							
1941 Bos-N	42	52	4	10	1	0	0	4	9	8	0	....	.192	.323	.212	.534	55	-3	4	2.42	-1	C-30	1	-0.3
• MONTGOMERY, Bob	Robert Edward Montgomery b: 4/16/1944, Nashville, TN BR/TR, 6'1", 203 lbs. Deb: 9/6/1970																							
1970 Bos-A	22	78	8	14	2	0	1	4	6	20	0	0	.179	.247	.244	.491	33	-7	4	1.65	0	C-22	1	-0.6
1971 Bos-A	67	205	19	49	11	2	2	24	16	43	1	0	.239	.304	.341	.645	77	-6	21	3.37	-4	C-66	5	-0.7
1972 Bos-A	24	77	7	22	1	0	2	7	3	17	0	0	.286	.313	.377	.689	99	-0	9	4.25	0	C-22	3	0.0
1973 Bos-A	34	128	18	41	6	2	7	25	7	36	0	0	.320	.356	.563	.918	146	7	23	6.75	1	C-33	6	1.0
1974 Bos-A	88	254	26	64	10	0	4	38	13	50	3	0	.252	.291	.339	.630	75	-8	24	3.09	-3	C-79/D-5	5	-0.8
1975*Bos-A	62	195	16	44	10	1	2	26	4	37	1	1	.226	.245	.318	.563	53	-13	15	2.45	0	C-53/1-6,D-3	3	-1.1
1976 Bos-A	31	93	10	23	3	1	3	13	5	20	0	1	.247	.286	.398	.684	88	-2	10	3.75	-1	C-30/D-1	3	-0.2
1977 Bos-A	17	40	6	12	2	0	2	7	4	9	0	0	.300	.378	.500	.878	122	1	8	6.83	0	C-15	2	0.2
1978 Bos-A	10	29	2	7	1	1	0	5	2	12	0	0	.241	.290	.345	.635	70	-1	3	3.11	0	C-10	1	-0.1
1979 Bos-A	32	86	13	30	4	1	0	7	4	24	1	0	.349	.378	.419	.796	109	1	13	5.72	-2	C-31	3	0.0
Total 10	**387**	**1185**	**125**	**306**	**50**	**8**	**23**	**156**	**64**	**268**	**6**	**2**	**.258**	**.300**	**.372**	**.672**	**83**	**-27**	**129**	**3.70**	**-9**	**C-361/D-9,1-6**	**32**	**-2.3**
• MONTGOMERY, Ray	Raymond James Montgomery b: 8/8/1969, Bronxville, NY BR/TR, 6'3", 195 lbs. Deb: 7/3/1996 Career OF: 8-3-18																							
1996 Hou-N	12	14	4	3	1	0	1	4	1	5	0	0	.214	.267	.500	.767	105	-0	2	4.75	0	/0-6(5-1-2)	1	0.0
1997 Hou-N	29	68	8	16	4	1	0	4	5	18	0	0	.235	.288	.324	.611	62	-4	6	2.94	1	0-18(2-2-15)	0	-0.3
1998 Hou-N	6	5	2	2	0	0	0	0	0	0	0	0	.400	.400	.400	.800	114	0	1	7.20	0	/0-2(1-0-1)	0	0.0
Total 3	**47**	**87**	**14**	**21**	**5**	**1**	**1**	**8**	**6**	**23**	**0**	**0**	**.241**	**.290**	**.356**	**.647**	**71**	**-4**	**9**	**3.40**	**1**	**/0-26**	**1**	**-0.4**
• MONTOYO, Charlie	Jose Carlos (Diaz) Montoyo b: 10/17/1965, Florida, Puerto Rico BR/TR, 5'10", 170 lbs. Deb: 9/7/1993																							
1993 Mon-N	4	5	1	2	1	0	0	3	0	0	0	0	.400	.400	.600	1.000	157	0	1	10.80	-2	/2-3	1	-0.1
• MONTREUIL, Al	Allan Arthur Montreuil b: 8/23/1943, New Orleans, LA BR/TR, 5'5", 158 lbs. Deb: 9/1/1972																							
1972 Chi-N	5	11	0	1	0	0	0	0	1	4	0	0	.091	.167	.091	.258	-23	-2	0	.26	0	/2-5	0	-0.2
• MONZON, Dan	Daniel Francisco Monzon b: 5/17/1946, Bronx, NY d: 1/21/1996, Santo Domingo, Dominican Republic BR/TR, 5'10", 182 lbs. Deb: 4/25/1972 Career OF: 2-0-0																							
1972 Min-A	55	55	13	15	1	0	0	5	8	12	1	0	.273	.365	.291	.656	92	0	7	4.17	0	2-13/3-5,S-3,0-1	2	0.1
1973 Min-A	39	76	10	17	1	1	0	4	11	9	1	0	.224	.330	.263	.593	66	-3	8	3.54	0	2-17,3-14/0-1	2	-0.2
Total 2	**94**	**131**	**23**	**32**	**2**	**1**	**0**	**9**	**19**	**21**	**2**	**0**	**.244**	**.344**	**.275**	**.619**	**77**	**-2**	**15**	**3.81**	**-0**	**/2-30,3-19,S-3,0-2**	**4**	**-0.1**
• MOOCK, Joe	Joseph Geoffrey Moock b: 3/12/1944, Plaquemine, LA BL/TR, 6'1", 180 lbs. Deb: 9/1/1967																							
1967 NY-N	13	40	2	9	2	0	0	5	0	7	0	0	.225	.225	.275	.500	43	-3	2	1.86	0	3-12	0	-0.4
• MOOLIC, George	George Henry "Prunes" Moolic b: 3/12/1867, Lawrence, MA d: 2/19/1915, Lawrence, MA BR/TR, 5'7", 145 lbs. Deb: 5/1/1886																							
1886 Chi-N	16	56	9	8	3	0	0	2	2	17	0	....	.143	.172	.196	.369	10	-6	2	1.09	0	C-15/0-2(0-0-2)	1	-0.5
• MOON, Wally	Wallace Wade Moon b: 4/3/1930, Bay, AR BL/TR, 6', 175 lbs. Deb: 4/13/1954 C Career OF: 621-212-394																							
1954 StL-N	151	635	106	193	29	9	12	76	71	73	18	10	.304	.375	.435	.809	109	10	106	6.06	2	*0-148(10-139-0)	20	0.4
1955 StL-N	152	593	86	175	24	8	19	76	47	65	11	11	.295	.350	.459	.809	112	8	91	5.59	-3	*0-100(34-44-28),1-51	18	-0.2
1956 StL-N	149	540	86	161	22	11	16	68	80	50	12	9	.298	.390	.469	.858	129	24	99	6.63	3	0-97(0-1-96),1-52	22	2.1
1957 StL-N★	142	516	86	152	28	5	24	73	62	57	5	6	.295	.371	.508	.879	131	22	94	6.47	-6	*0-133(89-13-48)	21	0.8
1958 StL-N	108	290	36	69	10	3	7	38	47	30	2	3	.238	.344	.366	.710	85	-6	37	4.18	-1	0-82(31-8-54)	6	-1.0
1959*LA-N★	145	543	93	164	26	**11**	19	74	81	64	15	6	.302	.396	.495	.891	126	24	111	7.42	-4	*0-143(128-4-29)/1-1	25	1.2
1960 LA-N	138	469	74	140	21	6	13	69	67	53	6	10	.299	.387	.452	.839	121	13	77	5.60	7	*0-127(115-0-18)	16	1.4
1961 LA-N	134	463	79	152	25	3	17	88	89	79	7	5	.328	**.438**	.505	.943	137	30	107	8.66	-2	*0-133(126-0-19)	25	2.1
1962 LA-N	95	244	36	59	9	1	4	31	30	33	5	2	.242	.327	.336	.663	83	-5	28	3.80	-1	0-36(24-0-12),1-32	6	-0.9
1963 LA-N	122	343	41	90	13	2	8	48	45	43	5	5	.262	.350	.382	.732	118	9	45	4.31	-3	0-96(48-3-60)	13	0.0
1964 LA-N	68	118	8	26	2	1	2	9	12	22	1	1	.220	.292	.305	.597	74	-4	10	2.72	-1	0-23(6-0-17)	1	-0.6
1965*LA-N	53	89	6	18	3	0	1	11	13	22	2	0	.202	.304	.270	.574	67	-3	8	2.74	0	0-23(10-0-13)	2	-0.4
Total 12	**1457**	**4843**	**737**	**1399**	**212**	**60**	**142**	**661**	**644**	**591**	**89**	**68**	**.289**	**.374**	**.445**	**.819**	**116**	**121**	**810**	**5.92**	**-9**	***0-1141,1-136**	**175**	**4.7**
• MOORE, Al	Albert James Moore b: 8/4/1902, Brooklyn, NY d: 11/29/1974, Atlantic Ocean BR/TR, 5'10", 174 lbs. Deb: 9/27/1925 Career OF: 7-16-0																							
1925 NY-N	2	8	0	1	0	0	0	0	1	2	0	1	.125	.222	.125	.347	-9	-2	0	.45	0	/0-2(2-0-0)	0	-0.2
1926 NY-N	28	81	12	18	4	0	0	10	5	7	2	....	.222	.267	.272	.539	46	-6	6	2.32	2	0-20(5-16-0)	1	-0.5
Total 2	**30**	**89**	**12**	**19**	**4**	**0**	**0**	**10**	**6**	**9**	**2**	**1**	**.213**	**.263**	**.258**	**.522**	**41**	**-8**	**6**	**2.12**	**2**	**/0-22**	**1**	**-0.7**
• MOORE, Anse	Anselm Winn Moore b: 9/22/1917, Delhi, LA d: 10/29/1993, Pearl, MS BL/TR, 6'1", 190 lbs. Deb: 4/17/1946																							
1946 Det-A	51	134	16	28	4	0	1	8	12	9	1	1	.209	.279	.261	.540	48	-9	11	2.63	1	0-32(17-0-15)	1	-1.1
• MOORE, Archie	Archie Francis Moore b: 8/30/1941, Upper Darby, PA BL/TL, 6'2", 190 lbs. Deb: 4/20/1964 Career OF: 1-5-8																							
1964 NY-A	31	23	4	4	2	0	0	1	2	9	0	0	.174	.240	.261	.501	39	-2	2	2.22	0	/0-8(0-5-3),1-7	0	-0.2
1965 NY-A	9	17	1	7	2	0	1	4	4	4	0	0	.412	.524	.706	1.230	248	4	6	14.94	0	/0-5(1-0-5)	1	0.3
Total 2	**40**	**40**	**5**	**11**	**4**	**0**	**1**	**5**	**6**	**13**	**0**	**0**	**.275**	**.370**	**.450**	**.820**	**134**	**2**	**8**	**6.89**	**0**	**/0-13,1-7**	**1**	**0.1**
• MOORE, Bill	William Henry "Willie" Moore b: 12/12/1901, Kansas City, MO d: 5/24/1972, Kansas City, MO BL/TR, 5'11", 170 lbs. Deb: 9/7/1926																							
1926 Bos-A	5	18	2	3	0	0	0	0	0	2	0	0	.167	.167	.167	.333	-13	-3	0	.85	1	/C-5	0	-0.2
1927 Bos-A	44	69	7	15	2	0	0	4	13	8	0	0	.217	.341	.246	.588	56	-4	7	3.26	0	C-42	1	-0.2
Total 2	**49**	**87**	**9**	**18**	**2**	**0**	**0**	**4**	**13**	**10**	**0**	**0**	**.207**	**.310**	**.230**	**.540**	**43**	**-7**	**7**	**2.74**	**1**	**/C-47**	**1**	**-0.4**
• MOORE, Bill	William Ross Moore b: 10/10/1960, Los Angeles, CA BR/TL, 6'1", 185 lbs. Deb: 7/19/1986																							
1986 Mon-N	6	12	0	2	0	0	0	0	0	4	0	0	.167	.167	.167	.333	-8	-2	0	.90	0	/1-3,0-1	0	-0.2
• MOORE, Bobby	Robert Vincent Moore b: 10/27/1965, Cincinnati, OH BR/TR, 5'11", 165 lbs. Deb: 9/5/1991																							
1991 KC-A	18	14	3	5	1	0	0	0	1	2	3	2	.357	.400	.429	.829	129	0	2	5.12	0	0-13(9-5-0)	0	0.0
• MOORE, Charley	Charles Wesley Moore b: 12/1/1884, Jackson County, IN d: 7/29/1970, Portland, OR BR/TR, 5'10", 160 lbs. Deb: 4/16/1912																							
1912 Chi-N	5	9	2	2	0	1	0	2	0	1	0	....	.222	.222	.444	.667	80	-0	1	3.02	0	/S-2,2-1,3-1	0	0.0
• MOORE, Charlie	Charles William Moore b: 6/21/1953, Birmingham, AL BR/TR, 5'11", 180 lbs. Deb: 9/8/1973 Career OF: 49-8-341																							
1973 Mil-A	8	27	0	5	0	1	0	3	2	4	0	0	.185	.241	.259	.501	42	-2	2	2.15	2	/C-8	1	0.1
1974 Mil-A	72	204	17	50	10	4	0	19	21	34	3	4	.245	.316	.333	.649	87	-4	21	3.50	2	C-61/D-6	6	0.0
1975 Mil-A	73	241	26	70	20	1	1	29	17	31	1	5	.290	.337	.394	.731	106	-0	30	4.30	-1	C-47,0-22(16-0-6)/D-1	7	-0.1
1976 Mil-A	87	241	33	46	7	4	3	16	43	45	1	2	.191	.316	.290	.606	80	-5	24	3.21	1	C-49,0-28(28-0-0)/D-2,3-1	5	-0.3

YEAR TM-L	G	AB	R	H	2B	3B	HR	RBI	BB	SO	SB	CS	AVG	OBP	SLG	OPS	OPS+	BR/A	RC	RC/G	FR	G/POS	WS	TPW
1977 Mil-A	138	375	42	93	15	6	5	45	31	39	1	7	.248	.307	.360	.667	81	-12	38	3.24	4	*C-137	8	-0.3
1978 Mil-A	96	268	30	72	7	1	5	31	12	24	4	2	.269	.300	.358	.658	84	-6	28	3.71	-1	C-95	7	-0.3
1979 Mil-A	111	337	45	101	16	2	5	38	29	32	8	5	.300	.357	.404	.761	105	2	46	4.88	4	*C-106	14	1.1
1980 Mil-A	111	320	42	93	13	2	2	30	24	28	10	5	.291	.340	.363	.703	96	-2	39	4.22	-2	*C-105	9	0.1
1981*Mil-A	48	156	16	47	8	3	1	9	12	13	1	4	.301	.351	.410	.761	125	3	21	4.64	-1	C-34/O-8(3-0-5),D-6	7	0.4
1982*Mil-A	133	456	53	116	22	4	6	45	29	49	2	10	.254	.300	.360	.660	86	-14	45	3.28	5	*O-115(0-0-115),C-20/2-1	8	-1.3
1983 Mil-A	151	529	65	150	27	6	2	49	55	42	11	4	.284	.355	.369	.724	108	8	71	4.60	-7	*O-150(0-0-150)/C-7,D-1	15	-0.7
1984 Mil-A	70	188	13	44	7	1	2	17	10	26	0	4	.234	.276	.314	.590	66	-11	14	2.42	0	O-61(0-7-56)/C-7	1	-1.3
1985 Mil-A	105	349	35	81	13	4	0	31	27	53	4	0	.232	.289	.292	.581	60	-18	29	2.72	0	*C-102/O-3(0-0-3)	5	-1.3
1986 Mil-A	80	235	24	61	12	3	3	39	21	38	5	5	.260	.320	.374	.695	86	-6	27	3.78	6	C-72/O-4(0-1-3),D-2,2-1	8	0.3
1987 Tor-A	51	107	15	23	10	1	1	7	13	12	0	0	.215	.306	.355	.661	73	-4	12	3.67	-1	C-44/O-5(2-0-3)	2	-0.4
Total 15	**1334**	**4033**	**456**	**1052**	**187**	**43**	**36**	**408**	**346**	**470**	**51**	**57**	**.261**	**.321**	**.355**	**.676**	**89**	**-72**	**447**	**3.73**	**11**	**C-894,O-396/D-18,2-2,3-1**	**103**	**-3.9**

• MOORE, Dee

D C Moore b: 4/6/1914, Hedley, TX d: 7/2/1997, Williston, ND BR/TR, 5'11", 190 lbs. Deb: 9/12/1936

YEAR TM-L	G	AB	R	H	2B	3B	HR	RBI	BB	SO	SB	CS	AVG	OBP	SLG	OPS	OPS+	BR/A	RC	RC/G	FR	G/POS	WS	TPW
1936 Cin-N	6	10	4	4	2	1	0	1	0	3	0	....	.400	.400	.800	1.200	230	2	3	14.76	0	/P-2,C-1	2	0.5
1937 Cin-N	7	13	2	1	0	0	0	0	1	2	0	....	.077	.200	.077	.277	-23	-2	0	.70	-1	/C-6	0	-0.2
1943 Bro-N	37	79	8	20	3	0	0	12	11	8	1	....	.253	.344	.291	.636	84	-1	9	4.04	-4	C-15/3-9	3	-0.4
Phi-N	37	113	13	27	4	1	1	8	15	8	0	....	.239	.328	.319	.647	91	-1	12	3.38	-1	C-21/O-6(6-0-0),3-5,1-1	3	-0.1
Yr.	74	192	21	47	7	1	1	20	26	16	1	....	.245	.335	.307	.642	88	-2	21	3.64	-5	C-36,3-14/O-6(6-0-0),1-1	6	-0.6
1946 Phi-N	11	13	2	1	0	0	0	1	7	3	0	....	.077	.400	.077	.477	40	-0	1	2.54	0	/C-6,1-2	0	0.0
Total 4	**98**	**228**	**29**	**53**	**9**	**2**	**1**	**22**	**34**	**24**	**1**	**....**	**.232**	**.335**	**.303**	**.637**	**84**	**-3**	**25**	**3.74**	**-5**	**/C-49,3-14,O-6,1-3,P-2**	**8**	**-0.3**

• MOORE, Eddie

Graham Edward Moore b: 1/18/1899, Barlow, KY d: 2/10/1976, Fort Myers, FL BR/TR, 5'7", 165 lbs. Deb: 9/25/1923 Career OF: 69-18-58

YEAR TM-L	G	AB	R	H	2B	3B	HR	RBI	BB	SO	SB	CS	AVG	OBP	SLG	OPS	OPS+	BR/A	RC	RC/G	FR	G/POS	WS	TPW
1923 Pit-N	6	26	6	7	1	0	0	1	2	3	1	0	.269	.321	.308	.629	65	-1	3	3.77	-2	/S-6	1	-0.2
1924 Pit-N	72	209	47	75	8	4	2	13	27	12	6	7	.359	.437	.464	.901	139	12	42	7.81	3	O-35(1-0-34),3-13/2-4	10	1.3
1925*Pit-N	142	547	106	163	29	8	6	77	73	26	19	7	.298	.383	.413	.796	97	2	92	5.92	2	*2-122,O-15(0-0-15)/3-3	18	0.6
1926 Pit-N	43	132	19	30	8	1	0	19	12	6	3	....	.227	.292	.303	.595	57	-8	12	2.89	-1	2-24/3-9,S-1	1	-0.8
Bos-N	54	184	17	49	3	2	0	15	16	12	6	....	.266	.325	.304	.629	77	-5	19	3.31	-5	2-39,S-14/3-1	3	-0.8
Yr.	97	316	36	79	11	3	0	34	28	18	9	....	.250	.311	.304	.615	69	-13	31	3.14	-6	2-63,S-15,3-10	4	-1.6
1927 Bos-N	112	411	53	124	14	4	1	32	39	17	5	....	.302	.364	.363	.726	103	3	54	4.74	-7	3-52,2-39,O-16(1-11-4)/S-1	11	-0.1
1928 Bos-N	68	215	27	51	9	0	2	18	19	12	7	....	.237	.299	.307	.606	62	-12	20	3.01	4	O-54(54-0-0)/2-1	2	-1.2
1929 Bro-N	111	402	48	119	18	6	0	48	44	16	3	....	.296	.370	.371	.740	86	-7	56	4.89	-7	2-74,S-36/O-2(0-0-2),3-1	9	-0.8
1930 Bro-N	76	196	24	55	13	1	1	20	21	7	1	....	.281	.356	.372	.729	77	-7	26	4.64	2	2-23,O-23(13-7-3),S-17/3-1	4	-0.3
1932 NY-N	37	87	9	23	3	0	1	6	9	6	1	....	.264	.340	.333	.674	84	-2	10	4.24	-3	S-21/3-6,2-5	2	-0.3
1934 Cle-A	27	65	4	10	2	0	0	8	10	4	0	0	.154	.267	.185	.451	18	-8	4	1.80	-2	2-18/3-3,S-2	1	-0.8
Total 10	**748**	**2474**	**360**	**706**	**108**	**26**	**13**	**257**	**272**	**121**	**52**	**14**	**.285**	**.359**	**.366**	**.725**	**89**	**-33**	**338**	**4.76**	**-15**	**2-349,O-145/S-98,3-89**	**62**	**-3.4**

• MOORE, Ferdie

Ferdinand Depage Moore b: 2/21/1896, Camden, NJ d: 5/6/1947, Atlantic City, NJ Deb: 10/2/1914

YEAR TM-L	G	AB	R	H	2B	3B	HR	RBI	BB	SO	SB	CS	AVG	OBP	SLG	OPS	OPS+	BR/A	RC	RC/G	FR	G/POS	WS	TPW
1914 Phi-A	2	4	1	2	0	0	0	1	0	2	0	....	.500	.500	.500	1.000	209	0	1	10.07	-1	/1-2	0	0.0

• MOORE, Gary

Gary Douglas Moore b: 2/24/1945, Tulsa, OK BR/TL, 5'10", 175 lbs. Deb: 5/3/1970

YEAR TM-L	G	AB	R	H	2B	3B	HR	RBI	BB	SO	SB	CS	AVG	OBP	SLG	OPS	OPS+	BR/A	RC	RC/G	FR	G/POS	WS	TPW
1970 LA-N	7	16	2	3	0	2	0	0	0	1	1	0	.188	.188	.438	.625	65	-1	0	.85	0	/O-5(0-0-5),1-1	0	-0.1

• MOORE, Gene

Eugene "Rowdy" Moore, Jr. b: 8/26/1909, Lancaster, TX d: 3/12/1978, Jackson, MS BL/TL, 5'11", 175 lbs. Deb: 9/19/1931 Career OF: 31-45-842

YEAR TM-L	G	AB	R	H	2B	3B	HR	RBI	BB	SO	SB	CS	AVG	OBP	SLG	OPS	OPS+	BR/A	RC	RC/G	FR	G/POS	WS	TPW
1931 Cin-N	4	14	2	2	1	0	0	1	0	0	0	....	.143	.143	.214	.357	-6	-2	0	.90	0	/O-3(3-0-0)	0	-0.2
1933 StL-N	11	38	6	15	3	2	0	8	4	10	1	....	.395	.452	.579	1.031	183	4	10	11.37	0	O-10(0-10-0)	3	0.4
1934 StL-N	9	18	2	5	1	0	0	1	2	2	0	....	.278	.350	.333	.683	79	-0	2	4.85	0	/O-3(0-3-0)	0	0.0
1935 StL-N	3	3	0	0	0	0	0	0	0	1	0	....	.000	.000	.000	.000	-96	-1	0	.00	0	....	0	-0.1
1936 Bos-N	151	637	91	185	38	12	13	67	40	80	6	....	.290	.335	.449	.784	117	13	100	5.77	18	*O-151(0-0-151)	22	2.0
1937 Bos-N★	148	561	88	159	29	10	16	70	61	73	11	....	.283	.358	.456	.814	131	24	96	6.23	14	*O-148(0-0-148)	27	2.9
1938 Bos-N	54	180	27	49	8	3	3	19	16	20	1	....	.272	.338	.400	.738	114	3	25	5.11	1	O-47(0-0-47)	7	0.1
1939 Bro-N	107	306	45	69	13	6	3	39	40	50	4	....	.225	.315	.337	.652	72	-12	35	3.82	-4	O-86(2-1-83)/1-1	6	-2.0
1940 Bro-N	10	26	3	7	2	0	0	2	1	3	0	....	.269	.296	.346	.642	72	-1	3	3.90	-1	/O-6(0-0-6)	1	-0.2
Bos-N	103	363	46	106	24	1	5	39	25	32	2	....	.292	.338	.405	.743	110	4	48	4.78	6	O-94(0-1-94)	11	0.5
Yr.	113	389	49	113	26	1	5	41	26	35	2	....	.290	.335	.401	.736	108	3	51	4.73	6	*O-100(0-1-100)	12	0.3
1941 Bos-N	129	397	42	108	17	8	5	43	45	37	5	....	.272	.349	.393	.742	114	7	57	5.13	4	*O-110(1-28-84)	13	0.6
1942 Was-A	1	2	0	0	0	0	0	0	0	1	0	0	.000	.000	.000	.000	-101	-1	0	.00	0	/O-1	0	-0.1
1943 Was-A	92	254	41	68	14	3	2	39	19	29	0	2	.268	.321	.370	.691	106	0	29	3.93	1	O-57(24-1-32)/1-1	7	-0.2
1944*StL-A	110	390	56	93	13	6	6	58	24	37	0	5	.238	.284	.349	.633	76	-15	37	3.24	1	O-98(0-0-98)/1-1	7	-2.2
1945 StL-A	110	354	48	92	16	2	5	50	40	26	1	3	.260	.337	.359	.695	97	-2	46	4.52	-2	*O-100(1-0-99)	11	-1.0
Total 14	**1042**	**3543**	**497**	**958**	**179**	**53**	**58**	**436**	**317**	**401**	**31**	**10**	**.270**	**.333**	**.400**	**.733**	**106**	**23**	**489**	**4.90**	**39**	**O-914/1-3**	**115**	**0.4**

• MOORE, Harry

Henry S. Moore Deb: 4/17/1884

YEAR TM-L	G	AB	R	H	2B	3B	HR	RBI	BB	SO	SB	CS	AVG	OBP	SLG	OPS	OPS+	BR/A	RC	RC/G	FR	G/POS	WS	TPW
1884 Was-U	111	461	77	155	23	5	1	....	19	....	....	....	.336	.363	.414	.777	167	32	71	6.49	-11	*O-105(102-2-1)/S-8	22	1.6

• MOORE, Jackie

Jackie Spencer Moore b: 2/19/1939, Jay, FL BR/TR, 6', 180 lbs. Deb: 4/18/1965 M/C

YEAR TM-L	G	AB	R	H	2B	3B	HR	RBI	BB	SO	SB	CS	AVG	OBP	SLG	OPS	OPS+	BR/A	RC	RC/G	FR	G/POS	WS	TPW
1965 Det-A	21	53	2	5	0	0	0	2	6	12	0	0	.094	.186	.094	.281	-18	-8	1	.47	-1	C-20	1	-0.8

• MOORE, Jerrie

Jeremiah S. Moore b: Detroit, MI d: 9/26/1890, Wayne, MI BL, 5'11", 170 lbs. Deb: 4/17/1884

YEAR TM-L	G	AB	R	H	2B	3B	HR	RBI	BB	SO	SB	CS	AVG	OBP	SLG	OPS	OPS+	BR/A	RC	RC/G	FR	G/POS	WS	TPW
1884 Alt-U	20	80	10	25	3	1	1	....	0	....	....	....	.313	.313	.413	.725	142	3	11	5.38	-7	C-12/O-9(1-2-6)	2	-0.2
Cle-N	9	30	1	6	0	0	0	10	0	5	....	....	.200	.200	.200	.400	25	-3	1	1.41	-2	/C-9	0	-0.4
1885 Det-N	6	23	2	4	1	0	0	0	1	3	....	....	.174	.208	.217	.426	38	-2	1	1.52	0	/C-6	0	-0.1
Total 2	**35**	**133**	**13**	**35**	**4**	**1**	**1**	**10**	**1**	**8**	**....**	**....**	**.263**	**.269**	**.331**	**.599**	**97**	**-1**	**13**	**3.66**	**-9**	**/C-27,O-9**	**2**	**-0.7**

• MOORE, Jimmy

James William Moore b: 4/24/1903, Paris, TN d: 3/7/1986, Memphis, TN BR/TR, 6'.5", 187 lbs. Deb: 4/17/1930 Career OF: 43-3-14

YEAR TM-L	G	AB	R	H	2B	3B	HR	RBI	BB	SO	SB	CS	AVG	OBP	SLG	OPS	OPS+	BR/A	RC	RC/G	FR	G/POS	WS	TPW
1930 Chi-A	16	39	4	8	2	0	0	2	6	3	0	0	.205	.326	.256	.582	52	-3	4	3.13	1	O-11(11-0-0)	0	-0.2
*Phi-A	15	50	10	19	3	0	2	12	2	4	1	1	.380	.404	.560	.964	136	2	11	8.88	0	O-13(8-1-4)	2	0.1
Yr.	31	89	14	27	5	0	2	14	8	7	1	1	.303	.367	.427	.794	96	-0	14	6.00	1	O-24(19-1-4)	2	-0.1
1931*Phi-A	49	143	18	32	5	1	2	21	11	13	0	1	.224	.284	.315	.599	54	-10	13	2.99	1	O-36(24-2-10)	1	-1.0
Total 2	**80**	**232**	**32**	**59**	**10**	**1**	**4**	**35**	**19**	**20**	**1**	**2**	**.254**	**.316**	**.358**	**.674**	**70**	**-10**	**27**	**4.07**	**2**	**/O-60**	**3**	**-1.1**

• MOORE, Johnny

John Francis Moore b: 3/23/1902, Waterville, CT d: 4/4/1991, Bradenton, FL BL/TR, 5'10.5", 175 lbs. Deb: 9/15/1928 Career OF: 221-163-359

YEAR TM-L	G	AB	R	H	2B	3B	HR	RBI	BB	SO	SB	CS	AVG	OBP	SLG	OPS	OPS+	BR/A	RC	RC/G	FR	G/POS	WS	TPW
1928 Chi-N	4	4	0	0	0	0	0	0	0	0	0	....	.000	.000	.000	.000	-101	-1	0	.00	0	....	0	-0.1
1929 Chi-N	37	63	13	18	1	0	2	8	4	6	0	....	.286	.338	.397	.735	81	-2	8	4.69	0	O-15(10-4-1)	1	-0.3
1931 Chi-N	39	104	19	25	3	1	2	16	7	5	1	....	.240	.288	.346	.634	69	-5	11	3.38	1	O-22(12-9-1)	1	-0.5
1932*Chi-N	119	443	59	135	24	5	13	64	22	38	4	....	.305	.342	.470	.811	117	9	71	5.90	1	*O-109(4-91-14)	18	0.7
1933 Cin-N	135	514	60	135	19	5	1	44	29	16	4	....	.263	.306	.325	.631	81	-12	52	3.50	2	*O-132(75-57-0)	11	-1.7
1934 Cin-N	16	42	5	8	1	1	0	5	3	2	0	....	.190	.244	.262	.506	36	-4	3	2.34	-1	O-10(0-0-10)	0	-0.5
Phi-N	116	458	68	157	34	6	11	93	40	18	7	....	.343	.397	.515	.912	125	17	97	8.37	5	*O-115(10-0-108)	17	1.5
Yr.	132	500	73	165	35	7	11	98	43	20	7	....	.330	.384	.494	.878	118	14	100	7.78	4	*O-125(10-0-118)	17	1.0
1935 Phi-N	153	600	84	194	33	3	19	93	45	50	4	....	.323	.375	.483	.859	117	15	114	7.38	-12	*O-150(2-0-148)	20	-0.6
1936 Phi-N	124	472	85	155	24	3	16	68	26	22	1	....	.328	.365	.494	.858	117	10	83	6.70	-9	*O-112(78-0-35)	11	-0.5
1937 Phi-N	96	307	46	98	16	2	9	59	18	18	2	....	.319	.357	.472	.829	114	5	52	6.47	-1	O-72(30-2-42)	8	0.1
1945 Chi-N	7	6	0	1	0	0	0	2	1	1	0	....	.167	.286	.167	.452	28	-0	0	1.94	0	....	0	0.0
Total 10	**846**	**3013**	**439**	**926**	**155**	**26**	**73**	**452**	**195**	**176**	**23**	**....**	**.307**	**.352**	**.449**	**.801**	**108**	**32**	**492**	**6.07**	**-13**	**O-737**	**87**	**-1.9**

• MOORE, Jo-Jo

Joseph Gregg "The Gause Ghost" Moore
b: 12/25/1908, Gause, TX d: 4/1/2001, Bryan, TX BL/TR, 5'11", 155 lbs. Deb: 9/17/1930 Career OF: 1248-47-0

YEAR TM-L	G	AB	R	H	2B	3B	HR	RBI	BB	SO	SB	CS	AVG	OBP	SLG	OPS	OPS+	BR/A	RC	RC/G	FR	G/POS	WS	TPW
1930 NY-N	3	5	1	1	0	0	0	0	0	1	0	....	.200	.200	.200	.400	-3	-1	0	1.21	0	/O-1	0	-0.1
1931 NY-N	4	8	0	2	1	0	0	3	0	1	1	....	.250	.250	.375	.625	67	-0	1	3.16	-0	/O-1	0	0.0
1932 NY-N	86	361	53	110	15	2	2	27	20	18	4	....	.305	.341	.374	.715	94	-3	47	4.82	-1	O-86(85-1-0)	8	-0.9

YEAR TM-L	G	AB	R	H	2B	3B	HR	RBI	BB	SO	SB	CS	AVG	OBP	SLG	OPS	OPS+	BR/A	RC	RC/G	FR	G/POS	WS	TPW
1933*NY-N	132	524	56	153	16	5	0	42	21	27	4	....	.292	.323	.342	.665	91	-6	59	4.23	13	*O-132(111-21-0)	17	0.0
1934 NY-N★	139	580	106	192	37	4	15	61	31	23	5	....	.331	.370	.486	.856	130	23	109	7.46	-3	*O-131(112-20-0)	26	1.3
1935 NY-N★	155	681	108	201	28	9	15	71	53	24	5	....	.295	.353	.429	.782	111	11	110	6.09	4	*O-155(155-0-0)	24	0.5
1936*NY-N★	152	649	110	205	29	9	7	63	37	27	2	....	.316	.358	.421	.779	110	9	103	6.19	18	*O-149(149-0-0)	23	1.7
1937*NY-N★	142	580	89	180	37	10	6	57	46	37	7	....	.310	.364	.440	.804	116	12	96	6.28	0	*O-140(140-0-0)	21	0.5
1938 NY-N★	125	506	76	153	23	6	11	56	22	27	2	....	.302	.335	.437	.772	110	5	77	5.87	-3	*O-114(114-0-0)	16	-0.5
1939 NY-N	138	562	80	151	23	2	10	47	45	17	5	....	.269	.324	.370	.694	85	-12	69	4.41	6	*O-136(136-0-0)	13	-1.4
1940 NY-N★	138	543	83	150	33	4	6	46	43	30	7	....	.276	.337	.385	.722	98	-1	72	4.74	1	*O-133(133-0-0)	13	-0.9
1941 NY-N	121	428	47	117	16	2	7	40	30	15	4	....	.273	.322	.369	.692	93	-5	52	4.33	-4	*O-116(112-4-0)	9	-1.6
Total 12	**1335**	**5427**	**809**	**1615**	**258**	**53**	**79**	**513**	**348**	**247**	**46**	**....**	**.298**	**.344**	**.408**	**.752**	**105**	**31**	**795**	**5.50**	**30**	***O-1294**	**170**	**-1.3**
• MOORE, Junior	Alvin Earl Moore b: 1/25/1953, Waskom, TX BR/TR, 5'11", 185 lbs. Deb: 8/2/1976 Career OF: 61-0-12																							
1976 Atl-N	20	26	1	7	1	0	0	2	4	4	0	0	.269	.387	.308	.695	93	0	4	4.97	0	/3-6,2-1,O-1	1	0.0
1977 Atl-N	112	361	41	94	9	3	5	34	33	29	4	5	.260	.324	.343	.668	71	-15	38	3.46	-1	*3-104/2-1	6	-1.8
1978 Chi-A	24	65	8	19	0	1	0	4	6	7	1	1	.292	.352	.323	.675	90	-1	7	3.44	0	D-12/3-6,O-5(5-0-0)	1	-0.1
1979 Chi-A	88	201	24	53	6	2	1	23	12	20	0	2	.264	.305	.328	.634	71	-9	18	3.01	0	O-61(52-0-12),D-10/2-2	2	-1.1
1980 Chi-A	45	121	9	31	4	1	1	10	7	11	0	2	.256	.297	.331	.627	72	-6	10	2.79	-1	3-34/O-3(3-0-0),D-2,1-1	1	-0.7
Total 5	**289**	**774**	**83**	**204**	**20**	**7**	**7**	**73**	**62**	**71**	**5**	**10**	**.264**	**.320**	**.335**	**.654**	**73**	**-31**	**77**	**3.28**	**-3**	**3-150/O-70,D-24,2-4,1-1**	**11**	**-3.8**
• MOORE, Kelvin	Kelvin Orlando Moore b: 9/26/1957, Leroy, AL BR/TL, 6'1", 195 lbs. Deb: 8/28/1981																							
1981*Oak-A	14	47	5	12	0	1	1	3	5	15	1	0	.255	.327	.362	.689	103	0	6	4.34	0	1-13	1	-0.1
1982 Oak-A	21	67	6	15	1	1	2	6	3	23	0	1	.224	.257	.358	.615	70	-3	5	2.55	-1	1-20	0	-0.6
1983 Oak-A	41	124	12	26	4	0	5	16	10	39	2	4	.210	.274	.363	.637	78	-5	11	2.78	-1	1-40	1	-0.9
Total 3	**76**	**238**	**23**	**53**	**5**	**2**	**8**	**25**	**18**	**77**	**3**	**5**	**.223**	**.280**	**.361**	**.642**	**81**	**-8**	**22**	**2.99**	**-3**	**/1-73**	**2**	**-1.5**
• MOORE, Kerwin	Kerwin Lamar Moore b: 10/29/1970, Detroit, MI BB/TR, 6'1", 190 lbs. Deb: 8/30/1996																							
1996 Oak-A	22	16	4	1	1	0	0	0	2	6	1	0	.063	.167	.125	.292	-25	-3	1	.91	0	O-18(0-18-0)/D-2	0	-0.3
• MOORE, Molly	Maurice Moore d: 2/24/1881, New York, NY Deb: 6/30/1875																							
1875 Atl-n	21	86	5	19	4	0	0	5	0	4	0	1	.221	.221	.267	.488	79	-1	5	2.26	-4	S-14/1-8,O-2(0-0-2),2-1,3,C	....	-0.5
• MOORE, Randy	Randolph Edward Moore b: 6/21/1906, Naples, TX d: 6/12/1992, Mount Pleasant, TX BL/TR, 6', 185 lbs. Deb: 4/12/1927 Career OF: 66-13-339																							
1927 Chi-A	6	15	0	0	0	0	0	0	0	2	0	0	.000	.000	.000	.000	-103	-4	0	.00	0	/O-4(0-0-4)	0	-0.4
1928 Chi-A	24	61	6	13	4	1	0	5	3	5	0	1	.213	.250	.311	.561	47	-5	5	2.33	0	O-16(2-0-14)	0	-0.7
1930 Bos-N	83	191	24	55	9	0	2	34	10	13	3	....	.288	.323	.366	.690	69	-10	22	4.10	0	O-34(11-12-11),3-13	4	-1.0
1931 Bos-N	83	192	19	50	8	1	3	34	13	3	1	....	.260	.311	.359	.670	83	-5	22	3.96	0	O-29(17-1-11),3-22/2-1	4	-0.6
1932 Bos-N	107	351	41	103	21	2	3	43	15	11	1	....	.293	.322	.390	.713	94	-4	44	4.55	-1	O-41(0-0-41),3-31,1-22/C-1	10	-0.7
1933 Bos-N	135	497	64	150	23	7	8	70	40	16	3	....	.302	.356	.425	.781	133	21	74	5.41	0	*O-122(12-0-110),1-10	22	1.3
1934 Bos-N	123	422	55	120	21	2	7	64	40	16	2	....	.284	.346	.393	.740	105	4	59	5.02	1	O-72(16-0-56),1-37	14	-0.2
1935 Bos-N	125	407	42	112	20	4	4	42	26	16	1	....	.275	.319	.373	.692	93	-5	48	4.23	-1	O-78(7-0-71),1-21	6	-1.2
1936 Bro-N	42	88	4	21	3	0	0	14	8	1	0	....	.239	.302	.273	.575	55	-5	7	2.79	-2	O-21(0-0-21)	0	-0.8
1937 Bro-N	13	22	3	3	1	0	0	2	3	2	0	....	.136	.240	.182	.422	16	-3	1	1.32	-1	C-10	0	-0.3
StL-N	8	7	0	0	0	0	0	0	0	0	0	....	.000	.000	.000	.000	-98	-2	0	.00	0	/O-1	0	-0.2
Yr.	21	29	3	3	1	0	0	2	3	2	0	....	.103	.188	.138	.325	-9	-4	1	.94	-1	C-10/O-1	0	-0.5
Total 10	**749**	**2253**	**258**	**627**	**110**	**17**	**27**	**308**	**158**	**85**	**11**	**1**	**.278**	**.326**	**.378**	**.705**	**96**	**-18**	**283**	**4.44**	**-5**	**O-418/1-90,3-66,C-11,2-1**	**60**	**-4.8**
• MOORE, Scrappy	William Allen Moore b: 12/16/1892, St. Louis, MO d: 10/13/1964, Little Rock, AR BR/TR, 5'8", 153 lbs. Deb: 6/21/1917																							
1917 StL-A	4	8	1	1	0	0	0	0	1	0	0	....	.125	.222	.125	.347	6	-1	0	.76	0	/3-2	0	-0.1
• MOORE, Terry	Terry Bluford Moore b: 5/27/1912, Vernon, AL d: 3/29/1995, Collinsville, IL BR/TR, 5'11", 195 lbs. Deb: 4/16/1935 M/C Career OF: 0-1189-1																							
1935 StL-N	119	456	63	131	34	3	6	53	15	40	13	....	.287	.314	.414	.729	91	-7	60	4.85	4	*O-117(0-117-0)	15	-0.6
1936 StL-N	143	590	85	156	39	4	5	47	37	52	9	....	.264	.309	.369	.678	82	-16	70	4.27	7	*O-133(0-133-0)	15	-1.2
1937 StL-N	115	461	76	123	17	3	5	43	32	41	13	....	.267	.317	.349	.666	79	-14	53	4.05	1	*O-106(0-106-0)	10	-1.5
1938 StL-N	94	312	49	85	21	3	4	21	46	19	9	....	.272	.366	.397	.763	104	3	49	5.46	3	O-75(0-75-0)/3-6	10	0.5
1939 StL-N★	130	417	65	123	25	2	17	77	43	38	6	....	.295	.362	.487	.849	119	11	73	6.09	5	*O-121(0-121-0)/P-1	17	1.4
1940 StL-N★	136	537	92	163	33	4	17	64	42	44	18	....	.304	.356	.475	.831	120	14	92	6.49	7	*O-133(0-133-0)	22	1.9
1941 StL-N★	122	493	86	145	26	4	6	68	52	31	3	....	.294	.364	.400	.763	108	6	74	5.48	5	*O-121(0-121-1)	20	0.8
1942*StL-N★	130	489	80	141	26	3	6	49	56	26	10	....	.288	.364	.391	.754	112	9	72	5.24	-6	*O-126(0-126-0)/3-1	20	0.0
1946*StL-N	91	278	32	73	14	1	3	28	18	26	0	....	.263	.312	.353	.665	85	-6	32	4.11	0	O-66(0-66-0)	7	-0.9
1947 StL-N	127	460	61	130	17	1	7	45	38	39	1	....	.283	.339	.370	.708	84	-11	58	4.48	-5	*O-120(0-120-0)	12	-1.8
1948 StL-N	91	207	30	48	11	0	4	18	27	12	0	....	.232	.321	.343	.664	75	-7	24	3.83	-3	O-71(0-71-0)	4	-1.2
Total 11	**1298**	**4700**	**719**	**1318**	**263**	**28**	**80**	**513**	**406**	**368**	**82**	**....**	**.280**	**.340**	**.399**	**.739**	**98**	**-19**	**656**	**5.01**	**19**	***O-1189/3-7,P-1**	**152**	**-2.7**
• MORA, Andres	Andres (Ibara) Mora b: 5/25/1955, Rio Bravo, Mexico BR/TR, 6', 180 lbs. Deb: 4/13/1976 Career OF: 158-0-3																							
1976 Bal-A	73	220	18	48	11	0	6	25	13	49	1	0	.218	.262	.350	.612	83	-5	20	2.98	0	D-34,O-31(30-0-2)	3	-0.9
1977 Bal-A	77	233	32	57	8	2	13	44	5	53	0	0	.245	.264	.464	.727	100	-2	27	4.01	-1	O-57(57-0-0)/D-5,3-1	6	-0.4
1978 Bal-A	76	229	21	49	8	0	8	14	13	47	0	1	.214	.259	.354	.613	75	-9	20	2.84	1	O-69(69-0-0)/D-1	3	-1.2
1980 Cle-A	9	18	0	2	0	0	0	0	0	0	0	0	.111	.111	.111	.222	-39	-3	0	.38	0	/O-3(2-0-1)	0	-0.4
Total 4	**235**	**700**	**71**	**156**	**27**	**2**	**27**	**83**	**31**	**149**	**1**	**1**	**.223**	**.258**	**.383**	**.641**	**83**	**-19**	**67**	**3.19**	**0**	**O-160/D-40,3-1**	**12**	**-2.8**
• MORA, Melvin	Melvin Mora b: 2/2/1972, Agua Negra, Venezuela BR/TR, 5'10", 180 lbs. Deb: 5/30/1999 Career OF: 170-158-29																							
1999*NY-N	66	31	6	5	0	0	0	1	4	7	2	1	.161	.278	.161	.439	15	-4	2	1.85	-4	O-45(28-11-8)/2-4,3-3,S-1	0	-0.8
2000 NY-N	79	215	35	56	13	2	6	30	18	48	7	3	.260	.323	.423	.747	90	-4	30	4.66	-2	S-44,O-28(12-16-3)/2-4,3-4	6	-0.2
Bal-A	53	199	25	58	9	3	2	17	17	32	5	8	.291	.359	.397	.756	96	-4	27	4.83	4	S-52/2-1	6	0.4
2001 Bal-A	128	436	49	109	28	0	7	48	41	91	11	4	.250	.334	.362	.696	88	-6	56	4.35	7	O-88(0-88-0),S-44/2-1	11	0.4
2002 Bal-A	149	557	86	130	30	4	19	64	70	108	16	10	.233	.340	.404	.744	102	2	81	4.85	18	*O-104(74-31-5),S-41,2-12/D	16	1.9
2003 Bal-A★	96	344	68	109	17	1	15	48	49	71	6	3	.317	.420	.503	.923	147	26	78	8.45	5	O-79(56-12-13),S-11/2-6,1	16	2.8
Total 5	**571**	**1782**	**269**	**467**	**97**	**10**	**49**	**208**	**199**	**357**	**47**	**29**	**.262**	**.353**	**.410**	**.764**	**104**	**11**	**274**	**5.27**	**26**	**O-344,S-193/2-28,3-7,D-3,1**	**55**	**4.5**
• MORALES, Jerry	Julio Ruben (Torres) Morales b: 2/18/1949, Yabucoa, Puerto Rico BR/TR, 5'10", 175 lbs. Deb: 9/5/1969 Career OF: 261-505-560																							
1969 SD-N	19	41	5	8	2	0	1	6	5	7	0	2	.195	.283	.317	.600	71	-3	3	2.33	1	O-19(10-9-1)	0	-0.2
1970 SD-N	28	58	6	9	0	1	1	4	3	11	0	0	.155	.197	.241	.438	17	-7	2	1.28	-1	O-26(23-0-4)	0	-0.9
1971 SD-N	12	17	1	2	0	0	0	1	2	2	1	0	.118	.211	.118	.328	-5	-2	0	.81	0	/O-7(4-1-2)	0	-0.3
1972 SD-N	115	347	38	83	15	7	4	18	35	54	4	6	.239	.309	.357	.666	96	-4	38	3.60	1	O-96(34-56-12)/3-4	9	-0.7
1973 SD-N	122	388	47	109	23	2	9	34	27	55	6	5	.281	.328	.420	.748	115	5	49	4.34	0	*O-100(31-50-27)	11	0.1
1974 Chi-N	151	534	70	146	21	7	15	82	46	63	2	12	.273	.333	.423	.757	106	-2	69	4.39	-3	*O-143(83-32-41)	12	-1.3
1975 Chi-N	153	578	62	156	21	0	12	91	50	65	3	7	.270	.333	.369	.702	90	-10	69	4.07	0	*O-151(0-20-136)	13	-1.7
1976 Chi-N	140	537	66	147	17	0	16	67	41	49	3	8	.274	.325	.395	.720	95	-7	62	3.94	-2	*O-136(3-8-131)	12	-1.7
1977 Chi-N★	136	490	56	142	34	5	11	69	43	75	0	3	.290	.350	.447	.796	101	-0	75	5.55	-1	*O-128(6-125-3)	15	-0.4
1978 StL-N	130	457	44	109	19	8	4	46	33	44	4	4	.239	.291	.341	.633	77	-16	43	3.12	-3	*O-126(0-34-94)	7	-2.6
1979 Det-A	129	440	50	93	23	1	14	56	30	56	10	4	.211	.265	.364	.628	65	-22	39	2.82	-6	*O-119(18-20-88)/D-7	4	-3.2
1980 NY-N	94	193	19	49	7	1	3	30	13	31	2	3	.254	.304	.347	.651	84	-6	20	3.48	-2	O-63(3-55-6)	4	-0.9
1981 Chi-N	84	245	27	70	6	2	1	25	22	29	1	1	.286	.347	.339	.686	91	-2	29	4.20	-6	O-72(17-49-8)	5	-1.0
1982 Chi-N	65	116	14	33	2	2	4	30	9	7	1	2	.284	.336	.440	.776	112	1	15	4.46	1	O-41(12-36-4)	3	0.2
1983 Chi-N	63	87	11	17	9	0	0	11	7	19	0	0	.195	.255	.299	.554	51	-6	7	2.57	-0	O-29(17-10-3)	0	-0.7
Total 15	**1441**	**4528**	**516**	**1173**	**199**	**36**	**95**	**570**	**366**	**567**	**37**	**57**	**.259**	**.316**	**.382**	**.698**	**91**	**-81**	**520**	**3.89**	**-19**	***O-1256/D-7,3-4**	**95**	**-15.2**
• MORALES, Jose	Jose Manuel (Hernandez) Morales b: 12/30/1944, Frederiksted, V.I. BR/TR, 5'11", 195 lbs. Deb: 8/13/1973 C Career OF: 7-0-0																							
1973 Oak-A	6	14	0	4	1	0	0	1	1	5	0	1	.286	.333	.357	.690	100	-0	1	3.25	0	/D-3	0	-0.1
Mon-N	5	5	0	2	0	0	0	0	0	0	0	0	.400	.400	.400	.800	118	0	1	7.20	0	....	0	0.0
1974 Mon-N	25	26	3	7	4	0	1	5	1	7	0	0	.269	.296	.538	.835	123	1	3	4.07	0	/C-2	1	0.0

YEAR TM-L	G	AB	R	H	2B	3B	HR	RBI	BB	SO	SB	CS	AVG	OBP	SLG	OPS	OPS+	BR/A	RC	RC/G	FR	G/POS	WS	TPW
1975 Mon-N	93	163	18	49	6	1	2	24	14	21	0	2	.301	.356	.387	.742	101	-0	20	4.40	3	1-27/O-6(6-0-0),C-5	3	0.1
1976 Mon-N	104	158	12	50	11	0	4	37	3	20	0	0	.316	.337	.462	.799	120	3	23	5.30	3	1-21,C-12	4	0.6
1977 Mon-N	65	74	3	15	4	1	1	9	5	12	0	0	.203	.253	.324	.577	55	-5	5	2.10	0	/1-8,C-8	0	-0.5
1978 Min-A	101	242	22	76	13	1	2	38	20	35	0	1	.314	.369	.401	.770	114	5	34	4.86	0	D-77/1-1,C-1,O-1	5	0.3
1979 Min-A	92	191	21	51	5	1	2	27	14	27	0	0	.267	.324	.335	.659	75	-6	19	3.23	0	D-77/1-1	1	-0.8
1980 Min-A	97	241	36	73	17	2	8	36	22	19	0	0	.303	.364	.490	.853	122	7	40	5.82	0	D-86/1-2,C-2	7	0.5
1981 Bal-A	38	86	6	21	3	0	2	14	3	13	0	0	.244	.270	.349	.619	77	-3	6	2.37	0	D-22/1-3	0	-0.4
1982 Bal-A	3	3	0	0	0	0	0	0	0	2	0	0	.000	.000	.000	.000	-100	-1	0	.00	0	....	0	-0.1
LA-N	35	30	1	9	1	0	1	8	4	8	0	0	.300	.382	.433	.816	131	2	5	6.08	0	....	1	0.2
1983*LA-N	47	53	4	15	3	0	3	8	1	11	0	0	.283	.296	.509	.806	120	1	7	4.77	-1	/1-4	2	0.0
1984 LA-N	22	19	0	3	0	0	0	0	1	2	0	0	.158	.200	.158	.358	2	-2	1	1.01	0	....	0	-0.2
Total 12	733	1305	126	375	68	6	26	207	89	182	0	4	.287	.336	.408	.744	102	0	164	4.35	4	D-265/1-67,C-30,O-7	24	-0.4

• MORALES, Rich Richard Angelo Morales b: 9/20/1943, San Francisco, CA BR/TR, 5'11", 170 lbs. Deb: 8/8/1967 C

YEAR TM-L	G	AB	R	H	2B	3B	HR	RBI	BB	SO	SB	CS	AVG	OBP	SLG	OPS	OPS+	BR/A	RC	RC/G	FR	G/POS	WS	TPW
1967 Chi-A	8	10	0	0	0	0	0	0	0	2	0	0	.000	.000	.000	.000	-104	-2	0	.00	0	/S-7	0	-0.3
1968 Chi-A	10	29	2	5	0	0	0	0	2	5	0	0	.172	.226	.172	.398	22	-3	1	1.15	0	/S-7,2-5	0	-0.3
1969 Chi-A	55	121	12	26	0	1	0	6	7	18	1	0	.215	.269	.231	.501	39	-10	8	2.09	1	2-38,S-13/3-1	2	-0.7
1970 Chi-A	62	112	6	18	2	0	1	2	9	16	1	0	.161	.230	.205	.435	20	-12	6	1.57	-5	S-24,3-20,2-12	1	-1.6
1971 Chi-A	84	185	19	45	8	0	2	14	22	26	2	3	.243	.336	.319	.655	84	-4	20	3.73	-2	S-57,3-18/2-3,O-1	4	-0.1
1972 Chi-A	110	287	24	59	7	1	2	20	19	49	2	3	.206	.262	.258	.520	54	-17	17	1.94	-7	S-86,2-16,3-14	3	-1.7
1973 Chi-A	7	4	1	0	0	0	0	1	1	1	0	0	.000	.200	.000	.200	-38	-1	0	.00	-1	/3-5,2-2	0	-0.1
SD-N	90	244	9	40	6	1	0	16	27	36	0	1	.164	.247	.197	.444	27	-24	13	1.62	1	2-79,S-10	3	-1.8
1974 SD-N	54	61	8	12	3	0	1	5	8	6	1	0	.197	.290	.295	.585	67	-2	6	2.71	-6	S-29,2-18/3-6,1-1	1	-0.6
Total 8	480	1053	81	205	26	3	6	64	95	159	7	7	.195	.268	.242	.510	46	-75	70	2.13	-19	S-233,2-173/3-64,1-1,O-1	14	-7.2

• MORALES, Willie William Anthony Morales b: 9/7/1972, Tucson, AZ BR/TR, 5'10", 185 lbs. Deb: 4/9/2000

YEAR TM-L	G	AB	R	H	2B	3B	HR	RBI	BB	SO	SB	CS	AVG	OBP	SLG	OPS	OPS+	BR/A	RC	RC/G	FR	G/POS	WS	TPW
2000 Bal-A	3	11	1	3	1	0	0	0	0	3	0	0	.273	.273	.364	.636	62	-1	1	3.68	1	/C-3	0	0.1

• MORAN, Al Richard Alan Moran b: 12/5/1938, Detroit, MI BR/TR, 6'1.5", 190 lbs. Deb: 4/9/1963

YEAR TM-L	G	AB	R	H	2B	3B	HR	RBI	BB	SO	SB	CS	AVG	OBP	SLG	OPS	OPS+	BR/A	RC	RC/G	FR	G/POS	WS	TPW
1963 NY-N	119	331	26	64	5	2	1	23	36	60	3	7	.193	.274	.230	.504	46	-24	21	2.00	-11	*S-116/3-1	3	-2.8
1964 NY-N	16	22	2	5	0	0	0	4	2	2	0	0	.227	.292	.227	.519	50	-1	1	2.06	-1	S-15/3-1	0	-0.1
Total 2	135	353	28	69	5	2	1	27	38	62	3	7	.195	.276	.229	.505	46	-25	22	2.01	-11	S-131/3-2	3	-2.9

• MORAN, Bill William L. Moran b: 10/10/1869, Joliet, IL d: 4/8/1916, Joliet, IL, 5'10.5", 175 lbs. Deb: 5/7/1892

YEAR TM-L	G	AB	R	H	2B	3B	HR	RBI	BB	SO	SB	CS	AVG	OBP	SLG	OPS	OPS+	BR/A	RC	RC/G	FR	G/POS	WS	TPW
1892 StL-N	24	81	2	11	1	0	0	5	2	12	0	....	.136	.157	.148	.305	-8	-11	2	.74	-3	C-22/O-2(2-0-0)	1	-1.1
1895 Chi-N	15	55	8	9	2	1	1	9	3	2	2	....	.164	.220	.291	.511	29	-6	4	2.39	-2	C-15	0	-0.5
Total 2	39	136	10	20	3	1	1	14	5	14	2	....	.147	.183	.206	.389	7	-17	6	1.39	-5	/C-37,O-2	1	-1.6

• MORAN, Billy William Nelson Moran b: 11/27/1933, Montgomery, AL BR/TR, 5'11", 185 lbs. Deb: 4/15/1958

YEAR TM-L	G	AB	R	H	2B	3B	HR	RBI	BB	SO	SB	CS	AVG	OBP	SLG	OPS	OPS+	BR/A	RC	RC/G	FR	G/POS	WS	TPW
1958 Cle-A	115	257	26	58	11	0	1	18	13	23	3	2	.226	.263	.280	.543	51	-18	18	2.25	-3	2-74,S-38	3	-1.4
1959 Cle-A	11	17	1	5	0	0	0	2	0	1	0	0	.294	.294	.294	.588	64	-1	1	3.31	-1	/2-6,S-5	0	-0.2
1961 LA-A	54	173	17	45	7	1	2	22	17	16	0	0	.260	.330	.347	.677	73	-6	20	3.84	-3	2-51/S-2	3	-0.5
1962 LA-A★	160	659	90	186	25	3	17	74	39	80	5	1	.282	.326	.407	.733	99	-2	89	4.79	12	*2-160	24	2.5
1963 LA-A	153	597	67	164	29	5	7	65	31	57	1	1	.275	.314	.375	.689	98	-4	68	3.96	6	*2-151	17	1.7
1964 LA-A	50	198	26	53	10	1	0	11	13	20	1	3	.268	.316	.328	.644	88	-5	18	3.00	-8	3-47/2-3,S-1	3	-1.3
Cle-A	69	151	14	31	6	0	1	10	18	16	0	1	.205	.294	.265	.559	57	-9	12	2.42	-3	3-42,2-15/1-2	2	-1.2
Yr.	119	349	40	84	16	1	1	21	31	36	1	4	.241	.306	.301	.607	75	-13	30	2.74	-11	3-89,2-18/1-2,S-1	5	-2.5
1965 Cle-A	22	24	1	3	0	0	0	0	2	5	0	0	.125	.222	.125	.347	1	-3	1	1.08	1	/2-7,S-1	0	-0.2
Total 7	634	2076	242	545	88	10	28	202	133	218	10	8	.263	.310	.355	.665	85	-47	227	3.72	2	2-467/3-89,S-47,1-2	52	-0.7

• MORAN, Charles Charles Vincent Moran b: 3/26/1879, Washington, DC d: 4/11/1934, Washington, DC TR Deb: 4/29/1903

YEAR TM-L	G	AB	R	H	2B	3B	HR	RBI	BB	SO	SB	CS	AVG	OBP	SLG	OPS	OPS+	BR/A	RC	RC/G	FR	G/POS	WS	TPW
1903 Was-A	98	373	41	84	14	5	1	24	33	....	8	....	.225	.297	.298	.594	77	-9	37	3.32	4	S-96/2-2	8	-0.2
1904 Was-A	62	243	27	54	10	0	0	7	23	....	7	....	.222	.289	.263	.553	77	-6	22	2.97	-6	S-61/3-1	4	-1.1
StL-A	82	272	15	47	3	1	0	14	25	....	2	....	.173	.242	.191	.434	40	-17	15	1.66	-6	3-81/O-1	1	-2.3
Yr.	144	515	42	101	13	1	0	21	48	....	9	....	.196	.265	.225	.490	57	-23	36	2.25	-11	3-82,S-61/O-1	5	-3.4
1905 StL-A	27	82	6	16	1	0	0	5	10	....	3	....	.195	.290	.207	.498	62	-3	7	2.52	-7	2-20/3-5	1	-1.0
Total 3	269	970	89	201	28	6	1	50	91	....	20	....	.207	.279	.252	.531	65	-35	81	2.68	-14	S-157/3-87,2-22,O-1	14	-4.6

• MORAN, Charlie Charles Barthell "Uncle Charlie" Moran b: 2/22/1878, Nashville, TN d: 6/14/1949, Horse Cave, KY BR/TR, 5'8", 180 lbs. Deb: 9/9/1903 U

YEAR TM-L	G	AB	R	H	2B	3B	HR	RBI	BB	SO	SB	CS	AVG	OBP	SLG	OPS	OPS+	BR/A	RC	RC/G	FR	G/POS	WS	TPW
1903 StL-N	4	14	2	6	0	0	0	1	0	....	1	....	.429	.429	.429	.857	149	2	3	10.19	-1	/P-3,S-1	1	-0.4
1908 StL-N	21	63	2	11	1	2	0	2	0	....	0	....	.175	.175	.254	.429	38	-5	3	1.27	-1	C-16	0	-0.5
Total 2	25	77	4	17	1	2	0	3	0	....	1	....	.221	.221	.286	.506	59	-3	6	2.46	-2	/C-16,P-3,S-1	1	-0.9

• MORAN, Herbie John Herbert Moran b: 2/16/1884, Costello, PA d: 9/21/1954, Clarkson, NY BL/TR, 5'5", 150 lbs. Deb: 4/16/1908 Career OF: 48-142-407

YEAR TM-L	G	AB	R	H	2B	3B	HR	RBI	BB	SO	SB	CS	AVG	OBP	SLG	OPS	OPS+	BR/A	RC	RC/G	FR	G/POS	WS	TPW
1908 Phi-A	19	59	4	9	0	0	0	4	6	....	1	....	.153	.242	.153	.395	27	-4	3	1.28	-1	O-19(0-10-9)	1	-0.7
Bos-N	8	29	3	8	0	0	0	2	2	....	1	....	.276	.364	.276	.639	106	0	3	3.96	3	/O-8(8-0-0)	1	0.3
1909 Bos-N	8	31	8	7	1	0	0	0	5	....	0	....	.226	.333	.258	.591	80	-0	3	2.81	0	/O-8(8-0-0)	1	-0.1
1910 Bos-N	20	67	11	8	0	0	0	3	13	14	6	....	.119	.280	.119	.400	17	-6	4	1.67	5	O-20(11-0-9)	1	-0.2
1912 Bro-N	130	508	77	140	18	10	1	40	69	38	28	....	.276	.368	.356	.724	102	4	76	5.16	3	*O-129(2-73-55)	13	0.0
1913 Bro-N	132	515	71	137	15	5	0	26	45	29	21	....	.266	.333	.315	.648	83	-10	58	3.83	0	*O-129(3-6-121)	9	-1.8
1914 Cin-N	107	395	43	93	10	5	1	35	41	29	26	....	.235	.312	.294	.606	78	-10	42	3.51	-3	*O-107(1-24-82)	8	-2.0
*Bos-N	41	154	24	41	3	1	0	4	17	11	4	....	.266	.347	.299	.646	93	-1	17	3.78	-3	O-41(0-17-30)	4	-0.6
Yr.	148	549	67	134	13	6	1	39	58	40	30	....	.244	.322	.295	.617	82	-11	59	3.58	-6	*O-148(1-41-112)	12	-2.6
1915 Bos-N	130	419	59	84	13	5	0	21	66	41	16	10	.200	.320	.255	.576	77	-9	38	2.85	1	*O-123(15-12-101)	8	-1.5
Total 7	595	2177	300	527	60	26	2	135	264	162	103	10	.242	.332	.296	.629	83	-36	244	3.69	6	O-584	46	-6.5

• MORAN, Pat Patrick Joseph Moran b: 2/7/1876, Fitchburg, MA d: 3/7/1924, Orlando, FL BR/TR, 5'10", 180 lbs. Deb: 5/15/1901 M/U Career OF: 0-0-4

YEAR TM-L	G	AB	R	H	2B	3B	HR	RBI	BB	SO	SB	CS	AVG	OBP	SLG	OPS	OPS+	BR/A	RC	RC/G	FR	G/POS	WS	TPW
1901 Bos-N	52	180	12	38	5	1	2	18	3	....	3	....	.211	.228	.283	.512	44	-14	13	2.37	-8	C-28,1-13/3-4,O-3(0-0-3),S,2	2	-1.9
1902 Bos-N	80	251	22	60	5	5	1	24	17	....	6	....	.239	.303	.311	.614	88	-3	27	3.62	0	C-71/1-3,O-1	9	0.4
1903 Bos-N	109	389	40	102	25	5	7	54	29	....	8	....	.262	.331	.406	.737	114	6	57	5.15	20	*C-107/1-1	17	3.5
1904 Bos-N	113	398	26	90	11	3	4	34	18	....	10	....	.226	.267	.299	.566	77	-11	36	2.98	8	C-72,3-39/1-2	9	0.4
1905 Bos-N	85	267	22	64	11	5	2	22	8	....	3	....	.240	.270	.341	.611	83	-7	26	3.33	6	C-78	7	0.8
1906*Chi-N	70	226	22	57	13	1	0	35	7	....	6	....	.252	.281	.319	.599	82	-6	23	3.43	-4	C-61	7	-0.3
1907*Chi-N	65	198	8	45	5	1	1	19	10	....	5	....	.227	.271	.278	.549	68	-8	17	2.85	-2	C-59	5	-0.5
1908 Chi-N	50	150	12	39	5	1	0	12	13	....	6	....	.260	.323	.307	.630	97	-0	17	3.77	-2	C-45	7	0.2
1909 Chi-N	77	246	18	54	11	1	1	23	16	....	2	....	.220	.278	.285	.563	73	-8	20	2.60	-4	C-74	7	-0.6
1910 Phi-N	68	199	13	47	7	1	0	11	17	16	6	....	.236	.306	.281	.587	69	-8	19	3.13	2	C-56	5	0.0
1911 Phi-N	34	103	2	19	3	0	0	8	3	13	0	....	.184	.208	.214	.421	18	-12	5	1.36	2	C-32	2	-0.7
1912 Phi-N	13	26	1	3	1	0	0	1	1	7	0	....	.115	.148	.154	.302	-16	-4	1	.59	-1	C-13	0	-0.4
1913 Phi-N	1	1	0	0	0	0	0	0	0	0	0	....	.000	.000	.000	.000	-96	-0	0	.00	0	....	0	0.0
1914 Phi-N	1	0	0	0	0	0	0	0	1	0	0	....	....	....	....	....	-94	0	0	....	-1	/C-1	0	-0.1
Total 14	818	2634	198	618	102	24	18	262	142	36	55	....	.235	.283	.312	.595	79	-75	260	3.29	16	C-697/3-43,1-19,O-4,S-3,2-1	77	0.8

• MORAN, Roy Roy Ellis "Deedle" Moran b: 9/17/1884, Vincennes, IN d: 7/18/1966, Atlanta, GA BR/TR, 5'8", 155 lbs. Deb: 9/3/1912

YEAR TM-L	G	AB	R	H	2B	3B	HR	RBI	BB	SO	SB	CS	AVG	OBP	SLG	OPS	OPS+	BR/A	RC	RC/G	FR	G/POS	WS	TPW
1912 Was-A	7	13	1	2	0	0	0	0	8	....	3	....	.154	.476	.154	.630	82	1	3	5.64	0	/O-6(5-0-0)	1	0.1

• MORANDINI, Mickey Michael Robert Morandini b: 4/22/1966, Kittanning, PA BL/TR, 5'11", 171 lbs. Deb: 9/1/1990

YEAR TM-L	G	AB	R	H	2B	3B	HR	RBI	BB	SO	SB	CS	AVG	OBP	SLG	OPS	OPS+	BR/A	RC	RC/G	FR	G/POS	WS	TPW
1990 Phi-N	25	79	9	19	4	0	1	3	6	19	3	0	.241	.294	.329	.623	71	-3	8	3.57	-0	2-25	1	-0.2
1991 Phi-N	98	325	38	81	11	4	1	20	29	45	13	2	.249	.315	.317	.632	79	-7	35	3.57	4	2-97	9	0.0
1992 Phi-N	127	422	47	112	8	8	3	30	25	64	8	3	.265	.306	.344	.650	84	-9	46	3.78	11	*2-124/S-3	9	0.5
1993*Phi-N	120	425	57	105	19	9	3	33	34	73	13	2	.247	.310	.355	.666	79	-11	49	3.95	4	*2-111	10	-0.2

YEAR TM-L	G	AB	R	H	2B	3B	HR	RBI	BB	SO	SB	CS	AVG	OBP	SLG	OPS	OPS+	BR/A	RC	RC/G	FR	G/POS	WS	TPW
1994 Phi-N	87	274	40	80	16	5	2	26	34	33	10	5	.292	.378	.409	.787	103	2	44	5.75	5	2-79	10	1.1
1995 Phi-N★	127	494	65	140	34	7	6	49	42	80	9	6	.283	.350	.417	.767	101	-0	71	5.13	9	*2-122	17	1.4
1996 Phi-N	140	539	64	135	24	6	3	32	49	87	26	5	.250	.323	.334	.657	73	-17	61	3.80	7	*2-137	10	-0.4
1997 Phi-N	150	553	83	163	40	2	1	39	62	91	16	13	.295	.374	.380	.754	98	-2	81	5.13	-8	*2-146/S-1	16	-0.2
1998*Chi-N	154	582	93	172	20	4	8	53	72	84	13	1	.296	.382	.385	.766	99	5	90	5.66	-5	*2-152	23	0.7
1999 Chi-N	144	456	60	110	18	5	4	37	48	61	6	6	.241	.322	.329	.651	66	-25	49	3.54	-2	*2-132	7	-2.0
2000 Phi-N	91	302	31	76	13	3	0	22	29	54	5	2	.252	.325	.315	.640	62	-17	31	3.38	-2	2-85	5	-1.4
Tor-A	35	107	10	29	2	1	0	7	7	23	1	0	.271	.316	.308	.624	57	-7	11	3.51	-1	2-35	2	-0.6
Total 11	**1298**	**4558**	**597**	**1222**	**209**	**54**	**32**	**351**	**437**	**714**	**123**	**45**	**.268**	**.340**	**.359**	**.698**	**84**	**-91**	**576**	**4.37**	**22**	***2-1245/S-4**	**119**	**-1.4**

• MORBAN, Jose Jose Morban b: 12/2/1979, Santiago, Dominican Republic BB/TR, 6'1", 170 lbs. Deb: 4/6/2003

YEAR TM-L	G	AB	R	H	2B	3B	HR	RBI	BB	SO	SB	CS	AVG	OBP	SLG	OPS	OPS+	BR/A	RC	RC/G	FR	G/POS	WS	TPW
2003 Bal-A	61	71	14	10	0	0	2	5	3	21	8	0	.141	.187	.225	.412	8	-8	4	1.73	-3	D-14,S-14,2-12/3-1	1	-1.0

• MORDECAI, Mike Michael Howard Mordecai b: 12/13/1967, Birmingham, AL BB/TR, 5'11", 175 lbs. Deb: 5/8/1994 Career OF: 1-1-2

YEAR TM-L	G	AB	R	H	2B	3B	HR	RBI	BB	SO	SB	CS	AVG	OBP	SLG	OPS	OPS+	BR/A	RC	RC/G	FR	G/POS	WS	TPW
1994 Atl-N	4	4	1	1	0	0	1	3	1	0	0	0	.250	.400	1.000	1.400	244	1	2	15.34	-1	/S-4	1	0.0
1995*Atl-N	69	75	10	21	6	0	3	11	9	16	0	0	.280	.357	.480	.837	115	2	14	6.52	-1	2-21/1-9,3-6,S-6,0-1	4	0.1
1996*Atl-N	66	108	12	26	5	0	2	8	9	24	1	0	.241	.299	.343	.642	65	-5	12	3.61	-4	2-20,3-10/S-6,1-1	1	-0.9
1997 Atl-N	61	81	8	14	2	1	0	3	6	16	0	1	.173	.230	.222	.452	19	-10	3	1.27	-2	3-19/2-4,S-4,1-3,D-1,0-1	0	-1.2
1998 Mon-N	73	119	12	24	4	2	3	10	9	20	1	0	.202	.258	.345	.602	57	-8	11	2.92	-3	S-30,2-21,3-11/1-1	1	-0.9
1999 Mon-N	109	226	29	53	10	2	5	25	20	31	2	5	.235	.300	.363	.662	68	-13	24	3.63	-2	2-38,S-38,3-32/1-1	4	-1.2
2000 Mon-N	86	169	20	48	16	0	4	16	12	34	2	2	.284	.335	.450	.785	93	-3	26	5.54	-4	3-58,S-10/2-9,1-3	3	-0.5
2001 Mon-N	96	254	28	71	17	2	3	32	19	53	2	2	.280	.332	.398	.730	86	-6	33	4.53	-10	3-42,2-32/S-4,1-1,C-1,D-1,0	6	-1.3
2002 Mon-N	55	74	9	15	4	0	0	4	8	14	1	1	.203	.289	.257	.546	44	-6	6	2.26	-2	3-28/2-4,1-3,S-3,0-1	0	-0.7
Fla-N	38	77	10	22	4	0	0	7	5	13	1	1	.286	.337	.338	.675	82	-2	9	4.00	2	S-24/3-7,1-1	2	0.1
Yr.	93	151	19	37	8	0	0	11	13	27	2	2	.245	.313	.298	.611	62	-8	15	3.07	0	3-35,S-27/1-4,2-4,0-1	2	-0.7
2003*Fla-N	65	89	11	19	4	0	2	8	8	21	3	0	.213	.278	.326	.604	59	-5	9	3.31	-5	S-14,2-12,3-12/1-1	1	-0.9
Total 10	**722**	**1276**	**150**	**314**	**72**	**7**	**23**	**127**	**106**	**242**	**13**	**12**	**.246**	**.306**	**.368**	**.674**	**73**	**-56**	**148**	**3.89**	**-31**	**3-225,2-161,S-143/1-24,0,D,C**	**23**	**-7.4**

• MOREHART, Ray Raymond Anderson Morehart b: 12/2/1899, Abner, TX d: 1/13/1989, Dallas, TX BL/TR, 5'9", 157 lbs. Deb: 8/9/1924

YEAR TM-L	G	AB	R	H	2B	3B	HR	RBI	BB	SO	SB	CS	AVG	OBP	SLG	OPS	OPS+	BR/A	RC	RC/G	FR	G/POS	WS	TPW
1924 Chi-A	31	100	10	20	4	2	0	8	17	7	3	1	.200	.316	.280	.596	56	-6	10	3.22	-6	S-27/2-2	1	-0.9
1926 Chi-A	73	192	27	61	10	3	0	21	11	15	3	11	.318	.358	.401	.759	101	-4	24	4.35	-2	2-48	4	-0.5
1927 NY-A	73	195	45	50	7	2	1	20	29	18	4	4	.256	.353	.328	.681	80	-5	24	4.10	0	2-53	5	-0.3
Total 3	**177**	**487**	**82**	**131**	**21**	**7**	**1**	**49**	**57**	**40**	**10**	**16**	**.269**	**.347**	**.347**	**.694**	**83**	**-15**	**58**	**4.00**	**-8**	**2-103/S-27**	**10**	**-1.7**

• MOREJON, Danny Daniel (Torres) Morejon b: 7/21/1930, Havana, Cuba BR/TR, 6'1", 175 lbs. Deb: 7/11/1958

YEAR TM-L	G	AB	R	H	2B	3B	HR	RBI	BB	SO	SB	CS	AVG	OBP	SLG	OPS	OPS+	BR/A	RC	RC/G	FR	G/POS	WS	TPW
1958 Cin-N	12	26	4	5	0	0	0	1	9	2	1	0	.192	.400	.192	.592	60	-1	3	3.42	-1	0-11(2-6-3)	0	-0.2

• MORELAND, Keith Bobby Keith Moreland b: 5/2/1954, Dallas, TX BR/TR, 6', 200 lbs. Deb: 10/1/1978 Career OF: 119-0-560

YEAR TM-L	G	AB	R	H	2B	3B	HR	RBI	BB	SO	SB	CS	AVG	OBP	SLG	OPS	OPS+	BR/A	RC	RC/G	FR	G/POS	WS	TPW
1978 Phi-N	1	2	0	0	0	0	0	0	0	0	0	0	.000	.000	.000	.000	-99	-1	0	.00	0	/C-1	0	-0.1
1979 Phi-N	14	48	3	18	3	2	0	8	3	5	0	0	.375	.412	.521	.933	148	3	10	8.81	-1	C-13	3	0.3
1980*Phi-N	62	159	13	50	8	0	4	29	8	14	3	1	.314	.347	.440	.788	112	2	22	5.05	-1	C-39/3-4,0-2(0-0-2)	6	0.3
1981*Phi-N	61	196	16	50	7	0	6	37	15	13	1	2	.255	.311	.383	.694	92	-3	20	3.41	-3	C-50/3-7,1-2,0-2(0-0-2)	4	-0.5
1982 Chi-N	138	476	50	124	17	2	15	68	46	71	0	6	.261	.330	.399	.729	100	-3	61	4.38	7	0-86(54-0-35),C-44/3-2	13	0.2
1983 Chi-N	154	533	76	161	30	3	16	70	68	73	0	3	.302	.384	.460	.844	127	20	93	6.16	-1	*0-151(0-0-151)/C-3	18	1.2
1984*Chi-N	140	495	59	138	17	3	16	80	34	71	1	4	.279	.329	.422	.751	101	-2	64	4.48	-6	*0-103(1-0-102),1-29/3-8,C	13	-1.6
1985 Chi-N	161	587	74	180	30	3	14	106	68	58	12	3	.307	.380	.440	.819	116	15	100	6.18	-8	*0-148(0-0-148),1-12,3-11/C	19	-0.1
1986 Chi-N	156	586	72	159	30	0	12	79	53	48	3	6	.271	.332	.384	.716	90	-10	72	4.19	-8	*0-121(0-0-120),3-24,C-13,1	11	-2.5
1987 Chi-N	153	563	63	150	29	1	27	88	39	66	3	3	.266	.314	.465	.779	99	-4	78	4.73	-2	*3-150/1-1	13	-0.8
1988 SD-N	143	511	40	131	23	0	5	64	40	51	2	3	.256	.310	.331	.641	86	-11	50	3.26	5	1-73,0-64(64-0-0)/3-2	9	-1.4
1989 Det-A	90	318	34	95	16	0	5	35	27	33	3	2	.299	.357	.396	.754	115	6	42	4.70	-4	D-51,1-31,3-12/C-1	6	-0.2
Bal-A	33	107	11	23	4	0	1	10	4	12	0	0	.215	.243	.280	.524	49	-8	6	1.66	0	D-29	0	-0.9
Yr.	123	425	45	118	20	0	6	45	31	45	3	2	.278	.330	.367	.697	99	-2	47	3.86	-4	D-80,1-31,3-12/C-1	6	-1.1
Total 12	**1306**	**4581**	**511**	**1279**	**214**	**14**	**121**	**674**	**405**	**515**	**28**	**33**	**.279**	**.339**	**.411**	**.751**	**103**	**5**	**616**	**4.67**	**-24**	**0-677,3-220,C-169,1-160/D-80**	**115**	**-5.8**

• MORELOCK, Harry A. Harry Morelock b: 11/1869, Philadelphia, PA Deb: 8/21/1891

YEAR TM-L	G	AB	R	H	2B	3B	HR	RBI	BB	SO	SB	CS	AVG	OBP	SLG	OPS	OPS+	BR/A	RC	RC/G	FR	G/POS	WS	TPW
1891 Phi-N	4	14	1	1	0	0	0	0	3	3	0	....	.071	.235	.071	.307	-9	-2	0	.50	-1	/S-4	0	-0.2
1892 Phi-N	1	3	0	0	0	0	0	0	1	0	0	....	.000	.250	.000	.250	-23	-0	0	.00	-1	/3-1	0	-0.1
Total 2	**5**	**17**	**1**	**1**	**0**	**0**	**0**	**0**	**4**	**3**	**0**	**....**	**.059**	**.238**	**.059**	**.297**	**-12**	**-2**	**0**	**.41**	**-2**	**/S-4,3-1**	**0**	**-0.3**

• MORENO, Jose Jose De Los Santos Moreno b: 11/1/1957, Santo Domingo, Dominican Republic BB/TR, 6', 175 lbs. Deb: 5/24/1980

YEAR TM-L	G	AB	R	H	2B	3B	HR	RBI	BB	SO	SB	CS	AVG	OBP	SLG	OPS	OPS+	BR/A	RC	RC/G	FR	G/POS	WS	TPW
1980 NY-N	37	46	6	9	2	1	2	9	3	12	1	0	.196	.245	.413	.658	83	-1	4	3.03	-1	/2-4,3-4	1	-0.2
1981 SD-N	34	48	5	11	2	0	0	6	1	8	4	1	.229	.245	.271	.516	50	-3	3	1.85	0	/0-9(4-0-5),2-1	0	-0.3
1982 Cal-A	11	3	3	0	0	0	0	0	2	0	0	2	.000	.400	.000	.400	21	-1	0	.00	0	/2-2,D-1	0	-0.1
Total 3	**82**	**97**	**14**	**20**	**4**	**1**	**2**	**15**	**6**	**20**	**5**	**3**	**.206**	**.252**	**.330**	**.582**	**64**	**-5**	**7**	**2.29**	**0**	**/0-9,2-7,3-4,D-1**	**1**	**-0.6**

• MORENO, Omar Omar Renan (Quintero) Moreno b: 10/24/1952, Puerto Armuelles, Panama BL/TL, 6'2", 180 lbs. Deb: 9/6/1975 Career OF: 22-1221-83

YEAR TM-L	G	AB	R	H	2B	3B	HR	RBI	BB	SO	SB	CS	AVG	OBP	SLG	OPS	OPS+	BR/A	RC	RC/G	FR	G/POS	WS	TPW
1975 Pit-N	6	6	1	1	0	0	0	0	1	1	1	0	.167	.286	.167	.452	28	-0	1	2.75	0	/0-1	0	-0.1
1976 Pit-N	48	122	24	33	4	1	2	12	16	24	15	5	.270	.360	.369	.729	106	3	19	5.23	1	0-42(0-41-0)	5	0.2
1977 Pit-N	150	492	69	118	19	9	7	34	38	102	53	16	.240	.296	.358	.653	72	-16	55	3.74	5	*0-147(0-147-0)	12	-1.2
1978 Pit-N	155	515	95	121	15	7	2	33	81	104	**71**	22	.235	.342	.303	.645	78	-7	65	3.93	3	*0-152(0-152-0)	18	-0.6
1979*Pit-N	162	695	110	196	21	12	8	69	51	104	**77**	21	.282	.334	.381	.715	90	-2	94	4.75	8	*0-162(0-162-0)	23	0.4
1980 Pit-N	162	676	87	168	20	**13**	2	36	57	101	96	33	.249	.309	.325	.634	76	-16	71	3.44	11	*0-162(0-162-0)	17	-0.7
1981 Pit-N	103	434	62	120	18	8	1	35	26	76	39	14	.276	.322	.362	.684	91	-4	53	4.31	0	*0-103(0-103-0)	11	-0.5
1982 Pit-N	158	645	82	158	18	9	3	44	44	121	60	26	.245	.294	.315	.609	68	-27	61	3.10	6	*0-157(0-157-0)	11	-2.4
1983 Hou-N	97	405	48	98	12	11	0	25	22	72	30	13	.242	.283	.326	.609	73	-15	38	3.17	5	0-97(0-97-0)	9	-1.2
NY-A	48	152	17	38	9	1	1	17	8	31	7	3	.250	.288	.342	.630	75	-5	14	3.09	1	0-48(0-48-0)	2	-0.5
1984 NY-A	117	355	37	92	12	6	4	38	18	48	20	11	.259	.297	.361	.657	84	-9	37	3.54	1	*0-108(0-108-0)/D-1	6	-1.0
1985 NY-A	34	66	12	13	4	1	1	4	1	16	1	1	.197	.209	.333	.542	47	-5	4	1.98	1	0-26(3-19-4)/D-1	1	-0.4
KC-A	24	70	9	17	1	3	2	12	3	8	0	1	.243	.284	.429	.712	91	-2	8	3.85	-1	0-21(0-13-8)	1	-0.3
Yr.	58	136	21	30	5	4	3	16	4	24	1	2	.221	.248	.382	.631	70	-7	12	2.92	1	0-47(3-32-12)/D-1	2	-0.7
1986 Atl-N	118	359	46	84	18	6	4	27	21	77	17	16	.234	.276	.351	.627	68	-20	32	2.91	1	0-97(18-12-71)	3	-2.4
Total 12	**1382**	**4992**	**699**	**1257**	**171**	**87**	**37**	**386**	**387**	**885**	**487**	**182**	**.252**	**.308**	**.343**	**.651**	**78**	**-124**	**553**	**3.69**	**42**	***0-1323/D-2**	**119**	**-10.7**

• MORGAN, Bill William Morgan b: 1856, Brooklyn, NY d: 9/9/1908, New York, NY Deb: 8/6/1883 Career OF: 18-6-14

YEAR TM-L	G	AB	R	H	2B	3B	HR	RBI	BB	SO	SB	CS	AVG	OBP	SLG	OPS	OPS+	BR/A	RC	RC/G	FR	G/POS	WS	TPW
1883 Pit-a	32	114	12	18	2	1	0	0	7	....	....	....	.158	.207	.193	.400	31	-8	5	1.36	-5	S-21/0-6(1-4-1),C-5,2-2	1	-1.0
1884 Was-a	45	162	8	28	1	1	0	0	8	....	....	....	.173	.216	.191	.408	38	-9	7	1.41	-6	0-31(17-2-13),C-12/2-2,S-2	0	-1.4
Total 2	**77**	**276**	**20**	**46**	**3**	**2**	**0**	**0**	**15**	**....**	**....**	**....**	**.167**	**.212**	**.192**	**.404**	**35**	**-17**	**12**	**1.39**	**-10**	**/0-37,S-23,C-17,2-4**	**1**	**-2.4**

• MORGAN, Bill Henry William Morgan b: Brooklyn, NY Deb: 8/17/1882 U Career OF: 0-0-14

YEAR TM-L	G	AB	R	H	2B	3B	HR	RBI	BB	SO	SB	CS	AVG	OBP	SLG	OPS	OPS+	BR/A	RC	RC/G	FR	G/POS	WS	TPW
1882 Pit-a	17	66	10	17	2	1	0	....	4	....	....	....	.258	.300	.318	.618	114	1	6	3.69	-6	0-11(0-0-11)/C-7	2	-0.4
1884 Ric-a	6	20	0	2	0	0	0	0	1	....	....	....	.100	.143	.100	.243	-20	-3	0	.45	-1	/C-3,0-2(0-0-2),2-1	0	-0.3
Bal-U	2	9	1	2	0	0	0	....	1	....	....	....	.222	.300	.222	.522	72	-0	1	2.46	-1	/2-1,C-1,0-1	0	-0.1
Total 2	**25**	**95**	**11**	**21**	**2**	**1**	**0**	**0**	**6**	**....**	**....**	**....**	**.221**	**.267**	**.263**	**.530**	**82**	**-2**	**7**	**2.78**	**-9**	**/0-14,C-11,2-2**	**2**	**-0.9**

• MORGAN, Bobby Robert Morris Morgan b: 6/29/1926, Oklahoma City, OK BR/TR, 5'9", 175 lbs. Deb: 4/18/1950

YEAR TM-L	G	AB	R	H	2B	3B	HR	RBI	BB	SO	SB	CS	AVG	OBP	SLG	OPS	OPS+	BR/A	RC	RC/G	FR	G/POS	WS	TPW
1950 Bro-N	67	199	38	45	10	3	7	21	32	43	0	....	.226	.342	.412	.754	95	-1	29	4.72	9	3-52,S-10	7	0.8
1952*Bro-N	67	191	36	45	8	0	7	16	46	35	2	2	.236	.392	.387	.779	115	6	33	5.68	0	3-60/2-5,S-4	9	0.7
1953*Bro-N	69	196	35	51	6	2	7	33	33	47	2	2	.260	.370	.418	.788	103	1	31	5.38	-2	3-36,S-21	7	0.1
1954 Phi-N	135	455	58	119	25	2	14	50	70	68	3	1	.262	.360	.418	.778	102	3	70	5.16	-3	*S-129/3-8,2-5	15	1.1
1955 Phi-N	136	483	61	112	20	2	10	49	73	72	6	4	.232	.333	.344	.676	81	-11	57	3.90	2	2-88,S-41/3-6,1-1	10	0.0
1956 Phi-N	8	25	1	5	0	0	0	1	6	4	0	0	.200	.355	.200	.555	55	-1	2	2.72	0	/3-5,2-3	0	-0.1

YEAR TM-L	G	AB	R	H	2B	3B	HR	RBI	BB	SO	SB	CS	AVG	OBP	SLG	OPS	OPS+	BR/A	RC	RC/G	FR	G/POS	WS	TPW
StL-N	61	113	14	22	7	0	3	20	15	24	0	2	.195	.289	.336	.625	67	-6	10	2.79	-4	2-13,3-11/S-6	1	-0.9
Yr.	69	138	15	27	7	0	3	21	21	28	0	2	.196	.302	.312	.613	65	-7	12	2.78	-3	2-16,3-16/S-6	1	-1.0
1957 Phi-N	2	0	0	0	0	0	0	0	0	0	0	0	....	....	....	....	-103	0	0	....	0	/2-1	0	0.0
Chi-N	125	425	43	88	20	2	5	27	52	87	5	0	.207	.295	.299	.594	61	-21	41	3.12	12	*2-116,3-12	7	-0.1
Yr.	127	425	43	88	20	2	5	27	52	87	5	0	.207	.295	.299	.594	61	-21	41	3.12	12	*2-117,3-12	7	-0.1
1958 Chi-N	1	1	0	0	0	0	0	0	0	1	0	0	.000	.000	.000	.000	-102	-0	0	.00	0	....	0	0.0
Total 8	671	2088	286	487	96	11	53	217	327	381	18	11	.233	.339	.366	.705	87	-30	272	4.30	15	2-231,S-211,3-190/1-1	56	1.7

• MORGAN, Chet — Chester Collins "Chick" Morgan b: 6/6/1910, Cleveland, MS d: 9/20/1991, Pasadena, TX BL/TR, 5'9", 160 lbs. Deb: 4/19/1935 Career OF: 10-68-0

YEAR TM-L	G	AB	R	H	2B	3B	HR	RBI	BB	SO	SB	CS	AVG	OBP	SLG	OPS	OPS+	BR/A	RC	RC/G	FR	G/POS	WS	TPW
1935 Det-A	14	23	2	4	1	0	0	1	5	0	0	0	.174	.321	.217	.539	43	-2	2	2.71	0	/0-4(4-0-0)	0	-0.2
1938 Det-A	74	306	50	87	6	1	0	27	20	12	5	6	.284	.330	.310	.641	58	-21	31	3.58	0	0-74(6-68-0)	4	-2.1
Total 2	88	329	52	91	7	1	0	28	25	12	5	6	.277	.330	.304	.634	57	-23	33	3.52	-1	/0-78	4	-2.3

• MORGAN, Ed — Edward Carre Morgan b: 5/22/1904, Cairo, IL d: 4/9/1980, New Orleans, LA BR/TR, 6'.5", 180 lbs. Deb: 4/11/1928 Career OF: 1-18-102

YEAR TM-L	G	AB	R	H	2B	3B	HR	RBI	BB	SO	SB	CS	AVG	OBP	SLG	OPS	OPS+	BR/A	RC	RC/G	FR	G/POS	WS	TPW
1928 Cle-A	76	265	42	83	24	6	4	54	21	17	5	5	.313	.366	.494	.860	123	7	47	6.31	1	1-36,0-21(0-18-3),3-14	8	0.6
1929 Cle-A	93	318	60	101	19	10	3	37	37	24	4	3	.318	.392	.469	.861	116	9	59	7.06	-5	0-80(0-0-80)	10	-0.1
1930 Cle-A	150	584	122	204	47	11	26	136	62	66	8	4	.349	.413	.601	1.014	148	42	144	9.50	-1	*1-129,0-19(0-0-19)	28	2.9
1931 Cle-A	131	462	87	162	33	4	11	86	83	46	4	5	.351	.451	.511	.961	144	35	110	9.39	0	*1-117/3-3	21	2.3
1932 Cle-A	144	532	96	156	32	7	4	68	94	44	7	6	.293	.402	.402	.804	102	6	92	6.25	-2	*1-142/3-1	15	-0.9
1933 Cle-A	39	121	10	32	3	3	1	13	7	9	1	1	.264	.305	.364	.668	73	-5	13	3.86	2	1-32/0-1	2	-0.6
1934 Bos-A	138	528	95	141	28	4	3	79	81	46	7	1	.267	.367	.352	.719	81	-12	74	5.00	-9	*1-137	11	-3.1
Total 7	771	2810	512	879	186	45	52	473	385	252	36	25	.313	.398	.467	.864	117	82	540	7.13	-13	1-593,0-121/3-18	95	1.1

• MORGAN, Eddie — Edwin Willis "Pepper" Morgan b: 11/19/1914, Brady Lake, OH d: 6/27/1982, Lakewood, OH BL/TL, 5'10", 160 lbs. Deb: 4/14/1936 Career OF: 1-1-9

YEAR TM-L	G	AB	R	H	2B	3B	HR	RBI	BB	SO	SB	CS	AVG	OBP	SLG	OPS	OPS+	BR/A	RC	RC/G	FR	G/POS	WS	TPW
1936 StL-N	8	18	4	5	0	0	1	3	2	4	0	....	.278	.350	.444	.794	113	0	3	6.34	-1	/0-4(0-0-4)	1	-0.1
1937 Bro-N	31	48	4	9	3	0	0	5	9	7	0	....	.188	.316	.250	.566	54	-3	5	3.15	-2	/1-7,0-7(1-1-5)	0	-0.6
Total 2	39	66	8	14	3	0	1	8	11	11	0	....	.212	.325	.303	.628	69	-2	8	3.92	-3	/0-11,1-7	1	-0.6

• MORGAN, Joe — Joseph Michael Morgan b: 11/19/1930, Walpole, MA BL/TR, 5'10", 170 lbs. Deb: 4/14/1959 M/C Career OF: 0-2-2

YEAR TM-L	G	AB	R	H	2B	3B	HR	RBI	BB	SO	SB	CS	AVG	OBP	SLG	OPS	OPS+	BR/A	RC	RC/G	FR	G/POS	WS	TPW
1959 Mil-N	13	23	2	5	1	0	0	1	2	4	0	0	.217	.280	.261	.541	49	-2	2	2.19	-1	/2-7	0	-0.3
KC-A	20	21	2	4	0	1	0	3	3	7	0	0	.190	.292	.286	.577	58	-1	2	2.54	0	/3-2	0	-0.1
1960 Phi-N	26	83	5	11	2	2	0	2	6	11	0	0	.133	.191	.205	.396	8	-11	3	1.04	0	3-24	1	-1.1
Cle-A	22	47	6	14	2	0	2	4	6	4	0	0	.298	.377	.468	.845	131	2	8	6.54	-1	3-12/0-2	2	0.1
1961 Cle-A	4	10	0	2	0	0	0	0	1	3	0	0	.200	.273	.200	.473	29	-1	1	2.08	0	/0-2(0-2-0)	0	-0.1
1964 StL-N	3	3	0	0	0	0	0	0	0	2	0	0	.000	.000	.000	.000	-92	-1	0	.00	0	....	0	-0.1
Total 4	88	187	15	36	5	3	2	10	18	31	0	0	.193	.263	.283	.547	51	-13	15	2.60	-3	/3-38,2-7,0-4	3	-1.6

• MORGAN, Joe — Joe Leonard Morgan b: 9/19/1943, Bonham, TX BL/TR, 5'7", 160 lbs. Deb: 9/21/1963 HOF: 1990 Career OF: 14-2-0

YEAR TM-L	G	AB	R	H	2B	3B	HR	RBI	BB	SO	SB	CS	AVG	OBP	SLG	OPS	OPS+	BR/A	RC	RC/G	FR	G/POS	WS	TPW
1963 Hou-N	8	25	5	6	0	1	0	3	5	5	1	0	.240	.367	.320	.687	106	1	4	5.12	-2	/2-7	1	-0.1
1964 Hou-N	10	37	4	7	0	0	0	0	6	7	0	1	.189	.302	.189	.492	45	-3	2	2.08	-1	2-10	0	-0.3
1965 Hou-N	157	601	100	163	22	12	14	40	**97**	77	20	9	.271	.375	.418	.793	132	30	103	6.05	1	*2-157	30	4.7
1966 Hou-N★	122	425	60	121	14	8	5	42	89	43	11	8	.285	.412	.391	.803	134	25	77	6.41	-12	*2-117	19	2.4
1967 Hou-N	133	494	73	136	27	11	6	42	81	51	29	5	.275	.380	.411	.790	130	28	88	6.43	-8	*2-130/0-1	26	3.4
1968 Hou-N	10	20	6	5	0	1	0	0	7	4	3	0	.250	.444	.350	.794	144	2	5	8.30	-1	/2-5,0-1	2	0.1
1969 Hou-N	147	535	94	126	18	5	15	43	110	74	49	14	.236	.367	.372	.739	110	17	86	5.28	-2	*2-132,0-14(12-2-0)	24	2.5
1970 Hou-N★	144	548	102	147	28	9	8	52	102	55	42	13	.268	.384	.396	.780	114	19	92	5.76	8	*2-142	24	3.7
1971 Hou-N	160	583	87	149	27	**11**	13	56	88	52	40	8	.256	.354	.407	.761	118	21	95	5.53	7	*2-157	29	4.2
1972*Cin-N★	149	552	**122**	161	23	4	16	73	**115**	44	58	17	.292	**.419**	.435	.854	152	**51**	117	7.50	8	*2-149	**39**	**7.5**
1973*Cin-N★	157	576	116	167	35	2	26	82	111	61	67	15	.290	.408	.493	.901	157	58	128	7.83	3	*2-154	**40**	**7.4**
1974 Cin-N★	149	512	107	150	31	3	22	67	120	69	58	12	.293	**.430**	.494	.924	160	**56**	125	**8.74**	11	*2-142	37	**7.9**
1975*Cin-N★	146	498	107	163	27	6	17	94	**132**	52	67	10	.327	**.471**	.508	**.979**	**168**	**67**	145	**11.07**	17	*2-142	**44**	**9.8**
1976*Cin-N★	141	472	113	151	30	5	27	111	114	41	60	9	.320	**.453**	**.576**	**1.029**	**186**	**69**	144	**11.27**	-8	*2-133	**37**	7.5
1977 Cin-N★	153	521	113	150	21	6	22	78	117	58	49	10	.288	.420	.478	.898	138	41	121	8.36	5	*2-151	30	5.4
1978 Cin-N★	132	441	68	104	27	0	13	75	79	40	19	5	.236	.354	.385	.740	107	8	67	5.05	-9	*2-124	17	0.6
1979*Cin-N★	127	436	70	109	26	1	9	32	93	45	28	6	.250	.383	.376	.759	107	13	72	5.55	-4	*2-121	18	1.5
1980*Hou-N	141	461	66	112	17	5	11	49	**93**	47	24	6	.243	.370	.373	.743	117	17	73	5.39	-3	*2-130	21	2.2
1981 SF-N	90	308	47	74	16	1	8	31	66	37	14	5	.240	.374	.377	.751	116	10	49	5.39	-6	2-87	14	1.0
1982 SF-N	134	463	68	134	19	4	14	61	85	60	24	4	.289	.402	.438	.840	135	29	92	7.34	-9	*2-120/3-3	29	2.8
1983*Phi-N	123	404	72	93	20	1	16	59	89	54	18	2	.230	.374	.403	.778	117	16	68	5.50	8	*2-117	19	3.1
1984 Oak-A	116	365	50	89	21	0	6	43	66	39	8	3	.244	.361	.351	.712	105	6	51	4.72	-3	*2-100/D-5	12	0.8
Total 22	2649	9277	1650	2517	449	96	268	1133	1865	1015	689	162	.271	.395	.427	.823	133	582	1804	6.79	0	*2-2527/0-16,D-5,3-3	512	78.1

• MORGAN, Kevin — Kevin Lee Morgan b: 12/3/1970, Lafayette, LA BR/TR, 6'1", 170 lbs. Deb: 6/15/1997

YEAR TM-L	G	AB	R	H	2B	3B	HR	RBI	BB	SO	SB	CS	AVG	OBP	SLG	OPS	OPS+	BR/A	RC	RC/G	FR	G/POS	WS	TPW
1997 NY-N	1	1	0	0	0	0	0	0	0	0	0	0	.000	.000	.000	.000	-104	-0	0	.00	0	/3-1	0	0.0

• MORGAN, Pidgey — Daniel Morgan b: 5/1853, MO d: 1/31/1910, St. Louis, MO Deb: 5/4/1875 ♦

YEAR TM-L	G	AB	R	H	2B	3B	HR	RBI	BB	SO	SB	CS	AVG	OBP	SLG	OPS	OPS+	BR/A	RC	RC/G	FR	G/POS	WS	TPW
1875 RS-n	19	69	11	18	4	0	0	1	5	4	2	1	.261	.311	.319	.630	132	3	8	4.34	-4	0-10(3-7-0)/3-7,P-7	....	-0.2
1878 Mil-N	14	56	2	11	0	0	0	5	3	9	....	....	.196	.237	.196	.434	41	-4	3	1.63	-3	0-13(0-1-12)/3-3,2-1	0	-0.6

• MORGAN, Ray — Raymond Caryll Morgan b: 6/14/1889, Baltimore, MD d: 2/15/1940, Baltimore, MD BR/TR, 5'8.5", 155 lbs. Deb: 8/7/1911

YEAR TM-L	G	AB	R	H	2B	3B	HR	RBI	BB	SO	SB	CS	AVG	OBP	SLG	OPS	OPS+	BR/A	RC	RC/G	FR	G/POS	WS	TPW
1911 Was-A	25	89	11	19	2	0	0	5	4	....	2	....	.213	.247	.236	.483	36	-8	6	2.03	-3	3-25	0	-1.0
1912 Was-A	81	273	40	65	10	7	1	30	29	....	11	....	.238	.318	.337	.655	87	-5	33	3.93	-12	2-76/S-4,3-1	7	-1.5
1913 Was-A	138	481	58	131	19	8	0	57	68	63	19	....	.272	.369	.345	.714	107	7	66	4.67	-5	*2-134/S-4	21	0.5
1914 Was-A	147	491	50	126	22	8	1	49	62	34	24	17	.257	.352	.340	.692	104	2	63	4.18	-2	*2-146	19	0.3
1915 Was-A	62	193	21	45	5	4	0	21	30	15	6	5	.233	.342	.301	.643	91	-2	22	3.56	3	2-57/3-2,S-2	6	0.2
1916 Was-A	99	315	41	84	12	4	1	29	59	29	14	....	.267	.398	.340	.738	123	13	50	5.34	-5	2-82/S-9,1-3,3-1	15	1.1
1917 Was-A	101	338	32	90	9	1	1	33	40	29	7	....	.266	.346	.308	.653	101	1	38	3.82	-2	2-95/3-3	12	0.2
1918 Was-A	88	300	25	70	11	1	0	30	28	14	4	....	.233	.311	.277	.588	79	-7	27	2.88	8	2-80/0-2(0-0-2)	6	0.2
Total 8	741	2480	278	630	90	33	4	254	320	184	87	22	.254	.348	.322	.670	99	2	304	4.05	-19	2-670/3-32,S-19,1-3,0-2	86	0.0

• MORGAN, Red — James Edward Morgan b: 10/6/1883, Neola, IA d: 3/25/1981, New York, NY BR/TR Deb: 6/20/1906

YEAR TM-L	G	AB	R	H	2B	3B	HR	RBI	BB	SO	SB	CS	AVG	OBP	SLG	OPS	OPS+	BR/A	RC	RC/G	FR	G/POS	WS	TPW
1906 Bos-A	88	307	20	66	6	3	1	21	16	....	7	....	.215	.270	.264	.534	67	-11	26	2.70	-18	3-88	2	-3.0

• MORGAN, Vern — Vernon Thomas Morgan b: 8/8/1928, Emporia, VA d: 11/8/1975, Minneapolis, MN BL/TR, 6'1", 190 lbs. Deb: 8/10/1954 C

YEAR TM-L	G	AB	R	H	2B	3B	HR	RBI	BB	SO	SB	CS	AVG	OBP	SLG	OPS	OPS+	BR/A	RC	RC/G	FR	G/POS	WS	TPW
1954 Chi-N	24	64	3	15	2	0	0	2	1	10	0	0	.234	.246	.266	.512	33	-6	4	1.95	-4	3-15	0	-1.0
1955 Chi-N	7	7	1	1	0	0	0	1	3	4	0	0	.143	.400	.143	.543	52	-0	1	3.20	-1	/3-2	0	-0.2
Total 2	31	71	4	16	2	0	0	3	4	14	0	0	.225	.267	.254	.520	35	-7	5	2.08	-5	/3-17	0	-1.2

• MORHARDT, Moe — Meredith Goodwin Morhardt b: 1/16/1937, Manchester, CT BL/TL, 6'1", 185 lbs. Deb: 9/7/1961

YEAR TM-L	G	AB	R	H	2B	3B	HR	RBI	BB	SO	SB	CS	AVG	OBP	SLG	OPS	OPS+	BR/A	RC	RC/G	FR	G/POS	WS	TPW
1961 Chi-N	7	18	3	5	0	0	0	1	3	5	0	0	.278	.381	.278	.659	77	-0	2	4.57	-1	/1-7	0	-0.2
1962 Chi-N	18	16	1	2	0	0	0	2	2	8	0	0	.125	.222	.125	.347	-4	-2	1	1.08	0	....	0	-0.2
Total 2	25	34	4	7	0	0	0	3	5	13	0	0	.206	.308	.206	.514	40	-3	3	2.76	-1	/1-7	0	-0.4

• MORIARITY, Gene — Eugene John Moriarity b: 1/5/1865, Holyoke, MA BL/TL, 5'8", 130 lbs. Deb: 6/18/1884 Career OF: 49-3-12

YEAR TM-L	G	AB	R	H	2B	3B	HR	RBI	BB	SO	SB	CS	AVG	OBP	SLG	OPS	OPS+	BR/A	RC	RC/G	FR	G/POS	WS	TPW
1884 Bos-N	4	16	1	1	0	0	0	0	0	8	....	....	.063	.063	.063	.125	-61	-3	0	.12	0	/0-4(1-3-0)	0	-0.3
Ind-a	10	37	4	8	0	2	0	4	0	....	....	....	.216	.216	.324	.541	76	-1	3	2.52	-1	/0-7(0-0-7),P-2,3-1	0	-0.5
1885 Det-N	11	39	1	1	1	0	0	0	0	10	....	....	.026	.026	.051	.077	-75	-7	0	.04	0	/0-6(1-0-5),3-4,P-1,S-1	0	-0.8
1892 StL-N	47	177	20	31	4	1	3	19	4	37	7	....	.175	.207	.260	.466	43	-13	11	2.07	-1	0-47(47-0-0)	0	-1.7
Total 3	72	269	26	41	5	3	3	23	4	55	7	....	.152	.174	.227	.401	25	-24	14	1.66	-2	/0-64,3-5,P-3,S-1	0	-3.2

YEAR TM-L	G	AB	R	H	2B	3B	HR	RBI	BB	SO	SB	CS	AVG	OBP	SLG	OPS	OPS+	BR/A	RC	RC/G	FR	G/POS	WS	TPW
• MORIARTY, Bill	William Joseph Moriarty b: 8/1883, Chicago, IL d: 12/25/1916, Elgin, IL BR/TR, 6'2", 180 lbs. Deb: 4/29/1909																							
1909 Cin-N	6	20	1	4	1	0	0	1	0	....	2	....	.200	.200	.250	.450	40	-2	1	2.02	0	/S-6	0	-0.1
• MORIARTY, Ed	Edward Jerome Moriarty b: 10/12/1912, Holyoke, MA d: 9/29/1991, Holyoke, MA BR/TR, 5'10.5", 180 lbs. Deb: 6/21/1935																							
1935 Bos-N	8	34	4	11	2	1	1	1	0	6	0	....	.324	.324	.529	.853	136	1	6	7.01	-2	/2-8	1	0.0
1936 Bos-N	6	6	1	1	0	0	0	0	0	1	0	....	.167	.167	.167	.333	-11	-1	0	.92	0	....	0	-0.1
Total 2	14	40	5	12	2	1	1	1	0	7	0	....	.300	.300	.475	.775	114	1	6	5.92	-2	/2-8	1	-0.1
• MORIARTY, George	George Joseph Moriarty b: 6/7/1884, Chicago, IL d: 4/8/1964, Miami, FL BR/TR, 6', 185 lbs. Deb: 9/27/1903 M/U Career OF: 30-9-5																							
1903 Chi-N	1	5	1	0	0	0	0	0	0	....	0	....	.000	.000	.000	.000	-103	-1	0	.00	0	/3-1	0	-0.1
1904 Chi-N	4	13	0	0	0	0	0	0	1	....	0	....	.000	.071	.000	.071	-77	-3	0	.00	-1	/3-2,0-2(0-2-0)	0	-0.4
1906 NY-A	65	197	22	46	7	7	0	23	17	....	8	....	.234	.298	.340	.638	90	-2	24	3.92	-1	3-39,0-15(14-2-0)/1-5,2-1	6	-0.3
1907 NY-A	126	437	51	121	16	5	0	43	25	....	28	....	.277	.320	.336	.657	101	0	59	4.77	-11	3-91,1-22/0-9(1-4-3),2-8,S	16	-1.0
1908 NY-A	101	348	25	82	12	1	0	27	11	....	22	....	.236	.269	.276	.545	76	-10	31	2.95	8	1-52,3-28,0-10(8-0-2)/2-4	7	-0.2
1909*Det-A	133	473	43	129	20	4	1	39	24	....	34	....	.273	.309	.338	.648	100	-1	59	4.28	4	*3-106,1-24	17	0.6
1910 Det-A	136	490	53	123	24	3	2	60	33	....	33	....	.251	.308	.324	.632	92	-5	58	3.98	4	*3-134	16	0.3
1911 Det-A	130	478	51	116	20	4	1	60	27	....	28	....	.243	.287	.308	.595	63	-26	51	3.40	-2	*3-129/1-1	8	-2.3
1912 Det-A	105	375	38	93	23	1	0	54	26	....	27	....	.248	.316	.315	.630	83	-8	46	3.99	-6	1-71,3-33	7	-1.5
1913 Det-A	104	347	29	83	5	2	0	30	24	25	33	....	.239	.302	.265	.567	67	-14	36	3.31	-5	3-94/0-7(7-0-0)	5	-1.8
1914 Det-A	132	465	56	118	19	5	1	40	39	27	34	15	.254	.318	.323	.641	90	-5	55	3.77	8	*3-126/1-3	15	0.7
1915 Det-A	31	38	2	8	1	0	0	0	5	7	1	1	.211	.318	.237	.555	63	-2	3	2.62	-1	3-12/1-1,2-1,0-1	1	-0.3
1916 Chi-A	7	5	1	1	0	0	0	0	2	0	0	....	.200	.429	.200	.629	88	0	0	2.79	0	/1-1,3-1	0	0.1
Total 13	1075	3671	372	920	147	32	5	376	234	59	248	16	.251	.303	.312	.616	84	-78	424	3.80	-3	3-796,1-180/0-44,2-14,S-1	98	-6.4
• MORIARTY, Mike	Michael Thomas Moriarty b: 3/8/1974, Camden, NJ BR/TR, 6', 188 lbs. Deb: 4/11/2002																							
2002 Bal-A	8	16	0	3	1	0	0	3	0	2	0	1	.188	.188	.250	.438	16	-2	0	.00	3	/S-4,2-2,3-1	0	0.1
• MORLEY, Bill	William M. Morley b: 1/23/1890, Holland, MI d: 5/14/1985, Lubbock, TX BR/TR, 5'11", 170 lbs. Deb: 9/8/1913																							
1913 Was-A	2	3	0	0	0	0	0	0	0	0	0	....	.000	.000	.000	.000	-98	-1	0	.00	-1	/2-1	0	-0.1
• MORMAN, Russ	Russell Lee Morman b: 4/28/1962, Independence, MO BR/TR, 6'4", 220 lbs. Deb: 8/3/1986 Career OF: 26-0-14																							
1986 Chi-A	49	159	18	40	5	0	4	17	16	36	1	0	.252	.328	.358	.686	84	-3	19	3.99	-2	1-47	3	-0.7
1988 Chi-A	40	75	8	18	2	0	0	3	3	17	0	0	.240	.269	.267	.536	51	-5	4	1.84	-2	1-22,0-10(10-0-0)/D-3	0	-0.8
1989 Chi-A	37	58	5	13	2	0	0	8	6	16	1	0	.224	.297	.259	.555	59	-3	5	2.72	0	1-35/D-1	0	-0.4
1990 KC-A	12	37	5	10	4	2	1	3	3	3	0	0	.270	.325	.568	.893	147	2	7	6.82	1	/0-8(8-0-0),1-3,D-1	1	0.3
1991 KC-A	12	23	1	6	0	0	0	1	1	5	0	0	.261	.292	.261	.553	54	-1	2	2.78	0	/1-8,0-2(2-0-0),D-1	0	-0.2
1994 Fla-N	13	33	2	7	0	1	1	2	2	9	0	0	.212	.278	.364	.641	64	-2	3	3.20	1	/1-8	0	-0.2
1995 Fla-N	34	72	9	20	2	1	3	7	3	12	0	0	.278	.316	.458	.774	101	-0	9	4.03	0	0-18(6-0-12)/1-3	1	-0.1
1996 Fla-N	6	6	0	1	1	0	0	0	1	2	0	0	.167	.286	.333	.619	65	-0	1	3.49	0	/1-2	0	-0.1
1997 Fla-N	4	7	3	2	1	0	1	2	0	2	1	0	.286	.286	.857	1.143	194	1	2	10.06	0	/0-2(0-0-2),1-1	1	0.1
Total 9	207	470	51	117	17	4	10	43	35	102	3	0	.249	.306	.366	.672	82	-12	51	3.64	-2	1-129/0-40,D-6	6	-2.0
• MORNEAU, Justin	Justin Ernest Morneau b: 5/15/1981, New Westminster, Canada BL/TR, 6'4", 205 lbs. Deb: 6/10/2003																							
2003 Min-A	40	106	14	24	4	0	4	16	9	30	0	0	.226	.287	.377	.664	73	-4	11	3.33	1	D-22/1-7	1	-0.5
• MORONKO, Jeff	Jeffrey Robert Moronko b: 8/17/1959, Houston, TX BR/TR, 6'2", 190 lbs. Deb: 9/1/1984																							
1984 Cle-A	7	19	1	3	1	0	0	3	3	5	0	0	.158	.273	.211	.483	35	-2	1	2.20	-1	/3-6,D-1	0	-0.3
1987 NY-A	7	11	0	1	0	0	0	0	0	2	0	0	.091	.167	.091	.258	-29	-2	0	.57	0	/3-3,0-2(1-0-1),S-2	0	-0.2
Total 2	14	30	1	4	1	0	0	3	3	7	0	0	.133	.235	.167	.402	13	-4	2	1.59	-1	/3-9,0-2,S-2,D-1	0	-0.4
• MORRILL, John	John Francis "Honest John" Morrill b: 2/19/1855, Boston, MA d: 4/2/1932, Brookline, MA BR/TR, 5'10.5", 155 lbs. Deb: 4/24/1876 M/U Career OF: 2-12-12 ♦																							
1876 Bos-N	66	281	38	73	5	2	0	26	3	5	....	....	.260	.270	.295	.565	87	-4	23	3.10	4	2-37,C-23/0-5(1-3-1),1-3	8	0.2
1877 Bos-N	61	242	47	73	5	1	0	28	6	15	....	....	.302	.319	.331	.649	101	0	26	4.25	-9	3-30,1-18,0-11(0-0-11)/2-3	6	-0.8
1878 Bos-N	60	233	26	56	5	1	0	23	5	16	....	....	.240	.256	.270	.527	68	-9	17	2.57	-4	*1-59/3-1,0-1	5	-1.4
1879 Bos-N	84	348	56	98	18	5	0	49	14	32	....	....	.282	.309	.362	.671	118	7	40	4.48	4	3-51,1-33	11	0.9
1880 Bos-N	86	342	51	81	16	8	2	44	11	37	....	....	.237	.261	.348	.609	108	3	32	3.35	-3	1-46,3-40/P-3	10	0.1
1881 Bos-N	81	311	47	90	19	3	1	39	12	30	....	....	.289	.316	.379	.695	123	8	38	4.67	10	*1-74/2-4,P-3,3-2	11	1.2
1882 Bos-N	83	349	73	101	19	11	2	54	18	29	....	....	.289	.324	.424	.748	137	14	49	5.45	2	*1-76/S-3,2-2,3-1,0-1,P-1	12	0.9
1883 Bos-N	97	404	83	129	33	16	6	68	15	68	....	....	.319	.344	.525	.868	155	26	75	7.47	4	*1-81/0-7(0-7-0),3-6,2-2,P,S	20	2.1
1884 Bos-N	111	438	80	114	19	7	3	61	30	87	....	....	.260	.308	.356	.664	109	5	49	4.18	7	*1-91,2-17/P-7,3-2,0-1	14	-0.7
1885 Bos-N	111	394	74	89	20	7	4	44	64	78	....	....	.226	.334	.343	.677	124	14	46	4.09	2	*1-92,2-17/3-2	14	0.8
1886 Bos-N	117	430	86	106	25	6	7	69	56	81	9	....	.247	.333	.381	.715	121	13	59	4.93	6	S-55,1-42,2-20/P-1	17	1.8
1887 Bos-N	127	541	79	178	32	6	12	81	37	86	19	....	.329	.330	.438	.769	115	9	81	5.93	-4	*1-127	13	-0.5
1888 Bos-N	135	486	60	96	18	7	4	39	55	68	21	....	.198	.282	.288	.570	79	-10	46	3.22	9	*1-133/2-2	8	-1.2
1889 Was-N	44	146	20	27	5	0	2	16	30	23	12	....	.185	.328	.260	.588	70	-4	17	3.74	-2	1-40/3-3,2-1,P-1	2	-0.8
1890 Bos-P	2	7	1	1	0	0	0	2	2	1	0	....	.143	.333	.143	.476	28	-1	0	1.54	-1	/1-1,S-1	0	-0.1
Total 15	1265	4952	821	1312	239	80	43	643	358	656	61	....	.265	.310	.367	.677	111	73	599	4.48	25	1-916,3-138,2-105/S-61,0,C,P	151	2.5
• MORRIS, Doyt	Doyt Theodore Morris b: 7/15/1916, Stanley, NC d: 7/4/1984, Gastonia, NC BR/TR, 6'4", 195 lbs. Deb: 6/6/1937																							
1937 Phi-A	6	13	0	2	0	0	0	0	0	3	0	0	.154	.154	.154	.308	-23	-2	0	.71	0	/0-3(2-1-0)	0	-0.2
• MORRIS, E.	E. Morris b: Trenton, NJ Deb: 9/11/1884																							
1884 Bal-U	1	3	0	0	0	0	0	....	0	....	....	....	.000	.000	.000	.000	-91	-1	0	.00	0	/0-1,P-1	0	-0.1
• MORRIS, Hal	William Harold Morris b: 4/9/1965, Fort Rucker, AL BL/TL, 6'3", 215 lbs. Deb: 7/29/1988 Career OF: 56-0-6																							
1988 NY-A	15	20	1	2	0	0	0	0	0	9	0	0	.100	.100	.100	.200	-44	-4	0	.30	0	/0-4(3-0-2),D-1	0	-0.4
1989 NY-A	15	18	2	5	0	0	0	4	1	4	0	0	.278	.316	.278	.594	69	-1	1	1.99	0	/0-5(2-0-3),1-2,D-1	0	-0.1
1990*Cin-N	107	309	50	105	22	3	7	36	21	32	9	3	.340	.384	.498	.882	135	15	55	6.67	-2	1-80/0-6(6-0-0)	11	0.8
1991 Cin-N	136	478	72	152	33	1	14	59	46	61	10	4	.318	.379	.479	.858	135	22	89	6.96	2	*1-128/0-1	15	1.6
1992 Cin-N	115	395	41	107	21	3	6	53	45	53	6	6	.271	.348	.385	.733	105	2	51	4.44	4	*1-109	13	-0.2
1993 Cin-N	101	379	48	120	18	0	7	49	34	51	2	2	.317	.376	.420	.795	112	7	61	6.02	-0	1-98	11	-0.2
1994 Cin-N	112	436	60	146	30	4	10	78	34	62	6	2	.335	.389	.491	.880	129	19	79	6.78	2	*1-112	15	1.0
1995*Cin-N	101	359	53	100	25	2	11	51	29	58	1	1	.279	.334	.451	.785	105	1	52	5.12	3	1-99	7	-0.4
1996 Cin-N	142	528	82	165	32	4	16	80	50	76	7	5	.313	.377	.479	.857	125	18	94	6.50	-5	*1-140	18	0.1
1997 Cin-N	96	333	42	92	20	1	1	33	23	43	3	1	.276	.329	.351	.680	77	-11	37	3.93	-2	1-89	4	-2.0
1998 KC-A	127	472	50	146	27	2	1	40	32	52	1	0	.309	.354	.381	.736	89	-7	61	4.71	0	1-46,D-39,0-39(39-0-0)	5	-1.3
1999 Cin-N	80	102	10	29	9	0	0	16	10	21	0	0	.284	.348	.373	.721	80	-3	14	5.03	0	1-25/0-4(4-0-0),D-1	3	-0.4
2000 Cin-N	59	63	9	14	2	1	2	6	12	10	0	0	.222	.355	.381	.736	84	-1	9	4.25	3	1-16/D-1,0-1	0	0.1
Det-A	40	106	15	33	7	0	1	8	19	16	0	0	.311	.416	.406	.822	112	3	19	6.57	2	1-38/0-1	2	0.2
Total 13	1246	3998	535	1216	246	21	76	513	356	548	45	24	.304	.364	.433	.797	111	60	622	5.64	6	1-982/0-61,D-43	104	-1.2
• MORRIS, John	John Daniel Morris b: 2/23/1961, North Bellmore, NY BL/TL, 6'1", 185 lbs. Deb: 8/5/1986 Career OF: 44-54-166																							
1986 StL-N	39	100	8	24	0	1	1	14	7	15	6	2	.240	.290	.290	.580	61	-5	8	2.83	0	0-31(5-4-26)	1	-0.7
1987*StL-N	101	157	22	41	6	4	3	23	11	22	5	2	.261	.314	.408	.721	88	-3	20	4.45	1	0-74(2-8-68)	4	-0.4
1988 StL-N	20	38	3	11	2	1	0	3	1	7	0	0	.289	.308	.395	.702	99	-0	5	4.70	-1	0-16(11-3-2)	0	-0.2
1989 StL-N	96	117	8	28	4	1	2	14	4	22	1	0	.239	.264	.342	.606	70	-5	10	2.74	0	0-51(10-11-32)	2	-0.6
1990 StL-N	18	18	0	2	0	0	0	0	3	6	0	0	.111	.238	.111	.349	-1	-2	1	1.12	0	/0-6(0-1-5)	0	-0.3
1991 Phi-N	85	127	15	28	2	1	1	6	12	25	2	0	.220	.293	.276	.568	61	-6	11	2.96	-1	0-57(11-27-24)	1	-0.8
1992 Cal-A	43	57	4	11	1	0	1	3	4	11	1	0	.193	.258	.263	.521	46	-4	4	2.49	0	0-14(5-0-9)/D-6	0	-0.4
Total 7	402	614	60	145	15	8	8	63	42	108	15	4	.236	.288	.326	.614	68	-25	59	3.25	-3	0-249/D-6	8	-3.5

YEAR TM-L	G	AB	R	H	2B	3B	HR	RBI	BB	SO	SB	CS	AVG	OBP	SLG	OPS	OPS+	BR/A	RC	RC/G	FR	G/POS	WS	TPW
• MORRIS, P.	P. Morris b: Rockford, IL Deb: 5/14/1884																							
1884 Was-U	1	3	0	0	0	0	0	....	0	....	....	....	.000	.000	.000	.000	-103	-1	0	.00	0	/S-1	0	-0.1
• MORRIS, Walter	John Walter Morris b: 1/31/1880, Rockwall, TX d: 8/2/1961, Dallas, TX BR/TR, 5'11" Deb: 8/31/1908																							
1908 StL-N	23	73	1	13	1	1	0	2	0	....	1	....	.178	.178	.219	.397	28	-6	3	1.24	-1	S-23	0	-0.8
• MORRIS, Warren	Warren Randall Morris b: 1/11/1974, Alexandria, LA BL/TR, 5'11", 179 lbs. Deb: 4/5/1999																							
1999 Pit-N	147	511	65	147	20	3	15	73	59	88	3	7	.288	.364	.427	.790	99	-3	78	5.36	-7	*2-144	16	-0.3
2000 Pit-N	144	528	68	137	31	2	3	43	65	78	7	10	.259	.343	.343	.686	75	-22	64	4.12	-1	*2-134	10	-1.6
2001 Pit-N	48	103	6	21	6	0	2	11	3	9	2	3	.204	.241	.320	.561	42	-10	7	2.12	-1	2-29/3-1	1	-1.0
2002 Min-A	4	7	0	0	0	0	0	0	0	1	0	0	.000	.000	.000	.000	-99	-2	0	.00	0	/2-4	0	-0.1
2003 Det-A	97	346	37	94	13	2	6	37	23	42	4	2	.272	.319	.373	.692	88	-6	41	4.15	6	2-89	8	0.4
Total 5	**440**	**1495**	**176**	**399**	**70**	**7**	**26**	**164**	**150**	**218**	**16**	**22**	**.267**	**.337**	**.375**	**.712**	**83**	**-43**	**190**	**4.37**	**-3**	**2-400/3-1**	**35**	**-2.6**
• MORRISON, Jim	James Forrest Morrison b: 9/23/1952, Pensacola, FL BR/TR, 5'11", 182 lbs. Deb: 9/18/1977 Career OF: 8-0-3																							
1977 Phi-N	5	7	3	3	0	0	0	1	1	1	0	0	.429	.500	.429	.929	145	1	2	11.00	0	/3-5	1	0.1
1978*Phi-N	53	108	12	17	1	1	3	10	10	21	1	1	.157	.235	.269	.504	40	-9	7	1.92	4	2-31/3-3,0-1	2	-0.3
1979 Chi-A	67	240	38	66	14	0	14	35	15	48	11	3	.275	.328	.508	.837	122	7	41	5.86	-1	2-48,3-29	9	0.8
1980 Chi-A	162	604	66	171	40	0	15	57	36	74	9	6	.283	.332	.424	.756	106	3	80	4.55	-15	*2-161/D-1,S-1	18	-0.3
1981 Chi-A	90	290	27	68	8	1	10	34	10	29	3	2	.234	.265	.372	.637	84	-8	26	2.87	8	3-87/2-1,D-1	4	0.0
1982 Chi-A	51	166	17	37	7	3	7	19	13	15	0	1	.223	.279	.428	.707	91	-3	18	3.63	-4	3-50/D-1	3	-0.7
Pit-N	44	86	10	24	4	1	4	15	5	14	2	0	.279	.319	.488	.807	119	2	12	4.65	-2	3-26/0-2(0-0-0),2-1,S-1	3	0.0
1983 Pit-N	66	158	16	48	7	2	6	25	9	25	2	6	.304	.349	.487	.836	126	3	24	5.21	-2	2-28,3-26/S-7	6	0.2
1984 Pit-N	100	304	38	87	14	2	11	45	20	52	0	1	.286	.332	.454	.786	119	6	43	5.02	-2	3-61,2-26/S-2,1-1	9	0.4
1985 Pit-N	92	244	17	62	10	0	4	22	8	44	3	0	.254	.281	.344	.625	75	-9	23	3.32	-10	3-59,2-15/0-1	3	-2.0
1986 Pit-N	154	537	58	147	35	4	23	88	47	88	9	8	.274	.337	.482	.819	120	11	86	5.70	-21	*3-151/2-1,S-1	16	-1.2
1987 Pit-N	96	348	41	92	22	1	9	46	27	57	8	5	.264	.319	.411	.730	91	-6	44	4.26	-1	3-82,S-17/2-9	8	-0.7
*Det-A	34	117	15	24	1	1	4	19	2	26	2	1	.205	.225	.333	.558	47	-9	9	2.39	3	3-16/D-8,2-3,0-3(1-0-2),S,1	1	-0.7
1988 Det-A	24	74	7	16	5	0	0	6	0	14	0	2	.216	.216	.284	.500	40	-7	3	1.48	-1	D-14/1-4,3-4,0-2(1-0-1),S	0	-0.8
Atl-N	51	92	6	14	2	0	2	13	10	13	0	1	.152	.235	.239	.474	35	-8	5	1.67	-2	3-20/0-4(4-0-0),P-3	1	-0.9
Total 12	**1089**	**3375**	**371**	**876**	**170**	**16**	**112**	**435**	**213**	**521**	**50**	**37**	**.260**	**.308**	**.419**	**.727**	**98**	**-26**	**424**	**4.25**	**-46**	**3-619,2-324/S-33,D-25,0,1,P**	**84**	**-6.1**
• MORRISON, Jon	Jonathan W. Morrison b: 1859, London, Canada BL, 5'9.5", 167 lbs. Deb: 8/1/1884 Career OF: 0-53-0																							
1884 Ind-a	44	182	26	48	6	8	1	0	7	....	....	....	.264	.306	.401	.707	132	6	23	4.69	-1	0-44(0-44-0)	6	0.4
1887 NY-a	9	40	7	10	0	0	0	3	6	....	0	....	.250	.268	.118	.386	10	-4	1	.99	-4	/0-9(0-9-0)	0	-0.7
Total 2	**53**	**222**	**33**	**58**	**6**	**8**	**1**	**3**	**13**	**....**	**0**	**....**	**.261**	**.299**	**.356**	**.656**	**111**	**3**	**24**	**4.02**	**-5**	**/0-53**	**6**	**-0.3**
• MORRISON, Tom	Thomas J. Morrison b: 8/1870, St. Louis, MO d: 3/27/1902, St. Louis, MO, 5'3", 145 lbs. Deb: 9/18/1895																							
1895 Lou-N	6	22	3	6	0	2	0	4	1	1	0	....	.273	.304	.455	.759	100	-0	3	5.10	0	/3-3,S-3	0	0.0
1896 Lou-N	8	27	3	4	1	0	0	0	4	4	0	....	.148	.258	.185	.443	19	-3	1	1.52	0	/3-5,0-2(0-0-2),S-1	0	-0.2
Total 2	**14**	**49**	**6**	**10**	**1**	**2**	**0**	**4**	**5**	**5**	**0**	**....**	**.204**	**.278**	**.306**	**.584**	**54**	**-3**	**5**	**3.04**	**0**	**/3-8,S-4,0-2**	**0**	**-0.3**
• MORRISSEY, Jack	John Albert "King" Morrissey b: 5/2/1876, Lansing, MI d: 10/30/1936, Lansing, MI BB/TR, 5'10", 160 lbs. Deb: 9/18/1902 Career OF: 7-2-0																							
1902 Cin-N	12	39	5	11	1	1	0	3	4	....	0	....	.282	.349	.359	.708	108	0	5	4.70	-1	2-11/0-1	1	0.0
1903 Cin-N	29	89	14	22	1	0	0	9	14	....	3	....	.247	.350	.258	.608	67	-3	10	3.72	-8	2-17/0-8(6-2-0),S-2	1	-1.1
Total 2	**41**	**128**	**19**	**33**	**2**	**1**	**0**	**12**	**18**	**....**	**3**	**....**	**.258**	**.349**	**.289**	**.638**	**79**	**-3**	**15**	**4.01**	**-9**	**/2-28,0-9,S-2**	**2**	**-1.1**
• MORRISSEY, John	John J. Morrissey b: 12/30/1856, Janesville, WI d: 4/29/1884, Janesville, WI Deb: 5/2/1881																							
1881 Buf-N	12	47	3	10	2	0	0	3	0	3	....	....	.213	.213	.255	.468	47	-3	3	1.91	-2	3-12	0	-0.5
1882 Det-N	2	7	1	2	0	0	0	0	0	2	....	....	.286	.286	.286	.571	84	-0	1	3.22	-1	/3-2	0	-0.1
Total 2	**14**	**54**	**4**	**12**	**2**	**0**	**0**	**3**	**0**	**5**	**....**	**....**	**.222**	**.222**	**.259**	**.481**	**52**	**-3**	**3**	**2.07**	**-3**	**/3-14**	**0**	**-0.6**
• MORRISSEY, Jo-Jo	Joseph Anselm Morrissey b: 1/16/1904, Warren, RI d: 5/2/1950, Worcester, MA BR/TR, 6'1.5", 178 lbs. Deb: 4/12/1932																							
1932 Cin-N	89	269	15	65	10	1	0	13	14	15	2	....	.242	.282	.286	.568	55	-17	22	2.80	3	S-45,2-42,3-12/0-1	3	-0.9
1933 Cin-N	148	534	43	123	20	0	0	26	20	22	5	....	.230	.261	.268	.529	52	-34	35	2.10	-9	2-88,S-63,3-15	4	-3.5
1936 Chi-A	17	38	3	7	1	0	0	6	2	3	0	0	.184	.225	.211	.436	8	-6	2	1.58	-2	/3-9,S-4,2-1	0	-0.7
Total 3	**254**	**841**	**61**	**195**	**31**	**1**	**0**	**45**	**36**	**40**	**7**	**0**	**.232**	**.266**	**.271**	**.537**	**51**	**-56**	**59**	**2.29**	**-8**	**2-131,S-112/3-36,0-1**	**7**	**-5.1**
• MORRISSEY, Tom	Thomas J. Morrissey b: 1861, Janesville, WI d: 9/23/1941, Janesville, WI, 5'11", 180 lbs. Deb: 9/27/1884																							
1884 Mil-U	12	47	3	8	2	0	0	....	0	....	....	....	.170	.170	.213	.383	29	-3	2	1.25	-1	3-12	0	-0.4
• MORSE, Bud	Newell Obediah Morse b: 9/4/1904, Berkeley, CA d: 4/6/1987, Sparks, NV BL/TR, 5'9", 150 lbs. Deb: 9/14/1929																							
1929 Phi-A	8	27	1	2	0	0	0	0	0	2	0	0	.074	.074	.074	.148	-60	-6	0	.15	0	/2-8	0	-0.6
• MORSE, Hap	Peter Raymond "Pete" Morse b: 12/6/1886, St. Paul, MN d: 6/19/1974, St. Paul, MN BR/TR, 5'8", 160 lbs. Deb: 4/18/1911																							
1911 StL-N	4	8	0	0	0	0	0	0	1	2	0	....	.000	.111	.000	.111	-70	-2	0	.00	-1	/S-2,0-1	0	-0.3
• MORTON, Bubba	Wycliffe Nathaniel Morton b: 12/13/1931, Washington, DC BR/TR, 5'10", 180 lbs. Deb: 4/19/1961 Career OF: 33-38-212																							
1961 Det-A	77	108	26	31	5	1	2	19	9	25	3	1	.287	.347	.407	.755	97	-0	16	5.30	0	0-30(8-2-20)	3	-0.2
1962 Det-A	90	195	30	51	6	3	4	17	32	32	1	1	.262	.366	.385	.750	99	0	28	5.09	0	0-62(1-30-33)/1-3	6	-0.2
1963 Det-A	6	11	2	1	0	0	0	2	2	1	0	0	.091	.231	.091	.322	-5	-2	0	.95	0	/0-3(0-3-0)	0	-0.2
Mil-N	15	28	1	5	0	0	0	4	2	3	0	0	.179	.258	.179	.437	28	-2	1	1.15	0	/0-9(6-3-0)	0	-0.3
1966 Cal-A	15	50	4	11	1	0	0	4	2	6	1	1	.220	.250	.240	.490	43	-4	3	1.80	0	0-14(0-0-14)	0	-0.5
1967 Cal-A	80	201	23	63	9	3	0	32	22	29	0	3	.313	.387	.388	.775	134	8	29	5.04	-1	0-61(9-0-55)	9	0.5
1968 Cal-A	81	163	13	44	6	0	1	18	14	18	2	1	.270	.343	.325	.668	107	2	18	3.77	0	0-50(3-0-47)/3-1	5	-0.1
1969 Cal-A	87	172	18	42	10	1	7	32	28	29	0	0	.244	.360	.436	.796	128	7	28	5.57	3	0-49(6-0-43)/1-1	8	0.8
Total 7	**451**	**928**	**117**	**248**	**37**	**8**	**14**	**128**	**111**	**143**	**7**	**7**	**.267**	**.352**	**.370**	**.722**	**107**	**10**	**124**	**4.57**	**1**	**0-278/1-4,3-1**	**31**	**-0.2**
• MORTON, Charlie	Charles Hazen Morton b: 10/12/1854, Kingsville, OH d: 12/9/1921, Massillon, OH BR/TR, 150 lbs. Deb: 5/2/1882 M/U Career OF: 15-27-1																							
1882 Pit-a	25	103	12	29	0	3	0	....	5	....	....	....	.282	.315	.340	.655	127	3	11	4.27	0	0-25(0-25-0)/3-3,S-1	3	0.2
StL-a	9	32	2	2	0	1	0	....	2	....	....	....	.063	.118	.125	.243	-17	-4	0	.45	-3	/2-7,0-3(1-2-0)	0	-0.6
Yr.	34	135	14	31	0	4	0	....	7	....	....	....	.230	.268	.289	.556	92	-1	12	3.17	-3	0-28(1-27-0)/2-7,3-3,S-1	3	-0.4
1884 Tol-a	32	111	11	18	6	2	0	0	7	....	....	....	.162	.212	.252	.464	49	-6	6	1.80	-1	3-16,0-15(14-0-1)/P-3,2-1	2	-0.5
1885 Det-N	22	79	9	14	1	2	0	3	5	10	....	....	.177	.226	.241	.467	51	-4	4	1.83	0	3-18/S-4	1	-0.4
Total 3	**88**	**325**	**34**	**63**	**7**	**8**	**0**	**3**	**19**	**10**	**....**	**....**	**.194**	**.238**	**.265**	**.503**	**67**	**-11**	**22**	**2.35**	**-5**	**/0-43,3-37,2-8,S-5,P-3**	**6**	**-1.3**
• MORTON, Moose	Guy "Moose" Morton, Jr. b: 11/4/1930, Tuscaloosa, AL BR/TR, 6'2", 200 lbs. Deb: 9/17/1954																							
1954 Bos-A	1	1	0	0	0	0	0	0	0	1	0	0	.000	.000	.000	.000	-90	-0	0	.00	0	....	0	0.0
• MORYN, Walt	Walter Joseph "Moose" Moryn b: 4/12/1926, St. Paul, MN d: 7/21/1996, Winfield, IL BL/TR, 6'2", 205 lbs. Deb: 6/29/1954 Career OF: 309-1-370																							
1954 Bro-N	48	91	16	25	4	2	2	14	7	11	0	0	.275	.333	.429	.762	94	-1	13	4.70	0	0-20(6-0-15)	2	-0.2
1955 Bro-N	11	19	3	5	1	0	1	3	5	4	0	0	.263	.417	.474	.890	132	1	4	8.07	-1	/0-7(1-0-6)	1	0.0
1956 Chi-N	147	529	69	151	27	3	23	67	50	67	4	2	.285	.351	.478	.829	122	16	89	6.09	4	*0-141(1-0-140)	19	1.6
1957 Chi-N	149	568	76	164	33	0	19	88	50	90	0	2	.289	.349	.447	.797	114	10	88	5.63	7	*0-147(0-0-147)	17	1.3
1958 Chi-N★	143	512	77	135	26	7	26	77	62	83	1	2	.264	.352	.494	.846	123	16	91	6.28	0	*0-141(141-0-0)	19	0.8
1959 Chi-N	117	381	41	89	14	1	14	48	44	66	0	2	.234	.318	.386	.704	87	-7	46	4.00	4	*0-104(97-1-9)	9	-0.8
1960 Chi-N	38	109	12	32	4	0	2	11	13	19	2	1	.294	.369	.385	.754	108	2	16	5.34	0	0-30(25-0-5)	3	0.0
StL-N	75	200	24	49	4	3	11	35	17	38	0	0	.245	.304	.460	.764	97	-1	26	4.44	-1	0-62(29-0-39)	5	-0.5
Yr.	113	309	36	81	8	3	13	46	30	57	2	1	.262	.327	.434	.761	101	0	42	4.74	-1	0-92(54-0-44)	8	-0.5
1961 StL-N	17	32	0	4	2	0	0	2	1	5	0	0	.125	.152	.188	.339	-10	-5	1	.71	-1	/0-7(3-0-4)	0	-0.6
Pit-N	40	65	6	13	1	0	3	9	2	10	0	0	.200	.235	.354	.589	53	-5	4	1.82	1	0-11(6-0-5)	0	-0.4

YEAR TM-L	G	AB	R	H	2B	3B	HR	RBI	BB	SO	SB	CS	AVG	OBP	SLG	OPS	OPS+	BR/A	RC	RC/G	FR	G/POS	WS	TPW
Yr.	57	97	6	17	3	0	3	11	3	15	0	0	.175	.208	.299	.507	33	-10	5	1.45	0	0-18(9-0-9)	0	-1.0
Total 8	**785**	**2506**	**324**	**667**	**116**	**16**	**101**	**354**	**251**	**393**	**7**	**7**	**.266**	**.338**	**.446**	**.784**	**108**	**27**	**377**	**5.28**	**14**	**0-670**	**75**	**1.2**
• MOSCHITTO, Ross	Rosaire Allen Moschitto b: 2/15/1945, Fresno, CA BR/TR, 6'2", 175 lbs. Deb: 4/15/1965 Career OF: 12-59-26																							
1965 NY-A	96	27	12	5	0	0	1	3	0	12	0	0	.185	.185	.296	.481	35	-2	2	1.79	-4	0-89(10-55-24)	0	-0.8
1967 NY-A	14	9	1	1	0	0	0	0	1	2	0	0	.111	.200	.111	.311	-6	-1	0	.97	-0	/0-8(2-4-2)	0	-0.1
Total 2	**110**	**36**	**13**	**6**	**0**	**0**	**1**	**3**	**1**	**14**	**0**	**0**	**.167**	**.189**	**.250**	**.439**	**23**	**-4**	**2**	**1.56**	**-4**	**/0-97**	**0**	**-1.0**
• MOSEBY, Lloyd	Lloyd Anthony Moseby b: 11/5/1959, Portland, AR BL/TR, 6'3", 200 lbs. Deb: 5/24/1980 Career OF: 101-1327-113																							
1980 Tor-A	114	389	44	89	24	1	9	46	25	85	4	6	.229	.282	.365	.647	73	-17	37	3.02	6	*0-104(12-6-86)/D-6	5	-1.6
1981 Tor-A	100	378	36	88	16	2	9	43	24	86	11	8	.233	.280	.357	.638	78	-13	37	3.22	-6	*0-100(0-80-21)	7	-2.1
1982 Tor-A	147	487	51	115	20	9	9	52	33	106	11	7	.236	.295	.370	.665	74	-18	52	3.54	-4	*0-145(0-145-0)	11	-2.4
1983 Tor-A	151	539	104	170	31	7	18	81	51	85	27	8	.315	.380	.499	.879	132	26	104	7.07	-5	*0-147(0-147-0)	25	1.9
1984 Tor-A	158	592	97	166	28	**15**	18	92	78	122	39	9	.280	.372	.470	.841	126	28	110	6.59	4	*0-156(0-156-0)	26	3.0
1985*Tor-A	152	584	92	151	30	7	18	70	76	91	37	15	.259	.348	.426	.774	108	9	89	5.14	-6	*0-152(0-152-0)	21	0.1
1986 Tor-A★	152	589	89	149	24	5	21	86	64	122	32	11	.253	.332	.418	.750	100	2	86	4.95	-5	*0-147(0-147-0)/D-3	17	-0.4
1987 Tor-A	155	592	106	167	27	4	26	96	70	124	39	7	.282	.360	.473	.833	116	19	106	6.37	-11	*0-153(0-153-0)/D-2	22	0.6
1988 Tor-A	128	472	77	113	17	7	10	42	70	93	31	8	.239	.345	.369	.714	100	5	66	4.70	-7	*0-125(11-117-6)/D-1	13	-0.4
1989*Tor-A	135	502	72	111	25	3	11	43	56	101	24	7	.221	.307	.349	.655	90	-4	58	3.77	-7	*0-120(0-120-0),D-14	12	-1.4
1990 Det-A	122	431	64	107	16	5	14	51	48	77	17	5	.248	.331	.406	.737	104	4	57	4.48	3	*0-116(14-104-0)/D-4	11	0.5
1991 Det-A	74	260	37	68	15	1	6	35	21	43	8	1	.262	.324	.396	.720	97	-0	35	4.74	-4	0-64(64-0-0)/D-7	7	-0.6
Total 12	**1588**	**5815**	**869**	**1494**	**273**	**66**	**169**	**737**	**616**	**1135**	**280**	**92**	**.257**	**.334**	**.414**	**.748**	**102**	**41**	**836**	**4.91**	**-40**	***0-1529/D-37**	**177**	**-2.9**
• MOSER, Arnie	Arnold Robert Moser b: 8/9/1915, Houston, TX d: 8/15/2002, Houston, TX BR/TR, 5'11", 165 lbs. Deb: 6/20/1937																							
1937 Cin-N	5	5	0	0	0	0	0	0	0	2	0	....	.000	.000	.000	.000	-105	-1	0	.00	0	....	0	-0.1
• MOSES, Jerry	Gerald Braheen Moses b: 8/9/1946, Yazoo City, MS BR/TR, 6'3", 210 lbs. Deb: 5/9/1965 Career OF: 1-0-1																							
1965 Bos-A	4	4	1	1	0	0	1	1	0	2	0	0	.250	.250	1.000	1.250	224	1	1	9.00	0	....	0	0.1
1968 Bos-A	6	18	2	6	0	0	2	4	1	4	0	1	.333	.368	.667	1.035	195	1	3	6.22	-1	/C-6	1	0.1
1969 Bos-A	53	135	13	41	9	1	4	17	5	23	0	1	.304	.333	.474	.807	117	2	21	5.70	-3	C-36	4	0.1
1970 Bos-A★	92	315	26	83	18	1	6	35	21	45	1	1	.263	.314	.384	.698	85	-7	37	4.12	-0	C-88/0-1	9	-0.2
1971 Cal-A	69	181	12	41	8	2	4	15	10	34	0	0	.227	.267	.359	.626	82	-5	15	2.63	0	C-63/0-1	4	-0.3
1972 Cle-A	52	141	9	31	3	0	4	14	11	29	0	0	.220	.290	.326	.617	80	-3	14	3.24	0	C-39/1-3	4	-0.2
1973 NY-A	21	59	5	15	2	0	0	3	2	6	0	0	.254	.279	.288	.567	62	-3	4	2.46	2	C-17/D-1	1	0.0
1974 Det-A	74	198	19	47	6	3	4	19	11	38	0	1	.237	.284	.359	.643	81	-6	19	3.20	-0	C-74	5	-0.3
1975 SD-N	13	19	1	3	2	0	0	1	2	3	0	0	.158	.238	.263	.501	41	-2	1	1.67	-1	/C-5	0	-0.2
Chi-A	2	2	1	1	0	1	0	0	0	0	0	0	.500	.500	1.500	2.000	441	1	2	40.50	0	/1-1,D-1	0	0.1
Total 9	**386**	**1072**	**89**	**269**	**48**	**8**	**25**	**109**	**63**	**184**	**1**	**4**	**.251**	**.297**	**.381**	**.678**	**88**	**-21**	**116**	**3.70**	**-3**	**C-328/1-4,D-2,0-2**	**28**	**-0.9**
• MOSES, John	John William Moses b: 8/9/1957, Los Angeles, CA BB/TL, 5'10", 170 lbs. Deb: 8/23/1982 C Career OF: 164-334-180 ♦																							
1982 Sea-A	22	44	7	14	5	1	1	3	4	5	5	1	.318	.375	.545	.920	145	3	10	8.53	1	0-19(8-3-9)	2	0.3
1983 Sea-A	93	130	19	27	4	1	0	6	12	20	11	5	.208	.280	.254	.534	46	-9	9	2.20	3	0-71(34-31-7),D-10	1	-0.7
1984 Sea-A	19	35	3	12	1	1	0	2	2	5	1	0	.343	.395	.429	.823	129	2	6	7.28	0	0-19(7-14-0)/D-1	2	0.2
1985 Sea-A	33	62	4	12	0	0	0	3	2	8	5	2	.194	.219	.194	.412	14	-7	2	1.04	0	0-29(1-28-0)	0	-0.8
1986 Sea-A	103	399	56	102	16	3	3	34	34	65	25	18	.256	.314	.333	.647	76	-16	40	3.25	2	0-93(2-91-0)/1-7,D-4	4	-1.5
1987 Sea-A	116	390	58	96	16	4	3	38	29	49	23	15	.246	.303	.331	.634	65	-22	38	3.16	-2	*0-100(0-97-4),1-16/D-5	4	-2.4
1988 Min-A	105	206	33	65	10	3	2	12	15	21	11	6	.316	.368	.422	.790	117	5	31	5.51	-1	0-82(29-20-43)/D-2	6	0.2
1989 Min-A	129	242	33	68	12	3	1	31	19	23	14	7	.281	.336	.368	.704	92	-3	30	4.18	-2	*0-108(39-26-63)/D-3,1-2,P	8	-0.6
1990 Min-A	115	172	26	38	3	1	1	14	19	19	2	3	.221	.306	.267	.573	58	-10	14	2.68	-1	0-85(16-23-52),D-10/1-6,P	1	-1.5
1991 Det-A	13	21	5	1	1	0	0	1	2	7	4	0	.048	.130	.095	.226	-36	-3	1	.82	0	0-12(11-0-1)	0	-0.3
1992 Sea-A	21	22	3	3	1	0	0	1	5	4	0	0	.136	.296	.182	.478	36	-2	2	2.25	0	0-18(17-1-1)/D-1	0	-0.2
Total 11	**769**	**1723**	**247**	**438**	**69**	**17**	**11**	**145**	**143**	**226**	**101**	**57**	**.254**	**.315**	**.333**	**.648**	**75**	**-61**	**183**	**3.51**	**0**	**0-636/D-36,1-31,P-3**	**28**	**-7.4**
• MOSES, Wally	Wallace Moses b: 10/8/1910, Uvalda, GA d: 10/10/1990, Vidalia, GA BL/TL, 5'10", 160 lbs. Deb: 4/17/1935 C Career OF: 10-204-1587																							
1935 Phi-A	85	345	60	112	21	3	5	35	25	18	3	4	.325	.375	.446	.822	113	5	57	6.37	-2	0-80(0-0-80)	9	-0.2
1936 Phi-A	146	585	98	202	35	11	7	66	62	32	12	6	.345	.410	.479	.888	121	21	117	7.82	-3	*0-144(0-136-9)	21	1.2
1937 Phi-A★	154	649	113	208	48	13	25	86	54	38	9	7	.320	.374	.550	.925	132	27	132	7.67	2	*0-154(0-0-154)	20	1.8
1938 Phi-A	142	589	86	181	29	8	8	49	58	31	15	5	.307	.369	.424	.794	101	2	95	6.04	-2	*0-139(0-0-139)	14	-0.7
1939 Phi-A	115	437	68	134	28	7	3	33	44	23	7	4	.307	.370	.423	.793	105	3	71	6.06	-4	*0-103(0-5-100)	12	-0.6
1940 Phi-A	142	537	91	166	41	9	9	50	75	44	6	4	.309	.396	.469	.865	126	23	108	7.58	1	*0-133(0-2-131)	21	1.5
1941 Phi-A	116	438	78	132	31	4	4	35	62	27	3	3	.301	.388	.418	.806	116	12	76	6.36	6	*0-109(0-0-109)	15	1.0
1942 Chi-A	146	577	73	156	28	4	7	49	74	27	16	10	.270	.353	.369	.722	106	5	81	5.02	7	*0-145(3-14-130)	20	0.4
1943 Chi-A	150	599	82	147	22	**12**	3	48	55	47	56	14	.245	.310	.337	.647	89	-2	69	3.91	7	*0-148(0-23-125)	18	-0.4
1944 Chi-A	136	535	82	150	26	9	3	34	52	22	21	7	.280	.345	.379	.725	108	8	77	5.30	-1	*0-134(0-0-134)	21	-0.2
1945 Chi-A★	140	569	79	168	**35**	15	2	50	69	33	11	5	.295	.373	.420	.793	134	26	97	6.36	8	*0-139(0-0-139)	28	2.6
1946 Chi-A	56	168	20	46	9	1	4	16	17	20	2	2	.274	.344	.411	.755	114	3	24	5.12	0	0-36(2-14-22)	6	0.2
*Bos-A	48	175	23	36	11	3	2	17	14	15	2	4	.206	.268	.337	.606	65	-10	16	2.96	0	0-44(0-2-43)	3	-1.2
Yr.	104	343	43	82	20	4	6	33	31	35	4	6	.239	.306	.373	.679	89	-7	40	3.97	0	0-80(2-16-65)	9	-1.0
1947 Bos-A	90	255	32	70	18	2	2	27	27	16	3	0	.275	.344	.384	.728	95	-1	35	4.91	-4	0-58(0-0-58)	7	-0.6
1948 Bos-A	78	189	26	49	12	1	2	29	21	19	5	0	.259	.340	.365	.705	83	-3	27	5.09	0	0-45(0-0-45)	5	-0.4
1949 Phi-A	110	308	49	85	19	3	1	25	51	19	1	3	.276	.381	.367	.747	102	2	48	5.40	-1	0-92(1-1-91)	10	-0.2
1950 Phi-A	88	265	47	70	16	5	2	21	40	17	0	1	.264	.365	.385	.750	94	-2	40	5.24	3	0-62(4-7-51)	6	-0.1
1951 Phi-A	70	136	17	26	6	0	0	9	21	9	2	1	.191	.304	.235	.539	46	-10	10	2.37	1	0-27(0-0-27)	1	-1.0
Total 17	**2012**	**7356**	**1124**	**2138**	**435**	**110**	**89**	**679**	**821**	**457**	**174**	**81**	**.291**	**.364**	**.416**	**.779**	**109**	**108**	**1179**	**5.84**	**21**	***0-1792**	**237**	**3.2**
• MOSKIMAN, Doc	William Bankhead Moskiman b: 12/20/1879, Oakland, CA d: 1/11/1953, San Leandro, CA BR/TR, 6', 170 lbs. Deb: 8/23/1910																							
1910 Bos-A	5	9	1	1	0	0	0	1	2		0	....	.111	.273	.111	.384	20	-1	0	.85	0	/1-2,0-1	0	0.0
• MOSOLF, Jim	James Frederick Mosolf b: 8/21/1905, Puyallup, WA d: 12/28/1979, Dallas, OR BL/TR, 5'10", 186 lbs. Deb: 9/9/1929 Career OF: 26-4-10 ♦																							
1929 Pit-N	8	13	3	6	1	1	0	2	1	1	0	....	.462	.500	.692	1.192	187	2	4	15.99	0	/0-3(3-0-0)	1	0.1
1930 Pit-N	40	51	16	17	2	1	0	9	8	7	0	....	.333	.424	.412	.835	103	1	9	6.78	-1	0-12(1-1-9)/P-1	1	-0.2
1931 Pit-N	39	44	7	11	1	0	1	8	8	5	0	....	.250	.365	.341	.706	92	-0	6	4.68	-0	/0-4(3-0-1)	1	0.0
1933 Chi-N	31	82	13	22	5	1	1	9	5	8	0	....	.268	.326	.390	.716	104	0	11	4.65	1	0-22(19-3-0)	3	0.0
Total 4	**118**	**190**	**39**	**56**	**9**	**3**	**2**	**28**	**22**	**21**	**0**	**....**	**.295**	**.374**	**.405**	**.779**	**106**	**3**	**31**	**5.75**	**-1**	**/0-41,P-1**	**6**	**-0.1**
• MOSQUERA, Julio	Julio Alberto (Cervantes) Mosquera b: 1/29/1972, Panama City, Panama BR/TR, 6', 165 lbs. Deb: 8/17/1996																							
1996 Tor-A	8	22	2	5	2	0	0	2	0	3	0	1	.227	.261	.318	.579	46	-2	2	2.37	-1	/C-8	0	-0.2
1997 Tor-A	3	8	0	2	1	0	0	0	0	2	0	0	.250	.250	.375	.625	60	-1	1	3.38	0	/C-3	0	0.0
Total 2	**11**	**30**	**2**	**7**	**3**	**0**	**0**	**2**	**0**	**5**	**0**	**1**	**.233**	**.258**	**.333**	**.591**	**49**	**-3**	**2**	**2.62**	**-1**	**/C-11**	**0**	**-0.3**
• MOSS, Charlie	Charles Crosby Moss b: 3/20/1911, Meridian, MS d: 10/9/1991, Meridian, MS BR/TR, 5'10", 160 lbs. Deb: 5/19/1934																							
1934 Phi-A	10	10	3	2	0	0	0	1	0	0	0	0	.200	.200	.200	.400	4	-1	0	1.27	-1	/C-6	0	-0.2
1935 Phi-A	4	3	1	1	0	0	0	1	1	0	0	0	.333	.500	.333	.833	120	0	1	8.01	0	/C-1	0	0.0
1936 Phi-A	33	44	2	11	1	1	0	10	6	5	1	0	.250	.340	.318	.658	65	-2	5	4.14	-1	C-19	0	-0.3
Total 3	**47**	**57**	**6**	**14**	**1**	**1**	**0**	**12**	**7**	**5**	**1**	**0**	**.246**	**.328**	**.298**	**.626**	**59**	**-3**	**6**	**3.79**	**-3**	**/C-26**	**0**	**-0.5**
• MOSS, Howie	Howard Glenn Moss b: 10/17/1919, Gastonia, NC d: 5/7/1989, Baltimore, MD BR/TR, 5'11.5", 185 lbs. Deb: 4/14/1942 Career OF: 2-1-6																							
1942 NY-N	7	14	0	0	0	0	0	0	0	4	0	....	.000	.000	.000	.000	-99	-4	0	.00	0	/0-3(2-1-0)	0	-0.4
1946 Cin-N	7	26	1	5	0	0	0	1	0	4	0	....	.192	.222	.192	.415	19	-3	1	1.50	0	/0-6(0-0-6)	0	-0.3

YEAR TM-L	G	AB	R	H	2B	3B	HR	RBI	BB	SO	SB	CS	AVG	OBP	SLG	OPS	OPS+	BR/A	RC	RC/G	FR	G/POS	WS	TPW
Cle-A	8	32	2	2	0	0	0	0	3	9	0	1	.063	.143	.063	.205	-44	-7	0	.13	1	/3-8	0	-0.6
Total 2	22	72	3	7	0	0	0	1	3	17	0	1	.097	.145	.097	.242	-32	-13	1	.52	1	/0-9,3-8	0	-1.3
• MOSS, Les	John Lester Moss b: 5/14/1925, Tulsa, OK BR/TR, 5'11", 205 lbs. Deb: 9/10/1946 M/C																							
1946 StL-A	12	35	4	13	3	0	0	5	3	5	1	0	.371	.436	.457	.893	142	2	8	9.61	-1	C-12	2	0.3
1947 StL-A	96	274	17	43	5	2	6	27	35	48	0	0	.157	.255	.255	.510	41	-22	20	2.25	-2	C-96	3	-2.0
1948 StL-A	107	335	35	86	12	1	14	46	39	50	0	0	.257	.334	.424	.758	98	-2	46	4.52	2	*C-103	8	0.5
1949 StL-A	97	278	28	81	11	0	10	39	49	32	0	1	.291	.399	.439	.838	117	8	51	6.50	1	C-83	10	1.3
1950 StL-A	84	222	24	59	6	0	8	34	26	32	0	1	.266	.343	.401	.744	87	-5	30	4.76	-3	C-60	5	-0.5
1951 StL-A	16	47	5	8	2	0	1	7	6	8	0	0	.170	.264	.277	.541	45	-4	3	1.99	0	C-12	0	-0.3
Bos-A	71	202	18	40	6	0	3	26	25	34	0	0	.198	.289	.272	.562	48	-15	16	2.47	-4	C-69	3	-1.5
Yr.	87	249	23	48	8	0	4	33	31	42	0	0	.193	.285	.273	.558	47	-18	19	2.38	-4	C-81	3	-1.8
1952 StL-A	52	118	11	29	3	0	3	12	15	13	0	1	.246	.331	.347	.678	86	-2	13	3.55	-1	C-39	2	-0.2
1953 StL-A	78	239	21	66	14	1	2	28	18	31	0	1	.276	.329	.368	.698	86	-5	27	3.99	-4	C-71	3	-0.6
1954 Bal-A	50	126	7	31	3	0	0	5	14	16	0	0	.246	.321	.270	.591	68	-5	11	3.10	-1	C-38	2	-0.4
1955 Bal-A	29	56	5	19	1	0	2	6	7	4	0	1	.339	.413	.464	.877	145	3	10	7.27	1	C-17	3	0.5
Chi-A	32	59	5	15	2	0	2	7	6	10	0	0	.254	.333	.390	.723	91	-1	8	4.86	-1	C-32	2	-0.1
Yr.	61	115	10	34	3	0	4	13	13	14	0	1	.296	.372	.426	.798	117	3	19	5.97	0	C-49	5	0.4
1956 Chi-A	56	127	20	31	4	0	10	22	18	15	0	0	.244	.338	.512	.850	120	3	20	5.20	-2	C-49	4	0.3
1957 Chi-A	42	115	10	31	3	0	2	12	20	18	0	0	.270	.378	.348	.726	99	1	16	4.73	-3	C-39	4	-0.1
1958 Chi-A	2	1	0	0	0	0	0	0	1	0	0	0	.000	.500	.000	.500	51	0	0	3.51	0	....	0	0.0
Total 13	824	2234	210	552	75	4	63	276	282	316	1	5	.247	.333	.369	.702	86	-43	280	4.21	-16	C-720	51	-2.8
• MOSTIL, Johnny	John Anthony "Bananas" Mostil b: 6/1/1896, Chicago, IL d: 12/10/1970, Midlothian, IL BR/TR, 5'8.5", 168 lbs. Deb: 6/20/1918 Career OF: 20-856-32																							
1918 Chi-A	10	33	4	9	2	2	0	4	1	6	1	....	.273	.294	.455	.749	125	1	4	4.55	-4	/2-9	1	-0.3
1921 Chi-A	100	326	43	98	21	7	3	42	28	35	10	12	.301	.379	.436	.814	109	2	53	5.60	-1	0-91(1-90-0)/2-1	9	-0.2
1922 Chi-A	132	458	74	139	28	14	7	70	38	39	14	10	.303	.375	.472	.846	120	13	81	6.26	-0	*0-123(18-105-0)	19	0.6
1923 Chi-A	153	546	91	159	37	15	3	64	62	51	41	16	.291	.376	.430	.806	113	15	93	5.81	15	*0-143(0-135-8)/3-5,S-1	20	2.3
1924 Chi-A	118	385	75	125	22	5	4	49	45	41	7	11	.325	.401	.439	.840	120	10	67	6.12	3	*0-102(1-90-12)	13	0.8
1925 Chi-A	153	605	**135**	181	36	16	2	50	**90**	52	**43**	20	.299	.400	.421	.822	115	20	109	6.35	3	*0-153(0-153-0)	23	1.5
1926 Chi-A	148	600	120	197	41	15	4	42	79	55	**35**	14	.328	.415	.467	.882	135	36	122	7.51	8	*0-147(0-147-0)	28	3.6
1927 Chi-A	13	16	3	2	0	0	0	1	0	1	1	0	.125	.176	.125	.301	-21	-3	0	.89	0	/0-6(0-6-0)	0	-0.2
1928 Chi-A	133	503	69	136	19	8	0	51	66	54	23	21	.270	.360	.340	.699	86	-11	63	4.14	10	*0-131(0-120-11)	14	-0.7
1929 Chi-A	12	35	4	8	3	0	0	3	6	2	1	1	.229	.341	.314	.656	71	-1	4	3.69	0	0-11(0-10-1)	1	-0.1
Total 10	972	3507	618	1054	209	82	23	376	415	336	176	105	.301	.386	.427	.812	113	80	596	5.93	35	0-907/2-10,3-5,S-1	128	7.3
• MOTA, Andy	Andres Alberto (Matos) Mota b: 3/4/1966, Santo Domingo, Dominican Republic BR/TR, 5'10", 180 lbs. Deb: 8/31/1991																							
1991 Hou-N	27	90	4	17	2	0	1	6	1	17	2	0	.189	.198	.244	.442	25	-9	5	1.70	2	2-27	1	-0.6
• MOTA, Jose	Jose Manuel (Matos) Mota b: 3/16/1965, Santo Domingo, Dominican Republic BB/TR, 5'9", 155 lbs. Deb: 5/24/1991																							
1991 SD-N	17	36	4	8	0	0	0	2	2	7	0	0	.222	.282	.222	.504	42	-3	3	2.37	-2	2-13/S-3	0	-0.5
1995 KC-A	2	2	0	0	0	0	0	0	0	0	0	0	.000	.000	.000	.000	-99	-1	0	.00	0	/2-2	0	-0.1
Total 2	19	38	4	8	0	0	0	2	2	7	0	0	.211	.268	.211	.479	36	-3	3	2.22	-2	/2-15,S-3	0	-0.5
• MOTA, Manny	Manuel Rafael (Geronimo) Mota b: 2/18/1938, Santo Domingo, Dominican Republic BR/TR, 5'10", 168 lbs. Deb: 4/16/1962 C Career OF: 725-270-118																							
1962 SF-N	47	74	9	13	1	0	0	9	7	8	3	2	.176	.256	.189	.445	22	-8	4	1.41	1	0-27(22-2-4)/3-7,2-3	1	-0.8
1963 Pit-N	59	126	20	34	2	3	0	7	7	18	0	2	.270	.313	.333	.647	86	-3	12	3.39	-2	0-37(35-2-2)/2-1	2	-0.8
1964 Pit-N	115	271	43	75	8	3	5	32	10	31	4	1	.277	.310	.384	.694	94	-2	32	4.04	-2	0-93(57-50-7)/2-1,C-1	6	-0.8
1965 Pit-N	121	294	47	82	7	6	4	29	22	32	2	2	.279	.333	.384	.718	101	0	37	4.43	2	0-95(35-60-15)	9	-0.1
1966 Pit-N	116	322	54	107	16	7	5	46	25	28	7	7	.332	.387	.472	.860	137	15	57	6.47	-1	0-96(45-52-12)/3-4	14	1.1
1967 Pit-N	120	349	53	112	14	8	4	56	14	46	3	2	.321	.351	.441	.792	124	10	52	5.38	4	0-99(48-48-13)/3-2	14	1.1
1968 Pit-N	111	331	35	93	10	2	1	33	20	19	4	2	.281	.324	.332	.656	99	-0	36	3.67	1	0-92(50-31-22)/2-1,3-1	9	-0.5
1969 Mon-N	31	89	6	28	1	1	0	0	6	11	1	3	.315	.358	.348	.706	98	-1	10	3.85	-2	0-22(1-17-5)	1	-0.4
LA-N	85	294	35	95	6	4	3	30	26	25	5	4	.323	.380	.401	.781	128	11	45	5.43	2	0-80(75-4-10)	11	0.9
Yr.	116	383	41	123	7	5	3	30	32	36	6	7	.321	.375	.389	.764	121	9	55	5.06	0	*0-102(76-21-15)	12	0.5
1970 LA-N	124	417	63	127	12	6	3	37	47	37	11	6	.305	.379	.384	.763	110	7	61	5.08	1	*0-111(109-1-4)/3-1	14	0.2
1971 LA-N	91	269	24	84	13	5	0	34	20	20	4	3	.312	.362	.398	.760	122	7	37	4.79	-2	0-80(62-0-24)	9	0.1
1972 LA-N	118	371	57	120	16	5	5	48	27	15	4	4	.323	.377	.434	.811	133	15	58	5.80	-3	0-99(96-3-0)	15	0.7
1973 LA-N★	89	293	33	92	11	2	0	23	25	12	1	3	.314	.370	.365	.735	109	3	37	4.47	-1	0-74(74-0-0)	8	-0.1
1974*LA-N	66	57	5	16	2	0	0	16	5	4	0	0	.281	.349	.316	.665	91	-1	7	3.83	0	/0-3(3-0-0)	1	-0.1
1975 LA-N	52	49	3	13	1	0	0	10	5	1	0	0	.265	.357	.286	.643	84	-1	5	3.22	0	/0-5(5-0-0)	1	-0.1
1976 LA-N	50	52	1	15	3	0	0	13	7	5	0	0	.288	.373	.346	.719	107	1	7	4.74	0	/0-6(6-0-0)	2	0.1
1977*LA-N	49	38	5	15	1	0	1	4	10	0	1	1	.395	.521	.500	1.021	176	5	10	10.29	-0	/0-1	2	0.5
1978*LA-N	37	33	2	10	1	0	0	6	3	4	0	0	.303	.361	.333	.694	95	0	4	4.76	0	....	1	0.0
1979 LA-N	47	42	1	15	0	0	0	3	3	4	0	0	.357	.400	.357	.757	110	1	6	4.99	0	/0-1	1	0.1
1980 LA-N	7	7	0	3	0	0	0	2	0	0	0	0	.429	.429	.429	.857	143	0	1	4.63	0	....	0	0.0
1982 LA-N	1	1	0	0	0	0	0	0	0	0	0	0	.000	.000	.000	.000	-103	-0	0	.00	0	....	0	0.0
Total 20	1536	3779	496	1149	125	52	31	438	289	320	50	42	.304	.358	.389	.747	112	59	517	4.81	-4	*0-1021/3-15,2-6,C-1	121	1.2
• MOTLEY, Darryl	Darryl De Wayne Motley b: 1/21/1960, Muskogee, OK BR/TR, 5'9", 196 lbs. Deb: 8/10/1981 Career OF: 159-6-239																							
1981 KC-A	42	125	15	29	4	0	2	8	7	15	1	3	.232	.278	.312	.590	70	-6	10	2.65	-1	0-39(2-0-38)	1	-0.9
1983 KC-A	19	68	9	16	1	2	3	11	2	8	2	1	.235	.268	.441	.709	91	-1	7	3.19	0	0-18(3-2-15)/D-1	1	-0.2
1984*KC-A	146	522	64	148	25	6	15	70	28	73	10	12	.284	.321	.441	.762	108	1	63	4.07	1	*0-138(105-3-45)	13	-0.5
1985*KC-A	123	383	45	85	20	1	17	49	18	57	6	4	.222	.261	.413	.673	80	-13	35	2.89	-2	*0-114(44-0-76)/D-7	4	-1.9
1986 KC-A	72	217	22	44	9	1	7	20	11	31	0	2	.203	.241	.350	.591	57	-15	16	2.28	-4	0-66(3-1-62)/D-2	1	-2.1
Atl-N	5	10	1	2	1	0	0	0	1	1	0	0	.200	.273	.300	.573	55	-1	1	2.76	0	/0-3(0-0-3)	0	-0.1
1987 Atl-N	6	8	0	0	0	0	0	1	0	1	0	0	.000	.000	.000	.000	-95	-2	0	.00	0	/0-2(2-0-0)	0	-0.2
Total 6	413	1333	156	324	60	10	44	159	67	186	19	22	.243	.282	.402	.684	86	-37	130	3.20	-5	0-380/D-10	20	-6.0
• MOTT, Bitsy	Elisha Matthew Mott b: 6/12/1918, Arcadia, FL d: 2/25/2001, Brandon, FL BR/TR, 5'8", 155 lbs. Deb: 4/17/1945																							
1945 Phi-N	90	289	21	64	8	0	0	22	27	25	2	....	.221	.290	.249	.539	52	-18	22	2.46	2	S-63,2-27/3-7	3	-1.1
• MOTTOLA, Chad	Charles Edward Mottola b: 10/15/1971, Augusta, GA BR/TR, 6'3", 220 lbs. Deb: 4/23/1996 Career OF: 2-2-37																							
1996 Cin-N	35	79	10	17	3	0	3	6	6	16	2	2	.215	.271	.367	.638	67	-5	8	3.27	-1	0-31(0-1-30)	1	-0.7
2000 Tor-A	3	9	1	2	0	0	0	2	0	4	0	0	.222	.300	.222	.522	34	-1	1	2.62	0	/0-3(0-0-3)	0	-0.1
2001 Fla-N	5	7	1	0	0	0	0	1	2	2	0	0	.000	.222	.000	.222	-36	-1	0	.70	1	/0-5(2-1-4)	0	0.0
Total 3	43	95	12	19	3	0	3	9	8	22	2	2	.200	.269	.326	.596	54	-7	9	2.95	0	/0-39	1	-0.8
• MOTTON, Curt	Curtell Howard Motton b: 9/24/1940, Darnell, LA BR/TR, 5'8", 175 lbs. Deb: 7/5/1967 C Career OF: 133-0-14																							
1967 Bal-A	27	65	5	13	2	0	2	9	5	14	0	1	.200	.278	.323	.601	78	-2	6	2.57	-1	0-18(18-0-1)	1	-0.5
1968 Bal-A	83	217	27	43	7	0	8	25	31	43	1	3	.198	.301	.341	.642	94	-2	22	3.12	1	0-54(54-0-0)	5	-0.5
1969*Bal-A	56	89	15	27	6	0	6	21	13	10	3	1	.303	.398	.573	.971	167	8	22	9.20	-1	0-20(16-0-4)	5	0.7
1970 Bal-A	52	84	16	19	3	1	3	19	18	20	1	2	.226	.369	.393	.762	109	1	14	5.30	0	0-21(20-0-2)	3	0.0
1971*Bal-A	38	53	13	10	1	0	4	8	10	12	0	0	.189	.317	.434	.751	112	1	8	4.57	0	0-16(12-0-5)	2	0.1
1972 Mil-A	6	6	1	1	0	0	1	2	1	2	0	0	.167	.286	.667	.952	181	1	1	6.57	0	/0-3(3-0-0)	0	0.0
Cal-A	42	39	6	6	1	0	0	1	5	12	0	0	.154	.250	.179	.429	31	-3	2	1.50	-1	/0-9(9-0-0)	0	-0.5
Yr.	48	45	7	7	1	0	1	3	6	14	0	0	.156	.255	.244	.499	52	-3	3	2.15	-1	0-12(12-0-0)	0	-0.5
1973 Bal-A	5	6	2	2	0	0	1	4	1	1	0	0	.333	.429	.833	1.262	250	1	2	15.22	0	/D-1,0-1	1	0.1
1974*Bal-A	7	8	0	0	0	0	0	0	2	2	0	0	.000	.200	.000	.200	-40	-1	0	.35	-0	/0-2(0-0-2),D-1	0	-0.2
Total 8	316	567	85	121	20	1	25	89	86	116	5	7	.213	.322	.384	.707	104	3	76	4.30	-2	0-144/D-2	17	-0.7

YEAR TM-L	G	AB	R	H	2B	3B	HR	RBI	BB	SO	SB	CS	AVG	OBP	SLG	OPS	OPS+	BR/A	RC	RC/G	FR	G/POS	WS	TPW
• MOTZ, Frank	Frank H. Motz b: 10/1/1869, Freeburg, PA d: 3/18/1944, Akron, OH, 6', 160 lbs. Deb: 8/27/1890																							
1890 Phi-N	1	2	1	0	0	0	0	0	1	1	1	....	.000	.333	.000	.333	-1	-0	0	4.53	0	/1-1	0	0.0
1893 Cin-N	43	156	16	40	7	1	2	25	19	10	3	....	.256	.352	.353	.705	85	-3	21	4.78	5	1-43	3	0.2
1894 Cin-N	18	69	8	14	4	0	0	12	9	1	2	....	.203	.304	.261	.565	36	-7	6	2.94	3	1-18	0	-0.4
Total 3	62	227	25	54	11	1	2	37	29	12	6	....	.238	.337	.322	.659	69	-11	27	4.19	8	/1-62	3	-0.2
• MOULTON, Allie	Albert Theodore Moulton b: 1/16/1886, Medway, MA d: 9/10/1968, Peabody, MA BR/TR, 5'6", 155 lbs. Deb: 9/25/1911																							
1911 StL-A	4	15	4	1	0	0	0	1	4	....	0	....	.067	.263	.067	.330	-6	-2	0	.47	0	/2-4	0	-0.2
• MOUNTAIN, Frank	Frank Henry Mountain b: 5/17/1860, Fort Edward, NY d: 11/19/1939, Schenectady, NY BR/TR, 5'11", 185 lbs. Deb: 7/19/1880 U Career OF: 18-16-2 ♦																							
1880 Tro-N	2	9	1	2	0	0	0	0	0	4	....	....	.222	.222	.222	.444	48	-0	0	1.79	0	/P-2	0	-0.5
1881 Det-N	7	25	0	4	1	1	0	4	2	8	....	....	.160	.222	.280	.502	54	-0	2	2.05	-1	/P-7	0	-1.5
1882 Wor-N	5	16	1	1	0	0	0	1	0	5	....	....	.063	.063	.063	.125	-58	-2	0	.12	-1	/P-5,S-1	0	-0.1
Phi-a	9	36	5	12	3	0	0	....	2	....	....	....	.333	.368	.417	.785	147	3	6	6.61	1	/P-8,0-1	5	-0.5
Wor-N	20	70	8	19	2	2	2	5	3	18	....	....	.271	.301	.443	.744	132	3	10	5.16	-2	P-13/0-6(1-5-0),1-2	3	-0.3
Yr.	25	86	9	20	2	2	2	6	3	23	....	....	.233	.258	.372	.631	98	0	10	4.02	-3	P-18/0-6(1-5-0),1-2,S-1	3	-0.4
1883 Col-a	70	276	36	60	14	5	3	0	9	....	....	....	.217	.242	.337	.579	92	7	23	2.99	0	P-59,0-12(8-4-0)	18	-1.9
1884 Col-a	58	210	26	50	7	3	4	0	9	....	....	....	.238	.283	.357	.640	116	11	22	3.73	4	P-42,0-17(9-7-1)	36	2.4
1885 Pit-a	5	20	1	2	0	1	0	1	1	....	....	....	.100	.143	.200	.343	7	-1	1	.88	0	/P-5	2	-0.6
1886 Pit-a	18	55	6	8	1	1	0	2	13	....	3	....	.145	.319	.200	.519	64	-1	5	2.63	-1	1-16/P-2	1	-1.0
Total 7	194	717	84	158	28	13	9	13	39	35	3	....	.220	.265	.333	.599	96	18	67	3.33	1	P-143/0-36,1-18,S-1	65	-4.1
• MOUTON, James	James Raleigh Mouton b: 12/29/1968, Denver, CO BR/TR, 5'9", 175 lbs. Deb: 4/4/1994 Career OF: 215-180-176																							
1994 Hou-N	99	310	43	76	11	0	2	16	27	69	24	5	.245	.316	.300	.616	65	-12	32	3.53	0	0-96(1-19-80)	3	-1.5
1995 Hou-N	104	298	42	78	18	2	4	27	25	59	25	8	.262	.327	.376	.703	91	-2	38	4.35	1	0-94(38-22-38)	6	-0.4
1996 Hou-N	122	300	40	79	15	1	3	34	38	55	21	9	.263	.346	.350	.696	91	-2	37	4.08	3	*0-108(79-29-5)	8	-0.2
1997 Hou-N	86	180	24	38	9	1	3	23	18	30	9	7	.211	.290	.322	.612	62	-11	16	2.85	1	0-61(9-39-14)	1	-1.1
1998 SD-N	55	63	8	12	2	1	0	7	7	11	4	3	.190	.271	.254	.525	42	-6	4	1.72	-1	0-33(16-4-14)/D-1	0	-0.7
1999 Mon-N	95	122	18	32	5	1	2	13	18	31	6	2	.262	.366	.369	.735	89	-1	18	4.99	0	0-56(32-16-11)/D-1	2	-0.1
2000 Mil-N	87	159	28	37	7	1	2	17	30	43	13	4	.233	.365	.327	.692	78	-3	22	4.30	1	0-45(19-23-7)	4	-0.3
2001 Mil-N	75	138	20	34	8	0	2	10	11	40	7	3	.246	.329	.348	.677	77	-4	17	4.17	2	0-53(21-28-7)/D-1	3	-0.3
Total 8	723	1570	223	386	75	7	18	147	174	338	109	41	.246	.330	.337	.667	78	-42	185	3.87	7	0-546/D-3	27	-4.6
• MOUTON, Lyle	Lyle Joseph Mouton b: 5/13/1969, Lafayette, LA BR/TR, 6'4", 240 lbs. Deb: 6/7/1995 Career OF: 103-1-135																							
1995 Chi-A	58	179	23	54	16	0	5	27	19	46	1	0	.302	.375	.475	.850	125	7	31	6.28	1	0-53(29-0-30)/D-2	5	0.5
1996 Chi-A	87	214	25	63	8	1	7	39	22	50	3	0	.294	.366	.439	.805	107	3	36	6.13	-1	0-47(22-0-28),D-28	6	0.0
1997 Chi-A	88	242	26	65	9	0	5	23	14	66	4	4	.269	.311	.368	.679	80	-9	25	3.54	-3	0-67(16-0-55),D-11	3	-1.4
1998 Bal-A	18	39	5	12	2	0	2	7	4	8	0	0	.308	.372	.513	.885	129	2	8	7.83	0	0-16(6-0-12)/D-2	2	0.1
1999 Mil-N	14	17	2	3	1	0	1	3	2	3	0	0	.176	.263	.412	.675	68	-1	2	3.82	0	/0-3(2-0-1)	0	-0.1
2000 Mil-N	42	97	14	27	7	1	2	16	10	29	1	0	.278	.352	.433	.785	99	-0	15	5.61	3	0-27(22-1-4)	4	0.2
2001 Fla-N	21	17	1	1	0	0	0	1	0	7	0	0	.059	.059	.059	.118	-72	-4	0	.10	-1	0-11(6-0-5)	0	-0.5
Total 7	328	805	96	225	43	2	22	116	71	209	9	4	.280	.342	.420	.762	99	-2	117	5.15	0	0-224/D-43	20	-1.2
• MOWE, Ray	Raymond Benjamin Mowe b: 7/12/1889, Rochester, IN d: 8/14/1968, Sarasota, FL BL/TR, 5'7.5", 160 lbs. Deb: 9/25/1913																							
1913 Bro-N	5	9	0	1	0	0	0	0	0	1	0	....	.111	.200	.111	.311	-10	-1	0	1.04	2	/S-2	0	0.1
• MOWREY, Mike	Harry Harlan Mowrey b: 4/20/1884, Brown's Mill, PA d: 3/20/1947, Chambersburg, PA BR/TR, 5'10", 180 lbs. Deb: 9/24/1905																							
1905 Cin-N	7	30	4	8	1	0	0	6	1	....	0	....	.267	.290	.300	.590	68	-1	3	3.17	-1	/3-7	0	-0.2
1906 Cin-N	21	53	3	17	3	0	0	6	5	....	2	....	.321	.379	.377	.757	130	2	9	6.18	1	3-15/2-1,S-1	2	0.3
1907 Cin-N	138	448	43	113	16	6	1	44	35	....	10	....	.252	.308	.321	.629	93	-4	51	3.74	-12	*3-127,S-11	11	-1.4
1908 Cin-N	77	227	17	50	9	1	0	23	12	....	5	....	.220	.266	.269	.534	73	-7	18	2.48	-4	3-56/0-3(3-0-0),S-3,2-1	5	-1.1
1909 Cin-N	38	115	10	22	5	0	0	5	20	....	2	....	.191	.311	.235	.546	70	-3	9	2.52	3	3-22,S-13	2	0.1
StL-N	12	29	3	7	1	0	0	4	4	....	1	....	.241	.333	.276	.609	95	0	3	3.46	-2	/2-7,3-2	1	-0.2
Yr.	50	144	13	29	6	0	0	9	24	....	3	....	.201	.315	.243	.559	75	-3	13	2.70	2	3-24,S-13/2-7	3	-0.1
1910 StL-N	143	489	69	138	24	6	2	70	67	38	21	....	.282	.375	.368	.744	121	16	76	5.36	6	*3-141	23	2.7
1911 StL-N	137	471	59	126	29	7	0	61	59	46	15	....	.268	.355	.359	.714	103	3	66	4.71	7	*3-134/S-1	18	1.4
1912 StL-N	114	408	59	104	13	8	2	50	46	29	19	....	.255	.335	.341	.675	87	-7	54	4.23	-2	*3-108	10	-0.6
1913 StL-N	132	450	61	117	18	4	0	33	53	40	21	....	.260	.342	.318	.660	90	-4	55	4.00	11	*3-131	14	1.1
1914 Pit-N	79	284	24	72	7	5	1	25	22	20	8	....	.254	.316	.324	.640	94	-2	31	3.62	2	3-78	9	0.2
1915 Pit-F	151	521	56	146	26	6	1	49	66	39	40	....	.280	.367	.359	.725	109	9	80	5.28	-10	*3-151	21	0.3
1916*Bro-N	144	495	57	121	22	6	0	60	50	60	16	....	.244	.320	.313	.633	92	-3	59	3.79	10	*3-144	17	1.3
1917 Bro-N	83	271	20	58	9	5	0	25	29	25	7	....	.214	.292	.284	.576	75	-7	24	2.82	2	3-80/2-2	6	-0.3
Total 13	1276	4291	485	1099	183	54	7	461	469	297	167	....	.256	.334	.329	.663	96	-9	539	4.13	11	*3-1196/S-29,2-11,0-3	139	3.8
• MOWRY, Joe	Joseph Aloysius Mowry b: 4/6/1908, St. Louis, MO d: 2/9/1994, St. Louis, MO BB/TR, 6', 198 lbs. Deb: 5/13/1933 Career OF: 82-7-40																							
1933 Bos-N	86	249	25	55	8	5	0	20	15	22	1	....	.221	.273	.293	.567	67	-11	21	2.75	0	0-64(48-5-11)	4	-1.5
1934 Bos-N	25	79	9	17	3	0	1	4	3	13	0	....	.215	.244	.291	.535	46	-6	6	2.57	2	0-20(4-0-16)/2-1	1	-0.5
1935 Bos-N	81	136	17	36	8	1	1	13	11	13	0	....	.265	.324	.360	.685	91	-2	17	4.27	1	0-45(30-2-13)	2	-0.2
Total 3	192	464	51	108	19	6	2	37	29	48	1	....	.233	.284	.313	.596	71	-18	44	3.15	3	0-129/2-1	7	-2.2
• MOYNAHAN, Mike	Michael Moynahan b: 1856, Chicago, IL d: 4/9/1899, Chicago, IL BL/TR Deb: 8/20/1880 Career OF: 33-1-2																							
1880 Buf-N	27	100	12	33	5	1	0	14	6	9	....	....	.330	.368	.400	.768	157	6	15	6.19	-7	S-27	5	0.0
1881 Cle-N	33	135	12	31	5	1	0	8	3	14	....	....	.230	.246	.281	.528	69	-5	10	2.49	-4	0-32(32-0-0)/3-1	2	-0.9
Det-N	1	4	1	1	0	0	0	0	0	1	....	....	.250	.250	.250	.500	55	-0	0	2.31	1	/3-1	0	0.0
Yr.	34	139	13	32	5	1	0	8	3	15	....	....	.230	.246	.281	.527	68	-5	10	2.49	-3	0-32(32-0-0)/3-2	2	-0.9
1883 Phi-a	95	400	90	124	18	10	1	67	31	....	....	....	.310	.360	.413	.772	137	16	61	6.17	1	*S-95	24	1.8
1884 Phi-a	1	4	0	0	0	0	0	0	0	....	....	....	.000	.000	.000	.000	-94	-1	0	.00	0	/0-1	0	-0.1
Cle-N	12	45	9	13	2	1	0	6	7	11	....	....	.289	.385	.378	.762	136	2	7	5.76	0	/2-6,0-3(1-0-2),S-3	1	0.2
Total 4	169	688	124	202	30	13	1	95	47	35	....	....	.294	.339	.379	.718	125	19	92	5.28	-10	S-125/0-36,2-6,3-2	32	0.9
• MUELLER, Bill	William Lawrence "Hawk" Mueller b: 11/9/1920, Bay City, MI d: 10/24/2001, Glenview, IL BR/TR, 6'1.5", 180 lbs. Deb: 8/29/1942 Career OF: 0-28-5																							
1942 Chi-A	26	85	5	14	1	0	0	5	12	9	2	1	.165	.276	.176	.452	29	-7	4	1.49	6	0-26(0-23-3)	2	-0.2
1945 Chi-A	13	9	3	0	0	0	0	0	2	1	1	0	.000	.182	.000	.182	-47	-1	0	.57	-1	/0-7(0-5-2)	0	-0.3
Total 2	39	94	8	14	1	0	0	5	14	10	3	1	.149	.266	.160	.426	21	-9	4	1.39	5	/0-33	2	-0.4
• MUELLER, Bill	William Richard Mueller b: 3/17/1971, Maryland Heights, MO BB/TR, 5'11", 175 lbs. Deb: 4/18/1996																							
1996 SF-N	55	200	31	66	15	1	0	19	24	26	0	0	.330	.404	.415	.819	122	7	36	7.03	4	3-45/2-8	9	1.2
1997*SF-N	128	390	51	114	26	3	7	44	48	71	4	3	.292	.374	.428	.802	113	8	63	5.67	-2	*3-122	14	0.8
1998 SF-N	145	534	93	157	27	0	9	59	79	83	3	3	.294	.386	.395	.781	113	12	85	5.72	-2	*3-137,2-10	18	1.3
1999 SF-N	116	414	61	120	24	0	2	36	65	52	4	2	.290	.390	.362	.752	99	2	62	5.29	-5	*3-108/2-3	12	-0.1
2000*SF-N	153	560	97	150	29	4	10	55	52	62	4	2	.268	.337	.388	.724	89	-10	73	4.44	1	*3-145/2-2	10	-0.7
2001 Chi-N	70	210	38	62	12	1	6	23	37	19	1	1	.295	.408	.448	.856	127	10	41	6.86	-1	3-64/2-1	8	1.0
2002 Chi-N	103	353	51	94	19	4	7	37	51	41	0	0	.266	.359	.402	.761	102	2	53	5.17	-2	*3-101	12	0.2
SF-N	8	13	0	2	0	0	0	1	1	1	0	0	.154	.214	.154	.368	-1	-2	0	.73	0	/3-3	0	-0.2
Yr.	111	366	51	96	19	4	7	38	52	42	0	0	.262	.354	.393	.748	99	0	53	4.99	-2	*3-104	12	0.0
2003*Bos-A	146	524	85	171	45	5	19	85	59	77	1	4	**.326**	.402	.540	.942	142	32	113	8.07	-8	*3-135,2-10/D-3,S-1	23	2.4
Total 8	924	3198	507	936	197	18	60	359	416	432	17	15	.293	.378	.422	.800	112	62	525	5.85	-15	3-860/2-34,D-3,S-1	106	5.9

• MUELLER, Don
Donald Frederick "Mandrake The Magician" Mueller b: 4/14/1927, St. Louis, MO BL/TR, 6', 185 lbs. Deb: 8/2/1948 Career OF: 34-1-1047

YEAR TM-L	G	AB	R	H	2B	3B	HR	RBI	BB	SO	SB	CS	AVG	OBP	SLG	OPS	OPS+	BR/A	RC	RC/G	FR	G/POS	WS	TPW
1948 NY-N	36	81	12	29	4	1	1	9	0	3	0	....	.358	.358	.469	.827	121	2	12	5.89	1	0-22(18-1-1)	3	0.2
1949 NY-N	51	56	5	13	4	0	0	1	5	6	0	....	.232	.295	.304	.599	61	-3	3	1.78	0	/0-6(2-0-4)	0	-0.3
1950 NY-N	132	525	60	153	15	6	7	84	10	26	1	....	.291	.309	.383	.691	80	-17	60	4.22	1	*0-125(3-0-122)	10	-1.9
1951 NY-N	122	469	58	130	10	7	16	69	19	13	1	1	.277	.307	.431	.737	95	-5	63	4.90	0	*0-115(0-0-115)	12	-0.9
1952 NY-N	126	456	61	128	14	7	12	49	34	24	2	1	.281	.333	.421	.754	107	4	65	5.18	0	*0-120(0-0-120)	15	0.0
1953 NY-N	131	480	56	160	12	2	6	60	19	13	2	0	.333	.360	.404	.764	97	-2	71	5.83	1	*0-122(11-0-111)	11	-0.5
1954*NY-N★	153	619	90	**212**	35	8	4	71	22	17	2	3	.342	.367	.444	.811	110	7	94	5.74	-2	*0-153(0-0-153)	19	0.0
1955 NY-N★	147	605	67	185	21	4	8	83	19	12	1	2	.306	.330	.393	.724	91	-9	75	4.53	-11	*0-146(0-0-146)	13	-2.6
1956 NY-N	138	453	38	122	12	1	5	41	15	7	0	1	.269	.293	.333	.626	68	-21	39	2.97	-6	*0-117(0-0-117)	3	-3.2
1957 NY-N	135	450	45	116	7	1	6	37	13	16	2	0	.258	.280	.318	.598	60	-25	39	3.07	2	*0-115(0-0-115)	4	-2.7
1958 Chi-A	70	166	7	42	5	0	0	16	11	9	0	0	.253	.299	.283	.583	62	-8	14	3.00	0	0-43(0-0-43)	2	-1.0
1959 Chi-A	4	4	0	2	0	0	0	0	0	0	0	0	.500	.500	.500	1.000	178	0	1	13.50	0	....	0	0.0
Total 12	**1245**	**4364**	**499**	**1292**	**139**	**37**	**65**	**520**	**167**	**146**	**11**	**8**	**.296**	**.324**	**.390**	**.713**	**89**	**-78**	**538**	**4.50**	**-16**	***0-1084**	**92**	**-12.9**

• MUELLER, Heinie
Clarence Francis Mueller b: 9/16/1899, St. Louis, MO d: 1/23/1975, De Soto, MO BL/TL, 5'8", 158 lbs. Deb: 9/25/1920 Career OF: 83-368-109

YEAR TM-L	G	AB	R	H	2B	3B	HR	RBI	BB	SO	SB	CS	AVG	OBP	SLG	OPS	OPS+	BR/A	RC	RC/G	FR	G/POS	WS	TPW
1920 StL-N	4	22	0	7	1	0	0	1	2	4	1	0	.318	.375	.364	.739	115	1	3	5.74	0	/0-4(1-0-4)	1	0.1
1921 StL-N	55	176	25	62	10	6	1	34	11	22	2	4	.352	.397	.494	.891	137	9	33	7.17	-2	0-54(0-51-3)	8	0.5
1922 StL-N	61	159	20	43	7	2	3	26	14	18	2	1	.270	.329	.396	.726	91	-2	21	4.61	1	0-44(10-34-0)	3	-0.3
1923 StL-N	78	265	39	91	16	9	5	41	18	16	4	3	.343	.392	.528	.920	144	16	54	7.90	1	0-74(0-71-3)	12	1.4
1924 StL-N	92	296	39	78	12	6	2	37	19	16	8	7	.264	.312	.365	.677	82	-8	33	3.82	-2	0-53(2-42-9),1-27	4	-1.4
1925 StL-N	78	243	33	76	16	4	1	26	17	11	0	3	.313	.365	.424	.789	99	-1	37	5.48	-2	0-72(2-57-13)	6	-0.6
1926 StL-N	52	191	36	51	7	5	3	28	11	6	8	....	.267	.330	.403	.733	93	-2	25	4.41	-0	0-51(0-21-30)	5	-0.5
NY-N	85	305	36	76	6	2	4	29	21	17	7	....	.249	.300	.321	.621	68	-14	29	3.24	1	0-82(10-38-35)	5	-1.8
Yr.	137	496	72	127	13	7	7	57	32	23	15	....	.256	.312	.353	.664	78	-16	54	3.70	1	*0-133(10-59-65)	10	-2.3
1927 NY-N	84	190	33	55	6	1	3	19	25	12	2	....	.289	.384	.379	.763	105	3	29	5.33	-3	0-56(49-5-2)/1-1	6	-0.4
1928 Bos-N	42	151	25	34	3	1	0	19	17	9	1	....	.225	.316	.258	.574	54	-9	14	2.76	3	0-41(4-37-0)	1	-0.8
1929 Bos-N	46	93	10	19	2	1	0	11	12	12	2	....	.204	.302	.247	.549	39	-9	8	2.56	0	0-24(4-11-10)	1	-0.8
1935 StL-A	16	27	0	5	1	0	0	1	1	4	0	0	.185	.214	.222	.437	12	-4	1	1.55	0	/1-3,0-2(1-1-0)	0	-0.4
Total 11	**693**	**2118**	**296**	**597**	**87**	**37**	**22**	**272**	**168**	**147**	**37**	**18**	**.282**	**.342**	**.389**	**.731**	**93**	**-21**	**287**	**4.73**	**-3**	**0-557/1-31**	**52**	**-5.0**

• MUELLER, Heinie
Emmett Jerome Mueller b: 7/20/1912, St. Louis, MO d: 10/3/1986, Orlando, FL BB/TR, 5'6", 167 lbs. Deb: 4/19/1938 Career OF: 33-1-35

YEAR TM-L	G	AB	R	H	2B	3B	HR	RBI	BB	SO	SB	CS	AVG	OBP	SLG	OPS	OPS+	BR/A	RC	RC/G	FR	G/POS	WS	TPW
1938 Phi-N	136	444	53	111	12	4	4	34	64	43	2	....	.250	.346	.322	.668	84	-7	55	4.29	-19	*2-111,3-21	10	-2.0
1939 Phi-N	115	341	46	95	19	4	9	43	33	34	4	....	.279	.342	.437	.779	113	5	49	5.02	1	2-51,3-17,0-17(4-0-13)/S-1	9	0.9
1940 Phi-N	97	263	24	65	13	2	3	28	37	23	2	....	.247	.344	.346	.690	95	-1	33	4.30	-5	2-34,0-31(29-0-2),3-13/1-2	6	-0.5
1941 Phi-N	93	233	21	53	11	1	1	22	22	24	2	....	.227	.302	.296	.598	72	-8	21	3.10	2	2-29,0-21(0-1-20),3-19	3	-0.6
Total 4	**441**	**1281**	**144**	**324**	**55**	**11**	**17**	**127**	**156**	**124**	**10**	**....**	**.253**	**.337**	**.353**	**.690**	**92**	**-11**	**159**	**4.26**	**-21**	**2-225/3-70,0-69,1-2,S-1**	**28**	**-2.1**

• MUELLER, Ray
Ray Coleman "Iron Man" Mueller b: 3/8/1912, Pittsburg, KS d: 6/29/1994, Lower Paxton Township, PA BR/TR, 5'9", 175 lbs. Deb: 5/11/1935 C

YEAR TM-L	G	AB	R	H	2B	3B	HR	RBI	BB	SO	SB	CS	AVG	OBP	SLG	OPS	OPS+	BR/A	RC	RC/G	FR	G/POS	WS	TPW
1935 Bos-N	42	97	10	22	5	0	3	11	3	11	0	....	.227	.250	.371	.621	70	-4	9	3.18	4	C-40	2	0.1
1936 Bos-N	24	71	5	14	4	0	0	5	5	17	0	....	.197	.250	.254	.504	38	-6	5	2.33	0	C-23	1	-0.5
1937 Bos-N	64	187	21	47	9	2	2	26	18	36	1	....	.251	.317	.353	.670	90	-3	21	3.68	5	C-57	7	0.5
1938 Bos-N	83	274	23	65	8	6	4	35	16	28	3	....	.237	.282	.354	.636	82	-8	27	3.35	4	C-75	9	0.1
1939 Pit-N	86	180	14	42	8	1	2	18	14	22	0	....	.233	.289	.322	.611	65	-9	18	3.18	0	C-81	4	-0.5
1940 Pit-N	4	3	1	1	0	0	0	1	2	0	0	....	.333	.600	.333	.933	165	1	1	12.31	0	/C-4	0	0.1
1943 Cin-N	141	427	50	111	19	4	8	52	56	42	1	....	.260	.347	.379	.726	111	7	59	4.70	20	*C-140	24	3.8
1944 Cin-N★	155	555	54	159	24	4	10	73	53	47	4	....	.286	.353	.398	.751	115	11	79	5.14	-8	*C-155	26	1.3
1946 Cin-N	114	378	35	96	18	4	8	48	27	37	0	....	.254	.309	.386	.695	100	-2	45	3.98	7	*C-100	12	1.1
1947 Cin-N	71	192	17	48	11	0	6	33	16	25	1	....	.250	.311	.401	.712	88	-4	22	3.91	3	C-55	5	0.2
1948 Cin-N	14	34	2	7	1	0	0	2	4	3	0	....	.206	.289	.235	.525	45	-3	2	2.29	0	C-10	0	-0.2
1949 Cin-N	32	106	7	29	4	0	1	13	5	13	1	....	.274	.319	.340	.658	76	-4	12	3.93	1	C-31	3	-0.1
NY-N	56	170	17	38	2	2	5	23	13	14	1	....	.224	.279	.347	.626	67	-9	15	2.79	-1	C-56	3	-0.7
Yr.	88	276	24	67	6	2	6	36	18	27	2	....	.243	.294	.344	.638	70	-12	27	3.21	0	C-87	6	-0.8
1950 NY-N	4	11	0	1	1	0	0	0	0	2	0	....	.091	.091	.182	.273	-30	-2	0	.00	0	/C-4	0	-0.2
Pit-N	67	156	17	42	7	0	6	24	11	14	2	....	.269	.321	.429	.751	92	-2	19	4.07	3	C-63	4	0.3
Yr.	71	167	17	43	8	0	6	24	11	16	2	....	.257	.307	.413	.720	85	-4	19	3.74	3	C-67	4	0.2
1951 Bos-N	28	70	8	11	2	0	1	9	7	11	0	0	.157	.234	.229	.462	27	-7	4	1.54	2	C-23	1	-0.4
Total 14	**985**	**2911**	**281**	**733**	**123**	**23**	**56**	**373**	**250**	**322**	**14**	**0**	**.252**	**.314**	**.368**	**.681**	**91**	**-43**	**337**	**3.92**	**40**	**C-917**	**101**	**4.8**

• MUELLER, Walter
Walter John Mueller b: 12/6/1894, Central, MO d: 8/16/1971, St. Louis, MO BR/TR, 5'8", 160 lbs. Deb: 5/7/1922 Career OF: 41-5-41

YEAR TM-L	G	AB	R	H	2B	3B	HR	RBI	BB	SO	SB	CS	AVG	OBP	SLG	OPS	OPS+	BR/A	RC	RC/G	FR	G/POS	WS	TPW
1922 Pit-N	32	122	21	33	5	1	2	18	5	7	1	0	.270	.305	.377	.682	74	-5	14	3.99	4	0-31(0-0-31)	2	-0.3
1923 Pit-N	40	111	11	34	4	4	0	20	4	6	2	2	.306	.336	.414	.751	95	-1	15	4.86	0	0-26(19-0-7)	3	-0.3
1924 Pit-N	30	50	6	13	1	1	0	8	4	4	1	0	.260	.327	.320	.647	73	-1	6	4.01	2	0-15(8-5-2)	1	0.0
1926 Pit-N	19	62	8	15	0	1	0	3	0	2	0	....	.242	.242	.274	.516	37	-6	4	2.12	0	0-15(14-0-1)	0	-0.7
Total 4	**121**	**345**	**46**	**95**	**10**	**7**	**2**	**49**	**13**	**19**	**4**	**2**	**.275**	**.307**	**.362**	**.670**	**74**	**-13**	**39**	**3.92**	**6**	**/0-87**	**6**	**-1.2**

• MULDOON, Mike
Michael D. Muldoon b: 4/9/1858, Westmeath County, Ireland, 5'8", 165 lbs. Deb: 5/1/1882 Career OF: 21-2-3

YEAR TM-L	G	AB	R	H	2B	3B	HR	RBI	BB	SO	SB	CS	AVG	OBP	SLG	OPS	OPS+	BR/A	RC	RC/G	FR	G/POS	WS	TPW
1882 Cle-N	84	341	50	84	17	5	6	45	10	28	....	....	.246	.268	.378	.646	108	3	35	3.79	2	*3-61,0-23(21-2-0)	12	0.5
1883 Cle-N	98	378	54	86	22	3	0	29	10	39	....	....	.228	.247	.302	.549	67	-15	29	2.72	-4	*3-98/0-2(0-0-2)	5	-1.4
1884 Cle-N	110	422	46	101	16	6	2	38	18	67	....	....	.239	.270	.320	.590	82	-9	37	3.21	-11	*3-109/2-1,0-1	6	-1.6
1885 Bal-a	102	410	47	103	20	6	2	52	20	....	....	....	.251	.293	.344	.637	102	1	42	3.72	-4	*3-101/2-1	11	-0.1
1886 Bal-a	101	381	57	76	13	8	0	23	34	....	12	....	.199	.269	.276	.544	72	-11	32	2.85	-5	2-57,3-44	10	-1.2
Total 5	**495**	**1932**	**254**	**450**	**88**	**28**	**10**	**187**	**92**	**134**	**12**	**....**	**.233**	**.270**	**.323**	**.593**	**86**	**-31**	**176**	**3.25**	**-21**	**3-413/2-59,0-26**	**44**	**-3.7**

• MULLANE, Tony
Anthony John "Count,The Apollo Of The Box" Mullane
b: 1/30/1859, Cork, Ireland d: 4/25/1944, Chicago, IL BB/TR, 5'10.5", 165 lbs. Deb: 8/27/1881 U Career OF: 57-59-39 ♦

YEAR TM-L	G	AB	R	H	2B	3B	HR	RBI	BB	SO	SB	CS	AVG	OBP	SLG	OPS	OPS+	BR/A	RC	RC/G	FR	G/POS	WS	TPW
1881 Det-N	5	19	0	5	0	0	0	1	0	0	....	....	.263	.263	.263	.526	63	-0	1	2.60	0	/P-5	0	-0.9
1882 Lou-a	77	303	46	78	13	1	0	....	13	....	....	....	.257	.288	.307	.595	106	11	27	3.42	12	*P-55,1-13,0-12(1-12-1)/2-2	**36**	3.6
1883 StL-a	83	307	38	69	11	6	0	33	13	....	....	....	.225	.256	.300	.556	74	-3	24	2.84	3	P-53,0-30(13-10-7)/2-3,1-2	**55**	3.0
1884 Tol-a	95	352	49	97	19	3	3	0	33	....	....	....	.276	.339	.372	.712	127	20	46	4.91	7	P-67,0-19(14-0-4)/1-7,3-6,2,S	**58**	**6.4**
1886 Cin-a	91	324	59	73	12	5	0	39	25	....	20	....	.225	.283	.293	.576	78	-1	33	3.59	0	P-63,0-27(2-23-2)/1-4,3-2,2,S	34	-1.6
1887 Cin-a	56	215	35	60	6	3	3	23	16	....	20	....	.279	.292	.327	.619	71	1	25	4.44	0	P-48/0-9(7-2-0)	46	2.9
1888 Cin-a	51	175	27	44	4	4	1	16	8	....	12	....	.251	.296	.337	.633	97	5	22	4.44	-1	P-44/1-4,0-3(0-0-3),2-2	33	0.9
1889 Cin-a	63	196	53	58	16	4	0	29	27	21	24	....	.296	.387	.418	.805	125	11	42	8.07	-3	P-33,3-18,0-12(4-5-3)/1-4	24	2.5
1890 Cin-N	81	286	41	79	9	8	0	34	39	30	19	....	.276	.375	.364	.738	116	12	47	6.05	-2	0-28(8-2-18),P-25,3-21,S-10/1	28	3.3
1891 Cin-N	64	209	16	31	1	2	0	10	18	33	4	....	.148	.229	.172	.402	17	-8	9	1.43	1	P-51,0-12(6-5-1)/3-4	24	-0.3
1892 Cin-N	39	118	14	20	3	1	0	9	9	8	4	....	.169	.246	.212	.458	39	-1	7	2.02	6	P-37/1-2	26	1.4
1893 Cin-N	16	52	11	15	0	0	1	6	5	3	1	....	.288	.383	.346	.729	92	3	7	5.35	0	P-15/3-1	10	0.5
Bal-N	38	114	15	26	2	1	0	14	5	14	5	....	.228	.261	.263	.524	39	-3	9	2.81	2	P-34/0-2(2-0-0),1-1	17	0.8
Yr.	54	166	26	41	2	1	1	20	10	17	6	....	.247	.302	.289	.591	57	-1	17	3.56	2	P-49/0-2(2-0-0),1-1,3-1	27	1.3
1894 Bal-N	21	53	3	21	3	0	0	9	6	3	2	....	.396	.475	.453	.928	120	5	13	10.29	-1	P-21	7	-0.7
Cle-N	4	13	0	1	0	0	0	0	4	2	1	....	.077	.294	.077	.371	-6	-1	1	1.31	2	/P-4	1	-0.7
Yr.	25	66	3	22	3	0	0	9	10	5	3	....	.333	.436	.379	.815	92	4	13	7.84	1	P-25	8	-1.4
Total 13	**784**	**2736**	**407**	**677**	**99**	**38**	**8**	**223**	**221**	**114**	**112**	**....**	**.247**	**.307**	**.316**	**.623**	**88**	**50**	**315**	**4.13**	**24**	**P-555,0-154/3-52,1-38,S-12,2**	**399**	**20.9**

• MULLEAVY, Greg
Gregory Thomas "Moe" Mulleavy b: 9/25/1905, Detroit, MI d: 2/1/1980, Arcadia, CA BR/TR, 5'9", 167 lbs. Deb: 7/4/1930 C

YEAR TM-L	G	AB	R	H	2B	3B	HR	RBI	BB	SO	SB	CS	AVG	OBP	SLG	OPS	OPS+	BR/A	RC	RC/G	FR	G/POS	WS	TPW
1930 Chi-A	77	289	27	76	14	5	0	28	20	23	5	2	.263	.311	.346	.657	69	-13	32	3.74	-15	S-73	3	-1.8
1932 Chi-A	1	3	0	0	0	0	0	0	0	0	0	0	.000	.000	.000	.000	-107	-1	0	.00	0	/2-1	0	-0.1

YEAR TM-L	G	AB	R	H	2B	3B	HR	RBI	BB	SO	SB	CS	AVG	OBP	SLG	OPS	OPS+	BR/A	RC	RC/G	FR	G/POS	WS	TPW
1933 Bos-A	1	0	1	0	0	0	0	0	0	0	0	0	....	....	....	....	-101	0	0	....	0	....	0	0.0
Total 3	79	292	28	76	14	5	0	28	20	23	5	2	.260	.308	.342	.650	67	-14	32	3.69	-15	/S-73,2-1	3	-1.9
• MULLEN,	Mullen Deb: 8/17/1872																							
1872 Cle-n	1	4	1	0	0	0	0	0	0	0	0	0	.000	.000	.000	.000	-106	-1	0	.00	0	/O-1	....	-0.1
• MULLEN, Billy	William John Mullen b: 1/23/1896, St. Louis, MO d: 5/4/1971, St. Louis, MO BR/TR, 5'8", 160 lbs. Deb: 10/2/1920																							
1920 StL-A	2	4	0	0	0	0	0	0	0	0	0	0	.000	.000	.000	.000	-97	-1	0	.00	0	/2-1	0	-0.1
1921 StL-A	4	4	0	0	0	0	0	0	2	1	0	0	.000	.333	.000	.333	-8	-1	0	1.10	-0	/3-2	0	0.0
1923 Bro-N	4	11	1	3	0	0	0	0	0	0	0	0	.273	.273	.273	.545	45	-1	1	2.48	0	/3-4	0	-0.1
1926 Det-A	11	13	2	1	0	0	0	0	5	1	1	0	.077	.333	.077	.410	11	-1	1	2.05	-1	/3-9	0	-0.2
1928 StL-A	15	18	2	7	1	0	0	2	3	4	0	0	.389	.476	.444	.921	139	1	4	8.95	-1	/3-6	1	0.1
Total 5	36	50	5	11	1	0	0	2	10	6	1	0	.220	.350	.240	.590	53	-2	6	3.83	-2	/3-21,2-1	1	-0.3
• MULLEN, Charlie	Charles George Mullen b: 3/15/1889, Seattle, WA d: 6/6/1963, Seattle, WA BR/TR, 5'10.5", 155 lbs. Deb: 5/18/1910 Career OF: 1-2-5																							
1910 Chi-A	41	123	15	24	2	1	0	13	4	....	4	....	.195	.220	.228	.448	43	-9	8	1.79	1	1-37/O-2(0-0-2)	1	-0.9
1911 Chi-A	20	59	7	12	2	1	0	5	5	....	1	....	.203	.266	.271	.537	51	-4	5	2.42	-1	1-20	0	-0.5
1914 NY-A	93	323	33	84	8	0	0	44	33	55	11	17	.260	.332	.285	.617	86	-10	32	3.07	2	1-93	6	-1.0
1915 NY-A	40	90	11	24	1	0	0	7	10	12	5	2	.267	.340	.278	.618	85	-1	10	3.68	1	1-27	2	0.0
1916 NY-A	59	146	11	39	9	1	0	18	9	13	7	....	.267	.310	.342	.652	94	-2	18	4.19	-5	2-20,1-17/O-6(1-2-3)	4	-0.8
Total 5	253	741	77	183	22	3	0	87	61	80	28	19	.247	.306	.285	.591	78	-25	72	3.06	-1	1-194/2-20,O-8	13	-3.2
• MULLEN, John	John Mullen b: Philadelphia, PA BL/TL Deb: 9/9/1876																							
1876 Phi-N	1	3	0	0	0	0	0	0	0	0	....	....	.000	.000	.000	.000	-101	-1	0	.00	0	/C-1	0	-0.1
• MULLEN, Moon	Ford Parker Mullen b: 2/9/1917, Olympia, WA BL/TR, 5'9", 165 lbs. Deb: 4/18/1944																							
1944 Phi-N	118	464	51	124	9	4	0	31	28	32	4	....	.267	.315	.304	.618	77	-14	46	3.59	-8	*2-114/3-1	8	-1.7
• MULLER, Freddie	Frederick William Muller b: 12/21/1907, Newark, CA d: 10/20/1976, Davis, CA BR/TR, 5'10", 170 lbs. Deb: 7/8/1933																							
1933 Bos-A	15	48	6	9	1	1	0	3	5	5	1	0	.188	.264	.250	.514	37	-4	4	2.38	-1	2-14	0	-0.4
1934 Bos-A	2	1	1	0	0	0	0	0	1	0	0	0	.000	.500	.000	.500	36	0	0	3.31	-1	/2-1,3-1	0	-0.1
Total 2	17	49	7	9	1	1	0	3	6	5	1	0	.184	.273	.245	.518	37	-4	4	2.40	-2	/2-15,3-1	0	-0.5
• MULLIGAN, Eddie	Edward Joseph Mulligan b: 8/27/1894, St. Louis, MO d: 3/15/1982, San Rafael, CA BR/TR, 5'9", 152 lbs. Deb: 9/23/1915																							
1915 Chi-N	11	22	5	8	1	0	0	2	5	1	2	2	.364	.481	.409	.891	170	2	5	6.78	-2	S-10/3-1	2	0.1
1916 Chi-N	58	189	13	29	3	4	0	9	8	30	1	....	.153	.200	.212	.412	24	-17	9	1.41	-5	S-58	1	-2.1
1921 Chi-A	151	609	82	153	21	12	1	45	32	53	13	18	.251	.293	.330	.623	59	-43	57	2.96	-25	*3-151/S-1	3	-5.4
1922 Chi-A	103	372	39	87	14	8	0	31	22	32	7	7	.234	.278	.315	.593	54	-27	33	2.73	4	3-84/S-7	4	-1.6
1928 Pit-N	27	43	4	10	2	0	0	1	3	4	0	....	.233	.283	.279	.562	45	-3	4	2.48	0	/3-6,2-4	0	-0.3
Total 5	350	1235	143	287	41	24	1	88	70	120	23	27	.232	.278	.307	.585	54	-88	107	2.69	-27	3-242/S-76,2-4	10	-9.2
• MULLIGAN, John	John Mulligan b: Philadelphia, PA Deb: 6/14/1884																							
1884 Was-U	1	4	2	1	0	0	0	....	0	....	....	....	.250	.250	.250	.500	72	-0	0	2.39	1	/3-1	0	0.1
• MULLIGAN, Sean	Sean Patrick Mulligan b: 4/25/1970, Lynwood, CA BR/TR, 6'2", 205 lbs. Deb: 9/1/1996																							
1996 SD-N	2	1	0	0	0	0	0	0	0	0	0	0	.000	.000	.000	.000	-106	-0	0	.00	0	....	0	0.0
• MULLIN, Henry	Henry J. Mullin b: 4/1862, St. John, Canada d: 11/8/1937, Beverly, MA BR, 5'9", 160 lbs. Deb: 6/4/1884																							
1884 Was-a	34	120	13	17	3	1	0	0	8	....	....	....	.142	.195	.183	.379	27	-8	4	1.18	-1	O-34(4-29-1)/3-1	0	-0.9
Bos-U	2	8	1	0	0	0	0	....	0	....	....	....	.000	.000	.000	.000	-102	-2	0	.00	2	/O-2(0-2-0)	0	0.1
• MULLIN, Jim	James Henry Mullin b: 10/16/1883, New York, NY d: 1/24/1925, Philadelphia, PA BR/TR, 5'10", 173 lbs. Deb: 6/1/1904																							
1904 Phi-A	22	52	5	14	1	0	1	5	3	....	2	....	.269	.321	.346	.668	106	1	7	4.56	-1	/1-7,2-5,S-2,O-1	2	0.0
Was-A	27	102	10	19	2	2	0	4	4	....	3	....	.186	.224	.245	.469	49	-6	7	2.07	2	2-27	1	-0.4
Phi-A	19	58	4	10	0	0	0	4	2	....	2	....	.172	.238	.172	.411	29	-4	3	1.69	0	1-19	0	-0.6
Yr.	68	212	19	43	3	2	1	13	9	....	7	....	203	.252	.250	.502	58	-10	17	2.52	1	2-32,1-26/S-2,O-1	3	-1.0
1905 Was-A	50	163	18	31	7	6	0	13	5	....	5	....	.190	.214	.307	.521	67	-7	13	2.42	-3	2-40/1-6	1	-1.1
Total 2	118	375	37	74	10	8	1	26	14	....	12	....	.197	.236	.275	.511	62	-17	29	2.47	-3	/2-72,1-32,S-2,O-1	4	-2.1
• MULLIN, Pat	Patrick Joseph Mullin b: 11/1/1917, Trotter, PA d: 8/14/1999, Brownsville, PA BL/TR, 6'2", 190 lbs. Deb: 9/18/1940 C Career OF: 228-87-335																							
1940 Det-A	4	4	0	0	0	0	0	0	0	0	0	0	.000	.000	.000	.000	-91	-1	0	.00	0	/O-1	0	-0.1
1941 Det-A	54	220	42	76	11	5	5	23	18	18	5	1	.345	.400	.509	.909	126	9	48	8.67	-4	O-51(0-51-0)	9	0.4
1946 Det-A	93	276	34	68	13	4	3	35	25	36	3	5	.246	.311	.355	.666	81	-9	31	3.76	-1	O-75(0-1-75)	6	-1.2
1947 Det-A★	116	398	62	102	28	6	15	62	63	66	3	8	.256	.359	.470	.829	126	11	69	5.93	6	*O-106(0-0-106)	15	1.4
1948 Det-A★	138	496	91	143	16	11	23	80	77	57	1	2	.288	.385	.504	.889	132	22	103	7.73	-3	*O-131(0-10-123)	22	1.5
1949 Det-A	104	310	55	83	8	6	12	59	42	29	1	2	.268	.357	.448	.805	112	4	52	5.91	1	O-79(61-18-3)	11	0.1
1950 Det-A	69	142	16	31	5	0	6	23	20	23	1	4	.218	.315	.380	.695	75	-7	18	4.13	2	O-32(21-0-13)	3	-0.6
1951 Det-A	110	295	41	83	11	6	12	51	40	38	2	2	.281	.367	.481	.849	127	11	55	6.85	-3	O-83(76-4-6)	11	0.3
1952 Det-A	97	255	29	64	13	5	7	35	31	30	4	2	.251	.332	.424	.756	108	3	36	4.69	3	O-65(60-2-5)	6	0.1
1953 Det-A	79	97	11	26	1	0	4	17	14	15	0	1	.268	.360	.402	.762	107	1	14	5.09	0	O-14(10-0-4)	3	0.0
Total 10	864	2493	381	676	106	43	87	385	330	312	20	27	.271	.358	.453	.811	115	43	426	6.05	1	O-637	86	1.8
• MULLINIKS, Rance	Steven Rance Mulliniks b: 1/15/1956, Tulare, CA BL/TR, 5'11", 170 lbs. Deb: 6/18/1977																							
1977 Cal-A	78	271	36	73	13	2	3	21	23	36	1	1	.269	.329	.365	.694	93	-3	34	4.38	1	S-77	9	0.7
1978 Cal-A	50	119	6	22	3	1	1	6	8	23	2	0	.185	.242	.252	.494	41	-9	7	1.96	0	S-47/D-2	1	-0.5
1979 Cal-A	22	68	7	10	0	0	1	8	4	14	0	0	.147	.205	.191	.397	8	-9	3	1.17	0	S-22	1	-0.7
1980 KC-A	36	54	8	14	3	0	0	6	7	10	0	0	.259	.344	.315	.659	81	-1	6	3.72	1	S-18,2-14	1	0.1
1981 KC-A	24	44	6	10	3	0	0	5	2	7	0	1	.227	.261	.295	.556	61	-3	3	1.93	-2	2-10/S-7,3-5	1	-0.4
1982 Tor-A	112	311	32	76	25	0	4	35	37	49	3	2	.244	.327	.363	.690	82	-7	36	3.92	-9	*3-102,S-16	6	-1.7
1983 Tor-A	129	364	54	100	34	3	10	49	57	43	0	2	.275	.374	.467	.841	122	12	62	5.87	-9	*3-116,S-15/2-2	14	0.3
1984 Tor-A	125	343	41	111	21	5	3	42	33	44	2	3	.324	.385	.440	.825	123	11	58	6.50	-1	*3-119/S-3,2-1	13	1.0
1985*Tor-A	129	366	55	108	26	1	10	57	55	54	2	0	.295	.387	.454	.841	126	16	66	6.49	-3	*3-119	15	1.1
1986 Tor-A	117	348	50	90	22	0	11	45	43	60	1	1	.259	.342	.417	.759	103	2	48	4.78	4	*3-110/D-5,2-1	10	0.4
1987 Tor-A	124	332	37	103	28	1	11	44	34	55	1	1	.310	.374	.500	.874	127	12	60	6.63	0	3-96,D-22/S-1	12	1.1
1988 Tor-A	119	337	49	101	21	1	12	48	56	57	1	0	.300	.399	.475	.874	143	22	65	7.00	0	*D-108/3-7	12	1.9
1989*Tor-A	103	273	25	65	11	2	3	29	34	40	0	0	.238	.322	.326	.648	88	-4	27	3.33	4	D-73,3-29	3	-0.2
1990 Tor-A	57	97	11	28	4	0	2	16	22	19	2	1	.289	.420	.392	.812	121	4	18	6.48	0	3-22,D-10/1-3	4	0.4
1991*Tor-A	97	240	27	60	12	1	2	24	44	44	0	0	.250	.366	.333	.700	92	-1	31	4.32	0	D-81/3-5	6	-0.3
1992 Tor-A	3	2	1	1	0	0	0	0	1	0	0	0	.500	.667	.500	1.167	221	1	1	22.68	0	/D-2	0	0.0
Total 16	1325	3569	445	972	226	17	73	435	460	555	15	12	.272	.357	.407	.763	107	44	526	5.13	-14	3-730,D-303,S-206/2-28,1-3	108	3.3
• MULLINS, Fran	Francis Joseph Mullins b: 5/14/1957, Oakland, CA BR/TR, 6', 180 lbs. Deb: 9/1/1980																							
1980 Chi-A	21	62	9	12	4	0	0	3	9	8	0	1	.194	.296	.258	.554	53	-4	4	2.19	1	3-21	0	-0.3
1984 SF-N	57	110	8	24	8	0	2	10	9	29	3	1	.218	.277	.345	.623	76	-4	10	3.04	1	3-28,S-28/2-4	2	-0.1
1986 Cle-A	28	40	3	7	4	0	0	5	2	11	0	0	.175	.214	.275	.489	33	-4	3	1.98	0	2-13,S-11/1-1,D-1	0	-0.2
Total 3	106	212	20	43	16	0	2	18	20	48	3	2	.203	.272	.307	.578	61	-12	17	2.58	3	/3-49,S-39,2-17,1-1,D-1	2	-0.6
• MULVEY, Joe	Joseph H. Mulvey b: 10/27/1858, Providence, RI d: 8/21/1928, Philadelphia, PA BR/TR, 5'11.5", 178 lbs. Deb: 5/31/1883 U																							
1883 Pro-N	4	16	1	2	1	0	0	2	0	1	....	....	.125	.125	.188	.313	-7	-2	0	.76	-1	/S-4	0	-0.3
Phi-N	3	12	2	6	1	0	0	3	0	1	....	....	.500	.500	.583	1.083	250	2	4	16.44	-1	/3-3	1	0.1
Yr.	7	28	3	8	2	0	0	5	0	2	....	....	.286	.286	.357	.643	103	0	4	5.46	-2	/S-4,3-3	1	-0.2
1884 Phi-N	100	401	47	92	11	2	2	32	4	49	....	....	.229	.237	.282	.519	65	-15	27	2.44	12	*3-100	7	-0.1

Total Baseball

YEAR TM-L	G	AB	R	H	2B	3B	HR	RBI	BB	SO	SB	CS	AVG	OBP	SLG	OPS	OPS+	BR/A	RC	RC/G	FR	G/POS	WS	TPW
1885 Phi-N	107	443	74	119	25	6	6	64	3	18	....	....	.269	.274	.393	.666	116	6	49	4.07	0	*3-107	15	0.8
1886 Phi-N	107	430	71	115	16	10	2	53	15	31	27	....	.267	.292	.365	.657	98	-2	55	4.72	-15	*3-107/0-1	14	-1.3
1887 Phi-N	111	495	93	157	21	6	2	78	21	14	43	....	.317	.321	.369	.690	86	-10	72	5.63	-11	*3-111	14	-1.6
1888 Phi-N	100	398	37	86	12	3	0	39	9	33	18	....	.216	.235	.261	.497	55	-21	29	2.55	-13	*3-100	4	-3.2
1889 Phi-N	129	544	77	157	21	9	6	77	23	25	23	....	.289	.319	.393	.712	91	-11	77	5.30	2	*3-129	15	-0.5
1890 Phi-P	120	519	96	149	26	16	5	87	27	36	20	....	.287	.326	.428	.754	98	-6	81	5.90	-13	*3-120	12	-1.3
1891 Phi-a	113	453	62	115	9	13	5	66	17	32	11	....	.254	.287	.364	.651	84	-14	52	4.06	3	*3-113	11	-0.8
1892 Phi-N	25	98	9	14	1	1	0	4	6	9	2	....	.143	.200	.173	.373	13	-10	4	1.25	3	3-25	1	-0.6
1893 Was-N	55	226	21	53	9	4	0	19	7	8	2	....	.235	.264	.310	.574	54	-16	19	2.98	-1	3-55	1	-1.3
1895 Bro-N	13	49	8	15	4	1	0	8	2	0	1	....	.306	.333	.429	.762	104	0	8	5.88	2	3-13	2	0.2
Total 12	987	4084	598	1080	157	71	28	532	134	257	147	....	.264	.287	.355	.642	84	-101	478	4.26	-32	3-983/S-4,0-1	97	-9.9

• **MUMPHREY, Jerry** Jerry Wayne Mumphrey b: 9/9/1952, Tyler, TX BB/TR, 6'2", 185 lbs. Deb: 9/10/1974 Career OF: 317-935-212

YEAR TM-L	G	AB	R	H	2B	3B	HR	RBI	BB	SO	SB	CS	AVG	OBP	SLG	OPS	OPS+	BR/A	RC	RC/G	FR	G/POS	WS	TPW
1974 StL-N	5	2	2	0	0	0	0	0	0	0	0	0	.000	.000	.000	.000	-101	-1	0	.00	0	/0-1	0	-0.1
1975 StL-N	11	16	2	6	2	0	0	1	4	3	0	0	.375	.500	.500	1.000	172	2	5	12.20	0	/0-3(0-0-3)	1	0.2
1976 StL-N	112	384	51	99	15	5	1	26	37	53	22	6	.258	.325	.331	.655	85	-5	46	4.13	4	0-94(15-77-12)	10	-0.4
1977 StL-N	145	463	73	133	20	10	2	38	47	70	22	15	.287	.354	.387	.741	100	-1	64	4.93	-2	*0-133(49-67-34)	16	-0.7
1978 StL-N	125	367	41	96	13	4	2	37	30	40	14	10	.262	.319	.335	.654	84	-9	37	3.41	3	*0-116(48-30-48)	7	-1.1
1979 StL-N	124	339	53	100	10	3	3	32	26	39	8	11	.295	.345	.369	.714	94	-6	41	4.15	-2	*0-114(83-19-20)	7	-1.2
1980 SD-N	160	564	61	168	24	3	4	59	49	90	52	5	.298	.354	.372	.726	109	17	79	4.99	4	*0-153(0-153-0)	19	1.9
1981*NY-A	80	319	44	98	11	5	6	32	24	27	14	9	.307	.356	.429	.785	127	10	47	5.16	2	0-79(0-79-0)	12	1.1
1982 NY-A	123	477	76	143	24	10	9	68	50	66	11	3	.300	.366	.449	.815	124	18	76	5.72	-1	*0-123(0-123-0)	17	1.5
1983 NY-A	83	267	41	70	11	4	7	36	28	33	2	3	.262	.332	.412	.744	107	2	34	4.18	3	0-83(0-83-0)	8	0.4
Hou-N	44	143	17	48	10	2	1	17	22	23	5	0	.336	.428	.455	.882	154	13	31	8.55	1	0-43(0-43-0)	9	1.3
1984 Hou-N★	151	524	66	152	20	3	9	83	56	79	15	7	.290	.359	.391	.750	119	14	74	5.02	0	*0-137(0-137-0)	19	0.9
1985 Hou-N	130	444	52	123	25	2	8	61	37	57	6	7	.277	.333	.396	.729	106	1	56	4.41	-1	*0-126(0-58-68)	14	-0.5
1986 Chi-N	111	309	37	94	11	2	5	32	26	45	2	3	.304	.358	.401	.760	101	-0	45	5.36	-2	0-92(39-65-21)	8	-0.5
1987 Chi-N	118	309	41	103	19	2	13	44	35	47	1	1	.333	.401	.534	.935	140	18	66	8.38	-2	0-85(78-1-6)	13	1.2
1988 Chi-N	63	66	3	9	2	0	0	9	7	16	0	0	.136	.219	.167	.386	12	-8	2	.99	0	/0-4(4-0-0)	0	-0.8
Total 15	1585	4993	660	1442	217	55	70	575	478	688	174	80	.289	.351	.396	.748	109	64	702	4.97	5	*0-1386	160	3.5

• **MUNCE, John** John Lewis "Big John" Munce b: 11/18/1857, Philadelphia, PA d: 3/15/1917, Philadelphia, PA, 5'8.5", 160 lbs. Deb: 8/19/1884

1884 Wil-U	7	21	1	4	0	0	0	....	1	....	....	....	.190	.227	.190	.418	41	-1	1	1.53	0	/0-7(0-2-6)	0	-0.1

• **MUNCH, Jake** Jacob Ferdinand Munch b: 11/16/1890, Morton, PA d: 6/8/1966, Lansdowne, PA BL/TL, 6'2.5", 170 lbs. Deb: 5/27/1918

1918 Phi-A	22	30	3	8	0	1	0	0	0	5	0	....	.267	.267	.333	.600	80	-1	2	2.86	-1	/0-3(0-1-2),1-2	0	-0.2

• **MUNDINGER, George** George Mundinger b: 11/20/1854, New Orleans, LA d: 10/12/1910, Covington, KY BR/TR, 6'2", 200 lbs. Deb: 5/9/1884

1884 Ind-a	3	8	1	2	0	0	0	3	0	....	....	....	.250	.250	.250	.500	65	-0	1	2.35	-1	/C-3	0	-0.1

• **MUNDY, Bill** William Edward Mundy b: 6/28/1889, Salineville, OH d: 9/23/1958, Kalamazoo, MI BL/TL, 5'10", 154 lbs. Deb: 8/17/1913

1913 Bos-A	16	47	4	12	0	0	0	4	4	12	0	....	.255	.314	.255	.569	65	-2	4	2.72	-3	1-14	0	-0.5

• **MUNN, Horatio** Horatio Brinsmade Munn b: 7/26/1851, Newark, NJ d: 2/17/1910, Brooklyn, NY Deb: 9/6/1875

1875 Atl-n	1	4	0	0	0	0	0	0	0	0	0	0	.000	.000	.000	.000	-115	-1	0	.00	0	/2-1	....	-0.1

• **MUNOZ, Jose** Jose Luis Munoz b: 11/11/1967, Chicago, IL BB/TR, 5'11", 165 lbs. Deb: 4/7/1996

1996 Chi-A	17	27	7	7	0	0	0	1	4	1	0	0	.259	.355	.259	.614	62	-1	2	2.86	-3	/2-7,D-2,S-2,3-1,0-1	0	-0.4

• **MUNOZ, Noe** Noe Munoz b: 11/11/1967, Escatepec, Mexico BR/TR, 6'2", 180 lbs. Deb: 4/30/1995

1995 LA-N	2	1	0	0	0	0	0	0	0	0	0	0	.000	.000	.000	.000	-110	-0	0	.00	0	/C-2	0	0.0

• **MUNOZ, Pedro** Pedro Javier (Gonzalez) Munoz b: 9/19/1968, Ponce, Puerto Rico BR/TR, 5'11", 207 lbs. Deb: 9/1/1990 Career OF: 127-0-273

YEAR TM-L	G	AB	R	H	2B	3B	HR	RBI	BB	SO	SB	CS	AVG	OBP	SLG	OPS	OPS+	BR/A	RC	RC/G	FR	G/POS	WS	TPW
1990 Min-A	22	85	13	23	4	1	0	5	2	16	3	0	.271	.287	.341	.629	70	-3	8	3.17	0	0-21(3-0-19)/D-1	1	-0.4
1991 Min-A	51	138	15	39	7	1	7	26	9	31	3	0	.283	.331	.500	.831	121	4	23	6.04	2	0-44(10-0-39)/D-2	6	0.4
1992 Min-A	127	418	44	113	16	3	12	71	17	90	4	5	.270	.300	.409	.710	94	-7	44	3.59	4	*0-122(7-0-117)/D-3	11	-0.6
1993 Min-A	104	326	34	76	11	1	13	38	25	97	1	2	.233	.294	.393	.686	82	-10	36	3.78	-1	*0-102(64-0-41)	5	-1.4
1994 Min-A	75	244	35	72	15	2	11	36	19	67	0	0	.295	.351	.508	.859	118	6	44	6.60	-3	0-58(42-0-19),D-12	7	0.0
1995 Min-A	104	376	45	113	17	0	18	58	19	86	0	3	.301	.339	.508	.829	112	3	56	5.39	-1	D-77,0-25(1-0-24)/1-3	7	-0.3
1996 Oak-A	34	121	17	31	5	0	6	18	9	31	0	0	.273	.308	.446	.754	90	-2	16	4.81	0	D-18,0-14(0-0-14)	3	-0.4
Total 7	517	1708	203	467	75	8	67	252	100	418	11	10	.273	.317	.444	.762	100	-9	228	4.68	0	0-386,D-113/1-3	40	-2.7

• **MUNSON, Eric** Eric Walter Munson b: 10/3/1977, San Diego, CA BL/TR, 6'3", 220 lbs. Deb: 7/18/2000

YEAR TM-L	G	AB	R	H	2B	3B	HR	RBI	BB	SO	SB	CS	AVG	OBP	SLG	OPS	OPS+	BR/A	RC	RC/G	FR	G/POS	WS	TPW
2000 Det-A	3	5	0	0	0	0	0	0	0	1	0	0	.000	.000	.000	.000	-103	-2	-1	.00	-1	/1-3	0	-0.2
2001 Det-A	17	66	4	10	3	1	1	6	3	21	0	1	.152	.188	.273	.461	20	-8	3	1.25	1	1-17	0	-0.9
2002 Det-A	18	59	3	11	0	0	2	5	6	11	0	0	.186	.273	.288	.561	52	-4	5	2.65	0	D-14/1-4	0	-0.5
2003 Det-A	99	313	28	75	9	0	18	50	35	61	3	0	.240	.318	.441	.759	105	3	46	4.95	-16	3-91/D-2	7	-1.2
Total 4	137	443	35	96	12	1	21	62	44	94	3	1	.217	.290	.391	.681	84	-11	53	3.96	-16	/3-91,1-24,D-16	7	-2.8

• **MUNSON, Joe** Joseph Martin Napoleon Munson b: 11/6/1899, Renovo, PA d: 2/24/1991, Drexel Hill, PA BL/TR, 5'9", 184 lbs. Deb: 9/18/1925 Career OF: 16-0-21

1925 Chi-N	9	35	5	13	3	1	0	3	3	1	1	1	.371	.436	.514	.950	140	2	8	8.51	0	/0-9(0-0-9)	2	0.1
1926 Chi-N	33	101	17	26	2	2	3	15	8	4	0	0	.257	.318	.406	.724	93	-1	13	4.15	-2	0-28(16-0-12)	2	-0.5
Total 2	42	136	22	39	5	3	3	18	11	5	1	1	.287	.349	.434	.783	105	1	21	5.15	-1	/0-37	4	-0.3

• **MUNSON, Red** Clarence Hanford Munson b: 7/31/1883, Cincinnati, OH d: 2/19/1957, Mishawaka, IN TR Deb: 8/28/1905

1905 Phi-N	9	26	1	3	1	0	0	2	0	....	0	....	.115	.115	.154	.269	-21	-4	1	.58	-2	/C-8	0	-0.5

• **MUNSON, Thurman** Thurman Lee "Tugboat, Squatty Body, The Wall" Munson
b: 6/7/1947, Akron, OH d: 8/2/1979, Canton, OH BR/TR, 5'11", 191 lbs. Deb: 8/8/1969 Career OF: 3-0-24

YEAR TM-L	G	AB	R	H	2B	3B	HR	RBI	BB	SO	SB	CS	AVG	OBP	SLG	OPS	OPS+	BR/A	RC	RC/G	FR	G/POS	WS	TPW
1969 NY-A	26	86	6	22	1	2	1	9	10	10	0	1	.256	.333	.349	.682	94	-1	9	3.35	0	C-25	2	0.1
1970 NY-A	132	453	59	137	25	4	6	53	57	56	5	7	.302	.389	.415	.804	128	18	72	5.67	6	*C-125	26	3.1
1971 NY-A★	125	451	71	113	15	4	10	42	52	65	6	5	.251	.337	.368	.705	106	4	57	4.28	3	*C-117/0-1	18	1.3
1972 NY-A	140	511	54	143	16	3	7	46	47	58	6	7	.280	.344	.364	.708	114	8	62	4.26	0	*C-132	19	1.7
1973 NY-A★	147	519	80	156	29	4	20	74	48	64	4	6	.301	.364	.487	.852	143	27	89	6.23	3	*C-142/D-1	25	3.8
1974 NY-A★	144	517	64	135	19	2	13	60	44	66	2	0	.261	.320	.381	.701	104	3	61	4.10	3	*C-137/D-4	17	1.3
1975 NY-A★	157	597	83	190	24	3	12	102	45	52	3	2	.318	.372	.429	.801	129	23	90	5.46	9	*C-130,D-22/1-2,0-2(1-0-1),3	23	3.7
1976*NY-A★	152	616	79	186	27	1	17	105	29	38	14	11	.302	.343	.432	.774	127	17	85	4.88	0	*C-121,D-21,0-11(2-0-9)	24	2.3
1977*NY-A★	149	595	85	183	28	5	18	100	39	55	5	6	.308	.352	.462	.814	121	15	90	5.55	-4	*C-136,D-10	22	1.7
1978*NY-A★	154	617	73	183	27	1	6	71	35	70	2	3	.297	.332	.373	.710	102	0	73	4.20	-3	*C-125,D-14,0-13(0-0-13)	19	0.2
1979 NY-A	97	382	42	110	18	3	3	42	32	37	1	2	.288	.343	.374	.717	95	-3	46	4.22	-1	C-88/D-5,1-3	11	0.0
Total 11	1423	5344	696	1558	229	32	113	701	438	571	48	50	.292	.350	.410	.760	117	110	735	4.87	15	*C-1278/D-77,0-27,1-5,3-1	206	19.2

• **MUNYAN, John** John B. Munyan b: 11/14/1860, Chester, PA d: 2/18/1945, Endicott, NY Deb: 7/12/1887 Career OF: 14-5-14

1887 Cle-a	16	61	9	17	1	1	0	6	3	....	....	4	.279	.279	.293	.572	61	-3	6	3.68	-1	0-12(3-3-6)/C-3,3-2	1	-0.4
1890 Col-a	2	7	1	1	0	0	0	0	0	....	....	0	.143	.250	.143	.393	17	-1	0	1.13	0	/0-2(0-2-0)	0	-0.1
StL-a	96	342	61	91	15	7	4	42	32	....	11	....	.266	.341	.386	.727	100	-2	50	5.28	-1	C-83/0-7(7-0-0),2-5,3-3,S	11	0.2
Yr.	98	349	62	92	15	7	4	42	32	....	11	....	.264	.339	.381	.720	98	-3	50	5.18	-1	C-83/0-9(7-2-0),2-5,3-3,S	11	0.2
1891 StL-a	62	182	44	42	4	3	0	20	43	39	13	....	.231	.389	.286	.674	81	-3	26	4.90	-5	C-45,0-12(4-0-8)/S-5,3-3	6	-0.5
Total 3	176	592	115	151	20	11	4	68	78	39	28	....	.255	.351	.343	.693	89	-9	82	4.94	-8	C-131/0-33,3-8-S,6-2-5	18	-0.6

• **MURCER, Bobby** Bobby Ray Murcer b: 5/20/1946, Oklahoma City, OK BL/TR, 5'11", 180 lbs. Deb: 9/8/1965 Career OF: 56-789-839

1965 NY-A	11	37	2	9	0	1	1	4	5	12	0	0	.243	.333	.378	.712	102	0	5	4.92	5	S-11	2	0.7

YEAR TM-L	G	AB	R	H	2B	3B	HR	RBI	BB	SO	SB	CS	AVG	OBP	SLG	OPS	OPS+	BR/A	RC	RC/G	FR	G/POS	WS	TPW
1966 NY-A	21	69	3	12	1	1	0	5	4	5	2	2	.174	.219	.217	.437	27	-7	3	1.50	-5	S-18	0	-1.2
1969 NY-A	152	564	82	146	24	4	26	82	50	103	7	5	.259	.323	.454	.776	119	11	82	5.07	-5	*0-118(0-27-99),3-31	20	0.0
1970 NY-A	159	581	95	146	23	3	23	78	87	100	15	10	.251	.351	.420	.771	118	14	89	5.22	4	*0-155(0-155-0)	27	1.5
1971 NY-A★	146	529	94	175	25	6	25	94	91	60	14	8	.331	**.429**	.543	**.972**	**185**	**62**	126	**9.10**	-5	*0-143(0-143-0)	**38**	**5.7**
1972 NY-A★	153	585	**102**	171	30	7	33	96	63	67	11	9	.292	.363	.537	.900	171	48	114	7.10	0	*0-151(0-151-0)	36	4.9
1973 NY-A★	160	616	83	187	29	2	22	95	50	67	6	7	.304	.359	.464	.823	135	25	100	6.00	1	*0-160(0-160-0)	25	2.2
1974 NY-A★	156	606	69	166	25	4	10	88	57	59	14	5	.274	.338	.378	.716	109	8	79	4.53	6	*0-156(0-59-101)	20	0.9
1975 SF-N★	147	526	80	157	29	4	11	91	91	45	9	5	.298	.404	.432	.835	126	23	97	6.56	-7	*0-144(0-2-143)	21	1.0
1976 SF-N	147	533	73	138	20	2	23	90	84	78	12	7	.259	.364	.433	.797	122	17	86	5.61	-1	*0-146(0-0-146)	21	0.9
1977 Chi-N	154	554	90	147	18	3	27	89	80	77	16	7	.265	.361	.455	.816	105	6	95	5.95	1	*0-150(0-0-150)/2-1,S-1	19	0.0
1978 Chi-N	146	499	66	140	22	6	9	64	80	57	14	5	.281	.380	.403	.783	106	8	79	5.60	-7	*0-138(0-33-121)	18	-0.5
1979 Chi-N	58	190	22	49	4	1	7	22	36	20	2	3	.258	.379	.400	.779	103	2	31	5.46	2	0-54(0-0-54)	7	0.1
NY-A	74	264	42	72	12	0	8	33	25	32	1	1	.273	.340	.409	.749	103	1	35	4.57	1	0-70(12-59-7)	8	0.1
1980*NY-A	100	297	41	80	9	1	13	57	34	28	2	0	.269	.348	.438	.786	116	7	45	5.14	-1	0-59(44-0-18),D-33	9	0.3
1981*NY-A	50	117	14	31	6	0	6	24	12	15	0	0	.265	.333	.470	.803	131	4	18	5.39	0	D-33	4	0.4
1982 NY-A	65	141	12	32	6	0	7	30	12	15	2	1	.227	.292	.418	.711	94	-2	16	3.82	0	D-47	2	-0.2
1983 NY-A	9	22	2	4	2	0	1	1	1	1	0	0	.182	.217	.409	.626	71	-1	1	1.04	0	/D-5	0	-0.1
Total 17	1908	6730	972	1862	285	45	252	1043	862	841	127	75	.277	.361	.445	.806	125	228	1103	5.76	-12	*0-1644,D-118/3-31,S-30,2-1	277	16.6

• MURCH, Simmy — Simeon Augustus Murch b: 11/21/1880, Castine, ME d: 6/6/1939, Exeter, NH BR/TR, 6'2", 220 lbs. Deb: 9/20/1904

YEAR TM-L	G	AB	R	H	2B	3B	HR	RBI	BB	SO	SB	CS	AVG	OBP	SLG	OPS	OPS+	BR/A	RC	RC/G	FR	G/POS	WS	TPW
1904 StL-N	13	51	3	7	1	0	0	1	1	....	0	....	.137	.154	.157	.311	-4	-6	1	.75	1	/2-6,3-6,S-1	1	-0.6
1905 StL-N	4	9	0	1	0	0	0	0	0	....	0	....	.111	.111	.111	.222	-35	-1	0	.51	-2	/2-2,S-1	0	-0.3
1908 Bro-N	6	11	1	2	1	0	0	0	1	....	0	....	.182	.250	.273	.523	70	-0	1	2.06	-1	/1-2	0	-0.1
Total 3	23	71	4	10	2	0	0	1	2	....	0	....	.141	.164	.169	.333	4	-8	2	.90	-2	/2-8,3-6,1-2,S-2	1	-1.0

• MURDOCH, Wilbur — Wilbur Edwin Murdoch b: 3/14/1875, Avon, NY d: 10/29/1941, Los Angeles, CA TR Deb: 8/29/1908

YEAR TM-L	G	AB	R	H	2B	3B	HR	RBI	BB	SO	SB	CS	AVG	OBP	SLG	OPS	OPS+	BR/A	RC	RC/G	FR	G/POS	WS	TPW
1908 StL-N	27	62	5	16	3	0	0	5	3	....	4	....	.258	.292	.306	.599	96	-0	7	3.62	-2	0-16(13-5-0)	2	-0.3

• MURNANE, Tim — Timothy Hayes Murnane
b: 6/4/1852, Naugatuck, CT d: 2/7/1917, Boston, MA BL/TR, 5'9.5", 172 lbs. Deb: 4/26/1872 M/U NA OF: 1-49-20 Career OF: 3-27-20

YEAR TM-L	G	AB	R	H	2B	3B	HR	RBI	BB	SO	SB	CS	AVG	OBP	SLG	OPS	OPS+	BR/A	RC	RC/G	FR	G/POS	WS	TPW
1872 Man-n	24	117	30	42	1	0	0	13	0	1	1	0	.359	.359	.368	.726	132	5	16	6.69	2	1-24	....	0.5
1873 Ath-n	41	176	53	39	3	0	1	10	8	13	7	2	.222	.255	.256	.511	49	-11	14	2.99	-2	0-30(0-24-6),1-10/2-6	....	-1.0
1874 Ath-n	21	82	11	17	2	0	0	11	1	3	0	1	.207	.217	.232	.449	40	-6	4	1.92	-3	0-14(0-1-13)/2-6,1-3	....	-0.7
1875 Phi-n	69	313	71	85	5	0	1	30	7	7	**30**	9	.272	.288	.297	.585	100	2	36	4.51	1	1-31,0-26(1-24-1),2-15	....	0.2
1876 Bos-N	69	316	60	87	4	3	2	34	8	12	....	....	.275	.301	.334	.635	109	3	32	4.02	-4	*1-65/0-3(2-1-0),2-1	10	-0.4
1877 Bos-N	35	140	23	39	7	1	1	15	6	7	....	....	.279	.308	.364	.673	107	1	16	4.39	-2	0-30(0-25-5)/1-5	4	-0.2
1878 Pro-N	49	188	35	45	6	1	0	14	8	12	....	....	.239	.270	.282	.552	82	-3	15	2.82	0	*1-48/0-1	4	-0.5
1884 Bos-U	76	311	55	73	5	2	0	....	22	....	....	....	.235	.285	.264	.549	88	-3	24	2.82	-4	1-63,0-16(1-0-15)	7	-1.1
Total 4 n	155	688	165	183	11	0	2	64	16	24	38	12	.266	.283	.291	.573	85	-11	70	4.09	-2	/0-70,1-68,2-27	....	-0.9
Total 4	229	955	173	244	22	7	3	63	44	31	....	....	.255	.291	.305	.596	96	-2	87	3.42	-10	1-181/0-50,2-1	25	-2.2

• MURPHY, — Murphy Deb: 8/16/1884

YEAR TM-L	G	AB	R	H	2B	3B	HR	RBI	BB	SO	SB	CS	AVG	OBP	SLG	OPS	OPS+	BR/A	RC	RC/G	FR	G/POS	WS	TPW
1884 Bos-U	1	3	0	0	0	0	0	....	1	....	....	....	.000	.250	.000	.250	-9	-0	0	.00	-1	/C-1,0-1	0	-0.1

• MURPHY, Billy — William Eugene Murphy b: 5/7/1944, Pineville, LA BR/TR, 6'1", 190 lbs. Deb: 4/15/1966

YEAR TM-L	G	AB	R	H	2B	3B	HR	RBI	BB	SO	SB	CS	AVG	OBP	SLG	OPS	OPS+	BR/A	RC	RC/G	FR	G/POS	WS	TPW
1966 NY-N	84	135	15	31	4	1	3	13	7	34	1	2	.230	.273	.341	.613	71	-6	12	2.82	2	0-57(8-48-1)	2	-0.5

• MURPHY, Buzz — Robert R. Murphy b: 4/26/1895, Denver, CO d: 5/11/1938, Denver, CO BL/TL, 5'8.5", 155 lbs. Deb: 7/14/1918 Career OF: 28-54-0

YEAR TM-L	G	AB	R	H	2B	3B	HR	RBI	BB	SO	SB	CS	AVG	OBP	SLG	OPS	OPS+	BR/A	RC	RC/G	FR	G/POS	WS	TPW
1918 Bos-N	9	32	6	12	2	3	1	9	3	5	0	....	.375	.429	.719	1.147	258	6	10	11.78	-2	/0-9(9-0-0)	3	0.4
1919 Was-A	79	252	19	66	7	4	0	28	19	32	5	....	.262	.326	.321	.648	83	-6	28	3.70	-2	0-73(19-54-0)	5	-1.2
Total 2	88	284	25	78	9	7	1	37	22	37	5	....	.275	.338	.366	.704	102	0	38	4.47	-4	/0-82	8	-0.8

• MURPHY, Clarence — Clarence Murphy Deb: 6/17/1886

YEAR TM-L	G	AB	R	H	2B	3B	HR	RBI	BB	SO	SB	CS	AVG	OBP	SLG	OPS	OPS+	BR/A	RC	RC/G	FR	G/POS	WS	TPW
1886 Lou-a	1	3	0	0	0	0	0	0	0	....	0	....	.000	.000	.000	.000	-95	-1	0	.00	0	/0-1	0	-0.1

• MURPHY, Connie — Cornelius David "Stone Face" Murphy b: 11/1/1870, Northfield, MA d: 12/14/1945, New Bedford, MA BL/TR, 5'8", 155 lbs. Deb: 9/17/1893

YEAR TM-L	G	AB	R	H	2B	3B	HR	RBI	BB	SO	SB	CS	AVG	OBP	SLG	OPS	OPS+	BR/A	RC	RC/G	FR	G/POS	WS	TPW
1893 Cin-N	6	17	3	3	1	0	0	2	1	2	0	....	.176	.222	.235	.458	21	-2	1	1.72	-1	/C-4	0	-0.2
1894 Cin-N	1	4	0	0	0	0	0	0	1	1	0	....	.000	.200	.000	.200	-46	-1	0	.00	-0	/C-1	0	-0.1
Total 2	7	21	3	3	1	0	0	2	2	3	0	....	.143	.217	.190	.408	6	-3	1	1.34	-1	/C-5	0	-0.3

• MURPHY, Dale — Dale Bryan Murphy b: 3/12/1956, Portland, OR BR/TR, 6'4", 215 lbs. Deb: 9/13/1976 Career OF: 101-1044-747

YEAR TM-L	G	AB	R	H	2B	3B	HR	RBI	BB	SO	SB	CS	AVG	OBP	SLG	OPS	OPS+	BR/A	RC	RC/G	FR	G/POS	WS	TPW
1976 Atl-N	19	65	3	17	6	0	0	9	7	9	0	0	.262	.333	.354	.687	89	-1	8	4.65	-1	C-19	2	-0.1
1977 Atl-N	18	76	5	24	8	1	2	14	0	8	0	1	.316	.316	.526	.842	108	0	11	5.08	-1	C-18	2	0.0
1978 Atl-N	151	530	66	120	14	3	23	79	42	145	11	7	.226	.287	.394	.681	80	-17	56	3.46	4	*1-129,C-21	7	-2.1
1979 Atl-N	104	384	53	106	7	2	21	57	38	67	6	1	.276	.344	.469	.813	111	7	60	5.51	-4	1-76,C-27	11	-0.1
1980 Atl-N★	156	569	98	160	27	2	33	89	59	133	9	6	.281	.350	.510	.859	133	23	101	6.38	0	*0-154(4-129-21)/1-1	28	2.1
1981 Atl-N	104	369	43	91	12	1	13	50	44	72	14	5	.247	.327	.390	.717	100	1	47	4.27	1	*0-103(0-102-1)/1-3	11	0.1
1982*Atl-N★	162	598	113	168	23	2	36	**109**	93	134	23	11	.281	.380	.507	.887	140	34	118	7.02	-6	*0-162(65-118-8)	32	2.5
1983 Atl-N★	162	589	131	178	24	4	36	**121**	90	110	30	4	.302	.396	**.540**	**.936**	146	43	131	**8.09**	1	*0-160(28-136-2)	32	4.3
1984 Atl-N★	162	607	94	176	32	8	**36**	100	79	134	19	7	.290	.374	**.547**	.920	145	37	123	7.33	-2	*0-160(0-160-0)	33	3.5
1985 Atl-N★	162	616	**118**	185	32	2	**37**	111	**90**	141	10	3	.300	.390	.539	.929	148	42	131	7.80	-8	*0-161(0-161-0)	31	3.3
1986 Atl-N★	160	614	89	163	29	7	29	83	75	141	7	7	.265	.347	.477	.825	119	13	102	5.86	-4	*0-159(0-155-6)	22	0.7
1987 Atl-N★	159	566	115	167	27	1	44	105	115	136	16	6	.295	.420	.580	1.000	154	49	143	9.14	8	*0-159(0-0-159)	29	4.8
1988 Atl-N	156	592	77	134	35	4	24	77	74	125	3	5	.226	.314	.421	.735	104	1	72	3.98	8	*0-156(0-0-156)	12	0.4
1989 Atl-N	154	574	60	131	16	0	20	84	65	142	3	2	.228	.309	.361	.670	88	-9	64	3.70	-2	*0-151(0-82-70)	14	-1.5
1990 Atl-N	97	349	38	81	14	0	17	55	41	84	9	2	.232	.315	.418	.733	94	-2	45	4.25	-2	0-97(0-0-97)	11	-0.7
Phi-N	57	214	22	57	9	1	7	28	20	46	0	1	.266	.329	.416	.745	104	0	26	4.13	0	0-55(1-1-53)	4	-0.1
Yr.	154	563	60	138	23	1	24	83	61	130	9	3	.245	.320	.417	.737	98	-2	71	4.21	-2	*0-152(1-1-150)	15	-0.9
1991 Phi-N	153	544	66	137	33	1	18	81	48	93	1	0	.252	.313	.415	.728	104	2	67	4.14	-4	*0-147(0-0-147)	13	-0.6
1992 Phi-N	18	62	5	10	1	0	2	7	1	13	0	0	.161	.175	.274	.449	25	-6	2	1.08	-1	0-16(1-0-16)	0	-0.8
1993 Col-N	26	42	1	6	1	0	0	7	5	15	0	0	.143	.234	.167	.401	8	-6	1	.70	1	0-13(2-0-11)	0	-0.5
Total 18	2180	7960	1197	2111	350	39	398	1266	986	1748	161	68	.265	.348	.469	.817	120	210	1307	5.70	-12	*0-1853,1-209/C-85	294	15.0

• MURPHY, Danny — Daniel Francis Murphy b: 8/11/1876, Philadelphia, PA d: 11/22/1955, Jersey City, NJ BR/TR, 5'9", 175 lbs. Deb: 9/17/1900 Career OF: 3-12-597

YEAR TM-L	G	AB	R	H	2B	3B	HR	RBI	BB	SO	SB	CS	AVG	OBP	SLG	OPS	OPS+	BR/A	RC	RC/G	FR	G/POS	WS	TPW
1900 NY-N	22	74	11	20	1	0	0	6	8	....	4	....	.270	.341	.284	.625	77	-2	9	4.28	-3	2-22	2	-0.3
1901 NY-N	5	20	0	4	0	0	0	0	1	....	0	....	.200	.238	.200	.438	29	-2	1	1.79	-2	/2-5	0	-0.3
1902 Phi-A	76	291	48	91	11	8	1	48	13	....	12	....	.313	.351	.416	.766	107	2	48	6.25	-16	2-76	9	-1.2
1903 Phi-A	133	513	66	140	31	11	1	60	13	....	17	....	.273	.295	.382	.677	97	-3	66	4.51	-13	*2-133	14	-1.6
1904 Phi-A	150	557	78	160	30	17	7	77	22	....	22	....	.287	.320	.440	.760	132	18	89	5.76	14	*2-150	26	3.7
1905*Phi-A	151	537	71	149	34	4	6	71	42	....	23	....	.277	.339	.389	.728	129	17	83	5.38	0	*2-151	23	2.1
1906 Phi-A	119	448	48	135	28	6	2	60	21	....	17	....	.301	.341	.404	.745	129	14	70	5.76	-10	*2-119	21	0.5
1907 Phi-A	124	469	51	127	23	3	2	57	30	....	11	....	.271	.317	.345	.663	109	4	58	4.32	15	*2-122	16	2.2
1908 Phi-A	142	525	51	139	28	7	4	66	32	....	16	....	.265	.309	.368	.677	112	6	65	4.11	11	0-84(2-12-70),2-56/1-2	18	1.5
1909 Phi-A	149	541	61	152	28	14	5	69	35	....	19	....	.281	.332	.412	.744	132	18	81	4.97	-4	*0-149(0-0-149)	23	0.7
1910*Phi-A	151	560	70	168	28	18	4	64	31	....	18	....	.300	.338	.436	.774	143	24	88	5.51	-4	*0-151(0-0-151)	24	1.5
1911*Phi-A	141	508	104	167	27	11	6	66	50	....	22	....	.329	.398	.461	.858	142	29	102	7.23	3	*0-136(0-0-136)/2-4	25	2.4
1912 Phi-A	36	130	27	42	6	2	2	20	16	....	8	....	.323	.401	.446	.848	148	8	26	7.46	-6	0-36(0-0-36)	6	0.1
1913 Phi-A	40	59	3	19	5	1	0	6	4	8	0	....	.322	.365	.441	.806	139	3	9	5.65	0	/0-9(0-0-9)	2	0.2
1914 Bro-F	52	161	16	49	9	0	4	32	17	16	4	....	.304	.374	.435	.809	129	6	28	5.78	0	0-46(1-0-45)	6	0.5

YEAR TM-L	G	AB	R	H	2B	3B	HR	RBI	BB	SO	SB	CS	AVG	OBP	SLG	OPS	OPS+	BR/A	RC	RC/G	FR	G/POS	WS	TPW
1915 Bro-F	5	6	0	1	0	0	0	0	0	0	0	....	.167	.167	.167	.333	-2	-1	0	.76	0	/2-1,0-1	0	-0.1
Total 16	1496	5399	705	1563	289	102	44	702	335	24	193	....	.289	.336	.405	.742	124	140	823	5.35	-14	2-839,0-612/1-2	215	11.7

• MURPHY, Danny Daniel Francis Murphy b: 8/23/1942, Beverly, MA BL/TR, 5'11", 185 lbs. Deb: 6/18/1960 Career OF: 2-17-15 ♦

YEAR TM-L	G	AB	R	H	2B	3B	HR	RBI	BB	SO	SB	CS	AVG	OBP	SLG	OPS	OPS+	BR/A	RC	RC/G	FR	G/POS	WS	TPW
1960 Chi-N	31	75	7	9	2	0	1	6	4	13	0	0	.120	.175	.187	.362	-1	-11	2	.92	0	0-21(0-16-5)	0	-1.1
1961 Chi-N	4	13	3	5	0	0	2	3	1	5	0	0	.385	.429	.846	1.275	225	2	5	16.29	0	/0-4(0-0-4)	1	0.2
1962 Chi-N	14	35	5	7	3	1	0	3	2	9	0	0	.200	.243	.343	.586	53	-2	3	2.94	0	/0-5(2-1-6)	0	-0.3
1969 Chi-A	17	1	0	0	0	0	0	0	2	0	0	0	.000	.667	.000	.667	95	1	0	9.36	0	P-17	5	0.8
1970 Chi-A	51	6	3	2	0	0	1	1	2	2	0	0	.333	.500	.833	1.333	252	2	2	11.18	-1	P-51	2	-1.3
Total 5	117	130	18	23	5	1	4	13	11	29	0	0	.177	.246	.323	.570	51	-8	13	3.07	-1	/P-68,0-30	8	-1.7

• MURPHY, Danny Daniel Joseph "Handsome Dan" Murphy b: 9/10/1864, Brooklyn, NY d: 12/14/1915, Brooklyn, NY, 156 lbs. Deb: 4/26/1892

YEAR TM-L	G	AB	R	H	2B	3B	HR	RBI	BB	SO	SB	CS	AVG	OBP	SLG	OPS	OPS+	BR/A	RC	RC/G	FR	G/POS	WS	TPW
1892 NY-N	8	26	2	3	0	0	0	0	5	4	0	....	.115	.258	.115	.373	14	-2	1	.93	-1	/C-8	0	-0.3

• MURPHY, Dave David Francis "Dirty Dave" Murphy b: 5/4/1876, Adams, MA d: 4/8/1940, Adams, MA TR Deb: 8/28/1905

YEAR TM-L	G	AB	R	H	2B	3B	HR	RBI	BB	SO	SB	CS	AVG	OBP	SLG	OPS	OPS+	BR/A	RC	RC/G	FR	G/POS	WS	TPW
1905 Bos-N	3	11	0	2	0	0	0	1	0	....	0	....	.182	.182	.182	.364	9	-1	0	1.21	-1	/S-2,3-1	0	-0.2

• MURPHY, Dick Richard Lee Murphy b: 10/25/1931, Cincinnati, OH BL/TL, 5'11", 170 lbs. Deb: 6/13/1954

YEAR TM-L	G	AB	R	H	2B	3B	HR	RBI	BB	SO	SB	CS	AVG	OBP	SLG	OPS	OPS+	BR/A	RC	RC/G	FR	G/POS	WS	TPW
1954 Cin-N	6	1	1	0	0	0	0	0	0	1	0	0	.000	.000	.000	.000	-97	-0	0	.00	0	....	0	0.0

• MURPHY, Dummy Herbert Courtland Murphy b: 12/18/1886, Olney, IL d: 8/10/1962, Tallahassee, FL BR/TR, 5'10", 165 lbs. Deb: 4/14/1914

YEAR TM-L	G	AB	R	H	2B	3B	HR	RBI	BB	SO	SB	CS	AVG	OBP	SLG	OPS	OPS+	BR/A	RC	RC/G	FR	G/POS	WS	TPW
1914 Phi-N	9	26	1	4	1	0	0	3	0	4	0	....	.154	.185	.192	.377	12	-3	1	1.06	-1	/S-9	0	-0.4

• MURPHY, Dwayne Dwayne Keith Murphy b: 3/18/1955, Merced, CA BL/TR, 6'1", 185 lbs. Deb: 4/8/1978 C Career OF: 57-1181-46

YEAR TM-L	G	AB	R	H	2B	3B	HR	RBI	BB	SO	SB	CS	AVG	OBP	SLG	OPS	OPS+	BR/A	RC	RC/G	FR	G/POS	WS	TPW
1978 Oak-A	60	52	15	10	2	0	0	5	7	14	0	1	.192	.288	.231	.519	50	-4	4	2.33	0	0-45(21-12-14)/D-5	1	-0.4
1979 Oak-A	121	388	57	99	10	4	11	40	84	80	15	11	.255	.389	.387	.776	116	12	62	5.15	-1	*0-118(2-115-3)	16	0.9
1980 Oak-A	159	573	86	157	18	2	13	68	102	96	26	15	.274	.386	.380	.766	119	20	90	5.19	8	*0-158(0-158-0)	27	2.5
1981*Oak-A	107	390	58	98	10	3	15	60	73	91	10	4	.251	.372	.408	.780	131	19	64	5.54	-1	*0-106(0-106-0)/D-1	20	1.7
1982 Oak-A	151	543	84	129	15	1	27	94	94	122	26	8	.238	.353	.418	.771	116	17	88	5.26	7	*0-147(0-147-0)/D-1,S-1	24	2.2
1983 Oak-A	130	471	55	107	17	2	17	75	62	105	7	5	.227	.317	.380	.697	97	-2	55	3.76	1	*0-124(0-124-0)/D-7	11	-0.3
1984 Oak-A	153	559	93	143	18	2	33	88	74	111	4	5	.256	.346	.472	.818	133	24	90	5.44	3	*0-153(0-153-0)	22	2.5
1985 Oak-A	152	523	77	122	21	3	20	59	84	123	4	5	.233	.343	.400	.742	111	8	73	4.59	-3	*0-150(0-150-0)	18	0.3
1986 Oak-A	98	329	50	83	11	3	9	39	56	80	3	1	.252	.368	.386	.754	114	9	51	5.29	7	0-97(0-97-0)/D-1	15	1.4
1987 Oak-A	82	219	39	51	7	0	8	35	58	61	4	4	.233	.394	.374	.768	113	7	36	5.28	-2	0-79(0-79-0)/1-1,2-1	8	0.4
1988 Det-A	49	144	14	36	5	0	4	19	24	26	1	1	.250	.361	.368	.729	109	2	21	5.17	1	0-43(4-35-10)/D-3	7	0.2
1989 Phi-N	98	156	20	34	5	0	9	27	29	44	0	1	.218	.341	.423	.764	117	4	24	5.12	-1	0-52(30-5-19)	4	0.2
Total 12	1360	4347	648	1069	139	20	166	609	747	953	100	61	.246	.359	.402	.761	116	116	659	5.00	18	*0-1272/D-18,1-1,2-1,S-1	173	11.6

• MURPHY, Ed Edward Joseph Murphy b: 8/23/1918, Joliet, IL d: 12/10/1991, Joliet, IL BR/TR, 5'11", 190 lbs. Deb: 9/10/1942

YEAR TM-L	G	AB	R	H	2B	3B	HR	RBI	BB	SO	SB	CS	AVG	OBP	SLG	OPS	OPS+	BR/A	RC	RC/G	FR	G/POS	WS	TPW
1942 Phi-N	13	28	2	7	2	0	0	4	2	4	0	....	.250	.300	.321	.621	86	-1	3	3.12	-1	/1-8	0	-0.2

• MURPHY, Eddie John Edward "Honest Eddie" Murphy
b: 10/2/1891, Hancock, NY d: 2/21/1969, Dunmore, PA BL/TR, 5'9", 155 lbs. Deb: 8/26/1912 Career OF: 10-0-558

YEAR TM-L	G	AB	R	H	2B	3B	HR	RBI	BB	SO	SB	CS	AVG	OBP	SLG	OPS	OPS+	BR/A	RC	RC/G	FR	G/POS	WS	TPW
1912 Phi-A	33	142	24	45	4	1	0	6	11	....	7	....	.317	.370	.359	.729	113	3	21	5.58	0	0-33(0-0-33)	5	0.1
1913*Phi-A	137	508	105	150	14	7	1	30	70	44	21	....	.295	.391	.356	.747	122	18	76	5.28	-14	*0-135(0-0-135)	22	-0.3
1914*Phi-A	148	573	101	156	12	9	3	43	87	46	36	32	.272	.379	.340	.720	121	13	77	4.42	-10	*0-148(0-0-148)	23	-0.5
1915 Phi-A	68	260	37	60	3	4	0	17	29	15	13	3	.231	.315	.273	.588	79	-5	25	3.28	-6	0-58(0-0-58)/3-6	5	-1.4
Chi-A	70	273	51	86	11	5	0	26	39	12	20	12	.315	.410	.392	.802	136	13	47	6.11	-1	0-70(3-0-67)	14	0.9
Yr.	138	533	88	146	14	9	0	43	68	27	33	15	.274	.365	.334	.698	109	8	72	4.69	-7	*0-128(3-0-125)/3-6	19	-0.5
1916 Chi-A	51	105	14	22	5	1	0	4	9	5	3	....	.210	.284	.276	.561	68	-4	9	2.83	-1	0-24(0-0-24)/3-1	1	-0.7
1917 Chi-A	53	51	9	16	2	1	0	16	5	1	4	....	.314	.386	.392	.778	135	2	9	6.21	-1	/0-9(1-0-8)	2	0.1
1918 Chi-A	91	286	36	85	9	3	0	23	22	18	6	....	.297	.350	.350	.699	110	3	37	4.40	-13	0-63(1-0-62)/2-8	8	-1.5
1919*Chi-A	30	35	8	17	4	0	0	5	7	0	0	....	.486	.571	.600	1.171	228	7	12	16.83	0	/0-6(2-0-4)	3	0.7
1920 Chi-A	58	118	22	40	2	1	0	19	12	4	1	3	.339	.405	.373	.777	107	1	18	5.64	2	0-19(0-0-19)/3-3	4	0.2
1921 Chi-A	6	5	1	1	0	0	0	0	0	0	0	0	.200	.200	.200	.400	2	-1	0	1.27	0	....	0	-0.1
1926 Pit-N	16	17	3	2	0	0	0	6	3	0	0	....	.118	.250	.118	.368	2	-2	1	1.20	0	/0-3(3-0-0)	0	-0.3
Total 11	761	2373	411	680	66	32	4	195	294	145	111	50	.287	.374	.346	.720	115	48	331	4.83	-44	0-568/3-10,2-8	87	-2.6

• MURPHY, Frank Francis Patrick Murphy b: 4/16/1875, North Tarrytown, NY d: 11/4/1912, Central Islip, NY BR Deb: 7/2/1901

YEAR TM-L	G	AB	R	H	2B	3B	HR	RBI	BB	SO	SB	CS	AVG	OBP	SLG	OPS	OPS+	BR/A	RC	RC/G	FR	G/POS	WS	TPW
1901 Bos-N	45	176	13	46	5	3	1	18	4	....	6	....	.261	.282	.341	.623	73	-7	19	3.85	4	0-45(45-0-0)	4	-0.5
NY-N	35	130	10	21	3	0	0	8	6	....	2	....	.162	.199	.185	.383	12	-14	5	1.30	-11	2-23,0-12(12-0-0)	0	-2.6
Yr.	80	306	23	67	8	3	1	26	10	....	8	....	.219	.246	.275	.521	47	-21	25	2.70	-7	0-57(57-0-0),2-23	4	-3.1

• MURPHY, Howard Howard Murphy b: 1/1/1882, Birmingham, AL d: 10/5/1926, Fort Worth, TX BL/TR, 5'8.5", 150 lbs. Deb: 8/4/1909

YEAR TM-L	G	AB	R	H	2B	3B	HR	RBI	BB	SO	SB	CS	AVG	OBP	SLG	OPS	OPS+	BR/A	RC	RC/G	FR	G/POS	WS	TPW
1909 StL-N	25	60	3	12	0	0	0	3	4	....	1	....	.200	.250	.200	.450	42	-4	3	1.75	-3	0-19(0-19-0)	0	-0.8

• MURPHY, John John Henry Murphy, 5'11", 165 lbs. Deb: 4/17/1884 ♦

YEAR TM-L	G	AB	R	H	2B	3B	HR	RBI	BB	SO	SB	CS	AVG	OBP	SLG	OPS	OPS+	BR/A	RC	RC/G	FR	G/POS	WS	TPW
1884 Wil-U	10	31	4	2	0	0	0	....	3	....	....	....	.065	.147	.065	.212	-25	-4	0	.29	-3	/P-7,0-2(0-0-2),S-2,3-1	1	-0.2
Alt-U	23	94	10	14	1	0	0	....	4	....	....	....	.149	.184	.160	.343	17	-7	3	.99	0	P-14,0-10(5-4-1)/2-4	5	-0.5
Yr.	33	125	14	16	1	0	0	....	7	....	....	....	.128	.174	.136	.310	6	-11	3	.80	-3	P-21,0-12(5-4-3)/2-4,S-2,3	6	-0.7

• MURPHY, John John Patrick "Soldier Boy" Murphy b: 1879, New Haven, CT d: 4/20/1949, Andover, MA, 5'7.5", 160 lbs. Deb: 9/10/1902

YEAR TM-L	G	AB	R	H	2B	3B	HR	RBI	BB	SO	SB	CS	AVG	OBP	SLG	OPS	OPS+	BR/A	RC	RC/G	FR	G/POS	WS	TPW
1902 StL-N	1	3	1	2	1	0	0	1	1	....	0	....	.667	.750	1.000	1.750	458	1	2	61.12	0	/3-1	1	0.1
1903 Det-A	5	22	1	4	1	0	0	1	0	....	0	....	.182	.182	.227	.409	23	-2	1	1.43	-1	/S-5	0	-0.3
Total 2	6	25	2	6	2	0	0	2	1	....	0	....	.240	.269	.320	.589	87	-1	3	4.41	-1	/S-5,3-1	1	-0.2

• MURPHY, Larry Patrick Lawrence Murphy b: 3/17/1857, Canada d: 10/6/1911, Indianapolis, IN BL, 5'8" Deb: 5/30/1891

YEAR TM-L	G	AB	R	H	2B	3B	HR	RBI	BB	SO	SB	CS	AVG	OBP	SLG	OPS	OPS+	BR/A	RC	RC/G	FR	G/POS	WS	TPW
1891 Was-a	101	400	73	106	15	3	1	35	63	27	29	....	.265	.372	.325	.697	104	6	61	5.46	-7	*0-101(69-3-30)	10	-0.3

• MURPHY, Leo Leo Joseph "Red" Murphy b: 1/7/1889, Terre Haute, IN d: 8/12/1960, Racine, WI BR/TR, 6'1", 179 lbs. Deb: 5/2/1915

YEAR TM-L	G	AB	R	H	2B	3B	HR	RBI	BB	SO	SB	CS	AVG	OBP	SLG	OPS	OPS+	BR/A	RC	RC/G	FR	G/POS	WS	TPW
1915 Pit-N	31	41	4	4	0	0	0	4	4	12	0	....	.098	.178	.098	.275	-16	-6	1	.59	0	C-20	0	-0.5

• MURPHY, Mike Michael Jerome Murphy b: 8/19/1888, Forestville, PA d: 10/26/1952, Johnson City, NY BR/TR, 5'9", 170 lbs. Deb: 5/17/1912

YEAR TM-L	G	AB	R	H	2B	3B	HR	RBI	BB	SO	SB	CS	AVG	OBP	SLG	OPS	OPS+	BR/A	RC	RC/G	FR	G/POS	WS	TPW
1912 StL-N	1	1	0	0	0	0	0	1	0	0	0	....	.000	.000	.000	.000	-102	-0	0	.00	0	/C-1	0	-0.1
1916 Phi-A	14	27	0	3	0	0	0	1	1	3	0	....	.111	.143	.111	.254	-25	-4	1	.55	1	C-12	0	-0.3
Total 2	15	28	0	3	0	0	0	2	1	3	0	....	.107	.138	.107	.245	-27	-4	1	.53	0	/C-13	0	-0.4

• MURPHY, Morgan Morgan Edward Murphy b: 2/14/1867, East Providence, RI d: 10/3/1938, Providence, RI BR/TR, 5'8", 160 lbs. Deb: 4/22/1890 U Career OF: 1-3-1

YEAR TM-L	G	AB	R	H	2B	3B	HR	RBI	BB	SO	SB	CS	AVG	OBP	SLG	OPS	OPS+	BR/A	RC	RC/G	FR	G/POS	WS	TPW
1890 Bos-P	68	246	38	56	10	2	2	32	24	31	16	....	.228	.301	.309	.610	59	-16	28	4.04	-5	C-67/S-2,3-1,0-1	5	-1.2
1891 Bos-a	106	402	60	87	11	4	4	54	36	58	17	....	.216	.289	.294	.582	68	-18	40	3.36	0	*C-104/0-4(1-2-1)	11	-0.8
1892 Cin-N	74	234	29	46	8	2	2	24	25	57	4	....	.197	.277	.274	.550	67	-9	19	2.77	-7	C-74	4	-0.8
1893 Cin-N	57	200	25	47	5	1	1	19	14	35	1	....	.235	.295	.285	.580	53	-14	18	3.04	-3	C-56/1-1	3	-1.0
1894 Cin-N	76	261	42	70	9	0	1	37	26	36	6	....	.268	.337	.314	.651	56	-19	30	4.14	0	C-74/3-1,S-1	4	-0.9
1895 Cin-N	25	82	15	22	2	0	0	16	11	8	6	....	.268	.355	.293	.648	65	-4	11	4.89	-1	C-25	2	-0.3
1896 StL-N	49	175	12	45	5	2	0	11	8	14	1	....	.257	.290	.309	.598	60	-10	17	3.33	-1	C-48	3	-0.6
1897 StL-N	63	211	13	36	2	0	0	12	6	....	1	....	.171	.197	.180	.377		-31	8	1.23	5	C-53/1-8	1	-1.8
1898 Pit-N	5	16	0	2	0	0	0	2	1	....	0	....	.125	.176	.125	.301	-14	-2	0	.82	1	/C-5	0	-0.1
Phi-N	25	86	6	17	3	0	0	11	6	....	0	....	.198	.258	.233	.491	43	-6	6	2.09	3	C-25	1	-0.1
Yr.	30	102	6	19	3	0	0	13	7	....	0	....	.186	.245	.216	.461	34	-9	6	1.87	4	C-30	1	-0.2
1900 Phi-N	11	36	2	10	0	1	0	3	0	....	0	....	.278	.278	.333	.611	69	-2	4	3.46	1	C-11	1	0.0
1901 Phi-A	9	28	5	6	1	0	0	6	0	....	1	....	.214	.214	.250	.464	27	-3	2	2.12	-2	/C-8,1-1	0	-0.3
Total 11	568	1977	247	444	56	12	10	227	157	239	53	....	.225	.286	.280	.567	54	-134	184	3.15	-8	C-550/1-10,0-5,S-3,3-2	35	-7.9

YEAR TM-L	G	AB	R	H	2B	3B	HR	RBI	BB	SO	SB	CS	AVG	OBP	SLG	OPS	OPS+	BR/A	RC	RC/G	FR	G/POS	WS	TPW
• MURPHY, Pat	Patrick J. Murphy b: 1/2/1857, Auburn, MA d: 5/16/1927, Worcester, MA TR, 5'10", 160 lbs. Deb: 9/2/1887																							
1887 NY-N	17	58	4	14	2	0	0	4	2	4	1	....	.241	.241	.250	.491	38	-5	4	2.24	-1	C-17	1	-0.4
1888*NY-N	28	106	11	18	1	0	0	4	6	11	3	....	.170	.214	.179	.394	27	-8	5	1.48	4	C-28	2	-0.2
1889 NY-N	9	28	5	10	1	1	1	4	2	0	0	....	.357	.400	.571	.971	170	2	7	9.66	0	/C-9	1	0.3
1890 NY-N	32	119	14	28	5	1	0	9	14	13	3	....	.235	.321	.294	.615	79	-3	12	3.64	-3	C-29/O-3(1-1-1),S-1	3	-0.4
Total 4	86	311	34	70	9	2	1	21	24	28	7	....	.225	.278	.272	.550	63	-13	28	3.05	-1	/C-83,O-3,S-1	7	-0.7
• MURPHY, Tony	Francis J. Murphy b: 7/1859, New York, NY d: 12/15/1915, New York, NY, 5'6", 145 lbs. Deb: 10/15/1884																							
1884 NY-a	1	3	1	1	0	0	0	0	0	....	....	....	.333	.333	.333	.667	121	0	0	4.70	0	/C-1	0	0.0
• MURPHY, Willie	William H. "Gentle Willie" Murphy b: 3/23/1864, Springfield, MA BL, 5'11", 198 lbs. Deb: 5/1/1884																							
1884 Cle-N	42	168	18	38	3	3	1	9	1	23	....	....	.226	.231	.298	.528	63	-8	12	2.50	-4	O-42(34-3-5)	1	-1.2
Was-a	5	21	3	10	0	0	0	0	1	....	....	....	.476	.542	.476	1.018	265	4	6	13.88	0	/O-4(4-0-0),2-1	2	0.4
• MURPHY, Yale	William Henry "Tot,Midget" Murphy b: 11/11/1869, Southville, MA d: 2/14/1906, Southville, MA BL/TR, 5'3", 125 lbs. Deb: 4/19/1894 U Career OF: 30-2-21																							
1894*NY-N	74	280	64	76	6	2	0	28	51	23	28	....	.271	.384	.307	.691	69	-11	45	5.71	-2	S-49,O-20(1-0-19)/3-3,1-1,2	7	-0.9
1895 NY-N	51	184	35	37	6	2	0	16	27	13	7	....	.201	.303	.255	.559	46	-14	17	3.10	-2	O-33(29-2-2)/3-8,S-8,2-1	1	-1.5
1897 NY-N	5	8	1	0	0	0	0	1	2	....	0	....	.000	.200	.000	.200	-46	-2	0	.00	-1	/S-3,2-2	0	-0.2
Total 3	130	472	100	113	12	4	0	45	80	36	35	....	.239	.350	.282	.631	58	-27	62	4.51	-5	/S-60,O-53,3-11,2-4,1-1	8	-2.7
• MURRAY, Bill	William Allenwood "Dasher" Murray b: 9/6/1893, Vinalhaven, ME d: 9/14/1943, Boston, MA BB/TR, 5'11", 165 lbs. Deb: 6/27/1917																							
1917 Was-A	8	21	2	3	0	1	0	4	2	2	1	....	.143	.217	.238	.455	39	-2	1	1.75	-1	/2-6,S-1	0	-0.3
• MURRAY, Bobby	Robert Hayes Murray b: 7/4/1898, St. Albans, VT d: 1/4/1979, Nashua, NH BL/TR, 5'7", 155 lbs. Deb: 9/24/1923																							
1923 Was-A	10	37	2	7	1	0	0	2	1	4	1	0	.189	.211	.216	.427	13	-4	2	1.55	1	3-10	0	-0.3
• MURRAY, Calvin	Calvin Duane Murray b: 7/30/1971, Dallas, TX BR/TR, 5'11", 190 lbs. Deb: 6/22/1999 Career OF: 10-251-4																							
1999 SF-N	15	19	1	5	2	0	0	5	2	4	1	0	.263	.333	.368	.702	83	-0	3	5.17	-1	/O-9(3-6-0)	1	-0.1
2000*SF-N	108	194	35	47	12	1	2	22	29	33	9	3	.242	.350	.345	.695	83	-4	27	4.78	0	*O-106(2-104-0)	6	-0.3
2001 SF-N	106	326	54	80	14	2	6	25	32	57	8	8	.245	.319	.356	.674	80	-11	37	3.78	3	*O-104(0-104-0)	7	-0.7
2002 SF-N	11	12	0	0	0	0	0	0	1	2	0	0	.000	.077	.000	.077	-81	-3	0	.05	1	O-10(5-4-3)	0	-0.3
Tex-A	37	77	16	13	5	1	0	1	6	15	4	0	.169	.238	.260	.498	31	-7	6	2.37	2	O-34(0-33-1)/D-1	1	-0.5
Total 4	277	628	106	145	33	4	8	53	70	111	22	11	.231	.315	.334	.649	72	-25	72	3.85	6	O-263/D-1	15	-1.8
• MURRAY, Ed	Edward Francis Murray b: 5/8/1895, Mystic, CT d: 11/8/1970, Cheyenne, WY BR/TR, 5'6", 145 lbs. Deb: 6/24/1917																							
1917 StL-A	1	1	0	0	0	0	0	0	0	1	0	....	.000	.000	.000	.000	-104	-0	0	.00	-1	/S-1	0	-0.1
• MURRAY, Eddie	Eddie Clarence "Steady Eddie" Murray b: 2/24/1956, Los Angeles, CA BB/TR, 6'2", 200 lbs. Deb: 4/7/1977 C HOF: 2003																							
1977 Bal-A	160	611	81	173	29	2	27	88	48	104	0	1	.283	.336	.470	.806	125	19	90	5.21	-6	*D-111,1-42/O-3(3-0-0)	21	0.6
1978 Bal-A★	161	610	85	174	32	3	27	95	70	97	6	5	.285	.360	.480	.840	143	34	104	6.01	-3	*1-157/3-3,D-1	28	2.2
1979*Bal-A	159	606	90	179	30	2	25	99	72	78	10	2	.295	.372	.475	.847	132	29	107	6.41	9	*1-157/D-2	25	2.7
1980 Bal-A	158	621	100	186	36	2	32	116	54	71	7	2	.300	.357	.519	.876	138	32	111	6.49	-14	*1-154/D-1	26	0.8
1981 Bal-A★	99	378	57	111	21	2	**22**	**78**	40	43	2	3	.294	.363	.534	.897	156	26	70	6.68	8	1-99	21	2.9
1982 Bal-A★	151	550	87	174	30	1	32	110	70	82	7	2	.316	.395	.549	.944	156	44	116	7.83	6	*1-149/D-2	29	4.1
1983*Bal-A★	156	582	115	178	30	3	33	111	86	90	5	1	.306	.398	.538	.936	**158**	49	127	8.00	7	*1-153/D-2	31	4.6
1984 Bal-A★	162	588	97	180	26	3	29	110	**107**	87	10	2	.306	**.415**	.509	.923	157	**52**	130	**8.23**	5	*1-159/D-3	33	4.8
1985 Bal-A★	156	583	111	173	37	1	31	124	84	68	5	2	.297	.387	.523	.910	150	42	122	7.68	10	*1-154/D-2	28	4.2
1986 Bal-A★	137	495	61	151	25	1	17	84	78	49	3	0	.305	.400	.463	.862	136	28	92	6.81	-1	*1-119,D-16	20	1.9
1987 Bal-A	160	618	89	171	28	3	30	91	73	80	1	2	.277	.353	.477	.830	121	17	103	5.95	9	*1-156/D-4	20	1.6
1988 Bal-A	161	603	75	171	27	2	28	84	75	78	5	2	.284	.363	.474	.837	136	30	101	5.98	6	*1-103,D-58	21	2.6
1989 LA-N	160	594	66	147	29	1	20	88	87	85	7	2	.247	.346	.401	.746	115	14	84	4.87	9	*1-159/3-2	21	1.2
1990 LA-N	155	558	96	184	22	3	26	95	82	64	8	5	.330	.417	.520	.936	160	47	118	7.90	-1	*1-150	31	3.7
1991 LA-N★	153	576	69	150	23	1	19	96	55	74	10	3	.260	.325	.403	.728	106	4	73	4.33	4	*1-149/3-1	16	-0.2
1992 NY-N	156	551	64	144	37	2	16	93	66	74	4	2	.261	.340	.423	.763	117	12	79	4.91	-5	*1-154	20	-0.4
1993 NY-N	154	610	77	174	28	1	27	100	40	61	2	2	.285	.329	.467	.796	112	7	86	4.91	-2	*1-154	15	-0.8
1994 Cle-A	108	433	57	110	21	1	17	76	31	53	8	4	.254	.304	.425	.729	85	-11	54	4.33	-2	D-82,1-26	9	-2.0
1995*Cle-A	113	436	68	141	21	0	21	82	39	65	5	1	.323	.379	.516	.895	128	18	83	7.17	4	D-95,1-18	16	1.3
1996 Cle-A	88	336	33	88	9	1	12	45	34	45	3	0	.262	.330	.402	.732	84	-8	43	4.36	0	D-87/1-1	2	-1.3
*Bal-A	64	230	36	59	12	0	10	34	27	42	1	0	.257	.335	.439	.774	94	-2	34	4.96	0	D-62	4	-0.6
Yr.	152	566	69	147	21	1	22	79	61	87	4	0	.260	.332	.417	.749	88	-10	76	4.61	0	*D-149/1-1	6	-1.8
1997 Ana-A	46	160	13	35	7	0	3	15	13	24	1	0	.219	.277	.319	.596	54	-11	13	2.55	0	D-45	0	-1.3
LA-N	9	7	0	2	0	0	0	3	2	2	0	0	.286	.444	.286	.730	104	0	1	2.16	0	....	0	0.0
Total 21	3026	11336	1627	3255	560	35	504	1917	1333	1516	110	43	.287	.363	.476	.839	130	472	1939	6.11	45	*1-2413,D-573/3-6,O-3	437	32.8
• MURRAY, Glenn	Glenn Everett Murray b: 11/23/1970, Manning, SC BR/TR, 6'2", 225 lbs. Deb: 5/10/1996																							
1996 Phi-N	38	97	8	19	3	0	2	6	7	36	1	1	.196	.250	.289	.539	41	-9	7	2.49	1	O-27(1-2-24)	0	-0.9
• MURRAY, Jim	James Oscar Murray b: 1/16/1878, Galveston, TX d: 4/25/1945, Galveston, TX BR/TL, 5'10", 180 lbs. Deb: 9/2/1902 Career OF: 18-2-49																							
1902 Chi-N	12	47	3	8	0	0	0	1	2	....	0	....	.170	.204	.170	.374	16	-5	2	1.19	-1	O-12(0-0-12)	0	-0.6
1911 StL-A	31	102	8	19	5	0	3	11	5	....	0	....	.186	.224	.324	.548	54	-7	7	2.18	0	O-25(0-1-24)	0	-0.9
1914 Bos-N	39	112	10	26	4	2	0	12	6	24	2	....	.232	.277	.304	.581	73	-4	10	2.81	-2	O-32(18-1-13)	1	-0.8
Total 3	82	261	21	53	9	2	3	24	13	24	2	....	.203	.244	.287	.531	56	-16	18	2.25	-3	/O-69	1	-2.3
• MURRAY, Larry	Larry Murray b: 4/1/1953, Chicago, IL BB/TR, 5'11", 179 lbs. Deb: 9/7/1974 Career OF: 59-56-84																							
1974 NY-A	6	1	1	0	0	0	0	0	0	0	0	1	.000	.000	.000	.000	-103	-1	0	.00	-1	/O-3(1-1-2)	0	-0.2
1975 NY-A	6	1	1	0	0	0	0	0	0	0	0	0	.000	.000	.000	.000	-103	-0	0	.00	0	/O-4(2-1-1)	0	-0.1
1976 NY-A	8	10	2	1	0	0	0	2	1	2	2	0	.100	.182	.100	.282	-16	-1	0	1.25	1	/O-7(0-6-1)	0	-0.1
1977 Oak-A	90	162	19	29	5	2	1	9	17	36	12	3	.179	.257	.253	.510	40	-12	12	2.35	2	O-78(27-36-22)/D-3,S-1	1	-1.1
1978 Oak-A	11	12	1	1	0	0	0	0	3	2	0	0	.083	.267	.083	.350	3	-1	0	1.17	0	/O-6(5-0-1)	0	-0.2
1979 Oak-A	105	226	25	42	11	2	2	20	28	34	6	6	.186	.276	.279	.554	53	-16	18	2.47	-2	O-90(24-12-57)/2-3	1	-2.1
Total 6	226	412	49	73	16	4	3	31	49	74	20	10	.177	.265	.257	.522	44	-31	31	2.33	-1	O-188/2-3,D-3,S-1	2	-3.7
• MURRAY, Miah	Jeremiah J. Murray b: 1/1/1865, Boston, MA d: 1/11/1922, Boston, MA BR/TR, 5'11.5", 170 lbs. Deb: 5/17/1884 U																							
1884 Pro-N	8	27	1	5	0	0	0	1	1	8	....	....	.185	.214	.185	.399	27	-2	1	1.37	-4	/C-7,1-1,O-1	0	-0.5
1885 Lou-a	12	43	4	8	0	0	0	3	2	....	....	....	.186	.239	.186	.425	36	-3	2	1.51	-1	C-12/1-2	0	-0.3
1888 Was-N	12	42	1	4	1	0	0	3	1	7	0	....	.095	.116	.119	.235	-26	-6	1	.42	0	C-10/1-2	0	-0.5
1891 Was-a	2	8	0	0	0	0	0	0	0	1	0	....	.000	.000	.000	.000	-105	-2	0	.00	0	/C-2	0	-0.2
Total 4	34	120	6	17	1	0	0	7	4	16	0	....	.142	.176	.150	.326	4	-13	4	.96	-6	/C-31,1-5,O-1	0	-1.5
• MURRAY, Ray	Raymond Lee "Deacon" Murray b: 10/12/1917, Spring Hope, NC d: 4/9/2003, Fort Worth, TX BR/TR, 6'3", 204 lbs. Deb: 4/25/1948																							
1948 Cle-A	4	4	0	0	0	0	0	0	0	3	0	0	.000	.000	.000	.000	-103	-1	0	.00	0	....	0	-0.1
1950 Cle-A	55	139	16	38	8	2	1	13	12	13	1	0	.273	.331	.381	.712	85	-3	16	3.81	0	C-45	3	-0.1
1951 Cle-A	1	1	0	1	0	0	0	1	0	0	0	0	1.000	1.000	1.000	2.000	468	0	1	∞	0	/C-1	0	0.1
Phi-A	40	122	10	26	6	0	0	13	14	8	0	0	.213	.294	.262	.556	50	-8	10	2.49	3	C-39	2	-0.4
Yr.	41	123	10	27	6	0	0	14	14	8	0	0	.220	.299	.268	.568	53	-8	11	2.49	3	C-40	2	-0.3
1952 Phi-A	44	136	14	28	5	0	1	10	9	13	0	0	.206	.255	.265	.520	42	-11	9	2.23	4	C-42	3	-0.5
1953 Phi-A	84	268	25	76	14	3	6	41	18	25	0	0	.284	.331	.425	.756	99	-1	38	5.11	8	C-78	9	1.0
1954 Bal-A	22	61	4	15	4	1	0	2	2	5	0	0	.246	.270	.344	.614	73	-3	6	3.10	1	C-21	1	-0.1
Total 6	250	731	69	184	37	6	8	80	55	67	1	0	.252	.305	.352	.657	75	-26	79	3.63	15	C-226	18	-0.1

YEAR TM-L	G	AB	R	H	2B	3B	HR	RBI	BB	SO	SB	CS	AVG	OBP	SLG	OPS	OPS+	BR/A	RC	RC/G	FR	G/POS	WS	TPW
• MURRAY, Red	John Joseph Murray	b: 3/4/1884, Arnot, PA	d: 12/4/1958, Sayre, PA	BR/TR, 5'10.5", 190 lbs.	Deb: 6/16/1906	Career OF: 318-149-718																		
1906 StL-N	46	144	18	37	9	7	1	16	9	....	5	....	.257	.305	.438	.743	137	5	21	5.17	0	0-34(4-11-20)/C-7	5	0.5
1907 StL-N	132	485	46	127	10	10	7	46	24	....	23	....	.262	.301	.367	.668	113	4	63	4.46	9	*0-131(124-1-6)	16	0.6
1908 StL-N	154	593	64	167	19	15	7	62	37	....	48	....	.282	.332	.400	.732	140	24	92	5.56	-3	*0-154(0-89-67)	27	1.7
1909 NY-N	149	570	74	150	15	12	**7**	91	45	....	48	....	.263	.319	.368	.688	112	6	81	4.83	6	*0-149(29-0-120)	19	0.5
1910 NY-N	149	553	78	153	27	8	4	87	52	51	57	....	.277	.345	.376	.721	110	7	91	5.60	9	*0-148(24-0-124)	17	1.0
1911*NY-N	140	488	70	142	27	15	3	78	43	37	48	....	.291	.354	.426	.781	115	8	89	6.49	-3	*0-131(50-2-83)	16	0.0
1912*NY-N	143	549	83	152	26	20	3	92	27	45	38	....	.277	.320	.413	.734	97	-6	83	5.12	9	*0-143(27-0-117)	17	-0.4
1913*NY-N	147	520	70	139	21	3	2	59	34	28	35	....	.267	.320	.331	.650	85	-10	63	4.05	7	*0-147(32-1-116)	14	-1.1
1914 NY-N	86	139	19	31	6	3	0	23	9	7	11	....	.223	.270	.309	.580	75	-5	14	3.17	-1	0-49(16-0-34)	2	-0.8
1915 NY-N	45	127	12	28	1	2	3	11	7	15	2	3	.220	.261	.331	.592	83	-4	10	2.71	0	0-34(1-30-3)	2	-0.7
Chi-N	51	144	20	43	6	1	0	11	8	8	6	5	.299	.340	.354	.694	110	1	18	4.28	1	0-40(7-11-25)/2-1	5	0.0
Yr.	96	271	32	71	7	3	3	22	15	23	8	8	.262	.303	.343	.646	98	-3	29	3.53	1	0-74(8-41-28)/2-1	7	-0.7
1917 NY-N	22	22	1	1	1	0	0	3	4	3	0	....	.045	.192	.091	.283	-12	-3	0	.57	0	0-11(4-4-3)/C-1	0	-0.4
Total 11	1264	4334	555	1170	168	96	37	579	299	194	321	8	.270	.323	.379	.702	109	27	627	4.95	35	*0-1171/C-8,2-1	140	0.9
• MURRAY, Rich	Richard Dale Murray	b: 7/6/1957, Los Angeles, CA	BR/TR, 6'4", 195 lbs.	Deb: 6/7/1980																				
1980 SF-N	53	194	19	42	8	2	4	24	11	48	2	1	.216	.259	.340	.599	67	-9	15	2.50	1	1-53	2	-1.2
1983 SF-N	4	10	0	2	0	0	0	1	0	3	0	0	.200	.200	.200	.400	11	-1	0	.60	0	/1-3	0	-0.2
Total 2	57	204	19	44	8	2	4	25	11	51	2	1	.216	.256	.333	.589	65	-11	15	2.40	1	/1-56	2	-1.4
• MURRAY, Tom	Thomas W. Murray	b: 1866, Paterson, NJ	BR, 5'7"	Deb: 6/20/1894																				
1894 Phi-N	1	2	0	0	0	0	0	0	0	2	0	....	.000	.000	.000	.000	-103	-1	0	.00	-1	/S-1	0	-0.1
• MURRAY, Tony	Anthony Joseph Murray	b: 4/30/1904, Chicago, IL	d: 3/19/1974, Chicago, IL	BR/TR, 5'10.5", 154 lbs.	Deb: 10/6/1923																			
1923 Chi-N	2	4	0	1	0	0	0	0	0	0	0	0	.250	.400	.250	.650	75	-0	0	4.27	0	/0-2(1-2-1)	0	0.0
• MURRELL, Ivan	Ivan Augustus (Peters) Murrell	b: 4/24/1945, Almirante, Panama	BR/TR, 6'2", 196 lbs.	Deb: 9/28/1963	Career OF: 175-112-73																			
1963 Hou-N	2	5	1	1	0	0	0	0	0	2	0	0	.200	.200	.200	.400	17	-1	0	1.35	-0	/0-2(0-2-0)	0	-0.1
1964 Hou-N	10	14	1	2	1	0	0	1	0	6	0	0	.143	.143	.214	.357	-1	-2	0	.97	0	/0-5(4-0-1)	0	-0.2
1967 Hou-N	10	29	2	9	0	0	0	1	1	9	1	0	.310	.333	.310	.644	88	-0	3	4.16	-1	/0-6(5-0-1)	1	-0.1
1968 Hou-N	32	59	3	6	1	1	0	3	1	17	0	0	.102	.117	.153	.269	-20	-9	1	.38	1	0-15(4-2-9)	0	-1.0
1969 SD-N	111	247	19	63	10	6	3	25	11	65	3	4	.255	.292	.381	.673	91	-5	26	3.60	-2	0-72(23-41-14)/1-2	4	-1.1
1970 SD-N	125	347	43	85	9	3	12	35	17	93	9	7	.245	.288	.392	.680	84	-11	36	3.52	0	*0-101(61-24-20)/1-1	5	-1.6
1971 SD-N	103	255	23	60	6	3	7	24	7	60	5	2	.235	.264	.365	.629	82	-7	22	2.90	-2	0-72(55-16-2)	3	-1.4
1972 SD-N	5	7	0	1	0	0	0	1	0	3	0	0	.143	.143	.143	.286	-20	-1	0	.64	-0	/0-1	0	-0.1
1973 SD-N	93	210	23	48	13	1	9	21	2	52	2	0	.229	.236	.429	.664	88	-5	20	3.17	-1	0-37(10-18-12),1-24	4	-0.9
1974 Atl-N	73	133	11	33	1	1	2	12	5	35	0	0	.248	.275	.316	.591	62	-7	11	2.96	0	0-32(13-9-13),1-13	2	-0.9
Total 10	564	1306	126	308	41	15	33	123	44	342	20	13	.236	.266	.366	.632	77	-48	120	3.09	-5	0-343/1-40	19	-7.5
• MURTAUGH, Danny	Daniel Edward Murtaugh	b: 10/8/1917, Chester, PA	d: 12/2/1976, Chester, PA	BR/TR, 5'9", 165 lbs.	Deb: 7/6/1941	M/C																		
1941 Phi-N	85	347	34	76	8	1	0	11	26	31	**18**	....	.219	.275	.248	.523	50	-23	25	2.45	1	2-85/S-1	3	-1.7
1942 Phi-N	144	506	48	122	16	4	0	27	49	39	13	....	.241	.311	.289	.599	80	-12	47	3.04	-2	S-60,3-53,2-32	8	-0.7
1943 Phi-N	113	451	65	123	17	4	1	35	57	23	4	....	.273	.357	.335	.692	104	5	57	4.44	5	*2-113	16	1.7
1946 Phi-N	6	19	1	4	1	0	1	3	2	2	0	....	.211	.286	.421	.707	102	-0	2	4.38	-1	/2-6	1	-0.1
1947 Bos-N	3	8	0	1	0	0	0	0	1	2	0	....	.125	.222	.125	.347	-6	-1	0	1.08	0	/2-2,3-2	0	-0.1
1948 Pit-N	146	514	56	149	21	5	1	71	60	40	10	....	.290	.365	.356	.721	94	-2	70	5.02	4	*2-146	19	1.0
1949 Pit-N	75	236	16	48	7	2	2	24	29	17	2	....	.203	.291	.275	.566	51	-16	21	2.90	-4	2-74	3	-1.6
1950 Pit-N	118	367	34	108	20	5	2	37	47	42	2	....	.294	.376	.392	.768	99	1	56	5.63	0	*2-108	10	0.7
1951 Pit-N	77	151	9	30	7	0	1	11	16	19	0	0	.199	.284	.265	.549	47	-11	11	2.40	-2	2-65/3-3	1	-1.1
Total 9	767	2599	263	661	97	21	8	219	287	215	49	0	.254	.331	.317	.648	81	-60	290	3.86	0	2-631/S-61,3-58	61	-2.0
• MUSER, Tony	Anthony Joseph Muser	b: 8/1/1947, Van Nuys, CA	BL/TL, 6'2", 190 lbs.	Deb: 9/14/1969	M/C	Career OF: 15-10-1																		
1969 Bos-A	2	9	0	1	0	0	0	1	1	1	0	0	.111	.200	.111	.311	-10	-1	0	.85	1	/1-2	0	-0.1
1971 Chi-A	11	16	2	5	0	1	0	0	1	1	0	0	.313	.353	.438	.790	119	0	2	3.55	0	/1-4	0	0.1
1972 Chi-A	44	61	6	17	2	2	1	9	2	6	1	1	.279	.302	.426	.728	112	0	7	4.28	-1	1-29/0-1	2	-0.2
1973 Chi-A	109	309	38	88	14	3	4	30	33	36	8	4	.285	.354	.388	.742	105	3	43	4.90	-1	1-89,D-13/0-2(2-0-0)	10	-0.5
1974 Chi-A	103	206	16	60	5	1	1	18	6	22	1	4	.291	.315	.340	.654	86	-5	20	3.29	-4	1-80,D-13	3	-1.4
1975 Chi-A	43	111	11	27	3	0	0	6	7	8	2	1	.243	.288	.270	.558	58	-6	8	2.30	-1	1-41	1	-0.9
Bal-A	80	82	11	26	3	0	0	11	8	9	0	0	.317	.378	.354	.731	115	2	11	4.79	-1	1-62	3	-0.1
Yr.	123	193	22	53	6	0	0	17	15	17	2	1	.275	.327	.306	.633	83	-4	19	3.30	-1	*1-103	4	-1.0
1976 Bal-A	136	326	25	74	7	1	1	30	21	34	1	1	.227	.274	.264	.538	62	-16	23	2.27	0	*1-109,0-12(8-4-0),D-10	2	-2.4
1977 Bal-A	120	118	14	27	6	0	0	7	13	16	1	2	.229	.305	.280	.585	65	-6	9	2.55	-1	1-77,0-11(5-6-0)/D-1	1	-0.9
1978 Mil-A	15	30	0	4	1	1	0	5	3	5	0	0	.133	.212	.233	.445	25	-3	1	1.41	0	1-12	0	-0.4
Total 9	663	1268	123	329	41	9	7	117	95	138	14	13	.259	.312	.323	.634	81	-32	124	3.30	-8	1-505/D-37,0-26	22	-6.8
• MUSIAL, Stan	Stanley Frank "Stan the Man" Musial	b: 11/21/1920, Donora, PA	BL/TL, 6', 175 lbs.	Deb: 9/17/1941	HOF: 1969	Career OF: 943-325-750																		
1941 StL-N	12	47	8	20	4	0	1	7	2	1	1	....	.426	.449	.574	1.023	175	4	12	12.36	0	0-11(3-0-8)	3	0.4
1942*StL-N	140	467	87	147	32	10	10	72	62	25	6	....	.315	.397	.490	.888	148	29	96	7.93	6	*0-135(133-2-2)	28	3.1
1943*StL-N★	157	617	108	**220**	**48**	**20**	13	81	72	18	9	....	**.357**	**.425**	**.562**	**.988**	**176**	**60**	147	**9.35**	7	*0-155(34-10-117)	**39**	**6.1**
1944*StL-N★	146	568	112	**197**	**51**	14	12	94	90	28	7	....	.347	**.440**	**.549**	**.990**	**174**	**60**	145	**10.23**	0	*0-146(1-38-124)	**38**	**5.2**
1946*StL-N★	156	624	**124**	**228**	**50**	**20**	16	103	73	31	7	....	**.365**	.434	**.587**	**1.021**	**180**	**65**	164	**10.91**	-5	*1-114,0-42(42-0-0)	**44**	**5.7**
1947 StL-N★	149	587	113	183	30	13	19	95	80	24	4	....	.312	.398	.504	.902	132	28	118	7.45	-1	*1-149	25	2.2
1948 StL-N★	155	611	**135**	**230**	**46**	**18**	39	**131**	79	34	7	....	**.376**	**.450**	**.702**	**1.152**	**196**	**82**	191	**12.89**	-2	*0-155(41-64-76)/1-2	**46**	**7.3**
1949 StL-N★	157	612	128	**207**	**41**	**13**	36	123	107	38	3	....	.338	**.438**	.624	1.062	174	67	173	11.20	-2	*0-156(3-72-117)/1-1	**40**	6.0
1950 StL-N★	146	555	105	192	41	7	28	109	87	36	5	....	**.346**	.437	**.596**	**1.034**	**161**	**52**	149	**10.75**	-6	0-77(56-14-10),1-69	**32**	3.9
1951 StL-N★	152	578	**124**	205	30	**12**	32	108	98	40	4	5	**.355**	.449	.614	1.063	**182**	**69**	169	**11.89**	4	0-91(84-10-1),1-60	**39**	6.4
1952 StL-N★	154	578	**105**	**194**	**42**	6	21	91	96	29	7	7	**.336**	.432	**.538**	**.970**	**167**	**56**	141	**9.47**	-7	*0-129(21-106-9),1-25/P-1	**37**	4.5
1953 StL-N★	157	593	127	200	**53**	9	30	113	**105**	32	3	4	.337	**.437**	.609	1.046	169	63	166	**11.03**	-8	*0-157(141-9-26)	33	4.3
1954 StL-N★	153	591	**120**	195	**41**	9	35	126	103	39	1	7	.330	.433	.607	1.040	166	58	153	9.58	1	*0-152(8-0-147),1-10	30	5.3
1955 StL-N★	154	562	97	179	30	5	33	108	80	39	5	4	.319	.411	.566	.977	156	47	131	8.72	8	*1-110,0-51(21-0-33)	29	4.6
1956 StL-N★	156	594	87	184	33	6	27	**109**	75	39	2	0	.310	.390	.522	.912	142	37	119	7.29	8	*1-103,0-53(3-0-51)	26	3.9
1957 StL-N★	134	502	82	176	38	3	29	102	66	34	1	1	**.351**	**.428**	.612	**1.040**	172	52	129	**9.99**	2	*1-130	30	4.8
1958 StL-N★	135	472	64	159	35	2	17	62	72	26	0	0	.337	.426	.528	.953	145	34	102	8.21	5	*1-124	21	3.2
1959 StL-N★	115	341	37	87	13	2	14	44	60	25	0	2	.255	.367	.428	.795	104	3	53	5.26	0	1-90/0-3(3-0-0)	8	-0.1
1960 StL-N★	116	331	49	91	17	1	17	63	41	34	1	1	.275	.358	.486	.845	118	9	59	6.33	-2	0-59(53-0-6),1-29	13	0.2
1961 StL-N★	123	372	46	107	22	4	15	70	52	35	0	0	.288	.376	.489	.866	116	10	69	6.71	6	*0-103(103-0-0)	14	1.1
1962 StL-N★	135	433	57	143	18	1	19	82	64	46	3	0	.330	.420	.508	.928	135	25	94	8.23	-2	*0-119(97-0-23)	19	1.7
1963 StL-N★	124	337	34	86	10	2	12	58	35	43	2	0	.255	.329	.404	.732	100	2	47	4.85	-2	0-96(96-0-0)	10	-0.4
Total 22	3026	10972	1949	3630	725	177	475	1951	1599	696	78	31	.331	.418	.559	.977	157	913	2625	9.20	12	*0-1890,1-1016/P-1	604	79.5
• MUSSER, Danny	William Daniel Musser	b: 9/5/1905, Zion, PA	d: 3/2/2000, Upper Sandusky, OH	BL/TR, 5'9.5", 160 lbs.	Deb: 9/18/1932																			
1932 Was-A	1	2	0	1	0	0	0	0	0	0	0	0	.500	.500	.500	1.000	162	0	0	12.72	0	/3-1	0	0.0
• MYATT, George	George Edward "Mercury,Stud,Foghorn" Myatt	b: 6/14/1914, Denver, CO	d: 9/14/2000, Orlando, FL	BL/TR, 5'11", 167 lbs.	Deb: 8/16/1938	M/C	Career OF: 1-0-34																	
1938 NY-N	43	170	27	52	2	1	3	10	14	13	10	....	.306	.362	.382	.745	104	1	24	5.03	3	S-24,3-19	6	0.7
1939 NY-N	22	53	7	10	2	0	0	3	6	6	2	....	.189	.271	.226	.498	35	-5	4	2.11	-2	3-14	0	-0.6
1943 Was-A	42	53	11	13	3	0	0	3	13	7	3	0	.245	.394	.302	.696	109	2	9	5.42	-4	2-11/3-2,S-2	2	-0.1
1944 Was-A	140	538	86	153	19	6	0	40	54	44	26	10	.284	.357	.342	.699	105	7	72	4.54	-17	*2-121,S-15/0-3(0-0-3)	17	-0.2

YEAR TM-L	G	AB	R	H	2B	3B	HR	RBI	BB	SO	SB	CS	AVG	OBP	SLG	OPS	OPS+	BR/A	RC	RC/G	FR	G/POS	WS	TPW
1945 Was-A	133	490	81	145	17	7	1	39	63	43	30	11	.296	.378	.365	.744	127	21	77	5.50	-1	2-94,0-32(1-0-31)/3-6,S-1	23	2.5
1946 Was-A	15	34	7	8	1	0	0	4	2	3	1	1	.235	.297	.265	.562	61	-2	3	2.84	-1	/3-7,2-2	1	-0.3
1947 Was-A	12	7	1	0	0	0	0	0	4	4	0	0	.000	.364	.000	.364	6	-1	0	1.46	0	/2-1	0	-0.1
Total 7	407	1345	220	381	44	14	4	99	156	120	72	22	.283	.362	.346	.708	109	25	188	4.81	-22	2-229/3-48,S-42,0-35	49	1.9

• MYATT, Glenn Glenn Calvin Myatt b: 7/9/1897, Argenta, AR d: 8/9/1969, Houston, TX BL/TR, 5'11", 165 lbs. Deb: 4/15/1920 Career OF: 2-0-36

YEAR TM-L	G	AB	R	H	2B	3B	HR	RBI	BB	SO	SB	CS	AVG	OBP	SLG	OPS	OPS+	BR/A	RC	RC/G	FR	G/POS	WS	TPW
1920 Phi-A	70	196	14	49	8	3	0	18	12	22	1	3	.250	.293	.321	.615	62	-11	18	3.10	0	0-37(1-0-36),C-22	2	-1.2
1921 Phi-A	44	69	6	14	2	0	0	5	6	7	1	0	.203	.267	.232	.499	28	-7	5	2.20	1	C-27	1	-0.5
1923 Cle-A	92	220	36	63	7	6	3	40	16	18	0	2	.286	.338	.414	.751	97	-2	30	4.95	-8	C-69	4	-0.7
1924 Cle-A	105	342	55	117	22	7	8	73	33	12	6	1	.342	.402	.518	.919	134	18	72	8.20	-1	C-95	15	2.1
1925 Cle-A	106	358	51	97	15	9	11	54	29	24	3	1	.271	.329	.455	.784	97	-3	54	5.34	-8	C-98/0-1	9	-0.5
1926 Cle-A	56	117	14	29	5	2	0	13	13	13	1	0	.248	.323	.325	.648	69	-5	13	3.86	-1	C-35	3	-0.4
1927 Cle-A	55	94	15	23	6	0	2	8	12	7	1	1	.245	.336	.372	.709	83	-2	12	4.41	1	C-26	2	0.0
1928 Cle-A	58	125	9	36	7	2	1	15	13	13	0	2	.288	.355	.400	.755	97	-1	17	5.08	0	C-30	3	0.0
1929 Cle-A	59	129	14	30	4	1	1	17	7	5	0	1	.233	.277	.302	.580	47	-11	11	2.77	0	C-41	1	-0.8
1930 Cle-A	86	265	30	78	23	2	2	37	18	17	2	3	.294	.342	.419	.760	88	-6	37	5.09	0	C-71	7	-0.1
1931 Cle-A	65	195	21	48	14	2	1	29	21	13	2	1	.246	.319	.354	.673	73	-7	23	4.07	-2	C-53	4	-0.5
1932 Cle-A	82	252	45	62	12	1	8	46	27	21	2	2	.246	.326	.397	.723	81	-8	34	4.43	-5	C-65	7	-0.8
1933 Cle-A	40	77	10	18	4	0	0	7	15	8	0	1	.234	.372	.286	.658	73	-2	9	4.05	0	C-27	2	-0.1
1934 Cle-A	36	107	18	34	6	1	0	12	13	5	1	0	.318	.392	.393	.784	101	1	17	6.20	-3	C-34	4	0.0
1935 Cle-A	10	36	1	3	1	0	0	2	4	3	0	0	.083	.175	.111	.286	-24	-7	1	.68	-1	C-10	0	-0.6
NY-N	13	18	2	4	0	1	1	6	0	3	0	....	.222	.222	.500	.722	90	-0	2	3.95	0	/C-4	0	0.0
1936 Det-A	27	78	5	17	1	0	0	5	9	4	0	0	.218	.299	.231	.530	32	-8	6	2.52	-1	C-27	1	-0.7
Total 16	1004	2678	346	722	137	37	38	387	248	195	20	18	.270	.334	.391	.725	85	-62	363	4.75	-27	C-734/0-38	65	-4.8

• MYER, Buddy Charles Solomon Myer b: 3/16/1904, Ellisville, MS d: 10/31/1974, Baton Rouge, LA BL/TR, 5'10.5", 163 lbs. Deb: 9/26/1925 Career OF: 12-0-1

YEAR TM-L	G	AB	R	H	2B	3B	HR	RBI	BB	SO	SB	CS	AVG	OBP	SLG	OPS	OPS+	BR/A	RC	RC/G	FR	G/POS	WS	TPW
1925★Was-A	4	8	1	2	0	0	0	0	0	1	0	0	.250	.250	.250	.500	28	-1	0	2.12	-1	/S-4	0	-0.1
1926 Was-A	132	434	66	132	18	6	1	62	45	19	10	11	.304	.370	.380	.750	98	-2	61	4.88	-11	*S-118/3-8	14	-0.1
1927 Was-A	15	51	7	11	1	0	0	7	8	3	3	1	.216	.322	.235	.557	47	-3	5	2.90	0	S-15	1	-0.2
Bos-A	133	469	59	135	22	11	2	47	48	15	9	5	.288	.359	.394	.753	97	-1	69	5.10	-3	*S-101,3-14,0-10(10-0-0)/2	14	0.7
Yr.	148	520	66	146	23	11	2	54	56	18	12	6	.281	.355	.379	.734	92	-4	74	4.86	-3	*S-116,3-14,0-10(10-0-0)/2	15	0.5
1928 Bos-A	147	536	78	168	26	6	1	44	53	28	**30**	16	.313	.379	.390	.769	104	5	82	5.29	-5	*3-144	18	0.9
1929 Was-A	141	563	80	169	29	10	3	82	63	33	18	7	.300	.373	.403	.776	99	2	88	5.67	-15	2-88,3-53	18	-0.6
1930 Was-A	138	541	97	164	18	8	2	61	58	31	14	11	.303	.373	.377	.750	90	-7	78	5.11	-2	*2-134/0-2(1-0-1)	14	-0.5
1931 Was-A	139	591	114	173	33	11	4	56	58	42	11	14	.293	.360	.406	.766	100	-0	85	5.13	-1	*2-137	20	0.8
1932 Was-A	143	577	120	161	38	16	5	52	69	33	12	7	.279	.360	.426	.786	104	4	91	5.57	-4	*2-139	20	0.9
1933★Was-A	131	530	95	160	29	15	4	61	60	29	6	8	.302	.374	.436	.810	115	11	87	5.93	13	*2-129	23	3.0
1934 Was-A	139	524	103	160	33	8	3	57	102	32	6	6	.305	.419	.416	.835	121	21	98	6.85	-14	*2-135	19	1.4
1935 Was-A★	151	616	115	215	36	11	5	100	96	40	7	6	**.349**	.440	.468	.907	139	41	132	8.49	-2	*2-151	33	4.5
1936 Was-A	51	156	31	42	5	2	0	15	42	11	7	2	.269	.427	.327	.754	94	3	27	5.95	3	2-43	6	0.8
1937 Was-A★	125	430	54	126	16	10	1	65	78	41	2	6	.293	.407	.384	.791	105	6	72	6.01	-2	*2-119/0-1	15	1.1
1938 Was-A	127	437	79	147	22	8	6	71	93	32	9	5	.336	.454	.465	.918	140	34	99	8.82	1	*2-121	24	3.8
1939 Was-A	83	258	33	78	10	3	1	32	40	18	4	1	.302	.396	.376	.772	106	5	42	6.10	3	2-65	9	1.2
1940 Was-A	71	210	28	61	14	4	0	29	34	10	6	3	.290	.389	.395	.785	111	5	34	5.81	1	2-54	8	0.9
1941 Was-A	53	107	14	27	3	1	0	9	18	10	2	0	.252	.360	.299	.659	80	-2	13	4.21	-1	2-24	2	-0.1
Total 17	1923	7038	1174	2131	353	130	38	850	965	428	156	109	.303	.389	.406	.795	108	121	1163	5.96	-38	*2-1340,S-238,3-219/0-13	258	18.3

• MYERS, Al James Albert "Cod" Myers b: 10/22/1863, Danville, IL d: 12/24/1927, Marshall, IL BR/TR, 5'8.5", 165 lbs. Deb: 9/27/1884

YEAR TM-L	G	AB	R	H	2B	3B	HR	RBI	BB	SO	SB	CS	AVG	OBP	SLG	OPS	OPS+	BR/A	RC	RC/G	FR	G/POS	WS	TPW
1884 Mil-U	12	46	6	15	6	0	0	....	0	....	....	....	.326	.326	.457	.783	162	3	7	6.34	3	2-12	2	0.5
1885 Phi-N	93	357	25	73	13	2	1	28	11	41	....	....	.204	.228	.261	.489	59	-16	22	2.07	-7	*2-93	5	-1.9
1886 KC-N	118	473	69	131	22	9	4	51	22	42	3	....	.277	.309	.387	.696	104	0	59	4.65	-17	*2-118	10	-1.1
1887 Was-N	105	402	45	124	9	5	2	36	40	26	18	....	.308	.312	.301	.613	75	-10	41	3.87	-12	2-78,S-27	7	-1.5
1888 Was-N	132	502	46	104	12	7	2	46	37	46	20	....	.207	.270	.271	.541	77	-11	43	2.93	-21	*2-132	8	-2.7
1889 Was-N	46	176	24	46	3	0	0	20	22	7	10	....	.261	.347	.278	.625	81	-3	21	4.27	-2	2-46	3	-0.3
Phi-N	75	305	52	82	14	2	0	28	36	9	8	....	.269	.354	.328	.681	84	-6	39	4.65	-9	2-75	6	-1.1
Yr.	121	481	76	128	17	2	0	48	58	16	18	....	.266	.351	.310	.661	83	-9	60	4.51	-11	*2-121	9	-1.4
1890 Phi-N	117	487	95	135	29	7	2	81	57	46	44	....	.277	.365	.378	.742	114	9	85	6.42	13	*2-117	18	2.4
1891 Phi-N	135	514	67	118	27	2	2	69	69	46	8	....	.230	.331	.302	.633	82	-10	55	3.77	-8	*2-135	13	-1.1
Total 8	833	3262	429	828	135	34	13	359	294	263	111	....	.254	.314	.320	.634	87	-44	372	4.09	-59	2-806/S-27	72	-6.9

• MYERS, Bert James Albert Myers b: 4/8/1874, Frederick, MD d: 10/12/1915, Washington, DC BR/TR, 5'10" Deb: 4/25/1896

YEAR TM-L	G	AB	R	H	2B	3B	HR	RBI	BB	SO	SB	CS	AVG	OBP	SLG	OPS	OPS+	BR/A	RC	RC/G	FR	G/POS	WS	TPW
1896 StL-N	122	454	47	116	12	8	0	37	40	32	8	....	.256	.320	.317	.637	71	-18	51	3.90	-13	*3-121/S-1	6	-2.5
1898 Was-N	31	110	14	29	1	4	0	13	13	....	2	....	.264	.341	.345	.687	97	-0	14	4.57	-6	3-31	2	-0.5
1900 Phi-N	7	28	5	5	1	0	0	2	3	....	1	....	.179	.258	.214	.472	31	-3	2	2.13	2	/3-7	0	-0.1
Total 3	160	592	66	150	14	12	0	52	56	32	11	....	.253	.321	.318	.639	74	-21	67	3.93	-17	3-159/S-1	8	-3.1

• MYERS, Billy William Harrison Myers b: 8/14/1910, Enola, PA d: 4/10/1995, Carlisle, PA BR/TR, 5'8", 168 lbs. Deb: 4/16/1935

YEAR TM-L	G	AB	R	H	2B	3B	HR	RBI	BB	SO	SB	CS	AVG	OBP	SLG	OPS	OPS+	BR/A	RC	RC/G	FR	G/POS	WS	TPW
1935 Cin-N	117	445	60	119	15	10	5	36	29	81	10	....	.267	.315	.380	.695	89	-8	55	4.36	-6	*S-112	11	-0.5
1936 Cin-N	98	323	45	87	9	6	6	27	28	56	6	....	.269	.328	.390	.718	99	-1	43	4.67	-7	S-98	10	-0.1
1937 Cin-N	124	335	35	84	13	3	7	43	44	57	0	....	.251	.339	.370	.710	97	-0	46	4.67	2	*S-121/2-6	11	1.0
1938 Cin-N	134	442	57	112	18	6	12	47	41	80	2	....	.253	.317	.403	.719	99	-1	58	4.48	3	*S-123,2-11	15	1.1
1939★Cin-N	151	509	79	143	18	6	9	56	71	90	4	....	.281	.369	.393	.762	104	5	81	5.56	7	*S-151	23	2.3
1940★Cin-N	90	282	33	57	14	2	5	30	30	56	0	....	.202	.283	.319	.603	65	-14	27	3.07	5	S-88	7	-0.3
1941 Chi-N	24	63	10	14	1	0	1	4	7	25	1	....	.222	.310	.286	.596	71	-2	6	3.13	1	S-19/2-1	2	0.0
Total 7	738	2399	319	616	88	33	45	243	250	445	23	....	.257	.328	.377	.706	93	-21	316	4.52	5	S-712/2-18	79	3.6

• MYERS, George George D. Myers b: 11/13/1860, Buffalo, NY d: 12/14/1926, Buffalo, NY BR/TR, 5'8", 170 lbs. Deb: 5/2/1884 U Career OF: 27-69-14

YEAR TM-L	G	AB	R	H	2B	3B	HR	RBI	BB	SO	SB	CS	AVG	OBP	SLG	OPS	OPS+	BR/A	RC	RC/G	FR	G/POS	WS	TPW
1884 Buf-N	78	325	34	59	9	2	2	32	13	33	....	....	.182	.213	.240	.453	41	-22	17	1.76	-16	C-49,0-34(16-18-0)	2	-3.2
1885 Buf-N	89	326	40	67	7	2	0	19	23	40	....	....	.206	.258	.239	.497	59	-14	21	2.15	-3	C-69,0-23(0-21-1)	4	-1.2
1886 StL-N	79	295	26	56	7	3	0	27	18	42	6	....	.190	.236	.234	.470	46	-18	18	2.05	-7	C-72/0-6(0-5-1),3-1	2	-1.7
1887 Ind-N	69	257	25	73	8	1	1	20	22	7	26	....	.284	.298	.272	.570	61	-11	27	3.96	-2	C-50,0-15(3-7-5)/1-6,3-1	3	-0.8
1888 Ind-N	66	248	36	59	9	0	2	16	16	14	28	....	.238	.292	.298	.591	87	-3	31	4.36	-2	C-47,3-14,0-10(2-1-7)/1-1	7	-0.2
1889 Ind-N	43	149	22	29	3	0	0	12	17	13	12	....	.195	.294	.215	.509	42	-11	13	2.93	5	0-23(6-17-0),C-18/1-1	1	-0.5
Total 6	424	1600	183	343	43	8	5	126	109	149	72	....	.214	.260	.250	.510	56	-80	127	2.72	-26	C-305,0-111/3-16,1-8	19	-7.6

• MYERS, Greg Gregory Richard Myers b: 4/14/1966, Riverside, CA BL/TR, 6'1", 205 lbs. Deb: 9/12/1987

YEAR TM-L	G	AB	R	H	2B	3B	HR	RBI	BB	SO	SB	CS	AVG	OBP	SLG	OPS	OPS+	BR/A	RC	RC/G	FR	G/POS	WS	TPW
1987 Tor-A	7	9	1	1	0	0	0	0	0	3	0	0	.111	.111	.111	.222	-40	-2	0	.00	0	/C-7	0	-0.1
1989 Tor-A	17	44	0	5	2	0	0	1	2	9	0	1	.114	.152	.159	.311	-13	-7	1	.42	1	C-11/D-6	0	-0.6
1990 Tor-A	87	250	33	59	7	1	5	22	22	33	0	1	.236	.298	.332	.630	72	-10	22	2.90	-0	C-87	4	-0.5
1991 Tor-A	107	309	25	81	22	0	8	36	21	45	0	0	.262	.309	.411	.720	94	-3	36	3.93	-3	*C-104	5	-0.2
1992 Tor-A	22	61	4	14	6	0	1	13	5	5	0	0	.230	.288	.377	.665	81	-2	6	3.35	1	C-18/D-1	1	0.0
Cal-A	8	17	0	4	1	0	0	0	0	6	0	0	.235	.235	.294	.529	47	-1	1	2.37	0	/C-8	0	-0.1
Yr.	30	78	4	18	7	0	1	13	5	11	0	0	.231	.277	.359	.636	74	-3	8	3.14	1	C-26/D-1	1	-0.1
1993 Cal-A	108	290	27	74	10	0	7	40	17	47	3	3	.255	.301	.362	.663	75	-11	30	3.44	1	C-97/D-2	3	-0.6
1994 Cal-A	45	126	10	31	6	0	2	8	10	27	0	2	.246	.301	.341	.643	64	-8	12	3.10	3	C-41/D-1	2	-0.2
1995 Cal-A	85	273	35	71	12	2	9	38	17	49	0	1	.260	.306	.418	.723	87	-7	34	4.39	1	C-61,D-16	6	-0.3
1996 Min-A	97	329	37	94	22	3	6	47	19	52	0	0	.286	.325	.426	.750	86	-8	42	4.56	-3	C-90	6	-0.5
1997 Min-A	62	165	24	44	11	1	5	28	16	29	0	0	.267	.331	.436	.768	97	-1	23	4.99	-2	C-38,D-10	3	-0.1
Atl-N	9	9	0	1	0	0	0	1	1	3	0	0	.111	.200	.111	.311	-16	-2	0	.85	0	/C-2	0	-0.1
1998★SD-N	69	171	19	42	10	0	4	20	17	36	0	1	.246	.314	.374	.688	86	-4	19	3.72	2	C-52	4	0.1

YEAR TM-L	G	AB	R	H	2B	3B	HR	RBI	BB	SO	SB	CS	AVG	OBP	SLG	OPS	OPS+	BR/A	RC	RC/G	FR	G/POS	WS	TPW
1999 SD-N	50	128	9	37	4	0	3	15	13	14	0	0	.289	.355	.391	.745	96	-1	17	4.74	-2	C-41	3	0.0
*Atl-N	34	72	10	16	2	0	2	9	13	16	0	0	.222	.341	.333	.675	72	-3	9	4.15	1	C-31	3	-0.1
Yr.	84	200	19	53	6	0	5	24	26	30	0	0	.265	.350	.370	.720	87	-4	26	4.52	-1	C-72	6	-0.1
2000 Bal-A	43	125	9	28	6	0	3	12	8	29	0	0	.224	.271	.344	.615	57	-9	10	2.54	1	C-28/D-9	1	-0.6
2001 Bal-A	25	74	11	20	2	0	4	18	8	17	0	0	.270	.341	.459	.801	114	1	11	5.21	-1	D-11/C-8	3	0.0
*Oak-A	33	87	13	16	1	0	7	13	13	21	0	0	.184	.290	.437	.727	88	-2	11	4.11	-2	C-28/D-2	3	-0.2
Yr.	58	161	24	36	3	0	11	31	21	38	0	0	.224	.313	.447	.760	100	-0	22	4.59	-2	C-36,D-13	6	-0.1
2002*Oak-A	65	144	15	32	5	0	6	21	26	36	0	0	.222	.341	.382	.723	92	-1	19	4.51	4	C-53/D-1	4	0.5
2003 Tor-A	121	329	51	101	19	0	15	52	37	57	0	3	.307	.377	.502	.879	127	12	58	6.27	-6	C-81,D-22	9	0.9
Total 16	**1094**	**3012**	**333**	**771**	**148**	**7**	**87**	**394**	**265**	**534**	**3**	**12**	**.256**	**.317**	**.396**	**.713**	**86**	**-68**	**362**	**4.08**	**-4**	**C-886/D-81**	**60**	**-2.5**

• MYERS, Hap Ralph Edward Myers b: 4/8/1888, San Francisco, CA d: 6/30/1967, San Francisco, CA BR/TR, 6'3", 175 lbs. Deb: 4/16/1910

YEAR TM-L	G	AB	R	H	2B	3B	HR	RBI	BB	SO	SB	CS	AVG	OBP	SLG	OPS	OPS+	BR/A	RC	RC/G	FR	G/POS	WS	TPW
1910 Bos-A	3	6	0	2	0	0	0	0	0	....	0	....	.333	.333	.333	.667	106	0	1	4.18	0	/O-2(0-0-2)	0	0.0
1911 StL-A	11	37	4	11	1	0	0	1	1	....	0	....	.297	.316	.324	.640	82	-1	4	3.61	-2	1-11	1	-0.3
Bos-A	13	38	3	14	2	0	0	0	4	....	4	....	.368	.429	.421	.850	139	2	8	9.12	-1	1-12	2	0.1
Yr.	24	75	7	25	3	0	0	1	5	....	4	....	.333	.375	.373	.748	111	1	12	6.15	-3	1-23	3	-0.2
1913 Bos-N	140	524	74	143	20	1	2	50	38	48	57	....	.273	.333	.326	.659	87	-8	73	4.55	4	*1-135	13	-0.7
1914 Bro-F	92	305	61	67	10	5	1	29	44	43	43	....	.220	.322	.295	.617	76	-8	40	4.11	1	1-88	7	-0.9
1915 Bro-F	118	341	61	98	9	1	1	36	32	39	28	....	.287	.352	.328	.680	103	2	49	4.76	-2	*1-107	9	-0.2
Total 5	**377**	**1251**	**203**	**335**	**42**	**7**	**4**	**116**	**119**	**130**	**132**	**....**	**.268**	**.338**	**.322**	**.660**	**90**	**-13**	**175**	**4.58**	**1**	**1-353/O-2**	**32**	**-1.9**

• MYERS, Henry Henry C. Myers b: 5/1858, Philadelphia, PA d: 4/18/1895, Philadelphia, PA BR/TR, 5'9", 159 lbs. Deb: 8/20/1881 M ♦

YEAR TM-L	G	AB	R	H	2B	3B	HR	RBI	BB	SO	SB	CS	AVG	OBP	SLG	OPS	OPS+	BR/A	RC	RC/G	FR	G/POS	WS	TPW
1881 Pro-N	1	4	0	0	0	0	0	0	0	2	....	....	.000	.000	.000	.000	-102	-1	0	.00	0	/S-1	0	-0.1
1882 Bal-a	69	294	43	53	3	0	0	....	12	....	....	....	.180	.212	.190	.403	40	-16	12	1.42	-8	*S-68/P-6	2	-2.9
1884 Wil-U	6	24	3	3	0	0	0	....	0	....	....	....	.125	.125	.125	.250	-15	-3	0	.51	2	/S-5,2-1	0	-0.1
Total 3	**76**	**322**	**46**	**56**	**3**	**0**	**0**	**0**	**12**	**2**	**....**	**....**	**.174**	**.204**	**.183**	**.387**	**34**	**-20**	**13**	**1.32**	**-6**	**/S-74,P-6,2-1**	**2**	**-3.0**

• MYERS, Hy Henry Harrison Myers b: 4/27/1889, East Liverpool, OH d: 5/1/1965, Minerva, OH BR/TR, 5'9.5", 175 lbs. Deb: 8/30/1909 Career OF: 5-1150-28

YEAR TM-L	G	AB	R	H	2B	3B	HR	RBI	BB	SO	SB	CS	AVG	OBP	SLG	OPS	OPS+	BR/A	RC	RC/G	FR	G/POS	WS	TPW
1909 Bro-N	6	22	1	5	1	0	0	6	2	....	1	....	.227	.292	.273	.564	78	-1	2	3.00	-1	/O-6(0-0-6)	0	-0.2
1911 Bro-N	13	43	2	7	1	0	0	0	2	3	1	....	.163	.200	.186	.386	9	-5	2	1.21	-1	O-13(0-12-1)	0	-0.7
1914 Bro-N	70	227	35	65	3	9	0	17	7	24	2	....	.286	.316	.379	.695	104	0	27	4.15	-6	O-60(4-45-12)	6	-1.0
1915 Bro-N	153	605	69	150	21	7	2	46	17	51	19	22	.248	.275	.316	.591	77	-24	52	2.78	-3	*O-153(0-153-0)	14	-4.1
1916*Bro-N	113	412	54	108	12	14	3	36	21	35	17	....	.262	.308	.381	.689	108	3	55	4.47	-8	*O-106(0-105-1)	15	-1.4
1917 Bro-N	120	471	37	126	15	10	1	41	18	25	5	....	.268	.294	.348	.643	94	-5	49	3.49	-5	O-66(0-62-4),1-22,2-19,3-15	12	-1.5
1918 Bro-N	107	407	36	104	9	8	4	40	20	26	17	....	.256	.292	.346	.638	95	-4	44	3.63	8	*O-107(0-107-0)	12	-0.4
1919 Bro-N	133	512	62	157	23	**14**	5	**73**	23	34	13	....	.307	.339	**.436**	.774	129	16	78	5.36	3	*O-131(0-131-0)	23	1.2
1920*Bro-N	154	582	83	177	36	**22**	4	80	35	54	9	13	.304	.345	.462	.807	126	16	88	5.20	-2	*O-152(0-152-0)/3-2	27	0.6
1921 Bro-N	144	549	51	158	14	4	4	68	22	51	8	6	.288	.318	.350	.667	74	-19	61	3.84	0	*O-124(0-124-0),2-21/3-1	12	-2.4
1922 Bro-N	153	618	82	196	20	9	6	89	13	26	9	10	.317	.331	.408	.739	90	-12	79	4.59	-3	*O-152(0-152-0)/2-1	17	-1.9
1923 StL-N	96	330	29	99	18	2	2	48	12	19	5	3	.300	.330	.385	.715	90	-5	42	4.50	4	O-87(0-87-0)	9	-0.4
1924 StL-N	43	124	12	26	5	1	1	15	3	10	1	2	.210	.228	.290	.519	39	-11	8	1.99	-3	O-22(1-17-4),3-12/2-3	1	-1.5
1925 StL-N	1	1	0	0	0	0	0	0	0	0	0	0	.000	.000	.000	.000	-98	-0	0	.00	0	....	0	0.0
Cin-N	3	6	1	1	1	0	0	0	0	0	0	0	.167	.167	.333	.500	25	-1	0	1.70	0	/O-3(0-3-0)	0	-0.1
StL-N	1	1	1	1	0	0	0	0	0	0	0	0	1.000	1.000	1.000	2.000	403	0	1	∞	0	....	0	0.0
Yr.	5	8	2	2	1	0	0	0	0	0	0	0	.250	.250	.375	.625	57	-1	1	1.41	0	/O-3(0-3-0)	0	-0.1
Total 14	**1310**	**4910**	**555**	**1380**	**179**	**100**	**32**	**559**	**195**	**358**	**107**	**56**	**.281**	**.312**	**.378**	**.690**	**96**	**-52**	**587**	**4.08**	**-17**	***O-1182/2-44,3-30,1-22**	**148**	**-13.7**

• MYERS, Lynn Lynnwood Lincoln Myers b: 2/23/1914, Enola, PA d: 1/19/2000, Harrisburg, PA BR/TR, 5'6.5", 145 lbs. Deb: 7/13/1938

YEAR TM-L	G	AB	R	H	2B	3B	HR	RBI	BB	SO	SB	CS	AVG	OBP	SLG	OPS	OPS+	BR/A	RC	RC/G	FR	G/POS	WS	TPW
1938 StL-N	70	227	18	55	10	2	1	19	9	25	9	....	.242	.271	.317	.588	58	-14	20	3.07	1	S-69	3	-0.8
1939 StL-N	74	117	24	28	6	1	0	10	12	23	1	....	.239	.310	.308	.618	63	-6	12	3.47	-2	S-36,3-13/2-5	2	-0.6
Total 2	**144**	**344**	**42**	**83**	**16**	**3**	**1**	**29**	**21**	**48**	**10**	**....**	**.241**	**.285**	**.314**	**.599**	**60**	**-20**	**32**	**3.21**	**-1**	**S-105/3-13,2-5**	**5**	**-1.4**

• MYERS, Richie Richard Myers b: 4/7/1930, Sacramento, CA BR/TR, 5'6", 150 lbs. Deb: 4/21/1956

YEAR TM-L	G	AB	R	H	2B	3B	HR	RBI	BB	SO	SB	CS	AVG	OBP	SLG	OPS	OPS+	BR/A	RC	RC/G	FR	G/POS	WS	TPW
1956 Chi-N	4	1	1	0	0	0	0	0	0	0	0	0	.000	.000	.000	.000	-102	-0	0	.00	0	....	0	0.0

• MYERS, Rod Roderick Demond Myers b: 1/14/1973, Conroe, TX BL/TL, 6', 190 lbs. Deb: 6/21/1996 Career OF: 16-24-11

YEAR TM-L	G	AB	R	H	2B	3B	HR	RBI	BB	SO	SB	CS	AVG	OBP	SLG	OPS	OPS+	BR/A	RC	RC/G	FR	G/POS	WS	TPW
1996 KC-A	22	63	9	18	7	0	1	11	7	16	3	2	.286	.357	.444	.802	101	-0	10	5.55	-1	O-19(4-15-1)	2	-0.1
1997 KC-A	31	101	14	26	7	0	2	9	17	22	4	0	.257	.370	.386	.756	95	1	16	5.55	0	O-26(12-9-10)	2	0.0
Total 2	**53**	**164**	**23**	**44**	**14**	**0**	**3**	**20**	**24**	**38**	**7**	**2**	**.268**	**.365**	**.409**	**.774**	**98**	**1**	**26**	**5.55**	**-1**	**/O-45**	**4**	**-0.1**

• NADY, Xavier Xavier Clifford Nady b: 11/14/1978, Salinas, CA BR/TR, 6'5", 180 lbs. Deb: 9/30/2000

YEAR TM-L	G	AB	R	H	2B	3B	HR	RBI	BB	SO	SB	CS	AVG	OBP	SLG	OPS	OPS+	BR/A	RC	RC/G	FR	G/POS	WS	TPW
2000 SD-N	1	1	1	1	0	0	0	0	0	0	0	0	1.000	1.000	1.000	2.000	438	1	1	∞	0	....	0	0.0
2003 SD-N	110	371	50	99	17	1	9	39	24	74	6	2	.267	.322	.391	.713	93	-4	44	4.09	0	*O-105(0-0-105)	7	-1.0
Total 2	**111**	**372**	**51**	**100**	**17**	**1**	**9**	**39**	**24**	**74**	**6**	**2**	**.269**	**.323**	**.392**	**.716**	**94**	**-4**	**45**	**4.09**	**0**	**O-105**	**7**	**-0.9**

• NAEHRING, Tim Timothy James Naehring b: 2/1/1967, Cincinnati, OH BR/TR, 6'2", 205 lbs. Deb: 7/15/1990

YEAR TM-L	G	AB	R	H	2B	3B	HR	RBI	BB	SO	SB	CS	AVG	OBP	SLG	OPS	OPS+	BR/A	RC	RC/G	FR	G/POS	WS	TPW
1990 Bos-A	24	85	10	23	6	0	2	12	8	15	0	0	.271	.333	.412	.745	102	0	11	4.84	-4	S-19/3-5,2-1	3	-0.2
1991 Bos-A	20	55	1	6	1	0	0	3	6	15	0	0	.109	.197	.127	.324	-8	-8	2	1.00	1	S-17/3-2,2-1	1	-0.6
1992 Bos-A	72	186	12	43	8	0	3	14	18	31	0	0	.231	.309	.323	.632	72	-7	20	3.64	1	S-30,2-23,3-10/D-4,O-1	6	-0.3
1993 Bos-A	39	127	14	42	10	0	1	17	10	26	1	0	.331	.380	.433	.813	111	2	21	6.14	1	2-15,D-10/3-9,S-4	4	0.3
1994 Bos-A	80	297	41	82	18	1	7	42	30	56	1	3	.276	.350	.414	.765	92	-5	41	4.67	6	2-49,3-11/1-8,S-8,D-7	8	0.3
1995*Bos-A	126	433	61	133	27	2	10	57	77	66	0	2	.307	.416	.448	.864	121	16	82	6.81	3	*3-124/D-1	17	1.9
1996 Bos-A	116	430	77	124	16	0	17	65	49	63	2	1	.288	.366	.444	.811	102	1	69	5.69	-2	*3-116/2-1	13	0.2
1997 Bos-A	70	259	38	74	18	1	9	40	38	40	1	1	.286	.379	.467	.846	117	7	45	6.13	0	3-68/D-1	7	0.8
Total 8	**547**	**1872**	**254**	**527**	**104**	**4**	**49**	**250**	**236**	**312**	**5**	**7**	**.282**	**.367**	**.420**	**.787**	**101**	**8**	**291**	**5.44**	**6**	**3-345/2-90,S-78,D-23,1-8,O**	**59**	**2.4**

• NAGEL, Bill William Taylor Nagel b: 8/19/1915, Memphis, TN d: 10/8/1981, Freehold, NJ BR/TR, 6'1", 190 lbs. Deb: 4/20/1939

YEAR TM-L	G	AB	R	H	2B	3B	HR	RBI	BB	SO	SB	CS	AVG	OBP	SLG	OPS	OPS+	BR/A	RC	RC/G	FR	G/POS	WS	TPW
1939 Phi-A	105	341	39	86	19	4	12	39	25	86	2	1	.252	.307	.437	.744	90	-7	42	4.05	-9	2-56,3-43/P-1	5	-1.2
1941 Phi-N	17	56	2	8	1	1	0	6	3	14	0	....	.143	.186	.196	.383	8	-7	2	1.11	1	2-12/O-2(2-0-0),3-1	0	-0.5
1945 Chi-A	67	220	21	46	10	3	3	27	15	41	3	1	.209	.263	.323	.585	71	-8	18	2.56	-5	1-57/3-1	2	-1.7
Total 3	**189**	**617**	**62**	**140**	**30**	**8**	**15**	**72**	**43**	**141**	**5**	**2**	**.227**	**.281**	**.374**	**.655**	**76**	**-22**	**61**	**3.22**	**-13**	**/2-68,1-57,3-45,O-2,P-1**	**7**	**-3.5**

• NAGELSEN, Lou Louis Marcellus Nagelsen b: 6/29/1887, Piqua, OH d: 10/21/1965, Fort Wayne, IN BR/TR, 6'2", 180 lbs. Deb: 9/10/1912

YEAR TM-L	G	AB	R	H	2B	3B	HR	RBI	BB	SO	SB	CS	AVG	OBP	SLG	OPS	OPS+	BR/A	RC	RC/G	FR	G/POS	WS	TPW
1912 Cle-A	2	3	0	0	0	0	0	0	0	....	0	....	.000	.000	.000	.000	-97	-1	0	.00	-1	/C-2	0	-0.1

• NAGELSON, Russ Russell Charles Nagelson b: 9/19/1944, Cincinnati, OH BL/TR, 6', 205 lbs. Deb: 9/11/1968 Career OF: 5-0-7

YEAR TM-L	G	AB	R	H	2B	3B	HR	RBI	BB	SO	SB	CS	AVG	OBP	SLG	OPS	OPS+	BR/A	RC	RC/G	FR	G/POS	WS	TPW
1968 Cle-A	5	3	0	1	0	0	0	0	2	2	0	0	.333	.600	.333	.933	192	1	1	12.31	0	....	0	0.1
1969 Cle-A	12	17	1	6	0	0	0	0	3	3	0	0	.353	.450	.353	.803	123	1	3	7.20	-0	/O-3(1-0-2),1-1	1	0.1
1970 Cle-A	17	24	3	3	1	0	1	2	3	9	0	0	.125	.222	.292	.514	39	-2	2	2.22	0	/O-4(1-0-3)	0	-0.2
Det-A	28	32	5	6	0	0	0	2	5	6	0	0	.188	.297	.188	.485	36	-3	2	2.26	0	/O-4(3-0-2),1-1	0	-0.3
Yr.	45	56	8	9	1	0	1	4	8	15	0	0	.161	.266	.232	.498	37	-5	4	2.25	0	/O-8(4-0-5),1-1	0	-0.5
Total 3	**62**	**76**	**9**	**16**	**1**	**0**	**1**	**4**	**13**	**20**	**0**	**0**	**.211**	**.326**	**.263**	**.589**	**65**	**-3**	**8**	**3.47**	**0**	**/O-11,1-2**	**1**	**-0.4**

• NAGLE, Tom Thomas Edward Nagle b: 10/30/1865, Milwaukee, WI d: 3/9/1946, Milwaukee, WI BR/TR, 5'10", 150 lbs. Deb: 4/22/1890 Career OF: 1-0-6

YEAR TM-L	G	AB	R	H	2B	3B	HR	RBI	BB	SO	SB	CS	AVG	OBP	SLG	OPS	OPS+	BR/A	RC	RC/G	FR	G/POS	WS	TPW
1890 Chi-N	38	144	21	39	5	1	1	11	7	24	4	....	.271	.318	.340	.658	88	-3	17	4.36	-6	C-33/O-6(0-0-6)	3	-0.6
1891 Chi-N	8	25	3	3	0	0	0	1	1	3	0	....	.120	.154	.120	.274	-20	-4	0	.58	-1	/C-7,O-1	0	-0.4
Total 2	**46**	**169**	**24**	**42**	**5**	**1**	**1**	**12**	**8**	**27**	**4**	**....**	**.249**	**.294**	**.308**	**.602**	**73**	**-7**	**18**	**3.71**	**-8**	**/C-40,O-7**	**3**	**-1.0**

• NAHORODNY, Bill William Gerard Nahorodny b: 8/31/1953, Hamtramck, MI BR/TR, 6'2", 200 lbs. Deb: 9/27/1976

YEAR TM-L	G	AB	R	H	2B	3B	HR	RBI	BB	SO	SB	CS	AVG	OBP	SLG	OPS	OPS+	BR/A	RC	RC/G	FR	G/POS	WS	TPW
1976 Phi-N	3	5	0	1	1	0	0	0	0	0	0	0	.200	.200	.400	.600	65	-0	0	2.70	0	/C-2	0	0.0
1977 Chi-A	7	23	3	6	1	0	1	4	2	3	0	0	.261	.320	.435	.755	104	0	3	4.22	1	/C-7	1	0.2

YEAR TM-L	G	AB	R	H	2B	3B	HR	RBI	BB	SO	SB	CS	AVG	OBP	SLG	OPS	OPS+	BR/A	RC	RC/G	FR	G/POS	WS	TPW
1978 Chi-A	107	347	29	82	11	2	8	35	23	52	1	0	.236	.288	.349	.636	77	-11	35	3.45	0	*C-104/1-4,D-1	7	-0.6
1979 Chi-A	65	179	20	46	10	0	6	29	18	23	0	1	.257	.325	.413	.738	98	-1	23	4.43	0	C-60/D-3	5	0.1
1980 Atl-N	59	157	14	38	12	0	5	18	8	21	0	2	.242	.287	.414	.701	91	-4	17	3.54	0	C-54/1-1	4	-0.2
1981 Atl-N	14	13	0	3	1	0	0	2	1	3	0	0	.231	.286	.308	.593	67	-1	1	3.09	0	/C-3,1-1	0	-0.1
1982 Cle-A	39	94	6	21	5	1	4	18	2	9	0	0	.223	.240	.426	.665	79	-3	8	2.94	1	C-35	2	-0.1
1983 Det-A	2	1	0	0	0	0	0	0	1	0	0	0	.000	.500	.000	.500	53	0	0	3.51	0	....	0	0.0
1984 Sea-A	12	25	2	6	0	0	1	3	1	7	0	1	.240	.321	.360	.681	89	-1	3	3.65	-1	C-10/1-1	1	-0.1
Total 9	308	844	74	203	41	3	25	109	56	118	1	4	.241	.292	.385	.678	85	-20	91	3.63	1	C-275/1-7,D-4	20	-0.9

• NALEWAY, Frank Frank "Chick" Naleway b: 7/5/1902, Chicago, IL d: 1/28/1949, Chicago, IL BR/TR, 5'9.5", 165 lbs. Deb: 9/16/1924

YEAR TM-L	G	AB	R	H	2B	3B	HR	RBI	BB	SO	SB	CS	AVG	OBP	SLG	OPS	OPS+	BR/A	RC	RC/G	FR	G/POS	WS	TPW
1924 Chi-A	1	2	0	0	0	0	0	0	1	0	0	0	.000	.333	.000	.333	-10	-0	0	1.63	-1	/S-1	0	-0.1

• NANCE, Doc William G. "Kid" Nance b: 8/2/1876, Fort Worth, TX d: 5/28/1958, Fort Worth, TX BR/TR, 5'7", 165 lbs. Deb: 8/19/1897 Career OF: 130-7-52

YEAR TM-L	G	AB	R	H	2B	3B	HR	RBI	BB	SO	SB	CS	AVG	OBP	SLG	OPS	OPS+	BR/A	RC	RC/G	FR	G/POS	WS	TPW
1897 Lou-N	35	120	25	29	5	3	3	17	20	....	3	....	.242	.355	.408	.763	105	1	19	5.44	4	O-35(0-7-28)	4	0.3
1898 Lou-N	22	76	13	24	5	0	1	16	12	....	2	....	.316	.416	.421	.837	142	5	15	7.25	2	O-22(0-0-22)	4	0.5
1901 Det-A	132	461	72	129	24	5	3	66	51	....	9	....	.280	.355	.373	.728	98	-1	69	5.14	6	*O-132(130-0-2)	13	-0.2
Total 3	189	657	110	182	34	8	7	99	83	....	14	....	.277	.362	.385	.748	104	5	103	5.42	11	O-189	21	0.5

• NAPLES, Al Aloysius Francis Naples b: 8/29/1927, St. George, NY BR/TR, 5'9", 168 lbs. Deb: 6/25/1949

YEAR TM-L	G	AB	R	H	2B	3B	HR	RBI	BB	SO	SB	CS	AVG	OBP	SLG	OPS	OPS+	BR/A	RC	RC/G	FR	G/POS	WS	TPW
1949 StL-A	2	7	0	1	1	0	0	0	0	1	0	0	.143	.143	.286	.429	12	-1	0	1.32	0	/S-2	0	-0.1

• NAPOLEON, Danny Daniel Napoleon b: 1/11/1942, Claysburg, PA BR/TR, 5'11", 190 lbs. Deb: 4/14/1965 Career OF: 24-0-1

YEAR TM-L	G	AB	R	H	2B	3B	HR	RBI	BB	SO	SB	CS	AVG	OBP	SLG	OPS	OPS+	BR/A	RC	RC/G	FR	G/POS	WS	TPW
1965 NY-N	68	97	5	14	1	1	0	7	8	23	0	0	.144	.224	.175	.400	15	-11	4	1.13	-2	O-15(14-0-1)/3-7	0	-1.4
1966 NY-N	12	33	2	7	2	0	0	0	1	10	0	1	.212	.235	.273	.508	42	-3	2	1.58	0	O-10(10-0-0)	0	-0.3
Total 2	80	130	7	21	3	1	0	7	9	33	0	1	.162	.227	.200	.427	21	-14	5	1.24	-2	/O-25,3-7	0	-1.8

• NARAGON, Hal Harold Richard Naragon b: 10/1/1928, Zanesville, OH BL/TR, 6', 175 lbs. Deb: 9/23/1951 C

YEAR TM-L	G	AB	R	H	2B	3B	HR	RBI	BB	SO	SB	CS	AVG	OBP	SLG	OPS	OPS+	BR/A	RC	RC/G	FR	G/POS	WS	TPW
1951 Cle-A	3	8	0	2	0	0	0	0	1	0	0	0	.250	.400	.250	.650	83	-0	1	4.63	0	/C-2	0	0.0
1954*Cle-A	46	101	10	24	2	2	0	12	9	12	0	0	.238	.300	.297	.597	63	-5	10	3.34	0	C-45	3	-0.3
1955 Cle-A	57	127	12	41	9	2	1	14	15	8	1	0	.323	.394	.449	.843	122	4	23	6.89	1	C-52	7	0.7
1956 Cle-A	53	122	11	35	3	1	3	18	13	9	0	0	.287	.360	.402	.762	99	-0	18	5.12	-2	C-48	4	-0.1
1957 Cle-A	57	121	12	31	1	1	0	8	12	9	0	0	.256	.328	.281	.609	69	-5	11	3.05	0	C-39	2	-0.4
1958 Cle-A	9	9	2	3	0	1	0	0	0	0	0	0	.333	.333	.556	.889	144	1	2	7.50	0	....	1	0.1
1959 Cle-A	14	36	6	10	4	1	0	5	3	2	0	0	.278	.350	.444	.794	121	1	6	6.00	0	C-10	2	0.1
Was-A	71	195	12	47	3	2	0	11	8	9	0	1	.241	.275	.277	.551	52	-13	14	2.47	-5	C-54	2	-1.6
Yr.	85	231	18	57	7	3	0	16	11	11	0	1	.247	.287	.303	.590	63	-12	20	2.99	-5	C-64	4	-1.4
1960 Was-A	33	92	7	19	2	0	0	5	8	4	0	0	.207	.277	.228	.505	38	-8	6	2.11	1	C-29	1	-0.6
1961 Min-A	57	139	10	42	2	1	2	11	4	8	0	0	.302	.326	.374	.700	82	-4	16	4.03	0	C-36	3	-0.2
1962 Min-A	24	35	1	8	1	0	0	3	3	1	0	0	.229	.289	.257	.547	47	-3	3	2.40	0	/C-9	0	-0.2
Total 10	424	985	83	262	27	11	6	87	76	62	1	1	.266	.323	.334	.657	77	-31	109	3.83	-5	C-324	25	-2.5

• NARLESKI, Bill William Edward "Cap" Narleski b: 6/9/1899, Perth Amboy, NJ d: 7/20/1964, Laurel Springs, NJ BR/TR, 5'9", 160 lbs. Deb: 4/18/1929

YEAR TM-L	G	AB	R	H	2B	3B	HR	RBI	BB	SO	SB	CS	AVG	OBP	SLG	OPS	OPS+	BR/A	RC	RC/G	FR	G/POS	WS	TPW
1929 Bos-A	96	260	30	72	16	1	0	25	21	22	4	4	.277	.333	.346	.679	77	-9	30	4.01	-4	S-51,2-29/3-7	5	-0.8
1930 Bos-A	39	98	11	23	9	0	0	7	7	5	0	0	.235	.306	.327	.632	63	-5	10	3.56	-2	S-19,3-14/2-5	1	-0.5
Total 2	135	358	41	95	25	1	0	32	28	27	4	4	.265	.326	.341	.666	73	-14	41	3.88	-6	/S-70,2-34,3-21	6	-1.3

• NARRON, Jerry Jerry Austin Narron b: 1/15/1956, Goldsboro, NC BL/TR, 6'3", 205 lbs. Deb: 4/13/1979 M/C

YEAR TM-L	G	AB	R	H	2B	3B	HR	RBI	BB	SO	SB	CS	AVG	OBP	SLG	OPS	OPS+	BR/A	RC	RC/G	FR	G/POS	WS	TPW
1979 NY-A	61	123	17	21	3	1	4	18	9	26	0	0	.171	.227	.309	.536	44	-10	9	2.18	-2	C-56/D-1	1	-1.0
1980 Sea-A	48	107	7	21	3	0	4	18	13	18	0	0	.196	.283	.336	.620	68	-5	11	3.12	-1	C-39/D-1	2	-0.4
1981 Sea-A	76	203	13	45	5	0	3	17	16	35	0	0	.222	.285	.291	.576	64	-9	17	2.84	-3	C-65	2	-1.0
1983 Cal-A	10	22	1	3	0	0	1	4	1	3	0	0	.136	.174	.273	.447	21	-2	1	1.55	0	/C-6,D-1	0	-0.3
1984 Cal-A	69	150	9	37	5	0	3	17	8	12	0	0	.247	.289	.340	.629	74	-5	13	2.89	-1	C-46/1-7	2	-0.5
1985 Cal-A	67	132	12	29	4	0	5	14	11	17	0	0	.220	.280	.364	.643	75	-5	13	3.44	1	C-45/D-7,1-1	4	-0.2
1986*Cal-A	57	95	5	21	3	1	1	8	9	14	0	0	.221	.295	.305	.601	65	-5	8	2.64	1	C-51/D-2	2	-0.3
1987 Sea-A	4	8	0	0	0	0	0	0	0	2	0	0	.000	.000	.000	.000	-95	-2	0	.00	0	/C-3	0	-0.2
Total 8	392	840	64	177	23	2	21	96	67	127	0	0	.211	.272	.318	.590	63	-43	72	2.78	-4	C-311/D-12,1-8	13	-3.8

• NARRON, Sam Samuel Woody Narron b: 8/25/1913, Middlesex, NC d: 12/31/1996, Raleigh, NC BR/TR, 5'10", 180 lbs. Deb: 9/15/1935 C

YEAR TM-L	G	AB	R	H	2B	3B	HR	RBI	BB	SO	SB	CS	AVG	OBP	SLG	OPS	OPS+	BR/A	RC	RC/G	FR	G/POS	WS	TPW
1935 StL-N	4	7	0	3	0	0	0	0	0	0	0	....	.429	.429	.429	.857	126	0	1	8.90	0	/C-1	0	0.0
1942 StL-N	10	10	0	4	0	0	0	1	0	0	0	....	.400	.400	.400	.800	125	0	2	7.20	0	/C-2	1	0.0
1943*StL-N	10	11	0	1	0	0	0	0	1	2	0	....	.091	.167	.091	.258	-24	-2	0	.57	-0	/C-3	0	-0.2
Total 3	24	28	0	8	0	0	0	1	1	2	0	....	.286	.310	.286	.596	64	-1	3	4.22	-1	/C-6	1	-0.2

• NASH, Billy William Mitchell Nash b: 6/24/1865, Richmond, VA d: 11/15/1929, East Orange, NJ BR/TR, 5'8.5", 167 lbs. Deb: 8/5/1884 M/U Career OF: 6-1-1

YEAR TM-L	G	AB	R	H	2B	3B	HR	RBI	BB	SO	SB	CS	AVG	OBP	SLG	OPS	OPS+	BR/A	RC	RC/G	FR	G/POS	WS	TPW
1884 Ric-a	45	166	31	33	8	8	1	0	12	....	....	....	.199	.281	.361	.643	109	2	17	3.57	5	3-45	5	0.8
1885 Bos-N	26	94	9	24	4	0	0	11	2	9	....	....	.255	.271	.298	.569	87	-1	8	3.00	-3	3-19/2-8	2	-0.4
1886 Bos-N	109	417	61	117	11	8	1	45	24	28	16	....	.281	.320	.353	.672	108	4	53	4.81	4	*3-90,S-17/O-2(1-1-0)	15	1.0
1887 Bos-N	121	535	100	200	24	12	6	94	60	30	43	....	.374	.376	.434	.810	128	20	96	7.59	7	*3-117/O-5(4-0-1)	19	2.5
1888 Bos-N	135	526	71	149	18	15	4	75	50	46	20	....	.283	.350	.397	.747	133	20	82	5.88	22	*3-105,2-31	23	**4.5**
1889 Bos-N	128	481	84	132	20	2	3	76	79	44	26	....	.274	.379	.343	.722	97	1	74	5.63	11	*3-128/P-1	20	1.3
1890 Bos-P	129	488	103	130	28	6	5	90	88	43	26	....	.266	.383	.379	.762	97	-1	83	6.24	16	*3-129/P-1	20	1.4
1891 Bos-N	140	537	92	148	24	9	5	95	74	50	28	....	.276	.369	.382	.750	106	4	88	6.11	-6	*3-140	20	0.1
1892*Bos-N	135	526	94	137	25	5	4	95	59	42	31	....	.260	.338	.350	.688	99	-1	75	5.18	28	*3-135/O-1	22	2.7
1893 Bos-N	128	485	115	141	27	6	10	123	85	29	30	....	.291	.399	.433	.832	112	9	98	7.55	8	*3-128	25	1.6
1894 Bos-N	132	512	132	148	23	6	8	87	91	23	20	....	.289	.399	.404	.804	84	-14	93	6.64	8	*3-132	17	-0.3
1895 Bos-N	133	513	97	147	24	6	10	108	74	19	18	....	.287	.380	.415	.795	101	1	92	6.66	-7	*3-132	17	-0.3
1896 Phi-N	65	227	29	56	9	1	3	30	34	21	3	....	.247	.355	.335	.690	83	-4	29	4.44	5	3-65	6	0.2
1897 Phi-N	104	337	45	87	20	2	0	39	60	....	4	....	.258	.373	.329	.703	89	-2	46	4.65	-4	3-79,S-19/2-4	9	-0.3
1898 Phi-N	20	70	9	17	2	1	0	9	11	....	0	....	.243	.346	.300	.646	89	-0	7	3.72	-1	3-20	2	-0.1
Total 15	1550	5914	1072	1666	267	87	60	977	803	384	265	....	.282	.366	.380	.746	104	37	942	5.89	91	*3-1464/2-43,S-36,O-8,P-2	222	14.5

• NASH, Cotton Charles Francis Nash b: 7/24/1942, Jersey City, NJ BR/TR, 6'6", 220 lbs. Deb: 9/1/1967

YEAR TM-L	G	AB	R	H	2B	3B	HR	RBI	BB	SO	SB	CS	AVG	OBP	SLG	OPS	OPS+	BR/A	RC	RC/G	FR	G/POS	WS	TPW
1967 Chi-A	3	3	1	0	0	0	0	0	1	0	0	0	.000	.250	.000	.250	-21	-0	0	.59	-1	/1-3	0	-0.1
1969 Min-A	6	9	0	2	0	0	0	0	1	2	0	0	.222	.300	.222	.522	47	-1	1	2.62	1	/1-6,O-1	0	0.0
1970 Min-A	4	4	1	1	0	0	0	2	1	1	0	1	.250	.400	.250	.650	82	-0	0	1.70	0	/1-2	0	-0.1
Total 3	13	16	2	3	0	0	0	2	3	3	0	1	.188	.316	.188	.503	42	-1	1	1.92	-0	/1-11,O-1	0	-0.2

• NASH, Ken Kenneth Leland Nash b: 7/14/1888, Weymouth, MA d: 2/16/1977, Epsom, NH BB/TR, 5'8", 140 lbs. Deb: 7/4/1912

YEAR TM-L	G	AB	R	H	2B	3B	HR	RBI	BB	SO	SB	CS	AVG	OBP	SLG	OPS	OPS+	BR/A	RC	RC/G	FR	G/POS	WS	TPW
1912 Cle-A	11	23	2	4	0	0	0	0	3	....	0	....	.174	.269	.174	.443	27	-2	1	1.41	-1	/S-8	0	-0.3
1914 StL-N	24	51	4	14	3	1	0	6	6	10	0	....	.275	.351	.373	.723	116	1	6	4.44	-4	3-10/2-6,S-3	2	-0.3
Total 2	35	74	6	18	3	1	0	6	9	10	0	....	.243	.325	.311	.636	89	-1	8	3.43	-5	/S-11,3-10,2-6	2	-0.6

• NATAL, Bob Robert Marcel Natal b: 11/13/1965, Long Beach, CA BR/TR, 5'11", 190 lbs. Deb: 7/18/1992

YEAR TM-L	G	AB	R	H	2B	3B	HR	RBI	BB	SO	SB	CS	AVG	OBP	SLG	OPS	OPS+	BR/A	RC	RC/G	FR	G/POS	WS	TPW
1992 Mon-N	5	6	0	0	0	0	0	0	1	1	0	0	.000	.143	.000	.143	-57	-1	0	.00	-1	/C-4	0	-0.2
1993 Fla-N	41	117	3	25	4	1	1	6	6	22	1	0	.214	.276	.291	.566	49	-8	9	2.30	0	C-38	2	-0.6
1994 Fla-N	10	29	2	8	2	0	0	2	5	5	1	0	.276	.382	.345	.727	89	-0	4	5.12	2	/C-8	1	0.3
1995 Fla-N	16	43	2	10	2	1	2	6	1	9	0	0	.233	.250	.465	.715	83	-1	5	3.93	0	C-13	1	-0.1
1996 Fla-N	44	90	4	12	1	1	0	2	15	31	0	1	.133	.257	.167	.424	15	-11	4	1.27	-2	C-43	1	-1.1
1997 Fla-N	4	4	2	2	1	0	1	3	2	0	0	0	.500	.667	1.500	2.167	468	2	4	36.21	0	/C-4	1	0.3
Total 6	120	289	13	57	10	3	4	19	30	68	2	1	.197	.282	.294	.576	54	-20	26	2.78	-0	C-110	6	-1.4

YEAR TM-L	G	AB	R	H	2B	3B	HR	RBI	BB	SO	SB	CS	AVG	OBP	SLG	OPS	OPS+	BR/A	RC	RC/G	FR	G/POS	WS	TPW
• NATON, Pete	Peter Alphonsus Naton b: 9/9/1931, Flushing, NY BR/TR, 6'1", 200 lbs. Deb: 6/16/1953																							
1953 Pit-N	6	12	2	2	0	0	0	1	2	1	0	0	.167	.286	.167	.452	22	-1	1	1.98	0	/C-4	0	-0.1
• NAVA, Sandy	Vincent Irwin Nava b: 4/12/1850, San Francisco, CA d: 6/15/1906, Baltimore, MD, 5'6", 155 lbs. Deb: 5/5/1882 Career OF: 1-0-2																							
1882 Pro-N	28	97	15	20	2	0	0	7	1	13	....	....	.206	.214	.227	.441	42	-6	5	1.73	-6	C-27/0-1	1	-0.9
1883 Pro-N	29	100	18	24	4	2	0	16	3	17	....	....	.240	.262	.320	.582	74	-3	9	3.11	0	C-27/0-2(1-0-1)	2	-0.1
1884 Pro-N	34	116	10	11	0	0	0	6	11	35	....	....	.095	.173	.095	.268	-14	-14	2	.51	-1	C-27/S-6,2-1	2	-1.1
1885 Bal-a	8	27	2	5	1	0	0	4	1	....	....	....	.185	.214	.222	.437	39	-2	1	1.62	-2	/C-8	0	-0.3
1886 Bal-a	2	5	0	1	0	0	0	0	0	....	1	....	.200	.200	.200	.400	26	-0	0	2.77	-1	/C-1,S-1	0	-0.1
Total 5	101	345	45	61	7	2	0	33	16	65	1	....	.177	.213	.209	.422	31	-26	17	1.65	-9	/C-90,S-7,0-3,2-1	5	-2.5
• NAVARRO, Tito	Norberto (Rodriguez) Navarro b: 9/12/1970, Rio Piedras, Puerto Rico BB/TR, 5'10", 165 lbs. Deb: 9/6/1993																							
1993 NY-N	12	17	1	1	0	0	0	1	0	4	0	0	.059	.059	.059	.118	-69	-4	0	.00	1	/S-2	0	-0.3
• NAYLOR, Earl	Earl Eugene Naylor b: 5/19/1919, Kansas City, MO d: 1/16/1990, Winter Haven, FL BR/TR, 6', 190 lbs. Deb: 4/15/1942 Career OF: 2-55-11 ♦																							
1942 Phi-N	76	168	9	33	4	1	0	14	11	18	1	....	.196	.246	.232	.478	42	-9	9	1.64	-1	0-34(2-22-11),P-20	0	-3.2
1943 Phi-N	33	120	12	21	2	0	3	14	12	16	1	....	.175	.256	.267	.522	53	-7	7	1.74	3	0-33(0-33-0)	1	-0.5
1946 Bro-N	3	2	1	0	0	0	0	0	0	1	0	....	.000	.000	.000	.000	-99	-1	0	.00	0	....	0	-0.1
Total 3	112	290	22	54	6	1	3	28	23	35	2	....	.186	.248	.245	.493	46	-17	16	1.67	2	/0-67,P-20	1	-3.7
• NEAGLE, Jack	John Henry Neagle b: 1/2/1858, Syracuse, NY d: 9/20/1904, Syracuse, NY BR/TR, 5'6", 155 lbs. Deb: 7/8/1879 Career OF: 14-12-14 ♦																							
1879 Cin-N	3	12	1	2	0	0	0	2	0	0	....	....	.167	.167	.167	.333	11	-1	0	.96	-1	/0-2(0-1-1),P-2	0	-0.3
1883 Phi-N	18	73	6	12	1	0	0	4	1	9	....	....	.164	.176	.178	.354	9	-6	2	1.06	-3	0-12(11-1-0)/P-8	0	-2.5
Bal-a	9	35	3	10	4	0	0	0	2	....	....	....	.286	.324	.400	.724	128	2	5	5.21	-1	/P-6,0-5(1-0-4)	2	-0.3
Pit-a	27	101	14	19	0	1	0	0	5	....	....	....	.188	.226	.208	.434	43	-4	5	1.66	-2	P-16,0-15(0-8-7)	1	-3.2
Yr.	36	136	17	29	4	1	0	0	7	....	....	....	.213	.252	.257	.509	65	-2	10	2.49	-3	P-22,0-20(1-8-11)	3	-3.5
1884 Pit-a	43	148	13	22	6	0	0	0	6	....	....	....	.149	.187	.189	.376	23	-7	5	1.17	-6	P-38/0-6(2-2-2)	14	-1.0
Total 3	100	369	37	65	11	1	0	6	14	9	....	....	.176	.208	.211	.420	35	-16	18	1.61	-13	/P-70,0-40	17	-7.3
• NEAL, Charlie	Charles Lenard Neal b: 1/30/1931, Longview, TX d: 11/18/1996, Dallas, TX BR/TR, 5'10", 165 lbs. Deb: 4/17/1956																							
1956*Bro-N	62	136	22	39	5	1	2	14	14	19	2	2	.287	.353	.382	.736	91	-2	18	4.93	1	2-51/S-1	5	0.1
1957 Bro-N	128	448	62	121	13	7	12	62	53	83	11	4	.270	.358	.411	.768	96	0	69	5.45	-2	*S-100,3-23/2-3	15	0.7
1958 LA-N	140	473	87	120	9	6	22	65	61	91	7	6	.254	.345	.438	.783	102	1	71	5.07	-3	*2-132/S-9	18	0.9
1959*LA-N★	151	616	103	177	30	**11**	19	83	43	86	17	6	.287	.338	.464	.802	103	3	91	5.02	10	*2-151/S-1	25	2.5
1960 LA-N★	139	477	60	122	23	2	8	40	48	75	5	5	.256	.325	.363	.688	83	-12	54	3.64	-25	*2-136/S-3	9	-2.7
1961 LA-N	108	341	40	80	6	1	10	48	30	49	3	2	.235	.298	.346	.644	65	-18	35	3.42	-2	*2-104	8	-1.1
1962 NY-N	136	508	59	132	14	9	11	58	56	90	2	8	.260	.333	.388	.721	91	-9	62	4.02	-8	2-85,S-39,3-12	7	-0.7
1963 NY-N	72	253	26	57	12	1	3	18	27	49	1	2	.225	.302	.316	.619	77	-7	25	3.44	1	3-66/S-8	6	-0.6
Cin-N	34	64	2	10	1	0	0	3	5	15	0	1	.156	.217	.172	.389	13	-7	3	1.24	-3	3-19/2-1,S-1	0	-1.1
Yr.	106	317	28	67	13	1	3	21	32	64	1	3	.211	.286	.287	.573	64	-15	28	2.96	-1	3-85/S-9,2-1	6	-1.7
Total 8	970	3316	461	858	113	38	87	391	337	557	48	36	.259	.331	.394	.725	89	-50	429	4.35	-30	2-663,S-162,3-120	93	-1.9
• NEAL, Offa	Theophilus Fountain Neal b: 6/5/1876, Logan, IL d: 4/12/1950, Mount Vernon, IL BL/TR, 6', 185 lbs. Deb: 9/30/1905																							
1905 NY-N	4	13	0	0	0	0	0	0	0	....	0	....	.000	.000	.000	.000	-98	-3	0	.00	0	/3-3,2-1	0	-0.3
• NEALE, Greasy	Alfred Earle Neale b: 11/5/1891, Parkersburg, WV d: 11/2/1973, Lake Worth, FL BL/TR, 6', 170 lbs. Deb: 4/12/1916 C Career OF: 268-110-364																							
1916 Cin-N	138	530	53	139	13	5	0	20	19	79	17	....	.262	.295	.306	.601	87	-9	54	3.48	9	*0-133(79-55-2)	9	-0.8
1917 Cin-N	121	385	40	113	14	9	3	33	24	36	25	....	.294	.343	.400	.743	133	14	58	5.39	1	*0-119(79-27-13)	16	1.1
1918 Cin-N	107	371	57	100	11	11	1	32	24	38	23	....	.270	.324	.367	.691	112	5	50	4.50	3	*0-102(78-12-12)	11	0.4
1919*Cin-N	139	500	57	121	10	12	1	54	47	51	28	....	.242	.316	.316	.632	93	-3	59	3.72	-2	*0-138(24-5-109)	15	-1.4
1920 Cin-N	150	530	55	135	10	7	3	46	45	48	29	12	.255	.322	.317	.639	85	-5	58	3.61	8	*0-150(0-3-148)	16	-0.5
1921 Phi-N	22	57	7	12	1	0	0	1	14	9	3	4	.211	.366	.228	.594	56	-4	5	2.90	-2	0-16(0-0-16)	0	-0.6
Cin-N	63	241	39	58	10	5	0	12	22	16	9	6	.241	.307	.324	.630	70	-10	24	3.33	-3	0-60(1-8-53)	3	-1.7
Yr.	85	298	46	70	11	5	0	13	36	25	12	10	.235	.319	.305	.625	67	-13	30	3.24	-5	0-76(1-8-69)	3	-2.3
1922 Cin-N	25	43	11	10	2	1	0	2	6	3	5	2	.233	.353	.326	.679	77	-1	6	4.16	-1	0-16(5-0-11)	1	-0.2
1924 Cin-N	3	4	0	0	0	0	0	0	0	1	0	0	.000	.000	.000	.000	-101	-1	0	.00	0	/0-2(2-0-0)	0	-0.1
Total 8	768	2661	319	688	71	50	8	200	201	281	139	24	.259	.319	.332	.651	95	-14	314	3.93	13	0-736	71	-3.9
• NEALE, Joe	Joseph Hunt Neale b: 5/7/1866, Wadsworth, OH d: 12/30/1913, Akron, OH BR/TR, 5'8", 153 lbs. Deb: 6/21/1886 Career OF: 2-0-1 ♦																							
1886 Lou-a	2	5	0	0	0	0	0	0	0	....	0	....	.000	.000	.000	.000	-95	-1	0	.00	1	/0-2(1-0-1),P-1	0	-0.4
1887 Lou-a	5	22	3	4	0	0	0	1	3	....	1	....	.182	.182	.053	.234	-32	-2	0	.56	-0	/P-5	0	-1.2
1890 StL-a	11	30	4	2	0	0	0	1	3	....	0	....	.067	.152	.067	.218	-31	-3	0	.29	-1	P-10/0-1	6	0.3
1891 StL-a	15	51	6	6	0	1	1	8	3	11	1	....	.118	.167	.216	.382	8	-3	2	1.21	2	P-15	7	-0.4
Total 4	33	108	13	12	0	1	1	10	9	11	2	....	.111	.158	.133	.291	-16	-10	3	.76	1	/P-31,0-3	13	-1.7
• NEALON, Jim	James Joseph Nealon b: 12/15/1884, Sacramento, CA d: 4/2/1910, San Francisco, CA BR/TR, 6'1.5" Deb: 4/12/1906																							
1906 Pit-N	154	556	82	142	21	12	3	**83**	53	....	15	....	.255	.327	.353	.679	107	4	73	4.38	2	*1-154	18	0.4
1907 Pit-N	105	381	29	98	10	8	0	47	23	....	11	....	.257	.301	.325	.627	95	-3	43	3.81	0	*1-104	9	-0.6
Total 2	259	937	111	240	31	20	3	130	76	....	26	....	.256	.317	.342	.658	102	1	116	4.15	2	1-258	27	-0.2
• NEEDHAM, Tom	Thomas Joseph "Deerfoot" Needham b: 5/17/1879, Steubenville, OH d: 12/14/1926, Steubenville, OH BR/TR, 5'10", 180 lbs. Deb: 5/12/1904 U Career OF: 0-5-0																							
1904 Bos-N	84	269	18	70	12	3	4	19	11	....	3	....	.260	.292	.372	.664	108	1	31	4.02	6	C-77/0-1	9	1.6
1905 Bos-N	83	271	21	59	6	1	2	17	24	....	3	....	.218	.293	.269	.563	70	-9	23	2.81	5	C-77/0-3(0-3-0),1-2	5	0.3
1906 Bos-N	83	285	11	54	8	2	1	12	13	....	3	....	.189	.230	.242	.472	49	-18	17	1.92	4	C-76/2-5,1-2,3-1,0-1	4	-0.7
1907 Bos-N	86	260	19	51	6	2	1	19	18	....	4	....	.196	.264	.246	.510	60	-12	19	2.32	0	C-78/1-1	3	-0.5
1908 NY-N	54	91	8	19	3	0	0	11	12	....	0	....	.209	.339	.242	.581	82	-1	8	2.76	-5	C-47	3	-0.3
1909 Chi-N	13	28	3	4	0	0	0	0	0	....	0	....	.143	.143	.143	.286	-11	-4	1	.55	-1	/C-7	0	-0.5
1910*Chi-N	31	76	9	14	3	1	0	10	10	10	1	....	.184	.287	.250	.537	57	-4	6	2.40	-2	C-27/1-1	2	-0.3
1911 Chi-N	27	62	4	12	2	0	0	5	9	14	2	....	.194	.315	.226	.541	52	-4	5	2.54	1	C-23	2	-0.1
1912 Chi-N	33	90	12	16	5	0	0	10	7	13	3	....	.178	.260	.233	.493	36	-8	6	2.10	1	C-32	2	-0.4
1913 Chi-N	20	42	5	10	4	1	0	11	4	8	0	....	.238	.304	.381	.685	95	-0	5	3.65	1	C-14/1-1	1	0.2
1914 Chi-N	9	17	3	2	1	0	0	3	1	4	1	....	.118	.167	.176	.343	2	-2	1	.99	0	/C-7	0	-0.2
Total 11	523	1491	113	311	50	10	8	117	109	49	20	....	.209	.274	.272	.546	67	-60	122	2.62	12	C-465/1-7,2-5,0-5,3-1	31	-1.0
• NEEL, Troy	Troy Lee Neel b: 9/14/1965, Freeport, TX BL/TR, 6'4", 210 lbs. Deb: 5/30/1992																							
1992 Oak-A	24	53	8	14	3	0	3	9	5	15	0	1	.264	.339	.491	.830	137	2	8	5.54	-1	/D-9,0-9(9-0-0),1-2	2	0.1
1993 Oak-A	123	427	59	124	21	0	19	63	49	101	3	5	.290	.369	.473	.842	132	18	74	6.33	0	D-85,1-34	13	1.0
1994 Oak-A	83	278	43	74	13	0	15	48	38	61	2	3	.266	.358	.475	.833	123	9	48	6.07	1	1-45,D-35	8	0.4
Total 3	230	758	110	212	37	0	37	120	92	177	5	9	.280	.363	.475	.838	129	29	131	6.18	0	D-129/1-81,0-9	23	1.5
• NEEMAN, Cal	Calvin Amandus Neeman b: 2/18/1929, Valmeyer, IL BR/TR, 6'1", 192 lbs. Deb: 4/16/1957																							
1957 Chi-N	122	415	37	107	17	1	10	39	22	87	0	0	.258	.300	.376	.676	81	-11	46	3.84	4	*C-118	11	-0.1
1958 Chi-N	76	201	30	52	7	0	12	29	21	41	0	0	.259	.338	.473	.810	113	4	32	5.54	-1	C-71	7	0.6
1959 Chi-N	44	105	7	17	2	0	3	9	11	23	0	0	.162	.241	.267	.508	35	-10	7	2.14	-2	C-38	0	-1.0
1960 Chi-N	9	13	0	2	1	0	0	0	0	5	0	0	.154	.154	.231	.385	4	-2	0	1.13	1	/C-9	0	-0.1
Phi-N	59	160	13	29	6	2	4	13	16	42	0	0	.181	.264	.319	.583	58	-9	13	2.57	2	C-52	2	-0.5
Yr.	68	173	13	31	7	2	4	13	16	47	0	0	.179	.257	.312	.569	55	-11	14	2.46	2	C-61	2	-0.6
1961 Phi-N	19	31	0	7	1	0	0	2	4	8	1	0	.226	.314	.258	.572	55	-2	2	2.46	0	C-19	0	-0.1
1962 Pit-N	24	50	5	9	1	1	1	5	3	10	0	0	.180	.226	.300	.526	40	-4	3	1.87	0	C-24	1	-0.4
1963 Cle-A	9	9	0	0	0	0	0	0	1	5	0	0	.000	.100	.000	.100	-70	-2	0	.19	0	/C-9	0	-0.2

YEAR TM-L	G	AB	R	H	2B	3B	HR	RBI	BB	SO	SB	CS	AVG	OBP	SLG	OPS	OPS+	BR/A	RC	RC/G	FR	G/POS	WS	TPW
Was-A	14	18	1	1	0	0	0	0	1	0	0	0	.056	.105	.056	.161	-54	-4	0	.21	0	C-12	0	-0.3
Yr.	23	27	1	1	0	0	0	0	2	5	0	0	.037	.103	.037	.140	-59	-6	0	.20	1	C-21	0	-0.5
Total 7	376	1002	93	224	35	4	30	97	79	221	1	0	.224	.286	.356	.642	72	-40	104	3.45	5	C-352	21	-2.1
• NEFF, Doug	Douglas Williams Neff b: 10/8/1891, Harrisonburg, VA d: 5/23/1932, Cape Charles, VA BR/TR, 5'9", 141 lbs. Deb: 6/26/1914																							
1914 Was-A	3	2	0	0	0	0	0	0	0	0	0	....	.000	.000	.000	.000	-96	-0	0	.00	0	/S-3	0	-0.1
1915 Was-A	30	60	1	10	1	0	0	4	4	6	1	2	.167	.219	.183	.402	20	-7	3	1.33	-5	3-12,2-10/S-7	0	-1.2
Total 2	33	62	1	10	1	0	0	4	4	6	1	2	.161	.212	.177	.390	17	-7	3	1.28	-5	/3-12,2-10,S-10	0	-1.3
• NEIGHBORS, Bob	Robert Otis Neighbors b: 11/9/1917, Talihina, OK d: 8/8/1952, North Korea BR/TR, 5'11", 165 lbs. Deb: 9/16/1939																							
1939 StL-A	7	11	3	2	0	0	1	1	0	1	0	0	.182	.182	.455	.636	56	-1	1	2.73	-1	/S-5	0	-0.1
• NEIGHBORS, Cy	Flemon Cecil Neighbors b: 9/23/1880, Fayetteville, MO d: 5/20/1964, Tacoma, WA BR, 5'10", 178 lbs. Deb: 4/29/1908																							
1908 Pit-N	1	0	0	0	0	0	0	0	0	....	0	....	....	....	....	....	-100	0	0	....	0	/O-1	0	0.0
• NEILL, Mike	Michael Robert Neill b: 4/27/1970, Martinsville, VA BR/TR, 6'2" Deb: 7/27/1998																							
1998 Oak-A	6	15	2	4	1	0	0	0	2	4	0	0	.267	.353	.333	.686	82	-0	2	4.78	0	/O-6(4-2-0)	0	0.0
• NEILL, Tommy	Thomas White Neill b: 11/7/1919, Hartselle, AL d: 9/22/1980, Houston, TX BL/TR, 6'2", 200 lbs. Deb: 9/10/1946 Career OF: 14-0-1																							
1946 Bos-N	13	45	8	12	2	0	0	7	2	1	0	....	.267	.298	.311	.609	72	-2	4	2.78	0	O-13(13-0-0)	1	-0.2
1947 Bos-N	7	10	1	2	0	1	0	0	1	2	0	....	.200	.333	.400	.733	96	-0	1	3.39	-0	/O-2(1-0-1)	0	0.0
Total 2	20	55	9	14	2	1	0	7	3	3	0	....	.255	.305	.327	.632	77	-2	5	2.90	0	/O-15	1	-0.2
• NEIS, Bernie	Bernard Edmund Neis b: 9/26/1895, Bloomington, IL d: 11/29/1972, Inverness, FL BB/TR, 5'7", 160 lbs. Deb: 4/14/1920 Career OF: 96-260-169																							
1920*Bro-N	95	249	38	63	11	2	2	22	26	35	9	9	.253	.329	.337	.666	89	-4	28	3.58	-1	O-83(11-7-65)	6	-1.0
1921 Bro-N	102	230	34	59	5	4	4	34	25	41	9	7	.257	.332	.365	.697	81	-6	28	4.00	1	O-77(11-24-45)/2-1	5	-0.9
1922 Bro-N	61	70	15	16	4	1	1	9	13	8	3	2	.229	.349	.357	.707	83	-1	9	4.31	-1	O-27(7-3-17)	2	-0.3
1923 Bro-N	126	445	78	122	17	4	5	37	36	38	8	8	.274	.330	.364	.694	85	-10	53	4.15	6	*O-111(13-87-11)	10	-0.9
1924 Bro-N	80	211	43	64	8	3	4	26	27	17	4	2	.303	.385	.427	.811	121	8	36	6.28	-4	O-62(19-22-22)	9	0.0
1925 Bos-N	106	355	47	101	20	2	5	45	38	19	8	10	.285	.354	.394	.748	99	-2	49	4.77	5	O-87(9-76-2)	10	-0.1
1926 Bos-N	30	93	16	20	5	2	0	8	8	10	4	....	.215	.277	.312	.589	64	-5	8	2.80	0	O-23(15-8-0)	1	-0.6
1927 Cle-A	32	96	17	29	9	0	4	18	18	9	0	1	.302	.412	.521	.933	140	6	21	7.42	3	O-29(5-24-0)	5	0.7
Chi-A	45	76	9	22	5	0	0	11	10	9	1	0	.289	.372	.355	.727	92	-0	11	5.14	0	O-21(6-9-7)	2	-0.1
Yr.	77	172	26	51	14	0	4	29	28	18	1	1	.297	.395	.448	.843	120	6	32	6.45	3	O-50(11-33-7)	7	0.6
Total 8	677	1825	297	496	84	18	25	210	201	186	46	39	.272	.346	.379	.724	94	-14	244	4.54	10	O-520/2-1	50	-3.2
• NEITZKE, Ernie	Ernest Fredrich Neitzke b: 11/13/1894, Toledo, OH d: 4/27/1977, Sylvania, OH BR/TR, 5'10", 180 lbs. Deb: 6/2/1921																							
1921 Bos-A	11	25	3	6	0	0	0	2	4	4	0	0	.240	.345	.240	.585	53	-1	2	3.25	0	/O-8(4-1-3),P-2	1	-0.4
• NELSON, Bry	Bryant Lawrence Nelson b: 1/27/1974, Crossett, AR BB/TR, 5'10", 205 lbs. Deb: 5/14/2002																							
2002 Bos-A	25	34	6	9	3	0	0	2	4	1	1	1	.265	.342	.353	.695	84	-1	4	3.83	0	2-11,O-11(7-2-2)/D-1	1	-0.1
• NELSON, Candy	John W. Nelson b: 3/14/1849, Portland, ME d: 9/4/1910, Brooklyn, NY BL/TR, 5'6", 145 lbs. Deb: 6/11/1872 U NA OF: 1-12-6 Career OF: 4-29-48																							
1872 Tro-n	4	20	2	7	0	0	0	4	0	2	0	0	.350	.350	.350	.700	114	0	3	5.99	-1	/O-3(0-3-0),S-1	....	0.0
Eck-n	18	76	12	19	2	0	0	8	2	2	1	0	.250	.269	.276	.546	80	0	6	3.30	-2	/2-9,O-8(0-8-0),3-3	....	-0.2
Yr.	22	96	14	26	2	0	0	12	2	4	1	0	.271	.286	.292	.577	87	0	9	3.80	-3	O-11(0-11-0)/2-9,3-3,S-1	....	-0.2
1873 Mut-n	36	168	28	55	4	1	0	22	1	2	2	0	.327	.331	.363	.694	107	2	21	5.78	0	2-27/O-6(0-0-6),3-5,1-1,C	....	0.0
1874 Mut-n	65	297	55	73	7	5	0	32	**9**	5	6	0	.246	.268	.303	.571	80	-6	26	3.53	-8	*2-51,S-14/O-1	....	-1.3
1875 Mut-n	70	276	28	55	7	1	0	23	9	0	4	2	.199	.225	.232	.456	56	-12	16	2.07	2	2-49,3-23/S-2,O-1	....	-1.2
1878 Ind-N	19	84	12	11	1	0	0	5	5	11	....	....	.131	.180	.143	.323	8	-7	2	.83	-5	S-19	0	-1.0
1879 Tro-N	28	106	17	28	7	1	0	10	8	4	....	....	.264	.316	.349	.665	127	4	12	4.30	0	S-24/O-4(4-0-0)	3	0.4
1881 Wor-N	24	103	13	29	1	0	1	15	5	6	....	....	.282	.315	.320	.635	94	-1	11	3.89	1	S-24	3	0.2
1883 NY-a	97	417	75	127	19	6	0	0	31	....	....	....	.305	.353	.379	.732	130	14	57	5.51	-4	*S-97	15	1.2
1884*NY-a	111	432	114	110	15	3	1	0	**74**	....	....	....	.255	.375	.310	.685	129	20	51	4.40	-10	*S-110/2-1	23	1.2
1885 NY-a	107	420	98	107	12	4	1	30	**61**	....	....	....	.255	.353	.310	.663	120	15	47	4.06	6	*S-107/3-1	21	2.3
1886 NY-a	109	413	89	93	7	2	0	23	64	....	14	....	.225	.332	.252	.584	88	-1	40	3.39	-6	S-73,O-36(0-28-8)	9	-0.5
1887 NY-a	68	305	61	111	5	1	0	24	48	....	29	....	.364	.380	.272	.653	87	1	39	5.37	7	O-37(0-1-36),S-32/2-1	7	0.6
NY-N	1	2	0	0	0	0	0	0	0	1	0	....	.000	.000	.000	.000	-105	-1	0	.00	0	/3-1	0	-0.1
1890 Bro-a	60	223	44	56	3	2	0	12	35	....	12	....	.251	.365	.283	.648	94	1	28	4.45	-10	S-57/O-4(0-0-4)	6	-0.6
Total 4 n	193	837	125	209	20	7	0	89	21	11	13	2	.250	.268	.290	.558	78	-16	72	3.45	-9	2-136/3-31,O-19,S-17,1-1,C	....	-2.6
Total 9	624	2505	523	672	70	19	3	119	331	22	55	....	.268	.349	.302	.650	107	46	287	4.28	-22	S-543/O-81,2-2,3-2	87	3.6
• NELSON, Dave	David Earl Nelson b: 6/20/1944, Fort Sill, OK BR/TR, 5'10", 160 lbs. Deb: 4/11/1968 C Career OF: 6-10-1																							
1968 Cle-A	88	189	26	44	4	5	0	19	17	35	23	7	.233	.300	.307	.606	85	-1	20	3.31	2	2-59,S-14	7	0.7
1969 Cle-A	52	123	11	25	0	0	0	6	9	26	4	3	.203	.263	.203	.466	31	-12	7	1.74	4	2-33/O-2(1-0-1)	1	-0.5
1970 Was-A	47	107	5	17	1	0	0	4	7	24	2	1	.159	.211	.168	.379	6	-14	4	1.13	2	2-33	1	-1.0
1971 Was-A	85	329	47	92	11	3	5	33	23	29	17	8	.280	.329	.377	.706	105	2	39	4.07	-8	3-84/2-1	9	-0.7
1972 Tex-A	145	499	68	113	16	3	2	28	67	81	51	17	.226	.324	.283	.607	85	-2	54	3.49	-11	*3-119,O-15(5-10-0)	15	-1.6
1973 Tex-A★	142	576	71	165	24	4	7	48	34	78	43	16	.286	.326	.378	.705	102	3	70	4.21	-4	*2-140	15	0.8
1974 Tex-A	121	474	71	112	13	1	3	42	34	72	25	13	.236	.293	.287	.580	69	-19	38	2.52	4	*2-120/D-1	7	-0.7
1975 Tex-A	28	80	9	17	1	0	2	10	8	10	6	0	.213	.292	.300	.592	68	-2	8	3.01	-2	2-23/D-1	1	-0.2
1976*KC-A	78	153	24	36	4	2	1	17	14	26	15	5	.235	.299	.307	.607	77	-3	16	3.31	1	2-46,D-22/1-3	3	-0.1
1977 KC-A	27	48	8	9	3	1	0	4	7	11	1	3	.188	.291	.292	.583	59	-4	4	2.24	-1	2-11/D-7	0	-0.4
Total 10	813	2578	340	630	77	19	20	211	220	392	187	73	.244	.307	.312	.619	81	-51	259	3.27	-13	2-466,3-203/D-31,O-17,S-14,1	59	-3.9
• NELSON, Jamie	James Victor Nelson b: 9/5/1959, Clinton, OK BR/TR, 5'11", 180 lbs. Deb: 7/21/1983																							
1983 Sea-A	40	96	9	21	3	0	1	5	13	12	4	2	.219	.312	.281	.593	62	-5	9	2.99	-1	C-39	2	-0.4
• NELSON, Ray	Raymond "Kell" Nelson b: 8/4/1875, Holyoke, MA d: 1/8/1961, Mount Vernon, NY BR/TR, 5'9", 150 lbs. Deb: 5/6/1901																							
1901 NY-N	39	130	12	26	2	0	0	7	10	....	3	....	.200	.262	.215	.478	41	-9	9	2.19	-12	2-39	0	-2.0
• NELSON, Ricky	Ricky Lee Nelson b: 5/8/1959, Eloy, AZ BL/TR, 6', 200 lbs. Deb: 5/17/1983 Career OF: 46-2-55																							
1983 Sea-A	98	291	32	74	13	3	5	36	17	50	7	4	.254	.295	.371	.667	79	-9	31	3.69	4	O-91(46-1-50)/D-1	4	-0.8
1984 Sea-A	9	15	2	3	0	0	1	2	2	4	0	0	.200	.294	.400	.694	91	-0	2	4.31	0	/D-3,O-2(0-0-2)	0	0.0
1985 Sea-A	6	2	2	0	0	0	0	0	0	1	0	0	.000	.000	.000	.000	-99	-1	0	.00	0	/O-3(0-0-3)	0	-0.1
1986 Sea-A	10	12	2	2	0	0	0	1	0	4	1	0	.167	.167	.167	.333	-9	-2	0	1.13	0	/D-5,O-1	0	-0.2
Total 4	123	320	38	79	13	3	6	39	19	59	8	4	.247	.289	.363	.652	76	-11	34	3.59	4	/O-97,D-9	4	-1.1
• NELSON, Rob	Robert Augustus Nelson b: 5/17/1964, Pasadena, CA BL/TL, 6'4", 215 lbs. Deb: 9/9/1986																							
1986 Oak-A	5	9	1	2	1	0	0	0	1	4	0	0	.222	.300	.333	.633	78	-0	1	3.77	0	/1-2,D-1	0	0.0
1987 Oak-A	7	24	1	4	1	0	0	0	0	12	0	0	.167	.167	.208	.375	-2	-4	1	1.14	2	/1-7	0	-0.2
SD-N	10	11	0	1	0	0	0	1	1	8	0	0	.091	.167	.091	.258	-31	-2	0	.57	0	/1-2	0	-0.3
1988 SD-N	7	21	4	4	0	0	1	3	2	9	0	0	.190	.261	.333	.594	71	-1	2	3.12	0	/1-5	0	-0.1
1989 SD-N	42	82	6	16	0	1	3	7	20	29	1	3	.195	.353	.329	.682	96	-1	10	3.75	2	1-31	3	0.0
1990 SD-N	5	5	0	0	0	0	0	0	0	4	0	0	.000	.000	.000	.000	-99	-1	0	.00	0	....	0	-0.1
Total 5	76	152	12	27	2	1	4	11	24	66	1	3	.178	.290	.283	.573	64	-9	14	2.86	4	/1-47,D-1	3	-0.7
• NELSON, Rocky	Glenn Richard Nelson b: 11/18/1924, Portsmouth, OH BL/TL, 5'10.5", 178 lbs. Deb: 4/27/1949 Career OF: 22-0-1																							
1949 StL-N	82	244	28	54	8	4	4	32	11	12	1	....	.221	.258	.336	.594	55	-16	20	2.78	-4	1-70	1	-2.3
1950 StL-N	76	235	27	58	10	4	1	20	26	9	4	....	.247	.324	.336	.661	71	-10	27	4.00	3	1-70	4	-0.9
1951 StL-N	9	18	3	4	1	0	0	1	1	0	0	0	.222	.263	.278	.541	45	-1	1	2.04	-1	/1-4,O-1	0	-0.2
Pit-N	71	195	29	52	7	4	1	14	10	7	1	1	.267	.302	.359	.661	75	-7	21	3.67	1	1-32,O-12(12-0-0)	3	-0.8

YEAR TM-L	G	AB	R	H	2B	3B	HR	RBI	BB	SO	SB	CS	AVG	OBP	SLG	OPS	OPS+	BR/A	RC	RC/G	FR	G/POS	WS	TPW
Yr.	80	213	32	56	8	4	1	15	11	7	1	1	.263	.299	.352	.651	72	-9	22	3.52	1	1-36,0-13(13-0-0)	3	-1.0
Chi-A	6	5	0	0	0	0	0	0	1	0	0	0	.000	.167	.000	.167	-53	-1	0	.23	0	....	0	-0.1
1952*Bro-N	37	39	6	10	1	0	0	3	7	4	0	0	.256	.370	.282	.652	82	-0	5	4.51	0	/1-5	1	-0.1
1954 Cle-A	4	4	0	0	0	0	0	0	0	1	0	0	.000	.000	.000	.000	-98	-1	0	.00	0	/1-2	0	-0.1
1956 Bro-N	31	96	7	20	2	0	4	15	4	10	0	0	.208	.240	.354	.594	53	-7	8	2.61	1	1-25	1	-0.7
StL-N	38	56	6	13	5	0	3	8	6	6	0	0	.232	.306	.482	.789	108	0	8	4.66	1	1-14/0-8(8-0-0)	1	0.1
Yr.	69	152	13	33	7	0	7	23	10	16	0	0	.217	.265	.401	.667	74	-6	15	3.34	2	1-39/0-8(8-0-0)	2	-0.6
1959 Pit-N	98	175	31	51	11	0	6	32	23	19	0	0	.291	.383	.457	.840	124	7	32	6.72	-6	1-56/0-2(1-0-1)	7	-0.1
1960*Pit-N	93	200	34	60	11	1	7	35	24	15	1	2	.300	.389	.470	.859	133	9	38	6.80	-2	1-73	9	0.4
1961 Pit-N	75	127	15	25	5	1	5	13	17	11	0	0	.197	.301	.370	.671	77	-4	14	3.71	-3	1-35	2	-0.9
Total 9	620	1394	186	347	61	14	31	173	130	94	7	3	.249	.318	.379	.698	85	-32	174	4.28	-10	1-386/0-23	29	-5.7
• NELSON, Tex	Robert Sidney "Babe" Nelson b: 8/7/1936, Dallas, TX BL/TL, 6'3", 220 lbs. Deb: 6/22/1955 Career OF: 17-0-22																							
1955 Bal-A	25	31	4	6	0	0	0	1	7	13	0	0	.194	.342	.194	.536	50	-2	3	2.89	1	/0-6(6-0-0),1-2	0	-0.1
1956 Bal-A	39	68	5	14	2	0	0	5	7	22	0	0	.206	.280	.235	.515	40	-6	5	2.17	1	0-24(9-0-16)	0	-0.5
1957 Bal-A	15	23	2	5	0	2	0	5	1	5	0	0	.217	.280	.391	.671	87	-0	3	4.00	0	/0-8(2-0-6)	1	-0.1
Total 3	79	122	11	25	2	2	0	11	15	40	0	0	.205	.297	.254	.551	51	-8	10	2.68	1	/0-38,1-2	1	-0.8
• NELSON, Tommy	Tom Cousineau Nelson b: 5/1/1917, Chicago, IL d: 9/24/1973, San Diego, CA BR/TR, 5'11.5", 180 lbs. Deb: 4/17/1945																							
1945 Bos-N	40	121	6	20	2	0	0	6	4	13	1	....	.165	.192	.182	.374	4	-16	3	.85	-3	3-20,2-12	1	-1.8
• NEN, Dick	Richard Le Roy Nen b: 9/24/1939, South Gate, CA BL/TL, 6'2", 205 lbs. Deb: 9/18/1963																							
1963 LA-N	7	8	2	1	0	0	1	1	3	3	0	0	.125	.364	.500	.864	157	1	1	4.16	-1	/1-5	0	0.0
1965 Was-A	69	246	18	64	7	1	6	31	19	47	1	2	.260	.316	.370	.686	95	-2	29	4.06	8	1-65	7	0.2
1966 Was-A	94	235	20	50	8	0	6	30	28	46	0	2	.213	.297	.323	.620	79	-7	21	2.88	-1	1-76	4	-1.3
1967 Was-A	110	238	21	52	7	1	6	29	21	39	0	1	.218	.282	.332	.614	84	-5	21	2.95	0	1-65/0-1	4	-1.0
1968 Chi-N	81	94	8	17	1	1	2	16	6	17	0	0	.181	.230	.277	.507	48	-6	6	2.16	-2	1-52	0	-1.0
1970 Was-A	6	5	1	1	0	0	0	0	0	0	0	0	.200	.200	.200	.400	11	-1	0	1.35	0	/1-1	0	0.0
Total 6	367	826	70	185	23	3	21	107	77	152	1	5	.224	.291	.335	.626	82	-20	79	3.15	4	1-264/0-1	15	-3.2
• NESS, Jack	John Charles Ness b: 11/11/1885, Chicago, IL d: 12/3/1957, DeLand, FL BR/TR, 6'2", 165 lbs. Deb: 5/9/1911																							
1911 Det-A	12	39	6	6	0	0	0	2	2	....	0	....	.154	.195	.154	.349	-2	-5	1	.91	0	1-12	0	-0.5
1916 Chi-A	75	258	32	69	7	5	1	34	9	32	4	....	.267	.310	.345	.655	96	-3	30	3.95	-3	1-69	6	-0.7
Total 2	87	297	38	75	7	5	1	36	11	32	4	....	.253	.295	.320	.615	83	-8	31	3.50	-2	/1-81	6	-1.2
• NETTLES, Graig	Graig Nettles b: 8/20/1944, San Diego, CA BL/TR, 6', 186 lbs. Deb: 9/6/1967 C Career OF: 58-2-13																							
1967 Min-A	3	3	0	1	1	0	0	0	0	0	0	0	.333	.333	.667	1.000	175	0	1	9.00	0	....	0	0.0
1968 Min-A	22	76	13	17	2	1	5	8	7	20	0	0	.224	.298	.474	.771	125	2	10	4.58	0	0-16(2-1-13)/3-5,1-3	3	0.1
1969*Min-A	96	225	27	50	9	2	7	26	32	47	1	2	.222	.322	.373	.695	92	-3	27	3.94	2	0-54(53-1-0),3-21	5	-0.4
1970 Cle-A	157	549	81	129	13	1	26	62	81	77	3	1	.235	.336	.404	.741	99	1	77	4.82	23	*3-154/0-3(3-0-0)	18	2.4
1971 Cle-A	158	598	78	156	18	1	28	86	82	56	7	4	.261	.353	.435	.788	112	11	93	5.34	40	*3-158	27	5.4
1972 Cle-A	150	557	65	141	28	0	17	70	57	50	2	3	.253	.327	.395	.722	110	7	73	4.53	4	*3-150	21	1.2
1973 NY-A	160	552	65	129	18	0	22	81	78	76	0	0	.234	.336	.386	.722	106	7	73	4.48	19	*3-157/D-2	19	2.6
1974 NY-A	155	566	74	139	21	1	22	75	59	75	1	0	.246	.320	.403	.723	110	7	75	4.51	15	*3-154/S-1	22	2.3
1975 NY-A★	157	581	71	155	24	4	21	91	51	88	1	3	.267	.328	.430	.758	116	10	82	4.94	19	*3-157	21	2.9
1976*NY-A	158	583	88	148	29	2	**32**	93	62	94	11	6	.254	.330	.475	.805	135	24	92	5.45	26	*3-158/S-1	28	**5.2**
1977*NY-A★	158	589	99	150	23	4	37	107	68	79	2	5	.255	.335	.496	.831	124	18	98	5.78	9	*3-156/D-1	25	2.4
1978*NY-A★	159	587	81	162	23	2	27	93	59	69	1	1	.276	.348	.460	.808	128	22	91	5.36	2	*3-159/S-2	26	2.3
1979 NY-A★	145	521	71	132	15	1	20	73	59	53	1	2	.253	.329	.401	.730	98	-2	68	4.43	2	*3-144	15	-0.2
1980*NY-A★	89	324	52	79	14	0	16	45	42	42	0	0	.244	.332	.435	.768	110	5	47	4.97	-6	3-88/S-1	10	-0.2
1981*NY-A	103	349	46	85	7	1	15	46	47	49	0	2	.244	.335	.398	.733	112	5	48	4.69	12	3-97/D-4	12	1.7
1982 NY-A	122	405	47	94	11	2	18	55	51	49	1	5	.232	.319	.402	.722	98	-3	50	4.10	2	*3-113/D-3	10	-0.2
1983 NY-A	129	462	56	123	17	3	20	75	51	65	0	1	.266	.343	.446	.789	120	12	71	5.46	0	*3-126/D-1	16	1.1
1984*SD-N	124	395	56	90	11	1	20	65	58	55	0	0	.228	.334	.413	.747	109	5	55	4.60	9	*3-119	16	1.3
1985 SD-N★	137	440	66	115	23	1	15	61	72	59	0	0	.261	.365	.420	.786	121	14	70	5.60	2	*3-130	17	1.6
1986 SD-N	126	354	36	77	9	0	16	55	41	62	0	1	.218	.302	.379	.681	88	-7	41	3.84	6	*3-114	9	-0.2
1987 Atl-N	112	177	16	37	8	1	5	33	22	25	1	0	.209	.296	.350	.647	67	-8	18	3.28	0	3-40/1-6	1	-0.9
1988 Mon-N	80	93	5	16	4	0	1	14	9	19	0	0	.172	.245	.247	.492	40	-7	5	1.70	-1	3-12/1-5	0	-0.9
Total 22	2700	8986	1193	2225	328	28	390	1314	1088	1209	32	36	.248	.332	.421	.753	110	119	1264	4.81	186	*3-2412/0-73,1-14,D-11,S-5	321	29.6
• NETTLES, Jim	James William Nettles b: 3/2/1947, San Diego, CA BL/TL, 6', 186 lbs. Deb: 9/7/1970 Career OF: 34-120-48																							
1970 Min-A	13	20	3	5	0	0	0	0	1	5	0	1	.250	.286	.250	.536	48	-2	1	2.11	0	0-11(5-1-5)	0	-0.2
1971 Min-A	70	168	17	42	5	1	6	24	19	24	3	2	.250	.326	.399	.725	101	0	22	4.43	-0	0-62(2-57-3)	5	-0.2
1972 Min-A	102	235	28	48	5	2	4	15	32	52	4	3	.204	.302	.294	.596	74	-7	21	2.97	0	0-78(12-58-8)/1-1	5	-1.1
1974 Det-A	43	141	20	32	5	1	6	17	15	26	3	4	.227	.306	.404	.710	99	-1	17	4.00	-2	0-41(8-4-30)	4	-0.6
1979 KC-A	11	23	0	2	0	0	0	1	3	2	0	0	.087	.192	.087	.279	-21	-4	1	.69	0	/0-8(7-0-1),1-1	0	-0.4
1981 Oak-A	1	0	0	0	0	0	0	0	0	0	0	0	....	....	....	....	-105	0	0	.00	0	/0-1	0	0.0
Total 6	240	587	68	129	15	4	16	57	70	109	10	10	.220	.305	.341	.646	83	-14	62	3.49	-3	0-201/1-2	14	-2.5
• NETTLES, Morris	Morris Nettles b: 1/26/1952, Los Angeles, CA BL/TL, 6'1", 170 lbs. Deb: 4/26/1974 Career OF: 42-75-31																							
1974 Cal-A	56	175	27	48	4	0	0	8	16	38	20	11	.274	.335	.297	.632	88	-3	18	3.31	-2	0-54(3-37-14)	3	-0.7
1975 Cal-A	112	294	50	68	11	0	0	23	26	57	22	15	.231	.296	.269	.565	65	-15	24	2.60	-1	0-90(39-38-17)/D-9	3	-2.0
Total 2	168	469	77	116	15	0	0	31	42	95	42	26	.247	.311	.279	.590	74	-17	41	2.86	-3	0-144/D-9	6	-2.7
• NETZEL, Milo	Miles A. Netzel b: 5/12/1886, Eldred, PA d: 3/18/1938, Oxnard, CA BL/TL Deb: 9/16/1909																							
1909 Cle-A	10	37	2	7	1	0	0	3	3	....	1	....	.189	.250	.216	.466	46	-2	2	1.85	-2	/3-6,0-2(2-0-0)	0	-0.5
• NEU, Otto	Otto Adam Neu b: 9/24/1894, Springfield, OH d: 9/19/1932, Kenton, OH BR/TR, 5'11", 170 lbs. Deb: 7/10/1917																							
1917 StL-A	1	0	0	0	0	0	0	0	0	0	0	....	....	....	....	....	-104	0	0	....	-1	/S-1	0	-0.1
• NEUN, Johnny	John Henry Neun b: 10/28/1900, Baltimore, MD d: 3/28/1990, Baltimore, MD BB/TL, 5'10.5", 175 lbs. Deb: 4/14/1925 M/C																							
1925 Det-A	60	75	15	20	3	3	0	4	9	12	2	3	.267	.345	.387	.732	87	-2	10	4.39	-1	1-13	1	-0.3
1926 Det-A	97	242	47	72	14	4	0	15	27	26	4	7	.298	.370	.388	.759	97	-2	34	5.03	-2	1-49	6	-0.7
1927 Det-A	79	204	38	66	9	4	0	27	35	13	22	7	.324	.427	.407	.834	116	9	40	6.92	-2	1-53	7	0.4
1928 Det-A	36	108	15	23	3	1	0	5	7	10	2	2	.213	.261	.259	.520	36	-10	7	2.19	-0	1-25	0	-1.1
1930 Bos-N	81	212	39	69	12	2	2	23	21	18	9	....	.325	.389	.429	.818	101	1	35	6.01	-1	1-55	6	-0.3
1931 Bos-N	79	104	17	23	1	3	0	11	11	14	2	....	.221	.302	.288	.590	62	-5	10	3.10	1	1-36	1	-0.6
Total 6	432	945	171	273	42	17	2	85	110	93	41	19	.289	.366	.376	.742	91	-10	136	5.02	-5	1-231	21	-2.7
• NEVIN, Alexander	Alexander Brown Nevin b: 10/3/1850, Allegheny City, PA d: 10/10/1921, Pensacola, FL Deb: 5/6/1873																							
1873 Res-n	13	53	7	11	1	2	0	2	0	3	0	0	.208	.208	.302	.509	54	-2	3	2.47	-8	3-12/0-1	....	-0.8
• NEVIN, Phil	Phillip Joseph Nevin b: 1/19/1971, Fullerton, CA BR/TR, 6'2", 180 lbs. Deb: 6/11/1995 Career OF: 81-0-38																							
1995 Hou-N	18	60	4	7	1	0	0	1	7	13	1	0	.117	.221	.133	.354	-4	-9	2	.99	-1	3-16	0	-1.0
Det-A	29	96	9	21	3	1	2	12	11	27	0	0	.219	.318	.333	.652	70	-4	10	3.59	-1	0-27(27-0-0)/D-2	2	-0.6
1996 Det-A	38	120	15	35	5	0	8	19	8	39	1	0	.292	.341	.533	.874	117	3	22	6.92	1	3-24/0-9(9-0-0),C-4,D-1	5	0.4
1997 Det-A	93	251	32	59	16	1	9	35	25	68	0	1	.235	.307	.414	.721	87	-6	32	4.28	3	0-40(40-0-0),D-30,3-17/1-7,C	6	-0.6
1998 Ana-A	75	237	27	54	8	1	8	27	17	67	0	0	.228	.293	.371	.665	71	-11	25	3.59	-2	C-69/D-3,1-2	2	-0.8
1999 SD-N	128	383	52	103	27	0	24	85	51	82	1	0	.269	.356	.527	.884	130	16	73	6.77	7	3-67,C-31,0-13(5-0-9),1-11/D	19	2.3
2000 SD-N	143	538	87	163	34	1	31	107	59	121	2	0	.303	.376	.543	.919	138	30	107	7.28	-8	*3-142	22	2.3
2001 SD-N★	149	546	97	167	31	0	41	126	71	147	4	4	.306	.390	.588	.978	162	49	123	8.35	3	*3-145/D-1	31	5.3

YEAR TM-L	G	AB	R	H	2B	3B	HR	RBI	BB	SO	SB	CS	AVG	OBP	SLG	OPS	OPS+	BR/A	RC	RC/G	FR	G/POS	WS	TPW
2002 SD-N	107	407	53	116	16	0	12	57	38	87	4	0	.285	.348	.413	.760	109	6	58	5.07	-3	3-71,1-36	12	0.0
2003 SD-N	59	226	30	63	8	0	13	46	21	44	2	0	.279	.340	.487	.827	124	7	35	5.51	-1	1-31,0-29(0-0-29)	9	0.2
Total 9	**839**	**2864**	**406**	**788**	**149**	**4**	**148**	**515**	**308**	**695**	**15**	**5**	**.275**	**.350**	**.485**	**.835**	**120**	**82**	**488**	**6.05**	**-2**	**3-482,0-118,C-105/1-87,D-38**	**108**	**7.6**

• NEWELL, John John A. Newell b: 1/14/1868, Wilmington, DE d: 1/28/1919, Wilmington, DE BR/TL, 5'9" Deb: 7/22/1891

YEAR TM-L	G	AB	R	H	2B	3B	HR	RBI	BB	SO	SB	CS	AVG	OBP	SLG	OPS	OPS+	BR/A	RC	RC/G	FR	G/POS	WS	TPW
1891 Pit-N	5	18	1	2	0	0	0	2	0	0	0	....	.111	.158	.111	.269	-22	-3	0	.55	1	/3-5	0	-0.2

• NEWELL, T.E. T. E. Newell b: St. Louis, MO Deb: 8/8/1877

YEAR TM-L	G	AB	R	H	2B	3B	HR	RBI	BB	SO	SB	CS	AVG	OBP	SLG	OPS	OPS+	BR/A	RC	RC/G	FR	G/POS	WS	TPW
1877 StL-N	1	3	0	0	0	0	0	0	0	0	....	....	.000	.000	.000	.000	-106	-1	0	.00	0	/S-1	0	-0.1

• NEWFIELD, Marc Marc Alexander Newfield b: 10/19/1972, Sacramento, CA BR/TR, 6'4", 205 lbs. Deb: 7/6/1993 Career OF: 212-0-24

YEAR TM-L	G	AB	R	H	2B	3B	HR	RBI	BB	SO	SB	CS	AVG	OBP	SLG	OPS	OPS+	BR/A	RC	RC/G	FR	G/POS	WS	TPW
1993 Sea-A	22	66	5	15	3	0	1	7	2	8	0	1	.227	.261	.318	.579	54	-5	5	2.35	-1	D-15/0-5(5-0-0)	0	-0.6
1994 Sea-A	12	38	3	7	1	0	1	4	2	4	0	0	.184	.225	.289	.514	31	-4	2	1.65	0	/D-9,0-3(3-0-0)	0	-0.4
1995 Sea-A	24	85	7	16	3	0	3	14	3	16	0	0	.188	.225	.329	.554	42	-8	6	2.21	0	0-24(23-0-1)	1	-0.8
SD-N	21	55	6	17	5	1	1	7	2	8	0	0	.309	.333	.491	.824	119	1	8	5.09	1	0-19(19-0-0)	2	0.1
1996 SD-N	84	191	27	48	11	0	5	26	16	44	1	1	.251	.316	.387	.703	90	-4	22	3.86	-1	0-51(30-0-23)/1-2	2	-0.6
Mil-A	49	179	21	55	15	0	7	31	11	26	0	1	.307	.361	.508	.869	112	2	33	6.90	0	0-49(49-0-0)	6	0.0
1997 Mil-A	50	157	14	36	8	0	1	18	14	27	0	0	.229	.301	.299	.600	57	-10	14	3.03	-1	0-28(28-0-0),D-18	1	-1.2
1998 Mil-N	93	186	15	44	7	0	3	25	19	29	0	1	.237	.311	.323	.633	67	-9	18	3.14	-1	0-55(55-0-0)/D-1	4	-1.2
Total 6	**355**	**957**	**98**	**238**	**53**	**1**	**22**	**132**	**69**	**162**	**1**	**4**	**.249**	**.307**	**.375**	**.682**	**77**	**-36**	**108**	**3.80**	**-4**	**0-234/D-43,1-2**	**16**	**-4.8**

• NEWHAN, David David Matthew Newhan b: 9/7/1973, Fullerton, CA BL/TR, 5'10", 180 lbs. Deb: 6/4/1999

YEAR TM-L	G	AB	R	H	2B	3B	HR	RBI	BB	SO	SB	CS	AVG	OBP	SLG	OPS	OPS+	BR/A	RC	RC/G	FR	G/POS	WS	TPW
1999 SD-N	32	43	7	6	1	0	2	6	1	11	2	1	.140	.159	.302	.461	14	-6	2	1.39	1	2-19/1-1,3-1	1	-0.4
2000 SD-N	14	20	5	3	1	0	1	2	6	7	0	0	.150	.346	.350	.696	82	-0	3	4.56	-1	/0-5(0-0-5),2-3,3-2	0	-0.1
Phi-N	10	17	3	3	0	0	0	0	2	6	0	0	.176	.263	.176	.440	14	-2	1	.94	4	/2-5	0	0.1
Yr.	24	37	8	6	1	0	1	2	8	13	0	0	.162	.311	.270	.581	53	-3	3	2.81	3	/2-8,0-5(0-0-5),3-2	0	0.0
2001 Phi-N	7	6	2	2	1	0	0	1	1	0	0	0	.333	.429	.500	.929	143	0	1	7.65	-1	/2-1	0	0.0
Total 3	**63**	**86**	**17**	**14**	**3**	**0**	**3**	**9**	**10**	**24**	**2**	**1**	**.163**	**.250**	**.302**	**.552**	**43**	**-8**	**7**	**2.41**	**3**	**/2-28,0-5,3-3,1-1**	**1**	**-0.5**

• NEWMAN, Al Albert Dwayne Newman b: 6/30/1960, Kansas City, MO BB/TR, 5'9", 183 lbs. Deb: 6/14/1985 C Career OF: 11-1-0

YEAR TM-L	G	AB	R	H	2B	3B	HR	RBI	BB	SO	SB	CS	AVG	OBP	SLG	OPS	OPS+	BR/A	RC	RC/G	FR	G/POS	WS	TPW
1985 Mon-N	25	29	7	5	1	0	0	1	3	4	2	1	.172	.250	.207	.457	31	-3	2	1.85	1	2-15/S-2	0	-0.1
1986 Mon-N	95	185	23	37	3	0	1	8	21	20	11	11	.200	.282	.232	.514	44	-16	12	1.84	0	2-59,S-22	2	-1.3
1987*Min-A	110	307	44	68	15	5	0	29	34	27	15	11	.221	.299	.303	.602	58	-20	28	2.88	8	S-55,2-47,3-12/D-5,0-2(2-0-0)	6	-0.6
1988 Min-A	105	260	35	58	7	0	0	19	29	34	12	3	.223	.301	.250	.551	55	-14	22	2.79	2	3-60,S-28,2-23/D-2	4	-1.0
1989 Min-A	141	446	62	113	18	2	0	38	59	46	25	12	.253	.343	.303	.646	78	-11	52	3.90	-7	2-84,3-37,S-31/0-4(4-1-0),D	11	-1.4
1990 Min-A	144	388	43	94	14	0	0	30	33	34	13	6	.242	.305	.278	.583	60	-20	35	2.94	-6	2-89,S-48,3-28/0-3(3-0-0)	5	-2.2
1991*Min-A	118	246	25	47	5	0	0	19	23	21	4	5	.191	.263	.211	.474	31	-24	14	1.76	-4	S-55,2-35,3-35/D-3,1-1,0-1	4	-2.4
1992 Tex-A	116	246	25	54	5	0	0	12	34	26	9	6	.220	.317	.240	.557	60	-12	21	2.66	-4	2-72,3-28,S-20/D-1,0-1	4	-1.4
Total 8	**854**	**2107**	**264**	**476**	**68**	**7**	**1**	**156**	**236**	**212**	**91**	**55**	**.226**	**.306**	**.266**	**.572**	**58**	**-119**	**185**	**2.81**	**-9**	**2-424,S-261,3-200/D-13,0-11,1**	**36**	**-10.4**

• NEWMAN, Charlie Charles "Decker" Newman b: 11/5/1868, Juda, WI d: 11/23/1947, San Diego, CA BR/TR, 5'11" Deb: 7/11/1892

YEAR TM-L	G	AB	R	H	2B	3B	HR	RBI	BB	SO	SB	CS	AVG	OBP	SLG	OPS	OPS+	BR/A	RC	RC/G	FR	G/POS	WS	TPW
1892 NY-N	3	12	1	4	0	0	0	1	2	0	3	....	.333	.429	.333	.762	133	1	3	10.38	0	/0-3(3-0-0)	1	0.0
Chi-N	16	61	4	10	0	0	0	2	1	6	2	....	.164	.177	.164	.341	3	-7	2	1.16	-2	0-16(16-0-0)	0	-1.0
Yr.	19	73	5	14	0	0	0	3	3	6	5	....	.192	.224	.192	.415	27	-7	5	2.41	-2	0-19(19-0-0)	1	-0.9

• NEWMAN, Jeff Jeffrey Lynn Newman b: 9/11/1948, Fort Worth, TX BR/TR, 6'2", 218 lbs. Deb: 6/30/1976 M/C

YEAR TM-L	G	AB	R	H	2B	3B	HR	RBI	BB	SO	SB	CS	AVG	OBP	SLG	OPS	OPS+	BR/A	RC	RC/G	FR	G/POS	WS	TPW
1976 Oak-A	43	77	5	15	4	0	0	4	4	12	0	0	.195	.235	.247	.481	43	-6	5	2.02	0	C-43	1	-0.4
1977 Oak-A	94	162	17	36	9	0	4	15	4	24	2	0	.222	.246	.352	.597	61	-9	14	2.84	0	C-94/P-1	3	-0.6
1978 Oak-A	105	268	25	64	7	1	9	32	18	40	0	3	.239	.289	.373	.662	90	-6	28	3.49	2	C-61,1-36/D-2	6	-0.3
1979 Oak-A★	143	516	53	119	17	2	22	71	27	88	2	1	.231	.270	.399	.669	82	-15	51	3.25	7	C-81,1-46/3-7,D-7	12	-0.7
1980 Oak-A	127	438	37	102	19	1	15	56	25	81	3	4	.233	.276	.384	.659	85	-12	43	3.24	-6	1-60,C-55/D-9,3-2,2-1	7	-1.9
1981*Oak-A	68	216	17	50	12	0	3	15	9	28	0	2	.231	.262	.329	.591	73	-9	16	2.48	1	C-37,1-30	3	-0.8
1982 Oak-A	72	251	19	50	11	0	6	30	14	49	0	1	.199	.242	.315	.556	54	-17	18	2.23	2	C-67/1-3,3-1,D-1	3	-1.2
1983 Bos-A	59	132	11	25	4	0	3	7	10	31	0	1	.189	.257	.288	.545	46	-10	9	2.17	2	C-51/D-6	2	-0.7
1984 Bos-A	24	63	5	14	2	0	1	3	5	16	0	0	.222	.279	.302	.581	58	-4	6	2.82	-1	C-24	1	-0.3
Total 9	**735**	**2123**	**189**	**475**	**85**	**4**	**63**	**233**	**116**	**369**	**7**	**12**	**.224**	**.266**	**.357**	**.622**	**73**	**-87**	**190**	**2.91**	**7**	**C-513,1-175/D-25,3-10,2-1,P**	**38**	**-6.9**

• NEWNAM, Patrick Patrick Henry Newnam b: 12/10/1880, Hempstead, TX d: 6/20/1938, San Antonio, TX BL/TR, 6', 180 lbs. Deb: 5/29/1910

YEAR TM-L	G	AB	R	H	2B	3B	HR	RBI	BB	SO	SB	CS	AVG	OBP	SLG	OPS	OPS+	BR/A	RC	RC/G	FR	G/POS	WS	TPW
1910 StL-A	103	384	45	83	3	8	2	26	29	....	16	....	.216	.275	.281	.556	79	-10	33	2.81	-7	*1-103	6	-2.1
1911 StL-A	20	62	11	12	4	0	0	5	12	....	4	....	.194	.351	.258	.609	74	-1	7	3.57	0	1-20	1	-0.1
Total 2	**123**	**446**	**56**	**95**	**7**	**8**	**2**	**31**	**41**	**....**	**20**	**....**	**.213**	**.287**	**.278**	**.565**	**78**	**-11**	**40**	**2.92**	**-7**	**1-123**	**7**	**-2.2**

• NEWSOME, Skeeter Lamar Ashby Newsome b: 10/18/1910, Phenix City, AL d: 8/31/1989, Columbus, GA BR/TR, 5'9", 170 lbs. Deb: 4/19/1935 Career OF: 1-0-1

YEAR TM-L	G	AB	R	H	2B	3B	HR	RBI	BB	SO	SB	CS	AVG	OBP	SLG	OPS	OPS+	BR/A	RC	RC/G	FR	G/POS	WS	TPW
1935 Phi-A	59	145	18	30	7	1	1	10	5	9	2	1	.207	.233	.290	.523	35	-15	10	2.20	0	S-24,2-13/3-4,0-1	1	-1.1
1936 Phi-A	127	471	41	106	15	2	0	46	25	27	13	4	.225	.266	.265	.531	32	-50	35	2.43	9	*S-123/2-2,3-1,0-1	6	-2.8
1937 Phi-A	122	438	53	111	22	1	1	30	37	22	11	5	.253	.312	.315	.627	59	-27	45	3.45	15	*S-122	8	-0.3
1938 Phi-A	17	48	7	13	4	0	0	7	1	4	1	1	.271	.286	.354	.640	61	-3	5	3.21	0	S-15	0	-0.2
1939 Phi-A	99	248	22	55	9	1	0	17	19	12	5	7	.222	.277	.266	.543	40	-24	17	2.06	-1	S-93/2-2	3	-1.9
1941 Bos-A	93	227	28	51	6	0	2	17	22	11	10	4	.225	.296	.278	.574	51	-15	20	2.78	-1	S-69,2-23	3	-1.2
1942 Bos-A	29	95	7	26	6	0	0	9	9	5	2	1	.274	.337	.337	.673	87	-1	11	4.14	0	3-12,2-10/S-7	2	0.0
1943 Bos-A	114	449	48	119	21	2	1	22	21	21	5	6	.265	.301	.327	.628	82	-12	43	3.27	7	S-98,3-15	11	0.3
1944 Bos-A	136	472	41	114	26	3	0	41	33	21	4	3	.242	.291	.309	.600	72	-18	43	2.98	4	*S-126/2-8,3-1	9	-0.3
1945 Bos-A	125	438	45	127	30	1	1	48	20	15	6	3	.290	.322	.370	.692	98	-2	51	3.99	-2	2-82,S-33,3-11	13	0.4
1946 Phi-N	112	375	35	87	10	2	1	23	30	23	4	....	.232	.289	.277	.566	63	-19	33	2.86	-8	*S-107/2-3,3-2	6	-2.1
1947 Phi-N	95	310	36	71	8	2	2	22	24	24	4	....	.229	.284	.287	.572	54	-21	26	2.83	1	S-85/2-6,3-3	5	-1.4
Total 12	**1128**	**3716**	**381**	**910**	**164**	**15**	**9**	**292**	**246**	**194**	**67**	**35**	**.245**	**.293**	**.304**	**.597**	**63**	**-208**	**338**	**3.01**	**25**	**S-902,2-149/3-49,0-2**	**67**	**-10.6**

• NEWSON, Warren Warren Dale Newson b: 7/3/1964, Newnan, GA BL/TL, 5'7", 202 lbs. Deb: 5/29/1991 Career OF: 108-3-216

YEAR TM-L	G	AB	R	H	2B	3B	HR	RBI	BB	SO	SB	CS	AVG	OBP	SLG	OPS	OPS+	BR/A	RC	RC/G	FR	G/POS	WS	TPW
1991 Chi-A	71	132	20	39	5	0	4	25	28	34	2	2	.295	.419	.424	.843	137	8	24	6.66	0	0-50(16-1-34)/D-3	6	0.8
1992 Chi-A	63	136	19	30	3	0	1	11	37	38	3	0	.221	.387	.265	.652	87	1	17	4.17	4	0-50(17-0-33)/D-4	3	0.4
1993*Chi-A	26	40	9	12	0	0	2	6	9	12	0	0	.300	.429	.450	.879	139	3	8	7.01	0	D-10/0-5(2-0-3)	2	0.2
1994 Chi-A	63	102	16	26	5	0	2	7	14	23	1	0	.255	.345	.363	.708	84	-2	13	4.38	0	0-34(9-0-26)/D-3	1	-0.3
1995 Chi-A	51	85	19	20	0	2	3	9	23	27	1	1	.235	.404	.388	.792	112	3	15	5.94	-1	0-24(12-0-14)/D-7	2	0.1
*Sea-A	33	72	15	21	2	0	2	6	16	18	1	0	.292	.420	.403	.823	114	3	14	7.15	0	0-23(18-2-4)	2	0.2
Yr.	84	157	34	41	2	2	5	15	39	45	2	1	.261	.411	.395	.806	113	5	29	6.47	-1	0-47(30-2-18)/D-7	4	0.2
1996*Tex-A	91	235	34	60	14	1	10	31	37	82	3	0	.255	.357	.451	.808	97	-0	40	6.10	-2	0-66(8-0-58)/D-9	5	-0.6
1997 Tex-A	81	169	23	36	10	1	10	23	31	53	3	0	.213	.335	.462	.797	100	1	27	5.37	-3	0-58(20-0-44)/D-9	4	-0.5
1998 Tex-A	10	21	1	4	1	0	0	2	1	5	0	0	.190	.227	.238	.465	20	-3	1	1.36	0	/0-6(6-0-0),D-3	0	-0.3
Total 8	**489**	**992**	**156**	**248**	**40**	**4**	**34**	**120**	**196**	**292**	**14**	**3**	**.250**	**.374**	**.401**	**.775**	**103**	**13**	**160**	**5.57**	**-3**	**0-316/D-48**	**25**	**0.0**

• NIARHOS, Gus Constantine Gregory Niarhos b: 12/6/1920, Birmingham, AL BR/TR, 6', 165 lbs. Deb: 6/9/1946 C

YEAR TM-L	G	AB	R	H	2B	3B	HR	RBI	BB	SO	SB	CS	AVG	OBP	SLG	OPS	OPS+	BR/A	RC	RC/G	FR	G/POS	WS	TPW
1946 NY-A	37	40	11	9	1	1	0	2	11	2	1	0	.225	.392	.300	.692	94	1	6	4.53	0	C-29	2	0.2
1948 NY-A	83	228	41	61	12	2	0	19	52	15	1	3	.268	.404	.338	.741	99	2	36	5.44	0	C-82	10	0.6
1949*NY-A	32	43	7	12	2	1	0	6	13	8	0	0	.279	.456	.372	.828	120	3	9	7.42	1	C-30	3	0.4
1950 NY-A	1	0	0	0	0	0	0	0	0	0	0	0	....	....	....	....	-103	0	0	....	0	....	0	0.0
Chi-A	41	105	17	34	4	0	0	16	14	6	0	0	.324	.408	.362	.770	101	1	16	5.94	0	C-36	4	0.3
Yr.	42	105	17	34	4	0	0	16	14	6	0	0	.324	.408	.362	.770	101	1	16	5.94	0	C-36	4	0.3
1951 Chi-A	66	168	27	43	6	0	1	10	47	9	4	3	.256	.419	.310	.728	101	4	26	5.19	2	C-59	7	0.8
1952 Bos-A	29	58	4	6	0	0	0	4	12	9	0	0	.103	.268	.103	.371	6	-7	3	1.26	0	C-25	1	-0.5
1953 Bos-A	16	35	6	7	1	1	0	2	4	4	0	1	.200	.300	.286	.586	56	-3	3	2.91	0	C-16	1	-0.2
1954 Phi-N	3	5	0	1	0	0	0	0	0	1	0	0	.200	.200	.200	.400	5	-1	0	1.35	0	/C-3	0	-0.1

YEAR TM-L	G	AB	R	H	2B	3B	HR	RBI	BB	SO	SB	CS	AVG	OBP	SLG	OPS	OPS+	BR/A	RC	RC/G	FR	G/POS	WS	TPW
1955 Phi-N	7	9	1	1	0	0	0	0	0	2	0	0	.111	.111	.111	.222	-42	-2	0	.00	0	/C-7	0	-0.1
Total 9	315	691	114	174	26	5	1	59	153	56	6	7	.252	.390	.308	.699	89	-2	99	4.84	4	C-287	28	1.4

• NICHOLAS, Don Donald Leigh Nicholas b: 10/30/1930, Phoenix, AZ BL/TR, 5'7", 150 lbs. Deb: 4/16/1952

YEAR TM-L	G	AB	R	H	2B	3B	HR	RBI	BB	SO	SB	CS	AVG	OBP	SLG	OPS	OPS+	BR/A	RC	RC/G	FR	G/POS	WS	TPW
1952 Chi-A	3	2	0	0	0	0	0	0	0	0	0	0	.000	.000	.000	.000	-99	-1	0	.00	0	....	0	-0.1
1954 Chi-A	7	0	3	0	0	0	0	0	1	0	0	1	....	1.000	....	1.000	185	-0	0	.00	0	....	0	0.0

• NICHOLL, Sam Samuel Anderson Nicholl b: 4/20/1869, County Antrim, Ireland d: 4/19/1937, Steubenville, OH BR/TR, 5'10", 178 lbs. Deb: 10/5/1888 Career OF: 14-8-0

YEAR TM-L	G	AB	R	H	2B	3B	HR	RBI	BB	SO	SB	CS	AVG	OBP	SLG	OPS	OPS+	BR/A	RC	RC/G	FR	G/POS	WS	TPW
1888 Pit-N	8	22	3	1	0	0	0	0	2	2	0	....	.045	.125	.045	.170	-47	-3	0	.16	0	/O-8(0-8-0)	0	-0.3
1890 Col-a	14	56	7	9	0	0	0	4	2	....	3	....	.161	.190	.161	.350	3	-7	2	1.32	2	O-14(14-0-0)	1	-0.4
Total 2	22	78	10	10	0	0	0	4	4	2	3	....	.128	.171	.128	.299	-11	-10	2	.96	3	/O-22	1	-0.7

• NICHOLLS, Simon Simon Burdette Nicholls b: 7/18/1882, Germantown, MD d: 3/12/1911, Baltimore, MD BL/TR, 5'11.5", 165 lbs. Deb: 9/18/1903

YEAR TM-L	G	AB	R	H	2B	3B	HR	RBI	BB	SO	SB	CS	AVG	OBP	SLG	OPS	OPS+	BR/A	RC	RC/G	FR	G/POS	WS	TPW
1903 Det-A	2	8	0	3	0	0	0	0	0	....	0	....	.375	.375	.375	.750	129	0	1	6.11	-2	/S-2	0	-0.2
1906 Phi-A	12	44	1	8	1	0	0	1	3	....	0	....	.182	.234	.205	.439	36	-3	2	1.59	1	S-12	0	-0.2
1907 Phi-A	124	460	75	139	12	2	0	23	24	....	13	....	.302	.338	.337	.675	113	6	62	4.66	-15	S-82,2-28,3-13	14	-0.6
1908 Phi-A	150	550	58	119	17	3	4	31	35	....	14	....	.216	.265	.280	.545	72	-18	46	2.57	-12	*S-120,2-23/3-7	9	-2.9
1909 Phi-A	21	71	10	15	2	1	0	3	3	....	0	....	.211	.243	.268	.511	60	-3	5	2.05	0	S-14/3-5,1-1	1	-0.4
1910 Cle-A	3	0	0	0	0	0	0	0	0	....	0	....	....	....	....	....	-99	0	0	....	-3	/S-3	0	-0.3
Total 6	312	1133	144	284	32	6	4	58	65	....	27	....	.251	.293	.300	.593	87	-18	116	3.33	-31	S-233/2-51,3-25,1-1	24	-4.5

• NICHOLS, Al Albert H. Nichols b: Brooklyn, NY, 5'11", 180 lbs. Deb: 4/24/1875

YEAR TM-L	G	AB	R	H	2B	3B	HR	RBI	BB	SO	SB	CS	AVG	OBP	SLG	OPS	OPS+	BR/A	RC	RC/G	FR	G/POS	WS	TPW
1875 Atl-n	32	131	4	20	2	0	0	9	0	6	0	0	.153	.153	.168	.321	13	-9	3	.91	7	3-32	....	-0.3
1876 NY-N	57	214	20	38	4	0	0	9	2	3	....	....	.178	.187	.198	.385	32	-12	8	1.29	5	*3-57	2	-0.5
1877 Lou-N	6	19	1	4	0	1	0	0	0	2	....	....	.211	.211	.316	.526	54	-1	1	2.37	2	/2-3,1-1,3-1,S-1	0	0.1
Total 2	63	233	21	42	4	1	0	9	2	5	....	....	.180	.189	.208	.397	34	-14	9	1.38	7	/3-58,2-3,1-1,S-1	2	-0.4

• NICHOLS, Art Arthur Francis Nichols b: 7/14/1871, Manchester, NH d: 8/9/1945, Willimantic, CT BR/TR, 5'10", 175 lbs. Deb: 9/16/1898 Career OF: 7-30-14

YEAR TM-L	G	AB	R	H	2B	3B	HR	RBI	BB	SO	SB	CS	AVG	OBP	SLG	OPS	OPS+	BR/A	RC	RC/G	FR	G/POS	WS	TPW
1898 Chi-N	14	42	7	12	1	0	0	6	4	....	6	....	.286	.388	.310	.697	101	1	8	6.57	-1	C-14	2	0.1
1899 Chi-N	17	47	5	12	2	0	1	11	0	....	3	....	.255	.286	.362	.647	79	-2	6	4.38	-2	C-15	1	-0.3
1900 Chi-N	8	25	1	5	0	0	0	0	3	....	1	....	.200	.286	.200	.486	36	-2	2	2.33	-1	/C-7	0	-0.2
1901 StL-N	93	308	50	75	11	3	1	33	10	....	14	....	.244	.290	.308	.598	77	-9	34	3.65	5	C-47,O-40(0-29-11)	6	-0.1
1902 StL-N	73	251	36	67	12	0	1	31	21	....	18	....	.267	.333	.327	.660	108	3	35	4.84	-3	1-56,C-11/O-4(0-1-3)	9	-0.1
1903 StL-N	36	120	13	23	2	0	0	9	12	....	9	....	.192	.281	.208	.490	42	-8	10	2.70	-4	1-25/O-7(7-0-0),C-2	0	-1.3
Total 6	241	793	112	194	28	3	3	90	50	....	51	....	.245	.308	.299	.606	82	-18	94	4.02	-6	/C-96,1-81,O-51	18	-1.8

• NICHOLS, Carl Carl Edward Nichols b: 10/14/1962, Los Angeles, CA BR/TR, 6', 208 lbs. Deb: 9/14/1986 Career OF: 1-0-3

YEAR TM-L	G	AB	R	H	2B	3B	HR	RBI	BB	SO	SB	CS	AVG	OBP	SLG	OPS	OPS+	BR/A	RC	RC/G	FR	G/POS	WS	TPW
1986 Bal-A	5	5	0	0	0	0	0	0	1	4	0	0	.000	.167	.000	.167	-51	-1	0	.00	0	/C-5	0	-0.1
1987 Bal-A	13	21	4	8	1	0	0	3	1	4	0	0	.381	.409	.429	.838	126	1	4	7.38	0	C-13	1	0.1
1988 Bal-A	18	47	2	9	1	0	0	1	3	10	0	0	.191	.240	.213	.453	29	-4	2	1.28	4	C-13/O-3(0-0-3)	1	0.0
1989 Hou-N	8	13	0	1	0	0	0	2	0	3	0	0	.077	.077	.077	.154	-58	-3	0	.17	0	/C-6	0	-0.3
1990 Hou-N	32	49	7	10	3	0	0	11	8	11	0	0	.204	.328	.265	.593	67	-2	5	3.08	0	C-15/1-3,O-1	2	-0.1
1991 Hou-N	20	51	3	10	3	0	0	1	5	17	0	0	.196	.268	.255	.523	51	-3	4	2.48	1	C-17	1	-0.2
Total 6	96	186	16	38	8	0	0	18	18	49	0	0	.204	.278	.247	.525	49	-13	15	2.50	5	/C-69,O-4,1-3	5	-0.5

• NICHOLS, Reid Thomas Reid Nichols b: 8/5/1958, Ocala, FL BR/TR, 5'11", 165 lbs. Deb: 9/16/1980 Career OF: 124-247-62

YEAR TM-L	G	AB	R	H	2B	3B	HR	RBI	BB	SO	SB	CS	AVG	OBP	SLG	OPS	OPS+	BR/A	RC	RC/G	FR	G/POS	WS	TPW
1980 Bos-A	12	36	5	8	0	1	0	3	3	8	0	1	.222	.282	.278	.560	51	-3	3	2.57	-0	/O-9(0-9-0),D-1	0	-0.3
1981 Bos-A	39	48	13	9	0	1	0	3	2	6	0	1	.188	.220	.229	.449	28	-5	3	1.54	1	O-27(1-25-1)/D-7,3-1	1	-0.5
1982 Bos-A	92	245	35	74	16	1	7	33	14	28	5	3	.302	.342	.461	.804	112	3	38	5.66	1	O-82(30-57-2)/D-4	9	0.2
1983 Bos-A	100	274	35	78	22	1	6	22	26	36	7	5	.285	.353	.438	.791	108	3	42	5.39	-1	O-72(11-32-30),D-18/S-1	8	-0.1
1984 Bos-A	74	124	14	28	5	1	1	14	12	18	2	1	.226	.309	.306	.616	68	-5	13	3.55	-2	O-48(17-26-4)/D-1	2	-0.8
1985 Bos-A	21	32	3	6	1	0	1	3	2	4	1	0	.188	.257	.313	.570	53	-2	3	2.48	-2	O-10(2-7-1)/D-4,2-3	0	-0.4
Chi-A	51	118	20	35	7	1	1	15	15	13	5	5	.297	.376	.398	.774	108	1	18	5.20	-1	O-48(25-27-8)/D-1	4	-0.1
Yr.	72	150	23	41	8	1	2	18	17	17	6	5	.273	.351	.380	.731	96	-1	20	4.55	-3	O-58(27-34-9)/D-5,2-3	4	-0.5
1986 Chi-A	74	136	9	31	4	0	2	18	11	23	5	4	.228	.286	.301	.587	58	-9	12	2.73	0	O-53(31-14-11)/D-3,2-2	2	-1.0
1987 Mon-N	77	147	22	39	8	2	4	20	14	13	2	1	.265	.333	.429	.762	97	-1	21	4.82	0	O-59(7-50-5)/3-3	5	-0.2
Total 8	540	1160	156	308	63	8	22	131	99	149	27	21	.266	.328	.391	.719	91	-17	151	4.45	-4	O-408/D-39,2-5,3-4,S-1	31	-3.1

• NICHOLS, Roy Roy Nichols b: 3/3/1921, Little Rock, AR d: 4/3/2002, Hot Springs, AR BR/TR, 5'11", 155 lbs. Deb: 5/6/1944

YEAR TM-L	G	AB	R	H	2B	3B	HR	RBI	BB	SO	SB	CS	AVG	OBP	SLG	OPS	OPS+	BR/A	RC	RC/G	FR	G/POS	WS	TPW
1944 NY-N	11	9	3	2	1	0	0	0	2	2	0	....	.222	.364	.333	.697	97	0	1	4.94	0	/2-1,3-1	0	0.0

• NICHOLSON, Bill William Beck "Swish" Nicholson
b: 12/11/1914, Chestertown, MD d: 3/8/1996, Chestertown, MD BL/TR, 6', 205 lbs. Deb: 6/13/1936 Career OF: 46-0-1427

YEAR TM-L	G	AB	R	H	2B	3B	HR	RBI	BB	SO	SB	CS	AVG	OBP	SLG	OPS	OPS+	BR/A	RC	RC/G	FR	G/POS	WS	TPW
1936 Phi-A	11	12	2	0	0	0	0	0	0	5	0	0	.000	.000	.000	.000	-102	-4	0	.00	-0	/O-1	0	-0.3
1939 Chi-N	58	220	37	65	12	5	5	38	20	29	0	....	.295	.354	.464	.818	116	4	38	6.38	-1	O-58(0-0-58)	9	0.0
1940 Chi-N★	135	491	78	146	27	7	25	98	50	67	2	....	.297	.366	.534	.899	148	31	97	7.45	3	*O-123(43-0-81)	20	2.6
1941 Chi-N★	147	532	74	135	26	1	26	98	82	91	1	....	.254	.357	.453	.810	132	23	90	6.03	1	*O-143(3-0-140)	21	1.6
1942 Chi-N	152	588	83	173	22	11	21	78	76	80	8	....	.294	.382	.476	.859	156	42	112	7.17	8	*O-151(0-0-151)	28	4.4
1943 Chi-N★	154	608	95	188	30	9	**29**	**128**	71	86	4	....	.309	.386	.531	.917	166	50	129	8.14	2	*O-154(0-0-154)	31	4.4
1944 Chi-N★	156	582	**116**	167	35	8	**33**	**122**	93	71	3	....	.287	.391	.545	.935	162	49	132	8.45	0	*O-156(0-0-156)	31	3.9
1945*Chi-N★	151	559	82	136	28	4	13	88	92	73	4	....	.243	.356	.377	.734	106	7	81	5.04	0	*O-151(0-0-151)	19	-0.3
1946 Chi-N	105	296	36	65	13	2	8	41	44	44	1	....	.220	.325	.358	.683	95	-1	37	4.21	2	O-80(0-0-80)	8	-0.2
1947 Chi-N	148	487	69	119	28	1	26	75	87	83	1	....	.244	.364	.466	.831	124	18	90	6.50	-1	*O-140(0-0-140)	18	1.3
1948 Chi-N	143	494	68	129	24	5	19	67	81	60	2	....	.261	.371	.445	.816	125	19	88	6.39	-1	*O-136(0-0-136)	17	1.4
1949 Phi-N	98	299	42	70	8	3	11	40	45	53	1	....	.234	.344	.391	.735	99	1	44	5.19	0	O-91(0-0-92)	9	-0.3
1950 Phi-N	41	58	3	13	2	1	3	10	8	16	0	....	.224	.318	.448	.766	101	-0	8	4.64	-1	O-15(0-0-15)	1	-0.1
1951 Phi-N	85	170	23	41	9	2	8	30	25	24	0	1	.241	.342	.459	.801	115	3	29	5.93	-3	O-41(0-0-41)	5	-0.1
1952 Phi-N	55	88	17	24	3	0	6	19	14	26	0	0	.273	.390	.511	.902	150	6	20	8.20	0	O-19(0-0-19)	5	0.6
1953 Phi-N	38	62	12	13	5	1	2	16	12	20	0	0	.210	.338	.419	.757	96	-0	9	4.90	0	O-12(0-0-12)	1	-0.1
Total 16	1677	5546	837	1484	272	60	235	948	800	828	27	1	.268	.365	.465	.830	133	248	1005	6.55	8	*O-1471	223	18.8

• NICHOLSON, Dave David Lawrence Nicholson b: 8/29/1939, St. Louis, MO BR/TR, 6'2", 215 lbs. Deb: 5/24/1960 Career OF: 327-38-113

YEAR TM-L	G	AB	R	H	2B	3B	HR	RBI	BB	SO	SB	CS	AVG	OBP	SLG	OPS	OPS+	BR/A	RC	RC/G	FR	G/POS	WS	TPW
1960 Bal-A	54	113	17	21	1	1	5	11	20	55	0	2	.186	.308	.345	.653	77	-4	12	3.46	2	O-44(34-0-11)	2	-0.4
1962 Bal-A	97	173	25	30	4	1	9	15	27	76	3	4	.173	.289	.364	.653	78	-7	19	3.35	1	O-80(34-20-27)	3	-0.8
1963 Chi-A	126	449	53	103	11	4	22	70	63	175	2	1	.229	.324	.419	.743	108	5	65	4.92	1	*O-123(123-0-0)	15	0.0
1964 Chi-A	97	294	40	60	6	1	13	39	52	126	0	2	.204	.330	.364	.693	95	-1	38	4.19	2	O-92(91-0-1)	9	-0.4
1965 Chi-A	54	85	11	13	2	1	2	12	9	40	0	0	.153	.234	.271	.505	46	-6	6	2.09	0	O-36(25-12-1)	0	-0.8
1966 Hou-N	100	280	36	69	8	4	10	31	46	92	1	1	.246	.359	.411	.769	121	10	45	5.66	2	O-90(13-5-73)	11	0.7
1967 Atl-N	10	25	2	5	0	0	0	1	2	9	0	0	.200	.259	.200	.459	34	-2	2	1.87	0	/O-7(7-1-0)	0	-0.3
Total 7	538	1419	184	301	32	12	61	179	219	573	6	10	.212	.320	.381	.701	97	-5	186	4.35	7	O-472	40	-2.1

• NICHOLSON, Fred Fred "Shoemaker" Nicholson b: 9/1/1894, Honey Grove, TX d: 1/23/1972, Kilgore, TX BR/TR, 5'10.5", 173 lbs. Deb: 4/11/1917 Career OF: 119-19-65

YEAR TM-L	G	AB	R	H	2B	3B	HR	RBI	BB	SO	SB	CS	AVG	OBP	SLG	OPS	OPS+	BR/A	RC	RC/G	FR	G/POS	WS	TPW
1917 Det-A	13	14	4	4	1	0	0	1	1	2	0	....	.286	.333	.357	.690	111	0	2	4.03	0	/O-3(1-0-2)	0	0.0
1919 Pit-N	30	66	8	18	2	2	1	6	6	11	2	....	.273	.333	.409	.742	118	1	9	4.87	-1	O-17(13-1-3)/1-1	2	0.0
1920 Pit-N	99	247	33	89	16	7	4	30	18	31	9	6	.360	.404	.530	.934	162	19	51	7.99	-1	O-58(28-18-13)	14	1.7
1921 Bos-N	83	245	36	80	11	7	5	41	17	29	5	4	.327	.370	.490	.860	133	11	43	6.45	0	O-59(57-0-3)/1-4,2-2	10	0.7
1922 Bos-N	78	222	31	56	4	5	2	29	23	24	5	7	.252	.336	.342	.678	79	-8	26	3.79	-3	O-63(20-0-44)	4	-1.5
Total 5	303	794	112	247	34	21	12	107	65	97	21	17	.311	.367	.452	.819	124	24	131	5.90	-6	O-200/1-5,2-2	30	0.9

YEAR TM-L	G	AB	R	H	2B	3B	HR	RBI	BB	SO	SB	CS	AVG	OBP	SLG	OPS	OPS+	BR/A	RC	RC/G	FR	G/POS	WS	TPW
• NICHOLSON, Kevin	Kevin Ronald Nicholson b: 3/29/1976, Vancouver, Canada BB/TR, 5'10", 190 lbs. Deb: 6/23/2000																							
2000 SD-N	37	97	7	21	6	1	1	8	4	31	1	0	.216	.255	.330	.585	50	-8	8	2.70	2	S-30/2-4	1	-0.3
• NICHOLSON, Ovid	Ovid Edward Nicholson b: 12/30/1888, Salem, IN d: 3/24/1968, Salem, IN BL/TR, 5'9.5", 155 lbs. Deb: 9/17/1912																							
1912 Pit-N	6	11	2	5	0	0	0	3	1	2	0	....	.455	.500	.455	.955	165	1	3	9.52	-1	/0-4(4-0-0)	1	0.0
• NICHOLSON, Parson	Thomas C. "Deacon" Nicholson b: 4/14/1863, Blaine, OH d: 2/28/1917, Bellaire, OH, 5'9", 190 lbs. Deb: 9/14/1888																							
1888 Det-N	24	85	11	22	2	3	1	9	2	7	6	....	.259	.284	.388	.672	113	1	11	4.87	-3	2-24	3	-0.1
1890 Tol-a	134	523	78	140	16	11	4	72	42	....	46	....	.268	.333	.363	.696	102	-1	80	5.57	-3	*2-134/C-1	14	0.1
1895 Was-N	10	38	7	7	2	1	0	5	7	4	6	....	.184	.311	.289	.601	56	-2	5	4.72	-3	S-10	0	-0.4
Total 3	168	646	96	169	20	15	5	86	51	11	58	....	.262	.325	.362	.688	100	-2	97	5.42	-9	2-158/S-10,C-1	17	-0.5
• NICOL, George	George Edward Nicol b: 10/17/1870, Barry, IL d: 8/4/1924, Milwaukee, WI TL, 5'7", 155 lbs. Deb: 9/23/1890 ♦																							
1890 StL-a	3	7	4	2	1	0	0	1	4	....	0	....	.286	.545	.429	.974	164	1	2	8.89	0	/P-3	1	0.0
1891 Chi-N	3	6	0	2	0	1	0	3	0	1	0	....	.333	.333	.667	1.000	189	1	1	9.23	-1	/P-3	0	-0.1
1894 Pit-N	8	20	8	9	1	0	0	3	0	1	0	....	.450	.450	.500	.950	130	2	5	10.90	-1	/P-8	3	-0.2
Lou-N	27	108	12	38	6	4	0	19	2	3	4	....	.352	.375	.481	.856	113	2	22	8.00	-4	0-26(0-0-26)/P-1	2	-0.6
Yr.	35	128	20	47	7	4	0	22	2	4	4	....	.367	.386	.484	.871	116	4	26	8.39	-5	0-26(0-0-26)/P-9	5	-0.8
Total 3	41	141	24	51	8	5	0	26	6	5	4	....	.362	.396	.489	.885	122	7	29	8.45	-6	/0-26,P-15	6	-0.8
• NICOL, Hugh	Hugh Nicol b: 1/1/1858, Campsie, Scotland d: 6/27/1921, Lafayette, IN BR/TR, 5'4", 145 lbs. Deb: 5/3/1881 M/U Career OF: 3-20-802																							
1881 Chi-N	26	108	13	22	2	0	0	7	4	12	....	....	.204	.232	.222	.454	41	-7	6	1.79	5	0-26(2-12-12)/S-1	2	-0.3
1882 Chi-N	47	186	19	37	9	1	1	16	7	29	....	....	.199	.228	.274	.502	60	-8	12	2.20	11	0-47(0-0-47)/S-8	3	0.2
1883 StL-a	94	368	73	105	13	3	0	39	18	....	....	....	.285	.319	.337	.656	105	1	41	4.31	14	*0-84(1-1-84),2-11	14	1.2
1884 StL-a	110	442	79	116	14	5	0	0	22	....	....	....	.262	.302	.317	.619	98	-1	43	3.65	21	*0-87(0-0-87),2-23/3-1,S-1	17	1.8
1885*StL-a	112	425	59	88	11	1	0	45	34	....	....	....	.207	.271	.238	.508	59	-20	28	2.24	13	*0-111(0-0-111)/3-1	12	-0.8
1886 StL-a	67	253	44	52	6	3	0	19	26	....	38	....	.206	.280	.253	.533	64	-11	29	3.93	-3	0-57(0-1-56)/S-8,2-4	4	-1.3
1887 Cin-a	125	561	122	188	18	2	1	34	86	....	**138**	....	.335	.341	.267	.608	69	-16	93	6.70	-1	*0-125(0-6-119)	9	-1.5
1888 Cin-a	135	548	112	131	10	2	1	35	67	....	103	....	.239	.330	.270	.600	88	-5	85	5.49	-1	*0-125(0-0-125),2-12/S-1	15	-0.7
1889 Cin-a	122	474	82	121	7	8	2	58	54	35	80	....	.255	.338	.316	.654	84	-9	80	5.98	2	*0-115(0-0-115)/2-7,3-3	12	-0.7
1890 Cin-N	50	186	28	39	1	4	0	19	19	12	24	....	.210	.283	.258	.541	58	-10	21	3.76	-3	0-46(0-0-46)/S-3,2-1	3	-1.2
Total 10	888	3551	631	899	91	29	5	272	337	88	383	....	.253	.307	.282	.589	78	-85	437	4.45	57	0-823/2-58,S-22,3-5	91	-3.4
• NICOSIA, Steve	Steven Richard Nicosia b: 8/6/1955, Paterson, NJ BR/TR, 5'10", 185 lbs. Deb: 7/8/1978																							
1978 Pit-N	3	5	0	0	0	0	0	0	1	0	0	0	.000	.167	.000	.167	-48	-1	0	.23	1	/C-1	0	0.0
1979*Pit-N	70	191	22	55	16	0	4	13	23	17	0	2	.288	.364	.435	.799	112	3	29	5.43	-2	C-65	8	0.3
1980 Pit-N	60	176	16	38	8	0	1	22	19	16	0	1	.216	.296	.278	.574	60	-10	14	2.53	-2	C-58	3	-0.9
1981 Pit-N	54	169	21	39	10	1	2	18	13	10	3	1	.231	.286	.337	.623	74	-6	15	2.88	-1	C-52	3	-0.5
1982 Pit-N	39	100	6	28	3	0	1	7	11	13	0	1	.280	.351	.340	.691	91	-1	12	4.25	0	C-35/0-3(3-0-0)	3	0.0
1983 Pit-N	21	46	4	6	2	0	1	1	1	7	0	0	.130	.149	.239	.388	6	-6	1	.29	-1	C-15	1	-0.7
SF-N	15	33	4	11	0	0	0	6	3	2	0	0	.333	.389	.333	.722	105	0	4	4.22	0	/C-9	1	0.1
Yr.	36	79	8	17	2	0	1	7	4	9	0	0	.215	.253	.278	.531	48	-6	4	1.65	-1	C-24	2	-0.6
1984 SF-N	48	132	9	40	11	2	2	19	8	14	1	1	.303	.343	.462	.805	128	4	20	5.42	-2	C-41	5	0.4
1985 Mon-N	42	71	4	12	2	0	0	1	7	11	1	0	.169	.244	.197	.441	26	-7	4	1.58	-1	C-23/1-2	1	-0.7
Tor-A	6	15	0	4	0	0	0	1	0	0	0	0	.267	.267	.267	.533	46	-1	1	2.62	0	/C-6	0	-0.1
Total 8	358	938	86	233	52	3	11	88	86	90	5	6	.248	.312	.345	.658	82	-25	99	3.52	-7	C-305/0-3,1-2	25	-2.0
• NIEBERGALL, Charlie	Charles Arthur "Nig" Niebergall b: 5/23/1899, New York, NY d: 8/29/1982, Holiday, FL BR/TR, 5'10", 160 lbs. Deb: 6/17/1921																							
1921 StL-N	5	6	1	1	0	0	0	0	0	0	0	0	.167	.167	.167	.333	-12	-1	0	.85	-1	/C-3	0	-0.1
1923 StL-N	9	28	2	3	1	0	0	1	2	2	0	0	.107	.167	.143	.310	-18	-5	1	.79	0	/C-7	0	-0.4
1924 StL-N	40	58	6	17	6	0	0	7	3	9	0	0	.293	.339	.397	.735	98	-0	8	4.78	-1	C-34	2	0.1
Total 3	54	92	9	21	7	0	0	8	5	11	0	0	.228	.276	.304	.580	56	-6	9	3.13	-1	/C-44	2	-0.5
• NIEHAUS, Al	Albert Bernard Niehaus b: 6/1/1899, Cincinnati, OH d: 10/14/1931, Cincinnati, OH BR/TR, 5'11", 175 lbs. Deb: 4/22/1925																							
1925 Pit-N	17	64	7	14	8	0	0	7	1	5	0	0	.219	.242	.344	.586	45	-6	5	2.71	-2	1-15	0	-0.8
Cin-N	51	147	16	44	10	2	0	14	13	10	1	4	.299	.360	.395	.755	95	-2	20	4.85	1	1-45	3	-0.3
Yr.	68	211	23	58	18	2	0	21	14	15	1	4	.275	.326	.379	.705	80	-8	25	4.16	0	1-60	3	-1.1
• NIEHOFF, Bert	John Albert Niehoff b: 5/13/1884, Louisville, CO d: 12/8/1974, Inglewood, CO BR/TR, 5'10.5", 170 lbs. Deb: 10/4/1913 C																							
1913 Cin-N	2	8	0	0	0	0	0	0	0	2	0	....	.000	.000	.000	.000	-100	-2	0	.00	2	/3-2	0	0.0
1914 Cin-N	142	484	46	117	16	9	4	49	38	77	20	....	.242	.298	.337	.635	86	-9	52	3.57	2	*3-134/2-3	11	-0.4
1915*Phi-N	148	529	61	126	27	2	2	49	30	63	21	11	.238	.280	.308	.588	77	-16	50	3.04	-4	*2-148	11	-1.9
1916 Phi-N	146	548	65	133	**42**	4	4	61	37	57	20	14	.243	.292	.356	.648	95	-6	60	3.43	1	*2-144/3-2	18	-0.3
1917 Phi-N	114	361	30	92	17	4	2	42	23	29	8	....	.255	.303	.341	.644	93	-3	39	3.57	8	2-96/1-7,3-6	11	0.7
1918 StL-N	22	84	5	15	2	0	0	5	3	10	2	....	.179	.207	.202	.409	26	-8	4	1.39	0	2-22	1	-0.8
NY-N	7	23	3	6	0	0	0	1	0	4	0	....	.261	.261	.261	.522	60	-1	1	2.21	-2	/2-7	0	-0.4
Yr.	29	107	8	21	2	0	0	6	3	14	2	....	.196	.218	.215	.433	33	-9	5	1.55	-2	2-29	1	-1.2
Total 6	581	2037	210	489	104	19	12	207	131	242	71	25	.240	.288	.327	.615	84	-46	206	3.27	6	2-420,3-144/1-7	52	-3.1
• NIEKRO, Lance	Lance Joseph Niekro b: 1/29/1979, Winter Haven, FL BR/TR, 6'3", 210 lbs. Deb: 9/5/2003																							
2003 SF-N	5	5	2	1	1	0	0	2	0	1	0	0	.200	.200	.400	.600	53	-0	0	2.70	0	/1-3	0	-0.1
• NIELSEN, Milt	Milton Robert Nielsen b: 2/8/1925, Tyler, MN BL/TL, 5'11", 190 lbs. Deb: 9/27/1949																							
1949 Cle-A	3	9	1	1	0	0	0	0	2	4	0	0	.111	.273	.111	.384	4	-1	0	1.42	0	/0-3(0-3-0)	0	-0.1
1951 Cle-A	16	6	1	0	0	0	0	0	1	1	0	0	.000	.143	.000	.143	-63	-1	0	.17	0	....	0	-0.1
Total 2	19	15	2	1	0	0	0	0	3	5	0	0	.067	.222	.067	.289	-22	-2	0	.88	0	/0-3	0	-0.3
• NIEMAN, Bob	Robert Charles Nieman b: 1/26/1927, Cincinnati, OH d: 3/10/1985, Corona, CA BR/TR, 5'11", 195 lbs. Deb: 9/14/1951 Career OF: 702-0-231																							
1951 StL-A	12	43	6	16	3	1	2	8	3	5	0	0	.372	.413	.628	1.041	173	4	11	10.33	-1	0-11(11-0-0)	3	0.3
1952 StL-A	131	478	66	138	22	2	18	74	46	73	0	4	.289	.352	.456	.808	120	11	75	5.54	1	*0-125(32-0-94)	15	0.7
1953 Det-A	142	508	72	143	32	5	15	69	57	57	0	3	.281	.354	.453	.807	118	11	82	5.74	0	*0-135(74-0-64)	16	0.5
1954 Det-A	91	251	24	66	14	1	8	35	22	32	0	2	.263	.322	.422	.745	105	-0	31	4.16	0	0-62(62-0-0)	6	-0.4
1955 Chi-A	99	272	36	77	11	2	11	53	36	37	1	0	.283	.371	.460	.831	119	8	46	5.94	2	0-78(29-0-52)	10	0.7
1956 Chi-A	14	40	3	12	1	0	2	4	4	4	0	1	.300	.364	.475	.839	118	1	5	3.99	0	0-10(0-0-10)	1	0.0
Bal-A	114	388	60	125	20	6	12	64	86	59	1	5	.322	.445	.497	.943	161	37	89	8.53	1	*0-114(114-0-0)	23	3.1
Yr.	128	428	63	137	21	6	14	68	90	63	1	6	.320	.438	.495	.934	157	38	94	8.05	1	*0-124(114-0-10)	24	3.1
1957 Bal-A	129	445	61	123	17	6	13	70	63	86	4	4	.276	.369	.429	.798	125	16	70	5.39	2	*0-120(116-0-4)	16	1.2
1958 Bal-A	105	366	56	119	20	2	16	60	44	57	2	8	.325	.398	.522	.919	159	27	71	7.03	-3	*0-100(100-0-0)	17	2.1
1959 Bal-A	118	360	49	105	18	2	21	60	42	55	1	2	.292	.369	.528	.897	146	22	67	6.63	4	0-97(97-0-0)	15	2.2
1960 StL-N	81	188	19	54	13	5	4	31	24	31	0	1	.287	.374	.473	.847	120	5	33	6.33	-3	0-55(53-0-2)	7	0.0
1961 StL-N	6	17	0	8	1	0	0	2	0	2	0	0	.471	.471	.529	1.000	150	1	4	12.71	0	/0-4(4-0-0)	1	0.1
Cle-A	39	65	2	23	6	0	2	10	7	4	1	0	.354	.417	.538	.955	157	6	16	10.00	0	0-12(7-0-5)	3	0.5
1962 Cle-A	2	1	0	0	0	0	0	1	0	1	0	0	.000	.000	.000	.000	-103	-0	0	.00	0	....	0	0.0
*SF-N	30	30	1	9	2	0	1	3	1	9	0	0	.300	.323	.467	.789	111	0	5	5.91	0	/0-3(3-0-0)	1	0.0
Total 12	1113	3452	455	1018	180	32	125	544	435	512	10	30	.295	.375	.474	.849	132	148	605	6.24	4	0-926	134	10.9
• NIEMAN, Butch	Elmer Le Roy Nieman b: 2/8/1918, Herkimer, KS d: 11/2/1993, Topeka, KS BL/TL, 6'2", 195 lbs. Deb: 5/2/1943 Career OF: 206-0-76																							
1943 Bos-N	101	335	39	84	15	8	7	46	39	39	4	....	.251	.331	.406	.737	114	5	47	5.02	6	0-93(77-0-16)	12	0.6
1944 Bos-N	134	468	65	124	16	6	16	65	47	47	5	....	.265	.332	.427	.759	108	4	69	5.31	0	*0-126(86-0-46)	15	-0.4

YEAR TM-L	G	AB	R	H	2B	3B	HR	RBI	BB	SO	SB	CS	AVG	OBP	SLG	OPS	OPS+	BR/A	RC	RC/G	FR	G/POS	WS	TPW
1945 Bos-N	97	247	43	61	15	0	14	56	43	33	11	....	.247	.361	.478	.839	131	11	44	6.29	-1	0-57(43-0-14)	7	0.5
Total 3	332	1050	147	269	46	14	37	167	129	119	20	....	.256	.339	.432	.771	116	20	161	5.45	5	0-276	34	0.8
• NIEMIEC, Al	Alfred Joseph Niemiec b: 5/18/1911, Meriden, CT d: 10/29/1995, Kirkland, WA BR/TR, 5'11", 158 lbs. Deb: 9/19/1934																							
1934 Bos-A	9	32	2	7	0	0	0	3	3	4	0	0	.219	.286	.219	.504	30	-3	2	2.23	2	/2-9	0	-0.1
1936 Phi-A	69	203	22	40	3	2	1	20	26	16	2	2	.197	.291	.246	.538	35	-21	16	2.51	4	2-52/S-5	2	-1.2
Total 2	78	235	24	47	3	2	1	23	29	20	2	2	.200	.291	.243	.533	34	-24	18	2.47	6	/2-61,S-5	2	-1.3
• NIETO, Tom	Thomas Andrew Nieto b: 10/27/1960, Downey, CA BR/TR, 6'1", 205 lbs. Deb: 5/10/1984																							
1984 StL-N	33	86	7	24	4	0	3	12	5	18	0	0	.279	.319	.430	.749	112	1	11	4.37	1	C-32	3	0.3
1985*StL-N	95	253	15	57	10	2	0	34	26	37	0	2	.225	.305	.281	.586	65	-12	21	2.63	-6	C-95	5	-1.5
1986 Mon-N	30	65	5	13	3	1	1	7	6	21	0	1	.200	.278	.323	.601	66	-4	5	2.42	-1	C-30	1	-0.4
1987 Min-A	41	105	7	21	7	1	1	12	8	24	0	0	.200	.276	.314	.590	54	-7	10	2.96	1	C-40/D-1	1	-0.4
1988 Min-A	24	60	1	4	0	0	0	0	1	17	0	0	.067	.097	.067	.163	-52	-12	0	.14	-1	C-24	1	-1.2
1989 Phi-N	11	20	1	3	0	0	0	0	6	7	0	0	.150	.370	.150	.520	54	-1	2	2.84	0	C-11	1	0.0
1990 Phi-N	17	30	1	5	0	0	0	4	3	11	0	0	.167	.265	.167	.431	21	-3	1	1.24	0	C-17	1	-0.3
Total 7	251	619	37	127	24	4	5	69	55	135	0	3	.205	.281	.281	.562	57	-38	50	2.54	-5	C-249/D-1	13	-3.4
• NIEVES, Jose	Jose Miguel (Pinto) Nieves b: 6/16/1975, Guacara, Venezuela BR/TR, 6'1", 180 lbs. Deb: 8/7/1998																							
1998 Chi-N	2	1	0	0	0	0	0	0	0	0	0	0	.000	.000	.000	.000	-97	-0	0	.00	-1	/S-1	0	-0.1
1999 Chi-N	54	181	16	45	9	1	2	18	8	25	0	2	.249	.295	.343	.638	62	-12	17	3.11	2	S-52	3	-0.6
2000 Chi-N	82	198	17	42	6	3	5	24	11	43	1	1	.212	.254	.348	.602	51	-16	15	2.45	0	3-39,S-24/2-7	2	-1.4
2001 Ana-A	29	53	5	13	3	1	2	3	2	20	0	1	.245	.298	.453	.751	92	-1	7	4.07	5	2-11,S-10/D-4,3-2,1-1	1	0.4
2002 Ana-A	45	97	17	28	2	0	0	6	2	14	1	1	.289	.303	.309	.612	63	-5	8	2.99	-4	2-18,S-13/3-5,1-3,D-2,0-2(0-1-1)	2	-0.8
Total 5	212	530	55	128	20	5	9	51	23	102	2	5	.242	.281	.349	.630	61	-35	47	2.92	1	S-100/3-46,2-36,D-6,1-4,0-2	8	-2.4
• NIEVES, Melvin	Melvin Ramos Nieves b: 12/28/1971, San Juan, Puerto Rico BB/TR, 6'2", 210 lbs. Deb: 9/1/1992 Career OF: 91-8-244																							
1992 Atl-N	12	19	0	4	1	0	0	1	2	7	0	0	.211	.286	.263	.549	53	-1	2	2.84	-1	/0-6(3-0-3)	0	-0.3
1993 SD-N	19	47	4	9	0	0	2	3	3	21	0	0	.191	.255	.319	.574	52	-3	4	2.91	-1	0-15(0-0-15)	0	-0.5
1994 SD-N	10	19	2	5	1	0	1	4	3	10	0	0	.263	.364	.474	.837	120	1	4	6.86	0	/0-6(2-0-4)	1	0.1
1995 SD-N	98	234	32	48	6	1	14	38	19	88	2	3	.205	.279	.419	.698	84	-7	25	3.29	2	0-79(62-6-15)/1-2	2	-0.7
1996 Det-A	120	431	71	106	23	4	24	60	44	158	1	2	.246	.324	.485	.809	101	-2	67	5.28	1	*0-105(21-0-84),D-11	9	-0.6
1997 Det-A	116	359	46	82	18	1	20	64	39	157	1	7	.228	.313	.451	.764	97	-6	50	4.64	-1	*0-101(0-2-101),D-10	10	-1.2
1998 Cin-N	83	119	8	30	4	0	2	17	26	42	0	0	.252	.386	.336	.722	91	-0	17	4.92	0	0-25(3-0-22)/D-3	2	-0.1
Total 7	458	1228	163	284	53	6	63	187	136	483	4	12	.231	.316	.438	.755	93	-19	167	4.55	0	0-337/D-24,1-2	24	-3.4
• NIEVES, Wil	Wilbert Nieves b: 9/25/1977, San Juan, Puerto Rico BR/TR, 5'11", 190 lbs. Deb: 7/21/2002																							
2002 SD-N	28	72	2	13	3	1	0	3	4	15	1	0	.181	.224	.250	.474	27	-8	4	1.75	1	C-27	1	-0.5
• NILAND, Tom	Thomas James "Honest Tom" Niland b: 4/14/1870, Brookfield, MA d: 4/30/1950, Lynn, MA BR/TR, 5'11", 160 lbs. Deb: 4/19/1896																							
1896 StL-N	18	68	3	12	0	1	0	3	5	4	0	....	.176	.243	.206	.449	20	-8	4	1.68	-2	0-13(6-0-7)/S-5	0	-0.9
• NILES, Bill	William E. Niles b: 1/11/1867, Covington, KY d: 7/3/1936, Springfield, OH, 160 lbs. Deb: 5/13/1895																							
1895 Pit-N	11	37	2	8	0	0	0	0	5	2	2	....	.216	.310	.216	.526	39	-3	3	2.99	0	3-10/2-1	1	-0.2
• NILES, Harry	Herbert Clyde Niles b: 9/10/1880, Buchanan, MI d: 4/18/1953, Sturgis, MI BR/TR, 5'8", 175 lbs. Deb: 4/24/1906 Career OF: 95-19-184																							
1906 StL-A	142	541	71	124	14	4	2	31	46	....	30	....	.229	.297	.281	.578	85	-8	57	3.51	14	*0-108(0-6-102),3-34	13	0.2
1907 StL-A	120	492	65	142	9	5	2	35	28	....	19	....	.289	.331	.339	.670	114	7	64	4.74	0	*2-116/0-1	16	0.9
1908 NY-A	96	362	43	90	14	6	4	24	25	....	18	....	.249	.304	.354	.658	112	4	44	4.04	-19	2-85/0-7(1-1-5)	12	-1.6
Bos-A	17	32	4	8	0	0	1	3	6	....	3	....	.250	.385	.344	.728	133	2	6	5.38	0	/2-8,S-2	2	0.2
Yr.	113	394	47	98	14	6	5	27	31	....	21	....	.249	.312	.353	.664	114	6	50	4.16	-19	2-93/0-7(1-1-5),S-2	14	-1.5
1909 Bos-A	145	546	65	134	12	5	1	38	39	....	27	....	.245	.311	.291	.602	88	-6	58	3.51	1	*0-117(77-12-28),3-13/S-9,2	14	-1.3
1910 Bos-A	18	57	6	12	3	0	1	3	4	....	1	....	.211	.262	.316	.578	79	-2	5	2.74	0	0-15(4-0-11)	1	-0.3
Cle-A	70	240	25	51	6	4	1	18	15	....	9	....	.213	.267	.283	.551	72	-8	20	2.70	-4	0-50(13-0-37)/S-7,3-5	3	-1.6
Yr.	88	297	31	63	9	4	2	21	19	....	10	....	.212	.266	.290	.556	73	-10	25	2.71	-4	0-65(17-0-48)/S-7,3-5	4	-1.9
Total 5	608	2270	279	561	58	24	12	152	163	....	107	....	.247	.306	.310	.616	96	-11	254	3.77	-8	0-298,2-214/3-52,S-18	61	-3.5
• NILL, Rabbit	George Charles Nill b: 7/14/1881, Fort Wayne, IN d: 5/24/1962, Fort Wayne, IN BR/TR, 5'7", 160 lbs. Deb: 9/27/1904 Career OF: 19-15-3																							
1904 Was-A	15	48	4	8	0	1	0	3	5	....	0	....	.167	.273	.208	.481	54	-2	3	1.90	-5	2-15	0	-0.7
1905 Was-A	103	319	46	58	7	3	3	31	33	....	12	....	.182	.269	.251	.520	68	-11	27	2.62	-2	3-52,2-33/S-6	5	-1.2
1906 Was-A	89	315	37	74	8	2	0	15	47	....	16	....	.235	.340	.273	.613	97	2	37	3.91	4	S-31,2-25,3-15,0-15(0-15-0)	11	0.8
1907 Was-A	66	215	21	47	7	3	0	25	15	....	6	....	.219	.282	.279	.561	86	-3	20	3.02	-1	2-39,0-18(17-0-1)/3-1	3	-0.6
Cle-A	12	43	5	12	1	0	0	2	3	....	2	....	.279	.326	.302	.628	100	0	5	4.26	-2	/3-7,S-4	2	-0.2
Yr.	78	258	26	59	8	3	0	27	18	....	8	....	.229	.289	.283	.572	88	-3	25	3.21	-3	2-39,0-18(17-0-1)/3-8,S-4	5	-0.8
1908 Cle-A	11	23	3	5	0	0	0	1	0	....	0	....	.217	.217	.217	.435	41	-2	1	1.56	-1	/S-6,0-3(2-0-2),2-1	0	-0.3
Total 5	296	963	116	204	23	9	3	77	103	....	36	....	.212	.297	.264	.561	82	-15	93	3.12	-7	2-113/3-75,S-47,0-36	21	-2.2
• NILSSON, Dave	David Wayne Nilsson b: 12/14/1969, Brisbane, Australia BL/TR, 6'3", 215 lbs. Deb: 5/18/1992 Career OF: 80-0-105																							
1992 Mil-A	51	164	15	38	8	0	4	25	17	18	2	2	.232	.304	.354	.658	85	-4	18	3.76	-1	C-46/1-3,D-2	5	-0.2
1993 Mil-A	100	296	35	76	10	2	7	40	37	36	3	6	.257	.339	.375	.714	93	-4	36	3.95	-5	C-91/1-4,D-4	6	-0.4
1994 Mil-A	109	397	51	109	28	3	12	69	34	61	1	0	.275	.332	.451	.783	95	-4	59	5.24	-5	C-60,D-43/1-5	9	-0.7
1995 Mil-A	81	263	41	73	12	1	12	53	24	41	2	0	.278	.343	.468	.810	103	1	41	5.36	2	0-58(15-0-47),D-14/1-7,C-2	6	0.0
1996 Mil-A	123	453	81	150	33	2	17	84	57	68	2	3	.331	.409	.525	.935	129	21	100	8.64	0	0-61(6-0-55),D-40,1-24/C-2	17	1.3
1997 Mil-A	156	554	71	154	33	0	20	81	65	88	2	3	.278	.356	.446	.802	107	5	90	5.80	-4	1-74,D-59,0-22(22-0-0)	12	-1.0
1998 Mil-N	102	309	39	83	14	1	12	56	33	48	2	2	.269	.341	.437	.778	103	1	44	4.82	-6	1-49,0-37(37-0-3)/C-7	10	-1.0
1999 Mil-N★	115	343	56	106	19	1	21	62	53	64	1	2	.309	.405	.554	.958	141	21	78	8.32	1	*C-101/D-1	15	2.7
Total 8	837	2779	389	789	157	10	105	470	320	424	15	18	.284	.360	.461	.821	110	37	464	5.94	-18	C-309,0-178,1-166,D-163	80	0.7
• NIVAR, Ramon	Ramon A. Nivar b: 2/22/1980, San Cristobal, Dominican Republic BR/TR, 5'10", 170 lbs. Deb: 7/30/2003																							
2003 Tex-A	28	90	9	19	1	2	0	7	4	10	4	2	.211	.253	.267	.519	34	-9	6	2.19	3	0-26(0-26-0)/D-1	1	-0.6
• NIX, Laynce	Layne Michael Nix b: 10/30/1980, Houston, TX BL/TL, 6', 190 lbs. Deb: 7/10/2003																							
2003 Tex-A	53	184	25	47	10	0	8	30	9	53	3	0	.255	.290	.440	.730	82	-5	24	4.67	3	0-52(5-21-37)/D-1	4	-0.3
• NIXON, Al	Albert Richard "Humpty Dumpty" Nixon b: 4/11/1886, Atlantic City, NJ d: 11/9/1960, Opelousas, LA BR/TL, 5'7.5", 164 lbs. Deb: 9/4/1915 Career OF: 105-226-41																							
1915 Bro-N	14	26	3	6	1	0	0	2	2	4	1	1	.231	.286	.269	.555	67	-1	2	2.57	1	0-14(8-1-1)	0	-0.1
1916 Bro-N	1	2	0	2	0	0	0	0	0	0	0	....	1.000	1.000	1.000	2.000	501	1	2	∞	0	/0-1	0	0.1
1918 Bro-N	6	11	1	5	0	0	0	0	0	0	0	....	.455	.455	.455	.909	178	1	2	9.42	0	/0-4(2-0-1)	1	0.1
1921 Bos-N	55	138	25	33	6	3	1	9	7	11	3	2	.239	.281	.348	.629	69	-6	13	3.16	0	0-43(22-10-13)	2	-0.8
1922 Bos-N	86	318	35	84	14	4	2	22	9	19	6	6	.264	.284	.352	.637	66	-17	30	3.27	-1	0-79(48-22-11)	4	-2.2
1923 Bos-N	88	321	53	88	12	4	0	19	24	14	2	3	.274	.334	.336	.671	81	-8	37	4.01	4	0-80(14-62-4)	6	-0.8
1926 Phi-N	93	311	38	91	18	2	4	41	13	20	5	....	.293	.323	.402	.725	90	-6	39	4.51	2	0-88(0-88-0)	6	-0.6
1927 Phi-N	54	154	18	48	7	0	0	18	5	5	1	....	.312	.333	.357	.690	84	-4	18	4.13	-1	0-44(0-43-1)	3	-0.6
1928 Phi-N	25	64	7	15	2	0	0	7	6	4	1	....	.234	.300	.266	.566	47	-5	5	2.72	-1	0-20(10-0-10)	0	-0.7
Total 9	422	1345	180	372	60	13	7	118	66	77	19	12	.277	.314	.356	.670	78	-45	148	3.80	4	0-373	22	-5.8
• NIXON, Donell	Robert Donell Nixon b: 12/31/1961, Evergreen, NC BR/TR, 6'1", 185 lbs. Deb: 4/7/1987 Career OF: 52-76-26																							
1987 Sea-A	46	132	17	33	4	0	3	12	13	28	21	7	.250	.327	.348	.675	75	-3	16	3.78	0	0-32(1-32-0)/D-6	2	-0.4
1988 SF-N	59	78	15	27	3	0	0	6	10	12	11	8	.346	.420	.385	.805	139	3	12	5.41	-1	0-46(32-15-0)	4	0.1
1989*SF-N	95	166	23	44	2	0	1	15	11	30	10	3	.265	.311	.295	.606	76	-4	15	3.22	-2	0-64(15-29-26)	3	-0.8

YEAR TM-L	G	AB	R	H	2B	3B	HR	RBI	BB	SO	SB	CS	AVG	OBP	SLG	OPS	OPS+	BR/A	RC	RC/G	FR	G/POS	WS	TPW
1990 Bal-A	8	20	1	5	2	0	0	2	1	7	5	0	.250	.286	.350	.636	79	1	3	5.07	0	/O-4(4-0-0),D-3	1	0.0
Total 4	208	396	56	109	11	0	4	35	35	77	47	18	.275	.337	.333	.671	89	-4	46	3.93	-4	O-146/D-9	10	-1.0

• NIXON, Otis Otis Junior Nixon b: 1/9/1959, Evergreen, NC BB/TR, 6'2", 180 lbs. Deb: 9/9/1983 Career OF: 357-1136-72

YEAR TM-L	G	AB	R	H	2B	3B	HR	RBI	BB	SO	SB	CS	AVG	OBP	SLG	OPS	OPS+	BR/A	RC	RC/G	FR	G/POS	WS	TPW
1983 NY-A	13	14	2	2	0	0	0	0	1	5	2	0	.143	.200	.143	.343	-4	-2	1	1.49	0	/O-9(0-4-5)	0	-0.2
1984 Cle-A	49	91	16	14	0	0	0	1	8	11	12	6	.154	.222	.154	.376	6	-11	3	1.01	1	O-46(43-4-0)	1	-1.2
1985 Cle-A	104	162	34	38	4	0	3	9	8	27	20	11	.235	.271	.315	.585	60	-10	12	2.38	-1	O-80(53-26-0),D-11	1	-1.2
1986 Cle-A	105	95	33	25	4	1	0	8	13	12	23	6	.263	.352	.326	.678	88	1	13	4.56	-1	O-95(84-14-0)/D-5	3	-0.1
1987 Cle-A	19	17	2	1	0	0	0	1	3	4	2	3	.059	.200	.059	.259	-26	-4	0	.20	0	O-17(11-7-0)/D-2	0	-0.4
1988 Mon-N	90	271	47	66	8	2	0	15	28	42	46	13	.244	.314	.288	.602	71	-6	30	3.60	-4	O-82(25-61-0)	7	-1.3
1989 Mon-N	126	258	41	56	7	2	0	21	33	36	37	12	.217	.306	.260	.566	62	-9	24	2.92	-4	O-98(13-92-1)	6	-1.6
1990 Mon-N	119	231	46	58	6	2	1	20	28	33	50	13	.251	.332	.307	.639	80	-0	29	4.04	0	O-88(21-71-0)/S-1	8	-0.2
1991 Atl-N	124	401	81	119	10	1	0	26	47	40	72	21	.297	.373	.327	.700	93	5	57	4.86	-1	*O-115(55-17-48)	15	0.0
1992*Atl-N	120	456	79	134	14	2	2	22	39	54	41	18	.294	.349	.346	.696	92	-3	58	4.47	5	*O-111(2-102-16)	16	0.0
1993*Atl-N	134	461	77	124	12	3	1	24	61	63	47	13	.269	.354	.315	.669	80	-6	58	4.22	3	*O-116(0-115-2)	13	-0.2
1994 Bos-A	103	398	60	109	15	1	0	25	55	65	42	10	.274	.362	.317	.679	74	-9	55	4.88	-1	*O-103(0-103-0)	10	-0.9
1995 Tex-A	139	589	87	174	21	2	0	45	58	85	50	21	.295	.359	.338	.696	81	-14	76	4.57	-1	*O-138(0-138-0)	13	-1.3
1996 Tor-A	125	496	87	142	15	1	1	29	71	68	54	13	.286	.377	.327	.703	80	-5	71	4.99	-1	*O-125(0-125-0)	12	-0.5
1997 Tor-A	103	401	54	105	12	1	1	26	52	54	47	10	.262	.347	.304	.651	71	-9	49	4.04	-6	*O-102(0-102-0)/D-1	8	-1.4
LA-N	42	175	30	48	6	2	1	18	13	24	12	2	.274	.324	.349	.673	83	-3	22	4.34	-1	O-42(0-42-0)	5	-0.3
1998 Min-A	110	448	71	133	6	6	1	20	44	56	37	7	.297	.362	.344	.706	84	-4	60	4.70	-7	*O-108(0-108-0)	8	-1.0
1999*Atl-N	84	151	31	31	2	1	0	8	23	15	26	7	.205	.310	.232	.542	40	-11	14	3.00	-2	O-52(50-5-0)	1	-1.4
Total 17	1709	5115	878	1379	142	27	11	318	585	694	620	186	.270	.345	.314	.660	76	-100	633	4.18	-22	*O-1527/D-19,S-1	127	-13.1

• NIXON, Russ Russell Eugene Nixon b: 2/19/1935, Cleves, OH BL/TR, 6'1", 200 lbs. Deb: 4/20/1957 M/C

YEAR TM-L	G	AB	R	H	2B	3B	HR	RBI	BB	SO	SB	CS	AVG	OBP	SLG	OPS	OPS+	BR/A	RC	RC/G	FR	G/POS	WS	TPW
1957 Cle-A	62	185	15	52	7	1	2	18	12	12	0	1	.281	.325	.362	.687	88	-3	20	3.78	0	C-57	5	-0.1
1958 Cle-A	113	376	42	113	17	4	9	46	13	38	0	3	.301	.324	.439	.763	111	2	47	4.38	-3	*C-101	11	0.4
1959 Cle-A	82	258	23	62	10	3	1	29	15	28	0	0	.240	.282	.314	.596	66	-12	21	2.73	-2	C-74	5	-1.2
1960 Cle-A	25	82	6	20	5	0	1	6	6	6	0	1	.244	.311	.341	.653	79	-3	8	3.17	0	C-25	2	-0.2
Bos-A	80	272	24	81	17	3	5	33	13	23	0	1	.298	.330	.438	.767	102	-1	36	4.64	0	C-74	7	0.3
Yr.	105	354	30	101	22	3	6	39	19	29	0	2	.285	.325	.415	.741	96	-4	44	4.27	0	C-99	9	0.1
1961 Bos-A	87	242	24	70	12	2	1	19	13	19	0	1	.289	.331	.368	.699	84	-6	29	4.24	-3	C-66	4	-0.6
1962 Bos-A	65	151	11	42	7	2	1	19	8	14	0	0	.278	.314	.371	.685	81	-4	17	3.94	-1	C-38	3	-0.4
1963 Bos-A	98	287	27	77	18	1	5	30	22	32	0	0	.268	.329	.390	.719	97	-1	36	4.37	-3	C-76	8	0.0
1964 Bos-A	81	163	10	38	7	0	1	20	14	29	0	0	.233	.302	.294	.596	63	-8	14	2.73	-1	C-45	1	-0.7
1965 Bos-A	59	137	11	37	5	1	0	11	6	23	0	0	.270	.301	.321	.622	72	-5	11	2.70	-2	C-38	1	-0.6
1966 Min-A	51	96	5	25	2	1	0	7	7	13	0	0	.260	.317	.302	.619	74	-3	9	3.30	-1	C-32	2	-0.3
1967 Min-A	74	170	16	40	6	1	1	22	18	29	0	0	.235	.309	.300	.609	74	-5	16	3.13	-1	C-69	5	-0.4
1968 Bos-A	29	85	1	13	2	0	0	6	7	13	0	0	.153	.217	.176	.394	19	-8	3	1.18	-2	C-27	1	-1.0
Total 12	906	2504	215	670	115	19	27	266	154	279	0	7	.268	.313	.361	.674	84	-57	266	3.65	-20	C-722	55	-4.8

• NIXON, Trot Christopher Trotman Nixon b: 4/11/1974, Durham, NC BL/TL, 6'1", 195 lbs. Deb: 9/21/1996 Career OF: 1-90-601

YEAR TM-L	G	AB	R	H	2B	3B	HR	RBI	BB	SO	SB	CS	AVG	OBP	SLG	OPS	OPS+	BR/A	RC	RC/G	FR	G/POS	WS	TPW
1996 Bos-A	2	4	2	2	1	0	0	0	0	1	1	0	.500	.500	.750	1.250	206	1	2	23.76	0	/O-2(0-0-2)	0	0.1
1998*Bos-A	13	27	3	7	1	0	0	0	1	3	0	0	.259	.286	.296	.582	51	-2	2	3.19	-0	/O-7(1-0-6),D-2	0	-0.2
1999*Bos-A	124	381	67	103	22	5	15	52	53	75	3	1	.270	.364	.472	.836	108	5	68	6.20	-7	*O-121(0-0-121)	10	-0.8
2000 Bos-A	123	427	66	118	27	8	12	60	63	85	8	1	.276	.372	.461	.833	106	6	76	6.19	3	*O-118(0-6-115)/D-1	14	0.3
2001 Bos-A	148	535	100	150	31	4	27	88	79	113	7	4	.280	.380	.505	.885	129	24	107	7.05	-5	*O-145(0-70-83)/D-1	20	1.5
2002 Bos-A	152	532	81	136	36	3	24	94	65	109	4	2	.256	.342	.470	.812	111	8	89	5.76	4	*O-152(0-13-145)	17	0.4
2003*Bos-A	134	441	81	135	24	6	28	87	65	96	4	2	.306	.399	.578	.977	150	33	106	9.12	-2	*O-130(0-1-129)	19	2.3
Total 7	696	2347	400	651	142	26	106	381	326	482	27	10	.277	.370	.496	.866	121	75	450	6.79	-8	O-675/D-4	80	3.6

• NOBLE, Ray Rafael Miguel (Magee) Noble b: 3/15/1919, Central Hatillo, Cuba d: 5/9/1998, Brooklyn, NY BR/TR, 5'11", 210 lbs. Deb: 4/18/1951

YEAR TM-L	G	AB	R	H	2B	3B	HR	RBI	BB	SO	SB	CS	AVG	OBP	SLG	OPS	OPS+	BR/A	RC	RC/G	FR	G/POS	WS	TPW
1951*NY-N	55	141	16	33	6	0	5	26	6	26	0	0	.234	.265	.383	.648	72	-6	13	3.01	-3	C-41	2	-0.7
1952 NY-N	6	5	0	0	0	0	0	0	0	1	0	0	.000	.000	.000	.000	-99	-1	0	.00	-1	/C-5	0	-0.2
1953 NY-N	46	97	15	20	0	1	4	14	19	14	1	0	.206	.353	.351	.703	83	-1	14	4.72	-1	C-41	3	-0.1
Total 3	107	243	31	53	6	1	9	40	25	41	1	0	.218	.299	.362	.661	73	-9	27	3.61	-5	/C-87	5	-1.0

• NOBOA, Junior Milciades Arturo (Diaz) Noboa b: 11/10/1964, Azua, Dominican Republic BR/TR, 5'10", 160 lbs. Deb: 8/22/1984 Career OF: 3-0-13

YEAR TM-L	G	AB	R	H	2B	3B	HR	RBI	BB	SO	SB	CS	AVG	OBP	SLG	OPS	OPS+	BR/A	RC	RC/G	FR	G/POS	WS	TPW
1984 Cle-A	23	11	3	4	0	0	0	0	0	2	1	0	.364	.364	.364	.727	100	0	1	3.78	-4	2-19/D-1	0	-0.3
1987 Cle-A	39	80	7	18	2	1	0	7	3	6	1	0	.225	.253	.275	.528	40	-7	6	2.31	0	2-21/S-8,3-5,D-1	0	-0.6
1988 Cal-A	21	16	4	1	0	0	0	0	0	1	0	0	.063	.063	.063	.125	-67	-4	0	.00	0	/2-9,S-3,3-2	0	-0.4
1989 Mon-N	21	44	3	10	0	0	0	1	1	3	0	0	.227	.244	.227	.472	35	-4	3	1.99	2	2-13/S-4,3-1	1	-0.1
1990 Mon-N	81	158	15	42	7	2	0	14	7	14	4	1	.266	.301	.335	.637	78	-5	16	3.51	-8	2-31/O-9(2-0-7),3-8,S-7,P	3	-1.2
1991 Mon-N	67	95	5	23	3	0	1	2	1	8	2	3	.242	.250	.305	.555	56	-7	6	2.22	-1	/O-7(1-0-6),2-6,3-2,S-2,1-1	0	-0.8
1992 NY-N	46	47	7	7	0	0	0	3	3	8	0	0	.149	.216	.149	.365	5	-6	1	.93	-2	2-16/3-3,S-2	0	-0.8
1994 Oak-A	17	40	3	13	1	1	0	6	2	5	1	0	.325	.357	.400	.757	104	0	6	6.09	-1	2-14/S-1	2	0.0
Pit-N	2	2	0	0	0	0	0	0	0	0	0	0	.000	.000	.000	.000	-99	-1	0	.00	0	/S-1	0	-0.1
Total 8	317	493	47	118	13	4	1	33	17	47	9	4	.239	.268	.288	.556	54	-31	40	2.67	-14	2-129/S-28,3-21,O-16,D-2,1,P	6	-4.2

• NOCE, Paul Paul David Noce b: 12/16/1959, San Francisco, CA BR/TR, 5'10", 175 lbs. Deb: 6/1/1987

YEAR TM-L	G	AB	R	H	2B	3B	HR	RBI	BB	SO	SB	CS	AVG	OBP	SLG	OPS	OPS+	BR/A	RC	RC/G	FR	G/POS	WS	TPW
1987 Chi-N	70	180	17	41	9	2	3	14	6	49	5	3	.228	.261	.350	.611	58	-12	16	2.91	-1	2-36,S-35/3-2	3	-0.9
1990 Cin-N	1	1	0	1	0	0	0	0	0	0	0	0	1.000	1.000	1.000	2.000	434	0	1	∞	0	....	0	0.0
Total 2	71	181	17	42	9	2	3	14	6	49	5	3	.232	.265	.354	.618	60	-12	17	2.91	-1	/2-36,S-35,3-2	3	-0.9

• NOFTSKER, George George Washington Noftsker b: 8/24/1859, Shippensburg, PA d: 5/8/1931, Shippensburg, PA BR/TR, 5'8", 135 lbs. Deb: 4/17/1884

YEAR TM-L	G	AB	R	H	2B	3B	HR	RBI	BB	SO	SB	CS	AVG	OBP	SLG	OPS	OPS+	BR/A	RC	RC/G	FR	G/POS	WS	TPW
1884 Alt-U	7	25	0	1	0	0	0	....	0	....	....	....	.040	.040	.040	.080	-72	-4	0	.05	-0	/O-5(0-1-4),C-3	0	-0.4

• NOKES, Matt Matthew Dodge Nokes b: 10/31/1963, San Diego, CA BL/TR, 6'1", 185 lbs. Deb: 9/3/1985 Career OF: 3-0-3

YEAR TM-L	G	AB	R	H	2B	3B	HR	RBI	BB	SO	SB	CS	AVG	OBP	SLG	OPS	OPS+	BR/A	RC	RC/G	FR	G/POS	WS	TPW
1985 SF-N	19	53	3	11	2	0	2	5	1	9	0	0	.208	.236	.358	.595	67	-3	4	2.40	-1	C-14	0	-0.4
1986 Det-A	7	24	2	8	1	0	1	2	1	1	0	0	.333	.360	.500	.860	131	1	4	6.10	0	/C-7	1	0.2
1987*Det-A★	135	461	69	133	14	2	32	87	35	70	2	1	.289	.347	.536	.882	135	21	82	6.39	-4	*C-109,D-19/O-3(3-0-1),3-2	20	2.0
1988 Det-A	122	382	53	96	18	0	16	53	34	58	0	1	.251	.314	.424	.738	109	3	49	4.31	0	*C-110/D-4	17	1.0
1989 Det-A	87	268	15	67	10	0	9	39	17	37	1	0	.250	.300	.388	.688	94	-3	30	3.86	1	C-51,D-33	8	0.0
1990 Det-A	44	111	12	30	5	1	3	8	4	14	0	0	.270	.308	.414	.722	99	-1	12	3.86	0	D-24,C-19	1	0.0
NY-A	92	240	21	57	4	0	8	32	20	33	2	2	.238	.307	.354	.661	84	-6	25	3.58	2	C-46,D-30/O-2(0-0-2)	6	-0.2
Yr.	136	351	33	87	9	1	11	40	24	47	2	2	.248	.307	.373	.680	89	-6	38	3.66	3	C-65,D-54/O-2(0-0-2)	7	-0.2
1991 NY-A	135	456	52	122	20	0	24	77	25	49	3	2	.268	.313	.469	.782	113	6	66	5.10	-2	*C-130/D-3	16	1.1
1992 NY-A	121	384	42	86	9	1	22	59	37	62	0	1	.224	.297	.424	.722	101	-1	45	3.84	2	*C-111	9	0.7
1993 NY-A	76	217	25	54	8	0	10	35	16	31	0	0	.249	.306	.424	.730	97	-2	28	4.43	-3	C-56,D-11	5	-0.2
1994 NY-A	28	79	11	23	3	0	7	19	5	16	0	0	.291	.333	.595	.928	138	4	16	7.22	-1	C-17/D-5,1-4	2	0.3
1995 Bal-A	26	49	4	6	1	0	2	6	4	11	0	0	.122	.189	.265	.454	16	-6	2	1.27	0	C-16/D-2	0	-0.6
Col-N	10	11	1	2	1	0	0	0	1	4	0	0	.182	.250	.273	.523	29	-1	1	1.35	-1	/C-3	0	-0.2
Total 11	902	2735	310	695	96	4	136	422	200	395	8	7	.254	.311	.441	.752	106	12	364	4.56	-7	C-689,D-131/O-5,1-4,3-2	85	3.8

• NOLAN, Joe Joseph William Nolan b: 5/12/1951, St. Louis, MO BL/TR, 5'11", 190 lbs. Deb: 9/21/1972

YEAR TM-L	G	AB	R	H	2B	3B	HR	RBI	BB	SO	SB	CS	AVG	OBP	SLG	OPS	OPS+	BR/A	RC	RC/G	FR	G/POS	WS	TPW
1972 NY-N	4	10	0	0	0	0	0	0	1	3	0	0	.000	.091	.000	.091	-74	-2	0	.06	0	/C-3	0	-0.3
1975 Atl-N	4	4	0	1	0	0	0	0	1	0	0	0	.250	.400	.250	.650	80	-0	1	4.54	-0	/C-1	0	0.0
1977 Atl-N	62	82	13	23	3	0	3	9	13	12	1	0	.280	.379	.427	.806	103	1	14	6.04	1	C-19	3	0.2
1978 Atl-N	95	213	22	49	7	3	4	22	34	28	3	2	.230	.339	.347	.686	83	-4	27	4.23	-3	C-61	5	-0.5
1979 Atl-N	89	230	28	57	9	3	4	21	27	28	1	3	.248	.335	.365	.700	85	-5	28	4.13	-4	C-74	5	-0.6

YEAR TM-L	G	AB	R	H	2B	3B	HR	RBI	BB	SO	SB	CS	AVG	OBP	SLG	OPS	OPS+	BR/A	RC	RC/G	FR	G/POS	WS	TPW
1980 Atl-N	17	22	2	6	1	0	0	2	2	4	0	0	.273	.333	.318	.652	80	-1	2	3.48	0	/C-6	1	0.0
Cin-N	53	154	14	48	7	0	3	24	13	8	0	0	.312	.365	.416	.781	117	4	24	5.43	-2	C-51	7	0.4
Yr.	70	176	16	54	8	0	3	26	15	12	0	0	.307	.361	.403	.765	113	3	26	5.19	-2	C-57	8	0.4
1981 Cin-N	81	236	25	73	18	1	1	26	24	19	1	2	.309	.375	.407	.782	120	6	35	5.36	-5	C-81	12	0.4
1982 Bal-A	77	219	24	51	7	1	6	35	16	35	1	1	.233	.285	.356	.641	75	-8	22	3.24	-3	C-72	5	-0.8
1983*Bal-A	73	184	25	51	11	1	5	24	16	31	0	0	.277	.342	.429	.771	113	3	26	5.17	-1	C-65	7	0.4
1984 Bal-A	35	62	2	18	1	1	1	9	12	10	0	0	.290	.405	.387	.793	123	3	11	6.38	0	D-11/C-6	2	0.3
1985 Bal-A	31	38	1	5	2	0	0	6	5	5	0	0	.132	.233	.184	.417	16	-4	2	1.35	0	/C-5,D-4	0	-0.4
Total 11	621	1454	156	382	66	10	27	178	164	183	7	8	.263	.340	.378	.718	95	-8	190	4.52	-17	C-444/D-15	47	-0.8

• NONNENKAMP, Red Leo William Nonnenkamp b: 7/7/1911, St. Louis, MO d: 12/3/2000, Little Rock, AR BL/TL, 5'11", 165 lbs. Deb: 9/6/1933 Career OF: 12-9-33

YEAR TM-L	G	AB	R	H	2B	3B	HR	RBI	BB	SO	SB	CS	AVG	OBP	SLG	OPS	OPS+	BR/A	RC	RC/G	FR	G/POS	WS	TPW
1933 Pit-N	1	1	0	0	0	0	0	0	0	1	0	....	.000	.000	.000	.000	-100	-0	0	.00	0	....	0	0.0
1938 Bos-A	87	180	37	51	4	1	0	18	21	13	6	1	.283	.358	.317	.675	67	-8	22	4.47	2	O-39(5-5-29)/1-5	3	-0.7
1939 Bos-A	58	75	12	18	2	1	0	5	12	6	0	1	.240	.345	.293	.638	62	-4	8	3.51	-1	O-15(7-4-4)	1	-0.5
1940 Bos-A	9	7	0	0	0	0	0	1	0	4	0	0	.000	.125	.000	.125	-62	-2	0	.13	0	....	0	-0.2
Total 4	155	263	49	69	6	2	0	24	33	24	6	2	.262	.347	.300	.647	62	-14	30	4.01	1	/O-54,1-5	4	-1.4

• NOONAN, Pete Peter John Noonan b: 11/24/1881, West Stockbridge, MA d: 2/11/1965, Great Barrington, MA BR/TR, 6', 180 lbs. Deb: 6/20/1904

YEAR TM-L	G	AB	R	H	2B	3B	HR	RBI	BB	SO	SB	CS	AVG	OBP	SLG	OPS	OPS+	BR/A	RC	RC/G	FR	G/POS	WS	TPW
1904 Phi-A	39	114	13	23	3	1	2	13	1	....	1	....	.202	.209	.298	.507	56	-6	8	2.18	-1	C-22,1-10	1	-0.6
1906 Chi-N	5	3	0	1	0	0	0	0	0	....	0	....	.333	.333	.333	.667	102	-0	0	4.44	0	/1-1	0	0.0
StL-N	44	125	8	21	1	3	1	9	11	....	1	....	.168	.235	.248	.483	53	-7	8	1.99	2	C-23,1-16	1	-0.4
Yr.	49	128	8	22	1	3	1	9	11	....	1	....	.172	.237	.250	.487	54	-7	9	2.03	2	C-23,1-17	1	-0.4
1907 StL-N	74	237	19	53	7	3	1	16	9	....	3	....	.224	.252	.291	.543	73	-9	19	2.64	1	C-70	3	-0.1
Total 3	162	479	40	98	11	7	4	38	21	....	5	....	.205	.238	.282	.520	64	-22	36	2.36	2	C-115/1-27	5	-1.0

• NORDBROOK, Tim Timothy Charles Nordbrook b: 7/7/1949, Baltimore, MD BR/TR, 6'1", 180 lbs. Deb: 9/13/1974

YEAR TM-L	G	AB	R	H	2B	3B	HR	RBI	BB	SO	SB	CS	AVG	OBP	SLG	OPS	OPS+	BR/A	RC	RC/G	FR	G/POS	WS	TPW
1974 Bal-A	6	15	4	4	0	0	0	1	2	2	1	0	.267	.353	.267	.620	83	0	2	4.37	1	/S-5,2-1	1	0.2
1975 Bal-A	40	34	6	4	1	0	0	0	7	7	0	0	.118	.268	.147	.415	21	-3	2	1.65	2	S-37/2-3	1	0.0
1976 Bal-A	27	22	4	5	0	0	0	0	3	5	0	0	.227	.320	.227	.547	66	-1	2	2.43	-4	2-14,S-12	1	-0.4
Cal-A	5	8	1	0	0	0	0	0	1	3	1	0	.000	.111	.000	.111	-70	-1	0	.39	-1	/S-4,2-1,D-1	0	-0.3
Yr.	32	30	5	5	0	0	0	0	4	8	1	0	.167	.265	.167	.431	27	-2	2	1.75	-6	S-16,2-15/D-1	1	-0.7
1977 Chi-A	15	20	2	5	0	0	0	1	7	4	1	0	.250	.444	.250	.694	95	1	3	5.51	-4	S-11/D-2,3-1	1	-0.2
Tor-A	24	63	9	11	0	1	0	1	4	11	1	0	.175	.224	.206	.430	18	-7	3	1.28	-2	S-24	1	-0.6
Yr.	39	83	11	16	0	1	0	2	11	15	2	0	.193	.287	.217	.504	41	-6	6	2.27	-6	S-35/D-2,3-1	2	-0.9
1978 Tor-A	7	0	1	0	0	0	0	0	0	0	0	0	....	1.000	....	1.000	200	0	0	∞	-2	/S-7	0	-0.1
Mil-A	2	5	0	0	0	0	0	0	1	1	0	0	.000	.167	.000	.167	-49	-1	0	.63	0	/S-2	0	-0.1
Yr.	9	5	1	0	0	0	0	0	1	1	0	0	.000	.286	.000	.286	-22	-1	0	.63	-1	/S-9	0	-0.2
1979 Mil-A	2	2	0	1	0	0	0	0	0	0	0	0	.500	.500	.500	1.000	171	0	1	13.50	-1	/S-2	0	-0.1
Total 6	128	169	27	30	1	1	0	3	25	33	4	0	.178	.287	.195	.482	37	-12	12	2.20	-10	S-104/2-19,D-3,3-1	5	-1.6

• NORDHAGEN, Wayne Wayne Oren Nordhagen b: 7/4/1948, Thief River Falls, MN BR/TR, 6'2", 205 lbs. Deb: 7/16/1976 Career OF: 125-3-139

YEAR TM-L	G	AB	R	H	2B	3B	HR	RBI	BB	SO	SB	CS	AVG	OBP	SLG	OPS	OPS+	BR/A	RC	RC/G	FR	G/POS	WS	TPW
1976 Chi-A	22	53	6	10	2	0	0	5	4	12	0	0	.189	.246	.226	.472	39	-4	3	1.81	0	O-10(0-0-10)/D-6,C-5	0	-0.5
1977 Chi-A	52	124	16	39	7	3	4	22	2	12	1	0	.315	.325	.516	.842	125	4	20	5.89	-4	O-46(12-2-34)/C-3,D-2	4	-0.2
1978 Chi-A	68	206	28	62	16	0	5	35	5	18	0	1	.301	.318	.451	.769	113	2	27	4.66	-1	O-36(19-0-18),D-16,C-12	6	0.0
1979 Chi-A	78	193	20	54	15	0	7	25	13	22	0	0	.280	.325	.466	.792	111	3	26	4.74	1	D-47,O-12(6-0-7)/C-5,P-2	4	0.1
1980 Chi-A	123	415	45	115	22	4	15	59	10	45	0	1	.277	.296	.458	.754	104	-1	51	4.32	1	O-74(45-0-33),D-32	9	-0.4
1981 Chi-A	65	208	19	64	8	1	6	33	10	25	0	1	.308	.342	.442	.785	127	6	29	4.96	-2	O-60(25-1-36)	6	0.2
1982 Tor-A	44	115	8	32	3	0	1	14	9	13	0	2	.278	.331	.330	.661	75	-4	11	3.41	1	D-32,O-10(10-0-1)	0	-0.5
Pit-N	1	4	0	2	0	0	0	2	0	1	0	0	.500	.500	.500	1.000	175	0	1	13.50	-0	/O-1	0	0.0
Tor-A	28	70	4	18	3	0	0	6	1	9	0	0	.257	.268	.300	.568	51	-5	5	2.52	0	D-28	1	-0.5
Yr.	72	185	12	50	6	0	1	20	10	22	0	2	.270	.308	.319	.627	66	-9	17	3.07	1	D-60,O-10(10-0-1)	1	-1.0
1983 Chi-N	21	35	1	5	1	0	1	4	0	5	0	0	.143	.167	.257	.424	15	-4	1	.87	0	/O-7(7-0-0)	0	-0.5
Total 8	502	1423	147	401	77	8	39	205	54	162	1	5	.282	.309	.429	.739	102	-3	174	4.28	-5	O-256,D-163/C-25,P-2	30	-2.3

• NORDYKE, Lou Louis Ellis Nordyke b: 8/7/1876, Brighton, IA d: 9/27/1945, Los Angeles, CA BR/TR, 6', 185 lbs. Deb: 4/18/1906

YEAR TM-L	G	AB	R	H	2B	3B	HR	RBI	BB	SO	SB	CS	AVG	OBP	SLG	OPS	OPS+	BR/A	RC	RC/G	FR	G/POS	WS	TPW
1906 StL-A	25	53	4	13	1	0	0	7	10	....	3	....	.245	.365	.264	.629	102	1	7	4.22	-2	1-12	2	-0.1

• NOREN, Irv Irving Arnold Noren b: 11/29/1924, Jamestown, NY BL/TL, 6', 190 lbs. Deb: 4/18/1950 C Career OF: 293-374-163

YEAR TM-L	G	AB	R	H	2B	3B	HR	RBI	BB	SO	SB	CS	AVG	OBP	SLG	OPS	OPS+	BR/A	RC	RC/G	FR	G/POS	WS	TPW
1950 Was-A	138	542	80	160	27	10	14	98	67	77	5	2	.295	.375	.459	.834	118	15	98	6.65	9	*O-121(0-121-0),1-17	22	1.9
1951 Was-A	129	509	82	142	33	5	8	86	51	35	10	7	.279	.345	.411	.755	105	2	72	4.93	5	*O-126(0-126-0)	18	0.3
1952 Was-A	12	49	4	12	3	1	0	2	6	3	1	0	.245	.327	.347	.674	91	-0	6	4.21	1	O-12(0-12-0)	2	0.1
*NY-A	93	272	36	64	13	2	5	21	26	34	4	2	.235	.316	.353	.669	91	-3	33	4.23	0	O-60(18-18-25),1-19	7	-0.6
Yr.	105	321	40	76	16	3	5	23	32	37	5	2	.237	.318	.352	.670	91	-3	39	4.23	1	O-72(18-30-25),1-19	9	-0.5
1953*NY-A	109	345	55	92	12	6	6	46	42	39	3	3	.267	.350	.388	.738	103	1	50	5.09	5	O-96(21-44-38)	11	0.2
1954 NY-A★	125	426	70	136	21	6	12	66	43	38	4	6	.319	.383	.481	.864	140	21	79	6.90	-0	*O-116(55-23-49)/1-1	21	1.6
1955*NY-A	132	371	49	94	19	1	8	59	43	33	5	2	.253	.336	.375	.710	92	-4	48	4.50	2	*O-126(117-10-3)	11	-0.9
1956 NY-A	29	37	4	8	1	0	0	6	12	7	0	0	.216	.408	.243	.651	78	-0	4	4.05	0	O-10(4-0-6)/1-1	1	0.0
1957 KC-A	81	160	8	34	8	0	2	16	11	19	0	0	.213	.267	.300	.567	54	-10	12	2.41	0	1-25/O-6(0-0-6)	1	-1.2
StL-N	17	30	3	11	4	1	1	10	4	6	0	1	.367	.441	.667	1.108	188	3	8	9.59	0	/O-8(1-0-7)	2	0.3
1958 StL-N	117	178	24	47	9	1	4	22	13	21	0	1	.264	.328	.393	.721	86	-4	23	4.52	-3	O-77(59-14-10)	4	-0.9
1959 StL-N	8	8	0	1	1	0	0	0	0	2	0	0	.125	.125	.250	.375	-3	-1	0	.00	0	/O-2(2-0-0),1-1	0	-0.2
Chi-N	65	156	27	50	6	2	4	19	13	24	2	0	.321	.384	.462	.845	125	6	29	7.34	2	O-40(16-6-18)/1-1	7	0.7
Yr.	73	164	27	51	7	2	4	19	13	26	2	0	.311	.372	.451	.823	119	5	29	6.83	2	O-42(18-6-18)/1-2	7	0.5
1960 Chi-N	12	11	0	1	0	0	0	1	3	4	0	0	.091	.286	.091	.377	9	-1	1	1.37	0	/1-1,O-1	0	-0.2
LA-N	26	25	1	5	0	0	1	1	1	8	0	0	.200	.231	.320	.551	46	-2	2	2.04	0	....	0	-0.2
Yr.	38	36	1	6	0	0	1	2	4	12	0	0	.167	.250	.250	.500	33	-3	2	1.83	0	/1-1,O-1	0	-0.3
Total 11	1093	3119	443	857	157	35	65	453	335	350	34	24	.275	.349	.410	.759	106	24	464	5.29	20	O-801/1-66	107	1.0

• NORMAN, Bill Henry Willis Patrick Norman b: 7/16/1910, St. Louis, MO d: 4/21/1962, Milwaukee, WI BR/TR, 6'2", 190 lbs. Deb: 8/8/1931 M/C Career OF: 4-25-1

YEAR TM-L	G	AB	R	H	2B	3B	HR	RBI	BB	SO	SB	CS	AVG	OBP	SLG	OPS	OPS+	BR/A	RC	RC/G	FR	G/POS	WS	TPW
1931 Chi-A	24	55	7	10	2	0	0	6	4	10	0	1	.182	.237	.218	.455	22	-6	3	1.59	-1	O-17(3-14-0)	0	-0.7
1932 Chi-A	13	48	6	11	3	1	0	2	2	3	0	0	.229	.260	.333	.593	56	-3	4	2.91	0	O-13(1-11-1)	0	-0.3
Total 2	37	103	13	21	5	1	0	8	6	13	0	1	.204	.248	.272	.520	38	-10	7	2.19	0	/O-30	0	-1.0

• NORMAN, Dan Daniel Edmund Norman b: 1/11/1955, Los Angeles, CA BR/TR, 6'2", 195 lbs. Deb: 9/27/1977 Career OF: 35-7-67

YEAR TM-L	G	AB	R	H	2B	3B	HR	RBI	BB	SO	SB	CS	AVG	OBP	SLG	OPS	OPS+	BR/A	RC	RC/G	FR	G/POS	WS	TPW
1977 NY-N	7	16	2	4	1	0	0	0	4	2	0	0	.250	.400	.313	.713	99	0	2	4.39	0	/O-6(0-1-6)	0	0.0
1978 NY-N	19	64	7	17	0	1	4	10	2	14	1	0	.266	.288	.484	.772	116	1	9	5.19	1	O-18(1-0-18)	2	0.1
1979 NY-N	44	110	9	27	3	1	3	11	10	26	2	0	.245	.314	.373	.687	90	-1	14	4.33	1	O-33(8-0-25)	2	-0.2
1980 NY-N	69	92	5	17	1	1	2	9	6	14	5	0	.185	.235	.283	.517	45	-6	7	2.41	0	O-19(9-0-10)	0	-0.6
1982 Mon-N	53	66	6	14	3	0	2	7	7	20	0	1	.212	.288	.348	.636	76	-3	7	3.46	-1	O-31(17-6-8)	1	-0.5
Total 5	192	348	29	79	8	3	11	37	29	76	8	1	.227	.288	.362	.650	81	-9	39	3.78	0	O-107	5	-1.2

• NORMAN, Les Leslie Eugene Norman b: 2/25/1969, Warren, MI BR/TR, 6'1", 185 lbs. Deb: 5/29/1995 Career OF: 19-8-28

YEAR TM-L	G	AB	R	H	2B	3B	HR	RBI	BB	SO	SB	CS	AVG	OBP	SLG	OPS	OPS+	BR/A	RC	RC/G	FR	G/POS	WS	TPW
1995 KC-A	24	40	6	9	0	1	0	4	6	6	0	1	.225	.326	.275	.601	58	-3	4	3.19	0	O-17(4-5-8)/D-5	1	-0.3
1996 KC-A	54	49	9	6	0	0	0	0	6	14	1	1	.122	.232	.122	.355	-7	-8	2	1.10	-1	O-38(15-3-20)/D-7	1	-0.9
Total 2	78	89	15	15	0	1	0	4	12	20	1	2	.169	.275	.191	.466	23	-11	6	1.99	-1	/O-55,D-12	2	-1.2

• NORMAN, Nelson Nelson Augusto Norman b: 5/23/1958, San Pedro de Macoris, Dominican Republic BB/TR, 6'2", 160 lbs. Deb: 5/20/1978

YEAR TM-L	G	AB	R	H	2B	3B	HR	RBI	BB	SO	SB	CS	AVG	OBP	SLG	OPS	OPS+	BR/A	RC	RC/G	FR	G/POS	WS	TPW
1978 Tex-A	23	34	1	9	2	0	0	1	0	5	0	0	.265	.265	.324	.588	64	-2	3	2.63	2	S-18/3-6	0	0.1
1979 Tex-A	147	343	36	76	9	3	0	21	19	41	4	1	.222	.262	.265	.528	43	-27	25	2.32	-25	*S-142/2-1	1	-3.9
1980 Tex-A	17	32	4	7	0	0	0	1	1	1	0	1	.219	.242	.219	.461	28	-4	1	1.07	-1	S-17	0	-0.3

YEAR TM-L	G	AB	R	H	2B	3B	HR	RBI	BB	SO	SB	CS	AVG	OBP	SLG	OPS	OPS+	BR/A	RC	RC/G	FR	G/POS	WS	TPW
1981 Tex-A	7	13	1	3	1	0	0	2	1	2	0	0	.231	.286	.308	.593	75	-0	1	3.13	1	/S-5	0	0.1
1982 Pit-N	3	3	0	0	0	0	0	0	0	0	0	0	.000	.000	.000	.000	-97	-1	0	.00	-1	/2-2,S-1	0	-0.2
1987 Mon-N	1	4	0	0	0	0	0	0	0	1	0	0	.000	.000	.000	.000	-97	-1	0	.00	-1	/S-1	0	-0.2
Total 6	198	429	42	95	12	3	0	25	21	50	4	2	.221	.258	.263	.521	43	-34	30	2.23	-25	S-184/3-6,2-3	1	-4.3
• NORRIS, Jim	James Francis Norris b: 12/20/1948, Brooklyn, NY BL/TL, 5'10", 175 lbs. Deb: 4/7/1977 Career OF: 83-121-185																							
1977 Cle-A	133	440	59	119	23	6	2	37	64	57	26	17	.270	.363	.364	.727	102	2	59	4.42	3	*O-124(3-74-49)/1-3	12	0.1
1978 Cle-A	113	315	41	89	14	5	2	27	42	20	12	7	.283	.367	.378	.745	111	6	45	4.92	2	O-78(26-5-51),D-15/1-6	10	0.4
1979 Cle-A	124	353	50	87	15	6	3	30	44	35	15	10	.246	.330	.348	.678	83	-9	39	3.58	-4	O-93(47-23-28),D-13	6	-1.7
1980 Tex-A	119	174	23	43	5	0	0	16	23	16	6	3	.247	.335	.276	.611	71	-6	15	2.72	-2	O-82(7-19-57),1-10/D-1	1	-0.9
Total 4	489	1282	173	338	57	17	7	110	173	128	59	37	.264	.351	.351	.702	95	-6	159	4.06	-1	O-377/D-29,1-19	29	-2.1
• NORRIS, Leo	Leo John Norris b: 5/17/1908, Bay St. Louis, MS d: 2/13/1987, Zachary, LA BR/TR, 5'11", 165 lbs. Deb: 4/14/1936																							
1936 Phi-N	154	581	64	154	27	4	11	76	39	79	4	....	.265	.315	.382	.697	79	-18	69	3.99	-6	*S-121,2-38	9	-1.3
1937 Phi-N	116	381	45	98	24	3	9	36	21	53	3	....	.257	.296	.407	.703	82	-11	48	4.37	-9	2-74,3-24,S-20	7	-1.4
Total 2	270	962	109	252	51	7	20	112	60	132	7	....	.262	.307	.392	.699	80	-29	117	4.14	-15	S-141,2-112/3-24	16	-2.7
• NORTH, Billy	William Alex North b: 5/15/1948, Seattle, WA BB/TR, 5'11", 185 lbs. Deb: 9/3/1971 Career OF: 16-1023-29																							
1971 Chi-N	8	16	3	6	0	0	0	0	4	6	1	1	.375	.524	.375	.899	138	1	4	8.84	0	/O-6(1-0-5)	1	0.1
1972 Chi-N	66	127	22	23	2	3	0	4	13	33	6	0	.181	.262	.244	.507	40	-9	9	2.36	-1	O-48(9-26-15)	1	-1.1
1973 Oak-A	146	554	98	158	10	5	5	34	78	89	53	20	.285	.376	.348	.725	111	15	81	5.06	14	*O-138(0-136-2)/D-6	25	2.5
1974*Oak-A	149	543	79	141	20	5	4	33	69	86	**54**	26	.260	.348	.337	.685	105	7	68	4.06	8	*O-138(0-138-0)/D-8	19	1.2
1975*Oak-A	140	524	74	143	17	5	1	43	81	80	30	12	.273	.374	.330	.705	103	8	73	4.71	7	*O-138(4-134-0)/D-1	22	1.2
1976 Oak-A	154	590	91	163	20	5	2	31	73	95	**75**	29	.276	.358	.337	.695	109	13	78	4.44	-3	*O-144(0-137-7)/D-8	21	0.6
1977 Oak-A	56	184	32	48	3	3	1	9	32	25	17	13	.261	.376	.326	.702	95	-1	24	4.24	-1	O-52(0-52-0)/D-1	5	-0.3
1978 Oak-A	24	52	5	11	4	0	0	5	9	13	3	2	.212	.349	.288	.638	86	-1	6	3.42	0	O-17(0-17-0)	1	-0.1
*LA-N	110	304	54	71	10	0	0	10	65	48	27	8	.234	.372	.266	.638	81	-1	38	4.14	-7	*O-103(1-102-0)	9	-1.0
1979 SF-N	142	460	87	119	15	4	5	30	96	84	58	24	.259	.388	.341	.729	108	13	71	5.14	5	*O-130(0-130-0)	20	1.7
1980 SF-N	128	415	73	104	12	1	1	19	81	78	45	19	.251	.374	.292	.666	90	1	54	4.34	-1	*O-115(1-114-0)	15	-0.2
1981 SF-N	46	131	22	29	7	0	1	12	26	28	26	8	.221	.354	.298	.652	88	2	18	4.22	-3	O-37(0-37-0)	4	-0.2
Total 11	1169	3900	640	1016	120	31	20	230	627	665	395	162	.261	.366	.323	.689	100	49	524	4.47	18	*O-1066/D-24	143	4.4
• NORTHEN, Hub	Hubbard Elwin Northen b: 8/16/1885, Atlanta, TX d: 10/1/1947, Shreveport, LA BL/TL, 5'8", 175 lbs. Deb: 9/10/1910 Career OF: 10-88-49																							
1910 StL-A	26	96	6	19	1	0	0	16	5	....	2	....	.198	.238	.208	.446	42	-6	5	1.71	-3	O-26(0-26-0)	0	-1.1
1911 Cin-N	1	0	0	0	0	0	0	0	0	0	0	....	....	....	....	....	-104	0	0	....	0	....	0	0.0
Bro-N	19	76	16	24	2	2	0	1	14	9	4	....	.316	.429	.395	.823	137	5	14	7.18	1	O-19(0-19-0)	4	0.4
Yr.	20	76	16	24	2	2	0	1	14	9	4	....	.316	.429	.395	.823	137	5	14	7.18	1	O-19(0-19-0)	4	0.4
1912 Bro-N	118	412	54	116	26	6	3	46	41	46	8	....	.282	.352	.396	.748	109	5	60	4.99	-6	*O-102(10-43-49)	10	-0.6
Total 3	164	584	76	159	29	8	3	63	60	55	14	....	.272	.345	.365	.710	102	3	79	4.65	-7	O-147	14	-1.3
• NORTHEY, Ron	Ronald James Northey b: 4/26/1920, Mahanoy City, PA d: 4/16/1971, Pittsburgh, PA BL/TR, 5'10", 195 lbs. Deb: 4/14/1942 C Career OF: 18-0-804																							
1942 Phi-N	127	402	31	101	13	2	5	31	28	33	2	....	.251	.300	.331	.631	89	-7	41	3.55	2	*O-109(0-0-109)	6	-1.2
1943 Phi-N	147	586	72	163	31	5	16	68	51	52	2	....	.278	.339	.430	.769	127	18	88	5.48	-4	*O-145(0-0-145)	22	0.4
1944 Phi-N	152	570	72	164	35	9	22	104	67	51	1	....	.288	.367	.496	.863	146	34	107	6.95	4	*O-151(0-0-151)	22	2.8
1946 Phi-N	128	438	55	109	24	6	16	62	39	59	1	....	.249	.313	.441	.754	116	6	61	4.92	-8	*O-111(0-0-111)	14	-0.5
1947 Phi-N	13	47	7	12	3	0	0	3	6	3	1	....	.255	.340	.319	.659	79	-1	6	4.34	0	O-13(0-0-13)	1	-0.1
StL-N	110	311	52	91	19	3	15	63	48	29	0	....	.293	.391	.518	.908	133	15	65	7.68	1	O-94(15-0-79)/3-2	13	1.4
Yr.	123	358	59	103	22	3	15	66	54	32	1	....	.288	.384	.492	.876	126	14	70	7.24	2	*O-107(15-0-92)/3-2	14	1.3
1948 StL-N	96	246	40	79	10	1	13	64	38	25	0	....	.321	.420	.528	.949	147	17	55	8.53	1	O-67(0-0-67)	13	1.7
1949 StL-N	90	265	28	69	18	2	7	50	31	15	0	....	.260	.338	.423	.760	98	-1	37	4.84	-2	O-73(0-0-73)	7	-0.4
1950 Cin-N	27	77	11	20	5	0	5	9	15	6	0	....	.260	.380	.519	.900	134	4	16	7.21	-1	O-24(0-0-24)	3	0.3
Chi-N	53	114	11	32	9	0	4	20	10	9	0	....	.281	.339	.465	.804	110	1	18	5.50	0	O-27(0-0-27)	3	0.0
Yr.	80	191	22	52	14	0	9	29	25	15	0	....	.272	.356	.487	.843	120	5	33	6.19	-1	O-51(0-0-51)	6	0.3
1952 Chi-N	1	1	0	0	0	0	0	0	0	0	0	0	.000	.000	.000	.000	-99	-0	0	.00	0	....	0	0.0
1955 Chi-A	14	14	1	5	2	0	1	4	3	3	0	0	.357	.471	.714	1.185	209	2	4	11.98	0	/O-2(0-0-2)	1	0.2
1956 Chi-A	53	48	4	17	2	0	3	23	8	1	0	0	.354	.446	.583	1.030	168	5	12	8.85	0	/O-4(3-0-3)	3	0.5
1957 Chi-A	40	27	0	5	1	0	0	7	11	5	0	0	.185	.421	.222	.643	80	1	4	3.95	0	....	1	0.1
Phi-N	33	26	1	7	0	0	1	5	6	6	0	0	.269	.406	.385	.791	118	1	5	6.52	0	....	1	0.1
Total 12	1084	3172	385	874	172	28	108	513	361	297	7	0	.276	.352	.450	.802	123	95	517	5.88	-6	O-820/3-2	110	5.3
• NORTHEY, Scott	Scott Richard Northey b: 10/15/1946, Philadelphia, PA BR/TR, 6', 175 lbs. Deb: 9/2/1969																							
1969 KC-A	20	61	11	16	2	2	1	7	7	19	6	3	.262	.338	.410	.748	108	1	9	4.95	0	O-18(0-18-0)	2	0.0
• NORTHRUP, Jim	James Thomas Northrup b: 11/24/1939, Breckenridge, MI BL/TR, 6'3", 190 lbs. Deb: 9/30/1964 Career OF: 310-466-708																							
1964 Det-A	5	12	1	1	1	0	0	0	0	3	1	0	.083	.083	.167	.250	-32	-2	0	.52	0	/O-2(0-2-1)	0	-0.2
1965 Det-A	80	219	20	45	12	3	2	16	12	50	1	1	.205	.253	.315	.568	60	-12	16	2.43	-3	O-54(10-6-38)	1	-1.9
1966 Det-A	123	419	53	111	24	6	16	58	33	52	4	7	.265	.325	.465	.790	121	9	56	4.49	5	*O-113(3-11-106)	14	0.7
1967 Det-A	144	495	63	134	18	6	10	61	43	83	7	1	.271	.333	.392	.725	110	8	63	4.51	-3	*O-143(65-94-39)	16	-0.2
1968*Det-A	154	580	76	153	29	7	21	90	50	87	4	5	.264	.326	.447	.773	129	18	82	4.84	0	*O-151(12-47-103)	24	0.9
1969 Det-A	148	543	79	160	31	5	25	66	52	83	4	2	.295	.360	.508	.868	135	24	100	6.81	-2	*O-143(29-89-49)	27	1.7
1970 Det-A	139	504	71	132	21	3	24	80	58	68	3	6	.262	.346	.458	.805	119	11	78	5.32	-3	*O-136(34-39-78)	17	0.2
1971 Det-A	136	459	72	124	27	2	16	71	60	43	7	4	.270	.357	.442	.799	120	13	71	5.40	-5	*O-108(42-68-39),1-32	18	0.2
1972*Det-A	134	426	40	111	15	2	8	42	38	47	4	7	.261	.324	.362	.686	100	-2	45	3.60	-2	*O-127(50-42-72)/1-2	11	-1.0
1973 Det-A	119	404	55	124	14	7	12	44	38	41	4	4	.307	.368	.465	.833	125	13	68	6.19	-2	*O-116(51-10-78)	16	0.6
1974 Det-A	97	376	41	89	12	1	11	42	36	46	0	0	.237	.303	.362	.665	88	-6	42	3.75	-1	O-97(0-2-97)	9	-1.3
Mon-N	21	54	3	13	1	0	2	8	5	9	0	0	.241	.305	.370	.675	84	-1	5	3.28	0	O-13(7-0-6)	1	-0.2
Bal-A	8	7	2	4	0	0	1	3	2	1	0	0	.571	.667	1.000	1.667	386	3	5	43.56	0	/O-6(4-0-2),D-1	1	0.3
Yr.	105	383	43	93	12	1	12	45	38	47	0	0	.243	.311	.373	.685	94	-3	46	4.15	-1	*O-103(4-2-99)/D-1	10	-1.0
1975 Bal-A	84	194	27	53	13	0	5	29	22	22	0	1	.273	.353	.418	.771	125	6	27	4.81	1	O-58(3-56-0)/D-3	6	0.6
Total 12	1392	4692	603	1254	218	42	153	610	449	635	39	38	.267	.335	.429	.765	115	81	659	4.88	-15	*O-1267/1-34,D-4	161	0.3
• NORTON, Frank	Frank Prescott Norton b: 6/1845, NY d: 8/1/1920, Greenwich, CT Deb: 5/5/1871 U																							
1871 Oly-n	1	1	0	0	0	0	0	0	0	1	0	0	.000	.000	.000	.000	-106	-0	0	.00	-1	/3-1,O-1	....	-0.1
• NORTON, Greg	Gregory Blakemoor Norton b: 7/6/1972, San Leandro, CA BB/TR, 6'1", 190 lbs. Deb: 8/18/1996 Career OF: 24-0-7																							
1996 Chi-A	11	23	4	5	0	0	2	3	4	6	0	1	.217	.333	.478	.812	107	-0	4	5.07	-1	/S-6,3-2,D-2	0	-0.1
1997 Chi-A	18	34	5	9	2	2	0	1	2	8	0	0	.265	.306	.441	.747	96	-0	5	4.95	-1	3-11/D-2	1	-0.1
1998 Chi-A	105	299	38	71	17	2	9	36	26	77	3	3	.237	.303	.398	.701	83	-9	33	3.67	-7	1-79,3-11/D-2,2-1	4	-2.1
1999 Chi-A	132	436	62	111	26	0	16	50	69	93	4	4	.255	.359	.424	.783	99	-1	68	5.32	6	*3-120,1-26/D-1	11	0.5
2000 Chi-A	71	201	25	49	6	1	6	28	26	47	1	0	.244	.336	.373	.709	78	-6	27	4.71	-9	3-47,1-17/D-3	3	-1.4
2001 Col-N	117	225	30	60	13	2	13	40	19	65	1	0	.267	.324	.516	.839	91	-3	36	5.65	-8	O-25(22-0-4),3-24,1-13/D-1	3	-1.2
2002 Col-N	113	168	19	37	8	1	7	37	24	52	2	3	.220	.318	.405	.722	77	-7	21	4.07	-4	3-22,1-15/O-2(2-0-0),D-1	2	-1.1
2003 Col-N	114	179	19	47	15	0	6	31	16	47	2	1	.263	.327	.447	.773	87	-4	26	5.04	-3	3-34/1-9,O-3(0-0-3)	4	-0.6
Total 8	681	1565	202	389	87	8	59	226	186	395	13	12	.249	.331	.427	.759	88	-30	220	4.78	-27	3-271,1-159/O-30,D-12,S-6,2	28	-6.2
• NORWOOD, Willie	Willie Norwood b: 11/7/1950, Greene County, AL BR/TR, 6', 185 lbs. Deb: 4/21/1977 Career OF: 104-83-57																							
1977 Min-A	39	83	15	19	3	0	3	9	6	17	6	1	.229	.281	.373	.654	78	-2	9	3.69	-2	O-28(3-20-8)/D-5	2	-0.5
1978 Min-A	125	428	56	109	22	3	8	46	28	64	25	10	.255	.305	.376	.681	89	-6	46	3.49	2	*O-115(101-14-4)/D-6	6	-0.9
1979 Min-A	96	270	32	67	13	3	6	30	20	51	9	5	.248	.300	.385	.685	80	-8	29	3.57	-1	O-71(0-44-28),D-14	4	-1.1

YEAR TM-L	G	AB	R	H	2B	3B	HR	RBI	BB	SO	SB	CS	AVG	OBP	SLG	OPS	OPS+	BR/A	RC	RC/G	FR	G/POS	WS	TPW
1980 Min-A	34	73	6	12	2	0	1	8	3	13	1	1	.164	.197	.233	.430	16	-9	3	1.10	0	O-17(0-5-17)/D-9	1	-0.9
Total 4	294	854	109	207	40	6	18	93	57	145	41	17	.242	.292	.367	.659	79	-25	87	3.31	-1	O-231/D-34	13	-3.5

• NOSSEK, Joe Joseph Rudolph Nossek b: 11/8/1940, Cleveland, OH BR/TR, 6', 178 lbs. Deb: 4/18/1964 C Career OF: 59-150-5

YEAR TM-L	G	AB	R	H	2B	3B	HR	RBI	BB	SO	SB	CS	AVG	OBP	SLG	OPS	OPS+	BR/A	RC	RC/G	FR	G/POS	WS	TPW
1964 Min-A	7	1	1	0	0	0	0	0	0	0	0	0	.000	.000	.000	.000	-99	-0	0	.00	0	/O-2(1-1-0)	0	-0.1
1965*Min-A	87	170	19	37	9	0	2	16	7	22	2	0	.218	.253	.306	.559	55	-10	13	2.37	1	O-48(2-46-2)/3-9	2	-1.1
1966 Min-A	4	0	0	0	0	0	0	0	0	0	0	0	....	....	....	....	-94	0	0	....	0	/O-2(0-2-0)	0	0.0
KC-A	87	230	13	60	10	3	1	27	8	21	4	2	.261	.286	.343	.629	82	-6	21	3.07	0	O-78(12-65-3)/3-1	5	-0.9
Yr.	91	230	13	60	10	3	1	27	8	21	4	2	.261	.286	.343	.629	82	-6	21	3.07	0	O-80(12-67-3)/3-1	5	-0.9
1967 KC-A	87	166	12	34	6	1	0	10	4	26	2	0	.205	.224	.253	.477	42	-12	9	1.86	-1	O-63(35-32-0)	1	-1.7
1969 Oak-A	13	6	0	0	0	0	0	0	0	0	0	0	.000	.000	.000	.000	-105	-2	0	.00	-1	O-12(9-3-0)	0	-0.2
StL-N	9	5	2	1	0	0	0	0	0	3	0	0	.200	.200	.200	.400	12	-1	0	1.35	0	/O-1	0	-0.1
1970 StL-N	1	1	0	0	0	0	0	0	0	0	0	0	.000	.000	.000	.000	-98	-0	0	.00	0	....	0	0.0
Total 6	295	579	47	132	25	4	3	53	19	72	8	2	.228	.254	.301	.554	60	-30	43	2.44	-1	O-206/3-10	8	-4.0

• NOVIKOFF, Lou Louis Alexander "The Mad Russian" Novikoff
b: 10/12/1915, Glendale, AZ d: 9/30/1970, South Gate, CA BR/TR, 5'10", 185 lbs. Deb: 4/15/1941 Career OF: 262-2-3

YEAR TM-L	G	AB	R	H	2B	3B	HR	RBI	BB	SO	SB	CS	AVG	OBP	SLG	OPS	OPS+	BR/A	RC	RC/G	FR	G/POS	WS	TPW
1941 Chi-N	62	203	22	49	8	0	5	24	11	15	0	....	.241	.284	.355	.638	82	-6	19	3.15	-2	O-54(51-0-3)	3	-1.1
1942 Chi-N	128	483	48	145	25	5	7	64	24	28	3	....	.300	.337	.416	.753	125	12	64	4.85	-2	*O-120(120-0-0)	14	0.4
1943 Chi-N	78	233	22	65	7	3	0	28	18	15	0	....	.279	.333	.335	.668	95	-2	24	3.67	-5	O-61(60-1-0)	4	-1.0
1944 Chi-N	71	139	15	39	4	2	3	19	10	11	1	....	.281	.329	.403	.732	106	1	19	4.82	-1	O-29(28-1-0)	4	-0.2
1946 Phi-N	17	23	0	7	1	0	0	3	1	2	0	....	.304	.333	.348	.681	96	-0	2	3.83	0	/O-3(3-0-0)	0	0.0
Total 5	356	1081	107	305	45	10	15	138	64	71	4	....	.282	.325	.384	.709	107	5	129	4.23	-10	O-267	25	-1.9

• NOVOTNEY, Rube Ralph Joseph Novotney b: 8/5/1924, Streator, IL d: 7/16/1987, Redondo Beach, CA BR/TR, 6', 187 lbs. Deb: 4/29/1949

YEAR TM-L	G	AB	R	H	2B	3B	HR	RBI	BB	SO	SB	CS	AVG	OBP	SLG	OPS	OPS+	BR/A	RC	RC/G	FR	G/POS	WS	TPW
1949 Chi-N	22	67	4	18	2	1	0	6	3	11	0	....	.269	.300	.328	.628	70	-3	6	3.04	-1	C-20	1	-0.3

• NUNAMAKER, Les Leslie Grant Nunamaker b: 1/25/1889, Malcolm, NE d: 11/14/1938, Hastings, NE BR/TR, 6'2", 190 lbs. Deb: 4/28/1911

YEAR TM-L	G	AB	R	H	2B	3B	HR	RBI	BB	SO	SB	CS	AVG	OBP	SLG	OPS	OPS+	BR/A	RC	RC/G	FR	G/POS	WS	TPW
1911 Bos-A	62	183	18	47	4	3	0	19	12	....	1	....	.257	.303	.311	.614	72	-7	18	3.21	-2	C-59	4	-0.5
1912 Bos-A	35	103	15	26	5	2	0	6	6	....	2	....	.252	.313	.340	.652	82	-3	12	3.74	-4	C-35	3	-0.4
1913 Bos-A	29	65	9	14	5	2	0	9	8	8	2	....	.215	.311	.354	.665	92	-1	8	3.63	-3	C-27	3	-0.2
1914 Bos-A	5	5	0	1	0	0	0	0	1	0	0	....	.200	.333	.200	.533	61	-0	0	2.21	0	/C-3,1-1	0	0.0
NY-A	87	257	19	68	10	3	2	29	22	34	11	9	.265	.327	.350	.678	104	-1	30	3.93	6	C-70/1-5	11	1.2
Yr.	92	262	19	69	10	3	2	29	23	34	11	9	.263	.328	.347	.675	103	-1	30	3.89	6	C-73/1-6	11	1.2
1915 NY-A	87	249	24	56	6	3	0	17	23	24	3	2	.225	.293	.273	.566	69	-10	21	2.77	-3	C-77/1-2	6	-0.7
1916 NY-A	91	260	25	77	14	7	0	28	34	21	4	....	.296	.380	.404	.784	133	11	41	5.84	1	C-79	15	2.0
1917 NY-A	104	310	22	81	9	2	0	33	21	25	5	....	.261	.310	.303	.613	86	-6	30	3.27	5	C-91	9	0.6
1918 StL-A	85	274	22	71	9	2	0	22	28	16	6	....	.259	.339	.307	.645	98	-0	30	3.62	2	C-81/1-1,O-1	9	0.9
1919 Cle-A	26	56	6	14	1	1	0	7	2	6	0	....	.250	.276	.304	.579	59	-3	5	2.72	-2	C-16	0	-0.5
1920*Cle-A	34	54	10	18	3	3	0	14	4	5	1	0	.333	.379	.500	.879	127	2	10	7.45	-1	C-17/1-6	2	0.2
1921 Cle-A	46	131	16	47	7	2	0	25	11	8	1	1	.359	.408	.443	.851	115	3	24	6.94	-2	C-46	6	0.4
1922 Cle-A	25	43	8	13	2	0	0	7	4	3	0	0	.302	.362	.349	.711	85	-1	6	4.71	-2	C-13	1	-0.2
Total 12	716	1990	194	533	75	30	2	216	176	150	36	12	.268	.332	.339	.670	95	-14	234	4.02	-5	C-614/1-15,O-1	69	2.9

• NUNEZ, Abraham Abraham Orlando (Adames) Nunez b: 3/16/1976, Santo Domingo, Dominican Republic BB/TR, 5'11", 160 lbs. Deb: 8/27/1997

YEAR TM-L	G	AB	R	H	2B	3B	HR	RBI	BB	SO	SB	CS	AVG	OBP	SLG	OPS	OPS+	BR/A	RC	RC/G	FR	G/POS	WS	TPW
1997 Pit-N	19	40	3	9	2	2	0	6	3	10	1	0	.225	.295	.375	.670	73	-1	5	3.73	1	S-12/2-9	1	0.1
1998 Pit-N	24	52	6	10	2	0	1	2	12	14	4	2	.192	.344	.288	.632	68	-2	6	3.47	0	S-23	1	-0.1
1999 Pit-N	90	259	25	57	8	0	0	17	28	54	9	1	.220	.299	.251	.550	41	-22	23	2.82	6	S-65,2-14	4	-1.0
2000 Pit-N	40	91	10	20	1	0	1	8	8	14	0	0	.220	.283	.264	.547	40	-8	7	2.38	1	S-21/2-6	1	-0.6
2001 Pit-N	115	301	30	79	11	4	1	21	28	53	8	2	.262	.327	.336	.663	71	-12	36	4.29	10	2-48,S-48/3-1,O-1	6	0.3
2002 Pit-N	112	253	28	59	14	1	2	15	27	44	3	4	.233	.312	.320	.632	66	-13	26	3.49	5	2-46,S-24/D-1	5	-0.5
2003 Pit-N	118	311	37	77	8	7	4	35	26	53	9	3	.248	.312	.357	.669	73	-12	35	3.67	-2	2-71,S-23/3-1	5	-1.0
Total 7	518	1307	139	311	46	14	9	104	132	242	34	12	.238	.312	.315	.627	62	-71	138	3.50	21	S-216,2-194/3-2,D-1,O-1	23	-2.8

• NUNEZ, Abraham Abraham Nunez b: 2/5/1977, Haina, Dominican Republic BB/TR, 6'3", 186 lbs. Deb: 9/3/2002

YEAR TM-L	G	AB	R	H	2B	3B	HR	RBI	BB	SO	SB	CS	AVG	OBP	SLG	OPS	OPS+	BR/A	RC	RC/G	FR	G/POS	WS	TPW
2002 Fla-N	19	17	2	2	0	0	0	1	0	5	0	1	.118	.118	.118	.235	-39	-4	0	.00	0	O-15(2-12-1)	0	-0.4

• NUNNALLY, Jon Jonathan Keith Nunnally b: 11/9/1971, Pelham, NC BL/TR, 5'10", 190 lbs. Deb: 4/26/1995 Career OF: 71-87-193

YEAR TM-L	G	AB	R	H	2B	3B	HR	RBI	BB	SO	SB	CS	AVG	OBP	SLG	OPS	OPS+	BR/A	RC	RC/G	FR	G/POS	WS	TPW
1995 KC-A	119	303	51	74	15	6	14	42	51	86	6	4	.244	.357	.472	.829	112	5	53	5.95	0	*O-107(16-7-92)/D-4	11	0.0
1996 KC-A	35	90	16	19	5	1	5	17	13	25	0	0	.211	.311	.456	.766	91	-2	14	5.12	-1	O-29(7-0-24)/D-4	2	-0.4
1997 KC-A	13	29	8	7	0	1	1	4	5	7	0	0	.241	.353	.414	.767	97	-0	5	5.76	0	/O-9(1-0-8)	1	0.0
Cin-N	65	201	38	64	12	3	13	35	26	51	7	3	.318	.402	.602	1.004	156	17	50	9.39	-2	O-60(14-46-11)	12	1.4
1998 Cin-N	74	174	29	36	9	0	7	20	34	38	3	4	.207	.340	.379	.719	88	-4	23	4.15	-3	O-70(6-24-53)	4	-0.8
1999 Bos-A	10	14	4	4	1	0	0	1	0	6	0	0	.286	.286	.357	.643	61	-1	1	3.86	0	/D-3,O-2(1-0-1)	0	-0.1
2000 NY-N	48	74	16	14	5	1	2	6	17	26	3	1	.189	.341	.365	.706	82	-2	11	4.53	3	O-34(26-10-4)	2	0.1
Total 6	364	885	162	218	47	12	42	125	146	239	19	12	.246	.356	.469	.825	111	14	157	6.02	-1	O-311/D-11	32	0.3

• NUNNARI, Talmadge Talmadge Raphael Nunnari b: 4/9/1975, Pensacola, FL BL/TL, 6'1", 200 lbs. Deb: 9/7/2000

YEAR TM-L	G	AB	R	H	2B	3B	HR	RBI	BB	SO	SB	CS	AVG	OBP	SLG	OPS	OPS+	BR/A	RC	RC/G	FR	G/POS	WS	TPW
2000 Mon-N	18	5	2	1	0	0	0	1	6	2	0	0	.200	.636	.200	.836	122	1	2	8.88	0	1-14	0	0.1

• NUSZ, Emory Emory Moberly Nusz b: 4/2/1866, Frederick, MD d: 8/3/1893, Point of Rocks, MD Deb: 4/26/1884

YEAR TM-L	G	AB	R	H	2B	3B	HR	RBI	BB	SO	SB	CS	AVG	OBP	SLG	OPS	OPS+	BR/A	RC	RC/G	FR	G/POS	WS	TPW
1884 Was-U	1	4	1	0	0	0	0	....	0	....	....	....	.000	.000	.000	.000	-103	-1	0	.00	0	/O-1	0	-0.1

• NUTTER, Dizzy Everett Clarence Nutter b: 8/27/1893, Roseville, OH d: 7/25/1958, Battle Creek, MI BL/TR, 5'9", 160 lbs. Deb: 9/7/1919

YEAR TM-L	G	AB	R	H	2B	3B	HR	RBI	BB	SO	SB	CS	AVG	OBP	SLG	OPS	OPS+	BR/A	RC	RC/G	FR	G/POS	WS	TPW
1919 Bos-N	18	52	4	11	0	0	0	3	4	5	1	....	.212	.268	.212	.479	47	-3	3	1.87	1	O-12(0-12-0)	0	-0.3

• NYCE, Charlie Charles Reiff Nyce b: 7/1/1870, Philadelphia, PA d: 5/9/1908, Philadelphia, PA, 5'8", 160 lbs. Deb: 5/28/1895

YEAR TM-L	G	AB	R	H	2B	3B	HR	RBI	BB	SO	SB	CS	AVG	OBP	SLG	OPS	OPS+	BR/A	RC	RC/G	FR	G/POS	WS	TPW
1895 Bos-N	9	35	7	8	5	0	2	9	4	2	0	....	.229	.325	.543	.868	115	0	6	6.33	0	/S-9	1	0.1

• NYMAN, Chris Christopher Curtis Nyman b: 6/6/1955, Pomona, CA BR/TR, 6'4", 200 lbs. Deb: 7/28/1982

YEAR TM-L	G	AB	R	H	2B	3B	HR	RBI	BB	SO	SB	CS	AVG	OBP	SLG	OPS	OPS+	BR/A	RC	RC/G	FR	G/POS	WS	TPW
1982 Chi-A	28	65	6	16	1	0	0	2	3	9	3	2	.246	.279	.262	.541	50	-5	4	1.97	-1	1-24/O-2(1-0-1)	0	-0.7
1983 Chi-A	21	28	12	8	0	0	2	4	4	7	2	2	.286	.394	.500	.894	139	1	5	6.68	-0	1-10,D-10	2	0.1
Total 2	49	93	18	24	1	0	2	6	7	16	5	4	.258	.317	.333	.650	78	-3	10	3.30	-1	/1-34,D-10,O-2	2	-0.6

• NYMAN, Nyls Nyls Wallace Rex Nyman b: 3/7/1954, Detroit, MI BL/TR, 6', 170 lbs. Deb: 9/6/1974 Career OF: 71-27-8

YEAR TM-L	G	AB	R	H	2B	3B	HR	RBI	BB	SO	SB	CS	AVG	OBP	SLG	OPS	OPS+	BR/A	RC	RC/G	FR	G/POS	WS	TPW
1974 Chi-A	5	14	5	9	2	1	0	4	0	1	1	0	.643	.667	.929	1.595	346	5	8	37.21	1	/O-3(3-0-0)	2	0.6
1975 Chi-A	106	327	36	74	6	3	2	28	11	34	10	4	.226	.256	.281	.537	51	-21	23	2.37	-3	O-94(62-26-8)/D-4	2	-3.0
1976 Chi-A	8	15	2	2	1	0	0	1	0	3	1	0	.133	.133	.200	.333	-3	-2	0	.97	0	/O-7(6-1-0)	0	-0.3
1977 Chi-A	1	1	0	0	0	0	0	0	0	0	0	0	.000	.000	.000	.000	-100	-0	0	.00	0	....	0	0.0
Total 4	120	357	43	85	9	4	2	33	11	38	12	4	.238	.267	.303	.569	60	-19	32	3.03	-3	O-104/D-4	4	-2.7

• OAKES, Rebel Ennis Telfair Oakes b: 12/17/1883, Lisbon, LA d: 3/1/1948, Lisbon, LA BL/TR, 5'8", 170 lbs. Deb: 4/14/1909 M Career OF: 8-945-17

YEAR TM-L	G	AB	R	H	2B	3B	HR	RBI	BB	SO	SB	CS	AVG	OBP	SLG	OPS	OPS+	BR/A	RC	RC/G	FR	G/POS	WS	TPW
1909 Cin-N	120	415	55	112	10	5	3	31	40	....	23	....	.270	.341	.340	.681	112	6	56	4.59	-5	*O-113(4-99-10)	15	-0.4
1910 StL-N	131	468	50	118	14	6	0	43	38	38	18	....	.252	.315	.308	.623	85	-9	51	3.64	-8	*O-127(3-118-6)	9	-2.4
1911 StL-N	154	551	69	145	13	6	2	59	41	35	25	....	.263	.320	.319	.639	81	-14	64	3.94	8	*O-151(1-150-0)	15	-1.6
1912 StL-N	136	495	57	139	19	5	3	58	31	24	26	....	.281	.328	.358	.686	90	-8	66	4.54	-4	*O-136(0-136-0)	11	-2.0
1913 StL-N	147	539	60	158	14	5	0	49	43	32	22	....	.293	.350	.338	.687	98	-0	71	4.43	-8	*O-145(0-145-0)	14	-1.8
1914 Pit-F	145	571	82	178	18	10	7	75	35	22	28	....	.312	.359	.415	.774	127	19	91	5.66	-6	*O-145(0-145-0)	21	0.4
1915 Pit-F	153	580	55	161	24	5	0	82	37	19	21	....	.278	.323	.336	.659	90	-8	69	4.01	-12	*O-153(0-152-1)	16	-3.1
Total 7	986	3619	428	1011	112	42	15	397	265	170	163	....	.279	.334	.346	.680	98	-15	469	4.40	-35	O-970	101	-11.0

YEAR	TM-L	G	AB	R	H	2B	3B	HR	RBI	BB	SO	SB	CS	AVG	OBP	SLG	OPS	OPS+	BR/A	RC	RC/G	FR	G/POS	WS	TPW
• OANA, Prince	Henry Kawaihoa Oana b: 1/22/1908, Waipahu, HI d: 6/19/1976, Austin, TX BR/TR, 6'2", 193 lbs. Deb: 4/22/1934 ♦																								
1934	Phi-N	6	21	3	5	1	0	0	3	0	1	0	....	.238	.238	.286	.524	35	-2	1	1.86	1	/0-4(4-0-0)	0	-0.1
1943	Det-A	20	26	5	10	2	1	1	7	1	2	0	0	.385	.407	.654	1.061	193	5	6	8.84	0	P-10	2	0.1
1945	Det-A	4	5	0	1	0	0	0	0	0	0	0	0	.200	.200	.200	.400	15	-0	0	1.38	0	/P-3	2	0.2
Total	3	30	52	8	16	3	1	1	10	1	3	0	0	.308	.321	.462	.782	114	2	7	5.03	0	/P-13,0-4	4	0.2
• OATES, Johnny	Johnny Lane Oates b: 1/21/1946, Sylva, NC BL/TR, 5'11", 188 lbs. Deb: 9/17/1970 M/C																								
1970	Bal-A	5	18	2	5	0	1	0	2	2	0	0	0	.278	.350	.389	.739	102	0	3	5.17	0	/C-4	1	0.1
1972	Bal-A	85	253	20	66	12	1	4	21	28	31	5	7	.261	.335	.364	.698	105	0	29	3.86	-1	C-82	10	0.3
1973	Atl-N	93	322	27	80	6	0	4	27	22	31	1	4	.248	.299	.304	.603	63	-18	28	2.87	5	C-86	4	-0.9
1974	Atl-N	100	291	22	65	10	0	1	21	23	24	2	3	.223	.280	.268	.548	52	-20	22	2.42	3	C-91	6	-1.3
1975	Atl-N	8	18	0	4	1	0	0	0	1	4	0	0	.222	.263	.278	.541	48	-1	1	2.67	0	/C-6	0	-0.1
	Phi-N	90	269	28	77	14	0	1	25	33	29	1	0	.286	.364	.349	.714	95	-0	35	4.60	4	C-82	10	0.7
	Yr.	98	287	28	81	15	0	1	25	34	33	1	0	.282	.358	.345	.703	92	-2	36	4.48	4	C-88	10	0.6
1976*	Phi-N	37	99	10	25	2	0	0	8	8	12	0	1	.253	.308	.273	.581	64	-5	7	2.48	-1	C-33	2	-0.4
1977*	LA-N	60	156	18	42	4	0	3	11	11	11	1	0	.269	.317	.353	.670	80	-4	17	3.88	3	C-56	5	0.1
1978*	LA-N	40	75	5	23	1	0	0	6	5	3	0	1	.307	.350	.320	.670	89	-1	8	4.31	-1	C-24	2	-0.1
1979	LA-N	26	46	4	6	2	0	0	2	4	1	0	1	.130	.200	.174	.374	3	-7	2	1.06	1	C-20	1	-0.5
1980	NY-A	39	64	6	12	3	0	1	3	2	3	1	2	.188	.224	.281	.505	38	-6	3	1.70	0	C-39	1	-0.5
1981	NY-A	10	26	4	5	1	0	0	0	2	0	0	0	.192	.250	.231	.481	40	-2	2	2.10	-2	C-10	0	-0.3
Total	11	593	1637	146	410	56	2	14	126	141	149	11	19	.250	.311	.313	.623	73	-64	158	3.24	13	C-533	42	-3.0
• OBANDO, Sherman	Sherman Omar (Gainor) Obando b: 1/23/1970, Bocas Del Toro, Panama BR/TR, 6'4", 215 lbs. Deb: 4/10/1993 Career OF: 2-0-75																								
1993	Bal-A	31	92	8	25	2	0	3	15	4	26	0	0	.272	.309	.391	.701	83	-2	11	4.43	0	D-21/0-8(1-0-7)	2	-0.4
1995	Bal-A	16	38	0	10	1	0	0	3	2	12	1	0	.263	.300	.289	.589	53	-2	4	3.42	0	/D-7,0-7(0-0-7)	0	-0.3
1996	Mon-N	89	178	30	44	9	0	8	22	22	48	2	0	.247	.333	.433	.766	98	-0	27	5.34	-1	0-47(0-0-47)	4	-0.3
1997	Mon-N	41	47	3	6	1	0	2	9	6	14	0	0	.128	.241	.277	.517	35	-5	4	2.35	0	0-15(1-0-14)/D-2	0	-0.5
Total	4	177	355	41	85	13	0	13	49	34	100	3	0	.239	.311	.386	.697	81	-10	46	4.47	-2	/0-77,D-30	6	-1.6
• OBERBECK, Henry	Henry A. Oberbeck b: 5/17/1858, St. Louis, MO d: 8/26/1921, St. Louis, MO Deb: 5/7/1883 U Career OF: 7-4-28 ♦																								
1883	Pit-a	2	9	1	2	1	0	0	0	0	....	....	....	.222	.222	.333	.556	80	-0	1	2.73	0	/1-2	0	0.0
	StL-a	4	14	0	0	0	0	0	0	0	....	....	....	.000	.000	.000	.000	-95	-3	0	.00	1	/0-4(3-1-0)	0	-0.2
	Yr.	6	23	1	2	1	0	0	0	0	....	....	....	.087	.087	.130	.217	-26	-3	1	.91	1	/0-4(3-1-0),1-2	0	-0.3
1884	Bal-U	33	125	19	23	4	0	0	....	3	....	....	....	.184	.203	.216	.419	38	-9	6	1.54	2	0-28(1-0-27)/3-8,P-2	1	-0.6
	KC-U	27	90	7	17	3	0	0	....	7	....	....	....	.189	.247	.222	.470	69	-1	5	1.95	4	3-15/0-7(3-3-1),P-6,1-3	1	-0.6
	Yr.	60	215	26	40	7	0	0	....	10	....	....	....	.186	.222	.219	.441	51	-10	11	1.71	6	0-35(4-3-28),3-23/P-8,1-3	2	-1.2
Total	2	66	238	27	42	8	0	0	0	10	....	....	....	.176	.210	.210	.420	44	-13	11	1.63	6	/0-39,3-23,P-8,1-5	2	-1.5
• OBERKFELL, Ken	Kenneth Ray Oberkfell b: 5/4/1956, Highland, IL BL/TR, 6', 210 lbs. Deb: 8/22/1977																								
1977	StL-N	9	9	0	1	0	0	0	1	0	3	0	0	.111	.111	.111	.222	-41	-2	0	.38	-1	/2-6	0	-0.3
1978	StL-N	24	50	7	6	1	0	0	0	3	1	0	0	.120	.170	.140	.310	-13	-8	1	.72	-1	2-17/3-4	0	-0.8
1979	StL-N	135	369	53	111	19	5	1	35	57	35	4	1	.301	.400	.388	.788	115	11	60	5.94	3	*2-117,3-17/S-2	15	2.0
1980	StL-N	116	422	58	128	27	6	3	46	51	23	4	4	.303	.380	.417	.797	118	11	66	5.59	-6	*2-101,3-16	15	1.1
1981	StL-N	102	376	43	110	12	6	2	45	37	28	13	5	.293	.356	.372	.728	104	3	49	4.62	7	*3-102/S-1	13	1.0
1982*	StL-N	137	470	55	136	22	5	2	34	40	31	11	9	.289	.346	.370	.717	99	-2	58	4.38	6	*3-135/2-1	15	0.3
1983	StL-N	151	488	62	143	26	5	3	38	61	27	12	6	.293	.373	.385	.758	110	9	71	5.21	3	*3-127,2-32/S-1	17	1.2
1984	StL-N	50	152	17	47	11	1	0	11	16	10	1	2	.309	.379	.395	.773	121	4	22	5.52	3	3-46/2-2,S-1	7	0.7
	Atl-N	50	172	21	40	8	1	1	10	15	17	1	3	.233	.294	.308	.602	65	-9	15	2.79	-2	3-45/2-4	2	-1.3
	Yr.	100	324	38	87	19	2	1	21	31	27	2	5	.269	.334	.349	.683	91	-5	37	3.97	1	3-91/2-6,S-1	9	-0.6
1985	Atl-N	134	412	30	112	19	4	3	35	51	38	1	2	.272	.360	.359	.720	96	-1	54	4.66	-10	*3-117,2-16	12	-1.2
1986	Atl-N	151	503	62	136	24	3	5	48	83	40	7	4	.270	.376	.360	.736	98	3	72	5.01	-7	*3-130,2-41	17	-0.4
1987	Atl-N	135	508	59	142	29	2	3	48	48	29	3	3	.280	.344	.362	.706	83	-12	63	4.34	-12	*3-126,2-11	10	-2.5
1988	Atl-N	120	422	42	117	20	4	3	40	32	28	4	5	.277	.331	.365	.696	95	-4	51	4.17	-7	*3-113/2-1	9	-1.1
	Pit-N	20	54	7	12	2	0	0	2	5	6	0	0	.222	.288	.259	.547	59	-3	4	2.33	-1	2-11/S-3,3-2,1-1	1	-0.3
	Yr.	140	476	49	129	22	4	3	42	37	34	4	5	.271	.326	.353	.679	91	-7	55	3.95	-7	*3-115,2-12/S-3,1-1	10	-1.4
1989	Pit-N	14	40	2	5	1	0	0	2	2	2	0	0	.125	.167	.150	.317	-9	-6	1	.88	0	/1-9,2-3	0	-0.7
	*SF-N	83	116	17	37	5	1	2	15	8	8	0	1	.319	.373	.431	.804	133	4	18	5.47	-1	3-38/1-7,2-7	4	0.3
	Yr.	97	156	19	42	6	1	2	17	10	10	0	1	.269	.321	.359	.680	97	-1	19	4.10	-1	3-38,1-16,2-10	4	-0.4
1990	Hou-N	77	150	10	31	6	1	1	12	15	17	1	1	.207	.283	.280	.563	57	-9	12	2.71	2	3-24,1-11,2-11	1	-0.8
1991	Hou-N	53	70	7	16	4	0	0	14	14	8	0	0	.229	.357	.286	.643	88	-0	8	4.04	0	1-13/3-4	2	-0.1
1992	Cal-A	41	91	6	24	1	0	0	10	8	5	0	1	.264	.323	.275	.598	69	-4	8	2.97	-3	2-21/D-5,1-2	1	-0.7
Total	16	1602	4874	558	1354	237	44	29	446	546	356	62	47	.278	.353	.362	.716	97	-14	636	4.56	-26	*3-1046,2-402/1-43,S-8,D-5	141	-3.5
• O'BERRY, Mike	Preston Michael O'Berry b: 4/20/1954, Birmingham, AL BR/TR, 6'2", 195 lbs. Deb: 4/8/1979																								
1979	Bos-A	43	59	8	10	1	0	1	4	5	16	0	0	.169	.246	.237	.483	29	-6	3	1.61	-3	C-43	0	-0.7
1980	Chi-N	19	48	7	10	1	0	0	5	5	13	0	0	.208	.283	.229	.512	41	-4	4	2.43	2	C-19	1	-0.1
1981	Cin-N	55	111	6	20	3	1	1	5	14	19	0	0	.180	.272	.252	.524	49	-7	8	2.24	-1	C-55	2	-0.7
1982	Cin-N	21	45	5	10	2	0	0	3	10	13	0	0	.222	.364	.267	.630	77	-1	5	3.78	2	C-21	1	0.1
1983	Cal-A	26	60	7	10	1	0	1	5	3	11	0	0	.167	.206	.233	.440	21	-7	3	1.49	1	C-26	1	-0.5
1984	NY-A	13	32	3	8	2	0	0	5	2	2	0	0	.250	.294	.313	.607	71	-1	3	3.48	0	C-12/3-1	1	-0.1
1985	Mon-N	20	21	2	4	0	0	0	0	4	3	1	0	.190	.320	.190	.510	49	-1	2	2.81	1	C-20	1	0.0
Total	7	197	376	38	72	10	1	3	27	43	77	1	0	.191	.276	.247	.524	46	-26	28	2.33	1	C-196/3-1	7	-2.0
• OBRADOVICH, Jim	James Thomas Obradovich b: 9/13/1949, Fort Campbell, KY BL/TL, 6'2", 200 lbs. Deb: 9/12/1978																								
1978	Hou-N	10	17	3	3	0	1	0	2	1	3	0	0	.176	.222	.294	.516	47	-1	1	2.14	0	/1-3	0	-0.2
• O'BRIEN, Billy	William Smith O'Brien b: 3/14/1860, Albany, NY d: 5/26/1911, Kansas City, MO BR/TR, 6', 185 lbs. Deb: 9/27/1884 ♦																								
1884	StP-U	8	30	1	7	3	0	0	....	0	....	....	....	.233	.233	.333	.567	89	-0	2	2.91	1	/3-8,P-2	2	0.2
	KC-U	4	17	2	4	0	0	0	....	0	....	....	....	.235	.235	.235	.471	68	-0	1	2.08	1	/3-3,1-1	0	0.0
	Yr.	12	47	3	11	3	0	0	....	0	....	....	....	.234	.234	.298	.532	82	-1	3	2.61	2	3-11/P-2,1-1	2	0.2
1887	Was-N	113	474	71	147	16	12	**19**	73	21	17	11	....	.310	.317	.492	.810	128	15	76	6.17	5	*1-104/3-4,0-4(1-3-0),2-2	13	1.0
1888	Was-N	133	528	42	119	15	2	9	66	9	70	10	....	.225	.238	.313	.551	79	-13	43	2.82	-6	*1-132/3-1	6	-3.0
1889	Was-N	2	8	1	0	0	0	0	0	1	1	0	....	.000	.111	.000	.111	-72	-2	0	.00	0	/1-2	0	-0.2
1890	Bro-a	96	388	47	108	25	8	4	67	28	....	5	....	.278	.332	.415	.747	124	9	56	5.34	-6	*1-96	10	-0.4
Total	5	356	1445	164	385	59	22	32	206	59	88	26	....	.266	.289	.395	.684	106	9	179	4.49	-5	1-335/3-16,0-4,2-2,P-2	31	-2.5
• O'BRIEN, Charlie	Charles Hugh O'Brien b: 5/1/1960, Tulsa, OK BR/TR, 6'2", 190 lbs. Deb: 6/2/1985																								
1985	Oak-A	16	11	3	3	1	0	0	1	3	3	0	0	.273	.429	.364	.792	129	1	2	6.91	-2	C-16	1	-0.1
1987	Mil-A	10	35	2	7	3	1	0	0	4	4	0	1	.200	.282	.343	.625	63	-2	3	3.05	5	C-10	1	0.3
1988	Mil-A	40	118	12	26	6	0	2	9	5	16	0	1	.220	.252	.322	.574	59	-7	9	2.38	1	C-40	3	-0.3
1989	Mil-A	62	188	22	44	10	0	6	35	21	11	0	0	.234	.339	.383	.722	104	2	23	3.86	2	C-62	9	0.8
1990	Mil-A	46	145	11	27	7	2	0	11	11	26	0	0	.186	.253	.262	.515	45	-11	10	2.11	3	C-46	2	-0.5
	NY-N	28	68	6	11	3	0	0	9	10	8	0	0	.162	.278	.206	.484	36	-6	5	2.03	2	C-28	1	-0.2
1991	NY-N	69	168	16	31	6	0	2	14	17	25	0	2	.185	.275	.256	.531	51	-12	12	2.15	2	C-67	4	-0.6
1992	NY-N	68	156	15	33	12	0	2	13	16	18	0	1	.212	.289	.327	.616	75	-6	15	2.98	3	C-64	2	0.0
1993	NY-N	67	188	15	48	11	0	4	23	14	14	1	1	.255	.314	.378	.691	85	-4	22	3.98	3	C-65	6	0.3
1994	Atl-N	51	152	24	37	11	0	8	28	15	24	0	0	.243	.324	.474	.797	102	0	22	4.97	0	C-48	6	0.3
1995*	Atl-N	67	198	18	45	7	0	9	23	29	40	0	1	.227	.343	.399	.742	92	-2	27	4.45	-3	C-64	3	-0.1
1996	Tor-A	109	324	33	77	17	0	13	44	29	68	0	1	.238	.332	.410	.743	87	-7	45	4.63	1	*C-105	11	0.0
1997	Tor-A	69	225	22	49	15	1	4	27	22	45	0	2	.218	.318	.347	.664	73	-9	25	3.53	11	C-69	9	0.6

YEAR TM-L	G	AB	R	H	2B	3B	HR	RBI	BB	SO	SB	CS	AVG	OBP	SLG	OPS	OPS+	BR/A	RC	RC/G	FR	G/POS	WS	TPW
1998 Chi-A	57	164	12	43	9	0	4	18	9	31	0	0	.262	.309	.390	.699	82	-5	20	4.10	0	C-57	4	-0.1
Ana-A	5	11	1	2	0	0	0	0	1	2	0	0	.182	.250	.182	.432	15	-1	1	1.70	0	/C-5	0	-0.1
Yr.	62	175	13	45	9	0	4	18	10	33	0	0	.257	.305	.377	.682	78	-6	20	3.94	0	C-62	4	-0.2
1999 Ana-A	27	62	3	6	0	0	1	4	1	12	0	0	.097	.138	.145	.284	-28	-12	1	.59	-1	C-27	1	-1.0
2000 Mon-N	9	19	1	4	1	0	1	2	2	7	0	0	.211	.286	.421	.707	73	-1	2	4.25	-2	/C-9	0	-0.2
Total 15	800	2232	216	493	119	4	56	261	209	354	1	10	.221	.305	.353	.658	75	-84	244	3.52	24	C-782	63	-1.1

• O'BRIEN, Darby William D. O'Brien b: 9/1/1863, Peoria, IL d: 6/15/1893, Peoria, IL BR/TR, 6'1", 186 lbs. Deb: 4/16/1887 U Career OF: 655-46-4 ♦

YEAR TM-L	G	AB	R	H	2B	3B	HR	RBI	BB	SO	SB	CS	AVG	OBP	SLG	OPS	OPS+	BR/A	RC	RC/G	FR	G/POS	WS	TPW
1887 NY-a	127	562	97	197	30	13	5	73	40	....	49	....	.351	.355	.437	.792	126	18	101	7.46	9	*O-121(121-1-0),1-10/S-2,3,P	18	1.8
1888 Bro-a	136	532	105	149	27	6	2	65	30	....	55	....	.280	.327	.365	.692	122	12	83	5.88	1	*O-136(136-0-0)	19	0.7
1889*Bro-a	136	567	146	170	30	11	5	80	61	76	91	....	.300	.384	.418	.802	128	22	129	8.61	-9	*O-136(136-0-0)	**30**	0.7
1890*Bro-N	85	350	78	110	28	6	2	63	32	43	38	....	.314	.378	.446	.824	139	17	75	8.30	2	O-85(44-42-0)	19	1.4
1891 Bro-N	103	395	79	100	18	6	5	57	39	53	31	....	.253	.331	.367	.698	104	2	60	5.47	-3	*O-103(103-0-0)	11	-0.4
1892 Bro-N	122	490	72	119	14	5	1	56	29	52	57	....	.243	.289	.298	.587	80	-12	60	4.38	2	*O-122(115-3-4)	12	-2.0
Total 6	709	2896	577	845	147	47	20	394	231	224	321	....	.292	.344	.387	.732	116	58	508	6.64	3	O-703/1-10,S-2,3-1,P-1	109	2.3

• O'BRIEN, Dink Frank Aloysius O'Brien b: 9/13/1894, San Francisco, CA d: 11/4/1971, Monterey Park, CA BR/TR, 5'8", 160 lbs. Deb: 4/26/1923

YEAR TM-L	G	AB	R	H	2B	3B	HR	RBI	BB	SO	SB	CS	AVG	OBP	SLG	OPS	OPS+	BR/A	RC	RC/G	FR	G/POS	WS	TPW
1923 Phi-N	15	21	3	7	2	0	0	0	2	1	0	0	.333	.391	.429	.820	104	0	4	6.77	0	/C-9	1	0.0

• O'BRIEN, Eddie Edward Joseph O'Brien b: 12/11/1930, South Amboy, NJ BR/TR, 5'9", 165 lbs. Deb: 4/25/1953 C Career OF: 6-57-0

YEAR TM-L	G	AB	R	H	2B	3B	HR	RBI	BB	SO	SB	CS	AVG	OBP	SLG	OPS	OPS+	BR/A	RC	RC/G	FR	G/POS	WS	TPW
1953 Pit-N	89	261	21	62	5	3	0	14	17	30	6	1	.238	.289	.280	.569	49	-18	23	2.96	-16	S-81	1	-2.7
1955 Pit-N	75	236	26	55	3	1	0	8	18	13	4	5	.233	.290	.254	.544	47	-19	18	2.51	0	O-56(1-56-0)/3-7,S-4	2	-2.1
1956 Pit-N	63	53	17	14	2	0	0	3	2	2	1	1	.264	.291	.302	.593	61	-3	5	3.02	0	S-23/O-6(5-1-0),3-4,2-2,P	2	-0.1
1957 Pit-N	3	4	0	0	0	0	0	0	0	0	0	0	.000	.000	.000	.000	-103	-1	0	.00	0	/P-3	1	0.2
1958 Pit-N	1	0	0	0	0	0	0	0	0	0	0	0	....	....	....	....	-103	0	0	....	0	/P-1	0	-0.2
Total 5	231	554	64	131	10	4	0	25	37	45	11	7	.236	.288	.269	.557	48	-41	45	2.74	-16	S-108/O-62,3-11,P-5,2-2	6	-4.9

• O'BRIEN, George George Joseph O'Brien b: 11/4/1889, Cleveland, OH d: 3/24/1966, Columbus, OH BR/TR, 6', 185 lbs. Deb: 8/16/1915

YEAR TM-L	G	AB	R	H	2B	3B	HR	RBI	BB	SO	SB	CS	AVG	OBP	SLG	OPS	OPS+	BR/A	RC	RC/G	FR	G/POS	WS	TPW
1915 StL-A	3	9	1	2	0	0	0	0	1	2	0	....	.222	.300	.222	.522	59	-0	1	2.27	0	/C-3	0	-0.1

• O'BRIEN, Jack John K. O'Brien b: 6/12/1860, Philadelphia, PA d: 11/20/1910, Philadelphia, PA BR/TR, 5'10", 184 lbs. Deb: 5/2/1882 Career OF: 5-36-31

YEAR TM-L	G	AB	R	H	2B	3B	HR	RBI	BB	SO	SB	CS	AVG	OBP	SLG	OPS	OPS+	BR/A	RC	RC/G	FR	G/POS	WS	TPW
1882 Phi-a	62	241	44	73	13	3	3	37	13	....	....	....	.303	.339	.419	.758	138	9	35	5.84	12	C-45,O-18(0-6-12)/1-1,3-1	14	2.2
1883 Phi-a	94	390	74	113	14	10	0	70	25	....	....	....	.290	.333	.377	.709	118	7	50	5.06	-5	C-58,O-25(0-25-0),3-19/S-1	19	0.5
1884 Phi-a	36	138	25	39	6	1	1	0	9	....	....	....	.283	.340	.362	.702	121	3	17	4.84	2	C-30/O-5(0-5-0),1-1	6	0.6
1885 Phi-a	62	225	35	60	9	1	2	30	20	....	....	....	.267	.340	.342	.682	109	3	27	4.39	-2	C-43/S-9,1-7,O-3(0-0-3),3	8	0.3
1886 Phi-a	105	423	65	107	25	7	0	56	38	....	23	....	.253	.325	.345	.670	109	5	56	4.81	-7	C-36,3-27,1-24,S-10/2-7,O	13	0.0
1887 Bro-a	30	129	18	34	4	1	1	17	6	....	8	....	.264	.264	.301	.564	56	-8	12	3.46	-3	C-25/O-4(1-0-3),2-1	2	-0.7
1888 Bal-a	57	196	25	44	11	5	0	18	17	....	14	....	.224	.300	.332	.631	105	2	24	4.31	-10	C-37,O-13(4-0-9)/1-7	6	-0.5
1890 Phi-a	109	433	80	113	24	14	4	80	52	....	31	....	.261	.356	.409	.765	128	16	76	6.29	3	*1-109/C-1,O-1	17	0.8
Total 8	555	2175	366	583	106	42	11	308	180	....	76	....	.268	.331	.369	.700	115	36	298	5.09	-11	C-275,1-149/O-72,3-49,S-20,2	85	3.2

• O'BRIEN, Jack John Joseph O'Brien b: 2/5/1873, Watervliet, NY d: 6/10/1933, Watervliet, NY BL/TR, 6'1", 165 lbs. Deb: 4/14/1899 Career OF: 165-68-62

YEAR TM-L	G	AB	R	H	2B	3B	HR	RBI	BB	SO	SB	CS	AVG	OBP	SLG	OPS	OPS+	BR/A	RC	RC/G	FR	G/POS	WS	TPW
1899 Was-N	127	468	68	132	11	5	6	51	31	....	17	....	.282	.331	.365	.696	92	-6	65	4.95	-4	*O-121(121-0-0)/3-4	9	-1.9
1901 Was-A	11	45	5	8	0	0	0	5	3	....	2	....	.178	.245	.178	.423	19	-5	3	1.88	-1	O-11(11-0-0)	0	-0.5
Cle-A	92	375	54	106	14	5	0	39	22	....	13	....	.283	.329	.347	.676	91	-4	49	4.73	-2	O-92(31-0-61)/3-1	8	-0.9
Yr.	103	420	59	114	14	5	0	44	25	....	15	....	.271	.320	.329	.649	83	-9	52	4.38	-2	*O-103(42-0-61)/3-1	8	-1.4
1903*Bos-A	96	338	44	71	14	4	3	38	21	....	10	....	.210	.262	.302	.564	65	-15	32	2.99	-5	O-71(2-68-1),3-11/2-4,S-1	5	-2.3
Total 3	326	1226	171	317	39	14	9	133	77	....	42	....	.259	.308	.335	.643	81	-30	149	4.17	-11	O-295/3-16,2-4,S-1	22	-5.7

• O'BRIEN, Jerry Jeremiah O'Brien d: 7/4/1911, Binghamton, NY Deb: 8/2/1887

YEAR TM-L	G	AB	R	H	2B	3B	HR	RBI	BB	SO	SB	CS	AVG	OBP	SLG	OPS	OPS+	BR/A	RC	RC/G	FR	G/POS	WS	TPW
1887 Was-N	1	4	0	0	0	0	0	0	0	2	0	....	.000	.000	.000	.000	-105	-1	0	.00	0	/2-1	0	-0.1

• O'BRIEN, John John E. O'Brien b: 10/22/1851, Columbus, OH d: 12/31/1914, Fall River, MA TR, 5'11.5", 187 lbs. Deb: 4/19/1884

YEAR TM-L	G	AB	R	H	2B	3B	HR	RBI	BB	SO	SB	CS	AVG	OBP	SLG	OPS	OPS+	BR/A	RC	RC/G	FR	G/POS	WS	TPW
1884 Bal-U	18	77	7	19	1	1	0	....	2	....	....	....	.247	.266	.286	.552	78	-2	6	2.89	0	O-18(3-14-1)	2	-0.3

• O'BRIEN, John John J. "Chewing Gum" O'Brien b: 7/14/1870, St. John, Canada d: 5/13/1913, Lewiston, ME BL/TR, 5'9", 175 lbs. Deb: 7/25/1891

YEAR TM-L	G	AB	R	H	2B	3B	HR	RBI	BB	SO	SB	CS	AVG	OBP	SLG	OPS	OPS+	BR/A	RC	RC/G	FR	G/POS	WS	TPW
1891 Bro-N	43	167	22	41	4	2	0	26	12	17	4	....	.246	.308	.293	.601	76	-5	17	3.58	-17	2-43	2	-1.9
1893 Chi-N	4	14	3	5	0	1	0	1	2	2	0	....	.357	.471	.500	.971	160	1	3	9.94	-1	/2-4	1	0.0
1895 Lou-N	128	539	82	138	10	4	1	50	45	20	15	....	.256	.325	.295	.620	65	-26	61	3.90	-2	*2-125/1-3	6	-1.8
1896 Lou-N	49	186	24	63	9	1	2	24	13	7	4	....	.339	.385	.430	.815	119	5	33	7.11	-8	2-49	5	-0.1
Was-N	73	270	38	72	6	3	4	33	27	12	4	....	.267	.344	.356	.700	85	-6	36	4.69	-2	2-73	6	-0.4
Yr.	122	456	62	135	15	4	6	57	40	19	8	....	.296	.361	.386	.747	98	-1	70	5.60	-10	*2-122	11	-0.5
1897 Was-N	86	320	37	78	12	2	3	45	19	....	6	....	.244	.309	.322	.630	67	-16	35	3.77	-6	*2-86	4	-1.5
1899 Bal-N	39	135	14	26	4	0	1	17	15	....	4	....	.193	.283	.244	.527	43	-11	11	2.64	7	2-39	2	-0.2
Pit-N	79	279	26	63	2	4	1	33	21	....	8	....	.226	.285	.272	.557	53	-18	26	3.03	-1	2-79	3	-1.4
Yr.	118	414	40	89	6	4	2	50	36	....	12	....	.215	.284	.263	.547	50	-29	37	2.90	6	*2-118	5	-1.6
Total 6	501	1910	246	486	47	17	12	229	154	58	45	....	.254	.322	.316	.637	71	-74	222	4.04	-30	2-498/1-3	29	-7.2

• O'BRIEN, Johnny John Thomas O'Brien b: 12/11/1930, South Amboy, NJ BR/TR, 5'9", 170 lbs. Deb: 4/19/1953 ♦

YEAR TM-L	G	AB	R	H	2B	3B	HR	RBI	BB	SO	SB	CS	AVG	OBP	SLG	OPS	OPS+	BR/A	RC	RC/G	FR	G/POS	WS	TPW
1953 Pit-N	89	279	28	69	13	2	2	22	21	36	1	1	.247	.309	.330	.639	67	-13	28	3.36	-4	2-77/S-1	4	-1.1
1955 Pit-N	84	278	22	83	15	2	1	25	20	19	1	1	.299	.348	.378	.726	94	-2	36	4.65	-5	2-78	9	-0.1
1956 Pit-N	73	104	13	18	1	0	0	3	5	7	0	0	.173	.211	.183	.394	7	-13	4	1.22	-2	2-53/P-8,S-1	1	-0.9
1957 Pit-N	34	35	7	11	2	1	0	1	1	4	0	0	.314	.368	.429	.797	117	2	5	5.64	-3	P-16/S-8,2-2	1	-1.0
1958 Pit-N	3	1	1	0	0	0	0	0	0	1	0	0	.000	.000	.000	.000	-103	-0	0	.00	0	....	0	0.0
StL-N	12	2	3	0	0	0	0	0	1	0	0	0	.000	.333	.000	.333	-2	-0	0	1.17	-3	/S-5,2-1,P-1	0	-0.7
Yr.	15	3	4	0	0	0	0	0	1	1	0	0	.000	.250	.000	.250	-27	-0	0	.78	-3	/S-5,2-1,P-1	0	-0.7
1959 Mil-N	44	116	16	23	4	0	1	8	11	15	0	0	.198	.273	.259	.532	46	-9	9	2.28	-1	2-37	1	-0.7
Total 6	339	815	90	204	35	5	4	59	59	82	2	2	.250	.307	.320	.628	67	-35	82	3.38	-17	2-248/P-25,S-15	16	-4.7

• O'BRIEN, Pete Peter J. O'Brien b: 6/17/1877, Binghamton, NY d: 1/31/1917, Jersey City, NJ BL/TR, 5'7", 170 lbs. Deb: 9/21/1901 U

YEAR TM-L	G	AB	R	H	2B	3B	HR	RBI	BB	SO	SB	CS	AVG	OBP	SLG	OPS	OPS+	BR/A	RC	RC/G	FR	G/POS	WS	TPW
1901 Cin-N	16	54	1	11	1	0	1	3	2	....	0	....	.204	.232	.278	.510	51	-3	4	2.20	-4	2-15	0	-0.7
1906 StL-A	151	524	44	122	9	4	2	57	42	....	25	....	.233	.293	.277	.570	82	-10	53	3.37	-26	*2-120,3-20,S-11	10	-3.8
1907 Cle-A	43	145	9	33	5	2	0	6	7	....	1	....	.228	.263	.290	.553	76	-4	12	2.76	0	2-15,3-12,S-12	3	-0.4
Was-A	39	134	6	25	3	1	0	12	12	....	4	....	.187	.259	.224	.482	59	-6	9	2.22	5	3-26,S-13/2-1	2	0.0
Yr.	82	279	15	58	8	3	0	18	19	....	5	....	.208	.261	.258	.519	67	-10	22	2.50	5	3-38,S-25,2-16	5	-0.4
Total 3	249	857	60	191	18	7	3	78	63	....	30	....	.223	.279	.271	.550	76	-23	79	3.01	-25	2-151/3-58,S-36	15	-4.9

• O'BRIEN, Pete Peter Michael O'Brien b: 2/9/1958, Santa Monica, CA BL/TL, 6'1", 198 lbs. Deb: 9/3/1982 Career OF: 40-0-21

YEAR TM-L	G	AB	R	H	2B	3B	HR	RBI	BB	SO	SB	CS	AVG	OBP	SLG	OPS	OPS+	BR/A	RC	RC/G	FR	G/POS	WS	TPW
1982 Tex-A	20	67	13	16	4	1	4	13	6	8	1	0	.239	.301	.507	.809	123	2	11	5.65	1	O-11(11-0-0)/D-4,1-3	2	0.2
1983 Tex-A	154	524	53	124	24	5	8	53	58	62	5	4	.237	.314	.347	.661	83	-12	57	3.68	11	*1-133,O-27(9-0-18)/D-1	10	-1.0
1984 Tex-A	142	520	57	149	26	2	18	80	53	50	3	5	.287	.353	.448	.801	116	10	80	5.48	8	*1-141/O-1	18	1.0
1985 Tex-A	159	573	69	153	34	3	22	92	69	53	5	10	.267	.347	.452	.799	115	9	85	4.98	3	*1-159	13	0.2
1986 Tex-A	156	551	86	160	23	3	23	90	87	66	4	4	.290	.387	.468	.855	128	24	98	6.37	6	*1-155	24	2.0
1987 Tex-A	159	569	84	163	26	1	23	88	59	61	0	4	.286	.354	.457	.810	113	8	91	5.75	16	*1-158/O-2(0-0-2),D-1	19	1.4
1988 Tex-A	156	547	57	149	24	1	16	71	72	73	1	4	.272	.357	.408	.765	111	8	80	5.10	14	*1-155/D-1	17	1.1
1989 Cle-A	155	554	75	144	24	1	12	55	83	48	3	1	.260	.358	.372	.730	104	6	77	4.87	6	*1-154/D-1	14	0.1
1990 Sea-A	108	366	32	82	18	0	5	27	44	33	0	0	.224	.311	.314	.625	74	-12	36	3.23	4	1-97/D-6,O-6(6-0-0)	2	-1.5
1991 Sea-A	152	560	58	139	29	3	17	88	44	61	0	1	.248	.304	.402	.706	93	-7	66	3.98	2	*1-132,D-18,O-13(13-0-0)	13	-1.5
1992 Sea-A	134	396	40	88	15	1	14	52	40	27	2	1	.222	.294	.371	.665	85	-9	43	3.57	1	1-81,D-36	6	-1.5
1993 Sea-A	72	210	30	54	7	0	7	27	26	21	0	0	.257	.339	.390	.729	94	-1	27	4.35	1	D-52/1-9,O-1	3	-0.4
Total 12	1567	5437	654	1421	254	21	169	736	641	563	24	34	.261	.340	.409	.749	104	27	752	4.76	71	*1-1377,D-120/O-61	141	0.2

YEAR TM-L	G	AB	R	H	2B	3B	HR	RBI	BB	SO	SB	CS	AVG	OBP	SLG	OPS	OPS+	BR/A	RC	RC/G	FR	G/POS	WS	TPW
• O'BRIEN, Pete	Peter James O'Brien b: 6/16/1867, Chicago, IL d: 6/30/1937, York, IL BR/TR, 5'9.5", 165 lbs. Deb: 4/29/1890																							
1890 Chi-N	27	106	15	30	7	0	3	16	5	10	4	....	.283	.315	.434	.749	113	1	16	5.63	0	2-27	4	0.2
• O'BRIEN, Ray	Raymond Joseph O'Brien b: 10/31/1892, St. Louis, MO d: 3/31/1942, St. Louis, MO BL/TL, 5'9", 175 lbs. Deb: 6/27/1916																							
1916 Pit-N	16	57	5	12	3	2	0	3	1	14	0	....	.211	.224	.333	.557	69	-2	5	2.49	0	0-14(7-0-7)	0	-0.3
• O'BRIEN, Syd	Sydney Lloyd O'Brien b: 12/18/1944, Compton, CA BR/TR, 6'1", 185 lbs. Deb: 4/15/1969																							
1969 Bos-A	100	263	47	64	10	5	9	29	15	37	2	3	.243	.287	.422	.709	91	-5	31	4.00	-3	3-53,S-15,2-12	6	-0.8
1970 Chi-A	121	441	48	109	13	2	8	44	22	62	3	3	.247	.286	.340	.626	69	-20	41	3.17	-16	3-68,2-43/S-5	5	-3.5
1971 Cal-A	90	251	25	50	8	1	5	21	15	33	0	2	.199	.247	.299	.546	58	-15	16	1.99	-6	S-52/2-7,3-6,1-1,0-1	2	-1.6
1972 Cal-A	36	39	10	7	2	0	1	1	6	10	0	0	.179	.289	.308	.597	82	-1	4	2.96	0	/3-8,S-4,2-3,1-1	1	0.0
Mil-A	31	58	5	12	2	0	1	5	2	13	0	1	.207	.233	.293	.526	57	-4	3	1.72	-2	/3-9,2-7	0	-0.6
Yr.	67	97	15	19	4	0	2	6	8	23	0	1	.196	.257	.299	.556	67	-4	7	2.19	-2	3-17,2-10/S-4,1-1	1	-0.7
Total 4	**378**	**1052**	**135**	**242**	**35**	**8**	**24**	**100**	**60**	**155**	**5**	**9**	**.230**	**.274**	**.347**	**.621**	**72**	**-45**	**95**	**2.97**	**-27**	**3-144/S-76,2-72,1-2,0-1**	**14**	**-6.5**
• O'BRIEN, Tom	Thomas J. O'Brien b: 2/20/1873, Verona, PA d: 2/4/1901, Phoenix, AZ, 5'11" Deb: 5/10/1897 Career OF: 168-61-32																							
1897*Bal-N	50	147	25	37	6	0	0	32	20	....	7	....	.252	.349	.293	.642	70	-5	18	4.31	0	1-25,0-24(13-1-10)	3	-0.6
1898 Bal-N	18	60	9	13	0	0	0	14	10	....	0	....	.217	.338	.217	.555	59	-3	5	2.59	-1	0-16(0-0-16)	1	-0.4
Pit-N	107	413	53	107	10	8	1	45	25	....	13	....	.259	.318	.329	.648	87	-7	51	4.15	-2	0-69(10-59-0),1-21/3-8,2-7,S	9	-1.2
Yr.	125	473	62	120	10	8	1	59	35	....	13	....	.254	.321	.315	.636	84	-10	56	3.95	-3	0-85(10-59-16),1-21/3-8,2,S	10	-1.6
1899 NY-N	151	577	101	171	22	10	6	77	44	....	23	....	.296	.350	.400	.751	109	7	92	5.93	0	*0-127(124-0-3),3-21/S-2,1,2	16	-0.4
1900*Pit-N	102	376	61	109	22	6	3	61	21	....	12	....	.290	.349	.404	.753	107	3	59	5.79	-6	1-65,0-25(21-1-3)/2-4,S-2	11	-0.4
Total 4	**428**	**1573**	**249**	**437**	**60**	**24**	**10**	**229**	**120**	**....**	**55**	**....**	**.278**	**.341**	**.366**	**.707**	**97**	**-5**	**225**	**5.10**	**-8**	**0-261,1-112/3-29,2-12,S-8**	**40**	**-3.0**
• O'BRIEN, Tom	Thomas H. O'Brien b: 6/22/1860, Salem, MA d: 4/21/1921, Worcester, MA BR/TR, 6'1", 185 lbs. Deb: 6/14/1882 Career OF: 19-13-3																							
1882 Wor-N	22	89	9	18	1	1	0	7	1	10	....	....	.202	.211	.236	.447	42	-6	5	1.76	-3	0-20(16-4-0)/2-2,3-1	0	-0.8
1883 Bal-a	33	138	16	37	6	4	0	0	5	....	....	....	.268	.294	.370	.663	109	1	15	4.26	-4	2-29/0-4(0-4-0)	3	-0.2
1884 Bos-U	103	449	80	118	31	8	4	....	12	....	....	....	.263	.282	.394	.676	128	13	51	4.33	-1	*2-99/0-3(1-1-1),1-2,C-1	18	1.3
1885 Bal-a	8	33	4	7	3	0	0	5	2	....	....	....	.212	.257	.303	.560	78	-1	3	2.74	1	/1-6,2-2	0	0.0
1887 NY-a	31	131	13	27	3	2	0	18	2	....	10	....	.206	.212	.248	.460	29	-12	9	2.37	-2	1-20/0-8(2-4-2),2-2,3-2,P	0	-1.3
1890 Roc-a	73	273	36	52	6	5	0	31	30	....	6	....	.190	.273	.249	.522	58	-13	21	2.48	-5	1-68/2-8	3	-2.1
Total 6	**270**	**1113**	**158**	**259**	**50**	**20**	**4**	**61**	**52**	**10**	**16**	**....**	**.233**	**.267**	**.323**	**.590**	**88**	**-18**	**104**	**3.34**	**-14**	**2-142/1-96,0-35,3-3,C-1,P-1**	**24**	**-3.2**
• O'BRIEN, Tommy	Thomas Edward "Obie" O'Brien b: 12/19/1918, Anniston, AL d: 11/5/1978, Anniston, AL BR/TR, 5'11", 195 lbs. Deb: 4/24/1943 Career OF: 49-12-125																							
1943 Pit-N	89	232	35	72	12	7	2	26	15	24	0	....	.310	.352	.448	.801	126	7	35	5.41	-2	0-48(17-0-31)/3-9	8	0.3
1944 Pit-N	85	156	27	39	6	2	3	20	21	12	1	....	.250	.343	.372	.714	97	-0	19	4.21	2	0-48(15-0-33)/3-1	4	0.0
1945 Pit-N	58	161	23	54	6	5	0	18	9	13	0	....	.335	.374	.435	.809	120	4	27	6.48	-1	0-45(12-0-33)	6	0.1
1949 Bos-A	49	125	24	28	5	0	3	10	21	12	1	0	.224	.336	.336	.672	73	-5	15	3.97	-1	0-32(0-8-25)	2	-0.6
1950 Bos-A	9	31	0	4	1	0	0	3	3	5	0	0	.129	.206	.161	.367	-5	-5	1	.81	0	/0-9(3-4-2)	0	-0.5
Was-A	3	9	1	1	0	0	0	1	1	0	0	0	.111	.200	.111	.311	-20	-2	0	.39	1	/0-3(2-0-1)	0	-0.1
Yr.	12	40	1	5	1	0	0	4	4	5	0	0	.125	.205	.150	.355	-8	-7	1	.71	1	0-12(5-4-3)	0	-0.6
Total 5	**293**	**714**	**110**	**198**	**30**	**14**	**8**	**78**	**70**	**66**	**2**	**0**	**.277**	**.344**	**.392**	**.736**	**101**	**-1**	**97**	**4.76**	**0**	**0-185/3-10**	**20**	**-0.8**
• OCHOA, Alex	Alex Ochoa b: 3/29/1972, Miami Lakes, FL BR/TR, 6', 185 lbs. Deb: 9/18/1995 Career OF: 206-24-488																							
1995 NY-N	11	37	7	11	1	0	0	0	2	10	1	0	.297	.333	.324	.658	77	-1	4	4.01	0	0-10(0-0-10)	0	-0.1
1996 NY-N	82	282	37	83	19	3	4	33	17	30	4	3	.294	.339	.426	.764	105	1	41	5.35	1	0-76(0-0-76)	8	-0.2
1997 NY-N	113	238	31	58	14	1	3	22	18	32	3	4	.244	.302	.349	.651	72	-11	23	3.25	3	0-88(0-4-84)/D-1	2	-1.0
1998 Min-A	94	249	35	64	14	2	2	25	10	35	6	3	.257	.288	.353	.642	65	-14	23	3.25	1	0-74(21-4-52)/D-3	3	-1.5
1999 Mil-N	119	277	47	83	16	3	8	40	45	43	6	4	.300	.407	.466	.872	121	10	55	7.32	1	0-85(50-9-31)/D-1	10	0.8
2000 Cin-N	118	244	50	77	21	3	13	58	24	27	8	4	.316	.384	.586	.970	137	13	53	7.80	1	0-95(74-3-37)	11	1.1
2001 Cin-N	90	349	48	101	20	4	7	35	24	53	12	9	.289	.339	.430	.768	93	-5	50	5.12	0	0-85(3-0-85)/D-1	7	-1.0
Col-N	58	187	25	47	10	3	1	17	21	23	5	4	.251	.333	.353	.686	64	-10	21	3.68	3	0-52(33-2-21)	2	-0.9
Yr.	148	536	73	148	30	7	8	52	45	76	17	13	.276	.337	.403	.740	82	-16	71	4.59	3	*0-137(36-2-106)/D-1	9	-1.9
2002 Mil-N	85	215	32	55	9	0	6	21	32	30	8	5	.256	.357	.381	.739	96	-1	29	4.57	4	0-72(18-2-61)	4	0.0
*Ana-A	37	65	8	18	7	0	2	10	10	5	2	2	.277	.373	.477	.850	124	2	12	6.62	0	0-36(7-0-31)	2	0.1
Total 8	**807**	**2143**	**320**	**597**	**131**	**19**	**46**	**261**	**203**	**288**	**55**	**38**	**.279**	**.346**	**.422**	**.768**	**97**	**-16**	**312**	**5.11**	**15**	**0-673/D-6**	**49**	**-2.8**
• OCK, Whitey	Harold David Ock b: 3/17/1912, Brooklyn, NY d: 3/18/1975, Mount Kisco, NY BR/TR, 5'11", 180 lbs. Deb: 9/29/1935																							
1935 Bro-N	1	3	0	0	0	0	0	0	1	2	0	....	.000	.250	.000	.250	-27	-1	0	.59	-0	/C-1	0	0.0
• O'CONNELL, Danny	Daniel Francis O'Connell b: 1/21/1927, Paterson, NJ d: 10/2/1969, Clifton, NJ BR/TR, 5'11", 180 lbs. Deb: 7/14/1950 C																							
1950 Pit-N	79	315	39	92	16	1	8	32	24	33	7	....	.292	.342	.425	.768	97	-2	45	5.13	15	S-65,3-12	8	1.7
1953 Pit-N	149	588	88	173	26	8	7	55	57	42	3	4	.294	.361	.401	.762	99	-1	87	5.37	-3	*3-104,2-47	16	0.0
1954 Mil-N	146	541	61	151	28	4	2	37	38	46	2	2	.279	.329	.357	.685	84	-13	64	4.04	4	*2-103,3-35/1-8,S-1	15	-0.2
1955 Mil-N	124	453	47	102	15	4	6	40	28	43	2	2	.225	.278	.316	.593	60	-27	40	2.94	7	*2-114/3-7,S-1	9	-1.1
1956 Mil-N	139	498	71	119	17	9	2	42	76	42	3	3	.239	.344	.321	.666	85	-8	61	4.05	1	*2-138/3-4,S-1	16	0.3
1957 Mil-N	48	183	29	43	9	1	1	8	19	20	1	0	.235	.314	.311	.625	74	-6	20	3.68	4	2-48	5	0.1
NY-N	95	364	57	97	18	3	7	28	33	30	8	3	.266	.331	.390	.721	93	-3	47	4.39	-1	2-68,3-30	11	0.1
Yr.	143	547	86	140	27	4	8	36	52	50	9	3	.256	.325	.364	.689	87	-9	66	4.16	3	*2-116,3-30	16	0.3
1958 SF-N	107	306	44	71	12	2	3	23	51	35	2	1	.232	.342	.314	.655	77	-8	36	3.82	1	*2-104/3-3	8	0.0
1959 SF-N	34	58	6	11	3	0	0	0	5	15	0	1	.190	.254	.241	.495	33	-6	4	2.03	-1	3-26/2-8	1	-0.7
1961 Was-A	138	493	61	128	30	1	1	37	77	62	15	5	.260	.363	.331	.694	91	-2	67	4.59	1	3-73,2-61	14	0.4
1962 Was-A	84	236	24	62	7	2	2	18	23	28	5	1	.263	.328	.335	.663	80	-6	27	3.81	4	3-41,2-22	4	0.0
Total 10	**1143**	**4035**	**527**	**1049**	**181**	**35**	**39**	**320**	**431**	**396**	**48**	**22**	**.260**	**.335**	**.351**	**.686**	**84**	**-80**	**496**	**4.20**	**31**	**2-713,3-335/S-68,1-8**	**107**	**0.8**
• O'CONNELL, Jimmy	James Joseph O'Connell b: 2/11/1901, Sacramento, CA d: 11/11/1976, Bakersfield, CA BL/TR, 5'10.5", 175 lbs. Deb: 4/17/1923 Career OF: 1-79-14																							
1923*NY-N	87	252	42	63	9	2	6	39	34	32	7	3	.250	.351	.373	.724	92	-1	35	4.82	-8	0-64(0-64-0)/1-8	8	-1.1
1924 NY-N	52	104	24	33	4	2	2	18	11	16	2	1	.317	.388	.452	.840	128	5	19	6.69	-1	0-29(1-15-14)/2-1	4	0.3
Total 2	**139**	**356**	**66**	**96**	**13**	**4**	**8**	**57**	**45**	**48**	**9**	**4**	**.270**	**.361**	**.396**	**.757**	**102**	**4**	**54**	**5.33**	**-9**	**/0-93,1-8,2-1**	**12**	**-0.8**
• O'CONNELL, John	John Charles O'Connell b: 6/13/1904, Verona, PA d: 10/17/1992, Canton, OH BR/TR, 6', 170 lbs. Deb: 8/16/1928																							
1928 Pit-N	1	1	0	0	0	0	0	0	0	0	0	....	.000	.000	.000	.000	-96	-0	0	.00	0	/C-1	0	0.0
1929 Pit-N	2	7	1	1	1	0	0	0	1	1	0	....	.143	.250	.286	.536	32	-1	1	2.28	0	/C-2	0	-0.1
Total 2	**3**	**8**	**1**	**1**	**1**	**0**	**0**	**0**	**1**	**1**	**0**	**....**	**.125**	**.222**	**.250**	**.472**	**17**	**-1**	**1**	**1.95**	**0**	**/C-3**	**0**	**-0.1**
• O'CONNELL, John	John Joseph O'Connell d: 5/14/1908, Derry, NH TR, 5'9.5", 170 lbs. Deb: 8/22/1891																							
1891 Bal-a	8	29	2	5	1	0	0	7	3	6	2	....	.172	.250	.207	.457	31	-3	2	2.26	-1	/2-3,S-3,0-2(0-0-2)	0	-0.3
1902 Det-A	8	22	1	4	0	0	0	0	3	....	0	....	.182	.280	.182	.462	29	-2	1	1.69	-1	/2-6,1-2	0	-0.2
Total 2	**16**	**51**	**3**	**9**	**1**	**0**	**0**	**7**	**6**	**6**	**2**	**....**	**.176**	**.263**	**.196**	**.459**	**30**	**-5**	**3**	**2.02**	**-2**	**/2-9,S-3,1-2,0-2**	**0**	**-0.6**
• O'CONNELL, Pat	Patrick H. O'Connell b: 6/10/1861, Bangor, ME d: 1/24/1943, Lewiston, ME BR/TR, 5'10", 175 lbs. Deb: 7/22/1886																							
1886 Bal-a	42	166	20	30	3	2	0	8	11	....	10	....	.181	.236	.223	.459	45	-10	11	2.26	-5	0-41(0-41-0)/1-1,P-1	1	-1.5
• O'CONNOR, Dan	Daniel Cornelius O'Connor b: 8/1868, Guelph, Canada d: 3/3/1942, Guelph, Canada BL/TR, 6'2", 185 lbs. Deb: 6/3/1890																							
1890 Lou-a	6	26	3	12	1	1	0	5	1	....	5	....	.462	.481	.577	1.058	217	4	10	18.68	0	/1-6	2	0.2
• O'CONNOR, Jack	John Joseph "Rowdy Jack,Peach Pie" O'Connor b: 6/2/1869, St. Louis, MO d: 11/14/1937, St. Louis, MO BR/TR, 5'10", 170 lbs. Deb: 4/20/1887 M/U Career OF: 42-113-217																							
1887 Cin-a	12	42	4	6	0	0	0	1	2	....	3	....	.143	.143	.100	.243	-31	-7	1	.77	2	/0-7(7-0-0),C-5	1	-0.4
1888 Cin-a	36	137	14	28	3	1	1	17	6	....	12	....	.204	.243	.263	.506	59	-7	12	2.96	-1	0-34(11-21-2)/C-2	2	-0.8
1889 Col-a	107	398	69	107	17	7	4	60	33	37	26	....	.269	.331	.377	.708	107	4	60	5.44	4	C-84,0-19(3-0-16)/2-4,1-3	12	1.2

YEAR TM-L	G	AB	R	H	2B	3B	HR	RBI	BB	SO	SB	CS	AVG	OBP	SLG	OPS	OPS+	BR/A	RC	RC/G	FR	G/POS	WS	TPW
1890 Col-a	121	457	89	148	14	10	2	66	38	....	29	....	.324	.377	.411	.788	142	24	84	7.19	3	*C-106/O-9(3-4-2),S-8,2-2,3	21	3.0
1891 Col-a	56	229	28	61	12	3	0	37	11	14	10	....	.266	.300	.345	.645	90	-4	27	4.32	4	O-40(7-0-33),C-21	5	0.1
1892*Cle-N	140	572	71	142	22	5	1	58	25	48	17	....	.248	.282	.309	.592	76	-20	56	3.52	2	*O-106(6-0-100),C-34	12	-1.9
1893 Cle-N	96	384	72	110	23	1	4	75	29	12	29	....	.286	.341	.383	.724	87	-9	62	5.96	1	C-56,O-44(2-27-15)	11	-0.4
1894 Cle-N	86	330	67	104	23	7	2	51	15	7	15	....	.315	.345	.445	.790	86	-10	57	6.59	-1	C-45,O-33(1-27-5)/1-7	9	-0.7
1895 Cle-N	90	343	52	100	14	10	0	58	31	22	11	....	.292	.355	.391	.746	87	-7	54	5.75	3	C-47,1-41/3-1	10	-0.1
1896*Cle-N	68	256	41	76	11	1	1	43	15	12	15	....	.297	.343	.359	.702	81	-8	38	5.45	1	C-37,1-17,O-12(0-3-9)	6	-0.3
1897 Cle-N	103	397	49	115	21	4	2	69	26	....	20	....	.290	.338	.378	.716	84	-10	60	5.48	-2	O-52(0-30-22),1-36,C-13	8	-1.3
1898 Cle-N	131	478	50	119	17	4	1	56	26	....	8	....	.249	.291	.308	.598	72	-18	48	3.40	10	1-69,C-48,O-15(2-1-12)	9	-0.5
1899 StL-N	84	289	33	73	5	6	0	43	15	....	7	....	.253	.299	.311	.610	66	-14	30	3.64	-2	C-57,1-26	4	-1.0
1900 StL-N	10	32	4	7	0	0	0	6	2	....	0	....	.219	.306	.219	.524	46	-2	2	2.32	0	C-10	0	-0.1
*Pit-N	43	147	15	35	4	1	0	19	3	....	5	....	.238	.263	.279	.542	49	-11	13	2.94	-5	C-40/1-2	1	-1.2
Yr.	53	179	19	42	4	1	0	25	5	....	5	....	.235	.271	.268	.539	49	-13	15	2.83	-5	C-50/1-2	1	-1.3
1901 Pit-N	61	202	16	39	7	3	0	22	10	....	2	....	.193	.238	.257	.496	42	-15	14	2.18	-7	C-59	2	-1.6
1902 Pit-N	49	170	13	50	1	2	1	28	3	....	2	....	.294	.306	.341	.648	96	-2	19	4.14	-5	C-42/1-6,O-1	5	-0.2
1903 NY-A	64	212	13	43	4	1	0	12	8	....	4	....	.203	.235	.231	.466	38	-16	13	2.02	-4	C-63/1-1	2	-1.4
1904 StL-A	14	47	4	10	1	0	0	2	2	....	0	....	.213	.245	.234	.479	55	-2	3	2.01	-1	C-14	1	-0.3
1906 StL-A	55	174	8	33	0	0	0	11	2	....	4	....	.190	.199	.190	.389	23	-16	8	1.49	2	C-51	2	-0.9
1907 StL-A	25	89	2	14	2	0	0	4	0	....	0	....	.157	.176	.180	.356	13	-9	3	1.04	1	C-25	1	-0.6
1910 StL-A	1	0	0	0	0	0	0	0	0	....	0	....	....	....	....	....	-107	0	0	....	0	/C-1	0	0.0
Total 21	1452	5385	714	1420	201	66	19	738	302	152	219	....	.264	.307	.336	.643	80	-161	664	4.38	6	C-860,O-372,1-208/S-8,2-6,3	124	-9.5

• O'CONNOR, Johnny John Charles "Bucky" O'Connor b: 12/1/1891, Cahirciveen, Ireland d: 5/30/1982, Bonner Springs, KS BR/TR, 5'9" Deb: 9/16/1916

YEAR TM-L	G	AB	R	H	2B	3B	HR	RBI	BB	SO	SB	CS	AVG	OBP	SLG	OPS	OPS+	BR/A	RC	RC/G	FR	G/POS	WS	TPW
1916 Chi-N	1	0	0	0	0	0	0	0	0	0	0	....	....	....	....	....	-90	0	0	....	-1	/C-1	0	-0.1

• O'CONNOR, Paddy Patrick Francis O'Connor b: 8/4/1879, County Kerry, Ireland d: 8/17/1950, Springfield, MA BR/TR, 5'8", 168 lbs. Deb: 4/17/1908 C

YEAR TM-L	G	AB	R	H	2B	3B	HR	RBI	BB	SO	SB	CS	AVG	OBP	SLG	OPS	OPS+	BR/A	RC	RC/G	FR	G/POS	WS	TPW
1908 Pit-N	12	16	1	3	0	0	0	2	0	....	0	....	.188	.188	.188	.375	20	-1	1	1.12	0	/C-4	0	-0.2
1909*Pit-N	9	16	1	5	1	0	0	3	0	....	0	....	.313	.313	.375	.688	108	0	2	4.25	-1	/C-3,3-1	1	-0.1
1910 Pit-N	6	4	0	1	0	0	0	0	1	1	0	....	.250	.400	.250	.650	85	0	0	3.41	0	/C-1	0	0.0
1914 StL-N	10	9	0	0	0	0	0	0	2	2	0	....	.000	.250	.000	.250	-24	-1	0	.00	0	/C-7	0	-0.2
1915 Pit-F	70	219	15	50	10	1	0	16	14	30	4	....	.228	.278	.283	.561	63	-11	18	2.65	3	C-66	6	-0.3
1918 NY-A	1	3	0	1	0	0	0	0	0	1	0	....	.333	.333	.333	.667	99	-0	0	4.00	0	/C-1	0	0.0
Total 6	108	267	17	60	11	1	0	21	17	34	4	....	.225	.276	.273	.550	60	-13	21	2.55	0	/C-82,3-1	7	-0.8

• O'DEA, Ken James Kenneth O'Dea b: 3/16/1913, Lima, NY d: 12/17/1985, Lima, NY BL/TR, 6', 180 lbs. Deb: 4/21/1935

YEAR TM-L	G	AB	R	H	2B	3B	HR	RBI	BB	SO	SB	CS	AVG	OBP	SLG	OPS	OPS+	BR/A	RC	RC/G	FR	G/POS	WS	TPW
1935*Chi-N	76	202	30	52	13	2	6	38	26	18	0	....	.257	.345	.431	.776	106	2	31	5.25	-2	C-63	8	0.3
1936 Chi-N	80	189	36	58	10	3	2	38	38	18	0	....	.307	.423	.423	.846	126	9	37	7.05	-3	C-55	9	0.9
1937 Chi-N	83	219	31	66	7	5	4	32	24	26	1	....	.301	.370	.434	.804	113	4	38	6.51	-3	C-64	11	0.5
1938*Chi-N	86	247	22	65	12	1	3	33	12	18	1	....	.263	.297	.356	.654	77	-8	25	3.43	-5	C-71	6	-0.9
1939 NY-N	52	97	7	17	1	0	3	11	10	16	0	....	.175	.252	.278	.531	42	-8	7	2.26	-1	C-30	1	-0.8
1940 NY-N	48	96	9	23	4	1	0	12	16	15	0	....	.240	.348	.302	.650	80	-2	11	3.89	4	C-31	3	0.3
1941 NY-N	59	89	13	19	5	1	3	17	8	20	0	....	.213	.278	.393	.672	86	-2	10	3.55	1	C-14	2	-0.1
1942*StL-N	58	192	22	45	7	1	5	32	17	23	0	....	.234	.297	.359	.656	85	-4	20	3.53	3	C-49	6	0.2
1943*StL-N	71	203	15	57	11	2	3	25	19	25	0	....	.281	.345	.399	.744	110	2	29	5.18	-1	C-56	8	0.5
1944*StL-N	85	265	35	66	11	2	6	37	37	29	1	....	.249	.343	.374	.717	100	1	37	4.81	0	C-69	11	0.5
1945 StL-N★	100	307	36	78	18	2	4	43	50	31	0	....	.254	.359	.365	.723	99	1	43	4.78	4	C-91	15	1.0
1946 StL-N	22	57	2	7	2	0	1	3	8	8	0	....	.123	.231	.211	.441	24	-6	3	1.20	-0	C-22	1	-0.5
Bos-N	12	32	4	7	0	0	0	2	8	4	0	....	.219	.375	.219	.594	70	-1	3	2.94	0	C-12	1	0.0
Yr.	34	89	6	14	2	0	1	5	16	12	0	....	.157	.286	.213	.499	41	-6	6	1.77	0	C-34	2	-0.5
Total 12	832	2195	262	560	101	20	40	323	273	251	3	....	.255	.338	.374	.712	95	-11	292	4.58	-4	C-627	82	1.9

• O'DEA, Paul Paul "Lefty" O'Dea b: 7/3/1920, Cleveland, OH d: 12/11/1978, Cleveland, OH BL/TL, 6', 200 lbs. Deb: 4/19/1944 Career OF: 36-0-58

YEAR TM-L	G	AB	R	H	2B	3B	HR	RBI	BB	SO	SB	CS	AVG	OBP	SLG	OPS	OPS+	BR/A	RC	RC/G	FR	G/POS	WS	TPW
1944 Cle-A	76	173	25	55	9	0	0	13	23	21	2	2	.318	.401	.370	.771	126	7	24	5.00	-1	O-41(36-0-5)/1-3,P-3	5	0.5
1945 Cle-A	87	221	21	52	2	2	1	21	20	26	3	0	.235	.299	.276	.575	70	-7	18	2.63	-1	O-53(0-0-53)/P-1	2	-1.5
Total 2	163	394	46	107	11	2	1	34	43	47	5	2	.272	.345	.317	.662	95	-0	43	3.61	-2	/O-94,P-4,1-3	7	-1.0

• ODOM, Heinie Herman Boyd Odom b: 10/13/1900, Rusk, TX d: 8/31/1970, Rusk, TX BB/TR, 6', 170 lbs. Deb: 4/22/1925

YEAR TM-L	G	AB	R	H	2B	3B	HR	RBI	BB	SO	SB	CS	AVG	OBP	SLG	OPS	OPS+	BR/A	RC	RC/G	FR	G/POS	WS	TPW
1925 NY-A	1	1	0	1	0	0	0	0	0	0	0	0	1.000	1.000	1.000	2.000	416	0	1	∞	0	/3-1	0	0.0

• O'DONNELL, Harry Harry Herman "Butch" O'Donnell b: 4/2/1894, Philadelphia, PA d: 1/31/1958, Philadelphia, PA BR/TR, 5'8", 175 lbs. Deb: 4/30/1927

YEAR TM-L	G	AB	R	H	2B	3B	HR	RBI	BB	SO	SB	CS	AVG	OBP	SLG	OPS	OPS+	BR/A	RC	RC/G	FR	G/POS	WS	TPW
1927 Phi-N	16	16	1	1	0	0	0	2	2	2	0	....	.063	.167	.063	.229	-36	-3	0	.41	0	C-12	0	-0.3

• O'DONNELL, John John O'Donnell b: Littlestown, PA Deb: 7/16/1884

YEAR TM-L	G	AB	R	H	2B	3B	HR	RBI	BB	SO	SB	CS	AVG	OBP	SLG	OPS	OPS+	BR/A	RC	RC/G	FR	G/POS	WS	TPW
1884 Phi-U	1	4	0	1	0	0	0	....	0	....	....	....	.250	.250	.250	.500	75	-0	0	2.39	-1	/C-1	0	0.0

• O'DOUL, Lefty Francis Joseph O'Doul b: 3/4/1897, San Francisco, CA d: 12/7/1969, San Francisco, CA BL/TL, 6', 180 lbs. Deb: 4/29/1919 Career OF: 744-1-59 ♦

YEAR TM-L	G	AB	R	H	2B	3B	HR	RBI	BB	SO	SB	CS	AVG	OBP	SLG	OPS	OPS+	BR/A	RC	RC/G	FR	G/POS	WS	TPW
1919 NY-A	19	16	2	4	0	0	0	1	1	2	1	....	.250	.294	.250	.544	53	-0	1	2.89	0	/P-3,O-1	0	-0.1
1920 NY-A	13	12	2	2	1	0	0	1	1	1	0	0	.167	.231	.250	.481	26	-1	1	1.91	0	/P-2,O-1	0	-0.1
1922 NY-A	8	9	0	3	1	0	0	4	0	2	0	0	.333	.333	.444	.778	99	1	1	5.65	0	/P-6	0	0.2
1923 Bos-A	36	35	2	5	0	0	0	4	2	3	0	0	.143	.189	.143	.332	-12	-3	1	.93	1	P-23/O-1	0	-1.0
1928 NY-N	114	354	67	113	19	4	8	46	30	8	9	....	.319	.372	.463	.836	117	8	60	6.27	-5	O-94(94-0-0)	12	-0.3
1929 Phi-N	154	638	152	**254**	35	6	32	122	76	19	2	....	**.398**	**.465**	.622	1.087	157	59	180	11.79	8	*O-154(139-0-15)	31	5.1
1930 Phi-N	140	528	122	202	37	7	22	97	63	21	3	....	.383	.453	.604	1.057	142	39	141	10.94	-6	*O-131(131-0-0)	20	2.1
1931 Bro-N	134	512	85	172	32	11	7	75	48	16	5	....	.336	.396	.482	.879	136	26	100	7.65	-2	*O-132(132-0-0)	22	1.6
1932 Bro-N	148	595	120	219	32	8	21	90	50	20	11	....	**.368**	.423	.555	.978	164	54	142	9.69	0	*O-148(148-0-0)	**33**	4.5
1933 Bro-N	43	159	14	40	5	1	5	21	15	6	2	....	.252	.320	.390	.710	106	1	21	4.54	-4	O-41(41-0-0)	4	-0.5
*NY-N★	78	229	31	70	9	1	9	35	29	17	1	....	.306	.388	.472	.860	147	15	43	6.95	2	O-63(32-0-31)	13	1.4
Yr.	121	388	45	110	14	2	14	56	44	23	3	....	.284	.361	.438	.799	131	16	63	5.93	-2	*O-104(73-0-31)	17	0.9
1934 NY-N	83	177	27	56	4	3	9	46	18	7	2	....	.316	.383	.525	.908	144	11	38	8.49	-1	O-38(27-0-11)	9	0.8
Total 11	970	3264	624	1140	175	41	113	542	333	122	36	0	.349	.413	.532	.945	141	211	730	8.78	-9	O-804/P-34	144	13.6

• ODWELL, Fred Frederick William "Fritz" Odwell
b: 9/25/1872, Downsville, NY d: 8/19/1948, Downsville, NY BL/TR, 5'9.5", 160 lbs. Deb: 4/16/1904 Career OF: 240-18-136

YEAR TM-L	G	AB	R	H	2B	3B	HR	RBI	BB	SO	SB	CS	AVG	OBP	SLG	OPS	OPS+	BR/A	RC	RC/G	FR	G/POS	WS	TPW
1904 Cin-N	129	468	75	133	22	10	1	58	26	....	30	....	.284	.333	.380	.713	110	5	72	5.40	12	*O-126(107-14-5)/2-1	19	0.9
1905 Cin-N	130	468	79	113	10	9	**9**	65	26	....	21	....	.241	.293	.359	.652	85	-11	59	4.08	5	*O-126(56-4-66)	11	-1.3
1906 Cin-N	58	202	20	45	5	4	0	21	15	....	11	....	.223	.286	.287	.573	75	-6	21	3.34	1	O-57(0-0-57)	3	-0.8
1907 Cin-N	94	274	24	74	5	7	0	24	22	....	10	....	.270	.336	.339	.675	107	2	37	4.53	0	O-84(77-0-8)/2-1	9	-0.3
Total 4	411	1412	198	365	42	30	10	168	89	....	72	....	.258	.313	.352	.665	96	-10	189	4.47	18	O-393/2-2	42	-1.5

• OERTEL, Chuck Charles Frank "Ducky,Snuffy" Oertel b: 3/12/1931, Coffeyville, KS d: 10/4/2000, Royal Oak, MI BL/TR, 5'8", 165 lbs. Deb: 9/1/1958

YEAR TM-L	G	AB	R	H	2B	3B	HR	RBI	BB	SO	SB	CS	AVG	OBP	SLG	OPS	OPS+	BR/A	RC	RC/G	FR	G/POS	WS	TPW
1958 Bal-A	14	12	4	2	0	0	1	1	1	1	0	0	.167	.231	.417	.647	78	-0	1	3.12	0	/O-2(2-0-1)	0	-0.1

• OESTER, Ron Ronald John Oester b: 5/5/1956, Cincinnati, OH BB/TR, 6'2", 190 lbs. Deb: 9/10/1978 C

YEAR TM-L	G	AB	R	H	2B	3B	HR	RBI	BB	SO	SB	CS	AVG	OBP	SLG	OPS	OPS+	BR/A	RC	RC/G	FR	G/POS	WS	TPW
1978 Cin-N	6	8	1	3	0	0	0	1	0	2	0	0	.375	.375	.375	.750	110	0	1	5.28	1	/S-6	0	0.1
1979 Cin-N	6	3	0	0	0	0	0	0	0	1	0	0	.000	.000	.000	.000	-99	-1	0	.00	0	/S-2	0	-0.1
1980 Cin-N	100	303	40	84	16	2	2	20	26	44	6	2	.277	.336	.363	.699	95	-1	37	4.27	0	2-79,S-17/3-3	10	0.3
1981 Cin-N	105	354	45	96	16	7	5	42	42	49	2	5	.271	.348	.398	.747	109	3	48	4.59	17	*2-103/S-9	15	2.8
1982 Cin-N	151	549	63	143	19	4	9	47	35	82	5	6	.260	.305	.359	.664	83	-15	56	3.42	6	*2-118,S-29,3-13	11	-0.1
1983 Cin-N	157	549	63	145	23	5	11	58	49	106	2	2	.264	.326	.384	.710	93	-6	66	4.06	-7	*2-154	14	-0.5
1984 Cin-N	150	553	54	134	26	3	3	38	41	97	7	2	.242	.296	.316	.612	69	-23	50	3.06	2	*2-147/S-1	8	-1.4
1985 Cin-N	152	526	59	155	26	3	1	34	51	65	5	0	.295	.357	.361	.718	97	-0	68	4.68	19	*2-149	21	2.9

YEAR TM-L	G	AB	R	H	2B	3B	HR	RBI	BB	SO	SB	CS	AVG	OBP	SLG	OPS	OPS+	BR/A	RC	RC/G	FR	G/POS	WS	TPW
1986 Cin-N	153	523	52	135	23	2	8	44	52	84	9	2	.258	.326	.356	.682	84	-10	59	3.81	15	*2-151	15	1.4
1987 Cin-N	69	237	28	60	9	6	2	23	22	51	2	3	.253	.317	.367	.684	77	-9	26	3.62	3	2-69	5	-0.2
1988 Cin-N	54	150	20	42	7	0	0	10	9	24	0	2	.280	.321	.327	.647	83	-4	15	3.53	0	2-49/S-5	3	-0.4
1989 Cin-N	109	305	23	75	15	0	1	14	32	47	1	0	.246	.318	.305	.622	76	-9	29	3.23	-1	*2-102/S-2	7	-0.7
1990*Cin-N	64	154	10	46	10	1	0	13	10	29	1	2	.299	.341	.377	.718	93	-2	20	4.57	-1	2-50/3-3	3	-0.3
Total 13	1276	4214	458	1118	190	33	42	344	369	681	40	26	.265	.325	.356	.681	87	-77	474	3.86	53	*2-1171/S-71,3-19	112	3.8

• O'FARRELL, Bob Robert Arthur O'Farrell b: 10/19/1896, Waukegan, IL d: 2/20/1988, Waukegan, IL BR/TR, 5'9.5", 180 lbs. Deb: 9/5/1915 M

YEAR TM-L	G	AB	R	H	2B	3B	HR	RBI	BB	SO	SB	CS	AVG	OBP	SLG	OPS	OPS+	BR/A	RC	RC/G	FR	G/POS	WS	TPW
1915 Chi-N	2	3	0	1	0	0	0	0	0	0	0	....	.333	.333	.333	.667	102	-0	0	4.42	-1	/C-2	0	-0.1
1916 Chi-N	1	0	0	0	0	0	0	0	0	0	0	....	....	....	....	....	-90	0	0	....	-1	/C-1	0	-0.1
1917 Chi-N	3	8	1	3	2	0	0	1	1	0	1	....	.375	.444	.625	1.069	210	1	2	12.98	0	/C-3	1	0.1
1918*Chi-N	52	113	9	32	7	3	1	14	10	15	0	....	.283	.347	.425	.772	132	4	16	5.05	0	C-45	7	0.7
1919 Chi-N	49	125	11	27	4	2	0	9	7	10	2	....	.216	.258	.280	.538	61	-6	9	2.36	1	C-38	2	-0.3
1920 Chi-N	94	270	29	67	11	4	3	19	34	23	1	0	.248	.332	.352	.684	95	0	34	4.23	-1	C-86	11	0.6
1921 Chi-N	96	260	32	65	12	7	4	32	18	14	2	0	.250	.299	.396	.695	82	-6	31	4.18	3	C-90	7	0.2
1922 Chi-N	128	392	68	127	18	8	4	60	79	34	5	3	.324	.439	.441	.880	125	21	82	7.83	16	*C-125	26	4.3
1923 Chi-N	131	452	73	144	25	4	12	84	67	38	10	3	.319	.408	.471	.879	131	25	91	7.62	4	*C-124	25	3.5
1924 Chi-N	71	183	25	44	6	2	3	28	30	13	2	0	.240	.347	.344	.692	85	-2	24	4.40	-2	C-57	6	0.0
1925 Chi-N	17	22	2	4	0	1	0	3	2	5	0	0	.182	.250	.273	.523	33	-2	2	2.30	0	/C-3	0	-0.2
StL-N	94	317	37	88	13	2	3	32	46	26	0	1	.278	.373	.360	.732	86	-4	45	5.14	0	C-92	10	0.1
Yr.	111	339	39	92	13	3	3	35	48	31	0	1	.271	.365	.354	.719	83	-7	47	4.94	0	C-95	10	-0.1
1926*StL-N	147	492	63	144	30	9	7	68	61	44	1	....	.293	.371	.433	.804	111	9	79	5.68	9	*C-146	23	2.7
1927 StL-N	61	178	19	47	10	1	0	18	23	22	3	....	.264	.348	.331	.680	80	-4	21	4.13	1	C-53	6	0.0
1928 StL-N	16	52	6	11	1	0	0	4	13	9	2	....	.212	.369	.231	.600	59	-2	5	3.35	0	C-14	2	-0.2
NY-N	75	133	23	26	6	0	2	20	34	16	2	....	.195	.359	.286	.645	70	-4	16	3.64	-2	C-63	3	-0.4
Yr.	91	185	29	37	7	0	2	24	47	25	4	....	.200	.362	.270	.632	67	-7	21	3.56	-3	C-77	5	-0.5
1929 NY-N	91	248	35	76	14	3	4	42	28	30	3	....	.306	.384	.435	.819	103	2	41	6.16	-10	C-84	8	-0.3
1930 NY-N	94	249	37	75	16	4	4	54	31	21	1	....	.301	.381	.446	.827	101	1	42	6.08	-2	C-69	9	0.3
1931 NY-N	85	174	11	39	8	3	1	19	21	23	0	....	.224	.311	.322	.633	72	-6	19	3.58	-3	C-80	5	-0.7
1932 NY-N	50	67	7	16	3	0	0	8	11	10	0	....	.239	.354	.284	.638	76	-2	8	3.84	-1	C-41	2	-0.1
1933 StL-N	55	163	16	39	4	2	2	20	15	25	0	....	.239	.303	.325	.629	75	-5	16	3.43	-4	C-50	3	-0.7
1934 Cin-N	44	123	10	30	8	3	1	9	11	19	0	....	.244	.306	.382	.688	85	-3	14	3.64	1	C-42	3	0.1
Chi-N	22	67	3	15	3	0	0	5	3	11	0	....	.224	.257	.269	.526	42	-6	5	2.36	1	C-22	2	-0.4
Yr.	66	190	13	45	11	3	1	14	14	30	0	....	.237	.289	.342	.631	70	-8	19	3.20	2	C-64	5	-0.3
1935 StL-N	14	10	0	0	0	0	0	0	2	0	0	....	.000	.167	.000	.167	-49	-2	0	.11	-1	/C-8	0	-0.3
Total 21	1492	4101	517	1120	201	58	51	549	547	408	35	7	.273	.360	.388	.748	97	9	604	5.15	8	*C-1338	161	9.1

• OFFERMAN, Jose Jose Antonio (Dono) Offerman b: 11/8/1968, San Pedro de Macoris, Dominican Republic BB/TR, 6', 165 lbs. Deb: 8/19/1990 Career OF: 5-1-3

YEAR TM-L	G	AB	R	H	2B	3B	HR	RBI	BB	SO	SB	CS	AVG	OBP	SLG	OPS	OPS+	BR/A	RC	RC/G	FR	G/POS	WS	TPW
1990 LA-N	29	58	7	9	0	0	1	7	4	14	1	0	.155	.210	.207	.417	15	-7	3	1.54	0	S-27	1	-0.6
1991 LA-N	52	113	10	22	2	0	0	3	25	32	3	2	.195	.345	.212	.558	62	-4	9	2.58	3	S-50	2	0.1
1992 LA-N	149	534	67	139	20	8	1	30	57	98	23	16	.260	.332	.333	.665	90	-8	61	3.87	-31	*S-149	10	-3.0
1993 LA-N	158	590	77	159	21	6	1	62	71	75	30	13	.269	.350	.331	.680	88	-6	73	4.02	-17	*S-158	14	-1.1
1994 LA-N	72	243	27	51	8	4	1	25	38	38	2	1	.210	.317	.288	.605	63	-12	24	3.11	-5	S-72	6	-1.1
1995*LA-N★	119	429	69	123	14	6	4	33	69	67	2	7	.287	.389	.375	.765	113	8	67	5.48	-1	*S-115	14	1.6
1996 KC-A	151	561	85	170	33	8	5	47	74	98	24	10	.303	.385	.417	.802	103	6	95	6.09	6	1-96,2-38,S-36/O-1	18	0.7
1997 KC-A	106	424	59	126	23	6	2	39	41	64	9	10	.297	.359	.394	.753	94	-5	60	5.04	-5	*2-101/D-1	9	-0.5
1998 KC-A	158	607	102	191	28	**13**	7	66	89	96	45	12	.315	.407	.438	.845	117	23	119	7.27	-1	*2-152/D-6	29	2.7
1999*Bos-A★	149	586	107	172	37	**11**	8	69	96	79	18	12	.294	.395	.435	.830	108	9	105	6.33	-10	*2-128,D-18/1-8	19	0.4
2000 Bos-A	116	451	73	115	14	3	9	41	70	70	0	8	.255	.356	.359	.716	80	-16	59	4.43	8	2-80,1-39/D-9	9	-0.7
2001 Bos-A	128	524	76	140	23	3	9	49	61	97	5	2	.267	.345	.374	.719	89	-7	70	4.70	5	2-91,1-43	14	-0.1
2002 Bos-A	72	237	39	55	10	0	4	27	33	29	8	5	.232	.328	.325	.653	73	-9	25	3.39	1	1-41,D-24/O-2(0-0-2)	4	-1.2
Sea-A	29	47	9	11	2	1	1	4	4	9	1	1	.234	.294	.383	.677	81	-2	4	2.85	2	1-11/O-6(5-0-1),D-4,2-1	0	0.0
Yr.	101	284	48	66	12	1	5	31	37	38	9	6	.232	.323	.335	.657	74	-10	29	3.30	4	1-52,D-28/O-8(5-0-3),2-1	4	-1.2
Total 13	1488	5404	807	1483	235	69	53	502	732	866	171	99	.274	.363	.373	.736	94	-30	772	4.94	-46	S-607,2-591,1-238/D-62,O-9	149	-2.8

• OFFICE, Rowland Rowland Johnie Office b: 10/25/1952, Sacramento, CA BL/TL, 6', 170 lbs. Deb: 8/5/1972 Career OF: 7-687-80

YEAR TM-L	G	AB	R	H	2B	3B	HR	RBI	BB	SO	SB	CS	AVG	OBP	SLG	OPS	OPS+	BR/A	RC	RC/G	FR	G/POS	WS	TPW
1972 Atl-N	2	5	1	2	0	0	0	0	1	2	0	0	.400	.500	.400	.900	145	0	1	10.17	-0	/O-1	0	0.0
1974 Atl-N	131	248	20	61	16	1	3	31	16	30	5	3	.246	.292	.355	.647	77	-9	23	3.11	-6	*O-119(1-118-0)	4	-1.7
1975 Atl-N	126	355	30	103	14	1	3	30	23	41	2	2	.290	.339	.361	.699	91	-5	42	4.16	-5	*O-107(1-106-0)	9	-1.3
1976 Atl-N	99	359	51	101	17	1	4	34	37	49	2	8	.281	.352	.368	.719	98	-3	46	4.48	-4	O-92(0-92-0)	10	-1.0
1977 Atl-N	124	428	42	103	13	1	5	39	23	58	2	4	.241	.284	.311	.595	53	-30	36	2.84	1	*O-104(1-103-0)/1-1	3	-3.0
1978 Atl-N	146	404	40	101	13	1	9	40	22	52	8	6	.250	.299	.354	.653	73	-16	41	3.44	-6	*O-136(0-138-0)	8	-2.5
1979 Atl-N	124	277	35	69	14	2	2	37	27	33	5	4	.249	.320	.336	.656	74	-10	30	3.70	-9	O-97(0-97-0)	5	-2.1
1980 Mon-N	116	292	36	78	13	4	6	30	36	39	3	3	.267	.348	.401	.748	108	3	42	4.90	-6	O-97(3-27-68)	9	-0.7
1981 Mon-N	26	40	4	7	0	0	0	0	4	6	0	0	.175	.250	.175	.425	22	-4	2	1.27	-1	O-15(0-3-12)	0	-0.6
1982 Mon-N	3	3	0	1	1	0	0	0	0	1	0	0	.333	.333	.667	1.000	170	0	1	9.00	0	/O-1	0	0.0
1983 NY-A	2	2	0	0	0	0	0	0	1	0	0	0	.000	.000	.000	.000	-104	-1	0	.00	-0	/O-2(0-2-0)	0	-0.1
Total 11	899	2413	259	626	101	11	32	242	189	311	27	30	.259	.317	.350	.668	80	-73	264	3.73	-35	O-771/1-1	48	-12.8

• OGLESBY, Jim James Dorn Oglesby b: 8/10/1905, Schofield, MO d: 9/1/1955, Tulsa, OK BL/TL, 6', 190 lbs. Deb: 4/14/1936

YEAR TM-L	G	AB	R	H	2B	3B	HR	RBI	BB	SO	SB	CS	AVG	OBP	SLG	OPS	OPS+	BR/A	RC	RC/G	FR	G/POS	WS	TPW
1936 Phi-A	3	11	0	2	0	0	0	2	2	0	0	0	.182	.308	.182	.490	24	-1	1	2.19	0	/1-3	0	-0.1

• OGLIVIE, Ben Benjamin Ambrosio (Palmer) Oglivie b: 2/11/1949, Colon, Panama BL/TL, 6'2", 170 lbs. Deb: 9/4/1971 Career OF: 1098-15-357

YEAR TM-L	G	AB	R	H	2B	3B	HR	RBI	BB	SO	SB	CS	AVG	OBP	SLG	OPS	OPS+	BR/A	RC	RC/G	FR	G/POS	WS	TPW
1971 Bos-A	14	38	2	10	3	0	0	4	0	5	0	0	.263	.263	.342	.605	66	-2	3	3.30	0	O-11(10-0-1)	1	-0.2
1972 Bos-A	94	253	27	61	10	2	8	30	18	61	1	1	.241	.294	.391	.685	97	-2	29	3.91	0	O-65(32-0-33)	7	-0.5
1973 Bos-A	58	147	16	32	9	1	2	9	9	32	1	1	.218	.272	.333	.605	66	-7	13	2.77	-1	O-32(4-0-28),D-13	1	-1.0
1974 Det-A	92	252	28	68	11	3	4	29	34	38	12	3	.270	.357	.385	.742	109	6	36	5.05	0	O-63(61-0-2),1-10/D-4	9	0.2
1975 Det-A	100	332	45	95	14	1	9	36	16	62	11	8	.286	.323	.416	.739	103	-1	40	4.17	0	O-86(76-0-10)/1-5,D-2	7	-0.7
1976 Det-A	115	305	36	87	12	3	15	47	11	44	9	4	.285	.317	.492	.808	129	9	43	4.80	-0	O-64(16-12-36)/1-9,D-1	11	0.6
1977 Det-A	132	450	63	118	24	2	21	61	40	80	9	9	.262	.327	.464	.791	107	2	64	4.87	3	*O-118(0-0-118)/D-2	11	-0.1
1978 Mil-A	128	469	71	142	29	4	18	72	52	69	11	7	.303	.372	.497	.869	142	26	85	6.55	-3	O-89(65-0-25),D-27,1-11	19	1.8
1979 Mil-A	139	514	88	145	30	4	29	81	48	56	12	5	.282	.346	.525	.871	131	21	91	6.24	-3	*O-120(102-0-23),D-13/1-9	20	1.2
1980 Mil-A★	156	592	94	180	26	2	**41**	118	54	71	11	9	.304	.367	.563	.930	156	42	121	7.49	11	*O-152(150-1-2)/D-4	27	4.4
1981*Mil-A	107	400	53	97	15	2	14	72	37	49	2	2	.243	.316	.395	.711	110	4	49	4.11	-5	*O-101(99-2-0)/D-6	13	-0.6
1982*Mil-A★	159	602	92	147	22	1	34	102	70	81	3	5	.244	.327	.453	.780	119	14	90	5.22	6	*O-159(159-0-0)	21	1.2
1983 Mil-A★	125	411	49	115	19	3	13	66	60	64	4	6	.280	.377	.436	.812	133	19	67	5.71	-1	*O-113(113-0-0)/D-8	16	1.2
1984 Mil-A	131	461	49	121	16	2	12	60	44	56	0	6	.262	.328	.384	.712	100	-2	55	4.11	0	*O-125(113-0-23)/D-1	11	-0.8
1985 Mil-A	101	341	40	99	17	2	10	61	37	51	0	2	.290	.363	.440	.803	119	9	54	5.50	-2	O-91(48-0-54)/D-4	12	0.2
1986 Mil-A	103	346	31	98	20	1	5	53	30	33	1	2	.283	.340	.390	.731	95	-3	45	4.61	1	O-50(50-0-2),D-42	8	-0.5
Total 16	1754	5913	784	1615	277	33	235	901	560	852	87	70	.273	.340	.450	.790	119	134	886	5.22	7	*O-1439,D-127/1-44	194	6.3

• OGRODOWSKI, Bruce Ambrose Francis "Brusie" Ogrodowski b: 2/17/1912, Hoytville, PA d: 3/5/1956, San Francisco, CA BR/TR, 5'11", 175 lbs. Deb: 4/14/1936

YEAR TM-L	G	AB	R	H	2B	3B	HR	RBI	BB	SO	SB	CS	AVG	OBP	SLG	OPS	OPS+	BR/A	RC	RC/G	FR	G/POS	WS	TPW
1936 StL-N	94	237	28	54	15	1	1	20	10	20	0	....	.228	.259	.312	.571	53	-16	18	2.44	-1	C-85	3	-1.3
1937 StL-N	90	279	37	65	10	3	3	31	11	17	2	....	.233	.267	.323	.590	58	-17	22	2.54	-2	C-87	4	-1.3
Total 2	184	516	65	119	25	4	4	51	21	37	2	....	.231	.263	.318	.581	56	-33	39	2.50	-3	C-172	7	-2.6

• O'HAGEN, Hal Harry P. O'Hagen b: 9/30/1873, Washington, DC d: 1/14/1913, Newark, NJ, 6', 173 lbs. Deb: 9/24/1892

YEAR TM-L	G	AB	R	H	2B	3B	HR	RBI	BB	SO	SB	CS	AVG	OBP	SLG	OPS	OPS+	BR/A	RC	RC/G	FR	G/POS	WS	TPW
1892 Was-N	1	4	1	1	0	0	0	0	0	2	0	....	.250	.250	.250	.500	53	-0	0	2.31	1	/C-1	0	0.0
1902 Chi-N	33	115	11	22	1	3	0	10	11	....	9	....	.191	.262	.252	.514	60	-5	10	2.84	2	1-31	1	-0.4
NY-N	4	11	0	1	0	0	0	0	0	....	0	....	.091	.091	.091	.182	-44	-2	0	.25	0	/O-4(0-3-1)	0	-0.2

YEAR TM-L	G	AB	R	H	2B	3B	HR	RBI	BB	SO	SB	CS	AVG	OBP	SLG	OPS	OPS+	BR/A	RC	RC/G	FR	G/POS	WS	TPW
Cle-A	3	13	2	5	2	0	0	1	0	....	2	....	.385	.385	.538	.923	160	1	4	11.75	1	/1-3	1	0.2
NY-N	22	73	5	11	2	1	0	8	2	....	3	....	.151	.195	.205	.400	24	-7	4	1.58	1	1-18/0-4(0-0-4)	1	-0.7
Yr.	59	199	16	34	3	4	0	18	13	....	12	....	.171	.229	.226	.455	42	-14	14	2.21	3	1-49/0-8(0-3-5)	2	-1.3
Total 2	**63**	**216**	**19**	**40**	**5**	**4**	**0**	**19**	**13**	**2**	**14**	**....**	**.185**	**.238**	**.245**	**.483**	**49**	**-13**	**18**	**2.63**	**4**	**/1-52,0-8,C-1**	**3**	**-1.1**
• O'HALLORAN, Greg	Gregory Joseph O'Halloran b: 5/21/1968, Toronto, Canada BL/TR, 6'2", 205 lbs. Deb: 5/16/1994																							
1994 Fla-N	12	11	1	2	0	0	0	1	0	1	0	0	.182	.182	.182	.364	-5	-2	0	1.13	0	/C-1	0	-0.2
• O'HARA, Bill	William Alexander O'Hara b: 8/14/1883, Toronto, Canada d: 6/13/1931, Jersey City, NJ BL/TR, 5'10", 165 lbs. Deb: 4/15/1909 Career OF: 11-93-11																							
1909 NY-N	115	360	48	85	9	3	1	30	41	....	31	....	.236	.318	.286	.604	86	-5	42	3.86	7	*0-111(11-89-11)	10	-0.4
1910 StL-N	9	20	1	3	0	0	0	2	1	3	0	....	.150	.190	.150	.340		-3	1	.98	0	/0-4(0-4-0),1-1,P-1	0	-0.2
Total 2	**124**	**380**	**49**	**88**	**9**	**3**	**1**	**32**	**42**	**3**	**31**	**....**	**.232**	**.311**	**.279**	**.590**	**82**	**-7**	**43**	**3.68**	**7**	**0-115/1-1,P-1**	**10**	**-0.6**
• O'HARA, Kid	James Francis O'Hara b: 12/19/1875, Wilkes-Barre, PA d: 12/1/1954, Canton, OH BB/TR, 5'7.5", 152 lbs. Deb: 9/15/1904																							
1904 Bos-N	8	29	3	6	0	0	0	0	4	....	1	....	.207	.303	.207	.510	60	-1	2	2.46	-0	/0-8(0-0-8)	0	-0.2
• O'HARA, Tom	Thomas F. O'Hara b: 7/13/1885, Waverly, NY d: 6/8/1954, Denver, CO Deb: 9/19/1906 Career OF: 38-0-23																							
1906 StL-N	14	53	8	16	1	0	0	0	3	....	3	....	.302	.339	.321	.660	110	1	7	4.85	-2	0-14(14-0-0)	1	-0.2
1907 StL-N	48	173	11	41	2	1	0	5	12	....	1	....	.237	.286	.260	.547	74	-5	14	2.69	1	0-47(24-0-23)	2	-0.7
Total 2	**62**	**226**	**19**	**57**	**3**	**1**	**0**	**5**	**15**	**....**	**4**	**....**	**.252**	**.299**	**.274**	**.573**	**82**	**-5**	**21**	**3.16**	**0**	**/0-61**	**3**	**-0.9**
• OJEDA, Augie	Octavio Augie Ojeda b: 12/20/1974, Los Angeles, CA BB/TR, 5'9", 165 lbs. Deb: 6/4/2000																							
2000 Chi-N	28	77	10	17	3	1	2	8	10	9	0	1	.221	.310	.364	.674	71	-4	9	3.72	0	S-25/2-4	2	-0.2
2001 Chi-N	78	144	16	29	5	1	1	12	12	20	1	0	.201	.272	.271	.543	43	-12	11	2.54	2	3-35,S-31,2-10	2	-0.7
2002 Chi-N	30	70	4	13	4	0	0	4	5	5	1	0	.186	.250	.243	.493	31	-7	5	1.92	0	S-16,2-10/3-5	1	-0.5
2003 Chi-N	12	25	2	3	0	0	0	0	1	5	0	0	.120	.185	.120	.305	-18	-4	0	.57	-1	/S-7,2-5,3-1	2	-0.5
Total 4	**148**	**316**	**32**	**62**	**12**	**2**	**3**	**24**	**28**	**39**	**2**	**1**	**.196**	**.270**	**.275**	**.545**	**43**	**-27**	**25**	**2.50**	**2**	**/S-79,3-41,2-29**	**7**	**-1.9**
• OJEDA, Miguel	Miguel Arturo Ojeda b: 1/29/1975, Sonora, Mexico BR/TR, 6'2", 190 lbs. Deb: 5/17/2003																							
2003 SD-N	61	141	13	33	6	0	4	22	18	26	1	1	.234	.333	.362	.695	89	-2	18	4.30	3	C-48/1-2	4	0.3
• OKRIE, Len	Leonard Joseph Okrie b: 7/16/1923, Detroit, MI BR/TR, 6', 185 lbs. Deb: 6/16/1948 C																							
1948 Was-A	19	42	1	10	0	1	0	1	1	7	0	0	.238	.256	.286	.542	45	-3	2	1.80	1	C-17	1	-0.2
1950 Was-A	17	27	1	6	0	0	0	2	6	7	0	0	.222	.382	.222	.605	61	-1	3	3.92	1	C-17	1	0.0
1951 Was-A	5	8	1	1	1	0	0	0	2	1	0	0	.125	.300	.250	.550	51	-0	1	2.84	-1	/C-5	0	-0.1
1952 Bos-A	1	1	0	0	0	0	0	0	0	1	0	0	.000	.000	.000	.000	-93	-0	0	.00	0	/C-1	0	0.0
Total 4	**42**	**78**	**3**	**17**	**1**	**1**	**0**	**3**	**9**	**16**	**0**	**0**	**.218**	**.307**	**.256**	**.563**	**50**	**-5**	**6**	**2.59**	**1**	**/C-40**	**2**	**-0.3**
• OLANDER, Jim	James Bentley Olander b: 2/21/1963, Tucson, AZ BR/TR, 6'2", 185 lbs. Deb: 9/20/1991																							
1991 Mil-A	12	9	2	0	0	0	0	0	2	5	0	0	.000	.182	.000	.182	-46	-2	0	.28	0	/0-9(2-5-1),D-2	0	-0.2
• OLDFIELD, Dave	David Oldfield b: 12/18/1864, Philadelphia, PA d: 8/28/1939, Philadelphia, PA BB/TL, 5'7", 175 lbs. Deb: 6/28/1883 Career OF: 0-4-8																							
1883 Bal-a	1	4	0	0	0	0	0	0	0	....	....	....	.000	.000	.000	.000	-97	-1	0	.00	-1	/C-1	0	-0.2
1885 Bro-a	10	25	2	8	1	0	0	2	3	....	....	....	.320	.414	.360	.774	145	2	4	6.06	-2	/C-9,0-2(0-1-1)	2	0.0
1886 Bro-a	14	55	7	13	1	0	0	5	2	....	1	....	.236	.263	.255	.518	62	-3	4	2.60	-3	C-13/0-1,S-1	1	-0.4
Was-N	21	71	2	10	2	0	0	2	5	15	0	....	.141	.197	.169	.366	13	-7	2	1.07	0	C-12/0-9(0-3-6)	0	-0.6
Total 3	**46**	**155**	**11**	**31**	**4**	**0**	**0**	**9**	**10**	**15**	**1**	**....**	**.200**	**.253**	**.226**	**.479**	**50**	**-9**	**10**	**2.24**	**-7**	**/C-35,0-12,S-1**	**3**	**-1.1**
• OLDHAM, John	John Hardin Oldham b: 11/6/1932, Salinas, CA BR/TL, 6'3", 198 lbs. Deb: 9/2/1956																							
1956 Cin-N	1	0	0	0	0	0	0	0	0	0	0	0	....	....	....	....	-94	0	0	....	0	....	0	0.0
• OLDIS, Bob	Robert Carl Oldis b: 1/5/1928, Preston, IA BR/TR, 6'1", 185 lbs. Deb: 4/28/1953 C																							
1953 Was-A	7	16	0	4	0	0	0	3	1	2	0	0	.250	.294	.250	.544	49	-1	1	2.13	0	/C-7	0	0.0
1954 Was-A	11	24	1	8	1	0	0	0	1	3	0	0	.333	.360	.375	.735	107	0	3	5.38	-2	/C-8,3-2	1	-0.2
1955 Was-A	6	6	1	0	0	0	0	0	1	0	0	0	.000	.143	.000	.143	-62	-1	0	.00	-0	/C-6	0	-0.1
1960*Pit-N	22	20	1	4	1	0	0	1	1	2	0	0	.200	.238	.250	.488	34	-2	1	2.11	-1	C-22	0	-0.2
1961 Pit-N	4	5	0	0	0	0	0	0	0	0	0	0	.000	.000	.000	.000	-100	-1	0	.00	1	/C-4	0	0.0
1962 Phi-N	38	80	9	21	1	0	1	10	13	10	0	1	.263	.366	.313	.678	86	-1	10	4.02	1	C-30	3	0.1
1963 Phi-N	47	85	8	19	3	0	0	8	3	5	0	0	.224	.250	.259	.509	47	-6	5	2.03	0	C-43	1	-0.5
Total 7	**135**	**236**	**20**	**56**	**6**	**0**	**1**	**22**	**20**	**22**	**0**	**1**	**.237**	**.297**	**.275**	**.572**	**60**	**-13**	**21**	**2.85**	**-1**	**C-120/3-2**	**5**	**-1.0**
• OLDRING, Rube	Reuben Henry Oldring b: 5/30/1884, New York, NY d: 9/9/1961, Bridgeton, NJ BR/TR, 5'10", 186 lbs. Deb: 10/2/1905 Career OF: 455-626-48																							
1905 NY-A	8	30	2	9	0	1	1	6	2	....	4	....	.300	.344	.467	.810	140	1	6	7.71	6	/S-8	3	0.9
1906 Phi-A	59	174	15	42	10	1	0	19	2	....	7	....	.241	.263	.310	.573	77	-5	17	3.29	-1	3-49/S-3,2-2,1-1	4	-0.6
1907 Phi-A	117	441	48	126	27	8	1	40	7	....	29	....	.286	.305	.390	.695	118	6	63	5.22	-8	*0-117(0-116-1)	17	-0.8
1908 Phi-A	116	434	38	96	14	2	1	39	18	....	13	....	.221	.267	.270	.536	70	-15	35	2.56	-8	*0-116(21-95-0)	7	-3.3
1909 Phi-A	90	326	39	75	13	8	1	28	20	....	17	....	.230	.287	.328	.615	92	-4	36	3.48	0	0-89(32-56-1)/1-1	9	-0.9
1910 Phi-A	134	546	79	168	27	14	4	57	23	....	17	....	.308	.340	.430	.771	142	23	85	5.53	-6	*0-134(1-130-3)	25	1.2
1911*Phi-A	121	495	84	147	11	14	3	59	21	....	21	....	.297	.332	.394	.726	104	0	72	4.99	-11	*0-119(0-119-0)	16	-1.7
1912 Phi-A	99	395	61	119	14	5	1	24	10	....	17	....	.301	.324	.370	.693	102	-1	53	4.65	-5	0-98(11-86-0)	11	-1.2
1913*Phi-A	137	538	101	152	27	9	5	71	34	37	40	....	.283	.328	.394	.722	113	6	78	4.94	-2	*0-131(131-0-0)/S-5	19	0.0
1914*Phi-A	119	466	68	129	21	7	3	49	18	35	14	16	.277	.308	.371	.679	108	-3	53	3.80	-6	*0-117(105-11-1)	13	-1.5
1915 Phi-A	107	408	49	101	23	3	6	42	22	21	11	6	.248	.293	.363	.655	100	-4	45	3.71	4	0-96(88-8-0)/3-8	10	-0.4
1916 Phi-A	40	146	10	36	8	3	0	14	9	9	1	....	.247	.290	.342	.633	95	-2	15	3.50	-2	0-40(40-0-0)	2	-0.6
NY-A	43	158	17	37	8	0	1	12	12	13	6	....	.234	.288	.304	.592	76	-5	16	3.30	-3	0-43(0-2-41)	3	-1.2
Yr.	83	304	27	73	16	3	1	26	21	22	7	....	.240	.289	.322	.612	85	-7	31	3.40	-5	0-83(40-2-41)	5	-1.8
1918 Phi-A	49	133	5	31	2	1	0	11	8	10	0	....	.233	.282	.263	.545	64	-6	10	2.39	-4	0-30(26-3-1)/2-2,3-2	1	-1.3
Total 13	**1239**	**4690**	**616**	**1268**	**205**	**76**	**27**	**471**	**206**	**125**	**197**	**22**	**.270**	**.307**	**.364**	**.671**	**104**	**-8**	**583**	**4.22**	**-45**	***0-1130/3-59,S-16,2-4,1-2**	**140**	**-11.3**
• O'LEARY, Charley	Charles Timothy O'Leary b: 10/15/1882, Chicago, IL d: 1/6/1941, Chicago, IL BR/TR, 5'7", 165 lbs. Deb: 4/14/1904 C																							
1904 Det-A	135	456	39	97	10	3	1	16	21	....	9	....	.213	.254	.254	.508	63	-19	35	2.43	2	*S-135	7	-1.5
1905 Det-A	148	512	47	109	13	1	0	33	29	....	13	....	.213	.259	.242	.501	59	-24	40	2.45	-4	*S-148	7	-2.6
1906 Det-A	128	443	34	97	13	2	2	34	17	....	8	....	.219	.253	.271	.524	62	-20	36	2.57	-10	*S-127	6	-2.9
1907*Det-A	139	465	61	112	19	1	0	34	32	....	11	....	.241	.298	.286	.584	83	-8	46	3.31	8	*S-138	16	0.5
1908*Det-A	65	211	21	53	9	3	0	17	9	....	4	....	.251	.295	.322	.617	96	-1	21	3.33	-13	S-64/2-1	7	-1.4
1909*Det-A	76	261	29	53	10	0	0	13	6	....	9	....	.203	.224	.241	.465	45	-17	16	1.91	-1	3-54,2-15/S-4,0-2(1-0-1)	3	-1.9
1910 Det-A	65	211	23	51	7	1	0	9	9	....	7	....	.242	.276	.284	.560	71	-8	19	2.86	0	2-38,S-18/3-6	3	-0.8
1911 Det-A	74	256	29	68	8	2	0	25	21	....	10	....	.266	.336	.313	.648	77	-7	32	3.98	8	2-67/3-6	6	0.2
1912 Det-A	3	10	1	2	0	0	0	1	0	....	0	....	.200	.200	.200	.400	15	-1	0	1.20	1	/2-3	0	0.0
1913 StL-N	121	406	32	88	15	5	0	31	20	34	3	....	.217	.260	.278	.539	55	-25	30	2.29	-16	*S-103,2-15	3	-3.5
1934 StL-A	1	1	1	1	0	0	0	0	0	0	0	0	1.000	1.000	1.000	2.000	385	0	1	∞	0	....	0	0.0
Total 11	**955**	**3232**	**317**	**731**	**104**	**18**	**3**	**213**	**164**	**34**	**74**	**0**	**.226**	**.270**	**.272**	**.543**	**67**	**-131**	**276**	**2.72**	**-27**	**S-737,2-139/3-66,0-2**	**58**	**-13.8**
• O'LEARY, Dan	Daniel "Hustling Dan" O'Leary b: 10/22/1856, Detroit, MI d: 6/24/1922, Chicago, IL BL, 5'10", 165 lbs. Deb: 9/3/1879 M Career OF: 22-18-5																							
1879 Pro-N	2	7	1	3	0	0	0	2	0	0	....	....	.429	.429	.429	.857	187	1	1	9.23	0	/0-2(0-0-2)	0	0.0
1880 Bos-N	3	12	1	3	2	0	0	1	0	3	....	....	.250	.250	.417	.667	125	0	1	3.91	0	/0-3(0-0-3)	1	0.0
1881 Det-N	2	8	0	0	0	0	0	0	0	2	....	....	.000	.000	.000	.000	-96	-2	0	.00	-1	/0-2(0-2-0)	0	-0.2
1882 Wor-N	6	22	2	4	1	0	0	2	5	5	....	....	.182	.333	.227	.561	82	-0	2	2.61	-2	/0-6(0-6-0)	0	-0.2
1884 Cin-U	32	132	14	34	0	2	1	....	5	....	....	....	.258	.285	.311	.595	94	-1	12	3.42	0	0-32(22-10-0)	4	-0.2
Total 5	**45**	**181**	**18**	**44**	**3**	**2**	**1**	**5**	**10**	**10**	**....**	**....**	**.243**	**.283**	**.298**	**.581**	**89**	**-2**	**16**	**3.31**	**-3**	**/0-45**	**5**	**-0.6**

YEAR TM-L	G	AB	R	H	2B	3B	HR	RBI	BB	SO	SB	CS	AVG	OBP	SLG	OPS	OPS+	BR/A	RC	RC/G	FR	G/POS	WS	TPW
• O'LEARY, Troy	Troy Franklin O'Leary b: 8/4/1969, Compton, CA BL/TL, 6', 196 lbs. Deb: 5/9/1993 Career OF: 732-30-403																							
1993 Mil-A	19	41	3	12	3	0	0	3	5	9	0	0	.293	.370	.366	.735	100	0	6	4.77	0	0-19(15-0-5)	1	0.0
1994 Mil-A	27	66	9	18	1	1	2	7	5	12	1	1	.273	.333	.409	.742	86	-2	9	5.04	2	0-21(13-0-10)/D-1	1	-0.1
1995 Bos-A	112	399	60	123	31	6	10	49	29	64	5	3	.308	.357	.491	.848	114	7	68	6.29	1	*0-105(16-13-91)/D-3	12	0.3
1996 Bos-A	149	497	68	129	28	5	15	81	47	80	3	2	.260	.328	.427	.755	87	-11	68	4.76	-4	*0-146(66-17-110)	12	-1.9
1997 Bos-A	146	499	65	154	32	4	15	80	39	70	0	5	.309	.361	.479	.840	115	8	81	5.97	-2	*0-142(24-0-119)/D-1	15	-0.2
1998*Bos-A	156	611	95	165	36	8	23	83	36	108	2	2	.270	.316	.468	.784	98	-5	85	4.90	-1	*0-155(155-0-0)	14	-1.1
1999*Bos-A	157	596	84	167	36	4	28	103	56	91	1	2	.280	.346	.495	.841	108	5	96	5.70	-1	*0-157(157-0-2)	19	-0.3
2000 Bos-A	138	513	68	134	30	4	13	70	44	76	0	2	.261	.322	.411	.733	81	-16	66	4.50	-3	*0-137(137-0-0)	11	-2.3
2001 Bos-A	104	341	50	82	16	6	13	50	25	73	1	3	.240	.302	.437	.739	91	-7	42	4.15	-1	0-89(52-0-41)/D-4	6	-1.2
2002 Mon-N	97	273	27	78	12	2	3	37	34	47	1	2	.286	.371	.377	.748	94	-2	39	5.06	1	0-70(69-0-1)/D-3	8	-0.4
2003*Chi-N	93	174	18	38	9	0	5	28	14	31	3	0	.218	.280	.356	.637	66	-9	16	2.93	1	0-51(28-0-24)	0	-0.9
Total 11	1198	4010	547	1100	234	40	127	591	334	661	17	22	.274	.334	.448	.782	97	-31	578	5.06	-7	*0-1092/D-12	99	-8.0
• OLERUD, John	John Garrett Olerud b: 8/5/1968, Seattle, WA BL/TL, 6'5", 220 lbs. Deb: 9/3/1989																							
1989 Tor-A	6	8	2	3	0	0	0	0	0	1	0	0	.375	.375	.375	.750	119	0	1	6.08	0	/1-5,D-1	0	0.0
1990 Tor-A	111	358	43	95	15	1	14	48	57	75	0	2	.265	.368	.430	.798	116	8	59	5.79	-1	D-90,1-18	11	0.4
1991*Tor-A	139	454	64	116	30	1	17	68	68	84	0	2	.256	.360	.438	.798	115	10	72	5.36	4	*1-135/D-1	13	0.5
1992*Tor-A	138	458	68	130	28	0	16	66	70	61	1	0	.284	.380	.450	.830	126	18	78	6.03	6	*1-133/D-1	16	1.6
1993*Tor-A★	158	551	109	200	**54**	2	24	107	114	65	0	2	**.363**	**.478**	.599	**1.077**	**186**	**74**	161	**11.70**	4	*1-137,D-20	**37**	**6.3**
1994 Tor-A	108	384	47	114	29	2	12	67	61	53	1	2	.297	.397	.477	.874	124	15	73	6.82	7	*1-104/D-3	14	1.2
1995 Tor-A	135	492	72	143	32	0	8	54	84	54	0	0	.291	.398	.404	.803	110	11	81	5.96	3	*1-133	11	0.2
1996 Tor-A	125	398	59	109	25	0	18	61	60	37	1	0	.274	.382	.472	.855	115	11	74	6.67	-2	*1-101,D-15	10	0.0
1997 NY-N	154	524	90	154	34	1	22	102	85	67	0	0	.294	.405	.489	.894	138	32	105	7.15	5	*1-146	27	2.4
1998 NY-N	160	557	91	197	36	4	22	93	96	73	2	2	.354	.452	.551	1.003	165	57	141	9.90	10	*1-157	34	5.3
1999*NY-N	162	581	107	173	39	0	19	96	125	66	3	0	.298	.431	.463	.894	130	35	122	7.56	7	*1-160	26	2.6
2000*Sea-A	159	565	84	161	45	0	14	103	102	96	0	2	.285	.398	.439	.837	118	19	101	6.29	14	*1-158	22	1.7
2001*Sea-A★	159	572	91	173	32	1	21	95	94	70	3	1	.302	.405	.472	.877	138	36	109	6.87	8	*1-158	21	2.9
2002 Sea-A	154	553	85	166	39	0	22	102	98	66	0	0	.300	.410	.490	.900	143	39	113	7.31	5	*1-152/D-2	27	2.9
2003 Sea-A	152	539	64	145	35	0	10	83	84	67	0	1	.269	.374	.390	.763	105	7	79	5.08	10	*1-152	15	0.4
Total 15	2020	6994	1076	2079	473	12	239	1145	1198	935	11	14	.297	.406	.471	.877	132	374	1371	7.06	80	*1-1849,D-133	284	28.2
• OLIN, Frank	Franklin Walter Olin b: 1/9/1860, Woodford, VT d: 5/20/1951, St. Louis, MO BL Deb: 7/4/1884																							
1884 Was-a	21	83	12	32	4	1	0	0	7	....	....	....	.386	.433	.458	.891	216	11	17	9.10	-6	2-12,0-11(1-7-3)	5	0.5
Was-U	1	4	0	0	0	0	0	....	0	....	....	....	.000	.000	.000	.000	-103	-1	0	.00	0	/0-1	0	-0.1
Tol-a	26	86	16	22	0	1	1	0	5	....	....	....	.256	.304	.314	.618	99	-0	8	3.62	2	0-26(26-0-0)	2	0.1
Yr.	47	169	28	54	4	2	1	0	12	....	....	....	.320	.368	.385	.753	156	11	25	6.05	-4	0-37(27-7-3),2-12	7	0.5
1885 Det-N	1	4	1	2	0	0	0	0	0	0	....	....	.500	.500	.500	1.000	224	1	1	13.84	0	/3-1	0	0.0
Total 2	49	177	29	56	4	2	1	0	12	0	....	....	.316	.363	.379	.742	152	10	26	5.98	-5	/0-38,2-12,3-1	7	0.5
• OLIVA, Jose	Jose (Galvez) Oliva b: 3/3/1971, San Pedro de Macoris, Dominican Republic d: 12/22/1997, San Cristobal, Dominican Republic BR/TR, 6'3", 150 lbs. Deb: 7/1/1994																							
1994 Atl-N	19	59	9	17	5	0	6	11	7	10	0	1	.288	.364	.678	1.042	160	4	13	7.98	1	3-16	3	0.6
1995 Atl-N	48	109	7	17	4	0	5	12	7	22	0	0	.156	.207	.330	.537	38	-11	7	2.06	-1	3-25/1-1	1	-1.1
StL-N	22	74	8	9	1	0	2	8	5	24	0	0	.122	.198	.216	.414	9	-10	3	1.14	0	3-18/1-2	0	-0.9
Yr.	70	183	15	26	5	0	7	20	12	46	0	0	.142	.203	.284	.487	26	-21	10	1.67	-1	3-43/1-3	1	-2.0
Total 2	89	242	24	43	10	0	13	31	19	56	0	1	.178	.243	.380	.624	59	-16	23	3.04	1	/3-59,1-3	4	-1.5
• OLIVA, Tony	Pedro (Lopez) Oliva b: 7/20/1940, Pinar del Rio, Cuba BL/TR, 6'1", 190 lbs. Deb: 9/9/1962 C Career OF: 10-39-1139																							
1962 Min-A	9	9	3	4	1	0	0	3	3	2	0	0	.444	.583	.556	1.139	201	2	3	18.21	0	/0-2(0-0-2)	1	0.2
1963 Min-A	7	7	0	3	0	0	0	1	0	2	0	0	.429	.429	.429	.857	138	0	1	8.68	0	....	0	0.0
1964 Min-A★	161	672	**109**	**217**	**43**	9	32	94	34	68	12	6	**.323**	.361	.557	.918	150	42	132	7.49	-0	*0-159(2-9-154)	27	3.2
1965*Min-A★	149	576	107	**185**	40	5	16	98	55	64	19	9	**.321**	.384	.491	.876	141	31	109	7.02	6	*0-147(0-8-143)	**33**	2.9
1966 Min-A★	159	622	99	**191**	32	7	25	87	42	72	13	7	.307	.356	.502	.857	135	27	106	6.17	5	*0-159(0-19-140)	28	2.3
1967 Min-A★	146	557	76	161	**34**	6	17	83	44	61	11	3	.289	.350	.463	.813	128	21	91	5.91	4	*0-146(0-0-146)	25	1.5
1968 Min-A★	128	470	54	136	24	5	18	68	45	61	10	9	.289	.360	.477	.837	145	24	77	5.82	4	*0-126(0-0-126)	21	2.2
1969*Min-A★	153	637	97	**197**	**39**	4	24	101	45	66	10	13	.309	.358	.496	.854	134	23	107	6.16	8	*0-152(0-0-152)	25	2.4
1970*Min-A★	157	628	96	**204**	**36**	7	23	107	38	67	5	4	.325	.366	.514	.881	138	30	112	6.74	9	*0-157(0-3-154)	30	3.2
1971 Min-A★	126	487	73	164	30	3	22	81	25	44	4	1	**.337**	.372	**.546**	.918	152	31	90	6.94	-3	*0-121(0-0-121)	23	2.5
1972 Min-A	10	28	1	9	1	0	0	1	2	5	0	0	.321	.367	.357	.724	110	0	4	4.73	0	/0-9(8-0-1)	1	0.0
1973 Min-A	146	571	63	166	20	0	16	92	45	44	2	1	.291	.347	.410	.757	108	6	79	5.06	0	*D-142	13	0.1
1974 Min-A	127	459	43	131	16	2	13	57	27	31	0	1	.285	.328	.414	.742	108	4	58	4.49	0	*D-112	9	0.0
1975 Min-A	131	455	46	123	10	0	13	58	41	45	0	1	.270	.348	.378	.726	103	3	60	4.62	0	*D-120	9	-0.1
1976 Min-A	67	123	3	26	3	0	1	16	2	13	0	0	.211	.236	.260	.496	44	-9	7	1.97	0	D-32	0	-1.0
Total 15	1676	6301	870	1917	329	48	220	947	448	645	86	55	.304	.356	.476	.832	130	234	1036	6.02	34	*0-1178,D-406	245	19.5
• OLIVARES, Ed	Edward (Balzac) Olivares b: 11/5/1938, Mayaguez, Puerto Rico BR/TR, 5'11", 180 lbs. Deb: 9/16/1960																							
1960 StL-N	3	5	0	0	0	0	0	0	0	3	0	0	.000	.000	.000	.000	-92	-1	0	.00	0	/3-1	0	-0.2
1961 StL-N	21	30	2	5	0	0	0	1	0	4	1	0	.167	.167	.167	.333	-10	-5	1	.78	0	0-10(5-0-5)	0	-0.5
Total 2	24	35	2	5	0	0	0	1	0	7	1	0	.143	.143	.143	.286	-22	-6	1	.66	0	/0-10,3-1	0	-0.7
• OLIVER, Al	Albert Oliver b: 10/14/1946, Portsmouth, OH BL/TL, 6', 195 lbs. Deb: 9/23/1968 Career OF: 481-835-80																							
1968 Pit-N	4	8	1	1	0	0	0	0	0	4	0	0	.125	.125	.125	.250	-25	-1	0	.48	0	/0-1	0	-0.1
1969 Pit-N	129	463	55	132	19	2	17	70	21	38	8	5	.285	.334	.445	.779	119	10	62	4.69	-4	*1-106,0-21(13-0-8)	13	-0.3
1970*Pit-N	151	551	63	149	33	5	12	83	35	35	1	1	.270	.330	.414	.744	101	-1	75	4.79	-1	0-80(28-0-54),1-77	15	-1.1
1971*Pit-N	143	529	69	149	31	7	14	64	27	72	4	3	.282	.323	.446	.769	115	8	72	4.76	-1	*0-116(0-116-0),1-25	18	0.2
1972*Pit-N★	140	565	88	176	27	4	12	89	34	44	2	4	.312	.356	.437	.793	127	17	85	5.51	-5	*0-138(0-138-0)/1-3	23	0.9
1973 Pit-N	158	654	90	191	38	7	20	99	22	52	6	0	.292	.320	.463	.783	118	13	92	5.07	-7	*0-109(0-109-0),1-50	22	-0.1
1974*Pit-N	147	617	96	198	38	12	11	85	33	58	10	1	.321	.360	.475	.835	137	29	101	6.12	-3	0-98(0-98-0),1-49	26	2.0
1975*Pit-N★	155	628	90	176	39	8	18	84	25	73	4	2	.280	.313	.454	.767	112	5	83	4.65	-4	*0-153(0-153-0)/1-4	21	-0.3
1976 Pit-N★	121	443	62	143	22	5	12	61	26	29	6	2	.323	.367	.476	.843	137	20	74	6.21	0	*0-106(0-106-0)/1-3	22	1.9
1977 Pit-N	154	568	75	175	29	6	19	82	40	38	13	16	.308	.358	.481	.838	119	10	91	5.70	-4	*0-148(128-36-0)	21	0.0
1978 Tex-A	133	525	65	170	35	5	14	89	31	41	8	9	.324	.364	.490	.853	138	22	90	6.38	3	*0-107(100-8-0),D-26	22	1.9
1979 Tex-A	136	492	69	159	28	4	12	76	34	34	4	5	.323	.372	.470	.841	127	17	81	6.08	1	*0-119(49-71-0),D-10	18	1.3
1980 Tex-A★	163	656	96	209	43	3	19	117	39	47	5	7	.319	.361	.480	.842	132	25	108	6.14	-3	*0-157(141-0-16)/D-4,1-1	21	1.5
1981 Tex-A★	102	421	53	130	29	1	4	55	24	28	3	0	.309	.349	.411	.760	125	13	56	4.86	0	*D-101/1-1	13	1.0
1982 Mon-N★	160	617	90	**204**	**43**	2	22	**109**	61	59	5	2	**.331**	.394	.514	.908	149	41	125	7.82	-6	*1-159	26	2.7
1983 Mon-N★	157	614	70	184	**38**	3	8	84	44	44	1	3	.300	.348	.410	.759	110	6	81	4.79	4	*1-153/0-1	14	0.1
1984 SF-N	91	339	27	101	19	2	0	34	20	27	2	2	.298	.339	.366	.705	101	-1	36	3.79	0	1-82	6	-0.6
Phi-N	28	93	9	29	7	0	0	14	7	9	1	2	.312	.360	.387	.747	108	0	11	4.38	-2	1-19/0-5(5-0-0)	2	-0.3
Yr.	119	432	36	130	26	2	0	48	27	36	3	4	.301	.343	.370	.714	103	-0	48	3.91	-2	*1-101/0-5(5-0-0)	8	-0.8
1985 LA-N	35	79	1	20	5	0	0	8	5	11	1	0	.253	.298	.316	.614	74	-3	7	3.03	1	0-17(17-0-0)	1	-0.3
*Tor-A	61	187	20	47	6	1	5	23	7	13	0	0	.251	.282	.374	.656	76	-7	17	3.15	0	D-59/1-1	1	-0.8
Total 18	2368	9049	1189	2743	529	77	219	1326	535	756	84	64	.303	.348	.451	.799	122	225	1348	5.40	-32	*0-1376,1-733,D-200	305	9.5
• OLIVER, Bob	Robert Lee Oliver b: 2/8/1943, Shreveport, LA BR/TR, 6'3", 215 lbs. Deb: 9/10/1965 Career OF: 15-48-165																							
1965 Pit-N	3	2	1	0	0	0	0	0	0	0	0	0	.000	.000	.000	.000	-100	-1	0	.00	-0	/0-3(3-0-0)	0	-0.1
1969 KC-A	118	394	43	100	8	4	13	43	21	74	5	5	.254	.295	.393	.688	90	-8	39	3.27	2	0-98(9-48-45),1-12/3-8	8	-1.0
1970 KC-A	160	612	83	159	24	6	27	99	42	126	3	3	.260	.311	.451	.761	107	3	82	4.63	-4	*1-115,3-46	16	-1.1
1971 KC-A	128	373	35	91	12	2	8	52	14	88	0	0	.244	.281	.351	.632	79	-12	34	3.02	-2	1-68,0-48(1-0-47)/3-2	5	-2.2

YEAR TM-L	G	AB	R	H	2B	3B	HR	RBI	BB	SO	SB	CS	AVG	OBP	SLG	OPS	OPS+	BR/A	RC	RC/G	FR	G/POS	WS	TPW
1972 KC-A	16	63	7	17	2	1	1	6	2	12	1	0	.270	.292	.381	.673	100	-0	7	3.68	2	0-16(0-0-16)	2	0.2
Cal-A	134	509	47	137	20	4	19	70	27	97	4	3	.269	.310	.436	.746	127	14	64	4.35	-6	*1-127/0-8(1-0-7)	21	-0.3
Yr.	150	572	54	154	22	5	20	76	29	109	5	3	.269	.308	.430	.738	124	13	70	4.28	-4	*1-127,0-24(1-0-23)	23	-0.1
1973 Cal-A	151	544	51	144	24	1	18	89	33	100	1	1	.265	.313	.412	.724	111	6	66	4.27	0	3-49,0-47(0-0-47),1-32,D-12	16	0.1
1974 Cal-A	110	359	22	89	9	1	8	55	16	51	2	1	.248	.282	.345	.627	84	-8	29	2.63	-10	1-57,3-46/0-4(1-0-3),D-1	3	-2.3
Bal-A	9	20	1	3	2	0	0	4	0	5	1	1	.150	.150	.250	.400	14	-3	1	.83	1	/1-4,D-1	0	-0.2
Yr.	119	379	23	92	11	1	8	59	16	56	3	2	.243	.275	.340	.616	81	-11	30	2.53	-9	1-61,3-46/0-4(1-0-3),D-2	3	-2.5
1975 NY-A	18	38	3	5	1	0	0	1	1	9	0	0	.132	.154	.158	.312	-12	-6	1	.50	0	/1-8,D-3,3-1	0	-0.6
Total 8	**847**	**2914**	**293**	**745**	**102**	**19**	**94**	**419**	**156**	**562**	**17**	**14**	**.256**	**.298**	**.400**	**.698**	**100**	**-14**	**322**	**3.75**	**-16**	**1-423,0-224,3-152/D-17**	**71**	**-7.6**

• OLIVER, Dave David Jacob Oliver b: 4/7/1951, Stockton, CA BL/TR, 5'11", 175 lbs. Deb: 9/25/1977 C

YEAR TM-L	G	AB	R	H	2B	3B	HR	RBI	BB	SO	SB	CS	AVG	OBP	SLG	OPS	OPS+	BR/A	RC	RC/G	FR	G/POS	WS	TPW
1977 Cle-A	7	22	2	7	0	1	0	3	4	0	0	0	.318	.444	.409	.854	139	2	5	7.45	0	/2-7	1	0.2

• OLIVER, Gene Eugene George Oliver b: 3/22/1935, Moline, IL BR/TR, 6'2", 225 lbs. Deb: 6/6/1959 Career OF: 87-0-6

YEAR TM-L	G	AB	R	H	2B	3B	HR	RBI	BB	SO	SB	CS	AVG	OBP	SLG	OPS	OPS+	BR/A	RC	RC/G	FR	G/POS	WS	TPW
1959 StL-N	68	172	14	42	9	0	6	28	7	41	3	2	.244	.274	.401	.675	72	-8	17	3.41	-1	0-42(41-0-3)/C-9,1-5	2	-1.0
1961 StL-N	22	52	8	14	2	0	4	9	6	10	0	0	.269	.367	.538	.905	124	2	10	6.55	1	C-15/0-1	3	0.3
1962 StL-N	122	345	42	89	19	1	14	45	50	59	5	2	.258	.354	.441	.794	102	2	54	5.44	-3	C-98/0-8(6-0-2),1-3	12	0.3
1963 StL-N	39	102	10	23	4	0	6	18	13	19	0	0	.225	.313	.441	.754	105	1	13	4.19	-2	C-35	3	0.0
Mil-N	95	296	34	74	12	2	11	47	27	59	4	4	.250	.323	.416	.739	112	4	38	4.36	-8	1-55,0-35(35-0-0)/C-2	8	-0.8
Yr.	134	398	44	97	16	2	17	65	40	78	4	4	.244	.321	.422	.743	110	5	52	4.31	-10	1-55,C-37,0-35(35-0-0)	11	-0.8
1964 Mil-N	93	279	45	77	15	1	13	49	17	41	3	7	.276	.320	.477	.797	120	4	37	4.57	-5	1-76/C-1	9	-0.6
1965 Mil-N	122	392	56	106	20	0	21	58	36	61	5	4	.270	.336	.482	.819	127	13	60	5.29	0	C-64,1-52/0-1	14	1.4
1966 Atl-N	76	191	19	37	9	1	8	24	16	43	2	0	.194	.256	.377	.633	72	-7	19	3.15	2	C-48/1-5,0-2(2-0-0)	4	-0.3
1967 Atl-N	17	51	8	10	2	0	3	6	6	8	0	0	.196	.281	.412	.692	97	-0	5	3.16	1	C-14	1	0.2
Phi-N	85	263	29	59	16	0	7	34	29	56	2	2	.224	.304	.365	.669	90	-4	29	3.67	-1	C-79/1-2	7	-0.1
Yr.	102	314	37	69	18	0	10	40	35	64	2	2	.220	.300	.373	.673	91	-4	34	3.58	0	C-93/1-2	8	0.0
1968 Bos-A	16	35	2	5	0	0	0	1	4	12	0	0	.143	.250	.143	.393	20	-3	2	1.36	-1	C-10/0-1	0	-0.4
Chi-N	8	11	1	4	0	0	0	1	3	2	0	0	.364	.500	.364	.864	152	1	2	6.91	1	/1-2,C-1,0-1	1	0.2
1969 Chi-N	23	27	0	6	3	0	0	0	1	9	0	0	.222	.276	.333	.609	62	-1	2	2.74	0	/C-6	0	-0.1
Total 10	**786**	**2216**	**268**	**546**	**111**	**5**	**93**	**320**	**215**	**420**	**24**	**21**	**.246**	**.317**	**.427**	**.744**	**103**	**3**	**289**	**4.40**	**-16**	**C-382,1-200/0-91**	**64**	**-0.9**

• OLIVER, Joe Joseph Melton Oliver b: 7/24/1965, Memphis, TN BR/TR, 6'3", 210 lbs. Deb: 7/15/1989 Career OF: 2-0-2

YEAR TM-L	G	AB	R	H	2B	3B	HR	RBI	BB	SO	SB	CS	AVG	OBP	SLG	OPS	OPS+	BR/A	RC	RC/G	FR	G/POS	WS	TPW
1989 Cin-N	49	151	13	41	8	0	3	23	6	28	0	0	.272	.304	.384	.688	92	-2	17	3.98	-1	C-47	4	0.0
1990*Cin-N	121	364	34	84	23	0	8	52	37	75	1	1	.231	.305	.360	.665	79	-11	40	3.68	-2	*C-118	12	-0.7
1991 Cin-N	94	269	21	58	11	0	11	41	18	53	0	0	.216	.265	.379	.644	76	-10	23	2.70	-3	C-90	4	-0.7
1992 Cin-N	143	485	42	131	25	1	10	57	35	75	2	3	.270	.321	.388	.708	97	-4	57	4.03	-4	*C-141/1-1	13	0.1
1993 Cin-N	139	482	40	115	28	0	14	75	27	91	0	0	.239	.280	.384	.664	76	-19	49	3.40	0	*C-133,1-12/0-1	14	-1.0
1994 Cin-N	6	19	1	4	0	0	1	5	2	3	0	0	.211	.286	.368	.654	70	-1	2	2.92	0	/C-6	0	0.0
1995 Mil-A	97	337	43	92	20	0	12	51	27	66	2	4	.273	.332	.439	.772	93	-5	46	4.71	-2	C-91/D-6,1-2	8	-0.2
1996 Cin-N	106	289	31	70	12	1	11	46	28	54	2	0	.242	.313	.405	.718	88	-5	36	4.18	2	C-97/1-3,0-3(2-0-1)	8	0.3
1997 Cin-N	111	349	28	90	13	0	14	43	25	58	1	3	.258	.317	.415	.732	88	-8	45	4.37	0	*C-106/1-4	9	-0.1
1998 Det-A	50	155	8	35	8	0	4	22	7	33	0	1	.226	.259	.355	.614	57	-11	13	2.65	-1	C-48/1-2	1	-0.8
Sea-A	29	85	12	19	3	0	2	10	10	15	1	0	.224	.305	.329	.635	65	-4	9	3.28	-1	C-29	1	-0.4
Yr.	79	240	20	54	11	0	6	32	17	48	1	1	.225	.276	.346	.622	60	-15	21	2.87	-2	C-77/1-2	2	-1.1
1999 Pit-N	45	134	10	27	8	0	1	13	10	33	2	0	.201	.257	.284	.541	37	-13	10	2.31	-1	C-44	3	-1.0
2000*Sea-A	69	200	33	53	13	1	10	35	14	38	2	1	.265	.313	.490	.803	105	0	29	4.89	-3	C-66/1-1,D-1	8	0.1
2001 NY-A	12	36	3	9	1	0	1	2	1	12	0	0	.250	.270	.361	.631	64	-2	4	3.33	1	C-12	0	0.0
Bos-A	5	12	1	3	1	0	0	1	1	3	0	0	.250	.308	.333	.641	68	-1	1	3.93	-2	/C-5	1	-0.2
Yr.	17	48	4	12	2	0	1	3	2	15	0	0	.250	.280	.354	.634	65	-3	5	3.47	0	C-17	1	-0.2
Total 13	**1076**	**3367**	**320**	**831**	**174**	**3**	**102**	**476**	**248**	**637**	**13**	**13**	**.247**	**.301**	**.391**	**.693**	**83**	**-95**	**379**	**3.78**	**-16**	***C-1033/1-25,D-7,0-4**	**86**	**-4.6**

• OLIVER, Nate Nathaniel "Pee Wee" Oliver b: 12/13/1940, St. Petersburg, FL BR/TR, 5'10", 160 lbs. Deb: 4/9/1963

YEAR TM-L	G	AB	R	H	2B	3B	HR	RBI	BB	SO	SB	CS	AVG	OBP	SLG	OPS	OPS+	BR/A	RC	RC/G	FR	G/POS	WS	TPW
1963 LA-N	65	163	23	39	2	3	1	9	13	25	3	4	.239	.299	.307	.606	80	-5	14	2.95	-5	2-57/S-2	4	-0.6
1964 LA-N	99	321	28	78	9	0	0	21	31	57	7	4	.243	.310	.271	.581	70	-12	26	2.70	-8	2-98/S-1	5	-1.1
1965 LA-N	8	1	3	1	0	0	0	0	0	0	1	0	1.000	1.000	1.000	2.000	498	1	1	27.54	0	/2-2	0	0.1
1966*LA-N	80	119	17	23	2	0	0	3	13	17	3	3	.193	.278	.210	.488	41	-9	7	1.75	-2	2-68/S-2,3-1	2	-0.8
1967 LA-N	77	232	18	55	6	2	0	7	13	50	3	2	.237	.283	.280	.564	67	-10	18	2.52	-8	2-39,S-32/0-1	3	-1.4
1968 SF-N	36	73	3	13	2	0	0	1	1	13	0	1	.178	.189	.205	.395	18	-8	3	1.19	-2	2-14,S-13/3-1	0	-1.0
1969 NY-A	1	1	0	0	0	0	0	0	0	0	0	0	.000	.000	.000	.000	-104	-0	0	.00	0	....	0	0.0
Chi-N	44	44	15	7	3	0	1	4	1	10	0	1	.159	.196	.295	.491	32	-5	2	1.38	1	2-13	1	-0.3
Total 7	**410**	**954**	**107**	**216**	**24**	**5**	**2**	**45**	**72**	**172**	**17**	**15**	**.226**	**.284**	**.268**	**.553**	**63**	**-48**	**71**	**2.41**	**-24**	**2-291/S-50,3-2,0-1**	**15**	**-5.2**

• OLIVER, Tom Thomas Noble "Rebel" Oliver b: 1/15/1903, Montgomery, AL d: 2/26/1988, Montgomery, AL BR/TR, 6', 168 lbs. Deb: 4/14/1930 C Career OF: 0-504-0

YEAR TM-L	G	AB	R	H	2B	3B	HR	RBI	BB	SO	SB	CS	AVG	OBP	SLG	OPS	OPS+	BR/A	RC	RC/G	FR	G/POS	WS	TPW
1930 Bos-A	154	646	86	189	34	2	0	46	42	25	6	6	.293	.339	.351	.690	78	-21	77	4.32	5	*0-154(0-154-0)	13	-2.0
1931 Bos-A	148	586	52	162	35	5	0	70	25	17	4	6	.276	.307	.353	.660	77	-19	62	3.76	14	*0-148(0-148-0)	12	-0.8
1932 Bos-A	122	455	39	120	23	3	0	37	25	12	1	6	.264	.305	.327	.632	66	-25	45	3.35	5	*0-116(0-116-0)	6	-2.2
1933 Bos-A	90	244	25	63	9	1	0	23	13	7	1	1	.258	.296	.303	.599	60	-14	22	3.14	3	0-86(0-86-0)	4	-1.3
Total 4	**514**	**1931**	**202**	**534**	**101**	**11**	**0**	**176**	**105**	**61**	**12**	**19**	**.277**	**.316**	**.340**	**.656**	**73**	**-80**	**206**	**3.77**	**27**	**0-504**	**35**	**-6.2**

• OLIVO, Miguel Miguel Eduardo (Pena) Olivo b: 7/15/1978, Villa Vasquez, Dominican Republic BR/TR, 6'1", 180 lbs. Deb: 9/15/2002

YEAR TM-L	G	AB	R	H	2B	3B	HR	RBI	BB	SO	SB	CS	AVG	OBP	SLG	OPS	OPS+	BR/A	RC	RC/G	FR	G/POS	WS	TPW
2002 Chi-A	6	19	2	4	1	0	1	5	2	5	0	0	.211	.286	.421	.707	82	-1	2	3.42	-1	/C-6	1	-0.1
2003 Chi-A	114	317	37	75	19	1	6	27	19	80	6	4	.237	.288	.360	.648	70	-15	33	3.51	7	*C-113	8	-0.1
Total 2	**120**	**336**	**39**	**79**	**20**	**1**	**7**	**32**	**21**	**85**	**6**	**4**	**.235**	**.288**	**.363**	**.651**	**71**	**-15**	**35**	**3.51**	**5**	**C-119**	**9**	**-0.3**

• OLMEDO, Ray Rainer Gustavo Olmedo b: 5/31/1981, Maracay, Venezuela BB/TR, 5'11", 155 lbs. Deb: 5/25/2003

YEAR TM-L	G	AB	R	H	2B	3B	HR	RBI	BB	SO	SB	CS	AVG	OBP	SLG	OPS	OPS+	BR/A	RC	RC/G	FR	G/POS	WS	TPW
2003 Cin-N	79	230	24	55	6	1	0	17	13	46	1	1	.239	.280	.274	.554	46	-19	18	2.57	-8	S-51,2-18	2	-2.2

• OLMO, Luis Luis Francisco Olmo b: 8/11/1919, Arecibo, Puerto Rico BR/TR, 5'11.5", 190 lbs. Deb: 7/23/1943 Career OF: 149-154-30

YEAR TM-L	G	AB	R	H	2B	3B	HR	RBI	BB	SO	SB	CS	AVG	OBP	SLG	OPS	OPS+	BR/A	RC	RC/G	FR	G/POS	WS	TPW
1943 Bro-N	57	238	39	72	6	4	4	37	8	20	3	....	.303	.325	.412	.737	112	2	29	4.35	-2	0-57(1-54-2)	7	-0.2
1944 Bro-N	136	520	65	134	20	5	9	85	17	37	10	....	.258	.284	.367	.651	84	-14	53	3.53	-10	0-64(3-61-1),2-42,3-31	9	-2.4
1945 Bro-N	141	556	62	174	27	**13**	10	110	36	33	15	....	.313	.356	.462	.818	127	18	90	6.15	-8	*0-106(100-6-0),3-31/2-1	22	0.4
1949*Bro-N	38	105	15	32	4	1	1	14	5	11	2	....	.305	.336	.390	.727	91	-2	12	4.04	-1	0-34(17-16-1)	2	-0.4
1950 Bos-N	69	154	23	35	7	1	5	22	18	23	3	....	.227	.308	.383	.691	86	-3	17	3.63	-2	0-55(18-11-24)/3-1	3	-0.6
1951 Bos-N	21	56	4	11	1	1	0	4	4	4	0	1	.196	.250	.250	.500	38	-5	4	2.11	0	0-16(10-6-2)	0	-0.5
Total 6	**462**	**1629**	**208**	**458**	**65**	**25**	**29**	**272**	**88**	**128**	**33**	**1**	**.281**	**.319**	**.405**	**.724**	**102**	**-5**	**204**	**4.48**	**-23**	**0-332/3-63,2-43**	**43**	**-3.8**

• OLSEN, Barney Bernard Charles Olsen b: 9/11/1919, Everett, MA d: 3/30/1977, Everett, MA BR/TR, 5'11", 179 lbs. Deb: 8/23/1941

YEAR TM-L	G	AB	R	H	2B	3B	HR	RBI	BB	SO	SB	CS	AVG	OBP	SLG	OPS	OPS+	BR/A	RC	RC/G	FR	G/POS	WS	TPW
1941 Chi-N	24	73	13	21	6	1	1	4	4	11	0	....	.288	.325	.438	.763	118	1	9	4.56	0	0-23(0-23-0)	2	0.0

• OLSON, Greg Gregory William Olson b: 9/6/1960, Marshall, MN BR/TR, 6', 200 lbs. Deb: 6/27/1989

YEAR TM-L	G	AB	R	H	2B	3B	HR	RBI	BB	SO	SB	CS	AVG	OBP	SLG	OPS	OPS+	BR/A	RC	RC/G	FR	G/POS	WS	TPW
1989 Min-A	3	2	0	1	0	0	0	0	0	0	0	0	.500	.500	.500	1.000	171	0	1	13.50	-1	/C-3	0	0.0
1990 Atl-N★	100	298	36	78	12	1	7	36	30	51	1	1	.262	.333	.379	.713	90	-4	37	4.33	-2	C-97/3-1	8	-0.1
1991*Atl-N	133	411	46	99	25	0	6	44	44	48	1	1	.241	.319	.345	.664	82	-10	45	3.63	-6	*C-127	12	-0.9
1992 Atl-N	95	302	27	72	14	2	3	27	34	31	2	1	.238	.318	.328	.645	78	-8	32	3.53	-3	C-94	8	-0.5
1993*Atl-N	83	262	23	59	10	0	4	24	29	27	1	0	.225	.305	.309	.614	64	-13	24	2.99	-3	C-81	5	-1.0
Total 5	**414**	**1275**	**132**	**309**	**61**	**3**	**20**	**131**	**137**	**157**	**5**	**3**	**.242**	**.319**	**.342**	**.661**	**79**	**-34**	**138**	**3.64**	**-14**	**C-402/3-1**	**33**	**-2.5**

• OLSON, Ivy Ivan Massie Olson b: 10/14/1885, Kansas City, MO d: 9/1/1965, Inglewood, CA BR/TR, 5'10.5", 175 lbs. Deb: 4/12/1911 C Career OF: 8-0-2

YEAR TM-L	G	AB	R	H	2B	3B	HR	RBI	BB	SO	SB	CS	AVG	OBP	SLG	OPS	OPS+	BR/A	RC	RC/G	FR	G/POS	WS	TPW
1911 Cle-A	140	545	89	142	20	8	1	50	34	....	20	....	.261	.311	.332	.643	78	-17	63	3.83	-15	*S-139/3-1	10	-2.2
1912 Cle-A	125	467	68	118	13	1	0	33	21	....	16	....	.253	.291	.285	.575	63	-24	45	3.08	5	S-56,3-36,2-21/0-3(3-0-0)	8	-1.3
1913 Cle-A	104	370	47	92	13	3	0	32	22	28	7	....	.249	.296	.300	.596	72	-14	35	3.02	3	3-73,1-21/2-1	8	-0.9

YEAR TM-L	G	AB	R	H	2B	3B	HR	RBI	BB	SO	SB	CS	AVG	OBP	SLG	OPS	OPS+	BR/A	RC	RC/G	FR	G/POS	WS	TPW
1914 Cle-A	89	310	22	75	6	2	1	20	13	24	15	9	.242	.275	.284	.559	65	-15	26	2.72	4	S-31,2-23,3-19/O-6(5-0-1),1	4	-1.0
1915 Cin-N	63	207	18	48	5	4	0	14	12	13	10	6	.232	.274	.295	.569	71	-8	18	2.78	4	2-39,3-15/1-7	4	-0.3
Bro-N	18	26	2	2	0	1	0	3	1	0	0	....	.077	.111	.154	.265	-20	-4	1	.68	-2	/S-7,2-1,3-1,0-1	0	-0.6
Yr.	81	233	20	50	5	5	0	17	13	13	10	6	.215	.256	.279	.535	60	-12	19	2.48	2	2-40,3-16/1-7,S-7,0-1	4	-1.0
1916*Bro-N	108	351	29	89	13	4	1	38	21	27	14	....	.254	.298	.322	.620	88	-5	40	3.70	-2	*S-103/2-3,1-1	10	0.0
1917 Bro-N	139	580	64	156	18	5	2	38	14	34	6	....	.269	.291	.328	.619	87	-11	55	3.26	4	*S-133/3-6	14	0.3
1918 Bro-N	126	506	63	121	16	4	1	17	27	18	21	....	.239	.286	.292	.578	77	-14	46	3.01	-24	*S-126	7	-3.3
1919 Bro-N	140	590	73	**164**	14	9	1	38	30	12	26	....	.278	.316	.337	.654	94	-4	67	4.00	-1	*S-140	19	0.5
1920*Bro-N	143	637	71	162	13	11	1	46	20	19	4	7	.254	.278	.314	.592	68	-27	54	2.91	3	*S-125,2-21	12	-1.6
1921 Bro-N	151	652	88	174	22	10	3	35	28	26	4	9	.267	.301	.345	.646	68	-31	66	3.49	-10	*S-133,2-20	12	-2.5
1922 Bro-N	136	551	63	150	26	6	1	47	25	10	8	5	.272	.306	.347	.653	69	-25	58	3.66	0	2-85,S-51	12	-1.6
1923 Bro-N	82	292	33	76	11	1	1	35	14	10	5	0	.260	.296	.315	.611	63	-14	29	3.34	1	2-72/3-4,1-2,S-2	5	-1.1
1924 Bro-N	10	27	0	6	1	0	0	0	3	1	0	0	.222	.300	.259	.559	53	-2	2	2.74	-1	/S-8,2-2	0	-0.2
Total 14	**1574**	**6111**	**730**	**1575**	**191**	**69**	**13**	**446**	**285**	**222**	**156**	**36**	**.258**	**.295**	**.318**	**.613**	**74**	**-215**	**605**	**3.32**	**-32**	***S-1054,2-288,3-155/1-34,0**	**125**	**-15.8**

• OLSON, Karl — Karl Arthur "Ole" Olson b: 7/6/1930, Kentfield, CA BR/TR, 6'3", 205 lbs. Deb: 6/30/1951 Career OF: 87-135-27

YEAR TM-L	G	AB	R	H	2B	3B	HR	RBI	BB	SO	SB	CS	AVG	OBP	SLG	OPS	OPS+	BR/A	RC	RC/G	FR	G/POS	WS	TPW
1951 Bos-A	5	10	0	1	0	0	0	0	0	3	0	0	.100	.100	.100	.200	-42	-2	0	.00	0	/O-5(2-0-3)	0	-0.2
1953 Bos-A	25	57	5	7	2	0	0	6	1	9	0	0	.123	.138	.211	.348	-7	-9	1	.43	-1	O-24(23-2-0)	0	-1.0
1954 Bos-A	101	227	25	59	12	2	1	20	12	23	2	1	.260	.297	.344	.641	68	-10	21	2.98	1	O-78(29-36-16)	2	-1.3
1955 Bos-A	26	48	7	12	1	2	0	1	1	10	0	0	.250	.265	.354	.619	60	-3	4	2.40	0	O-21(11-8-5)	1	-0.4
1956 Was-A	106	313	34	77	10	2	4	22	28	41	1	1	.246	.310	.329	.639	69	-14	30	3.14	-4	*O-101(16-84-3)	3	-2.2
1957 Was-A	8	12	2	2	0	0	0	0	1	2	0	0	.167	.231	.167	.397	10	-1	1	1.41	0	/O-6(2-4-0)	0	-0.2
Det-A	8	14	1	2	0	0	0	1	0	6	0	0	.143	.143	.143	.286	-21	-2	0	.70	-0	/O-5(4-1-0)	0	-0.3
Yr.	16	26	3	4	0	0	0	1	1	8	0	0	.154	.185	.154	.339	-7	-4	1	1.01	0	O-11(6-5-0)	0	-0.4
Total 6	**279**	**681**	**74**	**160**	**25**	**6**	**6**	**50**	**43**	**94**	**3**	**2**	**.235**	**.281**	**.316**	**.597**	**57**	**-42**	**56**	**2.64**	**-4**	**O-240**	**6**	**-5.6**

• OLSON, Marv — Marvin Clement "Sparky" Olson b: 5/28/1907, Gayville, SD d: 2/5/1998, Tyndall, SD BR/TR, 5'7", 160 lbs. Deb: 9/13/1931

YEAR TM-L	G	AB	R	H	2B	3B	HR	RBI	BB	SO	SB	CS	AVG	OBP	SLG	OPS	OPS+	BR/A	RC	RC/G	FR	G/POS	WS	TPW
1931 Bos-A	15	53	8	10	1	0	0	5	9	3	0	0	.189	.306	.208	.514	39	-4	4	2.41	1	2-15	0	-0.2
1932 Bos-A	115	403	58	100	14	6	0	25	61	26	1	5	.248	.347	.313	.660	74	-15	47	3.87	-19	*2-106/3-1	5	-2.5
1933 Bos-A	3	1	1	0	0	0	0	0	0	1	0	0	.000	.000	.000	.000	-101	-0	0	.00	-1	/2-1	0	-0.1
Total 3	**133**	**457**	**67**	**110**	**15**	**6**	**0**	**30**	**70**	**30**	**1**	**5**	**.241**	**.342**	**.300**	**.641**	**70**	**-19**	**51**	**3.68**	**-19**	**2-122/3-1**	**5**	**-2.8**

• O'MALLEY, Tom — Thomas Patrick O'Malley b: 12/25/1960, Orange, NJ BL/TR, 6', 190 lbs. Deb: 5/8/1982

YEAR TM-L	G	AB	R	H	2B	3B	HR	RBI	BB	SO	SB	CS	AVG	OBP	SLG	OPS	OPS+	BR/A	RC	RC/G	FR	G/POS	WS	TPW
1982 SF-N	92	291	26	80	12	4	2	27	33	39	0	3	.275	.351	.364	.715	100	-0	35	4.13	-3	3-83/2-1,S-1	8	-0.4
1983 SF-N	135	410	40	106	16	1	5	45	52	47	2	4	.259	.348	.339	.687	94	-3	49	4.01	1	*3-117	11	-0.3
1984 SF-N	13	25	2	3	0	0	0	0	2	2	0	0	.120	.185	.120	.305	-13	-4	1	.80	0	/3-7	0	-0.4
Chi-A	12	16	0	2	0	0	0	3	0	5	0	0	.125	.125	.125	.250	-29	-3	0	.23	-1	/3-6	0	-0.4
1985 Bal-A	8	14	1	1	0	0	1	2	0	2	0	0	.071	.071	.286	.357	-8	-2	0	.00	-1	/3-3	0	-0.3
1986 Bal-A	56	181	19	46	9	0	1	18	17	21	0	1	.254	.318	.320	.639	75	-6	18	3.48	1	3-55	3	-0.5
1987 Tex-A	45	117	10	32	8	0	1	12	15	9	0	0	.274	.356	.368	.724	92	-1	14	4.09	-3	3-40/2-1	2	-0.4
1988 Mon-N	14	27	3	7	0	0	0	2	3	4	0	0	.259	.333	.259	.593	69	-1	3	3.33	0	/3-7	1	-0.1
1989 NY-N	9	11	2	6	2	0	0	8	0	2	0	0	.545	.545	.727	1.273	274	2	4	23.56	0	/3-3	2	0.2
1990 NY-N	82	121	14	27	7	0	3	14	11	20	0	0	.223	.288	.355	.643	76	-4	13	3.61	-1	3-38/1-3	3	-0.5
Total 9	**466**	**1213**	**117**	**310**	**54**	**5**	**13**	**131**	**133**	**151**	**2**	**8**	**.256**	**.332**	**.340**	**.672**	**87**	**-22**	**136**	**3.82**	**-6**	**3-359/1-3,2-2,S-1**	**30**	**-3.2**

• O'MARA, Ollie — Oliver Edward O'Mara b: 3/8/1891, St. Louis, MO d: 10/24/1989, Reno, NV BR/TR, 5'9", 155 lbs. Deb: 9/8/1912

YEAR TM-L	G	AB	R	H	2B	3B	HR	RBI	BB	SO	SB	CS	AVG	OBP	SLG	OPS	OPS+	BR/A	RC	RC/G	FR	G/POS	WS	TPW
1912 Det-A	1	4	0	0	0	0	0	0	0	....	0	....	.000	.000	.000	.000	-103	-1	0	.00	0	/S-1	0	-0.1
1914 Bro-N	67	247	41	65	10	2	1	7	16	26	14	....	.263	.316	.332	.648	91	-3	29	3.98	-7	S-63	6	-0.6
1915 Bro-N	149	577	77	141	26	3	0	31	51	40	11	12	.244	.308	.300	.608	83	-14	56	3.17	-24	*S-149	14	-3.1
1916*Bro-N	72	193	18	39	5	2	0	15	12	20	10	....	.202	.249	.249	.497	52	-11	15	2.43	0	S-51	2	-0.9
1918 Bro-N	121	450	29	96	8	1	1	24	7	18	11	....	.213	.242	.242	.484	48	-29	29	2.02	-2	*3-121	6	-3.0
1919 Bro-N	2	7	1	0	0	0	0	0	0	0	0	....	.000	.000	.000	.000	-98	-2	0	.00	0	/3-2	0	-0.2
Total 6	**412**	**1478**	**166**	**341**	**49**	**8**	**2**	**77**	**86**	**104**	**46**	**12**	**.231**	**.280**	**.279**	**.559**	**68**	**-60**	**129**	**2.81**	**-34**	**S-264,3-123**	**28**	**-7.9**

• O'MEARA, Tom — Thomas Edward O'Meara b: 12/12/1872, Chicago, IL d: 2/16/1902, Fort Wayne, IN BR Deb: 9/29/1895

YEAR TM-L	G	AB	R	H	2B	3B	HR	RBI	BB	SO	SB	CS	AVG	OBP	SLG	OPS	OPS+	BR/A	RC	RC/G	FR	G/POS	WS	TPW
1895 Cle-N	1	1	1	0	0	0	0	0	1	0	0	....	.000	.500	.000	.500	34	0	0	.00	0	/C-1	0	0.0
1896 Cle-N	12	33	5	5	0	0	0	0	5	7	0	....	.152	.263	.152	.415	10	-4	1	1.28	-1	/C-9,1-1	0	-0.4
Total 2	**13**	**34**	**6**	**5**	**0**	**0**	**0**	**0**	**6**	**7**	**0**	**....**	**.147**	**.275**	**.147**	**.422**	**11**	**-4**	**1**	**1.23**	**-1**	**/C-10,1-1**	**0**	**-0.4**

• O'NEAL, — O'Neal b: Hartford, CT Deb: 10/23/1874

YEAR TM-L	G	AB	R	H	2B	3B	HR	RBI	BB	SO	SB	CS	AVG	OBP	SLG	OPS	OPS+	BR/A	RC	RC/G	FR	G/POS	WS	TPW
1874 Har-n	1	3	0	0	0	0	0	0	0	1	0	0	.000	.000	.000	.000	-95	-1	0	.00	1	/O-1	....	0.0

• O'NEIL, John — John Francis O'Neil b: 4/19/1920, Shelbiana, KY BR/TR, 5'9", 155 lbs. Deb: 4/16/1946

YEAR TM-L	G	AB	R	H	2B	3B	HR	RBI	BB	SO	SB	CS	AVG	OBP	SLG	OPS	OPS+	BR/A	RC	RC/G	FR	G/POS	WS	TPW
1946 Phi-N	46	94	12	25	3	0	0	9	5	12	0	....	.266	.303	.298	.601	73	-4	9	3.43	-4	S-32	2	-0.6

• O'NEIL, Mickey — George Michael O'Neil b: 4/12/1900, St. Louis, MO d: 4/8/1964, St. Louis, MO BR/TR, 5'10", 185 lbs. Deb: 9/12/1919 C

YEAR TM-L	G	AB	R	H	2B	3B	HR	RBI	BB	SO	SB	CS	AVG	OBP	SLG	OPS	OPS+	BR/A	RC	RC/G	FR	G/POS	WS	TPW
1919 Bos-N	11	28	3	6	0	0	0	1	1	7	0	....	.214	.241	.214	.456	39	-2	2	1.79	2	C-11	1	0.1
1920 Bos-N	112	304	19	86	5	4	0	28	21	20	4	4	.283	.339	.326	.665	96	-1	35	3.90	15	*C-105/2-1	12	2.3
1921 Bos-N	98	277	26	69	9	4	2	29	23	21	2	2	.249	.307	.332	.639	73	-10	29	3.46	8	C-95	9	0.4
1922 Bos-N	83	251	18	56	5	2	0	26	14	11	1	0	.223	.267	.259	.526	38	-22	18	2.40	3	C-79	3	-1.4
1923 Bos-N	96	306	29	65	7	4	0	20	17	14	3	2	.212	.258	.261	.520	39	-26	21	2.28	8	C-95	4	-1.2
1924 Bos-N	106	362	32	89	4	1	0	22	14	27	4	3	.246	.276	.262	.538	47	-26	26	2.48	11	*C-106	4	-0.9
1925 Bos-N	70	222	29	57	6	5	2	30	21	16	1	2	.257	.327	.356	.682	81	-6	26	4.08	-3	C-69	5	-0.5
1926 Bro-N	75	201	19	42	5	3	0	20	23	8	3	....	.209	.293	.264	.557	52	-13	17	2.57	0	C-74	4	-0.9
1927 Was-A	5	6	0	0	0	0	0	0	0	1	0	0	.000	.000	.000	.000	-101	-2	0	.00	0	/C-4	0	-0.2
NY-N	16	38	2	5	0	0	0	3	5	2	0	....	.132	.233	.132	.364		-5	1	1.07	0	C-16	1	-0.4
Total 9	**672**	**1995**	**177**	**475**	**41**	**23**	**4**	**179**	**139**	**127**	**18**	**13**	**.238**	**.292**	**.288**	**.579**	**59**	**-113**	**175**	**2.92**	**42**	**C-654/2-1**	**43**	**-2.7**

• O'NEILL, Bill — William John O'Neill b: 1/22/1880, St. John, Canada d: 7/20/1920, Woodhaven, NY BB/TR, 5'11", 175 lbs. Deb: 5/7/1904 Career OF: 22-87-87

YEAR TM-L	G	AB	R	H	2B	3B	HR	RBI	BB	SO	SB	CS	AVG	OBP	SLG	OPS	OPS+	BR/A	RC	RC/G	FR	G/POS	WS	TPW
1904 Bos-A	17	51	7	10	1	0	0	5	2	....	0	....	.196	.226	.216	.442	38	-4	3	1.65	-2	/O-9(8-1-0),S-2	0	-0.7
Was-A	95	365	33	89	10	1	1	16	22	....	22	....	.244	.294	.285	.579	85	-6	39	3.64	-15	O-93(14-79-0)/2-3	7	-2.8
Yr.	112	416	40	99	11	1	1	21	24	....	22	....	.238	.286	.276	.562	79	-10	41	3.39	-17	*O-102(22-80-0)/2-3,S-2	7	-3.5
1906*Chi-A	94	330	37	82	4	1	1	21	22	....	19	....	.248	.301	.276	.577	83	-6	35	3.62	2	O-93(0-7-87)	10	-0.9
Total 2	**206**	**746**	**77**	**181**	**15**	**2**	**2**	**42**	**46**	**....**	**41**	**....**	**.243**	**.293**	**.276**	**.569**	**81**	**-15**	**77**	**3.49**	**-15**	**O-195/2-3,S-2**	**17**	**-4.4**

• O'NEILL, Denny — Dennis O'Neill b: 11/22/1866, Holyoke, MA d: 11/15/1912, Rushville, IN BL/TL, 6'2.5", 200 lbs. Deb: 6/18/1893

YEAR TM-L	G	AB	R	H	2B	3B	HR	RBI	BB	SO	SB	CS	AVG	OBP	SLG	OPS	OPS+	BR/A	RC	RC/G	FR	G/POS	WS	TPW
1893 StL-N	7	25	3	3	0	0	0	2	4	0	3	....	.120	.241	.120	.361	-3	-4	1	1.79	-1	/1-7	0	-0.4

• O'NEILL, Fred — Frederick James "Tip" O'Neill b: 1865, London, Canada d: 3/7/1892, London, Canada, 5'7", 142 lbs. Deb: 5/3/1887

YEAR TM-L	G	AB	R	H	2B	3B	HR	RBI	BB	SO	SB	CS	AVG	OBP	SLG	OPS	OPS+	BR/A	RC	RC/G	FR	G/POS	WS	TPW
1887 NY-a	6	27	4	9	1	1	0	3	1	....	3	....	.333	.357	.423	.780	122	1	5	7.69	0	/O-6(0-1-5)	1	0.1

• O'NEILL, Harry — Harry Mink O'Neill b: 5/8/1917, Philadelphia, PA d: 3/6/1945, Iwo Jima, Marianas Islands BR/TR, 6'3", 205 lbs. Deb: 7/23/1939

YEAR TM-L	G	AB	R	H	2B	3B	HR	RBI	BB	SO	SB	CS	AVG	OBP	SLG	OPS	OPS+	BR/A	RC	RC/G	FR	G/POS	WS	TPW
1939 Phi-A	1	0	0	0	0	0	0	0	0	0	0	0	....	....	....	....	-102	0	0	....	0	/C-1	0	0.0

• O'NEILL, Jack — John Joseph O'Neill b: 1/10/1873, Galway, Ireland d: 6/25/1935, Scranton, PA BR/TR, 5'10", 165 lbs. Deb: 4/21/1902

YEAR TM-L	G	AB	R	H	2B	3B	HR	RBI	BB	SO	SB	CS	AVG	OBP	SLG	OPS	OPS+	BR/A	RC	RC/G	FR	G/POS	WS	TPW
1902 StL-N	63	192	13	27	1	1	0	12	13	....	2	....	.141	.214	.156	.371	15	-18	7	1.14	1	C-59	2	-1.2
1903 StL-N	75	246	23	58	9	1	0	27	13	....	11	....	.236	.288	.280	.568	64	-11	24	3.33	14	C-74	5	0.9
1904 Chi-N	51	168	8	36	5	0	1	19	6	....	1	....	.214	.258	.262	.520	61	-8	12	2.37	-2	C-49	3	-0.6
1905 Chi-N	53	172	16	34	4	2	0	12	8	....	6	....	.198	.277	.244	.522	54	-10	14	2.61	1	C-50	3	-0.4
1906 Bos-N	61	167	14	30	5	1	0	4	12	....	0	....	.180	.243	.222	.465	46	-10	10	1.81	6	C-48/1-2,0-1	3	0.1
Total 5	**303**	**945**	**74**	**185**	**24**	**5**	**1**	**74**	**52**	**....**	**20**	**....**	**.196**	**.258**	**.235**	**.493**	**48**	**-58**	**68**	**2.29**	**19**	**C-280/1-2,0-1**	**16**	**-1.1**

YEAR TM-L	G	AB	R	H	2B	3B	HR	RBI	BB	SO	SB	CS	AVG	OBP	SLG	OPS	OPS+	BR/A	RC	RC/G	FR	G/POS	WS	TPW
• O'NEILL, Jim	James Leo O'Neill b: 2/23/1893, Minooka, PA d: 9/5/1976, Chambersburg, PA BR/TR, 5'10.5", 165 lbs. Deb: 4/15/1920																							
1920 Was-A	86	294	27	85	17	7	1	40	13	30	7	3	.289	.324	.405	.728	95	-2	38	4.57	-6	S-80/2-2	8	-0.2
1923 Was-A	23	33	6	9	1	0	0	3	1	3	0	0	.273	.294	.303	.597	60	-2	3	3.20	-1	/2-8,3-4,0-1,S-1	1	-0.2
Total 2	109	327	33	94	18	7	1	43	14	33	7	3	.287	.321	.394	.715	91	-4	41	4.43	-7	/S-81,2-10,3-4,0-1	9	-0.4
• O'NEILL, John	John J. O'Neill b: New York, NY TR Deb: 9/6/1899																							
1899 NY-N	2	7	0	0	0	0	0	0	0	....	0	....	.000	.000	.000	.000	-104	-2	0	.00	0	/C-2	0	-0.1
1902 NY-N	2	8	0	0	0	0	0	0	0	....	0	....	.000	.000	.000	.000	-101	-2	0	.00	0	/C-2	0	-0.1
Total 2	4	15	0	0	0	0	0	0	0	....	0	....	.000	.000	.000	.000	-102	-4	0	.00	1	/C-4	0	-0.2
• O'NEILL, Mike	Michael Joyce O'Neill b: 9/7/1877, Maam, Ireland d: 8/12/1959, Scranton, PA BR/TR, 5'11", 185 lbs. Deb: 9/20/1901 U Career OF: 28-0-0 ♦																							
1901 StL-N	6	15	3	6	0	0	0	2	3	....	0	....	.400	.526	.400	.926	179	3	3	9.53	-1	/P-5	5	1.0
1902 StL-N	51	135	21	43	5	3	2	15	2	....	0	....	.319	.333	.444	.778	146	13	21	5.87	0	P-36/0-3(3-0-0)	18	1.4
1903 StL-N	41	110	12	25	2	2	0	6	8	....	3	....	.227	.303	.282	.585	69	1	11	3.30	0	P-19,0-13(13-0-0)	4	-0.9
1904 StL-N	30	91	9	21	7	2	0	16	5	....	0	....	.231	.286	.352	.637	101	6	10	3.44	1	P-25/0-3(3-0-0)	17	2.7
1907 Cin-N	9	29	5	2	0	2	0	2	2	....	1	....	.069	.129	.207	.336	5	-3	1	.92	-1	/0-9(9-0-0)	0	-0.5
Total 5	137	380	50	97	14	9	2	41	20	....	4	....	.255	.306	.355	.662	103	19	45	4.12	-1	/P-85,0-28	44	3.6
• O'NEILL, Paul	Paul Andrew O'Neill b: 2/25/1963, Columbus, OH BL/TL, 6'4", 215 lbs. Deb: 9/3/1985 Career OF: 99-23-1848																							
1985 Cin-N	5	12	1	4	1	0	0	1	0	2	0	0	.333	.333	.417	.750	103	-0	2	5.63	1	/0-2(2-0-0)	1	0.0
1986 Cin-N	3	2	0	0	0	0	0	0	1	1	0	0	.000	.333	.000	.333		-0	0	1.17	0	....	0	0.0
1987 Cin-N	84	160	24	41	14	1	7	28	18	29	2	1	.256	.331	.488	.819	109	2	26	5.66	-2	0-42(14-10-22)/1-2,P-1	5	-0.4
1988 Cin-N	145	485	58	122	25	3	16	73	38	65	8	6	.252	.309	.414	.723	102	-1	61	4.29	0	*0-118(0-8-114),1-21	13	-0.7
1989 Cin-N	117	428	49	118	24	2	15	74	46	64	20	5	.276	.349	.446	.795	122	14	69	5.68	-4	*0-115(0-4-115)	18	0.7
1990*Cin-N	145	503	59	136	28	0	16	78	53	103	13	11	.270	.342	.421	.764	105	1	69	4.73	6	*0-141(0-1-141)	16	0.3
1991 Cin-N★	152	532	71	136	36	0	28	91	73	107	12	7	.256	.347	.481	.828	126	18	89	5.86	5	*0-150(0-0-150)	19	1.9
1992 Cin-N	148	496	59	122	19	1	14	66	77	85	6	3	.246	.350	.373	.723	102	4	67	4.60	5	*0-143(0-0-143)	13	0.5
1993 NY-A	141	498	71	155	34	1	20	75	44	69	2	4	.311	.369	.504	.874	137	23	89	6.61	-2	*0-138(46-0-103)/D-2	15	1.4
1994 NY-A★	103	368	68	132	25	1	21	83	72	56	5	4	**.359**	.464	.603	1.067	179	46	100	10.46	3	0-99(12-0-90)/D-4	23	4.1
1995*NY-A★	127	460	82	138	30	4	22	96	71	76	1	2	.300	.395	.526	.921	138	26	89	6.70	-4	*0-121(25-0-107)/D-4	18	1.5
1996*NY-A	150	546	89	165	35	1	19	91	102	76	0	1	.302	.416	.474	.890	124	25	109	7.15	6	*0-146(0-0-146)/D-3,1-1	22	2.1
1997*NY-A★	149	553	89	179	42	0	21	117	75	92	10	7	.324	.404	.514	.918	139	32	113	7.51	4	*0-146(0-0-146)/1-2,D-2	28	2.7
1998*NY-A★	152	602	95	191	40	2	24	116	57	103	15	1	.317	.378	.510	.888	133	32	113	6.87	2	*0-150(0-0-150)/D-1	26	2.4
1999*NY-A	153	597	70	170	39	4	19	110	66	89	11	9	.285	.358	.459	.817	108	5	92	5.27	1	*0-151(0-0-151)	16	-0.2
2000*NY-A	142	566	79	160	26	0	18	100	51	90	14	9	.283	.342	.424	.766	93	-7	78	4.77	-1	*0-140(0-0-140)/D-2	13	-1.5
2001*NY-A	137	510	77	136	33	1	21	70	48	59	22	3	.267	.332	.459	.791	104	5	75	5.06	-11	*0-130(0-0-130)/D-6	13	-1.3
Total 17	2053	7318	1041	2105	451	21	281	1269	892	1166	141	73	.288	.367	.470	.837	121	223	1242	5.98	8	*0-1932/1-26,D-24,P-1	259	13.7
• O'NEILL, Peaches	Philip Bernard O'Neill b: 8/30/1879, Anderson, IN d: 8/2/1955, Anderson, IN BR/TR, 5'11", 165 lbs. Deb: 4/16/1904																							
1904 Cin-N	8	15	0	4	0	0	0	1	1	....	0	....	.267	.313	.267	.579	73	-0	1	3.03	-1	/C-5,1-1	0	-0.1
• O'NEILL, Steve	Stephen Francis O'Neill b: 7/6/1891, Minooka, PA d: 1/26/1962, Cleveland, OH BR/TR, 5'10", 165 lbs. Deb: 9/18/1911 M/C																							
1911 Cle-A	9	27	1	4	1	0	0	1	4	....	2	....	.148	.281	.185	.466	31	-2	2	2.20	3	/C-9	1	0.1
1912 Cle-A	69	215	17	49	4	0	0	14	12	....	2	....	.228	.272	.247	.518	47	-15	15	2.26	5	C-68	4	-0.5
1913 Cle-A	80	234	19	69	13	3	0	29	10	24	5	....	.295	.329	.376	.705	103	-0	30	4.39	5	C-80	10	1.1
1914 Cle-A	87	269	28	68	12	2	0	20	15	35	1	3	.253	.292	.312	.605	79	-9	24	3.11	5	C-82/1-1	6	0.3
1915 Cle-A	121	386	32	91	14	2	2	34	26	41	2	3	.236	.293	.298	.590	75	-14	35	3.00	10	*C-115	9	0.6
1916 Cle-A	130	378	30	89	23	0	0	29	24	33	2	....	.235	.288	.296	.584	71	-14	35	2.99	-1	*C-128	10	-0.6
1917 Cle-A	129	370	21	68	10	2	0	29	41	55	2	....	.184	.272	.222	.494	47	-23	24	1.94	1	*C-127	7	-1.3
1918 Cle-A	114	359	34	87	8	7	1	35	48	22	5	....	.242	.343	.312	.655	89	-3	39	3.57	1	*C-113	13	0.7
1919 Cle-A	125	398	46	115	35	7	2	47	48	21	4	....	.289	.373	.427	.800	117	10	63	5.60	-14	*C-123	18	0.6
1920*Cle-A	149	489	63	157	39	5	3	55	69	39	3	5	.321	.408	.440	.848	121	18	91	6.83	-7	*C-148	25	2.1
1921 Cle-A	106	335	39	108	22	1	1	50	57	22	0	1	.322	.424	.403	.827	110	9	61	6.80	2	*C-105	16	1.6
1922 Cle-A	133	392	33	122	27	4	2	65	73	25	2	2	.311	.423	.416	.839	118	16	74	7.01	-4	*C-130	16	1.9
1923 Cle-A	113	330	31	82	12	0	0	50	64	34	0	4	.248	.374	.285	.659	75	-9	39	4.02	-10	*C-111	5	-1.2
1924 Bos-A	106	307	29	73	15	1	0	38	63	23	0	0	.238	.371	.293	.664	73	-9	38	4.17	-1	C-92	6	-0.4
1925 NY-A	35	91	7	26	5	0	1	13	10	3	0	0	.286	.363	.374	.736	89	-1	13	5.12	0	C-31	3	0.1
1927 StL-A	74	191	14	44	7	0	1	22	20	6	0	3	.230	.303	.283	.586	51	-15	17	2.80	3	C-60	2	-0.7
1928 StL-A	10	24	4	7	1	0	0	6	8	0	0	0	.292	.485	.333	.818	115	2	5	6.95	-1	C-10	1	0.1
Total 17	1590	4795	448	1259	248	34	13	537	592	383	30	23	.263	.349	.337	.685	88	-61	604	4.30	-2	*C-1532/1-1	152	4.5
• O'NEILL, Tip	James Edward O'Neill b: 5/25/1858, Woodstock, Canada d: 12/31/1915, Montreal, Canada BR/TR, 6'1.5", 167 lbs. Deb: 5/5/1883 Career OF: 1012-6-6 ♦																							
1883 NY-N	23	76	8	15	3	0	0	5	3	15	....	....	.197	.228	.237	.465	42	-2	4	1.90	-2	P-19/0-7(0-1-6)	5	-1.7
1884 StL-a	78	297	49	82	13	11	3	54	12	....	....	....	.276	.309	.424	.733	132	12	40	5.10	-4	0-64(59-5-0),P-17/1-1	21	1.0
1885*StL-a	52	206	44	72	7	4	3	38	13	....	....	....	.350	.399	.466	.865	165	15	39	7.91	-1	0-52(52-0-0)	15	1.1
1886*StL-a	138	579	106	190	28	14	3	**107**	47	....	9	....	.328	.385	.440	.826	151	33	104	7.24	4	*0-138(138-0-0)	27	2.9
1887*StL-a	124	567	**167**	**275**	**52**	**19**	**14**	**123**	50	....	30	....	**.485**	**.490**	**.691**	**1.180**	**205**	**71**	194	**17.95**	-8	*0-124(124-0-0)	36	4.8
1888*StL-a	130	529	96	**177**	24	10	5	98	44	....	26	....	**.335**	.390	.446	.836	151	29	105	8.03	-4	*0-130(130-0-0)	28	1.9
1889 StL-a	134	534	123	179	33	8	9	110	72	37	28	....	.335	.419	.478	.897	137	26	122	9.07	-6	*0-134(134-0-0)	27	1.3
1890 Chi-P	137	577	112	174	20	16	3	75	65	36	29	....	.302	.377	.407	.784	105	4	102	6.84	-9	*0-137(137-0-0)	19	-0.8
1891 StL-a	127	514	111	166	28	4	10	95	61	33	25	....	.323	.404	.451	.855	126	16	106	8.11	-11	*0-129(129-0-0)	23	0.0
1892 Cin-N	109	419	63	105	14	6	2	52	53	25	14	....	.251	.339	.327	.666	103	3	52	4.51	-2	*0-109(109-0-0)	12	-0.9
Total 10	1052	4298	879	1435	222	92	52	757	420	146	161	....	.334	.392	.458	.851	139	205	869	8.16	-42	*0-1024/P-36,1-1	213	9.6
• ONIS, Ralph	Manuel Dominguez "Curly" Onis b: 10/24/1908, Tampa, FL d: 1/4/1995, Tampa, FL BR/TR, 5'9", 180 lbs. Deb: 4/27/1935																							
1935 Bro-N	1	1	0	1	0	0	0	0	0	0	0	....	1.000	1.000	1.000	2.000	449	0	1	∞	0	/C-1	0	0.0
• ONSLOW, Eddie	Edward Joseph Onslow b: 2/17/1893, Meadville, PA d: 5/8/1981, Dennison, OH BL/TL, 6', 170 lbs. Deb: 8/7/1912 C																							
1912 Det-A	36	128	11	29	1	2	1	13	3	....	3	....	.227	.250	.289	.539	56	-8	10	2.49	-2	1-35	0	-1.1
1913 Det-A	17	55	7	14	1	0	0	8	5	9	1	....	.255	.328	.273	.601	77	-1	5	3.12	0	1-17	1	-0.2
1918 Cle-A	2	6	0	1	0	0	0	0	0	1	0	....	.167	.167	.167	.333		-1	0	.75	0	/0-1	0	-0.1
1927 Was-A	9	18	1	4	1	0	0	1	1	0	0	0	.222	.263	.278	.541	41	-2	1	2.52	0	/1-5	0	-0.2
Total 4	64	207	19	48	3	2	1	22	9	10	4	0	.232	.271	.280	.551	59	-12	16	2.60	-3	/1-57,0-1	1	-1.6
• ONSLOW, Jack	John James Onslow b: 10/13/1888, Scottdale, PA d: 12/22/1960, Concord, MA BR/TR, 5'11", 180 lbs. Deb: 5/2/1912 M																							
1912 Det-A	36	69	7	11	1	0	0	4	10	....	1	....	.159	.284	.174	.458	33	-5	4	1.77	-3	C-35/0-1	0	-0.7
1917 NY-N	9	8	1	2	1	0	0	0	0	1	0	....	.250	.333	.375	.708	121	0	1	4.10	-1	/C-9	0	-0.1
Total 2	45	77	8	13	2	0	0	4	10	1	1	....	.169	.289	.195	.484	41	-5	5	1.97	-5	/C-44,0-1	0	-0.8
• ONTIVEROS, Steve	Steven Robert Ontiveros b: 10/26/1951, Bakersfield, CA BB/TR, 6', 185 lbs. Deb: 8/5/1973 Career OF: 7-3-11																							
1973 SF-N	24	33	3	8	0	0	1	5	4	7	0	0	.242	.324	.333	.658	79	-1	4	4.22	1	/1-5,0-1	1	0.0
1974 SF-N	120	343	45	91	15	1	4	33	57	41	0	0	.265	.375	.350	.725	99	2	46	4.75	1	3-75,1-19/0-2(1-0-1)	9	0.2
1975 SF-N	108	325	21	94	16	0	3	31	55	44	2	0	.289	.395	.366	.761	108	7	50	5.50	3	3-89/0-8(2-0-7),1-4	12	0.9
1976 SF-N	59	74	8	13	3	0	0	5	6	11	0	0	.176	.247	.216	.463	31	-7	4	1.70	-1	/3-7,0-7(4-3-2),1-4	0	-0.8
1977 Chi-N	156	546	54	163	32	3	10	68	81	69	3	3	.299	.392	.423	.815	107	9	92	6.13	-28	*3-155	18	-2.1
1978 Chi-N	82	276	34	67	14	4	1	22	34	33	0	2	.243	.326	.333	.659	75	-9	31	3.79	1	3-77/1-1	7	-1.0
1979 Chi-N	152	519	58	148	28	2	4	57	58	68	0	1	.285	.365	.370	.735	92	-3	69	4.68	-13	*3-142/1-1	13	-1.9
1980 Chi-N	31	77	7	16	3	0	1	3	14	17	0	0	.208	.330	.286	.615	68	-3	8	3.52	-1	3-24	1	-0.4
Total 8	732	2193	230	600	111	10	24	224	309	290	5	6	.274	.367	.366	.734	94	-5	305	4.88	-36	3-569/1-34,0-18	61	-5.0

YEAR TM-L	G	AB	R	H	2B	3B	HR	RBI	BB	SO	SB	CS	AVG	OBP	SLG	OPS	OPS+	BR/A	RC	RC/G	FR	G/POS	WS	TPW
• OQUENDO, Jose	Jose Manuel (Contreras) "Secret Weapon" Oquendo b: 7/4/1963, Rio Piedras, Puerto Rico BB/TR, 5'10", 160 lbs. Deb: 5/2/1983 C Career OF: 11-7-47																							
1983 NY-N	120	328	29	70	7	0	1	17	19	60	8	9	.213	.261	.244	.505	41	-29	19	1.79	-2	*S-116	5	-2.0
1984 NY-N	81	189	23	42	5	0	0	10	15	26	10	1	.222	.286	.249	.535	52	-10	16	2.71	3	S-67	4	-0.2
1986 StL-N	76	138	20	41	4	1	0	13	15	20	2	3	.297	.366	.341	.707	97	-1	17	4.23	-1	S-29,2-21/3-1,0-1	4	0.1
1987*StL-N	116	248	43	71	9	0	1	24	54	29	4	4	.286	.414	.335	.749	99	3	38	5.19	5	0-46(8-3-37),2-32,S-23/3-8,1,P	11	0.6
1988 StL-N	148	451	36	125	10	1	7	46	52	40	4	6	.277	.352	.350	.702	101	0	57	4.30	1	2-69,3-47,S-17,1-16,0-15(2-4-9)/C,P	14	0.3
1989 StL-N	163	556	59	162	28	7	1	48	79	59	3	5	.291	.380	.372	.752	112	11	81	5.13	14	*2-156/S-7,1-1	22	3.1
1990 StL-N	156	469	38	118	17	5	1	37	74	46	1	1	.252	.354	.316	.669	85	-7	57	4.16	-1	*2-150/S-4	13	-0.4
1991 StL-N	127	366	37	88	11	4	1	26	67	48	1	2	.240	.359	.301	.660	87	-3	43	4.01	16	*2-118,S-22/1-3,P-1	14	1.5
1992 StL-N	14	35	3	9	3	1	0	3	5	3	0	0	.257	.350	.400	.750	115	1	5	5.47	1	/2-9,S-5	2	0.3
1993 StL-N	46	73	7	15	0	0	0	4	12	8	0	0	.205	.318	.205	.523	44	-5	5	1.99	3	S-22,2-16	1	0.0
1994 StL-N	55	129	13	34	2	2	0	9	21	16	1	1	.264	.367	.310	.677	80	-3	15	3.77	-1	S-28,2-16	3	-0.2
1995 StL-N	88	220	31	46	8	3	2	17	35	21	1	1	.209	.318	.300	.618	64	-11	24	3.51	-0	2-62,S-24/3-2,0-1	6	-0.7
Total 12	**1190**	**3202**	**339**	**821**	**104**	**24**	**14**	**254**	**448**	**376**	**35**	**33**	**.256**	**.349**	**.317**	**.666**	**86**	**-55**	**375**	**3.95**	**38**	**2-649,S-364/0-63,3-58,1,P,C**	**99**	**2.3**
• ORAN, Tom	Thomas Oran b: 1847, CA d: 9/21/1886, St. Louis, MO Deb: 5/4/1875																							
1875 RS-n	19	81	7	15	3	1	0	10	1	1	3	2	.185	.195	.247	.442	58	-3	5	2.00	-3	0-19(0-2-17)/S-1	....	-0.4
• ORAVETZ, Ernie	Ernest Eugene Oravetz b: 1/24/1932, Johnstown, PA BB/TL, 5'4", 145 lbs. Deb: 4/11/1955 Career OF: 20-20-51																							
1955 Was-A	100	263	24	71	5	1	0	25	26	19	1	2	.270	.338	.297	.635	76	-9	27	3.59	-3	0-57(0-17-42)	4	-1.4
1956 Was-A	88	137	20	34	3	2	0	11	27	20	1	0	.248	.372	.299	.671	79	-2	18	4.54	-1	0-31(20-3-9)	3	-0.5
Total 2	**188**	**400**	**44**	**105**	**8**	**3**	**0**	**36**	**53**	**39**	**2**	**2**	**.263**	**.350**	**.298**	**.648**	**77**	**-11**	**45**	**3.92**	**-4**	**/0-88**	**7**	**-1.9**
• ORDAZ, Luis	Luis Javier Ordaz b: 8/12/1975, Maracaibo, Venezuela BR/TR, 5'11", 170 lbs. Deb: 9/3/1997																							
1997 StL-N	12	22	3	6	1	0	0	1	1	2	3	0	.273	.304	.318	.623	64	-1	3	4.53	0	S-11	1	0.0
1998 StL-N	57	153	9	31	5	0	0	8	12	18	2	0	.203	.261	.235	.496	32	-15	10	2.08	5	S-54/3-2,2-1	2	-0.6
1999 StL-N	10	9	3	1	0	0	0	2	1	2	1	0	.111	.200	.111	.311	-18	-1	0	1.25	-2	/S-8,2-1,3-1	0	-0.3
2000 KC-A	65	104	17	23	2	0	0	11	5	10	4	2	.221	.264	.240	.504	28	-12	6	1.63	-11	S-38,2-22	1	-1.8
2001 KC-A	28	56	8	14	3	0	0	4	3	8	0	0	.250	.300	.304	.604	55	-4	5	3.10	4	2-19/S-8,3-1,D-1	1	0.1
2002 KC-A	33	94	11	21	2	0	0	4	12	13	2	3	.223	.311	.245	.556	45	-8	8	2.44	-7	2-28/3-6,S-2	1	-1.3
Total 6	**205**	**438**	**51**	**96**	**13**	**0**	**0**	**30**	**34**	**53**	**12**	**5**	**.219**	**.278**	**.249**	**.527**	**37**	**-40**	**32**	**2.25**	**-10**	**S-121/2-71,3-10,D-1**	**6**	**-3.8**
• ORDENANA, Tony	Antonio (Rodriguez) "Mosquito" Ordenana b: 10/30/1918, Guanabacoa, Cuba d: 9/29/1988, Miami, FL BR/TR, 5'9", 158 lbs. Deb: 10/3/1943																							
1943 Pit-N	1	4	0	2	0	0	0	3	0	0	0	....	.500	.500	.500	1.000	183	0	1	13.50	1	/S-1	0	0.1
• ORDONEZ, Magglio	Magglio (Delgado) Ordonez b: 1/28/1974, Caracas, Venezuela BR/TR, 5'11", 170 lbs. Deb: 8/29/1997 Career OF: 0-27-919																							
1997 Chi-A	21	69	12	22	6	0	4	11	2	8	1	2	.319	.338	.580	.918	139	3	12	6.42	-0	0-19(0-0-19)	3	0.2
1998 Chi-A	145	535	70	151	25	2	14	65	28	53	9	7	.282	.329	.415	.744	94	-7	67	4.35	2	*0-145(0-22-136)	13	-1.1
1999 Chi-A★	157	624	100	188	34	3	30	117	47	64	13	6	.301	.351	.510	.861	116	13	103	5.91	1	*0-153(0-0-153)/D-2	20	0.5
2000*Chi-A★	153	588	102	185	34	3	32	126	60	64	18	4	.315	.380	.546	.926	129	27	114	6.86	-2	*0-152(0-0-152)	22	1.5
2001 Chi-A★	160	593	97	181	40	1	31	113	70	70	25	7	.305	.383	.533	.916	133	31	122	7.55	-3	*0-155(0-1-155)/D-3	25	1.9
2002 Chi-A	153	590	116	189	47	1	38	135	53	77	7	5	.320	.383	.597	.980	151	42	127	7.98	-5	*0-150(0-0-150)/D-1	26	2.7
2003 Chi-A★	160	606	95	192	46	3	29	99	57	73	9	5	.317	.382	.546	.928	142	36	121	7.40	4	*0-157(0-4-154)/D-2	23	3.0
Total 7	**949**	**3605**	**592**	**1108**	**232**	**13**	**178**	**666**	**317**	**409**	**82**	**36**	**.307**	**.368**	**.527**	**.895**	**128**	**144**	**667**	**6.68**	**-3**	**0-931/D-8**	**132**	**8.7**
• ORDONEZ, Rey	Reinaldo (Pereira) Ordonez b: 1/11/1971, Havana, Cuba BR/TR, 5'9", 160 lbs. Deb: 4/1/1996																							
1996 NY-N	151	502	51	129	12	4	1	30	22	53	1	3	.257	.290	.303	.592	59	-32	41	2.81	3	*S-150	7	-1.7
1997 NY-N	120	356	35	77	5	3	1	33	18	36	11	5	.216	.256	.256	.512	36	-34	23	1.97	8	*S-118	6	-1.6
1998 NY-N	153	505	46	124	20	2	1	42	23	60	3	6	.246	.280	.299	.579	53	-37	40	2.58	8	*S-151	9	-1.7
1999*NY-N	154	520	49	134	24	2	1	60	49	59	8	4	.258	.323	.317	.640	65	-28	53	3.35	13	*S-154	13	-0.2
2000 NY-N	45	133	10	25	5	0	0	9	17	16	0	0	.188	.280	.226	.506	31	-14	9	2.07	-2	S-44	1	-1.1
2001 NY-N	149	461	31	114	24	4	3	44	34	43	3	2	.247	.300	.336	.637	68	-23	43	3.08	5	*S-148	12	-0.6
2002 NY-N	144	460	53	117	25	2	1	42	24	46	2	2	.254	.294	.324	.618	65	-25	39	2.81	8	*S-142	9	-0.6
2003 TB-A	34	117	14	37	11	0	3	22	2	12	0	2	.316	.333	.487	.821	115	1	17	5.13	7	S-34	4	1.1
Total 8	**950**	**3054**	**289**	**757**	**126**	**17**	**11**	**282**	**189**	**325**	**28**	**24**	**.248**	**.293**	**.311**	**.605**	**59**	**-190**	**264**	**2.85**	**50**	**S-941**	**61**	**-6.5**
• ORENGO, Joe	Joseph Charles Orengo b: 11/29/1914, San Francisco, CA d: 7/24/1988, San Francisco, CA BR/TR, 6', 185 lbs. Deb: 4/18/1939																							
1939 StL-N	7	3	0	0	0	0	0	0	0	1	0	....	.000	.000	.000	.000	-94	-1	0	.00	-3	/S-7	0	-0.4
1940 StL-N	129	415	58	119	23	4	7	56	65	90	9	....	.287	.383	.412	.795	113	10	72	6.14	-4	2-77,3-34,S-19	17	1.4
1941 NY-N	77	252	23	54	11	2	4	25	28	49	1	....	.214	.298	.321	.619	73	-9	24	3.18	8	3-59/S-9,2-6	6	0.3
1943 NY-N	83	266	28	58	8	2	6	29	36	46	1	....	.218	.311	.331	.642	85	-5	28	3.41	1	1-82	5	-0.9
Bro-N	7	15	1	3	2	0	0	1	4	2	0	....	.200	.368	.333	.702	103	0	2	3.96	0	/3-6	1	0.0
Yr.	90	281	29	61	10	2	6	30	40	48	1	....	.217	.315	.331	.646	86	-5	30	3.44	1	1-82/3-6	6	-0.9
1944 Det-A	46	154	14	31	10	0	0	10	20	29	1	1	.201	.297	.266	.563	58	-8	13	2.70	-2	S-29,3-11/1-5,2-2	2	-0.8
1945 Chi-A	17	15	5	1	0	0	0	1	3	2	0	0	.067	.222	.067	.289	-15	-2	0	.88	-2	/3-7,2-1	0	-0.4
Total 6	**366**	**1120**	**129**	**266**	**54**	**8**	**17**	**122**	**156**	**219**	**12**	**1**	**.238**	**.332**	**.346**	**.678**	**88**	**-15**	**139**	**4.16**	**-2**	**3-117/1-87,2-86,S-64**	**31**	**-0.8**
• ORIE, Kevin	Kevin Leonard Orie b: 9/1/1972, West Chester, PA BR/TR, 6'4", 210 lbs. Deb: 4/1/1997																							
1997 Chi-N	114	364	40	100	23	5	8	44	39	57	2	2	.275	.353	.431	.784	102	1	54	5.06	10	*3-112/S-3	12	1.2
1998 Chi-N	64	204	24	37	14	0	2	21	18	35	1	1	.181	.258	.279	.537	40	-18	15	2.31	1	3-57	2	-1.7
Fla-N	48	175	23	46	8	1	6	17	14	24	1	0	.263	.335	.423	.758	102	0	25	5.01	3	3-48	5	0.4
Yr.	112	379	47	83	22	1	8	38	32	59	2	1	.219	.294	.346	.639	68	-18	40	3.47	4	*3-105	7	-1.2
1999 Fla-N	77	240	26	61	16	0	6	29	22	43	1	0	.254	.325	.396	.720	86	-6	30	4.29	-4	3-64/1-1	6	-0.8
2002 Chi-N	13	32	4	9	3	0	0	5	1	4	0	0	.281	.324	.375	.699	85	-1	4	3.91	-2	3-12	1	-0.3
Total 4	**316**	**1015**	**117**	**253**	**64**	**6**	**22**	**116**	**94**	**163**	**5**	**3**	**.249**	**.323**	**.389**	**.712**	**85**	**-24**	**127**	**4.23**	**9**	**3-293/S-3,1-1**	**26**	**-1.0**
• ORME, George	George William Orme b: 9/16/1891, Lebanon, IN d: 3/16/1962, Indianapolis, IN BR/TR, 5'10", 160 lbs. Deb: 9/14/1920																							
1920 Bos-A	4	6	4	2	0	0	0	1	3	0	0	0	.333	.556	.333	.889	146	1	1	9.82	0	/0-3(0-1-2)	1	0.1
• ORNDORFF, Jess	Jesse Walworth Thayer Orndorff b: 1/15/1881, Chicago, IL d: 9/28/1960, Cardiff-by-the-Sea, CA BB/TR, 6', 168 lbs. Deb: 4/18/1907																							
1907 Bos-N	5	17	0	2	0	0	0	0	0	....	0	....	.118	.118	.118	.235	-26	-2	0	.42	0	/C-5	0	-0.3
• O'ROURKE, Charlie	James Patrick O'Rourke b: 6/22/1937, Walla Walla, WA BR/TR, 6'2", 195 lbs. Deb: 6/16/1959																							
1959 StL-N	2	2	0	0	0	0	0	0	0	0	0	0	.000	.000	.000	.000	-94	-1	0	.00	0	....	0	-0.1
• O'ROURKE, Frank	James Francis "Blackie" O'Rourke b: 11/28/1894, Hamilton, Canada d: 5/14/1986, Chatham, NJ BR/TR, 5'10.5", 165 lbs. Deb: 6/12/1912																							
1912 Bos-N	61	196	11	24	3	1	0	16	11	50	1	....	.122	.177	.148	.325	-10	-30	6	.79	-18	S-59/3-1	1	-4.3
1917 Bro-N	64	198	18	47	7	1	0	15	14	25	11	....	.237	.294	.283	.577	75	-6	19	3.13	8	3-58	5	0.4
1918 Bro-N	4	12	0	2	0	0	0	2	1	3	0	....	.167	.231	.167	.397	22	-1	0	1.10	1	/2-2,0-1	0	0.0
1920 Was-A	14	54	8	16	1	0	0	5	2	5	2	1	.296	.321	.315	.636	71	-2	6	3.56	5	S-13/3-1	2	0.4
1921 Was-A	123	444	51	104	17	8	3	54	26	56	6	7	.234	.287	.329	.616	60	-29	42	3.10	-4	*S-122	8	-1.8
1922 Bos-A	67	216	28	57	14	3	1	17	20	28	6	6	.264	.335	.370	.705	84	-6	27	4.12	-10	S-49,3-20	4	-1.0
1924 Det-A	47	181	28	50	11	2	0	19	12	19	7	4	.276	.332	.359	.691	79	-6	22	4.03	4	2-40/S-7	4	0.1
1925 Det-A	124	482	88	141	40	7	5	57	32	37	5	8	.293	.350	.436	.786	100	-3	73	5.10	12	*2-118/3-6	14	1.2
1926 Det-A	111	363	43	88	16	1	1	41	35	33	8	6	.242	.321	.300	.621	62	-20	37	3.33	0	3-60,2-41,S-10	6	-1.4
1927 StL-A	140	538	85	144	25	3	1	39	64	43	18	8	.268	.358	.331	.689	77	-15	69	4.43	5	*3-121,2-16/1-3	12	-0.1
1928 StL-A	99	391	54	103	24	3	1	62	21	19	10	2	.263	.303	.348	.650	68	-17	43	3.62	-5	3-96/S-2	7	-1.5
1929 StL-A	154	585	81	147	23	9	2	62	41	28	14	7	.251	.306	.332	.637	62	-33	62	3.45	-15	*3-151/2-3,S-2	9	-3.6
1930 StL-A	115	400	52	107	15	4	1	41	35	30	11	9	.268	.326	.333	.659	65	-22	44	3.68	-1	3-84,S-23/1-3	6	-1.3

YEAR TM-L	G	AB	R	H	2B	3B	HR	RBI	BB	SO	SB	CS	AVG	OBP	SLG	OPS	OPS+	BR/A	RC	RC/G	FR	G/POS	WS	TPW
1931 StL-A	8	9	0	2	0	0	0	0	0	1	1	1	.222	.222	.222	.444	17	-1	0	.86	0	/S-2,1-1	0	-0.1
Total 14	1131	4069	547	1032	196	42	15	430	314	377	100	59	.254	.315	.333	.649	68	-190	449	3.64	-17	3-598,S-289,2-220/1-7,0-1	78	-13.2

• O'ROURKE, Jim

James Henry "Orator Jim" O'Rourke
b: 9/1/1850, Bridgeport, CT d: 1/8/1919, Bridgeport, CT BR/TR, 5'8", 185 lbs. Deb: 4/26/1872 M/U HOF: 1945 NA OF: 0-44-23 Career OF: 770-419-195 ♦

YEAR TM-L	G	AB	R	H	2B	3B	HR	RBI	BB	SO	SB	CS	AVG	OBP	SLG	OPS	OPS+	BR/A	RC	RC/G	FR	G/POS	WS	TPW
1872 Man-n	23	101	25	31	4	1	0	12	2	0	1	0	.307	.320	.366	.687	118	3	12	5.53	-6	S-16/C-8,3-2	....	-0.2
1873 Bos-n	57	280	79	98	19	3	1	48	14	1	4	2	.350	.381	.450	.831	135	11	51	8.41	1	1-32,0-22(0-0-22)/C-9	....	0.9
1874 Bos-n	70	331	82	104	15	8	**5**	61	4	5	11	1	.314	.322	.453	.776	138	14	53	7.00	2	*1-70	....	1.3
1875 Bos-n	75	358	97	106	13	7	**6**	72	9	6	17	5	.296	.313	.422	.735	148	18	54	6.19	-4	0-45(0-44-1),3-27/1-6,C-1	....	1.1
1876 Bos-N	70	327	61	102	17	3	2	43	15	17	....	....	.312	.358	.420	.778	156	18	48	6.41	-4	*0-68(9-60-0)/1-2,C-1	17	1.0
1877 Bos-N	61	265	**68**	96	14	4	0	23	**20**	9	....	....	.362	**.407**	.445	.852	162	19	49	8.01	-2	*0-60(23-35-3)/1-1	15	1.2
1878 Bos-N	60	255	44	71	17	7	1	29	5	21	....	....	.278	.292	.412	.704	120	4	31	4.70	2	*0-57(0-57-0)/1-2,C-2	12	0.3
1879 Pro-N	81	362	69	126	19	9	1	46	13	10	....	....	.348	**.371**	.459	.829	174	28	63	7.48	-5	*0-56(2-0-56),1-20/C-5,3-3	17	2.1
1880 Bos-N	86	363	71	100	20	11	**6**	45	21	8	....	....	.275	.315	.441	.756	158	22	52	5.40	-4	0-37(15-4-19),1-19,S-17,3-10/C	17	1.7
1881 Buf-N	83	348	71	105	21	7	0	30	27	18	....	....	.302	.352	.402	.754	138	16	51	5.61	-22	*3-56,0-18(18-0-0)/C-8,S-3,1	14	-0.5
1882 Buf-N	84	370	62	104	15	6	2	37	13	13	....	....	.281	.305	.370	.676	113	5	43	4.43	-4	*0-81(5-77-0)/C-2,S-2,3-1	11	-0.1
1883 Buf-N	94	436	102	143	29	8	1	38	15	13	....	....	.328	.350	.438	.788	135	17	69	6.44	-5	0-61(60-1-0),C-33/3-8,S-3,P	17	1.0
1884 Buf-N	108	467	119	**162**	33	7	5	63	35	17	....	....	**.347**	.392	.480	.872	167	36	90	8.12	-6	*0-86(86-0-0),1-18,C-10/P-4,3	25	2.3
1885 NY-N	112	477	119	143	21	**16**	5	42	40	21	....	....	.300	.354	.442	.796	158	31	77	6.19	-13	*0-112(0-112-0)/C-8	24	1.4
1886 NY-N	105	440	106	136	26	6	1	34	39	21	14	....	.309	.365	.402	.768	132	17	72	6.25	9	0-63(1-62-0),C-47/1-2	24	2.5
1887 NY-N	103	433	73	149	15	13	3	88	36	11	46	....	.344	.352	.411	.762	116	10	75	7.03	3	C-40,3-38,0-28(19-6-3)/2-2	13	1.3
1888*NY-N	107	409	50	112	16	6	4	50	24	30	25	....	.274	.319	.372	.690	121	10	58	5.26	4	0-87(75-3-9),C-15/1-4,3-2	17	1.2
1889*NY-N	128	502	89	161	36	7	3	81	40	34	33	....	.321	.372	.438	.810	126	16	96	7.50	-8	*0-128(128-0-0)/C-1	19	0.3
1890 NY-P	111	478	112	172	37	5	9	115	33	20	23	....	.360	.410	.515	.925	134	21	113	9.98	4	*0-111(10-1-100)	20	1.8
1891 NY-N	136	555	92	164	28	7	5	95	26	29	19	....	.295	.334	.398	.732	118	10	82	5.67	7	*0-126(126-1-0),C-14	17	1.3
1892 NY-N	115	448	62	136	28	5	0	56	30	30	16	....	.304	.354	.388	.742	126	13	69	5.97	-7	*0-111(106-0-5)/C-4,1-1	15	-0.3
1893 Was-N	129	547	75	157	22	5	2	95	49	26	15	....	.287	.354	.356	.711	92	-6	76	5.18	4	*0-87(87-0-0),1-33/C-9	11	-0.7
1904 NY-N	1	4	1	1	0	0	0	0	0	....	0	....	.250	.250	.250	.500	52	-0	0	2.22	-1	/C-1	0	-0.1
Total 4 n	225	1070	283	339	51	19	12	193	29	12	33	8	.317	.335	.434	.768	138	45	170	6.93	-7	1-108/0-67,3-29,C-18,S-16	....	3.1
Total 19	1774	7486	1446	2340	414	132	50	1010	481	348	191	....	.313	.355	.421	.776	134	289	1214	6.42	-46	*0-1377,C-209,3-119,1/S,P,2	305	17.7

• O'ROURKE, Joe

Joseph Leo O'Rourke, Jr. b: 10/28/1904, Philadelphia, PA d: 6/27/1990, Philadelphia, PA BL/TR, 5'7", 145 lbs. Deb: 4/19/1929

YEAR TM-L	G	AB	R	H	2B	3B	HR	RBI	BB	SO	SB	CS	AVG	OBP	SLG	OPS	OPS+	BR/A	RC	RC/G	FR	G/POS	WS	TPW
1929 Phi-N	3	3	0	0	0	0	0	0	0	1	0	....	.000	.000	.000	.000	-94	-1	0	.00	0	....	0	-0.1

• O'ROURKE, John

John O'Rourke b: 8/23/1849, Bridgeport, CT d: 6/23/1911, Boston, MA BL/TL, 6', 190 lbs. Deb: 5/1/1879 Career OF: 3-224-2

YEAR TM-L	G	AB	R	H	2B	3B	HR	RBI	BB	SO	SB	CS	AVG	OBP	SLG	OPS	OPS+	BR/A	RC	RC/G	FR	G/POS	WS	TPW
1879 Bos-N	72	317	69	108	17	11	6	**62**	8	32	....	....	.341	.357	**.521**	**.877**	181	27	60	**8.09**	1	*0-71(0-70-1)	17	2.2
1880 Bos-N	81	313	30	86	22	8	3	36	18	32	....	....	.275	.314	.425	.739	153	18	43	5.19	1	*0-81(3-78-1)	13	1.4
1883 NY-a	77	315	49	85	19	5	2	0	21		....	....	.270	.315	.381	.696	118	6	39	4.72	-5	*0-76(0-76-0)/1-1	10	-0.1
Total 3	230	945	148	279	58	24	11	98	47	64	....	....	.295	.329	.442	.771	150	50	142	5.94	-3	0-228/1-1	40	3.5

• O'ROURKE, Patsy

Joseph Leo O'Rourke, Sr. b: 4/13/1881, Philadelphia, PA d: 4/18/1956, Philadelphia, PA BR/TR, 5'7", 160 lbs. Deb: 4/16/1908

YEAR TM-L	G	AB	R	H	2B	3B	HR	RBI	BB	SO	SB	CS	AVG	OBP	SLG	OPS	OPS+	BR/A	RC	RC/G	FR	G/POS	WS	TPW
1908 StL-N	53	164	8	32	4	2	0	16	14	....	2	....	.195	.263	.244	.506	65	-6	11	2.13	-15	S-53	1	-2.3

• O'ROURKE, Queenie

James Stephen O'Rourke b: 12/26/1883, Bridgeport, CT d: 12/22/1955, Sparrows Point, MD BR/TR, 5'7", 150 lbs. Deb: 8/15/1908

YEAR TM-L	G	AB	R	H	2B	3B	HR	RBI	BB	SO	SB	CS	AVG	OBP	SLG	OPS	OPS+	BR/A	RC	RC/G	FR	G/POS	WS	TPW
1908 NY-A	34	108	5	25	1	0	0	3	4	....	4	....	.231	.259	.241	.500	62	-5	8	2.33	-1	0-14(14-0-0),S-11/2-4,3-3	1	-0.7

• O'ROURKE, Tim

Timothy Patrick "Voiceless Tim" O'Rourke
b: 5/18/1864, Chicago, IL d: 4/20/1938, Seattle, WA BL/TR, 5'10", 170 lbs. Deb: 5/27/1890 Career OF: 32-1-40

YEAR TM-L	G	AB	R	H	2B	3B	HR	RBI	BB	SO	SB	CS	AVG	OBP	SLG	OPS	OPS+	BR/A	RC	RC/G	FR	G/POS	WS	TPW
1890 Syr-a	87	332	48	94	13	6	1	46	36	....	22	....	.283	.360	.367	.728	128	13	53	5.92	-7	3-87	12	0.7
1891 Col-a	34	136	22	38	1	3	0	12	15	7	9	....	.279	.359	.331	.690	104	1	20	5.38	-1	3-34	5	0.1
1892 Bal-N	63	239	40	74	8	4	0	35	24	19	12	....	.310	.373	.377	.749	123	7	39	6.37	-15	S-58/0-4(2-1-1),3-1	7	-0.5
1893 Bal-N	31	135	22	49	4	1	0	19	12	4	5	....	.363	.423	.407	.830	119	4	26	8.01	-2	0-25(25-0-0)/3-5,S-1	4	0.0
Lou-N	92	352	80	99	8	4	0	53	77	15	22	....	.281	.421	.327	.748	108	12	59	6.19	-17	S-60,0-26(4-0-22)/3-6	13	-0.2
Yr.	123	487	102	148	12	5	0	72	89	19	27	....	.304	.422	.349	.771	111	17	85	6.65	-19	S-61,0-51(29-0-22),3-11	17	-0.1
1894 Lou-N	55	220	46	61	3	3	0	27	23	9	9	....	.277	.351	.318	.669	67	-10	28	4.65	-2	1-30,0-18(1-0-17)/3-3,S-3,2	3	-1.0
StL-N	18	71	10	20	4	1	0	10	8	3	2	....	.282	.354	.366	.721	74	-3	10	5.19	-1	3-18	1	-0.3
Was-N	7	25	4	5	2	1	0	2	2	1	0	....	.200	.259	.360	.619	50	-2	2	3.11	0	/2-4,S-3	0	-0.2
Yr.	80	316	60	86	9	5	0	39	33	13	11	....	.272	.345	.332	.677	67	-15	41	4.63	-4	1-30,3-21,0-18(1-0-17)/S-6,2	4	-1.5
Total 5	387	1510	272	440	43	23	1	204	197	58	81	....	.291	.380	.352	.732	107	22	238	5.90	-46	3-154,S-125/0-73,1-30,2-5	45	-1.4

• O'ROURKE, Tom

Thomas Joseph O'Rourke b: 10/1865, New York, NY d: 7/19/1929, New York, NY TR, 5'9", 158 lbs. Deb: 5/11/1887 Career OF: 0-0-2

YEAR TM-L	G	AB	R	H	2B	3B	HR	RBI	BB	SO	SB	CS	AVG	OBP	SLG	OPS	OPS+	BR/A	RC	RC/G	FR	G/POS	WS	TPW
1887 Bos-N	22	85	12	19	3	0	0	10	7	6	4	....	.224	.233	.192	.425	20	-8	5	1.82	-6	C-21/3-1,0-1	1	-1.0
1888 Bos-N	20	74	3	13	0	0	0	4	1	9	2	....	.176	.187	.176	.362	15	-7	3	1.27	2	C-20/0-1	1	-0.4
1890 NY-N	2	7	1	0	0	0	0	0	1	0	0	....	.000	.125	.000	.125	-63	-1	0	.00	0	/C-2	0	-0.1
Syr-a	41	153	16	33	8	0	0	12	12	....	2	....	.216	.277	.268	.545	68	-6	12	2.70	-7	C-40/1-1	3	-0.8
Total 3	85	319	32	65	11	0	0	26	21	15	8	....	.204	.242	.221	.463	40	-22	20	2.05	-11	/C-83,0-2,1-1,3-1	5	-2.3

• ORR, Billy

William John Orr b: 4/22/1891, San Francisco, CA d: 3/10/1967, St. Helena, CA BR/TR, 5'11", 168 lbs. Deb: 5/3/1913

YEAR TM-L	G	AB	R	H	2B	3B	HR	RBI	BB	SO	SB	CS	AVG	OBP	SLG	OPS	OPS+	BR/A	RC	RC/G	FR	G/POS	WS	TPW
1913 Phi-A	30	67	6	13	1	1	0	7	4	10	1	....	.194	.239	.239	.478	41	-5	4	1.76	-2	S-16/1-3,3-3,2-2	1	-0.6
1914 Phi-A	10	24	3	4	1	1	0	1	2	5	1	1	.167	.231	.292	.522	59	-2	2	1.90	-2	/S-6,3-1	0	-0.3
Total 2	40	91	9	17	2	2	0	8	6	15	2	1	.187	.237	.253	.490	46	-7	5	1.80	-3	/S-22,3-4,1-3,2-2	1	-1.0

• ORR, Dave

David L. Orr b: 9/29/1859, New York, NY d: 6/2/1915, Richmond Hill, NY BR/TR, 5'11", 250 lbs. Deb: 5/17/1883 M/U Career OF: 1-3-3

YEAR TM-L	G	AB	R	H	2B	3B	HR	RBI	BB	SO	SB	CS	AVG	OBP	SLG	OPS	OPS+	BR/A	RC	RC/G	FR	G/POS	WS	TPW
1883 NY-a	1	4	1	1	1	0	0	0	0	....	....	....	.250	.250	.500	.750	130	0	1	4.78	0	/1-1	0	0.0
NY-N	1	3	0	0	0	0	0	0	0	1	....	....	.000	.000	.000	.000	-101	-1	0	.00	0	/0-1	0	-0.1
NY-a	12	46	5	15	3	3	2	11	0	....	....	....	.326	.326	.652	.978	198	5	10	9.06	-1	1-12	3	0.3
Yr.	13	50	6	16	4	3	2	11	0	....	....	....	.320	.320	.640	.960	193	5	11	8.68	-1	1-13	3	0.3
1884*NY-a	110	458	82	**162**	32	13	9	**112**	5	....	....	....	**.354**	.362	.539	.901	**195**	**44**	92	8.52	7	*1-110/0-3(0-0-3)	27	3.8
1885 NY-a	107	444	76	152	29	**21**	6	77	8	....	....	....	.342	.358	**.543**	.901	**197**	47	88	8.18	-4	*1-107/P-3	27	2.6
1886 NY-a	136	571	93	**193**	25	**31**	7	91	17	....	16	....	.338	.363	**.527**	**.890**	**186**	**51**	118	8.41	8	*1-136	23	4.2
1887 NY-a	84	367	63	149	25	10	2	66	22	....	17	....	.406	.408	.516	.924	164	28	81	10.09	0	1-81/0-3(0-3-0)	16	1.8
1888 Bro-a	99	394	57	120	20	5	1	59	7	....	11	....	.305	.330	.388	.718	130	11	55	5.47	7	*1-99	13	0.9
1889 Col-a	134	560	70	183	31	12	4	87	9	38	12	....	.327	.340	.446	.786	130	17	91	6.41	7	*1-134	17	1.1
1890 Bro-P	107	464	89	172	32	13	6	124	30	11	10	....	.371	.414	.534	.948	143	25	109	10.11	-14	*1-107	19	0.2
Total 8	791	3311	536	1147	198	108	37	627	98	50	66	....	.346	.366	.502	.867	164	229	646	8.07	11	1-787/0-7,P-3	145	14.8

• ORSATTI, Ernie

Ernest Ralph Orsatti b: 9/8/1902, Los Angeles, CA d: 9/4/1968, Canoga Park, CA BL/TL, 5'7.5", 154 lbs. Deb: 9/4/1927 Career OF: 93-281-156

YEAR TM-L	G	AB	R	H	2B	3B	HR	RBI	BB	SO	SB	CS	AVG	OBP	SLG	OPS	OPS+	BR/A	RC	RC/G	FR	G/POS	WS	TPW
1927 StL-N	27	92	15	29	7	3	0	12	11	12	2	....	.315	.388	.457	.845	122	3	16	6.49	-1	0-26(0-6-20)	4	0.0
1928*StL-N	27	69	10	21	6	0	3	15	10	11	0	....	.304	.400	.522	.922	137	4	14	7.21	-1	0-17(2-0-15)/1-5	3	0.1
1929 StL-N	113	346	64	115	21	7	3	39	33	43	7	....	.332	.394	.460	.853	109	6	62	6.70	2	0-77(9-2-67),1-10	10	0.1
1930*StL-N	48	131	24	42	8	4	1	15	12	18	1	....	.321	.382	.466	.848	100	0	23	6.54	4	1-22,0-11(0-0-11)	4	0.1
1931*StL-N	70	158	27	46	16	6	0	19	14	16	1	....	.291	.349	.468	.817	113	3	26	5.97	-2	0-45(30-6-9)/1-1	6	-0.1
1932 StL-N	101	375	44	126	27	6	2	44	18	29	5	....	.336	.368	.456	.824	117	8	63	6.51	-9	0-96(40-55-1)/1-1	12	-0.4
1933 StL-N	120	436	55	130	21	6	0	38	33	33	14	....	.298	.348	.374	.721	101	1	58	4.76	-4	*0-107(6-96-5)/1-3	14	-0.6
1934*StL-N	105	337	39	101	14	4	0	31	27	31	6	....	.300	.353	.365	.718	87	-5	45	4.94	-3	0-90(0-90-0)	10	-1.0
1935 StL-N	90	221	28	53	9	3	1	24	18	25	10	....	.240	.297	.321	.618	64	-11	21	3.07	-4	0-60(6-26-28)	3	-1.7
Total 9	701	2165	306	663	129	39	10	237	176	218	46	....	.306	.360	.416	.776	102	8	328	5.51	-18	0-529/1-42	66	-3.5

• ORSINO, John

John Joseph "Horse" Orsino b: 4/22/1938, Teaneck, NJ BR/TR, 6'3", 215 lbs. Deb: 7/14/1961

YEAR TM-L	G	AB	R	H	2B	3B	HR	RBI	BB	SO	SB	CS	AVG	OBP	SLG	OPS	OPS+	BR/A	RC	RC/G	FR	G/POS	WS	TPW
1961 SF-N	25	83	5	23	3	2	4	12	3	13	0	0	.277	.310	.506	.816	116	1	13	6.01	-1	C-25	4	0.1

YEAR TM-L	G	AB	R	H	2B	3B	HR	RBI	BB	SO	SB	CS	AVG	OBP	SLG	OPS	OPS+	BR/A	RC	RC/G	FR	G/POS	WS	TPW
1962*SF-N	18	48	4	13	2	0	0	4	5	11	0	0	.271	.340	.313	.652	78	-1	5	3.54	-1	C-16	1	-0.2
1963 Bal-A	116	379	53	103	18	1	19	56	38	53	2	3	.272	.352	.475	.827	132	15	63	5.87	-1	*C-109/1-3	20	2.1
1964 Bal-A	81	248	21	55	10	0	8	23	23	55	0	0	.222	.293	.359	.652	81	-7	26	3.44	-3	C-66/1-5	6	-0.7
1965 Bal-A	77	232	30	54	10	2	9	28	23	51	1	0	.233	.315	.409	.725	102	1	26	3.64	-3	C-62/1-5	7	0.0
1966 Was-A	14	23	1	4	1	0	0	0	0	7	0	0	.174	.174	.217	.391	12	-3	1	1.24	0	/1-5,C-2	0	-0.3
1967 Was-A	1	1	0	0	0	0	0	0	0	1	0	0	.000	.000	.000	.000	-104	-0	0	.00	0	....	0	0.0
Total 7	332	1014	114	252	44	5	40	123	92	191	3	3	.249	.321	.420	.742	106	7	135	4.50	-10	C-280/1-18	38	0.9

• ORSULAK, Joe Joseph Michael Orsulak b: 5/31/1962, Glen Ridge, NJ BL/TL, 6'1", 196 lbs. Deb: 9/1/1983 Career OF: 449-216-669

YEAR TM-L	G	AB	R	H	2B	3B	HR	RBI	BB	SO	SB	CS	AVG	OBP	SLG	OPS	OPS+	BR/A	RC	RC/G	FR	G/POS	WS	TPW
1983 Pit-N	7	11	0	2	0	0	0	1	0	2	0	1	.182	.182	.182	.364	1	-2	0	.52	1	/O-4(0-4-0)	0	-0.1
1984 Pit-N	32	67	12	17	1	2	0	3	1	7	3	1	.254	.275	.328	.604	69	-3	6	3.17	0	O-25(7-12-5)	1	-0.3
1985 Pit-N	121	397	54	119	14	6	0	21	26	27	24	11	.300	.344	.365	.710	100	-0	51	4.47	3	*O-115(41-72-16)	9	-0.1
1986 Pit-N	138	401	60	100	19	6	2	19	28	38	24	11	.249	.300	.342	.642	75	-14	42	3.49	5	*O-120(9-46-73)	7	-1.3
1988 Bal-A	125	379	48	109	21	3	8	27	23	30	9	8	.288	.333	.422	.755	113	4	51	4.65	1	*O-117(36-14-76)	9	0.2
1989 Bal-A	123	390	59	111	22	5	7	55	41	35	5	3	.285	.356	.421	.776	122	11	59	5.23	2	*O-109(20-0-91)/D-5	14	1.0
1990 Bal-A	124	413	49	111	14	3	11	57	46	48	6	8	.269	.343	.397	.741	110	4	55	4.63	1	*O-109(30-0-80)/D-5	14	0.1
1991 Bal-A	143	486	57	135	22	1	5	43	28	45	6	2	.278	.322	.358	.680	92	-6	56	4.14	13	*O-132(85-1-68)/D-2	9	0.2
1992 Bal-A	117	391	45	113	18	3	4	39	28	34	5	4	.289	.343	.381	.724	100	-1	52	4.84	1	*O-110(14-0-98)/D-1	12	-0.3
1993 NY-N	134	409	59	116	15	4	8	35	28	25	5	4	.284	.333	.399	.731	96	-4	54	4.76	0	*O-114(66-40-23)/1-4	8	-0.7
1994 NY-N	96	292	39	76	3	0	8	42	16	21	4	2	.260	.305	.353	.658	72	-13	29	3.34	-1	O-90(18-13-63)/1-6	5	-1.7
1995 NY-N	108	290	41	82	19	2	1	37	19	35	1	3	.283	.329	.372	.701	87	-7	35	4.32	-1	O-86(56-0-31)/1-1	7	-1.1
1996 Fla-N	120	217	23	48	6	1	2	19	16	38	1	1	.221	.275	.286	.560	50	-16	17	2.60	0	O-59(30-14-19)/1-2	1	-1.8
1997 Mon-N	106	150	13	34	12	1	1	7	18	17	0	1	.227	.310	.340	.650	70	-7	16	3.65	0	O-63(37-0-26),1-15/D-1	1	-0.9
Total 14	1494	4293	559	1173	186	37	57	405	318	402	93	60	.273	.327	.374	.700	93	-53	523	4.24	25	*O-1253/1-28,D-14	97	-6.7

• ORTA, Jorge Jorge (Nunez) Orta b: 11/26/1950, Mazatlan, Mexico BL/TR, 5'10", 175 lbs. Deb: 4/15/1972 Career OF: 96-3-246

YEAR TM-L	G	AB	R	H	2B	3B	HR	RBI	BB	SO	SB	CS	AVG	OBP	SLG	OPS	OPS+	BR/A	RC	RC/G	FR	G/POS	WS	TPW
1972 Chi-A	51	124	20	25	3	1	3	11	6	37	3	3	.202	.244	.315	.559	64	-7	9	2.25	-1	S-18,2-14/3-9	1	-0.6
1973 Chi-A	128	425	46	113	9	10	6	40	37	87	8	8	.266	.326	.376	.703	94	-5	51	4.15	-27	*2-122/S-1	10	-2.5
1974 Chi-A	139	525	73	166	31	2	10	67	40	88	9	5	.316	.368	.440	.808	128	19	85	6.04	-6	*2-123,D-10/S-3	22	2.1
1975 Chi-A★	140	542	64	165	26	10	11	83	48	67	16	9	.304	.365	.450	.816	128	19	85	5.59	-16	*2-135/D-2	21	1.3
1976 Chi-A	158	636	74	174	29	8	14	72	38	77	24	8	.274	.320	.410	.730	112	9	81	4.45	-2	O-77(76-0-2),3-49,D-31	17	0.1
1977 Chi-A	144	564	71	159	27	8	11	84	46	49	4	4	.282	.338	.417	.755	105	3	78	4.89	-32	*2-139	14	-2.2
1978 Chi-A	117	420	45	115	19	2	13	53	42	39	1	2	.274	.345	.421	.767	114	7	61	5.05	-19	*2-114/D-2	15	-0.6
1979 Chi-A	113	325	49	85	18	3	11	46	44	33	1	5	.262	.351	.437	.788	111	4	50	5.20	-4	D-62,2-41	8	-0.1
1980 Cle-A★	129	481	78	140	18	3	10	64	71	44	6	5	.291	.384	.403	.788	116	13	78	5.81	4	*O-120(0-2-118)/D-7	18	1.0
1981 Cle-A	88	338	50	92	14	3	5	34	21	43	4	3	.272	.317	.376	.692	100	-1	38	3.76	0	O-86(0-1-86)	7	-0.5
1982 LA-N	86	115	13	25	5	0	2	8	12	13	0	1	.217	.297	.313	.610	73	-5	11	3.17	1	O-17(1-0-16)	1	-0.5
1983 Tor-A	103	245	30	58	6	3	10	38	19	29	1	2	.237	.292	.408	.700	85	-6	28	3.76	1	D-70,O-17(5-0-12)	3	-0.7
1984*KC-A	122	403	50	120	23	7	9	50	28	39	0	1	.298	.346	.457	.803	119	9	63	5.75	-1	D-83,O-26(14-0-12)/2-1	13	0.4
1985*KC-A	110	300	32	80	21	1	4	45	22	28	2	1	.267	.321	.383	.704	92	-4	36	4.10	0	D-85	5	-0.6
1986 KC-A	106	336	35	93	14	2	9	46	23	34	0	3	.277	.323	.411	.734	96	-4	42	4.37	0	D-87	5	-0.6
1987 KC-A	21	50	3	9	4	0	2	4	3	8	0	0	.180	.226	.380	.606	55	-3	4	2.91	0	D-12	0	-0.4
Total 16	1755	5829	733	1619	267	63	130	745	500	715	79	60	.278	.338	.412	.750	108	50	800	4.80	-104	2-689,D-451,O-343/3-58,S-22	160	-4.2

• ORTEGA, Bill William (Bobadilla) Ortega b: 7/24/1975, Havana, Cuba BR/TR, 6'4", 205 lbs. Deb: 9/7/2001

YEAR TM-L	G	AB	R	H	2B	3B	HR	RBI	BB	SO	SB	CS	AVG	OBP	SLG	OPS	OPS+	BR/A	RC	RC/G	FR	G/POS	WS	TPW
2001 StL-N	5	5	0	1	0	0	0	0	0	1	0	0	.200	.200	.200	.400	4	-1	0	1.35	0	....	0	-0.1

• ORTENZIO, Frank Frank Joseph Ortenzio b: 2/24/1951, Fresno, CA BR/TR, 6'2", 215 lbs. Deb: 9/9/1973

YEAR TM-L	G	AB	R	H	2B	3B	HR	RBI	BB	SO	SB	CS	AVG	OBP	SLG	OPS	OPS+	BR/A	RC	RC/G	FR	G/POS	WS	TPW
1973 KC-A	9	25	1	7	2	0	1	6	2	6	0	0	.280	.333	.480	.813	118	1	4	6.26	1	/1-7,D-1	1	0.1

• ORTH, Al Albert Lewis "Smiling Al,The Curveless Wonder" Orth
b: 9/5/1872, Tipton, IN d: 10/8/1948, Lynchburg, VA BL/TR, 6', 200 lbs. Deb: 8/15/1895 U Career OF: 20-21-14 ♦

YEAR TM-L	G	AB	R	H	2B	3B	HR	RBI	BB	SO	SB	CS	AVG	OBP	SLG	OPS	OPS+	BR/A	RC	RC/G	FR	G/POS	WS	TPW
1895 Phi-N	11	45	8	16	4	0	1	13	1	6	0	....	.356	.370	.511	.881	125	4	9	7.73	-1	P-11	9	1.0
1896 Phi-N	25	82	12	21	3	3	1	13	3	11	2	....	.256	.282	.402	.685	80	3	10	4.40	0	P-25	14	0.2
1897 Phi-N	53	152	26	50	7	4	1	17	3	....	5	....	.329	.342	.447	.789	110	9	26	6.57	0	P-36/O-6(3-3-0)	16	0.2
1898 Phi-N	39	123	17	36	6	4	1	14	3	....	1	....	.293	.310	.431	.740	116	9	18	5.01	0	P-32/O-1	18	2.1
1899 Phi-N	22	62	5	13	3	1	1	5	1	....	2	....	.210	.222	.339	.561	55	0	5	2.82	-4	P-21/O-1	14	1.6
1900 Phi-N	39	129	6	40	4	1	1	21	2	....	2	....	.310	.326	.380	.706	95	7	17	5.07	1	P-33/O-3(0-3-0)	18	0.3
1901 Phi-N	41	128	14	36	6	0	1	15	3	....	3	....	.281	.303	.352	.655	88	6	15	4.29	3	P-35/O-4(0-4-0)	29	4.0
1902 Was-A	56	175	20	38	3	2	2	10	9	....	2	....	.217	.255	.291	.547	51	-1	14	2.69	0	P-38,O-13(1-4-8)/1-1,S-1	19	-0.5
1903 Was-A	55	162	19	49	9	7	0	11	4	....	3	....	.302	.323	.444	.768	126	12	25	5.80	-3	P-36/S-7,O-4(2-0-2),1-2	15	-2.5
1904 Was-A	31	102	7	22	3	1	0	11	1	....	2	....	.216	.238	.265	.503	60	-3	7	2.34	-4	O-18(12-6-0),P-10	1	-2.5
NY-A	24	64	6	19	1	1	0	7	0	....	2	....	.297	.308	.344	.651	101	3	8	4.43	1	P-20/O-2(0-1-1)	14	0.0
Yr.	55	166	13	41	4	2	0	18	1	....	4	....	.247	.265	.295	.560	76	-0	15	3.10	-3	P-30,O-20(12-7-1)	15	-2.5
1905 NY-A	55	131	13	24	3	1	1	8	4	....	2	....	.183	.213	.244	.458	40	-1	8	1.86	0	P-40/1-1,O-1	18	0.6
1906 NY-A	47	135	12	37	2	2	1	17	6	....	2	....	.274	.305	.341	.646	93	6	15	4.03	0	P-45/O-1	36	3.7
1907 NY-A	44	105	11	34	6	0	1	13	4	....	1	....	.324	.355	.410	.764	133	9	16	5.89	2	P-36/O-1	16	1.9
1908 NY-A	38	69	4	20	1	2	0	4	2	....	0	....	.290	.310	.362	.672	117	5	8	3.91	-1	P-21	5	-0.7
1909 NY-A	22	34	3	9	0	1	0	5	5	....	1	....	.265	.359	.324	.683	115	1	4	4.35	-1	/2-6,P-1	1	-0.4
Total 15	602	1698	183	464	61	30	12	184	51	17	30	....	.273	.298	.366	.663	92	68	205	4.30	-9	P-440/O-55,S-8,2-6,1-4	243	9.2

• ORTIZ, David David Americo (Arias) Ortiz b: 11/18/1975, Santo Domingo, Dominican Republic BL/TL, 6'4", 230 lbs. Deb: 9/2/1997

YEAR TM-L	G	AB	R	H	2B	3B	HR	RBI	BB	SO	SB	CS	AVG	OBP	SLG	OPS	OPS+	BR/A	RC	RC/G	FR	G/POS	WS	TPW
1997 Min-A	15	49	10	16	3	0	1	6	2	19	0	0	.327	.353	.449	.802	106	0	8	5.96	1	1-11/D-1	2	0.1
1998 Min-A	86	278	47	77	20	0	9	46	39	72	1	0	.277	.376	.446	.822	111	6	48	6.03	2	1-70,D-10	9	0.2
1999 Min-A	10	20	1	0	0	0	0	0	5	12	0	0	.000	.200	.000	.200	-42	-4	0	.19	0	/D-5,1-1	0	-0.4
2000 Min-A	130	415	59	117	36	1	10	63	57	81	1	0	.282	.369	.446	.814	101	2	68	5.82	0	D-88,1-27	8	-0.5
2001 Min-A	89	303	46	71	17	1	18	48	40	68	1	0	.234	.326	.475	.801	105	2	47	5.29	0	D-78/1-8	7	-0.4
2002*Min-A	125	412	52	112	32	1	20	75	43	87	1	2	.272	.345	.500	.845	120	10	72	6.18	0	D-95,1-15	11	0.4
2003*Bos-A	128	448	79	129	39	2	31	101	58	83	0	0	.288	.371	.592	.962	145	29	98	8.04	0	D-74,1-45	15	1.9
Total 7	583	1925	294	522	147	5	89	339	244	422	4	2	.271	.356	.491	.848	116	44	341	6.26	4	D-351,1-177	52	1.2

• ORTIZ, Hector Hector (Montanez) Ortiz b: 10/14/1969, Rio Piedras, Puerto Rico BR/TR, 6', 205 lbs. Deb: 9/14/1998

YEAR TM-L	G	AB	R	H	2B	3B	HR	RBI	BB	SO	SB	CS	AVG	OBP	SLG	OPS	OPS+	BR/A	RC	RC/G	FR	G/POS	WS	TPW
1998 KC-A	4	4	1	0	0	0	0	0	0	0	0	0	.000	.000	.000	.000	-97	-1	0	.00	-1	/C-3,1-1	0	-0.2
2000 KC-A	26	88	15	34	6	0	0	5	8	8	0	0	.386	.443	.455	.898	124	4	19	9.03	-1	C-26	5	0.4
2001 KC-A	56	154	12	38	6	1	0	11	9	24	1	3	.247	.293	.299	.591	52	-12	12	2.59	4	C-55/D-1	2	-0.4
2002 Tex-A	7	14	1	3	1	0	1	2	1	1	0	0	.214	.267	.500	.767	93	-0	1	3.27	-2	/C-7	0	-0.2
Total 4	93	260	29	75	13	1	1	18	18	33	1	3	.288	.339	.358	.697	77	-9	32	4.40	0	/C-91,1-1,D-1	7	-0.4

• ORTIZ, Javier Javier Victor Ortiz b: 1/22/1963, Boston, MA BR/TR, 6'4", 220 lbs. Deb: 6/15/1990 Career OF: 35-1-20

YEAR TM-L	G	AB	R	H	2B	3B	HR	RBI	BB	SO	SB	CS	AVG	OBP	SLG	OPS	OPS+	BR/A	RC	RC/G	FR	G/POS	WS	TPW
1990 Hou-N	30	77	7	21	5	1	1	10	12	11	1	1	.273	.371	.403	.773	116	2	12	5.54	0	O-25(20-1-9)	2	0.1
1991 Hou-N	47	83	7	23	4	1	1	5	14	14	0	0	.277	.381	.386	.767	123	3	12	5.35	2	O-24(15-0-11)	2	0.5
Total 2	77	160	14	44	9	2	2	15	26	25	1	1	.275	.376	.394	.770	120	5	25	5.44	1	/O-49	4	0.5

• ORTIZ, Jose Jose Luis (Irizarry) Ortiz b: 6/25/1947, Ponce, Puerto Rico BR/TR, 5'9.5", 155 lbs. Deb: 9/4/1969 Career OF: 3-39-5

YEAR TM-L	G	AB	R	H	2B	3B	HR	RBI	BB	SO	SB	CS	AVG	OBP	SLG	OPS	OPS+	BR/A	RC	RC/G	FR	G/POS	WS	TPW
1969 Chi-A	16	11	0	3	1	0	0	2	1	0	0	0	.273	.333	.364	.697	90	-0	1	4.50	0	/O-8(2-5-2)	0	0.0
1970 Chi-A	15	24	4	8	1	0	0	1	2	2	1	0	.333	.407	.375	.782	113	1	4	6.75	2	/O-8(1-5-2)	1	0.2
1971 Chi-N	36	88	10	26	7	1	0	3	4	10	2	2	.295	.347	.398	.745	96	-1	12	5.15	-1	O-30(0-29-1)	3	-0.2
Total 3	67	123	14	37	9	1	0	6	7	12	3	2	.301	.358	.390	.748	99	0	18	5.39	1	/O-46	4	0.0

• ORTIZ, Jose Jose Daniel Ortiz b: 6/13/1977, Santo Domingo, Dominican Republic BR/TR, 5'9", 177 lbs. Deb: 9/15/2000

YEAR TM-L	G	AB	R	H	2B	3B	HR	RBI	BB	SO	SB	CS	AVG	OBP	SLG	OPS	OPS+	BR/A	RC	RC/G	FR	G/POS	WS	TPW
2000 Oak-A	7	11	4	2	0	0	0	1	2	3	0	0	.182	.308	.182	.490	29	-1	1	2.33	-1	/D-4,2-3	0	-0.2

YEAR TM-L	G	AB	R	H	2B	3B	HR	RBI	BB	SO	SB	CS	AVG	OBP	SLG	OPS	OPS+	BR/A	RC	RC/G	FR	G/POS	WS	TPW
2001 Oak-A	11	42	4	7	0	0	0	3	3	5	1	0	.167	.222	.167	.389	5	-6	1	.78	-3	2-10/D-1	0	-0.8
Col-N	53	204	38	52	8	1	13	35	14	36	3	1	.255	.315	.495	.810	86	-5	31	5.22	-4	2-51	4	-0.6
2002 Col-N	65	192	22	48	7	1	1	12	16	30	2	0	.250	.318	.313	.630	58	-11	20	3.62	-6	2-53/3-1	2	-1.4
Total 3	136	449	68	109	15	2	14	51	35	74	6	1	.243	.308	.379	.686	65	-22	53	3.98	-14	2-117/D-5,3-1	6	-3.1
• ORTIZ, Junior	Adalberto Colon Ortiz b: 10/24/1959, Humacao, Puerto Rico BR/TR, 5'11", 176 lbs. Deb: 9/20/1982																							
1982 Pit-N	7	15	1	3	1	0	0	0	1	3	0	0	.200	.250	.267	.517	43	-1	1	1.66	0	/C-7	0	-0.1
1983 Pit-N	5	8	1	1	0	0	0	0	1	0	0	0	.125	.222	.125	.347	-1	-1	0	1.20	0	/C-4	0	-0.1
NY-N	68	185	10	47	5	0	0	12	3	34	1	0	.254	.270	.281	.551	53	-12	14	2.74	-3	C-67	2	-1.2
Yr.	73	193	11	48	5	0	0	12	4	34	1	0	.249	.268	.275	.542	51	-13	15	2.66	-3	C-71	2	-1.3
1984 NY-N	40	91	6	18	3	0	0	11	5	15	1	0	.198	.240	.231	.470	33	-8	5	1.79	0	C-32	1	-0.7
1985 Pit-N	23	72	4	21	2	0	1	5	3	17	1	0	.292	.320	.361	.681	91	-1	8	4.25	2	C-23	2	0.2
1986 Pit-N	49	110	11	37	6	0	0	14	9	13	0	1	.336	.387	.391	.777	112	2	16	5.25	0	C-36	3	0.3
1987 Pit-N	75	192	16	52	8	1	1	22	15	23	0	2	.271	.324	.339	.662	75	-8	20	3.48	0	C-72	4	-0.5
1988 Pit-N	49	118	8	33	6	0	2	18	9	9	1	4	.280	.341	.381	.722	109	-0	13	3.54	1	C-40	2	0.3
1989 Pit-N	91	230	16	50	6	1	1	22	20	20	2	2	.217	.286	.265	.551	61	-12	17	2.26	0	C-84	2	-0.9
1990 Min-A	71	170	18	57	7	1	0	18	12	16	0	4	.335	.386	.388	.774	110	1	24	5.22	3	C-68/D-3	8	0.7
1991★Min-A	61	134	9	28	5	1	0	11	15	12	0	1	.209	.293	.261	.555	52	-9	10	2.30	-1	C-60	1	-0.8
1992 Cle-A	86	244	20	61	7	0	0	24	12	23	1	3	.250	.296	.279	.575	63	-13	19	2.61	-1	C-86	5	-1.0
1993 Cle-A	95	249	19	55	13	0	0	20	11	26	1	0	.221	.268	.273	.541	46	-19	17	2.19	8	C-95	5	-0.5
1994 Tex-A	29	76	3	21	2	0	0	9	5	11	0	1	.276	.329	.303	.632	65	-4	8	3.43	2	C-28	2	-0.1
Total 13	749	1894	142	484	71	4	5	186	121	222	8	18	.256	.306	.305	.612	69	-86	171	3.03	10	C-702/D-3	37	-4.4
• ORTIZ, Luis	Luis Albert (Galarza) Ortiz b: 5/25/1970, Santo Domingo, Dominican Republic BR/TR, 6', 190 lbs. Deb: 8/31/1993																							
1993 Bos-A	9	12	0	3	0	0	0	1	0	2	0	0	.250	.250	.250	.500	33	-1	1	2.25	0	/3-5,D-3	0	-0.1
1994 Bos-A	7	18	3	3	2	0	0	6	1	5	0	0	.167	.211	.278	.488	23	-2	1	1.81	0	/D-6	0	-0.2
1995 Tex-A	41	108	10	25	5	2	1	18	6	18	0	1	.231	.272	.343	.615	57	-8	8	2.29	-3	3-35/D-3	1	-1.0
1996 Tex-A	3	7	1	2	0	1	1	1	0	1	0	0	.286	.286	1.000	1.286	196	1	2	10.80	0	/D-1	0	0.1
Total 4	60	145	14	33	7	3	2	26	7	26	0	1	.228	.263	.359	.622	57	-10	12	2.56	-4	/3-40,D-13	1	-1.3
• ORTIZ, Roberto	Roberto Gonzalo (Nunez) Ortiz b: 6/30/1915, Camaguey, Cuba d: 9/15/1971, Miami, FL BR/TR, 6'4", 200 lbs. Deb: 9/6/1941 Career OF: 16-0-151																							
1941 Was-A	22	79	10	26	1	2	1	17	3	10	0	1	.329	.354	.430	.784	112	1	11	5.45	0	0-21(0-0-21)	2	-0.1
1942 Was-A	20	42	4	7	1	3	1	4	5	11	0	0	.167	.271	.405	.676	89	-1	5	3.97	0	/0-9(1-0-8)	1	-0.2
1943 Was-A	1	4	0	1	0	0	0	0	0	0	0	1	.250	.250	.250	.500	48	-1	0	.00	0	/0-1	0	-0.1
1944 Was-A	85	316	36	80	11	4	5	35	19	47	4	1	.253	.312	.361	.673	96	-2	38	4.25	-4	0-80(10-0-71)	8	-1.1
1949 Was-A	40	129	12	36	3	0	1	11	9	12	0	0	.279	.326	.326	.652	74	-5	13	3.75	1	0-32(4-0-28)	2	-0.4
1950 Was-A	39	75	4	17	2	1	0	8	7	12	0	0	.227	.301	.280	.581	52	-5	7	2.94	0	0-19(0-0-19)	0	-0.5
Phi-A	6	14	1	1	0	0	0	3	0	3	0	0	.071	.071	.071	.143	-65	-3	0	.00	0	/0-3(1-0-3)	0	-0.3
Yr.	45	89	5	18	2	1	0	11	7	15	0	0	.202	.268	.247	.515	34	-9	7	2.35	0	0-22(1-0-22)	0	-0.8
Total 6	213	659	67	168	18	10	8	78	43	95	4	3	.255	.310	.349	.659	85	-16	75	3.96	-3	0-165	13	-2.7
• ORTON, John	John Andrew Orton b: 12/8/1965, Santa Cruz, CA BR/TR, 6'1", 192 lbs. Deb: 8/20/1989																							
1989 Cal-A	16	39	4	7	1	0	0	4	2	17	0	0	.179	.220	.205	.425	21	-4	2	1.58	0	C-16	1	-0.3
1990 Cal-A	31	84	8	16	5	0	1	6	5	31	0	1	.190	.244	.286	.530	49	-6	5	2.03	1	C-31	1	-0.4
1991 Cal-A	29	69	7	14	4	0	0	3	10	17	0	1	.203	.313	.261	.573	60	-4	6	2.62	3	C-28/D-1	2	0.1
1992 Cal-A	43	114	11	25	3	0	2	12	7	32	1	1	.219	.276	.298	.575	61	-6	10	2.82	0	C-43	3	-0.3
1993 Cal-A	37	95	5	18	5	0	1	4	7	24	1	2	.189	.252	.274	.526	40	-9	6	2.14	-1	C-35/0-1	1	-0.7
Total 5	156	401	35	80	18	0	4	29	31	121	2	5	.200	.265	.274	.540	50	-29	30	2.33	4	C-153/D-1,0-1	8	-1.6
• ORWOLL, Ossie	Oswald Christian Orwoll b: 11/17/1900, Portland, OR d: 5/8/1967, Decorah, IA BL/TL, 6', 174 lbs. Deb: 4/13/1928 ♦																							
1928 Phi-A	64	170	28	52	13	2	0	22	16	24	3	1	.306	.366	.406	.771	100	4	26	5.56	0	1-34,P-27	10	-0.4
1929 Phi-A	30	51	6	13	2	1	0	6	2	11	0	0	.255	.283	.333	.616	56	-2	5	3.32	-1	P-12/0-9(1-8-0)	1	-0.4
Total 2	94	221	34	65	15	3	0	28	18	35	3	1	.294	.347	.389	.736	90	3	31	5.03	-1	/P-39,1-34,0-9	11	-0.8
• OSBORN, Fred	Wilferd Pearl Osborn b: 11/28/1883, Nevada, OH d: 9/2/1954, Upper Sandusky, OH BL/TR, 5'9" Deb: 6/8/1907 Career OF: 8-226-7																							
1907 Phi-N	56	163	22	45	2	3	0	9	3	....	4	....	.276	.298	.325	.623	97	-2	17	3.83	-1	0-36(8-26-1)/1-1	4	-0.4
1908 Phi-N	152	555	62	148	19	12	2	44	30	....	16	....	.267	.305	.355	.660	107	3	64	3.95	-3	*0-152(0-146-6)	19	-1.0
1909 Phi-N	58	189	14	35	4	1	0	19	12	....	6	....	.185	.238	.217	.455	41	-13	12	1.87	9	0-54(0-54-0)	3	-0.8
Total 3	266	907	98	228	25	16	2	72	45	....	26	....	.251	.290	.321	.611	91	-12	94	3.43	5	0-242/1-1	26	-2.1
• OSBORNE, Bobo	Lawrence Sidney Osborne b: 10/12/1935, Chattahoochee, GA BL/TR, 6'1" Deb: 6/27/1957 Career OF: 0-0-6																							
1957 Det-A	11	27	4	4	1	0	0	1	3	7	0	0	.148	.233	.185	.419	15	-3	1	1.58	0	/0-5(0-0-5),1-4	0	-0.4
1958 Det-A	2	2	0	0	0	0	0	0	0	0	0	0	.000	.000	.000	.000	-93	-1	0	.00	0	....	0	-0.1
1959 Det-A	86	209	27	40	7	1	3	21	16	41	1	0	.191	.256	.278	.533	44	-16	15	2.40	-1	1-56/0-1	1	-2.0
1961 Det-A	71	93	8	20	7	0	2	13	20	15	1	0	.215	.354	.355	.709	87	-1	13	4.83	-1	1-11/3-8	3	-0.2
1962 Det-A	64	74	12	17	1	0	0	7	16	25	0	0	.230	.374	.243	.617	68	-2	8	3.95	-2	3-13/1-7,C-1	1	-0.4
1963 Was-A	125	358	42	76	14	1	12	44	49	83	0	0	.212	.312	.358	.670	87	-5	42	3.89	-3	1-81,3-16	8	-1.4
Total 6	359	763	93	157	30	2	17	86	104	171	2	0	.206	.306	.317	.623	71	-28	81	3.50	-7	1-159/3-37,0-6,C-1	13	-4.5
• OSBORNE, Fred	Frederick W. Osborne b: 5/1865, TL Deb: 7/14/1890 ♦																							
1890 Pit-N	41	168	24	40	8	3	1	14	6	18	0	....	.238	.269	.339	.608	87	-2	16	3.25	-1	0-35(28-1-6)/P-8	1	-2.9
• OSIK, Keith	Keith Richard Osik b: 10/22/1968, Port Jefferson, NY BR/TR, 6', 185 lbs. Deb: 4/5/1996 Career OF: 3-0-1																							
1996 Pit-N	48	140	18	41	14	1	1	14	14	22	1	0	.293	.361	.429	.790	104	1	22	5.76	1	C-41/3-2,0-2(2-0-0)	4	0.4
1997 Pit-N	49	105	10	27	9	1	0	7	9	21	0	1	.257	.322	.362	.684	77	-4	12	4.08	-2	C-32/2-4,1-1,3-1	3	-0.4
1998 Pit-N	39	98	8	21	4	0	0	7	13	16	1	2	.214	.319	.255	.574	53	-7	8	2.47	4	C-26/3-7	1	-0.2
1999 Pit-N	66	167	12	31	3	1	2	13	11	30	0	0	.186	.240	.251	.492	25	-20	9	1.65	1	C-50/P-1	3	-1.8
2000 Pit-N	46	123	11	36	6	1	4	22	14	11	3	0	.293	.387	.455	.843	113	4	23	7.01	-5	C-26,3-12/1-5,D-1,P-1	5	-0.4
2001 Pit-N	56	120	9	25	4	0	2	13	13	24	1	0	.208	.301	.292	.593	53	-8	12	3.27	1	C-39/1-5,3-3,2-2,0-1	1	-0.4
2002 Pit-N	55	100	6	16	3	0	2	11	6	25	0	0	.160	.215	.250	.465	22	-12	5	1.64	6	C-27/3-4,1-3,2-1,0-1	1	-0.4
2003 Mil-N	80	241	22	60	12	0	2	21	31	44	0	1	.249	.342	.324	.665	77	-8	27	3.88	7	C-78	4	0.5
Total 8	439	1094	96	257	55	4	13	108	111	193	6	4	.235	.315	.328	.643	67	-53	119	3.63	13	C-319/3-29,1-14,2-7,0-4,P-2,D	22	-2.8
• OSTDIEK, Harry	Henry Girard Ostdiek b: 4/12/1881, Ottumwa, IA d: 5/6/1956, Minneapolis, MN BR/TR, 5'11", 185 lbs. Deb: 9/10/1904																							
1904 Cle-A	7	18	1	3	0	1	0	3	3	....	1	....	.167	.318	.278	.596	90	0	2	3.46	0	/C-7	0	0.0
1908 Bos-A	1	3	0	0	0	0	0	0	0	....	0	....	.000	.000	.000	.000	-97	-1	0	.00	0	/C-1	0	-0.1
Total 2	8	21	1	3	0	1	0	3	3	....	1	....	.143	.280	.238	.518	67	-1	2	2.88	0	/C-8	0	0.0
• OSTEEN, Champ	James Champlin Osteen b: 2/24/1877, Hendersonville, NC d: 12/14/1962, Greenville, SC BL/TR, 5'8", 150 lbs. Deb: 9/18/1903																							
1903 Was-A	10	40	4	8	0	2	0	4	2	....	0	....	.200	.256	.300	.556	65	-2	3	2.61	1	S-10	1	0.0
1904 NY-A	28	107	15	21	1	4	2	9	1	....	0	....	.196	.218	.336	.555	71	-4	8	2.48	0	3-17/S-8,1-4	2	-0.3
1908 StL-N	29	112	2	22	4	0	0	11	0	....	0	....	.196	.204	.232	.436	41	-8	5	1.44	-5	S-17,3-12	1	-1.4
1909 StL-N	16	45	6	9	1	0	0	7	7	....	1	....	.200	.308	.222	.530	69	-1	4	2.44	-7	S-16	1	-0.9
Total 4	83	304	27	60	6	6	2	31	10	....	1	....	.197	.233	.276	.509	59	-15	20	2.10	-10	/S-51,3-29,1-4	5	-2.6
• OSTERGARD, Red	Roy Lund Ostergard b: 5/16/1896, Denmark, WI d: 1/13/1977, Hemet, CA BR/TR, 5'10.5", 175 lbs. Deb: 6/14/1921																							
1921 Chi-A	12	11	2	4	0	0	0	0	0	2	0	0	.364	.364	.364	.727	87	-0	1	5.29	0	....	0	0.0
• OSTERHOUT, Charlie	Charles H. Osterhout b: 6/1856, Syracuse, NY d: 5/21/1933, Syracuse, NY TR Deb: 6/23/1879																							
1879 Syr-N	2	8	0	0	0	0	0	0	0	0	....	....	.000	.000	.000	.000	-113	-2	0	.00	0	/C-1,0-1	0	-0.2

YEAR TM-L	G	AB	R	H	2B	3B	HR	RBI	BB	SO	SB	CS	AVG	OBP	SLG	OPS	OPS+	BR/A	RC	RC/G	FR	G/POS	WS	TPW
• OSTROSSER, Brian	Brian Leonard Ostrosser b: 6/17/1949, Hamilton, Canada BL/TR, 6', 175 lbs. Deb: 8/5/1973																							
1973 NY-N	4	5	0	0	0	0	0	0	0	2	0	0	.000	.000	.000	.000	-102	-1	0	.00	0	/S-4	0	-0.2
• OSTROWSKI, Johnny	John Thaddeus Ostrowski b: 10/17/1917, Chicago, IL d: 11/13/1992, Chicago, IL BR/TR, 5'10.5", 170 lbs. Deb: 9/24/1943 Career OF: 87-9-15																							
1943 Chi-N	10	29	2	6	0	1	0	3	3	8	0	....	.207	.303	.276	.579	69	-1	2	2.37	-1	/0-5(5-0-0),3-4	0	-0.3
1944 Chi-N	8	13	2	2	1	0	0	2	1	4	0	....	.154	.214	.231	.445	25	-1	1	1.71	0	/0-2(2-0-0)	0	-0.2
1945 Chi-N	7	10	4	3	2	0	0	1	0	0	0	....	.300	.300	.500	.800	123	0	2	5.79	-1	/3-4	1	0.0
1946 Chi-N	64	160	20	34	4	2	3	12	20	31	1	....	.213	.300	.319	.619	77	-5	16	3.41	-1	3-50/2-1	3	-0.6
1948 Bos-A	1	1	0	0	0	0	0	0	0	1	0	0	.000	.000	.000	.000	-95	-0	0	.00	0	....	0	0.0
1949 Chi-A	49	158	19	42	9	4	5	31	15	41	4	3	.266	.333	.468	.802	115	2	24	5.24	-1	0-41(40-0-3)/3-8	4	-0.2
1950 Chi-A	21	45	9	10	1	1	2	2	9	8	0	0	.222	.364	.422	.786	104	0	8	5.59	0	0-14(6-1-8)	0	0.0
Was-A	55	141	16	32	2	1	4	23	20	31	2	0	.227	.327	.340	.668	75	-5	17	4.00	0	0-45(34-7-4)	3	-0.7
Chi-A	1	4	1	2	1	0	0	0	0	1	0	0	.500	.500	.750	1.250	223	1	2	20.76	-0	/0-1	1	0.1
Yr.	77	190	26	44	4	2	6	25	29	40	2	0	.232	.339	.368	.708	85	-4	26	4.61	0	0-60(40-9-12)	4	-0.6
Total 7	216	561	73	131	20	9	14	74	68	125	7	3	.234	.321	.376	.697	89	-9	71	4.25	-4	0-108/3-66,2-1	12	-2.0
• OTANEZ, Willis	Willis Alexander Otanez b: 4/19/1973, Vega Baja, Dominican Republic BR/TR, 6'1", 215 lbs. Deb: 8/25/1998																							
1998 Bal-A	3	5	0	1	0	0	0	0	0	2	0	0	.200	.200	.200	.400	5	-1	0	1.35	0	/0-2(0-0-2)	0	-0.1
1999 Bal-A	29	80	7	17	3	0	2	11	6	16	0	0	.213	.276	.325	.601	55	-6	7	2.70	-3	3-22/1-5,D-3	0	-0.8
Tor-A	42	127	21	32	8	0	5	13	9	30	0	0	.252	.307	.433	.740	85	-3	16	4.52	-2	3-24,1-13/D-4	1	-0.6
Yr.	71	207	28	49	11	0	7	24	15	46	0	0	.237	.295	.391	.686	73	-9	23	3.77	-4	3-46,1-18/D-7	1	-1.3
Total 2	74	212	28	50	11	0	7	24	15	48	0	0	.236	.293	.387	.679	71	-10	23	3.72	-4	/3-46,1-18,D-7,0-2	1	-1.4
• OTERO, Reggie	Regino Jose (Gomez) Otero b: 9/7/1915, Havana, Cuba d: 10/21/1988, Hialeah, FL BL/TR, 6', 165 lbs. Deb: 9/2/1945 C																							
1945 Chi-N	14	23	1	9	0	0	0	5	2	2	0	....	.391	.440	.391	.831	135	1	4	7.65	0	/1-8	1	0.1
• OTERO, Ricky	Ricardo (Figueroa) Otero b: 4/15/1972, Vega Baja, Puerto Rico BB/TR, 5'7", 150 lbs. Deb: 4/26/1995 Career OF: 16-149-1																							
1995 NY-N	35	51	5	7	2	0	0	1	3	10	2	1	.137	.185	.176	.362	-4	-8	2	.95	0	0-23(15-9-0)	0	-0.8
1996 Phi-N	104	411	54	112	11	7	2	32	34	30	16	10	.273	.331	.348	.679	79	-14	49	4.18	3	*0-100(0-100-0)	8	-0.9
1997 Phi-N	50	151	20	38	6	2	0	3	19	15	0	3	.252	.339	.318	.657	73	-7	17	3.72	2	0-42(1-40-1)	2	-0.4
Total 3	189	613	79	157	19	9	2	36	56	55	18	14	.256	.321	.326	.648	70	-28	67	3.75	6	0-165	10	-2.1
• OTIS, Amos	Amos Joseph Otis b: 4/26/1947, Mobile, AL BR/TR, 5'11.5", 166 lbs. Deb: 9/6/1967 C Career OF: 63-1825-46																							
1967 NY-N	19	59	6	13	2	0	0	1	5	13	0	4	.220	.292	.254	.547	59	-5	4	2.06	1	0-16(2-14-3)/3-1	0	-0.5
1969 NY-N	48	93	6	14	3	1	0	4	6	27	1	0	.151	.202	.204	.406	14	-11	4	1.44	1	0-35(16-18-1)/3-3	1	-1.1
1970 KC-A★	159	620	91	176	**36**	9	11	58	68	67	33	2	.284	.356	.424	.780	114	19	102	5.91	2	*0-159(0-159-0)	25	1.7
1971 KC-A★	147	555	80	167	26	4	15	79	40	74	**52**	8	.301	.350	.443	.793	124	25	87	5.54	9	*0-144(0-144-0)	27	3.2
1972 KC-A★	143	540	75	158	28	2	11	54	50	59	28	12	.293	.356	.413	.769	129	20	82	5.37	0	*0-137(0-137-0)	22	1.9
1973 KC-A★	148	583	89	175	21	4	26	93	63	47	13	9	.300	.369	.484	.853	129	22	103	6.48	-1	*0-135(0-135-0),D-14	29	1.6
1974 KC-A	146	552	87	157	31	9	12	73	58	67	18	5	.284	.355	.438	.793	120	17	86	5.31	1	*0-143(0-143-0)/D-2	22	1.4
1975 KC-A	132	470	87	116	26	6	9	46	66	48	39	11	.247	.344	.385	.730	103	7	68	4.82	-3	*0-130(0-130-0)	17	0.1
1976*KC-A★	153	592	93	165	**40**	2	18	86	55	100	26	7	.279	.345	.444	.789	129	23	92	5.38	-11	*0-152(0-152-0)	25	0.8
1977*KC-A	142	478	85	120	20	8	17	78	71	88	23	7	.251	.348	.433	.781	111	11	74	5.11	-3	*0-140(0-140-0)	18	0.6
1978*KC-A	141	486	74	145	30	7	22	96	66	54	32	8	.298	.387	.525	.911	150	37	102	7.45	-2	*0-136(0-136-0)/D-1	29	3.4
1979 KC-A	151	577	100	170	28	2	18	90	68	92	30	5	.295	.372	.444	.816	117	19	100	6.18	-3	*0-146(0-146-0)/D-4	23	1.4
1980*KC-A	107	394	56	99	16	3	10	53	39	70	16	1	.251	.323	.383	.707	92	-1	52	4.40	2	*0-105(0-105-0)	12	0.0
1981*KC-A	99	372	49	100	22	3	9	57	31	59	16	7	.269	.328	.417	.745	114	7	51	4.60	2	0-97(13-86-1)/D-1	12	0.8
1982 KC-A	125	475	73	136	25	3	11	88	37	65	9	5	.286	.340	.421	.762	108	5	64	4.66	-6	*0-125(0-125-0)	15	-0.3
1983 KC-A	98	356	35	93	16	3	4	41	27	63	5	2	.261	.313	.357	.670	84	-8	39	3.90	2	0-96(0-55-41)/D-1	8	-0.8
1984 Pit-N	40	97	6	16	4	0	0	10	7	15	0	0	.165	.221	.206	.427	21	-10	4	1.28	2	0-32(32-0-0)	1	-1.0
Total 17	1998	7299	1092	2020	374	66	193	1007	757	1008	341	93	.277	.347	.425	.773	115	177	1114	5.29	-6	*0-1928/D-23,3-4	286	13.3
• OTIS, Bill	Paul Franklin Otis b: 12/24/1889, Scituate, MA d: 12/15/1990, Duluth, MN BL/TR, 5'10.5", 150 lbs. Deb: 7/4/1912																							
1912 NY-A	4	17	1	1	0	0	0	2	3	....	0	....	.059	.200	.059	.259	-24	-3	0	.30	0	/0-4(0-4-0)	0	-0.3
• OTT, Billy	William Joseph Ott b: 11/23/1940, New York, NY BB/TR, 6'1", 180 lbs. Deb: 9/4/1962 Career OF: 0-0-17																							
1962 Chi-N	12	28	3	4	0	0	1	2	2	10	0	0	.143	.200	.250	.450	19	-3	1	1.35	0	/0-7(0-0-7)	0	-0.3
1964 Chi-N	20	39	4	7	3	0	0	1	3	10	0	1	.179	.238	.256	.495	38	-4	2	1.88	-0	0-10(0-0-10)	0	-0.4
Total 2	32	67	7	11	3	0	1	3	5	20	0	1	.164	.222	.254	.476	30	-7	4	1.66	0	/0-17	0	-0.8
• OTT, Ed	Nathan Edward Ott b: 7/11/1951, Muncy, PA BL/TR, 5'10", 198 lbs. Deb: 6/10/1974 C Career OF: 7-0-2																							
1974 Pit-N	7	5	1	0	0	0	0	0	0	1	0	0	.000	.000	.000	.000	-104	-1	0	.00	0	/0-2(0-0-2)	0	-0.2
1975 Pit-N	5	5	0	1	0	0	0	0	0	0	0	0	.200	.200	.200	.400	11	-1	0	1.35	-1	/C-2	0	-0.1
1976 Pit-N	27	39	2	12	2	0	0	5	3	5	0	0	.308	.357	.359	.716	103	0	5	5.06	1	/C-8	1	0.1
1977 Pit-N	104	311	40	82	14	3	7	38	32	41	7	7	.264	.336	.395	.732	93	-4	41	4.56	-4	C-90	10	-0.4
1978 Pit-N	112	379	49	102	18	4	9	38	27	56	4	1	.269	.318	.409	.727	97	-2	49	4.54	-6	C-97/0-4(4-0-0)	12	-0.4
1979*Pit-N	117	403	49	110	20	2	7	51	26	62	0	1	.273	.317	.385	.702	86	-9	48	4.13	-4	*C-116	13	-0.7
1980 Pit-N	120	392	35	102	14	0	8	41	33	47	1	6	.260	.318	.357	.675	87	-10	42	3.64	-1	*C-117/0-3(3-0-0)	10	-0.6
1981 Cal-A	75	258	20	56	8	1	2	22	17	42	2	1	.217	.268	.279	.547	58	-14	19	2.36	-1	C-72	3	-1.2
Total 8	567	1792	196	465	76	10	33	195	138	254	14	16	.259	.314	.368	.682	85	-40	203	3.90	-16	C-502/0-9	49	-3.4
• OTT, Mel	Melvin Thomas "Master Melvin" Ott b: 3/2/1909, Gretna, LA d: 11/21/1958, New Orleans, LA BL/TR, 5'9", 170 lbs. Deb: 4/27/1926 M HOF: 1951 Career OF: 29-128-2167																							
1926 NY-N	35	60	7	23	2	0	0	4	1	9	1	....	.383	.393	.417	.810	120	2	9	6.49	1	0-10(10-0-0)	2	0.2
1927 NY-N	82	163	23	46	7	3	1	19	13	9	2	....	.282	.335	.380	.716	91	-2	20	4.40	0	0-32(13-21-0)	4	-0.4
1928 NY-N	124	435	69	140	26	4	18	77	52	36	3	....	.322	.397	.524	.921	138	24	89	7.60	2	*0-115(5-1-108)/2-5,3-1	20	1.8
1929 NY-N	150	545	138	179	37	2	42	151	**113**	38	6	....	.328	.449	.635	1.084	166	60	157	10.85	15	*0-149(0-0-149)/2-1	31	5.8
1930 NY-N	148	521	122	182	34	5	25	119	103	35	9	....	.349	**.458**	.578	1.036	152	49	139	10.10	11	*0-146(0-0-146)	28	4.3
1931 NY-N	138	497	104	145	23	8	29	115	**80**	44	10	....	.292	.392	.545	.937	**153**	38	111	8.21	5	*0-137(0-71-66)	26	3.8
1932 NY-N	154	566	119	180	30	8	**38**	123	**100**	39	6	....	.318	**.424**	.601	1.025	**175**	**64**	151	10.10	3	*0-154(0-0-154)	**33**	**5.6**
1933*NY-N	152	580	98	164	36	1	23	103	**75**	48	1	....	.283	.367	.467	.834	139	31	105	6.58	5	*0-152(0-19-143)	31	2.9
1934 NY-N★	153	582	119	190	29	10	**35**	**135**	85	43	0	....	.326	.415	.591	1.006	**170**	**59**	150	**10.06**	-1	*0-153(0-16-137)	**38**	4.8
1935 NY-N★	152	593	113	191	33	6	31	114	82	58	7	....	.322	.407	.555	.962	159	51	144	9.47	8	*0-137(0-0-137),3-15	35	4.9
1936*NY-N★	150	534	120	175	28	6	**33**	135	111	41	6	....	.328	.448	**.588**	**1.036**	**179**	**65**	153	**10.97**	6	*0-148(0-0-148)	**36**	6.0
1937*NY-N★	151	545	99	160	28	2	**31**	95	**102**	69	7	....	.294	.408	.523	.931	149	41	128	8.81	3	0-91(0-0-91),3-60	32	4.0
1938 NY-N★	150	527	**116**	164	23	6	**36**	116	118	47	2	....	.311	**.442**	.583	1.024	**178**	**62**	149	**10.77**	-2	*3-113,0-37(0-0-37)	**36**	**6.3**
1939 NY-N★	125	396	85	122	23	2	27	80	100	50	2	....	.308	**.449**	.581	1.030	173	46	112	10.47	-5	0-96(0-0-96),3-20	28	3.6
1940 NY-N★	151	536	89	155	27	3	19	79	100	50	6	....	.289	.407	.457	.864	137	32	107	7.33	2	*0-111(0-0-111)/3-42	24	2.8
1941 NY-N★	148	525	89	150	29	0	27	90	100	68	5	....	.286	.403	.495	.898	149	38	115	8.09	0	*0-145(1-0-144)	26	3.0
1942 NY-N★	152	549	**118**	162	21	0	**30**	93	**109**	61	6	....	.295	.415	.497	**.912**	**165**	**50**	122	8.25	-2	*0-152(0-0-152)	35	4.2
1943 NY-N★	125	380	65	89	12	2	18	47	95	48	7	....	.234	.391	.418	.810	133	21	71	6.40	-1	*0-111(0-0-111)/3-1	16	1.3
1944 NY-N★	120	399	91	115	16	4	26	82	90	47	2	....	.288	.423	.544	.967	171	42	101	9.39	-3	*0-103(0-0-103)/3-4	25	3.3
1945 NY-N★	135	451	73	139	23	0	21	79	71	41	1	....	.308	.411	.499	.910	150	33	98	8.29	-1	*0-118(0-0-118)	22	2.4
1946 NY-N	31	68	2	5	1	0	1	4	8	15	0	....	.074	.171	.132	.303	-13	-10	2	.76	1	0-16(0-0-16)	0	-1.0
1947 NY-N	4	4	0	0	0	0	0	0	0	0	0	....	.000	.000	.000	.000	-99	-1	0	.00	0	....	0	-0.1
Total 22	2730	9456	1859	2876	488	72	511	1860	1708	896	89	....	.304	.414	.533	.947	155	794	2235	8.81	47	*0-2313,3-256/2-6	528	69.3
• OTTEN, John	John G. Otten b: 8/1870, Netherlands d: 10/17/1905, Chicago, IL TR, 175 lbs. Deb: 7/5/1895																							
1895 StL-N	26	87	8	21	0	0	0	8	5	8	2	....	.241	.283	.241	.524	36	-8	7	2.74	-2	C-24/0-2(1-1-0)	1	-0.7

YEAR TM-L	G	AB	R	H	2B	3B	HR	RBI	BB	SO	SB	CS	AVG	OBP	SLG	OPS	OPS+	BR/A	RC	RC/G	FR	G/POS	WS	TPW
• OTTERSON, Billy	William John Otterson b: 5/4/1862, Pittsburgh, PA d: 9/21/1940, Pittsburgh, PA BR/TR, 5'7", 124 lbs. Deb: 9/4/1887																							
1887 Bro-a	30	108	16	28	4	1	2	15	8	....	8	....	.259	.259	.320	.579	60	-6	11	3.59	3	S-30	2	-0.2
• OUELLETTE, Phil	Philip Roland Ouellette b: 11/10/1961, Salem, OR BB/TR, 6', 190 lbs. Deb: 9/10/1986																							
1986 SF-N	10	23	1	4	0	0	0	0	3	3	0	0	.174	.269	.174	.443	26	-2	1	.90	0	/C-9	0	-0.2
• OULLIBER, Johnny	John Andrew Oulliber b: 2/24/1911, New Orleans, LA d: 12/26/1980, New Orleans, LA BR/TR, 5'11", 165 lbs. Deb: 7/25/1933																							
1933 Cle-A	22	75	9	20	1	0	0	3	4	5	0	0	.267	.313	.280	.593	55	-5	7	3.18	0	0-18(12-0-6)	1	-0.5
• OUTEN, Chink	William Austin Outen b: 6/17/1905, Mount Holly, NC d: 9/11/1961, Durham, NC BL/TR, 6', 200 lbs. Deb: 4/16/1933																							
1933 Bro-N	93	153	20	38	10	0	4	17	20	15	1	....	.248	.335	.392	.727	112	3	22	4.98	1	C-56	6	0.6
• OUTLAW, Jimmy	James Paulus Outlaw b: 1/20/1913, Orme, TN BR/TR, 5'8", 168 lbs. Deb: 4/20/1937 Career OF: 229-61-104																							
1937 Cin-N	49	165	18	45	7	3	0	11	3	31	2	....	.273	.290	.352	.641	77	-6	17	3.81	4	3-41	3	0.0
1938 Cin-N	4	0	1	0	0	0	0	0	0	0	0	....	....	....	....	....	-103	0	0	....	0	....	0	0.0
1939 Bos-N	65	133	15	35	2	0	0	5	10	14	1	....	.263	.315	.278	.593	65	-6	13	3.42	-1	0-39(15-22-2)/3-2	2	-0.8
1943 Det-A	20	67	8	18	1	0	1	6	8	4	0	0	.269	.347	.328	.675	91	-0	8	4.38	0	0-16(4-3-9)	2	-0.1
1944 Det-A	139	535	69	146	20	6	3	57	41	40	7	8	.273	.327	.350	.677	88	-10	60	3.91	1	*0-137(71-6-60)	12	-1.8
1945*Det-A	132	446	56	121	16	5	0	34	45	33	6	7	.271	.338	.330	.668	88	-7	52	4.14	-1	*0-105(82-17-8),3-21	12	-1.4
1946 Det-A	92	299	36	78	14	2	2	31	29	24	5	4	.261	.328	.341	.669	82	-7	33	3.69	-6	0-43(26-10-9),3-38	6	-1.7
1947 Det-A	70	127	20	29	7	1	0	15	21	14	3	1	.228	.338	.299	.637	76	-3	15	3.84	-2	0-37(21-3-13)/3-9	2	-0.7
1948 Det-A	74	198	33	56	12	0	0	25	31	15	0	1	.283	.383	.343	.726	91	-1	27	4.77	-2	3-47,0-13(10-0-3)	5	-0.4
1949 Det-A	5	4	1	1	0	0	0	0	0	1	0	0	.250	.250	.250	.500	32	-0	0	.00	0	....	0	0.0
Total 10	**650**	**1974**	**257**	**529**	**79**	**17**	**6**	**184**	**188**	**176**	**24**	**21**	**.268**	**.333**	**.334**	**.668**	**84**	**-41**	**225**	**3.97**	**-7**	**0-390,3-158**	**44**	**-7.0**
• OVERBAY, Lyle	Lyle Stefan Overbay b: 1/28/1977, Centralia, WA BL/TL, 6'2", 215 lbs. Deb: 9/19/2001																							
2001 Ari-N	2	2	0	1	0	0	0	0	0	1	0	0	.500	.500	.500	1.000	151	0	1	13.50	0	....	0	0.0
2002 Ari-N	10	10	0	1	0	0	0	1	0	5	0	0	.100	.100	.100	.200	-43	-2	0	.30	0	....	0	-0.2
2003 Ari-N	86	254	23	70	20	0	4	28	35	67	1	0	.276	.368	.402	.769	92	-2	38	5.24	8	1-75	6	0.0
Total 3	**98**	**266**	**23**	**72**	**20**	**0**	**4**	**29**	**35**	**73**	**1**	**0**	**.271**	**.360**	**.391**	**.751**	**87**	**-4**	**38**	**5.06**	**8**	**/1-75**	**6**	**-0.2**
• OWEN, Dave	Dave Owen b: 4/25/1958, Cleburne, TX BB/TR, 6'2", 170 lbs. Deb: 9/6/1983																							
1983 Chi-N	16	22	1	2	0	1	0	2	2	7	1	0	.091	.167	.182	.348	-3	-3	1	1.15	0	S-14/3-3	0	-0.2
1984 Chi-N	47	93	8	18	2	2	1	10	8	15	1	2	.194	.272	.290	.562	53	-7	8	2.63	-1	S-35/3-6,2-4	1	-0.5
1985 Chi-N	22	19	6	7	0	0	0	4	1	5	1	1	.368	.400	.368	.768	105	-0	3	5.66	-3	/3-7,S-7,2-4	1	-0.3
1988 KC-A	7	5	0	0	0	0	0	0	0	3	0	0	.000	.000	.000	.000	-99	-1	0	.00	0	/S-7	0	-0.1
Total 4	**92**	**139**	**15**	**27**	**2**	**3**	**1**	**16**	**11**	**30**	**3**	**3**	**.194**	**.263**	**.273**	**.537**	**45**	**-11**	**11**	**2.57**	**-4**	**/S-63,3-16,2-8**	**2**	**-1.2**
• OWEN, Larry	Lawrence Thomas Owen b: 5/31/1955, Cleveland, OH BR/TR, 5'11", 185 lbs. Deb: 8/14/1981																							
1981 Atl-N	13	16	0	0	0	0	0	0	1	4	0	0	.000	.059	.000	.059	-80	-4	0	.03	1	C-10	0	-0.3
1982 Atl-N	2	3	1	1	1	0	0	0	0	1	0	0	.333	.333	.667	1.000	167	0	1	9.00	0	/C-2	0	0.0
1983 Atl-N	17	17	0	2	0	0	0	1	0	2	0	1	.118	.118	.118	.235	-32	-3	0	.20	-1	C-16	0	-0.4
1985 Atl-N	26	71	7	17	3	0	2	12	8	17	0	0	.239	.316	.366	.683	85	-1	8	3.70	-2	C-25	2	-0.2
1987 KC-A	76	164	17	31	6	0	5	14	16	51	0	0	.189	.261	.317	.578	51	-12	13	2.49	2	C-75	4	-0.7
1988 KC-A	37	81	5	17	1	0	1	3	9	23	0	0	.210	.304	.259	.564	59	-4	7	3.03	0	C-37	2	-0.2
Total 6	**171**	**352**	**30**	**68**	**11**	**0**	**8**	**30**	**34**	**98**	**0**	**1**	**.193**	**.268**	**.293**	**.561**	**52**	**-25**	**30**	**2.64**	**-1**	**C-165**	**8**	**-1.8**
• OWEN, Marv	Marvin James "Freck" Owen b: 3/22/1906, Agnew, CA d: 6/22/1991, Mountain View, CA BR/TR, 6'1", 175 lbs. Deb: 4/16/1931																							
1931 Det-A	105	377	35	84	11	6	3	39	29	38	2	2	.223	.282	.308	.590	53	-25	34	2.93	1	3-37,S-37,1-27/2-4	3	-2.0
1933 Det-A	138	550	77	144	24	9	2	65	44	56	2	2	.262	.321	.349	.670	76	-19	63	3.98	-8	*3-136	9	-2.1
1934*Det-A	154	565	79	179	34	9	8	96	59	37	3	3	.317	.385	.451	.837	115	12	100	6.66	-8	*3-154	23	0.9
1935*Det-A	134	483	52	127	24	5	2	71	43	37	1	4	.263	.326	.346	.672	76	-18	56	3.92	-6	*3-131	10	-1.8
1936 Det-A	154	583	72	172	20	4	9	105	53	41	9	6	.295	.361	.389	.750	85	-14	84	5.19	-5	*3-153/1-2	16	-1.2
1937 Det-A	107	396	48	114	22	5	1	45	41	24	3	4	.288	.358	.376	.734	83	-11	54	4.99	-3	*3-106	10	-0.9
1938 Chi-A	141	577	84	162	23	6	6	55	45	31	6	4	.281	.337	.373	.710	76	-23	74	4.60	-1	*3-140	12	-1.6
1939 Chi-A	58	194	22	46	9	0	0	15	16	15	4	5	.237	.302	.284	.585	49	-16	17	2.78	-2	3-55	2	-1.4
1940 Bos-A	20	57	4	12	0	0	0	6	8	4	0	0	.211	.308	.211	.518	36	-5	4	2.12	2	/3-9,1-8	0	-0.3
Total 9	**1011**	**3782**	**473**	**1040**	**167**	**44**	**31**	**497**	**338**	**283**	**30**	**30**	**.275**	**.339**	**.367**	**.706**	**80**	**-118**	**485**	**4.51**	**-30**	**3-921/1-37,S-37,2-4**	**85**	**-10.5**
• OWEN, Mickey	Arnold Malcolm Owen b: 4/4/1916, Nixa, MO BR/TR, 5'10", 190 lbs. Deb: 5/2/1937 C																							
1937 StL-N	80	234	17	54	4	2	0	20	15	13	1	....	.231	.277	.265	.542	47	-17	17	2.36	0	C-78	3	-1.3
1938 StL-N	122	397	45	106	25	2	4	36	32	14	2	....	.267	.325	.370	.695	86	-8	46	4.06	1	*C-116	9	0.0
1939 StL-N	131	344	32	89	18	2	3	35	43	28	6	....	.259	.344	.349	.693	82	-8	42	4.10	0	*C-126	9	-0.2
1940 StL-N	117	307	27	81	16	2	0	27	34	13	4	....	.264	.341	.329	.670	81	-7	35	3.88	-2	*C-113	8	-0.3
1941*Bro-N★	128	386	32	89	15	2	1	44	34	14	1	....	.231	.296	.288	.584	62	-19	33	2.73	2	*C-128	10	-1.1
1942 Bro-N★	133	421	53	109	16	3	0	44	44	17	10	....	.259	.330	.311	.642	87	-6	43	3.38	-1	*C-133	15	0.1
1943 Bro-N★	106	365	31	95	11	2	0	54	25	15	4	....	.260	.309	.301	.611	77	-11	34	3.21	1	*C-100/3-3,S-1	9	-0.5
1944 Bro-N★	130	461	43	126	20	3	1	42	36	17	4	....	.273	.326	.336	.662	88	-7	48	3.61	7	*C-125/2-1	11	0.7
1945 Bro-N	24	84	5	24	9	0	0	11	10	2	0	....	.286	.368	.393	.761	113	2	11	4.55	-1	C-24	3	0.2
1949 Chi-N	62	198	15	54	9	3	2	18	12	13	1	....	.273	.318	.379	.696	88	-4	24	4.40	0	C-59	5	0.0
1950 Chi-N	86	259	22	63	11	0	2	21	13	16	2	....	.243	.282	.309	.591	56	-17	21	2.77	1	C-86	4	-1.2
1951 Chi-N	58	125	10	23	6	0	0	15	19	13	1	0	.184	.292	.232	.524	42	-10	9	2.36	0	C-57	1	-0.7
1954 Bos-A	32	68	6	16	3	0	1	11	9	6	0	1	.235	.325	.324	.648	70	-3	7	3.08	1	C-30	1	-0.1
Total 13	**1209**	**3649**	**338**	**929**	**163**	**21**	**14**	**378**	**326**	**181**	**36**	**1**	**.255**	**.318**	**.322**	**.640**	**76**	**-115**	**371**	**3.43**	**9**	***C-1175/3-3,2-1,S-1**	**88**	**-4.3**
• OWEN, Spike	Spike Dee Owen b: 4/19/1961, Cleburne, TX BB/TR, 5'9", 170 lbs. Deb: 6/25/1983																							
1983 Sea-A	80	306	36	60	11	3	2	21	24	44	10	6	.196	.259	.271	.530	45	-24	23	2.34	-2	S-80	3	-1.8
1984 Sea-A	152	530	67	130	18	8	3	43	46	63	16	8	.245	.309	.326	.636	77	-16	56	3.58	8	*S-151	14	0.8
1985 Sea-A	118	352	41	91	10	6	6	37	34	27	11	5	.259	.324	.372	.696	89	-5	44	4.24	5	*S-117	11	1.2
1986 Sea-A	112	402	46	99	22	6	0	35	34	42	1	3	.246	.307	.331	.637	73	-16	40	3.28	11	*S-112	8	0.7
*Bos-A	42	126	21	23	2	1	1	10	17	9	3	1	.183	.285	.238	.523	44	-9	10	2.42	-2	S-42	1	-0.7
Yr.	154	528	67	122	24	7	1	45	51	51	4	4	.231	.301	.309	.610	66	-25	49	3.06	9	*S-154	9	0.0
1987 Bos-A	132	437	50	113	17	7	2	48	53	43	11	8	.259	.340	.343	.683	80	-13	52	4.00	-24	*S-130	9	-2.2
1988*Bos-A	89	257	40	64	14	1	5	18	27	27	0	1	.249	.325	.370	.695	90	-4	31	3.99	-3	S-76/D-7	4	-0.1
1989 Mon-N	142	437	52	102	17	4	6	41	76	44	3	2	.233	.351	.332	.683	95	0	53	4.02	-5	*S-142	15	0.7
1990 Mon-N	149	453	55	106	24	5	5	35	70	60	8	6	.234	.337	.342	.679	91	-5	55	4.04	0	*S-148	13	0.5
1991 Mon-N	139	424	39	108	22	8	3	26	42	61	2	6	.255	.323	.366	.689	95	-5	48	3.76	4	*S-133	11	0.9
1992 Mon-N	122	386	52	104	16	3	7	40	50	30	9	4	.269	.353	.381	.734	109	6	53	4.68	-8	*S-116	14	0.7
1993 NY-A	103	334	41	78	16	2	2	20	29	30	3	2	.234	.295	.311	.606	65	-17	31	3.12	0	S-96/D-2	5	-0.9
1994 Cal-A	82	268	30	83	17	2	3	37	49	17	2	8	.310	.418	.422	.840	116	6	48	6.54	3	3-70/S-5,1-4,D-2,2-1	11	0.9
1995 Cal-A	82	218	17	50	9	3	1	28	18	22	3	2	.229	.288	.312	.600	57	-14	19	2.81	0	3-29,S-25,2-16	3	-1.2
Total 13	**1544**	**4930**	**587**	**1211**	**215**	**59**	**46**	**439**	**569**	**519**	**82**	**62**	**.246**	**.326**	**.341**	**.667**	**83**	**-116**	**562**	**3.81**	**-14**	***S-1373/3-99,2-17,D-11,1-4**	**122**	**-0.6**
• OWENS, Eric	Eric Blake Owens b: 2/3/1971, Danville, VA BR/TR, 6'1", 185 lbs. Deb: 6/6/1995 Career OF: 291-201-251																							
1995 Cin-N	2	2	0	2	0	0	0	1	0	0	0	0	1.000	1.000	1.000	2.000	432	1	2	45.36	-1	/3-2	0	0.0
1996 Cin-N	88	205	26	41	6	0	0	9	23	38	16	2	.200	.284	.229	.513	38	-16	17	2.61	-1	0-52(52-0-0)/2-6,3-5	1	-1.7
1997 Cin-N	27	57	8	15	0	0	0	3	4	11	3	2	.263	.311	.263	.575	51	-4	4	2.54	-2	0-18(9-8-1)/2-2	0	-0.7
1998 Mil-N	34	40	5	5	2	0	1	4	2	6	0	0	.125	.167	.250	.417	8	-6	1	.71	-2	0-16(10-5-2)/2-4	0	-0.7
1999 SD-N	149	440	55	117	22	3	9	61	38	50	33	7	.266	.328	.391	.719	88	-4	58	4.50	-1	*0-116(69-47-27),1-12/3-4,2	11	-0.9
2000 SD-N	145	583	87	171	19	7	6	51	45	63	29	14	.293	.348	.381	.729	90	-9	75	4.54	4	*0-144(65-34-68)/2-1	15	-1.0
2001 Fla-N	119	400	51	101	16	1	5	28	29	59	8	6	.253	.303	.335	.638	67	-21	38	3.16	-5	*0-106(1-37-72)/D-1	3	-2.8

YEAR TM-L	G	AB	R	H	2B	3B	HR	RBI	BB	SO	SB	CS	AVG	OBP	SLG	OPS	OPS+	BR/A	RC	RC/G	FR	G/POS	WS	TPW
2002 Fla-N	131	385	44	104	15	5	4	37	31	33	26	9	.270	.325	.366	.691	85	-7	45	3.94	7	*O-121(75-22-39)	8	-0.4
2003 Ana-A	111	241	29	65	6	0	1	20	10	24	11	8	.270	.302	.307	.609	64	-14	21	2.97	0	O-97(10-48-42)/D-2	3	-1.5
Total 9	**806**	**2353**	**305**	**621**	**86**	**16**	**26**	**214**	**182**	**284**	**126**	**48**	**.264**	**.319**	**.347**	**.666**	**76**	**-79**	**260**	**3.75**	**-1**	**O-670/2-14,1-12,3-11,D-3**	**41**	**-9.6**

• OWENS, Frank Frank Walter "Yip" Owens b: 1/26/1886, Toronto, Canada d: 7/2/1958, Minneapolis, MN BR/TR, 6', 170 lbs. Deb: 9/11/1905

YEAR TM-L	G	AB	R	H	2B	3B	HR	RBI	BB	SO	SB	CS	AVG	OBP	SLG	OPS	OPS+	BR/A	RC	RC/G	FR	G/POS	WS	TPW
1905 Bos-A	1	2	0	0	0	0	0	0	0	....	0	....	.000	.000	.000	.000	-99	-0	0	.00	0	/C-1	0	-0.1
1909 Chi-A	64	174	12	35	4	1	0	17	8	....	3	....	.201	.245	.236	.480	54	-9	11	1.96	-7	C-57	2	-1.2
1914 Bro-F	58	184	15	51	7	3	2	20	9	16	2	....	.277	.314	.380	.695	96	-2	21	4.05	-3	C-58	5	-0.1
1915 Bal-F	99	334	32	84	14	7	3	28	17	34	4	....	.251	.290	.362	.652	85	-8	35	3.50	1	C-99	8	0.1
Total 4	**222**	**694**	**59**	**170**	**25**	**11**	**5**	**65**	**34**	**50**	**9**	**....**	**.245**	**.284**	**.334**	**.618**	**80**	**-19**	**67**	**3.21**	**-9**	**C-215**	**15**	**-1.2**

• OWENS, Jack Furman Lee Owens b: 5/6/1908, Converse, SC d: 11/14/1958, Greenville, SC BR/TR, 6'1", 186 lbs. Deb: 9/21/1935

YEAR TM-L	G	AB	R	H	2B	3B	HR	RBI	BB	SO	SB	CS	AVG	OBP	SLG	OPS	OPS+	BR/A	RC	RC/G	FR	G/POS	WS	TPW
1935 Phi-A	2	8	0	2	0	0	0	1	0	1	0	0	.250	.250	.250	.500	30	-1	0	2.12	0	/C-2	0	-0.1

• OWENS, Jayhawk Claude Jayhawk Owens b: 2/10/1969, Cincinnati, OH BR/TR, 6'1", 200 lbs. Deb: 6/6/1993

YEAR TM-L	G	AB	R	H	2B	3B	HR	RBI	BB	SO	SB	CS	AVG	OBP	SLG	OPS	OPS+	BR/A	RC	RC/G	FR	G/POS	WS	TPW
1993 Col-N	33	86	12	18	5	0	3	6	6	30	1	0	.209	.277	.372	.649	62	-5	9	3.57	-1	C-32	1	-0.4
1994 Col-N	6	12	4	3	0	1	0	1	3	3	0	0	.250	.400	.417	.817	97	0	2	5.20	1	/C-6	1	0.1
1995*Col-N	18	45	7	11	2	0	4	12	2	15	0	0	.244	.292	.556	.847	91	-1	8	5.80	0	C-16	2	0.0
1996 Col-N	73	180	31	43	9	1	4	17	27	56	4	1	.239	.341	.367	.708	70	-7	25	4.74	-3	C-68	2	-0.6
Total 4	**130**	**323**	**54**	**75**	**16**	**2**	**11**	**36**	**38**	**104**	**5**	**1**	**.232**	**.321**	**.396**	**.717**	**72**	**-13**	**44**	**4.59**	**-3**	**C-122**	**6**	**-0.9**

• OWENS, Red Thomas Llewellyn Owens b: 11/1/1874, Pottsville, PA d: 8/20/1952, Harrisburg, PA BR/TR Deb: 7/28/1899

YEAR TM-L	G	AB	R	H	2B	3B	HR	RBI	BB	SO	SB	CS	AVG	OBP	SLG	OPS	OPS+	BR/A	RC	RC/G	FR	G/POS	WS	TPW
1899 Phi-N	8	21	0	1	0	0	0	1	2	....	0	....	.048	.130	.048	.178	-52	-4	0	.28	-1	/2-8	0	-0.4
1905 Bro-N	43	168	14	36	6	2	1	20	6	....	1	....	.214	.241	.292	.533	63	-8	13	2.45	-1	2-43	1	-0.9
Total 2	**51**	**189**	**14**	**37**	**6**	**2**	**1**	**21**	**8**	**....**	**1**	**....**	**.196**	**.228**	**.265**	**.493**	**50**	**-13**	**13**	**2.16**	**-2**	**/2-51**	**1**	**-1.3**

• OXLEY, Henry Henry Havelock Oxley b: 1/4/1858, Covehead, Canada d: 10/12/1945, Somerville, MA, 5'11", 163 lbs. Deb: 7/30/1884

YEAR TM-L	G	AB	R	H	2B	3B	HR	RBI	BB	SO	SB	CS	AVG	OBP	SLG	OPS	OPS+	BR/A	RC	RC/G	FR	G/POS	WS	TPW
1884 NY-N	2	4	0	0	0	0	0	0	1	2	....	....	.000	.200	.000	.200	-31	-1	0	.00	1	/C-2	0	0.1
NY-a	1	3	0	0	0	0	0	0	0	....	....	....	.000	.000	.000	.000	-102	-1	0	.00	0	/C-1	0	-0.1

• OYLER, Andy Andrew Paul "Pepper" Oyler b: 5/5/1880, Newville, PA d: 10/24/1970, Cumberland County, PA BR/TR, 5'6.5", 138 lbs. Deb: 5/8/1902

YEAR TM-L	G	AB	R	H	2B	3B	HR	RBI	BB	SO	SB	CS	AVG	OBP	SLG	OPS	OPS+	BR/A	RC	RC/G	FR	G/POS	WS	TPW
1902 Bal-A	27	77	9	17	1	0	1	6	8	....	3	....	.221	.318	.273	.591	62	-4	8	3.47	-4	3-20/O-3(0-2-1),S-2,2-1	1	-0.6

• OYLER, Ray Raymond Francis Oyler b: 8/4/1938, Indianapolis, IN d: 1/26/1981, Redmond, WA BR/TR, 5'11", 165 lbs. Deb: 4/18/1965

YEAR TM-L	G	AB	R	H	2B	3B	HR	RBI	BB	SO	SB	CS	AVG	OBP	SLG	OPS	OPS+	BR/A	RC	RC/G	FR	G/POS	WS	TPW
1965 Det-A	82	194	22	36	6	0	5	13	21	61	1	0	.186	.265	.294	.559	58	-11	14	2.23	0	S-57,2-11/1-1,3-1	3	-0.6
1966 Det-A	71	210	16	36	8	3	1	9	23	62	0	0	.171	.263	.252	.515	48	-14	14	2.09	6	S-69	3	-0.3
1967 Det-A	148	367	33	76	14	2	1	29	37	91	0	2	.207	.283	.264	.548	61	-18	28	2.36	10	*S-146	7	0.3
1968*Det-A	111	215	13	29	6	1	1	12	20	59	0	2	.135	.215	.186	.401	22	-21	8	1.11	-1	*S-111	4	-1.7
1969 Sea-A	106	255	24	42	5	0	7	22	31	80	1	2	.165	.260	.267	.527	48	-18	17	2.06	-8	*S-106	2	-1.7
1970 Cal-A	24	24	2	2	0	0	0	1	3	6	0	0	.083	.185	.083	.269	-24	-4	1	.74	-2	S-13/3-2	0	-0.5
Total 6	**542**	**1265**	**110**	**221**	**39**	**6**	**15**	**86**	**135**	**359**	**2**	**6**	**.175**	**.259**	**.251**	**.510**	**47**	**-85**	**83**	**1.97**	**5**	**S-502/2-11,3-3,1-1**	**19**	**-4.5**

• OZUNA, Pablo Pablo Jose Ozuna b: 8/25/1974, Santo Domingo, Dominican Republic BR/TR, 6', 160 lbs. Deb: 4/23/2000 Career OF: 0-6-0

YEAR TM-L	G	AB	R	H	2B	3B	HR	RBI	BB	SO	SB	CS	AVG	OBP	SLG	OPS	OPS+	BR/A	RC	RC/G	FR	G/POS	WS	TPW
2000 Fla-N	14	24	2	8	1	0	0	0	0	2	1	0	.333	.333	.375	.708	82	-0	3	4.87	-1	/2-7	1	-0.1
2002 Fla-N	34	47	4	13	2	2	0	3	1	3	1	1	.277	.306	.404	.710	89	-1	5	3.51	-2	2-10/O-1	0	-0.2
2003 Col-N	17	40	5	8	1	0	0	2	2	6	3	0	.200	.273	.225	.498	28	-4	3	2.35	4	/2-8,O-5(O-5-0),S-3	1	0.0
Total 3	**65**	**111**	**11**	**29**	**4**	**2**	**0**	**5**	**3**	**11**	**5**	**1**	**.261**	**.299**	**.333**	**.632**	**65**	**-5**	**11**	**3.34**	**1**	**/2-25,O-6,S-3**	**2**	**-0.3**

• PABOR, Charlie Charles Henry Pabor b: 9/24/1846, Brooklyn, NY d: 4/23/1913, New Haven, CT BL/TL, 5'8", 155 lbs. Deb: 5/4/1871 M/U NA OF: 152-3-14 ♦

YEAR TM-L	G	AB	R	H	2B	3B	HR	RBI	BB	SO	SB	CS	AVG	OBP	SLG	OPS	OPS+	BR/A	RC	RC/G	FR	G/POS	WS	TPW
1871 Cle-n	29	142	24	42	2	4	0	18	1	3	1	0	.296	.301	.366	.667	96	-0	16	5.15	-5	*O-28(28-0-0)/P-7	....	-0.7
1872 Cle-n	21	92	12	19	0	0	0	7	0	0	0	0	.207	.207	.207	.413	29	-7	4	1.71	-2	O-20(19-0-1)/P-2	....	-0.4
1873 Atl-n	55	228	36	82	8	3	0	42	6	3	2	0	.360	.376	.421	.797	153	17	38	7.89	-0	*O-55(55-0-0)	....	1.3
1874 Phi-n	17	77	11	17	0	1	0	1	0	0	0	1	.221	.221	.247	.468	48	-5	4	2.11	-2	O-17(2-3-13)	....	-0.5
1875 Atl-n	42	153	14	36	2	2	0	11	1	1	0	0	.235	.240	.275	.515	90	0	10	2.61	0	O-42(42-0-0)/P-1	....	-0.1
NH-n	6	23	4	8	0	2	0	2	0	1	0	0	.348	.348	.522	.870	226	3	4	8.41	-1	/O-6(6-0-0)	....	0.2
Yr.	48	176	18	44	2	4	0	13	1	2	0	0	.250	.254	.307	.561	108	3	15	3.27	-1	O-48(48-0-0)/P-1	....	0.1
Total 5 n	**170**	**715**	**101**	**204**	**12**	**12**	**0**	**81**	**8**	**8**	**3**	**1**	**.285**	**.293**	**.336**	**.629**	**103**	**9**	**77**	**4.59**	**-10**	**O-168/P-10**	**....**	**-0.3**

• PABST, Ed Edward D. A. Pabst b: 1868, St. Louis, MO d: 6/19/1940, St. Louis, MO, 5'11", 170 lbs. Deb: 9/26/1890

YEAR TM-L	G	AB	R	H	2B	3B	HR	RBI	BB	SO	SB	CS	AVG	OBP	SLG	OPS	OPS+	BR/A	RC	RC/G	FR	G/POS	WS	TPW
1890 Phi-a	8	25	7	10	2	0	0	3	5	....	3	....	.400	.500	.480	.980	193	3	8	13.58	4	/O-8(8-0-0)	2	0.6
StL-a	4	14	1	2	0	1	0	0	0	....	0	....	.143	.143	.286	.429	23	-2	1	1.29	1	/O-4(4-0-0)	0	0.0
Yr.	12	39	8	12	2	1	0	3	5	....	3	....	.308	.386	.410	.797	139	2	8	8.12	5	O-12(12-0-0)	2	0.5

• PACIOREK, Jim James Joseph Paciorek b: 6/7/1960, Detroit, MI BR/TR, 6'3", 203 lbs. Deb: 4/9/1987

YEAR TM-L	G	AB	R	H	2B	3B	HR	RBI	BB	SO	SB	CS	AVG	OBP	SLG	OPS	OPS+	BR/A	RC	RC/G	FR	G/POS	WS	TPW
1987 Mil-A	48	101	16	23	5	0	2	10	12	20	1	0	.228	.310	.337	.646	69	-4	11	3.48	-5	1-21,3-15/O-5(4-0-1),D-2	1	-1.0

• PACIOREK, John John Francis Paciorek b: 2/11/1945, Detroit, MI BR/TR, 6'2", 200 lbs. Deb: 9/29/1963

YEAR TM-L	G	AB	R	H	2B	3B	HR	RBI	BB	SO	SB	CS	AVG	OBP	SLG	OPS	OPS+	BR/A	RC	RC/G	FR	G/POS	WS	TPW
1963 Hou-N	1	3	4	3	0	0	0	3	2	0	0	0	1.000	1.000	1.000	2.000	509	2	4	∞	-0	/O-1	1	0.2

• PACIOREK, Tom Thomas Marian Paciorek b: 11/2/1946, Detroit, MI BR/TR, 6'4", 215 lbs. Deb: 9/12/1970 Career OF: 476-73-281

YEAR TM-L	G	AB	R	H	2B	3B	HR	RBI	BB	SO	SB	CS	AVG	OBP	SLG	OPS	OPS+	BR/A	RC	RC/G	FR	G/POS	WS	TPW
1970 LA-N	8	9	2	2	1	0	0	0	0	3	0	0	.222	.300	.333	.633	73	-0	1	3.77	0	/O-3(1-0-2)	0	-0.1
1971 LA-N	2	2	0	1	0	0	0	1	0	0	0	0	.500	.500	.500	1.000	195	0	1	13.50	-0	/O-1	0	0.0
1972 LA-N	11	47	4	12	4	0	1	6	1	7	1	0	.255	.271	.404	.675	92	-1	5	3.71	1	/1-6,O-6(1-0-5)	1	0.0
1973 LA-N	96	195	26	51	8	0	5	18	11	35	3	3	.262	.304	.379	.684	92	-3	20	3.37	-1	O-77(36-22-25)/1-4	4	-0.8
1974*LA-N	85	175	23	42	8	6	1	24	10	32	1	3	.240	.285	.371	.656	86	-5	17	3.29	-3	O-77(44-23-15)/1-1	3	-1.1
1975 LA-N	62	145	14	28	8	0	1	5	11	29	4	3	.193	.250	.269	.519	46	-11	9	2.02	-2	O-54(30-2-25)	1	-1.6
1976 Atl-N	111	324	39	94	10	4	4	36	19	57	2	3	.290	.335	.383	.718	97	-2	40	4.37	-4	O-84(38-7-44),1-12/3-1	8	-1.1
1977 Atl-N	72	155	20	37	8	0	3	15	6	46	1	0	.239	.267	.348	.615	57	-10	15	3.24	-2	1-32/O-9(4-2-3),3-1	1	-1.3
1978 Atl-N	5	9	2	3	0	0	0	0	0	1	0	0	.333	.333	.333	.667	78	-0	1	4.50	0	/1-2	0	-0.1
Sea-A	70	251	32	75	20	3	4	30	15	39	2	2	.299	.338	.450	.789	121	6	36	5.28	-1	O-54(53-4-0),D-12/1-3	8	0.2
1979 Sea-A	103	310	38	89	23	4	6	42	28	62	6	4	.287	.356	.445	.801	113	5	49	5.58	1	O-75(47-0-29),1-15	8	0.2
1980 Sea-A	126	418	44	114	19	1	15	59	17	67	3	2	.273	.303	.431	.733	98	-3	50	4.17	1	O-60(19-1-41),1-36,D-23	8	-0.8
1981 Sea-A★	104	405	50	132	28	2	14	66	35	50	13	10	.326	.385	.509	.894	150	24	76	6.78	-1	*O-103(84-12-14)	17	1.9
1982 Chi-A	104	382	49	119	27	4	11	55	24	53	3	3	.312	.366	.490	.856	132	16	68	6.56	-2	*1-102/O-6(6-0-0)	15	0.8
1983*Chi-A	115	420	65	129	32	3	9	63	25	58	6	1	.307	.350	.462	.812	117	10	67	5.85	0	1-67,O-55(30-0-27)/D-2	16	0.5
1984 Chi-A	111	363	35	93	21	2	4	29	25	69	6	0	.256	.311	.358	.669	81	-8	42	4.04	-5	1-67,O-41(25-0-17)	6	-1.8
1985 Chi-A	46	122	14	30	2	0	0	9	8	22	2	0	.246	.298	.262	.560	53	-7	10	2.74	1	O-23(21-0-2),D-12/1-6	1	-0.8
NY-N	46	116	14	33	3	1	1	11	6	14	1	0	.284	.325	.353	.679	92	-1	13	4.19	-2	O-29(6-0-24)/1-8	3	-0.5
1986 Tex-A	88	213	17	61	7	0	4	22	3	41	1	3	.286	.306	.376	.682	82	-7	22	3.71	3	O-25(22-0-3),1-23,3-21/D-9,S	4	-0.6
1987 Tex-A	27	60	6	17	3	0	3	12	1	19	0	1	.283	.306	.483	.790	105	-0	7	3.95	0	1-12,O-12(8-0-5)/D-3	1	-0.1
Total 18	**1392**	**4121**	**494**	**1162**	**232**	**30**	**86**	**503**	**245**	**704**	**55**	**38**	**.282**	**.328**	**.415**	**.744**	**103**	**1**	**548**	**4.70**	**-18**	**O-794,1-396/D-61,3-23,S-1**	**105**	**-7.0**

• PACK, Frankie Frank Pack b: 4/10/1928, Morristown, TN d: 1/26/2000, Hendersonville, NC BL/TR, 6', 190 lbs. Deb: 6/5/1949

YEAR TM-L	G	AB	R	H	2B	3B	HR	RBI	BB	SO	SB	CS	AVG	OBP	SLG	OPS	OPS+	BR/A	RC	RC/G	FR	G/POS	WS	TPW
1949 StL-A	1	1	0	0	0	0	0	0	0	1	0	0	.000	.000	.000	.000	-96	-0	0	.00	0	....	0	0.0

• PADDEN, Dick Richard Joseph "Brains" Padden b: 9/17/1870, Martins Ferry, OH d: 10/31/1922, Martins Ferry, OH BR/TR, 5'10", 165 lbs. Deb: 7/15/1896

YEAR TM-L	G	AB	R	H	2B	3B	HR	RBI	BB	SO	SB	CS	AVG	OBP	SLG	OPS	OPS+	BR/A	RC	RC/G	FR	G/POS	WS	TPW
1896 Pit-N	61	219	33	53	4	8	2	24	14	9	8	....	.242	.294	.361	.654	75	-9	27	4.15	-9	2-61	4	-1.3
1897 Pit-N	134	517	84	146	16	10	2	58	38	....	18	....	.282	.350	.364	.714	92	-5	77	5.19	6	*2-134	14	0.6
1898 Pit-N	128	463	61	119	7	6	2	43	35	....	11	....	.257	.335	.311	.646	87	-6	54	4.09	-1	*2-128	13	-0.1
1899 Was-N	134	451	66	125	20	7	2	61	24	....	27	....	.277	.337	.366	.703	94	-4	67	5.34	-7	S-85,2-48	15	-0.4
1901 StL-N	123	489	71	125	17	7	2	62	31	....	26	....	.256	.315	.331	.646	92	-5	62	4.38	0	*2-115/S-8	13	-0.3
1902 StL-A	117	413	54	109	26	3	1	40	30	....	11	....	.264	.327	.349	.676	89	-6	53	4.50	16	*2-117	13	1.1

YEAR TM-L	G	AB	R	H	2B	3B	HR	RBI	BB	SO	SB	CS	AVG	OBP	SLG	OPS	OPS+	BR/A	RC	RC/G	FR	G/POS	WS	TPW
1903 StL-A	29	94	7	19	3	0	0	6	9	....	5	....	.202	.306	.234	.540	65	-3	9	3.00	2	2-29	2	-0.1
1904 StL-A	132	453	42	108	19	4	0	36	40	....	23	....	.238	.325	.298	.623	104	5	54	4.03	-18	*2-132	15	-1.3
1905 StL-A	16	58	5	10	1	1	0	4	3	....	3	....	.172	.213	.224	.437	41	-4	4	1.94	-3	2-16	0	-0.8
Total 9	**874**	**3157**	**423**	**814**	**113**	**46**	**11**	**334**	**224**	**9**	**132**	**....**	**.258**	**.326**	**.333**	**.660**	**90**	**-37**	**405**	**4.46**	**-14**	**2-780/S-93**	**89**	**-2.7**
• PADDEN, Tom	Thomas Francis Padden b: 10/6/1908, Manchester, NH d: 6/11/1973, Manchester, NH BR/TR, 5'11.5", 170 lbs. Deb: 5/29/1932																							
1932 Pit-N	47	118	13	31	6	1	0	10	9	7	0	....	.263	.315	.331	.645	75	-4	13	3.76	0	C-43	4	-0.2
1933 Pit-N	30	90	5	19	2	0	0	8	2	6	0	....	.211	.237	.233	.470	35	-8	5	1.77	3	C-27	2	-0.3
1934 Pit-N	82	237	27	76	12	2	0	22	30	23	3	....	.321	.399	.388	.787	109	5	37	5.70	-7	C-76	7	0.3
1935 Pit-N	97	302	35	82	9	1	1	30	48	26	1	....	.272	.371	.318	.689	84	-4	39	4.60	1	C-94	10	0.3
1936 Pit-N	88	281	22	70	9	2	1	31	22	41	0	....	.249	.304	.306	.610	63	-14	27	3.20	3	C-87	5	-0.6
1937 Pit-N	35	98	14	28	2	0	0	8	13	11	1	....	.286	.369	.306	.675	85	-1	12	4.43	1	C-34	3	0.2
1943 Phi-N	17	41	5	12	0	0	0	1	2	6	0	....	.293	.341	.293	.634	87	-1	4	3.29	1	C-16	1	0.2
Was-A	3	3	1	0	0	0	0	0	1	1	0	0	.000	.250	.000	.250	-25	-0	0	.59	0	/C-2	0	0.0
Total 7	**399**	**1170**	**122**	**318**	**40**	**6**	**2**	**110**	**127**	**121**	**5**	**0**	**.272**	**.345**	**.321**	**.666**	**80**	**-27**	**136**	**4.07**	**2**	**C-379**	**32**	**-0.3**
• PADDOCK, Del	Delmar Harold Paddock b: 6/8/1887, Volga, SD d: 2/6/1952, Remer, MN BL/TR, 5'9", 165 lbs. Deb: 4/14/1912																							
1912 Chi-A	1	1	0	0	0	0	0	0	0	....	0	....	.000	.000	.000	.000	-103	-0	0	.00	0	....	0	0.0
NY-A	46	156	26	45	5	3	1	14	23	....	9	....	.288	.393	.378	.772	114	4	27	6.10	-2	3-41/2-2,0-1	5	0.3
Yr.	47	157	26	45	5	3	1	14	23	....	9	....	.287	.391	.376	.767	113	4	27	6.05	-2	3-41/2-2,0-1	5	0.2
• PADGETT, Don	Don Wilson Padgett b: 12/5/1911, Caroleen, NC d: 12/9/1980, High Point, NC BL/TR, 6', 190 lbs. Deb: 4/23/1937 Career OF: 62-11-168																							
1937 StL-N	123	446	62	140	22	6	10	74	30	43	4	....	.314	.357	.457	.815	117	10	75	6.51	-5	*0-109(0-6-102)	16	-0.2
1938 StL-N	110	388	59	105	26	5	8	65	18	28	0	....	.271	.303	.425	.728	93	-6	48	4.34	4	0-71(3-5-63),1-16/C-6	7	-0.6
1939 StL-N	92	233	38	93	15	3	5	53	18	11	1	....	.399	.444	.554	.998	157	19	54	9.29	-3	C-61/1-6	12	1.9
1940 StL-N	93	240	24	58	15	1	6	41	26	14	1	....	.242	.321	.388	.708	89	-4	30	4.30	-4	C-72/1-2	6	-0.4
1941 StL-N	107	324	39	80	18	0	5	44	21	16	0	....	.247	.293	.349	.642	75	-12	32	3.41	-3	0-62(59-0-3),C-18/1-2	5	-1.8
1946 Bro-N	19	30	2	5	1	0	1	9	4	4	0	....	.167	.265	.300	.565	59	-2	2	2.45	0	C-10	0	-0.1
Bos-N	44	98	6	25	3	0	2	21	5	7	0	....	.255	.291	.347	.638	80	-3	10	3.77	-2	C-26	2	-0.5
Yr.	63	128	8	30	4	0	3	30	9	11	0	....	.234	.285	.336	.621	75	-5	13	3.43	-2	C-36	2	-0.6
1947 Phi-N	75	158	14	50	8	1	0	24	16	5	0	....	.316	.383	.380	.763	107	2	22	5.32	-1	C-39	4	0.3
1948 Phi-N	36	74	3	17	3	0	0	7	3	2	0	....	.230	.260	.270	.530	44	-6	5	2.37	-1	C-19	0	-0.7
Total 8	**699**	**1991**	**247**	**573**	**111**	**16**	**37**	**338**	**141**	**130**	**6**	**....**	**.288**	**.336**	**.415**	**.752**	**101**	**-1**	**279**	**5.09**	**-15**	**C-251,0-242/1-26**	**52**	**-2.1**
• PADGETT, Ernie	Ernest Kitchen "Red" Padgett b: 3/1/1899, Philadelphia, PA d: 4/15/1957, East Orange, NJ BR/TR, 5'8", 155 lbs. Deb: 10/3/1923																							
1923 Bos-N	4	11	3	2	0	0	0	0	2	0	0	0	.182	.308	.182	.490	33	-1	1	2.19	2	/S-2,2-1	0	0.2
1924 Bos-N	138	502	42	128	25	9	1	46	37	56	4	9	.255	.310	.347	.657	79	-16	53	3.60	-10	*3-113,2-29	12	-1.9
1925 Bos-N	86	256	31	78	9	7	0	29	14	14	3	5	.305	.341	.395	.735	96	-3	33	4.67	-13	2-47,S-18/3-7	6	-1.2
1926 Cle-A	36	62	7	13	0	1	0	6	8	3	1	0	.210	.300	.242	.542	42	-5	5	2.74	2	3-29/S-2	1	-0.2
1927 Cle-A	7	7	1	2	0	0	0	0	0	2	0	0	.286	.286	.286	.571	48	-1	1	2.91	-1	/2-4	0	-0.1
Total 5	**271**	**838**	**84**	**223**	**34**	**17**	**1**	**81**	**61**	**75**	**8**	**14**	**.266**	**.318**	**.351**	**.669**	**80**	**-26**	**92**	**3.82**	**-20**	**3-149/2-81,S-22**	**19**	**-3.3**
• PAEPKE, Dennis	Dennis Ray Paepke b: 4/17/1945, Long Beach, CA BR/TR, 6', 202 lbs. Deb: 6/2/1969 Career OF: 1-0-17																							
1969 KC-A	12	27	2	3	1	0	0	0	2	3	0	0	.111	.172	.148	.321	-10	-4	1	.67	1	/C-8	0	-0.3
1971 KC-A	60	152	11	31	6	0	2	14	8	29	0	0	.204	.244	.283	.527	49	-10	9	1.96	-1	C-32,0-17(1-0-16)	2	-1.1
1972 KC-A	2	6	0	0	0	0	0	0	1	2	0	0	.000	.143	.000	.143	-55	-1	0	.00	0	/C-2	0	-0.1
1974 KC-A	6	12	0	2	0	0	0	0	1	2	0	1	.167	.231	.167	.397	15	-2	0	.39	0	/C-4,0-1	0	-0.2
Total 4	**80**	**197**	**13**	**36**	**7**	**0**	**2**	**14**	**12**	**36**	**0**	**1**	**.183**	**.230**	**.249**	**.478**	**35**	**-17**	**10**	**1.59**	**0**	**/C-46,0-18**	**2**	**-1.7**
• PAFKO, Andy	Andrew "Handy Andy,Pruschka" Pafko b: 2/25/1921, Boyceville, WI BR/TR, 6', 190 lbs. Deb: 9/24/1943 C Career OF: 362-803-443																							
1943 Chi-N	13	58	7	22	3	0	0	10	2	5	1	....	.379	.400	.431	.831	142	3	9	6.65	0	0-13(0-13-0)	2	0.2
1944 Chi-N	128	469	47	126	16	2	6	62	28	23	2	....	.269	.315	.350	.665	87	-9	50	3.67	11	*0-123(0-123-1)	10	0.0
1945*Chi-N★	144	534	64	159	24	12	12	110	45	36	5	....	.298	.361	.455	.816	129	19	92	6.18	2	*0-140(0-140-0)	25	1.8
1946 Chi-N	65	234	18	66	6	4	3	39	27	15	4	....	.282	.366	.380	.746	114	5	33	4.76	5	0-64(0-64-0)	9	0.9
1947 Chi-N★	129	513	68	155	25	7	13	66	31	39	4	....	.302	.346	.454	.800	115	9	75	5.35	5	*0-127(0-127-0)	16	1.0
1948 Chi-N★	142	548	82	171	30	2	26	101	50	50	3	....	.312	.375	.516	.891	145	32	105	7.22	-3	*3-139	23	2.9
1949 Chi-N★	144	519	79	146	29	2	18	69	63	33	4	....	.281	.369	.449	.818	121	16	86	5.91	-8	0-98(1-89-9),3-49	19	0.6
1950 Chi-N★	146	514	95	156	24	8	36	92	69	32	4	....	.304	.397	.591	.989	158	43	124	9.11	8	*0-144(0-138-6)	27	4.7
1951 Chi-N	49	178	26	47	5	3	12	35	17	10	1	1	.264	.342	.528	.870	128	6	31	6.14	0	0-48(0-48-0)	7	0.5
Bro-N	84	277	42	69	11	0	18	58	35	27	1	4	.249	.350	.484	.834	120	6	47	5.72	1	0-76(70-9-0)	10	0.2
Yr.	133	455	68	116	16	3	30	93	52	37	2	5	.255	.347	.501	.848	123	12	78	5.88	1	*0-124(70-57-0)	17	0.8
1952*Bro-N	150	551	76	158	17	5	19	85	64	48	4	3	.287	.366	.439	.805	121	17	91	5.93	2	*0-139(105-12-38),3-13	21	1.2
1953 Mil-N	140	516	70	153	23	4	17	72	37	33	2	1	.297	.347	.455	.803	114	10	81	5.61	-6	*0-139(0-0-139)	18	-0.1
1954 Mil-N	138	510	61	146	22	4	14	69	37	36	1	2	.286	.339	.427	.767	105	2	72	4.85	-2	*0-138(0-7-131)	14	-0.5
1955 Mil-N	86	252	29	67	3	5	5	34	7	23	1	2	.266	.297	.377	.674	81	-8	26	3.46	-2	0-58(1-7-52),3-12	4	-1.2
1956 Mil-N	45	93	15	24	5	0	2	9	10	13	0	0	.258	.330	.376	.706	95	-1	12	4.81	0	0-37(33-0-5)	3	-0.2
1957*Mil-N	83	220	31	61	6	1	8	27	10	22	1	0	.277	.312	.423	.734	102	0	28	4.39	-2	0-69(32-1-36)	6	-0.5
1958*Mil-N	95	164	17	39	7	1	3	23	15	17	0	0	.238	.309	.348	.657	80	-5	18	3.68	1	0-93(80-3-17)	4	-0.6
1959 Mil-N	71	142	17	31	8	2	1	15	14	15	0	0	.218	.293	.324	.617	70	-6	13	3.10	-2	0-64(40-22-9)	2	-1.0
Total 17	**1852**	**6292**	**844**	**1796**	**264**	**62**	**213**	**976**	**561**	**477**	**38**	**13**	**.285**	**.351**	**.449**	**.800**	**117**	**141**	**992**	**5.62**	**12**	***0-1570,3-213**	**220**	**10.0**
• PAGAN, Jose	Jose Antonio (Rodriguez) Pagan b: 5/5/1935, Barceloneta, Puerto Rico BR/TR, 5'9", 165 lbs. Deb: 8/4/1959 C Career OF: 83-0-10																							
1959 SF-N	31	46	7	8	1	0	0	1	2	8	1	0	.174	.208	.196	.404	8	-6	2	1.49	-4	3-18/S-5,2-3	0	-0.9
1960 SF-N	18	49	8	14	2	2	0	2	1	6	2	2	.286	.300	.408	.708	97	-1	5	3.24	-2	S-11/3-1	1	-0.3
1961 SF-N	134	434	38	110	15	2	5	46	31	45	8	5	.253	.306	.332	.638	72	-18	42	3.23	-1	*S-132/0-4(3-0-2)	10	-0.8
1962*SF-N	164	580	73	150	25	6	7	57	47	77	13	9	.259	.315	.359	.674	82	-16	63	3.64	1	*S-164	16	-0.1
1963 SF-N	148	483	46	113	12	1	6	39	26	67	10	7	.234	.279	.300	.579	67	-21	40	2.78	3	*S-143/2-1,0-1	10	-0.7
1964 SF-N	134	367	33	82	10	1	1	28	35	66	5	4	.223	.293	.264	.557	57	-20	29	2.55	-17	*S-132/0-8(6-0-2)	4	-2.9
1965 SF-N	26	83	10	17	4	0	0	5	8	9	1	0	.205	.275	.253	.528	48	-5	6	2.18	-7	S-26	1	-1.1
Pit-N	42	38	6	9	1	0	0	1	1	7	1	0	.237	.275	.263	.538	52	-2	3	2.14	-2	3-15/S-7	0	-0.4
Yr.	68	121	16	26	5	0	0	6	9	16	2	0	.215	.275	.256	.531	50	-7	8	2.17	-9	S-33,3-15	1	-1.5
1966 Pit-N	109	368	44	97	15	6	4	54	13	38	0	2	.264	.296	.370	.666	84	-9	38	3.53	-6	3-83,S-18/2-3,0-3(3-0-0)	7	-1.5
1967 Pit-N	81	211	17	61	6	2	1	19	10	28	1	1	.289	.330	.351	.681	94	-2	24	4.04	2	3-25,0-23(23-0-0),S-16/2-2,C	6	0.1
1968 Pit-N	80	163	24	36	7	1	4	21	11	32	2	3	.221	.282	.350	.632	90	-3	15	2.98	-4	3-30,0-19(19-0-0)/S-8,2-2,1	3	-0.8
1969 Pit-N	108	274	29	78	11	4	9	42	17	46	1	0	.285	.329	.453	.781	119	6	41	5.42	-2	3-44,0-23(21-0-2)/2-1	10	0.3
1970*Pit-N	95	230	21	61	14	1	7	29	20	24	1	1	.265	.324	.426	.750	103	-0	31	4.65	-5	3-53/0-4(1-0-3),1-1,2-1	6	-0.6
1971*Pit-N	57	158	16	38	1	0	5	15	16	25	0	0	.241	.314	.342	.656	85	-3	17	3.64	-2	3-41/0-3(3-0-0),1-2	4	-0.6
1972 Pit-N	53	127	11	32	9	0	3	8	5	17	0	0	.252	.286	.394	.679	93	-2	14	3.91	-7	3-32/0-2(2-0-0)	3	-1.0
1973 Phi-N	46	78	4	16	5	0	0	5	1	15	0	1	.205	.215	.269	.484	33	-8	3	1.41	0	3-16/1-5,0-2(1-0-1),2-1	0	-0.8
Total 15	**1326**	**3689**	**387**	**922**	**138**	**26**	**52**	**372**	**244**	**510**	**46**	**35**	**.250**	**.300**	**.344**	**.644**	**79**	**-110**	**373**	**3.40**	**-54**	**S-662,3-358/0-92,2-14,1-9,C**	**81**	**-12.0**
• PAGE, Mike	Michael Randy Page b: 7/12/1940, Woodruff, SC BL/TR, 6'2.5", 210 lbs. Deb: 6/30/1968																							
1968 Atl-N	20	28	1	5	0	0	0	1	1	9	0	0	.179	.207	.179	.385	16	-3	1	1.02	-0	/0-6(1-0-5)	0	-0.3
• PAGE, Mitchell	Mitchell Otis Page b: 10/15/1951, Los Angeles, CA BL/TR, 6'2", 205 lbs. Deb: 4/9/1977 C Career OF: 254-0-10																							
1977 Oak-A	145	501	85	154	28	8	21	75	78	95	42	5	.307	.407	.521	.928	153	47	117	8.64	3	*0-133(131-0-5)/D-8	30	4.4
1978 Oak-A	147	516	62	147	25	7	17	70	53	95	23	19	.285	.356	.459	.815	135	20	82	5.49	0	*0-114(112-0-2),D-33	20	1.5
1979 Oak-A	133	478	51	118	11	2	9	42	52	93	17	16	.247	.325	.335	.659	83	-14	51	3.51	0	*D-126/0-4(4-0-0)	8	-1.8
1980 Oak-A	110	348	58	85	10	4	17	51	35	87	14	7	.244	.315	.443	.758	113	5	47	4.37	0	*D-101	8	0.2
1981 Oak-A	34	92	9	13	1	0	4	13	7	29	2	1	.141	.202	.283	.485	40	-7	5	1.73	0	D-29	0	-0.8
1982 Oak-A	31	78	14	20	5	0	4	7	7	24	3	4	.256	.333	.474	.808	124	1	10	4.27	0	D-24	2	0.1

YEAR TM-L	G	AB	R	H	2B	3B	HR	RBI	BB	SO	SB	CS	AVG	OBP	SLG	OPS	OPS+	BR/A	RC	RC/G	FR	G/POS	WS	TPW
1983 Oak-A	57	79	16	19	3	0	0	1	10	22	3	3	.241	.341	.278	.619	77	-3	8	3.14	0	D-34,0-10(7-0-3)	1	-0.3
1984 Pit-N	16	12	2	4	1	0	0	0	3	4	0	0	.333	.467	.417	.883	150	1	3	9.10	0	....	1	0.1
Total 8	673	2104	297	560	84	21	72	259	245	449	104	55	.266	.348	.429	.776	117	52	322	5.21	3	D-355,0-261	70	3.3

• PAGEL, Karl Karl Douglas Pagel b: 3/29/1955, Madison, WI BL/TL, 6'2", 190 lbs. Deb: 9/21/1978

YEAR TM-L	G	AB	R	H	2B	3B	HR	RBI	BB	SO	SB	CS	AVG	OBP	SLG	OPS	OPS+	BR/A	RC	RC/G	FR	G/POS	WS	TPW
1978 Chi-N	2	2	0	0	0	0	0	0	0	2	0	0	.000	.000	.000	.000	-89	-0	0	.00	0	....	0	-0.1
1979 Chi-N	1	1	0	0	0	0	0	0	0	1	0	0	.000	.000	.000	.000	-91	-0	0	.00	0	....	0	0.0
1981 Cle-A	14	15	3	4	0	2	1	4	4	1	0	0	.267	.421	.733	1.154	230	3	5	12.17	1	/1-6,D-1	2	0.4
1982 Cle-A	23	18	3	3	0	0	0	2	7	11	0	0	.167	.400	.167	.567	63	-0	2	3.28	0	1-10/D-1	0	-0.1
1983 Cle-A	8	20	1	6	0	0	0	1	0	5	0	0	.300	.300	.300	.600	63	-1	2	3.47	0	/D-5,0-1	0	-0.2
Total 5	48	56	7	13	0	2	1	7	11	20	0	0	.232	.358	.357	.715	104	1	9	5.39	1	/1-16,D-7,0-1	2	0.1

• PAGLIARONI, Jim James Vincent "Pag" Pagliaroni b: 12/8/1937, Dearborn, MI BR/TR, 6'4", 210 lbs. Deb: 8/13/1955

YEAR TM-L	G	AB	R	H	2B	3B	HR	RBI	BB	SO	SB	CS	AVG	OBP	SLG	OPS	OPS+	BR/A	RC	RC/G	FR	G/POS	WS	TPW
1955 Bos-A	1	0	0	0	0	0	0	1	0	0	0	0	....	....	....	....	-92	0	0	.00	0	/C-1	0	0.0
1960 Bos-A	28	62	7	19	5	2	2	9	13	11	0	0	.306	.434	.548	.983	158	6	16	10.04	0	C-18	4	0.6
1961 Bos-A	120	376	50	91	17	0	16	58	55	74	1	1	.242	.345	.415	.760	100	0	56	5.05	-2	*C-108	11	0.4
1962 Bos-A	90	260	39	67	14	0	11	37	36	55	2	1	.258	.359	.438	.797	110	4	43	5.73	-2	C-73	9	0.6
1963 Pit-N	92	252	27	58	5	0	11	26	36	57	0	0	.230	.331	.381	.712	104	2	31	4.02	0	C-85	8	0.7
1964 Pit-N	97	302	33	89	12	3	10	36	41	56	1	0	.295	.383	.454	.836	135	16	52	6.22	-7	C-96	15	1.5
1965 Pit-N	134	403	42	108	15	0	17	65	41	84	0	0	.268	.340	.432	.772	115	8	57	4.91	-3	*C-131	17	1.2
1966 Pit-N	123	374	37	88	20	0	11	49	50	71	0	5	.235	.332	.377	.709	96	-2	47	4.23	-5	*C-118	12	-0.2
1967 Pit-N	44	100	4	20	1	1	0	9	16	26	0	0	.200	.316	.230	.546	58	-4	7	2.37	0	C-38	2	-0.3
1968 Oak-A	66	199	19	49	4	0	6	20	24	42	0	0	.246	.333	.357	.690	115	4	25	4.25	-5	C-63	7	0.2
1969 Oak-A	14	27	1	4	1	0	1	2	5	2	0	0	.148	.303	.296	.599	71	-1	3	3.40	2	/C-7	1	0.2
Sea-A	40	110	10	29	4	1	5	14	13	16	0	0	.264	.341	.455	.796	123	3	18	5.59	-1	C-29/1-2,0-1	5	0.3
Yr.	54	137	11	33	5	1	6	16	18	18	0	0	.241	.333	.423	.757	112	2	21	5.13	1	C-36/1-2,0-1	6	0.5
Total 11	849	2465	269	622	98	7	90	326	330	494	4	7	.252	.346	.407	.754	109	37	355	4.93	-24	C-767/1-2,0-1	91	5.1

• PAGLIARULO, Mike Michael Timothy Pagliarulo b: 3/15/1960, Medford, MA BL/TR, 6'1", 195 lbs. Deb: 7/7/1984

YEAR TM-L	G	AB	R	H	2B	3B	HR	RBI	BB	SO	SB	CS	AVG	OBP	SLG	OPS	OPS+	BR/A	RC	RC/G	FR	G/POS	WS	TPW
1984 NY-A	67	201	24	48	15	3	7	34	15	46	0	0	.239	.292	.448	.739	105	1	25	4.24	1	3-67	6	0.1
1985 NY-A	138	380	55	91	16	2	19	62	45	86	0	0	.239	.326	.442	.768	111	5	56	5.05	-2	*3-134	13	0.2
1986 NY-A	149	504	71	120	24	3	28	71	54	120	4	1	.238	.317	.464	.781	111	7	74	5.02	9	*3-143/S-2	15	1.4
1987 NY-A	150	522	76	122	26	3	32	87	53	111	1	3	.234	.307	.479	.786	105	1	75	4.87	9	*3-147/1-1	17	0.7
1988 NY-A	125	444	46	96	20	1	15	67	37	104	1	0	.216	.280	.367	.647	80	-13	46	3.48	4	*3-124	13	-0.8
1989 NY-A	74	223	19	44	10	0	4	16	19	43	1	1	.197	.266	.296	.562	59	-13	18	2.71	-4	3-69/D-1	1	-1.6
SD-N	50	148	12	29	7	0	3	14	18	39	2	0	.196	.287	.304	.591	69	-5	14	2.97	1	3-49	3	-0.5
1990 SD-N	128	398	29	101	23	2	7	38	39	66	1	3	.254	.325	.374	.699	91	-6	47	3.97	0	*3-116	8	-0.5
1991*Min-A	121	365	38	102	20	0	6	36	21	55	1	2	.279	.324	.384	.707	91	-6	43	4.21	13	*3-118/2-1	9	0.8
1992 Min-A	42	105	10	21	4	0	0	9	1	17	1	0	.200	.215	.238	.453	26	-10	5	1.70	2	3-37/D-1	1	-0.8
1993 Min-A	83	253	31	74	16	4	3	23	18	34	6	6	.292	.351	.423	.774	107	1	36	5.05	5	3-79	9	0.7
Bal-A	33	117	24	38	9	0	6	21	8	15	0	0	.325	.373	.556	.929	140	6	24	8.02	1	3-28/1-4	5	0.7
Yr.	116	370	55	112	25	4	9	44	26	49	6	6	.303	.358	.465	.823	117	7	60	5.93	5	*3-107/1-4	14	1.3
1995 Tex-A	86	241	27	56	16	0	4	27	15	49	0	0	.232	.280	.349	.629	61	-15	21	2.88	-2	3-68,1-11	2	-1.5
Total 11	1246	3901	462	942	206	18	134	505	343	785	18	16	.241	.308	.407	.714	93	-47	486	4.23	38	*3-1179/1-16,D-2,S-2,2-1	102	-1.1

• PAGNOZZI, Tom Thomas Alan Pagnozzi b: 7/30/1962, Tucson, AZ BR/TR, 6', 190 lbs. Deb: 4/12/1987

YEAR TM-L	G	AB	R	H	2B	3B	HR	RBI	BB	SO	SB	CS	AVG	OBP	SLG	OPS	OPS+	BR/A	RC	RC/G	FR	G/POS	WS	TPW
1987*StL-N	27	48	8	9	1	0	2	9	4	13	1	0	.188	.250	.333	.583	52	-3	4	2.91	0	C-25/1-1	1	-0.3
1988 StL-N	81	195	17	55	9	0	0	15	11	32	0	0	.282	.320	.328	.649	86	-4	20	3.63	-3	1-28,C-28/3-5	4	-0.7
1989 StL-N	52	80	3	12	2	0	0	3	6	19	0	0	.150	.218	.175	.393	13	-9	2	.77	-1	C-38/1-2,3-1	0	-0.9
1990 StL-N	69	220	20	61	15	0	2	23	14	37	1	1	.277	.323	.373	.696	91	-4	28	4.60	3	C-63/1-2	8	0.4
1991 StL-N	140	459	38	121	24	5	2	57	36	63	9	13	.264	.323	.351	.673	89	-11	49	3.54	6	*C-139/1-3	17	0.4
1992 StL-N★	139	485	33	121	26	3	7	44	28	64	2	5	.249	.292	.359	.651	86	-12	46	3.16	-2	*C-138	11	-0.6
1993 StL-N	92	330	31	85	15	1	7	41	19	30	1	0	.258	.300	.373	.673	80	-10	36	3.76	0	C-92	7	-0.4
1994 StL-N	70	243	21	66	12	1	7	40	21	39	0	0	.272	.330	.416	.745	94	-2	34	4.98	4	C-70/1-1	9	0.6
1995 StL-N	62	219	17	47	14	1	2	15	11	31	0	1	.215	.255	.315	.570	50	-17	15	2.26	4	C-61	3	-0.9
1996*StL-N	119	407	48	110	23	0	13	55	24	78	4	1	.270	.314	.423	.737	93	-5	53	4.53	1	*C-116/1-1	14	0.4
1997 StL-N	25	50	4	11	3	0	1	8	1	7	0	0	.220	.235	.340	.575	49	-4	3	2.23	-1	C-13/1-2,3-1	0	-0.4
1998 StL-N	51	160	7	35	9	0	1	10	14	37	0	0	.219	.282	.294	.575	52	-11	13	2.71	-1	C-44	1	-0.9
Total 12	927	2896	247	733	153	11	44	320	189	450	18	21	.253	.301	.359	.660	80	-93	303	3.55	11	C-827/1-40,3-7	75	-3.5

• PALACIOS, Rey Robert Rey Palacios b: 11/8/1962, Brooklyn, NY BR/TR, 5'10", 190 lbs. Deb: 9/8/1988 Career OF: 0-0-2

YEAR TM-L	G	AB	R	H	2B	3B	HR	RBI	BB	SO	SB	CS	AVG	OBP	SLG	OPS	OPS+	BR/A	RC	RC/G	FR	G/POS	WS	TPW
1988 KC-A	5	11	2	1	0	0	0	0	0	4	0	0	.091	.091	.091	.182	-48	-2	0	.00	0	/C-3,3-1,D-1	0	-0.2
1989 KC-A	55	47	12	8	2	0	1	8	2	14	0	1	.170	.220	.277	.497	39	-4	3	1.60	-3	3-21,1-18,C-13/D-2,0-1	1	-0.8
1990 KC-A	41	56	8	13	3	0	2	9	5	24	2	2	.232	.295	.393	.688	92	-1	6	3.83	-2	C-27/1-7,3-3,0-1	1	-0.2
Total 3	101	114	22	22	5	0	3	17	7	42	2	3	.193	.246	.316	.562	57	-8	9	2.43	-6	/C-43,1-25,3-25,D-3,0-2	2	-1.3

• PALMEIRO, Orlando Orlando Palmeiro b: 1/19/1969, Hoboken, NJ BL/TL, 5'11", 155 lbs. Deb: 7/1/1995 Career OF: 261-110-219

YEAR TM-L	G	AB	R	H	2B	3B	HR	RBI	BB	SO	SB	CS	AVG	OBP	SLG	OPS	OPS+	BR/A	RC	RC/G	FR	G/POS	WS	TPW
1995 Cal-A	15	20	3	7	0	0	0	1	1	1	0	0	.350	.381	.350	.731	93	-0	3	5.74	-0	/0-7(3-4-0),D-1	1	0.0
1996 Cal-A	50	87	6	25	6	1	0	6	8	13	0	1	.287	.361	.379	.740	89	-2	12	5.02	0	0-31(7-17-8)/D-4	2	-0.2
1997 Ana-A	74	134	19	29	2	2	0	8	17	11	2	2	.216	.309	.261	.570	50	-10	11	2.62	-0	0-52(4-45-4),D-11	1	-1.0
1998 Ana-A	75	165	28	53	7	2	0	21	20	11	5	4	.321	.395	.388	.782	104	1	26	5.67	-2	0-54(46-6-4)/D-3	5	-0.3
1999 Ana-A	109	317	46	88	12	1	1	23	39	30	5	5	.278	.367	.331	.699	81	-9	41	4.52	-1	0-92(60-1-35),D-12	6	-1.3
2000 Ana-A	108	243	38	73	20	2	0	25	38	20	4	1	.300	.399	.399	.798	100	2	42	6.09	3	0-72(40-2-31),D-19	7	0.2
2001 Ana-A	104	230	29	56	10	1	2	23	25	24	6	6	.243	.326	.322	.647	70	-11	25	3.47	0	0-59(26-7-28),D-30	4	-1.4
2002*Ana-A	110	263	35	79	12	1	0	31	30	22	7	2	.300	.372	.354	.726	95	-0	36	4.85	1	0-86(33-11-47)/D-6	7	-0.3
2003 StL-N	141	317	37	86	13	1	3	33	32	31	3	3	.271	.342	.347	.689	84	-8	40	4.38	3	0-112(42-17-62)	6	-0.8
Total 9	786	1776	241	496	82	11	6	171	210	163	32	24	.279	.361	.348	.709	85	-35	237	4.59	3	0-565/D-86	39	-5.0

• PALMEIRO, Rafael Rafael (Corrales) Palmeiro b: 9/24/1964, Havana, Cuba BL/TL, 6', 188 lbs. Deb: 9/8/1986 Career OF: 208-2-8

YEAR TM-L	G	AB	R	H	2B	3B	HR	RBI	BB	SO	SB	CS	AVG	OBP	SLG	OPS	OPS+	BR/A	RC	RC/G	FR	G/POS	WS	TPW
1986 Chi-N	22	73	9	18	4	0	3	12	4	6	1	1	.247	.295	.425	.720	89	-2	8	3.41	-1	0-20(19-0-3)	1	-0.4
1987 Chi-N	84	221	32	61	15	1	14	30	20	26	2	2	.276	.339	.543	.882	124	6	40	6.37	-2	0-45(44-0-2),1-18	7	0.2
1988 Chi-N★	152	580	75	178	41	5	8	53	38	34	12	2	.307	.353	.436	.789	120	15	89	5.70	-2	*0-147(145-2-3)/1-5	17	0.9
1989 Tex-A	156	559	76	154	23	4	8	64	63	48	4	3	.275	.355	.374	.729	104	4	74	4.62	8	*1-147/D-6	17	0.2
1990 Tex-A	154	598	72	**191**	35	6	14	89	40	59	3	3	.319	.365	.468	.833	131	23	94	5.73	-4	*1-146/D-6	22	0.8
1991 Tex-A★	159	631	115	203	**49**	3	26	88	68	72	4	3	.322	.393	.532	.925	156	48	129	7.64	-4	*1-157/D-2	26	3.3
1992 Tex-A	159	608	84	163	27	4	22	85	72	83	2	3	.268	.355	.434	.789	124	20	96	5.53	3	*1-156/D-2	24	1.2
1993 Tex-A	160	597	**124**	176	40	2	37	105	73	85	22	3	.295	.376	.554	.931	153	47	128	7.83	13	*1-160	31	4.4
1994 Bal-A	111	436	82	139	32	0	23	76	54	63	7	3	.319	.396	.550	.947	134	23	95	8.08	2	*1-111	17	1.3
1995 Bal-A	143	554	89	172	30	2	39	104	62	65	3	1	.310	.383	.583	.966	145	35	123	8.31	10	*1-142	21	3.1
1996*Bal-A	162	626	110	181	40	2	39	142	95	96	8	0	.289	.385	.546	.932	133	33	137	8.03	2	*1-159/D-3	30	1.8
1997*Bal-A	158	614	95	156	24	2	38	110	67	109	5	2	.254	.332	.485	.818	113	11	98	5.53	4	*1-155/D-3	18	0.1
1998 Bal-A★	162	619	98	183	36	1	43	121	79	91	11	7	.296	.382	.565	.947	144	39	132	7.75	7	*1-159/D-3	24	3.1
1999*Tex-A★	158	565	96	183	30	1	47	148	97	69	2	4	.324	.426	.630	1.056	157	50	152	10.09	0	*D-135,1-28	31	3.6
2000 Tex-A	158	565	102	163	29	3	39	120	103	77	2	1	.288	.401	.558	.958	137	34	128	8.18	-8	*1-108,D-46	23	1.3
2001 Tex-A	160	600	98	164	33	0	47	123	101	90	1	1	.273	.384	.563	.948	140	37	135	8.11	-4	*1-113,D-46	25	1.9
2002 Tex-A	155	546	99	149	34	0	43	105	104	94	2	0	.273	.395	.571	.966	145	39	128	8.36	3	1-97,D-55	19	2.9
2003 Tex-A	154	561	92	146	21	2	38	112	84	77	2	0	.260	.362	.508	.870	116	14	108	6.83	4	D-96,1-55	19	0.6
Total 18	2567	9553	1548	2780	543	38	528	1687	1224	1244	93	39	.291	.376	.522	.898	134	476	1896	7.17	32	*1-1916,D-403,0-212	372	30.2

• PALMER, Dean Dean William Palmer b: 12/27/1968, Tallahassee, FL BR/TR, 6'1", 195 lbs. Deb: 9/1/1989 Career OF: 30-0-0

YEAR TM-L	G	AB	R	H	2B	3B	HR	RBI	BB	SO	SB	CS	AVG	OBP	SLG	OPS	OPS+	BR/A	RC	RC/G	FR	G/POS	WS	TPW
1989 Tex-A	16	19	0	2	2	0	0	1	0	12	0	0	.105	.105	.211	.316	-13	-3	0	.68	-1	/3-6,D-6,0-1,S-1	0	-0.4
1991 Tex-A	81	268	38	50	9	2	15	37	32	98	0	2	.187	.281	.403	.684	88	-6	31	3.67	-1	3-50,0-29(29-0-0)/D-5	7	-0.8
1992 Tex-A	152	541	74	124	25	0	26	72	62	154	10	4	.229	.313	.420	.733	107	5	73	4.51	-13	*3-150	16	-0.7
1993 Tex-A	148	519	88	127	31	2	33	96	53	154	11	10	.245	.324	.503	.827	124	13	84	5.51	-19	*3-148/S-1	16	-0.3
1994 Tex-A	93	342	50	84	14	2	19	59	26	89	3	4	.246	.303	.465	.768	94	-6	46	4.58	-4	3-91	7	-0.8
1995 Tex-A	36	119	30	40	6	0	9	24	21	21	1	1	.336	.451	.613	1.065	170	13	34	11.17	-1	3-36	7	1.2
1996*Tex-A	154	582	98	163	26	2	38	107	59	145	2	0	.280	.351	.527	.879	112	9	106	6.52	-18	*3-154/D-1	15	-0.6
1997 Tex-A	94	355	47	87	21	0	14	55	26	84	1	0	.245	.298	.423	.721	81	-11	45	4.44	-10	3-93	6	-1.9
KC-A	49	187	23	52	10	1	9	31	15	50	1	2	.278	.338	.487	.825	109	1	30	5.73	-3	3-48/D-1	5	-0.1
Yr.	143	542	70	139	31	1	23	86	41	134	2	2	.256	.312	.445	.757	91	-10	75	4.87	-13	*3-141/D-1	11	-1.9
1998 KC-A★	152	572	84	159	27	2	34	119	48	134	8	2	.278	.340	.510	.851	114	11	95	5.78	-18	*3-129,D-22	12	-0.7
1999 Det-A	150	560	92	147	25	2	38	100	57	153	3	3	.263	.341	.518	.859	114	10	97	6.07	-6	*3-141/D-9	17	0.4
2000 Det-A	145	524	73	134	22	2	29	102	66	146	4	2	.256	.343	.471	.815	106	4	87	5.71	-22	*3-115,1-20,D-14	15	-1.6
2001 Det-A	57	216	34	48	11	0	11	40	27	59	4	1	.222	.317	.426	.743	98	-0	31	4.81	0	D-57	6	-0.4
2002 Det-A	4	12	0	0	0	0	0	0	1	5	0	0	.000	.077	.000	.077	-82	-3	0	.00	0	/D-3	0	-0.3
2003 Det-A	26	86	3	12	2	0	0	6	9	28	0	0	.140	.237	.163	.400	9	-11	4	1.31	1	D-22/1-1,3-1	0	-1.1
Total 14	1357	4902	734	1229	231	15	275	849	502	1332	48	31	.251	.327	.472	.799	106	26	764	5.35	-115	*3-1162,D-140/0-30,1-21,S-2	129	-8.1

• PALMER, Eddie Edwin Henry "Baldy" Palmer b: 6/1/1893, Petty, TX d: 1/9/1983, Marlow, OK BR/TR, 5'9.5", 175 lbs. Deb: 9/6/1917

YEAR TM-L	G	AB	R	H	2B	3B	HR	RBI	BB	SO	SB	CS	AVG	OBP	SLG	OPS	OPS+	BR/A	RC	RC/G	FR	G/POS	WS	TPW
1917 Phi-A	16	52	7	11	1	0	0	5	7	7	1	....	.212	.305	.231	.536	65	-2	4	2.34	-1	3-13/S-1	1	-0.3

• PALMISANO, Joe Joseph Palmisano b: 11/19/1902, West Point, GA d: 11/5/1971, Albuquerque, NM BR/TR, 5'8", 160 lbs. Deb: 5/31/1931

YEAR TM-L	G	AB	R	H	2B	3B	HR	RBI	BB	SO	SB	CS	AVG	OBP	SLG	OPS	OPS+	BR/A	RC	RC/G	FR	G/POS	WS	TPW
1931 Phi-A	19	44	5	10	2	0	0	4	6	3	0	0	.227	.320	.273	.593	54	-3	4	3.25	-1	C-16/2-1	1	-0.3

• PALYS, Stan Stanley Francis Palys b: 5/1/1930, Blakely, PA BR/TR, 6'2", 190 lbs. Deb: 9/20/1953 Career OF: 65-4-14

YEAR TM-L	G	AB	R	H	2B	3B	HR	RBI	BB	SO	SB	CS	AVG	OBP	SLG	OPS	OPS+	BR/A	RC	RC/G	FR	G/POS	WS	TPW
1953 Phi-N	2	2	0	0	0	0	0	0	1	0	0	0	.000	.333	.000	.333	-4	-0	0	1.17	0	/0-1	0	0.0
1954 Phi-N	2	4	0	1	0	0	0	0	1	1	0	0	.250	.400	.250	.650	74	-0	1	4.54	-0	/0-1	0	0.0
1955 Phi-N	15	52	8	15	3	0	1	8	6	5	1	0	.288	.362	.404	.766	105	1	8	5.65	0	0-15(3-4-8)	2	0.0
Cin-N	79	222	29	51	14	0	7	30	12	35	1	1	.230	.272	.387	.660	68	-11	23	3.39	2	0-55(55-0-0)/1-1	2	-1.2
Yr.	94	274	37	66	17	0	8	38	18	40	2	1	.241	.290	.391	.681	75	-10	31	3.78	1	0-70(58-4-8)/1-1	4	-1.2
1956 Cin-N	40	53	5	12	0	0	2	5	6	13	0	0	.226	.305	.340	.645	69	-2	6	3.87	-1	0-10(7-0-4)	1	-0.3
Total 4	138	333	42	79	17	0	10	43	26	54	2	1	.237	.294	.378	.673	74	-13	37	3.79	1	/0-82,1-1	5	-1.6

• PANKOVITS, Jim James Franklin Pankovits b: 8/6/1955, Pennington Gap, VA BR/TR, 5'10", 195 lbs. Deb: 5/27/1984 Career OF: 28-0-20

YEAR TM-L	G	AB	R	H	2B	3B	HR	RBI	BB	SO	SB	CS	AVG	OBP	SLG	OPS	OPS+	BR/A	RC	RC/G	FR	G/POS	WS	TPW
1984 Hou-N	53	81	6	23	7	0	1	14	2	20	2	1	.284	.301	.407	.709	105	-0	10	4.19	-2	2-15/S-4,0-3(3-0-0)	2	-0.2
1985 Hou-N	75	172	24	42	3	0	4	14	17	29	1	0	.244	.316	.331	.647	84	-4	19	3.76	2	0-33(14-0-20),2-21/3-1,S-1	4	-0.3
1986*Hou-N	70	113	12	32	6	1	1	7	11	25	1	1	.283	.347	.381	.727	103	0	14	4.44	-2	2-26/0-5(5-0-0),C-1	3	-0.1
1987 Hou-N	50	61	7	14	2	0	1	8	6	13	2	0	.230	.299	.311	.610	64	-3	6	3.16	2	/2-9,0-6(6-0-0),3-4	1	-0.1
1988 Hou-N	68	140	13	31	7	1	2	12	8	28	2	1	.221	.273	.329	.602	75	-5	13	3.09	-2	2-31,3-11/1-2	2	-0.7
1990 Bos-A	2	0	0	0	0	0	0	0	0	0	0	0	....	....	....	....	-96	0	0	....	-1	/2-2	0	-0.1
Total 6	318	567	62	142	25	2	9	55	44	115	8	3	.250	.308	.349	.657	86	-11	61	3.71	-4	2-104/0-47,3-16,S-5,1-2,C-1	12	-1.4

• PAPE, Ken Kenneth Wayne Pape b: 10/1/1951, San Antonio, TX BR/TR, 5'11", 195 lbs. Deb: 5/17/1976

YEAR TM-L	G	AB	R	H	2B	3B	HR	RBI	BB	SO	SB	CS	AVG	OBP	SLG	OPS	OPS+	BR/A	RC	RC/G	FR	G/POS	WS	TPW
1976 Tex-A	21	23	7	5	1	0	1	4	3	2	0	1	.217	.357	.391	.748	117	0	3	3.63	-1	/S-6,3-4,D-3,2-1	1	0.0

• PAPI, Stan Stanley Gerard Papi b: 2/4/1951, Fresno, CA BR/TR, 6', 178 lbs. Deb: 4/11/1974

YEAR TM-L	G	AB	R	H	2B	3B	HR	RBI	BB	SO	SB	CS	AVG	OBP	SLG	OPS	OPS+	BR/A	RC	RC/G	FR	G/POS	WS	TPW
1974 StL-N	8	4	0	1	0	0	0	1	0	0	0	0	.250	.250	.250	.500	40	-0	0	2.25	-2	/S-7,2-1	0	-0.2
1977 Mon-N	13	43	5	10	2	1	0	4	1	9	1	0	.233	.250	.326	.576	55	-3	3	2.67	-1	3-10/S-2,2-1	0	-0.4
1978 Mon-N	67	152	15	35	11	0	0	11	10	28	0	0	.230	.287	.303	.589	65	-7	12	2.57	0	S-22,3-15/2-5	2	-0.6
1979 Bos-A	50	117	9	22	8	0	1	6	5	20	0	0	.188	.221	.282	.503	33	-11	8	2.13	3	2-26,S-21/D-1	2	-0.6
1980 Bos-A	1	0	0	0	0	0	0	0	0	0	0	0	....	....	....	....	-95	0	0	....	0	/3-1	0	0.0
Det-A	46	114	12	27	3	4	3	17	5	24	0	0	.237	.269	.412	.681	82	-3	12	3.44	-1	2-31,3-11/S-5,1-1	2	-0.3
Yr.	47	114	12	27	3	4	3	17	5	24	0	0	.237	.269	.412	.681	82	-3	12	3.44	-1	2-31,3-12/S-5,1-1	2	-0.3
1981 Det-A	40	93	8	19	2	1	3	12	3	18	1	0	.204	.229	.344	.573	61	-5	7	2.41	0	3-32/D-3,1-1,2-1,0-1	1	-0.6
Total 6	225	523	49	114	26	6	7	51	24	99	2	0	.218	.255	.331	.586	60	-30	42	2.63	-2	/3-69,2-65,S-57,D-4,1-2,0-1	7	-2.6

• PAPPAS, Erik Erik Daniel Pappas b: 4/25/1966, Chicago, IL BR/TR, 6', 190 lbs. Deb: 4/19/1991

YEAR TM-L	G	AB	R	H	2B	3B	HR	RBI	BB	SO	SB	CS	AVG	OBP	SLG	OPS	OPS+	BR/A	RC	RC/G	FR	G/POS	WS	TPW
1991 Chi-N	7	17	1	3	0	0	0	2	1	5	0	0	.176	.222	.176	.399	13	-2	1	1.40	0	/C-6	0	-0.2
1993 StL-N	82	228	25	63	12	0	1	28	35	35	1	3	.276	.373	.342	.715	95	-1	29	4.45	-1	C-63,0-16(1-0-15)/1-2	7	0.1
1994 StL-N	15	44	8	4	1	0	0	5	10	13	0	0	.091	.273	.114	.386	6	-6	2	1.40	-2	C-15	0	-0.6
Total 3	104	289	34	70	13	0	1	35	46	53	1	3	.242	.348	.298	.646	75	-9	32	3.70	-3	/C-84,0-16,1-2	7	-0.7

• PAQUETTE, Craig Craig Harold Paquette b: 3/28/1969, Long Beach, CA BR/TR, 6', 190 lbs. Deb: 6/1/1993 Career OF: 132-0-75

YEAR TM-L	G	AB	R	H	2B	3B	HR	RBI	BB	SO	SB	CS	AVG	OBP	SLG	OPS	OPS+	BR/A	RC	RC/G	FR	G/POS	WS	TPW
1993 Oak-A	105	393	35	86	20	4	12	46	14	108	4	2	.219	.246	.382	.627	70	-19	35	2.95	-7	*3-104/D-1,0-1	5	-2.4
1994 Oak-A	14	49	0	7	2	0	0	0	0	14	1	0	.143	.143	.184	.327	-18	-8	1	.88	1	3-14	0	-0.7
1995 Oak-A	105	283	42	64	13	1	13	49	12	88	5	2	.226	.260	.417	.677	77	-11	30	3.40	-4	3-75,0-20(18-0-2)/S-8,1-3	4	-1.4
1996 KC-A	118	429	61	111	15	1	22	67	23	101	5	3	.259	.300	.452	.752	87	-11	55	4.34	-5	3-51,0-47(47-0-0),1-19,S-11/D	5	-1.8
1997 KC-A	77	252	26	58	15	1	8	33	10	57	2	2	.230	.265	.393	.658	67	-14	22	2.75	-2	3-72/0-4(4-0-0)	2	-1.4
1998 NY-N	7	19	3	5	2	0	0	0	0	6	1	0	.263	.263	.368	.632	65	-1	1	1.26	0	/3-4,1-2,0-1	0	-0.1
1999 StL-N	48	157	21	45	6	0	10	37	6	38	1	0	.287	.313	.516	.829	104	0	23	5.12	0	0-27(3-0-25),3-10/2-7,1-6	5	0.0
2000*StL-N	134	384	47	94	24	2	15	61	27	83	4	3	.245	.298	.435	.733	82	-13	49	4.36	-3	3-86,0-31(18-0-16),1-28,2-13	8	-1.7
2001*StL-N	123	340	47	96	17	0	15	64	18	67	3	1	.282	.328	.465	.793	102	1	49	5.02	-4	0-57(33-0-26),3-33,1-23/2-4	12	-0.7
2002 Det-A	72	252	20	49	14	1	4	20	10	53	1	0	.194	.225	.306	.531	42	-21	16	2.03	-4	3-49,1-14/0-8(4-0-4),D-5	1	-2.5
2003 Det-A	11	33	2	5	0	0	0	0	0	5	0	0	.152	.152	.152	.303	-21	-6	0	.41	-1	/1-5,0-5(3-0-2)	0	-0.7
Total 11	814	2591	304	620	128	10	99	377	120	620	27	13	.239	.276	.411	.687	76	-104	280	3.61	-29	3-498,0-201,1-100/2-24,S-19,D	42	-13.2

• PARDO, Al Alberto Judas Pardo b: 9/8/1962, Oviedo, Spain BB/TR, 6'2", 187 lbs. Deb: 7/3/1985

YEAR TM-L	G	AB	R	H	2B	3B	HR	RBI	BB	SO	SB	CS	AVG	OBP	SLG	OPS	OPS+	BR/A	RC	RC/G	FR	G/POS	WS	TPW
1985 Bal-A	34	75	3	10	1	0	0	1	3	15	0	0	.133	.167	.147	.313	-14	-12	2	.82	-2	C-29	1	-1.2
1986 Bal-A	16	51	3	7	1	0	1	3	0	14	0	0	.137	.137	.216	.353	-6	-8	1	.63	-0	C-14/D-1	0	-0.7
1988 Phi-N	2	2	0	0	0	0	0	0	0	2	0	0	.000	.000	.000	.000	-98	-1	0	.00	-1	/C-2	0	-0.1
1989 Phi-N	1	1	0	0	0	0	0	0	0	0	0	0	.000	.000	.000	.000	-100	-0	0	.00	-0	/C-1	0	0.0
Total 4	53	129	6	17	2	0	1	4	3	31	0	0	.132	.152	.171	.322	-13	-20	3	.72	-2	/C-46,D-1	1	-2.0

• PAREDES, Johnny Johnny Alfonso (Isambert) Paredes b: 9/2/1962, Maracaibo, Venezuela BR/TR, 5'11", 165 lbs. Deb: 4/29/1988

YEAR TM-L	G	AB	R	H	2B	3B	HR	RBI	BB	SO	SB	CS	AVG	OBP	SLG	OPS	OPS+	BR/A	RC	RC/G	FR	G/POS	WS	TPW
1988 Mon-N	35	91	6	17	2	0	1	10	9	17	5	2	.187	.282	.242	.523	49	-6	7	2.44	4	2-28/0-1	2	-0.1
1990 Det-A	6	8	2	1	0	0	0	0	1	0	0	0	.125	.222	.125	.347		-1	0	1.08	0	/2-4	0	-0.1
Mon-N	3	6	0	2	1	0	0	1	1	0	0	0	.333	.429	.500	.929	161	1	1	8.68	0	/2-2	1	0.1
1991 Det-A	16	18	4	6	0	0	0	0	0	1	1	1	.333	.333	.333	.667	84	-1	2	3.76	-1	/2-7,D-2,3-1,S-1	0	-0.2
Total 3	60	123	12	26	3	0	1	11	11	18	6	3	.211	.292	.260	.552	56	-7	10	2.76	2	/2-41,D-2,3-1,0-1,S-1	3	-0.4

• PARENT, Freddy Frederick Alfred Parent b: 11/25/1875, Biddeford, ME d: 11/2/1972, Sanford, ME BR/TR, 5'7", 154 lbs. Deb: 7/14/1899 Career OF: 34-102-12

YEAR TM-L	G	AB	R	H	2B	3B	HR	RBI	BB	SO	SB	CS	AVG	OBP	SLG	OPS	OPS+	BR/A	RC	RC/G	FR	G/POS	WS	TPW
1899 StL-N	2	8	0	1	0	0	0	1	0	....	0	....	.125	.125	.125	.250	-31	-1	0	.49	0	/2-2	0	-0.2
1901 Bos-A	138	517	87	158	23	9	4	59	41	....	16	....	.306	.367	.408	.775	117	12	88	6.13	4	*S-138	21	1.9
1902 Bos-A	138	567	91	156	31	8	3	62	24	....	16	....	.275	.309	.374	.683	86	-12	74	4.59	5	*S-138	16	-0.3
1903*Bos-A	139	560	83	170	31	17	4	80	13	....	24	....	.304	.326	.441	.767	122	13	92	6.04	11	*S-139	26	2.9
1904 Bos-A	155	591	85	172	22	9	6	77	28	....	20	....	.291	.330	.389	.719	120	12	87	5.19	10	*S-155	29	3.1
1905 Bos-A	153	602	55	141	16	5	0	33	47	....	25	....	.234	.296	.277	.574	81	-12	63	3.35	-6	*S-153	15	-1.4
1906 Bos-A	149	600	67	141	14	10	1	49	31	....	16	....	.235	.277	.297	.574	80	-15	57	3.18	-12	*S-143/2-6	10	-2.5
1907 Bos-A	114	409	51	113	19	5	1	26	22	....	12	....	.276	.321	.355	.676	116	7	54	4.54	2	0-47(26-13-9),S-43/3-7,2-5	12	0.9
1908 Chi-A	119	391	28	81	7	5	0	35	50	....	9	....	.207	.300	.251	.551	81	-6	33	2.65	-7	*S-118	11	-1.1

YEAR TM-L	G	AB	R	H	2B	3B	HR	RBI	BB	SO	SB	CS	AVG	OBP	SLG	OPS	OPS+	BR/A	RC	RC/G	FR	G/POS	WS	TPW
1909 Chi-A	136	472	61	123	10	5	0	30	46	....	32	....	.261	.335	.303	.638	106	5	60	4.17	11	S-98,0-38(7-30-1)/2-1	23	2.0
1910 Chi-A	81	258	23	46	6	1	1	16	29	....	14	....	.178	.266	.221	.487	56	-12	19	2.26	-2	0-62(1-59-2),2-11/S-4,3-1	4	-1.8
1911 Chi-A	3	9	2	4	1	0	0	3	2	....	0	....	.444	.545	.556	1.101	212	2	3	12.35	0	/2-3	1	0.2
Total 12	1327	4984	633	1306	180	74	20	471	333	....	184	....	.262	.315	.340	.655	98	-8	631	4.29	15	*S-1129,0-147/2-28,3-8	168	3.7
• PARENT, Mark	Mark Alan Parent b: 9/16/1961, Ashland, OR BR/TR, 6'5", 225 lbs. Deb: 9/20/1986																							
1986 SD-N	8	14	1	2	0	0	0	0	1	3	0	0	.143	.200	.143	.343	-4	-2	0	.63	-1	/C-3	0	-0.3
1987 SD-N	12	25	0	2	0	0	0	2	0	9	0	0	.080	.080	.080	.160	-60	-6	0	.19	0	C-10	0	-0.5
1988 SD-N	41	118	9	23	3	0	6	15	6	23	0	0	.195	.234	.373	.607	73	-5	10	2.87	-1	C-36	3	-0.4
1989 SD-N	52	141	12	27	4	0	7	21	8	34	1	0	.191	.235	.369	.604	70	-6	11	2.40	0	C-41/1-1	2	-0.4
1990 SD-N	65	189	13	42	11	0	3	16	16	29	1	0	.222	.283	.328	.611	67	-9	18	3.23	3	C-60	4	-0.3
1991 Tex-A	3	1	0	0	0	0	0	0	0	1	0	0	.000	.000	.000	.000	-102	-0	0	.00	0	/C-3	0	-0.1
1992 Bal-A	17	34	4	8	1	0	2	4	3	7	0	0	.235	.316	.441	.757	107	0	5	4.94	0	C-16	1	0.1
1993 Bal-A	22	54	7	14	2	0	4	12	3	14	0	0	.259	.298	.519	.817	110	0	8	4.86	-1	C-21/D-1	1	0.1
1994 Chi-N	44	99	8	26	4	0	3	16	13	24	0	1	.263	.354	.394	.748	96	-1	13	4.24	1	C-37	3	0.2
1995 Pit-N	69	233	25	54	9	0	15	33	23	62	0	0	.232	.301	.464	.764	96	-3	32	4.66	2	C-67	6	0.3
Chi-N	12	32	5	8	2	0	3	5	3	7	0	0	.250	.314	.594	.908	135	1	6	6.10	0	C-10	1	0.2
Yr.	81	265	30	62	11	0	18	38	26	69	0	0	.234	.302	.479	.782	101	-1	38	4.83	2	C-77	7	0.5
1996 Det-A	38	104	13	25	6	0	7	17	3	27	0	0	.240	.262	.500	.762	87	-3	13	4.23	1	C-33/1-1	2	0.0
*Bal-A	18	33	4	6	1	0	2	6	2	10	0	0	.182	.229	.394	.623	54	-3	3	2.54	0	C-18	1	-0.2
Yr.	56	137	17	31	7	0	9	23	5	37	0	0	.226	.254	.474	.728	78	-6	16	3.79	1	C-51/1-1	3	-0.2
1997 Phi-N	39	113	4	17	3	0	0	8	7	39	0	1	.150	.200	.177	.377		-17	4	.99	-0	C-38	1	-1.5
1998 Phi-N	34	113	7	25	4	0	1	13	10	30	1	1	.221	.285	.283	.568	49	-9	10	2.79	-1	C-34	1	-0.8
Total 13	474	1303	112	279	50	0	53	168	98	319	3	3	.214	.270	.375	.645	71	-61	133	3.31	1	C-427/1-2,D-1	26	-3.5
• PARIS, Kelly	Kelly Jay Paris b: 10/17/1957, Encino, CA BR/TR, 6', 180 lbs. Deb: 9/1/1982																							
1982 StL-N	12	29	1	3	0	0	0	1	0	7	0	0	.103	.103	.103	.207	-42	-5	0	.23	-1	/3-5,S-4	0	-0.6
1983 Cin-N	56	120	13	30	6	0	0	7	15	22	8	2	.250	.338	.300	.638	75	-3	13	3.73	-3	3-16,2-10/S-7,1-3	3	-0.5
1985 Bal-A	5	9	0	0	0	0	0	0	0	1	0	0	.000	.000	.000	.000	-103	-2	0	.00	-1	/2-2,D-2	0	-0.3
1986 Bal-A	5	10	0	2	0	0	0	0	0	3	0	1	.200	.200	.200	.400	9	-2	0	.00	0	/3-3,D-2	0	-0.2
1988 Chi-A	14	44	6	11	0	0	3	6	0	6	0	0	.250	.250	.455	.705	93	-1	5	3.61	0	/1-9,3-4,D-1	1	-0.1
Total 5	92	212	20	46	6	0	3	14	15	39	8	3	.217	.272	.288	.560	54	-13	18	2.76	-5	/3-28,1-12,2-12,S-11,D-5	4	-1.8
• PARISSE, Tony	Louis Peter Parisse b: 6/25/1911, Philadelphia, PA d: 6/2/1956, Philadelphia, PA BR/TR, 5'10", 165 lbs. Deb: 9/22/1943																							
1943 Phi-A	6	17	0	3	0	0	0	1	2	2	0	0	.176	.263	.176	.440	30	-1	1	1.36	1	/C-5	0	0.0
1944 Phi-A	4	4	0	0	0	0	0	0	0	1	0	0	.000	.000	.000	.000	-101	-1	0	.00	-1	/C-2	0	-0.2
Total 2	10	21	0	3	0	0	0	1	2	3	0	0	.143	.217	.143	.360	7	-2	1	1.08	-0	/C-7	0	-0.2
• PARKER, Ace	Clarence McKay Parker b: 5/17/1912, Portsmouth, VA BR/TR, 6', 180 lbs. Deb: 4/24/1937																							
1937 Phi-A	38	94	8	11	0	1	2	13	4	17	0	0	.117	.153	.202	.355	-11	-17	3	.95	-2	S-19/2-9,0-5(2-3-0)	1	-1.6
1938 Phi-A	56	113	12	26	5	0	0	12	10	16	1	2	.230	.293	.274	.567	44	-10	9	2.64	-2	S-26/2-9,3-9	1	-0.9
Total 2	94	207	20	37	5	1	2	25	14	33	1	2	.179	.231	.242	.472	20	-27	12	1.84	-3	/S-45,2-18,3-9,0-5	2	-2.5
• PARKER, Billy	William David Parker b: 1/14/1947, Hayneville, AL d: 2/9/2003, Sun City West, AZ BR/TR, 5'8", 168 lbs. Deb: 9/9/1971																							
1971 Cal-A	20	70	4	16	0	1	1	6	2	20	1	1	.229	.250	.300	.550	59	-4	5	2.18	-4	2-20	1	-0.8
1972 Cal-A	36	80	11	17	2	0	2	8	9	17	0	2	.213	.292	.313	.605	85	-2	7	2.53	0	3-21/2-9,0-5(5-0-0),S-1	2	-0.2
1973 Cal-A	38	102	14	23	2	1	0	7	8	23	0	1	.225	.288	.265	.553	61	-6	8	2.47	-5	2-32/S-3,D-1	1	-0.9
Total 3	94	252	29	56	4	2	3	21	19	60	1	4	.222	.279	.290	.569	68	-12	19	2.41	-9	/2-61,3-21,0-5,S-4,D-1	4	-1.8
• PARKER, Dave	David Gene Parker b: 6/9/1951, Grenada, MS BL/TR, 6'5", 230 lbs. Deb: 7/12/1973 C Career OF: 49-30-1791																							
1973 Pit-N	54	139	17	40	9	1	4	14	2	27	1	1	.288	.308	.453	.761	111	1	18	4.84	-1	0-39(4-16-19)	4	-0.2
1974*Pit-N	73	220	27	62	10	3	4	29	10	53	3	3	.282	.322	.409	.731	107	0	28	4.62	1	0-49(11-14-27)/1-6	6	-0.1
1975*Pit-N	148	558	75	172	35	10	25	101	38	89	8	6	.308	.358	**.541**	.899	148	31	101	6.60	3	*0-141(0-0-141)	26	2.8
1976 Pit-N	138	537	82	168	28	10	13	90	30	80	19	7	.313	.351	.475	.826	132	21	85	5.76	2	*0-134(0-0-134)	23	1.6
1977 Pit-N★	159	637	107	**215**	**44**	8	21	88	58	107	17	19	**.338**	.399	.531	.929	143	34	130	7.79	24	*0-158(0-0-158)/2-1	**33**	5.1
1978 Pit-N	148	581	102	194	32	12	30	117	57	92	20	7	**.334**	.395	**.585**	**.981**	163	**49**	134	**8.94**	-1	*0-147(0-0-147)	**37**	4.3
1979*Pit-N★	158	622	109	193	45	7	25	94	67	101	20	4	.310	.385	.526	.911	139	37	131	7.86	0	*0-158(0-0-158)	31	3.0
1980 Pit-N★	139	518	71	153	31	1	17	79	25	69	10	7	.295	.330	.458	.788	116	8	75	5.27	-1	*0-130(0-0-130)	17	0.1
1981 Pit-N★	67	240	29	62	14	3	9	48	9	25	6	2	.258	.291	.454	.745	105	0	30	4.32	-3	0-60(0-0-60)	6	-0.6
1982 Pit-N	73	244	41	66	19	3	6	29	22	45	7	5	.270	.333	.447	.780	113	3	34	4.77	-1	0-63(0-0-63)	7	-0.1
1983 Pit-N	144	552	68	154	29	4	12	69	28	89	12	9	.279	.314	.411	.725	97	-6	67	4.26	1	*0-142(0-0-142)	12	-1.3
1984 Cin-N	156	607	73	173	28	0	16	94	41	89	11	10	.285	.331	.410	.741	103	-1	80	4.72	-1	*0-151(0-0-151)	17	-1.0
1985 Cin-N★	160	635	88	198	**42**	4	34	**125**	52	80	5	13	.312	.367	.551	.918	146	32	112	6.29	2	*0-159(0-0-159)	29	2.7
1986 Cin-N★	162	637	89	174	31	3	31	116	56	126	1	6	.273	.333	.477	.810	116	9	94	5.15	-8	*0-159(0-0-159)	20	-0.7
1987 Cin-N	153	589	77	149	28	0	26	97	44	104	7	3	.253	.314	.433	.747	91	-9	77	4.51	0	*0-142(0-0-142)/1-9	13	-1.7
1988*Oak-A	101	377	43	97	18	1	12	55	32	70	0	1	.257	.315	.406	.721	104	1	49	4.65	1	D-61,0-34(34-0-0)/1-1	10	-0.2
1989*Oak-A	144	553	56	146	27	0	22	97	38	91	0	0	.264	.313	.432	.745	112	6	68	4.23	-0	*D-140/0-1	15	0.0
1990 Mil-A★	157	610	71	176	30	3	21	92	41	102	4	7	.289	.337	.451	.788	119	12	86	4.90	-1	*D-153/1-3	15	0.4
1991 Cal-A	119	466	45	108	22	2	11	56	29	91	3	2	.232	.281	.358	.639	76	-17	46	3.32	0	*D-119	5	-2.2
Tor-A	13	36	2	12	4	0	0	3	4	7	0	1	.333	.400	.444	.844	129	1	6	6.90	0	D-11	1	0.1
Yr.	132	502	47	120	26	2	11	59	33	98	3	3	.239	.290	.365	.655	80	-16	52	3.55	0	*D-130	6	-2.1
Total 19	2466	9358	1272	2712	526	75	339	1493	683	1537	154	113	.290	.342	.471	.813	121	212	1452	5.56	16	*0-1867,D-484/1-19,2-1	327	12.1
• PARKER, Dixie	Douglas Woolley Parker b: 4/24/1895, Forest Home, AL d: 5/15/1972, Tuscaloosa, AL BL/TR, 5'11", 160 lbs. Deb: 7/28/1923																							
1923 Phi-N	4	5	0	1	0	0	0	1	0	1	0	0	.200	.200	.200	.400	5	-1	0	1.27	-1	/C-2	0	-0.1
• PARKER, Pat	Clarence Perkins Parker b: 5/22/1893, Somerville, MA d: 3/21/1967, Claremont, NH BR/TR, 5'7", 160 lbs. Deb: 8/10/1915																							
1915 StL-A	3	6	0	1	0	0	0	1	0	3	0	1	.167	.167	.167	.333		-1	0	.00	0	/0-2(0-0-2)	0	-0.2
• PARKER, Rick	Richard Alan Parker b: 3/20/1963, Kansas City, MO BR/TR, 6', 185 lbs. Deb: 5/4/1990 Career OF: 44-24-28																							
1990 SF-N	54	107	19	26	5	0	2	14	10	15	6	1	.243	.314	.346	.659	84	-1	13	4.04	-2	0-35(13-5-23)/2-2,3-1,S-1	2	-0.5
1991 SF-N	13	14	0	1	0	0	0	1	1	5	0	0	.071	.133	.071	.205	-42	-3	0	.35	0	/0-4(4-1-0)	0	-0.3
1993 Hou-N	45	45	11	15	3	0	0	4	3	8	1	2	.333	.375	.400	.775	112	0	6	4.37	-1	0-16(3-13-1)/2-1,S-1	1	-0.1
1994 NY-N	8	16	1	1	0	0	0	0	0	2	0	0	.063	.063	.063	.125	-68	-4	0	.18	0	/0-6(4-1-3)	0	-0.4
1995 LA-N	27	29	3	8	0	0	0	4	2	4	1	1	.276	.323	.276	.598	65	-2	2	2.64	0	0-21(19-1-1)/3-2,S-2	1	-0.2
1996 LA-N	16	14	2	4	1	0	0	1	0	2	1	0	.286	.333	.357	.690	89	0	2	3.78	0	/0-4(1-3-0)	0	0.0
Total 6	163	225	36	55	9	0	2	24	16	36	9	4	.244	.300	.311	.612	69	-10	23	3.29	-4	/0-86,S-4,2-3,3-3	4	-1.5
• PARKER, Salty	Francis James Parker b: 7/8/1913, East St. Louis, IL d: 7/27/1992, Houston, TX BR/TR, 6', 173 lbs. Deb: 8/13/1936 M/C																							
1936 Det-A	11	25	6	7	2	0	0	4	2	3	0	2	.280	.333	.360	.693	71	-2	2	3.04	0	/S-7,1-2	0	-0.2
• PARKER, Wes	Maurice Wesley Parker b: 11/13/1939, Evanston, IL BB/TL, 6'1", 180 lbs. Deb: 4/19/1964 Career OF: 34-51-76																							
1964 LA-N	124	214	29	55	7	1	3	10	14	45	5	4	.257	.306	.341	.647	88	-4	23	3.45	0	0-69(9-15-49),1-31	5	-0.9
1965*LA-N	154	542	80	129	24	7	8	51	75	95	13	7	.238	.336	.352	.688	101	3	70	4.21	-1	*1-154/0-1	20	-0.8
1966*LA-N	156	475	67	120	17	5	12	51	69	83	7	3	.253	.353	.385	.739	114	12	67	4.70	-3	*1-140,0-14(2-7-5)	17	0.1
1967 LA-N	139	413	56	102	16	5	5	31	65	83	10	5	.247	.359	.346	.705	112	10	55	4.37	5	*1-112,0-18(0-18-0)	15	1.0
1968 LA-N	135	468	42	112	22	2	3	27	49	87	4	6	.239	.314	.314	.628	96	-3	49	3.45	-1	*1-114,0-28(22-6-1)	12	-1.3
1969 LA-N	132	471	76	131	23	4	13	68	56	46	4	1	.278	.357	.427	.784	128	19	73	5.45	0	*1-128/0-2(0-1-1)	18	0.9
1970 LA-N	161	614	84	196	**47**	4	10	111	79	70	8	2	.319	.397	.458	.854	134	32	113	6.83	9	*1-161	29	2.8
1971 LA-N	157	533	69	146	24	1	6	62	63	63	6	1	.274	.352	.356	.708	107	8	69	4.52	5	*1-148,0-18(1-0-18)	18	0.2

YEAR TM-L	G	AB	R	H	2B	3B	HR	RBI	BB	SO	SB	CS	AVG	OBP	SLG	OPS	OPS+	BR/A	RC	RC/G	FR	G/POS	WS	TPW
1972 LA-N	130	427	45	119	14	3	4	59	62	43	3	5	.279	.371	.354	.725	109	7	57	4.54	2	*1-120/0-5(0-3-2)	14	-0.1
Total 9	**1288**	**4157**	**548**	**1110**	**194**	**32**	**64**	**470**	**532**	**615**	**60**	**34**	**.267**	**.353**	**.375**	**.729**	**112**	**83**	**575**	**4.72**	**17**	***1-1108,0-155**	**148**	**2.0**

• PARKINSON, Frank Frank Joseph "Parky" Parkinson b: 3/23/1895, Dickson City, PA d: 7/4/1960, Trenton, NJ BR/TR, 5'11", 175 lbs. Deb: 4/13/1921

YEAR TM-L	G	AB	R	H	2B	3B	HR	RBI	BB	SO	SB	CS	AVG	OBP	SLG	OPS	OPS+	BR/A	RC	RC/G	FR	G/POS	WS	TPW
1921 Phi-N	108	391	36	99	20	2	5	32	13	81	3	4	.253	.277	.353	.630	61	-22	37	3.20	-12	*S-105/3-1	3	-2.2
1922 Phi-N	141	545	86	150	18	6	15	70	55	93	3	4	.275	.344	.413	.757	86	-11	79	5.03	9	*2-139	12	0.2
1923 Phi-N	67	219	21	53	12	0	3	28	13	31	0	4	.242	.288	.338	.625	58	-15	20	3.11	-3	2-37,S-15,3-11	2	-1.5
1924 Phi-N	62	156	14	33	7	0	1	19	14	28	3	1	.212	.281	.276	.556	44	-12	13	2.68	1	3-28,S-21,2-10	1	-0.7
Total 4	**378**	**1311**	**157**	**335**	**57**	**8**	**24**	**149**	**95**	**233**	**9**	**13**	**.256**	**.308**	**.366**	**.674**	**69**	**-60**	**149**	**3.86**	**-4**	**2-186,S-141/3-40**	**18**	**-4.2**

• PARKS, Art Artie William Parks b: 11/1/1911, Paris, AR d: 12/6/1989, Little Rock, AR BL/TR, 5'9", 170 lbs. Deb: 9/25/1937 Career OF: 36-0-34

YEAR TM-L	G	AB	R	H	2B	3B	HR	RBI	BB	SO	SB	CS	AVG	OBP	SLG	OPS	OPS+	BR/A	RC	RC/G	FR	G/POS	WS	TPW
1937 Bro-N	7	16	2	5	2	0	0	0	2	2	0	....	.313	.389	.438	.826	122	1	3	7.35	1	/0-4(4-0-0)	1	0.1
1939 Bro-N	71	239	27	65	13	2	1	19	28	14	2	....	.272	.348	.356	.704	86	-4	30	4.35	-3	0-65(32-0-34)	6	-1.1
Total 2	**78**	**255**	**29**	**70**	**15**	**2**	**1**	**19**	**30**	**16**	**2**	**....**	**.275**	**.351**	**.361**	**.712**	**89**	**-3**	**33**	**4.52**	**-2**	**/0-69**	**7**	**-0.9**

• PARKS, Bill William Robert Parks b: 6/4/1849, Easton, PA d: 10/10/1911, Easton, PA BR/TR, 5'8", 150 lbs. Deb: 4/26/1875 M ♦

YEAR TM-L	G	AB	R	H	2B	3B	HR	RBI	BB	SO	SB	CS	AVG	OBP	SLG	OPS	OPS+	BR/A	RC	RC/G	FR	G/POS	WS	TPW
1875 Was-n	27	111	13	20	0	0	0	6	1	1	1	1	.180	.188	.180	.368	29	-6	4	1.29	2	0-17(16-1-0),P-14	....	-0.8
Phi-n	2	6	0	1	0	0	0	0	0	1	0	0	.167	.167	.167	.333	16	-0	0	1.01	-1	/0-2(2-0-0),P-2	....	-0.3
Yr.	29	117	13	21	0	0	0	6	1	2	1	1	.179	.186	.179	.366	29	-7	4	1.28	1	0-19(18-1-0),P-16	....	-1.1
1876 Bos-N	1	4	0	0	0	0	0	0	0	0	....	....	.000	.000	.000	.000	-98	-1	0	.00	0	/0-1	0	-0.1

• PARKS, Derek Derek Gavin Parks b: 9/29/1968, Covina, CA BR/TR, 6', 205 lbs. Deb: 9/11/1992

YEAR TM-L	G	AB	R	H	2B	3B	HR	RBI	BB	SO	SB	CS	AVG	OBP	SLG	OPS	OPS+	BR/A	RC	RC/G	FR	G/POS	WS	TPW
1992 Min-A	7	6	1	2	0	0	0	0	1	1	0	0	.333	.500	.333	.833	133	1	1	8.51	0	/C-7	0	0.1
1993 Min-A	7	20	3	4	0	0	0	1	1	2	0	0	.200	.238	.200	.438	19	-2	1	1.71	0	/C-7	0	-0.2
1994 Min-A	31	89	6	17	6	0	1	9	4	20	0	1	.191	.242	.292	.534	37	-9	6	2.08	1	C-31	1	-0.6
Total 3	**45**	**115**	**10**	**23**	**6**	**0**	**1**	**10**	**6**	**23**	**0**	**1**	**.200**	**.258**	**.278**	**.536**	**40**	**-11**	**8**	**2.28**	**1**	**/C-45**	**1**	**-0.7**

• PARRILLA, Sam Samuel (Monge) Parrilla b: 6/12/1943, Santurce, Puerto Rico d: 2/9/1994, Brooklyn, NY BR/TR, 5'11", 185 lbs. Deb: 4/11/1970

YEAR TM-L	G	AB	R	H	2B	3B	HR	RBI	BB	SO	SB	CS	AVG	OBP	SLG	OPS	OPS+	BR/A	RC	RC/G	FR	G/POS	WS	TPW
1970 Phi-N	11	16	0	2	1	0	0	0	1	4	0	0	.125	.176	.188	.364	-3	-2	1	1.11	0	/0-3(3-0-0)	0	-0.3

• PARRISH, Lance Lance Michael Parrish b: 6/15/1956, Clairton, PA BR/TR, 6'3", 220 lbs. Deb: 9/5/1977 C Career OF: 2-0-4

YEAR TM-L	G	AB	R	H	2B	3B	HR	RBI	BB	SO	SB	CS	AVG	OBP	SLG	OPS	OPS+	BR/A	RC	RC/G	FR	G/POS	WS	TPW
1977 Det-A	12	46	10	9	2	0	3	7	5	12	0	0	.196	.275	.435	.709	85	-1	5	3.47	2	C-12	1	0.2
1978 Det-A	85	288	37	63	11	3	14	41	11	71	0	0	.219	.255	.424	.679	85	-7	29	3.30	1	C-79	7	-0.2
1979 Det-A	143	493	65	136	26	3	19	65	49	105	6	7	.276	.344	.456	.800	110	5	73	5.16	6	*C-142	21	1.7
1980 Det-A★	144	553	79	158	34	6	24	82	31	109	6	4	.286	.327	.499	.826	120	12	80	5.06	2	*C-121,D-16/1-5,0-5(1-0-4)	20	1.9
1981 Det-A	96	348	39	85	18	2	10	46	34	52	2	3	.244	.312	.394	.705	98	-2	38	3.62	0	C-90/D-5	11	0.3
1982 Det-A★	133	486	75	138	19	2	32	87	40	99	3	4	.284	.340	.529	.868	134	20	86	6.50	8	*C-132/0-1	24	3.4
1983 Det-A★	155	605	80	163	42	3	27	114	44	106	1	3	.269	.320	.483	.803	121	13	86	4.84	5	*C-131,D-27	24	2.4
1984*Det-A★	147	578	75	137	16	2	33	98	41	120	2	3	.237	.290	.443	.733	100	-3	71	4.13	2	*C-127,D-22	19	0.5
1985 Det-A★	140	549	64	150	27	1	28	98	41	90	2	6	.273	.326	.479	.805	118	9	82	5.24	2	*C-120,D-22	20	1.6
1986 Det-A★	91	327	53	84	6	1	22	62	38	83	0	0	.257	.343	.483	.826	122	10	57	6.10	1	C-85/D-6	15	1.5
1987 Phi-N	130	466	42	114	21	0	17	67	47	104	0	1	.245	.315	.399	.714	85	-12	53	3.79	-2	*C-127	10	-0.7
1988 Phi-N★	123	424	44	91	17	2	15	60	47	93	0	0	.215	.296	.370	.666	88	-7	46	3.56	5	*C-117/1-1	12	0.6
1989 Cal-A	124	433	48	103	12	1	17	50	42	104	1	1	.238	.308	.388	.696	97	-3	51	3.99	-1	*C-122/D-2	12	0.3
1990 Cal-A★	133	470	54	126	14	0	24	70	46	107	2	2	.268	.340	.451	.791	122	13	71	5.29	11	*C-131/1-4,D-1	24	3.2
1991 Cal-A	119	402	38	87	12	0	19	51	35	117	0	1	.216	.287	.388	.675	85	-10	45	3.71	5	*C-111/D-5,1-3	15	0.2
1992 Cal-A	24	83	7	19	2	0	4	11	5	22	0	0	.229	.273	.398	.670	85	-2	9	3.61	-1	C-22/D-2	2	-0.2
Sea-A	69	192	19	45	11	1	8	21	19	48	1	1	.234	.307	.427	.734	103	-0	24	4.14	-3	C-34,1-16,D-14	3	-0.2
Yr.	93	275	26	64	13	1	12	32	24	70	1	1	.233	.297	.418	.715	98	-2	33	3.98	-3	C-56,1-16,D-16	5	-0.3
1993 Cle-A	10	20	2	4	1	0	1	2	4	5	1	0	.200	.333	.400	.733	96	0	2	3.59	0	C-10	1	0.1
1994 Pit-N	40	126	10	34	5	0	3	16	18	28	1	1	.270	.366	.381	.746	94	-1	17	4.68	-1	C-38/1-1	4	0.1
1995 Tor-A	70	178	15	36	9	0	4	22	15	52	0	0	.202	.268	.320	.588	53	-13	16	2.72	7	C-67/D-1	3	-0.2
Total 19	**1988**	**7067**	**856**	**1782**	**305**	**27**	**324**	**1070**	**612**	**1527**	**28**	**37**	**.252**	**.315**	**.440**	**.756**	**105**	**22**	**941**	**4.54**	**49**	***C-1818,D-123/1-30,0-6**	**248**	**16.4**

• PARRISH, Larry Larry Alton Parrish b: 11/10/1953, Winter Haven, FL BR/TR, 6'3", 215 lbs. Deb: 9/6/1974 M/C Career OF: 3-0-405

YEAR TM-L	G	AB	R	H	2B	3B	HR	RBI	BB	SO	SB	CS	AVG	OBP	SLG	OPS	OPS+	BR/A	RC	RC/G	FR	G/POS	WS	TPW
1974 Mon-N	25	69	9	14	5	0	0	4	6	19	0	0	.203	.286	.275	.561	54	-4	6	2.67	-2	3-24	1	-0.6
1975 Mon-N	145	532	50	146	32	5	10	65	28	74	4	5	.274	.316	.410	.725	96	-7	64	4.19	-10	*3-143/2-1,S-1	12	-1.8
1976 Mon-N	154	543	65	126	28	5	11	61	41	91	2	6	.232	.288	.363	.651	80	-18	54	3.27	-8	*3-153	8	-2.7
1977 Mon-N	123	402	50	99	19	2	11	46	37	71	2	4	.246	.316	.386	.702	90	-7	47	3.89	-7	*3-115	7	-1.6
1978 Mon-N	144	520	68	144	39	4	15	70	32	103	2	3	.277	.321	.454	.775	116	7	69	4.59	1	*3-139	15	0.7
1979 Mon-N★	153	544	83	167	39	2	30	82	41	101	5	1	.307	.358	.551	.909	146	32	106	7.29	1	*3-153	28	3.2
1980 Mon-N	126	452	55	115	27	3	15	72	36	80	2	6	.254	.315	.427	.742	105	-1	57	4.21	-6	*3-124	13	-0.9
1981*Mon-N	97	349	41	85	19	3	8	44	28	73	0	0	.244	.300	.384	.684	92	-5	39	3.71	-8	3-95	8	-1.5
1982 Tex-A	128	440	59	116	15	0	17	62	30	84	5	2	.264	.316	.414	.730	104	2	56	4.39	-3	*0-124(0-0-124)/3-3,D-2	10	-0.7
1983 Tex-A	145	555	76	151	26	4	26	88	46	91	0	0	.272	.331	.474	.805	121	14	82	5.10	-6	*0-132(0-0-132),D-13	16	0.2
1984 Tex-A	156	613	72	175	42	1	22	101	42	116	2	4	.285	.337	.465	.802	116	11	89	5.19	4	0-81(2-0-80),D-63,3-12	18	0.8
1985 Tex-A	94	346	44	86	11	1	17	51	33	77	0	2	.249	.316	.434	.749	101	-1	44	4.27	-2	0-69(0-0-69),D-22/3-2	5	-0.7
1986 Tex-A	129	464	67	128	22	1	28	94	52	114	3	1	.276	.351	.509	.860	127	17	80	5.99	-1	D-98,3-30	17	1.3
1987 Tex-A★	152	557	79	149	22	1	32	100	49	154	3	1	.268	.330	.483	.813	112	8	88	5.63	-3	*D-122,3-28/0-1	14	0.0
1988 Tex-A	68	248	22	47	9	1	7	26	20	79	0	0	.190	.256	.319	.574	58	-14	20	2.65	0	D-67	0	-1.7
*Bos-A	52	158	10	41	5	0	7	26	8	32	0	1	.259	.299	.424	.723	96	-2	19	4.11	2	1-36,D-14	4	-0.3
Yr.	120	406	32	88	14	1	14	52	28	111	0	1	.217	.272	.360	.632	73	-16	39	3.19	2	D-81,1-36	4	-2.0
Total 15	**1891**	**6792**	**850**	**1789**	**360**	**33**	**256**	**992**	**529**	**1359**	**30**	**36**	**.263**	**.321**	**.439**	**.760**	**106**	**33**	**919**	**4.67**	**-49**	***3-1021,0-407,D-401/1-36,2,S**	**176**	**-6.3**

• PARROTT, Jiggs Walter Edward Parrott b: 7/14/1871, Portland, OR d: 4/16/1898, Phoenix, AZ, 5'11", 160 lbs. Deb: 7/11/1892 Career OF: 1-0-4

YEAR TM-L	G	AB	R	H	2B	3B	HR	RBI	BB	SO	SB	CS	AVG	OBP	SLG	OPS	OPS+	BR/A	RC	RC/G	FR	G/POS	WS	TPW
1892 Chi-N	78	333	38	67	8	5	2	22	8	30	7	....	.201	.222	.273	.495	49	-23	22	2.27	-1	3-78	5	-2.0
1893 Chi-N	110	455	54	111	10	9	1	65	13	25	25	....	.244	.267	.312	.579	54	-32	46	3.51	8	*3-99/2-7,0-4(0-0-4)	6	-1.8
1894 Chi-N	126	525	82	130	17	9	3	65	16	35	30	....	.248	.274	.331	.605	43	-53	57	3.77	-10	*2-123/3-1	3	-4.4
1895 Chi-N	3	4	0	1	0	0	0	0	0	0	0	....	.250	.250	.250	.500	27	-0	0	2.40	0	/1-1,0-1,S-1	0	-0.1
Total 4	**317**	**1317**	**174**	**309**	**35**	**23**	**6**	**152**	**37**	**90**	**62**	**....**	**.235**	**.258**	**.310**	**.568**	**48**	**-109**	**126**	**3.28**	**-2**	**3-178,2-130/0-5,1-1,S-1**	**14**	**-8.3**

• PARROTT, Tom Thomas William "Tacky Tom" Parrott
b: 4/10/1868, Portland, OR d: 1/1/1932, Dundee, OR BR/TR, 5'10.5", 170 lbs. Deb: 6/18/1893 Career OF: 15-88-28 ♦

YEAR TM-L	G	AB	R	H	2B	3B	HR	RBI	BB	SO	SB	CS	AVG	OBP	SLG	OPS	OPS+	BR/A	RC	RC/G	FR	G/POS	WS	TPW
1893 Chi-N	7	27	4	7	1	0	0	3	1	2	0	....	.259	.286	.296	.582	56	-1	2	3.10	-1	/P-4,3-2,2-1	0	-0.5
Cin-N	24	68	5	13	1	1	1	9	1	9	0	....	.191	.203	.279	.482	27	-3	4	1.90	1	P-22/0-1	12	0.5
Yr.	31	95	9	20	2	1	1	12	2	11	0	....	.211	.227	.284	.511	35	-4	6	2.22	1	P-26/3-2,2-1,0-1	12	0.0
1894 Cin-N	68	229	51	74	12	6	4	40	17	10	4	....	.323	.372	.480	.853	101	8	44	7.30	4	P-41,0-13(9-2-2),1-12/2-1,3,S	22	0.4
1895 Cin-N	64	201	35	69	13	7	3	41	11	8	10	....	.343	.377	.522	.900	125	12	45	8.79	0	P-41,1-14/0-9(1-8-0)	18	-0.4
1896 StL-N	118	474	62	138	13	12	7	70	11	24	12	....	.291	.307	.414	.721	93	-7	67	5.06	8	*0-108(4-78-26)/P-7,1-6	10	-1.1
Total 4	**281**	**999**	**157**	**301**	**40**	**26**	**15**	**163**	**41**	**53**	**26**	**....**	**.301**	**.329**	**.438**	**.768**	**96**	**9**	**162**	**5.96**	**12**	**0-131,P-115/1-32,3-3,2-2,S**	**62**	**-1.1**

• PARSONS, Casey Casey Robert Parsons b: 4/14/1954, Wenatchee, WA BL/TR, 6'1", 180 lbs. Deb: 5/31/1981 Career OF: 3-4-22

YEAR TM-L	G	AB	R	H	2B	3B	HR	RBI	BB	SO	SB	CS	AVG	OBP	SLG	OPS	OPS+	BR/A	RC	RC/G	FR	G/POS	WS	TPW
1981 Sea-A	36	22	6	5	1	0	1	5	1	4	0	0	.227	.320	.409	.729	105	0	3	4.37	1	0-24(3-2-19)/1-1	1	0.0
1983 Chi-A	8	5	1	1	0	0	0	0	2	1	0	0	.200	.429	.200	.629	77	0	1	3.65	-0	/0-3(0-1-2),D-2	0	0.0
1984 Chi-A	1	1	0	0	0	0	0	0	0	1	0	0	.000	.000	.000	.000	-96	-0	0	.00	0	....	0	0.0
1987 Cle-A	18	25	2	4	0	0	1	5	0	5	0	0	.160	.160	.280	.440	13	-3	1	.66	0	/D-5,0-2(0-1-1),1-1	0	-0.3
Total 4	**63**	**53**	**9**	**10**	**1**	**0**	**2**	**10**	**3**	**11**	**0**	**0**	**.189**	**.259**	**.321**	**.579**	**61**	**-3**	**4**	**2.44**	**0**	**/0-29,D-7,1-2**	**1**	**-0.3**

• PARSONS, Dixie Edward Dixon Parsons b: 5/12/1916, Talladega, AL d: 10/31/1991, Longview, TX BR/TR, 6'2", 180 lbs. Deb: 8/16/1939

YEAR TM-L	G	AB	R	H	2B	3B	HR	RBI	BB	SO	SB	CS	AVG	OBP	SLG	OPS	OPS+	BR/A	RC	RC/G	FR	G/POS	WS	TPW
1939 Det-A	5	1	0	0	0	0	0	0	1	1	0	0	.000	.500	.000	.500	36	0	0	3.51	-1	/C-4	0	-0.1
1942 Det-A	63	188	8	37	4	0	2	11	13	22	1	0	.197	.249	.250	.499	37	-16	12	2.01	1	C-62	4	-1.1

YEAR TM-L	G	AB	R	H	2B	3B	HR	RBI	BB	SO	SB	CS	AVG	OBP	SLG	OPS	OPS+	BR/A	RC	RC/G	FR	G/POS	WS	TPW
1943 Det-A	40	106	2	15	3	0	0	4	6	16	0	0	.142	.188	.170	.357	4	-13	3	.83	2	C-40	2	-1.0
Total 3	108	295	10	52	7	0	2	15	20	39	1	0	.176	.229	.220	.449	25	-28	15	1.56	2	C-106	6	-2.2
• PARSONS, John	John S. Parsons b: Napoleon, OH, 5'6", 138 lbs. Deb: 10/15/1884																							
1884 Cin-a	1	3	0	0	0	0	0	0	0	....	....	....	.000	.000	.000	.000	-95	-1	0	.00	0	/O-1	0	-0.1
• PARTEE, Roy	Roy Robert Partee b: 9/7/1917, Los Angeles, CA d: 12/26/2000, Eureka, CA BR/TR, 5'10", 180 lbs. Deb: 4/23/1943																							
1943 Bos-A	96	299	30	84	14	2	0	31	39	33	0	0	.281	.368	.341	.709	106	4	40	4.67	0	C-91	10	1.0
1944 Bos-A	89	280	18	68	12	0	2	41	37	29	0	1	.243	.333	.307	.640	85	-5	30	3.50	0	C-85	7	0.0
1946*Bos-A	40	111	13	35	5	2	0	9	13	14	0	0	.315	.387	.396	.783	113	3	17	5.40	-4	C-38	4	0.0
1947 Bos-A	60	169	14	39	2	0	0	16	18	23	0	0	.231	.305	.243	.547	50	-11	14	2.64	-1	C-54	2	-1.0
1948 StL-A	82	231	14	47	8	1	0	17	25	21	2	2	.203	.284	.247	.531	41	-20	16	2.31	-3	C-76	3	-1.9
Total 5	367	1090	89	273	41	5	2	114	132	120	2	3	.250	.334	.303	.636	79	-28	116	3.59	-9	C-344	26	-1.8
• PARTENHEIMER, Steve	Harold Philip Partenheimer b: 8/30/1891, Greenfield, MA d: 6/16/1971, Mansfield, OH BR/TR, 5'8.5", 145 lbs. Deb: 6/28/1913																							
1913 Det-A	1	2	0	0	0	0	0	0	0	0	0	....	.000	.333	.000	.333	-1	-0	0	.00	0	/3-1	0	0.0
• PARTRIDGE, Jay	James Bugg Partridge b: 11/15/1902, Mountville, GA d: 1/14/1974, Nashville, TN BL/TR, 5'11", 160 lbs. Deb: 4/12/1927																							
1927 Bro-N	146	572	72	149	17	6	7	40	20	36	9	....	.260	.289	.348	.637	70	-26	56	3.29	-8	*2-140	7	-3.0
1928 Bro-N	37	73	18	18	0	1	0	12	13	6	2	....	.247	.368	.274	.642	71	-2	8	3.67	-3	2-18/3-2	1	-0.5
Total 2	183	645	90	167	17	7	7	52	33	42	11	....	.259	.299	.340	.639	70	-29	64	3.34	-11	2-158/3-2	8	-3.5
• PASCHAL, Ben	Benjamin Edwin Paschal b: 10/13/1895, Enterprise, AL d: 11/10/1974, Charlotte, NC BR/TR, 5'11", 185 lbs. Deb: 8/16/1915 Career OF: 67-44-114																							
1915 Cle-A	9	9	0	1	0	0	0	0	0	3	0	....	.111	.111	.111	.222	-33	-1	0	.37	0	....	0	-0.1
1920 Bos-A	9	28	5	10	0	0	0	5	5	2	1	0	.357	.455	.357	.812	122	2	5	7.59	1	/O-7(0-0-7)	1	0.2
1924 NY-A	4	12	2	3	1	0	0	3	1	0	0	0	.250	.308	.333	.641	65	-1	1	3.71	1	/O-4(0-4-0)	0	0.0
1925 NY-A	89	247	49	89	16	5	12	56	22	29	14	9	.360	.417	.611	1.028	161	21	60	9.36	-2	O-66(16-14-36)	10	1.4
1926*NY-A	96	258	46	74	12	3	7	32	26	35	7	6	.287	.354	.438	.792	108	2	40	5.25	-2	O-74(12-17-47)	7	-0.5
1927 NY-A	50	82	16	26	9	2	2	16	4	10	0	2	.317	.349	.549	.898	134	2	14	6.46	0	O-27(11-4-12)	3	0.1
1928*NY-A	65	79	12	25	6	1	1	15	8	11	1	0	.316	.379	.456	.835	122	3	14	6.57	0	O-25(16-1-8)	3	0.2
1929 NY-A	42	72	13	15	3	0	2	11	6	3	1	1	.208	.269	.333	.603	58	-5	7	2.84	0	O-20(12-4-4)	0	-0.6
Total 8	364	787	143	243	47	11	24	138	72	93	24	18	.309	.369	.488	.857	122	23	142	6.43	-4	O-223	24	0.6
• PASEK, Johnny	John Paul Pasek b: 6/25/1905, Niagara Falls, NY d: 3/13/1976, Niagara Falls, NY BR/TR, 5'10", 175 lbs. Deb: 7/28/1933																							
1933 Det-A	28	61	6	15	4	0	0	4	7	7	2	0	.246	.324	.311	.635	68	-2	7	3.86	0	C-28	1	-0.1
1934 Chi-A	4	9	1	3	0	0	0	0	1	1	0	0	.333	.400	.333	.733	88	-0	1	5.53	0	/C-4	0	0.0
Total 2	32	70	7	18	4	0	0	4	8	8	2	0	.257	.333	.314	.648	70	-2	8	4.05	0	/C-32	1	-0.1
• PASKERT, Dode	George Henry Paskert b: 8/28/1881, Cleveland, OH d: 2/12/1959, Cleveland, OH BR/TR, 5'11", 165 lbs. Deb: 9/21/1907 Career OF: 146-1461-35																							
1907 Cin-N	16	50	10	14	4	0	1	8	2	....	2	....	.280	.333	.420	.753	130	2	8	5.68	0	O-16(0-16-0)	2	0.1
1908 Cin-N	118	395	40	96	14	4	1	36	27	....	25	....	.243	.298	.306	.604	96	-2	44	3.60	-3	*O-116(77-34-5)	12	-1.4
1909 Cin-N	104	322	49	81	7	4	0	33	34	....	23	....	.252	.327	.298	.625	95	-1	39	4.03	-1	O-82(36-46-1)/1-6	10	-0.7
1910 Cin-N	144	506	63	152	21	5	2	46	70	60	51	....	.300	.389	.374	.762	128	21	93	6.55	6	*O-139(6-126-8)/1-2	24	2.1
1911 Phi-N	153	560	96	153	18	5	4	47	70	70	28	....	.273	.358	.345	.703	96	-1	81	4.82	3	*O-153(2-146-7)	18	-0.8
1912 Phi-N	145	540	102	170	37	5	2	43	91	67	36	....	.315	.420	.413	.833	120	20	108	7.26	1	*O-141(0-141-0)/2-2,3-1	24	1.3
1913 Phi-N	124	454	83	119	21	9	4	29	65	69	12	....	.262	.358	.374	.733	105	5	65	4.65	15	*O-120(1-119-0)	17	1.3
1914 Phi-N	132	451	59	119	25	6	3	44	56	68	23	....	.264	.349	.366	.715	106	4	64	4.75	5	*O-128(0-128-0)/S-4	15	0.2
1915*Phi-N	109	328	51	80	17	4	3	39	35	38	9	6	.244	.319	.348	.666	100	-0	41	3.84	-3	O-92(19-74-1)/1-5	11	-1.0
1916 Phi-N	149	555	82	155	30	7	8	46	54	76	22	21	.279	.346	.402	.748	125	12	77	4.63	-4	*O-146(2-145-0)/S-1	27	-0.1
1917 Phi-N	141	546	78	137	27	11	4	43	62	63	19	....	.251	.331	.363	.693	108	6	68	4.25	-4	*O-138(0-138-0)	19	-0.8
1918*Chi-N	127	461	69	132	24	3	3	59	53	49	20	....	.286	.362	.371	.733	121	13	68	5.06	-8	*O-121(0-121-0)/3-6	23	-0.3
1919 Chi-N	88	270	21	53	11	3	2	29	28	33	7	....	.196	.274	.281	.556	67	-10	22	2.57	-3	O-80(3-76-3)	4	-2.0
1920 Chi-N	139	487	57	136	22	10	5	71	64	58	16	14	.279	.366	.396	.763	117	12	72	5.00	0	*O-137(0-136-1)	20	0.4
1921 Cin-N	27	92	8	16	1	1	0	4	4	8	0	2	.174	.208	.207	.415	11	-12	4	1.23	0	O-24(0-15-9)	1	-1.4
Total 15	1716	6017	868	1613	279	77	42	577	715	659	293	43	.268	.350	.361	.711	108	68	855	4.75	2	*O-1633/1-13,3-7,S-5,2-2	227	-3.0
• PASLEY, Kevin	Kevin Patrick Pasley b: 7/22/1953, Brooklyn, NY BR/TR, 6', 185 lbs. Deb: 10/2/1974																							
1974 LA-N	1	0	0	0	0	0	0	0	0	0	0	0	....	....	....	....	-104	0	0	....	0	/C-1	0	0.0
1976 LA-N	23	52	4	12	2	0	0	2	3	7	0	0	.231	.273	.269	.542	55	-3	4	2.65	1	C-23	1	-0.1
1977 LA-N	2	3	0	1	0	0	0	0	0	0	0	0	.333	.333	.333	.667	80	-0	0	4.50	0	/C-2	0	0.0
Sea-A	4	13	1	5	0	0	0	2	1	2	0	0	.385	.429	.385	.813	125	1	2	6.94	0	/C-4	0	0.0
1978 Sea-A	25	54	3	13	5	0	1	5	2	4	0	0	.241	.268	.389	.657	83	-1	5	3.03	-2	C-25	1	-0.2
Total 4	55	122	8	31	7	0	1	9	6	13	0	0	.254	.289	.336	.625	76	-4	12	3.27	-1	/C-55	2	-0.3
• PASQUA, Dan	Daniel Anthony Pasqua b: 10/17/1961, Yonkers, NY BL/TL, 6', 203 lbs. Deb: 5/30/1985 Career OF: 322-0-289																							
1985 NY-A	60	148	17	31	3	1	9	25	16	38	0	0	.209	.291	.426	.717	95	-1	19	4.30	1	O-37(31-0-6),D-14	4	-0.2
1986 NY-A	102	280	44	82	17	0	16	45	47	78	2	0	.293	.400	.525	.925	151	22	62	8.23	-2	O-81(71-0-12)/1-5,D-3	14	1.6
1987 NY-A	113	318	42	74	7	1	17	42	40	99	0	2	.233	.320	.421	.742	96	-3	43	4.49	-1	O-74(61-0-14),D-20,1-12	7	-0.8
1988 Chi-A	129	422	48	96	16	2	20	50	46	100	1	0	.227	.308	.417	.725	101	0	54	4.29	5	*O-112(65-0-52)/1-7,D-2	9	0.1
1989 Chi-A	73	246	26	61	9	1	11	47	25	58	1	2	.248	.320	.427	.747	111	2	35	4.95	1	O-66(52-0-20)/D-5	9	0.1
1990 Chi-A	112	325	43	89	27	3	13	58	37	66	1	1	.274	.352	.495	.847	137	16	57	6.31	3	D-57,O-43(21-0-22)	15	1.5
1991 Chi-A	134	417	71	108	22	5	18	66	62	86	0	2	.259	.359	.465	.824	129	17	71	5.92	3	1-83,O-59(9-0-51)/D-8	14	1.4
1992 Chi-A	93	265	26	56	16	1	6	33	36	57	0	1	.211	.308	.347	.655	84	-6	30	3.68	-1	O-81(0-0-81)/1-5,D-1	5	-0.9
1993*Chi-A	78	176	22	36	10	1	5	20	26	51	2	2	.205	.307	.358	.665	80	-5	20	3.64	-1	O-37(11-0-26),1-32/D-6	2	-0.9
1994 Chi-A	11	23	2	5	2	0	2	4	0	9	0	0	.217	.217	.565	.783	95	-0	2	3.21	-1	/O-5(1-0-5),1-3	0	-0.2
Total 10	905	2620	341	638	129	15	117	390	335	642	7	10	.244	.333	.438	.771	112	41	393	5.14	7	O-595,1-147,D-116	79	1.7
• PASQUELLA, Mike	Michael John "Toney" Pasquella b: 11/7/1898, Philadelphia, PA d: 4/5/1965, Bridgeport, CT BR/TR, 5'11", 167 lbs. Deb: 7/9/1919																							
1919 Phi-N	1	1	1	1	0	0	0	0	0	0	0	....	1.000	1.000	1.000	2.000	469	0	1	∞	0	/1-1	0	0.0
StL-N	1	1	0	0	0	0	0	0	0	1	0	....	.000	.000	.000	.000	-107	-0	0	.00	0	....	0	0.0
Yr.	2	2	1	1	0	0	0	0	0	1	0	....	.500	.500	.500	1.000	181	0	1	.00	0	/1-1	0	0.0
• PASTORNICKY, Cliff	Clifford Scot Pastornicky b: 11/18/1958, Seattle, WA BR/TR, 5'10", 170 lbs. Deb: 6/14/1983																							
1983 KC-A	10	32	4	4	0	0	2	5	0	3	0	0	.125	.125	.313	.438	16	-4	0	.00	-1	3-10	0	-0.4
• PATE, Bob	Robert Wayne Pate b: 12/3/1953, Los Angeles, CA BR/TR, 6'3.5", 200 lbs. Deb: 6/2/1980 Career OF: 3-2-18																							
1980 Mon-N	23	39	3	10	2	0	0	5	3	6	0	1	.256	.310	.308	.617	73	-2	4	3.13	-1	O-18(2-0-16)	1	-0.4
1981 Mon-N	8	6	0	2	0	0	0	0	1	0	0	0	.333	.429	.333	.762	117	0	1	6.54	0	/O-5(1-2-2)	0	0.0
Total 2	31	45	3	12	2	0	0	5	4	6	0	1	.267	.327	.311	.638	79	-2	5	3.50	-2	/O-23	1	-0.4
• PATEK, Freddie	Frederick Joseph "The Flea" Patek b: 10/9/1944, Seguin, TX BR/TR, 5'5", 148 lbs. Deb: 6/3/1968																							
1968 Pit-N	61	208	31	53	4	2	2	18	12	37	18	7	.255	.302	.322	.624	89	-2	22	3.43	-1	S-52/O-5(2-0-3),3-1	6	0.1
1969 Pit-N	147	460	48	110	9	1	5	32	53	86	15	8	.239	.319	.296	.615	75	-14	43	3.06	-15	*S-146	8	-1.3
1970*Pit-N	84	237	42	58	10	5	1	19	29	46	8	2	.245	.327	.342	.669	82	-5	29	4.11	4	S-65	8	0.6
1971 KC-A	147	591	86	158	21	**11**	6	36	44	80	49	14	.267	.323	.371	.694	97	2	75	4.40	11	*S-147	24	3.2
1972 KC-A★	136	518	59	110	25	4	0	32	47	64	33	7	.212	.282	.276	.558	67	-16	44	2.75	20	*S-136	13	2.3
1973 KC-A	135	501	82	117	19	5	5	45	54	63	36	14	.234	.312	.321	.633	73	-15	53	3.42	25	*S-135	16	2.5
1974 KC-A	149	537	72	121	18	6	3	38	77	69	33	15	.225	.326	.298	.624	76	-13	58	3.48	10	*S-149	15	1.5
1975 KC-A	136	483	58	110	14	5	5	45	42	65	32	7	.228	.292	.308	.601	68	-16	47	3.15	0	*S-136/D-1	11	0.0
1976*KC-A★	144	432	58	104	19	3	1	43	50	63	51	15	.241	.322	.306	.628	84	-3	48	3.56	5	*S-143/D-1	14	1.9
1977*KC-A	154	497	72	130	26	6	5	60	41	84	**53**	13	.262	.324	.368	.692	88	-2	65	4.31	-5	*S-154	15	0.8

YEAR TM-L	G	AB	R	H	2B	3B	HR	RBI	BB	SO	SB	CS	AVG	OBP	SLG	OPS	OPS+	BR/A	RC	RC/G	FR	G/POS	WS	TPW
1978*KC-A★	138	440	54	109	23	1	2	46	42	56	38	11	.248	.315	.318	.633	76	-9	48	3.61	-3	*S-137	11	0.1
1979 KC-A	106	306	30	77	17	0	1	37	16	42	11	12	.252	.295	.317	.612	64	-18	26	2.74	-9	*S-104	3	-1.8
1980 Cal-A	86	273	41	72	10	5	5	34	15	26	7	6	.264	.304	.392	.696	92	-5	28	3.37	-4	S-81	5	-0.1
1981 Cal-A	27	47	3	11	1	1	0	5	1	6	1	0	.234	.250	.298	.548	57	-2	3	2.47	0	2-16/3-7,S-3	1	-0.2
Total 14	**1650**	**5530**	**736**	**1340**	**216**	**55**	**41**	**490**	**523**	**787**	**385**	**131**	**.242**	**.311**	**.324**	**.635**	**79**	**-120**	**592**	**3.49**	**38**	***S-1588/2-16,3-8,0-5,D-2**	**150**	**9.8**
• PATRICK, Bob	Robert Lee Patrick b: 10/27/1917, Fort Smith, AR d: 10/6/1999, Fort Smith, AR BR/TR, 6'2", 190 lbs. Deb: 9/20/1941 Career OF: 3-0-3																							
1941 Det-A	5	7	2	2	0	0	0	0	0	1	0	0	.286	.286	.286	.571	47	-1	1	3.16	-1	/0-3(3-0-0)	0	-0.1
1942 Det-A	4	8	1	2	1	0	1	3	1	0	0	0	.250	.333	.750	1.083	185	1	2	9.62	0	/0-3(0-0-3)	0	0.0
Total 2	**9**	**15**	**3**	**4**	**1**	**0**	**1**	**3**	**1**	**1**	**0**	**0**	**.267**	**.313**	**.533**	**.846**	**124**	**0**	**3**	**6.68**	**-1**	**/0-6**	**0**	**-0.1**
• PATTEE, Harry	Harry Ernest Pattee b: 1/17/1882, Charlestown, MA d: 7/17/1971, Lynchburg, VA BL/TR, 5'8", 149 lbs. Deb: 4/14/1908																							
1908 Bro-N	80	264	19	57	5	2	0	9	25	....	24	....	.216	.286	.250	.536	74	-7	26	3.09	7	2-74	6	0.1
• PATTERSON, Claire	Lorenzo Claire Patterson b: 10/5/1887, Arkansas City, KS d: 3/28/1913, Mohave, CA BL/TR, 6', 180 lbs. Deb: 9/5/1909																							
1909 Cin-N	4	8	0	1	0	0	0	1	0	....	0	....	.125	.125	.125	.250	-23	-1	0	.40	0	/0-2(2-0-0)	0	-0.2
• PATTERSON, Corey	Donald Corey Patterson b: 8/13/1979, Atlanta, GA BL/TR, 5'10", 180 lbs. Deb: 9/18/2000 Career OF: 13-285-1																							
2000 Chi-N	11	42	9	7	1	0	2	2	3	14	1	1	.167	.239	.333	.572	43	-4	3	2.50	0	0-11(0-11-0)	0	-0.4
2001 Chi-N	59	131	26	29	3	0	4	14	6	33	4	0	.221	.271	.336	.607	59	-7	13	3.25	0	0-54(13-45-1)	3	-0.7
2002 Chi-N	153	592	71	150	30	5	14	54	19	142	18	3	.253	.286	.392	.678	78	-19	67	3.91	-7	*0-147(0-147-0)	8	-2.5
2003 Chi-N	83	329	49	98	17	7	13	55	15	77	16	5	.298	.330	.511	.841	117	8	54	6.03	-2	0-82(0-82-0)	13	0.6
Total 4	**306**	**1094**	**155**	**284**	**51**	**12**	**33**	**125**	**43**	**266**	**39**	**9**	**.260**	**.296**	**.419**	**.714**	**86**	**-23**	**138**	**4.37**	**-10**	**0-294**	**24**	**-3.1**
• PATTERSON, Dan	Thomas W. Patterson b: 1846, New York, NY TL, 5'9", 143 lbs. Deb: 5/18/1871 U NA OF: 12-9-29																							
1871 Mut-n	32	151	31	31	2	0	0	13	1	0	2	1	.205	.211	.219	.429	26	-13	8	1.97	-2	*0-31(9-0-22)/2-2	....	-0.9
1872 Eck-n	12	47	5	9	2	0	0	4	0	1	0	0	.191	.191	.234	.426	36	-2	2	1.76	2	0-11(2-9-0)/1-1	....	0.0
1874 Mut-n	1	5	1	2	0	0	0	2	0	0	0	0	.400	.400	.400	.800	152	0	1	8.20	0	/1-1,0-1	....	0.0
1875 Atl-n	12	45	4	9	0	0	0	4	0	0	1	0	.200	.200	.200	.400	45	-2	2	1.68	-6	/2-7,0-7(0-0-7)	....	-0.6
Total 4 n	**57**	**248**	**41**	**51**	**4**	**0**	**0**	**23**	**1**	**1**	**3**	**1**	**.206**	**.209**	**.222**	**.431**	**34**	**-16**	**13**	**1.97**	**-6**	**/0-50,2-9,1-2**	**....**	**-1.5**
• PATTERSON, George	George Patterson Deb: 4/24/1884																							
1884 Phi-U	2	7	0	1	0	0	0	....	0	....	....	....	.143	.143	.143	.286	-3	-1	0	.68	0	/0-2(1-0-1)	0	-0.1
• PATTERSON, Ham	Hamilton Patterson b: 10/13/1877, Belleville, IL d: 11/25/1945, East St. Louis, IL BR/TR, 6'2", 185 lbs. Deb: 5/18/1909																							
1909 StL-A	17	49	2	10	1	0	0	5	0	....	1	....	.204	.204	.224	.429	38	-4	2	1.53	-1	/1-6,0-6(6-0-0)	0	-0.6
Chi-A	1	3	2	0	0	0	0	0	1	....	0	....	.000	.250	.000	.250	-21	-0	0	.00	1	/1-1	0	0.0
Yr.	18	52	4	10	1	0	0	5	1	....	1	....	.192	.208	.212	.419	34	-4	2	1.42	-1	/1-7,0-6(6-0-0)	0	-0.6
• PATTERSON, Hank	Henry Joseph Colquit Patterson b: 7/17/1907, San Francisco, CA d: 9/30/1970, Panorama City, CA BR/TR, 5'11.5", 170 lbs. Deb: 9/5/1932 C																							
1932 Bos-A	1	1	0	0	0	0	0	0	0	0	0	0	.000	.000	.000	.000	-103	-0	0	.00	0	/C-1	0	-0.1
• PATTERSON, Jarrod	Jarrod Lane Patterson b: 9/7/1973, Montgomery, AL BL/TR, 6'1", 195 lbs. Deb: 6/16/2001																							
2001 Det-A	13	41	6	11	1	1	2	4	0	4	0	1	.268	.302	.488	.790	108	-0	5	3.90	-4	3-13	0	-0.4
2003 KC-A	13	22	3	4	0	0	0	0	3	6	0	0	.182	.280	.182	.462	23	-2	1	1.90	-1	/3-4,D-4,1-2	0	-0.4
Total 2	**26**	**63**	**9**	**15**	**1**	**1**	**2**	**4**	**3**	**10**	**0**	**1**	**.238**	**.294**	**.381**	**.675**	**77**	**-3**	**6**	**3.20**	**-6**	**/3-17,D-4,1-2**	**0**	**-0.8**
• PATTERSON, John	John Allen Patterson b: 2/11/1967, Key West, FL BB/TR, 5'9", 160 lbs. Deb: 4/6/1992																							
1992 SF-N	32	103	10	19	1	1	0	4	5	24	5	1	.184	.229	.214	.443	28	-9	5	1.64	3	2-22/0-5(0-5-0)	1	-0.6
1993 SF-N	16	16	1	3	0	0	1	2	0	5	0	1	.188	.188	.375	.563	48	-2	1	1.45	0	....	0	-0.2
1994 SF-N	85	240	36	57	10	1	3	32	16	43	13	3	.238	.315	.325	.640	70	-9	27	3.68	1	2-63	7	-0.5
1995 SF-N	95	205	27	42	5	3	1	14	14	41	4	2	.205	.294	.273	.568	52	-14	17	2.56	-5	2-53	2	-1.7
Total 4	**228**	**564**	**74**	**121**	**16**	**5**	**5**	**52**	**35**	**113**	**22**	**7**	**.215**	**.289**	**.287**	**.576**	**56**	**-33**	**50**	**2.82**	**-1**	**2-138/0-5**	**10**	**-2.9**
• PATTERSON, Mike	Michael Lee Patterson b: 1/26/1958, Santa Monica, CA BL/TR, 5'10", 170 lbs. Deb: 4/15/1981 Career OF: 7-7-4																							
1981 Oak-A	12	23	4	8	1	1	0	1	2	5	0	1	.348	.400	.478	.878	160	1	4	6.84	0	/0-5(2-0-3),D-2	1	0.1
NY-A	4	9	2	2	0	2	0	0	0	0	0	0	.222	.222	.667	.889	150	0	1	5.14	0	/0-4(3-0-1)	0	0.0
Yr.	16	32	6	10	1	3	0	1	2	5	0	1	.313	.353	.531	.884	157	2	5	6.32	0	/0-9(5-0-4),D-2	1	0.1
1982 NY-A	11	16	3	3	1	0	1	1	2	6	1	0	.188	.278	.438	.715	94	0	2	4.64	-1	/0-9(2-7-0),D-1	0	-0.1
Total 2	**27**	**48**	**9**	**13**	**2**	**3**	**1**	**2**	**4**	**11**	**1**	**1**	**.271**	**.327**	**.500**	**.827**	**135**	**2**	**8**	**5.72**	**-1**	**/0-18,D-3**	**1**	**0.1**
• PATTERSON, Pat	William Jennings Bryan Patterson b: 1/29/1901, Belleville, IL d: 10/1/1977, St. Louis, MO BR/TR, 6', 175 lbs. Deb: 4/14/1921																							
1921 NY-N	23	35	5	14	0	0	1	5	2	5	0	1	.400	.432	.486	.918	142	2	7	8.21	-1	3-14/S-7	2	0.2
• PATTON, Bill	George William Patton b: 10/7/1912, Cornwall, PA d: 3/15/1986, Philadelphia, PA BR/TR, 6'2", 180 lbs. Deb: 6/29/1935																							
1935 Phi-A	9	10	1	3	1	0	0	2	2	3	0	0	.300	.417	.400	.817	113	0	2	6.84	1	/C-3	1	0.1
• PATTON, Gene	Gene Tunney Patton b: 7/8/1926, Coatesville, PA BL/TR, 5'10", 165 lbs. Deb: 6/17/1944																							
1944 Bos-N	1	0	0	0	0	0	0	0	0	0	0	....	....	....	....	....	-96	0	0	....	0	....	0	0.0
• PATTON, Tom	Thomas Allen Patton b: 9/5/1935, Honey Brook, PA BR/TR, 5'9.5", 185 lbs. Deb: 4/30/1957																							
1957 Bal-A	1	2	0	0	0	0	0	0	0	2	0	0	.000	.000	.000	.000	-107	-1	0	.00	0	/C-1	0	0.0
• PAUL, Josh	Joshua William Paul b: 5/19/1975, Evanston, IL BR/TR, 6'1", 200 lbs. Deb: 9/7/1999 Career OF: 2-0-0																							
1999 Chi-A	6	18	2	4	1	0	0	1	0	4	0	0	.222	.222	.278	.500	26	-2	1	2.14	0	/C-6	0	-0.1
2000*Chi-A	36	71	15	20	3	2	1	8	5	17	1	0	.282	.338	.423	.760	90	-1	10	4.65	1	C-34/0-1	3	0.1
2001 Chi-A	57	139	20	37	11	0	3	18	13	25	6	2	.266	.329	.410	.739	90	-2	19	4.67	1	C-56	4	0.3
2002 Chi-A	33	104	11	25	4	0	0	11	9	22	2	0	.240	.307	.279	.586	56	-6	10	3.22	1	C-32/0-1	2	-0.3
2003 Chi-A	13	17	6	6	0	0	0	4	3	3	0	0	.353	.450	.353	.803	117	1	3	7.49	-2	C-11/D-1	1	-0.1
Chi-N	3	6	0	0	0	0	0	0	0	3	0	0	.000	.000	.000	.000	-102	-2	0	.00	1	/C-3	0	-0.1
Total 5	**148**	**355**	**54**	**92**	**19**	**2**	**4**	**42**	**30**	**74**	**9**	**2**	**.259**	**.320**	**.358**	**.678**	**75**	**-12**	**43**	**4.10**	**1**	**C-142/0-2,D-1**	**10**	**-0.3**
• PAUL, Lou	Louis Paul BR/TR Deb: 9/5/1876																							
1876 Phi-N	3	12	2	2	1	0	0	0	0	0	....	....	.167	.167	.250	.417	37	-1	1	1.44	-2	/C-3	0	-0.2
• PAULA, Carlos	Carlos (Conill) Paula b: 11/28/1927, Havana, Cuba d: 4/25/1983, Miami, FL BR/TR, 6'3", 195 lbs. Deb: 9/6/1954 Career OF: 21-0-91																							
1954 Was-A	9	24	2	4	1	0	0	2	2	4	0	0	.167	.231	.208	.439	22	-3	1	1.72	1	/0-6(6-0-0)	0	-0.2
1955 Was-A	115	351	34	105	20	7	6	45	17	43	2	3	.299	.335	.447	.782	115	4	49	5.07	-4	0-85(6-0-80)	10	-0.2
1956 Was-A	33	82	8	15	2	1	3	13	8	15	0	2	.183	.256	.341	.597	56	-6	5	1.92	-1	0-20(9-0-11)	0	-0.8
Total 3	**157**	**457**	**44**	**124**	**23**	**8**	**9**	**60**	**27**	**62**	**2**	**5**	**.271**	**.315**	**.416**	**.731**	**99**	**-5**	**56**	**4.21**	**-4**	**0-111**	**10**	**-1.3**
• PAULETTE, Gene	Eugene Edward Paulette b: 5/26/1891, Centralia, IL d: 2/8/1966, Little Rock, AR BR/TR, 6', 150 lbs. Deb: 6/16/1911 Career OF: 1-3-10																							
1911 NY-N	10	12	1	2	0	0	0	1	0	1	0	....	.167	.167	.167	.333	-6	-2	0	.78	-1	/1-7,3-1,S-1	0	-0.3
1916 StL-A	5	4	1	2	0	0	0	0	1	1	0	....	.500	.600	.500	1.100	242	1	1	15.60	0	....	0	0.1
1917 StL-A	12	22	3	4	0	0	0	0	3	3	0	....	.182	.280	.182	.462	43	-1	1	1.67	-1	/1-5,2-3,3-1	0	-0.3
StL-N	95	332	32	88	21	7	0	34	16	16	9	....	.265	.303	.370	.673	109	2	38	3.93	3	1-93	11	0.4
1918 StL-N	125	461	33	126	15	3	0	52	27	16	11	....	.273	.316	.319	.635	97	-2	49	3.63	2	1-97,S-12/2-7,0-6(1-1-3),3,P	11	-0.1
1919 StL-N	43	144	11	31	6	0	0	11	9	6	4	....	.215	.261	.257	.518	60	-7	10	2.28	2	1-35/S-3	1	-0.6
Phi-N	67	243	20	63	8	3	1	31	19	10	10	....	.259	.316	.329	.645	88	-3	27	3.80	-7	2-58,0-10(0-2-7)/1-1	5	-1.1
Yr.	110	387	31	94	14	3	1	42	28	16	14	....	.243	.296	.302	.598	77	-10	37	3.21	-5	2-58,1-36,0-10(0-2-7)/S-3	6	-1.7
1920 Phi-N	143	562	59	162	16	6	1	36	33	16	9	8	.288	.332	.343	.676	90	-6	64	4.06	3	*1-139/S-2	11	-0.6
Total 6	**500**	**1780**	**160**	**478**	**66**	**19**	**2**	**165**	**108**	**69**	**43**	**8**	**.269**	**.314**	**.330**	**.644**	**92**	**-18**	**191**	**3.70**	**0**	**1-377/2-68,S-18,0-16,3-4,P**	**39**	**-2.6**

YEAR TM-L	G	AB	R	H	2B	3B	HR	RBI	BB	SO	SB	CS	AVG	OBP	SLG	OPS	OPS+	BR/A	RC	RC/G	FR	G/POS	WS	TPW
• PAUXTIS, Si	Simon Francis Pauxtis b: 7/20/1885, Pittston, PA d: 3/13/1961, Philadelphia, PA BR/TR, 6', 175 lbs. Deb: 9/18/1909																							
1909 Cin-N	4	8	2	1	0	0	0	0	0	....	0	....	.125	.222	.125	.347	8	-1	0	.78	0	/C-4	0	-0.1
• PAVLETICH, Don	Donald Stephen Pavletich b: 7/13/1938, Milwaukee, WI BR/TR, 5'11", 209 lbs. Deb: 4/20/1957																							
1957 Cin-N	1	1	0	0	0	0	0	0	0	0	0	0	.000	.000	.000	.000	-93	-0	0	.00	0	....	0	0.0
1959 Cin-N	1	0	1	0	0	0	0	0	0	0	0	0	....	....	....	....	-97	0	0	....	0	....	0	0.0
1962 Cin-N	34	63	7	14	3	0	1	7	8	18	0	0	.222	.310	.317	.627	67	-3	7	3.73	0	1-25/C-2	1	-0.4
1963 Cin-N	71	183	18	38	11	0	5	18	17	12	0	0	.208	.275	.350	.625	76	-6	18	3.16	-4	1-57,C-13	4	-1.2
1964 Cin-N	34	91	12	22	4	0	5	11	10	17	0	0	.242	.317	.451	.767	109	1	13	5.07	-1	C-27/1-1	4	0.1
1965 Cin-N	68	191	25	61	11	1	8	32	23	27	1	1	.319	.395	.513	.908	144	12	38	7.44	0	C-54/1-9	10	1.4
1966 Cin-N	83	235	29	69	13	2	12	38	18	37	1	0	.294	.346	.519	.866	125	8	41	6.46	0	C-55,1-10	10	1.1
1967 Cin-N	74	231	25	55	14	3	6	34	21	38	2	1	.238	.313	.403	.715	93	-2	26	3.59	1	C-66/1-6,3-1	7	0.2
1968 Cin-N	46	98	11	28	3	1	2	11	8	23	0	0	.286	.352	.398	.750	117	2	12	4.06	0	1-22/C-5	3	0.2
1969 Chi-A	78	188	26	46	12	0	6	33	28	45	0	0	.245	.343	.404	.747	103	1	28	5.06	-2	C-51,1-13	6	0.0
1970 Bos-A	32	65	4	9	1	1	0	6	10	15	1	0	.138	.253	.185	.438	21	-7	3	1.60	1	1-16,C-10	1	-0.6
1971 Bos-A	14	27	5	7	1	0	1	3	5	5	0	0	.259	.375	.407	.782	113	1	5	6.23	-1	/C-8	1	0.0
Total 12	**536**	**1373**	**163**	**349**	**73**	**8**	**46**	**193**	**148**	**237**	**5**	**2**	**.254**	**.330**	**.420**	**.750**	**103**	**8**	**190**	**4.75**	**-5**	**C-291,1-159/3-1**	**47**	**0.8**
• PAWELEK, Ted	Theodore John "Porky" Pawelek b: 8/15/1919, Chicago Heights, IL d: 2/12/1964, Chicago Heights, IL BL/TR, 5'10.5", 202 lbs. Deb: 9/13/1946																							
1946 Chi-N	4	4	0	1	1	0	0	0	0	0	0	....	.250	.250	.500	.750	112	0	1	4.50	0	/C-1	0	-0.1
• PAWLOSKI, Stan	Stanley Walter Pawloski b: 9/6/1931, Wanamie, PA BR/TR, 6'1", 175 lbs. Deb: 9/24/1955																							
1955 Cle-A	2	8	0	1	0	0	0	0	0	2	0	0	.125	.125	.125	.250	-32	-1	0	.48	1	/2-2	0	-0.1
• PAYNE, Fred	Frederick Thomas Payne b: 9/2/1880, Camden, NY d: 1/16/1954, Camden, NY BR/TR, 5'10", 162 lbs. Deb: 4/21/1906 Career OF: 4-13-11																							
1906 Det-A	72	222	23	60	5	5	0	20	13	....	4	....	.270	.316	.338	.654	102	0	27	4.16	5	C-47,0-17(1-12-4)	8	1.0
1907*Det-A	53	169	17	28	2	2	0	14	7	....	4	....	.166	.221	.201	.422	34	-13	9	1.66	4	C-46/0-5(3-1-1)	3	-0.5
1908 Det-A	20	45	3	3	0	0	0	2	3	....	1	....	.067	.176	.067	.243	-20	-6	1	.59	-1	C-17/0-1	1	-0.6
1909 Chi-A	32	82	8	20	2	0	0	12	5	....	0	....	.244	.295	.268	.564	82	-2	7	2.67	1	C-27/0-3(0-0-3)	2	0.2
1910 Chi-A	91	252	17	56	5	4	0	19	11	....	6	....	.222	.260	.274	.534	71	-9	20	2.48	-3	C-78/0-2(0-0-2)	6	-0.6
1911 Chi-A	66	133	14	27	2	1	1	19	8	....	6	....	.203	.259	.256	.514	45	-10	10	2.43	-5	C-56	2	-1.2
Total 6	**334**	**903**	**82**	**194**	**16**	**12**	**1**	**86**	**47**	**....**	**21**	**....**	**.215**	**.265**	**.262**	**.528**	**64**	**-39**	**74**	**2.59**	**2**	**C-271/0-28**	**22**	**-1.6**
• PAYNTER, George	George Washington Paynter b: 7/6/1871, Cincinnati, OH d: 10/1/1950, Cincinnati, OH BR/TR, 5'9", 125 lbs. Deb: 8/12/1894																							
1894 StL-N	1	4	0	0	0	0	0	0	1	0	1	....	.000	.200	.000	.200	-48	-1	0	1.33	1	/0-1	0	0.0
• PAYTON, Jay	Jason Lee Payton b: 11/22/1972, Zanesville, OH BR/TR, 5'10", 185 lbs. Deb: 9/1/1998 Career OF: 198-354-6																							
1998 NY-N	15	22	2	7	1	0	0	0	1	4	0	0	.318	.348	.364	.711	89	-0	3	5.17	0	/0-9(8-0-1)	0	0.0
1999 NY-N	13	8	1	2	1	0	0	1	0	2	1	2	.250	.333	.375	.708	81	-1	0	1.42	0	/0-6(5-2-0)	0	-0.1
2000*NY-N	149	488	63	142	23	1	17	62	30	60	5	11	.291	.336	.447	.783	99	-6	68	4.94	-2	*0-146(4-143-0)	14	-0.6
2001 NY-N	104	361	44	92	16	1	8	34	18	52	4	3	.255	.299	.371	.671	76	-14	37	3.54	1	*0-103(0-103-0)	3	-1.2
2002 NY-N	87	275	33	78	6	3	8	31	21	34	4	1	.284	.337	.415	.751	101	0	37	4.83	-2	0-82(0-82-0)	8	-0.1
Col-N	47	170	36	57	14	4	8	28	8	20	3	3	.335	.376	.606	.982	132	7	37	8.35	1	0-44(32-16-2)	7	0.7
Yr.	134	445	69	135	20	7	16	59	29	54	7	4	.303	.351	.488	.839	112	7	74	6.11	-1	*0-126(32-98-2)	15	0.6
2003 Col-N	157	600	93	181	32	5	28	89	43	77	6	4	.302	.355	.512	.867	108	6	99	5.85	1	*0-151(149-8-3)	15	0.1
Total 6	**572**	**1924**	**272**	**559**	**93**	**14**	**69**	**245**	**121**	**249**	**23**	**24**	**.291**	**.339**	**.461**	**.800**	**100**	**-9**	**282**	**5.20**	**0**	**0-541**	**47**	**-1.3**
• PEACOCK, Johnny	John Gaston Peacock b: 1/10/1910, Fremont, NC d: 10/17/1981, Wilson, NC BL/TR, 5'11", 165 lbs. Deb: 9/23/1937																							
1937 Bos-A	9	32	3	10	2	1	0	6	1	0	0	0	.313	.333	.438	.771	89	-1	5	5.50	1	/C-9	1	0.0
1938 Bos-A	72	195	29	59	7	1	1	39	17	4	4	1	.303	.358	.364	.723	78	-6	26	5.04	-4	C-57/1-1,0-1	5	-0.7
1939 Bos-A	92	274	33	76	11	4	0	36	29	11	1	1	.277	.347	.347	.693	75	-10	35	4.40	-2	C-84	8	-0.7
1940 Bos-A	63	131	20	37	4	1	0	13	23	10	1	1	.282	.390	.328	.718	85	-2	17	4.34	-3	C-48	3	-0.3
1941 Bos-A	79	261	28	74	20	1	0	27	21	3	2	1	.284	.339	.368	.707	85	-6	34	4.70	-1	C-70	8	-0.2
1942 Bos-A	88	286	17	76	7	3	0	25	21	11	1	1	.266	.316	.311	.627	74	-10	29	3.58	-1	C-82	7	-0.7
1943 Bos-A	48	114	7	23	3	1	0	7	10	9	1	1	.202	.266	.246	.512	49	-7	8	2.11	-1	C-32	1	-0.7
1944 Bos-A	4	4	0	0	0	0	0	0	0	0	0	0	.000	.000	.000	.000	-101	-1	0	.00	0	/C-2	0	-0.1
Phi-N	83	253	21	57	9	3	0	21	31	15	1	....	.225	.310	.285	.594	70	-9	23	3.09	2	C-73/2-1	4	-0.3
1945 Phi-N	33	74	6	15	6	0	0	6	6	0	1	....	.203	.263	.284	.546	53	-5	5	2.37	0	C-23	1	-0.4
Bro-N	48	110	11	28	5	1	0	14	24	10	2	....	.255	.388	.318	.706	98	1	16	5.11	-1	C-38	4	0.3
Yr.	81	184	17	43	11	1	0	20	30	10	3	....	.234	.341	.304	.645	81	-4	21	3.95	0	C-61	5	-0.1
Total 9	**619**	**1734**	**175**	**455**	**74**	**16**	**1**	**194**	**183**	**73**	**14**	**6**	**.262**	**.333**	**.325**	**.658**	**76**	**-55**	**197**	**3.96**	**-11**	**C-518/1-1,2-1,0-1**	**42**	**-3.8**
• PEAK, Elias	Elias Peak b: 5/23/1859, Philadelphia, PA d: 12/17/1916, Philadelphia, PA Deb: 4/19/1884																							
1884 Bos-U	1	3	2	2	0	0	0	....	1	....	....	....	.667	.750	.667	1.417	388	1	2	43.05	0	/0-1	1	0.1
Phi-U	54	215	35	42	6	4	0	....	7	....	....	....	.195	.221	.260	.481	67	-6	13	2.05	-10	2-47/0-5(4-0-1),S-2	2	-1.2
Yr.	55	218	37	44	6	4	0	....	8	....	....	....	.202	.230	.266	.496	73	-5	14	2.29	-10	2-47/0-6(4-0-2),S-2	3	-1.2
• PEARCE, Dickey	Richard J. Pearce b: 2/29/1836, Brooklyn, NY d: 9/18/1908, Onset, MA BR/TR, 5'3.5", 161 lbs. Deb: 5/18/1871 M/U																							
1871 Mut-n	33	163	31	44	5	0	0	20	4	1	0	0	.270	.287	.301	.588	76	-4	14	3.82	-3	*S-33	....	-0.5
1872 Mut-n	44	206	32	40	1	1	1	23	4	1	1	1	.194	.210	.223	.433	35	-13	10	1.87	7	*S-42/0-2(1-0-1)	....	-0.5
1873 Atl-n	55	262	42	72	5	0	1	26	8	2	2	0	.275	.296	.305	.602	88	1	25	4.00	-8	*S-55/1-1,2-1	....	-0.6
1874 Atl-n	56	255	48	75	1	0	0	25	6	1	1	0	.294	.310	.298	.608	108	5	24	4.08	1	*S-56/3-2,2-1	....	0.4
1875 StL-n	70	311	51	77	6	3	0	29	7	7	8	3	.248	.264	.286	.550	100	3	26	3.27	3	*S-70/P-2	....	0.3
1876 StL-N	25	105	12	21	1	0	0	10	3	5	....	....	.200	.229	.216	.444	51	-5	5	1.78	7	S-23/2-1,0-1	2	0.3
1877 StL-N	8	29	1	5	0	0	0	4	1	4	....	....	.172	.200	.172	.372	19	-2	1	1.17	3	/S-8	1	0.1
Total 5 n	**258**	**1197**	**204**	**308**	**18**	**4**	**2**	**123**	**29**	**12**	**12**	**4**	**.257**	**.275**	**.284**	**.559**	**85**	**-8**	**100**	**3.40**	**0**	**S-256/2-2,3-2,0-2,P-2,1-1**	**....**	**-0.9**
Total 2	**33**	**134**	**13**	**26**	**1**	**0**	**0**	**14**	**4**	**9**	**....**	**....**	**.194**	**.222**	**.206**	**.428**	**44**	**-7**	**6**	**1.64**	**10**	**/S-31,2-1,0-1**	**3**	**0.4**
• PEARCE, Ducky	William C. Pearce b: 3/17/1885, Corning, OH d: 5/22/1933, Brownstown, IN BR/TR, 6'1", 185 lbs. Deb: 7/1/1908																							
1908 Cin-N	2	2	0	0	0	0	0	0	0	....	0	....	.000	.000	.000	.000	-103	-0	0	.00	0	/C-2	0	0.0
1909 Cin-N	2	2	0	0	0	0	0	0	0	....	0	....	.000	.000	.000	.000	-101	-0	0	.00	0	/C-2	0	-0.1
Total 2	**4**	**4**	**0**	**0**	**0**	**0**	**0**	**0**	**0**	**....**	**0**	**....**	**.000**	**.000**	**.000**	**.000**	**-102**	**-1**	**0**	**.00**	**-0**	**/C-4**	**0**	**-0.1**
• PEARCE, Harry	Harry James Pearce b: 7/12/1889, Philadelphia, PA d: 1/8/1942, Philadelphia, PA BR/TR, 5'9", 158 lbs. Deb: 10/2/1917																							
1917 Phi-N	7	16	2	4	3	0	0	2	0	4	0	....	.250	.294	.438	.732	118	0	2	4.18	3	/S-4	1	0.4
1918 Phi-N	60	164	16	40	3	2	0	18	9	31	5	....	.244	.295	.287	.582	73	-5	15	3.00	-1	2-46/S-2,1-1,3-1	2	-0.6
1919 Phi-N	68	244	24	44	3	3	0	9	8	27	6	....	.180	.209	.217	.427	26	-22	12	1.49	-4	2-43,S-23/3-2	2	-2.6
Total 3	**135**	**424**	**42**	**88**	**9**	**5**	**0**	**29**	**17**	**62**	**11**	**....**	**.208**	**.247**	**.252**	**.499**	**48**	**-27**	**29**	**2.14**	**-2**	**/2-89,S-29,3-3,1-1**	**5**	**-2.8**
• PEARSON, Albie	Albert Gregory Pearson b: 9/12/1934, Alhambra, CA BL/TL, 5'5", 141 lbs. Deb: 4/14/1958 Career OF: 54-558-249																							
1958 Was-A	146	530	63	146	25	5	3	33	64	31	7	8	.275	.356	.358	.714	99	-0	69	4.46	-3	*0-141(0-136-6)	15	-1.0
1959 Was-A	25	80	9	15	1	0	0	2	14	3	1	1	.188	.309	.200	.509	43	-6	6	2.45	-1	0-21(0-11-10)	0	-0.8
Bal-A	80	138	22	32	4	2	0	6	13	5	4	0	.232	.298	.290	.588	64	-6	12	3.02	-0	0-50(22-16-16)	2	-0.8
Yr.	105	218	31	47	5	2	0	8	27	8	5	1	.216	.302	.257	.559	55	-12	19	2.80	-1	0-71(22-27-26)	2	-1.6
1960 Bal-A	48	82	17	20	2	0	1	6	17	3	4	0	.244	.374	.305	.679	87	0	11	4.41	0	0-32(11-7-15)	3	-0.1
1961 LA-A	144	427	92	123	21	3	7	41	96	40	11	3	.288	.422	.400	.823	109	12	84	7.07	0	*0-113(1-46-76)	15	0.6
1962 LA-A	160	614	**115**	160	29	6	5	42	95	36	15	6	.261	.361	.352	.712	96	1	85	4.85	2	*0-160(0-143-17)	21	-0.3
1963 LA-A★	154	578	92	176	26	5	6	47	92	37	17	10	.304	.403	.398	.801	133	30	100	6.33	3	*0-148(2-135-15)	28	2.9
1964 LA-A	107	265	34	59	5	1	2	16	35	22	6	4	.223	.316	.272	.587	72	-9	25	3.04	-2	0-66(10-52-7)	5	-1.5
1965 Cal-A	122	360	41	100	17	2	4	21	51	17	12	1	.278	.370	.369	.740	113	11	55	5.35	2	*0-101(7-12-87)	15	0.7

YEAR TM-L	G	AB	R	H	2B	3B	HR	RBI	BB	SO	SB	CS	AVG	OBP	SLG	OPS	OPS+	BR/A	RC	RC/G	FR	G/POS	WS	TPW
1966 Cal-A	2	3	0	0	0	0	0	0	0	1	0	0	.000	.000	.000	.000	-103	-1	0	.00	0	/0-1	0	-0.1
Total 9	988	3077	485	831	130	24	28	214	477	195	77	33	.270	.370	.355	.725	102	32	447	5.06	-1	0-833	104	-0.5

• PECHOUS, Charlie Charles Edward Pechous b: 10/5/1896, Chicago, IL d: 9/13/1980, Kenosha, WI BR/TR, 6', 170 lbs. Deb: 9/14/1915

YEAR TM-L	G	AB	R	H	2B	3B	HR	RBI	BB	SO	SB	CS	AVG	OBP	SLG	OPS	OPS+	BR/A	RC	RC/G	FR	G/POS	WS	TPW
1915 Chi-F	18	51	4	9	3	0	0	4	4	15	1	....	.176	.236	.235	.472	41	-4	3	1.89	0	3-18	1	-0.3
1916 Chi-N	22	69	5	10	1	1	0	4	3	21	1	....	.145	.181	.188	.369	12	-7	3	1.16	3	3-22	1	-0.4
1917 Chi-N	13	41	2	10	0	0	0	1	2	9	1	....	.244	.295	.244	.539	61	-2	3	2.52	-2	/3-7,S-5	1	-0.4
Total 3	53	161	11	29	4	1	0	9	9	45	3	....	.180	.228	.217	.445	34	-13	9	1.71	1	/3-47,S-5	3	-1.1

• PECK, Hal Harold Arthur Peck b: 4/20/1917, Big Bend, WI d: 4/13/1995, Milwaukee, WI BL/TL, 5'11", 175 lbs. Deb: 5/13/1943 Career OF: 4-0-253

YEAR TM-L	G	AB	R	H	2B	3B	HR	RBI	BB	SO	SB	CS	AVG	OBP	SLG	OPS	OPS+	BR/A	RC	RC/G	FR	G/POS	WS	TPW
1943 Bro-N	1	1	0	0	0	0	0	0	0	0	0	....	.000	.000	.000	.000	-100	-0	0	.00	0	....	0	0.0
1944 Phi-A	2	8	0	2	0	0	0	1	0	2	0	2	.250	.250	.250	.500	44	-2	0	.00	-0	/0-2(0-0-2)	0	-0.2
1945 Phi-A	112	449	51	124	22	9	5	39	37	28	5	3	.276	.331	.399	.730	112	6	61	4.87	-7	*0-110(0-0-110)	11	-1.0
1946 Phi-A	48	150	14	37	8	2	2	11	16	14	1	2	.247	.319	.367	.686	92	-2	18	4.11	1	0-35(0-0-35)	3	-0.2
1947 Cle-A	114	392	58	115	18	2	8	44	27	31	3	3	.293	.342	.411	.753	112	4	56	5.26	2	0-97(3-0-95)	12	0.4
1948*Cle-A	45	63	12	18	3	0	0	8	4	8	1	0	.286	.328	.333	.662	78	-2	8	4.48	0	/0-9(1-0-9)	1	-0.2
1949 Cle-A	33	29	1	9	1	0	0	9	3	3	0	0	.310	.375	.345	.720	93	-0	4	5.58	0	/0-2(0-0-2)	1	0.0
Total 7	355	1092	136	305	52	13	15	112	87	86	10	10	.279	.334	.392	.726	106	4	147	4.84	-4	0-255	28	-1.2

• PECKINPAUGH, Roger Roger Thorpe Peckinpaugh b: 2/5/1891, Wooster, OH d: 11/17/1977, Cleveland, OH BR/TR, 5'10.5", 165 lbs. Deb: 9/15/1910 M

YEAR TM-L	G	AB	R	H	2B	3B	HR	RBI	BB	SO	SB	CS	AVG	OBP	SLG	OPS	OPS+	BR/A	RC	RC/G	FR	G/POS	WS	TPW
1910 Cle-A	15	45	1	9	0	0	0	6	1	....	3	....	.200	.234	.200	.434	36	-3	3	1.96	-6	S-14	0	-1.0
1912 Cle-A	70	236	18	50	4	1	1	22	16	....	11	....	.212	.262	.250	.512	45	-17	18	2.45	-3	S-68	3	-1.5
1913 Cle-A	1	0	1	0	0	0	0	0	0	0	0	....	....	....	....	....	-97	0	0	....	0	....	0	0.0
NY-A	95	340	35	91	10	7	1	32	24	47	19	....	.268	.316	.347	.663	94	-4	41	4.07	-4	S-93	8	-0.1
Yr.	96	340	36	91	10	7	1	32	24	47	19	....	.268	.316	.347	.663	94	-4	41	4.07	-4	S-93	8	-0.1
1914 NY-A	157	570	55	127	14	6	3	51	51	73	38	17	.223	.288	.284	.572	72	-19	52	2.94	6	*S-157	16	-0.2
1915 NY-A	142	540	67	119	18	7	5	44	49	72	19	12	.220	.289	.307	.596	78	-17	53	3.04	13	*S-142	14	0.7
1916 NY-A	145	552	65	141	22	8	4	58	62	50	18	....	.255	.332	.346	.678	101	1	72	4.33	7	*S-145	21	2.1
1917 NY-A	148	543	63	141	24	7	0	41	64	46	17	....	.260	.340	.330	.670	103	3	66	4.04	8	*S-148	20	2.5
1918 NY-A	122	446	59	103	15	3	0	43	43	41	12	....	.231	.303	.278	.581	74	-14	42	2.92	26	*S-122	14	2.3
1919 NY-A	122	453	89	138	20	2	7	33	59	37	10	....	.305	.390	.404	.794	122	15	75	5.78	28	*S-121	24	5.5
1920 NY-A	139	534	109	144	26	6	8	54	72	47	8	12	.270	.356	.386	.742	93	-6	75	4.75	4	*S-137	21	0.8
1921*NY-A	149	577	128	166	25	7	8	71	84	44	2	2	.288	.380	.397	.777	96	0	93	5.52	-6	*S-149	20	1.0
1922 Was-A	147	520	62	132	14	4	2	48	55	36	11	6	.254	.329	.308	.636	70	-20	57	3.59	9	*S-147	14	0.5
1923 Was-A	154	568	73	150	18	4	2	62	64	30	10	8	.264	.340	.320	.660	78	-16	66	3.77	10	*S-154	17	1.1
1924*Was-A	155	523	72	142	20	5	2	73	72	45	9	6	.272	.360	.340	.700	84	-10	69	4.47	32	*S-155	22	3.6
1925*Was-A	126	422	67	124	16	4	4	64	49	23	13	4	.294	.367	.379	.746	91	-2	63	5.13	-1	*S-124/1-1	15	0.8
1926 Was-A	57	147	19	35	4	1	1	14	28	12	3	0	.238	.360	.299	.659	75	-3	18	4.25	0	S-46/1-1	4	0.1
1927 Chi-A	68	217	23	64	6	3	0	23	21	6	2	3	.295	.360	.350	.710	87	-4	28	4.55	4	S-60	6	0.6
Total 17	2012	7233	1006	1876	256	75	48	739	814	609	205	70	.259	.336	.335	.672	87	-117	891	4.08	128	*S-1982/1-2	239	18.7

• PECOTA, Bill William Joseph Pecota b: 2/16/1960, Redwood City, CA BR/TR, 6'2", 190 lbs. Deb: 9/19/1986 Career OF: 13-2-19

YEAR TM-L	G	AB	R	H	2B	3B	HR	RBI	BB	SO	SB	CS	AVG	OBP	SLG	OPS	OPS+	BR/A	RC	RC/G	FR	G/POS	WS	TPW
1986 KC-A	12	29	3	6	2	0	0	2	3	3	0	2	.207	.303	.276	.579	58	-2	2	1.97	1	3-12/D-4,S-2	1	-0.2
1987 KC-A	66	156	22	43	5	1	3	14	15	25	5	0	.276	.343	.378	.721	89	-1	21	4.98	0	S-36,3-17,2-15/D-1	5	0.2
1988 KC-A	90	178	25	37	3	3	1	15	18	34	7	2	.208	.288	.275	.563	58	-9	16	2.89	-4	S-41,3-21,1-11/0-9(3-0-6),D,2,C	4	-1.1
1989 KC-A	65	83	21	17	4	2	3	5	7	9	5	0	.205	.275	.410	.684	91	-0	9	3.38	-4	S-29,0-15(4-2-9),2-12/3-7,1,D	1	-0.3
1990 KC-A	87	240	43	58	15	2	5	20	33	39	8	5	.242	.336	.383	.719	102	1	32	4.32	2	2-50,S-21,3-11/0-6(4-0-3),1,D	8	0.5
1991 KC-A	125	398	53	114	23	2	6	45	41	45	16	7	.286	.356	.399	.756	108	5	56	4.84	1	*3-102,2-34/S-9,1-8,D-2,0,P	14	0.7
1992 NY-N	117	269	28	61	13	0	2	26	25	40	9	3	.227	.295	.297	.592	69	-10	24	2.89	-1	3-48,S-39,2-38/1-1,P-1	5	-1.0
1993*Atl-N	72	62	17	20	2	1	0	5	2	5	1	1	.323	.344	.387	.731	94	-1	8	5.07	-2	3-23/2-4,0-1	2	-0.3
1994 Atl-N	64	112	11	24	5	0	2	16	16	16	1	0	.214	.313	.313	.625	62	-6	12	3.34	4	3-31/2-1,0-1	2	-0.1
Total 9	698	1527	223	380	72	11	22	148	160	216	52	20	.249	.324	.354	.677	87	-24	180	3.92	-4	3-272,S-177,2-157/0,1,D,P,C	42	-1.5

• PEDEN, Les Leslie Earl "Gooch" Peden b: 9/17/1923, Azle, TX d: 2/11/2002, Jacksonville, FL BR/TR, 6'1.5", 212 lbs. Deb: 4/17/1953 C

YEAR TM-L	G	AB	R	H	2B	3B	HR	RBI	BB	SO	SB	CS	AVG	OBP	SLG	OPS	OPS+	BR/A	RC	RC/G	FR	G/POS	WS	TPW
1953 Was-A	9	28	4	7	1	0	1	1	4	3	0	0	.250	.344	.393	.737	101	0	4	5.25	1	/C-8	1	0.1

• PEDERSON, Stu Stuart Russell Pederson b: 1/28/1960, Palo Alto, CA BL/TL, 6', 185 lbs. Deb: 9/8/1985

YEAR TM-L	G	AB	R	H	2B	3B	HR	RBI	BB	SO	SB	CS	AVG	OBP	SLG	OPS	OPS+	BR/A	RC	RC/G	FR	G/POS	WS	TPW
1985 LA-N	8	4	1	0	0	0	0	1	0	2	0	0	.000	.000	.000	.000	-103	-1	0	.00	0	/0-5(3-0-2)	0	-0.1

• PEDRE, Jorge Jorge Enrique Pedre b: 10/12/1966, Culver City, CA BR/TR, 5'11", 210 lbs. Deb: 9/7/1991

YEAR TM-L	G	AB	R	H	2B	3B	HR	RBI	BB	SO	SB	CS	AVG	OBP	SLG	OPS	OPS+	BR/A	RC	RC/G	FR	G/POS	WS	TPW
1991 KC-A	10	19	2	5	1	1	0	3	3	5	0	0	.263	.364	.421	.785	116	0	3	6.16	0	/C-9,1-1	1	0.1
1992 Chi-N	4	4	0	0	0	0	0	0	0	1	0	0	.000	.000	.000	.000	-98	-1	0	.00	-1	/C-4	0	-0.2
Total 2	14	23	2	5	1	1	0	3	3	6	0	0	.217	.308	.348	.656	83	-1	3	4.79	-1	/C-13,1-1	1	-0.2

• PEDRIQUE, Al Alfredo Jose (Garcia) Pedrique b: 8/11/1960, Aragua, Venezuela BR/TR, 6', 155 lbs. Deb: 4/14/1987

YEAR TM-L	G	AB	R	H	2B	3B	HR	RBI	BB	SO	SB	CS	AVG	OBP	SLG	OPS	OPS+	BR/A	RC	RC/G	FR	G/POS	WS	TPW
1987 NY-N	5	6	1	0	0	0	0	0	1	2	0	0	.000	.143	.000	.143	-61	-1	0	.17	0	/S-4,2-1	0	-0.1
Pit-N	88	246	23	74	10	1	1	27	18	27	5	4	.301	.356	.362	.718	90	-4	31	4.34	-5	S-76/3-3,2-2	6	-0.2
Yr.	93	252	24	74	10	1	1	27	19	29	5	4	.294	.350	.353	.704	86	-5	31	4.21	-5	S-80/2-3,3-3	6	-0.3
1988 Pit-N	50	128	7	23	5	0	0	4	8	17	0	0	.180	.234	.219	.452	31	-12	6	1.51	-3	S-46/3-5	1	-1.2
1989 Det-A	31	69	1	14	3	0	0	5	2	15	0	0	.203	.225	.246	.472	34	-6	3	1.22	0	3-12,S-12/2-8	1	-0.5
Total 3	174	449	32	111	18	1	1	36	29	61	5	4	.247	.299	.298	.597	63	-23	39	2.91	-8	S-138/3-20,2-11	8	-2.0

• PEDROES, Chick Charles P. Pedroes b: 10/27/1869, Chicago, IL d: 8/6/1927, Chicago, IL Deb: 8/21/1902

YEAR TM-L	G	AB	R	H	2B	3B	HR	RBI	BB	SO	SB	CS	AVG	OBP	SLG	OPS	OPS+	BR/A	RC	RC/G	FR	G/POS	WS	TPW
1902 Chi-N	2	6	0	0	0	0	0	0	0	....	0	....	.000	.000	.000	.000	-103	-1	0	.00	0	/0-2(0-0-2)	0	-0.2

• PEEL, Homer Homer Hefner Peel b: 10/10/1902, Fort Sullivan, TX d: 4/8/1997, Shreveport, LA BR/TR, 5'9.5", 170 lbs. Deb: 9/13/1927 Career OF: 42-53-21

YEAR TM-L	G	AB	R	H	2B	3B	HR	RBI	BB	SO	SB	CS	AVG	OBP	SLG	OPS	OPS+	BR/A	RC	RC/G	FR	G/POS	WS	TPW
1927 StL-N	2	2	0	0	0	0	0	0	0	1	0	....	.000	.000	.000	.000	-97	-1	0	.00	0	/0-1	0	-0.1
1929 Phi-N	53	156	16	42	12	1	0	19	12	7	1	....	.269	.329	.359	.688	66	-8	18	4.03	-1	0-39(1-36-2)/1-1	2	-1.0
1930 StL-N	26	73	9	12	2	0	0	10	3	4	0	....	.164	.197	.192	.389	-5	-13	3	1.16	-2	0-21(6-0-15)	0	-1.4
1933*NY-N	84	148	16	38	1	1	1	12	14	10	0	....	.257	.325	.297	.622	80	-3	15	3.36	0	0-45(35-9-1)	3	-0.5
1934 NY-N	21	41	7	8	0	0	1	3	1	2	0	....	.195	.214	.268	.483	29	-4	2	1.48	-1	0-10(0-8-2)	0	-0.5
Total 5	186	420	48	100	15	2	2	44	30	24	1	....	.238	.294	.298	.591	55	-29	38	2.97	-3	0-116/1-1	5	-3.4

• PEERSON, Jack Jack Chiles Peerson b: 8/28/1910, Brunswick, GA d: 10/23/1966, Fort Walton Beach, FL BR/TR, 5'11", 175 lbs. Deb: 9/7/1935

YEAR TM-L	G	AB	R	H	2B	3B	HR	RBI	BB	SO	SB	CS	AVG	OBP	SLG	OPS	OPS+	BR/A	RC	RC/G	FR	G/POS	WS	TPW
1935 Phi-A	10	19	3	6	1	0	0	1	1	1	0	0	.316	.350	.368	.718	87	-0	2	4.71	-1	/S-4	0	-0.1
1936 Phi-A	8	34	7	11	1	1	0	5	0	3	0	1	.324	.324	.412	.735	82	-2	4	4.36	3	/S-7,2-1	1	0.2
Total 2	18	53	10	17	2	1	0	6	1	4	0	1	.321	.333	.396	.730	84	-2	6	4.49	3	/S-11,2-1	1	0.1

• PEETE, Charlie Charles "Mule" Peete b: 2/22/1929, Franklin, VA d: 11/27/1956, Caracas, Venezuela BL/TR, 5'9.5", 190 lbs. Deb: 7/17/1956

YEAR TM-L	G	AB	R	H	2B	3B	HR	RBI	BB	SO	SB	CS	AVG	OBP	SLG	OPS	OPS+	BR/A	RC	RC/G	FR	G/POS	WS	TPW
1956 StL-N	23	52	3	10	2	2	0	6	6	10	0	2	.192	.288	.308	.596	60	-4	3	1.47	1	0-21(0-21-0)	1	-0.4

• PEGUERO, Julio Julio Cesar Peguero b: 9/7/1968, San Isidro, Dominican Republic BB/TR, 6', 160 lbs. Deb: 4/8/1992

YEAR TM-L	G	AB	R	H	2B	3B	HR	RBI	BB	SO	SB	CS	AVG	OBP	SLG	OPS	OPS+	BR/A	RC	RC/G	FR	G/POS	WS	TPW
1992 Phi-N	14	9	3	2	0	0	0	0	3	3	0	0	.222	.417	.222	.639	86	0	1	4.28	-1	0-14(0-9-5)	0	-0.1

• PEGUES, Steve Steven Antone Pegues b: 5/21/1968, Pontotoc, MS BR/TR, 6'2", 190 lbs. Deb: 7/6/1994 Career OF: 39-6-26

YEAR TM-L	G	AB	R	H	2B	3B	HR	RBI	BB	SO	SB	CS	AVG	OBP	SLG	OPS	OPS+	BR/A	RC	RC/G	FR	G/POS	WS	TPW
1994 Cin-N	11	10	1	3	0	0	0	0	1	3	0	0	.300	.364	.300	.664	76	-0	1	4.57	0	/0-4(3-0-1)	0	-0.1
Pit-N	7	26	1	10	2	0	0	2	1	2	1	0	.385	.407	.462	.869	124	1	4	5.38	0	/0-7(5-2-0)	1	0.1
Yr.	18	36	2	13	2	0	0	2	2	5	1	0	.361	.395	.417	.811	110	1	5	5.16	-1	0-11(8-2-1)	1	0.0
1995 Pit-N	82	171	17	42	8	0	6	16	4	36	1	2	.246	.267	.398	.665	71	-9	17	3.30	-1	0-53(31-4-25)	0	-1.1
Total 2	100	207	19	55	10	0	6	18	6	41	2	2	.266	.290	.401	.691	78	-8	22	3.60	-1	/0-64	1	-1.1

YEAR	TM-L	G	AB	R	H	2B	3B	HR	RBI	BB	SO	SB	CS	AVG	OBP	SLG	OPS	OPS+	BR/A	RC	RC/G	FR	G/POS	WS	TPW
• PEITZ, Heinie	Henry Clement Peitz b: 11/28/1870, St. Louis, MO d: 10/23/1943, Cincinnati, OH BR/TR, 5'11", 165 lbs. Deb: 10/15/1892 C/U Career OF: 4-0-7																								
1892	StL-N	1	3	0	0	0	0	0	0	0	0	0	....	.000	.000	.000	.000	-105	-1	0	.00	0	/C-1	0	-0.1
1893	StL-N	96	362	53	92	12	9	1	45	54	20	12	....	.254	.353	.345	.698	86	-7	50	4.86	-2	C-74,S-11,O-10(4-0-6)/1-5	9	-0.1
1894	StL-N	99	338	52	89	19	9	3	49	43	21	14	....	.263	.348	.399	.748	80	-12	53	5.55	5	3-47,C-39,1-14/P-1	7	-0.3
1895	StL-N	90	334	44	95	14	12	2	65	29	20	9	....	.284	.345	.416	.761	97	-2	53	5.89	1	C-71,1-11,3-10	7	0.5
1896	Cin-N	68	211	33	63	12	5	2	34	30	15	7	....	.299	.386	.431	.817	108	3	40	6.80	-6	C-67	8	0.2
1897	Cin-N	77	266	35	78	11	7	1	44	18	....	3	....	.293	.340	.398	.739	89	-5	39	5.28	0	C-71/P-2	9	-0.2
1898	Cin-N	105	330	49	90	15	5	1	43	35	....	9	....	.273	.348	.358	.705	96	-2	46	4.97	-6	*C-101	13	0.1
1899	Cin-N	94	293	45	79	13	2	1	43	45	....	11	....	.270	.371	.338	.708	93	-1	43	5.12	-7	C-91/P-1	11	0.0
1900	Cin-N	91	294	34	75	14	1	2	34	20	....	5	....	.255	.318	.330	.648	81	-8	33	4.02	6	C-80/1-8	9	0.6
1901	Cin-N	82	269	24	82	13	5	1	24	23	....	3	....	.305	.364	.401	.765	130	11	42	5.84	5	C-49,2-21/3-6,1-2	11	2.0
1902	Cin-N	112	387	54	122	22	5	1	60	24	....	7	....	.315	.369	.406	.775	127	12	63	6.12	1	2-48,C-47/1-6,3-6	15	1.9
1903	Cin-N	105	358	45	93	15	3	0	42	37	....	7	....	.260	.331	.318	.649	77	-11	42	4.10	-6	C-78,1-11/3-9,2-4	9	-0.9
1904	Cin-N	84	272	32	66	13	2	1	30	14	....	1	....	.243	.282	.316	.598	78	-8	26	3.18	3	C-64,1-18/3-1	7	0.1
1905	Pit-N	88	278	18	62	10	0	0	27	24	....	2	....	.223	.289	.259	.548	62	-13	24	2.71	-4	C-87/2-1	5	-0.8
1906	Pit-N	40	125	13	30	8	0	0	20	13	....	1	....	.240	.321	.304	.625	91	-1	13	3.53	-2	C-38	4	0.1
1913	StL-N	3	4	1	1	0	1	0	0	0	0	0	....	.250	.250	.750	1.000	182	0	1	4.52	-1	/C-2,O-1	0	-0.1
Total	**16**	**1235**	**4124**	**532**	**1117**	**191**	**66**	**16**	**560**	**409**	**76**	**91**	**....**	**.271**	**.342**	**.361**	**.702**	**92**	**-43**	**567**	**4.87**	**-14**	**C-960/3-79,1-75,2-74,O-11,S,P**	**124**	**2.9**
• PEITZ, Joe	Joseph Peitz b: 11/8/1869, St. Louis, MO d: 12/4/1919, St. Louis, MO Deb: 6/28/1894																								
1894	StL-N	7	26	10	11	2	3	0	3	6	1	2	....	.423	.531	.731	1.262	202	5	11	19.82	0	/O-7(0-0-7)	2	0.3
• PELAEZ, Alex	Alejandro Pelaez b: 4/6/1976, San Diego, CA BR/TR, 5'9", 190 lbs. Deb: 5/16/2002																								
2002	SD-N	3	8	0	2	0	0	0	0	0	0	0	0	.250	.250	.250	.500	35	-1	0	.00	0	/1-1,2-1,3-1	0	-0.1
• PELLAGRINI, Eddie	Edward Charles Pellagrini b: 3/13/1918, Boston, MA BR/TR, 5'9", 165 lbs. Deb: 4/22/1946																								
1946	Bos-A	22	71	7	15	3	1	2	4	3	18	1	0	.211	.253	.366	.620	68	-3	6	2.69	-4	3-14/S-9	1	-0.7
1947	Bos-A	74	231	29	47	8	1	4	19	23	35	2	2	.203	.281	.299	.580	57	-14	21	2.87	-8	3-42,S-26	3	-2.2
1948	StL-A	105	290	31	69	8	3	2	27	34	40	1	2	.238	.320	.307	.627	65	-15	30	3.56	9	S-98	7	0.0
1949	StL-A	79	235	26	56	8	1	2	15	14	24	2	1	.238	.284	.306	.590	54	-16	21	2.87	-3	S-76	3	-1.4
1951	Phi-N	86	197	31	46	4	5	5	30	23	25	5	1	.234	.326	.381	.707	91	-2	26	4.41	-2	2-53/S-8,3-6	5	-0.1
1952	Cin-N	46	100	15	17	2	0	1	3	8	18	1	0	.170	.231	.220	.451	26	-10	5	1.70	-1	2-22/1-8,3-1,S-1	1	-1.0
1953	Pit-N	78	174	16	44	3	2	4	19	14	20	1	1	.253	.309	.362	.671	74	-7	21	4.17	-4	2-31,3-12/S-3	3	-0.9
1954	Pit-N	73	125	12	27	6	0	0	16	9	21	0	0	.216	.290	.264	.554	46	-10	11	2.77	-1	3-31/2-7,S-1	1	-1.0
Total	**8**	**563**	**1423**	**167**	**321**	**42**	**13**	**20**	**133**	**128**	**201**	**13**	**7**	**.226**	**.295**	**.316**	**.611**	**63**	**-76**	**140**	**3.26**	**-14**	**S-222,2-113,3-106/1-8**	**24**	**-7.2**
• PELLOW, Kit	Kit Donovan Pellow b: 8/28/1973, Kansas City, MO BR/TR, 6'1", 200 lbs. Deb: 8/14/2002																								
2002	KC-A	29	63	6	15	1	0	1	5	9	21	1	1	.238	.342	.302	.644	66	-3	7	3.53	1	3-12,1-10/D-4	1	-0.3
2003	Col-N	11	18	6	8	3	1	1	4	0	4	0	0	.444	.500	.889	1.389	222	3	8	19.92	-1	/C-7,1-1,O-1	1	0.2
Total	**2**	**40**	**81**	**12**	**23**	**4**	**1**	**2**	**9**	**9**	**25**	**1**	**1**	**.284**	**.376**	**.432**	**.808**	**101**	**0**	**15**	**6.44**	**-1**	**/3-12,1-11,C-7,D-4,O-1**	**2**	**-0.1**
• PELOUZE, Louis	Louis Henri Pelouze b: 9/10/1863, Fort Monroe, VA d: 1/9/1939, New York, NY BR/TR, 6', 175 lbs. Deb: 7/24/1886																								
1886	StL-N	1	3	0	0	0	0	0	0	0	2	0	....	.000	.000	.000	.000	-107	-1	0	.00	0	/O-1	0	0.0
• PELTIER, Dan	Daniel Edward Peltier b: 6/30/1968, Clifton Park, NY BL/TL, 6'1", 200 lbs. Deb: 6/26/1992 Career OF: 4-0-63																								
1992	Tex-A	12	24	1	4	0	0	0	2	0	3	0	0	.167	.167	.167	.333	-7	-3	1	.90	-1	O-10(1-0-9)	0	-0.4
1993	Tex-A	65	160	23	43	7	1	1	17	20	27	0	4	.269	.354	.344	.697	92	-3	19	4.10	0	O-55(2-0-54)/1-5	2	-0.5
1996	SF-N	31	59	3	15	2	0	0	9	7	9	0	0	.254	.333	.288	.621	69	-2	6	3.51	-1	1-13/O-1	1	-0.4
Total	**3**	**108**	**243**	**27**	**62**	**9**	**1**	**1**	**28**	**27**	**39**	**0**	**4**	**.255**	**.332**	**.313**	**.645**	**78**	**-9**	**26**	**3.63**	**-1**	**/O-66,1-18**	**3**	**-1.3**
• PELTZ, John	John Peltz b: 4/23/1861, New Orleans, LA d: 2/27/1906, New Orleans, LA BR/TR, 5'8", 175 lbs. Deb: 5/1/1884 Career OF: 107-123-0																								
1884	Ind-a	106	393	40	86	13	17	3	0	7	....	....	....	.219	.236	.361	.598	95	-3	34	3.08	3	*O-106(106-0-0)	5	-0.3
1888	Bal-a	1	4	1	1	0	0	0	0	0	....	1	....	.250	.250	.250	.500	62	-0	1	4.61	0	/O-1	0	-0.1
1890	Bro-a	98	384	55	87	9	6	1	33	32	....	10	....	.227	.289	.289	.579	73	-13	36	3.20	2	*O-98(0-98-0)	6	-1.3
	Syr-a	5	17	2	3	1	1	0	2	3	....	0	....	.176	.300	.353	.653	103	0	2	3.49	1	/O-5(0-5-0)	1	0.1
	Tol-a	20	73	8	18	2	2	0	13	3	....	7	....	.247	.286	.329	.614	79	-2	9	4.37	0	O-20(0-20-0)	1	-0.3
	Yr.	123	474	65	108	12	9	1	48	38	....	17	....	.228	.289	.297	.587	75	-16	47	3.39	3	*O-123(0-123-0)	8	-1.5
Total	**3**	**230**	**871**	**106**	**195**	**25**	**26**	**4**	**48**	**45**	**....**	**18**	**....**	**.224**	**.266**	**.326**	**.592**	**83**	**-19**	**82**	**3.26**	**5**	**O-230**	**13**	**-1.9**
• PEMBERTON, Brock	Brock Pemberton b: 11/6/1953, Tulsa, OK BB/TL, 6'3", 190 lbs. Deb: 9/10/1974																								
1974	NY-N	11	22	0	4	0	0	0	1	0	3	0	1	.182	.182	.182	.364	2	-3	1	.78	1	/1-4	0	-0.3
1975	NY-N	2	2	0	0	0	0	0	0	0	1	0	0	.000	.000	.000	.000	-105	-1	0	.00	0	....	0	-0.1
Total	**2**	**13**	**24**	**0**	**4**	**0**	**0**	**0**	**1**	**0**	**4**	**0**	**1**	**.167**	**.167**	**.167**	**.333**	**-7**	**-4**	**1**	**.70**	**1**	**/1-4**	**0**	**-0.4**
• PEMBERTON, Rudy	Rudy Hector (Perez) Pemberton b: 12/17/1969, San Pedro de Macoris, Dominican Republic BR/TR, 6'1", 185 lbs. Deb: 4/26/1995 Career OF: 7-0-37																								
1995	Det-A	12	30	3	9	3	1	0	3	1	5	0	0	.300	.344	.467	.810	109	0	4	4.08	0	/O-8(6-0-2),D-3	1	0.0
1996	Bos-A	13	41	11	21	8	0	1	10	2	4	3	1	.512	.556	.780	1.336	228	8	18	23.73	0	O-13(1-0-12)	4	0.7
1997	Bos-A	27	63	8	15	2	0	2	10	4	13	0	0	.238	.314	.365	.679	75	-2	8	4.39	0	O-23(0-0-23)	2	-0.3
Total	**3**	**52**	**134**	**22**	**45**	**13**	**1**	**3**	**23**	**7**	**22**	**3**	**1**	**.336**	**.395**	**.515**	**.909**	**129**	**6**	**30**	**8.68**	**0**	**/O-44,D-3**	**7**	**0.4**
• PENA, Angel	Angel Maria Pena b: 2/16/1975, San Pedro de Macoris, Dominican Republic BR/TR, 5'10", 228 lbs. Deb: 9/8/1998																								
1998	LA-N	6	13	1	3	0	0	0	0	0	6	0	0	.231	.231	.231	.462	23	-1	1	1.87	0	/C-4	0	-0.1
1999	LA-N	43	120	14	25	6	0	4	21	12	24	0	1	.208	.280	.358	.639	64	-8	11	2.72	2	C-43	2	-0.3
2001	LA-N	22	54	3	11	1	0	1	2	1	17	0	0	.204	.218	.278	.496	29	-6	3	2.04	6	C-15	1	0.1
Total	**3**	**71**	**187**	**18**	**39**	**7**	**0**	**5**	**23**	**13**	**47**	**0**	**1**	**.209**	**.260**	**.326**	**.586**	**51**	**-15**	**15**	**2.48**	**8**	**/C-62**	**3**	**-0.3**
• PENA, Bert	Adalberto (Rivera) Pena b: 7/11/1959, Santurce, Puerto Rico BR/TR, 5'11", 165 lbs. Deb: 9/14/1981																								
1981	Hou-N	4	2	0	1	0	0	0	0	0	0	0	0	.500	.500	.500	1.000	194	0	1	6.84	-1	/S-3	0	-0.1
1983	Hou-N	4	8	0	1	0	0	0	0	2	2	0	0	.125	.300	.125	.425	23	-1	0	1.76	-1	/S-4	0	-0.1
1984	Hou-N	24	39	3	8	1	0	1	4	3	8	0	0	.205	.262	.308	.570	64	-2	2	1.89	-1	S-21	1	-0.1
1985	Hou-N	20	29	7	8	2	0	0	4	1	6	0	0	.276	.300	.345	.645	82	-1	3	3.18	-1	/3-7,S-6,2-2	1	-0.2
1986	Hou-N	15	29	3	6	1	0	0	2	5	5	1	0	.207	.324	.241	.565	60	-1	2	2.03	-2	S-10/3-2,2-1	0	-0.3
1987	Hou-N	21	46	5	7	0	0	0	0	2	7	0	0	.152	.204	.152	.356	-4	-7	1	.71	-2	S-19/3-1	0	-0.7
Total	**6**	**88**	**153**	**18**	**31**	**4**	**0**	**1**	**10**	**13**	**28**	**1**	**0**	**.203**	**.269**	**.248**	**.518**	**47**	**-11**	**9**	**1.85**	**-7**	**/S-63,3-10,2-3**	**2**	**-1.4**
• PENA, Carlos	Carlos Felipe Pena b: 5/17/1978, Santo Domingo, Dominican Republic BL/TL, 6'2", 210 lbs. Deb: 9/5/2001																								
2001	Tex-A	22	62	6	16	4	1	3	12	10	17	0	0	.258	.361	.500	.861	120	2	12	6.70	1	1-16/D-1	3	0.1
2002	Oak-A	40	124	12	27	4	0	7	16	15	38	0	0	.218	.307	.419	.726	90	-2	16	4.45	6	1-40	4	0.1
	Det-A	75	273	31	69	13	4	12	36	26	73	2	2	.253	.322	.462	.784	111	3	40	5.12	-7	1-73/D-2	7	-1.0
	Yr.	115	397	43	96	17	4	19	52	41	111	2	2	.242	.317	.448	.766	105	2	57	4.90	-1	*1-113/D-2	11	-0.9
2003	Det-A	131	452	51	112	21	6	18	50	53	123	4	5	.248	.335	.440	.775	111	5	68	5.14	-4	*1-128/D-1	9	-1.0
Total	**3**	**268**	**911**	**100**	**224**	**42**	**11**	**40**	**114**	**104**	**251**	**6**	**7**	**.246**	**.329**	**.448**	**.777**	**109**	**9**	**136**	**5.14**	**-5**	**1-257/D-4**	**23**	**-1.8**
• PENA, Elvis	Elvis (Mendez) Pena b: 9/15/1976, San Pedro de Macoris, Dominican Republic BB/TR, 5'11", 155 lbs. Deb: 9/2/2000																								
2000	Col-N	10	9	1	3	1	0	0	1	1	1	1	0	.333	.400	.444	.844	90	0	1	3.23	0	/S-3,2-1	0	0.0
2001	Mil-N	15	40	5	9	2	0	0	6	6	6	2	0	.225	.340	.275	.615	64	-1	4	3.00	3	2-11	1	0.2
Total	**2**	**25**	**49**	**6**	**12**	**3**	**0**	**0**	**7**	**7**	**7**	**3**	**0**	**.245**	**.351**	**.306**	**.657**	**68**	**-1**	**5**	**3.05**	**3**	**/2-12,S-3**	**1**	**0.2**
• PENA, Geronimo	Geronimo (Martinez) Pena b: 3/29/1967, Los Alcarrizos, Dominican Republic BB/TR, 6'1", 195 lbs. Deb: 9/5/1990																								
1990	StL-N	18	45	5	11	2	0	0	2	4	14	1	1	.244	.320	.289	.609	69	-2	5	3.38	0	2-11	1	-0.2
1991	StL-N	104	185	38	45	8	3	5	17	18	45	15	5	.243	.327	.400	.727	103	2	27	4.82	8	2-83/O-4(4-0-0)	6	1.1

YEAR TM-L	G	AB	R	H	2B	3B	HR	RBI	BB	SO	SB	CS	AVG	OBP	SLG	OPS	OPS+	BR/A	RC	RC/G	FR	G/POS	WS	TPW
1992 StL-N	62	203	31	62	12	1	7	31	24	37	13	8	.305	.392	.478	.870	150	13	39	6.91	8	2-57	12	2.4
1993 StL-N	74	254	34	65	19	2	5	30	25	71	13	5	.256	.332	.406	.738	98	-0	36	4.77	-1	2-64	8	0.2
1994 StL-N	83	213	33	54	13	1	11	34	24	54	9	1	.254	.346	.479	.825	114	6	38	6.06	5	2-59/3-1	10	1.3
1995 StL-N	32	101	20	27	6	1	1	8	16	30	3	2	.267	.373	.376	.749	99	0	15	4.86	0	2-25	3	0.1
1996 Cle-A	5	9	1	1	0	0	1	2	1	4	0	0	.111	.200	.444	.644	57	-1	0	.00	-1	/3-3,2-1	0	-0.1
Total 7	378	1010	162	265	60	8	30	124	112	255	54	22	.262	.349	.427	.776	111	18	159	5.34	19	2-300/3-4,0-4	40	4.9

• PENA, Roberto Roberto Cesar "Baby" Pena
b: 4/17/1937, Santo Domingo, Dominican Republic d: 7/23/1982, Santiago, Dominican Republic BR/TR, 5'8", 175 lbs. Deb: 4/12/1965

YEAR TM-L	G	AB	R	H	2B	3B	HR	RBI	BB	SO	SB	CS	AVG	OBP	SLG	OPS	OPS+	BR/A	RC	RC/G	FR	G/POS	WS	TPW
1965 Chi-N	51	170	17	37	5	1	2	12	16	19	1	2	.218	.293	.294	.587	64	-8	14	2.71	-6	S-50	2	-1.1
1966 Chi-N	6	17	0	3	2	0	0	1	0	4	0	0	.176	.176	.294	.471	28	-2	1	1.70	-1	/S-5	0	-0.3
1968 Phi-N	138	500	56	130	13	2	1	38	34	63	3	5	.260	.310	.300	.610	84	-11	45	3.10	-5	*S-133	14	-0.5
1969 SD-N	139	472	44	118	16	3	4	30	21	63	0	3	.250	.286	.322	.608	73	-19	41	3.01	-5	S-65,2-33,3-27,1-12	6	-1.8
1970 Oak-A	19	58	4	15	1	0	0	3	3	4	1	1	.259	.295	.276	.571	60	-3	4	2.48	-1	S-12/3-5	1	-0.4
Mil-A	121	416	36	99	19	1	3	42	25	45	3	5	.238	.284	.310	.595	63	-23	34	2.64	-8	S-99,2-15/1-7	4	-1.9
Yr.	140	474	40	114	20	1	3	45	28	49	4	6	.241	.286	.306	.592	63	-26	38	2.62	-9	*S-111,2-15/1-7,3-5	5	-2.3
1971 Mil-A	113	274	17	65	9	3	3	28	15	37	2	1	.237	.279	.325	.604	71	-11	24	2.90	1	1-50,3-37,S-23/2-1	4	-1.1
Total 6	587	1907	174	467	65	10	13	154	114	235	10	17	.245	.291	.310	.601	72	-77	164	2.88	-26	S-387/1-69,3-69,2-49	31	-7.1

• PENA, Tony Antonio Francisco (Padilla) Pena b: 6/4/1957, Monte Cristi, Dominican Republic BR/TR, 6', 181 lbs. Deb: 9/1/1980 M Career OF: 0-0-3

YEAR TM-L	G	AB	R	H	2B	3B	HR	RBI	BB	SO	SB	CS	AVG	OBP	SLG	OPS	OPS+	BR/A	RC	RC/G	FR	G/POS	WS	TPW
1980 Pit-N	8	21	1	9	1	1	0	1	0	4	0	1	.429	.429	.571	1.000	174	1	4	7.71	0	/C-6	1	0.2
1981 Pit-N	66	210	16	63	9	1	2	17	8	23	1	2	.300	.329	.381	.710	98	-2	25	4.30	3	C-64	7	0.5
1982 Pit-N★	138	497	53	147	28	4	11	63	17	57	2	5	.296	.324	.435	.759	107	1	63	4.48	-2	*C-137	16	0.6
1983 Pit-N	151	542	51	163	22	3	15	70	31	73	6	7	.301	.339	.435	.774	110	4	75	4.96	-3	*C-149	21	0.9
1984 Pit-N★	147	546	77	156	27	2	15	78	36	79	12	8	.286	.334	.425	.759	112	6	74	4.76	7	*C-146	21	2.2
1985 Pit-N★	147	546	53	136	27	2	10	59	29	67	12	8	.249	.287	.361	.648	81	-17	51	3.05	13	*C-146/1-1	11	0.3
1986 Pit-N★	144	510	56	147	26	2	10	52	53	69	9	10	.288	.356	.406	.762	107	3	68	4.62	6	*C-139/1-4	15	1.7
1987*StL-N	116	384	40	82	13	4	5	44	36	54	6	1	.214	.283	.307	.590	55	-25	30	2.52	-7	*C-112/1-4,0-2(0-0-2)	6	-2.6
1988 StL-N	149	505	55	133	23	1	10	51	33	60	6	2	.263	.310	.372	.682	94	-5	56	3.86	4	*C-142/1-3	17	0.8
1989 StL-N★	141	424	36	110	17	2	4	37	35	33	5	3	.259	.319	.337	.656	85	-8	41	3.26	5	*C-134/0-1	10	0.5
1990*Bos-A	143	491	62	129	19	1	7	56	43	71	8	6	.263	.323	.348	.672	84	-11	50	3.43	6	*C-142/1-1	15	0.4
1991 Bos-A	141	464	45	107	23	2	5	48	37	53	8	3	.231	.293	.321	.614	66	-21	40	2.76	1	*C-140	9	-1.1
1992 Bos-A	133	410	39	99	21	1	1	38	24	61	3	2	.241	.285	.305	.590	61	-22	35	2.77	-2	*C-132	6	-1.5
1993 Bos-A	126	304	20	55	11	0	4	19	25	46	1	3	.181	.248	.257	.504	34	-30	18	1.75	-1	*C-125/D-1	7	-2.2
1994 Cle-A	40	112	18	33	8	1	2	10	9	11	0	1	.295	.347	.438	.785	100	-1	15	4.45	0	C-40	3	0.2
1995*Cle-A	91	263	25	69	15	0	5	28	14	44	1	0	.262	.302	.376	.679	74	-11	28	3.69	0	C-91	6	-0.5
1996*Cle-A	67	174	14	34	4	0	1	27	15	25	0	1	.195	.259	.236	.495	26	-20	10	1.72	2	C-67	3	-1.3
1997 Chi-A	31	67	4	11	1	0	0	8	8	13	0	0	.164	.253	.179	.432	16	-8	3	1.38	0	C-30/3-1	1	-0.6
*Hou-N	9	19	2	4	3	0	0	2	2	3	0	0	.211	.286	.368	.654	72	-1	2	3.70	1	/C-8	0	0.0
Total 18	1988	6489	667	1687	298	27	107	708	455	846	80	63	.260	.311	.364	.674	84	-166	687	3.56	35	*C-1950/1-13,0-3,3-1,D-1	175	-1.5

• PENA, Wily Mo Wily Mo Pena b: 1/23/1982, Laguna Salada, Dominican Republic BR/TR, 6'3", 215 lbs. Deb: 9/10/2002 Career OF: 11-26-15

YEAR TM-L	G	AB	R	H	2B	3B	HR	RBI	BB	SO	SB	CS	AVG	OBP	SLG	OPS	OPS+	BR/A	RC	RC/G	FR	G/POS	WS	TPW
2002 Cin-N	13	18	1	4	0	0	1	1	0	11	0	0	.222	.222	.389	.611	55	-1	2	3.00	0	/0-4(3-0-1)	0	-0.2
2003 Cin-N	80	165	20	36	6	1	5	16	12	53	3	2	.218	.283	.358	.641	67	-9	17	3.37	-4	0-47(8-26-14)/3-1	1	-1.3
Total 2	93	183	21	40	6	1	6	17	12	64	3	2	.219	.278	.361	.638	66	-10	18	3.34	-4	/0-51,3-1	1	-1.5

• PENCE, Elmer Elmer Clair Pence b: 8/17/1900, Valley Springs, CA d: 9/17/1968, San Francisco, CA BR/TR, 6', 185 lbs. Deb: 8/23/1922

YEAR TM-L	G	AB	R	H	2B	3B	HR	RBI	BB	SO	SB	CS	AVG	OBP	SLG	OPS	OPS+	BR/A	RC	RC/G	FR	G/POS	WS	TPW
1922 Chi-A	1	0	0	0	0	0	0	0	0	0	0	0	....	....	....	....	-101	0	0	....	0	/0-1	0	0.0

• PENDLETON, Jim James Edward Pendleton b: 1/7/1924, St. Charles, MO d: 3/20/1996, Houston, TX BR/TR, 6', 185 lbs. Deb: 4/17/1953 Career OF: 189-42-63

YEAR TM-L	G	AB	R	H	2B	3B	HR	RBI	BB	SO	SB	CS	AVG	OBP	SLG	OPS	OPS+	BR/A	RC	RC/G	FR	G/POS	WS	TPW
1953 Mil-N	120	251	48	75	12	4	7	27	7	36	6	5	.299	.323	.462	.785	108	1	35	5.11	4	*0-105(75-15-25)/S-7	9	0.2
1954 Mil-N	71	173	20	38	3	1	1	16	4	21	2	1	.220	.237	.266	.503	33	-17	11	2.06	0	0-50(23-18-11)	1	-2.0
1955 Mil-N	8	10	0	0	0	0	0	0	0	2	0	0	.000	.000	.000	.000	-105	-3	0	.00	-1	/3-1,0-1,S-1	0	-0.4
1956 Mil-N	14	11	0	0	0	0	0	0	1	3	0	0	.000	.083	.000	.083	-80	-3	0	.00	-2	/S-3,3-2,1-1,2-1	0	-0.4
1957 Pit-N	46	59	9	18	1	1	0	9	9	14	0	0	.305	.406	.356	.762	110	2	9	5.28	-1	/0-9(2-1-6),3-2,S-1	1	0.0
1958 Pit-N	3	3	0	1	0	0	0	0	0	0	0	0	.333	.333	.333	.667	79	-0	0	4.50	0	....	0	0.0
1959 Cin-N	65	113	13	29	2	0	3	9	8	18	3	0	.257	.311	.354	.665	74	-3	12	3.68	-1	0-24(24-0-0),3-16/S-3	2	-0.5
1962 Hou-N	117	321	30	79	12	2	8	36	14	57	0	0	.246	.282	.371	.653	79	-11	33	3.43	-5	0-90(65-7-21)/1-8,3-3,S-2	4	-2.0
Total 8	444	941	120	240	30	8	19	97	43	151	11	6	.255	.292	.365	.656	77	-34	100	3.64	-5	0-279/3-24,S-17,1-9,2-1	17	-5.1

• PENDLETON, Terry Terry Lee Pendleton b: 7/16/1960, Los Angeles, CA BB/TR, 5'9", 180 lbs. Deb: 7/18/1984

YEAR TM-L	G	AB	R	H	2B	3B	HR	RBI	BB	SO	SB	CS	AVG	OBP	SLG	OPS	OPS+	BR/A	RC	RC/G	FR	G/POS	WS	TPW
1984 StL-N	67	262	37	85	16	3	1	33	16	32	20	5	.324	.363	.420	.783	123	9	40	5.53	3	3-66	11	1.2
1985*StL-N	149	559	56	134	16	3	5	69	37	75	17	12	.240	.287	.306	.593	66	-28	45	2.63	30	*3-149	10	0.0
1986 StL-N	159	578	56	138	26	5	1	59	34	59	24	6	.239	.282	.306	.588	63	-28	50	2.88	37	*3-156/0-1	13	0.7
1987*StL-N	159	583	82	167	29	4	12	96	70	74	19	12	.286	.365	.412	.777	103	3	86	5.05	17	*3-158	21	1.8
1988 StL-N	110	391	44	99	20	2	6	53	21	51	3	3	.253	.295	.361	.655	86	-9	39	3.43	7	*3-101	9	-0.1
1989 StL-N	162	613	83	162	28	5	13	74	44	81	9	5	.264	.314	.390	.703	97	-4	72	4.07	26	*3-161	18	2.5
1990 StL-N	121	447	46	103	20	2	6	58	30	58	7	5	.230	.280	.324	.605	66	-23	38	2.81	6	*3-117	5	-1.7
1991*Atl-N	153	586	94	**187**	34	8	22	86	43	70	10	2	**.319**	.367	.517	.884	138	29	107	6.73	23	*3-148	27	5.5
1992*Atl-N★	160	640	98	**199**	39	1	21	105	37	67	5	2	.311	.349	.473	.822	123	18	101	5.79	19	*3-158	35	4.1
1993*Atl-N	161	633	81	172	33	1	17	84	36	97	5	1	.272	.314	.408	.722	91	-10	77	4.26	15	*3-161	16	0.8
1994 Atl-N	77	309	25	78	18	3	7	30	12	57	2	0	.252	.280	.398	.678	73	-13	32	3.61	6	3-77	6	-0.6
1995 Fla-N	133	513	70	149	32	1	14	78	38	84	1	2	.290	.342	.439	.780	104	1	76	5.47	4	*3-129	17	0.7
1996 Fla-N	111	406	30	102	20	1	7	58	26	75	0	2	.251	.301	.357	.658	75	-17	42	3.49	2	*3-108	9	-1.2
*Atl-N	42	162	21	33	6	0	4	17	15	36	2	1	.204	.271	.315	.586	51	-12	12	2.40	-2	3-41	0	-1.4
Yr.	153	568	51	135	26	1	11	75	41	111	2	3	.238	.292	.345	.638	68	-29	54	3.16	0	*3-149	9	-2.6
1997 Cin-N	50	113	11	28	9	0	1	17	12	14	2	1	.248	.320	.354	.674	75	-4	13	4.14	0	3-32	3	-0.4
1998 KC-A	79	237	17	61	10	0	3	29	15	49	1	0	.257	.302	.338	.639	64	-13	25	3.72	-2	D-40,3-23	2	-1.6
Total 15	1893	7032	851	1897	356	39	140	946	486	979	127	59	.270	.318	.391	.710	92	-100	856	4.22	190	*3-1785/D-40,0-1	202	10.2

• PENN, Shannon Shannon Dion Penn b: 9/11/1969, Cincinnati, OH BB/TR, 5'10", 160 lbs. Deb: 4/28/1995

YEAR TM-L	G	AB	R	H	2B	3B	HR	RBI	BB	SO	SB	CS	AVG	OBP	SLG	OPS	OPS+	BR/A	RC	RC/G	FR	G/POS	WS	TPW
1995 Det-A	3	9	0	3	0	0	0	0	1	2	0	0	.333	.400	.333	.733	94	-0	1	2.20	0	/2-3	0	0.0
1996 Det-A	6	14	0	1	0	0	0	1	0	3	0	0	.071	.071	.071	.143	-64	-4	0	.15	0	/D-4,0-1	0	-0.4
Total 2	9	23	0	4	0	0	0	1	1	5	0	0	.174	.208	.174	.382	2	-4	1	.93	0	/D-4,2-3,0-1	0	-0.3

• PENNYFEATHER, Will William Nathaniel Pennyfeather b: 5/25/1968, Perth Amboy, NJ BR/TR, 6'2", 195 lbs. Deb: 6/27/1992 Career OF: 3-21-7

YEAR TM-L	G	AB	R	H	2B	3B	HR	RBI	BB	SO	SB	CS	AVG	OBP	SLG	OPS	OPS+	BR/A	RC	RC/G	FR	G/POS	WS	TPW
1992 Pit-N	15	9	2	2	0	0	0	0	0	0	0	0	.222	.222	.222	.444	26	-1	0	.76	-1	0-10(1-6-5)	0	-0.2
1993 Pit-N	21	34	4	7	1	0	0	2	0	6	0	1	.206	.206	.235	.441	18	-4	1	1.10	-1	0-17(1-15-2)	0	-0.5
1994 Pit-N	4	3	0	0	0	0	0	0	0	0	0	0	.000	.000	.000	.000	-99	-1	0	.00	0	/0-1	0	-0.1
Total 3	40	46	6	9	1	0	0	2	0	6	0	1	.196	.196	.217	.413	12	-6	1	.94	-1	/0-28	0	-0.8

• PEOPLES, Jimmy James Elsworth Peoples b: 10/8/1863, Big Beaver, MI d: 8/29/1920, Detroit, MI TR, 5'8", 200 lbs. Deb: 5/29/1884 U Career OF: 5-6-24

YEAR TM-L	G	AB	R	H	2B	3B	HR	RBI	BB	SO	SB	CS	AVG	OBP	SLG	OPS	OPS+	BR/A	RC	RC/G	FR	G/POS	WS	TPW
1884 Cin-a	69	267	28	45	2	2	1	16	6	....	....	....	.169	.187	.202	.389	26	-22	10	1.28	0	S-47,C-14,0-10(0-4-6)/1-1,3	4	-1.8
1885 Cin-a	7	22	1	4	0	0	0	1	1	....	....	....	.182	.217	.182	.399	27	-1	1	1.34	-1	/C-5,P-2,0-1	0	-1.5
Bro-a	41	151	21	30	4	1	1	15	5	....	....	....	.199	.229	.258	.488	53	-8	9	2.05	4	C-37/S-2,1-3,1-0-1	2	-0.1
Yr.	48	173	22	34	4	1	1	16	6	....	....	....	.197	.228	.249	.476	50	-10	10	1.95	3	C-42/0-2(0-1-1),P-2,S-2,1,3	2	-1.6
1886 Bro-a	93	340	43	74	7	3	3	38	20	....	20	....	.218	.261	.282	.543	70	-13	31	3.15	9	C-76,S-14/0-8(4-1-3),3-1	9	0.2
1887 Bro-a	73	284	36	84	14	2	1	38	16	....	22	....	.296	.306	.332	.638	77	-9	35	4.69	0	C-57/0-8(1-0-7),1-4,S-4,2	6	-0.3
1888 Bro-a	32	103	15	20	5	3	0	17	8	....	10	....	.194	.259	.301	.560	79	-2	11	3.54	-1	C-25/S-5,0-2(0-0-2)	4	-0.1

YEAR TM-L	G	AB	R	H	2B	3B	HR	RBI	BB	SO	SB	CS	AVG	OBP	SLG	OPS	OPS+	BR/A	RC	RC/G	FR	G/POS	WS	TPW
1889 Col-a	29	100	13	23	6	2	1	16	6	8	3	....	.230	.274	.360	.634	84	-2	11	3.76	-3	C-22/0-5(0-0-5),2-2,S-1	2	-0.3
Total 6	**344**	**1267**	**157**	**280**	**38**	**13**	**7**	**141**	**62**	**8**	**55**	**....**	**.221**	**.252**	**.279**	**.531**	**61**	**-58**	**108**	**2.95**	**9**	**C-236/S-73,0-35,1-6,2-3,3-3,P**	**27**	**-3.9**
• PEPITONE, Joe	Joseph Anthony "Pepi" Pepitone b: 10/9/1940, Brooklyn, NY BL/TL, 6'2", 200 lbs. Deb: 4/10/1962 C Career OF: 36-386-83																							
1962 NY-A	63	138	14	33	3	2	7	17	3	21	1	1	.239	.255	.442	.697	86	-4	13	3.22	-0	0-32(14-7-13),1-16	2	-0.5
1963*NY-A★	157	580	79	157	16	3	27	89	23	63	3	5	.271	.307	.448	.755	109	3	76	4.63	1	*1-143,0-16(0-7-9)	18	-0.5
1964*NY-A★	160	613	71	154	12	3	28	100	24	63	2	1	.251	.283	.418	.700	90	-10	67	3.74	2	*1-155,0-30(0-28-3)	13	-1.9
1965 NY-A★	143	531	51	131	18	3	18	62	43	59	4	2	.247	.306	.394	.699	98	-3	62	4.01	-2	*1-115,0-41(2-3-36)	13	-1.4
1966 NY-A	152	585	85	149	21	4	31	83	29	58	4	3	.255	.292	.463	.755	118	10	74	4.37	4	*1-119,0-55(0-49-9)	17	0.6
1967 NY-A	133	501	45	126	18	3	13	64	34	62	1	3	.251	.303	.377	.680	104	0	53	3.59	0	*0-123(0-123-0)/1-6	14	-0.4
1968 NY-A	108	380	41	93	9	3	15	56	37	45	8	2	.245	.313	.403	.716	119	9	48	4.35	-6	0-92(4-88-0),1-12	15	0.0
1969 NY-A	135	513	49	124	16	3	27	70	30	42	8	6	.242	.285	.442	.727	105	-2	59	3.89	-3	*1-132	12	-1.5
1970 Hou-N	75	279	44	70	9	5	14	35	18	28	5	2	.251	.299	.470	.768	107	1	37	4.51	-2	1-50,0-28(15-3-13)	7	-0.5
Chi-N	56	213	38	57	9	2	12	44	15	15	0	2	.268	.316	.498	.813	102	-1	33	5.32	-1	0-56(0-56-0),1-13	7	-0.4
Yr.	131	492	82	127	18	7	26	79	33	43	5	4	.258	.306	.482	.788	105	-0	69	4.86	-2	0-84(15-59-13),1-63	14	-0.9
1971 Chi-N	115	427	50	131	19	4	16	61	24	41	1	2	.307	.349	.482	.832	116	8	67	5.67	0	1-95,0-23(1-22-0)	14	0.0
1972 Chi-N	66	214	23	56	5	0	8	21	13	22	1	2	.262	.313	.397	.710	91	-3	26	4.13	-2	1-66	5	-1.0
1973 Chi-N	31	112	16	30	3	0	3	18	8	6	3	1	.268	.322	.375	.697	86	-2	14	4.47	0	1-28	2	-0.4
Atl-N	3	11	0	4	0	0	0	1	1	1	0	0	.364	.417	.364	.780	110	0	1	3.20	-1	/1-3	0	-0.1
Yr.	34	123	16	34	3	0	3	19	9	7	3	1	.276	.331	.374	.705	88	-2	15	4.35	-1	1-31	2	-0.5
Total 12	**1397**	**5097**	**606**	**1315**	**158**	**35**	**219**	**721**	**302**	**526**	**41**	**32**	**.258**	**.303**	**.432**	**.735**	**105**	**7**	**629**	**4.26**	**-8**	**1-953,0-496**	**139**	**-8.1**
• PEPLOSKI, Henry	Henry Stephen "Pep" Peploski b: 9/15/1905, Garlin, Poland d: 1/28/1982, Dover, NJ BL/TR, 5'9", 155 lbs. Deb: 9/19/1929																							
1929 Bos-N	6	10	1	2	0	0	0	1	1	3	0	....	.200	.273	.200	.473	20	-1	1	1.83	0	/3-2	0	-0.1
• PEPLOSKI, Pepper	Joseph Aloysius Peploski b: 9/12/1891, Brooklyn, NY d: 7/13/1972, New York, NY BR/TR, 5'8", 155 lbs. Deb: 6/24/1913																							
1913 Det-A	2	4	1	2	0	0	0	0	0	0	0	....	.500	.500	.500	1.000	196	0	1	12.24	0	/3-2	0	0.0
• PEPPER, Don	Donald Hoyte Pepper b: 10/8/1943, Saratoga Springs, NY BL/TR, 6'4.5", 215 lbs. Deb: 9/10/1966																							
1966 Det-A	4	3	0	0	0	0	0	0	0	1	0	0	.000	.000	.000	.000	-98	-1	0	.00	0	/1-1	0	-0.1
• PEPPER, Ray	Raymond Watson Pepper b: 8/5/1905, Decatur, AL d: 3/24/1996, Belle Mina, AL BR/TR, 6'2", 195 lbs. Deb: 4/15/1932 Career OF: 148-46-39																							
1932 StL-N	21	57	3	14	2	1	0	7	5	13	1	....	.246	.306	.316	.622	66	-3	6	3.48	-1	0-17(16-0-1)	1	-0.4
1933 StL-N	3	9	2	2	0	0	1	2	0	1	0	....	.222	.222	.556	.778	110	0	1	1.92	0	/0-2(2-0-0)	0	0.0
1934 StL-A	148	564	71	168	24	6	7	101	29	67	1	4	.298	.333	.399	.732	81	-19	73	4.81	1	*0-136(101-37-1)	11	-2.3
1935 StL-A	92	261	20	66	15	3	4	37	20	32	0	2	.253	.306	.379	.685	73	-12	30	3.99	-2	0-57(27-4-26)	3	-1.6
1936 StL-A	75	124	13	35	5	0	2	23	5	23	0	2	.282	.310	.371	.681	66	-8	13	3.87	-1	0-18(2-5-11)	1	-0.9
Total 5	**339**	**1015**	**109**	**285**	**46**	**10**	**14**	**170**	**59**	**136**	**2**	**8**	**.281**	**.321**	**.387**	**.708**	**77**	**-42**	**123**	**4.37**	**-3**	**0-230**	**16**	**-5.2**
• PERALTA, Jhonny	Jhonny Antonio Peralta b: 5/28/1982, Santiago, Dominican Republic BR/TR, 6'1", 180 lbs. Deb: 6/12/2003																							
2003 Cle-A	77	242	24	55	10	1	4	21	20	65	1	3	.227	.297	.326	.623	67	-13	23	3.13	1	S-72/3-6	5	-0.6
• PERCONTE, Jack	John Patrick Perconte b: 8/31/1954, Joliet, IL BL/TR, 5'10", 160 lbs. Deb: 9/13/1980																							
1980 LA-N	14	17	2	4	0	0	0	2	2	1	3	0	.235	.316	.235	.551	57	-0	2	2.86	0	/2-9	1	0.0
1981 LA-N	8	9	2	2	0	1	0	1	2	2	1	1	.222	.364	.444	.808	133	0	1	4.64	3	/2-2	1	0.4
1982 Cle-A	93	219	27	52	4	4	0	15	22	25	9	3	.237	.307	.292	.599	66	-9	22	3.30	1	2-82/D-2	4	-0.5
1983 Cle-A	14	26	1	7	1	0	0	0	5	2	3	1	.269	.387	.308	.695	91	0	4	5.20	2	2-13	1	0.3
1984 Sea-A	155	612	93	180	24	4	0	31	57	47	29	6	.294	.359	.346	.705	97	4	84	4.96	-6	*2-150	20	0.6
1985 Sea-A	125	485	60	128	17	7	2	23	50	36	31	2	.264	.336	.340	.677	85	-3	62	4.48	1	*2-125	13	0.5
1986 Chi-A	24	73	6	16	1	0	0	4	11	10	2	0	.219	.321	.233	.554	52	-4	6	2.80	-1	2-24	1	-0.4
Total 7	**433**	**1441**	**191**	**389**	**47**	**16**	**2**	**76**	**149**	**123**	**78**	**13**	**.270**	**.342**	**.329**	**.671**	**86**	**-11**	**181**	**4.39**	**0**	**2-405/D-2**	**41**	**0.9**
• PEREZ, Antonio	Antonio Miguel Perez b: 1/26/1980, Bani, Dominican Republic BR/TR, 5'11", 170 lbs. Deb: 5/14/2003																							
2003 TB-A	48	125	19	31	6	1	2	12	18	34	4	1	.248	.347	.360	.707	89	-1	17	4.77	-9	2-31/3-6,S-6,D-2	3	-0.8
• PEREZ, Danny	Daniel Perez b: 2/26/1971, El Paso, TX BR/TR, 5'10", 188 lbs. Deb: 6/30/1996																							
1996 Mil-A	4	4	0	0	0	0	0	0	0	0	0	0	.000	.000	.000	.000	-96	-1	0	.00	0	/0-3(2-1-0)	0	-0.1
• PEREZ, Eddie	Eduardo Perez b: 5/4/1968, Ciudad Ojeda, Venezuela BR/TR, 6'1", 175 lbs. Deb: 9/10/1995																							
1995 Atl-N	7	13	1	4	1	0	1	4	0	2	0	0	.308	.308	.615	.923	132	0	2	7.38	0	/C-5,1-1	1	0.1
1996*Atl-N	68	156	19	40	9	1	4	17	8	19	0	0	.256	.297	.404	.701	78	-6	17	3.72	1	C-54/1-7	5	-0.2
1997*Atl-N	73	191	20	41	5	0	6	18	10	35	0	1	.215	.261	.335	.596	54	-14	15	2.44	-3	C-64/1-6	2	-1.4
1998*Atl-N	61	149	18	50	12	0	6	32	15	28	1	1	.336	.404	.537	.941	145	10	32	8.37	2	C-45/1-8,D-1	10	1.4
1999*Atl-N	104	309	30	77	17	0	7	30	17	40	0	1	.249	.301	.372	.673	69	-16	33	3.56	2	C-98/1-2	8	-0.8
2000 Atl-N	7	22	0	4	1	0	0	3	0	2	0	0	.182	.182	.227	.409	2	-3	1	1.36	-1	/C-7	0	-0.4
2001 Atl-N	5	10	0	3	0	0	0	0	0	2	0	0	.300	.300	.300	.600	55	-1	1	3.47	-1	/C-5	0	-0.2
2002 Cle-A	42	117	6	25	9	0	0	4	5	25	0	0	.214	.252	.291	.543	45	-9	7	1.98	1	C-42	2	-0.6
2003 Mil-N	107	350	26	95	17	1	11	45	17	47	0	1	.271	.305	.420	.725	88	-8	39	3.78	-3	*C-102	7	-0.4
Total 9	**474**	**1317**	**120**	**339**	**71**	**2**	**35**	**153**	**72**	**200**	**1**	**4**	**.257**	**.302**	**.394**	**.696**	**79**	**-47**	**148**	**3.79**	**-3**	**C-422/1-24,D-1**	**35**	**-2.5**
• PEREZ, Eduardo	Eduardo Atanasio Perez b: 9/11/1969, Cincinnati, OH BR/TR, 6'4", 215 lbs. Deb: 7/27/1993 Career OF: 39-0-94																							
1993 Cal-A	52	180	16	45	6	2	4	30	9	39	5	4	.250	.293	.372	.665	75	-7	18	3.42	8	3-45/D-3	4	0.1
1994 Cal-A	38	129	10	27	7	0	5	16	12	29	3	0	.209	.277	.380	.656	66	-6	13	3.21	-3	1-38	1	-1.2
1995 Cal-A	29	71	9	12	4	1	1	7	12	9	0	2	.169	.306	.296	.602	58	-5	6	2.55	0	3-23/D-1	0	-0.5
1996 Cin-N	18	36	8	8	0	0	3	5	5	9	0	0	.222	.317	.472	.789	106	0	5	4.36	1	/1-8,3-3	1	0.0
1997 Cin-N	106	297	44	75	18	0	16	52	29	76	5	1	.253	.323	.475	.798	104	1	46	5.35	-2	1-67,0-12(11-0-1)/3-8,D-1	8	-0.6
1998 Cin-N	84	172	20	41	4	0	4	30	21	45	0	1	.238	.328	.331	.660	73	-7	20	3.89	8	1-51/3-1,0-1	4	-0.2
1999 StL-N	21	32	6	11	2	0	1	9	7	6	0	0	.344	.462	.500	.962	142	3	8	10.57	1	/0-6(6-0-0),1-5	2	0.3
2000 StL-N	35	91	9	27	4	0	3	10	5	19	1	0	.297	.354	.440	.793	98	-0	14	5.59	2	1-24/0-4(4-0-0),3-2	1	0.0
2002*StL-N	96	154	22	31	9	0	10	26	17	36	0	0	.201	.293	.455	.748	96	-2	19	3.87	2	0-35(7-0-29),1-10/3-6,D-1	3	-0.1
2003 StL-N	105	253	47	72	16	0	11	41	29	53	5	2	.285	.367	.478	.845	123	9	44	6.20	-3	0-71(10-0-64),3-12/1-5,D-1	7	0.3
Total 10	**584**	**1415**	**191**	**349**	**70**	**3**	**58**	**226**	**146**	**321**	**19**	**10**	**.247**	**.325**	**.423**	**.748**	**94**	**-15**	**194**	**4.62**	**13**	**1-208,0-129,3-100/D-7**	**31**	**-2.0**
• PEREZ, Marty	Martin Roman Perez b: 2/28/1946, Visalia, CA BR/TR, 5'11", 160 lbs. Deb: 9/9/1969																							
1969 Cal-A	13	13	3	3	0	0	0	0	2	1	0	0	.231	.333	.231	.564	63	-1	1	2.30	0	/S-7,2-2,3-2	0	0.0
1970 Cal-A	3	3	0	0	0	0	0	1	0	0	0	0	.000	.000	.000	.000	-104	-1	0	.00	-1	/S-2	0	-0.1
1971 Atl-N	130	410	28	93	15	3	4	32	25	44	1	2	.227	.273	.307	.580	60	-22	32	2.50	-18	*S-126/2-1	4	-2.7
1972 Atl-N	141	479	33	109	13	1	1	28	30	55	0	3	.228	.277	.265	.542	50	-32	32	2.13	-21	*S-141	3	-4.0
1973 Atl-N	141	501	66	125	15	5	8	57	49	66	2	3	.250	.319	.347	.666	79	-15	54	3.51	-8	*S-139	8	-0.7
1974 Atl-N	127	447	51	116	20	5	2	34	35	51	2	0	.260	.315	.340	.655	80	-12	47	3.61	9	*2-102,S-14/3-6	12	0.4
1975 Atl-N	120	461	50	127	14	2	2	34	37	44	2	2	.275	.329	.328	.657	80	-13	48	3.57	-6	*2-116/S-7	11	-1.1
1976 Atl-N	31	96	12	24	4	0	1	6	8	9	0	0	.250	.308	.323	.631	74	-3	9	2.77	-2	2-18,S-17/3-2	1	-0.4
SF-N	93	332	37	86	13	1	2	26	30	28	3	4	.259	.320	.322	.643	80	-9	36	3.68	2	2-89/S-5	9	-0.1
Yr.	124	428	49	110	17	1	3	32	38	37	3	4	.257	.318	.322	.640	79	-13	45	3.46	0	*2-107,S-22/3-2	10	-0.5
1977 NY-A	1	4	0	2	0	0	0	0	0	1	0	0	.500	.500	.500	1.000	176	0	1	4.50	1	/3-1	0	0.1
Oak-A	115	373	32	86	14	5	2	23	29	65	1	3	.231	.291	.311	.602	65	-19	33	2.94	2	*2-105,3-12/S-4	6	-1.2
Yr.	116	377	32	88	14	5	2	23	29	66	1	3	.233	.293	.313	.606	66	-18	34	2.96	3	*2-105,3-13/S-4	6	-1.1
1978 Oak-A	16	12	1	0	0	0	0	0	0	5	0	0	.000	.000	.000	.000	-105	-3	0	.00	0	3-11/S-3,2-1	0	-0.3
Total 10	**931**	**3131**	**313**	**771**	**108**	**22**	**22**	**241**	**245**	**369**	**11**	**17**	**.246**	**.303**	**.316**	**.619**	**70**	**-129**	**291**	**3.08**	**-44**	**S-465,2-434/3-34**	**54**	**-10.3**
• PEREZ, Neifi	Neifi Neftali (Diaz) Perez b: 6/2/1973, Villa Mella, Dominican Republic BB/TR, 6', 175 lbs. Deb: 8/31/1996																							
1996 Col-N	17	45	4	7	2	0	0	3	0	8	2	2	.156	.156	.200	.356	-6	-8	1	.43	-1	S-14/2-4	0	-0.8

YEAR TM-L	G	AB	R	H	2B	3B	HR	RBI	BB	SO	SB	CS	AVG	OBP	SLG	OPS	OPS+	BR/A	RC	RC/G	FR	G/POS	WS	TPW
1997 Col-N	83	313	46	91	13	10	5	31	21	43	4	3	.291	.337	.444	.781	83	-8	47	5.33	4	S-45,2-41/3-2	9	0.1
1998 Col-N	162	647	80	177	25	9	9	59	38	70	5	6	.274	.315	.382	.697	67	-32	78	4.10	14	*S-162/C-1	12	-0.5
1999 Col-N	157	690	108	193	27	**11**	12	70	28	54	13	5	.280	.309	.403	.712	62	-42	87	4.53	5	*S-157	14	-2.2
2000 Col-N	162	651	92	187	39	11	10	71	30	63	3	6	.287	.319	.427	.746	69	-34	85	4.63	26	*S-162	15	0.4
2001 Col-N	87	382	65	114	19	8	7	47	16	49	6	2	.298	.327	.445	.772	79	-12	53	5.10	5	S-87	8	0.1
KC-A	49	199	18	48	7	1	1	12	10	19	3	4	.241	.281	.302	.582	49	-16	17	2.71	4	S-46/2-4	3	-0.7
2002 KC-A	145	554	65	131	20	4	3	37	20	53	8	9	.236	.263	.303	.566	45	-47	41	2.43	-1	*S-139/2-5	6	-3.4
2003*SF-N	120	328	27	84	19	4	1	31	14	23	3	2	.256	.287	.348	.634	66	-17	31	3.11	27	2-57,S-45/3-2	8	1.5
Total 8	**982**	**3809**	**505**	**1032**	**171**	**58**	**48**	**361**	**177**	**382**	**47**	**39**	**.271**	**.304**	**.384**	**.688**	**64**	**-216**	**439**	**3.98**	**84**	**S-857,2-111/3-4,C-1**	**75**	**-5.6**
• PEREZ, Robert	Robert Alexander (Jimenez) Perez b: 6/4/1969, Bolivar, Venezuela BR/TR, 6'3", 205 lbs. Deb: 7/20/1994 Career OF: 114-3-65																							
1994 Tor-A	4	8	0	1	0	0	0	0	0	1	0	0	.125	.125	.125	.250	-35	-2	0	.00	0	/O-4(2-0-2)	0	-0.1
1995 Tor-A	17	48	2	9	2	0	1	3	0	5	0	0	.188	.188	.292	.479	23	-6	2	1.58	-1	O-15(5-0-11)	0	-0.7
1996 Tor-A	86	202	30	66	10	0	2	21	8	17	3	0	.327	.355	.406	.761	92	-2	28	5.19	-3	O-79(59-0-25)/D-2	5	-0.7
1997 Tor-A	37	78	4	15	4	1	2	6	0	16	0	0	.192	.192	.346	.538	37	-8	5	1.87	0	O-25(17-0-9)/D-7	0	-0.8
1998 Sea-A	17	35	3	6	1	0	2	6	0	5	0	0	.171	.171	.371	.543	36	-4	2	1.67	0	O-17(2-0-15)	0	-0.4
Mon-N	52	106	9	25	1	0	1	8	2	23	0	0	.236	.257	.274	.530	40	-9	7	2.08	-1	O-29(29-0-0)	0	-1.0
2001 NY-A	6	15	1	4	1	0	0	0	1	7	0	1	.267	.313	.333	.646	70	-1	1	2.96	0	/O-5(0-3-2),D-1	0	-0.1
Mil-N	2	5	0	0	0	0	0	0	0	0	0	0	.000	.000	.000	.000	-103	-1	0	.00	0	/O-1	0	-0.1
Total 6	**221**	**497**	**49**	**126**	**19**	**1**	**8**	**44**	**11**	**74**	**3**	**1**	**.254**	**.273**	**.344**	**.617**	**58**	**-32**	**45**	**3.08**	**-3**	**O-175/D-10**	**5**	**-4.0**
• PEREZ, Santiago	Santiago Alberto Perez b: 12/30/1975, Santo Domingo, Dominican Republic BB/TR, 6'2", 185 lbs. Deb: 6/3/2000																							
2000 Mil-N	24	52	8	9	2	0	0	2	8	9	4	0	.173	.295	.212	.507	32	-4	4	2.52	-2	S-20	1	-0.4
2001 SD-N	43	81	13	16	1	0	0	4	15	29	5	1	.198	.323	.210	.533	46	-5	7	2.99	-4	O-26(9-10-8)/S-8,2-2	1	-0.8
Total 2	**67**	**133**	**21**	**25**	**3**	**0**	**0**	**6**	**23**	**38**	**9**	**1**	**.188**	**.312**	**.211**	**.523**	**40**	**-10**	**12**	**2.80**	**-5**	**/S-28,O-26,2-2**	**2**	**-1.3**
• PEREZ, Timo	Timoniel Perez b: 4/8/1975, Bani, Dominican Republic BL/TL, 5'9", 167 lbs. Deb: 9/1/2000 Career OF: 96-157-101																							
2000*NY-N	24	49	11	14	4	1	1	3	3	5	1	1	.286	.340	.469	.809	106	0	8	5.76	2	O-19(8-7-8)	2	0.1
2001 NY-N	85	239	26	59	9	1	5	22	12	25	1	6	.247	.289	.356	.644	69	-14	24	3.28	3	O-73(6-8-62)	4	-1.3
2002 NY-N	136	444	52	131	27	6	8	47	23	36	10	6	.295	.333	.437	.770	105	1	62	4.87	5	*O-122(24-93-17)	14	0.6
2003 NY-N	127	346	32	93	21	0	4	42	18	29	5	6	.269	.309	.364	.673	77	-14	38	3.65	-3	*O-104(58-49-14)	5	-1.8
Total 4	**372**	**1078**	**121**	**297**	**61**	**8**	**18**	**114**	**56**	**95**	**17**	**19**	**.276**	**.316**	**.397**	**.713**	**88**	**-27**	**131**	**4.15**	**8**	**O-318**	**25**	**-2.5**
• PEREZ, Tomas	Tomas Orlando Perez b: 12/29/1973, Barquisimeto, Venezuela BB/TR, 5'11", 165 lbs. Deb: 5/3/1995 ♦																							
1995 Tor-A	41	98	12	24	3	1	1	8	7	18	0	1	.245	.295	.327	.622	62	-6	8	2.56	-3	S-31/2-7,3-1	1	-0.6
1996 Tor-A	91	295	24	74	13	4	1	19	25	29	1	2	.251	.312	.332	.644	63	-17	29	3.29	9	2-75,3-11/S-5	3	-0.4
1997 Tor-A	40	123	9	24	3	2	0	9	11	28	1	1	.195	.267	.252	.519	36	-12	9	2.23	8	S-32/2-8	2	-0.1
1998 Tor-A	6	9	1	1	0	0	0	0	1	3	0	0	.111	.200	.111	.311	-16	-2	0	.44	0	/S-4,2-1	0	-0.2
2000 Phi-N	45	140	17	31	7	1	1	13	11	30	1	1	.221	.278	.307	.585	47	-12	12	2.75	-2	S-44	1	-1.0
2001 Phi-N	62	135	11	41	7	1	3	19	7	22	0	1	.304	.347	.437	.784	104	0	20	5.50	8	2-29/3-9,S-8,O-1	5	0.9
2002 Phi-N	92	212	22	53	13	1	5	20	21	40	1	0	.250	.321	.392	.712	91	-3	26	4.26	10	2-50,3-14,S-13/1-3,P-1	4	1.0
2003 Phi-N	125	298	39	79	18	1	5	33	23	54	0	1	.265	.318	.383	.700	87	-7	35	4.01	2	3-58,2-26/1-9,S-4	5	-0.3
Total 8	**502**	**1310**	**135**	**327**	**64**	**11**	**16**	**121**	**106**	**224**	**4**	**7**	**.250**	**.308**	**.352**	**.660**	**72**	**-58**	**138**	**3.56**	**33**	**2-196,S-141/3-93,1-12,O-1,P**	**21**	**-0.6**
• PEREZ, Tony	Atanasio (Rigal) Perez b: 5/14/1942, Camaguey, Cuba BR/TR, 6'2", 205 lbs. Deb: 7/26/1964 M/C HOF: 2000																							
1964 Cin-N	12	25	1	2	1	0	0	1	3	9	0	0	.080	.179	.120	.299	-14	-4	1	.79	-2	/1-6	0	-0.6
1965 Cin-N	104	281	40	73	14	4	12	47	21	67	0	2	.260	.316	.466	.782	109	2	38	4.55	-2	1-93	6	-0.5
1966 Cin-N	99	257	25	68	10	4	4	39	14	44	1	0	.265	.308	.381	.689	83	-6	27	3.56	-5	1-75	4	-1.5
1967 Cin-N★	156	600	78	174	28	7	26	102	33	102	0	3	.290	.331	.490	.821	118	12	91	5.47	-12	*3-139,1-18/2-1	23	-0.1
1968 Cin-N★	160	625	93	176	25	7	18	92	51	92	3	2	.282	.342	.430	.772	123	18	88	4.97	7	*3-160	25	2.8
1969 Cin-N★	160	629	103	185	31	2	37	122	63	131	4	2	.294	.360	.526	.886	138	31	114	6.49	9	*3-160	31	4.1
1970*Cin-N★	158	587	107	186	28	6	40	129	83	134	8	3	.317	.405	.589	.994	156	48	140	8.85	-3	*3-153/1-8	33	4.4
1971 Cin-N	158	609	72	164	22	3	25	91	51	120	4	1	.269	.327	.438	.765	121	15	86	5.03	15	*3-148,1-44	23	3.0
1972*Cin-N	136	515	64	146	33	7	21	90	55	121	4	2	.283	.353	.497	.850	148	31	90	6.27	-1	*1-136	25	2.0
1973*Cin-N	151	564	73	177	33	3	27	101	74	117	3	1	.314	.396	.527	.923	162	48	118	7.85	-6	*1-151	32	3.1
1974 Cin-N★	158	596	81	158	28	2	28	101	61	112	1	3	.265	.335	.460	.795	123	14	88	5.12	-4	*1-157	20	-0.1
1975*Cin-N★	137	511	74	144	28	3	20	109	54	101	1	2	.282	.354	.466	.820	124	15	83	5.79	-2	*1-132	19	0.2
1976*Cin-N★	139	527	77	137	32	6	19	91	50	88	10	5	.260	.330	.452	.782	117	10	78	5.13	0	*1-136	16	-0.1
1977 Mon-N	154	559	71	158	32	6	19	91	63	111	4	3	.283	.357	.463	.821	122	17	91	5.74	9	*1-148	17	1.7
1978 Mon-N	148	544	63	158	38	3	14	78	38	104	2	0	.290	.339	.449	.788	120	13	82	5.48	1	*1-145	18	0.6
1979 Mon-N	132	489	58	132	29	4	13	73	38	82	2	1	.270	.326	.425	.752	104	2	65	4.66	-3	*1-129	14	-1.0
1980 Bos-A	151	585	73	161	31	3	25	105	41	93	1	0	.275	.324	.467	.790	108	5	80	4.73	-3	*1-137,D-13	13	-0.7
1981 Bos-A	84	306	35	77	11	3	9	39	27	66	0	0	.252	.312	.395	.708	97	-1	37	4.10	1	1-56,D-23	7	-0.5
1982 Bos-A	69	196	18	51	14	2	6	31	19	48	0	1	.260	.326	.444	.769	103	0	27	4.74	0	D-46/1-2	4	-0.1
1983*Phi-N	91	253	18	61	11	2	6	43	28	57	1	0	.241	.319	.372	.691	92	-3	29	3.89	-2	1-69	6	-0.9
1984 Cin-N	71	137	9	33	6	1	2	15	11	21	0	0	.241	.297	.343	.640	76	-5	12	2.88	-1	1-31	1	-0.7
1985 Cin-N	72	183	25	60	8	0	6	33	22	22	0	2	.328	.400	.470	.870	136	8	35	7.30	-3	1-50	8	0.3
1986 Cin-N	77	200	14	51	12	1	2	29	25	25	0	0	.255	.338	.355	.693	87	-3	24	4.12	-3	1-55	4	-0.9
Total 23	**2777**	**9778**	**1272**	**2732**	**505**	**79**	**379**	**1652**	**925**	**1867**	**49**	**33**	**.279**	**.344**	**.463**	**.808**	**122**	**269**	**1523**	**5.51**	**-11**	***1-1778,3-760/D-82,2-1**	**349**	**14.9**
• PEREZCHICA, Tony	Antonio Llamas (Gonzales) Perezchica b: 4/20/1966, Mexicali, Mexico BR/TR, 5'11", 165 lbs. Deb: 9/7/1988																							
1988 SF-N	7	8	1	1	0	0	0	1	2	1	0	0	.125	.300	.125	.425	27	-1	1	1.88	0	/2-6	0	-0.1
1990 SF-N	4	3	1	1	0	0	0	0	1	2	0	0	.333	.500	.333	.833	139	0	1	8.51	-2	/2-2,S-2	0	-0.2
1991 SF-N	23	48	2	11	4	1	0	3	2	12	0	1	.229	.260	.354	.614	73	-2	4	2.99	0	S-13/2-6	0	-0.2
Cle-A	17	22	4	8	2	0	0	0	3	5	0	0	.364	.440	.455	.895	147	2	5	9.15	-2	/S-6,3-3,2-2,D-1	1	0.0
1992 Cle-A	18	20	2	2	1	0	0	1	2	6	0	0	.100	.182	.150	.332	-6	-3	1	1.03	-3	/3-9,2-4,S-4,D-1	0	-0.6
Total 4	**69**	**101**	**10**	**23**	**7**	**1**	**0**	**5**	**10**	**26**	**0**	**1**	**.228**	**.297**	**.317**	**.614**	**71**	**-4**	**11**	**3.59**	**-8**	**/S-25,2-20,3-12,D-2**	**1**	**-1.1**
• PERKINS, Broderick	Broderick Phillip Perkins b: 11/23/1954, Pittsburg, CA BL/TL, 5'10", 180 lbs. Deb: 7/7/1978 Career OF: 10-0-31																							
1978 SD-N	62	217	14	52	14	1	2	33	5	29	4	0	.240	.257	.341	.598	71	-9	18	2.81	3	1-59	3	-1.0
1979 SD-N	57	87	8	23	0	0	0	8	8	12	0	0	.264	.326	.264	.591	67	-4	7	2.89	-1	1-28	1	-0.6
1980 SD-N	43	100	18	37	9	0	2	14	11	10	2	1	.370	.432	.520	.952	175	10	24	9.94	-2	1-20,O-10(0-0-10)	6	0.7
1981 SD-N	92	254	27	71	18	3	2	40	14	16	0	4	.280	.317	.398	.715	110	-0	29	3.95	-5	1-80/O-3(1-0-2)	6	-1.0
1982 SD-N	125	347	32	94	10	4	2	34	26	20	2	1	.271	.327	.340	.667	92	-4	39	3.93	6	1-98,O-11(4-0-7)	9	-0.3
1983 Cle-A	79	184	23	50	10	0	0	24	9	19	1	5	.272	.306	.326	.632	71	-9	17	3.07	-2	1-19,O-17(5-0-12),D-16	1	-1.3
1984 Cle-A	58	66	5	13	1	0	0	4	7	10	0	0	.197	.284	.212	.496	39	-5	4	1.86	0	D-10/1-2	0	-0.6
Total 7	**516**	**1255**	**127**	**340**	**62**	**8**	**8**	**157**	**80**	**116**	**9**	**11**	**.271**	**.317**	**.352**	**.669**	**91**	**-21**	**138**	**3.80**	**-1**	**1-306/O-41,D-26**	**26**	**-4.0**
• PERKINS, Cy	Ralph Foster Perkins b: 2/27/1896, Gloucester, MA d: 10/2/1963, Philadelphia, PA BR/TR, 5'10.5", 158 lbs. Deb: 9/25/1915 M/C																							
1915 Phi-A	7	20	2	4	1	0	0	0	3	3	0	....	.200	.304	.250	.554	68	-1	2	2.66	1	/C-6	0	0.1
1917 Phi-A	6	18	1	3	0	0	0	2	2	1	0	....	.167	.250	.167	.417	28	-1	1	1.38	3	/C-6	0	0.3
1918 Phi-A	68	218	9	41	4	1	1	14	8	15	1	....	.188	.217	.229	.446	34	-18	11	1.48	13	C-60	4	-0.1
1919 Phi-A	101	305	22	77	12	7	2	29	27	22	2	....	.252	.313	.357	.671	87	-6	33	3.73	10	C-87/S-8	9	1.2
1920 Phi-A	148	492	40	128	24	6	5	52	28	35	5	6	.260	.303	.364	.667	75	-19	53	3.70	18	*C-146/2-1	13	1.0
1921 Phi-A	141	538	58	155	31	4	12	73	32	32	5	9	.288	.329	.428	.757	91	-11	73	4.80	10	*C-141	12	0.7
1922 Phi-A	148	505	58	135	20	6	6	69	40	30	1	7	.267	.322	.366	.689	77	-20	59	3.99	4	*C-141	12	-0.6
1923 Phi-A	143	500	53	135	34	5	2	65	65	30	1	3	.270	.356	.370	.726	90	-6	69	4.81	-5	*C-137	15	-0.2
1924 Phi-A	128	392	31	95	19	4	0	32	31	20	3	4	.242	.304	.311	.616	58	-25	38	3.28	-2	*C-128	7	-1.7
1925 Phi-A	65	140	21	43	10	0	1	18	26	6	0	0	.307	.426	.400	.826	104	3	26	6.66	-5	C-58/3-1	6	0.2
1926 Phi-A	63	148	14	43	6	0	0	19	18	7	0	2	.291	.371	.331	.702	80	-4	19	4.26	2	C-55	4	0.0

YEAR TM-L	G	AB	R	H	2B	3B	HR	RBI	BB	SO	SB	CS	AVG	OBP	SLG	OPS	OPS+	BR/A	RC	RC/G	FR	G/POS	WS	TPW
1927 Phi-A	59	137	11	35	7	2	1	15	12	8	0	2	.255	.315	.358	.673	70	-7	15	3.73	-1	C-54/1-1	3	-0.5
1928 Phi-A	19	29	1	5	0	0	0	1	1	1	0	1	.172	.200	.172	.372	-1	-5	1	.91	0	C-19	0	-0.4
1929 Phi-A	38	76	4	16	4	0	0	9	5	4	0	0	.211	.259	.263	.522	34	-8	5	2.30	1	C-38	1	-0.5
1930 Phi-A	20	38	1	6	2	0	0	4	2	3	0	0	.158	.200	.211	.411	4	-6	2	1.35	-1	C-19/1-1	1	-0.6
1931 NY-A	16	47	3	12	1	0	0	7	1	4	0	0	.255	.286	.277	.562	51	-3	4	2.81	-1	C-16	1	-0.3
1934 Det-A	1	1	0	0	0	0	0	0	0	0	0	0	.000	.000	.000	.000	-100	-0	0	.00	0	....	0	0.0
Total 17	**1171**	**3604**	**329**	**933**	**175**	**35**	**30**	**409**	**301**	**221**	**18**	**34**	**.259**	**.319**	**.352**	**.670**	**75**	**-137**	**411**	**3.88**	**47**	***C-1111/S-8,1-2,2-1,3-1**	**88**	**-1.7**
• PERLOZZO, Sam	Samuel Benedict Perlozzo b: 3/4/1951, Cumberland, MD BR/TR, 5'9", 170 lbs. Deb: 9/13/1977 C																							
1977 Min-A	10	24	6	7	0	2	0	0	2	3	0	0	.292	.346	.458	.804	119	1	4	6.02	0	2-10/3-1	1	0.1
1979 SD-N	2	2	0	0	0	0	0	0	1	0	0	0	.000	.333	.000	.333	-1	-0	0	1.17	-1	/2-2	0	-0.1
Total 2	**12**	**26**	**6**	**7**	**0**	**2**	**0**	**0**	**3**	**3**	**0**	**0**	**.269**	**.345**	**.423**	**.768**	**107**	**0**	**4**	**5.54**	**-1**	**/2-12,3-1**	**1**	**-0.1**
• PERRIN, John	John Stephenson Perrin b: 2/4/1898, Escanaba, MI d: 6/24/1969, Detroit, MI BL/TR, 5'9", 160 lbs. Deb: 7/11/1921																							
1921 Bos-A	4	13	3	3	0	0	0	1	0	3	0	0	.231	.231	.231	.462	18	-2	1	1.76	0	/O-4(0-0-4)	0	-0.2
• PERRINE, Nig	John Grover Perrine b: 1/14/1885, Clinton, WI d: 8/13/1948, Kansas City, MO BR/TR, 5'9", 160 lbs. Deb: 4/11/1907																							
1907 Was-A	44	146	13	25	4	1	0	15	13	....	10	....	.171	.253	.212	.465	53	-7	11	2.35	-3	2-24,S-18/3-2	1	-1.1
• PERRING, George	George Wilson Perring b: 8/13/1884, Sharon, WI d: 8/20/1960, Beloit, WI BR/TR, 6', 190 lbs. Deb: 4/25/1908 ♦																							
1908 Cle-A	89	310	23	67	8	5	0	19	16	....	8	....	.216	.255	.274	.529	71	-10	23	2.41	-9	S-48,3-41	6	-1.9
1909 Cle-A	88	283	26	63	10	9	0	20	19	....	6	....	.223	.283	.322	.605	87	-5	27	3.10	0	3-67,S-11/2-4	8	-0.2
1910 Cle-A	39	122	14	27	6	3	0	8	3	....	3	....	.221	.240	.320	.560	74	-4	10	2.59	-1	3-33/1-4	2	-0.5
1914 KC-F	144	496	68	138	28	10	2	69	59	39	7	....	.278	.355	.387	.742	117	12	69	4.73	3	*3-101,1-41/P-1,S-1	17	1.6
1915 KC-F	153	553	67	143	23	7	7	67	57	30	10	....	.259	.329	.363	.692	107	5	68	4.12	6	*3-102,1-31,2-31/S-1	22	1.4
Total 5	**513**	**1764**	**198**	**438**	**75**	**34**	**9**	**183**	**154**	**69**	**34**	**....**	**.248**	**.311**	**.345**	**.655**	**99**	**-3**	**197**	**3.70**	**-1**	**3-344/1-76,S-61,2-35,P-1**	**55**	**0.5**
• PERRY, Bob	Melvin Gray Perry b: 9/14/1934, New Bern, NC BR/TR, 6'2", 180 lbs. Deb: 5/17/1963 Career OF: 7-85-27																							
1963 LA-A	61	166	16	42	9	0	3	14	9	31	1	1	.253	.303	.361	.665	91	-3	18	3.58	-3	O-55(7-23-26)	3	-0.8
1964 LA-A	70	221	19	61	8	1	3	16	14	52	1	1	.276	.319	.362	.681	99	-1	25	4.07	-2	O-62(0-62-1)	6	-0.5
Total 2	**131**	**387**	**35**	**103**	**17**	**1**	**6**	**30**	**23**	**83**	**2**	**2**	**.266**	**.312**	**.362**	**.674**	**95**	**-4**	**43**	**3.85**	**-5**	**O-117**	**9**	**-1.3**
• PERRY, Boyd	Boyd Glenn Perry b: 3/21/1914, Snow Camp, NC d: 6/29/1990, Burlington, NC BR/TR, 5'10", 158 lbs. Deb: 5/23/1941																							
1941 Det-A	36	83	9	15	5	0	0	11	10	9	1	0	.181	.269	.241	.510	32	-8	6	2.12	0	S-25,2-11	1	-0.7
• PERRY, Chan	Chan Everett Perry b: 9/13/1972, Live Oak, FL BR/TR, 6'2", 200 lbs. Deb: 8/5/2000																							
2000 Cle-A	13	14	1	1	0	0	0	0	0	5	0	0	.071	.071	.071	.143	-62	-3	0	.00	-0	/O-7(1-0-6),D-4,1-1	0	-0.3
2002 KC-A	5	11	0	1	0	0	0	3	0	1	0	0	.091	.091	.091	.182	-46	-2	0	.00	0	/1-5	0	-0.3
Total 2	**18**	**25**	**1**	**2**	**0**	**0**	**0**	**3**	**0**	**6**	**0**	**0**	**.080**	**.080**	**.080**	**.160**	**-55**	**-6**	**0**	**.00**	**0**	**/O-7,1-6,D-4**	**0**	**-0.6**
• PERRY, Clay	Clayton Shields Perry b: 12/18/1881, Rice Lake, WI d: 1/16/1954, Rice Lake, WI BR/TR, 5'10.5", 175 lbs. Deb: 9/2/1908																							
1908 Det-A	7	17	0	2	0	0	0	0	0	....	0	....	.118	.167	.118	.284	-7	-2	0	.53	-2	/3-7	0	-0.4
• PERRY, Gerald	Gerald June Perry b: 10/30/1960, Savannah, GA BL/TR, 5'11", 190 lbs. Deb: 8/11/1983 C Career OF: 87-0-3																							
1983 Atl-N	27	39	5	14	2	0	1	6	5	4	0	1	.359	.432	.487	.919	143	2	8	7.58	-2	/1-7,O-1	2	0.0
1984 Atl-N	122	347	52	92	12	2	7	47	61	38	15	12	.265	.378	.372	.750	104	3	50	4.74	-3	1-64,O-53(53-0-0)	10	-0.5
1985 Atl-N	110	238	22	51	5	0	3	13	23	28	9	5	.214	.284	.273	.557	53	-15	18	2.43	-1	1-55/O-1	1	-2.1
1986 Atl-N	29	70	6	19	2	0	2	11	8	4	0	1	.271	.346	.386	.732	96	-1	8	3.82	-1	O-21(21-0-1)/1-1	1	-0.3
1987 Atl-N	142	533	77	144	35	2	12	74	48	63	42	16	.270	.332	.411	.742	91	-6	69	4.35	-7	*1-136/O-7(7-0-0)	10	-2.1
1988 Atl-N★	141	547	61	164	29	1	8	74	36	49	29	14	.300	.344	.400	.745	108	5	70	4.45	-1	*1-141	15	-0.7
1989 Atl-N	72	266	24	67	11	0	4	21	32	28	10	6	.252	.339	.338	.677	92	-2	31	3.98	-3	1-72	4	-1.1
1990 KC-A	133	465	57	118	22	2	8	57	39	56	17	4	.254	.316	.361	.677	90	-4	53	3.83	3	D-68,1-51	7	-0.7
1991 StL-N	109	242	29	58	8	4	6	36	22	34	15	8	.240	.303	.380	.683	90	-4	28	3.84	0	1-61/O-5(4-0-1)	7	-0.8
1992 StL-N	87	143	13	34	8	0	1	18	15	23	3	6	.238	.314	.315	.629	81	-5	13	2.91	-3	1-29	1	-1.0
1993 StL-N	96	98	21	33	5	0	4	16	18	23	1	1	.337	.440	.510	.950	156	9	22	8.36	-2	1-15/O-1	5	0.6
1994 StL-N	60	77	12	25	7	0	3	18	15	12	1	1	.325	.435	.532	.967	153	7	17	8.14	-1	1-13	3	0.4
1995 StL-N	65	79	4	13	4	0	0	5	6	12	0	0	.165	.224	.215	.439	16	-10	4	1.47	-1	1-11	0	-1.1
Total 13	**1193**	**3144**	**383**	**832**	**150**	**11**	**59**	**396**	**328**	**374**	**142**	**75**	**.265**	**.336**	**.376**	**.712**	**95**	**-23**	**391**	**4.19**	**-22**	**1-656/O-89,D-68**	**66**	**-9.4**
• PERRY, Hank	William Henry "Socks" Perry b: 7/28/1886, Howell, MI d: 7/18/1956, Pontiac, MI BL/TR, 5'11", 190 lbs. Deb: 4/12/1912																							
1912 Det-A	13	36	3	6	1	0	0	0	3	....	0	....	.167	.231	.194	.425	23	-4	2	1.38	2	/O-7(0-7-0)	0	-0.2
• PERRY, Herb	Herbert Edward Perry b: 9/15/1969, Live Oak, FL BR/TR, 6'2", 210 lbs. Deb: 5/3/1994 Career OF: 7-0-0																							
1994 Cle-A	4	9	1	1	0	0	0	1	3	1	0	0	.111	.385	.111	.496	36	-1	1	2.46	0	/1-2,3-2	0	-0.1
1995*Cle-A	52	162	23	51	13	1	3	23	13	28	1	3	.315	.380	.463	.843	116	3	27	5.86	2	1-45/D-6,3-1	5	0.1
1996 Cle-A	7	12	1	1	1	0	0	0	1	2	1	0	.083	.154	.167	.321	-19	-2	0	1.05	0	/1-5,3-1	0	-0.2
1999 TB-A	66	209	29	53	10	1	6	32	16	42	0	0	.254	.336	.397	.733	85	-5	25	3.95	-2	3-42,1-14,D-10/O-6(6-0-0)	3	-0.7
2000 TB-A	7	28	2	6	1	0	0	1	2	7	0	0	.214	.267	.250	.517	32	-3	2	2.46	-2	/3-7,1-1	0	-0.4
*Chi-A	109	383	69	118	29	1	12	61	22	68	4	1	.308	.360	.483	.843	109	5	64	6.03	9	*3-104/1-3,D-3	13	1.4
Yr.	116	411	71	124	30	1	12	62	24	75	4	1	.302	.354	.467	.821	104	2	66	5.77	7	*3-111/1-4,D-3	13	1.0
2001 Chi-A	92	285	38	73	21	1	7	32	23	55	2	2	.256	.327	.411	.738	90	-5	36	4.29	-7	3-68,1-12,D-10	5	-1.1
2002 Tex-A	132	450	64	124	24	1	22	77	34	66	4	2	.276	.335	.480	.815	107	4	68	5.20	-5	*3-112,1-12/D-4,O-1	10	-0.1
2003 Tex-A	11	24	1	4	1	0	0	2	0	3	0	0	.167	.167	.208	.375	-2	-4	1	1.13	0	/1-5,3-2	0	-0.3
Total 8	**480**	**1562**	**228**	**431**	**100**	**5**	**50**	**229**	**114**	**272**	**12**	**8**	**.276**	**.340**	**.442**	**.782**	**98**	**-7**	**223**	**4.94**	**-5**	**3-339/1-99,D-33,O-7**	**36**	**-1.5**
• PESKY, Johnny	John Michael Pesky b: 9/27/1919, Portland, OR BL/TR, 5'9", 168 lbs. Deb: 4/14/1942 M/C																							
1942 Bos-A	147	620	105	**205**	29	9	2	51	42	36	12	7	.331	.375	.416	.791	118	15	100	5.98	20	*S-147	28	4.7
1946*Bos-A★	153	621	115	**208**	43	4	2	55	65	29	9	8	.335	.401	.427	.827	124	22	111	6.79	13	*S-153	34	4.6
1947 Bos-A	155	638	106	**207**	27	8	0	39	72	22	12	9	.324	.393	.392	.785	110	11	103	6.08	-15	*S-133,3-22	25	0.5
1948 Bos-A	143	565	124	159	26	6	3	55	99	32	3	5	.281	.394	.365	.759	98	2	90	5.65	4	*3-141	20	0.5
1949 Bos-A	148	604	111	185	27	7	2	69	100	19	8	4	.306	.408	.384	.792	103	8	104	6.38	20	*3-148	23	2.6
1950 Bos-A	127	490	112	153	22	6	1	49	104	31	2	1	.312	.437	.388	.825	103	10	93	7.05	15	*3-116/S-8	19	2.3
1951 Bos-A	131	480	93	150	20	6	3	41	84	15	2	2	.313	.417	.398	.815	110	12	87	6.74	-5	*S-106,3-11/2-5	21	1.4
1952 Bos-A	25	67	10	10	2	0	0	2	15	5	0	3	.149	.313	.179	.492	36	-6	4	1.94	-3	3-19/S-2	0	-1.0
Det-A	69	177	26	45	4	0	1	9	41	11	1	2	.254	.394	.294	.688	93	1	25	4.72	-6	S-41,2-22/3-3	5	-0.2
Yr.	94	244	36	55	6	0	1	11	56	16	1	5	.225	.372	.262	.634	77	-6	29	3.87	-10	S-43,2-22,3-22	5	-1.2
1953 Det-A	103	308	43	90	22	1	2	24	27	10	3	7	.292	.353	.390	.743	101	-1	43	4.91	-3	2-73	9	0.0
1954 Det-A	20	17	5	3	0	0	1	1	3	1	0	0	.176	.300	.353	.653	80	-0	1	2.29	0	....	0	0.0
Was-A	49	158	17	40	4	3	0	9	10	7	1	1	.253	.298	.316	.614	72	-7	15	3.27	-2	2-37/S-1	3	-0.6
Yr.	69	175	22	43	4	3	1	10	13	8	1	1	.246	.298	.320	.618	73	-7	16	3.16	-2	2-37/S-1	3	-0.7
Total 10	**1270**	**4745**	**867**	**1455**	**226**	**50**	**17**	**404**	**662**	**218**	**53**	**49**	**.307**	**.394**	**.386**	**.780**	**106**	**64**	**777**	**5.98**	**37**	**S-591,3-460,2-137**	**187**	**14.8**
• PETAGINE, Roberto	Roberto Antonio (Guerra) Petagine b: 6/7/1971, Nueva Esparta, Venezuela BL/TL, 6'1", 170 lbs. Deb: 4/4/1994 Career OF: 3-0-16																							
1994 Hou-N	8	7	0	0	0	0	0	0	1	3	0	0	.000	.125	.000	.125	-67	-2	0	.13	0	/1-2	0	-0.2
1995 SD-N	89	124	15	29	8	0	3	17	26	41	0	0	.234	.367	.371	.738	99	1	19	5.07	-1	1-51/O-2(1-0-1)	3	-0.3
1996 NY-N	50	99	10	23	3	0	4	17	9	27	0	2	.232	.315	.384	.699	87	-3	11	3.46	2	1-40	1	-0.3
1997 NY-N	12	15	2	1	0	0	0	2	3	6	0	0	.067	.222	.067	.289	-21	-3	0	.76	1	/1-6,O-1	0	-0.2
1998 Cin-N	34	62	14	16	2	1	3	7	16	11	1	0	.258	.410	.468	.878	129	4	13	7.16	0	1-15,O-15(1-0-15)	2	0.2
Total 5	**193**	**307**	**41**	**69**	**13**	**1**	**10**	**43**	**55**	**88**	**1**	**2**	**.225**	**.348**	**.371**	**.719**	**92**	**-3**	**43**	**4.56**	**1**	**1-114/O-18**	**6**	**-0.8**

YEAR TM-L	G	AB	R	H	2B	3B	HR	RBI	BB	SO	SB	CS	AVG	OBP	SLG	OPS	OPS+	BR/A	RC	RC/G	FR	G/POS	WS	TPW
• PETERMAN, Bill	William David Peterman b: 3/20/1921, Philadelphia, PA d: 3/13/1999, Philadelphia, PA BR/TR, 6'2", 185 lbs. Deb: 4/26/1942																							
1942 Phi-N	1	1	0	1	0	0	0	0	0	0	0	....	1.000	1.000	1.000	2.000	512	0	1	∞	0	/C-1	0	0.0
• PETERS, John	John William "Big Pete,Shotgun" Peters b: 7/14/1893, Kansas City, KS d: 2/21/1932, Kansas City, MO BR/TR, 6', 192 lbs. Deb: 5/1/1915																							
1915 Det-A	1	3	0	0	0	0	0	0	0	1	0	....	.000	.000	.000	.000	-95	-1	0	.00	1	/C-1	0	0.0
1918 Cle-A	1	1	0	0	0	0	0	0	1	1	0	....	.000	.500	.000	.500	46	0	0	.00	-1	/C-1	0	-0.1
1921 Phi-N	55	155	7	45	4	0	3	23	6	13	1	0	.290	.329	.374	.703	79	-4	19	4.54	-7	C-44	2	-0.8
1922 Phi-N	55	143	15	35	9	1	4	24	9	18	0	1	.245	.308	.406	.713	75	-6	18	4.22	-3	C-39	2	-0.6
Total 4	112	302	22	80	13	1	7	47	16	33	1	1	.265	.317	.384	.701	76	-10	37	4.31	-10	/C-85	4	-1.5
• PETERS, John	John Paul Peters b: 4/8/1850, Louisiana, MO d: 1/4/1924, St. Louis, MO BR/TR, 5'7", 180 lbs. Deb: 5/23/1874 ♦																							
1874 Chi-n	55	239	39	69	10	0	1	25	2	11	2	2	.289	.295	.343	.638	103	-0	25	4.42	3	S-36,2-19	....	0.1
1875 Chi-n	69	297	40	85	16	2	0	34	0	3	12	6	.286	.286	.354	.640	120	5	34	4.64	4	*S-65/2-6	....	0.6
1876 Chi-N	66	319	70	111	14	2	1	47	3	2	....	....	.348	.357	.418	.775	141	12	48	6.60	5	*S-66/P-1	12	1.8
1877 Chi-N	60	265	45	84	10	3	0	41	1	7	....	....	.317	.320	.377	.697	106	0	33	4.98	18	*S-60	9	1.9
1878 Mil-N	55	246	33	76	6	1	0	22	5	8	....	....	.309	.323	.341	.664	111	2	28	4.49	9	2-34,S-22	5	1.3
1879 Chi-N	83	379	45	93	13	2	1	31	1	19	....	....	.245	.247	.298	.546	74	-11	29	2.81	-14	*S-83	7	-2.0
1880 Pro-N	86	359	30	82	5	0	0	24	5	15	....	....	.228	.239	.242	.481	66	-12	21	2.12	-3	*S-86	7	-1.1
1881 Buf-N	54	229	21	49	8	1	0	25	3	12	....	....	.214	.224	.258	.482	51	-13	14	2.03	1	S-53/O-1	3	-0.8
1882 Pit-a	78	333	46	96	10	1	0	....	4	....	....	....	.288	.297	.324	.621	115	5	33	3.88	3	*S-77/2-1	10	0.9
1883 Pit-a	8	28	3	3	0	0	0	0	0	....	....	....	.107	.107	.107	.214	-32	-4	0	.37	0	/S-8	0	-0.3
1884 Pit-a	1	4	0	0	0	0	0	0	0	....	....	....	.000	.000	.000	.000	-98	-1	0	.00	0	/S-1	0	-0.1
Total 2 n	124	536	79	154	26	2	1	59	2	14	14	8	.287	.290	.349	.639	112	5	60	4.55	7	S-101/2-25	....	0.7
Total 9	491	2162	293	594	66	10	2	190	22	63	....	....	.275	.282	.318	.600	93	-22	206	3.64	19	S-456/2-35,0-1,P-1	53	1.6
• PETERS, Rick	Richard Devin Peters b: 11/21/1955, Lynwood, CA BB/TR, 5'9", 170 lbs. Deb: 9/8/1979 Career OF: 39-167-22																							
1979 Det-A	12	19	3	5	0	0	0	2	5	3	0	0	.263	.417	.263	.680	85	0	3	4.91	-2	/3-3,D-3,2-2,O-1	1	-0.2
1980 Det-A	133	477	79	139	19	7	2	42	54	48	13	7	.291	.371	.373	.744	102	4	66	4.77	-9	*O-109(8-97-5),D-11	13	-0.8
1981 Det-A	63	207	26	53	7	3	0	15	29	28	1	6	.256	.353	.319	.672	91	-3	22	3.44	2	O-38(5-33-0),D-19	5	-0.3
1983 Oak-A	55	178	20	51	7	0	0	20	12	21	4	9	.287	.335	.326	.661	88	-6	18	3.34	1	O-47(6-30-16)/D-8	3	-0.7
1986 Oak-A	44	38	7	7	1	0	0	1	7	7	2	2	.184	.311	.211	.522	49	-3	2	1.82	0	O-27(19-7-1)/2-1	0	-0.4
Total 5	307	919	135	255	34	10	2	80	107	107	20	24	.277	.358	.343	.701	94	-8	111	4.04	-9	O-222/D-41,2-3,3-3	22	-2.3
• PETERS, Rusty	Russell Dixon Peters b: 12/14/1914, Roanoke, VA d: 2/21/2003, Harrisonburg, VA BR/TR, 5'11", 170 lbs. Deb: 4/14/1936 Career OF: 4-0-0																							
1936 Phi-A	45	119	12	26	3	2	3	16	4	28	1	1	.218	.244	.353	.597	47	-11	10	2.78	-2	S-25,3-10/O-2(2-0-0),2-1	1	-1.0
1937 Phi-A	116	339	39	88	17	6	3	43	41	59	4	4	.260	.339	.372	.711	80	-11	44	4.49	-5	2-70,3-31,S-13	6	-0.9
1938 Phi-A	2	7	0	0	0	0	0	0	0	1	0	0	.000	.000	.000	.000	-103	-2	0	.00	-1	/S-2	0	-0.3
1940 Cle-A	30	71	5	17	3	2	0	7	4	14	1	0	.239	.280	.338	.618	61	-4	7	3.20	-1	/2-9,3-6,S-6,1-1	1	-0.3
1941 Cle-A	29	63	6	13	2	0	0	2	7	10	0	1	.206	.286	.238	.524	42	-6	4	2.30	-2	S-11/3-9,2-3	1	-0.6
1942 Cle-A	34	58	6	13	5	1	0	2	2	14	0	0	.224	.250	.345	.595	70	-3	4	2.36	-1	S-24/2-1,3-1	1	-0.2
1943 Cle-A	79	215	22	47	6	2	1	19	18	29	1	1	.219	.282	.279	.561	68	-9	18	2.62	-6	3-46,S-14/2-6,O-2(2-0-0)	3	-1.5
1944 Cle-A	88	282	23	63	13	3	1	24	15	35	2	1	.223	.268	.301	.569	65	-14	23	2.64	-5	2-63,S-13/3-8	3	-1.6
1946 Cle-A	9	21	0	6	0	0	0	2	1	1	0	1	.286	.318	.286	.604	74	-1	2	2.95	1	/S-7	1	0.0
1947 StL-A	39	47	10	16	4	0	0	2	6	8	0	0	.340	.415	.426	.841	131	2	9	7.18	-2	2-13/S-2	2	0.1
Total 10	471	1222	123	289	53	16	8	117	98	199	9	9	.236	.295	.326	.620	69	-57	120	3.28	-23	2-166,S-117,3-111/O-4,1-1	19	-6.3
• PETERSEN, Chris	Christopher Ronald Petersen b: 11/6/1970, Boston, MA BR/TR, 5'11", 175 lbs. Deb: 5/25/1999																							
1999 Col-N	7	13	1	2	0	0	0	2	2	3	0	0	.154	.267	.154	.421	8	-2	1	1.65	1	/2-6,S-1	0	-0.1
• PETERSON, Bob	Robert A. Peterson b: 7/16/1884, Philadelphia, PA d: 11/27/1962, Evesham, NJ BR/TR, 6'1", 160 lbs. Deb: 4/18/1906																							
1906 Bos-A	39	118	10	24	1	1	1	9	11	....	1	....	.203	.277	.254	.531	67	-4	9	2.48	-4	C-30/2-3,1-2,O-1	2	-0.6
1907 Bos-A	4	13	1	1	0	0	0	0	0	....	0	....	.077	.077	.077	.154	-51	-2	0	.17	0	/C-4	0	-0.2
Total 2	43	131	11	25	1	1	1	9	11	....	1	....	.191	.259	.237	.495	56	-6	9	2.22	-4	/C-34,2-3,1-2,O-1	2	-0.8
• PETERSON, Buddy	Carl Francis Peterson b: 4/23/1925, Portland, OR BR/TR, 5'9.5", 170 lbs. Deb: 9/14/1955																							
1955 Chi-A	6	21	7	6	1	0	0	2	3	1	0	0	.286	.400	.333	.733	96	0	3	5.79	0	/S-6	1	0.0
1957 Bal-A	7	17	1	3	2	0	0	0	2	2	0	0	.176	.263	.294	.557	55	-1	1	2.09	0	/S-7	0	-0.1
Total 2	13	38	8	9	3	0	0	2	5	3	0	0	.237	.341	.316	.657	78	-1	4	3.94	-1	/S-13	1	-0.1
• PETERSON, Cap	Charles Andrew Peterson b: 8/15/1942, Tacoma, WA d: 5/16/1980, Tacoma, WA BR/TR, 6'2", 195 lbs. Deb: 9/12/1962 Career OF: 142-0-139																							
1962 SF-N	4	6	1	1	0	0	0	0	1	4	0	0	.167	.286	.167	.452	25	-1	0	1.94	0	/S-2	0	0.0
1963 SF-N	22	54	7	14	2	0	1	2	2	13	0	0	.259	.286	.352	.638	83	-1	6	3.70	-3	/2-8,3-5,O-3(2-0-1),S-1	1	-0.4
1964 SF-N	66	74	8	15	1	1	1	8	3	20	0	0	.203	.234	.284	.518	44	-6	5	2.30	-1	O-10(10-0-1)/1-2,2-1,3-1	0	-0.7
1965 SF-N	63	105	14	26	7	0	3	15	10	16	0	0	.248	.313	.400	.713	97	-0	12	3.92	0	O-27(23-0-4)	2	-0.1
1966 SF-N	89	190	13	45	6	1	2	19	11	32	2	0	.237	.282	.311	.593	63	-9	15	2.60	1	O-51(50-0-1)/1-2	2	-1.0
1967 Was-A	122	405	35	97	17	2	8	46	32	61	0	3	.240	.300	.351	.651	95	-4	41	3.42	-1	*O-101(18-0-88)	10	-1.3
1968 Was-A	94	226	20	46	8	1	3	18	18	31	2	1	.204	.265	.288	.553	70	-8	18	2.55	-2	O-53(14-0-39)	3	-1.6
1969 Cle-A	76	110	8	25	3	0	1	14	24	18	0	0	.227	.370	.282	.652	82	-1	12	3.64	-1	O-30(25-0-5)/3-4	2	-0.4
Total 8	536	1170	106	269	44	5	19	122	101	195	4	4	.230	.294	.325	.619	80	-30	109	3.11	-6	O-275/3-10,2-9,1-4,S-3	20	-5.5
• PETERSON, Hardy	Harding William Peterson b: 10/17/1929, Perth Amboy, NJ BR/TR, 6', 205 lbs. Deb: 5/5/1955																							
1955 Pit-N	32	81	7	20	6	0	1	10	7	7	0	0	.247	.315	.358	.673	79	-2	9	3.55	2	C-31	2	0.1
1957 Pit-N	30	73	10	22	2	1	2	11	9	10	0	1	.301	.378	.438	.816	122	2	10	4.68	1	C-30	2	0.5
1958 Pit-N	2	6	0	2	0	0	0	0	1	0	0	0	.333	.429	.333	.762	108	0	1	6.54	0	/C-2	0	0.0
1959 Pit-N	2	1	0	0	0	0	0	0	0	0	0	0	.000	.000	.000	.000	-101	-0	0	.00	0	/C-2	0	0.0
Total 4	66	161	17	44	8	1	3	21	17	17	0	1	.273	.346	.391	.738	99	-0	20	4.13	3	/C-65	4	0.5
• PETOSKEY, Ted	Frederick Lee Petoskey b: 1/5/1911, St. Charles, MI d: 11/30/1996, Elgin, SC BR/TR, 5'11.5", 183 lbs. Deb: 9/9/1934 Career OF: 1-3-0																							
1934 Cin-N	6	7	0	0	0	0	0	1	0	5	0	....	.000	.000	.000	.000	-103	-2	0	.00	1	/O-2(0-2-0)	0	-0.1
1935 Cin-N	4	5	0	2	0	0	0	0	0	1	1	....	.400	.400	.400	.800	119	0	1	7.38	0	/O-2(1-1-0)	0	0.0
Total 2	10	12	0	2	0	0	0	1	0	6	1	....	.167	.167	.167	.333	-10	-2	1	2.21	1	/O-4	0	-0.1
• PETRALLI, Geno	Eugene James Petralli b: 9/25/1959, Sacramento, CA BL/TR, 6'2", 185 lbs. Deb: 9/4/1982																							
1982 Tor-A	16	44	3	16	2	0	0	1	4	6	0	0	.364	.417	.409	.826	117	1	8	6.83	-1	C-12/3-3	2	0.1
1983 Tor-A	6	4	0	0	0	0	0	0	1	1	0	0	.000	.200	.000	.200	-37	-1	0	.35	-1	/C-5,D-1	0	-0.1
1984 Tor-A	3	3	0	0	0	0	0	0	0	0	0	0	.000	.000	.000	.000	-97	-1	0	.00	0	/C-1,D-1	0	-0.1
1985 Tex-A	42	100	7	27	2	0	0	11	8	12	1	0	.270	.330	.290	.620	71	-4	10	3.15	0	C-41	2	-0.2
1986 Tex-A	69	137	17	35	9	3	2	18	5	14	3	0	.255	.282	.409	.690	83	-3	14	3.39	-3	C-41,3-15/2-2,D-2	3	-0.5
1987 Tex-A	101	202	28	61	11	2	7	31	27	29	0	2	.302	.390	.480	.870	129	8	38	6.91	-7	C-63,3-17/1-5,2-4,O-3(1-0-2),D	7	0.3
1988 Tex-A	129	351	35	99	14	2	7	36	41	52	0	1	.282	.360	.393	.754	108	5	49	4.85	0	C-85,D-23/3-9,1-2,2-2	8	0.9
1989 Tex-A	70	184	18	56	7	0	4	23	17	24	0	0	.304	.369	.408	.777	117	4	28	5.51	-1	C-49,D-16	5	0.5
1990 Tex-A	133	325	28	83	13	1	0	21	50	49	0	2	.255	.360	.302	.661	87	-4	36	3.75	-5	*C-118/3-7,2-3	6	-0.3
1991 Tex-A	87	199	21	54	8	1	2	20	21	25	2	1	.271	.341	.352	.693	94	-1	25	4.22	-1	C-66/3-7,D-5	5	0.0
1992 Tex-A	94	192	11	38	12	0	1	18	20	34	0	0	.198	.274	.276	.550	56	-11	14	2.26	1	C-54,D-14/3-4,2-2	4	-0.8
1993 Tex-A	59	133	16	32	5	0	1	13	22	17	2	0	.241	.348	.301	.649	79	-2	15	3.69	-1	C-39/D-2,2-1,3-1	2	-0.1
Total 12	809	1874	184	501	83	9	24	192	216	263	8	6	.267	.346	.360	.706	94	-8	234	4.30	-20	C-574/D-66,3-63,2-14,1-7,O	44	-0.3
• PETRICK, Ben	Benjamin Wayne Petrick b: 4/7/1977, Salem, OR BR/TR, 6', 200 lbs. Deb: 9/1/1999 Career OF: 34-17-3																							
1999 Col-N	19	62	13	20	3	0	4	12	10	13	1	0	.323	.417	.565	.981	114	2	15	9.64	0	C-19	2	0.2
2000 Col-N	52	146	32	47	10	1	3	20	20	33	1	2	.322	.411	.466	.876	97	-0	29	7.35	-5	C-48	3	-0.2

YEAR TM-L	G	AB	R	H	2B	3B	HR	RBI	BB	SO	SB	CS	AVG	OBP	SLG	OPS	OPS+	BR/A	RC	RC/G	FR	G/POS	WS	TPW
2001 Col-N	85	244	41	58	15	3	11	39	31	67	3	3	.238	.331	.459	.790	83	-7	37	5.02	-5	C-77/1-2	4	-0.7
2002 Col-N	38	95	10	20	3	1	5	11	9	33	0	1	.211	.286	.421	.707	72	-5	11	3.94	0	0-16(15-2-0),C-14	1	-0.4
2003 Col-N	3	2	0	0	0	0	0	0	0	1	0	0	.000	.000	.000	.000	-88	-1	0	.00	1	/0-2(1-1-0),C-1	0	0.0
Det-A	43	120	18	27	6	0	4	12	8	30	0	0	.225	.273	.375	.648	74	-5	12	3.29	0	0-32(18-14-3)/C-6,1-2	1	-0.5
Total 5	240	669	114	172	37	5	27	94	78	177	5	6	.257	.340	.448	.788	85	-16	105	5.38	-10	C-165/0-50,1-4	11	-1.6

• PETROCELLI, Rico Americo Peter Petrocelli b: 6/27/1943, Brooklyn, NY BR/TR, 6', 185 lbs. Deb: 9/21/1963

YEAR TM-L	G	AB	R	H	2B	3B	HR	RBI	BB	SO	SB	CS	AVG	OBP	SLG	OPS	OPS+	BR/A	RC	RC/G	FR	G/POS	WS	TPW
1963 Bos-A	1	4	0	1	1	0	0	1	0	1	0	0	.250	.250	.500	.750	101	-0	1	4.50	0	/S-1	0	0.0
1965 Bos-A	103	323	38	75	15	2	13	33	36	71	0	2	.232	.311	.412	.723	98	-2	41	4.28	2	S-93	9	0.9
1966 Bos-A	139	522	58	124	20	1	18	59	41	99	1	1	.238	.297	.383	.680	85	-10	60	3.90	5	*S-127/3-5	15	0.5
1967*Bos-A★	142	491	53	127	24	2	17	66	49	93	2	4	.259	.332	.420	.752	112	7	70	4.92	8	*S-141	23	2.9
1968 Bos-A	123	406	41	95	17	2	12	46	31	73	0	1	.234	.295	.374	.669	95	-3	45	3.68	2	*S-117/1-1	15	1.1
1969 Bos-A★	154	535	92	159	32	2	40	97	98	68	3	5	.297	.407	.589	.996	167	48	129	8.65	-0	*S-153/3-1	37	**7.0**
1970 Bos-A	157	583	82	152	31	3	29	103	67	82	1	1	.261	.339	.473	.812	114	10	92	5.39	2	*S-141,3-18	23	3.0
1971 Bos-A	158	553	82	139	24	4	28	89	91	108	2	0	.251	.359	.461	.820	122	19	92	5.53	7	*3-156	27	2.7
1972 Bos-A	147	521	62	125	15	2	15	75	78	91	0	1	.240	.341	.363	.704	104	5	68	4.47	-4	*3-146	21	0.0
1973 Bos-A	100	356	44	87	13	1	13	45	47	64	0	0	.244	.334	.396	.730	99	0	47	4.54	15	3-99	11	1.6
1974 Bos-A	129	454	53	121	23	1	15	76	48	74	1	0	.267	.339	.421	.760	110	7	65	5.01	-4	*3-116/D-9	15	0.2
1975*Bos-A	115	402	31	96	15	1	7	59	41	66	0	2	.239	.314	.333	.647	76	-13	40	3.26	-1	*3-113/D-1	6	-1.4
1976 Bos-A	85	240	17	51	7	1	3	24	34	36	0	5	.213	.310	.288	.598	67	-11	20	2.63	-1	3-73/2-5,D-4,1-1,S-1	3	-1.3
Total 13	1553	5390	653	1352	237	22	210	773	661	926	10	22	.251	.336	.420	.755	108	57	769	4.85	31	S-774,3-727/D-14,2-5,1-2	205	17.2

• PETTEE, Pat Patrick E. Pettee b: 1/10/1863, Natick, MA d: 10/9/1934, Natick, MA BR/TR, 5'10", 170 lbs. Deb: 4/8/1891

YEAR TM-L	G	AB	R	H	2B	3B	HR	RBI	BB	SO	SB	CS	AVG	OBP	SLG	OPS	OPS+	BR/A	RC	RC/G	FR	G/POS	WS	TPW
1891 Lou-a	2	5	1	0	0	0	0	0	3	1	1	....	.000	.375	.000	.375	9	-0	0	2.04	-1	/2-2	0	-0.1

• PETTIGREW, Ned Jim Ned Pettigrew b: 8/25/1881, Honey Grove, TX d: 8/20/1952, Duncan, OK BR/TR, 5'11", 175 lbs. Deb: 4/23/1914

YEAR TM-L	G	AB	R	H	2B	3B	HR	RBI	BB	SO	SB	CS	AVG	OBP	SLG	OPS	OPS+	BR/A	RC	RC/G	FR	G/POS	WS	TPW
1914 Buf-F	2	2	0	0	0	0	0	0	0	0	0	....	.000	.000	.000	.000	-96	-0	0	.00	0	....	0	-0.1

• PETTINI, Joe Joseph Paul Pettini b: 1/26/1955, Wheeling, WV BR/TR, 5'9", 165 lbs. Deb: 7/10/1980 C

YEAR TM-L	G	AB	R	H	2B	3B	HR	RBI	BB	SO	SB	CS	AVG	OBP	SLG	OPS	OPS+	BR/A	RC	RC/G	FR	G/POS	WS	TPW
1980 SF-N	63	190	19	44	3	1	1	9	17	33	5	2	.232	.295	.274	.568	61	-10	17	2.76	0	S-42,3-18/2-8	3	-0.7
1981 SF-N	35	29	3	2	1	0	0	2	4	5	1	0	.069	.182	.103	.285	-18	-4	1	.86	-3	2-12,S-12/3-9	0	-0.7
1982 SF-N	29	39	5	8	1	0	0	2	3	4	0	1	.205	.262	.231	.493	39	-4	2	1.71	-3	S-26/3-1	0	-0.5
1983 SF-N	61	86	11	16	0	1	0	7	9	11	4	1	.186	.263	.209	.472	33	-7	5	1.78	-2	S-26,2-14,3-12	1	-0.7
Total 4	188	344	38	70	5	2	1	20	33	53	10	4	.203	.273	.238	.512	45	-25	25	2.22	-8	S-106/3-40,2-34	4	-2.7

• PETTIS, Gary Gary George Pettis b: 4/3/1958, Oakland, CA BB/TR, 6'1", 165 lbs. Deb: 9/13/1982 C Career OF: 1-1125-3

YEAR TM-L	G	AB	R	H	2B	3B	HR	RBI	BB	SO	SB	CS	AVG	OBP	SLG	OPS	OPS+	BR/A	RC	RC/G	FR	G/POS	WS	TPW
1982 Cal-A	10	5	5	1	0	0	1	1	0	2	0	0	.200	.200	.800	1.000	159	0	1	5.40	0	/0-8(1-6-1)	0	0.0
1983 Cal-A	22	85	19	25	2	3	3	6	7	15	8	3	.294	.348	.494	.842	130	4	15	6.07	2	0-21(0-20-1)	3	0.5
1984 Cal-A	140	397	63	90	11	6	2	29	60	115	48	17	.227	.333	.300	.632	77	-7	46	3.74	4	*0-134(0-135-0)	10	-0.5
1985 Cal-A	125	443	67	114	10	8	1	32	62	125	56	9	.257	.349	.323	.671	86	2	61	4.64	11	*0-122(0-122-0)	16	1.1
1986*Cal-A	154	539	93	139	23	4	5	58	69	132	50	13	.258	.342	.343	.685	88	-1	71	4.39	15	*0-153(0-153-0)/D-1	18	1.1
1987 Cal-A	133	394	49	82	13	2	1	17	52	124	24	5	.208	.302	.259	.561	53	-23	35	2.90	6	*0-131(0-131-0)	5	-1.7
1988 Det-A	129	458	65	96	14	4	3	36	47	85	44	10	.210	.285	.277	.562	60	-18	42	3.00	3	*0-126(0-126-0)/D-2	12	-1.8
1989 Det-A	119	444	77	114	8	6	1	18	84	106	43	15	.257	.375	.309	.684	97	6	58	4.30	-3	*0-119(0-119-0)	10	0.1
1990 Tex-A	136	423	66	101	16	8	3	31	57	118	38	15	.239	.335	.336	.670	88	-4	52	3.96	7	*0-128(0-128-0)/D-2	11	0.1
1991 Tex-A	137	282	37	61	7	5	0	19	54	91	29	13	.216	.342	.277	.619	75	-7	32	3.49	-3	*0-126(0-126-0)/D-3	6	-1.1
1992 SD-N	30	30	0	6	1	0	0	0	2	11	1	0	.200	.250	.233	.483	37	-2	2	2.26	0	0-14(0-13-1)	0	-0.3
Det-A	48	129	27	26	4	3	1	12	27	34	13	4	.202	.340	.302	.642	81	-1	16	3.74	0	0-46(0-46-0)	3	-0.2
Total 11	1183	3629	568	855	109	49	21	259	521	958	354	104	.236	.333	.310	.643	80	-51	432	3.87	41	*0-1128/D-8	94	-2.6

• PETTIT, Bob Robert Henry Pettit b: 7/19/1861, Williamstown, MA d: 11/1/1910, Derby, CT BL/TR, 5'9", 160 lbs. Deb: 9/3/1887 Career OF: 3-4-76 ♦

YEAR TM-L	G	AB	R	H	2B	3B	HR	RBI	BB	SO	SB	CS	AVG	OBP	SLG	OPS	OPS+	BR/A	RC	RC/G	FR	G/POS	WS	TPW
1887 Chi-N	32	146	29	44	3	3	2	12	8	15	16	....	.301	.301	.370	.671	75	-5	21	5.38	1	0-32(0-0-32)/C-1,P-1	2	-0.4
1888 Chi-N	43	169	23	43	1	4	4	23	7	9	7	....	.254	.288	.379	.667	104	0	21	4.49	1	0-43(0-2-42)	4	0.0
1891 Mil-a	21	80	10	14	4	0	1	5	7	7	2	....	.175	.267	.263	.529	43	-7	6	2.52	0	/2-9,0-7(3-2-2),3-6	1	-0.6
Total 3	96	395	62	101	8	7	7	40	22	31	25	....	.256	.288	.351	.640	80	-12	48	4.36	1	/0-82,2-9,3-6,C-1,P-1	7	-1.0

• PEVEY, Marty Marty Ashley Pevey b: 12/25/1962, Savannah, GA BL/TR, 6'1", 185 lbs. Deb: 5/16/1989 C

YEAR TM-L	G	AB	R	H	2B	3B	HR	RBI	BB	SO	SB	CS	AVG	OBP	SLG	OPS	OPS+	BR/A	RC	RC/G	FR	G/POS	WS	TPW
1989 Mon-N	13	41	2	9	1	1	0	3	0	8	0	0	.220	.220	.293	.512	45	-3	2	1.89	0	C-11/0-1	1	-0.3

• PEZOLD, Larry Lorenz Johannes Pezold b: 6/22/1893, New Orleans, LA d: 10/22/1957, Baton Rouge, LA BR/TR, 5'9.5", 175 lbs. Deb: 7/27/1914

YEAR TM-L	G	AB	R	H	2B	3B	HR	RBI	BB	SO	SB	CS	AVG	OBP	SLG	OPS	OPS+	BR/A	RC	RC/G	FR	G/POS	WS	TPW
1914 Cle-A	23	71	4	16	0	1	0	5	9	6	2	3	.225	.313	.254	.566	68	-3	6	2.54	-3	3-20/0-1	1	-0.6

• PFEFFER, Fred Nathaniel Frederick "Fritz,Dandelion" Pfeffer
b: 3/17/1860, Louisville, KY d: 4/10/1932, Chicago, IL BR/TR, 5'10.5", 184 lbs. Deb: 5/1/1882 M/U Career OF: 0-2-1 ♦

YEAR TM-L	G	AB	R	H	2B	3B	HR	RBI	BB	SO	SB	CS	AVG	OBP	SLG	OPS	OPS+	BR/A	RC	RC/G	FR	G/POS	WS	TPW
1882 Tro-N	85	330	26	72	7	4	1	43	1	24	....	....	.218	.221	.273	.493	60	-14	20	2.17	8	*S-83/2-2	5	-0.3
1883 Chi-N	96	371	41	87	22	7	1	45	8	50	....	....	.235	.251	.340	.590	71	-14	32	3.13	3	*2-79,S-18/1-1,3-1	8	-0.7
1884 Chi-N	112	467	105	135	10	10	25	101	25	47	....	....	.289	.325	.514	.839	147	23	80	6.63	24	*2-112/P-1	19	4.5
1885*Chi-N	112	469	90	113	12	7	5	73	26	47	....	....	.241	.281	.328	.609	84	-10	44	3.36	15	*2-109/P-5,0-1	18	0.9
1886*Chi-N	118	474	88	125	17	8	7	95	36	46	30	....	.264	.316	.378	.693	95	-5	68	5.23	1	*2-118/1-1	16	0.0
1887 Chi-N	123	513	95	167	21	6	16	89	34	20	57	....	.326	.327	.447	.774	100	-4	91	6.95	10	*2-123/0-2(0-2-0)	16	0.9
1888 Chi-N	135	517	90	129	22	10	8	57	32	38	64	....	.250	.297	.377	.674	106	2	79	5.49	20	*2-135	20	2.7
1889 Chi-N	134	531	85	121	15	7	7	77	53	51	45	....	.228	.302	.322	.624	71	-23	67	4.31	23	*2-134	13	0.4
1890 Chi-P	124	499	86	128	21	8	5	80	44	23	27	....	.257	.319	.361	.680	78	-18	68	4.93	21	*2-124	13	0.5
1891 Chi-N	137	498	93	123	12	9	7	77	79	60	40	....	.247	.353	.349	.703	105	6	78	5.58	15	*2-137	21	2.3
1892 Lou-N	124	470	78	121	14	9	2	76	67	36	27	....	.257	.353	.338	.691	118	14	67	5.20	-2	*2-116,1-10/P-1	20	1.7
1893 Lou-N	125	508	85	129	29	12	3	75	51	18	32	....	.254	.322	.376	.698	92	-6	74	5.15	-7	*2-125	13	-0.6
1894 Lou-N	105	414	70	128	12	15	5	61	30	14	31	....	.309	.357	.447	.804	100	-0	79	7.19	1	*2-90,S-15/P-1	11	0.6
1895 Lou-N	11	45	8	13	1	0	0	5	5	3	2	....	.289	.360	.311	.671	79	-1	6	4.98	-5	/S-5,1-3,2-3	1	-0.4
1896 NY-N	4	14	1	2	0	0	0	4	1	1	0	....	.143	.250	.143	.393	5	-2	1	1.13	-2	/2-4	0	-0.3
Chi-N	94	360	45	88	16	7	2	52	23	20	22	....	.244	.294	.344	.638	65	-20	44	4.26	10	*2-94	7	-0.5
Yr.	98	374	46	90	16	7	2	56	24	21	22	....	.241	.292	.337	.629	63	-22	45	4.13	8	*2-98	7	-0.8
1897 Chi-N	32	114	10	26	0	1	0	11	12	....	5	....	.228	.318	.246	.563	48	-8	11	3.26	-7	2-32	1	-1.2
Total 16	1671	6594	1096	1707	231	120	94	1021	527	498	382	....	.259	.312	.370	.682	93	-81	908	4.98	129	*2-1537,S-121/1-15,P-8,0-3,3	202	10.5

• PFEFFER, Monte Monte Pfeffer b: 10/8/1891, New York, NY d: 9/27/1941, New York, NY BR/TR, 5'4.5", 147 lbs. Deb: 9/29/1913

YEAR TM-L	G	AB	R	H	2B	3B	HR	RBI	BB	SO	SB	CS	AVG	OBP	SLG	OPS	OPS+	BR/A	RC	RC/G	FR	G/POS	WS	TPW
1913 Phi-A	1	3	0	0	0	0	0	0	0	1	0	....	.000	.250	.000	.250	-26	-0	0	.00	0	/S-1	0	-0.1

• PFEIL, Bobby Robert Raymond Pfeil b: 11/13/1943, Passaic, NJ BR/TR, 6'1", 180 lbs. Deb: 6/26/1969 Career OF: 4-0-1

YEAR TM-L	G	AB	R	H	2B	3B	HR	RBI	BB	SO	SB	CS	AVG	OBP	SLG	OPS	OPS+	BR/A	RC	RC/G	FR	G/POS	WS	TPW
1969 NY-N	62	211	20	49	9	0	0	10	7	27	0	1	.232	.260	.275	.535	49	-15	14	2.23	2	3-49,2-11/0-2(2-0-0)	2	-1.3
1971 Phi-N	44	70	5	19	3	0	2	9	6	9	1	1	.271	.329	.400	.729	106	0	8	3.99	1	3-15/C-4,0-3(2-0-1),1-1,2,S	2	0.1
Total 2	106	281	25	68	12	0	2	19	13	36	1	2	.242	.278	.306	.584	63	-15	22	2.66	3	/3-64,2-12,0-5,C-4,1-1,S-1	4	-1.2

• PFISTER, George George Edward Pfister b: 9/4/1918, Bound Brook, NJ d: 8/14/1997, Somerset, NJ BR/TR, 6', 200 lbs. Deb: 9/27/1941 C

YEAR TM-L	G	AB	R	H	2B	3B	HR	RBI	BB	SO	SB	CS	AVG	OBP	SLG	OPS	OPS+	BR/A	RC	RC/G	FR	G/POS	WS	TPW
1941 Bro-N	1	2	0	0	0	0	0	0	0	0	0	0	.000	.000	.000	.000	-96	-1	0	.00	0	/C-1	0	-0.1

• PFYL, Monte Meinhard Charles Pfyl b: 5/11/1884, St. Louis, MO d: 10/18/1945, San Francisco, CA BL/TL, 6'3", 190 lbs. Deb: 7/30/1907

YEAR TM-L	G	AB	R	H	2B	3B	HR	RBI	BB	SO	SB	CS	AVG	OBP	SLG	OPS	OPS+	BR/A	RC	RC/G	FR	G/POS	WS	TPW
1907 NY-N	1	0	0	0	0	0	0	0	0	....	0	....	....	....	....	....	-97	0	0	.00	0	/1-1	0	0.0

• PHELAN, Art Arthur Thomas "Dugan" Phelan b: 8/14/1887, Niantic, IL d: 12/27/1964, Fort Worth, TX BR/TR, 5'8", 160 lbs. Deb: 6/25/1910

YEAR TM-L	G	AB	R	H	2B	3B	HR	RBI	BB	SO	SB	CS	AVG	OBP	SLG	OPS	OPS+	BR/A	RC	RC/G	FR	G/POS	WS	TPW
1910 Cin-N	23	42	7	9	0	0	0	4	7	6	5	....	.214	.327	.214	.541	61	-2	5	3.50	0	/3-8,2-5,0-3(3-0-0),S-1	1	-0.2
1912 Cin-N	130	461	56	112	9	11	3	54	46	37	25	....	.243	.314	.330	.644	79	-14	56	3.88	2	*3-127/2-3	13	-0.8
1913 Chi-N	91	261	41	65	11	6	2	35	29	26	8	....	.249	.331	.360	.691	97	-1	33	4.10	1	2-46,3-38/S-1	9	0.2

YEAR	TM-L	G	AB	R	H	2B	3B	HR	RBI	BB	SO	SB	CS	AVG	OBP	SLG	OPS	OPS+	BR/A	RC	RC/G	FR	G/POS	WS	TPW
1914	Chi-N	25	46	5	13	2	1	0	3	4	3	0	....	.283	.340	.370	.710	111	1	6	4.30	-1	/3-7,2-3,S-2	2	0.0
1915	Chi-N	133	448	41	98	16	7	3	35	55	42	12	9	.219	.307	.306	.613	86	-8	45	3.19	-4	*3-110,2-24	11	-0.9
Total	**5**	**402**	**1258**	**150**	**297**	**38**	**25**	**8**	**131**	**141**	**114**	**50**	**9**	**.236**	**.317**	**.325**	**.642**	**85**	**-23**	**144**	**3.67**	**-2**	**3-290/2-81,S-4,0-3**	**36**	**-1.7**

• PHELAN, Dan Daniel T. Phelan b: 7/23/1864, Thomaston, CT d: 12/7/1945, West Haven, CT BL, 5'10" Deb: 4/18/1890

YEAR	TM-L	G	AB	R	H	2B	3B	HR	RBI	BB	SO	SB	CS	AVG	OBP	SLG	OPS	OPS+	BR/A	RC	RC/G	FR	G/POS	WS	TPW
1890	Lou-a	8	32	4	8	1	1	0	4	0	....	1	....	.250	.250	.344	.594	77	-1	3	3.40	1	/1-8	0	-0.1

• PHELAN, Dick James Dickson Phelan b: 12/10/1854, Towanda, PA d: 2/13/1931, San Antonio, TX BR Deb: 4/17/1884

YEAR	TM-L	G	AB	R	H	2B	3B	HR	RBI	BB	SO	SB	CS	AVG	OBP	SLG	OPS	OPS+	BR/A	RC	RC/G	FR	G/POS	WS	TPW
1884	Bal-U	101	402	63	99	13	3	3	....	12	....	....	....	.246	.268	.316	.584	88	-7	35	3.23	-13	*2-100/3-5,0-1	10	-1.5
1885	Buf-N	4	16	2	2	0	0	1	3	0	3	....	....	.125	.125	.313	.438	37	-1	1	1.24	0	/2-4	0	-0.1
	StL-N	2	4	1	1	1	0	0	1	0	2	....	....	.250	.250	.500	.750	147	0	1	4.61	0	/3-2	0	0.0
	Yr.	6	20	3	3	1	0	1	4	0	5	....	....	.150	.150	.350	.500	59	-1	1	1.83	-1	/2-4,3-2	0	-0.1
Total	**2**	**107**	**422**	**66**	**102**	**14**	**3**	**4**	**4**	**12**	**5**	**....**	**....**	**.242**	**.263**	**.318**	**.580**	**86**	**-8**	**36**	**3.15**	**-14**	**2-104/3-7,0-1**	**10**	**-1.7**

• PHELPS, Babe Ernest Gordon "Blimp" Phelps b: 4/16/1908, Odenton, MD d: 12/10/1992, Odenton, MD BL/TR, 6'2", 225 lbs. Deb: 9/17/1931

YEAR	TM-L	G	AB	R	H	2B	3B	HR	RBI	BB	SO	SB	CS	AVG	OBP	SLG	OPS	OPS+	BR/A	RC	RC/G	FR	G/POS	WS	TPW
1931	Was-A	3	3	0	1	0	0	0	0	0	0	0	0	.333	.333	.333	.667	75	-0	0	4.24	0	....	0	0.0
1933	Chi-N	3	7	0	2	0	0	0	2	0	1	0	....	.286	.286	.286	.571	64	-0	1	3.16	0	/C-2	0	0.0
1934	Chi-N	44	70	7	20	5	2	2	12	1	8	0	....	.286	.296	.500	.796	111	1	10	5.39	0	C-18	2	0.1
1935	Bro-N	47	121	17	44	7	2	5	22	9	10	0	....	.364	.408	.579	.986	165	11	28	9.62	0	C-34	7	1.3
1936	Bro-N	115	319	36	117	23	2	5	57	27	18	1	....	.367	.421	.498	.920	145	21	69	8.96	1	C-98/0-1	16	2.5
1937	Bro-N	121	409	42	128	37	3	7	58	25	28	2	....	.313	.357	.469	.826	121	11	67	6.10	2	*C-111	15	1.9
1938	Bro-N★	66	208	33	64	12	2	5	46	23	15	2	....	.308	.379	.457	.836	126	8	35	6.23	0	C-55	8	1.1
1939	Bro-N★	98	323	33	92	21	2	6	42	24	24	0	....	.285	.336	.418	.754	98	-2	43	4.62	2	C-92	11	0.5
1940	Bro-N★	118	370	47	109	24	5	13	61	30	27	2	....	.295	.349	.492	.841	122	10	59	5.67	-5	C-99/1-1	14	1.1
1941	Bro-N	16	30	3	7	3	0	2	4	1	2	0	....	.233	.258	.533	.791	114	0	4	4.93	-1	C-11	1	0.0
1942	Pit-N	95	257	21	73	11	1	9	41	20	24	2	....	.284	.345	.440	.785	126	8	39	5.58	0	C-72	11	1.3
Total	**11**	**726**	**2117**	**239**	**657**	**143**	**19**	**54**	**345**	**160**	**157**	**9**	**0**	**.310**	**.362**	**.472**	**.835**	**124**	**66**	**356**	**6.25**	**0**	**C-592/1-1,0-1**	**85**	**9.8**

• PHELPS, Ed Edward Jaykill "Yaller" Phelps b: 3/3/1879, Albany, NY d: 1/31/1942, East Greenbush, NY BR/TR, 5'11", 185 lbs. Deb: 9/3/1902 U

YEAR	TM-L	G	AB	R	H	2B	3B	HR	RBI	BB	SO	SB	CS	AVG	OBP	SLG	OPS	OPS+	BR/A	RC	RC/G	FR	G/POS	WS	TPW
1902	Pit-N	18	61	5	13	1	0	0	6	4	....	2	....	.213	.284	.230	.513	57	-3	5	2.63	-2	C-13/1-5	1	-0.4
1903*	Pit-N	81	273	32	77	7	3	2	31	17	....	2	....	.282	.338	.352	.689	94	-2	35	4.55	-8	C-76/1-3	8	-0.3
1904	Pit-N	94	302	29	73	5	3	0	28	15	....	2	....	.242	.289	.278	.567	73	-10	27	2.92	-8	C-91/1-1	6	-0.9
1905	Cin-N	44	156	18	36	5	3	0	18	12	....	4	....	.231	.306	.301	.608	73	-5	16	3.47	-2	C-44	4	-0.3
1906	Cin-N	12	40	3	11	0	2	1	5	3	....	2	....	.275	.326	.450	.776	136	1	7	5.63	1	C-12	2	0.3
	Pit-N	43	118	9	28	3	1	0	12	9	....	1	....	.237	.302	.280	.582	78	-3	11	3.06	-5	C-40	3	-0.5
	Yr.	55	158	12	39	3	3	1	17	12	....	3	....	.247	.308	.323	.631	93	-2	18	3.72	-5	C-52	5	-0.2
1907	Pit-N	43	113	11	24	1	0	0	12	9	....	1	....	.212	.282	.221	.503	57	-5	8	2.27	-2	C-35/1-1	2	-0.4
1908	Pit-N	34	64	3	15	2	2	0	11	2	....	0	....	.234	.269	.328	.597	90	-1	5	2.85	-2	C-20	2	-0.1
1909	StL-N	104	306	43	76	13	1	0	22	39	....	7	....	.248	.350	.297	.648	108	5	35	3.79	0	C-83	9	1.4
1910	StL-N	93	270	25	71	4	2	0	37	36	29	9	....	.263	.356	.293	.649	93	-1	32	3.99	-5	C-80	8	0.2
1912	Bro-N	52	111	8	32	4	3	0	23	16	15	1	....	.288	.388	.378	.766	114	3	17	5.20	2	C-32	4	0.7
1913	Bro-N	15	18	0	4	0	0	0	0	1	2	0	....	.222	.263	.222	.485	38	-1	1	1.78	-1	/C-4	0	-0.2
Total	**11**	**633**	**1832**	**186**	**460**	**45**	**20**	**3**	**205**	**163**	**46**	**31**	**....**	**.251**	**.325**	**.302**	**.627**	**88**	**-22**	**200**	**3.63**	**-31**	**C-530/1-10**	**49**	**-0.5**

• PHELPS, Josh Joshua Lee Phelps b: 5/12/1978, Anchorage, AK BR/TR, 6'3", 215 lbs. Deb: 6/13/2000

YEAR	TM-L	G	AB	R	H	2B	3B	HR	RBI	BB	SO	SB	CS	AVG	OBP	SLG	OPS	OPS+	BR/A	RC	RC/G	FR	G/POS	WS	TPW
2000	Tor-A	1	1	0	0	0	0	0	0	0	1	0	0	.000	.000	.000	.000	-97	-0	0	.00	0	/C-1	0	-0.1
2001	Tor-A	8	12	3	0	0	0	0	1	2	5	1	0	.000	.143	.000	.143	-56	-3	0	.15	0	/C-7	0	-0.2
2002	Tor-A	74	265	41	82	20	1	15	58	19	82	0	0	.309	.362	.562	.925	136	13	52	7.43	0	D-71/1-2	10	0.8
2003	Tor-A	119	396	57	106	18	1	20	66	39	115	1	2	.268	.358	.470	.828	114	8	66	5.81	-1	*D-105/1-8	10	0.0
Total	**4**	**202**	**674**	**101**	**188**	**38**	**2**	**35**	**125**	**60**	**203**	**2**	**2**	**.279**	**.355**	**.497**	**.852**	**119**	**18**	**118**	**6.26**	**-1**	**D-176/1-10,C-8**	**20**	**0.5**

• PHELPS, Ken Kenneth Allen Phelps b: 8/6/1954, Seattle, WA BL/TL, 6'1", 209 lbs. Deb: 9/20/1980

YEAR	TM-L	G	AB	R	H	2B	3B	HR	RBI	BB	SO	SB	CS	AVG	OBP	SLG	OPS	OPS+	BR/A	RC	RC/G	FR	G/POS	WS	TPW
1980	KC-A	3	4	0	0	0	0	0	0	0	2	0	0	.000	.000	.000	.000	-99	-1	0	.00	0	/1-2	0	-0.2
1981	KC-A	21	22	1	3	0	1	0	1	1	13	0	0	.136	.174	.227	.401	15	-2	1	1.30	0	/D-4,1-2	0	-0.2
1982	Mon-N	10	8	0	2	0	0	0	0	0	3	0	0	.250	.333	.250	.583	64	-0	1	3.39	0	....	0	0.0
1983	Sea-A	50	127	10	30	4	1	7	16	13	25	0	0	.236	.307	.449	.756	101	-0	19	4.99	2	1-22,D-19	3	0.0
1984	Sea-A	101	290	52	70	9	0	24	51	61	73	3	3	.241	.382	.521	.903	149	21	63	7.40	-1	D-84/1-9	13	1.7
1985	Sea-A	61	116	18	24	3	0	9	24	24	33	2	0	.207	.343	.466	.808	118	4	20	5.92	0	D-25/1-8	4	0.3
1986	Sea-A	125	344	69	85	16	4	24	64	88	96	2	3	.247	.409	.526	.935	151	28	81	8.08	-7	1-55,D-52	15	1.6
1987	Sea-A	120	332	68	86	13	1	27	68	80	75	1	1	.259	.414	.548	.962	145	25	81	8.45	0	*D-114/1-1	15	2.1
1988	Sea-A	72	190	37	54	8	0	14	32	51	35	1	0	.284	.438	.547	.985	167	20	50	9.58	0	D-68/1-3	10	1.9
	NY-A	45	107	17	24	5	0	10	22	19	26	0	0	.224	.341	.551	.893	147	7	20	6.22	0	D-24/1-1	4	0.6
	Yr.	117	297	54	78	13	0	24	54	70	61	1	0	.263	.405	.549	.954	160	27	70	8.30	-0	D-92/1-4	14	2.5
1989	NY-A	86	185	26	46	3	0	7	29	27	47	0	0	.249	.344	.378	.723	105	2	26	4.83	-1	D-55/1-8	5	-0.1
	*Oak-A	11	9	0	1	1	0	0	0	4	0	0	0	.111	.385	.222	.607	78	0	1	3.95	0	/1-1,D-1	0	0.0
	Yr.	97	194	26	47	4	0	7	29	31	47	0	0	.242	.347	.371	.718	103	2	27	4.79	-1	D-56/1-9	5	-0.1
1990	Oak-A	32	59	6	11	2	0	1	6	12	10	0	0	.186	.324	.271	.595	71	-2	6	3.20	0	D-15/1-5	1	-0.2
	Cle-A	24	61	4	7	0	0	0	0	10	11	1	0	.115	.239	.115	.354	2	-7	2	.90	1	1-14/D-6	0	-0.8
	Yr.	56	120	10	18	2	0	1	6	22	21	1	0	.150	.282	.192	.473	37	-9	8	1.97	1	D-21,1-19	1	-1.0
Total	**11**	**761**	**1854**	**308**	**443**	**64**	**7**	**123**	**313**	**390**	**449**	**10**	**7**	**.239**	**.377**	**.480**	**.857**	**132**	**93**	**369**	**6.81**	**-7**	**D-467,1-131**	**70**	**6.6**

• PHELPS, Nealy Cornelius Carman Phelps b: 11/19/1840, New York, NY d: 2/12/1885, New York, NY Deb: 7/1/1871 U NA OF: 0-0-9

YEAR	TM-L	G	AB	R	H	2B	3B	HR	RBI	BB	SO	SB	CS	AVG	OBP	SLG	OPS	OPS+	BR/A	RC	RC/G	FR	G/POS	WS	TPW
1871	Kek-n	1	3	0	0	0	0	0	0	1	0	0	0	.000	.250	.000	.250	-20	-0	0	.00	0	/1-1	....	0.0
1873	Mut-n	1	6	0	0	0	0	0	0	0	0	0	0	.000	.000	.000	.000	-101	-1	0	.00	0	/1-1,0-1	....	-0.1
1874	Mut-n	6	24	5	3	0	0	0	2	0	0	0	0	.125	.125	.125	.250	-19	-3	0	.55	1	/0-6(0-0-6)	....	-0.1
1875	Mut-n	2	6	1	2	1	0	0	0	0	1	0	0	.333	.333	.500	.833	176	0	1	7.56	1	/0-2(0-0-2)	....	0.1
1876	NY-N	1	3	0	0	0	0	0	0	0	1	....	....	.000	.000	.000	.000	-115	-1	0	.00	0	/0-1	0	-0.1
	Phi-N	1	4	0	0	0	0	0	0	0	0	....	....	.000	.000	.000	.000	-101	-1	0	.00	-1	/C-1	0	-0.2
	Yr.	2	7	0	0	0	0	0	0	0	1	....	....	.000	.000	.000	.000	-107	-1	0	.00	-2	/C-1,0-1	0	-0.3
Total	**4 n**	**10**	**39**	**6**	**5**	**1**	**0**	**0**	**2**	**1**	**1**	**0**	**0**	**.128**	**.150**	**.154**	**.304**	**-2**	**-5**	**1**	**1.23**	**1**	**/0-9,1-2**	**....**	**-0.2**

• PHILLEY, Dave David Earl Philley b: 5/16/1920, Paris, TX BB/TR, 6', 188 lbs. Deb: 9/6/1941 Career OF: 204-590-714

YEAR	TM-L	G	AB	R	H	2B	3B	HR	RBI	BB	SO	SB	CS	AVG	OBP	SLG	OPS	OPS+	BR/A	RC	RC/G	FR	G/POS	WS	TPW
1941	Chi-A	7	9	4	2	1	0	0	0	3	3	0	0	.222	.417	.333	.750	102	0	2	6.20	0	/0-2(2-0-0)	0	0.0
1946	Chi-A	17	68	10	24	2	3	0	17	4	4	5	0	.353	.389	.471	.859	145	5	14	8.02	5	0-17(16-1-0)	4	0.9
1947	Chi-A	143	551	55	142	25	11	2	45	35	39	21	16	.258	.303	.354	.657	85	-15	56	3.39	2	*0-133(39-95-0)/3-4	11	-2.0
1948	Chi-A	137	488	51	140	28	3	5	42	50	33	8	10	.287	.353	.387	.740	100	-3	67	4.77	13	*0-128(6-123-0)	13	0.6
1949	Chi-A	146	598	84	171	20	8	0	44	54	51	13	4	.286	.347	.346	.693	86	-10	76	4.55	3	*0-145(0-3-143)	12	-1.1
1950	Chi-A	156	619	69	150	21	5	14	80	52	57	6	3	.242	.302	.360	.662	71	-29	67	3.64	9	*0-154(0-70-103)	8	-2.3
1951	Chi-A	7	25	0	6	2	0	0	2	2	3	0	0	.240	.296	.320	.616	68	-1	2	3.05	0	/0-6(6-0-0)	0	-0.2
	Phi-A	125	468	71	123	18	7	7	59	63	38	9	6	.263	.354	.376	.730	95	-2	68	5.11	-2	*0-120(2-116-2)/3-2	13	-0.7
	Yr.	132	493	71	129	20	7	7	61	65	41	9	6	.262	.351	.373	.724	94	-3	70	5.00	-2	*0-126(8-116-2)/3-2	13	-0.9
1952	Phi-A	151	586	80	154	25	4	7	71	59	35	11	4	.263	.334	.355	.689	86	-9	67	3.78	5	*0-149(0-149-0)/3-2	15	-0.8
1953	Phi-A	157	620	80	188	30	9	9	59	51	35	13	5	.303	.358	.424	.782	106	6	92	5.39	-1	*0-157(0-31-129)/3-1	15	0.1
1954*	Cle-A	133	452	48	102	13	3	12	60	57	48	2	4	.226	.312	.347	.660	79	-14	48	3.37	-4	*0-129(1-0-129)	9	-2.3
1955	Cle-A	43	104	15	31	4	2	2	9	12	10	0	2	.298	.371	.433	.803	111	1	15	4.94	0	0-34(2-0-32)	3	0.0
	Bal-A	83	311	50	93	13	3	6	41	34	38	1	2	.299	.368	.418	.786	119	8	47	5.45	-3	0-82(46-2-48)/3-2	11	0.1
	Yr.	126	415	65	124	17	5	8	50	46	48	1	4	.299	.369	.422	.790	117	9	62	5.31	-2	*0-116(48-2-80)/3-2	14	0.2
1956	Bal-A	32	117	13	24	4	2	1	17	18	13	3	1	.205	.311	.299	.610	67	-5	10	2.71	0	0-31(23-0-16)/3-5	1	-0.6
	Chi-A	86	279	44	74	14	2	4	47	28	27	1	3	.265	.334	.373	.707	85	-7	33	4.02	-3	1-51,0-30(17-0-19)	5	-1.3
	Yr.	118	396	57	98	18	4	5	64	46	40	4	4	.247	.327	.351	.678	80	-12	44	3.61	-3	0-61(40-0-35),1-51/3-5	6	-1.9

YEAR TM-L	G	AB	R	H	2B	3B	HR	RBI	BB	SO	SB	CS	AVG	OBP	SLG	OPS	OPS+	BR/A	RC	RC/G	FR	G/POS	WS	TPW
1957 Chi-A	22	71	9	23	4	0	0	9	4	10	1	1	.324	.360	.380	.740	102	0	10	5.06	0	0-17(0-0-17)/1-2	2	-0.1
Det-A	65	173	15	49	8	1	2	16	7	16	3	1	.283	.311	.376	.687	85	-4	19	4.03	4	1-27,0-12(4-0-8)/3-1	3	-0.2
Yr.	87	244	24	72	12	1	2	25	11	26	4	2	.295	.325	.377	.703	90	-4	29	4.32	4	1-29,0-29(4-0-25)/3-1	5	-0.3
1958 Phi-N	91	207	30	64	11	4	3	31	15	20	1	1	.309	.359	.444	.803	112	3	31	5.36	-2	0-24(0-0-24),1-18	5	0.0
1959 Phi-N	99	254	32	74	18	2	7	37	18	27	0	0	.291	.341	.461	.801	109	3	40	5.75	0	0-34(0-0-34),1-24	8	0.1
1960 Phi-N	14	15	2	5	2	0	0	4	3	2	0	0	.333	.444	.467	.911	149	1	3	7.18	-1	/0-3(2-0-1),1-2	1	0.0
SF-N	39	61	5	10	0	0	1	7	6	14	0	0	.164	.239	.213	.452	26	-6	3	1.55	-2	0-10(10-0-0)/3-3	0	-0.9
Yr.	53	76	7	15	2	0	1	11	9	16	0	0	.197	.282	.263	.546	52	-5	6	2.52	-2	0-13(12-0-1)/3-3,1-2	1	-0.8
Bal-A	14	34	6	9	2	1	1	5	4	5	1	0	.265	.342	.471	.813	119	1	6	6.49	0	/0-8(6-0-2),3-1	2	0.0
1961 Bal-A	99	144	13	36	9	2	1	23	10	20	2	0	.250	.299	.361	.660	77	-5	13	3.03	0	0-25(22-0-3)/1-1	1	-0.6
1962 Bos-A	38	42	3	6	2	0	0	4	5	3	0	0	.143	.250	.190	.440	20	-5	1	.92	0	/0-4(0-0-4)	0	-0.5
Total 18	1904	6296	789	1700	276	72	84	729	594	551	101	63	.270	.335	.377	.711	91	-86	790	4.32	24	*0-1454,1-125/3-21	142	-11.6

• PHILLIPS, Adolfo Adolfo Emilio (Lopez) Phillips b: 12/16/1941, Bethania, Panama BR/TR, 6'1", 177 lbs. Deb: 9/2/1964 Career OF: 18-576-3

YEAR TM-L	G	AB	R	H	2B	3B	HR	RBI	BB	SO	SB	CS	AVG	OBP	SLG	OPS	OPS+	BR/A	RC	RC/G	FR	G/POS	WS	TPW
1964 Phi-N	13	13	4	3	0	0	0	0	3	3	0	0	.231	.375	.231	.606	76	-0	2	3.73	0	/0-4(3-2-1)	1	0.0
1965 Phi-N	41	87	14	20	4	0	3	5	5	34	3	3	.230	.272	.379	.651	83	-3	9	3.27	-2	0-32(2-30-0)	1	-0.6
1966 Phi-N	2	3	1	0	0	0	0	0	0	0	0	0	.000	.000	.000	.000	-100	-1	0	.00	0	/0-1	0	-0.1
Chi-N	116	416	68	109	29	1	16	36	43	135	32	15	.262	.348	.452	.800	119	12	66	5.42	8	*0-111(0-111-0)	14	1.7
Yr.	118	419	69	109	29	1	16	36	43	135	32	15	.260	.346	.449	.795	117	11	66	5.37	7	*0-112(0-112-0)	14	1.6
1967 Chi-N	144	448	66	120	20	7	17	70	80	93	24	10	.268	.386	.458	.843	134	25	82	6.22	9	*0-141(0-141-0)	26	3.2
1968 Chi-N	143	439	49	106	20	5	13	33	47	90	9	7	.241	.322	.399	.720	108	4	55	4.19	4	*0-141(0-141-0)	16	0.5
1969 Chi-N	28	49	5	11	3	1	0	1	16	15	1	3	.224	.424	.327	.751	100	0	7	4.41	-1	0-25(1-24-0)	2	-0.2
Mon-N	58	199	25	43	4	4	4	7	19	62	6	5	.216	.288	.337	.624	74	-8	19	3.17	-1	0-53(0-53-0)	2	-1.0
Yr.	86	248	30	54	7	5	4	8	35	77	7	8	.218	.319	.335	.654	80	-8	26	3.43	-2	0-78(1-77-0)	4	-1.2
1970 Mon-N	92	214	36	51	6	3	6	21	36	51	7	1	.238	.353	.379	.732	96	1	31	4.92	-3	0-75(6-71-0)	7	-0.4
1972 Cle-A	12	7	2	0	0	0	0	0	2	2	0	0	.000	.222	.000	.222	-29	-1	0	.45	0	0-10(6-2-2)	0	-0.2
Total 8	649	1875	270	463	86	21	59	173	251	485	82	44	.247	.344	.410	.754	110	30	270	4.84	15	0-593	69	3.0

• PHILLIPS, Bill William B. Phillips b: 1857, St. John, Canada d: 10/7/1900, Chicago, IL BR/TR, 6', 202 lbs. Deb: 5/1/1879

YEAR TM-L	G	AB	R	H	2B	3B	HR	RBI	BB	SO	SB	CS	AVG	OBP	SLG	OPS	OPS+	BR/A	RC	RC/G	FR	G/POS	WS	TPW
1879 Cle-N	81	365	58	99	15	4	0	29	2	20	....	....	.271	.275	.334	.609	101	-0	34	3.62	-4	*1-75,C-11/0-2(0-1-1)	7	-0.7
1880 Cle-N	85	334	41	85	14	10	1	36	6	29	....	....	.254	.268	.365	.633	114	5	33	3.70	1	*1-85	10	0.1
1881 Cle-N	85	357	51	97	18	10	1	44	5	19	....	....	.272	.282	.387	.668	114	5	40	4.14	-3	*1-85	8	-0.3
1882 Cle-N	78	335	40	87	17	7	4	47	7	18	....	....	.260	.275	.388	.663	114	5	37	4.06	1	*1-78/C-1	10	-0.1
1883 Cle-N	97	382	42	94	29	8	2	40	8	49	....	....	.246	.262	.380	.641	93	-3	39	3.71	-4	*1-97	7	-1.4
1884 Cle-N	111	464	58	128	25	12	3	46	18	80	....	....	.276	.303	.401	.704	115	7	58	4.73	-8	*1-111	8	-0.9
1885 Bro-a	99	391	65	118	16	11	3	63	27	....	....	....	.302	.364	.422	.786	147	21	62	6.08	1	*1-99	17	1.2
1886 Bro-a	141	585	68	160	26	15	0	72	33	....	13	....	.274	.313	.369	.683	113	6	74	4.67	-1	*1-141	18	-0.6
1887 Bro-a	132	578	82	187	34	11	2	101	45	....	16	....	.324	.330	.383	.713	97	-3	75	5.15	0	*1-132	12	-1.2
1888 KC-a	129	509	57	120	20	10	1	56	27	....	10	....	.236	.284	.320	.604	88	-9	50	3.49	3	*1-129	9	-1.6
Total 10	1038	4300	562	1175	214	98	17	534	178	215	39	....	.273	.299	.374	.673	109	34	501	4.37	-16	*1-1032/C-12,0-2	106	-5.5

• PHILLIPS, Brandon Brandon Emil Phillips b: 6/28/1981, Raleigh, NC BR/TR, 5'11", 185 lbs. Deb: 9/13/2002

YEAR TM-L	G	AB	R	H	2B	3B	HR	RBI	BB	SO	SB	CS	AVG	OBP	SLG	OPS	OPS+	BR/A	RC	RC/G	FR	G/POS	WS	TPW
2002 Cle-A	11	31	5	8	3	1	0	4	3	6	0	0	.258	.343	.419	.762	103	0	5	5.46	-1	2-11	1	0.0
2003 Cle-A	112	370	36	77	18	1	6	33	14	77	4	5	.208	.243	.311	.554	46	-31	24	2.09	7	*2-109	4	-1.8
Total 2	123	401	41	85	21	2	6	37	17	83	4	5	.212	.251	.319	.570	51	-31	29	2.32	6	2-120	5	-1.8

• PHILLIPS, Bubba John Melvin Phillips b: 2/24/1928, West Point, MS d: 6/22/1993, Hattiesburg, MS BR/TR, 5'9", 180 lbs. Deb: 4/30/1955 Career OF: 111-62-46

YEAR TM-L	G	AB	R	H	2B	3B	HR	RBI	BB	SO	SB	CS	AVG	OBP	SLG	OPS	OPS+	BR/A	RC	RC/G	FR	G/POS	WS	TPW
1955 Det-A	95	184	18	43	4	0	3	23	14	20	2	1	.234	.295	.304	.599	63	-10	17	3.07	-3	0-65(61-2-4)/3-4	2	-1.6
1956 Chi-A	67	99	16	27	6	0	2	11	6	12	1	2	.273	.321	.394	.715	87	-3	13	4.51	1	0-35(6-7-22)/3-2	3	-0.3
1957 Chi-A	121	393	38	106	13	3	7	42	28	32	5	3	.270	.323	.372	.695	89	-6	48	4.27	15	3-97,0-20(1-13-8)	13	0.7
1958 Chi-A	84	260	26	71	10	0	5	30	15	14	3	0	.273	.315	.369	.684	89	-3	29	3.69	-1	3-47,0-37(19-15-4)	6	-0.7
1959*Chi-A	117	379	43	100	27	1	5	40	27	28	1	1	.264	.320	.380	.699	92	-5	45	4.15	7	*3-100,0-23(8-14-1)	11	0.1
1960 Cle-A	113	304	34	63	14	1	4	33	14	37	1	0	.207	.252	.299	.551	50	-22	23	2.40	-3	3-85,0-25(15-3-7)/S-1	2	-2.6
1961 Cle-A	143	546	64	144	23	1	18	72	29	61	1	0	.264	.307	.408	.715	92	-8	66	4.17	-11	*3-143	12	-1.9
1962 Cle-A	148	562	53	145	26	0	10	54	20	55	4	0	.258	.292	.358	.650	76	-20	56	3.39	-14	*3-145/0-3(0-3-0),2-1	10	-3.4
1963 Det-A	128	464	42	114	11	2	5	45	19	42	6	2	.246	.281	.310	.592	63	-23	38	2.68	6	*3-117/0-5(0-5-0)	6	-1.8
1964 Det-A	46	87	14	22	1	0	3	6	10	13	1	2	.253	.330	.368	.698	92	-1	10	3.83	2	3-22/0-1	2	0.0
Total 10	1062	3278	348	835	135	8	62	356	182	314	25	11	.255	.300	.358	.658	79	-101	343	3.55	-3	3-762,0-214/2-1,S-1	67	-11.5

• PHILLIPS, Damon Damon Roswell "Dee" Phillips b: 6/8/1919, Corsicana, TX BR/TR, 6', 176 lbs. Deb: 7/19/1942

YEAR TM-L	G	AB	R	H	2B	3B	HR	RBI	BB	SO	SB	CS	AVG	OBP	SLG	OPS	OPS+	BR/A	RC	RC/G	FR	G/POS	WS	TPW
1942 Cin-N	28	84	4	17	2	0	0	6	7	5	0	....	.202	.264	.226	.490	44	-6	5	1.97	2	S-27	1	-0.2
1944 Bos-N	140	489	35	126	30	1	1	53	28	34	1	....	.258	.301	.329	.630	74	-18	49	3.47	-6	3-90,S-60	10	-1.9
1946 Bos-N	2	2	0	1	0	0	0	0	0	0	0	....	.500	.500	.500	1.000	182	0	1	13.50	0	....	0	0.0
Total 3	170	575	39	144	32	1	1	59	35	39	1	....	.250	.296	.315	.611	70	-23	55	3.26	-4	/3-90,S-87	11	-2.1

• PHILLIPS, Dick Richard Eugene Phillips b: 11/24/1931, Racine, WI d: 3/29/1998, Burnaby, Canada BL/TR, 6', 180 lbs. Deb: 4/15/1962 C

YEAR TM-L	G	AB	R	H	2B	3B	HR	RBI	BB	SO	SB	CS	AVG	OBP	SLG	OPS	OPS+	BR/A	RC	RC/G	FR	G/POS	WS	TPW
1962 SF-N	5	3	1	0	0	0	0	1	1	1	0	0	.000	.250	.000	.250	-27	-1	0	.59	0	/1-1	0	-0.1
1963 Was-A	124	321	33	76	8	0	10	32	29	35	1	0	.237	.304	.355	.659	84	-7	36	3.82	1	1-68/2-5,3-4	7	-1.0
1964 Was-A	109	234	17	54	6	1	2	23	27	22	1	2	.231	.313	.291	.604	69	-10	23	3.21	3	1-61/3-4	4	-1.0
1966 Was-A	25	37	3	6	0	0	0	4	2	5	0	0	.162	.225	.162	.387	14	-4	1	.93	0	/1-5	0	-0.5
Total 4	263	595	54	136	14	1	12	60	59	63	2	2	.229	.302	.316	.618	73	-21	60	3.36	4	1-135/3-8,2-5	11	-2.6

• PHILLIPS, Eddie Edward David Phillips b: 2/17/1901, Worcester, MA d: 1/26/1968, Buffalo, NY BR/TR, 6', 178 lbs. Deb: 5/4/1924

YEAR TM-L	G	AB	R	H	2B	3B	HR	RBI	BB	SO	SB	CS	AVG	OBP	SLG	OPS	OPS+	BR/A	RC	RC/G	FR	G/POS	WS	TPW
1924 Bos-N	3	3	0	0	0	0	0	0	0	2	0	0	.000	.000	.000	.000	-104	-1	0	.00	0	/C-1	0	-0.1
1929 Det-A	68	221	24	52	13	1	2	21	20	16	0	1	.235	.302	.330	.632	62	-13	23	3.41	-3	C-63	3	-1.1
1931 Pit-N	106	353	30	82	18	3	7	44	41	49	1	....	.232	.317	.360	.677	82	-8	43	4.06	-5	*C-103	10	-0.7
1932 NY-A	9	31	4	9	1	0	2	4	2	3	1	0	.290	.333	.516	.849	123	1	5	6.57	0	/C-9	2	0.2
1934 Was-A	56	169	6	33	6	1	2	16	26	24	1	0	.195	.306	.278	.584	54	-11	16	3.09	-4	C-53	2	-1.1
1935 Cle-A	70	220	18	60	16	1	1	41	15	21	0	0	.273	.319	.368	.687	76	-8	26	4.31	-10	C-69	4	-1.3
Total 6	312	997	82	236	54	6	14	126	104	115	3	1	.237	.312	.345	.657	72	-40	113	3.84	-21	C-298	21	-4.1

• PHILLIPS, Eddie Howard Edward Phillips b: 7/8/1931, St. Louis, MO BB/TR, 6'1", 180 lbs. Deb: 9/10/1953

YEAR TM-L	G	AB	R	H	2B	3B	HR	RBI	BB	SO	SB	CS	AVG	OBP	SLG	OPS	OPS+	BR/A	RC	RC/G	FR	G/POS	WS	TPW
1953 StL-N	9	0	4	0	0	0	0	0	0	0	0	0	....	....	....	....	-100	0	0	....	0	....	0	0.0

• PHILLIPS, J.R. Charles Gene Phillips b: 4/29/1970, West Covina, CA BL/TL, 6'2", 185 lbs. Deb: 9/3/1993 Career OF: 8-0-24

YEAR TM-L	G	AB	R	H	2B	3B	HR	RBI	BB	SO	SB	CS	AVG	OBP	SLG	OPS	OPS+	BR/A	RC	RC/G	FR	G/POS	WS	TPW
1993 SF-N	11	16	1	5	1	1	1	4	0	5	0	0	.313	.313	.688	1.000	164	1	3	8.44	0	/1-5	1	0.0
1994 SF-N	15	38	1	5	0	0	1	3	1	13	1	0	.132	.154	.211	.364	-7	-6	1	.90	1	1-10	0	-0.6
1995 SF-N	92	231	27	45	9	0	9	28	19	69	1	1	.195	.256	.351	.607	60	-15	21	2.91	1	1-79/0-1	2	-1.9
1996 SF-N	15	25	3	5	0	0	2	5	1	13	0	0	.200	.231	.440	.671	75	-1	3	3.51	-1	1-10	1	-0.3
Phi-N	35	79	9	12	5	0	5	10	10	38	0	0	.152	.256	.405	.661	70	-4	8	3.36	1	0-15(0-0-15),1-11	1	-0.5
Yr.	50	104	12	17	5	0	7	15	11	51	0	0	.163	.250	.413	.663	71	-5	11	3.39	0	1-21,0-15(0-0-15)	2	-0.7
1997 Hou-N	13	15	2	2	0	0	1	4	0	7	0	0	.133	.133	.333	.467	18	-2	1	1.33	0	/1-3,0-3(0-0-3)	0	-0.2
1998 Hou-N	36	58	4	11	0	0	2	9	7	22	0	0	.190	.277	.293	.570	51	-4	5	2.73	-1	1-12/0-6(6-0-0)	1	-0.6
1999 Col-N	25	39	5	9	4	0	2	4	0	13	0	0	.231	.250	.487	.737	63	-3	5	4.33	2	/0-7(1-0-6),1-4	0	-0.1
Total 7	242	501	52	94	19	1	23	67	38	180	2	1	.188	.248	.367	.615	58	-33	47	3.02	1	1-134/0-32	6	-4.1

• PHILLIPS, Jack Jack Dorn "Stretch" Phillips b: 9/6/1921, Clarence, NY BR/TR, 6'4", 193 lbs. Deb: 8/22/1947

YEAR TM-L	G	AB	R	H	2B	3B	HR	RBI	BB	SO	SB	CS	AVG	OBP	SLG	OPS	OPS+	BR/A	RC	RC/G	FR	G/POS	WS	TPW
1947*NY-A	16	36	5	10	0	1	1	2	3	5	0	0	.278	.333	.417	.750	109	0	5	5.59	-1	1-10	1	-0.1
1948 NY-A	1	2	0	0	0	0	0	0	0	1	0	0	.000	.000	.000	.000	-101	-1	0	.00	0	/1-1	0	-0.1
1949 NY-A	45	91	16	28	4	1	1	10	12	9	1	0	.308	.388	.407	.795	110	2	15	5.96	-3	1-38	4	-0.2

YEAR TM-L	G	AB	R	H	2B	3B	HR	RBI	BB	SO	SB	CS	AVG	OBP	SLG	OPS	OPS+	BR/A	RC	RC/G	FR	G/POS	WS	TPW
Pit-N	18	56	6	13	3	1	0	3	4	6	1	....	.232	.283	.321	.605	60	-3	5	3.12	0	1-16/3-1	1	-0.4
1950 Pit-N	69	208	25	61	7	6	5	34	20	17	1	....	.293	.355	.457	.812	108	2	35	6.25	0	1-54/3-3,P-1	5	-0.1
1951 Pit-N	70	156	12	37	7	3	0	12	15	17	1	2	.237	.304	.321	.625	66	-8	15	3.10	-1	1-53/3-4	1	-1.0
1952 Pit-N	1	1	0	0	0	0	0	0	0	0	0	0	.000	.000	.000	.000	-97	-0	0	.00	0	/1-1	0	0.0
1955 Det-A	55	117	15	37	8	2	1	20	10	12	0	0	.316	.370	.444	.815	121	3	19	5.91	-1	1-35/3-3	4	0.1
1956 Det-A	67	224	31	66	13	2	1	20	21	19	1	1	.295	.355	.384	.739	95	-2	28	4.43	0	1-56/2-1,0-1	4	-0.5
1957 Det-A	1	1	1	0	0	0	0	0	0	0	0	0	.000	.000	.000	.000	-98	-0	0	.00	0	....	0	0.0
Total 9	343	892	111	252	42	16	9	101	85	86	5	3	.283	.345	.396	.741	96	-6	122	4.86	-7	1-264/3-11,2-1,0-1,P-1	20	-2.4

• PHILLIPS, Jason Jason Phillips b: 9/27/1976, La Mesa, CA BR/TR, 6'1", 171 lbs. Deb: 9/19/2001

YEAR TM-L	G	AB	R	H	2B	3B	HR	RBI	BB	SO	SB	CS	AVG	OBP	SLG	OPS	OPS+	BR/A	RC	RC/G	FR	G/POS	WS	TPW
2001 NY-N	6	7	2	1	1	0	0	0	0	1	0	0	.143	.143	.286	.429	7	-1	0	1.29	0	/C-5	0	-0.1
2002 NY-N	11	19	4	7	0	0	1	3	1	1	0	0	.368	.429	.526	.955	156	2	4	7.74	-1	/C-7	1	0.1
2003 NY-N	119	403	45	120	25	0	11	58	39	50	0	1	.298	.374	.442	.816	116	9	62	5.45	-6	1-84,C-29	12	-0.2
Total 3	136	429	51	128	26	0	12	61	40	52	0	1	.298	.373	.443	.816	116	10	66	5.48	-7	/1-84,C-41	13	-0.2

• PHILLIPS, Marr Marr B. Phillips b: 6/16/1857, Pittsburgh, PA d: 4/1/1928, Pittsburgh, PA BR, 5'6.5", 164 lbs. Deb: 5/1/1884

YEAR TM-L	G	AB	R	H	2B	3B	HR	RBI	BB	SO	SB	CS	AVG	OBP	SLG	OPS	OPS+	BR/A	RC	RC/G	FR	G/POS	WS	TPW
1884 Ind-a	97	413	41	111	18	8	0	0	5	....	....	....	.269	.279	.351	.630	107	2	42	3.78	9	*S-97	11	1.4
1885 Det-N	33	139	13	29	5	0	0	17	0	13	....	....	.209	.209	.245	.453	46	-8	7	1.78	2	S-33	1	-0.5
Pit-a	4	15	1	4	0	0	0	2	2	....	....	....	.267	.353	.267	.620	99	0	1	3.55	-1	/S-4	0	-0.1
1890 Roc-a	64	257	18	53	8	0	0	34	16	....	10	....	.206	.261	.237	.498	51	-15	19	2.47	5	S-64	5	-0.7
Total 3	198	824	73	197	31	8	0	53	23	13	10	....	.239	.263	.296	.559	79	-21	69	3.00	16	S-198	17	0.2

• PHILLIPS, Mike Michael Dwaine Phillips b: 8/19/1950, Beaumont, TX BL/TR, 6', 185 lbs. Deb: 4/15/1973

YEAR TM-L	G	AB	R	H	2B	3B	HR	RBI	BB	SO	SB	CS	AVG	OBP	SLG	OPS	OPS+	BR/A	RC	RC/G	FR	G/POS	WS	TPW
1973 SF-N	63	104	18	25	3	4	1	9	6	17	0	3	.240	.288	.375	.663	79	-5	10	3.01	-2	3-28,S-20/2-7	1	-0.4
1974 SF-N	100	283	19	62	6	1	2	20	14	37	4	5	.219	.258	.269	.527	45	-23	19	2.19	-4	3-34,2-30,S-23	3	-2.3
1975 SF-N	10	31	3	6	0	0	0	1	6	4	1	0	.194	.324	.194	.518	44	-2	2	2.49	1	/2-6,3-6	0	-0.1
NY-N	116	383	31	98	10	7	1	28	25	47	3	0	.256	.303	.326	.630	78	-11	38	3.41	-2	*S-115/2-1	8	0.0
Yr.	126	414	34	104	10	7	1	29	31	51	4	0	.251	.305	.316	.621	75	-13	40	3.34	-1	*S-115/2-7,3-6	8	-0.1
1976 NY-N	87	262	30	67	4	6	4	29	25	29	2	2	.256	.321	.363	.683	99	-1	31	4.07	-2	S-53,2-19,3-10	8	0.3
1977 NY-N	38	86	5	18	2	1	1	3	2	15	0	1	.209	.244	.291	.535	45	-7	6	2.23	0	S-24/3-9,2-4	1	-0.6
StL-N	48	87	17	21	3	2	0	9	9	13	1	0	.241	.320	.322	.641	74	-3	10	3.85	2	2-31/3-5,S-5	3	0.1
Yr.	86	173	22	39	5	3	1	12	11	28	1	1	.225	.283	.306	.590	60	-10	15	3.02	2	2-35,S-29,3-14	4	-0.5
1978 StL-N	76	164	14	44	8	1	1	28	13	25	0	0	.268	.330	.348	.677	91	-2	19	3.90	-1	2-55,S-10/3-1	5	-0.1
1979 StL-N	44	97	10	22	3	1	1	6	10	9	0	0	.227	.306	.309	.615	68	-4	9	2.86	4	S-25,2-16/3-1	2	0.3
1980 StL-N	63	128	13	30	5	0	0	7	9	17	0	0	.234	.285	.273	.558	55	-8	9	2.19	6	S-37/2-9,3-8	2	0.2
1981 SD-N	14	29	1	6	0	1	0	0	0	3	1	0	.207	.207	.276	.483	39	-2	1	.92	-2	/2-9,S-1	0	-0.4
*Mon-N	34	55	5	12	2	0	0	4	5	15	0	1	.218	.283	.255	.538	53	-4	4	2.08	1	S-26/2-6	1	-0.1
Yr.	48	84	6	18	2	1	0	4	5	18	1	1	.214	.258	.262	.520	48	-6	5	1.67	-1	S-27,2-15	1	-0.5
1982 Mon-N	14	8	0	1	0	0	0	1	0	3	0	0	.125	.125	.125	.250	-29	-1	0	.57	-1	2-10/S-2	0	-0.2
1983 Mon-N	5	2	0	0	0	0	0	0	0	0	0	0	.000	.000	.000	.000	-101	-1	0	.00	-2	/S-3,3-2	0	-0.3
Total 11	712	1719	166	412	46	24	11	145	124	234	12	12	.240	.294	.314	.608	71	-73	156	3.03	-1	S-344,2-203,3-104	34	-3.6

• PHILLIPS, Tony Keith Anthony Phillips b: 4/25/1959, Atlanta, GA BB/TR, 5'9", 175 lbs. Deb: 5/10/1982 Career OF: 566-97-169

YEAR TM-L	G	AB	R	H	2B	3B	HR	RBI	BB	SO	SB	CS	AVG	OBP	SLG	OPS	OPS+	BR/A	RC	RC/G	FR	G/POS	WS	TPW
1982 Oak-A	40	81	11	17	2	2	0	8	12	26	2	3	.210	.326	.284	.610	73	-3	8	3.18	-2	S-39	2	-0.2
1983 Oak-A	148	412	54	102	12	3	4	35	48	70	16	5	.248	.329	.320	.649	85	-6	48	3.87	6	*S-101,2-63/3-4,D-1	12	1.2
1984 Oak-A	154	451	62	120	24	3	4	37	42	86	10	6	.266	.329	.359	.688	97	-2	55	4.20	8	S-91,2-90/0-1	15	1.8
1985 Oak-A	42	161	23	45	12	2	4	17	13	34	3	2	.280	.333	.453	.787	122	4	25	5.43	5	3-31,2-24	7	1.0
1986 Oak-A	118	441	76	113	14	5	5	52	76	82	15	10	.256	.369	.345	.714	103	5	63	4.84	8	2-88,3-30/0-4(0-4-0),D-2,S	17	1.7
1987 Oak-A	111	379	48	91	20	0	10	46	57	76	7	6	.240	.339	.372	.711	95	-3	49	4.28	0	2-87,3-11/S-9,0-2(1-0-1),D	9	0.3
1988*Oak-A	79	212	32	43	8	4	2	17	36	50	0	2	.203	.321	.307	.628	80	-6	22	3.27	-4	3-32,0-31(24-6-3),2-27,S-10/1,D	4	-1.0
1989*Oak-A	143	451	48	118	15	6	4	47	58	66	3	8	.262	.350	.348	.698	101	-1	53	3.86	12	2-84,3-49,S-17,0-16(13-0-4)/1	14	1.4
1990 Det-A	152	573	97	144	23	5	8	55	99	85	19	9	.251	.365	.351	.716	100	5	81	4.75	9	*3-104,2-47,S-11/0-8(4-1-4),D	22	1.7
1991 Det-A	146	564	87	160	28	4	17	72	79	95	10	5	.284	.375	.438	.813	122	19	97	6.14	6	0-56(25-9-23),3-46,2-36,D-18,S	23	2.6
1992 Det-A	159	606	**114**	167	32	3	10	64	114	93	12	10	.276	.391	.388	.779	118	19	98	5.57	-2	0-69(14-24-35),2-57,D-34,3/S	23	1.6
1993 Det-A	151	566	113	177	27	0	7	57	**132**	102	16	11	.313	.446	.398	.843	129	33	111	7.21	6	*0-108(70-9-34),2-51/D-4,3	25	3.6
1994 Det-A	114	438	91	123	19	3	19	61	95	105	13	5	.281	.411	.468	.879	126	22	91	7.46	5	*0-104(104-0-0),2-12/D-6	16	2.1
1995 Cal-A	139	525	119	137	21	1	27	61	113	135	13	10	.261	.395	.459	.854	122	20	103	6.85	9	3-88,0-48(47-8-0)/D-2	19	2.7
1996 Chi-A	153	581	119	161	29	3	12	63	**125**	132	13	8	.277	.408	.399	.808	111	16	105	6.43	6	*0-150(150-2-0)/2-2,1-1	21	1.4
1997 Chi-A	36	129	23	40	6	0	2	9	29	29	4	1	.310	.440	.403	.843	127	8	26	7.33	0	0-28(0-0-28)/3-9	6	0.6
Ana-A	105	405	73	107	28	2	6	48	73	89	9	9	.264	.379	.388	.767	100	1	62	5.21	-3	2-43,0-35(31-2-3),D-26/3-1	12	-0.3
Yr.	141	534	96	147	34	2	8	57	102	118	13	10	.275	.394	.391	.786	107	9	88	5.70	-3	0-63(31-2-31),2-43,D-26,3-10	18	0.3
1998 Tor-A	13	48	9	17	5	0	1	7	9	6	0	0	.354	.475	.521	.995	158	5	12	9.68	-1	0-13(11-0-4)	3	0.4
NY-N	52	188	25	42	11	0	3	14	38	44	1	1	.223	.354	.330	.684	83	-4	25	4.50	-1	0-51(43-0-15)	4	-0.7
1999 Oak-A	106	406	76	99	24	4	15	49	71	94	11	3	.244	.363	.433	.797	107	7	69	5.82	-1	2-66,0-62(28-32-15)/3-2,D,S	14	0.7
Total 18	2161	7617	1300	2023	360	50	160	819	1319	1499	177	114	.266	.377	.389	.766	109	140	1203	5.44	68	0-786,2-777,3-428,S-294,D/1	268	22.4

• PHYLE, Bill William Joseph Phyle b: 6/25/1875, Duluth, MN d: 8/6/1953, Los Angeles, CA TR Deb: 9/17/1898 ♦

YEAR TM-L	G	AB	R	H	2B	3B	HR	RBI	BB	SO	SB	CS	AVG	OBP	SLG	OPS	OPS+	BR/A	RC	RC/G	FR	G/POS	WS	TPW
1898 Chi-N	4	9	1	1	0	0	0	0	2	....	0	....	.111	.273	.111	.384	11	-0	0	.93	-1	/P-3	2	0.6
1899 Chi-N	10	34	2	6	0	0	0	1	0	....	0	....	.176	.176	.176	.353	-3	-2	1	1.03	1	P-10	2	-0.6
1901 NY-N	25	66	8	12	2	0	0	3	2	....	0	....	.182	.206	.212	.418	22	-1	3	1.45	0	P-24/S-1	3	-1.5
1906 StL-N	22	73	6	13	3	1	0	4	5	....	2	....	.178	.231	.247	.477	51	-4	5	2.06	0	3-21	1	-0.4
Total 4	61	182	17	32	5	1	0	8	9	....	2	....	.176	.215	.214	.429	29	-8	9	1.59	0	/P-37,3-21,S-1	8	-1.9

• PIATT, Adam Adam David Piatt b: 2/8/1976, Chicago, IL BR/TR, 6'2", 195 lbs. Deb: 4/24/2000 Career OF: 81-0-79

YEAR TM-L	G	AB	R	H	2B	3B	HR	RBI	BB	SO	SB	CS	AVG	OBP	SLG	OPS	OPS+	BR/A	RC	RC/G	FR	G/POS	WS	TPW
2000*Oak-A	60	157	24	47	5	5	5	23	23	44	0	1	.299	.392	.490	.883	125	6	32	7.59	-6	0-29(8-0-22),3-13,D-13/1-3	6	-0.1
2001 Oak-A	36	95	9	20	5	1	0	6	13	26	0	0	.211	.306	.284	.590	57	-6	8	2.62	1	0-32(0-0-32)/D-1	1	-0.6
2002*Oak-A	55	137	18	32	8	0	5	18	12	33	2	1	.234	.305	.401	.706	85	-3	17	4.36	-2	0-50(40-0-12)/1-1	3	-0.6
2003 Oak-A	47	100	6	24	10	0	4	15	6	30	1	2	.240	.283	.460	.743	90	-3	12	3.94	-1	0-38(32-0-7)/D-2,1-1	1	-0.5
TB-A	14	32	5	6	3	0	2	3	3	16	0	0	.188	.257	.469	.726	87	-1	4	4.08	-2	/0-7(1-0-6),D-3	0	-0.3
Yr.	61	132	11	30	13	0	6	18	9	46	1	2	.227	.277	.462	.739	90	-3	16	3.97	-2	0-45(33-0-13)/D-5,1-1	1	-0.7
Total 4	212	521	62	129	31	6	16	65	57	149	3	4	.248	.325	.422	.748	93	-6	73	4.79	-9	0-156/D-19,3-13,1-5	11	-2.1

• PIAZZA, Mike Michael Joseph Piazza b: 9/4/1968, Norristown, PA BR/TR, 6'3", 197 lbs. Deb: 9/1/1992

YEAR TM-L	G	AB	R	H	2B	3B	HR	RBI	BB	SO	SB	CS	AVG	OBP	SLG	OPS	OPS+	BR/A	RC	RC/G	FR	G/POS	WS	TPW
1992 LA-N	21	69	5	16	3	0	1	7	4	12	0	0	.232	.284	.319	.603	71	-3	6	3.15	0	C-16	1	-0.1
1993 LA-N★	149	547	81	174	24	2	35	112	46	86	3	4	.318	.374	.561	.935	155	39	112	7.70	7	*C-146/1-1	31	5.6
1994 LA-N★	107	405	64	129	18	0	24	92	33	65	1	3	.319	.371	.541	.912	143	23	77	7.09	-5	*C-104	21	2.5
1995*LA-N★	112	434	82	150	17	0	32	93	39	80	1	0	.346	.401	.606	1.007	**177**	46	103	**9.43**	0	*C-112	27	5.2
1996*LA-N★	148	547	87	184	16	0	36	105	81	93	0	3	.336	.423	.563	.986	171	56	125	8.65	-2	*C-146	33	6.3
1997 LA-N★	152	556	104	201	32	1	40	124	69	77	5	1	.362	.435	.638	1.073	**191**	**74**	150	10.68	-2	*C-139/D-7	**39**	**8.1**
1998 LA-N	37	149	20	42	5	0	9	30	11	27	0	0	.282	.331	.497	.828	121	4	24	5.77	2	C-37	9	0.9
Fla-N	5	18	1	5	0	1	0	5	0	0	0	0	.278	.278	.389	.667	76	-1	2	3.82	1	/C-4	0	0.0
NY-N★	109	394	67	137	33	0	23	76	47	53	1	0	.348	.420	.607	1.026	168	39	98	9.73	4	C-99/D-4	24	5.0
Yr.	151	561	88	184	38	1	32	111	58	80	1	0	.328	.393	.570	.963	153	43	124	8.41	7	*C-140/D-4	33	5.9
1999*NY-N★	141	534	100	162	25	0	40	124	51	70	2	2	.303	.365	.575	.940	137	27	101	6.65	-7	*C-137/D-1	21	2.8
2000*NY-N★	136	482	90	156	26	0	38	113	58	69	4	2	.324	.400	.614	1.014	158	41	115	8.97	-3	*C-124/D-5	28	4.4
2001 NY-N★	141	503	81	151	29	0	36	94	67	87	0	2	.300	.385	.573	.957	150	37	104	7.50	-3	*C-130/D-5	21	4.1
2002 NY-N★	135	478	69	134	23	2	33	98	57	82	0	3	.280	.361	.544	.905	140	25	84	6.02	-5	*C-121/D-6	19	2.8
2003 NY-N	68	234	37	67	13	0	11	34	35	40	0	0	.286	.381	.483	.864	128	10	41	6.19	0	C-64/1-1	10	1.4
Total 12	1461	5350	888	1708	264	6	358	1107	598	841	17	20	.319	.390	.572	.962	156	417	1141	7.93	-12	*C-1379/D-28,1-2	284	48.9

YEAR TM-L	G	AB	R	H	2B	3B	HR	RBI	BB	SO	SB	CS	AVG	OBP	SLG	OPS	OPS+	BR/A	RC	RC/G	FR	G/POS	WS	TPW
• PICCIOLO, Rob	Robert Michael Picciolo b: 2/4/1953, Santa Monica, CA BR/TR, 6'2", 185 lbs. Deb: 4/9/1977 C Career OF: 2-0-1																							
1977 Oak-A	148	419	35	84	12	3	2	22	9	55	1	4	.200	.219	.258	.477	30	-42	22	1.64	6	*S-148	5	-2.3
1978 Oak-A	78	93	16	21	1	0	2	7	2	13	1	1	.226	.242	.301	.543	55	-6	6	2.16	-6	S-41,2-19,3-13	1	-0.9
1979 Oak-A	115	348	37	88	16	2	2	27	3	45	2	1	.253	.261	.328	.589	61	-20	27	2.64	-9	*S-105/2-6,3-4,0-1	4	-1.9
1980 Oak-A	95	271	32	65	9	2	5	18	2	63	1	1	.240	.245	.343	.589	64	-15	21	2.56	-4	S-49,2-47/0-1	3	-1.2
1981*Oak-A	82	179	23	48	5	3	4	13	5	22	0	1	.268	.292	.397	.689	102	-1	19	3.42	-2	S-82	6	0.4
1982 Oak-A	18	49	3	11	1	0	0	3	1	10	1	0	.224	.240	.245	.485	35	-4	3	2.14	3	S-18	1	0.1
Mil-A	22	21	7	6	1	0	0	1	1	4	0	0	.286	.318	.333	.652	84	-0	2	4.00	-5	2-11/S-6,D-1	0	-0.4
Yr.	40	70	10	17	2	0	0	4	2	14	1	0	.243	.264	.271	.535	50	-5	6	2.66	-2	S-24,2-11/D-1	1	-0.4
1983 Mil-A	14	27	2	6	3	0	0	1	0	4	0	0	.222	.222	.333	.556	55	-2	2	2.44	0	/S-7,2-2,3-2,1-1,D-1	0	-0.2
1984 Cal-A	87	119	18	24	6	0	1	9	0	21	0	1	.202	.202	.277	.479	31	-12	6	1.56	0	S-66,3-13/2-9,0-1	2	-0.8
1985 Oak-A	71	102	19	28	2	0	1	8	2	17	3	2	.275	.288	.324	.612	73	-4	9	3.04	-3	3-19,2-17,1-13,D-10/S-9	1	-0.6
Total 9	**730**	**1628**	**192**	**381**	**56**	**10**	**17**	**109**	**25**	**254**	**9**	**11**	**.234**	**.247**	**.312**	**.559**	**56**	**-107**	**118**	**2.35**	**-19**	**S-531,2-111/3-51,1-14,D-12,0**	**23**	**-7.8**
• PICCIUTO, Nick	Nicholas Thomas Picciuto b: 8/27/1921, Newark, NJ d: 1/10/1997, Winchester, VA BR/TR, 5'8.5", 165 lbs. Deb: 5/11/1945																							
1945 Phi-N	36	89	7	12	6	0	0	6	6	17	0	....	.135	.189	.202	.392	9	-11	4	1.22	-7	3-30/2-4	0	-1.7
• PICINICH, Val	Valentine John Picinich b: 9/8/1896, New York, NY d: 12/5/1942, Nobleboro, ME BR/TR, 5'9", 165 lbs. Deb: 7/25/1916 C																							
1916 Phi-A	40	118	8	23	3	1	0	5	6	33	1	....	.195	.234	.237	.471	44	-9	7	1.90	3	C-37	1	-0.3
1917 Phi-A	2	6	0	2	0	0	0	0	1	2	0	....	.333	.429	.333	.762	135	0	1	5.34	-1	/C-2	0	-0.1
1918 Was-A	47	148	13	34	3	3	0	12	9	25	0	....	.230	.274	.291	.564	72	-6	12	2.50	-4	C-46	3	-0.7
1919 Was-A	80	212	18	58	12	3	3	22	17	43	6	....	.274	.330	.401	.731	106	1	30	4.67	8	C-69	7	1.4
1920 Was-A	48	133	14	27	6	2	3	14	9	33	0	0	.203	.259	.346	.605	61	-8	12	2.98	3	C-45	3	-0.1
1921 Was-A	45	141	10	39	9	0	0	12	16	21	0	3	.277	.354	.340	.695	82	-4	17	4.13	-3	C-45	4	-0.4
1922 Was-A	76	210	16	48	12	2	0	19	23	33	1	0	.229	.311	.305	.615	64	-10	22	3.36	1	C-76	5	-0.4
1923 Bos-A	87	268	33	74	21	1	2	31	46	32	3	5	.276	.386	.384	.770	103	2	42	5.31	4	C-81	10	1.0
1924 Bos-A	69	161	25	44	6	3	1	24	29	19	5	1	.273	.394	.366	.760	97	2	26	5.67	-2	C-52	5	0.3
1925 Bos-A	90	251	31	64	21	0	1	25	33	21	2	0	.255	.344	.351	.694	77	-7	33	4.39	-2	C-74/1-2	4	-0.4
1926 Cin-N	89	240	33	63	16	1	2	31	29	22	4	....	.263	.342	.363	.705	92	-2	30	4.26	-8	C-86	8	-0.5
1927 Cin-N	65	173	16	44	8	3	0	12	24	15	3	....	.254	.345	.335	.680	85	-3	21	3.98	-4	C-61	6	-0.3
1928 Cin-N	96	324	29	98	15	1	7	35	20	25	1	....	.302	.343	.420	.763	100	-1	45	4.90	1	C-93	13	0.6
1929 Bro-N	93	273	28	71	16	6	4	31	34	24	3	....	.260	.342	.407	.749	86	-6	38	4.74	4	C-85	8	0.3
1930 Bro-N	23	46	4	10	3	0	0	3	5	6	1	....	.217	.294	.283	.577	41	-4	4	2.78	-1	C-22	0	-0.4
1931 Bro-N	24	45	5	12	4	0	1	4	4	9	1	....	.267	.327	.422	.749	100	-0	6	5.01	-1	C-15	1	-0.1
1932 Bro-N	41	70	8	18	6	0	1	11	4	8	0	....	.257	.297	.386	.683	84	-2	8	4.06	0	C-24	2	-0.1
1933 Bro-N	6	6	1	1	1	0	0	0	0	1	0	....	.167	.167	.333	.500	42	-0	0	1.85	0	/C-6	0	-0.1
Pit-N	16	52	6	13	4	0	1	7	5	10	0	....	.250	.316	.385	.700	99	-0	7	4.16	0	C-16	2	0.0
Yr.	22	58	7	14	5	0	1	7	5	11	0	....	.241	.302	.379	.681	94	-1	7	3.92	-1	C-22	2	0.0
Total 18	**1037**	**2877**	**298**	**743**	**166**	**26**	**26**	**298**	**314**	**382**	**31**	**9**	**.258**	**.334**	**.361**	**.695**	**85**	**-57**	**362**	**4.22**	**-3**	**C-935/1-2**	**82**	**-0.2**
• PICK, Charlie	Charles Thomas Pick b: 4/10/1888, Brookneal, VA d: 6/26/1954, Lynchburg, VA BL/TR, 5'10", 160 lbs. Deb: 9/20/1914 Career OF: 13-4-1																							
1914 Was-A	10	23	0	9	0	0	0	1	4	4	1	2	.391	.481	.391	.873	157	1	4	6.55	0	/0-7(6-0-1)	2	0.1
1915 Was-A	3	2	0	0	0	0	0	0	0	0	0	....	.000	.000	.000	.000	-98	-0	0	.00	0	....	0	0.0
1916 Phi-A	121	398	29	96	10	3	0	20	40	24	25	16	.241	.315	.281	.597	83	-9	39	3.07	-12	*3-108/0-8(5-3-0)	6	-2.1
1918*Chi-N	29	89	13	29	4	1	0	12	14	4	7	....	.326	.417	.393	.811	144	6	17	6.90	-1	2-20/3-8	6	0.6
1919 Chi-N	75	269	27	65	8	6	0	18	14	12	17	....	.242	.292	.316	.608	82	-6	29	3.46	5	2-71/3-3	6	0.1
Bos-N	34	114	12	29	1	1	1	7	7	5	4	....	.254	.325	.307	.632	94	-0	12	3.63	-7	2-21/3-5,0-3(2-1-0),1-2	2	-0.8
Yr.	109	383	39	94	9	7	1	25	21	17	21	....	.245	.302	.313	.615	86	-6	41	3.51	-2	2-92/3-8,0-3(2-1-0),1-2	8	-0.7
1920 Bos-N	95	383	34	105	16	6	2	28	23	11	10	16	.274	.320	.363	.683	100	-4	41	3.51	-4	2-94	8	-0.6
Total 6	**367**	**1278**	**115**	**333**	**39**	**17**	**3**	**86**	**102**	**60**	**64**	**34**	**.261**	**.323**	**.325**	**.648**	**95**	**-13**	**143**	**3.63**	**-19**	**2-206,3-124/0-18,1-2**	**30**	**-2.8**
• PICK, Eddie	Edgar Everett Pick b: 5/7/1899, Attleboro, MA d: 5/13/1967, Santa Monica, CA BB/TR, 6', 185 lbs. Deb: 9/13/1923 Career OF: 5-0-1																							
1923 Cin-N	9	8	2	3	0	0	0	2	3	3	0	0	.375	.545	.375	.920	150	1	2	9.09	0	/0-4(4-0-0)	1	0.1
1924 Cin-N	3	2	0	0	0	0	0	0	0	1	0	0	.000	.000	.000	.000	-101	-1	0	.00	0	/0-1	0	-0.1
1927 Chi-N	54	181	23	31	5	2	2	15	20	26	0	....	.171	.254	.254	.508	36	-17	12	2.04	-6	3-49/2-1,0-1	1	-2.0
Total 3	**66**	**191**	**25**	**34**	**5**	**2**	**2**	**17**	**23**	**30**	**0**	**0**	**.178**	**.266**	**.257**	**.523**	**41**	**-16**	**15**	**2.27**	**-7**	**/3-49,0-6,2-1**	**2**	**-2.0**
• PICKERING, Calvin	Calvin Elroy Pickering b: 9/29/1976, St. Thomas, V.I. BL/TL, 6'5", 275 lbs. Deb: 9/12/1998																							
1998 Bal-A	9	21	4	5	0	0	2	3	3	4	1	0	.238	.333	.524	.857	120	1	3	4.61	-1	/1-5,D-3	0	-0.1
1999 Bal-A	23	40	4	5	1	0	1	5	11	16	0	0	.125	.314	.225	.539	42	-3	3	2.62	-1	/1-8,D-7	0	-0.4
2001 Cin-N	4	4	0	1	0	0	0	1	0	2	0	0	.250	.250	.250	.500	29	-0	0	2.25	0	....	0	0.0
Bos-A	17	50	4	14	1	0	3	7	8	13	0	0	.280	.379	.480	.859	123	2	8	5.46	0	1-12/D-2	1	0.0
Total 3	**53**	**115**	**12**	**25**	**2**	**0**	**6**	**16**	**22**	**35**	**1**	**0**	**.217**	**.343**	**.391**	**.734**	**90**	**-1**	**15**	**4.15**	**-2**	**/1-25,D-12**	**1**	**-0.5**
• PICKERING, Ollie	Oliver Daniel Pickering b: 4/9/1870, Olney, IL d: 1/20/1952, Vincennes, IN BL/TR, 5'11", 175 lbs. Deb: 8/9/1896 Career OF: 19-611-231																							
1896 Lou-N	45	165	28	50	6	4	1	22	12	11	13	....	.303	.350	.406	.756	103	0	29	6.58	2	0-45(3-44-0)	4	-0.1
1897 Lou-N	63	249	34	62	5	2	1	21	26	....	20	....	.249	.325	.297	.622	67	-11	32	4.41	5	0-62(0-61-1)	5	-0.8
Cle-N	46	182	33	64	5	2	1	22	11	....	18	....	.352	.392	.418	.809	108	2	38	8.33	-1	0-46(1-45-1)/2-1	7	-0.2
Yr.	109	431	67	126	10	4	2	43	37	....	38	....	.292	.352	.348	.700	84	-9	70	5.93	4	*0-108(1-106-2)/2-1	12	-1.0
1901 Cle-A	137	547	102	169	25	6	0	40	58	....	36	....	.309	.383	.377	.760	116	15	96	6.62	9	*0-137(2-110-25)	22	1.6
1902 Cle-A	69	293	46	75	5	2	3	26	19	....	22	....	.256	.306	.317	.623	76	-9	36	4.37	-1	0-64(3-57-4)/1-2	6	-1.2
1903 Phi-A	137	512	93	144	18	6	1	36	53	....	40	....	.281	.353	.346	.699	105	6	82	5.50	0	*0-135(0-134-1)	19	-0.1
1904 Phi-A	124	455	56	103	10	3	0	30	45	....	17	....	.226	.299	.262	.560	74	-12	44	3.16	-4	*0-121(10-111-0)	10	-2.4
1907 StL-A	151	576	63	159	15	10	0	60	35	....	15	....	.276	.321	.337	.658	110	6	71	4.32	-11	*0-151(0-22-128)	14	-1.3
1908 Was-A	113	373	45	84	7	4	2	30	28	....	13	....	.225	.285	.282	.566	92	-3	33	2.90	-7	0-98(0-27-71)	7	-1.6
Total 8	**885**	**3352**	**500**	**910**	**96**	**39**	**9**	**287**	**287**	**11**	**194**	**....**	**.271**	**.334**	**.331**	**.665**	**97**	**-6**	**460**	**4.83**	**-7**	**0-859/1-2,2-1**	**94**	**-6.1**
• PICKERING, Urbane	Urbane Henry "Pick" Pickering b: 6/3/1899, Hoxie, KS d: 5/13/1970, Modesto, CA BR/TR, 5'10", 180 lbs. Deb: 4/18/1931																							
1931 Bos-A	103	341	48	86	13	4	9	52	33	53	3	4	.252	.318	.393	.711	91	-4	43	4.33	-10	3-74,2-16	8	-1.0
1932 Bos-A	132	457	47	119	28	5	2	40	39	71	3	4	.260	.320	.357	.677	77	-16	53	4.00	-13	*3-126/C-1	6	-2.3
Total 2	**235**	**798**	**95**	**205**	**41**	**9**	**11**	**92**	**72**	**124**	**6**	**8**	**.257**	**.319**	**.372**	**.691**	**83**	**-21**	**95**	**4.14**	**-24**	**3-200/2-16,C-1**	**14**	**-3.4**
• PICKETT, Dave	David T. Pickett b: 5/26/1874, Brookline, MA d: 4/22/1950, Easton, MA, 5'7.5", 170 lbs. Deb: 7/21/1898																							
1898 Bos-N	14	43	3	12	1	0	0	3	6	....	2	....	.279	.380	.302	.682	91	-0	6	4.97	0	0-14(14-0-0)	1	-0.1
• PICKETT, John	John Thomas Pickett b: 2/20/1866, Chicago, IL d: 7/4/1922, Chicago, IL BR/TR, 5'10.5" Deb: 6/6/1889																							
1889 KC-a	53	201	20	45	7	0	0	12	11	21	7	....	.224	.271	.259	.530	48	-15	16	2.78	-9	0-28(23-4-1),3-14,2-11	1	-2.0
1890 Phi-P	100	407	82	114	7	9	4	64	40	17	12	....	.280	.347	.371	.718	90	-7	58	5.35	-20	*2-100	10	-1.8
1892 Bal-N	36	141	13	30	2	3	1	12	7	10	2	....	.213	.260	.291	.551	65	-7	11	2.79	-3	2-36	1	-0.8
Total 3	**189**	**749**	**115**	**189**	**16**	**12**	**5**	**88**	**58**	**48**	**21**	**....**	**.252**	**.311**	**.326**	**.637**	**74**	**-28**	**86**	**4.13**	**-32**	**2-147/0-28,3-14**	**12**	**-4.6**
• PICKUP, Ty	Clarence William Pickup b: 10/29/1897, Philadelphia, PA d: 8/2/1974, Philadelphia, PA BR/TR, 6', 180 lbs. Deb: 4/30/1918																							
1918 Phi-N	1	1	0	1	0	0	0	0	0	0	0	....	1.000	1.000	1.000	2.000	478	0	1	∞	0	/0-1	0	0.0
• PIERCE, Gracie	Grayson S. Pierce b: New York, NY d: 8/29/1894, New York, NY BR/TR, 5'11" Deb: 5/2/1882 U Career OF: 0-23-6																							
1882 Lou-a	9	33	3	10	1	0	0	....	1	....	....	....	.303	.324	.333	.657	129	1	4	4.44	0	/2-9	1	0.2
Bal-a	41	151	8	30	2	1	0	....	3	....	....	....	.199	.214	.225	.439	52	-7	7	1.73	-11	2-38/0-3(0-0-3),S-1	1	-1.5
Yr.	50	184	11	40	3	1	0	....	4	....	....	....	.217	.234	.245	.479	66	-6	11	2.16	-11	2-47/0-3(0-0-3),S-1	2	-1.4
1883 Col-a	11	41	5	7	0	0	0	0	0	....	....	....	.171	.171	.171	.341	11	-4	1	1.01	-2	/2-6,0-5(0-4-1)	0	-0.5
NY-N	18	62	3	5	0	1	0	2	1	9	....	....	.081	.095	.113	.208	-37	-10	1	.33	-3	0-18(0-17-1)/2-1	0	-1.2

YEAR TM-L	G	AB	R	H	2B	3B	HR	RBI	BB	SO	SB	CS	AVG	OBP	SLG	OPS	OPS+	BR/A	RC	RC/G	FR	G/POS	WS	TPW
1884 NY-a	5	20	2	5	1	0	0	0	0	....	....	....	.250	.250	.300	.550	80	-0	2	2.82	-4	/2-3,0-3(0-2-1)	0	-0.4
Total 3	84	307	21	57	4	2	0	2	5	9	....	....	.186	.199	.212	.410	39	-20	15	1.63	-20	/2-57,0-29,S-1	2	-3.5
• PIERCE, Jack	Lavern Jack Pierce b: 6/2/1948, Laurel, MS BL/TR, 6', 210 lbs. Deb: 4/27/1973																							
1973 Atl-N	11	20	0	1	0	0	0	0	1	8	0	0	.050	.095	.050	.145	-55	-4	0	.17	0	/1-6	0	-0.4
1974 Atl-N	6	9	1	1	0	0	0	0	1	0	0	0	.111	.200	.111	.311	-11	-1	0	.85	0	/1-2	0	-0.1
1975 Det-A	53	170	19	40	6	1	8	22	20	40	0	0	.235	.323	.424	.746	105	1	24	4.89	-3	1-49	5	-0.6
Total 3	70	199	20	42	6	1	8	22	22	48	0	0	.211	.296	.372	.668	85	-4	25	4.13	-3	/1-57	5	-1.2
• PIERCE, Maury	Maurice Pierce b: Washington, DC Deb: 4/23/1884																							
1884 Was-U	2	7	0	1	0	0	0	....	0	....	....	....	.143	.143	.143	.286	-3	-1	0	.68	0	/3-2	0	-0.1
• PIERCY, Andy	Andrew J. Piercy b: 8/1856, San Jose, CA d: 12/27/1932, San Jose, CA TR Deb: 5/12/1881																							
1881 Chi-N	2	8	1	2	0	0	0	0	0	1	....	....	.250	.250	.250	.500	54	-0	1	2.31	-1	/2-1,3-1	0	-0.1
• PIERRE, Juan	Juan D'Vaughn Pierre b: 8/14/1977, Mobile, AL BL/TL, 6', 180 lbs. Deb: 8/7/2000 Career OF: 0-514-0																							
2000 Col-N	51	200	26	62	2	0	0	20	13	15	7	6	.310	.355	.320	.675	58	-13	23	4.10	-1	0-50(0-50-0)	3	-1.3
2001 Col-N	156	617	108	202	26	11	2	55	41	29	**46**	17	.327	.379	.415	.794	86	-8	101	6.04	-3	*0-154(0-154-0)	17	-1.0
2002 Col-N	152	592	90	170	20	5	1	35	31	52	47	12	.287	.332	.343	.675	68	-23	72	4.34	-5	*0-149(0-149-0)	15	-2.6
2003*Fla-N	162	668	100	204	28	7	1	41	55	35	**65**	20	.305	.363	.373	.735	96	3	97	5.12	-3	*0-161(0-161-0)	20	0.2
Total 4	521	2077	324	638	76	23	4	151	140	131	165	55	.307	.358	.372	.730	82	-41	293	5.06	-11	0-514	55	-4.7
• PIERSALL, Jim	James Anthony Piersall b: 11/14/1929, Waterbury, CT BR/TR, 6', 175 lbs. Deb: 9/7/1950 C Career OF: 113-1214-305																							
1950 Bos-A	6	7	4	2	0	0	0	0	4	0	0	0	.286	.545	.286	.831	107	1	2	9.10	1	/0-2(0-2-0)	1	0.1
1952 Bos-A	56	161	28	43	8	0	1	16	28	26	3	3	.267	.379	.335	.714	93	-1	23	4.88	-2	S-30,0-22(0-1-21)/3-1	5	-0.2
1953 Bos-A	151	585	76	159	21	9	3	52	41	52	11	10	.272	.329	.354	.683	80	-18	69	3.98	15	*0-151(1-2-150)	12	-0.8
1954 Bos-A★	133	474	77	135	24	2	8	38	36	42	5	1	.285	.339	.395	.734	90	-5	63	4.69	2	*0-126(0-30-96)	10	-0.9
1955 Bos-A	149	515	68	146	25	5	13	62	67	52	6	1	.283	.368	.427	.795	104	5	82	5.50	4	*0-147(0-147-0)	20	0.1
1956 Bos-A★	155	601	91	176	**40**	6	14	87	58	48	7	7	.293	.356	.449	.805	99	-3	92	5.26	13	*0-155(0-155-0)	21	0.2
1957 Bos-A	151	609	103	159	27	5	19	63	62	54	14	6	.261	.333	.415	.749	98	-1	83	4.64	9	*0-151(0-151-0)	19	0.0
1958 Bos-A	130	417	55	99	13	5	8	48	42	43	12	2	.237	.307	.350	.657	75	-12	46	3.63	3	*0-125(0-125-0)	9	-1.6
1959 Cle-A	100	317	42	78	13	2	4	30	25	31	6	3	.246	.305	.338	.643	79	-9	34	3.67	-2	0-91(0-91-0)/3-1	9	-1.6
1960 Cle-A	138	486	70	137	12	4	18	66	24	38	18	5	.282	.316	.434	.750	104	2	62	4.36	3	*0-134(8-127-2)	15	-0.2
1961 Cle-A	121	484	81	156	26	7	6	40	43	46	8	2	.322	.380	.442	.822	122	16	79	5.99	5	*0-120(0-120-0)	18	1.8
1962 Was-A	135	471	38	115	20	4	4	31	39	53	12	7	.244	.302	.329	.631	70	-20	45	3.23	3	*0-132(0-132-0)	7	-2.1
1963 Was-A	29	94	9	23	1	0	1	5	6	11	4	0	.245	.290	.287	.577	63	-4	8	2.98	0	0-25(0-25-0)	1	-0.4
NY-N	40	124	13	24	4	1	1	10	10	14	1	2	.194	.254	.266	.520	49	-9	8	1.96	0	0-38(0-38-0)	1	-1.0
LA-A	20	52	4	16	1	0	0	4	5	5	0	1	.308	.368	.327	.695	103	-0	6	4.14	0	0-18(1-12-5)	1	-0.1
Yr.	49	146	13	39	2	0	1	9	11	16	4	1	.267	.318	.301	.620	77	-4	15	3.38	0	0-43(1-37-5)	2	-0.5
1964 LA-A	87	255	28	80	11	0	2	13	16	32	5	3	.314	.354	.380	.735	116	5	34	4.86	0	0-72(48-32-0)	9	0.2
1965 Cal-A	53	112	10	30	5	2	2	12	5	15	2	2	.268	.305	.402	.707	101	-1	13	3.76	-1	0-41(29-10-4)	3	-0.3
1966 Cal-A	75	123	14	26	5	0	0	14	13	19	1	2	.211	.287	.252	.539	58	-7	8	1.85	-0	0-63(25-14-27)	1	-1.0
1967 Cal-A	5	3	0	0	0	0	0	0	0	2	0	0	.000	.000	.000	.000	-104	-1	0	.00	0	/0-1	0	-0.1
Total 17	1734	5890	811	1604	256	52	104	591	524	583	115	57	.272	.334	.386	.721	92	-62	756	4.39	53	*0-1614/S-30,3-2	162	-7.8
• PIERSON, Dave	David P. Pierson b: 8/20/1855, Wilkes-Barre, PA d: 11/11/1922, Newark, NJ BR/TR, 5'7", 142 lbs. Deb: 4/25/1876																							
1876 Cin-N	57	234	33	55	4	1	0	13	1	9	....	....	.235	.239	.262	.501	78	-3	15	2.35	1	C-31,0-30(1-0-29)/2-1,3-1,P,S	1	-0.3
• PIERSON, Dick	Edmund Dana Pierson b: 10/24/1857, Wilkes-Barre, PA d: 7/20/1922, Newark, NJ TR Deb: 6/23/1885																							
1885 NY-a	3	9	1	1	0	0	0	0	2	....	....	....	.111	.273	.111	.384	27	-1	0	.94	-3	/2-3	0	-0.3
• PIERZYNSKI, A.J.	Anthony John Pierzynski b: 12/30/1976, Bridgehampton, NY BL/TR, 6'3", 220 lbs. Deb: 9/9/1998																							
1998 Min-A	7	10	1	3	0	0	0	1	1	2	0	0	.300	.417	.300	.717	89	-0	2	5.24	0	/C-6	1	0.0
1999 Min-A	9	22	3	6	2	0	0	3	1	4	0	0	.273	.333	.364	.697	75	-1	3	4.79	0	/C-9	0	-0.1
2000 Min-A	33	88	12	27	5	1	2	11	5	14	1	0	.307	.358	.455	.812	100	0	15	6.31	-4	C-32	3	-0.1
2001 Min-A	114	381	51	110	33	2	7	55	16	57	1	7	.289	.324	.441	.765	97	-6	50	4.68	-5	*C-110/D-1	15	-0.4
2002*Min-A★	130	440	54	132	31	6	6	49	13	61	1	2	.300	.336	.439	.775	103	0	60	4.95	-5	*C-124	17	0.3
2003*Min-A	137	487	63	152	35	3	11	74	24	55	3	1	.312	.363	.464	.827	115	11	79	6.00	-1	*C-135	22	1.8
Total 6	430	1428	184	430	106	12	26	193	60	193	6	10	.301	.344	.447	.791	105	4	209	5.31	-15	C-416/D-1	58	1.7
• PIET, Tony	Anthony Francis Piet b: 12/7/1906, Berwick, PA d: 12/1/1981, Hinsdale, IL BR/TR, 6', 175 lbs. Deb: 8/15/1931																							
1931 Pit-N	44	167	22	50	12	4	0	24	13	24	10	....	.299	.354	.419	.773	108	2	25	5.51	1	2-44/S-1	6	0.5
1932 Pit-N	154	574	66	162	25	8	7	85	46	56	19	....	.282	.343	.390	.733	98	-1	80	4.93	3	*2-154	17	1.2
1933 Pit-N	107	362	45	117	21	5	1	42	19	28	12	....	.323	.367	.417	.784	124	11	57	5.90	1	2-97	15	1.9
1934 Cin-N	106	421	58	109	20	5	1	38	23	44	6	....	.259	.307	.337	.644	74	-15	43	3.58	-13	3-51,2-49	6	-2.3
1935 Cin-N	6	5	2	1	1	0	0	2	0	0	0	....	.200	.200	.400	.600	59	-0	0	2.77	-0	/0-1	0	0.0
Chi-A	77	292	47	87	17	5	3	27	33	27	2	1	.298	.375	.421	.796	103	2	48	5.94	-1	2-59,3-17	9	0.5
1936 Chi-A	109	352	69	96	15	2	7	42	66	48	15	5	.273	.400	.386	.787	92	-0	61	6.10	-1	2-68,3-32	12	0.4
1937 Chi-A	100	332	34	78	15	1	4	38	32	36	14	6	.235	.314	.322	.636	61	-20	36	3.58	-4	3-86,2-13	6	-1.8
1938 Det-A	41	80	9	17	6	0	0	14	15	11	2	4	.213	.351	.288	.638	58	-6	8	3.34	1	3-18/2-1	1	-0.4
Total 8	744	2585	352	717	132	30	23	312	247	274	80	16	.277	.350	.378	.728	92	-27	359	4.90	-13	2-485,3-204/0-1,S-1	72	0.0
• PIEZ, Sandy	Charles William Piez b: 10/13/1892, New York, NY d: 12/29/1930, Atlantic City, NJ BR/TR, 5'10", 170 lbs. Deb: 4/17/1914																							
1914 NY-N	37	8	9	3	0	1	0	3	0	1	4	....	.375	.375	.625	1.000	202	1	3	15.51	0	/0-5(2-2-1)	1	0.0
• PIGNATANO, Joe	Joseph Benjamin Pignatano b: 8/4/1929, Brooklyn, NY BR/TR, 5'10", 180 lbs. Deb: 4/28/1957 C																							
1957 Bro-N	8	14	0	3	1	0	0	1	0	5	0	0	.214	.214	.286	.500	30	-1	1	1.25	0	/C-6	0	-0.1
1958 LA-N	63	142	18	31	4	0	9	17	16	26	4	1	.218	.306	.437	.743	91	-2	19	4.43	1	C-57	5	0.1
1959*LA-N	52	139	17	33	4	1	1	11	21	15	1	0	.237	.346	.302	.648	69	-5	16	3.93	1	C-49	5	-0.1
1960 LA-N	58	90	11	21	4	0	2	9	15	17	1	1	.233	.343	.344	.687	83	-2	12	4.45	0	C-40	4	0.0
1961 KC-A	92	243	31	59	10	3	4	22	36	42	2	2	.243	.350	.358	.708	89	-3	34	4.72	1	C-83/3-2	7	0.2
1962 SF-N	7	5	2	1	0	0	0	0	4	0	0	0	.200	.556	.200	.756	114	1	1	7.65	-1	/C-7	1	0.0
NY-N	27	56	2	13	2	0	0	2	2	11	0	0	.232	.259	.268	.526	41	-5	3	1.88	1	C-25	1	-0.3
Yr.	34	61	4	14	2	0	0	2	6	11	0	0	.230	.299	.262	.561	51	-4	4	2.35	0	C-32	2	-0.3
Total 6	307	689	81	161	25	4	16	62	94	116	8	4	.234	.332	.351	.684	80	-17	86	4.17	3	C-267/3-2	23	-0.2
• PIKE, Jay	Jacob Emanuel Pike b: Brooklyn, NY BL/TL Deb: 8/27/1877 U																							
1877 Har-N	1	4	0	1	0	0	0	0	0	0	....	....	.250	.250	.250	.500	65	-0	0	2.35	-1	/0-1	0	-0.1
• PIKE, Jess	Jess Willard Pike b: 7/31/1915, Dustin, OK d: 3/28/1984, San Diego, CA BL/TR, 6'3", 175 lbs. Deb: 4/18/1946																							
1946 NY-N	16	41	4	7	1	1	1	6	6	9	0	....	.171	.277	.317	.594	68	-2	4	3.20	-1	0-10(0-6-4)	1	-0.3
• PIKE, Lip	Lipman Emanuel Pike b: 5/25/1845, New York, NY d: 10/10/1893, Brooklyn, NY BL/TL, 5'8", 158 lbs. Deb: 5/9/1871 M/U NA OF: 7-98-88 Career OF: 0-137-0																							
1871 Tro-n	28	130	43	49	10	7	**4**	39	5	7	3	2	.377	.400	.654	1.054	193	14	36	13.69	0	0-18(0-0-18)/2-7,1-4	....	1.0
1872 Bal-n	56	288	67	84	15	5	**7**	**61**	3	6	8	1	.292	.299	.441	.740	119	6	41	6.26	-4	0-25(6-5-16),2-24/3-9	....	0.1
1873 Bal-n	56	286	71	90	14	8	**4**	50	7	4	8	1	.315	.331	.462	.793	134	13	48	7.36	-4	*0-56(0-2-54)/2-2	....	0.8
1874 Har-n	52	234	58	83	**22**	5	1	51	5	0	3	1	.355	.368	**.504**	.872	168	17	46	9.01	10	0-27(0-27-0),S-20/2-7,3-1	....	2.0
1875 StL-n	70	312	61	108	22	12	0	44	3	8	25	10	.346	.352	.494	.846	**210**	**36**	65	8.91	0	*0-64(1-64-0),2-10/3-2,S-1	....	3.0
1876 StL-N	63	290	55	91	19	10	1	50	8	9	....	....	.314	.341	.472	.813	178	23	47	6.82	-2	*0-62(0-62-0)/2-2	17	1.6
1877 Cin-N	58	262	45	78	12	4	**4**	23	9	7	....	....	.298	.321	.420	.741	148	15	36	5.41	-8	0-38(0-38-0),2-22/S-2	7	0.5
1878 Cin-N	31	145	28	47	5	1	0	11	4	9	....	....	.324	.342	.372	.715	149	8	19	5.32	-5	0-31(0-31-0)	6	0.1

YEAR TM-L	G	AB	R	H	2B	3B	HR	RBI	BB	SO	SB	CS	AVG	OBP	SLG	OPS	OPS+	BR/A	RC	RC/G	FR	G/POS	WS	TPW
Pro-N	5	22	4	5	0	1	0	4	1	1	....	....	.227	.261	.318	.579	90	-0	2	3.03	-3	/2-5	1	-0.3
Yr.	36	167	32	52	5	2	0	15	5	10	....	....	.311	.331	.365	.697	141	8	21	4.98	-9	0-31(0-31-0)/2-5	7	-0.2
1881 Wor-N	5	18	1	2	0	0	0	0	4	3	....	....	.111	.273	.111	.384	23	-1	1	.94	-1	/0-5(0-5-0)	0	-0.3
1887 NY-a	1	4	0	0	0	0	0	0	0	....	0	....	.000	.000	.000	.000	-105	-1	0	.00	0	/0-1	0	-0.1
Total 5 n	262	1250	300	414	83	37	**16**	245	23	25	47	15	.331	.343	.493	.836	162	85	235	8.40	2	0-190/2-50,S-21,3-12,1-4	....	6.9
Total 5	163	741	133	223	36	16	5	88	26	29	0	....	.301	.328	.417	.746	153	43	104	5.66	-20	0-137/2-29,S-2	31	1.6

• PILARCIK, Al Alfred James Pilarcik b: 7/3/1930, Whiting, IN BL/TL, 5'10", 180 lbs. Deb: 7/13/1956 Career OF: 11-176-382

YEAR TM-L	G	AB	R	H	2B	3B	HR	RBI	BB	SO	SB	CS	AVG	OBP	SLG	OPS	OPS+	BR/A	RC	RC/G	FR	G/POS	WS	TPW
1956 KC-A	69	239	28	60	10	1	4	22	30	32	9	2	.251	.335	.351	.686	81	-5	31	4.49	0	0-67(0-64-3)	5	-0.8
1957 Bal-A	142	407	52	113	16	3	9	49	53	28	14	7	.278	.366	.398	.764	116	11	62	5.14	4	*O-126(2-54-79)	15	1.0
1958 Bal-A	141	379	40	92	21	0	1	24	42	37	7	3	.243	.322	.306	.628	78	-10	39	3.50	-5	*O-119(4-32-104)	7	-1.9
1959 Bal-A	130	273	37	77	12	1	3	16	30	25	9	3	.282	.355	.366	.722	101	2	37	4.54	-4	*O-106(3-8-102)	8	-0.5
1960 Bal-A	104	194	30	48	5	1	4	17	15	16	0	2	.247	.315	.345	.660	79	-7	21	3.58	0	0-75(0-2-74)	4	-0.8
1961 KC-A	35	60	9	12	1	1	0	9	6	7	1	0	.200	.273	.250	.523	41	-5	4	2.03	0	0-21(0-2-19)	0	-0.5
Chi-A	47	62	9	11	1	0	1	6	9	5	1	1	.177	.282	.242	.524	42	-5	4	2.12	1	0-17(2-14-1)	0	-0.5
Yr.	82	122	18	23	2	1	1	15	15	12	2	1	.189	.277	.246	.523	41	-10	8	2.07	1	0-38(2-16-20)	0	-1.0
Total 6	668	1614	205	413	66	7	22	143	185	150	41	18	.256	.336	.346	.683	89	-19	198	4.12	-3	0-531	39	-4.0

• PILNEY, Andy Antone James Pilney b: 1/19/1913, Frontenac, KS d: 9/15/1996, Kenner, LA BR/TR, 5'11", 174 lbs. Deb: 6/12/1936

YEAR TM-L	G	AB	R	H	2B	3B	HR	RBI	BB	SO	SB	CS	AVG	OBP	SLG	OPS	OPS+	BR/A	RC	RC/G	FR	G/POS	WS	TPW
1936 Bos-N	3	2	0	0	0	0	0	0	0	1	0	....	.000	.000	.000	.000	-107	-1	0	.00	0	....	0	-0.1

• PINCKNEY, George George Burton Pinckney b: 1/11/1862, Orange Prairie, IL d: 11/10/1926, Peoria, IL BR/TR, 5'7", 160 lbs. Deb: 8/16/1884

YEAR TM-L	G	AB	R	H	2B	3B	HR	RBI	BB	SO	SB	CS	AVG	OBP	SLG	OPS	OPS+	BR/A	RC	RC/G	FR	G/POS	WS	TPW
1884 Cle-N	36	144	18	45	9	0	0	16	10	7	....	....	.313	.357	.375	.732	126	4	20	5.49	-9	2-25,S-11	4	-0.3
1885 Bro-a	110	447	77	124	16	5	0	42	27	....	....	....	.277	.328	.336	.664	109	5	51	4.22	-9	2-57,3-51/S-3	14	-0.1
1886 Bro-a	141	597	119	156	22	7	0	37	**70**	....	32	....	.261	.339	.322	.660	106	6	78	4.76	-15	*3-141/P-1	19	-0.5
1887 Bro-a	138	641	133	216	26	6	3	69	61	....	59	....	.337	.343	.348	.691	92	-5	92	5.83	9	*3-136/S-2	18	0.5
1888 Bro-a	143	575	**134**	156	18	8	4	52	66	....	51	....	.271	.358	.351	.710	128	21	93	5.99	-15	*3-143	23	0.9
1889*Bro-a	138	545	103	134	25	7	4	82	59	43	47	....	.246	.327	.339	.667	89	-7	78	5.02	-1	*3-138	22	-0.4
1890*Bro-N	126	485	115	150	20	9	7	83	80	19	47	....	.309	.411	.431	.842	145	31	108	8.54	-9	*3-126	**29**	2.2
1891 Bro-N	135	501	80	137	19	6	2	71	67	32	44	....	.273	.367	.347	.714	109	9	82	6.08	-10	*3-130/S-5	17	0.1
1892 StL-N	78	290	31	50	3	2	0	25	36	26	4	....	.172	.268	.197	.465	43	-18	17	1.89	-10	3-78	2	-2.5
1893 Lou-N	118	446	64	105	12	6	1	62	50	8	12	....	.235	.323	.296	.619	70	-16	48	3.71	-10	*3-118	9	-2.0
Total 10	1163	4671	874	1273	170	56	21	539	526	135	296	....	.273	.345	.338	.683	103	30	665	5.25	-78	*3-1061/2-82,S-21,P-1	157	-1.9

• PINELLI, Babe Ralph Arthur Pinelli b: 10/18/1895, San Francisco, CA d: 10/22/1984, Daly City, CA BR/TR, 5'9", 165 lbs. Deb: 8/3/1918 U

YEAR TM-L	G	AB	R	H	2B	3B	HR	RBI	BB	SO	SB	CS	AVG	OBP	SLG	OPS	OPS+	BR/A	RC	RC/G	FR	G/POS	WS	TPW
1918 Chi-A	24	78	7	18	1	1	1	7	7	8	3	....	.231	.302	.308	.610	83	-2	8	3.23	-7	3-24	1	-0.8
1920 Det-A	102	284	33	65	9	3	0	21	25	16	6	8	.229	.296	.282	.578	55	-19	24	2.62	-1	3-74,S-18/2-1	3	-1.6
1922 Cin-N	156	547	77	167	19	7	1	72	48	37	17	22	.305	.368	.371	.739	93	-9	73	4.55	21	*3-156	18	2.1
1923 Cin-N	117	423	44	117	14	5	0	51	27	29	10	14	.277	.320	.333	.653	74	-19	43	3.36	6	*3-116	9	-0.5
1924 Cin-N	144	510	61	156	16	7	0	70	32	32	23	17	.306	.353	.365	.718	94	-5	65	4.28	23	*3-143	15	2.7
1925 Cin-N	130	492	68	139	33	6	2	49	22	28	8	19	.283	.316	.386	.702	80	-22	55	3.57	18	*3-109,S-17	12	0.5
1926 Cin-N	71	207	26	46	7	4	0	24	15	5	2	....	.222	.284	.295	.579	58	-12	18	2.72	3	3-40,S-27/2-3	4	-0.6
1927 Cin-N	30	76	11	15	2	0	1	4	6	7	2	....	.197	.265	.263	.528	43	-6	5	2.26	0	3-15/S-9,2-5	1	-0.5
Total 8	774	2617	327	723	101	33	5	298	182	162	71	80	.276	.328	.346	.674	79	-93	292	3.64	63	3-677/S-71,2-9	63	1.3

• PINIELLA, Lou Louis Victor Piniella b: 8/28/1943, Tampa, FL BR/TR, 6', 198 lbs. Deb: 9/4/1964 M/C Career OF: 1126-6-275

YEAR TM-L	G	AB	R	H	2B	3B	HR	RBI	BB	SO	SB	CS	AVG	OBP	SLG	OPS	OPS+	BR/A	RC	RC/G	FR	G/POS	WS	TPW
1964 Bal-A	4	1	0	0	0	0	0	0	0	0	0	0	.000	.000	.000	.000	-100	-0	0	.00	0	....	0	0.0
1968 Cle-A	6	5	1	0	0	0	0	1	0	0	0	0	.000	.000	.000	.000	-102	-1	0	.00	0	/0-2(2-0-0)	0	-0.2
1969 KC-A	135	493	43	139	21	6	11	68	33	56	2	4	.282	.331	.416	.747	107	2	65	4.61	3	*O-129(126-3-0)	16	-0.3
1970 KC-A	144	542	54	163	24	5	11	88	35	42	3	6	.301	.345	.424	.770	111	5	74	4.93	-4	*O-139(139-0-0)/1-1	15	-0.8
1971 KC-A	126	448	43	125	21	5	3	51	21	43	5	3	.279	.314	.368	.683	94	-5	49	3.85	-2	*O-115(115-0-0)	11	-1.5
1972 KC-A★	151	574	65	179	**33**	4	11	72	34	59	7	2	.312	.359	.441	.800	138	26	84	5.26	-2	*O-150(150-0-0)	21	1.7
1973 KC-A	144	513	53	128	28	1	9	69	30	65	5	7	.250	.294	.361	.654	77	-18	47	3.00	-3	*O-128(128-0-0)/D-9	6	-2.9
1974 NY-A	140	518	71	158	26	0	9	70	32	58	1	8	.305	.348	.407	.755	120	9	66	4.46	8	*O-130(99-0-34)/D-6,1-1	17	1.0
1975 NY-A	74	199	7	39	4	1	0	22	16	22	0	0	.196	.266	.226	.492	41	-15	10	1.58	1	0-46(15-0-31),D-12	1	-1.6
1976*NY-A	100	327	36	92	16	6	3	38	18	34	0	1	.281	.323	.394	.717	110	3	41	4.53	0	0-49(10-0-39),D-38	9	-0.1
1977*NY-A	103	339	47	112	19	3	12	45	20	31	2	2	.330	.369	.510	.880	138	17	59	6.39	-1	0-51(24-0-27),D-43/1-1	13	1.3
1978*NY-A	130	472	67	148	34	5	6	69	34	36	3	1	.314	.362	.445	.807	129	18	74	5.83	-4	*O-103(78-2-25),D-23	19	0.8
1979 NY-A	130	461	49	137	22	2	11	69	17	31	3	2	.297	.325	.425	.750	103	0	58	4.40	7	*O-112(84-0-29),D-16	12	0.1
1980*NY-A	116	321	39	92	18	0	2	27	29	20	0	2	.287	.346	.361	.707	96	-2	36	3.83	1	*O-104(102-1-1)/D-7	7	-0.5
1981*NY-A	60	159	16	44	9	0	5	18	13	9	0	1	.277	.331	.428	.759	119	3	20	4.34	1	0-36(11-0-25),D-19	4	0.2
1982 NY-A	102	261	33	80	17	1	6	37	18	18	0	1	.307	.354	.448	.802	120	7	37	5.08	1	D-55,0-40(13-0-27)	7	0.5
1983 NY-A	53	148	19	43	9	1	2	16	11	12	1	1	.291	.344	.405	.749	109	2	20	4.82	1	0-43(15-0-28)/D-1	4	0.1
1984 NY-A	29	86	8	26	4	1	1	6	7	5	0	0	.302	.355	.407	.762	115	2	10	4.12	1	0-24(15-0-9)/D-2	2	0.2
Total 18	1747	5867	651	1705	305	41	102	766	368	541	32	41	.291	.336	.409	.745	109	51	750	4.49	9	*O-1401,D-231/1-3	164	-2.0

• PINKHAM, Ed Edward Pinkham b: 1849, Brooklyn, NY BL/TL, 5'7", 142 lbs. Deb: 5/8/1871

YEAR TM-L	G	AB	R	H	2B	3B	HR	RBI	BB	SO	SB	CS	AVG	OBP	SLG	OPS	OPS+	BR/A	RC	RC/G	FR	G/POS	WS	TPW
1871 Chi-n	24	95	27	25	5	5	1	17	**18**	3	5	2	.263	.381	.453	.833	125	3	19	8.19	8	3-18/O-8(0-0-8),P-3	....	0.8

• PINSON, Vada Vada Edward Pinson b: 8/11/1938, Memphis, TN d: 10/21/1995, Oakland, CA BL/TL, 5'11", 181 lbs. Deb: 4/15/1958 C Career OF: 234-1676-549

YEAR TM-L	G	AB	R	H	2B	3B	HR	RBI	BB	SO	SB	CS	AVG	OBP	SLG	OPS	OPS+	BR/A	RC	RC/G	FR	G/POS	WS	TPW
1958 Cin-N	27	96	20	26	7	0	1	8	11	18	2	1	.271	.352	.375	.727	88	-1	13	4.92	1	0-27(4-5-18)	3	-0.1
1959 Cin-N★	154	648	**131**	205	**47**	9	20	84	55	98	21	6	.316	.371	.509	.880	128	27	124	7.28	4	*O-154(0-154-0)	27	2.4
1960 Cin-N★	154	652	107	187	**37**	12	20	61	47	96	32	12	.287	.339	.472	.812	117	16	104	5.71	-5	*O-154(0-154-0)	21	0.3
1961*Cin-N	154	607	101	**208**	34	8	16	87	39	63	23	10	.343	.383	.504	.887	131	27	116	7.30	6	*O-153(0-153-0)	32	2.9
1962 Cin-N	155	619	107	181	31	7	23	100	45	68	26	8	.292	.344	.477	.821	114	13	101	5.84	-3	*O-152(0-152-0)	26	0.4
1963 Cin-N	162	652	96	**204**	37	**14**	22	106	36	80	27	8	.313	.350	.514	.864	141	35	113	6.37	-3	*O-162(0-147-17)	31	2.9
1964 Cin-N	156	625	99	166	23	11	23	84	42	99	8	2	.266	.317	.448	.765	109	7	89	5.07	-6	*O-156(0-156-0)	22	-0.4
1965 Cin-N	159	669	97	204	34	10	22	94	43	81	21	8	.305	.353	.484	.838	125	22	112	6.10	-4	*O-159(0-159-0)	24	1.4
1966 Cin-N	156	618	70	178	35	6	16	76	33	83	18	10	.288	.329	.442	.771	103	2	87	4.97	-13	*O-154(0-139-24)	19	-1.8
1967 Cin-N	158	650	90	187	28	**13**	18	66	26	86	26	8	.288	.318	.454	.772	106	6	94	5.27	-11	*O-157(0-157-0)	24	-1.1
1968 Cin-N	130	499	60	135	29	6	5	48	32	59	17	11	.271	.315	.383	.697	102	-0	59	4.07	-7	*O-123(1-120-3)	15	-1.3
1969 StL-N	132	495	58	126	22	6	10	70	35	63	4	4	.255	.308	.384	.692	92	-7	56	3.85	-1	*O-124(0-1-124)	11	-1.5
1970 Cle-A	148	574	74	164	28	6	24	82	28	69	7	6	.286	.322	.481	.803	113	6	84	5.21	4	*O-141(15-14-120)/1-7	14	0.3
1971 Cle-A	146	566	60	149	23	4	11	35	21	58	25	6	.263	.297	.376	.673	82	-12	63	3.91	-3	*O-141(9-100-39)/1-3	11	-2.2
1972 Cal-A	136	484	56	133	24	2	7	49	30	54	17	6	.275	.324	.376	.700	114	8	59	4.29	1	*O-134(104-15-29)/1-1	20	0.2
1973 Cal-A	124	466	56	121	14	6	8	57	20	55	5	5	.260	.290	.367	.657	91	-9	46	3.33	0	*O-120(75-32-25)	9	-1.5
1974 KC-A	115	406	46	112	18	2	6	41	21	45	21	5	.276	.315	.374	.689	92	-2	49	4.22	0	*O-110(14-6-91)/D-2,1-1	10	-0.8
1975 KC-A	103	319	38	71	14	5	4	22	10	21	5	6	.223	.251	.335	.586	63	-18	24	2.50	-1	0-82(12-12-59)/D-5,1-4	2	-2.3
Total 18	2469	9645	1366	2757	485	127	256	1170	574	1196	305	122	.286	.330	.442	.772	110	121	1394	5.15	-42	*O-2403/1-16,D-7	321	-2.0

• PIPP, Wally Walter Clement Pipp b: 2/17/1893, Chicago, IL d: 1/11/1965, Grand Rapids, MI BL/TL, 6'1", 180 lbs. Deb: 6/29/1913

YEAR TM-L	G	AB	R	H	2B	3B	HR	RBI	BB	SO	SB	CS	AVG	OBP	SLG	OPS	OPS+	BR/A	RC	RC/G	FR	G/POS	WS	TPW
1913 Det-A	12	31	3	5	0	3	0	5	2	6	0	....	.161	.235	.355	.590	73	-1	2	2.34	0	1-10	0	-0.1
1915 NY-A	136	479	59	118	20	13	4	60	66	81	18	7	.246	.339	.367	.706	111	8	65	4.48	5	*1-134	16	1.0
1916 NY-A	151	545	70	143	20	14	**12**	93	54	82	16	....	.262	.331	.417	.748	122	12	82	5.10	7	*1-148	20	1.8
1917 NY-A	155	587	82	143	29	12	**9**	70	60	66	11	....	.244	.320	.380	.700	112	7	72	4.10	2	*1-155	17	0.7
1918 NY-A	91	349	48	106	15	9	2	44	22	34	11	....	.304	.345	.415	.760	127	9	52	5.19	-7	1-91	13	0.1
1919 NY-A	138	523	74	144	23	10	7	50	39	42	9	....	.275	.330	.398	.728	103	1	71	4.54	-1	*1-138	14	-0.3
1920 NY-A	153	610	109	171	30	14	11	76	48	54	4	10	.280	.339	.430	.768	99	-4	87	4.89	6	*1-153	18	-0.1
1921*NY-A	153	588	96	174	35	9	8	97	45	28	17	10	.296	.347	.427	.774	94	-6	87	5.06	2	*1-153	15	-1.4
1922*NY-A	152	577	96	190	32	10	9	90	56	32	7	12	.329	.392	.466	.859	120	15	104	6.46	7	*1-152	22	1.1

YEAR TM-L	G	AB	R	H	2B	3B	HR	RBI	BB	SO	SB	CS	AVG	OBP	SLG	OPS	OPS+	BR/A	RC	RC/G	FR	G/POS	WS	TPW
1923*NY-A	144	569	79	173	19	8	6	108	36	28	6	13	.304	.352	.397	.749	95	-8	77	4.72	3	*1-144	14	-1.4
1924 NY-A	153	589	88	174	30	**19**	9	114	51	36	12	5	.295	.352	.457	.808	108	6	96	5.72	1	*1-153	18	-0.4
1925 NY-A	62	178	19	41	6	3	3	24	13	12	3	3	.230	.286	.348	.635	62	-11	18	3.18	8	1-47	2	-0.6
1926 Cin-N	155	574	72	167	22	15	6	99	49	26	8	....	.291	.352	.413	.765	108	6	83	5.02	9	*1-155	19	0.5
1927 Cin-N	122	443	49	115	19	6	2	41	32	11	2	....	.260	.309	.343	.653	77	-15	47	3.54	4	*1-114	8	-1.8
1928 Cin-N	95	272	30	77	11	3	2	26	23	13	1	....	.283	.341	.368	.709	87	-5	34	4.30	2	1-72	7	-0.8
Total 15	1872	6914	974	1941	311	148	90	997	596	551	125	60	.281	.341	.408	.749	104	12	977	4.83	48	*1-1819	203	-1.6
• PIRIE, Jim	James Moir Pirie b: 3/31/1853, Canada d: 6/2/1934, Dundas, Canada, 5'8", 169 lbs. Deb: 9/25/1883																							
1883 Phi-N	5	19	1	3	0	0	0	0	0	2	....	....	.158	.158	.158	.316	-4	-2	0	.83	-4	/S-5	0	-0.5
• PIRKL, Greg	Gregory Daniel Pirkl b: 8/7/1970, Long Beach, CA BR/TR, 6'5", 225 lbs. Deb: 8/13/1993																							
1993 Sea-A	7	23	1	4	0	0	1	4	0	4	0	0	.174	.174	.304	.478	25	-3	1	.78	1	/1-5,D-2	0	-0.2
1994 Sea-A	19	53	7	14	3	0	6	11	1	12	0	0	.264	.291	.660	.951	133	2	10	6.31	-2	D-10/1-7	1	-0.1
1995 Sea-A	10	17	2	4	0	0	0	0	1	7	0	0	.235	.278	.235	.513	35	-2	1	2.46	0	/1-6,D-1	0	-0.2
1996 Sea-A	7	21	2	4	1	0	1	1	0	3	0	0	.190	.190	.381	.571	40	-2	1	1.71	0	/D-3,1-2	0	-0.2
Bos-A	2	2	0	0	0	0	0	0	0	1	0	0	.000	.000	.000	.000	-98	-1	0	.00	0	....	0	-0.1
Yr.	9	23	2	4	1	0	1	1	0	4	0	0	.174	.174	.348	.522	28	-3	1	1.54	0	/D-3,1-2	0	-0.2
Total 4	45	116	12	26	4	0	8	16	2	27	0	0	.224	.244	.466	.709	78	-5	13	3.56	0	/1-20,D-16	1	-0.7
• PISONI, Jim	James Pete Pisoni b: 8/14/1929, St. Louis, MO BR/TR, 5'10", 169 lbs. Deb: 9/25/1953 Career OF: 32-63-5																							
1953 StL-A	3	12	1	1	0	0	1	1	0	5	0	0	.083	.083	.333	.417	8	-2	0	.84	0	/O-3(0-2-1)	0	-0.2
1956 KC-A	10	30	4	8	0	0	2	5	2	8	0	0	.267	.313	.467	.779	103	-0	4	3.94	4	/O-9(9-0-0)	1	0.3
1957 KC-A	44	97	14	23	2	2	3	12	10	17	0	0	.237	.321	.392	.713	92	-1	13	4.69	2	O-44(0-44-1)	3	0.0
1959 Mil-N	9	24	4	4	1	0	0	0	2	6	0	0	.167	.231	.208	.439	20	-3	1	1.36	-0	/O-9(2-8-0)	0	-0.3
NY-A	17	17	2	3	0	1	0	1	1	9	0	0	.176	.222	.294	.516	42	-1	1	2.13	0	O-15(9-3-3)	0	-0.2
1960 NY-A	20	9	1	1	0	0	0	1	1	2	0	0	.111	.200	.111	.311	-14	-1	0	.85	0	O-18(12-6-0)	0	-0.2
Total 5	103	189	26	40	3	3	6	20	16	47	0	0	.212	.280	.354	.635	70	-8	20	3.40	5	/O-98	4	-0.7
• PITKO, Alex	Alexander "Spunk" Pitko b: 11/22/1914, Burlington, NJ BR/TR, 5'10", 180 lbs. Deb: 9/11/1938 Career OF: 2-0-8																							
1938 Phi-N	7	19	2	6	1	0	0	2	3	3	1	....	.316	.409	.368	.778	115	1	3	5.06	-1	/O-7(0-0-7)	1	0.0
1939 Was-A	4	8	0	1	0	0	0	1	1	3	0	0	.125	.222	.125	.347	-10	-1	0	.47	-0	/O-3(2-0-1)	0	-0.1
Total 2	11	27	2	7	1	0	0	3	4	6	1	0	.259	.355	.296	.651	81	-1	3	3.53	-1	/O-10	1	-0.2
• PITLER, Jake	Jacob Albert Pitler b: 4/22/1894, New York, NY d: 2/3/1968, Binghamton, NY BR/TR, 5'8", 150 lbs. Deb: 5/30/1917 C																							
1917 Pit-N	109	382	39	89	8	5	0	23	30	24	6	....	.233	.297	.280	.577	75	-11	34	2.86	-3	*2-106/O-3(1-0-1)	6	-1.3
1918 Pit-N	2	1	1	0	0	0	0	0	1	0	2	....	.000	.500	.000	.500	55	0	1	21.66	-1	/2-1	0	-0.1
Total 2	111	383	40	89	8	5	0	23	31	24	8	....	.232	.298	.279	.578	75	-10	35	2.92	-4	2-107/O-3	6	-1.4
• PITTARO, Chris	Christopher Francis Pittaro b: 9/16/1961, Trenton, NJ BB/TR, 5'11", 170 lbs. Deb: 4/8/1985																							
1985 Det-A	28	62	10	15	3	1	0	7	5	13	1	1	.242	.299	.323	.621	71	-3	6	3.44	0	3-22/2-4,D-1	1	-0.3
1986 Min-A	11	21	0	2	0	0	0	0	0	8	0	0	.095	.095	.095	.190	-47	-4	0	.27	-1	/2-8,S-4	0	-0.5
1987 Min-A	14	12	6	4	0	0	0	0	1	0	1	0	.333	.385	.333	.718	90	0	2	6.20	0	/2-8,D-2	1	0.0
Total 3	53	95	16	21	3	1	0	7	6	21	2	1	.221	.267	.274	.541	49	-7	8	2.94	-2	/3-22,2-20,S-4,D-3	2	-0.8
• PITTENGER, Pinky	Clarke Alonzo Pittenger b: 2/24/1899, Hudson, MI d: 11/4/1977, Fort Lauderdale, FL BR/TR, 5'10", 160 lbs. Deb: 4/15/1921																							
1921 Bos-A	40	91	6	18	1	0	0	5	4	13	3	2	.198	.232	.209	.440	13	-12	5	1.54	0	O-27(19-4-4)/3-3,S-2,2-1	1	-1.2
1922 Bos-A	66	186	16	48	3	0	0	7	9	10	2	5	.258	.299	.274	.574	51	-15	15	2.63	-9	3-33,S-29	1	-1.8
1923 Bos-A	60	177	15	38	5	0	0	15	5	10	3	1	.215	.236	.243	.479	26	-19	10	1.91	-6	2-42,S-10/3-3	1	-2.2
1925 Chi-N	59	173	21	54	7	2	0	15	12	7	5	4	.312	.364	.376	.739	88	-3	24	4.80	-2	3-24,S-24	5	-0.1
1927 Cin-N	31	84	17	23	5	0	1	10	2	5	4	....	.274	.291	.369	.660	78	-3	9	3.45	-3	2-20/S-9,3-2	2	-0.4
1928 Cin-N	40	38	12	9	0	1	0	4	0	1	2	....	.237	.237	.289	.526	37	-4	2	2.17	0	S-12/2-4,3-4	0	-0.3
1929 Cin-N	77	210	31	62	11	0	0	27	5	4	8	....	.295	.318	.348	.666	68	-11	22	3.69	-1	S-50/3-8,2-4	4	-0.6
Total 7	373	959	118	252	32	3	1	83	37	50	27	12	.263	.294	.306	.600	55	-66	87	3.03	-20	S-136/3-77,2-71,O-27	14	-6.6
• PITTMAN, Joe	Joseph Wayne Pittman b: 1/1/1954, Houston, TX BR/TR, 6'1", 180 lbs. Deb: 4/25/1981																							
1981*Hou-N	52	135	11	38	4	2	0	7	11	16	4	4	.281	.336	.341	.676	97	-1	15	3.68	-2	2-35/3-4	3	-0.2
1982 Hou-N	15	10	0	2	1	0	0	0	0	2	0	0	.200	.200	.300	.500	41	-1	1	1.92	0	/3-3,O-1	0	-0.1
SD-N	55	118	16	30	2	0	0	7	9	13	8	3	.254	.307	.271	.578	66	-5	10	2.81	-1	2-30,S-13	2	-0.3
Yr.	70	128	16	32	3	0	0	7	9	15	8	3	.250	.299	.273	.573	64	-6	11	2.73	-1	2-30,S-13/3-3,O-1	2	-0.5
1984 SF-N	17	22	2	5	0	0	0	2	0	6	1	1	.227	.227	.227	.455	29	-2	1	1.06	-1	/S-6,2-5,3-2	0	-0.3
Total 3	139	285	29	75	7	2	0	16	20	37	13	8	.263	.311	.302	.613	77	-9	26	3.02	-4	/2-70,S-19,3-9,O-1	5	-1.0
• PITTS, Gaylen	Gaylen Richard Pitts b: 6/6/1946, Wichita, KS BR/TR, 6'1", 175 lbs. Deb: 5/12/1974 C																							
1974 Oak-A	18	41	4	10	3	0	0	3	5	4	0	0	.244	.326	.317	.643	92	-0	4	3.61	-1	3-11/2-6,1-1	1	-0.2
1975 Oak-A	10	3	1	1	1	0	0	1	0	0	0	0	.333	.333	.667	1.000	181	0	0	.00	-1	/3-6,S-2,2-1	0	-0.1
Total 2	28	44	5	11	4	0	0	4	5	4	0	0	.250	.327	.341	.667	97	-0	4	3.31	-2	/3-17,2-7,S-2,1-1	1	-0.2
• PITZ, Herman	Herman Pitz b: 7/18/1865, Brooklyn, NY d: 9/3/1924, Far Rockaway, NY, 5'6", 140 lbs. Deb: 4/18/1890																							
1890 Bro-a	61	189	26	26	0	0	0	6	45	....	25	....	.138	.312	.138	.450	34	-12	16	2.65	-5	C-34,3-16/O-9(5-0-4),S-2,2	2	-1.2
Syr-a	29	95	17	21	0	0	0	3	13	....	14	....	.221	.321	.221	.542	67	-3	12	4.13	2	C-27/O-1,S-1	2	0.2
Yr.	90	284	43	47	0	0	0	9	58	....	39	....	.165	.315	.165	.481	44	-15	28	3.11	-3	C-61,3-16,O-10(5-1-4)/S-3,2	4	-1.1
• PLANTIER, Phil	Phillip Alan Plantier b: 1/27/1969, Manchester, NH BL/TR, 6', 195 lbs. Deb: 8/21/1990 Career OF: 382-1-126																							
1990 Bos-A	14	15	1	2	1	0	0	3	4	6	0	0	.133	.350	.200	.550	55	-1	1	2.48	0	/D-4,O-1	0	-0.1
1991 Bos-A	53	148	27	49	7	1	11	35	23	38	1	0	.331	.424	.615	1.039	175	16	40	10.51	0	O-40(16-0-27)/D-5	9	1.4
1992 Bos-A	108	349	46	86	19	0	7	30	44	83	2	3	.246	.334	.361	.695	89	-5	42	4.05	4	O-76(13-0-63),D-23	5	-0.4
1993 SD-N	138	462	67	111	20	1	34	100	61	124	4	5	.240	.338	.509	.846	121	11	81	5.99	10	*O-134(134-0-0)	16	1.6
1994 SD-N	96	341	44	75	21	0	18	41	36	91	3	1	.220	.304	.440	.744	94	-4	45	4.38	2	O-91(91-0-0)	5	-0.6
1995 Hou-N	22	68	12	17	2	0	4	15	11	19	0	0	.250	.363	.456	.818	123	2	12	6.19	-1	O-20(8-0-12)	3	0.1
SD-N	54	148	21	38	4	0	5	19	17	29	1	1	.257	.333	.385	.718	93	-2	19	4.50	2	O-39(39-0-0)	4	-0.1
Yr.	76	216	33	55	6	0	9	34	28	48	1	1	.255	.343	.407	.750	103	1	31	5.04	2	O-59(47-0-12)	7	0.0
1996 Oak-A	73	231	29	49	8	1	7	31	28	56	2	2	.212	.305	.346	.652	66	-13	25	3.53	4	O-68(67-1-1)/D-1	2	-1.1
1997 SD-N	10	8	0	1	0	0	0	0	2	3	0	0	.125	.300	.125	.425	18	-1	0	1.76	-0	/O-3(3-0-0)	0	-0.1
StL-N	42	113	13	29	8	0	5	18	11	27	0	3	.257	.339	.460	.799	108	-0	15	4.40	-1	O-32(10-0-23)	2	-0.3
Yr.	52	121	13	30	8	0	5	18	13	30	0	3	.248	.336	.438	.774	101	-1	16	4.21	-1	O-35(13-0-23)	2	-0.4
Total 8	610	1883	260	457	90	3	91	292	237	476	13	15	.243	.335	.439	.773	104	4	282	5.07	20	O-504/D-33	46	0.5
• PLARSKI, Don	Donald Joseph Plarski b: 11/9/1929, Chicago, IL d: 12/29/1981, St. Louis, MO BR/TR, 5'6", 160 lbs. Deb: 7/20/1955																							
1955 KC-A	8	11	0	1	0	0	0	0	0	2	1	0	.091	.091	.091	.182	-50	-2	0	.37	0	/O-6(0-6-0)	0	-0.2
• PLASKETT, Elmo	Elmo Alexander Plaskett b: 6/27/1938, Frederiksted, V.I. BR/TR, 5'10", 195 lbs. Deb: 9/8/1962																							
1962 Pit-N	7	14	2	4	0	0	1	3	1	3	0	0	.286	.333	.500	.833	120	0	2	6.53	0	/C-4	0	0.0
1963 Pit-N	10	21	1	3	0	0	0	2	0	5	0	0	.143	.143	.143	.286	-17	-3	0	.64	0	/C-5,3-1	0	-0.3
Total 2	17	35	3	7	0	0	1	5	1	8	0	0	.200	.222	.286	.508	40	-3	3	2.75	0	/C-9,3-1	0	-0.3
• PLATT, Whitey	Mizell George Platt b: 8/21/1920, West Palm Beach, FL d: 7/27/1970, West Palm Beach, FL BR/TR, 6'1.5", 195 lbs. Deb: 9/16/1942 Career OF: 207-32-14																							
1942 Chi-N	4	16	1	1	0	0	0	2	0	3	0	....	.063	.063	.063	.125	-66	-3	0	.00	0	/O-4(2-2-0)	0	-0.3
1943 Chi-N	20	41	2	7	3	0	0	2	1	7	0	....	.171	.190	.244	.434	25	-4	2	1.32	-1	O-14(7-7-0)	0	-0.6
1946 Chi-A	84	247	28	62	8	5	3	32	17	34	1	7	.251	.307	.360	.667	89	-7	24	3.21	0	O-61(25-23-14)	4	-1.0

YEAR TM-L	G	AB	R	H	2B	3B	HR	RBI	BB	SO	SB	CS	AVG	OBP	SLG	OPS	OPS+	BR/A	RC	RC/G	FR	G/POS	WS	TPW
1948 StL-A	123	454	57	123	22	10	7	82	39	51	1	4	.271	.331	.410	.741	94	-7	60	4.56	-9	*O-114(114-0-0)	7	-2.4
1949 StL-A	102	244	29	63	8	2	3	29	24	27	0	1	.258	.325	.344	.669	74	-10	27	3.81	-3	O-59(59-0-0)/1-2	3	-1.7
Total 5	333	1002	117	256	41	17	13	147	81	122	2	12	.255	.314	.369	.684	83	-31	112	3.80	-13	O-252/1-2	14	-6.0
• PLATTE, Al	Alfred Frederick Joseph Platte b: 4/13/1890, Grand Rapids, MI d: 8/29/1976, Grand Rapids, MI BL/TL, 5'7", 160 lbs. Deb: 9/1/1913																							
1913 Det-A	9	18	1	2	1	0	0	0	1	1	0	....	.111	.158	.167	.325	-5	-2	1	.76	-1	/O-5(5-0-0)	0	-0.4
• PLESS, Rance	Rance Pless b: 12/6/1925, Greenville, TN BR/TR, 6', 145 lbs. Deb: 4/21/1956																							
1956 KC-A	48	85	4	23	3	1	0	9	10	13	0	1	.271	.354	.329	.684	81	-2	9	3.57	1	1-15/3-5	1	-0.3
• PLEWS, Herb	Herbert Eugene Plews b: 6/14/1928, Helena, MT BL/TR, 5'11", 160 lbs. Deb: 4/18/1956																							
1956 Was-A	91	256	24	69	10	7	1	25	26	40	1	2	.270	.339	.375	.714	88	-5	32	4.39	-10	2-66/S-5,3-2	5	-1.0
1957 Was-A	104	329	51	89	19	4	1	26	28	39	0	3	.271	.331	.362	.693	90	-5	38	3.92	-10	2-79,3-11/S-4	7	-1.1
1958 Was-A	111	380	46	98	12	6	2	29	17	45	2	3	.258	.291	.337	.628	74	-15	36	3.27	-10	2-64,3-36	6	-2.1
1959 Was-A	27	40	4	9	0	0	0	2	3	5	0	1	.225	.279	.225	.504	40	-4	2	1.63	-1	/2-6	0	-0.4
Bos-A	13	12	0	1	1	0	0	0	0	4	0	0	.083	.083	.167	.250	-32	-2	0	.00	-1	/2-2	0	-0.3
Yr.	40	52	4	10	1	0	0	2	3	9	0	1	.192	.236	.212	.448	25	-6	2	1.20	-1	/2-8	0	-0.7
Total 4	346	1017	125	266	42	17	4	82	74	133	3	9	.262	.314	.348	.662	81	-31	107	3.64	-31	2-217/3-49,S-9	18	-4.9
• PLOCK, Walter	Walter S. Plock b: 7/2/1869, Philadelphia, PA d: 4/28/1900, Richmond, VA, 6'3", 180 lbs. Deb: 8/21/1891																							
1891 Phi-N	2	5	2	2	0	0	0	0	0	1	0	....	.400	.500	.400	.900	159	0	1	9.23	-1	/O-2(0-2-0)	0	0.0
• PLUMMER, Bill	William Francis Plummer b: 3/21/1947, Oakland, CA BR/TR, 6'1", 200 lbs. Deb: 4/19/1968 M/C																							
1968 Chi-N	2	2	0	0	0	0	0	0	0	1	0	0	.000	.000	.000	.000	-94	-0	0	.00	0	/C-1	0	-0.1
1970 Cin-N	4	8	0	1	0	0	0	0	0	2	0	0	.125	.222	.125	.347	-4	-1	0	1.08	-1	/C-4	0	-0.2
1971 Cin-N	10	19	0	0	0	0	0	0	0	4	0	0	.000	.000	.000	.000	-106	-5	0	.00	1	/C-4,3-2	0	-0.5
1972 Cin-N	38	102	8	19	4	0	2	9	4	20	0	0	.186	.217	.284	.501	44	-8	6	1.72	-1	C-36/1-1,3-1	1	-0.8
1973 Cin-N	50	119	8	18	3	0	2	11	18	26	1	0	.151	.268	.227	.495	41	-9	8	2.07	-1	C-42/3-5	2	-0.9
1974 Cin-N	50	120	7	27	7	0	2	10	6	21	1	0	.225	.262	.333	.595	67	-6	10	2.65	-2	C-49/3-1	2	-0.6
1975 Cin-N	65	159	17	29	7	0	1	19	24	28	1	0	.182	.297	.245	.543	51	-10	14	2.81	0	C-63	4	-0.8
1976 Cin-N	56	153	16	38	6	1	4	19	14	36	0	2	.248	.311	.379	.690	93	-3	16	3.44	-1	C-54	4	-0.1
1977 Cin-N	51	117	10	16	5	0	1	7	17	34	1	1	.137	.246	.205	.451	22	-13	7	1.74	-2	C-50	1	-1.4
1978 Sea-A	41	93	6	20	5	0	2	7	12	19	0	0	.215	.305	.333	.638	80	-2	9	3.32	-3	C-40	2	-0.4
Total 10	367	892	72	168	37	1	14	82	95	191	4	3	.188	.269	.279	.549	53	-57	70	2.47	-10	C-343/3-9,1-1	16	-5.7
• POCOROBA, Biff	Biff Benedict Pocoroba b: 7/25/1953, Burbank, CA BB/TR, 5'10", 180 lbs. Deb: 4/25/1975																							
1975 Atl-N	67	188	15	48	7	1	1	22	20	11	0	0	.255	.327	.319	.646	77	-6	20	3.61	-3	C-62	4	-0.6
1976 Atl-N	54	174	16	42	7	0	0	14	19	12	1	0	.241	.316	.282	.598	66	-7	15	2.83	1	C-54	3	-0.3
1977 Atl-N	113	321	46	93	24	1	8	44	57	27	3	4	.290	.398	.445	.844	113	8	57	6.18	7	*C-100	14	1.9
1978 Atl-N★	92	289	21	70	8	0	6	34	29	14	0	3	.242	.316	.332	.648	73	-11	27	2.98	-1	C-79	5	-0.9
1979 Atl-N	28	38	6	12	4	0	0	4	7	0	1	1	.316	.422	.421	.843	122	1	6	5.82	-1	/C-7	1	0.1
1980 Atl-N	70	83	7	22	4	0	2	8	11	11	1	0	.265	.351	.386	.737	102	1	12	4.89	-1	C-10	2	0.0
1981 Atl-N	57	122	4	22	4	0	0	8	12	15	0	0	.180	.265	.213	.478	36	-10	7	1.73	-2	3-21/C-9	1	-1.2
1982*Atl-N	56	120	5	33	7	0	2	22	13	12	0	0	.275	.351	.383	.734	101	0	16	5.00	-1	C-36/3-2	5	0.1
1983 Atl-N	55	120	11	32	6	0	2	16	12	7	0	0	.267	.333	.367	.700	87	-2	14	4.22	-1	C-34	3	-0.2
1984 Atl-N	4	2	1	0	0	0	0	0	0	2	0	0	.000	.500	.000	.500	48	0	0	3.51	0	....	0	0.0
Total 10	596	1457	132	374	71	2	21	172	182	109	6	8	.257	.342	.351	.693	85	-26	175	4.04	-1	C-391/3-23	38	-1.1
• PODSEDNIK, Scott	Scott Eric Podsednik b: 3/18/1976, West, TX BL/TL, 6', 170 lbs. Deb: 7/6/2001 Career OF: 15-125-16																							
2001 Sea-A	5	6	1	1	0	1	0	3	0	1	0	0	.167	.167	.500	.667	70	-0	0	.00	0	/O-5(3-1-1)	0	-0.1
2002 Sea-A	14	20	2	4	0	0	1	5	4	6	0	0	.200	.333	.350	.683	85	-0	2	3.60	0	O-11(9-1-2)/D-1	1	0.0
2003 Mil-N	154	558	100	175	29	8	9	58	56	91	43	10	.314	.380	.443	.823	116	19	99	6.44	-5	*O-139(3-123-13)	22	1.5
Total 3	173	584	103	180	29	9	10	66	60	98	43	10	.308	.377	.440	.817	115	19	101	6.23	-5	O-155/D-1	23	1.3
• POEPPING, Mike	Michael Harold Poepping b: 8/7/1950, Little Falls, MN BR/TR, 6'6", 230 lbs. Deb: 9/6/1975																							
1975 Min-A	14	37	0	5	1	0	0	1	5	7	0	0	.135	.238	.162	.400	15	-4	1	1.10	-1	O-13(0-0-14)	0	-0.5
• POFAHL, Jimmy	James Willard Pofahl b: 6/18/1917, Fairbault, MN d: 9/14/1984, Owatonna, MN BR/TR, 5'11", 185 lbs. Deb: 4/16/1940																							
1940 Was-A	119	406	34	95	23	5	2	36	37	55	2	0	.234	.298	.330	.628	67	-19	41	3.36	-14	*S-112/2-4	6	-2.4
1941 Was-A	22	75	9	14	3	2	0	6	10	11	1	0	.187	.282	.280	.562	52	-5	7	2.90	-2	S-21	1	-0.6
1942 Was-A	84	283	22	59	7	2	0	28	29	30	4	3	.208	.282	.247	.529	50	-19	20	2.22	-1	S-49,2-15,3-14	2	-1.5
Total 3	225	764	65	168	33	9	2	70	76	96	7	3	.220	.290	.295	.585	59	-43	67	2.88	-18	S-182/2-19,3-14	9	-4.5
• POFF, John	John William Poff b: 10/23/1952, Chillicothe, OH BL/TL, 6'2", 190 lbs. Deb: 9/8/1979 Career OF: 4-0-7																							
1979 Phi-N	12	19	2	2	1	0	0	1	1	4	0	0	.105	.150	.158	.308	-15	-3	0	.49	-1	/O-4(4-0-0),1-1	0	-0.4
1980 Mil-A	19	68	7	17	1	2	1	7	3	7	0	0	.250	.282	.368	.649	79	-2	7	3.51	-1	/D-7,O-7(0-0-7),1-3	1	-0.4
Total 2	31	87	9	19	2	2	1	8	4	11	0	0	.218	.253	.322	.575	58	-5	7	2.73	-2	/O-11,D-7,1-4	1	-0.8
• POINTER, Aaron	Aaron Elton "Hawk" Pointer b: 4/19/1942, Little Rock, AR BR/TR, 6'2", 185 lbs. Deb: 9/22/1963 Career OF: 33-0-1																							
1963 Hou-N	2	5	0	1	0	0	0	0	0	1	0	0	.200	.200	.200	.400	17	-1	0	1.35	-0	/O-1	0	-0.1
1966 Hou-N	11	26	5	9	1	0	1	5	5	6	1	1	.346	.469	.500	.969	182	3	7	9.90	2	O-11(11-0-0)	2	0.5
1967 Hou-N	27	70	6	11	4	0	1	10	13	26	1	0	.157	.298	.257	.555	62	-3	6	2.77	0	O-22(22-0-0)	1	-0.4
Total 3	40	101	11	21	5	0	2	15	18	33	2	1	.208	.339	.317	.656	91	-0	13	4.21	2	/O-34	3	0.0
• POLANCO, Placido	Placido Enrique Polanco b: 10/10/1975, Santo Domingo, Dominican Republic BR/TR, 5'10", 168 lbs. Deb: 7/3/1998																							
1998 StL-N	45	114	10	29	3	2	1	11	5	9	2	0	.254	.292	.342	.634	67	-5	12	3.65	2	S-28,2-14	2	-0.1
1999 StL-N	88	220	24	61	9	3	1	19	15	24	1	3	.277	.323	.359	.682	72	-11	24	3.66	2	2-66/3-9,S-9	3	-0.6
2000*StL-N	118	323	50	102	12	3	5	39	16	26	4	4	.316	.350	.418	.768	93	-5	45	4.98	10	2-51,3-35,S-29/1-1	11	0.8
2001*StL-N	144	564	87	173	26	4	3	38	25	43	12	3	.307	.343	.383	.726	88	-9	70	4.38	24	*3-104,S-42,2-15/D-1	14	1.9
2002 StL-N	94	342	47	97	19	1	5	27	12	27	3	1	.284	.316	.389	.705	86	-8	39	3.94	8	3-78,S-13/2-6	9	0.3
Phi-N	53	206	28	61	13	1	4	22	14	14	2	2	.296	.353	.427	.780	109	2	31	5.45	12	3-53	7	1.5
Yr.	147	548	75	158	32	2	9	49	26	41	5	3	.288	.330	.403	.733	95	-6	70	4.50	20	*3-131,S-13/2-6	16	1.8
2003 Phi-N	122	492	87	142	30	3	14	63	42	38	14	2	.289	.354	.447	.801	114	12	77	5.50	7	2-99,3-21	18	2.4
Total 6	664	2261	333	665	112	17	33	219	129	181	38	15	.294	.339	.402	.741	94	-23	298	4.63	66	3-300,2-251,S-121/1-1,D-1	64	6.3
• POLAND, Hugh	Hugh Reid Poland b: 1/19/1913, Tompkinsville, KY d: 3/30/1984, Guthrie, KY BL/TR, 5'11.5", 185 lbs. Deb: 4/22/1943																							
1943 NY-N	4	12	1	1	0	1	0	2	1	0	0	....	.083	.154	.250	.404	16	-1	1	1.23	0	/C-4	0	-0.1
Bos-N	44	141	5	27	7	0	0	13	4	11	0	....	.191	.214	.241	.455	32	-13	7	1.56	-5	C-38	1	-1.6
Yr.	48	153	6	28	7	1	0	15	5	11	0	....	.183	.209	.242	.451	30	-14	7	1.53	-5	C-42	1	-1.8
1944 Bos-N	8	23	1	3	1	0	0	2	0	1	0	....	.130	.130	.174	.304	-14	-4	0	.45	0	/C-6	0	-0.3
1946 Bos-N	4	6	0	1	1	0	0	0	0	0	0	....	.167	.167	.333	.500	39	-1	0	1.80	0	/C-2	0	-0.1
1947 Phi-N	4	8	0	0	0	0	0	0	0	0	0	....	.000	.000	.000	.000	-104	-2	0	.00	0	/C-2	0	-0.2
Cin-N	16	18	1	6	1	0	0	2	1	4	0	....	.333	.368	.389	.757	102	0	3	6.02	-1	/C-3	1	-0.1
Yr.	20	26	1	6	1	0	0	2	1	4	0	....	.231	.259	.269	.528	41	-2	3	3.44	-1	/C-5	1	-0.3
1948 Cin-N	3	3	0	1	0	0	0	0	0	0	0	....	.333	.333	.333	.667	84	-0	0	4.50	0	....	0	0.0
Total 5	83	211	8	39	10	1	0	19	6	16	0	....	.185	.207	.242	.449	28	-21	11	1.67	-6	/C-55	2	-2.4
• POLCOVICH, Kevin	Kevin Michael Polcovich b: 6/28/1970, Auburn, NY BR/TR, 5'9", 170 lbs. Deb: 5/17/1997																							
1997 Pit-N	84	245	37	67	16	1	4	21	21	45	2	2	.273	.353	.396	.749	94	-2	32	4.46	-2	S-80/2-2,3-1	6	0.2
1998 Pit-N	81	212	18	40	12	0	0	14	15	33	4	3	.189	.259	.245	.504	33	-21	13	1.87	5	S-54,2-15/3-8	3	-1.2
Total 2	165	457	55	107	28	1	4	35	36	78	6	5	.234	.310	.326	.636	66	-23	45	3.18	3	S-134/2-17,3-9	9	-0.9

YEAR TM-L	G	AB	R	H	2B	3B	HR	RBI	BB	SO	SB	CS	AVG	OBP	SLG	OPS	OPS+	BR/A	RC	RC/G	FR	G/POS	WS	TPW
• POLHEMUS, Mark	Mark S. "Humpty Dumpty" Polhemus b: 10/4/1862, Brooklyn, NY d: 11/12/1923, Lynn, MA, 5'6.5", 185 lbs. Deb: 7/13/1887																							
1887 Ind-N	20	77	6	20	1	0	0	8	2	9	4	....	.260	.260	.253	.513	45	-5	6	2.85	0	0-20(0-0-20)	0	-0.5
• POLIDOR, Gus	Gustavo Adolfo (Gonzalez) Polidor b: 10/26/1961, Caracas, Venezuela d: 4/28/1995, Caracas, Venezuela BR/TR, 6', 170 lbs. Deb: 9/7/1985																							
1985 Cal-A	2	1	1	1	0	0	0	0	0	0	0	0	1.000	1.000	1.000	2.000	452	0	1	∞	0	/O-1,S-1	0	0.1
1986 Cal-A	6	19	1	5	1	0	0	1	1	0	0	0	.263	.300	.316	.616	69	-1	1	2.11	0	/2-4,3-1,S-1	0	-0.1
1987 Cal-A	63	137	12	36	3	0	2	15	2	15	0	0	.263	.279	.328	.607	62	-8	12	3.04	-2	S-46,3-11/2-3	2	-0.7
1988 Cal-A	54	81	4	12	3	0	0	4	3	11	0	0	.148	.179	.185	.364	2	-11	3	.95	-1	S-25,3-22/2-3,D-1	1	-1.1
1989 Mil-A	79	175	15	34	7	0	0	14	6	18	3	0	.194	.230	.234	.464	31	-16	9	1.61	-4	3-30,2-29,S-21/D-2	2	-1.8
1990 Mil-A	18	15	0	1	0	0	0	1	0	1	0	0	.067	.067	.067	.133	-63	-3	0	.13	-1	3-14/2-2,S-2	0	-0.5
1993 Fla-N	7	6	0	1	1	0	0	0	0	2	0	0	.167	.167	.333	.500	28	-1	0	1.80	-1	/2-1,3-1	0	-0.1
Total 7	229	434	33	90	15	0	2	35	12	47	3	0	.207	.234	.256	.490	35	-38	26	1.85	-10	/S-96,3-79,2-42,D-3,O-1	5	-4.2
• POLLY, Nick	Nicholas Polly b: 4/18/1917, Chicago, IL d: 1/17/1993, Chicago, IL BR/TR, 5'11", 190 lbs. Deb: 9/11/1937																							
1937 Bro-N	10	18	2	4	0	0	0	2	0	1	0	....	.222	.222	.222	.444	21	-2	1	1.76	-1	/3-7	0	-0.2
1945 Bos-A	4	7	0	1	0	0	0	1	0	1	0	0	.143	.143	.143	.286	-17	-1	0	.66	0	/3-2	0	-0.1
Total 2	14	25	2	5	0	0	0	3	0	2	0	0	.200	.200	.200	.400	10	-3	1	1.43	-1	/3-9	0	-0.3
• POLONIA, Luis	Luis Andrew (Almonte) Polonia b: 12/10/1964, Santiago, Dominican Republic BL/TL, 5'8", 152 lbs. Deb: 4/24/1987 Career OF: 927-87-54																							
1987 Oak-A	125	435	78	125	16	10	4	49	32	64	29	7	.287	.336	.398	.734	100	3	61	5.13	-1	*O-104(35-69-8),D-18	13	-0.1
1988*Oak-A	84	288	51	84	11	4	2	27	21	40	24	9	.292	.340	.378	.718	105	3	38	4.70	1	O-76(76-0-1)/D-2	10	0.1
1989 Oak-A	59	206	31	59	6	4	1	17	9	15	13	4	.286	.316	.369	.685	96	-1	23	3.98	3	O-55(55-0-0)	7	0.1
NY-A	66	227	39	71	11	2	2	29	16	29	9	4	.313	.363	.405	.769	118	5	32	5.03	2	O-53(53-0-0)/D-9	7	0.5
Yr.	125	433	70	130	17	6	3	46	25	44	22	8	.300	.341	.388	.729	107	5	55	4.53	5	*O-108(108-0-0)/D-9	14	0.6
1990 NY-A	11	22	2	7	0	0	0	3	0	1	1	0	.318	.318	.318	.636	78	-0	2	3.33	0	/D-4	0	-0.1
Cal-A	109	381	50	128	7	9	2	32	25	42	20	14	.336	.378	.417	.796	125	11	57	5.50	0	O-85(73-13-0),D-11	12	0.7
Yr.	120	403	52	135	7	9	2	35	25	43	21	14	.335	.375	.412	.787	122	10	59	5.37	0	O-85(73-13-0),D-15	12	0.7
1991 Cal-A	150	604	92	179	28	8	2	50	52	74	48	23	.296	.353	.379	.732	103	3	81	4.69	0	*O-143(143-1-0)/D-4	18	-0.2
1992 Cal-A	149	577	83	165	17	4	0	35	45	64	51	21	.286	.339	.329	.668	87	-7	63	3.68	0	O-99(99-0-0),D-47	13	-1.3
1993 Cal-A	152	576	75	156	17	6	1	32	48	53	55	24	.271	.329	.326	.655	74	-19	64	3.75	1	*O-141(141-0-0)/D-4	11	-2.3
1994 NY-A	95	350	62	109	21	6	1	36	37	36	20	12	.311	.384	.414	.798	110	5	56	5.71	3	O-84(84-0-0)/D-2	12	0.4
1995 NY-A	67	238	37	62	9	3	2	15	25	29	10	4	.261	.331	.349	.680	78	-7	29	4.14	3	O-64(64-0-0)/D-1	3	-0.7
*Atl-N	28	53	6	14	7	0	0	2	3	9	3	0	.264	.304	.396	.700	80	-1	7	4.80	0	O-15(11-4-1)	1	-0.2
1996 Bal-A	58	175	25	42	4	1	2	14	10	20	8	6	.240	.285	.309	.594	50	-15	12	2.19	-1	O-34(32-0-2),D-18	0	-1.6
*Atl-N	22	31	3	13	0	0	0	2	1	3	1	1	.419	.438	.419	.857	121	1	6	7.61	0	/O-7(7-0-0)	1	0.1
1999 Det-A	87	333	46	108	21	8	10	32	16	32	17	9	.324	.359	.526	.885	121	9	62	6.95	1	D-51,O-40(31-0-10)	10	0.5
2000 Det-A	80	267	37	73	10	5	6	25	22	25	8	5	.273	.331	.416	.747	90	-5	37	4.82	2	D-44,O-27(1-0-26)	5	-0.6
*NY-A	37	77	11	22	4	0	1	5	7	7	4	2	.286	.345	.377	.722	83	-2	10	4.42	-2	O-28(22-0-6)/D-7	1	-0.5
Yr.	117	344	48	95	14	5	7	30	29	32	12	7	.276	.334	.407	.741	88	-7	47	4.73	0	O-55(23-0-32),D-51	6	-1.1
Total 12	1379	4840	728	1417	189	70	36	405	369	543	321	145	.293	.345	.383	.728	97	-17	641	4.64	11	*O-1055,D-222	124	-5.2
• PONCE, Carlos	Carlos Antonio (Diaz) Ponce b: 2/7/1959, Rio Piedras, Puerto Rico BR/TR, 5'10", 170 lbs. Deb: 8/14/1985																							
1985 Mil-A	21	62	4	10	2	0	1	5	1	9	0	0	.161	.175	.242	.417	13	-8	2	.82	-1	1-10/O-6(5-0-1),D-3	0	-0.9
• POND, Ralph	Ralph Benjamin Pond b: 5/4/1888, Eau Claire, WI d: 9/8/1947, Cleveland, OH TR Deb: 6/8/1910																							
1910 Bos-A	1	4	0	1	0	0	0	0	0	....	1	....	.250	.250	.250	.500	55	-0	0	4.09	-1	/O-1	0	-0.1
• POOL, Harlin	Harold G "Samson" Pool b: 3/13/1908, Lakeport, CA d: 2/15/1963, Rodeo, CA BL/TR, 5'10", 195 lbs. Deb: 5/30/1934 Career OF: 91-0-21																							
1934 Cin-N	99	358	38	117	22	5	2	50	17	18	3	....	.327	.369	.433	.802	117	8	58	6.20	-1	O-94(76-0-18)	10	0.2
1935 Cin-N	28	68	8	12	6	2	0	11	2	2	0	....	.176	.200	.324	.524	39	-6	4	2.03	0	O-18(15-0-3)	0	-0.6
Total 2	127	426	46	129	28	7	2	61	19	20	3	....	.303	.343	.415	.758	105	2	62	5.43	-1	O-112	10	-0.4
• POOLE, Ed	Edward I. Poole b: 9/7/1874, Canton, OH d: 3/11/1919, Malvern, OH BR/TR, 5'10", 175 lbs. Deb: 10/6/1900 Career OF: 5-8-1 ♦																							
1900 Pit-N	2	4	1	2	0	1	1	3	0	....	0	....	.500	.500	1.750	2.250	504	2	4	47.53	0	/O-1,P-1	2	0.3
1901 Pit-N	26	78	6	16	4	0	1	4	4	....	1	....	.205	.244	.295	.539	54	-2	6	2.56	0	O-12(4-7-1),P-12/2-1,3-1	4	-0.7
1902 Pit-N	1	4	0	1	0	0	0	0	0	....	0	....	.250	.250	.250	.500	52	-0	0	2.26	0	/P-1	0	0.1
Cin-N	17	61	7	7	2	0	0	1	0	....	0	....	.115	.115	.148	.262	-18	-5	1	.52	-1	P-16/O-1	11	0.5
Yr.	18	65	7	8	2	0	0	1	0	....	0	....	.123	.123	.154	.277	-13	-5	1	.61	-1	P-17/O-1	11	0.7
1903 Cin-N	25	70	7	17	1	0	0	7	2	....	0	....	.243	.264	.257	.521	44	0	5	2.48	2	P-25	10	0.6
1904 Bro-N	25	62	3	8	1	0	0	0	0	....	0	....	.129	.129	.145	.274	-16	-3	1	.64	3	P-25	6	-1.6
Total 5	96	279	24	51	8	1	2	15	6	....	1	....	.183	.200	.240	.440	27	-8	18	1.99	4	/P-80,O-14,2-1,3-1	33	-0.7
• POOLE, Jim	James Robert "Easy" Poole b: 5/12/1895, Taylorsville, NC d: 1/2/1975, Hickory, NC BL/TR, 6', 175 lbs. Deb: 4/14/1925																							
1925 Phi-A	133	480	65	143	29	8	5	67	27	37	5	4	.298	.338	.423	.761	86	-12	68	5.08	-7	*1-123	9	-2.5
1926 Phi-A	112	361	49	106	23	5	8	63	23	25	4	3	.294	.339	.452	.791	99	-2	55	5.46	1	*1-101/O-1	9	-0.7
1927 Phi-A	38	99	4	22	2	0	0	10	9	6	0	0	.222	.287	.242	.529	36	-9	8	2.47	1	1-31	1	-0.9
Total 3	283	940	118	271	54	13	13	140	59	68	9	7	.288	.333	.415	.748	86	-23	130	4.92	-5	1-255/O-1	19	-4.1
• POOLE, Ray	Raymond Herman Poole b: 1/16/1920, Salisbury, NC BL/TR, 6', 180 lbs. Deb: 9/9/1941																							
1941 Phi-A	2	2	0	0	0	0	0	0	0	1	0	0	.000	.000	.000	.000	-103	-1	0	.00	0	....	0	-0.1
1947 Phi-A	13	13	1	3	0	0	0	1	1	4	0	0	.231	.286	.231	.516	44	-1	1	1.75	0	....	0	-0.1
• POORMAN, Tom	Thomas Iverson Poorman b: 10/14/1857, Lock Haven, PA d: 2/18/1905, Lock Haven, PA BL/TR, 5'7", 135 lbs. Deb: 5/5/1880 Career OF: 0-10-476 ♦																							
1880 Buf-N	19	70	5	11	1	0	0	1	0	13	....	....	.157	.157	.171	.329	11	-5	2	.90	-1	P-11,O-10(0-10-0)	0	-1.8
Chi-N	7	25	3	5	1	2	0	0	0	2	....	....	.200	.200	.400	.600	92	-0	2	2.82	-2	/O-7(0-0-7),P-2	2	-0.2
Yr.	26	95	8	16	2	2	0	1	0	15	....	....	.168	.168	.232	.400	32	-5	4	1.39	-3	O-17(0-10-7),P-13	2	-2.0
1884 Tol-a	94	382	56	89	8	7	0	0	10	....	....	....	.233	.254	.291	.545	75	-11	29	2.72	4	*O-93(0-0-93)/P-1	6	-0.8
1885 Bos-N	56	227	44	54	5	3	3	25	7	32	....	....	.238	.261	.326	.587	92	-2	20	3.09	-3	O-56(0-0-56)	4	-0.6
1886 Bos-N	88	371	72	97	16	6	3	41	19	52	31	....	.261	.297	.361	.659	103	1	50	4.96	-1	*O-88(0-0-88)	12	-0.1
1887 Phi-a	135	620	140	190	18	**19**	4	61	35	....	88	....	.306	.317	.381	.699	94	-6	101	6.35	-1	*O-135(0-0-135)/2-2,P-1	13	-1.0
1888 Phi-a	97	383	76	87	16	6	2	44	31	....	46	....	.227	.294	.316	.609	96	-1	50	4.58	-8	*O-97(0-0-97)	10	-1.0
Total 6	496	2078	396	533	65	43	12	172	102	99	165	....	.256	.285	.335	.620	90	-25	254	4.46	-12	O-486/P-15,2-2	47	-5.4
• POPE, Dave	David Pope b: 6/17/1921, Talladega, AL d: 8/28/1999, Cleveland, OH BL/TR, 5'10.5", 170 lbs. Deb: 7/1/1952 Career OF: 55-69-58																							
1952 Cle-A	12	34	9	10	1	1	1	4	1	7	0	0	.294	.314	.471	.785	125	1	5	5.89	0	O-10(0-0-10)	1	0.0
1954*Cle-A	60	102	21	30	2	1	4	13	10	22	2	1	.294	.357	.451	.808	118	2	16	5.77	0	O-29(18-6-5)	4	0.1
1955 Cle-A	35	104	17	31	5	0	6	22	12	31	0	0	.298	.376	.519	.895	134	5	21	7.60	-3	O-31(12-14-7)	5	0.0
Bal-A	86	222	21	55	8	4	1	30	16	34	5	2	.248	.304	.333	.638	77	-7	22	3.31	0	O-73(19-37-31)	4	-1.1
Yr.	121	326	38	86	13	4	7	52	28	65	5	2	.264	.328	.393	.720	95	-3	43	4.57	-4	*O-104(31-51-38)	9	-1.1
1956 Bal-A	12	19	1	3	0	0	0	1	0	7	0	0	.158	.200	.158	.358	-5	-3	1	1.14	0	/O-4(2-0-3)	0	-0.3
Cle-A	25	70	6	17	3	1	0	3	1	12	0	0	.243	.254	.314	.568	48	-6	6	2.85	0	O-18(4-12-2)	1	-0.6
Yr.	37	89	7	20	3	1	0	4	1	19	0	0	.225	.242	.281	.523	36	-8	6	2.44	-0	O-22(6-12-5)	1	-0.9
Total 4	230	551	75	146	19	7	12	73	40	113	7	3	.265	.319	.390	.710	92	-8	71	4.51	-4	O-165	15	-1.8
• POPOVICH, Paul	Paul Edward Popovich b: 8/18/1940, Flemington, WV BB/TR, 6', 175 lbs. Deb: 4/19/1964																							
1964 Chi-N	1	1	0	1	0	0	0	0	0	0	0	0	1.000	1.000	1.000	2.000	447	0	1	∞	0	....	0	0.0
1966 Chi-N	2	6	0	0	0	0	0	0	0	2	0	0	.000	.000	.000	.000	-99	-2	0	.00	-1	/2-2	0	-0.2
1967 Chi-N	49	159	18	34	4	0	0	2	9	12	0	1	.214	.265	.239	.504	43	-12	9	1.86	0	S-31,2-17/3-2	1	-1.0
1968 LA-N	134	418	35	97	8	1	2	25	29	37	1	3	.232	.283	.270	.554	72	-15	32	2.54	1	2-89,S-45/3-7	9	-0.4
1969 LA-N	28	50	5	10	0	0	0	4	1	4	0	0	.200	.216	.200	.416	18	-5	2	1.34	-1	2-23/S-3	1	-0.6
Chi-N	60	154	26	48	6	0	1	14	18	14	0	1	.312	.387	.370	.757	100	1	24	5.67	0	2-25/S-7,3-6,O-1	6	0.4

YEAR TM-L	G	AB	R	H	2B	3B	HR	RBI	BB	SO	SB	CS	AVG	OBP	SLG	OPS	OPS+	BR/A	RC	RC/G	FR	G/POS	WS	TPW
Yr.	88	204	31	58	6	0	1	18	19	18	0	1	.284	.348	.328	.677	81	-5	26	4.45	-1	2-48,S-10/3-6,O-1	7	-0.3
1970 Chi-N	78	186	22	47	5	1	4	20	18	18	0	1	.253	.325	.355	.680	73	-7	22	4.00	1	2-22,S-17,3-16	3	-0.4
1971 Chi-N	89	226	24	49	7	1	4	28	14	17	0	1	.217	.263	.310	.572	54	-14	17	2.44	-1	2-40,3-16/S-1	2	-1.4
1972 Chi-N	58	129	8	25	3	2	1	11	12	8	0	1	.194	.262	.271	.534	47	-9	9	2.11	4	2-36/S-8,3-1	2	-0.2
1973 Chi-N	99	280	24	66	6	3	2	24	18	27	3	2	.236	.284	.300	.584	58	-16	23	2.65	-5	2-84/S-9,3-1	5	-1.6
1974*Pit-N	59	83	9	18	2	1	0	5	5	10	0	0	.217	.261	.265	.526	49	-6	6	2.48	-1	2-12,S-10	1	-0.6
1975 Pit-N	25	40	5	8	1	0	0	1	3	2	0	0	.200	.273	.225	.498	40	-3	3	2.31	-1	/2-8,S-8	1	-0.4
Total 11	682	1732	176	403	42	9	14	134	127	151	4	10	.233	.288	.292	.580	62	-89	147	2.79	-5	2-358,S-139/3-49,O-1	31	-6.6

• POPPLEIN, George George J. Popplein b: 8/1840, Baltimore, MD d: 3/31/1901, Baltimore, MD Deb: 7/11/1873

YEAR TM-L	G	AB	R	H	2B	3B	HR	RBI	BB	SO	SB	CS	AVG	OBP	SLG	OPS	OPS+	BR/A	RC	RC/G	FR	G/POS	WS	TPW
1873 Mar-n	1	4	0	0	0	0	0	0	0	0	0	0	.000	.000	.000	.000	-130	-1	0	.00	-1	/O-1,S-1	....	-0.1

• POQUETTE, Tom Thomas Arthur Poquette b: 10/30/1951, Eau Claire, WI BL/TR, 5'10", 175 lbs. Deb: 9/1/1973 C Career OF: 241-39-105

YEAR TM-L	G	AB	R	H	2B	3B	HR	RBI	BB	SO	SB	CS	AVG	OBP	SLG	OPS	OPS+	BR/A	RC	RC/G	FR	G/POS	WS	TPW
1973 KC-A	21	28	4	6	1	0	0	3	1	4	1	1	.214	.267	.250	.517	43	-2	2	2.17	-1	O-20(0-2-18)	0	-0.4
1976*KC-A	104	344	43	104	18	10	2	34	29	31	6	5	.302	.363	.430	.794	131	12	52	5.44	-1	O-98(84-0-17)/D-2	14	0.7
1977*KC-A	106	342	43	100	23	6	2	33	19	21	1	4	.292	.339	.412	.751	103	-0	47	4.95	1	O-96(72-1-28)	11	-0.4
1978*KC-A	80	204	16	44	9	2	4	30	14	9	2	0	.216	.266	.338	.604	67	-9	18	2.77	-1	O-63(48-1-17)/D-1	3	-1.3
1979 KC-A	21	26	1	5	0	0	0	3	1	4	0	0	.192	.222	.192	.415	13	-3	1	1.52	1	O-10(2-0-8)	0	-0.3
Bos-A	63	154	14	51	9	0	2	23	8	7	2	2	.331	.376	.429	.804	110	2	25	5.94	-1	O-43(3-30-11)/D-4	4	0.0
Yr.	84	180	15	56	9	0	2	26	9	11	2	2	.311	.354	.394	.749	96	-1	26	5.22	0	O-53(5-30-19)/D-4	4	-0.3
1981 Bos-A	3	2	0	0	0	0	0	0	0	0	0	0	.000	.000	.000	.000	-94	-0	0	.00	0	/O-2(2-0-0)	0	-0.1
Tex-A	30	64	2	10	1	0	0	7	5	1	0	1	.156	.229	.172	.400	18	-7	2	1.01	-1	O-18(10-5-3)	0	-0.9
Yr.	33	66	2	10	1	0	0	7	5	1	0	1	.152	.222	.167	.389	15	-8	2	.98	-1	O-20(12-5-3)	0	-1.0
1982 KC-A	24	62	4	9	1	0	0	3	4	5	1	0	.145	.209	.161	.370	3	-8	3	1.28	0	O-23(20-0-3)	1	-0.9
Total 7	452	1226	127	329	62	18	10	136	81	82	13	13	.268	.321	.373	.694	93	-16	149	4.19	-3	O-373/D-7	33	-3.4

• PORTER, Bo Marquis Donnell Porter b: 7/5/1972, Newark, NJ BR/TR, 6'2", 195 lbs. Deb: 5/9/1999 Career OF: 35-17-29

YEAR TM-L	G	AB	R	H	2B	3B	HR	RBI	BB	SO	SB	CS	AVG	OBP	SLG	OPS	OPS+	BR/A	RC	RC/G	FR	G/POS	WS	TPW
1999 Chi-N	24	26	2	5	1	0	0	0	2	13	0	0	.192	.250	.231	.481	23	-3	1	1.71	-2	O-21(16-5-3)	0	-0.5
2000*Oak-A	17	13	3	2	0	0	1	2	2	5	0	0	.154	.267	.385	.651	64	-1	1	3.61	0	O-16(1-2-14)	0	-0.1
2001 Tex-A	48	87	18	20	4	2	1	6	9	34	3	2	.230	.302	.356	.658	70	-4	10	3.58	-1	O-40(18-10-12)/D-2	1	-0.5
Total 3	89	126	23	27	5	2	2	8	13	52	3	2	.214	.288	.333	.621	60	-8	12	3.17	-3	/O-77,D-2	1	-1.1

• PORTER, Bob Robert Lee Porter b: 7/22/1959, Yuma, AZ BL/TL, 5'10", 180 lbs. Deb: 5/13/1981

YEAR TM-L	G	AB	R	H	2B	3B	HR	RBI	BB	SO	SB	CS	AVG	OBP	SLG	OPS	OPS+	BR/A	RC	RC/G	FR	G/POS	WS	TPW
1981 Atl-N	17	14	2	4	1	0	0	4	2	1	0	0	.286	.375	.357	.732	106	0	2	5.59	0	....	0	0.0
1982 Atl-N	24	27	1	3	0	0	0	0	1	9	0	0	.111	.143	.111	.254	-27	-5	1	.56	0	/O-4(4-0-0),1-1	0	-0.5
Total 2	41	41	3	7	1	0	0	4	3	10	0	0	.171	.227	.195	.422	20	-4	3	2.00	0	/O-4,1-1	0	-0.5

• PORTER, Colin Colin F. Porter b: 11/23/1975, Tucson, AZ BL/TL, 6'2", 210 lbs. Deb: 5/30/2003

YEAR TM-L	G	AB	R	H	2B	3B	HR	RBI	BB	SO	SB	CS	AVG	OBP	SLG	OPS	OPS+	BR/A	RC	RC/G	FR	G/POS	WS	TPW
2003 Hou-N	24	32	5	6	0	0	0	0	1	17	1	0	.188	.212	.188	.400	5	-4	1	1.23	0	O-14(1-7-6)	0	-0.5

• PORTER, Dan Daniel Edward Porter b: 10/17/1931, Decatur, IL BL/TL, 6', 164 lbs. Deb: 8/16/1951

YEAR TM-L	G	AB	R	H	2B	3B	HR	RBI	BB	SO	SB	CS	AVG	OBP	SLG	OPS	OPS+	BR/A	RC	RC/G	FR	G/POS	WS	TPW
1951 Was-A	13	19	2	4	0	0	0	0	2	4	0	0	.211	.286	.211	.496	36	-2	1	2.38	0	/O-3(0-0-3)	0	-0.2

• PORTER, Darrell Darrell Ray Porter b: 1/17/1952, Joplin, MO d: 8/5/2002, Sugar Creek, MO BL/TR, 6', 193 lbs. Deb: 9/2/1971

YEAR TM-L	G	AB	R	H	2B	3B	HR	RBI	BB	SO	SB	CS	AVG	OBP	SLG	OPS	OPS+	BR/A	RC	RC/G	FR	G/POS	WS	TPW
1971 Mil-A	22	70	4	15	2	0	2	9	9	20	2	2	.214	.304	.329	.632	80	-2	7	3.44	2	C-22	2	0.1
1972 Mil-A	18	56	2	7	1	0	1	2	5	21	0	0	.125	.210	.196	.406	22	-5	2	1.32	3	C-18	1	-0.1
1973 Mil-A	117	350	50	89	19	2	16	67	57	85	5	2	.254	.365	.457	.822	133	17	61	6.04	3	C-90,D-19	16	2.4
1974 Mil-A★	131	432	59	104	15	4	12	56	50	88	8	7	.241	.326	.377	.704	103	1	54	4.24	2	*C-117/D-9	15	0.9
1975 Mil-A	130	409	66	95	12	5	18	60	89	77	2	5	.232	.376	.418	.794	123	15	68	5.50	5	*C-124/D-2	19	2.7
1976 Mil-A	119	389	43	81	14	1	5	32	51	61	2	0	.208	.302	.288	.590	75	-11	37	3.15	-3	*C-111/D-2	7	-0.9
1977*KC-A	130	425	61	117	21	3	16	60	53	70	1	0	.275	.357	.452	.809	118	12	71	5.96	-5	*C-125/D-1	18	1.3
1978*KC-A★	150	520	77	138	27	6	18	78	75	75	0	5	.265	.360	.444	.804	122	15	82	5.45	-3	*C-145/D-4	23	1.9
1979 KC-A★	157	533	101	155	23	10	20	112	**121**	65	3	4	.291	**.429**	.484	.913	143	39	119	7.82	2	*C-141,D-15	31	4.7
1980*KC-A★	118	418	51	104	14	2	7	51	69	50	1	1	.249	.358	.342	.700	92	-2	54	4.43	-2	C-81,D-34	12	-0.1
1981 StL-N	61	174	22	39	10	2	6	31	39	32	1	2	.224	.369	.408	.777	117	5	28	5.26	-2	C-52	8	0.6
1982*StL-N	120	373	46	86	18	5	12	48	66	66	1	1	.231	.349	.402	.751	108	6	55	4.95	-2	*C-111	16	1.0
1983 StL-N	145	443	57	116	24	3	15	66	68	94	1	3	.262	.365	.431	.796	120	12	71	5.63	-2	*C-133	17	1.7
1984 StL-N	127	422	56	98	16	3	11	68	60	79	5	3	.232	.335	.363	.697	98	0	52	4.13	-2	*C-122	14	0.5
1985*StL-N	84	240	30	53	12	2	10	36	41	48	6	1	.221	.337	.413	.749	109	4	36	5.04	-5	C-82	11	0.3
1986 Tex-A	68	155	21	41	6	0	12	29	22	51	1	1	.265	.360	.535	.895	136	8	30	6.90	0	C-25,D-19	8	0.8
1987 Tex-A	85	130	19	31	3	0	7	21	30	43	0	0	.238	.389	.423	.812	115	4	24	6.22	-1	D-35/C-7,1-5	4	0.2
Total 17	1782	5539	765	1369	237	48	188	826	905	1025	39	37	.247	.357	.409	.766	113	119	853	5.24	-11	*C-1506,D-140/1-5	222	17.8

• PORTER, Dick Richard Twilley "Wiggles,Twitches" Porter
b: 12/30/1901, Princess Anne, MD d: 9/24/1974, Philadelphia, PA BL/TR, 5'10", 170 lbs. Deb: 4/16/1929 Career OF: 12-0-589

YEAR TM-L	G	AB	R	H	2B	3B	HR	RBI	BB	SO	SB	CS	AVG	OBP	SLG	OPS	OPS+	BR/A	RC	RC/G	FR	G/POS	WS	TPW
1929 Cle-A	71	192	26	63	16	5	1	24	17	14	3	5	.328	.386	.479	.865	117	4	34	6.56	-4	O-28(4-0-24),2-20	6	-0.2
1930 Cle-A	119	480	100	168	43	8	4	57	55	31	3	3	.350	.420	.498	.918	127	22	102	8.21	-5	*O-118(0-0-118)	20	0.7
1931 Cle-A	114	414	82	129	24	3	1	38	56	36	6	9	.312	.395	.391	.786	102	3	65	5.75	-3	*O-109(0-0-109)/2-1	11	-0.6
1932 Cle-A	146	621	106	191	42	8	4	60	64	43	2	4	.308	.373	.420	.793	99	-1	99	5.85	-14	*O-145(0-0-145)	18	-2.2
1933 Cle-A	132	499	73	133	19	6	0	41	51	42	4	4	.267	.335	.329	.663	73	-19	57	3.95	0	*O-124(7-0-119)	10	-2.5
1934 Cle-A	13	44	9	10	2	1	1	6	4	5	0	0	.227	.292	.386	.678	73	-2	5	3.85	-1	O-10(0-0-10)	1	-0.3
Bos-A	80	265	30	80	13	6	0	56	21	15	5	2	.302	.355	.396	.752	88	-5	38	5.35	-6	O-65(1-0-64)	6	-1.4
Yr.	93	309	39	90	15	7	1	62	25	20	5	2	.291	.346	.395	.741	85	-7	43	5.11	-7	O-75(1-0-74)	7	-1.6
Total 6	675	2515	426	774	159	37	11	282	268	186	23	27	.308	.376	.414	.790	99	1	400	5.82	-31	O-599/2-21	72	-6.4

• PORTER, Irv Irving Marble Porter b: 5/17/1888, Lynn, MA d: 2/20/1971, Lynn, MA BB/TR, 5'9", 155 lbs. Deb: 8/20/1914

YEAR TM-L	G	AB	R	H	2B	3B	HR	RBI	BB	SO	SB	CS	AVG	OBP	SLG	OPS	OPS+	BR/A	RC	RC/G	FR	G/POS	WS	TPW
1914 Chi-A	1	4	1	1	0	0	0	0	0	1	0	....	.250	.250	.250	.500	51	-0	0	2.21	0	/O-1	0	0.0

• PORTER, Jay J W "Jay" Porter b: 1/17/1933, Shawnee, OK BR/TR, 6'2", 180 lbs. Deb: 7/30/1952 Career OF: 14-26-22

YEAR TM-L	G	AB	R	H	2B	3B	HR	RBI	BB	SO	SB	CS	AVG	OBP	SLG	OPS	OPS+	BR/A	RC	RC/G	FR	G/POS	WS	TPW
1952 StL-A	33	104	12	26	4	1	0	7	10	10	4	0	.250	.316	.308	.623	72	-3	11	3.44	0	O-29(3-26-0)/3-2	2	-0.4
1955 Det-A	24	55	6	13	2	0	0	3	8	15	0	0	.236	.333	.273	.606	66	-2	5	3.40	-1	/1-6,C-4,O-4(4-0-0)	1	-0.4
1956 Det-A	14	21	0	2	0	0	0	3	0	8	0	0	.095	.095	.095	.190	-49	-5	0	.15	0	/C-2,O-2(2-0-0)	0	-0.5
1957 Det-A	58	140	14	35	8	0	2	18	14	20	0	0	.250	.323	.350	.673	82	-3	17	4.21	0	O-27(5-0-22),C-12/1-3	3	-0.4
1958 Cle-A	40	85	13	17	1	0	4	19	9	23	0	0	.200	.284	.353	.637	76	-3	8	3.11	-1	C-20/1-4,3-1	1	-0.3
1959 Was-A	37	106	8	24	4	0	1	10	11	16	0	0	.226	.305	.292	.598	65	-5	10	2.96	1	C-34/1-2	2	-0.3
StL-N	23	33	5	7	3	0	1	2	1	4	0	0	.212	.257	.394	.651	66	-2	3	3.61	0	C-19/1-1	1	-0.1
Total 6	229	544	58	124	22	1	8	62	53	96	4	0	.228	.301	.316	.617	68	-22	54	3.33	-2	/C-91,O-62,1-16,3-3	10	-2.3

• PORTER, Matthew Matthew Sheldon Porter b: 1859, NY Deb: 6/27/1884 M

YEAR TM-L	G	AB	R	H	2B	3B	HR	RBI	BB	SO	SB	CS	AVG	OBP	SLG	OPS	OPS+	BR/A	RC	RC/G	FR	G/POS	WS	TPW
1884 KC-U	3	12	1	1	1	0	0	....	0	....	....	....	.083	.083	.167	.250	-20	-1	0	.43	1	/O-3(0-3-0)	0	-0.1

• POSADA, Jorge Jorge Rafael (Villeta) Posada b: 8/17/1971, Santurce, Puerto Rico BB/TR, 6'2", 190 lbs. Deb: 9/4/1995

YEAR TM-L	G	AB	R	H	2B	3B	HR	RBI	BB	SO	SB	CS	AVG	OBP	SLG	OPS	OPS+	BR/A	RC	RC/G	FR	G/POS	WS	TPW
1995*NY-A	1	0	0	0	0	0	0	0	0	0	0	0	....	....	....	....	-101	0	0	....	0	/C-1	0	0.0
1996 NY-A	8	14	1	1	0	0	0	0	1	6	0	0	.071	.133	.071	.205	-46	-3	0	.16	0	/C-4,D-3	0	-0.3
1997*NY-A	60	188	29	47	12	0	6	25	30	33	1	2	.250	.362	.410	.772	102	1	30	5.39	-3	C-60	6	0.1
1998*NY-A	111	358	56	96	23	0	17	63	47	92	0	1	.268	.353	.475	.828	117	8	57	5.49	3	C-99/D-6,1-1	15	1.6
1999*NY-A	112	379	50	93	19	2	12	57	53	91	1	0	.245	.343	.401	.744	90	-5	54	4.88	1	*C-109/1-1,D-1	10	0.3
2000*NY-A★	151	505	92	145	35	1	28	86	107	151	2	2	.287	.419	.527	.946	139	34	117	8.40	1	*C-142,1-12/D-4	29	4.0
2001*NY-A★	138	484	59	134	28	1	22	95	62	132	2	6	.277	.366	.475	.841	118	11	83	6.04	-5	*C-131/D-6,1-2	23	1.4
2002*NY-A★	143	511	79	137	40	1	20	99	81	143	1	0	.268	.371	.468	.839	122	18	86	5.82	1	*C-138/D-5	22	2.8

YEAR TM-L	G	AB	R	H	2B	3B	HR	RBI	BB	SO	SB	CS	AVG	OBP	SLG	OPS	OPS+	BR/A	RC	RC/G	FR	G/POS	WS	TPW
2003*NY-A★	142	481	83	135	24	0	30	101	93	110	2	4	.281	.408	.518	.925	145	34	104	7.67	8	*C-137/D-2	29	4.9
Total 9	866	2920	449	788	181	5	135	526	474	758	9	15	.270	.378	.474	.852	121	98	531	6.36	6	C-821/D-27,1-16	134	14.9
• POSADA, Leo	Leopoldo Jesus (Hernandez) Posada b: 4/15/1936, Havana, Cuba BR/TR, 5'11", 175 lbs. Deb: 9/21/1960 Career OF: 83-20-38																							
1960 KC-A	10	36	8	13	0	2	1	2	3	7	1	0	.361	.410	.556	.966	158	3	8	8.84	-0	/O-9(4-0-8)	2	0.3
1961 KC-A	116	344	37	87	10	4	7	53	36	84	0	0	.253	.331	.366	.697	86	-7	43	4.13	-2	*O-102(69-20-29)	7	-1.4
1962 KC-A	29	46	6	9	1	1	0	3	7	14	0	0	.196	.302	.261	.563	51	-3	4	2.73	1	O-11(10-0-1)	0	-0.3
Total 3	155	426	51	109	11	7	8	58	46	105	1	0	.256	.334	.371	.705	88	-7	55	4.32	-1	O-122	9	-1.4
• POSE, Scott	Scott Vernon Pose b: 2/11/1967, Davenport, IA BL/TR, 5'11", 165 lbs. Deb: 4/5/1993 Career OF: 55-14-30																							
1993 Fla-N	15	41	0	8	2	0	0	3	2	4	0	2	.195	.233	.244	.476	26	-5	2	1.51	0	O-10(6-8-0)	0	-0.5
1997*NY-A	54	87	19	19	2	1	0	5	9	11	3	1	.218	.292	.264	.556	47	-6	7	2.81	0	O-45(28-3-17)/D-5	1	-0.8
1999 KC-A	86	137	27	39	3	0	0	12	21	22	6	2	.285	.380	.307	.686	76	-3	18	4.54	1	O-25(18-1-6),D-20	2	-0.3
2000 KC-A	47	48	6	9	0	0	0	1	6	13	0	1	.188	.278	.188	.465	20	-6	3	1.67	-1	O-11(3-2-7)/D-4	0	-0.7
Total 4	202	313	52	75	7	1	0	21	38	50	9	6	.240	.322	.268	.590	54	-21	29	3.17	0	/O-91,D-29	3	-2.3
• POST, Lew	Lewis G. Post b: 4/12/1875, Woodland, MI d: 8/21/1944, Chicago, IL Deb: 9/21/1902																							
1902 Det-A	3	12	2	1	0	0	0	2	0	....	0	....	.083	.083	.083	.167	-53	-2	0	.21	-1	/O-3(0-0-3)	0	-0.3
• POST, Sam	Samuel Gilbert Post b: 11/17/1896, Richmond, VA d: 3/31/1971, Portsmouth, VA BL/TL, 6'1.5", 170 lbs. Deb: 4/22/1922																							
1922 Bro-N	9	25	3	7	0	0	0	4	1	4	1	0	.280	.308	.280	.588	53	-1	2	3.19	-1	/1-8	0	-0.3
• POST, Wally	Walter Charles Post b: 7/9/1929, St. Wendelin, OH d: 1/6/1982, St. Henry, OH BR/TR, 6'1", 203 lbs. Deb: 9/18/1949 Career OF: 215-16-826																							
1949 Cin-N	6	8	1	2	0	0	0	1	0	3	0	....	.250	.250	.250	.500	34	-1	0	.96	0	/O-3(1-1-1)	0	-0.1
1951 Cin-N	15	41	6	9	3	0	1	7	3	4	0	0	.220	.273	.366	.639	69	-2	4	2.92	0	/O-9(0-9-0)	1	-0.2
1952 Cin-N	19	58	5	9	1	0	2	7	4	20	0	0	.155	.222	.276	.498	37	-5	4	1.97	1	O-16(15-1-0)	0	-0.6
1953 Cin-N	11	33	3	8	1	0	1	4	4	6	1	0	.242	.324	.364	.688	78	-1	4	3.75	0	O-11(0-4-7)	1	-0.1
1954 Cin-N	130	451	46	115	21	3	18	83	26	70	2	2	.255	.300	.435	.735	86	-11	56	4.31	-1	*O-116(0-1-115)	8	-1.6
1955 Cin-N	154	601	116	186	33	3	40	109	60	102	7	4	.309	.374	.574	.948	139	33	125	7.72	-2	*O-154(0-0-154)	23	2.5
1956 Cin-N	143	539	94	134	25	3	36	83	37	124	6	0	.249	.302	.506	.808	105	3	81	5.23	7	*O-136(0-0-136)	16	0.5
1957 Cin-N	134	467	68	114	26	2	20	74	33	84	2	2	.244	.294	.437	.731	87	-10	57	4.09	5	*O-124(1-0-123)	9	-1.0
1958 Phi-N	110	379	51	107	21	3	12	62	32	74	0	2	.282	.343	.449	.792	109	4	59	5.63	-2	O-91(2-0-90)	10	-0.2
1959 Phi-N	132	468	62	119	17	6	22	94	36	101	0	0	.254	.312	.457	.769	100	-2	67	5.00	3	*O-120(2-0-118)	14	-0.3
1960 Phi-N	34	84	11	24	6	1	2	12	9	24	0	0	.286	.355	.452	.807	119	2	14	6.02	0	O-22(18-0-5)	3	0.1
Cin-N	77	249	36	70	14	0	17	38	28	51	0	2	.281	.354	.542	.896	138	12	43	6.01	1	O-67(44-0-23)	8	1.0
Yr.	111	333	47	94	20	1	19	50	37	75	0	2	.282	.354	.520	.874	134	14	57	6.01	1	O-89(62-0-28)	11	1.1
1961*Cin-N	99	282	44	83	16	3	20	57	22	61	0	1	.294	.348	.585	.933	140	14	55	7.12	-1	O-81(41-0-40)	13	0.9
1962 Cin-N	109	285	43	75	10	3	17	62	32	67	1	0	.263	.342	.498	.840	118	7	48	5.86	-4	O-90(88-0-2)	10	-0.1
1963 Cin-N	5	7	1	0	0	0	0	0	0	1	0	0	.000	.125	.000	.125	-59	-1	0	.00	0	/O-1	0	-0.1
Min-A	21	47	6	9	0	1	2	6	2	17	0	0	.191	.224	.362	.586	60	-3	4	2.48	-0	O-12(2-0-10)	0	-0.3
1964 Cle-A	5	8	1	0	0	0	0	0	3	4	0	0	.000	.273	.000	.273	-17	-1	0	.72	-1	/O-2(0-0-2)	0	-0.2
Total 15	1204	4007	594	1064	194	28	210	699	331	813	19	13	.266	.325	.485	.810	109	38	621	5.43	6	*O-1055	116	0.3
• POTTER, Mike	Michael Gary Potter b: 5/16/1951, Montebello, CA BR/TR, 6'1", 195 lbs. Deb: 9/6/1976 Career OF: 4-0-1																							
1976 StL-N	9	16	0	0	0	0	0	0	1	6	0	0	.000	.059	.000	.059	-82	-4	0	.03	0	/O-4(4-0-0)	0	-0.4
1977 StL-N	5	7	0	0	0	0	0	0	0	2	0	0	.000	.000	.000	.000	-102	-2	0	.00	0	/O-1	0	-0.2
Total 2	14	23	0	0	0	0	0	0	1	8	0	0	.000	.042	.000	.042	-87	-6	0	.02	0	/O-5	0	-0.7
• POTTS, Dan	Vivian Potts b: 1/1869, Bristol, PA d: 8/17/1934, Bristol, PA Deb: 10/3/1892																							
1892 Was-N	1	4	0	1	0	0	0	0	0	1	0	....	.250	.250	.250	.500	53	-0	0	2.31	1	/C-1	0	0.1
• POTTS, John	John Frederick "Fred" Potts b: 2/6/1887, Tipp City, OH d: 9/5/1962, Cleveland, OH BL/TR, 5'7", 165 lbs. Deb: 4/18/1914																							
1914 KC-F	41	102	14	27	4	0	1	9	25	13	7	....	.265	.414	.333	.747	120	5	17	5.40	-2	O-31(1-5-25)	4	0.2
• POULSEN, Ken	Ken Sterling Poulsen b: 8/4/1947, Van Nuys, CA BL/TR, 6'1", 190 lbs. Deb: 7/3/1967																							
1967 Bos-A	5	5	0	1	1	0	0	0	0	2	0	0	.200	.200	.400	.600	68	-0	0	2.70	-1	/3-2,S-1	0	-0.1
• POWELL, Abner	Charles Abner "Ab" Powell b: 12/15/1860, Shenandoah, PA d: 8/7/1953, New Orleans, LA BL/TR, 5'7", 160 lbs. Deb: 8/4/1884 Career OF: 8-18-21 ♦																							
1884 Was-U	48	191	36	54	10	5	0	....	3	....	....	....	.283	.294	.387	.681	133	7	22	4.55	0	O-30(0-12-18),P-18/3-2,2-1,S	12	0.3
1886 Bal-a	11	39	4	7	2	1	0	7	1	....	4	....	.179	.200	.282	.482	52	-1	3	2.59	1	/P-7,O-4(3-0-1)	1	-1.1
Cin-a	19	74	13	17	1	1	0	8	4	....	0	....	.230	.269	.270	.540	67	-3	6	2.61	0	O-13(5-6-2)/S-6,P-4	2	-0.4
Yr.	30	113	17	24	3	2	0	15	5	....	4	....	.212	.246	.274	.520	62	-4	9	2.61	0	O-17(8-6-3),P-11/S-6	3	-1.5
Total 2	78	304	53	78	13	7	0	15	8	....	4	....	.257	.276	.345	.621	106	3	31	3.79	0	/O-47,P-29,S-7,3-2,2-1	15	-1.2
• POWELL, Alonzo	Alonzo Sidney Powell b: 12/12/1964, San Francisco, CA BR/TR, 6'2", 190 lbs. Deb: 4/6/1987 Career OF: 34-6-16																							
1987 Mon-N	14	41	3	8	3	0	0	4	5	17	0	0	.195	.283	.268	.551	46	-3	3	2.84	0	O-11(10-0-1)	0	-0.4
1991 Sea-A	57	111	16	24	6	1	3	12	11	24	0	2	.216	.293	.369	.662	82	-4	12	3.50	-1	O-40(24-6-15)/1-7,D-7	1	-0.6
Total 2	71	152	19	32	9	1	3	16	16	41	0	2	.211	.290	.342	.632	72	-7	15	3.33	-1	/O-51,1-7,D-7	1	-1.0
• POWELL, Boog	John Wesley Powell b: 8/17/1941, Lakeland, FL BL/TR, 6'4.5", 240 lbs. Deb: 9/26/1961 Career OF: 431-0-1																							
1961 Bal-A	4	13	0	1	0	0	0	1	0	2	0	0	.077	.077	.077	.154	-60	-3	0	.17	0	/O-3(3-0-0)	0	-0.3
1962 Bal-A	124	400	44	97	13	2	15	53	38	79	1	1	.243	.311	.398	.709	94	-5	47	3.96	-1	*O-112(112-0-0)/1-1	8	-1.0
1963 Bal-A	140	491	67	130	22	2	25	82	49	87	1	2	.265	.331	.470	.802	124	14	74	5.23	0	*O-121(121-0-1),1-23	18	0.8
1964 Bal-A	134	424	74	123	17	0	39	99	76	91	0	0	.290	.400	**.606**	1.007	176	45	105	9.06	11	*O-124(124-0-0)/1-5	29	**5.3**
1965 Bal-A	144	472	54	117	20	2	17	72	71	93	1	1	.248	.351	.407	.758	112	9	71	5.12	5	1-78,O-71(71-0-0)	19	0.8
1966*Bal-A	140	491	78	141	18	0	34	109	67	125	0	4	.287	.374	.532	.905	159	37	97	7.15	-7	*1-136	26	2.3
1967 Bal-A	125	415	53	97	14	1	13	55	55	94	1	3	.234	.326	.366	.693	105	3	51	4.17	-10	*1-114	10	-1.5
1968 Bal-A★	154	550	60	137	21	1	22	85	73	97	7	1	.249	.340	.411	.751	127	20	79	4.91	-7	*1-149	22	0.5
1969*Bal-A★	152	533	83	162	25	0	37	121	72	76	1	1	.304	.388	.559	.947	161	43	112	7.60	-3	*1-144	27	3.0
1970*Bal-A★	154	526	82	156	28	0	35	114	104	80	1	1	.297	.417	.549	.967	163	49	123	8.48	-4	*1-145	31	3.4
1971*Bal-A★	128	418	59	107	19	0	22	92	82	64	1	0	.256	.383	.459	.842	139	25	77	6.39	-4	*1-124	19	1.3
1972 Bal-A	140	465	53	117	20	1	21	81	65	92	4	0	.252	.348	.434	.783	128	19	71	5.23	-5	*1-133	18	0.4
1973*Bal-A	114	370	52	98	13	1	11	54	85	64	0	2	.265	.402	.395	.797	126	17	62	5.73	-4	*1-111	13	0.5
1974*Bal-A	110	344	37	91	13	1	12	45	52	58	0	1	.265	.361	.413	.774	126	13	49	4.84	-2	*1-102/D-1	13	0.3
1975 Cle-A	134	435	64	129	18	0	27	86	59	72	1	3	.297	.382	.524	.906	154	30	89	7.47	-1	*1-121/D-5	23	2.0
1976 Cle-A	95	293	29	63	9	0	9	33	41	43	1	1	.215	.311	.338	.649	91	-3	31	3.34	-2	1-89	5	-1.3
1977 LA-N	50	41	0	10	0	0	0	5	12	9	0	0	.244	.415	.244	.659	82	-0	5	4.65	0	/1-4	1	-0.1
Total 17	2042	6681	889	1776	270	11	339	1187	1001	1226	20	21	.266	.364	.462	.826	134	314	1145	5.96	-33	*1-1479,O-431/D-6	282	16.6
• POWELL, Dante	Le Jon Dante Powell b: 8/25/1973, Long Beach, CA BR/TR, 6'2", 185 lbs. Deb: 4/15/1997 Career OF: 5-37-12																							
1997*SF-N	27	39	8	12	1	0	1	3	4	11	1	1	.308	.372	.410	.782	108	0	6	5.74	0	O-22(0-20-2)	2	0.0
1998 SF-N	8	4	2	2	0	0	1	1	3	0	0	0	.500	.714	1.250	1.964	429	2	4	55.74	-1	/O-8(0-8-0)	1	0.1
1999 Ari-N	22	25	4	4	3	0	0	1	2	6	2	1	.160	.222	.280	.502	26	-3	2	1.90	-1	O-15(0-8-7)	0	-0.3
2001 SF-N	13	6	5	2	0	0	0	0	0	0	0	0	.333	.333	.333	.667	79	-0	1	4.50	1	/O-9(5-1-3)	0	0.0
Total 4	70	74	19	20	4	0	2	5	9	17	3	2	.270	.349	.405	.755	105	-0	13	5.86	-1	/O-54	3	-0.2
• POWELL, Hosken	Hosken Powell b: 5/14/1955, Selma, AL BL/TL, 6'1", 185 lbs. Deb: 4/5/1978 Career OF: 33-0-480																							
1978 Min-A	121	381	55	94	20	2	3	31	45	31	11	5	.247	.326	.333	.660	84	-6	44	3.88	2	*O-117(0-0-117)	7	-1.0
1979 Min-A	104	338	49	99	17	3	2	36	33	25	5	1	.293	.361	.379	.740	96	-0	47	4.97	5	O-93(8-0-85)/D-5	8	0.1
1980 Min-A	137	485	58	127	17	5	6	35	32	46	14	3	.262	.312	.355	.666	76	-14	53	3.75	8	*O-129(0-0-129)	9	-1.2
1981 Min-A	80	264	30	63	11	3	2	25	17	31	7	4	.239	.287	.326	.613	71	-10	24	3.02	2	O-64(12-0-52)/D-8	3	-1.2

YEAR TM-L	G	AB	R	H	2B	3B	HR	RBI	BB	SO	SB	CS	AVG	OBP	SLG	OPS	OPS+	BR/A	RC	RC/G	FR	G/POS	WS	TPW
1982 Tor-A	112	265	43	73	13	4	3	26	12	23	4	4	.275	.307	.389	.696	82	-8	30	4.00	-3	0-75(8-0-68),D-19	5	-1.4
1983 Tor-A	40	83	6	14	0	0	1	7	5	8	2	0	.169	.216	.205	.421	16	-9	4	1.53	-1	0-33(5-0-29)/1-1,D-1	1	-1.1
Total 6	594	1816	241	470	78	17	17	160	144	164	43	17	.259	.316	.349	.664	79	-48	202	3.81	14	0-511/D-33,1-1	33	-5.7

• POWELL, Jake Alvin Jacob Powell b: 7/15/1908, Silver Spring, MD d: 11/4/1948, Washington, DC BR/TR, 5'11.5", 180 lbs. Deb: 8/3/1930 Career OF: 304-258-86

YEAR TM-L	G	AB	R	H	2B	3B	HR	RBI	BB	SO	SB	CS	AVG	OBP	SLG	OPS	OPS+	BR/A	RC	RC/G	FR	G/POS	WS	TPW
1930 Was-A	3	4	1	0	0	0	0	0	0	1	0	0	.000	.000	.000	.000	-100	-1	0	.00	-0	/0-2(1-0-1)	0	-0.1
1934 Was-A	9	35	6	10	2	0	0	1	4	2	1	1	.286	.359	.343	.702	85	-1	4	4.31	1	/0-9(0-9-0)	1	0.0
1935 Was-A	139	551	88	172	26	10	6	98	37	37	15	7	.312	.360	.428	.788	107	5	85	5.68	-5	*0-136(0-136-1)/2-2	17	-0.3
1936 Was-A	53	210	40	62	11	5	1	30	18	21	10	4	.295	.357	.410	.766	94	-2	31	5.44	-5	0-53(0-53-0)	5	-0.7
*NY-A	87	328	62	99	13	3	7	48	33	30	16	7	.302	.366	.424	.789	98	-1	52	5.76	0	0-84(42-42-0)	9	-0.4
Yr.	140	538	102	161	24	8	8	78	51	51	26	11	.299	.362	.418	.780	96	-2	83	5.63	-5	*0-137(42-95-0)	14	-1.1
1937*NY-A	97	365	54	96	22	3	3	45	25	36	7	5	.263	.314	.364	.678	70	-18	42	3.93	0	0-94(94-0-0)	6	-2.2
1938*NY-A	45	164	27	42	12	1	2	20	15	20	3	1	.256	.326	.378	.704	76	-6	21	4.45	-1	0-43(37-1-6)	3	-0.9
1939 NY-A	31	86	12	21	4	1	1	9	3	8	1	2	.244	.270	.349	.619	58	-7	7	2.88	0	0-23(19-2-3)	1	-0.7
1940 NY-A	12	27	3	5	0	0	0	2	1	4	0	0	.185	.214	.185	.399	5	-4	1	1.13	0	/0-7(3-2-2)	0	-0.4
1943 Was-A	37	132	14	35	10	2	0	20	5	13	3	5	.265	.297	.371	.668	99	-3	13	3.34	1	0-33(25-8-0)	3	-0.3
1944 Was-A	96	367	29	88	9	1	1	37	16	26	7	2	.240	.272	.278	.549	60	-19	29	2.69	-4	0-90(58-0-32)/3-1	3	-3.0
1945 Was-A	31	98	4	19	2	0	0	3	8	8	1	1	.194	.255	.214	.469	40	-8	6	1.90	0	0-27(21-0-6)	1	-1.0
Phi-N	48	173	13	40	5	0	1	14	8	13	1	....	.231	.265	.277	.543	52	-12	11	2.04	1	0-44(4-5-35)	1	-1.2
Total 11	688	2540	353	689	116	26	22	327	173	219	65	35	.271	.320	.363	.684	81	-75	303	4.15	-11	0-645/2-2,3-1	50	-11.2

• POWELL, Jim James Edwin Powell b: 8/30/1859, Richmond, VA d: 11/20/1929, Butte, MT, 5'10", 170 lbs. Deb: 8/5/1884

YEAR TM-L	G	AB	R	H	2B	3B	HR	RBI	BB	SO	SB	CS	AVG	OBP	SLG	OPS	OPS+	BR/A	RC	RC/G	FR	G/POS	WS	TPW
1884 Ric-a	41	151	23	37	8	4	0	0	7	....	....	....	.245	.296	.351	.647	112	2	16	3.88	-3	1-41	4	-0.4
1885 Phi-a	19	75	5	12	0	3	0	5	1	....	....	....	.160	.192	.240	.432	34	-6	4	1.52	-1	1-19	0	-0.7
Total 2	60	226	28	49	8	7	0	5	8	....	....	....	.217	.263	.314	.577	86	-4	20	3.04	-3	/1-60	4	-1.1

• POWELL, Leroy Robert Leroy Powell b: 10/17/1933, Flint, MI BR/TR, 6'1", 190 lbs. Deb: 9/16/1955

YEAR TM-L	G	AB	R	H	2B	3B	HR	RBI	BB	SO	SB	CS	AVG	OBP	SLG	OPS	OPS+	BR/A	RC	RC/G	FR	G/POS	WS	TPW
1955 Chi-A	1	0	0	0	0	0	0	0	0	0	0	0	....	....	....	....	-97	0	0	....	0	....	0	0.0
1957 Chi-A	1	0	1	0	0	0	0	0	0	0	0	0	....	....	....	....	-100	0	0	....	0	....	0	0.0

• POWELL, Martin Martin J. Powell b: 3/25/1856, Fitchburg, MA d: 2/5/1888, Fitchburg, MA BL/TL, 6', 170 lbs. Deb: 6/18/1881

YEAR TM-L	G	AB	R	H	2B	3B	HR	RBI	BB	SO	SB	CS	AVG	OBP	SLG	OPS	OPS+	BR/A	RC	RC/G	FR	G/POS	WS	TPW
1881 Det-N	55	219	47	74	9	4	1	38	15	9	....	....	.338	.380	.429	.810	148	12	37	6.82	-5	*1-55/C-1	8	0.4
1882 Det-N	80	338	44	81	13	0	0	29	19	27	....	....	.240	.280	.278	.558	80	-7	27	2.89	-10	*1-80	5	-2.2
1883 Det-N	101	421	76	115	17	5	1	48	28	23	....	....	.273	.318	.344	.663	106	5	47	4.25	-7	*1-101	11	-0.9
1884 Cin-U	43	185	46	59	4	2	1	....	13	....	....	....	.319	.364	.378	.742	140	7	26	5.80	-2	1-43	7	0.2
Total 4	279	1163	213	329	43	11	3	115	75	59	....	....	.283	.326	.347	.673	112	18	137	4.51	-24	1-279/C-1	31	-2.5

• POWELL, Paul Paul Ray Powell b: 3/19/1948, San Angelo, TX BR/TR, 5'11", 185 lbs. Deb: 4/7/1971 Career OF: 2-15-0

YEAR TM-L	G	AB	R	H	2B	3B	HR	RBI	BB	SO	SB	CS	AVG	OBP	SLG	OPS	OPS+	BR/A	RC	RC/G	FR	G/POS	WS	TPW
1971 Min-A	20	31	7	5	0	0	1	2	3	12	0	0	.161	.235	.258	.493	38	-3	2	1.79	0	0-15(0-15-0)	0	-0.3
1973 LA-N	2	1	0	0	0	0	0	0	0	1	0	0	.000	.000	.000	.000	-105	-0	0	.00	0	/0-1	0	0.0
1975 LA-N	8	10	2	2	1	0	0	0	1	2	0	0	.200	.273	.300	.573	61	-1	1	1.78	-0	/C-7,0-1	0	0.0
Total 3	30	42	9	7	1	0	1	2	4	15	0	0	.167	.239	.262	.501	41	-3	2	1.74	0	/0-17,C-7	0	-0.4

• POWELL, Ray Raymond Reath "Rabbit" Powell
b: 11/20/1888, Siloam Springs, AR d: 10/16/1962, Chillicothe, MO BL/TR, 5'9", 160 lbs. Deb: 4/16/1913 Career OF: 8-693-124

YEAR TM-L	G	AB	R	H	2B	3B	HR	RBI	BB	SO	SB	CS	AVG	OBP	SLG	OPS	OPS+	BR/A	RC	RC/G	FR	G/POS	WS	TPW
1913 Det-A	2	0	0	0	0	0	0	0	0	0	0	....	....	....	....	....	-102	0	0	....	0	/0-1	0	0.0
1917 Bos-N	88	357	42	97	10	4	4	30	24	54	12	....	.272	.318	.356	.673	113	5	42	4.09	3	0-88(0-88-0)	12	0.3
1918 Bos-N	53	188	31	40	7	5	0	20	29	30	2	....	.213	.321	.303	.624	95	0	19	3.17	0	0-53(0-53-0)	5	-0.3
1919 Bos-N	123	470	51	111	12	12	2	33	41	79	16	....	.236	.303	.326	.628	93	-4	49	3.45	3	*0-122(0-1-120)	8	-0.8
1920 Bos-N	147	609	69	137	12	12	6	29	44	83	10	18	.225	.282	.314	.595	74	-24	51	2.73	7	*0-147(0-147-1)	7	-2.7
1921 Bos-N	149	624	114	191	25	**18**	12	74	58	85	6	17	.306	.369	.462	.830	125	19	102	5.82	-4	*0-149(0-149-0)	24	0.9
1922 Bos-N	142	550	82	163	22	11	6	37	59	66	3	12	.296	.369	.409	.778	105	2	82	5.34	0	*0-136(0-136-0)	17	-0.3
1923 Bos-N	97	338	57	102	20	4	4	38	45	36	1	6	.302	.385	.420	.806	117	8	55	5.79	-6	0-84(1-83-0)	9	-0.1
1924 Bos-N	74	188	21	49	9	1	1	15	21	28	1	3	.261	.338	.335	.673	85	-4	22	3.96	4	0-46(7-36-3)	4	-0.2
Total 9	875	3324	467	890	117	67	35	276	321	461	51	56	.268	.336	.375	.711	102	2	421	4.35	8	0-826	86	-3.3

• POWER, Tom Thomas E. Power b: San Francisco, CA d: 2/25/1898, San Francisco, CA, 5'11", 164 lbs. Deb: 8/27/1890

YEAR TM-L	G	AB	R	H	2B	3B	HR	RBI	BB	SO	SB	CS	AVG	OBP	SLG	OPS	OPS+	BR/A	RC	RC/G	FR	G/POS	WS	TPW
1890 Bal-a	38	125	11	26	3	1	0	6	13	....	6	....	.208	.293	.248	.541	54	-8	11	2.97	-2	1-26,2-12	1	-1.0

• POWER, Vic Victor Pellot (Pove) Power b: 11/1/1927, Arecibo, Puerto Rico BR/TR, 6', 195 lbs. Deb: 4/13/1954 Career OF: 41-56-18

YEAR TM-L	G	AB	R	H	2B	3B	HR	RBI	BB	SO	SB	CS	AVG	OBP	SLG	OPS	OPS+	BR/A	RC	RC/G	FR	G/POS	WS	TPW
1954 Phi-A	127	462	36	118	17	5	8	38	19	19	2	1	.255	.288	.366	.654	78	-16	44	3.30	2	*0-101(33-56-12),1-21/3-1,S	7	-2.1
1955 KC-A★	147	596	91	190	34	10	19	76	35	27	0	2	.319	.357	.505	.862	128	19	103	6.51	11	*1-144	26	2.2
1956 KC-A★	127	530	77	164	21	5	14	63	24	16	2	2	.309	.341	.447	.788	106	2	80	5.74	8	1-76,2-47/0-7(7-0-0)	14	0.8
1957 KC-A	129	467	48	121	15	1	14	42	19	21	3	2	.259	.292	.385	.678	82	-13	50	3.72	14	*1-113/0-6(0-0-6),2-4	8	-0.6
1958 KC-A	52	205	35	62	13	4	4	27	7	3	1	1	.302	.325	.463	.789	112	2	28	4.81	6	1-50/2-1	6	0.6
Cle-A	93	385	63	122	24	6	12	53	13	11	2	1	.317	.341	.504	.845	133	15	65	6.34	7	3-42,1-41,2-27/S-2,0-1	16	2.3
Yr.	145	590	98	184	37	**10**	16	80	20	14	3	2	.312	.336	.490	.825	126	17	92	5.79	14	1-91,3-42,2-28/S-2,0-1	22	2.9
1959 Cle-A★	147	595	102	172	31	6	10	60	40	22	9	13	.289	.336	.412	.748	108	1	75	4.35	15	*1-121,2-21/3-7	19	1.1
1960 Cle-A★	147	580	69	167	26	3	10	84	24	20	9	5	.288	.316	.395	.711	94	-7	69	4.16	18	*1-147/S-5,3-4	15	0.2
1961 Cle-A	147	563	64	151	34	4	5	63	38	16	4	3	.268	.316	.369	.685	85	-14	62	3.68	20	*1-141/2-7	10	-0.2
1962 Min-A	144	611	80	177	28	2	16	63	22	35	7	1	.290	.318	.421	.738	93	-7	79	4.60	11	*1-142/2-2	15	-0.5
1963 Min-A	138	541	65	146	28	2	10	52	22	24	3	1	.270	.298	.384	.683	88	-10	59	3.72	5	*1-124,2-18/3-5	10	-1.0
1964 Min-A	19	45	6	10	2	0	0	1	1	3	0	0	.222	.239	.267	.506	40	-4	3	2.24	1	1-12/2-1	0	-0.3
LA-A	68	221	17	55	6	0	3	13	8	14	1	1	.249	.278	.317	.595	72	-9	18	2.70	2	1-48,3-28/2-5	3	-0.9
Yr.	87	266	23	65	8	0	3	14	9	17	1	1	.244	.272	.308	.580	67	-13	21	2.62	3	1-60,3-28/2-6	3	-1.3
Phi-N	18	48	1	10	4	0	0	3	2	3	0	0	.208	.240	.292	.532	49	-3	3	2.48	1	1-17	0	-0.3
1965 Cal-A	124	197	11	51	7	1	1	20	5	13	2	2	.259	.281	.320	.601	72	-8	17	2.93	5	*1-107/2-6,3-2	3	-0.6
Total 12	1627	6046	765	1716	290	49	126	658	279	247	45	35	.284	.317	.411	.728	97	-52	755	4.40	126	*1-1304,2-139,0-115/3-89,S	152	0.6

• POWERS, Doc Michael Riley Powers b: 9/22/1870, Pittsfield, MA d: 4/26/1909, Philadelphia, PA BR/TR Deb: 6/12/1898 U Career OF: 1-0-1

YEAR TM-L	G	AB	R	H	2B	3B	HR	RBI	BB	SO	SB	CS	AVG	OBP	SLG	OPS	OPS+	BR/A	RC	RC/G	FR	G/POS	WS	TPW
1898 Lou-N	34	99	13	27	4	3	1	19	5	....	1	....	.273	.308	.404	.712	105	-0	13	4.68	0	C-22/1-6,0-1	3	0.1
1899 Lou-N	49	169	15	35	8	2	0	22	6	....	1	....	.207	.239	.278	.517	42	-14	12	2.35	-7	C-38/1-7	2	-1.7
Was-N	14	38	3	10	2	0	0	3	1	....	0	....	.263	.282	.316	.598	64	-2	4	3.27	-1	C-12/1-1	0	-0.2
Yr.	63	207	18	45	10	2	0	25	7	....	1	....	.217	.247	.285	.532	46	-16	16	2.51	-8	C-50/1-8	2	-1.8
1901 Phi-A	116	431	53	108	26	5	1	47	18	....	10	....	.251	.292	.341	.633	72	-18	47	3.85	-2	*C-111/1-3	10	-0.9
1902 Phi-A	71	246	35	65	7	1	2	39	14	....	3	....	.264	.312	.325	.637	74	-9	27	3.88	5	C-68/1-3	8	0.2
1903 Phi-A	75	247	19	56	11	1	0	23	5	....	1	....	.227	.242	.279	.521	54	-14	18	2.43	3	C-66/1-7	5	-0.6
1904 Phi-A	57	184	11	35	3	0	0	11	6	....	3	....	.190	.220	.207	.426	34	-14	10	1.69	-6	C-56/0-1	2	-1.7
1905*Phi-A	21	60	6	10	0	0	0	5	0	....	2	....	.167	.180	.167	.347	10	-6	2	1.23	-3	C-21	0	-0.7
NY-A	11	33	3	6	1	0	0	2	1	....	0	....	.182	.206	.212	.418	29	-3	1	1.45	0	/1-7,C-4	0	-0.3
*Phi-A	19	61	2	8	0	0	0	5	3	....	2	....	.131	.172	.131	.303	-3	-7	2	1.00	1	C-19	2	-0.6
Yr.	51	154	11	24	1	0	0	12	4	....	4	....	.156	.182	.162	.345	8	-16	6	1.17	-2	C-44/1-7	2	-1.6
1906 Phi-A	58	185	5	29	1	0	0	7	1	....	2	....	.157	.170	.162	.332	4	-21	6	.99	7	C-57/1-1	4	-1.0
1907 Phi-A	59	159	9	29	3	0	0	9	7	....	1	....	.182	.217	.201	.418	33	-12	9	1.63	7	C-59	5	0.0
1908 Phi-A	62	172	8	31	6	1	0	7	5	....	1	....	.180	.217	.227	.443	41	-11	9	1.54	3	C-60/1-2	3	-0.4
1909 Phi-A	1	4	1	1	0	0	0	0	0	....	0	....	.250	.250	.250	.500	57	-0	0	2.04	0	/C-1	0	0.0
Total 11	647	2088	183	450	72	13	4	199	72	....	27	....	.216	.248	.268	.516	49	-132	161	2.52	6	C-594/1-37,0-2	44	-7.5

• POWERS, John John Calvin Powers b: 7/8/1929, Birmingham, AL d: 9/25/2001, Birmingham, AL BL/TR, 6'1", 190 lbs. Deb: 9/24/1955 Career OF: 18-0-27

YEAR TM-L	G	AB	R	H	2B	3B	HR	RBI	BB	SO	SB	CS	AVG	OBP	SLG	OPS	OPS+	BR/A	RC	RC/G	FR	G/POS	WS	TPW
1955 Pit-N	2	4	0	1	0	0	0	0	0	0	0	0	.250	.250	.250	.500	34	-0	0	2.25	0	/0-2(0-0-2)	0	0.0
1956 Pit-N	11	21	0	1	0	0	0	0	1	4	0	0	.048	.091	.048	.139	-63	-5	0	.00	-0	/0-5(4-0-1)	0	-0.5

YEAR TM-L	G	AB	R	H	2B	3B	HR	RBI	BB	SO	SB	CS	AVG	OBP	SLG	OPS	OPS+	BR/A	RC	RC/G	FR	G/POS	WS	TPW
1957 Pit-N	20	35	7	10	3	0	2	8	5	9	0	0	.286	.419	.543	.961	161	3	9	9.18	0	/0-9(4-0-4)	2	0.4
1958 Pit-N	57	82	6	15	1	0	2	2	8	19	0	0	.183	.256	.268	.524	40	-7	5	2.06	1	0-14(3-0-12)	0	-0.7
1959 Cin-N	43	43	8	11	2	1	2	4	3	13	0	0	.256	.319	.488	.808	108	0	7	5.93	0	/0-5(4-0-1)	1	0.0
1960 Bal-A	10	18	3	2	0	0	0	0	3	1	0	0	.111	.238	.111	.349	-2	-3	1	1.12	-1	/0-4(0-0-4)	0	-0.3
Cle-A	8	12	2	2	1	1	0	0	2	2	0	0	.167	.286	.417	.702	90	-0	1	2.90	0	/0-5(3-0-3)	0	-0.1
Yr.	18	30	5	4	1	1	0	0	5	3	0	0	.133	.257	.233	.490	35	-3	2	1.84	-1	/0-9(3-0-7)	0	-0.4
Total 6	151	215	26	42	7	2	6	14	22	48	0	0	.195	.282	.330	.612	65	-11	23	3.50	1	/0-44	3	-1.2

• POWERS, Les Leslie Edwin Powers b: 11/5/1909, Seattle, WA d: 11/13/1978, Santa Monica, CA BL/TL, 6', 175 lbs. Deb: 9/17/1938

YEAR TM-L	G	AB	R	H	2B	3B	HR	RBI	BB	SO	SB	CS	AVG	OBP	SLG	OPS	OPS+	BR/A	RC	RC/G	FR	G/POS	WS	TPW
1938 NY-N	2	3	0	0	0	0	0	0	0	1	0	....	.000	.000	.000	.000	-99	-1	0	.00	0	....	0	-0.1
1939 Phi-N	19	52	7	18	1	1	0	2	4	6	0	....	.346	.393	.404	.797	120	2	9	6.28	-2	1-13	2	-0.2
Total 2	21	55	7	18	1	1	0	2	4	7	0	....	.327	.373	.382	.755	109	1	9	5.82	-2	/1-13	2	-0.2

• POWERS, Mike Ellis Foree Powers b: 3/2/1906, Toddspoint, KY d: 12/2/1983, Louisville, KY BL/TL, 6'1", 185 lbs. Deb: 8/19/1932 Career OF: 4-0-16

YEAR TM-L	G	AB	R	H	2B	3B	HR	RBI	BB	SO	SB	CS	AVG	OBP	SLG	OPS	OPS+	BR/A	RC	RC/G	FR	G/POS	WS	TPW
1932 Cle-A	14	33	4	6	4	0	0	5	2	2	0	0	.182	.229	.303	.532	34	-3	2	2.27	-1	/0-8(0-0-8)	0	-0.4
1933 Cle-A	24	47	6	13	2	1	0	2	6	6	2	1	.277	.358	.362	.720	87	-1	6	4.84	-1	0-11(4-0-8)	1	-0.2
Total 2	38	80	10	19	6	1	0	7	8	8	2	1	.238	.307	.338	.644	66	-4	9	3.72	-2	/0-19	1	-0.6

• POWERS, Phil Philip B. "Grandmother" Powers b: 7/26/1854, New York, NY d: 12/22/1914, New York, NY BR/TR, 5'7", 166 lbs. Deb: 8/31/1878 Career OF: 1-3-16

YEAR TM-L	G	AB	R	H	2B	3B	HR	RBI	BB	SO	SB	CS	AVG	OBP	SLG	OPS	OPS+	BR/A	RC	RC/G	FR	G/POS	WS	TPW
1878 Chi-N	8	31	2	5	1	1	0	2	1	5	....	....	.161	.188	.258	.446	42	-2	2	1.63	3	/C-8	0	0.1
1880 Bos-N	37	126	11	18	5	0	0	10	5	15	....	....	.143	.176	.183	.358	22	-10	4	1.05	1	C-37/0-2(1-1-1)	1	-0.8
1881 Cle-N	5	15	1	1	0	0	0	0	1	2	....	....	.067	.125	.067	.192	-40	-2	0	.25	-0	/C-4,3-1	0	-0.2
1882 Cin-a	16	60	4	13	1	1	0	5	3	....	....	....	.217	.254	.267	.521	72	-2	4	2.48	2	C-10/1-5,0-1	1	0.0
1883 Cin-a	30	114	16	28	1	4	0	8	3	....	....	....	.246	.265	.325	.590	84	-2	10	3.27	1	C-17,0-13(0-2-11)	3	-0.1
1884 Cin-a	34	130	10	18	1	0	0	8	5	....	....	....	.138	.170	.146	.317	4	-14	3	.81	4	C-31/1-2,0-2(0-0-2)	3	-0.7
1885 Cin-a	15	60	6	16	2	0	0	7	0	....	....	....	.267	.267	.300	.567	77	-2	5	3.02	-2	C-15	1	-0.2
Bal-a	9	34	6	4	1	0	0	2	1	....	....	....	.118	.143	.147	.290	-8	-4	1	.66	-2	/C-8,0-1	0	-0.5
Yr.	24	94	12	20	3	0	0	9	1	....	....	....	.213	.221	.245	.466	46	-6	6	2.06	-4	C-23/0-1	1	-0.7
Total 7	154	570	56	103	12	6	0	42	19	22	....	....	.181	.207	.223	.430	39	-38	29	1.72	6	C-130/0-19,1-7,3-1	9	-2.3

• POWIS, Carl Carl Edgar "Jug" Powis b: 1/11/1928, Philadelphia, PA d: 5/10/1999, Houston, TX BR/TR, 6', 185 lbs. Deb: 4/15/1957

YEAR TM-L	G	AB	R	H	2B	3B	HR	RBI	BB	SO	SB	CS	AVG	OBP	SLG	OPS	OPS+	BR/A	RC	RC/G	FR	G/POS	WS	TPW
1957 Bal-A	15	41	4	8	3	1	0	2	7	9	2	0	.195	.327	.317	.644	82	-0	5	3.79	-1	0-13(0-0-13)	1	-0.1

• POZO, Arquimedez Arquimedez (Ortiz) Pozo b: 8/24/1973, Santo Domingo, Dominican Republic BR/TR, 5'10", 160 lbs. Deb: 9/12/1995

YEAR TM-L	G	AB	R	H	2B	3B	HR	RBI	BB	SO	SB	CS	AVG	OBP	SLG	OPS	OPS+	BR/A	RC	RC/G	FR	G/POS	WS	TPW
1995 Sea-A	1	1	0	0	0	0	0	0	0	0	0	0	.000	.000	.000	.000	-99	-0	0	.00	0	/2-1	0	0.0
1996 Bos-A	21	58	4	10	3	1	1	11	2	10	1	0	.172	.213	.310	.523	30	-6	4	2.07	-1	2-10,3-10	1	-0.7
1997 Bos-A	4	15	0	4	1	0	0	3	0	5	0	0	.267	.267	.333	.600	54	-1	1	2.95	3	/3-4	0	0.1
Total 3	26	74	4	14	4	1	1	14	2	15	1	0	.189	.221	.311	.532	33	-8	5	2.22	1	/3-14,2-11	1	-0.6

• PRAMESA, Johnny John Steven Pramesa b: 8/28/1925, Barton, OH d: 9/9/1996, Los Angeles, CA BR/TR, 6'2", 210 lbs. Deb: 4/24/1949

YEAR TM-L	G	AB	R	H	2B	3B	HR	RBI	BB	SO	SB	CS	AVG	OBP	SLG	OPS	OPS+	BR/A	RC	RC/G	FR	G/POS	WS	TPW
1949 Cin-N	17	25	2	6	1	0	1	2	3	5	0	....	.240	.321	.400	.721	91	-0	3	4.92	-1	C-13	1	-0.1
1950 Cin-N	74	228	14	70	10	1	5	30	19	15	0	....	.307	.363	.425	.788	106	2	34	5.42	-3	C-73	7	0.3
1951 Cin-N	72	227	12	52	5	2	6	22	5	17	0	0	.229	.246	.348	.594	57	-15	18	2.61	-5	C-63	2	-1.7
1952 Chi-N	22	46	1	13	1	0	1	5	4	4	0	0	.283	.340	.370	.710	96	-0	6	4.69	-1	C-17	1	0.0
Total 4	185	526	29	141	17	3	13	59	31	41	0	0	.268	.310	.386	.696	84	-13	61	4.06	-10	C-166	11	-1.5

• PRATT, Del Derrill Burnham Pratt b: 1/10/1888, Walhalia, SC d: 9/30/1977, Texas City, TX BR/TR, 5'11", 175 lbs. Deb: 4/11/1912 Career OF: 3-3-8

YEAR TM-L	G	AB	R	H	2B	3B	HR	RBI	BB	SO	SB	CS	AVG	OBP	SLG	OPS	OPS+	BR/A	RC	RC/G	FR	G/POS	WS	TPW
1912 StL-A	152	570	76	172	26	15	5	69	36	....	24	....	.302	.348	.426	.774	125	16	91	5.78	13	*2-122,S-21/0-8(0-3-5),3-1	19	3.2
1913 StL-A	155	592	60	175	31	13	2	87	40	57	37	....	.296	.341	.402	.743	121	12	89	5.23	0	*2-146/1-9	19	1.6
1914 StL-A	158	584	85	165	34	13	5	65	50	45	37	28	.283	.341	.411	.752	131	15	83	4.72	7	*2-152/0-5(2-0-3),S-1	26	2.7
1915 StL-A	159	602	61	175	31	11	3	78	26	43	32	23	.291	.323	.394	.717	119	6	80	4.37	11	*2-158	21	2.1
1916 StL-A	158	596	64	159	35	12	5	**103**	54	56	26	17	.267	.331	.391	.722	123	12	80	4.42	27	*2-158	24	4.7
1917 StL-A	123	450	40	111	22	8	1	53	33	36	18	....	.247	.301	.338	.639	98	-3	49	3.62	8	*2-119/1-2	12	0.8
1918 NY-A	126	477	65	131	19	7	2	55	35	26	12	....	.275	.327	.356	.683	104	1	59	4.07	11	*2-126	17	1.6
1919 NY-A	140	527	69	154	27	7	4	56	36	24	22	....	.292	.342	.393	.735	105	2	75	5.03	26	*2-140	20	3.3
1920 NY-A	154	574	84	180	37	8	4	97	50	24	12	10	.314	.372	.427	.798	107	6	91	5.61	12	*2-154	25	2.0
1921 Bos-A	135	521	80	169	36	10	5	102	44	10	8	10	.324	.378	.461	.839	116	10	89	6.35	-3	*2-134	20	1.0
1922 Bos-A	154	607	73	183	44	7	6	86	53	20	7	10	.301	.361	.427	.788	106	3	93	5.53	-12	*2-154	19	-0.5
1923 Det-A	101	297	43	92	18	3	0	40	25	9	6	1	.310	.375	.391	.766	104	4	46	5.54	-7	2-60,1-17,3-12	9	-0.2
1924 Det-A	121	429	56	130	32	3	1	77	31	10	6	9	.303	.353	.399	.751	95	-6	59	4.71	-6	2-65,1-51/3-4,0-1	11	-1.2
Total 13	1836	6826	856	1996	392	117	43	968	513	360	247	108	.292	.345	.403	.748	113	78	984	4.99	89	*2-1688/1-79,S-22,3-17,0-14	242	21.1

• PRATT, Frank Francis Bruce "Trackhorse" Pratt b: 8/24/1897, Blocton, AL d: 3/8/1974, Centreville, AL BL/TR, 5'9.5", 155 lbs. Deb: 5/13/1921

YEAR TM-L	G	AB	R	H	2B	3B	HR	RBI	BB	SO	SB	CS	AVG	OBP	SLG	OPS	OPS+	BR/A	RC	RC/G	FR	G/POS	WS	TPW
1921 Chi-A	1	1	0	0	0	0	0	0	0	0	0	0	.000	.000	.000	.000	-101	-0	0	.00	0	....	0	0.0

• PRATT, Larry Lester John Pratt b: 10/8/1886, Gibson City, IL d: 1/8/1969, Peoria, IL BR/TR, 6', 183 lbs. Deb: 9/19/1914

YEAR TM-L	G	AB	R	H	2B	3B	HR	RBI	BB	SO	SB	CS	AVG	OBP	SLG	OPS	OPS+	BR/A	RC	RC/G	FR	G/POS	WS	TPW
1914 Bos-A	5	4	0	0	0	0	0	0	0	4	0	....	.000	.000	.000	.000	-100	-1	0	.00	0	/C-5	0	-0.1
1915 Bro-F	20	49	5	9	1	0	1	2	2	18	2	....	.184	.216	.265	.481	42	-4	3	1.90	-1	C-17	0	-0.4
New-F	5	4	2	2	2	0	0	0	3	1	2	....	.500	.714	1.000	1.714	426	2	4	52.08	0	/C-3	1	0.2
Yr.	25	53	7	11	3	0	1	2	5	19	4	....	.208	.276	.321	.597	88	-2	7	4.23	-1	C-20	1	-0.2
Total 2	30	57	7	11	3	0	1	2	5	23	4	....	.193	.258	.298	.556	76	-3	7	3.87	-1	/C-25	1	-0.2

• PRATT, Todd Todd Alan Pratt b: 2/9/1967, Bellevue, NE BR/TR, 6'3", 225 lbs. Deb: 7/29/1992

YEAR TM-L	G	AB	R	H	2B	3B	HR	RBI	BB	SO	SB	CS	AVG	OBP	SLG	OPS	OPS+	BR/A	RC	RC/G	FR	G/POS	WS	TPW
1992 Phi-N	16	46	6	13	1	0	2	10	4	12	0	0	.283	.340	.435	.775	118	1	6	4.87	-1	C-11	2	0.1
1993*Phi-N	33	87	8	25	6	0	5	13	5	19	0	0	.287	.333	.529	.862	128	3	15	6.07	-2	C-26	4	0.3
1994 Phi-N	28	102	10	20	6	1	2	9	12	29	0	1	.196	.281	.333	.614	58	-7	9	2.86	-1	C-28	2	-0.6
1995 Chi-N	25	60	3	8	2	0	0	4	6	21	0	0	.133	.212	.167	.379	2	-9	2	1.15	-1	C-25	1	-0.8
1997 NY-N	39	106	12	30	6	0	2	19	13	32	0	1	.283	.372	.396	.768	105	1	16	5.65	1	C-36/D-1	5	0.3
1998 NY-N	41	69	9	19	9	1	2	18	2	20	0	0	.275	.296	.522	.818	111	1	11	5.83	-1	C-16/1-3	2	0.0
1999*NY-N	71	140	18	41	4	0	3	21	15	32	2	0	.293	.373	.386	.759	95	-0	22	5.83	-1	C-52/1-1,0-1	5	0.1
2000*NY-N	80	160	33	44	6	0	8	25	22	31	0	0	.275	.380	.463	.842	116	4	29	6.23	-5	C-71/D-1	5	0.3
2001 NY-N	45	80	6	13	5	0	2	4	15	36	1	0	.163	.309	.300	.609	62	-4	8	2.91	-7	C-31	0	-0.9
Phi-N	35	93	12	19	3	0	2	7	19	25	0	0	.204	.345	.301	.646	71	-3	11	3.78	-5	C-34/1-1	2	-0.6
Yr.	80	173	18	32	8	0	4	11	34	61	1	0	.185	.329	.301	.629	67	-7	19	3.36	-12	C-65/1-1	2	-1.5
2002 Phi-N	39	106	14	33	11	0	3	16	24	28	2	0	.311	.455	.500	.955	159	11	26	8.98	2	C-34/1-2	7	1.6
2003 Phi-N	43	125	16	34	10	1	4	20	22	38	0	0	.272	.405	.464	.869	134	8	25	7.04	-1	C-35/1-6	6	0.8
Total 11	495	1174	147	299	69	3	35	166	159	323	5	2	.255	.355	.408	.763	102	6	180	5.29	-21	C-399/1-13,D-2,0-1	41	0.8

• PRATT, Tom Thomas J. Pratt b: 1/26/1844, Chelsea, MA d: 9/28/1908, Philadelphia, PA TL, 5'7.5", 150 lbs. Deb: 10/18/1871 U

YEAR TM-L	G	AB	R	H	2B	3B	HR	RBI	BB	SO	SB	CS	AVG	OBP	SLG	OPS	OPS+	BR/A	RC	RC/G	FR	G/POS	WS	TPW
1871 Ath-n	1	6	2	2	0	0	0	1	0	0	0	0	.333	.333	.333	.667	93	-0	1	5.38	-1	/1-1	....	0.0

• PREIBISCH, Mel Melvin Adolphus "Primo" Preibisch b: 11/23/1914, Sealy, TX d: 4/12/1980, Sealy, TX BR/TR, 5'11", 185 lbs. Deb: 9/17/1940 Career OF: 1-12-1

YEAR TM-L	G	AB	R	H	2B	3B	HR	RBI	BB	SO	SB	CS	AVG	OBP	SLG	OPS	OPS+	BR/A	RC	RC/G	FR	G/POS	WS	TPW
1940 Bos-N	11	40	3	9	2	0	0	5	2	4	0	....	.225	.262	.275	.537	51	-3	3	2.60	0	0-11(0-11-0)	0	-0.3
1941 Bos-N	5	4	0	0	0	0	0	0	1	2	0	....	.000	.200	.000	.200	-42	-1	0	.35	0	/0-2(1-1-1)	0	-0.1
Total 2	16	44	3	9	2	0	0	5	3	6	0	....	.205	.255	.250	.505	41	-3	3	2.35	0	/0-13	0	-0.4

• PRESCOTT, Bobby George Bertrand Prescott b: 3/27/1931, Colon, Panama BR/TR, 5'11", 180 lbs. Deb: 6/17/1961

YEAR TM-L	G	AB	R	H	2B	3B	HR	RBI	BB	SO	SB	CS	AVG	OBP	SLG	OPS	OPS+	BR/A	RC	RC/G	FR	G/POS	WS	TPW
1961 KC-A	10	12	0	1	0	0	0	0	2	5	0	0	.083	.214	.083	.298	-17	-2	0	.49	0	/0-2(2-0-0)	0	-0.2

• PRESLEY, Jim James Arthur Presley b: 10/23/1961, Pensacola, FL BR/TR, 6'1", 200 lbs. Deb: 6/24/1984 C

YEAR TM-L	G	AB	R	H	2B	3B	HR	RBI	BB	SO	SB	CS	AVG	OBP	SLG	OPS	OPS+	BR/A	RC	RC/G	FR	G/POS	WS	TPW
1984 Sea-A	70	251	27	57	12	1	10	36	6	63	1	1	.227	.248	.402	.650	78	-9	24	3.19	-6	3-69/D-1	3	-1.6

YEAR TM-L	G	AB	R	H	2B	3B	HR	RBI	BB	SO	SB	CS	AVG	OBP	SLG	OPS	OPS+	BR/A	RC	RC/G	FR	G/POS	WS	TPW
1985 Sea-A	155	570	71	157	33	1	28	84	44	100	2	2	.275	.328	.484	.813	118	12	80	4.74	-5	*3-154	17	0.5
1986 Sea-A★	155	616	83	163	33	4	27	107	32	172	0	4	.265	.305	.463	.768	105	-1	80	4.46	-10	*3-155	14	-1.2
1987 Sea-A	152	575	78	142	23	6	24	88	38	157	2	0	.247	.298	.433	.731	86	-13	72	4.26	7	*3-148/S-4,D-1	12	-0.8
1988 Sea-A	150	544	50	125	26	0	14	62	36	114	3	5	.230	.283	.355	.637	74	-22	52	3.12	-16	*3-146/D-4	6	-3.7
1989 Sea-A	117	390	42	92	20	1	12	41	21	107	0	0	.236	.277	.385	.661	82	-11	39	3.31	-9	3-90,1-30/D-1	4	-2.1
1990 Atl-N	140	541	59	131	34	1	19	72	29	130	1	1	.242	.284	.414	.699	85	-14	62	3.93	-7	*3-133,1-17	7	-2.2
1991 SD-N	20	59	3	8	0	0	1	5	4	16	0	1	.136	.203	.186	.390	10	-8	2	.96	-2	3-16	0	-0.9
Total 8	**959**	**3546**	**413**	**875**	**181**	**14**	**135**	**495**	**210**	**859**	**9**	**14**	**.247**	**.292**	**.420**	**.712**	**90**	**-65**	**409**	**3.90**	**-48**	**3-911/1-47,D-7,S-4**	**63**	**-12.0**
• PRESTON, Walt	Walter B. Preston b: 4/6/1868, Richmond, VA d: 12/23/1937, New Orleans, LA BL/TR, 6', 175 lbs. Deb: 4/18/1895																							
1895 Lou-N	50	197	42	55	6	4	1	24	17	17	11	....	.279	.366	.365	.732	95	-0	31	5.91	-6	0-26(0-19-7),3-25	4	-0.6
• PRICE, Jackie	John Thomas Reid "Johnny" Price b: 11/13/1912, Winborn, MS d: 10/2/1967, San Francisco, CA BL/TR, 5'10.5", 150 lbs. Deb: 8/18/1946																							
1946 Cle-A	7	13	1	3	0	0	0	0	0	0	0	0	.231	.231	.231	.462	31	-1	1	1.16	0	/S-4	0	-0.1
• PRICE, Jim	Jimmie William Price b: 10/13/1941, Harrisburg, PA BR/TR, 6', 195 lbs. Deb: 4/11/1967																							
1967 Det-A	44	92	9	24	4	0	0	8	4	10	0	0	.261	.292	.304	.596	74	-3	7	2.66	-2	C-24	1	-0.4
1968*Det-A	64	132	12	23	4	0	3	13	13	14	0	0	.174	.253	.273	.526	58	-7	8	1.96	0	C-42	2	-0.6
1969 Det-A	72	192	21	45	8	0	9	28	18	20	0	0	.234	.300	.417	.717	95	-2	24	4.15	0	C-51	7	0.0
1970 Det-A	52	132	12	24	4	0	5	15	21	23	0	0	.182	.294	.326	.620	70	-5	13	2.89	-5	C-38	3	-0.9
1971 Det-A	29	54	4	13	2	0	1	7	6	3	0	0	.241	.328	.333	.661	84	-1	6	3.30	-1	C-25	1	-0.1
Total 5	**261**	**602**	**58**	**129**	**22**	**0**	**18**	**71**	**62**	**70**	**0**	**0**	**.214**	**.290**	**.341**	**.630**	**77**	**-18**	**58**	**3.07**	**-9**	**C-180**	**14**	**-2.0**
• PRICE, Joe	Joseph Preston "Lumber" Price b: 4/10/1897, Milligan College, TN d: 1/15/1961, Washington, DC BR/TR, 6'1.5", 187 lbs. Deb: 9/5/1928																							
1928 NY-N	1	1	0	0	0	0	0	0	0	1	0	....	.000	.000	.000	.000	-100	-0	0	.00	0	/0-1	0	0.0
• PRICHARD, Bob	Robert Alexander Prichard b: 10/21/1917, Paris, TX d: 9/25/1991, Abilene, TX BL/TL, 6'1", 195 lbs. Deb: 6/14/1939																							
1939 Was-A	26	85	8	20	5	0	0	8	19	16	0	2	.235	.375	.294	.669	79	-2	11	4.23	-1	1-26	2	-0.6
• PRIDDY, Jerry	Gerald Edward Priddy b: 11/9/1919, Los Angeles, CA d: 3/3/1980, North Hollywood, CA BR/TR, 5'11.5", 180 lbs. Deb: 4/17/1941																							
1941 NY-A	56	174	18	37	7	0	1	26	18	16	4	2	.213	.290	.270	.560	50	-12	14	2.55	6	2-31,3-14,1-10	2	-0.5
1942*NY-A	59	189	23	53	9	2	2	28	31	27	0	1	.280	.385	.381	.766	118	6	31	5.89	1	3-35,1-11/2-8,S-3	9	0.8
1943 Was-A	149	560	68	152	31	3	4	62	67	76	5	5	.271	.350	.359	.709	112	9	72	4.43	8	*2-134,S-15/3-1	20	2.8
1946 Was-A	138	511	54	130	22	8	6	58	57	73	9	3	.254	.332	.364	.696	100	2	64	4.29	4	*2-138	17	1.4
1947 Was-A	147	505	42	108	20	3	3	49	62	79	7	6	.214	.301	.283	.584	65	-24	44	2.79	-3	*2-146	9	-1.9
1948 StL-A	151	560	96	166	40	9	8	79	86	71	6	5	.296	.391	.443	.834	118	16	101	6.44	15	*2-146	20	3.8
1949 StL-A	145	544	83	158	26	4	11	63	80	81	5	3	.290	.382	.414	.796	106	6	89	5.82	1	*2-145	17	1.4
1950 Det-A	157	618	104	171	26	6	13	75	95	95	2	7	.277	.376	.401	.777	96	-4	95	5.23	24	*2-157	24	2.7
1951 Det-A	154	584	73	152	22	6	8	57	69	73	4	3	.260	.338	.360	.698	88	-9	73	4.22	-1	*2-154/S-1	16	-0.2
1952 Det-A	75	279	37	79	23	3	4	20	42	29	1	8	.283	.379	.430	.809	124	7	46	5.84	-10	2-75	9	0.1
1953 Det-A	65	196	14	46	6	2	1	24	17	19	1	1	.235	.299	.301	.600	63	-10	18	2.99	-5	2-45,1-11/3-2	2	-1.3
Total 11	**1296**	**4720**	**612**	**1252**	**232**	**46**	**61**	**541**	**624**	**639**	**44**	**44**	**.265**	**.353**	**.373**	**.725**	**97**	**-15**	**646**	**4.69**	**41**	***2-1179/3-52,1-32,S-19**	**145**	**9.3**
• PRIDE, Curtis	Curtis John Pride b: 12/17/1968, Washington, DC BL/TR, 6', 205 lbs. Deb: 9/14/1993 Career OF: 140-4-27																							
1993 Mon-N	10	9	3	4	1	1	1	5	0	3	1	0	.444	.444	1.111	1.556	288	2	5	25.25	0	/0-2(2-0-0)	2	0.2
1995 Mon-N	48	63	10	11	1	0	0	2	5	16	3	2	.175	.235	.190	.426	13	-8	3	1.27	-1	0-24(24-1-0)	0	-1.0
1996 Det-A	95	267	52	80	17	5	10	31	31	63	11	6	.300	.372	.513	.886	121	8	52	7.10	-2	0-48(45-0-5),D-31	9	0.2
1997 Det-A	79	162	21	34	4	4	2	19	24	45	6	4	.210	.316	.321	.636	67	-8	17	3.28	0	0-35(34-0-3),D-23	2	-0.9
Bos-A	2	2	1	1	0	0	1	1	0	1	0	0	.500	.500	2.000	2.500	502	1	2	54.00	0	....	0	0.1
Yr.	81	164	22	35	4	4	3	20	24	46	6	4	.213	.317	.341	.659	72	-7	19	3.64	0	0-35(34-0-3),D-23	2	-0.8
1998 Atl-N	70	107	19	27	6	1	3	9	9	29	4	0	.252	.328	.411	.739	93	-0	15	4.94	-0	0-22(8-0-14)/D-2	2	-0.1
2000 Bos-A	9	20	4	5	1	0	0	0	1	7	0	0	.250	.286	.300	.586	47	-2	2	3.22	0	/0-9(7-2-0),D-1	0	-0.1
2001 Mon-N	36	76	8	19	3	1	1	9	9	22	3	2	.250	.345	.355	.700	80	-2	9	3.71	0	0-23(19-1-3)/D-2	1	-0.2
2003 NY-A	4	12	1	1	0	0	1	1	0	2	0	0	.083	.083	.333	.417	3	-2	0	.00	0	/0-3(1-0-2)	0	-0.2
Total 8	**353**	**718**	**119**	**182**	**33**	**12**	**19**	**77**	**79**	**188**	**28**	**14**	**.253**	**.333**	**.412**	**.745**	**90**	**-10**	**104**	**4.90**	**-4**	**0-166/D-59**	**16**	**-2.2**
• PRIEST, Johnny	John Gooding Priest b: 6/23/1886, St. Joseph, MO d: 11/4/1979, Washington, DC BR/TR, 5'11", 170 lbs. Deb: 5/30/1911																							
1911 NY-A	8	21	2	3	0	0	0	2	2	....	3	....	.143	.250	.143	.393	10	-3	1	2.07	-2	/2-5,3-2	0	-0.4
1912 NY-A	2	2	1	1	0	0	0	1	0	....	0	....	.500	.500	.500	1.000	176	0	0	12.79	0	....	0	0.0
Total 2	**10**	**23**	**3**	**4**	**0**	**0**	**0**	**3**	**2**	**....**	**3**	**....**	**.174**	**.269**	**.174**	**.443**	**23**	**-2**	**2**	**2.63**	**-2**	**/2-5,3-2**	**0**	**-0.4**
• PRIETO, Alex	Alejandro Antonio Prieto b: 6/19/1976, Caracas, Venezuela BR/TR, 5'10", 200 lbs. Deb: 7/26/2003																							
2003 Min-A	8	11	1	1	0	0	0	0	0	4	0	0	.091	.091	.091	.182	-51	-2	0	.25	0	/2-5,S-1	0	-0.2
• PRINCE, Tom	Thomas Albert Prince b: 8/13/1964, Kankakee, IL BR/TR, 5'11", 185 lbs. Deb: 9/22/1987																							
1987 Pit-N	4	9	1	2	1	0	1	2	0	2	0	0	.222	.222	.667	.889	123	0	1	5.14	0	/C-4	0	0.1
1988 Pit-N	29	74	3	13	2	0	0	6	4	15	0	0	.176	.218	.203	.421	22	-8	3	1.02	-1	C-28	1	-0.8
1989 Pit-N	21	52	1	7	4	0	0	5	6	12	1	1	.135	.224	.212	.436	26	-5	2	1.40	-1	C-21	0	-0.5
1990 Pit-N	4	10	1	1	0	0	0	0	1	2	0	1	.100	.182	.100	.282	-21	-2	0	.31	0	/C-3	0	-0.2
1991 Pit-N	26	34	4	9	3	0	1	2	7	3	0	0	.265	.405	.441	.846	140	2	6	5.49	0	C-19/1-1	1	0.3
1992 Pit-N	27	44	1	4	2	0	0	5	6	9	1	1	.091	.200	.136	.336	-3	-6	1	.74	-1	C-19/3-1	1	-0.7
1993 Pit-N	66	179	14	35	14	0	2	24	13	38	1	1	.196	.276	.307	.584	56	-12	15	2.63	0	C-59	3	-0.8
1994 LA-N	3	6	2	2	0	0	0	1	1	3	0	0	.333	.429	.333	.762	109	0	1	6.54	0	/C-3	1	0.0
1995 LA-N	18	40	3	8	2	1	1	4	4	10	0	0	.200	.273	.375	.648	75	-2	4	3.69	1	C-17	1	0.0
1996 LA-N	40	64	6	19	6	0	1	11	6	15	0	0	.297	.375	.438	.813	123	2	11	6.09	0	C-35	3	0.4
1997 LA-N	47	100	17	22	5	0	3	14	5	15	0	0	.220	.278	.360	.638	71	-5	10	3.20	3	C-45	3	0.1
1998 LA-N	37	81	7	15	5	1	0	5	7	24	0	0	.185	.267	.272	.538	45	-7	7	2.60	2	C-32	2	-0.3
1999 Phi-N	4	6	1	1	0	0	0	0	1	1	0	0	.167	.286	.167	.452	18	-1	0	.81	-0	/C-4	0	-0.1
2000 Phi-N	46	122	14	29	9	0	2	16	13	31	1	0	.238	.321	.361	.682	71	-5	14	3.59	-1	C-46	2	-0.4
2001 Min-A	64	196	19	43	4	1	7	23	12	39	3	1	.219	.285	.357	.642	66	-10	20	3.31	8	C-64	6	0.3
2002*Min-A	51	125	14	28	7	1	4	16	14	26	1	3	.224	.322	.392	.714	88	-3	15	3.71	-2	C-50	5	-0.2
2003 Min-A	24	40	5	8	2	0	2	5	5	7	1	0	.200	.319	.400	.719	87	-0	6	4.71	0	C-22/D-2	1	0.0
KC-A	8	8	0	2	0	0	0	1	0	0	0	0	.250	.250	.250	.500	29	-1	0	.00	-1	/C-7	0	-0.2
Yr.	32	48	5	10	2	0	2	6	5	7	1	0	.208	.309	.375	.684	79	-1	6	3.81	-1	C-29/D-2	1	-0.1
Total 17	**519**	**1190**	**113**	**248**	**66**	**4**	**24**	**140**	**105**	**252**	**9**	**8**	**.208**	**.289**	**.331**	**.620**	**65**	**-61**	**116**	**3.07**	**6**	**C-478/D-2,1-1,3-1**	**30**	**-3.0**
• PRINCE, Walter	Walter Farr Prince b: 5/9/1861, Amherst, NH d: 3/2/1938, Bristol, NH BL/TR, 5'9", 150 lbs. Deb: 8/7/1883 Career OF: 0-0-9																							
1883 Lou-a	4	11	1	2	0	0	0	0	0	....	....	....	.182	.182	.182	.364	19	-1	0	1.16	-1	/1-2,0-2(0-0-2),S-1	0	-0.2
1884 Det-N	7	21	0	3	0	0	0	1	3	4	....	....	.143	.250	.143	.393	29	-1	1	1.17	-4	/0-7(0-0-7)	0	-0.5
Was-a	43	166	22	36	3	2	1	0	13	....	....	....	.217	.286	.277	.563	95	1	13	2.85	-9	1-43	3	-1.0
Was-U	1	4	0	1	0	0	0	....	0	....	....	....	.250	.250	.250	.500	72	-0	0	2.39	0	/1-1	0	-0.1
Total 2	**55**	**202**	**23**	**42**	**3**	**2**	**1**	**1**	**16**	**4**	**....**	**....**	**.208**	**.276**	**.257**	**.533**	**84**	**-2**	**15**	**2.56**	**-14**	**/1-46,0-9,S-1**	**3**	**-1.8**
• PRITCHARD, Buddy	Harold William Pritchard b: 1/25/1936, South Gate, CA BR/TR, 6'1", 195 lbs. Deb: 4/21/1957																							
1957 Pit-N	23	11	1	1	0	0	0	0	0	4	0	0	.091	.091	.091	.182	-53	-2	0	.31	-2	S-10/2-3	0	-0.4
• PRITCHETT, Chris	Christopher Davis Pritchett b: 1/31/1970, Merced, CA BL/TR, 6'4", 185 lbs. Deb: 9/6/1996																							
1996 Cal-A	5	13	1	2	0	0	0	1	0	3	0	0	.154	.154	.154	.308	-22	-2	0	.76	0	/1-5	0	-0.3
1998 Ana-A	31	80	12	23	2	1	2	8	4	16	2	0	.288	.321	.413	.734	89	-1	10	4.51	1	1-29/D-1	1	-0.2
1999 Ana-A	20	45	3	7	1	0	1	2	2	9	1	1	.156	.191	.244	.436	10	-7	2	1.41	1	1-15/D-5	0	-0.6

YEAR TM-L	G	AB	R	H	2B	3B	HR	RBI	BB	SO	SB	CS	AVG	OBP	SLG	OPS	OPS+	BR/A	RC	RC/G	FR	G/POS	WS	TPW
2000 Phi-N	5	11	0	1	0	0	0	0	1	3	0	0	.091	.167	.091	.258	-32	-2	0	.26	1	/1-3	0	-0.1
Total 4	61	149	16	33	3	1	3	11	7	31	3	1	.221	.256	.315	.572	46	-12	13	2.76	2	/1-52,D-6	1	-1.3

• PROESER, George George "Yatz" Proeser b: 5/30/1864, Cincinnati, OH d: 10/13/1941, New Burlington, OH BL/TL, 5'10", 190 lbs. Deb: 9/15/1888 ♦

YEAR TM-L	G	AB	R	H	2B	3B	HR	RBI	BB	SO	SB	CS	AVG	OBP	SLG	OPS	OPS+	BR/A	RC	RC/G	FR	G/POS	WS	TPW
1888 Cle-a	7	23	5	7	2	0	0	1	1	....	0	....	.304	.333	.391	.725	136	2	3	5.19	-1	/P-7	3	-0.2
1890 Syr-a	13	53	11	13	1	1	1	6	10	....	1	....	.245	.365	.358	.724	126	2	7	4.96	-2	0-13(0-0-13)	2	0.0
Total 2	20	76	16	20	3	1	1	7	11	....	1	....	.263	.356	.368	.725	129	4	11	5.02	-3	/0-13,P-7	5	-0.2

• PROPST, Jake William Jacob Propst b: 3/10/1895, Kennedy, AL d: 2/24/1967, Columbus, MS BL/TR, 5'10", 165 lbs. Deb: 8/7/1923

YEAR TM-L	G	AB	R	H	2B	3B	HR	RBI	BB	SO	SB	CS	AVG	OBP	SLG	OPS	OPS+	BR/A	RC	RC/G	FR	G/POS	WS	TPW
1923 Was-A	1	1	0	0	0	0	0	0	0	0	0	0	.000	.000	.000	.000	-105	-0	0	.00	0	....	0	0.0

• PROTHRO, Doc James Thompson Prothro b: 7/16/1893, Memphis, TN d: 10/14/1971, Memphis, TN BR/TR, 5'10.5", 170 lbs. Deb: 9/26/1920 M

YEAR TM-L	G	AB	R	H	2B	3B	HR	RBI	BB	SO	SB	CS	AVG	OBP	SLG	OPS	OPS+	BR/A	RC	RC/G	FR	G/POS	WS	TPW
1920 Was-A	6	13	2	5	0	0	0	2	0	4	0	0	.385	.385	.385	.769	107	0	2	6.12	0	/3-2,S-2	1	0.1
1923 Was-A	6	8	2	2	0	1	0	3	1	3	0	0	.250	.333	.500	.833	124	0	1	6.02	0	/3-6	0	0.1
1924 Was-A	46	159	17	53	11	5	0	24	15	11	4	4	.333	.394	.465	.860	125	5	29	6.45	-4	3-45	6	0.4
1925 Bos-A	119	415	44	130	23	3	0	51	52	21	9	11	.313	.390	.383	.773	97	-2	62	5.50	-10	*3-108/S-3	11	-0.5
1926 Cin-N	3	5	1	1	0	1	0	1	1	1	0	....	.200	.333	.600	.933	151	0	1	6.57	0	/3-2	0	0.0
Total 5	180	600	66	191	34	10	0	81	69	40	13	15	.318	.390	.408	.798	105	4	95	5.79	-12	3-163/S-5	18	0.2

• PRUESS, Earl Earl Henry "Gibby" Pruess b: 4/2/1895, Chicago, IL d: 8/28/1979, Branson, MO BR/TR, 5'10.5", 170 lbs. Deb: 9/15/1920

YEAR TM-L	G	AB	R	H	2B	3B	HR	RBI	BB	SO	SB	CS	AVG	OBP	SLG	OPS	OPS+	BR/A	RC	RC/G	FR	G/POS	WS	TPW
1920 StL-A	1	0	1	0	0	0	0	0	1	0	1	0	....	1.000	....	1.000	176	1	1	∞	-0	/0-1	0	0.0

• PRUETT, Jim James Calvin Pruett b: 12/16/1917, Nashville, TN d: 7/29/2003, Waukesha, WI BR/TR, 5'10", 178 lbs. Deb: 9/26/1944

YEAR TM-L	G	AB	R	H	2B	3B	HR	RBI	BB	SO	SB	CS	AVG	OBP	SLG	OPS	OPS+	BR/A	RC	RC/G	FR	G/POS	WS	TPW
1944 Phi-A	3	4	1	1	0	0	0	0	1	0	0	0	.250	.500	.250	.750	119	0	1	3.48	0	/C-2	0	0.1
1945 Phi-A	6	9	1	2	0	0	0	0	1	2	0	1	.222	.300	.222	.522	53	-1	0	1.56	0	/C-4	0	-0.1
Total 2	9	13	2	3	0	0	0	0	2	2	0	1	.231	.375	.231	.606	78	-1	1	2.20	0	/C-6	0	0.0

• PRUITT, Ron Ronald Ralph Pruitt b: 10/21/1951, Flint, MI BR/TR, 6', 185 lbs. Deb: 6/25/1975 Career OF: 83-6-77

YEAR TM-L	G	AB	R	H	2B	3B	HR	RBI	BB	SO	SB	CS	AVG	OBP	SLG	OPS	OPS+	BR/A	RC	RC/G	FR	G/POS	WS	TPW
1975 Tex-A	14	17	2	3	0	0	0	0	1	3	0	0	.176	.222	.176	.399	14	-2	1	.98	0	C-13/0-1	0	-0.1
1976 Cle-A	47	86	7	23	1	1	0	5	16	8	2	3	.267	.382	.302	.685	103	1	11	4.21	1	0-26(12-1-13)/3-6,C-6,D-4,1	3	0.1
1977 Cle-A	78	219	29	63	10	2	2	32	28	22	2	3	.288	.373	.379	.752	109	3	30	4.63	-4	0-69(27-3-42)/C-4,D-4,3-1	5	-0.3
1978 Cle-A	71	187	17	44	6	1	6	17	16	20	2	1	.235	.296	.374	.670	88	-3	21	3.74	-3	C-48,0-16(12-0-4)/D-5,3-2	4	-0.6
1979 Cle-A	64	166	23	47	7	0	2	21	19	21	2	0	.283	.357	.361	.718	94	-0	22	4.64	-1	0-29(19-0-11),D-14,C-11/3-3	4	-0.2
1980 Cle-A	23	36	1	11	1	0	0	4	4	6	0	0	.306	.375	.333	.708	95	-0	5	4.53	0	/0-6(0-1-5),3-2,D-2	1	0.0
Chi-A	33	70	8	21	2	0	2	11	8	7	0	0	.300	.372	.414	.786	116	2	10	4.96	-2	0-11(10-1-0)/D-7,C-5,3-3,1	2	-0.1
Yr.	56	106	9	32	3	0	2	15	12	13	0	0	.302	.373	.387	.760	109	2	15	4.81	-2	0-17(10-2-5)/D-9,3-5,C-5,1	3	-0.1
1981 Cle-A	5	9	0	0	0	0	0	0	1	2	0	0	.000	.100	.000	.100	-70	-2	0	.00	-1	/0-3(2-0-1),C-1,D-1	0	-0.3
1982 SF-N	5	4	1	2	1	0	0	2	1	1	0	0	.500	.600	.750	1.350	276	1	2	24.30	0	/C-1,0-1	0	0.1
1983 SF-N	1	1	0	0	0	0	0	0	0	0	0	0	.000	.000	.000	.000	-103	-0	0	.00	0	....	0	0.0
Total 9	341	795	88	214	28	4	12	92	94	90	8	7	.269	.348	.360	.708	97	-1	100	4.29	-9	0-162/C-89,D-37,3-17,1-2	19	-1.5

• PRYOR, Greg Gregory Russell Pryor b: 10/2/1949, Marietta, OH BR/TR, 6', 186 lbs. Deb: 6/4/1976

YEAR TM-L	G	AB	R	H	2B	3B	HR	RBI	BB	SO	SB	CS	AVG	OBP	SLG	OPS	OPS+	BR/A	RC	RC/G	FR	G/POS	WS	TPW
1976 Tex-A	5	8	2	3	0	0	0	1	0	1	0	0	.375	.375	.375	.750	118	0	1	5.28	0	/2-3,3-1,S-1	0	0.0
1978 Chi-A	82	222	27	58	11	0	2	15	11	18	3	1	.261	.299	.338	.637	78	-6	22	3.47	-1	2-35,S-28,3-20	5	-0.3
1979 Chi-A	143	476	60	131	23	3	3	34	35	41	3	4	.275	.327	.355	.683	84	-11	52	3.76	-4	*S-119,2-25,3-22	9	-0.3
1980 Chi-A	122	338	32	81	18	4	1	29	12	35	2	2	.240	.270	.325	.595	63	-19	28	2.63	8	S-76,3-41/2-5,D-1	6	-0.4
1981 Chi-A	47	76	4	17	1	0	0	6	6	8	0	0	.224	.298	.237	.534	57	-4	6	2.41	1	3-27,S-13/2-5	1	-0.3
1982 KC-A	73	152	23	41	10	1	2	12	10	20	2	0	.270	.315	.388	.703	92	-1	18	4.04	3	3-40,2-15,1-14/S-7	4	0.2
1983 KC-A	68	115	9	25	4	0	1	14	7	8	0	0	.217	.262	.278	.541	49	-8	8	2.31	1	3-60/1-6,2-3	1	-0.7
1984*KC-A	123	270	32	71	11	1	4	25	12	28	0	3	.263	.302	.356	.657	80	-9	26	3.29	5	*3-105,2-22/S-2,1-1,D-1	5	-0.4
1985*KC-A	63	114	8	25	3	0	1	3	8	12	0	1	.219	.270	.272	.542	49	-8	7	1.97	-1	3-26,2-20,S-13/1-1,D-1	1	-0.9
1986 KC-A	63	112	7	19	4	0	0	7	3	14	1	1	.170	.191	.205	.397	8	-15	3	.93	-1	3-35,S-17,2-12/1-1	1	-1.5
Total 10	789	1883	204	471	85	9	14	146	104	185	11	12	.250	.293	.327	.620	70	-82	172	3.03	10	3-377,S-276,2-145/1-23,D-3	33	-4.7

• PUCCINELLI, George George Lawrence "Pooch,Count" Puccinelli
b: 6/22/1907, San Francisco, CA d: 4/16/1956, San Francisco, CA BR/TR, 6'.5", 190 lbs. Deb: 7/17/1930 Career OF: 34-0-123

YEAR TM-L	G	AB	R	H	2B	3B	HR	RBI	BB	SO	SB	CS	AVG	OBP	SLG	OPS	OPS+	BR/A	RC	RC/G	FR	G/POS	WS	TPW
1930*StL-N	11	16	5	9	1	0	3	8	0	1	0	....	.563	.563	1.188	1.750	298	5	10	36.92	0	/0-3(3-0-1)	2	0.4
1932 StL-N	31	108	17	30	8	0	3	11	12	13	1	....	.278	.350	.435	.785	106	1	17	5.69	2	0-30(24-0-6)	3	0.1
1934 StL-A	10	26	4	6	1	0	2	5	1	8	0	0	.231	.286	.500	.786	92	-1	4	4.91	1	/0-6(6-0-0)	1	0.0
1936 Phi-A	135	457	83	127	30	3	11	78	65	70	2	3	.278	.369	.429	.798	98	-2	75	5.93	-1	*0-117(1-0-116)	10	-0.8
Total 4	187	607	109	172	40	3	19	102	78	92	3	3	.283	.367	.453	.820	104	4	105	6.33	1	0-156	16	-0.4

• PUCKETT, Kirby Kirby Puckett b: 3/14/1961, Chicago, IL BR/TR, 5'8", 210 lbs. Deb: 5/8/1984 HOF: 2001 Career OF: 10-1432-276

YEAR TM-L	G	AB	R	H	2B	3B	HR	RBI	BB	SO	SB	CS	AVG	OBP	SLG	OPS	OPS+	BR/A	RC	RC/G	FR	G/POS	WS	TPW
1984 Min-A	128	557	63	165	12	5	0	31	16	69	14	7	.296	.321	.336	.656	78	-16	58	3.76	15	*0-128(0-128-0)	16	-0.3
1985 Min-A	161	691	80	199	29	13	4	74	41	87	21	12	.288	.332	.385	.716	90	-10	88	4.55	10	*0-161(0-161-0)	19	-0.2
1986 Min-A★	161	680	119	223	37	6	31	96	34	99	20	12	.328	.366	.537	.903	138	33	127	7.07	-1	*0-160(0-160-0)	26	2.9
1987*Min-A★	157	624	96	**207**	32	5	28	99	32	91	12	7	.332	.370	.534	.904	131	26	116	7.05	-5	*0-147(0-147-0)/D-8	29	1.8
1988 Min-A★	158	657	109	**234**	42	5	24	121	23	83	6	7	.356	.380	.545	.925	151	40	126	7.48	3	*0-158(0-158-0)	32	4.1
1989 Min-A★	159	635	75	**215**	45	4	9	85	41	59	11	4	**.339**	.381	.465	.846	129	24	107	6.41	6	*0-157(0-157-0)/D-2	27	2.8
1990 Min-A★	146	551	82	164	40	3	12	80	57	73	5	4	.298	.367	.446	.813	119	14	88	5.78	2	*0-141(9-125-9)/D-4,2-1,3,S	22	1.4
1991*Min-A★	152	611	92	195	29	6	15	89	31	78	11	5	.319	.356	.460	.816	118	14	91	5.29	4	*0-152(0-144-19)	21	1.5
1992 Min-A★	160	639	104	**210**	38	4	19	110	44	97	17	7	.329	.377	.490	.867	137	31	114	6.67	2	*0-149(0-149-0)/D-9,2-2,3,S	31	3.0
1993 Min-A★	156	622	89	184	39	3	22	89	47	93	8	6	.296	.352	.474	.826	119	15	100	5.81	0	*0-139(1-95-47),D-17	18	1.1
1994 Min-A★	108	439	79	139	32	3	20	**112**	28	47	6	3	.317	.367	.540	.907	130	18	84	7.00	3	0-95(0-3-95),D-13	20	1.4
1995 Min-A★	137	538	83	169	39	0	23	99	56	89	3	2	.314	.382	.515	.897	130	23	102	7.06	-6	*0-109(0-5-106),D-28/2-1,3,S	20	1.0
Total 12	1783	7244	1071	2304	414	57	207	1085	450	965	134	76	.318	.363	.477	.839	123	211	1200	6.13	33	*0-1696/D-81,2-4,3-4,S-3	281	20.4

• PUHL, John John G. Puhl b: 7/10/1876, Brooklyn, NY d: 8/24/1900, Bayonne, NJ Deb: 10/13/1898

YEAR TM-L	G	AB	R	H	2B	3B	HR	RBI	BB	SO	SB	CS	AVG	OBP	SLG	OPS	OPS+	BR/A	RC	RC/G	FR	G/POS	WS	TPW
1898 NY-N	2	9	1	2	0	0	0	1	0	....	0	....	.222	.222	.222	.444	28	-1	0	1.72	-1	/3-2	0	-0.1
1899 NY-N	1	2	0	0	0	0	0	0	0	....	0	....	.000	.333	.000	.333	-6	-0	0	.00	0	/3-1	0	-0.1
Total 2	3	11	1	2	0	0	0	1	0	....	0	....	.182	.250	.182	.432	20	-1	0	1.34	-1	/3-3	0	-0.2

• PUHL, Terry Terry Stephen Puhl b: 7/8/1956, Melville, Canada BL/TR, 6'2", 200 lbs. Deb: 7/12/1977 Career OF: 235-343-787

YEAR TM-L	G	AB	R	H	2B	3B	HR	RBI	BB	SO	SB	CS	AVG	OBP	SLG	OPS	OPS+	BR/A	RC	RC/G	FR	G/POS	WS	TPW
1977 Hou-N	60	229	40	69	13	5	0	10	30	31	10	1	.301	.385	.402	.786	122	10	39	6.24	1	0-59(48-11-1)	9	0.9
1978 Hou-N★	149	585	87	169	25	6	3	35	48	46	32	14	.289	.347	.368	.714	108	7	75	4.52	1	*0-148(43-109-4)	19	0.4
1979 Hou-N	157	600	87	172	22	4	8	49	58	46	30	22	.287	.353	.377	.730	105	2	80	4.60	-5	*0-152(6-109-40)	23	-0.7
1980*Hou-N	141	535	75	151	24	5	13	55	60	52	27	11	.282	.359	.419	.778	126	20	85	5.67	5	*0-135(4-30-107)	23	2.0
1981*Hou-N	96	350	43	88	19	4	3	28	31	49	22	4	.251	.319	.354	.674	96	1	44	4.23	-1	0-88(0-20-71)	11	-0.4
1982 Hou-N	145	507	64	133	17	9	8	50	51	49	17	9	.262	.332	.379	.711	106	4	66	4.48	-4	*0-138(0-32-122)	15	-0.6
1983 Hou-N	137	465	66	136	25	7	8	44	36	48	24	11	.292	.346	.428	.774	121	12	70	5.36	-2	*0-124(0-13-118)	18	0.4
1984 Hou-N	132	449	66	135	19	7	9	55	59	45	13	8	.301	.383	.434	.817	139	24	77	6.17	-1	*0-126(8-0-123)	19	1.7
1985 Hou-N	57	194	34	55	14	3	2	23	18	23	6	2	.284	.347	.418	.765	116	4	30	5.47	2	0-53(1-0-53)	8	0.5
1986*Hou-N	81	172	17	42	10	0	3	14	15	24	3	2	.244	.305	.355	.659	84	-4	18	3.30	-2	0-47(5-0-42)	3	-0.8
1987 Hou-N	90	122	9	28	5	0	2	15	11	16	1	1	.230	.293	.320	.613	65	-7	11	3.06	-1	0-40(28-5-9)	1	-0.9
1988 Hou-N	113	234	42	71	7	2	3	19	35	30	22	4	.303	.396	.389	.785	131	14	42	6.78	-1	0-78(48-1-33)	12	1.2
1989 Hou-N	121	354	41	96	25	4	0	27	45	39	9	8	.271	.355	.364	.719	110	4	46	4.48	-3	*0-103(37-11-64)/1-3	13	-0.2
1990 Hou-N	37	41	5	12	1	0	0	8	5	7	1	2	.293	.383	.317	.700	98	-1	5	4.31	0	/0-8(6-2-0),1-1	2	-0.1
1991 KC-A	15	18	0	4	0	0	0	3	3	2	0	0	.222	.333	.222	.556	57	-1	1	2.32	0	/D-2,0-1	0	-0.1
Total 15	1531	4855	676	1361	226	56	62	435	505	507	217	99	.280	.351	.388	.740	113	90	690	4.97	-10	*0-1300/1-4,D-2	176	3.4

YEAR TM-L	G	AB	R	H	2B	3B	HR	RBI	BB	SO	SB	CS	AVG	OBP	SLG	OPS	OPS+	BR/A	RC	RC/G	FR	G/POS	WS	TPW
• PUIG, Rich	Richard Gerald Puig b: 3/16/1953, Tampa, FL BL/TR, 5'10", 165 lbs. Deb: 9/13/1974																							
1974 NY-N	4	10	0	0	0	0	0	0	1	2	0	0	.000	.091	.000	.091	-74	-2	0	.06	-1	/2-3,3-1	0	-0.3
• PUJOLS, Albert	Jose Alberto "Prince Albert,Phat Albert" Pujols b: 1/16/1980, Santo Domingo, Dominican Republic BR/TR, 6'3", 210 lbs. Deb: 4/2/2001 Career OF: 269-0-40																							
2001★StL-N★	161	590	112	194	47	4	37	130	69	93	1	3	.329	.407	.610	1.017	159	52	141	8.87	9	0-78(39-0-39),3-55,1-43/D-2	29	5.4
2002★StL-N	157	590	118	185	40	2	34	127	72	69	2	4	.314	.396	.561	.957	153	44	126	7.86	-3	*0-118(117-0-1),3-41,1-21/D,S	32	3.5
2003 StL-N★	157	591	**137**	**212**	**51**	1	43	124	79	65	5	1	**.359**	.443	.667	1.109	192	81	176	11.92	1	*0-113(113-0-0),1-62/D-1	**41**	7.3
Total 3	475	1771	367	591	138	7	114	381	220	227	8	8	.334	.416	.613	1.028	168	177	442	9.49	7	0-309,1-126/3-96,D-5,S-1	102	16.2
• PUJOLS, Luis	Luis Bienvenido (Toribio) Pujols b: 11/18/1955, Santiago Rodriguez, Dominican Republic BR/TR, 6'2", 195 lbs. Deb: 9/22/1977 M/C																							
1977 Hou-N	6	15	0	1	0	0	0	0	0	5	0	0	.067	.067	.067	.133	-70	-4	0	.13	0	/C-6	0	-0.3
1978 Hou-N	56	153	11	20	8	1	1	11	12	45	0	0	.131	.199	.216	.414	17	-17	6	1.14	-1	C-55/1-1	2	-1.7
1979 Hou-N	26	75	7	17	2	1	0	8	2	14	0	0	.227	.247	.280	.527	46	-6	5	1.97	-2	C-26	1	-0.7
1980★Hou-N	78	221	15	44	6	1	0	20	13	29	0	0	.199	.247	.235	.482	38	-19	13	1.83	-3	C-75/3-1	3	-1.9
1981★Hou-N	40	117	5	28	3	1	1	14	10	17	1	0	.239	.299	.308	.607	76	-3	10	2.96	-1	C-39	3	-0.3
1982 Hou-N	65	176	8	35	6	2	4	15	10	40	0	3	.199	.242	.324	.566	62	-11	12	2.17	0	C-64	2	-0.9
1983 Hou-N	40	87	4	17	2	0	0	12	5	14	0	0	.195	.239	.218	.458	29	-8	4	1.42	-4	C-39	1	-1.1
1984 KC-A	4	5	0	1	0	0	0	1	0	0	0	0	.200	.200	.200	.400	11	-1	0	1.35	0	/C-4	0	-0.1
1985 Tex-A	1	1	0	1	0	0	0	0	0	0	0	0	1.000	1.000	1.000	2.000	444	0	1	∞	0	/C-1	0	0.0
Total 9	316	850	50	164	27	6	6	81	52	164	1	3	.193	.241	.260	.501	43	-68	51	1.85	-11	C-309/1-1,3-1	12	-7.0
• PULLIAM, Harvey	Harvey Jerome Pulliam b: 10/20/1967, San Francisco, CA BR/TR, 6', 205 lbs. Deb: 8/10/1991 Career OF: 52-1-31																							
1991 KC-A	18	33	4	9	1	0	3	4	3	9	0	0	.273	.333	.576	.909	146	2	6	6.19	-1	0-15(11-0-5)	1	0.0
1992 KC-A	4	5	2	1	1	0	0	0	1	3	0	0	.200	.333	.400	.733	102	0	1	5.09	0	/D-2,0-1	0	0.0
1993 KC-A	27	62	7	16	5	0	1	6	2	14	0	0	.258	.292	.387	.679	76	-2	6	3.36	-1	0-26(12-0-16)	2	-0.4
1995 Col-N	5	5	1	2	1	0	1	3	0	2	0	0	.400	.400	1.200	1.600	234	1	2	21.60	0	/0-1	1	0.1
1996 Col-N	10	15	2	2	0	0	0	0	2	6	0	0	.133	.235	.133	.369		-2	0	.86	-0	/0-3(3-0-0)	0	-0.2
1997 Col-N	59	67	15	19	3	0	3	9	5	15	0	1	.284	.333	.463	.796	86	-2	9	4.99	-1	0-33(24-1-10)	1	-0.3
Total 6	123	187	31	49	11	0	8	22	13	49	0	1	.262	.313	.449	.763	91	-4	25	4.61	-3	/0-79,D-2	5	-0.8
• PUNTO, Nick	Nicholas Paul Punto b: 11/8/1977, San Diego, CA BB/TR, 5'9", 170 lbs. Deb: 9/9/2001																							
2001 Phi-N	4	5	0	2	0	0	0	0	0	0	0	0	.400	.400	.400	.800	111	0	1	7.20	-1	/S-1	0	0.0
2002 Phi-N	9	6	0	1	0	0	0	0	0	3	0	0	.167	.167	.167	.333	-13	-1	0	.98	0	/2-1,S-1	0	-0.1
2003 Phi-N	64	92	14	20	2	0	1	4	7	22	2	1	.217	.273	.272	.544	45	-7	7	2.68	2	2-16/3-9,S-7	1	-0.4
Total 3	77	103	14	23	2	0	1	4	7	25	2	1	.223	.273	.272	.545	45	-8	8	2.72	2	/2-17,3-9,S-9	1	-0.5
• PURCELL, Blondie	William Aloysius Purcell b: 3/16/1854, Paterson, NJ d: 2/20/1912, Trenton, NJ BR/TR, 5'9.5", 159 lbs. Deb: 5/1/1879 M Career OF: 480-92-430 ♦																							
1879 Syr-N	63	277	32	72	6	3	0	25	3	13	....	....	.260	.268	.303	.571	99	4	23	3.15	-19	0-47(0-10-37),P-22/C-1	9	-2.9
Cin-N	12	50	10	11	0	0	0	4	0	3	....	....	.220	.220	.220	.440	48	-2	2	1.78	0	0-10(0-7-3)/P-2	1	-0.6
Yr.	75	327	42	83	6	3	0	29	3	16	....	....	.254	.261	.291	.551	91	1	26	2.93	-19	*0-57(0-17-40),P-24/C-1	10	-3.4
1880 Cin-N	77	325	48	95	13	6	1	24	5	13	....	....	.292	.303	.378	.681	131	12	38	4.57	-6	*0-55(0-54-2),P-25/S-1	12	-0.7
1881 Cle-N	20	80	3	14	2	1	0	4	5	8	....	....	.175	.224	.225	.449	43	-5	4	1.69	-3	0-20(7-13-0)	0	-0.8
Buf-N	30	113	15	33	7	2	0	17	8	8	....	....	.292	.339	.389	.728	130	5	15	5.16	-5	0-25(25-0-0)/P-9	8	0.0
Yr.	50	193	18	47	9	3	0	21	13	16	....	....	.244	.291	.321	.613	94	0	19	3.59	-8	0-45(32-13-0)/P-9	8	-0.8
1882 Buf-N	84	380	79	105	18	6	2	40	14	27	....	....	.276	.302	.371	.673	112	5	44	4.37	-7	*0-82(78-5-0)/P-6	11	-1.1
1883 Phi-N	97	425	70	114	20	5	1	32	13	26	....	....	.268	.290	.346	.636	101	4	44	3.86	-1	3-46,0-44(44-0-0),P-11	7	-0.3
1884 Phi-N	103	428	67	108	11	7	1	31	29	30	....	....	.252	.300	.318	.618	99	1	42	3.59	-5	*0-103(103-0-0)/P-1	13	-0.6
1885 Phi-a	66	304	71	90	15	5	0	22	16		....	....	.296	.337	.378	.716	119	6	40	5.02	1	0-66(66-1-0)/P-1	9	0.2
Bos-N	21	87	9	19	1	1	0	3	3	15	....	....	.218	.244	.253	.497	63	-3	6	2.19	-2	0-21(21-0-0)	1	-0.6
1886 Bal-a	26	85	17	19	0	1	0	8	17	....	13	....	.224	.365	.247	.612	96	1	13	5.21	-1	0-26(25-1-0)/P-1,S-1	3	-0.1
1887 Bal-a	140	613	101	188	25	8	4	96	46	....	88	....	.307	.318	.344	.662	90	-6	92	5.86	-4	*0-140(0-0-140)/P-1	13	-1.4
1888 Bal-a	101	406	53	96	9	4	2	39	27	....	16	....	.236	.289	.293	.582	89	-5	40	3.48	-8	*0-100(7-1-95)/S-2,1-1	8	-1.3
Phi-a	18	66	10	11	3	1	0	6	5	....	10	....	.167	.236	.242	.479	54	-3	6	3.09	0	0-17(0-0-17)/3-1	1	-0.3
Yr.	119	472	63	107	12	5	2	45	32	....	26	....	.227	.281	.286	.568	84	-8	46	3.42	-8	*0-117(7-1-112)/S-2,1-1,3	9	-1.6
1889 Phi-a	129	507	72	160	19	7	0	85	50	27	22	....	.316	.383	.381	.763	119	14	84	6.44	-10	*0-129(0-0-129)	15	0.2
1890 Phi-a	110	463	110	128	28	3	2	59	43	....	48	....	.276	.343	.363	.706	110	6	76	6.01	-3	*0-110(104-0-7)	14	-0.1
Total 12	1097	4609	767	1263	177	60	13	495	284	170	197	....	.274	.314	.340	.654	103	33	569	4.60	-74	0-995/P-79,3-47,S-4,1-1,C-1	125	-10.3
• PURDY, Pid	Everett Virgil Purdy b: 6/15/1904, Beatrice, NE d: 1/16/1951, Beatrice, NE BL/TR, 5'6", 150 lbs. Deb: 9/7/1926 Career OF: 90-17-21																							
1926 Chi-A	11	33	5	6	2	1	0	6	2	1	0	1	.182	.229	.303	.532	39	-4	2	1.79	0	/0-9(0-0-9)	0	-0.4
1927 Cin-N	18	62	15	22	2	4	1	12	4	3	0	....	.355	.412	.565	.976	164	5	14	8.63	-2	0-16(0-16-0)	3	0.3
1928 Cin-N	70	223	32	69	11	1	0	25	23	13	1	....	.309	.377	.368	.744	97	-0	31	5.08	-1	0-61(56-1-4)	7	-0.6
1929 Cin-N	82	181	22	49	7	5	1	16	19	8	2	....	.271	.350	.381	.731	85	-4	24	4.64	1	0-42(34-0-8)	4	-0.5
Total 4	181	499	74	146	22	11	2	59	48	25	3	1	.293	.362	.393	.754	97	-2	72	5.04	-2	0-128	14	-1.3
• PURNELL, Jesse	Jesse Rhoades Purnell b: 5/11/1881, Glenside, PA d: 7/4/1966, Philadelphia, PA BL/TR, 5'5.5", 140 lbs. Deb: 10/1/1904																							
1904 Phi-N	7	19	2	2	0	0	0	1	4	....	1	....	.105	.292	.105	.397	25	-1	1	1.37	-1	/3-7	0	-0.3
• PURTELL, Billy	William Patrick Purtell b: 1/6/1886, Columbus, OH d: 3/17/1962, Bradenton, FL BR/TR, 5'9", 170 lbs. Deb: 4/16/1908																							
1908 Chi-A	26	69	3	9	2	0	0	3	2	....	2	....	.130	.155	.159	.314	2	-7	2	.88	3	3-25	2	-0.4
1909 Chi-A	103	361	34	93	9	3	0	40	19	....	14	....	.258	.302	.299	.601	94	-3	39	3.39	0	3-71,2-32	11	-0.1
1910 Chi-A	102	368	21	82	5	3	1	36	21	....	5	....	.223	.272	.261	.533	71	-13	28	2.43	1	*3-102	7	-1.0
Bos-A	49	168	15	35	1	2	1	15	18	....	2	....	.208	.289	.256	.545	69	-6	14	2.52	-2	3-41/S-8	2	-0.7
Yr.	151	536	36	117	6	5	2	51	39	....	7	....	.218	.278	.259	.537	70	-18	43	2.46	-2	*3-143/S-8	9	-1.7
1911 Bos-A	27	82	5	23	5	3	0	7	1	....	1	....	.280	.298	.415	.712	99	-1	10	4.36	-1	3-15/2-3,S-3,0-1	2	-0.1
1914 Det-A	28	76	4	13	4	0	0	3	2	7	0	2	.171	.203	.224	.426	27	-8	3	1.30	-1	3-16/S-2,2-1	1	-1.0
Total 5	335	1124	82	255	26	11	2	104	63	7	24	2	.227	.275	.275	.550	73	-38	97	2.68	-1	3-270/2-36,S-13,0-1	25	-3.3
• PUTMAN, Ed	Eddy William Putman b: 9/25/1953, Los Angeles, CA BR/TR, 6'1", 190 lbs. Deb: 9/7/1976																							
1976 Chi-N	5	7	0	3	0	0	0	0	0	0	0	0	.429	.429	.429	.857	132	0	0	1.93	-1	/C-3,1-1	0	-0.1
1978 Chi-N	17	25	2	5	0	0	0	3	4	6	0	0	.200	.310	.200	.510	40	-2	2	2.53	-2	/3-8,1-3,C-2	0	-0.4
1979 Det-A	21	39	4	9	3	0	2	4	4	12	0	1	.231	.302	.462	.764	99	-1	5	4.11	0	C-16/1-5	1	0.0
Total 3	43	71	6	17	3	0	2	7	8	18	0	1	.239	.316	.366	.683	81	-2	7	3.34	-2	/C-21,1-9,3-8	1	-0.5
• PUTNAM, Pat	Patrick Edward Putnam b: 12/3/1953, Bethel, VT BL/TR, 6', 214 lbs. Deb: 9/2/1977 Career OF: 17-0-1																							
1977 Tex-A	11	26	3	8	4	0	0	3	1	4	0	1	.308	.333	.462	.795	113	-0	3	4.20	0	/1-7,D-3	0	-0.1
1978 Tex-A	20	46	4	7	1	0	1	2	2	5	0	0	.152	.188	.239	.427	19	-5	2	1.46	-0	D-12/1-4	0	-0.6
1979 Tex-A	139	426	57	118	19	2	18	64	23	50	1	6	.277	.323	.458	.781	109	2	57	4.61	3	1-96,D-32	10	-0.1
1980 Tex-A	147	410	42	108	16	2	13	55	36	49	0	2	.263	.323	.407	.730	102	-0	51	4.22	2	*1-137/3-1,D-1	8	-0.5
1981 Tex-A	95	297	33	79	17	2	8	35	17	38	4	2	.266	.306	.418	.723	113	4	37	4.43	1	1-94/0-3(3-0-1)	9	0.0
1982 Tex-A	43	122	14	28	8	0	2	9	10	18	0	2	.230	.293	.344	.637	78	-5	11	3.11	1	1-39/3-1,0-1	1	-0.6
1983 Sea-A	144	469	58	126	23	2	19	67	39	57	2	1	.269	.329	.448	.777	107	4	67	4.99	2	*1-125,D-11	12	-0.2
1984 Sea-A	64	155	11	31	6	0	2	16	12	27	3	0	.200	.257	.277	.535	49	-10	11	2.25	1	D-30,0-13(13-0-0)/1-6	0	-1.0
Min-A	14	38	1	3	1	0	0	4	4	12	0	0	.079	.167	.105	.272	-22	-6	1	.68	0	D-11	0	-0.7
Yr.	78	193	12	34	7	0	2	20	16	39	3	0	.176	.239	.244	.483	34	-16	12	1.91	1	D-41,0-13(13-0-0)/1-6	0	-1.7
Total 8	677	1989	223	508	95	8	63	255	144	260	10	14	.255	.309	.406	.715	97	-17	241	4.13	9	1-508,D-100/0-17,3-2	40	-3.8
• PYBURN, Jim	James Edward Pyburn b: 11/1/1932, Fairfield, AL BR/TR, 6', 190 lbs. Deb: 4/17/1955 Career OF: 18-77-13																							
1955 Bal-A	39	98	5	20	2	2	0	7	8	24	1	1	.204	.271	.265	.536	48	-7	7	2.21	-2	3-33/0-1	0	-0.9

YEAR	TM-L	G	AB	R	H	2B	3B	HR	RBI	BB	SO	SB	CS	AVG	OBP	SLG	OPS	OPS+	BR/A	RC	RC/G	FR	G/POS	WS	TPW
1956	Bal-A	84	156	23	27	3	3	2	11	17	26	4	1	.173	.254	.269	.524	41	-13	11	2.19	2	0-77(11-64-3)	1	-1.3
1957	Bal-A	35	40	8	9	0	0	1	2	9	6	1	0	.225	.367	.300	.667	90	0	5	3.97	1	0-28(7-13-9)/C-1	1	0.0
Total	**3**	**158**	**294**	**36**	**56**	**5**	**5**	**3**	**20**	**34**	**56**	**6**	**2**	**.190**	**.277**	**.272**	**.549**	**51**	**-20**	**23**	**2.43**	**0**	**0-106/3-33,C-1**	**2**	**-2.3**
• PYE, Eddie	Robert Edward Pye b: 2/13/1967, Columbia, TN BR/TR, 5'10", 175 lbs. Deb: 6/3/1994																								
1994	LA-N	7	10	2	1	0	0	0	0	1	4	0	0	.100	.182	.100	.282	-26	-2	0	.80	1	/2-3,S-3	0	-0.1
1995	LA-N	7	8	0	0	0	0	0	0	0	4	0	0	.000	.000	.000	.000	-110	-2	0	.00	-1	/3-2	0	-0.3
Total	**2**	**14**	**18**	**2**	**1**	**0**	**0**	**0**	**0**	**1**	**8**	**0**	**0**	**.056**	**.105**	**.056**	**.161**	**-59**	**-4**	**0**	**.45**	**0**	**/2-3,S-3,3-2**	**0**	**-0.4**
• PYTLAK, Frankie	Frank Anthony Pytlak b: 7/30/1908, Buffalo, NY d: 5/8/1977, Buffalo, NY BR/TR, 5'7.5", 160 lbs. Deb: 4/22/1932																								
1932	Cle-A	12	29	5	7	1	1	0	4	3	2	0	0	.241	.333	.345	.678	71	-1	4	3.92	-1	C-12	1	-0.1
1933	Cle-A	80	248	36	77	10	6	2	33	17	10	3	4	.310	.355	.423	.778	101	-1	36	5.43	5	C-69	11	0.8
1934	Cle-A	91	289	46	75	12	4	0	35	36	11	11	2	.260	.352	.329	.680	75	-8	37	4.46	-6	C-88	9	-0.8
1935	Cle-A	55	149	14	44	6	1	1	12	11	4	3	2	.295	.348	.369	.717	84	-4	19	4.66	-5	C-48	4	-0.6
1936	Cle-A	75	224	35	72	15	4	0	31	24	11	5	2	.321	.394	.424	.819	101	1	39	6.54	-3	C-58	7	0.1
1937	Cle-A	125	397	60	125	15	6	1	44	52	15	16	5	.315	.404	.390	.794	100	5	68	6.31	2	*C-115	17	1.3
1938	Cle-A	113	364	46	112	14	7	1	43	36	15	9	5	.308	.376	.393	.769	95	-2	55	5.66	-3	C-99	13	0.0
1939	Cle-A	63	183	20	49	2	5	0	14	20	5	4	1	.268	.343	.333	.676	76	-5	22	4.13	2	C-51	6	-0.1
1940	Cle-A	62	149	16	21	2	1	0	16	17	5	0	1	.141	.234	.168	.401	6	-21	7	1.32	3	C-58/0-1	4	-1.4
1941	Bos-A	106	336	36	91	23	1	2	39	28	19	5	7	.271	.329	.363	.692	81	-11	40	4.08	-2	C-91	9	-0.8
1945	Bos-A	9	17	1	2	0	0	0	0	3	0	0	0	.118	.250	.118	.368	8	-2	1	1.27	1	/C-6	0	-0.1
1946	Bos-A	4	14	1	2	0	0	0	1	0	0	0	0	.143	.143	.143	.286	-19	-2	0	.66	1	/C-4	0	-0.1
Total	**12**	**795**	**2399**	**316**	**677**	**100**	**36**	**7**	**272**	**247**	**97**	**56**	**29**	**.282**	**.355**	**.363**	**.718**	**83**	**-51**	**328**	**4.83**	**-7**	**C-699/0-1**	**81**	**-1.7**
• PYZNARSKI, Tim	Timothy Matthew Pyznarski b: 2/4/1960, Chicago, IL BR/TR, 6'2", 195 lbs. Deb: 9/14/1986																								
1986	SD-N	15	42	3	10	1	0	0	0	4	11	2	0	.238	.319	.262	.581	63	-1	4	2.93	0	1-13	0	-0.3
• QUALLS, Jim	James Robert Qualls b: 10/9/1946, Exeter, CA BB/TR, 5'10", 158 lbs. Deb: 4/10/1969 Career OF: 2-36-0																								
1969	Chi-N	43	120	12	30	5	3	0	9	2	14	2	1	.250	.268	.342	.610	62	-6	11	3.28	0	0-35(0-35-0)/2-4	2	-0.7
1970	Mon-N	9	9	1	1	0	0	0	1	0	0	0	0	.111	.111	.111	.222	-40	-2	0	.38	0	/2-2,0-2(2-0-0)	0	-0.2
1972	Chi-A	11	10	0	0	0	0	0	0	0	2	0	0	.000	.000	.000	.000	-98	-2	0	.00	0	/0-1	0	-0.3
Total	**3**	**63**	**139**	**13**	**31**	**5**	**3**	**0**	**10**	**2**	**16**	**2**	**1**	**.223**	**.239**	**.302**	**.542**	**43**	**-11**	**11**	**2.75**	**0**	**/0-38,2-6**	**2**	**-1.2**
• QUEEN, Billy	William Eddleman "Doc" Queen b: 11/28/1928, Gastonia, NC BR/TR, 6'1", 185 lbs. Deb: 4/13/1954																								
1954	Mil-N	3	2	0	0	0	0	0	0	0	2	0	0	.000	.000	.000	.000	-107	-1	0	.00	-0	/0-1	0	-0.1
• QUEEN, Mel	Melvin Douglas Queen b: 3/26/1942, Johnson City, NY BL/TR, 6'1", 197 lbs. Deb: 4/13/1964 M/C Career OF: 2-0-52 ♦																								
1964	Cin-N	48	95	7	19	2	0	2	12	4	19	0	1	.200	.232	.284	.517	43	-8	5	1.70	0	0-20(0-0-20)	1	-1.0
1965	Cin-N	5	3	0	0	0	0	0	0	0	1	0	0	.000	.000	.000	.000	-94	-1	0	.00	-0	/0-1	0	-0.1
1966	Cin-N	56	55	4	7	1	0	0	5	10	12	0	0	.127	.262	.145	.407	15	-6	3	1.47	-2	0-32(2-0-31)/P-7	0	-1.1
1967	Cin-N	49	81	6	17	4	0	0	5	4	10	2	0	.210	.247	.259	.506	40	3	5	1.94	-2	P-31	17	2.8
1968	Cin-N	10	8	2	1	0	0	0	0	1	3	0	0	.125	.222	.125	.347	6	0	0	1.08	0	/P-5	0	-0.6
1969	Cin-N	2	6	0	1	0	0	0	1	0	2	0	0	.167	.167	.167	.333	-6	-0	0	.90	0	/P-2	1	0.2
1970	Cal-A	37	16	1	4	0	0	0	1	0	2	0	0	.250	.250	.250	.500	40	1	1	2.25	-1	P-34	3	-0.5
1971	Cal-A	45	8	0	0	0	0	0	1	1	0	0	0	.000	.111	.000	.111	-71	-1	0	.32	-1	P-44	7	1.0
1972	Cal-A	17	2	0	0	0	0	0	0	1	1	0	0	.000	.333	.000	.333	5	0	0	1.17	0	P-17	0	-0.6
Total	**9**	**269**	**274**	**20**	**49**	**7**	**0**	**2**	**25**	**21**	**50**	**2**	**1**	**.179**	**.237**	**.226**	**.464**	**28**	**-11**	**15**	**1.63**	**-6**	**P-140/0-53**	**29**	**0.1**
• QUELLICH, George	George William Quellich b: 2/10/1903, Johnsville, CA d: 8/21/1958, Johnsville, CA BR/TR, 6'1", 180 lbs. Deb: 8/1/1931																								
1931	Det-A	13	54	6	12	5	0	1	11	3	4	1	0	.222	.263	.370	.634	63	-3	5	3.40	2	0-13(13-0-0)	1	-0.2
• QUEST, Joe	Joseph L. Quest b: 11/16/1852, New Castle, PA d: 11/14/1924, San Diego, CA BR/TR, 5'6", 150 lbs. Deb: 8/30/1871 U																								
1871	Cle-n	3	13	1	3	1	0	0	2	1	0	0	0	.231	.286	.308	.593	75	-0	1	3.69	-1	/2-2,S-1	....	-0.1
1878	Ind-N	62	278	45	57	3	2	0	13	12	24	....	....	.205	.238	.230	.468	63	-8	16	1.94	3	*2-62	4	-0.2
1879	Chi-N	83	334	38	69	16	1	0	22	9	33	....	....	.207	.227	.260	.488	57	-16	20	2.14	9	*2-83	5	-0.3
1880	Chi-N	82	300	37	71	12	1	0	27	8	16	....	....	.237	.256	.283	.540	78	-7	22	2.68	4	*2-80/S-2,3-1	8	0.1
1881	Chi-N	78	293	35	72	6	0	1	26	2	29	....	....	.246	.251	.276	.527	61	-14	21	2.54	3	*2-77/S-1	6	-0.6
1882	Chi-N	42	159	24	32	5	2	0	15	8	16	....	....	.201	.240	.258	.497	59	-7	10	2.18	-2	2-41/S-1	2	-0.7
1883	Det-N	37	137	22	32	8	2	0	15	10	18	....	....	.234	.286	.321	.607	88	-1	13	3.37	-3	2-37	3	-0.2
	StL-a	19	78	12	20	3	1	0	10	1	....	....	....	.256	.266	.321	.586	83	-2	7	3.29	-3	2-19	2	-0.3
1884	StL-a	81	310	46	64	9	5	0	0	19	....	....	....	.206	.257	.268	.525	69	-11	22	2.44	-9	*2-81	6	-1.6
	Pit-a	12	43	2	9	3	0	0	0	0	....	....	....	.209	.227	.279	.506	63	-2	3	2.26	1	/2-7,S-5	1	0.0
	Yr.	93	353	48	73	12	5	0	0	19	....	....	....	.207	.253	.269	.522	68	-12	25	2.42	-8	*2-88/S-5	7	-1.6
1885	Det-N	55	200	24	39	8	2	0	21	14	25	....	....	.195	.248	.255	.503	63	-8	13	2.17	-4	2-39,S-15/0-1	2	-1.0
1886	Phi-a	42	150	14	31	4	1	0	10	20	....	5	....	.207	.300	.247	.547	71	-4	13	2.93	0	S-41/2-2	4	-0.3
Total	**9**	**593**	**2282**	**299**	**496**	**77**	**17**	**1**	**159**	**103**	**161**	**5**	**....**	**.217**	**.252**	**.267**	**.519**	**67**	**-80**	**159**	**2.45**	**-1**	**2-528/S-65,3-1,0-1**	**43**	**-5.2**
• QUICK, Hal	James Harold "Blondie" Quick b: 10/4/1917, Rome, GA d: 3/9/1974, Swansea, IL BR/TR, 5'10.5", 163 lbs. Deb: 9/7/1939																								
1939	Was-A	12	41	3	10	1	0	0	2	1	1	1	0	.244	.279	.268	.547	44	-3	3	2.29	-1	S-10	0	-0.3
• QUILICI, Frank	Francis Ralph "Guido" Quilici b: 5/11/1939, Chicago, IL BR/TR, 6'1", 175 lbs. Deb: 7/18/1965 M/C																								
1965*	Min-A	56	149	16	31	5	1	0	7	15	33	1	1	.208	.280	.255	.536	51	-10	11	2.31	5	2-52/S-4	2	-0.1
1967	Min-A	23	19	2	2	1	0	0	0	3	4	0	0	.105	.227	.158	.385	14	-2	1	1.03	-2	2-13/3-8,S-1	0	-0.4
1968	Min-A	97	229	22	56	11	4	1	22	21	45	0	0	.245	.311	.341	.651	93	-2	25	3.60	4	2-48,3-40/S-6,1-1	7	0.6
1969	Min-A	118	144	19	25	3	1	2	12	12	22	2	0	.174	.237	.250	.487	36	-12	9	2.00	-7	3-84,2-36/S-1	2	-1.8
1970*	Min-A	111	141	19	32	3	0	2	12	15	16	0	2	.227	.301	.291	.592	63	-8	11	2.51	-4	2-73,3-27/S-1	2	-0.9
Total	**5**	**405**	**682**	**78**	**146**	**23**	**6**	**5**	**53**	**66**	**120**	**3**	**3**	**.214**	**.284**	**.287**	**.572**	**63**	**-33**	**57**	**2.66**	**-5**	**2-222,3-159/S-13,1-1**	**13**	**-2.6**
• QUILLEN, Lee	Leon Abner Quillen b: 5/5/1882, North Branch, MN d: 5/14/1965, White Bear Lake, MN BR/TR, 5'10", 165 lbs. Deb: 9/30/1906																								
1906	Chi-A	4	9	1	3	0	0	0	0	0	....	1	....	.333	.333	.333	.667	112	0	1	5.51	-3	/S-3	0	-0.3
1907	Chi-A	49	151	17	29	5	0	0	14	10	....	8	....	.192	.256	.225	.481	56	-7	12	2.43	-6	3-48	3	-1.3
Total	**2**	**53**	**160**	**18**	**32**	**5**	**0**	**0**	**14**	**10**	**....**	**9**	**....**	**.200**	**.260**	**.231**	**.491**	**59**	**-7**	**13**	**2.59**	**-9**	**/3-48,S-3**	**3**	**-1.6**
• QUINLAN,	Quinlan Deb: 9/7/1874																								
1874	Phi-n	1	4	0	1	0	0	0	1	0	0	0	0	.250	.250	.250	.500	59	-0	0	2.56	0	/S-1	....	0.0
• QUINLAN, Finners	Thomas Finners Quinlan b: 10/21/1887, Scranton, PA d: 2/17/1966, Scranton, PA BL/TL, 5'8", 154 lbs. Deb: 9/6/1913 Career OF: 10-10-24																								
1913	StL-N	13	50	1	8	0	0	0	1	1	9	0	....	.160	.176	.160	.336	-4	-7	1	.76	2	0-12(1-0-11)	0	-0.6
1915	Chi-A	42	114	11	22	3	0	0	7	4	11	3	4	.193	.270	.219	.489	45	-9	7	1.91	1	0-32(9-10-13)	1	-0.9
Total	**2**	**55**	**164**	**12**	**30**	**3**	**0**	**0**	**8**	**5**	**20**	**3**	**4**	**.183**	**.243**	**.201**	**.444**	**31**	**-16**	**9**	**1.57**	**3**	**/0-44**	**1**	**-1.5**
• QUINLAN, Frank	Francis Patrick Quinlan b: 3/9/1869, Marlboro, MA d: 5/4/1904, Brockton, MA, 5'9", 180 lbs. Deb: 10/5/1891																								
1891	Bos-a	2	5	0	0	0	0	0	0	0	2	0	....	.000	.000	.000	.000	-101	-1	0	.00	0	/C-1,0-1	0	-0.1
• QUINLAN, Humberto	Humberto Quinlan b: 3/17/1977, St. Paul, MN BR/TR, 6'1", 190 lbs. Deb: 7/28/2003																								
2003	SD-N	12	23	1	5	0	0	0	2	1	6	0	0	.217	.250	.217	.467	26	-3	1	1.88	1	C-11	0	-0.1
• QUINLAN, Tom	Thomas Raymond Quinlan b: 3/27/1968, St. Paul, MN BR/TR, 6'3", 200 lbs. Deb: 9/4/1990																								
1990	Tor-A	1	2	0	1	0	0	0	0	0	1	0	0	.500	.667	.500	1.167	219	0	1	22.68	0	/3-1	0	0.1
1992	Tor-A	13	15	2	1	1	0	0	2	2	9	0	0	.067	.176	.133	.310	-12	-2	0	.86	-1	3-13	0	-0.3
1994	Phi-N	24	35	6	7	2	0	1	3	3	13	0	0	.200	.263	.343	.606	55	-2	3	3.11	0	3-20	0	-0.2

YEAR TM-L	G	AB	R	H	2B	3B	HR	RBI	BB	SO	SB	CS	AVG	OBP	SLG	OPS	OPS+	BR/A	RC	RC/G	FR	G/POS	WS	TPW
1996 Min-A	4	6	0	0	0	0	0	0	0	3	0	0	.000	.000	.000	.000	-99	-2	0	.00	-1	/3-4	0	-0.2
Total 4	42	58	8	9	3	0	1	5	5	26	0	0	.155	.234	.259	.493	31	-6	5	2.50	-1	/3-38	0	-0.7
• QUINN,	Quinn, 5'8" Deb: 9/9/1875																							
1875 Atl-n	2	8	2	1	0	0	0	0	0	0	0	0	.125	.125	.125	.250	-15	-1	0	.54	-1	/O-2(0-1-1),S-1	....	-0.2
• QUINN, Frank	Frank J. Quinn b: 1876, Grand Rapids, MI d: 2/17/1920, Camden, IN, 5'8" Deb: 8/9/1899																							
1899 Chi-N	12	34	6	6	0	1	0	1	6	....	1	....	.176	.300	.235	.535	49	-2	3	2.71	-1	O-10(4-6-0)/2-1	0	-0.3
• QUINN, Joe	Joseph Quinn d: 3/1893, , 162 lbs. Deb: 9/7/1881 U																							
1881 Bos-N	1	4	0	0	0	0	0	0	0	0	....	....	.000	.000	.000	.000	-105	-1	0	.00	0	/1-1	0	-0.1
Wor-N	2	7	0	1	0	0	0	1	1	2	....	....	.143	.250	.143	.393	25	-1	0	1.15	-2	/C-2	0	-0.3
Yr.	3	11	0	1	0	0	0	1	1	2	....	....	.091	.167	.091	.258	-18	-1	0	.69	-2	/C-2,1-1	0	-0.3
• QUINN, Joe	Joseph J. Quinn b: 12/25/1864, Sydney, Australia d: 11/12/1940, St. Louis, MO BR/TR, 5'7", 158 lbs. Deb: 4/26/1884 M Career OF: 31-66-27																							
1884 StL-U	103	429	74	116	21	1	0	....	9	....	....	....	.270	.285	.324	.609	102	-1	41	3.64	-2	*1-100/O-3(1-0-2),S-1	10	-1.0
1885 StL-N	97	343	27	73	8	2	0	15	9	38	....	....	.213	.233	.248	.481	59	-15	20	2.03	-4	O-57(27-13-17),3-31,1-11	3	-1.9
1886 StL-N	75	271	33	63	11	3	1	21	8	31	12	....	.232	.254	.306	.561	75	-8	25	3.22	-3	O-48(0-47-1),2-15/1-7,3-4,S	4	-1.2
1888 Bos-N	38	156	19	47	8	3	4	29	2	5	12	....	.301	.310	.468	.778	140	6	27	6.69	-5	2-38	6	0.2
1889 Bos-N	112	444	57	116	13	5	2	69	25	21	24	....	.261	.308	.327	.635	73	-18	53	4.31	-22	S-63,2-47/3-2	10	-3.2
1890 Bos-P	130	509	87	153	19	8	7	82	44	24	29	....	.301	.359	.411	.769	98	-4	87	6.63	14	*2-130	17	1.2
1891 Bos-N	124	508	70	122	8	10	3	63	28	28	24	....	.240	.288	.313	.601	67	-25	54	3.78	-15	*2-124	9	-3.2
1892*Bos-N	143	532	63	116	14	1	1	59	35	40	17	....	.218	.275	.254	.529	55	-31	43	2.78	5	*2-143	9	-1.8
1893 StL-N	135	547	68	126	18	6	0	71	33	7	24	....	.230	.279	.285	.564	50	-41	51	3.24	-15	*2-135	4	-4.1
1894 StL-N	106	405	59	116	18	1	4	61	24	8	25	....	.286	.328	.365	.693	67	-23	58	5.23	15	*2-106	8	-0.2
1895 StL-N	135	547	86	172	19	9	3	76	37	7	22	....	.314	.360	.399	.759	94	-6	87	6.05	-1	*2-134	10	-0.1
1896 StL-N	48	191	19	40	6	1	1	17	9	5	8	....	.209	.252	.267	.519	38	-17	16	2.69	0	2-48	1	-1.3
*Bal-N	24	82	22	27	1	1	0	5	6	1	6	....	.329	.375	.366	.741	94	-1	14	6.61	1	/2-8,O-8(1-1-6),3-5,S-1	2	0.0
Yr.	72	273	41	67	7	2	1	22	15	6	14	....	.245	.290	.297	.586	55	-18	30	3.71	1	2-56/O-8(1-1-6),3-5,S-1	3	-1.2
1897 Bal-N	75	285	33	74	11	4	1	45	13	....	12	....	.260	.299	.337	.636	68	-14	33	4.14	8	3-37,S-21,2-11/O-6(1-5-0),1	7	-0.4
1898 Bal-N	12	32	5	8	1	0	0	5	1	....	0	....	.250	.273	.281	.554	58	-2	3	2.80	-1	/3-8,2-1,O-1	1	-0.2
StL-N	103	375	35	94	10	5	0	36	24	....	13	....	.251	.301	.304	.605	72	-14	40	3.68	-10	2-62,S-41/O-1	3	-1.9
Yr.	115	407	40	102	11	5	0	41	25	....	13	....	.251	.299	.302	.601	71	-16	43	3.61	-11	2-63,S-41/3-8,O-2(1-0-1)	4	-2.1
1899 Cle-N	147	615	73	176	24	6	0	72	21	....	22	....	.286	.312	.345	.657	86	-13	75	4.51	-20	*2-147	5	-2.4
1900 StL-N	22	80	12	21	2	0	1	11	10	....	4	....	.263	.344	.325	.669	86	-1	11	4.76	-4	2-14/S-6,3-1	2	-0.4
Cin-N	74	266	18	73	5	2	0	25	16	....	7	....	.274	.316	.308	.624	74	-9	30	3.93	-19	2-74	5	-2.3
Yr.	96	346	30	94	7	2	1	36	26	....	11	....	.272	.323	.312	.635	77	-10	40	4.12	-23	2-88/S-6,3-1	7	-2.7
1901 Was-A	66	266	33	67	11	2	2	34	11	....	7	....	.252	.287	.331	.618	72	-11	28	3.70	-8	2-66	4	-1.6
Total 17	1769	6883	893	1800	228	70	30	796	365	215	268	....	.262	.302	.328	.631	75	-247	798	4.16	-87	*2-1303,S-135,O-124,1-120/3	120	-25.8
• QUINN, John	John Edward "Pick" Quinn b: 9/12/1885, Framingham, MA d: 4/9/1956, Marlboro, MA BR/TR, 5'11", 150 lbs. Deb: 10/9/1911																							
1911 Phi-N	1	2	0	0	0	0	0	0	0	0	0	....	.000	.000	.000	.000	-99	-1	0	.00	0	/C-1	0	0.0
• QUINN, Mark	Mark David Quinn b: 5/21/1974, La Mirada, CA BR/TR, 6'1", 195 lbs. Deb: 9/14/1999 Career OF: 142-1-70																							
1999 KC-A	17	60	11	20	4	1	6	18	4	11	1	0	.333	.385	.733	1.118	173	6	17	11.14	1	O-15(15-0-1)/D-1	3	0.6
2000 KC-A	135	500	76	147	33	2	20	78	35	91	5	2	.294	.344	.488	.832	104	2	82	5.95	3	O-81(78-1-4),D-48	13	-0.2
2001 KC-A	118	453	57	122	31	2	17	60	12	69	9	5	.269	.299	.459	.758	88	-10	55	4.23	3	O-99(49-0-50),D-18	6	-1.3
2002 KC-A	23	76	9	18	4	0	2	11	5	15	2	1	.237	.301	.368	.670	69	-4	8	3.36	-1	O-15(0-0-15)/D-7	0	-0.6
Total 4	293	1089	153	307	72	5	45	167	56	186	17	8	.282	.325	.481	.806	99	-6	162	5.28	5	O-210/D-74	22	-1.5
• QUINN, Paddy	Patrick J. Quinn b: 8/1849, Chicago, IL d: 1/2/1909, Chicago, IL, 5'8.5", 148 lbs. Deb: 7/26/1871 U																							
1871 Kek-n	5	17	8	4	0	0	0	2	4	0	3	1	.235	.381	.235	.616	81	-0	3	6.15	2	/C-5	....	0.1
1875 Wes-n	11	43	4	14	1	0	0	5	0	1	0	1	.326	.326	.349	.674	127	1	5	4.92	1	C-10/O-1	....	0.2
Har-n	5	13	1	3	0	0	0	1	1	3	0	1	.231	.286	.231	.516	78	-1	1	2.36	-1	/C-3,O-3(0-1-2)	....	-0.2
Chi-n	17	61	12	14	0	0	0	1	0	2	1	1	.230	.230	.230	.459	59	-3	4	2.17	-3	C-11,O-10(0-9-1)	....	-0.5
Yr.	33	117	17	31	1	0	0	7	1	6	1	3	.265	.271	.274	.545	86	-3	9	3.12	-4	C-24,O-14(0-11-3)	....	-0.5
1877 Chi-N	4	14	1	1	0	0	0	0	1	0	....	....	.071	.133	.071	.205	-30	-2	0	.29	0	/O-4(0-0-4)	0	-0.2
Total 2 n	38	134	25	35	1	0	0	9	5	6	4	4	.261	.288	.269	.556	85	-3	12	3.53	-2	/C-29,O-14	....	-0.4
• QUINN, Tom	Thomas Oscar Quinn b: 4/25/1864, Annapolis, MD d: 7/24/1932, Pittsburgh, PA BR/TR, 5'8", 180 lbs. Deb: 9/2/1886																							
1886 Pit-a	3	11	1	0	0	0	0	0	0	....	1	....	.000	.000	.000	.000	-101	-3	0	.00	-1	/C-3	0	-0.3
1889 Bal-a	55	194	18	34	2	1	1	15	19	22	6	....	.175	.252	.211	.464	33	-17	12	2.01	-2	C-55	3	-1.2
1890 Pit-P	55	207	23	44	4	3	1	15	17	8	1	....	.213	.282	.275	.557	53	-13	17	2.78	-3	C-55	2	-0.9
Total 3	113	412	42	78	6	4	2	30	36	30	8	....	.189	.261	.238	.499	40	-32	29	2.32	-6	C-113	5	-2.3
• QUINONES, Luis	Luis Raul Quinones b: 4/28/1962, Ponce, Puerto Rico BB/TR, 5'11", 175 lbs. Deb: 5/27/1983																							
1983 Oak-A	19	42	5	8	2	1	0	4	1	4	1	1	.190	.209	.286	.495	37	-4	2	1.79	0	/2-6,3-4,D-4,O-4(0-0-4),S-3	0	-0.4
1986 SF-N	71	106	13	19	1	3	0	11	3	17	3	1	.179	.209	.245	.454	26	-11	6	1.62	-3	S-33,3-31/2-8	1	-1.3
1987 Chi-N	49	101	12	22	6	0	0	8	10	16	0	0	.218	.288	.277	.566	49	-7	9	3.01	-2	S-28/2-4,3-1	1	-0.7
1988 Cin-N	23	52	4	12	3	0	1	11	2	11	1	1	.231	.259	.346	.605	70	-3	5	2.85	1	S-10/2-4,3-4	2	-0.1
1989 Cin-N	97	340	43	83	13	4	12	34	25	46	2	4	.244	.302	.412	.713	99	-3	42	4.16	1	2-53,3-50/S-5	10	0.0
1990*Cin-N	83	145	10	35	7	0	2	17	13	29	1	0	.241	.308	.331	.639	73	-5	15	3.46	0	3-22,2-13/S-9,1-1	3	-0.5
1991 Cin-N	97	212	15	47	4	3	4	20	21	31	1	2	.222	.298	.325	.623	72	-8	21	3.33	-2	2-33,3-19/S-5	2	-1.0
1992 Min-A	3	5	0	1	0	0	0	1	0	0	0	0	.200	.200	.200	.400	12	-1	0	1.37	-1	/3-1,D-1,S-1	0	-0.1
Total 8	442	1003	102	227	36	11	19	106	75	154	9	9	.226	.285	.341	.626	72	-42	100	3.29	-5	3-132,2-121/S-94,D-5,O-4,1	19	-4.0
• QUINONES, Rey	Rey Francisco (Santiago) Quinones b: 11/11/1963, Rio Piedras, Puerto Rico BR/TR, 5'11", 160 lbs. Deb: 5/17/1986																							
1986 Bos-A	62	190	26	45	12	1	2	15	19	26	3	2	.237	.316	.342	.658	79	-6	20	3.43	-10	S-62	4	-0.9
Sea-A	36	122	6	23	4	0	0	7	5	31	1	1	.189	.220	.221	.442	21	-14	6	1.65	1	S-36	1	-1.0
Yr.	98	312	32	68	16	1	2	22	24	57	4	3	.218	.280	.295	.575	57	-19	26	2.72	-9	S-98	5	-1.9
1987 Sea-A	135	478	55	132	18	2	12	56	26	71	1	3	.276	.319	.397	.716	84	-13	57	4.13	-8	*S-135	10	-0.6
1988 Sea-A	140	499	63	124	30	3	12	52	23	71	0	3	.248	.286	.393	.679	84	-14	52	3.57	0	*S-135/D-4	12	-0.3
1989 Sea-A	7	19	2	2	0	0	0	0	1	1	0	0	.105	.150	.105	.255	-26	-3	0	.64	-1	/S-7	0	-0.4
Pit-N	71	225	21	47	11	0	3	29	15	40	0	2	.209	.261	.298	.559	62	-13	17	2.33	-10	S-69	4	-1.9
Total 4	451	1533	173	373	75	6	29	159	89	240	5	11	.243	.290	.357	.646	74	-62	153	3.32	-28	S-444/D-4	31	-5.0
• QUINTANA, Carlos	Carlos Narcis (Hernandez) Quintana b: 8/26/1965, Estado Miranda, Venezuela BR/TR, 6', 195 lbs. Deb: 9/16/1988 Career OF: 6-1-85																							
1988 Bos-A	5	6	1	2	0	0	0	2	2	3	0	0	.333	.500	.333	.833	133	0	1	8.51	0	/O-3(0-0-3),D-1	1	0.0
1989 Bos-A	34	77	6	16	5	0	0	6	7	12	0	0	.208	.274	.273	.547	51	-5	5	2.00	-2	O-21(4-1-17)/D-7,1-1	0	-0.7
1990*Bos-A	149	512	56	147	28	0	7	67	52	74	1	2	.287	.355	.383	.738	102	2	67	4.63	9	*1-148/O-3(0-0-3)	13	0.1
1991 Bos-A	149	478	69	141	21	1	11	71	61	66	1	0	.295	.377	.412	.789	113	11	74	5.51	5	*1-138,O-13(1-0-12)/D-1	14	0.7
1993 Bos-A	101	303	31	74	5	0	1	19	31	52	1	0	.244	.318	.271	.589	57	-17	26	2.80	1	1-53,O-51(1-0-50)	2	-2.1
Total 5	438	1376	163	380	59	1	19	165	153	207	3	2	.276	.351	.362	.713	93	-9	173	4.36	14	1-340/O-91,D-9	30	-2.0
• QUINTERO, Robb	Robb William Quintero b: 8/2/1979, Maracaibo, Venezuela BR/TR, 6'1", 195 lbs. Deb: 9/3/2003																							
2003 Ana-A	38	94	13	27	4	2	0	4	6	16	1	2	.287	.330	.372	.702	88	-2	10	3.86	0	1-33/D-3,O-1	0	-0.4
• QUINTON, Marshall	Marshall J. Quinton b: Philadelphia, PA, 5'11", 190 lbs. Deb: 8/7/1884																							
1884 Ric-a	26	94	12	22	5	0	0	0	0	....	....	....	.234	.242	.287	.529	73	-3	7	2.56	0	C-14,O-10(0-0-10)/S-2	1	-0.2
1885 Phi-a	7	29	6	6	1	0	0	4	1	....	....	....	.207	.258	.241	.499	55	-2	2	2.17	-2	/C-7	0	-0.2
Total 2	33	123	18	28	6	0	0	4	1	....	....	....	.228	.246	.276	.522	68	-4	9	2.47	-2	/C-21,O-10,S-2	1	-0.5

YEAR TM-L	G	AB	R	H	2B	3B	HR	RBI	BB	SO	SB	CS	AVG	OBP	SLG	OPS	OPS+	BR/A	RC	RC/G	FR	G/POS	WS	TPW
• QUIRK, Jamie	James Patrick Quirk b: 10/22/1954, Whittier, CA BL/TR, 6'4", 200 lbs. Deb: 9/4/1975 C Career OF: 24-0-8																							
1975 KC-A	14	39	2	10	0	0	1	5	2	7	0	0	.256	.293	.333	.626	75	-1	4	3.20	0	0-10(10-0-0)/3-2,D-1	0	-0.2
1976*KC-A	64	114	11	28	6	0	1	15	2	22	0	0	.246	.259	.325	.583	70	-5	8	2.36	-6	D-19,S-12,3-11/1-2	0	-1.1
1977 Mil-A	93	221	16	48	14	1	3	13	8	47	0	1	.217	.251	.330	.581	57	-14	17	2.60	-1	D-53,0-10(10-0-0)/3-8	0	-1.6
1978 KC-A	17	29	3	6	2	0	0	2	5	4	0	0	.207	.324	.276	.599	68	-1	3	3.53	0	3-10/S-2,D-1	1	-0.1
1979 KC-A	51	79	8	24	6	1	1	11	5	13	0	0	.304	.353	.443	.796	111	1	13	6.33	-1	/C-9,D-9,S-5,3-3	3	0.0
1980 KC-A	62	163	13	45	5	0	5	21	7	24	3	2	.276	.310	.399	.709	92	-2	18	3.60	0	3-28,C-15/0-7(2-0-5),1-1,D	3	-0.2
1981 KC-A	46	100	8	25	7	0	0	10	6	17	0	2	.250	.299	.320	.619	79	-4	8	2.58	-1	C-22/3-8,2-1,0-1	1	-0.5
1982 KC-A	36	78	8	18	3	0	1	5	3	15	0	0	.231	.259	.308	.567	55	-5	6	2.51	0	C-29/1-6,3-1,0-1	1	-0.4
1983 StL-N	48	86	3	18	2	1	2	11	6	27	0	0	.209	.269	.326	.594	64	-4	7	2.84	-4	C-22/3-7,S-1	0	-0.8
1984 Chi-A	3	2	0	0	0	0	0	1	0	2	0	0	.000	.000	.000	.000	-96	-1	0	.00	0	/3-1	0	-0.1
Cle-A	1	1	1	1	0	0	1	1	0	0	0	0	1.000	1.000	4.000	5.000	1189	1	4	∞	0	/C-1	1	0.1
Yr.	4	3	1	1	0	0	1	2	0	2	0	0	.333	.333	1.333	1.667	225	1	4	.00	-1	/3-1,C-1	1	0.0
1985*KC-A	19	57	3	16	3	1	0	4	2	9	0	0	.281	.305	.368	.674	83	-1	6	3.99	-0	C-17/1-1	2	-0.1
1986 KC-A	80	219	24	47	10	0	8	26	17	41	0	1	.215	.274	.370	.644	72	-10	22	3.27	8	C-41,3-24/1-6,0-1	4	0.0
1987 KC-A	109	296	24	70	17	0	5	33	28	56	1	0	.236	.311	.345	.656	72	-12	32	3.60	-1	*C-108/S-1	6	-0.8
1988 KC-A	84	196	22	47	7	1	8	25	28	41	1	5	.240	.338	.408	.746	107	0	27	4.49	-1	C-79/1-1,3-1	6	0.4
1989 NY-A	13	24	0	2	0	0	0	0	3	5	0	1	.083	.185	.083	.269	-22	-4	0	.35	0	/C-6,D-1,S-1	0	-0.4
Oak-A	9	10	1	2	0	0	1	1	0	4	0	0	.200	.200	.500	.700	95	-0	1	3.38	-1	/3-3,C-2,1-1,0-1	0	-0.2
Bal-A	25	51	5	11	2	0	0	9	9	11	0	1	.216	.333	.255	.588	70	-2	4	2.48	-1	C-24	2	-0.1
Yr.	47	85	6	15	2	0	1	10	12	20	0	2	.176	.278	.235	.514	47	-7	6	1.92	-2	C-32/3-3,1-1,D-1,0-1,S-1	2	-0.7
1990*Oak-A	56	121	12	34	5	1	3	26	14	34	0	0	.281	.360	.413	.774	121	4	19	5.42	-2	C-37/1-8,3-8,D-1,0-1	8	0.3
1991 Oak-A	76	203	16	53	4	0	1	17	16	28	0	3	.261	.321	.296	.617	76	-8	18	2.98	1	C-54/1-8,3-1,D-1	4	-0.4
1992*Oak-A	78	177	13	39	7	1	2	11	16	28	0	0	.220	.296	.305	.601	72	-6	16	2.99	-1	C-59/1-9,3-2,D-1	2	-0.4
Total 18	984	2266	193	544	100	7	43	247	177	435	5	16	.240	.300	.347	.648	79	-74	234	3.37	-13	C-525,3-118/D-88,1-43,0,S,2	44	-6.6
• RAABE, Brian	Brian Charles Raabe b: 11/5/1967, New Ulm, MN BR/TR, 5'9", 177 lbs. Deb: 9/17/1995																							
1995 Min-A	6	14	4	3	0	0	0	1	1	0	0	0	.214	.267	.214	.481	27	-1	1	2.13	0	/2-4,3-2	0	-0.1
1996 Min-A	7	9	0	2	0	0	0	1	0	1	0	0	.222	.222	.222	.444	13	-1	1	1.70	-1	/3-6,2-1	0	-0.2
1997 Sea-A	2	3	0	0	0	0	0	0	1	2	0	0	.000	.250	.000	.250	-28	-1	0	.59	-1	/3-2,2-1	0	-0.1
Col-N	2	3	0	1	0	0	0	0	0	1	0	0	.333	.333	.333	.667	61	-0	0	3.42	0	/2-1	0	0.0
Total 3	17	29	4	6	0	0	0	2	2	4	0	0	.207	.258	.207	.465	20	-3	2	1.96	-1	/3-10,2-7	0	-0.4
• RABB, John	John Andrew Rabb b: 6/23/1960, Los Angeles, CA BR/TR, 6'1", 180 lbs. Deb: 9/4/1982 Career OF: 5-0-10																							
1982 SF-N	2	2	0	1	0	1	0	0	0	1	0	0	.500	.500	1.500	2.000	440	1	2	40.50	-0	/0-1	0	0.1
1983 SF-N	40	104	10	24	9	0	1	14	9	17	1	0	.231	.292	.346	.638	79	-3	10	3.16	0	C-31/0-2(0-0-2)	3	-0.2
1984 SF-N	54	82	10	16	1	0	3	9	10	33	1	1	.195	.283	.317	.600	70	-4	8	3.19	-1	1-13/0-8(3-0-6),C-6	1	-0.6
1985 Atl-N	3	2	0	0	0	0	0	0	0	1	0	0	.000	.000	.000	.000	-94	-1	0	.00	0	/0-1	0	-0.1
1988 Sea-A	9	14	2	5	2	0	0	4	0	1	0	0	.357	.357	.500	.857	131	0	3	7.50	-0	/D-5,0-2(0-0-2),1-1	1	0.0
Total 5	108	204	22	46	12	1	4	27	19	53	2	1	.225	.291	.353	.644	80	-6	22	3.60	-2	/C-37,1-14,0-14,D-5	5	-0.7
• RABBITT, Joe	Joseph Patrick Rabbitt b: 1/16/1900, Frontenac, KS d: 12/5/1969, Norwalk, CT BL/TR, 5'10", 165 lbs. Deb: 9/15/1922																							
1922 Cle-A	2	3	1	1	0	0	0	0	0	0	0	0	.333	.333	.333	.667	74	-0	0	4.24	0	/0-1	0	0.0
• RACKLEY, Marv	Marvin Eugene Rackley b: 7/25/1921, Seneca, SC BL/TL, 5'10", 170 lbs. Deb: 4/15/1947 Career OF: 47-81-2																							
1947 Bro-N	18	9	2	2	0	0	0	2	1	0	0	....	.222	.300	.222	.522	39	-1	1	2.62	0	/0-2(0-1-1)	0	0.0
1948 Bro-N	88	281	55	92	13	5	0	15	19	25	8	....	.327	.370	.409	.779	107	3	44	6.17	-1	0-74(43-33-1)	10	-0.2
1949*Bro-N	9	9	2	4	1	0	0	1	1	0	0	0	.444	.500	.556	1.056	176	1	3	11.82	0	/0-3(0-0-0)	0	0.1
Pit-N	11	35	5	11	2	0	0	2	2	3	1	....	.314	.351	.371	.723	92	-0	5	5.34	0	/0-8(0-8-0)	1	-0.1
*Bro-N	54	141	23	41	4	1	1	14	13	8	1	....	.291	.351	.355	.705	86	-3	18	4.74	-1	0-44(4-39-0)	4	-0.4
Yr.	74	185	30	56	7	1	1	17	16	11	2	0	.303	.358	.368	.726	92	-2	25	5.17	-1	0-55(4-47-0)	5	-0.4
1950 Cin-N	5	2	0	1	0	0	0	1	0	0	0	....	.500	.500	.500	1.000	163	0	1	13.50	0	....	0	0.0
Total 4	185	477	87	151	20	6	1	35	36	36	10	0	.317	.365	.390	.754	100	0	71	5.72	-2	0-131	15	-0.6
• RADBOURN, Charley	Charles Gardner "Old Hoss" Radbourn b: 12/11/1854, Rochester, NY d: 2/5/1897, Bloomington, IL BR/TR, 5'9", 168 lbs. Deb: 5/5/1880 HOF: 1939 Career OF: 15-12-92 ♦																							
1880 Buf-N	6	21	1	3	0	0	0	1	0	1	....	....	.143	.143	.143	.286	-3	-2	0	.67	3	/2-3,0-3(0-0-3)	0	0.1
1881 Pro-N	72	270	27	59	9	0	0	28	10	15	....	....	.219	.246	.252	.498	58	-7	17	2.20	-1	P-41,0-25(0-1-24),S-13	24	0.8
1882 Pro-N	83	326	30	78	11	0	1	32	12	22	....	....	.239	.266	.282	.548	76	-5	25	2.78	4	*P-55,0-31(1-0-30)/S-1	**50**	2.2
1883 Pro-N	89	381	59	108	11	3	3	48	14	16	....	....	.283	.309	.352	.661	98	11	42	4.27	5	*P-76,0-20(10-4-6)/1-2	**60**	5.0
1884*Pro-N	87	361	48	83	7	1	1	37	26	42	....	....	.230	.282	.263	.545	74	3	27	2.71	-3	*P-75/0-7(0-1-7),1-5,S-2,2	**89**	**8.5**
1885 Pro-N	66	249	34	58	9	2	0	22	36	27	....	....	.233	.330	.285	.615	104	12	24	3.39	0	P-49,0-16(2-4-10)/2-2	39	3.1
1886 Bos-N	66	253	30	60	5	1	2	22	17	36	5	....	.237	.285	.289	.574	78	8	23	3.19	0	P-58/0-6(1-0-5)	32	2.6
1887 Bos-N	51	193	25	58	2	2	1	24	18	21	6	....	.301	.308	.280	.588	66	3	17	3.40	-4	P-50/0-2(0-0-2)	22	-2.9
1888 Bos-N	24	79	6	17	1	0	0	6	3	14	4	....	.215	.262	.228	.490	55	1	6	2.57	-1	P-24	11	0.0
1889 Bos-N	35	122	17	23	1	0	1	13	9	19	3	....	.189	.256	.221	.477	32	-1	8	2.10	1	P-33/0-2(0-1-1),3-1	21	1.4
1890 Bos-P	45	154	20	39	6	0	0	16	9	20	7	....	.253	.299	.292	.591	54	-0	16	3.74	1	P-41/0-4(0-0-4),1-1	34	3.0
1891 Cin-N	29	96	11	17	2	2	0	10	4	11	1	....	.177	.225	.240	.465	35	-2	6	1.90	-3	P-26/0-2(1-1-0),3-1	9	-2.1
Total 12	653	2505	308	603	64	11	9	259	158	244	26	....	.241	.283	.281	.564	73	20	212	3.03	3	P-528,0-118/S-16,1-8,2-6,3	391	21.6
• RADCLIFF, Rip	Raymond Allen Radcliff b: 1/19/1906, Kiowa, OK d: 5/23/1962, Enid, OK BL/TL, 5'10", 170 lbs. Deb: 9/17/1934 Career OF: 745-0-143																							
1934 Chi-A	14	56	7	15	2	1	0	5	0	2	1	0	.268	.268	.339	.607	54	-4	5	3.19	0	0-14(0-0-14)	0	-0.4
1935 Chi-A	146	623	95	178	28	8	10	68	53	21	4	4	.286	.346	.404	.750	91	-9	88	5.16	-15	*0-142(142-0-0)	13	-3.0
1936 Chi-A★	138	618	120	207	31	7	8	82	44	12	6	3	.335	.381	.447	.828	100	-0	105	6.72	-12	*0-132(132-0-0)	17	-1.7
1937 Chi-A	144	584	105	190	38	10	4	79	53	25	6	1	.325	.383	.445	.829	108	9	102	6.76	2	*0-139(139-0-0)	21	0.2
1938 Chi-A	129	503	64	166	23	6	5	81	36	17	5	7	.330	.376	.429	.805	99	-3	80	6.05	0	0-99(99-0-0),1-23	13	-1.0
1939 Chi-A	113	397	49	105	25	2	2	53	26	21	6	4	.264	.313	.353	.666	68	-20	44	3.85	-5	0-78(10-0-69),1-20	6	-2.9
1940 StL-A	150	584	83	**200**	33	9	7	81	47	20	6	4	.342	.392	.466	.858	119	17	109	7.28	-4	*0-139(116-0-23)/1-4	20	0.5
1941 StL-A	19	71	12	20	2	2	2	14	10	1	1	1	.282	.370	.451	.821	112	1	12	6.33	-2	0-14(14-0-0)/1-3	2	-0.1
Det-A	96	379	47	120	14	5	3	40	19	13	4	4	.317	.351	.404	.755	90	-7	53	5.23	-3	0-87(85-0-2)	8	-1.4
Yr.	115	450	59	140	16	7	5	54	29	14	5	5	.311	.354	.411	.765	94	-5	66	5.40	-5	*0-101(99-0-2)/1-3	10	-1.5
1942 Det-A	62	144	13	36	5	0	1	20	9	6	0	1	.250	.294	.306	.600	64	-7	13	3.04	0	0-24(6-0-18)/1-4	2	-0.9
1943 Det-A	70	115	3	30	4	0	0	10	13	3	1	1	.261	.341	.296	.637	81	-2	12	3.59	1	0-19(2-0-17)/1-1	2	-0.3
Total 10	1081	4074	598	1267	205	50	42	533	310	141	40	30	.311	.362	.417	.779	96	-27	623	5.73	-37	0-887/1-55	104	-11.1
• RADCLIFFE, John	John Y. Radcliffe b: 6/29/1848, Philadelphia, PA d: 7/26/1911, Ocean City, NJ, 5'6", 140 lbs. Deb: 5/20/1871 U																							
1871 Ath-n	28	145	47	44	7	5	0	22	6	1	5	1	.303	.331	.421	.752	115	3	22	6.92	5	*S-28	....	0.5
1872 Bal-n	56	297	70	86	13	4	1	44	0	2	3	3	.290	.290	.370	.660	97	-3	34	4.86	8	*S-50/3-6,2-1	....	0.2
1873 Bal-n	45	245	59	70	7	0	0	33	3	2	0	0	.286	.294	.314	.609	81	-5	23	4.05	4	3-24,S-23/2-1	....	-0.1
1874 Phi-n	23	103	20	25	7	0	1	14	2	0	1	1	.243	.257	.340	.597	87	-2	9	3.60	-1	0-15(0-1-14)/2-4,3-3,S-3,1	....	-0.2
1875 Cen-n	5	23	2	4	0	0	0	0	1	0	0	0	.174	.208	.174	.382	37	-1	1	1.33	0	/S-5	....	-0.1
Total 5 n	157	813	198	229	34	9	2	113	12	5	9	5	.282	.292	.353	.645	93	-9	90	4.69	16	S-109/3-33,0-15,2-6,1-2	....	0.3
• RADER, Dave	David Martin Rader b: 12/26/1948, Claremore, OK BL/TR, 5'11", 165 lbs. Deb: 9/5/1971																							
1971 SF-N	3	4	0	0	0	0	0	0	0	0	0	0	.000	.000	.000	.000	-102	-1	0	.00	0	/C-1	0	-0.1
1972 SF-N	133	459	44	119	14	1	6	41	29	31	1	2	.259	.308	.333	.641	81	-12	45	3.41	-4	*C-127	10	-1.1
1973 SF-N	148	462	59	106	15	4	9	41	63	22	0	2	.229	.330	.338	.667	82	-10	51	3.57	-5	*C-148	12	-0.8
1974 SF-N	113	323	26	94	16	2	1	26	31	21	1	0	.291	.353	.362	.715	96	-1	41	4.49	-6	*C-109	9	-0.2
1975 SF-N	98	292	39	85	15	0	5	31	32	30	1	0	.291	.363	.394	.757	105	3	41	5.02	0	C-94	11	0.7
1976 SF-N	88	255	25	67	15	0	1	22	27	21	2	0	.263	.333	.333	.667	87	-3	27	3.55	-3	C-81	6	-0.3

YEAR TM-L	G	AB	R	H	2B	3B	HR	RBI	BB	SO	SB	CS	AVG	OBP	SLG	OPS	OPS+	BR/A	RC	RC/G	FR	G/POS	WS	TPW
1977 StL-N	66	114	15	30	7	1	1	16	9	10	1	0	.263	.317	.368	.685	85	-2	15	4.35	-3	C-38	3	-0.3
1978 Chi-N	116	305	29	62	13	3	3	36	34	26	1	1	.203	.285	.295	.580	56	-18	24	2.48	-1	*C-114	3	-1.6
1979 Phi-N	31	54	3	11	1	1	1	5	6	7	0	0	.204	.283	.315	.598	61	-3	4	2.49	-2	C-25	0	-0.5
1980 Bos-A	50	137	14	45	11	0	3	17	14	12	1	1	.328	.391	.474	.865	129	6	25	6.79	1	C-34/D-9	6	0.7
Total 10	846	2405	254	619	107	12	30	235	245	180	8	4	.257	.329	.349	.678	86	-42	272	3.84	-23	C-771/D-9	60	-3.5
• RADER, Don	Donald Russell Rader b: 9/5/1893, Wolcott, IN d: 6/26/1983, Walla Walla, WA BL/TR, 5'10", 164 lbs. Deb: 7/25/1913																							
1913 Chi-A	4	3	1	1	1	0	0	0	0	0	0	....	.333	.333	.667	1.000	193	0	1	7.99	-1	/3-1,0-1	0	0.0
1921 Phi-N	9	32	4	9	2	0	0	3	3	5	0	0	.281	.343	.344	.687	76	-1	4	4.34	-0	/S-9	1	0.0
Total 2	13	35	5	10	3	0	0	3	3	5	0	0	.286	.342	.371	.714	85	-1	5	4.62	-1	/S-9,3-1,0-1	1	-0.1
• RADER, Doug	Douglas Lee "Rojo,The Red Rooster" Rader b: 7/30/1944, Chicago, IL BR/TR, 6'2", 215 lbs. Deb: 7/31/1967 M/C																							
1967 Hou-N	47	162	24	54	10	4	2	26	7	31	0	3	.333	.368	.481	.850	146	8	27	6.06	-1	1-36/3-7	7	0.6
1968 Hou-N	98	333	42	89	16	4	6	43	31	51	2	2	.267	.332	.393	.725	119	8	43	4.43	-3	3-86/1-5	13	0.5
1969 Hou-N	155	569	62	140	25	3	11	83	62	103	1	5	.246	.327	.359	.685	94	-6	65	3.83	9	*3-154/1-4	16	0.3
1970 Hou-N	156	576	90	145	25	3	25	87	57	102	3	2	.252	.323	.436	.759	106	3	76	4.43	20	*3-154/1-1	19	2.2
1971 Hou-N	135	484	51	118	21	4	12	56	40	112	5	1	.244	.306	.378	.684	95	-3	56	3.95	5	*3-135	15	0.1
1972 Hou-N	152	553	70	131	24	7	22	90	57	120	5	5	.237	.314	.425	.739	110	5	70	4.14	12	*3-152	19	1.8
1973 Hou-N	154	574	79	146	26	0	21	89	46	97	4	3	.254	.313	.409	.722	99	-3	73	4.37	3	*3-152	18	0.0
1974 Hou-N	152	533	61	137	27	3	17	78	60	131	7	2	.257	.337	.415	.751	114	10	74	4.83	6	*3-152	18	1.6
1975 Hou-N	129	448	41	100	23	2	12	48	42	101	5	4	.223	.297	.364	.661	89	-9	47	3.49	1	*3-124/S-2	9	-0.9
1976 SD-N	139	471	45	121	22	4	9	55	55	102	3	4	.257	.338	.378	.716	112	7	60	4.31	8	*3-137	17	1.5
1977 SD-N	52	170	19	46	8	3	5	27	33	40	0	1	.271	.392	.441	.833	137	10	30	6.26	0	3-51	8	1.0
Tor-A	96	313	47	75	18	2	13	40	38	65	2	1	.240	.328	.435	.762	104	2	44	4.54	0	3-45,D-34/1-7,0-1	7	0.1
Total 11	1465	5186	631	1302	245	39	155	722	528	1055	37	33	.251	.325	.403	.728	106	32	665	4.34	61	*3-1349/1-53,D-34,S-2,0-1	166	8.7
• RADFORD, Paul	Paul Revere "Shorty" Radford b: 10/14/1861, Roxbury, MA d: 2/21/1945, Boston, MA BR/TR, 5'6", 148 lbs. Deb: 5/1/1883 Career OF: 33-153-724 ♦																							
1883 Bos-N	72	258	46	53	6	3	0	14	9	26	....	....	.205	.232	.252	.484	46	-17	15	2.08	-4	*0-72(1-24-50)	2	-2.0
1884*Pro-N	97	355	56	70	11	2	1	29	25	43	....	....	.197	.250	.248	.498	58	-15	23	2.18	4	*0-96(0-0-96)/P-2	7	-1.8
1885 Pro-N	105	371	55	90	12	5	0	32	33	43	....	....	.243	.304	.302	.606	101	2	35	3.36	2	*0-88(2-8-80),S-16/P-3,2-1	13	-0.7
1886 KC-N	122	493	78	113	17	5	0	20	58	48	39	....	.229	.310	.284	.594	77	-13	57	4.05	3	*0-92(0-0-92),S-30/2-1	7	-1.0
1887 NY-a	128	592	127	235	15	5	4	45	**106**	....	73	....	.397	.403	.342	.745	114	18	99	7.47	-13	S-76,0-37(1-1-36),2-18/P-2	18	0.0
1888 Bro-a	90	308	48	67	9	3	2	29	35	....	33	....	.218	.305	.286	.591	90	-2	38	4.24	4	0-88(0-83-5)/2-2	10	-0.1
1889 Cle-N	136	487	94	116	21	5	1	46	91	37	30	....	.238	.365	.308	.673	91	-1	67	4.81	2	*0-136(0-2-136)/3-1	13	-0.1
1890 Cle-P	122	466	98	136	24	12	2	62	82	28	25	....	.292	.406	.408	.814	128	25	90	7.33	8	0-80(6-35-39),S-36/3-7,2-4,P	17	2.5
1891 Bos-a	133	456	102	118	11	5	0	65	96	36	55	....	.259	.393	.305	.698	102	8	78	6.13	13	*S-131/0-4(4-0-0),P-1	22	2.2
1892 Was-N	137	510	93	130	19	4	1	37	86	47	35	....	.255	.366	.314	.679	109	11	73	5.19	-6	0-62(2-0-60),3-54,S-20/2-2	13	0.4
1893 Was-N	124	464	87	106	18	3	2	34	104	42	32	....	.228	.378	.293	.672	82	-5	65	4.82	8	*0-123(7-0-116)/2-1,P-1	10	-0.4
1894 Was-N	95	325	61	78	13	5	0	49	65	23	24	....	.240	.378	.311	.689	70	-12	48	5.10	-6	S-47,2-25,0-24(10-0-14)	6	-1.3
Total 12	1361	5085	945	1312	176	57	13	462	790	373	346	....	.258	.351	.308	.660	92	-0	688	4.89	12	0-902,S-356/3-62,2-54,P-10	138	-2.3
• RADMANOVICH, Ryan	Ryan Ashley Radmanovich b: 8/9/1971, Calgary, Canada BL/TR, 6'2" Deb: 4/13/1998																							
1998 Sea-A	25	69	5	15	4	0	2	10	4	25	1	1	.217	.260	.362	.623	60	-5	7	3.11	0	0-24(0-0-24)/1-1	0	-0.5
• RADTKE, Jack	Jack William Radtke b: 4/14/1913, Denver, CO BB/TR, 5'7", 160 lbs. Deb: 8/1/1936																							
1936 Bro-N	33	31	8	3	0	0	0	2	4	9	3	....	.097	.200	.097	.297	-18	-5	1	.79	-2	2-14/3-5,S-4	0	-0.7
• RAFTER, Jack	John Cornelius Rafter b: 2/20/1875, Troy, NY d: 1/5/1943, Troy, NY BR/TR, 5'8", 165 lbs. Deb: 9/24/1904																							
1904 Pit-N	1	3	0	0	0	0	0	0	0	....	0	....	.000	.000	.000	.000	-97	-1	0	.00	0	/C-1	0	-0.1
• RAFTERY, Tom	Thomas Francis Raftery b: 10/5/1881, Boston, MA d: 12/31/1954, Boston, MA BR/TR, 5'10.5", 175 lbs. Deb: 4/18/1909																							
1909 Cle-A	8	32	6	7	2	1	0	0	4	....	1	....	.219	.306	.344	.649	101	0	4	3.68	0	/0-8(1-1-6)	1	-0.1
• RAGLAND, Tom	Thomas Ragland b: 6/16/1946, Talladega, AL BR/TR, 5'10", 155 lbs. Deb: 4/5/1971																							
1971 Was-A	10	23	1	4	0	0	0	0	0	5	0	0	.174	.208	.174	.382	10	-3	0	.44	0	2-10	0	-0.2
1972 Tex-A	25	58	3	10	2	0	0	2	5	11	0	1	.172	.238	.207	.445	35	-5	3	1.49	-1	2-13/3-5,S-3	0	-0.5
1973 Cle-A	67	183	16	47	7	1	0	12	8	31	2	3	.257	.292	.306	.598	67	-9	16	2.88	1	2-65/S-2	3	-0.4
Total 3	102	264	20	61	9	1	0	14	13	47	2	4	.231	.272	.273	.545	55	-17	19	2.31	1	/2-88,3-5,S-5	3	-1.2
• RAINES, Larry	Lawrence Glenn Hope Raines b: 3/9/1930, St. Albans, VT d: 1/28/1978, Lansing, MI BR/TR, 5'10", 165 lbs. Deb: 4/16/1957																							
1957 Cle-A	96	244	39	64	14	0	2	16	19	40	5	2	.262	.318	.344	.662	82	-6	27	3.97	1	3-27,S-25,2-10/0-8(8-0-0)	6	-0.4
1958 Cle-A	7	9	1	0	0	0	0	0	0	5	0	1	.000	.000	.000	.000	-103	-3	0	.00	2	/2-2	0	-0.1
Total 2	103	253	40	64	14	0	2	16	19	45	5	3	.253	.308	.332	.640	76	-9	27	3.77	3	/3-27,S-25,2-12,0-8	6	-0.5
• RAINES, Tim	Timothy "Rock" Raines, Sr. b: 9/16/1959, Sanford, FL BB/TR, 5'8", 178 lbs. Deb: 9/11/1979 Career OF: 1966-165-1																							
1979 Mon-N	6	0	3	0	0	0	0	0	0	0	2	0	....	....	....	....	-101	0	0	....	0	....	0	0.0
1980 Mon-N	15	20	5	1	0	0	0	0	6	3	5	0	.050	.269	.050	.319	-6	-2	1	1.99	0	/2-7,0-1	0	-0.2
1981*Mon-N★	88	313	61	95	13	7	5	37	45	31	**71**	11	.304	.394	.438	.832	134	26	64	7.19	-7	0-81(81-0-0)/2-1	18	1.7
1982 Mon-N★	156	647	90	179	32	8	4	43	75	83	**78**	16	.277	.354	.369	.723	101	12	96	5.23	-5	*0-120(120-0-0),2-36	21	0.3
1983 Mon-N★	156	615	**133**	183	32	8	11	71	97	70	**90**	14	.298	.395	.429	.824	129	42	120	6.98	4	*0-154(153-2-0)/2-7	29	4.0
1984 Mon-N★	160	622	106	192	**38**	9	8	60	87	69	**75**	10	.309	.395	.437	.833	140	**48**	124	7.35	-7	*0-160(0-160-0)/2-2	32	4.1
1985 Mon-N★	150	575	115	184	30	13	11	41	81	60	70	9	.320	.407	.475	.881	155	56	124	8.10	3	*0-146(146-0-0)	**36**	5.4
1986 Mon-N★	151	580	91	194	35	10	9	62	78	60	70	9	**.334**	**.415**	.476	.891	146	**51**	130	**8.66**	2	*0-147(147-0-0)	**32**	**4.7**
1987 Mon-N★	139	530	**123**	175	34	8	18	68	90	52	50	5	.330	.431	.526	.958	148	49	132	9.57	2	*0-139(139-0-0)	**34**	4.3
1988 Mon-N	109	429	66	116	19	7	12	48	53	44	33	7	.270	.353	.431	.785	119	15	69	5.59	2	*0-108(108-0-0)	19	1.4
1989 Mon-N	145	517	76	148	29	6	9	60	93	48	41	9	.286	.398	.418	.816	132	31	96	6.60	0	*0-139(140-0-0)	25	2.8
1990 Mon-N	130	457	65	131	11	5	9	62	70	43	49	16	.287	.385	.392	.777	119	18	75	5.64	-7	*0-123(123-0-0)	19	0.6
1991 Chi-A	155	609	102	163	20	6	5	50	83	68	51	15	.268	.360	.345	.705	98	7	85	4.78	3	*0-133(134-1-0),D-19	19	0.4
1992 Chi-A	144	551	102	162	22	9	7	54	81	48	45	6	.294	.384	.405	.789	123	27	98	6.44	8	*0-129(129-1-0),D-14	28	3.0
1993*Chi-A	115	415	75	127	16	4	16	54	64	35	21	7	.306	.402	.480	.882	139	27	85	7.46	-1	*0-112(112-0-0)	19	2.1
1994 Chi-A	101	384	80	102	15	5	10	52	61	43	13	0	.266	.368	.409	.777	102	6	62	5.61	-3	0-96(97-0-0)	14	-0.2
1995 Chi-A	133	502	81	143	25	4	12	67	70	52	13	2	.285	.376	.422	.798	112	13	85	6.13	-3	*0-107(107-0-1),D-22	14	0.4
1996*NY-A	59	201	45	57	10	0	9	33	34	29	10	1	.284	.390	.468	.857	116	7	39	6.92	-2	0-51(51-0-0)/D-2	7	0.3
1997*NY-A	74	271	56	87	20	2	4	38	41	34	8	5	.321	.410	.454	.864	126	12	53	7.16	-3	0-57(57-0-0),D-13	9	0.6
1998*NY-A	109	321	53	93	13	1	5	47	55	49	8	3	.290	.398	.383	.782	109	8	54	6.07	2	D-56,0-47(47-0-0)	11	0.5
1999 Oak-A	58	135	20	29	5	0	4	17	26	17	4	1	.215	.342	.341	.682	78	-3	17	3.94	-1	0-38(38-1-0)/D-3	1	-0.5
2001 Mon-N	47	78	13	24	8	1	0	4	18	6	1	0	.308	.438	.436	.873	125	4	16	7.76	-2	/0-2(20-0-0)	3	0.2
Bal-A	4	11	1	3	0	0	1	5	0	3	0	0	.273	.273	.545	.818	114	0	2	4.89	0	0-20(2-0-0)/D-1	0	0.0
2002 Fla-N	98	89	9	17	3	0	1	7	22	19	0	0	.191	.357	.258	.616	68	-3	9	3.30	0	0-14(14-0-0)/D-1	0	-0.3
Total 23	2502	8872	1571	2605	430	113	170	980	1330	966	808	146	.294	.388	.425	.813	124	451	1636	6.62	-15	*0-2124,D-131/2-53	390	35.7
• RAINES, Tim	Timothy Raines, Jr. b: 8/31/1979, Memphis, TN BB/TR, 5'10", 183 lbs. Deb: 10/1/2001 Career OF: 1-24-0																							
2001 Bal-A	7	23	6	4	2	0	0	0	3	8	3	0	.174	.269	.261	.530	43	-1	2	3.10	-1	/0-7(0-7-0)	0	-0.2
2003 Bal-A	20	43	4	6	1	1	0	2	2	12	0	0	.140	.196	.209	.405	7	-6	1	1.03	2	0-18(1-17-0)/D-1	0	-0.4
Total 2	27	66	10	10	3	1	0	2	5	20	3	0	.152	.222	.227	.449	20	-7	4	1.73	1	/0-25,D-1	0	-0.6
• RAINEY, John	John Paul Rainey b: 7/26/1864, Birmingham, MI d: 11/11/1912, Detroit, MI BL/TR, 5'10", 164 lbs. Deb: 8/25/1887																							
1887 NY-N	17	63	6	22	3	0	0	12	5	6	0	....	.349	.349	.345	.694	98	0	7	4.63	-3	3-17	1	-0.2
1890 Buf-P	42	166	29	39	5	1	1	20	24	15	12	....	.235	.349	.295	.644	79	-3	22	4.64	-1	0-28(0-0-28)/S-7,3-6,2-2	3	-0.3
Total 2	59	229	35	61	8	1	1	32	29	21	12	....	.266	.349	.308	.657	84	-3	29	4.63	-4	/0-28,3-23,S-7,2-2	4	-0.5

YEAR TM-L	G	AB	R	H	2B	3B	HR	RBI	BB	SO	SB	CS	AVG	OBP	SLG	OPS	OPS+	BR/A	RC	RC/G	FR	G/POS	WS	TPW
• RAJSICH, Gary	Gary Louis Rajsich b: 10/28/1954, Youngstown, OH BL/TL, 6'2", 210 lbs. Deb: 4/9/1982																							
1982 NY-N	80	162	17	42	8	3	2	12	17	40	1	3	.259	.333	.383	.716	101	-1	20	4.33	-2	0-35(10-0-26)/1-2	4	-0.5
1983 NY-N	11	36	5	12	3	0	1	3	3	1	0	0	.333	.400	.500	.900	149	2	7	7.61	-1	1-10	2	0.1
1984 StL-N	7	7	1	1	0	0	0	2	2	1	0	0	.143	.333	.143	.476	39	-0	1	2.36	0	/1-3	0	-0.1
1985 SF-N	51	91	5	15	6	0	0	10	17	22	0	1	.165	.296	.231	.527	52	-6	7	2.45	-1	1-23	1	-0.8
Total 4	149	296	28	70	17	3	3	27	39	64	1	4	.236	.329	.345	.674	89	-5	35	3.99	-4	/1-38,0-35	7	-1.3
• RALSTON, Doc	Samuel Beryl Ralston b: 8/3/1885, Pierpont, OH d: 8/29/1950, Lancaster, PA BR/TR, 6', 185 lbs. Deb: 9/8/1910																							
1910 Was-A	21	73	4	15	1	0	0	3	3	....	2	....	.205	.256	.219	.476	52	-4	5	2.03	2	0-21(21-0-0)	1	-0.4
• RAMAZZOTTI, Bob	Robert Louis Ramazzotti b: 1/16/1917, Elanora, PA d: 2/15/2000, Altoona, PA BR/TR, 5'8.5", 175 lbs. Deb: 4/20/1946																							
1946 Bro-N	62	120	10	25	4	0	0	7	9	13	0	....	.208	.264	.242	.505	43	-9	8	2.24	0	3-30,2-16	1	-0.9
1948 Bro-N	4	3	0	0	0	0	0	0	0	1	0	....	.000	.000	.000	.000	-97	-1	0	.00	0	/3-2,2-1	0	-0.1
1949 Bro-N	5	13	1	2	0	0	1	3	0	3	0	....	.154	.154	.385	.538	38	-1	1	1.89	0	/3-3	0	-0.2
Chi-N	65	190	14	34	3	1	0	6	5	33	9	....	.179	.200	.205	.405	9	-25	6	.98	-2	3-36,S-12/2-4	1	-2.6
Yr.	70	203	15	36	3	1	1	9	5	36	9	....	.177	.197	.217	.414	11	-26	7	1.04	-2	3-39,S-12/2-4	1	-2.7
1950 Chi-N	61	145	19	38	3	3	1	6	4	16	3	....	.262	.287	.345	.631	66	-8	14	3.57	-7	2-31,3-10/S-3	2	-1.2
1951 Chi-N	73	158	13	39	5	2	1	15	10	23	0	0	.247	.292	.323	.614	64	-8	15	3.20	-3	S-51/2-6,3-1	3	-0.8
1952 Chi-N	50	183	26	52	5	3	1	12	14	14	3	1	.284	.338	.361	.699	93	-1	22	4.23	4	2-50	5	0.5
1953 Chi-N	26	39	3	6	2	0	0	4	3	4	0	0	.154	.214	.205	.419	10	-5	2	1.36	-4	2-18	0	-0.8
Total 7	346	851	86	196	22	9	4	53	45	107	15	1	.230	.271	.291	.562	52	-58	68	2.65	-12	2-126/3-82,S-66	12	-6.1
• RAMIREZ, Alex	Alexander Ramon Ramirez b: 10/3/1974, Caracas, Venezuela BR/TR, 5'11", 200 lbs. Deb: 9/19/1998 Career OF: 22-2-71																							
1998 Cle-A	3	8	1	1	0	0	0	0	0	3	0	0	.125	.125	.125	.250	-34	-2	0	.48	0	/0-3(2-0-1)	0	-0.2
1999 Cle-A	48	97	11	29	6	1	3	18	3	26	1	1	.299	.327	.474	.801	97	-1	15	5.56	0	0-30(5-1-23),D-14	2	-0.2
2000 Cle-A	41	112	13	32	5	1	5	12	5	17	1	0	.286	.316	.482	.798	96	-1	16	5.28	0	0-31(15-1-16)/D-6	1	-0.3
Pit-N	43	115	13	24	6	1	4	18	7	32	1	0	.209	.254	.383	.637	58	-8	9	2.59	0	0-31(0-0-31)/1-1	1	-0.9
Total 3	135	332	38	86	17	3	12	48	15	78	3	1	.259	.293	.437	.730	80	-12	40	4.21	-2	/0-95,D-20,1-1	4	-1.6
• RAMIREZ, Aramis	Aramis (Nin) Ramirez b: 6/25/1978, Santo Domingo, Dominican Republic BR/TR, 6'1", 219 lbs. Deb: 5/26/1998																							
1998 Pit-N	72	251	23	59	9	1	6	24	18	72	0	1	.235	.297	.351	.647	69	-12	27	3.62	-6	3-71	2	-1.7
1999 Pit-N	18	56	2	10	2	1	0	7	6	9	0	0	.179	.258	.250	.508	29	-6	4	2.33	-2	3-17	0	-0.7
2000 Pit-N	73	254	19	65	15	2	6	35	10	36	0	0	.256	.297	.402	.699	75	-11	28	3.74	-12	3-72	3	-2.0
2001 Pit-N	158	603	83	181	40	0	34	112	40	100	5	4	.300	.352	.536	.887	122	18	112	6.88	4	*3-157	27	2.3
2002 Pit-N	142	522	51	122	26	0	18	71	29	95	2	0	.234	.284	.387	.671	74	-21	54	3.42	-9	*3-131/D-3	6	-2.8
2003 Pit-N	96	375	44	105	25	1	12	67	25	68	1	1	.280	.337	.448	.785	100	-1	52	4.71	-2	3-96	9	-0.1
*Chi-N	63	232	31	60	7	1	15	39	17	31	1	1	.259	.317	.491	.809	109	2	36	5.35	-1	3-63	9	0.1
Yr.	159	607	75	165	32	2	27	106	42	99	2	2	.272	.329	.465	.794	104	1	87	4.95	-3	*3-159	18	0.0
Total 6	622	2293	253	602	124	6	91	355	145	411	9	7	.263	.316	.441	.757	93	-32	312	4.70	-27	3-607/D-3	56	-4.9
• RAMIREZ, Julio	Julio Cesar (Figueroa) Ramirez b: 8/10/1977, San Juan de la Maguana, Dominican Republic BR/TR, 5'11", 170 lbs. Deb: 9/10/1999 Career OF: 1-50-11																							
1999 Fla-N	15	21	3	3	1	0	0	2	1	6	0	1	.143	.182	.190	.372	-6	-4	1	.83	-1	0-11(0-11-0)	0	-0.4
2001 Chi-A	22	37	2	3	0	0	0	1	2	15	2	0	.081	.128	.081	.209	-42	-7	1	.46	3	0-21(1-21-0)	1	-0.4
2002 Ana-A	29	32	6	9	0	1	1	7	2	14	0	2	.281	.343	.438	.780	106	-1	4	4.56	1	0-23(0-15-9)/D-1	1	0.0
2003 Ana-A	6	2	1	0	0	0	0	0	0	0	0	0	.000	.000	.000	.000	-104	-1	0	.00	-0	/0-5(0-3-2),D-1	0	-0.1
Total 4	72	92	12	15	1	1	1	10	5	35	2	3	.163	.214	.228	.443	16	-12	5	1.80	3	/0-60,D-2	2	-0.9
• RAMIREZ, Manny	Manuel Aristides (Onelcida) Ramirez b: 5/30/1972, Santo Domingo, Dominican Republic BR/TR, 6', 190 lbs. Deb: 9/2/1993 Career OF: 247-0-905																							
1993 Cle-A	22	53	5	9	1	0	2	5	2	8	0	0	.170	.200	.302	.502	33	-5	2	1.38	0	D-20/0-1	0	-0.6
1994 Cle-A	91	290	51	78	22	0	17	60	42	72	4	2	.269	.361	.521	.882	124	10	55	6.63	1	0-84(0-0-84)/D-5	11	0.6
1995*Cle-A★	137	484	85	149	26	1	31	107	75	112	6	6	.308	.406	.558	.964	146	33	109	8.14	-2	*0-131(0-0-131)/D-5	25	2.2
1996*Cle-A	152	550	94	170	45	3	33	112	85	104	8	5	.309	.404	.582	.986	146	39	127	8.32	8	*0-149(0-0-149)/D-3	23	3.5
1997*Cle-A	150	561	99	184	40	0	26	88	79	115	2	3	.328	.417	.538	.956	142	37	124	8.33	-3	*0-146(0-0-146)/D-4	21	2.4
1998*Cle-A★	150	571	108	168	35	2	45	145	76	121	5	3	.294	.383	.599	.982	145	38	128	7.94	-3	*0-148(0-0-148)/D-2	25	2.5
1999*Cle-A★	147	522	131	174	34	3	44	**165**	96	131	2	4	.333	.448	**.663**	**1.111**	**171**	**59**	158	**11.41**	2	*0-146(0-0-146)/D-2	**35**	4.9
2000 Cle-A★	118	439	92	154	34	2	38	122	86	117	1	1	.351	.460	**.697**	**1.157**	184	59	144	**13.03**	-5	0-93(0-0-93),D-25	27	4.3
2001 Bos-A★	142	529	93	162	33	2	41	125	81	147	0	1	.306	.406	.609	1.015	161	48	132	9.41	-3	D-87,0-55(55-0-0)	25	3.5
2002 Bos-A★	120	436	84	152	31	0	33	107	73	85	0	0	**.349**	**.451**	.647	1.097	183	56	127	11.54	0	0-68(64-0-7),D-50	29	4.7
2003*Bos-A★	154	569	117	185	36	1	37	104	97	94	3	1	.325	**.430**	.587	1.017	161	55	141	9.23	-2	*0-128(128-0-0),D-26	27	4.4
Total 11	1383	5004	959	1585	337	14	347	1140	792	1106	31	26	.317	.416	.598	1.014	156	426	1247	9.25	-6	*0-1149,D-229	248	32.6
• RAMIREZ, Mario	Mario (Torres) Ramirez b: 9/12/1957, Yauco, Puerto Rico BR/TR, 5'9", 159 lbs. Deb: 4/25/1980																							
1980 NY-N	18	24	2	5	0	0	0	0	1	7	0	0	.208	.240	.208	.448	27	-2	1	1.43	0	/S-7,2-4,3-3	0	-0.2
1981 SD-N	13	13	1	1	0	0	0	1	2	5	0	0	.077	.200	.077	.277	-21	-2	0	.57	1	/3-2,S-2	0	-0.1
1982 SD-N	13	23	1	4	1	0	0	1	2	4	0	0	.174	.240	.217	.457	30	-2	1	1.88	0	/S-8,2-1,3-1	0	-0.1
1983 SD-N	55	107	11	21	6	3	0	12	20	23	0	0	.196	.328	.308	.637	80	-2	12	3.60	2	S-38/3-1	3	0.3
1984*SD-N	48	59	12	7	1	0	2	9	13	14	0	0	.119	.278	.237	.515	46	-4	4	2.14	0	S-33/3-6,2-2	1	-0.2
1985 SD-N	37	60	6	17	0	0	2	5	3	11	0	0	.283	.317	.383	.701	97	-1	8	4.74	-3	S-27/2-7	2	-0.2
Total 6	184	286	33	55	8	3	4	28	41	64	0	0	.192	.296	.283	.579	63	-13	27	2.99	0	S-115/2-14,3-13	6	-0.6
• RAMIREZ, Milt	Milton (Barboza) Ramirez b: 4/2/1950, Mayaguez, Puerto Rico BR/TR, 5'9", 150 lbs. Deb: 4/11/1970																							
1970 StL-N	62	79	8	15	2	1	0	3	8	9	0	1	.190	.264	.241	.505	35	-8	4	1.69	0	S-59/3-1	2	-0.5
1971 StL-N	4	11	2	3	0	0	0	0	2	1	0	0	.273	.385	.273	.657	86	-0	1	4.57	-1	/S-4	0	-0.1
1979 Oak-A	28	62	4	10	1	1	0	3	3	8	0	0	.161	.200	.210	.410	11	-8	3	1.30	-3	3-12,2-11/S-8	0	-0.9
Total 3	94	152	14	28	3	2	0	6	13	18	0	1	.184	.248	.230	.479	30	-15	8	1.70	-4	/S-71,3-13,2-11	2	-1.5
• RAMIREZ, Orlando	Orlando (Leal) Ramirez b: 12/18/1951, Cartagena, Colombia BR/TR, 5'10", 175 lbs. Deb: 7/6/1974																							
1974 Cal-A	31	86	4	14	0	0	0	7	6	23	2	1	.163	.217	.163	.380	11	-10	4	1.22	2	S-31	1	-0.5
1975 Cal-A	44	100	10	24	4	1	0	4	11	22	9	6	.240	.315	.300	.615	80	-3	9	2.89	-6	S-40	2	-0.5
1976 Cal-A	30	70	3	14	1	0	0	5	6	11	3	2	.200	.263	.214	.477	44	-5	4	1.69	-1	S-30	1	-0.3
1977 Cal-A	25	13	6	1	0	0	0	0	0	3	1	0	.077	.077	.077	.154	-60	-3	0	.26	0	/2-5,S-3,D-1	0	-0.2
1979 Cal-A	13	12	1	0	0	0	0	0	1	6	1	0	.000	.143	.000	.143	-60	-2	0	.43	-1	S-10/D-1	0	-0.2
Total 5	143	281	24	53	5	1	0	16	24	65	16	9	.189	.255	.214	.468	38	-23	17	1.82	-6	S-114/2-5,D-2	4	-1.8
• RAMIREZ, Rafael	Rafael Emilio (Peguero) Ramirez b: 2/18/1958, San Pedro de Macoris, Dominican Republic BR/TR, 6', 185 lbs. Deb: 8/4/1980																							
1980 Atl-N	50	165	17	44	6	1	2	11	2	33	2	1	.267	.292	.352	.644	76	-6	17	3.57	-3	S-46	4	-0.4
1981 Atl-N	95	307	30	67	16	2	2	20	24	47	7	3	.218	.277	.303	.580	63	-15	27	2.85	-3	S-95	5	-0.9
1982*Atl-N	157	609	74	169	24	4	10	52	36	49	27	14	.278	.321	.379	.700	91	-8	73	4.05	12	*S-157	21	2.1
1983 Atl-N	152	622	82	185	13	5	7	58	36	48	16	12	.297	.338	.368	.706	89	-11	76	4.42	0	*S-152	18	0.5
1984 Atl-N★	145	591	51	157	22	4	2	48	26	70	14	17	.266	.298	.327	.624	70	-29	53	3.06	-14	*S-145	8	-2.9
1985 Atl-N	138	568	54	141	25	4	5	58	20	63	2	6	.248	.274	.333	.607	65	-31	45	2.62	-5	*S-133	6	-2.3
1986 Atl-N	134	496	57	119	21	1	8	33	21	60	19	8	.240	.275	.335	.610	64	-25	42	2.76	-4	S-86,3-57/0-3(2-0-1)	6	-2.3
1987 Atl-N	56	179	22	47	12	0	1	21	8	16	6	3	.263	.302	.346	.648	68	-9	18	3.49	-2	S-38,3-12	3	-0.8
1988 Hou-N	155	566	51	156	30	5	6	59	18	61	3	2	.276	.302	.378	.680	98	-5	60	3.69	-9	*S-154	18	-0.2
1989 Hou-N	151	537	46	132	20	2	6	54	29	64	3	1	.246	.284	.324	.608	76	-18	49	3.16	-25	*S-149	9	-3.4
1990 Hou-N	132	445	44	116	19	3	2	37	24	46	10	5	.261	.300	.330	.630	75	-16	43	3.27	-4	*S-129	11	-1.1
1991 Hou-N	101	233	17	55	10	0	1	20	13	40	3	3	.236	.276	.292	.568	64	-12	18	2.67	-5	S-45,2-27/3-2	1	-1.5
1992 Hou-N	73	176	17	44	6	0	1	13	7	24	0	0	.250	.283	.301	.584	68	-8	14	2.75	0	S-57/3-1	3	-0.5
Total 13	1539	5494	562	1432	224	31	53	484	264	621	112	75	.261	.297	.342	.639	77	-193	536	3.32	-63	*S-1386/3-72,2-27,0-3	113	-13.6

YEAR TM-L	G	AB	R	H	2B	3B	HR	RBI	BB	SO	SB	CS	AVG	OBP	SLG	OPS	OPS+	BR/A	RC	RC/G	FR	G/POS	WS	TPW
• RAMOS, Bobby	Roberto Ramos b: 11/5/1955, Calabazar de Sagua, Cuba BR/TR, 5'11", 208 lbs. Deb: 9/26/1978 C																							
1978 Mon-N	2	4	0	0	0	0	0	0	0	1	0	0	.000	.000	.000	.000	-101	-1	0	.00	0	/C-1	0	-0.1
1980 Mon-N	13	32	5	5	2	0	0	2	5	5	0	0	.156	.270	.219	.489	38	-3	2	1.95	-0	C-12	1	-0.2
1981 Mon-N	26	41	4	8	1	0	1	3	3	5	0	0	.195	.250	.293	.543	53	-3	3	2.02	0	C-23	1	-0.3
1982 NY-A	4	11	1	1	0	0	1	2	0	3	0	0	.091	.091	.364	.455	18	-1	0	.98	0	/C-4	0	-0.1
1983 Mon-N	27	61	2	14	3	1	0	5	8	11	0	0	.230	.329	.311	.640	79	-2	7	3.98	1	C-25	2	0.0
1984 Mon-N	31	83	8	16	1	0	2	5	6	13	0	0	.193	.247	.277	.524	49	-6	5	1.73	1	C-31	2	-0.3
Total 6	**103**	**232**	**20**	**44**	**7**	**1**	**4**	**17**	**22**	**38**	**0**	**0**	**.190**	**.263**	**.280**	**.543**	**53**	**-15**	**17**	**2.26**	**2**	**/C-96**	**6**	**-1.0**
• RAMOS, Chucho	Jesus Manuel (Garcia) Ramos b: 4/12/1918, Maturin, Venezuela d: 9/2/1977, Caracas, Venezuela BR/TL, 5'10.5", 167 lbs. Deb: 5/7/1944																							
1944 Cin-N	4	10	1	5	1	0	0	0	0	0	0	....	.500	.500	.600	1.100	217	1	3	16.20	-0	/O-3(1-0-3)	1	0.1
• RAMOS, Domingo	Domingo Antonio (De Ramos) Ramos b: 3/29/1958, Santiago, Dominican Republic BR/TR, 5'10", 155 lbs. Deb: 9/8/1978																							
1978 NY-A	1	0	0	0	0	0	0	0	0	0	0	0	....	....	....	....	-102	0	0	....	-1	/S-1	0	-0.1
1980 Tor-A	5	16	0	2	0	0	0	0	2	5	0	0	.125	.222	.125	.347	-2	-2	1	1.08	1	/2-2,S-2,D-1	0	-0.1
1982 Sea-A	8	26	3	4	2	0	0	1	3	2	0	0	.154	.241	.231	.472	30	-2	2	2.00	-1	/S-8	0	-0.3
1983 Sea-A	53	127	14	36	4	0	2	10	7	12	3	1	.283	.326	.362	.688	86	-2	14	4.00	-3	S-28/2-8,3-8,D-2	3	-0.2
1984 Sea-A	59	81	6	15	2	0	0	2	5	12	2	2	.185	.233	.210	.442	24	-9	3	1.18	-5	3-38,S-13/1-5,2-3	1	-1.3
1985 Sea-A	75	168	19	33	6	0	1	15	17	23	0	1	.196	.270	.250	.520	43	-13	12	2.16	-4	S-36,2-20,1-14/3-7	1	-1.5
1986 Sea-A	49	99	8	18	2	0	0	5	8	13	0	1	.182	.250	.202	.452	25	-11	4	1.20	-1	S-21,2-16/3-8,D-2	1	-1.0
1987 Sea-A	42	103	9	32	6	0	2	11	3	12	0	1	.311	.336	.427	.764	96	-1	14	5.17	0	S-25/3-7,2-6,D-2	3	0.1
1988 Cle-A	22	46	7	12	1	0	0	5	3	7	0	0	.261	.320	.283	.603	68	-2	5	3.48	2	2-11/1-5,S-4,3-2	1	0.0
Cal-A	10	15	3	2	0	0	0	0	0	0	0	0	.133	.133	.133	.267	-26	-3	0	.00	-1	/3-8,O-1	0	-0.3
Yr.	32	61	10	14	1	0	0	5	3	7	0	0	.230	.277	.246	.523	47	-4	5	2.46	1	2-11,3-10/1-5,S-4,O-1	1	-0.3
1989*Chi-N	85	179	18	47	6	2	1	19	17	23	1	1	.263	.333	.335	.669	85	-3	18	3.30	1	S-42,3-30	6	0.1
1990 Chi-N	98	226	22	60	5	0	2	17	27	29	0	2	.265	.346	.314	.661	77	-7	25	3.69	-11	3-66,S-21/2-1	3	-1.6
Total 11	**507**	**1086**	**109**	**261**	**34**	**2**	**8**	**85**	**92**	**138**	**6**	**9**	**.240**	**.304**	**.297**	**.601**	**63**	**-56**	**97**	**2.93**	**-22**	**S-201,3-174/2-67,1-24,D-7,O**	**19**	**-6.2**
• RAMOS, John	John Joseph Ramos b: 8/6/1965, Tampa, FL BR/TR, 6', 190 lbs. Deb: 9/18/1991																							
1991 NY-A	10	26	4	8	1	0	0	3	1	3	0	0	.308	.333	.346	.679	88	-0	3	3.65	0	/C-5,D-4	0	0.0
• RAMOS, Ken	Kenneth Cecil Ramos b: 6/6/1967, Sidney, NE BL/TL, 6'1", 185 lbs. Deb: 5/16/1997																							
1997 Hou-N	14	12	0	0	0	0	0	1	2	0	0	0	.000	.143	.000	.143	-61	-3	0	.13	0	/O-2(1-0-1)	0	-0.3
• RAMSEY, Bill	William Thrace "Square Jaw" Ramsey b: 2/20/1920, Osceola, AR BR/TR, 6', 175 lbs. Deb: 4/19/1945																							
1945 Bos-N	78	137	16	40	8	0	1	12	4	22	1	....	.292	.326	.372	.699	93	-2	16	4.33	-2	O-43(30-13-0)	2	-0.5
• RAMSEY, Fernando	Fernando David (Ramsey) Ramsey b: 12/20/1965, Rainbow, Panama BR/TR, 6'1", 175 lbs. Deb: 9/7/1992																							
1992 Chi-N	18	25	0	3	0	0	0	2	0	6	0	0	.120	.120	.120	.240	-31	-4	0	.44	-1	O-15(0-15-0)	0	-0.6
• RAMSEY, Mike	Michael Jeffrey Ramsey b: 3/29/1954, Roanoke, VA BB/TR, 6'1", 170 lbs. Deb: 9/4/1978 Career OF: 4-0-0																							
1978 StL-N	12	5	4	1	0	0	0	0	0	1	0	0	.200	.200	.200	.400	12	-1	0	1.35	0	/S-4	0	0.0
1980 StL-N	59	126	11	33	8	1	0	8	3	17	0	0	.262	.279	.341	.620	70	-5	11	3.24	-2	2-24,S-20/3-8	2	-0.6
1981 StL-N	47	124	19	32	3	0	0	9	8	16	4	0	.258	.303	.282	.585	65	-5	10	2.75	6	S-35/3-5,2-1,O-1	2	0.4
1982*StL-N	112	256	18	59	8	2	1	21	22	34	6	5	.230	.294	.289	.583	63	-13	21	2.61	-1	2-43,3-28,S-22/O-2(2-0-0)	4	-1.1
1983 StL-N	97	175	25	46	4	3	1	16	12	23	4	2	.263	.314	.337	.651	80	-5	18	3.54	-2	2-66,S-20/3-8,O-1	4	-0.5
1984 StL-N	21	15	1	1	1	0	0	0	1	3	0	0	.067	.125	.133	.258	-28	-3	0	.62	0	/2-7,S-7,3-1	0	-0.3
Mon-N	37	70	2	15	1	0	0	3	0	13	0	0	.214	.214	.229	.443	26	-7	3	1.41	-1	S-26,2-12	1	-0.6
Yr.	58	85	3	16	2	0	0	3	1	16	0	0	.188	.198	.212	.409	15	-10	3	1.23	-1	S-33,2-19/3-1	1	-0.9
1985 LA-N	9	15	1	2	1	0	0	0	2	4	0	0	.133	.235	.200	.435	24	-2	1	1.72	-1	/S-4,2-2	0	-0.2
Total 7	**394**	**786**	**81**	**189**	**26**	**6**	**2**	**57**	**48**	**111**	**14**	**7**	**.240**	**.286**	**.296**	**.582**	**62**	**-40**	**65**	**2.74**	**-2**	**2-155,S-138/3-50,O-4**	**13**	**-2.8**
• RAMSEY, Mike	Michael James Ramsey b: 7/8/1960, Thomson, GA BB/TL, 6', 170 lbs. Deb: 4/6/1987																							
1987 LA-N	48	125	18	29	4	2	0	12	10	32	2	4	.232	.289	.296	.585	57	-9	10	2.49	-3	O-43(4-38-1)	1	-1.3
• RAND, Dick	Richard Hilton Rand b: 3/7/1931, South Gate, CA d: 1/22/1996, Moreno Valley, CA BR/TR, 6'2", 185 lbs. Deb: 9/16/1953																							
1953 StL-N	9	31	3	9	1	0	0	1	2	6	0	0	.290	.333	.323	.656	72	-1	4	4.29	2	/C-9	1	0.1
1955 StL-N	3	10	1	3	0	0	1	3	1	1	0	1	.300	.364	.600	.964	150	0	2	5.76	0	/C-3	0	0.0
1957 Pit-N	60	105	7	23	2	1	1	9	11	24	0	0	.219	.293	.286	.579	58	-6	10	3.05	-1	C-57	2	-0.5
Total 3	**72**	**146**	**11**	**35**	**3**	**1**	**2**	**13**	**14**	**31**	**0**	**1**	**.240**	**.306**	**.315**	**.621**	**67**	**-7**	**15**	**3.47**	**1**	**/C-69**	**3**	**-0.3**
• RANDA, Joe	Joseph Gregory "The Joker" Randa b: 12/18/1969, Milwaukee, WI BR/TR, 5'11", 190 lbs. Deb: 4/30/1995																							
1995 KC-A	34	70	6	12	2	0	1	5	6	17	0	1	.171	.237	.243	.480	25	-8	4	1.62	-1	3-22/2-9,D-2	1	-0.8
1996 KC-A	110	337	36	102	24	1	6	47	26	47	13	4	.303	.354	.433	.788	98	-0	50	5.33	-5	3-92,2-15/1-7,D-1	9	-0.4
1997 Pit-N	126	443	58	134	27	9	7	60	41	64	4	2	.302	.369	.451	.821	112	8	74	6.06	3	*3-120,2-13	16	1.3
1998 Det-A	138	460	56	117	21	2	9	50	41	70	8	7	.254	.325	.367	.692	79	-15	55	4.04	5	*3-118,2-20/1-1,D-1	9	-0.8
1999 KC-A	156	628	92	197	36	8	16	84	50	80	5	4	.314	.367	.473	.840	110	8	106	6.26	11	*3-156	17	2.0
2000 KC-A	158	612	88	186	29	4	15	106	36	66	6	3	.304	.349	.438	.787	94	-6	89	5.23	-1	*3-156/D-1	18	-0.5
2001 KC-A	151	581	59	147	34	2	13	83	42	80	3	2	.253	.310	.386	.696	75	-22	67	3.98	-7	*3-137,D-14/2-1	11	-2.7
2002 KC-A	151	549	63	155	36	5	11	80	46	69	2	1	.282	.348	.426	.774	93	-5	81	5.21	-5	*3-129,D-19	10	-0.8
2003 KC-A	131	502	80	146	31	1	16	72	41	61	1	0	.291	.353	.452	.805	97	-1	80	5.61	1	*3-129/D-2	14	0.2
Total 9	**1155**	**4182**	**538**	**1196**	**240**	**32**	**94**	**587**	**329**	**554**	**42**	**24**	**.286**	**.345**	**.426**	**.771**	**94**	**-42**	**606**	**5.13**	**2**	***3-1059/2-58,D-40,1-8**	**105**	**-2.5**
• RANDALL, Bob	Robert Lee Randall b: 6/6/1948, Norton, KS BR/TR, 6'2", 180 lbs. Deb: 4/13/1976 C																							
1976 Min-A	153	475	55	127	18	4	1	34	28	38	3	5	.267	.319	.328	.647	87	-9	51	3.62	0	*2-153	12	0.0
1977 Min-A	103	306	36	73	13	2	0	22	15	25	1	4	.239	.290	.294	.584	60	-18	27	2.83	1	*2-101/1-1,3-1,D-1	5	-1.2
1978 Min-A	119	330	36	89	11	3	0	21	24	22	5	3	.270	.331	.321	.652	82	-7	36	3.66	5	*2-116/3-2,D-1	9	0.3
1979 Min-A	80	199	25	49	7	0	0	14	15	17	2	2	.246	.299	.281	.580	55	-13	18	2.89	0	2-71/3-7,O-1,S-1	3	-1.0
1980 Min-A	5	15	2	3	1	0	0	0	1	0	0	0	.200	.250	.267	.517	39	-1	1	1.66	-0	/3-4,2-1	0	-0.1
Total 5	**460**	**1325**	**154**	**341**	**50**	**9**	**1**	**91**	**83**	**102**	**11**	**14**	**.257**	**.311**	**.311**	**.622**	**75**	**-48**	**132**	**3.31**	**5**	**2-442/3-14,D-2,1-1,O-1,S-1**	**29**	**-2.0**
• RANDALL, Newt	Newton J. Randall b: 2/3/1880, New Lowell, Canada d: 5/3/1955, Duluth, MN BR/TR, 5'10" Deb: 4/18/1907																							
1907 Chi-N	22	78	6	16	4	2	0	4	8	....	2	....	.205	.279	.308	.587	79	-2	8	3.12	1	O-21(1-1-21)	2	-0.2
Bos-N	75	258	16	55	6	3	0	15	19	....	4	....	.213	.285	.260	.545	71	-8	21	2.66	-7	O-73(59-3-12)	3	-2.2
Yr.	97	336	22	71	10	5	0	19	27	....	6	....	.211	.284	.271	.555	73	-10	28	2.77	-5	O-94(60-4-33)	5	-2.4
• RANDALL, Sap	James Odell Randall b: 8/19/1960, Mobile, AL BB/TR, 5'11", 195 lbs. Deb: 8/2/1988																							
1988 Chi-A	4	12	1	0	0	0	0	1	2	3	0	0	.000	.143	.000	.143	-57	-3	0	.29	0	/1-2,D-1,O-1	0	-0.2
• RANDLE, Len	Leonard Shenoff Randle b: 2/12/1949, Long Beach, CA BB/TR, 5'10", 169 lbs. Deb: 6/16/1971 Career OF: 62-85-6																							
1971 Was-A	75	215	27	47	11	0	2	13	24	56	1	1	.219	.300	.298	.598	74	-7	21	3.06	1	2-66	5	-0.2
1972 Tex-A	74	249	23	48	13	0	2	21	13	51	4	5	.193	.236	.269	.505	52	-17	14	1.69	-6	2-65/S-4,O-2(0-2-0)	1	-2.1
1973 Tex-A	10	29	3	6	1	1	1	1	0	2	0	2	.207	.207	.414	.621	74	-2	2	1.73	-2	/2-5,O-2(0-2-0)	0	-0.4
1974 Tex-A	151	520	65	157	17	4	1	49	29	43	26	17	.302	.341	.356	.697	103	0	61	4.00	-2	3-89,2-40,O-21(13-5-3)/D-2,S	16	0.0
1975 Tex-A	156	601	85	166	24	7	4	57	57	80	16	19	.276	.343	.359	.702	99	-4	73	4.14	2	2-79,O-66(7-61-0),3-17/D-3,C,S	17	0.1
1976 Tex-A	142	539	53	121	11	6	1	51	46	63	30	15	.224	.288	.273	.561	63	-24	45	2.73	-5	*2-113,O-30(28-1-1)/3-2,D	8	-2.5
1977 NY-N	136	513	78	156	22	7	5	27	65	70	33	21	.304	.384	.404	.788	117	13	78	5.28	13	*3-110,2-20/O-6(4-4-0),S-1	18	2.6
1978 NY-N	132	437	53	102	16	8	2	35	64	57	14	11	.233	.333	.320	.653	86	-8	49	3.65	-5	*3-124/2-5	10	-1.5
1979 NY-A	20	39	2	7	0	0	0	3	3	2	0	0	.179	.238	.179	.418	15	-5	2	1.36	1	O-11(4-7-0)/D-2	0	-0.4
1980 Chi-N	130	489	67	135	19	6	5	39	50	55	19	13	.276	.344	.370	.715	93	-5	61	4.21	-8	*3-111,2-17/O-6(4-2-0)	10	-1.5
1981 Sea-A	82	273	22	63	9	1	4	25	17	22	11	6	.231	.278	.315	.593	68	-12	24	2.90	4	3-59,2-21/O-5(2-1-2),S-3	4	-0.8

YEAR TM-L	G	AB	R	H	2B	3B	HR	RBI	BB	SO	SB	CS	AVG	OBP	SLG	OPS	OPS+	BR/A	RC	RC/G	FR	G/POS	WS	TPW
1982 Sea-A	30	46	10	8	2	0	0	1	4	4	2	2	.174	.240	.217	.457	26	-5	2	1.43	-1	D-13/3-9,2-6	0	-0.6
Total 12	1138	3950	488	1016	145	40	27	322	372	505	156	112	.257	.323	.335	.658	87	-76	430	3.62	-9	3-521,2-437,0-149/D-21,S-10,C	89	-7.3
• RANDOLPH, Willie	Willie Larry Randolph b: 7/6/1954, Holly Hill, SC BR/TR, 5'11", 166 lbs. Deb: 7/29/1975 C																							
1975*Pit-N	30	61	9	10	1	0	0	3	7	6	1	0	.164	.250	.180	.430	21	-6	3	1.36	1	2-14/3-1	1	-0.5
1976*NY-A★	125	430	59	115	15	4	1	40	58	39	37	12	.267	.358	.328	.686	103	7	55	4.31	24	*2-124	17	4.2
1977*NY-A★	147	551	91	151	28	11	4	40	64	53	13	6	.274	.351	.387	.737	102	4	77	4.87	24	*2-147	20	3.5
1978 NY-A	134	499	87	139	18	6	3	42	82	51	36	7	.279	.385	.357	.741	112	18	78	5.37	13	*2-134	23	3.9
1979 NY-A	153	574	98	155	15	13	5	61	95	39	33	12	.270	.376	.368	.744	104	10	82	4.79	-4	*2-153	23	1.4
1980*NY-A★	138	513	99	151	23	7	7	46	**119**	45	30	5	.294	.429	.407	.836	133	36	105	7.47	-8	*2-138	31	3.6
1981*NY-A★	93	357	59	83	14	3	2	24	57	24	14	5	.232	.338	.305	.643	88	-2	40	3.64	3	2-93	9	0.7
1982 NY-A	144	553	85	155	21	4	3	36	75	35	16	9	.280	.369	.349	.718	100	3	75	4.66	3	*2-142/D-1	19	1.4
1983 NY-A	104	420	73	117	21	1	2	38	53	32	12	4	.279	.361	.348	.708	100	3	55	4.62	5	*2-104	15	1.3
1984 NY-A	142	564	86	162	24	2	2	31	86	42	10	6	.287	.382	.348	.729	108	10	79	4.85	3	*2-142	21	2.2
1985 NY-A	143	497	75	137	21	2	5	40	85	39	16	9	.276	.386	.356	.742	107	9	69	4.61	21	*2-143	20	3.8
1986 NY-A	141	492	76	136	15	2	5	50	94	49	15	2	.276	.396	.346	.741	105	12	77	5.43	0	*2-139/D-1	18	1.9
1987 NY-A★	120	449	96	137	24	2	7	67	82	25	11	1	.305	.415	.414	.829	122	21	82	6.59	6	*2-119/D-1	22	3.2
1988 NY-A	110	404	43	93	20	1	2	34	55	39	8	4	.230	.325	.300	.625	77	-11	42	3.35	16	*2-110	13	0.8
1989 LA-N★	145	549	62	155	18	0	2	36	71	51	7	6	.282	.369	.326	.695	102	3	70	4.49	1	*2-140	20	0.9
1990 LA-N	26	96	15	26	4	0	1	9	13	9	1	0	.271	.364	.344	.707	98	0	13	4.50	-1	2-26	3	0.0
*Oak-A	93	292	37	75	9	3	1	21	32	25	6	1	.257	.332	.318	.651	86	-4	31	3.57	16	2-84/D-6	8	1.5
1991 Mil-A	124	431	60	141	14	3	0	54	75	38	4	2	.327	.427	.374	.800	127	21	72	6.25	18	*2-121/D-2	22	4.2
1992 NY-N	90	286	29	72	11	1	2	15	40	34	1	3	.252	.352	.318	.670	92	-2	34	3.97	-2	2-79	7	-0.3
Total 18	2202	8018	1239	2210	316	65	54	687	1243	675	271	94	.276	.375	.351	.727	105	134	1138	4.89	140	*2-2152/D-11,3-1	312	37.9
• RANEW, Merritt	Merritt Thomas Ranew b: 5/10/1938, Albany, GA BL/TR, 5'11", 180 lbs. Deb: 4/13/1962																							
1962 Hou-N	71	218	26	51	6	8	4	24	14	43	2	2	.234	.289	.390	.679	87	-5	24	3.77	-2	C-58	5	-0.4
1963 Chi-N	78	154	18	52	8	1	3	15	9	32	1	0	.338	.382	.461	.843	134	7	27	6.87	0	C-37/1-9	7	0.9
1964 Chi-N	16	33	0	3	0	0	0	1	2	6	0	0	.091	.167	.091	.258	-24	-5	1	.46	0	/C-9	0	-0.5
Mil-N	9	17	1	2	0	0	0	0	0	3	0	1	.118	.118	.118	.235	-33	-3	0	.20	0	/C-3	0	-0.3
Yr.	25	50	1	5	0	0	0	1	2	9	0	1	.100	.151	.100	.251	-27	-9	1	.37	1	C-12	0	-0.8
1965 Cal-A	41	91	12	19	4	0	1	10	7	22	0	0	.209	.265	.286	.551	58	-5	7	2.30	0	C-24	1	-0.5
1969 Sea-A	54	81	11	20	2	0	0	4	10	14	0	0	.247	.330	.272	.601	71	-3	7	2.81	-1	C-13/0-3(3-0-0),3-1	1	-0.3
Total 5	269	594	68	147	20	9	8	54	42	120	3	3	.247	.304	.352	.656	83	-15	66	3.75	-2	C-144/1-9,0-3,3-1	14	-1.2
• RANSOM, Cody	Bryan Cody Ransom b: 2/17/1976, Mesa, AZ BR/TR, 6'2", 190 lbs. Deb: 9/5/2001																							
2001 SF-N	9	7	1	0	0	0	0	0	0	5	0	0	.000	.000	.000	.000	-108	-2	0	.00	0	/S-6	0	-0.2
2002 SF-N	7	3	2	2	0	0	0	1	1	1	0	0	.667	.750	.667	1.417	290	1	2	40.50	0	/S-3	0	0.1
2003 SF-N	20	27	7	6	1	0	1	1	1	11	0	0	.222	.250	.370	.620	61	-2	3	3.30	-1	S-12	0	-0.2
Total 3	36	37	10	8	1	0	1	2	2	17	0	0	.216	.256	.324	.581	54	-3	4	3.78	-1	/S-21	0	-0.3
• RANSOM, Jeff	Jeffrey Dean Ransom b: 11/11/1960, Fresno, CA BR/TR, 5'11", 185 lbs. Deb: 9/5/1981																							
1981 SF-N	5	15	2	4	1	0	0	0	1	1	0	0	.267	.313	.333	.646	85	-0	1	2.81	1	/C-5	0	0.1
1982 SF-N	15	44	5	7	0	0	0	3	6	7	0	0	.159	.260	.159	.419	20	-5	2	1.17	1	C-14	1	-0.3
1983 SF-N	6	20	3	4	0	0	1	3	4	7	0	0	.200	.333	.350	.683	92	-0	2	3.72	-1	/C-6	0	0.0
Total 3	26	79	10	15	1	0	1	6	11	15	0	0	.190	.289	.241	.529	50	-5	5	2.07	1	/C-25	1	-0.3
• RAPP, Earl	Earl Wellington Rapp b: 5/20/1921, Corunna, MI d: 2/13/1992, Swedesboro, NJ BL/TR, 6'2", 185 lbs. Deb: 4/28/1949 Career OF: 11-0-44																							
1949 Det-A	1	0	0	0	0	0	0	0	1	0	0	0	....	1.000	....	1.000	175	0	0	∞	0	....	0	0.0
Chi-A	19	54	3	14	1	1	0	11	5	6	1	1	.259	.322	.315	.637	71	-2	6	3.56	2	0-13(11-0-2)	1	-0.1
Yr.	20	54	3	14	1	1	0	11	6	6	1	1	.259	.333	.315	.648	73	-2	6	3.56	2	0-13(11-0-2)	1	-0.1
1951 NY-N	13	11	0	1	0	0	0	1	2	3	0	0	.091	.231	.091	.322	-10	-2	0	.58	0	....	0	-0.2
StL-A	26	98	14	32	5	3	2	14	11	11	1	0	.327	.394	.500	.894	137	5	21	8.21	-0	0-25(0-0-25)	4	0.4
1952 StL-A	30	49	3	7	4	0	0	4	0	8	0	0	.143	.143	.224	.367	1	-7	1	.71	0	/0-7(0-0-7)	0	-0.7
Was-A	46	67	7	19	6	0	0	9	6	13	0	0	.284	.351	.373	.724	105	1	10	5.42	-1	0-10(0-0-10)	2	0.0
Yr.	76	116	10	26	10	0	0	13	6	21	0	0	.224	.268	.310	.579	64	-6	11	3.17	-1	0-17(0-0-17)	2	-0.8
Total 3	135	279	27	73	16	4	2	39	25	41	2	1	.262	.325	.369	.694	89	-5	38	4.72	1	/0-55	7	-0.6
• RAPP, Goldie	Joseph Aloysius Rapp b: 2/6/1894, Cincinnati, OH d: 7/1/1966, La Mesa, CA BB/TR, 5'10", 165 lbs. Deb: 4/13/1921																							
1921 NY-N	58	181	21	39	9	1	0	15	15	13	3	11	.215	.276	.276	.552	46	-17	12	1.99	7	3-56	3	-0.7
Phi-N	52	202	28	56	7	1	1	10	14	8	6	7	.277	.324	.337	.661	70	-10	21	3.55	-3	3-50/2-1	2	-1.0
Yr.	110	383	49	95	16	2	1	25	29	21	9	18	.248	.301	.308	.609	58	-27	33	2.76	4	*3-106/2-1	5	-1.6
1922 Phi-N	119	502	58	127	26	3	0	38	32	29	6	12	.253	.299	.317	.616	54	-38	46	3.03	-7	*3-117/S-2	4	-3.4
1923 Phi-N	47	179	27	47	5	0	1	10	14	14	1	1	.263	.320	.307	.627	59	-10	18	3.56	-2	3-45	2	-0.9
Total 3	276	1064	134	269	47	5	2	73	75	64	16	31	.253	.303	.312	.615	56	-75	97	3.01	-5	3-268/S-2,2-1	11	-6.0
• RARIDEN, Bill	William Angel "Bedford Bill" Rariden b: 2/4/1888, Bedford, IN d: 8/28/1942, Bedford, IN BR/TR, 5'10", 168 lbs. Deb: 8/12/1909																							
1909 Bos-N	13	42	1	6	1	0	0	1	4	....	1	....	.143	.217	.167	.384	18	-4	2	1.27	-1	C-13	0	-0.4
1910 Bos-N	49	137	15	31	5	1	1	14	12	22	1	....	.226	.293	.299	.593	70	-6	13	2.92	-1	C-49	2	-0.2
1911 Bos-N	70	246	22	56	9	0	0	21	21	18	3	....	.228	.288	.264	.553	51	-17	19	2.59	7	C-65/3-3,2-1	2	-0.4
1912 Bos-N	79	247	27	55	3	1	1	14	18	35	3	....	.223	.281	.255	.536	46	-18	19	2.39	4	C-73	2	-0.9
1913 Bos-N	95	246	31	58	9	2	3	30	30	21	5	....	.236	.324	.325	.649	84	-5	27	3.52	-2	C-87	8	0.0
1914 Ind-F	131	396	44	93	15	5	0	47	61	43	12	....	.235	.337	.298	.635	73	-12	43	3.49	9	*C-130	13	0.8
1915 New-F	142	444	49	120	30	7	0	40	60	29	8	....	.270	.361	.369	.730	122	14	60	4.70	17	*C-142	25	4.6
1916 NY-N	120	351	23	78	9	3	1	29	55	32	4	....	.222	.333	.274	.606	92	-0	34	3.19	-9	*C-119	12	0.0
1917*NY-N	101	266	20	72	10	1	0	25	42	17	3	....	.271	.372	.316	.688	116	8	32	4.14	-11	*C-100	12	0.3
1918 NY-N	69	183	15	41	5	1	0	17	15	15	1	....	.224	.283	.262	.545	68	-7	14	2.46	-5	C-63	4	-0.8
1919*Cin-N	74	218	16	47	6	3	1	24	17	19	4	....	.216	.275	.284	.560	70	-8	18	2.59	-1	C-70	6	-0.3
1920 Cin-N	39	101	9	25	3	0	0	10	5	0	2	0	.248	.283	.277	.560	62	-4	8	2.84	-1	C-37	3	-0.2
Total 12	982	2877	272	682	105	24	7	272	340	251	47	0	.237	.320	.298	.618	82	-58	289	3.29	6	C-948/3-3,2-1	89	2.4
• RATH, Morrie	Morris Charles Rath b: 12/25/1886, Mobeetie, TX d: 11/18/1945, Upper Darby, PA BL/TR, 5'8.5", 160 lbs. Deb: 9/28/1909																							
1909 Phi-A	7	26	4	7	1	0	0	3	2	....	1	....	.269	.387	.308	.695	117	1	3	4.67	2	/S-4,3-2	1	0.3
1910 Phi-A	18	26	3	4	0	0	0	1	5	....	0	....	.154	.290	.154	.444	40	-1	2	1.65	-5	3-11/2-3	0	-0.7
Cle-A	24	67	5	13	3	0	0	0	10	....	2	....	.194	.299	.239	.538	68	-2	5	2.52	-1	3-22/S-1	2	-0.3
Yr.	42	93	8	17	3	0	0	1	15	....	2	....	.183	.296	.215	.511	59	-4	7	2.25	-6	3-33/2-3,S-1	2	-0.9
1912 Chi-A	157	591	104	161	10	2	1	19	95	....	30	....	.272	.380	.301	.681	98	6	80	4.65	14	*2-157	26	2.3
1913 Chi-A	92	295	37	59	2	0	0	12	46	22	22	....	.200	.310	.207	.517	52	-15	26	2.63	0	2-86	6	-1.5
1919*Cin-N	138	537	77	142	13	1	1	29	64	24	17	....	.264	.343	.298	.641	96	0	61	3.78	29	*2-138	21	3.5
1920 Cin-N	129	506	61	135	7	4	2	28	36	24	10	11	.267	.319	.308	.628	82	-12	51	3.27	16	*2-126/3-1,0-1	14	0.7
Total 6	565	2048	291	521	36	7	4	92	258	70	82	11	.254	.342	.285	.626	85	-24	227	3.65	55	2-510/3-36,S-5,0-1	70	4.4
• RATLIFF, Gene	Kelly Eugene Ratliff b: 9/28/1945, Macon, GA BR/TR, 6'5", 185 lbs. Deb: 5/15/1965																							
1965 Hou-N	4	4	0	0	0	0	0	0	0	4	0	0	.000	.000	.000	.000	-107	-1	0	.00	0	....	0	-0.1
• RATLIFF, Paul	Paul Hawthorne Ratliff b: 1/23/1944, San Diego, CA BL/TR, 6'2", 190 lbs. Deb: 4/14/1963																							
1963 Min-A	10	21	2	4	1	0	1	3	2	7	0	0	.190	.292	.381	.673	85	-0	3	4.07	0	/C-7	1	0.0
1970*Min-A	69	149	19	40	7	2	5	22	15	51	0	0	.268	.363	.443	.806	119	4	25	6.23	-1	C-53	8	0.5
1971 Min-A	21	44	3	7	1	0	2	6	4	17	0	0	.159	.229	.318	.547	52	-3	3	2.44	1	C-15	1	-0.2
Mil-A	23	41	3	7	1	0	3	7	5	21	0	0	.171	.277	.415	.691	95	-0	5	4.02	0	C-13	1	0.0

YEAR TM-L	G	AB	R	H	2B	3B	HR	RBI	BB	SO	SB	CS	AVG	OBP	SLG	OPS	OPS+	BR/A	RC	RC/G	FR	G/POS	WS	TPW
Yr.	44	85	6	14	2	0	5	13	9	38	0	0	.165	.253	.365	.617	73	-3	8	3.19	0	C-28	2	-0.2
1972 Mil-A	22	42	1	3	0	0	1	4	2	23	0	0	.071	.114	.143	.256	-25	-6	1	.40	0	C-13	0	-0.7
Total 4	145	297	28	61	10	2	12	42	28	119	0	0	.205	.293	.374	.667	84	-6	37	4.17	0	C-101	11	-0.4

• RAUB, Tommy Thomas Jefferson Raub b: 12/1/1870, Raubsville, PA d: 2/15/1949, Phillipsburg, NJ BR/TR, 5'10", 155 lbs. Deb: 5/3/1903

YEAR TM-L	G	AB	R	H	2B	3B	HR	RBI	BB	SO	SB	CS	AVG	OBP	SLG	OPS	OPS+	BR/A	RC	RC/G	FR	G/POS	WS	TPW
1903 Chi-N	36	84	6	19	3	2	0	7	5	....	3	....	.226	.278	.310	.587	69	-4	8	3.36	-3	C-12/1-6,O-5(0-0-5),3-4	1	-0.6
1906 StL-N	24	78	9	22	2	4	0	2	4	....	2	....	.282	.325	.410	.736	135	3	11	5.26	0	C-22	3	0.5
Total 2	60	162	15	41	5	6	0	9	9	....	5	....	.253	.301	.358	.659	100	-1	20	4.22	-4	/C-34,1-6,O-5,3-4	4	-0.1

• RAUDMAN, Bob Robert Joyce "Shorty" Raudman b: 3/14/1942, Erie, PA BL/TL, 5'9.5", 185 lbs. Deb: 9/13/1966 Career OF: 8-0-8

YEAR TM-L	G	AB	R	H	2B	3B	HR	RBI	BB	SO	SB	CS	AVG	OBP	SLG	OPS	OPS+	BR/A	RC	RC/G	FR	G/POS	WS	TPW
1966 Chi-N	8	29	1	7	2	0	0	2	1	4	0	0	.241	.267	.310	.577	59	-2	2	2.54	0	/O-8(8-0-0)	0	-0.2
1967 Chi-N	8	26	0	4	0	0	0	1	1	4	0	0	.154	.185	.154	.339	-2	-3	0	.50	-0	/O-8(0-0-8)	0	-0.4
Total 2	16	55	1	11	2	0	0	3	2	8	0	0	.200	.228	.236	.464	30	-5	3	1.50	0	/O-16	0	-0.6

• RAWLINGS, Johnny John William "Red" Rawlings b: 8/17/1892, Bloomfield, IA d: 10/16/1972, Inglewood, CA BR/TR, 5'8", 158 lbs. Deb: 4/14/1914 Career OF: 8-1-23

YEAR TM-L	G	AB	R	H	2B	3B	HR	RBI	BB	SO	SB	CS	AVG	OBP	SLG	OPS	OPS+	BR/A	RC	RC/G	FR	G/POS	WS	TPW
1914 Cin-N	33	60	9	13	1	0	0	8	6	8	1	....	.217	.288	.233	.521	54	-3	5	2.37	0	3-10/2-7,S-5	1	-0.3
KC-F	61	193	19	41	3	0	0	15	22	25	6	....	.212	.296	.228	.524	53	-11	15	2.38	5	S-61	4	-0.2
1915 KC-F	120	399	40	86	9	2	2	24	27	40	17	....	.216	.269	.263	.532	58	-21	33	2.56	-14	*S-120	6	-2.9
1917 Bos-N	122	371	37	95	9	4	2	31	38	32	12	....	.256	.337	.318	.655	107	5	43	3.87	-4	2-96,S-17/3-1,O-1	14	0.4
1918 Bos-N	111	410	32	85	7	3	0	21	30	31	10	....	.207	.265	.239	.504	56	-21	29	2.18	-2	S-71,2-20,O-18(0-0-18)	5	-2.0
1919 Bos-N	77	275	30	70	8	2	1	16	16	20	10	....	.255	.298	.309	.607	86	-5	28	3.33	-11	2-58,O-10(7-1-5)/S-5	5	-1.6
1920 Bos-N	5	3	0	0	0	0	0	2	0	1	0	0	.000	.000	.000	.000	-105	-1	0	.00	0	/2-1	0	-0.1
Phi-N	98	384	39	90	19	2	3	30	22	25	9	6	.234	.278	.318	.595	67	-16	34	2.83	-8	2-97	4	-2.3
Yr.	103	387	39	90	19	2	3	32	22	26	9	6	.233	.276	.315	.591	65	-16	34	2.78	-8	2-98	4	-2.4
1921 Phi-N	60	254	20	74	14	2	1	16	8	12	4	5	.291	.318	.374	.692	76	-9	29	4.02	-1	2-60	4	-0.8
*NY-N	86	307	40	82	8	1	1	30	18	19	4	4	.267	.316	.309	.626	66	-14	31	3.36	6	2-86/S-1	6	-0.5
Yr.	146	561	60	156	22	3	2	46	26	31	8	9	.278	.317	.339	.656	71	-23	60	3.65	5	*2-146/S-1	10	-1.4
1922 NY-N	88	308	46	87	13	8	1	30	23	15	7	6	.282	.342	.386	.729	87	-6	41	4.56	3	2-77/3-5	8	-0.1
1923 Pit-N	119	461	53	131	18	4	1	45	25	29	9	0	.284	.322	.347	.669	75	-14	54	4.15	-8	*2-119	11	-1.8
1924 Pit-N	3	3	0	1	0	0	0	2	0	0	0	0	.333	.333	.333	.667	78	-0	0	4.24	0	....	0	0.0
1925 Pit-N	36	110	17	31	7	0	2	13	8	8	0	1	.282	.336	.400	.736	82	-3	15	4.78	3	2-29	3	0.0
1926 Pit-N	61	181	27	42	6	0	0	20	14	10	3	....	.232	.287	.265	.552	47	-13	15	2.45	3	2-59	2	-0.9
Total 12	1080	3719	409	928	122	28	14	303	257	275	92	22	.250	.303	.309	.611	72	-133	371	3.27	-28	2-709,S-280/O-29,3-16	73	-13.2

• RAY, Irv Irving Burton "Stubby" Ray b: 1/22/1864, Harrington, ME d: 2/21/1948, Harrington, ME BL/TR, 5'6", 165 lbs. Deb: 7/7/1888 Career OF: 0-0-70

YEAR TM-L	G	AB	R	H	2B	3B	HR	RBI	BB	SO	SB	CS	AVG	OBP	SLG	OPS	OPS+	BR/A	RC	RC/G	FR	G/POS	WS	TPW
1888 Bos-N	50	206	26	51	2	3	2	26	6	11	7	....	.248	.272	.316	.588	84	-4	20	3.50	-9	S-48/2-3	4	-1.2
1889 Bos-N	9	33	8	10	1	0	0	2	4	0	1	....	.303	.378	.333	.712	94	-0	5	5.36	-1	/S-5,3-4	1	-0.1
Bal-a	26	106	20	36	4	1	0	17	7	6	12	....	.340	.397	.396	.793	129	4	22	8.31	-8	S-20/O-6(0-0-6)	4	-0.2
1890 Bal-a	38	139	28	50	6	2	1	20	15	....	11	....	.360	.433	.453	.886	147	8	33	9.78	-8	S-38	6	0.1
1891 Bal-a	103	418	72	116	17	5	0	58	54	18	28	....	.278	.366	.342	.708	101	2	64	5.62	-13	O-64(0-0-64),S-40	12	-1.0
Total 4	226	902	154	263	30	11	3	123	86	35	59	....	.292	.360	.359	.720	108	10	144	5.97	-39	S-151/O-70,3-4,2-3	27	-2.4

• RAY, Johnny John Cornelius Ray b: 3/1/1957, Chouteau, OK BB/TR, 5'11", 185 lbs. Deb: 9/2/1981

YEAR TM-L	G	AB	R	H	2B	3B	HR	RBI	BB	SO	SB	CS	AVG	OBP	SLG	OPS	OPS+	BR/A	RC	RC/G	FR	G/POS	WS	TPW
1981 Pit-N	31	102	10	25	11	0	0	6	6	9	0	0	.245	.287	.353	.640	78	-3	10	3.22	4	2-31	2	0.3
1982 Pit-N	162	647	79	182	30	7	7	63	36	34	16	7	.281	.320	.382	.702	93	-7	80	4.32	4	*2-162	19	0.6
1983 Pit-N	151	576	68	163	**38**	7	5	53	35	26	18	9	.283	.324	.399	.723	97	-4	73	4.40	18	*2-151	20	2.3
1984 Pit-N	155	555	75	173	**38**	6	6	67	37	31	11	6	.312	.358	.434	.792	122	14	83	5.41	-5	*2-149	20	1.8
1985 Pit-N	154	594	67	163	33	3	7	70	46	24	13	9	.274	.328	.375	.703	97	-5	71	4.17	-19	*2-151	11	-1.7
1986 Pit-N	155	579	67	174	33	0	7	78	58	47	6	9	.301	.367	.394	.761	107	4	79	4.79	-2	*2-151	18	1.1
1987 Pit-N	123	472	48	129	19	3	5	54	41	36	4	2	.273	.331	.358	.689	82	-12	53	3.89	9	*2-119	10	0.3
Cal-A	30	127	16	44	11	0	0	15	3	10	0	0	.346	.362	.433	.795	113	2	19	5.62	4	2-29/D-1	4	0.7
1988 Cal-A★	153	602	75	184	42	7	6	83	36	38	4	1	.306	.349	.429	.777	120	15	90	5.46	-6	*2-104,O-40(40-0-0)/D-6	21	1.0
1989 Cal-A	134	530	52	153	16	3	5	62	36	30	6	3	.289	.334	.358	.692	97	-3	62	4.09	-3	*2-130	18	-0.2
1990 Cal-A	105	404	47	112	23	0	5	43	19	44	2	3	.277	.310	.371	.681	91	-7	44	3.79	-1	*2-100/D-1	10	-0.5
Total 10	1353	5188	604	1502	294	36	53	594	353	329	80	49	.290	.336	.391	.727	101	-5	662	4.51	4	*2-1277/O-40,D-8	153	5.8

• RAY, Larry Larry Dale Ray b: 3/11/1958, Madison, IN BL/TR, 6'1", 195 lbs. Deb: 9/10/1982

YEAR TM-L	G	AB	R	H	2B	3B	HR	RBI	BB	SO	SB	CS	AVG	OBP	SLG	OPS	OPS+	BR/A	RC	RC/G	FR	G/POS	WS	TPW
1982 Hou-N	5	6	0	1	0	0	0	1	0	4	0	0	.167	.167	.167	.333	-7	-1	0	.98	0	/O-1	0	-0.1

• RAYFORD, Floyd Floyd Kinnard Rayford b: 7/27/1957, Memphis, TN BR/TR, 5'10", 195 lbs. Deb: 4/17/1980

YEAR TM-L	G	AB	R	H	2B	3B	HR	RBI	BB	SO	SB	CS	AVG	OBP	SLG	OPS	OPS+	BR/A	RC	RC/G	FR	G/POS	WS	TPW
1980 Bal-A	8	18	1	4	0	0	0	1	0	5	0	0	.222	.222	.222	.444	22	-2	1	1.20	0	/3-4,2-1,D-1	0	-0.2
1982 Bal-A	34	53	7	7	0	0	3	5	6	14	0	1	.132	.220	.302	.522	42	-5	4	2.05	0	3-27/C-2,D-2	1	-0.6
1983 StL-N	56	104	5	22	4	0	3	14	10	27	1	0	.212	.281	.337	.617	70	-4	10	3.00	-2	3-33	1	-0.6
1984 Bal-A	86	250	24	64	14	0	4	27	12	51	0	3	.256	.298	.360	.658	83	-7	25	3.45	0	C-66,3-22/1-1	7	-0.4
1985 Bal-A	105	359	55	110	21	1	18	48	10	69	3	1	.306	.325	.521	.846	131	13	56	5.80	0	3-78,C-29/D-1	14	1.3
1986 Bal-A	81	210	15	37	4	0	8	19	15	50	0	0	.176	.231	.310	.541	46	-16	14	2.05	1	3-72,C-10/D-1	2	-1.6
1987 Bal-A	20	50	5	11	0	0	2	3	2	9	0	0	.220	.250	.340	.590	56	-3	4	2.44	0	C-17/3-1,D-1	1	-0.2
Total 7	390	1044	112	255	43	1	38	117	55	225	4	5	.244	.284	.397	.681	86	-25	113	3.67	-1	3-237,C-124/D-6,1-1,2-1	26	-2.3

• RAYMER, Fred Frederick Charles Raymer b: 11/12/1875, Leavenworth, KS d: 6/11/1957, Los Angeles, CA BR/TR, 5'11", 185 lbs. Deb: 4/24/1901

YEAR TM-L	G	AB	R	H	2B	3B	HR	RBI	BB	SO	SB	CS	AVG	OBP	SLG	OPS	OPS+	BR/A	RC	RC/G	FR	G/POS	WS	TPW
1901 Chi-N	120	463	41	108	14	2	0	43	11	....	18	....	.233	.257	.272	.529	56	-27	39	2.84	-19	3-82,S-29/1-5,2-3	3	-4.1
1904 Bos-N	114	419	28	88	12	3	1	27	13	....	17	....	.210	.236	.260	.496	55	-23	32	2.40	-12	*2-114	3	-3.6
1905 Bos-N	137	498	26	105	14	2	0	31	8	....	15	....	.211	.232	.247	.479	44	-36	34	2.19	-25	*2-134/1-1,O-1	3	-6.2
Total 3	371	1380	95	301	40	7	1	101	32	....	50	....	.218	.242	.259	.501	51	-86	105	2.47	-55	2-251/3-82,S-29,1-6,O-1	9	-13.9

• RAYMOND, Harry Harry H. "Jack" Raymond b: 2/20/1862, Utica, NY d: 3/21/1925, San Diego, CA, 5'9", 179 lbs. Deb: 9/9/1888 Career OF: 1-0-1

YEAR TM-L	G	AB	R	H	2B	3B	HR	RBI	BB	SO	SB	CS	AVG	OBP	SLG	OPS	OPS+	BR/A	RC	RC/G	FR	G/POS	WS	TPW
1888 Lou-a	32	123	8	26	2	0	0	13	1	....	7	....	.211	.218	.228	.445	44	-8	8	2.17	-2	3-31/O-1	1	-0.8
1889 Lou-a	130	515	58	123	12	9	0	47	19	45	19	....	.239	.270	.297	.567	62	-27	48	3.22	-16	*3-129/O-1,P-1	4	-3.0
1890*Lou-a	123	521	91	135	7	4	2	51	22	....	18	....	.259	.293	.299	.592	76	-17	52	3.59	0	*3-119/S-4	12	-1.3
1891 Lou-a	14	59	4	12	2	0	0	2	5	6	3	....	.203	.288	.237	.525	51	-4	5	2.83	4	S-14	1	0.0
1892 Pit-N	12	49	4	4	0	1	0	2	4	8	1	....	.082	.151	.122	.273	-17	-7	1	.65	-1	3-12	0	-0.7
Was-N	4	15	2	1	0	0	0	0	3	2	1	....	.067	.222	.067	.289	-12	-2	0	.88	1	/3-4	0	-0.1
Yr.	16	64	6	5	0	1	0	2	7	10	2	....	.078	.169	.109	.278	-16	-9	2	.70	0	3-16	0	-0.8
Total 5	315	1282	167	301	23	14	2	115	54	61	49	....	.235	.270	.279	.549	62	-64	114	3.09	-14	3-295/S-18,O-2,P-1	18	-6.0

• RAYMOND, Lou Louis Anthony Raymond b: 12/11/1894, Buffalo, NY d: 5/2/1979, Rochester, NY BR/TR, 5'10.5", 187 lbs. Deb: 5/2/1919

YEAR TM-L	G	AB	R	H	2B	3B	HR	RBI	BB	SO	SB	CS	AVG	OBP	SLG	OPS	OPS+	BR/A	RC	RC/G	FR	G/POS	WS	TPW
1919 Phi-N	1	2	0	1	0	0	0	0	0	0	0	....	.500	.500	.500	1.000	188	0	0	12.48	-1	/2-1	0	0.0

• REACH, Al Alfred James Reach b: 5/25/1840, London, England d: 1/14/1928, Atlantic City, NJ BL/TL, 5'6", 155 lbs. Deb: 5/20/1871 M/U NA OF: 0-4-39

YEAR TM-L	G	AB	R	H	2B	3B	HR	RBI	BB	SO	SB	CS	AVG	OBP	SLG	OPS	OPS+	BR/A	RC	RC/G	FR	G/POS	WS	TPW
1871 Ath-n	26	133	43	47	7	6	0	34	5	6	2	0	.353	.377	.496	.873	150	8	26	9.62	1	*2-26	....	0.5
1872 Ath-n	24	118	21	23	0	0	0	11	4	0	1	1	.195	.221	.195	.416	29	-10	5	1.76	4	O-20(0-0-20)/1-4	....	-0.3
1873 Ath-n	13	73	13	16	5	1	0	9	0	0	2	0	.219	.219	.315	.534	53	-4	6	3.01	5	/2-9,O-7(0-4-3)	....	0.0
1874 Ath-n	14	55	8	7	2	0	0	2	0	4	0	0	.127	.127	.164	.291	-7	-7	1	.73	4	O-14(0-0-14)	....	-0.2
1875 Ath-n	3	14	4	4	1	0	0	1	0	0	2	1	.286	.286	.357	.643	110	0	2	5.50	-1	/O-2(0-0-2),2-1	....	-0.1
Total 5 n	80	393	89	97	15	7	0	57	9	10	7	2	.247	.264	.321	.584	73	-12	41	4.24	13	/O-43,2-36,1-4	....	0.0

• REACH, Bob Robert Reach b: 8/28/1843, Brooklyn, NY d: 5/19/1922, Springfield, MA, 5'5", 155 lbs. Deb: 4/18/1872

YEAR TM-L	G	AB	R	H	2B	3B	HR	RBI	BB	SO	SB	CS	AVG	OBP	SLG	OPS	OPS+	BR/A	RC	RC/G	FR	G/POS	WS	TPW
1872 Oly-n	2	8	1	2	0	0	0	0	0	0	0	0	.250	.250	.250	.500	57	-0	1	2.65	-1	/S-2	....	-0.1
1873 Was-n	1	5	1	1	0	0	0	0	0	0	0	0	.200	.200	.200	.400	20	-0	0	1.56	-1	/S-1	....	-0.1
Total 2 n	3	13	2	3	0	0	0	0	0	0	0	0	.231	.231	.231	.462	43	-1	1	2.21	-2	/S-3	....	-0.2

YEAR	TM-L	G	AB	R	H	2B	3B	HR	RBI	BB	SO	SB	CS	AVG	OBP	SLG	OPS	OPS+	BR/A	RC	RC/G	FR	G/POS	WS	TPW
• READY, Randy	Randy Max Ready b: 1/8/1960, San Mateo, CA BR/TR, 5'11", 180 lbs. Deb: 9/4/1983 Career OF: 167-0-6																								
1983	Mil-A	12	37	8	15	3	2	1	6	6	3	0	1	.405	.488	.676	1.164	234	7	12	14.36	0	/D-6,3-4	3	0.6
1984	Mil-A	37	123	13	23	6	1	3	13	14	18	0	0	.187	.270	.325	.595	67	-6	11	2.91	0	3-36	2	-0.6
1985	Mil-A	48	181	29	48	9	5	1	21	14	23	0	0	.265	.321	.387	.708	93	-2	22	4.09	2	O-37(36-0-3)/3-7,2-3,D-2	4	-0.2
1986	Mil-A	23	79	8	15	4	0	1	4	9	9	2	0	.190	.273	.278	.551	49	-5	6	2.43	-1	O-11(11-0-0)/2-7,3-3,D-1	0	-0.6
	SD-N	1	3	0	0	0	0	0	0	0	1	0	0	.000	.000	.000	.000	-102	-1	0	.00	0	/3-1	0	-0.1
1987	SD-N	124	350	69	108	26	6	12	54	67	44	7	3	.309	.424	.520	.944	154	30	81	8.62	3	3-52,2-51,O-16(16-0-0)	18	3.4
1988	SD-N	114	331	43	88	16	2	7	39	39	38	6	2	.266	.349	.390	.738	114	7	48	5.10	-1	3-57,2-26,O-16(15-0-1)	13	0.7
1989	SD-N	28	67	4	17	2	1	0	5	11	6	0	0	.254	.359	.313	.672	94	-0	8	4.05	-1	3-18/2-2,O-1	2	-0.1
	Phi-N	72	187	33	50	11	1	8	21	31	31	4	3	.267	.377	.465	.843	139	10	35	6.46	0	O-36(36-0-0),3-14/2-7	6	0.9
	Yr.	100	254	37	67	13	2	8	26	42	37	4	3	.264	.372	.425	.798	127	10	43	5.81	-1	O-37(37-0-0),3-32/2-9	8	0.8
1990	Phi-N	101	217	26	53	9	1	1	26	29	35	3	2	.244	.336	.309	.645	79	-6	25	3.78	1	O-30(30-0-0),2-28	7	-0.5
1991	Phi-N	76	205	32	51	10	1	1	20	47	25	2	1	.249	.391	.322	.713	104	4	29	4.80	-1	2-66	8	0.5
1992*	Oak-A	61	125	17	25	2	0	3	17	25	23	1	0	.200	.333	.288	.621	80	-2	14	3.67	-1	D-24,O-24(22-0-2)/3-7,1-4,2	3	-0.4
1993	Mon-N	40	134	22	34	8	1	1	10	23	8	2	1	.254	.367	.351	.718	89	-1	18	4.65	1	2-28,1-13/3-3	4	0.1
1994	Phi-N	17	42	5	16	1	0	1	3	8	6	0	1	.381	.480	.476	.956	147	3	10	9.37	1	2-11/3-1	2	0.4
1995	Phi-N	23	29	3	4	0	0	0	0	3	6	0	1	.138	.219	.138	.357	-3	-5	1	.60	-1	/1-3,2-1	0	-0.6
Total	**13**	**777**	**2110**	**312**	**547**	**107**	**21**	**40**	**239**	**326**	**276**	**27**	**15**	**.259**	**.362**	**.387**	**.748**	**108**	**34**	**320**	**5.21**	**3**	**2-234,3-203,O-171/D-33,1-20**	**72**	**3.7**
• REAMS, Leroy	Leroy Reams b: 8/11/1943, Pine Bluff, AR BL/TR, 6'2", 175 lbs. Deb: 5/7/1969																								
1969	Phi-N	1	1	0	0	0	0	0	0	0	1	0	0	.000	.000	.000	.000	-103	-0	0	.00	0	....	0	0.0
• REARDON, Phil	Philip Michael Reardon b: 10/3/1883, Brooklyn, NY d: 9/28/1920, Brooklyn, NY BR/TR, 5'9", 160 lbs. Deb: 9/19/1906																								
1906	Bro-N	5	14	0	1	0	0	0	0	0	....	0	....	.071	.133	.071	.205	-39	-2	0	.27	1	/O-4(0-1-3)	0	-0.1
• REBEL, Art	Arthur Anthony Rebel b: 3/4/1915, Cincinnati, OH BL/TL, 5'8", 180 lbs. Deb: 4/19/1938 Career OF: 0-1-20																								
1938	Phi-N	7	9	2	2	0	0	0	1	1	1	0	....	.222	.300	.222	.522	45	-1	0	1.56	0	/O-3(0-1-2)	0	-0.1
1945	StL-N	26	72	12	25	4	0	0	5	6	4	1	....	.347	.397	.403	.800	120	2	11	5.83	2	O-18(0-0-18)	3	0.3
Total	**2**	**33**	**81**	**14**	**27**	**4**	**0**	**0**	**6**	**7**	**5**	**1**	**....**	**.333**	**.386**	**.383**	**.769**	**111**	**1**	**11**	**5.25**	**2**	**/O-21**	**3**	**0.2**
• REBOULET, Jeff	Jeffrey Allen Reboulet b: 4/30/1964, Dayton, OH BR/TR, 6', 169 lbs. Deb: 5/12/1992 Career OF: 7-3-15																								
1992	Min-A	73	137	15	26	7	1	1	16	23	26	3	2	.190	.311	.277	.588	64	-6	14	3.18	6	S-36,3-22,2-13/O-7(1-1-5),D	6	0.2
1993	Min-A	109	240	33	62	8	0	1	15	35	37	5	5	.258	.357	.304	.662	79	-6	27	3.80	-0	S-62,3-35,2-11/O-3(1-2-0),D	6	-0.2
1994	Min-A	74	189	28	49	11	1	3	23	18	23	0	0	.259	.327	.376	.703	81	-6	23	4.15	-5	S-42,2-14,1-10/3-6,O-4(1-0-3),D	5	-0.7
1995	Min-A	87	216	39	63	11	0	4	23	27	34	1	2	.292	.373	.398	.771	101	0	33	5.59	3	S-39,3-22,1-17,2-15/C-1	7	0.5
1996	Min-A	107	234	20	52	9	0	0	23	25	34	4	2	.222	.300	.261	.561	43	-20	18	2.44	3	S-37,3-36,2-22,1-13/O-7(2-0-6),D	2	-1.5
1997*	Bal-A	99	228	26	54	9	0	4	27	23	44	3	0	.237	.310	.329	.638	69	-10	25	3.60	-1	2-63,S-22,3-12/D-1,O-1	5	-0.8
1998	Bal-A	79	126	20	31	6	0	1	8	19	34	0	1	.246	.354	.317	.671	78	-4	15	3.88	-3	2-28,S-28,3-23	2	-0.5
1999	Bal-A	99	154	25	25	4	0	0	4	33	29	1	0	.162	.317	.188	.506	35	-14	12	2.51	3	3-56,2-36,S-10	2	-0.8
2000	KC-A	66	182	29	44	7	0	0	14	23	32	3	1	.242	.327	.280	.607	54	-12	17	2.98	6	2-50,3-11/S-5,D-1	3	-0.4
2001	LA-N	94	214	35	57	15	2	3	22	33	48	0	1	.266	.367	.397	.764	105	2	33	5.38	-4	S-56,2-22/3-7,O-2(2-0-0)	10	0.2
2002	LA-N	38	48	3	10	3	0	0	2	6	13	0	0	.208	.296	.271	.567	54	-3	4	2.70	-1	2-11/S-5,3-3,D-1	0	-0.3
2003	Pit-N	93	261	37	63	10	2	3	25	27	47	2	1	.241	.322	.330	.651	69	-11	29	3.63	4	2-76/3-7	6	-0.4
Total	**12**	**1018**	**2229**	**310**	**536**	**100**	**6**	**20**	**202**	**292**	**401**	**22**	**15**	**.240**	**.333**	**.318**	**.650**	**71**	**-90**	**251**	**3.71**	**10**	**2-361,S-342,3-240/1-40,O,D,C**	**54**	**-4.5**
• RECCIUS, John	John Reccius b: 10/29/1859, Louisville, KY d: 9/1/1930, Louisville, KY, 5'6.5" Deb: 5/2/1882 Career OF: 0-70-15 ♦																								
1882	Lou-a	74	266	46	63	12	3	1	....	23	....	....	....	.237	.298	.316	.613	113	7	26	3.53	0	*O-65(0-55-11),P-13	10	0.0
1883	Lou-a	18	63	10	9	2	0	0	3	7	....	....	....	.143	.229	.175	.403	34	-4	3	1.34	-1	O-18(0-15-4)/P-1	0	-0.5
Total	**2**	**92**	**329**	**56**	**72**	**14**	**3**	**1**	**3**	**30**	**....**	**....**	**....**	**.219**	**.284**	**.289**	**.573**	**98**	**3**	**28**	**3.07**	**-2**	**/O-83,P-14**	**10**	**-0.5**
• RECCIUS, Phil	Phillip Reccius b: 6/7/1862, Louisville, KY d: 2/15/1903, Louisville, KY, 5'9", 163 lbs. Deb: 9/25/1882 Career OF: 4-4-13 ♦																								
1882	Lou-a	4	15	0	2	0	0	0	....	0	....	....	....	.133	.133	.133	.267	-10	-2	0	.59	0	/O-4(0-4-0)	0	-0.2
1883	Lou-a	1	3	1	1	1	0	0	0	0	....	....	....	.333	.333	.667	1.000	231	0	1	9.57	0	/O-1	0	0.0
1884	Lou-a	73	263	23	63	9	2	3	21	5	....	....	....	.240	.267	.323	.591	96	1	23	3.20	-2	3-51,P-18,S-10	13	0.1
1885	Lou-a	102	402	57	97	8	10	1	38	13	....	....	....	.241	.267	.318	.585	84	-7	35	3.10	-3	*3-97/P-7	8	-1.0
1886	Lou-a	5	13	4	4	1	1	0	2	3	....	0	....	.308	.471	.538	1.009	204	2	3	10.13	1	/O-5(2-0-3),P-1	1	0.1
1887	Lou-a	11	45	9	17	2	0	0	4	8	....	3	....	.378	.391	.297	.689	92	0	6	5.41	2	O-10(2-0-8)/S-1	1	0.2
	Cle-a	62	253	23	71	6	3	0	29	24	....	9	....	.281	.295	.258	.552	56	-12	21	3.05	3	3-62/P-1	3	-0.9
	Yr.	73	298	32	88	8	3	0	33	32	....	12	....	.295	.309	.263	.572	62	-12	26	3.36	5	3-62,O-10(2-0-8)/P-1,S-1	4	-0.7
1888	Lou-a	2	9	0	2	1	0	0	4	1	....	0	....	.222	.300	.333	.633	105	0	1	3.56	0	/3-2	0	0.0
1890	Roc-a	1	4	0	0	0	0	0	1	0	....	0	....	.000	.000	.000	.000	-108	-1	0	.00	0	/O-1	0	-0.1
Total	**8**	**261**	**1007**	**117**	**257**	**28**	**16**	**4**	**99**	**54**	**....**	**12**	**....**	**.255**	**.280**	**.305**	**.585**	**81**	**-18**	**90**	**3.25**	**1**	**3-212/P-27,O-21,S-11**	**26**	**-1.7**
• REDER, Johnny	John Anthony Reder b: 9/24/1909, Lublin, Poland d: 4/12/1990, Fall River, MA BR/TR, 6', 184 lbs. Deb: 4/16/1932																								
1932	Bos-A	17	37	4	5	1	0	0	3	6	6	0	0	.135	.256	.162	.418	11	-5	2	1.54	0	1-10/3-1	0	-0.5
• REDFERN, Buck	George Howard Redfern b: 4/7/1902, Asheville, NC d: 9/8/1964, Asheville, NC BR/TR, 5'11", 165 lbs. Deb: 4/11/1928																								
1928	Chi-A	86	261	22	61	6	3	0	35	12	19	8	2	.234	.267	.280	.547	44	-20	21	2.56	-6	2-45,S-33/3-1	3	-2.1
1929	Chi-A	21	46	0	6	0	0	0	3	3	3	1	1	.130	.184	.130	.314	-18	-8	1	.74	-2	2-11/3-5,S-4	0	-0.9
Total	**2**	**107**	**307**	**22**	**67**	**6**	**3**	**0**	**38**	**15**	**22**	**9**	**3**	**.218**	**.255**	**.257**	**.512**	**35**	**-28**	**22**	**2.26**	**-8**	**/2-56,S-37,3-6**	**3**	**-3.0**
• REDFIELD, Joe	Joseph Randall Redfield b: 1/14/1961, Doylestown, PA BR/TR, 6'2", 190 lbs. Deb: 6/4/1988																								
1988	Cal-A	1	2	0	0	0	0	0	0	0	0	0	0	.000	.000	.000	.000	-103	-1	0	.00	0	/3-1	0	0.0
1991	Pit-N	11	18	1	2	0	0	0	0	4	1	0	1	.111	.273	.111	.384	12	-2	1	1.16	0	/3-9	0	-0.2
Total	**2**	**12**	**20**	**1**	**2**	**0**	**0**	**0**	**0**	**4**	**1**	**0**	**1**	**.100**	**.250**	**.100**	**.350**	**3**	**-3**	**1**	**1.04**	**0**	**/3-10**	**0**	**-0.3**
• REDMAN, Prentice	Prentice Montezz Redman b: 8/23/1979, Tuscaloosa, AL BR/TR, 6'3", 185 lbs. Deb: 8/24/2003																								
2003	NY-N	15	24	3	3	1	0	1	2	1	9	2	0	.125	.192	.292	.484	25	-2	1	1.58	-1	O-10(0-9-2)	0	-0.3
• REDMAN, Tike	Julian Jawonn Redman b: 3/10/1977, Tuscaloosa, AL BL/TL, 5'11", 166 lbs. Deb: 6/30/2000 Career OF: 2-82-11																								
2000	Pit-N	9	18	2	6	1	0	1	1	1	7	1	0	.333	.368	.556	.924	130	1	4	8.94	2	/O-6(2-0-4)	1	0.2
2001	Pit-N	37	125	8	28	4	1	1	4	4	25	3	5	.224	.248	.296	.544	39	-13	8	1.98	6	O-35(0-28-7)	1	-0.7
2003	Pit-N	56	230	36	76	16	5	3	19	14	18	7	3	.330	.374	.483	.857	119	6	43	7.18	-1	O-54(0-54-0)	9	0.5
Total	**3**	**102**	**373**	**46**	**110**	**21**	**6**	**5**	**24**	**19**	**50**	**11**	**8**	**.295**	**.332**	**.424**	**.756**	**93**	**-6**	**54**	**5.28**	**7**	**/O-95**	**11**	**0.1**
• REDMON, Glenn	Glenn Vincent Redmon b: 1/11/1948, Detroit, MI BR/TR, 5'11", 180 lbs. Deb: 9/8/1974																								
1974	SF-N	7	17	0	4	3	0	0	4	1	3	0	0	.235	.278	.412	.690	87	-0	2	3.95	-1	/2-4	0	-0.1
• REDMOND, Billy	William T. Redmond b: Brooklyn, NY BL/TL Deb: 5/4/1875																								
1875	RS-n	19	82	12	16	2	0	0	1	2	7	3	0	.195	.214	.220	.434	56	-2	5	2.06	6	S-19/C-2	....	0.3
1877	Cin-N	3	12	1	3	1	0	0	3	1	1	....	....	.250	.308	.333	.641	114	0	1	3.85	1	/S-3	0	0.2
1878	Mil-N	48	187	16	43	8	0	0	21	8	13	....	....	.230	.262	.273	.534	71	-6	14	2.61	-15	S-39/O-7(0-4-3),3-3,C-1	2	-1.8
Total	**2**	**51**	**199**	**17**	**46**	**9**	**0**	**0**	**24**	**9**	**14**	**....**	**....**	**.231**	**.264**	**.276**	**.541**	**74**	**-6**	**15**	**2.68**	**-13**	**/S-42,O-7,3-3,C-1**	**2**	**-1.6**
• REDMOND, Harry	Harry John Redmond b: 9/13/1887, Cleveland, OH d: 7/10/1960, Cleveland, OH BR/TR, 5'8", 170 lbs. Deb: 9/7/1909																								
1909	Bro-N	6	19	3	0	0	0	0	1	0	....	0	....	.000	.000	.000	.000	-104	-4	0	.00	3	/2-5	0	-0.2
• REDMOND, Jack	John McKittrick "Red" Redmond b: 9/3/1910, Florence, AZ d: 7/27/1968, Garland, TX BL/TR, 5'11", 185 lbs. Deb: 4/22/1935																								
1935	Was-A	22	34	8	6	1	0	1	7	3	1	0	0	.176	.243	.294	.537	40	-3	3	2.38	-1	C-15	0	-0.3
• REDMOND, Mike	Michael Patrick Redmond b: 5/5/1971, Seattle, WA BR/TR, 6'1", 185 lbs. Deb: 5/31/1998																								
1998	Fla-N	37	118	10	39	9	0	2	12	5	16	0	0	.331	.368	.458	.826	120	3	18	5.40	2	C-37	4	0.8

YEAR TM-L	G	AB	R	H	2B	3B	HR	RBI	BB	SO	SB	CS	AVG	OBP	SLG	OPS	OPS+	BR/A	RC	RC/G	FR	G/POS	WS	TPW
1999 Fla-N	84	242	22	73	9	0	1	27	26	34	0	0	.302	.381	.351	.732	92	-2	33	4.87	4	C-82	12	0.7
2000 Fla-N	87	210	17	53	8	1	0	15	13	19	0	0	.252	.320	.300	.620	61	-12	20	3.33	4	C-85	5	-0.3
2001 Fla-N	48	141	19	44	4	0	4	14	13	13	0	0	.312	.378	.426	.804	111	3	21	5.51	2	C-47	6	0.7
2002 Fla-N	89	256	19	78	15	0	2	28	21	34	0	2	.305	.375	.387	.762	105	2	37	5.33	8	C-80/1-2	12	1.5
2003*Fla-N	59	125	12	30	7	1	0	11	7	16	0	0	.240	.307	.312	.619	65	-6	13	3.35	-2	C-37/1-1,3-1	1	-0.6
Total 6	**404**	**1092**	**99**	**317**	**52**	**2**	**9**	**107**	**85**	**132**	**0**	**2**	**.290**	**.358**	**.366**	**.724**	**91**	**-13**	**142**	**4.62**	**18**	**C-368/1-3,3-1**	**40**	**2.7**
• REDMOND, Wayne	Howard Wayne Redmond b: 11/25/1945, Athens, AL BR/TR, 5'10", 165 lbs. Deb: 9/7/1965																							
1965 Det-A	4	4	1	0	0	0	0	0	1	1	0	0	.000	.200	.000	.200	-38	-1	0	.35	0	/O-2(1-1-0)	0	-0.1
1969 Det-A	5	3	0	0	0	0	0	0	0	2	0	0	.000	.000	.000	.000	-96	-1	0	.00	0	....	0	-0.1
Total 2	**9**	**7**	**1**	**0**	**0**	**0**	**0**	**0**	**1**	**3**	**0**	**0**	**.000**	**.125**	**.000**	**.125**	**-59**	**-1**	**0**	**.20**	**0**	**/O-2**	**0**	**-0.2**
• REDUS, Gary	Gary Eugene Redus b: 11/1/1956, Tanner, AL BR/TR, 6'1", 185 lbs. Deb: 9/7/1982 Career OF: 571-132-117																							
1982 Cin-N	20	83	12	18	3	2	1	7	5	21	11	2	.217	.261	.337	.599	65	-3	8	3.33	1	O-20(20-0-0)	1	-0.3
1983 Cin-N	125	453	90	112	20	9	17	51	71	111	39	14	.247	.353	.444	.797	115	13	76	5.59	-2	*O-120(120-0-0)	18	0.5
1984 Cin-N	123	394	69	100	21	3	7	22	52	71	48	11	.254	.342	.376	.718	97	5	58	4.91	-4	*O-114(93-24-1)	13	-0.4
1985 Cin-N	101	246	51	62	14	4	6	28	44	52	48	12	.252	.368	.415	.782	113	10	45	6.12	1	O-85(63-37-0)	12	0.9
1986 Phi-N	90	340	62	84	22	4	11	33	47	78	25	7	.247	.344	.432	.776	109	7	55	5.58	3	O-89(89-0-0)	13	0.5
1987 Chi-A	130	475	78	112	26	6	12	48	69	90	52	11	.236	.333	.392	.724	89	-0	69	4.80	6	*O-123(97-19-20)/D-4	13	0.0
1988 Chi-A	77	262	42	69	10	4	6	34	33	52	26	2	.263	.350	.401	.751	110	9	42	5.45	3	O-68(54-16-2)/D-2	10	1.1
Pit-N	30	71	12	14	2	0	2	4	15	19	5	2	.197	.345	.310	.655	91	0	9	3.98	1	O-19(11-1-7)	1	0.0
1989 Pit-N	98	279	42	79	18	7	6	33	40	51	25	6	.283	.375	.462	.837	143	19	52	6.50	5	1-72,O-16(2-1-12)	13	2.1
1990*Pit-N	96	227	32	56	15	3	6	23	33	38	11	5	.247	.347	.419	.766	114	5	36	5.29	-3	1-72/O-7(4-1-2)	7	-0.2
1991*Pit-N	98	252	45	62	12	2	7	24	28	39	17	3	.246	.329	.393	.721	104	4	37	5.03	-4	1-47,O-33(11-12-11)	6	-0.4
1992*Pit-N	76	176	26	45	7	3	3	12	17	25	11	4	.256	.321	.381	.702	99	0	23	4.52	-4	1-36,O-15(2-1-12)	5	-0.6
1993 Tex-A	77	222	28	64	12	4	6	31	23	35	4	4	.288	.355	.459	.815	122	6	36	5.77	-1	O-61(5-17-46)/1-5,2-1,D-1	8	0.2
1994 Tex-A	18	33	2	9	1	0	0	2	4	6	0	0	.273	.351	.303	.654	71	-1	3	2.91	0	/O-7(0-3-4),1-5	0	-0.2
Total 13	**1159**	**3513**	**591**	**886**	**183**	**51**	**90**	**352**	**481**	**688**	**322**	**83**	**.252**	**.345**	**.410**	**.755**	**107**	**73**	**548**	**5.28**	**1**	**O-777,1-237/D-7,2-1**	**120**	**3.3**
• REECE, Bob	Robert Scott Reece b: 1/5/1951, Sacramento, CA BR/TR, 6'1", 190 lbs. Deb: 4/22/1978																							
1978 Mon-N	9	11	2	2	1	0	0	3	0	4	0	0	.182	.182	.273	.455	26	-1	1	1.64	0	/C-9	0	-0.1
• REED, Billy	William Joseph Reed b: 11/12/1922, Shawano, WI BL/TR, 5'10.5", 175 lbs. Deb: 4/15/1952																							
1952 Bos-N	15	52	4	13	0	0	0	0	0	5	0	0	.250	.264	.250	.514	45	-4	3	2.00	-2	2-14	0	-0.5
• REED, Darren	Darren A. Douglas Reed b: 10/16/1965, Ojai, CA BR/TR, 6'1", 190 lbs. Deb: 5/1/1990 Career OF: 20-7-31																							
1990 NY-N	26	39	5	8	4	1	1	2	3	11	1	0	.205	.262	.436	.698	89	-1	5	4.17	0	O-14(2-7-6)	1	-0.1
1992 Mon-N	42	81	10	14	2	0	5	10	6	23	0	0	.173	.239	.383	.621	74	-3	7	2.55	0	O-29(8-0-21)	1	-0.4
Min-A	14	33	2	6	2	0	0	4	2	11	0	0	.182	.229	.242	.471	31	-3	2	1.92	0	O-13(10-0-4)/D-1	0	-0.3
Total 2	**82**	**153**	**17**	**28**	**8**	**1**	**6**	**16**	**11**	**45**	**1**	**0**	**.183**	**.242**	**.366**	**.608**	**68**	**-7**	**13**	**2.80**	**1**	**/O-56,D-1**	**2**	**-0.8**
• REED, Hugh	Hugh Reed b: 1837, Chicago, IL d: 11/3/1883, Chicago, IL Deb: 8/26/1874 U																							
1874 Bal-n	1	4	0	0	0	0	0	0	0	0	0	0	.000	.000	.000	.000	-101	-1	0	.00	-0	/O-1	....	-0.1
• REED, Jack	John Burwell Reed b: 2/2/1933, Silver City, MS BR/TR, 6', 185 lbs. Deb: 4/23/1961 Career OF: 46-83-63																							
1961*NY-A	28	13	4	2	0	0	0	1	1	1	0	0	.154	.214	.154	.368		-2	0	1.19	-2	O-27(12-14-1)	0	-0.4
1962 NY-A	88	43	17	13	2	1	1	4	4	7	2	1	.302	.362	.465	.827	125	1	7	5.71	-3	O-75(20-39-16)	2	-0.3
1963 NY-A	106	73	18	15	3	1	0	1	9	14	5	1	.205	.293	.274	.567	60	-3	7	3.01	0	O-89(14-30-46)	2	-0.5
Total 3	**222**	**129**	**39**	**30**	**5**	**2**	**1**	**6**	**14**	**22**	**7**	**2**	**.233**	**.308**	**.326**	**.633**	**76**	**-3**	**14**	**3.68**	**-5**	**O-191**	**4**	**-1.2**
• REED, Jeff	Jeffrey Scott Reed b: 11/12/1962, Joliet, IL BL/TR, 6'2", 190 lbs. Deb: 4/5/1984																							
1984 Min-A	18	21	3	3	3	0	0	1	2	6	0	0	.143	.217	.286	.503	36	-2	1	2.08	0	C-18	0	-0.2
1985 Min-A	7	10	2	2	0	0	0	0	0	3	0	0	.200	.200	.200	.400	9	-1	0	1.35	0	/C-7	0	-0.1
1986 Min-A	68	165	13	39	6	1	2	9	16	19	1	0	.236	.308	.321	.629	70	-7	17	3.58	-1	C-64	3	-0.4
1987 Mon-N	75	207	15	44	11	0	1	21	12	20	0	1	.213	.259	.280	.539	42	-18	14	2.06	-2	C-74	0	-1.7
1988 Mon-N	43	123	10	27	3	2	0	9	13	22	1	0	.220	.294	.276	.571	62	-6	10	2.77	1	C-39	2	-0.2
Cin-N	49	142	10	33	6	0	1	7	15	19	0	0	.232	.306	.296	.602	71	-5	13	3.27	-1	C-49	4	-0.3
Yr.	92	265	20	60	9	2	1	16	28	41	1	0	.226	.300	.287	.587	66	-11	24	3.03	1	C-88	6	-0.5
1989 Cin-N	102	287	16	64	11	0	3	23	34	46	0	0	.223	.310	.293	.602	71	-10	27	3.12	-0	C-99	7	-0.5
1990*Cin-N	72	175	12	44	8	1	3	16	24	26	0	0	.251	.342	.360	.702	89	-2	22	4.25	-3	C-70	5	-0.1
1991 Cin-N	91	270	20	72	15	2	3	31	23	38	0	1	.267	.327	.370	.697	92	-3	32	4.12	-2	C-89	5	0.0
1992 Cin-N	15	25	2	4	0	0	0	2	1	4	0	0	.160	.192	.160	.352	1	-3	1	.76	0	/C-6	0	-0.3
1993 SF-N	66	119	10	31	3	0	6	12	16	22	0	1	.261	.348	.437	.785	112	2	18	5.28	0	C-37	4	0.4
1994 SF-N	50	103	11	18	3	0	1	7	11	21	0	0	.175	.254	.233	.487	30	-11	6	1.81	-1	C-33	1	-0.9
1995 SF-N	66	113	12	30	2	0	0	9	20	17	0	0	.265	.376	.283	.659	79	-2	13	4.02	2	C-42	4	0.2
1996 Col-N	116	341	34	97	20	1	8	37	43	65	2	2	.284	.368	.419	.787	87	-6	53	5.43	-3	*C-111	9	-0.2
1997 Col-N	90	256	43	76	10	0	17	47	35	55	2	1	.297	.386	.535	.921	112	5	52	7.29	-2	C-78	11	0.9
1998 Col-N	113	259	43	75	17	1	9	39	37	57	0	0	.290	.380	.467	.848	100	1	47	6.47	-2	C-99	8	0.5
1999 Col-N	46	106	11	27	5	0	2	11	17	24	0	1	.255	.363	.358	.721	66	-6	14	4.53	1	C-36	2	-0.3
Chi-N	57	150	18	39	11	2	1	17	28	34	1	1	.260	.383	.380	.763	95	-0	23	5.37	-3	C-49/3-1,D-1	4	0.0
Yr.	103	256	29	66	16	2	3	28	45	58	1	2	.258	.375	.371	.746	83	-6	37	5.02	-2	C-85/3-1,D-1	6	-0.3
2000 Chi-N	90	229	26	49	10	0	4	25	44	68	0	1	.214	.343	.310	.653	68	-10	27	3.80	-2	C-71	5	-0.8
Total 17	**1234**	**3101**	**311**	**774**	**144**	**10**	**61**	**323**	**391**	**566**	**7**	**9**	**.250**	**.336**	**.361**	**.698**	**80**	**-85**	**392**	**4.29**	**-17**	***C-1071/3-1,D-1**	**74**	**-4.3**
• REED, Jody	Jody Eric Reed b: 7/26/1962, Tampa, FL BR/TR, 5'9", 165 lbs. Deb: 9/12/1987																							
1987 Bos-A	9	30	4	9	1	1	0	8	4	0	1	1	.300	.382	.400	.782	105	0	5	5.67	4	/S-4,2-2,3-1	1	0.4
1988*Bos-A	109	338	60	99	23	1	1	28	45	21	1	3	.293	.382	.376	.758	109	5	51	5.33	1	S-94,2-11/3-4,D-1	11	1.3
1989 Bos-A	146	524	76	151	42	2	3	40	73	44	4	5	.288	.379	.393	.772	111	10	81	5.36	-3	S-77,2-70/3-4,D-1,O-1	17	1.5
1990*Bos-A	155	598	70	173	**45**	0	5	51	75	65	4	4	.289	.372	.390	.762	108	9	87	5.07	0	*2-119,S-50/D-1	22	1.5
1991 Bos-A	153	618	87	175	42	2	5	60	60	53	6	5	.283	.350	.382	.732	98	-2	83	4.68	-1	*2-152/S-6	20	0.2
1992 Bos-A	143	550	64	136	27	1	3	40	62	44	7	8	.247	.324	.316	.640	75	-19	55	3.30	10	*2-142/D-1	12	-0.5
1993 LA-N	132	445	48	123	21	2	2	31	38	40	1	3	.276	.335	.346	.681	88	-9	49	3.66	13	*2-132	14	1.0
1994 Mil-A	108	399	48	108	22	0	2	37	57	34	5	4	.271	.365	.341	.705	80	-11	52	4.57	17	*2-106	12	1.1
1995 SD-N	131	445	58	114	18	1	4	40	59	38	6	4	.256	.350	.328	.678	83	-9	54	4.17	16	*2-130/S-5	14	1.3
1996*SD-N	146	495	45	121	20	0	2	49	59	53	2	5	.244	.329	.297	.626	71	-21	48	3.21	2	*2-145	11	-1.2
1997 Det-A	52	112	6	22	2	0	0	8	10	15	3	2	.196	.280	.214	.494	32	-11	7	2.05	2	2-41/D-5	2	-0.7
Total 11	**1284**	**4554**	**566**	**1231**	**263**	**10**	**27**	**392**	**542**	**407**	**40**	**44**	**.270**	**.352**	**.350**	**.702**	**90**	**-59**	**573**	**4.29**	**61**	***2-1050,S-236/3-9,D-9,O-1**	**136**	**5.8**
• REED, Milt	Milton D. Reed b: 7/4/1890, Atlanta, GA d: 7/27/1938, Atlanta, GA BL/TR, 5'9.5", 150 lbs. Deb: 9/9/1911																							
1911 StL-N	1	1	0	0	0	0	0	0	0	0	0	....	.000	.000	.000	.000	-103	-0	0	.00	0	....	0	0.0
1913 Phi-N	13	24	4	6	1	0	0	0	1	5	1	....	.250	.280	.292	.572	61	-1	2	2.93	-3	/S-9,2-3	0	-0.4
1914 Phi-N	44	107	10	22	2	1	0	2	10	13	4	....	.206	.280	.243	.523	52	-6	8	2.44	-10	S-22,2-11/3-1	0	-1.6
1915 Bro-F	10	31	2	9	1	1	0	8	2	0	2	....	.290	.353	.387	.740	120	1	5	5.27	-3	S-10	1	-0.1
Total 4	**68**	**163**	**16**	**37**	**4**	**2**	**0**	**10**	**13**	**18**	**7**	**....**	**.227**	**.292**	**.276**	**.568**	**66**	**-7**	**15**	**3.00**	**-15**	**/S-41,2-14,3-1**	**1**	**-2.1**
• REED, Ted	Ralph Edwin Reed b: 10/18/1890, Beaver, PA d: 2/16/1959, Beaver, PA BR/TR, 5'11", 190 lbs. Deb: 9/10/1915																							
1915 New-F	20	77	5	20	1	2	0	4	2	7	1	....	.260	.288	.325	.612	85	-2	8	3.18	-2	3-20	1	-0.4
• REEDER, Icicle	James Edward Reeder b: 1858, Cincinnati, OH d: 1/15/1913, Cincinnati, OH BR, 6' Deb: 6/24/1884 U																							
1884 Cin-a	3	14	0	2	0	0	0	0	0	....	....	....	.143	.143	.143	.286	-6	-2	0	.67	-0	/O-3(3-0-0)	0	-0.2
Was-U	3	12	0	2	0	0	0	....	0	....	....	....	.167	.167	.167	.333	13	-1	0	.96	-1	/O-3(0-1-2)	0	-0.2

YEAR TM-L	G	AB	R	H	2B	3B	HR	RBI	BB	SO	SB	CS	AVG	OBP	SLG	OPS	OPS+	BR/A	RC	RC/G	FR	G/POS	WS	TPW
• REEDER, Nick	Nicholas Reeder b: 3/22/1867, Louisville, KY d: 9/26/1894, Louisville, KY BR/TR, 5'9", 189 lbs. Deb: 4/11/1891																							
1891 Lou-a	1	2	0	0	0	0	0	0	0	1	0	....	.000	.000	.000	.000	-101	-1	0	.00	-0	/3-1	0	0.0
• REESE, Jimmie	James Herman Reese b: 10/1/1901, New York, NY d: 7/13/1994, Santa Ana, CA BL/TR, 5'11.5", 165 lbs. Deb: 4/19/1930 C																							
1930 NY-A	77	188	44	65	14	2	3	18	11	8	1	1	.346	.382	.489	.871	125	7	35	7.15	-1	2-48/3-5	7	0.6
1931 NY-A	65	245	41	59	10	2	3	26	17	10	2	3	.241	.293	.335	.627	68	-11	24	3.30	6	2-61	4	-0.1
1932 StL-N	90	309	38	82	15	0	2	26	20	19	4	....	.265	.314	.333	.648	72	-12	33	3.78	10	2-77	7	0.2
Total 3	**232**	**742**	**123**	**206**	**39**	**4**	**8**	**70**	**48**	**37**	**7**	**4**	**.278**	**.324**	**.373**	**.697**	**84**	**-16**	**92**	**4.40**	**15**	**2-186/3-5**	**18**	**0.8**
• REESE, Pee Wee	Harold Henry Reese b: 7/23/1918, Ekron, KY d: 8/14/1999, Louisville, KY BR/TR, 5'10", 175 lbs. Deb: 4/23/1940 C HOF: 1984																							
1940 Bro-N	84	312	58	85	8	4	5	28	45	42	15	....	.272	.366	.372	.738	98	1	47	5.45	9	S-83	13	1.6
1941*Bro-N	152	595	76	136	23	5	2	46	68	56	10	....	.229	.311	.294	.605	68	-24	59	3.36	25	*S-151	15	1.2
1942 Bro-N★	151	564	87	144	24	5	3	53	82	55	15	....	.255	.350	.332	.681	98	2	71	4.38	32	*S-151	27	**4.8**
1946 Bro-N★	152	542	79	154	16	10	5	60	87	71	10	....	.284	.384	.378	.762	115	15	85	5.55	7	*S-152	26	3.3
1947*Bro-N★	142	476	81	135	24	4	12	73	**104**	67	7	....	.284	.414	.426	.841	119	19	93	7.06	9	*S-142	26	3.6
1948 Bro-N★	151	566	96	155	31	4	9	75	79	63	25	....	.274	.363	.390	.753	100	2	82	5.08	19	*S-149	23	3.1
1949*Bro-N★	155	617	**132**	172	27	3	16	73	116	59	26	....	.279	.396	.410	.806	112	16	111	6.57	14	*S-155	32	3.9
1950 Bro-N★	141	531	97	138	21	5	11	52	91	62	17	....	.260	.369	.380	.750	96	-0	81	5.36	1	*S-134/3-7	20	0.9
1951 Bro-N★	154	616	94	176	20	8	10	84	81	57	20	14	.286	.371	.393	.763	103	4	91	5.07	-4	*S-154	22	1.0
1952*Bro-N★	149	559	94	152	18	8	6	58	86	59	**30**	5	.272	.369	.365	.734	103	11	84	5.11	0	*S-145	23	2.0
1953*Bro-N★	140	524	108	142	25	7	13	61	82	61	22	6	.271	.374	.420	.794	104	8	88	5.71	8	*S-135	21	2.6
1954 Bro-N★	141	554	98	171	35	8	10	69	90	62	8	5	.309	.408	.455	.863	121	21	104	6.65	0	*S-140	26	3.2
1955*Bro-N	145	553	99	156	29	4	10	61	78	60	8	7	.282	.374	.403	.777	103	5	82	4.99	-11	*S-142	18	0.5
1956*Bro-N	147	572	85	147	19	2	9	46	56	69	13	4	.257	.324	.344	.669	74	-18	66	3.83	-7	*S-136,3-12	14	-1.5
1957 Bro-N	103	330	33	74	3	1	1	29	39	32	5	2	.224	.308	.248	.557	47	-23	27	2.72	4	3-75,S-23	4	-1.7
1958 LA-N	59	147	21	33	7	2	4	17	26	15	1	2	.224	.341	.381	.722	88	-3	20	4.28	0	S-22,3-21	4	-0.1
Total 16	**2166**	**8058**	**1338**	**2170**	**330**	**80**	**126**	**885**	**1210**	**890**	**232**	**45**	**.269**	**.366**	**.377**	**.743**	**99**	**34**	**1191**	**5.12**	**104**	***S-2014,3-115**	**314**	**28.5**
• REESE, Pokey	Calvin Reese b: 6/10/1973, Columbia, SC BR/TR, 5'11", 180 lbs. Deb: 4/1/1997																							
1997 Cin-N	128	397	48	87	15	0	4	26	31	82	25	7	.219	.284	.287	.571	49	-27	36	3.04	3	*S-110/2-8,3-8	7	-1.5
1998 Cin-N	59	133	20	34	2	2	1	16	14	28	3	2	.256	.327	.323	.650	71	-6	14	3.56	-1	3-32,S-18/2-3	3	-0.5
1999 Cin-N	149	585	85	167	37	5	10	52	35	81	38	7	.285	.332	.417	.749	86	-9	84	5.12	30	*2-146,S-16	18	2.7
2000 Cin-N	135	518	76	132	20	6	12	46	45	86	29	3	.255	.322	.386	.708	76	-15	69	4.59	24	*2-133	11	1.4
2001 Cin-N	133	428	50	96	20	2	9	40	34	82	25	4	.224	.286	.343	.629	59	-23	45	3.42	3	S-78,2-51	7	-1.1
2002 Pit-N	119	421	46	111	25	0	4	50	41	81	12	1	.264	.333	.352	.685	80	-10	54	4.46	8	*2-117	15	0.4
2003 Pit-N	37	107	9	23	2	0	1	12	9	31	6	0	.215	.276	.262	.538	40	-8	9	2.65	10	2-33	2	0.4
Total 7	**760**	**2589**	**334**	**650**	**121**	**15**	**41**	**242**	**209**	**471**	**138**	**24**	**.251**	**.313**	**.357**	**.670**	**70**	**-98**	**311**	**4.10**	**77**	**2-491,S-222/3-40**	**63**	**1.6**
• REESE, Randy	Andrew Jackson Reese b: 2/7/1904, Tupelo, MS d: 1/10/1966, Tupelo, MS BR/TR, 5'11", 180 lbs. Deb: 4/15/1927 Career OF: 81-26-15																							
1927 NY-N	97	355	43	94	14	2	4	21	13	52	5	....	.265	.298	.349	.648	73	-14	36	3.46	-4	3-64,0-16(7-0-9)/1-1	6	-1.5
1928 NY-N	109	406	61	125	18	4	6	44	13	24	7	....	.308	.331	.416	.747	94	-5	53	4.73	-4	0-64(59-2-4),2-26/1-6,3-6,S	10	-1.3
1929 NY-N	58	209	36	55	11	3	0	21	15	19	8	....	.263	.316	.344	.660	64	-12	23	3.68	3	2-44/0-8(7-1-0),3-4	4	-0.7
1930 NY-N	67	172	26	47	4	2	4	25	10	12	1	....	.273	.313	.390	.703	70	-9	20	4.08	-3	0-32(8-23-2),3-10/1-1	2	-1.1
Total 4	**331**	**1142**	**166**	**321**	**47**	**11**	**14**	**111**	**51**	**107**	**21**	**....**	**.281**	**.315**	**.378**	**.694**	**78**	**-41**	**132**	**4.03**	**-8**	**0-120/3-84,2-70,1-8,S-6**	**22**	**-4.6**
• REESE, Rich	Richard Benjamin Reese b: 9/29/1941, Leipsic, OH BL/TL, 6'3", 200 lbs. Deb: 9/4/1964 Career OF: 73-0-2																							
1964 Min-A	10	7	0	0	0	0	0	0	0	1	0	0	.000	.000	.000	.000	-99	-2	0	.00	0	/1-1	0	-0.2
1965 Min-A	14	7	0	2	1	0	0	0	2	2	0	0	.286	.444	.429	.873	143	1	1	7.82	0	/1-6,0-1	1	0.0
1966 Min-A	3	2	0	0	0	0	0	0	1	2	0	0	.000	.333	.000	.333	5	-0	0	1.17	0	....	0	0.0
1967 Min-A	95	101	13	25	5	0	4	20	8	17	0	0	.248	.303	.416	.719	102	0	13	4.44	-2	1-36,0-10(10-0-0)	3	-0.3
1968 Min-A	126	332	40	86	15	2	4	28	18	36	3	1	.259	.303	.352	.656	93	-3	35	3.66	-4	1-87,0-15(15-0-0)	7	-1.3
1969*Min-A	132	419	52	135	24	4	16	69	23	57	1	5	.322	.365	.513	.878	140	19	76	6.82	-5	*1-117/0-5(5-0-0)	17	0.6
1970*Min-A	153	501	63	131	15	5	10	56	48	70	5	4	.261	.335	.371	.706	93	-5	64	4.43	1	*1-146	14	-1.5
1971 Min-A	120	329	40	72	8	3	10	39	20	35	7	4	.219	.274	.353	.627	74	-12	30	2.95	1	1-95/0-9(8-0-1)	5	-2.0
1972 Min-A	132	197	23	43	3	2	5	26	25	27	0	1	.218	.306	.330	.636	85	-4	20	3.38	0	1-98,0-13(13-0-0)	4	-0.9
1973 Det-A	59	102	10	14	1	0	2	4	7	17	0	0	.137	.193	.206	.399	11	-12	4	1.18	-1	1-37,0-21(21-0-1)	0	-1.5
Min-A	22	23	7	4	1	1	1	3	6	6	0	0	.174	.345	.435	.780	114	1	4	5.44	0	1-17	1	0.0
Yr.	81	125	17	18	2	1	3	7	13	23	0	0	.144	.225	.248	.473	33	-12	8	1.95	-1	1-54,0-21(21-0-1)	1	-1.5
Total 10	**866**	**2020**	**248**	**512**	**73**	**17**	**52**	**245**	**158**	**270**	**16**	**15**	**.253**	**.314**	**.384**	**.698**	**95**	**-17**	**247**	**4.20**	**-9**	**1-640/0-74**	**52**	**-7.0**
• REEVES, Bobby	Robert Edwin "Gunner" Reeves b: 6/24/1904, Hill City, TN d: 6/4/1993, Chattanooga, TN BR/TR, 5'11", 170 lbs. Deb: 6/9/1926																							
1926 Was-A	20	49	4	11	0	1	0	7	6	9	1	1	.224	.321	.265	.587	56	-3	4	3.04	-2	3-16/2-1,S-1	1	-0.4
1927 Was-A	112	380	37	97	11	5	1	39	21	53	3	1	.255	.296	.318	.614	60	-22	37	3.25	-2	S-96,3-12/2-2	6	-1.2
1928 Was-A	102	353	44	107	16	8	3	42	24	47	4	8	.303	.351	.419	.770	102	-2	50	4.97	-8	S-66,2-22/3-8,0-1	9	-0.1
1929 Bos-A	140	460	66	114	19	2	2	28	60	57	7	8	.248	.343	.311	.654	71	-18	52	3.82	1	*3-131/2-2,S-2,1-1	9	-0.9
1930 Bos-A	92	272	41	59	7	4	2	18	50	36	6	2	.217	.345	.294	.639	66	-11	32	3.82	2	3-62,S-15,2-11	5	-0.3
1931 Bos-A	36	84	11	14	2	2	0	1	14	16	0	1	.167	.293	.238	.531	43	-6	7	2.41	-9	2-29/P-1	1	-1.3
Total 6	**502**	**1598**	**203**	**402**	**55**	**22**	**8**	**135**	**175**	**218**	**21**	**21**	**.252**	**.331**	**.329**	**.660**	**72**	**-63**	**182**	**3.82**	**-18**	**3-229,S-180/2-67,1-1,0-1,P**	**31**	**-4.3**
• REGALADO, Rudy	Rudolph Valentino Regalado b: 5/21/1930, Los Angeles, CA BR/TR, 6'1", 185 lbs. Deb: 4/13/1954																							
1954*Cle-A	65	180	21	45	5	0	2	24	19	16	0	2	.250	.335	.311	.646	76	-6	19	3.48	-4	3-50/2-2	4	-1.1
1955 Cle-A	10	26	2	7	2	0	0	5	2	4	0	0	.269	.321	.346	.668	77	-1	3	4.35	0	/3-8,2-1	1	-0.1
1956 Cle-A	16	47	4	11	1	0	0	2	4	1	0	0	.234	.308	.255	.563	49	-3	4	2.80	-2	3-14/1-1	0	-0.6
Total 3	**91**	**253**	**27**	**63**	**8**	**0**	**2**	**31**	**25**	**21**	**0**	**2**	**.249**	**.329**	**.304**	**.633**	**71**	**-10**	**26**	**3.44**	**-7**	**/3-72,2-3,1-1**	**5**	**-1.7**
• REGAN, Bill	William Wright Regan b: 1/23/1899, Pittsburgh, PA d: 6/11/1968, Pittsburgh, PA BR/TR, 5'10", 155 lbs. Deb: 6/2/1926																							
1926 Bos-A	108	403	40	106	21	3	4	34	23	37	6	3	.263	.309	.360	.669	77	-14	45	3.87	-4	*2-106	6	-1.5
1927 Bos-A	129	468	43	128	37	10	2	66	26	51	10	10	.274	.315	.408	.723	88	-12	58	4.19	-8	*2-121	10	-1.6
1928 Bos-A	138	511	53	135	30	6	7	75	21	40	9	6	.264	.296	.387	.683	80	-17	58	3.79	3	*2-137/0-1	9	-1.1
1929 Bos-A	104	371	38	107	27	7	1	54	22	38	7	5	.288	.328	.407	.735	90	-6	49	4.60	-11	2-91,3-10/1-1	8	-1.4
1930 Bos-A	134	507	54	135	35	10	3	53	25	60	4	2	.266	.303	.393	.696	78	-18	60	4.16	-4	*2-127/3-2	8	-1.7
1931 Pit-N	28	104	8	21	8	0	1	10	5	19	2	....	.202	.239	.308	.546	46	-8	8	2.36	-2	2-28	1	-0.8
Total 6	**641**	**2364**	**236**	**632**	**158**	**36**	**18**	**292**	**122**	**245**	**38**	**26**	**.267**	**.306**	**.387**	**.694**	**81**	**-77**	**278**	**4.02**	**-27**	**2-610/3-12,1-1,0-1**	**42**	**-8.1**
• REGAN, Joe	Joseph Charles Regan b: 7/12/1872, Seymour, CT d: 11/18/1948, Hartford, CT BR/TR, 6'1" Deb: 9/21/1898																							
1898 NY-N	2	5	1	1	0	0	0	2	0	....	0	....	.200	.200	.200	.400	15	-1	0	1.36	-0	/0-2(0-0-2)	0	-0.1
• REGO, Tony	Antone Rego b: 10/31/1897, Wailuku, HI d: 1/6/1978, Tulsa, OK BR/TR, 5'4", 165 lbs. Deb: 6/21/1924																							
1924 StL-A	24	59	5	13	1	0	0	5	1	3	0	0	.220	.233	.237	.471	20	-7	3	1.83	-1	C-23	1	-0.6
1925 StL-A	20	32	5	13	2	1	0	3	3	2	0	0	.406	.472	.531	1.003	147	3	8	11.41	1	C-19	2	0.4
Total 2	**44**	**91**	**10**	**26**	**3**	**1**	**0**	**8**	**4**	**5**	**0**	**0**	**.286**	**.323**	**.341**	**.664**	**67**	**-4**	**11**	**4.59**	**0**	**/C-42**	**3**	**-0.2**
• REHG, Wally	Walter Phillip Rehg b: 8/31/1888, Summerfield, IL d: 4/5/1946, Burbank, CA BR/TR, 5'8", 160 lbs. Deb: 4/14/1912 Career OF: 54-6-140																							
1912 Pit-N	8	9	1	0	0	0	0	0	0	1	0	....	.000	.000	.000	.000	-102	-2	0	.00	0	/0-2(0-1-1)	0	-0.3
1913 Bos-A	30	101	13	28	3	2	0	9	2	7	4	....	.277	.291	.347	.638	84	-3	11	3.63	-2	0-26(8-3-15)	2	-0.6
1914 Bos-A	88	151	14	33	4	2	0	11	18	11	5	8	.219	.306	.272	.577	74	-7	12	2.48	0	0-43(16-0-27)	2	-0.9
1915 Bos-A	5	5	2	1	0	0	0	0	0	1	1	....	.200	.200	.200	.400	20	-1	0	2.45	-0	/0-1	0	-0.1
1917 Bos-N	87	341	48	92	12	6	1	31	24	32	13	....	.270	.320	.349	.669	111	4	41	4.07	-6	0-86(0-0-86)	10	-0.7
1918 Bos-N	40	133	6	32	5	1	1	12	5	14	3	....	.241	.268	.316	.584	81	-4	11	2.86	2	0-38(30-1-7)	2	-0.3

YEAR	TM-L	G	AB	R	H	2B	3B	HR	RBI	BB	SO	SB	CS	AVG	OBP	SLG	OPS	OPS+	BR/A	RC	RC/G	FR	G/POS	WS	TPW
1919	Cin-N	5	12	1	2	0	0	0	3	1	0	0	....	.167	.231	.167	.397	21	-1	1	1.33	0	/0-5(0-1-3)	0	-0.1
Total	**7**	**263**	**752**	**85**	**188**	**24**	**11**	**2**	**66**	**50**	**66**	**26**	**8**	**.250**	**.299**	**.319**	**.618**	**90**	**-13**	**76**	**3.34**	**-5**	**0-201**	**16**	**-2.9**
• REIBER, Frank	Frank Bernard "Tubby" Reiber b: 9/19/1909, Huntington, WV d: 12/26/2002, Bradenton, FL BR/TR, 5'8.5", 169 lbs. Deb: 4/13/1933																								
1933	Det-A	13	18	3	5	0	1	1	3	2	3	0	0	.278	.350	.556	.906	134	1	4	7.21	-1	/C-6	1	0.0
1934	Det-A	3	1	0	0	0	0	0	0	2	0	0	0	.000	.667	.000	.667	84	0	0	8.82	0	....	0	0.0
1935	Det-A	8	11	3	3	0	0	0	1	3	3	0	0	.273	.429	.273	.701	88	0	2	5.15	-0	/C-5	1	0.0
1936	Det-A	20	55	7	15	2	0	1	5	5	7	0	1	.273	.333	.364	.697	72	-3	7	4.12	-1	C-17/0-1	1	-0.3
Total	**4**	**44**	**85**	**13**	**23**	**2**	**1**	**2**	**9**	**12**	**13**	**0**	**1**	**.271**	**.361**	**.388**	**.749**	**87**	**-2**	**12**	**4.95**	**-2**	**/C-28,0-1**	**3**	**-0.3**
• REICH, Herman	Herman Charles Reich b: 11/23/1917, Bell, CA BR/TL, 6'2", 200 lbs. Deb: 5/3/1949																								
1949	Was-A	2	2	0	0	0	0	0	0	0	1	0	0	.000	.000	.000	.000	-102	-1	0	.00	0	....	0	-0.1
	Cle-A	1	2	0	1	0	0	0	0	1	0	0	0	.500	.667	.500	1.167	215	1	1	23.13	0	/0-1	0	0.0
	Yr.	3	4	0	1	0	0	0	0	1	1	0	0	.250	.400	.250	.650	88	-0	1	7.71	0	/0-1	0	0.0
	Chi-N	108	386	43	108	18	2	3	34	13	32	4	....	.280	.305	.360	.665	80	-12	41	3.73	9	1-85,0-16(0-0-16)	6	-0.7
• REICHARDT, Rick	Frederic Carl Reichardt b: 3/16/1943, Madison, WI BR/TR, 6'3", 215 lbs. Deb: 9/1/1964 Career OF: 713-158-39																								
1964	LA-A	11	37	0	6	0	0	0	0	1	12	1	0	.162	.184	.162	.346	-3	-5	1	.87	0	0-11(0-11-0)	1	-0.6
1965	Cal-A	20	75	8	20	4	0	1	6	5	12	4	1	.267	.321	.360	.681	95	-0	9	4.05	0	0-20(17-4-0)	2	-0.1
1966	Cal-A	89	319	48	92	5	4	16	44	27	61	8	4	.288	.368	.480	.847	145	19	57	6.41	1	0-87(77-20-0)	16	1.7
1967	Cal-A	146	498	56	132	14	2	17	69	35	90	5	3	.265	.322	.404	.726	118	10	61	4.25	5	*0-138(138-0-0)	18	0.8
1968	Cal-A	151	534	62	136	20	3	21	73	42	118	8	7	.255	.330	.421	.751	131	18	72	4.57	0	*0-148(148-0-0)	21	1.2
1969	Cal-A	137	493	60	125	11	4	13	68	43	100	3	6	.254	.324	.371	.695	99	-3	56	3.77	4	*0-136(136-0-0)/1-3	12	-0.8
1970	Cal-A	9	6	1	1	0	0	0	1	3	0	0	0	.167	.444	.167	.611	78	0	1	3.67	-0	/0-1	0	0.0
	Was-A	107	277	42	70	14	2	15	46	23	69	2	4	.253	.330	.480	.810	127	8	39	4.67	-3	0-79(38-18-31)/3-1	8	0.2
	Yr.	116	283	43	71	14	2	15	47	26	69	2	4	.251	.333	.473	.807	125	8	40	4.64	-3	0-80(38-18-32)/3-1	8	0.2
1971	Chi-A	138	496	53	138	14	2	19	62	37	90	5	10	.278	.336	.429	.765	112	4	67	4.70	-4	*0-128(117-15-0)/1-9	13	-0.7
1972	Chi-A	101	291	31	73	14	4	8	43	28	63	2	2	.251	.323	.409	.732	114	5	39	4.53	-6	0-90(11-84-0)	10	-0.4
1973	Chi-A	46	153	15	42	8	1	3	16	8	29	2	3	.275	.315	.399	.714	96	-2	18	4.10	0	0-37(30-6-1)/D-6	3	-0.4
	KC-A	41	127	15	28	5	2	3	17	11	28	0	1	.220	.283	.362	.645	75	-5	12	2.98	1	D-31/0-7(1-0-6)	1	-0.6
	Yr.	87	280	30	70	13	3	6	33	19	57	2	4	.250	.300	.382	.682	86	-7	30	3.56	1	0-44(31-6-7),D-37	4	-0.9
1974	KC-A	1	1	0	1	0	0	0	0	0	0	0	0	1.000	1.000	1.000	2.000	451	0	1	∞	0	....	0	0.0
Total	**11**	**997**	**3307**	**391**	**864**	**109**	**24**	**116**	**445**	**263**	**672**	**40**	**41**	**.261**	**.328**	**.414**	**.742**	**115**	**49**	**433**	**4.44**	**-1**	**0-882/D-37,1-12,3-1**	**105**	**0.4**
• REICHLE, Dick	Richard Wendell Reichle b: 11/23/1896, Lincoln, IL d: 6/13/1967, Richmond Heights, MO BL/TR, 6', 185 lbs. Deb: 9/19/1922 Career OF: 3-93-4																								
1922	Bos-A	6	24	3	6	1	0	0	0	0	2	0	0	.250	.280	.292	.572	49	-2	2	2.87	-1	/0-6(0-6-0)	0	-0.2
1923	Bos-A	122	361	40	93	17	3	1	39	22	34	3	6	.258	.315	.330	.644	69	-18	37	3.51	-3	0-93(3-87-4)/1-2	5	-2.3
Total	**2**	**128**	**385**	**43**	**99**	**18**	**3**	**1**	**39**	**22**	**36**	**3**	**6**	**.257**	**.313**	**.327**	**.640**	**68**	**-19**	**39**	**3.47**	**-4**	**/0-99,1-2**	**5**	**-2.6**
• REID, Billy	William Alexander Reid b: 5/17/1857, London, Canada d: 6/26/1940, London, Canada BL/TR, 6', 170 lbs. Deb: 5/1/1883																								
1883	Bal-a	24	97	14	27	3	0	0	0	4	....	....	....	.278	.307	.309	.616	96	-1	9	3.78	-5	2-23/S-1	2	-0.4
1884	Pit-a	19	70	11	17	2	0	0	0	4	....	....	....	.243	.293	.271	.565	84	-1	6	2.96	-4	0-17(17-0-0)/2-1,3-1	1	-0.5
Total	**2**	**43**	**167**	**25**	**44**	**5**	**0**	**0**	**0**	**8**	**....**	**....**	**....**	**.263**	**.301**	**.293**	**.595**	**91**	**-2**	**15**	**3.43**	**-9**	**/2-24,0-17,3-1,S-1**	**3**	**-0.9**
• REID, Jessie	Jessie Thomas Reid b: 6/1/1962, Honolulu, HI BL/TL, 6'1", 200 lbs. Deb: 9/9/1987																								
1987	SF-N	6	8	1	1	0	0	1	1	1	5	0	0	.125	.222	.500	.722	89	-0	1	3.65	0	/0-3(1-0-2)	0	0.0
1988	SF-N	2	2	0	0	0	0	0	0	0	1	0	0	.000	.000	.000	.000	-105	-0	0	.00	0	....	0	-0.1
Total	**2**	**8**	**10**	**1**	**1**	**0**	**0**	**1**	**1**	**1**	**6**	**0**	**0**	**.100**	**.182**	**.400**	**.582**	**54**	**-1**	**1**	**2.84**	**0**	**/0-3**	**0**	**-0.1**
• REID, Scott	Scott Donald Reid b: 1/7/1947, Chicago, IL BL/TR, 6'1", 195 lbs. Deb: 9/10/1969 Career OF: 5-16-5																								
1969	Phi-N	13	19	5	4	0	0	0	0	7	5	0	1	.211	.423	.211	.634	85	-0	2	3.06	0	/0-5(2-4-0)	0	0.0
1970	Phi-N	25	49	5	6	1	0	0	1	11	22	0	0	.122	.283	.143	.426	18	-5	3	1.61	3	0-18(3-12-5)	0	-0.3
Total	**2**	**38**	**68**	**10**	**10**	**1**	**0**	**0**	**1**	**18**	**27**	**0**	**1**	**.147**	**.326**	**.162**	**.487**	**38**	**-5**	**5**	**2.02**	**3**	**/0-23**	**0**	**-0.3**
• REILLEY, Charlie	Charles E. Reilley b: 1856, Hartford, CT BR/TR, 5'10", 165 lbs. Deb: 5/1/1879 Career OF: 3-15-6																								
1879	Tro-N	62	236	17	54	5	1	0	19	1	20	....	....	.229	.232	.258	.491	66	-8	15	2.23	-15	C-49,1-11/0-2(1-0-1)	2	-2.1
1880	Cin-N	30	103	8	21	1	0	0	9	0	5	....	....	.204	.204	.214	.417	42	-6	5	1.54	-2	0-16(1-14-1),C-13/3-4	1	-0.8
1881	Det-N	19	70	8	12	2	0	0	3	0	10	....	....	.171	.171	.200	.371	16	-7	2	1.15	-3	C-10/0-4(1-1-2),3-3,S-3,1	1	-0.9
	Wor-N	2	8	2	3	0	0	0	1	0	1	....	....	.375	.375	.375	.750	129	0	1	6.23	-1	/C-2	0	0.0
	Yr.	21	78	10	15	2	0	0	4	0	11	....	....	.192	.192	.218	.410	27	-7	4	1.55	-4	C-12/0-4(1-1-2),3-3,S-3,1	1	-1.0
1882	Pro-N	3	11	0	2	0	0	0	2	1	2	....	....	.182	.250	.182	.432	41	-1	1	1.57	-2	/C-3	0	-0.3
1884	Bos-U	3	11	1	0	0	0	0	....	1	....	....	....	.000	.083	.000	.083	-71	-2	0	.00	0	/0-2(0-0-2),3-1	0	-0.2
Total	**5**	**119**	**439**	**36**	**92**	**8**	**1**	**0**	**34**	**3**	**38**	**....**	**....**	**.210**	**.215**	**.232**	**.447**	**49**	**-23**	**23**	**1.86**	**-24**	**/C-77,0-24,1-12,3-8,S-3**	**4**	**-4.3**
• REILLEY, Duke	Alexander Aloysius "Midget" Reilley b: 8/25/1884, Chicago, IL d: 3/4/1968, Indianapolis, IN BB/TR, 5'4.5", 148 lbs. Deb: 8/28/1909																								
1909	Cle-A	20	62	10	13	0	0	0	0	4	....	5	....	.210	.258	.210	.467	46	-4	5	2.37	2	0-18(13-5-0)	1	-0.3
• REILLY, Arch	Archer Edwin Reilly b: 8/17/1891, Alton, IL d: 11/29/1963, Columbus, OH BR/TR, 5'10", 163 lbs. Deb: 6/1/1917																								
1917	Pit-N	1	0	0	0	0	0	0	0	0	0	0	....	....	....	....	....	-97	0	0	....	0	/3-1	0	0.0
• REILLY, Barney	Bernard Eugene Reilly b: 2/7/1884, Brockton, MA d: 11/15/1934, St. Joseph, MO BR/TR, 6', 175 lbs. Deb: 7/2/1909																								
1909	Chi-A	12	25	3	5	0	0	0	3	3	....	2	....	.200	.286	.200	.486	56	-1	2	2.56	-1	2-11/0-1	1	-0.3
• REILLY, Charlie	Charles Thomas "Princeton Charlie" Reilly b: 2/15/1867, Princeton, NJ d: 12/16/1937, Los Angeles, CA BB/TR, 5'11", 190 lbs. Deb: 10/9/1889 U Career OF: 10-11-4																								
1889	Col-a	6	23	5	11	1	0	3	6	2	2	9	....	.478	.538	.913	1.452	326	7	17	36.56	1	/3-6	3	0.7
1890	Col-a	137	530	75	141	23	3	4	77	35	....	43	....	.266	.319	.343	.662	102	1	74	5.01	32	*3-137	20	3.2
1891	Pit-N	114	415	43	91	8	5	3	44	29	58	20	....	.219	.277	.284	.561	65	-19	39	3.26	2	*3-99,S-11/0-4(1-3-0)	6	-1.3
1892	Phi-N	91	331	42	65	7	3	1	24	18	43	13	....	.196	.242	.245	.487	47	-22	23	2.37	12	3-70,0-15(5-8-2)/2-4	5	-0.9
1893	Phi-N	104	416	64	102	16	7	4	56	33	36	13	....	.245	.314	.346	.661	76	-16	51	4.27	0	*3-104	8	-1.2
1894	Phi-N	40	136	21	40	1	2	0	19	16	10	9	....	.294	.381	.331	.712	75	-4	21	5.71	5	3-28/0-5(4-0-1),2-4,1-1,S	3	0.1
1895	Phi-N	49	179	28	48	6	1	0	25	13	12	7	....	.268	.335	.313	.648	67	-8	23	4.39	-1	S-34,3-11/2-3,0-1	3	-0.6
1897	Was-N	101	351	64	97	18	3	2	60	34	....	18	....	.276	.359	.362	.720	91	-4	54	5.49	9	*3-101	10	0.6
Total	**8**	**642**	**2381**	**342**	**595**	**80**	**24**	**17**	**311**	**180**	**161**	**132**	**....**	**.250**	**.314**	**.325**	**.639**	**80**	**-66**	**302**	**4.45**	**60**	**3-556/S-46,0-25,2-11,1-1**	**58**	**0.5**
• REILLY, Hal	Harold John Reilly b: 4/1/1894, Oshkosh, WI d: 12/24/1957, Chicago, IL BR/TR, 6', 180 lbs. Deb: 6/19/1919																								
1919	Chi-N	1	3	0	0	0	0	0	0	0	1	0	....	.000	.000	.000	.000	-100	-1	0	.00	0	/0-1	0	-0.1
• REILLY, Joe	Joseph J. Reilly b: 1861, New York, NY, 5'10", 140 lbs. Deb: 6/8/1885																								
1885	NY-a	10	40	6	7	3	0	0	3	2	....	....	....	.175	.214	.250	.464	50	-2	2	1.80	0	/2-8,3-2	0	-0.2
• REILLY, John	John Good "Long John" Reilly b: 10/5/1858, Cincinnati, OH d: 5/31/1937, Cincinnati, OH BR/TR, 6'3", 178 lbs. Deb: 5/18/1880 Career OF: 27-27-24																								
1880	Cin-N	73	272	21	56	8	4	0	16	3	36	....	....	.206	.215	.265	.479	62	-10	16	2.02	-9	*1-72/0-3(0-0-3)	1	-2.2
1883	Cin-a	98	437	103	136	21	14	9	79	9	....	....	....	.311	.325	.485	.810	149	21	71	6.57	-2	*1-98/0-1	18	0.9
1884	Cin-a	105	448	114	152	24	19	**11**	91	5	....	....	....	.339	.366	**.551**	**.918**	186	40	93	**8.61**	-4	*1-103/0-3(0-0-3),S-1	25	2.5
1885	Cin-a	111	482	92	143	18	11	5	60	11	....	....	....	.297	.322	.411	.733	128	13	65	5.20	-7	*1-107/0-7(0-2-5)	16	-0.2
1886	Cin-a	115	441	92	117	12	11	6	79	31	....	19	....	.265	.321	.383	.704	116	7	62	5.15	-7	*1-110/0-6(0-5-1)	13	-0.9
1887	Cin-a	134	573	106	192	35	14	10	96	22	....	50	....	.335	.352	.477	.829	127	16	113	8.00	4	*1-127/0-9(1-6-2)	18	0.7
1888	Cin-a	127	527	112	169	28	14	**13**	**103**	17	....	82	....	.321	.363	**.501**	**.864**	**167**	36	129	**9.71**	0	*1-117,0-10(0-2-8)	25	2.3
1889	Cin-a	111	427	84	111	24	13	5	66	34	37	43	....	.260	.340	.412	.752	110	4	76	6.41	0	*1-109/0-2(1-1-0)	12	-0.4
1890	Cin-N	133	553	114	166	25	**26**	6	86	16	41	29	....	.300	.328	.472	.800	133	17	98	6.68	-1	*1-132/0-1	16	0.4

YEAR TM-L	G	AB	R	H	2B	3B	HR	RBI	BB	SO	SB	CS	AVG	OBP	SLG	OPS	OPS+	BR/A	RC	RC/G	FR	G/POS	WS	TPW
1891 Cin-N	135	546	60	132	20	13	4	64	9	42	22	....	.242	.267	.348	.615	78	-19	58	3.79	-4	*1-100,0-36(25-10-1)	7	-3.0
Total 10	1142	4706	898	1374	215	139	69	740	157	156	245	....	.292	.325	.438	.763	128	125	780	6.33	-31	*1-1075/0-78,S-1	151	0.1
• REILLY, Josh	William Henry Reilly b: 5/9/1868, San Francisco, CA d: 6/12/1938, San Francisco, CA BR/TR, 5'8" Deb: 5/2/1896																							
1896 Chi-N	9	42	6	9	1	0	0	2	1	1	2	....	.214	.233	.238	.471	23	-5	3	2.30	0	/2-8,S-1	0	-0.4
• REILLY, Tom	Thomas Henry Reilly b: 8/3/1884, St. Louis, MO d: 10/18/1918, New Orleans, LA BR/TR, 5'10" Deb: 7/27/1908																							
1908 StL-N	29	81	5	14	1	0	1	3	2	....	4	....	.173	.193	.222	.415	34	-6	4	1.53	-5	S-29	0	-1.3
1909 StL-N	5	7	0	2	0	1	0	2	0	....	0	....	.286	.286	.571	.857	176	0	1	5.67	0	/S-5	0	0.0
1914 Cle-A	1	1	0	0	0	0	0	0	0	0	0	....	.000	.000	.000	.000	-96	-0	0	.00	0	....	0	0.0
Total 3	35	89	5	16	1	1	1	5	2	0	4	....	.180	.198	.247	.445	43	-6	5	1.79	-6	/S-34	0	-1.3
• REIMER, Kevin	Kevin Michael Reimer b: 6/28/1964, Macon, GA BL/TR, 6'2", 225 lbs. Deb: 9/13/1988 Career OF: 205-0-21																							
1988 Tex-A	12	25	2	3	0	0	1	2	0	6	0	0	.120	.120	.240	.360	-2	-3	1	.88	0	/D-7,0-1	0	-0.4
1989 Tex-A	3	5	0	0	0	0	0	0	0	1	0	0	.000	.000	.000	.000	-98	-1	0	.00	0	/D-1	0	-0.1
1990 Tex-A	64	100	5	26	9	1	2	15	10	22	0	1	.260	.333	.430	.763	112	1	14	4.72	-1	D-21/0-9(5-0-5)	3	-0.1
1991 Tex-A	136	394	46	106	22	0	20	69	33	93	0	3	.269	.336	.477	.814	125	11	60	5.32	-3	0-66(61-0-6),D-56	13	0.4
1992 Tex-A	148	494	56	132	32	2	16	58	42	103	2	4	.267	.337	.437	.774	120	11	71	5.11	1	*0-110(110-0-0),D-32	12	0.7
1993 Mil-A	125	437	53	109	22	1	13	60	30	72	5	4	.249	.305	.394	.699	88	-9	50	3.85	-2	D-83,0-37(28-0-10)	5	-1.7
Total 6	488	1455	162	376	85	4	52	204	115	297	7	12	.258	.323	.430	.752	108	8	196	4.64	-5	0-223,D-200	33	-1.2
• REINBACH, Mike	Michael Wayne Reinbach b: 8/6/1949, San Diego, CA d: 5/20/1989, Palm Desert, CA BL/TR, 6'2", 195 lbs. Deb: 4/7/1974																							
1974 Bal-A	12	20	2	5	1	0	0	2	2	5	0	0	.250	.318	.300	.618	81	-0	2	3.48	-0	/D-3,0-3(1-0-2)	0	-0.1
• REINECKER, Wally	Walter Joseph Reinecker b: 4/21/1890, Pittsburgh, PA d: 4/18/1957, Pittsburgh, PA BR/TR, 5'6", 150 lbs. Deb: 9/17/1915																							
1915 Bal-F	3	8	0	1	0	0	0	0	0	0	0	....	.125	.222	.125	.347	3	-1	0	.76	-2	/3-3	0	-0.3
• REINHOLZ, Art	Arthur August Reinholz b: 1/27/1903, Detroit, MI d: 12/29/1980, New Port Richey, FL BR/TR, 5'10.5", 175 lbs. Deb: 9/27/1928																							
1928 Cle-A	2	3	0	1	0	0	0	0	1	0	0	0	.333	.500	.333	.833	122	0	1	8.01	0	/3-2	0	0.0
• REIPSCHLAGER, Charlie	Charles W. Reipschlager b: 2/1854, New York, NY d: 3/16/1910, Atlantic City, NJ BR/TR, 5'6.5", 160 lbs. Deb: 5/2/1883 Career OF: 8-18-5																							
1883 NY-a	37	145	8	27	4	2	0	0	4	....	....	....	.186	.208	.241	.449	42	-10	7	1.77	3	C-29/0-8(0-7-1)	3	-0.4
1884*NY-a	59	233	21	56	13	2	0	0	1	....	....	....	.240	.250	.313	.563	85	-4	19	2.91	12	C-51/0-8(5-2-1)	7	1.1
1885 NY-a	72	268	29	65	11	1	0	21	9	....	....	....	.243	.270	.291	.561	84	-4	22	2.87	12	C-59/3-6,0-6(2-3-1),2-1,S	6	1.1
1886 NY-a	65	232	21	49	4	6	0	25	9	....	2	....	.211	.244	.280	.524	67	-9	17	2.47	3	C-57/0-9(1-6-2)	4	-0.1
1887 Cle-a	63	242	20	60	8	3	0	17	11	....	7	....	.248	.251	.273	.524	47	-16	18	2.67	6	C-48,1-16	3	-0.6
Total 5	296	1120	99	257	40	14	0	63	34	....	9	....	.229	.248	.283	.531	67	-43	82	2.60	36	C-244/0-31,1-16,3-6,2-1,S-1	23	1.1
• REIS, Bobby	Robert Joseph Thomas Reis b: 1/2/1909, Woodside, NY d: 5/1/1973, St. Paul, MN BR/TR, 6'1", 175 lbs. Deb: 9/19/1931 Career OF: 19-17-15 ♦																							
1931 Bro-N	6	17	3	5	0	0	0	2	2	0	0	....	.294	.368	.294	.663	81	-0	2	3.93	-1	/3-6	0	-0.1
1932 Bro-N	1	4	0	1	0	0	0	0	0	1	0	....	.250	.250	.250	.500	36	-0	0	2.11	0	/3-1	0	-0.1
1935 Bro-N	52	85	10	21	3	2	0	4	6	13	2	....	.247	.297	.329	.626	70	-2	8	3.40	4	0-21(4-3-14),P-14/2-4,1-1,3	4	0.5
1936 Bos-N	37	60	3	13	2	0	0	5	3	6	0	....	.217	.254	.250	.504	39	0	4	2.36	3	P-35/0-2(0-2-0)	6	-1.1
1937 Bos-N	45	86	10	21	5	0	0	6	13	12	2	....	.244	.343	.302	.646	84	-1	10	3.91	-1	0-18(6-12-0)/1-4,P-4	3	-0.2
1938 Bos-N	34	49	6	9	0	0	0	4	1	3	1	....	.184	.200	.184	.384	7	-4	2	1.14	-1	P-16,0-10(9-0-1)/S-3,2-1,C	0	-1.6
Total 6	175	301	32	70	10	2	0	21	25	35	5	....	.233	.291	.279	.570	58	-7	26	2.95	4	/P-69,0-51,3-8,1-5,2-5,S-3,C	13	-2.6
• REISER, Pete	Harold Patrick Reiser b: 3/17/1919, St. Louis, MO d: 10/25/1981, Palm Springs, CA BL/TR, 5'11", 185 lbs. Deb: 7/23/1940 C Career OF: 209-413-17																							
1940 Bro-N	58	225	34	66	11	4	3	20	15	33	2	....	.293	.338	.418	.755	101	-0	31	5.18	3	3-30,0-17(5-1-9)/S-5	7	0.4
1941*Bro-N★	137	536	**117**	184	**39**	**17**	14	76	46	71	4	....	**.343**	.406	**.558**	**.964**	**163**	44	124	**9.17**	5	*0-133(0-133-2)	**34**	**4.7**
1942 Bro-N★	125	480	89	149	33	5	10	64	48	45	**20**	....	.310	.375	.463	.838	142	25	88	7.06	-9	*0-125(0-125-0)	28	1.3
1946 Bro-N★	122	423	75	117	21	5	11	73	55	58	**34**	....	.277	.361	.428	.789	122	12	70	6.02	7	0-97(69-28-0),3-15	19	1.5
1947*Bro-N	110	388	68	120	23	2	5	46	68	41	14	....	.309	.415	.418	.832	117	13	74	7.24	-1	*0-108(51-62-0)	18	0.7
1948 Bro-N	64	127	17	30	8	2	1	19	29	21	4	....	.236	.382	.354	.736	97	1	20	5.25	-1	0-30(17-10-5)/3-4	4	-0.1
1949 Bos-N	84	221	32	60	8	3	8	40	33	42	3	....	.271	.369	.443	.812	123	8	38	6.08	-2	0-63(27-36-0)/3-4	8	0.4
1950 Bos-N	53	78	12	16	2	0	1	10	18	22	1	....	.205	.367	.269	.637	75	-2	9	4.01	-2	0-24(16-6-0)/3-1	2	-0.4
1951 Pit-N	74	140	22	38	9	3	2	13	27	20	4	2	.271	.389	.421	.811	115	4	25	6.47	-2	0-27(20-6-1)/3-5	5	0.1
1952 Cle-A	34	44	7	6	1	0	3	7	4	16	1	1	.136	.208	.364	.572	61	-3	3	2.02	-1	0-10(4-6-0)	0	-0.4
Total 10	861	2662	473	786	155	41	58	368	343	369	87	3	.295	.380	.450	.829	127	102	483	6.74	-1	0-634/3-59,S-5	125	8.1
• REISING, Charlie	Charles "Pop" Reising b: 8/28/1861, Lanesville, IN d: 7/26/1915, Louisville, KY Deb: 7/19/1884																							
1884 Ind-a	2	8	0	0	0	0	0	0	1	....	....	....	.000	.111	.000	.111	-62	-1	0	.00	-1	/0-2(1-1-1)	0	-0.2
• REISS, Al	Albert Allen Reiss b: 1/8/1909, Elizabeth, NJ d: 5/13/1989, Red Bank, NJ BB/TR, 5'10.5", 165 lbs. Deb: 6/22/1932																							
1932 Phi-A	9	5	0	1	0	0	0	1	1	1	0	0	.200	.333	.200	.533	40	-0	0	2.67	-2	/S-6	0	-0.2
• REITZ, Heinie	Henry P. Reitz b: 6/29/1867, Chicago, IL d: 11/10/1914, Sacramento, CA BL/TR, 5'7", 158 lbs. Deb: 4/27/1893 U																							
1893 Bal-N	130	490	90	140	17	13	1	76	65	32	24	....	.286	.377	.380	.757	100	1	81	6.15	1	*2-130	14	0.6
1894*Bal-N	108	446	86	135	22	**31**	2	105	42	24	18	....	.303	.372	.504	.876	105	0	93	7.74	16	*2-97,3-12	17	1.6
1895 Bal-N	71	245	45	72	15	5	0	29	18	11	15	....	.294	.350	.396	.746	89	-5	41	6.10	3	2-48,3-18/S-1	6	0.1
1896*Bal-N	120	464	76	133	15	6	4	106	49	32	28	....	.287	.357	.371	.728	91	-6	75	5.77	-9	*2-118/S-3	13	-0.8
1897*Bal-N	128	477	76	138	15	6	2	84	50	....	23	....	.289	.370	.358	.728	93	-3	74	5.71	20	*2-128	17	1.9
1898 Was-N	132	489	62	148	20	2	2	47	32	....	11	....	.303	.357	.364	.721	107	4	71	5.30	1	*2-132	12	1.0
1899 Pit-N	35	133	12	35	4	2	0	16	10	....	3	....	.263	.315	.323	.638	75	-5	15	3.98	4	2-34	2	0.1
Total 7	724	2744	447	801	108	65	11	463	266	99	122	....	.292	.363	.391	.753	97	-12	450	5.99	36	2-687/3-30,S-4	81	4.5
• REITZ, Ken	Kenneth John Reitz b: 6/24/1951, San Francisco, CA BR/TR, 6', 185 lbs. Deb: 9/5/1972																							
1972 StL-N	21	78	5	28	4	0	0	10	2	4	0	1	.359	.375	.410	.785	124	2	10	4.92	-3	3-20	2	-0.1
1973 StL-N	147	426	40	100	20	2	6	42	9	25	0	1	.235	.257	.333	.591	63	-23	31	2.40	-3	*3-135/S-1	5	-2.8
1974 StL-N	154	579	48	157	28	2	7	54	23	63	0	0	.271	.301	.363	.664	86	-13	56	3.33	-11	*3-151/S-2,2-1	9	-2.6
1975 StL-N	161	592	43	159	25	1	5	63	22	54	1	1	.269	.300	.340	.640	75	-22	56	3.29	-16	*3-160	9	-4.0
1976 SF-N	155	577	40	154	21	1	5	66	24	48	5	4	.267	.297	.333	.630	76	-20	51	2.95	-7	*3-155/S-1	9	-3.0
1977 StL-N	157	587	58	153	36	1	17	79	19	74	2	6	.261	.292	.412	.704	88	-15	64	3.70	0	*3-157	15	-1.7
1978 StL-N	150	540	41	133	26	2	10	75	23	61	1	0	.246	.283	.357	.641	79	-17	52	3.29	-4	*3-150	12	-2.4
1979 StL-N	159	605	42	162	41	2	8	73	25	85	1	0	.268	.301	.382	.683	84	-15	67	3.89	-15	*3-158	11	-3.3
1980 StL-N★	151	523	39	141	33	0	8	58	22	44	0	1	.270	.303	.379	.682	86	-12	56	3.65	-9	*3-150	10	-2.4
1981 Chi-N	82	260	10	56	9	1	2	28	15	56	0	0	.215	.266	.281	.547	53	-16	18	2.25	-2	3-81	2	-2.1
1982 Pit-N	7	10	0	0	0	0	0	0	0	4	0	0	.000	.091	.000	.091	-70	-2	0	.06	0	/3-4	0	-0.2
Total 11	1344	4777	366	1243	243	12	68	548	184	518	10	14	.260	.293	.359	.651	79	-154	461	3.29	-70	*3-1321/S-4,2-1	84	-24.5
• RELAFORD, Desi	Desmond Lamont Relaford b: 9/16/1973, Valdosta, GA BB/TR, 5'8", 155 lbs. Deb: 8/1/1996 Career OF: 26-5-25																							
1996 Phi-N	15	40	2	7	2	0	0	1	3	9	1	0	.175	.233	.225	.458	21	-4	2	1.71	0	/S-9,2-4	0	-0.4
1997 Phi-N	15	38	3	7	1	2	0	6	5	6	3	0	.184	.279	.316	.595	55	-2	4	3.54	-1	S-12	1	-0.2
1998 Phi-N	142	494	45	121	25	3	5	41	33	87	9	5	.245	.296	.338	.634	65	-26	49	3.30	-14	*S-137	5	-2.8
1999 Phi-N	65	211	31	51	11	2	1	26	19	34	4	3	.242	.322	.327	.649	63	-12	23	3.50	2	S-63	4	-0.4
2000 Phi-N	83	253	29	56	12	3	3	30	48	45	5	0	.221	.365	.328	.693	76	-6	34	4.42	-4	S-81	7	-0.3
SD-N	45	157	26	32	2	0	2	16	27	26	8	0	.204	.332	.255	.586	55	-8	17	3.44	0	S-45	5	-0.4
Yr.	128	410	55	88	14	3	5	46	75	71	13	0	.215	.352	.300	.652	68	-14	50	4.04	-4	*S-126	12	-0.7
2001 NY-N	120	301	43	91	27	0	8	36	27	65	13	5	.302	.369	.472	.841	121	10	54	6.43	-7	2-54,S-25,3-20/P-1	13	0.7
2002 Sea-A	112	329	55	88	13	2	6	43	33	51	10	3	.267	.345	.374	.719	95	-1	45	4.66	0	S-40,3-38,0-35(25-0-10),2-11/D	9	0.1

YEAR TM-L	G	AB	R	H	2B	3B	HR	RBI	BB	SO	SB	CS	AVG	OBP	SLG	OPS	OPS+	BR/A	RC	RC/G	FR	G/POS	WS	TPW
2003 KC-A	141	500	70	127	27	5	8	59	40	70	20	4	.254	.317	.376	.693	72	-18	62	4.18	-2	2-89,3-33,0-20(1-5-15)/S-6,D	11	-1.5
Total 8	738	2323	304	580	120	17	33	258	235	393	73	20	.250	.329	.359	.687	78	-67	289	4.18	-27	S-418,2-158/3-91,0-55,D-6,P	55	-5.3

• REMENTER, Butch Willis J. H. Rementer b: 3/14/1878, Philadelphia, PA d: 9/23/1922, Philadelphia, PA BR/TR, 5'6.5" Deb: 10/8/1904

YEAR TM-L	G	AB	R	H	2B	3B	HR	RBI	BB	SO	SB	CS	AVG	OBP	SLG	OPS	OPS+	BR/A	RC	RC/G	FR	G/POS	WS	TPW
1904 Phi-N	1	2	0	0	0	0	0	0	0	....	0	....	.000	.000	.000	.000	-104	-0	0	.00	-0	/C-1	0	0.0

• REMSEN, Jack John Jay Remsen b: 1851, Brooklyn, NY BR/TR, 5'11", 189 lbs. Deb: 5/2/1872 U NA OF: 8-225-5 Career OF: 40-290-0

YEAR TM-L	G	AB	R	H	2B	3B	HR	RBI	BB	SO	SB	CS	AVG	OBP	SLG	OPS	OPS+	BR/A	RC	RC/G	FR	G/POS	WS	TPW
1872 Atl-n	37	164	25	40	4	5	0	13	2	6	1	2	.244	.253	.329	.582	66	-10	14	3.51	3	*0-37(0-37-0)	....	-0.5
1873 Atl-n	50	207	29	61	4	6	1	29	2	2	1	2	.295	.301	.386	.688	115	5	25	5.16	1	*0-50(0-50-0)	....	0.5
1874 Mut-n	64	284	52	65	9	3	2	37	0	5	6	0	.229	.229	.303	.532	67	-10	22	2.96	2	*0-63(8-57-0)/1-3	....	-0.6
1875 Har-n	86	358	70	96	10	4	0	34	5	4	6	3	.268	.278	.318	.597	102	-0	34	3.81	-0	*0-86(0-81-5)	....	0.0
1876 Har-N	69	325	62	89	12	5	1	30	1	15	....	....	.274	.277	.352	.629	100	-2	32	3.86	10	*0-69(3-66-0)	11	0.4
1877 StL-N	33	123	14	32	3	4	0	13	4	3	....	....	.260	.283	.350	.633	104	1	12	3.78	1	0-33(0-33-0)	4	0.0
1878 Chi-N	56	224	32	52	11	1	1	19	**17**	33	....	....	.232	.286	.304	.590	88	-3	20	3.19	6	*0-56(0-56-0)	5	0.1
1879 Chi-N	42	152	14	33	4	2	0	8	2	23	....	....	.217	.227	.270	.497	59	-7	10	2.25	-1	0-31(5-26-0),1-11	2	-0.9
1881 Cle-N	48	172	14	30	4	3	0	13	9	31	....	....	.174	.215	.233	.448	43	-10	9	1.68	-4	0-48(0-48-0)	2	-1.6
1884 Phi-N	12	43	9	9	2	0	0	3	6	9	....	....	.209	.306	.256	.562	82	-0	3	2.79	1	0-12(0-12-0)	1	0.0
Bro-a	81	301	45	67	6	6	3	0	23	....	....	....	.223	.278	.312	.590	91	-2	27	3.15	0	*0-81(32-49-0)	8	-0.5
Total 4 n	237	1013	176	262	27	18	3	113	9	17	14	7	.259	.265	.330	.595	89	-15	95	3.78	6	0-236/1-3	....	-0.7
Total 6	341	1340	190	312	42	21	5	86	62	114	....	....	.233	.267	.307	.574	84	-24	113	3.05	14	0-330/1-11	33	-2.4

• REMY, Jerry Gerald Peter Remy b: 11/8/1952, Fall River, MA BL/TR, 5'9", 165 lbs. Deb: 4/7/1975

YEAR TM-L	G	AB	R	H	2B	3B	HR	RBI	BB	SO	SB	CS	AVG	OBP	SLG	OPS	OPS+	BR/A	RC	RC/G	FR	G/POS	WS	TPW
1975 Cal-A	147	569	82	147	17	5	1	46	45	55	34	21	.258	.313	.311	.624	83	-15	53	3.03	15	*2-147	15	1.0
1976 Cal-A	143	502	64	132	14	3	0	28	38	43	35	16	.263	.315	.303	.618	87	-8	50	3.34	8	*2-133/D-5	17	1.0
1977 Cal-A	154	575	74	145	19	10	4	44	59	59	41	17	.252	.324	.341	.665	85	-9	67	3.77	-5	*2-152/3-1	14	-0.6
1978 Bos-A★	148	583	87	162	24	6	2	44	40	55	30	13	.278	.324	.350	.674	81	-13	66	3.80	6	*2-140/D-4,S-1	16	0.1
1979 Bos-A	80	306	49	91	11	2	0	29	26	25	14	9	.297	.352	.346	.699	85	-7	39	4.46	-7	2-76	7	-1.0
1980 Bos-A	63	230	24	72	7	2	0	9	10	14	14	6	.313	.342	.361	.703	88	-3	27	4.14	-4	2-60/0-1	6	-0.5
1981 Bos-A	88	358	55	110	9	1	0	31	36	30	9	2	.307	.371	.338	.709	99	3	48	4.77	-6	2-87	12	0.2
1982 Bos-A	155	636	89	178	22	3	0	47	55	77	16	9	.280	.339	.324	.663	79	-17	71	3.82	-23	*2-154	14	-3.2
1983 Bos-A	146	592	73	163	16	5	0	43	40	35	11	3	.275	.321	.319	.640	72	-21	62	3.63	-18	*2-144	11	-3.1
1984 Bos-A	30	104	8	26	1	1	0	8	7	11	4	3	.250	.297	.279	.576	58	-6	9	2.80	-2	2-24	1	-0.7
Total 10	1154	4455	605	1226	140	38	7	329	356	404	208	99	.275	.329	.328	.658	82	-96	492	3.73	-37	*2-1117/D-9,3-1,0-1,S-1	113	-6.8

• RENICK, Rick Warren Richard Renick b: 3/16/1944, London, OH BR/TR, 6', 190 lbs. Deb: 7/11/1968 C Career OF: 59-1-4

YEAR TM-L	G	AB	R	H	2B	3B	HR	RBI	BB	SO	SB	CS	AVG	OBP	SLG	OPS	OPS+	BR/A	RC	RC/G	FR	G/POS	WS	TPW
1968 Min-A	42	97	16	21	5	2	3	13	9	42	0	0	.216	.283	.402	.685	101	-0	11	3.76	-2	S-40	2	0.0
1969*Min-A	71	139	21	34	3	0	5	17	12	32	0	1	.245	.309	.374	.683	88	-3	15	3.69	-6	3-30,0-10(8-0-2)/S-6	2	-0.9
1970*Min-A	81	179	20	41	8	0	7	25	22	29	0	2	.229	.317	.391	.708	93	-3	21	3.86	1	3-30,0-25(25-1-0)/S-1	4	-0.2
1971 Min-A	27	45	4	10	2	0	1	8	5	14	0	0	.222	.314	.333	.647	81	-1	5	3.49	-2	/3-7,0-7(7-0-0)	1	-0.3
1972 Min-A	55	93	10	16	2	0	4	8	15	25	0	1	.172	.287	.323	.610	77	-3	8	2.52	-1	0-21(19-0-2)/1-6,3-4,S-1	1	-0.5
Total 5	276	553	71	122	20	2	20	71	63	142	0	4	.221	.304	.373	.676	89	-9	60	3.52	-9	/3-71,0-63,S-48,1-6	10	-1.9

• RENNA, Bill William Beneditto "Big Bill" Renna b: 10/14/1924, Hanford, CA BR/TR, 6'3", 218 lbs. Deb: 4/14/1953 Career OF: 81-6-192

YEAR TM-L	G	AB	R	H	2B	3B	HR	RBI	BB	SO	SB	CS	AVG	OBP	SLG	OPS	OPS+	BR/A	RC	RC/G	FR	G/POS	WS	TPW
1953 NY-A	61	121	19	38	6	3	2	13	13	31	0	1	.314	.385	.463	.848	133	5	22	6.81	-1	0-40(32-5-3)	5	0.3
1954 Phi-A	123	422	52	98	15	4	13	53	41	60	1	3	.232	.305	.379	.684	86	-10	49	3.87	4	*0-115(1-1-114)	8	-1.0
1955 KC-A	100	249	33	53	7	3	7	28	31	42	0	3	.213	.305	.349	.654	75	-10	27	3.54	0	0-79(8-0-72)	4	-1.2
1956 KC-A	33	48	12	13	3	0	2	5	3	10	1	0	.271	.314	.458	.772	101	-0	7	5.14	0	0-25(22-0-3)	1	0.0
1958 Bos-A	39	56	5	15	5	0	4	18	6	14	0	0	.268	.339	.571	.910	136	3	11	6.91	0	0-11(11-0-0)	2	0.2
1959 Bos-A	14	22	2	2	0	0	0	2	5	9	0	0	.091	.259	.091	.350		-3	1	1.16	0	/0-7(7-0-0)	0	-0.3
Total 6	370	918	123	219	36	10	28	119	99	166	2	7	.239	.317	.391	.708	91	-15	117	4.29	3	0-277	20	-2.2

• RENSA, Tony George Anthony "Pug" Rensa b: 9/29/1901, Parsons, PA d: 1/4/1987, Wilkes-Barre, PA BR/TR, 5'10", 180 lbs. Deb: 5/5/1930

YEAR TM-L	G	AB	R	H	2B	3B	HR	RBI	BB	SO	SB	CS	AVG	OBP	SLG	OPS	OPS+	BR/A	RC	RC/G	FR	G/POS	WS	TPW
1930 Det-A	20	37	6	10	2	1	1	3	6	7	1	0	.270	.386	.459	.846	111	1	7	6.81	-1	C-18	1	0.1
Phi-N	54	172	31	49	11	2	3	31	10	18	0	....	.285	.328	.424	.752	75	-8	23	4.82	-2	C-49	3	-0.6
1931 Phi-N	19	29	2	3	1	0	0	2	6	2	0	....	.103	.257	.138	.395	8	-4	1	1.38	1	C-17	1	-0.2
1933 NY-A	8	29	4	9	2	1	0	3	1	3	0	1	.310	.333	.448	.782	112	-0	4	4.63	0	/C-8	1	0.0
1937 Chi-A	26	57	10	17	5	1	0	5	8	6	3	0	.298	.385	.421	.806	103	1	10	6.76	0	C-23	3	0.2
1938 Chi-A	59	165	15	41	5	0	3	19	25	16	1	1	.248	.351	.333	.684	71	-7	21	4.38	2	C-57	4	-0.2
1939 Chi-A	14	25	3	5	0	0	0	2	1	2	0	0	.200	.231	.200	.431	11	-3	1	.72	0	C-13	0	-0.3
Total 6	200	514	71	134	26	5	7	65	57	54	5	2	.261	.338	.372	.710	74	-20	67	4.53	-1	C-185	13	-1.1

• RENTERIA, Edgar Edgar Enrique Renteria b: 8/7/1976, Barranquilla, Colombia BR/TR, 6'1", 172 lbs. Deb: 5/10/1996

YEAR TM-L	G	AB	R	H	2B	3B	HR	RBI	BB	SO	SB	CS	AVG	OBP	SLG	OPS	OPS+	BR/A	RC	RC/G	FR	G/POS	WS	TPW
1996 Fla-N	106	431	68	133	18	3	5	31	33	68	16	2	.309	.361	.399	.760	103	5	63	5.35	9	*S-106	15	2.2
1997*Fla-N	154	617	90	171	21	3	4	52	45	108	32	15	.277	.330	.340	.671	80	-18	69	3.68	3	*S-153	15	-0.3
1998 Fla-N★	133	517	79	146	18	2	3	31	48	78	41	22	.282	.348	.342	.690	86	-10	61	3.95	-14	*S-129	11	-1.3
1999 StL-N	154	585	92	161	36	2	11	63	53	82	37	8	.275	.338	.400	.738	85	-9	81	4.72	-8	*S-151	13	-0.5
2000*StL-N★	150	562	94	156	32	1	16	76	63	77	21	13	.278	.351	.423	.775	94	-6	80	4.75	2	*S-149	15	0.8
2001*StL-N	141	493	54	128	19	3	10	57	39	73	17	4	.260	.318	.371	.689	78	-14	57	3.90	7	*S-137/1-1,D-1	13	0.4
2002*StL-N	152	544	77	166	36	2	11	83	49	57	22	7	.305	.367	.439	.806	114	13	86	5.61	-10	*S-149	26	1.5
2003 StL-N★	157	587	96	194	47	1	13	100	65	54	34	7	.330	.398	.480	.879	133	34	112	6.99	-8	*S-156	25	3.8
Total 8	1147	4336	650	1255	227	17	73	493	395	597	220	78	.289	.352	.400	.752	97	-7	608	4.84	-18	*S-1130/1-1,D-1	133	6.6

• RENTERIA, Rich Richard Avina Renteria b: 12/25/1961, Harbor City, CA BR/TR, 5'9", 172 lbs. Deb: 9/14/1986 Career OF: 3-0-0

YEAR TM-L	G	AB	R	H	2B	3B	HR	RBI	BB	SO	SB	CS	AVG	OBP	SLG	OPS	OPS+	BR/A	RC	RC/G	FR	G/POS	WS	TPW
1986 Pit-N	10	12	2	3	1	0	0	1	0	4	0	0	.250	.250	.333	.583	58	-1	1	3.00	0	/3-1	0	-0.1
1987 Sea-A	12	10	2	1	1	0	0	0	1	2	1	0	.100	.182	.200	.382	1	-1	0	.68	-1	/2-4,D-4,S-1	0	-0.2
1988 Sea-A	31	88	6	18	9	0	0	6	2	8	1	3	.205	.222	.307	.529	45	-8	4	1.54	1	D-12,S-11/3-5,2-4	1	-0.7
1993 Fla-N	103	263	27	67	9	2	2	30	21	31	0	2	.255	.315	.327	.642	68	-13	26	3.33	4	2-45,3-25/0-1	6	-0.7
1994 Fla-N	28	49	5	11	0	0	2	4	1	4	0	1	.224	.269	.347	.616	57	-4	4	2.77	2	3-14/2-6,0-2(2-0-0)	0	-0.2
Total 5	184	422	42	100	20	2	4	41	25	49	2	6	.237	.286	.322	.608	60	-26	36	2.78	5	/2-59,3-45,D-16,S-12,0-3	7	-1.8

• REPASS, Bob Robert Willis Repass b: 11/6/1917, West Pittston, PA BR/TR, 6'1", 185 lbs. Deb: 9/18/1939

YEAR TM-L	G	AB	R	H	2B	3B	HR	RBI	BB	SO	SB	CS	AVG	OBP	SLG	OPS	OPS+	BR/A	RC	RC/G	FR	G/POS	WS	TPW
1939 StL-N	3	6	0	2	1	0	0	1	0	2	0	....	.333	.333	.500	.833	114	0	1	6.75	1	/2-2	0	0.1
1942 Was-A	81	259	30	62	11	1	2	23	33	30	6	1	.239	.328	.313	.640	81	-4	29	3.81	-6	2-33,3-29,S-11	7	-0.7
Total 2	84	265	30	64	12	1	2	24	33	32	6	1	.242	.328	.317	.645	82	-4	30	3.86	-6	/2-35,3-29,S-11	7	-0.6

• REPOZ, Roger Roger Allen Repoz b: 8/3/1940, Bellingham, WA BL/TL, 6'3", 195 lbs. Deb: 9/11/1964 Career OF: 54-357-242

YEAR TM-L	G	AB	R	H	2B	3B	HR	RBI	BB	SO	SB	CS	AVG	OBP	SLG	OPS	OPS+	BR/A	RC	RC/G	FR	G/POS	WS	TPW
1964 NY-A	11	1	1	0	0	0	0	0	1	1	0	0	.000	.500	.000	.500	52	0	0	3.51	-1	/0-9(0-0-9)	0	-0.1
1965 NY-A	79	218	34	48	7	4	12	28	25	57	1	1	.220	.300	.454	.755	112	3	30	4.67	-4	0-69(0-65-7)	7	-0.4
1966 NY-A	37	43	4	15	4	1	0	9	4	8	0	0	.349	.404	.488	.893	161	3	9	8.05	-1	0-30(0-28-5)	3	0.2
KC-A	101	319	40	69	10	3	11	34	44	80	3	3	.216	.315	.370	.685	99	-0	38	3.91	-3	0-52(8-41-3),1-45	10	-0.8
Yr.	138	362	44	84	14	4	11	43	48	88	3	3	.232	.325	.384	.709	106	3	47	4.33	-4	0-82(8-69-8),1-45	13	-0.6
1967 KC-A	40	87	9	21	6	1	2	8	12	20	4	2	.241	.340	.402	.742	122	3	12	4.82	1	0-31(16-9-6)	3	0.3
Cal-A	74	176	25	44	9	1	5	20	19	37	2	2	.250	.323	.398	.721	116	3	24	4.69	0	0-63(6-54-4)	7	0.1
Yr.	114	263	34	65	15	2	7	28	31	57	6	4	.247	.329	.399	.728	118	6	36	4.74	1	0-94(22-63-10)	10	0.4
1968 Cal-A	133	375	30	90	8	1	13	54	38	83	8	7	.240	.315	.371	.686	111	4	46	4.12	-1	*0-114(0-71-52)	13	-0.3
1969 Cal-A	103	219	25	36	1	1	8	19	32	52	1	3	.164	.271	.288	.559	59	-13	19	2.66	3	0-48(13-22-16),1-31	2	-1.4
1970 Cal-A	137	407	50	97	17	6	18	47	45	90	4	2	.238	.319	.442	.761	112	6	60	5.03	1	*0-110(6-42-68),1-18	17	0.1
1971 Cal-A	113	297	39	59	11	1	13	41	60	69	3	5	.199	.335	.374	.709	108	4	40	4.33	6	0-97(5-25-72),1-13	12	0.6
1972 Cal-A	3	3	0	1	0	0	0	0	0	2	0	0	.333	.333	.333	.667	105	0	0	4.50	0	....	0	0.0
Total 9	831	2145	257	480	73	19	82	260	280	499	26	25	.224	.316	.390	.706	106	12	279	4.32	1	0-623,1-107	74	-1.6

YEAR TM-L	G	AB	R	H	2B	3B	HR	RBI	BB	SO	SB	CS	AVG	OBP	SLG	OPS	OPS+	BR/A	RC	RC/G	FR	G/POS	WS	TPW
• REPULSKI, Rip	Eldon John Repulski b: 10/4/1927, Sauk Rapids, MN d: 2/10/1993, Waite Park, MN BR/TR, 6', 195 lbs. Deb: 4/14/1953 Career OF: 488-169-156																							
1953 StL-N	153	567	75	156	25	4	15	66	33	71	3	6	.275	.325	.413	.738	91	-11	74	4.58	-5	*0-153(0-153-0)	13	-2.1
1954 StL-N	152	619	99	175	39	5	19	79	43	75	8	10	.283	.333	.454	.787	102	-2	88	4.92	-4	*0-152(137-12-3)	14	-1.6
1955 StL-N	147	512	64	138	28	2	23	73	49	66	5	7	.270	.338	.467	.805	111	6	75	4.98	-4	*0-141(110-1-32)	14	-0.6
1956 StL-N★	112	376	44	104	18	3	11	55	24	46	2	2	.277	.332	.428	.760	102	1	50	4.60	-2	*0-100(99-1-1)	9	-0.7
1957 Phi-N	134	516	65	134	23	4	20	68	19	74	7	1	.260	.293	.436	.729	95	-4	64	4.32	-6	*0-130(54-0-84)	13	-1.7
1958 Phi-N	85	238	33	58	9	4	13	40	15	47	0	0	.244	.300	.479	.779	103	-0	31	4.38	-6	0-56(35-0-21)	4	-0.9
1959*LA-N	53	94	11	24	4	0	2	14	13	23	0	1	.255	.346	.362	.707	83	-2	11	4.08	-1	0-31(16-2-13)	2	-0.4
1960 LA-N	4	5	0	1	0	0	0	0	0	1	0	0	.200	.200	.200	.400	9	-1	0	.00	0	/0-2(0-0-2)	0	-0.1
Bos-A	73	136	14	33	6	1	3	20	10	25	0	0	.243	.295	.368	.662	75	-5	13	3.22	-2	0-33(33-0-0)	1	-0.8
1961 Bos-A	15	25	2	7	1	0	0	1	1	5	0	2	.280	.308	.320	.628	66	-2	2	2.57	0	/0-4(4-0-0)	0	-0.2
Total 9	928	3088	407	830	153	23	106	416	207	433	25	29	.269	.322	.436	.758	98	-21	409	4.55	-30	0-802	70	-9.2
• RESSLER, Larry	Lawrence P. Ressler b: 8/10/1848, France d: 6/12/1918, Reading, PA Deb: 4/26/1875																							
1875 Was-n	27	108	17	21	1	0	0	5	0	4	4	0	.194	.194	.204	.398	40	-5	5	1.76	4	0-20(0-3-17)/2-7	....	0.0
• RESTELLI, Dino	Dino Paul "Dingo" Restelli b: 9/23/1924, St. Louis, MO BR/TR, 6'1.5", 191 lbs. Deb: 6/14/1949 Career OF: 8-51-14																							
1949 Pit-N	72	232	41	58	11	0	12	40	35	26	3	....	.250	.358	.453	.811	113	5	38	5.53	-1	0-61(0-47-14)/1-1	8	0.2
1951 Pit-N	21	38	1	7	1	0	1	3	2	4	0	0	.184	.225	.289	.514	36	-4	3	2.31	-1	0-11(8-4-0)	0	-0.5
Total 2	93	270	42	65	12	0	13	43	37	30	3	0	.241	.341	.430	.770	103	1	41	5.07	-1	/0-72,1-1	8	-0.3
• RESTOVICH, Michael	Michael Jerome Restovich b: 1/3/1979, Rochester, MN BR/TR, 6'4", 233 lbs. Deb: 9/18/2002 Career OF: 7-0-15																							
2002 Min-A	8	13	3	4	0	0	1	1	1	4	1	0	.308	.357	.538	.896	132	1	2	4.09	0	/0-5(4-0-1),D-2	0	0.0
2003 Min-A	24	53	10	15	3	2	0	4	10	12	0	0	.283	.406	.415	.821	117	2	9	5.88	-1	0-17(3-0-14)/D-6	2	0.0
Total 2	32	66	13	19	3	2	1	5	11	16	1	0	.288	.397	.439	.837	119	3	11	5.50	-1	/0-22,D-8	2	0.0
• RETTENMUND, Merv	Mervin Weldon Rettenmund b: 6/6/1943, Flint, MI BR/TR, 5'10", 195 lbs. Deb: 4/14/1968 C Career OF: 228-155-436																							
1968 Bal-A	31	64	10	19	5	0	2	7	18	20	1	1	.297	.458	.469	.927	181	8	16	8.94	0	0-23(4-13-13)	5	0.8
1969*Bal-A	95	190	27	47	10	3	4	25	28	28	6	1	.247	.344	.395	.739	105	3	27	4.59	-3	0-78(45-18-21)	6	-0.3
1970*Bal-A	106	338	60	109	17	2	18	58	38	59	13	7	.322	.396	.544	.940	155	25	72	7.74	1	0-93(30-44-36)	19	2.2
1971*Bal-A	141	491	81	156	23	4	11	75	87	60	15	6	.318	.424	.448	.872	149	37	99	7.37	-2	*0-134(46-40-72)	27	3.1
1972 Bal-A	102	301	40	70	10	2	6	21	41	37	6	4	.233	.325	.339	.663	95	-1	33	3.58	0	0-98(6-23-79)	9	-0.5
1973*Bal-A	95	321	59	84	17	2	9	44	57	38	11	2	.262	.380	.411	.791	124	14	56	6.01	4	0-90(11-2-81)	14	1.4
1974 Cin-N	80	208	30	45	6	0	6	28	37	39	5	1	.216	.340	.332	.672	90	-1	25	3.89	0	0-69(0-9-60)	5	-0.4
1975*Cin-N	93	188	24	45	6	1	2	19	35	22	5	0	.239	.359	.314	.673	86	-1	23	4.16	-2	0-61(20-4-38)/3-1	5	-0.5
1976 SD-N	86	140	16	32	7	0	2	11	29	23	4	1	.229	.361	.321	.682	103	3	19	4.37	3	0-43(34-1-11)	5	0.4
1977 SD-N	107	126	23	36	6	1	4	17	33	28	1	2	.286	.438	.444	.882	153	11	27	7.30	0	0-27(23-1-3)/3-1	7	1.1
1978 Cal-A	50	108	16	29	5	1	1	14	30	13	0	3	.269	.436	.361	.797	131	6	19	5.81	-1	0-22(5-0-17),D-18	5	0.4
1979*Cal-A	35	76	7	20	2	0	1	10	11	14	1	0	.263	.364	.329	.693	91	-0	9	4.20	0	D-17/0-9(4-0-5)	2	-0.1
1980 Cal-A	2	4	0	1	0	0	0	0	1	1	0	0	.250	.400	.250	.650	84	-0	1	4.54	0	/D-1	0	0.0
Total 13	1023	2555	393	693	114	16	66	329	445	382	68	28	.271	.383	.406	.789	124	104	425	5.71	-1	0-747/D-36,3-2	109	7.5
• RETZER, Ken	Kenneth Leo Retzer b: 4/30/1934, Wood River, IL BL/TR, 6', 185 lbs. Deb: 9/9/1961																							
1961 Was-A	16	53	7	18	4	0	1	3	4	5	1	0	.340	.386	.472	.858	134	3	10	7.34	0	C-16	2	0.4
1962 Was-A	109	340	36	97	11	2	8	37	26	21	2	0	.285	.336	.400	.736	98	-1	45	4.74	-2	C-99	9	0.2
1963 Was-A	95	265	21	64	10	0	5	31	17	20	2	0	.242	.292	.336	.628	76	-8	26	3.43	-1	C-81	5	-0.6
1964 Was-A	17	32	1	3	0	0	0	1	5	4	0	0	.094	.237	.094	.331	-4	-4	1	.81	0	C-13	0	-0.4
Total 4	237	690	65	182	25	2	14	72	52	50	5	0	.264	.318	.367	.685	87	-11	82	4.18	-2	C-209	16	-0.4
• REVERING, Dave	David Alvin Revering b: 2/12/1953, Roseville, CA BL/TR, 6'4", 210 lbs. Deb: 4/8/1978																							
1978 Oak-A	152	521	49	141	21	3	16	46	26	55	0	1	.271	.305	.415	.720	106	2	63	4.23	11	*1-138/D-3	12	0.4
1979 Oak-A	125	472	63	136	25	5	19	77	34	65	1	4	.288	.337	.483	.820	125	13	75	5.76	0	*1-104,D-18	19	0.7
1980 Oak-A	106	376	48	109	21	5	15	62	32	37	1	0	.290	.346	.492	.838	136	18	64	6.21	8	1-95/D-5	14	1.9
1981 Oak-A	31	87	12	20	1	1	2	10	11	12	0	1	.230	.323	.333	.657	94	-1	9	3.54	-1	1-29/D-2	2	-0.4
*NY-A	45	119	8	28	4	1	2	7	11	20	0	1	.235	.300	.336	.636	84	-3	12	3.31	2	1-44	2	-0.3
Yr.	76	206	20	48	5	2	4	17	22	32	0	2	.233	.310	.335	.645	88	-4	21	3.41	1	1-73/D-2	4	-0.7
1982 NY-A	14	40	2	6	2	0	0	2	3	4	0	0	.150	.209	.200	.409	13	-5	1	.85	-3	1-13/D-1	0	-0.8
Tor-A	55	135	15	29	6	0	5	18	22	30	0	3	.215	.325	.370	.695	83	-4	16	3.91	-0	D-49/1-4	2	-0.5
Sea-A	29	82	8	17	3	1	3	12	9	17	0	0	.207	.286	.378	.664	78	-3	8	3.31	-1	1-27	1	-0.5
Yr.	98	257	25	52	11	1	8	32	34	51	0	3	.202	.296	.346	.642	71	-11	26	3.19	-4	D-50,1-44	3	-1.9
Total 5	557	1832	205	486	83	16	62	234	148	240	2	10	.265	.321	.430	.750	110	17	248	4.74	16	1-454/D-78	52	0.5
• REVILLE, Henry	Henry Reville b: Baltimore, MD Deb: 10/14/1874																							
1874 Bal-n	1	4	0	0	0	0	0	0	0	0	0	0	.000	.000	.000	.000	-101	-1	0	.00	1	/0-1	....	0.0
• REXTER, William	William H. Rexter b: Brooklyn, NY Deb: 9/25/1875																							
1875 Atl-n	1	4	0	0	0	0	0	0	0	0	0	0	.000	.000	.000	.000	-115	-1	0	.00	0	/0-1	....	-0.1
• REYES, Gilberto	Gilberto Rolando (Polanco) Reyes b: 12/10/1963, Santo Domingo, Dominican Republic BR/TR, 6'2", 203 lbs. Deb: 6/11/1983																							
1983 LA-N	19	31	1	5	2	0	0	0	0	5	0	0	.161	.188	.226	.413	14	-4	1	.63	-1	C-19	0	-0.4
1984 LA-N	4	5	0	0	0	0	0	0	0	3	0	0	.000	.000	.000	.000	-101	-1	0	.00	0	/C-2	0	-0.1
1985 LA-N	6	1	0	0	0	0	0	0	1	1	0	0	.000	.667	.000	.667	105	0	0	9.36	0	/C-6	1	0.0
1987 LA-N	1	0	0	0	0	0	0	0	0	0	0	0	....	....	....	....	-103	0	0	....	0	/C-1	0	0.0
1988 LA-N	5	9	1	1	0	0	0	0	0	3	0	0	.111	.111	.111	.222	-37	-2	0	.38	0	/C-5	0	-0.2
1989 Mon-N	4	5	0	1	0	0	0	1	0	1	0	0	.200	.200	.200	.400	14	-1	0	1.35	0	/C-4	0	0.0
1991 Mon-N	83	207	11	45	9	0	0	13	19	51	2	4	.217	.286	.261	.547	56	-13	15	2.43	4	C-80	4	-0.5
Total 7	122	258	13	52	11	0	0	14	20	64	2	4	.202	.267	.244	.511	45	-20	17	2.07	3	C-117	5	-1.2
• REYES, Jose	Jose Bernabe Reyes b: 6/11/1983, Villa Gonzalez, Dominican Republic BB/TR, 6', 160 lbs. Deb: 6/10/2003																							
2003 NY-N	69	274	47	84	12	4	5	32	13	36	13	3	.307	.338	.434	.772	103	2	42	5.69	6	S-69	12	1.3
• REYES, Nap	Napoleon Aguilera Reyes b: 11/24/1919, Santiago de Cuba, Cuba d: 9/15/1995, Miami, FL BR/TR, 6', 205 lbs. Deb: 5/19/1943																							
1943 NY-N	40	125	13	32	4	2	0	13	4	12	2	....	.256	.290	.320	.610	76	-4	12	3.30	-7	1-38/3-1	2	-1.4
1944 NY-N	116	374	38	108	16	5	8	53	15	24	2	....	.289	.325	.422	.747	110	3	49	4.68	-1	1-63,3-37/0-3(3-0-0)	11	-0.1
1945 NY-N	122	431	39	124	15	4	5	44	25	26	1	....	.288	.338	.376	.714	97	-3	53	4.30	-3	*3-115/1-5	11	-0.4
1950 NY-N	1	1	0	0	0	0	0	0	0	0	0	....	.000	.000	.000	.000	-99	-0	0	.00	0	/1-1	0	-0.1
Total 4	279	931	90	264	35	11	13	110	44	62	5	....	.284	.326	.387	.713	99	-4	113	4.31	-11	3-153,1-107/0-3	24	-1.9
• REYES, Rene	Rene Reyes b: 2/21/1978, Margarita, Venezuela BB/TR, 5'11", 213 lbs. Deb: 7/22/2003																							
2003 Col-N	53	116	13	30	7	1	2	7	5	19	2	1	.259	.289	.388	.677	65	-6	12	3.58	0	0-36(11-5-24)	0	-0.7
• REYNOLDS, Bill	William Dee Reynolds b: 8/14/1884, Eastland, TX d: 6/5/1924, Carnegie, OK BR/TR, 6', 185 lbs. Deb: 9/15/1913																							
1913 NY-A	5	5	0	0	0	0	0	0	0	1	0	....	.000	.000	.000	.000	-100	-1	0	.00	-1	/C-5	0	-0.2
1914 NY-A	4	5	0	2	0	0	0	0	0	3	0	....	.400	.400	.400	.800	141	0	1	7.07	0	/C-1	0	0.0
Total 2	9	10	0	2	0	0	0	0	0	4	0	....	.200	.200	.200	.400	21	-1	1	2.65	0	/C-6	0	-0.1
• REYNOLDS, Carl	Carl Nettles Reynolds b: 2/1/1903, LaRue, TX d: 5/29/1978, Houston, TX BR/TR, 6', 194 lbs. Deb: 9/1/1927 Career OF: 281-301-574																							
1927 Chi-A	14	42	5	9	3	0	1	7	5	7	1	2	.214	.313	.357	.670	75	-2	4	3.30	1	0-13(11-0-2)	1	-0.2
1928 Chi-A	84	291	51	94	21	11	2	36	17	13	15	3	.323	.371	.491	.862	126	13	54	6.97	0	0-74(15-1-58)	12	0.7
1929 Chi-A	131	517	81	164	24	12	11	67	20	37	19	9	.317	.348	.474	.821	111	7	83	5.79	1	*0-130(13-21-98)	15	-0.1
1930 Chi-A	138	563	103	202	25	18	22	104	20	39	16	4	.359	.388	.584	.973	148	40	126	8.83	5	*0-132(35-54-47)	25	3.3

YEAR TM-L	G	AB	R	H	2B	3B	HR	RBI	BB	SO	SB	CS	AVG	OBP	SLG	OPS	OPS+	BR/A	RC	RC/G	FR	G/POS	WS	TPW
1931 Chi-A	118	462	71	134	24	14	6	77	24	26	17	6	.290	.333	.442	.775	109	7	68	5.35	-7	*O-109(11-18-90)	14	-0.6
1932 Was-A	102	406	53	124	28	7	9	63	13	19	8	4	.305	.332	.475	.807	108	3	62	5.73	1	O-95(0-0-95)	13	-0.2
1933 StL-A	135	475	81	136	26	14	8	71	49	25	5	4	.286	.357	.451	.807	106	3	77	5.80	-4	*O-124(123-2-0)	10	-0.7
1934 Bos-A	113	413	61	125	26	9	4	86	27	28	5	3	.303	.350	.438	.788	96	-4	63	5.69	-1	*O-100(2-66-33)	13	-0.8
1935 Bos-A	78	244	33	66	13	4	6	35	24	20	4	1	.270	.336	.430	.766	91	-4	36	5.22	5	O-64(3-1-60)	7	-0.2
1936 Was-A	89	293	41	81	18	2	4	41	21	22	8	4	.276	.329	.392	.722	82	-9	38	4.63	1	O-72(0-4-69)	6	-1.1
1937 Chi-N	7	11	0	3	1	0	0	1	2	2	0	....	.273	.385	.364	.748	100	0	1	4.26	0	/O-2(2-0-0)	0	0.0
1938*Chi-N	125	497	59	150	28	10	3	67	22	32	9	....	.302	.335	.416	.752	103	0	69	5.13	0	*O-125(63-83-4)	18	-0.5
1939 Chi-N	88	281	33	69	10	6	4	44	16	38	5	....	.246	.298	.367	.665	76	-10	30	3.50	-2	O-72(3-51-18)	5	-1.4
Total 13	1222	4495	672	1357	247	107	80	699	260	308	112	40	.302	.346	.458	.804	107	44	713	5.78	1	*O-1112	139	-1.9
• REYNOLDS, Charlie	Charles E. Reynolds b: 7/31/1857, Allegany, NY d: 5/1/1913, Buffalo, NY Deb: 5/18/1882 ♦																							
1882 Phi-a	2	8	1	1	0	0	0	....	0	....	....	....	.125	.125	.125	.250	-14	-1	0	.51	-1	/P-2,O-1	0	-0.4
• REYNOLDS, Charlie	Charles Lawrence Reynolds b: 5/1/1865, Williamsburg, IN d: 7/3/1944, Denver, CO BR, 5'9", 175 lbs. Deb: 5/8/1889																							
1889 KC-a	1	4	1	1	0	0	0	1	0	1	0	....	.250	.250	.250	.500	40	-0	0	2.26	0	/C-1	0	-0.1
Bro-a	12	42	5	9	1	1	0	3	1	6	2	....	.214	.233	.286	.518	47	-3	3	2.68	-0	C-12	1	-0.2
Yr.	13	46	6	10	1	1	0	4	1	7	2	....	.217	.234	.283	.517	46	-3	4	2.65	0	C-13	1	-0.2
• REYNOLDS, Craig	Gordon Craig Reynolds b: 12/27/1952, Houston, TX BL/TR, 6'1", 175 lbs. Deb: 8/1/1975 Career OF: 3-0-1																							
1975*Pit-N	31	76	8	17	3	0	0	4	3	5	0	1	.224	.253	.263	.516	44	-6	5	2.07	1	S-30	1	-0.2
1976 Pit-N	7	4	1	1	0	0	1	1	0	0	0	0	.250	.250	1.000	1.250	241	1	1	9.00	-1	/S-4,2-1	0	0.0
1977 Sea-A	135	420	41	104	12	3	4	28	15	23	6	6	.248	.279	.319	.598	63	-23	36	2.78	4	*S-134	6	-0.6
1978 Sea-A★	148	548	57	160	16	7	5	44	36	41	9	6	.292	.339	.374	.713	101	0	71	4.65	-2	*S-146	17	1.4
1979 Hou-N★	146	555	63	147	20	9	0	39	21	49	12	6	.265	.294	.333	.627	75	-21	57	3.39	7	*S-143	17	0.1
1980*Hou-N	137	381	34	86	9	6	3	28	20	39	2	1	.226	.264	.304	.569	63	-20	32	2.69	12	*S-135	8	0.3
1981*Hou-N	87	323	43	84	10	**12**	4	31	12	31	3	3	.260	.287	.402	.689	99	-4	35	3.58	7	S-85	10	1.3
1982 Hou-N	54	118	16	30	2	3	1	7	11	9	3	1	.254	.323	.347	.671	95	-1	14	4.03	0	S-35/3-7	4	0.3
1983 Hou-N	65	98	10	21	3	0	1	6	6	10	0	1	.214	.260	.276	.535	51	-7	7	2.45	-5	2-26,3-15/S-8,O-1	1	-1.1
1984 Hou-N	146	527	61	137	15	11	6	60	22	53	7	1	.260	.290	.364	.654	89	-9	57	3.71	16	*S-143/3-1	16	2.2
1985 Hou-N	107	379	43	103	18	8	4	32	12	30	4	4	.272	.294	.393	.687	93	-7	42	3.95	11	*S-102/2-1	14	1.6
1986*Hou-N	114	313	32	78	7	3	6	41	12	31	3	1	.249	.277	.348	.625	73	-12	28	3.07	8	S-98/1-5,3-4,O-2(1-0-1),P	7	0.0
1987 Hou-N	135	374	35	95	17	3	4	28	30	44	5	1	.254	.309	.348	.657	77	-13	42	3.80	-10	*S-129/3-2	8	-1.1
1988 Hou-N	78	161	20	41	7	0	1	14	8	23	3	0	.255	.290	.317	.607	77	-5	15	3.41	-2	S-22,3-19,2-11,1-10	4	-0.6
1989 Hou-N	101	189	16	38	4	0	2	14	19	18	1	0	.201	.274	.254	.528	54	-11	14	2.42	-1	2-29,S-26,3-10/1-5,O-1,P-1	2	-1.3
Total 15	1491	4466	480	1142	143	65	42	377	227	406	58	32	.256	.293	.345	.638	80	-137	457	3.46	46	*S-1240/2-68,3-58,1-20,O-4,P	115	2.4
• REYNOLDS, Danny	Daniel Vance "Squirrel" Reynolds b: 11/27/1919, Stony Point, NC BR/TR, 5'11", 158 lbs. Deb: 5/26/1945																							
1945 Chi-A	29	72	6	12	2	1	0	4	3	8	1	2	.167	.200	.222	.422	23	-8	2	.87	1	S-14,2-11	1	-0.6
• REYNOLDS, Don	Donald Edward Reynolds b: 4/16/1953, Arkadelphia, AR BR/TR, 5'8", 178 lbs. Deb: 4/7/1978 Career OF: 29-5-5																							
1978 SD-N	57	87	8	22	2	0	0	10	15	14	1	0	.253	.363	.276	.639	87	-0	10	4.20	0	O-25(22-0-3)	2	-0.1
1979 SD-N	30	45	6	10	1	2	0	6	7	6	0	1	.222	.327	.333	.660	86	-1	4	2.83	0	O-14(7-5-2)	0	-0.1
Total 2	87	132	14	32	3	2	0	16	22	20	1	1	.242	.351	.295	.646	87	-2	14	3.68	0	/O-39	2	-0.2
• REYNOLDS, Harold	Harold Craig Reynolds b: 11/26/1960, Eugene, OR BB/TR, 5'11", 165 lbs. Deb: 9/2/1983																							
1983 Sea-A	20	59	8	12	4	1	0	1	2	9	0	2	.203	.230	.305	.535	44	-6	3	1.77	-1	2-18	1	-0.5
1984 Sea-A	10	10	3	3	0	0	0	0	0	1	1	1	.300	.364	.300	.664	87	-0	1	3.23	0	/2-6	0	0.0
1985 Sea-A	67	104	15	15	3	1	0	6	17	14	3	2	.144	.264	.192	.457	27	-10	7	1.91	-2	2-61	1	-1.1
1986 Sea-A	126	445	46	99	19	4	1	24	29	42	30	12	.222	.275	.290	.565	53	-28	37	2.65	8	*2-126	5	-1.3
1987 Sea-A★	160	530	73	146	31	8	1	35	39	34	**60**	20	.275	.327	.370	.697	80	-11	67	4.27	13	*2-160	15	1.0
1988 Sea-A★	158	598	61	169	26	**11**	4	41	51	51	35	29	.283	.341	.383	.724	98	-7	74	4.18	6	*2-158	17	0.4
1989 Sea-A	153	613	87	184	24	9	0	43	55	45	25	18	.300	.361	.369	.729	103	1	83	4.93	21	*2-151/D-1	20	2.7
1990 Sea-A	160	642	100	162	36	5	5	55	81	52	31	16	.252	.339	.347	.686	91	-6	80	4.17	10	*2-160	19	0.9
1991 Sea-A	161	631	95	160	34	6	3	57	72	63	28	8	.254	.335	.341	.675	87	-7	78	4.11	3	*2-159/D-1	21	0.1
1992 Sea-A	140	458	55	113	23	3	3	33	45	41	15	12	.247	.318	.330	.648	81	-13	47	3.31	-5	*2-134/D-1,O-1	8	-1.4
1993 Bal-A	145	485	64	122	20	4	4	47	66	47	12	11	.252	.346	.334	.680	80	-13	60	4.13	-2	*2-141/D-1	14	-0.9
1994 Cal-A	74	207	33	48	10	1	0	11	23	18	10	7	.232	.312	.290	.602	56	-14	19	2.90	-10	2-65/D-3	2	-2.0
Total 12	1374	4782	640	1233	230	53	21	353	480	417	250	138	.258	.329	.341	.670	83	-114	556	3.88	42	*2-1339/D-7,O-1	123	-2.1
• REYNOLDS, R.J.	Robert James Reynolds b: 4/19/1959, Sacramento, CA BB/TR, 6', 190 lbs. Deb: 9/1/1983 Career OF: 244-106-356																							
1983 LA-N	24	55	5	13	0	0	2	11	3	11	5	0	.236	.276	.345	.621	71	-1	6	3.42	0	O-18(9-7-5)	1	-0.1
1984 LA-N	73	240	24	62	12	2	2	24	14	38	7	5	.258	.302	.350	.652	84	-7	24	3.31	0	O-63(25-19-34)	4	-0.9
1985 LA-N	73	207	22	55	10	4	0	25	13	31	6	3	.266	.312	.353	.665	88	-4	23	3.76	0	O-54(31-5-24)	5	-0.6
Pit-N	31	130	22	40	5	3	3	17	9	18	12	2	.308	.357	.462	.819	129	6	22	6.14	1	O-31(29-8-0)	4	0.6
Yr.	104	337	44	95	15	7	3	42	22	49	18	5	.282	.330	.395	.724	104	3	45	4.64	1	O-85(60-13-24)	9	0.0
1986 Pit-N	118	402	63	108	30	2	9	48	40	78	16	9	.269	.336	.420	.757	105	2	55	4.67	-4	*O-112(84-12-44)	10	-0.8
1987 Pit-N	117	335	47	87	24	1	7	51	34	80	14	1	.260	.328	.400	.728	91	-2	46	4.81	1	O-99(29-0-72)	9	-0.5
1988 Pit-N	130	323	35	80	14	2	6	51	20	62	15	2	.248	.292	.359	.651	87	-4	35	3.71	-1	O-95(19-1-79)	8	-0.8
1989 Pit-N	125	363	45	98	16	2	6	48	34	66	22	5	.270	.334	.375	.709	106	5	45	4.20	0	O-98(5-30-72)	11	0.3
1990*Pit-N	95	215	25	62	10	1	0	19	23	35	12	2	.288	.357	.344	.701	98	2	26	4.11	-1	O-59(13-24-26)	4	0.0
Total 8	786	2270	288	605	121	17	35	294	190	419	109	29	.267	.325	.381	.706	97	-3	282	4.24	-3	O-629	56	-2.9
• REYNOLDS, Ronn	Ronn Dwayne Reynolds b: 9/28/1958, Wichita, KS BR/TR, 6', 200 lbs. Deb: 9/29/1982																							
1982 NY-N	2	4	0	0	0	0	0	0	1	1	0	0	.000	.200	.000	.200	-40	-1	0	.35	0	/C-2	0	-0.1
1983 NY-N	24	66	4	13	1	0	0	2	8	12	0	0	.197	.284	.212	.496	40	-5	4	2.00	-1	C-24	0	-0.6
1985 NY-N	28	43	4	9	2	0	0	1	0	18	0	0	.209	.227	.256	.483	36	-4	2	1.76	1	C-25	1	-0.3
1986 Phi-N	43	126	8	27	4	0	3	10	5	30	0	0	.214	.244	.317	.562	52	-9	9	2.30	-1	C-42	1	-0.8
1987 Hou-N	38	102	5	17	4	0	1	7	3	29	0	1	.167	.190	.235	.426	12	-14	4	1.15	-2	C-38	1	-1.4
1990 SD-N	8	15	1	1	1	0	0	1	1	6	0	0	.067	.125	.133	.258	-29	-3	0	.54	0	/C-8	0	-0.2
Total 6	143	356	22	67	12	0	4	21	18	96	0	1	.188	.229	.256	.485	32	-35	20	1.73	-3	C-139	3	-3.3
• REYNOLDS, Tommie	Tommie D Reynolds b: 8/15/1941, Arizona, LA BR/TR, 6'2", 190 lbs. Deb: 9/5/1963 C Career OF: 276-14-92																							
1963 KC-A	8	19	1	1	1	0	0	0	1	7	0	0	.053	.143	.105	.248	-28	-3	0	.34	-1	/O-5(5-0-0)	0	-0.5
1964 KC-A	31	94	11	19	1	0	2	9	10	22	0	0	.202	.292	.277	.569	58	-5	7	2.54	-1	O-25(25-0-0)/3-3	0	-0.8
1965 KC-A	90	270	34	64	11	3	1	22	36	41	9	2	.237	.327	.311	.638	83	-4	28	3.47	3	O-83(77-0-6)/3-1	5	-0.6
1967 NY-N	101	136	16	28	1	0	2	9	11	26	1	1	.206	.280	.257	.537	56	-8	10	2.33	1	O-72(42-13-21)/3-5,C-1	1	-1.0
1969 Oak-A	107	315	51	81	10	0	2	20	34	29	1	3	.257	.345	.308	.652	87	-5	34	3.69	1	O-89(81-0-8)	7	-1.0
1970 Cal-A	59	120	11	30	3	1	1	6	6	10	1	1	.250	.291	.317	.608	70	-5	10	2.77	0	O-32(4-1-28)/3-1	2	-0.8
1971 Cal-A	45	86	4	16	3	0	2	8	9	6	0	1	.186	.286	.291	.576	68	-4	6	2.07	2	O-26(6-0-23)/3-1	1	-0.4
1972 Mil-A	72	130	13	26	5	1	2	13	10	25	0	0	.200	.262	.300	.562	68	-5	10	2.45	-1	O-41(36-0-6)/1-1,3-1	1	-1.0
Total 8	513	1170	141	265	35	5	12	87	117	166	12	8	.226	.307	.296	.603	73	-39	106	2.96	2	O-373/3-12,1-1,C-1	17	-5.9
• RHAWN, Bobby	Robert John "Rocky" Rhawn b: 2/13/1919, Catawissa, PA d: 6/9/1984, Danville, PA BR/TR, 5'8", 180 lbs. Deb: 9/17/1947																							
1947 NY-N	13	45	7	14	3	0	1	3	8	1	0	....	.311	.415	.444	.860	127	2	9	7.19	1	/2-8,3-5	2	0.3
1948 NY-N	36	44	11	12	2	1	1	8	8	6	3	....	.273	.385	.432	.816	120	1	7	5.79	-2	S-14/3-7	2	0.0
1949 NY-N	14	29	8	5	0	0	0	2	7	2	1	....	.172	.333	.172	.506	40	-2	2	2.57	2	/2-8	0	0.0
Pit-N	3	7	0	1	0	0	0	0	0	0	0	....	.143	.143	.143	.286	-23	-1	0	.00	0	/3-2	0	-0.1
Yr.	17	36	8	6	0	0	0	2	7	2	1	....	.167	.302	.167	.469	29	-3	2	1.95	2	/2-8,3-2	0	-0.1

YEAR TM-L	G	AB	R	H	2B	3B	HR	RBI	BB	SO	SB	CS	AVG	OBP	SLG	OPS	OPS+	BR/A	RC	RC/G	FR	G/POS	WS	TPW
Chi-A	24	73	12	15	4	1	0	5	12	8	0	1	.205	.318	.288	.605	63	-4	7	3.24	1	3-19/S-3	1	-0.3
Total 3	90	198	38	47	9	2	2	18	35	17	4	1	.237	.352	.333	.685	83	-4	26	4.32	2	/3-33,S-17,2-16	5	0.0
• RHEAM, Cy	Kenneth Johnston Rheam b: 9/28/1893, Pittsburgh, PA d: 10/23/1947, Pittsburgh, PA BR/TR, 6', 175 lbs. Deb: 5/20/1914 Career OF: 13-4-6																							
1914 Pit-F	73	214	15	45	5	3	0	20	9	33	6	....	.210	.242	.262	.504	46	-16	15	2.11	-6	1-43,3-13,2-11/0-1	1	-2.2
1915 Pit-F	34	69	10	12	0	0	1	5	1	7	4	....	.174	.186	.217	.403	18	-7	4	1.48	-1	0-22(12-4-6)/1-1	1	-1.0
Total 2	107	283	25	57	5	3	1	25	10	40	10	....	.201	.229	.251	.480	39	-23	18	1.95	-6	/1-44,0-23,3-13,2-11	2	-3.2
• RHIEL, Billy	William Joseph Rhiel b: 8/16/1900, Youngstown, OH d: 8/16/1946, Youngstown, OH BR/TR, 5'11", 175 lbs. Deb: 4/20/1929 Career OF: 9-0-0																							
1929 Bro-N	76	205	27	57	9	4	4	25	19	25	0	....	.278	.339	.420	.759	89	-4	29	4.92	-2	2-47/3-7,S-2	4	-0.4
1930 Bos-N	20	47	3	8	4	0	0	4	2	5	0	....	.170	.204	.255	.459	11	-7	2	1.55	0	3-13/2-2	0	-0.6
1932 Det-A	85	250	30	70	13	3	3	38	17	23	2	0	.280	.328	.392	.720	82	-6	33	4.77	3	3-37,1-12/0-8(8-0-0),2-1	6	-0.4
1933 Det-A	19	17	1	3	0	1	0	1	5	4	0	0	.176	.364	.294	.658	75	-0	2	4.16	0	/0-1	0	0.0
Total 4	200	519	61	138	26	8	7	68	43	57	2	0	.266	.323	.387	.711	78	-18	66	4.47	1	/3-57,2-50,1-12,0-9,S-2	10	-1.4
• RHODES, Dusty	James Lamar Rhodes b: 5/13/1927, Mathews, AL BL/TR, 6', 180 lbs. Deb: 7/15/1952 Career OF: 244-4-51																							
1952 NY-N	67	176	34	44	8	1	10	36	23	33	1	0	.250	.340	.477	.817	123	6	29	5.76	-4	0-56(55-2-0)	7	-0.2
1953 NY-N	76	163	18	38	7	0	11	30	10	28	0	1	.233	.277	.479	.756	91	-4	21	4.39	1	0-47(25-0-22)	3	-0.5
1954*NY-N	82	164	31	56	7	3	15	50	18	25	1	0	.341	.410	.695	1.105	181	19	47	11.35	0	0-37(33-2-1)	11	1.8
1955 NY-N	94	187	22	57	5	2	6	32	27	26	1	1	.305	.393	.449	.842	122	7	35	7.14	1	0-45(45-0-0)	8	0.6
1956 NY-N	111	244	20	53	10	3	8	33	30	41	0	0	.217	.303	.381	.684	83	-6	27	3.63	1	0-68(64-0-5)	3	-0.8
1957 NY-N	92	190	20	39	5	1	4	19	18	34	0	0	.205	.278	.305	.583	57	-12	15	2.58	-2	0-44(22-0-23)	0	-1.5
1959 SF-N	54	48	1	9	2	0	0	7	5	9	0	0	.188	.264	.229	.493	34	-4	3	1.91	0	....	0	-0.4
Total 7	576	1172	146	296	44	10	54	207	131	196	3	2	.253	.329	.445	.775	104	7	178	5.27	-2	0-297	32	-1.1
• RHODES, Karl	Karl Derrick "Tuffy" Rhodes b: 8/21/1968, Cincinnati, OH BL/TL, 6', 170 lbs. Deb: 8/7/1990 Career OF: 53-101-53																							
1990 Hou-N	38	86	12	21	6	1	1	3	13	12	4	1	.244	.343	.372	.716	100	1	12	4.68	-1	0-30(19-9-5)	2	-0.1
1991 Hou-N	44	136	7	29	3	1	1	12	14	26	2	2	.213	.291	.272	.563	63	-7	11	2.56	1	0-44(0-0-44)	1	-0.8
1992 Hou-N	5	4	0	0	0	0	0	0	0	2	0	0	.000	.000	.000	.000	-105	-1	0	.00	0	/0-1	0	-0.2
1993 Hou-N	5	2	0	0	0	0	0	0	0	0	0	0	.000	.000	.000	.000	-104	-1	0	.00	0	/0-4(1-2-1)	0	-0.1
Chi-N	15	52	12	15	2	1	3	7	11	9	2	0	.288	.413	.538	.951	155	5	13	9.61	0	0-14(6-14-1)	4	0.5
Yr.	20	54	12	15	2	1	3	7	11	9	2	0	.278	.400	.519	.919	147	4	13	9.11	-1	0-18(7-16-2)	4	0.4
1994 Chi-N	95	269	39	63	17	0	8	19	33	64	6	4	.234	.320	.387	.707	84	-7	35	4.42	-4	0-76(15-67-1)	3	-1.0
1995 Chi-N	13	16	2	2	0	0	0	2	0	4	0	0	.125	.125	.125	.250	-34	-3	0	.25	-1	0-11(11-0-0)	0	-0.4
Bos-A	10	25	2	2	1	0	0	1	3	4	0	0	.080	.179	.120	.299	-20	-5	1	.61	-1	/0-9(0-9-0)	0	-0.5
Total 6	225	590	74	132	29	3	13	44	74	121	14	7	.224	.312	.349	.661	79	-17	72	4.03	-6	0-189	10	-2.6
• RHOMBERG, Kevin	Kevin Jay Rhomberg b: 11/22/1955, Dubuque, IA BR/TR, 6', 175 lbs. Deb: 9/1/1982 Career OF: 22-1-0																							
1982 Cle-A	16	18	3	6	0	0	1	1	2	4	0	2	.333	.400	.500	.900	146	0	3	5.51	0	/0-7(7-0-0),D-4,3-1	1	0.0
1983 Cle-A	12	21	2	10	0	0	0	2	2	4	1	1	.476	.522	.476	.998	170	2	5	11.00	0	/0-9(8-1-0),D-1	1	0.2
1984 Cle-A	13	8	0	2	0	0	0	0	0	3	0	0	.250	.250	.250	.500	38	-1	1	2.25	0	/0-7(7-0-0),1-1,2-1,D-1	0	-0.1
Total 3	41	47	5	18	0	0	1	3	4	11	1	3	.383	.431	.447	.878	141	2	9	7.08	0	/0-23,D-6,1-1,2-1,3-1	2	0.1
• RHYNE, Hal	Harold J. Rhyne b: 3/30/1899, Paso Robles, CA d: 1/7/1971, Orangevale, CA BR/TR, 5'8.5", 163 lbs. Deb: 4/18/1926																							
1926 Pit-N	109	366	46	92	14	3	2	39	35	21	1	....	.251	.327	.322	.649	71	-14	40	3.55	7	2-66,S-44/3-1	9	-0.1
1927*Pit-N	62	168	21	46	5	0	0	17	14	9	0	....	.274	.330	.304	.633	66	-8	17	3.31	-1	2-45,3-10/S-7	3	-0.7
1929 Bos-A	120	346	41	87	24	5	0	38	25	14	4	1	.251	.309	.350	.659	71	-14	39	3.80	-6	*S-113/3-1,0-1	7	-0.9
1930 Bos-A	107	296	34	60	8	5	0	23	25	19	1	4	.203	.269	.264	.533	37	-29	22	2.29	3	*S-107	4	-1.5
1931 Bos-A	147	565	75	154	34	3	0	51	57	41	3	3	.273	.341	.343	.685	85	-9	68	4.33	1	*S-147	14	0.2
1932 Bos-A	71	207	26	47	12	5	0	14	23	14	3	2	.227	.310	.333	.644	69	-9	22	3.64	5	S-55/3-4,2-1	4	-0.1
1933 Chi-A	39	83	9	22	1	1	0	10	5	9	1	1	.265	.315	.301	.616	67	-4	8	3.32	-4	2-19,3-13/S-2	1	-0.6
Total 7	655	2031	252	508	98	22	2	192	184	127	13	11	.250	.318	.323	.641	69	-87	217	3.58	5	S-475,2-131/3-29,0-1	42	-3.6
• RICE, Bob	Robert Turnbull Rice b: 5/28/1899, Philadelphia, PA d: 2/20/1986, Elizabethtown, PA BR/TR, 5'10", 170 lbs. Deb: 9/1/1926																							
1926 Phi-N	19	54	3	8	0	1	0	10	3	4	0	....	.148	.193	.185	.378	2	-8	2	1.10	-2	3-15/2-2,S-2	0	-0.9
• RICE, Del	Delbert Rice b: 10/27/1922, Portsmouth, OH d: 1/26/1983, Buena Park, CA BR/TR, 6'2", 190 lbs. Deb: 5/2/1945 M/C																							
1945 StL-N	83	253	27	66	17	3	1	28	16	33	0	....	.261	.313	.364	.676	85	-6	28	3.74	1	C-77	9	0.0
1946*StL-N	55	139	10	38	8	1	1	12	8	16	0	....	.273	.313	.367	.680	89	-3	15	3.70	-4	C-53	4	-0.4
1947 StL-N	97	261	28	57	7	3	12	44	36	40	1	....	.218	.315	.406	.722	86	-6	35	4.41	-3	C-94	8	-0.4
1948 StL-N	100	290	24	57	10	1	4	34	37	46	1	....	.197	.298	.279	.578	54	-18	26	2.88	2	C-99	8	-1.1
1949 StL-N	92	284	25	67	16	1	4	29	30	40	0	....	.236	.320	.342	.661	74	-10	32	3.80	-4	C-92	8	-1.0
1950 StL-N	130	414	39	101	20	3	9	54	43	65	0	....	.244	.323	.372	.694	78	-13	50	4.07	-1	*C-130	12	-0.8
1951 StL-N	122	374	34	94	13	1	9	47	34	26	0	0	.251	.319	.364	.682	83	-9	44	3.96	2	*C-120	12	-0.1
1952 StL-N	147	495	43	128	27	2	11	65	33	38	0	1	.259	.313	.388	.701	93	-6	60	4.22	0	*C-147	18	0.1
1953 StL-N★	135	419	32	99	22	1	6	37	48	49	0	0	.236	.323	.337	.660	72	-16	47	3.76	-4	*C-135	11	-1.3
1954 StL-N	56	147	13	37	10	1	2	16	16	21	0	1	.252	.325	.374	.699	81	-4	18	4.11	-3	C-52	4	-0.5
1955 StL-N	20	59	6	12	3	0	1	7	7	6	0	0	.203	.288	.305	.593	58	-4	5	2.76	-1	C-18	0	-0.4
Mil-N	27	71	5	14	0	1	2	7	6	12	0	0	.197	.260	.310	.570	53	-5	6	2.63	0	C-22	1	-0.4
Yr.	47	130	11	26	3	1	3	14	13	18	0	0	.200	.273	.308	.580	55	-8	11	2.69	-1	C-40	1	-0.8
1956 Mil-N	71	188	15	40	9	1	3	17	18	34	0	0	.213	.282	.319	.601	65	-9	16	2.84	-1	C-65	4	-0.8
1957*Mil-N	54	144	15	33	1	1	9	20	17	37	0	0	.229	.311	.438	.748	106	1	18	4.21	0	C-48	6	0.3
1958 Mil-N	43	121	10	27	7	0	1	8	8	30	0	0	.223	.271	.306	.577	57	-8	10	2.64	0	C-38	2	-0.6
1959 Mil-N	13	29	3	6	0	0	0	1	2	3	0	0	.207	.258	.207	.465	28	-3	1	1.37	-1	/C-9	0	-0.4
1960 Chi-N	18	52	2	12	3	0	0	4	2	7	0	0	.231	.259	.288	.548	50	-4	3	1.94	-1	C-18	0	-0.4
StL-N	1	2	0	0	0	0	0	0	1	0	0	0	.000	.333	.000	.333		-0	0	.00	-0	/C-1	0	0.0
Yr.	19	54	2	12	3	0	0	4	3	7	0	0	.222	.263	.278	.541	48	-4	3	1.81	-1	C-19	0	-0.4
Bal-A	1	1	0	0	0	0	0	0	0	0	0	0	.000	.000	.000	.000	-101	-0	0	.00	0	/C-1	0	-0.1
1961 LA-A	44	83	11	20	4	0	4	11	20	19	0	1	.241	.388	.434	.822	107	1	15	5.83	0	C-30	3	0.3
Total 17	1309	3826	342	908	177	20	79	441	382	522	2	3	.237	.312	.356	.668	78	-121	430	3.75	-18	*C-1249	110	-7.9
• RICE, Hal	Harold Housten "Hoot" Rice b: 2/11/1924, Morganette, WV d: 12/22/1997, Bloomington, IN BL/TR, 6'1", 195 lbs. Deb: 9/25/1948 Career OF: 271-4-50																							
1948 StL-N	8	31	3	10	1	2	0	3	2	4	0	....	.323	.364	.484	.848	121	1	6	7.26	0	/0-8(8-0-0)	1	0.0
1949 StL-N	40	46	3	9	2	1	1	9	3	7	0	....	.196	.245	.348	.593	55	-3	4	3.00	1	0-10(10-0-0)	0	-0.3
1950 StL-N	44	128	12	27	3	1	2	11	10	10	0	....	.211	.268	.297	.565	46	-10	11	2.79	-1	0-37(33-0-4)	1	-1.3
1951 StL-N	69	236	20	60	12	1	4	38	24	22	0	1	.254	.323	.364	.687	84	-6	27	3.97	1	0-63(48-0-16)	4	-0.8
1952 StL-N	98	295	37	85	14	5	7	45	16	26	1	3	.288	.325	.441	.765	110	2	39	4.78	-1	0-81(77-4-5)	8	-0.4
1953 StL-N	8	8	0	2	0	0	0	0	0	3	0	0	.250	.250	.250	.500	31	-1	1	2.31	0	....	0	-0.1
Pit-N	78	286	39	89	16	1	4	42	17	22	0	1	.311	.350	.416	.766	99	-1	42	5.50	11	0-70(68-0-2)	7	0.5
Yr.	86	294	39	91	16	1	4	42	17	25	0	1	.310	.347	.412	.759	98	-2	42	5.41	11	0-70(68-0-2)	7	0.4
1954 Pit-N	28	81	10	14	4	1	1	9	14	24	0	2	.173	.295	.284	.579	52	-6	7	2.55	2	0-24(24-0-2)	1	-0.5
Chi-N	51	72	5	11	0	0	0	5	8	15	0	0	.153	.238	.153	.390	4	-10	3	1.30	0	0-24(3-0-21)	0	-1.1
Yr.	79	153	15	25	4	1	1	14	22	39	0	2	.163	.269	.222	.491	30	-16	10	1.96	2	0-48(27-0-23)	1	-1.6
Total 7	424	1183	129	307	52	12	19	162	94	133	1	7	.260	.314	.372	.686	82	-35	139	4.11	13	0-317	22	-4.0
• RICE, Harry	Harry Francis Rice b: 11/22/1901, Ware Station, IL d: 1/1/1971, Portland, OR BL/TR, 5'9", 185 lbs. Deb: 4/18/1923 Career OF: 28-465-421																							
1923 StL-A	4	3	0	0	0	0	0	0	0	0	0	0	.000	.000	.000	.000	-95	-1	0	.00	0	....	0	-0.1
1924 StL-A	54	93	19	26	7	0	0	15	7	5	1	3	.280	.350	.355	.704	77	-4	11	4.12	-1	3-15/2-4,1-2,0-2(1-0-1),S	2	-0.3
1925 StL-A	103	354	87	127	25	8	11	47	54	15	8	7	.359	.450	.568	1.018	149	28	92	10.08	3	0-85(3-6-76)/1-3,2-1,3-1,C	19	2.2
1926 StL-A	148	578	86	181	27	10	9	59	63	40	10	11	.313	.384	.441	.826	110	7	98	6.22	7	*0-133(0-47-87)/3-8,2-4,S	19	0.6

YEAR TM-L	G	AB	R	H	2B	3B	HR	RBI	BB	SO	SB	CS	AVG	OBP	SLG	OPS	OPS+	BR/A	RC	RC/G	FR	G/POS	WS	TPW
1927 StL-A	137	520	90	149	26	9	7	68	50	21	5	4	.287	.351	.412	.763	94	-5	77	5.19	10	*O-130(0-44-87)/3-7	13	-0.3
1928 Det-A	131	510	87	154	21	12	6	81	44	27	20	13	.302	.360	.425	.785	104	2	78	5.33	-6	*O-129(0-129-0)/3-2	15	-0.9
1929 Det-A	130	536	97	163	33	7	6	69	61	23	6	10	.304	.379	.425	.805	106	4	87	5.82	2	*O-127(0-127-0)/3-3	15	0.1
1930 Det-A	37	128	16	39	6	0	2	24	19	8	0	3	.305	.403	.398	.801	102	0	21	5.78	-2	O-35(19-0-16)	3	-0.4
NY-A	100	346	62	103	17	5	7	74	31	21	3	3	.298	.361	.436	.797	106	3	55	5.68	-1	O-87(4-83-0)/1-6,3-1	10	-0.2
Yr.	137	474	78	142	23	5	9	98	50	29	3	6	.300	.372	.426	.799	105	3	76	5.71	-3	*O-122(23-83-16)/1-6,3-1	13	-0.6
1931 Was-A	47	162	32	43	5	6	0	15	12	10	2	1	.265	.320	.370	.690	81	-4	20	4.19	-2	O-42(1-19-23)	3	-0.7
1933 Cin-N	143	510	44	133	19	6	0	54	35	24	4	....	.261	.316	.322	.637	84	-10	53	3.50	3	*O-141(0-10-131)/3-1	11	-1.6
Total 10	1034	3740	620	1118	186	63	48	506	376	194	59	55	.299	.368	.421	.789	104	21	590	5.62	14	O-911/3-38,1-11,2-9,S-4,C-1	110	-1.5

• RICE, Jim

James Edward Rice b: 3/8/1953, Anderson, SC BR/TR, 6'2", 205 lbs. Deb: 8/19/1974 C Career OF: 1504-1-43

YEAR TM-L	G	AB	R	H	2B	3B	HR	RBI	BB	SO	SB	CS	AVG	OBP	SLG	OPS	OPS+	BR/A	RC	RC/G	FR	G/POS	WS	TPW
1974 Bos-A	24	67	6	18	2	1	1	13	4	12	0	0	.269	.319	.373	.693	92	-1	8	3.90	-1	D-16/O-3(3-0-0)	1	-0.2
1975 Bos-A	144	564	92	174	29	4	22	102	36	122	10	5	.309	.354	.491	.845	126	18	92	5.85	-1	O-90(90-0-0),D-54	20	1.1
1976 Bos-A	153	581	75	164	25	8	25	85	28	123	8	5	.282	.320	.482	.802	118	10	83	4.94	-7	O-98(98-0-0),D-54	17	-0.5
1977 Bos-A★	160	644	104	206	29	15	**39**	114	53	120	5	4	.320	.379	**.593**	.972	143	38	136	7.87	-0	*D-116,O-44(19-0-27)	26	3.1
1978 Bos-A★	163	677	121	**213**	25	**15**	**46**	**139**	58	126	7	5	.315	.373	**.600**	**.973**	153	**45**	147	**8.08**	1	*O-114(101-1-15),D-49	**36**	4.0
1979 Bos-A★	158	619	117	201	39	6	39	130	57	97	9	4	.325	.385	.596	.981	152	44	138	8.36	-4	*O-125(124-0-1),D-33	28	3.2
1980 Bos-A★	124	504	81	148	22	6	24	86	30	87	8	3	.294	.338	.504	.842	121	13	81	5.74	2	*O-109(109-0-0),D-15	16	0.9
1981 Bos-A	108	451	51	128	18	1	17	62	34	76	2	2	.284	.338	.441	.779	116	8	64	4.99	-1	*O-108(108-0-0)	15	0.2
1982 Bos-A	145	573	86	177	24	5	24	97	55	98	0	1	.309	.376	.494	.870	129	24	98	6.17	-4	*O-145(145-0-0)	21	1.3
1983 Bos-A★	155	626	90	191	34	1	**39**	**126**	52	102	0	2	.305	.364	.550	.914	137	30	113	6.43	7	*O-151(151-0-0)/D-4	24	2.9
1984 Bos-A★	159	657	98	184	25	7	28	122	44	102	4	0	.280	.326	.467	.793	112	10	88	4.60	5	*O-157(157-0-0)/D-2	17	0.7
1985 Bos-A★	140	546	85	159	20	3	27	103	51	75	2	0	.291	.354	.487	.841	123	17	83	5.18	-2	*O-130(130-0-0)/D-7	14	0.9
1986*Bos-A★	157	618	98	200	39	2	20	110	62	78	0	1	.324	.389	.490	.879	137	32	115	6.94	9	*O-156(156-0-0)/D-1	28	3.3
1987 Bos-A	108	404	66	112	14	0	13	62	45	77	1	1	.277	.360	.408	.768	100	1	55	4.69	3	O-94(94-0-0),D-12	8	0.0
1988*Bos-A	135	485	57	128	18	3	15	72	48	89	1	1	.264	.334	.406	.740	102	1	63	4.45	-1	*D-112,O-19(19-0-0)	9	-0.5
1989 Bos-A	56	209	22	49	10	2	3	28	13	39	1	0	.234	.283	.344	.627	71	-8	20	3.26	0	D-55	2	-1.1
Total 16	2089	8225	1249	2452	373	79	382	1451	670	1423	58	34	.298	.356	.502	.858	126	283	1382	6.00	7	*O-1543,D-530	282	19.2

• RICE, Len

Leonard Oliver Rice b: 9/2/1918, Lead, SD d: 6/13/1992, Sonora, CA BR/TR, 6', 175 lbs. Deb: 4/26/1944

YEAR TM-L	G	AB	R	H	2B	3B	HR	RBI	BB	SO	SB	CS	AVG	OBP	SLG	OPS	OPS+	BR/A	RC	RC/G	FR	G/POS	WS	TPW
1944 Cin-N	10	4	1	0	0	0	0	0	0	0	0	....	.000	.000	.000	.000	-104	-1	0	.00	-1	/C-5	0	-0.2
1945 Chi-N	32	99	10	23	3	0	0	7	5	8	2	....	.232	.269	.263	.532	49	-7	6	2.11	-3	C-29	1	-0.8
Total 2	42	103	11	23	3	0	0	7	5	8	2	....	.223	.259	.252	.512	44	-8	6	2.01	-3	/C-34	1	-1.0

• RICE, Sam

Edgar Charles Rice
b: 2/20/1890, Morocco, IN d: 10/13/1974, Rossmoor, MD BL/TR, 5'9", 150 lbs. Deb: 8/7/1915 HOF: 1963 Career OF: 47-601-1657 ♦

YEAR TM-L	G	AB	R	H	2B	3B	HR	RBI	BB	SO	SB	CS	AVG	OBP	SLG	OPS	OPS+	BR/A	RC	RC/G	FR	G/POS	WS	TPW
1915 Was-A	4	8	0	3	0	0	0	0	0	1	0	....	.375	.375	.375	.750	122	1	1	5.96	0	/P-4	2	0.3
1916 Was-A	58	197	26	59	8	3	1	17	15	13	4	....	.299	.352	.386	.738	123	6	28	5.26	0	O-46(4-0-42)/P-5	8	0.3
1917 Was-A	155	586	77	177	25	7	0	69	50	41	35	....	.302	.360	.369	.729	124	16	86	5.29	2	*O-155(0-0-155)	24	1.1
1918 Was-A	7	23	3	8	1	0	0	3	2	0	1	....	.348	.400	.391	.791	141	1	4	6.39	3	/O-6(0-0-6)	1	0.4
1919 Was-A	141	557	80	179	23	9	3	71	42	26	26	....	.321	.376	.411	.787	122	16	91	6.14	0	*O-141(0-0-141)	18	0.9
1920 Was-A	153	624	83	211	29	9	3	80	39	23	**63**	30	.338	.381	.428	.809	117	17	100	5.75	11	*O-153(0-153-0)	23	1.8
1921 Was-A	143	561	83	185	39	13	4	79	38	10	26	12	.330	.382	.467	.849	121	19	100	6.47	4	*O-141(0-137-4)	23	1.5
1922 Was-A	154	633	91	187	37	13	6	69	48	13	20	9	.295	.347	.423	.770	105	5	93	5.37	5	*O-154(0-154-0)	20	0.3
1923 Was-A	148	595	117	188	35	**18**	3	75	57	12	20	8	.316	.381	.450	.832	125	23	105	6.48	11	*O-147(0-0-147)	24	2.1
1924*Was-A	154	646	106	**216**	39	14	1	76	46	24	24	13	.334	.382	.443	.825	116	15	109	6.29	-1	*O-154(0-34-123)	24	0.3
1925*Was-A	152	649	111	227	31	13	1	87	37	10	26	11	.350	.388	.442	.831	112	14	112	6.54	6	*O-152(0-29-133)	24	0.8
1926 Was-A	152	641	98	**216**	32	14	3	76	42	20	24	23	.337	.380	.445	.824	117	11	103	5.85	5	*O-152(0-44-120)	23	0.4
1927 Was-A	142	603	98	179	33	14	2	65	36	11	19	6	.297	.336	.408	.744	94	-6	84	5.01	-3	*O-139(1-0-138)	17	-1.8
1928 Was-A	148	616	95	202	32	15	2	55	49	15	16	3	.328	.379	.438	.818	115	16	105	6.47	-6	*O-147(1-0-147)	19	-0.1
1929 Was-A	150	616	119	199	39	10	1	62	55	9	16	8	.323	.382	.424	.806	106	8	102	6.07	5	*O-147(0-0-147)	20	0.2
1930 Was-A	147	593	121	207	35	13	1	73	55	14	13	8	.349	.407	.457	.864	118	18	111	7.18	7	*O-145(0-15-133)	23	1.3
1931 Was-A	120	413	81	128	21	8	0	42	35	11	6	5	.310	.365	.400	.765	100	2	61	5.35	-1	*O-105(10-11-85)	13	-0.5
1932 Was-A	106	288	58	93	16	7	1	34	32	6	7	4	.323	.391	.438	.828	116	8	50	6.58	2	O-69(10-14-48)	11	0.6
1933*Was-A	73	85	19	25	4	3	1	12	2	7	0	2	.294	.326	.447	.773	104	-1	11	4.86	3	O-39(8-10-23)	3	0.1
1934 Cle-A	97	335	48	98	19	1	1	33	28	9	5	1	.293	.351	.364	.715	83	-7	44	4.89	-6	O-78(13-0-65)	7	-1.6
Total 20	2404	9269	1514	2987	498	184	34	1078	708	275	351	143	.322	.374	.427	.801	113	181	1501	5.97	47	*O-2270/P-9	327	8.4

• RICHARD, Chris

Christopher Robert Richard b: 6/7/1974, San Diego, CA BL/TL, 6'2", 190 lbs. Deb: 7/17/2000 Career OF: 4-36-72

YEAR TM-L	G	AB	R	H	2B	3B	HR	RBI	BB	SO	SB	CS	AVG	OBP	SLG	OPS	OPS+	BR/A	RC	RC/G	FR	G/POS	WS	TPW
2000 StL-N	6	16	1	2	0	0	1	1	2	2	0	0	.125	.222	.313	.535	33	-2	1	2.37	0	/O-3(1-0-2),1-2	0	-0.2
Bal-A	56	199	38	55	14	2	13	36	15	38	7	5	.276	.339	.563	.902	129	7	35	6.04	-6	1-53/D-1,O-1	6	-0.3
2001 Bal-A	136	483	74	128	31	3	15	61	45	100	11	9	.265	.338	.435	.772	107	3	67	4.70	3	O-96(0-36-69),D-20,1-18	12	0.0
2002 Bal-A	50	155	15	36	11	0	4	21	12	30	0	3	.232	.296	.381	.677	82	-6	17	3.59	-1	D-36/1-9	1	-0.9
2003 Col-N	19	27	3	6	1	1	1	3	3	6	0	1	.222	.300	.444	.744	80	-1	3	3.50	0	/O-3(3-0-0),1-1	0	-0.1
Total 4	267	880	131	227	57	6	34	122	77	176	18	18	.258	.327	.452	.780	106	1	123	4.72	-3	O-103/1-83,D-57	19	-1.5

• RICHARD, Lee

Lee Edward "Bee Bee" Richard b: 9/18/1948, Lafayette, LA BR/TR, 5'11", 165 lbs. Deb: 4/7/1971 Career OF: 0-22-1

YEAR TM-L	G	AB	R	H	2B	3B	HR	RBI	BB	SO	SB	CS	AVG	OBP	SLG	OPS	OPS+	BR/A	RC	RC/G	FR	G/POS	WS	TPW
1971 Chi-A	87	260	38	60	7	3	2	17	20	46	8	9	.231	.288	.304	.592	66	-14	21	2.62	-7	S-68,O-16(0-16-0)	3	-1.5
1972 Chi-A	11	29	5	7	0	0	0	1	0	7	1	0	.241	.241	.241	.483	43	-2	2	1.83	0	/O-6(0-6-0),S-1	0	-0.2
1974 Chi-A	32	67	5	11	1	0	0	1	5	8	0	0	.164	.222	.179	.401	16	-7	3	1.40	1	3-12/S-6,D-5,2-3,O-1	0	-0.6
1975 Chi-A	43	45	11	9	0	1	0	5	4	7	2	3	.200	.265	.244	.510	44	-4	3	1.85	-1	3-12/S-9,2-5,D-5	0	-0.5
1976 StL-N	66	91	12	16	4	2	0	5	4	9	1	0	.176	.211	.264	.474	34	-8	4	1.45	-3	2-26,S-12/3-1	1	-1.0
Total 5	239	492	71	103	12	6	2	29	33	77	12	12	.209	.260	.270	.531	50	-35	33	2.12	-10	/S-96,2-34,3-25,O-23,D-10	4	-3.7

• RICHARDS, Fred

Fred Charles "Fuzzy" Richards b: 11/3/1927, Warren, OH BL/TL, 6'1.5", 185 lbs. Deb: 9/15/1951

YEAR TM-L	G	AB	R	H	2B	3B	HR	RBI	BB	SO	SB	CS	AVG	OBP	SLG	OPS	OPS+	BR/A	RC	RC/G	FR	G/POS	WS	TPW
1951 Chi-N	10	27	1	8	2	0	0	4	2	3	0	0	.296	.345	.370	.715	91	-0	4	5.08	1	/1-9	1	0.1

• RICHARDS, Gene

Eugene Richards b: 9/29/1953, Monticello, SC BL/TL, 6', 175 lbs. Deb: 4/6/1977 Career OF: 634-170-23

YEAR TM-L	G	AB	R	H	2B	3B	HR	RBI	BB	SO	SB	CS	AVG	OBP	SLG	OPS	OPS+	BR/A	RC	RC/G	FR	G/POS	WS	TPW
1977 SD-N	146	525	79	152	16	11	5	32	60	80	56	12	.290	.365	.390	.755	114	20	81	5.52	5	*O-109(72-41-1),1-32	21	2.0
1978 SD-N	154	555	90	171	26	12	4	45	64	80	37	17	.308	.384	.420	.803	135	28	92	5.96	-5	*O-124(113-26-0),1-26	24	1.7
1979 SD-N	150	545	77	152	17	9	4	41	47	62	24	8	.279	.345	.365	.710	100	2	72	4.70	-1	*O-132(20-102-10)	16	-0.1
1980 SD-N	158	642	91	193	26	8	4	41	61	73	61	16	.301	.363	.385	.748	115	20	96	5.41	9	*O-156(156-0-1)	22	2.2
1981 SD-N	104	393	47	113	14	**12**	3	42	53	44	20	8	.288	.374	.407	.781	131	18	63	5.68	1	*O-102(101-0-0)	14	1.5
1982 SD-N	132	521	63	149	13	8	3	28	36	52	30	20	.286	.335	.359	.693	99	-4	62	4.16	-0	*O-103(103-0-0),1-25	16	-1.0
1983 SD-N	95	233	37	64	11	3	3	22	17	17	14	5	.275	.327	.386	.713	100	0	28	4.13	-1	O-54(54-0-0)	7	-0.3
1984 SF-N	87	135	18	34	4	0	0	4	18	28	5	3	.252	.340	.281	.621	79	-3	13	3.40	-2	O-26(15-1-11)	2	-0.7
Total 8	1026	3549	502	1028	127	63	26	255	356	436	247	89	.290	.358	.383	.741	113	82	508	5.08	6	O-806/1-83	122	5.4

• RICHARDS, Paul

Paul Rapier Richards b: 11/21/1908, Waxahachie, TX d: 5/4/1986, Waxahachie, TX BR/TR, 6'1.5", 180 lbs. Deb: 4/17/1932 M

YEAR TM-L	G	AB	R	H	2B	3B	HR	RBI	BB	SO	SB	CS	AVG	OBP	SLG	OPS	OPS+	BR/A	RC	RC/G	FR	G/POS	WS	TPW
1932 Bro-N	3	8	0	0	0	0	0	0	0	2	0	....	.000	.000	.000	.000	-102	-2	0	.00	2	/C-3	0	0.0
1933 NY-N	51	87	4	17	3	0	0	10	3	12	0	....	.195	.222	.230	.452	30	-8	4	1.28	1	C-36	1	-0.6
1934 NY-N	42	75	10	12	1	0	0	3	13	8	0	....	.160	.284	.173	.457	26	-7	4	1.82	1	C-37	2	-0.5
1935 NY-N	7	4	0	1	0	0	0	0	2	1	0	....	.250	.500	.250	.750	110	0	1	6.95	0	/C-4	0	0.1
Phi-A	85	257	31	63	10	1	4	29	24	12	0	0	.245	.310	.339	.648	68	-12	28	3.73	0	C-79	4	-0.8
1943 Det-A	100	313	32	69	7	1	5	33	38	35	1	0	.220	.307	.297	.604	71	-10	31	3.25	9	*C-100	11	0.5
1944 Det-A	95	300	24	71	13	0	3	37	35	30	8	3	.237	.318	.310	.628	76	-8	30	3.20	5	C-90	10	0.3
1945*Det-A	83	234	26	60	12	1	3	32	19	31	4	0	.256	.315	.355	.670	88	-3	29	4.40	5	C-83	11	0.3
1946 Det-A	57	139	13	28	5	2	0	11	23	18	2	0	.201	.315	.266	.581	60	-6	13	2.75	3	C-54	5	-0.1
Total 8	523	1417	140	321	51	5	15	155	157	149	15	3	.227	.305	.301	.606	68	-57	139	3.22	21	C-486	44	-0.7

YEAR TM-L	G	AB	R	H	2B	3B	HR	RBI	BB	SO	SB	CS	AVG	OBP	SLG	OPS	OPS+	BR/A	RC	RC/G	FR	G/POS	WS	TPW
• **RICHARDSON,**	Richardson b: Boston, MA, 5'4", 136 lbs. Deb: 7/10/1884																							
1884 CP-U	1	4	0	0	0	0	0	....	0	....	....	....	.000	.000	.000	.000	-107	-1	0	.00	0	/2-1	0	-0.1
• **RICHARDSON, Bill**	William Henry Richardson b: 9/24/1878, Salem, IN d: 11/6/1949, Sullivan, IN BR/TR, 5'11", 200 lbs. Deb: 9/20/1901																							
1901 StL-N	15	52	7	11	2	0	2	7	6	....	1	....	.212	.293	.365	.658	95	-0	6	3.84	-2	1-15	1	-0.2
• **RICHARDSON, Bobby**	Robert Clinton Richardson b: 8/19/1935, Sumter, SC BR/TR, 5'9", 170 lbs. Deb: 8/5/1955																							
1955 NY-A	11	26	2	4	0	0	0	3	2	0	1	1	.154	.214	.154	.368		-4	1	.83	-2	/2-6,S-4	0	-0.6
1956 NY-A	5	7	1	1	0	0	0	0	0	1	0	0	.143	.143	.143	.286	-25	-1	0	.64	-1	/2-5	0	-0.2
1957*NY-A★	97	305	36	78	11	1	0	19	9	26	1	3	.256	.277	.298	.575	58	-19	23	2.48	2	2-93	4	-1.2
1958*NY-A	73	182	18	45	6	2	0	14	8	5	1	3	.247	.279	.302	.581	62	-11	15	2.80	0	2-51,3-13/S-2	3	-0.7
1959 NY-A★	134	469	53	141	18	6	2	33	26	20	5	5	.301	.337	.377	.715	99	-2	60	4.66	-2	*2-109,S-14,3-12	14	0.5
1960*NY-A	150	460	45	116	12	3	1	26	35	19	6	6	.252	.305	.298	.603	67	-22	42	3.07	-3	*2-141,3-11	8	-1.6
1961*NY-A	162	662	80	173	17	5	3	49	30	23	9	7	.261	.295	.316	.611	67	-33	59	3.05	-4	*2-161	12	-2.3
1962*NY-A★	161	692	99	**209**	38	5	8	59	37	24	11	9	.302	.338	.406	.744	102	-1	92	4.70	2	*2-161	22	1.5
1963*NY-A★	151	630	72	167	20	6	3	48	25	22	15	1	.265	.295	.330	.625	76	-19	63	3.54	6	*2-150	18	0.1
1964*NY-A★	159	679	90	181	25	4	4	50	28	36	11	2	.267	.296	.333	.628	73	-24	66	3.32	-10	*2-157/S-1	15	-2.1
1965 NY-A★	160	664	76	164	28	2	6	47	37	39	7	5	.247	.288	.322	.610	74	-25	61	3.10	-15	*2-158	14	-2.8
1966 NY-A★	149	610	71	153	21	3	7	42	25	28	6	6	.251	.281	.330	.611	78	-20	52	2.87	-11	*2-147/3-2	10	-1.9
Total 12	1412	5386	643	1432	196	37	34	390	262	243	73	48	.266	.301	.335	.636	77	-181	534	3.41	-39	*2-1339/3-38,S-21	120	-11.3
• **RICHARDSON, Danny**	Daniel Richardson b: 1/25/1863, Elmira, NY d: 9/12/1926, New York, NY BR/TR, 5'8", 165 lbs. Deb: 5/22/1884 M Career OF: 41-51-51 ♦																							
1884 NY-N	74	277	36	70	8	1	1	27	16	17	....	....	.253	.294	.300	.593	85	-5	25	3.32	0	0-55(11-7-37),S-19	7	-0.5
1885 NY-N	49	198	26	52	9	3	0	25	10	14	....	....	.263	.298	.338	.636	107	3	20	3.79	3	0-22(10-2-12),3-21/P-9	14	0.5
1886 NY-N	68	237	43	55	9	1	1	27	17	21	12	....	.232	.283	.291	.575	74	-7	24	3.49	1	0-64(20-42-2)/P-5,2-1,3-1,S	5	-1.4
1887 NY-N	122	486	79	161	19	10	3	62	36	25	41	....	.331	.337	.384	.721	105	4	74	6.02	11	*2-108,3-14/P-1	14	1.6
1888*NY-N	135	561	82	127	16	7	8	61	15	35	35	....	.226	.248	.323	.570	82	-13	55	3.41	18	*2-135	15	0.9
1889*NY-N	125	497	88	139	22	8	7	100	46	37	32	....	.280	.342	.398	.740	106	3	81	5.97	16	*2-125	17	2.0
1890 NY-P	123	528	102	135	12	9	4	80	37	19	37	....	.256	.307	.335	.642	66	-30	67	4.62	26	S-68,2-56	13	0.0
1891 NY-N	123	516	85	139	18	5	4	51	33	27	28	....	.269	.313	.347	.660	96	-4	66	4.76	37	*2-114/S-9	17	3.4
1892 Was-N	142	551	48	132	13	4	3	58	25	45	25	....	.240	.274	.294	.568	74	-19	52	3.38	36	S-93,2-49/3-1	11	2.2
1893 Bro-N	54	206	36	46	6	2	0	27	13	18	7	....	.223	.279	.272	.551	49	-15	18	2.99	-10	2-46/3-5,S-3	2	-1.9
1894 Lou-N	116	430	51	109	17	2	1	40	35	31	8	....	.253	.317	.309	.626	55	-30	46	3.71	-8	*S-107,2-10	8	-2.5
Total 11	1131	4487	676	1165	149	52	32	558	283	289	225	....	.260	.301	.332	.633	82	-112	528	4.26	129	2-644,S-300,0-141/3-42,P-15	123	4.4
• **RICHARDSON, Hardy**	Abram Harding "Old True Blue" Richardson b: 4/21/1855, Clarksboro, NJ d: 1/14/1931, Utica, NY BR/TR, 5'9.5", 170 lbs. Deb: 5/1/1879 U Career OF: 375-158-11																							
1879 Buf-N	79	336	54	95	18	10	0	37	16	30	....	....	.283	.315	.396	.711	129	11	43	4.99	-3	*3-78/C-1	12	0.9
1880 Buf-N	83	343	48	89	18	8	0	17	14	37	....	....	.259	.289	.359	.647	115	5	36	3.94	-11	*3-81/C-5	11	-0.3
1881 Buf-N	83	344	62	100	18	9	2	53	12	27	....	....	.291	.315	.413	.727	128	11	46	5.07	23	*0-79(0-79-0)/2-5,3-1,S-1	15	2.8
1882 Buf-N	83	354	61	96	20	8	2	57	11	33	....	....	.271	.293	.390	.683	115	5	41	4.42	14	*2-83	11	2.0
1883 Buf-N	92	399	73	124	34	7	1	56	22	20	....	....	.311	.347	.439	.785	134	16	62	6.22	22	*2-92	17	3.6
1884 Buf-N	102	439	85	132	27	9	6	60	22	41	....	....	.301	.334	.444	.778	138	18	67	5.98	7	2-71,0-24(0-24-0)/3-5,1-3	19	2.3
1885 Buf-N	96	426	90	136	19	11	6	44	20	22	....	....	.319	.350	.458	.808	154	24	70	6.51	2	2-50,0-48(1-47-0)/P-1,S-1	19	2.4
1886 Det-N	125	538	125	**189**	27	11	**11**	61	46	27	42	....	.351	.402	.504	.906	169	44	129	9.99	14	0-80(80-0-0),2-42/P-4,S-3,3	32	5.0
1887*Det-N	120	574	131	209	25	18	8	94	31	40	29	....	.364	.366	.484	.851	130	20	110	7.96	21	2-64,0-59(58-1-0)	23	3.5
1888 Det-N	58	266	60	77	18	2	6	32	17	23	13	....	.289	.335	.440	.774	145	13	45	6.37	4	2-58	11	1.9
1889 Bos-N	132	536	122	163	33	10	6	79	48	44	47	....	.304	.367	.437	.803	117	10	106	7.50	11	2-86,0-46(46-0-0)	25	1.9
1890 Bos-P	130	555	126	181	26	14	13	**146**	52	46	42	....	.326	.384	.494	.878	125	16	124	8.98	2	*0-124(124-0-0)/S-6,1-1	20	1.1
1891 Bos-a	74	278	45	71	9	4	7	52	40	26	16	....	.255	.351	.392	.743	114	5	45	5.76	1	0-60(57-1-2)/3-9,S-4,1-3	10	0.3
1892 Was-N	10	37	2	4	0	0	0	0	5	3	2	....	.108	.214	.108	.322	-2	-4	1	1.08	0	/0-7(7-0-0),3-2,2-1	0	-0.5
NY-N	64	248	36	53	11	5	2	34	21	26	14	....	.214	.278	.323	.600	83	-6	27	3.71	3	2-33,0-17(2-6-9)/1-9,S-6	5	-0.2
Yr.	74	285	38	57	11	5	2	34	26	29	16	....	.200	.269	.295	.564	71	-10	28	3.33	3	2-34,0-24(9-6-9)/1-9,S-6,3	5	-0.6
Total 14	1331	5673	1120	1719	303	126	70	822	377	445	205	....	.303	.344	.435	.779	130	188	952	6.50	108	2-585,0-544,3-178/S-21,1,C,P	230	26.9
• **RICHARDSON, Jeff**	Jeffrey Scott Richardson b: 8/26/1965, Grand Island, NE BR/TR, 6'2", 175 lbs. Deb: 7/14/1989																							
1989 Cin-N	53	125	10	21	4	0	2	11	10	23	1	0	.168	.235	.248	.483	37	-10	8	1.84	0	S-39/3-8	1	-0.8
1991 Pit-N	6	4	0	1	0	0	0	0	0	3	0	0	.250	.250	.250	.500	42	-0	0	2.25	-2	/3-3,S-2	0	-0.2
1993 Bos-A	15	24	3	5	2	0	0	2	1	3	0	0	.208	.240	.292	.532	40	-2	2	2.37	2	/2-8,S-5,D-2,3-1	1	0.1
Total 3	74	153	13	27	6	0	2	13	11	29	1	0	.176	.236	.255	.491	38	-13	10	1.93	1	/S-46,3-12,2-8,D-2	2	-1.0
• **RICHARDSON, Ken**	Kenneth Franklin Richardson b: 5/2/1915, Orleans, IN d: 12/7/1987, Woodland Hills, CA BR/TR, 5'10.5", 187 lbs. Deb: 4/14/1942																							
1942 Phi-A	6	15	1	1	0	0	0	0	2	0	0	0	.067	.176	.067	.243	-30	-3	0	.62	0	/0-3(1-0-2),1-1,3-1	0	-0.3
1946 Phi-N	6	20	1	3	1	0	0	2	0	2	0	....	.150	.150	.200	.350	-1	-3	0	.60	-1	/2-6	0	-0.4
Total 2	12	35	2	4	1	0	0	2	2	2	0	0	.114	.162	.143	.305	-15	-5	1	.61	-1	/2-6,0-3,1-1,3-1	0	-0.7
• **RICHARDSON, Nolen**	Clifford Nolen Richardson b: 1/18/1903, Chattanooga, TN d: 9/25/1951, Athens, GA BR/TR, 6'1.5", 170 lbs. Deb: 4/16/1929																							
1929 Det-A	13	21	2	4	0	0	0	2	2	1	1	1	.190	.261	.190	.451	18	-3	1	1.55	-3	S-13	0	-0.5
1931 Det-A	38	148	13	40	9	2	0	16	6	3	2	1	.270	.299	.358	.657	70	-6	16	3.70	0	3-38	2	-0.5
1932 Det-A	69	155	13	34	5	2	0	12	9	13	5	2	.219	.262	.277	.540	38	-14	12	2.44	4	3-65/S-4	2	-0.8
1935 NY-A	12	46	3	10	1	1	0	5	3	1	0	0	.217	.265	.283	.548	44	-4	4	2.58	-2	S-12	0	-0.5
1938 Cin-N	35	100	8	29	4	0	0	10	3	4	0	....	.290	.311	.330	.641	78	-3	10	3.64	3	S-35	3	0.2
1939 Cin-N	1	3	0	0	0	0	0	0	0	0	0	....	.000	.000	.000	.000	-99	-1	0	.00	0	/S-1	0	0.0
Total 6	168	473	39	117	19	5	0	45	23	22	8	4	.247	.282	.309	.591	55	-31	42	3.01	2	3-103/S-65	7	-2.1
• **RICHARDSON, Tom**	Thomas Mitchell Richardson b: 8/7/1883, Louisville, IL d: 11/15/1939, Onawa, IA BR/TR, 6', 190 lbs. Deb: 8/2/1917																							
1917 StL-A	1	1	0	0	0	0	0	0	0	0	0	....	.000	.000	.000	.000	-104	-0	0	.00	0	....	0	0.0
• **RICHARDT, Mike**	Michael Anthony Richardt b: 5/24/1958, North Hollywood, CA BR/TR, 6', 170 lbs. Deb: 8/30/1980																							
1980 Tex-A	22	71	2	16	2	0	0	8	1	7	0	0	.225	.236	.254	.490	35	-6	4	1.96	1	2-20/D-1	1	-0.5
1982 Tex-A	119	402	34	97	10	0	3	43	23	42	9	1	.241	.284	.289	.573	61	-20	32	2.66	-8	2-98,D-15/0-6(6-0-0)	5	-2.3
1983 Tex-A	22	83	9	13	2	1	1	7	2	11	2	1	.157	.176	.241	.417	14	-10	3	1.12	2	2-20	1	-0.7
1984 Tex-A	6	9	0	1	0	0	0	0	1	1	0	1	.111	.200	.111	.311	-11	-2	0	.38	0	/2-4	0	-0.1
Hou-N	16	15	1	4	1	0	0	2	0	1	0	0	.267	.267	.333	.600	73	-0	1	3.27	0	....	0	-0.1
Total 4	185	580	46	131	15	1	4	60	27	62	11	3	.226	.262	.276	.537	50	-38	41	2.31	-5	2-142/D-16,0-6	7	-3.7
• **RICHBOURG, Lance**	Lance Clayton Richbourg b: 12/18/1897, DeFuniak Springs, FL d: 9/10/1975, Crestview, FL BL/TR, 5'10.5", 160 lbs. Deb: 7/4/1921 Career OF: 18-6-607																							
1921 Phi-N	10	5	2	1	1	0	0	0	0	3	1	1	.200	.200	.400	.600	51	-1	0	.00	-1	/2-4	0	-0.1
1924 Was-A	15	32	3	9	2	1	0	1	2	0	0	0	.281	.324	.406	.730	90	-1	4	4.67	1	/0-7(0-0-7)	1	0.0
1927 Bos-N	115	450	57	139	12	9	2	34	22	30	24	....	.309	.342	.389	.731	103	1	58	4.59	-6	*0-110(0-3-107)	11	-1.3
1928 Bos-N	148	612	105	206	26	12	2	52	62	39	11	....	.337	.399	.428	.828	123	22	104	6.49	0	*0-148(0-0-148)	20	1.0
1929 Bos-N	139	557	76	170	24	13	3	56	42	26	7	....	.305	.355	.411	.766	93	-6	80	5.14	4	*0-134(2-0-132)	13	-1.2
1930 Bos-N	130	529	81	161	23	8	3	54	19	31	13	....	.304	.331	.395	.726	77	-20	66	4.59	-5	*0-128(0-0-128)	11	-3.1
1931 Bos-N	97	286	32	82	11	6	2	29	19	14	9	....	.287	.331	.388	.719	96	-2	38	4.65	-1	0-71(15-0-56)	7	-0.8
1932 Chi-N	44	148	22	38	2	2	1	21	8	4	0	....	.257	.295	.318	.612	65	-7	14	3.28	-1	0-33(1-3-29)	2	-1.0
Total 8	698	2619	378	806	101	51	13	247	174	147	65	1	.308	.352	.400	.752	97	-14	364	5.04	-9	0-631/2-4	65	-6.4
• **RICHIE, Rob**	Robert Eugene Richie b: 9/5/1965, Reno, NV BL/TR, 6'2", 190 lbs. Deb: 8/19/1989																							
1989 Det-A	19	49	6	13	4	2	1	10	5	10	0	1	.265	.333	.490	.823	132	1	7	4.71	0	0-13(11-0-2)/D-4	2	0.1

YEAR TM-L	G	AB	R	H	2B	3B	HR	RBI	BB	SO	SB	CS	AVG	OBP	SLG	OPS	OPS+	BR/A	RC	RC/G	FR	G/POS	WS	TPW
• RICHMOND, Don	Donald Lester Richmond b: 10/27/1919, Gillett, PA d: 5/24/1981, Elmira, NY BL/TR, 6'1", 175 lbs. Deb: 9/16/1941																							
1941 Phi-A	9	35	3	7	1	1	0	5	0	1	0	2	.200	.200	.286	.486	28	-5	1	1.00	1	/3-9	0	-0.4
1946 Phi-A	16	62	3	18	3	0	1	9	0	10	1	0	.290	.290	.387	.677	89	-1	7	4.32	-1	3-16	1	-0.2
1947 Phi-A	19	21	2	4	1	1	0	4	3	3	0	0	.190	.292	.333	.625	72	-1	2	2.98	-2	/3-4,2-1	0	-0.3
1951 StL-N	12	34	3	3	1	0	1	4	3	3	0	1	.088	.162	.206	.368	-2	-5	1	.70	1	3-11	1	-0.4
Total 4	56	152	11	32	6	2	2	22	6	17	1	3	.211	.241	.316	.556	52	-12	11	2.37	0	/3-40,2-1	2	-1.2
• RICHMOND, John	John H. Richmond b: 3/5/1854, Philadelphia, PA TR, 5'9", 170 lbs. Deb: 4/22/1875 Career OF: 4-122-7																							
1875 Ath-n	29	125	29	25	2	0	0	12	1	4	1	0	.200	.206	.216	.422	42	-8	6	1.75	-2	2-17,0-11(2-3-6)/C-3	....	-0.9
1879 Syr-N	62	254	31	54	8	4	1	23	4	24	....	....	.213	.225	.287	.512	76	-5	17	2.35	-3	0-35(4-29-2),S-28/C-2	4	-0.7
1880 Bos-N	32	129	12	32	3	1	0	9	2	18	....	....	.248	.260	.287	.546	88	-2	10	2.79	-7	S-31/0-1	3	-0.7
1881 Bos-N	27	98	13	27	2	2	1	12	6	7	....	....	.276	.317	.367	.685	120	2	12	4.45	-1	0-25(0-24-1)/S-2	4	0.0
1882 Cle-N	41	140	12	24	6	2	0	11	11	27	....	....	.171	.232	.243	.475	54	-6	8	1.92	3	0-41(0-41-0)	1	-0.4
Phi-a	18	65	8	12	2	2	0	4	11	....	....	....	.185	.303	.277	.580	86	-1	6	2.95	0	0-18(0-17-1)	2	-0.1
1883 Col-a	92	385	63	109	7	8	0	0	25	....	....	....	.283	.327	.343	.670	126	13	44	4.49	21	*S-91/0-2(0-2-0)	14	**3.3**
1884 Col-a	105	398	57	100	13	7	3	0	35	....	....	....	.251	.317	.342	.658	124	13	44	4.07	-10	*S-105	16	0.6
1885 Pit-a	34	131	14	27	2	2	0	12	8	....	....	....	.206	.262	.252	.514	64	-5	9	2.30	-9	S-23,0-11(0-8-3)	2	-1.3
Total 7	411	1600	210	385	43	28	5	71	102	76	....	....	.241	.288	.312	.600	101	10	149	3.40	-6	S-280,0-133/C-2	46	0.6
• RICHMOND, Lee	J Lee Richmond b: 5/5/1857, Sheffield, OH d: 10/1/1929, Toledo, OH TL, 5'10", 155 lbs. Deb: 9/27/1879 U Career OF: 35-14-41 ♦																							
1879 Bos-N	1	6	0	2	0	0	0	1	0	1	....	....	.333	.333	.333	.667	118	0	1	4.78	0	/P-1	1	0.0
1880 Wor-N	77	309	44	70	8	4	0	34	9	32	....	....	.227	.248	.278	.527	72	-4	22	2.52	-7	*P-74,0-20(1-1-18)	42	1.3
1881 Wor-N	61	252	31	63	5	1	0	28	10	10	....	....	.250	.279	.278	.556	71	-1	20	2.86	-1	P-53,0-11(0-2-9)	26	-0.9
1882 Wor-N	55	228	50	64	8	9	2	28	9	11	....	....	.281	.308	.421	.729	128	10	30	5.08	1	P-48,0-11(1-1-9)	13	0.0
1883 Pro-N	49	194	41	55	8	6	1	19	15	19	....	....	.284	.335	.402	.737	119	6	27	5.30	-7	0-41(33-3-5),P-12	9	-0.6
1886 Cin-a	8	29	3	8	0	0	0	3	3	....	0	....	.276	.344	.276	.620	92	0	3	3.62	-3	/0-7(0-7-0),P-3	1	-1.0
Total 6	251	1018	169	262	29	20	3	113	46	73	0	....	.257	.289	.334	.623	94	13	102	3.71	-16	P-191/0-90	92	-1.2
• RICHTER, Al	Allen Gordon Richter b: 2/7/1927, Norfolk, VA BR/TR, 5'11", 165 lbs. Deb: 9/23/1951																							
1951 Bos-A	5	11	1	1	0	0	0	0	3	0	0	0	.091	.286	.091	.377	5	-1	0	.27	1	/S-3	0	0.0
1953 Bos-A	1	0	0	0	0	0	0	0	0	0	0	0	....	....	....	....	-95	0	0	....	0	/S-1	0	0.0
Total 2	6	11	1	1	0	0	0	0	3	0	0	0	.091	.286	.091	.377	5	-1	0	.27	1	/S-4	0	0.0
• RICHTER, John	John M. Richter b: 2/8/1873, Louisville, KY d: 10/4/1927, Louisville, KY, 6', 178 lbs. Deb: 10/6/1898																							
1898 Lou-N	3	13	1	2	0	0	0	0	0	....	0	....	.154	.154	.154	.308	-12	-2	0	.88	1	/3-3	0	-0.1
• RICKERT, Joe	Joseph Francis "Diamond Joe" Rickert b: 12/12/1876, London, OH d: 10/15/1943, Springfield, OH BR/TR, 5'10.5", 165 lbs. Deb: 10/12/1898 Career OF: 15-0-0																							
1898 Pit-N	2	6	0	1	0	0	0	0	0	....	0	....	.167	.167	.167	.333	-5	-1	0	1.12	1	/0-2(2-0-0)	0	0.0
1901 Bos-N	13	60	6	10	1	2	0	1	3	....	1	....	.167	.206	.250	.456	29	-6	3	1.81	2	0-13(13-0-0)	1	-0.4
Total 2	15	66	6	11	1	2	0	1	3	....	1	....	.167	.203	.242	.445	26	-7	4	1.74	3	/0-15	1	-0.4
• RICKERT, Marv	Marvin August "Twitch" Rickert b: 1/8/1921, Longbranch, WA d: 6/3/1978, Oakville, WA BL/TR, 6'2", 195 lbs. Deb: 9/10/1942 Career OF: 164-31-110																							
1942 Chi-N	8	26	5	7	0	0	0	1	1	5	0	....	.269	.296	.269	.566	69	-1	2	2.54	1	/0-6(0-6-0)	0	0.0
1946 Chi-N	111	392	44	103	18	3	7	47	28	54	3	....	.263	.314	.378	.691	97	-3	46	4.08	-2	*0-104(75-19-10)	10	-1.1
1947 Chi-N	71	137	7	20	0	0	2	15	15	17	0	....	.146	.230	.190	.420	13	-17	6	1.31	0	0-30(18-3-9)/1-7	1	-1.8
1948 Cin-N	8	6	0	1	0	0	0	0	0	0	0	....	.167	.167	.167	.333	-10	-1	0	.90	0	....	0	-0.1
*Bos-N	3	13	1	3	0	1	0	2	0	1	0	....	.231	.286	.385	.670	81	-0	2	4.06	1	/0-3(3-0-0)	0	0.0
Yr.	11	19	1	4	0	1	0	2	0	1	0	....	.211	.250	.316	.566	54	-1	2	3.01	1	/0-3(3-0-0)	0	0.0
1949 Bos-N	100	277	44	81	18	3	6	49	23	38	1	....	.292	.347	.444	.791	117	6	42	5.52	3	0-75(50-3-25),1-12	9	0.4
1950 Pit-N	17	20	0	3	0	0	0	4	0	4	0	....	.150	.150	.150	.300	-20	-4	0	.45	0	/0-3(0-0-3)	0	-0.4
Chi-A	84	278	38	66	9	2	4	27	21	42	0	1	.237	.291	.327	.618	60	-18	25	2.97	-1	0-78(18-0-63)/1-1	2	-2.0
Total 6	402	1149	139	284	45	9	19	145	88	161	4	1	.247	.302	.352	.653	79	-38	122	3.63	3	0-299/1-20	22	-4.9
• RICKETTS, Dave	David William Ricketts b: 7/12/1935, Pottstown, PA BB/TR, 6', 195 lbs. Deb: 9/25/1963 C																							
1963 StL-N	3	8	0	2	0	0	0	0	0	2	0	0	.250	.250	.250	.500	41	-1	1	2.25	0	/C-3	0	-0.1
1965 StL-N	11	29	1	7	0	0	0	0	1	3	0	0	.241	.267	.241	.508	40	-2	2	2.36	-1	C-11	0	-0.3
1967*StL-N	52	99	11	27	8	0	1	14	4	7	0	0	.273	.301	.384	.685	96	-1	11	3.75	0	C-21	3	0.0
1968*StL-N	20	22	1	3	0	0	0	1	0	3	0	0	.136	.136	.136	.273	-18	-3	0	.58	0	/C-1	0	-0.4
1969 StL-N	30	44	2	12	1	0	0	5	4	5	0	0	.273	.333	.295	.629	77	-1	5	3.49	-1	/C-8	1	-0.2
1970 Pit-N	14	11	0	2	0	0	0	0	1	3	0	0	.182	.250	.182	.432	18	-1	1	1.70	-1	/C-7	0	-0.2
Total 6	130	213	15	53	9	0	1	20	10	23	0	0	.249	.283	.305	.588	67	-9	19	2.99	-3	/C-51	4	-1.1
• RICKEY, Branch	Wesley Branch "The Mahatma" Rickey b: 12/20/1881, Flat, OH d: 12/9/1965, Columbia, MO BL/TR, 5'9", 175 lbs. Deb: 6/16/1905 M HOF: 1967 Career OF: 20-1-2																							
1905 StL-A	1	3	0	0	0	0	0	0	0	....	0	....	.000	.000	.000	.000	-106	-1	0	.00	0	/C-1	0	-0.1
1906 StL-A	65	201	22	57	7	3	3	24	16	....	4	....	.284	.345	.393	.738	137	8	30	5.37	-4	C-55/0-1	8	1.1
1907 NY-A	52	137	16	25	1	3	0	15	11	....	4	....	.182	.253	.234	.487	51	-7	10	2.23	-6	0-22(20-1-1),C-11/1-9	1	-1.5
1914 StL-A	2	2	0	0	0	0	0	0	0	1	0	....	.000	.000	.000	.000	-104	-0	0	.00	0	....	0	-0.1
Total 4	120	343	38	82	8	6	3	39	27	1	8	....	.239	.304	.324	.628	99	-0	39	3.92	-9	/C-67,0-23,1-9	9	-0.5
• RICKLEY, Chris	Christian Rickley b: 10/7/1859, Philadelphia, PA d: 10/25/1911, Philadelphia, PA, 5'8", 160 lbs. Deb: 6/9/1884																							
1884 Phi-U	6	25	5	5	2	0	0	....	2	....	....	....	.200	.259	.280	.539	89	-0	2	2.60	0	/S-6	1	0.0
• RICKS, John	John Ricks Deb: 9/21/1891																							
1891 StL-a	5	18	3	3	0	0	0	0	0	2	0	....	.167	.167	.167	.333	-4	-3	1	.91	-1	/3-5	0	-0.3
1894 StL-N	1	1	0	0	0	0	0	0	0	0	0	....	.000	.000	.000	.000	-100	-0	0	.00	-1	/3-1	0	-0.1
Total 2	6	19	3	3	0	0	0	0	0	2	0	....	.158	.158	.158	.316	-9	-3	1	.85	-3	/3-6	0	-0.5
• RICO, Art	Arthur Raymond Rico b: 7/23/1896, Roxbury, MA d: 1/3/1919, Boston, MA BR/TR, 5'9.5", 185 lbs. Deb: 7/31/1916																							
1916 Bos-N	4	4	0	0	0	0	0	0	0	0	0	....	.000	.000	.000	.000	-106	-1	0	.00	-1	/C-4	0	-0.2
1917 Bos-N	13	14	1	4	1	0	0	2	0	2	0	....	.286	.286	.357	.643	102	-0	1	3.45	-1	C-11/0-2(1-0-0)	0	-0.1
Total 2	17	18	1	4	1	0	0	2	0	2	0	....	.222	.222	.278	.500	56	-1	1	2.47	-2	/C-15,0-2	0	-0.3
• RICO, Fred	Alfredo (Cruz) Rico b: 7/4/1944, Jerome, AZ BR/TR, 5'10", 180 lbs. Deb: 9/1/1969																							
1969 KC-A	12	26	2	6	2	0	0	2	9	10	0	1	.231	.429	.308	.736	108	1	4	4.59	3	/0-9(0-2-7),3-1	2	0.3
• RICONDA, Harry	Henry Paul Riconda b: 5/17/1897, New York, NY d: 11/15/1958, Mahopac, NY BR/TR, 5'10", 175 lbs. Deb: 4/19/1923																							
1923 Phi-A	55	175	23	46	11	4	0	12	12	18	4	2	.263	.317	.371	.689	80	-5	21	4.01	1	3-47/S-2	4	-0.1
1924 Phi-A	83	281	34	71	16	3	1	21	27	43	3	4	.253	.323	.342	.664	71	-13	32	3.78	-6	3-73/S-2	5	-1.4
1926 Bos-N	4	12	1	2	0	0	0	0	2	2	0	....	.167	.286	.167	.452	27	-1	1	1.74	-2	/3-4	0	-0.3
1928 Bro-N	92	281	22	63	15	4	3	35	20	28	6	....	.224	.285	.338	.623	63	-16	27	3.10	-2	2-53,3-21,S-16	4	-1.5
1929 Pit-N	8	15	3	7	2	0	0	2	0	0	0	....	.467	.467	.600	1.067	158	1	4	9.88	-1	/S-4	1	0.0
1930 Cin-N	1	1	0	0	0	0	0	0	0	0	0	....	.000	.000	.000	.000	-105	-0	0	.00	0	....	0	0.0
Total 6	243	765	83	189	44	11	4	70	61	91	13	6	.247	.309	.349	.658	71	-34	84	3.64	-11	3-145/2-53,S-24	14	-3.2
• RIDDLE, John	John H. Riddle b: 2/1864, Philadelphia, PA d: 5/5/1931, Camden, NJ BR/TR Deb: 9/18/1889 Career OF: 9-3-2																							
1889 Was-N	11	37	3	8	3	0	0	3	2	8	0	....	.216	.256	.297	.554	58	-2	3	2.64	0	/C-9,0-2(0-0-2)	0	-0.1
1890 Phi-a	27	85	7	7	0	1	0	2	17	....	4	....	.082	.243	.106	.349	3	-10	3	1.10	-3	C-13,0-12(9-3-0)/2-2,3-1	0	-1.0
Total 2	38	122	10	15	3	1	0	5	19	8	4	....	.123	.246	.164	.410	18	-12	6	1.52	-3	/C-22,0-14,2-2,3-1	0	-1.1

YEAR TM-L	G	AB	R	H	2B	3B	HR	RBI	BB	SO	SB	CS	AVG	OBP	SLG	OPS	OPS+	BR/A	RC	RC/G	FR	G/POS	WS	TPW

• RIDDLE, Johnny John Ludy "Mutt" Riddle b: 10/3/1905, Clinton, SC d: 12/15/1998, Indianapolis, IN BR/TR, 5'11", 190 lbs. Deb: 4/17/1930 C

YEAR TM-L	G	AB	R	H	2B	3B	HR	RBI	BB	SO	SB	CS	AVG	OBP	SLG	OPS	OPS+	BR/A	RC	RC/G	FR	G/POS	WS	TPW
1930 Chi-A	25	58	7	14	3	1	0	4	3	6	0	0	.241	.290	.328	.618	58	-4	6	3.28	1	C-25	1	-0.1
1937 Was-A	8	26	2	7	0	0	0	3	0	2	0	0	.269	.296	.269	.566	46	-2	2	2.83	0	/C-8	0	-0.1
Bos-N	2	3	0	0	0	0	0	0	1	0	0	....	.000	.250	.000	.250	-29	-0	0	.59	0	/C-2	0	0.0
1938 Bos-N	19	57	6	16	1	0	0	2	4	2	0	....	.281	.328	.298	.626	81	-1	6	3.99	1	C-19	2	0.1
1941 Cin-N	10	10	2	3	0	0	0	0	0	1	0	....	.300	.300	.300	.600	69	-0	1	3.47	0	C-10	0	-0.1
1944 Cin-N	1	0	0	0	0	0	0	0	0	0	0	....	....	....	....	....	-104	0	0	....	0	/C-1	0	0.0
1945 Cin-N	23	45	0	8	0	0	0	2	4	6	0	....	.178	.245	.178	.423	19	-5	2	1.62	2	C-23	1	-0.2
1948 Pit-N	10	15	1	3	0	0	0	0	1	2	0	....	.200	.250	.200	.450	23	-2	1	1.29	0	C-10	0	-0.1
Total 7	98	214	18	51	4	1	0	11	13	19	0	0	.238	.288	.266	.555	51	-15	18	2.82	4	/C-98	4	-0.6

• RIEBE, Hank Harvey Donald Riebe b: 10/10/1921, Cleveland, OH d: 4/16/2001, Cleveland, OH BR/TR, 5'9.5", 175 lbs. Deb: 8/26/1942

YEAR TM-L	G	AB	R	H	2B	3B	HR	RBI	BB	SO	SB	CS	AVG	OBP	SLG	OPS	OPS+	BR/A	RC	RC/G	FR	G/POS	WS	TPW
1942 Det-A	11	35	1	11	2	0	0	2	0	6	0	0	.314	.314	.371	.686	85	-1	4	4.11	-0	C-11	1	0.0
1947 Det-A	8	7	0	0	0	0	0	2	0	2	0	0	.000	.000	.000	.000	-97	-2	0	.00	-1	/C-3	0	-0.3
1948 Det-A	25	62	0	12	0	0	0	5	3	5	0	1	.194	.231	.194	.424	13	-8	2	1.11	-1	C-24	1	-0.8
1949 Det-A	17	33	1	6	2	0	0	2	0	5	1	0	.182	.182	.242	.424	12	-4	1	.98	0	C-11	0	-0.4
Total 4	61	137	2	29	4	0	0	11	3	18	1	1	.212	.229	.241	.469	25	-15	7	1.66	-2	/C-49	2	-1.5

• RIESGO, Nikco Damon Nikco Riesgo b: 1/11/1967, Long Beach, CA BR/TR, 6'2", 185 lbs. Deb: 4/20/1991

YEAR TM-L	G	AB	R	H	2B	3B	HR	RBI	BB	SO	SB	CS	AVG	OBP	SLG	OPS	OPS+	BR/A	RC	RC/G	FR	G/POS	WS	TPW
1991 Mon-N	4	7	1	1	0	0	0	0	3	1	0	0	.143	.400	.143	.543	60	-0	1	2.06	0	/O-2(0-0-2)	0	0.0

• RIGGERT, Joe Joseph Aloysius Riggert b: 12/11/1886, Janesville, WI d: 12/10/1973, Kansas City, MO BR/TR, 5'9.5", 170 lbs. Deb: 5/12/1911 Career OF: 31-91-28

YEAR TM-L	G	AB	R	H	2B	3B	HR	RBI	BB	SO	SB	CS	AVG	OBP	SLG	OPS	OPS+	BR/A	RC	RC/G	FR	G/POS	WS	TPW
1911 Bos-A	50	146	19	31	4	4	2	13	12	....	5	....	.212	.290	.336	.626	75	-5	16	3.37	-2	O-39(21-11-6)	2	-0.9
1914 Bro-N	27	83	6	16	1	3	2	6	4	20	2	....	.193	.230	.349	.579	70	-4	7	2.52	-1	O-20(1-0-20)	1	-0.6
StL-N	34	89	9	19	5	2	0	8	5	14	4	....	.213	.255	.315	.570	70	-4	8	2.77	-1	O-30(9-19-2)	1	-0.6
Yr.	61	172	15	35	6	5	2	14	9	34	6	....	.203	.243	.331	.574	70	-7	15	2.65	-2	O-50(10-19-22)	2	-1.3
1919 Bos-N	63	240	34	68	8	5	4	17	25	30	9	....	.283	.356	.408	.764	135	10	36	5.37	1	O-61(0-61-0)	9	0.8
Total 3	174	558	68	134	18	14	8	44	46	64	20	....	.240	.305	.366	.671	99	-2	66	3.93	-4	O-150	13	-1.4

• RIGGS, Adam Adam David Riggs b: 10/4/1972, Steubenville, OH BR/TR, 6', 195 lbs. Deb: 8/7/1997

YEAR TM-L	G	AB	R	H	2B	3B	HR	RBI	BB	SO	SB	CS	AVG	OBP	SLG	OPS	OPS+	BR/A	RC	RC/G	FR	G/POS	WS	TPW
1997 LA-N	9	20	3	4	1	0	0	1	4	3	1	0	.200	.333	.250	.583	60	-1	2	3.54	0	/2-8	0	0.0
2001 SD-N	12	36	2	7	1	0	0	1	2	8	1	1	.194	.237	.222	.459	22	-4	2	1.45	-1	2-11/3-1	0	-0.5
2003 Ana-A	24	61	11	15	4	1	3	5	9	9	3	1	.246	.343	.492	.835	121	2	10	5.40	3	1-10/O-8(8-0-0),2-3,D-2	1	0.4
Total 3	45	117	16	26	6	1	3	7	15	20	5	2	.222	.311	.368	.678	82	-3	14	3.85	2	/2-22,1-10,O-8,D-2,3-1	1	-0.1

• RIGGS, Lew Lewis Sidney Riggs b: 4/22/1910, Mebane, NC d: 8/12/1975, Durham, NC BL/TR, 6', 175 lbs. Deb: 4/28/1934

YEAR TM-L	G	AB	R	H	2B	3B	HR	RBI	BB	SO	SB	CS	AVG	OBP	SLG	OPS	OPS+	BR/A	RC	RC/G	FR	G/POS	WS	TPW
1934 StL-N	2	1	0	0	0	0	0	0	0	1	0	....	.000	.000	.000	.000	-94	-0	0	.00	0	....	0	0.0
1935 Cin-N	142	532	73	148	26	8	5	46	43	32	8	....	.278	.334	.385	.720	96	-3	72	4.88	4	*3-135	16	0.6
1936 Cin-N★	141	538	69	138	20	12	6	57	38	33	5	....	.257	.314	.372	.686	90	-9	63	4.10	9	*3-140	15	0.6
1937 Cin-N	122	384	43	93	17	5	6	45	24	17	4	....	.242	.289	.359	.648	79	-12	40	3.62	14	*3-100/2-4,S-1	8	0.5
1938 Cin-N	142	531	53	134	21	13	2	55	40	28	3	....	.252	.311	.352	.663	84	-12	60	3.88	5	*3-140	13	-0.2
1939 Cin-N	22	38	5	6	1	0	0	1	5	4	1	....	.158	.256	.184	.440	20	-4	2	1.58	-1	3-11	0	-0.5
1940★Cin-N	41	72	8	21	7	1	1	9	2	4	0	....	.292	.311	.458	.769	109	0	10	5.17	1	3-11	2	0.2
1941★Bro-N	77	197	27	60	13	4	5	36	16	12	1	....	.305	.357	.487	.844	130	7	35	6.46	-5	3-43/1-1,2-1	8	0.3
1942 Bro-N	70	180	20	50	5	0	3	22	13	9	0	....	.278	.333	.356	.689	100	-0	22	4.30	-2	3-46/1-1	6	-0.1
1946 Bro-N	1	4	0	0	0	0	0	0	0	0	0	....	.000	.000	.000	.000	-99	-1	0	.00	0	/3-1	0	-0.1
Total 10	760	2477	298	650	110	43	28	271	181	140	22	....	.262	.317	.375	.692	91	-34	304	4.31	24	3-627/2-5,1-2,S-1	68	1.2

• RIGNEY, Bill William Joseph "Specs,The Cricket" Rigney b: 1/29/1918, Alameda, CA d: 2/20/2001, Walnut Creek, CA BR/TR, 6'1", 178 lbs. Deb: 4/16/1946 M/C

YEAR TM-L	G	AB	R	H	2B	3B	HR	RBI	BB	SO	SB	CS	AVG	OBP	SLG	OPS	OPS+	BR/A	RC	RC/G	FR	G/POS	WS	TPW
1946 NY-N	110	360	38	85	9	1	3	31	36	29	9	....	.236	.307	.292	.599	70	-14	34	3.15	1	3-73,S-33	5	-1.2
1947 NY-N	130	531	84	142	24	3	17	59	51	54	7	....	.267	.337	.420	.757	99	-2	76	5.06	1	2-72,3-41,S-24	16	0.4
1948 NY-N★	113	424	72	112	17	3	10	43	47	54	4	....	.264	.342	.389	.731	97	-2	58	4.79	-0	*2-105/S-7	13	0.4
1949 NY-N	122	389	53	108	19	6	6	47	47	38	3	....	.278	.356	.404	.759	103	2	56	5.15	-2	S-81,2-26,3-14	11	0.6
1950 NY-N	56	83	8	15	2	0	0	8	8	13	0	....	.181	.253	.205	.458	22	-9	4	1.60	0	2-23,3-11	1	-0.8
1951★NY-N	44	69	9	16	2	0	4	9	8	7	0	1	.232	.321	.435	.755	100	-1	10	4.94	1	3-12/2-9	2	0.1
1952 NY-N	60	90	15	27	5	1	1	14	11	6	2	3	.300	.388	.411	.799	121	2	14	5.58	-1	3-10/2-9,S-4,1-1	4	0.2
1953 NY-N	19	20	2	5	0	0	0	1	0	5	0	0	.250	.250	.250	.500	30	-2	1	2.31	-1	/3-2,2-1	0	-0.3
Total 8	654	1966	281	510	78	14	41	212	208	206	25	4	.259	.334	.376	.710	91	-25	254	4.49	0	2-245,3-163,S-149/1-1	52	-0.6

• RIGNEY, Topper Emory Elmo Rigney b: 1/7/1897, Groveton, TX d: 6/6/1972, San Antonio, TX BR/TR, 5'9", 150 lbs. Deb: 4/12/1922

YEAR TM-L	G	AB	R	H	2B	3B	HR	RBI	BB	SO	SB	CS	AVG	OBP	SLG	OPS	OPS+	BR/A	RC	RC/G	FR	G/POS	WS	TPW
1922 Det-A	155	536	68	161	17	7	2	63	68	44	17	8	.300	.380	.369	.750	99	3	81	5.10	-19	*S-155	15	0.1
1923 Det-A	129	470	63	148	24	11	1	74	55	35	7	5	.315	.389	.419	.808	115	12	80	5.86	-14	*S-129	16	1.2
1924 Det-A	147	499	81	144	29	9	4	94	102	39	11	11	.289	.410	.407	.817	113	14	90	6.00	-1	*S-146	22	2.7
1925 Det-A	62	146	21	36	5	2	2	18	21	15	2	2	.247	.341	.349	.691	77	-5	18	4.22	-5	S-51/3-4	3	-0.6
1926 Bos-A	148	525	71	142	32	6	4	53	108	31	6	8	.270	.395	.377	.772	105	8	85	5.43	-2	*S-146	17	2.1
1927 Bos-A	8	18	0	2	1	0	0	0	1	2	0	0	.111	.158	.167	.325	-16	-3	1	.85	0	/3-4,S-1	0	-0.3
Was-A	45	132	20	36	5	4	0	13	22	10	1	2	.273	.381	.371	.752	97	-0	20	5.22	-0	S-32/3-6	5	0.3
Yr.	53	150	20	38	6	4	0	13	23	12	1	2	.253	.356	.347	.703	84	-3	20	4.58	0	S-33,3-10	5	0.1
Total 6	694	2326	324	669	113	39	13	315	377	176	44	36	.288	.388	.387	.775	104	29	374	5.43	-41	S-660/3-14	78	5.6

• RIKARD, Culley Culley Rikard b: 5/9/1914, Oxford, MS d: 2/25/2000, Memphis, TN BL/TR, 5'11", 183 lbs. Deb: 9/20/1941 Career OF: 10-45-45

YEAR TM-L	G	AB	R	H	2B	3B	HR	RBI	BB	SO	SB	CS	AVG	OBP	SLG	OPS	OPS+	BR/A	RC	RC/G	FR	G/POS	WS	TPW
1941 Pit-N	6	20	1	4	1	0	0	0	1	1	0	....	.200	.238	.250	.488	38	-2	1	2.11	0	/O-5(3-3-0)	0	-0.2
1942 Pit-N	38	52	6	10	2	1	0	5	7	8	0	....	.192	.288	.269	.557	62	-2	4	2.69	-1	O-16(2-14-0)	0	-0.3
1947 Pit-N	109	324	57	93	16	4	4	32	50	39	1	....	.287	.384	.398	.782	105	4	51	5.74	-4	O-79(5-28-45)	9	-0.2
Total 3	153	396	64	107	19	5	4	37	58	48	1	....	.270	.365	.374	.739	96	0	57	5.11	-4	O-100	9	-0.7

• RILES, Ernest Ernest Riles b: 10/2/1960, Cairo, GA BL/TR, 6'1", 180 lbs. Deb: 5/14/1985

YEAR TM-L	G	AB	R	H	2B	3B	HR	RBI	BB	SO	SB	CS	AVG	OBP	SLG	OPS	OPS+	BR/A	RC	RC/G	FR	G/POS	WS	TPW
1985 Mil-A	116	448	54	128	12	7	5	45	36	54	2	2	.286	.342	.377	.719	97	-2	55	4.29	-8	*S-115/D-1	13	0.2
1986 Mil-A	145	524	69	132	24	2	9	47	54	80	7	7	.252	.323	.357	.680	82	-14	59	3.79	-17	*S-142	11	-1.6
1987 Mil-A	83	276	38	72	11	1	4	38	30	47	3	4	.261	.336	.351	.687	80	-8	33	3.96	-6	3-65,S-21	6	-1.3
1988 Mil-A	41	127	7	32	6	1	1	9	7	26	2	2	.252	.291	.339	.630	75	-5	12	3.12	-1	3-28/S-9,D-5	2	-0.5
SF-N	79	187	26	55	7	2	3	28	10	33	1	2	.294	.330	.401	.731	114	2	23	4.34	7	3-30,2-17,S-16	7	1.0
1989★SF-N	122	302	43	84	13	2	7	40	28	50	0	6	.278	.343	.404	.747	116	3	39	4.51	3	3-83,2-18/S-7,O-5(2-0-3)	11	0.8
1990 SF-N	92	155	22	31	2	1	8	21	26	26	0	0	.200	.315	.381	.696	94	-1	20	4.16	2	S-26,2-24,3-10	4	0.2
1991 Oak-A	108	281	30	60	8	4	5	32	31	42	3	2	.214	.294	.324	.618	75	-10	27	3.01	-3	3-69,S-20/2-7,1-5	7	-1.2
1992 Hou-N	39	61	5	16	1	0	1	4	2	11	1	0	.262	.286	.328	.614	77	-2	6	3.56	-2	/S-6,3-5,1-4,2-2	1	-0.4
1993 Bos-A	94	143	15	27	8	0	5	20	20	40	1	3	.189	.297	.350	.647	69	-7	15	3.12	3	2-20,D-15,3-11/1-1	1	-0.4
Total 9	919	2504	309	637	92	20	48	284	244	409	20	28	.254	.323	.365	.687	90	-44	288	3.87	-23	S-362,3-301/2-88,D-21,1-10,O-5	63	-3.2

• RILEY, Billy William James "Pigtail Billy" Riley b: 1855, Cincinnati, OH d: 11/9/1887, Cincinnati, OH BR/TR, 5'10", 160 lbs. Deb: 5/5/1875 U

YEAR TM-L	G	AB	R	H	2B	3B	HR	RBI	BB	SO	SB	CS	AVG	OBP	SLG	OPS	OPS+	BR/A	RC	RC/G	FR	G/POS	WS	TPW
1875 Wes-n	8	33	4	5	1	0	0	1	1	1	0	0	.152	.176	.182	.358	23	-3	1	1.14	0	/O-8(0-0-8)	....	-0.2
1879 Cle-N	43	161	14	23	2	0	0	9	2	26	....	....	.143	.153	.155	.309	2	-16	4	.80	4	O-43(43-0-0)	1	-1.3

• RILEY, Jim James Norman Riley b: 5/25/1895, Bayfield, Canada d: 5/25/1969, Seguin, TX BL/TR, 5'10.5", 185 lbs. Deb: 7/3/1921

YEAR TM-L	G	AB	R	H	2B	3B	HR	RBI	BB	SO	SB	CS	AVG	OBP	SLG	OPS	OPS+	BR/A	RC	RC/G	FR	G/POS	WS	TPW
1921 StL-A	4	11	0	0	0	0	0	0	1	3	0	0	.000	.083	.000	.083	-73	-3	0	.05	-1	/2-4	0	-0.4
1923 Was-A	2	3	1	0	0	0	0	0	2	0	0	0	.000	.400	.000	.400	12	-0	0	1.76	-1	/1-2	0	-0.1
Total 2	6	14	1	0	0	0	0	0	3	3	0	0	.000	.176	.000	.176	-48	-3	0	.42	-2	/2-4,1-2	0	-0.5

• RILEY, Jim James Joseph Riley b: 11/10/1886, Buffalo, NY d: 3/25/1949, Buffalo, NY BR/TR, 6', 165 lbs. Deb: 8/2/1910

YEAR TM-L	G	AB	R	H	2B	3B	HR	RBI	BB	SO	SB	CS	AVG	OBP	SLG	OPS	OPS+	BR/A	RC	RC/G	FR	G/POS	WS	TPW
1910 Bos-N	1	1	0	0	0	0	0	0	1	1	0	....	.000	.500	.000	.500	46	0	0	.00	0	/O-1	0	0.0

• RILEY, Lee Leon Francis Riley b: 8/20/1906, Princeton, NE d: 9/13/1970, Schenectady, NY BL/TR, 6'1", 185 lbs. Deb: 4/19/1944

YEAR TM-L	G	AB	R	H	2B	3B	HR	RBI	BB	SO	SB	CS	AVG	OBP	SLG	OPS	OPS+	BR/A	RC	RC/G	FR	G/POS	WS	TPW
1944 Phi-N	4	12	1	1	1	0	0	1	0	0	0	....	.083	.083	.167	.250	-32	-2	0	.41	0	/0-3(3-0-0)	0	-0.2

• RINGO, Frank Frank C. Ringo b: 10/12/1860, Parkville, MO d: 4/12/1889, Kansas City, MO BR, 5'11", 175 lbs. Deb: 5/1/1883 Career OF: 3-11-0

YEAR TM-L	G	AB	R	H	2B	3B	HR	RBI	BB	SO	SB	CS	AVG	OBP	SLG	OPS	OPS+	BR/A	RC	RC/G	FR	G/POS	WS	TPW
1883 Phi-N	60	221	24	42	10	1	0	12	6	34	....	....	.190	.211	.244	.456	42	-14	12	1.80	-5	C-39,0-11(3-8-0)/S-6,3-5,2	1	-1.3
1884 Phi-N	26	91	4	12	2	0	0	6	3	19	....	....	.132	.160	.154	.313	-1	-10	2	.80	-11	C-26	0	-1.7
Phi-a	2	6	0	0	0	0	0	0	0	....	....	....	.000	.000	.000	.000	-94	-1	0	.00	-1	/C-2	0	-0.2
1885 Det-N	17	65	12	16	3	0	0	2	0	7	....	....	.246	.246	.292	.538	73	-2	5	2.64	1	/3-8,C-8,0-1	1	0.0
Pit-a	3	11	0	2	0	0	0	0	0	....	....	....	.182	.182	.182	.364	15	-1	0	1.12	1	/C-3	0	0.0
1886 Pit-a	15	56	3	12	2	2	0	5	1	....	0	....	.214	.228	.321	.549	72	-2	4	2.58	1	/1-9,C-6	1	-0.1
KC-N	16	56	6	13	7	0	0	7	5	10	0	....	.232	.295	.357	.652	92	-1	6	3.80	-1	C-13/0-2(0-2-0),3-1	1	-0.1
Total 4	**139**	**506**	**49**	**97**	**24**	**3**	**0**	**32**	**15**	**70**	**0**	**....**	**.192**	**.215**	**.251**	**.466**	**45**	**-31**	**29**	**1.96**	**-15**	**/C-97,3-14,0-14,1-9,S-6,2-2**	**4**	**-3.4**

• RINKER, Bob Robert John Rinker b: 4/21/1921, Audenried, PA d: 12/19/2002, Hazleton, PA BR/TR, 6', 190 lbs. Deb: 9/6/1950

YEAR TM-L	G	AB	R	H	2B	3B	HR	RBI	BB	SO	SB	CS	AVG	OBP	SLG	OPS	OPS+	BR/A	RC	RC/G	FR	G/POS	WS	TPW
1950 Phi-A	3	3	0	1	0	0	0	0	0	0	0	0	.333	.333	.333	.667	72	-0	0	4.61	0	/C-1	0	0.0

• RIOS, Armando Armando Rios b: 9/13/1971, Santurce, Puerto Rico BL/TL, 5'9", 185 lbs. Deb: 9/1/1998 Career OF: 68-29-248

YEAR TM-L	G	AB	R	H	2B	3B	HR	RBI	BB	SO	SB	CS	AVG	OBP	SLG	OPS	OPS+	BR/A	RC	RC/G	FR	G/POS	WS	TPW
1998 SF-N	12	7	3	4	0	0	2	3	3	2	0	0	.571	.700	1.429	2.129	469	4	8	67.91	0	/0-5(2-1-2)	2	0.4
1999 SF-N	72	150	32	49	9	0	7	29	24	35	7	4	.327	.423	.527	.950	149	12	34	8.35	2	0-53(14-2-39)	7	1.1
2000*SF-N	115	233	38	62	15	5	10	50	31	43	3	2	.266	.352	.502	.854	122	7	39	5.64	4	0-93(19-0-76)/1-1	11	0.7
2001 SF-N	93	316	38	82	17	3	14	49	34	73	3	2	.259	.331	.465	.797	111	4	50	5.59	6	0-87(13-3-76)	10	0.6
Pit-N	2	3	0	1	0	0	0	1	2	1	0	0	.333	.600	.333	.933	148	1	1	4.59	-1	/0-2(0-0-2)	0	0.0
Yr.	95	319	38	83	17	3	14	50	36	74	3	2	.260	.335	.464	.799	111	5	51	5.58	5	0-89(13-3-78)	10	0.5
2002 Pit-N	76	208	20	55	11	0	1	24	16	39	1	1	.264	.320	.332	.652	71	-9	21	3.43	2	0-56(11-0-47)	2	-0.9
2003 Chi-A	49	104	4	22	3	0	2	11	5	13	0	1	.212	.248	.298	.546	43	-9	6	1.77	-1	0-32(9-23-6)/D-4	1	-1.0
Total 6	**419**	**1021**	**135**	**275**	**55**	**8**	**36**	**167**	**115**	**206**	**14**	**10**	**.269**	**.344**	**.445**	**.789**	**108**	**10**	**158**	**5.33**	**12**	**0-328/D-4,1-1**	**33**	**0.8**

• RIOS, Juan Juan Onofre Velez Rios b: 7/14/1942, Mayaguez, Puerto Rico d: 8/28/1995, Mayaguez, Puerto Rico BR/TR, 6'3", 185 lbs. Deb: 4/9/1969

YEAR TM-L	G	AB	R	H	2B	3B	HR	RBI	BB	SO	SB	CS	AVG	OBP	SLG	OPS	OPS+	BR/A	RC	RC/G	FR	G/POS	WS	TPW
1969 KC-A	87	196	20	44	5	1	1	5	7	19	1	3	.224	.262	.276	.538	50	-15	12	2.07	-7	2-46,S-32/3-4	1	-1.9

• RIPKEN, Billy William Oliver Ripken b: 12/16/1964, Havre de Grace, MD BR/TR, 6'1", 186 lbs. Deb: 7/11/1987

YEAR TM-L	G	AB	R	H	2B	3B	HR	RBI	BB	SO	SB	CS	AVG	OBP	SLG	OPS	OPS+	BR/A	RC	RC/G	FR	G/POS	WS	TPW
1987 Bal-A	58	234	27	72	9	0	2	20	21	23	4	1	.308	.365	.372	.737	99	0	33	5.32	-2	2-58	7	0.2
1988 Bal-A	150	512	52	106	18	1	2	34	33	63	8	2	.207	.262	.258	.520	47	-35	35	2.16	-2	*2-149/3-2,D-1	4	-3.3
1989 Bal-A	115	318	31	76	11	2	2	26	22	53	1	2	.239	.288	.305	.593	69	-14	27	2.58	13	*2-114/D-1	6	0.2
1990 Bal-A	129	406	48	118	28	1	3	38	28	43	5	2	.291	.342	.387	.729	107	4	55	4.68	13	*2-127	16	2.1
1991 Bal-A	104	287	24	62	11	1	0	14	15	31	0	1	.216	.255	.261	.516	45	-22	17	1.80	-4	*2-103	3	-2.4
1992 Bal-A	111	330	35	76	15	0	4	36	18	26	2	3	.230	.276	.312	.588	63	-18	27	2.59	12	*2-108/D-2	7	-0.3
1993 Tex-A	50	132	12	25	4	0	0	11	11	19	0	2	.189	.272	.220	.492	35	-13	8	1.68	-1	2-34,S-18/3-1	2	-1.1
1994 Tex-A	32	81	9	25	5	0	0	6	3	11	2	0	.309	.333	.370	.704	81	-2	10	4.53	-2	3-18,2-12/S-2,1-1	2	-0.3
1995 Cle-A	8	17	4	7	0	0	2	3	0	3	0	0	.412	.412	.765	1.176	195	2	5	14.45	-1	/2-7,3-1	0	0.2
1996 Bal-A	57	135	19	31	8	0	2	12	9	18	0	0	.230	.283	.333	.616	55	-10	12	3.01	2	2-30,3-25/1-1	2	-0.5
1997 Tex-A	71	203	18	56	9	1	3	24	9	32	0	1	.276	.307	.374	.681	73	-9	21	3.57	2	S-31,2-25,3-13/1-9	3	-0.4
1998 Det-A	27	74	8	20	3	0	0	5	5	10	3	2	.270	.325	.311	.636	66	-4	7	3.31	-2	S-21/1-2,2-2,3-2,D-1	1	-0.4
Total 12	**912**	**2729**	**287**	**674**	**121**	**6**	**20**	**229**	**174**	**332**	**25**	**16**	**.247**	**.296**	**.318**	**.614**	**69**	**-120**	**256**	**3.08**	**30**	**2-769/S-72,3-62,1-13,D-5**	**53**	**-6.1**

• RIPKEN, Cal Calvin Edwin "Iron Man" Ripken, Jr. b: 8/24/1960, Havre de Grace, MD BR/TR, 6'4", 225 lbs. Deb: 8/10/1981

YEAR TM-L	G	AB	R	H	2B	3B	HR	RBI	BB	SO	SB	CS	AVG	OBP	SLG	OPS	OPS+	BR/A	RC	RC/G	FR	G/POS	WS	TPW
1981 Bal-A	23	39	1	5	0	0	0	0	1	8	0	0	.128	.150	.128	.278	-19	-6	0	.19	0	S-12/3-6	0	-0.6
1982 Bal-A	160	598	90	158	32	5	28	93	46	95	3	3	.264	.320	.475	.795	115	10	87	5.01	9	S-94,3-71	23	2.9
1983*Bal-A★	162	663	**121**	**211**	**47**	2	27	102	58	97	0	4	.318	.373	.517	.890	145	37	120	6.67	19	*S-162	**35**	**7.4**
1984 Bal-A★	162	641	103	195	37	7	27	86	71	89	2	1	.304	.375	.510	.885	146	40	122	7.08	28	*S-162	**37**	**8.6**
1985 Bal-A★	161	642	116	181	32	5	26	110	67	68	2	3	.282	.351	.469	.820	125	21	96	5.17	6	*S-161	25	4.4
1986 Bal-A★	162	627	98	177	35	1	25	81	70	60	4	2	.282	.358	.461	.819	123	20	102	5.75	10	*S-162	28	**4.6**
1987 Bal-A★	162	624	97	157	28	3	27	98	81	77	3	5	.252	.339	.436	.774	106	4	90	4.85	-7	*S-162	20	1.4
1988 Bal-A★	161	575	87	152	25	1	23	81	102	69	2	2	.264	.377	.431	.808	129	26	99	6.00	-4	*S-161	25	3.5
1989 Bal-A★	162	646	80	166	30	0	21	93	57	72	3	2	.257	.320	.401	.721	105	3	79	4.18	13	*S-162	26	2.9
1990 Bal-A★	161	600	78	150	28	4	21	84	82	66	3	1	.250	.345	.415	.760	115	14	88	5.04	-10	*S-161	20	1.6
1991 Bal-A★	162	650	99	210	46	5	34	114	53	46	6	1	.323	.379	.566	.945	164	55	134	7.71	16	*S-162	**34**	**8.4**
1992 Bal-A★	162	637	73	160	29	1	14	72	64	50	4	3	.251	.326	.366	.692	91	-7	76	4.12	-2	*S-162	21	0.4
1993 Bal-A★	162	641	87	165	26	3	24	90	65	58	1	4	.257	.331	.420	.751	96	-5	86	4.60	-7	*S-162	17	0.1
1994 Bal-A★	112	444	71	140	19	3	13	75	32	41	1	0	.315	.367	.459	.826	106	4	71	5.87	-1	*S-112	18	1.1
1995 Bal-A★	144	550	71	144	33	2	17	88	52	59	0	1	.262	.328	.422	.750	92	-8	74	4.63	9	*S-144	16	1.2
1996*Bal-A★	163	640	94	178	40	1	26	102	59	78	1	2	.278	.343	.466	.808	102	-0	94	5.14	-2	*S-158/3-6	22	1.0
1997*Bal-A★	162	615	79	166	30	0	17	84	56	73	1	0	.270	.336	.402	.737	94	-5	81	4.59	7	*3-162/S-3	18	0.4
1998 Bal-A★	161	601	65	163	27	1	14	61	51	68	0	2	.271	.332	.389	.722	88	-12	78	4.69	-9	*3-161	13	-1.7
1999 Bal-A★	86	332	51	113	27	0	18	57	13	31	0	1	.340	.371	.584	.955	144	19	65	7.26	-1	3-85	12	1.8
2000 Bal-A★	83	309	43	79	16	0	15	56	23	37	0	0	.256	.313	.453	.767	95	-3	42	4.62	7	3-73,D-10	8	0.4
2001 Bal-A★	128	477	43	114	16	0	14	68	26	63	0	2	.239	.281	.361	.642	71	-22	45	3.09	4	*3-111,D-14	9	-1.7
Total 21	**3001**	**11551**	**1647**	**3184**	**603**	**44**	**431**	**1695**	**1129**	**1305**	**36**	**39**	**.276**	**.344**	**.447**	**.791**	**113**	**184**	**1728**	**5.25**	**85**	***S-2302,3-675/D-24**	**427**	**48.1**

• RIPPLE, Jimmy James Albert Ripple b: 10/14/1909, Export, PA d: 7/16/1959, Greensburg, PA BL/TR, 5'10", 170 lbs. Deb: 4/20/1936 Career OF: 66-151-242

YEAR TM-L	G	AB	R	H	2B	3B	HR	RBI	BB	SO	SB	CS	AVG	OBP	SLG	OPS	OPS+	BR/A	RC	RC/G	FR	G/POS	WS	TPW
1936*NY-N	96	311	42	95	17	2	7	47	28	15	1	....	.305	.365	.441	.805	117	7	51	6.13	1	0-76(0-75-1)	12	0.7
1937*NY-N	121	426	70	135	23	3	5	66	29	20	3	....	.317	.362	.420	.782	110	6	65	5.67	-2	*0-111(0-54-57)	14	0.0
1938 NY-N	134	501	68	131	21	3	10	60	49	21	2	....	.261	.333	.375	.709	94	-4	62	4.18	0	*0-131(0-17-115)	10	-1.1
1939 NY-N	66	123	10	28	4	0	1	12	8	7	0	....	.228	.286	.285	.570	53	-8	10	2.61	1	0-23(9-4-10)	0	-0.9
Bro-N	28	106	18	35	8	4	0	22	11	8	0	....	.330	.398	.481	.879	131	5	19	6.53	-1	0-28(12-1-15)	4	0.2
Yr.	94	229	28	63	12	4	1	34	19	15	0	....	.275	.339	.376	.714	90	-3	29	4.35	-1	0-51(21-5-25)	4	-0.7
1940 Bro-N	7	13	0	3	0	0	0	0	2	2	0	....	.231	.333	.231	.564	55	-1	1	3.17	1	/0-3(1-0-2)	0	0.0
*Cin-N	32	101	15	31	10	0	4	20	13	5	1	....	.307	.397	.525	.921	151	7	22	8.07	0	0-30(27-0-3)	6	0.6
Yr.	39	114	15	34	10	0	4	20	15	7	1	....	.298	.389	.491	.881	140	7	23	7.48	0	0-33(28-0-5)	6	0.5
1941 Cin-N	38	102	10	22	6	1	1	9	9	4	0	....	.216	.279	.324	.603	69	-4	10	3.26	0	0-25(7-0-18)	2	-0.6
1943 Phi-A	32	126	8	30	3	1	0	15	7	7	0	0	.238	.284	.278	.561	65	-6	11	2.87	-3	0-31(10-0-21)	1	-1.1
Total 7	**554**	**1809**	**241**	**510**	**92**	**14**	**28**	**251**	**156**	**89**	**7**	**0**	**.282**	**.343**	**.395**	**.738**	**101**	**3**	**252**	**4.91**	**-4**	**0-458**	**49**	**-2.3**

• RISBERG, Swede Charles August Risberg b: 10/13/1894, San Francisco, CA d: 10/13/1975, Red Bluff, CA BR/TR, 6', 175 lbs. Deb: 4/11/1917

YEAR TM-L	G	AB	R	H	2B	3B	HR	RBI	BB	SO	SB	CS	AVG	OBP	SLG	OPS	OPS+	BR/A	RC	RC/G	FR	G/POS	WS	TPW
1917*Chi-A	149	474	59	96	20	8	1	45	59	65	16	....	.203	.297	.285	.582	76	-13	45	2.93	-15	*S-146	14	-2.0
1918 Chi-A	82	273	36	70	12	3	1	27	23	32	5	....	.256	.321	.333	.654	96	-2	30	3.63	-6	S-30,3-24,2-12/1-7,0-3(0-0-3)	8	-0.5
1919*Chi-A	119	414	48	106	19	6	2	38	35	38	19	....	.256	.317	.345	.662	86	-8	49	4.00	-8	S-97,1-22	12	-1.0
1920 Chi-A	126	458	53	122	21	10	2	65	31	45	12	10	.266	.316	.369	.685	81	-14	53	3.86	9	*S-124	15	0.4
Total 4	**476**	**1619**	**196**	**394**	**72**	**27**	**6**	**175**	**148**	**180**	**52**	**10**	**.243**	**.311**	**.332**	**.644**	**83**	**-37**	**177**	**3.57**	**-20**	**S-397/1-29,3-24,2-12,0-3**	**49**	**-3.1**

• RISING, Pop Percival Sumner Rising b: 1/2/1872, Industry, PA d: 1/28/1938, Rochester, PA TR Deb: 8/10/1905

YEAR TM-L	G	AB	R	H	2B	3B	HR	RBI	BB	SO	SB	CS	AVG	OBP	SLG	OPS	OPS+	BR/A	RC	RC/G	FR	G/POS	WS	TPW
1905 Bos-A	11	29	2	3	1	1	0	2	2	....	0	....	.103	.161	.207	.368	16	-3	1	1.06	0	/0-6(0-0-6),3-1	0	-0.3

• RITCHEY, Claude Claude Cassius "Little All Right" Ritchey
b: 10/5/1873, Emlenton, PA d: 11/8/1951, Emlenton, PA BB/TR, 5'6.5", 167 lbs. Deb: 4/22/1897 Career OF: 10-1-12

YEAR TM-L	G	AB	R	H	2B	3B	HR	RBI	BB	SO	SB	CS	AVG	OBP	SLG	OPS	OPS+	BR/A	RC	RC/G	FR	G/POS	WS	TPW
1897 Cin-N	101	337	58	95	12	4	0	41	42	....	11	....	.282	.370	.341	.711	83	-7	50	5.16	-4	S-70,0-22(10-1-11)/2-8	9	-0.8
1898 Lou-N	151	551	65	140	10	4	5	51	46	....	19	....	.254	.322	.314	.636	84	-11	67	4.04	-6	S-80,2-71	13	-0.9
1899 Lou-N	148	540	66	162	15	7	4	73	49	....	21	....	.300	.369	.376	.745	105	5	87	5.81	-4	*2-137,S-11	15	0.6
1900*Pit-N	123	476	62	139	17	8	1	67	29	....	18	....	.292	.339	.368	.707	94	-4	69	5.17	11	*2-123	16	1.1
1901 Pit-N	140	540	66	160	20	4	1	74	47	....	15	....	.296	.358	.354	.712	104	4	78	5.19	13	*2-139/S-1	19	1.8
1902 Pit-N	115	405	54	112	13	1	2	55	53	....	10	....	.277	.370	.328	.698	112	9	57	4.86	12	*2-114/0-1	17	2.4

YEAR TM-L	G	AB	R	H	2B	3B	HR	RBI	BB	SO	SB	CS	AVG	OBP	SLG	OPS	OPS+	BR/A	RC	RC/G	FR	G/POS	WS	TPW
1903*Pit-N	138	506	66	145	28	10	0	59	55	....	15	....	.287	.360	.381	.741	108	6	78	5.56	23	*2-137	21	2.8
1904 Pit-N	156	544	79	143	22	12	0	51	59	....	12	....	.263	.338	.347	.686	109	7	72	4.48	-2	*2-156/S-2	22	0.6
1905 Pit-N	153	533	54	136	29	6	0	52	51	....	12	....	.255	.324	.332	.656	93	-4	64	4.09	-4	*2-153/S-2	17	-0.7
1906 Pit-N	152	484	46	130	21	5	1	62	68	....	6	....	.269	.369	.339	.708	116	12	68	4.68	5	*2-151	23	2.1
1907 Bos-N	144	499	45	127	17	4	2	51	50	....	8	....	.255	.329	.317	.645	103	2	58	3.90	-2	*2-144	16	0.2
1908 Bos-N	121	421	44	115	10	3	2	36	50	....	7	....	.273	.361	.325	.687	122	13	54	4.28	6	*2-120	17	2.3
1909 Bos-N	30	87	4	15	1	0	0	3	8	....	1	....	.172	.242	.184	.426	31	-7	4	1.46	-3	2-25	0	-1.1
Total 13	**1672**	**5923**	**709**	**1619**	**215**	**68**	**18**	**675**	**607**	**....**	**155**	**....**	**.273**	**.348**	**.342**	**.690**	**102**	**24**	**808**	**4.69**	**44**	***2-1478,S-166/0-23**	**205**	**10.3**
• RITTER, Charlie	Charles J. Ritter Deb: 9/21/1885																							
1885 Buf-N	2	6	0	1	0	0	0	0	0	2	....	....	.167	.167	.167	.333	8	-1	0	.92	-1	/2-2	0	-0.1
• RITTER, Floyd	Floyd Alexander Ritter b: 6/1/1870, Dorset, OH d: 2/7/1943, Stevenson, WA BR/TR, 5'8", 155 lbs. Deb: 6/4/1890																							
1890 Tol-a	1	3	0	0	0	0	0	0	0	....	0	....	.000	.000	.000	.000	-97	-1	0	.00	0	/C-1	0	-0.1
• RITTER, Lew	Lewis Elmer "Old Dog" Ritter b: 9/7/1875, Liverpool, PA d: 5/27/1952, Harrisburg, PA BR/TR, 5'9", 150 lbs. Deb: 9/10/1902 Career OF: 6-2-8																							
1902 Bro-N	16	57	5	12	1	0	0	2	1	....	2	....	.211	.237	.228	.465	43	-4	4	2.18	1	C-16	1	-0.2
1903 Bro-N	78	259	26	61	9	6	0	37	19	....	9	....	.236	.290	.317	.607	75	-9	28	3.60	-13	C-74/0-2(1-1-0)	4	-1.4
1904 Bro-N	72	214	23	53	4	1	0	19	20	....	17	....	.248	.318	.276	.593	86	-3	25	3.98	8	C-57/2-5,3-1	7	1.2
1905 Bro-N	92	311	32	68	10	5	1	28	15	....	16	....	.219	.255	.293	.547	68	-13	29	2.98	2	C-84/0-4(0-1-3),3-2	5	-0.3
1906 Bro-N	73	226	22	47	1	3	0	15	16	....	6	....	.208	.263	.239	.502	61	-10	17	2.38	-0	C-53/0-9(5-0-5),1-3,3-2	4	-0.6
1907 Bro-N	93	271	15	55	6	1	0	17	18	....	5	....	.203	.255	.232	.488	57	-13	19	2.18	-2	C-89	4	-0.7
1908 Bro-N	38	99	6	19	2	1	0	2	7	....	0	....	.192	.245	.232	.478	55	-5	6	1.77	2	C-37	2	-0.1
Total 7	**462**	**1437**	**129**	**315**	**33**	**17**	**1**	**120**	**96**	**....**	**55**	**....**	**.219**	**.271**	**.268**	**.539**	**67**	**-57**	**127**	**2.87**	**-2**	**C-410/0-15,2-5,3-5,1-3**	**27**	**-2.1**
• RITTERSON, Whitey	Edward West Ritterson b: 4/26/1855, Philadelphia, PA d: 7/28/1917, Bucks County, PA BR/TR, 5'8" Deb: 5/3/1876																							
1876 Phi-N	16	52	8	13	3	0	0	4	0	2	....	....	.250	.250	.308	.558	85	-1	4	2.94	-6	C-14/0-4(0-2-2),3-1	1	-0.6
• RITZ, Jim	James L. Ritz b: 1874, Pittsburgh, PA d: 11/10/1896, Pittsburgh, PA, 5'8" Deb: 7/20/1894																							
1894 Pit-N	1	4	1	0	0	0	0	0	0	0	1	....	.000	.200	.000	.200	-49	-1	0	1.33	0	/3-1	0	-0.1
• RIVAS, Luis	Luis Wilfredo Rivas b: 8/30/1979, La Guaira, Venezuela BR/TR, 5'10", 175 lbs. Deb: 9/16/2000																							
2000 Min-A	16	58	8	18	4	1	0	6	2	4	2	0	.310	.333	.414	.747	84	-1	8	4.56	-3	2-14/S-2	1	-0.3
2001 Min-A	153	563	70	150	21	6	7	47	40	99	31	11	.266	.322	.362	.684	78	-16	65	3.92	-38	*2-150	8	-4.6
2002*Min-A	93	316	46	81	23	4	4	35	19	51	9	4	.256	.305	.392	.697	83	-8	35	3.62	-14	2-93	6	-1.7
2003*Min-A	135	475	69	123	16	9	8	43	30	65	17	7	.259	.310	.381	.691	80	-14	51	3.56	-13	*2-134	6	-1.9
Total 4	**397**	**1412**	**193**	**372**	**64**	**20**	**19**	**131**	**91**	**219**	**59**	**22**	**.263**	**.314**	**.377**	**.692**	**80**	**-39**	**159**	**3.76**	**-68**	**2-391/S-2**	**21**	**-8.5**
• RIVERA, Bombo	Jesus Manuel (Torres) Rivera b: 8/2/1952, Ponce, Puerto Rico BR/TR, 5'10", 187 lbs. Deb: 4/17/1975 Career OF: 153-1-168																							
1975 Mon-N	5	9	1	1	0	0	0	0	2	3	0	0	.111	.273	.111	.384	9	-1	0	.83	0	/0-5(4-0-2)	0	-0.2
1976 Mon-N	68	185	22	51	11	4	2	19	13	32	1	0	.276	.323	.411	.734	103	0	24	4.58	3	0-56(44-0-15)	5	0.1
1978 Min-A	101	251	35	68	8	2	3	23	35	47	5	3	.271	.365	.355	.719	101	2	35	4.84	1	0-94(32-0-72)/D-1	7	0.0
1979 Min-A	112	263	37	74	13	5	2	31	17	40	5	5	.281	.325	.392	.717	89	-5	32	4.03	6	*0-105(61-1-50)/D-2	5	-0.3
1980 Min-A	44	113	13	25	7	0	3	10	4	20	0	0	.221	.248	.363	.611	61	-7	9	2.64	0	0-37(10-0-28)/D-1	1	-0.8
1982 KC-A	5	10	1	1	0	0	0	0	0	2	0	0	.100	.100	.100	.200	-45	-2	0	.30	0	/0-3(2-0-1)	0	-0.2
Total 6	**335**	**831**	**109**	**220**	**39**	**11**	**10**	**83**	**71**	**144**	**11**	**8**	**.265**	**.324**	**.374**	**.698**	**90**	**-13**	**100**	**4.10**	**10**	**0-300/D-4**	**18**	**-1.5**
• RIVERA, Carlos	Carlos Alberto Rivera b: 6/10/1978, Fajardo, Puerto Rico BL/TL, 5'11", 245 lbs. Deb: 6/22/2003																							
2003 Pit-N	78	95	12	21	5	0	3	10	8	28	0	0	.221	.288	.368	.657	68	-5	10	3.43	-2	1-60	0	-0.8
• RIVERA, German	German (Diaz) Rivera b: 7/6/1960, Santurce, Puerto Rico BR/TR, 6'2", 195 lbs. Deb: 9/2/1983																							
1983 LA-N	13	17	1	6	1	0	0	0	2	2	0	1	.353	.421	.412	.833	132	0	3	6.23	0	/3-8	1	0.1
1984 LA-N	94	227	20	59	12	2	2	17	21	30	1	0	.260	.325	.357	.682	92	-2	23	3.30	0	3-90	5	-0.3
1985 Hou-N	13	36	3	7	2	1	0	2	4	8	0	0	.194	.275	.306	.581	64	-2	3	2.28	1	3-11	1	-0.1
Total 3	**120**	**280**	**24**	**72**	**15**	**3**	**2**	**19**	**27**	**40**	**1**	**1**	**.257**	**.325**	**.354**	**.678**	**91**	**-3**	**28**	**3.31**	**1**	**3-109**	**7**	**-0.4**
• RIVERA, Jim	Manuel Joseph "Jungle Jim" Rivera b: 7/22/1922, New York, NY BL/TL, 6', 196 lbs. Deb: 4/15/1952 Career OF: 98-392-594																							
1952 StL-A	97	336	45	86	13	6	4	30	29	59	8	7	.256	.319	.366	.685	88	-7	40	4.14	2	0-88(8-81-0)	8	-0.8
Chi-A	53	201	27	50	7	3	3	18	21	27	13	2	.249	.320	.358	.678	88	-1	26	4.57	1	0-53(0-53-0)	7	-0.2
Yr.	150	537	72	136	20	9	7	48	50	86	21	9	.253	.319	.363	.682	88	-8	67	4.30	2	*0-141(8-134-0)	15	-1.1
1953 Chi-A	156	567	79	147	26	**16**	11	78	53	70	22	15	.259	.329	.420	.749	98	-4	76	4.46	-2	*0-156(0-153-3)	20	-1.3
1954 Chi-A	145	490	62	140	16	8	13	61	49	68	18	10	.286	.358	.431	.788	111	7	77	5.55	-9	*0-143(3-28-128)	17	-0.7
1955 Chi-A	147	454	71	120	24	4	10	52	62	59	**25**	16	.264	.354	.401	.755	100	-1	66	4.86	13	*0-143(2-50-115)	15	0.7
1956 Chi-A	139	491	76	125	23	5	12	66	49	75	20	9	.255	.326	.395	.721	88	-9	66	4.60	0	*0-134(0-14-122)	12	-1.3
1957 Chi-A	125	402	51	103	21	6	14	52	40	80	18	2	.256	.328	.443	.771	108	7	59	5.01	-3	0-86(1-4-83),1-31	13	0.0
1958 Chi-A	116	276	37	62	8	4	9	35	24	49	21	3	.225	.289	.380	.669	84	-3	31	3.63	1	0-99(54-1-45)	7	-0.6
1959*Chi-A	80	177	18	39	9	4	4	19	11	19	5	3	.220	.270	.384	.654	78	-6	18	3.40	1	0-69(21-0-48)	4	-0.8
1960 Chi-A	48	17	17	5	0	0	1	1	3	3	4	0	.294	.400	.471	.871	136	2	4	9.77	0	0-24(9-1-14)	1	0.1
1961 Chi-A	1	0	0	0	0	0	0	0	0	0	0	1	....	....	....	....	-102	-0	0	.00	0	....	0	0.0
KC-A	64	141	20	34	8	0	2	10	24	14	6	2	.241	.352	.340	.692	86	-2	18	4.44	-2	0-43(0-7-36)	3	-0.5
Yr.	65	141	20	34	8	0	2	10	24	14	6	3	.241	.352	.340	.692	86	-2	18	4.40	-2	0-43(0-7-36)	3	-0.6
Total 10	**1171**	**3552**	**503**	**911**	**155**	**56**	**83**	**422**	**365**	**523**	**160**	**70**	**.256**	**.330**	**.402**	**.731**	**96**	**-17**	**484**	**4.61**	**3**	***0-1038/1-31**	**107**	**-5.4**
• RIVERA, Juan	Juan Luis Rivera b: 7/3/1978, Guarenas, Venezuela BR/TR, 6'2", 170 lbs. Deb: 9/4/2001 Career OF: 49-1-39																							
2001 NY-A	3	4	0	0	0	0	0	0	0	0	0	0	.000	.000	.000	.000	-99	-1	0	.00	0	/0-3(0-1-2)	0	-0.2
2002*NY-A	28	83	9	22	5	0	1	6	6	10	1	1	.265	.315	.361	.676	80	-3	8	3.32	0	0-28(15-0-15)	1	-0.4
2003*NY-A	57	173	22	46	14	0	7	26	10	27	0	0	.266	.306	.468	.774	102	-0	22	4.31	-2	0-56(34-0-22)	4	-0.4
Total 3	**88**	**260**	**31**	**68**	**19**	**0**	**8**	**32**	**16**	**37**	**1**	**1**	**.262**	**.304**	**.427**	**.731**	**92**	**-4**	**30**	**3.91**	**-2**	**/0-87**	**5**	**-0.9**
• RIVERA, Luis	Luis Antonio (Pedraza) Rivera b: 1/3/1964, Cidra, Puerto Rico BR/TR, 5'9", 170 lbs. Deb: 8/3/1986																							
1986 Mon-N	55	166	20	34	11	1	0	13	17	33	1	1	.205	.286	.283	.570	58	-10	15	2.90	-10	S-55	1	-1.5
1987 Mon-N	18	32	0	5	2	0	0	1	1	8	0	0	.156	.182	.219	.401	5	-4	1	1.32	-1	S-15	0	-0.5
1988 Mon-N	123	371	35	83	17	3	4	30	24	69	3	4	.224	.273	.318	.591	66	-18	30	2.66	-3	*S-116	5	-1.4
1989 Bos-A	93	323	35	83	17	1	5	29	20	60	2	3	.257	.302	.362	.665	81	-9	34	3.59	-10	S-90/2-1,D-1	6	-1.3
1990*Bos-A	118	346	38	78	20	0	7	45	25	58	4	3	.225	.280	.344	.624	70	-15	32	2.92	-10	*S-112/2-3,3-1	6	-1.6
1991 Bos-A	129	414	64	107	22	3	8	40	35	86	4	4	.258	.321	.384	.705	90	-7	50	4.02	-2	*S-129	9	0.2
1992 Bos-A	102	288	17	62	11	1	0	29	26	56	4	3	.215	.287	.260	.547	51	-19	22	2.54	-1	S-93/D-2,2-1,3-1,0-1	5	-1.3
1993 Bos-A	62	130	13	27	8	1	1	7	11	36	1	2	.208	.275	.308	.582	53	-9	11	2.68	4	2-27,S-27/D-7,3-2	2	-0.3
1994 NY-N	32	43	11	12	2	1	3	5	4	14	0	1	.279	.367	.581	.949	144	2	9	7.10	-1	S-11/2-5	2	0.2
1997 Hou-N	7	13	2	3	0	1	0	3	1	6	0	0	.231	.286	.385	.670	76	-1	2	3.78	-1	/S-6,2-1	0	-0.1
1998 KC-A	42	89	14	22	4	0	0	7	7	17	1	1	.247	.302	.292	.594	54	-6	8	3.08	2	S-30/2-6,3-6	3	-0.2
Total 11	**781**	**2215**	**249**	**516**	**114**	**12**	**28**	**209**	**171**	**443**	**20**	**22**	**.233**	**.292**	**.333**	**.625**	**70**	**-97**	**214**	**3.17**	**-32**	**S-684/2-44,3-10,D-10,0-1**	**39**	**-7.9**
• RIVERA, Mike	Michael R. Rivera b: 9/8/1976, Rio Piedras, Puerto Rico BR/TR, 6', 190 lbs. Deb: 9/18/2001																							
2001 Det-A	4	12	2	4	2	0	0	1	0	2	0	0	.333	.333	.500	.833	121	0	2	6.75	1	/C-4	0	0.2
2002 Det-A	39	132	11	30	8	1	1	11	4	35	0	0	.227	.255	.326	.581	56	-9	10	2.44	3	C-37/D-1	1	-0.3
2003 SD-N	19	53	2	9	1	0	1	2	5	11	0	0	.170	.241	.245	.487	30	-6	2	1.39	4	C-19/1-1	0	0.0
Total 3	**62**	**197**	**15**	**43**	**11**	**1**	**2**	**14**	**9**	**48**	**0**	**0**	**.218**	**.256**	**.315**	**.571**	**53**	**-14**	**14**	**2.34**	**8**	**/C-60,1-1,D-1**	**1**	**-0.2**
• RIVERA, Ruben	Ruben (Moreno) Rivera b: 11/14/1973, Chorrera, Panama BR/TR, 6'3", 200 lbs. Deb: 9/3/1995 Career OF: 52-455-123																							
1995 NY-A	5	1	0	0	0	0	0	0	0	1	0	0	.000	.000	.000	.000	-101	-0	0	.00	0	/0-4(4-0-0)	0	-0.1

YEAR TM-L	G	AB	R	H	2B	3B	HR	RBI	BB	SO	SB	CS	AVG	OBP	SLG	OPS	OPS+	BR/A	RC	RC/G	FR	G/POS	WS	TPW
1996*NY-A	46	88	17	25	6	1	2	16	13	26	6	2	.284	.388	.443	.832	110	2	17	6.50	1	0-45(13-14-19)	4	0.2
1997 SD-N	17	20	2	5	1	0	0	1	2	9	2	1	.250	.318	.300	.618	69	-1	2	3.48	0	/0-7(2-4-4)	1	-0.1
1998*SD-N	95	172	31	36	7	2	6	29	28	52	5	1	.209	.327	.378	.705	91	-1	24	4.62	-3	0-91(13-13-73)	6	-0.6
1999 SD-N	147	411	65	80	16	1	23	48	55	143	18	7	.195	.297	.406	.704	82	-12	51	3.89	4	*0-143(0-143-0)	6	-0.6
2000 SD-N	135	423	62	88	18	6	17	57	44	137	8	4	.208	.298	.400	.697	79	-15	51	3.95	4	*0-132(1-131-0)	10	-1.0
2001 Cin-N	117	263	37	67	13	1	10	34	21	83	6	3	.255	.322	.426	.748	87	-5	35	4.56	1	0-99(10-70-21)	5	-0.5
2002 Tex-A	69	158	17	33	4	0	4	14	17	45	4	2	.209	.306	.310	.616	61	-9	16	3.29	5	0-67(0-67-0)/D-1	3	-0.3
2003 SF-N	31	50	6	9	2	0	2	4	5	14	1	0	.180	.255	.340	.595	55	-3	5	3.11	2	0-27(9-13-6)	1	-0.1
Total 9	662	1586	237	343	67	11	64	203	185	510	50	20	.216	.309	.393	.703	82	-44	200	4.13	14	0-615/D-1	36	-3.1
• RIVERS, Mickey	John Milton "Mick the Quick" Rivers b: 10/31/1948, Miami, FL BL/TL, 5'10", 165 lbs. Deb: 8/4/1970 Career OF: 78-1145-40																							
1970 Cal-A	17	25	6	8	2	0	0	3	3	5	1	0	.320	.414	.400	.814	130	1	5	7.25	0	/0-5(0-0-5)	2	0.1
1971 Cal-A	79	268	31	71	12	2	1	12	19	38	13	1	.265	.316	.336	.652	91	-1	32	4.22	4	0-76(4-61-18)	9	0.0
1972 Cal-A	58	159	18	34	6	2	0	7	8	26	4	3	.214	.256	.277	.533	62	-8	11	2.14	-1	0-48(6-38-7)	1	-1.2
1973 Cal-A	30	129	26	45	6	4	0	16	8	11	8	3	.349	.391	.457	.849	150	9	24	7.06	-3	0-29(0-29-0)	7	0.5
1974 Cal-A	118	466	69	133	19	**11**	3	31	39	47	30	13	.285	.342	.393	.735	117	11	64	4.75	3	*0-116(0-116-0)	16	1.2
1975 Cal-A	155	616	70	175	17	**13**	1	53	43	42	**70**	14	.284	.333	.359	.692	103	12	81	4.66	1	*0-152(27-125-0)/D-1	22	0.8
1976*NY-A★	137	590	95	184	31	8	8	67	13	51	43	7	.312	.330	.432	.762	123	20	88	5.64	-0	*0-136(0-136-0)	26	1.7
1977*NY-A	138	565	79	184	18	5	12	69	18	45	22	14	.326	.351	.439	.790	115	9	86	5.72	-1	*0-136(0-136-0)/D-1	22	0.6
1978*NY-A	141	559	78	148	25	8	11	48	29	51	25	5	.265	.305	.397	.702	98	0	69	4.26	7	*0-138(0-138-0)	19	0.6
1979 NY-A	74	286	37	82	18	5	3	25	13	21	3	7	.287	.320	.416	.736	99	-4	36	4.36	0	0-69(0-69-0)/D-1	7	-0.4
Tex-A	58	247	35	74	9	3	6	25	9	18	7	2	.300	.327	.433	.760	104	1	35	5.22	1	0-57(0-57-0)	8	0.1
Yr.	132	533	72	156	27	8	9	50	22	39	10	9	.293	.323	.424	.747	101	-2	71	4.75	1	*0-126(0-126-0)/D-1	15	-0.3
1980 Tex-A	147	630	96	210	32	6	7	60	20	34	18	7	.333	.355	.437	.791	119	15	98	6.01	1	*0-141(0-141-0)/D-4	20	1.4
1981 Tex-A	99	399	62	114	21	2	3	26	24	31	9	5	.286	.328	.371	.699	107	3	49	4.47	8	0-97(0-97-0)	14	0.9
1982 Tex-A	19	68	6	16	1	1	1	4	0	7	0	0	.235	.235	.324	.559	54	-4	5	2.45	0	D-16	0	-0.5
1983 Tex-A	96	309	37	88	17	0	1	20	11	21	9	4	.285	.312	.350	.661	83	-7	35	4.00	0	D-53,0-23(15-0-8)	5	-1.0
1984 Tex-A	102	313	40	94	13	1	4	33	9	23	5	5	.300	.320	.387	.706	91	-5	38	4.48	2	D-48,0-30(26-2-2)	7	-0.6
Total 15	1468	5629	785	1660	247	71	61	499	266	471	267	90	.295	.329	.397	.726	106	52	756	4.85	22	*0-1253,D-124	185	4.3
• RIZZO, Johnny	John Costa Rizzo b: 7/30/1912, Houston, TX d: 12/4/1977, Houston, TX BR/TR, 6', 190 lbs. Deb: 4/19/1938 Career OF: 331-31-130																							
1938 Pit-N	143	555	97	167	31	9	23	111	54	61	1	....	.301	.368	.514	.882	139	28	105	6.98	-6	*0-140(140-0-0)	23	1.4
1939 Pit-N	94	330	49	86	23	3	6	55	42	27	0	....	.261	.349	.403	.752	103	2	46	4.60	-3	0-86(86-0-0)	8	-0.6
1940 Pit-N	9	28	1	5	1	0	0	2	5	5	0	....	.179	.324	.214	.538	51	-2	2	2.50	-1	/0-7(7-0-0)	0	-0.3
Cin-N	31	110	17	31	6	0	4	17	14	14	1	....	.282	.363	.445	.808	121	3	19	6.30	5	0-30(30-0-0)	5	0.6
Phi-N	103	367	53	107	12	2	20	53	37	31	2	....	.292	.358	.499	.857	139	19	67	6.82	4	0-91(56-23-15)/3-7	14	1.8
Yr.	143	505	71	143	19	2	24	72	56	50	3	....	.283	.357	.471	.828	130	20	88	6.43	7	*0-128(93-23-15)/3-7	19	2.1
1941 Phi-N	99	235	20	51	9	2	4	24	24	34	1	....	.217	.295	.323	.618	77	-7	22	3.04	-1	0-62(3-8-53)/3-2	2	-1.2
1942 Bro-N	78	217	31	50	8	0	4	27	24	25	2	....	.230	.307	.323	.630	83	-5	21	3.26	1	0-70(9-0-62)	5	-0.8
Total 5	557	1842	268	497	90	16	61	289	200	197	7	....	.270	.345	.435	.781	115	39	282	5.38	-2	0-486/3-9	57	0.9
• RIZZUTO, Phil	Philip Francis "Scooter" Rizzuto b: 9/25/1917, Brooklyn, NY BR/TR, 5'6", 160 lbs. Deb: 4/15/1941 HOF: 1994																							
1941*NY-A	133	515	65	158	20	9	3	46	27	36	14	5	.307	.343	.398	.741	97	-3	70	4.95	28	*S-128	21	3.4
1942*NY-A★	144	553	79	157	24	7	4	68	44	40	22	6	.284	.343	.374	.718	104	5	74	4.71	30	*S-144	25	4.6
1946 NY-A	126	471	53	121	17	1	2	38	34	39	14	7	.257	.315	.310	.625	74	-16	48	3.43	13	*S-125	12	0.5
1947*NY-A	153	549	78	150	26	9	2	60	57	31	11	6	.273	.350	.364	.714	100	1	76	4.87	33	*S-151	26	4.5
1948 NY-A	128	464	65	117	13	2	6	50	60	24	6	5	.252	.340	.328	.668	79	-14	57	4.12	5	*S-128	15	0.0
1949*NY-A	153	614	110	169	22	7	5	65	72	34	18	6	.275	.352	.358	.711	88	-8	82	4.47	14	*S-152	22	1.5
1950*NY-A★	155	617	125	200	36	7	7	66	92	39	12	8	.324	.418	.439	.857	123	25	124	7.44	22	*S-155	**35**	**5.3**
1951*NY-A★	144	540	87	148	21	6	2	43	58	27	18	3	.274	.350	.346	.696	92	-2	73	4.55	18	*S-144	23	2.5
1952*NY-A★	152	578	89	147	24	10	2	43	67	42	17	6	.254	.337	.341	.678	95	-1	73	4.21	18	*S-152	21	2.7
1953*NY-A★	134	413	54	112	21	3	2	54	71	39	4	3	.271	.383	.351	.734	103	6	63	5.20	12	*S-133	18	2.8
1954 NY-A	127	307	47	60	11	0	2	15	41	23	3	2	.195	.292	.251	.543	51	-20	25	2.46	8	*S-126/2-1	6	-0.4
1955*NY-A	81	143	19	37	4	1	1	9	22	18	7	1	.259	.369	.322	.691	88	0	20	4.52	-4	S-79/2-1	6	0.0
1956 NY-A	31	52	6	12	0	0	0	6	6	6	3	0	.231	.310	.231	.541	46	-3	5	2.76	2	S-30	1	0.0
Total 13	1661	5816	877	1588	239	62	38	563	651	398	149	58	.273	.351	.355	.706	93	-29	789	4.64	197	*S-1647/2-2	231	27.3
• ROACH, Mel	Melvin Earl Roach b: 1/25/1933, Richmond, VA BR/TR, 6'1", 190 lbs. Deb: 7/31/1953 Career OF: 41-0-3																							
1953 Mil-N	5	2	1	0	0	0	0	0	0	1	0	0	.000	.000	.000	.000	-107	-1	0	.00	-1	/2-1	0	-0.1
1954 Mil-N	3	4	0	0	0	0	0	0	0	1	0	0	.000	.000	.000	.000	-107	-1	0	.00	0	/1-1	0	-0.1
1957 Mil-N	7	6	1	1	0	0	0	0	0	3	0	0	.167	.167	.167	.333	-11	-1	0	.98	-1	/2-5	0	-0.2
1958 Mil-N	44	136	14	42	7	0	3	10	6	15	0	0	.309	.338	.426	.764	110	1	20	5.37	-1	2-27/0-7(4-0-3),1-1	5	0.3
1959 Mil-N	19	31	1	3	0	0	0	0	2	4	0	0	.097	.152	.097	.248	-35	-6	1	.51	-2	/2-8,0-4(4-0-0),3-1	0	-0.7
1960 Mil-N	48	140	12	42	12	0	3	18	6	19	0	0	.300	.333	.450	.783	121	3	17	4.12	-3	0-21(21-0-0),2-20/1-1,3-1	4	0.1
1961 Mil-N	13	36	3	6	0	0	1	6	2	4	0	0	.167	.250	.250	.500	35	-3	3	2.23	-1	/0-9(9-0-0),1-2	0	-0.4
Chi-N	23	39	1	5	2	0	0	1	3	9	1	0	.128	.190	.179	.370	-1	-5	1	.72	-3	/1-7,2-7	0	-0.8
Yr.	36	75	4	11	2	0	1	7	5	13	1	0	.147	.220	.213	.433	17	-9	4	1.42	-3	/1-9,0-9(9-0-0),2-7	0	-1.2
1962 Phi-N	65	105	9	20	4	0	0	8	5	19	0	0	.190	.227	.229	.456	23	-11	5	1.64	-1	3-26/2-9,1-4,0-3(3-0-0)	1	-1.2
Total 8	227	499	42	119	25	0	7	43	24	75	1	0	.238	.278	.331	.608	68	-24	47	3.08	-11	/2-77,0-44,3-28,1-16	10	-3.3
• ROACH, Mike	Michael Stephen Roach b: 12/23/1869, Driftwood, PA d: 11/12/1916, New York, NY, 5'7", 145 lbs. Deb: 8/10/1899																							
1899 Was-N	24	78	7	17	1	0	0	7	3	....	3	....	.218	.265	.231	.496	37	-7	6	2.49	-2	C-20/1-3	1	-0.6
• ROACH, Roxey	Wilbur Charles Roach b: 11/28/1882, Anita, PA d: 12/26/1947, Bay City, MI BR/TR, 5'11", 160 lbs. Deb: 5/2/1910																							
1910 NY-A	70	220	27	47	9	2	0	20	29	....	15	....	.214	.313	.273	.586	79	-4	24	3.42	-3	S-58/0-9(9-0-0)	7	-0.7
1911 NY-A	13	40	4	10	2	1	0	2	6	....	0	....	.250	.348	.350	.698	89	-0	5	4.08	-2	/S-8,2-5	1	-0.2
1912 Was-A	2	2	1	1	0	0	1	1	0	....	0	....	.500	.500	2.000	2.500	601	1	2	51.17	-1	/S-2	1	0.0
1915 Buf-F	92	346	35	93	20	3	2	31	17	34	11	....	.269	.303	.361	.664	95	-4	39	3.91	12	S-92	12	1.6
Total 4	177	608	67	151	31	6	3	54	52	34	26	....	.248	.311	.334	.645	90	-7	70	3.83	6	S-160/0-9,2-5	21	0.8
• ROARKE, Mike	Michael Thomas Roarke b: 11/8/1930, West Warwick, RI BR/TR, 6'2", 195 lbs. Deb: 4/19/1961 C																							
1961 Det-A	86	229	21	51	6	1	2	22	20	31	0	0	.223	.285	.284	.569	51	-16	18	2.64	-3	C-85	4	-1.5
1962 Det-A	56	136	11	29	4	1	4	14	13	17	0	0	.213	.287	.346	.632	67	-7	13	3.17	1	C-53	3	-0.3
1963 Det-A	23	44	5	14	0	0	0	1	2	3	0	0	.318	.362	.318	.680	89	-0	5	4.31	0	C-16	1	0.0
1964 Det-A	29	82	4	19	1	0	0	7	10	10	0	0	.232	.315	.244	.559	57	-4	7	2.89	0	C-27	2	-0.3
Total 4	194	491	41	113	11	2	6	44	45	61	0	0	.230	.297	.297	.595	60	-27	43	2.96	-2	C-181	10	-2.2
• ROAT, Fred	Frederick R. Roat b: 11/10/1867, Oregon, IL d: 9/24/1913, Oregon, IL TR Deb: 5/10/1890																							
1890 Pit-N	57	215	18	48	2	0	2	17	16	22	7	....	.223	.286	.260	.547	67	-8	18	2.93	-2	3-44/1-9,0-4(0-0-4)	2	-0.8
1892 Chi-N	8	31	4	6	0	1	0	2	2	3	2	....	.194	.242	.258	.500	51	-2	2	2.68	-3	/2-8	0	-0.4
Total 2	65	246	22	54	2	1	2	19	18	25	9	....	.220	.281	.260	.541	65	-10	21	2.90	-4	/3-44,1-9,2-8,0-4	2	-1.2
• ROBELLO, Tony	Thomas Vardasco Robello b: 2/9/1913, San Leandro, CA d: 12/25/1994, Fort Worth, TX BR/TR, 5'10.5", 175 lbs. Deb: 8/13/1933																							
1933 Cin-N	14	30	1	7	3	0	0	3	1	5	0	....	.233	.258	.333	.591	69	-1	3	3.18	0	2-11/3-2	1	-0.1
1934 Cin-N	2	2	0	0	0	0	0	0	0	1	0	....	.000	.000	.000	.000	-103	-1	0	.00	0	....	0	-0.1
Total 2	16	32	1	7	3	0	0	3	1	6	0	....	.219	.242	.313	.555	58	-2	3	2.93	0	/2-11,3-2	1	-0.1
• ROBERGE, Skippy	Joseph Albert Armand Roberge b: 5/19/1917, Lowell, MA d: 6/7/1993, Lowell, MA BR/TR, 5'11", 185 lbs. Deb: 7/18/1941																							
1941 Bos-N	55	167	12	36	6	0	0	15	9	18	0	....	.216	.256	.251	.507	45	-12	12	2.33	2	2-46/3-5,S-2	1	-0.8
1942 Bos-N	74	172	10	37	7	0	1	12	9	19	1	....	.215	.258	.273	.531	57	-10	13	2.38	-3	2-29,3-27/S-6	2	-1.1

YEAR TM-L	G	AB	R	H	2B	3B	HR	RBI	BB	SO	SB	CS	AVG	OBP	SLG	OPS	OPS+	BR/A	RC	RC/G	FR	G/POS	WS	TPW
1946 Bos-N	48	169	13	39	6	2	2	20	7	12	1	....	.231	.270	.325	.595	67	-8	15	2.91	2	3-48	4	-0.6
Total 3	177	508	35	112	19	2	3	47	25	49	2	....	.220	.261	.283	.545	56	-30	39	2.53	1	/3-80,2-75,S-8	7	-2.5

• ROBERSON, Kevin Kevin Lynn Roberson b: 1/29/1968, Decatur, IL BB/TR, 6'4", 210 lbs. Deb: 7/15/1993 Career OF: 25-0-61

YEAR TM-L	G	AB	R	H	2B	3B	HR	RBI	BB	SO	SB	CS	AVG	OBP	SLG	OPS	OPS+	BR/A	RC	RC/G	FR	G/POS	WS	TPW
1993 Chi-N	62	180	23	34	4	1	9	27	12	48	0	1	.189	.251	.372	.624	65	-10	17	3.03	0	0-51(14-0-42)	2	-1.2
1994 Chi-N	44	55	8	12	4	0	4	9	2	14	0	0	.218	.271	.509	.780	99	-1	6	3.76	0	/0-9(0-0-9)	1	-0.1
1995 Chi-N	32	38	5	7	1	0	4	6	6	14	0	1	.184	.311	.526	.837	118	0	6	4.76	0	0-11(10-0-1)	0	0.0
1996 NY-N	27	36	8	8	1	0	3	9	7	17	0	0	.222	.364	.500	.864	131	2	7	6.61	0	0-10(1-0-9)	1	0.1
Total 4	165	309	44	61	10	1	20	51	27	93	0	2	.197	.277	.430	.707	87	-9	36	3.80	-1	/0-81	4	-1.2

• ROBERTS, Bip Leon Joseph Roberts b: 10/27/1963, Berkeley, CA BB/TR, 5'7", 165 lbs. Deb: 4/7/1986 Career OF: 382-72-25

YEAR TM-L	G	AB	R	H	2B	3B	HR	RBI	BB	SO	SB	CS	AVG	OBP	SLG	OPS	OPS+	BR/A	RC	RC/G	FR	G/POS	WS	TPW
1986 SD-N	101	241	34	61	5	2	1	12	14	29	14	12	.253	.294	.303	.597	66	-14	20	2.76	3	2-87	4	-0.8
1988 SD-N	5	9	1	3	0	0	0	0	1	2	0	2	.333	.400	.333	.733	115	-1	1	2.20	0	/3-2,2-1	0	-0.1
1989 SD-N	117	329	81	99	15	8	3	25	49	45	21	11	.301	.393	.422	.816	133	16	58	6.24	2	0-54(34-1-21),3-37,S-14/2-9	18	1.9
1990 SD-N	149	556	104	172	36	3	9	44	55	65	46	12	.309	.378	.433	.811	121	22	97	6.30	5	0-75(75-0-0),3-56,S-18/2-8	22	2.7
1991 SD-N	117	424	66	119	13	3	3	32	37	71	26	11	.281	.344	.347	.691	92	-3	53	4.35	-3	2-68,0-46(19-29-0)	14	-0.5
1992 Cin-N★	147	532	92	172	34	6	4	45	62	54	44	16	.323	.396	.432	.828	131	26	96	6.69	-3	0-79(69-16-0),2-42,3-36	28	2.3
1993 Cin-N	83	292	46	70	13	0	1	18	38	46	26	6	.240	.333	.295	.628	70	-8	34	3.96	1	2-64,0-11(11-1-0)/3-3,S-1	5	-0.5
1994 SD-N	105	403	52	129	15	5	2	31	39	57	21	7	.320	.384	.397	.781	107	7	64	5.94	-10	2-90,0-20(16-5-0)	13	0.1
1995 SD-N	73	296	40	90	14	0	2	25	17	36	20	2	.304	.346	.372	.718	93	0	42	5.34	5	0-50(48-4-0),2-25/S-7	11	0.5
1996 KC-A	90	339	39	96	21	2	0	52	25	38	12	9	.283	.336	.357	.693	76	-14	39	3.91	5	2-63,D-16,0-11(8-2-1)	8	-0.7
1997 KC-A	97	346	44	107	17	2	1	36	21	53	15	3	.309	.351	.379	.729	88	-4	47	5.05	-1	0-84(82-2-0),3-10	6	-0.8
*Cle-A	23	85	19	23	3	0	3	8	7	14	3	0	.271	.340	.412	.752	92	-0	13	5.36	0	2-13,0-10(10-0-0)	2	0.0
Yr.	120	431	63	130	20	2	4	44	28	67	18	3	.302	.348	.385	.734	89	-4	60	5.11	-1	0-94(92-2-0),2-13,3-10	8	-0.8
1998 Det-A	34	113	17	28	6	0	0	9	16	14	6	1	.248	.351	.301	.652	72	-3	13	4.04	0	D-29/0-2(2-0-0),2-1	2	-0.4
Oak-A	61	182	28	51	11	0	1	15	15	24	10	3	.280	.342	.357	.699	84	-3	23	4.43	-2	2-30,0-22(8-12-3)/3-3	5	-0.4
Yr.	95	295	45	79	17	0	1	24	31	38	16	4	.268	.345	.336	.681	79	-6	36	4.28	-2	2-31,D-29,0-24(10-12-3)/3-3	7	-0.8
Total 12	1202	4147	663	1220	203	31	30	352	396	548	264	95	.294	.360	.380	.740	100	21	600	5.16	2	2-501,0-464,3-147/D-45,S-40	138	3.3

• ROBERTS, Brian Brian M. Roberts b: 10/9/1977, Durham, NC BB/TR, 5'9", 170 lbs. Deb: 6/14/2001

YEAR TM-L	G	AB	R	H	2B	3B	HR	RBI	BB	SO	SB	CS	AVG	OBP	SLG	OPS	OPS+	BR/A	RC	RC/G	FR	G/POS	WS	TPW
2001 Bal-A	75	273	42	69	12	3	2	17	13	36	12	3	.253	.287	.341	.627	68	-12	28	3.44	-1	S-51,2-12/D-7	3	-0.8
2002 Bal-A	38	128	18	29	6	0	1	11	15	21	9	2	.227	.313	.297	.609	67	-5	13	3.29	2	2-25/D-7	2	-0.2
2003 Bal-A	112	460	65	124	22	4	5	41	46	58	23	6	.270	.337	.367	.705	89	-4	60	4.52	2	*2-107/D-3,S-2	13	0.2
Total 3	225	861	125	222	40	7	8	69	74	115	44	11	.258	.318	.348	.666	79	-21	100	3.98	2	2-144/S-53,D-17	18	-0.8

• ROBERTS, Curt Curtis Benjamin Roberts b: 8/16/1929, Pineland, TX d: 11/14/1969, Oakland, CA BR/TR, 5'8", 165 lbs. Deb: 4/13/1954

YEAR TM-L	G	AB	R	H	2B	3B	HR	RBI	BB	SO	SB	CS	AVG	OBP	SLG	OPS	OPS+	BR/A	RC	RC/G	FR	G/POS	WS	TPW
1954 Pit-N	134	496	47	115	18	7	1	36	55	49	6	3	.232	.311	.302	.613	61	-27	50	3.38	-8	*2-131	8	-2.4
1955 Pit-N	6	17	1	2	1	0	0	0	2	1	0	0	.118	.211	.176	.387	4	-2	1	1.33	0	/2-6	0	-0.2
1956 Pit-N	31	62	6	11	5	2	0	4	5	12	1	0	.177	.239	.323	.561	50	-4	5	2.51	1	2-27	1	-0.2
Total 3	171	575	54	128	24	9	1	40	62	62	7	3	.223	.300	.301	.601	59	-34	56	3.21	-7	2-164	9	-2.9

• ROBERTS, Dave David Ray Roberts b: 5/31/1972, Okinawa, Japan BL/TL, 5'10", 180 lbs. Deb: 8/7/1999 Career OF: 25-265-3

YEAR TM-L	G	AB	R	H	2B	3B	HR	RBI	BB	SO	SB	CS	AVG	OBP	SLG	OPS	OPS+	BR/A	RC	RC/G	FR	G/POS	WS	TPW
1999*Cle-A	41	143	26	34	4	0	2	12	9	16	11	3	.238	.283	.308	.591	48	-10	14	3.23	-1	0-39(1-38-0)	2	-1.0
2000 Cle-A	19	10	1	2	0	0	0	0	2	2	1	1	.200	.333	.200	.533	39	-1	1	2.22	0	0-17(12-5-1)	0	-0.1
2001 Cle-A	15	12	3	4	1	0	0	2	1	2	0	1	.333	.385	.417	.801	110	-0	2	4.86	0	0-13(9-2-2)/D-2	0	-0.1
2002 LA-N	127	422	63	117	14	7	3	34	48	51	45	10	.277	.354	.365	.719	96	4	63	5.28	-1	*0-118(3-115-0)	19	0.5
2003 LA-N	107	388	56	97	6	5	2	16	43	39	40	14	.250	.331	.307	.638	72	-12	46	3.97	1	*0-105(0-105-0)	8	-1.0
Total 5	309	975	149	254	25	12	7	64	103	110	97	29	.261	.335	.332	.667	79	-19	125	4.40	0	0-292/D-2	29	-1.7

• ROBERTS, Dave David Wayne Roberts b: 2/17/1951, Lebanon, OR BR/TR, 6'3", 215 lbs. Deb: 6/7/1972 C Career OF: 3-6-10

YEAR TM-L	G	AB	R	H	2B	3B	HR	RBI	BB	SO	SB	CS	AVG	OBP	SLG	OPS	OPS+	BR/A	RC	RC/G	FR	G/POS	WS	TPW
1972 SD-N	100	418	38	102	17	0	5	33	18	64	7	2	.244	.275	.321	.596	74	-15	37	3.04	-4	3-84,2-20/S-3,C-1	8	-2.0
1973 SD-N	127	479	56	137	20	3	21	64	17	83	11	2	.286	.312	.472	.784	124	14	70	5.29	1	*3-111,2-12	19	1.5
1974 SD-N	113	318	26	53	10	1	5	18	32	69	2	0	.167	.247	.252	.499	41	-25	20	1.92	-6	*3-103/S-3,0-1	2	-3.2
1975 SD-N	33	113	7	32	2	0	2	12	13	19	3	1	.283	.367	.354	.721	107	2	16	4.95	-4	3-30/2-5	4	-0.2
1977 SD-N	82	186	15	41	14	1	1	23	11	32	2	1	.220	.268	.323	.590	64	-10	16	2.75	-2	C-63/2-2,3-2,S-1	2	-1.0
1978 SD-N	54	97	7	21	4	1	1	7	12	25	0	0	.216	.309	.309	.618	79	-3	9	3.17	-2	C-41/1-8,0-2(1-1-0)	2	-0.3
1979 Tex-A	44	84	12	22	2	1	3	14	7	17	1	0	.262	.319	.417	.735	98	-0	11	4.32	2	C-14,0-11(1-5-5)/2-8,1-6,D,3	3	0.2
1980 Tex-A	101	235	27	56	4	0	10	30	13	38	0	1	.238	.281	.383	.664	83	-7	24	3.47	-6	3-37,S-33,C-22/0-5(0-0-5),1,2	4	-1.1
1981*Hou-N	27	54	4	13	3	0	1	5	3	6	1	0	.241	.281	.352	.633	83	-1	5	3.33	-2	1-10/3-7,2-3,C-1	1	-0.4
1982 Phi-N	28	33	2	6	1	0	0	2	2	8	0	1	.182	.229	.212	.441	23	-4	2	1.46	-2	3-11,C-10/2-7	0	-0.6
Total 10	709	2017	194	483	77	7	49	208	128	361	27	8	.239	.288	.357	.645	83	-49	210	3.51	-25	3-386,C-152/2-61,S-40,1,0,D	45	-7.1

• ROBERTS, Dave David Leonard Roberts b: 6/30/1933, Panama City, Panama BL/TL, 6', 172 lbs. Deb: 9/5/1962 Career OF: 10-0-6

YEAR TM-L	G	AB	R	H	2B	3B	HR	RBI	BB	SO	SB	CS	AVG	OBP	SLG	OPS	OPS+	BR/A	RC	RC/G	FR	G/POS	WS	TPW
1962 Hou-N	16	53	3	13	3	0	1	10	8	8	0	0	.245	.355	.358	.713	99	0	8	5.03	-1	0-12(6-0-6)/1-6	1	-0.1
1964 Hou-N	61	125	9	23	4	1	1	7	14	28	0	1	.184	.271	.256	.527	52	-8	9	2.28	4	1-34/0-4(4-0-0)	1	-0.6
1966 Pit-N	14	16	3	2	1	0	0	0	0	7	0	0	.125	.125	.188	.313	-15	-2	0	.34	0	/1-2	0	-0.3
Total 3	91	194	15	38	8	1	2	17	22	43	0	1	.196	.284	.278	.563	61	-10	17	2.79	3	/1-42,0-16	2	-1.0

• ROBERTS, Leon Leon Kauffman Roberts b: 1/22/1951, Vicksburg, MI BR/TR, 6'3", 200 lbs. Deb: 9/3/1974 C Career OF: 243-29-533

YEAR TM-L	G	AB	R	H	2B	3B	HR	RBI	BB	SO	SB	CS	AVG	OBP	SLG	OPS	OPS+	BR/A	RC	RC/G	FR	G/POS	WS	TPW
1974 Det-A	17	63	5	17	3	2	0	7	3	10	0	2	.270	.303	.381	.684	93	-2	6	2.95	-2	0-17(0-1-16)	1	-0.5
1975 Det-A	129	447	51	115	17	5	10	38	36	94	3	7	.257	.318	.385	.703	94	-6	53	3.99	2	*0-127(0-0-127)/D-1	9	-1.1
1976 Hou-N	87	235	31	68	11	2	7	33	19	43	1	0	.289	.350	.443	.793	136	10	38	5.93	-1	0-60(49-0-12)	11	0.7
1977 Hou-N	19	27	1	2	0	0	0	2	1	8	0	0	.074	.107	.074	.181	-55	-6	0	.17	1	/0-9(4-0-6)	0	-0.5
1978 Sea-A	134	472	78	142	21	7	22	92	41	52	6	3	.301	.367	.515	.881	146	28	90	6.99	3	*0-128(0-0-128)/D-2	21	2.6
1979 Sea-A	140	450	61	122	24	6	15	54	56	64	3	3	.271	.354	.451	.805	114	9	73	5.64	0	*0-136(67-0-69)/D-1	13	0.2
1980 Sea-A	119	374	48	94	18	3	10	33	43	59	8	4	.251	.330	.396	.726	97	-1	48	4.25	-2	*0-104(20-20-70)/D-4	8	-0.8
1981 Tex-A	72	233	26	65	17	2	4	31	25	38	3	4	.279	.351	.421	.772	128	8	33	4.69	-1	0-71(25-3-46)	9	0.3
1982 Tex-A	31	73	7	17	3	0	1	6	4	14	0	0	.233	.282	.315	.597	67	-3	6	2.46	-1	0-28(11-2-17)/D-1	0	-0.6
Tor-A	40	105	6	24	4	0	1	5	7	16	1	1	.229	.277	.295	.572	52	-7	8	2.54	-1	D-21,0-16(16-0-0)	0	-0.9
Yr.	71	178	13	41	7	0	2	11	11	30	1	1	.230	.279	.303	.582	58	-10	14	2.51	-2	0-44(27-2-17),D-22	0	-1.4
1983 KC-A	84	213	24	55	7	0	8	24	17	27	1	1	.258	.316	.404	.720	96	-2	26	4.11	-1	0-76(41-3-35)/D-1	5	-0.6
1984 KC-A	29	45	4	10	1	1	0	3	4	3	0	0	.222	.300	.289	.589	63	-2	4	3.00	0	0-16(10-0-7)/D-3,P-1	1	-0.5
Total 11	901	2737	342	731	126	28	78	328	256	428	26	25	.267	.335	.419	.754	109	26	383	4.81	-3	0-788/D-34,P-1	78	-1.6

• ROBERTS, Red Charles Emory Roberts b: 8/8/1918, Carrollton, GA d: 12/2/1998, Atlanta, GA BR/TR, 6', 170 lbs. Deb: 9/3/1943

YEAR TM-L	G	AB	R	H	2B	3B	HR	RBI	BB	SO	SB	CS	AVG	OBP	SLG	OPS	OPS+	BR/A	RC	RC/G	FR	G/POS	WS	TPW
1943 Was-A	9	23	1	6	1	0	1	3	4	2	0	0	.261	.370	.435	.805	140	1	4	6.64	-4	/S-6,3-1	1	-0.3

• ROBERTS, Skipper Clarence Ashley Roberts b: 1/11/1888, Wardner, ID d: 12/24/1963, Long Beach, CA BL/TR, 5'10.5", 175 lbs. Deb: 6/12/1913

YEAR TM-L	G	AB	R	H	2B	3B	HR	RBI	BB	SO	SB	CS	AVG	OBP	SLG	OPS	OPS+	BR/A	RC	RC/G	FR	G/POS	WS	TPW
1913 StL-N	26	41	4	6	2	0	0	3	3	13	1	....	.146	.205	.195	.400	15	-5	2	1.20	-3	C-16	0	-0.7
1914 Pit-F	33	55	7	12	2	1	0	4	1	11	2	....	.218	.246	.291	.537	55	-3	4	2.39	-1	C-14	0	-0.4
Chi-F	4	3	0	1	0	0	0	1	1	1	0	....	.333	.500	.333	.833	148	0	0	6.18	0	....	0	0.0
Pit-F	19	39	5	10	2	1	1	4	1	8	1	....	.256	.293	.436	.729	112	0	5	4.30	-1	/C-9,0-1	1	0.0
Yr.	56	97	12	23	4	2	1	9	3	20	3	....	.237	.275	.351	.625	82	-3	9	3.23	-2	C-23/0-1	1	-0.3
Total 2	82	138	16	29	6	2	1	12	6	33	4	....	.210	.253	.304	.558	62	-7	11	2.58	-5	/C-39,0-1	1	-1.1

• ROBERTSON, Andre Andre Levett Robertson b: 10/2/1957, Orange, TX BR/TR, 5'10", 160 lbs. Deb: 9/3/1981

YEAR TM-L	G	AB	R	H	2B	3B	HR	RBI	BB	SO	SB	CS	AVG	OBP	SLG	OPS	OPS+	BR/A	RC	RC/G	FR	G/POS	WS	TPW
1981*NY-A	10	19	1	5	1	0	0	0	0	3	1	1	.263	.263	.316	.579	67	-1	1	2.47	1	/S-8,2-3	0	0.0
1982 NY-A	44	118	16	26	5	0	2	9	8	19	0	0	.220	.270	.314	.583	61	-6	9	2.59	-3	S-27,2-15/3-2	2	-0.6
1983 NY-A	98	322	37	80	16	3	1	22	8	54	2	4	.248	.273	.326	.599	67	-17	26	2.69	9	S-78,2-29	7	0.1
1984 NY-A	52	140	10	30	5	1	0	6	4	20	0	1	.214	.236	.264	.500	40	-12	6	1.27	-4	S-49/2-6	2	-1.1

YEAR TM-L	G	AB	R	H	2B	3B	HR	RBI	BB	SO	SB	CS	AVG	OBP	SLG	OPS	OPS+	BR/A	RC	RC/G	FR	G/POS	WS	TPW
1985 NY-A	50	125	16	41	5	0	2	17	6	24	1	2	.328	.364	.416	.780	116	2	18	5.18	-2	3-33,S-14/2-2	4	0.1
Total 5	**254**	**724**	**80**	**182**	**32**	**4**	**5**	**54**	**26**	**120**	**4**	**8**	**.251**	**.281**	**.327**	**.609**	**69**	**-35**	**61**	**2.75**	**0**	**S-176/2-55,3-35**	**15**	**-1.6**

• ROBERTSON, Bob Robert Eugene Robertson b: 10/2/1946, Frostburg, MD BR/TR, 6'1", 210 lbs. Deb: 9/18/1967 Career OF: 26-0-0

YEAR TM-L	G	AB	R	H	2B	3B	HR	RBI	BB	SO	SB	CS	AVG	OBP	SLG	OPS	OPS+	BR/A	RC	RC/G	FR	G/POS	WS	TPW
1967 Pit-N	9	35	4	6	0	0	2	4	3	12	0	0	.171	.237	.343	.580	64	-2	3	2.82	0	/1-9	0	-0.3
1969 Pit-N	32	96	7	20	4	1	1	9	8	30	1	0	.208	.269	.302	.571	61	-5	7	2.32	0	1-26	0	-0.7
1970*Pit-N	117	390	69	112	19	4	27	82	51	98	4	1	.287	.372	.564	.937	152	28	83	7.58	-4	1-99/3-5,0-3(3-0-0)	18	1.6
1971*Pit-N	131	469	65	127	18	2	26	72	60	101	1	2	.271	.358	.484	.842	135	21	83	6.31	9	*1-126	20	2.2
1972*Pit-N	115	306	25	59	11	0	12	41	41	84	1	1	.193	.294	.346	.641	83	-7	33	3.49	7	1-89,0-23(23-0-0),3-11	5	-0.6
1973 Pit-N	119	397	43	95	16	0	14	40	55	77	0	4	.239	.333	.385	.719	101	-0	50	4.19	3	*1-107	10	-0.7
1974*Pit-N	91	236	25	54	11	0	16	48	33	48	0	0	.229	.323	.479	.802	127	7	36	4.99	-1	1-63	8	0.2
1975*Pit-N	75	124	17	34	4	0	6	18	23	25	0	0	.274	.396	.452	.848	136	7	25	7.22	2	1-27	6	0.7
1976 Pit-N	61	129	10	28	5	1	2	25	16	23	0	1	.217	.303	.318	.621	76	-4	13	3.39	0	1-29	2	-0.8
1978 Sea-A	64	174	17	40	5	2	8	28	24	39	0	0	.230	.327	.420	.746	109	2	24	4.51	-1	D-29,1-18	4	0.0
1979 Tor-A	15	29	1	3	0	0	1	1	3	9	0	0	.103	.188	.207	.394	6	-4	1	1.32	1	/1-9,D-4	0	-0.3
Total 11	**829**	**2385**	**283**	**578**	**93**	**10**	**115**	**368**	**317**	**546**	**7**	**9**	**.242**	**.334**	**.434**	**.769**	**114**	**45**	**357**	**5.09**	**15**	**1-602/D-33,0-26,3-16**	**73**	**1.3**

• ROBERTSON, Daryl Daryl Berdene Robertson b: 1/5/1936, Cripple Creek, CO BR/TR, 6', 184 lbs. Deb: 5/4/1962

YEAR TM-L	G	AB	R	H	2B	3B	HR	RBI	BB	SO	SB	CS	AVG	OBP	SLG	OPS	OPS+	BR/A	RC	RC/G	FR	G/POS	WS	TPW
1962 Chi-N	9	19	0	2	0	0	0	2	2	10	0	0	.105	.190	.105	.296	-18	-3	1	.83	0	/S-6,3-1	0	-0.3

• ROBERTSON, Dave Davis Aydelotte Robertson b: 9/25/1889, Portsmouth, VA d: 11/5/1970, Virginia Beach, VA BL/TL, 6', 186 lbs. Deb: 6/5/1912 Career OF: 171-38-519

YEAR TM-L	G	AB	R	H	2B	3B	HR	RBI	BB	SO	SB	CS	AVG	OBP	SLG	OPS	OPS+	BR/A	RC	RC/G	FR	G/POS	WS	TPW
1912 NY-N	3	2	0	1	0	0	0	1	0	1	1	....	.500	.500	.500	1.000	168	0	1	25.09	0	/1-1,0-1	0	0.0
1914 NY-N	82	256	25	68	12	3	2	32	10	26	9	....	.266	.299	.359	.658	99	-2	29	3.83	2	0-71(15-0-56)	7	-0.3
1915 NY-N	141	544	72	160	17	10	3	58	22	52	22	10	.294	.326	.379	.705	120	11	71	4.63	0	*0-138(16-0-123)	21	0.4
1916 NY-N	150	587	88	180	18	8	**12**	69	14	56	21	17	.307	.326	.426	.752	137	18	82	4.83	2	*0-144(0-0-144)	24	1.4
1917*NY-N	142	532	64	138	16	9	**12**	54	10	47	17	....	.259	.276	.391	.667	107	0	59	3.73	-2	*0-140(0-1-140)	16	-1.0
1919 NY-N	1	0	0	0	0	0	0	0	0	0	0	....	....	....	....	....	-101	0	0	....	0	....	0	0.0
Chi-N	27	96	8	20	2	0	1	10	1	10	3	....	.208	.224	.260	.485	45	-7	6	1.93	-2	0-25(1-24-0)	1	-1.1
Yr.	28	96	8	20	2	0	1	10	1	10	3	....	.208	.224	.260	.485	45	-7	6	1.93	-2	0-25(1-24-0)	1	-1.1
1920 Chi-N	134	500	68	150	29	11	10	75	40	44	17	23	.300	.353	.462	.815	130	14	75	5.12	-9	*0-134(134-0-0)	20	-0.1
1921 Chi-N	22	36	7	8	3	0	0	14	1	3	0	2	.222	.243	.306	.549	44	-4	2	1.78	0	/0-7(1-6-0)	0	-0.4
Pit-N	60	230	29	74	18	3	6	48	12	16	4	5	.322	.361	.504	.865	123	7	40	6.24	-7	0-58(2-1-55)	9	-0.5
Yr.	82	266	36	82	21	3	6	62	13	19	4	7	.308	.345	.477	.823	113	3	42	5.54	-7	0-65(3-7-55)	9	-0.9
1922 NY-N	42	47	5	13	2	0	1	3	3	7	0	0	.277	.320	.383	.703	80	-1	6	4.50	0	/0-8(1-6-1)	1	-0.1
Total 9	**804**	**2830**	**366**	**812**	**117**	**44**	**47**	**364**	**113**	**262**	**94**	**57**	**.287**	**.318**	**.409**	**.727**	**117**	**37**	**370**	**4.51**	**-17**	**0-726/1-1**	**99**	**-1.8**

• ROBERTSON, Don Donald Alexander Robertson b: 10/15/1930, Harvey, IL BL/TL, 5'10", 180 lbs. Deb: 4/13/1954

YEAR TM-L	G	AB	R	H	2B	3B	HR	RBI	BB	SO	SB	CS	AVG	OBP	SLG	OPS	OPS+	BR/A	RC	RC/G	FR	G/POS	WS	TPW
1954 Chi-N	14	6	2	0	0	0	0	0	0	2	0	0	.000	.000	.000	.000	-99	-2	0	.00	-1	/0-6(0-0-6)	0	-0.3

• ROBERTSON, Gene Eugene Edward Robertson b: 12/25/1898, St. Louis, MO d: 10/21/1981, Fallon, NV BL/TR, 5'7", 152 lbs. Deb: 7/4/1919

YEAR TM-L	G	AB	R	H	2B	3B	HR	RBI	BB	SO	SB	CS	AVG	OBP	SLG	OPS	OPS+	BR/A	RC	RC/G	FR	G/POS	WS	TPW
1919 StL-A	5	7	1	1	0	0	0	0	1	2	0	....	.143	.250	.143	.393	11	-1	0	1.01	-1	/S-2	0	-0.1
1922 StL-A	18	27	2	8	2	1	0	1	1	1	1	0	.296	.321	.444	.766	95	-0	4	5.50	-1	/3-7,S-6,2-1	1	0.0
1923 StL-A	78	251	36	62	10	1	0	17	21	7	4	2	.247	.310	.295	.605	57	-15	25	3.16	-5	3-74/2-1	3	-1.5
1924 StL-A	121	439	70	140	25	4	4	52	36	14	3	5	.319	.373	.421	.795	98	-2	69	5.86	1	*3-111/2-2	14	0.5
1925 StL-A	154	582	97	158	26	5	14	76	81	30	10	7	.271	.364	.405	.770	90	-7	90	5.36	-2	*3-154/S-1	17	0.0
1926 StL-A	78	247	23	62	12	6	1	19	17	10	5	1	.251	.302	.360	.662	69	-11	28	3.79	-4	3-55,S-10/2-3	4	-1.0
1928*NY-A	83	251	29	73	9	0	1	36	14	6	2	4	.291	.328	.339	.667	78	-9	28	3.78	-10	3-70/2-3	5	-1.4
1929 NY-A	90	309	45	92	15	6	0	35	28	6	3	3	.298	.358	.385	.743	98	-1	43	5.01	-6	3-77	8	-0.2
Bos-N	8	28	1	8	0	0	0	6	1	0	1	....	.286	.310	.286	.596	51	-2	2	2.93	-2	/3-6,S-1	0	-0.3
1930 Bos-N	21	59	7	11	1	0	0	7	5	3	0	....	.186	.250	.203	.453	12	-8	3	1.66	0	3-17	1	-0.7
Total 9	**656**	**2200**	**311**	**615**	**100**	**23**	**20**	**249**	**205**	**79**	**29**	**22**	**.280**	**.344**	**.373**	**.717**	**82**	**-57**	**292**	**4.61**	**-30**	**3-571/S-20,2-10**	**53**	**-4.8**

• ROBERTSON, Jim Alfred James Robertson b: 1/29/1928, Chicago, IL BR/TR, 5'9", 183 lbs. Deb: 4/15/1954

YEAR TM-L	G	AB	R	H	2B	3B	HR	RBI	BB	SO	SB	CS	AVG	OBP	SLG	OPS	OPS+	BR/A	RC	RC/G	FR	G/POS	WS	TPW
1954 Phi-A	63	147	9	27	8	0	0	8	23	25	0	0	.184	.298	.238	.536	48	-10	12	2.61	0	C-50	1	-0.8
1955 KC-A	6	8	1	2	0	0	0	0	1	2	0	0	.250	.333	.250	.583	58	-0	1	3.39	0	/C-4	0	0.0
Total 2	**69**	**155**	**10**	**29**	**8**	**0**	**0**	**8**	**24**	**27**	**0**	**0**	**.187**	**.300**	**.239**	**.539**	**49**	**-10**	**13**	**2.64**	**0**	**/C-54**	**1**	**-0.8**

• ROBERTSON, Mike Michael Francis Robertson b: 10/9/1970, Norwich, CT BL/TL, 6', 180 lbs. Deb: 9/6/1996

YEAR TM-L	G	AB	R	H	2B	3B	HR	RBI	BB	SO	SB	CS	AVG	OBP	SLG	OPS	OPS+	BR/A	RC	RC/G	FR	G/POS	WS	TPW
1996 Chi-A	6	7	0	1	1	0	0	0	0	1	0	0	.143	.143	.286	.429	5	-1	0	1.29	0	/1-2,D-2	0	-0.1
1997 Phi-N	22	38	3	8	2	1	0	4	0	6	1	0	.211	.268	.316	.584	52	-3	4	3.21	-1	/1-5,0-5(4-0-1),D-1	1	-0.4
1998 Ari-N	11	13	0	2	0	0	0	0	0	2	0	0	.154	.154	.154	.308	-19	-2	0	.76	0	/D-2	0	-0.2
Total 3	**39**	**58**	**3**	**11**	**3**	**1**	**0**	**4**	**0**	**9**	**1**	**0**	**.190**	**.230**	**.276**	**.505**	**32**	**-6**	**4**	**2.39**	**-1**	**/1-7,D-5,0-5**	**1**	**-0.7**

• ROBERTSON, Sherry Sherrard Alexander Robertson b: 1/1/1919, Montreal, Canada d: 10/23/1970, Houghton, SD BL/TR, 6', 180 lbs. Deb: 9/8/1940 C Career OF: 57-1-105

YEAR TM-L	G	AB	R	H	2B	3B	HR	RBI	BB	SO	SB	CS	AVG	OBP	SLG	OPS	OPS+	BR/A	RC	RC/G	FR	G/POS	WS	TPW
1940 Was-A	10	33	4	7	0	1	0	0	5	6	0	0	.212	.316	.273	.589	58	-2	3	3.45	-1	S-10	1	-0.2
1941 Was-A	1	3	0	0	0	0	0	0	0	3	0	0	.000	.000	.000	.000	-105	-1	0	.00	0	/3-1	0	-0.1
1943 Was-A	59	120	22	26	4	1	3	14	17	19	0	2	.217	.319	.342	.661	97	-1	14	3.86	-4	3-27/S-1	3	-0.4
1946 Was-A	74	230	30	46	6	3	6	19	30	42	6	2	.200	.292	.330	.623	78	-6	25	3.65	-1	3-38,2-14,S-12/0-1	5	-0.6
1947 Was-A	95	266	25	62	9	3	1	23	32	52	4	5	.233	.318	.301	.618	74	-10	27	3.39	-1	0-55(55-0-0),3-10/2-4	4	-1.6
1948 Was-A	71	187	19	46	11	3	2	22	24	26	8	0	.246	.335	.369	.704	90	-1	27	4.92	-2	0-51(1-1-49)	5	-0.4
1949 Was-A	110	374	59	94	17	3	11	42	42	35	10	3	.251	.329	.401	.730	95	-4	52	4.84	-10	2-71,3-19,0-13(0-0-13)	9	-0.9
1950 Was-A	71	123	19	32	3	3	2	16	22	18	1	1	.260	.372	.382	.755	98	0	19	5.50	-3	0-14(0-0-14),2-12/3-1	3	-0.2
1951 Was-A	62	111	14	21	2	1	1	10	9	22	2	1	.189	.256	.252	.508	38	-10	8	2.27	1	0-22(1-0-21)	0	-0.9
1952 Was-A	1	0	0	0	0	0	0	0	0	0	0	0	....	....	....	....	-104	0	0	....	0	....	0	0.0
Phi-A	43	60	8	12	3	0	0	5	21	15	1	2	.200	.407	.250	.657	81	-1	8	4.19	-2	/2-8,0-7(0-0-7),3-2	2	-0.3
Yr.	44	60	8	12	3	0	0	5	21	15	1	2	.200	.407	.250	.657	81	-1	8	4.19	-2	/2-8,0-7(0-0-7),3-2	2	-0.3
Total 10	**597**	**1507**	**200**	**346**	**55**	**18**	**26**	**151**	**202**	**238**	**32**	**16**	**.230**	**.323**	**.342**	**.664**	**83**	**-34**	**184**	**4.11**	**-22**	**0-163,2-109/3-98,S-23**	**32**	**-5.7**

• ROBIDOUX, Billy Jo William Joseph Robidoux b: 1/13/1964, Ware, MA BL/TR, 6'1", 200 lbs. Deb: 9/11/1985 Career OF: 12-0-0

YEAR TM-L	G	AB	R	H	2B	3B	HR	RBI	BB	SO	SB	CS	AVG	OBP	SLG	OPS	OPS+	BR/A	RC	RC/G	FR	G/POS	WS	TPW
1985 Mil-A	18	51	5	9	2	0	3	8	12	16	0	0	.176	.333	.392	.725	98	0	7	4.61	1	0-11(11-0-0)/1-6,D-1	2	0.0
1986 Mil-A	56	181	15	41	8	0	1	21	33	36	0	0	.227	.346	.287	.633	72	-6	19	3.38	-1	1-43,D-10	2	-0.9
1987 Mil-A	23	62	9	12	0	0	0	4	8	17	0	1	.194	.286	.194	.479	30	-7	4	1.99	-1	1-10,D-10	0	-0.8
1988 Mil-A	33	91	9	23	5	0	0	5	8	14	1	1	.253	.313	.308	.621	74	-3	8	2.95	2	1-30/D-1	1	-0.4
1989 Chi-A	16	39	2	5	2	0	0	1	4	9	0	0	.128	.209	.179	.389	11	-5	2	1.34	0	1-15/0-1	0	-0.6
1990 Bos-A	27	44	3	8	4	0	1	4	6	14	0	0	.182	.294	.341	.635	74	-2	4	2.96	0	1-11/D-4	0	-0.2
Total 6	**173**	**468**	**43**	**98**	**21**	**0**	**5**	**43**	**71**	**106**	**1**	**2**	**.209**	**.315**	**.286**	**.601**	**65**	**-21**	**44**	**3.03**	**-0**	**1-115/D-26,0-12**	**5**	**-2.8**

• ROBINSON, Aaron Aaron Andrew Robinson b: 6/23/1915, Lancaster, SC d: 3/9/1966, Lancaster, SC BL/TR, 6'2", 205 lbs. Deb: 5/6/1943

YEAR TM-L	G	AB	R	H	2B	3B	HR	RBI	BB	SO	SB	CS	AVG	OBP	SLG	OPS	OPS+	BR/A	RC	RC/G	FR	G/POS	WS	TPW
1943 NY-A	1	1	0	0	0	0	0	0	0	1	0	0	.000	.000	.000	.000	-99	-0	0	.00	0	....	0	0.0
1945 NY-A	50	160	19	45	6	1	8	24	21	23	0	0	.281	.368	.481	.849	139	8	30	6.76	-2	C-45	8	0.9
1946 NY-A	100	330	32	98	17	2	16	64	48	39	0	1	.297	.388	.506	.894	146	21	69	7.79	-1	C-95	19	2.6
1947*NY-A★	82	252	23	68	11	5	5	36	40	26	0	1	.270	.370	.413	.783	118	7	41	5.81	-1	C-74	12	1.0
1948 Chi-A	98	326	47	82	14	2	8	39	46	30	0	1	.252	.344	.380	.724	96	-2	45	4.73	0	C-92	8	0.3
1949 Det-A	110	331	38	89	12	0	13	56	73	21	0	2	.269	.402	.423	.825	118	11	60	6.13	-7	*C-108	15	0.9
1950 Det-A	107	283	37	64	7	0	9	37	75	35	0	1	.226	.388	.346	.735	86	-3	45	5.41	-3	*C-103	13	-0.1
1951 Det-A	36	82	3	17	6	0	0	9	17	9	0	0	.207	.343	.280	.624	70	-3	8	3.32	1	C-35	2	-0.1
Bos-A	26	74	9	15	1	1	2	7	17	10	0	0	.203	.352	.324	.676	76	-2	10	4.45	0	C-25	2	-0.1
Yr.	62	156	12	32	7	1	2	16	34	19	0	0	.205	.347	.301	.649	73	-5	18	3.84	0	C-60	4	-0.2
Total 8	**610**	**1839**	**208**	**478**	**74**	**11**	**61**	**272**	**337**	**194**	**0**	**6**	**.260**	**.375**	**.412**	**.787**	**112**	**37**	**307**	**5.84**	**-14**	**C-577**	**79**	**5.4**

• ROBINSON, Bill William Henry Robinson b: 6/26/1943, McKeesport, PA BR/TR, 6'2", 205 lbs. Deb: 9/20/1966 C Career OF: 479-280-364

YEAR TM-L	G	AB	R	H	2B	3B	HR	RBI	BB	SO	SB	CS	AVG	OBP	SLG	OPS	OPS+	BR/A	RC	RC/G	FR	G/POS	WS	TPW
1966 Atl-N	6	11	1	3	0	1	0	3	0	1	0	0	.273	.273	.455	.727	96	-0	1	4.60	0	/0-5(2-0-3)	0	-0.1
1967 NY-A	116	342	31	67	6	1	7	29	28	56	2	2	.196	.261	.281	.541	62	-16	24	2.14	2	*0-102(20-33-53)	2	-2.2
1968 NY-A	107	342	34	82	16	7	6	40	26	54	7	6	.240	.297	.380	.677	107	1	36	3.36	-2	0-98(6-51-44)	10	-0.7
1969 NY-A	87	222	23	38	11	2	3	21	16	39	3	1	.171	.227	.279	.506	42	-18	13	1.87	0	0-62(17-19-29)/1-1	1	-2.2
1972 Phi-N	82	188	19	45	9	1	8	21	5	30	2	3	.239	.259	.426	.685	89	-5	16	2.79	1	0-72(13-30-32)	2	-0.6
1973 Phi-N	124	452	62	130	32	1	25	65	27	91	5	4	.288	.329	.529	.858	131	15	74	5.76	-1	*0-113(13-44-75),3-14	16	1.0
1974 Phi-N	100	280	32	66	14	1	5	29	17	61	5	3	.236	.282	.346	.628	72	-12	24	2.72	2	0-87(40-40-19)	3	-1.4
1975*Pit-N	92	200	26	56	12	2	6	33	11	36	3	1	.280	.318	.450	.768	112	2	27	4.59	0	0-57(31-15-13)	6	-0.1
1976 Pit-N	122	393	55	119	22	3	21	64	16	73	2	4	.303	.332	.534	.866	142	17	62	5.61	-4	0-78(24-27-29),3-37/1-3	17	1.0
1977 Pit-N	137	507	74	154	32	1	26	104	25	92	12	6	.304	.340	.525	.865	125	15	88	6.29	-7	1-86,0-43(41-2-1),3-17	18	0.2
1978 Pit-N	136	499	70	123	36	2	14	80	35	105	14	11	.246	.302	.411	.713	93	-8	60	3.96	2	*0-127(111-19-10),3-29/1-3	14	-1.2
1979*Pit-N	148	421	59	111	17	6	24	75	24	81	13	2	.264	.305	.504	.808	111	6	60	4.88	-3	*0-125(119-0-6),1-28/3-3	12	-0.3
1980 Pit-N	100	272	28	78	10	1	12	36	15	45	1	4	.287	.324	.463	.787	115	3	36	4.58	-4	1-49,0-41(28-0-14)	7	-0.5
1981 Pit-N	39	88	8	19	3	0	2	8	5	18	1	0	.216	.258	.318	.576	61	-5	7	2.64	-1	1-23/0-7(1-0-6),3-1	0	-0.8
1982 Pit-N	31	71	8	17	3	0	4	12	5	19	0	1	.239	.289	.451	.740	101	-1	8	3.53	-1	0-22(12-0-11)	2	-0.2
Phi-N	35	69	6	18	6	0	3	19	7	15	1	1	.261	.329	.478	.807	121	1	10	4.91	1	0-19(0-0-19)/1-5	2	0.2
Yr.	66	140	14	35	9	0	7	31	12	34	1	2	.250	.309	.464	.773	111	1	18	4.21	1	0-41(12-0-30)/1-5	4	0.0
1983 Phi-N	10	7	0	1	0	0	0	2	1	4	0	0	.143	.250	.143	.393	12	-1	0	.61	-1	/1-3,3-2,0-1	0	-0.2
Total 16	1472	4364	536	1127	229	29	166	641	263	820	71	49	.258	.303	.438	.741	103	-5	545	4.20	-17	*0-1059,1-201,3-103	112	-8.1

• ROBINSON, Brooks Brooks Calbert Robinson b: 5/18/1937, Little Rock, AR BR/TR, 6'1", 190 lbs. Deb: 9/17/1955 C HOF: 1983

YEAR TM-L	G	AB	R	H	2B	3B	HR	RBI	BB	SO	SB	CS	AVG	OBP	SLG	OPS	OPS+	BR/A	RC	RC/G	FR	G/POS	WS	TPW
1955 Bal-A	6	22	0	2	0	0	0	1	0	10	0	0	.091	.091	.091	.182	-55	-5	0	.25	-1	/3-6	0	-0.6
1956 Bal-A	15	44	5	10	4	0	1	1	1	5	0	0	.227	.244	.386	.631	70	-2	4	3.35	-1	3-14/2-1	1	-0.3
1957 Bal-A	50	117	13	28	6	1	2	14	7	10	1	0	.239	.288	.359	.647	81	-3	11	3.29	0	3-47	2	-0.3
1958 Bal-A	145	463	31	110	16	3	3	32	31	51	1	2	.238	.293	.305	.597	68	-21	38	2.70	14	*3-140,2-16	7	-0.7
1959 Bal-A	88	313	29	89	15	2	4	24	17	37	2	2	.284	.325	.383	.709	96	-3	38	4.42	4	3-87/2-1	9	0.1
1960 Bal-A★	152	595	74	175	27	9	14	88	35	49	2	2	.294	.333	.440	.774	109	4	78	4.45	14	*3-152/2-3	21	1.8
1961 Bal-A★	163	668	89	192	38	7	7	61	47	57	1	3	.287	.338	.397	.735	97	-4	85	4.46	-4	*3-163/2-2,S-1	18	-0.8
1962 Bal-A★	162	634	77	192	29	9	23	86	42	70	3	1	.303	.347	.486	.833	127	22	102	5.75	8	*3-162/S-3,2-2	27	3.0
1963 Bal-A★	161	589	67	148	26	4	11	67	46	84	2	3	.251	.307	.365	.672	89	-10	66	3.86	8	*3-160/S-1	19	-0.2
1964 Bal-A★	163	612	82	194	35	3	28	**118**	51	64	1	0	.317	.373	.521	.895	146	37	115	6.88	1	*3-163	33	4.1
1965 Bal-A★	144	559	81	166	25	2	18	80	47	47	3	0	.297	.354	.445	.799	123	17	86	5.59	-1	*3-143	26	1.7
1966*Bal-A★	157	620	91	167	35	2	23	100	56	36	2	3	.269	.335	.444	.778	123	18	88	4.96	8	*3-157	24	2.8
1967 Bal-A★	158	610	88	164	25	5	22	77	54	54	1	3	.269	.332	.434	.767	126	18	83	4.63	32	*3-158	24	5.5
1968 Bal-A★	162	608	65	154	36	6	17	75	44	55	1	1	.253	.308	.416	.724	118	11	76	4.30	19	*3-162	25	3.4
1969*Bal-A★	156	598	73	140	21	3	23	84	56	55	2	1	.234	.303	.395	.698	93	-7	69	3.77	30	*3-156	17	2.3
1970*Bal-A★	158	608	84	168	31	4	18	94	53	53	1	1	.276	.338	.429	.768	109	7	85	4.94	8	*3-156	21	1.5
1971*Bal-A★	156	589	67	160	21	1	20	92	63	50	0	0	.272	.345	.413	.758	115	12	83	4.99	17	*3-156	23	3.0
1972 Bal-A★	153	556	48	139	23	2	8	64	43	45	1	0	.250	.306	.342	.648	90	-6	58	3.57	14	*3-152	16	0.8
1973*Bal-A★	155	549	53	141	17	2	9	72	55	50	2	0	.257	.328	.344	.672	90	-6	61	3.76	14	*3-154	12	0.8
1974*Bal-A★	153	553	46	159	27	0	7	59	56	47	2	0	.288	.356	.374	.731	114	12	74	4.77	21	*3-153	23	3.4
1975 Bal-A	144	482	50	97	15	1	6	53	44	33	0	0	.201	.269	.274	.543	57	-27	37	2.49	2	*3-143	6	-2.5
1976 Bal-A	71	218	16	46	8	2	3	11	8	24	0	0	.211	.242	.307	.550	64	-11	16	2.30	1	3-71	2	-1.0
1977 Bal-A	24	47	3	7	2	0	1	4	4	4	0	0	.149	.216	.255	.471	30	-5	2	1.47	2	3-15	0	-0.3
Total 23	2896	10654	1232	2848	482	68	268	1357	860	990	28	22	.267	.325	.401	.726	105	49	1358	4.40	211	*3-2870/2-25,S-5	356	27.3

• ROBINSON, Bruce Bruce Philip Robinson b: 4/16/1954, La Jolla, CA BL/TR, 6'1", 185 lbs. Deb: 8/19/1978

YEAR TM-L	G	AB	R	H	2B	3B	HR	RBI	BB	SO	SB	CS	AVG	OBP	SLG	OPS	OPS+	BR/A	RC	RC/G	FR	G/POS	WS	TPW
1978 Oak-A	28	84	5	21	3	1	0	8	3	8	0	0	.250	.276	.310	.585	68	-4	7	2.79	1	C-28	2	-0.1
1979 NY-A	6	12	0	2	0	0	0	2	1	0	0	0	.167	.231	.167	.397	9	-2	1	1.41	-1	/C-6	0	-0.2
1980 NY-A	4	5	0	0	0	0	0	0	0	4	0	0	.000	.000	.000	.000	-102	-1	0	.00	0	/C-3	0	-0.2
Total 3	38	101	5	23	3	1	0	10	4	12	0	0	.228	.257	.277	.534	53	-7	7	2.45	-0	/C-37	2	-0.5

• ROBINSON, Charlie Charles Henry Robinson b: 7/27/1856, Westerly, RI d: 5/18/1913, Providence, RI BL/TR Deb: 8/2/1884

YEAR TM-L	G	AB	R	H	2B	3B	HR	RBI	BB	SO	SB	CS	AVG	OBP	SLG	OPS	OPS+	BR/A	RC	RC/G	FR	G/POS	WS	TPW
1884 Ind-a	20	80	11	23	2	0	0	0	3	....	....	....	.288	.313	.313	.626	108	1	8	3.87	2	C-17/S-3,0-1	2	0.4
1885 Bro-a	11	40	5	6	2	1	0	4	3	....	....	....	.150	.209	.250	.459	44	-3	2	1.70	-1	C-11	0	-0.2
Total 2	31	120	16	29	4	1	0	4	6	....	....	....	.242	.278	.292	.569	86	-2	10	3.06	2	/C-28,S-3,0-1	2	0.2

• ROBINSON, Craig Craig George Robinson b: 8/21/1948, Abington, PA BR/TR, 5'10", 165 lbs. Deb: 9/9/1972

YEAR TM-L	G	AB	R	H	2B	3B	HR	RBI	BB	SO	SB	CS	AVG	OBP	SLG	OPS	OPS+	BR/A	RC	RC/G	FR	G/POS	WS	TPW
1972 Phi-N	5	15	0	3	1	0	0	0	1	2	0	0	.200	.250	.267	.517	46	-1	1	2.40	1	/S-4	0	0.0
1973 Phi-N	46	146	11	33	7	0	0	7	0	25	1	1	.226	.226	.274	.500	37	-13	8	1.93	-5	S-42/2-4	2	-1.4
1974 Atl-N	145	452	52	104	4	6	0	29	30	57	11	2	.230	.282	.265	.548	52	-28	34	2.37	-7	*S-142	6	-1.9
1975 Atl-N	10	17	1	1	0	0	0	0	0	5	0	0	.059	.059	.059	.118	-65	-4	0	.00	-1	/S-7	0	-0.5
SF-N	29	29	4	2	1	0	0	0	2	6	0	0	.069	.129	.103	.232	-34	-5	0	.35	-2	S-12/2-9	0	-0.7
Yr.	39	46	5	3	1	0	0	0	2	11	0	0	.065	.104	.087	.191	-44	-9	0	.22	-4	S-19/2-9	0	-1.2
1976 SF-N	15	13	4	4	1	0	0	2	3	4	0	1	.308	.438	.385	.822	131	0	2	5.46	0	/2-7,3-2,S-1	1	0.1
Atl-N	15	17	4	4	0	0	0	3	5	2	0	0	.235	.409	.235	.644	81	0	2	4.39	-2	/2-5,S-2,3-1	1	-0.1
Yr.	30	30	8	8	1	0	0	5	8	6	0	1	.267	.421	.300	.721	102	0	5	4.86	-2	2-12/3-3,S-3	2	-0.1
1977 Atl-N	27	29	4	6	1	0	0	1	1	6	0	0	.207	.233	.241	.475	25	-3	2	1.99	-1	S-23	0	-0.3
Total 6	292	718	80	157	15	6	0	42	42	107	12	4	.219	.265	.256	.521	44	-54	50	2.21	-17	S-233/2-25,3-3	10	-4.8

• ROBINSON, Dave David Tanner Robinson b: 5/22/1946, Minneapolis, MN BB/TL, 6'1", 186 lbs. Deb: 9/10/1970

YEAR TM-L	G	AB	R	H	2B	3B	HR	RBI	BB	SO	SB	CS	AVG	OBP	SLG	OPS	OPS+	BR/A	RC	RC/G	FR	G/POS	WS	TPW
1970 SD-N	15	38	5	12	2	0	2	6	5	4	2	0	.316	.395	.526	.922	151	3	8	7.43	1	0-13(12-1-0)	2	0.3
1971 SD-N	7	6	0	0	0	0	0	0	1	3	0	0	.000	.143	.000	.143	-61	-1	0	.17	0	....	0	-0.1
Total 2	22	44	5	12	2	0	2	6	6	7	2	0	.273	.360	.455	.815	121	2	8	6.15	1	/0-13	2	0.2

• ROBINSON, Earl Earl John Robinson b: 11/3/1936, New Orleans, LA BR/TR, 6'1", 190 lbs. Deb: 9/10/1958 Career OF: 23-21-94

YEAR TM-L	G	AB	R	H	2B	3B	HR	RBI	BB	SO	SB	CS	AVG	OBP	SLG	OPS	OPS+	BR/A	RC	RC/G	FR	G/POS	WS	TPW
1958 LA-N	8	15	3	3	0	0	0	0	1	4	0	0	.200	.250	.200	.450	20	-2	0	.79	1	/3-6	0	-0.1
1961 Bal-A	96	222	37	59	12	3	8	30	31	54	4	3	.266	.356	.455	.811	117	5	36	5.59	2	0-82(6-1-78)	9	0.2
1962 Bal-A	29	63	12	18	3	1	1	4	8	10	2	0	.286	.366	.413	.779	115	2	10	5.81	0	0-17(1-0-16)	2	0.1
1964 Bal-A	37	121	11	33	5	1	3	10	7	24	1	2	.273	.313	.405	.717	98	-1	15	4.13	2	0-34(16-20-0)	4	0.0
Total 4	170	421	63	113	20	5	12	44	47	92	7	5	.268	.342	.425	.767	108	4	61	5.00	5	0-133/3-6	15	0.2

• ROBINSON, Eddie William Edward Robinson b: 12/15/1920, Paris, TX BL/TR, 6'2.5", 210 lbs. Deb: 9/9/1942 C

YEAR TM-L	G	AB	R	H	2B	3B	HR	RBI	BB	SO	SB	CS	AVG	OBP	SLG	OPS	OPS+	BR/A	RC	RC/G	FR	G/POS	WS	TPW
1942 Cle-A	8	8	1	1	0	0	0	2	1	0	0	0	.125	.222	.125	.347	-1	-1	0	1.10	0	/1-1	0	-0.1
1946 Cle-A	8	30	6	12	1	0	3	4	2	4	0	0	.400	.438	.733	1.171	239	5	10	13.40	-2	/1-8	3	0.3
1947 Cle-A	95	318	52	78	10	1	14	52	30	18	1	0	.245	.314	.415	.729	104	1	41	4.38	0	1-87	8	-0.2
1948*Cle-A	134	493	53	125	18	5	16	83	36	42	1	0	.254	.307	.408	.715	91	-9	61	4.25	3	*1-131	9	-1.0
1949 Was-A★	143	527	66	155	27	3	18	78	67	30	3	4	.294	.381	.459	.840	124	17	93	6.36	1	*1-143	18	1.3
1950 Was-A	36	129	21	30	4	2	1	13	25	4	0	0	.233	.365	.318	.683	80	-3	17	4.49	0	1-36	3	-0.4
Chi-A	119	424	62	133	11	2	20	73	60	28	0	0	.314	.405	.491	.895	132	22	90	8.09	-10	*1-119	15	0.7
Yr.	155	553	83	163	15	4	21	86	85	32	0	0	.295	.395	.450	.846	119	19	107	7.18	-10	*1-155	18	0.3
1951 Chi-A★	151	564	85	159	23	5	29	117	77	54	2	5	.282	.371	.495	.866	135	26	107	6.76	-6	*1-147	19	1.4
1952 Chi-A★	155	594	79	176	33	1	22	104	70	49	2	0	.296	.382	.466	.848	134	29	113	7.10	-8	*1-155	25	1.6
1953 Phi-A★	156	615	64	152	28	4	22	102	63	56	1	2	.247	.322	.413	.735	94	-7	84	4.71	-10	*1-155	12	-2.6
1954 NY-A	85	142	11	37	9	0	3	27	19	21	0	0	.261	.348	.387	.735	105	1	21	5.14	-1	1-29	5	-0.1
1955*NY-A	88	173	25	36	1	0	16	42	36	26	0	0	.208	.360	.491	.851	129	8	31	5.72	-4	1-46	7	0.1
1956 NY-A	26	54	7	12	1	0	5	11	5	3	0	1	.222	.323	.519	.841	123	1	9	5.74	-1	1-14	2	-0.1
KC-A	75	172	13	34	5	1	2	12	26	20	0	0	.198	.310	.273	.583	55	-11	15	2.75	-3	1-47	1	-1.6
Yr.	101	226	20	46	6	1	7	23	31	23	0	1	.204	.313	.332	.645	71	-10	24	3.43	-4	1-61	3	-1.7

YEAR TM-L	G	AB	R	H	2B	3B	HR	RBI	BB	SO	SB	CS	AVG	OBP	SLG	OPS	OPS+	BR/A	RC	RC/G	FR	G/POS	WS	TPW
1957 Det-A	13	9	0	0	0	0	0	0	3	0	0	0	.000	.308	.000	.308	-9	-1	0	.49	0	/1-1	0	-0.1
Cle-A	19	27	1	6	1	0	1	3	0	3	0	0	.222	.250	.370	.620	68	-1	2	2.09	0	/1-7	0	-0.2
Bal-A	4	3	0	0	0	0	0	0	1	1	0	0	.000	.250	.000	.250	-28	-0	0	.59	0	....	0	0.0
Yr.	36	39	1	6	1	0	1	3	4	4	0	0	.154	.267	.256	.523	38	-3	2	1.54	0	/1-8	0	-0.3
Total 13	1315	4282	546	1146	172	24	172	723	521	359	10	12	.268	.354	.440	.793	114	77	694	5.70	-41	*1-1126	127	-0.8
• ROBINSON, Floyd	Floyd Andrew Robinson b: 5/9/1936, Prescott, AR BL/TR, 5'9", 175 lbs. Deb: 8/10/1960 Career OF: 242-5-723																							
1960 Chi-A	22	46	7	13	0	0	0	1	11	8	2	3	.283	.431	.283	.714	98	0	7	4.81	-1	0-17(1-4-12)	1	-0.1
1961 Chi-A	132	432	69	134	20	7	11	59	52	32	7	4	.310	.389	.465	.855	129	19	82	7.10	-1	*0-106(0-0-106)	19	1.0
1962 Chi-A	156	600	89	187	**45**	10	11	109	72	47	4	2	.312	.387	.475	.862	131	28	113	7.00	-4	*0-155(114-0-75)	27	1.4
1963 Chi-A	146	527	71	149	21	6	13	71	62	43	4	3	.283	.363	.419	.782	120	15	81	5.50	0	*0-137(36-0-119)	20	0.7
1964 Chi-A	141	525	83	158	17	3	11	59	70	41	9	5	.301	.388	.408	.796	125	21	87	6.08	1	*0-138(54-0-112)	25	1.4
1965 Chi-A	156	577	70	153	15	6	14	66	76	51	4	1	.265	.356	.385	.740	117	16	83	5.01	-3	*0-153(6-1-148)	24	0.2
1966 Chi-A	127	342	44	81	11	2	5	35	44	32	8	2	.237	.332	.325	.657	96	1	41	4.11	-3	*0-113(4-0-111)	11	-0.9
1967 Cin-N	55	130	19	31	6	2	1	10	14	14	3	1	.238	.313	.338	.651	77	-3	14	3.76	-1	0-39(4-0-35)	3	-0.7
1968 Oak-A	53	81	5	20	5	0	1	14	4	10	0	0	.247	.282	.346	.628	94	-1	8	3.49	0	0-18(18-0-0)	2	-0.1
Bos-A	23	24	1	3	0	0	0	2	3	4	1	0	.125	.250	.125	.375	15	-2	1	1.20	-1	0-10(5-0-5)	0	-0.4
Yr.	76	105	6	23	5	0	1	16	7	14	1	0	.219	.274	.295	.570	75	-3	9	2.90	0	0-28(23-0-5)	2	-0.5
Total 9	1011	3284	458	929	140	36	67	426	408	282	42	21	.283	.367	.409	.775	118	93	517	5.64	-12	0-886	132	2.4
• ROBINSON, Frank	Frank Robinson b: 8/31/1935, Beaumont, TX BR/TR, 6'1", 195 lbs. Deb: 4/17/1956 M/C HOF: 1982 Career OF: 820-99-1281																							
1956 Cin-N★	152	572	**122**	166	27	6	38	83	64	95	8	4	.290	.381	.558	.939	139	33	121	7.52	-3	*0-152(143-10-0)	26	2.1
1957 Cin-N★	150	611	97	197	29	5	29	75	44	92	10	2	.322	.379	.529	.908	131	29	122	7.50	9	*0-136(106-32-1),1-24	27	2.9
1958 Cin-N	148	554	90	149	25	6	31	83	62	80	10	1	.269	.350	.504	.854	116	15	99	6.35	-1	*0-138(83-53-0),3-11	20	0.6
1959 Cin-N★	146	540	106	168	31	4	36	125	69	93	18	8	.311	.397	.583	.980	152	42	122	8.16	-2	*1-125,0-40(40-0-0)	25	3.1
1960 Cin-N	139	464	86	138	33	6	31	83	82	67	13	6	.297	.413	**.595**	**1.007**	169	47	113	**8.51**	3	1-78,0-51(51-0-0)/3-1	23	4.4
1961*Cin-N★	153	545	117	176	32	7	37	124	71	64	22	3	.323	.411	**.611**	**1.022**	164	**55**	137	**9.32**	1	*0-150(52-3-99)/3-1	34	4.7
1962 Cin-N★	162	609	**134**	208	**51**	2	39	136	76	62	18	9	.342	**.424**	**.624**	**1.048**	**171**	**63**	160	**10.08**	1	*0-161(9-0-155)	**41**	5.2
1963 Cin-N	140	482	79	125	19	3	21	91	81	69	26	10	.259	.381	.442	.823	132	26	87	6.21	-1	*0-139(116-1-31)/1-1	23	1.8
1964 Cin-N	156	568	103	174	38	6	29	96	79	67	23	5	.306	.399	.548	.947	158	49	127	8.18	-3	*0-156(77-0-102)	33	3.8
1965 Cin-N★	156	582	109	172	33	5	33	113	70	100	13	9	.296	.388	.540	.928	148	38	120	7.41	-7	*0-155(7-0-152)	26	2.2
1966*Bal-A★	155	576	**122**	182	34	2	**49**	**122**	87	90	8	5	**.316**	**.415**	**.637**	**1.052**	**200**	**77**	146	**9.17**	-4	*0-151(20-0-135)/1-3	**41**	**6.8**
1967 Bal-A★	129	479	83	149	23	7	30	94	71	84	2	3	.311	.408	.576	.984	189	54	113	8.73	-1	*0-126(31-0-95)/1-2	30	5.1
1968 Bal-A	130	421	69	113	27	1	15	52	73	84	11	2	.268	.391	.444	.835	153	33	77	6.32	-4	*0-117(55-0-78)/1-3	24	2.5
1969*Bal-A★	148	539	111	166	19	5	32	100	88	62	9	3	.308	.417	.540	.957	164	51	126	8.68	-1	*0-134(1-0-134),1-19	32	4.4
1970*Bal-A★	132	471	88	144	24	1	25	78	69	70	2	1	.306	.402	.520	.922	151	35	99	7.73	1	*0-120(0-0-120)/1-7	26	3.0
1971*Bal-A★	133	455	82	128	16	2	28	99	72	62	3	0	.281	.390	.510	.900	154	35	88	6.69	-6	0-92(1-0-91),1-37	23	2.4
1972 LA-N	103	342	41	86	6	1	19	59	55	76	2	3	.251	.358	.442	.800	129	14	55	5.42	2	0-95(9-0-88)	14	1.2
1973 Cal-A	147	534	85	142	29	0	30	97	82	93	1	1	.266	.374	.489	.863	153	39	99	6.54	3	*D-127,0-17(17-0-0)	26	3.8
1974 Cal-A★	129	427	75	107	26	2	20	63	75	85	5	1	.251	.375	.461	.836	148	30	77	6.19	0	*D-123/0-1	17	2.8
Cle-A	15	50	6	10	1	1	2	5	10	10	0	1	.200	.333	.380	.713	106	0	7	4.10	-1	D-11/1-4	1	-0.1
Yr.	144	477	81	117	27	3	22	68	85	95	5	2	.245	.371	.453	.823	143	31	84	5.96	-1	*D-134/1-4,0-1	18	2.7
1975 Cle-A	49	118	19	28	5	0	9	24	29	15	0	0	.237	.388	.508	.896	152	9	25	7.19	0	D-42	6	0.8
1976 Cle-A	36	67	5	15	0	0	3	10	11	12	0	0	.224	.333	.358	.692	104	1	8	3.84	0	D-18/1-2,0-1	1	0.0
Total 21	2808	10006	1829	2943	528	72	586	1812	1420	1532	204	77	.294	.392	.537	.929	154	775	2127	7.63	-12	*0-2132,D-321,1-305/3-13	519	63.3
• ROBINSON, Fred	Frederic Henry Robinson b: 7/6/1856, South Acton, MA d: 12/18/1933, Hudson, MA BR/TR Deb: 4/17/1884																							
1884 Cin-U	3	13	1	3	0	0	0	....	0	....	....	....	.231	.231	.231	.462	52	-1	1	1.99	0	/2-3	0	-0.1
• ROBINSON, Jack	John W. "Bridgeport" Robinson b: 7/15/1880, Portland, ME d: 7/22/1921, Macon, GA TR Deb: 9/6/1902																							
1902 NY-N	4	9	0	0	0	0	0	0	0	....	0	....	.000	.000	.000	.000	-101	-2	0	.00	0	/C-3	0	-0.2
• ROBINSON, Jackie	Jack Roosevelt Robinson b: 1/31/1919, Cairo, GA d: 10/24/1972, Stamford, CT BR/TR, 5'11.5", 204 lbs. Deb: 4/15/1947 HOF: 1962 Career OF: 161-0-1																							
1947*Bro-N	151	590	125	175	31	5	12	48	74	36	**29**	....	.297	.383	.427	.810	111	11	104	6.27	-3	*1-151	21	0.3
1948 Bro-N	147	574	108	170	38	8	12	85	57	37	22	....	.296	.367	.453	.820	117	13	99	6.36	12	*2-116,1-30/3-6	25	3.1
1949*Bro-N★	156	593	122	203	38	12	16	124	86	27	**37**	....	**.342**	.432	.528	.960	150	46	135	8.51	11	*2-156	36	**6.5**
1950 Bro-N★	144	518	99	170	39	4	14	81	80	24	12	....	.328	.423	.500	.923	139	33	114	8.34	15	*2-144	29	5.4
1951 Bro-N★	153	548	106	185	33	7	19	88	79	27	25	8	.338	.429	.527	.957	153	46	133	9.29	25	*2-150	38	**8.0**
1952*Bro-N★	149	510	104	157	17	3	19	75	106	40	24	7	.308	**.440**	.465	.904	149	45	116	8.18	18	*2-146	34	**7.4**
1953*Bro-N★	136	484	109	159	34	7	12	95	74	30	17	4	.329	.425	.502	.927	137	33	111	8.54	8	0-76(76-0-0),3-44/2-9,1-6,S	25	3.5
1954 Bro-N★	124	386	62	120	22	4	15	59	63	20	7	3	.311	.417	.505	.922	134	23	83	7.69	2	0-74(73-0-1),3-50/2-4	20	2.1
1955*Bro-N	105	317	51	81	6	2	8	36	61	18	12	3	.256	.381	.363	.743	96	3	49	5.12	14	3-84,0-10(10-0-0)/1-1,2-1	12	1.6
1956*Bro-N	117	357	61	98	15	2	10	43	60	32	12	5	.275	.383	.412	.795	106	6	60	5.67	16	3-72,2-22/1-9,0-2(2-0-0)	17	2.4
Total 10	1382	4877	947	1518	273	54	137	734	740	291	197	30	.311	.410	.474	.883	131	259	1002	7.49	118	2-748,3-256,1-197,0-162/S-1	257	40.2
• ROBINSON, Kerry	Kerry Keith Robinson b: 10/3/1973, St. Louis, MO BL/TL, 6', 175 lbs. Deb: 9/22/1998 Career OF: 134-52-73																							
1998 TB-A	2	3	0	0	0	0	0	0	0	1	0	0	.000	.000	.000	.000	-98	-1	0	.00	-0	/0-2(2-0-0)	0	-0.1
1999 Cin-N	9	1	4	0	0	0	0	0	0	1	0	1	.000	.000	.000	.000	-97	-1	0	.00	0	/0-2(2-0-0)	0	-0.1
2001*StL-N	114	186	34	53	6	1	1	15	12	20	11	2	.285	.335	.344	.679	77	-5	24	4.49	3	0-74(42-22-17)	4	-0.3
2002*StL-N	124	181	27	47	7	4	1	15	11	29	7	4	.260	.302	.359	.661	75	-7	20	3.74	1	0-76(52-10-17)	4	-0.8
2003 StL-N	116	208	19	52	6	3	1	16	8	27	6	1	.250	.281	.322	.603	59	-12	19	3.13	-3	0-88(36-20-39)	3	-1.7
Total 5	365	579	84	152	19	8	3	46	31	78	24	8	.263	.303	.339	.642	69	-25	62	3.72	0	0-242	11	-2.9
• ROBINSON, Rabbit	William Clyde Robinson b: 3/5/1882, Wellsburg, WV d: 4/9/1915, Waterbury, CT BR/TR, 5'6", 148 lbs. Deb: 4/22/1903 Career OF: 7-14-29																							
1903 Was-A	103	373	41	79	10	8	1	20	33	....	16	....	.212	.279	.290	.569	70	-13	36	3.20	2	2-45,0-30(0-14-16),S-24/3-5	6	-1.1
1904 Det-A	101	320	30	77	13	6	0	37	29	....	14	....	.241	.314	.319	.632	103	2	39	4.02	4	S-30,3-26,0-20(7-0-13),2-19	11	0.8
1910 Cin-N	2	7	0	0	0	0	0	1	1	0	0	....	.000	.125	.000	.125	-66	-1	0	.00	0	/3-2	0	-0.1
Total 3	206	700	71	156	23	14	1	58	63	0	30	....	.223	.294	.300	.594	84	-13	75	3.54	6	/2-64,S-54,0-50,3-33	17	-0.5
• ROBINSON, Val	Alfred Valentine "Miley" Robinson b: 8/31/1848, Washington, DC d: 8/2/1896, Washington, DC Deb: 5/1/1872 U																							
1872 Oly-n	7	30	6	6	0	0	0	4	1	1	0	0	.200	.226	.200	.426	34	-2	1	1.79	0	/0-7(0-0-7)	....	-0.1
• ROBINSON, Wilbert	Wilbert "Uncle Robbie" Robinson b: 6/29/1863, Bolton, MA d: 8/8/1934, Atlanta, GA BR/TR, 5'8.5", 215 lbs. Deb: 4/19/1886 M/C/U HOF: 1945 Career OF: 0-5-3																							
1886 Phi-a	87	342	57	69	11	3	1	30	21	....	33	....	.202	.254	.260	.514	61	-16	32	3.14	1	C-61,1-22/0-5(0-4-1)	5	-1.0
1887 Phi-a	68	278	28	74	6	2	1	24	14	....	15	....	.266	.269	.277	.545	52	-17	24	3.21	6	C-67/1-3,0-1	4	-0.5
1888 Phi-a	66	254	32	62	7	2	1	31	9	....	11	....	.244	.270	.299	.569	83	-6	24	3.39	13	C-65/1-1	9	1.2
1889 Phi-a	69	264	31	61	13	2	0	28	6	34	9	....	.231	.251	.295	.546	56	-16	22	2.92	5	C-69	5	-0.5
1890 Phi-a	82	329	32	78	13	4	4	42	16	....	20	....	.237	.279	.337	.616	83	-9	37	3.95	-7	C-82	8	-0.8
Bal-a	14	48	7	13	1	0	0	4	3	....	1	....	.271	.314	.292	.605	72	-2	5	3.65	-1	C-11/1-3	1	-0.2
Yr.	96	377	39	91	14	4	4	46	19	....	21	....	.241	.283	.332	.615	82	-11	42	3.91	-8	*C-93/1-3	9	-1.0
1891 Bal-a	93	334	25	72	8	5	2	46	16	37	18	....	.216	.251	.287	.539	53	-23	29	2.97	-12	C-92/0-1	5	-2.3
1892 Bal-N	90	330	36	88	14	4	2	57	15	35	5	....	.267	.303	.352	.654	95	-4	38	4.19	-5	C-87/1-2,0-1	6	-0.2
1893 Bal-N	95	359	49	120	21	3	3	57	26	22	17	....	.334	.382	.435	.817	115	7	68	7.52	-9	*C-93/1-1	12	0.5
1894*Bal-N	109	414	69	146	21	4	1	98	46	18	12	....	.353	.421	.430	.851	101	2	82	7.96	-7	*C-109	15	0.4
1895*Bal-N	77	282	38	74	19	1	0	48	12	19	11	....	.262	.295	.337	.632	61	-18	33	4.13	5	C-75	6	-0.5
1896*Bal-N	67	245	43	85	9	6	2	38	14	13	9	....	.347	.385	.457	.842	120	6	48	7.77	-9	C-67	9	0.4
1897 Bal-N	48	181	25	57	9	0	0	23	8	....	0	....	.315	.347	.365	.712	88	-3	24	5.01	-5	C-48	4	-0.3
1898 Bal-N	79	289	29	80	12	2	0	38	16	....	3	....	.277	.317	.332	.649	84	-7	33	4.06	-2	C-77	6	-0.2
1899 Bal-N	108	356	40	101	15	2	0	47	31	....	5	....	.284	.344	.337	.682	83	-8	45	4.57	-15	*C-105	6	-1.3

YEAR TM-L	G	AB	R	H	2B	3B	HR	RBI	BB	SO	SB	CS	AVG	OBP	SLG	OPS	OPS+	BR/A	RC	RC/G	FR	G/POS	WS	TPW
1900 StL-N	60	210	26	52	5	1	0	28	11	....	7	....	.248	.291	.281	.572	59	-12	20	3.31	3	C-54	3	-0.3
1901 Bal-A	68	239	32	72	12	3	0	26	10	....	9	....	.301	.335	.377	.711	93	-3	34	5.35	-8	C-67	5	-0.3
1902 Bal-A	91	335	38	98	16	7	1	57	12	....	11	....	.293	.321	.391	.712	93	-5	47	5.19	-9	C-87	7	-0.5
Total 17	**1371**	**5089**	**637**	**1402**	**212**	**51**	**18**	**722**	**286**	**178**	**196**	**....**	**.275**	**.316**	**.346**	**.662**	**82**	**-134**	**645**	**4.61**	**-54**	***C-1316/1-32,0-8**	**116**	**-6.3**
• ROBINSON, Yank	William H. Robinson b: 9/19/1859, Philadelphia, PA d: 8/25/1894, St. Louis, MO BR/TR, 5'6.5", 170 lbs. Deb: 8/24/1882 Career OF: 52-2-2 ♦																							
1882 Det-N	11	39	1	7	1	0	3	2	1	13	....	....	.179	.200	.205	.405	97	-0	3	2.99	-3	S-10/0-1,P-1	0	-0.2
1884 Bal-U	102	415	101	111	24	4	3	....	**37**	....	....	....	.267	.327	.359	.686	120	8	50	4.61	11	3-71,S-14,C-11,P-11/2-3	24	2.1
1885*StL-a	78	287	63	75	8	8	0	35	29	....	....	....	.261	.344	.345	.689	113	5	35	4.44	1	0-52(52-0-0),2-19/C-5,3-2,1	16	0.5
1886*StL-a	133	481	89	132	26	9	3	71	64	....	51	....	.274	.377	.385	.761	132	21	91	7.05	8	*2-125/3-6,0-1,P-1,S-1	20	3.0
1887*StL-a	125	522	102	223	32	4	1	74	92	....	75	....	.427	.445	.405	.850	125	20	114	10.26	4	*2-117/3-6,0-2(0-0-2),S-2,C,P	20	2.3
1888*StL-a	134	455	111	105	17	6	3	53	**116**	....	56	....	.231	**.400**	.314	.714	117	17	82	6.29	-11	*2-102,S-34	21	0.9
1889 StL-a	132	452	97	94	17	3	5	70	**118**	55	39	....	.208	.378	.292	.671	81	-7	66	4.91	-21	*2-132	13	-2.0
1890 Pit-P	98	306	59	70	10	3	0	38	101	33	17	....	.229	.434	.281	.715	101	13	46	5.24	-19	*2-98	10	-0.2
1891 Cin-a	97	342	48	61	9	4	1	37	68	51	23	....	.178	.328	.237	.565	57	-18	35	3.29	-12	*2-97	5	-2.3
StL-a	1	3	0	0	0	0	0	0	0	0	0	....	.000	.000	.000	.000	-87	-1	0	.00	-1	/2-1	0	-0.1
Yr.	98	345	48	61	9	4	1	37	68	51	23	....	.177	.325	.235	.560	56	-19	35	3.26	-13	*2-98	5	-2.4
1892 Was-N	67	218	26	39	4	3	0	19	38	29	11	....	.179	.301	.225	.526	61	-8	18	2.79	-7	3-58/S-5,2-4	2	-1.3
Total 10	**978**	**3520**	**697**	**917**	**148**	**44**	**19**	**399**	**664**	**181**	**272**	**....**	**.261**	**.375**	**.323**	**.698**	**104**	**50**	**540**	**5.60**	**-50**	**2-698,3-143/S-66,0-56,C,P,1**	**131**	**2.6**
• ROBLES, Rafael	Rafael Orlando (Natera) Robles b: 10/20/1947, San Pedro de Macoris, Dominican Republic d: 8/13/1998, New York, NY BR/TR, 6', 170 lbs. Deb: 4/8/1969																							
1969 SD-N	6	20	1	2	0	0	0	0	1	3	1	1	.100	.143	.100	.243	-32	-4	0	.18	-2	/S-6	0	-0.5
1970 SD-N	23	89	5	19	1	0	0	3	5	11	3	0	.213	.263	.225	.488	33	-8	6	2.21	2	S-23	1	-0.3
1972 SD-N	18	24	1	4	0	0	0	0	0	3	0	0	.167	.167	.167	.333	-5	-3	1	.64	-2	S-15/3-1	0	-0.5
Total 3	**47**	**133**	**7**	**25**	**1**	**0**	**0**	**3**	**6**	**17**	**4**	**1**	**.188**	**.229**	**.195**	**.424**	**17**	**-15**	**7**	**1.57**	**-1**	**/S-44,3-1**	**1**	**-1.3**
• ROBLES, Sergio	Sergio (Valenzuela) Robles b: 4/16/1946, Magdalena, Mexico BR/TR, 6'2", 190 lbs. Deb: 8/27/1972																							
1972 Bal-A	2	5	0	1	0	0	0	0	0	0	0	0	.200	.200	.200	.400	19	-1	0	1.35	-0	/C-1	0	-0.1
1973 Bal-A	8	13	0	1	0	0	0	0	3	1	0	0	.077	.250	.077	.327	-4	-2	0	1.00	0	/C-8	0	-0.2
1976 LA-N	6	3	0	0	0	0	0	0	0	2	0	0	.000	.000	.000	.000	-102	-1	0	.00	-1	/C-6	0	-0.2
Total 3	**16**	**21**	**0**	**2**	**0**	**0**	**0**	**0**	**3**	**3**	**0**	**0**	**.095**	**.208**	**.095**	**.304**	**-12**	**-3**	**1**	**.92**	**-1**	**/C-15**	**0**	**-0.4**
• ROBSON, Tom	Thomas James Robson b: 1/15/1946, Rochester, NY BR/TR, 6'3", 215 lbs. Deb: 9/14/1974 C																							
1974 Tex-A	6	13	2	3	1	0	0	2	4	3	0	0	.231	.412	.308	.719	112	1	2	4.37	0	/D-5,1-1	0	0.0
1975 Tex-A	17	35	3	7	0	0	0	2	1	3	0	0	.200	.222	.200	.422	20	-4	1	1.10	0	/1-5,D-4	0	-0.4
Total 2	**23**	**48**	**5**	**10**	**1**	**0**	**0**	**4**	**5**	**6**	**0**	**0**	**.208**	**.283**	**.229**	**.512**	**49**	**-3**	**3**	**1.95**	**0**	**/D-9,1-6**	**0**	**-0.4**
• ROCAP, Adam	Adam Rocap b: 1854, Philadelphia, PA d: 3/26/1892, Philadelphia, PA, 5'9", 170 lbs. Deb: 5/5/1875 U																							
1875 Ath-n	16	69	13	12	1	0	0	4	1	7	3	2	.174	.186	.188	.374	27	-6	3	1.52	-2	0-12(0-5-7)/2-4	....	-0.6
• ROCCO, Mickey	Michael Dominick Rocco b: 3/2/1916, St. Paul, MN d: 6/1/1997, St. Paul, MN BL/TL, 5'11", 188 lbs. Deb: 6/5/1943																							
1943 Cle-A	108	405	43	97	14	4	5	46	51	40	1	2	.240	.328	.331	.658	99	0	47	3.89	-4	*1-108	11	-1.1
1944 Cle-A	155	653	87	174	29	7	13	70	56	51	4	8	.266	.325	.392	.717	108	3	84	4.45	8	*1-155	15	0.3
1945 Cle-A	143	565	81	149	28	6	10	56	52	40	0	4	.264	.326	.388	.713	111	5	72	4.38	8	*1-141	15	0.6
1946 Cle-A	34	98	8	24	2	0	2	14	15	15	1	1	.245	.345	.327	.672	94	-0	12	4.06	4	1-27	3	0.3
Total 4	**440**	**1721**	**219**	**444**	**73**	**17**	**30**	**186**	**174**	**146**	**6**	**15**	**.258**	**.327**	**.372**	**.700**	**106**	**8**	**215**	**4.27**	**16**	**1-431**	**44**	**0.2**
• ROCHE, Jack	John Joseph "Red" Roche b: 11/22/1890, Los Angeles, CA d: 3/30/1983, Peoria, AZ BR/TR, 6'1", 178 lbs. Deb: 5/24/1914																							
1914 StL-N	12	9	1	6	2	1	0	3	0	1	1	....	.667	.700	1.111	1.811	441	4	7	64.13	-4	/C-9	2	0.0
1915 StL-N	46	39	2	8	0	1	0	6	4	8	1	....	.205	.295	.256	.552	67	-1	3	2.80	0	/C-4	1	-0.2
1917 StL-N	1	1	0	0	0	0	0	0	0	0	0	....	.000	.000	.000	.000	-103	-0	0	.00	-1	/C-1	0	-0.1
Total 3	**59**	**49**	**3**	**14**	**2**	**2**	**0**	**9**	**4**	**9**	**2**	**....**	**.286**	**.364**	**.408**	**.772**	**131**	**2**	**11**	**7.83**	**-5**	**/C-14**	**3**	**-0.3**
• ROCHEFORT, Ben	Bennett Harold Rochefort b: 8/15/1896, Camden, NJ d: 4/2/1981, Red Bank, NJ BL/TR, 6'2", 185 lbs. Deb: 10/3/1914																							
1914 Phi-A	1	2	0	1	0	0	0	0	0	1	0	....	.500	.500	.500	1.000	209	0	1	13.25	0	/1-1	0	0.1
• ROCHELLI, Lou	Louis Joseph Rochelli b: 1/11/1919, Staunton, IL d: 10/23/1992, Victoria, TX BR/TR, 6'1", 175 lbs. Deb: 8/25/1944																							
1944 Bro-N	5	17	0	3	0	1	0	2	2	6	0	....	.176	.263	.294	.557	58	-1	1	2.80	0	/2-5	0	-0.1
• ROCK, Les	Lester Henry Rock b: 8/19/1912, Springfield, MN d: 9/9/1991, Davis, CA BL/TR, 6'2", 184 lbs. Deb: 9/11/1936																							
1936 Chi-A	2	1	0	0	0	0	0	1	0	0	0	0	.000	.000	.000	.000	-97	-0	0	.00	0	/1-2	0	0.0
• ROCKENFIELD, Ike	Isaac Broc Rockenfield b: 11/3/1876, Omaha, NE d: 2/21/1927, San Diego, CA BR/TR, 5'7", 150 lbs. Deb: 5/5/1905																							
1905 StL-A	95	322	40	70	12	0	0	16	46	....	11	....	.217	.340	.255	.595	95	2	36	3.48	-20	2-95	8	-1.9
1906 StL-A	27	89	3	21	4	0	0	8	1	....	0	....	.236	.277	.281	.557	78	-2	8	2.80	-3	2-26	1	-0.6
Total 2	**122**	**411**	**43**	**91**	**16**	**0**	**0**	**24**	**47**	**....**	**11**	**....**	**.221**	**.328**	**.260**	**.588**	**91**	**-0**	**44**	**3.34**	**-23**	**2-121**	**9**	**-2.5**
• ROCKETT, Pat	Patrick Edward Rockett b: 1/9/1955, San Antonio, TX BR/TR, 5'11", 170 lbs. Deb: 9/17/1976																							
1976 Atl-N	4	5	0	1	0	0	0	0	0	1	0	0	.200	.200	.200	.400	13	-1	0	1.35	-1	/S-2	0	-0.1
1977 Atl-N	93	264	27	67	10	0	1	24	27	32	1	2	.254	.330	.303	.633	63	-13	26	3.42	-13	S-84	3	-1.8
1978 Atl-N	55	142	6	20	2	0	0	4	13	12	1	2	.141	.213	.155	.368	4	-19	4	.85	-7	S-51	1	-2.3
Total 3	**152**	**411**	**33**	**88**	**12**	**0**	**1**	**28**	**40**	**45**	**2**	**4**	**.214**	**.289**	**.251**	**.539**	**43**	**-33**	**31**	**2.41**	**-20**	**S-137**	**4**	**-4.2**
• RODGERS, Andre	Kenneth Andre Ian "Andy" Rodgers b: 12/2/1934, Nassau, Bahamas BR/TR, 6'3", 200 lbs. Deb: 4/16/1957 Career OF: 5-0-2																							
1957 NY-N	32	86	8	21	2	1	3	9	9	21	0	0	.244	.323	.395	.718	92	-1	12	4.85	-1	S-20/3-8	3	-0.1
1958 SF-N	22	63	7	13	3	1	2	11	4	14	0	0	.206	.254	.381	.635	67	-3	6	2.80	-2	S-18	1	-0.4
1959 SF-N	71	228	32	57	12	1	6	24	32	50	2	1	.250	.345	.390	.735	97	-0	32	4.73	-7	S-66	7	-0.1
1960 SF-N	81	217	22	53	8	5	2	22	24	44	1	1	.244	.328	.355	.683	92	-2	25	3.84	1	S-41,3-21/1-6,0-2(2-0-0)	6	0.1
1961 Chi-N	73	214	27	57	17	0	6	23	25	54	1	1	.266	.346	.430	.776	103	1	31	5.09	-2	1-42,S-24/0-2(0-0-2),2-1	5	-0.2
1962 Chi-N	138	461	40	128	20	8	5	44	44	93	5	6	.278	.344	.388	.733	93	-6	60	4.54	-7	*S-133/1-1	10	-0.2
1963 Chi-N	150	516	51	118	17	4	5	33	65	90	5	7	.229	.325	.306	.632	79	-13	52	3.26	-18	*S-150	11	-1.9
1964 Chi-N	129	448	50	107	17	3	12	46	53	88	5	1	.239	.319	.371	.690	90	-4	55	4.11	-9	*S-126	11	-0.3
1965 Pit-N	75	178	17	51	12	0	2	25	18	28	2	1	.287	.352	.388	.740	108	2	24	4.64	-1	S-33,3-15/1-6,2-1	6	0.3
1966 Pit-N	36	49	6	9	1	0	0	4	8	7	0	1	.184	.298	.204	.502	43	-4	3	1.70	-2	/S-5,3-3,0-3(3-0-0),1-2	0	-0.5
1967 Pit-N	47	61	8	14	3	0	2	4	8	18	1	1	.230	.319	.377	.696	98	-0	7	3.68	1	/1-9,3-5,S-3,2-2	1	0.1
Total 11	**854**	**2521**	**268**	**628**	**112**	**23**	**45**	**245**	**290**	**507**	**22**	**20**	**.249**	**.331**	**.365**	**.696**	**90**	**-30**	**305**	**4.08**	**-48**	**S-619/1-66,3-52,0-7,2-4**	**61**	**-3.2**
• RODGERS, Bill	William Sherman Rodgers b: 12/5/1922, Harrisburg, PA BL/TL, 6', 162 lbs. Deb: 9/27/1944																							
1944 Pit-N	2	4	1	1	0	0	0	0	0	1	0	....	.250	.250	.250	.500	39	-0	0	2.25	0	/0-1	0	-0.1
1945 Pit-N	1	1	0	1	0	0	0	0	0	0	0	....	1.000	1.000	1.000	2.000	440	0	1	∞	0	....	0	0.0
Total 2	**3**	**5**	**1**	**2**	**0**	**0**	**0**	**0**	**0**	**1**	**0**	**....**	**.400**	**.400**	**.400**	**.800**	**119**	**0**	**1**	**2.25**	**0**	**/0-1**	**0**	**0.0**
• RODGERS, Bill	Wilbur Kincaid "Rawmeat Bill" Rodgers b: 4/18/1887, Pleasant Ridge, OH d: 12/24/1978, Goliad, TX BL/TR, 5'9.5", 170 lbs. Deb: 4/15/1915																							
1915 Cle-A	16	45	8	14	2	0	0	7	8	7	3	3	.311	.415	.356	.771	128	1	7	5.15	-3	2-13	1	-0.2
Bos-A	11	6	2	0	0	0	0	0	3	2	0	....	.000	.333	.000	.333		-0	0	.00	0	/2-6	0	-0.1
Yr.	27	51	10	14	2	0	0	7	11	9	3	3	.275	.403	.314	.717	110	1	7	4.41	-3	2-19	1	-0.2
Cin-N	72	213	20	51	13	4	0	12	11	29	8	5	.239	.299	.338	.637	91	-3	22	3.47	4	2-56/S-6,3-1,0-1	6	0.3
1916 Cin-N	3	4	0	0	0	0	0	0	0	2	0	....	.000	.000	.000	.000	-102	-1	0	.00	-0	/S-1	0	-0.1
Total 2	**102**	**268**	**30**	**65**	**15**	**4**	**0**	**19**	**22**	**40**	**11**	**8**	**.243**	**.316**	**.328**	**.645**	**92**	**-3**	**29**	**3.59**	**1**	**/2-75,S-7,3-1,0-1**	**7**	**0.0**

YEAR TM-L	G	AB	R	H	2B	3B	HR	RBI	BB	SO	SB	CS	AVG	OBP	SLG	OPS	OPS+	BR/A	RC	RC/G	FR	G/POS	WS	TPW
• RODGERS, Buck	Robert Leroy Rodgers b: 8/16/1938, Delaware, OH BB/TR, 6'2", 195 lbs. Deb: 9/8/1961 M/C																							
1961 LA-A	16	56	8	18	2	0	2	13	1	6	0	0	.321	.333	.464	.798	99	-0	7	4.85	0	C-14	1	0.1
1962 LA-A	155	565	65	146	34	6	6	61	45	68	1	8	.258	.313	.372	.685	86	-15	61	3.60	2	*C-150	15	-0.6
1963 LA-A	100	300	24	70	6	0	4	23	29	35	2	2	.233	.305	.293	.598	73	-11	28	3.03	3	C-85	6	-0.4
1964 LA-A	148	514	38	125	18	3	4	54	40	71	4	3	.243	.303	.313	.616	80	-15	47	3.03	6	*C-146	14	-0.1
1965 Cal-A	132	411	33	86	14	3	1	32	35	61	4	5	.209	.276	.265	.541	56	-25	28	2.13	-1	*C-128	6	-2.1
1966 Cal-A	133	454	45	107	20	3	7	48	29	57	3	4	.236	.285	.339	.624	81	-13	41	3.03	-2	*C-133	12	-0.9
1967 Cal-A	139	429	29	94	13	3	6	41	34	55	1	4	.219	.280	.305	.585	75	-15	35	2.60	0	*C-134/O-1	10	-0.8
1968 Cal-A	91	258	13	49	6	0	1	14	16	48	2	1	.190	.245	.225	.470	45	-17	15	1.81	2	C-87	3	-1.2
1969 Cal-A	18	46	4	9	1	0	0	2	5	8	0	0	.196	.288	.217	.506	45	-3	3	2.38	1	C-18	1	-0.1
Total 9	932	3033	259	704	114	18	31	288	234	409	17	27	.232	.291	.312	.603	73	-114	265	2.86	14	C-895/O-1	68	-6.1
• RODIN, Eric	Eric Chapman Rodin b: 2/5/1930, Orange, NJ d: 1/4/1991, Somerville, NJ BR/TR, 6'2", 215 lbs. Deb: 9/7/1954																							
1954 NY-N	5	6	0	0	0	0	0	0	0	2	0	0	.000	.000	.000	.000	-99	-2	0	.00	-0	/O-3(0-2-1)	0	-0.2
• RODRIGUEZ, Alex	Alexander Emmanuel "A-Rod" Rodriguez b: 7/27/1975, New York, NY BR/TR, 6'3", 190 lbs. Deb: 7/8/1994																							
1994 Sea-A	17	54	4	11	0	0	0	2	3	20	3	0	.204	.246	.204	.449	17	-6	3	2.05	-3	S-17	0	-0.7
1995*Sea-A	48	142	15	33	6	2	5	19	6	42	4	2	.232	.264	.408	.672	71	-7	15	3.72	-4	S-46/D-1	2	-0.7
1996 Sea-A★	146	601	**141**	215	**54**	1	36	123	59	104	15	4	**.358**	.419	.631	1.049	160	56	157	10.12	7	*S-146	**34**	**6.9**
1997*Sea-A★	141	587	100	176	40	3	23	84	41	99	29	6	.300	.351	.496	.846	119	18	101	6.28	-2	*S-140/D-1	22	2.7
1998 Sea-A★	161	686	123	**213**	35	5	42	124	45	121	46	13	.310	.362	.560	.921	135	37	138	7.40	-2	*S-160/D-1	30	4.5
1999 Sea-A	129	502	110	143	25	0	42	111	56	109	21	7	.285	.362	.586	.948	134	25	105	7.33	6	*S-129	23	3.8
2000*Sea-A★	148	554	134	175	34	2	41	132	100	121	15	4	.316	.427	.606	1.033	167	61	150	10.02	15	*S-148	37	**8.1**
2001 Tex-A★	162	632	**133**	201	34	1	**52**	135	75	131	18	3	.318	.404	.622	1.026	159	58	159	9.36	4	*S-161/D-1	37	**7.2**
2002 Tex-A★	162	624	125	187	27	2	**57**	**142**	87	122	9	4	.300	.394	.623	1.017	156	52	153	9.02	0	*S-162	**35**	**6.2**
2003 Tex-A★	161	607	**124**	181	30	6	**47**	118	87	126	17	3	.298	.399	**.600**	.999	146	44	148	8.84	-7	*S-158/D-1	31	4.8
Total 10	1275	4989	1009	1535	285	22	345	990	559	995	177	46	.308	.385	.581	.966	144	338	1131	8.30	13	*S-1267/D-5	251	42.6
• RODRIGUEZ, Aurelio	Aurelio (Ituarte) Rodriguez b: 12/28/1947, Cananea, Mexico d: 9/23/2000, Detroit, MI BR/TR, 5'10", 180 lbs. Deb: 9/1/1967																							
1967 Cal-A	29	130	14	31	3	1	1	8	2	21	1	0	.238	.250	.300	.550	64	-6	10	2.61	5	3-29	2	-0.2
1968 Cal-A	76	223	14	54	10	1	1	16	17	36	0	2	.242	.299	.309	.608	88	-4	19	2.96	-4	3-70/2-2	4	-0.9
1969 Cal-A	159	561	47	130	17	2	7	49	32	88	5	3	.232	.276	.307	.582	66	-27	45	2.68	7	*3-159	9	-2.2
1970 Cal-A	17	63	6	17	2	2	0	7	3	6	0	1	.270	.313	.365	.679	90	-1	6	3.56	4	3-17	2	0.2
Was-A	142	547	64	135	31	5	19	76	37	81	15	5	.247	.303	.426	.729	104	2	67	4.11	5	*3-136/S-7	15	0.7
Yr.	159	610	70	152	33	7	19	83	40	87	15	6	.249	.304	.420	.724	102	0	73	4.05	8	*3-153/S-7	17	0.9
1971 Det-A	154	604	68	153	30	7	15	39	27	93	4	6	.253	.289	.401	.689	90	-12	65	3.66	9	*3-153/S-1	14	-0.3
1972*Det-A	153	601	65	142	23	5	13	56	28	104	2	3	.236	.273	.356	.629	83	-15	55	3.06	25	*3-153/S-2	14	1.0
1973 Det-A	160	555	46	123	27	3	9	58	31	85	3	1	.222	.267	.330	.596	63	-28	48	2.89	11	*3-160/S-1	9	-1.8
1974 Det-A	159	571	54	127	23	5	5	49	26	70	2	0	.222	.258	.306	.564	60	-30	43	2.45	19	*3-159	8	-1.2
1975 Det-A	151	507	47	124	20	6	13	60	30	63	1	1	.245	.287	.385	.671	85	-12	55	3.71	13	*3-151	13	0.0
1976 Det-A	128	480	40	115	13	2	8	50	19	61	0	4	.240	.270	.325	.595	71	-21	37	2.45	2	*3-128	5	-2.0
1977 Det-A	96	306	30	67	14	1	10	32	16	36	1	1	.219	.258	.369	.627	65	-16	27	2.92	13	3-95/S-1	5	-0.3
1978 Det-A	134	385	40	102	25	2	7	43	19	37	0	1	.265	.305	.395	.699	93	-5	44	3.99	1	*3-131	10	-0.5
1979 Det-A	106	343	27	87	18	0	5	36	11	40	0	2	.254	.279	.350	.629	66	-18	31	3.03	7	*3-106/1-1	6	-1.1
1980 SD-N	89	175	7	35	7	2	2	13	6	26	1	1	.200	.227	.297	.524	48	-13	11	1.92	0	3-88/S-2	1	-1.4
*NY-A	52	164	14	36	6	1	3	14	7	35	0	0	.220	.251	.323	.575	57	-10	12	2.21	-4	3-49/2-6	1	-1.4
1981*NY-A	27	52	4	18	2	0	2	8	2	10	0	0	.346	.370	.500	.870	151	3	9	7.01	1	3-20/2-3,D-2,1-1	2	0.4
1982 Chi-A	118	257	24	62	15	1	3	31	11	35	0	0	.241	.275	.342	.618	68	-12	23	2.96	-8	*3-112/2-3,S-2	3	-2.0
1983 Bal-A	45	67	0	8	0	0	0	2	0	13	0	0	.119	.132	.119	.252	-31	-12	1	.53	0	3-45	1	-1.2
*Chi-A	22	20	1	4	1	0	1	1	0	3	0	0	.200	.200	.400	.600	58	-1	1	1.83	2	3-22	0	0.1
Yr.	67	87	1	12	1	0	1	3	0	16	0	0	.138	.148	.184	.332	-10	-13	2	.82	2	3-67	1	-1.2
Total 17	2017	6611	612	1570	287	46	124	648	324	943	35	31	.237	.276	.351	.627	75	-239	610	3.07	109	*3-1983/S-16,2-14,1-2,D-2	124	-14.3
• RODRIGUEZ, Carlos	Carlos (Marquez) Rodriguez b: 11/1/1967, Mexico City, Mexico BB/TR, 5'9", 160 lbs. Deb: 6/16/1991																							
1991 NY-A	15	37	1	7	0	0	0	2	1	2	0	0	.189	.211	.189	.400	11	-4	1	.79	0	S-11/2-3	1	-0.3
1994 Bos-A	57	174	15	50	14	1	1	13	11	13	1	0	.287	.330	.397	.726	82	-5	23	4.63	3	S-32,2-20/3-4	6	0.1
1995 Bos-A	13	30	5	10	2	0	0	5	2	2	0	0	.333	.394	.400	.794	104	0	5	6.08	0	/2-7,S-6,3-1	1	0.1
Total 3	85	241	21	67	16	1	1	20	14	17	1	0	.278	.320	.365	.685	75	-9	29	4.12	3	/S-49,2-30,3-5	8	-0.1
• RODRIGUEZ, Edwin	Edwin (Morales) Rodriguez b: 8/14/1960, Ponce, Puerto Rico BR/TR, 5'11", 175 lbs. Deb: 9/28/1982																							
1982 NY-A	3	9	2	3	0	0	0	1	1	1	0	0	.333	.400	.333	.733	106	0	1	5.87	0	/2-3	0	0.0
1983 SD-N	7	12	1	2	1	0	0	0	1	3	0	0	.167	.231	.250	.481	34	-1	1	1.99	-1	/2-5,S-2,3-1	0	-0.2
1985 SD-N	1	1	0	0	0	0	0	0	0	0	0	0	.000	.000	.000	.000	-102	-0	0	.00	0	....	0	0.0
Total 3	11	22	3	5	1	0	0	1	2	4	0	0	.227	.292	.273	.564	57	-1	2	3.17	-1	/2-8,S-2,3-1	0	-0.2
• RODRIGUEZ, Ellie	Eliseo (Delgado) Rodriguez b: 5/24/1946, Fajardo, Puerto Rico BR/TR, 5'11", 185 lbs. Deb: 5/26/1968																							
1968 NY-A	9	24	1	5	0	0	0	1	3	3	0	0	.208	.296	.208	.505	57	-1	2	2.43	0	/C-9	1	-0.1
1969 KC-A★	95	267	27	63	10	0	2	20	31	26	3	2	.236	.333	.296	.629	77	-7	27	3.37	-1	C-90	5	-0.5
1970 KC-A	80	231	25	52	8	2	1	15	27	35	2	1	.225	.317	.290	.607	68	-9	21	2.86	2	C-75	4	-0.3
1971 Mil-A	115	319	28	67	10	1	1	30	41	51	1	1	.210	.315	.257	.572	64	-13	27	2.65	8	*C-114	8	0.0
1972 Mil-A★	116	355	31	101	14	2	2	35	52	43	1	4	.285	.386	.352	.739	123	12	51	5.02	-3	*C-114	17	1.6
1973 Mil-A	94	290	30	78	8	1	0	30	41	28	4	3	.269	.378	.303	.682	96	1	36	4.21	3	C-75,D-14	9	0.8
1974 Cal-A	140	395	48	100	20	0	7	36	69	56	4	5	.253	.376	.357	.733	119	13	56	4.74	2	*C-137/D-1	18	2.2
1975 Cal-A	90	226	20	53	6	0	3	27	49	37	2	2	.235	.384	.301	.685	103	5	30	4.21	-2	C-90	9	0.6
1976 LA-N	36	66	10	14	0	0	0	9	19	12	0	0	.212	.409	.212	.621	82	0	8	3.86	2	C-33	3	0.4
Total 9	775	2173	220	533	76	6	16	203	332	291	17	18	.245	.359	.308	.667	95	1	258	3.91	11	C-737/D-15	74	4.7
• RODRIGUEZ, Hector	Hector Antonio (Ordenana) "Oh Henry!" Rodriguez b: 6/13/1920, Alquizar, Cuba BR/TR, 5'8", 165 lbs. Deb: 4/15/1952																							
1952 Chi-A	124	407	55	108	14	0	1	40	47	22	7	6	.265	.346	.307	.653	82	-9	45	3.82	12	*3-113	11	0.3
• RODRIGUEZ, Henry	Henry Anderson (Lorenzo) Rodriguez b: 11/8/1967, Santo Domingo, Dominican Republic BL/TL, 6'1", 200 lbs. Deb: 7/5/1992 Career OF: 682-0-95																							
1992 LA-N	53	146	11	32	7	0	3	14	8	30	0	0	.219	.260	.329	.589	67	-7	12	2.85	2	O-48(17-0-31)/1-1	1	-0.6
1993 LA-N	76	176	20	39	10	0	8	23	11	39	1	0	.222	.267	.415	.682	84	-5	20	3.87	0	O-48(26-0-23),1-13	3	-0.7
1994 LA-N	104	306	33	82	14	2	8	49	17	58	0	1	.268	.311	.405	.716	91	-6	36	4.08	0	O-86(85-0-6),1-17	9	-0.9
1995 LA-N	21	80	6	21	4	1	1	10	5	17	0	1	.263	.306	.375	.681	86	-2	8	3.41	0	O-20(0-0-20)/1-1	1	-0.4
Mon-N	24	58	7	12	0	0	1	5	6	11	0	0	.207	.281	.259	.540	42	-5	4	2.32	0	1-10/O-8(4-0-4)	0	-0.6
Yr.	45	138	13	33	4	1	2	15	11	28	0	1	.239	.295	.326	.621	67	-7	12	2.93	0	O-28(4-0-24),1-11	1	-1.0
1996 Mon-N★	145	532	81	147	42	1	36	103	37	160	2	0	.276	.327	.562	.889	126	16	95	6.46	-5	O-90(89-0-2),1-51	19	0.4
1997 Mon-N	132	476	55	116	28	3	26	83	42	149	3	3	.244	.308	.479	.787	103	-2	70	5.06	-1	*O-126(126-0-1)/1-3	16	-0.8
1998*Chi-N	128	415	56	104	21	1	31	85	54	113	1	3	.251	.337	.530	.867	119	9	74	6.16	9	*O-114(114-0-0)/D-5	16	1.3
1999 Chi-N	130	447	72	136	29	0	26	87	56	113	2	4	.304	.382	.544	.925	132	20	91	7.60	-1	*O-123(123-0-0)/D-2	17	1.3
2000 Chi-N	76	259	37	65	15	1	18	51	22	76	1	2	.251	.317	.525	.842	110	2	42	5.61	0	O-70(70-0-1)	8	-0.1
Fla-N	36	108	10	29	6	0	2	10	14	23	0	0	.269	.358	.380	.737	91	-1	16	5.30	-1	O-29(24-0-6)	3	-0.3
Yr.	112	367	47	94	21	1	20	61	36	99	1	2	.256	.329	.482	.812	104	0	58	5.52	-1	O-99(94-0-7)	11	-0.5
2001 NY-A	5	8	0	0	0	0	0	0	0	6	0	0	.000	.000	.000	.000	-99	-2	0	.00	0	/D-1	0	-0.2
2002 Mon-N	20	20	1	1	0	0	0	3	4	8	0	0	.050	.208	.050	.258	-26	-4	1	.69	-1	/O-5(4-0-1)	0	-0.5
Total 11	950	3031	389	784	176	9	160	523	276	803	10	14	.259	.323	.481	.804	107	14	470	5.42	2	O-767/1-96,D-8	93	-2.0
• RODRIGUEZ, Ivan	Ivan (Torres) "Pudge,I-Rod" Rodriguez b: 11/27/1971, Manati, Puerto Rico BR/TR, 5'9", 205 lbs. Deb: 6/20/1991																							
1991 Tex-A	88	280	24	74	16	0	3	27	5	42	0	1	.264	.277	.354	.631	75	-11	24	2.95	6	C-88	6	0.0

YEAR TM-L	G	AB	R	H	2B	3B	HR	RBI	BB	SO	SB	CS	AVG	OBP	SLG	OPS	OPS+	BR/A	RC	RC/G	FR	G/POS	WS	TPW
1992 Tex-A★	123	420	39	109	16	1	8	37	24	73	0	0	.260	.301	.360	.661	87	-8	42	3.42	10	*C-116/D-2	13	0.9
1993 Tex-A★	137	473	56	129	28	4	10	66	29	70	8	7	.273	.320	.412	.732	99	-3	57	4.07	1	*C-134/D-1	15	0.7
1994 Tex-A★	99	363	56	108	19	1	16	57	31	42	6	3	.298	.364	.488	.852	117	9	63	6.22	0	C-99	15	1.5
1995 Tex-A★	130	492	56	149	32	2	12	67	16	48	0	2	.303	.330	.449	.779	98	-4	69	5.15	3	*C-127/D-1	16	0.7
1996*Tex-A★	153	639	116	192	47	3	19	86	38	55	5	0	.300	.344	.473	.816	98	-2	101	5.85	7	*C-146/D-6	23	1.3
1997 Tex-A★	150	597	98	187	34	4	20	77	38	89	7	3	.313	.362	.484	.846	112	10	100	6.19	5	*C-143/D-5	26	2.4
1998*Tex-A★	145	579	88	186	40	4	21	91	32	88	9	0	.321	.360	.513	.873	119	16	102	6.68	4	*C-139/D-6	27	2.8
1999*Tex-A★	144	600	116	199	29	1	35	113	24	64	25	12	.332	.358	.558	.917	124	18	102	6.16	7	*C-141/D-1	28	3.3
2000 Tex-A★	91	363	66	126	27	4	27	83	19	48	5	5	.347	.381	.667	1.048	156	27	80	8.17	4	C-87/D-1	19	3.4
2001 Tex-A★	111	442	70	136	24	2	25	65	23	73	10	3	.308	.348	.541	.888	125	15	78	6.56	12	*C-106/D-5	18	3.2
2002 Tex-A	108	408	67	128	32	2	19	60	25	71	5	4	.314	.356	.542	.898	127	14	73	6.52	3	*C-100/D-6	11	2.3
2003*Fla-N	144	511	90	152	36	3	16	85	55	92	10	6	.297	.372	.474	.846	124	18	87	6.01	-4	*C-138/D-1	25	2.2
Total 13	1623	6167	942	1875	380	31	231	914	359	855	90	46	.304	.347	.488	.835	113	98	979	5.73	58	*C-1564/D-35	242	24.7

• RODRIGUEZ, Jose Jose "El Hombre Goma" Rodriguez b: 2/23/1894, Havana, Cuba d: 1/21/1953, Havana, Cuba BR/TR, 5'8", 150 lbs. Deb: 10/5/1916

YEAR TM-L	G	AB	R	H	2B	3B	HR	RBI	BB	SO	SB	CS	AVG	OBP	SLG	OPS	OPS+	BR/A	RC	RC/G	FR	G/POS	WS	TPW
1916 NY-N	1	0	0	0	0	0	0	0	0	0	0	....	....	....	....	....	-106	0	0	....	0	....	0	0.0
1917 NY-N	7	20	2	4	0	1	0	2	2	1	2	....	.200	.273	.300	.573	78	-1	2	3.19	-1	/1-7	0	-0.1
1918 NY-N	50	125	15	20	0	2	0	15	12	3	6	....	.160	.239	.192	.431	33	-10	7	1.68	-2	2-40/1-8,3-2	1	-1.2
Total 3	58	145	17	24	0	3	0	17	14	4	8	....	.166	.244	.207	.451	39	-10	9	1.87	-3	/2-40,1-15,3-2	1	-1.4

• RODRIGUEZ, Liu Liubiemithz Rodriguez b: 11/5/1976, Caracas, Venezuela BB/TR, 5'9", 170 lbs. Deb: 6/9/1999

YEAR TM-L	G	AB	R	H	2B	3B	HR	RBI	BB	SO	SB	CS	AVG	OBP	SLG	OPS	OPS+	BR/A	RC	RC/G	FR	G/POS	WS	TPW
1999 Chi-A	39	93	8	22	2	2	1	12	12	11	0	0	.237	.343	.333	.676	73	-3	11	3.59	-2	2-22,S-14/3-1	3	-0.3

• RODRIGUEZ, Ruben Ruben Dario (Martinez) Rodriguez b: 8/4/1964, Cabrera, Dominican Republic BR/TR, 6', 190 lbs. Deb: 9/15/1986

YEAR TM-L	G	AB	R	H	2B	3B	HR	RBI	BB	SO	SB	CS	AVG	OBP	SLG	OPS	OPS+	BR/A	RC	RC/G	FR	G/POS	WS	TPW
1986 Pit-N	2	3	0	0	0	0	0	0	0	1	0	0	.000	.000	.000	.000	-98	-1	0	.00	0	/C-2	0	-0.1
1988 Pit-N	2	5	1	1	0	1	0	1	0	2	0	0	.200	.200	.600	.800	123	0	1	4.05	0	/C-2	0	0.0
Total 2	4	8	1	1	0	1	0	1	0	3	0	0	.125	.125	.375	.500	40	-1	1	2.31	0	/C-4	0	-0.1

• RODRIGUEZ, Steve Steven James Rodriguez b: 11/29/1970, Las Vegas, NV BR/TR, 5'8", 170 lbs. Deb: 4/30/1995

YEAR TM-L	G	AB	R	H	2B	3B	HR	RBI	BB	SO	SB	CS	AVG	OBP	SLG	OPS	OPS+	BR/A	RC	RC/G	FR	G/POS	WS	TPW
1995 Bos-A	6	8	1	1	0	0	0	0	1	1	1	0	.125	.222	.125	.347	-6	-1	0	1.53	-2	/S-4,2-1,D-1	0	-0.2
Det-A	12	31	4	6	1	0	0	0	5	9	1	2	.194	.306	.226	.531	41	-3	2	1.88	-1	2-12/S-1	0	-0.4
Yr.	18	39	5	7	1	0	0	0	6	10	2	2	.179	.289	.205	.494	32	-4	2	1.81	-3	2-13/S-5,D-1	0	-0.6

• RODRIGUEZ, Tony Luis Antonio Rodriguez b: 8/15/1970, Rio Piedras, Puerto Rico BR/TR, 5'11", 165 lbs. Deb: 7/6/1996

YEAR TM-L	G	AB	R	H	2B	3B	HR	RBI	BB	SO	SB	CS	AVG	OBP	SLG	OPS	OPS+	BR/A	RC	RC/G	FR	G/POS	WS	TPW
1996 Bos-A	27	67	7	16	1	0	1	9	4	8	0	0	.239	.292	.299	.590	49	-5	6	2.56	-1	S-21/3-5	1	-0.4

• RODRIGUEZ, Vic Victor Manuel (Rivera) Rodriguez b: 7/14/1961, New York, NY BR/TR, 5'11", 173 lbs. Deb: 9/5/1984

YEAR TM-L	G	AB	R	H	2B	3B	HR	RBI	BB	SO	SB	CS	AVG	OBP	SLG	OPS	OPS+	BR/A	RC	RC/G	FR	G/POS	WS	TPW
1984 Bal-A	11	17	4	7	3	0	0	2	0	2	0	0	.412	.412	.588	1.000	177	2	4	11.12	-1	/2-7,D-1	1	0.1
1989 Min-A	6	11	2	5	2	0	0	0	0	1	0	0	.455	.455	.636	1.091	191	1	3	14.32	0	/3-5,D-1	0	0.1
Total 2	17	28	6	12	5	0	0	2	0	3	0	0	.429	.429	.607	1.036	183	3	7	12.32	-1	/2-7,3-5,D-2	1	0.2

• ROENICKE, Gary Gary Steven Roenicke b: 12/5/1954, Covina, CA BR/TR, 6'3", 205 lbs. Deb: 6/8/1976 Career OF: 693-113-236

YEAR TM-L	G	AB	R	H	2B	3B	HR	RBI	BB	SO	SB	CS	AVG	OBP	SLG	OPS	OPS+	BR/A	RC	RC/G	FR	G/POS	WS	TPW
1976 Mon-N	29	90	9	20	3	1	2	5	4	18	0	0	.222	.263	.344	.608	68	-4	8	3.08	1	0-25(3-0-22)	1	-0.5
1978 Bal-A	27	58	5	15	3	0	3	15	8	3	0	1	.259	.358	.466	.824	138	3	9	4.77	1	0-20(20-0-0)	2	0.3
1979*Bal-A	133	376	60	98	16	1	25	64	61	74	1	3	.261	.381	.508	.889	143	23	73	6.69	2	*0-130(114-26-8)/D-2	19	2.0
1980 Bal-A	118	297	40	71	13	0	10	28	41	49	2	0	.239	.343	.384	.727	100	2	40	4.46	-1	*0-113(86-13-38)	9	-0.4
1981 Bal-A	85	219	31	59	16	0	3	20	23	29	1	2	.269	.344	.384	.728	110	3	26	3.91	-2	0-83(45-13-54)	6	-0.3
1982 Bal-A	137	393	58	106	25	1	21	74	70	73	6	7	.270	.392	.499	.891	143	25	79	7.01	2	*0-125(80-34-42),1-10	20	2.1
1983*Bal-A	115	323	45	84	13	0	19	64	30	35	2	2	.260	.331	.477	.807	121	8	49	5.12	-1	*0-100(79-8-23)/1-7,3-2,D	11	0.4
1984 Bal-A	121	326	36	73	19	1	10	44	58	43	1	2	.224	.348	.380	.728	104	3	45	4.47	3	*0-117(85-6-32)	10	0.2
1985 Bal-A	114	225	36	49	9	0	15	43	44	36	2	2	.218	.346	.458	.804	121	7	37	5.31	2	0-89(76-9-9),D-17	8	0.6
1986 NY-A	69	136	11	36	5	0	3	18	27	30	1	1	.265	.390	.368	.758	109	3	22	5.74	1	0-37(33-3-2),D-15/3-3,1-2	4	0.3
1987 Atl-N	67	151	25	33	8	0	9	28	32	23	0	0	.219	.359	.450	.809	107	2	26	5.60	-1	0-44(40-0-4)/1-9	4	-0.1
1988 Atl-N	49	114	11	26	5	0	1	7	8	15	0	0	.228	.279	.298	.577	63	-6	9	2.60	-2	0-35(32-1-2)/1-1	0	-0.9
Total 12	1064	2708	367	670	135	4	121	410	406	428	16	20	.247	.354	.434	.788	117	69	424	5.24	4	0-918/D-36,1-29,3-5	94	3.6

• ROENICKE, Ron Ronald Jon Roenicke b: 8/19/1956, Covina, CA BB/TL, 6', 180 lbs. Deb: 9/2/1981 C Career OF: 100-169-141

YEAR TM-L	G	AB	R	H	2B	3B	HR	RBI	BB	SO	SB	CS	AVG	OBP	SLG	OPS	OPS+	BR/A	RC	RC/G	FR	G/POS	WS	TPW
1981 LA-N	22	47	6	11	0	0	0	0	6	8	1	1	.234	.321	.234	.555	61	-2	4	2.86	0	0-20(5-6-10)	1	-0.4
1982 LA-N	109	143	18	37	8	0	1	12	21	32	5	0	.259	.361	.336	.697	99	2	20	4.76	-1	0-72(21-18-39)	4	0.0
1983 LA-N	81	145	12	32	4	0	2	12	14	26	3	2	.221	.289	.290	.579	61	-8	12	2.54	-1	0-62(9-17-44)	2	-1.1
Sea-A	59	198	23	50	12	0	4	23	33	22	6	2	.253	.365	.374	.739	100	2	30	5.21	6	0-54(16-38-4)/1-8,D-1	7	0.6
1984*SD-N	12	20	4	6	1	0	1	2	2	5	0	0	.300	.364	.500	.864	141	1	4	7.20	0	0-10(7-2-2)	1	0.1
1985 SF-N	65	133	23	34	9	1	3	13	35	27	6	2	.256	.411	.406	.817	136	9	26	6.70	-1	0-35(9-6-20)	7	0.7
1986 Phi-N	102	275	42	68	13	1	5	42	61	52	2	2	.247	.384	.356	.740	102	3	42	5.17	-1	0-83(24-63-8)	10	0.0
1987 Phi-N	63	78	9	13	3	1	1	4	14	15	1	0	.167	.293	.269	.563	49	-5	7	2.73	0	0-26(9-15-4)	0	-0.6
1988 Cin-N	14	37	4	5	1	0	0	5	4	8	0	0	.135	.238	.162	.400	16	-4	2	1.28	-0	0-14(0-4-10)	0	-0.5
Total 8	527	1076	141	256	51	3	17	113	190	195	24	9	.238	.355	.338	.693	93	-2	146	4.53	1	0-376/1-8,D-1	32	-1.2

• ROETTGER, Oscar Oscar Frederick Louis "Okkie" Roettger b: 2/19/1900, St. Louis, MO d: 7/4/1986, St. Louis, MO BR/TR, 6', 170 lbs. Deb: 7/7/1923 ♦

YEAR TM-L	G	AB	R	H	2B	3B	HR	RBI	BB	SO	SB	CS	AVG	OBP	SLG	OPS	OPS+	BR/A	RC	RC/G	FR	G/POS	WS	TPW
1923 NY-A	5	2	0	0	0	0	0	0	0	0	0	0	.000	.000	.000	.000	-98	-0	0	.00	0	/P-5	0	-0.6
1924 NY-A	1	0	0	0	0	0	0	0	0	0	0	0	....	....	....	....	-100	0	0	....	-0	/P-1	0	0.0
1927 Bro-N	5	4	0	0	0	0	0	0	1	1	0	....	.000	.333	.000	.333	-4	-0	0	1.05	0	/0-1	0	-0.1
1932 Phi-A	26	60	7	14	1	0	0	6	5	4	0	0	.233	.292	.250	.542	40	-5	5	2.62	-1	1-15	0	-0.7
Total 4	37	66	7	14	1	0	0	6	6	5	0	0	.212	.288	.227	.515	33	-6	5	2.40	-1	/1-15,P-6,0-1	0	-1.4

• ROETTGER, Wally Walter Henry Roettger b: 8/28/1902, St. Louis, MO d: 9/14/1951, Champaign, IL BR/TR, 6'1.5", 190 lbs. Deb: 5/1/1927 Career OF: 231-100-183

YEAR TM-L	G	AB	R	H	2B	3B	HR	RBI	BB	SO	SB	CS	AVG	OBP	SLG	OPS	OPS+	BR/A	RC	RC/G	FR	G/POS	WS	TPW
1927 StL-N	5	1	0	0	0	0	0	0	1	0	0	....	.000	.500	.000	.500	42	0	0	3.14	-1	/0-3(3-0-0)	0	-0.1
1928 StL-N	68	261	27	89	17	4	6	44	10	22	2	....	.341	.372	.506	.878	125	8	47	6.72	-4	0-66(33-0-34)	10	-0.1
1929 StL-N	79	269	27	68	11	3	3	42	13	27	0	....	.253	.287	.349	.637	56	-19	26	3.28	-1	0-69(7-0-62)	2	-2.2
1930 NY-N	121	420	51	119	15	5	5	51	25	29	1	....	.283	.330	.379	.708	72	-19	51	4.31	-1	*0-114(28-85-4)	8	-2.3
1931 Cin-N	44	185	25	65	11	4	1	20	7	9	1	....	.351	.378	.470	.849	135	8	33	6.84	0	0-44(18-2-24)	7	0.6
*StL-N	45	151	16	43	12	2	0	17	9	14	0	....	.285	.337	.391	.728	92	-2	21	4.70	-2	0-42(8-7-27)	4	-0.5
Yr.	89	336	41	108	23	6	1	37	16	23	1	....	.321	.360	.435	.794	115	6	53	5.82	-1	0-86(26-9-51)	11	0.1
1932 Cin-N	106	347	26	96	18	3	3	43	23	24	0	....	.277	.323	.372	.695	89	-5	43	4.32	0	0-94(89-5-0)	7	-1.0
1933 Cin-N	84	209	13	50	7	1	1	17	8	10	0	....	.239	.267	.297	.564	62	-11	15	2.30	0	0-55(26-1-28)	1	-1.4
1934 Pit-N	47	106	7	26	5	1	0	11	3	8	0	....	.245	.266	.311	.577	53	-7	8	2.69	-1	0-23(19-0-4)	1	-1.0
Total 8	599	1949	192	556	96	23	19	245	99	143	4	....	.285	.324	.387	.711	86	-47	244	4.38	-9	0-510	40	-8.0

• ROETZ, Ed Edward Bernard Roetz b: 8/6/1905, Philadelphia, PA d: 3/16/1965, Philadelphia, PA BR/TR, 5'10", 160 lbs. Deb: 5/26/1929

YEAR TM-L	G	AB	R	H	2B	3B	HR	RBI	BB	SO	SB	CS	AVG	OBP	SLG	OPS	OPS+	BR/A	RC	RC/G	FR	G/POS	WS	TPW
1929 StL-A	16	45	7	11	4	1	0	5	4	6	0	0	.244	.306	.378	.684	72	-2	5	3.96	-2	/S-8,1-5,2-2,3-1	1	-0.3

• ROGELL, Billy William George Rogell b: 11/24/1904, Springfield, IL d: 8/9/2003, Sterling Heights, MI BB/TR, 5'10.5", 163 lbs. Deb: 4/14/1925 Career OF: 3-2-4

YEAR TM-L	G	AB	R	H	2B	3B	HR	RBI	BB	SO	SB	CS	AVG	OBP	SLG	OPS	OPS+	BR/A	RC	RC/G	FR	G/POS	WS	TPW
1925 Bos-A	58	169	12	33	5	1	0	17	11	17	0	3	.195	.244	.237	.481	22	-21	10	1.77	-1	2-49/S-6	1	-1.9
1927 Bos-A	82	207	35	55	14	6	2	28	24	28	3	1	.266	.342	.420	.762	99	-0	31	5.18	1	3-53/2-2,0-2(1-0-1)	6	0.4
1928 Bos-A	102	296	33	69	10	4	0	29	22	47	2	6	.233	.295	.294	.589	56	-21	26	2.76	0	S-67,2-22/0-6(1-2-3),3-3	3	-1.4
1930 Det-A	54	144	20	24	4	2	0	9	15	23	1	2	.167	.250	.222	.472	20	-18	9	1.81	2	S-33,3-13/0-1	2	-1.1
1931 Det-A	48	185	21	56	12	3	2	24	24	17	8	8	.303	.383	.432	.815	110	2	30	5.71	11	S-48	6	1.6
1932 Det-A	144	554	88	150	29	6	9	61	50	38	14	6	.271	.332	.394	.726	84	-13	74	4.70	13	*S-139/3-4	17	0.9
1933 Det-A	155	587	67	173	42	11	0	57	79	33	6	9	.295	.381	.404	.785	106	6	93	5.72	22	*S-155	25	3.7
1934*Det-A	154	592	114	175	32	8	3	100	74	36	13	3	.296	.374	.392	.766	98	-1	92	5.64	6	*S-154	24	1.7
1935*Det-A	150	560	88	154	23	11	6	71	80	29	3	6	.275	.367	.388	.754	99	-1	83	5.22	16	*S-150	23	2.5

YEAR TM-L	G	AB	R	H	2B	3B	HR	RBI	BB	SO	SB	CS	AVG	OBP	SLG	OPS	OPS+	BR/A	RC	RC/G	FR	G/POS	WS	TPW
1936 Det-A	146	585	85	160	27	5	6	68	73	41	14	10	.274	.357	.368	.725	79	-20	80	4.79	1	*S-146/3-1	16	-0.7
1937 Det-A	146	536	85	148	30	7	8	64	83	48	5	5	.276	.376	.403	.779	94	-3	86	5.63	6	*S-146	18	1.2
1938 Det-A	136	501	76	130	22	8	3	55	86	37	9	2	.259	.373	.353	.727	78	-13	73	5.13	3	*S-134	16	0.0
1939 Det-A	74	174	24	40	6	3	2	23	26	14	3	1	.230	.330	.333	.663	65	-9	21	4.01	-2	S-43,3-21/2-2	4	-0.7
1940 Chi-N	33	59	7	8	0	0	1	3	2	8	1	....	.136	.164	.186	.350	-4	-8	2	1.02	-5	S-14/3-9,2-3	0	-1.3
Total 14	**1482**	**5149**	**755**	**1375**	**256**	**75**	**42**	**609**	**649**	**416**	**82**	**62**	**.267**	**.351**	**.370**	**.722**	**84**	**-118**	**709**	**4.77**	**73**	***S-1235,3-104/2-78,0-9**	**161**	**4.9**

• ROGERS, Eddie Edward Antonio Rogers b: 8/29/1978, San Pedro de Macoris, Dominican Republic BR/TR, 6'1", 172 lbs. Deb: 9/5/2002

YEAR TM-L	G	AB	R	H	2B	3B	HR	RBI	BB	SO	SB	CS	AVG	OBP	SLG	OPS	OPS+	BR/A	RC	RC/G	FR	G/POS	WS	TPW
2002 Bal-A	5	3	0	0	0	0	0	0	0	0	0	0	.000	.000	.000	.000	-105	-1	0	.00	1	/S-4	0	0.0

• ROGERS, Emmett Emmett E. Rogers b: 10/11/1870, Hot Springs, AR d: 10/24/1941, Fort Smith, AR BB, 5'10", 165 lbs. Deb: 4/19/1890

YEAR TM-L	G	AB	R	H	2B	3B	HR	RBI	BB	SO	SB	CS	AVG	OBP	SLG	OPS	OPS+	BR/A	RC	RC/G	FR	G/POS	WS	TPW
1890 Tol-a	35	110	18	19	3	3	0	7	14	....	2	....	.173	.266	.255	.521	52	-7	8	2.38	-4	C-34/0-1	2	-0.7

• ROGERS, Fraley Fraley W. Rogers b: 1850, Brooklyn, NY d: 5/10/1881, New York, NY, 5'8", 184 lbs. Deb: 4/30/1872

YEAR TM-L	G	AB	R	H	2B	3B	HR	RBI	BB	SO	SB	CS	AVG	OBP	SLG	OPS	OPS+	BR/A	RC	RC/G	FR	G/POS	WS	TPW
1872 Bos-n	45	204	39	56	7	1	1	28	1	4	2	0	.275	.278	.333	.611	83	-5	20	4.18	0	*0-41(4-0-38)/1-6	....	-0.1
1873 Bos-n	1	6	1	2	1	0	0	2	0	1	0	0	.333	.333	.500	.833	133	0	1	7.82	0	/1-1	....	0.0
Total 2 n	**46**	**210**	**40**	**58**	**8**	**1**	**1**	**30**	**1**	**5**	**2**	**0**	**.276**	**.280**	**.338**	**.618**	**84**	**-5**	**21**	**4.27**	**-0**	**/0-41,1-7**	**....**	**-0.1**

• ROGERS, Jay Jay Lewis Rogers b: 8/3/1888, Sandusky, NY d: 7/1/1964, Carlisle, NY BR/TR, 5'11.5", 178 lbs. Deb: 5/22/1914

YEAR TM-L	G	AB	R	H	2B	3B	HR	RBI	BB	SO	SB	CS	AVG	OBP	SLG	OPS	OPS+	BR/A	RC	RC/G	FR	G/POS	WS	TPW
1914 NY-A	5	8	0	0	0	0	0	0	0	4	0	....	.000	.000	.000	.000	-100	-2	0	.00	0	/C-4	0	-0.2

• ROGERS, Jim James F. Rogers b: 4/9/1872, Hartford, CT d: 1/21/1900, Bridgeport, CT, 5'7.5", 180 lbs. Deb: 4/17/1896 M

YEAR TM-L	G	AB	R	H	2B	3B	HR	RBI	BB	SO	SB	CS	AVG	OBP	SLG	OPS	OPS+	BR/A	RC	RC/G	FR	G/POS	WS	TPW
1896 Was-N	38	154	21	43	6	4	1	30	10	9	3	....	.279	.323	.390	.713	87	-3	21	4.95	-3	3-32/2-6,0-1	3	-0.5
Lou-N	72	290	39	75	8	6	0	38	15	14	13	....	.259	.297	.328	.625	67	-14	33	4.05	-2	1-60,S-12	3	-1.3
Yr.	110	444	60	118	14	10	1	68	25	23	16	....	.266	.306	.349	.655	74	-18	54	4.36	-5	1-60,3-32,S-12/2-6,0-1	6	-1.9
1897 Lou-N	42	153	22	22	3	2	2	22	23	....	4	....	.144	.260	.229	.489	31	-15	11	2.18	-8	2-39/1-3	1	-1.8
Total 2	**152**	**597**	**82**	**140**	**17**	**12**	**3**	**90**	**48**	**23**	**20**	**....**	**.235**	**.294**	**.318**	**.612**	**62**	**-33**	**66**	**3.71**	**-13**	**/1-63,2-45,3-32,S-12,0-1**	**7**	**-3.7**

• ROGERS, Packy Stanley Frank "Packy" Rogers b: 4/26/1913, Swoyersville, PA d: 5/15/1998, Elmira, NY BR/TR, 5'8", 175 lbs. Deb: 7/12/1938

YEAR TM-L	G	AB	R	H	2B	3B	HR	RBI	BB	SO	SB	CS	AVG	OBP	SLG	OPS	OPS+	BR/A	RC	RC/G	FR	G/POS	WS	TPW
1938 Bro-N	23	37	3	7	1	1	0	5	6	6	0	....	.189	.302	.270	.573	57	-2	3	2.25	-2	/S-9,3-8,2-3,0-1	0	-0.3

• ROGODZINSKI, Mike Michael George Rogodzinski b: 2/22/1948, Evanston, IL BL/TR, 6', 185 lbs. Deb: 5/4/1973 Career OF: 7-0-14

YEAR TM-L	G	AB	R	H	2B	3B	HR	RBI	BB	SO	SB	CS	AVG	OBP	SLG	OPS	OPS+	BR/A	RC	RC/G	FR	G/POS	WS	TPW
1973 Phi-N	66	80	13	19	3	0	2	7	12	19	0	0	.238	.337	.350	.687	88	-1	10	4.09	0	0-16(5-0-13)	2	-0.1
1974 Phi-N	17	15	1	1	0	0	0	1	2	3	0	0	.067	.176	.067	.243	-29	-3	0	.52	0	/0-1	0	-0.3
1975 Phi-N	16	19	3	5	1	0	0	4	3	2	0	1	.263	.364	.316	.679	86	-1	2	3.88	0	/0-2(2-0-0)	0	-0.1
Total 3	**99**	**114**	**17**	**25**	**4**	**0**	**2**	**12**	**17**	**24**	**0**	**1**	**.219**	**.321**	**.307**	**.628**	**73**	**-4**	**12**	**3.52**	**0**	**/0-19**	**2**	**-0.5**

• ROHDE, Dave David Grant Rohde b: 5/8/1964, Los Altos, CA BB/TR, 6'2", 180 lbs. Deb: 4/9/1990

YEAR TM-L	G	AB	R	H	2B	3B	HR	RBI	BB	SO	SB	CS	AVG	OBP	SLG	OPS	OPS+	BR/A	RC	RC/G	FR	G/POS	WS	TPW
1990 Hou-N	59	98	8	18	4	0	0	5	9	20	0	0	.184	.286	.224	.510	44	-7	7	2.11	4	2-32/3-4,S-2	1	-0.3
1991 Hou-N	29	41	3	5	0	0	0	0	5	8	0	0	.122	.217	.122	.339	-2	-5	1	.95	1	/2-4,3-3,S-3,1-1	0	-0.5
1992 Cle-A	5	7	0	0	0	0	0	0	2	3	0	0	.000	.222	.000	.222	-34	-1	0	.22	0	/3-5	0	-0.2
Total 3	**93**	**146**	**11**	**23**	**4**	**0**	**0**	**5**	**16**	**31**	**0**	**0**	**.158**	**.263**	**.185**	**.448**	**27**	**-14**	**8**	**1.67**	**4**	**/2-36,3-12,S-5,1-1**	**1**	**-1.0**

• ROHE, George George Anthony "Whitey" Rohe b: 9/15/1875, Cincinnati, OH d: 6/10/1957, Cincinnati, OH BR/TR, 5'9", 165 lbs. Deb: 5/7/1901

YEAR TM-L	G	AB	R	H	2B	3B	HR	RBI	BB	SO	SB	CS	AVG	OBP	SLG	OPS	OPS+	BR/A	RC	RC/G	FR	G/POS	WS	TPW
1901 Bal-A	14	36	7	10	2	0	0	4	5	....	1	....	.278	.381	.333	.714	95	0	5	5.17	-2	/1-8,3-6	1	-0.2
1905 Chi-A	34	113	14	24	1	0	1	12	12	....	2	....	.212	.310	.248	.558	81	-2	10	2.89	-5	2-17,3-17	3	-0.6
1906*Chi-A	77	225	14	58	5	1	0	25	16	....	8	....	.258	.316	.289	.604	92	-2	25	3.74	1	3-57/2-5,0-1	9	0.1
1907 Chi-A	144	494	46	105	11	2	2	51	39	....	16	....	.213	.274	.255	.529	71	-15	42	2.75	-21	3-76,2-39,S-30	10	-3.6
Total 4	**269**	**868**	**81**	**197**	**19**	**3**	**3**	**92**	**72**	**....**	**27**	**....**	**.227**	**.294**	**.266**	**.561**	**79**	**-18**	**82**	**3.11**	**-27**	**3-156/2-61,S-30,1-8,0-1**	**23**	**-4.3**

• ROHN, Dan Daniel Jay Rohn b: 1/10/1956, Alpena, MI BL/TR, 5'8", 165 lbs. Deb: 9/2/1983

YEAR TM-L	G	AB	R	H	2B	3B	HR	RBI	BB	SO	SB	CS	AVG	OBP	SLG	OPS	OPS+	BR/A	RC	RC/G	FR	G/POS	WS	TPW
1983 Chi-N	23	31	3	12	3	2	0	6	2	2	1	0	.387	.424	.613	1.037	176	3	8	11.43	-2	/2-6,S-1	2	0.2
1984 Chi-N	25	31	1	4	0	0	1	3	1	6	0	0	.129	.156	.226	.382	6	-4	1	.88	-3	/3-7,2-5,S-5	0	-0.7
1986 Cle-A	6	10	1	2	0	0	0	2	1	1	0	0	.200	.273	.200	.473	32	-1	1	2.08	-1	/2-2,3-2,S-1	0	-0.2
Total 3	**54**	**72**	**5**	**18**	**3**	**2**	**1**	**11**	**4**	**9**	**1**	**0**	**.250**	**.289**	**.389**	**.678**	**83**	**-2**	**10**	**4.75**	**-5**	**/2-13,3-9,S-7**	**2**	**-0.7**

• ROHRMEIER, Dan Daniel Rohrmeier b: 9/27/1965, Cincinnati, OH BR/TR, 6', 185 lbs. Deb: 9/3/1997

YEAR TM-L	G	AB	R	H	2B	3B	HR	RBI	BB	SO	SB	CS	AVG	OBP	SLG	OPS	OPS+	BR/A	RC	RC/G	FR	G/POS	WS	TPW
1997 Sea-A	7	9	4	3	0	0	0	2	2	4	0	0	.333	.455	.333	.788	111	0	2	7.20	0	/D-4,1-3	1	0.0

• ROHWER, Ray Ray Rohwer b: 6/5/1895, Dixon, CA d: 1/24/1988, Davis, CA BL/TL, 5'10", 155 lbs. Deb: 4/13/1921 Career OF: 0-5-35

YEAR TM-L	G	AB	R	H	2B	3B	HR	RBI	BB	SO	SB	CS	AVG	OBP	SLG	OPS	OPS+	BR/A	RC	RC/G	FR	G/POS	WS	TPW
1921 Pit-N	30	40	6	10	3	2	0	6	4	8	0	1	.250	.318	.425	.743	93	-1	5	4.26	-1	0-10(0-3-7)	1	-0.2
1922 Pit-N	53	129	19	38	6	3	3	22	10	17	1	0	.295	.350	.457	.807	105	1	21	5.81	-1	0-30(0-2-28)	4	-0.2
Total 2	**83**	**169**	**25**	**48**	**9**	**5**	**3**	**28**	**14**	**25**	**1**	**1**	**.284**	**.342**	**.450**	**.792**	**102**	**1**	**26**	**5.43**	**-2**	**/0-40**	**5**	**-0.4**

• ROIG, Tony Anton Ambrose Roig b: 12/23/1927, New Orleans, LA BR/TR, 6'1", 180 lbs. Deb: 9/13/1953

YEAR TM-L	G	AB	R	H	2B	3B	HR	RBI	BB	SO	SB	CS	AVG	OBP	SLG	OPS	OPS+	BR/A	RC	RC/G	FR	G/POS	WS	TPW
1953 Was-A	3	8	0	1	1	0	0	0	0	1	0	0	.125	.125	.250	.375	-1	-1	0	.99	1	/2-2	0	0.0
1955 Was-A	29	57	3	13	1	1	0	4	2	15	0	0	.228	.254	.281	.535	46	-4	4	2.12	0	S-21/3-8,2-1	1	-0.4
1956 Was-A	44	119	11	25	5	2	0	7	20	29	2	0	.210	.324	.286	.609	62	-6	11	3.02	-2	2-27,S-19	1	-0.5
Total 3	**76**	**184**	**14**	**39**	**7**	**3**	**0**	**11**	**22**	**45**	**2**	**0**	**.212**	**.296**	**.283**	**.579**	**55**	**-11**	**15**	**2.66**	**-2**	**/S-40,2-30,3-8**	**2**	**-0.9**

• ROJAS, Cookie Octavio Victor (Rivas) Rojas b: 3/6/1939, Havana, Cuba BR/TR, 5'10", 170 lbs. Deb: 4/10/1962 M/C Career OF: 79-124-10

YEAR TM-L	G	AB	R	H	2B	3B	HR	RBI	BB	SO	SB	CS	AVG	OBP	SLG	OPS	OPS+	BR/A	RC	RC/G	FR	G/POS	WS	TPW
1962 Cin-N	39	86	9	19	2	0	0	6	9	4	1	1	.221	.302	.244	.546	47	-6	6	2.36	-2	2-30/3-1	1	-0.7
1963 Phi-N	64	77	18	17	0	1	1	2	3	8	4	1	.221	.259	.286	.545	57	-4	5	2.21	1	2-25/0-1	1	-0.1
1964 Phi-N	109	340	58	99	19	5	2	31	22	17	1	3	.291	.338	.394	.732	107	2	42	4.24	-3	0-70(23-54-1),2-20,S-18/3-1,C	11	-0.1
1965 Phi-N★	142	521	78	158	25	3	3	42	42	33	5	5	.303	.359	.380	.739	110	7	71	4.94	-1	2-84,0-55(11-41-5),S-11/C-2,1	19	1.2
1966 Phi-N	156	626	77	168	18	1	6	55	35	46	4	6	.268	.311	.329	.640	78	-19	63	3.45	-7	*2-106,0-56(30-28-3)/S-2	13	-2.0
1967 Phi-N	147	528	60	137	21	2	4	45	30	58	8	4	.259	.299	.330	.629	79	-14	50	3.17	-12	*2-137/0-9(8-1-1),C-3,S-2,3,P	12	-1.6
1968 Phi-N	152	621	53	144	19	0	9	48	16	55	4	8	.232	.251	.306	.557	67	-29	43	2.29	-1	*2-150/C-1	10	-2.0
1969 Phi-N	110	391	35	89	11	1	4	30	23	28	1	6	.228	.272	.292	.564	60	-24	28	2.30	-10	2-95/0-2(2-0-0)	2	-2.9
1970 StL-N	23	47	2	5	0	0	0	2	3	4	0	0	.106	.176	.106	.283	-22	-8	1	.59	1	2-10/0-3(3-0-0),S-2	1	-0.7
KC-A	98	384	36	100	13	3	2	28	20	29	3	7	.260	.297	.326	.623	72	-18	34	3.06	3	2-97	7	-0.8
1971 KC-A★	115	414	56	124	22	2	6	59	39	35	8	3	.300	.363	.406	.768	118	11	60	5.20	-10	*2-111/S-2,0-1	18	0.9
1972 KC-A★	137	487	49	127	25	0	3	53	41	35	2	8	.261	.319	.331	.650	94	-6	47	3.22	-5	*2-131/3-6,S-2	12	-0.3
1973 KC-A★	139	551	78	152	29	3	6	69	37	38	18	4	.276	.323	.372	.695	88	-7	65	4.12	-4	*2-137	16	-0.2
1974 KC-A★	144	542	52	147	17	1	6	60	30	43	8	4	.271	.313	.339	.653	83	-12	52	3.23	-12	*2-141	10	-1.6
1975 KC-A	120	406	34	103	18	2	2	37	30	24	4	5	.254	.305	.323	.628	75	-14	37	3.00	-3	*2-117/D-1	8	-1.1
1976*KC-A	63	132	11	32	6	0	0	16	8	15	2	0	.242	.286	.288	.574	68	-5	11	2.59	1	2-40/D-9,3-6,1-1	1	-0.4
1977*KC-A	64	156	8	39	9	1	0	10	8	17	1	3	.250	.287	.321	.607	65	-9	12	2.65	3	3-31,2-16/D-6	2	-0.6
Total 16	**1822**	**6309**	**714**	**1660**	**254**	**25**	**54**	**593**	**396**	**489**	**74**	**68**	**.263**	**.309**	**.337**	**.646**	**83**	**-156**	**630**	**3.37**	**-62**	***2-1447,0-197/3-46,S,D,C,1,P**	**144**	**-12.8**

• ROJEK, Stan Stanley Andrew Rojek b: 4/21/1919, North Tonawanda, NY d: 7/9/1997, North Tonawanda, NY BR/TR, 5'10", 170 lbs. Deb: 9/22/1942

YEAR TM-L	G	AB	R	H	2B	3B	HR	RBI	BB	SO	SB	CS	AVG	OBP	SLG	OPS	OPS+	BR/A	RC	RC/G	FR	G/POS	WS	TPW
1942 Bro-N	1	0	1	0	0	0	0	0	0	0	0	....	....	....	....	....	-98	0	0	....	0	....	0	0.0
1946 Bro-N	45	47	11	13	2	1	0	2	4	1	1	....	.277	.333	.362	.695	96	-0	5	3.55	0	S-15/2-6,3-4	1	0.1
1947 Bro-N	32	80	7	21	0	1	0	7	7	3	1	....	.263	.322	.288	.609	61	-4	7	3.09	4	S-17/3-9,2-7	2	0.1
1948 Pit-N	156	641	85	186	27	5	4	51	61	41	24	....	.290	.355	.367	.721	93	-5	87	4.98	-8	*S-156	21	-0.3
1949 Pit-N	144	557	72	136	19	2	0	31	50	31	4	....	.244	.309	.285	.594	59	-32	52	3.11	-11	*S-144	9	-3.3
1950 Pit-N	76	230	28	59	12	1	0	17	18	13	2	....	.257	.313	.317	.631	64	-12	23	3.53	-12	S-68/2-3	3	-2.0
1951 Pit-N	8	16	0	3	0	0	0	0	0	1	0	0	.188	.188	.188	.375	1	-2	1	1.22	-1	/S-8	0	-0.3
StL-N	51	186	21	51	7	3	0	14	10	10	0	3	.274	.318	.344	.662	78	-7	19	3.37	0	S-51	4	-0.4
Yr.	59	202	21	54	7	3	0	14	10	11	0	3	.267	.308	.332	.640	72	-9	19	3.18	-1	S-59	4	-0.7

YEAR TM-L	G	AB	R	H	2B	3B	HR	RBI	BB	SO	SB	CS	AVG	OBP	SLG	OPS	OPS+	BR/A	RC	RC/G	FR	G/POS	WS	TPW
1952 StL-A	9	7	0	1	0	0	0	0	2	0	0	0	.143	.333	.143	.476	35	-0	0	1.32	0	/S-4,2-1	0	-0.1
Total 8	522	1764	225	470	67	13	4	122	152	100	32	3	.266	.327	.326	.653	75	-63	193	3.82	-28	S-463/2-17,3-13	40	-6.2

• ROLEN, Scott Scott Bruce Rolen b: 4/4/1975, Evansville, IN BR/TR, 6'4", 210 lbs. Deb: 8/1/1996

YEAR TM-L	G	AB	R	H	2B	3B	HR	RBI	BB	SO	SB	CS	AVG	OBP	SLG	OPS	OPS+	BR/A	RC	RC/G	FR	G/POS	WS	TPW
1996 Phi-N	37	130	10	33	7	0	4	18	13	27	0	2	.254	.326	.400	.726	89	-3	16	4.09	-4	3-37	2	-0.6
1997 Phi-N	156	561	93	159	35	3	21	92	76	138	16	6	.283	.382	.469	.850	121	20	107	6.84	16	*3-155	29	3.8
1998 Phi-N	160	601	120	174	45	4	31	110	93	141	14	7	.290	.394	.532	.927	139	36	131	7.84	7	*3-159	30	4.5
1999 Phi-N	112	421	74	113	28	1	26	77	67	114	12	2	.268	.373	.525	.898	120	15	86	7.19	13	*3-112	15	2.8
2000 Phi-N	128	483	88	144	32	6	26	89	51	99	8	1	.298	.371	.551	.922	128	21	102	7.97	15	*3-128	18	3.5
2001 Phi-N	151	554	96	160	39	1	25	107	74	127	16	5	.289	.385	.498	.884	129	28	113	7.29	23	*3-151	29	5.2
2002 Phi-N★	100	375	52	97	21	4	17	66	52	68	5	2	.259	.361	.472	.833	123	13	64	5.86	9	*3-100	16	2.4
*StL-N	55	205	37	57	8	4	14	44	20	34	3	2	.278	.354	.561	.915	140	11	37	6.22	13	3-55	12	2.5
Yr.	155	580	89	154	29	8	31	110	72	102	8	4	.266	.358	.503	.862	129	24	101	5.99	23	*3-155	28	4.9
2003 StL-N★	154	559	98	160	49	1	28	104	82	104	13	3	.286	.386	.528	.914	141	36	114	7.21	5	*3-153	25	4.3
Total 8	1053	3889	668	1097	264	24	192	707	528	852	87	30	.282	.377	.510	.888	129	176	770	7.05	98	*3-1050	176	28.3

• ROLFE, Red Robert Abial Rolfe b: 10/17/1908, Penacook, NH d: 7/8/1969, Gilford, NH BL/TR, 5'11.5", 170 lbs. Deb: 6/29/1931 M/C

YEAR TM-L	G	AB	R	H	2B	3B	HR	RBI	BB	SO	SB	CS	AVG	OBP	SLG	OPS	OPS+	BR/A	RC	RC/G	FR	G/POS	WS	TPW
1931 NY-A	1	0	0	0	0	0	0	0	0	0	0	0	....	....	....	....	-106	0	0	....	-1	/S-1	0	-0.1
1934 NY-A	89	279	54	80	13	2	0	18	26	16	2	3	.287	.348	.348	.695	86	-6	34	4.40	9	S-46,3-26	8	0.6
1935 NY-A	149	639	108	192	33	9	5	67	57	39	7	3	.300	.361	.404	.764	103	4	95	5.51	10	*3-136,S-17	22	1.8
1936*NY-A	135	568	116	181	39	**15**	10	70	68	38	3	0	.319	.392	.493	.884	121	20	113	7.52	11	*3-133	24	3.1
1937*NY-A★	154	648	143	179	34	10	4	62	90	53	4	2	.276	.365	.378	.743	87	-10	94	5.29	11	*3-154	19	0.5
1938*NY-A★	151	631	132	196	36	8	10	80	74	44	13	1	.311	.386	.441	.826	107	10	113	6.75	-12	*3-151	22	0.4
1939*NY-A★	152	648	**139**	**213**	**46**	10	14	80	81	41	7	6	.329	.404	.495	.899	131	30	134	8.08	-3	*3-152	30	3.0
1940 NY-A★	139	588	102	147	26	6	10	53	50	48	4	2	.250	.311	.366	.677	78	-20	71	4.25	2	*3-138	14	-1.1
1941*NY-A	136	561	106	148	22	5	8	42	57	38	3	2	.264	.332	.364	.695	85	-12	73	4.69	-1	*3-134	16	-0.8
1942*NY-A	69	265	42	58	8	2	8	25	23	18	1	1	.219	.281	.355	.636	80	-8	28	3.61	5	3-60	7	-0.1
Total 10	1175	4827	942	1394	257	67	69	497	526	335	44	20	.289	.360	.413	.773	100	7	756	5.75	31	*3-1084/S-64	162	7.4

• ROLISON, Nate Nathan Mardis Rolison b: 3/27/1977, Hattiesburg, MS BL/TR, 6'5", 240 lbs. Deb: 9/5/2000

YEAR TM-L	G	AB	R	H	2B	3B	HR	RBI	BB	SO	SB	CS	AVG	OBP	SLG	OPS	OPS+	BR/A	RC	RC/G	FR	G/POS	WS	TPW
2000 Fla-N	8	13	0	1	0	0	0	2	1	4	0	0	.077	.143	.077	.220	-45	-3	0	.55	0	/1-4	0	-0.3

• ROLLING, Ray Raymond Copeland Rolling b: 9/8/1886, Martinsburg, MO d: 8/25/1966, St. Paul, MN BR/TR, 5'10.5", 160 lbs. Deb: 9/6/1912

YEAR TM-L	G	AB	R	H	2B	3B	HR	RBI	BB	SO	SB	CS	AVG	OBP	SLG	OPS	OPS+	BR/A	RC	RC/G	FR	G/POS	WS	TPW
1912 StL-N	5	15	0	3	0	0	0	0	0	5	0	....	.200	.200	.200	.400	10	-2	1	1.18	-1	/2-4	0	-0.3

• ROLLINGS, Red William Russell Rollings b: 3/31/1904, Mobile, AL d: 12/31/1964, Mobile, AL BL/TR, 5'11", 167 lbs. Deb: 4/17/1927

YEAR TM-L	G	AB	R	H	2B	3B	HR	RBI	BB	SO	SB	CS	AVG	OBP	SLG	OPS	OPS+	BR/A	RC	RC/G	FR	G/POS	WS	TPW
1927 Bos-A	82	184	19	49	4	1	0	9	12	10	3	1	.266	.325	.299	.624	64	-9	19	3.53	-3	3-44,1-10/2-2	3	-1.0
1928 Bos-A	50	48	7	11	3	1	0	9	6	8	0	0	.229	.315	.333	.648	72	-2	5	3.62	-3	/1-5,2-4,0-4(2-0-2),3-1	0	-0.5
1930 Bos-N	52	123	10	29	6	0	0	10	9	5	2	....	.236	.288	.285	.572	40	-12	10	2.69	1	3-28,2-10	2	-0.8
Total 3	184	355	36	89	13	2	0	28	27	23	5	1	.251	.311	.299	.609	57	-23	35	3.25	-6	/3-73,2-16,1-15,0-4	5	-2.3

• ROLLINS, Jimmy James Calvin Rollins b: 11/27/1978, Oakland, CA BB/TR, 5'8", 160 lbs. Deb: 9/17/2000

YEAR TM-L	G	AB	R	H	2B	3B	HR	RBI	BB	SO	SB	CS	AVG	OBP	SLG	OPS	OPS+	BR/A	RC	RC/G	FR	G/POS	WS	TPW
2000 Phi-N	14	53	5	17	1	1	0	5	2	7	3	0	.321	.345	.377	.723	82	-1	8	5.72	-2	S-13	1	-0.1
2001 Phi-N★	158	656	97	180	29	**12**	14	54	48	108	**46**	8	.274	.326	.419	.745	93	-1	96	5.16	-7	*S-157	20	0.5
2002 Phi-N★	154	637	82	156	33	**10**	11	60	54	103	31	13	.245	.308	.380	.688	84	-15	74	3.84	4	*S-152/2-1	16	0.1
2003 Phi-N	156	628	85	165	42	6	8	62	54	113	20	12	.263	.321	.387	.708	89	-12	78	4.27	3	*S-154	18	0.4
Total 4	482	1974	269	518	105	29	33	181	158	331	100	33	.262	.319	.395	.714	88	-29	255	4.45	-2	S-476/2-1	55	0.8

• ROLLINS, Rich Richard John "Red" Rollins b: 4/16/1938, Mount Pleasant, PA BR/TR, 5'10", 185 lbs. Deb: 6/16/1961

YEAR TM-L	G	AB	R	H	2B	3B	HR	RBI	BB	SO	SB	CS	AVG	OBP	SLG	OPS	OPS+	BR/A	RC	RC/G	FR	G/POS	WS	TPW
1961 Min-A	13	17	3	5	1	0	0	3	2	2	0	0	.294	.400	.353	.753	98	0	3	6.10	0	/2-5,3-4	1	0.0
1962 Min-A★	159	624	96	186	23	5	16	96	75	61	3	1	.298	.379	.428	.807	112	13	104	6.02	-9	*3-159/S-1	23	0.5
1963 Min-A	136	531	75	163	23	1	16	61	36	59	2	0	.307	.360	.444	.804	122	16	84	5.77	2	*3-132/2-1	19	1.9
1964 Min-A	148	596	87	161	25	**10**	12	68	53	80	2	5	.270	.335	.406	.741	104	2	80	4.66	3	*3-146	14	0.5
1965*Min-A	140	469	59	117	22	1	5	32	37	54	4	0	.249	.310	.333	.642	79	-12	48	3.44	-1	*3-112,2-16	10	-1.2
1966 Min-A	90	269	30	66	7	1	10	40	13	34	0	2	.245	.290	.390	.681	88	-5	28	3.39	-2	3-65/2-2,0-1	5	-0.8
1967 Min-A	109	339	31	83	11	2	6	39	27	58	1	1	.245	.306	.342	.648	84	-6	34	3.41	-4	3-97	7	-1.1
1968 Min-A	93	203	14	49	5	0	6	30	10	34	3	1	.241	.287	.355	.642	89	-3	20	3.24	2	3-56	4	-0.1
1969 Sea-A	58	187	15	42	7	0	4	21	7	19	2	0	.225	.271	.326	.598	68	-8	16	2.94	2	3-47/S-1	3	-0.7
1970 Mil-A	14	25	3	5	1	0	0	5	3	4	0	0	.200	.286	.240	.526	46	-2	2	2.59	1	/3-7	0	0.0
Cle-A	42	43	6	10	0	0	2	4	3	5	0	0	.233	.283	.372	.655	75	-2	5	3.88	-1	/3-5	1	-0.3
Yr.	56	68	9	15	1	0	2	9	6	9	0	0	.221	.284	.324	.607	64	-3	7	3.38	1	3-12	1	-0.3
Total 10	1002	3303	419	887	125	20	77	399	266	410	17	10	.269	.330	.388	.719	98	-7	424	4.45	-6	3-830/2-24,S-2,0-1	87	-1.4

• ROLLINSON, Bill William Rollinson b: 6/10/1856, Fairfield, ME d: 9/28/1938, Bristow, VA Deb: 6/17/1884

YEAR TM-L	G	AB	R	H	2B	3B	HR	RBI	BB	SO	SB	CS	AVG	OBP	SLG	OPS	OPS+	BR/A	RC	RC/G	FR	G/POS	WS	TPW
1884 Was-U	1	3	0	0	0	0	0	....	0	....	....	....	.000	.000	.000	.000	-103	-1	0	.00	0	/C-1	0	0.0

• ROLLS, Damian Damian Michael Rolls b: 9/15/1977, Manhattan, KS BR/TR, 6'2", 205 lbs. Deb: 9/3/2000 Career OF: 17-22-46

YEAR TM-L	G	AB	R	H	2B	3B	HR	RBI	BB	SO	SB	CS	AVG	OBP	SLG	OPS	OPS+	BR/A	RC	RC/G	FR	G/POS	WS	TPW
2000 TB-A	4	3	0	1	0	0	0	0	0	1	0	0	.333	.333	.333	.667	70	-0	0	4.50	0	/3-1,D-1	0	0.0
2001 TB-A	81	237	33	62	11	1	2	12	10	47	12	4	.262	.291	.342	.633	67	-11	23	3.34	-1	2-42,0-25(7-18-0)/D-4,3-1	2	-1.0
2002 TB-A	21	89	15	26	6	1	0	6	3	16	2	5	.292	.330	.382	.712	90	-3	10	3.74	0	0-21(4-4-13)	0	-0.4
2003 TB-A	107	373	43	95	20	0	7	46	19	84	11	3	.255	.303	.365	.668	76	-12	42	3.91	9	3-73,0-37(6-0-33)/2-2	7	-0.4
Total 4	213	702	91	184	37	2	9	64	32	148	25	12	.262	.303	.359	.662	75	-26	75	3.70	8	/0-83,3-75,2-44,D-5	9	-1.7

• ROMAN, Bill William Anthony Roman b: 10/11/1938, Detroit, MI BL/TL, 6'4", 190 lbs. Deb: 9/30/1964

YEAR TM-L	G	AB	R	H	2B	3B	HR	RBI	BB	SO	SB	CS	AVG	OBP	SLG	OPS	OPS+	BR/A	RC	RC/G	FR	G/POS	WS	TPW
1964 Det-A	3	8	2	3	0	0	1	1	0	2	0	0	.375	.375	.750	1.125	201	1	2	12.15	0	/1-2	1	0.1
1965 Det-A	21	27	0	2	0	0	0	0	2	7	0	0	.074	.138	.074	.212	-38	-5	0	.27	-1	/1-6	0	-0.6
Total 2	24	35	2	5	0	0	1	1	2	9	0	0	.143	.189	.229	.418	14	-4	3	2.19	-1	/1-8	1	-0.5

• ROMANO, Jason Jason Anthony Romano b: 6/24/1979, Tampa, FL BR/TR, 6', 185 lbs. Deb: 4/17/2002 Career OF: 20-28-2

YEAR TM-L	G	AB	R	H	2B	3B	HR	RBI	BB	SO	SB	CS	AVG	OBP	SLG	OPS	OPS+	BR/A	RC	RC/G	FR	G/POS	WS	TPW
2002 Tex-A	29	54	8	11	4	0	0	4	4	13	2	0	.204	.259	.278	.536	41	-4	5	2.72	1	0-18(11-8-0)/2-8,D-4,3-1	1	-0.3
Col-N	18	37	9	12	0	1	0	1	3	11	4	1	.324	.375	.378	.753	86	-0	6	5.93	-2	2-12/S-5,0-3(0-3-0),3-1	1	-0.2
2003 LA-N	37	36	3	3	0	0	0	0	1	8	2	0	.083	.108	.083	.191	-52	-8	0	.18	0	0-28(9-17-2)/2-1,D-1	0	-0.8
Total 2	84	127	20	26	4	1	0	5	8	32	8	1	.205	.252	.252	.504	29	-12	11	2.70	-1	/0-49,2-21,D-5,S-5,3-2	2	-1.3

• ROMANO, John John Anthony "Honey" Romano b: 8/23/1934, Hoboken, NJ BR/TR, 5'11", 205 lbs. Deb: 9/12/1958 Career OF: 8-0-0

YEAR TM-L	G	AB	R	H	2B	3B	HR	RBI	BB	SO	SB	CS	AVG	OBP	SLG	OPS	OPS+	BR/A	RC	RC/G	FR	G/POS	WS	TPW
1958 Chi-A	4	7	1	2	0	0	0	1	1	0	0	0	.286	.375	.286	.661	86	-0	1	4.58	0	/C-2	0	0.0
1959*Chi-A	53	126	20	37	5	1	5	25	23	18	0	0	.294	.407	.468	.875	141	8	25	7.00	1	C-38	8	1.0
1960 Cle-A	108	316	40	86	12	2	16	52	37	50	0	0	.272	.354	.475	.829	126	11	53	5.96	-1	C-99	15	1.4
1961 Cle-A★	142	509	76	152	29	1	21	80	61	60	0	0	.299	.379	.483	.862	132	24	95	6.90	1	*C-141	25	3.2
1962 Cle-A★	135	459	71	120	19	3	25	81	73	64	0	1	.261	.369	.479	.848	130	20	82	6.08	3	*C-130	26	3.0
1963 Cle-A	89	255	28	55	5	2	10	34	38	49	4	3	.216	.322	.369	.691	94	-2	32	4.10	0	C-71/0-4(4-0-0)	10	0.1
1964 Cle-A	106	352	46	85	18	1	19	47	51	83	2	2	.241	.349	.460	.809	124	12	54	5.08	-4	C-96/1-1	15	1.4
1965 Chi-A	122	356	39	86	11	0	18	48	59	74	0	2	.242	.357	.424	.781	129	14	54	5.01	6	*C-111/0-4(4-0-0),1-2	20	2.6
1966 Chi-A	122	329	33	76	12	0	15	47	58	72	0	0	.231	.348	.404	.752	124	12	50	5.15	3	*C-102	16	2.1
1967 StL-N	24	58	1	7	1	0	0	2	13	15	1	0	.121	.282	.138	.420	24	-5	3	1.65	-2	C-20	1	-0.6
Total 10	905	2767	355	706	112	10	129	417	414	485	7	9	.255	.358	.443	.801	123	95	450	5.56	6	C-810/0-8,1-3	136	14.2

• ROMANO, Tom Thomas Michael Romano b: 10/25/1958, Syracuse, NY BR/TR, 5'10", 170 lbs. Deb: 9/1/1987

YEAR TM-L	G	AB	R	H	2B	3B	HR	RBI	BB	SO	SB	CS	AVG	OBP	SLG	OPS	OPS+	BR/A	RC	RC/G	FR	G/POS	WS	TPW
1987 Mon-N	7	3	1	0	0	0	0	0	0	1	0	0	.000	.000	.000	.000	-97	-1	0	.00	0	/0-3(3-0-0)	0	-0.1

YEAR TM-L	G	AB	R	H	2B	3B	HR	RBI	BB	SO	SB	CS	AVG	OBP	SLG	OPS	OPS+	BR/A	RC	RC/G	FR	G/POS	WS	TPW
• ROMERO, Ed	Edgardo Ralph (Rivera) Romero b: 12/9/1957, Santurce, Puerto Rico BR/TR, 5'11", 175 lbs. Deb: 7/16/1977 Career OF: 17-1-14																							
1977 Mil-A	10	25	4	7	1	0	0	2	4	3	0	0	.280	.379	.320	.699	93	0	3	4.30	0	S-10	1	0.1
1980 Mil-A	42	104	20	27	7	0	1	10	9	11	2	0	.260	.319	.356	.674	87	-1	12	3.91	-3	S-22,2-15/3-3	3	-0.2
1981*Mil-A	44	91	6	18	3	0	1	10	4	9	0	2	.198	.232	.264	.495	45	-7	4	1.43	2	S-22,2-18/3-3	2	-0.3
1982 Mil-A	52	144	18	36	8	0	1	7	8	16	0	0	.250	.289	.326	.616	73	-5	13	3.07	-1	2-39,S-10/3-2,0-1	3	-0.4
1983 Mil-A	59	145	17	46	7	0	1	18	8	8	1	0	.317	.353	.386	.739	112	2	20	5.13	-3	S-22,0-15(14-0-1)/3-5,D-5,2	5	0.1
1984 Mil-A	116	357	36	90	12	0	1	31	29	25	3	3	.252	.310	.294	.604	71	-14	31	2.91	-5	3-59,S-39,2-11/1-4,D-2,0-1	6	-1.6
1985 Mil-A	88	251	24	63	11	1	0	21	26	20	1	1	.251	.321	.303	.624	72	-9	26	3.55	7	S-43,2-31,0-14(2-0-12)/3-1	7	0.4
1986*Bos-A	100	233	41	49	11	0	2	23	18	16	2	0	.210	.273	.283	.556	51	-15	19	2.56	-10	S-75,3-18/2-4,0-1	2	-1.9
1987 Bos-A	88	235	23	64	5	0	0	14	18	22	0	2	.272	.324	.294	.618	64	-13	21	3.05	-1	2-29,3-24,S-24/1-8	3	-1.1
1988*Bos-A	31	75	3	18	3	0	0	5	3	8	0	0	.240	.278	.280	.558	55	-5	5	2.17	0	3-15/S-8,2-5,1-1,D-1	1	-0.3
1989 Bos-A	46	113	14	24	4	0	0	6	7	7	0	2	.212	.264	.248	.512	42	-9	7	2.08	3	2-22,3-14,S-10	2	-0.6
Atl-N	7	19	1	5	1	0	1	1	0	0	0	0	.263	.263	.474	.737	104	-0	2	3.41	2	/2-4,S-2,3-1	1	0.2
Mil-A	15	50	3	10	3	0	0	3	0	10	0	0	.200	.200	.260	.460	29	-5	2	1.14	1	2-11/3-4,D-2,S-1	0	-0.4
Yr.	61	163	17	34	7	0	0	9	7	17	0	2	.209	.246	.252	.497	39	-14	9	1.79	3	2-33,3-18,S-11/D-2	2	-1.0
1990 Det-A	32	70	8	16	3	0	0	4	6	4	0	0	.229	.289	.271	.561	57	-4	6	2.87	3	3-27/D-3	1	-0.1
Total 12	730	1912	218	473	79	1	8	155	140	159	9	10	.247	.300	.302	.603	68	-86	172	2.99	-5	S-288,2-192,3-176/0-32,1-13,D	37	-6.1
• ROMERO, Mandy	Armando Romero b: 10/29/1967, Miami, FL BR/TR, 5'11", 200 lbs. Deb: 7/15/1997																							
1997 SD-N	21	48	7	10	0	0	2	4	2	18	1	0	.208	.240	.333	.573	53	-3	4	2.60	0	C-19	1	-0.2
1998 SD-N	6	9	1	0	0	0	0	0	1	3	0	0	.000	.100	.000	.100	-76	-2	0	.08	0	/C-6	0	-0.2
Bos-A	12	13	2	3	1	0	0	1	3	3	0	0	.231	.375	.308	.683	79	-0	1	3.67	0	/C-4,D-3	0	0.0
2003 Col-N	3	7	2	3	1	0	0	0	0	1	0	0	.429	.556	.571	1.127	171	1	2	10.85	1	/C-2	0	0.2
Total 3	42	77	12	16	2	0	2	5	6	25	1	0	.208	.282	.312	.594	55	-5	7	3.07	1	/C-31,D-3	1	-0.3
• ROMINE, Kevin	Kevin Andrew Romine b: 5/23/1961, Exeter, NH BR/TR, 5'11", 185 lbs. Deb: 9/5/1985 Career OF: 53-112-130																							
1985 Bos-A	24	28	3	6	2	0	0	1	1	4	1	0	.214	.241	.286	.527	42	-2	2	2.05	0	0-23(12-1-12)/D-1	0	-0.2
1986 Bos-A	35	35	6	9	2	0	0	2	3	9	2	0	.257	.316	.314	.630	72	-1	4	3.63	0	0-33(0-28-5)	1	-0.1
1987 Bos-A	9	24	5	7	2	0	0	2	2	6	0	0	.292	.346	.375	.721	89	-0	3	5.23	1	/0-7(1-4-3),D-2	0	0.0
1988*Bos-A	57	78	17	15	2	1	1	6	7	15	2	0	.192	.259	.282	.541	49	-5	6	2.27	-2	0-45(5-9-38)/D-5	0	-0.7
1989 Bos-A	92	274	30	75	13	0	1	23	21	53	1	1	.274	.330	.332	.662	82	-6	28	3.54	0	0-89(9-48-32)/D-2	4	-0.8
1990 Bos-A	70	136	21	37	7	0	2	14	12	27	4	0	.272	.336	.368	.703	92	-0	16	4.02	-2	0-64(16-18-30)/D-1	2	-0.4
1991 Bos-A	44	55	7	9	2	0	1	7	3	10	1	1	.164	.207	.255	.461	26	-6	3	1.48	-1	0-23(10-4-10),D-14	0	-0.7
Total 7	331	630	89	158	30	1	5	55	49	124	11	2	.251	.308	.325	.633	73	-21	62	3.27	-3	0-284/D-25	7	-2.9
• RONAN, Marc	Edward Marcus Ronan b: 9/19/1969, Ozark, AL BL/TR, 6'2", 190 lbs. Deb: 9/21/1993																							
1993 StL-N	6	12	0	1	0	0	0	0	0	5	0	0	.083	.083	.083	.167	-56	-3	0	.20	-1	/C-6	0	-0.3
• RONDEAU, Henri	Henri Joseph Rondeau b: 5/5/1887, Danielson, CT d: 5/28/1943, Woonsocket, RI BL/TR, 5'10.5", 175 lbs. Deb: 4/11/1913 Career OF: 42-0-17																							
1913 Det-A	36	70	5	13	2	0	0	5	14	16	1	....	.186	.321	.214	.536	58	-3	5	2.26	2	C-16/1-6	1	0.0
1915 Was-A	14	40	3	7	0	0	0	4	4	3	1	2	.175	.250	.175	.425	27	-4	2	1.39	2	0-11(11-0-0)	1	-0.3
1916 Was-A	50	162	20	36	5	3	1	28	18	18	7	....	.222	.311	.309	.620	87	-2	18	3.62	0	0-48(31-0-17)	4	-0.5
Total 3	100	272	28	56	7	3	1	37	36	37	9	2	.206	.305	.265	.570	70	-10	25	2.89	4	/0-59,C-16,1-6	6	-0.8
• ROOF, Gene	Eugene Lawrence Roof b: 1/13/1958, Paducah, KY BB/TR, 6'2", 180 lbs. Deb: 9/3/1981 C Career OF: 25-1-6																							
1981 StL-N	23	60	11	18	6	0	0	3	12	16	5	1	.300	.417	.400	.817	129	4	11	6.84	-2	0-20(20-0-0)	3	0.1
1982 StL-N	11	15	3	4	0	0	0	2	1	4	2	0	.267	.313	.267	.579	63	-0	1	2.98	-0	/0-5(4-0-2)	0	0.0
1983 StL-N	6	3	1	0	0	0	0	0	0	0	0	0	.000	.000	.000	.000	-100	-1	0	.00	0	/0-1	0	-0.1
Mon-N	8	12	2	2	2	0	0	1	1	3	0	0	.167	.231	.333	.564	55	-1	1	2.65	0	/0-5(0-1-4)	0	-0.1
Yr.	14	15	3	2	2	0	0	1	1	3	0	0	.133	.188	.267	.454	26	-2	1	2.04	0	/0-6(1-1-4)	0	-0.2
Total 3	48	90	17	24	8	0	0	6	14	23	7	1	.267	.365	.356	.721	103	2	14	5.29	-3	/0-31	3	-0.2
• ROOF, Phil	Phillip Anthony Roof b: 3/5/1941, Paducah, KY BR/TR, 6'2", 210 lbs. Deb: 4/29/1961 C																							
1961 Mil-N	1	0	0	0	0	0	0	0	0	0	0	0	....	....	....	....	-106	0	0	....	-0	/C-1	0	0.0
1964 Mil-N	1	2	0	0	0	0	0	0	0	1	0	0	.000	.000	.000	.000	-99	-1	0	.00	0	/C-1	0	0.0
1965 Cal-A	9	22	1	3	0	0	0	0	0	6	0	0	.136	.136	.136	.273	-23	-4	0	.37	1	/C-9	1	-0.2
Cle-A	43	52	3	9	1	0	0	3	5	13	0	0	.173	.259	.192	.451	30	-5	3	1.70	2	C-41	2	-0.2
Yr.	52	74	4	12	1	0	0	3	5	19	0	0	.162	.225	.176	.401	16	-8	3	1.30	3	C-50	3	-0.4
1966 KC-A	127	369	33	77	14	3	7	44	37	95	2	5	.209	.286	.320	.606	76	-13	31	2.58	5	*C-123/1-2	7	-0.2
1967 KC-A	114	327	23	67	14	5	6	24	23	85	4	1	.205	.268	.333	.601	79	-8	30	3.04	2	*C-113	7	-0.1
1968 Oak-A	34	64	5	12	0	0	1	2	2	15	1	0	.188	.212	.234	.446	37	-5	3	1.46	-3	C-32	0	-0.7
1969 Oak-A	106	247	19	58	6	1	2	19	33	55	1	0	.235	.337	.291	.628	80	-5	25	3.37	-5	*C-106	7	-0.6
1970 Mil-A	110	321	39	73	7	1	13	37	32	72	3	2	.227	.307	.377	.684	87	-6	36	3.71	2	*C-107/1-1	9	0.1
1971 Mil-A	41	114	6	22	2	1	1	10	8	28	0	0	.193	.252	.254	.506	44	-8	7	1.83	2	C-39	2	-0.6
Min-A	31	87	6	21	4	0	0	6	8	18	0	1	.241	.305	.287	.593	67	-4	6	2.32	2	C-29	2	-0.1
Yr.	72	201	12	43	6	1	1	16	16	46	0	1	.214	.275	.269	.544	54	-12	13	2.04	3	C-68	4	-0.7
1972 Min-A	61	146	16	30	11	1	3	12	6	27	0	1	.205	.237	.356	.593	71	-6	12	2.66	-3	C-61	2	-0.8
1973 Min-A	47	117	10	23	4	1	1	15	13	27	0	0	.197	.277	.274	.550	53	-7	9	2.39	0	C-47	2	-0.5
1974 Min-A	44	97	10	19	1	0	2	13	6	24	0	0	.196	.257	.268	.525	49	-6	6	1.67	3	C-44	3	-0.2
1975 Min-A	63	126	18	38	2	0	7	21	9	28	0	0	.302	.353	.484	.837	132	5	22	6.06	2	C-63	7	0.9
1976 Min-A	18	46	1	10	3	0	0	4	2	6	0	0	.217	.250	.283	.533	54	-3	3	2.26	2	C-12/D-1	1	0.0
Chi-A	4	9	0	1	0	0	0	0	0	3	0	0	.111	.111	.111	.222	-35	-2	0	.00	1	/C-4	0	-0.1
Yr.	22	55	1	11	3	0	0	4	2	9	0	0	.200	.228	.255	.483	40	-4	3	1.82	3	C-16/D-1	1	-0.1
1977 Tor-A	3	5	0	0	0	0	0	0	0	1	0	0	.000	.000	.000	.000	-99	-1	0	.00	0	/C-3	0	-0.1
Total 15	857	2151	190	463	69	13	43	210	184	504	11	10	.215	.284	.319	.604	73	-78	193	2.87	12	C-835/1-3,D-1	52	-3.5
• ROOKS, George	George Brinton McClellan Rooks b: 10/21/1863, Chicago, IL d: 3/11/1935, Chicago, IL BR/TR, 5'11", 170 lbs. Deb: 5/12/1891																							
1891 Bos-N	5	16	1	2	0	0	0	0	4	1	0	....	.125	.300	.125	.425	23	-1	1	1.19	1	/0-5(5-0-0)	0	-0.1
• ROOMES, Rolando	Rolando Audley Roomes b: 2/15/1962, Kingston, Jamaica BR/TR, 6'3", 180 lbs. Deb: 4/12/1988 Career OF: 64-31-46																							
1988 Chi-N	17	16	3	3	0	0	0	0	0	4	0	1	.188	.188	.188	.375	8	-2	0	.72	-1	/0-5(4-0-1)	0	-0.3
1989 Cin-N	107	315	36	83	18	5	7	34	13	100	12	8	.263	.299	.419	.718	100	-2	38	4.23	-4	*0-100(45-29-37)	8	-0.9
1990 Cin-N	30	61	5	13	0	0	2	7	0	20	0	0	.213	.213	.311	.525	41	-5	3	1.85	1	0-19(12-0-7)	0	-0.5
Mon-N	16	14	1	4	0	1	0	1	1	6	0	2	.286	.333	.429	.762	112	-1	1	2.70	0	/0-6(3-2-1)	0	-0.1
Yr.	46	75	6	17	0	1	2	8	1	26	0	2	.227	.237	.333	.570	55	-6	5	2.01	1	0-25(15-2-8)	0	-0.6
Total 3	170	406	45	103	18	6	9	42	14	130	12	11	.254	.284	.394	.678	88	-11	43	3.65	-3	0-130	8	-1.9
• ROONEY, Frank	Frank Rooney b: 10/12/1884, Podebrady, Austria-Hungary d: 4/6/1977, Bessemer, MI Deb: 4/18/1914																							
1914 Ind-F	12	35	1	7	0	1	1	8	1	0	2	....	.200	.222	.343	.565	54	-2	3	2.52	-2	/1-9	0	-0.4
• ROONEY, Pat	Patrick Eugene Rooney b: 11/28/1957, Chicago, IL BR/TR, 6'1", 190 lbs. Deb: 9/9/1981																							
1981 Mon-N	4	5	0	0	0	0	0	0	0	3	0	0	.000	.000	.000	.000	-99	-1	0	.00	0	/0-2(0-0-2)	0	-0.2
• ROQUE, Jorge	Jorge (Vargas) Roque b: 4/28/1950, Ponce, Puerto Rico BR/TR, 5'10", 158 lbs. Deb: 9/4/1970 Career OF: 2-47-3																							
1970 StL-N	5	1	2	0	0	0	0	0	0	1	0	0	.000	.500	.000	.500	45	0	0	3.51	0	/0-1	0	0.0
1971 StL-N	3	10	2	3	0	0	0	1	0	3	1	0	.300	.300	.300	.600	68	-0	1	3.72	0	/0-3(0-3-0)	0	0.0
1972 StL-N	32	67	3	7	2	1	1	5	6	19	1	1	.104	.178	.209	.387	10	-8	2	.84	-1	0-24(0-21-3)	1	-1.1
1973 Mon-N	25	61	7	9	2	0	1	6	4	17	2	2	.148	.212	.230	.442	22	-7	2	1.19	-3	0-24(1-23-0)	0	-1.2
Total 4	65	139	14	19	4	1	2	12	10	40	4	3	.137	.205	.223	.428	19	-16	6	1.19	-5	/0-52	1	-2.3

• ROSADO, Luis Luis (Robles) Rosado b: 12/6/1955, Santurce, Puerto Rico BR/TR, 6', 180 lbs. Deb: 9/8/1977

YEAR TM-L	G	AB	R	H	2B	3B	HR	RBI	BB	SO	SB	CS	AVG	OBP	SLG	OPS	OPS+	BR/A	RC	RC/G	FR	G/POS	WS	TPW
1977 NY-N	9	24	1	5	1	0	0	3	1	3	0	0	.208	.269	.250	.519	42	-2	2	1.99	0	/1-7,C-1	0	-0.3
1980 NY-N	2	4	0	0	0	0	0	0	0	1	0	0	.000	.000	.000	.000	-103	-1	0	.00	0	/1-1	0	-0.1
Total 2	11	28	1	5	1	0	0	3	1	4	0	0	.179	.233	.214	.448	24	-3	2	1.62	0	/1-8,C-1	0	-0.4

• ROSAR, Buddy Warren Vincent Rosar b: 7/3/1914, Buffalo, NY d: 3/13/1994, Rochester, NY BR/TR, 5'9", 190 lbs. Deb: 4/29/1939

YEAR TM-L	G	AB	R	H	2B	3B	HR	RBI	BB	SO	SB	CS	AVG	OBP	SLG	OPS	OPS+	BR/A	RC	RC/G	FR	G/POS	WS	TPW
1939 NY-A	43	105	18	29	5	1	0	12	13	10	4	0	.276	.356	.343	.699	81	-2	14	4.57	-2	C-35	3	-0.1
1940 NY-A	73	228	34	68	11	3	4	37	19	11	7	1	.298	.357	.425	.783	106	3	36	5.63	-1	C-63	10	0.6
1941*NY-A	67	209	25	60	17	2	1	36	22	10	0	0	.287	.355	.402	.757	101	1	29	5.01	-2	C-60	9	0.2
1942*NY-A★	69	209	18	48	10	0	2	34	17	20	1	2	.230	.288	.306	.594	68	-10	17	2.65	1	C-58	5	-0.5
1943 Cle-A★	115	382	53	108	17	1	1	41	33	12	0	4	.283	.340	.340	.680	106	1	44	4.03	9	*C-114	15	1.8
1944 Cle-A	99	331	29	87	9	3	0	30	34	17	1	2	.263	.339	.308	.647	89	-4	37	3.81	4	C-98	9	0.6
1945 Phi-A	92	300	23	63	12	1	1	25	20	16	2	1	.210	.262	.267	.528	54	-18	20	2.14	1	C-85	2	-1.3
1946 Phi-A★	121	424	34	120	22	2	2	47	36	17	1	3	.283	.339	.358	.698	95	-3	48	3.92	11	*C-117	11	1.5
1947 Phi-A★	102	359	40	93	20	2	1	33	40	13	1	3	.259	.335	.334	.669	85	-8	41	3.81	10	*C-102	12	0.8
1948 Phi-A★	90	302	30	77	13	0	4	41	39	12	0	2	.255	.344	.338	.682	81	-8	38	4.38	2	C-90	11	-0.2
1949 Phi-A	32	95	7	19	2	0	0	6	16	5	0	0	.200	.315	.221	.536	45	-7	8	2.52	-1	C-31	1	-0.6
1950 Bos-A	27	84	13	25	2	0	1	12	7	4	0	0	.298	.352	.357	.709	75	-3	10	4.52	-2	C-25	2	-0.4
1951 Bos-A	58	170	11	39	7	0	1	13	19	14	0	0	.229	.307	.288	.595	56	-10	16	3.21	-2	C-56	4	-0.9
Total 13	988	3198	335	836	147	15	18	367	315	161	17	18	.261	.330	.334	.663	84	-67	358	3.82	29	C-934	94	1.5

• ROSARIO, Jimmy Angel Ramon (Ferrer) Rosario b: 5/5/1945, Bayamon, Puerto Rico BB/TR, 5'10", 155 lbs. Deb: 4/8/1971 Career OF: 20-63-1

YEAR TM-L	G	AB	R	H	2B	3B	HR	RBI	BB	SO	SB	CS	AVG	OBP	SLG	OPS	OPS+	BR/A	RC	RC/G	FR	G/POS	WS	TPW
1971*SF-N	92	192	26	43	6	1	0	13	33	35	7	4	.224	.341	.266	.606	75	-5	20	3.31	0	0-67(9-60-1)	5	-0.7
1972 SF-N	7	2	1	0	0	0	0	0	0	0	0	1	.000	.000	.000	.000	-99	-1	0	.00	0	/0-1	0	-0.1
1976 Mil-A	15	37	4	7	0	0	1	5	3	8	1	3	.189	.250	.270	.520	53	-3	2	1.62	0	0-12(11-2-0)/D-2	0	-0.5
Total 3	114	231	31	50	6	1	1	18	36	43	8	8	.216	.325	.264	.589	70	-9	22	2.97	-1	/0-80,D-2	5	-1.3

• ROSARIO, Mel Melvin Gregorio Rosario b: 5/25/1973, Santo Domingo, Dominican Republic BB/TR, 6', 191 lbs. Deb: 9/11/1997

YEAR TM-L	G	AB	R	H	2B	3B	HR	RBI	BB	SO	SB	CS	AVG	OBP	SLG	OPS	OPS+	BR/A	RC	RC/G	FR	G/POS	WS	TPW
1997 Bal-A	4	3	0	0	0	0	0	0	0	1	0	0	.000	.000	.000	.000	-103	-1	0	.00	-1	/C-4	0	-0.2

• ROSARIO, Santiago Santiago Rosario b: 7/25/1939, Guayanilla, Puerto Rico BL/TL, 5'11", 165 lbs. Deb: 6/23/1965

YEAR TM-L	G	AB	R	H	2B	3B	HR	RBI	BB	SO	SB	CS	AVG	OBP	SLG	OPS	OPS+	BR/A	RC	RC/G	FR	G/POS	WS	TPW
1965 KC-A	81	85	8	20	3	0	2	8	6	16	0	0	.235	.293	.341	.635	81	-2	8	3.32	0	1-31/0-3(2-0-1)	1	-0.4

• ROSARIO, Victor Victor Manuel (Rivera) Rosario b: 8/26/1966, Hato Mayor del Rey, Dominican Republic BR/TR, 5'11", 155 lbs. Deb: 9/6/1990

YEAR TM-L	G	AB	R	H	2B	3B	HR	RBI	BB	SO	SB	CS	AVG	OBP	SLG	OPS	OPS+	BR/A	RC	RC/G	FR	G/POS	WS	TPW
1990 Atl-N	9	7	3	1	0	0	0	0	1	1	0	0	.143	.250	.143	.393	10	-1	0	1.42	-1	/S-3,2-1	0	-0.2

• ROSE, Bobby Robert Richard Rose b: 3/15/1967, Covina, CA BR/TR, 5'11", 170 lbs. Deb: 8/12/1989

YEAR TM-L	G	AB	R	H	2B	3B	HR	RBI	BB	SO	SB	CS	AVG	OBP	SLG	OPS	OPS+	BR/A	RC	RC/G	FR	G/POS	WS	TPW
1989 Cal-A	14	38	4	8	1	2	1	3	2	10	0	0	.211	.268	.421	.689	93	-1	4	3.03	0	3-10/2-3	0	-0.1
1990 Cal-A	7	13	5	5	0	0	1	2	2	1	0	0	.385	.467	.615	1.082	204	2	4	11.87	-1	/2-4,3-3	1	0.1
1991 Cal-A	22	65	5	18	5	1	1	8	3	13	0	0	.277	.309	.431	.740	102	-0	8	4.68	1	/2-8,0-7(6-0-1),3-4,1-3	3	0.1
1992 Cal-A	30	84	10	18	5	0	2	10	8	9	1	1	.214	.298	.345	.643	79	-3	9	3.26	-2	2-28/1-2	3	-0.4
Total 4	73	200	24	49	11	3	5	23	15	33	1	1	.245	.307	.405	.712	98	-1	25	4.12	-3	/2-43,3-17,0-7,1-5	7	-0.4

• ROSE, Pete Peter Edward Rose, Jr. b: 11/16/1969, Cincinnati, OH BL/TR, 6'1", 180 lbs. Deb: 9/1/1997

YEAR TM-L	G	AB	R	H	2B	3B	HR	RBI	BB	SO	SB	CS	AVG	OBP	SLG	OPS	OPS+	BR/A	RC	RC/G	FR	G/POS	WS	TPW
1997 Cin-N	11	14	2	2	0	0	0	0	2	9	0	0	.143	.250	.143	.393	6	-2	1	1.42	-1	/3-2,1-1	0	-0.3

• ROSE, Pete Peter Edward "Charlie Hustle" Rose, Sr. b: 4/14/1941, Cincinnati, OH BB/TR, 5'11", 200 lbs. Deb: 4/8/1963 M Career OF: 671-70-594

YEAR TM-L	G	AB	R	H	2B	3B	HR	RBI	BB	SO	SB	CS	AVG	OBP	SLG	OPS	OPS+	BR/A	RC	RC/G	FR	G/POS	WS	TPW
1963 Cin-N	157	623	101	170	25	9	6	41	55	72	13	15	.273	.337	.371	.708	100	-2	77	4.28	-9	*2-157/0-1	19	0.4
1964 Cin-N	136	516	64	139	13	2	4	34	36	51	4	10	.269	.319	.326	.645	79	-17	53	3.57	2	*2-128	12	-0.4
1965 Cin-N★	162	670	117	**209**	35	11	11	81	69	76	8	3	.312	.383	.446	.829	124	25	118	6.60	-1	*2-162	27	4.0
1966 Cin-N	156	654	97	205	38	5	16	70	37	61	4	9	.313	.351	.460	.811	113	9	100	5.67	8	*2-140,3-16	25	3.1
1967 Cin-N★	148	585	86	176	32	8	12	76	56	66	11	6	.301	.365	.444	.809	117	15	95	6.03	-1	*0-123(123-1-0),2-35	24	1.1
1968 Cin-N★	149	626	94	**210**	42	6	10	49	56	76	3	7	**.335**	**.394**	.470	.863	149	37	113	6.94	3	*0-148(0-7-144)/2-3,1-1	32	3.3
1969 Cin-N★	156	627	**120**	218	33	11	16	82	88	65	7	10	**.348**	.432	.512	.944	155	48	138	8.46	-7	*0-156(0-56-101)/2-2	37	3.7
1970*Cin-N★	159	649	120	**205**	37	9	15	52	73	64	12	7	.316	.387	.470	.857	123	22	121	7.05	0	*0-159(1-5-155)	29	1.4
1971 Cin-N★	160	632	86	192	27	4	13	44	68	50	13	9	.304	.374	.421	.795	132	26	100	5.86	1	*0-158(0-1-158)	28	2.1
1972*Cin-N	154	645	107	**198**	31	11	6	57	73	46	10	3	.307	.383	.417	.801	135	33	109	6.37	7	*0-154(154-0-0)	32	3.2
1973*Cin-N★	160	680	115	**230**	36	8	5	64	65	42	10	7	**.338**	.401	.437	.838	139	37	119	6.81	5	*0-159(159-0-0)	34	3.3
1974 Cin-N★	163	652	**110**	185	**45**	7	3	51	106	54	2	4	.284	.388	.388	.776	119	20	104	5.76	6	*0-163(163-0-0)	27	1.7
1975*Cin-N★	162	662	**112**	210	**47**	4	7	74	89	50	0	1	.317	.407	.432	.839	130	31	120	6.95	-9	*3-137,0-35(35-0-0)	31	2.1
1976*Cin-N★	162	665	**130**	**215**	**42**	6	10	63	86	54	9	5	.323	.406	.450	.855	139	37	123	6.99	4	*3-159/0-1	30	4.3
1977 Cin-N★	162	655	95	204	38	7	9	64	66	42	16	4	.311	.379	.432	.811	115	17	111	6.41	-6	*3-161	23	0.9
1978 Cin-N★	159	655	103	198	**51**	3	7	52	62	30	13	9	.302	.365	.421	.787	119	16	102	5.71	-10	*3-156/0-7(7-0-0),1-2	27	0.4
1979 Phi-N★	163	628	90	208	40	5	4	59	95	32	20	11	.331	.421	.430	.851	128	30	116	6.87	-7	*1-159/3-5,2-1	27	1.4
1980*Phi-N★	162	655	95	185	**42**	1	1	64	66	33	12	8	.282	.354	.354	.708	93	-5	83	4.51	-1	*1-162	17	-1.7
1981*Phi-N★	107	431	73	**140**	18	5	0	33	46	26	4	4	.325	.394	.390	.784	118	11	67	5.91	-1	*1-107	17	0.5
1982 Phi-N★	162	634	80	172	25	4	3	54	66	32	8	8	.271	.347	.338	.684	90	-8	75	4.13	-2	*1-162	17	-2.1
1983*Phi-N	151	493	52	121	14	3	0	45	52	28	7	7	.245	.320	.286	.606	70	-20	46	3.10	-2	*1-112,0-35(0-0-35)	7	-3.1
1984 Mon-N	95	278	34	72	6	2	0	23	31	20	1	1	.259	.335	.295	.630	82	-6	27	3.33	7	1-40,0-28(28-0-0)	4	-0.3
Cin-N	26	96	9	35	9	0	0	11	9	7	0	0	.365	.430	.458	.888	143	6	20	8.53	-2	1-23	4	0.3
Yr.	121	374	43	107	15	2	0	34	40	27	1	1	.286	.360	.337	.697	98	0	47	4.47	5	1-63,0-28(28-0-0)	8	0.0
1985 Cin-N★	119	405	60	107	12	2	2	46	86	35	8	1	.264	.398	.319	.716	98	6	59	5.05	-1	*1-110	14	-0.1
1986 Cin-N	72	237	15	52	8	2	0	25	30	31	3	0	.219	.317	.270	.587	61	-11	23	3.32	-2	1-61	3	-1.7
Total 24	3562	14053	2165	**4256**	746	135	160	1314	1566	1143	198	149	.303	.377	.409	.786	117	357	2220	5.80	-17	*0-1327,1-939,3-634,2-628	547	27.8

• ROSEBORO, Johnny John Junior Roseboro b: 5/13/1933, Ashland, OH d: 8/16/2002, Los Angeles, CA BL/TR, 5'11.5", 190 lbs. Deb: 6/14/1957 C

YEAR TM-L	G	AB	R	H	2B	3B	HR	RBI	BB	SO	SB	CS	AVG	OBP	SLG	OPS	OPS+	BR/A	RC	RC/G	FR	G/POS	WS	TPW
1957 Bro-N	35	69	6	10	2	0	2	6	10	20	0	0	.145	.253	.261	.514	35	-6	5	2.33	-1	C-19/1-5	1	-0.7
1958 LA-N★	114	384	52	104	11	9	14	43	36	56	11	8	.271	.336	.456	.792	104	1	58	5.21	-3	*C-104/0-5(4-1-0)	14	0.3
1959*LA-N	118	397	39	92	14	7	10	38	52	69	7	5	.232	.325	.378	.703	81	-11	50	4.12	1	*C-117	15	-0.4
1960 LA-N	103	287	22	61	15	3	8	42	44	53	7	6	.213	.325	.369	.695	84	-6	37	4.19	1	C-87/1-1,3-1	10	-0.1
1961 LA-N★	128	394	59	99	16	6	18	59	56	62	6	4	.251	.350	.459	.810	104	2	67	5.90	3	*C-125	20	1.2
1962 LA-N★	128	389	45	97	16	7	7	55	50	60	12	3	.249	.345	.380	.726	101	3	54	4.64	-0	*C-128	16	0.9
1963*LA-N	135	470	50	111	13	7	9	49	36	50	7	6	.236	.295	.351	.646	91	-6	48	3.36	-3	*C-134	16	-0.3
1964 LA-N	134	414	42	119	24	1	3	45	44	61	3	3	.287	.361	.372	.733	115	9	57	4.84	2	*C-128	19	1.9
1965*LA-N	136	437	42	102	10	0	8	57	34	51	1	6	.233	.292	.311	.603	75	-17	39	2.99	-5	*C-131/3-1	13	-1.6
1966*LA-N	142	445	47	123	23	2	9	53	44	51	3	2	.276	.346	.398	.743	115	10	60	4.73	1	*C-138	21	1.9
1967 LA-N	116	334	37	91	18	2	4	24	38	33	2	4	.272	.350	.374	.725	117	7	43	4.42	2	*C-107	13	1.5
1968 Min-A	135	380	31	82	12	0	8	39	46	57	2	3	.216	.304	.311	.614	82	-8	37	3.14	-2	*C-117	10	-0.4
1969*Min-A★	115	361	33	95	12	0	3	32	39	44	5	5	.263	.335	.321	.656	82	-9	39	3.72	2	*C-111	10	-0.2
1970 Was-A	46	86	7	20	4	0	1	6	18	10	1	1	.233	.365	.314	.679	94	0	11	4.25	-1	C-30	3	0.0
Total 14	1585	4847	512	1206	190	44	104	548	547	677	67	56	.249	.329	.371	.700	95	-31	604	4.21	0	*C-1476/1-6,0-5,3-2	181	3.9

• ROSELLI, Bob Robert Edward Roselli b: 12/10/1931, San Francisco, CA BR/TR, 5'11", 185 lbs. Deb: 8/16/1955

YEAR TM-L	G	AB	R	H	2B	3B	HR	RBI	BB	SO	SB	CS	AVG	OBP	SLG	OPS	OPS+	BR/A	RC	RC/G	FR	G/POS	WS	TPW
1955 Mil-N	6	9	1	2	1	0	0	0	1	4	0	0	.222	.364	.333	.697	91	-0	1	4.94	0	/C-2	0	0.0
1956 Mil-N	4	2	1	1	0	0	1	1	0	1	0	0	.500	.500	2.000	2.500	563	1	2	54.00	0	/C-3	1	0.2
1958 Mil-N	1	1	0	0	0	0	0	0	0	0	0	0	.000	.000	.000	.000	-109	-0	0	.00	0	....	0	0.0
1961 Chi-A	22	38	2	10	3	0	0	4	0	11	0	0	.263	.263	.342	.605	61	-2	3	2.81	-0	C-10	1	-0.2
1962 Chi-A	35	64	4	12	3	1	1	5	11	15	1	0	.188	.316	.313	.628	70	-2	7	3.60	0	C-20	2	-0.2
Total 5	68	114	8	25	7	1	2	10	12	31	1	0	.219	.305	.351	.656	75	-4	13	3.95	0	/C-35	4	-0.2

YEAR TM-L	G	AB	R	H	2B	3B	HR	RBI	BB	SO	SB	CS	AVG	OBP	SLG	OPS	OPS+	BR/A	RC	RC/G	FR	G/POS	WS	TPW
• ROSELLO, Dave	David (Rodriguez) Rosello b: 6/26/1950, Mayaguez, Puerto Rico BR/TR, 5'11", 160 lbs. Deb: 9/10/1972																							
1972 Chi-N	5	12	2	3	0	0	1	3	3	2	0	0	.250	.400	.500	.900	139	1	3	8.14	-2	/S-5	1	-0.1
1973 Chi-N	16	38	4	10	2	0	0	2	2	4	2	2	.263	.300	.316	.616	66	-2	2	1.94	-3	2-13/S-1	1	-0.4
1974 Chi-N	62	148	9	30	7	0	0	10	10	28	1	1	.203	.253	.250	.503	39	-12	10	2.22	-5	2-49,S-12	1	-1.5
1975 Chi-N	19	58	7	15	2	0	1	8	9	8	0	1	.259	.358	.345	.703	92	-1	7	4.08	-4	S-19	1	-0.3
1976 Chi-N	91	227	27	55	5	1	1	11	41	33	1	2	.242	.361	.286	.647	78	-5	25	3.80	-7	S-86/2-1	7	-0.3
1977 Chi-N	56	82	18	18	2	1	1	9	12	12	0	0	.220	.319	.305	.624	61	-4	9	3.54	-4	3-21,S-10/2-3	1	-0.8
1979 Cle-A	59	107	20	26	6	1	3	14	15	27	1	0	.243	.336	.402	.738	98	0	16	4.44	-3	2-33,3-14,S-11	4	-0.1
1980 Cle-A	71	117	16	29	3	0	2	12	9	19	0	0	.248	.302	.325	.626	71	-5	12	3.35	-7	2-43,3-22/S-3,D-1	2	-1.0
1981 Cle-A	43	84	11	20	4	0	1	7	7	12	0	1	.238	.297	.321	.618	79	-3	8	2.95	-6	2-26/3-8,D-4,S-4	2	-0.8
Total 9	**422**	**873**	**114**	**206**	**31**	**3**	**10**	**76**	**108**	**145**	**5**	**7**	**.236**	**.321**	**.313**	**.633**	**74**	**-31**	**92**	**3.44**	**-41**	**2-168,S-151/3-65,D-5**	**20**	**-5.3**
• ROSEMAN, Chief	James John Roseman b: 7/4/1856, Brooklyn, NY d: 7/4/1938, Brooklyn, NY BR/TR, 5'7", 167 lbs. Deb: 5/1/1882 M Career OF: 123-351-189																							
1882 Tro-N	82	331	41	78	21	6	1	29	3	41	....	....	.236	.243	.344	.587	90	-3	28	3.08	-4	*0-82(1-0-81)	6	-0.8
1883 NY-a	93	398	48	100	13	6	0	0	11	....	....	....	.251	.271	.314	.585	84	-8	35	3.27	-2	*0-91(3-8-80)/1-2	8	-1.1
1884*NY-a	107	436	97	130	16	11	4	0	21	....	....	....	.298	.339	.413	.752	147	23	63	5.62	-3	*0-107(4-103-0)	21	1.5
1885 NY-a	101	410	72	114	13	14	4	46	25	....	....	....	.278	.335	.407	.742	145	23	57	5.23	-7	*0-101(1-99-1)/P-1	19	0.9
1886 NY-a	134	559	90	127	19	10	5	53	24	....	6	....	.227	.269	.324	.593	89	-7	52	3.22	-2	*0-134(88-44-3)/P-1	10	-1.4
1887 Phi-a	21	83	16	26	2	1	0	8	10	....	3	....	.313	.352	.274	.626	76	-2	8	3.93	-2	0-21(0-21-0)	2	-0.3
NY-a	60	250	30	64	10	1	1	27	9	....	3	....	.256	.265	.290	.555	57	-14	20	2.88	-7	0-59(9-36-14)/1-3,P-2	2	-2.1
Bro-a	1	3	2	1	0	0	0	1	0	....	0	....	.333	.500	.333	.833	133	0	1	6.92	-1	/0-1	0	0.0
Yr.	82	336	48	91	12	2	1	36	19	....	6	....	.271	.290	.287	.577	63	-15	29	3.16	-10	0-81(9-57-23)/1-3,P-2	4	-2.4
1890 StL-a	80	302	47	103	26	0	2	58	30	....	7	....	.341	.449	.447	.896	144	19	65	8.70	-6	0-58(17-40-1),1-22	13	0.8
Lou-a	2	8	0	2	0	0	0	0	0	....	0	....	.250	.250	.250	.500	48	-1	1	2.26	-1	/1-2	0	-0.1
Yr.	82	310	47	105	26	0	2	58	30	....	7	....	.339	.444	.442	.886	142	18	66	8.51	-7	0-58(17-40-1),1-24	13	0.7
Total 7	**681**	**2780**	**443**	**745**	**120**	**49**	**17**	**222**	**133**	**41**	**19**	**....**	**.268**	**.312**	**.360**	**.672**	**110**	**30**	**329**	**4.39**	**-35**	**0-654/1-29,P-4**	**81**	**-2.7**
• ROSEN, Al	Albert Leonard "Flip" Rosen b: 2/29/1924, Spartanburg, SC BR/TR, 5'10.5", 180 lbs. Deb: 9/10/1947																							
1947 Cle-A	7	9	1	1	0	0	0	0	0	3	0	0	.111	.111	.111	.222	-39	-2	0	.38	0	/3-2,0-1	0	-0.2
1948*Cle-A	5	5	0	1	0	0	0	0	0	2	0	0	.200	.200	.200	.400	7	-1	0	.00	0	/3-2	0	-0.1
1949 Cle-A	23	44	3	7	2	0	0	5	7	4	0	1	.159	.275	.205	.479	28	-5	3	1.80	-1	3-10	0	-0.6
1950 Cle-A	155	554	100	159	23	4	**37**	116	100	72	5	7	.287	.405	.543	.948	146	38	120	7.50	9	*3-154	29	4.3
1951 Cle-A	154	573	82	152	30	1	24	102	85	71	7	5	.265	.362	.447	.809	125	20	96	5.89	-10	*3-154	25	0.9
1952 Cle-A★	148	567	101	171	32	5	28	**105**	75	54	8	6	.302	.387	.524	.911	162	46	115	7.35	-16	*3-147/1-4,S-3	31	3.1
1953 Cle-A★	155	599	**115**	201	27	5	**43**	**145**	85	48	8	7	.336	.422	**.613**	**1.034**	**181**	**67**	155	**9.86**	-2	*3-154/1-1,S-1	**42**	**6.5**
1954*Cle-A★	137	466	76	140	20	2	24	102	85	43	6	2	.300	.412	.506	.918	148	34	100	7.66	-5	3-87,1-46/2-1,S-1	27	2.8
1955 Cle-A★	139	492	61	120	13	1	21	81	92	44	4	2	.244	.367	.402	.770	103	5	76	5.21	-2	*3-106,1-41	16	0.1
1956 Cle-A	121	416	64	111	18	2	15	61	58	44	1	3	.267	.357	.428	.784	104	2	62	5.14	-3	*3-116	15	-0.1
Total 10	**1044**	**3725**	**603**	**1063**	**165**	**20**	**192**	**717**	**587**	**385**	**39**	**33**	**.285**	**.386**	**.495**	**.882**	**139**	**204**	**729**	**6.90**	**-29**	**3-932/1-92,S-5,2-1,0-1**	**185**	**16.7**
• ROSEN, Goody	Goodwin George Rosen b: 8/28/1912, Toronto, Canada d: 4/6/1994, Toronto, Canada BL/TL, 5'9.5", 155 lbs. Deb: 9/14/1937 Career OF: 23-330-121																							
1937 Bro-N	22	77	10	24	5	1	0	6	6	6	2	....	.312	.361	.403	.764	105	1	12	6.14	0	0-21(8-13-0)	3	0.0
1938 Bro-N	138	473	75	133	17	11	4	51	65	43	0	....	.281	.368	.389	.757	106	6	74	5.73	6	*0-113(13-43-59)	16	0.6
1939 Bro-N	54	183	22	46	6	4	1	12	23	21	4	....	.251	.335	.344	.679	80	-5	23	4.41	-2	0-47(1-40-7)	5	-0.8
1944 Bro-N	89	264	38	69	8	3	0	23	26	27	0	....	.261	.330	.314	.644	83	-5	29	3.96	5	0-65(1-62-3)	6	-0.2
1945 Bro-N★	145	606	126	197	24	11	12	75	50	36	4	....	.325	.379	.460	.840	134	26	110	6.94	-5	*0-141(0-141-0)	31	1.7
1946 Bro-N	3	3	0	1	0	0	0	0	0	1	0	....	.333	.333	.333	.667	88	-0	0	4.50	0	/0-1	0	0.0
NY-N	100	310	39	87	11	4	5	30	48	32	2	....	.281	.377	.390	.767	117	8	47	5.33	-2	0-84(0-30-52)	10	0.4
Yr.	103	313	39	88	11	4	5	30	48	33	2	....	.281	.377	.390	.767	117	8	47	5.33	-2	0-85(0-31-52)	10	0.4
Total 6	**551**	**1916**	**310**	**557**	**71**	**34**	**22**	**197**	**218**	**166**	**12**	**....**	**.291**	**.364**	**.398**	**.762**	**111**	**31**	**295**	**5.66**	**2**	**0-472**	**71**	**1.8**
• ROSENBERG, Harry	Harry Rosenberg b: 6/22/1908, San Francisco, CA d: 4/13/1997, San Mateo, CA BR/TR, 5'10", 160 lbs. Deb: 7/15/1930																							
1930 NY-N	9	5	1	0	0	0	0	0	1	4	0	....	.000	.167	.000	.167	-56	-1	0	.21	0	/0-3(0-2-1)	0	-0.1
• ROSENBERG, Lou	Louis Rosenberg b: 3/5/1904, San Francisco, CA d: 9/8/1991, San Francisco, CA BR/TR, 5'7", 155 lbs. Deb: 5/22/1923																							
1923 Chi-A	3	4	0	1	0	0	0	0	0	1	0	1	.250	.250	.250	.500	32	-1	0	.00	-1	/2-2	0	-0.2
• ROSENFELD, Max	Max Rosenfeld b: 12/23/1902, New York, NY d: 3/10/1969, Miami, FL BR/TR, 5'8", 175 lbs. Deb: 4/21/1931 Career OF: 2-14-19																							
1931 Bro-N	3	9	0	2	1	0	0	0	1	1	0	....	.222	.300	.333	.633	70	-0	1	3.53	-0	/0-3(0-3-0)	0	0.0
1932 Bro-N	34	39	8	14	3	0	2	7	0	10	2	....	.359	.359	.590	.949	153	3	8	8.36	0	0-30(1-10-19)	2	0.2
1933 Bro-N	5	9	0	1	0	0	0	0	1	1	0	....	.111	.200	.111	.311	-10	-1	0	.39	0	/0-2(1-1-0)	0	-0.1
Total 3	**42**	**57**	**8**	**17**	**4**	**0**	**2**	**7**	**2**	**12**	**2**	**....**	**.298**	**.322**	**.474**	**.796**	**111**	**1**	**9**	**5.79**	**0**	**/0-35**	**2**	**0.0**
• ROSENTHAL, Larry	Lawrence John Rosenthal b: 5/21/1910, St. Paul, MN d: 3/4/1992, Woodbury, MN BL/TL, 6'.5", 190 lbs. Deb: 6/20/1936 Career OF: 109-177-131																							
1936 Chi-A	85	317	71	89	15	8	3	46	59	37	2	0	.281	.394	.407	.801	95	-0	55	6.28	6	0-80(0-80-0)	11	0.3
1937 Chi-A	58	97	20	28	5	3	0	9	9	20	1	0	.289	.355	.402	.757	90	-1	14	5.45	2	0-25(0-25-0)	3	0.0
1938 Chi-A	61	105	14	30	5	1	1	12	12	13	0	1	.286	.359	.381	.740	83	-3	15	5.01	1	0-22(0-22-2)	2	-0.2
1939 Chi-A	107	324	50	86	21	5	10	51	53	46	6	4	.265	.369	.454	.822	106	3	58	6.11	-3	0-93(0-20-75)	11	-0.5
1940 Chi-A	107	276	46	83	14	5	6	42	64	32	2	3	.301	.432	.453	.885	128	15	61	7.99	2	0-92(68-15-11)	14	1.2
1941 Chi-A	20	59	9	14	4	0	0	1	12	5	0	0	.237	.366	.305	.671	80	-1	7	3.93	-1	0-18(0-2-16)	1	-0.3
Cle-A	45	75	10	14	3	1	1	8	9	10	1	0	.187	.274	.293	.567	53	-5	7	2.85	0	0-14(5-8-1)/1-1	1	-0.5
Yr.	65	134	19	28	7	1	1	9	21	15	1	0	.209	.316	.299	.615	65	-6	14	3.32	-1	0-32(5-10-17)/1-1	2	-0.8
1944 NY-A	36	101	9	20	3	0	0	9	19	15	1	0	.198	.325	.228	.553	57	-4	9	3.03	2	0-26(10-5-11)	2	-0.4
Phi-A	32	54	5	11	2	0	1	6	5	9	0	0	.204	.271	.296	.567	63	-3	5	2.92	0	0-19(5-0-15)	1	-0.4
Yr.	68	155	14	31	5	0	1	15	24	24	1	0	.200	.307	.252	.559	59	-7	14	2.99	1	0-45(15-5-26)	3	-0.9
1945 Phi-A	28	75	6	15	3	2	0	5	9	8	0	1	.200	.286	.293	.579	68	-3	7	2.97	0	0-21(21-0-0)	1	-0.5
Total 8	**579**	**1483**	**240**	**390**	**75**	**25**	**22**	**189**	**251**	**195**	**13**	**9**	**.263**	**.370**	**.392**	**.762**	**95**	**-3**	**237**	**5.57**	**9**	**0-410/1-1**	**47**	**-1.2**
• ROSENTHAL, Si	Simon Rosenthal b: 11/13/1903, Boston, MA d: 4/7/1969, Boston, MA BL/TL, 5'9", 165 lbs. Deb: 9/8/1925 Career OF: 55-0-29																							
1925 Bos-A	19	72	6	19	5	2	0	8	7	3	1	0	.264	.329	.389	.718	82	-2	10	4.79	0	0-17(7-0-10)	1	-0.3
1926 Bos-A	104	285	34	76	12	3	4	34	19	18	4	1	.267	.317	.372	.689	82	-8	34	4.21	-8	0-67(48-0-19)	4	-1.9
Total 2	**123**	**357**	**40**	**95**	**17**	**5**	**4**	**42**	**26**	**21**	**5**	**1**	**.266**	**.319**	**.375**	**.695**	**82**	**-9**	**44**	**4.32**	**-8**	**/0-84**	**5**	**-2.2**
• ROSER, Bunny	John William Joseph "Jack" Roser b: 11/15/1901, St. Louis, MO d: 5/6/1979, Rocky Hill, CT BL/TL, 5'11", 175 lbs. Deb: 8/24/1922																							
1922 Bos-N	32	113	13	27	3	4	0	16	10	19	2	1	.239	.306	.336	.643	69	-5	12	3.45	-2	0-32(32-0-0)	2	-0.9
• ROSKOS, John	John Edward Roskos b: 11/19/1974, Victorville, CA BR/TR, 5'11", 195 lbs. Deb: 4/20/1998																							
1998 Fla-N	10	10	1	1	0	0	0	0	0	5	0	0	.100	.100	.100	.200	-49	-2	0	.30	0	/1-1	0	-0.2
1999 Fla-N	13	12	0	2	2	0	0	1	1	7	0	0	.167	.231	.333	.564	43	-1	1	2.65	0	/C-1	0	-0.1
2000 SD-N	14	27	0	1	1	0	0	1	3	7	0	0	.037	.133	.074	.207	-49	-6	0	.28	-1	/0-6(4-0-2),1-2	0	-0.7
Total 3	**37**	**49**	**1**	**4**	**3**	**0**	**0**	**2**	**4**	**19**	**0**	**0**	**.082**	**.151**	**.143**	**.294**	**-27**	**-10**	**1**	**.80**	**-1**	**/0-6,1-3,C-1**	**0**	**-1.0**
• ROSS, Chet	Chester James Ross b: 4/1/1917, Buffalo, NY d: 2/21/1989, Buffalo, NY BR/TR, 6'1", 195 lbs. Deb: 9/15/1939 Career OF: 312-1-28																							
1939 Bos-N	11	31	4	10	1	1	0	0	2	10	0	....	.323	.364	.419	.783	118	1	5	6.32	1	/0-8(1-1-7)	1	0.1
1940 Bos-N	149	569	84	160	23	14	17	89	59	127	4	....	.281	.352	.460	.812	129	22	96	6.22	5	*0-149(149-0-0)	24	1.8
1941 Bos-N	29	50	1	6	1	0	0	4	9	17	0	....	.120	.254	.140	.394	14	-5	2	1.21	0	0-12(12-0-0)	0	-0.6
1942 Bos-N	76	220	20	43	7	2	5	19	16	37	0	....	.195	.250	.314	.564	66	-10	17	2.54	0	0-57(52-0-6)	2	-1.4
1943 Bos-N	94	285	27	62	12	2	7	32	26	67	1	....	.218	.285	.347	.633	84	-7	28	3.26	6	0-73(73-0-0)	5	-0.6
1944 Bos-N	54	154	20	35	9	2	5	26	12	23	1	....	.227	.287	.409	.697	91	-3	18	3.93	4	0-38(25-0-15)	3	-0.1
Total 6	**413**	**1309**	**156**	**316**	**53**	**21**	**34**	**170**	**124**	**281**	**6**	**....**	**.241**	**.309**	**.392**	**.701**	**99**	**-3**	**166**	**4.39**	**16**	**0-337**	**35**	**-0.8**

YEAR TM-L	G	AB	R	H	2B	3B	HR	RBI	BB	SO	SB	CS	AVG	OBP	SLG	OPS	OPS+	BR/A	RC	RC/G	FR	G/POS	WS	TPW
• ROSS, Cody	Cody J. Ross b: 12/23/1980, Portales, NM BR/TL, 5'11", 180 lbs. Deb: 7/4/2003																							
2003 Det-A	6	19	1	4	1	0	1	5	1	3	0	0	.211	.286	.421	.707	90	-0	2	4.16	0	/O-6(0-0-6)	1	-0.1
• ROSS, Dave	David Wade Ross b: 3/19/1977, Bainbridge, GA BR/TR, 6'2", 205 lbs. Deb: 6/29/2002																							
2002 LA-N	8	10	2	2	1	0	1	2	2	4	0	0	.200	.385	.600	.985	165	1	3	8.80	0	/C-6	1	0.1
2003 LA-N	40	124	19	32	7	0	10	18	13	42	0	0	.258	.338	.556	.895	136	6	23	6.28	-2	C-38	4	0.7
Total 2	48	134	21	34	8	0	11	20	15	46	0	0	.254	.342	.560	.902	138	7	25	6.47	-2	/C-44	5	0.8
• ROSS, Don	Donald Raymond Ross b: 7/16/1914, Pasadena, CA d: 3/28/1996, Arcadia, CA BR/TR, 6'1", 200 lbs. Deb: 4/19/1938 Career OF: 11-0-104																							
1938 Det-A	77	265	22	69	7	1	1	30	29	11	1	0	.260	.333	.306	.639	58	-17	29	3.82	3	3-75	5	-1.0
1940 Bro-N	10	38	4	11	2	0	1	8	3	3	1	....	.289	.341	.421	.763	103	0	6	5.73	0	3-10	1	0.1
1942 Det-A	87	226	29	62	10	2	3	30	36	16	2	1	.274	.379	.376	.755	104	3	34	5.34	-3	O-38(5-0-33),3-20	6	-0.1
1943 Det-A	89	247	19	66	13	0	0	18	20	3	2	0	.267	.325	.320	.644	82	-5	27	3.79	-4	O-38(6-0-32),S-18/2-7,3-1	5	-1.0
1944 Det-A	66	167	14	35	5	0	2	15	14	9	2	1	.210	.275	.275	.550	54	-10	13	2.44	1	O-37(0-0-37)/S-2,1-1	1	-1.2
1945 Det-A	8	29	3	11	4	0	0	4	5	1	2	0	.379	.471	.517	.988	175	4	8	11.11	0	/3-8	2	0.4
Cle-A	106	363	26	95	15	1	2	43	42	15	0	4	.262	.340	.325	.665	98	-2	41	3.78	-6	*3-106	9	-0.6
Yr.	114	392	29	106	19	1	2	47	47	16	2	4	.270	.350	.339	.689	103	2	49	4.22	-6	*3-114	11	-0.3
1946 Cle-A	55	153	12	41	7	0	3	14	17	12	0	0	.268	.341	.373	.714	106	1	20	4.71	-3	3-41/O-2(0-0-2)	5	-0.2
Total 7	498	1488	129	390	63	4	12	162	166	70	10	6	.262	.338	.334	.672	87	-24	177	4.12	-12	3-261,O-115/S-20,2-7,1-1	34	-3.8
• ROSSI, Joe	Joseph Anthony Rossi b: 3/13/1921, Oakland, CA d: 2/20/1999, Oakland, CA BR/TR, 6'1", 205 lbs. Deb: 4/20/1952																							
1952 Cin-N	55	145	14	32	0	1	1	6	20	20	1	0	.221	.319	.255	.574	61	-6	13	3.08	1	C-46	3	-0.3
• ROSSMAN, Claude	Claude R. Rossman b: 6/17/1881, Philmont, NY d: 1/16/1928, Poughkeepsie, NY BL/TL, 6', 188 lbs. Deb: 9/16/1904 Career OF: 0-2-18																							
1904 Cle-A	18	62	5	13	5	0	0	6	0	....	0	....	.210	.210	.290	.500	58	-3	4	2.11	-2	O-17(0-1-16)	0	-0.7
1906 Cle-A	118	396	49	122	13	2	1	53	17	....	11	....	.308	.338	.359	.697	120	8	55	5.02	-4	*1-105/O-1	10	0.2
1907*Det-A	153	571	60	158	21	8	0	69	33	....	20	....	.277	.318	.342	.660	107	3	73	4.42	-14	*1-153	17	-1.5
1908*Det-A	138	524	45	154	33	13	2	71	27	....	8	....	.294	.330	.418	.748	137	19	74	4.96	4	*1-138	23	2.2
1909 Det-A	82	287	16	75	8	3	0	39	13	....	10	....	.261	.293	.310	.603	87	-5	29	3.39	-2	1-75	6	-1.0
StL-A	2	8	0	1	0	0	0	0	0	....	0	....	.125	.125	.125	.250	-23	-1	0	.40	0	/O-2(0-0-2)	0	-0.2
Yr.	84	295	16	76	8	3	0	39	13	....	10	....	.258	.289	.305	.594	84	-6	29	3.30	-2	1-75/O-2(0-0-2)	6	-1.1
Total 5	511	1848	175	523	80	26	3	238	90	....	49	....	.283	.318	.359	.677	113	20	236	4.42	-18	1-471/O-20	56	-0.8
• ROSSY, Rico	Elam Jose (Ramos) Rossy b: 2/16/1964, San Juan, Puerto Rico BR/TR, 5'10", 175 lbs. Deb: 9/11/1991																							
1991 Atl-N	5	1	0	0	0	0	0	0	0	1	0	0	.000	.000	.000	.000	-94	-0	0	.00	-1	/S-1	0	-0.1
1992 KC-A	59	149	21	32	8	1	1	12	20	20	0	3	.215	.312	.302	.614	71	-7	13	2.71	-1	S-51/3-9,2-3	3	-0.4
1993 KC-A	46	86	10	19	4	0	2	12	9	11	0	0	.221	.302	.337	.639	68	-4	10	3.81	0	2-24,3-16,S-11	2	-0.3
1998 Sea-A	37	81	12	16	6	0	1	4	6	13	0	0	.198	.253	.309	.562	45	-7	7	2.75	3	3-25/2-6,S-4,D-1	1	-0.3
Total 4	147	317	43	67	18	1	4	28	35	45	0	3	.211	.294	.312	.606	63	-18	30	2.99	1	/S-67,3-50,2-33,D-1	6	-1.0
• ROTH, Braggo	Robert Frank Roth b: 8/28/1892, Burlington, WI d: 9/11/1936, Chicago, IL BR/TR, 5'7.5", 170 lbs. Deb: 9/1/1914 Career OF: 42-135-550																							
1914 Chi-A	34	126	14	37	4	6	1	10	8	25	3	3	.294	.355	.444	.800	142	5	20	5.56	3	O-34(0-12-22)	6	0.7
1915 Chi-A	70	240	44	60	6	10	3	35	29	50	12	6	.250	.338	.396	.734	116	4	34	4.71	-11	3-35,O-30(29-1-0)	9	-0.8
Cle-A	39	144	23	43	4	7	4	20	22	22	14	4	.299	.399	.507	.906	168	13	32	7.82	-5	O-39(0-39-0)	6	0.7
Yr.	109	384	67	103	10	17	**7**	55	51	72	26	10	.268	.361	.438	.799	136	17	66	5.85	-16	O-69(29-40-0),3-35	15	-0.1
1916 Cle-A	125	409	50	117	19	7	4	72	38	48	29	14	.286	.350	.396	.746	117	8	62	4.97	5	*O-112(0-9-103)	15	0.7
1917 Cle-A	145	495	69	141	30	9	1	72	52	73	51	....	.285	.355	.388	.743	118	11	82	5.71	6	*O-135(0-0-135)	19	1.1
1918 Cle-A	106	375	53	106	21	12	1	59	53	41	35	....	.283	.383	.411	.794	127	14	69	6.27	-5	*O-106(2-0-104)	16	0.5
1919 Phi-A	48	195	33	63	13	8	5	29	15	21	11	....	.323	.377	.549	.926	156	13	42	8.15	-4	O-48(0-0-48)	7	0.7
Bos-A	63	227	32	58	9	4	0	23	24	32	9	....	.256	.337	.330	.668	93	-1	27	4.07	-6	O-58(1-57-0)	6	-1.1
Yr.	111	422	65	121	22	12	5	52	39	53	20	....	.287	.355	.431	.787	122	12	69	5.84	-9	*O-106(1-57-48)	13	-0.4
1920 Was-A	138	468	80	136	23	8	9	92	75	57	24	12	.291	.395	.432	.827	122	20	85	6.30	-17	*O-128(7-0-121)	18	-0.3
1921 NY-A	43	152	29	43	9	2	2	10	19	20	1	2	.283	.370	.408	.778	96	-1	24	5.46	-3	O-37(3-17-17)	4	-0.6
Total 8	811	2831	427	804	138	73	30	422	335	389	189	41	.284	.367	.416	.783	123	86	477	5.79	-36	O-727/3-35	106	1.6
• ROTH, Frank	Francis Charles Roth b: 10/11/1878, Chicago, IL d: 3/27/1955, Burlington, WI BR/TR, 5'10", 160 lbs. Deb: 4/18/1903 C/U																							
1903 Phi-N	68	220	27	60	11	4	0	22	9	....	3	....	.273	.304	.359	.663	92	-3	26	4.23	1	C-60/3-1	5	0.3
1904 Phi-N	81	229	28	59	8	1	1	20	12	....	8	....	.258	.298	.314	.612	92	-2	25	3.72	3	C-67/1-1,2-1	6	0.6
1905 StL-A	35	107	9	25	3	0	0	7	6	....	1	....	.234	.274	.262	.536	74	-3	8	2.66	2	C-29	2	0.1
1906 Chi-A	16	51	4	10	1	1	0	7	3	....	1	....	.196	.241	.255	.496	57	-3	4	2.28	2	C-15	1	0.1
1909 Cin-N	56	147	12	35	7	2	0	16	6	....	5	....	.238	.287	.313	.600	87	-3	14	3.24	-5	C-54	4	-0.3
1910 Cin-N	26	29	3	7	2	0	0	3	0	2	1	....	.241	.267	.310	.577	71	-1	3	3.00	-1	/C-4,0-1	0	-0.2
Total 6	282	783	83	196	32	8	1	75	36	2	19	....	.250	.289	.315	.605	85	-16	80	3.48	2	C-229/1-1,2-1,3-1,O-1	18	0.6
• ROTHEL, Bob	Robert Burton Rothel b: 9/17/1923, Columbia Station, OH d: 3/21/1984, Huron, OH BR/TR, 5'10.5", 170 lbs. Deb: 4/22/1945																							
1945 Cle-A	4	10	0	2	0	0	0	0	3	1	0	0	.200	.385	.200	.585	75	-0	1	2.61	0	/3-4	0	0.0
• ROTHERMEL, Bobby	Edward Hill Rothermel b: 12/18/1870, Fleetwood, PA d: 2/11/1927, Detroit, MI, 5'6.5" Deb: 6/18/1899																							
1899 Bal-N	10	21	1	2	0	0	0	3	1	....	0	....	.095	.136	.095	.232	-34	-4	0	.48	-2	/2-5,3-2,S-1	0	-0.5
• ROTHFUSS, Jack	John Albert Rothfuss b: 4/18/1872, Newark, NJ d: 4/20/1947, Basking Ridge, NJ BR/TR, 5'11.5", 195 lbs. Deb: 8/2/1897																							
1897 Pit-N	35	115	20	36	3	1	2	18	5	....	3	....	.313	.352	.409	.761	105	0	18	6.02	0	1-32	3	0.0
• ROTHGEB, Claude	Claude James Rothgeb b: 1/1/1880, Milford, IL d: 7/6/1944, Manitowic, WI BB, 6'.5", 200 lbs. Deb: 6/17/1905																							
1905 Was-A	7	16	2	2	0	0	0	0	0	....	1	....	.125	.125	.125	.250	-22	-2	0	.80	0	/O-4(0-0-4)	0	-0.2
• ROTHROCK, Jack	John Huston Rothrock b: 3/14/1905, Long Beach, CA d: 2/2/1980, San Bernardino, CA BB/TR, 5'11.5", 165 lbs. Deb: 7/28/1925 Career OF: 138-194-311																							
1925 Bos-A	22	55	6	19	3	3	0	7	3	7	0	0	.345	.379	.509	.888	124	2	10	7.71	-4	S-22	2	-0.1
1926 Bos-A	15	17	3	5	1	0	0	2	3	1	0	0	.294	.400	.353	.753	101	0	3	4.90	-2	/S-2	0	-0.1
1927 Bos-A	117	428	61	111	24	8	1	36	24	46	5	5	.259	.302	.360	.662	73	-19	46	3.68	-2	S-40,2-36,3-20,1-13	8	-1.5
1928 Bos-A	117	344	52	92	9	4	3	22	33	40	12	6	.267	.333	.343	.676	79	-9	41	4.10	-4	O-53(26-12-19),3-17,1-16,S/2,C,P	6	-1.5
1929 Bos-A	143	473	70	142	19	7	6	59	43	47	23	13	.300	.361	.408	.769	100	0	70	5.21	0	*O-128(0-126-2)	13	-0.4
1930 Bos-A	45	65	4	18	3	1	0	4	2	9	0	2	.277	.299	.354	.652	67	-4	6	3.28	0	/O-9(1-0-8),3-1	0	-0.4
1931 Bos-A	133	475	81	132	32	3	4	42	47	48	13	7	.278	.343	.383	.726	96	-0	64	4.79	-2	O-79(75-2-2),2-23/1-8,3-2,S	10	-0.5
1932 Bos-A	12	48	3	10	1	0	0	0	5	5	3	0	.208	.283	.229	.512	35	-4	4	2.63	2	O-12(12-0-0)	0	-0.2
Chi-A	39	64	8	12	2	1	0	6	5	9	1	0	.188	.246	.250	.496	31	-6	4	2.15	-3	O-19(12-1-6)/3-8,1-1	0	-0.9
Yr.	51	112	11	22	3	1	0	6	10	14	4	0	.196	.262	.241	.503	33	-10	8	2.35	-2	O-31(24-1-6)/3-8,1-1	0	-1.1
1934*StL-N	154	647	106	184	35	3	11	72	49	56	10	....	.284	.336	.399	.734	90	-9	91	5.13	1	*O-154(5-0-149)/2-1	18	-1.7
1935 StL-N	129	502	76	137	18	5	3	56	57	29	7	....	.273	.347	.347	.694	84	-10	66	4.56	-6	*O-127(1-1-125)	13	-2.3
1937 Phi-A	88	232	28	62	15	0	0	21	28	15	1	0	.267	.346	.332	.678	73	-9	28	4.39	-3	O-58(6-52-0)/2-1	3	-1.2
Total 11	1014	3350	498	924	162	35	28	327	299	312	75	33	.276	.336	.370	.706	85	-68	433	4.56	-22	O-639/S-78,2-63,3-48,1-38,C,P	73	-10.8
• ROUSH, Edd	Edd J Roush b: 5/8/1893, Oakland City, IN d: 3/21/1988, Bradenton, FL BL/TL, 5'11", 170 lbs. Deb: 8/20/1913 C HOF: 1962 Career OF: 81-1754-13																							
1913 Chi-A	9	10	2	1	0	0	0	0	0	2	0	....	.100	.100	.100	.200	-42	-2	0	.42	0	/O-2(0-2-0)	0	-0.2
1914 Ind-F	74	166	26	54	8	4	1	30	6	20	12	....	.325	.353	.440	.792	112	2	30	5.89	1	O-43(38-4-1)/1-2	6	0.1
1915 New-F	145	551	73	164	20	11	3	60	38	25	28	....	.298	.350	.390	.740	124	16	82	5.23	-2	*O-144(0-143-1)	22	0.5
1916 NY-N	39	69	4	13	0	1	0	5	1	4	4	....	.188	.200	.217	.417	30	-6	4	1.73	0	O-15(0-5-10)	0	-0.8
Cin-N	69	272	34	78	7	14	0	15	13	19	15	....	.287	.336	.415	.751	133	10	43	5.57	2	O-69(0-69-0)	10	0.9
Yr.	108	341	38	91	7	15	0	20	14	23	19	....	.267	.309	.375	.685	113	4	47	4.73	2	O-84(0-74-10)	10	0.1

YEAR TM-L	G	AB	R	H	2B	3B	HR	RBI	BB	SO	SB	CS	AVG	OBP	SLG	OPS	OPS+	BR/A	RC	RC/G	FR	G/POS	WS	TPW
1917 Cin-N	136	522	82	178	19	14	4	67	27	24	21	....	**.341**	.379	.454	.833	162	36	94	6.82	-7	*O-134(0-134-0)	30	2.3
1918 Cin-N	113	435	61	145	18	10	5	62	22	10	24	....	.333	.368	**.455**	**.823**	**153**	25	80	**6.46**	-3	*O-113(0-113-0)	22	1.8
1919*Cin-N	133	504	73	162	19	12	4	71	42	19	20	....	**.321**	.380	.431	.811	147	29	88	6.30	3	*O-133(0-133-0)	**33**	2.7
1920 Cin-N	149	579	81	196	22	16	4	90	42	22	36	24	.339	.386	.453	.839	142	31	98	5.99	3	*O-139(0-139-0),1-11/2-1	33	2.6
1921 Cin-N	112	418	68	147	27	12	4	71	31	8	19	17	.352	.403	.502	.905	145	25	80	7.18	-6	*O-108(0-108-0)	18	1.4
1922 Cin-N	49	165	29	58	7	4	1	24	19	5	5	3	.352	.428	.461	.888	132	9	33	7.89	1	O-43(0-43-0)	9	0.7
1923 Cin-N	138	527	88	185	**41**	18	6	88	46	16	10	15	.351	.406	.531	.938	148	33	109	7.72	-6	*O-137(0-137-0)	28	2.1
1924 Cin-N	121	483	67	168	23	**21**	3	72	22	11	17	13	.348	.376	.501	.877	135	21	86	6.69	-4	*O-119(0-119-0)	20	1.2
1925 Cin-N	134	540	91	183	28	16	8	83	35	14	22	20	.339	.383	.494	.878	125	17	97	6.60	2	*O-134(0-134-0)	23	1.3
1926 Cin-N	144	563	95	182	37	10	7	79	38	17	8	....	.323	.366	.462	.828	125	18	92	5.82	-10	*O-143(0-143-0)/1-1	21	0.2
1927 NY-N	140	570	83	173	27	4	7	58	26	15	18	....	.304	.335	.402	.737	97	-4	74	4.64	-2	*O-138(0-137-1)	16	-1.1
1928 NY-N	46	163	20	41	5	3	2	13	14	8	1	....	.252	.315	.356	.670	75	-6	18	3.81	2	O-39(0-39-0)	3	-0.6
1929 NY-N	115	450	76	146	19	7	8	52	45	16	6	....	.324	.390	.451	.841	108	6	78	6.45	2	*O-107(0-107-0)	15	0.4
1931 Cin-N	101	376	46	102	12	5	1	41	17	5	2	....	.271	.308	.338	.646	78	-12	40	3.72	-2	O-88(43-45-0)	5	-1.7
Total 18	**1967**	**7363**	**1099**	**2376**	**339**	**182**	**68**	**981**	**484**	**260**	**268**	**92**	**.323**	**.369**	**.446**	**.815**	**128**	**248**	**1226**	**6.02**	**-24**	***O-1848/1-14,2-1**	**314**	**13.9**

• ROUTCLIFFE, Phil

Philip John "Chicken" Routcliffe b: 10/24/1870, Oswego, NY d: 10/4/1918, Oswego, NY BR/TR, 6', 175 lbs. Deb: 4/21/1890

YEAR TM-L	G	AB	R	H	2B	3B	HR	RBI	BB	SO	SB	CS	AVG	OBP	SLG	OPS	OPS+	BR/A	RC	RC/G	FR	G/POS	WS	TPW
1890 Pit-N	1	4	1	1	0	0	0	1	0	0	1	....	.250	.400	.250	.650	102	0	1	7.24	0	/O-1	0	0.0

• ROWAN, Dave

David Rowan b: 12/6/1882, Elora, Canada d: 7/30/1955, Toronto, Canada BL/TL, 5'11", 175 lbs. Deb: 5/27/1911

YEAR TM-L	G	AB	R	H	2B	3B	HR	RBI	BB	SO	SB	CS	AVG	OBP	SLG	OPS	OPS+	BR/A	RC	RC/G	FR	G/POS	WS	TPW
1911 StL-A	18	65	7	25	1	1	0	11	4	....	0	....	.385	.420	.431	.851	143	4	12	7.39	-2	1-18	2	0.2

• ROWAND, Aaron

Aaron Ryan Rowand b: 8/29/1977, Portland, OR BR/TR, 6'1", 200 lbs. Deb: 6/16/2001 Career OF: 98-173-30

YEAR TM-L	G	AB	R	H	2B	3B	HR	RBI	BB	SO	SB	CS	AVG	OBP	SLG	OPS	OPS+	BR/A	RC	RC/G	FR	G/POS	WS	TPW
2001 Chi-A	63	123	21	36	5	0	4	20	15	28	5	1	.293	.387	.431	.818	112	3	22	6.29	3	O-61(34-32-11)	5	0.5
2002 Chi-A	126	302	41	78	16	2	7	29	12	54	0	1	.258	.300	.394	.694	80	-10	34	3.76	3	*O-120(40-76-7)	7	-0.6
2003 Chi-A	93	157	22	45	8	0	6	24	7	21	0	0	.287	.329	.452	.782	104	0	24	5.56	2	O-87(24-65-12)/D-1	6	0.2
Total 3	**282**	**582**	**84**	**159**	**29**	**2**	**17**	**73**	**34**	**103**	**5**	**2**	**.273**	**.328**	**.418**	**.745**	**94**	**-6**	**80**	**4.75**	**7**	**O-268/D-1**	**18**	**0.1**

• ROWDON, Wade

Wade Lee Rowdon b: 9/7/1960, Riverhead, NY BR/TR, 6'2", 180 lbs. Deb: 9/8/1984 Career OF: 11-0-0

YEAR TM-L	G	AB	R	H	2B	3B	HR	RBI	BB	SO	SB	CS	AVG	OBP	SLG	OPS	OPS+	BR/A	RC	RC/G	FR	G/POS	WS	TPW
1984 Cin-N	4	7	0	2	0	0	0	0	0	1	0	0	.286	.286	.286	.571	58	-0	1	3.09	1	/3-1,S-1	0	0.0
1985 Cin-N	5	9	2	2	0	0	0	2	2	1	0	0	.222	.364	.222	.586	64	-0	1	3.53	-1	/3-4	0	-0.1
1986 Cin-N	38	80	9	20	5	1	0	10	9	17	2	0	.250	.333	.338	.671	82	-1	10	4.50	-3	/3-7,S-6,O-5(6-0-0),2-3	2	-0.4
1987 Chi-N	11	31	2	7	1	1	1	4	3	10	0	2	.226	.294	.419	.713	83	-2	3	2.84	-2	/3-9	0	-0.3
1988 Bal-A	20	30	1	3	0	0	0	0	0	6	1	1	.100	.100	.100	.200	-45	-6	0	.00	0	/3-8,D-5,O-5(5-0-0)	0	-0.6
Total 5	**78**	**157**	**14**	**34**	**6**	**2**	**1**	**16**	**14**	**35**	**3**	**3**	**.217**	**.285**	**.299**	**.584**	**58**	**-10**	**15**	**3.00**	**-4**	**/3-29,O-10,S-7,D-5,2-3**	**2**	**-1.4**

• ROWE, Dave

David Elwood Rowe b: 10/9/1854, Harrisburg, PA d: 12/9/1930, Glendale, CA BR/TR, 5'9", 180 lbs. Deb: 5/30/1877 M Career OF: 9-246-51

YEAR TM-L	G	AB	R	H	2B	3B	HR	RBI	BB	SO	SB	CS	AVG	OBP	SLG	OPS	OPS+	BR/A	RC	RC/G	FR	G/POS	WS	TPW
1877 Chi-N	2	7	0	2	0	0	0	0	0	3	....	....	.286	.286	.286	.571	72	-0	1	3.22	0	/O-2(0-0-2),P-1	0	-0.2
1882 Cle-N	24	97	13	25	4	3	1	17	4	9	....	....	.258	.287	.392	.679	119	2	11	4.27	-2	O-23(3-20-1)/P-1	3	-0.9
1883 Bal-a	59	256	40	80	11	6	0	0	2	....	....	....	.313	.318	.402	.720	126	6	34	5.34	-7	O-50(2-0-48)/S-7,1-3,P-1	6	-0.7
1884 StL-U	109	485	95	142	32	11	4	....	10	....	....	....	.293	.307	.429	.736	141	18	65	5.34	-5	*O-92(0-92-0),S-14/1-2,2-2,P	22	0.9
1885 StL-N	16	62	8	10	3	0	0	3	5	8	....	....	.161	.224	.210	.434	44	-3	3	1.55	-2	O-16(0-16-0)	0	-0.6
1886 KC-N	105	429	53	103	24	8	3	57	15	43	2	....	.240	.266	.354	.620	82	-12	42	3.47	-11	*O-90(4-86-0),S-11/2-4	5	-2.3
1888 KC-a	32	122	14	21	3	4	0	13	6	....	2	....	.172	.217	.262	.479	50	-7	8	2.02	3	O-32(0-32-0)	1	-0.5
Total 7	**347**	**1458**	**223**	**383**	**77**	**32**	**8**	**90**	**42**	**63**	**4**	**....**	**.263**	**.284**	**.376**	**.660**	**107**	**4**	**163**	**4.20**	**-24**	**O-305/S-32,2-6,1-5,P-4**	**37**	**-4.2**

• ROWE, Harland

Harland Stimson "Hypie" Rowe b: 4/20/1896, Springvale, ME d: 5/26/1969, Springvale, ME BL/TR, 6'1", 170 lbs. Deb: 6/23/1916

YEAR TM-L	G	AB	R	H	2B	3B	HR	RBI	BB	SO	SB	CS	AVG	OBP	SLG	OPS	OPS+	BR/A	RC	RC/G	FR	G/POS	WS	TPW
1916 Phi-A	17	36	2	5	1	0	0	3	2	8	0	....	.139	.184	.167	.351	6	-4	1	.93	-1	/3-8,O-1	0	-0.6

• ROWE, Jack

John Charles Rowe b: 12/8/1856, Hamburg, PA d: 4/26/1911, St. Louis, MO BL/TR, 5'8", 170 lbs. Deb: 9/6/1879 M/U Career OF: 47-32-26

YEAR TM-L	G	AB	R	H	2B	3B	HR	RBI	BB	SO	SB	CS	AVG	OBP	SLG	OPS	OPS+	BR/A	RC	RC/G	FR	G/POS	WS	TPW
1879 Buf-N	8	34	8	12	1	0	0	8	0	1	....	....	.353	.353	.382	.735	139	1	5	5.99	1	/C-6,O-2(0-0-2)	1	0.2
1880 Buf-N	79	326	43	82	10	6	1	36	6	17	....	....	.252	.265	.328	.593	98	-1	29	3.28	-11	*C-60,O-25(2-6-19)/3-3	8	-1.0
1881 Buf-N	64	246	30	82	11	**11**	1	43	1	12	....	....	.333	.336	.480	.816	155	14	41	6.69	-9	C-46/3-7,S-7,O-5(0-1-4)	12	0.7
1882 Buf-N	75	308	43	82	14	5	1	42	12	0	....	....	.266	.294	.354	.648	105	1	33	3.99	-12	C-46,S-22/3-7,O-1	9	-0.5
1883 Buf-N	87	374	65	104	18	7	1	38	15	14	....	....	.278	.306	.372	.678	102	1	44	4.44	-14	C-49,O-28(28-0-0),S-18/3-3	11	-0.9
1884 Buf-N	93	400	85	126	14	14	4	61	23	14	....	....	.315	.352	.450	.802	145	20	65	6.52	-8	C-65,O-30(17-12-1)/S-6	19	1.5
1885 Buf-N	98	421	62	122	28	8	2	51	13	19	....	....	.290	.311	.409	.720	127	11	55	4.95	-18	S-65,C-23,O-12(0-12-0)	15	-0.3
1886 Det-N	111	468	97	142	21	9	6	87	26	27	12	....	.303	.340	.425	.765	128	14	74	6.09	-8	*S-110/C-3	18	0.9
1887*Det-N	124	576	135	210	30	10	6	96	39	11	22	....	.365	.368	.445	.813	121	14	98	7.13	-18	*S-124	20	0.0
1888 Det-N	105	451	62	125	19	8	2	74	19	28	10	....	.277	.311	.368	.679	116	7	56	4.64	-7	*S-105	14	0.3
1889 Pit-N	75	317	57	82	14	3	2	32	22	16	5	....	.259	.313	.341	.654	91	-3	36	4.09	-2	S-75	9	-0.2
1890 Buf-P	125	504	77	126	22	7	2	76	48	18	10	....	.250	.324	.333	.657	82	-10	59	4.22	-14	*S-125	8	-1.6
Total 12	**1044**	**4425**	**764**	**1295**	**202**	**88**	**28**	**644**	**224**	**177**	**59**	**....**	**.293**	**.323**	**.392**	**.715**	**115**	**69**	**594**	**5.13**	**-118**	**S-657,C-298,O-103/3-20**	**144**	**-0.9**

• ROWELL, Bama

Carvel William Rowell b: 1/13/1916, Citronelle, AL d: 8/16/1993, Citronelle, AL BL/TR, 5'11", 185 lbs. Deb: 9/4/1939 Career OF: 191-32-18

YEAR TM-L	G	AB	R	H	2B	3B	HR	RBI	BB	SO	SB	CS	AVG	OBP	SLG	OPS	OPS+	BR/A	RC	RC/G	FR	G/POS	WS	TPW
1939 Bos-N	21	59	5	11	2	2	0	6	1	4	0	....	.186	.200	.288	.488	32	-6	3	1.53	0	O-16(0-13-3)	0	-0.7
1940 Bos-N	130	486	46	148	19	8	3	58	18	22	12	....	.305	.331	.395	.726	105	2	64	4.98	-4	*2-115/O-7(0-1-6)	15	0.4
1941 Bos-N	138	483	49	129	23	6	7	60	39	36	11	....	.267	.322	.383	.705	102	0	61	4.52	-12	*2-112,O-14(7-2-6)/3-2	14	-0.5
1946 Bos-N	95	293	37	82	12	6	3	31	29	15	5	....	.280	.345	.392	.737	107	2	41	4.92	2	O-85(71-14-0)	11	-0.1
1947 Bos-N	113	384	48	106	23	2	5	40	18	14	7	....	.276	.310	.385	.696	86	-10	47	4.32	-6	*O-100(99-2-0)/2-7,3-4	9	-2.2
1948 Phi-N	77	196	15	47	16	2	1	22	8	14	2	....	.240	.270	.357	.627	70	-9	18	3.24	-4	3-18,O-17(14-0-3),2-12	2	-1.4
Total 6	**574**	**1901**	**200**	**523**	**95**	**26**	**19**	**217**	**113**	**105**	**37**	**....**	**.275**	**.316**	**.382**	**.699**	**95**	**-21**	**233**	**4.41**	**-25**	**2-246,O-239/3-24**	**51**	**-4.4**

• ROWEN, Ed

W. Edward Rowen b: 10/22/1857, Bridgeport, CT d: 2/22/1892, Bridgeport, CT, 5'6", 155 lbs. Deb: 5/1/1882 Career OF: 0-5-51

YEAR TM-L	G	AB	R	H	2B	3B	HR	RBI	BB	SO	SB	CS	AVG	OBP	SLG	OPS	OPS+	BR/A	RC	RC/G	FR	G/POS	WS	TPW
1882 Bos-N	83	327	36	81	7	4	1	43	19	18	....	....	.248	.289	.303	.592	90	-3	29	3.28	-12	O-48(0-0-48),C-34/S-6,3-1	8	-1.2
1883 Phi-a	49	196	28	43	10	1	0	21	11	....	....	....	.219	.261	.281	.541	69	-7	15	2.69	-8	C-44/O-8(0-5-3),2-1,3-1	5	-1.0
1884 Phi-a	4	15	4	6	1	0	0	1	1	....	....	....	.400	.471	.467	.937	194	2	3	10.32	-1	/C-4	1	0.1
Total 3	**136**	**538**	**68**	**130**	**18**	**5**	**1**	**65**	**31**	**18**	**....**	**....**	**.242**	**.284**	**.299**	**.583**	**85**	**-9**	**47**	**3.21**	**-22**	**/C-82,O-56,S-6,3-2,2-1**	**14**	**-2.2**

• ROWLAND, Chuck

Charlie Leland Rowland b: 7/23/1899, Warrentown, NC d: 1/21/1992, Raleigh, NC BR/TR, 6'1", 185 lbs. Deb: 5/11/1923

YEAR TM-L	G	AB	R	H	2B	3B	HR	RBI	BB	SO	SB	CS	AVG	OBP	SLG	OPS	OPS+	BR/A	RC	RC/G	FR	G/POS	WS	TPW
1923 Phi-A	5	6	0	0	0	0	0	0	0	2	0	0	.000	.000	.000	.000	-99	-2	0	.00	-0	/C-4	0	-0.2

• ROWLAND, Rich

Richard Garnet Rowland b: 2/25/1964, Cloverdale, CA BR/TR, 6'1", 215 lbs. Deb: 9/7/1990

YEAR TM-L	G	AB	R	H	2B	3B	HR	RBI	BB	SO	SB	CS	AVG	OBP	SLG	OPS	OPS+	BR/A	RC	RC/G	FR	G/POS	WS	TPW
1990 Det-A	7	19	3	3	1	0	0	0	2	4	0	0	.158	.238	.211	.449	26	-2	1	1.29	-1	/C-5,D-2	0	-0.2
1991 Det-A	4	4	0	1	0	0	0	1	1	2	0	0	.250	.400	.250	.650	83	-0	1	4.01	0	/C-2,D-1	0	0.0
1992 Det-A	6	14	2	3	0	0	0	0	3	3	0	0	.214	.353	.214	.567	62	-1	1	2.50	-0	/C-3,D-2,1-1,3-1	0	-0.1
1993 Det-A	21	46	2	10	3	0	0	4	5	16	0	0	.217	.294	.283	.577	56	-3	4	2.84	0	C-17/D-3	1	-0.2
1994 Bos-A	46	118	14	27	3	0	9	20	11	35	0	0	.229	.295	.483	.778	92	-2	17	4.85	-3	C-39/D-4,1-1	3	-0.3
1995 Bos-A	14	29	1	5	1	0	0	1	0	11	0	0	.172	.172	.207	.379	-2	-4	1	1.16	0	C-11/D-3	0	-0.4
Total 6	**98**	**230**	**22**	**49**	**8**	**0**	**9**	**26**	**22**	**71**	**0**	**0**	**.213**	**.282**	**.365**	**.647**	**66**	**-12**	**24**	**3.48**	**-3**	**/C-77,D-15,1-2,3-1**	**4**	**-1.1**

• ROXBURGH, Jim

James A. Roxburgh b: 1/17/1858, San Francisco, CA d: 2/21/1934, San Francisco, CA BR/TR, 5'10", 170 lbs. Deb: 5/30/1884

YEAR TM-L	G	AB	R	H	2B	3B	HR	RBI	BB	SO	SB	CS	AVG	OBP	SLG	OPS	OPS+	BR/A	RC	RC/G	FR	G/POS	WS	TPW
1884 Bal-a	2	4	1	2	0	0	0	0	1	....	....	....	.500	.667	.500	1.167	275	1	1	18.79	-1	/C-2	1	0.0
1887 Phi-a	2	8	0	1	0	0	0	0	0	....	0	....	.125	.125	.125	.250	-30	-1	0	.49	-1	/C-2,2-1	0	-0.2
Total 2	**4**	**12**	**1**	**3**	**0**	**0**	**0**	**0**	**1**	**....**	**0**	**....**	**.250**	**.357**	**.250**	**.607**	**101**	**-0**	**1**	**4.56**	**-2**	**/C-4,2-1**	**1**	**-0.2**

• ROYER, Stan

Stanley Dean Royer b: 8/31/1967, Olney, IL BR/TR, 6'3", 195 lbs. Deb: 9/11/1991

YEAR TM-L	G	AB	R	H	2B	3B	HR	RBI	BB	SO	SB	CS	AVG	OBP	SLG	OPS	OPS+	BR/A	RC	RC/G	FR	G/POS	WS	TPW
1991 StL-N	9	21	1	6	1	0	0	1	1	2	0	0	.286	.318	.333	.652	83	-1	2	4.16	0	/3-5	0	-0.1
1992 StL-N	13	31	6	10	2	0	2	9	1	4	0	0	.323	.344	.581	.924	162	2	6	7.68	0	/3-5,1-4	2	0.2
1993 StL-N	24	46	4	14	2	0	1	8	2	14	0	1	.304	.333	.413	.746	100	-1	5	4.08	-1	3-10/1-2	2	-0.2
1994 StL-N	39	57	3	10	5	0	1	2	0	18	0	0	.175	.175	.316	.491	25	-7	3	1.60	0	1-11/3-5	0	-0.7

YEAR TM-L	G	AB	R	H	2B	3B	HR	RBI	BB	SO	SB	CS	AVG	OBP	SLG	OPS	OPS+	BR/A	RC	RC/G	FR	G/POS	WS	TPW
Bos-A	4	9	0	1	0	0	0	1	0	3	0	0	.111	.111	.111	.222	-41	-2	0	.38	-1	/3-3,1-1	0	-0.2
Total 4	89	164	14	41	10	0	4	21	4	41	0	1	.250	.268	.384	.652	77	-7	17	3.55	-3	/3-28,1-18	4	-1.0
• ROYSTER, Jerry	Jeron Kennis Royster b: 10/18/1952, Sacramento, CA BR/TR, 6', 165 lbs. Deb: 8/14/1973 M/C Career OF: 123-21-9																							
1973 LA-N	10	19	1	4	0	0	0	2	0	5	1	0	.211	.211	.211	.421	18	-2	1	1.71	-1	/3-6,2-1	0	-0.3
1974 LA-N	6	0	2	0	0	0	0	0	0	0	0	0	....	....	....	....	-104	0	0	....	0	/2-1,3-1,0-1	0	0.0
1975 LA-N	13	36	2	9	2	1	0	1	1	3	1	0	.250	.270	.361	.631	77	-1	3	3.23	0	/0-7(1-0-6),2-4,3-3,S-1	1	-0.1
1976 Atl-N	149	533	65	132	13	1	5	45	52	53	24	13	.248	.316	.304	.620	72	-19	52	3.19	12	*3-148/S-2	13	-0.8
1977 Atl-N	140	445	64	96	10	2	6	28	38	67	28	10	.216	.279	.288	.567	47	-32	36	2.59	-9	3-56,S-51,2-38/0-1	3	-3.7
1978 Atl-N	140	529	67	137	17	8	2	35	56	49	27	17	.259	.333	.333	.666	78	-16	60	3.76	-10	2-75,S-60/3-1	11	-1.6
1979 Atl-N	154	601	103	164	25	6	3	51	62	59	35	8	.273	.341	.349	.690	83	-9	78	4.52	8	3-80,2-77	17	0.2
1980 Atl-N	123	392	42	95	17	5	1	20	37	48	22	13	.242	.309	.319	.628	73	-15	39	3.28	-5	2-49,3-48,0-41(41-0-0)	8	-2.1
1981 Atl-N	64	93	13	19	4	1	0	9	7	14	7	5	.204	.260	.269	.529	49	-7	6	1.88	-4	3-24,2-13	1	-1.1
1982*Atl-N	108	261	43	77	13	2	2	25	22	36	14	6	.295	.354	.383	.738	102	1	37	4.95	-5	3-62,0-25(25-0-0),2-16,S-10	9	-0.4
1983 Atl-N	91	268	32	63	10	3	3	30	28	35	11	7	.235	.307	.328	.636	71	-11	25	2.89	-1	3-47,2-26,0-18(18-0-0),S-13	4	-1.2
1984 Atl-N	81	227	22	47	13	2	1	21	15	41	6	4	.207	.259	.295	.554	52	-16	16	2.16	-1	2-29,3-17,S-16,0-11(10-0-0)	3	-1.5
1985 SD-N	90	249	31	70	13	2	5	31	32	31	6	5	.281	.365	.410	.775	118	6	37	5.15	6	2-58,3-29/S-7,0-2(0-1-1)	10	1.6
1986 SD-N	118	257	31	66	12	0	5	26	32	45	3	5	.257	.339	.362	.701	95	-3	31	3.99	4	3-59,S-24,2-21/0-7(7-0-0)	7	0.3
1987 Chi-A	55	154	25	37	11	0	7	23	19	28	2	1	.240	.328	.448	.776	101	-0	23	5.09	-1	3-30,0-13(13-0-0)/2-5,D-4	4	-0.2
NY-A	18	42	1	15	2	0	0	4	4	4	2	1	.357	.413	.405	.818	120	1	6	5.28	3	3-13/2-1,0-1,S-1	1	0.4
Yr.	73	196	26	52	13	0	7	27	23	32	4	2	.265	.345	.439	.784	105	1	30	5.13	2	3-43,0-14(14-0-0)/2-6,D-4,S	5	0.3
1988 Atl-N	68	102	8	18	3	0	0	1	6	16	0	0	.176	.222	.206	.428	22	-10	5	1.43	-2	0-26(7-19-1),3-10/2-2,S-2	1	-1.3
Total 16	1428	4208	552	1049	165	33	40	352	411	534	189	95	.249	.318	.333	.650	76	-132	456	3.57	-6	3-634,2-416,S-187,0-153/D-4	93	-11.7
• ROYSTER, Willie	Willie Arthur Royster b: 4/11/1954, Clarksville, VA BR/TR, 5'11", 180 lbs. Deb: 9/3/1981																							
1981 Bal-A	4	4	0	0	0	0	0	0	0	2	0	0	.000	.000	.000	.000	-100	-1	0	.00	-1	/C-4	0	-0.2
• ROZNOVSKY, Vic	Victor Joseph Roznovsky b: 10/19/1938, Shiner, TX BL/TR, 6', 180 lbs. Deb: 6/28/1964																							
1964 Chi-N	35	76	2	15	1	0	0	2	5	18	0	1	.197	.247	.211	.457	29	-7	4	1.77	1	C-26	1	-0.6
1965 Chi-N	71	172	9	38	4	1	3	15	16	30	1	0	.221	.298	.308	.607	69	-6	17	3.22	1	C-63	4	-0.3
1966 Bal-A	41	97	4	23	5	0	1	10	9	11	0	0	.237	.308	.320	.628	82	-2	10	3.27	-1	C-34	3	-0.1
1967 Bal-A	45	97	7	20	5	0	0	10	1	20	0	0	.206	.214	.258	.472	39	-8	4	1.46	-0	C-23	1	-0.7
1969 Phi-N	13	13	0	3	0	0	0	1	1	4	0	0	.231	.286	.231	.516	47	-1	1	2.51	-0	/C-2	0	-0.1
Total 5	205	455	22	99	15	1	4	38	32	83	1	1	.218	.275	.281	.556	59	-24	36	2.58	1	C-148	9	-1.9
• RUAN, Wilkin	Wilkin Chal Ruan b: 11/18/1978, Guaymate, Dominican Republic BR/TR, 6', 170 lbs. Deb: 9/1/2002 Career OF: 0-25-0																							
2002 LA-N	12	11	2	3	1	0	0	3	0	2	0	0	.273	.273	.364	.636	70	-1	1	3.68	0	/0-5(0-5-0)	1	-0.1
2003 LA-N	21	41	2	9	2	1	0	2	0	7	1	0	.220	.220	.317	.537	40	-4	3	2.50	1	0-20(0-20-0)	1	-0.3
Total 2	33	52	4	12	3	1	0	5	0	9	1	0	.231	.231	.327	.558	46	-4	4	2.74	0	/0-25	2	-0.3
• RUBELING, Al	Albert William Rubeling b: 5/10/1913, Baltimore, MD d: 1/28/1988, Baltimore, MD BR/TR, 6', 185 lbs. Deb: 4/16/1940																							
1940 Phi-A	108	376	49	92	16	6	4	38	48	58	4	5	.245	.330	.351	.681	78	-12	45	4.08	-7	3-98,2-10	7	-1.4
1941 Phi-A	6	19	0	5	0	0	0	2	2	1	0	0	.263	.333	.263	.596	61	-1	2	3.63	-2	/3-6	0	-0.2
1943 Pit-N	47	168	23	44	8	4	0	9	8	17	0	....	.262	.295	.357	.653	85	-4	17	3.40	0	2-44/3-1	3	-0.1
1944 Pit-N	92	184	22	45	7	2	4	30	19	19	4	....	.245	.322	.370	.692	90	-2	23	4.25	2	0-18(9-0-9),2-17,3-16	5	-0.1
Total 4	253	747	94	186	31	12	8	79	77	95	8	5	.249	.321	.355	.676	82	-20	87	3.96	-6	3-121/2-71,0-18	15	-1.9
• RUBERTO, Sonny	John Edward Ruberto b: 1/2/1946, Staten Island, NY BR/TR, 5'11", 175 lbs. Deb: 5/25/1969 C																							
1969 SD-N	19	21	3	3	0	0	0	0	1	7	0	0	.143	.182	.143	.325	-8	-3	1	.89	1	C-15	0	-0.1
1972 Cin-N	2	3	0	0	0	0	0	0	0	1	0	0	.000	.250	.000	.250	-25	-0	0	.59	0	/C-2	0	-0.1
Total 2	21	24	3	3	0	0	0	0	1	8	0	0	.125	.192	.125	.317	-11	-3	1	.85	1	/C-17	0	-0.2
• RUBLE, Art	William Arthur "Speedy" Ruble b: 3/11/1903, Knoxville, TN d: 11/1/1983, Maryville, TN BL/TR, 5'10.5", 168 lbs. Deb: 4/18/1927 Career OF: 28-14-17																							
1927 Det-A	56	91	16	15	4	2	0	11	14	15	2	2	.165	.283	.253	.536	39	-8	8	2.32	0	0-43(24-13-7)	1	-1.0
1934 Phi-N	19	54	7	15	4	0	0	8	7	3	0	....	.278	.361	.352	.713	81	-1	7	4.20	-1	0-14(4-1-10)	1	-0.3
Total 2	75	145	23	30	8	2	0	19	21	18	2	2	.207	.311	.290	.601	54	-10	14	2.95	-1	/0-57	2	-1.2
• RUCKER, Johnny	John Joel Rucker b: 1/15/1917, Crabapple, GA d: 8/7/1985, Moultrie, GA BL/TR, 6'2", 175 lbs. Deb: 4/16/1940 Career OF: 0-603-6																							
1940 NY-N	86	277	38	82	7	5	4	23	7	32	4	....	.296	.313	.401	.714	95	-3	34	4.60	-5	0-57(0-57-0)	6	-0.9
1941 NY-N	143	622	95	179	38	9	1	42	29	61	8	....	.288	.320	.383	.702	95	-6	76	4.49	-2	*0-142(0-142-0)	13	-1.3
1943 NY-N	132	505	56	138	19	4	2	46	22	44	4	....	.273	.304	.339	.642	85	-12	53	3.78	-1	*0-117(0-117-0)	9	-1.7
1944 NY-N	144	587	79	143	14	8	6	39	24	48	8	....	.244	.275	.325	.600	69	-27	54	3.20	-13	*0-139(0-139-0)	7	-4.4
1945 NY-N	105	429	58	117	19	11	7	51	20	36	7	....	.273	.305	.417	.722	98	-4	55	4.68	-1	0-98(0-98-0)	11	-0.8
1946 NY-N	95	197	28	52	8	2	1	13	7	27	4	....	.264	.300	.340	.640	81	-6	20	3.63	-5	0-54(0-50-6)	3	-1.2
Total 6	705	2617	354	711	105	39	21	214	109	248	35	....	.272	.302	.366	.668	87	-57	293	4.03	-27	0-607	49	-10.3
• RUDDERHAM, John	John Edmund Rudderham b: 8/30/1863, Quincy, MA d: 4/3/1942, Randolph, MA BR/TR, 5'8", 170 lbs. Deb: 9/18/1884 U																							
1884 Bos-U	1	4	0	1	0	0	0	....	0	....	....	....	.250	.250	.250	.500	70	-0	0	2.39	-1	/0-1	0	-0.1
• RUDI, Joe	Joseph Oden Rudi b: 9/7/1946, Modesto, CA BR/TR, 6'2", 200 lbs. Deb: 4/11/1967 C Career OF: 1160-2-47																							
1967 KC-A	19	43	4	8	2	0	0	1	3	7	0	0	.186	.239	.233	.472	41	-3	2	1.76	-1	/1-9,0-6(6-0-0)	0	-0.6
1968 Oak-A	68	181	10	32	5	1	1	12	12	32	1	1	.177	.236	.232	.468	44	-12	10	1.72	-1	0-56(55-1-1)	1	-1.8
1969 Oak-A	35	122	10	23	3	1	2	6	5	16	1	1	.189	.220	.279	.499	41	-10	7	1.75	1	0-18(18-0-0),1-11	1	-1.2
1970 Oak-A	106	350	40	108	23	2	11	42	16	61	3	1	.309	.342	.480	.822	129	12	54	5.59	1	0-63(58-1-12),1-28	13	0.9
1971*Oak-A	127	513	62	137	23	4	10	52	28	62	3	2	.267	.306	.386	.692	97	-4	57	3.80	2	*0-121(115-0-9)/1-5	15	-1.1
1972*Oak-A★	147	593	94	**181**	32	**9**	19	75	37	62	3	4	.305	.348	.486	.834	154	35	95	5.68	-6	*0-147(147-0-0)/3-1	29	2.3
1973*Oak-A	120	437	53	118	25	1	12	66	30	72	0	0	.270	.320	.414	.734	111	5	55	4.33	-1	*0-117(117-0-0)/1-1,D-1	13	-0.3
1974*Oak-A★	158	593	73	174	**39**	4	22	99	34	92	2	3	.293	.337	.484	.821	143	29	94	5.78	-6	*0-140(140-0-0),1-27/D-2	24	1.5
1975*Oak-A★	126	468	66	130	26	6	21	75	40	56	2	1	.278	.339	.494	.832	136	20	76	5.77	-4	1-91,0-44(44-0-0)/D-2	20	0.8
1976 Oak-A	130	500	54	135	32	3	13	94	41	71	6	1	.270	.329	.424	.753	124	15	68	4.67	-4	*0-126(126-0-1)/1-2,D-2	16	0.3
1977 Cal-A	64	242	48	64	13	2	13	53	22	48	1	0	.264	.336	.496	.832	128	9	42	6.09	2	0-61(61-0-0)/D-3	10	0.8
1978 Cal-A	133	497	58	127	27	1	17	79	28	82	2	1	.256	.298	.416	.714	103	-0	60	4.14	-1	*0-111(111-0-0),D-11,1-10	14	-0.7
1979 Cal-A	90	330	35	80	11	3	11	61	24	61	0	0	.242	.296	.394	.690	87	-7	38	3.87	-1	0-80(69-0-12)/1-5,D-3	6	-1.2
1980 Cal-A	104	372	42	88	17	1	16	53	17	84	1	0	.237	.279	.417	.696	90	-7	41	3.70	-2	0-90(89-0-1)/1-6,D-3	7	-1.3
1981 Bos-A	49	122	14	22	3	0	6	24	8	29	0	0	.180	.242	.352	.595	66	-6	10	2.68	-1	D-21/1-5,0-1	1	-0.8
1982 Oak-A	71	193	21	41	6	1	5	18	24	35	0	0	.212	.303	.332	.634	78	-6	21	3.56	-6	1-49,0-14(4-0-10)/D-3	3	-1.5
Total 16	1547	5556	684	1468	287	39	179	810	369	870	25	15	.264	.314	.427	.741	113	70	730	4.53	-27	*0-1195,1-249/D-51,3-1	173	-3.9
• RUDOLPH, Dutch	John Herman Rudolph b: 7/10/1882, Natrona, PA d: 4/17/1967, Natrona, PA BL/TL, 5'10", 160 lbs. Deb: 7/3/1903																							
1903 Phi-N	1	1	0	0	0	0	0	0	0	....	0	....	.000	.000	.000	.000	-103	-0	0	.00	0	....	0	0.0
1904 Chi-N	2	3	0	1	0	0	0	0	0	....	0	....	.333	.333	.333	.667	106	0	0	4.44	0	/0-2(0-0-2)	0	0.0
Total 2	3	4	0	1	0	0	0	0	0	....	0	....	.250	.250	.250	.500	54	-0	0	2.96	0	/0-2	0	0.0
• RUDOLPH, Ken	Kenneth Victor Rudolph b: 12/29/1946, Rockford, IL BR/TR, 6'1", 185 lbs. Deb: 4/20/1969																							
1969 Chi-N	27	34	7	7	1	0	1	6	6	11	0	0	.206	.325	.324	.649	73	-1	4	3.63	0	C-11/0-3(3-0-0)	1	-0.1
1970 Chi-N	20	40	1	4	1	0	0	2	1	12	0	0	.100	.122	.125	.247	-30	-8	1	.39	0	C-16	1	-0.7
1971 Chi-N	25	76	5	15	3	0	0	7	6	20	0	0	.197	.265	.237	.502	38	-6	5	1.90	3	C-25	2	-0.2
1972 Chi-N	42	106	10	25	1	1	2	9	6	14	1	2	.236	.283	.321	.604	64	-6	8	2.55	0	C-41	2	-0.5
1973 Chi-N	64	170	12	35	8	1	2	17	7	25	1	4	.206	.242	.300	.542	46	-14	10	1.83	0	C-64	3	-1.3
1974 SF-N	57	158	11	41	3	0	0	10	21	15	0	0	.259	.350	.278	.628	74	-4	15	3.36	-1	C-56	4	-0.3
1975 StL-N	44	80	5	16	2	0	1	6	3	10	0	0	.200	.229	.263	.491	35	-7	4	1.56	-1	C-31	1	-0.7

YEAR TM-L	G	AB	R	H	2B	3B	HR	RBI	BB	SO	SB	CS	AVG	OBP	SLG	OPS	OPS+	BR/A	RC	RC/G	FR	G/POS	WS	TPW
1976 StL-N	27	50	1	8	3	0	0	5	1	7	0	0	.160	.176	.220	.396	12	-6	2	.95	-2	C-14	0	-0.8
1977 SF-N	11	15	1	3	0	0	0	0	1	3	0	0	.200	.250	.200	.450	22	-2	1	1.69	0	C-11	0	-0.1
Bal-A	11	14	2	4	1	0	0	2	0	4	0	0	.286	.286	.357	.643	79	-0	1	3.86	0	C-11	1	0.0
Total 9	328	743	55	158	23	2	6	64	52	121	2	6	.213	.268	.273	.541	48	-55	51	2.17	0	C-280/0-3	15	-4.6

• RUEL, Muddy Herold Dominic Ruel b: 2/20/1896, St. Louis, MO d: 11/13/1963, Palo Alto, CA BR/TR, 5'9", 150 lbs. Deb: 5/29/1915 M/C

YEAR TM-L	G	AB	R	H	2B	3B	HR	RBI	BB	SO	SB	CS	AVG	OBP	SLG	OPS	OPS+	BR/A	RC	RC/G	FR	G/POS	WS	TPW
1915 StL-A	10	14	0	0	0	0	0	1	5	5	0	....	.000	.263	.000	.263	-22	-2	0	.00	-1	/C-6	0	-0.2
1917 NY-A	6	17	1	2	0	0	0	1	2	2	1	....	.118	.211	.118	.328		-2	1	1.10	0	/C-6	0	-0.2
1918 NY-A	3	6	0	2	0	0	0	0	2	1	1	....	.333	.500	.333	.833	148	1	1	8.81	0	/C-2	0	0.1
1919 NY-A	79	233	18	56	6	0	0	31	34	26	4	....	.240	.340	.266	.606	71	-7	22	3.15	-7	C-79	6	-0.8
1920 NY-A	82	261	30	70	14	1	1	15	15	18	4	2	.268	.310	.341	.651	70	-11	28	3.72	-6	C-80	6	-1.0
1921 Bos-A	113	358	41	99	21	1	1	45	41	15	2	7	.277	.353	.349	.702	82	-11	45	4.26	-5	*C-109	11	-0.8
1922 Bos-A	116	361	34	92	15	1	0	28	41	26	4	2	.255	.333	.302	.634	67	-16	39	3.67	6	*C-112	9	-0.3
1923 Was-A	136	449	63	142	24	3	0	54	55	21	4	6	.316	.394	.383	.778	111	9	70	5.59	17	*C-133	23	3.4
1924*Was-A	149	501	50	142	20	2	0	57	62	20	7	11	.283	.370	.331	.702	84	-11	65	4.31	2	*C-147	17	0.0
1925*Was-A	127	393	55	122	9	2	0	54	63	16	4	5	.310	.411	.344	.754	95	1	60	5.52	7	*C-126/1-1	18	1.5
1926 Was-A	117	368	42	110	22	4	1	53	61	14	7	6	.299	.401	.389	.790	109	8	61	5.86	3	*C-117	18	1.8
1927 Was-A	131	428	61	132	16	5	1	52	63	18	9	6	.308	.403	.376	.779	104	6	69	5.92	2	*C-128	20	1.5
1928 Was-A	108	350	31	90	18	2	0	55	44	14	12	10	.257	.342	.320	.662	75	-12	40	3.79	4	*C-101/1-2	8	-0.2
1929 Was-A	69	188	16	46	4	2	0	20	31	7	0	4	.245	.352	.287	.639	66	-10	20	3.55	5	C-62	5	-0.1
1930 Was-A	66	198	18	50	3	4	0	26	24	13	1	0	.253	.342	.308	.650	66	-9	23	3.97	0	C-60	5	-0.4
1931 Bos-A	33	83	6	25	5	0	0	6	9	6	0	0	.301	.370	.361	.731	98	1	12	5.18	-1	C-30	3	0.1
Det-A	14	50	1	6	1	0	0	3	5	1	0	0	.120	.200	.140	.340	-9	-8	2	.96	3	C-14	1	-0.4
Yr.	47	133	7	31	6	0	0	9	14	7	0	0	.233	.306	.278	.584	58	-7	13	3.38	2	C-44	4	-0.2
1932 Det-A	51	136	10	32	4	2	0	18	17	6	1	0	.235	.320	.294	.614	58	-8	14	3.49	-0	C-49	3	-0.5
1933 StL-A	36	63	13	12	2	0	0	8	24	4	0	0	.190	.414	.222	.636	68	-1	8	4.18	3	C-28	2	0.3
1934 Chi-A	22	57	4	12	3	0	0	7	8	5	0	0	.211	.308	.263	.571	47	-4	5	2.93	1	C-21	1	-0.2
Total 19	1468	4514	494	1242	187	29	4	534	606	238	61	59	.275	.365	.332	.697	84	-86	585	4.46	34	*C-1410/1-3	156	3.6

• RUFER, Rudy Rudolph Joseph Rufer b: 10/28/1926, Ridgewood, NJ BR/TR, 6'.5", 165 lbs. Deb: 9/22/1949

YEAR TM-L	G	AB	R	H	2B	3B	HR	RBI	BB	SO	SB	CS	AVG	OBP	SLG	OPS	OPS+	BR/A	RC	RC/G	FR	G/POS	WS	TPW
1949 NY-N	7	15	1	1	0	0	0	2	2	0	0	....	.067	.176	.067	.243	-32	-3	0	.52	-0	/S-7	0	-0.3
1950 NY-N	15	11	1	1	0	0	0	0	0	1	1	....	.091	.091	.091	.182	-52	-2	0	.25	-2	/S-8	0	-0.4
Total 2	22	26	2	2	0	0	0	2	2	1	1	....	.077	.143	.077	.220	-40	-5	0	.40	-2	/S-15	0	-0.6

• RUIZ, Chico Manuel (Cruz) Ruiz b: 11/1/1951, Santurce, Puerto Rico BR/TR, 5'11.5", 170 lbs. Deb: 7/29/1978

YEAR TM-L	G	AB	R	H	2B	3B	HR	RBI	BB	SO	SB	CS	AVG	OBP	SLG	OPS	OPS+	BR/A	RC	RC/G	FR	G/POS	WS	TPW
1978 Atl-N	18	46	3	13	3	0	0	2	2	4	0	0	.283	.313	.348	.660	76	-2	5	3.77	-1	2-14/3-1	1	-0.2
1980 Atl-N	25	26	3	8	2	1	0	2	3	7	0	1	.308	.379	.462	.841	129	1	4	6.26	-3	3-16/S-4,2-2	1	-0.2
Total 2	43	72	6	21	5	1	0	4	5	11	0	1	.292	.338	.389	.727	96	-1	9	4.66	-4	/3-17,2-16,S-4	2	-0.4

• RUIZ, Chico Hiraldo (Sablon) Ruiz b: 12/5/1938, Santo Domingo, Cuba d: 2/9/1972, San Diego, CA BB/TR, 6', 173 lbs. Deb: 4/13/1964 Career OF: 11-0-3

YEAR TM-L	G	AB	R	H	2B	3B	HR	RBI	BB	SO	SB	CS	AVG	OBP	SLG	OPS	OPS+	BR/A	RC	RC/G	FR	G/POS	WS	TPW
1964 Cin-N	77	311	33	76	13	2	2	16	7	41	11	3	.244	.270	.318	.589	63	-14	28	2.97	3	3-49,2-30	5	-0.9
1965 Cin-N	29	18	7	2	1	0	0	1	0	5	1	2	.111	.111	.167	.278	-21	-4	0	.00	-2	/3-4,S-3	0	-0.5
1966 Cin-N	82	110	13	28	2	1	0	5	5	14	1	2	.255	.287	.291	.578	56	-7	9	2.93	-3	3-27/0-8(7-0-1),S-6	1	-1.1
1967 Cin-N	105	250	32	55	12	4	0	13	11	35	9	4	.220	.259	.300	.559	53	-15	18	2.28	1	2-56,3-13,S-11/0-5(3-0-2)	3	-1.0
1968 Cin-N	85	139	15	36	2	1	0	9	12	18	4	3	.259	.318	.288	.606	78	-4	13	3.06	2	2-34,1-16/3-5,S-3	3	0.0
1969 Cin-N	88	196	19	48	4	1	0	13	14	28	4	2	.245	.295	.276	.571	58	-11	17	2.89	-1	2-39,S-29/3-7,1-2,0-1	3	-0.8
1970 Cal-A	68	107	10	26	3	1	0	12	7	16	3	0	.243	.296	.290	.585	64	-4	9	2.77	0	3-27/2-3,S-3,1-2,C-1	2	-0.5
1971 Cal-A	31	19	4	5	0	0	0	0	2	7	1	0	.263	.333	.263	.596	76	-0	2	3.52	-1	/3-3,2-2	0	-0.1
Total 8	565	1150	133	276	37	10	2	69	58	164	34	16	.240	.281	.295	.575	60	-59	96	2.74	-2	2-164,3-135/S-55,1-20,0-14,C	17	-4.9

• RULLO, Joe Joseph Vincent Rullo b: 6/16/1916, New York, NY d: 10/28/1969, Philadelphia, PA BR/TR, 5'11", 168 lbs. Deb: 9/22/1943

YEAR TM-L	G	AB	R	H	2B	3B	HR	RBI	BB	SO	SB	CS	AVG	OBP	SLG	OPS	OPS+	BR/A	RC	RC/G	FR	G/POS	WS	TPW
1943 Phi-A	16	55	2	16	3	0	0	6	8	7	0	0	.291	.381	.345	.726	114	1	8	5.22	-1	2-16	2	0.2
1944 Phi-A	35	96	5	16	0	0	0	5	6	19	1	0	.167	.223	.167	.390	12	-11	4	1.12	0	2-33/1-1,0-1	1	-1.0
Total 2	51	151	7	32	3	0	0	11	14	26	1	0	.212	.283	.232	.515	51	-9	12	2.45	-1	/2-49,1-1,0-1	3	-0.8

• RUMLER, William William George Rumler b: 3/27/1891, Milford, NE d: 5/26/1966, Lincoln, NE BR/TR, 6'1", 190 lbs. Deb: 5/4/1914 Career OF: 3-0-12

YEAR TM-L	G	AB	R	H	2B	3B	HR	RBI	BB	SO	SB	CS	AVG	OBP	SLG	OPS	OPS+	BR/A	RC	RC/G	FR	G/POS	WS	TPW
1914 StL-A	34	46	2	8	1	0	0	6	3	12	2	2	.174	.240	.196	.436	32	-4	3	1.54	1	C-10/0-6(0-0-6)	0	-0.4
1916 StL-A	27	37	6	12	3	0	0	10	3	7	0	....	.324	.375	.405	.780	141	2	6	5.80	0	/C-9	2	0.3
1917 StL-A	78	88	7	23	3	4	1	16	8	9	2	....	.261	.323	.420	.743	131	3	12	4.70	0	/0-9(3-0-6)	3	0.2
Total 3	139	171	15	43	7	4	1	32	14	28	4	2	.251	.312	.357	.669	106	0	20	3.90	1	/C-19,0-15	5	0.1

• RUNGE, Paul Paul William Runge b: 5/21/1958, Kingston, NY BR/TR, 6', 175 lbs. Deb: 9/25/1981

YEAR TM-L	G	AB	R	H	2B	3B	HR	RBI	BB	SO	SB	CS	AVG	OBP	SLG	OPS	OPS+	BR/A	RC	RC/G	FR	G/POS	WS	TPW
1981 Atl-N	10	27	2	7	1	0	0	2	4	4	0	0	.259	.355	.296	.651	84	-0	3	3.75	-1	S-10	1	0.0
1982 Atl-N	4	2	0	0	0	0	0	0	0	0	0	0	.000	.000	.000	.000	-96	-1	0	.00	0	....	0	-0.1
1983 Atl-N	5	8	0	2	0	0	0	1	1	4	0	0	.250	.333	.250	.583	59	-0	1	3.22	0	/2-2	0	0.0
1984 Atl-N	28	90	5	24	3	1	0	3	10	14	5	3	.267	.340	.322	.662	81	-2	10	3.67	1	2-22/S-7,3-3	3	0.1
1985 Atl-N	50	87	15	19	3	0	1	5	18	18	0	1	.218	.352	.287	.640	76	-2	10	3.40	-6	3-28/S-5,2-2	2	-0.8
1986 Atl-N	7	8	1	2	0	0	0	0	2	4	0	0	.250	.400	.250	.650	79	-0	1	2.92	0	/2-5	0	0.0
1987 Atl-N	27	47	9	10	1	0	3	8	5	10	0	1	.213	.288	.426	.714	82	-2	5	3.54	-3	3-10/S-9,2-2	1	-0.5
1988 Atl-N	52	76	11	16	5	0	0	7	14	21	0	0	.211	.333	.276	.610	73	-2	7	2.99	-4	3-19/2-7,S-6	1	-0.6
Total 8	183	345	43	80	13	1	4	26	54	75	5	5	.232	.336	.310	.646	77	-10	37	3.38	-12	/3-60,2-40,S-37	8	-1.9

• RUNNELLS, Tom Thomas William Runnells b: 4/17/1955, Greeley, CO BB/TR, 6', 175 lbs. Deb: 8/9/1985 M/C

YEAR TM-L	G	AB	R	H	2B	3B	HR	RBI	BB	SO	SB	CS	AVG	OBP	SLG	OPS	OPS+	BR/A	RC	RC/G	FR	G/POS	WS	TPW
1985 Cin-N	28	35	3	7	1	0	0	0	3	4	0	0	.200	.263	.229	.492	37	-3	2	1.90	1	S-11/2-1	0	-0.2
1986 Cin-N	12	11	1	1	1	0	0	0	0	2	0	0	.091	.091	.182	.273	-26	-2	0	.00	0	/2-4,3-3	0	-0.2
Total 2	40	46	4	8	2	0	0	0	3	6	0	0	.174	.224	.217	.442	24	-5	2	1.43	0	/S-11,2-5,3-3	0	-0.4

• RUNNELS, Pete James Edward Runnels b: 1/28/1928, Lufkin, TX d: 5/20/1991, Pasadena, TX BL/TR, 6', 170 lbs. Deb: 7/1/1951 M/C

YEAR TM-L	G	AB	R	H	2B	3B	HR	RBI	BB	SO	SB	CS	AVG	OBP	SLG	OPS	OPS+	BR/A	RC	RC/G	FR	G/POS	WS	TPW
1951 Was-A	78	273	31	76	12	2	0	25	31	24	0	3	.278	.354	.337	.691	89	-4	34	4.40	-4	S-73	8	-0.5
1952 Was-A	152	555	70	158	18	3	1	64	72	55	0	10	.285	.368	.333	.701	99	-2	69	4.38	7	*S-147/2-1	22	1.5
1953 Was-A	137	486	64	125	15	5	2	50	64	36	3	4	.257	.347	.321	.668	83	-10	55	3.84	-5	*S-121,2-11	12	-0.5
1954 Was-A	139	488	75	131	17	15	3	56	78	60	2	3	.268	.369	.383	.752	112	10	72	5.22	-12	*S-107,2-27/0-1	18	0.9
1955 Was-A	134	503	66	143	16	4	2	49	55	51	3	9	.284	.356	.344	.700	94	-6	60	4.13	-9	*2-132/S-2	14	-0.5
1956 Was-A	147	578	72	179	29	9	8	76	58	64	5	5	.310	.375	.433	.807	113	10	91	5.71	-9	1-81,2-69/S-3	18	0.2
1957 Was-A	134	473	53	109	18	4	2	35	55	51	2	3	.230	.313	.298	.611	69	-20	46	3.28	0	1-72,3-32,2-23	7	-2.3
1958 Bos-A	147	568	103	183	32	5	8	59	87	49	1	2	.322	.418	.438	.856	127	26	107	7.13	-7	*2-106,1-42	26	2.6
1959 Bos-A★	147	560	95	176	33	6	6	57	95	48	6	5	.314	.415	.427	.841	126	24	102	6.69	-2	*2-101,1-44/S-9	24	2.9
1960 Bos-A★	143	528	80	169	29	2	2	35	71	51	5	2	**.320**	.403	.394	.797	112	13	86	5.97	2	*2-129,1-57/3-3	20	2.4
1961 Bos-A	143	360	49	114	20	3	3	38	46	32	5	1	.317	.399	.414	.812	115	10	60	6.17	-1	*1-113,3-11/2-7,S-1	14	0.5
1962 Bos-A★	152	562	80	183	33	5	10	60	79	57	3	4	**.326**	.411	.456	.867	129	25	110	7.53	-3	*1-151	24	1.3
1963 Hou-N	124	388	35	98	9	1	2	23	45	42	2	0	.253	.335	.296	.631	89	-3	38	3.17	4	1-70,2-36/3-3	9	0.0
1964 Hou-N	22	51	3	10	1	0	0	3	8	7	0	0	.196	.305	.216	.521	53	-3	3	2.00	-1	1-14	0	-0.5
Total 14	1799	6373	876	1854	282	64	49	630	844	627	37	51	.291	.376	.378	.755	106	72	934	5.22	-41	1-644,2-642,S-463/3-49,0-1	216	7.9

• RUSHFORD, Jim James Thomas Rushford b: 3/24/1974, Chicago, IL BL/TL, 6'1", 190 lbs. Deb: 9/3/2002

YEAR TM-L	G	AB	R	H	2B	3B	HR	RBI	BB	SO	SB	CS	AVG	OBP	SLG	OPS	OPS+	BR/A	RC	RC/G	FR	G/POS	WS	TPW
2002 Mil-N	23	77	8	11	2	0	1	6	6	9	0	0	.143	.214	.208	.422	12	-10	3	1.25	-1	0-22(1-0-21)	0	-1.3

• RUSS, John John Russ b: 4/1/1858, Cannelton, IN d: 1/18/1912, Louisville, KY Deb: 7/4/1882

YEAR TM-L	G	AB	R	H	2B	3B	HR	RBI	BB	SO	SB	CS	AVG	OBP	SLG	OPS	OPS+	BR/A	RC	RC/G	FR	G/POS	WS	TPW
1882 Bal-a	1	3	0	1	0	0	0	....	0	....	....	....	.333	.333	.333	.667	136	0	0	4.78	0	/0-1,P-1	0	0.0

YEAR TM-L	G	AB	R	H	2B	3B	HR	RBI	BB	SO	SB	CS	AVG	OBP	SLG	OPS	OPS+	BR/A	RC	RC/G	FR	G/POS	WS	TPW
• RUSSELL, Bill	William Ellis Russell b: 10/21/1948, Pittsburg, KS BR/TR, 6', 175 lbs. Deb: 4/7/1969 M/C Career OF: 62-75-179																							
1969 LA-N	98	212	35	48	6	2	5	15	22	45	4	1	.226	.302	.344	.646	87	-3	23	3.66	1	0-86(7-24-62)	5	-0.6
1970 LA-N	81	278	30	72	11	9	0	28	16	28	9	1	.259	.306	.363	.670	82	-6	32	3.93	5	0-79(2-23-57)/S-1	7	-0.5
1971 LA-N	91	211	29	48	7	4	2	15	11	39	6	3	.227	.266	.327	.593	71	-9	18	2.90	-7	2-41,0-40(3-8-35)/S-6	4	-1.5
1972 LA-N	129	434	47	118	19	5	4	34	34	64	14	7	.272	.328	.366	.694	99	-1	53	4.29	5	*S-121/0-6(1-1-4)	16	2.1
1973 LA-N★	162	615	55	163	26	3	4	56	34	63	15	7	.265	.305	.337	.641	81	-17	62	3.46	15	*S-162	17	1.9
1974*LA-N	160	553	61	149	18	6	5	65	53	53	14	5	.269	.338	.351	.689	97	-1	64	3.89	-7	*S-160/0-1	16	1.1
1975 LA-N	84	252	24	52	9	2	0	14	23	28	5	0	.206	.278	.258	.536	52	-15	19	2.42	1	S-83	3	-0.5
1976 LA-N★	149	554	53	152	17	3	5	65	21	46	15	5	.274	.304	.343	.647	85	-11	55	3.45	9	*S-149	15	1.5
1977*LA-N	153	634	84	176	28	6	4	51	24	43	16	7	.278	.306	.360	.666	78	-20	64	3.44	8	*S-153	15	0.4
1978*LA-N	155	625	72	179	32	4	3	46	30	34	10	6	.286	.321	.365	.686	92	-9	69	3.86	19	*S-155	18	2.8
1979 LA-N	153	627	72	170	26	4	7	56	24	43	6	9	.271	.299	.359	.658	80	-22	60	3.23	-12	*S-150	10	-1.8
1980 LA-N★	130	466	38	123	23	2	3	34	18	44	13	2	.264	.296	.341	.637	79	-13	48	3.59	-2	*S-129	12	-0.1
1981*LA-N	82	262	20	61	9	2	0	22	19	20	2	1	.233	.287	.282	.570	64	-12	19	2.34	6	S-80	5	0.2
1982 LA-N	153	497	64	136	20	2	3	46	63	30	10	2	.274	.360	.340	.700	99	3	63	4.39	-1	*S-150	16	1.9
1983*LA-N	131	451	47	111	13	1	1	30	33	31	13	9	.246	.303	.286	.589	64	-23	40	2.97	4	*S-127	11	-0.6
1984 LA-N	89	262	25	70	12	1	0	19	25	24	4	4	.267	.331	.321	.652	85	-6	28	3.49	-2	S-65,0-18(0-18-0)/2-5	7	-0.3
1985 LA-N	76	169	19	44	6	1	0	13	18	9	4	0	.260	.335	.308	.643	83	-2	19	3.98	-4	S-23,0-21(21-0-0)/2-8,3-5	4	-0.5
1986 LA-N	105	216	21	54	11	0	0	18	15	23	7	0	.250	.305	.301	.606	73	-7	21	3.16	-1	0-48(28-1-20),S-32/2-8,3-1	4	-0.6
Total 18	2181	7318	796	1926	293	57	46	627	483	667	167	69	.263	.312	.338	.650	83	-174	759	3.52	36	*S-1746,0-299/2-62,3-6	185	4.9
• RUSSELL, Harvey	Harvey Holmes Russell b: 1/10/1887, Marshall, VA d: 1/8/1980, Alexandria, VA BL/TR, 5'9.5", 163 lbs. Deb: 4/17/1914																							
1914 Bal-F	81	168	18	39	3	2	0	13	18	17	2	....	.232	.310	.274	.584	67	-7	14	2.79	-8	C-47/0-1,S-1	3	-1.2
1915 Bal-F	53	73	5	19	1	2	0	11	14	5	1	....	.260	.407	.329	.735	109	2	11	4.76	0	C-21	3	0.4
Total 2	134	241	23	58	4	4	0	24	32	22	3	....	.241	.342	.290	.632	82	-4	25	3.41	-7	/C-68,0-1,S-1	6	-0.8
• RUSSELL, Jim	James William Russell b: 10/1/1918, Fayette City, PA d: 11/24/1987, Pittsburgh, PA BB/TR, 6'1", 181 lbs. Deb: 9/12/1942 Career OF: 568-360-25																							
1942 Pit-N	5	14	2	1	0	0	0	0	1	4	0	....	.071	.133	.071	.205	-38	-2	0	.35	0	/0-3(0-3-0)	0	-0.2
1943 Pit-N	146	533	79	138	19	11	4	44	77	67	12	....	.259	.354	.358	.712	102	4	70	4.62	2	*0-134(133-2-2)/1-6	16	-0.3
1944 Pit-N	152	580	109	181	34	14	8	66	79	63	6	....	.312	.399	.460	.859	136	30	112	7.42	9	*0-149(139-6-4)	31	3.0
1945 Pit-N	146	510	88	145	24	8	12	77	71	40	15	....	.284	.377	.433	.810	120	15	88	6.34	4	*0-140(139-1-0)	21	1.1
1946 Pit-N	146	516	68	143	29	6	8	50	67	54	11	....	.277	.362	.403	.765	114	10	78	5.39	-9	*0-134(67-68-0)/1-5	16	-0.5
1947 Pit-N	128	478	68	121	21	8	8	51	63	58	7	....	.253	.343	.381	.723	89	-7	64	4.62	-2	*0-119(1-102-19)	10	-1.2
1948 Bos-N	89	322	44	85	18	1	9	54	46	31	4	....	.264	.361	.410	.771	110	5	49	5.37	-1	0-84(2-82-0)	11	0.2
1949 Bos-N	130	415	57	96	22	1	8	54	64	68	3	....	.231	.337	.347	.684	88	-5	52	4.18	-9	*0-120(30-93-0)	9	-1.8
1950 Bro-N	77	214	37	49	8	2	10	32	31	36	1	....	.229	.329	.425	.755	95	-2	30	4.78	4	0-55(53-3-0)	6	-0.2
1951 Bro-N	16	13	2	0	0	0	0	0	4	6	0	0	.000	.278	.000	.278	-18	-2	0	.39	0	/0-4(4-0-0)	0	-0.2
Total 10	1035	3595	554	959	175	51	67	428	503	427	59	0	.267	.360	.400	.760	108	47	544	5.36	-2	0-942/1-11	120	-0.1
• RUSSELL, John	John William Russell b: 1/5/1961, Oklahoma City, OK BR/TR, 6', 200 lbs. Deb: 6/22/1984 C Career OF: 88-0-36																							
1984 Phi-N	39	99	11	28	8	1	2	11	12	33	0	1	.283	.360	.444	.805	123	3	16	5.48	0	0-29(14-0-18)/C-2	3	0.1
1985 Phi-N	81	216	22	47	12	0	9	23	18	72	2	0	.218	.278	.398	.676	85	-5	24	3.65	-1	0-49(49-0-0),1-18	4	-0.9
1986 Phi-N	93	315	35	76	21	2	13	60	25	103	0	1	.241	.303	.444	.748	100	-2	42	4.48	-6	C-89	9	-0.3
1987 Phi-N	24	62	5	9	1	0	3	8	3	17	0	1	.145	.185	.306	.491	26	-7	2	.99	-1	0-10(10-0-0)/C-7	0	-0.8
1988 Phi-N	22	49	5	12	1	0	2	4	3	15	0	0	.245	.302	.388	.690	95	-0	5	3.66	-1	C-15	0	0.0
1989 Atl-N	74	159	14	29	2	0	2	9	8	53	0	0	.182	.226	.233	.459	31	-15	8	1.59	1	C-45,0-14(1-0-15)/1-2,3-2,P	2	-1.2
1990 Tex-A	68	128	16	35	4	0	2	8	11	41	1	0	.273	.331	.352	.682	91	-1	15	4.14	-2	C-31,D-19/0-6(6-0-0),1-3,3	1	-0.3
1991 Tex-A	22	27	3	3	0	0	0	1	1	7	0	0	.111	.143	.111	.254	-29	-5	1	.56	-1	/0-8(6-0-2),C-5,D-5	0	-0.5
1992 Tex-A	7	10	1	1	0	0	0	2	1	4	0	0	.100	.250	.100	.350	2	-1	0	1.27	0	/C-4,0-2(1-0-1),D-1	0	-0.1
1993 Tex-A	18	22	1	5	1	0	1	3	2	10	0	0	.227	.292	.409	.701	90	-0	3	4.41	-2	C-11/1-1,3-1,0-1	0	-0.2
Total 10	448	1087	113	245	50	3	34	129	84	355	3	3	.225	.285	.371	.655	80	-34	115	3.51	-13	C-209,0-119/D-25,1-24,3-4,P	19	-4.4
• RUSSELL, Lloyd	Lloyd Opal Russell b: 4/10/1913, Atoka, OK d: 5/24/1968, Waco, TX BR/TR, 5'11", 166 lbs. Deb: 4/26/1938																							
1938 Cle-A	2	0	0	0	0	0	0	0	0	0	0	0	....	....	....	....	-102	0	0	....	0	....	0	0.0
• RUSSELL, Paul	Paul A. Russell b: 1870, Reading, PA d: Pottstown, PA Deb: 7/29/1894																							
1894 StL-N	3	10	1	1	0	0	0	0	0	2	0	....	.100	.100	.100	.200	-52	-3	0	.30	0	/2-1,3-1,0-1	0	-0.2
• RUSSELL, Reb	Ewell Albert Russell b: 4/12/1889, Jackson, MS d: 9/30/1973, Indianapolis, IN BL/TL, 5'11", 185 lbs. Deb: 4/18/1913 Career OF: 5-0-133 ♦																							
1913 Chi-A	54	106	9	20	5	3	1	7	1	29	0	....	.189	.204	.321	.524	53	3	7	1.88	-4	P-52	32	4.0
1914 Chi-A	46	64	6	17	1	1	0	7	1	14	0	....	.266	.277	.313	.589	78	3	6	3.12	0	P-38	9	0.0
1915 Chi-A	45	86	11	21	2	3	0	7	4	14	1	....	.244	.293	.337	.631	86	4	9	3.58	-2	P-41	16	1.7
1916 Chi-A	56	91	9	13	2	0	0	6	0	18	1	....	.143	.152	.165	.317	-5	-4	3	.85	-1	P-56	20	0.3
1917*Chi-A	39	68	5	19	3	3	0	9	2	10	0	....	.279	.300	.412	.712	115	5	8	4.09	-1	P-35/0-1	18	2.3
1918 Chi-A	27	50	2	7	3	0	0	3	0	6	0	....	.140	.157	.200	.357	8	-2	2	.93	-2	P-19/0-1	7	0.1
1919 Chi-A	1	0	0	0	0	0	0	0	0	0	0	....	....	....	....	....	-100	0	0	....	-0	/P-1	0	0.0
1922 Pit-N	60	220	51	81	14	8	12	75	14	18	4	2	.368	.423	.668	1.091	175	24	61	10.79	-5	0-60(0-0-60)	12	1.3
1923 Pit-N	94	291	49	84	18	7	9	58	20	21	3	1	.289	.341	.491	.832	115	6	49	6.10	-1	0-76(4-0-72)	10	-0.1
Total 9	422	976	142	262	48	25	22	172	42	130	9	3	.268	.309	.436	.745	102	38	144	5.09	-17	P-242,0-138	124	9.7
• RUSSELL, Rip	Glen David Russell b: 1/26/1915, Los Angeles, CA d: 9/26/1976, Los Alamitos, CA BR/TR, 6'1", 180 lbs. Deb: 5/5/1939																							
1939 Chi-N	143	542	55	148	24	5	9	79	36	56	2	....	.273	.318	.386	.704	87	-11	66	4.20	-3	*1-143	12	-2.8
1940 Chi-N	68	215	15	53	7	2	5	33	8	23	1	....	.247	.277	.367	.644	78	-7	20	3.15	-7	1-51/3-3	2	-2.0
1941 Chi-N	6	17	1	5	1	0	0	1	1	5	0	....	.294	.333	.353	.686	97	-0	2	4.45	0	/1-5	0	0.0
1942 Chi-N	102	302	32	73	9	0	8	41	17	21	0	....	.242	.282	.351	.633	88	-6	29	3.29	-9	1-35,2-24,3-10/0-3(3-0-0)	4	-1.8
1946*Bos-A	80	274	22	57	10	1	6	35	13	30	1	1	.208	.247	.318	.564	54	-18	19	2.22	1	3-70/2-3	2	-1.8
1947 Bos-A	26	52	8	8	1	0	1	3	8	7	0	0	.154	.267	.231	.497	36	-4	3	1.61	-1	3-13	0	-0.5
Total 6	425	1402	133	344	52	8	29	192	83	142	4	1	.245	.289	.356	.644	77	-47	140	3.32	-18	1-234/3-96,2-27,0-3	20	-8.9
• RUSZKOWSKI, Hank	Henry Alexander Ruszkowski b: 11/10/1925, Cleveland, OH d: 5/31/2000, Cleveland, OH BR/TR, 6', 190 lbs. Deb: 9/26/1944																							
1944 Cle-A	3	8	1	3	0	0	0	1	0	1	0	0	.375	.375	.375	.750	119	0	1	3.46	0	/C-2	0	0.1
1945 Cle-A	14	49	2	10	0	0	0	5	4	9	0	0	.204	.264	.204	.468	38	-4	3	1.68	2	C-14	1	-0.1
1947 Cle-A	23	27	5	7	2	0	3	4	2	6	0	0	.259	.310	.667	.977	172	2	6	7.95	-1	C-16	2	0.2
Total 3	40	84	8	20	2	0	3	10	6	16	0	0	.238	.289	.369	.658	88	-1	9	3.71	2	/C-32	3	0.2
• RUTH, Babe	George Herman "The Bambino,The Sultan Of Swat" Ruth b: 2/6/1895, Baltimore, MD d: 8/16/1948, New York, NY BL/TL, 6'2", 215 lbs. Deb: 7/11/1914 C HOF: 1936 Career OF: 1057-64-1131 ♦																							
1914 Bos-A	5	10	1	2	1	0	0	2	0	4	0	....	.200	.200	.300	.500	50	0	1	1.99	0	/P-4	1	-0.4
1915*Bos-A	42	92	16	29	10	1	4	21	9	23	0	....	.315	.376	.576	.952	191	15	20	8.23	2	P-32	23	2.3
1916*Bos-A	67	136	18	37	5	3	3	15	10	23	0	....	.272	.322	.419	.741	122	13	19	4.78	1	P-44	37	6.0
1917 Bos-A	52	123	14	40	6	3	2	12	12	18	0	....	.325	.385	.472	.857	163	17	22	6.45	3	P-41	36	3.9
1918*Bos-A	95	317	50	95	26	11	**11**	66	58	58	6	....	.300	.411	.555	.966	195	41	72	8.14	6	0-59(47-12-0),P-20,1-13	40	5.3
1919 Bos-A	130	432	**103**	139	34	12	**29**	**114**	101	58	7	....	.322	**.456**	**.657**	**1.114**	**224**	**79**	128	**11.25**	11	*0-111(111-0-0),P-17/1-5	**43**	**8.9**
1920 NY-A	142	458	**158**	172	36	9	**54**	**137**	**150**	80	14	14	.376	**.532**	**.847**	**1.379**	**252**	**108**	212	**18.42**	2	*0-141(36-20-85)/1-2,P-1	**51**	**10.0**
1921*NY-A	152	540	**177**	204	44	16	**59**	**171**	**145**	81	17	13	.378	**.512**	**.846**	**1.359**	**236**	**117**	239	**17.91**	4	*0-152(134-18-0)/1-2,P-2	**53**	**9.8**
1922*NY-A	110	406	94	128	24	8	35	99	84	80	2	5	.315	.434	**.672**	**1.106**	**181**	48	120	11.11	1	*0-110(71-0-40)/1-1	29	4.0
1923*NY-A	152	522	**151**	205	45	13	**41**	**131**	**170**	93	17	21	.393	**.545**	**.764**	**1.309**	**238**	**114**	223	**17.36**	14	*0-148(68-7-73)/1-4	**55**	**11.2**
1924 NY-A	153	529	**143**	200	39	7	**46**	121	**142**	81	9	13	**.378**	**.513**	**.739**	**1.252**	**221**	**100**	205	**15.61**	2	*0-152(50-7-99)	**45**	**8.5**
1925 NY-A	98	359	61	104	12	2	25	66	59	68	2	4	.290	.393	.543	.936	138	20	78	7.80	4	0-98(33-0-66)	13	1.5
1926*NY-A	152	495	**139**	184	30	5	**47**	**146**	**144**	76	11	9	.372	**.516**	**.737**	**1.253**	**228**	**101**	196	**15.76**	-3	*0-149(82-0-68)/1-2	**45**	**8.4**

YEAR TM-L	G	AB	R	H	2B	3B	HR	RBI	BB	SO	SB	CS	AVG	OBP	SLG	OPS	OPS+	BR/A	RC	RC/G	FR	G/POS	WS	TPW
1927*NY-A	151	540	**158**	192	29	8	**60**	164	**137**	89	7	6	.356	**.486**	**.772**	**1.258**	**229**	**107**	208	**14.97**	5	*O-151(56-0-95)	**45**	**9.5**
1928*NY-A	154	536	**163**	173	29	8	**54**	**142**	**137**	87	4	5	.323	.463	**.709**	**1.172**	**211**	**91**	183	**12.87**	-7	*O-154(55-0-99)	**45**	**6.9**
1929 NY-A	135	499	121	172	26	6	**46**	154	72	60	5	3	.345	.430	**.697**	**1.128**	**199**	**72**	150	**11.61**	0	*O-133(55-0-78)	32	**6.0**
1930 NY-A	145	518	150	186	28	9	**49**	153	**136**	61	10	10	.359	**.493**	**.732**	**1.225**	**216**	**98**	191	**13.97**	-2	*O-144(53-0-91)/P-1	38	**7.8**
1931 NY-A	145	534	149	199	31	3	**46**	163	**128**	51	5	4	.373	**.495**	**.700**	**1.195**	**223**	**105**	192	**15.04**	-3	*O-142(51-0-91)/1-1	**38**	**8.8**
1932*NY-A	133	457	120	156	13	5	41	137	**130**	62	2	2	.341	**.489**	.661	1.150	**206**	81	157	13.75	2	*O-128(44-0-87)/1-1	36	7.0
1933 NY-A★	137	459	97	138	21	3	34	103	**114**	90	4	5	.301	.442	.582	1.023	180	58	124	10.11	1	*O-132(55-0-78)/1-1,P-1	29	4.9
1934 NY-A★	125	365	78	105	17	4	22	84	104	63	1	3	.288	.448	.537	.985	164	40	95	9.57	-1	*O-111(34-0-77)	20	3.1
1935 Bos-N	28	72	13	13	0	0	6	12	20	24	0	....	.181	.359	.431	.789	121	3	12	5.51	0	O-26(22-0-4)	2	0.2
Total 22	2503	8399	2174	2873	506	136	714	2213	2062	1330	123	117	.342	.474	.690	1.164	209	**1429**	2849	13.09	40	*O-2241,P-163/1-32	**756**	**133.6**

• RUTHERFORD, Jim James Hollis Rutherford b: 9/26/1886, Stillwater, MN d: 9/18/1956, Lakewood, OH BL/TR, 6'1", 180 lbs. Deb: 7/12/1910

YEAR TM-L	G	AB	R	H	2B	3B	HR	RBI	BB	SO	SB	CS	AVG	OBP	SLG	OPS	OPS+	BR/A	RC	RC/G	FR	G/POS	WS	TPW
1910 Cle-A	1	2	0	1	0	0	0	0	0	....	0	....	.500	.500	.500	1.000	211	0	0	12.79	-0	/O-1	0	0.0

• RUTNER, Mickey Milton Rutner b: 3/18/1920, Hempstead, NY BR/TR, 5'11", 190 lbs. Deb: 9/11/1947

YEAR TM-L	G	AB	R	H	2B	3B	HR	RBI	BB	SO	SB	CS	AVG	OBP	SLG	OPS	OPS+	BR/A	RC	RC/G	FR	G/POS	WS	TPW
1947 Phi-A	12	48	4	12	1	0	1	4	3	2	0	0	.250	.294	.333	.627	73	-2	4	2.47	0	3-11	0	-0.2

• RYAL, Mark Mark Dwayne Ryal b: 8/28/1960, Henryetta, OK BL/TL, 6'1", 185 lbs. Deb: 9/7/1982 Career OF: 26-2-25

YEAR TM-L	G	AB	R	H	2B	3B	HR	RBI	BB	SO	SB	CS	AVG	OBP	SLG	OPS	OPS+	BR/A	RC	RC/G	FR	G/POS	WS	TPW
1982 KC-A	6	13	0	1	0	0	0	0	1	3	0	0	.077	.143	.077	.220	-38	-2	0	.41	0	/O-5(4-1-0)	0	-0.3
1985 Chi-A	12	33	4	5	3	0	0	3	3	3	0	0	.152	.222	.242	.465	26	-3	2	1.31	-0	O-12(12-1-0)	0	-0.4
1986 Cal-A	13	32	6	12	0	0	2	5	2	4	1	0	.375	.412	.563	.974	164	3	7	9.23	-1	/O-6(0-0-6),1-4,D-2	2	0.2
1987 Cal-A	58	100	7	20	6	0	5	18	3	15	0	0	.200	.223	.410	.633	65	-6	8	2.44	-2	O-21(6-0-15)/D-5,1-4	0	-0.8
1989 Phi-N	29	33	2	8	2	0	0	5	1	6	0	0	.242	.265	.303	.568	62	-2	3	2.93	0	/1-4,O-4(2-0-2)	0	-0.3
1990 Pit-N	9	12	0	1	0	0	0	0	0	3	0	0	.083	.083	.083	.167	-56	-3	0	.20	-0	/O-4(2-0-2)	0	-0.3
Total 6	127	223	19	47	11	0	7	31	10	34	1	0	.211	.245	.354	.599	60	-13	19	2.82	-3	/O-52,1-12,D-7	2	-1.8

• RYAN, Blondy John Collins Ryan b: 1/4/1906, Lynn, MA d: 11/28/1959, Swampscott, MA BR/TR, 6'1", 178 lbs. Deb: 7/13/1930

YEAR TM-L	G	AB	R	H	2B	3B	HR	RBI	BB	SO	SB	CS	AVG	OBP	SLG	OPS	OPS+	BR/A	RC	RC/G	FR	G/POS	WS	TPW
1930 Chi-A	28	87	9	18	0	4	1	10	6	13	2	0	.207	.258	.333	.591	50	-6	8	2.98	-1	3-23/S-2,2-1	1	-0.6
1933*NY-N	146	525	47	125	10	5	3	48	15	62	0	....	.238	.259	.293	.553	58	-29	38	2.43	3	*S-146	8	-1.7
1934 NY-N	110	385	35	93	19	0	2	41	19	68	3	....	.242	.277	.306	.584	57	-23	31	2.64	2	3-65,S-30,2-25	5	-1.6
1935 Phi-N	39	129	13	34	3	0	1	10	7	20	1	....	.264	.312	.310	.622	61	-7	12	3.09	-1	S-35/2-1,3-1	2	-0.5
NY-A	30	105	12	25	1	3	0	11	3	10	0	0	.238	.259	.305	.564	48	-8	8	2.69	-3	S-30	1	-0.9
1937*NY-N	21	75	10	18	3	1	1	13	6	8	0	....	.240	.296	.347	.643	73	-3	7	3.26	1	S-19/2-1,3-1	2	0.0
1938 NY-N	12	24	1	5	0	0	0	0	1	3	0	....	.208	.240	.208	.448	24	-2	1	.80	0	/2-5,3-3,S-2	0	-0.2
Total 6	386	1330	127	318	36	13	8	133	57	184	6	0	.239	.271	.304	.575	57	-80	105	2.62	1	S-264/3-93,2-33	19	-5.5

• RYAN, Buddy John Budd Ryan b: 10/6/1885, Denver, CO d: 7/9/1956, Sacramento, CA BL/TR, 5'9.5", 172 lbs. Deb: 4/11/1912 Career OF: 59-65-34

YEAR TM-L	G	AB	R	H	2B	3B	HR	RBI	BB	SO	SB	CS	AVG	OBP	SLG	OPS	OPS+	BR/A	RC	RC/G	FR	G/POS	WS	TPW
1912 Cle-A	93	328	53	89	12	9	1	31	30	....	12	....	.271	.343	.372	.715	101	0	46	4.78	3	O-90(56-0-34)	9	0.0
1913 Cle-A	73	243	26	72	6	1	0	32	11	13	9	....	.296	.332	.329	.661	91	-3	29	4.08	-2	O-68(3-65-0)/1-1	6	-0.9
Total 2	166	571	79	161	18	10	1	63	41	13	21	....	.282	.339	.354	.692	97	-3	75	4.48	2	O-158/1-1	15	-1.0

• RYAN, Connie Cornelius Joseph Ryan b: 2/27/1920, New Orleans, LA d: 1/3/1996, Metairie, LA BR/TR, 5'11", 175 lbs. Deb: 4/14/1942 M/C

YEAR TM-L	G	AB	R	H	2B	3B	HR	RBI	BB	SO	SB	CS	AVG	OBP	SLG	OPS	OPS+	BR/A	RC	RC/G	FR	G/POS	WS	TPW
1942 NY-N	11	27	4	5	0	0	0	2	4	3	1	....	.185	.290	.185	.476	40	-2	2	2.17	1	2-11	0	0.0
1943 Bos-N	132	457	52	97	10	2	1	24	58	56	7	....	.212	.301	.249	.550	61	-21	38	2.70	-20	*2-100,3-30	5	-3.8
1944 Bos-N★	88	332	56	98	18	5	4	25	36	40	13	....	.295	.364	.416	.780	114	7	50	5.21	9	2-80,3-14	13	2.1
1946 Bos-N	143	502	55	121	28	8	1	48	55	63	7	....	.241	.317	.335	.652	84	-11	56	3.75	-1	*2-120,3-24	14	-0.6
1947 Bos-N	150	544	60	144	33	5	5	69	71	60	5	....	.265	.351	.371	.722	94	-3	74	4.70	-0	*2-150/S-1	17	0.5
1948*Bos-N	51	122	14	26	3	0	0	10	21	16	0	....	.213	.333	.238	.571	58	-6	11	3.03	2	2-40/3-4	3	-0.2
1949 Bos-N	85	208	28	52	13	1	6	20	21	30	1	....	.250	.319	.409	.727	99	-1	27	4.51	-1	3-25,S-18,2-16/1-3	6	0.0
1950 Bos-N	20	72	12	14	2	0	3	6	12	9	0	....	.194	.326	.347	.673	82	-2	8	3.65	2	2-20	2	0.2
Cin-N	106	367	45	95	18	5	3	43	52	46	4	....	.259	.352	.360	.712	88	-5	48	4.52	8	*2-103	10	0.9
Yr.	126	439	57	109	20	5	6	49	64	55	4	....	.248	.348	.358	.705	87	-7	57	4.37	11	*2-123	12	1.1
1951 Cin-N	136	473	75	112	17	4	16	53	79	72	11	6	.237	.350	.391	.741	97	0	69	4.81	4	*2-121/3-3,1-2,O-1	15	1.1
1952 Phi-N	154	577	81	139	24	6	12	49	69	72	13	5	.241	.327	.366	.693	93	-4	73	4.26	5	*2-154	17	1.0
1953 Phi-N	90	247	47	73	14	6	5	26	30	35	5	1	.296	.372	.462	.833	116	7	45	6.65	4	2-65/1-2	11	1.5
Chi-A	17	54	6	12	1	0	0	6	9	12	2	0	.222	.333	.241	.574	55	-2	5	2.65	-2	3-16	1	-0.5
1954 Cin-N	1	0	0	0	0	0	0	0	1	0	0	0	....	1.000	....	1.000	182	0	0	∞	0	....	0	0.0
Total 12	1184	3982	535	988	181	42	56	381	518	514	69	12	.248	.337	.357	.694	90	-43	506	4.29	11	2-980,3-116/S-19,1-7,O-1	114	2.2

• RYAN, Cyclone Daniel R. Ryan b: 1866, Capperwhite, Ireland d: 1/30/1917, Medfield, MA TR, 6', 200 lbs. Deb: 8/8/1887 ♦

YEAR TM-L	G	AB	R	H	2B	3B	HR	RBI	BB	SO	SB	CS	AVG	OBP	SLG	OPS	OPS+	BR/A	RC	RC/G	FR	G/POS	WS	TPW
1887 NY-a	8	35	4	10	1	0	0	3	3	....	1	....	.286	.286	.250	.536	52	-2	3	2.85	-0	/1-8,P-2	0	-0.6
1891 Bos-N	1	1	0	0	0	0	0	0	0	0	0	....	.000	.000	.000	.000	-89	-0	0	.00	0	/P-1	1	0.1
Total 2	9	36	4	10	1	0	0	3	3	0	1	....	.278	.278	.242	.520	48	-2	3	2.74	0	/1-8,P-3	1	-0.5

• RYAN, Jack John Francis Ryan b: 5/5/1905, West Mineral, KS d: 9/2/1967, Rochester, MN BR/TR, 6', 185 lbs. Deb: 6/18/1929

YEAR TM-L	G	AB	R	H	2B	3B	HR	RBI	BB	SO	SB	CS	AVG	OBP	SLG	OPS	OPS+	BR/A	RC	RC/G	FR	G/POS	WS	TPW
1929 Bos-A	2	3	0	0	0	0	0	0	0	0	0	0	.000	.000	.000	.000	-102	-1	0	.00	0	/O-2(1-0-1)	0	-0.1

• RYAN, Jack John Bernard Ryan b: 11/12/1868, Haverhill, MA d: 8/21/1952, Boston, MA BR/TR, 5'10.5", 165 lbs. Deb: 9/2/1889 C Career OF: 4-4-7

YEAR TM-L	G	AB	R	H	2B	3B	HR	RBI	BB	SO	SB	CS	AVG	OBP	SLG	OPS	OPS+	BR/A	RC	RC/G	FR	G/POS	WS	TPW
1889 Lou-a	21	79	8	14	1	0	0	2	3	17	2	....	.177	.207	.190	.397	14	-9	4	1.47	0	C-15/O-4(0-3-1),3-2	0	-0.7
1890*Lou-a	93	337	43	73	16	4	0	35	12	....	6	....	.217	.244	.288	.531	58	-20	26	2.58	4	C-89/O-3(1-0-2),1-1,S-1	6	-0.8
1891 Lou-a	75	253	24	57	5	4	2	25	15	40	3	....	.225	.271	.300	.572	64	-13	22	2.97	0	C-56,1-11/3-6,O-4(3-1-0),2	3	-0.8
1894 Bos-N	53	201	39	54	12	7	1	29	13	16	3	....	.269	.316	.413	.729	66	-14	28	4.93	-2	C-51/1-2	4	-0.9
1895 Bos-N	49	189	22	55	7	0	0	18	6	6	3	....	.291	.313	.328	.641	62	-12	22	4.15	1	C-43/2-5,O-1	4	-0.5
1896 Bos-N	8	32	2	3	1	0	0	0	0	1	0	....	.094	.094	.125	.219	-40	-7	0	.35	0	/C-8	1	-0.5
1898 Bro-N	87	301	39	57	11	4	0	24	15	....	5	....	.189	.233	.252	.485	39	-25	20	2.11	1	C-84/3-4,1-1	4	-1.5
1899 Bal-N	2	4	0	2	1	0	0	1	0	....	1	....	.500	.500	.750	1.250	229	1	2	27.16	1	/C-2	0	0.1
1901 StL-N	83	300	27	59	6	5	0	31	7	....	5	....	.197	.218	.250	.468	37	-24	19	2.00	5	C-65/2-9,1-5,O-3(0-0-3)	3	-1.3
1902 StL-N	76	267	23	48	4	4	0	14	4	....	2	....	.180	.195	.225	.420	31	-22	14	1.55	2	C-66/1-4,3-4,2-2,S-1	3	-1.5
1903 StL-N	67	227	18	54	5	1	1	10	10	....	2	....	.238	.273	.282	.555	60	-12	19	2.85	3	C-47,1-18/S-2	2	-0.6
1912 Was-A	1	1	0	0	0	0	0	0	0	....	0	....	.000	.000	.000	.000	-99	-0	0	.00	0	/3-1	0	0.0
1913 Was-A	1	1	0	0	0	0	0	0	0	0	0	....	.000	.000	.000	.000	-98	-0	0	.00	0	/C-1	0	0.0
Total 13	616	2192	245	476	69	29	4	189	85	80	32	....	.217	.249	.281	.529	48	-157	175	2.64	13	C-527/1-42,2-19,3-17,O-15,S	30	-8.9

• RYAN, Jimmy James Edward "Pony" Ryan
b: 2/11/1863, Clinton, MA d: 10/26/1923, Chicago, IL BR/TL, 5'9", 162 lbs. Deb: 10/8/1885 U Career OF: 393-956-607 ♦

YEAR TM-L	G	AB	R	H	2B	3B	HR	RBI	BB	SO	SB	CS	AVG	OBP	SLG	OPS	OPS+	BR/A	RC	RC/G	FR	G/POS	WS	TPW
1885 Chi-N	3	13	2	6	1	0	0	2	1	1	....	....	.462	.500	.538	1.038	205	2	4	13.84	1	/S-2,O-1	1	0.2
1886*Chi-N	84	327	58	100	17	6	4	53	12	28	10	....	.306	.330	.431	.762	113	3	51	6.08	4	O-70(38-8-24)/3-6,S-6,2-5,P	14	0.1
1887 Chi-N	126	561	117	198	23	10	11	74	53	19	50	....	.353	.360	.435	.795	106	4	100	7.30	1	*O-122(1-97-24)/P-8,2-3	18	0.1
1888 Chi-N	129	549	115	**182**	**33**	10	**16**	64	35	50	60	....	.332	.377	**.515**	.892	170	43	133	**9.75**	8	*O-128(0-127-1)/P-8	**34**	4.4
1889 Chi-N	135	576	140	177	31	14	17	72	70	62	45	....	.307	.388	.498	.886	140	29	132	8.77	7	*O-106(0-105-1),S-29	25	2.9
1890 Chi-P	118	486	99	165	32	5	6	89	60	36	30	....	.340	.416	.463	.879	129	21	109	9.15	1	*O-118(0-118-0)	23	1.4
1891 Chi-N	118	505	110	140	22	15	9	66	53	38	27	....	.277	.355	.434	.789	129	18	90	6.62	5	*O-117(43-74-0)/P-2,S-2	22	1.8
1892 Chi-N	128	505	105	148	21	11	10	65	61	41	27	....	.293	.375	.438	.812	144	27	95	7.21	0	*O-120(0-120-0)/S-9	25	1.8
1893 Chi-N	83	341	82	102	21	7	3	30	59	25	8	....	.299	.407	.428	.835	124	14	64	7.12	-3	O-73(1-73-1),S-10/P-1	12	0.7
1894 Chi-N	110	482	133	172	37	7	3	62	51	24	11	....	.357	.422	.481	.903	112	9	105	8.81	5	*O-108(0-5-104)	13	0.6
1895 Chi-N	108	438	83	139	22	8	6	49	48	22	18	....	.317	.392	.445	.837	109	5	86	7.67	2	*O-108(0-0-108)	14	0.2
1896 Chi-N	128	489	83	149	24	10	3	86	46	16	29	....	.305	.369	.413	.782	102	1	89	6.70	0	*O-128(0-0-128)	14	-0.5
1897 Chi-N	136	520	103	156	33	17	5	85	50	....	27	....	.300	.369	.458	.827	113	8	101	7.18	10	*O-136(0-0-136)	16	0.9
1898 Chi-N	144	572	122	185	32	13	4	79	73	....	29	....	.323	.405	.446	.850	144	34	119	7.98	-5	*O-144(134-0-10)	28	1.6
1899 Chi-N	125	525	91	158	20	10	3	68	43	....	9	....	.301	.357	.394	.752	109	6	80	5.69	3	*O-125(125-0-0)	17	-0.2
1900 Chi-N	105	415	66	115	25	4	5	59	29	....	19	....	.277	.329	.393	.722	102	0	62	5.39	-4	*O-105(49-9-57)	12	-0.9

YEAR TM-L	G	AB	R	H	2B	3B	HR	RBI	BB	SO	SB	CS	AVG	OBP	SLG	OPS	OPS+	BR/A	RC	RC/G	FR	G/POS	WS	TPW
1902 Was-A	120	484	92	155	32	6	6	44	43	....	10	....	.320	.384	.448	.832	129	20	90	7.12	-3	*0-120(2-105-13)	19	1.0
1903 Was-A	114	437	42	109	25	4	7	46	17	....	9	....	.249	.290	.373	.663	96	-3	52	4.08	-3	*0-114(0-114-0)	9	-1.2
Total 18	2014	8225	1643	2556	451	157	118	1093	804	362	418	....	.311	.374	.443	.817	123	241	1560	7.26	30	*0-1943/S-58,P-24,2-8,3-6	316	15.0
• RYAN, Johnny	John Joseph Ryan b: 10/1853, Philadelphia, PA d: 3/22/1902, Philadelphia, PA, 5'7.5", 150 lbs. Deb: 8/19/1873 NA OF: 77-1-0 Career OF: 64-6-0 ♦																							
1873 Phi-n	2	8	1	2	0	0	0	1	0	0	0	0	.250	.250	.250	.500	47	-1	1	2.61	0	/1-1,0-1	....	0.0
1874 Bal-n	47	181	29	35	8	1	0	19	5	13	3	0	.193	.215	.249	.464	48	-9	11	2.17	13	*0-47(47-0-0)/P-1	....	0.3
1875 NH-n	37	146	17	23	2	2	0	8	3	12	10	4	.158	.174	.199	.373	34	-6	7	1.62	-5	0-30(30-0-0),P-10/C-4,S-1	....	-1.1
1876 Lou-N	64	247	32	61	5	1	1	18	6	23	....	....	.247	.271	.295	.566	75	-8	20	3.07	-4	*0-64(63-1-0)/P-1	5	-1.6
1877 Cin-N	6	26	2	4	0	1	0	2	1	5	....	....	.154	.185	.231	.416	34	-2	1	1.42	-1	/0-6(1-5-0)	0	-0.2
Total 3 n	86	335	47	60	10	3	0	28	8	25	13	4	.179	.198	.227	.425	42	-16	18	1.93	9	/0-78,P-11,C-4,1-1,S-1	....	-0.9
Total 2	70	273	34	65	5	2	1	20	7	28	....	....	.238	.263	.288	.551	71	-10	21	2.89	-5	/0-70,P-1	5	-1.8
• RYAN, Michael	Michael Sean Ryan b: 7/6/1977, Indiana, PA BL/TR, 5'10", 185 lbs. Deb: 9/20/2002 Career OF: 8-3-12																							
2002 Min-A	7	11	3	1	0	0	0	0	0	2	0	0	.091	.091	.091	.182	-51	-2	0	.25	-1	/0-5(4-3-0),D-1	0	-0.3
2003*Min-A	27	61	13	24	7	0	5	13	6	12	2	1	.393	.448	.754	1.202	207	9	18	11.34	3	0-16(4-0-12)/D-4	4	1.1
Total 2	34	72	16	25	7	0	5	13	6	14	2	1	.347	.397	.653	1.050	171	7	18	9.25	2	/0-21,D-5	4	0.7
• RYAN, Mike	J. Ryan b: St. Louis, MO Deb: 7/25/1895																							
1895 StL-N	2	2	0	0	0	0	0	0	0	0	0	....	.000	.000	.000	.000	-101	-1	0	.00	-1	/3-2	0	-0.1
• RYAN, Mike	Michael James Ryan b: 11/25/1941, Haverhill, MA BR/TR, 6'2", 205 lbs. Deb: 10/3/1964 C																							
1964 Bos-A	1	3	0	1	0	0	0	2	1	0	0	0	.333	.500	.333	.833	131	0	1	6.75	-0	/C-1	0	0.0
1965 Bos-A	33	107	7	17	0	1	3	9	5	19	0	0	.159	.196	.262	.458	27	-11	4	1.16	-1	C-33	1	-1.0
1966 Bos-A	116	369	27	79	15	3	2	32	29	68	1	0	.214	.271	.287	.559	55	-21	28	2.50	0	*C-114	5	-1.6
1967*Bos-A	79	226	21	45	4	2	2	27	26	42	2	0	.199	.285	.261	.546	57	-11	17	2.36	-2	C-79	4	-0.9
1968 Phi-N	96	296	12	53	6	1	1	15	15	59	0	3	.179	.219	.216	.435	31	-26	12	1.20	2	C-96	4	-2.2
1969 Phi-N	133	446	41	91	17	2	12	44	30	66	1	1	.204	.257	.332	.589	66	-22	36	2.62	9	*C-132	7	-0.7
1970 Phi-N	46	134	14	24	8	0	2	11	16	24	0	0	.179	.267	.284	.550	49	-10	9	2.01	0	C-46	2	-0.8
1971 Phi-N	43	134	9	22	5	1	3	6	10	32	0	0	.164	.222	.284	.506	42	-11	8	1.99	5	C-43	2	-0.4
1972 Phi-N	46	106	6	19	4	0	2	10	10	25	0	0	.179	.256	.274	.530	49	-7	7	1.96	2	C-46	1	-0.4
1973 Phi-N	28	69	7	16	1	2	1	5	6	19	0	0	.232	.293	.348	.641	75	-2	6	2.82	1	C-27	1	-0.1
1974 Pit-N	15	30	2	3	0	0	0	0	4	16	0	0	.100	.206	.100	.306	-13	-4	1	.55	1	C-15	1	-0.3
Total 11	636	1920	146	370	60	12	28	161	152	370	4	4	.193	.253	.280	.534	51	-124	128	2.11	16	C-632	28	-8.6
• RYAN, Rob	Robert James Ryan b: 6/24/1973, Havre, MT BL/TL, 5'11", 192 lbs. Deb: 8/20/1999 Career OF: 1-4-7																							
1999 Ari-N	20	29	4	7	1	0	2	5	1	8	0	0	.241	.267	.483	.749	84	-1	4	4.67	0	/0-5(1-0-4)	1	-0.1
2000 Ari-N	27	27	4	8	1	1	0	2	4	7	0	0	.296	.406	.407	.814	103	0	5	7.10	0	/0-2(0-0-2),D-1	1	0.0
2001 Ari-N	1	1	0	0	0	0	0	0	0	1	0	0	.000	.000	.000	.000	-94	-0	0	.00	0	....	0	0.0
Oak-A	7	7	0	0	0	0	0	0	0	5	0	0	.000	.000	.000	.000	-100	-2	0	.00	0	/0-5(0-4-1),D-1	0	-0.2
Total 3	55	64	8	15	2	1	2	7	5	21	0	0	.234	.300	.391	.691	72	-3	9	4.85	-1	/0-12,D-2	2	-0.4
• RYDER, Tom	Thomas Ryder b: 5/9/1863, Dubuque, IA d: 7/18/1935, Dubuque, IA BL Deb: 7/22/1884																							
1884 StL-U	8	28	4	7	1	0	0	....	2	....	....	....	.250	.300	.286	.586	95	-0	2	3.28	0	/0-8(5-3-0)	0	-0.1
• RYE, Gene	Eugene Rudolph "Half Pint" Rye b: 11/15/1906, Chicago, IL d: 1/21/1980, Park Ridge, IL BL/TR, 5'6", 165 lbs. Deb: 4/22/1931																							
1931 Bos-A	17	39	3	7	0	0	0	1	2	5	....	0	.179	.220	.179	.399	6	-5	2	1.31	-1	0-10(10-0-0)	0	-0.6
• SABO, Alex	Alexander "Giz" Sabo b: 2/14/1910, New Brunswick, NJ d: 1/3/2001, Tuckerton, NJ BR/TR, 6', 192 lbs. Deb: 8/1/1936																							
1936 Was-A	4	8	1	3	0	0	0	1	0	2	0	0	.375	.375	.375	.750	91	-0	1	5.72	0	/C-4	0	0.0
1937 Was-A	1	0	0	0	0	0	0	0	0	0	0	0	....	....	....	....	-105	0	0		0	/C-1	0	0.0
Total 2	5	8	1	3	0	0	0	1	0	2	0	0	.375	.375	.375	.750	91	-0	1	5.72	0	/C-5	0	0.0
• SABO, Chris	Christopher Andrew "Spuds" Sabo b: 1/19/1962, Detroit, MI BR/TR, 5'11", 185 lbs. Deb: 4/4/1988																							
1988 Cin-N★	137	538	74	146	40	2	11	44	29	52	46	14	.271	.316	.414	.730	104	4	69	4.39	18	*3-135/S-2	17	2.5
1989 Cin-N	82	304	40	79	21	1	6	29	25	33	14	9	.260	.318	.395	.713	99	-2	38	4.26	2	3-76	9	0.1
1990*Cin-N★	148	567	95	153	38	2	25	71	61	58	25	10	.270	.345	.476	.821	118	14	94	5.85	-2	*3-146	20	1.4
1991 Cin-N★	153	582	91	175	35	3	26	88	44	79	19	6	.301	.356	.505	.861	134	26	103	6.41	-10	*3-151	22	1.8
1992 Cin-N	96	344	42	84	19	3	12	43	30	54	4	5	.244	.307	.422	.728	102	-2	41	3.87	0	3-93	8	-0.1
1993 Cin-N	148	552	86	143	33	2	21	82	43	105	6	4	.259	.319	.440	.760	101	-2	77	4.77	-12	*3-148	16	-1.1
1994 Bal-A	68	258	41	66	15	3	11	42	20	38	1	1	.256	.322	.465	.787	95	-3	37	4.82	0	3-37,0-22(9-0-13),D-10	7	-0.4
1995 Chi-A	20	71	10	18	5	0	1	8	3	12	2	0	.254	.303	.366	.669	77	-2	9	4.11	0	D-15/1-1,3-1	1	-0.3
StL-N	5	13	0	2	1	0	0	3	1	2	1	0	.154	.214	.231	.445	17	-1	1	1.22	0	/1-2,3-1	0	-0.1
1996 Cin-N	54	125	15	32	7	1	3	16	18	27	2	0	.256	.354	.400	.754	99	1	18	5.05	5	3-43	4	0.6
Total 9	911	3354	494	898	214	17	116	426	274	460	120	49	.268	.329	.445	.774	109	34	487	5.00	1	3-831/D-25,0-22,1-3,S-2	104	4.2
• SACKA, Frank	Frank Sacka b: 8/30/1924, Romulus, MI d: 12/7/1994, Dearborn, MI BR/TR, 6', 195 lbs. Deb: 4/29/1951																							
1951 Was-A	7	16	1	4	0	0	0	3	0	5	0	0	.250	.250	.250	.500	36	-1	1	2.31	0	/C-6	0	-0.1
1953 Was-A	7	18	2	5	0	0	0	3	3	1	0	0	.278	.381	.278	.659	82	-0	2	3.68	1	/C-6	1	0.1
Total 2	14	34	3	9	0	0	0	6	3	6	0	0	.265	.324	.265	.589	63	-2	3	3.07	1	/C-12	1	0.0
• SADEK, Mike	Michael George Sadek b: 5/30/1946, Minneapolis, MN BR/TR, 5'9", 165 lbs. Deb: 4/13/1973																							
1973 SF-N	39	66	6	11	1	1	0	4	11	8	1	0	.167	.286	.212	.498	38	-5	5	2.28	-3	C-35	1	-0.7
1975 SF-N	42	106	14	25	5	2	0	9	14	14	1	0	.236	.325	.321	.646	76	-3	10	3.21	0	C-38	3	-0.1
1976 SF-N	55	93	8	19	2	0	0	7	11	10	0	0	.204	.295	.226	.521	48	-6	7	2.31	-3	C-51	1	-0.7
1977 SF-N	61	126	12	29	7	0	1	15	12	5	2	1	.230	.297	.310	.607	63	-6	12	3.16	2	C-57	3	-0.2
1978 SF-N	40	109	15	26	3	0	2	9	10	11	1	0	.239	.303	.321	.624	77	-3	11	3.39	-1	C-37	3	-0.3
1979 SF-N	63	126	14	30	5	0	1	11	15	24	1	0	.238	.324	.302	.626	77	-3	12	3.07	0	C-60/0-1	3	-0.1
1980 SF-N	64	151	14	38	4	1	1	16	27	18	0	0	.252	.365	.311	.676	93	-0	19	4.16	-2	C-59	6	0.1
1981 SF-N	19	36	5	6	3	0	0	3	8	7	0	0	.167	.318	.250	.568	64	-1	4	3.11	2	C-19	2	0.1
Total 8	383	813	88	184	30	4	5	74	108	97	6	1	.226	.319	.292	.610	71	-28	80	3.18	-5	C-356/0-1	22	-2.0
• SADLER, Donnie	Donnie Lamont Sadler b: 6/17/1975, Clifton, TX BR/TR, 5'6", 175 lbs. Deb: 4/1/1998 Career OF: 47-61-25																							
1998*Bos-A	58	124	21	28	4	4	3	15	6	28	4	0	.226	.278	.395	.673	71	-5	15	3.84	-3	2-50/D-4,S-4	3	-0.6
1999*Bos-A	49	107	18	30	5	1	0	4	5	20	2	1	.280	.313	.346	.658	66	-6	12	3.86	-2	S-14,2-10/3-9,0-8(1-6-1),D	1	-0.6
2000 Bos-A	49	99	14	22	5	0	1	10	5	18	3	1	.222	.267	.303	.570	43	-9	9	2.68	1	S-19,0-17(3-13-1),2-12/3-3,D	2	-0.6
2001 Cin-N	39	84	9	17	3	0	1	3	9	20	3	3	.202	.280	.274	.553	42	-8	6	2.12	-1	2-15,S-12/0-8(6-2-2)	0	-0.8
KC-A	54	101	19	13	3	0	0	2	9	17	4	1	.129	.214	.158	.373	1	-14	5	1.33	14	0-16(5-4-7),3-15,2-13/S-6	2	0.0
2002 KC-A	35	68	10	13	1	1	0	5	4	12	3	1	.191	.236	.235	.471	23	-7	4	1.99	-3	0-15(11-0-4),3-11/2-4,S-4,D	0	-1.0
Tex-A	38	30	6	3	1	0	0	2	3	7	2	2	.100	.229	.133	.362		-5	1	.83	1	0-18(2-14-3),S-12/3-4,2-2	1	-0.3
Yr.	73	98	16	16	2	1	0	7	7	19	5	3	.163	.234	.204	.438	15	-12	5	1.58	-2	0-33(13-14-7),S-16,3-15/2-6,D	1	-1.4
2003 Tex-A	77	131	27	26	5	2	1	5	13	34	4	3	.198	.281	.290	.571	47	-11	11	2.71	-3	0-41(19-22-7),3-23,S-19/2-1	1	-1.3
Total 6	399	744	124	152	27	8	6	46	54	156	25	12	.204	.267	.286	.554	42	-65	62	2.61	3	0-123,2-107/S-90,3-65,D-11	10	-5.2
• SADOWSKI, Bob	Robert Frank "Bo" Sadowski b: 1/15/1937, St. Louis, MO BL/TR, 6', 175 lbs. Deb: 9/16/1960																							
1960 StL-N	1	1	0	0	0	0	0	0	1	0	0	0	.000	.500	.000	.500	47	0	0	3.51	-1	/2-1	0	-0.1
1961 Phi-N	16	54	4	7	0	0	0	0	4	7	1	0	.130	.203	.130	.333	-9	-8	1	.82	0	3-14	0	-0.8
1962 Chi-A	79	130	22	30	3	3	6	24	13	22	0	0	.231	.301	.438	.739	97	-1	17	4.32	0	3-16,2-12	3	0.0
1963 LA-A	88	144	12	36	6	0	1	22	15	34	2	1	.250	.321	.313	.633	83	-3	15	3.68	-2	0-25(1-0-24)/3-6,2-4	3	-0.6
Total 4	184	329	38	73	9	3	7	46	33	63	3	1	.222	.295	.331	.626	73	-12	34	3.41	-2	/3-36,0-25,2-17	6	-1.5

YEAR TM-L	G	AB	R	H	2B	3B	HR	RBI	BB	SO	SB	CS	AVG	OBP	SLG	OPS	OPS+	BR/A	RC	RC/G	FR	G/POS	WS	TPW
• SADOWSKI, Ed	Edward Roman Sadowski b: 1/19/1931, Pittsburgh, PA d: 11/6/1993, Garden Grove, CA BR/TR, 5'11", 175 lbs. Deb: 4/20/1960																							
1960 Bos-A	38	93	10	20	2	0	3	8	8	13	0	0	.215	.284	.333	.618	64	-5	8	2.67	0	C-36	1	-0.3
1961 LA-A	69	164	16	38	13	0	4	12	11	33	2	3	.232	.280	.384	.664	68	-9	16	3.30	-1	C-56	3	-0.8
1962 LA-A	27	55	4	11	4	0	1	3	2	14	1	0	.200	.228	.327	.555	49	-4	4	2.41	-2	C-18	1	-0.5
1963 LA-A	80	174	24	30	1	1	4	15	17	33	2	1	.172	.246	.259	.505	44	-13	11	1.95	6	C-68	3	-0.4
1966 Atl-N	3	9	1	1	0	0	0	1	1	1	0	0	.111	.200	.111	.311	-11	-1	0	.85	0	/C-3	0	-0.1
Total 5	**217**	**495**	**55**	**100**	**20**	**1**	**12**	**39**	**39**	**94**	**5**	**4**	**.202**	**.262**	**.319**	**.581**	**55**	**-32**	**39**	**2.55**	**4**	**C-181**	**8**	**-2.0**
• SAENZ, Olmedo	Olmedo (Sanchez) Saenz b: 10/8/1970, Chitre Herrera, Panama BR/TR, 6'2", 185 lbs. Deb: 5/28/1994																							
1994 Chi-A	5	14	2	2	0	1	0	0	0	5	0	0	.143	.143	.286	.429	7	-2	0	.58	0	/3-5	0	-0.2
1999 Oak-A	97	255	41	70	18	0	11	41	22	47	1	1	.275	.366	.475	.841	117	7	45	6.22	-1	3-56,1-28/D-8	7	0.4
2000*Oak-A	76	214	40	67	12	2	9	33	25	40	1	0	.313	.402	.514	.916	133	12	45	7.84	-1	D-27,3-18,1-17	8	0.7
2001*Oak-A	106	305	33	67	21	1	9	32	19	64	0	1	.220	.294	.384	.677	76	-12	33	3.56	0	D-56,1-28,3-14	1	-1.5
2002*Oak-A	68	156	15	43	10	1	6	18	13	31	1	1	.276	.358	.468	.826	117	4	27	6.13	1	1-34,3-15/D-7	5	0.2
Total 5	**352**	**944**	**131**	**249**	**61**	**5**	**35**	**124**	**79**	**187**	**3**	**3**	**.264**	**.347**	**.450**	**.798**	**106**	**9**	**150**	**5.52**	**-1**	**3-108,1-107/D-98**	**21**	**-0.3**
• SAFFELL, Tom	Thomas Judson Saffell b: 7/26/1921, Etowah, TN BL/TR, 5'11", 170 lbs. Deb: 7/2/1949 Career OF: 7-153-11																							
1949 Pit-N	73	205	36	66	7	1	2	25	21	27	5	....	.322	.385	.395	.780	107	3	32	5.89	-1	0-53(0-52-2)	7	0.0
1950 Pit-N	67	182	18	37	7	0	2	6	14	34	1	....	.203	.264	.275	.539	41	-16	14	2.55	2	0-43(0-42-2)	2	-1.5
1951 Pit-N	49	65	11	13	0	0	1	5	5	18	1	1	.200	.257	.246	.503	35	-6	4	2.07	-1	0-17(1-13-3)	0	-0.8
1955 Pit-N	73	113	21	19	1	0	1	3	15	22	1	0	.168	.266	.204	.469	27	-11	7	1.96	-1	0-47(6-37-4)	1	-1.4
KC-A	9	37	5	8	0	0	0	1	4	7	1	0	.216	.293	.216	.509	38	-3	3	2.31	-1	/0-9(0-9-0)	0	-0.4
Total 4	**271**	**602**	**91**	**143**	**15**	**1**	**6**	**40**	**59**	**108**	**9**	**1**	**.238**	**.307**	**.296**	**.602**	**60**	**-34**	**61**	**3.39**	**-2**	**0-169**	**10**	**-4.0**
• SAGE, Harry	Harry "Doc" Sage b: 3/16/1864, Rock Island, IL d: 5/27/1947, Rock Island, IL BR/TR, 5'10", 185 lbs. Deb: 4/17/1890 U																							
1890 Tol-a	81	275	40	41	8	4	2	25	29	....	10	....	.149	.235	.229	.464	36	-23	18	1.99	19	C-80/O-1	5	0.2
• SAGER, Pony	Samuel B. Sager b: 1847, Marshalltown, IA, 140 lbs. Deb: 5/6/1871																							
1871 Rok-n	8	39	9	11	0	0	0	5	2	2	5	1	.282	.317	.282	.599	77	-0	5	5.65	-3	/O-4(4-0-0),S-4	....	-0.2
• SAGMOEN, Marc	Marc Richard Sagmoen b: 4/16/1971, Seattle, WA BL/TL, 5'11", 185 lbs. Deb: 4/15/1997																							
1997 Tex-A	21	43	2	6	2	0	1	4	2	13	0	0	.140	.178	.256	.434	11	-6	2	1.27	-1	O-17(2-0-16)/1-1,D-1	0	-0.7
• SAIER, Vic	Victor Sylvester Saier b: 5/4/1891, Lansing, MI d: 5/14/1967, East Lansing, MI BL/TR, 5'11", 185 lbs. Deb: 5/3/1911																							
1911 Chi-N	86	259	42	67	15	1	1	37	25	37	11	....	.259	.340	.336	.676	89	-3	34	4.33	-4	1-73	6	-0.9
1912 Chi-N	122	451	74	130	25	14	2	61	34	65	11	....	.288	.340	.419	.759	107	3	67	5.12	-7	*1-120	13	-0.6
1913 Chi-N	149	519	94	150	15	**21**	14	92	62	62	26	....	.289	.370	.480	.850	141	28	97	6.49	-5	*1-149	26	2.0
1914 Chi-N	153	537	87	129	24	8	18	72	94	61	19	....	.240	.357	.415	.773	130	22	85	5.13	0	*1-153	24	2.1
1915 Chi-N	144	497	74	131	35	11	11	64	64	62	29	9	.264	.350	.445	.795	140	26	83	5.77	-4	*1-139	24	2.2
1916 Chi-N	147	498	60	126	25	3	7	50	79	68	20	17	.253	.356	.357	.714	108	5	66	4.26	5	*1-147	13	0.9
1917 Chi-N	6	21	5	5	1	0	0	2	2	1	0	....	.238	.304	.286	.590	75	-1	2	2.79	2	/1-6	0	0.1
1919 Pit-N	58	166	19	37	3	3	2	17	18	13	5	....	.223	.306	.313	.620	83	-3	17	3.29	-1	1-51	4	-0.5
Total 8	**865**	**2948**	**455**	**775**	**143**	**61**	**55**	**395**	**378**	**369**	**121**	**26**	**.263**	**.351**	**.409**	**.760**	**120**	**77**	**450**	**5.11**	**-14**	**1-838**	**110**	**5.3**
• SAKATA, Lenn	Lenn Haruki Sakata b: 6/8/1954, Honolulu, HI BR/TR, 5'9", 160 lbs. Deb: 7/21/1977																							
1977 Mil-A	53	154	13	25	2	0	2	12	9	22	1	3	.162	.209	.214	.423	16	-19	7	1.34	6	2-53	2	-1.1
1978 Mil-A	30	78	8	15	4	0	0	3	8	11	1	0	.192	.267	.244	.511	44	-5	5	2.03	-4	2-29	1	-0.8
1979 Mil-A	4	14	1	7	2	0	0	1	0	1	0	0	.500	.500	.643	1.143	206	2	5	17.36	1	/2-4	1	0.3
1980 Bal-A	43	83	12	16	3	2	1	9	6	10	2	1	.193	.247	.313	.560	53	-6	6	2.18	-1	2-34/S-4,D-1	1	-0.5
1981 Bal-A	61	150	19	34	4	0	5	15	11	18	4	0	.227	.284	.353	.637	83	-3	15	3.25	0	S-42,2-20	5	0.1
1982 Bal-A	136	343	40	89	18	1	6	31	30	39	7	4	.259	.326	.370	.697	91	-4	42	4.07	-4	2-83,S-56	10	0.0
1983*Bal-A	66	134	23	34	7	0	3	12	16	17	8	4	.254	.338	.373	.711	97	-0	17	4.14	-2	2-60/C-1,D-1	4	0.0
1984 Bal-A	81	157	23	30	1	0	3	11	6	15	4	1	.191	.221	.255	.476	32	-14	8	1.66	-3	2-76/O-1	2	-1.5
1985 Bal-A	55	97	15	22	3	0	3	6	6	15	3	2	.227	.279	.351	.629	73	-4	9	2.89	-5	2-50/D-1	1	-0.8
1986 Oak-A	17	34	4	12	2	0	0	5	3	6	0	1	.353	.405	.412	.817	133	1	5	5.65	1	2-16/D-1	1	0.3
1987 NY-A	19	45	5	12	0	1	2	4	2	4	0	1	.267	.313	.444	.757	99	-1	5	3.90	1	3-12/2-6	1	0.0
Total 11	**565**	**1289**	**163**	**296**	**46**	**4**	**25**	**109**	**97**	**158**	**30**	**17**	**.230**	**.288**	**.330**	**.617**	**71**	**-53**	**123**	**3.10**	**-10**	**2-431,S-102/3-12,D-4,C-1,O**	**29**	**-3.8**
• SALAS, Mark	Mark Bruce Salas b: 3/8/1961, Montebello, CA BL/TR, 6', 205 lbs. Deb: 6/19/1984 Career OF: 3-0-1																							
1984 StL-N	14	20	1	2	1	0	0	1	0	3	0	0	.100	.100	.150	.250	-31	-4	0	.48	0	/C-4,O-3(2-0-1)	0	-0.4
1985 Min-A	120	360	51	108	20	5	9	41	18	37	0	1	.300	.335	.458	.793	108	3	53	5.44	0	*C-115/D-3	13	0.8
1986 Min-A	91	258	28	60	7	4	8	33	18	32	3	1	.233	.285	.384	.669	78	-8	27	3.37	-1	C-69/D-8	3	-0.7
1987 Min-A	22	45	8	17	2	0	3	9	5	6	0	1	.378	.440	.622	1.062	171	4	12	10.95	-1	C-14	3	0.4
NY-A	50	115	13	23	4	0	3	12	10	17	0	0	.200	.281	.313	.594	58	-7	11	2.97	-1	C-41/D-4,O-1	2	-0.6
Yr.	72	160	21	40	6	0	6	21	15	23	0	1	.250	.326	.400	.726	90	-3	23	4.87	-2	C-55/D-4,O-1	5	-0.2
1988 Chi-A	75	196	17	49	7	0	3	9	12	17	0	0	.250	.303	.332	.635	78	-6	20	3.56	2	C-69/D-1	3	-0.1
1989 Cle-A	30	77	4	17	4	1	2	7	5	13	0	0	.221	.277	.377	.654	81	-2	8	3.34	-1	D-20/C-5	1	-0.4
1990 Det-A	74	164	18	38	3	0	9	24	21	28	0	0	.232	.323	.415	.737	104	1	22	4.67	1	C-57/D-3,3-1	5	0.4
1991 Det-A	33	57	2	5	1	0	1	7	0	10	0	0	.088	.119	.158	.277	-24	-10	1	.60	0	C-11/D-8,1-5	0	-1.0
Total 8	**509**	**1292**	**142**	**319**	**49**	**10**	**38**	**143**	**89**	**163**	**3**	**3**	**.247**	**.302**	**.389**	**.690**	**85**	**-29**	**154**	**4.08**	**-2**	**C-385/D-47,1-5,O-4,3-1**	**30**	**-1.5**
• SALAZAR, Angel	Argenis Antonio (Yepez) Salazar b: 11/4/1961, Anaco, Venezuela BR/TR, 6', 173 lbs. Deb: 8/10/1983																							
1983 Mon-N	36	37	5	8	1	1	0	1	1	8	0	0	.216	.237	.297	.534	47	-3	2	2.08	-2	S-34	0	-0.3
1984 Mon-N	80	174	12	27	4	2	0	12	4	38	1	1	.155	.179	.201	.380	7	-22	6	1.08	-5	S-80	2	-2.2
1986 KC-A	117	298	24	73	20	2	0	24	7	47	1	1	.245	.267	.326	.593	59	-18	26	2.95	0	*S-115/2-1	4	-0.8
1987 KC-A	116	317	24	65	7	0	2	21	6	46	4	4	.205	.220	.246	.466	23	-37	16	1.58	5	*S-116	5	-2.0
1988 Chi-N	34	60	4	15	1	1	0	1	1	11	0	0	.250	.262	.300	.562	58	-3	5	2.55	-1	S-29/2-2,3-1	1	-0.3
Total 5	**383**	**886**	**69**	**188**	**33**	**6**	**2**	**59**	**19**	**150**	**6**	**6**	**.212**	**.231**	**.270**	**.501**	**35**	**-83**	**55**	**1.99**	**-3**	**S-374/2-3,3-1**	**12**	**-5.7**
• SALAZAR, Luis	Luis Ernesto (Garcia) Salazar b: 5/19/1956, Barcelona, Venezuela BR/TR, 5'9", 180 lbs. Deb: 8/15/1980 Career OF: 161-114-36																							
1980 SD-N	44	169	28	57	4	7	1	25	9	25	11	2	.337	.374	.462	.836	140	10	29	6.50	-2	3-42/O-4(0-3-1)	7	0.8
1981 SD-N	109	400	37	121	19	6	3	38	16	72	11	8	.303	.331	.403	.733	116	5	51	4.53	-3	3-94,O-23(1-10-14)	11	-0.1
1982 SD-N	145	524	55	127	15	5	8	62	23	80	32	9	.242	.277	.336	.613	75	-17	48	3.04	20	*3-129,S-18/O-1	12	0.4
1983 SD-N	134	481	52	124	16	2	14	45	17	80	24	9	.258	.286	.387	.673	88	-9	53	3.74	20	*3-118,S-19	15	1.1
1984*SD-N	93	228	20	55	7	2	3	17	6	38	11	7	.241	.261	.329	.590	65	-12	17	2.49	6	3-58,O-24(4-19-2)/S-4	4	-0.7
1985 Chi-A	122	327	39	80	18	2	10	45	12	60	14	4	.245	.271	.404	.675	79	-10	35	3.51	-3	O-84(26-68-1),3-39/D-8,1-6	7	-1.5
1986 Chi-A	4	7	1	1	0	0	0	0	1	3	0	0	.143	.250	.143	.393	10	-1	0	1.42	0	/D-2	0	-0.1
1987 SD-N	84	189	13	48	5	0	3	17	14	30	3	3	.254	.305	.328	.633	70	-9	19	3.42	-2	3-38,S-22,O-10(4-6-2)/P-2,1	3	-0.9
1988 Det-A	130	452	61	122	14	1	12	62	21	70	6	0	.270	.307	.385	.692	96	-3	52	3.91	3	O-68(60-5-5),S-37,3-31/2-5,1	15	0.0
1989 SD-N	95	246	27	66	7	2	8	22	11	44	1	3	.268	.302	.411	.713	102	-2	29	4.01	3	3-72,O-14(2-2-10)/S-9,1-2	6	0.1
*Chi-N	26	80	7	26	5	0	1	12	4	13	0	1	.325	.357	.425	.782	114	1	11	5.34	-2	3-25/O-2(2-0-0)	4	-0.1
Yr.	121	326	34	92	12	2	9	34	15	57	1	4	.282	.316	.414	.730	105	-1	40	4.33	0	3-97,O-16(4-2-10)/S-9,1-2	10	0.0
1990 Chi-N	115	410	44	104	13	3	12	47	19	59	3	1	.254	.293	.388	.681	80	-13	47	4.05	-20	3-91,O-28(28-0-0)	7	-3.4
1991 Chi-N	103	333	34	86	14	1	14	38	15	45	0	3	.258	.292	.432	.725	97	-4	39	4.01	-11	3-86/1-7,O-1	6	-1.5
1992 Chi-N	98	255	20	53	7	2	5	25	11	34	1	1	.208	.241	.310	.550	53	-17	17	2.04	1	3-40,O-34(33-0-1),S-12/1-5	2	-1.7
Total 13	**1302**	**4101**	**438**	**1070**	**144**	**33**	**94**	**455**	**179**	**653**	**117**	**51**	**.261**	**.294**	**.381**	**.675**	**88**	**-80**	**446**	**3.71**	**9**	**3-863,O-293,S-121/1-25,D,2,P**	**99**	**-7.6**
• SALAZAR, Oscar	Oscar Enrique Salazar b: 6/27/1978, Maracay, Venezuela BR/TR, 5'11", 178 lbs. Deb: 4/10/2002																							
2002 Det-A	8	21	2	4	1	0	1	3	1	2	0	0	.190	.227	.381	.608	61	-1	2	2.86	-3	/2-6,3-1,S-1	1	-0.3

YEAR TM-L	G	AB	R	H	2B	3B	HR	RBI	BB	SO	SB	CS	AVG	OBP	SLG	OPS	OPS+	BR/A	RC	RC/G	FR	G/POS	WS	TPW
• SALES, Ed	Edward A. Sales b: 1861, Harrisburg, PA d: 8/10/1912, New Haven, CT BL/TR Deb: 7/15/1890																							
1890 Pit-N	51	189	19	43	7	3	1	23	16	15	3	....	.228	.298	.312	.610	88	-2	19	3.44	-16	S-51	2	-1.5
• SALKELD, Bill	William Franklin Salkeld b: 3/8/1917, Pocatello, ID d: 4/22/1967, Los Angeles, CA BL/TR, 5'10", 190 lbs. Deb: 4/18/1945																							
1945 Pit-N	95	267	45	83	16	1	15	52	50	16	2	....	.311	.420	.547	.966	161	23	63	8.82	-2	C-86	18	2.6
1946 Pit-N	69	160	18	47	8	0	3	19	39	16	2	....	.294	.432	.400	.832	133	10	32	7.45	1	C-51	8	1.4
1947 Pit-N	47	61	5	13	2	0	0	8	6	8	0	....	.213	.284	.246	.529	41	-5	4	2.26	0	C-15	0	-0.5
1948*Bos-N	78	198	26	48	8	1	8	28	42	37	1	....	.242	.378	.414	.792	116	6	34	5.74	2	C-59	10	1.1
1949 Bos-N	66	161	17	41	5	0	5	25	44	24	1	....	.255	.417	.379	.796	121	8	29	6.07	0	C-63	8	1.1
1950 Chi-A	1	3	0	0	0	0	0	0	1	0	0	0	.000	.250	.000	.250	-33	-1	0	.59	-0	/C-1	0	-0.1
Total 6	356	850	111	232	39	2	31	132	182	101	6	0	.273	.402	.433	.835	129	42	162	6.72	0	C-275	44	5.6
• SALMON, Chico	Ruthford Eduardo Salmon b: 12/3/1940, Colon, Panama d: 9/17/2000, Bocas Del Toro, Panama BR/TR, 5'10", 170 lbs. Deb: 6/28/1964 Career OF: 56-5-64																							
1964 Cle-A	86	283	43	87	17	2	4	25	13	37	10	6	.307	.342	.424	.766	113	4	41	5.30	-2	O-53(1-0-52),2-32,1-13	10	0.0
1965 Cle-A	79	120	20	29	8	0	3	12	5	19	7	4	.242	.283	.383	.667	87	-3	12	3.23	-2	1-28,O-17(10-1-6)/2-5,3-5	2	-0.7
1966 Cle-A	126	422	46	108	13	2	7	40	21	41	10	1	.256	.291	.346	.637	82	-8	44	3.63	-7	S-61,2-28,1-24,O-10(9-0-1)/3	12	-1.0
1967 Cle-A	90	203	19	46	13	1	2	19	17	29	10	4	.227	.290	.330	.620	82	-4	20	3.14	-1	O-28(24-4-3),1-24,2-24,S-14/3	5	-0.4
1968 Cle-A	103	276	24	59	8	1	3	12	12	30	7	7	.214	.254	.283	.537	63	-14	19	2.13	2	2-45,3-18,S-15,O-13(11-0-2),1	3	-1.0
1969*Bal-A	52	91	18	27	5	0	3	12	10	22	0	0	.297	.379	.451	.829	130	4	16	6.63	-3	1-17/2-9,S-9,3-3,O-1	4	0.2
1970*Bal-A	63	172	19	43	4	0	7	22	8	30	2	2	.250	.287	.395	.683	85	-5	19	3.67	-3	S-33,2-12,3-11/1-2	4	-0.5
1971 Bal-A	42	84	11	15	1	0	2	7	3	21	0	0	.179	.207	.262	.469	32	-8	4	1.46	-3	/1-9,2-9,3-6,S-5	0	-1.1
1972 Bal-A	17	16	2	1	1	0	0	0	0	4	0	0	.063	.063	.125	.188	-44	-3	0	.00	0	/1-2,3-1	0	-0.3
Total 9	658	1667	202	415	70	6	31	149	89	233	46	24	.249	.291	.354	.645	84	-37	174	3.52	-19	2-164,S-137,1-130,O-122/3-54	40	-4.8
• SALMON, Tim	Timothy James Salmon b: 8/24/1968, Long Beach, CA BR/TR, 6'3", 220 lbs. Deb: 8/21/1992 Career OF: 0-1-1254																							
1992 Cal-A	23	79	8	14	1	0	2	6	11	23	1	1	.177	.286	.266	.552	55	-5	6	2.58	0	O-21(0-0-21)	0	-0.6
1993 Cal-A	142	515	93	146	35	1	31	95	82	135	5	6	.283	.387	.536	.923	141	30	110	7.65	7	*O-140(0-1-140)/D-1	24	2.8
1994 Cal-A	100	373	67	107	18	2	23	70	54	102	1	3	.287	.384	.531	.915	131	17	79	7.76	3	O-99(0-0-99)	13	1.3
1995 Cal-A	143	537	111	177	34	3	34	105	91	111	5	5	.330	.432	.594	1.026	165	53	142	10.14	3	*O-142(0-0-142)/D-1	29	4.5
1996 Cal-A	156	581	90	166	27	4	30	98	93	125	4	2	.286	.388	.501	.889	125	24	118	7.45	3	*O-153(0-0-153)/D-3	22	1.6
1997 Ana-A	157	582	95	172	28	1	33	129	95	142	9	12	.296	.401	.517	.918	136	30	124	7.58	8	*O-153(0-0-153)/D-4	29	2.8
1998 Ana-A	136	463	84	139	28	1	26	88	90	100	0	1	.300	.417	.533	.951	144	33	110	8.79	1	*D-111,O-19(0-0-19)	22	2.5
1999 Ana-A	98	353	60	94	24	2	17	69	63	82	4	1	.266	.377	.490	.867	120	12	69	6.78	4	O-89(0-0-89)/D-9	14	1.0
2000 Ana-A	158	568	108	165	36	2	34	97	104	139	0	2	.290	.406	.540	.946	133	31	128	8.19	7	*O-124(0-0-124),D-33	23	2.6
2001 Ana-A	137	475	63	108	21	1	17	49	96	121	9	3	.227	.366	.383	.749	96	1	73	5.13	6	*O-125(0-0-125),D-12	11	0.0
2002*Ana-A	138	483	84	138	37	1	22	88	71	102	6	3	.286	.385	.503	.888	134	25	98	7.34	-5	*O-111(0-0-111),D-25	22	1.3
2003 Ana-A	148	528	78	145	35	4	19	72	77	93	3	1	.275	.377	.464	.841	125	22	96	6.43	-3	O-78(0-0-78),D-68	18	1.0
Total 12	1536	5537	941	1571	324	22	288	966	927	1275	47	40	.284	.392	.506	.899	131	273	1153	7.49	32	*O-1254,D-267	227	20.7
• SALTZGAVER, Jack	Otto Hamlin Saltzgaver b: 1/23/1903, Croton, IA d: 2/1/1978, Keokuk, IA BL/TR, 5'11", 165 lbs. Deb: 4/12/1932																							
1932 NY-A	20	47	10	6	2	1	0	5	10	10	1	1	.128	.281	.213	.493	31	-5	4	2.07	-1	2-16	1	-0.4
1934 NY-A	94	350	64	95	8	1	6	36	48	28	8	1	.271	.359	.351	.711	90	-2	48	4.85	-3	3-84/1-4	9	-0.3
1935 NY-A	61	149	17	39	6	0	3	18	23	12	0	2	.262	.368	.362	.730	95	-1	21	4.87	-2	2-25,3-18/1-6	4	-0.1
1936 NY-A	34	90	14	19	5	0	1	13	13	18	0	0	.211	.311	.300	.611	53	-7	9	3.34	-1	3-16/2-6,1-4	1	-0.6
1937 NY-A	17	11	6	2	0	0	0	0	3	4	0	0	.182	.357	.182	.539	40	-1	1	2.81	0	/1-4	0	-0.1
1945 Pit-N	52	117	20	38	5	3	0	10	8	8	0	....	.325	.368	.419	.787	114	2	18	6.14	-2	2-31/3-1	4	0.1
Total 6	278	764	131	199	26	5	10	82	105	80	9	4	.260	.351	.347	.698	85	-13	101	4.60	-10	3-119/2-78,1-18	19	-1.5
• SAMCOFF, Ed	Edward William Samcoff b: 9/1/1924, Sacramento, CA BR/TR, 5'10", 165 lbs. Deb: 4/21/1951																							
1951 Phi-A	4	11	0	0	0	0	0	0	1	2	0	0	.000	.083	.000	.083	-75	-3	0	.05	0	/2-3	0	-0.2
• SAMFORD, Ron	Ronald Edward Samford b: 2/28/1930, Dallas, TX BR/TR, 5'11", 156 lbs. Deb: 4/15/1954																							
1954 NY-N	12	5	2	0	0	0	0	0	0	1	0	1	.000	.000	.000	.000	-99	-2	0	.00	0	/2-3	0	-0.2
1955 Det-A	1	1	0	0	0	0	0	0	0	1	0	0	.000	.000	.000	.000	-102	-0	0	.00	0	/S-1	0	0.0
1957 Det-A	54	91	6	20	1	2	0	5	6	15	1	0	.220	.276	.275	.550	49	-6	7	2.71	0	S-35,2-11/3-4	2	-0.4
1959 Was-A	91	237	23	53	13	0	5	22	11	29	1	0	.224	.264	.342	.606	65	-12	19	2.61	-4	S-64,2-23	3	-1.1
Total 4	158	334	31	73	14	2	5	27	17	46	2	1	.219	.263	.317	.580	58	-20	27	2.56	-5	S-100/2-37,3-4	5	-1.7
• SAMPLE, Bill	William Amos Sample b: 4/2/1955, Roanoke, VA BR/TR, 5'9", 175 lbs. Deb: 9/2/1978 Career OF: 532-99-97																							
1978 Tex-A	8	15	2	7	2	0	0	3	0	3	0	0	.467	.467	.600	1.067	197	2	4	14.18	0	/D-3,O-2(2-0-0)	1	0.1
1979 Tex-A	128	325	60	95	21	2	5	35	37	28	8	6	.292	.368	.415	.784	112	6	50	5.34	2	*O-103(91-10-5)/D-9	11	0.3
1980 Tex-A	99	204	29	53	10	0	4	19	18	15	8	5	.260	.338	.368	.705	96	-1	26	4.16	-4	O-72(15-18-40)/D-4	4	-0.7
1981 Tex-A	66	230	36	65	16	0	3	25	17	21	4	1	.283	.350	.391	.742	120	7	33	5.10	0	O-64(62-5-0)	10	0.4
1982 Tex-A	97	360	56	94	14	2	10	29	27	35	10	2	.261	.318	.394	.712	99	1	47	4.55	-2	O-91(85-9-0)/D-1	9	-0.6
1983 Tex-A	147	554	80	152	28	3	12	57	44	46	44	8	.274	.333	.401	.734	103	8	79	5.01	5	*O-146(144-2-1)	17	0.7
1984 Tex-A	130	489	67	121	20	2	5	33	29	46	18	6	.247	.290	.327	.617	68	-20	46	3.19	-7	*O-122(72-51-3)/D-2	7	-3.1
1985 NY-A	59	139	18	40	5	0	1	15	9	10	2	1	.288	.340	.345	.685	90	-2	17	4.29	0	O-55(51-4-0)	3	-0.3
1986 Atl-N	92	200	23	57	11	0	6	14	14	26	4	2	.285	.341	.430	.771	105	1	31	5.57	-1	O-56(10-0-48)/2-1	6	-0.2
Total 9	826	2516	371	684	127	9	46	230	195	230	98	31	.272	.331	.384	.715	98	1	334	4.60	-7	O-711/D-19,2-1	68	-3.5
• SAMUEL, Amado	Amado Ruperto Samuel b: 12/6/1938, San Pedro de Macoris, Dominican Republic BR/TR, 6'1", 170 lbs. Deb: 4/10/1962																							
1962 Mil-N	76	209	16	43	10	0	3	20	12	54	0	2	.206	.249	.297	.546	47	-17	15	2.30	0	S-36,2-28/3-3	2	-1.3
1963 Mil-N	15	17	0	3	1	0	0	0	0	4	0	1	.176	.176	.235	.412	18	-2	1	.85	-2	/S-7,2-4	0	-0.4
1964 NY-N	53	142	7	33	7	0	0	5	4	24	0	1	.232	.264	.282	.545	55	-9	10	2.41	3	S-34,3-17/2-3	1	-0.4
Total 3	144	368	23	79	18	0	3	25	16	82	0	4	.215	.251	.288	.539	49	-28	26	2.27	1	/S-77,2-35,3-20	3	-2.1
• SAMUEL, Juan	Juan Milton Samuel b: 12/9/1960, San Pedro de Macoris, Dominican Republic BR/TR, 5'11", 170 lbs. Deb: 8/24/1983 Career OF: 34-197-40																							
1983*Phi-N	18	65	14	18	1	2	2	5	4	16	3	2	.277	.329	.446	.775	114	1	9	4.79	-2	2-18	2	0.0
1984 Phi-N★	160	701	105	191	36	**19**	15	69	28	168	72	15	.272	.307	.442	.749	107	11	99	5.03	-16	*2-160	19	0.4
1985 Phi-N	161	663	101	175	31	13	19	74	33	141	53	19	.264	.305	.436	.741	102	1	87	4.50	-0	*2-159	21	1.0
1986 Phi-N	145	591	90	157	36	12	16	78	26	142	42	14	.266	.306	.448	.754	102	1	80	4.65	-5	*2-143	18	0.4
1987 Phi-N★	160	655	113	178	37	**15**	28	100	60	162	35	15	.272	.338	.502	.840	115	12	109	5.76	-3	*2-160	22	1.8
1988 Phi-N	157	629	68	153	32	9	12	67	39	151	33	10	.243	.300	.380	.680	92	-6	73	3.97	-18	*2-152/O-3(0-2-1),3-1	18	-2.0
1989 Phi-N	51	199	32	49	3	1	8	20	18	45	11	3	.246	.312	.392	.704	100	1	26	4.43	1	O-50(0-50-0)	5	0.1
NY-N	86	333	37	76	13	1	3	28	24	75	31	9	.228	.300	.300	.600	76	-7	33	3.23	1	O-84(0-84-0)	7	-0.8
Yr.	137	532	69	125	16	2	11	48	42	120	42	12	.235	.304	.335	.639	85	-7	58	3.66	2	*O-134(0-134-0)	12	-0.7
1990 LA-N	143	492	62	119	24	3	13	52	51	126	38	20	.242	.319	.382	.701	95	-5	60	3.92	-8	*2-108,O-31(0-31-0)	12	-1.1
1991 LA-N★	153	594	74	161	22	6	12	58	49	133	23	8	.271	.330	.389	.719	104	4	78	4.58	-1	*2-152	20	0.8
1992 LA-N	47	122	7	32	3	1	0	15	7	22	2	2	.262	.308	.303	.611	75	-5	12	3.27	1	2-38/O-1	2	-0.4
KC-A	29	102	15	29	5	3	0	8	7	27	6	1	.284	.336	.392	.729	101	1	14	4.93	-2	O-18(0-0-18),2-10	3	-0.1
1993 Cin-N	103	261	31	60	10	4	4	26	23	53	9	7	.230	.300	.345	.644	72	-12	27	3.45	0	2-70/1-6,3-4,O-3(2-0-1)	6	-0.9
1994 Det-A	59	136	32	42	9	5	5	21	10	26	5	2	.309	.369	.559	.928	134	7	27	7.13	0	O-27(2-25-0),D-10/2-8,1-2	5	0.6
1995 Det-A	76	171	28	48	10	1	10	34	24	38	5	4	.281	.376	.526	.902	132	7	34	6.97	-3	1-37,D-16/O-9(9-0-0),2-6	8	0.1
KC-A	15	34	3	6	0	0	2	5	5	11	1	0	.176	.282	.353	.635	63	-2	4	3.69	0	/D-7,O-5(5-0-0),1-1	1	-0.2
Yr.	91	205	31	54	10	1	12	39	29	49	6	4	.263	.360	.498	.858	121	6	38	6.39	-4	1-38,D-23,O-14(14-0-0)/2-6	9	-0.2
1996 Tor-A	69	188	34	48	8	3	8	26	15	65	9	1	.255	.320	.457	.778	94	-1	29	5.47	-3	D-24,O-24(8-5-15),1-17	4	-0.6
1997 Tor-A	45	95	13	27	5	4	3	15	10	28	5	3	.284	.364	.516	.880	126	3	17	6.35	0	D-15/3-9,1-7,2-4,O-2(0-0-2)	3	0.2
1998 Tor-A	43	50	14	9	2	0	1	2	7	13	13	8	.180	.293	.280	.573	50	-4	4	1.92	-1	D-11,O-10(8-0-2)/1-3,2-2	0	-0.6
Total 16	1720	6081	873	1578	287	102	161	703	440	1442	396	143	.259	.317	.420	.737	100	8	821	4.62	-58	*2-1190,O-267/D-83,1-73,3-14	176	-1.3

YEAR TM-L	G	AB	R	H	2B	3B	HR	RBI	BB	SO	SB	CS	AVG	OBP	SLG	OPS	OPS+	BR/A	RC	RC/G	FR	G/POS	WS	TPW
• **SAMUELS, Ike**	Samuel Earl Samuels b: 2/20/1874, Quincy, IL d: 2/22/1964, New York, NY BR/TR Deb: 8/3/1895																							
1895 StL-N	24	74	5	17	2	0	0	5	5	7	5	....	.230	.278	.257	.535	39	-7	7	3.24	-7	3-21/S-3	0	-1.1
• **SANCHEZ, Alejandro**	Alejandro (Pimentel) Sanchez b: 2/14/1959, San Pedro de Macoris, Dominican Republic BR/TR, 6', 185 lbs. Deb: 9/6/1982 Career OF: 9-2-40																							
1982 Phi-N	7	14	3	4	1	0	2	4	0	4	0	0	.286	.286	.786	1.071	186	1	3	8.49	0	/O-4(0-0-4)	1	0.1
1983 Phi-N	8	7	2	2	0	0	0	2	0	2	0	0	.286	.286	.286	.571	59	-0	0	1.29	0	/O-2(0-0-2)	0	-0.1
1984 SF-N	13	41	3	8	0	1	0	2	0	12	2	3	.195	.195	.244	.439	23	-5	1	1.01	0	O-11(3-0-9)	0	-0.6
1985 Det-A	71	133	19	33	6	2	6	12	0	39	2	2	.248	.248	.459	.707	89	-3	13	3.21	-1	O-31(5-2-24),D-28	1	-0.6
1986 Min-A	8	16	1	2	0	0	0	1	1	8	0	0	.125	.176	.125	.301	-16	-3	0	.22	0	/D-3,O-1	0	-0.3
1987 Oak-A	2	3	0	0	0	0	0	0	0	1	0	0	.000	.000	.000	.000	-107	-1	0	.00	-0	/D-1,O-1	0	-0.1
Total 6	**109**	**214**	**28**	**49**	**7**	**3**	**8**	**21**	**1**	**66**	**4**	**5**	**.229**	**.233**	**.402**	**.634**	**71**	**-11**	**18**	**2.67**	**-2**	**/O-50,D-32**	**2**	**-1.5**
• **SANCHEZ, Alex**	Alexis Sanchez b: 8/26/1976, Havana, Cuba BL/TL, 5'10", 179 lbs. Deb: 6/15/2001 Career OF: 19-235-3																							
2001 Mil-N	30	68	7	14	3	2	0	4	5	13	6	2	.206	.260	.309	.569	47	-5	6	2.85	-1	O-19(3-14-3)	0	-0.6
2002 Mil-N	112	394	55	114	10	7	1	33	31	62	37	14	.289	.344	.358	.702	86	-6	51	4.53	3	*O-100(16-86-0)	11	-0.2
2003 Mil-N	43	163	15	46	10	3	0	10	7	28	8	6	.282	.320	.380	.700	83	-5	19	4.06	2	O-36(0-36-0)	3	-0.3
Det-A	101	394	43	114	13	5	1	22	18	46	44	18	.289	.322	.355	.677	85	-7	45	3.93	1	O-99(0-99-0)	6	-0.5
Total 3	**286**	**1019**	**120**	**288**	**36**	**17**	**2**	**69**	**61**	**149**	**95**	**40**	**.283**	**.326**	**.357**	**.683**	**83**	**-23**	**122**	**4.10**	**6**	**O-254**	**20**	**-1.6**
• **SANCHEZ, Celerino**	Celerino (Perez) Sanchez b: 2/3/1944, Veracruz, Mexico d: 5/1/1992, Leon, Mexico BR/TR, 5'11", 160 lbs. Deb: 6/13/1972																							
1972 NY-A	71	250	18	62	8	3	0	22	12	30	0	0	.248	.293	.304	.597	80	-6	21	2.82	-2	3-68	4	-1.0
1973 NY-A	34	64	12	14	3	0	1	9	2	12	1	1	.219	.242	.313	.555	57	-4	5	2.51	1	3-11,D-11/O-2(0-0-2),S-2	0	-0.3
Total 2	**105**	**314**	**30**	**76**	**11**	**3**	**1**	**31**	**14**	**42**	**1**	**1**	**.242**	**.283**	**.306**	**.589**	**76**	**-10**	**26**	**2.76**	**-1**	**/3-79,D-11,O-2,S-2**	**4**	**-1.3**
• **SANCHEZ, Freddy**	Frederick P. Sanchez b: 12/21/1977, Hollywood, CA BR/TR, 5'11", 185 lbs. Deb: 9/10/2002																							
2002 Bos-A	12	16	3	3	0	0	0	2	2	3	0	0	.188	.278	.188	.465	27	-2	1	2.03	-1	/2-5,S-5,D-1	0	-0.2
2003 Bos-A	20	34	6	8	2	0	0	2	0	8	0	0	.235	.235	.294	.529	38	-3	2	2.44	2	/3-7,S-6,2-3	1	-0.1
Total 2	**32**	**50**	**9**	**11**	**2**	**0**	**0**	**4**	**2**	**11**	**0**	**0**	**.220**	**.250**	**.260**	**.510**	**34**	**-5**	**3**	**2.31**	**1**	**/S-11,2-8,3-7,D-1**	**1**	**-0.3**
• **SANCHEZ, Orlando**	Orlando (Marquez) Sanchez b: 9/7/1956, Canovanas, Puerto Rico BL/TR, 6'1", 195 lbs. Deb: 5/6/1981																							
1981 StL-N	27	49	5	14	2	1	0	6	2	6	1	0	.286	.314	.367	.681	90	-1	5	3.69	-3	C-18	1	-0.3
1982 StL-N	26	37	6	7	0	1	0	3	5	5	0	0	.189	.286	.243	.529	49	-2	3	2.63	0	C-15	1	-0.2
1983 StL-N	6	6	0	0	0	0	0	0	0	4	0	0	.000	.000	.000	.000	-100	-2	0	.00	0	/C-1	0	-0.2
1984 KC-A	10	10	0	1	1	0	0	2	0	2	0	0	.100	.100	.200	.300	-19	-2	0	.00	0	/C-1	0	-0.2
Bal-A	4	8	0	2	0	0	0	1	0	2	0	0	.250	.250	.250	.500	40	-1	1	2.25	0	/C-4	0	0.0
Yr.	14	18	0	3	1	0	0	3	0	4	0	0	.167	.167	.222	.389	7	-2	1	.84	0	/C-5	0	-0.2
Total 4	**73**	**110**	**11**	**24**	**3**	**2**	**0**	**12**	**7**	**19**	**1**	**0**	**.218**	**.265**	**.282**	**.547**	**53**	**-7**	**9**	**2.59**	**-3**	**/C-39**	**2**	**-0.9**
• **SANCHEZ, Rey**	Rey Francisco (Guadalupe) Sanchez b: 10/5/1967, Rio Piedras, Puerto Rico BR/TR, 5'10", 170 lbs. Deb: 9/8/1991																							
1991 Chi-N	13	23	1	6	0	0	0	2	4	3	0	0	.261	.370	.261	.631	77	-0	3	4.14	0	S-10/2-2	1	0.0
1992 Chi-N	74	255	24	64	14	3	1	19	10	17	2	1	.251	.287	.341	.628	75	-9	24	3.12	1	S-68/2-4	5	-0.3
1993 Chi-N	105	344	35	97	11	2	0	28	15	22	1	1	.282	.318	.326	.643	74	-13	34	3.48	13	S-98	9	0.7
1994 Chi-N	96	291	26	83	13	1	0	24	20	29	2	5	.285	.346	.337	.683	80	-10	32	3.80	6	2-50,S-30,3-17	7	0.1
1995 Chi-N	114	428	57	119	22	2	3	27	14	48	6	4	.278	.302	.360	.662	75	-17	44	3.60	14	*2-111/S-4	7	0.2
1996 Chi-N	95	289	28	61	9	0	1	12	22	42	7	1	.211	.274	.253	.526	39	-25	21	2.33	16	S-92	5	-0.1
1997 Chi-N	97	205	14	51	9	0	1	12	11	26	4	2	.249	.287	.307	.594	54	-14	17	2.71	-3	S-63,2-32/3-1	2	-1.3
*NY-A	38	138	21	43	12	0	1	15	5	21	0	4	.312	.340	.420	.761	98	-3	18	4.68	0	2-37/S-6	5	0.0
1998 SF-N	109	316	44	90	14	2	2	30	16	47	0	0	.285	.327	.361	.688	86	-7	35	3.97	5	S-76,2-36	8	0.5
1999 KC-A	134	479	66	141	18	6	2	56	22	48	11	5	.294	.331	.370	.700	77	-17	56	4.08	25	*S-134	12	1.7
2000 KC-A	143	509	68	139	18	2	1	38	28	55	7	3	.273	.316	.322	.638	60	-31	50	3.33	11	*S-143	9	-0.7
2001 KC-A	100	390	46	118	14	5	0	28	11	34	9	1	.303	.325	.364	.689	75	-13	45	4.08	23	*S-100	10	1.7
*Atl-N	49	154	10	35	4	1	0	9	4	15	2	0	.227	.247	.266	.513	32	-15	8	1.70	9	S-48	3	-0.2
2002 Bos-A	107	357	46	102	12	3	1	38	17	31	2	2	.286	.322	.345	.666	76	-13	38	3.73	2	*2-100,S-10	9	-0.5
2003 NY-N	56	174	11	36	3	1	0	12	8	18	1	1	.207	.242	.236	.477	26	-19	9	1.58	1	S-42,2-12	2	-1.4
Sea-A	46	170	22	50	5	1	0	11	8	21	1	0	.294	.333	.335	.669	80	-5	19	4.04	4	S-46	4	0.3
Total 13	**1376**	**4522**	**519**	**1235**	**178**	**29**	**13**	**361**	**215**	**477**	**55**	**30**	**.273**	**.311**	**.334**	**.645**	**69**	**-210**	**454**	**3.44**	**127**	**S-970,2-384/3-18**	**98**	**0.6**
• **SAND, Heinie**	John Henry Sand b: 7/3/1897, San Francisco, CA d: 11/3/1958, San Francisco, CA BR/TR, 5'8", 160 lbs. Deb: 4/17/1923																							
1923 Phi-N	132	470	85	107	16	5	4	32	82	56	7	3	.228	.347	.309	.656	66	-19	57	3.99	-13	*S-120,3-11	9	-1.7
1924 Phi-N	137	539	79	132	21	6	6	40	52	57	5	4	.245	.316	.340	.655	67	-23	60	3.78	-8	*S-137	10	-1.7
1925 Phi-N	148	496	69	138	30	7	3	55	64	65	1	1	.278	.364	.385	.749	84	-9	73	5.23	-6	*S-143	13	-0.1
1926 Phi-N	149	567	99	154	30	5	4	37	66	56	2	....	.272	.350	.363	.713	88	-8	73	4.44	-17	*S-149	13	-1.0
1927 Phi-N	141	535	87	160	22	8	1	49	58	59	5	....	.299	.369	.376	.744	98	1	75	4.84	-8	S-86,3-58	15	0.4
1928 Phi-N	141	426	38	90	26	1	0	38	60	47	1	....	.211	.310	.277	.587	53	-28	40	2.88	-18	*S-137	3	-3.2
Total 6	**848**	**3033**	**457**	**781**	**145**	**32**	**18**	**251**	**382**	**340**	**21**	**8**	**.258**	**.343**	**.344**	**.688**	**77**	**-87**	**378**	**4.21**	**-70**	**S-772/3-69**	**63**	**-7.1**
• **SANDBERG, Gus**	Gustave E. Sandberg b: 2/23/1896, Long Island City, NY d: 2/3/1930, Los Angeles, CA BR/TR, 6'1", 189 lbs. Deb: 5/11/1923																							
1923 Cin-N	7	17	1	3	1	0	0	1	1	1	0	0	.176	.222	.235	.458	21	-2	1	1.72	-0	/C-5	0	-0.2
1924 Cin-N	24	52	1	9	0	0	0	3	2	7	0	0	.173	.204	.173	.377	2	-7	2	1.17	-1	C-24	1	-0.7
Total 2	**31**	**69**	**2**	**12**	**1**	**0**	**0**	**4**	**3**	**8**	**0**	**0**	**.174**	**.208**	**.188**	**.397**	**7**	**-9**	**3**	**1.30**	**-1**	**/C-29**	**1**	**-0.8**
• **SANDBERG, Jared**	Jared Lawrence Sandberg b: 3/2/1978, Olympia, WA BR/TR, 6'3", 185 lbs. Deb: 8/7/2001																							
2001 TB-A	39	136	13	28	7	0	1	15	10	45	1	0	.206	.265	.279	.545	45	-11	11	2.54	-0	3-38/1-1	1	-1.0
2002 TB-A	102	358	55	82	21	1	18	54	39	139	3	2	.229	.307	.444	.751	98	-2	48	4.54	2	3-97/1-3,D-2	8	0.1
2003 TB-A	55	136	15	29	10	1	6	23	16	52	0	0	.213	.305	.434	.739	93	-2	18	4.38	2	3-50/1-1,S-1	3	0.1
Total 3	**196**	**630**	**83**	**139**	**38**	**2**	**25**	**92**	**65**	**236**	**4**	**2**	**.221**	**.298**	**.406**	**.704**	**86**	**-15**	**77**	**4.07**	**4**	**3-185/1-5,D-2,S-1**	**12**	**-0.8**
• **SANDBERG, Ryne**	Ryne Dee "Ryno" Sandberg b: 9/18/1959, Spokane, WA BR/TR, 6'1", 180 lbs. Deb: 9/2/1981																							
1981 Phi-N	13	6	2	1	0	0	0	0	0	1	0	0	.167	.167	.167	.333	-5	-1	0	.90	-1	/S-5,2-1	0	-0.2
1982 Chi-N	156	635	103	172	33	5	7	54	36	90	32	12	.271	.314	.372	.686	89	-9	75	4.12	-1	*3-133,2-24	17	-1.1
1983 Chi-N	158	633	94	165	25	4	8	48	51	79	37	11	.261	.319	.351	.669	81	-13	75	4.04	17	*2-157/S-1	18	1.3
1984*Chi-N★	156	636	**114**	200	36	**19**	19	84	52	101	32	7	.314	.369	.520	.889	135	32	126	**7.41**	16	*2-156	**38**	**5.9**
1985 Chi-N★	153	609	113	186	31	6	26	83	57	97	54	11	.305	.366	.504	.870	127	28	117	7.00	-5	*2-153/S-1	28	3.2
1986 Chi-N★	154	627	68	178	28	5	14	76	46	79	34	11	.284	.333	.411	.744	97	-2	86	4.84	-3	*2-153	20	0.4
1987 Chi-N★	132	523	81	154	25	2	16	59	59	79	21	2	.294	.368	.442	.810	109	11	89	6.23	0	*2-131	20	1.8
1988 Chi-N★	155	618	77	163	23	8	19	69	54	91	25	10	.264	.324	.419	.743	107	5	82	4.59	0	*2-153	22	1.0
1989*Chi-N★	157	606	**104**	176	25	5	30	76	59	85	15	5	.290	.357	.497	.854	132	26	109	6.57	8	*2-155	28	4.0
1990 Chi-N★	155	615	**116**	188	30	3	**40**	100	50	84	25	7	.306	.359	.559	.918	138	32	124	7.41	2	*2-154	34	3.9
1991 Chi-N★	158	585	104	170	32	2	26	100	87	89	22	8	.291	.384	.485	.870	136	32	114	6.98	3	*2-157	**37**	4.1
1992 Chi-N★	158	612	100	186	32	8	26	87	68	73	17	6	.304	.374	.510	.884	145	37	117	7.11	7	*2-157	33	5.2
1993 Chi-N★	117	456	67	141	20	0	9	45	37	62	9	2	.309	.364	.412	.776	109	7	68	5.47	-4	*2-115	14	0.9
1994 Chi-N	57	223	36	53	9	5	5	24	23	40	2	3	.238	.312	.390	.702	83	-7	26	3.92	10	2-57	7	0.6
1996 Chi-N	150	554	85	135	28	4	25	92	54	116	12	8	.244	.319	.444	.763	96	-6	78	4.76	0	*2-146	19	0.1
1997 Chi-N	135	447	54	118	26	0	12	64	28	94	7	4	.264	.310	.403	.713	83	-13	56	4.41	-8	*2-126/D-1	11	-1.5
Total 16	**2164**	**8385**	**1318**	**2386**	**403**	**76**	**282**	**1061**	**761**	**1260**	**344**	**107**	**.285**	**.347**	**.452**	**.798**	**113**	**158**	**1342**	**5.71**	**41**	***2-1995,3-133/S-7,D-1**	**346**	**29.5**
• **SANDERS, Anthony**	Anthony Marcus Sanders b: 3/2/1974, Tucson, AZ BR/TR, 6'2", 200 lbs. Deb: 4/26/1999 Career OF: 9-0-2																							
1999 Tor-A	3	7	1	2	1	0	0	2	0	2	0	0	.286	.286	.429	.714	78	-0	0	1.93	-0	/D-2,O-1	0	0.0
2000 Sea-A	1	1	1	1	0	0	0	0	0	0	0	0	1.000	1.000	1.000	2.000	433	0	1	∞	0	/O-1	0	0.1

YEAR TM-L	G	AB	R	H	2B	3B	HR	RBI	BB	SO	SB	CS	AVG	OBP	SLG	OPS	OPS+	BR/A	RC	RC/G	FR	G/POS	WS	TPW
2001 Sea-A	9	17	1	3	2	0	0	2	2	3	0	0	.176	.263	.294	.557	49	-1	1	2.80	0	/O-9(8-0-1)	0	-0.1
Total 3	**13**	**25**	**3**	**6**	**3**	**0**	**0**	**4**	**2**	**5**	**0**	**0**	**.240**	**.296**	**.360**	**.656**	**71**	**-1**	**3**	**2.54**	**0**	**/O-11,D-2**	**0**	**-0.1**
• SANDERS, Ben	Alexander Bennett Sanders b: 2/16/1865, Catharpin, VA d: 8/29/1930, Memphis, TN BR/TR, 6', 210 lbs. Deb: 6/6/1888 U Career OF: 24-11-36 ♦																							
1888 Phi-N	57	236	26	58	11	2	1	25	8	12	13	....	.246	.276	.322	.598	86	4	25	3.83	4	P-31,O-25(13-6-7)/3-1	35	4.0
1889 Phi-N	44	169	21	47	8	2	0	21	6	11	4	....	.278	.307	.349	.656	76	6	20	4.30	-3	P-44/O-3(1-2-0)	28	4.4
1890 Phi-P	52	189	31	59	6	6	0	30	10	10	2	....	.312	.347	.407	.754	99	9	28	5.83	0	P-43,O-10(0-3-7)	28	2.3
1891 Phi-a	40	156	24	39	6	4	1	19	7	12	2	....	.250	.291	.359	.650	83	-0	17	3.92	-5	O-22(10-0-13),P-19	13	-0.3
1892 Lou-N	54	198	30	54	12	2	3	18	16	17	6	....	.273	.330	.399	.729	131	13	29	5.39	-3	P-31,1-15/O-9(0-0-9)	22	0.5
Total 5	**247**	**948**	**132**	**257**	**43**	**16**	**5**	**113**	**47**	**62**	**27**	**....**	**.271**	**.310**	**.366**	**.676**	**96**	**32**	**119**	**4.63**	**-6**	**P-168/O-69,1-15,3-1**	**126**	**11.0**
• SANDERS, Deion	Deion Luwynn Sanders b: 8/9/1967, Fort Myers, FL BL/TL, 6'1", 195 lbs. Deb: 5/31/1989 Career OF: 139-403-11																							
1989 NY-A	14	47	7	11	2	0	2	7	3	8	1	0	.234	.280	.404	.684	92	-1	6	4.21	0	O-14(3-11-0)	1	-0.1
1990 NY-A	57	133	24	21	2	2	3	9	13	27	8	2	.158	.238	.271	.509	42	-10	9	2.13	0	O-42(29-15-0)/D-4	1	-1.1
1991 Atl-N	54	110	16	21	1	2	4	13	12	23	11	3	.191	.270	.345	.616	68	-4	11	3.23	0	O-44(41-5-1)	3	-0.5
1992*Atl-N	97	303	54	92	6	**14**	8	28	18	52	26	9	.304	.347	.495	.842	128	12	51	6.09	1	O-75(12-60-9)	13	1.3
1993*Atl-N	95	272	42	75	18	6	6	28	16	42	19	7	.276	.323	.452	.775	104	1	40	5.09	0	O-60(5-55-0)	11	0.2
1994 Atl-N	46	191	32	55	10	0	4	21	16	28	19	7	.288	.346	.403	.749	92	-1	27	4.82	-2	O-46(0-46-0)	7	-0.3
Cin-N	46	184	26	51	7	4	0	7	16	35	19	9	.277	.342	.359	.700	84	-4	24	4.42	0	O-45(0-45-0)	4	-0.4
Yr.	92	375	58	106	17	4	4	28	32	63	38	16	.283	.344	.381	.725	88	-5	50	4.62	-3	O-91(0-91-0)	11	-0.7
1995 Cin-N	33	129	19	31	2	3	1	10	9	18	16	3	.240	.300	.326	.626	65	-4	15	3.85	1	O-33(0-33-0)	3	-0.3
SF-N	52	214	29	61	9	5	5	18	18	42	8	6	.285	.346	.444	.790	110	2	33	5.54	-4	O-52(0-52-0)	7	-0.2
Yr.	85	343	48	92	11	8	6	28	27	60	24	9	.268	.329	.399	.728	93	-3	48	4.87	-3	O-85(0-85-0)	10	-0.5
1997 Cin-N	115	465	53	127	13	7	5	23	34	67	56	13	.273	.331	.363	.694	80	-7	62	4.66	-6	*O-113(37-77-0)	10	-1.4
2001 Cin-N	32	75	6	13	2	0	1	4	4	10	3	4	.173	.235	.240	.475	22	-10	3	1.34	3	O-16(12-4-1)/D-2	0	-0.7
Total 9	**641**	**2123**	**308**	**558**	**72**	**43**	**39**	**168**	**159**	**352**	**186**	**63**	**.263**	**.320**	**.392**	**.713**	**88**	**-26**	**281**	**4.53**	**-7**	**O-540/D-6**	**60**	**-3.6**
• SANDERS, John	John Frank Sanders b: 11/20/1945, Grand Island, NE BR/TR, 6'2", 200 lbs. Deb: 4/13/1965																							
1965 KC-A	1	0	0	0	0	0	0	0	0	0	0	0	....	....	....	....	-102	0	0	....	0	....	0	0.0
• SANDERS, Ray	Raymond Floyd Sanders b: 12/4/1916, Bonne Terre, MO d: 10/28/1983, Washington, MO BL/TR, 6'2", 185 lbs. Deb: 4/14/1942																							
1942*StL-N	95	282	37	71	17	2	5	39	42	31	2	....	.252	.351	.379	.730	106	3	39	4.77	-4	1-77	9	-0.8
1943*StL-N	144	478	69	134	21	5	11	73	77	33	1	....	.280	.381	.414	.796	124	17	80	5.85	-8	*1-141	18	0.2
1944*StL-N	154	601	87	177	34	9	12	102	71	50	2	....	.295	.371	.441	.812	125	21	101	6.10	-6	*1-152	22	0.7
1945 StL-N	143	537	85	148	29	3	8	78	83	55	3	....	.276	.375	.385	.760	109	9	84	5.62	2	*1-142	19	0.4
1946 Bos-N	80	259	43	63	12	0	6	35	50	38	0	....	.243	.368	.359	.727	105	4	38	5.09	5	1-77	9	0.6
1948*Bos-N	5	4	0	1	0	0	0	2	1	0	0	....	.250	.400	.250	.650	81	0	0	1.70	0	....	0	0.0
1949 Bos-N	9	21	0	3	1	0	0	0	4	9	0	....	.143	.280	.190	.470	30	-2	1	2.12	2	/1-7	0	0.0
Total 7	**630**	**2182**	**321**	**597**	**114**	**19**	**42**	**329**	**328**	**216**	**8**	**....**	**.274**	**.370**	**.401**	**.771**	**115**	**53**	**344**	**5.58**	**-10**	**1-596**	**77**	**1.0**
• SANDERS, Reggie	Reginald Jerome Sanders b: 9/9/1949, Birmingham, AL BR/TR, 6'2", 205 lbs. Deb: 9/1/1974																							
1974 Det-A	26	99	12	27	7	0	3	10	5	20	1	0	.273	.308	.434	.742	108	1	13	4.61	1	1-25/D-1	3	0.0
• SANDERS, Reggie	Reginald Laverne Sanders b: 12/1/1967, Florence, SC BR/TR, 6', 186 lbs. Deb: 8/22/1991 Career OF: 258-210-1001																							
1991 Cin-N	9	40	6	8	0	0	1	3	0	9	1	1	.200	.200	.275	.475	31	-4	2	1.37	0	/O-9(0-9-0)	0	-0.5
1992 Cin-N	116	385	62	104	26	6	12	36	48	98	16	7	.270	.357	.462	.819	127	14	65	5.97	4	*O-110(53-77-0)	14	1.7
1993 Cin-N	138	496	90	136	16	4	20	83	51	118	27	10	.274	.348	.444	.791	110	8	77	5.33	-5	*O-137(0-4-135)	17	-0.4
1994 Cin-N	107	400	66	105	20	8	17	62	41	114	21	9	.263	.334	.480	.814	110	5	66	5.76	7	*O-104(0-0-104)	13	0.7
1995*Cin-N★	133	484	91	148	36	6	28	99	69	122	36	12	.306	.401	.579	.980	155	42	115	8.59	0	*O-130(0-16-125)	27	3.5
1996 Cin-N	81	287	49	72	17	1	14	33	44	86	24	8	.251	.354	.463	.818	114	8	48	5.58	1	O-80(0-0-80)	7	0.4
1997 Cin-N	86	312	52	79	19	2	19	56	42	93	13	7	.253	.347	.510	.857	119	8	53	5.77	1	O-85(0-0-85)	13	0.5
1998 Cin-N	135	481	83	129	18	6	14	59	51	137	20	9	.268	.347	.418	.765	99	-0	71	5.06	-7	*O-131(0-88-57)	14	-0.9
1999 SD-N	133	478	92	136	24	7	26	72	65	108	36	13	.285	.377	.527	.904	136	28	97	7.14	-4	*O-129(97-15-41)/D-1	19	1.8
2000*Atl-N	103	340	43	79	23	1	11	37	32	78	21	4	.232	.302	.403	.705	76	-11	42	4.08	1	O-96(69-1-27)	6	-1.3
2001*Ari-N	126	441	84	116	21	3	33	90	46	126	14	10	.263	.339	.549	.888	117	9	82	6.50	1	*O-119(0-0-119)	14	0.3
2002*SF-N	140	505	75	126	23	6	23	85	47	121	18	6	.250	.328	.455	.783	109	6	76	5.12	5	*O-137(0-0-137)	14	0.4
2003 Pit-N	130	453	74	129	27	4	31	87	38	110	15	5	.285	.347	.567	.914	131	19	87	6.89	1	*O-120(39-0-91)/D-2	18	1.4
Total 13	**1437**	**5102**	**867**	**1367**	**270**	**54**	**249**	**802**	**574**	**1320**	**262**	**101**	**.268**	**.349**	**.488**	**.837**	**117**	**133**	**882**	**5.98**	**6**	***O-1387/D-3**	**176**	**7.6**
• SANDLOCK, Mike	Michael Joseph Sandlock b: 10/17/1915, Old Greenwich, CT BB/TR, 6'1", 185 lbs. Deb: 9/19/1942																							
1942 Bos-N	2	1	1	1	0	0	0	0	0	0	0	....	1.000	1.000	1.000	2.000	496	0	1	∞	-1	/S-2	0	-0.1
1944 Bos-N	30	30	1	3	0	0	0	2	5	3	0	....	.100	.250	.100	.350	1	-4	1	1.02	-1	3-22/S-7	1	-0.5
1945 Bro-N	80	195	21	55	14	2	2	17	18	19	2	....	.282	.346	.405	.751	109	2	28	5.15	-2	C-47,S-22/2-4,3-2	7	0.4
1946 Bro-N	19	34	1	5	0	0	0	0	3	4	0	....	.147	.216	.147	.363	4	-4	1	1.22	1	C-17/3-1	1	-0.3
1953 Pit-N	64	186	10	43	5	0	0	12	12	19	0	0	.231	.281	.258	.539	42	-16	14	2.57	6	C-64	2	-0.6
Total 5	**195**	**446**	**34**	**107**	**19**	**2**	**2**	**31**	**38**	**45**	**2**	**0**	**.240**	**.304**	**.305**	**.609**	**66**	**-21**	**46**	**3.39**	**2**	**C-128/S-31,3-25,2-4**	**11**	**-1.1**
• SANDS, Charlie	Charles Duane Sands b: 12/17/1947, Newport News, VA BL/TR, 6'2", 215 lbs. Deb: 6/21/1967																							
1967 NY-A	1	1	0	0	0	0	0	0	0	1	0	0	.000	.000	.000	.000	-104	-0	0	.00	0	....	0	0.0
1971*Pit-N	28	25	4	5	2	0	1	5	7	6	0	0	.200	.375	.400	.775	118	1	4	5.11	0	/C-3	1	0.1
1972 Pit-N	1	1	0	0	0	0	0	0	0	0	0	0	.000	.000	.000	.000	-102	-0	0	.00	0	....	0	0.0
1973 Cal-A	17	33	5	9	2	1	1	5	5	10	0	0	.273	.368	.485	.853	150	2	6	7.06	-1	C-10	2	0.1
1974 Cal-A	43	83	6	16	2	0	4	13	23	17	0	0	.193	.374	.361	.735	119	4	12	4.72	0	D-21/C-5	3	0.3
1975 Oak-A	3	2	0	1	0	0	0	0	1	1	0	0	.500	.667	.500	1.167	239	1	1	22.68	0	/D-1	0	0.1
Total 6	**93**	**145**	**15**	**31**	**6**	**1**	**6**	**23**	**36**	**35**	**0**	**0**	**.214**	**.374**	**.393**	**.767**	**125**	**7**	**24**	**5.33**	**-1**	**/D-22,C-18**	**6**	**0.6**
• SANDT, Tommy	Thomas James Sandt b: 12/22/1950, Brooklyn, NY BR/TR, 5'11", 175 lbs. Deb: 6/29/1975 C																							
1975 Oak-A	1	0	0	0	0	0	0	0	0	0	0	0	....	....	....	....	-102	0	0	....	-1	/2-1	0	-0.1
1976 Oak-A	41	67	6	14	1	0	0	3	7	9	0	0	.209	.284	.224	.508	52	-4	5	2.27	-2	S-29/2-9,3-2	1	-0.3
Total 2	**42**	**67**	**6**	**14**	**1**	**0**	**0**	**3**	**7**	**9**	**0**	**0**	**.209**	**.284**	**.224**	**.508**	**52**	**-4**	**5**	**2.27**	**-2**	**/S-29,2-10,3-2**	**1**	**-0.4**
• SANFORD, Chance	Chance Steven Sanford b: 6/2/1972, Houston, TX BL/TR, 5'10", 175 lbs. Deb: 4/30/1998																							
1998 Pit-N	14	28	3	4	1	1	0	3	1	6	0	0	.143	.172	.250	.422	9	-4	1	1.08	-2	/3-5,2-1,S-1	0	-0.5
1999 LA-N	5	8	1	2	0	0	0	2	0	1	0	0	.250	.250	.250	.500	29	-1	1	2.25	-1	/2-2	0	-0.1
Total 2	**19**	**36**	**4**	**6**	**1**	**1**	**0**	**5**	**1**	**7**	**0**	**0**	**.167**	**.189**	**.250**	**.439**	**13**	**-5**	**2**	**1.31**	**-2**	**/3-5,2-3,S-1**	**0**	**-0.7**
• SANFORD, Jack	John Doward Sanford b: 6/23/1917, Chatham, VA BR/TR, 6'3", 195 lbs. Deb: 8/24/1940																							
1940 Was-A	34	122	5	24	4	2	0	10	6	17	0	0	.197	.234	.262	.497	30	-13	8	2.22	-2	1-34	0	-1.7
1941 Was-A	3	5	1	2	0	1	0	0	1	1	0	0	.400	.500	.800	1.300	251	1	2	19.62	0	/1-1	1	0.1
1946 Was-A	10	26	7	6	0	1	0	1	2	6	0	0	.231	.286	.308	.593	70	-1	2	3.36	-1	/1-6	0	-0.3
Total 3	**47**	**153**	**13**	**32**	**4**	**4**	**0**	**11**	**9**	**24**	**0**	**0**	**.209**	**.253**	**.288**	**.541**	**45**	**-13**	**13**	**2.84**	**-4**	**/1-41**	**1**	**-1.9**
• SANGUILLEN, Manny	Manuel De Jesus (Magan) Sanguillen b: 3/21/1944, Colon, Panama BR/TR, 6', 193 lbs. Deb: 7/23/1967 Career OF: 2-0-68																							
1967 Pit-N	30	96	6	26	4	0	0	8	4	12	0	1	.271	.300	.313	.613	75	-4	8	2.98	0	C-28	2	-0.3
1969 Pit-N	129	459	62	139	21	6	5	57	12	48	8	4	.303	.325	.407	.732	106	2	56	4.42	-1	*C-113	14	0.7
1970*Pit-N	128	486	63	158	19	9	7	61	17	45	2	3	.325	.348	.444	.792	114	7	69	5.25	7	*C-125	19	1.9
1971*Pit-N★	138	533	60	170	26	5	7	81	19	32	6	4	.319	.346	.426	.772	116	9	70	4.85	6	*C-135	24	2.4
1972*Pit-N★	136	520	55	155	18	8	7	71	21	38	1	2	.298	.325	.404	.729	108	3	65	4.57	-6	*C-127/O-2(2-0-0)	18	0.4
1973 Pit-N	149	589	64	166	26	7	12	65	17	29	2	5	.282	.305	.411	.716	99	-5	67	3.95	4	C-89,O-59(0-0-59)	15	0.0
1974*Pit-N	151	596	77	171	21	4	7	68	21	27	2	2	.287	.317	.371	.688	95	-7	65	3.85	-2	*C-151	16	-0.1
1975*Pit-N★	133	481	60	158	24	4	9	58	48	31	5	4	.328	.393	.451	.844	135	22	83	6.53	-6	*C-132	23	2.4

YEAR TM-L	G	AB	R	H	2B	3B	HR	RBI	BB	SO	SB	CS	AVG	OBP	SLG	OPS	OPS+	BR/A	RC	RC/G	FR	G/POS	WS	TPW
1976 Pit-N	114	389	52	113	16	6	2	36	28	18	2	4	.290	.341	.378	.719	103	-0	46	4.10	-4	*C-111	13	0.1
1977 Oak-A	152	571	42	157	17	5	6	58	22	35	2	5	.275	.304	.354	.658	80	-18	57	3.53	3	C-77,D-58/O-9(0-0-9),1-7	9	-1.5
1978 Pit-N	85	220	15	58	5	1	3	16	9	10	2	2	.264	.299	.336	.635	74	-9	21	3.27	-3	1-40,C-18	4	-1.4
1979*Pit-N	56	74	8	17	5	2	0	4	2	5	0	0	.230	.250	.351	.601	59	-4	6	2.37	-1	/C-8,1-5	0	-0.5
1980 Pit-N	47	48	2	12	3	0	0	2	3	1	3	2	.250	.294	.313	.607	68	-2	4	2.66	0	/1-5	0	-0.3
Total 13	1448	5062	566	1500	205	57	65	585	223	331	35	38	.296	.329	.398	.727	103	-6	616	4.36	-3	*C-1114/O-70,D-58,1-57	157	3.7
• SANICKI, Ed	Edward Robert "Butch" Sanicki b: 7/7/1923, Wallington, NJ d: 7/6/1998, Old Bridge, NJ BR/TR, 5'9.5", 175 lbs. Deb: 9/14/1949 Career OF: 10-1-5																							
1949 Phi-N	7	13	4	3	0	0	3	7	1	4	0	....	.231	.286	.923	1.209	217	2	3	8.37	0	/O-6(0-1-5)	1	0.1
1951 Phi-N	13	4	1	2	1	0	0	1	1	1	1	0	.500	.600	.750	1.350	265	1	2	31.23	-2	O-10(10-0-0)	1	-0.1
Total 2	20	17	5	5	1	0	3	8	2	5	1	0	.294	.368	.882	1.251	229	3	6	11.88	-2	/O-16	2	0.1
• SANKEY, Ben	Benjamin Turner Sankey b: 9/2/1907, Nauvoo, AL d: 10/14/2001, Washington, GA BR/TR, 5'10", 155 lbs. Deb: 10/5/1929																							
1929 Pit-N	2	7	1	1	0	0	0	0	0	1	0	....	.143	.143	.143	.286	-28	-1	0	.63	0	/S-2	0	-0.1
1930 Pit-N	13	30	6	5	0	0	0	0	2	3	0	....	.167	.219	.167	.385	-5	-5	1	1.17	-2	/S-6,2-4	0	-0.5
1931 Pit-N	57	132	14	30	2	5	0	14	14	10	0	....	.227	.301	.318	.620	67	-6	14	3.30	-1	S-49/2-2,3-2	3	-0.4
Total 3	72	169	21	36	2	5	0	14	16	14	0	....	.213	.281	.284	.565	51	-13	15	2.78	-3	/S-57,2-6,3-2	3	-1.1
• SANTANA, Andres	Andres Confesor (Belonis) Santana b: 2/5/1968, San Pedro de Macoris, Dominican Republic BB/TR, 5'11", 160 lbs. Deb: 9/16/1990																							
1990 SF-N	6	2	0	0	0	0	0	1	0	0	0	0	.000	.000	.000	.000	-104	-1	0	.00	-1	/S-3	0	-0.1
• SANTANA, Pedro	Pedro Santana b: 9/21/1976, San Pedro de Macoris, Dominican Republic BR/TR, 5'11", 160 lbs. Deb: 7/16/2001																							
2001 Det-A	1	0	0	0	0	0	0	0	0	0	0	0	....	....	....	....	-105	0	0	....	-0	/2-1	0	0.0
• SANTANA, Rafael	Rafael Francisco (De La Cruz) Santana b: 1/31/1958, La Romana, Dominican Republic BR/TR, 6'1", 165 lbs. Deb: 4/5/1983 C																							
1983 StL-N	30	14	1	3	0	0	0	2	2	2	0	1	.214	.353	.214	.567	61	-1	1	2.50	-7	/2-9,S-6,3-4	0	-0.8
1984 NY-N	51	152	14	42	11	1	1	12	9	17	0	3	.276	.317	.382	.698	97	-3	17	3.90	0	S-50	5	0.2
1985 NY-N	154	529	41	136	19	1	1	29	29	54	1	0	.257	.296	.302	.598	69	-22	45	2.94	4	*S-153	11	-0.3
1986*NY-N	139	394	38	86	11	0	1	28	36	43	0	0	.218	.287	.254	.541	52	-25	27	2.25	15	*S-137/2-1	8	0.2
1987 NY-N	139	439	41	112	21	2	5	44	29	57	1	1	.255	.303	.346	.649	75	-17	44	3.48	4	*S-138	11	0.1
1988 NY-A	148	480	50	115	12	1	4	38	33	61	1	2	.240	.290	.294	.584	64	-24	38	2.65	-8	*S-148	7	-2.0
1990 Cle-A	7	13	3	3	0	0	1	3	0	0	0	0	.231	.231	.462	.692	89	-0	1	2.27	1	/S-7	1	0.0
Total 7	668	2021	188	497	74	5	13	156	138	234	3	7	.246	.296	.307	.603	68	-92	173	2.91	9	S-639/2-10,3-4	43	-2.5
• SANTANGELO, F.P.	Frank-Paul Santangelo b: 10/24/1967, Livonia, MI BB/TR, 5'10", 165 lbs. Deb: 8/2/1995 Career OF: 217-195-88																							
1995 Mon-N	35	98	11	29	5	1	1	9	12	9	1	1	.296	.384	.398	.782	103	1	16	6.17	-4	O-25(20-2-7)/2-5	3	-0.4
1996 Mon-N	152	393	54	109	20	5	7	56	49	61	5	2	.277	.373	.407	.780	103	4	64	5.61	5	*O-124(33-76-18),3-23/2-5,S	18	0.8
1997 Mon-N	130	350	56	87	19	5	5	31	50	73	8	5	.249	.381	.374	.755	99	2	58	5.47	0	O-99(40-13-51),3-32/2-7,S	10	0.0
1998 Mon-N	122	383	53	82	18	0	4	23	44	72	7	3	.214	.331	.292	.624	67	-16	42	3.57	-5	O-92(72-23-1),2-35/3-1	6	-2.2
1999 SF-N	113	254	49	66	17	3	3	26	53	54	12	4	.260	.409	.386	.795	111	9	48	6.47	-2	O-81(26-49-9),2-11/3-3,S-1	10	0.7
2000 LA-N	81	142	19	28	4	0	1	9	21	33	3	2	.197	.325	.246	.572	50	-10	13	2.71	-3	O-50(26-27-1)/2-7	1	-1.2
2001*Oak-A	32	71	16	14	4	0	0	8	11	17	1	1	.197	.345	.254	.598	61	-4	7	3.30	-2	2-20/O-6(0-5-1),3-3,D-1	2	-0.5
Total 7	665	1691	258	415	87	14	21	162	240	319	37	18	.245	.366	.351	.717	89	-15	248	4.88	-11	O-477/2-90,3-62,S-3,D-1	50	-2.9
• SANTIAGO, Benito	Benito (Rivera) Santiago b: 3/9/1965, Ponce, Puerto Rico BR/TR, 6'1", 182 lbs. Deb: 9/14/1986 Career OF: 2-0-0																							
1986 SD-N	17	62	10	18	2	0	3	6	2	12	0	1	.290	.313	.468	.780	115	0	9	5.15	-2	C-17	2	-0.1
1987 SD-N	146	546	64	164	33	2	18	79	16	112	21	12	.300	.326	.467	.793	111	4	77	5.06	-3	*C-146	15	0.8
1988 SD-N	139	492	49	122	22	2	10	46	24	82	15	7	.248	.284	.362	.646	86	-11	46	3.04	0	*C-136	10	-0.3
1989 SD-N★	129	462	50	109	16	3	16	62	26	89	11	6	.236	.278	.387	.666	88	-9	47	3.42	-2	*C-127	13	-0.4
1990 SD-N★	100	344	42	93	8	5	11	53	27	55	5	5	.270	.329	.419	.747	103	-1	47	4.75	-0	C-98	12	0.6
1991 SD-N★	152	580	60	155	22	3	17	87	23	114	8	10	.267	.300	.403	.703	93	-10	61	3.55	2	*C-151/O-1	16	0.1
1992 SD-N★	106	386	37	97	21	0	10	42	21	52	2	5	.251	.290	.383	.673	88	-10	38	3.26	-2	*C-103	7	-0.5
1993 Fla-N	139	469	49	108	19	6	13	50	37	88	10	7	.230	.294	.380	.673	74	-19	51	3.61	-6	*C-136/O-1	8	-1.6
1994 Fla-N	101	337	35	92	14	2	11	41	25	57	1	2	.273	.325	.424	.749	91	-6	44	4.46	8	C-97	12	0.8
1995*Cin-N	81	266	40	76	20	0	11	44	24	48	2	2	.286	.354	.485	.839	119	6	44	5.95	-1	C-75/1-8	12	1.0
1996 Phi-N	136	481	71	127	21	2	30	85	49	104	2	0	.264	.333	.503	.836	116	9	81	6.00	-3	*C-114,1-14	19	1.3
1997 Tor-A	97	341	31	83	10	0	13	42	17	80	1	0	.243	.283	.387	.670	72	-15	35	3.48	-5	C-95/D-1	9	-1.3
1998 Tor-A	15	29	3	9	5	0	0	4	1	6	0	0	.310	.333	.483	.816	108	0	4	5.50	0	C-15	1	0.1
1999 Chi-N	109	350	28	87	18	3	7	36	32	71	1	1	.249	.315	.377	.692	75	-14	39	3.78	-2	*C-107/1-1	7	-0.9
2000 Cin-N	89	252	22	66	11	1	8	45	19	45	2	2	.262	.316	.409	.725	80	-9	31	4.12	-1	C-84	6	-0.5
2001 SF-N	133	477	39	125	25	4	6	45	23	78	5	4	.262	.299	.369	.668	77	-18	47	3.29	3	*C-130/1-2	10	-0.7
2002*SF-N★	126	478	56	133	24	5	16	74	27	73	4	2	.278	.320	.450	.769	105	1	62	4.46	-8	*C-125	15	0.2
2003*SF-N	108	401	53	112	21	2	11	56	29	69	0	1	.279	.331	.424	.755	98	-3	53	4.71	-11	*C-106	13	-0.6
Total 18	1923	6753	739	1776	312	40	211	897	422	1235	90	67	.263	.310	.415	.725	93	-104	816	4.13	-34	*C-1862/1-25,O-2,D-1	187	-2.0
• SANTIAGO, Ramon	Ramon D. Santiago b: 8/31/1979, Las Matas de Farfan, Dominican Republic BB/TR, 5'11", 150 lbs. Deb: 5/17/2002																							
2002 Det-A	65	222	33	54	5	5	4	20	13	48	8	5	.243	.309	.365	.674	83	-6	26	3.82	1	S-63/D-1	4	0.0
2003 Det-A	141	444	41	100	18	1	2	29	33	66	10	4	.225	.294	.284	.577	58	-26	39	2.81	-11	S-85,2-53	5	-2.6
Total 2	206	666	74	154	23	6	6	49	46	114	18	9	.231	.299	.311	.609	66	-32	65	3.13	-10	S-148/2-53,D-1	9	-2.6
• SANTO, Ron	Ronald Edward Santo b: 2/25/1940, Seattle, WA BR/TR, 6', 190 lbs. Deb: 6/26/1960 Career OF: 7-0-1																							
1960 Chi-N	95	347	44	87	24	2	9	44	31	44	0	3	.251	.312	.409	.721	97	-3	42	4.09	-17	3-94	6	-2.2
1961 Chi-N	154	578	84	164	32	6	23	83	73	77	2	3	.284	.364	.479	.843	120	17	95	5.74	-3	*3-153	18	1.3
1962 Chi-N	162	604	44	137	20	4	17	83	65	94	4	1	.227	.304	.358	.662	74	-22	65	3.58	6	*3-157/S-8	9	-1.5
1963 Chi-N★	162	630	79	187	29	6	25	99	42	92	6	4	.297	.345	.481	.826	128	22	99	5.65	4	*3-162	26	2.8
1964 Chi-N★	161	592	94	185	33	**13**	30	114	**86**	96	3	4	.313	**.401**	.564	.966	162	50	135	8.55	2	*3-161	36	5.6
1965 Chi-N★	164	608	88	173	30	4	33	101	88	109	3	1	.285	.379	.510	.889	144	38	121	7.22	8	*3-164	32	4.9
1966 Chi-N★	155	561	93	175	21	8	30	94	**95**	78	4	5	.312	**.417**	.538	.955	161	50	127	8.20	25	*3-152/S-8	30	**7.9**
1967 Chi-N	161	586	107	176	23	4	31	98	**96**	103	1	5	.300	.401	.512	.913	152	42	120	7.29	32	*3-161	**38**	**8.1**
1968 Chi-N★	162	577	86	142	17	3	26	98	**96**	106	3	4	.246	.357	.421	.778	124	20	87	5.09	12	*3-162	28	3.6
1969 Chi-N★	160	575	97	166	18	4	29	123	96	97	1	3	.289	.392	.485	.877	128	24	108	6.55	-3	*3-160	26	2.1
1970 Chi-N	154	555	83	148	30	4	26	114	92	108	2	0	.267	.372	.476	.848	112	11	100	6.24	5	*3-152/O-1	19	1.6
1971 Chi-N★	154	555	77	148	22	1	21	88	79	95	4	0	.267	.358	.423	.781	105	7	84	5.20	-9	*3-149/O-6(6-0-0)	19	-0.3
1972 Chi-N★	133	464	68	140	25	5	17	74	69	75	1	4	.302	.397	.487	.884	135	23	89	6.87	-2	*3-129/2-3,O-1,S-1	21	2.2
1973 Chi-N★	149	536	65	143	29	2	20	77	63	97	1	2	.267	.348	.440	.789	109	7	76	4.83	-26	*3-146	13	-2.1
1974 Chi-A	117	375	29	83	12	1	5	41	37	72	0	2	.221	.295	.299	.593	69	-15	31	2.66	-1	D-47,2-39,3-28/1-3,S-1	3	-1.5
Total 15	2243	8143	1138	2254	365	67	342	1331	1108	1343	35	41	.277	.366	.464	.830	124	272	1379	5.92	33	*3-2130/D-47,2-42,S-18,O-8,1	324	32.5
• SANTO DOMINGO, Rafael	Rafael (Molina) Santo Domingo b: 11/24/1955, Orocovis, Puerto Rico BB/TR, 6' Deb: 9/7/1979																							
1979 Cin-N	7	6	0	1	0	0	0	0	1	3	0	0	.167	.286	.167	.452	26	-1	0	1.94	0	....	0	-0.1
• SANTOS, Angel	Angel Ramon Santos b: 8/14/1979, Rio Piedras, Puerto Rico BB/TR, 5'11", 185 lbs. Deb: 9/8/2001																							
2001 Bos-A	9	16	2	2	1	0	0	1	2	7	0	0	.125	.222	.188	.410	10	-2	0	.68	-1	/2-6	0	-0.3
2003 Cle-A	32	76	9	17	3	1	3	6	3	18	1	1	.224	.253	.408	.661	73	-4	8	3.45	-1	2-28/3-4	1	-0.3
Total 2	41	92	11	19	4	1	3	7	5	25	1	1	.207	.247	.370	.617	61	-6	8	2.85	-2	/2-34,3-4	1	-0.6
• SANTOS, Francisco	Francisco Alejandro Santos b: 3/9/1974, Santo Domingo, Dominican Republic BL/TL, 6'1", 175 lbs. Deb: 6/18/2003																							
2003 SF-N	8	15	2	3	2	0	1	1	0	3	0	0	.200	.200	.533	.733	85	-1	2	3.60	0	/O-3(0-0-3),1-1	0	-0.1
• SANTOVENIA, Nelson	Nelson Gil (Mayol) Santovenia b: 7/27/1961, Pinar del Rio, Cuba BR/TR, 6'3", 215 lbs. Deb: 9/16/1987																							
1987 Mon-N	2	1	0	0	0	0	0	0	0	0	0	0	.000	.000	.000	.000	-97	-0	0	.00	0	/C-1	0	-0.1

YEAR TM-L	G	AB	R	H	2B	3B	HR	RBI	BB	SO	SB	CS	AVG	OBP	SLG	OPS	OPS+	BR/A	RC	RC/G	FR	G/POS	WS	TPW
1988 Mon-N	92	309	26	73	20	2	8	41	24	77	2	3	.236	.298	.392	.689	92	-5	36	3.85	4	C-86/1-1	8	0.5
1989 Mon-N	97	304	30	76	14	1	5	31	24	37	2	1	.250	.311	.352	.663	88	-5	31	3.43	3	C-89/1-1	7	0.4
1990 Mon-N	59	163	13	31	3	1	6	28	8	31	0	3	.190	.228	.331	.559	54	-13	10	1.92	0	C-51	1	-1.0
1991 Mon-N	41	96	7	24	5	0	2	14	2	18	0	0	.250	.265	.365	.630	76	-3	8	2.70	1	C-30/1-7	2	-0.2
1992 Chi-A	2	3	1	1	0	0	1	2	0	0	0	0	.333	.333	1.333	1.667	351	1	1	18.00	0	/C-2	1	0.1
1993 KC-A	4	8	0	1	0	0	0	0	1	2	0	0	.125	.222	.125	.347	-4	-1	0	1.08	0	/C-4	0	-0.1
Total 7	**297**	**884**	**77**	**206**	**42**	**4**	**22**	**116**	**59**	**165**	**4**	**7**	**.233**	**.286**	**.364**	**.650**	**82**	**-27**	**87**	**3.21**	**6**	**C-263/1-9**	**19**	**-0.5**

• SANTRY, Edward Edward Santry b: 1861, Chicago, IL d: 3/6/1899, Chicago, IL Deb: 8/7/1884

YEAR TM-L	G	AB	R	H	2B	3B	HR	RBI	BB	SO	SB	CS	AVG	OBP	SLG	OPS	OPS+	BR/A	RC	RC/G	FR	G/POS	WS	TPW
1884 Det-N	6	22	1	4	0	0	0	0	1	2	....	....	.182	.217	.182	.399	29	-2	1	1.36	0	/S-5,2-1	0	-0.2

• SARDINHA, Dane Dane K.A.A. Sardinha b: 4/8/1979, Honolulu, HI BR/TR, 6', 215 lbs. Deb: 9/6/2003

YEAR TM-L	G	AB	R	H	2B	3B	HR	RBI	BB	SO	SB	CS	AVG	OBP	SLG	OPS	OPS+	BR/A	RC	RC/G	FR	G/POS	WS	TPW
2003 Cin-N	1	2	0	0	0	0	0	0	0	1	0	0	.000	.000	.000	.000	-102	-1	0	.00	0	/C-1	0	-0.1

• SARGENT, Joe Joseph Alexander "Horse Belly" Sargent b: 9/24/1893, Rochester, NY d: 7/5/1950, Rochester, NY BR/TR, 5'10", 165 lbs. Deb: 4/27/1921

YEAR TM-L	G	AB	R	H	2B	3B	HR	RBI	BB	SO	SB	CS	AVG	OBP	SLG	OPS	OPS+	BR/A	RC	RC/G	FR	G/POS	WS	TPW
1921 Det-A	66	178	21	45	8	5	2	22	24	26	2	3	.253	.342	.388	.729	86	-4	24	4.44	-5	2-24,3-23,S-19	4	-0.6

• SARNI, Bill William Florine Sarni b: 9/19/1927, Los Angeles, CA d: 4/15/1983, Creve Coeur, MO BR/TR, 5'11", 187 lbs. Deb: 5/9/1951 C

YEAR TM-L	G	AB	R	H	2B	3B	HR	RBI	BB	SO	SB	CS	AVG	OBP	SLG	OPS	OPS+	BR/A	RC	RC/G	FR	G/POS	WS	TPW
1951 StL-N	36	86	7	15	1	0	0	2	9	13	1	0	.174	.253	.186	.439	20	-9	4	1.47	0	C-35	1	-0.8
1952 StL-N	3	5	0	1	0	0	0	0	0	1	0	0	.200	.200	.200	.400	11	-1	0	1.38	0	/C-3	0	-0.1
1954 StL-N	123	380	40	114	18	4	9	70	25	42	3	3	.300	.343	.439	.783	101	-1	55	5.11	-1	*C-118	13	0.3
1955 StL-N	107	325	32	83	15	2	3	34	27	33	1	1	.255	.314	.342	.656	74	-12	33	3.37	-3	C-99	5	-1.0
1956 StL-N	43	148	12	43	7	2	5	22	8	15	1	0	.291	.331	.466	.797	111	2	22	5.32	2	C-41	6	0.7
NY-N	78	238	16	55	9	3	5	23	20	31	0	1	.231	.293	.357	.651	74	-9	25	3.47	5	C-78	6	-0.1
Yr.	121	386	28	98	16	5	10	45	28	46	1	1	.254	.308	.399	.707	88	-7	47	4.14	7	*C-119	12	0.6
Total 5	**390**	**1182**	**107**	**311**	**50**	**11**	**22**	**151**	**89**	**135**	**6**	**5**	**.263**	**.316**	**.380**	**.696**	**83**	**-29**	**139**	**3.99**	**3**	**C-374**	**31**	**-0.9**

• SASSER, Mackey Mack Daniel Sasser b: 8/3/1962, Fort Gaines, GA BL/TR, 6'1", 210 lbs. Deb: 7/17/1987 Career OF: 41-0-28

YEAR TM-L	G	AB	R	H	2B	3B	HR	RBI	BB	SO	SB	CS	AVG	OBP	SLG	OPS	OPS+	BR/A	RC	RC/G	FR	G/POS	WS	TPW
1987 SF-N	2	4	0	0	0	0	0	0	0	0	0	0	.000	.000	.000	.000	-105	-1	0	.00	0	/C-1	0	-0.1
Pit-N	12	23	2	5	0	0	0	2	0	2	0	0	.217	.217	.217	.435	16	-3	1	1.24	0	/C-5	0	-0.3
Yr.	14	27	2	5	0	0	0	2	0	2	0	0	.185	.185	.185	.370	-2	-4	1	1.02	0	/C-6	0	-0.4
1988*NY-N	60	123	9	35	10	1	1	17	6	9	0	0	.285	.318	.407	.724	112	1	15	4.18	-2	C-42/3-1,0-1	4	0.2
1989 NY-N	72	182	17	53	14	2	1	22	7	15	0	1	.291	.317	.407	.724	111	1	22	4.45	-1	C-62/3-1	6	0.4
1990 NY-N	100	270	31	83	14	0	6	41	15	19	0	0	.307	.346	.426	.772	111	3	38	5.19	0	C-87/1-1	9	0.8
1991 NY-N	96	228	18	62	14	2	5	35	9	19	0	2	.272	.303	.417	.719	101	-2	26	3.96	0	C-43,0-21(7-0-14),1-10	7	-0.1
1992 NY-N	92	141	7	34	6	0	2	18	3	10	0	0	.241	.257	.326	.583	65	-7	11	2.55	-2	C-27,1-12/0-9(7-0-2)	0	-0.9
1993 Sea-A	83	188	18	41	10	2	1	21	15	30	1	0	.218	.279	.309	.588	57	-11	15	2.60	-1	0-37(26-0-11),D-19/C-4,1-1	0	-1.4
1994 Sea-A	3	4	0	0	0	0	0	0	0	0	0	0	.000	.000	.000	.000	-98	-1	0	.00	-1	/C-1,0-1	0	-0.2
1995 Pit-N	14	26	1	4	1	0	0	0	0	0	0	0	.154	.154	.192	.346	-9	-4	1	.94	0	C-11	0	-0.3
Total 9	**534**	**1189**	**103**	**317**	**69**	**7**	**16**	**156**	**55**	**104**	**1**	**3**	**.267**	**.301**	**.377**	**.678**	**89**	**-24**	**128**	**3.74**	**-6**	**C-283/0-69,1-24,D-19,3-2**	**26**	**-2.0**

• SASSER, Rob Robert Doffell Sasser b: 3/9/1975, Philadelphia, PA BR/TR, 6'3" Deb: 7/31/1998

YEAR TM-L	G	AB	R	H	2B	3B	HR	RBI	BB	SO	SB	CS	AVG	OBP	SLG	OPS	OPS+	BR/A	RC	RC/G	FR	G/POS	WS	TPW
1998 Tex-A	1	1	0	0	0	0	0	0	0	0	0	0	.000	.000	.000	.000	-96	-0	0	.00	0	....	0	0.0

• SATRIANO, Tom Thomas Victor Nicholas Satriano b: 8/28/1940, Pittsburgh, PA BL/TR, 6'1", 190 lbs. Deb: 7/23/1961

YEAR TM-L	G	AB	R	H	2B	3B	HR	RBI	BB	SO	SB	CS	AVG	OBP	SLG	OPS	OPS+	BR/A	RC	RC/G	FR	G/POS	WS	TPW
1961 LA-A	35	96	15	19	5	1	1	8	12	16	2	0	.198	.294	.302	.596	53	-6	10	3.27	-4	3-23,2-10/S-1	1	-0.9
1962 LA-A	10	19	4	8	2	0	2	6	0	1	0	0	.421	.421	.842	1.263	238	3	6	13.26	0	/3-5	1	0.3
1963 LA-A	23	50	1	9	1	0	0	2	9	10	0	0	.180	.305	.200	.505	48	-3	4	2.37	0	3-13/C-2,1-1	1	-0.3
1964 LA-A	108	255	18	51	9	0	1	17	30	37	0	2	.200	.284	.247	.531	55	-16	17	2.03	-2	3-38,1-32,C-25/S-2,2-1	2	-1.9
1965 Cal-A	47	79	8	13	2	0	1	4	10	10	1	1	.165	.258	.228	.486	40	-6	5	1.83	0	3-15,2-12,C-12/1-3	1	-0.6
1966 Cal-A	103	226	16	54	5	3	0	24	27	32	3	3	.239	.320	.288	.608	78	-6	21	3.15	-5	C-43,1-36,3-25/2-4	5	-1.1
1967 Cal-A	90	201	13	45	7	0	4	21	28	25	1	0	.224	.319	.318	.637	92	-1	21	3.53	0	3-38,C-23,2-15/1-5	6	0.0
1968 Cal-A	111	297	20	75	9	0	8	35	37	44	0	0	.253	.337	.364	.701	117	7	37	4.35	0	C-85,2-14,3-11/1-1	12	1.2
1969 Cal-A	41	108	5	28	2	0	1	16	18	15	0	2	.259	.370	.306	.676	95	-1	13	3.87	1	C-36/1-5,2-2	4	0.2
Bos-A	47	127	9	24	2	0	0	11	22	12	0	0	.189	.318	.205	.523	46	-8	9	2.11	-3	C-44	1	-1.0
Yr.	88	235	14	52	4	0	1	27	40	27	0	2	.221	.342	.251	.593	69	-9	22	2.87	-2	C-80/1-5,2-2	5	-0.7
1970 Bos-A	59	165	21	39	9	1	3	13	21	23	0	0	.236	.326	.358	.684	83	-3	19	3.68	-1	C-51	4	-0.2
Total 10	**674**	**1623**	**130**	**365**	**53**	**5**	**21**	**157**	**214**	**225**	**7**	**8**	**.225**	**.317**	**.303**	**.620**	**80**	**-40**	**160**	**3.23**	**-15**	**C-321,3-168/1-83,2-58,S-3**	**38**	**-4.2**

• SATURRIA, Luis Luis Arturo Saturria b: 7/21/1976, San Pedro de Macoris, Dominican Republic BR/TR, 6'2", 165 lbs. Deb: 9/11/2000 Career OF: 3-8-7

YEAR TM-L	G	AB	R	H	2B	3B	HR	RBI	BB	SO	SB	CS	AVG	OBP	SLG	OPS	OPS+	BR/A	RC	RC/G	FR	G/POS	WS	TPW
2000 StL-N	12	5	1	0	0	0	0	0	1	3	0	0	.000	.167	.000	.167	-53	-1	0	.23	-1	/0-9(0-5-4)	0	-0.2
2001 StL-N	13	5	0	1	1	0	0	1	0	1	1	0	.200	.200	.400	.600	50	-0	1	3.40	0	/0-9(3-3-3)	0	0.0
Total 2	**25**	**10**	**1**	**1**	**1**	**0**	**0**	**1**	**1**	**4**	**1**	**0**	**.100**	**.182**	**.200**	**.382**	**-6**	**-1**	**1**	**1.64**	**-1**	**/0-18**	**0**	**-0.2**

• SAUCIER, Frank Francis Field Saucier b: 5/28/1926, Leslie, MO BL/TR, 6'1", 180 lbs. Deb: 7/21/1951

YEAR TM-L	G	AB	R	H	2B	3B	HR	RBI	BB	SO	SB	CS	AVG	OBP	SLG	OPS	OPS+	BR/A	RC	RC/G	FR	G/POS	WS	TPW
1951 StL-A	18	14	4	1	1	0	0	1	3	4	0	0	.071	.278	.143	.421	16	-2	1	1.32	-1	/0-3(1-0-2)	0	-0.2

• SAUER, Ed Edward "Horn" Sauer b: 1/3/1919, Pittsburgh, PA d: 7/1/1988, Thousand Oaks, CA BR/TR, 6'1", 188 lbs. Deb: 9/17/1943 Career OF: 79-22-35

YEAR TM-L	G	AB	R	H	2B	3B	HR	RBI	BB	SO	SB	CS	AVG	OBP	SLG	OPS	OPS+	BR/A	RC	RC/G	FR	G/POS	WS	TPW
1943 Chi-N	14	55	3	15	3	0	0	9	3	6	1	....	.273	.322	.327	.649	89	-1	6	3.48	2	0-13(13-0-0)	1	0.0
1944 Chi-N	23	50	3	11	4	0	0	5	2	6	0	....	.220	.250	.300	.550	55	-3	4	2.39	-1	0-12(12-0-0)	0	-0.5
1945*Chi-N	49	93	8	24	4	1	2	11	8	23	2	....	.258	.317	.387	.704	97	-1	12	4.37	1	0-26(21-2-3)	3	-0.1
1949 StL-N	24	45	5	10	2	1	0	1	3	8	0	....	.222	.271	.311	.582	53	-3	4	2.73	0	0-10(4-0-7)	0	-0.3
Bos-N	79	214	26	57	12	0	3	31	17	34	0	....	.266	.323	.364	.688	89	-4	25	4.12	-2	0-71(29-20-25)	5	-0.8
Yr.	103	259	31	67	14	1	3	32	20	42	0	....	.259	.314	.355	.669	83	-7	29	3.87	-1	0-81(33-20-32)	5	-1.1
Total 4	**189**	**457**	**45**	**117**	**25**	**2**	**5**	**57**	**33**	**77**	**3**	**....**	**.256**	**.309**	**.352**	**.661**	**83**	**-11**	**50**	**3.75**	**0**	**0-132**	**9**	**-1.7**

• SAUER, Hank Henry John "The Honker" Sauer
b: 3/17/1917, Pittsburgh, PA d: 8/24/2001, Burlingame, CA BR/TR, 6'3", 199 lbs. Deb: 9/9/1941 C Career OF: 1029-0-208

YEAR TM-L	G	AB	R	H	2B	3B	HR	RBI	BB	SO	SB	CS	AVG	OBP	SLG	OPS	OPS+	BR/A	RC	RC/G	FR	G/POS	WS	TPW
1941 Cin-N	9	33	4	10	4	0	0	5	1	4	0	....	.303	.324	.424	.748	109	0	4	4.72	1	/0-8(8-0-0)	1	0.1
1942 Cin-N	7	20	4	5	0	0	2	4	2	2	0	....	.250	.318	.550	.868	152	1	4	6.60	1	/1-4	1	0.1
1945 Cin-N	31	116	18	34	1	0	5	20	6	16	2	....	.293	.328	.431	.759	112	1	17	5.57	0	0-28(28-0-0)/1-3	4	-0.1
1948 Cin-N	145	530	78	138	22	1	35	97	60	85	2	....	.260	.340	.504	.844	130	20	92	6.10	3	*0-132(132-0-0),1-12	19	1.3
1949 Cin-N	42	152	22	36	6	0	4	16	18	19	0	....	.237	.318	.355	.673	79	-4	16	3.46	3	0-39(39-0-0)/1-1	2	-0.4
Chi-N	96	357	59	104	17	1	27	83	37	47	0	....	.291	.363	.571	.934	151	24	75	7.82	5	0-96(96-0-0)	17	2.1
Yr.	138	509	81	140	23	1	31	99	55	66	0	....	.275	.349	.507	.856	129	19	91	6.41	8	*0-135(135-0-0)/1-1	19	1.7
1950 Chi-N★	145	540	85	148	32	2	32	103	60	67	1	....	.274	.350	.519	.868	127	19	96	6.39	1	*0-125(125-0-0),1-18	18	1.0
1951 Chi-N	141	525	77	138	19	4	30	89	45	77	2	1	.263	.325	.486	.810	113	7	84	5.68	10	*0-132(131-0-1)	18	0.8
1952 Chi-N★	151	567	89	153	31	3	**37**	**121**	77	92	1	2	.270	.361	.531	.892	143	32	111	6.96	9	*0-151(151-0-0)	28	3.1
1953 Chi-N	108	395	61	104	16	5	19	60	50	56	0	0	.263	.349	.473	.822	109	5	66	5.89	-4	*0-105(42-0-64)	12	-0.4
1954 Chi-N	142	520	98	150	18	1	41	103	70	68	2	1	.288	.379	.563	.943	140	31	114	7.95	-1	*0-141(9-0-140)	22	2.5
1955 Chi-N	79	261	29	55	8	1	12	28	26	47	0	0	.211	.287	.387	.674	77	-9	28	3.53	1	0-68(67-0-1)	5	-1.1
1956 StL-N	75	151	11	45	4	0	5	24	25	31	0	0	.298	.408	.424	.832	124	7	27	6.42	1	0-37(35-0-2)	6	0.6
1957 NY-N	127	378	46	98	14	1	26	76	49	59	1	0	.259	.344	.508	.852	125	14	67	6.27	-1	0-98(98-0-0)	13	0.8
1958 SF-N	88	236	27	59	8	0	12	46	35	37	0	0	.250	.356	.436	.793	111	5	39	5.69	0	0-67(67-0-0)	8	0.1
1959 SF-N	13	15	1	1	0	0	1	1	0	7	0	0	.067	.067	.267	.333	-17	-3	0	.51	0	/0-1	0	-0.3
Total 15	**1399**	**4796**	**709**	**1278**	**200**	**19**	**288**	**876**	**561**	**714**	**11**	**4**	**.266**	**.347**	**.496**	**.844**	**123**	**149**	**840**	**6.21**	**29**	***0-1228/1-38**	**174**	**10.3**

• SAUNDERS, Doug Douglas Long Saunders b: 12/13/1969, Yorba Linda, CA BR/TR, 6', 172 lbs. Deb: 6/13/1993

YEAR TM-L	G	AB	R	H	2B	3B	HR	RBI	BB	SO	SB	CS	AVG	OBP	SLG	OPS	OPS+	BR/A	RC	RC/G	FR	G/POS	WS	TPW
1993 NY-N	28	67	8	14	2	0	0	0	3	4	0	0	.209	.243	.239	.482	30	-7	4	1.75	-2	2-22/3-4,S-1	0	-0.8

YEAR TM-L	G	AB	R	H	2B	3B	HR	RBI	BB	SO	SB	CS	AVG	OBP	SLG	OPS	OPS+	BR/A	RC	RC/G	FR	G/POS	WS	TPW
• SAUNDERS, Rusty	Russell Collier Saunders b: 3/12/1906, Trenton, NJ d: 11/24/1967, Trenton, NJ BR/TR, 6'2", 205 lbs. Deb: 9/24/1927																							
1927 Phi-A	5	15	2	2	1	0	0	2	3	2	0	0	.133	.278	.200	.478	24	-2	1	2.05	-0	/O-4(4-0-0)	0	-0.2
• SAUTER, Al	Albert C. Sauter b: 9/2/1868, Philadelphia, PA d: 7/15/1928, Ocean City, NJ Deb: 9/8/1890																							
1890 Phi-a	14	41	1	4	0	0	0	0	11	....	0	....	.098	.288	.098	.386	14	-4	1	.85	-3	3-11/2-2,O-2(0-2-0)	0	-0.5
• SAVAGE, Don	Donald Anthony Savage b: 3/5/1919, Bloomfield, NJ d: 12/25/1961, Montclair, NJ BR/TR, 6', 180 lbs. Deb: 4/18/1944																							
1944 NY-A	71	239	31	63	7	5	4	24	20	41	1	1	.264	.323	.385	.708	99	-1	29	4.19	-4	3-60	5	-0.4
1945 NY-A	34	58	5	13	1	0	0	3	3	14	1	0	.224	.262	.241	.504	44	-4	4	2.06	-1	3-14/O-2(2-0-0)	0	-0.5
Total 2	**105**	**297**	**36**	**76**	**8**	**5**	**4**	**27**	**23**	**55**	**2**	**1**	**.256**	**.312**	**.357**	**.668**	**88**	**-5**	**33**	**3.76**	**-5**	**/3-74,O-2**	**5**	**-0.9**
• SAVAGE, Jimmie	James Harold Savage b: 8/29/1883, Southington, CT d: 6/26/1940, New Castle, PA BB/TR, 5'5", 150 lbs. Deb: 9/3/1912 Career OF: 22-5-69																							
1912 Phi-N	2	3	1	0	0	0	0	0	1	0	0	....	.000	.250	.000	.250	-27	-1	0	.00	0	/2-1	0	-0.1
1914 Pit-F	132	479	81	136	9	9	1	26	67	32	17	....	.284	.372	.347	.718	111	10	66	4.75	-3	O-93(22-5-66),3-29,S-11/2-3	15	0.4
1915 Pit-F	14	21	0	3	0	0	0	0	1	0	0	....	.143	.182	.143	.325	-4	-3	0	.71	-1	/O-3(0-0-3),3-1	0	-0.4
Total 3	**148**	**503**	**82**	**139**	**9**	**9**	**1**	**26**	**69**	**32**	**17**	**....**	**.276**	**.364**	**.336**	**.700**	**106**	**7**	**66**	**4.52**	**-4**	**/O-96,3-30,S-11,2-4**	**15**	**0.0**
• SAVAGE, Ted	Theodore Edmund Savage b: 2/21/1937, Venice, IL BR/TR, 6'1", 185 lbs. Deb: 4/9/1962 Career OF: 219-81-172																							
1962 Phi-N	127	335	54	89	11	2	7	39	40	66	16	5	.266	.347	.373	.721	96	0	46	4.69	-2	*O-109(92-12-10)	10	-0.7
1963 Pit-N	85	149	22	29	2	1	5	14	14	31	4	3	.195	.268	.322	.590	69	-6	11	2.29	-1	O-47(36-9-2)	1	-0.9
1965 StL-N	30	63	7	10	3	0	1	4	6	9	1	1	.159	.232	.254	.486	34	-6	3	1.62	0	O-20(0-0-20)	0	-0.8
1966 StL-N	16	29	4	5	2	1	0	3	4	7	4	0	.172	.273	.310	.583	62	-1	3	3.17	-0	/O-7(0-2-5)	0	-0.1
1967 StL-N	9	8	1	1	0	0	0	0	1	3	0	0	.125	.222	.125	.347	2	-1	0	1.08	0	....	0	-0.1
Chi-N	96	225	40	49	10	1	5	33	40	54	7	6	.218	.348	.338	.686	93	-1	27	3.79	0	O-86(0-23-66)/3-1	7	-0.5
Yr.	105	233	41	50	10	1	5	33	41	57	7	6	.215	.344	.330	.675	90	-2	27	3.69	0	O-86(0-23-66)/3-1	7	-0.6
1968 Chi-N	3	8	0	2	0	0	0	0	0	1	0	1	.250	.250	.250	.500	47	-1	0	.96	0	/O-2(0-1-2)	0	-0.1
LA-N	61	126	7	26	6	1	2	7	10	20	1	2	.206	.270	.317	.588	82	-4	9	2.20	2	O-39(18-0-24)	1	-0.5
Yr.	64	134	7	28	6	1	2	7	10	21	1	3	.209	.269	.313	.582	80	-4	9	2.12	2	O-41(18-1-26)	1	-0.6
1969 Cin-N	68	110	20	25	7	0	2	11	20	27	3	0	.227	.346	.345	.692	90	-0	15	4.53	-3	O-42(28-12-4)/2-1	4	-0.4
1970 Mil-A	114	276	43	77	10	5	12	50	57	44	10	6	.279	.406	.482	.888	143	18	57	7.02	-5	O-82(34-22-33)/1-1	13	1.1
1971 Mil-A	14	17	2	3	0	0	0	1	5	4	1	0	.176	.364	.176	.540	58	-0	2	3.38	0	/O-6(6-0-1)	0	-0.1
KC-A	19	29	2	5	0	0	0	1	3	6	2	0	.172	.250	.172	.422	22	-2	1	1.33	1	/O-9(5-0-5)	0	-0.2
Yr.	33	46	4	8	0	0	0	2	8	10	3	0	.174	.296	.174	.470	36	-3	3	2.05	1	O-15(11-0-6)	0	-0.3
Total 9	**642**	**1375**	**202**	**321**	**51**	**11**	**34**	**163**	**200**	**272**	**49**	**24**	**.233**	**.335**	**.361**	**.696**	**95**	**-3**	**175**	**4.13**	**-8**	**O-449/1-1,2-1,3-1**	**36**	**-3.4**
• SAVERINE, Bob	Robert Paul "Rabbit" Saverine b: 6/2/1941, Norwalk, CT BB/TR, 5'10", 165 lbs. Deb: 9/12/1959 Career OF: 8-60-4																							
1959 Bal-A	1	0	1	0	0	0	0	0	0	0	0	0	....	....	....	....	-102	0	0	....	0	....	0	0.0
1962 Bal-A	8	21	2	5	2	0	0	3	1	3	0	2	.238	.273	.333	.606	65	-2	1	1.37	1	/2-7	0	-0.1
1963 Bal-A	115	167	21	39	1	2	1	12	25	44	8	3	.234	.333	.281	.615	76	-4	17	3.37	1	O-59(1-58-0),2-19,S-13	5	-0.1
1964 Bal-A	46	34	14	5	1	0	0	0	3	6	3	1	.147	.216	.176	.393	11	-4	1	.95	0	S-15/O-2(0-2-0)	0	-0.4
1966 Was-A	120	406	54	102	10	4	5	24	27	62	4	3	.251	.301	.333	.634	83	-9	41	3.38	0	2-70,3-26,S-11/O-9(5-0-4)	10	-0.4
1967 Was-A	89	233	22	55	13	0	0	8	17	34	8	0	.236	.288	.292	.580	75	-5	20	2.93	-2	2-48,S-10/3-8,O-2(2-0-0)	5	-0.4
Total 6	**379**	**861**	**114**	**206**	**27**	**6**	**6**	**47**	**73**	**149**	**23**	**9**	**.239**	**.300**	**.305**	**.606**	**76**	**-25**	**81**	**3.09**	**-1**	**2-144/O-72,S-49,3-34**	**20**	**-1.5**
• SAWATSKI, Carl	Carl Ernest "Swats,Swisher,Swish" Sawatski b: 11/4/1927, Shickshinny, PA d: 11/24/1991, Little Rock, AR BL/TR, 5'10", 210 lbs. Deb: 9/29/1948																							
1948 Chi-N	2	2	0	0	0	0	0	0	0	0	0	....	.000	.000	.000	.000	-104	-1	0	.00	0	....	0	-0.1
1950 Chi-N	38	103	4	18	1	0	1	7	11	19	0	....	.175	.254	.214	.468	25	-11	6	1.83	2	C-32	2	-0.7
1953 Chi-N	43	59	5	13	3	0	1	5	7	7	0	0	.220	.303	.322	.625	62	-3	6	3.27	-1	C-15	0	-0.3
1954 Chi-A	43	109	6	20	3	3	1	12	15	20	0	0	.183	.282	.294	.576	56	-7	9	2.68	-1	C-33	2	-0.6
1957*Mil-N	58	105	13	25	4	0	6	17	10	15	0	0	.238	.316	.448	.764	110	1	15	4.84	2	C-28	4	0.5
1958 Mil-N	10	10	1	1	0	0	0	1	2	5	0	0	.100	.250	.100	.350	-3	-1	0	.77	0	/C-3	0	-0.1
Phi-N	60	183	12	42	4	1	5	12	16	42	0	0	.230	.302	.344	.646	71	-7	19	3.59	-1	C-53	3	-0.6
Yr.	70	193	13	43	4	1	5	13	18	47	0	0	.223	.299	.332	.631	67	-9	20	3.39	0	C-56	3	-0.7
1959 Phi-N	74	198	15	58	10	0	9	43	32	36	0	0	.293	.394	.480	.874	129	9	38	6.90	0	C-69	9	1.2
1960 StL-N	78	179	16	41	4	0	6	27	22	24	0	0	.229	.313	.352	.665	75	-6	19	3.60	2	C-67	6	-0.1
1961 StL-N	86	174	23	52	8	0	10	33	25	17	0	0	.299	.387	.517	.904	125	7	35	7.39	1	C-60/O-1	8	1.0
1962 StL-N	85	222	26	56	9	1	13	42	36	38	0	0	.252	.357	.477	.834	111	4	39	6.16	-3	C-70	9	0.4
1963 StL-N	56	105	12	25	0	0	6	14	15	28	2	0	.238	.333	.410	.743	103	1	15	5.19	-1	C-27	4	0.2
Total 11	**633**	**1449**	**133**	**351**	**46**	**5**	**58**	**213**	**191**	**251**	**2**	**0**	**.242**	**.333**	**.401**	**.734**	**92**	**-14**	**202**	**4.77**	**1**	**C-457/O-1**	**47**	**0.6**
• SAWYER, Carl	Carl Everett "Huck" Sawyer b: 10/19/1890, Seattle, WA d: 1/17/1957, Los Angeles, CA BR/TR, 5'11", 160 lbs. Deb: 9/11/1915																							
1915 Was-A	10	32	8	8	1	0	0	3	4	5	2	....	.250	.351	.281	.633	88	-0	4	4.15	-2	/2-6,S-4	1	-0.2
1916 Was-A	16	31	3	6	1	0	0	2	4	4	3	....	.194	.306	.226	.531	60	-1	3	3.09	-1	/2-6,S-5,3-1	1	-0.3
Total 2	**26**	**63**	**11**	**14**	**2**	**0**	**0**	**5**	**8**	**9**	**5**	**....**	**.222**	**.329**	**.254**	**.583**	**74**	**-2**	**7**	**3.60**	**-3**	**/2-12,S-9,3-1**	**2**	**-0.4**
• SAX, Dave	David John Sax b: 9/22/1958, Sacramento, CA BR/TR, 6', 185 lbs. Deb: 9/1/1982 Career OF: 3-0-2																							
1982 LA-N	2	2	0	0	0	0	0	0	0	0	0	0	.000	.000	.000	.000	-103	-1	0	.00	-0	/O-1	0	-0.1
1983 LA-N	7	8	0	0	0	0	0	1	0	0	0	0	.000	.000	.000	.000	-101	-2	0	.00	-1	/C-4	0	-0.3
1985 Bos-A	22	36	2	11	3	0	0	6	3	3	0	1	.306	.359	.389	.748	101	-0	5	4.59	-2	C-16/O-4(2-0-2)	1	-0.1
1986 Bos-A	4	11	1	5	1	0	1	1	0	1	0	0	.455	.455	.818	1.273	237	2	4	18.41	-0	/C-2,1-1	1	0.2
1987 Bos-A	2	3	0	0	0	0	0	0	0	1	0	0	.000	.000	.000	.000	-97	-1	0	.00	0	/C-2	0	-0.1
Total 5	**37**	**60**	**3**	**16**	**4**	**0**	**1**	**8**	**3**	**5**	**0**	**1**	**.267**	**.302**	**.383**	**.685**	**84**	**-2**	**9**	**5.06**	**-2**	**/C-24,O-5,1-1**	**2**	**-0.4**
• SAX, Ollie	Erik Oliver Sax b: 11/5/1904, Branford, CT d: 3/21/1982, Newark, NJ BR/TR, 5'8", 164 lbs. Deb: 4/13/1928																							
1928 StL-A	16	17	4	3	0	0	0	0	5	3	0	0	.176	.364	.176	.540	44	-1	2	2.84	0	/3-9	0	0.0
• SAX, Steve	Stephen Louis Sax b: 1/29/1960, Sacramento, CA BR/TR, 5'11", 185 lbs. Deb: 8/18/1981 Career OF: 27-0-6																							
1981*LA-N	31	119	15	33	2	0	2	9	7	14	5	7	.277	.317	.345	.662	91	-4	12	3.41	2	2-29	3	0.0
1982 LA-N★	150	638	88	180	23	7	4	47	49	53	49	19	.282	.335	.359	.694	97	-1	79	4.28	-9	*2-149	18	-0.2
1983*LA-N★	155	623	94	175	18	5	5	41	58	73	56	30	.281	.343	.350	.693	93	-6	76	4.11	-28	*2-152	17	-2.7
1984 LA-N	145	569	70	138	24	4	1	35	47	53	34	19	.243	.301	.304	.606	71	-23	51	2.95	-3	*2-141	11	-1.9
1985*LA-N	136	488	62	136	8	4	1	42	54	43	27	11	.279	.354	.318	.672	92	-2	56	3.92	-16	*2-135/3-1	12	-1.2
1986 LA-N★	157	633	91	210	43	4	6	56	59	58	40	17	.332	.391	.441	.832	139	35	110	6.45	-14	*2-154	31	3.0
1987 LA-N	157	610	84	171	22	7	6	46	44	61	37	11	.280	.332	.369	.701	88	-8	76	4.35	-5	*2-152/3-1,O-1	18	-0.6
1988*LA-N	160	632	70	175	19	4	5	57	45	51	42	12	.277	.326	.343	.669	95	-1	73	4.04	-18	*2-158	24	-1.6
1989 NY-A★	158	651	88	205	26	3	5	63	52	44	43	17	.315	.366	.387	.754	114	14	91	4.97	-12	*2-158	21	0.7
1990 NY-A★	155	615	70	160	24	2	4	42	49	46	43	9	.260	.319	.325	.644	80	-10	68	3.75	-22	*2-154	14	-2.8
1991 NY-A	158	652	85	198	38	2	10	56	41	38	31	11	.304	.348	.414	.762	110	9	92	5.09	-7	*2-149/3-5,D-4	24	0.6
1992 Chi-A	143	567	74	134	26	4	4	47	43	42	30	12	.236	.292	.317	.610	72	-21	51	2.89	-20	*2-141/D-1	5	-3.7
1993 Chi-A	57	119	20	28	5	0	1	8	8	6	7	3	.235	.283	.303	.586	59	-7	11	2.95	-1	O-32(26-0-6),D-21/2-1	0	-0.9
1994 Oak-A	7	24	2	6	0	1	0	1	0	2	0	0	.250	.250	.333	.583	53	-2	2	3.00	2	/2-6	0	0.0
Total 14	**1769**	**6940**	**913**	**1949**	**278**	**47**	**54**	**550**	**556**	**584**	**444**	**178**	**.281**	**.336**	**.358**	**.694**	**95**	**-27**	**847**	**4.22**	**-151**	***2-1679/O-33,D-26,3-7**	**198**	**-11.2**
• SAY, Jimmy	James I. Say b: 1862, Baltimore, MD d: 6/23/1894, Baltimore, MD Deb: 7/22/1882																							
1882 Lou-a	1	4	1	1	1	0	0	....	0	....	....	....	.250	.250	.250	.500	73	-0	0	2.39	-1	/3-1	0	-0.1
Phi-a	22	82	12	17	2	0	1	....	1	....	....	....	.207	.217	.268	.485	56	-4	5	2.11	1	S-22	2	-0.2
Yr.	23	86	13	18	2	0	1	....	1	....	....	....	.209	.218	.267	.486	57	-4	5	2.12	0	S-22/3-1	2	-0.3
1884 Wil-U	16	59	3	13	1	2	0	....	1	....	....	....	.220	.233	.305	.538	78	-1	4	2.62	-5	3-16	0	-0.5
KC-U	2	8	0	2	0	0	0	....	0	....	....	....	.250	.250	.250	.500	80	-0	1	2.39	-1	/3-2	0	-0.1
Yr.	18	67	3	15	1	2	0	....	1	....	....	....	.224	.235	.299	.534	79	-2	5	2.59	-6	3-18	0	-0.7

YEAR TM-L	G	AB	R	H	2B	3B	HR	RBI	BB	SO	SB	CS	AVG	OBP	SLG	OPS	OPS+	BR/A	RC	RC/G	FR	G/POS	WS	TPW
1887 Cle-a	16	65	9	25	5	3	0	12	1	....	0	....	.385	.385	.547	.931	163	5	14	9.31	-5	3-16	2	0.0
Total 3	57	218	25	58	8	5	1	12	3	....	0	....	.266	.273	.359	.632	95	-1	24	4.07	-11	/3-35,S-22	4	-1.0

• SAY, Lou Louis I. Say b: 2/4/1854, Baltimore, MD d: 6/5/1930, Fallston, MD BR/TR, 5'7", 145 lbs. Deb: 4/14/1873 U NA OF: 0-1-1

YEAR TM-L	G	AB	R	H	2B	3B	HR	RBI	BB	SO	SB	CS	AVG	OBP	SLG	OPS	OPS+	BR/A	RC	RC/G	FR	G/POS	WS	TPW
1873 Mar-n	3	12	1	2	0	0	0	2	0	0	0	0	.167	.167	.167	.333	-1	-1	0	1.04	-1	/S-2,0-1	....	-0.1
1874 Bal-n	18	66	4	14	3	0	0	5	0	1	0	0	.212	.212	.258	.470	50	-4	4	2.13	2	S-18	....	-0.2
1875 Was-n	11	38	4	10	0	0	0	2	0	7	0	0	.263	.263	.263	.526	86	-0	3	2.84	-3	/S-8,2-2,0-1	....	-0.3
1880 Cin-N	48	191	14	38	8	1	0	15	4	31	....	....	.199	.215	.251	.467	58	-8	11	1.90	1	S-48	2	-0.4
1882 Phi-a	49	199	35	45	4	3	1	28	8	....	....	....	.226	.256	.291	.547	75	-6	15	2.77	1	S-49	6	-0.3
1883 Bal-a	74	324	52	83	13	2	1	0	10	....	....	....	.256	.278	.318	.596	89	-5	29	3.42	3	*S-74	6	0.1
1884 Bal-U	78	339	65	81	14	2	2	....	11	....	....	....	.239	.263	.310	.573	84	-7	28	3.07	-3	*S-78	9	-0.7
KC-U	17	70	6	14	2	0	1	....	2	....	....	....	.200	.222	.271	.494	76	-1	4	2.16	6	S-16/2-1	1	0.5
Yr.	95	409	71	95	16	2	3	....	13	....	....	....	.232	.256	.303	.559	83	-8	33	2.91	3	*S-94/2-1	10	-0.2
Total 3 n	32	116	9	26	3	0	0	9	0	8	0	0	.224	.224	.250	.474	57	-5	7	2.23	-2	/S-28,2-2,0-2	....	-0.6
Total 4	266	1123	172	261	41	8	5	43	35	31	....	....	.232	.256	.297	.552	79	-27	88	2.85	9	S-265/2-1	24	-0.8

• SCALA, Jerry Gerald Michael Scala b: 9/27/1924, Bayonne, NJ d: 12/14/1993, Fallston, MD BL/TR, 5'11", 178 lbs. Deb: 4/22/1948 Career OF: 3-59-0

YEAR TM-L	G	AB	R	H	2B	3B	HR	RBI	BB	SO	SB	CS	AVG	OBP	SLG	OPS	OPS+	BR/A	RC	RC/G	FR	G/POS	WS	TPW
1948 Chi-A	3	6	1	0	0	0	0	0	0	3	0	0	.000	.000	.000	.000	-104	-2	0	.00	-0	/0-2(0-2-0)	0	-0.2
1949 Chi-A	37	120	17	30	7	1	1	13	17	19	3	3	.250	.348	.350	.698	88	-3	16	4.63	-1	0-37(2-35-0)	3	-0.4
1950 Chi-A	40	67	8	13	2	1	0	6	10	10	0	0	.194	.299	.254	.552	44	-6	5	2.63	0	0-23(1-22-0)	1	-0.5
Total 3	80	193	26	43	9	2	1	19	27	32	3	3	.223	.321	.306	.627	67	-10	22	3.74	-1	/0-62	4	-1.2

• SCALZI, Johnny John Anthony Scalzi b: 3/22/1907, Stamford, CT d: 9/27/1962, Port Chester, NY BR/TR, 5'7", 170 lbs. Deb: 6/19/1931

YEAR TM-L	G	AB	R	H	2B	3B	HR	RBI	BB	SO	SB	CS	AVG	OBP	SLG	OPS	OPS+	BR/A	RC	RC/G	FR	G/POS	WS	TPW
1931 Bos-N	2	1	0	0	0	0	0	0	0	1	0	....	.000	.000	.000	.000	-104	-0	0	.00	0	....	0	0.0

• SCALZI, Skeeter Frank John Scalzi b: 6/16/1913, Lafferty, OH d: 8/25/1984, Pittsburgh, PA BR/TR, 5'6", 160 lbs. Deb: 7/21/1939

YEAR TM-L	G	AB	R	H	2B	3B	HR	RBI	BB	SO	SB	CS	AVG	OBP	SLG	OPS	OPS+	BR/A	RC	RC/G	FR	G/POS	WS	TPW
1939 NY-N	11	18	3	6	0	0	0	0	3	2	1	....	.333	.429	.333	.762	106	0	2	4.36	-1	/S-5,3-1	0	-0.1

• SCANLAN, Mort Mortimer J. Scanlan b: 3/18/1861, Chicago, IL d: 12/29/1928, Chicago, IL, 6'1", 186 lbs. Deb: 4/21/1890

YEAR TM-L	G	AB	R	H	2B	3B	HR	RBI	BB	SO	SB	CS	AVG	OBP	SLG	OPS	OPS+	BR/A	RC	RC/G	FR	G/POS	WS	TPW
1890 NY-N	3	10	0	0	0	0	0	0	2	5	1	....	.000	.167	.000	.167	-50	-2	0	.45	0	/1-3	0	-0.2

• SCANLON, Pat James Patrick Scanlon b: 9/23/1952, Minneapolis, MN BL/TR, 6', 180 lbs. Deb: 9/27/1974

YEAR TM-L	G	AB	R	H	2B	3B	HR	RBI	BB	SO	SB	CS	AVG	OBP	SLG	OPS	OPS+	BR/A	RC	RC/G	FR	G/POS	WS	TPW
1974 Mon-N	2	4	1	1	0	0	0	0	0	1	0	0	.250	.250	.250	.500	38	-0	0	2.25	0	/3-1	0	0.0
1975 Mon-N	60	109	5	20	3	1	2	15	17	25	0	1	.183	.294	.284	.578	58	-6	9	2.74	1	3-28/1-1	1	-0.6
1976 Mon-N	11	27	2	5	1	0	1	2	2	5	0	0	.185	.241	.333	.575	59	-2	2	2.26	-2	/3-7,1-1	0	-0.4
1977 SD-N	47	79	9	15	3	0	1	11	12	20	0	0	.190	.297	.266	.563	58	-4	6	2.21	-2	2-15,3-11/0-1	0	-0.6
Total 4	120	219	17	41	7	1	4	28	31	51	0	1	.187	.288	.283	.571	58	-13	17	2.48	-3	/3-47,2-15,1-2,0-1	1	-1.6

• SCANLON, Patrick Patrick J. Scanlon b: 3/25/1861, Canada d: 7/17/1913, Springfield, MA Deb: 7/4/1884

YEAR TM-L	G	AB	R	H	2B	3B	HR	RBI	BB	SO	SB	CS	AVG	OBP	SLG	OPS	OPS+	BR/A	RC	RC/G	FR	G/POS	WS	TPW
1884 Bos-U	6	24	2	7	1	0	0		0	....	....	....	.292	.292	.333	.625	112	0	2	3.94	0	/0-6(6-0-0)	1	0.0

• SCARRITT, Russ Stephen Russell Mallory Scarritt
b: 1/14/1903, Pensacola, FL d: 12/4/1994, Pensacola, FL BL/TR, 5'10.5", 165 lbs. Deb: 4/18/1929 Career OF: 254-1-10

YEAR TM-L	G	AB	R	H	2B	3B	HR	RBI	BB	SO	SB	CS	AVG	OBP	SLG	OPS	OPS+	BR/A	RC	RC/G	FR	G/POS	WS	TPW
1929 Bos-A	151	540	69	159	26	17	1	71	34	38	13	11	.294	.337	.411	.749	94	-7	73	4.73	-1	*0-145(134-1-10)	11	-1.8
1930 Bos-A	113	447	48	129	17	8	2	48	12	49	4	7	.289	.312	.376	.688	76	-19	50	3.92	-0	*0-110(110-0-0)	6	-2.5
1931 Bos-A	10	39	2	6	1	0	0	1	2	2	0	0	.154	.195	.179	.375	-1	-5	1	1.13	1	/0-9(9-0-0)	0	-0.5
1932 Phi-N	11	11	0	2	0	0	0	0	1	2	0	....	.182	.250	.182	.432	16	-1	1	1.58	0	/0-1	0	-0.1
Total 4	285	1037	119	296	44	25	3	120	49	91	17	18	.285	.320	.385	.705	82	-33	125	4.20	0	0-265	17	-4.9

• SCARSELLA, Les Leslie George Scarsella b: 11/23/1913, Santa Cruz, CA d: 12/16/1958, San Francisco, CA BL/TL, 5'11", 185 lbs. Deb: 9/15/1935

YEAR TM-L	G	AB	R	H	2B	3B	HR	RBI	BB	SO	SB	CS	AVG	OBP	SLG	OPS	OPS+	BR/A	RC	RC/G	FR	G/POS	WS	TPW
1935 Cin-N	6	10	4	2	1	0	0	0	3	1	0	....	.200	.385	.300	.685	89	0	1	5.00	1	/1-2	1	0.1
1936 Cin-N	115	485	63	152	21	9	3	65	14	36	6	....	.313	.335	.412	.748	107	3	66	5.18	-4	*1-115	13	-1.2
1937 Cin-N	110	329	35	81	11	4	3	34	17	26	5	....	.246	.285	.331	.617	70	-14	30	3.08	-8	1-65,0-14(12-0-2)	3	-2.8
1939 Cin-N	16	14	0	2	0	0	0	2	0	2	0	....	.143	.143	.143	.286	-23	-2	0	.32	0	....	0	-0.2
1940 Bos-N	18	60	7	18	1	3	0	8	3	5	2	....	.300	.344	.417	.760	115	1	9	5.75	-2	1-15	2	-0.2
Total 5	265	898	109	255	34	16	6	109	37	70	13	....	.284	.315	.378	.693	92	-13	107	4.28	-13	1-197/0-14	19	-4.4

• SCARSONE, Steve Steven Wayne Scarsone b: 4/11/1966, Anaheim, CA BR/TR, 6'2", 195 lbs. Deb: 5/15/1992

YEAR TM-L	G	AB	R	H	2B	3B	HR	RBI	BB	SO	SB	CS	AVG	OBP	SLG	OPS	OPS+	BR/A	RC	RC/G	FR	G/POS	WS	TPW
1992 Phi-N	7	13	1	2	0	0	0	0	1	6	0	0	.154	.214	.154	.368	6	-2	0	1.19	0	/2-3	0	-0.2
Bal-A	11	17	2	3	0	0	0	0	1	6	0	0	.176	.222	.176	.399	13	-2	1	1.43	-1	/2-5,3-2,S-1	0	-0.2
1993 SF-N	44	103	16	26	9	0	2	15	4	32	0	1	.252	.280	.398	.678	82	-4	12	3.76	0	2-20/3-8,1-6	3	-0.3
1994 SF-N	52	103	21	28	8	0	2	13	10	20	0	2	.272	.336	.408	.744	97	-1	14	4.53	4	2-22/3-8,1-6,S-1	4	0.4
1995 SF-N	80	233	33	62	10	3	11	29	18	82	3	2	.266	.335	.476	.811	114	4	38	5.73	0	3-50,2-13,1-11	7	0.4
1996 SF-N	105	283	28	62	12	1	5	23	25	91	2	3	.219	.287	.322	.609	63	-17	26	2.94	-2	2-74,3-14/1-1,S-1	2	-1.5
1997 StL-N	5	10	0	1	0	0	0	0	2	5	1	0	.100	.250	.100	.350	-4	-1	1	1.53	-1	/2-2,0-2(1-1-0),3-1	0	-0.2
1999 KC-A	46	68	2	14	5	0	0	6	9	24	1	0	.206	.299	.279	.578	48	-5	7	3.21	-1	S-16,1-12/2-9,3-3,D-2	1	-0.5
Total 7	350	830	103	198	44	4	20	86	70	266	7	8	.239	.304	.373	.677	80	-28	98	3.92	1	2-148/3-86,1-36,S-19,D-2,0	17	-2.1

• SCHAAL, Paul Paul Schaal b: 3/3/1943, Pittsburgh, PA BR/TR, 5'11", 180 lbs. Deb: 9/3/1964

YEAR TM-L	G	AB	R	H	2B	3B	HR	RBI	BB	SO	SB	CS	AVG	OBP	SLG	OPS	OPS+	BR/A	RC	RC/G	FR	G/POS	WS	TPW
1964 LA-A	17	32	3	4	0	0	0	0	2	5	0	1	.125	.176	.125	.301	-16	-5	1	.48	-2	/2-9,3-9	0	-0.7
1965 Cal-A	155	483	48	108	12	2	9	45	61	88	6	3	.224	.312	.313	.625	80	-12	50	3.38	-16	*3-153/2-1	9	-3.0
1966 Cal-A	138	386	59	94	15	7	6	24	68	56	6	4	.244	.364	.365	.729	113	10	55	4.82	-2	*3-131	15	0.8
1967 Cal-A	99	272	31	51	9	1	6	20	38	39	2	2	.188	.289	.294	.584	76	-8	25	2.89	-2	3-88/S-2,2-1	6	-1.1
1968 Cal-A	60	219	22	46	7	1	2	16	29	25	5	7	.210	.308	.279	.587	82	-6	19	2.81	10	3-58	5	0.5
1969 KC-A	61	205	22	54	6	0	1	13	25	27	2	1	.263	.349	.307	.656	84	-3	24	4.09	-6	3-49/2-6,S-6	5	-0.9
1970 KC-A	124	380	50	102	12	3	5	35	43	39	7	4	.268	.344	.355	.700	93	-3	47	4.28	-10	3-97,S-10/2-6	9	-1.2
1971 KC-A	161	548	80	150	31	6	11	63	103	51	7	5	.274	.391	.412	.803	129	25	95	6.11	-15	*3-161	26	1.1
1972 KC-A	127	435	47	99	19	3	6	41	61	59	1	3	.228	.325	.326	.652	95	-2	46	3.51	-22	*3-123/S-1	9	-2.7
1973 KC-A	121	396	61	114	14	3	8	42	63	45	5	6	.288	.392	.399	.791	114	10	63	5.52	-23	*3-121	15	-1.4
1974 KC-A	12	34	3	6	2	0	1	4	5	5	0	0	.176	.300	.324	.624	75	-1	3	2.35	-1	3-12	0	-0.2
Cal-A	53	165	10	41	5	0	2	20	18	27	2	2	.248	.322	.315	.638	89	-2	16	3.37	-10	3-51	3	-1.3
Yr.	65	199	13	47	7	0	3	24	23	32	2	2	.236	.318	.317	.635	86	-3	19	3.16	-10	3-63	3	-1.4
Total 11	1128	3555	436	869	132	26	57	323	516	466	43	38	.244	.344	.344	.688	98	3	444	4.19	-98	*3-1053/2-23,S-19	102	-10.1

• SCHAEFER, Germany Herman A. Schaefer b: 2/4/1877, Chicago, IL d: 5/16/1919, Saranac Lake, NY BR/TR, 5'9", 175 lbs. Deb: 10/5/1901 C Career OF: 18-13-46

YEAR TM-L	G	AB	R	H	2B	3B	HR	RBI	BB	SO	SB	CS	AVG	OBP	SLG	OPS	OPS+	BR/A	RC	RC/G	FR	G/POS	WS	TPW
1901 Chi-N	2	5	0	3	1	0	0	0	2	....	0	....	.600	.714	.800	1.514	352	2	3	38.80	1	/2-1,3-1	1	0.3
1902 Chi-N	81	291	32	57	2	3	0	14	19	....	12	....	.196	.250	.223	.473	48	-18	21	2.28	-9	3-75/1-3,0-2(0-0-2),S-1	1	-2.5
1905 Det-A	153	554	64	135	17	9	2	47	45	....	19	....	.244	.302	.318	.619	96	-3	64	3.77	10	*2-151/S-3	18	1.0
1906 Det-A	124	446	48	106	14	3	2	42	32	....	31	....	.238	.290	.296	.586	81	-10	51	3.74	4	*2-114/S-7	11	-0.5
1907*Det-A	109	372	44	96	12	3	1	32	30	....	21	....	.258	.313	.315	.628	97	-1	46	4.19	3	2-74,S-18,3-14/0-1	13	0.4
1908*Det-A	153	584	96	151	20	10	3	52	37	....	40	....	.259	.304	.342	.646	105	2	74	4.05	3	S-68,2-58,3-29	23	1.0
1909 Det-A	87	280	26	70	12	0	0	22	14	....	12	....	.250	.286	.293	.579	79	-7	27	3.16	8	2-86/0-1	7	0.1
Was-A	37	128	13	31	5	1	1	4	6	....	2	....	.242	.281	.320	.602	94	-1	12	3.09	0	2-32/3-1	3	-0.1
Yr.	124	408	39	101	17	1	1	26	20	....	14	....	.248	.284	.301	.586	84	-9	39	3.13	7	*2-118/3-1,0-1	10	0.0
1910 Was-A	74	229	27	63	6	5	0	14	25	....	17	....	.275	.352	.345	.697	124	7	34	5.04	1	2-35,0-26(8-13-5)/3-2	8	0.8
1911 Was-A	125	440	73	147	14	7	0	45	57	....	22	....	.334	.412	.398	.809	129	20	82	6.85	-1	*1-108/0-7(7-0-0)	19	1.6
1912 Was-A	60	166	21	41	7	3	0	19	23	....	11	....	.247	.342	.325	.667	90	-1	22	4.46	-8	0-19(0-0-19),1-15,2-15/P-1	5	-1.0
1913 Was-A	54	100	17	32	1	1	0	7	15	12	6	....	.320	.419	.350	.769	123	4	17	6.01	-3	2-16/1-6,3-2,0-1,P-1	5	-0.1
1914 Was-A	30	29	6	7	1	0	0	2	3	5	4	1	.241	.313	.276	.588	74	-0	3	3.69	0	/2-3,0-3(0-0-3)	1	-0.1
1915 New-F	59	154	26	33	5	3	0	8	25	11	3	....	.214	.328	.286	.613	86	-2	15	3.15	0	0-17(3-0-14),1-13/3-9,2-2	3	-0.3
1916 NY-A	1	1	0	0	0	0	0	0	0	0	0	....	.000	.000	.000	.000	-98	-0	0	.00	0	/0-1	0	-0.1

YEAR TM-L	G	AB	R	H	2B	3B	HR	RBI	BB	SO	SB	CS	AVG	OBP	SLG	OPS	OPS+	BR/A	RC	RC/G	FR	G/POS	WS	TPW
1918 Cle-A	1	5	2	0	0	0	0	0	0	0	1	....	.000	.000	.000	.000	-91	-1	0	.00	0	/2-1	0	-0.1
Total 15	1150	3784	495	972	117	48	9	308	333	28	201	1	.257	.319	.320	.639	97	-10	471	4.13	9	2-588,1-145,3-133/S-97,0-78,P	118	0.5

• SCHAEFER, Jeff Jeffrey Scott Schaefer b: 5/31/1960, Patchogue, NY BR/TR, 5'10", 170 lbs. Deb: 4/7/1989

YEAR TM-L	G	AB	R	H	2B	3B	HR	RBI	BB	SO	SB	CS	AVG	OBP	SLG	OPS	OPS+	BR/A	RC	RC/G	FR	G/POS	WS	TPW
1989 Chi-A	15	10	2	1	0	0	0	0	0	2	1	1	.100	.100	.100	.200	-45	-2	0	.00	-3	/S-5,2-4,3-4,D-1	0	-0.5
1990 Sea-A	55	107	11	22	3	0	0	6	3	11	4	1	.206	.241	.234	.475	33	-9	7	1.95	-2	3-26,S-24/2-3	2	-0.9
1991 Sea-A	84	164	19	41	7	1	1	11	5	25	3	1	.250	.272	.323	.595	64	-8	13	2.52	0	S-46,3-30,2-11/D-1	2	-0.5
1992 Sea-A	65	70	5	8	2	0	1	3	2	10	0	1	.114	.139	.186	.325	-10	-11	1	.57	-6	S-33,3-21/2-7,D-2	1	-1.5
1994 Oak-A	6	8	0	1	0	0	0	0	0	1	0	0	.125	.125	.125	.250	-39	-2	0	.48	-2	/3-3,S-2,1-1	0	-0.3
Total 5	225	359	37	73	12	1	2	20	10	49	8	4	.203	.229	.259	.488	35	-32	21	1.79	-12	S-110/3-84,2-25,D-4,1-1	5	-3.8

• SCHAFER, Harry Harry C. "Silk Stockings" Schafer
b: 8/14/1846, Philadelphia, PA d: 2/28/1935, Philadelphia, PA BR/TR, 5'9.5", 143 lbs. Deb: 5/5/1871 U NA OF: 18-1-0 Career OF: 1-0-24

YEAR TM-L	G	AB	R	H	2B	3B	HR	RBI	BB	SO	SB	CS	AVG	OBP	SLG	OPS	OPS+	BR/A	RC	RC/G	FR	G/POS	WS	TPW
1871 Bos-n	31	149	38	42	7	5	0	28	3	1	13	4	.282	.296	.396	.692	94	-2	22	6.20	1	*3-31	....	-0.1
1872 Bos-n	48	225	51	65	10	4	1	37	0	8	2	0	.289	.289	.382	.671	99	-1	26	5.05	2	*3-43/0-5(5-0-0),C-2	....	0.0
1873 Bos-n	60	295	65	79	12	3	2	46	3	1	3	4	.268	.275	.349	.624	78	-11	30	4.14	-17	*3-47,0-13(13-0-0)	....	-2.0
1874 Bos-n	71	327	69	87	10	2	1	45	1	5	2	4	.266	.268	.318	.586	82	-9	29	3.58	1	*3-71/S-1	....	-0.7
1875 Bos-n	52	222	49	64	9	0	0	17	1	8	3	2	.288	.291	.329	.620	111	2	23	4.19	3	*3-51/0-1	....	0.3
1876 Bos-N	70	290	47	72	11	0	0	35	4	11	....	....	.248	.262	.290	.552	82	-5	22	2.92	1	*3-70	8	-0.2
1877 Bos-N	33	141	20	39	5	2	0	13	0	7	....	....	.277	.277	.340	.617	90	-2	14	3.67	-11	0-23(1-0-22)/3-9,S-1	2	-1.1
1878 Bos-N	2	8	0	1	0	0	0	0	0	1	....	....	.125	.125	.125	.250	-16	-1	0	.50	-1	/0-2(0-0-2)	0	-0.2
Total 5 n	262	1218	272	337	48	14	4	173	8	23	23	14	.277	.281	.349	.630	91	-22	130	4.42	-10	3-243/0-19,C-2,S-1	....	-2.4
Total 3	105	439	67	112	16	2	0	48	4	19	....	....	.255	.264	.303	.568	83	-8	36	3.10	-11	/3-79,0-25,S-1	10	-1.5

• SCHAFFER, Jimmie Jimmie Ronald Schaffer b: 4/5/1936, Limeport, PA BR/TR, 5'9", 185 lbs. Deb: 5/20/1961 C

YEAR TM-L	G	AB	R	H	2B	3B	HR	RBI	BB	SO	SB	CS	AVG	OBP	SLG	OPS	OPS+	BR/A	RC	RC/G	FR	G/POS	WS	TPW
1961 StL-N	68	153	15	39	7	0	1	16	9	29	0	0	.255	.301	.320	.621	59	-9	14	3.09	2	C-68	4	-0.5
1962 StL-N	70	66	7	16	2	1	0	6	6	16	1	0	.242	.306	.303	.609	58	-4	6	3.12	-3	C-69	1	-0.5
1963 Chi-N	57	142	17	34	7	0	7	19	11	35	0	0	.239	.294	.437	.731	102	0	16	3.88	1	C-54	5	0.3
1964 Chi-N	54	122	9	25	6	1	2	9	17	17	2	4	.205	.307	.320	.627	74	-5	10	2.60	-2	C-43	1	-0.6
1965 Chi-A	17	31	2	6	3	1	0	1	3	4	0	0	.194	.265	.355	.620	79	-1	2	2.00	1	C-14	1	0.1
NY-N	24	37	0	5	2	0	0	0	1	15	0	0	.135	.158	.189	.347	-3	-5	1	.61	-1	C-21	0	-0.6
1966 Phi-N	8	15	2	2	1	0	1	4	1	7	0	0	.133	.188	.400	.588	58	-1	1	2.44	0	/C-6	0	-0.1
1967 Phi-N	2	2	1	0	0	0	0	0	1	1	0	0	.000	.333	.000	.333	3	-0	0	.00	0	/C-1	0	0.0
1968 Cin-N	4	6	0	1	0	0	0	1	0	3	0	0	.167	.167	.167	.333		-1	0	.90	0	/C-2	0	-0.1
Total 8	304	574	53	128	28	3	11	56	49	127	3	4	.223	.286	.340	.626	69	-25	51	2.88	-2	C-278	12	-1.9

• SCHAIVE, Johnny John Edward Schaive b: 2/25/1934, Springfield, IL BR/TR, 5'8", 175 lbs. Deb: 9/19/1958

YEAR TM-L	G	AB	R	H	2B	3B	HR	RBI	BB	SO	SB	CS	AVG	OBP	SLG	OPS	OPS+	BR/A	RC	RC/G	FR	G/POS	WS	TPW
1958 Was-A	7	24	1	6	0	0	0	1	1	4	0	0	.250	.280	.250	.530	48	-2	1	1.29	-1	/2-6	0	-0.2
1959 Was-A	16	59	3	9	2	0	0	2	0	7	0	0	.153	.167	.186	.353	-3	-8	2	1.02	-1	2-16	1	-0.8
1960 Was-A	6	12	1	3	1	0	0	0	0	3	0	0	.250	.250	.333	.583	56	-1	1	1.80	0	/2-4	0	-0.1
1962 Was-A	82	225	20	57	15	1	6	29	6	25	0	1	.253	.273	.409	.682	81	-8	21	3.04	3	3-49/2-6	3	-0.4
1963 Was-A	3	3	0	0	0	0	0	0	0	1	0	0	.000	.000	.000	.000	-100	-1	0	.00	0	....	0	-0.1
Total 5	114	323	25	75	18	1	6	32	7	40	0	1	.232	.251	.350	.601	61	-19	24	2.44	1	/3-49,2-32	4	-1.6

• SCHALK, Ray Raymond William "Cracker" Schalk b: 8/12/1892, Harvel, IL d: 5/19/1970, Chicago, IL BR/TR, 5'9", 165 lbs. Deb: 8/11/1912 M/C HOF: 1955

YEAR TM-L	G	AB	R	H	2B	3B	HR	RBI	BB	SO	SB	CS	AVG	OBP	SLG	OPS	OPS+	BR/A	RC	RC/G	FR	G/POS	WS	TPW
1912 Chi-A	23	63	7	18	2	0	0	8	3	....	2	....	.286	.357	.317	.675	96	-0	8	4.37	-2	C-23	3	0.0
1913 Chi-A	129	401	38	98	15	5	1	38	27	36	14	....	.244	.297	.314	.611	80	-11	40	3.25	-5	*C-125	13	-0.7
1914 Chi-A	136	392	30	106	13	2	0	36	38	24	24	11	.270	.347	.314	.661	100	2	50	4.13	3	*C-125	17	1.6
1915 Chi-A	135	413	46	110	14	4	1	54	62	21	15	18	.266	.366	.327	.693	104	-0	51	4.03	-10	*C-134	18	0.1
1916 Chi-A	129	410	36	95	12	9	0	41	41	31	30	13	.232	.311	.305	.616	84	-7	45	3.38	7	*C-124	16	1.1
1917*Chi-A	140	424	48	96	12	5	2	51	59	27	19	....	.226	.331	.292	.623	88	-4	47	3.53	-1	*C-139	20	0.8
1918 Chi-A	108	333	35	73	6	3	0	22	36	22	12	....	.219	.301	.255	.556	67	-12	29	2.72	-8	*C-106	7	-1.3
1919*Chi-A	131	394	57	111	9	3	0	34	51	25	11	....	.282	.367	.320	.687	93	-1	50	4.37	-2	*C-129	17	0.8
1920 Chi-A	151	485	64	131	25	5	1	61	68	19	10	4	.270	.362	.348	.711	89	-3	67	4.66	-3	*C-151	21	0.6
1921 Chi-A	128	416	32	105	24	4	0	47	40	36	3	4	.252	.328	.329	.658	69	-19	47	3.82	11	*C-126	11	0.0
1922 Chi-A	142	442	57	124	22	3	4	60	67	36	12	4	.281	.379	.371	.750	96	2	68	5.25	16	*C-142	22	2.7
1923 Chi-A	123	382	42	87	12	2	1	44	39	28	7	4	.228	.306	.277	.583	55	-24	35	2.97	-0	*C-121	7	-1.5
1924 Chi-A	57	153	15	30	4	2	1	11	21	10	1	5	.196	.301	.268	.569	49	-13	13	2.53	6	C-56	2	-0.3
1925 Chi-A	125	343	44	94	18	1	0	52	57	27	11	5	.274	.382	.332	.714	87	-2	49	4.83	3	*C-125	12	0.8
1926 Chi-A	82	226	26	60	9	1	0	32	27	11	5	1	.265	.349	.314	.663	77	-6	27	4.14	-5	C-80	5	-0.6
1927 Chi-A	16	26	2	6	2	0	0	2	2	1	0	0	.231	.286	.308	.593	55	-2	2	3.02	1	C-15	0	0.0
1928 Chi-A	2	1	0	1	0	0	0	1	0	0	1	0	1.000	1.000	1.000	2.000	433	1	1	∞	0	/C-1	0	0.1
1929 NY-N	5	2	0	0	0	0	0	0	0	1	0	....	.000	.000	.000	.000	-100	-1	0	.00	0	/C-5	0	-0.1
Total 18	1762	5306	579	1345	199	49	11	594	638	355	177	69	.253	.340	.316	.656	84	-100	630	3.89	13	*C-1727	191	4.0

• SCHALK, Roy Le Roy John Schalk b: 11/9/1908, Chicago, IL d: 3/11/1990, Gainesville, TX BR/TR, 5'10", 168 lbs. Deb: 9/17/1932

YEAR TM-L	G	AB	R	H	2B	3B	HR	RBI	BB	SO	SB	CS	AVG	OBP	SLG	OPS	OPS+	BR/A	RC	RC/G	FR	G/POS	WS	TPW
1932 NY-A	3	12	3	3	1	0	0	0	2	2	0	0	.250	.357	.333	.690	84	-0	2	4.56	0	/2-3	0	0.0
1944 Chi-A	146	587	47	129	14	4	1	44	45	52	5	4	.220	.276	.262	.539	55	-35	43	2.33	-12	*2-142/S-5	5	-4.0
1945 Chi-A	133	513	50	127	23	1	1	65	32	41	3	6	.248	.293	.302	.595	75	-19	45	2.83	-6	*2-133	9	-1.8
Total 3	282	1112	100	259	38	5	2	109	79	95	8	10	.233	.285	.281	.566	64	-54	90	2.58	-18	2-278/S-5	14	-5.8

• SCHALL, Gene Eugene David Schall b: 6/5/1970, Abington, PA BR/TR, 6'3", 190 lbs. Deb: 6/16/1995

YEAR TM-L	G	AB	R	H	2B	3B	HR	RBI	BB	SO	SB	CS	AVG	OBP	SLG	OPS	OPS+	BR/A	RC	RC/G	FR	G/POS	WS	TPW
1995 Phi-N	24	65	2	15	2	0	0	5	6	16	0	0	.231	.306	.262	.567	51	-4	5	2.87	0	1-14/0-4(4-0-0)	0	-0.6
1996 Phi-N	28	66	7	18	5	1	2	10	12	15	0	0	.273	.392	.470	.862	125	3	13	6.82	-1	1-19	3	0.0
Total 2	52	131	9	33	7	1	2	15	18	31	0	0	.252	.351	.366	.717	90	-2	18	4.82	-1	/1-33,0-4	3	-0.6

• SCHALLER, Biff Walter Schaller b: 9/23/1889, Chicago, IL d: 10/9/1939, Emeryville, CA BL/TR, 5'11", 168 lbs. Deb: 4/30/1911 Career OF: 39-9-0

YEAR TM-L	G	AB	R	H	2B	3B	HR	RBI	BB	SO	SB	CS	AVG	OBP	SLG	OPS	OPS+	BR/A	RC	RC/G	FR	G/POS	WS	TPW
1911 Det-A	40	60	8	8	0	1	1	7	4	....	1	....	.133	.200	.217	.417	15	-7	3	1.32	1	0-16(7-9-0)/1-1	0	-0.7
1913 Chi-A	36	96	12	21	3	0	0	4	20	16	5	....	.219	.353	.250	.603	78	-1	10	3.33	-4	0-32(32-0-0)	2	-0.7
Total 2	76	156	20	29	3	1	1	11	24	16	6	....	.186	.298	.237	.536	56	-9	13	2.52	-3	/0-48,1-1	2	-1.3

• SCHANG, Bobby Robert Martin Schang b: 12/7/1886, Wales Center, NY d: 8/29/1966, Sacramento, CA BR/TR, 5'7", 165 lbs. Deb: 9/23/1914

YEAR TM-L	G	AB	R	H	2B	3B	HR	RBI	BB	SO	SB	CS	AVG	OBP	SLG	OPS	OPS+	BR/A	RC	RC/G	FR	G/POS	WS	TPW
1914 Pit-N	11	35	0	8	1	1	0	1	0	10	0	....	.229	.229	.314	.543	64	-2	2	2.23	-1	C-10	0	-0.2
1915 Pit-N	56	125	13	23	6	3	0	4	14	32	2	2	.184	.271	.280	.551	68	-5	10	2.48	1	C-45	2	-0.2
NY-N	12	21	1	3	0	0	0	1	4	5	1	....	.143	.280	.143	.423	31	-1	1	1.76	-2	/C-6	0	-0.3
Yr.	68	146	14	26	6	3	0	5	18	37	3	2	.178	.273	.260	.533	62	-7	12	2.38	-1	C-51	2	-0.5
1927 StL-N	3	5	0	1	0	0	0	0	0	0	0	....	.200	.200	.200	.400	7	-1	0	1.21	0	/C-3	0	-0.1
Total 3	82	186	14	35	7	4	0	6	18	47	3	2	.188	.263	.269	.532	61	-9	14	2.32	-1	/C-64	2	-0.7

• SCHANG, Wally Walter Henry Schang b: 8/22/1889, South Wales, NY d: 3/6/1965, St. Louis, MO BB/TR, 5'10", 180 lbs. Deb: 5/1/1913 C Career OF: 97-65-5

YEAR TM-L	G	AB	R	H	2B	3B	HR	RBI	BB	SO	SB	CS	AVG	OBP	SLG	OPS	OPS+	BR/A	RC	RC/G	FR	G/POS	WS	TPW
1913*Phi-A	79	207	32	55	16	3	3	30	34	44	4	....	.266	.392	.415	.807	139	12	34	5.62	-5	C-72	13	1.4
1914*Phi-A	107	307	44	88	11	8	3	45	32	33	7	7	.287	.371	.404	.775	138	13	47	5.31	-4	*C-100	19	1.9
1915 Phi-A	116	359	64	89	9	11	1	44	66	47	18	3	.248	.385	.343	.728	122	17	55	5.08	2	3-43,0-41(20-21-0),C-26	17	2.2
1916 Phi-A	110	338	41	90	15	8	7	38	38	44	14	....	.266	.358	.420	.778	140	16	57	5.68	10	0-61(58-3-0),C-36	12	2.9
1917 Phi-A	118	316	41	90	14	9	3	36	29	24	6	....	.285	.362	.415	.776	139	14	49	5.31	4	C-80,3-12/0-6(2-0-4)	15	2.6
1918*Bos-A	88	225	36	55	7	1	0	20	46	35	4	....	.244	.377	.284	.662	101	4	26	3.73	-7	C-57,0-16(14-2-0)/3-5,S-1	10	0.0
1919 Bos-A	113	330	43	101	16	3	0	55	71	42	15	....	.306	.436	.373	.809	136	22	58	6.44	4	*C-103	19	3.6
1920 Bos-A	122	387	58	118	30	7	4	51	64	37	7	7	.305	.413	.450	.862	134	22	75	7.00	2	C-73,0-40(0-39-1)	20	2.6
1921*NY-A	134	424	77	134	30	5	6	55	78	35	7	4	.316	.428	.453	.881	122	19	88	7.75	-10	*C-132	20	1.7
1922*NY-A	124	408	46	130	21	7	1	53	53	36	12	6	.319	.405	.412	.816	111	10	72	6.23	-7	*C-119	18	1.1

YEAR TM-L	G	AB	R	H	2B	3B	HR	RBI	BB	SO	SB	CS	AVG	OBP	SLG	OPS	OPS+	BR/A	RC	RC/G	FR	G/POS	WS	TPW
1923*NY-A	84	272	39	75	8	2	2	29	27	17	5	2	.276	.360	.342	.702	84	-4	36	4.64	-7	C-81	8	-0.6
1924 NY-A	114	356	46	104	19	7	5	52	48	43	2	6	.292	.382	.427	.809	109	4	59	5.79	-4	*C-108	16	0.7
1925 NY-A	73	167	17	40	8	1	2	24	17	9	2	1	.240	.310	.335	.645	65	-9	18	3.59	4	C-58	4	-0.2
1926 StL-A	103	285	36	94	19	5	8	50	32	20	5	5	.330	.405	.516	.921	133	13	59	7.61	4	C-82/O-3(3-0-0)	14	2.1
1927 StL-A	97	264	40	84	15	2	5	42	41	33	3	2	.318	.414	.447	.861	119	9	51	7.30	4	C-75	12	1.6
1928 StL-A	91	245	41	70	10	5	3	39	68	26	8	2	.286	.448	.404	.852	121	15	52	7.46	-8	C-82	14	1.1
1929 StL-A	94	249	43	59	10	5	5	36	74	22	1	4	.237	.424	.378	.802	104	6	46	6.15	-4	C-85	11	0.7
1930 Phi-A	45	92	16	16	4	1	1	9	17	15	0	0	.174	.309	.272	.581	47	-7	9	2.98	0	C-36	2	-0.5
1931 Det-A	30	76	9	14	2	0	0	2	14	11	1	0	.184	.311	.211	.522	38	-6	6	2.57	1	C-30	1	-0.3
Total 19	1842	5307	769	1506	264	90	59	710	849	573	121	49	.284	.393	.401	.794	118	171	898	5.90	-20	*C-1435,O-167/3-60,S-1	245	24.6

• SCHAREIN, Art Arthur Otto "Scoop" Scharein b: 6/30/1905, Decatur, IL d: 7/2/1969, San Antonio, TX BR/TR, 5'11", 155 lbs. Deb: 7/6/1932

YEAR TM-L	G	AB	R	H	2B	3B	HR	RBI	BB	SO	SB	CS	AVG	OBP	SLG	OPS	OPS+	BR/A	RC	RC/G	FR	G/POS	WS	TPW
1932 StL-A	81	303	43	92	19	2	0	42	25	10	4	8	.304	.363	.380	.742	87	-7	41	4.82	15	3-77/S-3,2-2	8	1.0
1933 StL-A	123	471	49	96	13	3	0	26	41	21	7	9	.204	.269	.244	.513	35	-46	32	2.15	14	3-95,S-24/2-7	5	-2.6
1934 StL-A	1	2	0	1	0	0	0	2	0	0	0	0	.500	.500	.500	1.000	146	0	0	12.72	0		0	0.0
Total 3	205	776	92	189	32	5	0	70	66	31	11	17	.244	.306	.298	.604	55	-54	73	3.13	28	3-172/S-27,2-9	13	-1.7

• SCHAREIN, George George Albert "Tom" Scharein b: 11/21/1914, Decatur, IL d: 12/23/1981, Decatur, IL BR/TR, 6'1", 174 lbs. Deb: 4/19/1937

YEAR TM-L	G	AB	R	H	2B	3B	HR	RBI	BB	SO	SB	CS	AVG	OBP	SLG	OPS	OPS+	BR/A	RC	RC/G	FR	G/POS	WS	TPW
1937 Phi-N	146	511	44	123	20	1	0	57	36	47	13	....	.241	.293	.284	.577	53	-33	44	2.90	-3	*S-146	6	-2.5
1938 Phi-N	117	390	47	93	16	4	1	29	16	33	11	....	.238	.268	.308	.576	58	-23	32	2.76	-11	S-77,2-39/3-1	4	-2.7
1939 Phi-N	118	399	35	95	17	1	1	33	13	40	4	....	.238	.262	.293	.555	51	-28	31	2.55	-8	*S-117	3	-2.8
1940 Phi-N	7	17	0	5	0	0	0	0	0	3	0	....	.294	.294	.294	.588	65	-1	1	3.31	-3	/S-7	0	-0.3
Total 4	388	1317	126	316	53	6	2	119	65	123	28	....	.240	.277	.294	.571	54	-86	108	2.76	-25	S-347/2-39,3-1	13	-8.4

• SCHARF, Nick Edward T. Scharf b: 7/1858, Baltimore, MD d: 3/12/1937, Baltimore, MD TR Deb: 5/18/1882

YEAR TM-L	G	AB	R	H	2B	3B	HR	RBI	BB	SO	SB	CS	AVG	OBP	SLG	OPS	OPS+	BR/A	RC	RC/G	FR	G/POS	WS	TPW
1882 Bal-a	10	39	4	8	1	1	1	....	0	....	....	....	.205	.205	.359	.564	94	-0	3	2.66	-2	/O-9(1-7-1),3-1	1	-0.2
1883 Bal-a	3	13	1	2	1	0	0	0	1	....	....	....	.154	.214	.231	.445	42	-1	1	1.68	-2	/S-3	0	-0.2
Total 2	13	52	5	10	2	1	1	0	1	....	....	....	.192	.208	.327	.534	80	-1	4	2.40	-4	/O-9,S-3,3-1	1	-0.5

• SCHEER, Al Allan G. Scheer b: 10/21/1888, Dayton, OH d: 5/6/1959, Logansport, IN BL/TR, 5'9", 165 lbs. Deb: 8/2/1913 Career OF: 201-2-60

YEAR TM-L	G	AB	R	H	2B	3B	HR	RBI	BB	SO	SB	CS	AVG	OBP	SLG	OPS	OPS+	BR/A	RC	RC/G	FR	G/POS	WS	TPW
1913 Bro-N	6	22	3	5	0	0	0	0	2	4	1	....	.227	.292	.227	.519	48	-1	2	2.40	0	/O-6(0-0-6)	0	-0.2
1914 Ind-F	120	363	63	111	23	6	3	45	49	39	9	....	.306	.396	.427	.823	121	12	63	6.17	-2	*O-102(46-2-54)/2-4,S-1	14	0.5
1915 New-F	155	546	75	146	25	14	2	60	65	38	31	....	.267	.353	.375	.728	121	16	80	5.01	-3	*O-155(155-0-0)	20	0.6
Total 3	281	931	141	262	48	20	5	105	116	81	41	....	.281	.368	.392	.760	119	26	144	5.38	-6	O-263/2-4,S-1	34	1.0

• SCHEER, Heinie Henry William Scheer b: 7/31/1900, New York, NY d: 3/21/1976, New Haven, CT BR/TR, 5'8", 146 lbs. Deb: 4/20/1922

YEAR TM-L	G	AB	R	H	2B	3B	HR	RBI	BB	SO	SB	CS	AVG	OBP	SLG	OPS	OPS+	BR/A	RC	RC/G	FR	G/POS	WS	TPW
1922 Phi-A	51	135	10	23	3	0	4	12	3	25	1	0	.170	.188	.281	.470	20	-16	7	1.64	1	2-30,3-10	1	-1.3
1923 Phi-A	69	210	26	50	8	1	2	21	17	41	3	4	.238	.301	.314	.616	61	-13	21	3.02	-1	2-61	3	-1.2
Total 2	120	345	36	73	11	1	6	33	20	66	4	4	.212	.259	.301	.560	46	-29	28	2.47	0	/2-91,3-10	4	-2.5

• SCHEEREN, Fritz Frederick "Dutch" Scheeren b: 9/8/1891, Kokomo, IN d: 6/17/1973, Oil City, PA BR/TR, 6', 180 lbs. Deb: 9/14/1914 Career OF: 0-5-7

YEAR TM-L	G	AB	R	H	2B	3B	HR	RBI	BB	SO	SB	CS	AVG	OBP	SLG	OPS	OPS+	BR/A	RC	RC/G	FR	G/POS	WS	TPW
1914 Pit-N	11	31	4	9	0	1	1	2	1	6	1	....	.290	.313	.452	.764	132	1	4	5.14	-2	O-10(0-4-7)	1	-0.2
1915 Pit-N	4	3	0	0	0	0	0	0	0	0	0	....	.000	.000	.000	.000	-101	-1	0	.00	0	/O-1	0	-0.1
Total 2	15	34	4	9	0	1	1	2	1	6	1	....	.265	.286	.412	.697	112	0	4	4.53	-2	/O-11	1	-0.3

• SCHEFFING, Bob Robert Boden Scheffing b: 8/11/1913, Overland, MO d: 10/26/1985, Phoenix, AZ BR/TR, 6'2", 189 lbs. Deb: 4/27/1941 M/C

YEAR TM-L	G	AB	R	H	2B	3B	HR	RBI	BB	SO	SB	CS	AVG	OBP	SLG	OPS	OPS+	BR/A	RC	RC/G	FR	G/POS	WS	TPW
1941 Chi-N	51	132	9	32	8	0	1	20	5	19	2	....	.242	.270	.326	.596	70	-6	10	2.65	-2	C-34	1	-0.6
1942 Chi-N	44	102	7	20	3	0	2	12	7	11	2	....	.196	.248	.284	.532	58	-6	7	2.16	1	C-32	2	-0.3
1946 Chi-N	63	115	8	32	4	1	0	18	12	18	0	....	.278	.346	.330	.677	94	-1	13	3.99	-1	C-40	4	0.0
1947 Chi-N	110	363	33	96	11	5	5	50	25	25	2	....	.264	.312	.364	.675	82	-10	39	3.73	1	C-97	8	-0.4
1948 Chi-N	102	293	23	88	18	2	5	45	22	27	0	....	.300	.351	.427	.778	114	5	44	5.55	0	C-78	10	0.8
1949 Chi-N	55	149	12	40	6	1	3	19	9	9	0	....	.268	.314	.383	.697	88	-3	16	3.68	0	C-40	3	-0.1
1950 Chi-N	12	16	0	3	1	0	0	1	0	2	0	....	.188	.188	.250	.438	14	-2	1	1.56	0	/C-3	0	-0.2
Cin-N	21	47	4	13	0	0	2	6	4	2	0	....	.277	.333	.404	.738	93	-1	5	3.63	-1	C-11	1	-0.1
Yr.	33	63	4	16	1	0	2	7	4	4	0	....	.254	.299	.365	.664	74	-3	6	3.10	-1	C-14	1	-0.3
1951 Cin-N	47	122	9	31	2	0	2	14	16	9	0	0	.254	.345	.320	.665	79	-3	15	4.27	-3	C-41	3	-0.4
StL-N	12	18	0	2	0	0	0	2	3	5	0	0	.111	.238	.111	.349	-3	-3	1	.91	0	C-11	0	-0.2
Yr.	59	140	9	33	2	0	2	16	19	14	0	0	.236	.331	.293	.624	68	-6	15	3.72	-4	C-52	3	-0.7
Total 8	517	1357	105	357	53	9	20	187	103	127	6	0	.263	.316	.360	.676	86	-29	150	3.84	-5	C-387	32	-1.6

• SCHEFFLER, Ted Theodore J. Scheffler b: 4/5/1864, New York, NY d: 2/24/1949, Jamaica, NY BR/TR, 5'10", 160 lbs. Deb: 8/7/1888 Career OF: 6-23-117

YEAR TM-L	G	AB	R	H	2B	3B	HR	RBI	BB	SO	SB	CS	AVG	OBP	SLG	OPS	OPS+	BR/A	RC	RC/G	FR	G/POS	WS	TPW
1888 Det-N	27	94	17	19	3	1	0	4	9	9	4	....	.202	.286	.255	.541	73	-2	8	2.95	-5	O-27(4-23-0)	1	-0.8
1890 Roc-a	119	445	111	109	12	6	3	34	78	....	77	....	.245	.374	.319	.693	113	14	84	6.63	8	*O-119(2-0-117)/C-1	16	1.7
Total 2	146	539	128	128	15	7	3	38	87	9	81	....	.237	.360	.308	.668	106	12	92	5.96	3	O-146/C-1	17	1.0

• SCHEIBECK, Frank Frank S. Scheibeck b: 6/28/1865, Detroit, MI d: 10/22/1956, Detroit, MI BR/TR, 5'7", 145 lbs. Deb: 5/9/1887

YEAR TM-L	G	AB	R	H	2B	3B	HR	RBI	BB	SO	SB	CS	AVG	OBP	SLG	OPS	OPS+	BR/A	RC	RC/G	FR	G/POS	WS	TPW
1887 Cle-a	3	11	2	4	0	0	0	0	2	....	0	....	.364	.364	.222	.586	67	-0	1	2.88	-2	/3-1,P-1,S-1	0	-0.7
1888 Det-N	1	4	0	0	0	0	0	0	0	0	0	....	.000	.000	.000	.000	-100	-1	0	.00	-1	/S-1	0	-0.2
1890 Tol-a	134	485	72	117	13	5	1	49	76	....	57	....	.241	.350	.295	.645	88	-5	72	5.16	4	*S-134	14	0.3
1894 Pit-N	28	102	20	36	2	3	1	10	11	9	7	....	.353	.416	.461	.877	112	2	23	9.07	-3	S-11/O-9(8-1-0),3-3,2-2	3	-0.1
Was-N	52	196	49	45	2	4	0	17	45	24	11	....	.230	.384	.281	.664	64	-8	26	4.47	7	S-52	4	0.1
Yr.	80	298	69	81	4	7	1	27	56	33	18	....	.272	.394	.342	.736	80	-6	49	5.87	4	S-63/O-9(8-1-0),3-3,2-2	7	0.0
1895 Was-N	49	172	18	31	5	2	0	25	17	23	5	....	.180	.258	.233	.490	27	-19	12	2.31	-5	S-44/2-2,3-2	1	-1.8
1899 Was-N	27	94	19	27	4	1	0	9	11	....	5	....	.287	.368	.351	.719	99	0	15	5.58	-2	S-27	3	0.0
1901 Cle-A	93	329	33	70	11	3	0	38	18	....	3	....	.213	.258	.264	.522	47	-23	25	2.46	-13	S-92	2	-3.0
1906 Det-A	3	10	1	1	0	0	0	0	2	....	0	....	.100	.250	.100	.350	11	-1	0	1.09	0	/2-3	0	-0.1
Total 8	390	1403	214	331	37	18	2	148	182	56	88	....	.236	.328	.291	.620	69	-55	174	4.21	-15	S-362/O-9,2-7,3-6,P-1	27	-5.5

• SCHEINBLUM, Richie Richard Alan Scheinblum b: 11/5/1942, New York, NY BB/TR, 6'1", 180 lbs. Deb: 9/1/1965 Career OF: 60-3-241

YEAR TM-L	G	AB	R	H	2B	3B	HR	RBI	BB	SO	SB	CS	AVG	OBP	SLG	OPS	OPS+	BR/A	RC	RC/G	FR	G/POS	WS	TPW
1965 Cle-A	4	1	1	0	0	0	0	0	0	0	0	0	.000	.000	.000	.000	-99	-0	0	.00	0	....	0	0.0
1967 Cle-A	18	66	8	21	4	2	0	6	5	10	0	2	.318	.366	.439	.806	136	2	10	5.63	-1	O-18(0-0-18)	3	0.0
1968 Cle-A	19	55	3	12	5	0	0	5	5	8	0	0	.218	.295	.309	.604	84	-1	5	2.83	0	O-16(6-0-11)	1	-0.3
1969 Cle-A	102	199	13	37	5	1	1	13	19	30	0	2	.186	.257	.236	.493	37	-18	11	1.72	0	O-50(32-3-15)	1	-2.1
1971 Was-A	27	49	5	7	3	0	0	4	8	5	0	0	.143	.263	.204	.467	36	-4	3	1.69	3	O-13(7-0-6)	0	-0.2
1972 KC-A★	134	450	60	135	21	4	8	66	58	40	0	1	.300	.385	.418	.803	139	24	71	5.59	-2	*O-119(2-0-119)	18	1.8
1973 Cin-N	29	54	5	12	2	0	1	8	10	4	0	0	.222	.344	.315	.659	88	-0	6	3.94	1	O-19(1-0-18)	2	-0.1
Cal-A	77	229	28	75	10	2	3	21	35	27	0	0	.328	.419	.428	.847	151	17	42	6.97	0	O-54(6-0-49)/D-7	12	1.4
1974 Cal-A	10	26	1	4	0	0	0	2	1	2	0	0	.154	.185	.154	.339	-2	-3	0	.53	0	/O-8(4-0-5),D-1	0	-0.4
KC-A	36	83	7	15	2	0	0	2	8	8	0	1	.181	.253	.205	.458	31	-8	4	1.40	0	D-17/O-2(2-0-0)	0	-0.9
Yr.	46	109	8	19	2	0	0	4	9	10	0	1	.174	.237	.193	.430	24	-11	4	1.18	-1	D-18,O-10(6-0-5)	0	-1.3
StL-N	6	6	0	2	0	0	0	0	0	1	0	0	.333	.333	.333	.667	88	-0	1	4.50	0	....	0	0.0
Total 8	462	1218	131	320	52	9	13	127	149	135	0	6	.263	.346	.352	.698	106	9	153	4.28	-1	O-299/D-25	37	-0.7

• SCHELL, Danny Clyde Daniel Schell b: 12/26/1927, Fostoria, MI d: 5/11/1972, Mayville, MI BR/TR, 6'1", 195 lbs. Deb: 4/13/1954

YEAR TM-L	G	AB	R	H	2B	3B	HR	RBI	BB	SO	SB	CS	AVG	OBP	SLG	OPS	OPS+	BR/A	RC	RC/G	FR	G/POS	WS	TPW
1954 Phi-N	92	272	25	77	14	3	7	33	17	31	0	3	.283	.330	.434	.764	97	-3	34	4.31	-2	O-69(60-3-6)	5	-0.9
1955 Phi-N	2	2	0	0	0	0	0	0	0	1	0	0	.000	.000	.000	.000	-102	-1	0	.00	0	....	0	-0.1
Total 2	94	274	25	77	14	3	7	33	17	32	0	3	.281	.328	.431	.758	96	-4	34	4.27	-2	/O-69	5	-1.0

• SCHELLHASE, Al Albert Herman "Schelley" Schellhase b: 9/13/1864, Evansville, IN d: 1/3/1919, Evansville, IN BR/TR, 5'8", 148 lbs. Deb: 5/7/1890

YEAR TM-L	G	AB	R	H	2B	3B	HR	RBI	BB	SO	SB	CS	AVG	OBP	SLG	OPS	OPS+	BR/A	RC	RC/G	FR	G/POS	WS	TPW
1890 Bos-N	9	29	1	4	0	0	0	1	1	10	0	....	.138	.167	.138	.305	-10	-4	1	.72	-1	/O-5(0-0-5),C-2,3-1,S-1	0	-0.4

YEAR TM-L	G	AB	R	H	2B	3B	HR	RBI	BB	SO	SB	CS	AVG	OBP	SLG	OPS	OPS+	BR/A	RC	RC/G	FR	G/POS	WS	TPW
1891 Lou-a	6	16	3	2	0	0	0	0	1	1	2	....	.125	.176	.125	.301	-14	-2	1	1.37	1	/C-7	0	-0.1
Total 2	**15**	**45**	**4**	**6**	**0**	**0**	**0**	**1**	**2**	**11**	**2**	**....**	**.133**	**.170**	**.133**	**.304**	**-11**	**-7**	**1**	**.96**	**0**	**/C-9,0-5,3-1,S-1**	**0**	**-0.5**
• SCHEMER, Mike	Michael "Lefty" Schemer b: 11/20/1917, Baltimore, MD d: 4/22/1983, Miami, FL BL/TL, 6', 180 lbs. Deb: 8/8/1945																							
1945 NY-N	31	108	10	36	3	1	1	10	6	1	2	....	.333	.368	.407	.776	114	2	14	4.98	3	1-27	3	0.4
1946 NY-N	1	1	0	0	0	0	0	0	0	0	0	....	.000	.000	.000	.000	-99	-0	0	.00	0	....	0	0.0
Total 2	**32**	**109**	**10**	**36**	**3**	**1**	**1**	**10**	**6**	**1**	**2**	**....**	**.330**	**.365**	**.404**	**.769**	**112**	**2**	**14**	**4.92**	**3**	**/1-27**	**3**	**0.3**
• SCHENCK, Bill	William G. Schenck b: 7/1854, Brooklyn, NY d: 1/29/1934, Brooklyn, NY, 5'7", 171 lbs. Deb: 5/29/1882																							
1882 Lou-a	60	231	37	60	11	3	0	....	8	....	....	....	.260	.285	.333	.618	114	4	22	3.68	-7	*3-58/P-2,S-2	8	0.0
1884 Ric-a	42	151	14	31	4	0	3	0	1	....	....	....	.205	.216	.291	.507	65	-6	10	2.23	-8	S-40/2-2	1	-1.1
1885 Bro-a	1	4	0	0	0	0	0	0	0	....	....	....	.000	.000	.000	.000	-99	-1	0	.00	-0	/3-1	0	-0.1
Total 3	**103**	**386**	**51**	**91**	**15**	**3**	**3**	**0**	**9**	**....**	**....**	**....**	**.236**	**.255**	**.313**	**.569**	**93**	**-3**	**32**	**3.04**	**-15**	**/3-59,S-42,2-2,P-2**	**9**	**-1.2**
• SCHENZ, Hank	Henry Leonard Schenz b: 4/11/1919, New Richmond, OH d: 5/12/1988, Cincinnati, OH BR/TR, 5'9.5", 175 lbs. Deb: 9/18/1946																							
1946 Chi-N	6	11	0	2	0	0	0	1	0	0	1	....	.182	.182	.182	.364	3	-1	0	1.09	0	/3-5	0	-0.1
1947 Chi-N	7	14	2	1	0	0	0	0	2	1	0	....	.071	.235	.071	.307	-16	-2	1	.99	0	/3-5	0	-0.2
1948 Chi-N	96	337	43	88	17	1	1	14	18	15	3	....	.261	.306	.326	.633	74	-13	34	3.53	-9	2-78/3-5	5	-1.8
1949 Chi-N	7	14	2	6	0	0	0	1	1	0	2	....	.429	.467	.429	.895	145	1	3	9.86	1	/3-5	1	0.2
1950 Pit-N	58	101	17	23	4	2	1	5	6	7	0	....	.228	.271	.337	.608	57	-7	8	2.74	2	2-21,3-12/S-4	1	-0.4
1951 Pit-N	25	61	5	13	1	0	0	3	0	2	0	2	.213	.226	.230	.455	22	-8	3	1.53	-1	2-19/3-2	0	-0.8
*NY-N	8	0	1	0	0	0	0	0	0	0	0	0	....	....	....	....	-99	0	0	....	0	....	0	0.0
Yr.	33	61	6	13	1	0	0	3	0	2	0	2	.213	.226	.230	.455	22	-8	3	1.53	-1	2-19/3-2	0	-0.8
Total 6	**207**	**538**	**70**	**133**	**22**	**3**	**2**	**24**	**27**	**25**	**6**	**2**	**.247**	**.291**	**.310**	**.601**	**63**	**-30**	**49**	**3.12**	**-8**	**2-118/3-34,S-4**	**7**	**-3.2**
• SCHEPNER, Joe	Joseph Maurice "Gentleman Joe" Schepner b: 8/10/1895, Aliquippa, PA d: 7/25/1959, Mobile, AL BR/TR, 5'10", 160 lbs. Deb: 9/11/1919																							
1919 StL-A	14	48	2	10	4	0	0	6	1	5	0	....	.208	.224	.292	.516	43	-4	3	1.99	0	3-13	0	-0.3
• SCHERBARTH, Bob	Robert Elmer Scherbarth b: 1/18/1926, Milwaukee, WI BR/TR, 6', 180 lbs. Deb: 4/23/1950																							
1950 Bos-A	1	0	0	0	0	0	0	0	0	0	0	0	....	....	....	....	-91	0	0	....	0	/C-1	0	0.0
• SCHERER, Harry	Harry Scherer b: Baltimore, MD Deb: 7/24/1889																							
1889 Lou-a	1	3	0	1	0	0	0	0	0	0	0	....	.333	.333	.333	.667	92	-0	0	4.53	-1	/O-1	0	-0.1
• SCHIAPPACASSE, Lou	Louis Joseph Schiappacasse b: 3/29/1881, Ann Arbor, MI d: 9/20/1910, Ann Arbor, MI BR/TR Deb: 9/7/1902																							
1902 Det-A	2	5	0	0	0	0	0	1	1	....	0	....	.000	.167	.000	.167	-50	-1	0	.00	-1	/O-2(0-0-2)	0	-0.1
• SCHICK, Morrie	Maurice Francis Schick b: 4/17/1892, Chicago, IL d: 10/25/1979, Hazel Crest, IL BR/TR, 5'11", 170 lbs. Deb: 4/15/1917																							
1917 Chi-N	14	34	3	5	0	0	0	3	3	10	0	....	.147	.216	.147	.363	11	-3	1	1.05	1	O-12(2-10-0)	0	-0.3
• SCHILLING, Chuck	Charles Thomas Schilling b: 10/25/1937, Brooklyn, NY BR/TR, 5'10", 170 lbs. Deb: 4/11/1961																							
1961 Bos-A	158	646	87	167	25	2	5	62	78	77	7	6	.259	.340	.327	.667	77	-20	76	4.08	9	*2-158	19	0.3
1962 Bos-A	119	413	48	95	17	1	7	35	29	48	1	0	.230	.287	.327	.614	63	-22	38	2.99	-4	*2-118	6	-1.6
1963 Bos-A	146	576	63	135	25	0	8	33	41	72	3	2	.234	.291	.319	.610	69	-24	54	3.15	-5	*2-143	9	-1.8
1964 Bos-A	47	163	18	32	6	0	0	7	15	22	0	1	.196	.264	.233	.497	38	-14	11	2.08	-3	2-42	1	-1.4
1965 Bos-A	71	171	14	41	3	2	3	9	13	17	0	1	.240	.293	.333	.627	73	-7	15	2.82	0	2-41	1	-0.4
Total 5	**541**	**1969**	**230**	**470**	**76**	**5**	**23**	**146**	**176**	**236**	**11**	**10**	**.239**	**.305**	**.317**	**.622**	**68**	**-87**	**193**	**3.29**	**-4**	**2-502**	**36**	**-4.8**
• SCHINDLER, Bill	Williams Gibbons Schindler b: 7/10/1896, Perryville, MO d: 2/6/1979, Perryville, MO BR/TR, 5'11", 160 lbs. Deb: 9/3/1920																							
1920 StL-N	1	2	0	0	0	0	0	0	0	1	0	0	.000	.000	.000	.000	-102	-1	0	.00	0	/C-1	0	-0.1
• SCHIRICK, Dutch	Harry Ernest Schirick b: 6/15/1890, Ruby, NY d: 11/12/1968, Kingston, NY BR/TR, 5'8", 160 lbs. Deb: 9/17/1914																							
1914 StL-A	1	0	0	0	0	0	0	0	1	0	2	....	....	1.000	....	1.000	211	0	2	∞	0	....	0	0.0
• SCHLAFLY, Larry	Harry Linton Schlafly b: 9/20/1878, Port Washington, OH d: 6/27/1919, Canton, OH BR/TR, 5'11", 182 lbs. Deb: 9/18/1902 M Career OF: 1-0-5																							
1902 Chi-N	10	31	5	10	0	3	0	5	6	....	2	....	.323	.432	.516	.949	198	4	8	10.07	-3	/O-5(0-0-5),2-4,3-2	2	0.1
1906 Was-A	123	426	60	105	13	8	2	30	50	....	29	....	.246	.345	.329	.674	117	11	62	4.84	11	*2-123	19	2.6
1907 Was-A	24	74	10	10	0	0	1	4	22	....	7	....	.135	.354	.176	.529	75	0	8	3.11	-7	2-24	2	-0.7
1914 Buf-F	51	127	16	33	7	1	2	19	12	22	3	....	.260	.338	.378	.716	99	-0	16	4.39	2	2-23/1-7,3-1,C-1,O-1	4	0.2
Total 4	**208**	**658**	**91**	**158**	**20**	**12**	**5**	**58**	**90**	**22**	**41**	**....**	**.240**	**.349**	**.330**	**.679**	**112**	**16**	**95**	**4.75**	**3**	**2-174/1-7,O-6,3-3,C-1**	**27**	**2.2**
• SCHLEI, Admiral	George Henry Schlei b: 1/12/1878, Cincinnati, OH d: 1/24/1958, Huntington, WV BR/TR, 5'8.5", 179 lbs. Deb: 4/24/1904																							
1904 Cin-N	97	291	25	69	8	3	0	32	17	....	7	....	.237	.297	.285	.583	74	-9	28	3.22	2	C-88	9	0.2
1905 Cin-N	99	314	32	71	8	3	1	36	22	....	9	....	.226	.285	.280	.566	62	-15	30	3.04	7	C-89/1-6	7	0.1
1906 Cin-N	116	388	44	95	13	8	4	54	29	....	7	....	.245	.304	.351	.655	100	-1	46	3.93	6	C-91,1-21	11	1.5
1907 Cin-N	84	246	28	67	3	2	0	27	28	....	5	....	.272	.347	.301	.648	99	1	29	4.07	4	C-67/1-3,O-2(1-0-1)	9	1.3
1908 Cin-N	92	300	31	66	6	4	1	22	22	....	2	....	.220	.278	.277	.554	79	-7	24	2.54	-4	C-88	7	-0.3
1909 NY-N	92	279	25	68	12	0	0	30	40	....	4	....	.244	.343	.287	.629	94	-0	30	3.48	-3	C-89	10	0.7
1910 NY-N	55	99	10	19	2	1	0	8	14	10	4	....	.192	.304	.232	.537	57	-5	9	2.65	1	C-49	2	-0.1
1911 NY-N	1	1	0	0	0	0	0	0	0	1	0	....	.000	.000	.000	.000	-98	-0	0	.00	0	....	0	0.0
Total 8	**636**	**1918**	**195**	**455**	**52**	**21**	**6**	**209**	**172**	**11**	**38**	**....**	**.237**	**.307**	**.296**	**.603**	**83**	**-37**	**195**	**3.33**	**12**	**C-561/1-30,O-2**	**55**	**3.4**
• SCHLESINGER, Rudy	William Cordes Schlesinger b: 11/5/1941, Cincinnati, OH BR/TR, 6'2", 175 lbs. Deb: 5/4/1965																							
1965 Bos-A	1	1	0	0	0	0	0	0	0	0	0	0	.000	.000	.000	.000	-94	-0	0	.00	0	....	0	0.0
• SCHLIEBNER, Dutch	Frederick Paul Schliebner b: 5/19/1891, Charlottenburg, Germany d: 4/15/1975, Toledo, OH BR/TR, 5'10", 180 lbs. Deb: 4/17/1923																							
1923 Bro-N	19	76	11	19	4	0	0	4	5	7	1	0	.250	.296	.303	.599	60	-4	7	3.19	2	1-19	1	-0.3
StL-A	127	444	50	122	19	6	4	52	39	60	3	2	.275	.339	.372	.710	82	-11	58	4.52	-4	*1-127	8	-2.3
• SCHLUETER, Jay	Jay D Schlueter b: 7/31/1949, Phoenix, AZ BR/TR, 6', 182 lbs. Deb: 6/18/1971																							
1971 Hou-N	7	3	1	1	0	0	0	0	0	1	0	0	.333	.333	.333	.667	92	-0	0	4.50	-0	/O-2(2-0-0)	0	0.0
• SCHLUETER, Norm	Norman John "Duke" Schlueter b: 9/25/1916, Belleville, IL BR/TR, 5'10", 175 lbs. Deb: 5/28/1938																							
1938 Chi-A	35	118	11	27	5	1	0	7	4	15	1	0	.229	.254	.288	.542	35	-12	9	2.53	-2	C-34	1	-1.1
1939 Chi-A	34	56	5	13	2	1	0	8	1	11	2	0	.232	.246	.304	.549	39	-5	3	1.79	-2	C-32	1	-0.5
1944 Cle-A	49	122	2	15	4	0	0	11	12	22	0	2	.123	.201	.156	.357	3	-16	4	.90	-1	C-43	1	-1.6
Total 3	**118**	**296**	**18**	**55**	**11**	**2**	**0**	**26**	**17**	**48**	**3**	**2**	**.186**	**.230**	**.236**	**.467**	**22**	**-33**	**16**	**1.66**	**-5**	**C-109**	**3**	**-3.2**
• SCHMANDT, Ray	Raymond Henry Schmandt b: 1/25/1896, St. Louis, MO d: 2/2/1969, St. Louis, MO BR/TR, 6'1", 175 lbs. Deb: 6/24/1915																							
1915 StL-A	3	4	0	0	0	0	0	0	0	1	0	....	.000	.000	.000	.000	-104	-1	0	.00	0	/1-1	0	-0.1
1918 Bro-N	34	114	11	35	5	4	0	18	7	7	1	....	.307	.347	.421	.768	134	4	16	5.26	-2	2-34	5	0.3
1919 Bro-N	47	127	8	21	4	0	0	10	4	13	0	....	.165	.191	.197	.388	16	-13	4	1.05	-5	2-18,1-12/3-6	1	-2.0
1920*Bro-N	28	63	7	15	2	1	0	7	3	4	1	1	.238	.273	.302	.574	63	-3	5	2.60	2	1-20	1	-0.1
1921 Bro-N	95	350	42	107	8	5	1	43	11	22	3	4	.306	.329	.366	.694	81	-10	41	4.16	-1	1-92	7	-1.7
1922 Bro-N	110	396	54	106	17	3	2	44	21	28	6	6	.268	.306	.341	.647	67	-20	41	3.52	0	*1-110	6	-2.6
Total 6	**317**	**1054**	**122**	**284**	**36**	**13**	**3**	**122**	**46**	**75**	**11**	**11**	**.269**	**.301**	**.337**	**.638**	**72**	**-42**	**108**	**3.50**	**-7**	**1-235/2-52,3-6**	**20**	**-6.2**
• SCHMEES, George	George Edward "Rocky" Schmees b: 9/6/1924, Cincinnati, OH d: 10/30/1998, San Jose, CA BL/TL, 6', 190 lbs. Deb: 4/15/1952																							
1952 StL-A	34	61	9	8	1	1	0	3	2	18	0	0	.131	.159	.180	.339	-6	-9	2	.95	-1	O-19(9-2-8)/1-2	0	-1.1
Bos-A	42	64	8	13	3	0	0	3	10	11	0	1	.203	.311	.250	.561	53	-4	5	2.73	1	O-29(0-18-11)/1-2,P-2	1	-0.4
Yr.	76	125	17	21	4	1	0	6	12	29	0	1	.168	.241	.216	.457	26	-13	7	1.85	-1	O-48(9-20-19)/1-4,P-2	1	-1.5

YEAR TM-L	G	AB	R	H	2B	3B	HR	RBI	BB	SO	SB	CS	AVG	OBP	SLG	OPS	OPS+	BR/A	RC	RC/G	FR	G/POS	WS	TPW
• SCHMIDT, Bob	Robert Benjamin Schmidt b: 4/22/1933, St. Louis, MO BR/TR, 6'2", 205 lbs. Deb: 4/16/1958																							
1958 SF-N★	127	393	46	96	20	2	14	54	33	59	0	1	.244	.308	.412	.720	90	-7	44	3.75	1	*C-123	10	0.0
1959 SF-N	71	181	17	44	7	1	5	20	13	24	0	2	.243	.297	.376	.673	80	-6	19	3.54	3	C-70	5	-0.1
1960 SF-N	110	344	31	92	12	1	8	37	26	51	0	3	.267	.319	.378	.697	96	-4	39	3.98	-5	*C-108	8	-0.4
1961 SF-N	2	6	0	1	0	0	0	1	0	1	0	0	.167	.167	.167	.333	-12	-1	0	.98	1	/C-2	0	0.0
Cin-N	27	70	4	9	0	0	1	4	8	14	0	0	.129	.218	.171	.389	5	-10	2	.88	0	C-27	1	-0.9
Yr.	29	76	4	10	0	0	1	5	8	15	0	0	.132	.214	.171	.385	4	-11	2	.89	1	C-29	1	-0.9
1962 Was-A	88	256	28	62	14	0	10	31	14	37	0	0	.242	.284	.414	.698	86	-6	30	4.04	2	C-88	6	-0.1
1963 Was-A	9	15	3	3	1	0	0	0	3	5	0	0	.200	.333	.267	.600	71	-0	1	2.76	0	/C-6	0	-0.1
1965 NY-A	20	40	4	10	1	0	1	3	3	8	0	0	.250	.302	.350	.652	85	-1	4	3.79	-1	C-20	1	-0.1
Total 7	454	1305	133	317	55	4	39	150	100	199	0	6	.243	.299	.381	.680	84	-35	141	3.63	1	C-444	31	-1.5
• SCHMIDT, Boss	Charles Schmidt b: 9/12/1880, Coal Hill, AR d: 11/14/1932, Clarksville, AR BB/TR, 5'11", 200 lbs. Deb: 4/30/1906 U Career OF: 0-0-2																							
1906 Det-A	68	216	13	47	4	3	0	10	6	....	1	....	.218	.242	.264	.506	57	-11	15	2.28	8	C-67	5	0.3
1907*Det-A	104	349	32	85	6	6	0	23	5	....	8	....	.244	.269	.295	.564	77	-10	32	3.07	1	*C-103	9	0.1
1908*Det-A	122	419	45	111	14	3	1	38	16	....	5	....	.265	.297	.320	.617	96	-3	41	3.32	5	*C-121	15	1.6
1909*Det-A	84	253	21	53	8	2	1	28	7	....	7	....	.209	.240	.269	.508	58	-13	19	2.22	-6	C-81/O-1	4	-1.2
1910 Det-A	71	197	22	51	7	7	1	23	2	....	2	....	.259	.277	.381	.658	99	-2	21	3.58	0	C-66	6	0.4
1911 Det-A	28	46	4	13	2	1	0	2	0	....	0	....	.283	.298	.370	.667	82	-1	5	3.82	0	/C-9,O-1	1	-0.1
Total 6	477	1480	137	360	41	22	3	124	36	....	23	....	.243	.270	.307	.577	79	-41	133	2.95	7	C-447/O-2	40	1.1
• SCHMIDT, Butch	Charles John "Butcher Boy" Schmidt b: 7/19/1886, Baltimore, MD d: 9/4/1952, Baltimore, MD BL/TL, 6'1.5", 200 lbs. Deb: 5/11/1909																							
1909 NY-A	1	2	0	0	0	0	0	0	0	....	0	....	.000	.000	.000	.000	-99	-0	0	.00	0	/P-1	0	-0.3
1913 Bos-N	22	78	6	24	2	2	1	14	2	5	1	....	.308	.333	.423	.756	113	1	11	4.99	1	1-22	3	0.2
1914*Bos-N	147	537	67	153	17	9	1	71	43	55	14	....	.285	.350	.356	.706	111	8	71	4.54	-4	*1-147	19	0.0
1915 Bos-N	127	458	46	115	26	7	2	60	36	59	3	10	.251	.318	.352	.670	104	-2	52	3.68	-6	*1-127	12	-1.1
Total 4	297	1075	119	292	45	18	4	145	81	119	18	10	.272	.335	.358	.693	108	7	134	4.18	-10	1-296/P-1	34	-1.2
• SCHMIDT, Dave	David Frederick Schmidt b: 12/22/1956, Mesa, AZ BR/TR, 6'1", 190 lbs. Deb: 4/28/1981																							
1981 Bos-A	15	42	6	10	1	0	2	3	7	17	0	0	.238	.347	.405	.752	109	1	6	5.03	0	C-15	1	0.1
• SCHMIDT, Mike	Michael Jack Schmidt b: 9/27/1949, Dayton, OH BR/TR, 6'2", 203 lbs. Deb: 9/12/1972 HOF: 1995																							
1972 Phi-N	13	34	2	7	0	0	1	3	5	15	0	0	.206	.325	.294	.619	75	-1	4	3.76	2	3-11/2-1	1	0.1
1973 Phi-N	132	367	43	72	11	0	18	52	62	136	8	2	.196	.326	.373	.700	91	-2	48	4.22	6	*3-125/2-4,1-2,S-2	10	0.3
1974 Phi-N★	162	568	108	160	28	7	**36**	116	106	138	23	12	.282	.398	**.546**	.944	156	44	130	8.12	24	*3-162	**39**	7.1
1975 Phi-N	158	562	93	140	34	3	**38**	95	101	180	29	12	.249	.367	.523	.890	139	31	113	6.82	27	*3-151,S-10	28	6.1
1976*Phi-N★	160	584	112	153	31	4	**38**	107	100	149	14	9	.262	.380	.524	.904	150	39	121	7.18	32	*3-160	35	**7.5**
1977*Phi-N★	154	544	114	149	27	11	38	101	104	122	15	8	.274	.399	.574	.972	151	42	129	8.25	22	*3-149/S-2,2-1	**33**	**6.3**
1978*Phi-N	145	513	93	129	27	2	21	78	91	103	19	6	.251	.368	.435	.803	122	20	90	6.03	9	*3-139/S-1	23	2.9
1979 Phi-N★	160	541	109	137	25	4	45	114	**120**	115	9	5	.253	.392	.564	.955	153	42	123	7.70	20	*3-157/S-2	**33**	6.3
1980*Phi-N★	150	548	104	157	25	8	**48**	**121**	89	119	12	5	.286	.388	**.624**	**1.012**	**169**	**51**	137	**8.89**	18	*3-149	**37**	**7.1**
1981*Phi-N★	102	354	**78**	112	19	2	**31**	**91**	**73**	71	12	4	.316	**.439**	**.644**	**1.083**	**195**	**48**	102	**10.66**	21	*3-101	**30**	**7.3**
1982 Phi-N★	148	514	108	144	26	3	35	87	**107**	131	14	7	.280	**.407**	**.547**	**.954**	**161**	46	118	**8.08**	14	*3-148	**37**	**6.1**
1983*Phi-N★	154	534	104	136	16	4	**40**	109	**128**	148	7	8	.255	**.402**	.524	.926	**156**	**44**	117	7.55	15	*3-153/S-2	**35**	5.9
1984 Phi-N★	151	528	93	146	23	3	**36**	**106**	92	116	5	7	.277	.388	.536	**.924**	**155**	38	108	7.10	16	*3-145/1-2,S-1	26	5.5
1985 Phi-N	158	549	89	152	31	5	33	93	87	117	1	3	.277	.379	.532	.911	148	35	113	7.30	1	*1-106,3-54/S-1	26	3.1
1986 Phi-N★	160	552	97	160	29	1	**37**	**119**	89	84	1	2	.290	.395	**.547**	**.942**	**152**	40	122	8.01	4	*3-124,1-35	31	4.3
1987 Phi-N★	147	522	88	153	28	0	35	113	83	80	2	1	.293	.392	.548	.940	141	32	111	7.60	22	*3-138/1-9,S-3	26	5.2
1988 Phi-N	108	390	52	97	21	2	12	62	49	42	3	0	.249	.342	.405	.747	111	7	55	4.75	5	*3-104/1-3	14	1.3
1989 Phi-N★	42	148	19	30	7	0	6	28	21	17	0	1	.203	.302	.372	.673	91	-2	16	3.29	0	3-42	3	-0.2
Total 18	2404	8352	1506	2234	408	59	548	1595	1507	1883	174	92	.267	.384	.527	.912	147	554	1757	7.31	259	*3-2212,1-157/S-24,2-6	467	82.3
• SCHMIDT, Walter	Walter Joseph Schmidt b: 3/20/1887, Coal Hill, AR d: 7/4/1973, Modesto, CA BR/TR, 5'9", 159 lbs. Deb: 4/13/1916																							
1916 Pit-N	64	184	16	35	1	2	2	15	10	13	3	....	.190	.236	.250	.486	49	-11	12	2.07	4	C-57	3	-0.3
1917 Pit-N	72	183	9	45	7	0	0	17	11	11	4	....	.246	.296	.284	.580	76	-5	16	2.94	4	C-61	3	0.4
1918 Pit-N	105	323	31	77	6	3	0	27	17	19	7	....	.238	.281	.276	.556	67	-13	27	2.69	12	*C-104	10	0.9
1919 Pit-N	85	267	23	67	9	2	0	29	23	9	5	....	.251	.310	.300	.610	81	-6	26	3.24	-3	C-85	8	-0.2
1920 Pit-N	94	310	22	86	8	4	0	20	24	15	9	3	.277	.337	.329	.666	89	-2	36	4.07	-5	C-92	11	0.1
1921 Pit-N	114	393	30	111	9	3	0	38	12	13	10	6	.282	.307	.321	.628	65	-19	38	3.41	-2	*C-111	10	-1.4
1922 Pit-N	40	152	21	50	11	1	0	22	1	5	2	1	.329	.333	.414	.748	91	-2	20	5.06	-3	C-40	5	-0.3
1923 Pit-N	97	335	39	83	7	2	0	37	22	12	10	5	.248	.300	.281	.581	53	-22	29	2.96	-1	C-96	6	-1.6
1924 Pit-N	58	177	16	43	3	2	1	20	13	5	6	1	.243	.295	.299	.594	59	-9	17	3.19	-3	C-57	4	-0.8
1925 StL-N	37	87	9	22	2	1	0	9	4	3	1	0	.253	.293	.299	.592	51	-6	8	3.10	2	C-31	2	-0.2
Total 10	766	2411	216	619	63	20	3	234	137	105	57	16	.257	.301	.303	.604	69	-94	231	3.23	6	C-734	62	-3.4
• SCHMULBACH, Hank	Harry Alrives Schmulbach b: 1/17/1925, East St. Louis, IL d: 5/3/2001, Belleville, IL BL/TR, 5'11", 165 lbs. Deb: 9/27/1943																							
1943 StL-A	1	0	1	0	0	0	0	0	0	0	0	0	....	....	....	....	-98	0	0	....	0	....	0	0.0
• SCHNECK, Dave	David Lee Schneck b: 6/18/1949, Allentown, PA BL/TL, 5'10", 200 lbs. Deb: 7/14/1972 Career OF: 24-88-25																							
1972 NY-N	37	123	7	23	3	2	3	10	10	26	0	1	.187	.254	.317	.571	63	-7	10	2.51	-1	O-33(1-17-16)	1	-1.0
1973 NY-N	13	36	2	7	0	1	0	0	1	4	0	0	.194	.216	.250	.466	29	-4	1	1.27	0	O-12(0-12-0)	0	-0.4
1974 NY-N	93	254	23	52	11	1	5	25	16	43	4	1	.205	.255	.315	.570	60	-14	21	2.81	-2	O-84(23-59-9)	3	-2.0
Total 3	143	413	32	82	14	4	8	35	27	73	4	2	.199	.251	.310	.561	58	-25	32	2.57	-3	O-129	4	-3.4
• SCHNEIDER, Brian	Brian Duncan Schneider b: 11/26/1976, Jacksonville, FL BL/TR, 6'1", 200 lbs. Deb: 5/26/2000																							
2000 Mon-N	45	115	6	27	6	0	0	11	7	24	0	1	.235	.279	.287	.566	42	-11	9	2.69	0	C-43	1	-0.8
2001 Mon-N	27	41	4	13	3	0	1	6	6	3	0	0	.317	.404	.463	.868	121	2	8	7.67	2	C-14	2	0.5
2002 Mon-N	73	207	21	57	19	2	5	29	21	41	1	2	.275	.342	.459	.801	105	1	30	4.97	-3	C-65/O-2(1-0-1)	8	0.2
2003 Mon-N	108	335	34	77	26	1	9	46	37	75	0	2	.230	.310	.394	.704	69	-16	38	3.76	10	C-98/D-2	13	0.1
Total 4	253	698	65	174	54	3	15	92	71	143	1	5	.249	.320	.400	.720	79	-25	86	4.14	10	C-220/D-2,O-2	24	-0.1
• SCHOENDIENST, Red	Albert Fred Schoendienst b: 2/2/1923, Germantown, IL BB/TR, 6', 170 lbs. Deb: 4/17/1945 M/C HOF: 1989 Career OF: 119-4-0																							
1945 StL-N	137	565	89	157	22	6	1	47	21	17	**26**	....	.278	.305	.343	.648	78	-19	59	3.78	1	*O-118(118-0-0),S-10/2-1	11	-2.5
1946*StL-N★	142	606	94	170	28	5	0	34	37	27	12	....	.281	.322	.343	.665	85	-13	67	3.97	1	*2-128,3-12/S-4	19	-0.5
1947 StL-N	151	659	91	167	25	9	3	48	48	27	6	....	.253	.304	.332	.636	66	-33	65	3.45	-1	*2-142/3-5,O-1	13	-2.6
1948 StL-N★	119	408	64	111	21	4	4	36	28	16	1	....	.272	.319	.373	.691	82	-11	49	4.31	5	2-96	12	-0.1
1949 StL-N★	151	640	102	190	25	2	3	54	51	18	8	....	.297	.351	.356	.707	86	-12	82	4.71	20	*2-138,S-14/3-6,O-2(0-2-0)	20	1.6
1950 StL-N★	153	642	81	177	**43**	9	7	63	33	32	3	....	.276	.313	.403	.717	83	-18	79	4.28	-2	*2-143,S-10/3-1	18	-1.1
1951 StL-N★	135	553	88	160	32	7	6	54	35	23	0	1	.289	.335	.405	.740	97	-3	75	4.84	5	*2-124/S-8	17	0.9
1952 StL-N★	152	620	91	188	40	7	7	67	42	30	9	6	.303	.347	.424	.772	113	9	89	5.18	16	*2-142,3-11/S-3	25	3.5
1953 StL-N★	146	564	107	193	35	5	15	79	60	23	3	3	.342	.405	.502	.907	135	30	114	7.76	12	*2-140	27	5.1
1954 StL-N★	148	610	98	192	38	8	5	79	54	22	4	2	.315	.371	.428	.799	107	7	96	5.72	16	*2-144	21	3.4
1955 StL-N★	145	553	68	148	21	3	11	51	54	28	7	7	.268	.337	.376	.713	89	-9	70	4.47	-14	*2-142	16	-1.2
1956 StL-N	40	153	22	48	9	0	0	15	13	5	0	1	.314	.367	.373	.740	100	-0	21	5.20	-3	2-36	5	0.0
NY-N	92	334	39	99	12	3	2	14	28	10	1	2	.296	.354	.368	.723	95	-2	42	4.50	-5	2-85	10	-0.1
Yr.	132	487	61	147	21	3	2	29	41	15	1	3	.302	.358	.370	.728	97	-2	63	4.71	-8	*2-121	15	-0.1
1957 NY-N	57	254	35	78	8	4	9	33	10	8	2	1	.307	.338	.476	.815	116	5	40	5.91	-4	2-57	10	0.6
*Mil-N★	93	394	56	122	23	4	6	32	23	7	2	3	.310	.349	.434	.783	117	8	59	5.47	7	2-92/O-2(0-2-0)	16	2.2
Yr.	150	648	91	**200**	31	8	15	65	33	15	4	4	.309	.345	.451	.796	117	13	99	5.64	3	*2-149/O-2(0-2-0)	26	2.8
1958*Mil-N	106	427	47	112	23	1	1	24	31	21	3	1	.262	.314	.328	.642	77	-14	44	3.63	-2	*2-105	11	-0.8

YEAR TM-L	G	AB	R	H	2B	3B	HR	RBI	BB	SO	SB	CS	AVG	OBP	SLG	OPS	OPS+	BR/A	RC	RC/G	FR	G/POS	WS	TPW
1959 Mil-N	5	3	0	0	0	0	0	0	0	0	0	0	.000	.000	.000	.000	-109	-1	0	.00	-2	/2-4	0	-0.3
1960 Mil-N	68	226	21	58	9	1	1	19	17	13	1	0	.257	.311	.319	.630	79	-6	23	3.58	0	2-62	5	-0.3
1961 StL-N	72	120	9	36	9	0	1	12	12	6	1	0	.300	.364	.400	.764	93	-1	18	5.73	-3	2-32	3	-0.2
1962 StL-N	98	143	21	43	4	0	2	12	9	12	0	0	.301	.346	.371	.717	84	-3	17	4.31	2	2-21/3-4	3	0.0
1963 StL-N	6	5	0	0	0	0	0	0	0	1	0	0	.000	.000	.000	.000	-91	-1	0	.00	0	....	0	-0.1
Total 19	2216	8479	1223	2449	427	78	84	773	606	346	89	27	.289	.338	.387	.725	93	-87	1109	4.71	49	*2-1834,0-123/S-49,3-39	262	7.6
• SCHOENECK, Jumbo	Lewis N. Schoeneck b: 3/3/1862, Chicago, IL d: 1/20/1930, Chicago, IL BR/TR, 6'2", 223 lbs. Deb: 4/20/1884																							
1884 CP-U	90	366	56	116	22	2	2	....	8	....	....	....	.317	.332	.404	.736	157	22	50	5.63	11	*1-90	14	2.1
Bal-U	16	60	5	15	2	0	0	....	0	....	....	....	.250	.250	.283	.533	72	-2	4	2.71	1	1-16	1	-0.2
Yr.	106	426	61	131	24	2	2	....	8	....	....	....	.308	.320	.387	.708	146	20	55	5.19	12	*1-106	15	2.0
1888 Ind-N	48	169	15	40	4	0	0	20	9	24	11	....	.237	.283	.260	.544	73	-5	16	3.34	-2	1-48/P-2	3	-0.9
1889 Ind-N	16	62	3	15	2	2	0	8	3	3	1	....	.242	.299	.339	.637	76	-2	7	3.80	1	1-16	1	-0.2
Total 3	170	657	79	186	30	4	2	28	20	27	12	....	.283	.308	.350	.658	120	12	77	4.54	11	1-170/P-2	19	0.8
• SCHOFIELD, Dick	Richard Craig Schofield b: 11/21/1962, Springfield, IL BR/TR, 5'10", 178 lbs. Deb: 9/8/1983																							
1983 Cal-A	21	54	4	11	2	0	3	4	6	8	0	0	.204	.295	.407	.702	92	-1	6	3.69	-1	S-21	1	0.0
1984 Cal-A	140	400	39	77	10	3	4	21	33	79	5	2	.193	.264	.263	.527	47	-28	29	2.31	8	*S-140	8	-0.7
1985 Cal-A	147	438	50	96	19	3	8	41	35	70	11	4	.219	.289	.331	.620	70	-18	43	3.18	10	*S-147	12	0.6
1986*Cal-A	139	458	67	114	17	6	13	57	48	55	23	5	.249	.327	.397	.724	97	1	63	4.54	11	*S-137	18	2.7
1987 Cal-A	134	479	52	120	17	3	9	46	37	63	19	3	.251	.307	.355	.662	77	-13	56	4.01	-8	*S-131/2-2,D-1	13	-0.6
1988 Cal-A	155	527	61	126	11	6	6	34	40	57	20	5	.239	.304	.317	.621	76	-14	55	3.51	10	*S-155	14	0.8
1989 Cal-A	91	302	42	69	11	2	4	26	28	47	9	3	.228	.300	.318	.618	76	-9	31	3.31	-3	S-90	8	-0.5
1990 Cal-A	99	310	41	79	8	1	1	18	52	61	3	4	.255	.365	.297	.662	89	-3	38	4.07	-3	S-99	9	0.2
1991 Cal-A	134	427	44	96	9	3	0	31	50	69	8	4	.225	.310	.260	.570	60	-22	39	3.01	-2	*S-133	8	-1.4
1992 Cal-A	1	3	0	1	0	0	0	0	1	0	0	0	.333	.500	.333	.833	137	0	1	8.51	0	/S-1	0	0.0
NY-N	142	420	52	86	18	2	4	36	60	82	11	4	.205	.311	.286	.597	71	-14	41	3.02	9	*S-141	13	0.7
1993 Tor-A	36	110	11	21	1	2	0	5	16	25	3	0	.191	.294	.236	.530	44	-8	9	2.70	4	S-36	3	-0.1
1994 Tor-A	95	325	38	83	14	1	4	32	34	62	7	7	.255	.333	.342	.675	74	-14	39	4.03	-3	S-95	8	-0.8
1995 LA-N	9	10	0	1	0	0	0	0	1	3	0	0	.100	.182	.100	.282	-25	-2	0	.69	1	/S-3,3-1	0	-0.1
Cal-A	12	20	1	5	0	0	0	2	4	2	0	0	.250	.375	.250	.625	67	-1	2	3.27	1	S-12	1	0.0
1996 Cal-A	13	16	3	4	0	0	0	0	1	1	1	0	.250	.294	.250	.544	40	-1	1	3.16	-2	/S-7,2-2,3-1,D-1	0	-0.2
Total 14	1368	4299	505	989	137	32	56	353	446	684	120	41	.230	.309	.316	.625	73	-144	455	3.46	32	*S-1348/2-4,3-2,D-2	116	0.7
• SCHOFIELD, Dick	John Richard "Ducky" Schofield b: 1/7/1935, Springfield, IL BB/TR, 5'9", 165 lbs. Deb: 7/3/1953 Career OF: 5-0-7																							
1953 StL-N	33	39	9	7	0	0	2	4	2	11	0	0	.179	.220	.333	.553	42	-4	3	2.56	-1	S-15	0	-0.4
1954 StL-N	43	7	17	1	0	1	0	1	0	3	1	1	.143	.143	.429	.571	42	-1	0	.00	-5	S-11	0	-0.5
1955 StL-N	12	4	3	0	0	0	0	0	0	1	0	0	.000	.000	.000	.000	-100	-1	0	.00	-1	/S-3	0	-0.2
1956 StL-N	16	30	3	3	2	0	0	1	0	6	0	0	.100	.100	.167	.267	-30	-5	0	.32	-1	/S-9	0	-0.6
1957 StL-N	65	56	10	9	0	0	0	1	7	13	1	3	.161	.254	.161	.415	14	-8	2	1.04	0	S-23	1	-0.7
1958 StL-N	39	108	16	23	4	0	1	8	23	15	0	2	.213	.351	.278	.629	67	-5	12	3.59	-6	S-27	2	-0.8
Pit-N	26	27	4	4	0	1	0	2	3	6	0	1	.148	.233	.222	.456	22	-4	1	1.53	0	/S-5,3-2	0	-0.3
Yr.	65	135	20	27	4	1	1	10	26	21	0	3	.200	.329	.267	.596	58	-9	13	3.14	-6	S-32/3-2	2	-1.2
1959 Pit-N	81	145	21	34	10	1	1	9	16	22	1	1	.234	.311	.338	.648	73	-6	16	3.67	0	2-28/S-8,0-3(0-0-3)	4	-0.3
1960*Pit-N	65	102	9	34	4	1	0	10	16	20	0	1	.333	.429	.392	.821	126	4	18	6.75	0	S-23,2-10/3-1	6	0.7
1961 Pit-N	60	78	16	15	2	1	0	2	10	19	0	1	.192	.284	.244	.528	42	-7	6	2.33	0	3-11/S-9,2-5,0-3(2-0-2)	1	-0.6
1962 Pit-N	54	104	19	30	3	0	2	10	17	22	0	1	.288	.388	.375	.763	106	1	17	5.83	-2	3-20/2-2,S-1	4	0.0
1963 Pit-N	138	541	54	133	18	2	3	32	69	83	2	4	.246	.334	.303	.638	84	-9	58	3.63	-3	*S-117,2-20/3-1	14	0.0
1964 Pit-N	121	398	50	98	22	5	3	36	54	60	1	2	.246	.346	.349	.696	97	0	52	4.54	-2	*S-111	14	0.8
1965 Pit-N	31	109	13	25	5	0	0	6	15	19	1	0	.229	.323	.275	.598	70	-4	11	3.24	3	S-28	3	0.2
SF-N	101	379	39	77	10	1	2	19	33	50	2	4	.203	.272	.251	.523	47	-27	26	2.23	-2	S-93	4	-2.2
Yr.	132	488	52	102	15	1	2	25	48	69	3	4	.209	.284	.256	.540	52	-31	37	2.45	2	*S-121	7	-1.9
1966 SF-N	11	16	4	1	0	0	0	0	2	2	0	0	.063	.167	.063	.229	-32	-3	0	.46	0	/S-8	0	-0.3
NY-A	25	58	5	9	2	0	0	2	9	8	0	0	.155	.269	.190	.458	36	-4	4	1.99	-3	S-19	0	-0.6
LA-N	20	70	10	18	0	0	0	4	8	8	1	1	.257	.350	.257	.607	78	-2	7	3.18	-1	3-19/S-3	1	-0.3
Yr.	31	86	14	19	0	0	0	4	10	10	1	1	.221	.316	.221	.537	58	-4	7	2.62	-2	3-19,S-11	1	-0.6
1967 LA-N	84	232	23	50	10	1	2	15	31	40	1	2	.216	.308	.293	.601	79	-6	20	2.78	-1	S-69/2-4,3-2	5	-0.1
1968*StL-N	69	127	14	28	7	1	1	8	13	31	1	2	.220	.303	.315	.618	87	-2	12	3.27	-1	S-43,2-23	5	0.1
1969 Bos-A	94	226	30	58	9	3	2	20	29	44	0	2	.257	.351	.350	.701	92	-2	29	4.49	3	2-37,S-11/3-9,0-5(3-0-2)	7	0.4
1970 Bos-A	76	139	16	26	1	2	1	14	21	26	0	1	.187	.298	.245	.543	48	-10	10	2.10	-2	2-15,3-15/S-3	1	-1.1
1971 StL-N	34	60	7	13	2	0	1	6	10	9	0	0	.217	.347	.300	.647	81	-1	7	3.72	2	S-17,2-13/3-3	2	0.3
Mil-A	23	28	2	3	2	0	0	1	2	8	0	0	.107	.194	.179	.372	6	-3	1	1.21	-2	3-12/S-4,2-2	0	-0.6
Total 19	1321	3083	394	699	113	20	21	211	390	526	12	29	.227	.319	.297	.615	73	-107	312	3.35	-24	S-660,2-159/3-95,0-11	74	-7.2
• SCHOMBERG, Otto	Otto H. Schomberg b: 11/14/1864, Milwaukee, WI d: 5/3/1927, Ottawa, KS BL/TL Deb: 7/7/1886 Career OF: 0-0-16																							
1886 Pit-a	72	246	53	67	6	6	1	29	57	....	7	....	.272	.417	.358	.775	144	18	41	6.12	-9	1-72	12	0.3
1887 Ind-N	112	475	91	185	18	16	5	83	56	32	21	....	.389	.397	.463	.860	143	27	88	8.00	-14	*1-112/0-1	15	0.3
1888 Ind-N	30	112	11	24	5	1	1	10	10	12	6	....	.214	.290	.304	.594	88	-1	12	3.65	-3	1-15,0-15(0-0-15)	2	-0.5
Total 3	214	833	155	276	29	23	7	122	123	44	34	....	.331	.389	.407	.796	136	44	140	6.71	-26	1-199/0-16	29	0.0
• SCHOONMAKER, Jerry	Jerald Lee Schoonmaker b: 12/14/1933, Seymour, MO BR/TR, 5'11", 190 lbs. Deb: 6/11/1955 Career OF: 10-11-7																							
1955 Was-A	20	46	5	7	0	1	1	4	5	11	1	0	.152	.235	.261	.496	35	-4	3	2.00	0	0-15(5-3-7)	0	-0.4
1957 Was-A	30	23	5	2	1	0	0	0	2	11	0	0	.087	.160	.130	.290	-20	-4	1	.72	0	0-13(5-8-0)	0	-0.5
Total 2	50	69	10	9	1	1	1	4	7	22	1	0	.130	.211	.217	.428	17	-8	4	1.57	0	/0-28	0	-0.9
• SCHRAMKA, Paul	Paul Edward Schramka b: 3/22/1928, Milwaukee, WI BL/TL, 6', 185 lbs. Deb: 4/14/1953																							
1953 Chi-N	2	0	0	0	0	0	0	0	0	0	0	0	....	....	....	....	-98	0	0	....	0	/0-1	0	0.0
• SCHRECKENGOST, Ossee	Ossee Freeman Schreckengost b: 4/11/1875, New Bethlehem, PA d: 7/9/1914, Philadelphia, PA BR/TR, 5'10", 180 lbs. Deb: 9/8/1897 U Career OF: 0-1-2																							
1897 Lou-N	1	3	0	0	0	0	0	0	0	....	0	....	.000	.000	.000	.000	-104	-1	0	.00	0	/C-1	0	-0.1
1898 Cle-N	10	35	5	11	2	3	0	10	0	....	1	....	.314	.314	.543	.857	146	2	6	7.11	-1	/C-9	2	0.1
1899 StL-N	6	8	0	0	0	0	0	0	1	....	0	....	.000	.111	.000	.111	-67	-2	0	.00	0	/1-1,0-1	0	-0.2
Cle-N	43	150	15	47	8	3	0	10	6	....	4	....	.313	.348	.407	.755	115	3	23	5.94	3	C-39/1-1,0-1,S-1	2	0.9
StL-N	66	269	42	77	12	2	2	37	14	....	14	....	.286	.324	.368	.692	88	-6	38	5.17	-3	1-41,C-25/2-1	5	-0.6
Yr.	115	427	57	124	20	5	2	47	21	....	18	....	.290	.328	.375	.703	94	-5	61	5.29	0	C-64,1-43/0-2(0-0-2),2-1,S	7	0.1
1901 Bos-A	86	280	37	85	13	5	0	38	19	....	6	....	.304	.356	.386	.742	108	3	42	5.61	3	C-72/1-4	11	1.2
1902 Cle-A	18	74	5	25	0	0	0	9	0	....	2	....	.338	.338	.338	.676	91	-1	9	5.06	-0	1-17	1	-0.1
Phi-A	79	284	45	92	17	2	2	43	9	....	3	....	.324	.347	.419	.766	107	2	44	5.86	13	C-71/1-7,0-1	13	2.1
Yr.	97	358	50	117	17	2	2	52	9	....	5	....	.327	.345	.402	.747	104	1	54	5.71	13	C-71,1-24/0-1	14	2.0
1903 Phi-A	92	306	26	78	13	4	3	30	11	....	0	....	.255	.285	.353	.638	86	-6	32	3.66	5	C-77,1-10	10	0.8
1904 Phi-A	95	311	23	58	9	1	1	21	5	....	3	....	.186	.199	.232	.431	34	-24	16	1.64	-7	C-84/1-9	4	-2.5
1905*Phi-A	123	420	30	114	19	6	0	45	3	....	9	....	.271	.278	.345	.624	96	-5	44	3.79	-6	*C-114/1-2	14	0.1
1906 Phi-A	98	338	29	96	20	1	1	41	10	....	5	....	.284	.305	.358	.663	104	0	40	4.29	7	C-89/1-4	15	1.7
1907 Phi-A	101	356	30	97	16	3	0	38	17	....	4	....	.272	.306	.334	.640	102	-0	39	3.94	10	C-99/1-2	16	2.2
1908 Phi-A	71	207	16	46	7	1	0	16	6	....	1	....	.222	.248	.266	.513	63	-9	14	2.14	5	C-65/1-1	5	0.3
Chi-A	6	16	1	3	0	0	0	0	1	....	0	....	.188	.235	.188	.423	38	-1	1	1.54	3	/C-6	0	0.3
Yr.	77	223	17	49	7	1	0	16	7	....	1	....	.220	.247	.260	.507	61	-10	15	2.09	8	C-71/1-1	5	0.6
Total 11	895	3057	304	829	136	31	9	338	102	....	52	....	.271	.297	.345	.642	90	-45	349	4.06	32	C-751/1-99,0-3,2-1,S-1	98	6.1

YEAR TM-L	G	AB	R	H	2B	3B	HR	RBI	BB	SO	SB	CS	AVG	OBP	SLG	OPS	OPS+	BR/A	RC	RC/G	FR	G/POS	WS	TPW
• SCHREIBER, Hank	Henry Walter Schreiber b: 7/12/1891, Cleveland, OH d: 2/23/1968, Indianapolis, IN BR/TR, 5'11", 165 lbs. Deb: 4/14/1914																							
1914 Chi-A	1	2	0	0	0	0	0	0	0	1	0	....	.000	.000	.000	.000	-101	-0	0	.00	0	/O-1	0	-0.1
1917 Bos-N	2	7	1	2	0	0	0	0	0	1	0	....	.286	.286	.286	.571	80	-0	1	2.76	-1	/3-1,S-1	0	-0.1
1919 Cin-N	19	58	5	13	4	0	0	4	0	12	0	....	.224	.224	.293	.517	56	-3	4	2.04	4	3-17/S-2	1	0.2
1921 NY-N	4	6	2	2	0	0	0	2	1	1	0	0	.333	.429	.333	.762	104	0	1	6.16	-2	/2-2,S-2,3-1	0	-0.1
1926 Chi-N	10	18	2	1	1	0	0	0	0	1	0	....	.056	.056	.111	.167	-55	-4	0	.19	0	/3-3,S-3,2-1	0	-0.4
Total 5	36	91	10	18	5	0	0	6	1	16	0	0	.198	.207	.253	.459	35	-8	5	1.79	2	/3-22,S-8,2-3,O-1	1	-0.5
• SCHREIBER, Ted	Theodore Henry Schreiber b: 7/11/1938, Brooklyn, NY BR/TR, 5'11", 175 lbs. Deb: 4/14/1963																							
1963 NY-N	39	50	1	8	0	0	0	2	4	14	0	1	.160	.236	.160	.396	16	-6	2	1.14	0	3-17/S-9,2-3	1	-0.6
• SCHRIVER, Pop	William Frederick Schriver b: 7/11/1865, Brooklyn, NY d: 12/27/1932, Brooklyn, NY BR/TR, 5'9.5", 172 lbs. Deb: 4/29/1886 U Career OF: 8-10-5																							
1886 Bro-a	8	21	2	1	0	0	0	0	2	....	0	....	.048	.130	.048	.178	-43	-3	0	.18	0	/O-5(2-0-3),C-3	0	-0.3
1888 Phi-N	40	134	15	26	5	2	1	23	7	21	2	....	.194	.250	.284	.534	66	-5	10	2.56	-6	C-27/3-6,S-6,O-1	2	-0.9
1889 Phi-N	55	211	24	56	10	0	1	19	16	8	5	....	.265	.323	.327	.650	75	-8	25	4.19	1	C-48/2-6,3-1	5	-0.2
1890 Phi-N	57	223	37	61	9	6	0	35	22	15	9	....	.274	.339	.368	.706	103	0	32	5.17	-5	C-34,1-10/3-8,2-3,O-2(2-0-0)	6	-0.2
1891 Chi-N	27	90	15	30	1	4	1	21	10	9	1	....	.333	.412	.467	.878	156	7	18	8.17	-1	C-27/1-2	5	0.7
1892 Chi-N	92	326	40	73	10	6	1	34	27	25	4	....	.224	.297	.301	.598	80	-8	31	3.32	1	C-82,O-10(0-10-0)	9	0.0
1893 Chi-N	64	229	49	65	8	3	4	34	14	9	4	....	.284	.336	.397	.733	96	-2	33	5.29	0	C-56/O-5(4-0-1)	6	0.2
1894 Chi-N	98	354	56	97	12	3	3	49	32	21	9	....	.274	.344	.350	.695	65	-22	47	4.75	4	*C-88/3-3,S-3,1-2	6	-0.8
1895 NY-N	24	92	16	29	2	1	1	16	9	10	3	....	.315	.382	.391	.774	102	1	15	6.51	0	C-18/1-6	3	0.2
1897 Cin-N	61	178	29	54	12	4	1	30	19	....	3	....	.303	.374	.433	.806	105	1	31	6.45	-1	C-53	7	0.4
1898 Pit-N	95	315	25	72	15	3	0	32	23	....	0	....	.229	.287	.295	.583	68	-13	29	3.01	1	C-92/1-1	7	-0.4
1899 Pit-N	92	302	31	85	19	5	1	49	24	....	4	....	.281	.344	.387	.732	101	0	44	5.12	0	C-78/1-8	10	0.6
1900*Pit-N	37	92	12	27	7	0	1	12	10	....	0	....	.293	.381	.402	.783	115	2	14	5.89	-6	C-24/1-1	3	-0.1
1901 StL-N	53	166	17	45	7	3	1	23	12	....	2	....	.271	.335	.367	.703	109	2	23	4.67	5	C-24,1-19	5	0.9
Total 14	803	2733	368	721	117	40	16	377	227	118	46	....	.264	.330	.353	.683	88	-49	352	4.56	-7	C-654/1-49,O-23,3-18,2-9,S	74	0.2
• SCHRODER, Bob	Robert James Schroder b: 12/30/1944, Ridgefield, NJ BL/TR, 6', 175 lbs. Deb: 4/20/1965																							
1965 SF-N	31	9	4	2	0	0	0	1	1	1	0	0	.222	.300	.222	.522	48	-1	1	2.62	0	/2-4,3-1	0	0.0
1966 SF-N	10	33	0	8	0	0	0	2	0	2	0	0	.242	.242	.242	.485	34	-3	2	1.74	-1	/S-9	0	-0.3
1967 SF-N	62	135	20	31	4	0	0	7	15	15	1	0	.230	.307	.259	.566	64	-5	12	2.96	3	2-45/3-4	3	0.0
1968 SF-N	35	44	5	7	1	1	0	2	7	3	0	0	.159	.288	.227	.516	56	-2	3	2.30	-2	2-12/S-4,3-2	0	-0.4
Total 4	138	221	29	48	5	1	0	12	23	21	1	0	.217	.294	.249	.543	58	-11	18	2.61	1	/2-61,S-13,3-7	3	-0.7
• SCHROEDER, Bill	Alfred William Schroeder b: 9/7/1958, Baltimore, MD BR/TR, 6'2", 200 lbs. Deb: 7/13/1983																							
1983 Mil-A	23	73	7	13	2	1	3	7	3	23	0	1	.178	.221	.356	.577	60	-5	6	2.44	-1	C-23	0	-0.5
1984 Mil-A	61	210	29	54	6	0	14	25	8	54	0	1	.257	.291	.486	.777	115	3	27	4.32	0	C-58/D-3,1-1	7	0.5
1985 Mil-A	53	194	18	47	8	0	8	25	12	61	0	1	.242	.293	.407	.700	90	-4	22	3.81	2	C-48/D-4,1-1	4	0.0
1986 Mil-A	64	217	32	46	14	0	7	19	9	59	1	0	.212	.263	.373	.636	69	-10	22	3.25	2	C-35,1-19,D-10	4	-0.8
1987 Mil-A	75	250	35	83	12	0	14	42	16	56	5	2	.332	.379	.548	.927	138	13	52	8.13	1	C-67/1-4,D-2	13	1.6
1988 Mil-A	41	122	9	19	2	0	5	10	6	36	0	0	.156	.208	.295	.503	39	-10	6	1.52	3	C-30,1-10/D-1	2	-0.7
1989 Cal-A	41	138	16	28	2	0	6	15	3	44	0	0	.203	.220	.348	.568	59	-8	10	2.28	5	C-33/1-8	2	-0.2
1990 Cal-A	18	58	7	13	3	0	4	9	1	10	0	0	.224	.237	.483	.720	98	-1	5	2.96	1	C-15/1-3	2	0.1
Total 8	376	1262	153	303	49	1	61	152	58	343	6	5	.240	.282	.426	.708	90	-22	149	3.98	13	C-309/1-46,D-20	34	0.2
• SCHU, Rick	Richard Spencer Schu b: 1/26/1962, Philadelphia, PA BR/TR, 6', 170 lbs. Deb: 9/1/1984																							
1984 Phi-N	17	29	12	8	2	1	2	5	6	6	0	0	.276	.400	.621	1.021	180	3	8	9.58	1	3-15	2	0.4
1985 Phi-N	112	416	54	105	21	4	7	24	38	78	8	6	.252	.318	.373	.691	90	-7	49	4.06	-8	*3-111	9	-1.7
1986 Phi-N	92	208	32	57	10	1	8	25	18	44	2	2	.274	.338	.447	.785	111	2	32	5.48	-5	3-58	7	-0.4
1987 Phi-N	92	196	24	46	6	3	7	23	20	36	0	2	.235	.312	.403	.715	85	-6	25	4.42	-2	3-45,1-28	4	-0.9
1988 Bal-A	89	270	22	69	9	4	4	20	21	49	6	4	.256	.316	.363	.679	92	-3	30	3.81	-4	3-72/D-9,1-4	5	-0.8
1989 Bal-A	1	0	0	0	0	0	0	0	0	0	0	0	....	....	....	....	-103	0	0	....	0	/2-1	0	0.0
Det-A	98	266	25	57	11	0	7	21	24	37	1	2	.214	.279	.335	.614	74	-10	24	2.98	-3	3-83/D-9,2-5,1-3,S-3	1	-1.3
Yr.	99	266	25	57	11	0	7	21	24	37	1	2	.214	.279	.335	.614	74	-10	24	2.98	-3	3-83/D-9,2-6,1-3,S-3	1	-1.4
1990 Cal-A	61	157	19	42	8	0	6	14	11	25	0	0	.268	.315	.433	.749	110	1	21	4.66	-2	3-38,1-15/O-4(4-0-0),2-1	2	-0.1
1991 Phi-N	17	22	1	2	0	0	0	2	1	7	0	0	.091	.130	.091	.221	-37	-4	0	.28	-1	/3-3,1-1	0	-0.5
1996 Mon-N	1	4	0	0	0	0	0	0	0	0	0	0	.000	.000	.000	.000	-98	-1	0	.00	0	/3-1	0	-0.1
Total 9	580	1568	189	386	67	13	41	134	139	282	17	16	.246	.311	.384	.695	91	-25	189	4.13	-25	3-426/1-51,D-18,2-7,O-4,S-3	30	-5.5
• SCHUBLE, Heinie	Henry George Schuble b: 11/1/1906, Houston, TX d: 10/2/1990, Baytown, TX BR/TR, 5'9", 152 lbs. Deb: 7/8/1927																							
1927 StL-N	65	218	29	56	6	2	4	28	7	27	0	....	.257	.283	.358	.641	69	-11	21	3.35	-4	S-65	5	-0.8
1929 Det-A	92	258	35	60	11	7	2	28	19	23	3	2	.233	.288	.353	.640	64	-15	27	3.43	-20	S-86/3-2	3	-2.5
1932 Det-A	102	340	58	92	20	6	5	52	24	37	14	5	.271	.319	.409	.728	84	-8	45	4.59	5	3-76,S-16	9	0.1
1933 Det-A	49	96	12	21	4	1	0	6	5	17	2	0	.219	.257	.281	.539	42	-8	7	2.52	-1	3-23/S-2,2-1	1	-0.8
1934 Det-A	11	15	2	4	2	0	0	2	1	4	0	0	.267	.313	.400	.713	83	-0	2	4.23	0	/S-3,3-2,2-1	0	0.0
1935 Det-A	11	8	3	2	0	0	0	0	1	0	0	0	.250	.333	.250	.583	55	-0	1	3.19	-1	/3-2,2-1	0	-0.1
1936 StL-N	2	0	0	0	0	0	0	0	0	0	0	....	....	....	....	....	-100	0	0	....	0	/3-1	0	0.0
Total 7	332	935	139	235	43	16	11	116	57	108	19	7	.251	.296	.367	.663	70	-42	103	3.74	-21	S-172,3-106/2-3	18	-4.0
• SCHULMERICH, Wes	Edward Wesley Schulmerich b: 4/21/1901, Hillsboro, OR d: 6/26/1985, Corvallis, OR BR/TR, 5'11", 210 lbs. Deb: 5/1/1931 Career OF: 113-0-262																							
1931 Bos-N	95	327	36	101	17	7	2	43	28	30	0	....	.309	.363	.422	.785	115	7	51	5.82	-3	O-87(0-0-87)	11	-0.2
1932 Bos-N	119	404	47	105	22	5	11	57	27	61	5	....	.260	.314	.421	.735	99	-1	55	4.70	2	*O-101(0-0-101)	12	-0.5
1933 Bos-N	29	85	10	21	6	1	1	13	5	10	0	....	.247	.289	.376	.665	97	-1	10	3.89	1	O-21(0-0-21)	3	-0.1
Phi-N	97	365	53	122	19	4	8	59	32	45	1	....	.334	.394	.474	.868	130	16	69	7.30	-2	O-97(97-0-0)	12	0.8
Yr.	126	450	63	143	25	5	9	72	37	55	1	....	.318	.375	.456	.830	124	15	78	6.60	-2	*O-118(97-0-21)	15	0.7
1934 Phi-N	15	52	2	13	1	0	0	1	4	8	0	....	.250	.316	.269	.585	51	-3	4	2.89	0	O-13(3-0-10)	0	-0.4
Cin-N	74	209	21	55	8	3	5	19	22	43	1	....	.263	.333	.402	.735	98	-0	28	4.67	-4	O-56(13-0-43)	4	-0.7
Yr.	89	261	23	68	9	3	5	20	26	51	1	....	.261	.330	.375	.705	89	-4	33	4.32	-4	O-69(16-0-53)	4	-1.2
Total 4	429	1442	169	417	73	20	27	192	118	197	7	....	.289	.347	.424	.771	109	17	217	5.44	-7	O-375	42	-1.2
• SCHULT, Art	Arthur William "Dutch" Schult b: 6/20/1928, Brooklyn, NY BR/TR, 6'3", 220 lbs. Deb: 5/17/1953 Career OF: 36-1-23																							
1953 NY-A	7	0	3	0	0	0	0	0	0	0	0	0	....	....	....	....	-104	0	0	....	0	....	0	0.0
1956 Cin-N	5	7	3	3	0	0	0	2	1	1	0	0	.429	.500	.429	.929	144	1	2	11.00	0	/O-1	1	0.0
1957 Cin-N	21	34	4	9	2	0	0	4	0	2	0	0	.265	.286	.324	.609	59	-2	3	3.01	0	/O-5(5-0-0)	0	-0.2
Was-A	77	247	30	65	14	0	4	35	14	30	0	1	.263	.305	.368	.674	84	-6	26	3.60	-3	1-35,O-31(14-1-17)	4	-1.3
1959 Chi-N	42	118	17	32	7	0	2	14	7	14	0	0	.271	.323	.381	.704	87	-2	13	3.74	-2	1-23,O-15(12-0-6)	2	-0.5
1960 Chi-N	12	15	1	2	1	0	0	1	1	3	0	0	.133	.188	.200	.388	6	-2	1	1.17	0	/O-4(4-0-0),1-1	0	-0.2
Total 5	164	421	58	111	24	0	6	56	23	50	0	1	.264	.308	.363	.671	81	-12	44	3.59	-5	/1-59,O-56	7	-2.2
• SCHULTE, Frank	Frank M. "Wildfire" Schulte b: 9/17/1882, Cohocton, NY d: 10/2/1949, Oakland, CA BL/TR, 5'11", 170 lbs. Deb: 9/21/1904 Career OF: 544-9-1189																							
1904 Chi-N	20	84	16	24	4	3	2	13	2	....	1	....	.286	.310	.476	.787	141	3	13	5.65	0	O-20(20-0-0)	5	0.3
1905 Chi-N	123	493	67	135	15	14	1	47	32	....	16	....	.274	.326	.367	.693	102	0	68	4.69	-6	*O-123(107-0-16)	16	-1.3
1906*Chi-N	146	563	77	158	18	**13**	7	60	31	....	25	....	.281	.324	.396	.720	118	9	85	5.09	1	*O-146(0-0-146)	24	0.4
1907*Chi-N	97	342	44	98	14	7	2	32	22	....	7	....	.287	.339	.386	.725	120	7	51	4.98	0	O-92(1-0-91)	14	0.3
1908*Chi-N	102	386	42	91	20	2	1	43	29	....	15	....	.236	.294	.306	.600	88	-5	40	3.28	-3	*O-102(12-1-89)	11	-1.6
1909 Chi-N	140	538	57	142	16	11	4	60	24	....	23	....	.264	.298	.357	.655	101	-3	64	3.94	-10	*O-140(0-0-140)	18	-2.2
1910*Chi-N	151	559	93	168	29	15	**10**	68	39	57	22	....	.301	.349	.460	.809	137	22	97	6.03	-4	*O-150(0-0-150)	26	1.1
1911 Chi-N	154	577	105	173	30	21	**21**	**107**	76	71	23	....	.300	.384	**.534**	.918	**155**	**41**	127	7.58	-3	*O-154(0-0-154)	**31**	2.9
1912 Chi-N	139	553	90	146	27	11	12	64	53	70	17	....	.264	.336	.418	.754	106	3	83	4.96	-1	*O-139(0-0-139)	17	-0.6

YEAR TM-L	G	AB	R	H	2B	3B	HR	RBI	BB	SO	SB	CS	AVG	OBP	SLG	OPS	OPS+	BR/A	RC	RC/G	FR	G/POS	WS	TPW
1913 Chi-N	132	497	85	138	28	6	9	68	39	68	21	....	.278	.336	.412	.749	113	7	73	4.96	-4	*O-130(1-0-129)	18	-0.3
1914 Chi-N	137	465	54	112	22	7	5	61	39	55	16	....	.241	.306	.351	.657	95	-4	53	3.74	-11	*O-134(134-0-2)	13	-2.1
1915 Chi-N	151	550	66	137	20	6	12	62	49	68	19	17	.249	.313	.373	.686	107	0	66	3.85	5	*O-147(146-0-4)	17	-0.1
1916 Chi-N	72	230	31	68	11	1	5	27	20	35	9	....	.296	.352	.417	.769	123	6	37	5.82	0	O-67(66-0-1)	8	0.4
Pit-N	55	177	12	45	5	3	0	14	17	19	5	....	.254	.323	.316	.639	96	-0	20	3.84	-4	O-48(20-0-28)	4	-0.8
Yr.	127	407	43	113	16	4	5	41	37	54	14	....	.278	.339	.373	.713	111	6	57	4.93	-4	*O-115(86-0-29)	12	-0.3
1917 Pit-N	30	103	11	22	5	1	0	7	10	14	5	....	.214	.283	.282	.565	71	-3	9	2.84	-1	O-28(3-0-25)	1	-0.7
Phi-N	64	149	21	32	10	0	1	15	16	22	4	....	.215	.299	.302	.601	81	-3	14	3.06	-5	O-42(20-7-15)	3	-1.0
Yr.	94	252	32	54	15	1	1	22	26	36	9	....	.214	.293	.294	.587	77	-6	23	2.97	-6	O-70(23-7-40)	4	-1.7
1918 Was-A	93	267	35	77	14	3	0	44	47	36	5	....	.288	.406	.363	.770	135	15	41	5.29	1	O-75(14-1-60)	13	1.3
Total 15	1806	6533	906	1766	288	124	92	792	545	515	233	17	.270	.332	.395	.726	114	94	942	4.83	-45	*O-1737	239	-3.9

• SCHULTE, Fred Fred William "Fritz" Schulte b: 1/13/1901, Belleville, IL d: 5/20/1983, Belleville, IL BR/TR, 6'1", 183 lbs. Deb: 4/15/1927 Career OF: 17-1016-28

YEAR TM-L	G	AB	R	H	2B	3B	HR	RBI	BB	SO	SB	CS	AVG	OBP	SLG	OPS	OPS+	BR/A	RC	RC/G	FR	G/POS	WS	TPW
1927 StL-A	60	189	32	60	16	5	3	34	20	14	5	3	.317	.383	.503	.885	124	6	36	6.94	-3	O-49(0-49-0)	7	0.1
1928 StL-A	146	556	90	159	44	6	7	85	51	60	6	5	.286	.347	.424	.771	99	-2	83	5.19	7	*O-143(0-143-0)	19	-0.1
1929 StL-A	121	446	63	137	24	5	3	71	59	44	8	3	.307	.389	.404	.793	101	4	74	6.02	7	*O-116(0-116-0)	18	0.5
1930 StL-A	113	392	59	109	23	5	5	62	41	44	12	8	.278	.348	.401	.748	86	-9	55	4.93	-4	O-98(0-98-0)/1-5	9	-1.5
1931 StL-A	134	553	100	168	32	7	9	65	56	49	6	8	.304	.369	.436	.805	107	6	89	5.92	0	*O-134(0-134-0)	16	0.3
1932 StL-A	146	565	106	166	35	6	9	73	71	44	5	9	.294	.373	.425	.797	100	-1	90	5.80	-6	*O-129(3-126-0)/1-5	15	-0.9
1933*Was-A	144	550	98	162	30	7	5	87	61	27	10	12	.295	.366	.402	.768	104	2	81	5.22	10	*O-142(0-142-0)	21	0.8
1934 Was-A	136	524	72	156	32	6	3	73	53	34	3	7	.298	.363	.399	.762	100	-2	76	5.24	-2	*O-134(0-134-0)	13	-0.7
1935 Was-A	76	226	33	60	6	4	2	23	26	22	0	3	.265	.344	.354	.698	83	-6	28	4.32	-1	O-56(12-19-26)	4	-0.9
1936 Pit-N	74	238	28	62	7	3	1	17	20	20	1	....	.261	.320	.328	.648	73	-9	26	3.91	-4	O-55(1-54-0)	4	-1.4
1937 Pit-N	29	20	5	2	0	0	0	3	4	3	0	....	.100	.280	.100	.380	7	-2	1	1.41	0	/O-4(1-1-2)	0	-0.3
Total 11	1179	4259	686	1241	249	54	47	593	462	361	56	58	.291	.362	.408	.770	98	-12	639	5.37	3	*O-1060/1-10	126	-4.1

• SCHULTE, Ham Herman Joseph Schulte b: 9/1/1912, St. Louis, MO d: 12/21/1993, St. Charles, MO BR/TR, 5'8.5", 158 lbs. Deb: 4/16/1940

YEAR TM-L	G	AB	R	H	2B	3B	HR	RBI	BB	SO	SB	CS	AVG	OBP	SLG	OPS	OPS+	BR/A	RC	RC/G	FR	G/POS	WS	TPW
1940 Phi-N	120	436	44	103	18	2	1	21	32	30	3	....	.236	.288	.294	.582	63	-22	40	3.01	-11	*2-119/S-1	5	-2.6

• SCHULTE, Jack John Herman Frank Schulte b: 11/15/1881, Cincinnati, OH d: 8/17/1975, Roseville, MI BR/TR, 5'9", 180 lbs. Deb: 8/19/1906

YEAR TM-L	G	AB	R	H	2B	3B	HR	RBI	BB	SO	SB	CS	AVG	OBP	SLG	OPS	OPS+	BR/A	RC	RC/G	FR	G/POS	WS	TPW
1906 Bos-N	2	7	0	0	0	0	0	0	0	....	0	....	.000	.000	.000	.000	-103	-2	0	.00	0	/S-2	0	-0.2

• SCHULTE, Johnny John Clement Schulte b: 9/8/1896, Fredericktown, MD d: 6/28/1978, St. Louis, MO BL/TR, 5'11", 190 lbs. Deb: 4/18/1923 C

YEAR TM-L	G	AB	R	H	2B	3B	HR	RBI	BB	SO	SB	CS	AVG	OBP	SLG	OPS	OPS+	BR/A	RC	RC/G	FR	G/POS	WS	TPW
1923 StL-A	7	3	1	0	0	0	0	1	4	0	0	0	.000	.571	.000	.571	56	0	1	5.04	0	/1-1,C-1	0	0.1
1927 StL-N	64	156	35	45	8	2	9	32	47	19	1	....	.288	.456	.538	.994	160	17	41	9.24	-3	C-59	12	1.7
1928 Phi-N	65	113	14	28	2	2	4	17	15	12	0	....	.248	.336	.407	.743	90	-2	16	4.63	1	C-34	2	0.1
1929 Chi-N	31	69	6	18	3	0	0	9	7	11	0	....	.261	.329	.304	.633	58	-4	7	3.47	-0	C-30	2	-0.3
1932 StL-A	15	24	2	5	2	0	0	3	1	6	0	0	.208	.240	.292	.532	35	-2	2	2.33	-1	/C-6	0	-0.3
Bos-N	10	9	1	2	0	0	1	2	2	1	0	....	.222	.364	.556	.919	149	1	2	6.34	0	C-10	1	0.1
Total 5	192	374	59	98	15	4	14	64	76	49	1	0	.262	.388	.436	.824	114	9	68	6.17	-2	C-140/1-1	17	1.4

• SCHULTE, Len Leonard Bernard Schulte b: 12/5/1916, St. Charles, MO d: 5/6/1986, Orlando, FL BR/TR, 5'10", 160 lbs. Deb: 9/27/1944

YEAR TM-L	G	AB	R	H	2B	3B	HR	RBI	BB	SO	SB	CS	AVG	OBP	SLG	OPS	OPS+	BR/A	RC	RC/G	FR	G/POS	WS	TPW
1944 StL-A	1	0	0	0	0	0	0	0	1	0	0	0	....	1.000	....	1.000	188	0	0	∞	0	....	0	0.0
1945 StL-A	119	430	37	106	16	1	0	36	24	35	0	3	.247	.286	.288	.575	64	-21	36	2.81	-2	3-71,2-37,S-14	6	-2.1
1946 StL-A	4	5	1	2	0	0	0	2	0	0	0	0	.400	.400	.400	.800	118	0	0	2.77	-0	/2-1,3-1	0	0.0
Total 3	124	435	38	108	16	1	0	38	25	35	0	3	.248	.289	.290	.579	65	-21	37	2.81	-2	/3-72,2-38,S-14	6	-2.1

• SCHULTZ, Howie Howard Henry "Stretch,Steeple" Schultz b: 7/3/1922, St. Paul, MN BR/TR, 6'6", 200 lbs. Deb: 8/16/1943

YEAR TM-L	G	AB	R	H	2B	3B	HR	RBI	BB	SO	SB	CS	AVG	OBP	SLG	OPS	OPS+	BR/A	RC	RC/G	FR	G/POS	WS	TPW
1943 Bro-N	45	182	20	49	12	0	1	34	6	24	3	....	.269	.300	.352	.652	88	-4	18	3.54	3	1-45	4	-0.3
1944 Bro-N	138	526	59	134	32	3	11	83	24	67	6	....	.255	.290	.390	.680	92	-9	55	3.60	5	*1-136	10	-1.1
1945 Bro-N	39	142	18	34	8	2	1	19	10	14	2	....	.239	.294	.345	.639	78	-5	14	3.28	3	1-38	2	-0.4
1946 Bro-N	90	249	27	63	14	1	3	27	16	34	2	....	.253	.298	.353	.652	83	-6	26	3.62	5	1-87	4	-0.4
1947 Bro-N	2	1	0	0	0	0	0	0	0	0	0	....	.000	.000	.000	.000	-96	-0	0	.00	0	/1-1	0	0.0
Phi-N	114	403	30	90	19	1	6	35	21	70	0	....	.223	.264	.320	.584	56	-27	33	2.69	-1	*1-114	2	-3.1
Yr.	116	404	30	90	19	1	6	35	21	70	0	....	.223	.263	.319	.582	56	-27	33	2.67	-1	*1-115	2	-3.1
1948 Phi-N	6	13	0	1	0	0	0	1	1	2	0	....	.077	.143	.077	.220	-40	-3	0	.41	0	/1-3	0	-0.2
Cin-N	36	72	9	12	0	0	2	9	4	7	2	....	.167	.211	.250	.461	25	-8	4	1.65	-3	1-26	0	-1.1
Yr.	42	85	9	13	0	0	2	10	5	9	2	....	.153	.200	.224	.424	15	-10	4	1.45	-3	1-29	0	-1.4
Total 6	470	1588	163	383	85	7	24	208	82	218	15	....	.241	.281	.349	.630	75	-61	150	3.20	11	1-450	22	-6.8

• SCHULTZ, Joe Joseph Charles "Germany" Schultz, Sr.
b: 7/24/1893, Pittsburgh, PA d: 4/13/1941, Columbia, SC BR/TR, 5'11.5", 172 lbs. Deb: 9/28/1912 Career OF: 104-9-307

YEAR TM-L	G	AB	R	H	2B	3B	HR	RBI	BB	SO	SB	CS	AVG	OBP	SLG	OPS	OPS+	BR/A	RC	RC/G	FR	G/POS	WS	TPW
1912 Bos-N	4	12	1	3	1	0	0	4	0	2	0	....	.250	.250	.333	.583	58	-1	1	2.67	-1	/2-4	0	-0.1
1913 Bos-N	9	18	2	4	0	0	0	1	2	7	0	....	.222	.333	.222	.556	59	-1	2	2.62	0	/O-5(0-2-3),2-1	0	-0.1
1915 Bro-N	56	120	13	35	3	2	0	4	10	18	3	4	.292	.346	.350	.696	109	0	14	4.18	-3	3-27/S-1	5	-0.2
Chi-N	7	8	1	2	0	0	0	3	0	2	0	....	.250	.250	.250	.500	51	-0	1	2.21	-1	/2-2	0	-0.1
Yr.	63	128	14	37	3	2	0	7	10	20	3	4	.289	.341	.344	.684	106	-0	15	4.06	-4	3-27/2-2,S-1	5	-0.3
1916 Pit-N	77	204	18	53	8	2	0	22	7	14	6	....	.260	.298	.319	.616	88	-3	22	3.61	-12	2-24,3-24/O-6(4-0-3),S-1	4	-1.6
1919 StL-N	88	229	24	58	9	1	2	21	11	7	4	....	.253	.288	.328	.615	90	-3	22	3.21	-1	O-49(2-2-46)/2-6,3-1	4	-0.7
1920 StL-N	99	320	38	84	5	5	0	32	21	11	5	4	.263	.308	.309	.617	79	-8	31	3.27	-2	O-80(2-0-79)	4	-1.5
1921 StL-N	92	275	37	85	20	3	6	45	15	11	4	3	.309	.347	.469	.816	116	6	44	5.65	1	O-67(0-0-67)/3-3,1-2	9	0.2
1922 StL-N	112	344	50	108	13	4	2	64	19	10	3	1	.314	.350	.392	.742	96	-1	48	5.10	-2	O-89(33-3-53)	9	-1.0
1923 StL-N	2	7	0	2	0	0	0	1	1	0	0	0	.286	.375	.286	.661	78	-0	1	3.91	0	/O-2(0-0-2)	0	0.0
1924 StL-N	12	12	0	2	0	0	0	2	3	0	0	0	.167	.333	.167	.500	39	-1	1	2.38	0	/O-2(1-1-0)	0	-0.1
Phi-N	88	284	35	80	15	1	5	29	20	18	6	2	.282	.329	.394	.723	83	-6	37	4.66	-3	O-76(54-1-25)	5	-1.4
Yr.	100	296	35	82	15	1	5	31	23	18	6	2	.277	.329	.385	.714	81	-7	38	4.55	-3	O-78(55-2-25)	5	-1.5
1925 Phi-N	24	64	10	22	6	0	0	8	4	1	1	1	.344	.382	.438	.820	100	-0	10	6.43	-1	O-20(3-0-17)	2	-0.2
Cin-N	33	62	6	20	3	1	0	13	3	1	3	1	.323	.354	.403	.757	95	-0	9	5.36	0	O-15(5-0-12)/2-1	2	-0.1
Yr.	57	126	16	42	9	1	0	21	7	2	4	2	.333	.368	.421	.789	98	-0	19	5.89	-1	O-35(8-0-29)/2-1	4	-0.3
Total 11	703	1959	235	558	83	19	15	249	116	102	35	16	.285	.327	.370	.696	92	-18	242	4.33	-26	O-411/3-55,2-38,1-2,S-2	44	-7.0

• SCHULTZ, Joe Joseph Charles "Dode" Schultz, Jr. b: 8/29/1918, Chicago, IL d: 1/10/1996, St. Louis, MO BL/TR, 5'11", 184 lbs. Deb: 9/27/1939 M/C

YEAR TM-L	G	AB	R	H	2B	3B	HR	RBI	BB	SO	SB	CS	AVG	OBP	SLG	OPS	OPS+	BR/A	RC	RC/G	FR	G/POS	WS	TPW
1939 Pit-N	4	14	3	4	2	0	0	2	2	0	0	....	.286	.375	.429	.804	117	0	2	6.60	1	/C-4	1	0.2
1940 Pit-N	16	36	2	7	0	1	0	4	2	1	0	....	.194	.237	.250	.487	35	-3	2	2.10	-1	C-13	0	-0.4
1941 Pit-N	2	2	1	1	0	0	0	0	0	0	0	....	.500	.500	.500	1.000	183	0	1	13.50	-1	/C-2	0	0.0
1943 StL-A	46	92	6	22	5	0	0	8	9	8	0	1	.239	.307	.293	.600	74	-3	8	2.77	-1	C-26	1	-0.4
1944 StL-A	3	8	1	2	0	0	0	0	0	1	0	0	.250	.250	.250	.500	41	-1	1	2.31	-1	/C-3	0	-0.1
1945 StL-A	41	44	1	13	2	0	0	8	3	1	0	0	.295	.340	.341	.681	93	-0	5	4.35	-1	/C-4	1	-0.1
1946 StL-A	42	57	1	22	4	0	0	14	11	2	0	0	.386	.485	.456	.941	156	5	14	10.16	-1	C-17	4	0.5
1947 StL-A	43	38	3	7	0	0	1	1	4	5	0	0	.184	.262	.263	.525	45	-2	3	2.27	0	....	0	-0.3
1948 StL-A	43	37	0	7	0	0	0	9	6	3	0	0	.189	.302	.189	.492	32	-3	2	2.12	0	....	0	-0.3
Total 9	240	328	18	85	13	1	1	46	37	21	0	1	.259	.334	.314	.648	81	-7	38	4.01	-4	/C-69	7	-0.8

• SCHULZ, Jeff Jeffrey Alan Schulz b: 6/2/1961, Evansville, IN BL/TR, 6'1", 190 lbs. Deb: 9/2/1989 Career OF: 12-0-16

YEAR TM-L	G	AB	R	H	2B	3B	HR	RBI	BB	SO	SB	CS	AVG	OBP	SLG	OPS	OPS+	BR/A	RC	RC/G	FR	G/POS	WS	TPW
1989 KC-A	7	9	0	2	0	0	0	1	0	2	0	0	.222	.222	.222	.444	26	-1	0	1.71	-0	/O-5(4-0-0)	0	-0.1
1990 KC-A	30	66	5	17	5	1	0	6	6	13	0	0	.258	.319	.364	.683	92	-1	7	3.82	-2	O-22(8-0-16)/D-1	0	-0.3
1991 Pit-N	3	3	0	0	0	0	0	0	0	2	0	0	.000	.000	.000	.000	-102	-1	0	.00	0	....	0	-0.1
Total 3	40	78	5	19	5	1	0	7	6	17	0	0	.244	.298	.333	.631	78	-2	8	3.40	-2	/O-27,D-1	0	-0.5

YEAR TM-L	G	AB	R	H	2B	3B	HR	RBI	BB	SO	SB	CS	AVG	OBP	SLG	OPS	OPS+	BR/A	RC	RC/G	FR	G/POS	WS	TPW
• SCHULZE, John	John Schulze b: 4/1866, St. Louis, MO d: 5/19/1941, St. Louis, MO Deb: 8/7/1891																							
1891 StL-a	1	2	0	0	0	0	0	0	0	0	0	....	.000	.000	.000	.000	-87	-1	0	.00	0	/C-1	0	0.0
• SCHUSTER, Bill	William Charles "Broadway Bill" Schuster b: 8/4/1912, Buffalo, NY d: 6/28/1987, El Monte, CA BR/TR, 5'9", 164 lbs. Deb: 9/29/1937																							
1937 Pit-N	3	6	2	3	0	0	0	1	1	0	0	....	.500	.571	.500	1.071	193	1	2	17.15	1	/S-2	1	0.2
1939 Bos-N	2	3	0	0	0	0	0	0	0	1	0	....	.000	.000	.000	.000	-108	-1	0	.00	-1	/3-1,S-1	0	-0.2
1943 Chi-N	13	51	3	15	2	1	0	0	3	2	0	....	.294	.333	.373	.706	105	0	6	4.16	7	S-13	2	0.9
1944 Chi-N	60	154	14	34	7	1	1	14	12	16	4	....	.221	.277	.299	.576	62	-8	12	2.53	-1	S-38/2-6	2	-0.6
1945★Chi-N	45	47	8	9	2	1	0	2	7	4	2	....	.191	.296	.277	.573	61	-2	4	2.31	-3	S-22/2-3,3-1	1	-0.4
Total 5	123	261	27	61	11	3	1	17	23	23	6	....	.234	.296	.310	.606	72	-10	23	2.94	3	/S-76,2-9,3-2	6	-0.1
• SCHWARTZ, Bill	William Charles "Blab" Schwartz b: 4/22/1884, Cleveland, OH d: 8/29/1961, Nashville, TN BR/TR, 6'2", 185 lbs. Deb: 5/2/1904																							
1904 Cle-A	24	86	5	13	2	0	0	0	0	....	4	....	.151	.151	.174	.326	3	-10	3	1.09	-4	1-22/3-1	0	-1.6
• SCHWARTZ, Bill	William August "Pop,Scooper Bill" Schwartz b: 4/3/1864, Jamestown, KY d: 12/22/1940, Newport, KY BR/TR, 6'1", 195 lbs. Deb: 5/3/1883																							
1883 Col-a	2	4	0	1	0	0	0	0	0	....	....	....	.250	.250	.250	.500	67	-0	0	2.39	-1	/1-1,C-1	0	-0.1
1884 Cin-U	29	106	14	25	4	0	1	....	3	....	....	....	.236	.257	.302	.559	82	-2	8	2.91	-9	C-25/O-3(2-1-1),3-1	3	-0.8
Total 2	31	110	14	26	4	0	1	0	3	....	....	....	.236	.257	.300	.557	81	-3	9	2.89	-10	/C-26,O-3,1-1,3-1	3	-0.9
• SCHWARTZ, Randy	Douglas Randall Schwartz b: 2/9/1944, Los Angeles, CA BL/TL, 6'3", 230 lbs. Deb: 9/8/1965																							
1965 KC-A	6	7	0	2	0	0	0	1	0	4	0	0	.286	.286	.286	.571	64	-0	1	3.09	1	/1-2	0	0.0
1966 KC-A	10	11	0	1	0	0	0	1	1	3	0	0	.091	.167	.091	.258	-24	-2	0	.57	0	/1-2	0	-0.2
Total 2	16	18	0	3	0	0	0	2	1	7	0	0	.167	.211	.167	.377	8	-2	1	1.41	0	/1-4	0	-0.2
• SCHWEITZER, Al	Albert Caspar "Cheese" Schweitzer b: 12/23/1882, Cleveland, OH d: 1/27/1969, Newark, OH BR/TR, 5'7.5", 170 lbs. Deb: 4/30/1908 Career OF: 16-75-163																							
1908 StL-A	64	182	22	53	4	2	1	14	20	....	6	....	.291	.374	.352	.725	135	8	27	5.07	6	O-55(0-28-27)	10	1.3
1909 StL-A	27	76	7	17	2	0	0	2	5	....	3	....	.224	.298	.250	.548	79	-2	6	2.79	-1	O-22(6-7-9)	2	-0.4
1910 StL-A	113	379	37	87	11	2	2	37	36	....	26	....	.230	.303	.285	.588	90	-4	40	3.47	-1	*O-109(1-32-76)	9	-1.1
1911 StL-A	76	237	31	51	11	4	0	34	43	....	12	....	.215	.338	.295	.633	80	-4	28	3.77	1	O-68(9-8-51)	5	-0.7
Total 4	280	874	97	208	28	8	3	87	104	....	47	....	.238	.327	.299	.626	96	-1	101	3.81	4	O-254	26	-0.9
• SCHWERT, Pi	Pius Louis Schwert b: 11/22/1892, Angola, NY d: 3/11/1941, Washington, DC BR/TR, 5'10.5", 160 lbs. Deb: 8/20/1914																							
1914 NY-A	3	6	0	0	0	0	0	0	2	3	0	....	.000	.250	.000	.250	-24	-1	0	.00	1	/C-3	0	0.0
1915 NY-A	9	18	6	5	3	0	0	6	1	6	0	....	.278	.316	.444	.760	128	0	3	5.15	0	/C-9	1	0.1
Total 2	12	24	6	5	3	0	0	6	3	9	0	....	.208	.296	.333	.630	83	-0	3	3.52	0	/C-12	1	0.1
• SCHWIND, Art	Arthur Edwin Schwind b: 11/4/1889, Fort Wayne, IN d: 1/13/1968, Sullivan, IL BB/TR, 5'8", 150 lbs. Deb: 10/3/1912																							
1912 Bos-N	1	2	0	1	0	0	0	0	0	0	0	....	.500	.500	.500	1.000	171	0	0	12.55	0	/3-1	0	0.0
• SCHYPINSKI, Jerry	Gerald Albert Schypinski b: 9/16/1931, Detroit, MI BL/TR, 5'10", 170 lbs. Deb: 8/31/1955																							
1955 KC-A	22	69	7	15	2	0	0	5	1	6	0	0	.217	.229	.246	.475	27	-7	4	1.82	-2	S-21/2-2	0	-0.8
• SCIOSCIA, Mike	Michael Lorri Scioscia b: 11/27/1958, Upper Darby, PA BL/TR, 6'2", 220 lbs. Deb: 4/20/1980 M/C																							
1980 LA-N	54	134	8	34	5	1	1	8	12	9	1	0	.254	.315	.328	.643	81	-3	15	3.64	2	C-54	5	0.1
1981★LA-N	93	290	27	80	10	0	2	29	36	18	0	2	.276	.358	.331	.689	100	0	34	4.07	-5	C-91	11	0.0
1982 LA-N	129	365	31	80	11	1	5	38	44	31	2	0	.219	.305	.296	.601	70	-13	34	3.06	-5	*C-123	8	-1.3
1983 LA-N	12	35	3	11	3	0	1	7	5	2	0	0	.314	.400	.486	.886	145	2	7	7.31	0	C-11	2	0.3
1984 LA-N	114	341	29	93	18	0	5	38	52	26	2	1	.273	.371	.370	.740	110	6	48	4.87	0	*C-112	15	1.3
1985★LA-N	141	429	47	127	26	3	7	53	77	21	3	3	.296	.409	.420	.829	136	24	78	6.37	1	*C-139	26	3.3
1986 LA-N	122	374	36	94	18	1	5	26	62	23	3	3	.251	.362	.345	.707	103	3	49	4.35	-2	*C-119	13	0.8
1987 LA-N	142	461	44	122	26	1	6	38	55	23	7	4	.265	.344	.364	.709	90	-6	58	4.29	3	*C-138	18	0.4
1988★LA-N	130	408	29	105	18	0	3	35	38	31	0	3	.257	.321	.324	.644	88	-8	40	3.28	4	*C-123	14	0.4
1989 LA-N★	133	408	40	102	16	0	10	44	52	29	0	2	.250	.339	.363	.702	102	1	52	4.40	9	*C-130	16	2.0
1990 LA-N★	135	435	46	115	25	0	12	66	55	31	4	1	.264	.351	.405	.756	110	7	62	4.98	3	*C-132	20	1.9
1991 LA-N	119	345	39	91	16	2	8	40	47	32	4	3	.264	.357	.391	.748	113	7	51	5.05	1	*C-115	14	1.5
1992 LA-N	117	348	19	77	6	3	3	24	32	31	3	2	.221	.289	.282	.570	63	-17	28	2.64	7	*C-108	6	-0.4
Total 13	1441	4373	398	1131	198	12	68	446	567	307	29	24	.259	.347	.356	.703	99	5	555	4.32	18	*C-1395	168	10.2
• SCOFFIC, Lou	Louis "Weaser" Scoffic b: 5/20/1913, Herrin, IL d: 8/28/1997, Herrin, IL BR/TR, 5'10", 182 lbs. Deb: 4/16/1936																							
1936 StL-N	4	7	2	3	0	0	0	2	1	2	0	....	.429	.500	.429	.929	153	1	2	11.26	0	/O-3(0-0-3)	1	0.0
• SCONIERS, Daryl	Daryl Anthony Sconiers b: 10/3/1958, San Bernardino, CA BL/TL, 6'2", 195 lbs. Deb: 9/13/1981																							
1981 Cal-A	15	52	6	14	1	1	1	7	1	10	0	0	.269	.283	.385	.668	91	-1	6	4.07	1	1-12/D-3	1	-0.1
1982 Cal-A	12	13	0	2	0	0	0	2	2	1	0	0	.154	.267	.154	.421	19	-1	0	.70	0	/1-3,D-1	0	-0.2
1983 Cal-A	106	314	49	86	19	3	8	46	17	41	4	2	.274	.311	.430	.741	102	-0	39	4.38	-6	1-57,D-27/O-1	7	-1.0
1984 Cal-A	57	160	14	39	4	0	4	17	13	17	1	2	.244	.301	.344	.644	78	-5	15	3.11	-1	1-41/D-1	2	-0.9
1985 Cal-A	44	98	14	28	6	1	2	12	15	18	2	1	.286	.381	.429	.809	122	3	17	5.94	-1	D-20/1-6	4	0.2
Total 5	234	637	83	169	30	5	15	84	48	87	7	5	.265	.317	.399	.716	97	-4	77	4.17	-8	1-119/D-52,O-1	14	-2.0
• SCOTT,	Scott Deb: 7/16/1884																							
1884 Bal-U	13	53	10	12	1	1	1	....	2	....	....	....	.226	.255	.340	.594	90	-1	5	3.21	-1	O-13(0-0-13)/3-1	1	-0.1
• SCOTT, Dick	Richard Edward Scott b: 7/19/1962, Ellsworth, ME BR/TR, 6'1", 170 lbs. Deb: 5/19/1989																							
1989 Oak-A	3	2	0	0	0	0	0	1	0	0	0	0	.000	.000	.000	.000	-104	-1	0	.00	-2	/S-3	0	-0.2
• SCOTT, Donnie	Donald Malcolm Scott b: 8/16/1961, Dunedin, FL BB/TR, 5'11", 185 lbs. Deb: 9/30/1983																							
1983 Tex-A	2	4	0	0	0	0	0	0	0	0	0	0	.000	.000	.000	.000	-102	-1	0	.00	0	/C-2	0	-0.1
1984 Tex-A	81	235	16	52	9	0	3	20	20	44	0	1	.221	.282	.298	.580	59	-13	20	2.72	-2	C-80	3	-1.2
1985 Sea-A	80	185	18	41	13	0	4	23	15	41	1	1	.222	.280	.357	.637	72	-8	19	3.27	0	C-74	4	-0.5
1991 Cin-N	10	19	0	3	0	0	0	0	0	2	0	0	.158	.158	.158	.316	-11	-3	0	.80	0	/C-8	0	-0.3
Total 4	173	443	34	96	22	0	7	43	35	87	1	2	.217	.274	.314	.588	61	-25	39	2.83	-2	C-164	7	-2.0
• SCOTT, Everett	Lewis Everett "Deacon" Scott b: 11/19/1892, Bluffton, IN d: 11/2/1960, Fort Wayne, IN BR/TR, 5'8", 148 lbs. Deb: 4/14/1914																							
1914 Bos-A	144	539	66	129	15	6	2	37	32	43	9	14	.239	.286	.301	.586	76	-22	48	2.82	8	*S-143	13	-0.3
1915★Bos-A	100	359	25	72	11	0	0	28	17	21	4	7	.201	.237	.231	.468	41	-29	22	1.82	5	*S-100	6	-1.8
1916★Bos-A	123	366	37	85	19	2	0	27	23	24	8	....	.232	.283	.295	.578	73	-13	37	3.09	8	*S-121/2-1,3-1	11	0.3
1917 Bos-A	157	528	40	127	24	7	0	50	20	46	12	....	.241	.268	.313	.581	78	-17	49	2.86	14	*S-157	15	0.9
1918★Bos-A	126	443	40	98	11	5	0	43	12	16	11	....	.221	.242	.269	.510	55	-27	32	2.17	15	*S-126	9	-0.3
1919 Bos-A	138	507	41	141	19	0	0	38	19	26	8	....	.278	.306	.316	.621	79	-16	50	3.41	2	*S-138	14	-0.4
1920 Bos-A	154	569	41	153	21	12	4	61	21	15	4	11	.269	.300	.369	.669	80	-21	60	3.54	12	*S-154	15	0.2
1921 Bos-A	154	576	65	151	21	9	1	62	27	21	5	9	.262	.295	.335	.630	62	-36	55	3.25	38	*S-154	16	1.7
1922★NY-A	154	557	64	150	23	5	3	45	23	22	2	3	.269	.304	.345	.649	67	-28	59	3.56	26	*S-154	16	1.4
1923★NY-A	152	533	48	131	16	4	6	60	13	19	1	3	.246	.266	.325	.591	54	-38	45	2.83	2	*S-152	9	-2.0
1924 NY-A	153	548	56	137	12	6	4	64	21	15	3	7	.250	.278	.316	.593	53	-42	47	2.84	16	*S-153	11	-0.9
1925 NY-A	22	60	3	13	0	0	0	4	2	2	0	1	.217	.242	.217	.459	17	-8	3	1.62	2	S-18	1	-0.4
Was-A	33	103	10	28	6	1	0	18	4	4	1	2	.272	.299	.350	.649	65	-6	10	3.39	-2	S-30/3-2	2	-0.5
Yr.	55	163	13	41	6	1	0	22	6	6	1	3	.252	.278	.301	.579	47	-14	13	2.70	-0	S-48/3-2	3	-0.8
1926 Chi-A	40	143	15	36	10	1	0	13	9	8	1	3	.252	.296	.336	.632	67	-8	14	3.14	5	S-39	3	0.1
Cin-N	4	6	1	4	0	0	0	1	0	0	0	....	.667	.667	.667	1.333	267	1	2	32.24	-2	/S-4	1	0.0
Total 13	1654	5837	552	1455	208	58	20	551	243	282	69	60	.249	.281	.315	.596	66	-309	532	2.97	150	*S-1643/3-3,2-1	142	-1.9

YEAR TM-L	G	AB	R	H	2B	3B	HR	RBI	BB	SO	SB	CS	AVG	OBP	SLG	OPS	OPS+	BR/A	RC	RC/G	FR	G/POS	WS	TPW
• SCOTT, Gary	Gary Thomas Scott b: 8/22/1968, New Rochelle, NY BR/TR, 6', 175 lbs. Deb: 4/9/1991																							
1991 Chi-N	31	79	8	13	3	0	1	5	13	14	0	1	.165	.305	.241	.546	53	-5	6	2.37	-1	3-31	1	-0.6
1992 Chi-N	36	96	8	15	2	0	2	11	5	14	0	1	.156	.198	.240	.438	23	-10	4	1.21	-3	3-29/S-2	0	-1.4
Total 2	67	175	16	28	5	0	3	16	18	28	0	2	.160	.250	.240	.490	37	-15	10	1.73	-4	/3-60,S-2	1	-2.1
• SCOTT, George	George Charles "Boomer" Scott b: 3/23/1944, Greenville, MS BR/TR, 6'2", 215 lbs. Deb: 4/12/1966																							
1966 Bos-A★	162	601	73	147	18	7	27	90	65	152	4	0	.245	.326	.433	.759	105	6	81	4.48	-2	*1-158/3-5	16	-0.6
1967*Bos-A	159	565	74	171	21	7	19	82	63	119	10	8	.303	.377	.465	.842	136	26	97	6.20	0	*1-152/3-2	23	1.9
1968 Bos-A	124	350	23	60	14	0	3	25	26	88	3	5	.171	.239	.237	.476	42	-26	18	1.54	-1	*1-112/3-6	1	-3.8
1969 Bos-A	152	549	63	139	14	5	16	52	61	74	4	3	.253	.332	.384	.717	95	-4	69	4.31	-9	*3-109,1-53	15	-1.8
1970 Bos-A	127	480	50	142	24	5	16	63	44	95	4	11	.296	.357	.467	.824	117	7	74	5.45	-3	3-68,1-59	15	0.0
1971 Bos-A	146	537	72	141	16	4	24	78	41	102	0	3	.263	.321	.441	.762	106	2	69	4.32	0	*1-143	15	-1.0
1972 Mil-A	152	578	71	154	24	4	20	88	43	130	16	4	.266	.322	.426	.747	123	17	76	4.53	4	*1-139,3-23	21	1.2
1973 Mil-A	158	604	98	185	30	4	24	107	61	94	9	5	.306	.372	.488	.860	144	34	106	6.36	14	*1-157/D-1	24	3.7
1974 Mil-A	158	604	74	170	36	2	17	82	59	90	9	9	.281	.348	.432	.780	124	17	84	4.76	9	*1-148/D-9	19	1.5
1975 Mil-A★	158	617	86	176	26	4	**36**	**109**	51	97	6	5	.285	.343	.515	.858	139	28	99	5.61	3	*1-144,D-12/3-5	23	2.0
1976 Mil-A	156	606	73	166	21	5	18	77	53	118	0	1	.274	.337	.414	.752	122	15	82	4.71	6	*1-155	19	0.9
1977 Bos-A★	157	584	103	157	26	5	33	95	57	112	1	1	.269	.340	.500	.840	112	10	93	5.47	4	*1-157	15	0.5
1978 Bos-A	120	412	51	96	16	4	12	54	44	86	1	1	.233	.307	.379	.686	83	-9	44	3.46	-10	*1-113/D-7	6	-2.7
1979 Bos-A	45	156	18	35	9	1	4	23	17	22	0	0	.224	.301	.372	.672	76	-5	14	2.89	-2	1-41	1	-1.0
KC-A	44	146	19	39	8	2	1	20	12	32	1	1	.267	.331	.370	.701	87	-3	15	3.22	-2	1-41/D-2,3-1	1	-0.7
NY-A	16	44	9	14	3	1	1	6	2	7	1	0	.318	.348	.500	.848	128	2	8	6.99	0	D-15/1-1	2	0.1
Yr.	105	346	46	88	20	4	6	49	31	61	2	1	.254	.319	.387	.707	87	-6	37	3.47	-5	1-83,D-17/3-1	4	-1.6
Total 14	2034	7433	957	1992	306	60	271	1051	699	1418	69	57	.268	.335	.435	.770	113	117	1027	4.73	13	*1-1773,3-219/D-46	216	0.2
• SCOTT, Jim	James Walter Scott b: 9/22/1888, Shenandoah, PA d: 5/12/1972, South Pasadena, FL BR/TR, 5'9.5", 165 lbs. Deb: 4/22/1914																							
1914 Pit-F	8	24	2	6	1	0	0	1	5	0	1	....	.250	.379	.292	.671	98	0	3	4.03	-2	/S-8	1	-0.1
• SCOTT, John	John Henry Scott b: 1/24/1952, Jackson, MS BR/TR, 6'2", 165 lbs. Deb: 9/7/1974 Career OF: 32-44-1																							
1974 SD-N	14	15	3	1	0	0	0	0	0	4	1	0	.067	.067	.067	.133	-65	-3	0	.00	1	/0-8(5-2-1)	0	-0.3
1975 SD-N	25	9	6	0	0	0	0	0	0	2	2	0	.000	.000	.000	.000	-107	-2	0	.00	0	/0-1	0	-0.2
1977 Tor-A	79	233	26	56	9	0	2	15	8	39	10	8	.240	.266	.305	.570	54	-16	17	2.37	-3	0-67(27-41-0)/D-2	1	-2.1
Total 3	118	257	35	57	9	0	2	15	8	45	13	8	.222	.245	.280	.525	42	-21	17	2.11	-2	/0-76,D-2	1	-2.6
• SCOTT, Le Grant	Le Grant Edward Scott b: 7/25/1910, Cleveland, OH d: 11/12/1993, Birmingham, AL BL/TL, 5'8.5", 170 lbs. Deb: 4/19/1939																							
1939 Phi-N	76	232	31	65	15	1	1	26	22	14	5	....	.280	.343	.366	.709	95	-2	29	4.41	-3	0-55(1-1-54)	5	-0.8
• SCOTT, Milt	Milton Parker "Mikado Milt" Scott b: 1/17/1866, Chicago, IL d: 11/3/1938, Baltimore, MD BR, 5'9", 160 lbs. Deb: 9/30/1882																							
1882 Chi-N	1	5	1	2	0	0	0	0	0	0	....	....	.400	.400	.400	.800	156	0	1	7.52	0	/1-1	0	0.0
1884 Det-N	110	438	29	108	17	5	3	50	9	62	....	....	.247	.262	.329	.591	90	-5	39	3.22	3	*1-110	7	-1.0
1885 Det-N	38	148	14	39	7	0	0	12	4	16	....	....	.264	.283	.311	.594	92	-2	13	3.30	1	1-38	2	-0.4
Pit-a	55	210	15	52	7	1	0	18	5	....	....	....	.248	.272	.290	.562	79	-5	17	2.91	6	1-55	3	-0.3
1886 Bal-a	137	484	48	92	11	4	2	52	22	....	11	....	.190	.239	.242	.481	52	-26	31	2.16	14	*1-137/P-1	8	-2.1
Total 4	341	1285	107	293	42	10	5	132	40	78	11	....	.228	.257	.288	.545	74	-38	101	2.77	25	1-341/P-1	20	-3.7
• SCOTT, Pete	Floyd John Scott b: 12/21/1898, Woodland, CA d: 5/3/1953, Daly City, CA BR/TR, 5'11.5", 175 lbs. Deb: 4/13/1926 Career OF: 64-1-77																							
1926 Chi-N	77	189	34	54	13	1	3	34	22	31	3	....	.286	.363	.413	.776	107	2	29	5.06	2	0-59(34-0-29)/3-1	6	0.0
1927 Chi-N	71	156	28	49	18	1	0	21	19	18	1	....	.314	.392	.442	.834	123	6	27	6.35	0	0-36(1-1-35)	6	0.3
1928 Pit-N	60	177	33	55	10	4	5	33	18	14	1	....	.311	.378	.497	.875	122	5	33	6.57	3	0-42(29-0-13)/1-8	7	0.5
Total 3	208	522	95	158	41	6	8	88	59	63	5	....	.303	.377	.450	.827	117	13	88	5.93	5	0-137/1-8,3-1	19	0.8
• SCOTT, Rodney	Rodney Darrell Scott b: 10/16/1953, Indianapolis, IN BB/TR, 6', 160 lbs. Deb: 4/11/1975 Career OF: 0-10-1																							
1975 KC-A	48	15	13	1	0	0	0	0	1	3	4	2	.067	.125	.067	.192	-43	-3	0	.00	-4	D-22/2-9,S-8	0	-0.6
1976 Mon-N	7	10	3	4	0	0	0	0	1	1	2	0	.400	.455	.400	.855	138	1	2	10.84	-2	/2-6,S-3	1	-0.1
1977 Oak-A	133	364	56	95	4	4	0	20	43	50	33	18	.261	.344	.294	.638	77	-10	41	3.74	-5	2-71,S-70/3-5,D-1,0-1	9	-0.8
1978 Chi-N	78	227	41	64	5	1	0	15	43	41	27	10	.282	.403	.313	.716	91	2	35	5.06	-6	3-59,0-10(0-10-0)/2-6,S-6	8	-0.4
1979 Mon-N	151	562	69	134	12	5	3	42	66	82	39	12	.238	.321	.294	.614	69	-19	61	3.57	4	*2-113,S-39	14	-0.5
1980 Mon-N	154	567	84	127	13	**13**	0	46	70	75	63	13	.224	.310	.293	.603	69	-14	60	3.40	-4	*2-129,S-21	13	-0.9
1981*Mon-N	95	336	43	69	9	3	0	26	50	35	30	7	.205	.310	.250	.560	60	-13	32	2.90	5	2-93	7	-0.3
1982 Mon-N	14	25	2	5	0	0	0	1	3	2	5	0	.200	.286	.200	.486	37	-1	2	3.23	0	2-12	0	-0.1
NY-A	10	26	5	5	0	0	0	0	4	2	2	0	.192	.300	.192	.492	39	-2	2	2.30	0	/S-6,2-4	1	-0.1
Total 8	690	2132	316	504	43	26	3	150	281	291	205	62	.236	.328	.285	.613	70	-58	235	3.56	-11	2-443,S-153/3-64,D-23,0-11	53	-3.7
• SCOTT, Tony	Anthony Scott b: 9/18/1951, Cincinnati, OH BB/TR, 6', 175 lbs. Deb: 9/1/1973 C Career OF: 125-653-106																							
1973 Mon-N	11	1	2	0	0	0	0	0	0	1	0	0	.000	.000	.000	.000	-97	-0	0	.00	-1	/0-3(1-1-1)	0	-0.1
1974 Mon-N	19	7	2	2	0	0	0	1	1	3	1	1	.286	.375	.286	.661	82	-0	1	3.13	-1	0-16(2-1-14)	0	-0.2
1975 Mon-N	92	143	19	26	4	2	0	11	12	38	5	6	.182	.259	.238	.497	37	-14	8	1.67	1	0-71(45-4-28)	1	-1.6
1977 StL-N	95	292	38	85	16	3	3	41	33	48	13	10	.291	.369	.397	.766	107	3	42	5.10	-1	0-89(3-82-6)	12	0.0
1978 StL-N	96	219	28	50	5	2	1	14	14	41	5	6	.228	.281	.283	.564	59	-14	16	2.39	-1	0-77(38-31-10)	1	-1.8
1979 StL-N	153	587	69	152	22	10	6	68	34	92	37	17	.259	.305	.361	.666	80	-16	62	3.54	10	*0-151(0-140-14)	13	-0.9
1980 StL-N	143	415	51	104	19	3	0	28	35	68	22	10	.251	.310	.311	.621	72	-15	40	3.22	0	*0-134(0-134-0)	7	-1.8
1981 StL-N	45	176	21	40	5	2	2	17	5	22	10	7	.227	.253	.313	.565	58	-11	12	2.24	0	0-44(0-44-0)	2	-1.3
*Hou-N	55	225	28	66	13	2	2	22	15	32	8	3	.293	.338	.396	.733	113	4	31	5.07	-2	0-55(0-55-0)	9	0.1
Yr.	100	401	49	106	18	4	4	39	20	54	18	10	.264	.301	.359	.660	89	-8	43	3.74	-2	0-99(0-99-0)	11	-1.2
1982 Hou-N	132	460	43	110	16	3	1	29	15	56	18	4	.239	.265	.293	.558	61	-23	35	2.52	-2	*0-129(2-125-3)	5	-2.9
1983 Hou-N	80	186	20	42	6	1	2	17	11	39	5	4	.226	.269	.301	.570	61	-11	16	2.74	1	0-61(17-30-28)	2	-1.2
1984 Hou-N	25	21	2	4	1	0	0	0	4	3	0	0	.190	.320	.238	.558	63	-1	2	2.91	0	/0-6(1-5-0)	0	-0.1
Mon-N	45	71	8	18	4	0	0	5	7	21	1	1	.254	.321	.310	.630	81	-2	7	3.45	-0	0-17(16-1-2)	1	-0.3
Yr.	70	92	10	22	5	0	0	5	11	24	1	1	.239	.320	.293	.614	77	-3	9	3.32	0	0-23(17-6-2)	1	-0.4
Total 11	991	2803	331	699	111	28	17	253	186	464	125	69	.249	.300	.327	.627	75	-102	272	3.25	4	0-853	53	-12.0
• SCRANTON, Jim	James Dean Scranton b: 4/5/1960, Torrance, CA BR/TR, 6', 175 lbs. Deb: 9/5/1984																							
1984 KC-A	2	2	0	0	0	0	0	0	0	0	0	0	.000	.000	.000	.000	-99	-1	0	.00	0	/3-1,S-1	0	-0.1
1985 KC-A	6	4	1	0	0	0	0	0	0	0	0	0	.000	.000	.000	.000	-100	-1	0	.00	0	/S-5	0	0.0
Total 2	8	6	1	0	0	0	0	0	0	0	0	0	.000	.000	.000	.000	-100	-2	0	.00	0	/S-6,3-1	0	-0.1
• SCRIVENER, Chuck	Wayne Allison Scrivener b: 10/3/1947, Alexandria, VA BR/TR, 5'9", 170 lbs. Deb: 9/18/1975																							
1975 Det-A	4	16	0	4	1	0	0	0	0	1	1	0	.250	.250	.313	.563	56	-1	1	3.11	0	/3-3,S-2	0	0.0
1976 Det-A	80	222	28	49	7	1	2	16	19	34	1	0	.221	.282	.288	.570	65	-10	19	2.91	-3	2-43,S-37/3-5	4	-0.7
1977 Det-A	61	72	10	6	0	0	0	2	5	9	0	0	.083	.143	.083	.226	-35	-13	1	.43	0	S-50/2-8,3-3	1	-1.1
Total 3	145	310	38	59	8	1	2	18	24	44	2	0	.190	.249	.242	.490	41	-24	22	2.25	-3	/S-89,2-51,3-11	5	-1.8
• SCRUGGS, Tony	Anthony Raymond Scruggs b: 3/19/1966, Riverside, CA BR/TR, 6'1", 210 lbs. Deb: 4/8/1991																							
1991 Tex-A	5	6	1	0	0	0	0	0	0	1	0	0	.000	.000	.000	.000	-102	-2	0	.00	-0	/0-5(5-1-0)	0	-0.2
• SCUTARO, Marco	Marcos Scutaro b: 10/30/1975, San Felipe, Venezuela BR/TR, 5'10", 170 lbs. Deb: 7/21/2002																							
2002 NY-N	27	36	2	8	0	1	1	6	0	11	0	1	.222	.222	.361	.583	52	-3	2	1.87	-2	2-12/S-6,3-3,0-1	0	-0.4
2003 NY-N	48	75	10	16	4	0	2	6	13	14	2	0	.213	.337	.347	.684	82	-1	10	4.33	-5	2-39/S-1	2	-0.5
Total 2	75	111	12	24	4	1	3	12	13	25	2	1	.216	.304	.351	.655	73	-4	12	3.49	-6	/2-51,S-7,3-3,0-1	2	-0.9

YEAR TM-L	G	AB	R	H	2B	3B	HR	RBI	BB	SO	SB	CS	AVG	OBP	SLG	OPS	OPS+	BR/A	RC	RC/G	FR	G/POS	WS	TPW
• SEABOL, Scott	Scott Anthony Seabol b: 5/17/1975, McKeesport, PA BR/TR, 6'4", 200 lbs. Deb: 4/8/2001																							
2001 NY-A	1	1	0	0	0	0	0	0	0	0	0	0	.000	.000	.000	.000	-99	-0	0	.00	0	/D-1	0	0.0
• SEARS, Ken	Kenneth Eugene "Ziggy" Sears b: 7/6/1917, Streator, IL d: 7/17/1968, Bridgeport, TX BL/TR, 6'1", 200 lbs. Deb: 5/2/1943																							
1943 NY-A	60	187	22	52	7	0	2	22	11	18	1	3	.278	.328	.348	.676	97	-2	21	4.05	-2	C-50	7	-0.1
1946 StL-A	7	15	1	5	0	0	0	1	3	0	0	0	.333	.444	.333	.778	114	1	2	5.64	0	/C-4	0	0.0
Total 2	**67**	**202**	**23**	**57**	**7**	**0**	**2**	**23**	**14**	**18**	**1**	**3**	**.282**	**.338**	**.347**	**.684**	**98**	**-1**	**23**	**4.16**	**-2**	**/C-54**	**7**	**-0.1**
• SEARS, Todd	Todd Andrew Sears b: 10/23/1975, Des Moines, IA BL/TR, 6'5", 215 lbs. Deb: 9/17/2002																							
2002 Min-A	7	12	2	4	2	0	0	0	0	1	0	0	.333	.333	.500	.833	116	0	2	6.75	0	/1-6	0	0.0
2003 Min-A	24	65	7	16	2	0	2	11	7	15	0	0	.246	.329	.369	.698	83	-2	7	3.59	1	1-14/D-6	2	-0.2
SD-N	9	8	2	2	1	0	0	0	0	3	0	0	.250	.250	.375	.625	66	-0	1	3.38	-0	/1-1	0	0.0
Total 2	**40**	**85**	**11**	**22**	**5**	**0**	**2**	**11**	**7**	**19**	**0**	**0**	**.259**	**.323**	**.388**	**.711**	**86**	**-2**	**10**	**3.95**	**1**	**/1-21,D-6**	**2**	**-0.2**
• SEBRING, Jimmy	James Dennison Sebring b: 3/22/1882, Liberty, PA d: 12/22/1909, Williamsport, PA BL/TR, 6', 180 lbs. Deb: 9/8/1902 Career OF: 0-22-339																							
1902 Pit-N	19	80	15	26	4	4	0	15	5	....	2	....	.325	.365	.475	.840	153	5	15	7.25	4	0-19(0-0-19)	4	0.8
1903*Pit-N	124	506	71	140	16	13	4	64	32	....	20	....	.277	.325	.383	.708	98	-3	72	5.13	12	*0-124(0-0-124)	16	0.3
1904 Pit-N	80	305	28	82	11	7	0	32	17	....	8	....	.269	.307	.351	.658	100	-1	36	4.23	7	0-80(0-0-80)	10	0.3
Cin-N	56	222	22	50	9	2	0	24	14	....	8	....	.225	.271	.284	.555	65	-9	20	2.98	3	0-56(0-0-56)	4	-1.0
Yr.	136	527	50	132	20	9	0	56	31	....	16	....	.250	.292	.323	.615	86	-10	56	3.68	10	*0-136(0-0-136)	14	-0.7
1905 Cin-N	58	217	31	62	10	5	2	28	14	....	11	....	.286	.329	.406	.735	107	1	34	5.43	-3	0-56(0-0-56)	7	-0.5
1909 Bro-N	25	81	11	8	1	1	0	5	11	....	3	....	.099	.207	.136	.342	7	-9	3	.99	-1	0-25(0-21-4)	0	-1.1
Was-A	1	0	0	0	0	0	0	0	0	....	0	....	....	....	....	....	-105	0	0	....	0	/0-1	0	0.0
Total 5	**363**	**1411**	**178**	**368**	**51**	**32**	**6**	**168**	**93**	**....**	**52**	**....**	**.261**	**.308**	**.355**	**.663**	**93**	**-16**	**180**	**4.46**	**22**	**0-361**	**41**	**-1.2**
• SECORY, Frank	Frank Edward Secory b: 8/24/1912, Mason City, IA d: 4/7/1995, Port Huron, MI BR/TR, 6'1", 200 lbs. Deb: 4/28/1940 U Career OF: 38-1-2																							
1940 Det-A	1	1	0	0	0	0	0	0	0	1	0	0	.000	.000	.000	.000	-91	-0	0	.00	0	....	0	0.0
1942 Cin-N	2	5	1	0	0	0	0	1	3	2	0	0	.000	.375	.000	.375	14	-0	0	1.58	0	/0-2(2-0-0)	0	0.0
1944 Chi-N	22	56	10	18	1	0	4	17	6	8	1	....	.321	.387	.554	.941	163	5	13	8.10	0	0-17(17-1-0)	3	0.3
1945*Chi-N	35	57	4	9	1	0	0	6	2	7	0	....	.158	.186	.175	.362	1	-8	2	.89	0	0-12(10-0-2)	0	-0.8
1946 Chi-N	33	43	6	10	3	0	3	12	6	6	0	....	.233	.327	.512	.838	139	2	7	5.73	-1	/0-9(9-0-0)	2	0.1
Total 5	**93**	**162**	**21**	**37**	**5**	**0**	**7**	**36**	**17**	**24**	**1**	**0**	**.228**	**.302**	**.389**	**.691**	**95**	**-2**	**22**	**4.37**	**-1**	**/0-40**	**5**	**-0.5**
• SEE, Charlie	Charles Henry "Chad" See b: 10/13/1896, Pleasantville, NY d: 7/19/1948, Bridgeport, CT BL/TR, 5'10.5", 175 lbs. Deb: 8/6/1919 Career OF: 2-27-22																							
1919 Cin-N	8	14	1	4	0	0	0	1	1	0	0	....	.286	.333	.286	.619	89	-0	1	3.38	-1	/0-4(2-2-0)	1	-0.1
1920 Cin-N	47	82	9	25	4	0	0	15	1	7	2	4	.305	.329	.354	.683	97	-1	9	3.47	2	0-17(0-14-4)/P-1	2	-0.3
1921 Cin-N	37	106	11	26	5	1	1	7	7	5	3	2	.245	.298	.340	.638	72	-4	11	3.39	-1	0-30(0-11-18)	2	-0.7
Total 3	**92**	**202**	**21**	**55**	**9**	**1**	**1**	**23**	**9**	**12**	**5**	**6**	**.272**	**.313**	**.342**	**.655**	**83**	**-6**	**21**	**3.42**	**0**	**/0-51,P-1**	**5**	**-1.0**
• SEE, Larry	Ralph Laurence See b: 6/20/1960, Norwalk, CA BR/TR, 6'1", 195 lbs. Deb: 9/3/1986																							
1986 LA-N	13	20	1	5	2	0	0	2	2	7	0	0	.250	.318	.350	.668	90	-0	2	4.31	1	/1-9	0	0.0
1988 Tex-A	13	23	0	3	0	0	0	0	1	8	0	0	.130	.167	.130	.297	-15	-4	1	.78	-1	/D-7,1-2,C-2,3-1	0	-0.5
Total 2	**26**	**43**	**1**	**8**	**2**	**0**	**0**	**2**	**3**	**15**	**0**	**0**	**.186**	**.239**	**.233**	**.472**	**34**	**-4**	**3**	**2.25**	**0**	**/1-11,D-7,C-2,3-1**	**0**	**-0.5**
• SEEDS, Bob	Ira Robert "Suitcase Bob" Seeds b: 2/24/1907, Ringgold, TX d: 10/28/1993, Shamrock, TX BR/TR, 6', 180 lbs. Deb: 4/19/1930 Career OF: 194-160-131																							
1930 Cle-A	85	277	37	79	11	3	3	32	12	22	1	3	.285	.315	.379	.694	72	-13	32	4.08	0	0-70(48-21-1)	4	-1.6
1931 Cle-A	48	134	26	41	4	1	1	10	11	11	1	0	.306	.359	.373	.732	88	-1	18	5.20	-1	0-33(3-1-29)/1-2	3	-0.4
1932 Cle-A	2	4	0	0	0	0	0	0	0	0	0	0	.000	.000	.000	.000	-94	-1	0	.00	0	/0-1	0	-0.1
Chi-A	116	434	53	126	18	6	2	45	31	37	5	7	.290	.342	.373	.715	91	-7	55	4.51	-3	*0-112(34-34-53)	8	-1.5
Yr.	118	438	53	126	18	6	2	45	31	37	5	7	.288	.339	.370	.709	89	-8	55	4.45	-3	*0-113(34-34-54)	8	-1.6
1933 Bos-A	82	230	26	56	13	4	0	23	21	20	1	3	.243	.310	.335	.644	71	-10	24	3.53	0	1-41,0-32(17-0-16)	3	-1.4
1934 Bos-A	8	6	0	1	0	0	0	1	0	1	0	0	.167	.167	.167	.333	-13	-1	0	.85	0	/0-1	0	-0.1
Cle-A	61	186	28	46	8	1	0	18	21	13	2	1	.247	.327	.301	.628	62	-10	20	3.58	-2	0-48(26-2-21)	2	-1.4
Yr.	69	192	28	47	8	1	0	19	21	14	2	1	.245	.322	.297	.619	60	-11	20	3.49	-3	0-49(26-2-22)	2	-1.5
1936*NY-A	13	42	12	11	1	0	4	10	5	3	3	1	.262	.340	.571	.912	126	2	8	6.82	0	/0-9(1-0-8),3-3	2	0.1
1938 NY-N	81	296	35	86	12	3	9	52	20	33	0	....	.291	.338	.443	.780	112	4	44	5.34	-2	0-76(37-40-1)	8	-0.1
1939 NY-N	63	173	33	46	5	1	5	26	22	31	1	....	.266	.352	.393	.745	99	0	25	5.12	-1	0-50(12-38-0)	5	-0.2
1940 NY-N	56	155	18	45	5	2	4	16	17	19	0	....	.290	.371	.426	.797	118	4	25	5.79	0	0-40(16-24-0)	5	0.3
Total 9	**615**	**1937**	**268**	**537**	**77**	**21**	**28**	**233**	**160**	**190**	**14**	**15**	**.277**	**.336**	**.382**	**.718**	**89**	**-34**	**251**	**4.59**	**-9**	**0-472/1-43,3-3**	**40**	**-6.4**
• SEEREY, Pat	James Patrick Seerey b: 3/17/1923, Wilburton, OK d: 4/28/1986, Jennings, MO BR/TR, 5'10", 200 lbs. Deb: 6/9/1943 Career OF: 291-100-140																							
1943 Cle-A	26	72	8	16	3	0	1	5	4	19	0	0	.222	.263	.306	.569	70	-3	5	2.41	2	0-16(16-0-0)	1	-0.3
1944 Cle-A	101	342	39	80	16	0	15	39	19	99	0	2	.234	.276	.412	.689	99	-4	36	3.56	3	0-86(63-19-4)	6	-0.6
1945 Cle-A	126	414	56	98	22	2	14	56	66	97	1	2	.237	.342	.401	.743	120	11	60	4.89	-7	*0-117(38-28-68)	13	-0.1
1946 Cle-A	117	404	57	91	17	2	26	62	65	101	2	3	.225	.334	.470	.804	132	16	64	5.21	-5	*0-115(39-40-43)	15	0.7
1947 Cle-A	82	216	24	37	4	1	11	29	34	66	0	1	.171	.284	.352	.636	78	-7	22	3.15	-0	0-68(53-1-16)	3	-1.1
1948 Cle-A	10	23	7	6	0	0	1	6	7	8	0	0	.261	.433	.391	.825	123	1	4	5.54	-0	/0-7(0-0-7)	1	0.1
Chi-A	95	340	44	78	11	0	18	64	61	94	0	0	.229	.347	.421	.767	107	4	53	5.27	4	0-93(82-12-0)	9	0.2
Yr.	105	363	51	84	11	0	19	70	68	102	0	0	.231	.353	.419	.771	108	5	57	5.29	4	*0-100(82-12-7)	10	0.3
1949 Chi-A	4	4	1	0	0	0	0	0	3	1	0	0	.000	.429	.000	.429	19	-0	0	2.26	0	/0-2(0-0-2)	0	0.0
Total 7	**561**	**1815**	**236**	**406**	**73**	**5**	**86**	**261**	**259**	**485**	**3**	**8**	**.224**	**.321**	**.412**	**.733**	**109**	**18**	**246**	**4.47**	**-3**	**0-504**	**48**	**-1.2**
• SEERY, Emmett	John Emmett Seery b: 2/13/1861, Princeville, IL d: 8/7/1930, Saranac Lake, NY BL/TR, 5'7", 145 lbs. Deb: 4/17/1884 Career OF: 778-2-138																							
1884 Bal-U	105	463	113	144	25	7	2	....	20	....	....	....	.311	.340	.408	.748	138	16	66	5.77	7	*0-103(99-0-5)/C-3,3-2	21	1.7
KC-U	1	4	2	2	1	0	0	....	1	....	....	....	.500	.600	.750	1.350	407	1	2	25.83	0	/0-1	1	0.1
Yr.	106	467	115	146	26	7	2	....	21	....	....	....	.313	.342	.411	.753	140	17	68	5.90	7	*0-104(100-0-5)/C-3,3-2	22	1.8
1885 StL-N	59	216	20	35	7	0	1	14	16	37	....	....	.162	.220	.208	.428	42	-13	10	1.51	4	0-59(49-0-10)/3-1	1	-1.0
1886 StL-N	126	453	73	108	22	6	2	48	57	82	24	....	.238	.324	.327	.650	105	6	57	4.46	-3	*0-126(126-0-0)/P-2	11	-0.4
1887 Ind-N	122	536	104	175	18	15	4	28	71	68	48	....	.326	.331	.353	.684	93	-1	72	5.29	6	*0-122(122-1-1)/S-1	10	0.0
1888 Ind-N	133	500	87	110	20	10	5	50	64	73	80	....	.220	.316	.330	.646	104	5	79	5.49	6	*0-133(133-0-0)/S-1	17	0.7
1889 Ind-N	127	526	123	165	26	12	8	59	67	59	19	....	.314	.401	.454	.856	136	27	106	7.79	1	*0-127(127-0-0)	18	2.1
1890 Bro-P	104	394	78	88	12	7	1	50	70	36	44	....	.223	.348	.297	.645	69	-17	57	5.06	6	*0-104(104-0-0)	10	-1.1
1891 Cin-a	97	372	77	106	15	10	4	36	81	52	19	....	.285	.423	.411	.834	128	17	75	7.43	3	*0-97(17-1-80)	15	1.6
1892 Lou-N	42	154	18	31	6	1	0	15	24	19	6	....	.201	.309	.253	.562	76	-3	14	3.13	3	0-42(0-0-42)	3	-0.2
Total 9	**916**	**3618**	**695**	**964**	**152**	**68**	**27**	**300**	**471**	**426**	**240**	**....**	**.266**	**.345**	**.356**	**.701**	**106**	**39**	**538**	**5.46**	**34**	**0-914/3-3,C-3,P-2,S-2**	**107**	**3.4**
• SEFCIK, Kevin	Kevin John Sefcik b: 2/10/1971, Tinley Park, IL BR/TR, 5'11", 175 lbs. Deb: 9/8/1995 Career OF: 91-47-46																							
1995 Phi-N	5	4	1	0	0	0	0	0	0	2	0	0	.000	.000	.000	.000	-99	-1	0	.00	-0	/3-2	0	-0.1
1996 Phi-N	44	116	10	33	5	3	0	9	9	16	3	0	.284	.346	.379	.726	90	-1	15	4.54	-0	S-21,3-20/2-1	2	0.1
1997 Phi-N	61	119	11	32	3	0	2	6	4	9	1	2	.269	.298	.345	.643	68	-7	11	2.97	-3	2-22,S-10/3-4	1	-0.8
1998 Phi-N	104	169	27	53	7	2	3	20	25	32	4	2	.314	.423	.432	.855	124	8	33	7.21	-1	0-60(35-8-20)/3-2,2-1	7	0.5
1999 Phi-N	111	209	28	58	15	3	1	11	29	24	9	4	.278	.368	.392	.761	90	-2	32	5.29	-2	0-64(31-19-17),2-15	3	-0.5
2000 Phi-N	99	153	15	36	6	2	0	10	13	19	4	2	.235	.304	.301	.604	53	-11	14	3.02	-1	0-50(25-20-9)/D-1	1	-1.2
2001 Col-N	1	1	0	0	0	0	0	0	0	0	0	0	.000	.000	.000	.000	-82	-0	0	.00	0	....	0	0.0
Total 7	**425**	**771**	**92**	**212**	**36**	**10**	**6**	**56**	**80**	**102**	**21**	**10**	**.275**	**.353**	**.371**	**.724**	**86**	**-15**	**105**	**4.68**	**-7**	**0-174/2-39,S-31,3-28,D-1**	**14**	**-2.0**
• SEGRIST, Kal	Kal Hill Segrist b: 4/14/1931, Greenville, TX BR/TR, 6', 180 lbs. Deb: 7/16/1952																							
1952 NY-A	13	23	3	1	0	0	0	1	3	1	0	0	.043	.154	.043	.197	-46	-4	0	.40	0	2-11/3-1	0	-0.4
1955 Bal-A	7	9	1	3	0	0	0	0	2	0	0	0	.333	.455	.333	.788	123	0	1	4.94	0	/3-3,1-2,2-1	0	0.1
Total 2	**20**	**32**	**4**	**4**	**0**	**0**	**0**	**1**	**5**	**1**	**0**	**0**	**.125**	**.243**	**.125**	**.368**	**3**	**-4**	**2**	**1.46**	**0**	**/2-12,3-4,1-1**	**0**	**-0.4**

YEAR TM-L	G	AB	R	H	2B	3B	HR	RBI	BB	SO	SB	CS	AVG	OBP	SLG	OPS	OPS+	BR/A	RC	RC/G	FR	G/POS	WS	TPW
• SEGUI, David	David Vincent Segui b: 7/19/1966, Kansas City, KS BB/TL, 6'1", 202 lbs. Deb: 5/8/1990 Career OF: 71-0-29																							
1990 Bal-A	40	123	14	30	7	0	2	15	11	15	0	0	.244	.311	.350	.661	87	-2	10	2.59	0	1-36/D-4	2	-0.4
1991 Bal-A	86	212	15	59	7	0	2	22	12	19	1	1	.278	.317	.340	.657	85	-5	21	3.49	1	1-42,0-33(28-0-5)/D-4	3	-0.7
1992 Bal-A	115	189	21	44	9	0	1	17	20	23	1	0	.233	.306	.296	.603	68	-8	18	3.15	1	1-95,0-18(3-0-15)	2	-1.0
1993 Bal-A	146	450	54	123	27	0	10	60	58	53	2	1	.273	.356	.400	.756	99	1	63	4.74	2	*1-144/D-1	10	-0.9
1994 NY-N	92	336	46	81	17	1	10	43	33	43	0	0	.241	.311	.387	.698	81	-10	41	4.14	0	1-78,0-21(19-0-2)	5	-1.7
1995 NY-N	33	73	9	24	3	1	2	11	12	9	1	3	.329	.430	.479	.910	144	4	15	6.54	1	0-18(18-0-0)/1-7	1	0.4
Mon-N	97	383	59	117	22	3	10	57	28	38	1	4	.305	.356	.457	.813	109	3	60	5.70	2	1-97/0-2(2-0-0)	12	-0.4
Yr.	130	456	68	141	25	4	12	68	40	47	2	7	.309	.369	.461	.829	115	7	74	5.84	3	*1-104,0-20(20-0-0)	13	0.0
1996 Mon-N	115	416	69	119	30	1	11	58	60	54	4	4	.286	.376	.442	.818	112	8	70	6.13	2	*1-113	15	0.0
1997 Mon-N	125	459	75	141	22	3	21	68	57	66	1	0	.307	.385	.505	.890	131	22	90	7.29	0	*1-125	16	1.1
1998 Sea-A	143	522	79	159	36	1	19	84	49	80	3	1	.305	.364	.487	.851	119	14	91	6.41	10	*1-134/0-1	15	1.2
1999 Sea-A	90	345	43	101	22	3	9	39	32	43	1	2	.293	.354	.452	.807	102	-0	53	5.58	1	1-90	7	-0.7
Tor-A	31	95	14	30	5	0	5	13	8	17	0	0	.316	.369	.526	.895	123	3	19	7.54	0	D-25/1-4	3	0.1
Yr.	121	440	57	131	27	3	14	52	40	60	1	2	.298	.358	.468	.826	106	3	72	5.98	1	1-94,D-25	10	-0.5
2000 Tex-A	93	351	52	118	29	1	11	57	34	51	0	1	.336	.395	.519	.913	127	14	69	7.43	1	D-52,1-38	11	0.7
Cle-A	57	223	41	74	13	0	8	46	19	33	0	0	.332	.387	.498	.885	119	7	41	6.97	2	1-36,D-16/0-7(0-0-7)	7	0.4
Yr.	150	574	93	192	42	1	19	103	53	84	0	1	.334	.392	.510	.902	124	21	110	7.26	3	1-74,D-68/0-7(0-0-7)	18	1.1
2001 Bal-A	82	292	48	88	18	1	10	46	49	61	1	1	.301	.409	.473	.881	139	18	60	7.63	-6	1-65,D-16	14	0.6
2002 Bal-A	26	95	10	25	4	0	2	16	11	22	0	0	.263	.340	.368	.708	93	-1	13	4.91	0	D-19/1-7	2	-0.2
2003 Bal-A	67	224	26	59	10	1	5	25	26	47	1	0	.263	.343	.384	.727	95	-1	29	4.49	1	D-52/1-8	4	-0.4
Total 14	1438	4788	675	1392	281	16	138	677	519	674	17	18	.291	.362	.443	.804	109	66	762	5.71	19	*1-1119,D-189,0-100	129	-2.0
• SEGUIGNOL, Fernando	Fernando Alfredo Seguignol b: 1/19/1975, Bocas Del Toro, Panama BB/TR, 6'5", 230 lbs. Deb: 9/5/1998 Career OF: 38-0-25																							
1998 Mon-N	16	42	6	11	4	0	2	3	3	15	0	0	.262	.311	.500	.811	111	0	6	5.16	1	/0-9(8-0-1),1-7	0	0.1
1999 Mon-N	35	105	14	27	9	0	5	10	5	33	0	0	.257	.333	.486	.819	107	1	18	5.84	-1	1-23/0-8(6-0-3)	2	-0.2
2000 Mon-N	76	162	22	45	8	0	10	22	9	46	0	1	.278	.328	.512	.840	105	-0	25	5.50	-3	0-31(17-0-14),1-30/D-1	2	-0.5
2001 Mon-N	46	50	0	7	2	0	0	5	2	17	0	0	.140	.189	.180	.369	-4	-8	1	.63	1	0-13(7-0-7)/1-7	0	-0.7
2003 NY-A	5	7	0	1	0	0	0	0	1	3	0	0	.143	.250	.143	.393	8	-1	0	1.42	1	/1-3,D-1	0	0.0
Total 5	178	366	42	91	23	0	17	40	20	114	0	1	.249	.307	.451	.758	90	-8	51	4.67	-2	/1-70,0-61,D-2	4	-1.5
• SEIBERT, Kurt	Kurt Elliott Seibert b: 10/16/1955, Cheverly, MD BB/TR, 6', 165 lbs. Deb: 9/3/1979																							
1979 Chi-N	7	2	2	0	0	0	0	0	0	1	0	0	.000	.000	.000	.000	-91	-1	0	.00	0	/2-1	0	-0.1
• SEIBOLD, Socks	Harry Seibold b: 4/3/1896, Philadelphia, PA d: 9/21/1965, Philadelphia, PA BR/TR, 5'8.5", 162 lbs. Deb: 9/18/1915 Career OF: 2-1-0 ♦																							
1915 Phi-A	10	26	3	3	1	0	0	2	4	4	0	....	.115	.233	.154	.387	16	-3	1	1.08	-5	/S-7	0	-0.7
1916 Phi-A	5	12	0	2	1	0	0	1	0	4	0	....	.167	.167	.250	.417	26	-0	1	1.30	2	/P-3,0-1	0	-0.3
1917 Phi-A	36	59	6	13	1	1	0	5	4	8	1	....	.220	.281	.271	.552	70	2	5	2.62	-1	P-33/0-2(2-0-0)	3	-1.9
1919 Phi-A	15	13	1	2	0	0	0	1	0	4	0	....	.154	.154	.154	.308	-13	-1	0	.86	0	P-14	0	-0.9
1929 Bos-N	33	70	6	20	2	0	0	9	6	6	0	....	.286	.342	.314	.656	66	5	8	3.79	-1	P-33	13	0.4
1930 Bos-N	36	90	6	19	2	0	1	5	6	6	0	....	.211	.260	.267	.527	29	0	6	2.25	-3	P-36	20	2.0
1931 Bos-N	33	70	3	9	0	0	0	2	1	9	0	....	.129	.141	.129	.269	-28	-4	2	.60	0	P-33	5	-2.3
1932 Bos-N	28	46	2	7	0	0	0	2	2	0	0	....	.152	.188	.152	.340	-8	-2	1	.95	2	P-28	0	-1.6
1933 Bos-N	11	9	0	1	0	0	0	0	2	2	0	....	.111	.273	.111	.384	14	0	0	1.42	0	P-11	1	-0.2
Total 9	207	395	27	76	7	1	1	27	25	43	1	....	.192	.242	.223	.465	25	-3	24	1.88	-6	P-191/S-7,0-3	42	-5.4
• SEILHEIMER, Ricky	Ricky Allen Seilheimer b: 8/30/1960, Brenham, TX BL/TR, 5'11", 185 lbs. Deb: 7/5/1980																							
1980 Chi-A	21	52	4	11	3	1	1	3	4	15	1	0	.212	.268	.365	.633	72	-2	5	3.52	-1	C-21	1	-0.2
• SEITZER, Kevin	Kevin Lee Seitzer b: 3/26/1962, Springfield, IL BR/TR, 5'11", 190 lbs. Deb: 9/3/1986 Career OF: 14-1-1																							
1986 KC-A	28	96	16	31	4	1	2	11	19	14	0	0	.323	.440	.448	.888	139	7	21	8.80	1	1-22/0-5(5-0-0),3-3	5	0.6
1987 KC-A★	161	641	105	**207**	33	8	15	83	80	85	12	7	.323	.400	.470	.869	126	26	120	7.03	-1	*3-141,1-25/0-3(3-0-0),D-1	23	2.2
1988 KC-A	149	559	90	170	32	5	5	60	72	64	10	8	.304	.389	.406	.795	122	18	89	5.75	3	*3-147/D-1,0-1	21	2.2
1989 KC-A	160	597	78	168	17	2	4	48	102	76	17	8	.281	.391	.337	.727	107	12	85	4.93	-8	*3-159/S-6,0-3(2-1-0),1-2	22	0.5
1990 KC-A	158	622	91	171	31	5	6	38	67	66	7	5	.275	.347	.370	.717	102	3	82	4.66	-2	*3-152,2-10	21	0.2
1991 KC-A	85	234	28	62	11	3	1	25	29	21	4	1	.265	.351	.350	.701	94	-0	30	4.59	0	3-68/D-3	7	0.0
1992 Mil-A	148	540	74	146	35	1	5	71	57	44	13	11	.270	.342	.367	.709	101	-1	66	4.07	-3	*3-146/2-2,1-1	16	-0.3
1993 Oak-A	73	255	24	65	10	2	4	27	27	33	4	7	.255	.329	.357	.685	90	-6	28	3.63	-2	3-46,1-24/D-3,0-3(3-0-0),2,P,S	3	-0.9
Mil-A	47	162	21	47	6	0	7	30	17	15	3	0	.290	.361	.457	.818	120	5	26	5.64	1	3-33/1-7,D-3,2-1,0-1	7	0.6
Yr.	120	417	45	112	16	2	11	57	44	48	7	7	.269	.341	.396	.737	101	-0	54	4.37	-1	3-79,1-31/D-6,0-4(3-0-1),2,P,S	10	-0.3
1994 Mil-A	80	309	44	97	24	2	5	49	30	38	2	1	.314	.378	.453	.831	108	4	53	6.32	-4	3-43,1-35/D-4	11	-0.2
1995 Mil-A★	132	492	56	153	33	3	5	69	64	57	2	0	.311	.397	.421	.818	107	8	85	6.35	2	3-88,1-36,D-14	17	0.7
1996 Mil-A	132	490	74	155	25	3	12	62	73	68	6	1	.316	.409	.453	.862	113	14	95	7.17	0	1-65,D-56,3-12	14	0.5
*Cle-A	22	83	11	32	10	0	1	16	14	11	0	0	.386	.480	.542	1.022	159	9	22	11.38	3	D-17/1-5	4	0.9
Yr.	154	573	85	187	35	3	13	78	87	79	6	1	.326	.420	.466	.886	120	23	117	7.72	3	D-73,1-70,3-12	18	1.4
1997*Cle-A	64	198	27	53	14	0	2	24	18	25	0	0	.268	.329	.369	.697	79	-6	24	4.10	0	D-24,1-19,3-13	3	-0.9
Total 12	1439	5278	739	1557	285	35	74	613	669	617	80	49	.295	.378	.404	.782	110	93	826	5.60	-10	*3-1051,1-241,D-126/0,2,S,P	174	6.1
• SELBACH, Kip	Albert Karl Selbach b: 3/24/1872, Columbus, OH d: 2/17/1956, Columbus, OH BR/TR, 5'7", 190 lbs. Deb: 4/24/1894 Career OF: 1355-65-148																							
1894 Was-N	97	372	69	114	21	17	7	71	51	20	21	....	.306	.390	.511	.901	120	11	84	8.50	-9	0-80(45-2-33),S-19	9	-0.2
1895 Was-N	130	519	116	168	22	**22**	6	55	71	28	31	....	.324	.406	.486	.892	131	25	118	8.96	11	*0-118(117-0-1)/S-6,2-5	14	2.1
1896 Was-N	127	487	100	148	17	13	5	100	76	28	49	....	.304	.405	.423	.828	118	16	107	8.16	5	*0-126(124-0-2)	18	0.9
1897 Was-N	124	486	113	152	25	16	5	59	80	....	46	....	.313	.414	.461	.875	131	25	115	8.98	13	*0-124(124-0-0)	19	2.3
1898 Was-N	132	515	88	156	28	11	3	60	64	....	25	....	.303	.383	.417	.801	130	21	95	6.89	13	*0-131(127-4-0)/S-1	17	2.1
1899 Cin-N	141	525	105	156	28	11	3	87	70	....	38	....	.297	.385	.410	.795	114	12	101	6.82	7	*0-140(101-39-0)	23	0.6
1900 NY-N	141	523	98	176	29	12	4	68	72	....	36	....	.337	.425	.461	.885	151	40	121	9.07	15	*0-141(141-0-0)	27	4.0
1901 NY-N	125	502	89	145	29	6	1	56	45	....	8	....	.289	.350	.376	.726	115	10	71	5.21	-7	*0-125(125-0-0)	15	-0.4
1902 Bal-A	128	503	86	161	27	9	3	60	58	....	22	....	.320	.393	.427	.820	122	17	97	7.27	0	*0-127(127-0-0)	16	0.9
1903 Was-A	140	533	68	134	23	12	3	49	41	....	20	....	.251	.305	.356	.661	96	-3	67	4.32	-7	*0-140(120-0-20)/3-1	11	-1.8
1904 Was-A	48	178	15	49	8	4	0	14	24	....	9	....	.275	.361	.365	.727	132	8	28	5.60	1	0-48(48-0-0)	9	0.6
Bos-A	98	376	50	97	19	8	0	30	48	....	10	....	.258	.347	.351	.698	114	8	52	4.76	-1	0-98(98-0-0)	17	0.2
Yr.	146	554	65	146	27	12	0	44	72	....	19	....	.264	.351	.356	.707	120	16	79	5.02	0	*0-146(146-0-0)	26	0.8
1905 Bos-A	121	418	54	103	16	6	4	47	67	....	12	....	.246	.355	.342	.697	120	13	58	4.71	-3	*0-112(0-20-92)	17	0.5
1906 Bos-A	60	228	15	48	9	2	0	23	18	....	7	....	.211	.277	.268	.545	71	-7	20	2.85	1	0-58(58-0-0)	3	-1.1
Total 13	1612	6165	1066	1807	301	149	44	779	785	76	334	....	.293	.377	.412	.788	121	197	1134	6.73	40	*0-1568/S-26,2-5,3-1	215	10.7
• SELBY, Bill	William Frank Selby b: 6/11/1970, Monroeville, AL BL/TR, 5'9", 190 lbs. Deb: 4/19/1996 Career OF: 24-0-11																							
1996 Bos-A	40	95	12	26	4	0	3	6	9	11	1	1	.274	.337	.411	.747	86	-2	12	4.54	-2	2-14,3-14/0-6(6-0-0)	1	-0.4
2000 Cle-A	30	46	8	11	1	0	0	4	1	9	0	0	.239	.271	.261	.532	35	-5	3	2.35	-1	0-10(4-0-6)/2-6,3-4,D-3	0	-0.5
2001 Cin-N	36	92	7	21	7	1	2	12	5	13	0	0	.228	.276	.391	.667	67	-5	10	3.64	-2	2-21/3-8,1-2	1	-0.6
2002 Cle-A	65	159	15	34	7	2	6	21	15	27	0	1	.214	.282	.396	.678	79	-6	17	3.45	-4	3-33,0-18(13-0-5)/2-6	3	-0.9
2003 Cle-A	27	39	3	4	1	0	0	5	3	11	0	0	.103	.167	.128	.295	-21	-7	1	.79	3	3-10/D-2,1-1,2-1,0-1	0	-0.3
Total 5	198	431	45	96	20	3	11	48	33	71	1	2	.223	.281	.360	.641	64	-24	43	3.33	-6	/3-69,2-48,0-35,D-5,1-3	5	-2.7
• SELKIRK, George	George Alexander "Twinkletoes" Selkirk b: 1/4/1908, Huntsville, Canada d: 1/19/1987, Fort Lauderdale, FL BL/TR, 6'1", 182 lbs. Deb: 8/12/1934 Career OF: 340-2-437																							
1934 NY-A	46	176	23	55	7	1	5	38	15	17	1	1	.313	.370	.449	.819	118	4	29	6.36	1	0-46(43-0-7)	6	0.2
1935 NY-A	128	491	64	153	29	12	11	94	44	36	2	7	.312	.372	.487	.859	128	16	87	6.62	4	*0-127(0-0-127)	19	1.2
1936*NY-A★	137	493	93	152	28	9	18	107	94	60	13	7	.308	.420	.511	.931	133	29	111	8.37	1	*0-135(18-0-118)	21	1.9
1937*NY-A	78	256	49	84	13	5	18	68	34	24	8	2	.328	.411	.629	1.040	157	23	68	10.25	3	0-69(0-0-69)	14	2.0

YEAR TM-L	G	AB	R	H	2B	3B	HR	RBI	BB	SO	SB	CS	AVG	OBP	SLG	OPS	OPS+	BR/A	RC	RC/G	FR	G/POS	WS	TPW
1938*NY-A	99	335	58	85	12	5	10	62	68	52	9	4	.254	.384	.409	.793	99	2	58	5.99	2	0-95(95-0-0)	11	-0.1
1939*NY-A★	128	418	103	128	17	4	21	101	103	49	12	5	.306	.452	.517	.969	149	39	110	9.69	-3	*0-124(86-0-38)	25	2.6
1940 NY-A	118	379	68	102	17	5	19	71	84	43	3	6	.269	.406	.491	.896	137	22	83	7.73	-2	*0-111(79-2-31)	17	1.4
1941*NY-A	70	164	30	36	5	0	6	25	28	30	1	0	.220	.340	.360	.700	86	-2	22	4.58	1	0-47(19-0-28)	4	-0.4
1942*NY-A	42	78	15	15	3	0	0	10	16	8	0	0	.192	.330	.231	.561	60	-3	7	3.03	-1	0-19(0-0-19)	1	-0.5
Total 9	846	2790	503	810	131	41	108	576	486	319	49	32	.290	.400	.483	.883	128	130	575	7.51	6	0-773	118	8.2

• SELLERS, Rube Oliver Sellers b: 3/7/1881, Duquesne, PA d: 1/14/1952, Pittsburgh, PA BR/TR, 5'10", 180 lbs. Deb: 8/12/1910

YEAR TM-L	G	AB	R	H	2B	3B	HR	RBI	BB	SO	SB	CS	AVG	OBP	SLG	OPS	OPS+	BR/A	RC	RC/G	FR	G/POS	WS	TPW
1910 Bos-N	12	32	3	5	0	0	0	2	6	5	1	....	.156	.289	.156	.446	29	-3	2	1.70	0	/0-9(8-0-1)	0	-0.3

• SELLMAN, Frank Charles Francis Sellman b: 1852, Baltimore, MD d: 5/6/1907, Baltimore, MD Deb: 5/4/1871 U

YEAR TM-L	G	AB	R	H	2B	3B	HR	RBI	BB	SO	SB	CS	AVG	OBP	SLG	OPS	OPS+	BR/A	RC	RC/G	FR	G/POS	WS	TPW
1871 Kek-n	14	65	14	15	3	0	1	10	4	0	1	0	.231	.275	.323	.598	70	-3	6	3.91	0	3-14/C-5,S-2	....	-0.2
1872 Oly-n	9	42	3	10	2	0	0	1	0	1	0	2	.238	.238	.286	.524	64	-2	3	2.67	-1	/C-7,3-2	....	-0.2
1873 Mar-n	1	3	1	1	0	0	0	0	0	0	0	0	.333	.333	.333	.667	129	0	0	5.21	0	/P-1	....	-0.2
1874 Bal-n	12	54	9	16	3	2	0	5	0	2	2	0	.296	.296	.426	.722	129	2	8	5.99	-12	/C-6,S-6,2-2,3-2,0-2(0-1-1)	....	-0.7
1875 Was-n	1	3	0	1	0	0	0	0	0	0	0	0	.333	.333	.333	.667	137	0	0	5.04	0	/1-1	....	0.0
Total 5 n	37	167	27	43	8	2	1	16	4	3	3	2	.257	.275	.347	.622	89	-3	17	4.24	-13	/3-18,C-18,S-8,2-2,0-2,1-1,P	....	-1.3

• SELPH, Carey Carey Isom Selph b: 12/5/1901, Donaldson, AR d: 2/24/1976, Houston, TX BR/TR, 5'9.5", 175 lbs. Deb: 5/25/1929

YEAR TM-L	G	AB	R	H	2B	3B	HR	RBI	BB	SO	SB	CS	AVG	OBP	SLG	OPS	OPS+	BR/A	RC	RC/G	FR	G/POS	WS	TPW
1929 StL-N	25	51	8	12	1	1	0	7	6	4	1	....	.235	.316	.294	.610	52	-4	5	3.15	0	2-16	1	-0.3
1932 Chi-A	116	396	50	112	19	8	0	51	31	9	7	6	.283	.341	.371	.712	90	-6	50	4.54	-12	3-71,2-26	8	-1.3
Total 2	141	447	58	124	20	9	0	58	37	13	8	6	.277	.338	.362	.701	86	-10	55	4.37	-12	/3-71,2-42	9	-1.6

• SEMBER, Mike Michael David Sember b: 2/24/1953, Hammond, IN BR/TR, 6', 185 lbs. Deb: 8/18/1977

YEAR TM-L	G	AB	R	H	2B	3B	HR	RBI	BB	SO	SB	CS	AVG	OBP	SLG	OPS	OPS+	BR/A	RC	RC/G	FR	G/POS	WS	TPW
1977 Chi-N	3	4	0	1	0	0	0	0	0	2	0	0	.250	.250	.250	.500	31	-0	0	2.25	0	/2-1	0	0.0
1978 Chi-N	9	3	2	1	0	0	0	0	1	1	0	0	.333	.500	.333	.833	122	0	1	8.51	-2	/3-7,S-1	0	-0.2
Total 2	12	7	2	2	0	0	0	0	1	3	0	0	.286	.375	.286	.661	77	-0	1	4.75	-2	/3-7,2-1,S-1	0	-0.2

• SEMINICK, Andy Andrew Wasil Seminick b: 9/12/1920, Pierce, WV d: 2/22/2004, Melbourne, FL BR/TR, 5'11", 187 lbs. Deb: 9/14/1943 C Career OF: 9-0-0

YEAR TM-L	G	AB	R	H	2B	3B	HR	RBI	BB	SO	SB	CS	AVG	OBP	SLG	OPS	OPS+	BR/A	RC	RC/G	FR	G/POS	WS	TPW
1943 Phi-N	22	72	9	13	2	0	2	5	7	22	0	....	.181	.253	.292	.545	60	-4	5	2.10	-0	C-22/0-1	1	-0.3
1944 Phi-N	22	63	9	14	2	1	0	4	6	17	2	....	.222	.300	.286	.586	68	-3	5	2.85	1	C-11/0-7(7-0-0)	1	-0.1
1945 Phi-N	80	188	18	45	7	2	6	26	18	38	3	....	.239	.313	.394	.706	98	-1	23	4.15	1	C-70/3-4,0-1	5	0.3
1946 Phi-N	124	406	55	107	15	5	12	52	39	86	2	....	.264	.334	.414	.748	115	7	52	4.44	7	*C-118	15	2.0
1947 Phi-N	111	337	48	85	16	2	13	50	58	69	4	....	.252	.370	.427	.797	115	9	56	5.68	-1	*C-107	11	1.3
1948 Phi-N	125	391	49	88	11	3	13	44	58	68	4	....	.225	.328	.368	.696	90	-5	49	4.16	4	*C-124	11	0.6
1949 Phi-N★	109	334	52	81	11	2	24	68	69	74	0	....	.243	.380	.503	.883	138	20	67	6.76	5	C-98	18	3.0
1950*Phi-N	130	393	55	113	15	3	24	68	68	50	0	....	.288	.400	.524	.925	143	27	84	7.80	-2	*C-124	22	3.0
1951 Phi-N	101	291	42	66	8	1	11	37	63	67	1	0	.227	.370	.375	.744	102	4	46	5.32	1	C-91	11	1.0
1952 Cin-N	108	336	38	86	16	1	14	50	35	65	1	3	.256	.330	.435	.764	111	3	48	5.01	1	C-99	12	0.9
1953 Cin-N	119	387	46	91	12	0	19	64	49	82	2	2	.235	.323	.413	.736	89	-7	53	4.60	0	*C-112	10	-0.1
1954 Cin-N	86	247	25	58	9	4	7	30	48	39	0	0	.235	.364	.389	.752	93	-1	37	4.99	3	C-82	10	0.6
1955 Cin-N	6	15	1	2	0	0	1	1	0	3	0	0	.133	.133	.333	.467	18	-2	1	1.38	0	/C-5	0	-0.2
Phi-N	93	289	32	71	12	1	11	34	32	59	1	2	.246	.333	.408	.742	97	-1	39	4.54	8	C-88	11	1.1
Yr.	99	304	33	73	12	1	12	35	32	62	1	2	.240	.325	.405	.729	94	-3	39	4.37	8	C-93	11	0.9
1956 Phi-N	60	161	16	32	3	1	7	23	31	38	3	0	.199	.332	.360	.692	88	-1	19	3.74	-2	C-54	4	-0.1
1957 Phi-N	8	11	0	1	0	0	0	0	1	3	0	0	.091	.167	.091	.258	-29	-2	0	.26	0	/C-8	0	-0.2
Total 15	1304	3921	495	953	139	26	164	556	582	780	23	7	.243	.347	.417	.764	107	43	584	5.05	24	*C-1213/0-9,3-4	142	12.8

• SENERCHIA, Sonny Emanuel Robert Senerchia b: 4/6/1931, Newark, NJ d: 11/1/2003, Freehold, NJ BR/TR, 6'1", 195 lbs. Deb: 8/22/1952

YEAR TM-L	G	AB	R	H	2B	3B	HR	RBI	BB	SO	SB	CS	AVG	OBP	SLG	OPS	OPS+	BR/A	RC	RC/G	FR	G/POS	WS	TPW
1952 Pit-N	29	100	5	22	5	0	3	11	4	21	0	3	.220	.250	.360	.610	65	-6	8	2.80	-4	3-28	1	-1.1

• SENSENDERFER, Count John Phillips Jenkins Sensenderfer b: 12/28/1847, Philadelphia, PA d: 5/3/1903, Philadelphia, PA, 5'9", 170 lbs. Deb: 5/20/1871 U NA OF: 0-45-5

YEAR TM-L	G	AB	R	H	2B	3B	HR	RBI	BB	SO	SB	CS	AVG	OBP	SLG	OPS	OPS+	BR/A	RC	RC/G	FR	G/POS	WS	TPW
1871 Ath-n	25	127	38	41	5	2	0	23	0	1	5	3	.323	.323	.394	.717	106	0	18	6.44	-2	*0-25(0-25-0)	....	-0.1
1872 Ath-n	1	5	2	2	0	0	0	1	0	0	0	1	.400	.400	.400	.800	146	-0	1	6.36	0	/0-1	....	0.0
1873 Ath-n	20	86	12	24	1	0	0	8	0	2	0	2	.279	.279	.291	.570	65	-5	7	3.41	0	0-19(0-19-0)/1-1	....	-0.4
1874 Ath-n	5	16	3	3	0	0	0	2	0	0	0	0	.188	.188	.188	.375	19	-2	1	1.33	-1	/0-5(0-1-4)	....	-0.2
Total 4 n	51	234	55	70	6	2	0	34	0	3	5	6	.299	.299	.342	.641	86	-7	27	4.91	-3	/0-50,1-1	....	-0.7

• SENTELL, Paul Leopold Theodore Sentell b: 8/27/1879, New Orleans, LA d: 4/27/1923, Cincinnati, OH BR/TR, 5'9", 176 lbs. Deb: 4/12/1906 U Career OF: 0-0-3

YEAR TM-L	G	AB	R	H	2B	3B	HR	RBI	BB	SO	SB	CS	AVG	OBP	SLG	OPS	OPS+	BR/A	RC	RC/G	FR	G/POS	WS	TPW
1906 Phi-N	63	192	19	44	5	1	1	14	14	....	15	....	.229	.292	.281	.573	79	-5	22	3.58	-5	3-33,2-19/0-2(0-0-2),S-1	4	-1.0
1907 Phi-N	3	3	0	0	0	0	0	0	1	....	0	....	.000	.250	.000	.250	-22	-0	0	.00	-1	/S-2,0-1	0	-0.1
Total 2	66	195	19	44	5	1	1	14	15	....	15	....	.226	.291	.277	.568	77	-5	22	3.51	-6	/3-33,2-19,0-3,S-3	4	-1.2

• SEPKOWSKI, Ted Theodore Walter Sepkowski b: 11/9/1923, Baltimore, MD d: 3/8/2002, Severna Park, MD BL/TR, 5'11", 190 lbs. Deb: 9/9/1942

YEAR TM-L	G	AB	R	H	2B	3B	HR	RBI	BB	SO	SB	CS	AVG	OBP	SLG	OPS	OPS+	BR/A	RC	RC/G	FR	G/POS	WS	TPW
1942 Cle-A	5	10	0	1	0	0	0	0	0	3	0	0	.100	.100	.100	.200	-46	-2	0	.31	0	/2-2	0	-0.2
1946 Cle-A	2	8	2	4	1	0	0	1	0	0	0	0	.500	.500	.625	1.125	228	1	3	17.30	-1	/3-2	1	0.1
1947 Cle-A	10	8	0	1	1	0	0	0	1	1	0	0	.125	.222	.250	.472	32	-1	1	1.98	0	/0-1	0	-0.1
NY-A	2	0	1	0	0	0	0	0	0	0	0	1	....	....	....	....	-101	-0	0	.00	0	....	0	0.0
Yr.	12	8	1	1	1	0	0	0	1	1	0	1	.125	.222	.250	.472	32	-1	1	1.73	0	/0-1	0	-0.1
Total 3	19	26	3	6	2	0	0	1	1	4	0	1	.231	.259	.308	.567	61	-2	3	4.09	-1	/2-2,3-2,0-1	1	-0.2

• SERENA, Bill William Robert Serena b: 10/2/1924, Alameda, CA d: 4/17/1996, Hayward, CA BR/TR, 5'9.5", 175 lbs. Deb: 9/16/1949

YEAR TM-L	G	AB	R	H	2B	3B	HR	RBI	BB	SO	SB	CS	AVG	OBP	SLG	OPS	OPS+	BR/A	RC	RC/G	FR	G/POS	WS	TPW
1949 Chi-N	12	37	3	8	3	0	1	7	7	9	0	....	.216	.341	.378	.719	95	-0	5	4.53	-2	3-11	1	-0.3
1950 Chi-N	127	435	56	104	20	4	17	61	65	75	1	....	.239	.339	.421	.760	100	0	64	5.04	-15	*3-125	10	-1.5
1951 Chi-N	13	39	8	13	3	1	1	4	11	4	0	2	.333	.490	.538	1.029	173	4	11	10.72	-3	3-12	2	0.1
1952 Chi-N	122	390	49	107	21	5	15	61	39	83	1	0	.274	.345	.469	.814	122	12	62	5.60	-3	3-58,2-49	15	1.1
1953 Chi-N	93	275	30	69	10	5	10	52	41	46	0	0	.251	.350	.433	.783	100	1	43	5.33	-5	2-49,3-28	7	-0.1
1954 Chi-N	41	63	8	10	0	1	4	13	14	18	0	0	.159	.321	.381	.701	81	-2	8	3.99	-2	3-12/2-2	1	-0.4
Total 6	408	1239	154	311	57	16	48	198	177	235	2	2	.251	.348	.439	.787	108	15	193	5.36	-31	3-246,2-100	36	-1.0

• SERNA, Paul Paul David Serna b: 11/16/1958, El Centro, CA BR/TR, 5'8", 170 lbs. Deb: 9/1/1981

YEAR TM-L	G	AB	R	H	2B	3B	HR	RBI	BB	SO	SB	CS	AVG	OBP	SLG	OPS	OPS+	BR/A	RC	RC/G	FR	G/POS	WS	TPW
1981 Sea-A	30	94	11	24	2	0	4	9	3	11	2	3	.255	.293	.404	.697	95	-2	11	3.88	-1	S-23/2-7	2	0.0
1982 Sea-A	65	169	15	38	3	0	3	8	4	13	0	5	.225	.247	.296	.543	47	-15	10	1.91	-1	S-31,2-18,3-15/D-2	2	-1.3
Total 2	95	263	26	62	5	0	7	17	7	24	2	8	.236	.264	.335	.598	64	-16	21	2.58	-2	/S-54,2-25,3-15,D-2	4	-1.3

• SERVAIS, Scott Scott Daniel Servais b: 6/4/1967, La Crosse, WI BR/TR, 6'2", 195 lbs. Deb: 7/12/1991

YEAR TM-L	G	AB	R	H	2B	3B	HR	RBI	BB	SO	SB	CS	AVG	OBP	SLG	OPS	OPS+	BR/A	RC	RC/G	FR	G/POS	WS	TPW
1991 Hou-N	16	37	0	6	3	0	0	6	4	8	0	0	.162	.244	.243	.487	40	-3	3	2.12	0	C-14	1	-0.3
1992 Hou-N	77	205	12	49	9	0	0	15	11	25	0	0	.239	.294	.283	.577	67	-9	17	2.64	0	C-73	3	-0.6
1993 Hou-N	85	258	24	63	11	0	11	32	22	45	0	0	.244	.316	.415	.731	97	-2	34	4.39	1	C-82	9	0.5
1994 Hou-N	78	251	27	49	15	1	9	41	10	44	0	0	.195	.238	.371	.608	58	-17	21	2.61	-3	C-78	4	-1.4
1995 Hou-N	28	89	7	20	10	0	1	12	9	15	0	1	.225	.303	.371	.674	82	-3	9	3.18	0	C-28	2	-0.1
Chi-N	52	175	31	50	12	0	12	35	23	37	2	1	.286	.375	.560	.935	145	11	36	7.23	0	C-52	8	1.4
Yr.	80	264	38	70	22	0	13	47	32	52	2	2	.265	.351	.496	.847	124	8	45	5.76	-1	C-80	10	1.3
1996 Chi-N	129	445	42	118	20	0	11	63	30	75	0	2	.265	.331	.384	.716	86	-10	53	4.03	2	*C-128/1-1	13	0.1
1997 Chi-N	122	385	36	100	21	0	6	45	24	56	0	1	.260	.313	.361	.674	74	-15	43	3.84	5	*C-118/D-2,1-1	10	-0.3
1998*Chi-N	113	325	35	72	15	1	7	36	26	51	1	0	.222	.289	.338	.628	62	-18	30	3.02	3	*C-110/1-1	4	-0.9
1999 SF-N	69	198	21	54	10	0	5	21	13	31	0	0	.273	.327	.399	.726	89	-4	24	4.29	-1	C-62/1-1	5	-0.1
2000 Col-N	33	101	6	22	4	0	1	13	7	16	0	1	.218	.275	.287	.562	34	-11	8	2.60	6	C-32	1	-0.3
SF-N	7	8	1	2	0	0	0	0	2	1	0	0	.250	.400	.250	.650	75	-0	1	4.07	0	/C-6	0	0.0
Yr.	40	109	7	24	4	0	1	13	9	17	0	1	.220	.286	.284	.570	37	-11	9	2.70	6	C-38	1	-0.3

YEAR TM-L	G	AB	R	H	2B	3B	HR	RBI	BB	SO	SB	CS	AVG	OBP	SLG	OPS	OPS+	BR/A	RC	RC/G	FR	G/POS	WS	TPW
2001 Hou-N	11	16	1	6	0	0	0	0	2	3	0	0	.375	.444	.375	.819	109	0	3	7.82	1	/C-9	0	0.2
Total 11	820	2493	243	611	130	2	63	319	183	407	3	6	.245	.309	.375	.683	80	-80	281	3.77	13	C-792/1-4,D-2	60	-1.7

• SESSI, Walter Walter Anthony "Watsie" Sessi b: 7/23/1918, Finleyville, PA d: 4/18/1998, Mobile, AL BL/TL, 6'3", 225 lbs. Deb: 9/18/1941

YEAR TM-L	G	AB	R	H	2B	3B	HR	RBI	BB	SO	SB	CS	AVG	OBP	SLG	OPS	OPS+	BR/A	RC	RC/G	FR	G/POS	WS	TPW
1941 StL-N	5	13	2	0	0	0	0	0	1	2	0	....	.000	.071	.000	.071	-74	-3	0	.00	-1	/O-3(0-0-3)	0	-0.4
1946 StL-N	15	14	2	2	0	0	1	2	1	4	0	....	.143	.200	.357	.557	54	-1	1	2.37	0	....	0	-0.1
Total 2	20	27	4	2	0	0	1	2	2	6	0	....	.074	.138	.185	.323	-8	-4	1	1.09	-1	/O-3	0	-0.5

• SEVCIK, John John Joseph Sevcik b: 7/11/1942, Oak Park, IL BR/TR, 6'2", 205 lbs. Deb: 4/24/1965

YEAR TM-L	G	AB	R	H	2B	3B	HR	RBI	BB	SO	SB	CS	AVG	OBP	SLG	OPS	OPS+	BR/A	RC	RC/G	FR	G/POS	WS	TPW
1965 Min-A	12	16	1	1	1	0	0	0	1	5	0	0	.063	.118	.125	.243	-30	-3	0	.25	1	C-11	1	-0.2

• SEVEREID, Hank Henry Levai Severeid b: 6/1/1891, Story City, IA d: 12/17/1968, San Antonio, TX BR/TR, 6', 175 lbs. Deb: 5/15/1911 Career OF: 6-1-0

YEAR TM-L	G	AB	R	H	2B	3B	HR	RBI	BB	SO	SB	CS	AVG	OBP	SLG	OPS	OPS+	BR/A	RC	RC/G	FR	G/POS	WS	TPW
1911 Cin-N	37	56	5	17	6	1	0	10	3	6	0	....	.304	.350	.446	.796	127	2	8	5.66	-2	C-22	2	0.1
1912 Cin-N	50	114	10	27	0	3	0	13	8	11	0	....	.237	.287	.289	.576	60	-6	10	2.68	-4	C-20/1-7,O-6(5-1-0)	2	-0.9
1913 Cin-N	8	6	0	0	0	0	0	0	1	1	0	....	.000	.143	.000	.143	-58	-1	0	.00	-1	/C-2,O-1	0	-0.2
1915 StL-A	80	203	12	45	6	1	1	22	16	25	2	1	.222	.279	.276	.554	69	-8	16	2.64	-2	C-64	2	-0.7
1916 StL-A	100	293	23	80	8	2	0	34	26	17	3	....	.273	.341	.314	.655	102	1	33	3.95	-7	C-89/1-1,3-1	8	0.0
1917 StL-A	143	501	45	133	23	4	1	57	28	20	6	....	.265	.306	.333	.639	98	-3	51	3.50	-3	*C-139/1-1	12	0.6
1918 StL-A	51	133	8	34	4	0	0	11	18	4	4	....	.256	.357	.286	.643	97	1	14	3.65	-3	C-42	4	0.1
1919 StL-A	112	351	16	87	12	2	0	36	21	13	2	....	.248	.298	.293	.591	65	-17	30	2.91	1	*C-103	8	-0.8
1920 StL-A	123	422	46	117	14	5	2	49	33	11	5	3	.277	.336	.348	.684	79	-11	51	4.27	-1	*C-117	11	-0.2
1921 StL-A	143	472	66	153	23	7	2	78	42	9	7	2	.324	.379	.415	.795	97	-0	76	6.00	1	*C-126	18	0.8
1922 StL-A	137	517	49	166	32	7	3	78	28	12	1	4	.321	.356	.427	.783	100	-2	77	5.53	1	*C-133	18	0.8
1923 StL-A	122	432	50	133	27	6	3	51	31	11	3	0	.308	.356	.419	.775	98	-1	66	5.52	5	*C-116	16	1.1
1924 StL-A	137	432	37	133	23	2	4	48	36	15	1	6	.308	.362	.398	.761	90	-8	62	4.92	0	*C-130	16	0.0
1925 StL-A	34	109	15	40	9	0	1	21	11	2	0	2	.367	.425	.477	.902	122	3	22	7.72	2	C-31	6	0.6
*Was-A	50	110	11	39	8	1	0	14	13	6	0	0	.355	.423	.445	.868	123	5	21	7.74	-1	C-35	6	0.6
Yr.	84	219	26	79	17	1	1	35	24	8	0	2	.361	.424	.461	.885	122	8	43	7.73	1	C-66	12	1.2
1926 Was-A	22	34	2	7	1	0	0	4	3	2	0	0	.206	.270	.235	.506	33	-3	2	2.24	0	C-16	1	-0.3
*NY-A	41	127	13	34	8	1	0	13	13	4	1	1	.268	.336	.346	.682	79	-4	15	4.20	1	C-40	4	-0.1
Yr.	63	161	15	41	9	1	0	17	16	6	1	1	.255	.322	.323	.645	70	-7	17	3.77	1	C-56	5	-0.3
Total 15	1390	4312	408	1245	204	42	17	539	331	169	35	19	.289	.342	.367	.709	91	-54	556	4.56	-12	*C-1225/1-9,O-7,3-1	134	1.6

• SEVERSON, Rich Richard Allen Severson b: 1/18/1945, Artesia, CA BR/TR, 6', 174 lbs. Deb: 4/10/1970

YEAR TM-L	G	AB	R	H	2B	3B	HR	RBI	BB	SO	SB	CS	AVG	OBP	SLG	OPS	OPS+	BR/A	RC	RC/G	FR	G/POS	WS	TPW
1970 KC-A	77	240	22	60	11	1	1	22	16	33	0	0	.250	.300	.317	.616	70	-10	23	3.24	5	S-50,2-25	5	0.2
1971 KC-A	16	30	4	9	0	2	0	1	3	5	0	0	.300	.364	.433	.797	126	1	5	6.44	1	/2-6,S-6,3-1	2	0.3
Total 2	93	270	26	69	11	3	1	23	19	38	0	0	.256	.307	.330	.637	76	-9	28	3.56	6	/S-56,2-31,3-1	7	0.5

• SEWARD, Ed Edward William Seward b: 6/29/1867, Cleveland, OH d: 7/30/1947, Cleveland, OH TR, 5'7", 175 lbs. Deb: 9/30/1885 U Career OF: 5-33-7 ♦

YEAR TM-L	G	AB	R	H	2B	3B	HR	RBI	BB	SO	SB	CS	AVG	OBP	SLG	OPS	OPS+	BR/A	RC	RC/G	FR	G/POS	WS	TPW
1885 Pro-N	1	3	0	0	0	0	0	0	0	2	....	....	.000	.000	.000	.000	-104	-0	0	.00	1	/P-1	1	0.1
1887 Phi-a	74	282	31	66	10	0	5	28	16	....	14	....	.234	.239	.282	.521	45	-10	22	2.73	-3	P-55,O-21(2-19-0)	33	-0.5
1888 Phi-a	64	225	27	32	3	3	2	14	18	....	12	....	.142	.215	.209	.424	36	-6	13	1.82	4	P-57/O-7(2-1-4)	42	4.6
1889 Phi-a	46	143	22	31	5	3	2	17	22	19	6	....	.217	.333	.336	.669	92	6	18	4.37	-3	P-39/O-8(0-6-2),2-1	21	-1.0
1890 Phi-a	26	72	7	10	4	0	0	2	8	....	3	....	.139	.244	.194	.438	30	-2	4	1.82	-1	P-21/O-6(0-6-0)	6	-0.7
1891 Cle-N	7	19	2	4	2	0	0	1	3	4	0	....	.211	.318	.316	.634	81	0	2	3.52	-1	/O-3(1-1-1),P-3,1-1	1	-0.1
Total 6	218	744	89	143	24	6	9	62	67	25	35	....	.192	.253	.261	.514	51	-12	60	2.66	-3	P-176/O-45,1-1,2-1	104	2.5

• SEWARD, George George T. Seward b: St. Louis, MO d: 3/28/1904, St. Louis, MO, 5'7.5", 145 lbs. Deb: 5/19/1875

YEAR TM-L	G	AB	R	H	2B	3B	HR	RBI	BB	SO	SB	CS	AVG	OBP	SLG	OPS	OPS+	BR/A	RC	RC/G	FR	G/POS	WS	TPW
1875 StL-n	25	96	12	24	2	0	0	8	1	1	1	0	.250	.258	.271	.529	92	0	7	2.92	1	C-18/O-7(3-1-3),2-2	....	0.2
1876 NY-N	1	3	0	0	0	0	0	0	0	0	....	....	.000	.000	.000	.000	-115	-1	0	.00	-0	/2-1	0	-0.1
1882 StL-a	38	144	23	31	1	1	0	....	12	....	....	....	.215	.276	.236	.512	71	-4	10	2.38	-1	O-35(6-2-27)/C-5	3	-0.5
Total 2	39	147	23	31	1	1	0	0	12	0	....	....	.211	.270	.231	.502	68	-5	10	2.32	-1	/O-35,C-5,2-1	3	-0.5

• SEWELL, Joe Joseph Wheeler Sewell b: 10/9/1898, Titus, AL d: 3/6/1990, Mobile, AL BL/TR, 5'6.5", 155 lbs. Deb: 9/10/1920 C HOF: 1977

YEAR TM-L	G	AB	R	H	2B	3B	HR	RBI	BB	SO	SB	CS	AVG	OBP	SLG	OPS	OPS+	BR/A	RC	RC/G	FR	G/POS	WS	TPW
1920*Cle-A	22	70	14	23	4	1	0	12	9	4	1	0	.329	.413	.414	.827	116	3	13	6.81	-1	S-22	4	0.3
1921 Cle-A	154	572	101	182	36	12	4	93	80	17	7	6	.318	.412	.444	.856	116	18	109	6.97	6	*S-154	26	3.8
1922 Cle-A	153	558	80	167	28	7	2	83	73	20	10	12	.299	.386	.385	.771	101	2	86	5.38	3	*S-139,2-12	21	2.0
1923 Cle-A	153	553	98	195	41	10	3	109	98	12	9	6	.353	.456	.479	.935	147	45	128	8.74	-3	*S-151	29	5.6
1924 Cle-A	153	594	99	188	**45**	5	4	106	67	13	3	3	.316	.388	.429	.817	109	10	102	6.25	14	*S-153	22	3.8
1925 Cle-A	155	608	78	204	37	7	1	98	64	4	7	6	.336	.402	.424	.827	109	11	106	6.51	17	*S-153/2-3	24	4.1
1926 Cle-A	154	578	91	187	41	5	4	85	65	6	17	7	.324	.399	.433	.832	116	17	104	6.59	12	*S-154	29	4.5
1927 Cle-A	153	569	83	180	48	5	1	92	51	7	3	16	.316	.382	.424	.805	108	2	89	5.51	-1	*S-153	21	1.7
1928 Cle-A	155	588	79	190	40	2	4	70	58	9	7	1	.323	.391	.418	.809	111	14	100	6.28	11	*S-137,3-19	23	3.9
1929 Cle-A	152	578	90	182	38	3	7	73	48	4	6	6	.315	.372	.427	.800	102	2	93	5.57	1	*3-152	21	1.2
1930 Cle-A	109	353	44	102	17	6	0	48	41	3	1	4	.289	.374	.371	.745	86	-7	51	5.04	-8	3-97	9	-0.8
1931 NY-A	130	484	102	146	22	1	6	64	61	8	1	1	.302	.390	.388	.778	111	13	78	5.80	5	*3-121/2-1	15	2.1
1932*NY-A	125	503	95	137	21	3	11	68	56	3	0	2	.272	.349	.392	.740	96	-2	71	4.93	7	*3-123	17	0.9
1933 NY-A	135	524	87	143	18	1	2	54	71	4	2	2	.273	.361	.323	.683	87	-6	65	4.41	8	*3-131	16	0.6
Total 14	1903	7132	1141	2226	436	68	49	1055	842	114	74	72	.312	.391	.413	.804	109	120	1196	6.03	71	*S-1216,3-643/2-16	277	33.9

• SEWELL, Luke James Luther Sewell b: 1/5/1901, Titus, AL d: 5/14/1987, Akron, OH BR/TR, 5'9", 160 lbs. Deb: 6/30/1921 M/C Career OF: 4-0-5

YEAR TM-L	G	AB	R	H	2B	3B	HR	RBI	BB	SO	SB	CS	AVG	OBP	SLG	OPS	OPS+	BR/A	RC	RC/G	FR	G/POS	WS	TPW
1921 Cle-A	3	6	0	0	0	0	0	1	0	3	0	0	.000	.000	.000	.000	-98	-2	0	.00	0	/C-3	0	-0.1
1922 Cle-A	41	87	14	23	5	0	0	10	5	8	1	1	.264	.312	.322	.634	65	-5	9	3.48	-3	C-39	1	-0.5
1923 Cle-A	10	10	2	2	0	1	0	1	1	0	0	0	.200	.273	.400	.673	76	-0	1	3.69	0	/C-7	0	-0.1
1924 Cle-A	63	165	27	48	9	1	0	17	22	13	1	0	.291	.387	.358	.745	92	-0	25	5.48	-2	C-57	5	0.1
1925 Cle-A	74	220	30	51	10	2	0	18	33	18	6	2	.232	.337	.295	.633	61	-11	25	3.70	-1	C-66/O-2(2-0-0)	4	-0.8
1926 Cle-A	126	433	41	103	16	4	0	46	36	27	9	3	.238	.302	.293	.596	55	-27	42	3.09	-6	*C-125	8	-2.4
1927 Cle-A	128	470	52	138	27	6	0	53	20	23	4	8	.294	.328	.377	.705	82	-16	56	4.16	3	*C-126	11	-0.4
1928 Cle-A	122	411	52	111	16	9	3	52	26	27	3	4	.270	.318	.375	.693	81	-13	49	4.05	10	*C-118	10	0.5
1929 Cle-A	124	406	41	96	16	3	1	39	29	26	6	6	.236	.287	.298	.585	49	-32	36	2.80	-4	*C-124	5	-2.6
1930 Cle-A	76	292	40	75	21	2	1	43	14	9	5	2	.257	.293	.353	.646	61	-18	30	3.55	-2	C-76	5	-1.3
1931 Cle-A	108	375	45	103	30	4	1	53	36	17	1	1	.275	.341	.384	.725	86	-6	51	4.76	-8	*C-104	10	-0.8
1932 Cle-A	87	300	36	76	20	2	2	52	38	24	4	5	.253	.337	.353	.691	74	-12	37	4.17	-5	C-84	8	-1.1
1933*Was-A	141	474	65	125	30	4	2	61	48	24	7	2	.264	.335	.357	.692	84	-9	60	4.37	-8	*C-141	16	-0.8
1934 Was-A	72	207	21	49	7	3	2	21	22	10	0	1	.237	.313	.329	.642	68	-10	22	3.64	0	C-50/O-7(2-0-5),1-6,2-1,3	3	-0.7
1935 Chi-A	118	421	52	120	19	3	2	67	32	18	3	2	.285	.336	.359	.694	78	-14	51	4.42	10	*C-112	12	0.3
1936 Chi-A	128	451	59	113	20	5	5	73	54	16	11	2	.251	.332	.350	.682	66	-23	56	4.34	11	*C-126	14	-0.4
1937 Chi-A★	122	412	51	111	21	6	1	61	46	18	4	5	.269	.343	.357	.700	77	-16	51	4.43	3	*C-118	13	-0.5
1938 Chi-A	65	211	23	45	4	1	0	27	20	20	0	0	.213	.284	.242	.526	32	-22	16	2.45	5	C-65	3	-1.2
1939 Cle-A	16	20	1	3	1	0	0	1	3	1	0	0	.150	.261	.200	.461	20	-2	1	1.98	0	C-15/1-1	0	-0.2
1942 StL-A	6	12	1	1	0	0	0	0	1	5	0	0	.083	.154	.083	.237	-32	-2	0	.22	0	/C-6	0	-0.1
Total 20	1630	5383	653	1393	272	56	20	696	486	307	65	44	.259	.323	.341	.665	70	-240	618	3.92	2	*C-1562/O-9,1-7,2-1,3-1	128	-13.2

• SEWELL, Tommy Thomas Wesley Sewell b: 4/16/1906, Titus, AL d: 7/30/1956, Montgomery, AL BL/TR, 5'7.5", 155 lbs. Deb: 6/21/1927

YEAR TM-L	G	AB	R	H	2B	3B	HR	RBI	BB	SO	SB	CS	AVG	OBP	SLG	OPS	OPS+	BR/A	RC	RC/G	FR	G/POS	WS	TPW
1927 Chi-N	1	1	0	0	0	0	0	0	0	0	0	....	.000	.000	.000	.000	-100	-0	0	.00	0	....	0	0.0

• SEXSON, Richie Richmond Lockwood Sexson b: 12/29/1974, Portland, OR BR/TR, 6'6", 205 lbs. Deb: 9/14/1997 Career OF: 109-0-3

YEAR TM-L	G	AB	R	H	2B	3B	HR	RBI	BB	SO	SB	CS	AVG	OBP	SLG	OPS	OPS+	BR/A	RC	RC/G	FR	G/POS	WS	TPW
1997 Cle-A	5	11	1	3	0	0	0	0	0	2	0	0	.273	.273	.273	.545	41	-1	0	.74	0	/1-2,D-1	0	-0.1
1998*Cle-A	49	174	28	54	14	1	11	35	6	42	1	1	.310	.344	.592	.936	133	7	34	7.43	3	1-45/O-3(3-0-0),D-2	5	0.6
1999*Cle-A	134	479	72	122	17	7	31	116	34	117	3	3	.255	.309	.514	.823	100	-3	69	4.80	5	1-61,O-49(48-0-3),D-25	10	-0.6
2000 Cle-A	91	324	45	83	16	1	16	44	25	96	1	0	.256	.317	.460	.777	92	-5	46	4.96	0	O-58(58-0-0),1-27,D-10	5	-1.0

YEAR TM-L	G	AB	R	H	2B	3B	HR	RBI	BB	SO	SB	CS	AVG	OBP	SLG	OPS	OPS+	BR/A	RC	RC/G	FR	G/POS	WS	TPW
Mil-N	57	213	44	63	14	0	14	47	34	63	1	0	.296	.400	.559	.959	142	14	50	8.75	10	1-57	11	1.8
2001 Mil-N	158	598	94	162	24	3	45	125	60	178	2	4	.271	.343	.547	.890	128	22	106	6.16	9	*1-158	19	1.6
2002 Mil-N★	157	570	86	159	37	2	29	102	70	136	0	0	.279	.366	.504	.869	128	23	104	6.49	7	*1-154/D-1	22	1.6
2003 Mil-N★	162	606	97	165	28	2	45	124	98	151	2	3	.272	.381	.548	.929	142	37	126	7.31	10	*1-162	26	3.1
Total 7	813	2975	467	811	150	16	191	593	327	785	10	11	.273	.352	.526	.878	124	94	535	6.31	42	1-666,0-110/D-39	98	6.9

• SEXTON, Chris Christopher Philip Sexton b: 8/3/1971, Cincinnati, OH BR/TR, 5'11", 185 lbs. Deb: 5/3/1999

YEAR TM-L	G	AB	R	H	2B	3B	HR	RBI	BB	SO	SB	CS	AVG	OBP	SLG	OPS	OPS+	BR/A	RC	RC/G	FR	G/POS	WS	TPW
1999 Col-N	35	59	9	14	0	1	1	7	11	10	4	2	.237	.357	.322	.679	58	-4	7	3.91	-2	0-13(3-9-1),2-10/S-6	1	-0.5
2000 Cin-N	35	100	9	21	4	0	0	10	13	12	4	2	.210	.313	.250	.563	44	-8	8	2.41	-3	S-14,2-12/3-3	1	-0.9
Total 2	70	159	18	35	4	1	1	17	24	22	8	4	.220	.330	.277	.606	49	-12	15	2.94	-4	/2-22,S-20,0-13,3-3	2	-1.3

• SEXTON, Jimmy Jimmy Dale Sexton b: 12/15/1951, Mobile, AL BR/TR, 5'10", 175 lbs. Deb: 9/2/1977

YEAR TM-L	G	AB	R	H	2B	3B	HR	RBI	BB	SO	SB	CS	AVG	OBP	SLG	OPS	OPS+	BR/A	RC	RC/G	FR	G/POS	WS	TPW
1977 Sea-A	14	37	5	8	1	1	1	3	2	6	1	1	.216	.256	.378	.635	71	-2	3	2.63	1	S-12	0	0.0
1978 Hou-N	88	141	17	29	3	2	2	6	13	28	16	2	.206	.273	.298	.571	64	-4	14	3.27	-5	S-58/3-8,2-3	3	-0.6
1979 Hou-N	52	43	8	9	0	0	0	1	7	7	1	3	.209	.320	.209	.529	50	-4	3	2.15	-1	S-11/3-4,2-2	1	-0.4
1981 Oak-A	7	3	3	0	0	0	0	0	0	2	2	0	.000	.000	.000	.000	-105	-0	0	.00	0	/3-1,D-1	0	0.0
1982 Oak-A	69	139	19	34	4	0	2	14	9	24	16	0	.245	.295	.317	.612	71	-2	16	4.03	-3	S-47/3-8,D-5	5	-0.1
1983 StL-N	6	9	1	1	1	0	0	0	1	4	0	0	.111	.200	.222	.422	17	-1	0	1.35	1	/S-4,3-2	0	0.0
Total 6	236	372	53	81	9	3	5	24	32	71	36	6	.218	.281	.298	.580	63	-13	37	3.26	-7	S-132/3-23,D-6,2-5	9	-1.1

• SEXTON, Tom Thomas William Sexton b: 3/14/1865, Rock Island, IL d: 2/8/1934, Rock Island, IL BL Deb: 9/27/1884

YEAR TM-L	G	AB	R	H	2B	3B	HR	RBI	BB	SO	SB	CS	AVG	OBP	SLG	OPS	OPS+	BR/A	RC	RC/G	FR	G/POS	WS	TPW
1884 Mil-U	12	47	9	11	2	0	0	....	4	....	....	....	.234	.294	.277	.571	94	-0	4	3.05	-2	S-12	1	-0.1

• SEYBOLD, Socks Ralph Orlando Seybold b: 11/23/1870, Washingtonville, OH d: 12/22/1921, Greensburg, PA BR/TR, 5'11", 175 lbs. Deb: 8/20/1899 Career OF: 5-42-889

YEAR TM-L	G	AB	R	H	2B	3B	HR	RBI	BB	SO	SB	CS	AVG	OBP	SLG	OPS	OPS+	BR/A	RC	RC/G	FR	G/POS	WS	TPW
1899 Cin-N	22	85	13	19	5	1	0	8	6	....	2	....	.224	.283	.306	.588	60	-5	8	3.26	0	0-22(3-0-19)	1	-0.6
1901 Phi-A	114	449	74	150	24	14	8	90	40	....	15	....	.334	.397	.503	.901	142	25	99	8.54	-4	*0-100(2-25-74),1-14	21	1.5
1902 Phi-A	137	522	91	165	27	12	**16**	97	43	....	6	....	.316	.375	.506	.881	137	24	105	7.59	1	*0-136(0-16-120)	24	1.8
1903 Phi-A	137	522	76	156	**45**	8	8	84	38	....	5	....	.299	.353	.462	.815	137	23	89	6.42	-3	*0-120(0-1-119),1-18	22	1.5
1904 Phi-A	143	510	56	149	26	9	3	64	42	....	12	....	.292	.351	.396	.747	129	18	79	5.54	1	*0-129(0-0-129),1-13	21	1.4
1905*Phi-A	133	492	64	135	37	4	6	59	42	....	5	....	.274	.341	.402	.744	133	18	73	5.18	8	*0-133(0-0-133)	21	2.2
1906 Phi-A	116	411	41	130	23	2	5	59	30	....	9	....	.316	.367	.418	.786	141	19	70	6.26	-4	*0-114(0-0-114)	19	1.1
1907 Phi-A	147	564	58	153	29	4	5	92	40	....	10	....	.271	.324	.363	.687	116	10	75	4.52	4	*0-147(0-0-147)	19	0.7
1908 Phi-A	48	130	5	28	2	0	0	3	12	....	2	....	.215	.287	.231	.517	64	-5	9	2.28	-4	0-34(0-0-34)	1	-1.1
Total 9	997	3685	478	1085	218	54	51	556	293	....	66	....	.294	.353	.424	.777	129	128	607	5.96	-1	0-935/1-45	149	8.6

• SEYMOUR, Cy James Bentley Seymour b: 12/9/1872, Albany, NY d: 9/20/1919, New York, NY BL/TL, 6', 200 lbs. Deb: 4/22/1896 Career OF: 20-1094-224 ♦

YEAR TM-L	G	AB	R	H	2B	3B	HR	RBI	BB	SO	SB	CS	AVG	OBP	SLG	OPS	OPS+	BR/A	RC	RC/G	FR	G/POS	WS	TPW
1896 NY-N	12	32	2	7	0	0	0	0	0	7	0	....	.219	.219	.219	.438	16	-2	2	1.66	0	P-11/0-1	0	-1.6
1897 NY-N	45	141	13	34	5	1	2	14	4	....	3	....	.241	.262	.333	.595	58	-1	14	3.32	7	P-38/0-6(2-4-0)	21	2.0
1898 NY-N	80	297	41	82	5	2	4	23	9	....	8	....	.276	.300	.347	.646	88	3	34	4.19	7	P-45,0-35(10-12-15)/2-1	26	1.2
1899 NY-N	50	159	25	52	3	2	2	27	4	....	2	....	.327	.344	.409	.752	110	9	24	5.71	3	P-32/0-8(2-1-5),1-3,3-1	21	1.0
1900 NY-N	23	40	9	12	0	0	0	2	3	....	0	....	.300	.349	.300	.649	84	1	4	4.06	0	P-13/0-3(1-1-2),1-1	1	-1.8
1901 Bal-A	134	547	84	166	19	8	1	77	28	....	38	....	.303	.337	.373	.710	93	-7	85	5.74	5	*0-133(4-0-131)/1-1	14	-0.7
1902 Bal-A	72	280	38	75	8	8	3	41	18	....	12	....	.268	.317	.386	.702	90	-5	40	4.93	-3	0-72(0-3-70)	4	-1.0
Cin-N	62	244	27	83	8	2	2	37	12	....	8	....	.340	.378	.414	.792	132	9	43	6.89	2	0-61(0-61-0)/3-1,P-1	10	0.6
1903 Cin-N	135	558	85	191	25	15	7	72	33	....	25	....	.342	.382	.478	.861	130	19	116	8.06	3	*0-135(0-135-0)	24	1.6
1904 Cin-N	131	531	71	166	26	13	5	58	29	....	11	....	.313	.352	.439	.790	132	18	89	6.20	7	*0-130(0-130-0)	26	1.9
1905 Cin-N	149	581	95	**219**	**40**	**21**	8	**121**	51	....	21	....	**.377**	.429	**.559**	**.988**	**175**	**52**	153	10.71	14	*0-149(0-149-0)	42	6.2
1906 Cin-N	79	307	35	79	7	2	4	38	24	....	9	....	.257	.317	.332	.650	98	-1	37	4.10	6	0-79(0-79-0)	10	0.2
NY-N	72	269	35	86	12	3	4	42	18	....	20	....	.320	.365	.431	.796	145	13	51	7.07	1	0-72(0-72-0)	15	1.2
Yr.	151	576	70	165	19	5	8	80	42	....	29	....	.286	.339	.378	.718	120	12	88	5.44	8	*0-151(0-151-0)	25	1.3
1907 NY-N	131	473	46	139	25	8	3	75	36	....	21	....	.294	.350	.400	.750	131	16	77	5.76	-4	*0-126(0-126-0)	20	0.6
1908 NY-N	156	587	60	157	23	2	5	92	30	....	18	....	.267	.306	.339	.645	101	-1	67	3.79	11	*0-155(0-155-0)	19	0.3
1909 NY-N	80	280	37	87	12	5	1	30	25	....	14	....	.311	.369	.400	.769	137	12	46	5.96	4	0-74(1-71-1)	13	1.3
1910 NY-N	79	287	32	76	9	4	1	40	23	18	10	....	.265	.324	.334	.658	92	-3	34	4.04	-4	0-76(0-76-0)	6	-1.2
1913 Bos-N	39	73	2	13	2	0	0	10	7	7	2	....	.178	.259	.205	.465	33	-6	4	1.78	1	0-18(0-18-0)	0	-0.6
Total 16	1529	5686	737	1724	229	96	52	799	354	32	222	....	.303	.347	.405	.752	117	127	920	5.88	61	*0-1333,P-140/1-5,3-2,2-1	272	11.1

• SHAFER, Orator George W. Shafer
b: 10/1851, Philadelphia, PA d: 1/21/1922, Philadelphia, PA BL/TR, 5'9", 165 lbs. Deb: 5/23/1874 NA OF: 11-8-3 Career OF: 9-23-807

YEAR TM-L	G	AB	R	H	2B	3B	HR	RBI	BB	SO	SB	CS	AVG	OBP	SLG	OPS	OPS+	BR/A	RC	RC/G	FR	G/POS	WS	TPW
1874 Har-n	9	35	6	8	0	0	1	3	0	4	0	0	.229	.229	.314	.543	69	-1	3	2.86	-2	/0-9(8-0-1)	....	-0.2
Mut-n	1	5	1	1	0	0	0	0	0	0	0	0	.200	.200	.200	.400	28	-0	0	1.54	0	/0-1	....	0.0
Yr.	10	40	7	9	0	0	1	3	0	4	0	0	.225	.225	.300	.525	63	-2	3	2.69	-2	0-10(8-0-2)	....	-0.3
1875 Phi-n	19	70	10	17	2	1	0	6	0	4	2	0	.243	.243	.300	.543	84	-1	6	3.19	-2	0-12(3-8-1)/3-5,1-2	....	-0.2
1877 Lou-N	61	260	38	74	9	5	3	34	9	17	....	....	.285	.309	.392	.701	101	-1	32	4.77	15	*0-60(0-1-60)/1-1	7	1.2
1878 Ind-N	63	266	48	90	19	6	0	30	13	20	....	....	.338	.369	.455	.824	**196**	**28**	46	7.15	6	*0-63(1-0-63)	13	**3.2**
1879 Chi-N	73	316	53	96	13	0	0	35	6	28	....	....	.304	.317	.345	.662	111	3	35	4.50	22	*0-72(0-0-72)/3-1	12	2.3
1880 Cle-N	83	338	62	90	14	9	0	21	17	36	....	....	.266	.301	.361	.662	126	9	38	4.18	15	*0-83(0-0-83)	14	2.4
1881 Cle-N	85	343	48	88	13	6	1	34	23	20	....	....	.257	.303	.338	.641	107	4	36	3.82	-2	*0-85(0-0-85)	8	0.2
1882 Cle-N	84	313	37	67	14	2	3	28	27	27	....	....	.214	.276	.300	.577	88	-3	27	2.98	-7	*0-84(2-1-83)	6	-1.0
1883 Buf-N	95	401	67	117	11	3	0	41	27	39	....	....	.292	.336	.334	.671	103	2	46	4.47	17	*0-95(0-0-95)	12	1.5
1884 StL-U	106	467	130	168	**40**	10	2	....	30	....	....	....	.360	.398	.501	.899	195	45	96	8.95	1	*0-100(6-0-96)/2-7,1-1	28	3.9
1885 StL-N	69	257	30	50	11	2	0	18	19	31	....	....	.195	.250	.253	.503	67	-8	17	2.17	11	0-69(0-1-68)	3	0.1
Phi-a	2	9	1	2	0	1	0	1	1	....	....	....	.222	.300	.444	.744	125	0	1	4.74	0	/0-2(0-2-0)	0	0.0
1886 Phi-a	21	82	15	22	3	3	0	8	8	....	3	....	.268	.333	.378	.711	122	2	12	5.23	-1	0-21(0-18-4)	3	0.0
1890 Phi-a	100	390	55	110	15	5	1	58	47	....	29	....	.282	.367	.354	.720	115	9	63	5.94	-4	*0-98(0-0-98)/1-3	14	0.3
Total 2 n	29	110	17	26	2	1	1	9	0	8	2	0	.236	.236	.300	.536	77	-3	9	3.00	-4	/0-22,3-5,1-2	....	-0.5
Total 11	842	3442	584	974	162	52	10	308	227	218	32	....	.283	.328	.369	.697	123	91	448	4.98	74	0-832/2-7,1-5,3-1	120	14.1

• SHAFER, Ralph Ralph Newton Shafer b: 3/17/1894, Cincinnati, OH d: 2/5/1950, Akron, OH, 5'11" Deb: 7/25/1914

YEAR TM-L	G	AB	R	H	2B	3B	HR	RBI	BB	SO	SB	CS	AVG	OBP	SLG	OPS	OPS+	BR/A	RC	RC/G	FR	G/POS	WS	TPW
1914 Pit-N	1	0	0	0	0	0	0	0	0	0	0	....	....	....	....	....	-105	0	0	....	0	....	0	0.0

• SHAFER, Taylor Zachary Taylor Shafer b: 7/13/1866, Philadelphia, PA d: 10/27/1945, Glendale, CA BL, 5'7" Deb: 4/24/1884

YEAR TM-L	G	AB	R	H	2B	3B	HR	RBI	BB	SO	SB	CS	AVG	OBP	SLG	OPS	OPS+	BR/A	RC	RC/G	FR	G/POS	WS	TPW
1884 Alt-U	19	74	11	21	2	0	0	....	3	....	....	....	.284	.312	.311	.622	110	1	7	3.88	-3	0-17(9-7-1)/C-2,3-1	1	-0.2
KC-U	44	164	18	28	3	2	0	....	15	....	....	....	.171	.240	.213	.454	63	-4	9	1.77	-2	0-41(0-0-41)/C-2,2-1,3-1,S	1	-0.6
Bal-U	3	13	1	1	0	0	0	....	0	....	....	....	.077	.077	.077	.154	-43	-2	0	.18	0	/0-3(1-0-3)	0	-0.2
Yr.	66	251	30	50	5	2	0	....	18	....	....	....	.199	.253	.235	.488	71	-5	16	2.24	-5	0-61(10-7-45)/C-4,3-2,2-1,S	2	-1.0
1890 Phi-a	69	261	28	45	3	4	0	21	28	....	19	....	.172	.258	.215	.472	40	-19	20	2.43	-8	2-69	2	-2.2
Total 2	135	512	58	95	8	6	0	21	46	....	19	....	.186	.255	.225	.480	55	-24	36	2.34	-13	/2-70,0-61,C-4,3-2,S-1	4	-3.1

• SHAFER, Tillie Arthur Joseph Shafer b: 3/22/1889, Los Angeles, CA d: 1/10/1962, Los Angeles, CA BB/TR, 5'10", 165 lbs. Deb: 4/24/1909 Career OF: 4-13-1

YEAR TM-L	G	AB	R	H	2B	3B	HR	RBI	BB	SO	SB	CS	AVG	OBP	SLG	OPS	OPS+	BR/A	RC	RC/G	FR	G/POS	WS	TPW
1909 NY-N	38	84	11	15	2	1	0	7	14	....	6	....	.179	.296	.226	.522	61	-3	8	2.72	-6	3-16,2-13/0-2(0-1-1)	1	-0.9
1910 NY-N	29	21	5	4	1	0	0	1	0	6	0	....	.190	.190	.238	.429	25	-2	1	1.34	-1	/3-8,2-2,S-2	0	-0.3
1912*NY-N	78	163	48	47	4	1	0	23	30	19	22	....	.288	.408	.325	.733	99	2	31	6.44	-3	S-31,3-16,2-15	7	0.1
1913*NY-N	138	508	74	146	17	12	5	52	61	55	32	....	.287	.369	.398	.767	118	14	82	5.63	-1	3-79,2-25,S-16,0-15(4-12-0)	23	1.6
Total 4	283	776	138	212	24	14	5	83	105	80	60	....	.273	.366	.360	.725	105	10	122	5.32	-12	3-119/2-55,S-49,0-17	31	0.4

• SHAFFER, Shaffer Deb: 9/15/1875

YEAR TM-L	G	AB	R	H	2B	3B	HR	RBI	BB	SO	SB	CS	AVG	OBP	SLG	OPS	OPS+	BR/A	RC	RC/G	FR	G/POS	WS	TPW
1875 Atl-n	1	4	0	0	0	0	0	0	0	0	0	0	.000	.000	.000	.000	-115	-1	0	.00	0	/0-1	....	-0.1

• SHAMSKY, Art Arthur Louis Shamsky b: 10/14/1941, St. Louis, MO BL/TL, 6'1", 175 lbs. Deb: 4/17/1965 Career OF: 166-0-229

YEAR TM-L	G	AB	R	H	2B	3B	HR	RBI	BB	SO	SB	CS	AVG	OBP	SLG	OPS	OPS+	BR/A	RC	RC/G	FR	G/POS	WS	TPW
1965 Cin-N	64	96	13	25	4	3	2	10	10	29	1	0	.260	.330	.427	.757	104	1	15	5.54	0	0-18(3-0-15)/1-1	3	-0.1

YEAR TM-L	G	AB	R	H	2B	3B	HR	RBI	BB	SO	SB	CS	AVG	OBP	SLG	OPS	OPS+	BR/A	RC	RC/G	FR	G/POS	WS	TPW
1966 Cin-N	96	234	41	54	5	0	21	47	32	45	0	2	.231	.323	.521	.845	119	5	39	5.44	-3	0-74(42-0-33)	8	-0.2
1967 Cin-N	76	147	6	29	3	1	3	13	15	34	0	1	.197	.276	.293	.569	56	-8	12	2.71	0	0-40(18-0-25)	2	-1.1
1968 NY-N	116	345	30	82	14	4	12	48	21	58	1	0	.238	.295	.406	.701	108	3	41	4.00	4	0-82(71-0-12),1-17	10	0.2
1969*NY-N	100	303	42	91	9	3	14	47	36	32	1	2	.300	.380	.488	.869	139	16	57	6.81	-2	0-78(16-0-63)/1-9	17	1.0
1970 NY-N	122	403	48	118	19	2	11	49	49	33	1	1	.293	.374	.432	.805	115	9	64	5.78	1	0-58(4-0-54),1-56	13	0.3
1971 NY-N	68	135	13	25	6	2	5	18	21	18	1	1	.185	.299	.370	.670	90	-2	14	3.28	2	0-38(12-0-27)/1-1	3	-0.1
1972 Chi-N	15	16	1	2	0	0	0	1	3	3	0	0	.125	.263	.125	.388	12	-2	1	1.41	0	/1-4	0	-0.2
Oak-A	8	7	0	0	0	0	0	0	1	2	0	0	.000	.125	.000	.125	-64	-1	0	.13	0	....	0	-0.1
Total 8	**665**	**1686**	**194**	**426**	**60**	**15**	**68**	**233**	**188**	**254**	**5**	**7**	**.253**	**.333**	**.427**	**.760**	**109**	**21**	**243**	**4.95**	**2**	**0-388/1-88**	**56**	**-0.3**

• SHANER, Wally

Walter Dedaker "Skinny" Shaner
b: 5/24/1900, Lynchburg, VA d: 11/13/1992, Las Vegas, NV BR/TR, 6'2", 195 lbs. Deb: 5/4/1923 Career OF: 137-25-10

YEAR TM-L	G	AB	R	H	2B	3B	HR	RBI	BB	SO	SB	CS	AVG	OBP	SLG	OPS	OPS+	BR/A	RC	RC/G	FR	G/POS	WS	TPW
1923 Cle-A	3	4	1	1	0	0	0	0	1	1	0	0	.250	.400	.250	.650	74	-0	0	4.27	0	/0-2(2-0-0),3-1	0	0.0
1926 Bos-A	69	191	20	54	12	2	0	21	17	13	1	0	.283	.348	.366	.714	89	-2	25	4.82	2	0-48(48-0-0)	4	-0.4
1927 Bos-A	122	406	54	111	33	6	3	49	21	35	11	4	.273	.311	.406	.717	87	-9	51	4.44	-2	*0-108(85-25-10)/1-1	7	-1.7
1929 Cin-N	13	28	5	9	0	0	1	4	4	5	1	....	.321	.406	.429	.835	112	1	5	6.74	-1	/1-8,0-2(2-0-0)	1	0.0
Total 4	**207**	**629**	**80**	**175**	**45**	**8**	**4**	**74**	**43**	**54**	**13**	**4**	**.278**	**.327**	**.394**	**.722**	**89**	**-11**	**82**	**4.64**	**-1**	**0-160/1-9,3-1**	**12**	**-2.3**

• SHANKS, Howie

Howard Samuel "Hawk" Shanks b: 7/21/1890, Chicago, IL d: 7/30/1941, Monaca, PA BR/TR, 5'11", 170 lbs. Deb: 5/9/1912 C Career OF: 602-55-44

YEAR TM-L	G	AB	R	H	2B	3B	HR	RBI	BB	SO	SB	CS	AVG	OBP	SLG	OPS	OPS+	BR/A	RC	RC/G	FR	G/POS	WS	TPW
1912 Was-A	116	399	52	92	14	7	1	48	40	....	21	....	.231	.305	.308	.614	75	-13	45	3.56	2	*0-114(111-0-2)	9	-1.6
1913 Was-A	109	390	38	99	11	5	1	37	15	40	24	....	.254	.287	.315	.602	75	-14	39	3.36	6	*0-109(109-0-0)	10	-1.3
1914 Was-A	143	500	44	112	22	10	4	64	29	51	18	16	.224	.269	.332	.601	78	-20	47	2.86	-3	*0-139(94-43-2)	10	-3.3
1915 Was-A	141	492	52	123	19	8	0	47	30	42	12	14	.250	.297	.321	.618	83	-16	48	3.17	5	0-80(75-1-4),3-49,2-10	12	-1.4
1916 Was-A	140	471	51	119	15	7	1	48	41	34	23	12	.253	.317	.321	.637	92	-5	54	3.58	6	0-88(72-3-13),3-31/S-8,1-7	13	-0.3
1917 Was-A	126	430	45	87	15	5	0	28	33	37	15	....	.202	.269	.260	.529	62	-20	35	2.46	17	S-90,0-26(21-5-0)/1-2	8	0.3
1918 Was-A	120	436	42	112	19	4	1	56	31	21	23	....	.257	.312	.326	.638	94	-4	50	3.73	7	0-64(54-2-8),2-48/3-3	12	0.1
1919 Was-A	135	491	33	122	8	7	1	54	25	48	13	....	.248	.289	.299	.588	66	-23	47	3.06	3	S-94,2-34/0-6(6-0-0)	7	-1.4
1920 Was-A	128	444	56	119	16	7	4	37	29	43	11	6	.268	.316	.363	.678	82	-11	51	3.95	0	3-63,0-35(32-0-3),1-14/2-5,S	9	-1.1
1921 Was-A	154	562	81	170	24	**18**	7	69	57	38	11	10	.302	.370	.447	.816	113	10	93	5.79	8	*3-154/2-1	21	2.6
1922 Was-A	84	272	35	77	10	9	1	32	25	25	6	0	.283	.352	.397	.749	100	2	41	5.17	3	3-54,0-27(21-0-6)	9	0.6
1923 Bos-A	131	464	38	118	19	5	3	57	19	37	6	6	.254	.285	.336	.621	63	-27	44	3.15	-16	3-83,2-38/0-6(4-1-1),S-1	6	-3.6
1924 Bos-A	72	193	22	50	16	3	0	25	21	12	1	0	.259	.332	.373	.705	81	-5	25	4.40	6	S-41,3-22/0-4(0-0-4),1-2,2	5	0.5
1925 NY-A	66	155	15	40	3	1	1	18	20	15	1	0	.258	.343	.310	.653	68	-6	18	3.90	-4	3-26,2-21/0-4(3-0-1)	3	-0.8
Total 14	**1665**	**5699**	**604**	**1440**	**211**	**96**	**25**	**620**	**415**	**443**	**185**	**64**	**.253**	**.308**	**.337**	**.644**	**82**	**-154**	**637**	**3.64**	**40**	**0-702,3-485,S-235,2-159/1-25**	**134**	**-10.6**

• SHANLEY, Doc

Harry Root Shanley b: 1/30/1889, Granbury, TX d: 12/13/1934, St. Petersburg, FL BR/TR, 6', 174 lbs. Deb: 9/15/1912

YEAR TM-L	G	AB	R	H	2B	3B	HR	RBI	BB	SO	SB	CS	AVG	OBP	SLG	OPS	OPS+	BR/A	RC	RC/G	FR	G/POS	WS	TPW
1912 StL-A	5	8	1	0	0	0	0	1	2	....	0	....	.000	.200	.000	.200	-43	-1	0	.00	-1	/S-4	0	-0.2

• SHANLEY, Jim

James H. Shanley b: 5/4/1854, Brooklyn, NY d: 11/4/1904, Brooklyn, NY Deb: 5/3/1876

YEAR TM-L	G	AB	R	H	2B	3B	HR	RBI	BB	SO	SB	CS	AVG	OBP	SLG	OPS	OPS+	BR/A	RC	RC/G	FR	G/POS	WS	TPW
1876 NY-N	2	8	0	1	0	0	0	0	0	0	....	....	.125	.125	.125	.250	-19	-1	0	.51	-1	/0-2(0-1-1)	0	-0.2

• SHANNABROOK, Warren

Warren H. Shannabrook b: 11/30/1880, Massillon, OH d: 3/10/1964, North Canton, OH BR/TR, 6', 170 lbs. Deb: 8/13/1906

YEAR TM-L	G	AB	R	H	2B	3B	HR	RBI	BB	SO	SB	CS	AVG	OBP	SLG	OPS	OPS+	BR/A	RC	RC/G	FR	G/POS	WS	TPW
1906 Was-A	1	2	0	0	0	0	0	0	0	....	0	....	.000	.000	.000	.000	-105	-0	0	.00	0	/3-1	0	0.0

• SHANNON, Dan

Daniel Webster Shannon b: 3/23/1865, Bridgeport, CT d: 10/24/1913, Bridgeport, CT, 5'9", 175 lbs. Deb: 4/17/1889 M

YEAR TM-L	G	AB	R	H	2B	3B	HR	RBI	BB	SO	SB	CS	AVG	OBP	SLG	OPS	OPS+	BR/A	RC	RC/G	FR	G/POS	WS	TPW
1889 Lou-a	121	498	90	128	22	12	4	48	42	52	26	....	.257	.315	.373	.688	97	-3	68	4.90	-13	*2-121	8	-1.1
1890 Phi-P	19	75	15	18	5	1	1	16	4	12	4	....	.240	.278	.373	.652	72	-4	9	4.33	-1	2-19	1	-0.3
NY-P	83	324	59	70	7	8	3	44	25	34	21	....	.216	.274	.315	.589	52	-25	35	3.68	5	2-77/S-6	5	-1.4
Yr.	102	399	74	88	12	9	4	60	29	46	25	....	.221	.275	.326	.601	56	-29	44	3.80	4	*2-96/S-6	6	-1.7
1891 Was-a	19	67	7	9	2	0	0	3	6	9	3	....	.134	.205	.164	.370	6	-8	3	1.35	-2	S-14/2-5	1	-0.8
Total 3	**242**	**964**	**171**	**225**	**36**	**21**	**8**	**111**	**77**	**107**	**54**	**....**	**.233**	**.291**	**.339**	**.630**	**74**	**-40**	**115**	**4.16**	**-11**	**2-222/S-20**	**15**	**-3.6**

• SHANNON, Frank

John Francis Shannon b: 12/3/1873, San Francisco, CA d: 2/27/1934, Boston, MA, 5'3", 155 lbs. Deb: 10/1/1892

YEAR TM-L	G	AB	R	H	2B	3B	HR	RBI	BB	SO	SB	CS	AVG	OBP	SLG	OPS	OPS+	BR/A	RC	RC/G	FR	G/POS	WS	TPW
1892 Was-N	1	4	0	1	0	0	0	2	0	2	0	....	.250	.250	.250	.500	53	-0	0	2.31	-1	/S-1	0	-0.1
1896 Lou-N	31	115	14	18	1	1	1	15	13	15	3	....	.157	.248	.209	.457	22	-13	7	1.94	-12	S-28/3-3	0	-2.0
Total 2	**32**	**119**	**14**	**19**	**1**	**1**	**1**	**17**	**13**	**17**	**3**	**....**	**.160**	**.248**	**.210**	**.458**	**23**	**-13**	**8**	**1.95**	**-13**	**/S-29,3-3**	**0**	**-2.1**

• SHANNON, Joe

Joseph Aloysius Shannon b: 2/11/1897, Jersey City, NJ d: 7/28/1955, Jersey City, NJ BR/TR, 5'11", 170 lbs. Deb: 7/7/1915

YEAR TM-L	G	AB	R	H	2B	3B	HR	RBI	BB	SO	SB	CS	AVG	OBP	SLG	OPS	OPS+	BR/A	RC	RC/G	FR	G/POS	WS	TPW
1915 Bos-N	5	10	3	2	0	0	0	1	0	3	0	....	.200	.200	.200	.400	22	-1	1	1.53	0	/0-4(1-1-0),2-1	0	-0.2

• SHANNON, Mike

Thomas Michael "Moonman" Shannon b: 7/15/1939, St. Louis, MO BR/TR, 6'3", 195 lbs. Deb: 9/11/1962 Career OF: 44-30-294

YEAR TM-L	G	AB	R	H	2B	3B	HR	RBI	BB	SO	SB	CS	AVG	OBP	SLG	OPS	OPS+	BR/A	RC	RC/G	FR	G/POS	WS	TPW
1962 StL-N	10	15	3	2	0	0	0	0	1	3	0	0	.133	.188	.133	.321	-11	-2	0	.88	0	/0-7(5-0-2)	0	-0.2
1963 StL-N	32	26	3	8	0	0	1	2	0	6	0	1	.308	.333	.423	.756	106	-0	3	3.79	0	0-26(13-1-12)	1	-0.1
1964*StL-N	88	253	30	66	8	2	9	43	19	54	4	0	.261	.313	.415	.728	95	-1	32	4.33	0	0-88(9-6-76)	7	-0.5
1965 StL-N	124	244	32	54	17	3	3	25	28	46	2	1	.221	.307	.352	.659	78	-7	26	3.45	2	*0-101(1-14-87)/C-4	5	-1.1
1966 StL-N	137	459	61	132	20	6	16	64	37	106	8	4	.288	.341	.462	.803	121	13	70	5.46	3	*0-129(14-7-112)/C-1	18	0.7
1967*StL-N	130	482	53	118	18	3	12	77	37	89	2	4	.245	.304	.369	.673	93	-6	52	3.62	-4	*3-122/0-6(2-2-5)	12	-1.0
1968*StL-N	156	576	62	153	29	2	15	79	37	114	1	2	.266	.312	.401	.713	114	8	70	4.26	4	*3-156	23	1.4
1969 StL-N	150	551	51	140	15	5	12	55	49	87	1	4	.254	.316	.365	.681	90	-9	63	3.96	-12	*3-149	12	-2.2
1970 StL-N	55	174	18	37	9	2	0	22	16	20	1	1	.213	.279	.287	.566	51	-12	14	2.63	-13	3-51	0	-2.6
Total 9	**882**	**2780**	**313**	**710**	**116**	**23**	**68**	**367**	**224**	**525**	**19**	**17**	**.255**	**.313**	**.387**	**.700**	**97**	**-16**	**331**	**4.08**	**-19**	**3-478,0-357/C-5**	**78**	**-5.7**

• SHANNON, Owen

Owen Dennis Ignatius Shannon b: 12/22/1879, Omaha, NE d: 4/10/1918, Omaha, NE BR/TR Deb: 9/6/1903

YEAR TM-L	G	AB	R	H	2B	3B	HR	RBI	BB	SO	SB	CS	AVG	OBP	SLG	OPS	OPS+	BR/A	RC	RC/G	FR	G/POS	WS	TPW
1903 StL-A	9	28	1	6	2	0	0	3	1	....	0	....	.214	.241	.286	.527	59	-1	2	2.38	-1	/C-8,1-1	0	-0.2
1907 Was-A	4	7	0	1	0	0	0	0	0	....	0	....	.143	.143	.143	.286	-10	-1	0	.65	1	/C-4	0	0.0
Total 2	**13**	**35**	**1**	**7**	**2**	**0**	**0**	**3**	**1**	**....**	**0**	**....**	**.200**	**.222**	**.257**	**.479**	**46**	**-2**	**2**	**2.01**	**0**	**/C-12,1-1**	**0**	**-0.1**

• SHANNON, Red

Maurice Joseph Shannon b: 2/11/1897, Jersey City, NJ d: 4/12/1970, Jersey City, NJ BB/TR, 5'11", 170 lbs. Deb: 10/7/1915

YEAR TM-L	G	AB	R	H	2B	3B	HR	RBI	BB	SO	SB	CS	AVG	OBP	SLG	OPS	OPS+	BR/A	RC	RC/G	FR	G/POS	WS	TPW
1915 Bos-N	1	3	0	0	0	0	0	0	0	0	0	....	.000	.000	.000	.000	-102	-1	0	.00	0	/2-1	0	-0.1
1917 Phi-A	11	35	8	10	0	0	0	7	6	9	2	....	.286	.390	.286	.676	108	1	4	4.54	-2	S-10	1	-0.1
1918 Phi-A	72	225	23	54	6	5	0	16	42	52	5	....	.240	.367	.311	.678	103	3	28	3.92	-7	S-45,2-26	7	0.0
1919 Phi-A	39	155	14	42	7	2	0	14	12	28	4	....	.271	.331	.342	.673	88	-2	18	4.06	-5	2-37	3	-0.7
Bos-A	80	290	36	75	11	7	0	17	17	42	7	....	.259	.313	.345	.658	90	-5	32	3.78	-6	2-79	7	-1.0
Yr.	119	445	50	117	18	9	0	31	29	70	11	....	.263	.320	.344	.663	89	-7	50	3.87	-11	*2-116	10	-1.6
1920 Was-A	63	222	30	64	8	7	0	30	22	32	2	5	.288	.352	.387	.740	99	-1	30	4.67	-6	S-31,2-16,3-15	6	-0.5
Phi-A	24	88	4	15	1	1	0	3	4	12	1	1	.170	.207	.205	.411	9	-12	4	1.32	0	S-24	1	-0.9
Yr.	87	310	34	79	9	8	0	33	26	44	3	6	.255	.313	.335	.648	74	-13	34	3.62	-6	S-55,2-16,3-15	7	-1.5
1921 Phi-A	1	1	0	0	0	0	0	0	0	0	0	0	.000	.000	.000	.000	-99	-0	0	.00	0	....	0	0.0
1926 Chi-N	19	51	9	17	5	0	0	4	6	3	0	....	.333	.414	.431	.845	126	2	9	6.48	0	S-13	2	0.4
Total 7	**310**	**1070**	**124**	**277**	**38**	**22**	**0**	**91**	**109**	**178**	**21**	**6**	**.259**	**.334**	**.336**	**.670**	**90**	**-15**	**125**	**3.93**	**-26**	**2-159,S-123/3-15**	**27**	**-2.9**

• SHANNON, Spike

William Porter Shannon b: 2/7/1878, Pittsburgh, PA d: 5/16/1940, Minneapolis, MN BB/TR, 5'11", 180 lbs. Deb: 4/15/1904 U Career OF: 532-23-139

YEAR TM-L	G	AB	R	H	2B	3B	HR	RBI	BB	SO	SB	CS	AVG	OBP	SLG	OPS	OPS+	BR/A	RC	RC/G	FR	G/POS	WS	TPW
1904 StL-N	134	500	84	140	10	3	1	26	50	....	34	....	.280	.349	.318	.667	111	9	73	4.87	8	*0-133(13-3-117)	17	1.1
1905 StL-N	140	544	73	146	16	3	0	41	47	....	27	....	.268	.327	.309	.635	92	-4	68	4.22	-5	*0-140(140-0-0)	13	-1.8
1906 StL-N	80	302	36	78	4	0	0	25	36	....	15	....	.258	.337	.272	.609	94	-1	35	3.89	7	0-80(80-0-0)	7	0.2
NY-N	76	287	42	73	5	1	0	25	34	....	18	....	.254	.342	.279	.620	91	-1	35	4.16	-2	0-76(76-0-0)	8	-0.8
Yr.	156	589	78	151	9	1	0	50	70	....	33	....	.256	.339	.275	.614	93	-2	71	4.02	5	*0-156(156-0-0)	15	-0.7
1907 NY-N	155	585	**104**	155	12	5	1	33	82	....	33	....	.265	.363	.308	.671	107	9	81	4.77	-2	*0-155(155-0-0)	21	-0.2
1908 NY-N	77	268	34	60	2	1	1	21	28	....	13	....	.224	.314	.250	.564	77	-5	26	3.06	-1	0-74(60-0-15)	6	-1.2
Pit-N	32	127	10	25	0	2	0	12	9	....	5	....	.197	.250	.228	.478	53	-7	8	2.08	-1	0-32(8-20-7)	2	-1.1

YEAR TM-L	G	AB	R	H	2B	3B	HR	RBI	BB	SO	SB	CS	AVG	OBP	SLG	OPS	OPS+	BR/A	RC	RC/G	FR	G/POS	WS	TPW
Yr.	109	395	44	85	2	3	1	33	37	....	18	....	.215	.294	.243	.537	69	-12	34	2.74	-2	*0-106(68-20-22)	8	-2.4
Total 5	**694**	**2613**	**383**	**677**	**49**	**15**	**3**	**183**	**286**	**....**	**145**	**....**	**.259**	**.337**	**.293**	**.630**	**96**	**0**	**327**	**4.18**	**4**	**0-690**	**74**	**-3.9**
• SHANNON, Wally	Walter Charles Shannon b: 1/23/1933, Cleveland, OH d: 2/8/1992, Creve Coeur, MO BL/TR, 6', 178 lbs. Deb: 7/9/1959																							
1959 StL-N	47	95	5	27	5	0	0	5	0	12	0	0	.284	.292	.337	.629	63	-5	9	3.74	-3	S-21,2-10	1	-0.7
1960 StL-N	18	23	2	4	0	0	0	1	3	6	0	0	.174	.296	.174	.470	30	-2	1	2.01	2	2-15/S-1	0	0.0
Total 2	**65**	**118**	**7**	**31**	**5**	**0**	**0**	**6**	**3**	**18**	**0**	**0**	**.263**	**.293**	**.305**	**.598**	**55**	**-7**	**11**	**3.36**	**-1**	**/2-25,S-22**	**1**	**-0.7**
• SHANTZ, Billy	Wilmer Ebert Shantz b: 7/31/1927, Pottstown, PA d: 12/13/1993, Lauderhill, FL BR/TR, 6'1", 160 lbs. Deb: 4/13/1954																							
1954 Phi-A	51	164	13	42	9	3	1	17	17	23	0	0	.256	.326	.366	.692	89	-2	19	4.09	1	C-51	4	0.1
1955 KC-A	79	217	18	56	4	1	1	12	11	14	0	0	.258	.294	.300	.593	59	-13	18	2.89	2	C-78	3	-0.8
1960 NY-A	1	0	0	0	0	0	0	0	0	0	0	0	....	....	....	....	-106	0	0	....	0	/C-1	0	0.0
Total 3	**131**	**381**	**31**	**98**	**13**	**4**	**2**	**29**	**28**	**37**	**0**	**0**	**.257**	**.308**	**.328**	**.636**	**72**	**-15**	**38**	**3.40**	**3**	**C-130**	**7**	**-0.7**
• SHARMAN, Ralph	Ralph Edward "Bally" Sharman b: 4/11/1895, Cleveland, OH d: 5/24/1918, Camp Sheridan, AL BR/TR, 5'11", 176 lbs. Deb: 9/10/1917																							
1917 Phi-A	13	37	2	11	2	1	0	2	3	2	1	....	.297	.366	.405	.771	137	2	6	5.40	-1	0-10(2-3-5)	1	0.0
• SHARON, Dick	Richard Louis Sharon b: 4/15/1950, San Mateo, CA BR/TR, 6'2", 195 lbs. Deb: 5/13/1973 Career OF: 81-33-97																							
1973 Det-A	91	178	20	43	9	0	7	16	10	31	2	0	.242	.282	.410	.692	87	-3	20	3.73	-1	0-91(19-7-71)	4	-0.8
1974 Det-A	60	129	12	28	4	0	2	10	14	29	4	4	.217	.294	.295	.588	67	-6	11	2.65	0	0-56(23-14-19)	2	-0.9
1975 SD-N	91	160	14	31	7	0	4	20	26	35	0	2	.194	.306	.313	.619	77	-6	15	2.90	-3	0-57(39-12-7)	2	-1.2
Total 3	**242**	**467**	**46**	**102**	**20**	**0**	**13**	**46**	**50**	**95**	**6**	**6**	**.218**	**.294**	**.345**	**.639**	**78**	**-15**	**46**	**3.13**	**-5**	**0-204**	**8**	**-2.8**
• SHARP, Bill	William Howard Sharp b: 1/18/1950, Lima, OH BL/TL, 5'10", 178 lbs. Deb: 5/26/1973 Career OF: 80-159-156																							
1973 Chi-A	77	196	23	54	8	3	4	22	19	28	2	3	.276	.349	.408	.757	109	2	28	5.02	3	0-70(11-59-0)/D-1	7	0.3
1974 Chi-A	100	320	45	81	13	2	4	24	25	37	0	3	.253	.311	.344	.655	86	-7	33	3.38	-5	0-99(13-7-85)	5	-1.8
1975 Chi-A	18	35	1	7	0	0	0	4	2	3	0	0	.200	.243	.200	.443	26	-3	2	1.77	-1	0-14(2-1-11)	0	-0.5
Mil-A	125	373	37	95	27	3	1	34	19	26	0	3	.255	.293	.351	.644	81	-12	36	3.21	0	*0-124(43-82-23)	7	-1.6
Yr.	143	408	38	102	27	3	1	38	21	29	0	3	.250	.288	.338	.627	76	-15	38	3.09	0	*0-138(45-83-34)	7	-2.1
1976 Mil-A	78	180	16	44	4	0	0	11	10	15	1	3	.244	.288	.267	.555	64	-9	13	2.48	3	0-56(11-10-37)/D-7	2	-0.9
Total 4	**398**	**1104**	**122**	**281**	**52**	**8**	**9**	**95**	**75**	**109**	**3**	**12**	**.255**	**.306**	**.341**	**.647**	**83**	**-29**	**113**	**3.40**	**0**	**0-363/D-8**	**21**	**-4.5**
• SHARPE, Bud	Bayard Heston Sharpe b: 8/6/1881, West Chester, PA d: 5/31/1916, Haddock, GA BL/TR, 6'1" Deb: 4/14/1905																							
1905 Bos-N	46	170	8	31	3	2	0	11	7	....	0	....	.182	.215	.224	.438	31	-15	9	1.59	4	0-42(0-0-42)/C-3,1-1	1	-1.3
1910 Bos-N	115	439	30	105	14	3	0	29	14	31	4	....	.239	.264	.285	.549	58	-26	34	2.54	0	*1-113	2	-2.9
Pit-N	4	16	2	3	0	1	0	1	0	2	0	....	.188	.188	.313	.500	43	-1	1	1.72	0	/1-4	0	-0.1
Yr.	119	455	32	108	14	4	0	30	14	33	4	....	.237	.262	.286	.547	57	-27	35	2.51	1	*1-117	2	-3.0
Total 2	**165**	**625**	**40**	**139**	**17**	**6**	**0**	**41**	**21**	**33**	**4**	**....**	**.222**	**.249**	**.269**	**.518**	**50**	**-42**	**44**	**2.25**	**5**	**1-118/0-42,C-3**	**3**	**-4.2**
• SHARPERSON, Mike	Michael Tyrone Sharperson b: 10/4/1961, Orangeburg, SC d: 5/26/1996, Las Vegas, NV BR/TR, 6'3", 191 lbs. Deb: 4/6/1987																							
1987 Tor-A	32	96	4	20	4	1	0	9	7	15	2	1	.208	.269	.271	.540	43	-8	7	2.38	-4	2-32	1	-1.0
LA-N	10	33	7	9	2	0	0	1	4	5	0	0	.273	.351	.333	.685	85	-1	4	4.13	2	/3-7,2-6	1	0.1
1988*LA-N	46	59	8	16	1	0	0	4	1	12	0	1	.271	.295	.288	.583	70	-3	5	2.68	-2	2-20/3-6,S-4	1	-0.4
1989 LA-N	27	28	2	7	3	0	0	5	4	7	0	1	.250	.344	.357	.701	102	-0	3	3.38	-1	/2-4,1-2,3-2,S-1	1	-0.1
1990 LA-N	129	357	42	106	14	2	3	36	46	39	15	6	.297	.379	.373	.751	111	7	54	5.32	5	*3-106,S-15/2-9,1-6	14	1.4
1991 LA-N	105	216	24	60	11	2	2	20	25	24	1	3	.278	.355	.375	.730	108	2	30	4.74	1	3-68,S-16,1-10/2-5	6	0.4
1992 LA-N★	128	317	48	95	21	0	3	36	47	33	2	2	.300	.390	.394	.784	125	12	50	5.61	3	2-63,3-60/S-2	13	1.7
1993 LA-N	73	90	13	23	4	0	2	10	5	17	2	0	.256	.302	.367	.669	83	-2	10	3.88	-2	2-17/3-6,S-3,1-1,0-1	2	-0.3
1995 Atl-N	7	7	1	1	1	0	0	2	0	2	0	0	.143	.143	.286	.429	9	-1	0	1.29	0	/3-1	0	-0.1
Total 8	**557**	**1203**	**149**	**337**	**61**	**5**	**10**	**123**	**139**	**154**	**22**	**14**	**.280**	**.357**	**.364**	**.721**	**104**	**6**	**163**	**4.69**	**2**	**3-256,2-156/S-41,1-19,0-1**	**39**	**1.6**
• SHARROTT, Jack	John Henry Sharrott b: 8/13/1869, Bangor, ME d: 12/31/1927, Los Angeles, CA BR/TR, 5'9", 165 lbs. Deb: 4/22/1890 Career OF: 29-9-12 ♦																							
1890 NY-N	32	109	16	22	3	2	0	14	0	14	6	....	.202	.202	.266	.468	36	-5	7	2.21	0	P-25/0-9(5-0-4)	11	0.4
1891 NY-N	10	30	5	10	2	0	1	7	1	2	3	....	.333	.355	.500	.855	154	4	7	8.84	1	P-10	6	0.7
1892 NY-N	4	8	1	1	0	0	0	0	0	1	0	....	.125	.125	.125	.250	-25	-1	0	.49	-1	/0-3(0-0-3),P-1	0	-0.2
1893 Phi-N	50	152	25	38	4	3	1	22	8	14	6	....	.250	.288	.336	.623	65	-7	17	3.90	-2	0-33(24-9-5),P-12	4	-0.9
Total 4	**96**	**299**	**47**	**71**	**9**	**5**	**2**	**43**	**9**	**31**	**15**	**....**	**.237**	**.260**	**.321**	**.581**	**62**	**-9**	**31**	**3.58**	**-2**	**/P-48,0-45**	**21**	**0.0**
• SHAUGHNESSY, Shag	Francis Joseph Shaughnessy b: 4/8/1883, Amboy, IL d: 5/15/1969, Montreal, Canada BR/TR, 6'1.5", 185 lbs. Deb: 4/17/1905 C Career OF: 0-8-1																							
1905 Was-A	1	3	0	0	0	0	0	0	0	....	0	....	.000	.250	.000	.250	-19	-0	0	.00	0	/0-1	0	-0.1
1908 Phi-A	8	29	2	9	0	0	0	1	2	....	3	....	.310	.355	.310	.665	109	0	4	5.15	-2	/0-8(0-8-0)	1	-0.2
Total 2	**9**	**32**	**2**	**9**	**0**	**0**	**0**	**1**	**2**	**....**	**3**	**....**	**.281**	**.343**	**.281**	**.624**	**95**	**0**	**4**	**4.53**	**-2**	**/0-9**	**1**	**-0.3**
• SHAVE, Jon	Jonathan Taylor Shave b: 11/4/1967, Waycross, GA BR/TR, 6', 185 lbs. Deb: 5/15/1993																							
1993 Tex-A	17	47	3	15	2	0	0	7	0	8	1	3	.319	.319	.362	.681	86	-2	5	3.13	-1	/S-9,2-8	1	-0.2
1998 Min-A	19	40	7	10	3	0	1	5	3	10	1	2	.250	.302	.400	.702	79	-2	4	3.73	0	3-15/1-1,D-1,S-1	1	-0.2
1999 Tex-A	43	73	10	21	4	0	0	9	5	17	1	0	.288	.350	.342	.692	74	-2	10	4.79	-1	S-24/1-9,3-6,D-3,2-1	3	-0.2
Total 3	**79**	**160**	**20**	**46**	**9**	**0**	**1**	**21**	**8**	**35**	**3**	**5**	**.288**	**.329**	**.363**	**.692**	**79**	**-7**	**19**	**4.00**	**-1**	**/S-34,3-21,1-10,2-9,D-4**	**5**	**-0.6**
• SHAW, Al	Albert Simpson Shaw b: 3/1/1881, Toledo, IL d: 12/30/1974, Danville, IL BL/TR, 5'8.5", 165 lbs. Deb: 9/28/1907 Career OF: 122-272-24																							
1907 StL-N	9	25	2	7	0	0	0	1	3	....	1	....	.280	.379	.280	.659	110	1	4	4.45	-1	/0-9(0-9-0)	1	0.0
1908 StL-N	107	367	40	97	13	4	1	19	25	....	9	....	.264	.311	.330	.641	110	3	40	3.73	5	0-91(2-67-22)/S-4,3-1	11	0.5
1909 StL-N	114	331	45	82	12	7	2	34	55	....	15	....	.248	.355	.344	.699	125	12	45	4.66	-6	0-92(0-90-2)	12	0.1
1914 Bro-F	112	376	81	122	27	7	5	49	44	59	24	....	.324	.395	.473	.869	145	23	76	7.37	-1	*0-102(0-102-0)	19	1.7
1915 KC-F	132	448	67	126	22	10	6	67	46	45	15	....	.281	.348	.415	.763	128	15	67	5.24	-7	*0-124(120-4-0)	21	0.3
Total 5	**474**	**1547**	**235**	**434**	**74**	**28**	**14**	**170**	**173**	**104**	**64**	**....**	**.281**	**.353**	**.392**	**.745**	**127**	**53**	**232**	**5.22**	**-10**	**0-418/S-4,3-1**	**64**	**2.5**
• SHAW, Al	Alfred "Shoddy" Shaw b: 10/3/1874, Burslem, England d: 3/25/1958, Uhrichsville, OH BR/TR, 5'8", 170 lbs. Deb: 6/8/1901																							
1901 Det-A	55	171	20	46	7	0	1	23	10	....	2	....	.269	.321	.327	.648	76	-6	20	4.01	-5	C-42/1-9,3-2,S-1	3	-0.6
1907 Bos-A	76	198	10	38	1	3	0	7	18	....	4	....	.192	.269	.227	.497	59	-8	14	2.26	6	C-73/1-1	4	0.5
1908 Chi-A	32	49	0	4	1	0	0	2	2	....	0	....	.082	.118	.102	.220	-29	-7	1	.32	-6	C-29	1	-1.2
1909 Bos-N	18	41	1	4	0	0	0	0	5	....	0	....	.098	.213	.098	.310	-3	-5	1	.56	1	C-14	0	-0.2
Total 4	**181**	**459**	**31**	**92**	**9**	**3**	**1**	**32**	**35**	**....**	**6**	**....**	**.200**	**.267**	**.240**	**.507**	**51**	**-26**	**35**	**2.47**	**-3**	**C-158/1-10,3-2,S-1**	**8**	**-1.5**
• SHAW, Ben	Benjamin Nathaniel Shaw b: 6/18/1893, La Center, KY d: 3/16/1959, Cleveland, OH BR/TR, 5'11.5", 190 lbs. Deb: 4/11/1917																							
1917 Pit-N	2	2	0	0	0	0	0	0	0	0	0	....	.000	.000	.000	.000	-97	-0	0	.00	0	....	0	-0.1
1918 Pit-N	21	36	5	7	1	0	0	2	2	2	0	....	.194	.275	.222	.497	50	-2	2	1.84	-1	/1-9,C-5	0	-0.3
Total 2	**23**	**38**	**5**	**7**	**1**	**0**	**0**	**2**	**2**	**2**	**0**	**....**	**.184**	**.262**	**.211**	**.472**	**43**	**-2**	**2**	**1.72**	**-1**	**/1-9,C-5**	**0**	**-0.4**
• SHAW, Hunky	Royal N Shaw b: 9/29/1884, Yakima, WA d: 7/3/1969, Yakima, WA BB/TR, 5'8", 165 lbs. Deb: 5/16/1908																							
1908 Pit-N	1	1	0	0	0	0	0	0	0	....	0	....	.000	.000	.000	.000	-100	-0	0	.00	0	....	0	0.0
• SHAY, Danny	Daniel C. Shay b: 11/8/1876, Springfield, OH d: 12/1/1927, Kansas City, MO BR/TR, 5'10" Deb: 4/30/1901																							
1901 Cle-A	19	75	4	17	2	2	0	10	2	....	0	....	.227	.266	.307	.572	61	-4	6	2.87	-3	S-19	1	-0.6
1904 StL-N	99	340	45	87	11	1	1	18	39	....	36	....	.256	.338	.303	.641	103	3	49	4.90	-6	S-97/2-2	14	0.0
1905 StL-N	78	281	30	67	12	1	0	28	35	....	11	....	.238	.331	.288	.620	88	-2	32	3.80	-17	2-39,S-39	7	-1.8
1907 NY-N	35	79	10	15	1	1	1	6	12	....	5	....	.190	.304	.266	.570	76	-2	8	3.30	-5	2-13/S-9,0-2(0-2-0)	2	-0.7
Total 4	**231**	**775**	**89**	**186**	**26**	**5**	**2**	**62**	**88**	**....**	**52**	**....**	**.240**	**.325**	**.294**	**.620**	**91**	**-5**	**95**	**4.13**	**-31**	**S-164/2-54,0-2**	**24**	**-3.1**
• SHAY, Marty	Arthur Joseph Shay b: 4/25/1896, Boston, MA d: 2/20/1951, Worcester, MA BR/TR, 5'7.5", 148 lbs. Deb: 9/16/1916																							
1916 Chi-N	2	7	0	2	0	0	0	0	0	1	0	....	.286	.286	.286	.571	68	-0	1	2.97	0	/S-2	0	0.0

YEAR TM-L	G	AB	R	H	2B	3B	HR	RBI	BB	SO	SB	CS	AVG	OBP	SLG	OPS	OPS+	BR/A	RC	RC/G	FR	G/POS	WS	TPW
1924 Bos-N	19	68	4	16	3	1	0	2	5	5	2	1	.235	.297	.309	.606	65	-3	6	3.21	-4	2-19/S-1	1	-0.7
Total 2	21	75	4	18	3	1	0	2	5	6	2	1	.240	.296	.307	.603	66	-3	7	3.19	-4	/2-19,S-3	1	-0.7
• SHEA, Gerry	Gerald J. Shea b: 7/26/1881, St. Louis, MO d: 5/3/1964, Berkeley, MO TR, 5'7", 160 lbs. Deb: 10/1/1905																							
1905 StL-N	2	6	0	2	0	0	0	0	0	....	0	....	.333	.333	.333	.667	102	-0	1	4.44	0	/C-2	0	0.0
• SHEA, Merv	Mervyn David John Shea b: 9/5/1900, San Francisco, CA d: 1/27/1953, Sacramento, CA BR/TR, 5'11", 175 lbs. Deb: 4/23/1927 C																							
1927 Det-A	34	85	5	15	6	3	0	9	7	15	0	0	.176	.239	.318	.557	43	-8	7	2.47	-3	C-31	1	-0.9
1928 Det-A	39	85	8	20	2	3	0	9	9	11	2	2	.235	.316	.329	.645	69	-4	9	3.47	0	C-30	2	-0.3
1929 Det-A	50	162	23	47	6	0	3	24	19	18	2	1	.290	.365	.383	.747	92	-1	23	5.32	0	C-46	4	0.1
1933 Bos-A	16	56	1	8	3	0	0	8	4	7	0	0	.143	.200	.196	.396	5	-8	2	1.28	2	C-16	1	-0.5
StL-A	94	279	26	73	11	1	1	27	43	26	2	0	.262	.360	.319	.679	76	-7	35	4.47	7	C-85	8	0.5
Yr.	110	335	27	81	14	1	1	35	47	33	2	0	.242	.335	.299	.634	65	-15	38	3.87	9	*C-101	9	0.1
1934 Chi-A	62	176	8	28	3	0	0	5	24	19	0	1	.159	.260	.176	.436	14	-23	9	1.63	4	C-60	2	-1.5
1935 Chi-A	46	122	8	28	2	0	0	13	30	9	0	0	.230	.382	.246	.627	64	-5	14	3.88	3	C-43	4	0.1
1936 Chi-A	14	24	3	3	0	0	0	2	6	5	0	0	.125	.300	.125	.425	8	-3	1	1.71	0	C-14	1	-0.2
1937 Chi-A	25	71	7	15	1	0	0	5	15	10	1	0	.211	.349	.225	.574	48	-5	7	3.24	1	C-25	2	-0.2
1938 Bro-N	48	120	14	22	5	0	0	12	28	20	1	....	.183	.338	.225	.563	56	-6	11	3.06	0	C-47	2	-0.3
1939 Det-A	4	2	0	0	0	0	0	0	0	1	0	0	.000	.000	.000	.000	-93	-1	0	.00	-2	/C-4	0	-0.2
1944 Phi-N	7	15	2	4	0	0	1	1	4	4	0	....	.267	.421	.467	.888	155	1	3	6.66	0	/C-6	1	0.1
Total 11	439	1197	105	263	39	7	5	115	189	145	8	4	.220	.327	.277	.603	58	-68	123	3.41	12	C-407	28	-3.1
• SHEA, Nap	John Edward "Napoleon,Shorty,Red" Shea b: 5/23/1874, Ware, MA d: 7/8/1968, Bloomfield Hills, MI BR/TR, 5'5", 155 lbs. Deb: 9/11/1902																							
1902 Phi-N	3	8	1	1	0	0	0	0	1	....	0	....	.125	.300	.125	.425	32	-0	0	1.16	0	/C-3	0	0.0
• SHEAFFER, Danny	Danny Todd Sheaffer b: 8/2/1961, Jacksonville, FL BR/TR, 6', 202 lbs. Deb: 4/9/1987 Career OF: 20-2-9																							
1987 Bos-A	25	66	5	8	1	0	1	5	0	14	0	0	.121	.121	.182	.303	-21	-12	1	.50	-1	C-25	1	-1.1
1989 Cle-A	7	16	1	1	0	0	0	0	2	2	0	0	.063	.167	.063	.229	-32	-3	0	.54	0	/D-3,3-2,0-1	0	-0.3
1993 Col-N	82	216	26	60	9	1	4	32	8	15	2	3	.278	.307	.384	.691	72	-10	22	3.40	1	C-65/1-7,0-2(2-0-0),3-1	5	-0.5
1994 Col-N	44	110	11	24	4	0	1	12	10	11	0	2	.218	.283	.282	.565	41	-10	8	2.52	2	C-30/1-2,0-1	2	-0.6
1995 StL-N	76	208	24	48	10	1	5	30	23	38	0	0	.231	.307	.361	.668	76	-8	22	3.51	5	C-67/1-3,3-1	6	0.1
1996*StL-N	79	198	10	45	9	3	2	20	9	25	3	3	.227	.271	.333	.605	59	-13	14	2.18	1	C-47,3-17/1-6,0-3(3-0-0)	3	-0.9
1997 StL-N	76	132	10	33	5	0	0	11	8	17	1	0	.250	.298	.288	.586	55	-9	10	2.26	-2	3-30,0-22(13-2-9)/C-9,2-3	1	-1.0
Total 7	389	946	87	219	38	5	13	110	60	122	6	8	.232	.281	.323	.604	56	-64	77	2.61	6	C-243/3-51,0-29,1-18,2-3,D	18	-4.4
• SHEAN, Dave	David William Shean b: 7/9/1883, Arlington, MA d: 5/22/1963, Boston, MA BR/TR, 5'11", 175 lbs. Deb: 9/10/1906																							
1906 Phi-A	22	75	7	16	3	2	0	3	5	....	6	....	.213	.280	.307	.587	81	-2	9	3.71	0	2-22	2	-0.2
1908 Phi-N	14	48	4	7	2	0	0	2	1	....	1	....	.146	.180	.188	.368	17	-5	2	1.12	-3	S-14	0	-0.9
1909 Phi-N	36	112	14	26	2	2	0	4	14	....	3	....	.232	.323	.286	.609	88	-1	11	3.32	-2	2-14,1-11/0-3(0-3-0),S-1	2	-0.4
Bos-N	75	267	32	66	11	4	1	29	17	....	14	....	.247	.297	.330	.627	90	-4	31	3.69	1	2-72	6	-0.2
Yr.	111	379	46	92	13	6	1	33	31	....	17	....	.243	.305	.317	.622	90	-5	42	3.58	-1	2-86,1-11/0-3(0-3-0),S-1	8	-0.7
1910 Bos-N	150	543	52	130	12	7	3	36	42	45	16	....	.239	.294	.304	.598	71	-21	53	3.21	24	*2-148	9	0.4
1911 Chi-N	54	145	17	28	4	0	0	15	8	15	4	....	.193	.240	.221	.461	29	-14	9	1.87	2	2-23,S-19/3-1	2	-1.1
1912 Bos-N	4	10	1	3	0	0	0	0	1	2	0	....	.300	.417	.300	.717	96	0	1	4.48	-0	/S-4	0	0.0
1917 Cin-N	131	442	36	93	9	5	2	35	22	39	10	....	.210	.249	.267	.516	61	-21	31	2.23	13	*2-131	5	-0.6
1918*Bos-A	115	425	58	112	16	3	0	34	40	25	11	....	.264	.331	.315	.646	97	-2	51	3.69	-10	*2-115	15	-1.0
1919 Bos-A	29	100	4	14	0	0	0	8	5	7	1	....	.140	.189	.140	.329	-7	-14	3	.86	-1	2-29	1	-1.6
Total 9	630	2167	225	495	59	23	6	166	155	133	66	....	.228	.284	.285	.569	71	-83	200	2.92	23	2-554/S-38,1-11,0-3,3-1	42	-5.6
• SHEARER, Ray	Ray Solomon Shearer b: 9/19/1929, Jacobus, PA d: 2/21/1982, York, PA BR/TR, 6', 200 lbs. Deb: 9/18/1957																							
1957 Mil-N	2	2	1	1	0	0	0	0	1	1	0	0	.500	.667	.500	1.167	237	1	1	22.68	0	/0-1	0	0.0
• SHEARON, John	John M. Shearon b: 1870, Pittsburgh, PA d: 2/1/1923, Bradford, PA Deb: 7/28/1891 Career OF: 4-14-26 ♦																							
1891 Cle-N	30	124	10	30	1	1	0	13	1	15	6	....	.242	.248	.266	.514	48	-7	10	2.85	-1	0-25(4-14-10)/P-6	2	-0.7
1896 Cle-N	16	64	6	11	0	1	0	3	4	6	3	....	.172	.221	.203	.424	11	-9	4	1.81	-3	0-16(0-0-16)	0	-1.0
Total 2	46	188	16	41	1	2	0	16	5	21	9	....	.218	.238	.245	.483	35	-16	14	2.47	-4	/0-41,P-6	2	-1.8
• SHECKARD, Jimmy	Samuel James Tilden Sheckard b: 11/23/1878, Upper Chanceford, PA d: 1/15/1947, Lancaster, PA BL/TR, 5'9", 175 lbs. Deb: 9/14/1897 Career OF: 1843-22-214																							
1897 Bro-N	13	49	12	14	3	2	3	14	6	....	5	....	.286	.364	.612	.976	164	4	13	9.88	-4	S-11/0-2(0-0-2)	2	0.0
1898 Bro-N	105	408	51	113	17	9	4	64	37	....	8	....	.277	.349	.392	.741	113	6	61	5.36	-2	*0-105(101-4-0)/3-1	13	-0.5
1899 Bal-N	147	536	104	158	18	10	3	75	56	....	**77**	....	.295	.380	.382	.763	104	5	111	7.63	14	*0-146(0-1-146)/1-1	21	1.0
1900 Bro-N	85	273	74	82	19	10	1	39	42	....	30	....	.300	.416	.454	.870	132	14	66	8.98	0	0-78(67-6-5)	15	0.7
1901 Bro-N	133	554	116	196	29	**19**	11	104	47	....	35	....	.354	.409	**.534**	.944	168	47	139	10.21	4	*0-121(120-1-0),3-12	33	4.3
1902 Bal-A	4	15	3	4	1	0	0	0	1	....	2	....	.267	.313	.333	.646	76	-1	2	5.40	0	/0-4(0-4-0)	0	-0.1
Bro-N	123	486	86	129	20	10	4	37	57	....	23	....	.265	.349	.372	.721	122	14	74	5.37	6	*0-123(122-1-0)	25	1.3
1903 Bro-N	139	515	99	171	29	9	**9**	75	75	....	**67**	....	.332	.423	.476	.899	161	**44**	137	9.97	12	*0-139(139-0-0)	33	4.6
1904 Bro-N	143	507	70	121	23	6	1	46	56	....	21	....	.239	.317	.314	.630	97	-0	61	3.91	4	*0-141(141-0-0)/2-2	11	-0.5
1905 Bro-N	130	480	58	140	20	11	3	41	61	....	23	....	.292	.380	.398	.777	142	28	85	6.24	15	*0-129(129-0-0)	21	3.6
1906*Chi-N	149	549	90	144	27	10	1	45	67	....	30	....	.262	.349	.353	.702	112	10	85	4.97	1	*0-149(149-0-0)	25	0.2
1907*Chi-N	143	484	76	129	23	1	1	36	76	....	31	....	.267	.373	.324	.697	112	11	77	5.12	-4	*0-142(142-0-0)	23	-0.1
1908*Chi-N	115	403	54	93	18	3	2	22	62	....	18	....	.231	.336	.305	.641	101	3	49	3.84	0	*0-115(115-0-0)	15	-0.5
1909 Chi-N	148	525	81	134	29	5	1	43	72	....	15	....	.255	.346	.335	.681	109	8	70	4.18	0	*0-148(148-0-0)	23	-0.2
1910*Chi-N	144	507	82	130	27	6	5	51	83	53	22	....	.256	.366	.363	.729	114	12	78	4.96	9	*0-143(143-0-0)	23	1.3
1911 Chi-N	156	539	**121**	149	26	11	4	50	**147**	58	32	....	.276	**.434**	.388	.822	130	33	106	6.79	19	*0-156(156-0-0)	30	4.6
1912 Chi-N	146	523	85	128	22	10	3	47	**122**	81	15	....	.245	.392	.342	.735	102	9	76	4.81	12	*0-146(146-0-0)	21	1.5
1913 StL-N	52	136	18	27	2	1	0	17	41	25	5	....	.199	.388	.228	.616	79	-0	14	3.15	1	0-46(16-0-36)	3	-0.1
Cin-N	47	116	16	22	1	3	0	7	27	16	6	....	.190	.343	.250	.593	71	-3	12	3.13	0	0-38(9-5-25)	2	-0.5
Yr.	99	252	34	49	3	4	0	24	68	41	11	....	.194	.368	.238	.606	76	-3	26	3.14	1	0-84(25-5-61)	5	-0.6
Total 17	2122	7605	1296	2084	354	136	56	813	1135	233	465	....	.274	.375	.378	.753	120	243	1316	5.93	85	*0-2071/3-13,S-11,2-2,1-1	339	20.7
• SHEEHAN, Biff	Timothy James Sheehan b: 2/13/1868, Hartford, CT d: 10/21/1923, Hartford, CT BL/TR, 5'9", 165 lbs. Deb: 7/22/1895 Career OF: 1-2-44																							
1895 StL-N	52	180	24	57	3	6	1	18	20	6	7	....	.317	.394	.417	.811	111	4	34	7.15	-1	0-41(0-2-39),1-11	4	0.1
1896 StL-N	6	19	0	3	0	0	0	1	4	0	0	....	.158	.304	.158	.462	25	-2	1	1.55	0	/0-6(1-0-5)	0	-0.2
Total 2	58	199	24	60	3	6	1	19	24	6	7	....	.302	.385	.392	.777	102	2	35	6.53	-1	/0-47,1-11	4	-0.2
• SHEEHAN, Jack	John Thomas Sheehan b: 4/15/1893, Chicago, IL d: 5/29/1987, West Palm Beach, FL BB/TR, 5'8.5", 165 lbs. Deb: 9/11/1920																							
1920*Bro-N	3	5	0	2	1	0	0	0	1	0	0	0	.400	.500	.600	1.100	208	1	2	13.82	-1	/S-2,3-1	0	0.0
1921 Bro-N	5	12	2	0	0	0	0	0	0	1	0	0	.000	.000	.000	.000	-97	-3	0	.00	-1	/2-2,3-1,S-1	0	-0.4
Total 2	8	17	2	2	1	0	0	0	1	1	0	0	.118	.167	.176	.343	5	-3	2	2.76	-2	/S-3,2-2,3-2	0	-0.4
• SHEEHAN, Jim	James Thomas "Big Jim" Sheehan b: 6/3/1913, New Haven, CT d: 12/2/2003, New Haven, CT BR/TR, 6'2", 196 lbs. Deb: 9/26/1936																							
1936 NY-N	1	4	0	0	0	0	0	0	0	2	0	....	.000	.000	.000	.000	-101	-1	0	.00	0	/C-1	0	-0.1
• SHEEHAN, John	John M. Sheehan b: Washington, DC Deb: 4/19/1884																							
1884 Was-U	7	28	2	4	0	1	0	....	1	....	....	....	.143	.172	.214	.387	31	-2	1	1.24	-1	/0-7(2-3-2),3-1	0	-0.3
Wil-U	2	6	0	1	0	0	0	....	1	....	....	....	.167	.286	.167	.452	55	-0	0	1.64	0	/0-2(1-1-0)	0	0.0
Yr.	9	34	2	5	0	1	0	....	2	....	....	....	.147	.194	.206	.400	36	-2	1	1.31	-1	/0-9(3-4-2),3-1	0	-0.3
• SHEEHAN, Tommy	Thomas H. Sheehan b: 11/6/1877, Sacramento, CA d: 5/22/1959, Panama City, Panama BR/TR, 5'8", 160 lbs. Deb: 8/2/1900																							
1900 NY-N	1	2	0	0	0	0	0	0	0	....	0	....	.000	.000	.000	.000	-105	-1	0	.00	-1	/S-1	0	-0.1

YEAR TM-L	G	AB	R	H	2B	3B	HR	RBI	BB	SO	SB	CS	AVG	OBP	SLG	OPS	OPS+	BR/A	RC	RC/G	FR	G/POS	WS	TPW
1906 Pit-N	95	315	28	76	6	3	1	34	18	....	13	....	.241	.284	.289	.573	75	-10	32	3.28	-1	3-90	8	-0.9
1907 Pit-N	75	226	23	62	2	3	0	25	23	....	10	....	.274	.341	.310	.651	103	1	30	4.37	2	3-57,S-10	9	0.6
1908 Bro-N	146	468	45	100	18	2	0	29	53	....	9	....	.214	.302	.261	.562	83	-7	42	2.75	-9	*3-145	10	-1.3
Total 4	317	1011	96	238	26	8	1	88	94	....	32	....	.235	.305	.280	.585	85	-16	104	3.25	-8	3-292/S-11	27	-1.7

• SHEELY, Bud Hollis Kimball Sheely b: 11/26/1920, Spokane, WA d: 10/17/1985, Sacramento, CA BL/TR, 6'1", 200 lbs. Deb: 7/26/1951

YEAR TM-L	G	AB	R	H	2B	3B	HR	RBI	BB	SO	SB	CS	AVG	OBP	SLG	OPS	OPS+	BR/A	RC	RC/G	FR	G/POS	WS	TPW
1951 Chi-A	34	89	2	16	2	0	0	7	6	7	0	0	.180	.240	.202	.442	21	-10	5	1.60	-0	C-33	1	-0.8
1952 Chi-A	36	75	1	18	2	0	0	3	12	7	0	1	.240	.352	.267	.619	73	-2	8	3.40	0	C-31	1	-0.1
1953 Chi-A	31	46	4	10	1	0	0	2	9	8	0	0	.217	.345	.239	.585	58	-2	5	3.23	0	C-17	1	-0.2
Total 3	101	210	7	44	5	0	0	12	27	22	0	1	.210	.305	.233	.539	49	-14	17	2.57	-1	/C-81	3	-1.2

• SHEELY, Earl Earl Homer "Whitey" Sheely b: 2/12/1893, Bushnell, IL d: 9/16/1952, Seattle, WA BR/TR, 6'3.5", 195 lbs. Deb: 4/14/1921

YEAR TM-L	G	AB	R	H	2B	3B	HR	RBI	BB	SO	SB	CS	AVG	OBP	SLG	OPS	OPS+	BR/A	RC	RC/G	FR	G/POS	WS	TPW
1921 Chi-A	154	563	68	171	25	6	11	95	57	34	4	9	.304	.375	.428	.803	106	3	90	5.70	2	*1-154	15	-0.4
1922 Chi-A	149	526	72	167	37	4	6	80	60	27	4	6	.317	.393	.437	.830	116	14	92	6.21	4	*1-149	19	0.7
1923 Chi-A	156	570	74	169	25	3	4	88	79	30	5	5	.296	.387	.372	.759	102	5	87	5.36	2	*1-156	16	-0.3
1924 Chi-A	146	535	84	171	34	3	3	103	95	28	7	4	.320	.426	.411	.837	120	23	102	6.80	-8	*1-146	19	0.5
1925 Chi-A	153	600	93	189	43	3	9	111	68	23	3	3	.315	.389	.442	.831	117	17	106	6.40	1	*1-153	20	0.7
1926 Chi-A	145	525	77	157	40	2	6	89	75	13	3	1	.299	.394	.417	.811	116	16	92	6.26	-3	*1-144	18	0.3
1927 Chi-A	45	129	11	27	3	0	2	16	20	5	1	3	.209	.320	.279	.599	58	-8	13	2.96	-3	1-36	1	-1.2
1929 Pit-N	139	485	63	142	22	4	6	88	75	24	6	....	.293	.392	.392	.784	93	-2	77	5.53	1	*1-139	13	-1.0
1931 Bos-N	147	538	30	147	15	2	1	77	34	21	0	....	.273	.319	.314	.633	73	-20	56	3.61	1	*1-143	8	-3.1
Total 9	1234	4471	572	1340	244	27	48	747	563	205	33	31	.300	.383	.399	.782	104	48	716	5.64	-1	*1-1220	129	-3.8

• SHEERIN, Chuck Charles Joseph Sheerin b: 4/17/1909, Brooklyn, NY d: 9/27/1986, Valley Stream, NY BR/TR, 5'11.5", 198 lbs. Deb: 4/21/1936

YEAR TM-L	G	AB	R	H	2B	3B	HR	RBI	BB	SO	SB	CS	AVG	OBP	SLG	OPS	OPS+	BR/A	RC	RC/G	FR	G/POS	WS	TPW
1936 Phi-N	39	72	4	19	4	0	0	4	7	18	0	....	.264	.329	.319	.649	68	-3	8	3.75	1	2-17,3-13/S-5	1	-0.2

• SHEETS, Andy Andrew Mark Sheets b: 11/19/1971, Baton Rouge, LA BR/TR, 6'2", 180 lbs. Deb: 4/22/1996

YEAR TM-L	G	AB	R	H	2B	3B	HR	RBI	BB	SO	SB	CS	AVG	OBP	SLG	OPS	OPS+	BR/A	RC	RC/G	FR	G/POS	WS	TPW
1996 Sea-A	47	110	18	21	8	0	0	9	10	41	2	0	.191	.264	.264	.528	34	-11	8	2.39	2	3-25,2-18/S-7	1	-0.7
1997*Sea-A	32	89	18	22	3	0	4	9	7	34	2	0	.247	.302	.416	.718	86	-2	12	4.30	-2	3-21/S-9,2-2	1	-0.2
1998*SD-N	88	194	31	47	5	3	7	29	21	62	7	2	.242	.319	.407	.727	96	-1	26	4.44	-3	S-39,3-23,2-22/1-2	10	0.0
1999 Ana-A	87	244	22	48	10	0	3	29	14	59	1	2	.197	.240	.275	.515	31	-27	15	1.94	-16	S-76/2-7,3-1	1	-3.4
2000 Bos-A	12	21	1	2	0	0	0	1	0	3	0	0	.095	.095	.095	.190	-50	-5	0	.13	1	S-10/D-2,1-1	0	-0.3
2001 TB-A	49	153	10	30	8	0	1	14	12	35	2	0	.196	.255	.268	.523	39	-13	12	2.46	2	S-49	2	-0.7
2002 TB-A	41	149	18	37	4	0	4	22	12	41	2	3	.248	.304	.356	.660	76	-6	16	3.66	6	2-26,S-11/3-4	4	0.2
Total 7	356	960	118	207	38	3	19	113	76	275	16	7	.216	.275	.321	.595	56	-64	89	2.98	-10	S-201/2-75,3-74,1-3,D-2	19	-5.2

• SHEETS, Larry Larry Kent Sheets b: 12/6/1959, Staunton, VA BL/TR, 6'3", 225 lbs. Deb: 9/18/1984 Career OF: 192-0-144

YEAR TM-L	G	AB	R	H	2B	3B	HR	RBI	BB	SO	SB	CS	AVG	OBP	SLG	OPS	OPS+	BR/A	RC	RC/G	FR	G/POS	WS	TPW
1984 Bal-A	8	16	3	7	1	0	1	2	1	3	0	0	.438	.471	.688	1.158	221	3	5	15.90	1	/O-7(0-0-7)	1	0.3
1985 Bal-A	113	328	43	86	8	0	17	50	28	52	0	1	.262	.324	.442	.766	110	4	43	4.42	0	D-93/O-9(1-0-8),1-1	7	0.0
1986 Bal-A	112	338	42	92	17	1	18	60	21	56	2	0	.272	.319	.488	.807	117	7	47	4.79	1	D-58,O-32(21-0-11)/C-6,1-4,3	8	0.5
1987 Bal-A	135	469	74	148	23	0	31	94	31	67	1	1	.316	.362	.563	.925	144	27	90	7.05	-2	*O-124(72-0-58)/D-7,1-3	18	1.9
1988 Bal-A	136	452	38	104	19	1	10	47	42	72	1	6	.230	.304	.343	.647	83	-13	45	3.31	3	O-76(42-0-36),D-50/1-3	6	-1.4
1989 Bal-A	102	304	33	74	12	1	7	33	26	58	1	1	.243	.309	.359	.668	90	-4	34	3.82	0	D-88	5	-0.7
1990 Det-A	131	360	40	94	17	2	10	52	24	42	1	3	.261	.311	.403	.714	97	-3	41	3.87	4	O-79(56-0-23),D-44	7	-0.3
1993 Sea-A	11	17	0	2	1	0	0	1	2	1	0	0	.118	.250	.176	.426	17	-2	1	.90	-0	/D-5,O-1	0	-0.2
Total 8	748	2284	273	607	98	5	94	339	175	351	6	12	.266	.323	.437	.760	108	18	305	4.61	7	D-345,O-328/1-11,C-6,3-2	52	0.1

• SHEFFIELD, Gary Gary Antonian Sheffield b: 11/18/1968, Tampa, FL BR/TR, 5'11", 190 lbs. Deb: 9/3/1988 Career OF: 428-0-847

YEAR TM-L	G	AB	R	H	2B	3B	HR	RBI	BB	SO	SB	CS	AVG	OBP	SLG	OPS	OPS+	BR/A	RC	RC/G	FR	G/POS	WS	TPW
1988 Mil-A	24	80	12	19	1	0	4	12	7	7	3	1	.238	.299	.400	.699	93	-1	8	3.20	-3	S-24	2	-0.3
1989 Mil-A	95	368	34	91	18	0	5	32	27	33	10	6	.247	.306	.337	.643	82	-10	39	3.58	-1	S-70,3-21/D-4	6	-0.6
1990 Mil-A	125	487	67	143	30	1	10	67	44	41	25	10	.294	.356	.421	.777	117	12	73	5.22	-1	*3-125	20	1.2
1991 Mil-A	50	175	25	34	12	2	2	22	19	15	5	5	.194	.284	.320	.604	69	-9	16	2.77	-9	3-43/D-5	1	-1.7
1992 SD-N★	146	557	87	184	34	3	33	100	48	40	5	6	**.330**	.390	.580	.969	168	47	118	7.86	12	*3-144	32	6.4
1993 SD-N	68	258	34	76	12	2	10	36	18	30	5	1	.295	.348	.473	.821	115	6	41	5.62	-6	3-67	8	0.1
Fla-N★	72	236	33	69	8	3	10	37	29	34	12	4	.292	.384	.479	.863	122	9	46	7.00	-6	3-66	8	0.4
Yr.	140	494	67	145	20	5	20	73	47	64	17	5	.294	.365	.476	.841	119	15	87	6.28	-12	*3-133	16	0.5
1994 Fla-N	87	322	61	89	16	1	27	78	51	50	12	6	.276	.385	.584	.969	144	21	71	7.51	-5	O-87(0-0-87)	15	1.2
1995 Fla-N	63	213	46	69	8	0	16	46	55	45	19	4	.324	.471	.587	1.057	176	30	66	11.63	-2	O-61(3-0-59)	13	2.4
1996 Fla-N★	161	519	118	163	33	1	42	120	142	66	16	9	.314	**.469**	.624	**1.094**	**192**	78	159	11.06	-11	*O-161(0-0-161)	34	5.8
1997*Fla-N	135	444	86	111	22	1	21	71	121	79	11	7	.250	.426	.446	.872	135	31	95	7.35	0	*O-132(0-0-132)/D-1	22	2.3
1998 Fla-N	40	136	21	37	11	1	6	28	26	16	4	2	.272	.396	.500	.896	139	9	28	7.19	1	O-37(0-0-37)	8	0.8
LA-N★	90	301	52	95	16	1	16	57	69	30	18	5	.316	.452	.535	.987	168	37	80	9.75	0	O-89(0-0-89)	22	3.2
Yr.	130	437	73	132	27	2	22	85	95	46	22	7	.302	.435	.524	.959	160	45	108	8.92	2	*O-126(0-0-126)	30	4.0
1999 LA-N★	152	549	103	165	20	0	34	101	101	64	11	5	.301	.413	.523	.936	143	39	124	8.24	-1	*O-145(145-0-0)/D-3	24	3.1
2000 LA-N★	141	501	105	163	24	3	43	109	101	71	4	6	.325	.442	.643	1.085	180	63	143	10.67	-4	*O-139(139-0-0)/D-2	31	5.0
2001 LA-N	143	515	98	160	28	2	36	100	94	67	10	4	.311	.421	.583	1.003	168	56	129	9.28	-3	*O-141(141-0-2)/D-2	30	4.5
2002*Atl-N	135	492	82	151	26	0	25	84	72	53	12	2	.307	.407	.512	.919	139	32	105	7.81	-1	*O-127(0-0-127)/D-4	26	2.4
2003*Atl-N★	155	576	126	190	37	2	39	132	86	55	18	4	.330	.424	.604	1.028	164	59	150	9.76	1	*O-153(0-0-153)	35	5.0
Total 16	1882	6729	1190	2009	356	23	379	1232	1110	796	200	87	.299	.405	.527	.933	148	509	1491	7.94	-38	*O-1272,3-466/S-94,D-21	337	41.3

• SHELBY, John John T. Shelby b: 2/23/1958, Lexington, KY BB/TR, 6'1", 175 lbs. Deb: 9/15/1981 C Career OF: 114-781-85

YEAR TM-L	G	AB	R	H	2B	3B	HR	RBI	BB	SO	SB	CS	AVG	OBP	SLG	OPS	OPS+	BR/A	RC	RC/G	FR	G/POS	WS	TPW
1981 Bal-A	7	2	2	0	0	0	0	0	0	1	2	0	.000	.000	.000	.000	-100	-0	0	.00	-1	/O-4(0-4-0)	0	-0.1
1982 Bal-A	26	35	8	11	3	0	1	2	0	5	0	1	.314	.314	.486	.800	116	0	5	5.25	-0	O-24(0-24-0)	1	0.0
1983*Bal-A	126	325	52	84	15	2	5	27	18	64	15	2	.258	.297	.363	.660	82	-6	37	4.02	0	*O-115(0-115-0)/D-1	8	-0.7
1984 Bal-A	128	383	44	80	12	5	6	30	20	71	12	4	.209	.248	.313	.561	55	-23	31	2.55	3	*O-124(0-118-9)	4	-2.2
1985 Bal-A	69	205	28	58	6	2	7	27	7	44	5	1	.283	.307	.434	.741	103	1	26	4.64	-2	O-59(9-43-10)/D-3,2-1	5	-0.3
1986 Bal-A	135	404	54	92	14	4	11	49	18	75	18	6	.228	.264	.364	.628	70	-17	39	3.27	-2	*O-121(49-56-31)/D-2	5	-2.2
1987 Bal-A	21	32	4	6	0	0	1	3	1	13	0	1	.188	.212	.281	.493	30	-4	2	1.66	0	O-19(0-4-15)/D-1	0	-0.4
LA-N	120	476	61	132	26	0	21	69	31	97	16	6	.277	.323	.464	.787	108	4	70	5.10	3	*O-117(0-117-0)	15	0.5
1988*LA-N	140	494	65	130	23	6	10	64	44	128	16	5	.263	.323	.395	.718	109	6	62	4.31	0	*O-140(0-140-0)	19	0.3
1989 LA-N	108	345	28	63	11	1	1	12	25	92	10	7	.183	.238	.229	.467	35	-31	18	1.66	-2	O-98(0-98-0)	2	-3.6
1990 LA-N	25	24	2	6	1	0	0	2	0	7	1	0	.250	.250	.292	.542	50	-2	2	2.23	0	O-12(7-1-4)	0	-0.2
Det-A	78	222	22	55	9	3	4	20	10	51	3	5	.248	.280	.369	.650	80	-8	20	2.97	2	O-68(24-35-13)/D-5	3	-0.8
1991 Det-A	53	143	19	22	8	1	3	8	8	23	0	2	.154	.204	.287	.491	34	-14	7	1.58	1	O-47(25-26-3)/D-4	1	-1.4
Total 11	1036	3090	389	739	128	24	70	313	182	671	98	40	.239	.282	.364	.646	79	-95	320	3.46	1	O-948/D-16,2-1	63	-11.3

• SHELDON, Bob Bob Mitchell Sheldon b: 11/27/1950, Montebello, CA BL/TR, 6', 170 lbs. Deb: 4/10/1974

YEAR TM-L	G	AB	R	H	2B	3B	HR	RBI	BB	SO	SB	CS	AVG	OBP	SLG	OPS	OPS+	BR/A	RC	RC/G	FR	G/POS	WS	TPW
1974 Mil-A	10	17	4	2	1	1	0	0	4	2	0	1	.118	.286	.294	.580	67	-1	2	2.31	-0	/D-4,2-3	0	-0.1
1975 Mil-A	53	181	17	52	3	3	0	14	13	14	0	3	.287	.342	.337	.679	92	-3	20	3.78	7	2-44/D-6	4	0.6
1977 Mil-A	31	64	9	13	4	1	0	3	6	9	0	0	.203	.271	.297	.568	55	-4	6	2.80	0	D-17/2-5	0	-0.4
Total 3	94	262	30	67	8	5	0	17	23	25	0	4	.256	.321	.324	.645	81	-8	27	3.40	7	/2-52,D-27	4	0.1

• SHELDON, Scott Scott Patrick Sheldon b: 11/28/1968, Hammond, IN BR/TR, 6'3", 185 lbs. Deb: 5/18/1997 Career OF: 4-1-2

YEAR TM-L	G	AB	R	H	2B	3B	HR	RBI	BB	SO	SB	CS	AVG	OBP	SLG	OPS	OPS+	BR/A	RC	RC/G	FR	G/POS	WS	TPW
1997 Oak-A	13	24	2	6	0	0	1	2	1	6	0	0	.250	.308	.375	.683	79	-1	3	4.23	-2	S-12/2-1,3-1	1	-0.2
1998 Tex-A	7	16	0	2	0	0	0	1	1	6	0	0	.125	.176	.125	.301	-19	-3	0	.48	2	/3-3,S-2,1-1,D-1	0	-0.1
1999 Tex-A	2	1	0	0	0	0	0	0	0	0	0	0	.000	.000	.000	.000	-96	-0	0	.00	-0	/3-2	0	0.0
2000 Tex-A	58	124	21	35	11	0	4	19	10	37	0	0	.282	.341	.468	.808	101	-0	20	5.72	1	S-22,3-15,2-12,1-10/C-3,O,D,P	3	0.2
2001 Tex-A	61	120	11	24	5	0	3	11	3	35	1	1	.200	.220	.317	.536	38	-12	8	2.05	5	3-38,S-16/O-3(2-0-1),C-1	1	-0.6
Total 5	141	285	34	67	16	0	8	33	15	84	1	1	.235	.278	.375	.654	66	-16	31	3.60	5	/3-59,S-52,2-13,1-11,O,C,D,P	5	-0.7

YEAR	TM-L	G	AB	R	H	2B	3B	HR	RBI	BB	SO	SB	CS	AVG	OBP	SLG	OPS	OPS+	BR/A	RC	RC/G	FR	G/POS	WS	TPW

• SHELLEY, Hugh   Hubert Leneirre Shelley   b: 10/26/1910, Rogers, TX   d: 6/16/1978, Beaumont, TX   BR/TR, 6', 170 lbs.   Deb: 6/25/1935

| 1935 | Det-A | 7 | 8 | 1 | 2 | 0 | 0 | 0 | 1 | 2 | 1 | 0 | 0 | .250 | .400 | .250 | .650 | 74 | -0 | 1 | 4.27 | -0 | /O-5(3-1-1) | 0 | 0.0 |

• SHELTON, Ben   Benjamin Davis Shelton   b: 9/21/1969, Chicago, IL   BR/TL, 6'3.5", 210 lbs.   Deb: 6/16/1993

| 1993 | Pit-N | 15 | 24 | 3 | 6 | 1 | 0 | 2 | 7 | 3 | 3 | 0 | 0 | .250 | .333 | .542 | .875 | 130 | 1 | 4 | 4.82 | 0 | /O-6(6-0-0),1-2 | 1 | 0.1 |

• SHELTON, Skeeter   Andrew Kemper Shelton   b: 6/29/1888, Huntington, WV   d: 1/9/1954, Huntington, WV   BR/TR, 5'11", 175 lbs.   Deb: 8/25/1915

| 1915 | NY-A | 10 | 40 | 1 | 1 | 0 | 0 | 0 | 0 | 2 | 10 | 0 | 0 | .025 | .071 | .025 | .096 | -71 | -8 | 0 | .09 | 0 | O-10(0-10-0) | 0 | -1.0 |

• SHEMO, Steve   Stephen Michael Shemo   b: 4/9/1915, Swoyersville, PA   d: 4/13/1992, Eden, NC   BR/TR, 5'11", 175 lbs.   Deb: 4/18/1944

1944	Bos-N	18	31	3	9	2	0	0	1	1	3	0	....	.290	.313	.355	.667	84	-1	4	3.96	0	2-16/3-2	1	0.0
1945	Bos-N	17	46	4	11	1	0	0	7	1	3	0	....	.239	.255	.261	.516	43	-4	3	2.41	-3	2-12/3-3,S-1	0	-0.6
Total 2		35	77	7	20	3	0	0	8	2	6	0	....	.260	.278	.299	.577	61	-4	7	3.06	-3	2-28,3-5,S-1	1	-0.6

• SHEPARD, Jack   Jack Leroy Shepard   b: 5/13/1931, Clovis, CA   d: 12/31/1994, Atherton, CA   BR/TR, 6'2", 195 lbs.   Deb: 6/19/1953

1953	Pit-N	2	4	0	1	0	0	0	2	0	0	0	0	.250	.250	.250	.500	31	0	0	2.31	-1	/C-2	0	-0.1
1954	Pit-N	82	227	24	69	8	2	3	22	26	33	0	0	.304	.375	.396	.772	103	2	33	4.96	6	C-67	8	1.1
1955	Pit-N	94	264	24	63	10	2	2	23	33	25	1	0	.239	.323	.314	.638	71	-10	27	3.46	2	C-77	5	-0.5
1956	Pit-N	100	256	24	62	11	2	7	30	25	37	1	1	.242	.310	.383	.692	87	-5	29	3.71	1	C-86/1-2	7	0.0
Total 4		278	751	72	195	29	6	12	75	84	97	2	1	.260	.334	.362	.696	86	-13	90	3.99	8	C-232/1-2	20	0.5

• SHEPARDSON, Ray   Raymond Francis Shepardson   b: 5/3/1897, Little Falls, NY   d: 11/8/1975, Little Falls, NY   BR/TR, 5'11.5", 170 lbs.   Deb: 9/19/1924

| 1924 | StL-N | 3 | 6 | 1 | 0 | 0 | 0 | 0 | 0 | 0 | 3 | 0 | 0 | .000 | .000 | .000 | .000 | -102 | -2 | 0 | .00 | 0 | /C-3 | 0 | -0.1 |

• SHEPHERD, Ron   Ronald Wayne Shepherd   b: 10/27/1960, Longview, TX   BR/TR, 6'4", 175 lbs.   Deb: 9/5/1984   Career OF: 20-23-12

1984	Tor-A	12	4	0	0	0	0	0	0	0	3	0	1	.000	.000	.000	.000	-97	-1	0	.00	0	/O-5(5-0-0),D-4	0	-0.1
1985	Tor-A	38	35	7	4	2	0	0	1	2	13	3	0	.114	.162	.171	.334	-8	-5	1	.92	0	0-16(3-13-1),D-15	0	-0.5
1986	Tor-A	65	69	16	14	4	0	2	4	3	22	0	0	.203	.236	.348	.584	55	-5	6	2.63	-1	0-32(12-10-1),D-16	0	-0.6
Total 3		115	108	23	18	6	0	2	5	5	37	3	1	.167	.204	.278	.481	29	-11	7	1.91	-1	/O-53,D-35	0	-1.2

• SHEPPARD, John   John Sheppard   b: Baltimore, MD   Deb: 6/27/1873

| 1873 | Mar-n | 3 | 11 | 1 | 0 | 0 | 0 | 0 | 0 | 0 | 1 | 0 | 0 | .000 | .000 | .000 | .000 | -130 | -2 | 0 | .00 | -1 | /O-2(1-0-1),C-1 | .... | -0.2 |

• SHERIDAN,   Sheridan   Deb: 10/9/1875

| 1875 | Atl-n | 1 | 4 | 0 | 0 | 0 | 0 | 0 | 0 | 0 | 1 | 0 | 0 | .000 | .000 | .000 | .000 | -115 | -1 | 0 | .00 | 0 | /O-1 | .... | -0.1 |

• SHERIDAN, Neill   Neill Rawlins "Wild Horse" Sheridan   b: 11/20/1921, Sacramento, CA   BR/TR, 6'1.5", 195 lbs.   Deb: 9/19/1948

| 1948 | Bos-A | 2 | 1 | 0 | 0 | 0 | 0 | 0 | 0 | 0 | 0 | 0 | 0 | .000 | .000 | .000 | .000 | -95 | -0 | 0 | .00 | 0 | | 0 | 0.0 |

• SHERIDAN, Pat   Patrick Arthur Sheridan   b: 12/4/1957, Ann Arbor, MI   BL/TR, 6'3", 175 lbs.   Deb: 9/16/1981   Career OF: 162-173-481

1981	KC-A	3	1	0	0	0	0	0	0	0	1	0	0	.000	.000	.000	.000	-101	-0	0	.00	0	/O-3(1-0-2)	0	0.0
1983	KC-A	109	333	43	90	12	2	7	36	20	64	12	3	.270	.312	.381	.693	89	-4	41	4.37	1	*O-100(28-36-48)	9	-0.7
1984*	KC-A	138	481	64	136	24	4	8	53	41	91	19	6	.283	.340	.399	.740	103	-4	68	5.00	3	*O-134(0-35-101)	16	0.2
1985*	KC-A	78	206	18	47	9	2	3	17	23	38	11	3	.228	.309	.335	.644	76	-5	23	3.58	-4	0-69(0-0-69)/D-1	4	-0.9
1986	Det-A	98	236	41	56	9	1	6	19	21	57	9	2	.237	.302	.360	.662	80	-6	27	3.84	-3	0-90(11-51-32)/D-5	5	-1.1
1987*	Det-A	141	421	57	109	19	3	6	49	44	90	18	13	.259	.330	.361	.692	87	-9	50	3.96	-3	*O-137(0-26-124)	8	-1.6
1988	Det-A	127	347	47	88	9	5	11	47	44	64	8	6	.254	.341	.403	.744	112	5	48	4.68	-2	*O-111(92-9-12)/D-3	12	0.0
1989	Det-A	50	120	16	29	3	0	3	15	17	21	4	0	.242	.336	.342	.677	93	0	15	4.37	1	0-35(19-7-9)/D-8	3	0.0
*SF-N		70	161	20	33	3	4	3	14	13	45	4	1	.205	.264	.329	.594	71	-6	15	3.06	-2	0-66(8-3-58)	2	-1.0
1991	NY-A	62	113	13	23	3	0	4	7	13	30	1	1	.204	.286	.336	.622	71	-5	10	2.65	1	0-34(3-6-26)/D-2	0	-0.4
Total 9		876	2419	319	611	91	21	51	257	236	501	86	35	.253	.321	.371	.691	91	-27	296	4.16	-5	0-779/D-19	59	-5.7

• SHERIDAN, Red   Eugene Anthony Sheridan   b: 11/14/1896, Brooklyn, NY   d: 11/25/1975, Queens Village, NY   BR/TR, 5'10.5", 160 lbs.   Deb: 7/3/1918

1918	Bro-N	2	4	0	1	0	0	0	0	1	0	1	....	.250	.400	.250	.650	100	0	1	6.16	0	/2-2	0	0.0
1920	Bro-N	3	2	0	0	0	0	0	0	0	1	0	0	.000	.000	.000	.000	-97	-0	0	.00	0	/S-3	0	0.0
Total 2		5	6	0	1	0	0	0	0	1	1	1	0	.167	.286	.167	.452	44	-0	1	3.69	0	/S-3,2-2	0	0.0

• SHERLING, Ed   Edward Creech "Shine" Sherling   b: 7/17/1897, Coalburg, AL   d: 11/16/1965, Enterprise, AL   BR/TR, 6'1", 185 lbs.   Deb: 8/13/1924

| 1924 | Phi-A | 4 | 2 | 2 | 1 | 1 | 0 | 0 | 0 | 0 | 0 | 0 | 0 | .500 | .500 | 1.000 | 1.500 | 278 | 0 | 1 | 25.44 | 0 | .... | 0 | 0.0 |

• SHERLOCK, Monk   John Clinton Sherlock   b: 10/26/1904, Buffalo, NY   d: 11/26/1985, Buffalo, NY   BR/TR, 5'10", 175 lbs.   Deb: 4/20/1930

| 1930 | Phi-N | 92 | 299 | 51 | 97 | 18 | 2 | 0 | 38 | 27 | 28 | 0 | .... | .324 | .380 | .398 | .778 | 83 | -7 | 45 | 5.52 | -2 | 1-70/2-5,0-1 | 5 | -1.2 |

• SHERLOCK, Vince   Vincent Thomas "Baldy" Sherlock   b: 3/27/1910, Buffalo, NY   d: 5/11/1997, Cheektowaga, NY   BR/TR, 6', 180 lbs.   Deb: 9/18/1935

| 1935 | Bro-N | 9 | 26 | 4 | 12 | 1 | 0 | 0 | 6 | 1 | 2 | 1 | .... | .462 | .481 | .500 | .981 | 168 | 2 | 7 | 12.61 | -3 | /2-8 | 2 | 0.0 |

• SHERMAN, Darrell   Darrell Edward Sherman   b: 12/4/1967, Los Angeles, CA   BL/TL, 5'9", 160 lbs.   Deb: 4/8/1993

| 1993 | SD-N | 37 | 63 | 8 | 14 | 1 | 0 | 0 | 2 | 6 | 8 | 2 | 1 | .222 | .319 | .238 | .558 | 51 | -4 | 6 | 3.00 | 0 | 0-26(24-6-1) | 0 | -0.5 |

• SHERRILL, Dennis   Dennis Lee Sherrill   b: 5/3/1956, Miami, FL   BR/TR, 6', 165 lbs.   Deb: 9/4/1978

1978	NY-A	2	1	0	0	0	0	0	0	1	0	0	0	.000	.000	.000	.000	-102	-0	0	.00	0	/3-1,D-1	0	-0.1
1980	NY-A	3	4	1	1	0	0	0	0	0	1	0	0	.250	.250	.250	.500	38	-0	0	.00	-1	/S-2,2-1	0	-0.1
Total 2		5	5	1	1	0	0	0	0	1	1	0	0	.200	.200	.200	.400	10	-1	0	.00	-1	/S-2,2-1,3-1,D-1	0	-0.2

• SHERRY, Norm   Norman Burt Sherry   b: 7/16/1931, New York, NY   BR/TR, 5'11", 181 lbs.   Deb: 4/12/1959   M/C

1959	LA-N	2	3	0	1	0	0	0	2	0	0	0	0	.333	.500	.333	.833	119	0	0	2.84	0	/C-2	0	0.0
1960	LA-N	47	138	22	39	4	1	8	19	12	29	0	0	.283	.353	.500	.853	122	4	25	6.49	0	C-44	7	0.6
1961	LA-N	47	121	10	31	2	0	5	21	9	30	0	0	.256	.308	.397	.704	78	-4	13	3.52	1	C-45	4	-0.1
1962	LA-N	35	88	7	16	2	0	3	16	6	17	0	0	.182	.242	.307	.549	49	-7	6	2.30	-1	C-34	0	-0.5
1963	NY-N	63	147	6	20	1	0	2	11	10	26	1	0	.136	.184	.204	.390	13	-16	5	1.05	1	C-61	1	-1.1
Total 5		194	497	45	107	9	1	18	69	37	102	1	0	.215	.280	.346	.627	67	-22	49	3.22	2	C-186	13	-1.3

• SHETRONE, Barry   Barry Stevan Shetrone   b: 7/6/1938, Baltimore, MD   d: 7/18/2001, Bowie, MD   BL/TR, 6'2", 190 lbs.   Deb: 7/27/1959   Career OF: 8-21-2

1959	Bal-A	33	79	8	16	1	1	0	5	5	9	0	0	.203	.250	.241	.491	36	-6	6	2.28	-1	0-23(5-17-1)	0	-0.8
1960	Bal-A	1	0	1	0	0	0	0	0	0	0	0	0	....	....	....		-101	0	0	....	0		0	0.0
1961	Bal-A	3	7	0	1	0	0	0	1	0	2	0	0	.143	.143	.143	.286	-24	-1	0	.64	0	/O-2(0-2-0)	0	-0.1
1962	Bal-A	21	24	3	6	1	0	1	1	0	5	0	0	.250	.250	.417	.667	80	-1	3	3.75	-0	/O-6(3-2-1)	0	-0.1
1963	Was-A	2	2	0	0	0	0	0	0	0	0	0	0	.000	.000	.000	.000	-100	-1	0	.00	0		0	-0.1
Total 5		60	112	12	23	2	1	1	7	5	16	3	0	.205	.239	.268	.507	39	-9	8	2.41	-1	/O-31	0	-1.1

• SHETZLINE, John   John Henry Shetzline   b: 1850, Philadelphia, PA   d: 12/15/1892, Philadelphia, PA   5'11.5", 190 lbs.   Deb: 5/2/1882

| 1882 | Bal-a | 73 | 282 | 23 | 62 | 8 | 5 | 0 | | 5 | | | .... | .220 | .233 | .270 | .503 | 75 | -6 | 18 | 2.31 | 1 | 3-52,2-20/0-1,S-1 | 6 | -0.2 |

• SHEVLIN, Jimmy   James Cornelius Shevlin   b: 7/9/1909, Cincinnati, OH   d: 10/30/1974, Fort Lauderdale, FL   BL/TL, 5'10.5", 155 lbs.   Deb: 6/29/1930

1930	Det-A	28	14	4	2	0	0	0	2	3	0	2	....	.143	.250	.143	.393	-2	-1	1	1.34	-1	1-25	0	-0.3
1932	Cin-N	7	24	3	5	2	0	0	4	4	0	4	....	.208	.345	.292	.636	76	-1	3	3.80	0	/1-7	0	-0.1
1934	Cin-N	18	39	6	12	2	0	0	6	5	8	2	....	.308	.356	.308	.759	107	1	5	4.80	1	/1-10	1	0.1
Total 3		53	77	13	19	4	0	0	12	12	8	4	0	.247	.356	.299	.654	79	-2	9	4.25	0	/1-42	1	-0.3

• SHIELDS, Pete   Francis Leroy Shields   b: 9/21/1891, Swiftwater, MS   d: 2/11/1961, Jackson, MS   BR/TR, 6', 175 lbs.   Deb: 4/14/1915

| 1915 | Cle-A | 23 | 72 | 4 | 15 | 6 | 0 | 0 | 6 | 4 | 14 | 3 | 3 | .208 | .250 | .292 | .542 | 61 | -5 | 5 | 2.21 | -1 | 1-23 | 0 | -0.6 |

YEAR TM-L	G	AB	R	H	2B	3B	HR	RBI	BB	SO	SB	CS	AVG	OBP	SLG	OPS	OPS+	BR/A	RC	RC/G	FR	G/POS	WS	TPW
• SHIELDS, Tommy	Thomas Charles Shields b: 8/14/1964, Fairfax, VA BL/TR, 6', 180 lbs. Deb: 7/25/1992																							
1992 Bal-A	2	0	0	0	0	0	0	0	0	0	0	0	....	....	....	....	-98	0	0	....	0	....	0	0.0
1993 Chi-N	20	34	4	6	1	0	0	1	2	10	0	0	.176	.222	.206	.428	16	-4	1	1.36	1	/2-7,3-7,1-1,0-1	0	-0.3
Total 2	22	34	4	6	1	0	0	1	2	10	0	0	.176	.222	.206	.428	16	-4	1	1.36	1	/2-7,3-7,1-1,0-1	0	-0.3
• SHILLING, Jim	James Robert Shilling b: 5/14/1914, Tulsa, OK d: 9/12/1986, Tulsa, OK BR/TR, 5'11", 175 lbs. Deb: 4/21/1939																							
1939 Cle-A	31	98	8	27	7	2	0	12	7	9	1	0	.276	.324	.388	.712	84	-2	12	4.30	-1	2-27/S-3	2	-0.1
Phi-N	11	33	3	10	1	3	0	4	1	4	0	....	.303	.324	.515	.839	128	1	5	4.93	-1	/2-5,3-3,S-3,0-1	1	0.0
• SHINAULT, Ginger	Enoch Erskine Shinault b: 9/7/1892, Benton, AR d: 12/29/1930, Denver, CO BR/TR, 5'11", 170 lbs. Deb: 7/4/1921																							
1921 Cle-A	22	29	5	11	1	0	0	4	6	5	1	0	.379	.486	.414	.900	129	2	7	9.22	0	C-20	2	0.3
1922 Cle-A	13	15	1	2	1	0	0	0	0	2	0	0	.133	.133	.200	.333	-14	-3	0	.78	-4	C-11	0	-0.6
Total 2	35	44	6	13	2	0	0	4	6	7	1	0	.295	.380	.341	.721	87	-0	7	5.79	-4	/C-31	2	-0.4
• SHINDLE, Billy	William Shindle b: 12/5/1860, Gloucester, NJ d: 6/3/1936, Lakeland, NJ BR/TR, 5'8.5", 155 lbs. Deb: 10/5/1886																							
1886 Det-N	7	26	4	7	0	0	0	4	0	5	2	....	.269	.269	.269	.538	62	-1	2	3.53	0	/S-7	1	-0.1
1887 Det-N	22	91	17	31	3	2	0	12	7	10	13	....	.341	.341	.369	.710	94	-1	15	6.79	-2	3-21/0-1	3	-0.2
1888 Bal-a	135	514	61	107	14	8	1	53	20	....	52	....	.208	.249	.272	.521	69	-18	49	3.25	36	*3-135	15	2.0
1889 Bal-a	138	567	122	178	24	7	3	64	42	37	56	....	.314	.369	.397	.765	120	15	106	7.23	26	*3-138	27	3.7
1890 Phi-P	132	584	127	189	21	21	10	90	40	30	51	....	.324	.371	.483	.854	124	16	127	8.66	10	*S-130/3-2	26	2.4
1891 Phi-N	103	415	68	87	13	1	0	38	33	39	17	....	.210	.278	.246	.523	51	-26	34	2.79	6	*3-100/S-3	7	-1.6
1892 Bal-N	143	619	100	156	20	18	3	50	35	34	24	....	.252	.301	.357	.658	96	-6	75	4.40	21	*3-134/S-9	15	1.6
1893 Bal-N	125	521	100	136	22	11	1	75	66	17	17	....	.261	.353	.351	.704	86	-10	72	4.98	7	*3-125	14	-0.1
1894 Bro-N	117	480	94	142	22	9	4	96	29	21	19	....	.296	.344	.404	.748	86	-11	75	5.77	7	*3-116	13	-0.1
1895 Bro-N	117	481	92	135	21	2	3	69	47	28	17	....	.281	.358	.351	.709	91	-3	69	5.30	4	*3-116	16	0.2
1896 Bro-N	131	516	75	144	24	9	1	61	24	20	24	....	.279	.316	.366	.682	84	-13	71	4.82	-13	*3-131	12	-2.0
1897 Bro-N	134	542	83	154	32	6	4	105	35	....	23	....	.284	.336	.387	.723	96	-4	82	5.34	-9	*3-134	14	-0.9
1898 Bro-N	120	466	50	105	10	3	1	41	10	....	3	....	.225	.249	.266	.516	48	-33	34	2.41	-5	*3-120	4	-3.3
Total 13	1424	5822	993	1571	226	97	31	758	388	241	318	....	.270	.323	.357	.680	88	-95	813	5.03	89	*3-1272,S-149/0-1	167	1.7
• SHINES, Razor	Anthony Raymond "Ray" Shines b: 7/18/1956, Durham, NC BB/TR, 6'1", 210 lbs. Deb: 9/9/1983																							
1983 Mon-N	3	2	0	1	0	0	0	0	0	0	0	0	.500	.500	.500	1.000	179	0	1	13.50	0	/0-1	0	0.0
1984 Mon-N	12	20	0	6	1	0	0	2	0	3	0	0	.300	.300	.350	.650	86	-0	2	3.87	-1	/1-3,3-1	0	-0.2
1985 Mon-N	47	50	0	6	0	0	0	3	4	9	0	1	.120	.185	.120	.305	-14	-8	1	.52	0	/1-5,P-1	0	-0.8
1987 Mon-N	6	9	0	2	0	0	0	0	1	0	1	0	.222	.364	.222	.586	58	-0	1	2.80	0	/1-2	0	0.0
Total 4	68	81	0	15	1	0	0	5	5	12	1	1	.185	.241	.198	.439	23	-8	4	1.67	-1	/1-10,3-1,0-1,P-1	0	-1.0
• SHINJO, Tsuyoshi	Tsuyoshi Shinjo b: 1/28/1972, Osaka, Japan BR/TR, 6'1", 185 lbs. Deb: 4/3/2001 Career OF: 54-211-50																							
2001 NY-N	123	400	46	107	23	1	10	56	25	70	4	5	.268	.322	.405	.727	91	-7	50	4.35	12	*0-119(46-53-39)	11	0.1
2002*SF-N	118	362	42	86	15	3	9	37	24	46	5	0	.238	.296	.370	.666	78	-12	41	3.86	9	*0-117(1-108-10)	8	-0.2
2003 NY-N	62	114	10	22	3	0	1	7	6	12	0	1	.193	.240	.246	.485	28	-13	7	1.98	5	0-54(7-50-1)	1	-0.7
Total 3	303	876	98	215	41	4	20	100	55	128	9	6	.245	.301	.370	.670	77	-32	98	3.82	26	0-290	20	-0.7
• SHINNERS, Ralph	Ralph Peter Shinners b: 10/4/1895, Monches, WI d: 7/23/1962, Milwaukee, WI BR/TR, 6', 180 lbs. Deb: 4/12/1922 Career OF: 6-87-16																							
1922 NY-N	56	135	16	34	4	2	0	15	5	22	3	5	.252	.308	.311	.619	60	-9	12	2.97	-3	0-37(1-30-6)	1	-1.3
1923 NY-N	33	13	5	2	1	0	0	0	2	1	0	0	.154	.267	.231	.497	33	-1	1	2.17	0	/0-6(2-1-3)	0	-0.2
1925 StL-N	74	251	39	74	9	2	7	36	12	19	8	5	.295	.330	.430	.760	90	-4	35	4.80	-3	0-66(3-56-7)	6	-1.0
Total 3	163	399	60	110	14	4	7	51	19	42	11	10	.276	.320	.383	.703	78	-15	48	4.06	-6	0-109	7	-2.4
• SHINNICK, Tim	Timothy James "Dandy,Good-Eye" Shinnick b: 11/6/1867, Exeter, NH d: 5/18/1944, Exeter, NH BB/TR, 5'9", 150 lbs. Deb: 4/19/1890																							
1890*Lou-a	133	493	87	126	16	11	1	82	62	....	62	....	.256	.348	.339	.687	105	5	82	5.90	-20	*2-130/3-3	15	-0.9
1891 Lou-a	126	436	77	96	9	11	1	52	54	46	36	....	.220	.315	.298	.613	73	-16	52	3.97	-20	*2-120/3-7,S-1	9	-2.7
Total 2	259	929	164	222	25	22	2	134	116	46	98	....	.239	.332	.320	.652	90	-11	134	4.96	-39	2-250/3-10,S-1	24	-3.6
• SHIPKE, Bill	William Martin "Skipper Bill,Muskrat Bill" Shipke b: 11/18/1882, St. Louis, MO d: 9/10/1940, Omaha, NE BR/TR, 5'7", 145 lbs. Deb: 4/23/1906																							
1906 Cle-A	2	6	0	0	0	0	0	0	0	....	0	....	.000	.000	.000	.000	-101	-1	0	.00	1	/2-2	0	0.0
1907 Was-A	64	189	17	37	3	2	1	9	15	....	6	....	.196	.262	.249	.511	68	-6	15	2.50	5	3-63	3	0.0
1908 Was-A	111	341	40	71	7	8	0	20	38	....	15	....	.208	.297	.276	.573	94	-1	34	3.01	-9	*3-110/2-1	8	-0.8
1909 Was-A	9	16	2	2	1	0	0	0	2	....	0	....	.125	.222	.188	.410	31	-1	1	1.28	-1	/3-6,S-2	0	-0.2
Total 4	186	552	59	110	11	10	1	29	55	....	21	....	.199	.280	.261	.541	82	-9	50	2.75	-4	3-179/2-3,S-2	11	-1.0
• SHIPLEY, Craig	Craig Barry Shipley b: 1/7/1963, Parramatta, Australia BR/TR, 6'1", 185 lbs. Deb: 6/22/1986 Career OF: 4-4-4																							
1986 LA-N	12	27	3	3	1	0	0	4	2	5	0	0	.111	.200	.148	.348	-3	-4	1	.84	-2	S-10/2-1,3-1	0	-0.5
1987 LA-N	26	35	3	9	1	0	0	2	0	6	0	0	.257	.257	.286	.543	45	-3	2	1.93	-1	S-18/3-6	0	-0.3
1989 NY-N	4	7	3	1	0	0	0	0	0	1	0	0	.143	.143	.143	.286	-19	-1	0	.64	0	/S-3,3-2	0	-0.2
1991 SD-N	37	91	6	25	3	0	1	6	2	14	0	1	.275	.298	.341	.639	77	-3	9	3.46	-1	S-19,2-14	2	-0.3
1992 SD-N	52	105	7	26	6	0	0	7	2	21	1	1	.248	.262	.305	.566	59	-6	8	2.51	-0	S-23,2-11/3-8	2	-0.5
1993 SD-N	105	230	25	54	9	0	4	22	10	31	12	3	.235	.276	.326	.602	59	-13	21	3.13	-3	S-38,3-37,2-12/0-5(2-3-0)	3	-1.3
1994 SD-N	81	240	32	80	14	4	4	30	9	28	6	6	.333	.365	.475	.840	120	5	40	6.11	-4	3-53,S-14,2-13/0-2(1-1-0),1	7	0.3
1995 Hou-N	92	232	23	61	8	1	3	24	8	28	6	1	.263	.293	.345	.638	73	-9	20	2.89	-3	3-65,S-11/2-4,1-1	2	-1.0
1996 SD-N	33	92	13	29	5	0	1	7	2	15	7	0	.315	.344	.402	.746	102	2	14	5.86	1	2-17/S-7,3-4,0-3(0-0-3)	3	0.3
1997 SD-N	63	139	22	38	9	0	5	19	7	20	1	1	.273	.308	.446	.754	103	-0	19	4.88	-5	S-21,2-16/1-4,3-2	4	-0.4
1998 Ana-A	77	147	18	38	7	1	2	17	5	22	0	4	.259	.306	.361	.666	72	-8	15	3.29	2	3-48,2-11/1-8,S-5,0-2(1-0-1)	3	-0.6
Total 11	582	1345	155	364	63	6	20	138	47	191	33	17	.271	.304	.371	.675	81	-41	149	3.82	-18	3-226,S-169/2-99,1-14,0-12	26	-4.5
• SHIRES, Art	Charles Arthur "Art The Great" Shires b: 8/13/1907, Italy, TX d: 7/13/1967, Italy, TX BL/TR, 6'1", 195 lbs. Deb: 8/20/1928																							
1928 Chi-A	33	123	20	42	6	1	1	11	13	10	0	3	.341	.409	.431	.840	122	3	21	6.64	3	1-32	5	0.4
1929 Chi-A	100	353	41	110	20	7	3	41	32	20	4	5	.312	.370	.433	.804	107	3	56	5.88	-2	1-90/2-3	9	-0.4
1930 Chi-A	37	128	14	33	5	1	1	18	6	6	2	0	.258	.291	.336	.627	61	-7	13	3.39	-1	1-33	1	-1.0
Was-A	38	84	11	31	5	0	1	19	5	5	1	3	.369	.404	.464	.869	119	1	15	6.65	0	1-21	3	0.0
Yr.	75	212	25	64	10	1	2	37	11	11	3	3	.302	.336	.387	.723	83	-6	28	4.57	-1	1-54	4	-1.0
1932 Bos-N	82	298	32	71	9	3	5	30	25	21	1	....	.238	.299	.339	.638	74	-11	32	3.55	-2	1-80	5	-2.0
Total 4	290	986	118	287	45	12	11	119	81	62	8	11	.291	.347	.395	.741	94	-10	137	4.94	-3	1-256/2-3	23	-3.0
• SHIRLEY, Bart	Barton Arvin Shirley b: 1/4/1940, Corpus Christi, TX BR/TR, 5'10", 183 lbs. Deb: 9/14/1964																							
1964 LA-N	18	62	6	17	1	1	0	7	4	8	0	0	.274	.318	.323	.641	87	-1	5	2.91	2	3-10/S-8	1	0.1
1966 LA-N	12	5	2	1	0	0	0	0	0	2	0	0	.200	.200	.200	.400	13	-1	0	1.35	-1	/S-5	0	-0.2
1967 NY-N	6	12	1	0	0	0	0	0	0	5	0	0	.000	.000	.000	.000	-102	-3	0	.00	0	/2-3	0	-0.3
1968 LA-N	39	83	6	15	3	0	0	4	10	13	0	1	.181	.269	.217	.486	51	-5	4	1.52	0	S-21,2-18	1	-0.3
Total 4	75	162	15	33	4	1	0	11	14	28	0	1	.204	.267	.241	.508	53	-10	10	1.87	1	/S-34,2-21,3-10	2	-0.6
• SHIRLEY, Mule	Ernest Raeford Shirley b: 5/21/1901, Snow Hill, NC d: 8/3/1955, Goldsboro, NC BL/TL, 5'11", 180 lbs. Deb: 5/6/1924																							
1924*Was-A	30	77	12	18	2	2	0	16	3	7	0	0	.234	.263	.312	.574	49	-6	7	2.64	1	1-25	0	-0.6
1925 Was-A	14	23	2	3	1	0	0	2	1	7	0	0	.130	.167	.174	.341	-14	-4	1	.90	0	/1-9	0	-0.4
Total 2	44	100	14	21	3	2	0	18	4	14	0	0	.210	.240	.280	.520	36	-10	7	2.23	0	/1-34	0	-1.1
• SHIVER, Ivey	Ivey Merwin "Chick" Shiver b: 1/22/1907, Sylvester, GA d: 8/31/1972, Savannah, GA BR/TR, 6'1.5", 190 lbs. Deb: 4/14/1931 Career OF: 0-2-15																							
1931 Det-A	2	9	2	1	0	0	0	0	0	3	0	0	.111	.111	.111	.222	-40	-2	0	.35	0	/0-2(0-2-0)	0	-0.2
1934 Cin-N	19	59	6	12	1	0	2	6	3	15	1	....	.203	.242	.322	.564	51	-4	5	2.82	-1	0-15(0-0-15)	0	-0.6
Total 2	21	68	8	13	1	0	2	6	3	18	1	0	.191	.225	.294	.519	39	-6	5	2.46	-2	/0-17	0	-0.8

YEAR TM-L	G	AB	R	H	2B	3B	HR	RBI	BB	SO	SB	CS	AVG	OBP	SLG	OPS	OPS+	BR/A	RC	RC/G	FR	G/POS	WS	TPW
• SHOCH, George	George Quintus Shoch b: 1/6/1859, Philadelphia, PA d: 9/30/1937, Philadelphia, PA BR/TR, 5'6", 158 lbs. Deb: 9/10/1886 Career OF: 99-41-159																							
1886 Was-N	26	95	11	28	2	1	1	18	2	13	2	....	.295	.309	.368	.678	112	1	12	4.73	-3	0-25(1-0-24)/S-1	2	-0.2
1887 Was-N	70	285	47	84	9	1	1	18	21	16	29	....	.295	.304	.292	.596	70	-9	33	4.36	5	0-63(11-3-49)/S-6,2-1	4	-0.5
1888 Was-N	90	317	46	58	6	3	2	24	25	22	23	....	.183	.262	.240	.502	64	-11	27	2.77	6	S-52,0-35(9-0-26)/2-1,P-1	6	-0.3
1889 Was-N	30	109	12	26	2	0	0	11	20	5	9	....	.239	.385	.257	.642	86	0	15	4.66	3	0-29(16-0-13)/S-1	3	0.2
1891 Mil-a	34	127	29	40	7	1	1	16	18	5	12	....	.315	.435	.409	.845	118	4	29	8.69	4	S-25/3-9	7	0.7
1892 Bal-N	76	308	42	85	15	3	1	50	24	19	14	....	.276	.340	.354	.694	107	2	43	5.19	-11	S-57,0-12(8-4-0)/3-7	7	-0.6
1893 Bro-N	94	327	53	86	17	1	2	54	48	13	9	....	.263	.366	.339	.705	92	-1	45	4.95	-1	0-46(32-0-15),3-37,S-11/2-3	10	-0.4
1894 Bro-N	65	243	47	77	6	5	1	37	26	6	16	....	.317	.394	.395	.789	101	2	46	7.37	3	0-35(1-28-6),3-14/2-9,S-6	8	0.3
1895 Bro-N	61	216	49	56	9	7	0	29	32	6	7	....	.259	.368	.366	.733	97	1	33	5.45	1	0-39(16-2-21),2-13/S-6,3-3	7	0.1
1896 Bro-N	76	250	36	73	7	4	1	28	33	10	11	....	.292	.381	.364	.745	103	3	41	5.88	-2	2-62,0-10(2-3-5)/3-3,S-1	8	0.3
1897 Bro-N	85	284	42	79	9	2	0	38	49	....	6	....	.278	.393	.324	.717	96	2	42	5.08	8	2-68,S-13/0-4(3-1-0)	9	1.2
Total 11	707	2561	414	692	89	28	10	323	298	115	138	....	.270	.354	.333	.687	93	-5	364	5.13	12	0-298,S-179,2-157/3-73,P-1	71	0.7
• SHOCKLEY, Costen	John Costen Shockley b: 2/8/1942, Georgetown, DE BL/TL, 6'2", 200 lbs. Deb: 7/17/1964																							
1964 Phi-N	11	35	4	8	0	0	1	2	2	8	0	0	.229	.270	.314	.585	65	-2	3	2.65	0	/1-9	0	-0.2
1965 Cal-A	40	107	5	20	2	0	2	17	9	16	0	0	.187	.256	.262	.518	49	-7	7	2.21	0	1-31/0-1	1	-0.9
Total 2	51	142	9	28	2	0	3	19	11	24	0	0	.197	.260	.275	.534	53	-9	10	2.32	0	/1-40,0-1	1	-1.2
• SHOEMAKER, Charlie	Charles Landis Shoemaker b: 8/10/1939, Los Angeles, CA d: 5/31/1990, Mount Penn, PA BL/TR, 5'10", 155 lbs. Deb: 9/9/1961																							
1961 KC-A	7	26	5	10	2	0	0	1	2	2	0	0	.385	.429	.462	.890	137	1	5	7.81	0	/2-6	1	0.2
1962 KC-A	5	11	1	2	0	0	0	0	0	2	0	0	.182	.182	.182	.364	-2	-2	0	1.09	0	/2-4	0	-0.1
1964 KC-A	16	52	6	11	2	2	0	3	0	9	0	0	.212	.212	.327	.538	46	-4	4	2.37	-2	2-14	0	-0.5
Total 3	28	89	12	23	4	2	0	4	2	13	0	0	.258	.275	.348	.623	68	-4	9	3.58	-1	/2-24	1	-0.4
• SHOFNER, Strick	Frank Strickland Shofner b: 7/23/1919, Crawford, TX d: 10/10/1998, Crawford, TX BL/TR, 5'10.5", 187 lbs. Deb: 4/19/1947																							
1947 Bos-A	5	13	1	2	0	1	0	0	0	3	0	0	.154	.154	.308	.462	25	-1	1	1.55	0	/3-4	0	-0.1
• SHOKES, Eddie	Edward Christopher Shokes b: 1/27/1920, Charleston, SC d: 9/14/2002, Winchester, VA BL/TL, 6', 170 lbs. Deb: 6/9/1941																							
1941 Cin-N	1	1	0	0	0	0	0	0	0	1	0	....	.000	.000	.000	.000	-100	-0	0	.00	0	....	0	0.0
1946 Cin-N	31	83	3	10	1	0	0	5	18	21	1	....	.120	.277	.133	.410	19	-8	4	1.57	-1	1-29	0	-1.0
Total 2	32	84	3	10	1	0	0	5	18	22	1	....	.119	.275	.131	.405	18	-8	4	1.55	-1	/1-29	0	-1.1
• SHOOK, Ray	Raymond Curtis Shook b: 11/18/1889, Ferry, OH d: 9/16/1970, South Bend, IN BR/TR, 5'7.5", 155 lbs. Deb: 4/16/1916																							
1916 Chi-A	1	0	0	0	0	0	0	0	0	0	0	....	....	....	....	....	-99	0	0	....	0	....	0	0.0
• SHOOP, Ron	Ronald Lee Shoop b: 9/19/1931, Rural Valley, PA BR/TR, 5'11", 180 lbs. Deb: 8/22/1959																							
1959 Det-A	3	7	1	1	0	0	0	1	0	1	0	0	.143	.143	.143	.286	-20	-1	0	.00	0	/C-3	0	-0.1
• SHOPAY, Tom	Thomas Michael Shopay b: 2/21/1945, Bristol, CT BL/TR, 5'9.5", 160 lbs. Deb: 9/17/1967 Career OF: 53-36-37																							
1967 NY-A	8	27	2	8	1	0	2	6	1	5	2	0	.296	.321	.556	.877	160	2	5	6.94	1	/0-7(7-0-0)	1	0.3
1969 NY-A	28	48	2	4	0	1	0	0	2	10	0	1	.083	.120	.125	.245	-33	-9	1	.29	0	0-11(7-0-5)	0	-1.0
1971*Bal-A	47	74	10	19	2	0	0	5	3	7	2	1	.257	.286	.284	.569	62	-4	6	2.55	0	0-13(4-0-9)	1	-0.4
1972 Bal-A	49	40	3	9	0	0	0	2	5	12	0	0	.225	.311	.225	.536	60	-2	3	2.79	0	/0-3(3-0-0)	0	-0.2
1975 Bal-A	40	31	4	5	1	0	0	2	4	7	3	0	.161	.257	.194	.451	31	-2	2	1.65	1	0-13(1-6-6)/D-3,C-1	0	-0.1
1976 Bal-A	14	20	4	4	0	0	0	1	3	3	1	0	.200	.304	.200	.504	53	-1	2	2.72	0	0-11(6-2-3)/C-1	1	-0.1
1977 Bal-A	67	69	15	13	3	0	1	4	8	7	3	3	.188	.273	.275	.548	53	-5	5	2.39	1	0-52(25-28-14)/D-2	0	-0.5
Total 7	253	309	40	62	7	1	3	20	26	51	11	5	.201	.263	.259	.522	50	-20	23	2.39	2	0-110/D-5,C-2	3	-2.2
• SHORT, Dave	Davis Orvis Short b: 5/11/1917, Magnolia, AR d: 11/22/1983, Shreveport, LA BL/TR, 5'11.5", 162 lbs. Deb: 9/16/1940																							
1940 Chi-A	4	3	1	1	0	0	0	0	1	2	0	0	.333	.500	.333	.833	119	0	1	8.67	0	....	0	0.0
1941 Chi-A	3	8	0	0	0	0	0	0	2	1	0	0	.000	.200	.000	.200	-44	-2	0	.35	0	/0-2(2-0-0)	0	-0.2
Total 2	7	11	1	1	0	0	0	0	3	3	0	0	.091	.286	.091	.377	3	-1	1	2.02	0	/0-2	0	-0.2
• SHORTEN, Chick	Charles Henry Shorten b: 4/19/1892, Scranton, PA d: 10/23/1965, Scranton, PA BL/TL, 6', 175 lbs. Deb: 9/22/1915 Career OF: 47-144-162																							
1915 Bos-A	6	14	1	3	1	0	0	0	0	2	0	....	.214	.214	.286	.500	51	-1	1	2.06	1	/0-5(0-4-1)	0	-0.1
1916*Bos-A	53	112	14	33	2	1	0	11	10	8	1	....	.295	.352	.330	.683	105	1	14	4.40	-2	0-33(13-19-1)	4	-0.2
1917 Bos-A	69	168	12	30	4	2	0	16	10	10	2	....	.179	.229	.226	.455	39	-13	9	1.68	-2	0-43(16-20-7)	1	-1.9
1919 Det-A	95	270	37	85	9	3	0	22	22	13	5	....	.315	.366	.370	.737	110	4	40	5.00	-7	0-75(0-18-57)	9	-0.8
1920 Det-A	116	364	35	105	9	6	1	40	28	14	2	4	.288	.339	.354	.694	86	-7	44	4.17	2	0-99(0-31-68)	9	-1.0
1921 Det-A	92	217	33	59	11	3	0	23	20	11	2	3	.272	.333	.350	.684	75	-8	26	4.06	-3	0-51(3-36-12)	3	-1.3
1922 StL-A	55	131	22	36	12	5	2	16	16	8	0	1	.275	.354	.489	.842	114	2	23	5.98	-1	0-31(4-16-12)	4	0.0
1924 Cin-N	41	69	7	19	3	0	0	6	4	2	0	0	.275	.315	.319	.634	71	-3	7	3.61	0	0-15(11-0-4)	1	-0.3
Total 8	527	1345	161	370	51	20	3	134	110	68	12	8	.275	.330	.349	.680	87	-26	163	4.11	-12	0-352	31	-5.6
• SHOTTON, Burt	Burton Edwin "Barney" Shotton b: 10/18/1884, Brownhelm, OH d: 7/29/1962, Lake Wales, FL BL/TR, 5'11", 175 lbs. Deb: 9/13/1909 M/C Career OF: 598-607-72																							
1909 StL-A	17	61	5	16	0	1	0	0	5	....	3	....	.262	.328	.295	.623	104	0	7	3.81	0	0-17(2-15-0)	2	-0.1
1911 StL-A	139	572	84	146	11	8	0	36	51	....	26	....	.255	.317	.302	.620	76	-18	62	3.72	-1	*0-139(18-121-0)	11	-2.6
1912 StL-A	154	580	87	168	15	8	2	40	86	....	35	....	.290	.390	.353	.743	117	18	92	5.75	0	*0-154(0-154-0)	19	0.9
1913 StL-A	147	549	105	163	23	8	1	28	**99**	63	43	....	.297	.405	.373	.779	132	28	95	6.17	7	*0-146(0-146-0)	23	2.7
1914 StL-A	154	579	82	156	19	9	0	38	64	66	40	29	.269	.344	.333	.678	108	2	69	3.98	-8	*0-152(0-152-0)	19	-1.7
1915 StL-A	156	559	93	158	18	11	1	30	118	62	43	32	.283	.409	.360	.769	135	27	87	5.26	-4	*0-154(138-5-11)	24	1.8
1916 StL-A	156	614	97	174	23	6	1	36	**110**	65	41	28	.283	.392	.345	.738	128	23	88	4.85	11	*0-156(156-0-0)	26	3.1
1917 StL-A	118	398	48	89	9	1	1	20	62	47	16	....	.224	.330	.259	.589	83	-5	38	3.11	-13	*0-107(107-0-0)	8	-2.5
1918 Was-A	126	505	68	132	16	7	0	21	67	28	25	....	.261	.349	.321	.670	104	4	61	4.15	7	*0-122(67-1-54)	16	0.6
1919 StL-N	85	270	35	77	13	5	1	20	22	25	16	....	.285	.341	.381	.723	125	8	39	5.03	-1	0-67(67-0-0)	9	0.5
1920 StL-N	62	180	28	41	5	0	1	12	18	14	5	1	.228	.305	.272	.577	68	-5	17	3.06	2	0-51(41-2-6)	3	-0.5
1921 StL-N	38	48	9	12	1	1	1	7	7	4	0	2	.250	.357	.375	.732	96	-1	6	4.32	1	0-11(1-10-0)	1	-0.1
1922 StL-N	34	30	5	6	1	0	0	2	4	6	0	1	.200	.294	.233	.527	39	-3	2	2.17	0	/0-3(1-1-1)	0	-0.3
1923 StL-N	1	0	1	0	0	0	0	0	0	0	0	0	....	....	....	....	-102	0	0	....	0	....	0	0.0
Total 14	1387	4945	747	1338	154	65	9	290	713	380	293	93	.271	.365	.333	.698	110	80	663	4.59	1	*0-1279	161	1.8
• SHOUPE, John	John F. Shoupe b: 9/30/1851, Cincinnati, OH d: 2/13/1920, Cincinnati, OH BL/TL, 5'7", 140 lbs. Deb: 5/3/1879																							
1879 Tro-N	11	44	5	4	0	0	0	1	0	3	....	....	.091	.091	.091	.182	-43	-6	0	.26	-6	S-10/2-1	0	-1.0
1882 StL-a	2	7	1	0	0	0	0	....	0	....	....	....	.000	.000	.000	.000	-96	-1	0	.00	1	/2-2	0	-0.1
1884 Was-U	1	4	1	3	0	0	0	....	0	....	....	....	.750	.750	.750	1.500	422	1	2	64.58	2	/0-1	1	0.3
Total 3	14	55	7	7	0	0	0	1	0	3	....	....	.127	.127	.127	.255	-16	-6	3	1.56	-3	/S-10,2-3,0-1	1	-0.8
• SHOVLIN, John	John Joseph "Brode" Shovlin b: 1/14/1891, Drifton, PA d: 2/16/1976, Bethesda, MD BR/TR, 5'7", 163 lbs. Deb: 6/21/1911																							
1911 Pit-N	2	1	1	0	0	0	0	0	0	1	0	....	.000	.000	.000	.000	-96	-0	0	.00	-1	....	0	0.0
1919 StL-A	9	35	4	7	0	0	0	1	5	2	0	....	.200	.300	.200	.500	41	-3	2	2.03	-1	/2-9	0	-0.4
1920 StL-A	7	7	2	2	0	0	0	2	0	0	0	0	.286	.286	.286	.571	50	-0	1	2.91	0	/S-5	0	-0.1
Total 3	18	43	7	9	0	0	0	3	5	3	0	0	.209	.292	.209	.501	39	-3	3	2.09	-1	/2-9,S-5	0	-0.4
• SHUBA, George	George Thomas "Shotgun" Shuba b: 12/13/1924, Youngstown, OH BL/TR, 5'11", 180 lbs. Deb: 7/2/1948 Career OF: 205-3-10																							
1948 Bro-N	63	161	21	43	6	0	4	32	34	31	1	....	.267	.395	.379	.774	107	3	27	5.90	-4	0-56(55-2-1)	6	-0.4
1949 Bro-N	1	1	0	0	0	0	0	0	0	0	0	....	.000	.000	.000	.000	-96	-0	0	.00	0	....	0	0.0
1950 Bro-N	34	111	15	23	8	2	3	12	13	22	2	....	.207	.302	.396	.698	80	-3	14	4.27	4	0-27(27-0-0)	2	-0.1
1952*Bro-N	94	256	40	78	12	1	9	40	38	29	1	3	.305	.395	.465	.859	136	13	47	6.75	-2	0-67(66-0-1)	11	0.6

YEAR TM-L	G	AB	R	H	2B	3B	HR	RBI	BB	SO	SB	CS	AVG	OBP	SLG	OPS	OPS+	BR/A	RC	RC/G	FR	G/POS	WS	TPW
1953*Bro-N	74	169	19	43	12	1	5	23	17	20	1	2	.254	.326	.426	.752	92	-3	23	4.57	0	O-44(43-0-1)	4	-0.4
1954 Bro-N	45	65	3	10	5	0	2	10	7	10	0	0	.154	.247	.323	.570	46	-5	5	2.55	-1	O-13(7-0-5)	0	-0.7
1955*Bro-N	44	51	8	14	2	0	1	8	11	10	0	0	.275	.422	.373	.794	110	2	9	5.98	-1	/O-9(7-1-2)	2	0.1
Total 7	355	814	106	211	45	4	24	125	120	122	5	5	.259	.359	.413	.771	104	6	125	5.33	-4	O-216	25	-1.0
• SHUGART, Frank	Frank Harry Shugart b: 12/10/1866, Luthersburg, PA d: 9/9/1944, Clearfield, PA BL/TR, 5'8", 170 lbs. Deb: 8/23/1890 Career OF: 0-164-19																							
1890 Chi-P	29	106	8	20	5	5	0	15	5	13	5	....	.189	.232	.330	.562	47	-9	10	2.99	-2	S-25/O-5(0-1-4)	1	-0.9
1891 Pit-N	75	320	57	88	19	8	3	33	20	26	21	....	.275	.324	.413	.736	117	5	51	5.91	2	S-75	10	0.8
1892 Pit-N	137	554	94	148	19	14	0	62	47	48	28	....	.267	.329	.352	.681	105	3	75	5.00	2	*S-134/C-2,O-1	22	1.1
1893 Pit-N	52	210	37	55	7	3	1	32	19	15	12	....	.262	.332	.338	.670	80	-6	28	4.83	-2	S-51	5	-0.5
StL-N	59	246	41	69	10	4	0	28	22	10	13	....	.280	.354	.354	.708	88	-4	36	5.43	-2	O-28(0-19-9),S-23/3-9	5	-0.5
Yr.	111	456	78	124	17	7	1	60	41	25	25	....	.272	.344	.346	.690	84	-10	65	5.15	-4	S-74,O-28(0-19-9)/3-9	10	-1.0
1894 StL-N	133	527	103	154	19	18	7	72	38	37	21	....	.292	.350	.436	.787	89	-12	90	6.28	-7	*O-122(0-122-0)/3-7,S-7	12	-2.1
1895 Lou-N	113	473	61	125	14	13	4	70	31	25	14	....	.264	.315	.374	.689	82	-13	62	4.77	-26	*S-88,O-27(0-22-5)	6	-3.0
1897 Phi-N	40	163	20	41	8	2	5	25	8	....	5	....	.252	.287	.417	.704	87	-4	22	4.64	-4	S-40	3	-0.5
1901 Chi-A	107	415	62	104	9	12	2	47	28	....	12	....	.251	.301	.345	.646	81	-11	49	4.05	-7	*S-107	10	-1.3
Total 8	745	3014	483	804	110	79	22	384	218	174	131	....	.267	.323	.378	.700	90	-52	423	5.06	-47	S-550,O-183/3-16,C-2	74	-6.8
• SHUMPERT, Terry	Terrance Darnell Shumpert b: 8/16/1966, Paducah, KY BR/TR, 5'11", 185 lbs. Deb: 5/1/1990 Career OF: 84-9-15																							
1990 KC-A	32	91	7	25	6	1	0	8	2	17	3	3	.275	.298	.363	.661	85	-3	8	2.86	-1	2-27/D-3	2	-0.3
1991 KC-A	144	369	45	80	16	4	5	34	30	75	17	11	.217	.285	.322	.607	67	-18	32	2.71	-1	*2-144	6	-1.5
1992 KC-A	36	94	6	14	5	1	1	11	3	17	2	2	.149	.175	.255	.431	19	-11	4	1.11	-3	2-33/D-1,S-1	1	-1.4
1993 KC-A	8	10	0	1	0	0	0	0	2	2	1	0	.100	.250	.100	.350	-2	-1	1	1.53	0	/2-8	0	-0.1
1994 KC-A	64	183	28	44	6	2	8	24	13	39	18	3	.240	.291	.426	.717	79	-4	25	4.58	-5	2-38,3-24/D-2,S-1	5	-0.7
1995 Bos-A	21	47	6	11	3	0	0	3	4	13	3	1	.234	.294	.298	.592	53	-3	5	3.33	2	/2-8,3-5,S-3,D-1	1	0.0
1996 Chi-N	27	31	5	7	1	0	2	6	2	11	0	1	.226	.294	.452	.746	91	-1	4	4.09	-2	3-10/2-4,S-1	1	-0.3
1997 SD-N	13	33	4	9	3	0	1	6	3	4	0	0	.273	.333	.455	.788	114	1	5	5.03	-3	/2-7,O-3(2-0-1),3-2	1	-0.2
1998 Col-N	23	26	3	6	1	0	1	2	2	8	0	0	.231	.286	.385	.670	61	-2	3	4.06	1	/2-6	0	0.0
1999 Col-N	92	262	58	91	26	3	10	37	31	41	14	0	.347	.420	.584	1.004	119	11	69	10.30	0	2-54,O-19(6-9-4),3-14/S-2	10	1.3
2000 Col-N	115	263	52	68	11	7	9	40	28	40	8	4	.259	.343	.456	.800	80	-9	43	5.60	-3	O-40(40-0-0),2-23,3-15/S-7,1,D	5	-1.2
2001 Col-N	114	242	37	70	14	5	4	24	15	44	14	3	.289	.338	.438	.776	81	-5	38	5.58	-0	2-41,O-24(24-0-0),3-12/S-4	5	-0.5
2002 Col-N	106	234	30	55	12	1	6	21	21	41	4	1	.235	.309	.372	.681	68	-11	26	3.57	-2	2-60/O-8(7-0-1),S-3,3-1	1	-1.1
2003 TB-A	59	84	14	16	5	2	2	7	10	17	1	0	.190	.292	.369	.661	74	-3	10	3.89	-2	2-14,O-14(5-0-9),D-13,3-11/S	1	-0.5
Total 14	854	1969	295	497	109	26	49	223	166	369	85	29	.252	.318	.409	.727	78	-59	272	4.62	-19	2-467,O-108/3-94,S-23,D-21,1	39	-6.5
• SHUPE, Vince	Vincent William Shupe b: 9/5/1921, East Canton, OH d: 4/5/1962, Canton, OH BL/TL, 5'11", 180 lbs. Deb: 7/7/1945																							
1945 Bos-N	78	283	22	76	8	0	0	15	17	16	3	....	.269	.312	.297	.609	69	-12	26	3.16	2	1-77	2	-1.4
• SICKING, Ed	Edward Joseph Sicking b: 3/30/1897, St. Bernard, OH d: 8/30/1978, Madeira, OH BR/TR, 5'9.5", 165 lbs. Deb: 8/26/1916																							
1916 Chi-N	1	1	0	0	0	0	0	0	0	0	0	....	.000	.000	.000	.000	-90	-0	0	.00	0	....	0	0.0
1918 NY-N	46	132	9	33	4	0	0	12	6	11	2	....	.250	.283	.280	.563	73	-4	10	2.70	-6	3-24,2-18/S-3	3	-1.1
1919 NY-N	6	15	2	5	0	0	0	3	1	0	0	....	.333	.412	.333	.745	127	1	2	5.15	2	/S-6	1	0.3
Phi-N	61	185	16	40	2	1	0	15	8	17	4	....	.216	.253	.238	.490	45	-12	12	2.06	-3	S-35,2-22	2	-1.4
Yr.	67	200	18	45	2	1	0	18	9	17	4	....	.225	.265	.245	.510	51	-12	14	2.27	-1	S-41,2-22	3	-1.1
1920 NY-N	46	134	11	23	3	1	0	9	10	10	6	2	.172	.234	.209	.443	28	-11	7	1.68	-6	3-28,2-15/S-3	1	-1.7
Cin-N	37	123	12	33	3	0	0	17	13	5	2	3	.268	.338	.293	.631	83	-2	12	3.48	1	2-25/S-9,3-2	4	0.0
Yr.	83	257	23	56	6	1	0	26	23	15	8	5	.218	.285	.249	.534	55	-14	20	2.48	-4	2-40,3-30,S-12	5	-1.7
1927 Pit-N	6	7	1	1	1	0	0	3	1	0	0	....	.143	.250	.286	.536	40	-1	1	2.28	0	/2-5	0	0.0
Total 5	203	597	51	135	13	2	0	59	39	43	14	5	.226	.277	.255	.532	57	-31	45	2.45	-11	/2-85,S-56,3-54	11	-3.9
• SIDDALL, Joe	Joseph Todd Siddall b: 10/25/1967, Windsor, Canada BL/TR, 6'1", 197 lbs. Deb: 7/28/1993 Career OF: 1-0-1																							
1993 Mon-N	19	20	0	2	1	0	0	1	1	5	0	0	.100	.143	.150	.293	-21	-3	0	.64	0	C-15/1-1,O-1	0	-0.3
1995 Mon-N	7	10	4	3	0	0	0	1	3	3	0	0	.300	.500	.300	.800	113	1	2	7.79	-1	/C-7	1	0.0
1996 Fla-N	18	47	0	7	1	0	0	3	2	8	0	0	.149	.184	.170	.354	-6	-7	2	1.06	0	C-18	0	-0.6
1998 Det-A	29	65	3	12	3	0	1	6	7	25	0	0	.185	.264	.277	.541	41	-6	5	2.45	2	C-27/O-1	1	-0.2
Total 4	73	142	7	24	5	0	1	11	13	41	0	0	.169	.244	.225	.469	24	-16	9	2.03	1	/C-67,O-2,1-1	2	-1.2
• SIEBERN, Norm	Norman Leroy Siebern b: 7/26/1933, St. Louis, MO BL/TR, 6'2", 205 lbs. Deb: 6/15/1956 Career OF: 402-16-11																							
1956*NY-A	54	162	27	33	1	4	4	21	19	38	1	1	.204	.287	.333	.621	66	-9	16	3.16	-3	O-51(51-0-0)	2	-1.4
1958*NY-A	134	460	79	138	19	5	14	55	66	87	5	8	.300	.389	.454	.843	136	23	82	6.49	2	*O-133(127-11-0)	21	1.7
1959 NY-A	120	380	52	103	17	0	11	53	41	71	3	1	.271	.345	.403	.748	108	5	56	5.21	-3	O-93(82-5-9)/1-2	12	-0.4
1960 KC-A	144	520	69	145	31	6	19	69	72	68	0	0	.279	.369	.471	.840	125	19	93	6.41	1	O-75(75-0-0),1-69	21	1.2
1961 KC-A	153	560	68	166	36	5	18	98	82	91	2	4	.296	.387	.475	.862	129	23	108	7.15	-5	*1-109,O-47(47-0-0)	23	1.0
1962 KC-A★	162	600	114	185	25	6	25	117	110	88	3	1	.308	.416	.495	.911	140	39	129	7.98	6	*1-162	27	3.5
1963 KC-A★	152	556	80	151	25	2	16	83	79	82	1	4	.272	.362	.410	.772	111	9	85	5.34	7	*1-131,O-16(16-0-1)	18	0.8
1964 Bal-A★	150	478	92	117	24	2	12	56	**106**	87	2	3	.245	.384	.379	.763	113	14	78	5.56	1	*1-149	20	0.6
1965 Bal-A	106	297	44	76	13	4	8	32	50	49	1	2	.256	.365	.407	.772	117	8	47	5.54	-1	1-76	13	0.3
1966 Cal-A	125	336	29	83	14	1	5	41	63	61	0	1	.247	.366	.339	.705	107	6	45	4.60	2	1-99	12	0.3
1967 SF-N	46	58	6	9	1	1	0	4	14	13	0	0	.155	.319	.207	.526	54	-3	5	2.75	0	1-15/O-2(2-0-0)	1	-0.4
*Bos-A	33	44	2	9	0	2	0	7	6	8	0	0	.205	.300	.295	.595	71	-1	4	3.00	1	1-13/O-1	1	-0.1
1968 Bos-A	27	30	0	2	0	0	0	0	0	5	0	0	.067	.067	.067	.133	-56	-6	0	.06	0	/1-2,O-2(1-0-1)	0	-0.7
Total 12	1406	4481	662	1217	206	38	132	636	708	748	18	25	.272	.372	.423	.795	118	127	749	5.91	8	1-827,O-420	171	6.4
• SIEBERT, Dick	Richard Walther Siebert b: 2/19/1912, Fall River, MA d: 12/9/1978, Minneapolis, MN BL/TL, 6', 170 lbs. Deb: 9/7/1932 Career OF: 42-0-18																							
1932 Bro-N	6	7	1	2	0	0	0	0	2	2	0	....	.286	.444	.286	.730	103	0	1	5.64	0	/1-2	0	0.0
1936 Bro-N	2	2	0	0	0	0	0	0	0	0	0	....	.000	.000	.000	.000	-99	-1	0	.00	1	/O-1	0	0.0
1937 StL-N	22	38	3	7	2	0	0	2	4	8	1	....	.184	.279	.237	.516	40	-3	3	2.56	0	/1-7	0	-0.4
1938 StL-N	1	1	0	1	0	0	0	0	0	0	0	....	1.000	1.000	1.000	2.000	427	0	1	∞	0	....	0	0.0
Phi-A	48	194	24	55	8	3	0	28	10	9	2	3	.284	.329	.356	.684	73	-9	22	4.09	7	1-46	2	-0.5
1939 Phi-A	101	402	58	118	28	3	6	47	21	22	4	1	.294	.329	.423	.751	93	-6	56	5.00	9	1-99	9	-0.6
1940 Phi-A	154	595	69	170	31	6	5	77	33	34	8	6	.286	.325	.383	.709	85	-15	74	4.41	8	*1-154	10	-2.0
1941 Phi-A	123	467	63	156	28	8	5	79	37	22	1	3	.334	.385	.460	.846	126	16	82	6.68	8	*1-123	15	1.2
1942 Phi-A	153	612	57	159	25	7	2	74	24	17	4	5	.260	.291	.333	.624	76	-23	59	3.41	0	*1-152	10	-3.8
1943 Phi-A★	146	558	50	140	26	7	1	72	33	21	6	7	.251	.295	.328	.623	83	-15	50	3.05	9	*1-145	9	-1.5
1944 Phi-A	132	468	52	143	27	5	6	52	62	17	2	0	.306	.387	.423	.810	133	23	83	6.71	4	1-74,O-58(42-0-17)	20	2.1
1945 Phi-A	147	573	62	153	29	1	7	51	50	33	2	7	.267	.328	.358	.686	99	-3	69	4.19	2	*1-147	12	-1.0
Total 11	1035	3917	439	1104	204	40	32	482	276	185	30	32	.282	.332	.379	.710	96	-35	500	4.55	46	1-949/O-59	87	-6.4
• SIEFKE, Fred	Frederick Edwin Siefke b: 3/5/1870, New York, NY d: 4/18/1893, New York, NY, 5'11", 168 lbs. Deb: 5/2/1890																							
1890 Bro-a	16	58	1	8	2	0	0	3	5	....	2	....	.138	.206	.172	.379	12	-6	3	1.35	-2	3-16	0	-0.7
• SIEGEL, John	John Siegel b: York, PA Deb: 6/9/1884																							
1884 Phi-U	8	31	4	7	2	0	0	....	1	....	....	....	.226	.250	.290	.540	89	-0	2	2.69	-4	/3-8	0	-0.4
• SIEGLE, Johnny	John Herbert Siegle b: 7/8/1874, Urbana, OH d: 2/12/1968, Urbana, OH BR/TR, 5'10", 165 lbs. Deb: 9/15/1905 Career OF: 7-14-16																							
1905 Cin-N	17	56	9	17	1	2	1	8	7	....	0	....	.304	.391	.446	.837	135	3	10	6.44	-1	O-16(0-0-16)	3	0.1
1906 Cin-N	22	68	4	8	2	2	0	7	3	....	0	....	.118	.178	.206	.384	19	-7	3	1.24	-1	O-21(7-14-0)	1	-0.9
Total 2	39	124	13	25	3	4	1	15	10	....	0	....	.202	.277	.315	.592	72	-4	14	3.24	-2	/O-37	4	-0.8
• SIEMER, Oscar	Oscar Sylvester "Cotton" Siemer b: 8/14/1901, St. Louis, MO d: 12/5/1959, St. Louis, MO BR/TR, 5'9", 162 lbs. Deb: 5/20/1925																							
1925 Bos-N	16	46	5	14	0	1	1	6	1	0	0	0	.304	.319	.413	.732	94	-1	6	4.76	-1	C-16	1	-0.1

YEAR TM-L	G	AB	R	H	2B	3B	HR	RBI	BB	SO	SB	CS	AVG	OBP	SLG	OPS	OPS+	BR/A	RC	RC/G	FR	G/POS	WS	TPW
1926 Bos-N	31	73	3	15	1	0	0	5	2	7	0	....	.205	.227	.219	.446	22	-8	4	1.55	-3	C-30	1	-1.0
Total 2	47	119	8	29	1	1	1	11	3	7	0	0	.244	.262	.294	.556	50	-8	10	2.69	-5	/C-46	2	-1.1

• SIERRA, Ruben Ruben Angel (Garcia) Sierra b: 10/6/1965, Rio Piedras, Puerto Rico BB/TR, 6'1", 200 lbs. Deb: 6/1/1986 Career OF: 186-31-1393

YEAR TM-L	G	AB	R	H	2B	3B	HR	RBI	BB	SO	SB	CS	AVG	OBP	SLG	OPS	OPS+	BR/A	RC	RC/G	FR	G/POS	WS	TPW
1986 Tex-A	113	382	50	101	13	10	16	55	22	65	7	8	.264	.306	.476	.783	106	-0	51	4.54	0	*O-107(44-21-68)/D-3	11	-0.5
1987 Tex-A	158	643	97	169	35	4	30	109	39	114	16	11	.263	.307	.470	.777	102	-3	85	4.45	3	*O-157(0-4-156)	15	-0.7
1988 Tex-A	156	615	77	156	32	2	23	91	44	91	18	4	.254	.305	.424	.729	99	-0	77	4.29	5	*O-153(0-0-153)/D-1	16	0.0
1989 Tex-A★	162	634	101	194	35	**14**	29	**119**	43	82	8	2	.306	.352	**.543**	.895	146	36	122	7.16	2	*O-162(0-2-161)	**34**	3.4
1990 Tex-A	159	608	70	170	37	2	16	96	49	86	9	0	.280	.334	.426	.760	111	10	85	5.00	-4	*O-151(0-0-151)/D-7	21	0.1
1991 Tex-A★	161	661	110	203	44	5	25	116	56	91	16	4	.307	.361	.502	.863	139	35	117	6.49	-1	*O-161(0-3-161)	28	2.9
1992 Tex-A★	124	500	66	139	30	6	14	70	31	59	12	4	.278	.320	.446	.766	117	9	70	4.94	-8	*O-119(0-0-119)/D-4	15	-0.3
*Oak-A	27	101	17	28	4	1	3	17	14	9	2	0	.277	.365	.426	.791	128	4	16	5.65	-2	O-25(0-0-25)/D-2	6	0.2
Yr.	151	601	83	167	34	7	17	87	45	68	14	4	.278	.328	.443	.771	119	14	86	5.06	-10	*O-144(0-0-144)/D-6	21	-0.1
1993 Oak-A	158	630	77	147	23	5	22	101	52	97	25	5	.233	.292	.390	.682	87	-10	70	3.67	-1	*O-133(0-0-133),D-25	13	-1.9
1994 Oak-A★	110	426	71	114	21	1	23	92	23	64	8	5	.268	.305	.484	.789	108	2	56	4.42	-6	O-98(0-1-97),D-10	13	-0.9
1995 Oak-A	70	264	40	70	17	0	12	42	24	42	4	4	.265	.326	.466	.792	110	2	40	5.32	-4	O-62(0-0-62)/D-7	6	-0.5
*NY-A	56	215	33	56	15	0	7	44	22	34	1	0	.260	.329	.428	.757	96	-2	30	4.74	0	D-46,O-10(0-0-10)	7	-0.5
Yr.	126	479	73	126	32	0	19	86	46	76	5	4	.263	.328	.449	.776	104	0	70	5.06	-4	O-72(0-0-72),D-53	13	-1.0
1996 NY-A	96	360	39	93	17	1	11	52	40	58	1	3	.258	.333	.403	.735	85	-10	46	4.35	1	D-61,O-33(32-0-1)	5	-1.3
Det-A	46	158	22	35	9	1	1	20	20	25	3	1	.222	.309	.310	.619	57	-10	16	3.45	1	O-23(4-0-19),D-20	1	-1.1
Yr.	142	518	61	128	26	2	12	72	60	83	4	4	.247	.325	.375	.700	76	-20	63	4.07	2	D-81,O-56(36-0-20)	6	-2.4
1997 Cin-N	25	90	6	22	5	1	2	7	6	21	0	0	.244	.292	.389	.681	75	-4	10	3.99	1	O-24(12-0-12)	1	-0.3
Tor-A	14	48	4	10	0	2	1	5	3	13	0	0	.208	.255	.354	.609	57	-3	5	3.12	0	/O-7(6-0-2),D-6	0	-0.4
1998 Chi-A	27	74	7	16	4	1	4	11	3	11	2	0	.216	.247	.459	.706	80	-2	8	3.56	0	O-14(2-0-12)/D-5	1	-0.2
2000 Tex-A	20	60	5	14	0	0	1	7	4	9	1	0	.233	.281	.283	.565	43	-5	5	2.83	0	D-14	1	-0.5
2001 Tex-A	94	344	55	100	22	1	23	67	19	52	2	0	.291	.328	.561	.889	124	10	58	5.96	-4	D-50,O-36(1-0-35)	6	0.1
2002 Sea-A	122	419	47	113	23	0	13	60	31	66	4	0	.270	.320	.418	.738	97	-1	52	4.32	-4	O-60(59-0-1),D-52	7	-1.0
2003 Tex-A	43	133	14	35	9	0	3	12	14	27	1	1	.263	.333	.398	.732	85	-3	18	4.76	-3	O-23(20-0-4),D-15	2	-0.7
*NY-A	63	174	19	48	8	1	6	31	13	20	1	0	.276	.326	.437	.763	101	0	23	4.60	-1	D-30,O-17(6-0-11)	3	-0.3
Yr.	106	307	33	83	17	1	9	43	27	47	2	1	.270	.329	.420	.750	94	-3	41	4.67	-4	D-45,O-40(26-0-15)	5	-1.0
Total 17	2004	7539	1027	2033	403	58	285	1224	572	1136	141	52	.270	.322	.452	.774	107	54	1060	4.89	-24	*O-1575,D-358	212	-4.4

• SIEVERS, Roy Roy Edward "Squirrel" Sievers b: 11/18/1926, St. Louis, MO BR/TR, 6'1", 195 lbs. Deb: 4/21/1949 C Career OF: 676-163-4

YEAR TM-L	G	AB	R	H	2B	3B	HR	RBI	BB	SO	SB	CS	AVG	OBP	SLG	OPS	OPS+	BR/A	RC	RC/G	FR	G/POS	WS	TPW
1949 StL-A	140	471	84	144	28	1	16	91	70	75	1	5	.306	.398	.471	.869	124	15	89	6.90	-4	*O-125(51-76-0)/3-7	16	0.6
1950 StL-A	113	370	46	88	20	4	10	57	34	42	1	3	.238	.305	.395	.700	75	-17	43	3.92	-2	O-78(10-68-0),3-21	6	-2.0
1951 StL-A	31	89	10	20	2	1	1	11	9	21	0	0	.225	.303	.303	.606	62	-5	8	2.94	-1	O-25(9-19-0)	1	-0.7
1952 StL-A	11	30	3	6	3	0	0	5	1	4	0	0	.200	.226	.300	.526	44	-2	2	1.95	-1	/1-7	0	-0.4
1953 StL-A	92	285	37	77	15	0	8	35	32	47	0	1	.270	.344	.407	.751	100	-0	40	4.82	-7	1-76	5	-1.1
1954 Was-A	145	514	75	119	26	6	24	102	80	77	2	1	.232	.337	.446	.783	120	14	78	4.92	5	*O-133(133-0-0)/1-8	16	1.1
1955 Was-A	144	509	74	138	20	8	25	106	73	66	1	2	.271	.367	.489	.856	136	25	90	6.15	-6	*O-129(129-0-0),1-17/3-2	20	1.1
1956 Was-A★	152	550	92	139	27	2	29	95	100	88	0	0	.253	.373	.467	.840	121	18	100	6.32	-3	O-78(78-0-0),1-76	20	0.6
1957 Was-A★	152	572	99	172	23	5	**42**	**114**	76	55	1	1	.301	.389	.579	.968	163	50	131	8.58	-1	*O-130(130-0-0),1-21	32	4.2
1958 Was-A	148	550	85	162	18	1	39	108	53	63	3	1	.295	.361	.544	.904	148	35	106	7.02	-5	*O-114(114-0-0),1-33	26	2.1
1959 Was-A★	115	385	55	93	19	0	21	49	53	62	1	1	.242	.336	.455	.791	116	8	59	5.17	9	1-93,O-13(13-0-0)	12	1.1
1960 Chi-A	127	444	87	131	22	0	28	93	74	69	1	1	.295	.399	.534	.933	151	33	95	7.76	-6	*1-114/O-6(6-0-0)	22	2.0
1961 Chi-A★	141	492	76	145	26	6	27	92	61	62	1	0	.295	.379	.537	.916	144	31	101	7.54	-2	*1-132	23	2.1
1962 Phi-N	144	477	61	125	19	5	21	80	56	80	2	1	.262	.348	.455	.803	117	12	78	5.75	0	*1-130/O-7(3-0-4)	17	0.4
1963 Phi-N	138	450	46	108	19	2	19	82	43	72	0	2	.240	.313	.418	.731	110	5	60	4.46	-4	*1-126	13	-0.6
1964 Phi-N	49	120	7	22	3	1	4	16	13	20	0	0	.183	.269	.325	.594	67	-5	10	2.44	0	1-33	1	-0.8
Was-A	33	58	5	10	1	0	4	11	9	14	0	0	.172	.284	.397	.680	87	-1	7	3.67	2	1-15	1	0.0
1965 Was-A	12	21	3	4	1	0	0	0	4	3	0	0	.190	.320	.238	.558	62	-1	2	2.54	-1	/1-7	0	-0.2
Total 17	1887	6387	945	1703	292	42	318	1147	841	920	14	19	.267	.357	.475	.831	125	214	1097	6.00	-29	1-888,O-838/3-30	231	9.5

• SIFFELL, Frank Frank Siffell b: 1861, Germany d: 10/26/1909, Philadelphia, PA Deb: 6/14/1884

YEAR TM-L	G	AB	R	H	2B	3B	HR	RBI	BB	SO	SB	CS	AVG	OBP	SLG	OPS	OPS+	BR/A	RC	RC/G	FR	G/POS	WS	TPW
1884 Phi-a	7	17	3	3	1	0	0	3	0	....	....	....	.176	.222	.235	.458	46	-1	1	1.79	-1	/C-7	0	-0.1
1885 Phi-a	3	10	0	1	0	0	0	0	0	....	....	....	.100	.100	.100	.200	-35	-2	0	.31	-2	/C-2,O-1	0	-0.3
Total 2	10	27	3	4	1	0	0	3	0	....	....	....	.148	.179	.185	.364	17	-3	1	1.21	-2	/C-9,O-1	0	-0.4

• SIGAFOOS, Frank Francis Leonard Sigafoos b: 3/21/1904, Easton, PA d: 4/12/1968, Indianapolis, IN BR/TR, 5'9", 170 lbs. Deb: 9/3/1926

YEAR TM-L	G	AB	R	H	2B	3B	HR	RBI	BB	SO	SB	CS	AVG	OBP	SLG	OPS	OPS+	BR/A	RC	RC/G	FR	G/POS	WS	TPW
1926 Phi-A	13	43	4	11	0	0	0	2	0	3	0	0	.256	.256	.256	.512	32	-4	3	2.22	0	S-12	0	-0.3
1929 Det-A	14	23	3	4	1	0	0	2	5	4	0	2	.174	.321	.217	.539	41	-3	2	1.90	-2	/3-6,S-5	0	-0.4
Chi-A	7	3	1	1	0	0	0	1	2	1	0	0	.333	.600	.333	.933	148	1	1	8.61	0	/2-6	0	0.0
Yr.	21	26	4	5	1	0	0	3	7	5	0	2	.192	.364	.231	.594	59	-2	3	2.71	-3	/2-6,3-6,S-5	0	-0.4
1931 Cin-N	21	65	6	11	2	0	0	8	0	6	0	....	.169	.182	.200	.382	3	-9	3	1.14	-3	3-15/S-2	0	-1.1
Total 3	55	134	14	27	3	0	0	13	7	14	0	2	.201	.246	.224	.470	25	-15	8	1.79	-6	/3-21,S-19,2-6	0	-1.8

• SIGLIN, Paddy Wesley Peter Siglin b: 9/24/1891, Aurelia, IA d: 8/5/1956, Oakland, CA BR/TR, 5'10", 160 lbs. Deb: 9/12/1914

YEAR TM-L	G	AB	R	H	2B	3B	HR	RBI	BB	SO	SB	CS	AVG	OBP	SLG	OPS	OPS+	BR/A	RC	RC/G	FR	G/POS	WS	TPW
1914 Pit-N	14	39	4	6	0	0	0	2	4	6	1	....	.154	.233	.154	.386	16	-4	2	1.23	-4	2-11	0	-0.8
1915 Pit-N	6	7	1	2	0	0	0	0	1	2	1	....	.286	.375	.286	.661	103	0	1	5.66	0	/2-1	0	0.0
1916 Pit-N	3	4	0	1	0	0	0	0	0	2	0	....	.250	.250	.250	.500	53	-0	0	2.17	0	/2-3	0	-0.1
Total 3	23	50	5	9	0	0	0	2	5	10	2	....	.180	.255	.180	.435	31	-4	3	1.83	-4	/2-15	0	-0.9

• SIGMAN, Tripp Wesley Triplett Sigman b: 1/17/1899, Mooresville, NC d: 3/8/1971, Augusta, GA BL/TR, 6', 180 lbs. Deb: 9/18/1929 Career OF: 8-21-0

YEAR TM-L	G	AB	R	H	2B	3B	HR	RBI	BB	SO	SB	CS	AVG	OBP	SLG	OPS	OPS+	BR/A	RC	RC/G	FR	G/POS	WS	TPW
1929 Phi-N	10	29	8	15	1	0	2	9	3	1	0	....	.517	.563	.759	1.321	210	5	12	22.13	-1	O-10(5-5-0)	2	0.4
1930 Phi-N	52	100	15	27	4	1	4	6	6	9	1	....	.270	.324	.450	.774	79	-4	14	4.99	0	O-19(3-16-0)	1	-0.4
Total 2	62	129	23	42	5	1	6	15	9	10	1	....	.326	.379	.519	.898	109	1	26	7.72	-1	/O-29	3	0.0

• SILBER, Eddie Edward James Silber b: 6/6/1914, Philadelphia, PA d: 10/26/1976, Dunedin, FL BR/TR, 5'11", 170 lbs. Deb: 9/3/1937

YEAR TM-L	G	AB	R	H	2B	3B	HR	RBI	BB	SO	SB	CS	AVG	OBP	SLG	OPS	OPS+	BR/A	RC	RC/G	FR	G/POS	WS	TPW
1937 StL-A	22	83	10	26	2	0	0	4	5	13	0	2	.313	.352	.337	.690	74	-4	9	4.12	-3	O-21(2-6-15)	0	-0.7
1939 StL-A	1	1	0	0	0	0	0	0	0	1	0	0	.000	.000	.000	.000	-98	-0	0	.00	0	....	0	0.0
Total 2	23	84	10	26	2	0	0	4	5	14	0	2	.310	.348	.333	.682	72	-4	9	4.05	-3	/O-21	0	-0.7

• SILCH, Ed Edward "Baldy" Silch b: 2/22/1865, St. Louis, MO d: 1/15/1895, St. Louis, MO TR, 6'2", 180 lbs. Deb: 4/29/1888

YEAR TM-L	G	AB	R	H	2B	3B	HR	RBI	BB	SO	SB	CS	AVG	OBP	SLG	OPS	OPS+	BR/A	RC	RC/G	FR	G/POS	WS	TPW
1888 Bro-a	14	48	5	13	4	0	0	3	4	....	4	....	.271	.327	.354	.681	118	1	7	5.43	-1	O-14(0-6-8)	1	-0.1

• SILVA, Danny Daniel James Silva b: 10/5/1896, Everett, MA d: 4/4/1974, Hyannis, MA BR/TR, 6', 170 lbs. Deb: 8/11/1919

YEAR TM-L	G	AB	R	H	2B	3B	HR	RBI	BB	SO	SB	CS	AVG	OBP	SLG	OPS	OPS+	BR/A	RC	RC/G	FR	G/POS	WS	TPW
1919 Was-A	1	4	0	1	0	0	0	0	0	0	0	....	.250	.250	.250	.500	41	-0	0	1.99	1	/3-1	0	0.1

• SILVERA, Al Aaron Albert Silvera b: 8/26/1935, San Diego, CA d: 7/24/2002, Los Angeles, CA BR/TR, 6', 180 lbs. Deb: 6/12/1955

YEAR TM-L	G	AB	R	H	2B	3B	HR	RBI	BB	SO	SB	CS	AVG	OBP	SLG	OPS	OPS+	BR/A	RC	RC/G	FR	G/POS	WS	TPW
1955 Cin-N	13	7	3	1	0	0	0	2	0	1	0	0	.143	.143	.143	.286	-23	-1	0	.64	0	/O-1	0	-0.1
1956 Cin-N	1	0	0	0	0	0	0	0	0	0	0	0	....	....	....	....	-94	0	0	....	0	....	0	0.0
Total 2	14	7	3	1	0	0	0	2	0	1	0	0	.143	.143	.143	.286	-23	-1	0	.64	0	/O-1	0	-0.1

• SILVERA, Charlie Charles Anthony Ryan "Swede" Silvera b: 10/13/1924, San Francisco, CA BR/TR, 5'10", 175 lbs. Deb: 9/29/1948 C

YEAR TM-L	G	AB	R	H	2B	3B	HR	RBI	BB	SO	SB	CS	AVG	OBP	SLG	OPS	OPS+	BR/A	RC	RC/G	FR	G/POS	WS	TPW
1948 NY-A	4	14	1	8	0	1	0	1	0	1	0	0	.571	.571	.714	1.286	243	3	6	26.36	-0	/C-4	1	0.3
1949*NY-A	58	130	8	41	2	0	0	13	18	5	2	1	.315	.403	.331	.733	95	0	18	5.16	3	C-51	6	0.5
1950 NY-A	18	25	2	4	0	0	0	1	1	2	0	0	.160	.192	.160	.352	-9	-4	1	1.08	-1	C-15	0	-0.4
1951 NY-A	18	51	5	14	3	0	1	7	5	3	0	0	.275	.339	.392	.731	101	0	5	3.18	0	C-18	2	0.1
1952 NY-A	20	55	4	18	3	0	0	11	5	2	0	3	.327	.383	.382	.765	121	0	7	4.76	0	C-20	2	0.1
1953 NY-A	42	82	11	23	3	1	0	12	9	5	0	1	.280	.352	.341	.693	91	-1	11	4.61	1	C-39/3-1	4	0.1
1954 NY-A	20	37	1	10	1	0	0	4	3	2	0	1	.270	.341	.297	.639	79	-1	3	2.87	-1	C-18	1	-0.2

YEAR TM-L	G	AB	R	H	2B	3B	HR	RBI	BB	SO	SB	CS	AVG	OBP	SLG	OPS	OPS+	BR/A	RC	RC/G	FR	G/POS	WS	TPW
1955 NY-A	14	26	1	5	0	0	0	1	6	4	0	0	.192	.344	.192	.536	48	-2	2	2.90	0	C-11	1	-0.1
1956 NY-A	7	9	0	2	0	0	0	0	2	3	0	0	.222	.364	.222	.586	60	-0	1	2.32	-1	/C-7	0	-0.1
1957 Chi-N	26	53	1	11	3	0	0	2	4	5	0	0	.208	.263	.264	.527	43	-4	3	2.10	1	C-26	1	-0.3
Total 10	227	482	34	136	15	2	1	52	53	32	2	6	.282	.356	.328	.683	86	-10	58	4.16	3	C-209/3-1	18	0.0

• SILVERIO, Luis Luis Pascual (Delmonte) Silverio b: 10/23/1956, Villa Gonzalez, Dominican Republic BR/TR, 5'11", 165 lbs. Deb: 9/9/1978

YEAR TM-L	G	AB	R	H	2B	3B	HR	RBI	BB	SO	SB	CS	AVG	OBP	SLG	OPS	OPS+	BR/A	RC	RC/G	FR	G/POS	WS	TPW
1978 KC-A	8	11	7	6	2	1	0	3	2	3	1	1	.545	.615	.909	1.524	315	3	6	22.29	0	/O-6(4-0-2),D-2	1	0.3

• SILVERIO, Tom Tomas Roberto (Veloz) Silverio b: 10/14/1945, Santiago, Dominican Republic BL/TL, 5'10", 170 lbs. Deb: 4/30/1970 Career OF: 3-6-1

YEAR TM-L	G	AB	R	H	2B	3B	HR	RBI	BB	SO	SB	CS	AVG	OBP	SLG	OPS	OPS+	BR/A	RC	RC/G	FR	G/POS	WS	TPW
1970 Cal-A	15	15	1	0	0	0	0	0	2	4	0	1	.000	.118	.000	.118	-67	-4	0	.03	-1	/O-5(1-4-0),1-1	0	-0.5
1971 Cal-A	3	3	0	1	0	0	0	0	0	0	0	0	.333	.333	.333	.667	96	-0	0	4.50	0	/O-1	0	0.0
1972 Cal-A	13	12	1	2	0	0	0	0	0	5	0	0	.167	.167	.167	.333	-1	-1	0	.90	0	/O-4(2-1-1)	0	-0.2
Total 3	31	30	2	3	0	0	0	0	2	9	0	1	.100	.156	.100	.256	-27	-5	1	.66	-1	/O-10,1-1	0	-0.7

• SILVESTRI, Dave David Joseph Silvestri b: 9/29/1967, St. Louis, MO BR/TR, 6', 196 lbs. Deb: 4/27/1992 Career OF: 5-1-0

YEAR TM-L	G	AB	R	H	2B	3B	HR	RBI	BB	SO	SB	CS	AVG	OBP	SLG	OPS	OPS+	BR/A	RC	RC/G	FR	G/POS	WS	TPW
1992 NY-A	7	13	3	4	0	2	0	1	0	3	0	0	.308	.308	.615	.923	154	1	2	4.98	0	/S-6	0	0.1
1993 NY-A	7	21	4	6	1	0	1	4	5	3	0	0	.286	.423	.476	.899	146	2	4	7.33	0	/S-4,3-3	1	0.2
1994 NY-A	12	18	3	2	0	1	1	2	4	9	0	1	.111	.273	.389	.662	71	-1	2	2.79	-1	/2-9,3-2,S-1	0	-0.2
1995 NY-A	17	21	4	2	0	0	1	4	4	9	0	0	.095	.269	.238	.507	34	-2	2	1.95	0	/2-7,1-4,D-4,S-1	1	-0.2
Mon-N	39	72	12	19	6	0	2	7	9	27	2	0	.264	.346	.431	.776	100	0	11	5.26	-2	/S-9,3-8,1-4,2-3,O-3(3-0-0)	2	-0.1
1996 Mon-N	86	162	16	33	4	0	1	17	34	41	2	1	.204	.342	.247	.589	57	-9	15	2.99	0	3-47,S-10/O-2(1-1-0),1-1,2	2	-0.8
1997 Tex-A	2	4	0	0	0	0	0	0	0	1	0	0	.000	.000	.000	.000	-95	-1	0	.00	0	/3-1,S-1	0	-0.1
1998 TB-A	8	14	0	1	0	0	0	0	0	2	0	0	.071	.071	.071	.143	-62	-3	0	.00	0	/3-3,2-2,D-2,S-1	0	-0.4
1999 Ana-A	3	11	0	1	1	0	0	1	0	1	0	0	.091	.091	.182	.273	-33	-2	0	.00	0	/2-1,O-1,S-1	0	-0.2
Total 8	181	336	42	68	12	3	6	36	56	96	4	2	.202	.318	.310	.628	66	-16	36	3.36	-3	/3-64,S-34,2-23,1-9,D-6,O-6	6	-1.6

• SILVESTRI, Ken Kenneth Joseph "Hawk" Silvestri b: 5/3/1916, Chicago, IL d: 3/31/1992, Tallahassee, FL BB/TR, 6'1", 200 lbs. Deb: 4/18/1939 M/C

YEAR TM-L	G	AB	R	H	2B	3B	HR	RBI	BB	SO	SB	CS	AVG	OBP	SLG	OPS	OPS+	BR/A	RC	RC/G	FR	G/POS	WS	TPW
1939 Chi-A	22	75	6	13	3	0	2	5	6	13	0	1	.173	.244	.293	.537	36	-8	6	2.35	0	C-20	1	-0.6
1940 Chi-A	28	24	5	6	2	0	2	10	4	7	0	0	.250	.357	.583	.940	137	1	4	5.94	0	/C-1	1	0.1
1941 NY-A	17	40	6	10	5	0	1	4	7	6	0	0	.250	.362	.450	.812	115	1	7	6.01	0	C-13	2	0.2
1946 NY-A	13	21	4	6	1	0	0	1	3	7	0	0	.286	.375	.333	.708	98	0	3	5.37	0	C-12	1	0.0
1947 NY-A	3	10	0	2	0	0	0	0	2	2	0	0	.200	.333	.200	.533	51	-1	1	2.89	0	/C-3	0	0.0
1949 Phi-N	4	4	1	0	0	0	0	0	2	1	0	....	.000	.333	.000	.333	-3	-0	0	1.17	0	/2-1,C-1,S-1	0	0.0
1950*Phi-N	11	20	2	5	0	1	0	4	4	3	0	....	.250	.400	.350	.750	101	0	3	4.07	0	/C-9	1	0.0
1951 Phi-N	4	9	2	2	0	0	0	1	3	2	0	0	.222	.417	.222	.639	78	-0	1	4.55	-1	/C-3,2-1	0	-0.1
Total 8	102	203	26	44	11	1	5	25	31	41	0	1	.217	.326	.355	.681	79	-6	25	4.01	-1	/C-62,2-2,S-1	6	-0.5

• SIMMONS, Al Aloysius Harry "Bucketfoot Al" Simmons
b: 5/22/1902, Milwaukee, WI d: 5/26/1956, Milwaukee, WI BR/TR, 5'11", 190 lbs. Deb: 4/15/1924 C HOF: 1953 Career OF: 1377-771-1

YEAR TM-L	G	AB	R	H	2B	3B	HR	RBI	BB	SO	SB	CS	AVG	OBP	SLG	OPS	OPS+	BR/A	RC	RC/G	FR	G/POS	WS	TPW
1924 Phi-A	152	594	69	183	31	9	8	102	30	60	16	15	.308	.343	.431	.774	98	-7	84	5.01	2	*O-152(51-101-0)	17	-1.2
1925 Phi-A	153	654	122	**253**	43	12	24	129	35	41	7	14	.387	.419	.599	1.018	146	39	155	9.74	-2	*O-153(0-153-0)	**34**	2.8
1926 Phi-A	147	583	90	199	53	10	19	109	48	49	11	3	.341	.392	.564	.957	139	33	129	8.62	-7	*O-147(0-147-0)	27	1.9
1927 Phi-A	106	406	86	159	36	11	15	108	31	30	10	2	.392	.436	.645	1.081	168	41	113	11.15	-2	*O-105(10-94-1)	26	3.2
1928 Phi-A	119	464	78	163	33	9	15	107	31	30	1	4	.351	.396	.558	.954	144	27	100	8.36	0	*O-114(114-0-0)	23	1.7
1929*Phi-A	143	581	114	212	41	9	34	**157**	31	38	4	2	.365	.398	.642	1.040	158	46	145	9.90	16	*O-142(142-0-0)	**34**	4.9
1930*Phi-A	138	554	**152**	211	41	16	36	165	39	34	9	2	**.381**	.423	.708	1.130	173	60	163	11.90	1	*O-136(129-7-0)	36	4.5
1931*Phi-A	128	513	105	200	37	13	22	128	47	45	3	3	**.390**	.444	.641	1.085	172	54	145	12.13	3	*O-128(125-3-0)	34	4.6
1932 Phi-A	154	670	144	**216**	28	9	35	151	47	76	4	2	.322	.368	.548	.915	129	26	134	7.77	-7	*O-154(154-1-0)	24	0.9
1933 Chi-A★	146	605	85	200	29	10	14	119	39	49	5	1	.331	.373	.481	.854	130	25	109	7.05	12	*O-145(144-1-0)	25	2.7
1934 Chi-A★	138	558	102	192	36	7	18	104	53	58	3	2	.344	.403	.530	.933	135	28	120	8.62	4	*O-138(136-2-0)	23	2.3
1935 Chi-A★	128	525	68	140	22	7	16	79	33	43	4	6	.267	.313	.427	.739	87	-14	68	4.61	1	*O-126(11-115-0)	13	-1.6
1936 Det-A	143	568	96	186	38	6	13	112	49	35	6	4	.327	.383	.484	.867	112	9	105	7.21	-4	*O-138(7-134-0)/1-1	20	0.1
1937 Was-A	103	419	60	117	21	10	8	84	27	35	3	2	.279	.329	.434	.763	95	-5	60	5.16	3	*O-102(98-4-0)	11	-0.7
1938 Was-A	125	470	79	142	23	6	21	95	38	40	2	1	.302	.357	.511	.868	123	14	86	6.86	-3	*O-117(112-8-0)	16	0.5
1939 Bos-N	93	330	39	93	17	5	7	43	22	40	0	....	.282	.331	.427	.758	110	3	43	4.61	4	O-82(81-1-0)	9	0.3
*Cin-N	9	21	0	3	0	0	0	1	2	3	0	....	.143	.217	.143	.360	-1	-3	1	1.15	1	/O-5(5-0-0)	0	-0.2
Yr.	102	351	39	96	17	5	7	44	24	43	0	....	.274	.324	.410	.734	103	0	44	4.38	5	O-87(86-1-0)	9	0.1
1940 Phi-A	37	81	7	25	4	0	1	19	4	8	0	0	.309	.341	.395	.736	92	-1	10	4.48	1	O-18(18-0-0)	2	-0.1
1941 Phi-A	9	24	1	3	1	0	0	1	1	2	0	0	.125	.160	.167	.327	-14	-4	0	.41	0	/O-5(5-0-0)	0	-0.4
1943 Bos-A	40	133	9	27	5	0	1	12	8	21	0	1	.203	.248	.263	.511	49	-9	8	2.05	0	O-33(33-0-0)	1	-1.2
1944 Phi-A	4	6	1	3	0	0	0	2	0	0	0	0	.500	.500	.500	1.000	189	1	1	6.92	0	/O-2(2-0-0)	0	0.1
Total 20	2215	8759	1507	2927	539	149	307	1827	615	737	88	64	.334	.380	.535	.915	131	364	1777	7.82	23	*O-2142/1-1	375	25.3

• SIMMONS, Brian Brian Lee Simmons b: 9/4/1973, Lebanon, PA BB/TR, 6'2", 190 lbs. Deb: 9/21/1998 Career OF: 49-27-16

YEAR TM-L	G	AB	R	H	2B	3B	HR	RBI	BB	SO	SB	CS	AVG	OBP	SLG	OPS	OPS+	BR/A	RC	RC/G	FR	G/POS	WS	TPW
1998 Chi-A	5	19	4	7	0	0	2	6	0	2	0	1	.368	.368	.684	1.053	170	1	4	8.53	0	/O-5(2-4-0)	2	0.1
1999 Chi-A	54	126	14	29	3	3	4	17	9	30	4	0	.230	.281	.397	.678	70	-5	14	3.81	0	O-46(28-11-9)/D-3	2	-0.6
2001 Tor-A	60	107	8	19	5	0	2	8	8	26	1	0	.178	.241	.280	.522	36	-10	8	2.42	2	O-37(19-12-7)/D-1	1	-0.8
Total 3	119	252	26	55	8	3	8	31	17	58	5	1	.218	.270	.369	.639	63	-14	26	3.50	2	/O-88,D-4	5	-1.3

• SIMMONS, Hack George Washington Simmons b: 1/29/1885, Brooklyn, NY d: 4/26/1942, Arverne, NY BR/TR, 5'8", 179 lbs. Deb: 4/15/1910 Career OF: 74-1-13

YEAR TM-L	G	AB	R	H	2B	3B	HR	RBI	BB	SO	SB	CS	AVG	OBP	SLG	OPS	OPS+	BR/A	RC	RC/G	FR	G/POS	WS	TPW
1910 Det-A	42	110	12	25	3	1	0	9	10	....	1	....	.227	.303	.273	.576	75	-3	10	2.81	0	1-22/3-7,O-2(0-1-1)	2	-0.4
1912 NY-A	110	401	45	96	17	2	0	41	33	....	19	....	.239	.308	.292	.600	68	-17	41	3.44	-19	2-88,1-13/S-4	4	-3.4
1914 Bal-F	114	352	50	95	16	5	1	38	32	26	7	....	.270	.341	.352	.693	98	-0	43	4.16	-2	O-73(61-0-12),2-26/1-4,S-2,3	9	-0.5
1915 Bal-F	39	88	8	18	7	1	1	14	10	9	1	....	.205	.293	.341	.634	80	-2	9	3.18	-2	2-13,O-13(13-0-0)	1	-0.5
Total 4	305	951	115	234	43	9	2	102	85	35	28	....	.246	.318	.317	.635	81	-22	103	3.60	-23	2-127/O-88,1-39,3-8,S-6	16	-4.8

• SIMMONS, Joe Joseph S. Simmons b: 6/13/1845, New York, NY d: 7/24/1901, Jersey City, NJ, 5'9", 166 lbs. Deb: 5/8/1871 M/U NA OF: 1-18-20

YEAR TM-L	G	AB	R	H	2B	3B	HR	RBI	BB	SO	SB	CS	AVG	OBP	SLG	OPS	OPS+	BR/A	RC	RC/G	FR	G/POS	WS	TPW
1871 Chi-n	27	129	29	28	6	1	0	17	1	0	4	1	.217	.223	.279	.502	39	-12	9	2.82	1	*O-25(0-9-17)/1-2	....	-0.7
1872 Cle-n	18	90	11	23	5	1	0	9	1	2	1	0	.256	.264	.333	.597	87	-1	8	3.88	-1	1-15/O-3(1-0-2)	....	-0.1
1875 Wes-n	13	53	5	9	1	0	0	4	0	2	1	2	.170	.170	.189	.358	23	-5	2	1.23	-1	O-10(0-9-1)/1-3	....	-0.5
Total 3 n	58	272	45	60	12	2	0	30	2	4	6	3	.221	.226	.279	.506	52	-17	19	2.81	-1	/O-38,1-20	....	-1.3

• SIMMONS, John John Earl Simmons b: 7/7/1924, Birmingham, AL BR/TR, 6'1.5", 192 lbs. Deb: 4/22/1949

YEAR TM-L	G	AB	R	H	2B	3B	HR	RBI	BB	SO	SB	CS	AVG	OBP	SLG	OPS	OPS+	BR/A	RC	RC/G	FR	G/POS	WS	TPW
1949 Was-A	62	93	12	20	0	0	0	5	11	6	0	0	.215	.298	.215	.513	38	-8	6	2.12	-1	O-26(18-0-8)	0	-1.0

• SIMMONS, Nelson Nelson Bernard Simmons b: 6/27/1963, Washington, DC BB/TR, 6'1", 185 lbs. Deb: 9/4/1984 Career OF: 27-0-30

YEAR TM-L	G	AB	R	H	2B	3B	HR	RBI	BB	SO	SB	CS	AVG	OBP	SLG	OPS	OPS+	BR/A	RC	RC/G	FR	G/POS	WS	TPW
1984 Det-A	9	30	4	13	2	0	0	3	2	5	1	0	.433	.469	.500	.969	169	3	6	9.11	0	/O-5(2-0-4),D-4	2	0.3
1985 Det-A	75	251	31	60	11	0	10	33	26	41	1	0	.239	.310	.402	.713	94	-2	32	4.32	-1	O-38(25-0-13),D-31	4	-0.6
1987 Bal-A	16	49	3	13	1	1	1	4	3	8	0	1	.265	.308	.388	.695	85	-2	5	2.97	1	O-13(0-0-13)/D-1	0	-0.1
Total 3	100	330	38	86	14	1	11	40	31	54	2	1	.261	.324	.409	.733	99	-1	43	4.45	0	/O-56,D-36	6	-0.4

• SIMMONS, Ted Ted Lyle Simmons b: 8/9/1949, Highland Park, MI BB/TR, 5'11", 200 lbs. Deb: 9/21/1968 Career OF: 37-0-3

YEAR TM-L	G	AB	R	H	2B	3B	HR	RBI	BB	SO	SB	CS	AVG	OBP	SLG	OPS	OPS+	BR/A	RC	RC/G	FR	G/POS	WS	TPW
1968 StL-N	2	3	0	1	0	0	0	0	1	1	0	0	.333	.500	.333	.833	156	0	1	8.51	0	/C-2	0	0.0
1969 StL-N	5	14	0	3	0	1	0	3	1	1	0	0	.214	.267	.357	.624	73	-1	1	3.25	-1	/C-4	0	-0.2
1970 StL-N	82	284	29	69	8	2	3	24	37	37	2	2	.243	.334	.317	.651	74	-10	31	3.79	-1	C-79	6	-0.7
1971 StL-N	133	510	64	155	32	4	7	77	36	50	1	3	.304	.353	.424	.777	115	9	71	4.88	-5	*C-130	20	1.1
1972 StL-N★	152	594	70	180	36	6	16	96	29	57	1	3	.303	.338	.465	.802	127	17	86	5.29	7	*C-135,1-15	23	3.2
1973 StL-N★	161	619	62	192	36	2	13	91	61	47	2	2	.310	.374	.438	.812	125	21	94	5.43	4	*C-153/1-6,O-2(0-0-2)	28	3.3
1974 StL-N★	152	599	66	163	33	6	20	103	47	35	0	0	.272	.331	.447	.779	117	11	83	4.82	-2	*C-141,1-12	21	1.6
1975 StL-N	157	581	80	193	32	3	18	100	63	35	1	3	.332	.398	.491	.889	141	31	108	7.04	-7	*C-154/1-2,O-2(2-0-0)	28	3.3
1976 StL-N	150	546	60	159	35	3	5	75	73	35	0	7	.291	.375	.394	.769	117	12	80	5.30	1	*C-113,1-30/O-7(7-0-0),3-2	20	1.6

YEAR TM-L	G	AB	R	H	2B	3B	HR	RBI	BB	SO	SB	CS	AVG	OBP	SLG	OPS	OPS+	BR/A	RC	RC/G	FR	G/POS	WS	TPW
1977 StL-N★	150	516	82	164	25	3	21	95	79	37	2	6	.318	.410	.500	.910	145	34	100	7.10	-7	*C-143/0-1	28	3.4
1978 StL-N★	152	516	71	148	40	5	22	80	77	39	1	1	.287	.383	.512	.894	150	35	98	6.69	4	*C-134,0-23(23-0-0)	30	**4.6**
1979 StL-N★	123	448	68	127	22	0	26	87	61	34	0	1	.283	.374	.507	.881	137	23	84	6.69	-4	*C-122	20	2.6
1980 StL-N	145	495	84	150	33	2	21	98	59	45	1	0	.303	.379	.505	.885	140	27	94	6.95	-2	*C-129/0-5(5-0-0)	22	3.3
1981*Mil-A★	100	380	45	82	13	3	14	61	23	32	0	1	.216	.266	.376	.642	88	-8	36	3.07	0	C-75,D-22/1-4	8	-0.5
1982*Mil-A	137	539	73	145	29	0	23	97	32	40	0	0	.269	.312	.451	.763	114	8	70	4.46	3	*C-121,D-15	19	1.6
1983 Mil-A★	153	600	76	185	39	3	13	108	41	51	4	2	.308	.355	.448	.803	129	22	89	5.36	-1	C-86,D-66	20	2.3
1984 Mil-A	132	497	44	110	23	2	4	52	30	40	3	0	.221	.270	.300	.570	60	-27	36	2.36	-4	D-77,1-37,3-14	1	-3.6
1985 Mil-A	143	528	60	144	28	2	12	76	57	32	1	1	.273	.345	.402	.746	104	3	71	4.70	-1	D-99,1-28,C-15/3-2	13	-0.2
1986 Atl-N	76	127	14	32	5	0	4	25	12	14	1	0	.252	.321	.386	.707	89	-2	16	4.43	-3	1-14,C-10/3-9	3	-0.5
1987 Atl-N	73	177	20	49	8	0	4	30	21	23	1	1	.277	.354	.390	.743	92	-2	24	4.86	3	1-28,C-15/3-2	4	0.0
1988 Atl-N	78	107	6	21	6	0	2	11	15	9	0	0	.196	.295	.308	.603	70	-4	10	2.85	-1	1-19,C-10	1	-0.6
Total 21	2456	8680	1074	2472	483	47	248	1389	855	694	21	33	.285	.352	.437	.789	118	201	1284	5.22	-16	*C-1771,D-279,1-195/0-40,3	315	25.8
• SIMMS, Mike	Michael Howard Simms b: 1/12/1967, Orange, CA BR/TR, 6'4", 185 lbs. Deb: 9/5/1990 Career OF: 15-0-126																							
1990 Hou-N	12	13	3	4	1	0	1	2	0	4	0	0	.308	.308	.615	.923	152	1	2	4.98	0	/1-6	0	0.1
1991 Hou-N	49	123	18	25	5	0	3	16	18	38	1	0	.203	.305	.317	.622	80	-3	13	3.43	0	0-41(1-0-41)	2	-0.4
1992 Hou-N	15	24	1	6	1	0	1	3	2	9	0	0	.250	.333	.417	.750	116	1	3	4.54	1	/0-9(0-0-9),1-1	0	0.1
1994 Hou-N	6	12	1	1	1	0	0	0	0	5	1	0	.083	.083	.167	.250	-39	-2	0	.52	0	/0-3(0-0-3)	0	-0.3
1995 Hou-N	50	121	14	31	4	0	9	24	13	28	1	2	.256	.343	.512	.855	131	4	20	5.75	-2	1-25,0-12(0-0-12)	4	0.0
1996 Hou-N	49	68	6	12	2	1	1	8	4	16	1	0	.176	.233	.279	.512	37	-6	5	2.16	0	0-12(9-0-3)/1-5	1	-0.7
1997 Tex-A	59	111	13	28	8	0	5	22	8	27	0	1	.252	.303	.459	.762	90	-2	14	4.32	-1	D-28,0-19(2-0-17)/1-2	3	-0.5
1998*Tex-A	86	186	36	55	11	0	16	46	24	47	0	1	.296	.385	.613	.998	148	13	44	8.55	-1	0-43(3-0-40),D-26,1-16	8	0.8
1999 Tex-A	4	2	0	1	0	0	0	0	0	1	0	0	.500	.500	.500	1.000	150	0	1	13.50	0	/D-2,1-1,0-1	0	0.0
Total 9	330	660	92	163	33	1	36	121	69	175	4	4	.247	.326	.464	.789	107	5	102	5.25	-4	0-140/1-56,D-56	18	-0.9
• SIMON, Hank	Henry Joseph Simon b: 8/25/1862, Hawkinsville, NY d: 1/1/1925, Albany, NY BR/TR, 5'6", 155 lbs. Deb: 10/7/1887 Career OF: 128-2-0																							
1887 Cle-a	3	10	1	1	0	0	0	0	0	....	0	....	.100	.100	.100	.200	-45	-2	0	.31	-0	/0-3(3-0-0)	0	-0.2
1890 Bro-a	89	373	66	96	17	11	0	38	34	....	23	....	.257	.323	.362	.685	105	2	52	5.00	5	0-89(89-0-0)	9	0.3
Syr-a	38	156	33	47	5	3	2	23	17	....	12	....	.301	.370	.410	.780	145	9	29	7.01	-3	0-38(36-2-0)	6	0.4
Yr.	127	529	99	143	22	14	2	61	51	....	35	....	.270	.337	.376	.713	117	11	81	5.57	2	*0-127(125-2-0)	15	0.8
Total 2	130	539	100	144	22	14	2	61	51	....	35	....	.267	.333	.371	.704	114	9	81	5.45	2	0-130	15	0.6
• SIMON, Mike	Michael Edward Simon b: 4/13/1883, Hayden, IN d: 6/10/1963, Los Angeles, CA BR/TR, 5'11", 188 lbs. Deb: 6/27/1909																							
1909 Pit-N	12	18	2	3	0	0	0	2	1	....	0	....	.167	.211	.167	.377	16	-2	1	1.27	-2	/C-9	0	-0.3
1910 Pit-N	22	50	3	10	0	1	0	5	1	2	1	....	.200	.216	.240	.456	31	-5	3	1.72	-1	C-14	1	-0.5
1911 Pit-N	71	215	19	49	4	3	0	22	10	14	1	....	.228	.275	.274	.550	52	-14	16	2.49	-6	C-68	4	-1.5
1912 Pit-N	42	113	10	34	2	1	0	11	5	9	1	....	.301	.331	.336	.667	84	-3	12	4.02	-2	C-40	4	-0.2
1913 Pit-N	92	255	23	63	6	2	1	17	10	15	3	....	.247	.281	.298	.579	68	-11	21	2.75	8	C-92	7	0.4
1914 StL-F	93	276	21	57	11	2	0	21	18	21	2	....	.207	.263	.261	.523	46	-20	19	2.14	5	C-78	4	-0.9
1915 Bro-F	47	142	7	25	5	1	0	12	9	12	1	....	.176	.225	.225	.451	33	-12	7	1.55	1	C-45	1	-0.9
Total 7	379	1069	85	241	28	10	1	90	54	73	9	....	.225	.269	.273	.542	53	-66	80	2.40	3	C-346	21	-3.8
• SIMON, Randall	Randall Carlito Simon b: 5/26/1975, Willemstad, Curacao BL/TL, 6', 180 lbs. Deb: 9/1/1997																							
1997 Atl-N	13	14	2	6	1	0	0	1	1	2	0	0	.429	.467	.500	.967	150	1	3	8.71	0	/1-6	1	0.1
1998 Atl-N	7	16	2	3	0	0	0	4	0	1	0	0	.188	.188	.188	.375	-1	-2	1	1.20	-1	/1-4	0	-0.3
1999 Atl-N	90	218	26	69	16	0	5	25	17	25	2	2	.317	.369	.459	.827	108	2	33	5.52	-1	1-70	4	-0.4
2001 Det-A	81	256	28	78	14	2	6	37	15	28	0	1	.305	.343	.445	.788	110	3	36	5.09	-1	1-43,D-27	7	-0.3
2002 Det-A	130	482	51	145	17	1	19	82	13	30	0	1	.301	.325	.459	.783	111	5	67	5.02	-4	D-65,1-59	12	-0.8
2003 Pit-N	91	307	34	84	14	0	10	51	12	30	0	0	.274	.305	.417	.722	84	-8	38	4.44	-0	1-80	6	-1.4
*Chi-N	33	103	13	29	3	0	6	21	4	7	0	0	.282	.321	.485	.807	108	1	16	5.69	2	1-29	5	0.0
Yr.	124	410	47	113	17	0	16	72	16	37	0	0	.276	.309	.434	.743	90	-7	54	4.75	1	*1-109	11	-1.4
Total 6	445	1396	156	414	65	3	46	221	62	123	2	4	.297	.331	.446	.777	104	1	193	5.01	-5	1-291/D-92	35	-3.2
• SIMON, Syl	Sylvester Adam "Sammy" Simon b: 12/14/1897, Evansville, IN d: 2/28/1973, Chandler, IN BR/TR, 5'10.5", 170 lbs. Deb: 10/1/1923																							
1923 StL-A	1	1	0	0	0	0	0	0	0	0	0	0	.000	.000	.000	.000	-95	-0	0	.00	0	....	0	0.0
1924 StL-A	23	32	5	8	1	1	0	6	3	5	0	0	.250	.314	.344	.658	66	-2	4	3.92	-1	/3-6,S-5	1	-0.2
Total 2	24	33	5	8	1	1	0	6	3	5	0	0	.242	.306	.333	.639	61	-2	4	3.77	-1	/3-6,S-5	1	-0.2
• SIMONS, Mel	Melbern Ellis "Butch" Simons b: 7/1/1900, Carlyle, IL d: 11/10/1974, Paducah, KY BL/TR, 5'10", 175 lbs. Deb: 4/14/1931 Career OF: 19-47-0																							
1931 Chi-A	68	189	24	52	9	0	0	12	12	17	1	1	.275	.318	.323	.641	73	-7	20	3.63	-1	0-59(15-45-0)	3	-0.8
1932 Chi-A	7	5	0	0	0	0	0	0	0	1	0	0	.000	.000	.000	.000	-107	-1	0	.00	-1	/0-6(4-2-0)	0	-0.2
Total 2	75	194	24	52	9	0	0	12	12	18	1	1	.268	.311	.314	.625	69	-8	20	3.51	-2	/0-65	3	-1.0
• SIMPSON, Dick	Richard Charles Simpson b: 7/28/1943, Washington, DC BR/TR, 6'4", 176 lbs. Deb: 9/21/1962 Career OF: 31-72-113																							
1962 LA-A	6	8	1	2	1	0	0	1	2	3	0	0	.250	.400	.375	.775	114	0	1	6.34	0	/0-4(4-0-1)	0	0.0
1964 LA-A	21	50	11	7	1	0	2	4	8	15	2	2	.140	.259	.280	.539	55	-3	4	2.08	0	0-16(0-16-0)	0	-0.4
1965 Cal-A	8	27	2	6	1	0	0	3	2	8	1	0	.222	.276	.259	.535	54	-1	2	2.34	-1	/0-8(0-8-0)	0	-0.2
1966 Cin-N	92	84	26	20	2	0	4	14	10	32	0	1	.238	.333	.405	.738	95	-1	12	4.81	-4	0-64(9-10-46)	2	-0.6
1967 Cin-N	44	54	8	14	3	0	1	6	7	11	0	1	.259	.344	.370	.715	94	-1	7	4.25	0	0-26(1-4-21)	2	-0.2
1968 StL-N	26	56	11	13	0	0	3	8	8	21	0	1	.232	.328	.393	.721	117	1	7	4.13	0	0-22(0-0-22)	2	0.0
Hou-N	59	177	25	33	7	2	3	11	20	61	4	4	.186	.284	.299	.583	77	-5	15	2.77	-2	0-49(13-16-23)	3	-1.1
Yr.	85	233	36	46	7	2	6	19	28	82	4	5	.197	.294	.322	.616	86	-4	23	3.09	-2	0-71(13-16-45)	5	-1.1
1969 NY-A	6	11	2	3	2	0	0	4	3	6	0	0	.273	.429	.455	.883	153	1	2	8.36	1	/0-5(3-2-0)	1	0.1
Sea-A	26	51	8	9	2	0	2	5	4	17	3	1	.176	.236	.333	.570	59	-3	4	2.14	-1	0-17(1-16-0)	0	-0.4
Yr.	32	62	10	12	4	0	2	9	7	23	3	1	.194	.275	.355	.630	78	-2	6	3.08	0	0-22(4-18-0)	1	-0.2
Total 7	288	518	94	107	19	2	15	56	64	174	10	10	.207	.301	.338	.639	84	-12	54	3.37	-7	0-211	10	-2.8
• SIMPSON, Harry	Harry Leon "Suitcase,Goody" Simpson b: 12/3/1925, Atlanta, GA d: 4/3/1979, Akron, OH BL/TR, 6'1", 180 lbs. Deb: 4/21/1951 Career OF: 44-136-415																							
1951 Cle-A	122	332	51	76	7	0	7	24	45	48	6	4	.229	.325	.313	.638	77	-10	36	3.63	-3	0-68(5-8-58),1-50	6	-1.6
1952 Cle-A	146	545	66	145	21	10	10	65	56	82	5	3	.266	.337	.396	.733	111	7	75	4.89	-3	*0-127(0-11-117),1-28	18	0.0
1953 Cle-A	82	242	25	55	3	1	7	22	18	27	0	0	.227	.284	.335	.618	68	-11	23	3.18	-5	0-69(1-7-62)/1-2	3	-1.8
1955 Cle-A	3	1	1	0	0	0	0	0	2	0	0	0	.000	.667	.000	.667	88	0	0	9.36	0	....	0	0.0
KC-A	112	396	42	119	16	7	5	52	34	61	3	5	.301	.359	.414	.773	106	2	57	5.15	-5	*0-100(4-91-10)/1-3	12	-0.8
Yr.	115	397	43	119	16	7	5	52	36	61	3	5	.300	.361	.413	.774	106	2	57	5.17	-5	*0-100(4-91-10)/1-3	12	-0.8
1956 KC-A★	141	543	76	159	22	**11**	21	105	47	82	2	3	.293	.350	.490	.840	119	12	87	5.70	-10	*0-111(0-19-96),1-32	14	-0.4
1957 KC-A	50	179	24	53	9	6	6	24	12	28	0	0	.296	.340	.514	.854	128	6	28	5.47	2	1-27,0-21(0-0-21)	6	0.6
*NY-A	75	224	27	56	7	3	7	39	19	36	1	0	.250	.309	.402	.710	94	-2	27	4.13	-1	0-42(16-0-26),1-21	6	-0.6
Yr.	125	403	51	109	16	**9**	13	63	31	64	1	1	.270	.323	.452	.774	109	4	55	4.71	1	0-63(16-0-47),1-48	12	0.0
1958 NY-A	24	51	1	11	2	1	0	6	6	12	0	0	.216	.310	.294	.604	70	-2	5	3.25	0	0-15(8-0-9)	1	-0.3
KC-A	78	212	21	56	7	1	7	27	26	33	0	2	.264	.345	.406	.750	104	1	31	5.16	-3	1-43,0-11(9-0-2)	7	-0.5
Yr.	102	263	22	67	9	2	7	33	32	45	0	2	.255	.338	.384	.722	97	-1	36	4.77	-3	1-43,0-26(17-0-11)	8	-0.8
1959 KC-A	8	14	1	4	0	0	1	2	2	4	0	0	.286	.412	.500	.912	146	1	3	7.92	-0	/1-4	1	0.1
Chi-A	38	75	5	14	5	1	2	13	4	14	0	0	.187	.228	.360	.588	60	-5	6	2.63	-1	0-12(0-0-12)/1-1	1	-0.7
Yr.	46	89	6	18	5	1	3	15	6	18	0	0	.202	.260	.382	.642	76	-4	9	3.43	-1	0-12(0-0-12)/1-5	2	-0.6
Pit-N	9	15	3	4	2	0	0	2	0	2	0	0	.267	.267	.400	.667	75	-1	2	3.93	0	/0-3(1-0-2)	0	-0.1
Total 8	888	2829	343	752	101	41	73	381	271	429	17	18	.266	.332	.408	.740	101	-2	380	4.68	-29	0-579,1-211	75	-6.0
• SIMPSON, Joe	Joe Allen Simpson b: 12/31/1951, Purcell, OK BL/TL, 6'3", 175 lbs. Deb: 9/2/1975 Career OF: 100-226-198																							
1975 LA-N	9	6	3	2	0	0	0	0	0	2	0	0	.333	.333	.333	.667	89	-0	1	4.50	0	/0-6(0-6-0)	0	0.0

YEAR TM-L	G	AB	R	H	2B	3B	HR	RBI	BB	SO	SB	CS	AVG	OBP	SLG	OPS	OPS+	BR/A	RC	RC/G	FR	G/POS	WS	TPW
1976 LA-N	23	30	2	4	1	0	0	0	1	6	0	1	.133	.161	.167	.328	-7	-5	1	.68	0	0-20(5-6-9)	0	-0.6
1977 LA-N	29	23	2	4	0	0	0	1	2	6	1	1	.174	.240	.174	.414	13	-3	1	1.04	0	0-28(5-7-16)/1-1	0	-0.4
1978 LA-N	10	5	1	2	0	0	0	1	0	2	0	0	.400	.400	.400	.800	125	0	1	7.20	0	0-10(3-2-6)	0	0.0
1979 Sea-A	120	265	29	75	11	0	2	27	11	21	6	3	.283	.314	.347	.661	77	-9	28	3.72	4	*0-105(27-5-73)/D-3	3	-0.9
1980 Sea-A	129	365	42	91	15	3	3	34	28	43	17	4	.249	.305	.332	.636	73	-11	39	3.51	1	*0-119(24-36-63)/1-3	5	-1.5
1981 Sea-A	91	288	32	64	11	3	2	30	15	41	12	3	.222	.263	.302	.565	60	-14	24	2.73	-1	0-88(0-86-2)	2	-1.7
1982 Sea-A	105	296	39	76	14	4	2	23	22	48	8	14	.257	.313	.351	.664	80	-13	30	3.42	0	0-97(32-59-10)	5	-1.5
1983 KC-A	91	119	16	20	2	2	0	8	11	21	1	1	.168	.250	.218	.468	30	-11	7	1.84	2	1-54,0-38(4-19-19)/P-2,D-1	1	-1.1
Total 9	**607**	**1397**	**166**	**338**	**54**	**12**	**9**	**124**	**90**	**190**	**45**	**27**	**.242**	**.291**	**.317**	**.608**	**66**	**-65**	**132**	**3.12**	**5**	**0-511/1-58,D-4,P-2**	**16**	**-7.6**

• SIMPSON, Marty Martin Simpson b: Baltimore, MD Deb: 5/14/1873

YEAR TM-L	G	AB	R	H	2B	3B	HR	RBI	BB	SO	SB	CS	AVG	OBP	SLG	OPS	OPS+	BR/A	RC	RC/G	FR	G/POS	WS	TPW
1873 Mar-n	4	15	4	2	0	0	0	2	0	0	0	0	.133	.133	.133	.267	-27	-2	0	.64	0	/2-3,C-1	....	-0.1

• SIMS, Duke Duane B. Sims b: 6/5/1941, Salt Lake City, UT BL/TR, 6'2", 205 lbs. Deb: 9/22/1964 Career OF: 35-0-19

YEAR TM-L	G	AB	R	H	2B	3B	HR	RBI	BB	SO	SB	CS	AVG	OBP	SLG	OPS	OPS+	BR/A	RC	RC/G	FR	G/POS	WS	TPW
1964 Cle-A	2	6	0	0	0	0	0	0	0	2	0	0	.000	.000	.000	.000	-101	-2	0	.00	1	/C-1	0	-0.1
1965 Cle-A	48	118	9	21	0	0	6	15	15	33	0	0	.178	.271	.331	.601	69	-5	11	2.95	1	C-40	3	-0.3
1966 Cle-A	52	133	12	35	2	2	6	19	11	31	0	1	.263	.338	.444	.781	123	4	19	5.15	-3	C-48	5	0.3
1967 Cle-A	88	272	25	55	8	2	12	37	30	64	3	3	.202	.295	.379	.674	97	-1	30	3.58	1	C-85	10	0.4
1968 Cle-A	122	361	48	90	21	0	11	44	62	68	1	3	.249	.367	.399	.766	134	17	54	5.18	2	C-84,1-31/0-4(2-0-2)	18	2.3
1969 Cle-A	114	326	40	77	8	0	18	45	66	80	1	2	.236	.374	.426	.801	119	11	57	6.08	5	*C-102/0-3(2-0-1),1-1	17	2.1
1970 Cle-A	110	345	46	91	12	0	23	56	46	59	0	4	.264	.360	.499	.859	128	12	63	6.40	1	C-39,0-36(26-0-10),1-29	12	1.1
1971 LA-N	90	230	23	63	7	2	6	25	30	39	0	1	.274	.360	.400	.760	122	7	34	5.21	2	C-74	11	1.3
1972 LA-N	51	151	7	29	7	0	2	11	17	23	0	0	.192	.278	.278	.556	60	-8	11	2.35	-2	C-48	2	-0.8
*Det-A	38	98	11	31	4	0	4	19	19	18	0	0	.316	.432	.480	.912	166	9	22	8.45	-1	C-25/0-4(0-0-4)	8	1.0
1973 Det-A	80	252	31	61	10	0	8	30	30	36	1	2	.242	.327	.377	.704	92	-3	32	4.22	3	C-68/0-6(5-0-1)	9	0.3
NY-A	4	9	3	3	0	0	1	1	3	1	0	0	.333	.500	.667	1.167	234	2	3	15.26	1	/D-2,C-1	1	0.3
Yr.	84	261	34	64	10	0	9	31	33	37	1	2	.245	.334	.387	.721	98	-1	35	4.54	3	C-69/0-6(5-0-1),D-2	10	0.6
1974 NY-A	5	15	1	2	1	0	0	2	1	5	0	0	.133	.188	.200	.388	12	-2	1	1.27	-0	/D-3,C-1	0	-0.2
Tex-A	39	106	7	22	0	0	3	6	8	24	0	0	.208	.282	.292	.575	67	-4	9	2.66	1	C-30/D-2,0-1	2	-0.2
Yr.	44	121	8	24	1	0	3	8	9	29	0	0	.198	.271	.281	.552	61	-6	9	2.48	1	C-31/D-5,0-1	2	-0.4
Total 11	**843**	**2422**	**263**	**580**	**80**	**6**	**100**	**310**	**338**	**483**	**6**	**16**	**.239**	**.341**	**.401**	**.742**	**111**	**36**	**346**	**4.87**	**11**	**C-646/1-61,0-54,D-7**	**98**	**7.6**

• SIMS, Greg Gregory Emmett Sims b: 6/28/1946, San Francisco, CA BB/TR, 6', 190 lbs. Deb: 4/15/1966

YEAR TM-L	G	AB	R	H	2B	3B	HR	RBI	BB	SO	SB	CS	AVG	OBP	SLG	OPS	OPS+	BR/A	RC	RC/G	FR	G/POS	WS	TPW
1966 Hou-N	7	6	1	1	0	0	0	0	1	3	0	0	.167	.286	.167	.452	32	-1	0	1.94	0	/0-1	0	-0.1

• SINATRO, Matt Matthew Stephen Sinatro b: 3/22/1960, Hartford, CT BR/TR, 5'9", 175 lbs. Deb: 9/22/1981 C

YEAR TM-L	G	AB	R	H	2B	3B	HR	RBI	BB	SO	SB	CS	AVG	OBP	SLG	OPS	OPS+	BR/A	RC	RC/G	FR	G/POS	WS	TPW
1981 Atl-N	12	32	4	9	1	1	0	4	5	4	1	0	.281	.378	.375	.753	111	1	5	6.02	2	C-12	2	0.3
1982 Atl-N	37	81	10	11	2	0	1	4	4	9	0	1	.136	.176	.198	.374	4	-11	2	.81	3	C-35	2	-0.8
1983 Atl-N	7	12	0	2	0	0	0	2	2	1	0	0	.167	.286	.167	.452	26	-1	1	1.94	0	/C-7	0	-0.1
1984 Atl-N	2	4	0	0	0	0	0	0	0	0	0	0	.000	.000	.000	.000	-93	-1	0	.00	0	/C-2	0	-0.1
1987 Oak-A	6	3	0	0	0	0	0	0	0	1	0	0	.000	.000	.000	.000	-107	-1	0	.00	-2	/C-6	0	-0.3
1988 Oak-A	10	9	1	3	2	0	0	5	0	1	0	0	.333	.333	.556	.889	149	0	1	1.66	0	/C-9	1	0.1
1989 Det-A	13	25	2	3	0	0	0	1	1	3	0	0	.120	.185	.120	.305	-13	-4	1	.61	-0	C-13	0	-0.3
1990 Sea-A	30	50	2	15	1	0	0	4	4	10	1	0	.300	.352	.320	.672	88	-0	5	3.53	1	C-28	2	0.2
1991 Sea-A	5	8	1	2	0	0	0	1	1	1	0	0	.250	.333	.250	.583	64	-0	1	3.39	0	/C-5	1	0.0
1992 Sea-A	18	28	0	3	0	0	0	0	0	5	0	0	.107	.107	.107	.214	-40	-5	0	.22	0	C-18	0	-0.5
Total 10	**140**	**252**	**20**	**48**	**6**	**1**	**1**	**21**	**17**	**35**	**2**	**1**	**.190**	**.244**	**.234**	**.479**	**36**	**-22**	**16**	**1.89**	**4**	**C-135**	**8**	**-1.4**

• SINER, Hosea Hosea John Siner b: 3/20/1885, Shelburn, IN d: 6/10/1948, Sullivan, IN BR/TR, 5'10.5", 185 lbs. Deb: 7/28/1909

YEAR TM-L	G	AB	R	H	2B	3B	HR	RBI	BB	SO	SB	CS	AVG	OBP	SLG	OPS	OPS+	BR/A	RC	RC/G	FR	G/POS	WS	TPW
1909 Bos-N	10	23	1	3	0	0	0	1	2	....	0	....	.130	.200	.130	.330	3	-3	1	.73	-1	/3-5,2-1,S-1	0	-0.4

• SINGLETON, Chris Christopher Verdell Singleton b: 8/15/1972, Martinez, CA BL/TL, 6'2", 210 lbs. Deb: 4/10/1999 Career OF: 53-613-12

YEAR TM-L	G	AB	R	H	2B	3B	HR	RBI	BB	SO	SB	CS	AVG	OBP	SLG	OPS	OPS+	BR/A	RC	RC/G	FR	G/POS	WS	TPW
1999 Chi-A	133	496	72	149	31	6	17	72	22	45	20	5	.300	.331	.490	.821	106	4	78	5.69	6	*0-127(11-121-1)/D-2	18	1.0
2000*Chi-A	147	511	83	130	22	5	11	62	35	85	22	7	.254	.303	.382	.685	71	-22	61	4.00	7	*0-145(19-143-0)/D-1	11	-1.4
2001 Chi-A	140	392	57	117	21	5	7	45	20	61	12	11	.298	.334	.431	.765	96	-5	54	4.69	10	*0-133(19-121-3)/D-1	12	0.5
2002 Bal-A	136	466	67	122	30	6	9	50	21	83	20	2	.262	.299	.410	.709	90	-4	58	4.31	-8	*0-126(0-126-0)/D-1	9	-1.1
2003*Oak-A	120	306	38	75	24	1	1	36	26	55	7	2	.245	.306	.340	.646	70	-13	34	3.76	-7	*0-113(4-102-8)	6	-1.8
Total 5	**676**	**2171**	**317**	**593**	**128**	**23**	**45**	**265**	**124**	**329**	**81**	**27**	**.273**	**.315**	**.415**	**.730**	**87**	**-41**	**285**	**4.53**	**8**	**0-644/D-5**	**56**	**-2.9**

• SINGLETON, Duane Duane Earl Singleton b: 8/6/1972, Staten Island, NY BL/TR, 6'1", 170 lbs. Deb: 8/4/1994 Career OF: 6-26-0

YEAR TM-L	G	AB	R	H	2B	3B	HR	RBI	BB	SO	SB	CS	AVG	OBP	SLG	OPS	OPS+	BR/A	RC	RC/G	FR	G/POS	WS	TPW
1994 Mil-A	2	0	0	0	0	0	0	0	0	0	0	0	....	....	....	....	-96	0	0	....	-0	/0-2(0-2-0)	0	0.0
1995 Mil-A	13	31	0	2	0	0	0	0	1	10	1	0	.065	.094	.065	.158	-55	-7	0	.24	0	0-11(3-9-0)	0	-0.6
1996 Det-A	18	56	5	9	1	0	0	3	4	15	0	2	.161	.230	.179	.408	5	-9	2	.98	2	0-15(3-15-0)	0	-0.6
Total 3	**33**	**87**	**5**	**11**	**1**	**0**	**0**	**3**	**5**	**25**	**1**	**2**	**.126**	**.183**	**.138**	**.321**	**-16**	**-16**	**2**	**.71**	**3**	**/0-28**	**0**	**-1.2**

• SINGLETON, Ken Kenneth Wayne Singleton b: 6/10/1947, New York, NY BB/TR, 6'4", 213 lbs. Deb: 6/24/1970 Career OF: 242-4-1313

YEAR TM-L	G	AB	R	H	2B	3B	HR	RBI	BB	SO	SB	CS	AVG	OBP	SLG	OPS	OPS+	BR/A	RC	RC/G	FR	G/POS	WS	TPW
1970 NY-N	69	198	22	52	8	0	5	26	30	48	1	1	.263	.362	.379	.741	99	0	28	4.86	-3	0-51(26-0-26)	5	-0.5
1971 NY-N	115	298	34	73	5	0	13	46	61	64	0	1	.245	.377	.393	.769	120	10	45	4.99	-2	0-96(10-3-85)	11	0.5
1972 Mon-N	142	507	77	139	23	2	14	50	70	99	5	10	.274	.364	.410	.775	118	11	75	5.09	0	*0-137(111-0-29)	18	0.3
1973 Mon-N	162	560	100	169	26	2	23	103	123	91	2	8	.302	**.429**	.479	.908	146	39	113	7.04	4	*0-161(2-0-161)	28	3.6
1974 Mon-N	148	511	68	141	20	2	9	74	93	84	5	2	.276	.387	.376	.763	108	10	77	5.23	-9	*0-143(0-0-143)	16	-0.7
1975 Bal-A	155	586	88	176	37	4	15	55	118	82	3	5	.300	.418	.454	.872	156	49	118	7.36	-3	*0-155(0-0-155)	**33**	3.9
1976 Bal-A	154	544	62	151	25	2	13	70	79	76	2	2	.278	.369	.403	.772	134	25	82	5.35	0	*0-134(80-0-63),D-19	24	1.9
1977 Bal-A★	152	536	90	176	24	0	24	99	107	101	0	1	.328	.442	.507	.949	168	57	124	8.76	4	*0-150(0-0-150)/D-1	36	5.5
1978 Bal-A	149	502	67	147	21	2	20	81	98	94	0	0	.293	.410	.462	.872	**154**	42	100	7.17	-1	*0-140(4-0-139)/D-5	28	3.6
1979*Bal-A★	159	570	93	168	29	1	35	111	109	118	3	1	.295	.409	.533	.942	158	51	127	8.02	0	*0-143(7-0-136),D-16	32	4.3
1980 Bal-A	156	583	85	177	28	3	24	104	92	94	0	2	.304	.399	.485	.885	143	37	113	7.09	-6	*0-151(0-0-151)/D-5	27	2.4
1981 Bal-A★	103	363	48	101	16	1	13	49	61	59	0	0	.278	.382	.435	.817	135	19	57	5.40	2	0-72(0-1-72),D-30	15	1.8
1982 Bal-A	156	561	71	141	27	2	14	77	86	93	0	1	.251	.353	.381	.734	102	4	75	4.45	-0	*D-148/0-5(2-0-3)	12	-0.1
1983*Bal-A	151	507	52	140	21	3	18	84	99	83	0	2	.276	.395	.436	.831	131	25	86	5.89	0	*D-150	17	2.1
1984 Bal-A	111	363	28	78	7	1	6	36	37	60	0	0	.215	.288	.289	.577	61	-18	27	2.37	0	*D-103	0	-2.2
Total 15	**2082**	**7189**	**985**	**2029**	**317**	**25**	**246**	**1065**	**1263**	**1246**	**21**	**36**	**.282**	**.391**	**.436**	**.827**	**133**	**362**	**1247**	**6.09**	**-14**	***0-1538,D-477**	**302**	**26.3**

• SINGTON, Fred Frederic William Sington b: 2/24/1910, Birmingham, AL d: 8/20/1998, Birmingham, AL BR/TR, 6'2", 215 lbs. Deb: 9/23/1934 Career OF: 26-0-115

YEAR TM-L	G	AB	R	H	2B	3B	HR	RBI	BB	SO	SB	CS	AVG	OBP	SLG	OPS	OPS+	BR/A	RC	RC/G	FR	G/POS	WS	TPW
1934 Was-A	9	35	2	10	2	0	0	6	4	3	0	1	.286	.359	.343	.702	85	-1	4	4.25	0	/0-9(3-0-6)	0	-0.1
1935 Was-A	20	22	1	4	0	0	0	3	5	1	0	0	.182	.333	.182	.515	38	-2	2	2.50	0	/0-4(2-0-2)	0	-0.1
1936 Was-A	25	94	13	30	8	0	1	28	15	9	0	0	.319	.413	.436	.849	116	3	18	7.37	-1	0-25(0-0-25)	3	0.0
1937 Was-A	78	228	27	54	15	4	3	36	37	33	1	1	.237	.348	.377	.726	87	-4	32	4.80	-1	0-64(14-0-50)	5	-0.8
1938 Bro-N	17	53	10	19	6	1	2	5	13	5	1	....	.358	.493	.623	1.115	200	8	18	14.22	-1	0-17(0-0-17)	4	0.7
1939 Bro-N	32	84	13	23	5	0	1	7	15	15	0	....	.274	.384	.369	.753	99	1	11	4.55	0	0-22(7-0-15)	2	-0.1
Total 6	**181**	**516**	**66**	**140**	**36**	**5**	**7**	**85**	**89**	**66**	**2**	**2**	**.271**	**.382**	**.401**	**.783**	**104**	**5**	**85**	**5.89**	**-2**	**0-141**	**14**	**-0.4**

• SIPEK, Dick Richard Francis Sipek b: 1/16/1923, Chicago, IL BL/TR, 5'9", 170 lbs. Deb: 4/28/1945

YEAR TM-L	G	AB	R	H	2B	3B	HR	RBI	BB	SO	SB	CS	AVG	OBP	SLG	OPS	OPS+	BR/A	RC	RC/G	FR	G/POS	WS	TPW
1945 Cin-N	82	156	14	38	6	2	0	13	9	15	0	....	.244	.302	.308	.609	71	-6	14	3.15	-1	0-31(14-0-17)	2	-0.9

• SIPIN, John John White Sipin b: 8/29/1946, Watsonville, CA BR/TR, 6'1.5", 175 lbs. Deb: 5/24/1969

YEAR TM-L	G	AB	R	H	2B	3B	HR	RBI	BB	SO	SB	CS	AVG	OBP	SLG	OPS	OPS+	BR/A	RC	RC/G	FR	G/POS	WS	TPW
1969 SD-N	68	229	22	51	12	2	2	9	8	44	2	0	.223	.252	.319	.571	61	-12	18	2.70	3	2-60	3	-0.5

• SISCO, Steve Steven Michael Sisco b: 12/2/1969, Thousand Oaks, CA BR/TR, 5'10", 190 lbs. Deb: 5/6/2000

YEAR TM-L	G	AB	R	H	2B	3B	HR	RBI	BB	SO	SB	CS	AVG	OBP	SLG	OPS	OPS+	BR/A	RC	RC/G	FR	G/POS	WS	TPW
2000 Atl-N	25	27	4	5	0	0	1	2	3	4	0	0	.185	.267	.296	.563	42	-2	2	2.40	0	/0-6(5-0-1),2-5,3-2,D-1	0	-0.2

• SISLER, Dick Richard Allan Sisler b: 11/2/1920, St. Louis, MO d: 11/20/1998, Nashville, TN BL/TR, 6'2", 205 lbs. Deb: 4/16/1946 M/C Career OF: 285-0-4

YEAR TM-L	G	AB	R	H	2B	3B	HR	RBI	BB	SO	SB	CS	AVG	OBP	SLG	OPS	OPS+	BR/A	RC	RC/G	FR	G/POS	WS	TPW
1946*StL-N	83	235	17	61	11	2	3	42	14	28	0	....	.260	.307	.362	.668	85	-5	26	3.80	1	1-37,0-29(29-0-0)	5	-0.8
1947 StL-N	46	74	4	15	2	1	0	9	3	8	0	....	.203	.234	.257	.491	29	-8	5	2.12	0	1-10/0-5(5-0-0)	0	-0.8
1948 Phi-N	121	446	60	122	21	3	11	56	47	46	1	....	.274	.344	.408	.752	105	3	66	5.28	-1	*1-120	13	-0.3
1949 Phi-N	121	412	42	119	19	6	7	50	25	38	0	....	.289	.333	.415	.748	102	-0	57	5.08	-9	1-96	11	-1.2
1950*Phi-N★	141	523	79	155	29	4	13	83	64	50	1	....	.296	.373	.442	.815	115	12	88	6.17	-1	*0-137(137-0-0)	20	0.2
1951 Phi-N	125	428	46	123	20	5	8	52	40	39	1	0	.287	.351	.414	.765	106	4	63	5.29	-3	*0-111(111-0-0)	12	-0.7
1952 Cin-N	11	27	3	5	1	1	0	4	3	5	0	0	.185	.267	.296	.563	56	-2	2	2.94	0	/0-7(3-0-4)	0	-0.2
StL-N	119	418	48	109	14	5	13	60	29	35	3	3	.261	.312	.411	.723	99	-2	53	4.50	-4	*1-114	10	-1.0
Yr.	130	445	51	114	15	6	13	64	32	40	3	3	.256	.309	.404	.713	96	-4	56	4.40	-4	*1-114/0-7(3-0-4)	10	-1.2
1953 StL-N	32	43	3	11	1	1	0	4	1	4	0	0	.256	.273	.326	.598	55	-3	4	2.99	1	1-10	0	-0.2
Total 8	799	2606	302	720	118	28	55	360	226	253	6	3	.276	.336	.406	.743	101	-1	365	5.00	-17	1-387,0-289	71	-5.1

• SISLER, George George Harold "Gorgeous George" Sisler b: 3/24/1893, Manchester, OH d: 3/26/1973, Richmond Heights, MO BL/TL, 5'11", 170 lbs. Deb: 6/28/1915 M/C HOF: 1939 Career OF: 12-10-15 ♦

YEAR TM-L	G	AB	R	H	2B	3B	HR	RBI	BB	SO	SB	CS	AVG	OBP	SLG	OPS	OPS+	BR/A	RC	RC/G	FR	G/POS	WS	TPW
1915 StL-A	81	274	28	78	10	2	3	29	7	27	10	9	.285	.307	.369	.676	106	-0	32	3.87	-5	1-36,0-29(6-8-15),P-15	10	-0.8
1916 StL-A	151	580	83	177	21	11	4	76	40	37	34	26	.305	.355	.400	.755	133	17	84	4.89	-4	*1-141/0-3(1-2-0),P-3,3-2	25	1.7
1917 StL-A	135	539	60	190	30	9	2	52	30	19	37	....	.353	.390	.453	.843	163	37	104	7.44	-3	*1-133/2-2	29	3.5
1918 StL-A	114	452	69	154	21	9	2	41	40	17	**45**	....	.341	.400	.440	.841	**158**	31	92	**7.64**	13	*1-114/P-2	22	**4.6**
1919 StL-A	132	511	96	180	31	15	10	83	27	20	28	....	.352	.390	.530	.921	153	33	112	8.31	6	*1-131	24	3.9
1920 StL-A	154	631	137	**257**	49	18	19	122	46	19	42	17	**.407**	.449	.632	1.082	179	72	176	11.52	9	*1-154/P-1	33	7.6
1921 StL-A	138	582	125	216	38	**18**	12	104	34	27	**35**	11	.371	.411	.560	.971	137	35	133	9.03	3	*1-138	27	2.7
1922 StL-A	142	586	**134**	**246**	42	**18**	8	105	49	14	**51**	19	**.420**	.467	.594	1.061	169	**63**	162	11.45	0	*1-141	29	**5.2**
1924 StL-A	151	636	94	194	27	10	9	74	31	29	19	17	.305	.340	.421	.762	90	-14	87	4.87	-8	*1-151	11	-3.0
1925 StL-A	150	649	100	224	21	15	12	105	27	24	11	12	.345	.371	.479	.851	109	4	110	6.49	0	*1-150/P-1	19	-0.5
1926 StL-A	150	613	78	178	21	12	7	71	30	30	12	8	.290	.327	.398	.725	84	-16	79	4.54	-9	*1-149/P-1	11	-3.4
1927 StL-A	149	614	87	201	32	8	5	97	24	15	**27**	7	.327	.357	.430	.787	100	2	95	5.74	-3	*1-149	16	-1.1
1928 Was-A	20	49	1	12	1	0	0	2	1	2	0	1	.245	.260	.265	.525	38	-5	3	2.11	-1	/1-5,0-5(5-0-0)	0	-0.6
Bos-N	118	491	71	167	26	4	4	68	30	15	11	....	.340	.380	.434	.814	118	13	78	6.04	8	*1-118/P-1	15	1.3
1929 Bos-N	154	629	67	205	40	8	2	79	33	17	6	....	.326	.363	.424	.788	98	-2	94	5.49	-7	*1-154	13	-1.8
1930 Bos-N	116	431	54	133	15	7	3	67	23	15	7	....	.309	.346	.397	.743	82	-13	58	4.79	3	*1-107	8	-1.5
Total 15	2055	8267	1284	2812	425	164	102	1175	472	327	375	127	.340	.379	.468	.847	125	258	1498	6.77	3	*1-1971/0-37,P-24,2-2,3-2	292	17.8

• SISTI, Sibby Sebastian Daniel Sisti b: 7/26/1920, Buffalo, NY BR/TR, 5'11", 175 lbs. Deb: 7/21/1939 C Career OF: 29-14-35

YEAR TM-L	G	AB	R	H	2B	3B	HR	RBI	BB	SO	SB	CS	AVG	OBP	SLG	OPS	OPS+	BR/A	RC	RC/G	FR	G/POS	WS	TPW
1939 Bos-N	63	215	19	49	7	1	1	11	12	38	4	....	.228	.269	.284	.552	52	-15	16	2.47	-3	2-34,3-17,S-10	2	-1.4
1940 Bos-N	123	459	73	115	19	5	6	34	36	64	4	....	.251	.311	.353	.664	87	-8	53	3.99	-4	*3-102,2-16	12	-0.7
1941 Bos-N	140	541	72	140	24	3	1	45	38	76	7	....	.259	.309	.320	.628	81	-15	54	3.53	-10	*3-137/2-2,S-2	9	-2.0
1942 Bos-N	129	407	50	86	11	4	4	35	45	55	5	....	.211	.296	.287	.584	73	-14	36	2.86	-8	*2-124/0-1	7	-1.5
1946 Bos-N	1	0	0	0	0	0	0	0	0	0	0	....	....	....	....	....	-99	0	0	....	0	/3-1	0	0.0
1947 Bos-N	56	153	22	43	8	0	2	15	20	17	2	....	.281	.371	.373	.744	100	1	22	4.99	-5	S-51/2-1	5	-0.2
1948*Bos-N	83	221	30	54	6	2	0	21	31	34	0	....	.244	.340	.290	.630	73	-7	24	3.62	0	2-44,S-26	5	-0.3
1949 Bos-N	101	268	39	69	12	0	5	22	34	42	1	....	.257	.343	.358	.701	93	-2	33	4.17	-5	0-48(21-13-17),2-21,S-18/3	6	-0.7
1950 Bos-N	69	105	21	18	3	1	2	11	16	19	1	....	.171	.287	.276	.563	52	-7	9	2.62	-10	S-23,2-19,3-13/1-1,0-1	1	-1.5
1951 Bos-N	114	362	46	101	20	2	2	38	32	50	4	5	.279	.341	.362	.703	96	-3	46	4.53	-4	S-55,2-52/3-6,1-1,0-1	10	-0.2
1952 Bos-N	90	245	19	52	10	1	4	24	14	43	2	0	.212	.255	.310	.565	58	-14	19	2.37	-11	2-33,0-23(8-0-16),S-18/3-9	2	-2.4
1953 Mil-N	38	23	8	5	1	0	0	4	5	2	0	0	.217	.357	.261	.618	69	-1	2	3.40	-4	2-13/S-6,3-4	0	-0.4
1954 Mil-N	9	0	2	0	0	0	0	0	0	0	0	0	....	....	....	....	-107	0	0	....	0	....	0	0.0
Total 13	1016	2999	401	732	121	19	27	260	283	440	30	5	.244	.313	.324	.637	79	-84	315	3.54	-63	2-359,3-290,S-209/0-74,1-2	59	-11.4

• SIXSMITH, Ed Edward Sixsmith b: 2/26/1863, Philadelphia, PA d: 12/12/1926, Philadelphia, PA BR/TR Deb: 9/11/1884

YEAR TM-L	G	AB	R	H	2B	3B	HR	RBI	BB	SO	SB	CS	AVG	OBP	SLG	OPS	OPS+	BR/A	RC	RC/G	FR	G/POS	WS	TPW
1884 Phi-N	1	2	0	0	0	0	0	0	0	0	....	....	.000	.000	.000	.000	-105	-0	0	.00	-1	/C-1	0	-0.1

• SIZEMORE, Ted Ted Crawford Sizemore b: 4/15/1945, Gadsden, AL BR/TR, 5'10", 165 lbs. Deb: 4/7/1969 Career OF: 16-0-10

YEAR TM-L	G	AB	R	H	2B	3B	HR	RBI	BB	SO	SB	CS	AVG	OBP	SLG	OPS	OPS+	BR/A	RC	RC/G	FR	G/POS	WS	TPW
1969 LA-N	159	590	69	160	20	5	4	46	45	40	5	5	.271	.328	.342	.670	95	-5	66	3.91	-8	*2-118,S-46/0-1	17	0.1
1970 LA-N	96	340	40	104	10	1	1	34	34	19	5	1	.306	.369	.350	.719	98	1	42	4.48	-3	2-86/0-9(8-0-1),S-2	11	0.3
1971 StL-N	135	478	53	126	14	5	3	42	42	26	4	6	.264	.324	.333	.657	83	-12	50	3.55	2	2-93,S-39,0-15(7-0-8)/3-1	13	0.0
1972 StL-N	120	439	53	116	17	4	2	38	37	36	8	3	.264	.327	.335	.662	89	-5	49	3.79	9	*2-111	11	1.3
1973 StL-N	142	521	69	147	22	1	1	54	68	34	6	4	.282	.367	.334	.701	96	-0	69	4.49	23	*2-139/3-3	22	3.4
1974 StL-N	129	504	68	126	17	0	2	47	70	37	8	4	.250	.341	.296	.637	80	-11	55	3.60	25	*2-128/0-1,S-1	15	2.4
1975 StL-N	153	562	56	135	23	1	3	49	45	37	1	5	.240	.299	.301	.600	64	-29	51	2.95	-11	*2-153	8	-3.2
1976 LA-N	84	266	18	64	8	1	0	18	15	22	2	3	.241	.281	.278	.559	60	-15	21	2.51	3	2-71/3-3,C-2	4	-0.8
1977*Phi-N	152	519	64	146	20	3	4	47	52	40	8	11	.281	.348	.355	.702	85	-12	56	3.65	2	*2-152	14	-0.2
1978*Phi-N	108	351	38	77	12	0	0	25	25	29	8	1	.219	.273	.254	.527	48	-23	23	2.12	13	*2-107	5	-0.6
1979 Chi-N	98	330	36	82	17	0	2	24	32	25	3	3	.248	.321	.318	.639	68	-14	34	3.38	8	2-96	8	-0.1
Bos-A	26	88	12	23	7	0	1	6	4	5	1	0	.261	.301	.375	.676	77	-3	8	3.13	1	2-26/C-2	2	0.0
1980 Bos-A	9	23	1	5	1	0	0	0	0	0	0	0	.217	.217	.261	.478	29	-2	1	1.48	-1	/2-8	0	-0.3
Total 12	1411	5011	577	1311	188	21	23	430	469	350	59	46	.262	.327	.321	.649	80	-131	526	3.52	63	*2-1288/S-88,0-26,3-7,C-4	130	2.1

• SKAFF, Frank Francis Michael Skaff b: 9/30/1910, La Crosse, WI d: 4/12/1988, Towson, MD BR/TR, 5'10", 185 lbs. Deb: 9/11/1935 M/C

YEAR TM-L	G	AB	R	H	2B	3B	HR	RBI	BB	SO	SB	CS	AVG	OBP	SLG	OPS	OPS+	BR/A	RC	RC/G	FR	G/POS	WS	TPW
1935 Bro-N	6	11	4	6	1	1	0	3	0	2	0	....	.545	.545	.818	1.364	267	2	4	18.87	-1	/3-3	1	0.2
1943 Phi-A	32	64	8	18	2	1	1	8	6	11	0	0	.281	.343	.391	.733	115	1	9	5.38	1	1-18/3-3,S-1	2	0.2
Total 2	38	75	12	24	3	2	1	11	6	13	0	0	.320	.370	.453	.824	135	4	14	6.91	1	/1-18,3-6,S-1	3	0.4

• SKAGGS, Dave David Lindsey Skaggs b: 6/12/1951, Santa Monica, CA BR/TR, 6'2", 200 lbs. Deb: 4/17/1977

YEAR TM-L	G	AB	R	H	2B	3B	HR	RBI	BB	SO	SB	CS	AVG	OBP	SLG	OPS	OPS+	BR/A	RC	RC/G	FR	G/POS	WS	TPW
1977 Bal-A	80	216	22	62	9	1	1	24	20	34	0	0	.287	.347	.352	.699	97	-0	28	4.57	0	C-80	9	0.4
1978 Bal-A	36	86	6	13	1	1	0	2	9	14	0	1	.151	.232	.186	.418	20	-9	4	1.39	0	C-35	2	-0.8
1979*Bal-A	63	137	9	34	8	0	1	14	13	14	0	0	.248	.313	.328	.642	76	-4	13	3.03	0	C-63	4	-0.2
1980 Bal-A	2	5	0	1	0	0	0	0	0	1	0	0	.200	.200	.200	.400	10	-1	0	1.35	0	/C-2	0	0.0
Cal-A	24	66	7	13	0	0	1	9	9	13	0	0	.197	.293	.242	.536	50	-4	5	2.55	-1	C-24	0	-0.5
Yr.	26	71	7	14	0	0	1	9	9	14	0	0	.197	.288	.239	.527	47	-5	5	2.47	-1	C-26	0	-0.5
Total 4	205	510	44	123	18	2	3	49	51	76	0	1	.241	.310	.302	.612	71	-19	50	3.25	0	C-204	15	-1.1

• SKETCHLEY, Bud Harry Clement Sketchley b: 3/30/1919, Virden, Canada d: 12/19/1979, Los Angeles, CA BL/TL, 5'10", 180 lbs. Deb: 4/14/1942

YEAR TM-L	G	AB	R	H	2B	3B	HR	RBI	BB	SO	SB	CS	AVG	OBP	SLG	OPS	OPS+	BR/A	RC	RC/G	FR	G/POS	WS	TPW
1942 Chi-A	13	36	1	7	1	0	0	3	7	4	0	1	.194	.326	.222	.548	57	-2	3	2.70	0	0-12(0-0-12)	0	-0.2

• SKIDMORE, Roe Robert Roe Skidmore b: 10/30/1945, Decatur, IL BR/TR, 6'3", 188 lbs. Deb: 9/17/1970

YEAR TM-L	G	AB	R	H	2B	3B	HR	RBI	BB	SO	SB	CS	AVG	OBP	SLG	OPS	OPS+	BR/A	RC	RC/G	FR	G/POS	WS	TPW
1970 Chi-N	1	1	0	1	0	0	0	0	0	0	0	0	1.000	1.000	1.000	2.000	390	0	1	∞	0	....	0	0.0

• SKIFF, Bill William Franklin Skiff b: 10/16/1895, New Rochelle, NY d: 12/25/1976, Bronxville, NY BR/TR, 5'10", 170 lbs. Deb: 5/17/1921

YEAR TM-L	G	AB	R	H	2B	3B	HR	RBI	BB	SO	SB	CS	AVG	OBP	SLG	OPS	OPS+	BR/A	RC	RC/G	FR	G/POS	WS	TPW
1921 Pit-N	16	45	7	13	2	0	0	11	0	4	1	1	.289	.289	.333	.622	63	-3	4	3.07	-1	C-13	1	-0.3
1926 NY-A	6	11	0	1	0	0	0	0	0	1	0	0	.091	.091	.091	.182	-53	-2	0	.23	0	/C-6	0	-0.2
Total 2	22	56	7	14	2	0	0	11	0	5	1	1	.250	.250	.286	.536	41	-5	4	2.44	-1	/C-19	1	-0.5

• SKINNER, Alexander Alexander Skinner d: 3/5/1901, Washington, MA Deb: 7/12/1884

YEAR TM-L	G	AB	R	H	2B	3B	HR	RBI	BB	SO	SB	CS	AVG	OBP	SLG	OPS	OPS+	BR/A	RC	RC/G	FR	G/POS	WS	TPW
1884 Bal-U	1	3	0	1	0	0	0	....	0	....	....	....	.333	.333	.333	.667	114	0	0	4.78	0	/0-1	0	0.0
CP-U	1	3	1	1	0	0	0	....	0	....	....	....	.333	.333	.333	.667	134	0	0	4.78	0	/0-1	0	0.0
Yr.	2	6	1	2	0	0	0	....	0	....	....	....	.333	.333	.333	.667	124	0	1	4.78	0	/0-2(0-1-1)	0	0.0

• SKINNER, Bob Robert Ralph Skinner b: 10/3/1931, La Jolla, CA BL/TR, 6'4", 190 lbs. Deb: 4/13/1954 M/C Career OF: 893-0-58

YEAR TM-L	G	AB	R	H	2B	3B	HR	RBI	BB	SO	SB	CS	AVG	OBP	SLG	OPS	OPS+	BR/A	RC	RC/G	FR	G/POS	WS	TPW
1954 Pit-N	132	470	67	117	15	9	8	46	47	59	4	0	.249	.317	.370	.687	80	-13	56	4.03	-4	*1-118/0-2(0-0-2)	8	-2.4
1956 Pit-N	113	233	29	47	8	3	5	29	26	50	1	1	.202	.285	.326	.611	65	-12	22	2.99	-3	0-36(26-0-10),1-23/3-1	2	-1.7

YEAR TM-L	G	AB	R	H	2B	3B	HR	RBI	BB	SO	SB	CS	AVG	OBP	SLG	OPS	OPS+	BR/A	RC	RC/G	FR	G/POS	WS	TPW
1957 Pit-N	126	387	58	118	12	6	13	45	38	50	10	4	.305	.370	.468	.838	127	16	70	6.73	2	0-93(93-0-0)/1-9,3-1	14	1.2
1958 Pit-N★	144	529	93	170	33	9	13	70	58	55	12	4	.321	.390	.491	.882	135	29	102	7.25	9	*0-141(141-0-0)	25	3.1
1959 Pit-N	143	547	78	153	18	4	13	61	67	65	10	7	.280	.358	.399	.757	102	2	81	5.30	-5	*0-142(142-0-0)/1-1	18	-1.2
1960*Pit-N★	145	571	83	156	33	6	15	86	59	86	11	8	.273	.342	.431	.773	109	7	82	4.98	4	*0-141(141-0-0)	18	0.2
1961 Pit-N	119	381	61	102	20	3	3	42	51	49	3	5	.268	.360	.360	.720	91	-4	51	4.63	-1	0-97(97-0-0)	9	-1.1
1962 Pit-N	144	510	87	154	29	7	20	75	76	89	10	4	.302	.397	.504	.901	140	31	106	7.59	-2	*0-139(139-0-0)	26	2.2
1963 Pit-N	34	122	18	33	5	5	0	8	13	22	4	1	.270	.341	.393	.734	110	2	16	4.41	0	0-32(32-0-0)	3	0.1
Cin-N	72	194	25	49	10	2	3	17	21	42	1	2	.253	.332	.371	.703	99	-0	23	4.07	0	0-51(51-0-0)	5	-0.3
Yr.	106	316	43	82	15	7	3	25	34	64	5	3	.259	.335	.380	.715	103	2	39	4.20	1	0-83(83-0-0)	8	-0.2
1964 Cin-N	25	59	6	13	3	0	3	5	4	12	0	0	.220	.270	.424	.694	89	-1	7	3.80	0	0-12(12-0-0)	1	-0.2
*StL-N	55	118	10	32	5	0	1	16	11	20	0	0	.271	.333	.339	.672	83	-2	14	4.43	-1	0-31(4-0-27)	3	-0.6
Yr.	80	177	16	45	8	0	4	21	15	32	0	0	.254	.313	.367	.680	85	-3	21	4.21	-1	0-43(16-0-27)	4	-0.8
1965 StL-N	80	152	25	47	5	4	5	26	12	30	1	0	.309	.360	.493	.853	126	5	26	6.31	-2	0-33(15-0-19)	5	0.2
1966 StL-N	49	45	2	7	1	0	1	5	2	17	0	0	.156	.208	.244	.453	25	-4	2	1.74	0	....	0	-0.4
Total 12	1381	4318	642	1198	197	58	103	531	485	646	67	36	.277	.353	.421	.774	108	55	656	5.39	-3	0-950,1-151/3-2	137	-0.8

• SKINNER, Camp Elisha Harrison Skinner b: 6/25/1897, Douglasville, GA d: 8/4/1944, Douglasville, GA BL/TR, 5'11", 165 lbs. Deb: 5/2/1922 Career OF: 1-5-0

YEAR TM-L	G	AB	R	H	2B	3B	HR	RBI	BB	SO	SB	CS	AVG	OBP	SLG	OPS	OPS+	BR/A	RC	RC/G	FR	G/POS	WS	TPW
1922 NY-A	27	33	1	6	0	0	0	2	0	4	1	0	.182	.206	.182	.388	2	-5	1	1.31	0	/0-4(1-3-0)	0	-0.5
1923 Bos-A	7	13	1	3	2	0	0	1	0	0	0	0	.231	.231	.385	.615	60	-1	1	2.94	0	/0-2(0-2-0)	0	-0.1
Total 2	34	46	2	9	2	0	0	3	0	4	1	0	.196	.213	.239	.452	18	-5	2	1.75	-1	/0-6	0	-0.6

• SKINNER, Joel Joel Patrick Skinner b: 2/21/1961, La Jolla, CA BR/TR, 6'4", 204 lbs. Deb: 6/12/1983 M/C

YEAR TM-L	G	AB	R	H	2B	3B	HR	RBI	BB	SO	SB	CS	AVG	OBP	SLG	OPS	OPS+	BR/A	RC	RC/G	FR	G/POS	WS	TPW
1983 Chi-A	6	11	2	3	0	0	0	1	0	1	0	0	.273	.273	.273	.545	49	-1	0	.74	0	/C-6	0	0.0
1984 Chi-A	43	80	4	17	2	0	0	3	7	19	1	0	.213	.276	.238	.513	42	-6	5	2.24	-1	C-43	1	-0.5
1985 Chi-A	22	44	9	15	4	1	1	5	5	13	0	0	.341	.408	.545	.954	153	3	9	7.84	0	C-21	3	0.4
1986 Chi-A	60	149	17	30	5	1	4	20	9	43	1	0	.201	.252	.329	.580	55	-10	13	2.74	1	C-60	3	-0.7
NY-A	54	166	6	43	4	0	1	17	7	40	0	4	.259	.289	.301	.590	62	-11	13	2.58	-1	C-54	2	-0.9
Yr.	114	315	23	73	9	1	5	37	16	83	1	4	.232	.271	.314	.585	58	-20	25	2.66	0	*C-114	5	-1.6
1987 NY-A	64	139	9	19	4	0	3	14	8	46	0	0	.137	.189	.230	.419	11	-18	5	.92	-1	C-64	3	-1.6
1988 NY-A	88	251	23	57	15	0	4	23	14	72	0	0	.227	.268	.335	.603	68	-11	22	2.85	-5	C-85/0-2(1-0-1),1-1	3	-1.2
1989 Cle-A	79	178	10	41	10	0	1	13	9	42	1	1	.230	.271	.303	.575	61	-10	14	2.73	-1	C-79	2	-0.7
1990 Cle-A	49	139	16	35	4	1	2	16	7	44	0	0	.252	.288	.338	.626	75	-5	13	3.41	0	C-49	4	-0.3
1991 Cle-A	99	284	23	69	14	0	1	24	14	67	0	2	.243	.281	.303	.584	61	-16	23	2.63	-4	C-99	4	-1.4
Total 9	564	1441	119	329	62	3	17	136	80	387	3	7	.228	.271	.311	.582	60	-85	117	2.66	-12	C-560/0-2,1-1	25	-7.0

• SKIZAS, Lou Louis Peter "The Nervous Greek" Skizas b: 6/2/1932, Chicago, IL BR/TR, 5'11", 175 lbs. Deb: 4/19/1956 Career OF: 80-0-89

YEAR TM-L	G	AB	R	H	2B	3B	HR	RBI	BB	SO	SB	CS	AVG	OBP	SLG	OPS	OPS+	BR/A	RC	RC/G	FR	G/POS	WS	TPW
1956 NY-A	6	6	0	1	0	0	0	1	0	2	0	0	.167	.167	.167	.333	-12	-1	0	.90	0	....	0	-0.1
KC-A	83	297	39	94	11	3	11	39	15	17	3	1	.316	.349	.485	.834	118	6	45	5.53	3	0-74(57-0-18)	8	0.5
Yr.	89	303	39	95	11	3	11	40	15	19	3	1	.314	.346	.479	.824	115	5	46	5.43	3	0-74(57-0-18)	8	0.5
1957 KC-A	119	376	34	92	14	1	18	44	27	15	5	2	.245	.299	.431	.730	95	-4	47	4.20	-2	0-76(14-0-69),3-32	9	-0.9
1958 Det-A	23	33	4	8	2	0	1	2	5	1	0	0	.242	.342	.394	.736	95	-0	4	4.60	-1	/0-5(4-0-1),3-4	1	-0.1
1959 Chi-A	8	13	3	1	0	0	0	0	3	2	0	0	.077	.250	.077	.327	-6	-2	0	.69	0	/0-6(5-0-1)	0	-0.2
Total 4	239	725	80	196	27	4	30	86	50	37	8	3	.270	.319	.443	.762	101	-0	97	4.63	1	0-161/3-36	18	-0.7

• SKOWRON, Bill William Joseph "Moose" Skowron b: 12/18/1930, Chicago, IL BR/TR, 5'11", 195 lbs. Deb: 4/13/1954

YEAR TM-L	G	AB	R	H	2B	3B	HR	RBI	BB	SO	SB	CS	AVG	OBP	SLG	OPS	OPS+	BR/A	RC	RC/G	FR	G/POS	WS	TPW
1954 NY-A	87	215	37	73	12	9	7	41	19	18	2	1	.340	.396	.577	.972	170	19	47	8.21	-2	1-61/3-5,2-2	13	1.6
1955*NY-A	108	288	46	92	17	3	12	61	21	32	1	1	.319	.372	.524	.896	141	15	52	6.72	-3	1-74/3-3	12	0.8
1956*NY-A	134	464	78	143	21	6	23	90	50	60	4	4	.308	.383	.528	.911	143	27	90	7.05	2	*1-120/3-2	21	2.1
1957*NY-A★	122	457	54	139	15	5	17	88	31	60	3	2	.304	.352	.470	.823	125	14	70	5.48	5	*1-115	17	1.2
1958*NY-A★	126	465	61	127	22	3	14	73	28	69	1	1	.273	.320	.424	.744	107	3	59	4.41	-4	*1-118/3-2	12	-0.8
1959 NY-A★	74	282	39	84	13	5	15	59	20	47	1	0	.298	.351	.539	.890	145	16	50	6.42	-1	1-72	11	1.1
1960*NY-A★	146	538	63	166	34	3	26	91	38	95	2	3	.309	.356	.528	.884	144	29	95	6.44	2	*1-142	24	2.3
1961*NY-A★	150	561	76	150	23	4	28	89	35	108	0	0	.267	.320	.472	.792	114	9	78	4.84	-6	*1-149	17	-0.6
1962*NY-A	140	478	63	129	16	6	23	80	36	99	0	1	.270	.328	.473	.800	116	8	71	5.20	-8	*1-135	14	-0.7
1963*LA-N	89	237	19	48	8	0	4	19	13	49	0	1	.203	.253	.287	.540	59	-13	15	2.00	-2	1-66/3-1	1	-2.1
1964 Was-A	73	262	28	71	10	0	13	41	11	56	0	0	.271	.308	.458	.766	110	2	35	4.70	0	1-66	8	-0.1
Chi-A	73	273	19	80	11	3	4	38	19	36	0	0	.293	.341	.399	.741	108	3	36	4.78	0	1-70	9	-0.2
Yr.	146	535	47	151	21	3	17	79	30	92	0	0	.282	.325	.428	.753	109	5	71	4.74	0	*1-136	17	-0.3
1965 Chi-A★	146	559	63	153	24	3	18	78	32	77	1	3	.274	.319	.424	.743	116	8	68	4.20	-5	*1-145	17	-0.5
1966 Chi-A	120	337	27	84	15	2	6	29	26	45	1	1	.249	.309	.359	.668	98	-1	35	3.57	2	1-98	7	-0.4
1967 Chi-A	8	8	0	0	0	0	0	1	0	1	0	0	.000	.000	.000	.000	-104	-2	0	.00	0	....	0	-0.2
Cal-A	62	123	8	27	2	1	1	10	4	18	0	0	.220	.267	.276	.544	63	-6	8	2.19	-1	1-32	0	-0.9
Yr.	70	131	8	27	2	1	1	11	4	19	0	0	.206	.252	.260	.511	54	-8	8	2.01	-1	1-32	0	-1.1
Total 14	1658	5547	681	1566	243	53	211	888	383	870	16	18	.282	.335	.459	.794	120	132	810	5.14	-21	*1-1463/3-13,2-2	183	2.7

• SKUBE, Bob Robert Jacob Skube b: 10/8/1957, Northridge, CA BL/TL, 6', 180 lbs. Deb: 9/17/1982 Career OF: 0-5-4

YEAR TM-L	G	AB	R	H	2B	3B	HR	RBI	BB	SO	SB	CS	AVG	OBP	SLG	OPS	OPS+	BR/A	RC	RC/G	FR	G/POS	WS	TPW
1982 Mil-A	4	3	0	2	0	0	0	0	0	0	0	0	.667	.667	.667	1.333	285	1	1	36.00	0	/D-1,0-1	0	0.1
1983 Mil-A	12	25	2	5	1	1	0	9	4	7	0	0	.200	.310	.320	.630	80	-1	2	2.68	-1	/0-8(0-4-4),D-2,1-1	0	-0.1
Total 2	16	28	2	7	1	1	0	9	4	7	0	0	.250	.344	.357	.701	99	0	4	4.13	-1	/0-9,D-3,1-1	0	-0.1

• SLADE, Gordon Gordon Leigh "Oskie" Slade b: 10/9/1904, Salt Lake City, UT d: 1/2/1974, Long Beach, CA BR/TR, 5'10.5", 160 lbs. Deb: 4/21/1930

YEAR TM-L	G	AB	R	H	2B	3B	HR	RBI	BB	SO	SB	CS	AVG	OBP	SLG	OPS	OPS+	BR/A	RC	RC/G	FR	G/POS	WS	TPW
1930 Bro-N	25	37	8	8	2	0	1	2	3	5	0	....	.216	.275	.351	.626	51	-3	4	3.00	3	S-21	1	0.1
1931 Bro-N	85	272	27	65	13	2	1	29	23	28	2	....	.239	.310	.313	.623	68	-12	28	3.45	4	S-82/3-2	8	-0.2
1932 Bro-N	79	250	23	60	15	1	1	23	11	26	3	....	.240	.280	.320	.600	62	-13	23	3.07	-1	S-55,3-23	4	-1.0
1933 StL-N	39	62	6	7	1	0	0	3	6	7	1	....	.113	.191	.129	.320	-7	-9	2	.69	0	S-31/2-1	1	-0.7
1934 Cin-N	138	555	61	158	19	8	4	52	25	34	6	....	.285	.320	.369	.690	86	-11	66	4.23	0	S-97,2-39	12	-0.3
1935 Cin-N	71	196	22	55	10	0	1	14	16	16	0	....	.281	.341	.347	.688	88	-3	24	4.27	-2	S-30,2-19/0-8(8-0-0),3-7	5	-0.2
Total 6	437	1372	147	353	60	11	8	123	84	116	12	....	.257	.307	.335	.641	73	-51	146	3.64	4	S-316/2-59,3-32,0-8	31	-2.3

• SLADEN, Art Arthur Sladen b: 10/28/1860, Lowell, MA d: 2/28/1914, Dracut, MA Deb: 8/22/1884

YEAR TM-L	G	AB	R	H	2B	3B	HR	RBI	BB	SO	SB	CS	AVG	OBP	SLG	OPS	OPS+	BR/A	RC	RC/G	FR	G/POS	WS	TPW
1884 Bos-U	2	7	0	0	0	0	0	....	0	....	....	....	.000	.000	.000	.000	-102	-1	0	.00	-0	/0-2(0-0-2)	0	-0.1

• SLAGLE, Jimmy James Franklin "Rabbit,Shorty" Slagle
b: 7/11/1873, Worthville, PA d: 5/10/1956, Chicago, IL BL/TR, 5'7", 144 lbs. Deb: 4/17/1899 Career OF: 567-666-61

YEAR TM-L	G	AB	R	H	2B	3B	HR	RBI	BB	SO	SB	CS	AVG	OBP	SLG	OPS	OPS+	BR/A	RC	RC/G	FR	G/POS	WS	TPW
1899 Was-N	147	599	92	163	15	8	0	41	55	....	22	....	.272	.338	.324	.662	83	-13	76	4.54	8	*0-146(0-146-0)	11	-1.3
1900 Phi-N	141	574	115	165	16	9	0	45	60	....	34	....	.287	.358	.347	.705	95	-2	89	5.41	-2	*0-141(141-0-0)	15	-1.5
1901 Phi-N	48	183	20	37	6	2	1	20	16	....	5	....	.202	.277	.273	.550	59	-10	17	2.86	6	0-48(48-0-0)	3	-0.6
Bos-N	66	255	35	69	7	0	0	7	34	....	14	....	.271	.359	.298	.657	84	-4	34	4.69	-2	0-66(0-5-61)	7	-0.9
Yr.	114	438	55	106	13	2	1	27	50	....	19	....	.242	.325	.288	.613	73	-13	51	3.88	3	*0-114(48-5-61)	10	-1.5
1902 Chi-N	117	463	66	146	11	4	0	28	53	....	41	....	.315	.386	.356	.742	133	20	82	6.73	8	*0-113(94-20-0)	23	2.3
1903 Chi-N	139	543	104	162	20	6	0	44	81	....	33	....	.298	.393	.357	.751	118	18	94	6.27	1	*0-139(115-24-0)	25	1.0
1904 Chi-N	120	481	73	125	12	10	1	31	41	....	28	....	.260	.322	.333	.655	102	1	63	4.50	-1	*0-120(102-18-0)	19	-0.7
1905 Chi-N	155	568	96	153	19	4	0	37	97	....	27	....	.269	.379	.317	.696	104	9	82	5.01	3	*0-155(33-123-0)	25	0.4
1906 Chi-N	127	498	71	119	8	6	0	33	63	....	25	....	.239	.324	.279	.604	83	-8	56	3.74	1	*0-127(4-123-0)	19	-1.4
1907*Chi-N	136	489	71	126	6	6	0	32	76	....	28	....	.258	.359	.294	.653	99	3	65	4.52	-6	*0-136(4-132-0)	22	-1.0
1908 Chi-N	104	352	38	78	4	1	0	26	43	....	17	....	.222	.306	.239	.545	71	-9	33	2.88	-6	*0-101(26-75-0)	8	-2.4
Total 10	1300	5005	781	1343	124	56	2	344	619	....	274	....	.268	.352	.317	.668	97	7	690	4.78	9	*0-1292	177	-6.2

• SLATTERY, Jack John Terrence Slattery b: 1/6/1878, South Boston, MA d: 7/17/1949, Boston, MA BR/TR, 6'2", 191 lbs. Deb: 9/28/1901 M/C

YEAR TM-L	G	AB	R	H	2B	3B	HR	RBI	BB	SO	SB	CS	AVG	OBP	SLG	OPS	OPS+	BR/A	RC	RC/G	FR	G/POS	WS	TPW
1901 Bos-A	1	3	1	1	0	0	0	1	1	....	0	....	.333	.500	.333	.833	137	0	1	6.79	0	/C-1	0	0.1

YEAR TM-L	G	AB	R	H	2B	3B	HR	RBI	BB	SO	SB	CS	AVG	OBP	SLG	OPS	OPS+	BR/A	RC	RC/G	FR	G/POS	WS	TPW
1903 Cle-A	4	11	1	0	0	0	0	0	0	....	0	....	.000	.000	.000	.000	-102	-3	0	.00	-1	/1-2	0	-0.3
Chi-A	63	211	8	46	3	2	0	20	2	....	2	....	.218	.233	.251	.484	47	-14	13	2.12	-5	C-56/1-5	2	-1.4
Yr.	67	222	9	46	3	2	0	20	2	....	2	....	.207	.221	.239	.460	40	-16	13	1.99	-6	C-56/1-7	2	-1.8
1906 StL-N	3	7	0	2	0	0	0	0	1	....	0	....	.286	.375	.286	.661	111	0	1	3.96	0	/C-2	0	0.0
1909 Was-A	32	56	4	12	2	0	0	6	2	....	1	....	.214	.254	.250	.504	62	-2	4	2.14	0	1-11/C-6	0	-0.3
Total 4	103	288	14	61	5	2	0	27	6	....	3	....	.212	.236	.243	.479	48	-18	19	2.12	-6	/C-65,1-18	2	-2.0

• SLATTERY, Mike Michael J. Slattery b: 11/26/1866, Boston, MA d: 10/16/1904, Boston, MA BL/TL, 6'2", 210 lbs. Deb: 4/17/1884 Career OF: 69-281-19

YEAR TM-L	G	AB	R	H	2B	3B	HR	RBI	BB	SO	SB	CS	AVG	OBP	SLG	OPS	OPS+	BR/A	RC	RC/G	FR	G/POS	WS	TPW
1884 Bos-U	106	413	60	86	6	2	0	....	4	....	....	....	.208	.216	.232	.448	52	-20	21	1.82	4	*O-96(1-96-0),1-11	6	-1.8
1888*NY-N	103	391	50	96	12	6	1	35	13	28	26	....	.246	.272	.315	.586	87	-6	41	3.80	1	*O-103(4-90-9)	12	-0.8
1889*NY-N	12	48	7	14	2	0	1	12	4	3	2	....	.292	.346	.396	.742	107	0	7	5.81	-1	O-12(4-7-1)	1	-0.1
1890 NY-P	97	411	80	126	20	11	5	67	27	25	18	....	.307	.352	.445	.798	103	-2	73	6.88	-13	*O-97(53-39-9)	12	-1.4
1891 Cin-N	41	158	24	33	3	2	1	16	10	10	1	....	.209	.256	.272	.528	53	-10	12	2.49	0	O-41(4-37-0)	1	-1.1
Was-a	15	60	8	17	1	0	0	5	4	5	6	....	.283	.358	.300	.658	93	-0	9	5.43	-2	O-15(3-12-0)	1	-0.2
Total 5	374	1481	229	372	44	21	8	135	62	71	53	....	.251	.284	.325	.610	80	-38	163	3.98	-11	O-364/1-11	33	-5.4

• SLAUGHT, Don Donald Martin Slaught b: 9/11/1958, Long Beach, CA BR/TR, 6'1", 190 lbs. Deb: 7/6/1982

YEAR TM-L	G	AB	R	H	2B	3B	HR	RBI	BB	SO	SB	CS	AVG	OBP	SLG	OPS	OPS+	BR/A	RC	RC/G	FR	G/POS	WS	TPW
1982 KC-A	43	115	14	32	6	0	3	8	9	12	0	0	.278	.331	.409	.739	102	0	15	4.66	-3	C-43	4	-0.1
1983 KC-A	83	276	21	86	13	4	0	28	11	27	3	1	.312	.338	.388	.726	99	-1	34	4.58	-6	C-79/D-1	7	-0.3
1984*KC-A	124	409	48	108	27	4	4	42	20	55	0	0	.264	.302	.379	.681	86	-8	46	3.82	-5	*C-123/D-1	10	-0.7
1985 Tex-A	102	343	34	96	17	4	8	35	20	41	5	4	.280	.331	.423	.753	103	0	46	4.77	-6	*C-102	8	0.0
1986 Tex-A	95	314	39	83	17	1	13	46	16	59	3	2	.264	.310	.449	.759	101	-1	42	4.55	0	C-91/D-2	12	0.3
1987 Tex-A	95	237	25	53	15	2	8	16	24	51	0	3	.224	.298	.405	.703	84	-7	27	3.62	-1	C-85/D-5	3	-0.5
1988 NY-A	97	322	33	91	25	1	9	43	24	54	1	0	.283	.338	.450	.788	120	8	47	5.10	-8	C-94/D-1	9	0.6
1989 NY-A	117	350	34	88	21	3	5	38	30	57	1	1	.251	.319	.371	.691	95	-3	41	3.97	4	*C-105/D-3	11	0.7
1990*Pit-N	84	230	27	69	18	3	4	29	27	27	0	1	.300	.381	.457	.837	134	11	42	6.58	0	C-78	12	1.5
1991*Pit-N	77	220	19	65	17	1	1	29	21	32	1	0	.295	.365	.395	.760	116	5	32	5.19	-2	C-69/3-1	10	0.7
1992*Pit-N	87	255	26	88	17	3	4	37	17	23	2	2	.345	.391	.482	.873	147	15	46	6.73	-3	C-79	12	1.8
1993 Pit-N	116	377	34	113	19	2	10	55	29	56	2	1	.300	.359	.440	.800	113	7	57	5.41	0	*C-105	14	1.4
1994 Pit-N	76	240	21	69	7	0	2	21	34	31	0	0	.288	.383	.342	.724	90	-2	33	5.06	2	C-74	7	0.5
1995 Pit-N	35	112	13	34	6	0	0	13	9	8	0	0	.304	.361	.357	.718	88	-2	14	4.34	-1	C-33	3	0.0
1996 Cal-A	62	207	23	67	9	0	6	32	13	20	0	0	.324	.369	.454	.823	109	3	31	5.42	2	C-59/D-1	7	0.8
Chi-A	14	36	2	9	1	0	0	4	2	2	0	0	.250	.289	.278	.567	47	-3	2	1.67	-1	C-12/D-1	1	-0.3
Yr.	76	243	25	76	10	0	6	36	15	22	0	0	.313	.358	.428	.786	100	-0	33	4.78	1	C-71/D-2	8	0.5
1997 SD-N	20	20	2	0	0	0	0	0	5	4	0	0	.000	.200	.000	.200	-46	-4	0	.34	0	/C-6	0	-0.4
Total 16	1327	4063	415	1151	235	28	77	476	311	559	18	15	.283	.341	.412	.752	104	18	555	4.79	-26	*C-1237/D-15,3-1	130	6.1

• SLAUGHTER, Enos Enos Bradsher "Country" Slaughter
b: 4/27/1916, Roxboro, NC d: 8/12/2002, Durham, NC BL/TR, 5'9.5", 192 lbs. Deb: 4/19/1938 HOF: 1985 Career OF: 513-21-1541

YEAR TM-L	G	AB	R	H	2B	3B	HR	RBI	BB	SO	SB	CS	AVG	OBP	SLG	OPS	OPS+	BR/A	RC	RC/G	FR	G/POS	WS	TPW
1938 StL-N	112	395	59	109	20	10	8	58	32	38	1	....	.276	.330	.438	.768	104	1	57	5.08	-1	O-92(1-20-75)	9	-0.4
1939 StL-N	149	604	95	193	**52**	5	12	86	44	53	2	....	.320	.371	.482	.852	120	16	108	6.71	11	*O-149(0-0-149)	23	1.8
1940 StL-N	140	516	96	158	25	13	17	73	50	35	8	....	.306	.370	.504	.874	131	21	99	7.38	0	*O-132(0-0-132)	22	1.3
1941 StL-N★	113	425	71	132	22	9	13	76	53	28	4	....	.311	.390	.496	.886	139	22	86	7.64	-8	*O-108(0-0-108)	20	0.8
1942*StL-N★	152	591	100	**188**	31	**17**	13	98	88	30	9	....	.318	.412	.494	.906	153	42	128	**8.38**	0	*O-151(0-0-151)	**37**	3.6
1946*StL-N★	156	609	100	183	30	8	18	**130**	69	41	9	....	.300	.374	.465	.838	131	25	110	6.76	4	*O-156(0-0-156)	29	2.5
1947 StL-N★	147	551	100	162	31	13	10	86	59	27	4	....	.294	.366	.452	.818	111	9	93	6.22	4	*O-142(110-0-32)	20	0.3
1948 StL-N★	146	549	91	176	27	11	11	90	81	29	4	....	.321	.409	.470	.879	130	26	110	7.58	1	*O-146(107-0-39)	26	1.7
1949 StL-N★	151	568	92	191	34	**13**	13	96	79	37	3	....	.336	.418	.511	.929	141	36	127	8.77	2	*O-150(150-0-0)	29	2.6
1950 StL-N★	148	556	82	161	26	7	10	101	66	33	3	....	.290	.367	.415	.782	101	2	87	5.65	0	*O-145(20-0-125)	16	-0.3
1951 StL-N★	123	409	48	115	17	8	4	64	67	25	7	2	.281	.386	.391	.777	109	9	67	5.86	6	*O-106(0-0-106)	14	1.3
1952 StL-N★	140	510	73	153	17	12	11	101	70	25	6	1	.300	.386	.445	.831	129	24	93	6.69	3	*O-137(0-0-137)	23	2.3
1953 StL-N★	143	492	64	143	34	9	6	89	80	28	4	4	.291	.395	.433	.828	116	14	90	6.67	1	*O-137(0-0-137)	17	1.1
1954 NY-A	69	125	19	31	4	2	1	19	28	8	0	2	.248	.386	.336	.722	102	1	18	5.13	-1	O-30(3-0-29)	5	0.0
1955 NY-A	10	9	1	1	0	0	0	1	1	1	0	0	.111	.200	.111	.311	-15	-1	0	.85	0	....	0	-0.1
KC-A	108	267	49	86	12	4	5	34	40	17	2	3	.322	.414	.453	.867	132	13	50	6.84	-1	O-77(0-0-77)	12	1.0
Yr.	118	276	50	87	12	4	5	35	41	18	2	3	.315	.408	.442	.850	127	11	50	6.61	-1	O-77(0-0-77)	12	0.8
1956 KC-A	91	223	37	62	14	3	2	23	29	20	1	0	.278	.364	.395	.758	100	1	33	5.23	-3	O-56(19-1-37)	5	-0.4
*NY-A	24	83	15	24	4	2	0	4	5	6	1	1	.289	.330	.386	.715	91	-2	11	4.78	-0	O-20(17-0-4)	2	-0.2
Yr.	115	306	52	86	18	5	2	27	34	26	2	1	.281	.355	.392	.747	98	-1	44	5.11	-3	O-76(36-1-41)	7	-0.6
1957*NY-A	96	209	24	53	7	1	5	34	40	19	0	2	.254	.373	.368	.742	105	3	30	4.79	-5	O-64(56-0-9)	7	-0.6
1958*NY-A	77	138	21	42	4	1	4	19	21	16	2	0	.304	.396	.435	.831	133	8	25	6.79	-1	O-35(16-0-20)	6	0.6
1959 NY-A	74	99	10	17	2	0	6	21	13	19	1	0	.172	.268	.374	.642	77	-3	10	3.21	-1	O-26(9-0-18)	1	-0.5
Mil-N	11	18	0	3	0	0	0	1	3	3	0	0	.167	.286	.167	.452	26	-2	1	1.94	0	/O-5(5-0-0)	0	-0.2
Total 19	2380	7946	1247	2383	413	148	169	1304	1018	538	71	15	.300	.382	.453	.835	122	264	1432	6.66	12	*O-2064	323	17.9

• SLAYBACK, Scottie Elbert Slayback b: 10/5/1901, Paducah, KY d: 11/30/1979, Cincinnati, OH BR/TR, 5'8", 165 lbs. Deb: 9/26/1926

YEAR TM-L	G	AB	R	H	2B	3B	HR	RBI	BB	SO	SB	CS	AVG	OBP	SLG	OPS	OPS+	BR/A	RC	RC/G	FR	G/POS	WS	TPW
1926 NY-N	2	8	0	0	0	0	0	0	0	0	0	....	.000	.000	.000	.000	-101	-2	0	.00	-1	/2-2	0	-0.3

• SLOAN, Bruce Bruce Adams "Fatso" Sloan b: 10/4/1914, McAlester, OK d: 9/24/1973, Oklahoma City, OK BL/TL, 5'9", 195 lbs. Deb: 4/29/1944

YEAR TM-L	G	AB	R	H	2B	3B	HR	RBI	BB	SO	SB	CS	AVG	OBP	SLG	OPS	OPS+	BR/A	RC	RC/G	FR	G/POS	WS	TPW
1944 NY-N	59	104	7	28	4	1	1	9	13	8	0	....	.269	.350	.356	.706	99	0	13	4.27	-2	O-21(3-0-18)	2	-0.2

• SLOAN, Tod Yale Yeastman Sloan b: 12/24/1890, Madisonville, TN d: 9/12/1956, Akron, OH BL/TR, 6', 175 lbs. Deb: 9/22/1913 Career OF: 16-1-87

YEAR TM-L	G	AB	R	H	2B	3B	HR	RBI	BB	SO	SB	CS	AVG	OBP	SLG	OPS	OPS+	BR/A	RC	RC/G	FR	G/POS	WS	TPW
1913 StL-A	7	26	2	7	1	0	0	2	1	9	1	....	.269	.321	.308	.629	87	-0	3	3.60	2	/O-7(0-0-7)	1	0.1
1917 StL-A	109	313	32	72	6	2	2	25	28	34	8	....	.230	.307	.281	.589	83	-6	28	2.98	-2	O-77(16-1-60)	5	-1.3
1919 StL-A	27	63	9	15	1	3	0	6	12	3	0	....	.238	.368	.349	.718	99	1	8	4.24	0	O-20(0-0-20)	2	0.0
Total 3	143	402	43	94	8	5	2	33	41	46	9	....	.234	.319	.294	.612	86	-6	39	3.22	0	O-104	8	-1.2

• SLOCUM, Ron Ronald Reece Slocum b: 7/2/1945, Modesto, CA BR/TR, 6'2", 185 lbs. Deb: 9/8/1969

YEAR TM-L	G	AB	R	H	2B	3B	HR	RBI	BB	SO	SB	CS	AVG	OBP	SLG	OPS	OPS+	BR/A	RC	RC/G	FR	G/POS	WS	TPW
1969 SD-N	13	24	6	7	1	0	1	5	0	5	0	0	.292	.292	.458	.750	112	0	3	4.84	0	/2-4,3-4,S-1	1	0.0
1970 SD-N	60	71	8	10	2	2	1	11	8	24	0	1	.141	.238	.268	.505	36	-7	4	1.77	-4	C-19,S-17,3-11/2-9	1	-0.9
1971 SD-N	7	18	1	0	0	0	0	0	0	8	0	0	.000	.053	.000	.053	-90	-4	0	.06	0	/3-6	0	-0.5
Total 3	80	113	15	17	3	2	2	16	8	37	0	1	.150	.220	.265	.485	31	-11	8	1.99	-4	/3-21,C-19,S-18,2-13	2	-1.4

• SMAJSTRLA, Craig Craig Lee Smajstrla b: 6/19/1962, Houston, TX BB/TR, 5'9", 165 lbs. Deb: 9/6/1988

YEAR TM-L	G	AB	R	H	2B	3B	HR	RBI	BB	SO	SB	CS	AVG	OBP	SLG	OPS	OPS+	BR/A	RC	RC/G	FR	G/POS	WS	TPW
1988 Hou-N	8	3	2	0	0	0	0	0	0	1	0	0	.000	.000	.000	.000	-104	-1	0	.00	-1	/2-2	0	-0.2

• SMALL, Charlie Charles Albert Small b: 10/24/1905, Auburn, ME d: 1/14/1953, Auburn, ME BL/TR, 5'11", 180 lbs. Deb: 7/7/1930

YEAR TM-L	G	AB	R	H	2B	3B	HR	RBI	BB	SO	SB	CS	AVG	OBP	SLG	OPS	OPS+	BR/A	RC	RC/G	FR	G/POS	WS	TPW
1930 Bos-A	25	18	1	3	1	0	0	0	2	5	1	0	.167	.250	.222	.472	22	-2	1	2.06	-0	/O-1	0	-0.2

• SMALL, Hank George Henry Small b: 7/31/1953, Atlanta, GA BR/TR, 6'3", 205 lbs. Deb: 9/27/1978

YEAR TM-L	G	AB	R	H	2B	3B	HR	RBI	BB	SO	SB	CS	AVG	OBP	SLG	OPS	OPS+	BR/A	RC	RC/G	FR	G/POS	WS	TPW
1978 Atl-N	1	4	0	0	0	0	0	0	0	0	0	0	.000	.000	.000	.000	-90	-1	0	.00	0	/1-1	0	-0.1

• SMALL, Jim James Arthur Patrick Small b: 3/8/1937, Portland, OR BL/TL, 6'1.5", 180 lbs. Deb: 6/22/1955 Career OF: 15-13-17

YEAR TM-L	G	AB	R	H	2B	3B	HR	RBI	BB	SO	SB	CS	AVG	OBP	SLG	OPS	OPS+	BR/A	RC	RC/G	FR	G/POS	WS	TPW
1955 Det-A	12	4	2	0	0	0	0	0	1	1	0	0	.000	.200	.000	.200	-44	-1	0	.35	0	/O-4(3-0-1)	0	0.0
1956 Det-A	58	91	13	29	4	2	0	10	6	10	0	0	.319	.361	.407	.767	102	0	14	5.65	-2	O-26(4-12-10)	2	-0.2
1957 Det-A	36	42	7	9	2	0	0	0	2	11	0	2	.214	.250	.262	.512	39	-4	2	1.57	0	O-14(8-1-5)	0	-0.5
1958 KC-A	2	4	0	0	0	0	0	0	1	0	0	0	.000	.200	.000	.200	-39	-1	0	.35	0	/O-1	0	-0.1
Total 4	108	141	22	38	6	2	0	10	10	22	0	2	.270	.318	.340	.658	74	-6	16	3.91	-1	/O-45	2	-0.9

• SMALLEY, Roy Roy Frederick Smalley, III b: 10/25/1952, Los Angeles, CA BB/TR, 6'1", 185 lbs. Deb: 4/30/1975

YEAR TM-L	G	AB	R	H	2B	3B	HR	RBI	BB	SO	SB	CS	AVG	OBP	SLG	OPS	OPS+	BR/A	RC	RC/G	FR	G/POS	WS	TPW
1975 Tex-A	78	250	22	57	8	0	3	33	30	42	4	0	.228	.311	.296	.607	73	-7	25	3.24	0	S-59,2-19/C-1	5	0.0

YEAR TM-L	G	AB	R	H	2B	3B	HR	RBI	BB	SO	SB	CS	AVG	OBP	SLG	OPS	OPS+	BR/A	RC	RC/G	FR	G/POS	WS	TPW
1976 Tex-A	41	129	15	29	2	0	1	8	29	27	2	0	.225	.367	.264	.631	85	-0	15	3.64	-4	2-38/S-5	4	-0.1
Min-A	103	384	46	104	16	3	2	36	47	79	0	4	.271	.353	.344	.697	102	1	49	4.20	5	*S-103	14	2.0
Yr.	144	513	61	133	18	3	3	44	76	106	2	4	.259	.357	.324	.681	97	1	63	4.05	2	*S-108,2-38	18	1.9
1977 Min-A	150	584	93	135	21	5	6	56	74	89	5	5	.231	.319	.315	.634	75	-19	62	3.41	7	*S-150	13	0.4
1978 Min-A	158	586	80	160	31	3	19	77	85	70	2	8	.273	.366	.433	.800	122	16	92	5.20	6	*S-157	22	**4.0**
1979 Min-A★	162	621	94	168	28	3	24	95	80	80	2	3	.271	.357	.441	.799	110	9	101	5.59	7	*S-161/1-1	24	3.3
1980 Min-A	133	486	64	135	24	1	12	63	65	63	3	3	.278	.365	.405	.771	103	4	72	5.11	12	*S-125/1-3,D-3	19	2.8
1981 Min-A	56	167	24	44	7	1	7	22	31	24	0	0	.263	.379	.443	.822	128	7	27	5.56	-10	S-37,D-15/1-1	6	0.0
1982 Min-A	4	13	2	2	1	0	0	0	3	4	0	0	.154	.313	.231	.543	51	-1	1	2.70	2	/S-4	0	0.1
NY-A	142	486	55	125	14	2	20	67	68	100	0	1	.257	.348	.418	.766	111	8	75	5.35	5	S-89,3-53/D-4,2-1	19	2.1
Yr.	146	499	57	127	15	2	20	67	71	104	0	1	.255	.347	.413	.760	109	8	76	5.28	7	S-93,3-53/D-4,2-1	19	2.3
1983 NY-A	130	451	70	124	24	1	18	62	58	68	3	3	.275	.360	.452	.812	127	17	75	5.78	1	S-91,3-26,1-22	20	2.4
1984 NY-A	67	209	17	50	8	1	7	26	15	35	2	1	.239	.290	.388	.678	89	-4	23	3.63	-1	3-35,S-13/1-5,D-5	4	-0.5
Chi-A	47	135	15	23	4	0	4	13	22	30	1	1	.170	.287	.289	.576	57	-8	12	2.91	-4	3-38/S-3,D-2,1-1	1	-1.2
Yr.	114	344	32	73	12	1	11	39	37	65	3	2	.212	.289	.349	.638	76	-11	35	3.34	-5	3-73,S-16/D-7,1-6	5	-1.7
1985 Min-A	129	388	57	100	20	0	12	45	60	65	0	2	.258	.359	.402	.761	102	2	58	5.17	3	D-56,S-49,3-14/1-1	12	0.6
1986 Min-A	143	459	59	113	20	4	20	57	68	80	1	3	.246	.343	.438	.781	108	5	70	5.19	1	*D-114,S-19/3-8	10	0.3
1987*Min-A	110	309	32	85	16	1	8	34	36	52	2	0	.275	.353	.411	.764	98	0	46	5.32	-3	D-73,3-14/S-4	8	-0.5
Total 13	1653	5657	745	1454	244	25	163	694	771	908	27	34	.257	.348	.395	.743	103	31	801	4.79	27	*S-1069,D-272,3-188/2-58,1,C	181	15.9

• SMALLEY, Roy Roy Frederick Smalley, Jr. b: 6/9/1926, Springfield, MO BR/TR, 6'3", 190 lbs. Deb: 4/20/1948

YEAR TM-L	G	AB	R	H	2B	3B	HR	RBI	BB	SO	SB	CS	AVG	OBP	SLG	OPS	OPS+	BR/A	RC	RC/G	FR	G/POS	WS	TPW
1948 Chi-N	124	361	25	78	11	4	4	36	23	76	0	....	.216	.265	.302	.567	55	-24	27	2.49	-2	*S-124	4	-1.9
1949 Chi-N	135	477	57	117	21	10	8	35	36	77	2	....	.245	.304	.382	.685	85	-12	54	3.90	-10	*S-132	10	-1.3
1950 Chi-N	154	557	58	128	21	9	21	85	49	114	2	....	.230	.297	.413	.710	85	-14	68	4.12	-2	*S-154	12	-0.6
1951 Chi-N	79	238	24	55	7	4	8	31	25	53	0	0	.231	.304	.395	.699	85	-5	29	4.08	-7	S-74	6	-0.8
1952 Chi-N	87	261	36	58	14	1	5	30	29	58	0	0	.222	.305	.341	.646	78	-7	29	3.70	-14	S-82	5	-1.7
1953 Chi-N	82	253	20	63	9	0	6	25	28	57	0	0	.249	.329	.356	.684	77	-8	32	4.30	-8	S-77	5	-1.0
1954 Mil-N	25	36	5	8	0	0	1	7	4	9	0	0	.222	.317	.306	.623	67	-2	3	2.92	1	/S-9,2-7,1-2	1	0.0
1955 Phi-N	92	260	33	51	11	1	7	39	39	58	0	0	.196	.306	.327	.633	69	-11	26	3.09	-6	S-87/2-1,3-1	4	-1.0
1956 Phi-N	65	168	14	38	9	3	0	16	23	29	0	0	.226	.323	.315	.638	74	-5	18	3.52	2	S-60	5	0.1
1957 Phi-N	28	31	5	5	0	1	1	1	1	9	0	0	.161	.212	.323	.535	42	-3	2	2.32	0	S-20	0	-0.2
1958 Phi-N	1	2	0	0	0	0	0	0	0	1	0	0	.000	.000	.000	.000	-101	-1	0	.00	0	/S-1	0	-0.1
Total 11	872	2644	277	601	103	33	61	305	257	541	4	0	.227	.300	.360	.661	76	-92	288	3.64	-45	S-820/2-8,1-2,3-1	52	-8.5

• SMALLEY, Will William Darwin "Deacon" Smalley b: 6/27/1871, Oakland, CA d: 10/11/1891, Bay City, MI BR/TR Deb: 4/19/1890

YEAR TM-L	G	AB	R	H	2B	3B	HR	RBI	BB	SO	SB	CS	AVG	OBP	SLG	OPS	OPS+	BR/A	RC	RC/G	FR	G/POS	WS	TPW
1890 Cle-N	136	502	62	107	11	1	0	42	60	44	10	....	.213	.303	.239	.542	60	-23	40	2.71	14	*3-136	8	-0.6
1891 Was-a	11	38	5	6	0	1	0	3	5	2	0	....	.158	.256	.211	.466	35	-3	2	1.74	-2	/3-9,2-2	0	-0.4
Total 2	147	540	67	113	11	2	0	45	65	46	10	....	.209	.300	.237	.537	58	-26	43	2.64	12	3-145/2-2	8	-1.0

• SMAZA, Joe Joseph Paul Smaza b: 7/7/1923, Detroit, MI d: 5/30/1979, Royal Oak, MI BL/TL, 5'11", 175 lbs. Deb: 9/18/1946

YEAR TM-L	G	AB	R	H	2B	3B	HR	RBI	BB	SO	SB	CS	AVG	OBP	SLG	OPS	OPS+	BR/A	RC	RC/G	FR	G/POS	WS	TPW
1946 Chi-A	2	5	2	1	0	0	0	0	0	0	0	0	.200	.200	.200	.400	12	-1	0	1.38	0	/O-1	0	-0.1

• SMILEY, Bill William B. Smiley b: 1856, Baltimore, MD d: 7/11/1884, Baltimore, MD Deb: 10/13/1874

YEAR TM-L	G	AB	R	H	2B	3B	HR	RBI	BB	SO	SB	CS	AVG	OBP	SLG	OPS	OPS+	BR/A	RC	RC/G	FR	G/POS	WS	TPW
1874 Bal-n	2	7	0	0	0	0	0	0	0	0	0	0	.000	.000	.000	.000	-101	-1	0	.00	-1	/3-2	....	-0.2
1882 StL-a	59	240	30	51	4	2	0	....	6	....	....	....	.213	.232	.246	.478	59	-11	14	2.08	-10	*2-57/O-2(1-0-1)	4	-1.7
Bal-a	16	61	3	9	0	0	0	....	0	....	....	....	.148	.148	.148	.295		-6	1	.73	0	2-16/S-2	0	-0.5
Yr.	75	301	33	60	4	2	0	....	6	....	....	....	.199	.215	.226	.441	47	-17	15	1.79	-10	*2-73/O-2(1-0-1),S-2	4	-2.2

• SMITH, Al Alphonse Eugene "Fuzzy" Smith b: 2/7/1928, Kirkwood, MO d: 1/3/2002, Hammond, IN BR/TR, 6'.5", 191 lbs. Deb: 7/10/1953 Career OF: 399-87-679

YEAR TM-L	G	AB	R	H	2B	3B	HR	RBI	BB	SO	SB	CS	AVG	OBP	SLG	OPS	OPS+	BR/A	RC	RC/G	FR	G/POS	WS	TPW
1953 Cle-A	47	150	28	36	9	0	3	14	20	25	2	0	.240	.341	.360	.701	92	-1	21	5.04	-4	O-39(4-0-35)/3-2	4	-0.6
1954*Cle-A	131	481	101	135	29	6	11	50	88	65	2	9	.281	.399	.435	.834	126	18	90	6.64	-6	*O-109(98-0-17),3-21/S-4	25	0.5
1955 Cle-A★	154	607	**123**	186	27	4	22	77	93	77	11	6	.306	.411	.473	.884	132	32	128	7.81	-10	*O-120(7-9-111),3-45/S-5,2	29	1.8
1956 Cle-A	141	526	87	144	26	5	16	71	84	72	6	3	.274	.382	.433	.815	112	12	90	5.93	-7	*O-122(50-23-58),3-28/2-1	21	0.0
1957 Cle-A	135	507	78	125	23	5	11	49	79	70	12	6	.247	.353	.377	.729	100	3	73	4.79	-7	3-84,O-58(18-41-6)	17	-0.7
1958 Chi-A	139	480	61	121	23	5	12	58	48	77	3	3	.252	.326	.396	.722	100	-0	59	4.15	-3	*O-138(77-2-63)/3-1	13	-1.1
1959*Chi-A	129	472	65	112	16	4	17	55	46	74	7	5	.237	.312	.396	.708	94	-5	58	4.09	4	*O-128(84-3-45)/3-1	14	-0.8
1960 Chi-A★	142	536	80	169	31	3	12	72	50	65	8	3	.315	.377	.451	.828	124	19	89	6.07	-5	*O-141(3-5-139)	20	0.8
1961 Chi-A	147	532	88	148	29	4	28	93	56	67	4	4	.278	.352	.506	.858	128	19	91	5.93	-8	3-80,O-71(10-3-59)	20	0.6
1962 Chi-A	142	511	62	149	23	8	16	82	57	60	3	3	.292	.366	.462	.828	122	15	83	5.83	-10	*3-105,O-39(38-0-2)	18	0.4
1963 Bal-A	120	368	45	100	17	1	10	39	32	74	9	0	.272	.335	.405	.740	109	6	49	4.63	0	O-97(7-0-92)	11	0.0
1964 Cle-A	61	136	15	22	1	1	4	9	8	32	0	1	.162	.214	.272	.486	34	-13	7	1.51	-2	O-48(1-1-46)/3-1	0	-1.8
Bos-A	29	51	10	11	4	0	2	7	13	10	0	0	.216	.385	.412	.796	116	2	9	5.99	-1	3-10/O-8(2-0-6)	2	0.0
Yr.	90	187	25	33	5	1	6	16	21	42	0	1	.176	.267	.310	.577	59	-11	16	2.64	-3	O-56(3-1-52),3-11	2	-1.8
Total 12	1517	5357	843	1458	258	46	164	676	674	768	67	43	.272	.360	.429	.790	113	107	846	5.51	-60	*O-1118,3-378/S-9,2-2	194	-0.9

• SMITH, Aleck Alexander Benjamin "Broadway Aleck" Smith b: 1871, New York, NY d: 7/9/1919, New York, NY TR Deb: 4/23/1897 Career OF: 35-13-10

YEAR TM-L	G	AB	R	H	2B	3B	HR	RBI	BB	SO	SB	CS	AVG	OBP	SLG	OPS	OPS+	BR/A	RC	RC/G	FR	G/POS	WS	TPW
1897 Bro-N	66	237	36	71	13	1	1	39	4	....	12	....	.300	.317	.376	.692	87	-5	33	5.15	2	C-43,O-18(14-2-2)/1-6	6	-0.1
1898 Bro-N	52	199	25	52	6	5	0	23	3	....	7	....	.261	.276	.342	.618	77	-7	22	3.77	-5	O-26(17-5-5),C-20/2-2,3-2,1	3	-1.1
1899 Bro-N	17	61	6	11	0	1	0	6	2	....	0	....	.180	.206	.213	.419	15	-7	3	1.49	-2	C-17	1	-0.8
Bal-N	41	120	17	46	6	4	0	25	4	....	7	....	.383	.417	.500	.917	144	7	29	9.95	-8	C-36/O-2(0-0-2),1-1	5	0.2
Yr.	58	181	23	57	6	5	0	31	6	....	7	....	.315	.347	.403	.751	101	-1	32	6.58	-11	C-53/O-2(0-0-2),1-1	6	-0.6
1900 Bro-N	7	25	2	6	0	0	0	3	1	....	2	....	.240	.269	.240	.509	39	-2	2	3.07	-1	/3-6,C-1	0	-0.2
1901 NY-N	26	78	5	11	0	0	0	6	0	....	2	....	.141	.141	.141	.282	-19	-12	2	.76	-1	C-24	1	-1.1
1902 Bal-A	41	145	10	34	3	0	0	21	8	....	5	....	.234	.275	.255	.530	45	-11	12	2.84	-2	C-27/1-7,O-4(4-0-0),2-3,3	1	-1.0
1903 Bos-A	11	33	4	10	1	0	0	4	0	....	0	....	.303	.303	.333	.636	86	-1	3	3.94	-1	C-10	1	-0.1
1904 Chi-N	10	29	2	6	1	0	0	1	3	....	1	....	.207	.281	.241	.523	62	-1	2	2.61	-1	/O-6(0-6-0),3-1,C-1	1	-0.3
1906 NY-N	16	28	0	5	0	0	0	2	1	....	1	....	.179	.207	.179	.385	20	-3	1	1.54	0	/C-8,1-3,O-1	0	-0.2
Total 9	287	955	107	252	30	11	1	130	26	....	37	....	.264	.288	.321	.609	69	-42	111	4.03	-19	C-187/O-57,1-18,3-10,2-5	19	-4.6

• SMITH, Bernie Calvin Bernard Smith b: 9/4/1941, Ponchatoula, LA BR/TR, 5'9", 164 lbs. Deb: 7/31/1970 Career OF: 5-12-36

YEAR TM-L	G	AB	R	H	2B	3B	HR	RBI	BB	SO	SB	CS	AVG	OBP	SLG	OPS	OPS+	BR/A	RC	RC/G	FR	G/POS	WS	TPW
1970 Mil-A	44	76	8	21	3	1	1	6	11	12	1	3	.276	.382	.382	.764	110	1	11	4.97	-2	O-39(2-11-27)	2	-0.3
1971 Mil-A	15	36	1	5	1	0	1	3	0	5	0	0	.139	.162	.250	.412	15	-4	1	1.06	0	O-12(3-1-9)	0	-0.5
Total 2	59	112	9	26	4	1	2	9	11	17	1	3	.232	.317	.339	.657	83	-4	12	3.61	-2	/O-51	2	-0.7

• SMITH, Bill William E. Smith b: 3/1860, East Liverpool, OH d: 8/9/1886, Toronto, Canada, 5'11" Deb: 9/17/1884 U

YEAR TM-L	G	AB	R	H	2B	3B	HR	RBI	BB	SO	SB	CS	AVG	OBP	SLG	OPS	OPS+	BR/A	RC	RC/G	FR	G/POS	WS	TPW
1884 Cle-N	1	3	0	0	0	0	0	0	0	2	....	....	.000	.000	.000	.000	-97	-1	0	.00	0	/O-1	0	-0.1

• SMITH, Bill William J. Smith b: Baltimore, MD d: 8/9/1886, Deb: 4/14/1873 M

YEAR TM-L	G	AB	R	H	2B	3B	HR	RBI	BB	SO	SB	CS	AVG	OBP	SLG	OPS	OPS+	BR/A	RC	RC/G	FR	G/POS	WS	TPW
1873 Mar-n	6	23	2	4	0	0	0	1	0	0	0	0	.174	.174	.174	.348	5	-2	1	1.14	-2	/O-3(0-3-0),C-2,2-1	....	-0.3

• SMITH, Billy Billy Edward Smith b: 7/14/1953, Hodge, LA BB/TR, 6'2.5", 185 lbs. Deb: 4/13/1975

YEAR TM-L	G	AB	R	H	2B	3B	HR	RBI	BB	SO	SB	CS	AVG	OBP	SLG	OPS	OPS+	BR/A	RC	RC/G	FR	G/POS	WS	TPW
1975 Cal-A	59	143	10	29	5	1	0	14	12	27	1	3	.203	.265	.252	.516	50	-10	10	2.22	-9	S-50/1-6,D-4,3-2	1	-1.5
1976 Cal-A	13	8	0	3	0	0	0	0	0	2	0	0	.375	.375	.375	.750	128	0	1	5.28	-4	S-10/D-1	0	-0.4
1977 Bal-A	109	367	44	79	12	2	5	29	33	71	3	2	.215	.282	.300	.582	62	-19	33	2.93	4	*2-104/S-5,1-2,3-1	9	-0.9
1978 Bal-A	85	250	29	65	12	2	5	30	27	40	3	0	.260	.335	.384	.719	108	4	34	4.82	-5	2-83/S-2	10	0.2
1979*Bal-A	68	189	18	47	9	4	6	33	15	33	1	0	.249	.311	.434	.745	102	0	27	4.78	1	2-63/S-5	7	0.4
1981 SF-N	36	61	6	11	0	0	1	5	9	16	0	0	.180	.286	.230	.515	48	-4	5	2.34	-1	S-21/2-5,3-3	1	-0.4
Total 6	370	1018	107	234	38	9	17	111	96	189	8	5	.230	.299	.335	.634	79	-29	110	3.59	-15	2-255/S-93,1-8,3-6,D-5	28	-2.6

• SMITH, Bob Robert Eldridge Smith b: 4/22/1895, Rogersville, TN d: 7/19/1987, Waycross, GA BR/TR, 5'10", 175 lbs. Deb: 4/19/1923 ♦

YEAR TM-L	G	AB	R	H	2B	3B	HR	RBI	BB	SO	SB	CS	AVG	OBP	SLG	OPS	OPS+	BR/A	RC	RC/G	FR	G/POS	WS	TPW
1923 Bos-N	115	375	30	94	16	3	0	40	17	35	4	9	.251	.285	.309	.594	59	-25	32	2.76	6	*S-101/2-8	6	-0.8

YEAR	TM-L	G	AB	R	H	2B	3B	HR	RBI	BB	SO	SB	CS	AVG	OBP	SLG	OPS	OPS+	BR/A	RC	RC/G	FR	G/POS	WS	TPW
1924	Bos-N	106	347	32	79	12	3	2	38	15	26	5	2	.228	.260	.297	.556	51	-23	27	2.59	-3	S-80,3-23	4	-1.6
1925	Bos-N	58	174	17	49	9	4	0	23	5	6	2	2	.282	.302	.379	.681	80	-2	19	3.93	-1	S-21,2-15,P-13/0-1	8	-0.6
1926	Bos-N	40	84	10	25	6	2	0	13	2	4	0	....	.298	.314	.417	.731	105	7	10	4.50	3	P-33	14	0.5
1927	Bos-N	54	109	10	27	3	1	1	10	2	4	0	....	.248	.261	.321	.582	60	4	9	2.71	2	P-41	14	0.8
1928	Bos-N	39	92	11	23	2	0	1	8	1	6	2	....	.250	.258	.304	.562	49	3	7	2.42	2	P-38	10	1.3
1929	Bos-N	39	99	12	17	4	2	1	8	2	8	1	....	.172	.188	.283	.471	16	-2	5	1.55	2	P-34/S-5	13	0.0
1930	Bos-N	39	81	7	19	2	0	0	4	0	5	0	....	.235	.235	.259	.494	20	-1	5	1.88	2	P-38	17	1.4
1931	Chi-N	36	87	7	19	2	0	0	4	5	2	0	....	.218	.261	.241	.502	35	1	6	2.13	1	P-36	17	2.1
1932*	Chi-N	36	42	5	10	4	1	0	4	0	2	1	....	.238	.238	.381	.619	64	2	4	3.01	1	P-34/2-2	6	-1.0
1933	Cin-N	23	25	2	5	1	0	0	1	1	0	1	....	.200	.231	.240	.471	35	0	1	1.58	-1	P-16/S-1	6	1.1
	Bos-N	14	20	1	4	0	1	0	2	0	1	0	....	.200	.200	.300	.500	45	1	1	2.08	1	P-14	4	0.0
	Yr.	37	45	3	9	1	1	0	3	1	1	1	....	.200	.217	.267	.484	39	1	3	1.79	0	P-30/S-1	10	1.1
1934	Bos-N	42	36	5	9	1	0	0	3	0	1	0	....	.250	.250	.278	.528	44	1	3	2.49	1	P-39	5	-1.0
1935	Bos-N	47	63	3	17	0	0	0	4	1	5	0	....	.270	.281	.270	.551	53	2	4	2.19	-1	P-46	9	0.6
1936	Bos-N	35	45	1	10	2	0	0	4	0	4	0	....	.222	.222	.267	.489	33	0	3	1.82	1	P-35	10	0.0
1937	Bos-N	19	10	1	2	0	0	0	0	1	1	0	....	.200	.273	.200	.473	33	0	1	2.13	-1	P-18	2	-0.3
Total	**15**	**742**	**1689**	**154**	**409**	**64**	**17**	**5**	**166**	**52**	**110**	**16**	**13**	**.242**	**.265**	**.309**	**.574**	**54**	**-31**	**136**	**2.66**	**15**	**P-435,S-208/2-25,3-23,0-1**	**145**	**2.3**

• SMITH, Bobby — Robert Eugene Smith b: 4/10/1974, Oakland, CA BR/TR, 6'3", 190 lbs. Deb: 4/3/1998

YEAR	TM-L	G	AB	R	H	2B	3B	HR	RBI	BB	SO	SB	CS	AVG	OBP	SLG	OPS	OPS+	BR/A	RC	RC/G	FR	G/POS	WS	TPW
1998	TB-A	117	370	44	102	15	3	11	55	34	110	5	3	.276	.346	.422	.768	97	-2	54	5.08	2	3-97/D-7,S-7,2-6	8	0.1
1999	TB-A	68	199	18	36	4	1	3	19	16	64	4	4	.181	.245	.256	.502	28	-23	11	1.68	-1	3-59,2-13	2	-2.1
2000	TB-A	49	175	21	41	8	0	6	26	14	59	2	2	.234	.295	.383	.678	70	-9	18	3.43	-1	2-45/3-5	3	-0.7
2001	TB-A	6	19	1	2	0	0	0	1	3	10	0	0	.105	.227	.105	.333	-8	-3	1	.76	-2	/2-6	0	-0.4
2002	TB-A	18	63	4	11	2	0	1	6	3	25	0	0	.175	.212	.254	.466	24	-7	4	1.85	1	3-10/1-6,0-2(1-0-1),D-1	0	-0.6
Total	**5**	**258**	**826**	**88**	**192**	**29**	**4**	**21**	**107**	**70**	**268**	**11**	**9**	**.232**	**.299**	**.354**	**.652**	**67**	**-44**	**87**	**3.47**	**0**	**3-171/2-70,D-8,S-7,1-6,0-2**	**13**	**-3.7**

• SMITH, Bobby Gene — Bobby Gene Smith b: 5/28/1934, Hood River, OR BR/TR, 5'11", 185 lbs. Deb: 4/16/1957 Career OF: 189-123-60

YEAR	TM-L	G	AB	R	H	2B	3B	HR	RBI	BB	SO	SB	CS	AVG	OBP	SLG	OPS	OPS+	BR/A	RC	RC/G	FR	G/POS	WS	TPW
1957	StL-N	93	185	24	39	7	1	3	18	13	35	1	1	.211	.263	.308	.571	52	-13	14	2.46	2	0-79(0-61-18)	2	-1.4
1958	StL-N	28	88	8	25	3	0	2	5	2	18	1	0	.284	.308	.386	.694	79	-3	11	4.37	2	0-27(0-25-2)	2	-0.2
1959	StL-N	43	60	11	13	1	1	1	7	1	9	0	0	.217	.230	.317	.546	41	-5	4	2.09	1	0-32(11-6-15)	0	-0.5
1960	Phi-N	98	217	24	62	5	2	4	27	10	28	2	3	.286	.317	.382	.700	90	-4	24	3.89	0	0-70(65-6-0)/3-1	4	-0.8
1961	Phi-N	79	174	16	44	7	0	2	18	15	32	0	1	.253	.316	.328	.643	72	-7	17	3.39	4	0-47(33-3-12)	2	-0.6
1962	NY-N	8	22	1	3	0	1	0	2	3	2	0	1	.136	.240	.227	.467	26	-3	1	1.19	0	/0-6(0-3-4)	0	-0.3
	Chi-N	13	29	3	5	0	0	1	2	2	6	0	1	.172	.226	.276	.502	33	-3	2	1.76	0	/0-7(0-6-1)	0	-0.3
	StL-N	91	130	13	30	9	0	0	12	7	14	1	1	.231	.270	.300	.570	48	-10	9	2.36	0	0-80(66-13-7)	1	-1.2
	Yr.	112	181	17	38	9	1	1	16	12	22	1	3	.210	.259	.287	.546	43	-16	12	2.10	1	0-93(66-22-12)	1	-1.8
1965	Cal-A	23	57	1	13	3	0	0	5	2	10	0	1	.228	.267	.281	.547	57	-4	4	2.48	0	0-15(14-0-1)	1	-0.4
Total	**7**	**476**	**962**	**101**	**234**	**35**	**5**	**13**	**96**	**55**	**154**	**5**	**9**	**.243**	**.286**	**.331**	**.617**	**64**	**-52**	**86**	**3.00**	**10**	**0-363/3-1**	**12**	**-5.7**

• SMITH, Brick — Brick Dudley Smith b: 5/2/1959, Charlotte, NC BR/TR, 6'4", 225 lbs. Deb: 9/13/1987

YEAR	TM-L	G	AB	R	H	2B	3B	HR	RBI	BB	SO	SB	CS	AVG	OBP	SLG	OPS	OPS+	BR/A	RC	RC/G	FR	G/POS	WS	TPW
1987	Sea-A	5	8	1	1	0	0	0	0	2	4	0	0	.125	.300	.125	.425	18	-1	0	1.76	0	/1-3,D-1	0	-0.1
1988	Sea-A	4	10	1	1	0	0	0	1	0	1	0	0	.100	.100	.100	.200	-42	-2	0	.30	1	/1-4	0	-0.1
Total	**2**	**9**	**18**	**2**	**2**	**0**	**0**	**0**	**1**	**2**	**5**	**0**	**0**	**.111**	**.200**	**.111**	**.311**	**-12**	**-3**	**1**	**.94**	**1**	**/1-7,D-1**	**0**	**-0.3**

• SMITH, Bull — Lewis Oscar Smith b: 8/20/1880, Plum, WV d: 5/1/1928, Charleston, WV BR/TR, 6', 180 lbs. Deb: 8/30/1904

YEAR	TM-L	G	AB	R	H	2B	3B	HR	RBI	BB	SO	SB	CS	AVG	OBP	SLG	OPS	OPS+	BR/A	RC	RC/G	FR	G/POS	WS	TPW
1904	Pit-N	13	42	2	6	0	1	0	0	1	....	0	....	.143	.163	.190	.353	9	-5	1	.96	-1	0-13(11-0-2)	0	-0.6
1906	Chi-N	1	1	0	0	0	0	0	0	0	....	0	....	.000	.000	.000	.000	-95	-0	0	.00	0	....	0	0.0
1911	Was-A	1	0	0	0	0	0	0	0	0	....	0	....	....	....	....	....	-102	0	0	....	0	....	0	0.0
Total	**3**	**15**	**43**	**2**	**6**	**0**	**1**	**0**	**0**	**1**	**....**	**0**	**....**	**.140**	**.159**	**.186**	**.345**	**6**	**-5**	**1**	**.94**	**-1**	**/0-13**	**0**	**-0.7**

• SMITH, Carr — Emanuel Carr Smith b: 4/8/1901, Kernersville, NC d: 4/14/1989, Miami, FL BR/TR, 6'1", 175 lbs. Deb: 9/23/1923 Career OF: 0-4-4

YEAR	TM-L	G	AB	R	H	2B	3B	HR	RBI	BB	SO	SB	CS	AVG	OBP	SLG	OPS	OPS+	BR/A	RC	RC/G	FR	G/POS	WS	TPW
1923	Was-A	5	9	0	1	1	0	0	1	0	0	0	0	.111	.111	.222	.333	-14	-2	0	.71	0	/0-4(0-4-0)	0	-0.2
1924	Was-A	5	10	1	2	0	0	0	0	0	3	0	0	.200	.200	.200	.400	3	-1	0	1.27	0	/0-4(0-0-4)	0	-0.2
Total	**2**	**10**	**19**	**1**	**3**	**1**	**0**	**0**	**1**	**0**	**3**	**0**	**0**	**.158**	**.158**	**.211**	**.368**	**-5**	**-3**	**1**	**.99**	**0**	**/0-8**	**0**	**-0.3**

• SMITH, Charley — Charles William Smith b: 9/15/1937, Charleston, SC d: 11/29/1994, Reno, NV BR/TR, 6'1", 177 lbs. Deb: 9/8/1960

YEAR	TM-L	G	AB	R	H	2B	3B	HR	RBI	BB	SO	SB	CS	AVG	OBP	SLG	OPS	OPS+	BR/A	RC	RC/G	FR	G/POS	WS	TPW
1960	LA-N	18	60	2	10	1	1	0	5	1	15	0	0	.167	.180	.217	.397	8	-8	3	1.30	1	3-18	1	-0.7
1961	LA-N	9	24	4	6	1	0	2	3	1	6	0	0	.250	.280	.542	.822	102	-0	4	5.57	0	/3-4,S-3	1	0.0
	Phi-N	112	411	43	102	13	4	9	47	23	76	3	4	.248	.296	.365	.661	75	-16	43	3.52	-5	3-94,S-14	6	-2.0
	Yr.	121	435	47	108	14	4	11	50	24	82	3	4	.248	.295	.375	.670	77	-16	47	3.62	-5	3-98,S-17	7	-2.0
1962	Chi-A	65	145	11	30	4	0	2	17	9	32	0	1	.207	.258	.276	.534	44	-12	9	1.99	-1	3-54	1	-1.3
1963	Chi-A	4	7	0	2	0	1	0	1	0	2	0	0	.286	.286	.571	.857	136	0	1	2.57	2	/S-1	0	0.2
1964	Chi-A	2	7	1	1	0	1	0	0	1	1	0	0	.143	.250	.429	.679	87	-0	0	1.57	3	/3-2	0	0.3
	NY-N	127	443	44	106	12	0	20	58	19	101	2	2	.239	.275	.402	.677	90	-8	47	3.60	-8	3-85,S-36,0-13(13-0-0)	9	-1.5
1965	NY-N	135	499	49	122	20	3	16	62	17	123	2	1	.244	.275	.393	.668	89	-9	50	3.38	7	*3-131/S-6,2-1	10	-0.3
1966	StL-N	116	391	34	104	13	4	10	43	22	81	0	2	.266	.305	.396	.702	93	-5	45	3.98	-3	*3-107/S-1	10	-0.8
1967	NY-A	135	425	38	95	15	3	9	38	32	110	0	2	.224	.279	.336	.616	84	-10	37	2.83	1	*3-115	8	-0.9
1968	NY-A	46	70	2	16	4	1	1	7	5	18	0	0	.229	.280	.357	.637	95	-1	7	3.08	1	3-13	2	0.0
1969	Chi-N	2	2	0	0	0	0	0	0	0	0	0	0	.000	.000	.000	.000	-89	-0	0	.00	0	....	0	-0.1
Total	**10**	**771**	**2484**	**228**	**594**	**83**	**18**	**69**	**281**	**130**	**565**	**7**	**12**	**.239**	**.281**	**.370**	**.651**	**82**	**-69**	**246**	**3.29**	**-4**	**3-623/S-61,0-13,2-1**	**48**	**-7.2**

• SMITH, Charlie — Charles J. Smith b: 12/11/1840, Brooklyn, NY d: 11/15/1897, Great Neck, NY, 5'10.5", 150 lbs. Deb: 5/18/1871

YEAR	TM-L	G	AB	R	H	2B	3B	HR	RBI	BB	SO	SB	CS	AVG	OBP	SLG	OPS	OPS+	BR/A	RC	RC/G	FR	G/POS	WS	TPW
1871	Mut-n	14	72	15	19	2	1	0	5	1	1	6	0	.264	.274	.319	.593	77	-0	8	4.84	-0	3-12/2-3	....	0.0

• SMITH, Chris — Christopher William Smith b: 7/18/1957, Torrance, CA BB/TR, 6', 185 lbs. Deb: 5/14/1981

YEAR	TM-L	G	AB	R	H	2B	3B	HR	RBI	BB	SO	SB	CS	AVG	OBP	SLG	OPS	OPS+	BR/A	RC	RC/G	FR	G/POS	WS	TPW
1981	Mon-N	7	7	0	0	0	0	0	0	0	2	0	0	.000	.000	.000	.000	-99	-2	0	.00	0	/2-1	0	-0.2
1982	Mon-N	2	2	0	0	0	0	0	0	0	1	0	0	.000	.000	.000	.000	-98	-1	0	.00	0	....	0	-0.1
1983	SF-N	22	67	13	22	6	1	1	11	7	12	0	0	.328	.408	.493	.900	153	5	14	8.41	-1	1-15/0-4(4-0-0),3-1	4	0.3
Total	**3**	**31**	**76**	**13**	**22**	**6**	**1**	**1**	**11**	**7**	**15**	**0**	**0**	**.289**	**.365**	**.434**	**.799**	**127**	**3**	**14**	**7.04**	**-1**	**/1-15,0-4,2-1,3-1**	**4**	**0.1**

• SMITH, Dick — Richard Kelly Smith b: 8/25/1944, Lincolnton, NC BR/TR, 6'5", 200 lbs. Deb: 8/20/1969

YEAR	TM-L	G	AB	R	H	2B	3B	HR	RBI	BB	SO	SB	CS	AVG	OBP	SLG	OPS	OPS+	BR/A	RC	RC/G	FR	G/POS	WS	TPW
1969	Was-A	21	28	2	3	0	0	0	0	4	7	0	0	.107	.242	.107	.350	1	-4	1	1.06	-1	/0-9(9-0-0)	0	-0.5

• SMITH, Dick — Richard Arthur Smith b: 5/17/1939, Lebanon, OR BR/TR, 6'2", 205 lbs. Deb: 7/20/1963 Career OF: 20-12-2

YEAR	TM-L	G	AB	R	H	2B	3B	HR	RBI	BB	SO	SB	CS	AVG	OBP	SLG	OPS	OPS+	BR/A	RC	RC/G	FR	G/POS	WS	TPW
1963	NY-N	20	42	4	10	0	1	0	3	5	10	3	2	.238	.319	.286	.605	74	-1	4	3.15	-1	0-10(3-7-0)/1-2	1	-0.2
1964	NY-N	46	94	14	21	6	1	0	3	1	29	6	2	.223	.247	.309	.556	57	-5	7	2.38	-1	1-18,0-13(12-1-1)	1	-0.8
1965	LA-N	10	6	0	0	0	0	0	1	0	3	0	0	.000	.000	.000	.000	-107	-2	0	.00	-1	/0-9(5-4-1)	0	-0.3
Total	**3**	**76**	**142**	**18**	**31**	**6**	**2**	**0**	**7**	**6**	**42**	**9**	**4**	**.218**	**.260**	**.289**	**.549**	**55**	**-8**	**11**	**2.46**	**-3**	**/0-32,1-20**	**2**	**-1.3**

• SMITH, Dick — Richard Harrison Smith b: 7/21/1927, Blandburg, PA BR/TR, 5'8", 160 lbs. Deb: 9/14/1951

YEAR	TM-L	G	AB	R	H	2B	3B	HR	RBI	BB	SO	SB	CS	AVG	OBP	SLG	OPS	OPS+	BR/A	RC	RC/G	FR	G/POS	WS	TPW
1951	Pit-N	12	46	2	8	0	0	0	4	8	8	0	2	.174	.296	.174	.470	29	-5	3	1.80	1	3-12	0	-0.4
1952	Pit-N	29	66	8	7	1	0	0	5	9	3	0	0	.106	.213	.121	.335	-5	-9	2	.95	0	3-16/2-4,S-4	1	-0.9
1953	Pit-N	13	43	4	7	0	1	0	2	6	6	0	1	.163	.265	.209	.475	26	-5	2	1.72	4	S-13	0	0.0
1954	Pit-N	12	31	2	3	1	1	0	0	6	5	0	0	.097	.243	.194	.437	16	-4	2	1.52	0	/3-9	0	-0.4
1955	Pit-N	4	0	1	0	0	0	0	0	1	0	0	0	....	1.000	....	1.000	198	0	0	∞	-1	/S-1	0	0.0
Total	**5**	**70**	**186**	**17**	**25**	**2**	**2**	**0**	**11**	**30**	**22**	**0**	**3**	**.134**	**.255**	**.167**	**.421**	**15**	**-23**	**9**	**1.43**	**4**	**/3-37,S-18,2-4**	**1**	**-1.8**

• SMITH, Dwight — John Dwight Smith b: 11/8/1963, Tallahassee, FL BL/TR, 5'11", 175 lbs. Deb: 5/1/1989 Career OF: 238-98-173

YEAR	TM-L	G	AB	R	H	2B	3B	HR	RBI	BB	SO	SB	CS	AVG	OBP	SLG	OPS	OPS+	BR/A	RC	RC/G	FR	G/POS	WS	TPW
1989*	Chi-N	109	343	52	111	19	6	9	52	31	51	9	4	.324	.383	.493	.876	138	17	66	7.27	3	*0-102(75-0-32)	16	1.9
1990	Chi-N	117	290	34	76	15	0	6	27	28	46	11	6	.262	.331	.376	.707	88	-5	36	4.19	1	0-81(59-3-22)	6	-0.7
1991	Chi-N	90	167	16	38	7	2	3	21	11	32	2	3	.228	.279	.347	.627	72	-8	16	3.11	-1	0-42(5-13-28)	4	-1.0

YEAR TM-L	G	AB	R	H	2B	3B	HR	RBI	BB	SO	SB	CS	AVG	OBP	SLG	OPS	OPS+	BR/A	RC	RC/G	FR	G/POS	WS	TPW
1992 Chi-N	109	217	28	60	10	3	3	24	13	40	9	8	.276	.320	.392	.712	98	-3	26	4.23	-2	0-63(20-27-22)	6	-0.6
1993 Chi-N	111	310	51	93	17	5	11	35	25	51	8	6	.300	.358	.494	.852	127	10	54	6.39	-2	0-89(14-53-28)	10	0.7
1994 Cal-A	45	122	19	32	5	1	5	18	7	20	2	3	.262	.302	.443	.745	88	-4	15	4.39	0	0-31(31-0-0)/D-2	2	-0.5
Bal-A	28	74	12	23	2	1	3	12	5	17	0	1	.311	.363	.486	.849	111	1	12	6.06	-2	0-22(20-2-1)/D-3	2	-0.2
Yr.	73	196	31	55	7	2	8	30	12	37	2	4	.281	.325	.459	.785	96	-3	28	5.00	-2	0-53(51-2-1)/D-5	4	-0.6
1995*Atl-N	103	131	16	33	8	2	3	21	13	35	0	3	.252	.329	.412	.741	91	-3	17	4.42	-1	0-25(11-0-14)	3	-0.5
1996 Atl-N	101	153	16	31	5	0	3	16	17	42	1	3	.203	.287	.294	.581	51	-12	13	2.72	1	0-29(3-0-26)	1	-1.2
Total 8	813	1807	244	497	88	20	46	226	150	334	42	37	.275	.335	.422	.757	102	-6	255	4.97	-2	0-484/D-5	50	-2.0

• SMITH, Earl Earl Calvin Smith b: 3/14/1928, Sunnyside, WA BR/TR, 6', 185 lbs. Deb: 4/14/1955

YEAR TM-L	G	AB	R	H	2B	3B	HR	RBI	BB	SO	SB	CS	AVG	OBP	SLG	OPS	OPS+	BR/A	RC	RC/G	FR	G/POS	WS	TPW
1955 Pit-N	5	16	1	1	0	0	0	0	4	2	0	0	.063	.286	.063	.348	-1	-2	1	1.18	0	/0-5(0-5-0)	0	-0.2

• SMITH, Earl Earl Sutton "Oil" Smith b: 2/14/1897, Hot Springs, AR d: 6/8/1963, Little Rock, AR BL/TR, 5'10.5", 180 lbs. Deb: 4/24/1919

YEAR TM-L	G	AB	R	H	2B	3B	HR	RBI	BB	SO	SB	CS	AVG	OBP	SLG	OPS	OPS+	BR/A	RC	RC/G	FR	G/POS	WS	TPW
1919 NY-N	21	36	5	9	2	1	0	8	3	3	1	....	.250	.308	.361	.669	102	0	4	3.85	-1	C-14/2-1	1	-0.1
1920 NY-N	91	262	20	77	7	1	1	30	18	16	5	2	.294	.344	.340	.684	98	1	31	4.39	-3	C-82	10	0.4
1921*NY-N	89	229	35	77	8	4	10	51	27	8	4	3	.336	.409	.537	.946	148	17	50	8.40	-4	C-78	14	1.7
1922*NY-N	90	234	29	65	11	4	9	39	37	12	1	1	.278	.383	.474	.858	119	8	44	6.89	-6	C-75	10	0.6
1923 NY-N	24	34	2	7	1	1	1	4	4	1	0	0	.206	.289	.382	.672	77	-1	4	3.73	0	C-12	1	-0.1
Bos-N	72	191	22	55	15	1	3	19	22	10	0	1	.288	.364	.424	.789	112	4	30	5.74	5	C-54	6	1.1
Yr.	96	225	24	62	16	2	4	23	26	11	0	1	.276	.353	.418	.771	107	3	34	5.40	5	C-66	7	1.0
1924 Bos-N	33	59	1	16	3	0	0	8	6	3	0	1	.271	.338	.322	.660	81	-2	6	3.79	0	C-13	1	-0.1
Pit-N	39	111	12	41	10	1	4	21	13	4	2	0	.369	.435	.586	1.021	168	12	29	10.36	-4	C-35	8	1.0
Yr.	72	170	13	57	13	1	4	29	19	7	2	1	.335	.402	.494	.896	139	10	35	7.88	-3	C-48	9	1.0
1925*Pit-N	109	329	34	103	22	3	8	64	31	13	4	1	.313	.374	.471	.845	107	5	59	6.74	-2	C-96	15	0.9
1926 Pit-N	105	292	29	101	17	2	2	46	28	7	1	....	.346	.407	.438	.845	121	10	52	6.70	-3	C-98	14	1.3
1927*Pit-N	66	189	16	51	3	1	5	25	21	11	0	....	.270	.346	.376	.722	87	-3	25	4.36	-2	C-61	6	-0.2
1928 Pit-N	32	85	8	21	6	0	2	11	11	7	0	....	.247	.333	.388	.722	85	-2	11	4.34	-1	C-28	2	-0.2
*StL-N	24	58	3	13	2	0	0	7	5	4	0	....	.224	.286	.259	.544	42	-5	4	2.48	-1	C-18	1	-0.5
Yr.	56	143	11	34	8	0	2	18	16	11	0	....	.238	.314	.336	.650	68	-7	16	3.58	-2	C-46	3	-0.6
1929 StL-N	57	145	9	50	8	0	1	22	18	6	0	....	.345	.417	.421	.838	107	3	26	6.91	-2	C-50	5	0.3
1930 StL-N	8	10	0	0	0	0	0	0	3	1	0	....	.000	.231	.000	.231	-36	-2	0	.44	-1	/C-6	0	-0.2
Total 12	860	2264	225	686	115	19	46	355	247	106	18	9	.303	.374	.432	.806	111	43	377	6.07	-25	C-720/2-1	94	6.0

• SMITH, Earl Earl Leonard "Sheriff" Smith b: 1/20/1891, Oak Hill, OH d: 3/14/1943, Portsmouth, OH BB/TR, 5'11", 170 lbs. Deb: 9/12/1916 Career OF: 136-68-114

YEAR TM-L	G	AB	R	H	2B	3B	HR	RBI	BB	SO	SB	CS	AVG	OBP	SLG	OPS	OPS+	BR/A	RC	RC/G	FR	G/POS	WS	TPW
1916 Chi-N	14	27	2	7	1	1	0	4	2	5	1	....	.259	.310	.370	.681	98	-0	4	4.35	0	/0-7(6-0-1)	0	-0.1
1917 StL-A	52	199	31	56	7	7	0	10	15	21	5	....	.281	.332	.387	.719	124	5	27	4.58	5	0-51(22-29-0)	7	0.7
1918 StL-A	89	286	28	77	10	5	0	32	13	16	13	....	.269	.303	.339	.642	97	-3	33	3.71	2	0-81(54-25-2)	7	-0.6
1919 StL-A	88	252	21	63	12	5	1	36	18	27	1	....	.250	.300	.349	.649	80	-7	27	3.45	8	0-68(0-4-64)	5	-0.3
1920 StL-A	103	353	45	108	21	8	3	55	13	18	11	4	.306	.336	.436	.772	100	0	51	5.29	-2	3-70,0-15(4-2-9)	8	-0.1
1921 StL-A	25	78	7	26	4	2	2	14	3	4	0	0	.333	.366	.513	.879	115	2	14	7.21	-3	3-13/0-4(0-4-0)	3	-0.1
Was-A	59	180	20	39	5	2	2	12	10	19	1	0	.217	.266	.300	.566	46	-14	15	2.72	4	0-43(3-4-36)/3-1	1	-1.2
Yr.	84	258	27	65	9	4	4	26	13	23	1	0	.252	.296	.364	.660	67	-13	29	3.92	1	0-47(3-8-36),3-14	4	-1.3
1922 Was-A	65	205	22	53	12	2	1	23	8	17	4	4	.259	.293	.351	.644	71	-10	20	3.34	4	0-49(47-0-2)/3-2	3	-0.9
Total 7	495	1580	176	429	72	32	9	186	82	127	36	8	.272	.311	.375	.686	90	-28	191	4.10	17	0-318/3-86	34	-2.5

• SMITH, Edgar Edgar Eugene Smith b: 6/12/1862, Providence, RI d: 11/3/1892, Providence, RI BR/TR, 5'10", 160 lbs. Deb: 5/25/1883 U Career OF: 3-0-14 ♦

YEAR TM-L	G	AB	R	H	2B	3B	HR	RBI	BB	SO	SB	CS	AVG	OBP	SLG	OPS	OPS+	BR/A	RC	RC/G	FR	G/POS	WS	TPW
1883 Pro-N	2	9	2	2	1	0	0	1	0	2	....	....	.222	.222	.333	.556	64	-0	1	2.68	-0	/1-2,0-2(2-0-0)	0	0.0
Phi-N	1	4	1	3	0	0	0	1	0	0	....	....	.750	.750	.750	1.500	393	1	2	63.42	-1	/0-1,P-1	1	-0.7
Yr.	3	13	3	5	1	0	0	2	0	2	....	....	.385	.385	.462	.846	165	1	3	10.28	-1	/0-3(3-0-0),1-2,P-1	1	-0.7
1884 Was-a	14	57	5	5	0	1	0	0	1	....	....	....	.088	.103	.123	.226	-30	-7	1	.39	3	0-12(0-0-12)/P-3	0	-0.6
1885 Pro-N	1	4	0	1	0	0	0	0	0	0	....	....	.250	.250	.250	.500	65	0	0	2.31	0	/P-1	1	0.2
1890 Cle-N	8	24	2	7	0	1	0	4	4	1	0	....	.292	.393	.375	.768	126	2	4	5.65	1	/P-6,0-2(0-0-2)	3	-0.1
Total 4	26	98	10	18	1	2	0	6	5	3	0	....	.184	.223	.235	.458	41	-4	8	2.57	4	/0-17,P-11,1-2	5	-1.3

• SMITH, Edgar (AE) Albert Edgar Smith b: 10/15/1860, North Haven, CT TR, 6', 200 lbs. Deb: 6/20/1883 U

YEAR TM-L	G	AB	R	H	2B	3B	HR	RBI	BB	SO	SB	CS	AVG	OBP	SLG	OPS	OPS+	BR/A	RC	RC/G	FR	G/POS	WS	TPW
1883 Bos-N	30	115	10	25	5	3	0	16	5	11	....	....	.217	.250	.313	.563	68	-4	9	2.82	0	0-30(0-30-0)/C-1	2	-0.5

• SMITH, Elmer Elmer Ellsworth Smith b: 3/23/1868, Pittsburgh, PA d: 11/5/1945, Pittsburgh, PA BL/TL, 5'11", 178 lbs. Deb: 9/10/1886 Career OF: 924-39-123 ♦

YEAR TM-L	G	AB	R	H	2B	3B	HR	RBI	BB	SO	SB	CS	AVG	OBP	SLG	OPS	OPS+	BR/A	RC	RC/G	FR	G/POS	WS	TPW
1886 Cin-a	9	28	6	8	1	1	0	2	9	....	0	....	.286	.459	.393	.852	163	4	5	6.99	-2	/P-9,0-1	5	0.2
1887 Cin-a	52	197	26	58	10	6	0	23	11	....	5	....	.294	.298	.371	.669	84	4	23	4.39	-4	P-52/0-2(0-2-0)	54	4.5
1888 Cin-a	40	129	15	29	4	1	0	9	20	....	2	....	.225	.329	.271	.600	88	5	12	3.37	-5	P-40/0-2(0-2-0)	30	1.2
1889 Cin-a	29	83	12	23	3	1	2	17	7	18	1	....	.277	.348	.410	.757	112	5	12	5.51	-5	P-29	9	-1.5
1892 Pit-N	138	511	86	140	16	14	4	63	82	43	22	....	.274	.375	.384	.759	129	24	84	6.11	-2	*0-124(115-2-7),P-17	31	0.3
1893 Pit-N	128	518	121	179	26	23	7	103	77	23	26	....	.346	.435	.525	.960	158	44	133	10.39	5	*0-128(128-0-0)	25	3.1
1894 Pit-N	126	490	128	175	33	19	6	74	68	12	34	....	.357	.440	.539	.979	136	30	134	11.03	2	*0-125(120-5-0)/P-1	19	1.6
1895 Pit-N	125	484	89	146	15	12	1	81	55	25	34	....	.302	.380	.388	.768	104	6	86	6.89	1	*0-123(123-0-0)	16	-0.4
1896 Pit-N	122	484	121	175	21	14	6	94	74	18	33	....	.362	.454	.500	.954	158	45	129	10.82	6	*0-122(122-0-0)	26	3.4
1897 Pit-N	123	467	99	145	19	17	6	54	70	....	25	....	.310	.408	.463	.871	135	26	102	8.20	-1	*0-123(123-0-0)	20	1.2
1898 Cin-N	123	486	79	166	21	10	1	66	69	....	20	....	.342	.425	.432	.858	136	26	101	8.22	-0	*0-123(123-0-0)/P-1	27	1.2
1899 Cin-N	88	343	65	101	13	6	1	24	47	....	10	....	.294	.381	.376	.757	106	4	55	5.89	-4	0-87(37-28-22)	12	-0.6
1900 Cin-N	29	111	14	31	4	4	1	18	18	....	5	....	.279	.389	.414	.804	125	5	20	6.74	1	0-27(27-0-0)	5	0.2
NY-N	85	312	47	81	9	7	2	34	24	....	14	....	.260	.317	.353	.669	88	-5	41	4.56	-4	0-83(0-0-83)	6	-1.2
Yr.	114	423	61	112	13	11	3	52	42	....	19	....	.265	.337	.369	.706	98	-0	62	5.10	-3	*0-110(27-0-83)	11	-1.0
1901 Pit-N	4	4	0	0	0	0	0	0	2	....	0	....	.000	.333	.000	.333	1	-0	0	.00	-0	/0-1	0	0.0
Bos-N	16	57	5	10	2	1	0	3	6	....	2	....	.175	.254	.246	.500	41	-4	4	2.37	-3	0-15(4-0-11)	0	-0.8
Yr.	20	61	5	10	2	1	0	3	8	....	2	....	.164	.261	.230	.490	38	-5	4	2.18	-3	0-16(5-0-11)	0	-0.8
Total 14	1237	4704	913	1467	197	136	37	665	639	139	233	....	.312	.398	.434	.831	126	219	942	7.64	-17	*0-1086,P-149	285	12.4

• SMITH, Elmer Elmer John Smith b: 9/21/1892, Sandusky, OH d: 8/3/1984, Columbia, KY BL/TR, 5'10", 165 lbs. Deb: 9/20/1914 Career OF: 123-16-732

YEAR TM-L	G	AB	R	H	2B	3B	HR	RBI	BB	SO	SB	CS	AVG	OBP	SLG	OPS	OPS+	BR/A	RC	RC/G	FR	G/POS	WS	TPW
1914 Cle-A	13	53	5	17	3	0	0	8	2	11	1	1	.321	.345	.377	.723	113	0	7	4.86	0	0-13(0-13-0)	2	0.0
1915 Cle-A	144	476	37	118	23	12	3	67	36	75	10	11	.248	.301	.366	.666	98	-7	53	3.66	1	*0-123(21-0-102)	8	-1.4
1916 Cle-A	79	213	25	59	15	3	3	40	18	35	3	....	.277	.336	.418	.754	119	4	32	5.15	1	0-57(1-0-56)	7	0.3
Was-A	45	168	12	36	10	3	2	27	18	28	4	....	.214	.298	.345	.643	94	-2	19	3.62	0	0-45(10-0-35)	4	-0.4
Yr.	124	381	37	95	25	6	5	67	36	63	7	....	.249	.319	.386	.705	108	2	51	4.44	1	*0-102(11-0-91)	11	-0.1
1917 Was-A	35	117	8	26	4	3	0	17	5	14	1	....	.222	.260	.308	.568	74	-4	10	2.58	-1	0-29(27-0-2)	1	-0.7
Cle-A	64	161	21	42	5	1	3	22	13	18	6	....	.261	.316	.360	.676	99	-1	20	4.08	2	0-40(8-0-32)	4	-0.1
Yr.	99	278	29	68	9	4	3	39	18	32	7	....	.245	.293	.338	.631	89	-5	29	3.43	1	0-69(35-0-34)	5	-0.8
1919 Cle-A	114	395	60	110	24	6	9	54	41	30	15	....	.278	.354	.438	.792	115	7	64	5.62	-4	*0-111(0-0-111)	15	-0.2
1920*Cle-A	129	456	82	144	37	10	12	103	53	35	5	4	.316	.391	.520	.910	135	24	93	7.53	-7	*0-129(0-0-129)	21	1.0
1921 Cle-A	129	431	98	125	28	9	16	85	56	46	0	2	.290	.374	.508	.882	121	13	83	6.82	-5	*0-127(1-0-126)	16	-0.1
1922 Bos-A	73	231	43	66	13	6	6	32	25	21	0	3	.286	.358	.472	.830	116	4	39	5.88	3	0-58(0-1-57)	8	0.2
*NY-A	21	27	1	5	0	0	1	5	3	5	0	0	.185	.267	.296	.563	45	-2	2	2.65	0	0-11(2-0-9)	0	-0.2
Yr.	94	258	44	71	13	6	7	37	28	26	0	3	.275	.348	.453	.802	108	2	41	5.50	3	0-69(2-1-66)	8	0.0
1923 NY-A	70	183	30	56	6	2	7	35	21	21	3	1	.306	.377	.475	.853	121	6	34	6.76	0	0-47(0-0-47)	7	0.3
1925 Cin-N	96	284	47	77	13	7	8	46	28	20	6	5	.271	.339	.451	.789	102	0	43	5.21	2	0-80(53-2-26)	8	-0.3
Total 10	1012	3195	469	881	181	62	70	541	319	359	54	27	.276	.344	.437	.781	112	42	499	5.39	-8	0-870	101	-1.8

• SMITH, Ernie Ernest Henry "Kansas City Kid" Smith b: 10/11/1899, Totowa, NJ d: 4/6/1973, Brooklyn, NY BR/TR, 5'8", 155 lbs. Deb: 4/17/1930

YEAR TM-L	G	AB	R	H	2B	3B	HR	RBI	BB	SO	SB	CS	AVG	OBP	SLG	OPS	OPS+	BR/A	RC	RC/G	FR	G/POS	WS	TPW
1930 Chi-A	24	79	5	19	3	0	0	3	5	6	2	0	.241	.286	.278	.564	45	-6	7	2.90	-6	S-21	0	-0.9

YEAR TM-L	G	AB	R	H	2B	3B	HR	RBI	BB	SO	SB	CS	AVG	OBP	SLG	OPS	OPS+	BR/A	RC	RC/G	FR	G/POS	WS	TPW
• SMITH, Frank	Frank L. Smith b: 11/24/1857, Canada d: 10/11/1928, Canandaigua, NY Deb: 8/6/1884																							
1884 Pit-a	10	36	3	9	0	1	0	0	0	....	....	....	.250	.250	.306	.556	79	-1	3	2.87	-2	/C-7,0-3(1-1-1)	1	-0.2
• SMITH, Fred	Fred Vincent Smith b: 7/29/1891, Cleveland, OH d: 5/28/1961, Cleveland, OH BR/TR, 5'11.5", 185 lbs. Deb: 4/17/1913																							
1913 Bos-N	92	285	35	65	9	3	0	27	29	55	7	....	.228	.302	.281	.582	65	-12	26	2.88	-9	3-59,2-14,S-11/0-4(4-0-0)	4	-1.9
1914 Buf-F	145	473	48	104	12	10	2	45	49	78	24	....	.220	.297	.300	.597	67	-20	47	3.15	0	*3-127,S-19/1-1	10	-1.5
1915 Buf-F	35	114	8	27	2	4	0	11	13	15	2	....	.237	.320	.325	.645	90	-1	12	3.50	0	S-32/3-1	4	0.1
Bro-F	110	385	41	95	16	6	5	58	25	49	21	....	.247	.298	.358	.656	95	-4	46	3.87	-8	S-94,3-15	9	-0.5
Yr.	145	499	49	122	18	10	5	69	38	64	23	....	.244	.303	.351	.654	94	-5	57	3.79	-8	*S-126,3-16	13	-0.4
1917 StL-N	56	165	11	30	0	2	1	17	17	22	4	....	.182	.262	.224	.487	51	-9	10	1.94	1	3-51/2-2,S-1	2	-0.8
Total 4	438	1422	143	321	39	25	8	158	133	219	58	....	.226	.296	.305	.601	74	-47	141	3.17	-15	3-253,S-157/2-16,0-4,1-1	29	-4.6
• SMITH, George	George Cornelius Smith b: 7/7/1937, St. Petersburg, FL d: 6/15/1987, St. Petersburg, FL BR/TR, 5'10", 170 lbs. Deb: 8/4/1963																							
1963 Det-A	52	171	16	37	8	2	0	17	18	34	4	0	.216	.298	.287	.585	63	-7	16	3.00	7	2-52	3	0.5
1964 Det-A	5	7	1	2	0	0	0	2	1	4	1	0	.286	.375	.286	.661	86	0	1	5.63	0	/2-3	0	0.1
1965 Det-A	32	53	6	5	0	0	1	1	3	18	0	0	.094	.143	.151	.294	-16	-8	1	.51	-1	2-22/3-3,S-3	1	-0.9
1966 Bos-A	128	403	41	86	19	4	8	37	37	86	4	0	.213	.284	.340	.624	71	-14	39	3.21	0	*2-109,S-19	7	-0.3
Total 4	217	634	64	130	27	6	9	57	59	142	9	0	.205	.278	.309	.587	62	-29	57	2.92	7	2-186/S-22,3-3	11	-0.6
• SMITH, Germany	George J. Smith b: 4/21/1863, Pittsburgh, PA d: 12/1/1927, Altoona, PA BR/TR, 6', 175 lbs. Deb: 4/17/1884 Career OF: 1-0-1																							
1884 Alt-U	25	108	9	34	8	1	0	....	1	....	....	....	.315	.321	.407	.729	143	4	14	5.48	7	S-25/P-1	3	1.0
Cle-N	72	291	31	74	14	4	4	26	2	45	....	....	.254	.259	.371	.631	93	-4	29	3.64	4	2-42,S-30	6	0.3
1885 Bro-a	108	419	63	108	17	11	4	62	10	....	....	....	.258	.275	.379	.655	104	0	45	3.89	36	*S-108	15	3.6
1886 Bro-a	105	426	66	105	17	6	2	45	19	....	22	....	.246	.279	.329	.607	89	-7	46	3.89	14	*S-105/C-1,0-1	14	0.9
1887 Bro-a	103	448	79	141	19	16	4	72	13	....	26	....	.315	.316	.439	.755	108	1	70	6.19	22	*S-101/3-2	16	2.2
1888 Bro-a	103	402	47	86	10	7	3	61	22	....	27	....	.214	.255	.296	.551	76	-12	38	3.26	14	*S-103/2-1	12	0.6
1889*Bro-a	121	446	89	103	22	3	3	53	40	42	35	....	.231	.296	.314	.610	73	-16	53	4.10	3	*S-120/0-1	15	-0.8
1890*Bro-N	129	481	76	92	6	5	1	47	42	23	24	....	.191	.260	.231	.491	43	-35	36	2.46	11	*S-129	10	-1.8
1891 Cin-N	138	512	50	103	11	5	3	53	38	32	16	....	.201	.258	.260	.517	50	-34	39	2.60	5	*S-138	7	-2.2
1892 Cin-N	139	506	58	123	13	6	8	63	42	52	19	....	.243	.301	.340	.641	95	-4	59	4.16	27	*S-139	20	2.7
1893 Cin-N	130	500	63	118	18	6	4	56	38	20	14	....	.236	.293	.320	.613	61	-31	52	3.62	17	*S-130	14	-0.6
1894 Cin-N	129	492	73	130	34	5	3	79	41	28	15	....	.264	.323	.372	.695	65	-31	66	4.71	0	*S-127	10	-1.9
1895 Cin-N	127	503	75	151	23	6	4	74	34	24	13	....	.300	.345	.394	.738	86	-12	75	5.69	2	*S-127	14	-0.3
1896 Cin-N	120	456	65	131	21	9	3	71	28	22	22	....	.287	.330	.393	.722	84	-13	69	5.48	1	*S-120	14	-0.5
1897 Bro-N	112	428	47	86	17	3	0	29	14	....	1	....	.201	.233	.255	.488	30	-43	27	2.06	-5	*S-112	5	-3.7
1898 StL-N	51	157	16	25	2	1	1	9	24	....	1	....	.159	.275	.204	.479	37	-12	10	1.90	-12	S-51	0	-2.0
Total 15	1712	6575	907	1610	252	94	47	800	408	288	235	....	.245	.289	.332	.621	75	-249	728	3.91	146	*S-1665/2-43,3-2,0-2,C-1,P	175	-2.5
• SMITH, Greg	Gregory Alan Smith b: 4/5/1967, Baltimore, MD BB/TR, 5'11", 170 lbs. Deb: 9/2/1989																							
1989 Chi-N	4	5	1	2	0	0	0	2	0	0	0	0	.400	.500	.400	.900	149	0	1	10.17	-1	/2-2	1	-0.1
1990 Chi-N	18	44	4	9	2	1	0	5	2	5	1	0	.205	.239	.295	.535	43	-3	3	2.23	0	/2-7,S-7	1	-0.3
1991 LA-N	5	3	1	0	0	0	0	0	0	2	0	0	.000	.000	.000	.000	-102	-1	0	.00	-1	/2-1	0	-0.1
Total 3	27	52	6	11	2	1	0	7	2	7	1	0	.212	.255	.288	.543	44	-4	4	2.56	-2	/2-10,S-7	2	-0.5
• SMITH, Hal	Harold Wayne Smith b: 12/7/1930, West Frankfort, IL BR/TR, 6', 195 lbs. Deb: 4/11/1955																							
1955 Bal-A	135	424	41	115	23	4	4	52	30	21	1	3	.271	.322	.373	.695	93	-7	47	3.76	3	*C-125	10	0.2
1956 Bal-A	77	229	16	60	14	0	3	18	17	22	1	0	.262	.316	.362	.678	85	-5	22	3.17	5	C-71	6	0.3
KC-A	37	142	15	39	9	2	2	24	3	12	1	1	.275	.290	.408	.698	82	-5	16	3.97	3	C-37	3	0.0
Yr.	114	371	31	99	23	2	5	42	20	34	2	1	.267	.306	.380	.686	84	-10	38	3.46	8	*C-108	9	0.3
1957 KC-A	107	360	41	109	26	0	13	41	14	44	2	2	.303	.331	.483	.814	118	7	52	5.13	-1	*C-103	12	1.1
1958 KC-A	99	315	32	86	19	2	5	46	25	47	0	0	.273	.330	.394	.724	97	-1	41	4.56	-3	3-43,C-31,1-14	10	-0.3
1959 KC-A	108	292	36	84	12	0	5	31	34	39	0	3	.288	.368	.380	.748	104	1	42	5.20	-2	3-77,C-22	9	0.0
1960*Pit-N	77	258	37	76	18	2	11	45	22	48	1	1	.295	.355	.508	.862	132	11	45	6.36	-3	C-71	13	1.1
1961 Pit-N	67	193	12	43	10	0	3	26	11	38	0	0	.223	.268	.321	.590	55	-13	16	2.66	-5	C-65	2	-1.5
1962 Hou-N	109	345	32	81	14	0	12	35	24	55	0	0	.235	.288	.380	.668	84	-9	35	3.35	3	C-92/3-6,1-2	7	-0.1
1963 Hou-N	31	58	1	14	2	0	0	2	4	15	0	0	.241	.290	.276	.566	68	-2	4	2.13	-1	C-11	0	-0.3
1964 Cin-N	32	66	6	8	1	0	0	3	12	20	1	0	.121	.256	.136	.393	14	-7	2	.93	0	C-20	1	-0.6
Total 10	879	2682	269	715	148	10	58	323	196	361	7	10	.267	.320	.394	.714	94	-30	323	4.11	0	C-648,3-126/1-16	73	0.0
• SMITH, Hal	Harold Raymond "Cura" Smith b: 6/1/1931, Barling, AR BR/TR, 5'10.5", 189 lbs. Deb: 5/2/1956 C																							
1956 StL-N	75	227	27	64	12	0	5	23	15	22	1	0	.282	.326	.401	.727	94	-2	28	4.46	-1	C-66	7	0.1
1957 StL-N★	100	333	25	93	12	3	2	37	18	18	2	2	.279	.316	.351	.668	78	-11	35	3.71	1	C-97	9	-0.6
1958 StL-N	77	220	13	50	4	1	1	24	14	14	0	0	.227	.274	.268	.542	42	-18	16	2.33	0	C-71	3	-1.5
1959 StL-N★	142	452	35	122	15	3	13	50	15	28	2	6	.270	.295	.403	.698	78	-17	47	3.61	4	*C-141	10	-0.7
1960 StL-N	127	337	20	77	16	0	2	28	29	33	1	0	.228	.292	.294	.585	56	-20	27	2.66	5	*C-124	9	-1.0
1961 StL-N	45	125	6	31	4	1	0	10	11	12	0	0	.248	.314	.296	.610	57	-7	12	3.11	3	C-45	4	-0.2
1965 Pit-N	4	3	0	0	0	0	0	0	0	1	0	0	.000	.000	.000	.000	-100	-1	0	.00	0	/C-4	0	-0.1
Total 7	570	1697	126	437	63	8	23	172	102	128	6	8	.258	.301	.345	.646	69	-76	165	3.32	12	C-548	42	-4.0
• SMITH, Happy	Henry Joseph Smith b: 7/14/1883, Coquille, OR d: 2/26/1961, San Jose, CA BL/TR, 6', 185 lbs. Deb: 4/15/1910																							
1910 Bro-N	35	76	6	18	2	0	0	5	4	14	4	....	.237	.275	.263	.538	59	-4	6	2.82	2	0-16(0-5-11)	1	-0.3
• SMITH, Harry	Harry Thomas Smith b: 10/31/1874, Yorkshire, England d: 2/17/1933, Salem, NJ BR/TR, 5'8.5" Deb: 7/11/1901 M/U Career OF: 2-0-3																							
1901 Phi-A	11	34	3	11	1	0	0	3	2	....	1	....	.324	.378	.353	.731	99	0	5	5.73	0	/C-9,0-1	1	0.0
1902 Pit-N	50	185	14	35	4	1	0	12	4	....	4	....	.189	.211	.222	.432	32	-15	10	1.76	-7	C-50	2	-1.8
1903*Pit-N	61	212	15	37	3	2	0	19	12	....	2	....	.175	.222	.208	.430	22	-22	12	1.66	-7	C-60/0-1	3	-2.2
1904 Pit-N	47	141	17	35	3	1	0	18	16	....	5	....	.248	.346	.284	.629	92	-0	16	3.92	1	C-44/0-3(2-0-1)	5	0.5
1905 Pit-N	1	3	0	0	0	0	0	1	0	....	1	....	.000	.000	.000	.000	-98	-1	0	.00	0	/C-1	0	0.0
1906 Pit-N	1	1	0	0	0	0	0	0	0	....	0	....	.000	.000	.000	.000	-96	-0	0	.00	-1	/C-1	0	-0.1
1907 Pit-N	18	38	4	10	1	0	0	1	4	....	0	....	.263	.364	.289	.653	103	1	4	3.83	-1	C-18	2	0.1
1908 Bos-N	41	130	13	32	2	2	1	16	7	....	2	....	.246	.295	.315	.610	96	-1	13	3.22	2	C-38	4	0.6
1909 Bos-N	43	113	9	19	4	1	0	4	5	....	3	....	.168	.203	.221	.425	30	-10	5	1.48	3	C-31	1	-0.4
1910 Bos-N	70	147	8	35	4	0	1	15	5	14	5	....	.238	.263	.286	.549	57	-9	12	2.72	-1	C-38	1	-0.7
Total 10	343	1004	83	214	22	7	2	89	55	14	23	....	.213	.262	.255	.517	55	-57	78	2.49	-12	C-290/0-5	19	-4.1
• SMITH, Harry	James Harry Smith b: 5/15/1890, Brooklyn, NY d: 4/1/1922, Charlotte, NC BR/TR, 5'10", 180 lbs. Deb: 9/21/1914 Career OF: 0-1-1																							
1914 NY-N	5	7	0	3	0	0	0	2	3	1	1	....	.429	.600	.429	1.029	215	1	2	14.66	0	/C-4	1	0.2
1915 NY-N	21	32	1	4	0	1	0	3	6	12	0	1	.125	.263	.188	.451	40	-3	1	1.30	-1	C-18	0	-0.3
Bro-F	28	65	5	13	0	0	1	4	7	16	2	....	.200	.278	.246	.524	56	-3	5	2.33	-2	C-19/0-1	1	-0.4
1917 Cin-N	8	17	0	2	0	0	0	1	2	7	0	....	.118	.211	.118	.328	2	-2	1	.85	1	/C-7	0	0.0
1918 Cin-N	13	27	4	5	1	2	0	4	3	6	1	....	.185	.267	.370	.637	95	-0	3	3.19	0	/C-6,0-1	1	0.0
Total 4	75	148	10	27	1	3	1	14	21	42	4	1	.182	.284	.250	.534	62	-7	12	2.45	-2	/C-54,0-2	3	-0.6
• SMITH, Harry	Harry W. Smith b: 2/5/1856, North Vernon, IN d: 6/4/1898, Queensville, IN BR/TR, 6', 175 lbs. Deb: 5/8/1877 Career OF: 0-11-3																							
1877 Chi-N	24	94	7	19	1	0	0	3	4	6	....	....	.202	.235	.213	.447	37	-7	5	1.76	-9	2-14,0-10(0-7-3)	0	-1.4
Cin-N	10	36	4	9	2	1	0	3	1	5	....	....	.250	.270	.361	.631	109	1	4	3.67	1	/C-8,2-3,0-3(0-3-0)	1	0.1
Yr.	34	130	11	28	3	1	0	6	5	11	....	....	.215	.244	.254	.498	57	-6	8	2.27	-8	2-17,0-13(0-10-3)/C-8	1	-1.3
1889 Lou-a	1	2	0	1	0	0	0	1	0	1	0	....	.500	.500	.500	1.000	188	0	1	13.58	-1	/C-1,0-1	0	-0.1
Total 2	35	132	11	29	3	1	0	7	5	12	0	....	.220	.248	.258	.506	59	-6	9	2.38	-9	/2-17,0-14,C-9	1	-1.3

YEAR TM-L	G	AB	R	H	2B	3B	HR	RBI	BB	SO	SB	CS	AVG	OBP	SLG	OPS	OPS+	BR/A	RC	RC/G	FR	G/POS	WS	TPW
• SMITH, Harvey	Harvey Fetterhoff Smith b: 7/24/1871, Union Deposit, PA d: 11/12/1962, Harrisburg, PA BL/TR, 5'8", 160 lbs. Deb: 8/19/1896																							
1896 Was-N	36	131	21	36	7	2	0	17	12	7	9	....	.275	.345	.359	.704	86	-3	20	5.43	-2	3-36	3	-0.3
• SMITH, Heinie	George Henry Smith b: 10/24/1871, Pittsburgh, PA d: 6/25/1939, Buffalo, NY BR/TR, 5'9.5", 160 lbs. Deb: 9/8/1897 M/U																							
1897 Lou-N	21	76	7	20	3	0	1	7	3	....	1	....	.263	.300	.342	.642	72	-3	8	3.92	-5	2-21	1	-0.6
1898 Lou-N	35	121	14	23	4	0	0	13	6	....	6	....	.190	.246	.223	.469	35	-10	9	2.29	-4	2-33	0	-1.2
1899 Pit-N	15	53	9	15	3	1	0	12	5	....	2	....	.283	.345	.377	.722	98	-0	8	5.37	-4	2-15/S-1	1	-0.3
1901 NY-N	9	29	5	6	2	1	1	4	1	....	1	....	.207	.233	.448	.682	99	0	3	3.76	-3	/2-7,P-2	1	-0.9
1902 NY-N	140	517	48	129	19	2	0	34	17	....	32	....	.250	.275	.294	.569	76	-16	52	3.53	-1	*2-138	9	-1.6
1903 Det-A	93	336	36	75	11	3	1	22	19	....	12	....	.223	.271	.283	.554	68	-13	32	3.02	-2	2-93	5	-1.5
Total 6	**313**	**1132**	**119**	**268**	**42**	**7**	**3**	**92**	**51**	**....**	**54**	**....**	**.237**	**.275**	**.294**	**.569**	**71**	**-42**	**113**	**3.34**	**-18**	**2-307/P-2,S-1**	**17**	**-6.1**
• SMITH, Jack	Jack Smith b: 6/23/1895, Chicago, IL d: 5/2/1972, Westchester, IL BL/TL, 5'8", 165 lbs. Deb: 9/30/1915 Career OF: 207-587-447																							
1915 StL-N	4	16	2	3	0	1	0	0	1	5	0	....	.188	.235	.313	.548	65	-1	1	2.40	0	/0-4(3-1-0)	0	-0.1
1916 StL-N	130	357	43	87	6	5	6	34	20	50	24	16	.244	.291	.339	.630	94	-5	37	3.19	-5	*0-120(1-109-11)	8	-1.9
1917 StL-N	137	462	64	137	16	11	3	34	38	65	25	....	.297	.351	.398	.750	133	18	70	5.39	-2	*0-128(27-65-37)	21	1.0
1918 StL-N	42	166	24	35	2	1	0	4	7	21	5	....	.211	.260	.235	.495	53	-9	11	2.12	3	0-42(0-42-0)	1	-0.9
1919 StL-N	119	408	47	91	16	3	0	15	26	29	30	....	.223	.271	.277	.548	69	-15	37	2.89	6	*0-111(1-36-76)	4	-1.7
1920 StL-N	91	313	53	104	22	5	1	28	25	23	14	9	.332	.385	.444	.829	141	17	53	6.26	3	0-83(18-57-14)	13	1.7
1921 StL-N	116	411	86	135	22	9	7	33	21	24	11	6	.328	.361	.477	.838	122	13	69	6.34	-1	*0-103(0-19-84)	15	0.5
1922 StL-N	143	510	117	158	23	12	8	46	50	30	18	7	.310	.375	.449	.824	117	16	88	6.23	-6	*0-136(17-79-40)	17	0.2
1923 StL-N	124	407	98	126	16	6	5	41	27	20	32	11	.310	.356	.415	.771	105	6	61	5.42	4	*0-109(77-10-23)	12	0.2
1924 StL-N	124	459	91	130	18	6	2	33	33	27	24	16	.283	.333	.362	.694	88	-8	54	4.06	4	*0-114(25-14-77)	8	-1.2
1925 StL-N	80	243	53	61	11	4	4	31	19	13	20	2	.251	.308	.379	.687	73	-7	31	4.27	-2	0-64(5-38-28)	5	-1.1
1926 StL-N	1	1	0	0	0	0	0	0	0	1	0	....	.000	.000	.000	.000	-96	-0	0	.00	0	....	0	0.0
Bos-N	96	322	46	100	15	2	2	25	28	12	11	....	.311	.369	.388	.758	114	7	46	5.20	1	0-83(10-59-15)	11	0.3
Yr.	97	323	46	100	15	2	2	25	28	13	11	....	.310	.368	.387	.755	114	7	46	5.18	1	0-83(10-59-15)	11	0.3
1927 Bos-N	84	183	27	58	6	4	1	24	16	12	8	....	.317	.375	.410	.785	119	5	28	5.48	-1	0-48(3-14-32)	6	0.1
1928 Bos-N	96	254	30	71	9	2	1	32	21	14	6	....	.280	.335	.343	.677	81	-7	29	3.86	-2	0-65(18-40-7)	4	-1.1
1929 Bos-N	19	20	2	5	0	0	0	2	2	2	0	....	.250	.318	.250	.568	45	-2	2	2.67	-1	/0-9(2-4-3)	0	-0.3
Total 15	**1406**	**4532**	**783**	**1301**	**182**	**71**	**40**	**382**	**334**	**348**	**228**	**67**	**.287**	**.339**	**.385**	**.724**	**103**	**27**	**618**	**4.73**	**1**	***0-1219**	**125**	**-4.2**
• SMITH, Jack	John Joseph Smith b: 8/8/1893, Oswayo, PA d: 12/4/1962, New York, NY BR/TR, 5'9" Deb: 5/18/1912																							
1912 Det-A	1	0	0	0	0	0	0	0	0	....	0	....	....	....	....	....	-103	0	0	....	0	/3-1	0	0.0
• SMITH, Jason	Jason William Smith b: 7/24/1977, Meridian, MS BL/TR, 6'3", 195 lbs. Deb: 6/17/2001																							
2001 Chi-N	2	1	0	0	0	0	0	0	0	1	0	0	.000	.000	.000	.000	-105	-0	0	.00	0	/S-1	0	0.0
2002 TB-A	26	65	9	13	1	2	1	6	2	24	3	0	.200	.224	.323	.547	44	-5	5	2.62	-2	3-12/S-9,2-1,D-1	0	-0.5
2003 TB-A	1	4	0	1	0	0	0	0	0	0	0	0	.250	.250	.250	.500	33	-0	0	2.25	0	/3-1	0	-0.1
Total 3	**29**	**70**	**9**	**14**	**1**	**2**	**1**	**6**	**2**	**25**	**3**	**0**	**.200**	**.222**	**.314**	**.537**	**41**	**-5**	**5**	**2.56**	**-1**	**/3-13,S-10,2-1,D-1**	**0**	**-0.6**
• SMITH, Jim	James Lorne Smith b: 9/8/1954, Santa Monica, CA BR/TR, 6'3", 185 lbs. Deb: 4/12/1982																							
1982 Pit-N	42	42	5	10	2	1	0	4	5	7	0	1	.238	.319	.333	.652	80	-1	5	3.42	-2	S-29/2-3,3-1	1	-0.2
• SMITH, Jimmy	James Lawrence "Greenfield Jimmy,Bluejacket" Smith b: 5/15/1895, Pittsburgh, PA d: 1/1/1974, Pittsburgh, PA BB/TR, 5'9", 152 lbs. Deb: 9/26/1914 Career OF: 3-3-4																							
1914 Chi-F	3	6	1	3	1	0	0	1	0	0	0	....	.500	.500	.667	1.167	245	1	2	16.32	1	/S-3	1	0.2
1915 Chi-F	95	318	32	69	11	4	4	30	14	65	4	....	.217	.250	.314	.564	70	-14	25	2.51	-9	S-92/2-1	6	-1.7
Bal-F	33	108	9	19	1	1	1	11	11	23	3	....	.176	.258	.231	.490	41	-8	7	1.96	-4	S-33	1	-1.1
Yr.	128	426	41	88	12	5	5	41	25	88	7	....	.207	.252	.293	.546	62	-22	31	2.37	-13	*S-125/2-1	7	-2.8
1916 Pit-N	36	96	4	18	1	1	0	5	6	22	0	....	.188	.257	.219	.476	46	-6	6	1.83	-1	S-27/3-6	1	-0.6
1917 NY-N	36	96	12	22	5	1	0	9	9	18	6	....	.229	.295	.302	.597	86	-1	10	3.33	1	2-29/S-7	3	0.0
1918 Bos-N	34	102	8	23	3	4	1	14	3	13	1	....	.225	.255	.363	.617	91	-2	10	2.93	-3	2-10/S-9,0-6(2-3-1),3-5	2	-0.5
1919*Cin-N	28	40	9	11	1	3	1	10	4	8	1	....	.275	.341	.525	.866	163	3	7	5.89	-2	/3-6,S-5,2-4,0-4(1-0-3)	3	0.1
1921 Phi-N	67	247	31	57	8	1	4	22	11	28	2	8	.231	.266	.320	.586	50	-20	19	2.44	3	2-66	2	-1.5
1922 Phi-N	38	114	13	25	1	0	1	6	5	9	1	3	.219	.258	.254	.513	30	-13	7	1.97	-3	S-23,2-13/3-1	1	-1.3
Total 8	**370**	**1127**	**119**	**247**	**32**	**15**	**12**	**108**	**63**	**186**	**18**	**11**	**.219**	**.265**	**.306**	**.571**	**64**	**-60**	**93**	**2.60**	**-18**	**S-199,2-123/3-18,0-10**	**20**	**-6.4**
• SMITH, Joe	Salvatore Smith b: 12/29/1893, New York, NY d: 6/12/1974, Yonkers, NY BR/TR, 5'7", 170 lbs. Deb: 7/7/1913																							
1913 NY-A	14	32	1	5	0	0	0	2	1	14	1	....	.156	.182	.156	.338	-1	-4	1	1.06	0	C-14	0	-0.3
• SMITH, John	John Marshall Smith b: 9/27/1906, Washington, DC d: 5/9/1982, Silver Spring, MD BB/TR, 6'1", 180 lbs. Deb: 9/17/1931																							
1931 Bos-A	4	15	2	2	0	0	0	1	2	1	1	0	.133	.235	.133	.369	-1	-2	1	1.40	-1	/1-4	0	-0.3
• SMITH, John	John Joseph Smith b: 1858, New York, NY d: 1/6/1899, San Francisco, CA, 5'11", 210 lbs. Deb: 5/1/1882																							
1882 Tro-N	35	149	27	36	4	3	0	14	3	24	....	....	.242	.257	.309	.565	84	-2	12	2.94	-1	1-35	2	-0.6
Wor-N	19	70	10	17	3	2	0	5	5	10	....	....	.243	.293	.343	.636	101	0	7	3.74	1	1-19	1	-0.1
Yr.	54	219	37	53	7	5	0	19	8	34	....	....	.242	.269	.320	.588	90	-2	19	3.20	0	1-54	3	-0.6
• SMITH, John	John Smith b: Baltimore, MD Deb: 4/14/1873																							
1873 Mar-n	5	19	2	2	0	0	0	1	0	1	0	0	.105	.105	.105	.211	-49	-2	0	.39	-2	/S-3,0-2(2-0-0)	....	-0.3
1874 Bal-n	6	21	2	4	1	0	0	1	0	1	0	0	.190	.190	.238	.429	37	-1	1	1.72	-2	/S-6	....	-0.3
1875 NH-n	1	3	0	0	0	0	0	0	1	0	0	0	.000	.250	.000	.250	-6	-0	0	.00	-1	/S-1	....	-0.1
Total 3 n	**12**	**43**	**4**	**6**	**1**	**0**	**0**	**2**	**1**	**2**	**0**	**0**	**.140**	**.159**	**.163**	**.322**	**-4**	**-4**	**1**	**.97**	**-5**	**/S-10,0-2**	**....**	**-0.7**
• SMITH, Jud	Grant Judson Smith b: 1/13/1869, Green Oak, MI d: 12/7/1947, Los Angeles, CA BR/TR, 6' Deb: 5/21/1893																							
1893 Cin-N	17	43	7	10	1	0	1	5	9	5	1	....	.233	.365	.326	.691	82	-1	6	4.51	-2	/0-9(1-0-8),3-6,S-1	1	-0.2
StL-N	4	13	1	1	0	0	0	0	1	2	0	....	.077	.200	.077	.277	-25	-2	0	.45	0	/3-4	0	-0.2
Yr.	21	56	8	11	1	0	1	5	10	7	1	....	.196	.328	.268	.596	58	-3	6	3.43	-1	3-10/0-9(1-0-8),S-1	1	-0.4
1896 Pit-N	10	35	6	12	2	1	0	4	2	2	3	....	.343	.395	.457	.852	129	1	8	8.59	1	3-10	1	0.2
1898 Was-N	66	234	33	71	7	5	3	28	22	....	11	....	.303	.378	.415	.792	127	9	42	6.69	-7	3-47,S-10/1-7,2-1	7	0.2
1901 Pit-N	6	21	1	3	1	0	0	0	3	....	0	....	.143	.250	.190	.440	28	-2	1	1.51	1	/3-6	0	-0.1
Total 4	**103**	**346**	**48**	**97**	**11**	**6**	**4**	**37**	**37**	**9**	**15**	**....**	**.280**	**.363**	**.382**	**.745**	**110**	**5**	**57**	**5.93**	**-6**	**/3-73,S-11,0-9,1-7,2-1**	**9**	**0.0**
• SMITH, Keith	Patrick Keith Smith b: 10/20/1961, Los Angeles, CA BB/TR, 6'1", 175 lbs. Deb: 4/12/1984																							
1984 NY-A	2	4	0	0	0	0	0	0	0	2	0	0	.000	.200	.000	.200	-41	-1	0	.35	1	/S-2	0	0.1
1985 NY-A	4	0	1	0	0	0	0	0	0	0	0	0	....	....	....	....	-102	0	0	....	-1	/S-3	0	-0.1
Total 2	**6**	**4**	**1**	**0**	**0**	**0**	**0**	**0**	**0**	**2**	**0**	**0**	**.000**	**.200**	**.000**	**.200**	**-41**	**-1**	**0**	**.35**	**-0**	**/S-5**	**0**	**0.0**
• SMITH, Keith	Keith Lavarne Smith b: 5/3/1953, Palmetto, FL BR/TR, 5'9", 178 lbs. Deb: 8/2/1977 Career OF: 31-1-2																							
1977 Tex-A	23	67	13	16	4	0	2	6	4	7	2	0	.239	.301	.388	.689	85	-1	9	4.24	0	0-22(22-0-0)	2	-0.2
1979 StL-N	6	13	1	3	0	0	0	0	0	1	0	1	.231	.231	.231	.462	26	-2	0	1.13	1	/0-5(5-0-0)	0	-0.1
1980 StL-N	24	31	3	4	1	0	0	2	2	2	0	0	.129	.182	.161	.343	-3	-4	1	.59	0	/0-7(4-1-2)	0	-0.5
Total 3	**53**	**111**	**17**	**23**	**5**	**0**	**2**	**8**	**6**	**10**	**2**	**1**	**.207**	**.261**	**.306**	**.567**	**56**	**-7**	**10**	**2.78**	**1**	**/0-34**	**2**	**-0.8**
• SMITH, Ken	Kenneth Earl Smith b: 2/12/1958, Youngstown, OH BL/TR, 6'1", 195 lbs. Deb: 9/22/1981																							
1981 Atl-N	5	3	0	1	1	0	0	0	0	1	0	0	.333	.333	.667	1.000	174	0	1	9.00	0	/1-4	0	0.0
1982 Atl-N	48	41	6	12	1	0	0	3	6	13	0	0	.293	.383	.317	.700	94	0	6	5.19	-1	/1-6,0-3(3-0-0)	1	-0.1
1983 Atl-N	30	12	2	2	0	0	1	2	1	5	1	0	.167	.231	.417	.647	71	-0	1	3.60	1	1-13	0	0.0
Total 3	**83**	**56**	**8**	**15**	**2**	**0**	**1**	**5**	**7**	**19**	**1**	**0**	**.268**	**.349**	**.357**	**.706**	**93**	**-0**	**8**	**4.99**	**0**	**/1-23,0-3**	**1**	**0.0**

YEAR TM-L	G	AB	R	H	2B	3B	HR	RBI	BB	SO	SB	CS	AVG	OBP	SLG	OPS	OPS+	BR/A	RC	RC/G	FR	G/POS	WS	TPW
• SMITH, Klondike	Armstrong Frederick Smith b: 1/4/1887, London, England d: 11/15/1959, Springfield, MA BL/TL, 5'9", 160 lbs. Deb: 9/28/1912																							
1912 NY-A	7	27	0	5	1	0	0	0	0	....	1	....	.185	.185	.222	.407	15	-3	1	1.43	-1	/O-7(0-5-2)	0	-0.4
• SMITH, L.	L. Smith Deb: 9/7/1882																							
1882 Bal-a	1	3	0	0	0	0	0	....	0	....	....	....	.000	.000	.000	.000	-108	-1	0	.00	0	/O-1	0	-0.1
• SMITH, Leo	Lionel H. Smith b: 5/13/1859, Brooklyn, NY d: 8/30/1935, Brooklyn, NY, 5'6", 142 lbs. Deb: 8/28/1890																							
1890 Roc-a	35	112	11	21	1	3	0	11	14	....	1	....	.188	.283	.250	.533	62	-5	8	2.45	4	S-35	3	0.1
• SMITH, Lonnie	Lonnie "Skates" Smith b: 12/22/1955, Chicago, IL BR/TR, 5'9", 170 lbs. Deb: 9/2/1978 Career OF: 1257-77-54																							
1978 Phi-N	17	4	6	0	0	0	0	0	4	3	4	0	.000	.500	.000	.500	50	1	2	10.53	-0	O-11(10-1-1)	1	0.1
1979 Phi-N	17	30	4	5	2	0	0	3	1	7	2	1	.167	.194	.233	.427	15	-4	1	1.39	0	O-11(3-5-4)	0	-0.3
1980★Phi-N	100	298	69	101	14	4	3	20	26	48	33	13	.339	.399	.443	.842	128	13	54	6.68	-4	O-82(52-9-23)	13	0.7
1981*Phi-N	62	176	40	57	14	3	2	11	18	14	21	10	.324	.402	.472	.874	141	10	35	7.02	6	O-51(8-23-24)	9	1.5
1982*StL-N★	156	592	**120**	182	35	8	8	69	64	74	68	26	.307	.383	.434	.818	127	26	102	6.07	4	*O-149(135-36-0)	26	2.5
1983 StL-N	130	492	83	158	31	5	8	45	41	55	43	18	.321	.384	.453	.837	131	22	85	6.25	4	*O-126(126-0-0)	19	2.2
1984 StL-N	145	504	77	126	20	4	6	49	70	90	50	13	.250	.352	.341	.693	98	7	70	4.64	3	*O-140(140-0-0)	16	0.4
1985 StL-N	28	96	15	25	2	2	0	7	15	20	12	6	.260	.377	.323	.700	98	1	13	4.36	1	O-28(29-0-0)	3	0.0
*KC-A	120	448	77	115	23	4	6	41	41	69	40	7	.257	.325	.366	.691	88	-1	60	4.70	4	*O-119(119-0-0)	12	-0.2
1986 KC-A	134	508	80	146	25	7	8	44	46	78	26	9	.287	.358	.411	.770	107	7	77	5.40	2	*O-118(118-0-0),D-10	14	0.3
1987 KC-A	48	167	26	42	7	1	3	8	24	31	9	4	.251	.359	.359	.718	89	-2	24	4.93	-2	O-32(32-0-0),D-15	3	-0.6
1988 Atl-N	43	114	14	27	3	0	3	9	10	25	4	2	.237	.298	.342	.640	79	-3	12	3.71	-2	O-35(35-0-0)	2	-0.7
1989 Atl-N	134	482	89	152	34	4	21	79	76	95	25	12	.315	**.420**	.533	.953	166	45	113	8.54	1	*O-132(132-0-0)	27	4.4
1990 Atl-N	135	466	72	142	27	9	9	42	58	69	10	10	.305	.389	.459	.848	125	15	86	6.79	-1	*O-122(122-0-0)	15	1.1
1991*Atl-N	122	353	58	97	19	1	7	44	50	64	9	5	.275	.379	.394	.772	111	7	57	5.69	0	O-99(99-0-0)	13	0.5
1992*Atl-N	84	158	23	39	8	2	6	33	17	37	4	0	.247	.331	.437	.768	109	3	25	5.42	-1	O-35(35-0-0)	8	0.0
1993 Pit-N	94	199	35	57	5	4	6	24	43	42	9	4	.286	.425	.442	.867	133	12	42	7.31	-2	O-60(58-3-0)	8	0.8
Bal-A	9	24	8	5	1	0	2	3	8	10	0	0	.208	.406	.500	.906	136	2	6	8.13	1	/D-5,O-4(4-0-0)	1	0.2
1994 Bal-A	35	59	13	12	3	0	0	2	11	18	1	0	.203	.338	.254	.592	53	-4	6	3.16	1	D-30/O-2(0-0-2)	0	-0.4
Total 17	**1613**	**5170**	**909**	**1488**	**273**	**58**	**98**	**533**	**623**	**849**	**370**	**140**	**.288**	**.374**	**.420**	**.794**	**118**	**160**	**869**	**5.93**	**13**	***O-1356/D-60**	**190**	**12.6**
• SMITH, Mark	Mark Edward Smith b: 5/7/1970, Pasadena, CA BR/TR, 6'3", 205 lbs. Deb: 5/14/1994 Career OF: 160-6-91																							
1994 Bal-A	3	7	0	1	0	0	0	2	0	2	0	0	.143	.143	.143	.286	-25	-1	0	.64	0	/O-3(0-0-3)	0	-0.1
1995 Bal-A	37	104	11	24	5	0	3	15	12	22	3	0	.231	.316	.365	.682	76	-3	12	3.75	0	O-32(15-0-17)/D-3	3	-0.4
1996 Bal-A	27	78	9	19	2	0	4	10	3	20	0	2	.244	.298	.423	.721	80	-4	9	4.19	1	O-20(12-0-8)/D-6	1	-0.4
1997 Pit-N	71	193	29	55	13	1	9	35	28	36	3	1	.285	.376	.503	.878	125	8	38	7.13	0	O-42(21-0-22)/1-9,D-5	9	0.5
1998 Pit-N	59	128	18	25	6	0	2	13	10	26	7	0	.195	.270	.289	.559	46	-9	12	2.96	-0	O-24(16-0-9)/1-6,D-3	1	-1.0
2000 Fla-N	104	192	22	47	8	1	5	27	17	54	2	0	.245	.313	.375	.688	76	-7	24	4.29	2	O-49(29-0-25)/D-1	4	-0.6
2001 Mon-N	80	194	28	47	13	1	6	18	23	38	0	2	.242	.329	.412	.741	88	-4	27	4.63	1	O-60(55-6-4)/1-1	3	-0.5
2003 Mil-N	33	63	8	15	4	0	3	10	4	13	0	0	.238	.284	.444	.728	88	-1	6	3.00	-1	O-15(12-0-3)	1	-0.3
Total 8	**414**	**959**	**125**	**233**	**51**	**3**	**32**	**130**	**97**	**211**	**15**	**5**	**.243**	**.320**	**.403**	**.722**	**85**	**-22**	**128**	**4.51**	**3**	**O-245/D-18,1-16**	**22**	**-2.9**
• SMITH, Mayo	Edward Mayo Smith b: 1/17/1915, New London, MO d: 11/24/1977, Boynton Beach, FL BL/TR, 6', 183 lbs. Deb: 6/24/1945 M																							
1945 Phi-A	73	203	18	43	5	0	0	11	36	13	0	1	.212	.333	.236	.570	67	-7	19	3.11	-2	O-65(33-27-7)	3	-1.3
• SMITH, Mike	Elwood Hope Smith b: 11/16/1904, Norfolk, VA d: 5/31/1981, Chesapeake, VA BL/TR, 5'11.5", 170 lbs. Deb: 9/4/1926																							
1926 NY-N	4	7	0	1	0	0	0	0	0	2	0	....	.143	.143	.143	.286	-23	-1	0	.58	0	/O-1	0	-0.1
• SMITH, Milt	Milton Smith b: 3/27/1929, Columbus, GA d: 4/11/1997, San Diego, CA BR/TR, 5'10", 165 lbs. Deb: 7/21/1955																							
1955 Cin-N	36	102	15	20	3	1	3	8	13	24	2	2	.196	.293	.333	.626	62	-6	10	2.98	0	3-28/2-5	1	-0.6
• SMITH, Nate	Nathaniel Beverly Smith b: 4/26/1935, Chicago, IL BR/TR, 5'11", 170 lbs. Deb: 9/19/1962																							
1962 Bal-A	5	9	3	2	1	0	0	0	1	4	0	0	.222	.364	.333	.697	93	0	1	4.94	0	/C-3	0	0.0
• SMITH, Ollie	Oliver H. Smith b: 1868, Mount Vernon, OH BL/TL Deb: 7/11/1894																							
1894 Lou-N	39	137	27	41	6	1	3	20	29	15	13	....	.299	.432	.423	.855	115	6	31	8.51	-2	O-38(0-0-38)	4	0.1
• SMITH, Ozzie	Osborne Earl Smith b: 12/26/1954, Mobile, AL BB/TR, 5'11", 150 lbs. Deb: 4/7/1978 HOF: 2002																							
1978 SD-N	159	590	69	152	17	6	1	46	47	43	40	12	.258	.312	.312	.624	81	-11	61	3.37	18	*S-159	20	2.4
1979 SD-N	156	587	77	124	18	6	0	27	37	37	28	7	.211	.260	.262	.523	46	-41	42	2.27	12	*S-155	7	-1.3
1980 SD-N	158	609	67	140	18	5	0	35	71	49	57	15	.230	.315	.276	.591	70	-16	62	3.24	30	*S-158	17	3.3
1981 SD-N★	110	450	53	100	11	2	0	21	41	37	22	12	.222	.294	.256	.550	61	-22	36	2.53	18	*S-110	8	0.9
1982*StL-N★	140	488	58	121	24	1	2	43	68	32	25	5	.248	.342	.314	.656	84	-5	58	3.98	28	*S-139	19	4.0
1983 StL-N★	159	552	69	134	30	6	3	50	64	36	34	7	.243	.323	.335	.658	82	-8	65	3.92	19	*S-158	18	2.9
1984 StL-N★	124	412	53	106	20	5	1	44	56	17	35	7	.257	.349	.337	.686	96	4	55	4.42	16	*S-124	19	3.5
1985*StL-N★	158	537	70	148	22	3	6	54	65	27	31	8	.276	.356	.361	.717	102	6	73	4.66	22	*S-158	25	4.8
1986 StL-N★	153	514	67	144	19	4	0	54	79	27	31	7	.280	.378	.333	.711	99	7	73	4.91	9	*S-144	23	3.3
1987*StL-N★	158	600	104	182	40	4	0	75	89	36	43	9	.303	.394	.383	.778	105	14	102	6.09	19	*S-158	33	4.9
1988 StL-N★	153	575	80	155	27	1	3	51	74	43	57	9	.270	.354	.336	.689	98	9	80	4.77	15	*S-150	22	3.9
1989 StL-N★	155	593	82	162	30	8	2	50	55	37	29	7	.273	.337	.361	.698	96	1	76	4.45	-1	*S-153	20	1.3
1990 StL-N★	143	512	61	130	21	1	1	50	61	33	32	6	.254	.336	.305	.640	77	-10	60	3.89	-10	*S-140	11	-1.0
1991 StL-N★	150	550	96	157	30	3	3	50	83	36	35	9	.285	.380	.367	.747	110	15	86	5.55	-8	*S-150	25	2.0
1992 StL-N★	132	518	73	153	20	2	0	31	59	34	43	9	.295	.367	.342	.709	105	11	72	4.87	21	*S-132	20	4.6
1993 StL-N	141	545	75	157	22	6	1	53	43	18	21	8	.288	.341	.356	.697	89	-7	67	4.32	25	*S-134	19	2.8
1994 StL-N★	98	381	51	100	18	3	3	30	38	26	6	3	.262	.329	.349	.678	79	-12	46	4.17	-6	S-96	9	-0.9
1995 StL-N★	44	156	16	31	5	1	0	11	17	12	4	3	.199	.286	.244	.529	41	-14	11	2.10	0	S-41	2	-1.0
1996*StL-N★	82	227	36	64	10	2	2	18	25	9	7	5	.282	.358	.370	.728	93	-2	31	4.58	8	S-52	8	1.0
Total 19	**2573**	**9396**	**1257**	**2460**	**402**	**69**	**28**	**793**	**1072**	**589**	**580**	**148**	**.262**	**.339**	**.328**	**.668**	**87**	**-81**	**1155**	**4.14**	**236**	***S-2511**	**325**	**41.3**
• SMITH, Paddy	Lawrence Patrick Smith b: 5/16/1894, Pelham, NY d: 12/2/1990, New Rochelle, NY BL/TR, 6', 195 lbs. Deb: 7/6/1920																							
1920 Bos-A	2	2	0	0	0	0	0	0	0	1	0	0	.000	.000	.000	.000	-104	-1	0	.00	0	/C-1	0	-0.1
• SMITH, Paul	Paul Stoner Smith b: 5/7/1888, Mount Zion, IL d: 7/3/1958, Decatur, IL BL/TR, 6'1", 190 lbs. Deb: 9/19/1916																							
1916 Cin-N	10	44	5	10	0	1	0	1	1	8	3	....	.227	.244	.273	.517	60	-2	4	2.72	0	O-10(10-0-0)	0	-0.3
• SMITH, Paul	Paul Leslie Smith b: 3/19/1931, New Castle, PA BL/TL, 5'8", 165 lbs. Deb: 4/14/1953 Career OF: 35-1-20																							
1953 Pit-N	118	389	41	110	12	7	4	44	24	23	3	0	.283	.329	.380	.710	85	-8	50	4.54	-3	1-74,O-19(19-0-0)	6	-1.5
1957 Pit-N	81	150	12	38	4	0	3	11	12	17	0	2	.253	.313	.340	.653	78	-5	15	3.25	0	O-33(16-1-20)/1-1	2	-0.7
1958 Pit-N	6	3	0	1	0	0	0	0	3	0	0	0	.333	.667	.333	1.000	180	1	1	16.02	0	....	0	0.1
Chi-N	18	20	1	3	0	0	0	1	3	4	0	0	.150	.261	.150	.411	13	-2	1	1.57	0	/1-4	0	-0.2
Yr.	24	23	1	4	0	0	0	1	6	4	0	0	.174	.345	.174	.519	47	-1	2	3.09	0	/1-4	0	-0.1
Total 3	**223**	**562**	**54**	**152**	**16**	**7**	**7**	**56**	**42**	**44**	**3**	**2**	**.270**	**.326**	**.361**	**.687**	**81**	**-15**	**67**	**4.12**	**-2**	**/1-79,O-52**	**8**	**-2.3**
• SMITH, Pop	Charles Marvin Smith b: 10/12/1856, Digby, Canada d: 4/18/1927, Boston, MA BR/TR, 5'11", 170 lbs. Deb: 5/1/1880 U Career OF: 2-6-6																							
1880 Cin-N	83	334	35	69	10	9	0	27	6	36	....	....	.207	.221	.290	.511	72	-9	22	2.28	-5	*2-83	3	-1.0
1881 Cle-N	10	34	1	4	0	0	0	3	0	8	....	....	.118	.118	.118	.235	-27	-5	0	.43	-2	3-10	0	-0.6
Buf-N	3	11	3	0	0	0	0	1	3	5	....	....	.000	.214	.000	.214	-28	-1	0	.00	0	/2-3	0	-0.2
Wor-N	11	41	1	3	0	0	0	2	3	5	....	....	.073	.136	.073	.210	-31	-6	0	.30	2	/O-8(1-4-3),2-3	0	-0.4
Yr.	24	86	5	7	0	0	0	6	6	18	....	....	.081	.141	.081	.223	-29	-12	1	.31	0	3-10/O-8(1-4-3),2-6	0	-1.1
1882 Phi-a	20	65	10	6	0	0	0	2	12	....	....	....	.092	.234	.092	.326	12	-6	1	.68	1	3-11/S-4,O-3(0-2-1),2-2	1	-0.4
Lou-a	3	11	1	2	0	0	0	....	0	....	....	....	.182	.182	.182	.364	24	-1	0	1.16	-1	/S-3	0	-0.1
Yr.	23	76	11	8	0	0	0	2	12	....	....	....	.105	.227	.105	.333	14	-7	2	.75	0	3-11/S-7,O-3(0-2-1),2-2	1	-0.6

YEAR TM-L	G	AB	R	H	2B	3B	HR	RBI	BB	SO	SB	CS	AVG	OBP	SLG	OPS	OPS+	BR/A	RC	RC/G	FR	G/POS	WS	TPW
1883 Col-a	97	405	82	106	14	**17**	4	0	22	....	....	....	.262	.300	.410	.710	137	18	51	4.78	10	*2-73,3-24/P-3	15	2.6
1884 Col-a	108	445	78	106	18	10	6	0	20	....	....	....	.238	.289	.364	.653	121	12	48	3.90	27	*2-108	18	3.9
1885 Pit-a	106	453	85	113	11	13	0	35	25	....	....	....	.249	.293	.331	.624	98	-1	45	3.58	38	*2-106	13	3.7
1886 Pit-a	126	483	75	105	20	9	2	57	42	....	38	....	.217	.288	.308	.597	87	-7	55	3.94	25	*S-98,2-28/C-1	18	2.0
1887 Pit-N	122	486	69	128	12	7	2	54	30	48	30	....	.263	.283	.285	.568	62	-21	46	3.43	8	*2-89,S-33	8	-0.8
1888 Pit-N	131	481	61	99	15	2	4	52	22	78	37	....	.206	.248	.270	.518	70	-15	42	3.00	6	S-75,2-56	12	-0.4
1889 Pit-N	72	258	26	54	10	2	5	27	24	38	12	....	.209	.292	.322	.613	79	-6	28	3.69	-2	S-58/2-9,3-3,O-3(1-0-2)	7	-0.5
Bos-N	59	208	21	54	13	4	0	32	23	30	11	....	.260	.345	.361	.705	92	-2	30	5.23	-3	S-59	7	-0.3
Yr.	131	466	47	108	23	6	5	59	47	68	23	....	.232	.315	.339	.655	85	-9	59	4.35	-5	*S-117/2-9,3-3,O-3(1-0-2)	14	-0.8
1890 Bos-N	134	463	82	106	16	12	1	53	80	81	39	....	.229	.353	.322	.675	90	-4	68	5.05	-10	*2-134/S-1	12	-0.8
1891 Was-a	27	90	13	16	2	2	0	13	13	16	2	....	.178	.295	.244	.540	57	-5	7	2.60	0	2-19/S-5,3-4	1	-0.3
Total 12	1112	4268	643	971	141	87	24	358	325	345	169	....	.228	.287	.313	.600	86	-59	447	3.66	94	2-713,S-336/3-52,O-14,P-3,C	115	6.3

• SMITH, Ray Raymond Edward Smith b: 9/18/1955, Glendale, CA BR/TR, 6'1", 185 lbs. Deb: 4/9/1981

YEAR TM-L	G	AB	R	H	2B	3B	HR	RBI	BB	SO	SB	CS	AVG	OBP	SLG	OPS	OPS+	BR/A	RC	RC/G	FR	G/POS	WS	TPW
1981 Min-A	15	40	4	8	1	0	1	1	0	3	0	0	.200	.200	.300	.500	40	-3	2	2.03	0	C-15	0	-0.3
1982 Min-A	9	23	1	5	0	1	0	1	1	3	0	0	.217	.250	.304	.554	50	-2	2	2.72	0	/C-9	0	-0.1
1983 Min-A	59	152	11	34	5	0	0	8	10	12	1	0	.224	.276	.257	.533	46	-11	11	2.34	2	C-59	2	-0.6
Total 3	83	215	16	47	6	1	1	10	11	18	1	0	.219	.260	.270	.530	45	-16	15	2.32	2	/C-83	2	-1.0

• SMITH, Red Willard Jehu Smith b: 4/11/1892, Logansport, IN d: 7/17/1972, Noblesville, IN BR/TR, 5'8", 165 lbs. Deb: 9/17/1917

YEAR TM-L	G	AB	R	H	2B	3B	HR	RBI	BB	SO	SB	CS	AVG	OBP	SLG	OPS	OPS+	BR/A	RC	RC/G	FR	G/POS	WS	TPW
1917 Pit-N	11	21	1	3	1	0	0	2	3	4	1	....	.143	.250	.190	.440	35	-2	1	1.63	1	/C-6	0	0.0
1918 Pit-N	15	24	1	4	1	0	0	3	3	0	0	....	.167	.259	.208	.468	42	-2	1	1.69	-1	C-10	0	-0.2
Total 2	26	45	2	7	2	0	0	5	6	4	1	....	.156	.255	.200	.455	38	-3	2	1.66	1	/C-16	0	-0.2

• SMITH, Red James Carlisle Smith b: 4/6/1890, Greenville, SC d: 10/11/1966, Atlanta, GA BR/TR, 5'11", 165 lbs. Deb: 9/5/1911

YEAR TM-L	G	AB	R	H	2B	3B	HR	RBI	BB	SO	SB	CS	AVG	OBP	SLG	OPS	OPS+	BR/A	RC	RC/G	FR	G/POS	WS	TPW
1911 Bro-N	28	111	10	29	6	1	0	19	5	13	5	....	.261	.299	.333	.632	80	-3	12	3.80	-2	3-28	2	-0.4
1912 Bro-N	128	486	75	139	28	6	4	57	54	51	22	....	.286	.362	.393	.755	111	8	77	5.41	6	*3-125	16	1.8
1913 Bro-N	151	540	70	160	**40**	10	6	76	45	67	22	....	.296	.358	.441	.799	124	16	90	5.72	5	*3-151	19	2.6
1914 Bro-N	90	330	39	81	10	8	4	48	30	26	11	....	.245	.310	.361	.671	97	-2	39	3.90	14	3-90	12	1.6
Bos-N	60	207	30	65	17	1	3	37	28	24	4	....	.314	.401	.449	.850	153	14	39	6.53	8	3-60	14	2.7
Yr.	150	537	69	146	27	9	7	85	58	50	15	....	.272	.346	.395	.741	120	13	78	4.88	22	*3-150	26	4.2
1915 Bos-N	157	549	66	145	34	4	2	65	67	49	10	5	.264	.345	.352	.697	113	10	71	4.41	-3	*3-157	24	1.4
1916 Bos-N	150	509	48	132	16	10	3	60	53	55	13	....	.259	.333	.348	.680	115	10	66	4.32	-4	*3-150	24	1.2
1917 Bos-N	147	505	60	149	31	6	2	62	53	61	16	....	.295	.369	.392	.761	141	26	78	5.35	-22	*3-147	22	0.9
1918 Bos-N	119	429	55	128	20	3	2	65	45	47	8	....	.298	.373	.373	.746	133	19	63	5.07	-1	*3-119	21	2.4
1919 Bos-N	87	241	24	59	6	0	1	25	40	22	6	....	.245	.359	.282	.641	98	2	27	3.65	2	O-48(17-30-3),3-23	7	0.2
Total 9	1117	3907	477	1087	208	49	27	514	420	415	117	5	.278	.353	.377	.731	120	101	562	4.89	3	*3-1050/O-48	161	14.4

• SMITH, Red Marvin Harold Smith b: 7/17/1899, Ashley, IL d: 2/19/1961, Los Angeles, CA BL/TR, 5'7", 165 lbs. Deb: 4/14/1925

YEAR TM-L	G	AB	R	H	2B	3B	HR	RBI	BB	SO	SB	CS	AVG	OBP	SLG	OPS	OPS+	BR/A	RC	RC/G	FR	G/POS	WS	TPW
1925 Phi-A	20	14	1	4	0	0	0	1	2	5	0	0	.286	.375	.286	.661	65	-1	2	4.11	-4	S-16/3-2	0	-0.3

• SMITH, Red Richard Paul Smith b: 5/18/1904, Brokaw, WI d: 5/8/1978, Sylvania, OH BR/TR, 5'10", 185 lbs. Deb: 5/31/1927 C

YEAR TM-L	G	AB	R	H	2B	3B	HR	RBI	BB	SO	SB	CS	AVG	OBP	SLG	OPS	OPS+	BR/A	RC	RC/G	FR	G/POS	WS	TPW
1927 NY-N	1	0	0	0	0	0	0	0	0	0	0	....	....	....	....	....	-100	0	0	....	0	/C-1	0	0.0

• SMITH, Reggie Carl Reginald Smith b: 4/2/1945, Shreveport, LA BB/TR, 6', 195 lbs. Deb: 9/18/1966 C Career OF: 3-808-874

YEAR TM-L	G	AB	R	H	2B	3B	HR	RBI	BB	SO	SB	CS	AVG	OBP	SLG	OPS	OPS+	BR/A	RC	RC/G	FR	G/POS	WS	TPW
1966 Bos-A	6	26	1	4	1	0	0	0	0	5	0	0	.154	.154	.192	.346	-1	-3	1	.96	0	/O-6(0-6-0)	0	-0.4
1967*Bos-A	158	565	78	139	24	6	15	61	57	95	16	6	.246	.316	.389	.706	99	1	71	4.33	2	*O-144(0-144-0)/2-6	19	-0.1
1968 Bos-A	155	558	78	148	**37**	5	15	69	64	77	22	18	.265	.345	.430	.775	125	15	80	4.86	-2	*O-155(0-155-0)	25	0.9
1969 Bos-A★	143	543	87	168	29	7	25	93	54	67	7	13	.309	.373	.527	.900	142	25	99	6.51	-4	*O-139(3-136-0)	24	1.8
1970 Bos-A	147	580	109	176	32	7	22	74	51	60	10	7	.303	.364	.497	.860	126	19	102	6.43	3	*O-145(0-145-0)	25	1.9
1971 Bos-A	159	618	85	175	**33**	2	30	96	63	82	11	3	.283	.354	.489	.843	128	23	106	6.16	-3	*O-159(0-87-74)	29	1.5
1972 Bos-A★	131	467	75	126	25	4	21	74	68	63	15	4	.270	.367	.475	.843	141	27	85	6.41	-5	*O-129(0-4-125)	26	1.8
1973 Bos-A	115	423	79	128	23	2	21	69	68	49	3	2	.303	.400	.515	.916	148	29	88	7.66	1	*O-104(0-104-0)/D-8,1-1	23	2.8
1974 StL-N★	143	517	79	160	26	9	23	100	71	70	4	3	.309	.394	.528	.922	158	39	105	7.39	0	*O-132(0-0-132)/1-1	25	3.3
1975 StL-N★	135	477	67	144	26	3	19	76	63	59	9	7	.302	.387	.488	.875	137	23	87	6.48	-2	O-69(0-1-68),1-66/3-1	20	1.4
1976 StL-N	47	170	20	37	7	1	8	23	14	28	1	2	.218	.281	.412	.693	94	-3	18	3.57	5	1-17,O-16(0-3-13),3-13	4	0.0
LA-N	65	225	35	63	8	4	10	26	18	42	2	0	.280	.336	.484	.821	133	9	36	5.89	1	O-58(0-1-57)/3-1	10	0.8
Yr.	112	395	55	100	15	5	18	49	32	70	3	2	.253	.312	.453	.766	116	6	55	4.84	6	O-74(0-4-70),1-17,3-14	14	0.8
1977*LA-N★	148	488	104	150	27	4	32	87	104	76	7	5	.307	**.432**	.576	1.008	**168**	52	129	**9.75**	-6	*O-140(0-9-138)	29	4.0
1978*LA-N★	128	447	82	132	27	2	29	93	70	90	12	5	.295	.392	.559	.951	**164**	39	102	8.11	-2	*O-126(0-1-126)	24	3.3
1979 LA-N	68	234	41	64	13	1	10	32	31	50	6	5	.274	.363	.466	.829	126	8	39	5.78	2	O-62(0-5-59)	9	0.7
1980 LA-N★	92	311	47	100	13	0	15	55	41	63	5	6	.322	.402	.508	.910	155	22	64	7.53	9	O-84(0-7-82)	17	2.9
1981*LA-N	41	35	5	7	1	0	1	8	7	8	0	0	.200	.333	.314	.648	88	-0	3	2.36	0	/1-2	0	0.0
1982 SF-N	106	349	51	99	11	0	18	56	46	46	7	0	.284	.367	.470	.837	133	17	61	6.30	4	1-99	16	1.7
Total 17	1987	7033	1123	2020	363	57	314	1092	890	1030	137	86	.287	.370	.489	.859	137	342	1277	6.46	3	*O-1668,1-186/3-15,D-8,2-6	325	28.1

• SMITH, Skyrocket Samuel J. Smith b: 3/19/1868, Baltimore, MD d: 4/26/1916, St. Louis, MO BR, 6'2", 170 lbs. Deb: 4/18/1888

YEAR TM-L	G	AB	R	H	2B	3B	HR	RBI	BB	SO	SB	CS	AVG	OBP	SLG	OPS	OPS+	BR/A	RC	RC/G	FR	G/POS	WS	TPW
1888 Lou-a	58	206	27	49	9	4	1	31	24	....	5	....	.238	.349	.335	.683	122	7	26	4.55	-1	1-58	6	0.1

• SMITH, Stub James A. Smith b: 11/26/1876, Elmwood, IL BL/TR, 5'6", 145 lbs. Deb: 9/10/1898

YEAR TM-L	G	AB	R	H	2B	3B	HR	RBI	BB	SO	SB	CS	AVG	OBP	SLG	OPS	OPS+	BR/A	RC	RC/G	FR	G/POS	WS	TPW
1898 Bos-N	3	10	1	1	0	0	0	0	0	....	0	....	.100	.100	.100	.200	-41	-2	0	.30	0	/S-3	0	-0.1

• SMITH, Syd Sydney E. Smith b: 8/31/1883, Smithville, SC d: 6/5/1961, Orangeburg, SC BR/TR, 5'10", 190 lbs. Deb: 4/14/1908

YEAR TM-L	G	AB	R	H	2B	3B	HR	RBI	BB	SO	SB	CS	AVG	OBP	SLG	OPS	OPS+	BR/A	RC	RC/G	FR	G/POS	WS	TPW
1908 Phi-A	46	128	8	26	8	0	1	10	4	....	0	....	.203	.233	.289	.522	65	-5	8	2.08	3	C-31/1-6,O-1	3	0.0
StL-A	27	76	6	14	4	0	0	5	4	....	2	....	.184	.225	.237	.462	50	-4	4	1.77	3	C-24	1	0.2
Yr.	73	204	14	40	12	0	1	15	8	....	2	....	.196	.230	.270	.500	59	-10	13	1.97	6	C-55/1-6,O-1	4	0.2
1910 Cle-A	9	27	1	9	1	0	0	3	3	....	0	....	.333	.400	.370	.770	140	1	4	5.66	1	/C-9	1	0.3
1911 Cle-A	58	154	8	46	8	1	1	21	11	....	0	....	.299	.353	.383	.736	104	1	21	4.80	2	C-48/1-1,3-1	6	0.7
1914 Pit-N	5	11	1	3	0	0	0	1	0	1	0	....	.273	.273	.273	.545	65	-1	1	2.46	0	/C-3	0	0.0
1915 Pit-N	1	1	0	0	0	0	0	0	0	0	0	....	.000	.000	.000	.000	-101	-0	0	.00	0	....	0	0.0
Total 5	146	397	24	98	21	1	2	40	22	1	2	....	.247	.291	.320	.611	83	-8	38	3.23	9	C-115/1-7,3-1,O-1	11	1.1

• SMITH, Tom Thomas N. Smith b: 1851, Guelph, Canada d: 3/28/1889, Detroit, MI, 5'8" Deb: 9/15/1875

YEAR TM-L	G	AB	R	H	2B	3B	HR	RBI	BB	SO	SB	CS	AVG	OBP	SLG	OPS	OPS+	BR/A	RC	RC/G	FR	G/POS	WS	TPW
1875 Atl-n	3	13	0	1	0	0	0	1	0	0	0	0	.077	.077	.077	.154	-53	-2	0	.19	0	/2-3	....	-0.2

• SMITH, Tommy Tommy Alexander Smith b: 8/1/1948, Albemarle, NC BL/TR, 6'4", 215 lbs. Deb: 9/6/1973 Career OF: 24-15-59

YEAR TM-L	G	AB	R	H	2B	3B	HR	RBI	BB	SO	SB	CS	AVG	OBP	SLG	OPS	OPS+	BR/A	RC	RC/G	FR	G/POS	WS	TPW
1973 Cle-A	14	41	6	10	2	0	2	3	1	2	1	0	.244	.262	.439	.701	93	-0	4	3.77	-1	O-13(1-11-1)	1	-0.2
1974 Cle-A	23	31	4	3	1	0	0	0	2	7	0	0	.097	.176	.129	.306	-11	-4	1	.80	0	O-17(9-4-4)/D-1	0	-0.6
1975 Cle-A	8	8	0	1	0	0	0	2	0	1	0	0	.125	.125	.125	.250	-29	-1	0	.57	0	/D-3,O-3(1-0-2)	0	-0.2
1976 Cle-A	55	164	17	42	3	1	2	12	8	8	8	0	.256	.291	.323	.614	80	-3	16	3.35	0	O-50(12-0-38)/D-2	3	-0.5
1977 Sea-A	21	27	1	7	1	1	0	4	0	6	0	1	.259	.259	.370	.630	70	-2	2	2.86	2	O-14(1-0-14)	0	0.0
Total 5	121	271	28	63	7	2	4	21	11	24	9	1	.232	.265	.317	.582	67	-11	23	2.92	0	/O-97,D-6	4	-1.5

• SMITH, Tony Anthony Smith b: 5/14/1884, Chicago, IL d: 2/27/1964, Galveston, TX BR/TR, 5'9", 150 lbs. Deb: 8/12/1907

YEAR TM-L	G	AB	R	H	2B	3B	HR	RBI	BB	SO	SB	CS	AVG	OBP	SLG	OPS	OPS+	BR/A	RC	RC/G	FR	G/POS	WS	TPW
1907 Was-A	51	139	12	26	1	1	0	8	18	....	3	....	.187	.285	.209	.493	63	-5	11	2.36	-5	S-51	1	-0.9
1910 Bro-N	106	321	31	58	10	1	1	16	69	53	9	....	.181	.329	.227	.556	65	-10	30	2.72	17	*S-101/3-6	10	1.1
1911 Bro-N	13	40	3	6	1	0	0	2	8	7	1	....	.150	.292	.175	.467	33	-3	2	1.72	-1	S-10/2-3	0	-0.4
Total 3	170	500	46	90	12	2	1	26	95	60	13	....	.180	.314	.218	.532	62	-18	43	2.54	11	S-162/3-6,2-3	11	-0.2

• SMITH, Vinnie Vincent Ambrose Smith b: 12/7/1915, Richmond, VA d: 12/14/1979, Virginia Beach, VA BR/TR, 6'1", 176 lbs. Deb: 9/10/1941 U

YEAR TM-L	G	AB	R	H	2B	3B	HR	RBI	BB	SO	SB	CS	AVG	OBP	SLG	OPS	OPS+	BR/A	RC	RC/G	FR	G/POS	WS	TPW
1941 Pit-N	9	33	3	10	1	0	0	5	1	5	0	....	.303	.324	.333	.657	86	-1	3	2.75	-1	/C-9	1	-0.1

YEAR TM-L	G	AB	R	H	2B	3B	HR	RBI	BB	SO	SB	CS	AVG	OBP	SLG	OPS	OPS+	BR/A	RC	RC/G	FR	G/POS	WS	TPW
1946 Pit-N	7	21	2	4	0	0	0	0	1	5	0	....	.190	.227	.190	.418	19	-2	1	1.16	-0	/C-7	0	-0.2
Total 2	16	54	5	14	1	0	0	5	2	10	0	....	.259	.286	.278	.563	59	-3	3	2.10	-1	/C-16	1	-0.3

• SMITH, Wally Wallace H. Smith b: 3/13/1888, Philadelphia, PA d: 6/10/1930, Florence, AZ BR/TR, 5'11.5", 180 lbs. Deb: 4/17/1911 Career OF: 0-1-1

YEAR TM-L	G	AB	R	H	2B	3B	HR	RBI	BB	SO	SB	CS	AVG	OBP	SLG	OPS	OPS+	BR/A	RC	RC/G	FR	G/POS	WS	TPW
1911 StL-N	81	194	23	42	6	5	2	19	21	33	5	....	.216	.303	.330	.633	79	-6	21	3.44	1	3-26,S-25/2-8,0-1	4	-0.3
1912 StL-N	75	219	22	56	5	5	0	26	29	27	4	....	.256	.351	.324	.675	87	-3	26	4.00	0	3-32,S-22/1-6	6	0.0
1914 Was-A	45	97	11	19	4	1	0	8	3	12	3	4	.196	.235	.258	.493	46	-8	6	1.77	-4	2-12/1-7,S-7,3-5,0-1	1	-1.3
Total 3	201	510	56	117	15	11	2	53	53	72	12	4	.229	.312	.314	.625	77	-16	53	3.33	-3	/3-63,S-54,2-20,1-13,0-2	11	-1.6

• SMITH, Wib Wilbur Floyd Smith b: 8/30/1886, Evart, MI d: 11/18/1959, Fargo, ND BL/TR, 5'10.5", 165 lbs. Deb: 5/31/1909

YEAR TM-L	G	AB	R	H	2B	3B	HR	RBI	BB	SO	SB	CS	AVG	OBP	SLG	OPS	OPS+	BR/A	RC	RC/G	FR	G/POS	WS	TPW
1909 StL-A	17	42	3	8	0	0	0	2	0	....	0	....	.190	.190	.190	.381	22	-4	2	1.14	-3	C-13/1-1	0	-0.7

• SMITH, Willie Willie Smith b: 2/11/1939, Anniston, AL BL/TL, 6', 190 lbs. Deb: 6/18/1963 Career OF: 288-3-56 ♦

YEAR TM-L	G	AB	R	H	2B	3B	HR	RBI	BB	SO	SB	CS	AVG	OBP	SLG	OPS	OPS+	BR/A	RC	RC/G	FR	G/POS	WS	TPW
1963 Det-A	17	8	2	1	0	0	0	0	0	1	0	0	.125	.125	.125	.250	-29	-0	0	.48	0	P-11	1	-0.3
1964 LA-A	118	359	46	108	14	6	11	51	8	39	7	5	.301	.320	.465	.785	128	12	49	4.96	-1	0-87(58-3-31),P-15	14	0.7
1965 Cal-A	136	459	52	120	14	9	14	57	32	60	9	8	.261	.311	.423	.734	109	2	58	4.41	4	*0-123(123-0-1)/1-2	14	0.0
1966 Cal-A	90	195	18	36	3	2	1	20	12	37	1	0	.185	.243	.236	.479	39	-15	12	2.05	1	0-52(32-0-22)	1	-1.8
1967 Cle-A	21	32	0	7	2	0	0	2	1	10	0	2	.219	.242	.281	.524	54	-3	1	1.35	-1	/0-4(4-0-0),1-3	0	-0.4
1968 Cle-A	33	42	1	6	2	0	0	3	3	14	0	0	.143	.217	.190	.408	25	-3	2	1.23	0	/1-7,P-2,0-1	0	-0.3
Chi-N	55	142	13	39	8	2	5	25	12	33	0	0	.275	.335	.465	.800	129	5	23	5.78	0	0-38(38-0-0)/1-4,P-1	7	0.5
1969 Chi-N	103	195	21	48	9	1	9	25	25	49	1	0	.246	.332	.441	.773	102	1	29	5.20	-1	0-33(32-0-1),1-24	6	-0.3
1970 Chi-N	87	167	15	36	9	1	5	24	11	32	2	1	.216	.268	.371	.639	62	-10	17	3.30	-6	1-43/0-1	1	-1.8
1971 Cin-N	31	55	3	9	2	0	1	4	3	9	0	0	.164	.207	.255	.461	32	-5	2	1.10	1	1-10	0	-0.5
Total 9	691	1654	171	410	63	21	46	211	107	284	20	16	.248	.297	.395	.692	94	-17	194	4.01	-4	0-339/1-93,P-29	44	-4.3

• SMITHERMAN, Stephen Stephen Lydell Smitherman b: 9/1/1978, McAlester, OK BR/TR, 6'4", 235 lbs. Deb: 7/1/2003

YEAR TM-L	G	AB	R	H	2B	3B	HR	RBI	BB	SO	SB	CS	AVG	OBP	SLG	OPS	OPS+	BR/A	RC	RC/G	FR	G/POS	WS	TPW
2003 Cin-N	21	44	3	7	2	0	1	6	3	9	1	0	.159	.213	.273	.485	26	-5	3	2.06	-1	0-14(14-0-0)	0	-0.6

• SMOOT, Homer Homer Vernon "Doc" Smoot b: 3/23/1878, Galestown, MD d: 3/25/1928, Salisbury, MD BL/TR, 5'10", 180 lbs. Deb: 4/17/1902 Career OF: 4-643-31

YEAR TM-L	G	AB	R	H	2B	3B	HR	RBI	BB	SO	SB	CS	AVG	OBP	SLG	OPS	OPS+	BR/A	RC	RC/G	FR	G/POS	WS	TPW
1902 StL-N	129	518	58	161	19	4	3	48	23	....	20	....	.311	.350	.380	.730	130	17	80	5.65	-2	*0-129(0-129-0)	21	0.9
1903 StL-N	129	500	67	148	22	8	4	49	32	....	17	....	.296	.342	.396	.738	114	8	77	5.54	-3	*0-129(0-129-0)	13	-0.1
1904 StL-N	137	520	58	146	23	6	3	66	37	....	23	....	.281	.331	.365	.696	120	12	74	4.95	-2	*0-137(0-137-0)	19	0.4
1905 StL-N	139	534	73	166	21	16	4	58	33	....	21	....	.311	.359	.433	.791	140	24	94	6.42	-5	*0-138(0-138-0)	23	1.3
1906 StL-N	86	343	41	85	9	10	0	31	11	....	3	....	.248	.289	.332	.622	98	-3	36	3.48	1	0-86(0-55-31)	6	-0.6
Cin-N	60	220	11	57	8	1	1	17	13	....	0	....	.259	.315	.318	.633	93	-2	23	3.61	-1	0-59(4-55-0)	5	-0.6
Yr.	146	563	52	142	17	11	1	48	24	....	3	....	.252	.300	.327	.626	96	-4	59	3.53	0	*0-145(4-110-31)	11	-1.2
Total 5	680	2635	308	763	102	45	15	269	149	....	84	....	.290	.336	.380	.715	120	56	384	5.17	-11	0-678	87	1.2

• SMOYER, Henry Henry Neitz "Hennie" Smoyer b: 4/25/1890, Fredericksburg, PA d: 2/28/1958, Du Bois, PA BR/TR, 5'6" Deb: 8/14/1912

YEAR TM-L	G	AB	R	H	2B	3B	HR	RBI	BB	SO	SB	CS	AVG	OBP	SLG	OPS	OPS+	BR/A	RC	RC/G	FR	G/POS	WS	TPW
1912 StL-A	6	14	1	3	0	0	0	0	2	....	0	....	.214	.313	.214	.527	53	-1	1	2.14	1	/S-4,3-2	0	0.1

• SMYKAL, Frank Frank John Smykal b: 10/13/1889, Chicago, IL d: 8/11/1950, Chicago, IL BR/TR, 5'7", 150 lbs. Deb: 8/30/1916

YEAR TM-L	G	AB	R	H	2B	3B	HR	RBI	BB	SO	SB	CS	AVG	OBP	SLG	OPS	OPS+	BR/A	RC	RC/G	FR	G/POS	WS	TPW
1916 Pit-N	6	10	1	3	0	0	0	2	3	1	1	....	.300	.500	.300	.800	147	1	2	7.13	0	/S-5,3-1	1	0.1

• SMYRES, Clancy Clarence Melvin Smyres b: 5/24/1922, Culver City, CA BB/TR, 5'11.5", 175 lbs. Deb: 4/18/1944

YEAR TM-L	G	AB	R	H	2B	3B	HR	RBI	BB	SO	SB	CS	AVG	OBP	SLG	OPS	OPS+	BR/A	RC	RC/G	FR	G/POS	WS	TPW
1944 Bro-N	5	2	1	0	0	0	0	0	0	0	0	....	.000	.000	.000	.000	-102	-1	0	.00	0	....	0	-0.1

• SMYTH, Red James Daniel Smyth b: 1/30/1891, Holly Springs, MS d: 4/14/1958, Inglewood, CA BL/TR, 5'9", 152 lbs. Deb: 8/11/1915 Career OF: 20-8-28

YEAR TM-L	G	AB	R	H	2B	3B	HR	RBI	BB	SO	SB	CS	AVG	OBP	SLG	OPS	OPS+	BR/A	RC	RC/G	FR	G/POS	WS	TPW
1915 Bro-N	19	22	3	3	1	0	0	3	4	2	1	2	.136	.269	.182	.451	37	-2	1	1.35	0	/0-9(6-2-1)	0	-0.3
1916 Bro-N	2	5	0	0	0	0	0	0	0	3	0	....	.000	.000	.000	.000	-97	-1	0	.00	-1	/2-2	0	-0.2
1917 Bro-N	29	24	5	3	0	0	0	1	4	6	0	....	.125	.250	.125	.375	16	-2	1	1.15	-2	/3-4,0-2(0-2-0)	0	-0.5
StL-N	38	72	5	15	0	2	0	4	4	9	3	....	.208	.269	.264	.533	66	-3	5	2.47	-2	0-23(12-4-5)	1	-0.7
Yr.	67	96	10	18	0	2	0	5	8	15	3	....	.188	.264	.229	.493	52	-5	6	2.09	-4	0-25(12-6-5)/3-4	1	-1.2
1918 StL-N	40	113	19	24	1	2	0	4	16	11	3	....	.212	.315	.257	.572	78	-2	10	2.79	-1	0-25(2-0-22),2-11	2	-0.5
Total 4	128	236	32	45	2	4	0	12	28	31	7	2	.191	.285	.233	.518	60	-11	17	2.27	-6	/0-59,2-13,3-4	3	-2.1

• SNEAD, Esix Esix Snead b: 6/7/1976, Fort Myers, FL BB/TR, 5'10", 175 lbs. Deb: 9/3/2002

YEAR TM-L	G	AB	R	H	2B	3B	HR	RBI	BB	SO	SB	CS	AVG	OBP	SLG	OPS	OPS+	BR/A	RC	RC/G	FR	G/POS	WS	TPW
2002 NY-N	17	13	3	4	0	0	1	3	1	4	4	3	.308	.357	.538	.896	137	0	1	3.00	0	/0-6(1-5-0)	1	0.0

• SNEED, John Jonathon L. Sneed b: 1861, Shelby County, TN d: 1/4/1899, Memphis, TN BL, 5'8", 160 lbs. Deb: 5/1/1884 U Career OF: 26-24-211

YEAR TM-L	G	AB	R	H	2B	3B	HR	RBI	BB	SO	SB	CS	AVG	OBP	SLG	OPS	OPS+	BR/A	RC	RC/G	FR	G/POS	WS	TPW
1884 Ind-a	27	102	14	22	4	0	1	0	6	....	....	....	.216	.259	.284	.544	79	-2	8	2.65	-1	0-27(0-21-6)	1	-0.4
1890 Tol-a	9	30	3	6	0	0	0	4	8	....	5	....	.200	.368	.200	.568	66	-1	4	4.59	2	/0-9(0-0-9)	1	0.1
Col-a	128	484	114	141	13	15	2	65	63	....	39	....	.291	.383	.393	.776	138	26	90	6.95	-6	*0-126(26-3-97)/S-2	19	1.5
Yr.	137	514	117	147	13	15	2	69	71	....	44	....	.286	.382	.381	.763	133	25	94	6.79	-4	*0-135(26-3-106)/S-2	20	1.7
1891 Col-a	99	366	66	94	9	6	1	61	55	29	24	....	.257	.366	.322	.688	103	5	53	5.19	-3	*0-99(0-0-99)	11	0.1
Total 3	263	982	197	263	26	21	4	130	132	29	68	....	.268	.364	.349	.714	117	28	155	5.73	-7	0-261/S-2	32	1.4

• SNELL, Charlie Charles Anthony Snell b: 11/29/1893, Hampstead, MD d: 4/4/1988, Reading, PA BR/TR, 5'11", 160 lbs. Deb: 7/19/1912

YEAR TM-L	G	AB	R	H	2B	3B	HR	RBI	BB	SO	SB	CS	AVG	OBP	SLG	OPS	OPS+	BR/A	RC	RC/G	FR	G/POS	WS	TPW
1912 StL-A	8	19	0	4	1	0	0	0	3	....	0	....	.211	.348	.263	.611	78	-0	2	2.94	0	/C-8	0	0.0

• SNELL, Wally Walter Henry "Doc" Snell b: 5/19/1889, West Bridgewater, MA d: 7/23/1980, Providence, RI BR/TR, 5'10", 170 lbs. Deb: 8/1/1913

YEAR TM-L	G	AB	R	H	2B	3B	HR	RBI	BB	SO	SB	CS	AVG	OBP	SLG	OPS	OPS+	BR/A	RC	RC/G	FR	G/POS	WS	TPW
1913 Bos-A	6	12	1	3	0	0	0	0	0	1	1	....	.250	.250	.250	.500	45	-1	1	2.51	-0	/C-2	0	-0.1

• SNELLING, Chris Christopher Doyle Snelling b: 12/3/1981, North Miami, FL BL/TL, 5'10", 165 lbs. Deb: 5/25/2002

YEAR TM-L	G	AB	R	H	2B	3B	HR	RBI	BB	SO	SB	CS	AVG	OBP	SLG	OPS	OPS+	BR/A	RC	RC/G	FR	G/POS	WS	TPW
2002 Sea-A	8	27	2	4	0	0	1	3	2	4	0	0	.148	.207	.259	.466	24	-3	1	1.12	0	/0-8(6-0-2)	0	-0.3

• SNIDER, Duke Edwin Donald "The Silver Fox" Snider b: 9/19/1926, Los Angeles, CA BL/TR, 6', 190 lbs. Deb: 4/17/1947 C HOF: 1980 Career OF: 78-1590-293

YEAR TM-L	G	AB	R	H	2B	3B	HR	RBI	BB	SO	SB	CS	AVG	OBP	SLG	OPS	OPS+	BR/A	RC	RC/G	FR	G/POS	WS	TPW
1947 Bro-N	40	83	6	20	3	1	0	5	3	24	2	....	.241	.276	.301	.577	51	-6	7	3.03	-1	0-25(4-13-7)	1	-0.8
1948 Bro-N	53	160	22	39	6	6	5	21	12	27	4	....	.244	.297	.450	.747	96	-2	21	4.43	2	0-47(0-41-7)	5	-0.1
1949*Bro-N	146	552	100	161	28	7	23	92	56	92	12	....	.292	.361	.493	.854	122	16	100	6.73	6	*0-145(0-145-0)	24	1.9
1950 Bro-N★	152	620	109	**199**	31	10	31	107	58	79	16	....	.321	.379	.553	.932	139	33	131	8.11	-1	*0-151(0-151-0)	29	2.7
1951 Bro-N★	150	606	96	168	26	6	29	101	62	97	14	10	.277	.344	.483	.828	118	13	96	5.43	-3	*0-150(0-150-0)	22	0.5
1952*Bro-N★	144	534	80	162	25	7	21	92	55	77	7	4	.303	.368	.494	.863	136	25	96	6.45	-6	*0-141(0-141-0)	25	1.6
1953*Bro-N★	153	590	**132**	198	38	4	42	126	82	90	16	7	.336	.419	**.627**	**1.046**	164	57	161	10.52	-10	*0-151(0-151-0)	37	3.9
1954 Bro-N★	149	584	**120**	199	39	10	40	130	84	96	6	6	.341	.427	.647	1.074	170	60	161	**10.64**	-10	*0-148(0-148-0)	39	4.2
1955*Bro-N★	148	538	**126**	166	34	6	42	**136**	104	87	9	7	.309	.421	.628	1.050	169	56	145	9.81	-1	*0-146(0-146-0)	36	4.8
1956*Bro-N★	151	542	112	158	33	2	**43**	101	**99**	101	3	3	.292	**.402**	**.598**	**1.000**	152	**42**	128	**8.39**	2	*0-150(0-150-0)	**34**	3.8
1957 Bro-N	139	508	91	139	25	7	40	92	77	104	3	4	.274	.370	.587	.957	139	27	106	7.22	-8	*0-136(0-136-0)	25	1.3
1958 LA-N	106	327	45	102	12	3	15	58	32	49	2	2	.312	.375	.505	.880	126	12	59	6.54	-5	0-92(6-78-11)	13	0.4
1959*LA-N	126	370	59	114	11	2	23	88	58	71	1	5	.308	.402	.535	.937	137	19	78	7.65	-4	*0-107(0-53-71)	18	1.2
1960 LA-N	101	235	38	57	13	5	14	36	46	54	1	0	.243	.369	.519	.888	131	12	46	6.56	-2	0-75(0-48-35)	9	0.7
1961 LA-N	85	233	35	69	8	3	16	56	29	43	1	1	.296	.376	.562	.939	133	11	48	7.52	2	0-66(0-24-51)	11	0.9
1962 LA-N	80	158	28	44	11	3	5	30	36	32	2	0	.278	.418	.481	.899	150	14	34	7.61	0	0-39(15-2-24)	9	1.2
1963 NY-N★	129	354	44	86	8	3	14	45	56	74	0	1	.243	.348	.401	.749	113	8	53	5.19	-2	*0-106(34-13-62)	13	0.1
1964 SF-N	91	167	16	35	7	0	4	17	22	40	0	0	.210	.302	.323	.625	74	-5	17	3.44	-1	0-43(19-0-25)	2	-0.8
Total 18	2143	7161	1259	2116	358	85	407	1333	971	1237	99	50	.295	.381	.540	.921	138	393	1487	7.51	-42	*0-1918	352	27.5

• SNIDER, Van Van Voorhees Snider b: 8/11/1963, Birmingham, AL BL/TR, 6'3", 185 lbs. Deb: 9/2/1988 Career OF: 11-0-5

YEAR TM-L	G	AB	R	H	2B	3B	HR	RBI	BB	SO	SB	CS	AVG	OBP	SLG	OPS	OPS+	BR/A	RC	RC/G	FR	G/POS	WS	TPW
1988 Cin-N	11	28	4	6	1	0	1	6	0	13	0	1	.214	.214	.357	.571	59	-2	2	2.04	0	/0-8(6-0-3)	1	-0.3
1989 Cin-N	8	7	1	1	0	0	0	0	0	5	0	0	.143	.143	.143	.286	-18	-1	0	.64	0	/0-6(5-0-2)	0	-0.1
Total 2	19	35	5	7	1	0	1	6	0	18	0	1	.200	.200	.314	.514	44	-3	2	1.76	0	/0-14	1	-0.4

YEAR TM-L	G	AB	R	H	2B	3B	HR	RBI	BB	SO	SB	CS	AVG	OBP	SLG	OPS	OPS+	BR/A	RC	RC/G	FR	G/POS	WS	TPW
• SNIPES, Roxy	Wyatt Eure "Roxy,Rock" Snipes b: 10/28/1896, Marion, SC d: 5/1/1941, Fayetteville, NC BL/TR, 6', 185 lbs. Deb: 7/15/1923																							
1923 Chi-A	1	1	0	0	0	0	0	0	0	0	0	0	.000	.000	.000	.000	-101	-0	0	.00	0	....	0	0.0
• SNODGRASS, Chappie	Amzie Beal Snodgrass b: 3/18/1870, Springfield, OH d: 9/9/1951, New York, NY BR/TR, 5'10", 165 lbs. Deb: 5/15/1901																							
1901 Bal-A	3	10	0	1	0	0	0	1	0	....	0	....	.100	.100	.100	.200	-43	-2	0	.30	-1	/O-2(2-0-0)	0	-0.3
• SNODGRASS, Fred	Frederick Carlisle "Snow" Snodgrass b: 10/19/1887, Ventura, CA d: 4/5/1974, Ventura, CA BR/TR, 5'11.5", 175 lbs. Deb: 6/4/1908 Career OF: 108-666-73																							
1908 NY-N	6	4	2	1	0	0	0	1	0	....	1	....	.250	.250	.250	.500	57	-0	0	4.09	0	/C-3	0	-0.1
1909 NY-N	28	70	10	21	5	0	1	6	7	....	10	....	.300	.388	.414	.802	146	4	15	7.63	0	O-20(15-3-1)/C-2,1-1	4	0.3
1910 NY-N	123	396	69	127	22	8	2	44	71	52	33	....	.321	.440	.432	.871	154	33	90	8.31	-3	*O-101(31-70-22)/1-9,3-1,C	23	2.5
1911*NY-N	151	534	83	157	27	10	1	77	72	59	51	....	.294	.393	.388	.781	116	15	102	6.61	10	*O-149(1-149-0)/1-1,3-1	23	1.6
1912*NY-N	146	535	91	144	24	9	3	69	70	65	43	....	.269	.362	.364	.727	96	-1	87	5.36	-3	*O-116(52-66-5),1-27/2-1	18	-1.0
1913*NY-N	141	457	65	133	21	6	3	49	53	44	27	....	.291	.373	.383	.756	115	11	72	5.50	-3	*O-133(0-133-0)/1-3,2-1	21	0.0
1914 NY-N	113	392	54	103	20	4	0	44	37	43	25	....	.263	.336	.334	.670	103	2	50	4.34	3	O-96(9-47-40),1-14/2-1,3-1	12	0.0
1915 NY-N	80	252	36	49	9	0	0	20	35	33	11	12	.194	.307	.230	.537	68	-11	19	2.26	-1	O-75(0-68-5)	3	-1.8
Bos-N	23	79	10	22	2	0	0	9	7	9	0	4	.278	.352	.304	.656	101	-1	8	3.29	-2	O-18(0-20-0)/1-5	2	-0.5
Yr.	103	331	46	71	11	0	0	29	42	42	11	16	.215	.318	.248	.565	76	-12	27	2.50	-3	O-93(0-88-5)/1-5	5	-2.3
1916 Bos-N	112	382	33	95	13	5	1	32	34	54	14	....	.249	.318	.317	.635	101	1	45	3.85	10	*O-110(0-110-0)	16	0.4
Total 9	923	3101	453	852	143	42	11	351	386	359	215	16	.275	.367	.359	.725	110	52	488	5.32	11	O-818/1-60,C-6,2-3,3-3	122	1.4
• SNOPEK, Chris	Christopher Charles Snopek b: 9/20/1970, Cynthiana, KY BR/TR, 6'1", 185 lbs. Deb: 7/31/1995																							
1995 Chi-A	22	68	12	22	4	0	1	7	9	12	1	0	.324	.403	.426	.829	122	3	12	6.75	1	3-17/S-6	2	0.4
1996 Chi-A	46	104	18	27	6	1	6	18	6	16	0	1	.260	.306	.510	.816	106	-0	14	4.40	1	3-27,S-12/D-3	3	0.2
1997 Chi-A	86	298	27	65	15	0	5	35	18	51	3	2	.218	.265	.319	.584	54	-21	25	2.78	-4	3-82/S-4	2	-2.3
1998 Chi-A	53	125	17	26	2	0	1	4	14	24	3	0	.208	.293	.248	.541	44	-9	10	2.52	-1	S-33,2-12/3-3,1-1,D-1,O-1	1	-0.7
Bos-A	8	12	2	2	0	0	0	2	2	5	0	0	.167	.286	.167	.452	21	-1	1	1.94	-1	/2-3,3-3,D-2	0	-0.2
Yr.	61	137	19	28	2	0	1	6	16	29	3	0	.204	.292	.241	.533	42	-11	10	2.47	-2	S-33,2-15/3-6,D-3,1-1,O-1	1	-0.9
Total 4	215	607	76	142	27	1	13	66	49	108	7	3	.234	.294	.346	.640	68	-29	62	3.38	-4	3-132/S-55,2-15,D-6,1-1,O-1	8	-2.6
• SNOW, Charlie	Charles M. Snow b: 8/3/1849, Lowell, MA Deb: 10/1/1874																							
1874 Atl-n	1	1	0	1	0	0	0	0	0	0	0	0	1.000	1.000	1.000	2.000	614	1	1	∞	-1	/C-1	....	0.0
• SNOW, J.T.	Jack Thomas Snow b: 2/26/1968, Long Beach, CA BL/TL, 6'2", 202 lbs. Deb: 9/20/1992																							
1992 NY-A	7	14	1	2	1	0	0	2	5	5	0	0	.143	.368	.214	.583	67	-0	1	3.35	0	/1-6,D-1	0	-0.1
1993 Cal-A	129	419	60	101	18	2	16	57	55	88	3	0	.241	.332	.408	.740	95	-2	58	4.63	-2	*1-129	9	-1.4
1994 Cal-A	61	223	22	49	4	0	8	30	19	48	0	1	.220	.290	.345	.635	62	-14	23	3.46	0	1-61	3	-1.8
1995 Cal-A	143	544	80	157	22	1	24	102	52	91	2	1	.289	.354	.465	.819	112	9	87	5.73	-14	*1-143	15	-1.8
1996 Cal-A	155	575	69	148	20	1	17	67	56	96	1	6	.257	.329	.384	.713	81	-19	68	4.04	0	*1-154	7	-3.0
1997*SF-N	157	531	81	149	36	1	28	104	96	124	6	4	.281	.392	.510	.902	139	32	110	7.40	-6	*1-156	28	1.1
1998 SF-N	138	435	65	108	29	1	15	79	58	84	1	2	.248	.337	.423	.760	104	2	62	4.78	3	*1-136	13	-0.5
1999 SF-N	161	570	93	156	25	2	24	98	86	121	0	4	.274	.374	.451	.825	116	13	96	5.88	9	*1-160	18	0.8
2000*SF-N	155	536	82	152	33	2	19	96	66	129	1	3	.284	.374	.459	.833	118	14	89	5.74	-1	*1-153	16	0.0
2001 SF-N	101	285	43	70	12	1	8	34	55	81	0	0	.246	.375	.379	.754	103	4	45	5.48	0	1-92	6	-0.3
2002*SF-N	143	422	47	104	26	2	6	53	59	90	0	0	.246	.348	.360	.709	91	-4	55	4.44	3	*1-135	11	-1.1
2003*SF-N	103	330	48	90	18	3	8	51	55	55	1	2	.273	.389	.418	.807	114	9	57	6.10	5	1-98	14	0.5
Total 12	1453	4884	691	1286	244	16	173	773	662	1012	15	23	.263	.357	.426	.783	106	43	753	5.32	-5	*1-1423/D-1	140	-7.8
• SNYDER, Bernie	Bernard Austin Snyder b: 8/25/1913, Philadelphia, PA d: 4/15/1999, Havertown, PA BR/TR, 6', 165 lbs. Deb: 9/15/1935																							
1935 Phi-A	10	32	5	11	1	0	0	3	1	2	0	0	.344	.364	.375	.739	92	-0	4	5.22	-3	/2-5,S-4	1	-0.3
• SNYDER, Charles	Charles Snyder b: Camden, NJ d: 3/3/1901, Philadelphia, PA BR/TR Deb: 9/19/1890																							
1890 Phi-a	9	33	5	9	1	0	0	4	2	....	0	....	.273	.314	.303	.617	84	-1	3	3.56	-3	/C-5,O-5(1-0-4)	1	-0.3
• SNYDER, Cooney	Frank C. Snyder b: Toronto, Canada d: 3/9/1917, Toronto, Canada, 6'3", 180 lbs. Deb: 5/19/1898																							
1898 Lou-N	17	61	4	10	0	0	0	6	3	....	0	....	.164	.215	.164	.379	9	-7	3	1.26	-1	C-17	0	-0.6
• SNYDER, Cory	James Cory Snyder b: 11/11/1962, Inglewood, CA BR/TR, 6'4", 185 lbs. Deb: 6/13/1986 Career OF: 99-17-793																							
1986 Cle-A	103	416	58	113	21	1	24	69	16	123	2	3	.272	.299	.500	.799	115	5	58	4.99	-2	O-74(6-0-70),S-34,3-11/D-1	13	0.2
1987 Cle-A	157	577	74	136	24	2	33	82	31	166	5	1	.236	.276	.456	.732	89	-12	74	4.41	-3	*O-139(15-0-134),S-18	11	-1.9
1988 Cle-A	142	511	71	139	24	3	26	75	42	101	5	1	.272	.329	.483	.812	121	13	79	5.49	4	*O-141(1-3-139)/D-1	18	1.3
1989 Cle-A	132	489	49	105	17	0	18	59	23	134	6	5	.215	.253	.360	.613	70	-23	41	2.76	11	*O-125(0-0-125)/S-7,D-2	8	-1.6
1990 Cle-A	123	438	46	102	27	3	14	55	21	118	1	4	.233	.271	.404	.675	87	-12	44	3.30	-2	*O-120(0-0-120)/S-5	7	-1.7
1991 Chi-A	50	117	10	22	4	0	3	11	6	41	0	0	.188	.228	.299	.527	46	-9	7	1.81	-1	O-29(13-0-17),1-18	1	-1.2
Tor-A	21	49	4	7	0	1	0	6	3	19	0	0	.143	.192	.184	.376	4	-6	2	1.08	1	O-14(0-0-14)/1-4,3-3,D-3	0	-0.6
Yr.	71	166	14	29	4	1	3	17	9	60	0	0	.175	.217	.265	.482	33	-15	9	1.59	-1	O-43(13-0-31),1-22/3-3,D-3	1	-1.8
1992 SF-N	124	390	48	105	22	2	14	57	23	96	4	4	.269	.313	.444	.757	119	6	51	4.51	3	O-70(22-13-48),1-27,3-14/2,S	11	0.6
1993 LA-N	143	516	61	137	33	1	11	56	47	147	4	1	.266	.332	.397	.729	100	-0	69	4.80	0	*O-115(2-1-113),3-23,1-12/S	12	-0.6
1994 LA-N	73	153	18	36	6	0	6	18	14	47	1	0	.235	.304	.392	.696	85	-3	17	3.77	-3	O-50(40-0-13)/1-9,3-6,S-4,2	4	-0.7
Total 9	1068	3656	439	902	178	13	149	488	226	992	28	19	.247	.293	.425	.718	96	-41	442	4.14	6	O-877/S-73,1-70,3-57,2-7,D	85	-6.2
• SNYDER, Earl	Earl Clifford Snyder b: 5/6/1976, New Britain, CT BR/TR, 6', 207 lbs. Deb: 4/28/2002																							
2002 Cle-A	18	55	5	11	2	0	1	4	6	21	0	0	.200	.279	.291	.570	53	-4	5	2.74	0	1-12/3-2,D-1	0	-0.5
• SNYDER, Frank	Frank Elton "Pancho" Snyder b: 5/27/1893, San Antonio, TX d: 1/5/1962, San Antonio, TX BR/TR, 6'2", 185 lbs. Deb: 8/25/1912 C																							
1912 StL-N	11	18	2	2	0	0	0	0	2	7	1	....	.111	.200	.111	.311	-14	-3	1	.89	0	C-11	0	-0.3
1913 StL-N	7	21	1	4	0	1	0	2	0	4	0	....	.190	.190	.286	.476	35	-2	1	1.58	1	/C-7	0	-0.1
1914 StL-N	100	326	19	75	15	4	1	25	13	28	1	....	.230	.262	.310	.572	70	-13	27	2.60	2	C-98	7	-0.4
1915 StL-N	144	473	41	141	22	7	2	55	39	49	3	6	.298	.353	.387	.740	123	11	65	4.95	12	*C-142	24	3.7
1916 StL-N	132	406	23	105	12	4	0	39	18	31	7	....	.259	.290	.308	.598	84	-8	39	3.30	11	C-72,1-46/S-1	11	0.8
1917 StL-N	115	313	18	74	9	2	1	33	27	43	4	....	.236	.301	.288	.589	83	-6	27	2.90	4	C-94/2-1	10	0.6
1918 StL-N	39	112	5	28	7	1	0	10	6	13	4	....	.250	.288	.330	.618	92	-1	11	3.37	2	C-27/1-3	3	0.3
1919 StL-N	50	154	7	28	4	2	0	14	5	13	2	....	.182	.213	.234	.446	36	-12	8	1.56	6	C-48/1-1	2	-0.3
NY-N	32	92	7	21	6	0	0	11	8	9	1	....	.228	.297	.293	.591	79	-2	8	2.88	-1	C-31	2	-0.1
Yr.	82	246	14	49	10	2	0	25	13	22	3	....	.199	.245	.256	.501	53	-14	16	2.03	5	C-79/1-1	4	-0.4
1920 NY-N	87	264	26	66	13	4	3	27	17	18	2	2	.250	.295	.364	.659	90	-3	29	3.58	-1	C-84	8	0.2
1921*NY-N	108	309	36	99	13	2	8	45	27	24	3	4	.320	.382	.453	.835	120	10	53	6.48	-0	*C-101	16	1.5
1922*NY-N	104	318	34	109	21	5	5	51	23	25	1	5	.343	.387	.487	.875	123	9	58	6.76	-5	C-97	13	0.9
1923*NY-N	120	402	37	103	13	6	5	63	24	29	5	3	.256	.298	.356	.654	73	-16	43	3.66	0	*C-112	12	-0.8
1924*NY-N	118	354	37	107	18	3	5	53	30	43	3	0	.302	.357	.412	.769	109	6	53	5.59	-5	*C-110	14	0.7
1925 NY-N	107	325	21	78	9	1	11	51	20	49	0	0	.240	.286	.375	.662	70	-15	35	3.71	4	C-96	11	-0.5
1926 NY-N	55	148	10	32	3	2	5	16	13	13	0	....	.216	.280	.365	.644	73	-6	15	3.30	0	C-55	2	-0.3
1927 StL-N	63	194	7	50	5	0	1	30	9	18	0	....	.258	.291	.299	.590	56	-12	17	2.86	-1	C-62	4	-1.0
Total 16	1392	4229	331	1122	170	44	47	525	281	416	37	20	.265	.313	.360	.672	89	-64	489	3.99	26	*C-1247/1-50,2-1,S-1	139	5.0
• SNYDER, Jack	John William Snyder b: 10/6/1886, Lincoln, PA d: 12/13/1981, Brownsville, PA BR/TR, 5'9", 168 lbs. Deb: 6/13/1914																							
1914 Buf-F	1	0	0	0	0	0	0	0	1	0	0	....	....	1.000	....	1.000	189	0	0	....	-1	/C-1	0	0.0
1917 Bro-N	7	11	1	3	0	0	0	1	0	2	0	....	.273	.273	.273	.545	66	-0	1	2.46	0	/C-5	0	0.0
Total 2	8	11	1	3	0	0	0	1	1	2	0	....	.273	.333	.273	.606	76	-0	1	2.46	0	/C-6	0	0.0

YEAR TM-L	G	AB	R	H	2B	3B	HR	RBI	BB	SO	SB	CS	AVG	OBP	SLG	OPS	OPS+	BR/A	RC	RC/G	FR	G/POS	WS	TPW
• SNYDER, Jerry	Gerald George Snyder b: 7/21/1929, Jenks, OK BR/TR, 6', 170 lbs. Deb: 5/8/1952																							
1952 Was-A	36	57	5	9	2	0	0	2	5	8	1	0	.158	.226	.193	.419	18	-6	3	1.52	0	2-19/S-4	1	-0.6
1953 Was-A	29	62	10	21	4	0	0	4	5	8	1	1	.339	.388	.403	.791	117	1	9	5.78	-1	S-17/2-4	3	0.2
1954 Was-A	64	154	17	36	3	1	0	17	15	18	3	0	.234	.302	.266	.568	60	-7	13	2.83	-2	S-48/2-3	3	-0.6
1955 Was-A	46	107	7	24	5	0	0	5	6	6	1	1	.224	.265	.271	.537	47	-8	7	2.08	-6	2-22,S-20	1	-1.2
1956 Was-A	43	148	14	40	3	1	2	14	10	9	1	0	.270	.321	.345	.665	76	-5	15	3.61	-1	S-35/2-7	2	-0.3
1957 Was-A	42	93	6	14	1	0	1	4	4	9	0	1	.151	.186	.194	.379	4	-13	3	.90	2	S-15,2-13/3-1	1	-1.0
1958 Was-A	6	9	1	1	0	0	0	1	1	1	0	0	.111	.200	.111	.311	-12	-1	0	.85	-1	/2-2,S-1	0	-0.3
Total 7	266	630	60	145	18	2	3	47	46	59	7	3	.230	.284	.279	.563	54	-40	51	2.65	-10	S-140/2-70,3-1	11	-3.7
• SNYDER, Jim	James C. A. Snyder b: 9/15/1847, Brooklyn, NY d: 12/1/1922, Rockaway Beach, NY, 5'7", 130 lbs. Deb: 5/7/1872																							
1872 Eck-n	26	107	16	28	2	2	0	11	0	1	0	0	.262	.262	.318	.579	91	1	9	3.58	0	S-25/C-1,0-1	....	0.0
• SNYDER, Jim	James Robert Snyder b: 8/15/1932, Dearborn, MI BR/TR, 6'1", 185 lbs. Deb: 9/15/1961 M/C																							
1961 Min-A	3	5	0	0	0	0	0	0	0	1	0	0	.000	.000	.000	.000	-95	-1	0	.00	0	/2-3	0	-0.1
1962 Min-A	12	10	1	1	0	0	0	1	0	0	0	1	.100	.100	.100	.200	-44	-2	0	.00	-1	/2-5,1-1	0	-0.3
1964 Min-A	26	71	3	11	2	0	1	9	4	11	0	0	.155	.211	.225	.436	21	-8	3	1.14	0	2-25	1	-0.6
Total 3	41	86	4	12	2	0	1	10	4	12	0	1	.140	.187	.198	.384	9	-11	3	.95	-1	/2-33,1-1	1	-1.0
• SNYDER, Josh	Joshua M. Snyder b: 3/1844, Brooklyn, NY d: 4/21/1881, Brooklyn, NY Deb: 5/18/1872																							
1872 Eck-n	9	37	2	6	2	0	0	1	1	1	0	0	.162	.184	.216	.400	27	-2	2	1.51	1	/O-9(9-0-0)	....	0.0
• SNYDER, Pop	Charles N. Snyder b: 10/6/1854, Washington, DC d: 10/29/1924, Washington, DC BR/TR, 5'11.5", 184 lbs. Deb: 6/16/1873 M/U Career OF: 0-4-13																							
1873 Was-n	28	108	16	21	2	0	0	4	3	3	0	1	.194	.216	.213	.429	29	-9	5	1.77	7	C-28/O-3(0-3-0)	....	-0.1
1874 Bal-n	39	151	24	33	4	0	1	17	1	2	0	0	.219	.224	.265	.489	56	-7	9	2.33	5	C-39	....	-0.1
1875 Phi-n	66	263	38	64	8	2	1	25	4	4	3	8	.243	.255	.300	.555	89	-6	21	3.05	-4	*C-66/1-1	....	-0.8
1876 Lou-N	56	226	21	44	4	1	1	9	2	7	....	....	.195	.204	.237	.440	39	-16	11	1.72	6	*C-55/O-4(0-3-1)	4	-0.8
1877 Lou-N	61	248	23	64	7	2	2	28	3	14	....	....	.258	.267	.327	.594	73	-9	22	3.31	8	*C-61/O-1,S-1	6	0.0
1878 Bos-N	60	226	21	48	5	0	0	14	1	19	....	....	.212	.216	.235	.450	44	-14	12	1.81	6	*C-58/O-2(0-0-2)	6	-0.6
1879 Bos-N	81	329	42	78	16	3	2	35	5	31	....	....	.237	.249	.322	.571	85	-6	27	3.01	21	*C-80/O-2(0-0-2)	12	1.6
1881 Bos-N	62	219	14	50	8	0	0	16	3	23	....	....	.228	.239	.265	.504	61	-10	14	2.27	2	*C-60/2-1,O-1,S-1	4	-0.6
1882 Cin-a	72	309	49	90	12	2	1	50	9	....	....	....	.291	.311	.353	.664	117	4	35	4.45	13	*C-70/1-2,O-1	13	2.1
1883 Cin-a	58	250	38	64	14	6	0	34	8	....	....	....	.256	.279	.360	.639	99	-1	26	3.88	4	C-57/S-2	9	0.7
1884 Cin-a	67	268	32	69	9	9	0	39	7	....	....	....	.257	.276	.358	.635	101	-1	27	3.76	18	C-65/1-2,O-1	13	2.1
1885 Cin-a	39	152	13	36	4	3	1	19	6	....	....	....	.237	.270	.322	.593	85	-3	14	3.16	1	C-38/1-1	5	0.1
1886 Cin-a	60	220	33	41	8	3	0	28	13	....	11	....	.186	.242	.250	.492	52	-13	16	2.46	1	C-41,1-19/O-1	3	-0.8
1887 Cle-a	74	291	33	81	12	6	0	27	9	....	5	....	.278	.281	.340	.621	75	-10	29	3.74	11	C-63,1-13	7	0.5
1888 Cle-a	64	237	22	51	7	3	0	14	6	....	9	....	.215	.238	.270	.508	64	-10	18	2.58	9	C-58/1-4,O-3(0-0-3)	5	0.4
1889 Cle-N	22	83	5	16	3	0	0	12	2	12	4	....	.193	.221	.229	.450	26	-8	5	2.06	3	C-22	1	-0.3
1890 Cle-P	13	48	5	9	1	0	0	12	1	9	1	....	.188	.220	.208	.428	16	-6	2	1.72	1	C-13	0	-0.3
1891 Was-a	8	27	4	5	0	1	0	2	0	3	0	....	.185	.241	.259	.501	45	-2	2	2.09	0	/1-4,C-3,O-1	0	-0.1
Total 3 n	133	522	78	118	14	2	2	46	8	9	3	9	.226	.238	.272	.510	67	-22	36	2.57	8	C-133/O-3,1-1	....	-1.0
Total 15	797	3133	355	746	110	39	7	339	75	118	30	....	.238	.256	.303	.559	74	-104	260	3.00	105	C-744/1-45,O-17,S-4,2-1	88	4.1
• SNYDER, Redleg	Emanuel Sebastian Snyder b: 12/12/1854, Camden, NJ d: 11/11/1933, Camden, NJ BR/TR, 5'10", 175 lbs. Deb: 4/25/1876 Career OF: 55-0-1																							
1876 Cin-N	55	206	10	31	3	1	0	12	1	19	....	....	.150	.155	.176	.331	12	-16	6	.92	1	*O-55(54-0-1)	0	-1.6
1884 Wil-U	17	52	4	10	0	0	0	....	1	....	....	....	.192	.208	.192	.400	35	-4	2	1.42	0	1-16/O-1	0	-0.4
Total 2	72	258	14	41	3	1	0	12	2	19			.159	.166	.179	.345	16	-19	8	1.02	1	/O-56,1-16	0	-2.0
• SNYDER, Russ	Russell Henry Snyder b: 6/22/1934, Oak, NE BL/TR, 6'1", 190 lbs. Deb: 4/18/1959 Career OF: 442-424-390																							
1959 KC-A	73	243	41	76	13	2	3	21	19	29	6	2	.313	.367	.420	.787	113	5	38	5.86	4	O-64(27-30-12)	8	0.6
1960 KC-A	125	304	45	79	10	5	4	26	20	28	7	3	.260	.308	.365	.673	81	-9	34	3.94	-4	O-91(21-16-62)	6	-1.6
1961 Bal-A	115	312	46	91	13	5	1	13	20	32	5	3	.292	.334	.375	.709	91	-5	39	4.50	-4	*O-108(75-28-22)	8	-1.3
1962 Bal-A	139	416	47	127	19	4	9	40	17	46	7	4	.305	.336	.435	.771	111	4	58	5.07	2	*O-121(43-41-45)	13	0.1
1963 Bal-A	148	429	51	110	21	2	7	36	40	48	18	5	.256	.323	.364	.686	94	-1	53	4.28	-4	*O-130(32-74-57)	13	-1.2
1964 Bal-A	56	93	11	27	3	0	1	7	11	22	0	2	.290	.365	.355	.720	102	-0	12	4.52	0	O-40(31-8-3)	3	-0.1
1965 Bal-A	132	345	49	93	11	2	1	29	27	38	3	4	.270	.324	.322	.646	83	-9	36	3.65	2	*O-106(36-36-52)	9	-1.2
1966*Bal-A	117	373	66	114	21	5	3	41	38	37	2	1	.306	.370	.413	.783	127	14	57	5.54	-3	*O-104(59-86-4)	15	0.7
1967 Bal-A	108	275	40	65	8	2	4	23	32	48	5	2	.236	.318	.324	.642	91	-2	31	3.81	0	O-69(24-25-27)	7	-0.6
1968 Chi-A	38	82	2	11	2	0	1	5	4	16	0	0	.134	.174	.195	.370	12	-9	3	.94	0	O-22(9-1-16)	0	-1.1
Cle-A	68	217	30	61	8	2	2	23	25	21	1	1	.281	.355	.364	.719	120	6	29	4.66	1	O-54(5-11-43)/1-1	9	0.4
Yr.	106	299	32	72	10	2	3	28	29	37	1	1	.241	.308	.318	.626	92	-3	31	3.51	1	O-76(14-12-59)/1-1	9	-0.8
1969 Cle-A	122	266	26	66	10	0	2	24	25	33	3	2	.248	.313	.308	.621	72	-10	26	3.29	-4	O-84(37-28-21)	4	-1.8
1970 Mil-A	124	276	34	64	11	0	4	31	16	40	1	3	.232	.274	.315	.589	62	-16	23	2.66	-6	*O-106(43-40-26)	2	-2.6
Total 12	1365	3631	488	984	150	29	42	319	294	438	58	32	.271	.327	.363	.690	94	-32	441	4.22	-16	*O-1099/1-1	97	-9.9
• SOCKALEXIS, Chief	Louis Francis Sockalexis b: 10/24/1871, Old Town, ME d: 12/24/1913, Burlington, ME BL/TR, 5'11", 185 lbs. Deb: 4/22/1897 Career OF: 4-5-79																							
1897 Cle-N	66	278	43	94	9	8	3	42	18	....	16	....	.338	.385	.460	.845	116	6	57	8.06	0	O-66(0-1-66)	9	0.2
1898 Cle-N	21	67	11	15	2	0	0	10	1	....	0	....	.224	.246	.254	.500	44	-5	4	2.19	3	O-16(4-4-8)	0	-0.3
1899 Cle-N	7	22	0	6	1	0	0	3	1	....	0	....	.273	.304	.318	.623	76	-1	2	3.62	0	/O-5(0-0-5)	0	-0.1
Total 3	94	367	54	115	12	8	3	55	20	....	16	....	.313	.355	.414	.770	101	-0	64	6.59	3	/O-87	9	-0.2
• SODD, Bill	William Sodd b: 9/18/1914, Fort Worth, TX d: 5/14/1998, Fort Worth, TX BR/TR, 6'2", 210 lbs. Deb: 9/27/1937																							
1937 Cle-A	1	1	0	0	0	0	0	0	0	1	0	0	.000	.000	.000	.000	-99	-0	0	.00	0	....	0	0.0
• SODERHOLM, Eric	Eric Thane Soderholm b: 9/24/1948, Cortland, NY BR/TR, 5'11", 187 lbs. Deb: 9/3/1971																							
1971 Min-A	21	64	9	10	4	0	1	4	10	17	0	1	.156	.299	.266	.564	59	-4	6	2.63	2	3-20	0	-0.2
1972 Min-A	93	287	28	54	10	0	13	39	19	48	3	3	.188	.246	.359	.605	75	-11	24	2.63	-3	3-79	5	-1.6
1973 Min-A	35	111	22	33	7	2	1	9	21	16	1	2	.297	.414	.423	.837	131	5	20	6.19	-3	3-33/S-1	4	0.2
1974 Min-A	141	464	63	128	18	3	10	51	48	68	7	3	.276	.350	.392	.742	109	7	63	4.76	-4	*3-130/S-1	15	0.3
1975 Min-A	117	419	62	120	17	2	11	58	53	66	3	5	.286	.367	.415	.782	118	10	62	5.20	8	*3-113/D-3	14	1.7
1977 Chi-A	130	460	77	129	20	3	25	67	47	47	2	4	.280	.352	.500	.852	129	17	77	5.83	11	*3-126/D-3	20	2.7
1978 Chi-A	143	457	57	118	17	1	20	67	39	44	2	2	.258	.322	.431	.753	109	4	61	4.54	13	*3-128,D-11/2-1	16	1.7
1979 Chi-A	56	210	31	53	8	2	6	34	19	19	0	1	.252	.314	.395	.710	90	-4	24	3.80	16	3-56	5	1.2
Tex-A	63	147	15	40	6	0	4	19	12	9	0	0	.272	.331	.395	.726	96	-1	19	4.30	2	3-37,D-14/1-2	3	0.0
Yr.	119	357	46	93	14	2	10	53	31	28	0	1	.261	.321	.395	.716	93	-4	42	4.01	18	3-93,D-14/1-2	8	1.2
1980*NY-A	95	275	38	79	13	1	11	35	27	25	0	0	.287	.353	.462	.815	123	9	43	5.67	-2	D-51,3-37	9	0.5
Total 9	894	2894	402	764	120	14	102	383	295	359	18	21	.264	.337	.421	.758	109	34	398	4.71	41	3-759/D-82,1-2,S-2,2-1	91	6.6
• SOFIELD, Rick	Richard Michael Sofield b: 12/16/1956, Cheyenne, WY BL/TR, 6'1", 195 lbs. Deb: 4/6/1979 Career OF: 114-55-32																							
1979 Min-A	35	93	8	28	5	0	0	12	12	27	2	3	.301	.381	.355	.736	96	-1	12	4.69	0	O-35(7-6-22)	2	-0.2
1980 Min-A	131	417	52	103	18	4	9	49	24	92	4	5	.247	.291	.374	.665	75	-16	46	3.64	-1	*O-126(74-49-9)/D-2	8	-2.2
1981 Min-A	41	102	9	18	2	0	0	5	8	22	3	2	.176	.236	.196	.432	24	-10	4	1.22	1	O-34(33-0-1)	1	-1.0
Total 3	207	612	69	149	25	4	9	66	44	141	9	10	.243	.296	.342	.638	70	-27	62	3.34	0	O-195/D-2	11	-3.4
• SOJO, Luis	Luis Beltran (Sojo) Sojo b: 1/3/1965, Caracas, Venezuela BR/TR, 5'11", 174 lbs. Deb: 7/14/1990 Career OF: 12-0-0																							
1990 Tor-A	33	80	14	18	3	0	1	9	5	5	1	1	.225	.271	.300	.571	56	-5	6	2.69	-2	2-15/O-5(5-0-0),S-5,3-4,D	1	-0.7
1991 Cal-A	113	364	38	94	14	1	3	20	14	26	4	2	.258	.295	.327	.622	72	-14	33	2.98	2	*2-107/S-2,3-1,D-1,O-1	5	-1.0
1992 Cal-A	106	368	37	100	12	3	7	43	14	24	7	11	.272	.300	.378	.678	88	-11	35	3.11	-4	2-96/3-9,S-5	11	-1.2
1993 Tor-A	19	47	5	8	2	0	0	6	4	2	0	0	.170	.235	.213	.448	21	-5	2	1.26	0	/2-8,S-8,3-3	1	-0.4

YEAR TM-L	G	AB	R	H	2B	3B	HR	RBI	BB	SO	SB	CS	AVG	OBP	SLG	OPS	OPS+	BR/A	RC	RC/G	FR	G/POS	WS	TPW
1994 Sea-A	63	213	32	59	9	2	6	22	8	25	2	1	.277	.309	.423	.732	85	-6	28	4.67	0	2-40,S-24/D-2,3-1	4	-0.2
1995*Sea-A	102	339	50	98	18	2	7	39	23	19	4	2	.289	.336	.416	.752	93	-4	46	4.78	-3	S-80,2-19/O-6(6-0-0)	9	-0.1
1996 Sea-A	77	247	20	52	8	1	1	16	10	13	2	2	.211	.244	.263	.507	28	-28	14	1.85	1	3-33,2-27,S-19	2	-2.2
*NY-A	18	40	3	11	2	0	0	5	1	4	0	0	.275	.293	.325	.618	56	-3	3	2.67	2	2-14/S-4,3-1	1	-0.1
Yr.	95	287	23	63	10	1	1	21	11	17	2	2	.220	.251	.272	.523	32	-31	18	1.96	3	2-41,3-34,S-23	3	-2.2
1997 NY-A	77	215	27	66	6	1	2	25	16	14	3	1	.307	.358	.372	.730	92	-2	29	4.81	-2	2-72/S-4,3-3,1-2	7	-0.2
1998*NY-A	54	147	16	34	3	1	0	14	4	15	1	0	.231	.252	.265	.517	36	-14	9	2.02	0	S-20,1-19/2-8,3-6,D-2	1	-1.2
1999*NY-A	49	127	20	32	6	0	2	16	4	17	1	0	.252	.275	.346	.621	58	-8	11	3.00	-1	3-20,2-16/S-6,1-4,D-2	2	-0.8
2000 Pit-N	61	176	14	50	11	0	5	20	11	16	1	0	.284	.330	.432	.762	91	-3	24	4.77	0	3-50/2-1	3	-0.2
*NY-A	34	125	19	36	7	1	2	17	6	6	1	0	.288	.321	.408	.729	83	-3	15	4.20	0	2-25,3-10/1-7,S-2	3	-0.2
2001*NY-A	39	79	5	13	2	0	0	9	4	12	1	0	.165	.214	.190	.404	8	-10	4	1.47	0	3-17/1-8,2-7,S-5,D-1	1	-0.9
2003 NY-A	3	4	0	0	0	0	0	0	0	0	0	0	.000	.000	.000	.000	-102	-1	0	.00	0	/1-1,2-1	0	-0.1
Total 13	**848**	**2571**	**300**	**671**	**103**	**12**	**36**	**261**	**124**	**198**	**28**	**20**	**.261**	**.298**	**.352**	**.651**	**71**	**-118**	**259**	**3.40**	**-7**	**2-456,S-184,3-158/1-41,O-12,D**	**51**	**-9.3**
• SOLAITA, Tony	Tolia Solaita b: 1/15/1947, Nuuuli, American Samoa d: 2/10/1990, Tafuna, American Samoa BL/TL, 6', 215 lbs. Deb: 9/16/1968																							
1968 NY-A	1	1	0	0	0	0	0	0	0	1	0	0	.000	.000	.000	.000	-103	-0	0	.00	0	/1-1	0	0.0
1974 KC-A	96	239	31	64	12	0	7	30	35	70	0	3	.268	.364	.406	.769	114	5	36	5.40	3	1-65,D-14/O-1	7	0.3
1975 KC-A	93	231	35	60	11	0	16	44	39	79	0	1	.260	.371	.515	.886	144	14	45	6.68	3	D-37,1-35	10	1.4
1976 KC-A	31	68	4	16	4	0	0	9	6	17	0	0	.235	.297	.294	.591	73	-2	7	3.24	0	D-14/1-5	1	-0.3
Cal-A	63	215	25	58	9	0	9	33	34	44	1	1	.270	.369	.437	.807	145	13	36	5.88	6	1-54/D-7	11	1.5
Yr.	94	283	29	74	13	0	9	42	40	61	1	1	.261	.353	.403	.756	128	10	43	5.22	6	1-59,D-21	12	1.2
1977 Cal-A	116	324	40	78	15	0	14	53	56	77	1	3	.241	.353	.417	.769	113	7	49	5.08	0	1-91/D-6	10	0.2
1978 Cal-A	60	94	10	21	3	0	1	14	16	25	0	0	.223	.336	.287	.624	80	-2	10	3.48	0	D-18,1-11	2	-0.2
1979 Mon-N	29	42	5	12	4	0	1	7	11	16	0	0	.286	.434	.452	.886	143	3	9	8.54	0	1-13	2	0.3
Tor-A	36	102	14	27	8	1	2	13	17	16	0	0	.265	.370	.422	.791	112	2	17	5.75	0	D-26/1-6	3	0.2
Total 7	**525**	**1316**	**164**	**336**	**66**	**1**	**50**	**203**	**214**	**345**	**2**	**8**	**.255**	**.361**	**.421**	**.782**	**121**	**39**	**209**	**5.48**	**13**	**1-281,D-122/O-1**	**46**	**3.3**
• SOLOMON, Mose	Mose Hirsch "The Rabbi Of Swat" Solomon b: 12/8/1900, New York, NY d: 6/25/1966, Miami, FL BL/TL, 5'9.5", 180 lbs. Deb: 9/30/1923																							
1923 NY-N	2	8	0	3	1	0	0	1	0	1	0	0	.375	.375	.500	.875	131	0	1	7.63	0	/O-2(0-0-2)	0	0.0
• SOLTERS, Moose	Julius Joseph Solters b: 3/22/1906, Pittsburgh, PA d: 9/28/1975, Pittsburgh, PA BR/TR, 6', 190 lbs. Deb: 4/17/1934 Career OF: 687-76-67																							
1934 Bos-A	101	365	61	109	25	4	7	58	18	50	9	4	.299	.333	.447	.780	93	-5	54	5.45	-2	O-89(6-57-26)	10	-1.0
1935 Bos-A	24	79	15	19	6	1	0	8	2	7	1	1	.241	.268	.342	.610	53	-6	7	2.96	2	O-21(10-0-11)	1	-0.5
StL-A	127	552	79	182	39	6	18	104	34	35	10	1	.330	.369	.520	.889	122	17	106	7.53	11	*O-127(116-12-0)	19	2.0
Yr.	151	631	94	201	45	7	18	112	36	42	11	2	.319	.356	.498	.854	113	11	113	6.87	13	*O-148(126-12-11)	20	1.5
1936 StL-A	152	628	100	183	45	7	17	134	41	76	3	0	.291	.336	.467	.802	93	-10	99	5.79	8	*O-147(145-6-0)	12	-0.9
1937 Cle-A	152	589	90	190	42	11	20	109	42	56	6	9	.323	.372	.533	.905	125	17	113	7.18	5	*O-149(149-0-0)	21	1.2
1938 Cle-A	67	199	30	40	6	3	2	22	13	28	4	1	.201	.250	.291	.541	36	-20	15	2.46	2	O-46(40-0-6)	1	-1.9
1939 Cle-A	41	102	19	28	7	2	2	19	9	15	2	1	.275	.333	.441	.775	100	-0	15	5.42	-2	O-25(17-0-8)	3	-0.3
StL-A	40	131	14	27	6	1	0	14	10	20	1	0	.206	.262	.267	.530	35	-13	9	2.41	0	O-30(22-1-7)	0	-1.4
Yr.	81	233	33	55	13	3	2	33	19	35	3	1	.236	.294	.343	.637	64	-13	25	3.67	-2	O-55(39-1-15)	3	-1.7
1940 Chi-A	116	428	65	132	28	3	12	80	27	54	3	3	.308	.351	.472	.823	110	4	70	6.06	5	*O-107(107-0-0)	14	0.4
1941 Chi-A	76	251	24	65	9	4	4	43	18	31	3	2	.259	.311	.375	.686	82	-7	28	3.87	0	O-63(62-0-1)	6	-1.0
1943 Chi-A	42	97	6	15	0	0	1	8	7	5	0	1	.155	.212	.186	.397	17	-11	3	.89	-1	O-21(13-0-8)	0	-1.4
Total 9	**938**	**3421**	**503**	**990**	**213**	**42**	**83**	**599**	**221**	**377**	**42**	**23**	**.289**	**.334**	**.449**	**.783**	**96**	**-34**	**519**	**5.51**	**28**	**O-825**	**87**	**-4.8**
• SOMERLOTT, Jock	John Wesley Somerlott b: 10/26/1882, Flint, IN d: 4/21/1965, Butler, IN BR/TR, 6', 160 lbs. Deb: 9/19/1910																							
1910 Was-A	16	63	6	14	0	0	0	2	3	....	2	....	.222	.258	.222	.480	53	-3	4	2.08	0	1-16	0	-0.4
1911 Was-A	13	40	2	7	0	0	0	2	0	....	2	....	.175	.195	.175	.370	4	-5	2	1.33	1	1-12	0	-0.4
Total 2	**29**	**103**	**8**	**21**	**0**	**0**	**0**	**4**	**3**	**....**	**4**	**....**	**.204**	**.234**	**.204**	**.438**	**33**	**-9**	**6**	**1.77**	**1**	**/1-28**	**0**	**-0.8**
• SOMERVILLE, Ed	Edward G. Somerville b: 3/1/1853, Philadelphia, PA d: 10/1/1877, London, Canada BR/TR, 5'7" Deb: 4/30/1875																							
1875 Cen-n	14	57	6	13	3	0	0	6	1	3	1	0	.228	.241	.281	.522	88	-0	4	2.82	-6	2-14/S-1	....	-0.6
NH-n	33	136	14	29	5	0	0	7	1	3	1	2	.213	.219	.250	.469	72	-3	8	2.13	7	2-29/3-2,1-1,S-1	....	0.2
Yr.	47	193	20	42	8	0	0	13	2	6	2	2	.218	.226	.259	.485	76	-3	12	2.33	0	2-43/3-2,S-2,1-1	....	-0.4
1876 Lou-N	64	257	29	48	5	1	0	14	1	6	....	....	.187	.191	.215	.406	29	-21	11	1.45	34	*2-64	4	1.4
• SOMMER, Joe	Joseph John Sommer b: 11/20/1858, Covington, KY d: 1/16/1938, Cincinnati, OH BR/TR Deb: 7/8/1880 U Career OF: 567-15-132 ♦																							
1880 Cin-N	24	88	10	16	1	0	0	6	0	2	....	....	.182	.182	.193	.375	27	-6	3	1.21	0	O-22(14-8-0)/3-1,C-1,S-1	0	-0.7
1882 Cin-a	80	354	82	102	12	6	1	29	24	....	....	....	.288	.333	.364	.698	128	10	44	4.90	3	*O-80(80-0-0)	16	1.0
1883 Cin-a	97	413	79	115	5	7	3	52	20	....	....	....	.278	.312	.346	.658	106	2	46	4.29	-4	*O-94(82-0-12)/3-3,P-1	13	-0.5
1884 Bal-a	107	479	96	129	11	10	4	0	8	....	....	....	.269	.293	.359	.652	107	2	52	4.06	6	*3-97/O-9(0-2-7),2-1	17	0.9
1885 Bal-a	110	471	84	118	23	6	1	44	24	....	....	....	.251	.291	.331	.622	98	-1	47	3.56	9	*O-107(105-2-0)/3-2,P-2,S,1	10	0.3
1886 Bal-a	139	560	79	117	18	4	1	52	24	....	31	....	.209	.245	.261	.506	60	-26	45	2.71	2	*O-95(95-0-0),2-32,3-11/S-3,P	9	-2.8
1887 Bal-a	131	526	88	186	11	5	0	65	63	....	29	....	.354	.358	.311	.670	93	1	64	5.05	-4	*O-110(110-0-0),2-13,3-10/S,P	13	-0.6
1888 Bal-a	79	297	31	65	10	0	0	35	18	....	13	....	.219	.266	.253	.518	68	-10	24	2.79	-4	O-44(30-0-14),S-34/2-2,1-1	5	-1.3
1889 Bal-a	106	386	51	85	13	2	1	36	42	49	18	....	.220	.298	.272	.570	64	-17	38	3.31	5	*O-105(4-3-99)/S-1	6	-1.2
1890 Cle-N	9	35	4	8	1	0	0	0	2	2	0	....	.229	.270	.257	.527	55	-2	2	2.45	-2	/O-9(9-0-0),P-1	0	-0.3
Bal-a	38	129	13	33	4	2	0	23	13	....	10	....	.256	.324	.318	.642	81	-4	17	4.67	0	O-38(38-0-0)	3	-0.4
Total 10	**920**	**3738**	**617**	**974**	**109**	**42**	**11**	**342**	**238**	**53**	**101**	**....**	**.261**	**.297**	**.309**	**.607**	**88**	**-52**	**380**	**3.75**	**12**	**O-713,3-124/2-48,S-43,P-6,1,C**	**92**	**-5.8**
• SOMMERS, Bill	William Dunn Sommers b: 2/17/1923, Brooklyn, NY d: 9/22/2000, Palm City, FL BR/TR, 6', 180 lbs. Deb: 4/25/1950																							
1950 StL-A	65	137	24	35	5	1	0	14	25	14	0	1	.255	.370	.307	.677	72	-5	17	3.97	-5	3-37,2-21	2	-0.9
• SOMMERS, Pete	Joseph Andrews Sommers b: 10/26/1866, Cleveland, OH d: 7/22/1908, Cleveland, OH BR/TR, 5'11.5", 181 lbs. Deb: 4/27/1887 Career OF: 0-3-4																							
1887 NY-a	33	123	9	28	3	0	1	12	7	....	6	....	.228	.234	.233	.467	32	-10	8	2.25	-4	C-31/1-1,O-1	1	-1.0
1888 Bos-N	4	13	1	3	1	0	0	0	0	3	0	....	.231	.231	.308	.538	68	-1	1	2.55	-1	/C-4	0	-0.1
1889 Chi-N	12	45	5	10	5	0	0	8	2	8	0	....	.222	.271	.333	.604	65	-2	4	3.15	-3	C-11/O-1	0	-0.4
Ind-N	23	84	12	21	2	2	2	14	1	16	2	....	.250	.267	.393	.660	82	-3	10	4.04	-5	C-21/O-2(0-2-0)	1	-0.6
Yr.	35	129	17	31	7	2	2	22	3	24	2	....	.240	.269	.372	.641	76	-5	14	3.72	-9	C-32/O-3(0-2-1)	1	-1.0
1890 NY-N	17	47	4	5	1	1	0	1	4	13	0	....	.106	.192	.170	.363	6	-6	2	.99	-1	C-11/1-5,O-2(0-0-2)	0	-0.6
Cle-N	9	34	4	7	1	1	0	1	2	3	0	....	.206	.250	.294	.544	60	-2	3	2.52	1	/C-8,O-1	0	0.0
Yr.	26	81	8	12	2	2	0	2	6	16	0	....	.148	.216	.222	.438	28	-8	4	1.59	-0	C-19/1-5,O-3(0-1-2)	0	-0.6
Total 4	**98**	**346**	**35**	**74**	**13**	**4**	**3**	**36**	**16**	**43**	**8**	**....**	**.214**	**.242**	**.286**	**.528**	**49**	**-24**	**27**	**2.62**	**-14**	**/C-86,O-7,1-6**	**2**	**-2.6**
• SORENSEN, Zach	Zach Hart Sorensen b: 1/3/1977, Salt Lake City, UT BB/TR, 6', 190 lbs. Deb: 6/3/2003																							
2003 Cle-A	36	37	2	5	1	0	1	2	7	13	0	3	.135	.273	.243	.516	39	-5	2	1.71	-2	2-14/S-3,3-1,O-1	0	-0.6
• SORIANO, Alfonso	Alfonso Guilleard Soriano b: 1/7/1978, San Pedro de Macoris, Dominican Republic BR/TR, 6'1", 180 lbs. Deb: 9/14/1999																							
1999 NY-A	9	8	2	1	0	0	1	1	0	3	0	1	.125	.125	.500	.625	50	-1	0	.00	0	/D-6,S-1	0	-0.1
2000 NY-A	22	50	5	9	3	0	2	3	1	15	2	0	.180	.196	.360	.556	37	-5	4	2.41	-4	3-10/S-9,2-1,D-1	0	-0.8
2001*NY-A	158	574	77	154	34	3	18	73	29	125	43	14	.268	.307	.432	.739	91	-7	76	4.57	-13	*2-156/D-2	16	-1.2
2002*NY-A★	156	696	**128**	**209**	51	2	39	102	23	157	**41**	13	.300	.336	.547	.883	130	30	126	6.61	-9	*2-155/D-1	30	2.7
2003*NY-A★	156	682	114	198	36	5	38	91	38	130	35	8	.290	.339	.525	.864	126	26	123	6.60	0	*2-155	28	3.3
Total 5	**501**	**2010**	**326**	**571**	**124**	**10**	**98**	**270**	**91**	**430**	**121**	**36**	**.284**	**.324**	**.502**	**.826**	**115**	**43**	**329**	**5.85**	**-27**	**2-467/3-10,D-10,S-10**	**74**	**3.8**
• SORRELL, Bill	William Sorrell b: 10/14/1940, Morehead, KY BL/TR, 6', 190 lbs. Deb: 9/2/1965 Career OF: 7-0-2																							
1965 Phi-N	10	13	2	5	0	0	1	2	2	1	0	0	.385	.467	.615	1.082	205	2	4	13.42	0	/3-1	1	0.2
1967 SF-N	18	17	1	3	1	0	0	1	3	2	0	0	.176	.300	.235	.535	56	-1	2	2.73	0	/O-5(5-0-0)	0	-0.1
1970 KC-A	57	135	12	36	2	0	4	14	10	13	1	0	.267	.317	.370	.688	89	-2	15	3.82	-4	3-29/O-4(2-0-2),1-3	2	-0.7
Total 3	**85**	**165**	**15**	**44**	**3**	**0**	**5**	**17**	**15**	**16**	**1**	**0**	**.267**	**.328**	**.376**	**.704**	**95**	**-1**	**20**	**4.30**	**-5**	**/3-30,O-9,1-3**	**3**	**-0.7**

YEAR TM-L	G	AB	R	H	2B	3B	HR	RBI	BB	SO	SB	CS	AVG	OBP	SLG	OPS	OPS+	BR/A	RC	RC/G	FR	G/POS	WS	TPW
• SORRELLS, Chick	Raymond Edwin Sorrells b: 7/31/1896, Stringtown, OK d: 7/20/1983, Terrell, TX BR/TR, 5'9", 155 lbs. Deb: 9/18/1922																							
1922 Cle-A	2	1	0	0	0	0	0	0	0	0	0	0	.000	.000	.000	.000	-99	-0	0	.00	0	/S-1	0	0.0
• SORRENTO, Paul	Paul Anthony Sorrento b: 11/17/1965, Somerville, MA BL/TR, 6'2", 200 lbs. Deb: 9/8/1989 Career OF: 61-0-17																							
1989 Min-A	14	21	2	5	0	0	0	1	5	4	0	0	.238	.385	.238	.623	74	-0	2	3.86	0	/1-5,D-5	0	-0.1
1990 Min-A	41	121	11	25	4	1	5	13	12	31	1	1	.207	.284	.380	.664	79	-4	13	3.39	-1	D-23,1-15	1	-0.6
1991*Min-A	26	47	6	12	2	0	4	13	4	11	0	0	.255	.314	.553	.867	129	2	7	4.80	1	1-13/D-2	1	0.2
1992 Cle-A	140	458	52	123	24	1	18	60	51	89	0	3	.269	.343	.443	.786	121	11	67	5.10	0	*1-121,D-11	11	0.2
1993 Cle-A	148	463	75	119	26	1	18	65	58	121	3	1	.257	.342	.434	.776	108	5	69	5.21	1	*1-144/0-3(0-0-3),D-1	12	-0.5
1994 Cle-A	95	322	43	90	14	0	14	62	34	68	0	1	.280	.348	.453	.802	104	1	50	5.54	0	1-86/D-8	9	-0.7
1995*Cle-A	104	323	50	76	14	0	25	79	51	71	1	1	.235	.340	.511	.850	116	6	55	5.67	1	1-91,D-11	11	-0.1
1996 Sea-A	143	471	67	136	32	1	23	93	57	103	0	2	.289	.374	.507	.881	120	13	89	6.79	1	*1-138	15	0.3
1997*Sea-A	146	457	68	123	19	0	31	80	51	112	0	2	.269	.346	.514	.861	122	13	78	6.02	3	*1-139/D-1	11	0.5
1998 TB-A	137	435	40	98	27	0	17	57	54	133	2	3	.225	.315	.405	.720	84	-12	56	4.32	1	D-86,1-27,0-18(4-0-14)	4	-1.8
1999 TB-A	99	294	40	69	14	1	11	42	49	101	1	1	.235	.352	.401	.753	90	-4	45	5.21	-4	0-57(57-0-0),1-27/D-9	7	-1.1
Total 11	1093	3412	454	876	176	5	166	565	426	844	8	15	.257	.343	.457	.800	108	32	531	5.39	2	1-806,D-157/0-78	82	-3.8
• SOSA, Juan	Juan Luis (Encarnacion) Sosa b: 8/19/1975, San Francisco de Macoris, Dominican Republic BR/TR, 6'1", 175 lbs. Deb: 9/10/1999																							
1999 Col-N	11	9	3	2	0	0	0	0	2	2	0	0	.222	.364	.222	.586	42	-1	1	3.53	-1	/0-6(1-5-0),S-2	0	-0.2
2001 Ari-N	2	1	0	0	0	0	0	0	0	1	0	0	.000	.000	.000	.000	-94	-0	0	.00	0	/3-1	0	0.0
Total 2	13	10	3	2	0	0	0	0	2	3	0	0	.200	.333	.200	.533	30	-1	1	3.09	-1	/0-6,S-2,3-1	0	-0.2
• SOSA, Sammy	Samuel Peralta Sosa b: 11/12/1968, San Pedro de Macoris, Dominican Republic BR/TR, 6', 185 lbs. Deb: 6/16/1989 Career OF: 13-233-1809																							
1989 Tex-A	25	84	8	20	3	0	1	3	0	20	0	2	.238	.238	.310	.548	52	-7	5	1.77	0	0-19(12-8-1)	0	-0.8
Chi-A	33	99	19	27	5	0	3	10	11	27	7	3	.273	.357	.414	.771	120	3	15	4.83	-2	0-33(1-25-9)/D-6	2	0.0
Yr.	58	183	27	47	8	0	4	13	11	47	7	5	.257	.306	.366	.672	90	-4	19	3.38	-2	0-52(13-33-10)/D-6	2	-0.7
1990 Chi-A	153	532	72	124	26	10	15	70	33	150	32	16	.233	.285	.404	.690	93	-7	58	3.54	7	*0-152(0-1-152)	13	-0.5
1991 Chi-A	116	316	39	64	10	1	10	33	14	98	13	6	.203	.241	.335	.576	59	-19	24	2.45	0	*0-111(0-13-102)/D-2	4	-2.2
1992 Chi-N	67	262	41	68	7	2	8	25	19	63	15	7	.260	.319	.393	.712	98	-1	33	4.21	-5	0-67(0-67-0)	7	-0.7
1993 Chi-N	159	598	92	156	25	5	33	93	38	135	36	11	.261	.309	.485	.794	111	9	86	4.96	4	*0-158(0-70-114)	15	0.8
1994 Chi-N	105	426	59	128	17	6	25	70	25	92	22	13	.300	.342	.545	.887	128	14	75	6.23	2	*0-105(0-15-98)	15	1.0
1995 Chi-N★	144	564	89	151	17	3	36	119	58	134	34	7	.268	.341	.500	.841	121	19	99	6.24	7	*0-143(0-0-143)	25	1.8
1996 Chi-N	124	498	84	136	21	2	40	100	34	134	18	5	.273	.326	.564	.890	126	17	87	6.09	7	*0-124(0-0-124)	18	1.7
1997 Chi-N	162	642	90	161	31	4	36	119	45	174	22	12	.251	.302	.480	.782	98	-6	86	4.52	0	*0-161(0-0-161)	14	-1.5
1998*Chi-N★	159	643	**134**	198	20	0	66	**158**	73	171	18	9	.308	.379	.647	1.026	158	52	149	8.41	3	*0-159(0-7-156)	35	4.5
1999 Chi-N★	162	625	114	180	24	2	63	141	78	171	7	8	.288	.370	.635	1.005	150	42	140	7.95	-2	*0-162(0-25-146)	26	3.0
2000 Chi-N★	156	604	106	193	38	1	**50**	138	91	168	7	4	.320	.410	.634	1.044	162	57	157	9.75	-10	*0-156(0-2-156)	30	3.6
2001 Chi-N★	160	577	**146**	189	34	5	64	**160**	116	153	0	2	.328	.445	.737	1.181	208	95	193	12.79	3	*0-160(0-0-160)	42	8.7
2002 Chi-N★	150	556	**122**	160	19	2	**49**	108	103	144	2	0	.288	.402	.594	.995	161	51	135	8.80	-2	*0-150(0-0-150)	27	4.1
2003*Chi-N	137	517	99	144	22	0	40	103	62	143	0	1	.279	.361	.553	.914	136	26	101	6.94	-5	*0-137(0-0-137)	21	1.3
Total 15	2012	7543	1314	2099	319	43	539	1450	800	1977	233	106	.278	.352	.546	.898	134	346	1443	6.72	4	*0-1997/D-8	294	25.0
• SOTHERN, Denny	Dennis Elwood Sothern b: 1/20/1904, Washington, DC d: 12/7/1977, Durham, NC BR/TR, 5'11", 175 lbs. Deb: 9/10/1926 Career OF: 27-293-8																							
1926 Phi-N	14	53	5	13	1	0	3	10	4	10	0	....	.245	.310	.434	.744	94	-1	7	4.45	1	0-13(11-3-0)	1	-0.1
1928 Phi-N	141	579	82	165	27	5	5	38	34	53	17	....	.285	.327	.375	.702	80	-18	69	4.30	5	*0-136(8-127-1)	8	-1.8
1929 Phi-N	76	294	52	90	21	3	5	27	16	24	13	....	.306	.346	.449	.795	90	-6	44	5.45	0	0-71(2-63-6)	7	-0.8
1930 Phi-N	90	347	66	97	26	1	5	36	22	37	6	....	.280	.326	.403	.730	70	-18	45	4.46	7	0-84(3-81-0)	4	-1.3
Pit-N	17	51	4	9	4	0	1	4	3	4	2	....	.176	.222	.314	.536	28	-6	3	2.15	-1	0-13(0-12-1)	0	-0.7
Yr.	107	398	70	106	30	1	6	40	25	41	8	....	.266	.313	.392	.705	65	-24	48	4.13	6	0-97(3-93-1)	4	-1.9
1931 Bro-N	19	31	10	5	1	0	0	0	4	8	0	....	.161	.257	.194	.451	23	-3	2	1.77	0	0-10(3-7-0)	0	-0.4
Total 5	357	1355	219	379	80	9	19	115	83	136	38	....	.280	.325	.394	.719	77	-51	170	4.43	11	0-327	20	-5.1
• SOUCHOCK, Steve	Stephen "Bud" Souchock b: 3/3/1919, Yatesboro, PA d: 7/28/2002, Westland, MI BR/TR, 6'2.5", 203 lbs. Deb: 5/25/1946 Career OF: 133-1-114																							
1946 NY-A	47	86	15	26	3	3	2	10	7	13	0	3	.302	.362	.477	.838	131	2	15	6.23	-3	1-20	3	-0.2
1948 NY-A	44	118	11	24	3	1	3	11	7	13	3	0	.203	.248	.322	.570	51	-8	9	2.50	-1	1-32	1	-1.0
1949 Chi-A	84	252	29	59	13	5	7	37	25	38	5	2	.234	.303	.409	.712	90	-5	32	4.30	1	0-39(39-0-0),1-30	5	-0.8
1951 Det-A	91	188	33	46	10	3	11	28	18	27	0	2	.245	.314	.505	.819	118	2	27	4.77	-1	0-59(30-0-29)/3-3,1-1,2-1	5	-0.1
1952 Det-A	92	265	40	66	16	4	13	45	21	28	1	0	.249	.304	.487	.791	117	4	34	4.23	-1	0-56(16-1-41),3-13/1-9	5	0.1
1953 Det-A	89	278	29	84	13	3	11	46	8	35	5	1	.302	.326	.489	.816	119	6	42	5.44	1	0-80(39-0-44)/1-1	8	0.4
1954 Det-A	25	39	6	7	0	1	3	8	2	10	1	1	.179	.220	.462	.681	84	-2	3	2.58	0	/0-9(9-0-0),3-2	0	-0.2
1955 Det-A	1	1	0	1	0	0	0	1	0	0	0	0	1.000	1.000	1.000	2.000	449	0	1	∞	0	....	0	0.0
Total 8	473	1227	163	313	58	20	50	186	88	164	15	9	.255	.307	.457	.764	106	0	163	4.48	-4	0-243/1-93,3-18,2-1	27	-1.7
• SOUTHWICK, Clyde	Clyde Aubra Southwick b: 11/3/1886, Maxwell, IA d: 10/14/1961, Freeport, IL BL/TR, 6', 180 lbs. Deb: 8/22/1911																							
1911 StL-A	4	12	3	3	0	0	0	0	1	....	0	....	.250	.308	.250	.558	58	-1	1	2.57	-0	/C-4	0	0.0
• SOUTHWORTH, Bill	William Frederick Southworth b: 11/10/1945, Madison, WI BR/TR, 6'2", 205 lbs. Deb: 10/2/1964																							
1964 Mil-N	3	7	2	2	0	0	1	2	0	3	0	0	.286	.444	.714	1.159	219	1	2	13.25	0	/3-2	1	0.1
• SOUTHWORTH, Billy	William Harrison Southworth b: 3/9/1893, Harvard, NE d: 11/15/1969, Columbus, OH BL/TR, 5'9", 170 lbs. Deb: 8/4/1913 M/C Career OF: 93-214-805																							
1913 Cle-A	1	0	0	0	0	0	0	0	0	0	0	....	....	....	....	....	-97	0	0	....	0	/0-1	0	0.0
1915 Cle-A	60	177	25	39	2	5	0	8	36	12	2	4	.220	.352	.288	.640	90	-2	18	3.29	1	0-44(10-30-4)	4	-0.4
1918 Pit-N	64	246	37	84	5	7	2	43	26	9	19	....	.341	.409	.443	.852	154	17	49	7.83	8	0-64(0-0-64)	14	2.4
1919 Pit-N	121	453	56	127	14	**14**	4	61	32	22	23	....	.280	.329	.400	.729	114	7	64	4.90	-2	*0-121(75-0-46)	17	0.0
1920 Pit-N	146	546	64	155	17	13	2	53	52	20	23	25	.284	.348	.374	.722	104	0	68	4.18	4	*0-142(0-0-142)	17	-0.4
1921 Bos-N	141	569	86	175	25	15	7	79	36	13	22	20	.308	.351	.441	.792	115	9	84	4.94	6	*0-141(0-0-141)	19	0.4
1922 Bos-N	43	158	27	51	4	4	4	18	18	1	4	1	.323	.392	.475	.867	128	8	30	7.07	3	0-41(0-0-41)	7	0.7
1923 Bos-N	153	611	95	195	29	16	6	78	61	23	14	16	.319	.383	.448	.831	124	19	103	6.06	1	*0-151(0-0-151)/2-2	17	0.7
1924*NY-N	94	281	40	72	13	0	3	36	32	16	1	6	.256	.332	.335	.667	81	-8	32	3.68	-7	0-75(1-51-19)	5	-1.9
1925 NY-N	123	473	79	138	19	5	6	44	51	11	6	13	.292	.363	.391	.754	97	-5	66	4.87	-10	*0-119(0-117-2)	12	-1.9
1926 NY-N	36	116	23	38	6	1	5	30	7	1	1	....	.328	.366	.526	.892	139	6	21	6.76	-1	0-29(7-16-8)	5	0.3
*StL-N	99	391	76	124	22	6	11	69	26	9	13	....	.317	.364	.488	.853	123	11	67	6.11	-7	0-99(0-0-99)	15	-0.3
Yr.	135	507	99	162	28	7	16	99	33	10	14	....	.320	.365	.497	.862	127	17	88	6.25	-8	*0-128(7-16-107)	20	0.0
1927 StL-N	92	306	52	92	15	5	2	39	23	7	10	....	.301	.350	.402	.752	98	-1	42	4.85	-3	0-83(0-0-83)	9	-1.0
1929 StL-N	19	32	1	6	2	0	0	3	2	4	0	....	.188	.235	.250	.485	20	-4	2	1.86	0	/0-5(0-0-5)	0	-0.4
Total 13	1192	4359	661	1296	173	91	52	561	402	148	138	85	.297	.359	.415	.773	112	57	647	5.16	-7	*0-1115/2-2	141	-1.8
• SOWDERS, Len	Leonard Sowders b: 6/29/1861, Louisville, KY d: 11/19/1888, Indianapolis, IN, 5'11.5", 172 lbs. Deb: 9/10/1886																							
1886 Bal-a	23	76	10	20	3	1	0	14	12	....	6	....	.263	.364	.329	.693	121	3	12	5.57	1	0-23(0-23-0)/1-1	3	0.2
• SPALDING, Al	Albert Goodwill Spalding b: 9/2/1850, Byron, IL d: 9/9/1915, San Diego, CA BR/TR, 6'1", 170 lbs. Deb: 5/5/1871 M HOF: 1939 NA OF: 1-44-9 ♦																							
1871 Bos-n	31	144	43	39	10	1	1	31	8	1	2	0	.271	.309	.375	.684	92	0	18	5.32	-1	*P-31/0-9(0-9-0)	....	1.2
1872 Bos-n	48	237	60	84	11	5	0	47	3	1	3	0	.354	.363	.443	.806	139	16	40	8.13	8	*P-48/0-7(0-7-0)	....	**4.5**
1873 Bos-n	60	322	83	106	18	2	1	60	3	1	1	0	.329	.335	.407	.742	110	16	45	6.41	10	*P-60,0-13(0-13-0)	....	**4.4**
1874 Bos-n	71	362	80	119	13	1	0	54	3	0	2	1	.329	.334	.370	.704	119	17	47	5.73	6	*P-71/0-6(0-6-0)	....	**6.7**
1875 Bos-n	74	343	68	107	15	3	0	56	3	3	2	2	.312	.318	.373	.691	134	16	42	5.25	3	*P-72,0-18(1-9-9)/1-4	....	3.5
1876 Chi-N	66	298	54	91	14	2	0	44	6	3	....	....	.305	.326	.373	.699	118	8	36	5.07	4	*P-61,0-10(9-1-0)/1-3,S-1	**57**	2.1
1877 Chi-N	60	254	29	65	7	6	0	35	3	16	....	....	.256	.265	.331	.595	77	-8	23	3.31	7	*1-45,2-13/P-4,3-2	5	-0.3

YEAR TM-L	G	AB	R	H	2B	3B	HR	RBI	BB	SO	SB	CS	AVG	OBP	SLG	OPS	OPS+	BR/A	RC	RC/G	FR	G/POS	WS	TPW
1878 Chi-N	1	4	0	2	0	0	0	0	0	0	....	....	.500	.500	.500	1.000	215	0	1	14.09	-2	/2-1	0	-0.1
Total 5 n	284	1408	334	455	67	12	2	248	20	6	10	3	.323	.333	.392	.725	121	65	192	6.10	26	P-282/O-53,1-4	....	**20.3**
Total 3	127	556	83	158	21	8	0	79	9	19	....	....	.284	.299	.355	.653	100	0	60	4.27	9	/P-65,1-48,2-14,O-10,3-2,S-1	62	1.7
• SPALDING, Dick	Charles Harry Spalding b: 10/13/1893, Philadelphia, PA d: 2/3/1950, Philadelphia, PA BL/TL, 5'11", 185 lbs. Deb: 4/18/1927 C Career OF: 121-0-3																							
1927 Phi-N	115	442	68	131	16	3	0	25	38	40	5	....	.296	.352	.346	.698	86	-7	54	4.31	-2	*O-113(113-0-0)	7	-1.8
1928 Was-A	16	23	1	8	0	0	0	0	0	4	0	2	.348	.348	.348	.696	84	-1	2	2.90	-0	O-11(8-0-3)	0	-0.2
Total 2	131	465	69	139	16	3	0	25	38	44	5	2	.299	.352	.346	.698	86	-9	56	4.23	-2	O-124	7	-1.9
• SPANGLER, Al	Albert Donald "Spanky" Spangler b: 7/8/1933, Philadelphia, PA BL/TL, 6', 175 lbs. Deb: 9/16/1959 C Career OF: 446-137-151																							
1959 Mil-N	6	12	3	5	0	1	0	0	1	1	1	0	.417	.462	.583	1.045	192	2	4	12.01	0	/O-4(1-3-0)	1	0.2
1960 Mil-N	101	105	26	28	5	2	0	6	14	17	6	2	.267	.358	.352	.711	103	2	15	4.84	1	O-92(90-1-1)	4	-0.1
1961 Mil-N	68	97	23	26	2	0	0	6	28	9	4	2	.268	.432	.289	.721	102	3	15	5.67	-3	O-44(23-21-1)	4	-0.1
1962 Hou-N	129	418	51	119	10	9	5	35	70	46	7	6	.285	.391	.388	.779	119	14	69	5.97	-1	*O-121(93-28-0)	15	0.7
1963 Hou-N	120	430	52	121	25	4	4	27	50	38	5	8	.281	.358	.386	.744	122	11	60	4.90	-2	*O-113(87-33-3)	18	0.4
1964 Hou-N	135	449	51	110	18	5	4	38	41	43	7	8	.245	.314	.334	.648	88	-8	48	3.54	-5	*O-127(113-18-0)	10	-2.0
1965 Hou-N	38	112	18	24	1	1	1	7	14	8	1	1	.214	.302	.268	.569	66	-5	10	2.87	0	O-33(31-1-1)	1	-0.7
Cal-A	51	96	17	25	1	0	0	1	8	9	4	0	.260	.317	.271	.588	70	-3	10	3.64	0	O-24(4-17-6)	2	-0.4
1966 Cal-A	6	9	2	6	0	0	0	0	2	2	0	0	.667	.727	.667	1.394	312	3	5	42.68	0	/O-3(0-0-3)	1	0.3
1967 Chi-N	62	130	18	33	7	0	0	13	23	17	2	2	.254	.366	.308	.674	90	-1	16	4.26	-2	O-41(0-7-34)	4	-0.5
1968 Chi-N	88	177	21	48	9	3	2	18	20	24	0	1	.271	.348	.390	.738	114	3	24	4.69	-1	O-48(1-7-42)	6	0.0
1969 Chi-N	82	213	23	45	8	1	4	23	21	16	0	2	.211	.285	.315	.600	60	-12	20	3.10	-3	O-58(0-1-57)	2	-1.9
1970 Chi-N	21	14	2	2	1	0	1	1	3	3	0	0	.143	.294	.429	.723	81	-0	2	4.49	-0	/O-6(3-0-3)	0	-0.1
1971 Chi-N	5	5	0	2	0	0	0	0	0	1	0	0	.400	.400	.400	.800	111	0	1	7.20	0	....	0	0.0
Total 13	912	2267	307	594	87	26	21	175	295	234	37	32	.262	.350	.351	.701	101	8	298	4.55	-16	O-714	68	-4.2
• SPEAKE, Bob	Robert Charles "Spook" Speake b: 8/22/1930, Springfield, MO BL/TL, 6'1", 178 lbs. Deb: 4/16/1955 Career OF: 79-40-8																							
1955 Chi-N	95	261	36	57	9	5	12	43	28	71	3	4	.218	.301	.429	.730	91	-5	34	4.41	1	O-55(49-0-8)/1-8	6	-0.7
1957 Chi-N	129	418	65	97	14	5	16	50	38	68	5	6	.232	.301	.404	.705	89	-9	51	4.15	3	O-60(20-40-0),1-39	9	-1.2
1958 SF-N	66	71	9	15	3	0	3	10	13	15	0	1	.211	.333	.380	.714	90	-1	9	4.34	1	O-10(10-0-0)	2	-0.1
1959 SF-N	15	11	0	1	0	0	0	1	1	4	0	0	.091	.167	.091	.258	-30	-2	0	.31	0	....	0	-0.2
Total 4	305	761	110	170	26	10	31	104	80	158	8	11	.223	.302	.406	.708	88	-17	95	4.18	5	O-125/1-47	17	-2.1
• SPEAKER, Tris	Tristram E "The Grey Eagle" Speaker b: 4/4/1888, Hubbard, TX d: 12/8/1958, Lake Whitney, TX BL/TL, 5'11.5", 193 lbs. Deb: 9/12/1907 M HOF: 1937 Career OF: 2-2690-6																							
1907 Bos-A	7	19	0	3	0	0	0	1	1	....	0	....	.158	.200	.158	.358	14	-2	1	1.02	1	/O-4(0-0-4)	0	-0.1
1908 Bos-A	31	116	12	26	2	2	0	9	4	....	3	....	.224	.262	.276	.538	73	-4	9	2.53	4	O-31(1-30-0)	2	-0.1
1909 Bos-A	143	544	73	168	26	13	7	77	38	....	35	....	.309	.362	.443	.805	151	30	99	6.52	21	*O-142(0-142-0)	34	5.0
1910 Bos-A	141	538	92	183	20	14	7	65	52	....	35	....	.340	.404	.468	.873	169	43	115	8.13	7	*O-140(0-140-0)	34	4.8
1911 Bos-A	141	500	88	167	34	13	8	70	59	....	25	....	.334	.418	.502	.920	158	40	115	8.54	3	*O-138(0-138-0)	27	3.4
1912*Bos-A	153	580	136	222	**53**	12	**10**	90	82	....	52	....	.383	**.464**	.567	1.031	185	67	175	12.46	14	*O-153(0-153-0)	**51**	7.1
1913 Bos-A	141	520	94	189	35	22	3	71	65	22	46	....	.363	.441	.533	.974	180	54	136	9.99	11	*O-139(0-139-0)	36	6.0
1914 Bos-A	158	571	101	**193**	**46**	18	4	90	77	25	42	29	.338	.423	**.503**	**.926**	178	52	124	7.82	17	*O-156(0-156-0)/1-1,P-1	**45**	6.5
1915*Bos-A	150	547	108	176	25	12	0	69	81	14	29	25	.322	.416	.411	.827	152	34	97	6.21	6	*O-150(0-150-0)	36	3.2
1916 Cle-A	151	546	102	**211**	**41**	8	2	79	82	20	35	27	**.386**	**.470**	**.502**	**.972**	**181**	54	132	9.11	9	*O-151(0-151-0)	**41**	**6.0**
1917 Cle-A	142	523	90	184	42	11	2	60	67	14	30	....	.352	.432	.486	.918	167	45	118	8.68	10	*O-142(0-142-0)	37	5.1
1918 Cle-A	127	471	73	150	**33**	11	0	61	64	9	27	....	.318	**.403**	.435	.839	139	25	90	6.89	7	*O-127(0-127-0)	27	2.7
1919 Cle-A	134	494	83	146	38	12	2	63	73	12	15	....	.296	.395	.433	.828	125	19	89	6.28	13	*O-134(0-134-0)	27	2.5
1920*Cle-A	150	552	137	214	**50**	11	8	107	97	13	10	13	.388	.483	.562	1.045	171	61	152	10.85	7	*O-148(0-148-0)	39	5.7
1921 Cle-A	132	506	107	183	**52**	14	3	75	68	12	2	4	.362	.439	.538	.977	146	37	121	9.45	6	*O-128(0-128-0)	27	3.5
1922 Cle-A	131	426	85	161	**48**	8	11	71	77	11	8	3	.378	**.474**	.606	1.080	178	54	127	**11.99**	2	*O-109(0-109-0)	**30**	5.0
1923 Cle-A	150	574	133	218	**59**	11	17	130	93	15	8	9	.380	.469	.610	1.079	183	71	166	11.34	6	*O-150(0-150-0)	35	6.8
1924 Cle-A	135	486	94	167	36	9	9	65	72	13	5	7	.344	.432	.510	.943	141	31	109	8.53	-1	*O-128(0-127-1)	21	2.3
1925 Cle-A	117	429	79	167	35	5	12	87	70	12	5	2	.389	**.479**	.578	1.057	166	48	123	**11.67**	3	*O-109(0-109-0)	25	**4.3**
1926 Cle-A	150	539	96	164	52	8	7	86	94	15	6	1	.304	.408	.469	.877	127	26	110	7.22	5	*O-149(0-149-0)	29	2.4
1927 Was-A	141	523	71	171	43	6	2	73	55	8	9	8	.327	.395	.444	.839	119	15	93	6.55	-5	*O-120(0-119-1),1-17	21	0.4
1928 Phi-A	64	191	28	51	22	2	3	30	10	5	5	1	.267	.310	.450	.761	95	-2	27	4.77	0	O-50(1-49-0)	6	-0.4
Total 22	2789	10195	1882	3514	**792**	222	117	1529	1381	220	432	129	.345	.428	.500	.928	157	796	2325	8.56	147	*O-2698/1-18,P-1	630	82.0
• SPEED, Horace	Horace Arthur Speed b: 10/4/1951, Los Angeles, CA BR/TR, 6'1", 180 lbs. Deb: 4/10/1975 Career OF: 27-26-38																							
1975 SF-N	17	15	2	2	1	0	0	1	1	8	0	0	.133	.235	.200	.435	21	-2	1	1.72	-1	/O-9(5-0-5)	0	-0.3
1978 Cle-A	70	106	13	24	4	1	0	4	14	31	2	4	.226	.322	.283	.605	72	-5	9	2.52	-1	O-61(12-23-30)/D-3	1	-0.7
1979 Cle-A	26	14	6	2	0	0	0	1	5	7	2	1	.143	.368	.143	.511	44	-1	1	2.85	-1	O-16(10-3-3)/D-4	0	-0.2
Total 3	113	135	21	28	5	1	0	6	20	46	4	5	.207	.318	.259	.578	64	-7	11	2.47	-3	/O-86,D-7	1	-1.2
• SPEHR, Tim	Timothy Joseph Spehr b: 7/2/1966, Excelsior Springs, MO BR/TR, 6'2", 200 lbs. Deb: 7/18/1991 Career OF: 2-0-1																							
1991 KC-A	37	74	7	14	5	0	3	14	9	18	1	0	.189	.286	.378	.664	82	-2	8	3.40	0	C-37	2	0.0
1993 Mon-N	53	87	14	20	6	0	2	10	6	20	2	0	.230	.287	.368	.655	71	-3	10	3.80	-2	C-49	2	-0.3
1994 Mon-N	52	36	8	9	3	1	0	5	4	11	2	0	.250	.325	.389	.714	84	-0	5	5.08	-2	C-46/O-2(2-0-0)	2	-0.2
1995 Mon-N	41	35	4	9	5	0	1	3	6	7	0	0	.257	.366	.486	.852	118	1	7	6.39	2	C-38	1	0.4
1996 Mon-N	63	44	4	4	1	0	1	3	3	15	1	0	.091	.167	.182	.348	-8	-7	1	.93	-7	C-58/O-1	1	-1.3
1997 KC-A	17	35	3	6	0	0	1	2	2	12	0	0	.171	.237	.257	.494	28	-4	2	2.16	0	C-17	0	-0.2
Atl-N	8	14	2	3	1	0	1	4	0	4	1	0	.214	.214	.500	.714	78	-0	2	3.96	-1	/C-7	1	-0.1
1998 NY-N	21	51	3	7	1	0	0	3	7	16	1	0	.137	.267	.157	.424	15	-6	3	1.73	1	C-21/1-1	2	-0.3
KC-A	11	25	5	6	2	0	1	2	8	3	0	0	.240	.457	.440	.897	131	2	6	7.56	0	C-11	2	0.2
1999 KC-A	60	155	26	32	7	0	9	26	22	47	1	0	.206	.328	.426	.754	88	-3	24	4.93	-4	C-59	4	-0.3
Total 8	363	556	76	110	31	1	19	72	67	153	9	0	.198	.300	.360	.660	71	-22	68	3.91	-13	C-343/O-3,1-1	17	-2.0
• SPEIER, Chris	Chris Edward Speier b: 6/28/1950, Alameda, CA BR/TR, 6'1", 182 lbs. Deb: 4/7/1971 C																							
1971*SF-N	157	601	74	141	17	6	8	46	56	90	4	7	.235	.307	.323	.630	80	-18	58	3.22	10	*S-156	16	1.1
1972 SF-N★	150	562	74	151	25	2	15	71	82	92	9	4	.269	.365	.400	.765	116	15	87	5.44	11	*S-150	25	4.7
1973 SF-N★	153	542	58	135	17	4	11	71	66	69	4	5	.249	.333	.356	.689	87	-9	63	3.88	3	*S-150/2-1	15	1.2
1974 SF-N★	141	501	55	125	19	5	9	53	62	64	3	2	.250	.337	.361	.698	91	-5	64	4.37	10	*S-135/2-4	17	2.1
1975 SF-N	141	487	60	132	30	5	10	69	70	50	4	5	.271	.364	.415	.779	111	7	73	5.23	0	*S-136/3-1	20	2.5
1976 SF-N	145	495	51	112	18	4	3	40	60	52	2	2	.226	.315	.297	.612	72	-17	47	3.08	-3	*S-135/2-7,3-5,1-1	11	-0.4
1977 SF-N	6	17	1	3	1	0	0	0	0	3	0	0	.176	.176	.235	.412	9	-2	1	1.36	1	/S-5	0	-0.1
Mon-N	139	531	58	125	30	6	5	38	67	78	1	2	.235	.322	.343	.665	81	-14	59	3.74	-3	*S-138	11	-0.2
Yr.	145	548	59	128	31	6	5	38	67	81	1	2	.234	.318	.339	.658	79	-16	60	3.67	-3	*S-143	11	-0.3
1978 Mon-N	150	501	47	126	18	3	5	51	60	75	1	0	.251	.333	.329	.662	87	-8	56	3.78	11	*S-148	15	2.0
1979 Mon-N	113	344	31	78	13	1	7	26	43	45	0	0	.227	.318	.331	.649	78	-10	35	3.39	4	*S-112	9	0.6
1980 Mon-N	128	388	35	103	14	4	1	32	52	38	0	3	.265	.352	.330	.682	91	-4	45	3.95	8	*S-127/3-1	12	1.7
1981*Mon-N	96	307	33	69	10	2	2	25	38	29	1	2	.225	.310	.290	.600	70	-12	27	2.89	8	S-96	8	0.7
1982 Mon-N	156	530	41	136	26	4	7	60	47	67	1	6	.257	.318	.360	.679	88	-11	58	3.71	4	*S-155	14	1.0
1983 Mon-N	88	261	31	67	12	2	2	22	29	37	2	1	.257	.336	.341	.677	88	-4	31	4.12	-6	S-74,3-12/2-2	7	-0.2
1984 Mon-N	25	40	1	6	0	0	0	1	1	8	0	0	.150	.171	.150	.321	-10	-6	1	.74	1	S-13/3-4	0	-0.4
StL-N	38	118	9	21	7	1	3	8	9	19	0	0	.178	.242	.331	.573	61	-7	9	2.32	7	S-34/3-2	2	0.4
Yr.	63	158	10	27	7	1	3	9	10	27	0	0	.171	.225	.285	.510	43	-12	10	1.90	8	S-47/3-6	2	-0.1
Min-A	12	33	2	7	0	0	0	1	3	7	0	0	.212	.278	.212	.490	36	-3	2	1.95	0	S-12	0	-0.2
1985 Chi-N	106	218	16	53	11	0	4	24	17	34	1	3	.243	.298	.349	.646	72	-9	21	3.13	3	S-58,3-31,2-13	3	-0.2
1986 Chi-N	95	155	21	44	8	0	6	23	15	32	2	2	.284	.351	.452	.802	111	2	24	5.23	1	3-53,S-23/2-7	5	0.4

YEAR TM-L	G	AB	R	H	2B	3B	HR	RBI	BB	SO	SB	CS	AVG	OBP	SLG	OPS	OPS+	BR/A	RC	RC/G	FR	G/POS	WS	TPW
1987*SF-N	111	317	39	79	13	0	11	39	42	51	4	7	.249	.343	.394	.737	99	-2	43	4.69	5	2-55,3-44,S-22	11	0.5
1988 SF-N	82	171	26	37	9	1	3	18	23	39	3	3	.216	.313	.333	.646	89	-3	17	3.08	4	2-45,3-22,S-12	4	0.3
1989 SF-N	28	37	7	9	4	0	0	2	5	9	0	0	.243	.333	.351	.685	99	0	4	3.53	0	/3-9,S-9,2-4,1-1	1	0.0
Total 19	2260	7156	770	1759	302	50	112	720	847	988	42	54	.246	.329	.349	.678	88	-119	826	3.88	77	*S-1900,3-184,2-138/1-2	206	17.4

• SPENCE, Bob John Robert Spence b: 2/10/1946, San Diego, CA BL/TR, 6'4", 215 lbs. Deb: 9/5/1969

YEAR TM-L	G	AB	R	H	2B	3B	HR	RBI	BB	SO	SB	CS	AVG	OBP	SLG	OPS	OPS+	BR/A	RC	RC/G	FR	G/POS	WS	TPW
1969 Chi-A	12	26	0	4	1	0	0	3	0	9	0	0	.154	.154	.192	.346	-4	-4	1	.96	0	/1-6	0	-0.4
1970 Chi-A	46	130	11	29	4	1	4	15	11	32	0	0	.223	.289	.362	.650	75	-5	14	3.42	2	1-37	2	-0.6
1971 Chi-A	14	27	2	4	0	0	0	1	5	6	0	0	.148	.281	.148	.429	24	-2	1	1.52	-1	/1-7	0	-0.4
Total 3	72	183	13	37	5	1	4	19	16	47	0	0	.202	.270	.306	.576	57	-11	16	2.75	0	/1-50	2	-1.5

• SPENCE, Stan Stanley Orville Spence b: 3/20/1915, South Portsmouth, KY d: 1/9/1983, Kingston, NC BL/TL, 5'10.5", 180 lbs. Deb: 6/8/1940 Career OF: 90-801-104

YEAR TM-L	G	AB	R	H	2B	3B	HR	RBI	BB	SO	SB	CS	AVG	OBP	SLG	OPS	OPS+	BR/A	RC	RC/G	FR	G/POS	WS	TPW
1940 Bos-A	51	68	5	19	2	1	2	13	4	9	0	1	.279	.319	.426	.746	88	-2	9	4.75	-1	0-15(6-0-9)	1	-0.3
1941 Bos-A	86	203	22	47	10	3	2	28	18	14	1	0	.232	.304	.340	.643	68	-9	22	3.74	3	0-52(27-10-16)/1-1	3	-0.8
1942 Was-A★	149	629	94	203	27	**15**	4	79	62	16	5	2	.323	.384	.432	.817	131	27	111	6.81	-16	*0-149(0-149-0)	29	0.7
1943 Was-A	149	570	72	152	23	10	12	88	84	39	8	1	.267	.366	.405	.771	130	26	93	5.80	-2	*0-148(0-148-0)	28	2.2
1944 Was-A★	153	592	83	187	31	8	18	100	69	28	3	7	.316	.391	.486	.877	157	41	118	7.56	12	*0-150(0-150-0)/1-3	33	5.2
1946 Was-A★	152	578	83	169	50	10	16	87	62	31	1	7	.292	.365	.497	.861	148	33	104	6.39	1	*0-150(0-150-0)	30	3.1
1947 Was-A★	147	506	62	141	22	6	16	73	81	41	2	2	.279	.378	.441	.819	130	22	89	6.36	2	*0-142(0-142-0)	25	2.2
1948 Bos-A	114	391	71	92	17	4	12	61	82	33	0	2	.235	.368	.391	.759	97	-0	62	5.39	-1	0-92(24-0-70),1-14	12	-0.6
1949 Bos-A	7	20	3	3	1	0	0	1	6	1	0	0	.150	.346	.200	.546	43	-1	2	3.11	1	/0-5(0-2-3)	0	-0.1
StL-A	104	314	46	77	13	3	13	45	52	36	1	1	.245	.356	.430	.786	103	1	50	5.29	0	0-87(33-50-6)/1-1	8	-0.2
Yr.	111	334	49	80	14	3	13	46	58	37	1	1	.240	.355	.416	.771	99	-0	52	5.15	1	0-92(33-52-9)/1-1	8	-0.3
Total 9	1112	3871	541	1090	196	60	95	575	520	248	21	23	.282	.369	.437	.806	127	137	660	6.13	0	0-990/1-19	169	11.4

• SPENCER, Spencer Deb: 6/3/1872

YEAR TM-L	G	AB	R	H	2B	3B	HR	RBI	BB	SO	SB	CS	AVG	OBP	SLG	OPS	OPS+	BR/A	RC	RC/G	FR	G/POS	WS	TPW
1872 Nat-n	1	4	1	0	0	0	0	0	0	0	0	0	.000	.000	.000	.000	-86	-1	0	.00	-1	/S-1	....	-0.1

• SPENCER, Ben Lloyd Benjamin Spencer b: 5/15/1890, Patapsco, MD d: 9/1/1970, Finksburg, MD BL/TL, 5'8", 160 lbs. Deb: 9/8/1913

YEAR TM-L	G	AB	R	H	2B	3B	HR	RBI	BB	SO	SB	CS	AVG	OBP	SLG	OPS	OPS+	BR/A	RC	RC/G	FR	G/POS	WS	TPW
1913 Was-A	8	21	2	6	1	1	0	2	2	4	0	....	.286	.348	.429	.776	124	1	3	5.04	0	/0-8(7-1-0)	1	0.0

• SPENCER, Chet Chester Arthur Spencer b: 3/4/1883, South Webster, OH d: 11/10/1938, Portsmouth, OH BL/TR, 6', 180 lbs. Deb: 8/22/1906

YEAR TM-L	G	AB	R	H	2B	3B	HR	RBI	BB	SO	SB	CS	AVG	OBP	SLG	OPS	OPS+	BR/A	RC	RC/G	FR	G/POS	WS	TPW
1906 Bos-N	8	27	1	4	1	0	0	0	0	....	0	....	.148	.148	.185	.333	4	-3	1	.86	0	/0-8(1-3-3)	0	-0.4

• SPENCER, Daryl Daryl Dean "Dee,Big Dee" Spencer b: 7/13/1929, Wichita, KS BR/TR, 6'2.5", 190 lbs. Deb: 9/17/1952

YEAR TM-L	G	AB	R	H	2B	3B	HR	RBI	BB	SO	SB	CS	AVG	OBP	SLG	OPS	OPS+	BR/A	RC	RC/G	FR	G/POS	WS	TPW
1952 NY-N	7	17	0	5	0	1	0	3	1	4	0	0	.294	.333	.412	.745	105	0	2	5.58	0	/3-3,S-3	1	0.1
1953 NY-N	118	408	55	85	18	5	20	56	42	74	0	1	.208	.287	.424	.711	81	-14	49	3.95	-10	S-53,3-36,2-32	7	-1.7
1956 NY-N	146	489	46	108	13	2	14	42	35	65	1	3	.221	.277	.342	.619	65	-25	45	3.03	-11	2-70,S-66,3-12	8	-2.6
1957 NY-N	148	534	65	133	31	2	11	50	50	50	3	1	.249	.315	.376	.691	85	-11	62	3.98	-1	*S-110,2-36/3-6	14	0.0
1958 SF-N	148	539	71	138	20	5	17	74	73	60	1	0	.256	.348	.406	.754	101	3	77	4.83	0	*S-134,2-17	18	1.4
1959 SF-N	152	555	59	147	20	1	12	62	58	67	5	0	.265	.334	.369	.704	89	-7	69	4.36	1	*2-151/S-4	15	0.6
1960 StL-N	148	507	70	131	20	3	16	58	81	74	1	1	.258	.366	.404	.770	102	4	77	5.25	-16	*S-138,2-16	19	0.0
1961 StL-N	37	130	19	33	4	0	4	21	23	17	1	0	.254	.366	.377	.743	89	-1	17	4.41	-0	S-37	3	0.2
LA-N	60	189	27	46	7	0	8	27	20	35	0	1	.243	.329	.407	.736	86	-4	25	4.43	5	3-57/S-3	6	0.1
Yr.	97	319	46	79	11	0	12	48	43	52	1	1	.248	.344	.395	.739	87	-5	42	4.42	5	3-57,S-40	9	0.3
1962 LA-N	77	157	24	37	5	1	2	12	32	31	0	0	.236	.365	.318	.684	91	-0	19	3.96	1	3-57,S-10	5	0.1
1963 LA-N	7	9	0	1	0	0	0	0	3	2	0	0	.111	.333	.111	.444	37	-1	1	1.43	0	/3-3	0	-0.1
Cin-N	50	155	21	37	7	0	1	23	31	37	1	0	.239	.369	.303	.672	93	1	21	4.61	4	3-48	6	0.5
Yr.	57	164	21	38	7	0	1	23	34	39	1	0	.232	.367	.293	.660	89	0	22	4.37	4	3-51	6	0.5
Total 10	1098	3689	457	901	145	20	105	428	449	516	13	7	.244	.329	.380	.709	88	-54	465	4.26	-26	S-558,2-322,3-222	102	-1.3

• SPENCER, Jim James Lloyd "Spence" Spencer b: 7/30/1946, Hanover, PA d: 2/10/2002, Fort Lauderdale, FL BL/TL, 6'2", 195 lbs. Deb: 9/7/1968

YEAR TM-L	G	AB	R	H	2B	3B	HR	RBI	BB	SO	SB	CS	AVG	OBP	SLG	OPS	OPS+	BR/A	RC	RC/G	FR	G/POS	WS	TPW
1968 Cal-A	19	68	2	13	1	0	0	5	3	10	0	0	.191	.236	.206	.442	36	-5	3	1.49	3	1-19	0	-0.4
1969 Cal-A	113	386	39	98	14	3	10	31	26	53	1	0	.254	.304	.383	.688	96	-3	45	4.03	4	*1-107	10	-0.8
1970 Cal-A	146	511	61	140	20	4	12	68	28	61	0	2	.274	.312	.399	.711	98	-4	61	4.23	-1	*1-142	15	-1.7
1971 Cal-A	148	510	50	121	21	2	18	59	48	63	0	1	.237	.307	.392	.699	104	1	59	3.81	2	*1-145	14	-0.9
1972 Cal-A	82	212	13	47	5	0	1	14	12	25	0	1	.222	.263	.259	.523	59	-11	13	2.00	1	1-35,0-24(24-0-0)	1	-1.5
1973 Cal-A	29	87	10	21	4	2	2	11	9	9	0	0	.241	.320	.402	.722	111	1	11	4.13	-2	1-26/D-2	3	-0.3
Tex-A★	102	352	35	94	12	3	4	43	34	41	0	3	.267	.333	.352	.686	97	-2	40	4.00	4	1-99/D-1	8	-0.5
Yr.	131	439	45	115	16	5	6	54	43	50	0	3	.262	.331	.362	.693	100	-1	51	4.02	2	*1-125/D-3	11	-0.8
1974 Tex-A	118	352	36	98	11	4	7	44	22	27	1	2	.278	.326	.392	.718	109	3	44	4.34	-1	1-60,D-54	10	-0.4
1975 Tex-A	132	403	50	107	18	1	11	47	35	43	0	1	.266	.327	.397	.724	105	2	51	4.48	1	1-99,D-25	11	-0.5
1976 Chi-A	150	518	53	131	13	2	14	70	49	52	6	4	.253	.319	.367	.685	100	-1	60	3.91	4	*1-143/D-2	12	-0.8
1977 Chi-A	128	470	56	116	16	1	18	69	36	50	1	2	.247	.303	.400	.703	90	-8	55	3.94	5	*1-125	9	-1.0
1978*NY-A	71	150	12	34	9	1	7	24	15	32	0	1	.227	.297	.440	.737	107	1	18	4.09	0	D-35,1-15	4	-0.1
1979 NY-A	106	295	60	85	15	3	23	53	38	25	0	2	.288	.369	.593	.963	158	22	60	7.08	-1	D-71,1-26	14	1.7
1980*NY-A	97	259	38	61	9	0	13	43	30	44	1	0	.236	.317	.421	.738	102	1	34	4.43	-1	1-75,D-15	7	-0.5
1981 NY-A	25	63	6	9	2	0	2	4	9	7	0	0	.143	.250	.270	.520	50	-4	4	1.86	1	1-25	1	-0.4
*Oak-A	54	171	14	35	6	0	2	9	10	20	1	0	.205	.249	.275	.523	53	-10	11	2.10	2	1-48	1	-1.1
Yr.	79	234	20	44	8	0	4	13	19	27	1	0	.188	.249	.274	.523	52	-14	15	2.03	3	1-73	2	-1.5
1982 Oak-A	33	101	6	17	3	1	2	5	3	20	0	0	.168	.192	.277	.470	28	-10	5	1.44	1	1-32	0	-1.1
Total 15	1553	4908	541	1227	179	27	146	599	407	582	11	19	.250	.310	.387	.696	98	-28	574	3.97	22	*1-1221,D-205/0-24	120	-10.2

• SPENCER, Roy Roy Hampton Spencer b: 2/22/1900, Scranton, NC d: 2/8/1973, Port Charlotte, FL BR/TR, 5'10", 168 lbs. Deb: 4/19/1925

YEAR TM-L	G	AB	R	H	2B	3B	HR	RBI	BB	SO	SB	CS	AVG	OBP	SLG	OPS	OPS+	BR/A	RC	RC/G	FR	G/POS	WS	TPW
1925 Pit-N	14	28	1	6	1	0	0	2	1	3	1	0	.214	.241	.250	.491	24	-3	2	2.17	-1	C-11	0	-0.3
1926 Pit-N	28	43	5	17	3	0	0	4	1	0	0	....	.395	.409	.465	.874	128	2	8	7.16	-1	C-12	2	0.1
1927*Pit-N	38	92	9	26	3	1	0	13	3	3	0	....	.283	.305	.337	.642	67	-4	9	3.48	-2	C-34	2	-0.4
1929 Was-A	50	116	18	18	4	0	1	9	8	15	0	0	.155	.222	.216	.438	13	-15	6	1.59	0	C-41	1	-1.3
1930 Was-A	93	321	32	82	11	4	0	36	18	27	3	0	.255	.303	.315	.618	57	-20	32	3.44	-2	C-93	7	-1.4
1931 Was-A	145	483	48	133	16	3	1	60	35	21	0	0	.275	.327	.327	.654	72	-17	53	3.93	-7	*C-145	12	-1.4
1932 Was-A	102	317	28	78	9	0	1	41	24	17	0	1	.246	.301	.284	.585	53	-22	28	3.02	-3	C-98	6	-1.8
1933 Cle-A	75	227	26	46	5	2	0	23	23	17	0	0	.203	.282	.242	.524	38	-20	17	2.42	0	C-72	5	-1.5
1934 Cle-A	5	7	0	1	1	0	0	2	0	1	0	0	.143	.143	.286	.429	8	-1	0	1.21	0	/C-4	0	-0.1
1936 NY-N	19	18	3	5	1	0	0	3	2	3	0	....	.278	.350	.333	.683	86	-0	2	4.62	0	C-14	1	0.0
1937 Bro-N	51	117	5	24	2	2	0	4	8	17	0	....	.205	.256	.256	.512	39	-10	8	2.10	3	C-45	2	-0.5
1938 Bro-N	16	45	2	12	1	1	0	6	5	6	0	....	.267	.340	.333	.673	84	-1	5	4.24	-1	C-16	1	-0.1
Total 12	636	1814	177	448	57	13	3	203	128	130	4	1	.247	.301	.298	.598	56	-112	171	3.20	-14	C-585	39	-8.7

• SPENCER, Shane Michael Shane Spencer b: 2/20/1972, Key West, FL BR/TR, 5'11", 225 lbs. Deb: 4/10/1998 Career OF: 238-0-169

YEAR TM-L	G	AB	R	H	2B	3B	HR	RBI	BB	SO	SB	CS	AVG	OBP	SLG	OPS	OPS+	BR/A	RC	RC/G	FR	G/POS	WS	TPW
1998*NY-A	27	67	18	25	6	0	10	27	5	12	0	1	.373	.417	.910	1.327	241	13	25	15.31	1	0-22(9-0-15)/D-4,1-1	6	1.2
1999*NY-A	71	205	25	48	8	0	8	20	18	51	0	4	.234	.302	.390	.692	76	-10	24	3.96	2	0-64(46-0-22)/D-3	3	-1.0
2000 NY-A	73	248	33	70	11	3	9	40	19	45	1	2	.282	.338	.460	.798	100	-1	38	5.38	2	0-40(33-0-7),D-33	6	-0.2
2001*NY-A	80	283	40	73	14	2	10	46	21	58	4	1	.258	.318	.428	.746	93	-3	39	4.86	2	0-68(44-0-28),D-14	8	-0.1
2002*NY-A	94	288	32	71	15	2	6	34	31	62	0	3	.247	.328	.375	.703	87	-6	36	4.15	-6	0-91(40-0-55)/D-1	5	-1.1
2003 Cle-A	64	210	23	57	10	0	8	26	18	52	2	0	.271	.332	.433	.765	103	1	30	4.96	-1	0-43(16-0-30),1-11/D-7	5	-0.3
Tex-A	55	185	16	42	10	0	4	23	27	40	0	0	.227	.332	.346	.678	73	-7	23	4.26	0	0-54(50-0-12)/D-1	3	-0.9
Yr.	119	395	39	99	20	0	12	49	45	92	2	0	.251	.332	.392	.724	89	-6	53	4.62	-1	0-97(66-0-42),1-11/D-8	8	-1.2
Total 6	464	1486	187	386	74	7	55	216	139	320	7	11	.260	.329	.430	.759	96	-14	215	5.01	8	0-382/D-63,1-12	36	-2.5

• SPENCER, Tom Hubert Thomas Spencer b: 2/28/1951, Gallipolis, OH BR/TR, 6', 170 lbs. Deb: 7/17/1978 C

YEAR TM-L	G	AB	R	H	2B	3B	HR	RBI	BB	SO	SB	CS	AVG	OBP	SLG	OPS	OPS+	BR/A	RC	RC/G	FR	G/POS	WS	TPW
1978 Chi-A	29	65	3	12	1	0	0	4	2	9	0	1	.185	.209	.200	.409	15	-8	2	1.19	1	0-27(6-19-2)/D-2	1	-0.8

YEAR TM-L	G	AB	R	H	2B	3B	HR	RBI	BB	SO	SB	CS	AVG	OBP	SLG	OPS	OPS+	BR/A	RC	RC/G	FR	G/POS	WS	TPW
• SPENCER, Tubby	Edward Russell Spencer b: 1/26/1884, Oil City, PA d: 2/1/1945, San Francisco, CA BR/TR, 5'10", 215 lbs. Deb: 7/23/1905																							
1905 StL-A	35	115	6	27	1	2	0	11	7	....	2	....	.235	.285	.278	.563	83	-2	10	3.00	1	C-34	2	0.2
1906 StL-A	58	188	15	33	6	1	0	17	7	....	4	....	.176	.205	.218	.423	34	-15	10	1.65	-6	C-54	2	-1.7
1907 StL-A	71	230	27	61	11	1	1	25	7	....	1	....	.265	.299	.335	.634	102	-0	24	3.74	-4	C-63	6	0.3
1908 StL-A	91	286	19	60	6	1	0	28	17	....	1	....	.210	.254	.238	.492	60	-13	17	1.95	2	C-88	5	-0.3
1909 Bos-A	28	74	6	12	1	0	0	9	6	....	2	....	.162	.225	.176	.401	26	-6	3	1.38	0	C-26	1	-0.5
1911 Phi-N	11	32	2	5	1	0	1	3	3	7	0	....	.156	.229	.281	.510	42	-3	2	1.87	-1	C-11	0	-0.3
1916 Det-A	19	54	7	20	1	1	1	10	6	6	2	....	.370	.443	.481	.924	172	5	13	8.84	0	C-19	4	0.6
1917 Det-A	70	192	13	46	8	3	0	22	15	15	0	....	.240	.324	.313	.637	95	-1	19	3.29	-3	C-62	6	0.1
1918 Det-A	66	155	11	34	8	1	0	8	19	18	1	....	.219	.313	.284	.596	83	-3	14	2.81	-2	C-48/1-1	4	-0.2
Total 9	449	1326	106	298	43	10	3	133	87	46	13	....	.225	.281	.279	.560	76	-37	112	2.79	-13	C-405/1-1	30	-1.7
• SPENCER, Vern	Vernon Murray Spencer b: 2/4/1894, Wixom, MI d: 6/3/1971, Wixom, MI BL/TR, 5'7", 165 lbs. Deb: 7/4/1920																							
1920 NY-N	45	140	15	28	2	3	0	19	11	17	4	3	.200	.258	.257	.515	49	-9	9	2.15	4	O-40(38-1-2)	1	-0.7
• SPERAW, Paul	Paul Bachman "Polly,Birdie" Speraw b: 10/5/1893, Annville, PA d: 2/22/1962, Cedar Rapids, IA BR/TR, 5'8.5", 145 lbs. Deb: 9/15/1920																							
1920 StL-A	1	2	0	0	0	0	0	0	0	0	0	0	.000	.000	.000	.000	-97	-1	0	.00	0	/3-1	0	-0.1
• SPERBER, Ed	Edwin George Sperber b: 1/21/1895, Cincinnati, OH d: 1/5/1976, Cincinnati, OH BL/TL, 5'11", 175 lbs. Deb: 4/16/1924																							
1924 Bos-N	24	59	8	17	2	0	1	12	10	9	3	1	.288	.400	.373	.773	113	2	10	5.61	-2	O-17(2-1-14)	2	-0.1
1925 Bos-N	2	2	0	0	0	0	0	0	0	0	0	0	.000	.000	.000	.000	-110	-1	0	.00	0	....	0	-0.1
Total 2	26	61	8	17	2	0	1	12	10	9	3	1	.279	.389	.361	.750	107	2	10	5.39	-2	/O-17	2	-0.2
• SPERRING, Rob	Robert Walter Sperring b: 10/10/1949, San Francisco, CA BR/TR, 6'1", 185 lbs. Deb: 8/11/1974 Career OF: 5-0-6																							
1974 Chi-N	42	107	9	22	3	0	1	5	9	28	1	2	.206	.267	.262	.529	46	-8	8	2.37	-6	2-35/S-8	0	-1.3
1975 Chi-N	65	144	25	30	4	1	1	9	16	31	0	2	.208	.292	.271	.563	54	-10	11	2.49	-8	3-22,2-17,S-16/O-8(2-0-6)	1	-1.6
1976 Chi-N	43	93	8	24	3	0	0	7	9	25	0	2	.258	.324	.290	.614	69	-4	9	3.00	-2	3-20,S-15/2-4,O-3(3-0-0)	1	-0.6
1977 Hou-N	58	129	6	24	3	0	1	9	12	23	0	0	.186	.255	.233	.488	35	-12	8	1.83	-3	S-22,2-20,3-11	1	-1.2
Total 4	208	473	48	100	13	1	3	30	46	107	1	6	.211	.283	.262	.545	50	-34	35	2.38	-19	/2-76,S-61,3-53,O-11	3	-4.8
• SPERRY, Stan	Stanley Kenneth Sperry b: 2/19/1914, Evansville, WI d: 9/27/1962, Evansville, WI BL/TR, 5'10.5", 164 lbs. Deb: 7/28/1936																							
1936 Phi-N	20	37	2	5	3	0	0	4	3	5	0	....	.135	.200	.216	.416	11	-5	2	1.29	-3	2-15	0	-0.7
1938 Phi-A	60	253	28	69	6	3	0	27	15	9	1	2	.273	.313	.320	.634	61	-16	25	3.53	-1	2-60	2	-1.2
Total 2	80	290	30	74	9	3	0	31	18	14	1	2	.255	.299	.307	.606	54	-21	27	3.19	-3	/2-75	2	-1.9
• SPIERS, Bill	William James Spiers b: 6/5/1966, Orangeburg, SC BL/TR, 6'2", 190 lbs. Deb: 4/7/1989 Career OF: 33-11-20																							
1989 Mil-A	114	345	44	88	9	3	4	33	21	63	10	2	.255	.300	.333	.633	79	-9	37	3.70	-7	S-89,3-12/2-4,D-4,1-2	9	-1.0
1990 Mil-A	112	363	44	88	15	3	2	36	16	45	11	6	.242	.276	.317	.593	66	-18	29	2.60	0	*S-111	5	-1.0
1991 Mil-A	133	414	71	117	13	6	8	54	34	55	14	8	.283	.340	.401	.741	107	3	56	4.58	-11	*S-128/D-2,O-1	16	0.2
1992 Mil-A	12	16	2	5	2	0	0	2	1	4	1	1	.313	.353	.438	.790	123	0	2	4.79	-2	/S-5,2-4,3-1,D-1	0	-0.2
1993 Mil-A	113	340	43	81	8	4	2	36	29	51	9	8	.238	.306	.303	.609	65	-18	30	2.80	-6	*2-104/O-7(2-2-4),S-4,D-1	3	-1.9
1994 Mil-A	73	214	27	54	10	1	0	17	19	42	7	1	.252	.316	.308	.625	59	-12	22	3.49	0	3-35,S-35/D-3,O-2(0-0-2),1	3	-0.9
1995 NY-N	63	72	5	15	2	1	0	11	12	15	0	1	.208	.321	.264	.585	58	-4	7	3.10	-3	3-11/2-6	1	-0.7
1996 Hou-N	122	218	27	55	10	1	6	26	20	34	7	0	.252	.321	.390	.711	94	-1	29	4.64	1	3-77/2-7,1-4,S-4,O-2(0-1-1)	7	0.1
1997*Hou-N	132	291	51	93	27	4	4	48	61	42	10	5	.320	.439	.481	.920	146	23	66	8.54	-2	3-84,S-28/1-8,2-4	18	2.4
1998*Hou-N	123	384	66	105	27	4	4	43	45	62	11	2	.273	.357	.396	.753	101	3	57	5.23	-2	3-99/2-9,1-7,S-2	13	0.2
1999*Hou-N	127	393	56	113	18	5	4	39	47	45	10	5	.288	.364	.389	.753	92	-4	56	5.07	4	3-71,O-31(25-7-9),S-13/2-4,1	12	0.1
2000 Hou-N	124	355	41	107	17	3	3	43	49	38	7	4	.301	.388	.392	.779	93	-2	56	5.69	10	3-51,S-27,2-26,O-10(6-0-4)	11	1.0
2001 Hou-N	4	3	0	1	0	0	0	0	1	0	0	0	.333	.500	.333	.833	116	0	1	6.75	0	....	0	0.0
Total 13	1252	3408	477	922	158	35	37	388	355	496	97	43	.271	.343	.370	.713	91	-38	447	4.52	-18	S-446,3-441,2-168/O-53,1-23,D	98	-1.6
• SPIES, Harry	Henry Spies b: 6/12/1866, New Orleans, LA d: 7/7/1942, Los Angeles, CA BR/TR, 5'11.5", 170 lbs. Deb: 4/20/1895																							
1895 Cin-N	14	50	2	11	0	1	0	5	3	2	0	....	.220	.264	.260	.524	34	-5	4	2.46	2	C-12/1-2	1	-0.1
Lou-N	72	276	42	74	14	7	2	35	11	19	4	....	.268	.313	.391	.704	86	-6	36	4.80	-3	1-47,C-26/S-1	4	-0.6
Yr.	86	326	44	85	14	8	2	40	14	21	4	....	.261	.305	.371	.677	78	-11	40	4.42	0	1-49,C-38/S-1	5	-0.7
• SPIEZIO, Ed	Edward Wayne Spiezio b: 10/31/1941, Joliet, IL BR/TR, 5'11", 180 lbs. Deb: 7/23/1964 Career OF: 7-0-15																							
1964 StL-N	12	12	0	4	0	0	0	0	0	1	0	0	.333	.333	.333	.667	81	-0	1	4.50	0	....	0	0.0
1965 StL-N	10	18	0	3	0	0	0	5	1	4	0	0	.167	.250	.167	.417	18	-2	1	1.58	0	/3-3	0	-0.2
1966 StL-N	26	73	4	16	5	1	2	10	5	11	1	0	.219	.269	.397	.666	82	-2	6	2.70	-3	3-19	1	-0.5
1967*StL-N	55	105	9	22	2	0	3	10	7	18	2	1	.210	.265	.314	.580	66	-5	8	2.58	0	3-19/O-7(2-0-6)	1	-0.5
1968*StL-N	29	51	1	8	0	0	0	2	5	6	1	1	.157	.232	.157	.389	19	-5	2	1.17	1	O-11(3-0-9)/3-2	0	-0.6
1969 SD-N	121	355	29	83	9	0	13	43	38	64	1	2	.234	.315	.369	.684	95	-3	41	3.90	-5	3-98/O-1	8	-0.9
1970 SD-N	110	316	45	90	18	1	12	42	43	42	4	0	.285	.377	.462	.839	129	15	57	6.48	-0	3-93	13	1.4
1971 SD-N	97	308	16	71	10	1	7	36	22	50	6	5	.231	.290	.338	.628	83	-8	29	3.03	6	3-91/O-1	5	-0.3
1972 SD-N	20	29	2	4	2	0	0	4	1	6	1	0	.138	.167	.207	.374	6	-3	1	.68	0	/3-5	0	-0.4
Chi-A	74	277	20	66	10	1	2	22	13	43	0	1	.238	.277	.303	.581	71	-11	22	2.62	4	3-74	5	-0.8
Total 9	554	1544	126	367	56	4	39	174	135	245	16	10	.238	.306	.355	.661	88	-24	168	3.64	2	3-404/O-20	33	-2.8
• SPIEZIO, Scott	Scott Edward Spiezio b: 9/21/1972, Joliet, IL BB/TR, 6'2", 205 lbs. Deb: 9/14/1996 Career OF: 30-0-19																							
1996 Oak-A	9	29	6	9	2	0	2	8	4	4	0	1	.310	.394	.586	.980	147	2	6	7.57	-1	/3-5,D-4	2	0.0
1997 Oak-A	147	538	58	131	28	4	14	65	44	75	9	3	.243	.302	.388	.690	80	-16	62	3.89	-16	*2-146/3-1	10	-2.4
1998 Oak-A	114	406	54	105	19	1	9	50	44	56	1	3	.259	.334	.377	.711	87	-9	51	4.24	-5	*2-112/D-1	10	-0.8
1999 Oak-A	89	247	31	60	24	0	8	33	29	36	0	0	.243	.327	.437	.765	97	-2	36	4.93	0	2-42,3-31,1-10/D-6	6	0.0
2000 Ana-A	123	297	47	72	11	2	17	49	40	56	1	2	.242	.338	.465	.803	98	-2	48	5.41	-2	D-50,1-29,3-15,O-10(9-0-2)/2	6	-0.7
2001 Ana-A	139	457	57	124	29	4	13	54	34	65	5	2	.271	.329	.438	.766	97	-3	66	5.15	8	*1-105,O-18(10-0-8),D-16,3	9	-0.4
2002*Ana-A	153	491	80	140	34	2	12	82	67	52	6	7	.285	.375	.436	.811	115	11	80	5.71	-3	*1-143,3-20,O-10(8-0-2)/2-1	17	-0.4
2003 Ana-A	158	521	69	138	36	7	16	83	46	66	6	3	.265	.330	.453	.783	108	5	76	5.07	-8	*1-114,3-52,O-10(3-0-7)	13	-1.0
Total 8	932	2986	402	779	183	20	91	424	308	410	28	21	.261	.334	.427	.761	98	-14	425	4.90	-28	1-401,2-303,3-134/D-77,O-48	73	-5.8
• SPIKES, Charlie	Leslie Charles Spikes b: 1/23/1951, Bogalusa, LA BR/TR, 6'3", 220 lbs. Deb: 9/1/1972 Career OF: 136-0-398																							
1972 NY-A	14	34	2	5	1	0	0	3	1	13	0	1	.147	.171	.176	.348	4	-5	1	.80	1	/O-9(0-0-9)	0	-0.5
1973 Cle-A	140	506	68	120	12	3	23	73	45	103	5	3	.237	.306	.409	.715	98	-2	62	4.13	3	*O-111(90-0-22),D-26	12	-0.7
1974 Cle-A	155	568	63	154	23	1	22	80	34	100	10	7	.271	.320	.431	.752	116	9	74	4.55	2	*O-154(0-0-154)	19	0.4
1975 Cle-A	111	345	41	79	13	3	11	33	30	51	7	6	.229	.291	.380	.670	88	-7	35	3.29	4	*O-103(31-0-72)/D-2	6	-0.8
1976 Cle-A	101	334	34	79	11	5	3	31	23	50	5	6	.237	.296	.326	.622	83	-9	32	3.20	0	O-98(2-0-96)/D-2	6	-1.5
1977 Cle-A	32	95	13	22	2	0	3	11	11	17	0	2	.232	.324	.347	.671	86	-2	10	3.31	-2	O-27(0-0-27)/D-2	1	-0.5
1978 Det-A	10	28	1	7	1	0	0	2	2	6	0	0	.250	.344	.286	.629	77	-1	3	3.88	0	/O-9(0-0-9)	0	-0.1
1979 Atl-N	66	93	12	26	8	0	3	21	5	30	0	0	.280	.316	.462	.779	102	-0	13	4.73	-2	O-15(12-0-3)	2	-0.2
1980 Atl-N	41	36	6	10	1	0	0	2	3	18	0	0	.278	.350	.306	.656	82	-1	4	4.19	0	/O-7(1-0-6)	1	-0.1
Total 9	670	2039	240	502	72	12	65	256	154	388	27	25	.246	.306	.389	.695	96	-18	233	3.87	6	O-533/D-32	47	-4.1
• SPILMAN, Harry	William Harry Spilman b: 7/18/1954, Albany, GA BL/TR, 6'1", 190 lbs. Deb: 9/11/1978 C Career OF: 4-0-0																							
1978 Cin-N	4	4	1	1	0	0	0	0	0	1	0	0	.250	.250	.250	.500	40	-0	0	2.25	0	....	0	0.0
1979*Cin-N	43	56	7	12	3	0	0	5	7	5	0	0	.214	.323	.268	.591	63	-3	5	3.11	0	1-12/3-4	1	-0.3
1980 Cin-N	65	101	14	27	4	0	4	19	9	19	0	0	.267	.333	.426	.759	110	1	14	4.92	1	1-18/O-2(2-0-0),3-1,C-1	3	0.1
1981 Cin-N	23	24	4	4	1	0	0	3	3	7	0	0	.167	.259	.208	.468	33	-2	1	1.66	-1	/3-3,1-2	0	-0.3
*Hou-N	28	34	5	10	0	0	0	1	2	3	0	1	.294	.333	.294	.627	83	-1	3	3.03	0	1-13	1	-0.2
Yr.	51	58	9	14	1	0	0	4	5	10	0	1	.241	.302	.259	.560	61	-3	4	2.40	-1	1-15/3-3	1	-0.5
1982 Hou-N	38	61	7	17	2	0	3	11	5	10	0	0	.279	.333	.459	.792	129	2	9	5.59	0	1-11	2	0.1
1983 Hou-N	42	78	7	13	3	0	1	9	5	12	0	0	.167	.217	.244	.460	29	-8	4	1.57	0	1-19/C-6	0	-0.9

YEAR TM-L	G	AB	R	H	2B	3B	HR	RBI	BB	SO	SB	CS	AVG	OBP	SLG	OPS	OPS+	BR/A	RC	RC/G	FR	G/POS	WS	TPW
1984 Hou-N	32	72	14	19	2	0	2	15	12	10	0	0	.264	.369	.375	.744	118	2	11	5.17	-2	1-18/C-8	3	-0.1
1985 Hou-N	44	66	3	9	1	0	1	4	3	7	0	0	.136	.174	.197	.371	4	-9	2	.91	-3	1-19/C-2	0	-1.3
1986 Det-A	24	49	6	12	2	0	3	8	3	8	0	0	.245	.288	.469	.758	102	-0	6	4.44	0	D-11/3-2,1-1,C-1	1	-0.1
SF-N	58	94	12	27	7	0	2	22	12	13	0	0	.287	.368	.426	.793	124	3	16	6.28	0	1-19/3-5,2-1,C-1,0-1	4	0.3
1987*SF-N	83	90	5	24	5	0	1	14	9	20	1	1	.267	.333	.356	.689	87	-2	10	3.87	-2	3-10/1-9,C-1	1	-0.4
1988 SF-N	40	40	4	7	1	1	1	3	4	6	0	0	.175	.250	.325	.575	67	-2	3	2.82	0	/1-6,C-2,0-1	0	-0.2
Hou-N	7	5	0	0	0	0	0	0	0	3	0	0	.000	.000	.000	.000	-104	-1	0	.00	0	/1-1	0	-0.2
Yr.	47	45	4	7	1	1	1	3	4	9	0	0	.156	.224	.289	.513	49	-3	3	2.45	0	/1-7,C-2,0-1	0	-0.4
1989 Hou-N	32	36	7	10	3	0	0	3	7	2	0	0	.278	.395	.361	.756	122	1	5	5.42	0	/1-9,C-1	1	0.1
Total 12	**563**	**810**	**96**	**192**	**34**	**1**	**18**	**117**	**81**	**126**	**1**	**2**	**.237**	**.309**	**.348**	**.657**	**85**	**-18**	**92**	**3.81**	**-8**	**1-157/3-25,C-23,D-11,0-4,2**	**17**	**-3.4**

• SPINDEL, Hal Harold Stewart Spindel b: 5/27/1913, Chandler, OK d: 7/28/2002, San Clemente, CA BR/TR, 6', 185 lbs. Deb: 4/23/1939

YEAR TM-L	G	AB	R	H	2B	3B	HR	RBI	BB	SO	SB	CS	AVG	OBP	SLG	OPS	OPS+	BR/A	RC	RC/G	FR	G/POS	WS	TPW
1939 StL-A	48	119	13	32	3	1	0	11	8	7	0	2	.269	.315	.311	.626	59	-8	11	3.14	0	C-32	1	-0.6
1945 Phi-N	36	87	7	20	3	0	0	8	6	7	0	....	.230	.280	.264	.544	53	-6	7	2.61	1	C-31	1	-0.3
1946 Phi-N	1	3	0	1	0	0	0	1	0	0	0	....	.333	.333	.333	.667	92	-0	0	.00	-0	/C-1	0	0.0
Total 3	**85**	**209**	**20**	**53**	**6**	**1**	**0**	**20**	**14**	**14**	**0**	**2**	**.254**	**.300**	**.292**	**.592**	**57**	**-14**	**17**	**2.86**	**1**	**/C-64**	**2**	**-0.8**

• SPIVEY, Junior Ernest Lee Spivey b: 1/28/1975, Oklahoma City, OK BR/TR, 6', 185 lbs. Deb: 6/2/2001

YEAR TM-L	G	AB	R	H	2B	3B	HR	RBI	BB	SO	SB	CS	AVG	OBP	SLG	OPS	OPS+	BR/A	RC	RC/G	FR	G/POS	WS	TPW
2001 Ari-N	72	163	33	42	6	3	5	21	23	47	3	0	.258	.356	.423	.780	95	-0	26	5.46	-1	2-66/S-1	6	0.1
2002*Ari-N★	143	538	103	162	34	6	16	78	65	100	11	6	.301	.393	.476	.868	117	16	103	7.00	4	*2-143	23	2.7
2003 Ari-N	106	365	52	93	22	2	13	50	33	95	4	3	.255	.328	.433	.761	88	-7	52	4.91	-2	2-98/0-1	10	-0.5
Total 3	**321**	**1066**	**188**	**297**	**62**	**11**	**34**	**149**	**121**	**242**	**18**	**9**	**.279**	**.366**	**.453**	**.819**	**104**	**8**	**182**	**6.02**	**1**	**2-307/0-1,S-1**	**39**	**2.3**

• SPOGNARDI, Andy Andrea Ettore Spognardi b: 10/18/1908, Boston, MA d: 1/1/2000, Dedham, MA BR/TR, 5'9.5", 160 lbs. Deb: 9/2/1932

YEAR TM-L	G	AB	R	H	2B	3B	HR	RBI	BB	SO	SB	CS	AVG	OBP	SLG	OPS	OPS+	BR/A	RC	RC/G	FR	G/POS	WS	TPW
1932 Bos-A	17	34	9	10	1	0	0	1	6	6	0	0	.294	.400	.324	.724	92	0	5	5.33	0	/2-9,S-3,3-2	1	0.1

• SPOHRER, Al Alfred Ray Spohrer b: 12/3/1902, Philadelphia, PA d: 7/17/1972, Plymouth, NH BR/TR, 5'10.5", 175 lbs. Deb: 4/13/1928

YEAR TM-L	G	AB	R	H	2B	3B	HR	RBI	BB	SO	SB	CS	AVG	OBP	SLG	OPS	OPS+	BR/A	RC	RC/G	FR	G/POS	WS	TPW
1928 NY-N	2	2	0	0	0	0	0	0	0	0	0	....	.000	.000	.000	.000	-100	-1	0	.00	0	/C-2	0	-0.1
Bos-N	51	124	15	27	3	0	0	9	5	11	1	....	.218	.254	.242	.496	32	-12	7	2.00	-1	C-48	1	-1.1
Yr.	53	126	15	27	3	0	0	9	5	11	1	....	.214	.250	.238	.488	30	-13	7	1.96	-1	C-50	1	-1.2
1929 Bos-N	114	342	42	93	21	8	2	48	26	35	1	....	.272	.327	.398	.725	82	-10	44	4.37	0	*C-109	7	-0.4
1930 Bos-N	112	356	44	113	22	8	2	37	22	24	3	....	.317	.361	.441	.802	96	-3	55	5.68	-8	*C-108	11	-0.4
1931 Bos-N	114	350	23	84	17	5	0	27	22	27	2	....	.240	.285	.317	.602	64	-18	32	3.16	1	*C-111	6	-1.1
1932 Bos-N	104	335	31	90	12	2	0	33	15	26	2	....	.269	.300	.316	.616	68	-15	32	3.37	3	*C-100	9	-0.5
1933 Bos-N	67	184	11	46	6	1	1	12	11	13	3	....	.250	.292	.310	.602	78	-5	17	3.20	-4	C-65	5	-0.6
1934 Bos-N	100	265	25	59	15	0	0	17	14	18	1	....	.223	.262	.279	.541	48	-19	19	2.33	0	C-98	4	-1.4
1935 Bos-N	92	260	22	63	7	1	1	16	9	12	0	....	.242	.273	.288	.562	55	-16	20	2.59	-1	C-90	2	-1.2
Total 8	**756**	**2218**	**213**	**575**	**103**	**25**	**6**	**199**	**124**	**166**	**13**	**....**	**.259**	**.301**	**.336**	**.637**	**69**	**-100**	**226**	**3.51**	**-10**	**C-731**	**45**	**-6.9**

• SPOTTS, Jim James Russell Spotts b: 4/10/1909, Honey Brook, PA d: 6/15/1964, Medford, NJ BR/TR, 5'10.5", 175 lbs. Deb: 4/23/1930

YEAR TM-L	G	AB	R	H	2B	3B	HR	RBI	BB	SO	SB	CS	AVG	OBP	SLG	OPS	OPS+	BR/A	RC	RC/G	FR	G/POS	WS	TPW
1930 Phi-N	3	2	1	0	0	0	0	0	0	1	0	....	.000	.000	.000	.000	-93	-1	0	.00	0	/C-2	0	-0.1

• SPRAGUE, Charlie Charles Wellington Sprague
b: 10/10/1864, Cleveland, OH d: 12/31/1912, Des Moines, IA BL/TL, 5'11", 150 lbs. Deb: 9/17/1887 U Career OF: 24-11-6 ♦

YEAR TM-L	G	AB	R	H	2B	3B	HR	RBI	BB	SO	SB	CS	AVG	OBP	SLG	OPS	OPS+	BR/A	RC	RC/G	FR	G/POS	WS	TPW
1887 Chi-N	3	13	0	2	0	0	0	0	0	2	0	....	.154	.154	.154	.308	-13	-1	0	.76	-1	/P-3,0-1	1	-0.2
1889 Cle-N	2	7	2	1	0	0	0	1	1	0	1	....	.143	.250	.143	.393	11	-0	1	2.26	0	/P-2	0	-0.8
1890 Tol-a	55	199	25	47	5	6	1	19	16	....	10	....	.236	.303	.337	.639	86	-1	24	4.17	-3	0-40(24-10-6),P-19	11	-0.4
Total 3	**60**	**219**	**27**	**50**	**5**	**6**	**1**	**20**	**17**	**2**	**11**	**....**	**.228**	**.293**	**.320**	**.613**	**78**	**-2**	**25**	**3.88**	**-4**	**/0-41,P-24**	**12**	**-1.4**

• SPRAGUE, Ed Edward Nelson Sprague, Jr. b: 7/25/1967, Castro Valley, CA BR/TR, 6'2", 210 lbs. Deb: 5/7/1991 Career OF: 14-0-2

YEAR TM-L	G	AB	R	H	2B	3B	HR	RBI	BB	SO	SB	CS	AVG	OBP	SLG	OPS	OPS+	BR/A	RC	RC/G	FR	G/POS	WS	TPW
1991 Tor-A	61	160	17	44	7	0	4	20	19	43	0	3	.275	.363	.394	.756	105	0	23	5.07	-1	3-35,1-22/C-2,D-2	5	-0.1
1992*Tor-A	22	47	6	11	2	0	1	7	3	7	0	0	.234	.280	.340	.620	70	-2	5	3.52	-1	C-15/1-4,D-2,3-1	2	-0.2
1993*Tor-A	150	546	50	142	31	1	12	73	32	85	1	0	.260	.313	.386	.699	86	-11	61	3.80	-6	*3-150	7	-1.5
1994 Tor-A	109	405	38	97	19	1	11	44	23	95	1	0	.240	.298	.373	.671	72	-18	44	3.66	-8	*3-107/1-3	4	-2.3
1995 Tor-A	144	521	77	127	27	2	18	74	58	96	0	0	.244	.337	.407	.744	93	-5	70	4.52	6	*3-139/1-7,D-2	9	0.2
1996 Tor-A	159	591	88	146	35	2	36	101	60	146	0	0	.247	.329	.496	.825	105	2	99	5.83	-9	*3-148,D-10	17	-0.5
1997 Tor-A	138	504	63	115	29	4	14	48	51	102	0	1	.228	.307	.385	.692	79	-17	60	4.04	-8	*3-129/D-8	6	-2.3
1998 Tor-A	105	382	49	91	20	0	17	51	24	73	0	2	.238	.302	.424	.726	86	-10	45	3.89	-6	*3-105	5	-1.4
Oak-A	27	87	8	13	5	0	3	7	2	17	1	0	.149	.187	.310	.497	27	-10	5	1.79	-2	3-23/1-1	1	-1.0
Yr.	132	469	57	104	25	0	20	58	26	90	1	2	.222	.281	.403	.684	75	-20	50	3.48	-8	*3-128/1-1	6	-2.4
1999 Pit-N★	137	490	71	131	27	2	22	81	50	93	3	6	.267	.355	.465	.821	106	2	79	5.59	-11	*3-134	15	-0.7
2000 SD-N	53	117	17	32	10	0	10	25	10	28	0	0	.274	.341	.615	.956	145	7	25	7.88	-1	1-24/3-5,0-5(4-0-1)	0	0.4
Bos-A	33	111	11	24	4	0	2	9	12	18	0	0	.216	.293	.306	.599	50	-9	10	3.11	1	3-31/1-3,D-1	1	-0.7
SD-N	20	40	2	9	2	0	0	2	3	12	0	0	.225	.295	.275	.570	49	-3	3	2.77	-1	/3-5,0-2(2-0-0),1-1,2-1	5	-0.4
Yr.	73	157	19	41	12	0	10	27	13	40	0	0	.261	.329	.529	.858	121	4	29	6.51	-2	1-25,3-10/0-7(6-0-1),2-1	5	0.0
2001*Sea-A	45	94	9	28	7	0	2	16	11	18	0	0	.298	.377	.436	.814	121	3	15	5.92	-1	1-12/D-9,3-8,0-2(8-0-1),C	3	0.0
Total 11	**1203**	**4095**	**506**	**1010**	**225**	**12**	**152**	**558**	**358**	**833**	**6**	**12**	**.247**	**.321**	**.419**	**.740**	**90**	**-70**	**546**	**4.54**	**-49**	***3-1020/1-77,D-34,C-18,0-9,2**	**80**	**-10.5**

• SPRATT, Harry Henry Lee Spratt b: 7/10/1888, Broadford, VA d: 7/3/1969, Washington, DC BL/TR, 5'8.5", 175 lbs. Deb: 4/13/1911

YEAR TM-L	G	AB	R	H	2B	3B	HR	RBI	BB	SO	SB	CS	AVG	OBP	SLG	OPS	OPS+	BR/A	RC	RC/G	FR	G/POS	WS	TPW
1911 Bos-N	62	154	22	37	4	4	2	13	13	25	1	....	.240	.299	.357	.657	77	-5	17	3.56	-14	S-26/2-5,3-4,0-4(0-3-1)	2	-1.8
1912 Bos-N	27	89	6	23	3	2	3	15	7	11	2	....	.258	.313	.438	.751	102	-0	12	4.77	-8	S-23	1	-0.7
Total 2	**89**	**243**	**28**	**60**	**7**	**6**	**5**	**28**	**20**	**36**	**3**	**....**	**.247**	**.304**	**.387**	**.691**	**86**	**-6**	**29**	**3.99**	**-22**	**/S-49,2-5,3-4,0-4**	**3**	**-2.5**

• SPRIGGS, George George Herman Spriggs b: 5/22/1941, Jewell, MD BL/TR, 5'11", 175 lbs. Deb: 9/15/1965 Career OF: 14-1-41

YEAR TM-L	G	AB	R	H	2B	3B	HR	RBI	BB	SO	SB	CS	AVG	OBP	SLG	OPS	OPS+	BR/A	RC	RC/G	FR	G/POS	WS	TPW
1965 Pit-N	9	2	5	1	0	0	0	0	0	0	2	0	.500	.500	.500	1.000	182	1	1	27.54	0	/0-1	0	0.1
1966 Pit-N	9	7	0	1	0	0	0	0	0	3	0	0	.143	.143	.143	.286	-20	-1	0	.64	0	....	0	-0.1
1967 Pit-N	38	57	14	10	1	1	0	5	6	20	3	0	.175	.254	.228	.482	39	-4	4	2.31	-0	0-13(10-0-3)	0	-0.5
1969 KC-A	23	29	4	4	2	1	0	0	3	8	0	0	.138	.242	.276	.518	44	-2	2	2.37	0	/0-6(4-1-1)	0	-0.3
1970 KC-A	51	130	12	27	2	3	1	7	14	32	4	3	.208	.285	.292	.577	59	-8	12	2.93	1	0-36(0-0-36)	1	-0.8
Total 5	**130**	**225**	**35**	**43**	**5**	**5**	**1**	**12**	**23**	**63**	**9**	**3**	**.191**	**.269**	**.271**	**.540**	**51**	**-14**	**19**	**2.75**	**1**	**/0-56**	**1**	**-1.6**

• SPRINGER, Steve Steven Michael Springer b: 2/11/1961, Long Beach, CA BR/TR, 6', 190 lbs. Deb: 5/22/1990

YEAR TM-L	G	AB	R	H	2B	3B	HR	RBI	BB	SO	SB	CS	AVG	OBP	SLG	OPS	OPS+	BR/A	RC	RC/G	FR	G/POS	WS	TPW
1990 Cle-A	4	12	1	2	0	0	0	1	0	6	0	0	.167	.167	.167	.333	-7	-2	0	.95	0	/3-3,D-1	0	-0.2
1992 NY-N	4	5	0	2	1	0	0	0	0	1	0	0	.400	.400	.600	1.000	182	0	1	10.80	0	/2-1,3-1	0	0.0
Total 2	**8**	**17**	**1**	**4**	**1**	**0**	**0**	**1**	**0**	**7**	**0**	**0**	**.235**	**.235**	**.294**	**.529**	**46**	**-1**	**2**	**3.06**	**-1**	**/3-4,2-1,D-1**	**0**	**-0.2**

• SPRINZ, Joe Joseph Conrad "Mule" Sprinz b: 8/3/1902, St. Louis, MO d: 1/11/1994, Fremont, CA BR/TR, 5'11", 185 lbs. Deb: 7/16/1930

YEAR TM-L	G	AB	R	H	2B	3B	HR	RBI	BB	SO	SB	CS	AVG	OBP	SLG	OPS	OPS+	BR/A	RC	RC/G	FR	G/POS	WS	TPW
1930 Cle-A	17	45	5	8	1	0	0	2	4	4	0	0	.178	.245	.200	.445	14	-6	2	1.70	1	C-17	1	-0.3
1931 Cle-A	1	3	0	0	0	0	0	0	0	0	0	0	.000	.000	.000	.000	-95	-1	0	.00	0	/C-1	0	-0.1
1933 StL-N	3	5	1	1	0	0	0	0	1	1	0	....	.200	.333	.200	.533	53	-0	0	1.16	0	/C-3	0	0.0
Total 3	**21**	**53**	**6**	**9**	**1**	**0**	**0**	**2**	**5**	**5**	**0**	**0**	**.170**	**.241**	**.189**	**.430**	**13**	**-7**	**3**	**1.52**	**1**	**/C-21**	**1**	**-0.4**

• SPURGEON, Freddy Fred Spurgeon b: 10/9/1900, Wabash, IN d: 11/5/1970, Kalamazoo, MI BR/TR, 5'11.5", 160 lbs. Deb: 9/19/1924

YEAR TM-L	G	AB	R	H	2B	3B	HR	RBI	BB	SO	SB	CS	AVG	OBP	SLG	OPS	OPS+	BR/A	RC	RC/G	FR	G/POS	WS	TPW
1924 Cle-A	3	7	0	1	1	0	0	0	0	0	0	0	.143	.250	.286	.536	37	-1	1	2.40	-1	/2-3	0	-0.2
1925 Cle-A	107	376	50	108	9	3	0	32	15	21	8	5	.287	.315	.327	.642	62	-22	39	3.56	-2	3-56,2-46/S-3	4	-1.7
1926 Cle-A	149	614	101	181	31	3	0	49	27	36	7	2	.295	.327	.355	.682	77	-20	73	4.10	4	*2-149	15	-1.2
1927 Cle-A	57	179	30	45	6	1	1	19	18	14	8	1	.251	.323	.313	.636	65	-7	21	3.52	-8	2-52	3	-1.3
Total 4	**316**	**1176**	**181**	**335**	**47**	**7**	**1**	**100**	**60**	**71**	**23**	**8**	**.285**	**.322**	**.339**	**.661**	**70**	**-50**	**133**	**3.82**	**-6**	**2-250/3-56,S-3**	**22**	**-4.4**

YEAR TM-L	G	AB	R	H	2B	3B	HR	RBI	BB	SO	SB	CS	AVG	OBP	SLG	OPS	OPS+	BR/A	RC	RC/G	FR	G/POS	WS	TPW
• SPURNEY, Ed	Edward Frederick Spurney b: 1/9/1872, Cleveland, OH d: 10/12/1932, Cleveland, OH Deb: 6/26/1891																							
1891 Pit-N	3	7	2	2	1	0	0	0	2	1	0	....	.286	.444	.429	.873	159	1	1	7.38	0	/S-3	0	0.1
• SQUIRES, Mike	Michael Lynn "Spanky" Squires b: 3/5/1952, Kalamazoo, MI BL/TL, 5'11", 185 lbs. Deb: 9/1/1975 C Career OF: 2-1-1																							
1975 Chi-A	20	65	5	15	0	0	0	4	8	5	3	0	.231	.315	.231	.546	55	-3	5	2.69	-1	1-20	1	-0.5
1977 Chi-A	3	3	0	0	0	0	0	0	0	1	0	0	.000	.000	.000	.000	-100	-1	0	.00	0	/1-1	0	-0.1
1978 Chi-A	46	150	25	42	9	2	0	19	16	21	4	4	.280	.349	.367	.716	101	-0	20	4.53	0	1-45	5	-0.3
1979 Chi-A	122	295	44	78	10	1	2	22	22	9	15	5	.264	.320	.325	.645	74	-9	30	3.40	1	*1-110/O-1	4	-1.3
1980 Chi-A	131	343	38	97	11	3	2	33	33	24	8	9	.283	.347	.350	.697	92	-5	41	4.11	2	*1-114/C-2	8	-0.9
1981 Chi-A	92	294	35	78	9	0	0	25	22	17	7	2	.265	.316	.296	.612	79	-7	29	3.30	0	1-88/O-1	5	-1.2
1982 Chi-A	116	195	33	52	9	3	1	21	14	13	3	3	.267	.316	.359	.675	85	-5	21	3.72	2	*1-109	3	-0.6
1983*Chi-A	143	153	21	34	4	1	1	11	22	11	3	3	.222	.328	.281	.609	67	-7	15	3.23	3	*1-124/D-5,3-1	3	-0.7
1984 Chi-A	104	82	9	15	1	0	0	6	6	7	2	2	.183	.239	.195	.434	21	-9	4	1.45	0	1-77,3-13/O-3(O-1-1),P-1	1	-1.1
1985 Chi-A	2	0	1	0	0	0	0	0	0	0	0	0	....	....	....	....	-96	0	0	....	0		0	0.0
Total 10	**779**	**1580**	**211**	**411**	**53**	**10**	**6**	**141**	**143**	**108**	**45**	**28**	**.260**	**.323**	**.318**	**.641**	**78**	**-45**	**166**	**3.51**	**7**	**1-688/3-14,D-5,O-5,C-2,P-1**	**30**	**-6.7**
• ST. CLAIRE, Ebba	Edward Joseph St. Claire b: 8/5/1921, Whitehall, NY d: 8/22/1982, Whitehall, NY BB/TR, 6'1", 219 lbs. Deb: 4/17/1951																							
1951 Bos-N	72	220	22	62	17	2	1	25	12	24	2	0	.282	.322	.391	.713	98	-1	29	4.89	-1	C-62	7	0.2
1952 Bos-N	39	108	5	23	2	0	2	4	8	12	0	1	.213	.267	.287	.554	56	-7	8	2.38	-1	C-34	1	-0.6
1953 Mil-N	33	80	7	16	3	0	2	5	3	9	0	0	.200	.229	.313	.541	42	-7	6	2.55	1	C-27	1	-0.5
1954 NY-N	20	42	5	11	1	0	2	6	12	7	0	0	.262	.436	.429	.865	126	3	9	7.54	-1	C-16	3	0.3
Total 4	**164**	**450**	**39**	**112**	**23**	**2**	**7**	**40**	**35**	**52**	**2**	**1**	**.249**	**.306**	**.356**	**.662**	**81**	**-12**	**52**	**4.05**	**-1**	**C-139**	**12**	**-0.7**
• STABELL, Joe	Joseph F. Stabell b: Buffalo, NY d: 7/10/1923, Buffalo, NY Deb: 9/19/1885																							
1885 Buf-N	7	22	0	1	0	0	0	0	0	9	....	....	.045	.045	.045	.091	-68	-4	0	.06	-3	/O-6(O-6-1),2-1	0	-0.7
• STAEHLE, Marv	Marvin Gustave Staehle b: 3/13/1942, Oak Park, IL BL/TR, 5'10", 172 lbs. Deb: 9/15/1964																							
1964 Chi-A	6	5	0	2	0	0	0	2	0	0	1	0	.400	.400	.400	.800	127	0	1	6.84	0	....	0	0.0
1965 Chi-A	7	7	0	3	0	0	0	2	0	0	0	0	.429	.429	.429	.857	154	0	1	8.68	0	....	0	0.1
1966 Chi-A	8	15	2	2	0	0	0	0	4	2	1	0	.133	.316	.133	.449	37	-1	1	2.33	1	/2-6	0	0.1
1967 Chi-A	32	54	1	6	1	0	0	1	4	8	1	1	.111	.172	.130	.302	-10	-8	1	.56	-2	2-17/S-5	1	-0.9
1969 Mon-N	6	17	4	7	2	0	1	1	2	0	0	0	.412	.474	.706	1.180	226	3	6	16.01	-0	/2-4	1	0.3
1970 Mon-N	104	321	41	70	9	1	0	26	39	21	1	3	.218	.309	.252	.561	52	-22	27	2.69	-6	2-91/S-1	3	-2.2
1971 Atl-N	22	36	5	4	0	0	0	1	5	4	0	0	.111	.238	.111	.349	2	-5	1	.84	3	/2-7,3-1	1	-0.2
Total 7	**185**	**455**	**53**	**94**	**12**	**1**	**1**	**33**	**54**	**35**	**4**	**4**	**.207**	**.296**	**.244**	**.540**	**49**	**-31**	**38**	**2.68**	**-4**	**2-125/S-6,3-1**	**6**	**-2.8**
• STAFFORD, Bob	Robert M. Stafford b: 6/26/1872, Oak Ridge, NC d: 8/20/1916, Moores Springs, NC, 6' Deb: 10/12/1890																							
1890 Phi-a	1	2	0	0	0	0	0	0	0	....	0	....	.000	.000	.000	.000	-102	-1	0	.00	0	/O-1	0	-0.1
• STAFFORD, General	James Joseph "Jamsey" Stafford b: 7/9/1868, Webster, MA d: 9/18/1923, Worcester, MA BR/TR, 5'8", 165 lbs. Deb: 8/27/1890 Career OF: 96-111-44 ♦																							
1890 Buf-P	15	49	11	7	1	0	0	3	7	8	2	....	.143	.250	.163	.413	12	-2	3	1.65	-2	P-12/O-4(1-1-2)	2	-1.1
1893 NY-N	67	281	58	79	7	4	5	27	25	31	19	....	.281	.344	.388	.732	94	-3	45	5.92	-6	O-67(O-67-0)	6	-1.1
1894 NY-N	14	46	10	10	1	1	0	4	10	7	2	....	.217	.368	.283	.651	59	-3	6	4.09	-3	/3-6,O-5(O-0-5),1-1,2-1	1	-0.4
1895 NY-N	123	463	79	129	12	5	3	73	40	32	42	....	.279	.344	.346	.689	80	-13	71	5.75	-15	*2-109,O-12(12-0-0)/3-2	11	-2.0
1896 NY-N	59	230	28	66	9	1	0	40	13	18	15	....	.287	.333	.335	.668	78	-7	32	5.06	-2	O-53(53-0-0)/S-6	4	-1.1
1897 NY-N	7	23	0	2	0	0	0	3	3	....	0	....	.087	.192	.087	.279	-26	-4	0	.50	-2	/O-5(5-0-0),S-2	0	-0.6
Lou-N	113	441	68	122	16	5	7	54	31	....	15	....	.277	.328	.383	.712	91	-7	63	5.05	-21	*S-103/O-7(4-2-1),3-1	9	-2.0
Yr.	120	464	68	124	16	5	7	57	34	....	15	....	.267	.321	.369	.690	85	-11	63	4.78	-24	*S-105,O-12(9-2-1)/3-1	9	-2.6
1898 Lou-N	49	181	26	54	3	0	1	25	19	....	7	....	.298	.368	.331	.700	102	1	26	5.21	-2	2-28,O-22(6-7-9)/3-1	5	0.0
Bos-N	37	123	21	32	2	0	1	8	4	....	3	....	.260	.289	.301	.590	66	-6	12	3.44	-3	O-35(9-1-25)/1-1	2	-1.0
Yr.	86	304	47	86	5	0	2	33	23	....	10	....	.283	.337	.319	.656	88	-5	38	4.47	-4	O-57(15-8-34),2-28/1-1,3-1	7	-1.0
1899 Bos-N	55	182	29	55	4	2	3	40	7	....	9	....	.302	.328	.396	.724	89	-4	28	5.41	-6	O-41(6-33-2)/2-5,S-5	5	-1.1
Was-N	31	118	11	29	5	1	1	14	5	....	4	....	.246	.276	.331	.607	67	-6	12	3.61	-3	2-17,S-13/3-2	2	-0.7
Yr.	86	300	40	84	9	3	4	54	12	....	13	....	.280	.308	.370	.678	81	-10	41	4.70	-9	O-41(6-33-2),2-22,S-18/3-2	7	-1.8
Total 8	**570**	**2137**	**341**	**585**	**60**	**19**	**21**	**291**	**164**	**96**	**118**	**....**	**.274**	**.330**	**.349**	**.680**	**82**	**-54**	**299**	**5.00**	**-65**	**O-251,2-160,S-129/3-12,P-12,1**	**47**	**-11.1**
• STAFFORD, Heinie	Henry Alexander Stafford b: 11/1/1891, Orleans, VT d: 1/29/1972, Lake Worth, FL BR/TR, 5'7", 160 lbs. Deb: 10/5/1916																							
1916 NY-N	1	1	0	0	0	0	0	0	0	0	0	....	.000	.000	.000	.000	-106	-0	0	.00	0	....	0	0.0
• STAFFORD, John	John Henry "Doc" Stafford b: 4/8/1870, Dudley, MA d: 7/3/1940, Worcester, MA BR/TR, 5'10", 170 lbs. Deb: 6/15/1893																							
1893 Cle-N	2	4	0	0	0	0	0	0	0	0	0	....	.000	.000	.000	.000	-94	-1	0	.00	0	/P-2,O-1	0	-0.7
• STAGGS, Steve	Stephen Robert Staggs b: 5/6/1951, Anchorage, AK BR/TR, 5'9", 150 lbs. Deb: 7/1/1977																							
1977 Tor-A	72	290	37	75	11	6	2	28	36	38	5	9	.259	.340	.359	.699	90	-6	36	4.20	-14	2-72	5	-1.6
1978 Oak-A	47	78	10	19	2	2	0	0	19	17	2	3	.244	.392	.321	.712	108	1	11	4.87	-3	2-40/3-2,D-2,S-2	3	0.0
Total 2	**119**	**368**	**47**	**94**	**13**	**8**	**2**	**28**	**55**	**55**	**7**	**12**	**.255**	**.352**	**.351**	**.703**	**94**	**-5**	**47**	**4.34**	**-16**	**2-112/3-2,D-2,S-2**	**8**	**-1.5**
• STAHL, Chick	Charles Sylvester Stahl b: 1/10/1873, Avilla, IN d: 3/28/1907, West Baden, IN BL/TL, 5'10", 160 lbs. Deb: 4/19/1897 M Career OF: 74-777-446																							
1897*Bos-N	114	469	112	166	30	13	4	97	38	....	18	....	.354	.406	.499	.905	130	19	105	9.06	-4	*O-111(1-0-110)	20	0.8
1898 Bos-N	125	467	72	144	21	8	3	52	46	....	6	....	.308	.375	.407	.782	118	11	77	6.09	0	*O-125(8-0-118)	19	0.3
1899 Bos-N	148	576	122	202	23	19	7	52	72	....	33	....	.351	.426	.493	.919	138	32	139	9.65	6	*O-148(1-1-146)/P-1	32	2.6
1900 Bos-N	136	553	88	163	23	16	5	82	34	....	27	....	.295	.336	.421	.757	96	-6	90	5.99	4	*O-135(64-1-71)	15	-1.1
1901 Bos-A	131	515	105	156	20	16	6	72	54	....	29	....	.303	.377	.439	.816	128	21	101	7.04	0	*O-131(0-130-1)	24	1.3
1902 Bos-A	127	508	92	164	22	11	2	58	37	....	24	....	.323	.375	.421	.796	117	12	93	6.89	-3	*O-125(0-125-0)	20	0.3
1903*Bos-A	77	299	60	82	12	6	2	44	28	....	10	....	.274	.338	.375	.713	108	3	43	5.13	-2	O-74(0-74-0)	12	-0.2
1904 Bos-A	157	587	83	170	27	**19**	3	67	64	....	11	....	.290	.366	.416	.782	139	28	99	5.94	-22	*O-157(0-157-0)	31	-0.2
1905 Bos-A	134	500	61	129	17	4	0	47	50	....	18	....	.258	.332	.308	.640	102	3	60	4.16	-7	*O-134(0-134-0)	17	-1.1
1906 Bos-A	155	595	63	170	24	6	4	51	47	....	13	....	.286	.346	.366	.713	123	17	84	5.05	8	*O-155(0-155-0)	21	1.8
Total 10	**1304**	**5069**	**858**	**1546**	**219**	**118**	**36**	**622**	**470**	**....**	**189**	**....**	**.305**	**.369**	**.416**	**.785**	**121**	**139**	**892**	**6.47**	**-20**	***O-1295/P-1**	**211**	**4.5**
• STAHL, Jake	Garland Stahl b: 4/13/1879, Elkhart, IL d: 9/18/1922, Monrovia, CA BR/TR, 6'2", 195 lbs. Deb: 4/20/1903 M Career OF: 65-27-0																							
1903 Bos-A	40	92	14	22	3	5	2	8	4	....	1	....	.239	.286	.446	.731	111	1	12	4.66	-1	C-28/O-1	4	0.2
1904 Was-A	142	520	54	136	29	12	3	50	21	....	25	....	.262	.309	.381	.690	119	10	72	4.82	1	*1-119,O-23(O-23-0)	18	0.9
1905 Was-A	141	501	66	125	22	12	5	66	28	....	41	....	.250	.311	.371	.683	121	11	74	5.02	-14	*1-140	21	-0.6
1906 Was-A	137	482	38	107	9	8	0	51	21	....	30	....	.222	.266	.274	.540	73	-16	46	3.11	-2	*1-136	8	-2.2
1908 NY-A	75	274	34	70	18	5	2	42	11	....	17	....	.255	.304	.380	.683	120	5	36	4.41	2	O-68(64-4-0)/1-6	10	0.3
Bos-A	78	262	29	64	9	11	0	23	20	....	13	....	.244	.333	.363	.696	123	7	36	4.51	-5	1-78	11	0.1
Yr.	153	536	63	134	27	16	2	65	31	....	30	....	.250	.319	.371	.690	122	13	72	4.46	-3	1-84,O-68(64-4-0)	21	0.4
1909 Bos-A	127	435	62	128	19	12	6	60	43	....	16	....	.294	.377	.434	.812	153	27	77	6.27	-12	*1-126	23	1.4
1910 Bos-A	144	531	68	144	19	16	**10**	77	42	....	22	....	.271	.334	.424	.758	134	19	82	5.25	-2	*1-142	19	1.6
1912*Bos-A	95	326	40	98	21	6	3	60	31	....	13	....	.301	.372	.429	.801	123	9	57	6.08	1	1-92	13	0.9
1913 Bos-A	2	2	0	0	0	0	0	0	0	1	0	....	.000	.000	.000	.000	-98	-0	0	.00	0	....	0	-0.1
Total 9	**981**	**3425**	**405**	**894**	**149**	**87**	**31**	**437**	**221**	**1**	**178**	**....**	**.261**	**.323**	**.382**	**.706**	**120**	**74**	**492**	**4.89**	**-32**	**1-839/O-92,C-28**	**127**	**2.6**
• STAHL, Larry	Larry Floyd Stahl b: 6/29/1941, Belleville, IL BL/TL, 6', 185 lbs. Deb: 9/11/1964 Career OF: 217-106-160																							
1964 KC-A	15	46	7	12	1	0	3	6	1	10	0	0	.261	.277	.478	.755	102	-0	6	4.89	0	O-10(5-4-1)	1	0.0
1965 KC-A	28	81	9	16	2	1	4	14	5	16	1	0	.198	.253	.395	.648	82	-2	8	3.33	0	O-21(8-12-4)	2	-0.3
1966 KC-A	119	312	37	78	11	5	5	34	17	63	5	3	.250	.291	.365	.656	90	-5	34	3.83	0	O-94(69-2-27)	9	-1.0
1967 NY-N	71	155	9	37	5	0	1	18	8	25	2	2	.239	.285	.290	.575	66	-7	12	2.71	1	O-43(3-32-8)	2	-0.9
1968 NY-N	53	183	15	43	7	2	3	10	21	38	3	0	.235	.314	.344	.658	97	1	22	4.11	2	O-47(13-30-19)/1-9	6	-0.1

YEAR TM-L	G	AB	R	H	2B	3B	HR	RBI	BB	SO	SB	CS	AVG	OBP	SLG	OPS	OPS+	BR/A	RC	RC/G	FR	G/POS	WS	TPW
1969 SD-N	95	162	10	32	6	2	3	10	17	31	3	3	.198	.278	.315	.593	68	-8	13	2.56	4	0-37(27-4-5),1-13	1	-0.6
1970 SD-N	52	66	5	12	2	0	0	3	2	14	2	2	.182	.206	.212	.418	13	-9	3	1.32	0	0-20(17-0-4)	0	-0.9
1971 SD-N	114	308	27	78	13	4	8	36	26	59	4	3	.253	.311	.399	.711	107	1	37	4.05	4	0-75(46-8-26)/1-7	8	0.0
1972 SD-N	107	297	31	67	9	3	7	20	31	67	1	3	.226	.299	.347	.646	89	-6	31	3.53	-2	0-76(26-10-42)/1-1	7	-1.2
1973*Cin-N	76	111	17	25	2	2	2	12	14	34	1	0	.225	.317	.333	.651	85	-2	13	3.88	1	0-29(3-4-24)/1-2	2	-0.1
Total 10	730	1721	167	400	58	19	36	163	142	357	22	16	.232	.293	.351	.644	86	-36	180	3.52	11	0-452/1-32	38	-5.0

• STAHOVIAK, Scott Scott Edmund Stahoviak b: 3/6/1970, Waukegan, IL BL/TR, 6'5", 210 lbs. Deb: 9/10/1993

YEAR TM-L	G	AB	R	H	2B	3B	HR	RBI	BB	SO	SB	CS	AVG	OBP	SLG	OPS	OPS+	BR/A	RC	RC/G	FR	G/POS	WS	TPW
1993 Min-A	20	57	1	11	4	0	0	1	3	22	0	2	.193	.233	.263	.496	33	-6	3	1.42	0	3-19	1	-0.6
1995 Min-A	94	263	28	70	19	0	3	23	30	61	5	1	.266	.344	.373	.716	86	-4	36	4.87	7	1-69,3-22/D-1	6	-0.2
1996 Min-A	130	405	72	115	30	3	13	61	59	114	3	3	.284	.378	.469	.847	111	7	72	6.41	9	*1-114/D-9	12	0.5
1997 Min-A	91	275	33	63	17	0	10	33	24	73	5	2	.229	.305	.400	.705	81	-8	33	3.99	4	1-81/D-5	4	-1.0
1998 Min-A	9	19	1	2	0	0	1	1	0	7	0	0	.105	.105	.263	.368	-8	-3	1	.84	0	/0-9(0-0-1),1-4	0	-0.3
Total 5	344	1019	135	261	70	3	27	119	116	277	13	8	.256	.337	.410	.748	90	-15	145	4.91	20	1-268/3-41,D-15,0-9	23	-1.6

• STAIGER, Roy Roy Joseph Staiger b: 1/6/1950, Tulsa, OK BR/TR, 6', 195 lbs. Deb: 9/12/1975

YEAR TM-L	G	AB	R	H	2B	3B	HR	RBI	BB	SO	SB	CS	AVG	OBP	SLG	OPS	OPS+	BR/A	RC	RC/G	FR	G/POS	WS	TPW
1975 NY-N	13	19	2	3	1	0	0	0	0	4	0	0	.158	.158	.211	.368	2	-3	0	.32	0	3-13	0	-0.2
1976 NY-N	95	304	23	67	8	1	2	26	25	35	3	3	.220	.282	.273	.555	61	-16	23	2.41	18	3-93/S-1	6	0.2
1977 NY-N	40	123	16	31	9	0	2	11	4	20	1	0	.252	.276	.374	.650	76	-4	12	3.50	3	3-36/S-1	2	-0.1
1979 NY-A	4	11	1	3	1	0	0	1	1	0	0	0	.273	.333	.364	.697	90	-0	1	2.98	0	/3-4	0	0.0
Total 4	152	457	42	104	19	1	4	38	30	59	4	3	.228	.277	.300	.576	64	-23	36	2.60	22	3-146/S-2	8	-0.2

• STAINBACK, Tuck George Tucker Stainback b: 8/4/1911, Los Angeles, CA d: 11/29/1992, Camarillo, CA BR/TR, 5'11.5", 175 lbs. Deb: 4/17/1934 Career OF: 182-284-168

YEAR TM-L	G	AB	R	H	2B	3B	HR	RBI	BB	SO	SB	CS	AVG	OBP	SLG	OPS	OPS+	BR/A	RC	RC/G	FR	G/POS	WS	TPW
1934 Chi-N	104	359	47	110	14	3	2	46	8	42	7	....	.306	.327	.379	.706	90	-6	45	4.70	-2	0-96(60-22-15)/3-1	8	-1.2
1935 Chi-N	47	94	16	24	4	0	3	11	0	13	1	....	.255	.271	.394	.664	76	-4	9	3.37	-1	0-28(1-1-26)	1	-0.6
1936 Chi-N	44	75	13	13	3	0	1	5	6	14	1	....	.173	.235	.253	.488	31	-7	5	2.00	-0	0-26(15-6-5)	1	-0.8
1937 Chi-N	72	160	18	37	7	1	0	14	7	16	3	....	.231	.268	.288	.555	49	-12	12	2.45	-1	0-49(9-39-1)	1	-1.4
1938 StL-N	6	10	2	0	0	0	0	0	0	3	0	....	.000	.000	.000	.000	-95	-3	0	.00	0	/0-2(1-1-0)	0	-0.2
Phi-N	30	81	9	21	3	0	1	11	3	3	1	....	.259	.294	.333	.627	72	-3	8	3.59	0	0-25(13-4-9)	1	-0.5
Bro-N	35	104	15	34	6	3	0	20	2	4	1	....	.327	.346	.442	.788	113	1	16	5.98	-2	0-23(2-21-0)	4	-0.1
Yr.	71	195	26	55	9	3	1	31	5	10	2	....	.282	.307	.374	.681	85	-5	24	4.52	-2	0-50(16-26-9)	5	-0.8
1939 Bro-N	68	201	22	54	7	0	3	19	4	23	0	....	.269	.290	.348	.638	68	-10	21	3.78	-5	0-55(10-39-7)	3	-1.6
1940 Det-A	15	40	4	9	2	0	0	1	1	9	0	0	.225	.262	.275	.537	36	-4	3	2.03	3	/0-9(1-8-0)	1	-0.1
1941 Det-A	94	200	19	49	8	1	2	10	3	21	6	3	.245	.260	.325	.585	49	-16	18	2.96	-4	0-80(39-6-36)	1	-2.2
1942*NY-A	15	10	0	2	0	0	0	0	0	2	0	0	.200	.200	.200	.400	13	-1	0	1.38	0	/0-3(2-0-1)	0	-0.1
1943*NY-A	71	231	31	60	11	2	0	10	7	16	3	3	.260	.285	.325	.609	77	-8	21	3.14	0	0-60(12-43-5)	4	-1.1
1944 NY-A	30	78	13	17	3	0	0	5	3	7	1	0	.218	.247	.256	.503	42	-6	6	2.33	-2	0-24(4-4-17)	0	-0.9
1945 NY-A	95	327	40	84	12	2	5	32	13	20	0	4	.257	.289	.352	.641	82	-10	33	3.42	4	0-83(2-72-9)	7	-0.9
1946 Phi-A	91	291	35	71	10	2	0	20	7	20	3	2	.244	.264	.292	.556	56	-18	23	2.79	-2	0-66(11-18-37)	2	-2.3
Total 13	817	2261	284	585	90	14	17	204	64	213	27	12	.259	.284	.333	.618	69	-105	219	3.38	-11	0-629/3-1	34	-14.1

• STAIRS, Matt Matthew Wade Stairs b: 2/27/1968, Fredericton, Canada BL/TR, 5'9", 175 lbs. Deb: 5/29/1992 Career OF: 148-2-440

YEAR TM-L	G	AB	R	H	2B	3B	HR	RBI	BB	SO	SB	CS	AVG	OBP	SLG	OPS	OPS+	BR/A	RC	RC/G	FR	G/POS	WS	TPW
1992 Mon-N	13	30	2	5	2	0	0	5	7	7	0	0	.167	.324	.233	.558	61	-1	3	3.06	0	0-10(10-0-0)	1	-0.2
1993 Mon-N	6	8	1	3	1	0	0	2	0	1	0	0	.375	.375	.500	.875	126	0	1	4.50	-0	/0-1	0	0.0
1995*Bos-A	39	88	8	23	7	1	1	17	4	14	0	1	.261	.301	.398	.699	77	-4	9	3.39	0	0-23(17-0-6)/D-2	1	-0.4
1996 Oak-A	61	137	21	38	5	1	10	23	19	23	1	1	.277	.369	.547	.917	131	6	28	7.37	6	/D-5,1-1,0-1	4	1.0
1997 Oak-A	133	352	62	105	19	0	27	73	50	60	3	2	.298	.390	.582	.973	153	27	81	8.46	-4	0-44(28-0-63),D-16/1-7	15	1.8
1998 Oak-A	149	523	88	154	33	1	26	106	59	93	8	3	.294	.372	.511	.883	130	23	99	6.86	4	*D-120,0-89(11-0-2)/1-6	20	1.7
1999 Oak-A	146	531	94	137	26	3	38	102	89	124	2	7	.258	.367	.533	.900	131	22	105	6.90	-2	0-12(0-1-139)/D-5,1-1	20	1.2
2000*Oak-A	143	476	74	108	26	0	21	81	78	122	5	2	.227	.337	.414	.751	91	-6	71	4.96	-4	*0-139(0-1-102),D-37/1-1	10	-1.6
2001 Chi-N	128	340	48	85	21	0	17	61	52	76	2	3	.250	.361	.462	.823	116	8	59	5.99	2	*0-103(22-0-1),1-89/D-2,2	11	0.3
2002 Mil-N	107	270	41	66	15	0	16	41	36	50	2	0	.244	.350	.478	.828	117	7	46	5.87	0	0-22(35-0-51)	7	0.3
2003 Pit-N	121	305	49	89	20	1	20	57	45	64	0	1	.292	.392	.561	.952	142	19	68	8.08	-6	0-55(8-0-47),1-31/D-2	13	0.8
Total 11	1046	3060	488	813	175	7	176	568	439	634	23	20	.266	.364	.500	.864	123	103	570	6.53	-4	0-499,D-189,1-136/2-1	102	5.0

• STALEY, Gale George Gaylord Staley b: 5/2/1899, De Pere, WI d: 4/19/1989, Walnut Creek, CA BL/TR, 5'8.5", 167 lbs. Deb: 9/16/1925

YEAR TM-L	G	AB	R	H	2B	3B	HR	RBI	BB	SO	SB	CS	AVG	OBP	SLG	OPS	OPS+	BR/A	RC	RC/G	FR	G/POS	WS	TPW
1925 Chi-N	7	26	2	11	2	0	0	3	2	1	0	1	.423	.464	.500	.964	144	1	6	9.21	2	/2-7	1	0.3

• STALLCUP, Virgil Thomas Virgil "Red" Stallcup b: 1/3/1922, Ravensford, NC d: 5/2/1989, Greenville, SC BR/TR, 6'3", 185 lbs. Deb: 4/18/1947

YEAR TM-L	G	AB	R	H	2B	3B	HR	RBI	BB	SO	SB	CS	AVG	OBP	SLG	OPS	OPS+	BR/A	RC	RC/G	FR	G/POS	WS	TPW
1947 Cin-N	8	1	1	0	0	0	0	0	0	1	0	....	.000	.000	.000	.000	-101	-0	0	.00	-1	/S-1	0	-0.1
1948 Cin-N	149	539	40	123	30	4	3	65	18	52	2	....	.228	.253	.315	.569	55	-36	40	2.48	-5	*S-148	6	-3.2
1949 Cin-N	141	575	49	146	28	5	3	45	9	44	1	....	.254	.268	.336	.604	60	-35	49	2.98	-5	*S-141	8	-3.0
1950 Cin-N	136	483	44	121	23	2	8	54	17	39	4	....	.251	.276	.356	.632	65	-27	44	3.10	1	*S-136	9	-1.7
1951 Cin-N	121	428	33	103	17	2	8	49	6	40	2	4	.241	.251	.346	.597	58	-28	34	2.73	3	*S-117	8	-1.8
1952 Cin-N	2	1	0	0	0	0	0	0	0	0	0	0	.000	.000	.000	.000	-100	-0	0	.00	-1	/S-1	0	-0.1
StL-N	29	31	4	4	1	0	0	1	1	5	0	0	.129	.156	.161	.318	-12	-5	1	.65	1	S-12	0	-0.4
Yr.	31	32	4	4	1	0	0	1	1	5	0	0	.125	.152	.156	.308	-15	-5	1	.63	0	S-13	0	-0.4
1953 StL-N	1	1	0	0	0	0	0	0	0	0	0	0	.000	.000	.000	.000	-100	-0	0	.00	0	....	0	0.0
Total 7	587	2059	171	497	99	13	22	214	51	181	9	4	.241	.260	.334	.595	58	-131	168	2.78	-5	S-556	31	-10.2

• STALLER, George George Walborn "Stopper" Staller b: 4/1/1916, Rutherford Heights, PA d: 7/3/1992, Harrisburg, PA BL/TL, 5'11", 190 lbs. Deb: 9/14/1943 C

YEAR TM-L	G	AB	R	H	2B	3B	HR	RBI	BB	SO	SB	CS	AVG	OBP	SLG	OPS	OPS+	BR/A	RC	RC/G	FR	G/POS	WS	TPW
1943 Phi-A	21	85	14	23	1	3	3	12	5	6	1	0	.271	.326	.459	.785	129	3	13	5.64	-1	0-20(0-0-20)	3	0.0

• STALLINGS, George George Tweedy "Gentleman George" Stallings b: 11/17/1867, Augusta, GA d: 5/13/1929, Haddock, GA BR/TR, 6'1", 187 lbs. Deb: 5/22/1890 M

YEAR TM-L	G	AB	R	H	2B	3B	HR	RBI	BB	SO	SB	CS	AVG	OBP	SLG	OPS	OPS+	BR/A	RC	RC/G	FR	G/POS	WS	TPW
1890 Bro-N	4	11	1	0	0	0	0	0	1	3	0	....	.000	.154	.000	.154	-54	-2	0	.00	-1	/C-4	0	-0.2
1897 Phi-N	2	9	1	2	1	0	0	0	0	....	0	....	.222	.222	.333	.556	47	-1	1	2.59	1	/1-1,0-1	0	0.0
1898 Phi-N	1	0	1	0	0	0	0	0	0	....	0	....	....	....	....	....	-104	0	0	....	0	....	0	0.0
Total 3	7	20	3	2	1	0	0	0	1	3	0	....	.100	.182	.150	.332	-13	-3	1	1.01	-0	/C-4,1-1,0-1	0	-0.2

• STANAGE, Oscar Oscar Harland Stanage b: 3/17/1883, Tulare, CA d: 11/11/1964, Detroit, MI BR/TR, 5'11", 185 lbs. Deb: 5/19/1906 C

YEAR TM-L	G	AB	R	H	2B	3B	HR	RBI	BB	SO	SB	CS	AVG	OBP	SLG	OPS	OPS+	BR/A	RC	RC/G	FR	G/POS	WS	TPW
1906 Cin-N	1	1	0	0	0	0	0	0	0	....	0	....	.000	.000	.000	.000	-96	-0	0	.00	0	/C-1	0	-0.1
1909*Det-A	77	252	17	66	8	6	0	21	11	....	2	....	.262	.298	.341	.639	98	-2	26	3.51	-7	C-77	8	-0.1
1910 Det-A	88	275	24	57	7	4	2	25	20	....	1	....	.207	.266	.284	.550	68	-11	21	2.42	2	C-84	5	-0.1
1911 Det-A	141	503	45	133	13	7	3	51	20	....	3	....	.264	.297	.336	.633	73	-21	51	3.42	-7	*C-141	9	-1.6
1912 Det-A	121	394	35	103	9	4	0	41	34	....	3	....	.261	.326	.305	.631	83	-8	40	3.47	-11	*C-120	6	-1.0
1913 Det-A	80	241	19	54	13	2	0	21	21	35	5	....	.224	.292	.295	.586	73	-9	22	2.85	-2	C-77	3	-0.5
1914 Det-A	122	400	16	77	8	4	0	25	24	58	2	1	.193	.242	.233	.474	41	-30	25	1.94	-9	*C-122	3	-3.1
1915 Det-A	100	300	27	67	9	2	1	31	20	41	5	1	.223	.274	.277	.551	62	-15	25	2.71	-11	*C-100	5	-1.9
1916 Det-A	94	291	16	69	17	3	0	30	17	48	3	....	.237	.286	.316	.602	78	-9	28	3.19	-11	C-94	6	-1.3
1917 Det-A	99	297	19	61	14	1	0	30	20	35	3	....	.205	.263	.259	.522	59	-15	21	2.20	-5	C-95	5	-1.4
1918 Det-A	54	186	9	47	4	0	1	14	11	18	2	....	.253	.294	.290	.585	80	-5	16	2.84	-2	C-47/1-5,S-1	4	-0.4
1919 Det-A	38	120	9	29	4	1	1	15	7	12	1	....	.242	.295	.317	.611	73	-5	11	3.10	1	C-36/1-1	3	-0.1
1920 Det-A	78	238	12	55	17	0	0	17	14	21	0	0	.231	.277	.303	.579	55	-15	21	2.86	-3	C-77	2	-1.2
1925 Det-A	3	5	0	1	0	0	0	0	0	0	0	0	.200	.200	.200	.400	2	-1	0	1.27	-1	/C-3	0	-0.1
Total 14	1096	3503	248	819	123	34	8	321	219	268	30	2	.234	.284	.295	.579	69	-144	305	2.86	-66	*C-1074/1-6,S-1	59	-13.0

• STANDAERT, Jerry Jerome John Standaert b: 11/2/1901, Chicago, IL d: 8/4/1964, Chicago, IL BR/TR, 5'10", 168 lbs. Deb: 4/16/1925

YEAR TM-L	G	AB	R	H	2B	3B	HR	RBI	BB	SO	SB	CS	AVG	OBP	SLG	OPS	OPS+	BR/A	RC	RC/G	FR	G/POS	WS	TPW
1925 Bro-N	1	1	0	0	0	0	0	0	0	1	0	0	.000	.000	.000	.000	-103	-0	0	.00	0	....	0	0.0
1926 Bro-N	66	113	13	39	8	2	0	14	5	7	0	....	.345	.378	.451	.829	124	4	19	6.17	-5	2-21,3-14/S-6	4	0.0

YEAR TM-L	G	AB	R	H	2B	3B	HR	RBI	BB	SO	SB	CS	AVG	OBP	SLG	OPS	OPS+	BR/A	RC	RC/G	FR	G/POS	WS	TPW
1929 Bos-A	19	18	1	3	2	0	0	4	3	2	0	0	.167	.286	.278	.563	47	-1	2	2.80	0	1-10	0	-0.2
Total 3	86	132	14	42	10	2	0	18	8	10	0	0	.318	.362	.424	.786	111	2	20	5.57	-5	/2-21,3-14,1-10,S-6	4	-0.2
• STANICEK, Pete	Peter Louis Stanicek b: 4/18/1963, Harvey, IL BB/TR, 5'11", 175 lbs. Deb: 9/1/1987																							
1987 Bal-A	30	113	9	31	3	0	0	9	8	19	8	1	.274	.333	.301	.634	72	-3	13	3.95	-2	2-19,D-10/3-2	2	-0.4
1988 Bal-A	83	261	29	60	7	1	4	17	28	45	12	6	.230	.314	.310	.624	78	-7	25	3.09	-1	0-65(65-0-0),2-16/D-1	3	-1.0
Total 2	113	374	38	91	10	1	4	26	36	64	20	7	.243	.320	.307	.627	76	-10	38	3.33	-3	/0-65,2-35,D-11,3-2	5	-1.4
• STANICEK, Steve	Stephen Blair Stanicek b: 6/19/1961, Lake Forest, IL BR/TR, 6', 190 lbs. Deb: 9/16/1987																							
1987 Mil-A	4	7	2	2	0	0	0	0	0	2	0	0	.286	.286	.286	.571	51	-1	1	3.09	0	/D-1	0	0.0
1989 Phi-N	9	9	0	1	0	0	0	1	0	3	0	0	.111	.111	.111	.222	-36	-2	0	.38	0	....	0	-0.2
Total 2	13	16	2	3	0	0	0	1	0	5	0	0	.188	.188	.188	.375	2	-2	1	1.42	0	/D-1	0	-0.2
• STANKARD, Tom	Thomas Francis Stankard b: 3/20/1882, Waltham, MA d: 6/13/1958, Waltham, MA BR/TR, 6', 190 lbs. Deb: 7/2/1904																							
1904 Pit-N	2	2	0	0	0	0	0	0	0	....	0	....	.000	.000	.000	.000	-97	-0	0	.00	0	/3-1,S-1	0	-0.1
• STANKIEWICZ, Andy	Andrew Neal "Stanky" Stankiewicz b: 8/10/1964, Inglewood, CA BR/TR, 5'9", 165 lbs. Deb: 4/11/1992																							
1992 NY-A	116	400	52	107	22	2	2	25	38	42	9	5	.268	.339	.348	.686	93	-3	47	3.94	11	S-81,2-34/D-1	12	1.5
1993 NY-A	16	9	5	0	0	0	0	0	1	1	0	0	.000	.100	.000	.100	-73	-2	0	.08	0	/2-6,3-4,D-1,S-1	0	-0.2
1994 Hou-N	37	54	10	14	3	0	1	5	12	12	1	1	.259	.403	.370	.773	109	1	9	5.20	0	S-17/2-6,3-1	2	0.2
1995 Hou-N	43	52	6	6	1	0	0	7	12	19	4	2	.115	.281	.135	.416	15	-6	3	1.52	1	S-14/2-6,3-3	1	-0.4
1996 Mon-N	64	77	12	22	5	1	0	9	6	12	1	0	.286	.360	.377	.737	92	-0	11	5.18	0	2-19,S-13/3-1	2	0.0
1997 Mon-N	76	107	11	24	9	0	1	5	4	22	1	1	.224	.252	.336	.589	53	-8	9	2.65	2	2-25,S-14/3-3,D-2	1	-0.5
1998 Ari-N	77	145	9	30	5	0	0	8	7	33	1	0	.207	.253	.241	.495	31	-14	9	2.02	-3	2-61	1	-1.6
Total 7	429	844	105	203	45	3	4	59	80	141	17	9	.241	.314	.315	.630	72	-33	87	3.40	10	2-157,S-140/3-12,D-4	19	-0.9
• STANKY, Eddie	Edward Raymond "The Brat,Muggsy" Stanky b: 9/3/1916, Philadelphia, PA d: 6/6/1999, Fairhope, AL BR/TR, 5'8", 170 lbs. Deb: 4/21/1943 M/C																							
1943 Chi-N	142	510	92	125	15	1	0	47	92	42	4	....	.245	.363	.278	.641	88	-2	58	3.80	14	*2-131,S-12/3-2	14	2.1
1944 Chi-N	13	25	4	6	0	1	0	0	2	2	1	....	.240	.296	.320	.616	74	-1	2	2.91	0	/2-3,3-3,S-3	0	-0.1
Bro-N	89	261	32	72	9	2	0	16	44	13	3	....	.276	.382	.326	.708	102	4	37	4.93	-8	2-58,S-35/3-1	9	0.1
Yr.	102	286	36	78	9	3	0	16	46	15	4	....	.273	.375	.325	.701	100	3	39	4.74	-8	2-61,S-38/3-4	9	0.0
1945 Bro-N	153	555	**128**	143	29	5	1	39	**148**	42	6	....	.258	.417	.333	.751	111	20	93	5.73	22	*2-153/S-1	27	5.0
1946 Bro-N	144	483	98	132	24	7	0	36	**137**	56	8	....	.273	**.436**	.352	.788	123	27	90	6.44	4	*2-141	28	4.1
1947★Bro-N★	146	559	97	141	24	5	3	53	103	39	3	....	.252	.373	.329	.702	85	-7	78	4.81	19	*2-146	20	2.0
1948★Bos-N★	67	247	49	79	14	2	2	29	61	13	3	....	.320	.455	.417	.872	140	19	52	7.98	10	2-66	14	3.2
1949 Bos-N	138	506	90	144	24	5	1	42	113	41	3	....	.285	.417	.358	.775	116	20	86	6.14	-6	*2-135	21	2.1
1950 NY-N★	152	527	115	158	25	5	8	51	**144**	50	9	....	.300	**.460**	.412	.872	131	37	116	8.13	13	*2-151	30	**5.6**
1951★NY-N	145	515	88	127	17	2	14	43	127	63	8	5	.247	.401	.369	.770	108	14	90	6.06	7	*2-140	24	2.9
1952 StL-N	53	83	13	19	4	0	0	7	19	9	0	0	.229	.373	.277	.650	82	-1	11	4.39	2	2-20	3	0.2
1953 StL-N	17	30	5	8	0	0	0	1	6	4	0	0	.267	.405	.267	.672	80	-0	4	4.69	1	/2-8	1	0.1
Total 11	1259	4301	811	1154	185	35	29	364	996	374	48	5	.268	.410	.348	.758	109	127	717	5.83	78	*2-1152/S-51,3-6	191	27.4
• STANLEY, Fred	Frederick Blair Stanley b: 8/13/1947, Farnhamville, IA BR/TR, 5'10", 167 lbs. Deb: 9/11/1969 C																							
1969 Sea-A	17	43	2	12	2	1	0	4	3	8	1	0	.279	.326	.372	.698	96	-0	6	4.69	-2	S-15/2-1	1	0.0
1970 Mil-A	6	0	1	0	0	0	0	0	0	0	0	0	....	....	....	....	-99	0	0	....	-1	/2-2	0	-0.1
1971 Cle-A	60	129	14	29	4	0	2	12	27	25	1	0	.225	.363	.302	.665	83	-1	16	3.98	-3	S-55/2-3	4	0.2
1972 Cle-A	6	12	1	2	1	0	0	0	2	3	0	0	.167	.286	.250	.536	58	-1	1	1.82	-1	/S-5,2-1	0	-0.2
SD-N	39	85	15	17	2	0	0	2	12	19	1	0	.200	.306	.224	.530	57	-4	7	2.75	-3	2-21,S-17/3-4	2	-0.5
1973 NY-A	26	66	6	14	0	1	1	5	7	16	0	0	.212	.288	.288	.576	65	-3	6	3.06	-1	S-21/2-3	1	-0.1
1974 NY-A	33	38	2	7	0	0	0	3	3	2	1	2	.184	.244	.184	.428	25	-4	1	.95	2	S-19,2-15	1	-0.1
1975 NY-A	117	252	34	56	5	1	0	15	21	27	3	1	.222	.285	.250	.535	54	-15	18	2.30	4	S-83,2-33/3-1	4	-0.1
1976★NY-A	110	260	32	62	2	2	1	20	34	29	1	0	.238	.329	.273	.602	78	-5	26	3.28	-2	*S-110/2-3	7	0.3
1977★NY-A	48	46	6	12	0	0	1	7	8	6	1	1	.261	.370	.326	.696	93	-0	6	4.62	-1	S-42/3-3,2-2	2	0.1
1978★NY-A	81	160	14	35	7	0	1	9	25	31	0	0	.219	.324	.281	.606	73	-5	16	3.31	-1	S-71,2-11/3-4	4	-0.1
1979 NY-A	57	100	9	20	1	0	2	14	5	17	0	1	.200	.238	.270	.508	38	-9	6	2.01	2	S-31,3-16/2-8,1-1,0-1	2	-0.5
1980 NY-A	49	86	13	18	3	0	0	5	5	5	0	0	.209	.269	.244	.513	42	-7	6	2.42	0	S-19,2-17,3-12	1	-0.5
1981★Oak-A	66	145	15	28	4	0	0	7	15	23	2	0	.193	.269	.221	.489	45	-9	11	2.27	-5	S-62/2-6	3	-1.0
1982 Oak-A	101	228	33	44	7	0	2	17	29	32	0	1	.193	.287	.250	.537	51	-15	17	2.47	-3	S-98/2-2	3	-0.9
Total 14	816	1650	197	356	38	5	10	120	196	243	11	6	.216	.302	.263	.565	62	-78	144	2.82	-14	S-648,2-128/3-40,1-1,0-1	35	-3.6
• STANLEY, Jim	James Francis Stanley b: 1889, Chicago, IL BB/TR, 5'6", 148 lbs. Deb: 4/19/1914																							
1914 Chi-F	54	98	13	19	3	0	0	4	19	14	2	....	.194	.347	.224	.572	68	-2	8	2.64	-3	S-40/3-3,2-1,0-1	2	-0.4
• STANLEY, Joe	Joseph Bernard Stanley b: 4/2/1881, Washington, DC d: 9/13/1967, Detroit, MI BB/TR, 5'9.5", 150 lbs. Deb: 9/11/1897 Career OF: 33-52-106																							
1897 Was-N	1	1	0	0	0	0	0	0	0	....	0	....	.000	.000	.000	.000	-101	-0	0	.00	-0	/P-1	0	0.0
1902 Was-A	3	12	2	4	0	0	0	1	0	....	0	....	.333	.333	.333	.667	85	-0	1	4.53	0	/0-3(3-0-0)	0	-0.1
1903 Bos-N	86	308	40	77	12	5	1	47	18	....	10	....	.250	.306	.331	.637	85	-6	36	4.02	3	0-77(11-32-34)/P-1,S-1	6	-0.8
1904 Bos-N	3	8	0	0	0	0	0	0	0	....	0	....	.000	.000	.000	.000	-104	-2	0	.00	1	/0-3(1-0-2)	0	-0.2
1905 Was-A	28	92	13	24	2	1	1	17	7	....	4	....	.261	.313	.337	.650	111	1	12	4.32	1	0-27(13-9-5)	3	0.0
1906 Was-A	73	221	18	36	0	4	0	9	20	....	6	....	.163	.236	.199	.435	38	-15	14	1.84	-4	0-63(0-7-56)/P-1	0	-2.7
1909 Chi-N	22	52	4	7	1	0	0	2	6	....	0	....	.135	.224	.154	.378	17	-5	2	1.07	-1	0-16(5-4-9)	0	-0.7
Total 7	216	694	77	148	15	10	2	76	51	....	20	....	.213	.275	.272	.547	65	-27	65	2.99	-1	0-189/P-3,S-1	9	-4.4
• STANLEY, Joe	Joseph Stanley b: NJ Deb: 4/24/1884																							
1884 Bal-U	6	21	3	5	1	0	0	....	0	....	....	....	.238	.238	.286	.524	69	-1	1	2.56	-2	/0-6(0-4-2)	0	-0.3
• STANLEY, Mickey	Mitchell Jack Stanley b: 7/20/1942, Grand Rapids, MI BR/TR, 6'1", 195 lbs. Deb: 9/13/1964 Career OF: 44-1171-82																							
1964 Det-A	4	11	3	3	0	0	0	1	0	1	0	0	.273	.273	.273	.545	51	-1	1	1.64	-0	/0-4(3-1-1)	0	-0.1
1965 Det-A	30	117	14	28	6	0	3	13	3	12	1	0	.239	.258	.368	.626	75	-4	11	3.15	0	0-29(0-29-0)	2	-0.5
1966 Det-A	92	235	28	68	15	4	3	19	17	20	2	1	.289	.337	.426	.763	115	4	33	5.15	4	0-82(0-82-0)	9	0.7
1967 Det-A	145	333	38	70	7	3	7	24	29	46	9	2	.210	.273	.312	.586	71	-11	30	2.91	-2	*0-129(2-126-2)/1-8	6	-1.9
1968★Det-A	153	583	88	151	16	6	11	60	42	57	4	3	.259	.313	.364	.677	101	0	62	3.58	-1	*0-130(0-130-0),1-15/S-9,2	18	-0.5
1969 Det-A	149	592	73	139	28	1	16	70	52	56	8	4	.235	.299	.367	.665	82	-16	64	3.62	-9	*0-101(0-98-3),S-59/1-4	13	-2.2
1970 Det-A	142	568	83	143	21	11	13	47	45	56	10	1	.252	.307	.396	.703	92	-6	67	3.95	-4	*0-132(0-132-0)/1-9	13	-1.5
1971 Det-A	139	401	43	117	14	5	7	41	24	44	1	3	.292	.332	.404	.736	103	0	52	4.65	5	*0-139(0-139-0)	13	0.2
1972★Det-A	142	435	45	102	16	6	14	55	29	49	1	0	.234	.282	.395	.678	97	-3	45	3.37	0	*0-139(0-139-0)	12	-0.8
1973 Det-A	157	602	81	147	23	5	17	57	48	65	0	4	.244	.300	.384	.684	86	-14	68	3.79	4	*0-157(0-157-0)	15	-1.5
1974 Det-A	99	394	40	87	13	2	8	34	26	63	5	3	.221	.271	.325	.596	68	-17	32	2.58	1	0-91(1-90-0),1-12/2-1	5	-1.9
1975 Det-A	52	164	26	42	7	3	3	19	15	27	1	1	.256	.322	.390	.712	96	-1	21	4.47	-1	0-28(14-15-0),1-14/3-7,D-1	4	-0.5
1976 Det-A	84	214	34	55	17	1	4	29	14	19	2	0	.257	.303	.402	.705	101	-0	25	3.98	-0	0-38(15-19-4),1-17,3-11/S-3,2,D	6	-0.2
1977 Det-A	75	222	30	51	9	1	8	23	18	30	0	0	.230	.288	.387	.675	78	-7	24	3.55	-3	0-57(7-10-44)/1-3,S-3,D-2	3	-1.2
1978 Det-A	53	151	15	40	9	0	3	8	9	19	0	1	.265	.306	.384	.690	90	-3	17	3.98	-2	0-34(2-4-28),1-12	3	-0.7
Total 15	1516	5022	641	1243	201	48	117	500	371	564	44	23	.248	.300	.377	.677	90	-77	549	3.70	-8	*0-1290/1-94,S-74,3-18,D-5,2	122	-12.5
• STANLEY, Mike	Robert Michael Stanley b: 6/25/1963, Fort Lauderdale, FL BR/TR, 6'1", 185 lbs. Deb: 6/24/1986 Career OF: 4-0-0																							
1986 Tex-A	15	30	4	10	3	0	1	1	3	7	1	0	.333	.394	.533	.927	146	2	7	9.20	0	/3-7,C-4,D-3,0-1	2	0.3
1987 Tex-A	78	216	34	59	8	1	6	37	31	48	3	0	.273	.367	.403	.770	104	3	33	5.37	-3	C-61,1-12/D-5,0-1	5	0.1
1988 Tex-A	94	249	21	57	8	0	3	27	37	62	0	0	.229	.329	.297	.626	75	-7	26	3.46	-2	C-64,D-18/1-6,3-2	5	-0.7
1989 Tex-A	67	122	9	30	3	1	1	11	12	29	1	0	.246	.324	.311	.635	78	-3	12	3.33	-2	C-25,D-21/1-7,3-3	1	-0.5
1990 Tex-A	103	189	21	47	8	1	2	19	30	25	1	0	.249	.352	.333	.685	92	-1	24	4.24	-3	C-63,D-14/3-8,1-6	5	-0.1
1991 Tex-A	95	181	25	45	13	1	3	25	34	44	0	0	.249	.373	.381	.754	111	4	29	5.41	-1	C-58,1-12/3-6,D-6,0-1	6	0.5

YEAR TM-L	G	AB	R	H	2B	3B	HR	RBI	BB	SO	SB	CS	AVG	OBP	SLG	OPS	OPS+	BR/A	RC	RC/G	FR	G/POS	WS	TPW
1992 NY-A	68	173	24	43	7	0	8	27	33	45	0	0	.249	.372	.428	.800	124	7	28	5.64	0	C-55/D-6,1-4	6	1.0
1993 NY-A	130	423	70	129	17	1	26	84	57	85	1	1	.305	.394	.534	.928	152	32	90	7.79	-7	*C-122/D-2	24	3.2
1994 NY-A	82	290	54	87	20	0	17	57	39	56	0	0	.300	.387	.545	.932	142	18	60	7.53	-3	C-72/1-7,D-4	14	1.8
1995*NY-A★	118	399	63	107	29	1	18	83	57	106	1	1	.268	.367	.481	.848	120	12	70	5.96	-3	*C-107,D-10	16	1.4
1996 Bos-A	121	397	73	107	20	1	24	69	69	62	2	0	.270	.384	.506	.891	120	14	81	7.29	-7	*C-105,D-10	12	1.2
1997 Bos-A	97	260	45	78	17	0	13	53	39	50	0	1	.300	.403	.515	.919	135	14	54	7.34	-1	D-53,1-31,C-15	10	0.9
*NY-A	28	87	16	25	8	0	3	12	15	22	0	0	.287	.392	.483	.875	128	4	16	6.39	-1	D-16,1-12	4	0.2
Yr.	125	347	61	103	25	0	16	65	54	72	0	1	.297	.400	.507	.908	133	18	70	7.10	-1	D-69,1-43,C-15	14	1.0
1998 Tor-A	98	341	49	82	13	0	22	47	56	86	2	1	.240	.356	.472	.828	112	7	60	6.02	0	0-84(1-0-0),D-73,1-22	8	0.0
*Bos-A	47	156	25	45	12	0	7	32	26	43	1	0	.288	.397	.500	.897	129	8	31	6.95	-1	D-34,1-13	7	0.4
Yr.	145	497	74	127	25	0	29	79	82	129	3	1	.256	.369	.481	.849	118	15	91	6.31	-1	*D-107,0-84(1-0-0),1-35	15	0.4
1999*Bos-A	136	427	59	120	22	0	19	72	70	94	0	0	.281	.396	.466	.862	115	13	83	7.06	0	*1-111,D-22	14	0.2
2000 Bos-A	58	185	22	41	5	0	10	28	30	44	0	0	.222	.330	.411	.741	84	-5	27	5.00	4	1-39,D-18	3	-0.5
Oak-A	32	97	11	26	7	0	4	18	14	21	0	0	.268	.366	.464	.830	111	2	17	5.98	1	1-19/D-8	3	0.0
Yr.	90	282	33	67	12	0	14	46	44	65	0	0	.238	.343	.429	.772	93	-3	44	5.33	4	1-58,D-26	6	-0.4
Total 15	**1467**	**4222**	**625**	**1138**	**220**	**7**	**187**	**702**	**652**	**929**	**13**	**4**	**.270**	**.373**	**.458**	**.831**	**117**	**123**	**749**	**6.20**	**-28**	**C-751,D-323,1-301/0-87,3-26**	**145**	**9.4**

• STANSBURY, Jack John James Stansbury b: 12/6/1885, Phillipsburg, NJ d: 12/26/1970, Easton, PA BR/TR, 5'9", 165 lbs. Deb: 6/30/1918

YEAR TM-L	G	AB	R	H	2B	3B	HR	RBI	BB	SO	SB	CS	AVG	OBP	SLG	OPS	OPS+	BR/A	RC	RC/G	FR	G/POS	WS	TPW
1918 Bos-A	20	47	3	6	1	0	0	2	6	3	0	....	.128	.241	.149	.390	18	-4	2	1.23	0	3-18/O-2(0-2-0)	1	-0.5

• STANTON, Buck George Washington Stanton b: 6/19/1906, Stantonsburg, NC d: 1/1/1992, San Antonio, TX BL/TL, 5'10", 150 lbs. Deb: 9/5/1931

YEAR TM-L	G	AB	R	H	2B	3B	HR	RBI	BB	SO	SB	CS	AVG	OBP	SLG	OPS	OPS+	BR/A	RC	RC/G	FR	G/POS	WS	TPW
1931 StL-A	13	15	3	3	2	0	0	0	0	6	0	0	.200	.200	.333	.533	37	-1	1	2.03	0	/0-1	0	-0.1

• STANTON, Harry Harry Andrew Stanton b: St. Louis, MO TR Deb: 10/14/1900

YEAR TM-L	G	AB	R	H	2B	3B	HR	RBI	BB	SO	SB	CS	AVG	OBP	SLG	OPS	OPS+	BR/A	RC	RC/G	FR	G/POS	WS	TPW
1900 StL-N	1	0	0	0	0	0	0	0	0	....	0	....	....	....	....	....	-101	0	0	....	0	/C-1	0	0.0

• STANTON, Leroy Leroy Bobby Stanton b: 4/10/1946, Latta, SC BR/TR, 6'1", 195 lbs. Deb: 9/10/1970 Career OF: 107-49-553

YEAR TM-L	G	AB	R	H	2B	3B	HR	RBI	BB	SO	SB	CS	AVG	OBP	SLG	OPS	OPS+	BR/A	RC	RC/G	FR	G/POS	WS	TPW
1970 NY-N	4	4	0	1	0	1	0	0	0	0	0	0	.250	.250	.750	1.000	157	0	0	.00	0	/0-1	0	0.0
1971 NY-N	5	21	2	4	1	0	0	2	2	4	0	0	.190	.261	.238	.499	43	-2	1	1.72	0	/0-5(0-0-5)	0	-0.2
1972 Cal-A	127	402	44	101	15	3	12	39	22	100	2	3	.251	.297	.393	.690	110	2	42	3.48	2	*0-124(0-2-123)	12	-0.2
1973 Cal-A	119	306	41	72	9	2	8	34	27	88	3	3	.235	.301	.356	.658	92	-4	31	3.34	-1	*0-107(36-0-76)	6	-1.0
1974 Cal-A	118	415	48	111	21	2	11	62	33	107	10	8	.267	.329	.407	.736	117	7	54	4.37	1	*0-114(0-10-110)	12	0.3
1975 Cal-A	137	440	67	115	20	3	14	82	52	85	18	6	.261	.347	.416	.763	124	16	66	5.10	2	*0-131(0-5-127)/D-1	17	1.2
1976 Cal-A	93	231	12	44	13	1	2	25	24	57	2	6	.190	.270	.281	.551	66	-12	16	2.01	-1	0-79(33-31-27)/D-4	2	-1.7
1977 Sea-A	133	454	56	125	24	1	27	90	42	115	0	1	.275	.343	.511	.854	131	18	79	6.26	2	0-91(8-0-84),D-33	19	1.5
1978 Sea-A	93	302	24	55	11	0	3	24	34	80	1	0	.182	.267	.248	.515	46	-21	21	2.24	-1	D-59,0-30(30-0-1)	0	-2.6
Total 9	**829**	**2575**	**294**	**628**	**114**	**13**	**77**	**358**	**236**	**636**	**36**	**27**	**.244**	**.313**	**.388**	**.701**	**103**	**5**	**310**	**4.01**	**5**	**0-682/D-97**	**68**	**-2.6**

• STANTON, Tom Thomas Patrick Stanton b: 10/25/1874, St. Louis, MO d: 1/17/1957, St. Louis, MO BB/TR, 5'10", 175 lbs. Deb: 4/19/1904

YEAR TM-L	G	AB	R	H	2B	3B	HR	RBI	BB	SO	SB	CS	AVG	OBP	SLG	OPS	OPS+	BR/A	RC	RC/G	FR	G/POS	WS	TPW
1904 Chi-N	1	3	0	0	0	0	0	0	0	....	0	....	.000	.000	.000	.000	-100	-1	0	.00	0	/C-1	0	-0.1

• STAPLETON, Dave David Leslie Stapleton b: 1/16/1954, Fairhope, AL BR/TR, 6'1", 178 lbs. Deb: 5/30/1980 Career OF: 1-4-2

YEAR TM-L	G	AB	R	H	2B	3B	HR	RBI	BB	SO	SB	CS	AVG	OBP	SLG	OPS	OPS+	BR/A	RC	RC/G	FR	G/POS	WS	TPW
1980 Bos-A	106	449	61	144	33	5	7	45	13	32	3	2	.321	.341	.463	.805	112	6	67	5.58	4	2-94/1-8,0-6(0-4-2),D-3,3	15	1.4
1981 Bos-A	93	355	45	101	17	1	10	42	21	22	0	4	.285	.326	.423	.749	108	1	45	4.40	-8	S-33,3-25,2-23,1-12/D-3	10	-0.4
1982 Bos-A	150	538	66	142	28	1	14	65	31	40	2	4	.264	.308	.398	.705	87	-12	58	3.61	3	*1-106,S-27/2-9,3-5,D-4,0	10	-1.2
1983 Bos-A	151	542	54	134	31	1	10	66	40	44	1	1	.247	.301	.363	.665	76	-18	56	3.43	-2	*1-145/2-5	7	-2.8
1984 Bos-A	13	39	4	9	2	0	0	1	3	3	0	0	.231	.286	.282	.568	55	-2	3	2.29	0	1-10/D-1	0	-0.3
1985 Bos-A	30	66	4	15	6	0	0	2	4	11	0	0	.227	.271	.318	.590	58	-4	6	2.91	-1	2-14/1-8,D-5	1	-0.4
1986*Bos-A	39	39	4	5	1	0	0	3	2	10	0	0	.128	.171	.154	.325	-11	-6	1	.75	0	1-29/2-6,3-2	0	-0.7
Total 7	**582**	**2028**	**238**	**550**	**118**	**8**	**41**	**224**	**114**	**162**	**6**	**11**	**.271**	**.312**	**.398**	**.710**	**90**	**-35**	**236**	**3.98**	**-3**	**1-318,2-151/S-60,3-34,D-16,0**	**43**	**-4.3**

• STARGELL, Willie Wilver Dornel "Pops" Stargell
b: 3/6/1940, Earlsboro, OK d: 4/9/2001, Wilmington, NC BL/TL, 6'2", 225 lbs. Deb: 9/16/1962 C HOF: 1988 Career OF: 1225-8-72

YEAR TM-L	G	AB	R	H	2B	3B	HR	RBI	BB	SO	SB	CS	AVG	OBP	SLG	OPS	OPS+	BR/A	RC	RC/G	FR	G/POS	WS	TPW
1962 Pit-N	10	31	1	9	3	1	0	4	3	10	0	1	.290	.353	.452	.805	114	0	5	5.51	0	/0-9(2-1-6)	1	-0.1
1963 Pit-N	108	304	34	74	11	6	11	47	19	85	0	2	.243	.292	.428	.720	104	-0	36	4.07	-4	0-65(35-6-24),1-16	7	-0.9
1964 Pit-N★	117	421	53	115	19	7	21	78	17	92	1	1	.273	.305	.501	.806	123	10	62	5.29	-8	0-59(57-1-2),1-50	13	-0.4
1965 Pit-N★	144	533	68	145	25	8	27	107	39	127	1	1	.272	.330	.501	.831	130	19	87	5.86	5	*0-137(125-0-19)/1-7	21	1.7
1966 Pit-N★	140	485	84	153	30	0	33	102	48	109	2	3	.315	.384	.581	.965	164	41	107	8.21	-4	*0-127(121-0-7),1-15	25	3.1
1967 Pit-N	134	462	54	125	18	6	20	73	67	103	1	0	.271	.367	.465	.832	136	24	78	5.99	1	0-98(92-0-6),1-37	20	2.0
1968 Pit-N	128	435	57	103	15	1	24	67	47	105	5	0	.237	.320	.441	.761	128	16	61	4.67	1	*0-113(108-0-5),1-13	16	1.2
1969 Pit-N	145	522	89	160	31	6	29	92	61	120	1	0	.307	.385	.556	.941	164	45	112	8.03	-2	*0-116(115-0-1),1-23	27	3.7
1970*Pit-N	136	474	70	125	18	3	31	85	44	119	0	1	.264	.333	.511	.843	127	15	77	5.59	9	*0-125(123-0-2)/1-1	17	1.6
1971*Pit-N★	141	511	104	151	26	0	**48**	125	83	154	0	0	.295	.401	.628	1.029	186	59	131	9.51	-2	*0-138(138-0-0)	35	**5.2**
1972*Pit-N★	138	495	75	145	28	2	33	112	65	129	1	1	.293	.377	.558	.935	166	42	105	7.79	-13	*1-101,0-32(32-0-0)	26	2.1
1973 Pit-N★	148	522	106	156	**43**	3	**44**	**119**	80	129	0	0	.299	.395	**.646**	**1.041**	**189**	**62**	136	**9.75**	2	*0-142(142-0-0)	36	5.9
1974*Pit-N	140	508	90	153	37	4	25	96	87	106	0	2	.301	.409	.537	**.947**	**169**	48	115	8.39	-5	*0-135(135-0-0)/1-1	29	3.7
1975*Pit-N	124	461	71	136	32	2	22	90	58	109	0	0	.295	.377	.516	.894	147	29	91	7.26	-8	*1-122	22	1.1
1976 Pit-N	117	428	54	110	20	3	20	65	50	101	2	0	.257	.342	.458	.800	124	14	70	5.80	-10	*1-111	17	-0.5
1977 Pit-N	63	186	29	51	12	0	13	35	31	55	0	1	.274	.386	.548	.935	143	12	39	7.49	-2	1-55	8	0.7
1978 Pit-N★	122	390	60	115	18	2	28	97	50	93	3	2	.295	.385	.567	.951	156	29	85	7.98	0	*1-112	22	2.4
1979*Pit-N	126	424	60	119	19	0	32	82	47	105	0	1	.281	.357	.552	.908	138	21	81	6.82	-7	*1-113	18	0.7
1980 Pit-N	67	202	28	53	10	1	11	38	26	52	0	0	.262	.352	.485	.837	129	8	35	6.27	-1	1-54	7	0.4
1981 Pit-N	38	60	2	17	4	0	0	9	5	9	0	0	.283	.338	.350	.688	93	-1	8	4.61	-2	/1-9	1	-0.3
1982 Pit-N	74	73	6	17	4	0	3	17	10	24	0	0	.233	.325	.411	.736	102	0	10	4.67	0	/1-8	2	0.0
Total 21	**2360**	**7927**	**1195**	**2232**	**423**	**55**	**475**	**1540**	**937**	**1936**	**17**	**16**	**.282**	**.363**	**.529**	**.892**	**148**	**492**	**1531**	**6.96**	**-48**	***0-1296,1-848**	**370**	**33.3**

• STARK, Dolly Monroe Randolph Stark b: 1/19/1885, Ripley, MS d: 12/1/1924, Memphis, TN BR/TR, 5'9", 160 lbs. Deb: 9/12/1909

YEAR TM-L	G	AB	R	H	2B	3B	HR	RBI	BB	SO	SB	CS	AVG	OBP	SLG	OPS	OPS+	BR/A	RC	RC/G	FR	G/POS	WS	TPW
1909 Cle-A	19	60	4	12	0	0	0	1	6	....	4	....	.200	.273	.200	.473	48	-3	4	2.30	-7	S-19	1	-1.1
1910 Bro-N	30	103	7	17	3	0	0	8	7	19	2	....	.165	.225	.194	.419	23	-10	5	1.46	-1	S-30	1	-1.0
1911 Bro-N	70	193	25	57	4	1	0	19	20	24	6	....	.295	.370	.326	.697	100	1	26	4.70	-5	S-34,2-18/3-3	6	-0.1
1912 Bro-N	8	22	2	4	0	0	0	2	1	3	2	....	.182	.217	.182	.399	10	-3	1	1.78	-1	/S-7	0	-0.4
Total 4	**127**	**378**	**38**	**90**	**7**	**1**	**0**	**30**	**34**	**46**	**14**	**....**	**.238**	**.308**	**.262**	**.570**	**66**	**-15**	**37**	**3.16**	**-14**	**/S-90,2-18,3-3**	**8**	**-2.6**

• STARK, Matt Matthew Scott Stark b: 1/21/1965, Whittier, CA BR/TR, 6'4", 225 lbs. Deb: 4/8/1987

YEAR TM-L	G	AB	R	H	2B	3B	HR	RBI	BB	SO	SB	CS	AVG	OBP	SLG	OPS	OPS+	BR/A	RC	RC/G	FR	G/POS	WS	TPW
1987 Tor-A	5	12	0	1	0	0	0	0	0	0	0	0	.083	.083	.083	.167	-55	-3	0	.00	-0	/C-5	0	-0.2
1990 Chi-A	8	16	0	4	1	0	0	3	1	6	0	0	.250	.294	.313	.607	71	-1	1	1.73	0	/D-6	0	-0.1
Total 2	**13**	**28**	**0**	**5**	**1**	**0**	**0**	**3**	**1**	**6**	**0**	**0**	**.179**	**.207**	**.214**	**.421**	**21**	**-3**	**1**	**.93**	**-0**	**/D-6,C-5**	**0**	**-0.3**

• STARNAGLE, George George Henry Starnagle b: 10/6/1873, Belleville, IL d: 2/15/1946, Belleville, IL BR/TR, 5'11", 175 lbs. Deb: 9/14/1902

YEAR TM-L	G	AB	R	H	2B	3B	HR	RBI	BB	SO	SB	CS	AVG	OBP	SLG	OPS	OPS+	BR/A	RC	RC/G	FR	G/POS	WS	TPW
1902 Cle-A	1	3	0	0	0	0	0	0	0	....	0	....	.000	.000	.000	.000	-104	-1	0	.00	-1	/C-1	0	-0.1

• STARR, Bill William Starr b: 2/26/1911, Brooklyn, NY d: 8/12/1991, La Jolla, CA BR/TR, 6'1", 175 lbs. Deb: 8/23/1935

YEAR TM-L	G	AB	R	H	2B	3B	HR	RBI	BB	SO	SB	CS	AVG	OBP	SLG	OPS	OPS+	BR/A	RC	RC/G	FR	G/POS	WS	TPW
1935 Was-A	12	24	1	5	0	0	0	1	0	1	0	0	.208	.208	.208	.417	8	-3	1	1.39	-0	C-12	0	-0.3
1936 Was-A	1	0	0	0	0	0	0	0	0	0	0	0	....	....	....	....	-106	0	0	....	0	/C-1	0	0.0
Total 2	**13**	**24**	**1**	**5**	**0**	**0**	**0**	**1**	**0**	**1**	**0**	**0**	**.208**	**.208**	**.208**	**.417**	**8**	**-3**	**1**	**1.39**	**0**	**/C-13**	**0**	**-0.3**

• STARR, Charlie Charles Watkin Starr b: 8/30/1878, Pike County, OH d: 10/18/1937, Pasadena, CA TR, 5'10.5", 165 lbs. Deb: 4/29/1905

YEAR TM-L	G	AB	R	H	2B	3B	HR	RBI	BB	SO	SB	CS	AVG	OBP	SLG	OPS	OPS+	BR/A	RC	RC/G	FR	G/POS	WS	TPW
1905 StL-A	26	97	9	20	0	0	0	6	7	....	0	....	.206	.260	.206	.466	51	-5	6	1.94	-2	2-18/3-6	0	-0.7
1908 Pit-N	20	59	8	11	2	0	0	8	13	....	6	....	.186	.342	.220	.563	80	-0	7	3.47	-2	2-12/S-5,3-2	2	-0.2
1909 Bos-N	61	216	16	48	2	3	0	6	31	....	7	....	.222	.333	.259	.593	80	-3	22	3.20	-6	2-54/S-6,3-3	4	-1.0
Phi-N	3	3	0	0	0	0	0	0	0	....	0	....	.000	.000	.000	.000	-99	-1	0	.00	0	....	0	-0.1

YEAR TM-L	G	AB	R	H	2B	3B	HR	RBI	BB	SO	SB	CS	AVG	OBP	SLG	OPS	OPS+	BR/A	RC	RC/G	FR	G/POS	WS	TPW
Yr.	64	219	16	48	2	3	0	6	31	....	7	....	.219	.329	.256	.585	78	-4	22	3.14	-6	2-54/S-6,3-3	4	-1.0
Total 3	110	375	33	79	4	3	0	20	51	....	13	....	.211	.315	.237	.552	72	-9	34	2.88	-10	/2-84,3-11,S-11	6	-2.0
• START, Joe	Joseph "Old Reliable,Rocks" Start b: 10/14/1842, New York, NY d: 3/27/1927, Providence, RI BL/TL, 5'9", 165 lbs. Deb: 5/18/1871 M NA OF: 1-1-2																							
1871 Mut-n	33	161	35	58	5	1	1	34	3	0	4	2	.360	.372	.422	.794	140	9	27	8.24	-2	*1-33	....	0.5
1872 Mut-n	55	282	62	76	4	0	0	50	0	0	3	3	.270	.270	.284	.553	75	-7	23	3.40	-4	*1-55	....	-0.7
1873 Mut-n	53	251	42	67	8	3	1	28	4	0	1	0	.267	.278	.335	.613	82	-5	24	4.02	1	*1-53/O-2(0-0-2)	....	-0.2
1874 Mut-n	63	306	67	96	13	3	2	45	4	0	5	0	.314	.323	.395	.718	125	8	42	5.95	3	*1-63/O-2(1-1-0)	....	1.0
1875 Mut-n	69	314	58	90	10	5	4	30	3	0	1	4	.287	.293	.389	.682	128	6	37	4.79	0	*1-69	....	0.6
1876 NY-N	56	265	40	73	6	0	0	21	1	2	....	....	.275	.279	.299	.578	106	3	23	3.31	0	*1-56	9	0.1
1877 Har-N	60	271	55	90	3	6	1	21	6	2	....	....	.332	.347	.399	.745	150	16	38	5.83	0	*1-60	11	1.1
1878 Chi-N	61	285	58	**100**	12	5	1	27	2	3	....	....	.351	.355	.439	.794	150	14	46	6.77	-2	*1-61	10	0.8
1879 Pro-N	66	317	70	101	11	5	2	37	7	4	....	....	.319	.333	.404	.737	144	15	44	5.67	3	*1-65/O-1	12	1.3
1880 Pro-N	82	345	53	96	14	6	0	27	13	20	....	....	.278	.304	.354	.658	126	10	38	4.20	1	*1-82	12	0.6
1881 Pro-N	79	348	56	114	12	6	0	29	9	7	....	....	.328	.345	.397	.741	134	13	49	5.62	-1	*1-79	16	0.8
1882 Pro-N	82	356	58	117	8	10	0	48	11	7	....	....	.329	.349	.407	.756	142	16	52	5.96	8	*1-82	14	1.5
1883 Pro-N	87	370	63	105	16	7	1	57	22	16	....	....	.284	.324	.373	.697	108	4	46	4.76	0	*1-87	10	-0.4
1884*Pro-N	93	381	80	105	10	5	2	32	35	25	....	....	.276	.337	.344	.680	117	9	45	4.50	1	*1-93	14	0.2
1885 Pro-N	101	374	47	103	11	4	0	41	39	10	....	....	.275	.344	.326	.670	122	12	43	4.28	1	*1-101	15	0.3
1886 Was-N	31	122	10	27	4	1	0	17	5	13	4	....	.221	.252	.270	.522	62	-5	10	2.72	-2	1-31	1	-0.9
Total 5 n	273	1314	264	387	40	12	8	187	14	0	14	9	.295	.302	.361	.663	109	12	153	4.97	-1	1-273/O-4	....	1.1
Total 11	798	3434	590	1031	107	55	7	357	150	109	4	....	.300	.330	.370	.699	127	105	432	4.94	10	1-797/O-1	124	5.5
• STATON, Dave	David Alan Staton b: 4/12/1968, Seattle, WA BR/TR, 6'5", 215 lbs. Deb: 9/8/1993																							
1993 SD-N	17	42	7	11	3	0	5	9	3	12	0	0	.262	.326	.690	1.017	161	3	8	6.95	3	1-12	2	0.5
1994 SD-N	29	66	6	12	2	0	4	6	10	18	0	0	.182	.289	.394	.683	78	-2	7	3.39	3	1-20	0	0.0
Total 2	46	108	13	23	5	0	9	15	13	30	0	0	.213	.303	.509	.813	109	1	16	4.69	7	/1-32	2	0.5
• STATON, Joe	Joseph Staton b: 3/8/1948, Seattle, WA BL/TL, 6'3", 175 lbs. Deb: 9/5/1972																							
1972 Det-A	6	2	1	0	0	0	0	0	0	1	0	1	.000	.000	.000	.000	-97	-1	0	.00	0	/1-2	0	-0.1
1973 Det-A	9	17	2	4	0	0	0	3	0	3	1	0	.235	.235	.235	.471	31	-1	1	2.21	1	/1-5	0	0.0
Total 2	15	19	3	4	0	0	0	3	0	4	1	1	.211	.211	.211	.421	17	-2	1	1.79	1	/1-7	0	-0.2
• STATZ, Jigger	Arnold John Statz b: 10/20/1897, Waukegan, IL d: 3/16/1988, Corona Del Mar, CA BR/TR, 5'7.5", 150 lbs. Deb: 7/30/1919 Career OF: 8-618-12																							
1919 NY-N	21	60	7	18	2	1	0	6	3	8	2	....	.300	.333	.367	.700	111	1	7	4.61	-3	O-18(3-7-8)/2-5	3	-0.4
1920 NY-N	16	30	0	4	0	1	0	5	2	9	0	1	.133	.188	.200	.388	11	-4	1	.97	-3	O-12(0-12-0)	0	-0.8
Bos-A	2	3	0	0	0	0	0	0	0	0	0	0	.000	.000	.000	.000	-104	-1	0	.00	0	/O-2(0-0-2)	0	-0.1
1922 Chi-N	110	462	77	137	19	5	1	34	41	31	16	13	.297	.355	.366	.721	85	-11	60	4.62	2	*O-110(0-110-0)	12	-1.3
1923 Chi-N	154	655	110	209	33	8	10	70	56	42	29	23	.319	.375	.440	.815	114	12	105	5.83	12	*O-154(0-154-0)	26	1.7
1924 Chi-N	135	549	69	152	22	5	3	49	37	50	13	9	.277	.325	.352	.676	80	-14	63	3.98	9	*O-131(0-131-0)/2-1	16	-1.0
1925 Chi-N	38	148	21	38	6	3	2	14	11	16	4	0	.257	.317	.378	.695	76	-4	19	4.32	1	O-37(0-37-0)	3	-0.5
1927 Bro-N	130	507	64	139	24	7	1	21	26	43	10	....	.274	.310	.355	.665	77	-17	54	3.69	10	*O-122(3-118-1)/2-1	12	-1.3
1928 Bro-N	77	171	28	40	8	1	0	16	18	12	3	....	.234	.311	.292	.603	59	-10	16	3.03	-3	O-52(2-49-1)/2-1	2	-1.4
Total 8	683	2585	376	737	114	31	17	215	194	211	77	46	.285	.337	.373	.710	87	-49	325	4.40	24	O-638/2-8	74	-5.1
• STAUB, Rusty	Daniel Joseph "Le Grand Orange" Staub b: 4/1/1944, New Orleans, LA BL/TR, 6'2", 200 lbs. Deb: 4/9/1963 C Career OF: 75-11-1604																							
1963 Hou-N	150	513	43	115	17	4	6	45	59	58	0	0	.224	.310	.308	.618	84	-8	51	3.31	2	*1-109,O-49(0-1-48)	12	-1.7
1964 Hou-N	89	292	26	63	10	2	8	35	21	31	1	1	.216	.275	.346	.621	78	-9	27	3.06	-1	1-49,O-38(0-7-31)	5	-1.6
1965 Hou-N	131	410	43	105	20	1	14	63	52	57	3	0	.256	.343	.412	.755	120	12	56	4.64	-2	*O-112(1-2-110)/1-1	13	0.2
1966 Hou-N	153	554	60	155	28	3	13	81	58	61	2	1	.280	.349	.412	.761	118	15	79	5.00	-1	*O-148(55-1-105)/1-1	18	0.4
1967 Hou-N★	149	546	71	182	**44**	1	10	74	60	47	0	4	.333	.402	.473	.875	155	39	100	6.84	-4	*O-144(0-0-144)	28	2.6
1968 Hou-N★	161	591	54	172	37	1	6	72	73	57	2	0	.291	.376	.387	.763	132	27	88	5.42	0	*1-147,O-15(0-0-15)	28	2.0
1969 Mon-N★	158	549	89	166	26	5	29	79	110	61	3	4	.302	.427	.526	.953	165	53	128	8.53	2	*O-156(0-0-156)	27	4.9
1970 Mon-N★	160	569	98	156	23	7	30	94	112	93	12	11	.274	.396	.497	.894	138	32	117	7.10	6	*O-160(0-0-160)	30	3.0
1971 Mon-N★	162	599	94	186	34	6	19	97	74	42	9	5	.311	.394	.482	.877	146	39	111	6.72	2	*O-162(1-0-162)	32	3.5
1972 NY-N	66	239	32	70	11	0	9	38	31	13	0	1	.293	.379	.452	.831	139	12	41	6.14	-2	O-65(0-0-65)	12	0.7
1973*NY-N	152	585	77	163	36	1	15	76	74	52	1	1	.279	.363	.421	.783	118	16	89	5.43	8	*O-152(0-0-152)	23	1.7
1974 NY-N	151	561	65	145	22	2	19	78	77	39	2	1	.258	.351	.406	.757	113	11	78	4.75	6	*O-147(0-0-147)	17	0.9
1975 NY-N	155	574	93	162	30	4	19	105	77	55	2	0	.282	.376	.448	.823	134	28	97	5.94	0	*O-153(0-0-153)	25	2.1
1976 Det-A★	161	589	73	176	28	3	15	96	83	49	3	1	.299	.392	.433	.825	136	31	99	5.98	-4	*O-126(0-0-126),D-36	26	2.0
1977 Det-A	158	623	84	173	34	3	22	101	59	47	1	1	.278	.341	.448	.789	107	7	89	4.88	0	*D-156	12	0.1
1978 Det-A	162	642	75	175	30	1	24	121	76	35	3	1	.273	.352	.435	.787	117	16	96	5.11	0	*D-162	16	1.0
1979 Det-A	68	246	32	58	12	1	9	40	32	18	1	0	.236	.336	.402	.738	95	-1	33	4.45	0	D-66	5	-0.3
Mon-N	38	86	9	23	3	0	3	14	14	10	0	0	.267	.370	.407	.777	113	2	13	5.21	-1	1-22/O-1	3	0.0
1980 Tex-A	109	340	42	102	23	2	9	55	39	18	1	1	.300	.375	.459	.834	131	15	55	5.69	-2	D-57,1-30,O-14(3-0-11)	10	0.9
1981 NY-N	70	161	9	51	9	0	5	21	22	12	1	0	.317	.402	.466	.868	148	11	30	6.84	-2	1-41	6	0.7
1982 NY-N	112	219	11	53	9	0	3	27	24	10	0	0	.242	.317	.324	.641	80	-5	22	3.19	2	O-27(12-0-15),1-18	3	-0.6
1983 NY-N	104	115	5	34	6	0	3	28	14	10	0	0	.296	.377	.426	.803	123	4	18	5.62	0	/1-5,O-5(3-0-2)	4	0.4
1984 NY-N	78	72	2	19	4	0	1	18	4	9	0	0	.264	.303	.361	.664	87	-1	8	3.67	0	/1-3	1	-0.2
1985 NY-N	54	45	2	12	3	0	1	8	10	4	0	0	.267	.400	.400	.800	128	2	8	6.01	-0	/O-1	2	0.2
Total 23	2951	9720	1189	2716	499	47	292	1466	1255	888	47	33	.279	.366	.431	.797	125	345	1534	5.52	8	*O-1675,D-477,1-426	358	22.8
• STEARNS, Ecky	Daniel Eckford Stearns b: 10/17/1861, Buffalo, NY d: 6/28/1944, Glendale, CA BL/TR, 6'1", 185 lbs. Deb: 8/17/1880 U Career OF: 7-3-28																							
1880 Buf-N	28	104	8	19	6	1	0	13	3	23	....	....	.183	.206	.260	.465	55	-5	6	1.84	-5	O-20(6-1-15)/C-8,3-5,S-1	0	-0.9
1881 Det-N	3	11	1	1	1	0	0	0	0	2	....	....	.091	.091	.182	.273	-16	-1	0	.50	-1	/S-3	0	-0.2
1882 Cin-a	49	214	28	55	10	2	0	35	6	....	....	....	.257	.277	.322	.600	96	-1	20	3.45	-4	1-35,O-12(0-0-12)/2-2,S-1	5	-0.8
1883 Bal-a	93	382	54	94	10	9	1	0	**34**	....	....	....	.246	.308	.327	.635	101	1	39	3.83	2	*1-92/O-1	6	-0.4
1884 Bal-a	100	396	61	94	12	3	3	0	28	....	....	....	.237	.298	.306	.603	93	-2	37	3.36	-1	*1-100/2-1	11	-1.1
1885 Bal-a	67	253	40	47	3	8	1	29	38	....	....	....	.186	.306	.273	.579	85	-2	22	2.84	-2	1-63/O-3(0-2-1),C-2	6	-0.9
Buf-N	30	105	7	21	6	1	0	9	8	23	....	....	.200	.257	.276	.533	70	-3	8	2.45	-7	S-19,1-12/C-2	1	-1.0
1889 KC-a	139	560	96	160	24	12	3	87	56	69	67	....	.286	.351	.388	.738	104	1	102	6.76	3	*1-135/3-4	16	-0.6
Total 7	509	2025	295	491	72	36	8	173	173	117	67	....	.242	.306	.325	.631	93	-13	233	4.12	-15	1-437/O-36,S-24,C-12,3-9,2	45	-5.9
• STEARNS, John	John Hardin "Bad Dude" Stearns b: 8/21/1951, Denver, CO BR/TR, 6', 185 lbs. Deb: 9/22/1974 C																							
1974 Phi-N	1	2	0	1	0	0	0	0	0	0	0	0	.500	.500	.500	1.000	173	0	1	13.50	0	/C-1	0	0.0
1975 NY-N	59	169	25	32	5	1	3	10	17	15	4	1	.189	.271	.284	.555	57	-10	13	2.34	6	C-54	4	-0.1
1976 NY-N	32	103	13	27	6	0	2	10	16	11	1	2	.262	.367	.379	.745	119	2	14	4.54	1	C-30	4	0.5
1977 NY-N★	139	431	52	108	25	1	12	55	77	76	9	8	.251	.373	.397	.770	112	9	64	4.96	0	*C-127/1-6	15	1.5
1978 NY-N	143	477	65	126	24	1	15	73	70	57	25	13	.264	.368	.413	.781	122	16	75	5.26	8	*C-141/3-1	22	3.2
1979 NY-N★	155	538	58	131	29	2	9	66	52	57	15	15	.243	.315	.355	.670	85	-14	54	3.25	10	*C-121,1-16,3-11/O-6(6-0-0)	11	0.0
1980 NY-N★	91	319	42	91	25	1	0	45	33	24	7	3	.285	.354	.370	.724	105	3	44	4.79	5	C-74,1-16/3-1	12	1.1
1981 NY-N	80	273	25	74	12	1	1	24	24	17	12	2	.271	.330	.333	.663	90	-2	30	3.72	3	C-66/1-9,3-4	6	0.4
1982 NY-N★	98	352	46	103	25	3	4	28	30	35	17	7	.293	.352	.415	.766	114	7	51	5.07	3	C-81,3-12	14	1.5
1983 NY-N	4	0	2	0	0	0	0	0	0	0	0	0	....	....	....	....	-101	0	0	....	0	....	0	0.0
1984 NY-N	8	17	6	3	1	0	0	1	4	2	1	0	.176	.333	.235	.569	63	-0	2	3.57	0	/C-4,1-2	1	0.0
Total 11	810	2681	334	696	152	10	46	312	323	294	91	51	.260	.345	.375	.720	102	12	347	4.32	36	C-699/1-49,3-29,O-6	89	8.2
• STEDRONSKY, John	John Stedronsky b: Cleveland, OH Deb: 9/26/1879																							
1879 Chi-N	4	12	0	1	0	0	0	0	0	3	....	....	.083	.083	.083	.167	-42	-2	0	.22	0	/3-4	0	-0.1

YEAR TM-L	G	AB	R	H	2B	3B	HR	RBI	BB	SO	SB	CS	AVG	OBP	SLG	OPS	OPS+	BR/A	RC	RC/G	FR	G/POS	WS	TPW
• STEELMAN, Farmer	Morris James Steelman b: 6/29/1875, Millville, NJ d: 9/16/1944, Merchantville, NJ TR Deb: 9/15/1899 Career OF: 0-0-17																							
1899 Lou-N	4	15	2	1	0	1	0	2	2	....	0	....	.067	.176	.200	.376	3	-2	1	1.13	-1	/C-4	0	-0.2
1900 Bro-N	1	4	0	0	0	0	0	0	0	....	0	....	.000	.000	.000	.000	-94	-1	0	.00	0	/C-1	0	-0.1
1901 Bro-N	1	3	0	1	0	0	0	0	0	....	0	....	.333	.333	.333	.667	91	-0	0	4.53	0	/C-1	0	0.0
Phi-A	27	88	5	23	2	0	0	7	10	....	4	....	.261	.350	.284	.634	74	-3	11	4.23	4	C-14,O-12(0-0-12)	2	0.2
1902 Phi-A	10	32	1	6	1	0	0	6	2	....	2	....	.188	.235	.219	.454	25	-3	2	2.24	1	/C-5,O-5(0-0-5)	1	-0.2
Total 4	**43**	**142**	**8**	**31**	**3**	**1**	**0**	**15**	**14**	**....**	**6**	**....**	**.218**	**.297**	**.254**	**.551**	**52**	**-9**	**14**	**3.23**	**4**	**/C-25,O-17**	**3**	**-0.3**
• STEELS, Jim	James Earl Steels b: 5/30/1961, Jackson, MS BL/TL, 5'10", 185 lbs. Deb: 4/6/1987 Career OF: 26-7-15																							
1987 SD-N	62	68	9	13	1	1	0	6	11	14	3	2	.191	.304	.235	.539	47	-5	5	2.35	0	O-28(17-6-7)	0	-0.6
1988 Tex-A	36	53	4	10	1	0	0	5	0	15	2	0	.189	.189	.208	.396	11	-6	2	1.43	-0	O-17(9-1-7)/1-7,D-7	0	-0.7
1989 SF-N	13	12	0	1	0	0	0	0	2	4	0	0	.083	.214	.083	.298	-12	-2	0	.66	0	/1-3,O-1	0	-0.2
Total 3	**111**	**133**	**13**	**24**	**2**	**1**	**0**	**11**	**13**	**33**	**5**	**2**	**.180**	**.253**	**.211**	**.464**	**28**	**-13**	**8**	**1.84**	**0**	**/O-46,1-10,D-7**	**0**	**-1.4**
• STEERE, Gene	Frederick Eugene Steere b: 8/16/1872, South Scituate, RI d: 3/13/1942, San Mateo, CA Deb: 8/29/1894																							
1894 Pit-N	10	39	3	8	0	0	0	4	2	1	2	....	.205	.244	.205	.449	9	-6	3	2.10	-1	S-10	0	-0.5
• STEFERO, John	John Robert Stefero b: 9/22/1959, Sumter, SC BL/TR, 5'8", 185 lbs. Deb: 6/24/1983																							
1983 Bal-A	9	11	2	5	1	0	0	4	3	2	0	0	.455	.571	.545	1.117	213	2	4	17.43	-1	/C-9	1	0.2
1986 Bal-A	52	120	14	28	2	0	2	13	16	25	0	1	.233	.324	.300	.624	72	-5	12	3.54	0	C-50/2-1	3	-0.3
1987 Mon-N	18	56	4	11	0	0	1	3	3	17	0	0	.196	.237	.250	.487	28	-6	3	1.70	0	C-17	0	-0.5
Total 3	**79**	**187**	**20**	**44**	**3**	**0**	**3**	**20**	**22**	**44**	**0**	**1**	**.235**	**.316**	**.299**	**.615**	**69**	**-8**	**19**	**3.52**	**-1**	**/C-76,2-1**	**4**	**-0.6**
• STEGMAN, Dave	David William Stegman b: 1/30/1954, Inglewood, CA BR/TR, 5'11", 190 lbs. Deb: 9/4/1978 Career OF: 30-89-40																							
1978 Det-A	8	14	3	4	2	0	1	3	1	2	0	0	.286	.333	.643	.976	164	1	2	5.03	0	/O-7(0-5-3)	1	0.0
1979 Det-A	12	31	6	6	0	0	3	5	2	3	1	1	.194	.242	.484	.726	88	-1	3	3.53	0	O-12(0-11-1)	1	-0.1
1980 Det-A	65	130	12	23	5	0	2	9	14	23	1	1	.177	.257	.262	.518	41	-11	10	2.37	-2	O-57(14-27-23)/D-2	1	-1.4
1982 NY-A	2	0	0	0	0	0	0	0	0	0	0	0	....	....	....	....	-102	0	0	....	0	/D-1	0	0.0
1983 Chi-A	30	53	5	9	2	0	0	4	10	9	0	1	.170	.302	.208	.509	42	-4	4	2.15	0	O-29(5-19-5)	0	-0.4
1984 Chi-A	55	92	13	24	1	2	2	11	4	18	3	0	.261	.306	.380	.687	85	-1	11	4.37	0	O-46(11-27-8)/D-3	2	-0.3
Total 6	**172**	**320**	**39**	**66**	**10**	**2**	**8**	**32**	**31**	**55**	**5**	**3**	**.206**	**.280**	**.325**	**.605**	**63**	**-16**	**31**	**3.09**	**-3**	**O-151/D-6**	**5**	**-2.2**
• STEIN, Bill	William Allen Stein b: 1/21/1947, Battle Creek, MI BR/TR, 5'10", 170 lbs. Deb: 9/6/1972 Career OF: 15-0-14																							
1972 StL-N	14	35	2	11	0	1	2	3	0	7	1	0	.314	.314	.543	.857	141	2	6	6.10	0	/3-4,O-4(4-0-1)	1	0.2
1973 StL-N	32	55	4	12	2	0	0	2	7	18	0	0	.218	.306	.255	.561	57	-3	5	3.04	-1	O-10(2-0-8)/1-2,3-1	1	-0.5
1974 Chi-A	13	43	5	12	1	0	0	5	7	8	0	0	.279	.380	.302	.682	96	0	5	3.59	-2	3-11/D-2	1	-0.2
1975 Chi-A	76	226	23	61	7	1	3	21	18	32	2	2	.270	.327	.350	.676	90	-3	25	3.87	-5	2-28,3-24,D-18/O-1	4	-0.7
1976 Chi-A	117	392	32	105	15	2	4	36	22	67	4	2	.268	.310	.347	.657	92	-5	41	3.69	-4	2-58,3-58/1-1,D-1,O-1,S-1	8	-0.6
1977 Sea-A	151	556	53	144	26	5	13	67	29	79	3	4	.259	.302	.394	.696	89	-11	62	3.83	-14	*3-147/D-3,S-2	11	-2.6
1978 Sea-A	114	403	41	105	24	4	4	37	37	56	1	0	.261	.323	.370	.692	95	-2	48	4.08	-12	*3-111/D-1	9	-1.6
1979 Sea-A	88	250	28	62	9	2	7	27	17	28	1	2	.248	.301	.384	.685	82	-7	26	3.35	-2	3-67,2-17/S-3	4	-0.9
1980 Sea-A	67	198	16	53	5	1	5	27	16	25	1	1	.268	.326	.379	.704	91	-3	24	4.01	-1	3-34,2-14/1-8,D-5	5	-0.4
1981 Tex-A	53	115	21	38	6	0	2	22	7	15	1	2	.330	.369	.435	.804	138	5	16	4.96	-1	1-20/O-8(7-0-1),3-7,2-3,S	4	0.3
1982 Tex-A	85	184	14	44	8	0	1	16	12	23	0	0	.239	.293	.299	.592	66	-8	16	2.98	0	2-34,3-28/S-6,D-3,1-2,O-1	3	-0.7
1983 Tex-A	78	232	21	72	15	1	2	33	8	31	2	3	.310	.333	.409	.743	105	0	30	4.69	0	2-32,1-23,3-10/D-6	6	0.0
1984 Tex-A	27	43	3	12	1	0	0	3	5	9	0	0	.279	.354	.302	.656	81	-1	5	3.88	-2	2-11/D-4,1-3,3-3	1	-0.3
1985 Tex-A	44	79	5	20	3	1	1	12	1	15	0	0	.253	.272	.354	.626	69	-4	7	3.09	-0	3-11/1-8,D-6,2-3,O-3(0-0-3)	1	-0.4
Total 14	**959**	**2811**	**268**	**751**	**122**	**18**	**44**	**311**	**186**	**413**	**16**	**16**	**.267**	**.316**	**.370**	**.686**	**91**	**-40**	**316**	**3.86**	**-42**	**3-516,2-200/1-67,D-49,O-28,S**	**59**	**-8.3**
• STEIN, Justin	Justin Marion "Ott" Stein b: 8/9/1911, St. Louis, MO d: 5/1/1992, Creve Coeur, MO BR/TR, 5'11", 180 lbs. Deb: 5/28/1938																							
1938 Phi-N	11	39	6	10	0	1	0	2	2	4	0	....	.256	.293	.308	.600	65	-2	4	3.49	0	/3-7,2-3	1	-0.2
Cin-N	11	18	3	6	1	0	0	1	0	1	0	....	.333	.333	.389	.722	101	-0	2	3.91	-1	/S-7,2-2	0	0.0
Yr.	22	57	9	16	1	1	0	3	2	5	0	....	.281	.305	.333	.638	76	-2	6	3.63	-1	/3-7,S-7,2-5	1	-0.2
• STEINBACH, Terry	Terry Lee Steinbach b: 3/2/1962, New Ulm, MN BR/TR, 6'1", 195 lbs. Deb: 9/12/1986 Career OF: 7-0-8																							
1986 Oak-A	6	15	3	5	0	0	2	4	1	0	0	0	.333	.375	.733	1.108	208	2	4	11.40	0	/C-5	1	0.2
1987 Oak-A	122	391	66	111	16	3	16	56	32	66	1	2	.284	.352	.463	.815	122	11	62	5.64	-4	*C-107,3-10/D-8,1-1	15	1.1
1988*Oak-A★	104	351	42	93	19	1	9	51	33	47	3	0	.265	.338	.402	.740	110	6	47	4.52	0	C-84/3-9,1-8,D-7,O-1	13	1.0
1989*Oak-A★	130	454	37	124	13	1	7	42	30	66	1	2	.273	.321	.352	.673	93	-6	49	3.75	-5	*C-103,O-14(6-0-8),1-10/D-4,3	13	-0.5
1990*Oak-A	114	379	32	95	15	2	9	57	19	66	0	1	.251	.294	.372	.666	88	-8	39	3.46	-3	C-83,D-25/1-3	11	-0.7
1991 Oak-A	129	456	50	125	31	1	6	67	22	70	2	2	.274	.318	.386	.703	99	-2	52	3.95	-3	*C-117/1-9,D-2	13	0.1
1992*Oak-A	128	438	48	122	20	1	12	53	45	58	2	3	.279	.347	.411	.758	118	9	58	4.55	5	*C-124/1-5,D-2	20	2.1
1993 Oak-A★	104	389	47	111	19	1	10	43	25	65	3	3	.285	.333	.416	.750	107	2	50	4.61	1	C-86,1-15/D-6	9	0.6
1994 Oak-A	103	369	51	105	21	2	11	57	26	62	2	1	.285	.332	.442	.773	106	2	52	4.96	6	C-93/1-6,D-6	15	1.3
1995 Oak-A	114	406	43	113	26	1	15	65	25	74	1	3	.278	.325	.458	.783	108	1	55	4.68	4	*C-111/1-2	16	1.2
1996 Oak-A	145	514	79	140	25	1	35	100	49	115	0	1	.272	.343	.529	.872	119	12	89	6.13	-4	*C-137/D-4,1-1	18	1.6
1997 Min-A	122	447	60	111	27	1	12	54	35	106	6	1	.248	.304	.394	.698	79	-14	52	3.92	-2	*C-116/1-2,D-1	7	-0.8
1998 Min-A	124	422	45	102	25	2	14	54	38	89	0	1	.242	.310	.410	.720	84	-11	50	4.02	-3	*C-119/D-3	10	-0.6
1999 Min-A	101	338	35	96	16	4	4	42	38	54	2	2	.284	.360	.391	.750	88	-6	47	5.02	-6	C-96/D-1	12	-0.5
Total 14	**1546**	**5369**	**638**	**1453**	**273**	**21**	**162**	**745**	**418**	**938**	**23**	**22**	**.271**	**.329**	**.420**	**.749**	**102**	**-0**	**706**	**4.57**	**-15**	***C-1381/D-69,1-62,3-22,O-15**	**173**	**6.3**
• STEINBACHER, Hank	Henry John Steinbacher b: 3/22/1913, Sacramento, CA d: 4/3/1977, Sacramento, CA BL/TR, 5'11", 180 lbs. Deb: 4/21/1937 Career OF: 16-8-114																							
1937 Chi-A	26	73	13	19	4	1	1	9	4	7	2	0	.260	.299	.384	.682	71	-3	9	4.23	-1	O-15(15-0-0)	1	-0.4
1938 Chi-A	106	399	59	132	23	8	4	61	41	19	1	3	.331	.393	.459	.852	110	6	72	6.98	-3	*O-101(0-8-93)	12	-0.3
1939 Chi-A	71	111	16	19	2	1	1	15	21	8	0	0	.171	.303	.234	.537	38	-10	9	2.69	-1	O-22(1-0-21)	1	-1.1
Total 3	**203**	**583**	**88**	**170**	**29**	**10**	**6**	**85**	**66**	**34**	**3**	**3**	**.292**	**.364**	**.407**	**.770**	**91**	**-8**	**90**	**5.67**	**-4**	**O-138**	**14**	**-1.8**
• STEINBRENNER, Gene	Eugene Gass Steinbrenner b: 11/17/1892, Pittsburgh, PA d: 4/25/1970, Pittsburgh, PA BR/TR, 5'8.5", 155 lbs. Deb: 4/25/1912																							
1912 Phi-N	3	9	0	2	1	0	0	1	0	3	0	....	.222	.222	.333	.556	48	-1	1	2.27	0	/2-3	0	-0.1
• STEINECKE, Bill	William Robert Steinecke b: 2/7/1907, Cincinnati, OH d: 7/20/1986, St. Augustine, FL BR/TR, 5'8.5", 175 lbs. Deb: 9/16/1931																							
1931 Pit-N	4	4	0	0	0	0	0	0	0	1	0	....	.000	.000	.000	.000	-101	-1	0	.00	0	/C-1	0	-0.1
• STEINER, Ben	Benjamin Saunders Steiner b: 7/28/1921, Alexandria, VA d: 10/27/1988, Venice, FL BL/TR, 5'11", 165 lbs. Deb: 4/17/1945																							
1945 Bos-A	78	304	39	78	8	3	3	20	31	29	10	6	.257	.327	.332	.660	89	-4	35	3.90	-6	2-77	7	-0.6
1946 Bos-A	3	4	1	1	0	0	0	0	0	0	0	0	.250	.250	.250	.500	38	-0	0	2.31	0	/3-1	0	-0.1
1947 Det-A	1	0	1	0	0	0	0	0	0	0	0	0	....	....	....	....	-97	0	0	....	0		0	0.0
Total 3	**82**	**308**	**41**	**79**	**8**	**3**	**3**	**20**	**31**	**29**	**10**	**6**	**.256**	**.326**	**.331**	**.658**	**89**	**-4**	**35**	**3.88**	**-6**	**/2-77,3-1**	**7**	**-0.7**
• STEINER, Red	James Harry Steiner b: 1/7/1915, Los Angeles, CA d: 11/16/2001, Gardena, CA BL/TR, 6', 185 lbs. Deb: 5/11/1945																							
1945 Cle-A	12	20	0	3	0	0	0	2	1	4	0	0	.150	.190	.150	.340	-1	-3	0	.71	1	/C-4	0	-0.2
Bos-A	26	59	6	12	1	0	0	4	14	2	0	0	.203	.356	.220	.577	67	-1	6	3.05	0	C-24	2	0.0
Yr.	38	79	6	15	1	0	0	6	15	6	0	0	.190	.319	.203	.522	52	-4	6	2.44	1	C-28	2	-0.2
• STEINFELDT, Harry	Harry M. Steinfeldt b: 9/29/1877, St. Louis, MO d: 8/17/1914, Bellevue, KY BR/TR, 5'9.5", 180 lbs. Deb: 4/22/1898 U Career OF: 15-16-4																							
1898 Cin-N	88	308	47	91	18	6	0	43	27	....	9	....	.295	.354	.393	.747	107	2	49	5.55	-6	2-31,O-29(14-15-0),3-22/S-5,1	10	-0.4
1899 Cin-N	108	390	63	96	16	8	0	43	40	....	19	....	.246	.326	.328	.654	77	-12	49	4.35	-2	3-59,2-40/S-8,O-2(0-1-1)	9	-1.0
1900 Cin-N	134	510	57	125	29	7	2	66	27	....	14	....	.245	.292	.341	.633	76	-18	58	3.83	26	3-67,2-64/O-2(0-0-2),S-2	11	1.2
1901 Cin-N	105	382	40	95	18	7	6	47	28	....	10	....	.249	.303	.380	.683	104	1	49	4.40	5	3-55,2-50	11	0.8
1902 Cin-N	129	479	53	133	20	7	1	49	24	....	12	....	.278	.316	.355	.671	98	-3	60	4.48	21	*3-129/O-1	14	2.3
1903 Cin-N	118	439	71	137	**32**	12	6	83	47	....	6	....	.312	.386	.481	.867	132	18	87	7.35	11	*3-104,S-14	21	3.1

YEAR TM-L	G	AB	R	H	2B	3B	HR	RBI	BB	SO	SB	CS	AVG	OBP	SLG	OPS	OPS+	BR/A	RC	RC/G	FR	G/POS	WS	TPW
1904 Cin-N	99	349	35	85	11	6	1	52	29	....	16	....	.244	.313	.318	.631	87	-5	42	3.97	-5	3-98	9	-0.8
1905 Cin-N	114	384	49	104	16	9	1	39	30	....	15	....	.271	.329	.367	.696	97	-2	54	4.80	5	*3-103/1-1,2-1,0-1	13	0.6
1906*Chi-N	151	539	81	**176**	27	10	3	**83**	47	....	29	....	.327	.395	.430	.825	149	31	109	7.27	-9	*3-150/2-1	33	2.9
1907*Chi-N	152	542	52	144	25	5	1	70	37	....	19	....	.266	.323	.336	.659	100	-0	70	4.28	-6	*3-151	20	-0.2
1908*Chi-N	150	539	63	130	20	6	1	62	36	....	12	....	.241	.294	.306	.600	88	-8	54	3.16	-10	*3-150	16	-1.5
1909 Chi-N	151	528	73	133	27	6	2	59	57	....	22	....	.252	.331	.337	.668	105	4	68	4.14	5	*3-151	25	1.4
1910*Chi-N	129	448	70	113	21	1	2	58	36	29	10	....	.252	.323	.317	.640	88	-7	51	3.65	3	*3-128	15	-0.1
1911 Bos-N	19	63	5	16	4	0	1	8	6	3	1	....	.254	.338	.365	.703	89	-1	8	4.36	-7	3-19	1	-0.8
Total 14	1647	5900	759	1578	284	90	27	762	471	32	194	....	.267	.330	.360	.690	101	-0	809	4.64	33	*3-1386,2-187/0-35,S-29,1-5	208	7.8

• STELLBAUER, Bill William Jennings Stellbauer b: 3/20/1894, Bremond, TX d: 2/16/1974, New Braunfels, TX BR/TR, 5'10", 175 lbs. Deb: 4/12/1916

YEAR TM-L	G	AB	R	H	2B	3B	HR	RBI	BB	SO	SB	CS	AVG	OBP	SLG	OPS	OPS+	BR/A	RC	RC/G	FR	G/POS	WS	TPW
1916 Phi-A	25	48	2	13	2	1	0	5	6	7	2	....	.271	.352	.354	.706	118	1	7	4.83	-3	0-14(14-0-0)	1	-0.3

• STELMASZEK, Rick Richard Francis Stelmaszek b: 10/8/1948, Chicago, IL BL/TR, 6'1", 195 lbs. Deb: 6/25/1971 C

YEAR TM-L	G	AB	R	H	2B	3B	HR	RBI	BB	SO	SB	CS	AVG	OBP	SLG	OPS	OPS+	BR/A	RC	RC/G	FR	G/POS	WS	TPW
1971 Was-A	6	9	0	0	0	0	0	0	0	3	0	0	.000	.000	.000	.000	-106	-2	0	.00	-0	/C-3	0	-0.3
1973 Tex-A	7	9	0	1	0	0	0	0	1	2	0	0	.111	.200	.111	.311	-11	-1	0	.85	0	/C-7	0	-0.1
Cal-A	22	26	2	4	1	0	0	3	6	7	0	0	.154	.313	.192	.505	49	-1	2	2.17	0	C-22	0	-0.1
Yr.	29	35	2	5	1	0	0	3	7	9	0	0	.143	.286	.171	.457	35	-3	2	1.84	0	C-29	0	-0.2
1974 Chi-N	25	44	2	10	2	0	1	7	10	6	0	0	.227	.370	.341	.711	96	0	6	4.26	-1	C-16	1	0.0
Total 3	60	88	4	15	3	0	1	10	17	18	0	0	.170	.305	.239	.543	55	-5	8	2.79	-1	/C-48	1	-0.5

• STEM, Fred Frederick Boothe Stem b: 9/22/1885, Oxford, NC d: 9/5/1964, Darlington, SC BL/TR, 6'2", 160 lbs. Deb: 9/15/1908

YEAR TM-L	G	AB	R	H	2B	3B	HR	RBI	BB	SO	SB	CS	AVG	OBP	SLG	OPS	OPS+	BR/A	RC	RC/G	FR	G/POS	WS	TPW
1908 Bos-N	20	72	9	20	0	1	0	3	2	....	1	....	.278	.297	.306	.603	94	-1	7	3.27	-2	1-19	1	-0.4
1909 Bos-N	73	245	13	51	2	3	0	11	12	....	5	....	.208	.254	.241	.495	51	-14	17	2.12	8	1-68	1	-0.9
Total 2	93	317	22	71	2	4	0	14	14	....	6	....	.224	.263	.256	.519	61	-15	24	2.35	5	/1-87	2	-1.3

• STENGEL, Casey Charles Dillon "The Old Perfessor" Stengel
b: 7/30/1890, Kansas City, MO d: 9/29/1975, Glendale, CA BL/TL, 5'11", 175 lbs. Deb: 9/17/1912 M/C HOF: 1966 Career OF: 8-275-901

YEAR TM-L	G	AB	R	H	2B	3B	HR	RBI	BB	SO	SB	CS	AVG	OBP	SLG	OPS	OPS+	BR/A	RC	RC/G	FR	G/POS	WS	TPW
1912 Bro-N	17	57	9	18	1	0	1	13	15	9	5	....	.316	.466	.386	.852	140	5	13	8.05	-3	0-17(0-17-0)	3	0.1
1913 Bro-N	124	438	60	119	16	8	7	43	56	58	19	....	.272	.356	.393	.748	111	7	65	5.06	-7	*0-119(0-117-2)	13	-0.7
1914 Bro-N	126	412	55	130	13	10	4	60	56	55	19	....	.316	**.404**	.425	.829	143	24	76	6.73	-8	*0-121(0-2-119)	20	1.1
1915 Bro-N	132	459	52	109	20	12	3	50	34	46	5	10	.237	.294	.353	.647	94	-8	48	3.37	-3	*0-129(1-0-128)	14	-1.9
1916*Bro-N	127	462	66	129	27	8	8	53	33	51	11	....	.279	.329	.424	.753	127	13	70	5.20	4	*0-121(0-0-121)	19	1.3
1917 Bro-N	150	549	69	141	23	12	6	73	60	62	18	....	.257	.336	.375	.711	115	11	72	4.47	10	*0-150(0-1-149)	20	1.5
1918 Pit-N	39	122	18	30	4	1	1	12	16	14	11	....	.246	.343	.320	.663	99	1	16	4.44	2	0-37(0-0-37)	4	0.1
1919 Pit-N	89	321	38	94	10	10	4	43	35	35	12	....	.293	.364	.424	.788	131	13	53	5.69	-4	0-87(0-0-87)	15	0.4
1920 Phi-N	129	445	53	130	25	6	9	50	38	35	7	13	.292	.356	.436	.792	121	10	66	5.13	-1	*0-118(1-5-113)	13	0.4
1921 Phi-N	24	59	7	18	3	1	0	4	6	7	1	1	.305	.369	.390	.759	94	-0	9	5.27	2	0-15(0-0-15)	1	0.1
NY-N	18	22	4	5	1	0	0	2	1	5	0	1	.227	.261	.273	.534	41	-2	1	1.92	-1	/0-8(0-2-6)	0	-0.3
Yr.	42	81	11	23	4	1	0	6	7	12	1	2	.284	.341	.358	.699	80	-3	10	4.29	2	0-23(0-2-21)	1	-0.2
1922*NY-N	84	250	48	92	8	10	7	48	21	17	4	2	.368	.436	.564	1.000	155	22	62	10.08	-1	0-77(0-75-2)	14	1.7
1923*NY-N	75	218	39	74	11	5	5	43	20	18	6	2	.339	.400	.505	.905	139	13	45	7.79	-4	0-57(6-51-0)	11	0.7
1924 Bos-N	131	461	57	129	20	6	5	39	45	39	13	13	.280	.348	.382	.730	100	-1	61	4.54	-9	*0-126(0-5-121)	12	-1.9
1925 Bos-N	12	13	0	1	0	0	0	2	1	2	0	1	.077	.143	.077	.220	-46	-3	0	.21	-0	/0-1	0	-0.3
Total 14	1277	4288	575	1219	182	89	60	535	437	453	131	43	.284	.356	.410	.766	119	104	654	5.32	-21	*0-1183	159	2.1

• STENHOUSE, Mike Michael Steven Stenhouse b: 5/29/1958, Pueblo, CO BL/TR, 6'1", 195 lbs. Deb: 10/3/1982 Career OF: 43-0-37

YEAR TM-L	G	AB	R	H	2B	3B	HR	RBI	BB	SO	SB	CS	AVG	OBP	SLG	OPS	OPS+	BR/A	RC	RC/G	FR	G/POS	WS	TPW
1982 Mon-N	1	1	0	0	0	0	0	0	0	1	0	0	.000	.000	.000	.000	-98	-0	0	.00	0	....	0	0.0
1983 Mon-N	24	40	2	5	1	0	0	2	4	10	0	0	.125	.205	.150	.355		-5	1	.82	0	/0-9(3-0-7),1-5	0	-0.6
1984 Mon-N	80	175	14	32	8	0	4	16	26	32	0	0	.183	.292	.297	.589	69	-7	16	2.80	0	0-48(30-0-19),1-14	2	-0.9
1985 Min-A	81	179	23	40	5	0	5	21	29	18	1	0	.223	.332	.335	.667	79	-4	22	4.07	1	D-27,0-16(8-0-9)/1-8	3	-0.5
1986 Bos-A	21	21	1	2	1	0	0	1	12	5	0	0	.095	.424	.143	.567	63	-0	3	3.26	0	/0-4(2-0-2),1-3	0	0.0
Total 5	207	416	40	79	15	0	9	40	71	66	1	0	.190	.309	.291	.600	66	-17	41	3.13	2	/0-77,1-30,D-27	5	-2.0

• STENNETT, Rennie Renaldo Antonio (Porte) Stennett b: 4/5/1951, Colon, Panama BR/TR, 5'11", 175 lbs. Deb: 7/10/1971 Career OF: 34-5-14

YEAR TM-L	G	AB	R	H	2B	3B	HR	RBI	BB	SO	SB	CS	AVG	OBP	SLG	OPS	OPS+	BR/A	RC	RC/G	FR	G/POS	WS	TPW
1971 Pit-N	50	153	24	54	5	4	1	15	7	9	1	1	.353	.381	.458	.839	135	6	26	6.65	-1	2-36	7	0.8
1972*Pit-N	109	370	43	106	14	5	3	30	9	43	4	3	.286	.307	.376	.683	95	-4	37	3.53	12	2-49,0-41(31-5-10)/S-6	10	1.0
1973 Pit-N	128	466	45	113	18	3	10	55	16	63	2	3	.242	.268	.358	.626	74	-19	42	3.06	7	2-84,S-43/0-5(3-0-2)	9	-0.4
1974*Pit-N	157	673	84	196	29	3	7	56	32	51	8	9	.291	.325	.374	.700	99	-6	77	4.02	17	*2-154/0-2(0-0-2)	20	2.2
1975*Pit-N	148	616	89	176	25	7	7	62	33	42	5	4	.286	.326	.383	.709	97	-5	74	4.26	21	*2-144	21	2.7
1976 Pit-N	157	654	59	168	31	9	2	60	19	32	18	6	.257	.279	.341	.620	75	-23	59	3.10	20	*2-157/S-4	16	0.8
1977 Pit-N	116	453	53	152	20	4	5	51	29	24	28	18	.336	.378	.430	.809	113	7	71	5.76	5	*2-113	18	1.8
1978 Pit-N	106	333	30	81	9	2	3	35	13	22	2	1	.243	.276	.309	.585	60	-18	26	2.69	2	2-80/3-6	5	-1.3
1979*Pit-N	108	319	31	76	13	2	0	24	24	25	1	4	.238	.292	.292	.583	57	-20	25	2.53	10	*2-102	5	-0.6
1980 SF-N	120	397	34	97	13	2	2	37	22	31	4	4	.244	.287	.302	.590	66	-20	32	2.73	-12	*2-111	6	-2.7
1981 SF-N	38	87	8	20	0	0	1	7	3	6	2	1	.230	.264	.264	.528	51	-6	6	2.09	-4	2-19	1	-0.9
Total 11	1237	4521	500	1239	177	41	41	432	207	348	75	54	.274	.308	.359	.667	85	-109	475	3.65	77	*2-1049/S-53,0-48,3-6	118	3.6

• STENSON, Dernell Dernell Renuald Stenson b: 6/17/1978, La Grange, GA d: 11/5/2003, Phoenix, AZ BL/TL, 6'1", 230 lbs. Deb: 8/13/2003

YEAR TM-L	G	AB	R	H	2B	3B	HR	RBI	BB	SO	SB	CS	AVG	OBP	SLG	OPS	OPS+	BR/A	RC	RC/G	FR	G/POS	WS	TPW
2003 Cin-N	37	81	14	20	5	0	3	13	11	24	0	0	.247	.337	.420	.757	98	-0	12	5.43	1	0-22(18-0-7)/1-1	2	0.0

• STENZEL, Jake Jacob Charles Stenzel b: 6/24/1867, Cincinnati, OH d: 1/6/1919, Cincinnati, OH BR/TR, 5'10", 168 lbs. Deb: 6/16/1890 Career OF: 18-690-33

YEAR TM-L	G	AB	R	H	2B	3B	HR	RBI	BB	SO	SB	CS	AVG	OBP	SLG	OPS	OPS+	BR/A	RC	RC/G	FR	G/POS	WS	TPW
1890 Chi-N	11	41	3	11	1	0	0	3	1	0	0	....	.268	.286	.293	.578	66	-2	4	3.10	-1	/C-6,0-6(0-0-6)	0	-0.2
1892 Pit-N	3	9	0	0	0	0	0	0	1	3	1	....	.000	.100	.000	.100	-69	-2	0	.31	1	/0-2(1-1-0),C-1	0	-0.1
1893 Pit-N	60	224	57	81	13	4	4	37	24	17	16	....	.362	.423	.509	.932	150	16	56	10.45	-4	0-45(4-18-23),C-12/2-1,S-1	10	0.8
1894 Pit-N	132	525	150	185	39	20	13	121	76	13	61	....	.352	.440	.577	1.017	145	40	164	12.55	-4	*0-131(5-126-0)	24	2.0
1895 Pit-N	130	518	114	192	38	13	7	97	57	25	53	....	.371	.444	.535	.978	160	49	151	12.24	-4	*0-129(0-129-0)	28	2.9
1896 Pit-N	114	479	104	173	26	14	2	82	32	13	57	....	.361	.410	.486	.897	141	28	122	10.40	-8	*0-114(0-114-0)/1-1	22	1.1
1897*Bal-N	131	536	113	189	**43**	7	4	116	36	....	69	....	.353	.404	.481	.885	133	25	136	10.26	-12	*0-131(0-131-0)	24	0.3
1898 Bal-N	35	138	33	35	5	2	0	22	12	....	4	....	.254	.340	.319	.659	87	-2	17	4.30	-1	0-35(0-35-0)	3	-0.4
StL-N	108	404	64	114	15	11	1	33	41	....	21	....	.282	.367	.381	.748	112	7	67	5.92	-4	*0-108(0-108-0)	10	-0.4
Yr.	143	542	97	149	20	13	1	55	53	....	25	....	.275	.360	.365	.725	106	5	84	5.50	-5	*0-143(0-143-0)	13	-0.8
1899 StL-N	35	128	21	35	9	0	1	19	16	....	8	....	.273	.367	.367	.735	99	0	21	5.78	0	0-33(8-21-4)	4	-0.2
Cin-N	9	29	5	9	1	0	0	3	4	....	2	....	.310	.412	.345	.757	106	1	5	6.71	-1	/0-7(0-7-0)	1	0.0
Yr.	44	157	26	44	10	0	1	22	20	....	10	....	.280	.376	.363	.739	101	1	26	5.93	-1	0-40(8-28-4)	5	-0.2
Total 9	768	3031	664	1024	190	71	32	533	300	71	292	....	.338	.408	.479	.887	134	160	743	9.66	-38	0-741/C-19,1-1,2-1,S-1	126	5.7

• STEPHENS, Gene Glen Eugene Stephens b: 1/20/1933, Gravette, AR BL/TR, 6'3.5", 175 lbs. Deb: 4/16/1952 Career OF: 566-136-126

YEAR TM-L	G	AB	R	H	2B	3B	HR	RBI	BB	SO	SB	CS	AVG	OBP	SLG	OPS	OPS+	BR/A	RC	RC/G	FR	G/POS	WS	TPW
1952 Bos-A	21	53	10	12	5	0	0	5	3	8	4	2	.226	.268	.321	.589	59	-3	4	2.63	0	0-13(2-0-11)	0	-0.3
1953 Bos-A	78	221	30	45	6	2	3	18	29	56	3	3	.204	.302	.290	.591	57	-13	22	3.21	-3	0-72(71-0-3)	2	-2.0
1955 Bos-A	109	157	25	46	9	4	3	18	20	34	0	0	.293	.380	.459	.838	114	4	29	6.80	1	0-75(71-4-0)	6	0.2
1956 Bos-A	104	63	22	17	2	0	1	7	12	12	0	1	.270	.387	.349	.736	85	-1	9	5.09	-1	0-71(69-2-2)	2	-0.4
1957 Bos-A	120	173	25	46	6	4	3	26	26	20	0	2	.266	.362	.399	.761	102	0	26	5.28	2	0-90(75-6-11)	5	0.0
1958 Bos-A	134	270	38	59	10	1	9	25	22	46	1	2	.219	.280	.363	.643	71	-12	27	3.28	-1	*0-110(92-26-3)	4	-1.8
1959 Bos-A	92	270	34	75	13	1	3	39	29	33	5	2	.278	.356	.367	.723	95	-1	38	4.93	2	0-85(62-17-7)	8	-0.3
1960 Bos-A	35	109	9	25	4	0	2	11	14	22	5	1	.229	.317	.321	.638	71	-4	13	3.99	-1	0-31(21-4-8)	2	-0.7
Bal-A	84	193	38	46	11	0	5	11	25	25	4	2	.238	.329	.373	.702	90	-2	26	4.64	1	0-77(36-19-42)	7	-0.4
Yr.	119	302	47	71	15	0	7	22	39	47	9	3	.235	.325	.354	.679	83	-6	39	4.40	0	*0-108(57-23-50)	9	-1.1
1961 Bal-A	32	58	4	11	2	0	0	2	14	7	1	1	.190	.347	.224	.571	57	-3	6	3.22	1	0-30(27-5-5)	1	-0.3
KC-A	62	183	22	38	6	1	4	26	16	27	3	2	.208	.279	.317	.596	59	-11	17	2.99	1	0-54(6-28-25)	2	-1.3
Yr.	94	241	26	49	8	1	4	28	30	34	4	3	.203	.297	.295	.591	58	-14	22	3.04	2	0-84(33-33-30)	3	-1.6

YEAR TM-L	G	AB	R	H	2B	3B	HR	RBI	BB	SO	SB	CS	AVG	OBP	SLG	OPS	OPS+	BR/A	RC	RC/G	FR	G/POS	WS	TPW
1962 KC-A	5	4	0	0	0	0	0	0	1	1	0	0	.000	.200	.000	.200	-40	-1	0	.35	0	....	0	-0.1
1963 Chi-A	6	18	5	7	0	0	1	2	1	3	0	0	.389	.421	.556	.977	174	2	4	9.70	1	/O-5(2-0-3)	1	0.2
1964 Chi-A	82	141	21	33	4	2	3	17	21	28	1	2	.234	.341	.355	.696	97	-1	18	4.21	0	O-59(32-25-6)	5	-0.3
Total 12	964	1913	283	460	78	15	37	207	233	322	27	20	.240	.327	.355	.682	82	-46	239	4.24	3	O-772	45	-7.5

• STEPHENS, Jim James Walter "Little Nemo" Stephens b: 12/10/1883, Salineville, OH d: 1/2/1965, Oxford, AL BR/TR, 5'6.5", 157 lbs. Deb: 4/11/1907

YEAR TM-L	G	AB	R	H	2B	3B	HR	RBI	BB	SO	SB	CS	AVG	OBP	SLG	OPS	OPS+	BR/A	RC	RC/G	FR	G/POS	WS	TPW
1907 StL-A	58	173	15	35	6	3	0	11	15	....	3	....	.202	.270	.272	.542	73	-5	14	2.68	-2	C-56	3	-0.3
1908 StL-A	47	150	14	30	4	1	0	6	9	....	0	....	.200	.255	.240	.495	61	-6	9	1.92	1	C-45	2	-0.1
1909 StL-A	79	223	18	49	5	0	3	18	13	....	5	....	.220	.278	.283	.561	83	-4	18	2.71	7	C-72	7	1.0
1910 StL-A	99	289	24	62	3	7	0	23	16	....	2	....	.215	.261	.273	.534	72	-10	22	2.33	15	C-96	5	1.5
1911 StL-A	70	212	11	49	5	5	0	17	17	....	1	....	.231	.300	.302	.602	71	-8	19	3.01	4	C-66	3	0.0
1912 StL-A	75	205	13	51	7	5	0	22	7	....	3	....	.249	.274	.332	.605	75	-8	19	3.10	5	C-66	3	0.2
Total 6	428	1252	95	276	30	21	3	97	77	....	14	....	.220	.273	.285	.558	73	-42	102	2.63	28	C-401	23	2.3

• STEPHENS, Ray Carl Ray Stephens b: 9/22/1962, Houston, TX BR/TR, 6', 190 lbs. Deb: 9/20/1990

YEAR TM-L	G	AB	R	H	2B	3B	HR	RBI	BB	SO	SB	CS	AVG	OBP	SLG	OPS	OPS+	BR/A	RC	RC/G	FR	G/POS	WS	TPW
1990 StL-N	5	15	2	2	1	0	1	1	0	3	0	0	.133	.133	.400	.533	41	-1	0	.00	0	/C-5	0	-0.1
1991 StL-N	6	7	0	2	0	0	0	0	1	3	0	0	.286	.375	.286	.661	88	-0	1	4.58	0	/C-6	0	0.0
1992 Tex-A	8	13	0	2	0	0	0	0	0	5	0	0	.154	.154	.154	.308	-14	-2	0	.81	0	/C-6,D-1	0	-0.2
Total 3	19	35	2	6	1	0	1	1	1	11	0	0	.171	.194	.286	.480	30	-3	1	1.02	1	/C-17,D-1	0	-0.2

• STEPHENS, Vern Vernon Decatur "Junior,Buster" Stephens b: 10/23/1920, McAllister, NM d: 11/4/1968, Long Beach, CA BR/TR, 5'10", 185 lbs. Deb: 9/13/1941

YEAR TM-L	G	AB	R	H	2B	3B	HR	RBI	BB	SO	SB	CS	AVG	OBP	SLG	OPS	OPS+	BR/A	RC	RC/G	FR	G/POS	WS	TPW
1941 StL-A	3	2	0	1	0	0	0	0	0	0	0	0	.500	.500	.500	1.000	160	0	1	13.84	0	/S-1	0	0.0
1942 StL-A	145	575	84	169	26	6	14	92	41	53	1	3	.294	.341	.433	.774	115	8	83	5.26	-11	*S-144	19	0.8
1943 StL-A★	137	512	75	148	27	3	22	91	54	73	3	2	.289	.357	.482	.839	141	25	90	6.35	-20	*S-123,O-11(9-0-3)	23	1.6
1944*StL-A★	145	559	91	164	32	1	20	**109**	62	54	2	2	.293	.365	.462	.826	128	20	101	6.70	-2	*S-143	34	3.1
1945 StL-A★	149	571	90	165	27	3	**24**	89	55	70	2	1	.289	.352	.473	.825	132	22	98	6.23	-3	*S-144/3-4	27	3.4
1946 StL-A★	115	450	67	138	19	4	14	64	35	49	0	1	.307	.357	.460	.817	121	11	73	6.01	-4	*S-112	20	1.6
1947 StL-A	150	562	74	157	18	4	15	83	70	61	8	4	.279	.359	.406	.765	110	9	88	5.66	8	*S-149	23	2.8
1948 Bos-A★	155	635	114	171	25	8	29	137	77	56	1	0	.269	.350	.471	.821	111	8	103	5.68	2	*S-155	25	2.0
1949 Bos-A★	155	610	113	177	31	2	39	**159**	101	73	2	2	.290	.391	.539	.930	135	29	132	7.84	1	*S-155	32	3.9
1950 Bos-A★	149	628	125	185	34	6	30	**144**	65	43	1	0	.295	.361	.511	.872	110	7	114	6.66	-9	*S-146	22	0.7
1951 Bos-A★	109	377	62	113	21	2	17	78	38	33	1	2	.300	.364	.501	.865	120	9	62	5.86	13	3-89/S-2	14	2.2
1952 Bos-A	92	295	35	75	13	2	7	44	39	31	2	2	.254	.343	.383	.726	95	-2	40	4.65	-2	S-53,3-29	9	0.0
1953 Chi-A	44	129	14	24	6	0	1	14	13	18	2	0	.186	.261	.256	.516	39	-11	9	2.28	1	3-38/S-3	1	-1.0
StL-A	46	165	16	53	8	0	4	17	18	24	0	0	.321	.388	.442	.830	121	5	28	6.17	-0	3-46	5	0.5
Yr.	90	294	30	77	14	0	5	31	31	42	2	0	.262	.332	.361	.693	85	-5	37	4.34	1	3-84/S-3	6	-0.4
1954 Bal-A	101	365	31	104	17	1	8	46	17	36	0	3	.285	.317	.403	.719	104	-2	46	4.41	-1	3-96	9	-0.3
1955 Bal-A	3	6	0	1	0	0	0	0	0	0	0	0	.167	.286	.167	.452	26	-1	0	1.94	0	/3-2	0	-0.1
Chi-A	22	56	10	14	3	0	3	7	7	11	0	0	.250	.333	.464	.798	109	1	9	5.33	0	3-18	2	0.0
Yr.	25	62	10	15	3	0	3	7	7	11	0	0	.242	.329	.435	.764	101	-0	9	4.99	0	3-20	2	0.0
Total 15	1720	6497	1001	1859	307	42	247	1174	692	685	25	22	.286	.355	.460	.816	118	141	1076	5.96	-27	*S-1330,3-322/O-11	265	21.2

• STEPHENSON, Bob Robert Lloyd Stephenson b: 8/11/1928, Blair, OK BR/TR, 6', 165 lbs. Deb: 4/14/1955

YEAR TM-L	G	AB	R	H	2B	3B	HR	RBI	BB	SO	SB	CS	AVG	OBP	SLG	OPS	OPS+	BR/A	RC	RC/G	FR	G/POS	WS	TPW
1955 StL-N	67	111	19	27	3	0	0	6	5	18	2	1	.243	.276	.270	.546	46	-9	8	2.27	-2	S-48/2-7,3-1	1	-0.8

• STEPHENSON, Dummy Reuben Crandol Stephenson b: 9/22/1869, Petersburg, NJ d: 12/1/1924, Trenton, NJ BR/TR, 5'11.5", 180 lbs. Deb: 9/9/1892

YEAR TM-L	G	AB	R	H	2B	3B	HR	RBI	BB	SO	SB	CS	AVG	OBP	SLG	OPS	OPS+	BR/A	RC	RC/G	FR	G/POS	WS	TPW
1892 Phi-N	8	37	4	10	3	0	0	5	0	2	0	....	.270	.289	.351	.641	94	-1	4	3.86	-1	/O-8(0-8-0)	0	-0.2

• STEPHENSON, Joe Joseph Chester Stephenson b: 6/30/1921, Detroit, MI d: 9/20/2001, Fullerton, CA BR/TR, 6'2", 185 lbs. Deb: 9/19/1943

YEAR TM-L	G	AB	R	H	2B	3B	HR	RBI	BB	SO	SB	CS	AVG	OBP	SLG	OPS	OPS+	BR/A	RC	RC/G	FR	G/POS	WS	TPW
1943 NY-N	9	24	4	6	1	0	0	1	0	5	0	....	.250	.250	.292	.542	56	-1	2	2.63	1	/C-6	0	0.0
1944 Chi-N	4	8	1	1	0	0	0	0	1	3	1	....	.125	.222	.125	.347	-1	-1	0	.47	0	/C-3	0	-0.1
1947 Chi-A	16	35	3	5	0	0	0	3	1	7	0	0	.143	.211	.143	.353	-1	-5	1	1.12	-1	C-13	0	-0.5
Total 3	29	67	8	12	1	0	0	4	2	15	1	0	.179	.225	.194	.419	18	-7	3	1.51	1	/C-22	0	-0.6

• STEPHENSON, John John Herman Stephenson b: 4/13/1941, South Portsmouth, KY BL/TR, 5'11", 180 lbs. Deb: 4/14/1964 Career OF: 7-3-2

YEAR TM-L	G	AB	R	H	2B	3B	HR	RBI	BB	SO	SB	CS	AVG	OBP	SLG	OPS	OPS+	BR/A	RC	RC/G	FR	G/POS	WS	TPW
1964 NY-N	37	57	2	9	0	0	1	2	4	18	0	0	.158	.226	.211	.436	24	-6	3	1.69	-2	3-14/O-8(5-3-0)	0	-0.8
1965 NY-N	62	121	9	26	5	0	4	15	8	19	0	1	.215	.264	.355	.619	75	-5	9	2.33	0	C-47/O-2(0-0-2)	1	-0.4
1966 NY-N	63	143	17	28	1	1	1	11	8	28	0	0	.196	.248	.238	.486	37	-12	7	1.64	1	C-52/O-1	1	-1.0
1967 Chi-N	18	49	3	11	3	1	0	5	1	6	0	0	.224	.255	.327	.581	62	-2	4	2.61	0	C-13	1	-0.2
1968 Chi-N	2	2	0	0	0	0	0	0	0	0	0	0	.000	.000	.000	.000	-94	-0	0	.00	0	....	0	-0.1
1969 SF-N	22	27	2	6	2	0	0	3	0	4	0	0	.222	.222	.296	.519	45	-2	1	1.35	-2	/C-9,3-1	0	-0.4
1970 SF-N	23	43	3	3	1	0	0	6	2	7	0	0	.070	.111	.093	.204	-45	-9	0	.28	1	/C-9,O-1	0	-0.7
1971 Cal-A	98	279	24	61	17	0	3	25	22	21	0	0	.219	.283	.312	.595	74	-10	24	2.75	-1	C-88	6	-0.8
1972 Cal-A	66	146	14	40	3	1	2	17	11	8	0	0	.274	.342	.349	.691	112	2	16	3.82	-1	C-56	6	0.3
1973 Cal-A	60	122	9	30	5	0	1	9	7	7	0	0	.246	.292	.311	.604	76	-4	11	2.90	-4	C-56	2	-0.6
Total 10	451	989	83	214	37	3	12	93	63	118	0	1	.216	.272	.296	.568	65	-48	75	2.45	-10	C-330/3-15,O-12	17	-4.7

• STEPHENSON, Phil Phillip Raymond Stephenson b: 9/19/1960, Guthrie, OK BL/TL, 6'1", 195 lbs. Deb: 4/5/1989 Career OF: 13-0-6

YEAR TM-L	G	AB	R	H	2B	3B	HR	RBI	BB	SO	SB	CS	AVG	OBP	SLG	OPS	OPS+	BR/A	RC	RC/G	FR	G/POS	WS	TPW
1989 Chi-N	17	21	0	3	0	0	0	0	2	3	1	0	.143	.217	.143	.360	5	-2	1	1.32	0	/O-3(3-0-0)	0	-0.3
SD-N	10	17	4	6	0	0	2	2	3	2	0	0	.353	.450	.706	1.156	225	3	6	11.74	0	/1-8	1	0.3
Yr.	27	38	4	9	0	0	2	2	5	5	1	0	.237	.326	.395	.720	112	0	7	5.69	0	/1-8,O-3(3-0-0)	1	0.0
1990 SD-N	103	182	26	38	9	1	4	19	30	43	2	1	.209	.321	.335	.656	80	-5	21	3.82	2	1-60	2	-0.5
1991 SD-N	11	7	0	2	0	0	0	0	2	3	0	0	.286	.444	.286	.730	106	0	1	6.05	0	....	0	0.0
1992 SD-N	53	71	5	11	2	1	0	8	10	11	0	0	.155	.259	.211	.471	34	-6	5	2.05	0	O-15(10-0-6)/1-7	1	-0.7
Total 4	194	298	35	60	11	2	6	29	47	62	3	1	.201	.310	.312	.622	74	-10	34	3.65	2	/1-75,O-18	4	-1.2

• STEPHENSON, Riggs Jackson Riggs "Old Hoss" Stephenson
b: 1/5/1898, Akron, AL d: 11/15/1985, Tuscaloosa, AL BR/TR, 5'10", 185 lbs. Deb: 4/13/1921 Career OF: 885-0-28

YEAR TM-L	G	AB	R	H	2B	3B	HR	RBI	BB	SO	SB	CS	AVG	OBP	SLG	OPS	OPS+	BR/A	RC	RC/G	FR	G/POS	WS	TPW
1921 Cle-A	65	206	45	68	17	2	2	34	23	15	4	1	.330	.408	.461	.869	119	8	40	7.35	-3	2-54/3-2	8	0.6
1922 Cle-A	86	233	47	79	24	5	2	32	27	18	3	0	.339	.421	.511	.932	141	16	52	8.92	-4	3-34,2-25/O-3(2-0-1)	12	1.4
1923 Cle-A	91	301	48	96	20	6	5	65	15	25	5	5	.319	.357	.475	.832	118	6	49	6.00	7	2-66/O-3(0-0-3),3-2	11	1.4
1924 Cle-A	71	240	33	89	20	0	4	44	27	10	1	2	.371	.439	.504	.943	141	15	53	9.08	-14	2-58/O-7(0-0-7)	10	0.2
1925 Cle-A	19	54	8	16	3	1	1	9	7	3	1	1	.296	.387	.444	.832	110	1	10	6.16	0	O-16(0-0-16)	2	0.0
1926 Chi-N	82	281	40	95	18	3	3	44	31	16	2	....	.338	.404	.456	.859	129	12	51	6.72	-2	O-74(73-0-1)	11	0.5
1927 Chi-N	152	579	101	199	**46**	9	7	82	65	28	8	....	.344	.415	.491	.906	141	36	117	7.63	5	*O-146(146-0-0)/3-6	27	3.0
1928 Chi-N	137	512	75	166	36	9	8	90	68	29	8	....	.324	.407	.477	.883	132	26	99	7.29	3	*O-135(135-0-0)	23	1.8
1929*Chi-N	136	495	91	179	36	6	17	110	67	21	10	....	.362	.445	.562	1.006	147	39	123	9.69	0	*O-130(130-0-0)	26	2.7
1930 Chi-N	109	341	56	125	21	1	5	68	32	20	2	....	.367	.421	.478	.899	116	10	67	7.75	-3	O-80(80-0-0)	11	0.1
1931 Chi-N	80	263	34	84	14	4	1	52	37	14	1	....	.319	.405	.414	.820	119	9	47	6.77	-2	O-66(66-0-0)	10	0.3
1932*Chi-N	147	583	86	189	49	4	4	85	54	27	3	....	.324	.383	.443	.826	122	20	102	6.63	-1	*O-147(147-0-0)	23	1.0
1933 Chi-N	97	346	45	114	17	4	4	51	34	16	5	....	.329	.397	.436	.834	138	19	60	6.61	1	O-91(91-0-0)	16	1.6
1934 Chi-N	38	74	5	16	0	0	0	7	7	5	0	....	.216	.293	.216	.509	39	-6	5	2.23	2	O-15(15-0-0)	0	-0.4
Total 14	1310	4508	714	1515	321	54	63	773	494	247	53	9	.336	.407	.473	.880	130	210	876	7.39	-11	O-913,2-203/3-44	190	14.0

• STEPHENSON, Walter Walter McQueen "Tarzan" Stephenson b: 3/27/1911, Saluda, NC d: 7/4/1993, Shreveport, LA BR/TR, 6', 180 lbs. Deb: 4/29/1935

YEAR TM-L	G	AB	R	H	2B	3B	HR	RBI	BB	SO	SB	CS	AVG	OBP	SLG	OPS	OPS+	BR/A	RC	RC/G	FR	G/POS	WS	TPW
1935*Chi-N	16	26	2	10	1	1	0	2	1	5	0	....	.385	.407	.500	.907	142	1	6	9.34	1	/C-6	1	0.3
1936 Chi-N	6	12	0	1	0	0	0	1	0	5	0	....	.083	.083	.083	.167	-54	-3	0	.00	0	/C-4	0	-0.2
1937 Phi-N	10	23	1	6	0	0	0	2	2	3	0	....	.261	.320	.261	.581	55	-1	2	2.80	0	/C-7	0	-0.1
Total 3	32	61	3	17	1	1	0	5	3	13	0	....	.279	.313	.328	.640	71	-2	7	4.34	1	/C-17	1	-0.1

YEAR TM-L	G	AB	R	H	2B	3B	HR	RBI	BB	SO	SB	CS	AVG	OBP	SLG	OPS	OPS+	BR/A	RC	RC/G	FR	G/POS	WS	TPW
• STERRETT, Dutch	Charles Hurlbut Sterrett b: 10/1/1889, Milroy, PA d: 12/8/1965, Baltimore, MD BR/TR, 5'11.5", 165 lbs. Deb: 6/20/1912																							
1912 NY-A	66	230	30	61	4	7	1	32	11	....	8	....	.265	.310	.357	.667	85	-5	28	4.09	-5	0-37(0-31-6),1-17,C-10/2-1	4	-1.3
1913 NY-A	21	35	0	6	0	0	0	3	1	5	1	....	.171	.216	.171	.388	14	-4	1	1.26	0	/1-6,C-1	0	-0.5
Total 2	**87**	**265**	**30**	**67**	**4**	**7**	**1**	**35**	**12**	**5**	**9**	**....**	**.253**	**.298**	**.332**	**.630**	**76**	**-9**	**29**	**3.67**	**-6**	**/0-37,1-23,C-11,2-1**	**4**	**-1.7**
• STEVENS, Bobby	Robert Jordan Stevens b: 4/17/1907, Chevy Chase, MD BL/TR, 5'8", 149 lbs. Deb: 7/3/1931																							
1931 Phi-N	12	35	3	12	0	0	0	4	2	2	0	....	.343	.410	.343	.753	97	0	5	5.54	-3	S-10	1	-0.2
• STEVENS, Chuck	Charles Augustus Stevens b: 7/20/1918, Van Houten, NM BB/TL, 6'1", 180 lbs. Deb: 9/16/1941																							
1941 StL-A	4	13	2	2	0	0	0	2	0	1	0	0	.154	.154	.154	.308	-18	-2	0	.77	-1	/1-4	0	-0.3
1946 StL-A	122	432	53	107	17	4	3	27	47	62	4	6	.248	.324	.326	.651	78	-13	46	3.61	1	*1-120	8	-1.7
1948 StL-A	85	287	34	75	12	4	1	26	41	26	2	2	.261	.354	.341	.695	83	-6	39	4.48	-3	1-85	5	-1.1
Total 3	**211**	**732**	**89**	**184**	**29**	**8**	**4**	**55**	**88**	**89**	**6**	**8**	**.251**	**.333**	**.329**	**.663**	**79**	**-22**	**86**	**3.90**	**-3**	**1-209**	**13**	**-3.2**
• STEVENS, Ed	Edward Lee "Big Ed" Stevens b: 1/12/1925, Galveston, TX BL/TL, 6'1", 190 lbs. Deb: 8/9/1945 C																							
1945 Bro-N	55	201	29	55	14	3	4	29	32	20	0	....	.274	.376	.433	.809	125	8	35	6.19	1	1-55	8	0.6
1946 Bro-N	103	310	34	75	13	7	10	60	27	44	2	....	.242	.303	.426	.728	104	-0	40	4.54	-4	1-99	8	-0.7
1947 Bro-N	5	13	0	2	1	0	0	0	1	5	0	....	.154	.214	.231	.445	17	-2	1	1.71	1	/1-4	0	-0.1
1948 Pit-N	128	429	47	109	19	6	10	69	35	53	4	....	.254	.313	.396	.710	89	-8	54	4.44	3	*1-117	10	-0.9
1949 Pit-N	67	221	22	58	10	1	4	32	22	24	1	....	.262	.332	.371	.703	86	-4	29	4.60	9	1-58	5	0.3
1950 Pit-N	17	46	2	9	2	0	0	3	4	5	0	....	.196	.260	.239	.499	31	-5	3	2.05	0	1-12	0	-0.4
Total 6	**375**	**1220**	**134**	**308**	**59**	**17**	**28**	**193**	**121**	**151**	**7**	**....**	**.252**	**.322**	**.398**	**.719**	**96**	**-11**	**162**	**4.65**	**10**	**1-345**	**31**	**-1.3**
• STEVENS, Lee	De Wain Lee Stevens b: 7/10/1967, Kansas City, MO BL/TL, 6'4", 219 lbs. Deb: 7/16/1990 Career OF: 20-0-39																							
1990 Cal-A	67	248	28	53	10	0	7	32	22	75	1	1	.214	.278	.339	.616	73	-10	22	2.85	-6	1-67	3	-2.0
1991 Cal-A	18	58	8	17	7	0	0	9	6	12	1	2	.293	.359	.414	.773	113	0	8	5.08	0	1-11/0-9(1-0-8)	1	-0.1
1992 Cal-A	106	312	25	69	19	0	7	37	29	64	1	4	.221	.289	.349	.639	78	-11	31	3.29	-5	1-91/D-2	6	-2.2
1996 Tex-A	27	78	6	18	2	3	3	12	6	22	0	0	.231	.294	.449	.743	80	-3	10	4.28	1	1-18/0-1	2	-0.3
1997 Tex-A	137	426	58	128	24	2	21	74	23	83	1	3	.300	.338	.514	.852	112	5	66	5.48	1	1-62,D-38/0-5(3-0-19)	11	-0.2
1998*Tex-A	120	344	52	91	17	4	20	59	31	93	0	2	.265	.325	.512	.837	109	2	56	5.73	-1	D-72,1-37,0-22(0-0-7)	8	-0.5
1999*Tex-A	146	517	76	146	31	1	24	81	52	132	2	3	.282	.348	.485	.833	105	2	81	5.50	-3	*1-133/D-8	11	-1.2
2000 Mon-N	123	449	60	119	27	2	22	75	48	105	0	0	.265	.339	.481	.820	101	-1	73	5.72	3	*1-123	11	-0.8
2001 Mon-N	152	542	77	133	35	1	25	95	74	157	2	1	.245	.341	.452	.793	101	1	83	5.13	-0	*1-152	13	-1.2
2002 Mon-N	63	205	28	39	6	1	10	31	39	57	1	0	.190	.320	.376	.695	80	-6	26	4.14	2	1-58	4	-0.9
Cle-A	53	153	22	34	7	1	5	26	15	32	0	0	.222	.292	.379	.671	78	-5	16	3.45	-1	1-25/0-7(11-0-5),D-2	3	-0.9
Total 10	**1012**	**3332**	**440**	**847**	**185**	**15**	**144**	**531**	**345**	**832**	**9**	**16**	**.254**	**.326**	**.448**	**.774**	**97**	**-25**	**472**	**4.84**	**-10**	**1-777,D-122/0-44**	**73**	**-10.4**
• STEVENS, R.C.	R C Stevens b: 7/22/1934, Moultrie, GA BR/TL, 6'5", 219 lbs. Deb: 4/15/1958																							
1958 Pit-N	59	90	16	24	3	1	7	18	5	25	0	0	.267	.320	.556	.875	129	3	17	6.77	1	1-52	4	0.3
1959 Pit-N	3	7	2	2	0	0	1	1	0	0	0	0	.286	.286	.714	1.000	157	0	1	7.71	0	/1-1	0	0.0
1960 Pit-N	9	3	1	0	0	0	0	0	0	1	0	0	.000	.000	.000	.000	-99	-1	0	.00	0	/1-7	0	-0.1
1961 Was-A	33	62	2	8	1	0	0	2	7	15	1	0	.129	.217	.145	.363	-1	-9	2	.93	3	1-25	0	-0.6
Total 4	**104**	**162**	**21**	**34**	**4**	**1**	**8**	**21**	**12**	**41**	**1**	**0**	**.210**	**.273**	**.395**	**.668**	**75**	**-6**	**20**	**4.11**	**5**	**/1-85**	**4**	**-0.4**
• STEVENS, Robert	Robert Stevens Deb: 5/4/1875																							
1875 Was-n	1	4	0	1	0	0	0	0	0	0	0	0	.250	.250	.250	.500	77	-0	0	2.52	0	/0-1	....	0.0
• STEVERSON, Todd	Todd Anthony Steverson b: 11/15/1971, Los Angeles, CA BR/TR, 6'2", 195 lbs. Deb: 4/28/1995																							
1995 Det-A	30	42	11	11	0	0	2	6	6	10	2	0	.262	.354	.405	.759	97	0	7	5.74	0	0-27(17-1-10)/D-1	1	0.0
1996 SD-N	1	1	0	0	0	0	0	0	0	1	0	0	.000	.000	.000	.000	-106	-0	0	.00	0	....	0	0.0
Total 2	**31**	**43**	**11**	**11**	**0**	**0**	**2**	**6**	**6**	**11**	**2**	**0**	**.256**	**.347**	**.395**	**.742**	**93**	**0**	**7**	**5.57**	**0**	**/0-27,D-1**	**1**	**0.0**
• STEWART, Ace	Asa Stewart b: 2/14/1869, Terre Haute, IN d: 4/17/1912, Terre Haute, IN BR/TR, 5'10", 176 lbs. Deb: 4/18/1895																							
1895 Chi-N	97	365	52	88	8	10	8	76	39	40	14	....	.241	.314	.384	.698	75	-16	50	4.81	-13	*2-97	7	-2.0
• STEWART, Andy	Andrew David Stewart b: 12/5/1970, Oshawa, Canada BR/TR, 5'11", 205 lbs. Deb: 9/6/1997																							
1997 KC-A	5	8	1	2	1	0	0	0	0	0	0	0	.250	.250	.375	.625	59	-1	0	1.45	0	/C-4,D-1	0	0.0
• STEWART, Bill	William Wayne Stewart b: 4/12/1928, Bay City, MI BR/TR, 5'11", 200 lbs. Deb: 4/17/1955																							
1955 KC-A	11	18	2	2	1	0	0	0	1	6	0	0	.111	.158	.167	.325	-13	-3	1	.87	1	/0-6(4-0-2)	0	-0.2
• STEWART, Bud	Edward Perry Stewart b: 6/15/1916, Sacramento, CA d: 6/21/2000, Palo Alto, CA BL/TR, 5'11", 170 lbs. Deb: 4/19/1941 Career OF: 281-58-222																							
1941 Pit-N	73	172	27	46	7	0	0	10	12	17	3	....	.267	.315	.308	.623	76	-5	18	3.65	2	0-41(15-4-24)	3	-0.6
1942 Pit-N	82	183	21	40	8	4	0	20	22	16	2	....	.219	.302	.306	.608	76	-5	18	3.25	-2	0-34(19-0-16),3-10/2-6	3	-0.9
1948 NY-A	6	5	1	1	1	0	0	0	0	0	0	0	.200	.200	.400	.600	58	-0	0	2.77	0	....	0	0.0
Was-A	118	401	56	112	17	13	7	69	49	27	8	9	.279	.361	.439	.800	115	6	66	5.74	-3	*0-114(10-37-72)	15	-0.1
Yr.	124	406	57	113	18	13	7	69	49	27	8	9	.278	.359	.438	.797	115	6	66	5.70	-3	*0-114(10-37-72)	15	-0.1
1949 Was-A	118	388	58	110	23	4	8	43	49	33	6	4	.284	.368	.425	.793	112	6	65	6.01	-4	*0-105(75-16-20)	13	-0.3
1950 Was-A	118	378	46	101	15	6	4	35	46	33	5	4	.267	.348	.370	.719	88	-7	53	4.96	2	*0-100(42-0-66)	9	-0.9
1951 Chi-A	95	217	40	60	13	5	6	40	29	9	1	6	.276	.367	.465	.832	127	6	36	5.66	0	0-63(52-1-14)	7	0.2
1952 Chi-A	92	225	23	60	10	0	5	30	28	17	3	0	.267	.350	.378	.728	102	2	34	5.33	-1	0-60(57-0-3)	7	-0.2
1953 Chi-A	53	59	16	16	2	0	2	13	14	3	1	0	.271	.411	.407	.818	118	3	11	7.01	0	0-16(11-0-5)	3	0.2
1954 Chi-A	18	13	0	1	0	0	0	0	3	2	0	0	.077	.250	.077	.327	-7	-2	0	.20	0	/0-2(0-0-2)	0	-0.2
Total 9	**773**	**2041**	**288**	**547**	**96**	**32**	**32**	**260**	**252**	**157**	**29**	**23**	**.268**	**.351**	**.393**	**.744**	**102**	**2**	**301**	**5.16**	**-6**	**0-535/3-10,2-6**	**60**	**-2.8**
• STEWART, Glen	Glen Weldon "Gabby" Stewart b: 9/29/1912, Tullahoma, TN d: 2/11/1997, Memphis, TN BR/TR, 6', 175 lbs. Deb: 6/26/1940																							
1940 NY-N	15	29	1	4	1	0	0	0	1	2	0	....	.138	.167	.172	.339	-6	-4	1	.53	0	/3-6,S-5	0	-0.4
1943 Phi-N	110	336	23	71	10	1	2	24	32	41	1	....	.211	.284	.265	.549	61	-16	26	2.51	-12	S-77,2-18/1-8,C-1	3	-2.3
1944 Phi-N	118	377	32	83	11	5	0	29	28	40	0	....	.220	.274	.276	.550	57	-22	27	2.31	-7	3-83,S-32/2-1	3	-2.6
Total 3	**243**	**742**	**56**	**158**	**22**	**6**	**2**	**53**	**61**	**83**	**1**	**....**	**.213**	**.275**	**.267**	**.541**	**57**	**-42**	**54**	**2.32**	**-20**	**S-114/3-89,2-19,1-8,C-1**	**6**	**-5.4**
• STEWART, Jimmy	James Franklin Stewart b: 6/11/1939, Opelika, AL BB/TR, 6', 165 lbs. Deb: 9/3/1963 Career OF: 176-43-11																							
1963 Chi-N	13	37	1	11	2	0	0	1	1	7	1	1	.297	.316	.351	.667	87	-1	4	3.89	1	/S-9,2-1	1	0.0
1964 Chi-N	132	415	59	105	17	0	3	33	49	61	10	8	.253	.335	.316	.650	81	-10	47	3.73	-3	2-61,S-45/0-4(0-4-0),3-1	9	-0.5
1965 Chi-N	116	282	26	63	9	4	0	19	30	53	13	3	.223	.303	.284	.586	65	-11	27	3.20	-1	0-55(47-8-0),S-48	4	-1.4
1966 Chi-N	57	90	4	16	4	1	0	4	7	12	1	1	.178	.253	.244	.497	38	-8	6	1.93	-2	0-15(4-11-1)/2-4,3-2,S-2	0	-1.1
1967 Chi-N	6	6	1	1	0	0	0	1	0	0	0	0	.167	.167	.167	.333	-4	-1	0	.90	0	....	0	-0.1
Chi-A	24	18	5	3	0	0	0	1	1	6	1	0	.167	.211	.167	.377	13	-2	1	1.45	-2	/0-6(6-0-0),2-5,S-2	0	-0.3
1969 Cin-N	119	221	26	56	3	4	4	24	19	33	4	2	.253	.313	.357	.670	83	-5	25	3.87	2	0-66(55-10-1),2-18/3-6,S-1	5	-0.5
1970*Cin-N	101	105	15	28	3	1	1	8	8	13	5	3	.267	.325	.343	.667	76	-4	12	3.70	-2	0-48(41-2-5),2-18/3-9,1-1,C	2	-0.7
1971 Cin-N	80	82	7	19	2	2	0	9	9	12	3	1	.232	.308	.305	.613	78	-2	8	3.19	-2	0-19(11-6-3)/3-9,2-6	1	-0.4
1972 Hou-N	68	96	14	21	5	2	0	9	6	9	0	1	.219	.265	.313	.577	65	-5	8	2.76	-2	0-11(9-2-1)/1-9,2-8,3-2	1	-0.8
1973 Hou-N	61	68	6	13	0	0	0	3	9	12	0	0	.191	.295	.191	.486	37	-5	5	2.10	1	/3-8,0-3(3-0-0),2-1	0	-0.5
Total 10	**777**	**1420**	**164**	**336**	**45**	**14**	**8**	**112**	**139**	**218**	**38**	**20**	**.237**	**.308**	**.305**	**.613**	**71**	**-52**	**142**	**3.31**	**-10**	**0-227,2-122,S-107/3-37,1-10,C**	**23**	**-6.1**
• STEWART, Mark	Mark "Big Stick" Stewart b: 10/11/1889, Whitlock, TN d: 1/17/1932, Memphis, TN BL/TR, 6'1", 180 lbs. Deb: 10/4/1913																							
1913 Cin-N	1	1	0	0	0	0	0	0	0	0	0	....	.000	.000	.000	.000	-100	-0	0	.00	0	/C-1	0	-0.1
• STEWART, Neb	Walter Nesbitt Stewart b: 5/21/1918, South Charleston, OH d: 6/8/1990, London, OH BR/TR, 6'1", 195 lbs. Deb: 9/8/1940																							
1940 Phi-N	10	31	3	4	0	0	0	0	1	5	0	....	.129	.156	.129	.285	-21	-5	1	.51	1	/0-9(8-1-0)	0	-0.5

YEAR TM-L	G	AB	R	H	2B	3B	HR	RBI	BB	SO	SB	CS	AVG	OBP	SLG	OPS	OPS+	BR/A	RC	RC/G	FR	G/POS	WS	TPW
• STEWART, Shannon	Shannon Harold Stewart b: 2/25/1974, Cincinnati, OH BR/TR, 6', 175 lbs. Deb: 9/2/1995 Career OF: 745-110-14																							
1995 Tor-A	12	38	2	8	0	0	0	1	5	5	2	0	.211	.318	.211	.529	41	-3	3	3.04	0	O-12(0-12-0)	0	-0.3
1996 Tor-A	7	17	2	3	1	0	0	2	1	4	1	0	.176	.222	.235	.458	16	-2	1	1.43	-1	O-16(0-6-0)	0	-0.2
1997 Tor-A	44	168	25	48	13	7	0	22	19	24	10	3	.286	.372	.446	.818	112	4	29	6.18	-2	/O-6(2-40-0),D-1	7	0.2
1998 Tor-A	144	516	90	144	29	3	12	55	67	77	51	18	.279	.378	.417	.795	106	10	89	6.00	-3	O-42(110-44-0)	18	0.3
1999 Tor-A	145	608	102	185	28	2	11	67	59	83	37	14	.304	.373	.411	.785	99	2	96	5.70	-10	*O-144(141-7-0)/D-2	17	-1.3
2000 Tor-A	136	583	107	186	43	5	21	69	37	79	20	5	.319	.366	.518	.884	117	15	110	7.06	3	*O-143(136-1-0)	17	1.1
2001 Tor-A	155	640	103	202	44	7	12	60	46	72	27	10	.316	.372	.463	.834	115	16	112	6.59	-1	*O-136(142-0-0),D-11	18	0.7
2002 Tor-A	141	577	103	175	38	6	10	45	54	60	14	2	.303	.372	.442	.814	111	13	95	6.09	-5	*O-142(99-0-0),D-38	17	0.1
2003 Tor-A	71	303	47	89	22	2	7	35	27	30	1	2	.294	.355	.449	.804	108	3	48	5.61	1	O-69(69-0-0)/D-2	9	0.1
*Min-A	65	270	43	87	22	0	6	38	25	36	3	4	.322	.388	.470	.858	124	9	49	6.78	1	O-58(46-0-14)/D-6	9	0.7
Yr.	136	573	90	176	44	2	13	73	52	66	4	6	.307	.371	.459	.830	116	12	97	6.15	2	*O-127(115-0-14)/D-8	18	0.7
Total 9	920	3720	624	1127	240	32	79	394	340	470	166	58	.303	.371	.448	.819	109	67	632	6.20	-18	O-768/D-60	112	1.3
• STEWART, Stuffy	John Franklin Stewart b: 1/31/1894, Jasper, FL d: 9/30/1980, Lake City, FL BR/TR, 5'9.5", 160 lbs. Deb: 9/3/1916																							
1916 StL-N	9	17	0	3	0	0	0	1	0	3	0	....	.176	.176	.176	.353	9	-2	1	.98	-2	/2-8	0	-0.4
1917 StL-N	13	9	4	0	0	0	0	0	0	4	0	....	.000	.000	.000	.000	-103	-2	0	.00	-1	/O-7(2-3-2),2-2	0	-0.4
1922 Pit-N	3	13	3	2	0	0	0	0	0	1	0	0	.154	.154	.154	.308	-20	-2	0	.71	-1	/2-3	0	-0.3
1923 Bro-N	4	11	3	4	1	0	1	1	1	1	0	0	.364	.417	.727	1.144	202	2	3	12.51	-1	/2-3	1	0.0
1925 Was-A	7	17	3	6	1	0	0	3	1	2	1	0	.353	.389	.412	.801	105	0	3	6.99	0	/3-5,2-1	1	0.1
1926 Was-A	62	63	27	17	6	1	0	9	6	6	8	4	.270	.333	.397	.730	92	-1	8	4.01	2	2-25/3-1	1	0.1
1927 Was-A	56	129	24	31	6	2	0	4	8	15	12	2	.240	.285	.318	.603	57	-7	13	3.31	1	2-37/3-2	2	-0.4
1929 Was-A	22	6	10	0	0	0	0	0	1	0	0	1	.000	.143	.000	.143	-60	-2	0	.00	0	/2-3	0	-0.2
Total 8	176	265	74	63	14	3	1	18	17	32	21	7	.238	.284	.325	.608	61	-14	28	3.44	-2	/2-82,3-8,O-7	5	-1.4
• STEWART, Tuffy	Charles Eugene Stewart b: 7/31/1883, Chicago, IL d: 11/18/1934, Chicago, IL BL/TL, 5'10", 167 lbs. Deb: 8/8/1913																							
1913 Chi-N	9	8	1	1	1	0	0	2	2	5	1	....	.125	.300	.250	.550	58	-0	1	2.95	-0	/O-1	0	0.0
1914 Chi-N	2	1	0	0	0	0	0	0	0	0	0	....	.000	.000	.000	.000	-100	-0	0	.00	0	....	0	0.0
Total 2	11	9	1	1	1	0	0	2	2	5	1	....	.111	.273	.222	.495	43	-1	1	2.58	-0	/O-1	0	-0.1
• STILLMAN, Royle	Royle Eldon Stillman b: 1/2/1951, Santa Monica, CA BL/TL, 5'11", 180 lbs. Deb: 6/22/1975 Career OF: 19-1-9																							
1975 Bal-A	13	14	1	6	0	0	0	1	1	3	0	0	.429	.467	.429	.895	165	1	3	9.86	-0	/O-2(0-1-1)	1	0.1
1976 Bal-A	20	22	0	2	0	0	0	1	3	4	0	0	.091	.200	.091	.291	-14	-3	1	.68	0	/D-5,1-2	0	-0.4
1977 Chi-A	56	119	18	25	7	1	3	13	17	21	2	1	.210	.309	.361	.670	82	-3	14	3.96	-3	O-26(19-0-8),D-13/1-1	2	-0.7
Total 3	89	155	19	33	7	1	3	15	21	28	2	1	.213	.307	.329	.636	76	-4	18	3.81	-3	/O-28,D-18,1-3	3	-0.9
• STILLWELL, Kurt	Kurt Andrew Stillwell b: 6/4/1965, Glendale, CA BB/TR, 5'11", 175 lbs. Deb: 4/13/1986																							
1986 Cin-N	104	279	31	64	6	1	0	26	30	47	6	2	.229	.309	.258	.567	56	-16	24	2.88	-6	S-80	5	-1.5
1987 Cin-N	131	395	54	102	20	7	4	33	32	50	4	6	.258	.317	.375	.692	79	-14	46	4.06	-2	S-51,2-37,3-20	8	-1.0
1988 KC-A★	128	459	63	115	28	5	10	53	47	76	6	5	.251	.324	.399	.723	100	-1	60	4.45	-8	*S-124	16	0.0
1989 KC-A	130	463	52	121	20	7	7	54	42	64	9	6	.261	.327	.380	.707	99	-2	60	4.49	-25	*S-130	15	-1.7
1990 KC-A	144	506	60	126	35	4	3	51	39	60	0	2	.249	.308	.352	.660	85	-11	54	3.62	-11	*S-141	12	-1.3
1991 KC-A	122	385	44	102	17	1	6	51	33	56	3	4	.265	.325	.361	.686	89	-7	44	3.93	-7	*S-118	10	-0.6
1992 SD-N	114	379	35	86	15	3	2	24	26	58	4	1	.227	.278	.298	.576	62	-19	32	2.77	-13	*2-111	4	-3.1
1993 SD-N	57	121	9	26	4	0	1	11	11	22	4	3	.215	.286	.273	.558	49	-9	9	2.51	-5	S-30/3-3	1	-1.2
Cal-A	22	61	2	16	2	2	0	3	4	11	2	0	.262	.308	.361	.668	76	-2	7	3.67	-5	2-18/S-7	1	-0.5
1996 Tex-A	46	77	12	21	4	0	1	4	10	11	0	0	.273	.364	.364	.727	81	-2	11	5.09	-3	2-21/S-9,3-6,1-1,D-1	1	-0.4
Total 9	998	3125	362	779	151	30	34	310	274	455	38	29	.249	.313	.349	.663	82	-82	348	3.78	-84	S-690,2-187/3-29,1-1,D-1	73	-11.2
• STILLWELL, Ron	Ronald Roy Stillwell b: 12/3/1939, Los Angeles, CA BR/TR, 5'11", 165 lbs. Deb: 7/3/1961																							
1961 Was-A	8	16	3	2	1	0	0	1	1	4	0	0	.125	.176	.188	.364	-3	-2	1	1.11	0	/S-5	0	-0.2
1962 Was-A	6	22	5	6	0	0	0	2	2	2	0	0	.273	.333	.273	.606	66	-1	2	3.58	0	/2-6,S-1	0	-0.1
Total 2	14	38	8	8	1	0	0	3	3	6	0	0	.211	.268	.237	.505	38	-3	3	2.46	-0	/2-6,S-6	0	-0.3
• STIMAC, Craig	Craig Steven Stimac b: 11/18/1954, Oak Park, IL BR/TR, 6'2", 185 lbs. Deb: 8/12/1980																							
1980 SD-N	20	50	5	11	2	0	0	7	1	6	0	0	.220	.235	.260	.495	40	-4	3	2.09	2	C-11/3-2	0	-0.2
1981 SD-N	9	9	0	1	0	0	0	0	0	3	0	0	.111	.111	.111	.222	-40	-2	0	.38	0	....	0	-0.2
Total 2	29	59	5	12	2	0	0	7	1	9	0	0	.203	.217	.237	.454	29	-6	4	1.82	2	/C-11,3-2	0	-0.3
• STINNETT, Kelly	Kelly Lee Stinnett b: 2/14/1970, Lawton, OK BR/TR, 5'11", 195 lbs. Deb: 4/5/1994																							
1994 NY-N	47	150	20	38	6	2	2	14	11	28	2	0	.253	.325	.360	.685	79	-4	18	4.23	-2	C-44	4	-0.3
1995 NY-N	77	196	23	43	8	1	4	18	29	65	2	0	.219	.338	.332	.669	80	-4	24	4.18	-5	C-67	4	-0.5
1996 Mil-A	14	26	1	2	0	0	0	0	2	11	0	0	.077	.172	.077	.249	-33	-5	0	.54	-1	C-14/D-1	0	-0.5
1997 Mil-A	30	36	2	9	4	0	0	3	3	9	0	0	.250	.308	.361	.669	73	-1	4	4.24	0	C-25/D-1	1	0.0
1998 Ari-N	92	274	35	71	14	1	11	34	35	74	0	1	.259	.356	.438	.794	108	3	42	5.27	0	C-86/D-1	10	0.9
1999*Ari-N	88	284	36	66	13	0	14	38	24	83	2	1	.232	.304	.426	.730	81	-9	37	4.43	-2	C-86	6	-0.5
2000 Ari-N	76	240	22	52	7	0	8	33	19	56	0	1	.217	.291	.346	.636	58	-17	24	3.30	4	C-74	5	-0.7
2001 Cin-N	63	187	27	48	11	0	9	25	17	61	2	2	.257	.335	.460	.795	98	-1	28	5.07	-3	C-59/D-1	5	0.0
2002 Cin-N	34	93	10	21	5	0	3	13	15	25	2	0	.226	.333	.376	.710	84	-2	13	4.76	3	C-30	4	0.3
2003 Cin-N	60	179	14	41	13	0	3	19	13	51	0	0	.229	.296	.352	.648	69	-8	19	3.53	-2	C-50	3	-0.7
Phi-N	7	7	0	3	0	0	0	0	1	1	0	0	.429	.500	.429	.929	155	1	2	11.00	1	/C-1	1	0.1
Yr.	67	186	14	44	13	0	3	19	14	52	0	0	.237	.304	.355	.659	73	-8	20	3.74	-2	C-51	4	-0.6
Total 10	588	1672	190	394	81	4	54	197	169	464	10	5	.236	.320	.386	.706	81	-49	211	4.29	-7	C-536/D-4	43	-2.0
• STINSON, Bob	Gorrell Robert Stinson b: 10/11/1945, Elkin, NC BB/TR, 5'11", 185 lbs. Deb: 9/23/1969 Career OF: 3-0-4																							
1969 LA-N	4	8	1	3	0	0	0	2	0	2	0	1	.375	.375	.375	.750	119	-0	0	1.32	-1	/C-4	0	-0.1
1970 LA-N	4	3	1	0	0	0	0	0	0	1	0	0	.000	.000	.000	.000	-105	-1	0	.00	-1	/C-3	0	-0.2
1971 StL-N	17	19	3	4	1	0	0	1	1	7	0	0	.211	.250	.263	.513	44	-1	1	2.37	-1	/C-6,O-3(1-0-2)	0	-0.2
1972 Hou-N	27	35	3	6	1	0	0	2	1	6	0	0	.171	.216	.200	.416	19	-4	2	1.52	-1	C-12/O-3(2-0-1)	0	-0.5
1973 Mon-N	48	111	12	29	6	1	3	12	17	15	0	0	.261	.374	.414	.788	114	2	18	5.50	-2	C-35/3-1	4	0.2
1974 Mon-N	38	87	4	15	2	0	1	6	15	16	1	1	.172	.294	.230	.524	45	-6	6	2.14	2	C-29	2	-0.3
1975 KC-A	63	147	18	39	9	1	1	9	18	29	1	0	.265	.349	.361	.710	98	1	20	4.77	1	C-59/1-1,2-1,D-1,O-1	6	0.4
1976*KC-A	79	209	26	55	7	1	2	25	25	29	3	1	.263	.345	.335	.680	99	1	25	4.07	-3	C-79	8	0.1
1977 Sea-A	105	297	27	80	11	1	8	32	37	50	0	3	.269	.362	.394	.756	107	3	41	4.72	-2	C-99/D-1	10	0.6
1978 Sea-A	124	364	46	94	14	3	11	55	45	42	2	1	.258	.349	.404	.753	112	7	52	4.89	-4	*C-123/D-1	13	0.9
1979 Sea-A	95	247	19	60	8	0	6	28	33	38	1	2	.243	.342	.348	.690	85	-5	30	3.96	-5	C-91	5	-0.5
1980 Sea-A	48	107	6	23	2	0	1	8	9	19	0	0	.215	.282	.262	.544	49	-7	8	2.51	-2	C-45	1	-0.8
Total 12	652	1634	166	408	61	7	33	180	201	254	8	10	.250	.340	.356	.696	94	-10	205	4.18	-19	C-585/O-7,D-3,1-1,2-1,3-1	49	-0.5
• STIRES, Gat	Garrett Stires b: 10/13/1849, Hunterdon County, NJ d: 6/13/1933, Byron, IL BL/TR, 5'8", 180 lbs. Deb: 5/6/1871 U																							
1871 Rok-n	25	110	23	30	4	6	2	24	7	5	3	0	.273	.316	.473	.789	129	5	18	7.02	1	*O-25(0-0-25)	....	0.5
• STIRNWEISS, Snuffy	George Henry Stirnweiss b: 10/26/1918, New York, NY d: 9/15/1958, Newark Bay, NJ BR/TR, 5'8.5", 175 lbs. Deb: 4/22/1943																							
1943*NY-A	83	274	34	60	8	4	1	25	47	37	11	9	.219	.333	.288	.622	82	-6	28	3.16	-2	S-68/2-4	7	-0.2
1944 NY-A	154	643	**125**	**205**	35	**16**	8	43	73	87	**55**	11	.319	.389	.460	.849	138	40	128	7.52	32	*2-154	**35**	**8.4**
1945 NY-A★	152	632	**107**	**195**	32	**22**	10	64	78	62	**33**	17	**.309**	.385	**.476**	**.862**	**143**	**35**	121	6.96	36	*2-152	**34**	**8.5**
1946 NY-A★	129	487	75	122	19	7	0	37	66	58	18	6	.251	.340	.318	.658	83	-7	57	3.97	9	3-79,2-46/S-4	13	0.4
1947*NY-A	148	571	102	146	18	8	5	41	89	47	5	3	.256	.358	.342	.700	96	0	76	4.55	12	*2-148	20	2.1
1948 NY-A	141	515	90	130	20	7	3	32	86	62	5	4	.252	.360	.336	.696	87	-7	68	4.46	13	*2-141	17	1.3
1949*NY-A	70	157	29	41	8	2	0	11	29	20	3	2	.261	.380	.338	.717	91	-1	23	5.05	1	2-51/3-4	6	0.3

YEAR TM-L	G	AB	R	H	2B	3B	HR	RBI	BB	SO	SB	CS	AVG	OBP	SLG	OPS	OPS+	BR/A	RC	RC/G	FR	G/POS	WS	TPW
1950 NY-A	7	2	0	0	0	0	0	0	0	0	0	0	.000	.000	.000	.000	-103	-1	0	.00	-1	/2-4	0	-0.2
StL-A	93	326	32	71	16	2	1	24	51	49	3	3	.218	.324	.288	.612	56	-22	33	3.34	-4	2-62,3-31/S-5	4	-2.1
Yr.	100	328	32	71	16	2	1	24	51	49	3	3	.216	.322	.287	.608	55	-22	33	3.32	-6	2-66,3-31/S-5	4	-2.3
1951 Cle-A	50	88	10	19	1	0	1	4	22	25	1	0	.216	.373	.261	.634	78	-1	11	4.00	5	2-25/3-2	3	0.5
1952 Cle-A	1	0	0	0	0	0	0	0	0	0	0	0	....	....	....	....	-107	0	0	....	0	/3-1	0	0.0
Total 10	1028	3695	604	989	157	68	29	281	541	447	134	55	.268	.362	.371	.733	102	31	545	5.10	100	2-787,3-117/S-77	139	19.0

• STIVETTS, Jack

John Elmer "Happy Jack" Stivetts
b: 3/31/1868, Ashland, PA d: 4/18/1930, Ashland, PA BR/TR, 6'2", 185 lbs. Deb: 6/26/1889 U Career OF: 41-33-69 ♦

YEAR TM-L	G	AB	R	H	2B	3B	HR	RBI	BB	SO	SB	CS	AVG	OBP	SLG	OPS	OPS+	BR/A	RC	RC/G	FR	G/POS	WS	TPW
1889 StL-a	27	79	12	18	2	2	0	7	3	13	0	....	.228	.265	.304	.569	55	-1	7	2.83	0	P-26/O-1	21	3.1
1890 StL-a	67	226	36	65	15	6	7	43	16	....	2	....	.288	.337	.500	.837	128	15	40	6.55	2	P-54,O-10(0-10-0)/1-3	41	4.5
1891 StL-a	85	302	45	92	10	2	7	54	10	32	4	....	.305	.331	.421	.752	100	9	44	5.61	4	P-64,O-24(1-0-23)	46	6.1
1892*Bos-N	71	240	40	71	14	2	3	36	27	28	8	....	.296	.369	.408	.778	124	16	40	6.41	1	P-54,O-18(16-2-0)/1-1	49	2.3
1893 Bos-N	50	172	32	51	5	6	3	25	12	14	6	....	.297	.342	.448	.790	101	6	29	6.38	-3	P-38/O-8(3-0-5),3-3	25	1.5
1894 Bos-N	68	244	55	80	12	7	8	64	16	21	3	....	.328	.369	.533	.902	102	9	50	7.98	-3	P-45,O-16(8-2-6)/1-4	33	2.7
1895 Bos-N	46	158	20	30	6	4	0	24	6	18	1	....	.190	.220	.278	.498	26	-10	10	2.15	-1	P-38/1-5,O-2(0-1-1)	18	-0.1
1896 Bos-N	67	221	42	76	9	6	3	49	12	10	4	....	.344	.380	.480	.860	119	14	43	7.70	-6	P-42,O-12(3-2-7)/1-5,3-1	29	1.5
1897*Bos-N	61	199	41	73	9	9	2	37	15	....	2	....	.367	.417	.533	.949	141	15	46	9.65	-1	O-29(6-10-14),P-18/1-2,2-2	20	2.0
1898 Bos-N	41	111	16	28	1	1	2	16	10	....	1	....	.252	.314	.333	.647	81	-3	13	3.88	-2	O-14(2-5-8),1-10/S-4,2-2,P	2	-1.1
1899 Cle-N	18	39	8	8	1	1	0	2	6	....	0	....	.205	.326	.282	.608	73	0	4	3.14	1	/O-7(2-1-4),P-7,3-1,S-1	1	-0.7
Total 11	601	1991	347	592	84	46	35	357	133	136	31	....	.297	.344	.438	.783	104	70	327	6.14	-9	P-388,O-141/1-30,3-5,S-5,2	285	21.9

• STOCK, Milt

Milton Joseph Stock b: 7/11/1893, Chicago, IL d: 7/16/1977, Fairhope, AL BR/TR, 5'8", 154 lbs. Deb: 9/29/1913 C

YEAR TM-L	G	AB	R	H	2B	3B	HR	RBI	BB	SO	SB	CS	AVG	OBP	SLG	OPS	OPS+	BR/A	RC	RC/G	FR	G/POS	WS	TPW
1913 NY-N	7	17	2	3	1	0	0	1	2	1	2	....	.176	.263	.235	.498	43	-1	1	2.55	-1	/S-7	0	-0.2
1914 NY-N	115	365	52	96	17	1	3	41	34	21	11	....	.263	.333	.340	.672	103	2	44	4.06	10	*3-113/S-1	15	1.7
1915*Phi-N	69	227	37	59	7	3	1	15	22	26	6	2	.260	.325	.330	.656	98	0	26	3.97	-1	3-55/S-4	8	0.1
1916 Phi-N	132	509	61	143	25	6	1	43	27	33	21	26	.281	.320	.360	.679	105	-5	56	3.61	0	*3-117,S-15	21	-0.1
1917 Phi-N	150	564	76	149	27	6	3	53	51	34	25	....	.264	.326	.349	.676	103	2	71	4.19	-17	*3-133,S-19	19	-1.0
1918 Phi-N	123	481	62	132	14	1	1	42	35	22	20	....	.274	.325	.314	.639	89	-6	54	3.84	-4	*3-123	13	-0.7
1919 StL-N	135	492	56	151	16	4	0	52	49	21	17	....	.307	.371	.356	.727	127	18	70	5.06	6	2-77,3-58	20	2.9
1920 StL-N	155	639	85	204	28	6	0	76	40	27	15	17	.319	.360	.382	.742	116	11	86	4.72	-8	*3-155	20	0.8
1921 StL-N	149	587	96	180	27	6	3	84	48	26	11	3	.307	.360	.388	.748	100	5	85	5.08	-19	*3-149	17	-0.4
1922 StL-N	151	581	85	177	33	9	5	79	42	29	7	12	.305	.352	.418	.770	103	-1	83	4.97	-7	*3-149/S-1	17	0.1
1923 StL-N	151	603	63	174	33	3	2	96	40	21	9	6	.289	.334	.363	.697	86	-12	74	4.28	-5	*3-150/2-1	15	-0.7
1924 Bro-N	142	561	66	136	14	4	2	52	26	32	3	8	.242	.277	.292	.570	54	-37	45	2.62	-21	*3-142	4	-4.9
1925 Bro-N	146	615	98	202	28	9	1	62	38	28	8	1	.328	.368	.408	.776	101	3	93	5.85	-11	*2-141/3-5	19	-0.3
1926 Bro-N	3	8	0	0	0	0	0	0	1	0	0	....	.000	.111	.000	.111	-69	-2	0	.19	0	/2-3	0	-0.2
Total 14	1628	6249	839	1806	270	58	22	696	455	321	155	75	.289	.339	.361	.700	98	-23	789	4.37	-79	*3-1349,2-222/S-47	188	-2.9

• STOCKER, Kevin

Kevin Douglas Stocker b: 2/13/1970, Spokane, WA BB/TR, 6', 175 lbs. Deb: 7/7/1993

YEAR TM-L	G	AB	R	H	2B	3B	HR	RBI	BB	SO	SB	CS	AVG	OBP	SLG	OPS	OPS+	BR/A	RC	RC/G	FR	G/POS	WS	TPW
1993*Phi-N	70	259	46	84	12	3	2	31	30	43	5	0	.324	.411	.417	.828	124	12	45	6.52	9	S-70	10	2.7
1994 Phi-N	82	271	38	74	11	2	2	28	44	41	2	2	.273	.388	.351	.739	92	-1	41	5.21	7	S-82	10	1.3
1995 Phi-N	125	412	42	90	14	3	1	32	43	75	6	1	.218	.306	.274	.580	54	-26	38	2.96	12	*S-125	8	-0.4
1996 Phi-N	119	394	46	100	22	6	5	41	43	89	6	4	.254	.339	.378	.717	88	-7	52	4.51	16	*S-119	12	1.8
1997 Phi-N	149	504	51	134	23	5	4	40	51	91	11	6	.266	.336	.355	.691	81	-14	59	4.06	-12	*S-147	12	-1.4
1998 TB-A	112	336	37	70	11	3	6	25	27	80	5	3	.208	.283	.313	.596	54	-24	30	2.86	13	*S-110	5	-0.2
1999 TB-A	79	254	39	76	11	2	1	27	24	41	9	7	.299	.369	.370	.739	88	-5	35	4.91	-10	S-76	7	-0.8
2000 TB-A	40	114	20	30	7	1	2	8	19	27	1	2	.263	.378	.395	.773	97	-0	17	5.18	-9	S-40	3	-0.6
Ana-A	70	229	21	45	13	3	0	16	32	54	0	3	.197	.300	.279	.580	47	-20	19	2.57	7	S-69	3	-0.7
Yr.	110	343	41	75	20	4	2	24	51	81	1	5	.219	.327	.318	.644	64	-20	37	3.37	-2	*S-109	6	-1.3
Total 8	846	2773	340	703	124	28	23	248	313	541	45	28	.254	.340	.343	.683	78	-84	337	4.10	33	S-838	70	1.8

• STOCKWELL, Len

Leonard Clark Stockwell b: 8/25/1859, Cordova, IL d: 1/28/1905, Niles, CA BR/TR, 5'11", 165 lbs. Deb: 5/17/1879 Career OF: 2-2-1

YEAR TM-L	G	AB	R	H	2B	3B	HR	RBI	BB	SO	SB	CS	AVG	OBP	SLG	OPS	OPS+	BR/A	RC	RC/G	FR	G/POS	WS	TPW
1879 Cle-N	2	6	0	0	0	0	0	0	0	2	....	....	.000	.000	.000	.000	-101	-1	0	.00	1	/O-2(0-1-1)	0	0.0
1884 Lou-a	2	9	0	1	0	0	0	0	0	....	....	....	.111	.111	.111	.222	-29	-1	0	.39	0	/O-2(1-1-0),C-1	0	-0.1
1890 Cle-N	2	7	2	2	1	0	0	0	0	3	0	....	.286	.286	.429	.714	109	0	1	4.66	0	/1-1,O-1	0	0.0
Total 3	6	22	2	3	1	0	0	0	0	5	0	....	.136	.136	.182	.318	-4	-2	1	1.39	1	/O-5,1-1,C-1	0	-0.1

• STODDARD,

Stoddard Deb: 9/25/1875

YEAR TM-L	G	AB	R	H	2B	3B	HR	RBI	BB	SO	SB	CS	AVG	OBP	SLG	OPS	OPS+	BR/A	RC	RC/G	FR	G/POS	WS	TPW
1875 Atl-n	2	9	1	1	1	0	0	0	0	1	0	0	.111	.111	.222	.333	15	-1	0	.84	0	/O-2(1-1-0)	....	-0.1

• STOKES, Al

Albert John Stokes b: 1/1/1900, Chicago, IL d: 12/19/1986, Grantham, NH BR/TR, 5'9", 175 lbs. Deb: 5/10/1925

YEAR TM-L	G	AB	R	H	2B	3B	HR	RBI	BB	SO	SB	CS	AVG	OBP	SLG	OPS	OPS+	BR/A	RC	RC/G	FR	G/POS	WS	TPW
1925 Bos-A	17	52	7	11	0	1	0	1	4	8	0	0	.212	.268	.250	.518	32	-5	4	2.33	2	C-17	0	-0.2
1926 Bos-A	30	86	7	14	3	3	0	6	8	28	0	0	.163	.234	.267	.501	32	-9	6	2.07	-1	C-29	1	-0.8
Total 2	47	138	14	25	3	4	0	7	12	36	0	0	.181	.247	.261	.508	32	-14	9	2.16	1	/C-46	1	-1.0

• STONE, Gene

Eugene Daniel Stone b: 1/16/1944, Burbank, CA BL/TL, 5'11", 190 lbs. Deb: 5/13/1969

YEAR TM-L	G	AB	R	H	2B	3B	HR	RBI	BB	SO	SB	CS	AVG	OBP	SLG	OPS	OPS+	BR/A	RC	RC/G	FR	G/POS	WS	TPW
1969 Phi-N	18	28	4	6	0	1	0	0	4	9	0	0	.214	.313	.286	.598	70	-1	3	3.37	-1	/1-5	0	-0.2

• STONE, George

George Robert Stone b: 9/3/1877, Lost Nation, IA d: 1/3/1945, Clinton, IA BL/TL, 5'9", 175 lbs. Deb: 4/20/1903 Career OF: 813-1-23

YEAR TM-L	G	AB	R	H	2B	3B	HR	RBI	BB	SO	SB	CS	AVG	OBP	SLG	OPS	OPS+	BR/A	RC	RC/G	FR	G/POS	WS	TPW
1903 Bos-A	2	2	0	0	0	0	0	0	0	....	0	....	.000	.000	.000	.000	-95	-0	0	.00	0	....	0	0.0
1905 StL-A	154	632	76	**187**	25	13	7	52	44	....	26	....	.296	.347	.410	.756	147	32	102	5.96	9	*O-154(154-0-0)	27	**3.5**
1906 StL-A	154	581	91	208	25	20	6	71	52	....	35	....	**.358**	**.417**	**.501**	**.918**	**195**	**63**	141	**9.56**	-2	*O-154(154-0-0)	**38**	5.8
1907 StL-A	155	596	77	191	13	11	4	59	59	....	23	....	.320	.387	.399	.787	151	36	105	6.69	-3	*O-155(155-0-0)	27	2.7
1908 StL-A	148	588	89	165	21	8	5	31	55	....	20	....	.281	.345	.369	.714	131	21	81	4.83	1	*O-148(148-0-0)	26	1.5
1909 StL-A	83	310	33	89	5	4	1	15	24	....	8	....	.287	.340	.339	.679	123	8	39	4.31	0	O-81(63-0-18)	11	0.3
1910 StL-A	152	562	60	144	17	12	0	40	48	....	20	....	.256	.315	.329	.644	109	5	65	3.83	-2	*O-145(139-1-5)	17	-0.6
Total 7	848	3271	426	984	106	68	23	268	282	....	132	....	.301	.360	.396	.756	145	165	534	5.91	3	O-837	146	13.1

• STONE, Jeff

Jeffrey Glen Stone b: 12/26/1960, Kennett, MO BL/TR, 6', 175 lbs. Deb: 9/9/1983 Career OF: 191-36-12

YEAR TM-L	G	AB	R	H	2B	3B	HR	RBI	BB	SO	SB	CS	AVG	OBP	SLG	OPS	OPS+	BR/A	RC	RC/G	FR	G/POS	WS	TPW
1983 Phi-N	9	4	2	3	0	2	0	3	0	1	4	0	.750	.750	1.750	2.500	580	3	7	183.87	0	/O-1	1	0.3
1984 Phi-N	51	185	27	67	4	6	1	15	9	26	27	5	.362	.398	.465	.863	139	13	37	7.86	-4	O-46(46-0-0)	8	0.8
1985 Phi-N	88	264	36	70	4	3	3	11	15	50	15	5	.265	.307	.337	.644	78	-7	28	3.73	-2	O-69(69-0-0)	4	-1.2
1986 Phi-N	82	249	32	69	6	4	6	19	20	52	19	6	.277	.341	.406	.746	101	2	36	5.10	3	O-58(37-25-0)	8	0.3
1987 Phi-N	66	125	19	32	7	1	1	16	8	38	3	1	.256	.316	.352	.668	74	-5	14	4.01	1	O-25(20-5-1)	2	-0.4
1988 Bal-A	26	61	4	10	1	0	0	1	4	11	4	1	.164	.215	.180	.396	12	-7	2	1.07	2	O-21(18-0-3)/D-1	0	-0.6
1989 Tex-A	22	36	5	6	1	2	0	5	3	5	2	1	.167	.250	.306	.556	55	-2	2	1.84	0	D-15/O-3(1-1-1)	0	-0.3
Bos-A	18	15	3	3	0	0	0	1	1	2	1	0	.200	.250	.200	.450	27	-1	1	1.37	0	O-11(0-4-7)/D-3	0	-0.2
Yr.	40	51	8	9	1	2	0	6	4	7	3	1	.176	.250	.275	.525	47	-3	3	1.71	-1	D-18,O-14(1-5-8)	0	-0.5
1990 Bos-A	10	2	1	1	0	0	0	1	0	1	0	1	.500	.500	.500	1.000	172	-0	0	.00	0	/D-2	0	0.0
Total 8	372	941	129	261	23	18	11	72	60	186	75	20	.277	.328	.375	.703	92	-4	128	4.76	0	O-234/D-21	23	-1.2

• STONE, John

John Thomas "Rocky" Stone
b: 10/10/1905, Lynchburg, TN d: 11/30/1955, Shelbyville, TN BL/TR, 6'1", 178 lbs. Deb: 8/31/1928 Career OF: 599-100-447

YEAR TM-L	G	AB	R	H	2B	3B	HR	RBI	BB	SO	SB	CS	AVG	OBP	SLG	OPS	OPS+	BR/A	RC	RC/G	FR	G/POS	WS	TPW
1928 Det-A	26	113	20	40	10	3	2	21	5	8	1	0	.354	.387	.549	.935	141	6	24	8.28	-1	O-26(26-0-0)	5	0.4
1929 Det-A	51	150	23	39	11	2	2	15	11	13	1	1	.260	.311	.400	.711	81	-5	19	4.32	0	O-36(35-0-2)	2	-0.7
1930 Det-A	127	425	60	132	29	11	3	56	32	49	6	9	.311	.360	.452	.812	102	-1	67	5.72	-6	*O-109(93-11-6)	11	-1.4
1931 Det-A	147	584	86	191	28	11	10	76	56	48	13	13	.327	.388	.464	.852	119	16	103	6.67	7	*O-147(143-5-0)	17	1.4
1932 Det-A	145	582	106	173	35	12	17	108	58	64	2	1	.297	.361	.486	.847	113	10	103	6.63	0	*O-142(90-53-0)	22	0.4
1933 Det-A	148	574	86	161	33	11	11	80	54	37	1	4	.280	.344	.434	.778	103	1	86	5.43	-1	*O-141(18-0-124)	16	-0.9
1934 Was-A	113	419	77	132	28	7	7	67	52	26	1	2	.315	.395	.465	.860	126	16	79	7.01	5	*O-112(0-16-98)	14	1.4

YEAR TM-L	G	AB	R	H	2B	3B	HR	RBI	BB	SO	SB	CS	AVG	OBP	SLG	OPS	OPS+	BR/A	RC	RC/G	FR	G/POS	WS	TPW
1935 Was-A	125	455	78	143	27	18	1	78	39	29	4	5	.314	.372	.459	.832	118	10	77	6.43	1	*0-114(19-7-90)	15	0.5
1936 Was-A	123	437	95	149	22	11	15	90	60	26	8	0	.341	.421	.545	.965	145	33	104	9.48	6	*0-114(109-0-6)	21	2.9
1937 Was-A	139	542	84	179	33	15	6	88	66	36	6	4	.330	.403	.480	.883	127	23	107	7.68	6	*0-137(37-7-95)	22	1.9
1938 Was-A	56	213	24	52	12	4	3	28	30	16	2	1	.244	.337	.380	.718	85	-5	29	4.68	-1	0-53(29-1-26)	4	-0.8
Total 11	**1200**	**4494**	**739**	**1391**	**268**	**105**	**77**	**707**	**463**	**352**	**45**	**40**	**.310**	**.376**	**.467**	**.843**	**116**	**106**	**797**	**6.64**	**17**	***0-1131**	**149**	**5.2**
• STONE, Ron	Harry Ronald Stone b: 9/9/1942, Corning, CA BL/TL, 6'2", 195 lbs. Deb: 4/13/1966 Career OF: 118-6-123																							
1966 KC-A	26	22	2	6	1	0	0	0	0	2	1	1	.273	.273	.318	.591	71	-1	2	2.71	0	/0-4(2-2-1),1-3	0	-0.2
1969 Phi-N	103	222	22	53	7	1	1	24	29	28	3	1	.239	.335	.293	.627	79	-5	21	3.08	1	0-69(37-2-32)	3	-0.6
1970 Phi-N	123	321	30	84	12	5	3	39	38	45	5	6	.262	.342	.358	.700	90	-5	40	4.25	-3	0-99(51-0-48)/1-6	7	-1.3
1971 Phi-N	95	185	16	42	8	1	2	23	25	36	2	2	.227	.319	.314	.633	80	-5	19	3.36	0	0-51(22-1-33)/1-3	3	-0.7
1972 Phi-N	41	54	3	9	0	1	0	3	9	11	0	0	.167	.286	.204	.489	40	-4	3	1.76	2	0-15(6-1-9)	0	-0.3
Total 5	**388**	**804**	**73**	**194**	**28**	**8**	**6**	**89**	**101**	**122**	**11**	**10**	**.241**	**.329**	**.318**	**.647**	**81**	**-20**	**85**	**3.49**	**0**	**0-238/1-12**	**13**	**-3.1**
• STONE, Tige	William Arthur Stone b: 9/18/1901, Macon, GA d: 1/1/1960, Jacksonville, FL BR/TR, 5'8", 145 lbs. Deb: 8/23/1923																							
1923 StL-N	5	1	0	1	0	0	0	0	2	0	0	0	1.000	1.000	1.000	2.000	438	1	1	∞	-1	/0-4(2-2-0),P-1	0	-0.2
• STONEHAM, John	John Andrew Stoneham b: 11/8/1908, Wood River, IL BL/TR, 5'9.5", 168 lbs. Deb: 9/18/1933																							
1933 Chi-A	10	25	4	3	0	0	1	3	2	2	0	0	.120	.185	.240	.425	12	-3	1	1.39	-1	/0-9(1-1-7)	0	-0.4
• STORIE, Howie	Howard Edward "Sponge" Storie b: 5/15/1911, Pittsfield, MA d: 7/27/1968, Pittsfield, MA BR/TR, 5'10", 175 lbs. Deb: 9/7/1931																							
1931 Bos-A	6	17	2	2	0	0	0	0	3	2	0	0	.118	.250	.118	.368	-1	-2	1	1.18	0	/C-6	0	-0.2
1932 Bos-A	6	8	0	3	0	0	0	0	0	0	0	0	.375	.375	.375	.750	97	-0	1	5.72	0	/C-5	0	0.0
Total 2	**12**	**25**	**2**	**5**	**0**	**0**	**0**	**0**	**3**	**2**	**0**	**0**	**.200**	**.286**	**.200**	**.486**	**27**	**-2**	**2**	**2.32**	**0**	**/C-11**	**0**	**-0.2**
• STORKE, Alan	Alan Marshall Storke b: 9/27/1884, Auburn, NY d: 3/18/1910, Newton, MA BR/TR, 6'1" Deb: 9/24/1906																							
1906 Pit-N	5	12	1	3	1	0	0	1	1	....	1	....	.250	.308	.333	.641	96	-0	2	4.56	1	/3-2,S-1	1	0.1
1907 Pit-N	112	357	24	92	6	6	1	39	16	....	6	....	.258	.295	.317	.612	90	-5	37	3.52	-5	3-67,1-23/2-7,S-5	9	-0.9
1908 Pit-N	64	202	20	51	5	3	1	12	9	....	4	....	.252	.284	.322	.606	93	-2	20	3.21	-3	1-49/3-6,2-1	5	-0.7
1909 Pit-N	37	118	12	30	5	2	0	12	7	....	1	....	.254	.302	.331	.632	92	-2	12	3.40	0	1-18,3-14	3	-0.2
StL-N	48	174	11	49	5	0	0	10	12	....	5	....	.282	.328	.310	.638	105	1	19	3.87	-2	S-44/2-4,1-1	4	0.0
Yr.	85	292	23	79	10	2	0	22	19	....	6	....	.271	.317	.318	.636	99	-1	32	3.67	-2	S-44,1-19,3-14/2-4	7	-0.2
Total 4	**266**	**863**	**68**	**225**	**22**	**11**	**2**	**74**	**45**	**....**	**17**	**....**	**.261**	**.300**	**.319**	**.619**	**94**	**-8**	**90**	**3.51**	**-9**	**/1-91,3-89,S-50,2-12**	**22**	**-1.7**
• STORTI, Lin	Lindo Ivan Storti b: 12/5/1906, Santa Monica, CA d: 7/24/1982, Ontario, CA BB/TR, 5'11", 165 lbs. Deb: 9/18/1930																							
1930 StL-A	7	28	6	9	1	1	0	2	2	6	0	0	.321	.367	.429	.795	97	-0	4	6.15	1	/2-6	1	0.1
1931 StL-A	86	273	32	60	15	4	3	26	15	50	0	2	.220	.263	.337	.600	55	-19	24	2.88	-2	3-67/2-7	2	-1.7
1932 StL-A	53	193	19	50	11	2	3	26	5	20	1	0	.259	.278	.383	.661	66	-10	20	3.65	0	3-51	3	-0.8
1933 StL-A	70	210	26	41	7	4	3	21	25	31	2	2	.195	.281	.310	.590	53	-15	19	2.90	2	3-32,2-24	2	-1.0
Total 4	**216**	**704**	**83**	**160**	**34**	**11**	**9**	**75**	**47**	**107**	**3**	**4**	**.227**	**.277**	**.345**	**.622**	**59**	**-44**	**68**	**3.20**	**1**	**3-150/2-37**	**8**	**-3.4**
• STOUCH, Tom	Thomas Carl Stouch b: 12/2/1869, Perrysville, OH d: 10/7/1956, Lancaster, PA BR/TR, 6'2", 165 lbs. Deb: 7/7/1898																							
1898 Lou-N	4	16	4	5	1	0	0	6	1	....	0	....	.313	.353	.375	.728	110	0	2	5.23	-1	/2-4	0	-0.1
• STOVALL, Da Rond	DaRond Tyrone Stovall b: 1/3/1973, St. Louis, MO BB/TL, 6'1" Deb: 4/1/1998																							
1998 Mon-N	62	78	11	16	2	1	2	6	6	29	1	0	.205	.262	.333	.595	56	-5	7	3.01	-2	*0-100(27-14-7)	0	-0.7
• STOVALL, George	George Thomas "Firebrand" Stovall b: 11/23/1877, Leeds, MO d: 11/5/1951, Burlington, IA BR/TR, 6'2", 180 lbs. Deb: 7/4/1904 M Career OF: 2-9-0																							
1904 Cle-A	52	181	18	54	10	1	1	31	2	....	3	....	.298	.317	.381	.698	121	4	24	4.81	-2	1-38/2-9,0-3(2-1-0),3-1	5	0.1
1905 Cle-A	112	423	41	115	31	1	1	47	13	....	13	....	.272	.295	.357	.652	105	0	50	4.23	1	1-60,2-46/0-4(0-3-0)	11	0.0
1906 Cle-A	116	443	54	121	19	5	0	37	8	....	15	....	.273	.288	.339	.626	97	-4	50	3.94	1	1-55,3-30,2-19	8	-0.3
1907 Cle-A	124	466	38	110	17	6	1	36	18	....	13	....	.236	.267	.305	.572	82	-11	44	3.15	0	*1-122/3-2	9	-1.4
1908 Cle-A	138	534	71	156	29	6	2	45	17	....	14	....	.292	.316	.380	.697	126	12	69	4.39	9	*1-132/0-5(0-5-0),S-1	21	2.1
1909 Cle-A	145	565	60	139	17	10	2	49	6	....	25	....	.246	.259	.322	.581	80	-16	53	3.06	7	*1-145	9	-1.3
1910 Cle-A	142	521	49	136	19	4	0	52	14	....	16	....	.261	.284	.313	.597	86	-11	52	3.24	6	*1-132/2-2	10	-0.8
1911 Cle-A	126	458	48	124	17	7	0	79	21	....	11	....	.271	.306	.338	.644	79	-15	50	3.77	5	*1-118/2-2	7	-1.2
1912 StL-A	116	398	35	101	17	5	0	45	14	....	11	....	.254	.286	.322	.608	76	-14	39	3.31	0	1-94	4	-1.5
1913 StL-A	89	303	34	87	14	3	1	24	7	23	7	....	.287	.305	.363	.669	98	-3	34	3.91	6	1-76	6	0.2
1914 KC-F	124	450	51	128	20	5	7	75	23	35	6	....	.284	.325	.398	.723	110	4	58	4.43	2	*1-116/3-1	12	0.5
1915 KC-F	130	480	48	111	21	3	0	44	29	36	8	....	.231	.283	.288	.571	70	-18	40	2.74	11	*1-129	9	-1.1
Total 12	**1414**	**5222**	**547**	**1382**	**231**	**56**	**15**	**564**	**172**	**94**	**142**	**....**	**.265**	**.292**	**.339**	**.631**	**93**	**-72**	**563**	**3.66**	**47**	***1-1217/2-78,3-34,0-12,S-1**	**111**	**-4.8**
• STOVEY, Harry	Harry Duffield Stovey b: 12/20/1856, Philadelphia, PA d: 9/20/1937, New Bedford, MA BR/TR, 5'11.5", 175 lbs. Deb: 5/1/1880 M Career OF: 519-176-251																							
1880 Wor-N	83	355	76	94	21	**14**	**6**	28	12	46	....	....	.265	.289	.454	.742	135	12	48	5.02	-5	0-46(5-42-0),1-37/P-2	13	0.2
1881 Wor-N	75	341	57	92	25	7	2	30	12	23	....	....	.270	.295	.402	.696	110	3	41	4.49	-3	*1-57,0-18(1-0-17)	9	-0.3
1882 Wor-N	84	360	90	104	13	10	5	26	22	34	....	....	.289	.330	.422	.752	136	14	51	5.52	4	1-43,0-41(41-0-0)	10	1.2
1883 Phi-a	94	421	**110**	128	**31**	6	**14**	66	27	....	....	....	.304	.346	**.506**	.852	158	26	76	7.22	4	*1-93/0-3(0-3-0),P-1	25	1.7
1884 Phi-a	104	448	**124**	146	22	**23**	10	83	26	....	....	....	.326	.368	.545	.913	182	39	92	8.39	0	*1-104	22	2.7
1885 Phi-a	112	486	**130**	153	27	9	**13**	75	39	....	....	....	.315	.371	.488	.858	160	32	90	7.30	3	*1-82,0-30(0-30-0)	23	2.4
1886 Phi-a	123	489	115	144	28	11	7	59	64	....	**68**	....	.294	.377	.440	.817	154	32	109	**8.56**	-2	0-63(0-46-17),1-62/P-1	24	1.8
1887 Phi-a	124	553	125	198	31	12	4	77	56	....	74	....	.358	.366	.421	.787	119	13	106	8.08	7	0-80(49-29-2),1-46	17	1.1
1888 Phi-a	130	530	127	152	25	**20**	9	65	62	....	87	....	.287	.365	.460	.825	165	**39**	124	8.84	6	*0-118(118-0-0),1-13	28	**3.7**
1889 Phi-a	137	556	**152**	171	38	13	**19**	**119**	77	68	63	....	.308	.393	**.525**	.918	162	45	143	9.84	18	*0-137(137-0-0)/1-1	28	**4.9**
1890 Bos-P	118	481	142	144	25	11	12	84	81	38	**97**	....	.299	.406	.472	.878	125	18	135	10.79	2	*0-117(1-0-116)/1-1	20	1.4
1891 Bos-N	134	544	118	152	31	**20**	**16**	95	79	69	57	....	.279	.373	**.498**	.871	137	23	125	8.63	5	*0-134(39-0-96)/1-1	26	2.2
1892 Bos-N	38	146	21	24	8	1	0	12	14	19	20	....	.164	.252	.233	.484	43	-11	14	3.08	0	0-38(38-0-0)	3	-1.3
Bal-N	74	283	58	77	14	11	4	55	40	32	20	....	.272	.364	.442	.806	140	13	54	7.09	-4	0-64(64-0-0),1-10	9	0.3
Yr.	112	429	79	101	22	12	4	67	54	51	40	....	.235	.326	.371	.697	107	3	68	5.60	-3	*0-102(102-0-0),1-10	12	-0.9
1893 Bal-N	8	26	4	4	2	0	0	5	8	3	1	....	.154	.353	.231	.584	55	-1	3	3.05	0	/0-7(7-0-0)	0	-0.1
Bro-N	48	175	43	44	6	6	1	29	44	11	22	....	.251	.402	.371	.773	111	6	36	7.25	-4	0-48(19-26-3)	8	-0.1
Yr.	56	201	47	48	8	6	1	34	52	14	23	....	.239	.395	.353	.748	104	4	38	6.64	-4	0-55(26-26-3)	8	-0.3
Total 14	**1486**	**6194**	**1492**	**1827**	**347**	**174**	**122**	**908**	**663**	**343**	**509**	**....**	**.295**	**.361**	**.461**	**.822**	**142**	**302**	**1247**	**7.73**	**31**	**0-944,1-550/P-4**	**265**	**21.7**
• STOVIAK, Ray	Raymond Thomas Stoviak b: 6/6/1915, Scottdale, PA BL/TL, 6'1", 195 lbs. Deb: 6/5/1938																							
1938 Phi-N	10	10	1	0	0	0	0	0	0	3	0	....	.000	.000	.000	.000	-100	-3	0	.00	0	/0-4(0-0-4)	0	-0.2
• STOWERS, Chris	Christopher James Stowers b: 8/18/1974, St. Louis, MO BL/TL, 6'3", 195 lbs. Deb: 7/10/1999																							
1999 Mon-N	4	2	0	0	0	0	0	0	0	0	0	0	.000	.000	.000	.000	-103	-1	0	.00	0	0-47(0-1-1)	0	-0.1
• STRAIN, Joe	Joseph Allan Strain b: 4/30/1954, Denver, CO BR/TR, 5'10", 169 lbs. Deb: 6/28/1979																							
1979 SF-N	67	257	27	62	8	1	1	12	13	21	8	4	.241	.286	.292	.578	62	-14	22	2.71	-6	2-67/3-1	4	-1.6
1980 SF-N	77	189	26	54	6	0	0	16	10	10	1	2	.286	.322	.317	.639	81	-6	18	3.10	-3	2-42/3-6,S-1	3	-0.8
1981 Chi-N	25	74	7	14	1	0	0	1	5	7	0	0	.189	.250	.203	.453	28	-7	4	1.74	2	2-20	1	-0.4
Total 3	**169**	**520**	**60**	**130**	**15**	**1**	**1**	**29**	**28**	**38**	**9**	**6**	**.250**	**.293**	**.288**	**.582**	**64**	**-26**	**43**	**2.71**	**-7**	**2-129/3-7,S-1**	**8**	**-2.8**
• STRAND, Paul	Paul Edward Strand b: 12/19/1893, Carbonado, WA d: 7/2/1974, Salt Lake City, UT BL/TL, 6'.5", 190 lbs. Deb: 5/15/1913 Career OF: 2-40-5 ♦																							
1913 Bos-N	7	6	0	1	0	0	0	0	0	0	0	....	.167	.167	.167	.333	-5	-0	0	.75	0	/P-7	1	0.2
1914 Bos-N	18	24	2	8	2	0	0	3	0	2	0	....	.333	.333	.417	.750	123	2	3	5.09	0	P-16	5	0.2
1915 Bos-N	24	22	3	2	0	0	0	2	0	4	0	....	.091	.091	.091	.182	-46	-3	0	.24	-1	/P-6,0-5(2-1-0)	1	-0.2

YEAR TM-L	G	AB	R	H	2B	3B	HR	RBI	BB	SO	SB	CS	AVG	OBP	SLG	OPS	OPS+	BR/A	RC	RC/G	FR	G/POS	WS	TPW
1924 Phi-A	47	167	15	38	9	4	0	13	4	9	3	3	.228	.254	.329	.584	49	-14	13	2.63	-6	0-44(0-39-5)	1	-2.0
Total 4	96	219	20	49	11	4	0	18	4	15	3	3	.224	.244	.311	.555	47	-15	17	2.53	-7	/0-49,P-29	8	-1.8
• STRANDS, Larry	John Lawrence Strands b: 12/5/1885, Chicago, IL d: 1/19/1957, Forest Park, IL BR/TR, 5'10.5", 165 lbs. Deb: 4/25/1915																							
1915 New-F	35	75	7	14	3	1	1	11	6	11	1	....	.187	.247	.293	.540	62	-4	6	2.31	-9	3-12/2-9,0-2(0-0-2)	0	-1.3
• STRANG, Sammy	Samuel Nicklin "The Dixie Thrush" Strang b: 12/16/1876, Chattanooga, TN d: 3/13/1932, Chattanooga, TN BB/TR, 5'8", 160 lbs. Deb: 7/10/1896 Career OF: 11-63-92																							
1896 Lou-N	14	46	6	12	0	0	0	7	6	6	4	....	.261	.346	.261	.607	64	-2	6	4.42	-5	S-14	1	-0.5
1900 Chi-N	27	102	15	29	3	0	0	9	8	....	1	....	.284	.348	.314	.662	86	-1	12	4.26	-4	3-16/S-9,2-2	2	-0.4
1901 NY-N	135	493	55	139	14	6	1	34	59	....	40	....	.282	.364	.341	.705	109	9	80	5.69	-6	3-91,2-37/0-5(0-0-5),S-4	20	0.6
1902 Chi-A	137	536	108	158	18	5	3	46	76	....	38	....	.295	.387	.364	.751	114	15	94	6.41	6	*3-137	25	2.4
Chi-N	3	11	1	4	0	0	0	0	0	....	1	....	.364	.364	.364	.727	128	0	2	7.06	-1	/2-2,3-2	1	-0.1
1903 Bro-N	135	508	101	138	21	5	0	38	75	....	46	....	.272	.376	.333	.709	106	9	84	5.89	-30	*3-124/0-8(0-8-0),2-3	19	-1.7
1904 Bro-N	77	271	28	52	11	0	1	9	45	....	16	....	.192	.316	.244	.559	75	-5	27	3.16	-24	2-63,3-12/S-1	4	-2.9
1905*NY-N	111	294	51	76	9	4	3	29	58	....	23	....	.259	.389	.347	.736	117	10	52	5.84	-1	2-47,0-38(4-7-27)/S-9,1-1,3	14	0.8
1906 NY-N	113	313	50	100	16	4	4	49	54	....	21	....	.319	.423	.435	.857	164	26	69	8.15	0	2-57,0-39(5-17-17)/S-4,3-3,1	23	2.8
1907 NY-N	123	306	56	77	20	4	4	30	60	....	21	....	.252	.388	.382	.770	137	17	55	6.18	0	0-70(1-28-41),2-13/3-7,1-5,S	16	1.6
1908 NY-N	28	53	8	5	0	0	0	2	23	....	5	....	.094	.385	.094	.479	52	-0	4	2.21	-3	2-14/0-5(1-3-2),S-3	1	-0.4
Total 10	903	2933	479	790	112	28	16	253	464	6	216	....	.269	.377	.343	.720	113	78	486	5.76	-66	3-393,2-238,0-165/S-45,1-7	126	2.2
• STRANGE, Alan	Alan Cochrane "Inky" Strange b: 11/7/1906, Philadelphia, PA d: 6/27/1994, Seattle, WA BR/TR, 5'9", 162 lbs. Deb: 4/17/1934																							
1934 StL-A	127	430	39	100	17	2	1	45	48	28	3	1	.233	.310	.288	.598	51	-31	41	3.23	3	*S-125	8	-1.8
1935 StL-A	49	147	8	34	6	1	0	17	17	7	0	0	.231	.311	.286	.597	53	-10	14	3.19	0	S-49	2	-0.6
Was-A	20	54	3	10	2	1	0	5	4	1	0	0	.185	.241	.259	.501	30	-6	4	2.09	0	S-16	1	-0.4
Yr.	69	201	11	44	8	2	0	22	21	8	0	0	.219	.293	.279	.571	47	-16	18	2.89	0	S-65	3	-1.0
1940 StL-A	54	167	26	31	8	3	0	6	22	12	2	1	.186	.284	.269	.554	43	-14	14	2.51	3	S-35/2-4	2	-0.7
1941 StL-A	45	112	14	26	4	0	0	11	15	5	1	0	.232	.323	.268	.591	56	-6	10	2.80	-2	S-32/1-2,3-1	1	-0.6
1942 StL-A	19	37	3	10	2	0	0	5	3	1	0	1	.270	.325	.324	.649	82	-1	4	3.35	-1	3-10/S-3,2-1	1	-0.1
Total 5	314	947	93	211	39	7	1	89	109	54	6	3	.223	.304	.282	.586	50	-68	86	2.97	5	S-260/3-11,2-5,1-2	15	-4.2
• STRANGE, Doug	Joseph Douglas Strange b: 4/13/1964, Greenville, SC BB/TR, 6'2", 185 lbs. Deb: 7/13/1989 Career OF: 18-0-2																							
1989 Det-A	64	196	16	42	4	1	1	14	17	36	3	3	.214	.280	.260	.541	54	-12	14	2.25	-6	3-54/2-9,S-9,D-1	1	-1.8
1991 Chi-N	3	9	0	4	1	0	0	1	0	1	1	0	.444	.500	.556	1.056	187	1	3	12.89	-1	/3-3	1	0.1
1992 Chi-N	52	94	7	15	1	0	1	5	10	15	1	0	.160	.240	.202	.443	26	-9	5	1.60	-3	3-33,2-12	1	-1.3
1993 Tex-A	145	484	58	124	29	0	7	60	43	69	6	4	.256	.321	.360	.680	86	-10	55	3.85	-17	*2-135/3-9,S-1	12	-2.0
1994 Tex-A	73	226	26	48	12	1	5	26	15	38	1	3	.212	.270	.341	.611	56	-17	19	2.72	-8	2-53,3-13/0-3(2-0-1)	1	-2.0
1995*Sea-A	74	155	19	42	9	2	2	21	10	25	0	3	.271	.323	.394	.717	85	-5	18	4.16	-1	3-41/2-5,0-4(4-0-0),D-1	3	-0.6
1996 Sea-A	88	183	19	43	7	1	3	23	14	31	1	0	.235	.293	.333	.626	58	-12	18	3.40	-1	3-39,D-10/1-3,2-3,0-2(10-0-1)	1	-1.2
1997 Mon-N	118	327	40	84	16	2	12	47	36	76	0	2	.257	.334	.428	.762	98	-2	47	4.97	-1	*3-105,0-11(2-0-0)/2-3,1-1	11	-0.2
1998 Pit-N	90	185	9	32	8	0	0	14	10	39	1	0	.173	.219	.216	.436	15	-23	9	1.43	-5	3-42/2-9,1-3	1	-2.7
Total 9	707	1859	194	434	87	7	31	211	155	330	14	15	.233	.297	.338	.635	69	-89	189	3.35	-43	3-339,2-229/0-20,D-12,S-10,1	32	-11.7
• STRATTON, Asa	Asa Evans Stratton b: 2/10/1853, Grafton, MA d: 8/14/1925, Fitchburg, MA Deb: 6/17/1881																							
1881 Wor-N	1	4	0	1	0	0	0	0	0	2	....	....	.250	.250	.250	.500	54	-0	0	2.31	-1	/S-1	0	-0.1
• STRATTON, Scott	C. Scott Stratton b: 10/2/1869, Campbellsburg, KY d: 3/8/1939, Louisville, KY BL/TR, 6', 180 lbs. Deb: 4/21/1888 Career OF: 41-23-68 ♦																							
1888 Lou-a	67	249	35	64	8	1	1	29	12	....	10	....	.257	.310	.309	.619	101	6	28	4.03	-3	0-38(28-7-3),P-33	11	-0.6
1889 Lou-a	62	229	30	66	7	5	4	34	13	36	10	....	.288	.332	.415	.747	114	6	36	5.81	5	0-29(10-4-15),P-19,1-17	7	1.6
1890*Lou-a	55	189	29	61	3	5	0	24	16	....	8	....	.323	.385	.392	.776	132	17	32	6.69	6	P-50/0-5(0-5-0)	51	7.6
1891 Pit-N	2	8	1	1	0	0	0	0	0	3	0	....	.125	.125	.125	.250	-28	-1	0	.49	1	/P-2	1	0.1
Lou-a	34	115	9	27	2	0	0	8	11	13	8	....	.235	.307	.252	.559	61	-1	12	3.51	3	P-20/1-8,0-6(2-3-1)	9	-0.9
1892 Lou-N	63	219	22	56	2	9	0	23	17	21	9	....	.256	.318	.347	.665	110	12	28	4.59	2	P-42,0-17(1-0-16)/1-6	29	1.4
1893 Lou-N	61	221	34	50	8	5	0	16	25	15	6	....	.226	.308	.308	.615	67	-1	23	3.50	4	P-37,0-24(0-0-23)/1-1	16	-2.7
1894 Lou-N	13	37	9	12	1	2	0	4	4	2	1	....	.324	.390	.459	.850	112	2	7	7.49	1	/P-7,0-5(0-0-5)	1	-1.0
Chi-N	24	99	30	37	5	4	3	23	7	1	3	....	.374	.421	.596	1.017	131	9	26	10.61	-1	P-15/0-5(0-0-5),1-2	8	0.8
Yr.	37	136	39	49	6	6	3	27	11	3	4	....	.360	.412	.559	.971	126	11	33	9.72	0	P-22,0-10(0-0-10)/1-2	9	-0.2
1895 Chi-N	10	24	3	7	1	1	0	2	4	2	1	....	.292	.393	.417	.810	102	1	5	6.84	0	/P-5,0-4(0-4-0)	1	-1.2
Total 8	391	1390	202	381	37	32	8	163	109	93	56	....	.274	.335	.364	.699	101	50	195	5.13	17	P-230,0-133/1-34	134	5.2
• STRAUB, Joe	Joseph J. Straub b: 1/19/1858, Milwaukee, WI d: 2/13/1929, Pueblo, CO BR/TR, 5'10", 160 lbs. Deb: 6/24/1880 Career OF: 0-1-1																							
1880 Tro-N	3	12	1	3	0	0	0	3	1	3	....	....	.250	.308	.250	.558	87	-0	1	2.89	1	/C-3	0	0.1
1882 Phi-a	8	32	2	6	2	0	0	1	1	....	....	....	.188	.212	.250	.462	49	-2	2	1.87	-1	/C-7,0-1	0	-0.2
1883 Col-a	27	100	4	13	0	0	0	0	4	....	....	....	.130	.163	.130	.293	-5	-11	2	.70	-1	C-14,1-12/0-1	0	-1.0
Total 3	38	144	7	22	2	0	0	4	6	3	....	....	.153	.187	.167	.353	15	-13	5	1.11	-1	/C-24,1-12,0-2	0	-1.1
• STRAUSS, Joe	Joseph "Dutch,The Socker" Strauss b: 11/16/1858, Cincinnati, OH d: 6/24/1906, Cincinnati, OH BR/TR Deb: 7/27/1884 Career OF: 83-8-1																							
1884 KC-U	16	60	4	12	3	0	0	....	1	....	....	....	.200	.213	.250	.463	64	-2	3	1.91	-1	0-10(8-2-0)/C-3,2-2,3-1	0	-0.2
1885 Lou-a	2	6	0	1	0	0	0	0	0	....	....	....	.167	.167	.167	.333	6	-1	0	.92	-1	/C-1,0-1	0	-0.2
1886 Lou-a	74	297	36	64	5	6	1	31	8	....	25	....	.215	.239	.283	.521	60	-16	27	3.09	7	0-73(67-6-1)/P-2,C-1	3	-1.0
Bro-a	9	36	6	9	1	1	0	5	1	....	4	....	.250	.270	.333	.604	88	-1	4	4.43	0	/0-7(7-0-0),C-2	1	0.0
Yr.	83	333	42	73	6	7	1	36	9	....	29	....	.219	.242	.288	.530	63	-16	31	3.23	7	0-80(74-6-1)/C-3,P-2	4	-1.0
Total 3	101	399	46	86	9	7	1	36	10	....	29	....	.216	.237	.281	.517	62	-19	35	2.99	6	/0-91,C-7,2-2,P-2,3-1	4	-1.4
• STRAWBERRY, Darryl	Darryl Eugene Strawberry b: 3/12/1962, Los Angeles, CA BL/TL, 6'6", 200 lbs. Deb: 5/6/1983 Career OF: 54-48-1308																							
1983 NY-N	122	420	63	108	15	7	26	74	47	128	19	6	.257	.338	.512	.849	134	19	74	6.16	-1	*0-117(0-0-117)	18	1.3
1984 NY-N★	147	522	75	131	27	4	26	97	75	131	27	8	.251	.345	.467	.812	128	22	87	5.71	-2	*0-146(0-21-134)	24	1.4
1985 NY-N★	111	393	78	109	15	4	29	79	73	96	26	11	.277	.392	.557	.949	167	37	87	7.62	-6	*0-110(0-27-100)	24	2.7
1986*NY-N★	136	475	76	123	27	5	27	93	72	141	28	12	.259	.363	.507	.871	142	28	92	6.56	-1	*0-131(1-0-130)	25	2.1
1987 NY-N★	154	532	108	151	32	5	39	104	97	122	36	12	.284	.401	.583	.984	165	54	132	8.91	-2	*0-151(0-0-151)	30	4.4
1988*NY-N★	153	543	101	146	27	3	**39**	101	85	127	29	14	.269	.371	**.545**	**.916**	**168**	48	111	7.06	2	*0-150(0-0-150)	30	**4.9**
1989 NY-N★	134	476	69	107	26	1	29	77	61	105	11	4	.225	.314	.466	.781	126	16	72	5.12	-1	*0-131(0-0-131)	18	1.1
1990 NY-N★	152	542	92	150	18	1	37	108	70	110	15	8	.277	.364	.518	.882	140	29	104	6.86	2	*0-149(0-0-149)	26	2.8
1991 LA-N★	139	505	86	134	22	4	28	99	75	125	10	8	.265	.364	.491	.855	141	27	92	6.31	-8	*0-136(0-0-136)	24	1.5
1992 LA-N	43	156	20	37	8	0	5	25	19	34	3	1	.237	.324	.385	.708	101	1	20	4.44	-1	0-42(2-0-40)	6	-0.1
1993 LA-N	32	100	12	14	2	0	5	12	16	19	1	0	.140	.271	.310	.581	58	-6	10	2.90	-2	0-29(4-0-25)	0	-0.9
1994 SF-N	29	92	13	22	3	1	4	17	19	22	0	3	.239	.369	.424	.793	111	1	14	4.91	0	0-27(0-0-27)	3	-0.1
1995*NY-A	32	87	15	24	4	1	3	13	10	22	0	0	.276	.364	.448	.812	111	1	15	6.52	0	D-15,0-11(1-0-10)	4	0.0
1996*NY-A	63	202	35	53	13	0	11	36	31	55	6	5	.262	.363	.490	.853	113	3	36	6.07	-1	D-26/0-2(26-0-8)	6	0.0
1997 NY-A	11	29	1	3	1	0	0	2	3	9	0	0	.103	.188	.138	.325	-13	-5	1	.58	0	0-34(4-0-0)/D-4	0	-0.5
1998 NY-A	101	295	44	73	11	2	24	57	46	90	8	7	.247	.355	.542	.897	134	13	58	6.81	-1	D-81/0-4(16-0-0)	11	0.7
1999*NY-A	24	49	10	16	5	0	3	6	17	16	2	0	.327	.500	.612	1.112	184	8	18	14.51	0	D-17	3	0.7
Total 17	1583	5418	898	1401	256	38	335	1000	816	1352	221	99	.259	.360	.505	.865	140	296	1023	6.52	-21	*0-1370,D-143	252	22.1
• STREET, Gabby	Charles Evard "Old Sarge" Street b: 9/30/1882, Huntsville, AL d: 2/6/1951, Joplin, MO BR/TR, 5'11", 180 lbs. Deb: 9/13/1904 M/C																							
1904 Cin-N	11	33	1	4	1	0	0	0	1	....	2	....	.121	.147	.152	.299	-7	-4	1	.95	1	C-11	1	-0.2
1905 Cin-N	2	2	0	0	0	0	0	0	2	....	0	....	.000	.500	.000	.500	48	0	0	.00	0	/C-1	0	0.0
Bos-N	3	12	0	2	0	0	0	0	0	....	1	....	.167	.167	.167	.333	-1	-1	1	1.33	-1	/C-3	0	-0.3
Cin-N	29	91	8	23	5	1	0	8	6	....	1	....	.253	.306	.330	.636	81	-2	10	3.72	3	C-26	3	0.4
Yr.	34	105	8	25	5	1	0	8	8	....	2	....	.238	.298	.305	.603	71	-4	10	3.33	2	C-30	3	0.1
1908 Was-A	131	394	31	81	12	7	1	32	40	....	5	....	.206	.289	.279	.568	92	-2	33	2.67	5	*C-128	11	1.7

YEAR TM-L	G	AB	R	H	2B	3B	HR	RBI	BB	SO	SB	CS	AVG	OBP	SLG	OPS	OPS+	BR/A	RC	RC/G	FR	G/POS	WS	TPW
1909 Was-A	137	407	25	86	12	1	0	29	26	....	2	....	.211	.262	.246	.508	63	-17	27	2.11	11	*C-137	6	0.8
1910 Was-A	89	257	13	52	6	0	1	16	23	....	1	....	.202	.273	.237	.510	63	-11	17	2.11	5	C-86	4	0.3
1911 Was-A	72	216	16	48	7	1	0	14	14	....	4	....	.222	.279	.264	.543	53	-14	17	2.54	7	C-71	4	-0.1
1912 NY-A	29	88	4	16	1	1	0	6	7	....	1	....	.182	.258	.216	.474	34	-8	5	1.79	1	C-29	1	-0.4
1931 StL-N	1	1	0	0	0	0	0	0	0	0	0	....	.000	.000	.000	.000	-96	-0	0	.00	0	/C-1	0	0.0
Total 8	504	1501	98	312	44	11	2	105	119	0	17	....	.208	.273	.256	.529	67	-59	111	2.35	31	C-493	30	2.1
• STREULI, Walt	Walter Herbert Streuli b: 9/26/1935, Memphis, TN BR/TR, 6'2", 195 lbs. Deb: 9/25/1954																							
1954 Det-A	1	0	0	0	0	0	0	0	1	0	0	0	....	1.000	....	1.000	195	0	0	∞	0	/C-1	0	0.0
1955 Det-A	2	4	1	1	1	0	0	1	0	0	0	0	.250	.250	.500	.750	100	-0	1	3.40	0	/C-2	0	0.0
1956 Det-A	3	8	0	2	1	0	0	1	1	2	0	0	.250	.333	.375	.708	86	-0	1	4.89	0	/C-3	0	0.0
Total 3	6	12	1	3	2	0	0	2	2	2	0	0	.250	.357	.417	.774	98	0	2	4.29	-1	/C-6	0	0.0
• STRICK, John	John Quincy Adams Strick b: 9/15/1858, Erie, PA d: 11/18/1933, Erie, PA Deb: 5/18/1882																							
1882 Lou-a	32	110	17	18	6	1	0	....	9	....	....	....	.164	.227	.236	.463	60	-4	6	1.84	-1	C-21/2-6,0-6(0-6-0),1-1,S	2	-0.3
• STRICKER, Cub	John A. Stricker b: 6/8/1859, Philadelphia, PA d: 11/19/1937, Philadelphia, PA BR/TR, 5'3", 138 lbs. Deb: 5/2/1882 M/U Career OF: 0-1-19 ♦																							
1882 Phi-a	72	272	34	59	6	1	0	18	15	....	....	....	.217	.258	.246	.504	63	-11	18	2.33	19	*2-72/P-2,0-1	7	1.1
1883 Phi-a	89	330	67	90	8	0	1	40	19	....	....	....	.273	.312	.306	.618	92	-3	32	3.77	-20	*2-88/C-2	11	-1.8
1884 Phi-a	107	399	59	92	16	11	1	0	19	....	....	....	.231	.267	.333	.601	89	-6	36	3.26	-38	*2-107/C-1,0-1,P-1	7	-3.7
1885 Phi-a	106	398	71	93	9	3	1	41	21	....	....	....	.234	.284	.279	.563	74	-12	32	2.86	-25	*2-106	7	-3.0
1887 Cle-a	131	587	122	194	19	4	2	53	53	....	86	....	.330	.334	.326	.660	87	-7	89	6.11	-9	*2-126/S-6,P-3	12	-0.9
1888 Cle-a	127	493	80	115	13	6	1	33	50	....	60	....	.233	.311	.290	.602	96	0	65	4.63	9	*2-122/0-6(0-0-6),P-2	15	1.1
1889 Cle-N	136	566	83	142	10	4	1	47	58	18	32	....	.251	.323	.288	.611	73	-19	64	4.03	6	*2-135/S-1	12	-0.7
1890 Cle-P	127	544	93	133	19	8	2	65	54	16	24	....	.244	.318	.320	.638	77	-15	65	4.25	-2	*2-109,S-20	9	-1.0
1891 Bos-a	139	514	96	111	15	4	0	46	63	34	54	....	.216	.309	.261	.569	64	-23	59	3.91	15	*2-139	13	-0.3
1892 StL-N	28	98	12	20	1	0	0	11	10	7	5	....	.204	.297	.214	.512	58	-4	8	2.74	-0	2-27/S-1	1	-0.3
Bal-N	75	269	45	71	5	5	3	37	32	18	13	....	.264	.344	.353	.698	108	3	38	5.20	-11	2-75	7	-0.5
Yr.	103	367	57	91	6	5	3	48	42	25	18	....	.248	.332	.316	.648	95	-1	46	4.50	-11	*2-102/S-1	8	-0.8
1893 Was-N	59	218	28	39	7	1	0	20	20	12	4	....	.179	.248	.220	.468	25	-23	13	1.96	-1	2-39,0-12(0-0-12)/3-4,S-4	1	-1.9
Total 11	1196	4688	790	1159	128	47	12	411	414	105	278	....	.247	.306	.294	.600	78	-121	520	3.98	-58	*2-1145/S-32,0-20,P-8,3-4,C	102	-12.0
• STRICKLAND, George	George Bevan "Bo" Strickland b: 1/10/1926, New Orleans, LA BR/TR, 6'1", 180 lbs. Deb: 5/7/1950 M/C																							
1950 Pit-N	23	27	0	3	0	0	0	2	3	8	0	....	.111	.226	.111	.337	-8	-4	1	1.08	-2	S-19/3-1	0	-0.6
1951 Pit-N	138	454	59	98	12	7	9	47	65	83	4	2	.216	.318	.333	.651	73	-16	52	3.78	-7	*S-125,2-13	9	-1.4
1952 Pit-N	76	232	17	41	6	2	5	22	21	45	4	2	.177	.248	.284	.533	46	-17	17	2.26	3	2-45,S-28/1-1,3-1	2	-1.1
Cle-A	31	88	8	19	4	0	1	8	14	15	0	0	.216	.324	.295	.619	78	-2	10	3.81	4	S-30/2-1	3	0.4
1953 Cle-A	123	419	43	119	17	4	5	47	51	52	0	0	.284	.362	.379	.741	103	3	63	5.37	11	*S-122/1-1	20	2.4
1954*Cle-A	112	361	42	77	12	3	6	37	55	62	2	1	.213	.319	.313	.632	72	-12	39	3.35	0	*S-112	10	-0.3
1955 Cle-A	130	388	34	81	9	5	2	34	49	60	1	0	.209	.302	.273	.575	54	-24	35	2.87	11	*S-128	10	-0.3
1956 Cle-A	85	171	22	36	1	2	3	17	22	27	0	1	.211	.301	.292	.593	56	-11	15	2.75	4	2-28,S-28,3-26	4	-0.3
1957 Cle-A	89	201	21	47	8	2	1	19	26	29	0	3	.234	.325	.308	.633	74	-8	20	3.30	1	2-48,S-23,3-19	5	-0.2
1959 Cle-A	132	441	55	105	15	2	3	48	51	64	1	1	.238	.317	.302	.619	74	-15	45	3.41	4	3-80,S-50/2-4	11	-0.7
1960 Cle-A	32	42	4	7	0	0	1	3	4	8	0	0	.167	.255	.238	.493	35	-4	3	1.94	1	S-14,3-12/2-2	0	-0.2
Total 10	971	2824	305	633	84	27	36	284	361	453	12	10	.224	.314	.311	.626	70	-111	299	3.47	30	S-679,2-141,3-139/1-2	74	-2.3
• STRIEF, George	George Andrew Strief b: 10/16/1856, Cincinnati, OH d: 4/1/1946, Cleveland, OH BR/TR, 5'7", 172 lbs. Deb: 5/1/1879 Career OF: 61-60-8																							
1879 Cle-N	71	264	24	46	7	1	0	15	10	23	....	....	.174	.204	.208	.413	37	-17	12	1.48	-12	*0-55(1-54-1),2-16	1	-2.8
1882 Pit-a	79	297	45	58	9	6	2	....	13	....	....	....	.195	.229	.286	.515	76	-6	20	2.34	-2	*2-78/S-1	5	-0.5
1883 StL-a	82	302	22	68	9	0	1	22	12	....	....	....	.225	.255	.265	.520	64	-13	21	2.50	10	*2-67,0-15(11-1-3)	6	0.0
1884 StL-a	48	184	22	37	5	2	2	0	13	....	....	....	.201	.254	.283	.536	72	-6	14	2.53	-2	0-44(43-1-0)/2-3,1-1	4	-0.8
KC-U	15	56	5	6	5	0	0	....	4	....	....	....	.107	.167	.196	.363	26	-3	2	1.05	3	2-15	0	0.1
CP-U	15	53	6	11	5	0	0	....	3	....	....	....	.208	.250	.302	.552	91	-0	4	2.73	-2	2-15	0	-0.1
Yr.	30	109	11	17	10	0	0	....	7	....	....	....	.156	.207	.248	.455	57	-4	6	1.82	2	2-30	0	-0.1
Cle-N	8	29	2	7	2	0	0	0	0	5	....	....	.241	.241	.310	.552	70	-1	2	2.78	1	/0-6(6-0-0),3-2	0	0.0
1885 Phi-a	44	175	19	48	8	5	0	27	9	....	....	....	.274	.310	.377	.687	110	1	21	4.46	-1	3-19,S-10/0-8(0-4-4),2-7	5	0.1
Total 5	362	1360	145	281	50	14	5	64	64	28	....	....	.207	.242	.275	.517	68	-45	95	2.44	-3	2-201,0-128/3-21,S-11,1-1	21	-4.2
• STRIKE, John	John Strike b: 1865, Philadelphia, PA Deb: 9/24/1886 ♦																							
1886 Phi-N	2	7	0	0	0	0	0	0	0	4	0	....	.000	.000	.000	.000	-99	-1	0	.00	-1	/P-2,0-1	0	-0.3
• STRINGER, Lou	Louis Bernard Stringer b: 5/13/1917, Grand Rapids, MI BR/TR, 5'11", 173 lbs. Deb: 4/15/1941																							
1941 Chi-N	145	512	59	126	31	4	5	53	59	86	3	....	.246	.324	.352	.676	94	-4	62	4.18	16	*2-137/S-7	16	2.1
1942 Chi-N	121	406	45	96	10	5	9	41	31	55	3	....	.236	.292	.352	.644	92	-6	42	3.45	-7	*2-113/3-1	8	-0.6
1946 Chi-N	80	209	26	51	3	1	3	19	26	34	0	....	.244	.328	.311	.639	83	-4	22	3.55	-11	2-62/3-1,S-1	5	-1.2
1948 Bos-A	4	11	1	1	0	0	1	1	0	3	0	0	.091	.091	.364	.455	17	-1	0	.00	3	/2-2	0	0.2
1949 Bos-A	35	41	10	11	4	0	1	6	5	10	0	0	.268	.348	.439	.787	100	-0	6	5.61	1	/2-9	1	0.1
1950 Bos-A	24	17	7	5	1	0	0	2	0	4	1	0	.294	.294	.353	.647	59	-1	2	3.26	-1	/3-3,2-1,S-1	0	-0.1
Total 6	409	1196	148	290	49	10	19	122	121	192	7	0	.242	.313	.348	.660	90	-17	135	3.80	2	2-324/S-9,3-5	30	0.4
• STRIPP, Joe	Joseph Valentine "Jersey Joe" Stripp b: 2/3/1903, Harrison, NJ d: 6/10/1989, Orlando, FL BR/TR, 5'11.5", 175 lbs. Deb: 7/2/1928 Career OF: 10-0-12																							
1928 Cin-N	42	139	18	40	7	3	1	17	8	8	0	....	.288	.340	.403	.743	95	-1	19	4.76	-3	0-21(10-0-11),3-17/S-1	4	-0.4
1929 Cin-N	64	187	24	40	3	2	3	20	24	15	2	....	.214	.313	.299	.613	55	-13	19	3.19	1	3-55/2-2	3	-0.8
1930 Cin-N	130	464	74	142	37	6	3	64	51	37	15	....	.306	.377	.431	.808	100	1	75	5.80	2	1-75,3-48	13	0.1
1931 Cin-N	105	426	71	138	26	2	3	42	21	31	5	....	.324	.359	.415	.774	114	8	64	5.66	3	3-96/1-9	15	1.4
1932 Bro-N	138	534	94	162	36	9	6	64	36	30	14	....	.303	.350	.438	.788	113	9	84	5.53	8	3-93,1-43	19	1.7
1933 Bro-N	141	537	69	149	20	7	1	51	26	23	5	....	.277	.312	.346	.658	92	-7	59	3.85	9	*3-140	14	0.8
1934 Bro-N	104	384	50	121	19	6	1	40	22	20	2	....	.315	.354	.404	.757	108	4	55	5.23	-7	3-96/1-7,S-1	11	-0.1
1935 Bro-N	109	373	44	114	13	5	3	43	22	15	2	....	.306	.344	.391	.736	99	-0	49	4.67	5	3-88,1-15/0-1	11	0.6
1936 Bro-N	110	439	51	139	31	1	1	60	22	12	2	....	.317	.351	.399	.749	100	-0	62	5.13	11	*3-106	13	1.4
1937 Bro-N	90	300	37	73	10	2	1	26	20	18	1	....	.243	.291	.300	.591	60	-17	25	2.73	-3	3-66,1-14/S-3	2	-1.8
1938 StL-N	54	199	24	57	7	0	0	18	18	10	0	....	.286	.349	.322	.670	81	-5	23	3.92	-2	3-51	4	-0.5
Bos-N	59	229	19	63	10	0	1	19	10	7	2	....	.275	.305	.332	.637	84	-6	24	3.61	1	3-58	7	-0.3
Yr.	113	428	43	120	17	0	1	37	28	17	2	....	.280	.326	.327	.653	82	-10	46	3.76	-1	*3-109	11	-0.8
Total 11	1146	4211	575	1238	219	43	24	464	280	226	50	....	.294	.340	.384	.724	96	-27	555	4.66	25	3-914,1-163/0-22,S-5,2-2	116	2.1
• STRITTMATTER, Mark	Mark Arthur Strittmatter b: 4/4/1969, Huntington, NY BR/TR, 6'1" Deb: 9/3/1998																							
1998 Col-N	4	4	0	0	0	0	0	0	0	3	0	0	.000	.000	.000	.000	-82	-1	0	.00	0	/C-3	0	-0.1
• STROBEL, Allie	Albert Irving Strobel b: 6/11/1884, Boston, MA d: 2/10/1955, Hollywood, FL BR/TR, 6', 160 lbs. Deb: 8/29/1905 Career OF: 1-1-0																							
1905 Bos-N	5	19	1	2	0	0	0	2	0	....	0	....	.105	.105	.105	.211	-38	-3	0	.46	0	/3-4,0-1	0	-0.3
1906 Bos-N	100	317	28	64	10	3	1	24	29	....	2	....	.202	.273	.262	.535	69	-11	25	2.49	-18	2-93/S-6,0-1	3	-3.2
Total 2	105	336	29	66	10	3	1	26	29	....	2	....	.196	.264	.253	.517	63	-15	26	2.35	-18	/2-93,S-6,3-4,0-2	3	-3.5
• STRONER, Jim	James Melvin Stroner b: 5/29/1901, Chicago, IL d: 12/6/1975, Tarboro, NC BR/TR, 5'10", 175 lbs. Deb: 5/1/1929																							
1929 Pit-N	6	8	0	3	1	0	0	0	1	0	0	....	.375	.444	.500	.944	130	0	2	9.16	-1	/3-2	0	0.0
• STRONG, Jamal	Jamal Najar Strong b: 8/5/1978, Pasadena, CA BR/TR, 5'10", 180 lbs. Deb: 9/2/2003																							
2003 Sea-A	12	2	2	0	0	0	0	0	0	0	0	0	.000	.000	.000	.000	-103	-1	0	.00	0	/D-4,0-2(0-2-0)	0	-0.1

YEAR TM-L	G	AB	R	H	2B	3B	HR	RBI	BB	SO	SB	CS	AVG	OBP	SLG	OPS	OPS+	BR/A	RC	RC/G	FR	G/POS	WS	TPW
• STROUD, Ed	Edwin Marvin Stroud b: 10/31/1939, Lapine, AL BL/TR, 5'11", 180 lbs. Deb: 9/11/1966 Career OF: 86-215-157																							
1966 Chi-A	12	36	3	6	2	0	0	1	2	8	3	0	.167	.231	.222	.453	33	-2	2	2.15	-0	0-11(4-0-7)	0	-0.3
1967 Chi-A	20	27	6	8	0	1	0	3	1	5	7	2	.296	.345	.370	.715	115	1	3	3.44	1	0-12(11-0-5)	1	0.2
Was-A	87	204	36	41	5	3	1	10	25	29	8	6	.201	.291	.270	.561	69	-8	17	2.53	-5	0-79(1-79-0)	3	-1.7
Yr.	107	231	42	49	5	4	1	13	26	34	15	8	.212	.297	.281	.579	74	-7	19	2.64	-4	0-91(12-79-5)	4	-1.4
1968 Was-A	105	306	41	73	10	10	4	23	20	50	9	3	.239	.285	.376	.661	102	0	30	3.29	-4	0-84(25-7-58)	8	-1.1
1969 Was-A	123	206	35	52	5	6	4	29	30	33	12	2	.252	.353	.393	.746	114	6	31	5.02	-3	0-85(28-1-58)	7	0.1
1970 Was-A	129	433	69	115	11	5	5	32	40	79	29	8	.266	.332	.349	.681	92	-1	51	4.03	2	*0-118(9-106-9)	11	-0.2
1971 Chi-A	53	141	19	25	4	3	0	2	11	20	4	5	.177	.237	.248	.485	36	-13	7	1.60	-1	0-44(8-22-20)	1	-1.6
Total 6	**529**	**1353**	**209**	**320**	**37**	**28**	**14**	**100**	**129**	**224**	**72**	**26**	**.237**	**.307**	**.336**	**.643**	**88**	**-16**	**141**	**3.44**	**-10**	**0-433**	**31**	**-4.7**
• STROUGHTER, Steve	Stephen Lewis Stroughter b: 3/15/1952, Visalia, CA BL/TR, 6'2", 190 lbs. Deb: 4/7/1982																							
1982 Sea-A	26	47	4	8	1	0	1	3	3	9	0	0	.170	.235	.255	.491	34	-4	3	2.08	1	/D-9,0-3(3-0-0)	0	-0.4
• STRUEVE, Al	Albert Frederick Strueve b: 6/26/1860, Cincinnati, OH d: 1/28/1929, Ross County, OH Deb: 6/22/1884																							
1884 StL-a	2	7	2	2	0	0	0	0	0	....	....	....	.286	.286	.286	.571	84	-0	1	3.22	1	/C-1,0-1	0	0.1
• STRUNK, Amos	Amos Aaron Strunk b: 1/22/1889, Philadelphia, PA d: 7/22/1979, Llanerch, PA BL/TL, 5'11.5", 175 lbs. Deb: 9/24/1908 Career OF: 143-954-228																							
1908 Phi-A	12	34	4	8	1	0	0	0	4	....	0	....	.235	.316	.265	.580	83	-0	3	2.82	-0	0-11(1-10-0)	1	-0.1
1909 Phi-A	11	35	1	4	0	0	0	2	1	....	2	....	.114	.139	.114	.253	-20	-5	1	.62	1	/0-9(1-8-0)	0	-0.4
1910*Phi-A	16	48	9	16	0	1	0	2	3	....	4	....	.333	.373	.375	.748	135	2	8	6.37	0	0-14(0-14-0)	3	0.2
1911*Phi-A	74	215	42	55	7	2	1	21	35	....	13	....	.256	.363	.321	.683	93	-0	31	4.59	-2	0-62(19-43-0)/1-2	7	-0.5
1912 Phi-A	122	412	58	119	13	12	3	63	47	....	29	....	.289	.366	.400	.766	124	13	72	5.87	9	*0-116(65-51-0)	18	1.6
1913*Phi-A	94	292	30	89	11	12	0	46	29	23	14	....	.305	.368	.425	.792	135	12	49	5.83	-3	0-81(0-80-0)	14	0.4
1914*Phi-A	122	404	58	111	15	3	2	45	57	38	25	22	.275	.364	.342	.706	117	6	53	4.23	1	*0-120(12-108-0)	17	0.0
1915 Phi-A	132	485	76	144	28	16	1	45	56	45	17	19	.297	.371	.427	.798	144	20	78	5.37	10	*0-111(0-59-52),1-19	21	2.5
1916 Phi-A	150	544	71	172	30	9	3	49	66	59	21	23	.316	.393	.421	.814	152	29	91	5.69	3	*0-143(6-119-18)/1-7	23	2.6
1917 Phi-A	148	540	83	152	26	7	1	45	68	37	16	....	.281	.363	.361	.724	123	16	76	4.80	-2	*0-146(0-146-0)	20	0.5
1918*Bos-A	114	413	50	106	18	9	0	35	36	13	20	....	.257	.316	.344	.660	101	-1	50	3.91	-2	*0-113(1-112-0)	16	-1.0
1919 Bos-A	48	184	27	50	11	3	0	17	13	13	3	....	.272	.323	.364	.687	98	-1	22	4.09	-3	0-48(0-48-0)	5	-0.7
Phi-A	60	194	15	41	6	4	0	13	23	15	3	....	.211	.298	.284	.582	63	-9	17	2.80	0	0-52(0-10-42)	1	-1.3
Yr.	108	378	42	91	17	7	0	30	36	28	6	....	.241	.310	.323	.633	80	-10	39	3.41	-3	*0-100(0-58-42)	6	-2.0
1920 Phi-A	58	202	23	60	9	3	0	20	21	9	0	6	.297	.363	.371	.735	94	-3	26	4.46	-4	0-54(6-10-38)	3	-1.0
Chi-A	53	188	33	45	8	1	1	16	28	15	1	0	.239	.338	.309	.646	72	-6	21	3.93	-3	0-49(3-7-38)	4	-1.1
Yr.	111	390	56	105	17	4	1	36	49	24	1	6	.269	.351	.341	.692	83	-9	48	4.20	-7	*0-103(9-17-76)	7	-2.1
1921 Chi-A	121	401	68	133	19	10	3	69	38	27	7	10	.332	.391	.451	.842	116	8	69	6.29	-2	*0-111(9-69-33)	12	0.0
1922 Chi-A	92	311	36	90	11	4	0	33	33	28	9	6	.289	.358	.350	.708	85	-6	40	4.54	4	0-74(14-56-4)/1-7	8	-0.6
1923 Chi-A	54	54	7	17	0	0	0	8	8	5	1	0	.315	.403	.315	.718	92	0	8	5.17	0	/0-5(2-3-0),1-2	1	0.0
1924 Chi-A	1	1	0	0	0	0	0	0	0	0	0	0	.000	.000	.000	.000	-103	-0	0	.00	0	....	0	0.0
Phi-A	30	42	5	6	0	0	0	1	7	4	0	0	.143	.265	.143	.408	7	-6	2	1.47	0	/0-8(4-1-3)	0	-0.6
Yr.	31	43	5	6	0	0	0	1	7	4	0	0	.140	.260	.140	.400	5	-6	2	1.43	0	/0-8(4-1-3)	0	-0.6
Total 17	**1512**	**4999**	**696**	**1418**	**213**	**96**	**15**	**530**	**573**	**331**	**185**	**86**	**.284**	**.359**	**.374**	**.732**	**114**	**69**	**720**	**4.84**	**6**	***0-1327/1-37**	**174**	**0.2**
• STUART, Bill	William Alexander "Chauncey" Stuart b: 8/28/1873, Boalsburg, PA d: 10/14/1928, Fort Worth, TX, 5'11", 170 lbs. Deb: 8/15/1895																							
1895 Pit-N	19	77	5	19	3	0	0	10	2	6	2	....	.247	.275	.286	.561	47	-6	7	3.15	0	S-17/2-2	1	-0.4
1899 NY-N	1	3	0	0	0	0	0	0	0	....	0	....	.000	.000	.000	.000	-104	-1	0	.00	0	/2-1	0	-0.1
Total 2	**20**	**80**	**5**	**19**	**3**	**0**	**0**	**10**	**2**	**6**	**2**	**....**	**.238**	**.265**	**.275**	**.540**	**42**	**-7**	**7**	**2.99**	**-0**	**/S-17,2-3**	**1**	**-0.5**
• STUART, Dick	Richard Lee "Stu,Dr. Strangeglove" Stuart b: 11/7/1932, San Francisco, CA d: 12/15/2002, Redwood City, CA BR/TR, 6'4", 212 lbs. Deb: 7/10/1958 Career OF: 2-0-0																							
1958 Pit-N	67	254	38	68	12	5	16	48	11	75	0	0	.268	.311	.543	.854	124	7	41	5.73	0	1-64	8	0.3
1959 Pit-N	118	397	64	118	15	2	27	78	42	86	1	1	.297	.367	.549	.916	141	22	78	6.98	-4	*1-105/0-1	17	1.3
1960*Pit-N	122	438	48	114	17	5	23	83	39	107	0	0	.260	.321	.479	.800	115	8	63	4.96	-6	*1-108	13	-0.4
1961 Pit-N★	138	532	83	160	28	8	35	117	34	121	0	3	.301	.347	.581	.928	140	27	97	6.47	-10	*1-132/0-1	19	0.9
1962 Pit-N	114	394	52	90	11	4	16	64	32	94	0	1	.228	.290	.398	.688	82	-12	44	3.75	-4	*1-101	6	-2.1
1963 Bos-A	157	612	81	160	25	4	42	**118**	44	144	0	0	.261	.312	.521	.833	125	17	91	5.14	0	*1-155	16	0.8
1964 Bos-A	156	603	73	168	27	1	33	114	37	130	0	0	.279	.323	.491	.814	117	12	93	5.56	-3	*1-155	18	0.0
1965 Phi-N	149	538	53	126	19	1	28	95	39	136	1	0	.234	.290	.429	.719	101	-1	66	4.14	-1	*1-143/3-1	13	-0.9
1966 NY-N	31	87	7	19	0	0	4	13	9	26	0	1	.218	.292	.356	.648	81	-3	8	2.74	-2	1-23	1	-0.6
*LA-N	38	91	4	24	1	0	3	9	11	17	0	1	.264	.356	.374	.729	112	1	12	4.51	3	1-25	3	0.3
Yr.	69	178	11	43	1	0	7	22	20	43	0	2	.242	.325	.365	.690	97	-1	19	3.61	1	1-48	4	-0.3
1969 Cal-A	22	51	3	8	2	0	1	4	3	21	0	0	.157	.204	.255	.459	29	-5	2	1.38	-1	1-13	0	-0.7
Total 10	**1112**	**3997**	**506**	**1055**	**157**	**30**	**228**	**743**	**301**	**957**	**2**	**7**	**.264**	**.319**	**.489**	**.808**	**116**	**75**	**595**	**5.16**	**-27**	***1-1024/0-2,3-1**	**114**	**-1.2**
• STUART, Luke	Luther Lane Stuart b: 5/23/1892, Alamance County, NC d: 6/15/1947, Winston-Salem, NC BR/TR, 5'8", 165 lbs. Deb: 7/28/1921																							
1921 StL-A	3	3	2	1	0	0	1	2	0	1	0	0	.333	.333	1.333	1.667	291	1	1	16.96	-1	/2-3	0	0.0
• STUBBS, Franklin	Franklin Lee Stubbs b: 10/21/1960, Richland, NC BL/TL, 6'2", 215 lbs. Deb: 4/28/1984 Career OF: 247-32-49																							
1984 LA-N	87	217	22	42	2	3	8	17	24	63	2	2	.194	.274	.341	.615	73	-9	22	3.22	1	1-51,0-20(6-3-13)	3	-1.2
1985 LA-N	10	9	0	2	0	0	0	2	0	3	0	0	.222	.222	.222	.444	25	-1	0	1.71	0	/1-4	0	-0.1
1986 LA-N	132	420	55	95	11	1	23	58	37	107	7	1	.226	.292	.421	.713	101	-0	51	4.03	1	*0-124(108-23-15),1-13	11	-0.4
1987 LA-N	129	386	48	90	16	3	16	52	31	85	8	1	.233	.292	.415	.706	87	-8	47	4.07	0	*1-111,0-18(13-0-6)	9	-1.4
1988*LA-N	115	242	30	54	13	0	8	34	23	61	11	3	.223	.293	.376	.669	94	-2	28	3.68	4	1-84,0-13(7-1-6)	6	-0.3
1989 LA-N	69	103	11	30	6	0	4	15	16	27	3	2	.291	.387	.466	.853	145	6	18	6.27	2	0-28(22-5-3)/1-7	5	0.7
1990 Hou-N	146	448	59	117	23	2	23	71	48	114	19	6	.261	.335	.475	.811	124	15	74	5.82	2	1-72,0-71(67-0-5)	16	1.1
1991 Mil-A	103	362	48	77	16	2	11	38	35	71	13	4	.213	.286	.359	.645	79	-10	39	3.52	5	1-92/D-4,0-4(4-0-0)	4	-1.2
1992 Mil-A	92	288	37	66	11	1	9	42	27	68	11	8	.229	.297	.368	.666	87	-7	32	3.59	7	1-68,D-16/0-1	7	-0.4
1995 Det-A	62	116	13	29	11	0	2	19	19	27	0	1	.250	.360	.397	.757	97	-0	17	4.96	-4	1-20,0-20(20-0-0)/D-3	4	-0.6
Total 10	**945**	**2591**	**323**	**602**	**109**	**12**	**104**	**348**	**260**	**626**	**74**	**28**	**.232**	**.305**	**.404**	**.709**	**97**	**-16**	**327**	**4.22**	**16**	**1-522,0-299/D-23**	**65**	**-3.9**
• STUBING, Moose	Lawrence George Stubing b: 3/31/1938, Bronx, NY BL/TL, 6'3", 220 lbs. Deb: 8/14/1967 M/C																							
1967 Cal-A	5	5	0	0	0	0	0	0	0	4	0	0	.000	.000	.000	.000	-104	-1	0	.00	0	....	0	-0.1
• STUDLEY, Seem	Seymour L. "Warhorse" Studley b: 5/1841, Byron, NY d: 7/9/1901, Grand Island, NE, 5'7.5" Deb: 4/20/1872																							
1872 Nat-n	5	21	3	2	0	0	0	2	0	1	0	0	.095	.095	.095	.190	-35	-4	0	.32	-2	/0-5(0-5-0)	....	-0.4
• STUMPF, Bill	William Frederick Stumpf b: 3/21/1892, Baltimore, MD d: 2/14/1966, Crownsville, MD BR/TR, 6'.5", 175 lbs. Deb: 5/11/1912 Career OF: 0-1-1																							
1912 NY-A	42	129	8	31	0	0	0	10	6	....	5	....	.240	.279	.240	.520	46	-9	10	2.59	-10	S-26/2-8,3-5,1-1,0-1	1	-1.7
1913 NY-A	12	29	5	6	1	0	0	1	3	3	0	....	.207	.281	.241	.523	53	-2	2	2.04	-3	/S-6,2-4,0-1	0	-0.4
Total 2	**54**	**158**	**13**	**37**	**1**	**0**	**0**	**11**	**9**	**3**	**5**	**....**	**.234**	**.280**	**.241**	**.520**	**47**	**-11**	**12**	**2.49**	**-13**	**/S-32,2-12,3-5,0-2,1-1**	**1**	**-2.1**
• STUMPF, George	George Frederick Stumpf b: 12/15/1910, New Orleans, LA d: 3/6/1993, Metairie, LA BL/TL, 5'8", 155 lbs. Deb: 9/19/1931 Career OF: 30-12-36																							
1931 Bos-A	7	28	2	7	1	1	0	4	1	2	0	0	.250	.276	.357	.633	69	-1	3	3.43	0	/0-7(6-2-0)	0	-0.2
1932 Bos-A	79	169	18	34	2	2	1	18	18	21	1	1	.201	.278	.254	.533	40	-15	13	2.45	-3	0-51(17-2-32)	1	-1.9
1933 Bos-A	22	41	8	14	3	0	0	5	4	2	4	0	.341	.400	.415	.815	117	2	8	7.58	0	0-15(3-8-4)	2	0.1
1936 Chi-A	10	22	3	6	1	0	0	5	2	1	0	0	.273	.333	.318	.652	59	-1	2	3.85	1	/0-4(4-0-0)	0	-0.1
Total 4	**118**	**260**	**31**	**61**	**7**	**3**	**1**	**32**	**25**	**26**	**5**	**1**	**.235**	**.302**	**.296**	**.598**	**57**	**-15**	**26**	**3.35**	**-3**	**/0-77**	**3**	**-2.0**
• STURDY, Guy	Guy R. Sturdy b: 8/7/1899, Sherman, TX d: 5/4/1965, Marshall, TX BL/TL, 6'.5", 180 lbs. Deb: 9/30/1927																							
1927 StL-A	5	21	5	9	1	0	0	5	1	0	2	0	.429	.455	.476	.931	137	2	5	10.87	-1	/1-5	1	0.1

YEAR TM-L	G	AB	R	H	2B	3B	HR	RBI	BB	SO	SB	CS	AVG	OBP	SLG	OPS	OPS+	BR/A	RC	RC/G	FR	G/POS	WS	TPW
1928 StL-A	54	45	3	10	1	0	1	8	8	4	1	0	.222	.340	.311	.651	70	-1	5	4.03	0	/1-1	1	-0.1
Total 2	**59**	**66**	**8**	**19**	**2**	**0**	**1**	**13**	**9**	**4**	**3**	**0**	**.288**	**.373**	**.364**	**.737**	**89**	**0**	**10**	**5.74**	**-1**	**/1-6**	**2**	**-0.1**
• STURGEON, Bobby	Robert Howard Sturgeon b: 8/6/1919, Clinton, IN BR/TR, 6', 175 lbs. Deb: 4/16/1940																							
1940 Chi-N	7	21	1	4	1	0	0	2	0	1	0	....	.190	.190	.238	.429	18	-2	1	1.07	-2	/S-7	0	-0.4
1941 Chi-N	129	433	45	106	15	3	0	25	9	30	5	....	.245	.260	.293	.553	58	-26	31	2.43	-3	*S-126/2-1,3-1	6	-2.1
1942 Chi-N	63	162	8	40	7	1	0	7	4	13	2	....	.247	.269	.302	.572	70	-7	13	2.80	3	2-32,S-29/3-2	3	0.0
1946 Chi-N	100	294	26	87	12	2	1	21	10	18	0	....	.296	.319	.361	.680	94	-4	33	4.09	-7	S-72,2-21	8	-0.6
1947 Chi-N	87	232	16	59	10	5	0	21	7	12	0	....	.254	.276	.341	.617	65	-13	19	2.82	-1	S-45,2-30/3-5	3	-1.0
1948 Bos-N	34	78	10	17	3	1	0	4	4	5	0	....	.218	.256	.282	.538	46	-6	5	2.29	-2	2-18/3-4,S-4	1	-0.7
Total 6	**420**	**1220**	**106**	**313**	**48**	**12**	**1**	**80**	**34**	**79**	**7**	**....**	**.257**	**.277**	**.318**	**.595**	**68**	**-57**	**103**	**2.90**	**-12**	**S-283,2-102/3-12**	**21**	**-4.8**
• STURGIS, Dean	Dean Donnell Sturgis b: 12/1/1892, Beloit, WI d: 6/4/1950, Uniontown, PA BR/TR, 6'1", 180 lbs. Deb: 5/1/1914																							
1914 Phi-A	4	4	1	1	0	0	0	0	1	2	0	....	.250	.400	.250	.650	100	0	0	3.53	0	/C-1	0	0.0
• STURM, Johnny	John Peter Joseph Sturm b: 1/23/1916, St. Louis, MO BL/TL, 6'1", 185 lbs. Deb: 4/15/1941																							
1941★NY-A	124	524	58	125	17	3	3	36	37	50	3	5	.239	.293	.300	.592	58	-34	46	2.98	-5	*1-124	4	-4.9
• STUTZ, George	George "Kid,Satan" Stutz b: 2/12/1893, Philadelphia, PA d: 12/29/1930, Philadelphia, PA BL/TR, 5'5", 150 lbs. Deb: 8/17/1926																							
1926 Phi-N	6	9	0	0	0	0	0	0	0	2	0	....	.000	.000	.000	.000	-95	-2	0	.00	-1	/S-5	0	-0.3
• STYLES, Lena	William Graves Styles b: 11/27/1899, Gurley, AL d: 3/14/1956, Huntsville, AL BR/TR, 6'1", 185 lbs. Deb: 9/10/1919																							
1919 Phi-A	8	22	0	6	1	0	0	5	1	6	0	....	.273	.304	.318	.623	74	-1	2	3.28	0	/C-8	1	0.0
1920 Phi-A	24	50	5	13	3	1	0	5	6	7	1	0	.260	.339	.360	.699	84	-1	7	4.68	1	/C-9,1-7	1	0.1
1921 Phi-A	4	5	0	1	0	0	0	0	0	2	0	0	.200	.200	.200	.400	2	-1	0	1.27	-1	/C-2	0	-0.2
1930 Cin-N	7	12	2	3	0	1	0	1	1	2	0	....	.250	.357	.417	.774	91	-0	2	5.30	-1	/C-5,1-1	0	0.0
1931 Cin-N	34	87	7	21	3	0	0	5	8	7	0	....	.241	.313	.276	.588	63	-4	8	3.09	-3	C-31	1	-0.5
Total 5	**77**	**176**	**14**	**44**	**7**	**2**	**0**	**16**	**16**	**24**	**1**	**0**	**.250**	**.320**	**.313**	**.632**	**71**	**-7**	**19**	**3.64**	**-4**	**/C-55,1-8**	**3**	**-0.7**
• STYNES, Chris	Christopher Desmond Stynes b: 1/19/1973, Queens, NY BR/TR, 5'9", 170 lbs. Deb: 5/19/1995 Career OF: 134-2-22																							
1995 KC-A	22	35	7	6	1	0	0	2	4	3	0	0	.171	.256	.200	.456	20	-4	1	1.22	1	2-17/D-2	1	-0.2
1996 KC-A	36	92	8	27	6	0	0	6	2	5	5	2	.293	.309	.359	.667	68	-4	10	3.92	-2	O-16(19-0-0)/2-5,D-3,3-2	1	-0.6
1997 Cin-N	49	198	31	69	7	1	6	28	11	13	11	2	.348	.394	.485	.879	126	9	38	7.46	4	O-19(38-0-0)/2-8,3-3	10	1.1
1998 Cin-N	123	347	52	88	10	1	6	27	32	36	15	1	.254	.324	.340	.664	74	-10	42	4.18	3	O-38(64-2-20),3-22,2-11/S-2	5	-0.9
1999 Cin-N	73	113	18	27	1	0	2	14	12	13	5	2	.239	.312	.301	.613	55	-8	11	3.24	2	O-80(4-0-0),2-43/3-8	2	-0.5
2000 Cin-N	119	380	71	127	24	1	12	40	32	54	5	2	.334	.389	.497	.886	119	11	74	7.56	-1	3-77,2-15/O-4(6-0-2)	13	1.1
2001 Bos-A	96	361	52	101	19	2	8	33	20	56	4	5	.280	.323	.410	.733	91	-7	44	4.21	-5	3-46,2-43/O-8(3-0-0)	8	-0.9
2002 Chi-N	98	195	25	47	9	1	5	26	21	29	1	1	.241	.318	.374	.692	83	-5	23	3.88	-3	3-40,2-20	5	-0.7
2003 Col-N	138	443	71	113	31	3	11	73	48	76	3	1	.255	.336	.413	.749	82	-11	63	4.96	-1	*3-119/2-5	10	-1.0
Total 9	**754**	**2164**	**335**	**605**	**108**	**9**	**50**	**249**	**182**	**285**	**49**	**16**	**.280**	**.341**	**.407**	**.748**	**90**	**-29**	**307**	**5.01**	**-2**	**3-317,2-167,O-165/D-5,S-2**	**55**	**-2.6**
• STYNES, Neil	Cornelius William Stynes b: 12/10/1868, Arlington, MA d: 3/26/1944, Somerville, MA BR/TR, 6', 165 lbs. Deb: 9/8/1890																							
1890 Cle-P	2	8	0	0	0	0	0	0	0	0	0	....	.000	.000	.000	.000	-109	-2	0	.00	-1	/C-2	0	-0.3
• SUAREZ, Ken	Kenneth Raymond Suarez b: 4/12/1943, Tampa, FL BR/TR, 5'9", 175 lbs. Deb: 4/14/1966																							
1966 KC-A	35	69	5	10	0	1	0	2	15	26	2	0	.145	.298	.174	.472	41	-4	5	2.18	2	C-34	1	-0.1
1967 KC-A	39	63	7	15	5	0	2	9	16	21	1	0	.238	.392	.413	.805	142	5	12	6.08	1	C-36	4	0.8
1968 Cle-A	17	10	1	1	0	0	0	0	1	3	0	0	.100	.182	.100	.282	-13	-1	0	.31	-3	C-12/2-1,3-1,O-1	0	-0.4
1969 Cle-A	36	85	7	25	5	0	1	9	15	12	1	0	.294	.400	.388	.788	117	3	13	5.14	2	C-36	4	0.7
1971 Cle-A	50	123	10	25	7	0	1	9	18	15	0	1	.203	.315	.285	.599	65	-5	12	3.06	1	C-48	3	-0.2
1972 Tex-A	25	33	2	5	1	0	0	4	1	4	0	0	.152	.176	.182	.358	7	-4	1	.88	-1	C-17	0	-0.5
1973 Tex-A	93	278	25	69	11	0	1	27	33	16	1	2	.248	.339	.299	.637	84	-5	29	3.38	0	C-90	6	0.0
Total 7	**295**	**661**	**57**	**150**	**29**	**1**	**5**	**60**	**99**	**97**	**5**	**3**	**.227**	**.334**	**.297**	**.630**	**81**	**-12**	**71**	**3.46**	**3**	**C-273/2-1,3-1,O-1**	**18**	**0.2**
• SUAREZ, Luis	Luis Abelardo Suarez b: 8/24/1916, Alto Songo, Cuba d: 6/5/1991, Havana, Cuba BR/TR, 5'11", 170 lbs. Deb: 5/28/1944																							
1944 Was-A	1	2	0	0	0	0	0	0	0	0	0	0	.000	.000	.000	.000	-105	-1	0	.00	0	/3-1	0	0.0
• SUCK, Tony	Anthony Suck b: 6/11/1858, Chicago, IL d: 1/29/1895, Chicago, IL, 5'9", 164 lbs. Deb: 8/9/1883 Career OF: 2-10-1																							
1883 Buf-N	2	7	1	0	0	0	0	0	1	4	....	....	.000	.125	.000	.125	-56	-1	0	.00	-1	/C-1,O-1	0	-0.2
1884 CP-U	53	188	18	28	2	0	0	....	13	....	....	....	.149	.204	.160	.364	26	-13	6	1.10	-1	C-28,S-15,O-12(1-10-1)/3-1	2	-1.0
Bal-U	3	10	2	3	0	0	0	....	0	....	....	....	.300	.300	.300	.600	94	-0	1	3.69	0	/C-3	1	0.0
Yr.	56	198	20	31	2	0	0	....	13	....	....	....	.157	.209	.167	.375	29	-13	7	1.21	-2	C-31,S-15,O-12(1-10-1)/3-1	3	-1.1
Total 2	**58**	**205**	**21**	**31**	**2**	**0**	**0**	**0**	**14**	**4**	**....**	**....**	**.151**	**.205**	**.161**	**.366**	**26**	**-14**	**7**	**1.16**	**-3**	**/C-32,S-15,O-13,3-1**	**3**	**-1.3**
• SUDAKIS, Bill	William Paul "Suds" Sudakis b: 3/27/1946, Joliet, IL BB/TR, 6'1", 190 lbs. Deb: 9/3/1968 Career OF: 1-0-6																							
1968 LA-N	24	87	11	24	4	2	3	12	15	14	1	0	.276	.382	.471	.854	168	8	15	6.24	3	3-24	6	1.3
1969 LA-N	132	462	50	108	17	5	14	53	40	94	3	2	.234	.296	.383	.679	96	-4	52	3.78	9	*3-121	13	0.5
1970 LA-N	94	269	37	71	11	0	14	44	35	46	4	0	.264	.355	.461	.816	122	9	45	5.80	4	C-38,3-37/O-3(0-0-3),1-1	12	1.4
1971 LA-N	41	83	10	16	3	0	3	7	12	22	0	1	.193	.302	.337	.639	86	-2	8	2.89	1	C-19/3-3,1-1,O-1	2	0.0
1972 NY-N	18	49	3	7	0	0	1	7	6	14	0	0	.143	.236	.204	.440	27	-5	3	1.59	1	/1-7,C-5	1	-0.5
1973 Tex-A	82	235	32	60	11	0	15	43	23	53	0	1	.255	.322	.494	.815	132	9	36	5.19	-3	3-29,1-24/C-9,D-8,O-2(0-0-2)	8	0.4
1974 NY-A	89	259	26	60	8	0	7	39	25	48	0	0	.232	.302	.344	.645	88	-4	29	3.69	0	D-39,1-33/3-3,C-1	5	-0.8
1975 Cal-A	30	58	4	7	2	0	1	6	12	15	1	1	.121	.282	.207	.489	43	-4	4	2.10	-1	D-13/C-5,1-2	0	-0.5
Cle-A	20	46	4	9	0	0	1	3	4	7	0	1	.196	.260	.261	.521	48	-4	3	2.18	0	1-12/C-6	0	-0.5
Yr.	50	104	8	16	2	0	2	9	16	22	1	2	.154	.273	.231	.503	45	-8	7	2.13	-1	1-14,D-13,C-11	0	-1.0
Total 8	**530**	**1548**	**177**	**362**	**56**	**7**	**59**	**214**	**172**	**313**	**9**	**6**	**.234**	**.313**	**.393**	**.707**	**102**	**4**	**194**	**4.20**	**14**	**3-217/C-83,1-80,D-60,O-6**	**47**	**1.4**
• SUDER, Pete	Peter "Pecky" Suder b: 4/16/1916, Aliquippa, PA BR/TR, 6', 175 lbs. Deb: 4/15/1941																							
1941 Phi-A	139	531	45	130	20	9	4	52	19	47	1	3	.245	.271	.339	.610	62	-32	43	2.66	-5	*3-136/S-3	5	-3.1
1942 Phi-A	128	476	46	122	20	4	4	54	24	39	4	4	.256	.293	.340	.634	78	-16	43	3.01	0	S-69,3-34,2-31	8	-0.8
1943 Phi-A	131	475	30	105	14	5	3	41	14	40	1	1	.221	.243	.291	.534	56	-28	31	2.16	-13	2-95,3-32/S-5	4	-3.8
1946 Phi-A	128	455	38	128	20	3	2	50	18	37	1	1	.281	.309	.352	.660	85	-11	48	3.66	3	S-67,3-33,2-12/1-3,O-2(0-0-2)	7	-0.3
1947 Phi-A	145	528	45	127	28	4	5	60	35	44	0	3	.241	.290	.337	.627	73	-22	51	3.16	-6	*2-140/S-3,3-2	9	-2.0
1948 Phi-A	148	519	64	125	23	5	7	60	60	60	1	3	.241	.321	.345	.666	77	-19	60	3.87	0	*2-148	15	-1.0
1949 Phi-A	118	445	44	119	24	6	10	75	23	35	0	1	.267	.306	.416	.722	93	-8	52	3.93	7	2-89,3-36/S-2	12	0.3
1950 Phi-A	77	248	34	61	10	0	8	35	23	31	2	2	.246	.310	.383	.693	78	-10	29	3.86	0	2-47,3-11,S-10/1-4	4	-0.7
1951 Phi-A	123	440	46	108	18	1	1	42	30	42	5	5	.245	.295	.298	.593	59	-26	37	2.79	-7	*2-103,S-18/3-3	5	-2.6
1952 Phi-A	74	228	22	55	7	2	1	20	16	17	1	1	.241	.291	.303	.594	61	-12	21	3.02	-4	2-43,S-17,3-16	3	-1.4
1953 Phi-A	115	454	44	130	11	3	4	35	17	35	3	3	.286	.312	.350	.662	76	-17	48	3.83	8	3-72,2-38/S-7	8	-0.6
1954 Phi-A	69	205	8	41	11	1	0	16	7	16	0	0	.200	.226	.263	.490	34	-19	11	1.75	1	2-35,3-20/S-2	2	-1.6
1955 KC-A	26	81	3	17	4	1	0	1	2	13	0	1	.210	.229	.284	.513	37	-8	5	1.97	-2	2-24	1	-0.8
Total 13	**1421**	**5085**	**469**	**1268**	**210**	**44**	**49**	**541**	**288**	**456**	**19**	**28**	**.249**	**.291**	**.337**	**.627**	**71**	**-228**	**478**	**3.15**	**-18**	**2-805,3-395,S-203/1-7,O-2**	**83**	**-18.4**
• SUDHOFF, Willie	John William "Wee Willie" Sudhoff b: 9/17/1874, St. Louis, MO d: 5/25/1917, St. Louis, MO BR/TR, 5'7", 165 lbs. Deb: 8/20/1897 Career OF: 3-11-3 ♦																							
1897 StL-N	11	42	7	10	1	0	0	3	1	....	0	....	.238	.256	.262	.518	38	-1	3	2.41	2	P-11	2	0.2
1898 StL-N	41	120	5	19	2	1	0	4	5	....	0	....	.158	.198	.192	.390	12	-6	5	1.30	6	P-41	14	-1.3
1899 Cle-N	11	31	1	2	0	1	0	6	4	....	0	....	.065	.171	.129	.300	-18	-2	1	.78	1	P-11	2	-2.7
StL-N	25	64	9	13	1	0	0	0	8	....	0	....	.203	.292	.219	.510	40	-0	5	2.34	5	P-25	14	0.1
Yr.	36	95	10	15	1	1	0	6	12	....	0	....	.158	.252	.189	.442	21	-2	6	1.78	6	P-36	16	-2.5
1900 StL-N	35	106	15	20	1	1	0	6	11	....	8	....	.189	.271	.217	.488	36	-5	9	2.66	0	P-16,O-12(0-10-2)/3-7	9	0.9

YEAR TM-L	G	AB	R	H	2B	3B	HR	RBI	BB	SO	SB	CS	AVG	OBP	SLG	OPS	OPS+	BR/A	RC	RC/G	FR	G/POS	WS	TPW
1901 StL-N	38	108	11	19	2	3	1	17	10	....	0	....	.176	.252	.278	.530	56	3	8	2.33	2	P-38	14	-1.3
1902 StL-A	31	77	6	13	2	0	0	5	4	....	3	....	.169	.220	.195	.414	16	-2	4	1.73	3	P-30/0-1	19	1.1
1903 StL-A	41	110	12	20	1	2	0	6	3	....	1	....	.182	.204	.227	.431	30	-1	6	1.63	3	P-38/0-1	25	2.0
1904 StL-A	29	85	5	14	3	0	0	7	6	....	0	....	.165	.237	.200	.437	41	-0	4	1.57	5	P-27/0-3(3-0-0)	4	-3.3
1905 StL-A	32	86	6	16	3	1	0	3	7	....	1	....	.186	.247	.244	.491	59	2	6	2.11	4	P-32	8	-0.7
1906 Was-A	9	7	0	3	0	0	0	0	0	....	0	....	.429	.429	.429	.857	177	1	1	8.73	1	/P-9	0	-1.4
Total 10	303	836	77	149	16	9	1	57	59	....	13	....	.178	.238	.222	.460	35	-11	52	1.94	32	P-278/0-17,3-7	111	-6.4

• SUERO, William William (Urban) Suero
b: 11/7/1966, Santo Domingo, Dominican Republic d: 11/30/1995, Santo Domingo, Dominican Republic BR/TR, 5'9", 175 lbs. Deb: 4/9/1992

YEAR TM-L	G	AB	R	H	2B	3B	HR	RBI	BB	SO	SB	CS	AVG	OBP	SLG	OPS	OPS+	BR/A	RC	RC/G	FR	G/POS	WS	TPW
1992 Mil-A	18	16	4	3	1	0	0	0	2	1	1	1	.188	.316	.250	.566	62	-1	1	1.41	1	2-15/D-2,S-1	0	0.0
1993 Mil-A	15	14	0	4	0	0	0	0	1	3	0	1	.286	.333	.286	.619	69	-1	1	1.92	0	/2-8,3-1	0	-0.1
Total 2	33	30	4	7	1	0	0	0	3	4	1	2	.233	.324	.267	.590	65	-2	2	1.63	1	/2-23,D-2,3-1,S-1	0	-0.1

• SUGDEN, Joe Joseph Sugden b: 7/31/1870, Philadelphia, PA d: 6/28/1959, Philadelphia, PA BB/TR, 5'10", 180 lbs. Deb: 7/20/1893 C/U Career OF: 0-6-18

YEAR TM-L	G	AB	R	H	2B	3B	HR	RBI	BB	SO	SB	CS	AVG	OBP	SLG	OPS	OPS+	BR/A	RC	RC/G	FR	G/POS	WS	TPW
1893 Pit-N	27	92	20	24	4	3	0	12	10	11	1	....	.261	.340	.370	.709	90	-1	12	4.75	1	C-27	2	0.1
1894 Pit-N	39	139	23	46	13	2	2	23	14	2	3	....	.331	.404	.496	.900	117	4	30	8.33	-3	C-31/3-4,S-3,0-1	5	0.3
1895 Pit-N	50	158	28	48	4	1	1	17	16	12	4	....	.304	.379	.361	.739	96	0	25	5.71	1	C-49	5	0.5
1896 Pit-N	80	301	42	89	5	7	0	36	19	9	5	....	.296	.348	.359	.706	90	-4	42	4.94	0	C-70/1-7,0-4(0-4-0)	9	0.2
1897 Pit-N	84	288	31	64	6	4	0	38	18	....	9	....	.222	.275	.271	.546	46	-22	26	2.92	-2	C-81/1-3	4	-1.4
1898 StL-N	89	289	29	73	7	1	0	34	23	....	5	....	.253	.314	.284	.598	70	-11	29	3.45	7	C-60,0-15(0-1-14)/1-8	4	0.1
1899 Cle-N	76	250	19	69	5	1	0	14	11	....	2	....	.276	.307	.304	.611	73	-9	25	3.58	9	C-66/0-4(0-0-4),1-3,3-1	3	0.5
1901 Chi-A	48	153	21	42	7	1	0	19	13	....	4	....	.275	.339	.333	.673	89	-2	20	4.53	-1	C-42/1-5	5	0.1
1902 StL-A	68	200	25	50	7	2	0	15	20	....	2	....	.250	.330	.305	.635	78	-5	23	3.78	-2	C-61/1-4,P-1	5	-0.1
1903 StL-A	79	241	18	51	4	0	0	22	25	....	4	....	.212	.288	.228	.517	58	-11	19	2.52	4	C-66/1-8	5	0.0
1904 StL-A	105	348	25	93	6	3	0	30	28	....	6	....	.267	.331	.302	.632	107	4	39	3.91	4	C-79,1-28	13	1.7
1905 StL-A	90	266	21	46	4	0	0	23	23	....	3	....	.173	.247	.188	.435	41	-17	15	1.70	9	C-76/1-9	4	0.0
1912 Det-A	1	4	1	1	0	0	0	0	0	....	0	....	.250	.250	.250	.500	44	-0	0	2.04	1	/1-1	0	0.1
Total 13	836	2729	303	696	72	25	3	283	220	34	48	....	.255	.318	.303	.621	77	-75	304	3.80	29	C-708/1-76,0-24,3-5,S-3,P-1	64	2.2

• SUHR, Gus August Richard Suhr b: 1/3/1906, San Francisco, CA BL/TR, 6', 180 lbs. Deb: 4/15/1930

YEAR TM-L	G	AB	R	H	2B	3B	HR	RBI	BB	SO	SB	CS	AVG	OBP	SLG	OPS	OPS+	BR/A	RC	RC/G	FR	G/POS	WS	TPW
1930 Pit-N	151	542	93	155	26	14	17	107	80	56	11	....	.286	.380	.480	.860	106	6	99	6.46	-8	*1-151	17	-1.0
1931 Pit-N	87	270	26	57	13	4	4	32	38	25	4	....	.211	.308	.333	.642	73	-10	30	3.61	3	1-76	4	-1.4
1932 Pit-N	154	581	78	153	31	16	5	81	63	39	7	....	.263	.337	.398	.735	98	-0	82	4.87	-3	*1-154	15	-1.8
1933 Pit-N	154	566	72	151	31	11	10	75	72	52	2	....	.267	.350	.413	.763	117	14	87	5.28	-3	*1-154	20	-0.3
1934 Pit-N	151	573	67	162	36	13	13	103	66	52	4	....	.283	.360	.459	.819	115	13	98	6.11	-1	*1-151	19	-0.2
1935 Pit-N	153	529	68	144	33	12	10	81	70	54	6	....	.272	.357	.437	.794	109	8	89	6.05	-1	*1-149/0-2(0-0-2)	16	-0.7
1936 Pit-N★	156	583	111	182	33	12	11	118	95	34	8	....	.312	.410	.467	.877	132	31	119	7.63	6	*1-156	25	2.1
1937 Pit-N	151	575	69	160	28	14	5	97	83	42	2	....	.278	.369	.402	.771	109	10	92	5.75	-2	*1-151	19	-0.7
1938 Pit-N	145	530	82	156	35	14	3	64	87	37	4	....	.294	.394	.430	.824	126	22	97	6.69	-10	*1-145	21	-0.2
1939 Pit-N	63	204	23	59	10	2	1	31	25	23	4	....	.289	.367	.373	.739	101	1	31	5.45	-4	1-52	5	-0.8
Phi-N	60	198	21	63	12	2	3	24	34	14	1	....	.318	.421	.444	.865	139	13	40	7.98	-1	1-60	9	0.7
Yr.	123	402	44	122	22	4	4	55	59	37	5	....	.303	.394	.408	.802	120	14	71	6.65	-4	*1-112	14	-0.1
1940 Phi-N	10	25	4	4	0	0	2	5	5	5	0	....	.160	.300	.400	.700	95	-0	3	4.36	-2	/1-7	0	-0.2
Total 11	1435	5176	714	1446	288	114	84	818	718	433	53	....	.279	.368	.428	.796	112	107	867	5.98	-27	*1-1406/0-2	170	-4.5

• SUKEFORTH, Clyde Clyde Leroy "Sukey" Sukeforth b: 11/30/1901, Washington, ME d: 9/3/2000, Waldoboro, ME BL/TR, 5'10", 155 lbs. Deb: 5/23/1926 M/C

YEAR TM-L	G	AB	R	H	2B	3B	HR	RBI	BB	SO	SB	CS	AVG	OBP	SLG	OPS	OPS+	BR/A	RC	RC/G	FR	G/POS	WS	TPW
1926 Cin-N	1	1	0	0	0	0	0	0	0	1	0	....	.000	.000	.000	.000	-103	-0	0	.00	0	....	0	0.0
1927 Cin-N	38	58	12	11	2	0	0	2	7	2	2	....	.190	.277	.224	.501	37	-5	4	2.07	-1	C-24	1	-0.5
1928 Cin-N	33	53	5	7	2	1	0	3	3	5	0	....	.132	.179	.208	.386	1	-8	2	1.11	-1	C-26	1	-0.8
1929 Cin-N	84	237	31	84	16	2	1	33	17	6	8	....	.354	.398	.451	.849	115	6	41	6.66	0	C-76	9	0.9
1930 Cin-N	94	296	30	84	9	3	1	19	17	12	1	....	.284	.325	.345	.669	65	-16	33	3.84	1	C-82	4	-0.9
1931 Cin-N	112	351	22	90	15	4	0	25	38	13	0	....	.256	.334	.322	.656	82	-8	40	3.97	-3	*C-106	6	-0.4
1932 Bro-N	59	111	14	26	4	4	0	12	6	10	1	....	.234	.280	.342	.622	68	-5	11	3.26	-0	C-36	2	-0.4
1933 Bro-N	20	36	1	2	0	0	0	0	2	1	0	....	.056	.105	.056	.161	-55	-7	0	.12	1	C-18	1	-0.6
1934 Bro-N	27	43	5	7	1	0	0	1	1	6	0	....	.163	.182	.186	.368	-1	-6	1	.98	0	C-18	0	-0.5
1945 Bro-N	18	51	2	15	1	0	0	1	4	1	0	....	.294	.345	.314	.659	85	-1	6	4.41	-2	C-13	1	-0.2
Total 10	486	1237	122	326	50	14	2	96	95	57	12	....	.264	.319	.331	.650	71	-51	138	3.84	-4	C-399	25	-3.4

• SULARZ, Guy Guy Patrick Sularz b: 11/7/1955, Minneapolis, MN BR/TR, 5'11", 165 lbs. Deb: 9/2/1980

YEAR TM-L	G	AB	R	H	2B	3B	HR	RBI	BB	SO	SB	CS	AVG	OBP	SLG	OPS	OPS+	BR/A	RC	RC/G	FR	G/POS	WS	TPW
1980 SF-N	25	65	3	16	1	1	0	3	9	6	1	0	.246	.338	.292	.630	79	-1	7	3.46	1	2-21/3-5	2	0.1
1981 SF-N	10	20	0	4	0	0	0	2	2	4	0	1	.200	.304	.200	.504	46	-2	1	1.99	1	/2-6,3-1	0	0.0
1982 SF-N	63	101	15	23	3	0	1	7	9	11	3	0	.228	.291	.287	.578	62	-4	9	3.01	-1	S-37,3-14/2-9	2	-0.3
1983 SF-N	10	20	3	2	0	0	0	0	3	2	0	0	.100	.217	.100	.317	-10	-3	0	.69	-1	/S-6,3-4	0	-0.3
Total 4	108	206	21	45	4	1	1	12	23	23	4	1	.218	.300	.262	.562	59	-10	18	2.79	1	/S-43,2-36,3-24	4	-0.5

• SULIK, Ernie Ernest Richard "Dave" Sulik b: 7/7/1910, San Francisco, CA d: 5/31/1963, Oakland, CA BL/TL, 5'10", 178 lbs. Deb: 4/15/1936

YEAR TM-L	G	AB	R	H	2B	3B	HR	RBI	BB	SO	SB	CS	AVG	OBP	SLG	OPS	OPS+	BR/A	RC	RC/G	FR	G/POS	WS	TPW
1936 Phi-N	122	404	69	116	14	4	6	36	40	22	4	....	.287	.353	.386	.739	90	-5	57	5.00	-4	*0-105(41-65-1)	7	-1.2

• SULLIVAN, Sullivan b: Bristol, RI Deb: 5/15/1875

YEAR TM-L	G	AB	R	H	2B	3B	HR	RBI	BB	SO	SB	CS	AVG	OBP	SLG	OPS	OPS+	BR/A	RC	RC/G	FR	G/POS	WS	TPW
1875 NH-n	2	8	3	3	0	0	0	2	0	1	1	0	.375	.375	.375	.750	185	1	2	9.07	0	/0-2(0-0-2)	....	0.1

• SULLIVAN, Andy Andrew R. Sullivan b: 8/30/1884, Southborough, MA d: 2/14/1920, Framingham, MA TR Deb: 9/13/1904

YEAR TM-L	G	AB	R	H	2B	3B	HR	RBI	BB	SO	SB	CS	AVG	OBP	SLG	OPS	OPS+	BR/A	RC	RC/G	FR	G/POS	WS	TPW
1904 Bos-N	1	1	0	0	0	0	0	0	1	....	0	....	.000	.500	.000	.500	61	0	0	.00	0	/S-1	0	0.0

• SULLIVAN, Bill William Sullivan b: 7/4/1853, Ireland d: 11/13/1884, Holyoke, MA Deb: 8/9/1878

YEAR TM-L	G	AB	R	H	2B	3B	HR	RBI	BB	SO	SB	CS	AVG	OBP	SLG	OPS	OPS+	BR/A	RC	RC/G	FR	G/POS	WS	TPW
1878 Chi-N	2	6	1	1	0	0	0	0	0	0	....	....	.167	.167	.167	.333	9	-1	0	.94	0	/0-2(2-0-0)	0	-0.1

• SULLIVAN, Billy William Joseph Sullivan, Sr. b: 2/1/1875, Oakland, WI d: 1/28/1965, Newberg, OR BR/TR, 5'9", 155 lbs. Deb: 9/13/1899 M

YEAR TM-L	G	AB	R	H	2B	3B	HR	RBI	BB	SO	SB	CS	AVG	OBP	SLG	OPS	OPS+	BR/A	RC	RC/G	FR	G/POS	WS	TPW
1899 Bos-N	22	74	10	20	2	0	2	12	1	....	2	....	.270	.308	.378	.686	80	-3	9	4.64	-2	C-22	2	-0.2
1900 Bos-N	72	238	36	65	6	0	8	41	9	....	4	....	.273	.302	.399	.702	83	-8	31	4.67	4	C-66/2-1,S-1	6	0.1
1901 Chi-A	98	367	54	90	15	6	4	56	10	....	12	....	.245	.271	.351	.623	74	-14	40	3.69	-4	C-97/3-1	9	-0.7
1902 Chi-A	76	263	36	64	12	3	1	26	6	....	11	....	.243	.268	.323	.592	66	-13	27	3.48	1	C-70/1-2,0-2(1-0-1)	6	-0.5
1903 Chi-A	32	111	10	21	4	0	1	7	5	....	3	....	.189	.224	.252	.476	45	-7	7	2.11	-1	C-31	1	-0.5
1904 Chi-A	108	371	29	85	18	4	1	44	12	....	11	....	.229	.255	.307	.562	81	-9	34	3.02	-4	*C-107	9	-0.2
1905 Chi-A	98	323	25	65	10	3	2	26	13	....	14	....	.201	.239	.269	.508	64	-14	26	2.55	-6	C-92/1-2,3-1	7	-1.2
1906★Chi-A	118	387	37	83	18	4	2	33	22	....	10	....	.214	.262	.297	.559	77	-11	36	2.93	-11	*C-118	11	-1.1
1907 Chi-A	112	329	30	59	8	4	0	36	21	....	6	....	.179	.235	.228	.463	49	-19	21	1.96	-5	*C-108/2-1	6	-1.5
1908 Chi-A	137	430	40	82	8	4	0	29	22	....	15	....	.191	.235	.228	.463	51	-23	27	1.92	-15	*C-137	7	-2.9
1909 Chi-A	97	265	11	43	3	0	0	16	17	....	9	....	.162	.226	.174	.400	28	-21	13	1.47	-2	C-97	4	-1.6
1910 Chi-A	45	142	10	26	4	1	0	6	7	....	0	....	.183	.227	.225	.452	44	-9	7	1.54	3	C-45	3	-0.2
1911 Chi-A	89	256	26	55	9	3	0	31	16	....	1	....	.215	.266	.273	.540	52	-17	19	2.37	-4	C-89	4	-1.5
1912 Chi-A	41	91	9	19	2	1	0	15	9	....	0	....	.209	.287	.253	.540	56	-5	7	2.39	3	C-41	2	0.1
1914 Chi-A	1	0	0	0	0	0	0	0	0	0	0	....	....	....	....	....	-101	0	0	....	0	/C-1	0	0.0
1916 Det-A	1	0	0	0	0	0	0	0	0	0	0	....	....	....	....	....	-97	0	0	....	0	/C-1	0	-0.1
Total 16	1147	3647	363	777	119	33	21	378	170	0	98	....	.213	.254	.281	.535	62	-173	306	2.69	-43	*C-1122/1-4,2-2,3-2,0-2,S-1	77	-12.0

• SULLIVAN, Billy William Joseph Sullivan, Jr. b: 10/23/1910, Chicago, IL d: 1/4/1994, Sarasota, FL BL/TR, 6', 170 lbs. Deb: 6/9/1931 Career OF: 33-0-33

YEAR TM-L	G	AB	R	H	2B	3B	HR	RBI	BB	SO	SB	CS	AVG	OBP	SLG	OPS	OPS+	BR/A	RC	RC/G	FR	G/POS	WS	TPW
1931 Chi-A	92	363	48	100	16	5	2	33	20	14	4	4	.275	.315	.364	.679	83	-9	41	3.97	-3	3-83/0-2(0-0-2),1-1	7	-0.9
1932 Chi-A	93	307	31	97	16	1	1	45	20	9	1	3	.316	.358	.384	.742	99	-1	41	5.13	-3	1-52,3-17/C-5,0-3(1-0-2)	7	-0.7
1933 Chi-A	54	125	9	24	0	1	0	13	10	5	0	0	.192	.252	.208	.460	24	-13	7	1.82	-2	1-22/C-8	0	-1.6

YEAR TM-L	G	AB	R	H	2B	3B	HR	RBI	BB	SO	SB	CS	AVG	OBP	SLG	OPS	OPS+	BR/A	RC	RC/G	FR	G/POS	WS	TPW
1935 Cin-N	85	241	29	64	9	4	2	36	19	16	4	....	.266	.324	.361	.685	87	-4	29	4.24	4	1-40,3-15/2-6	5	-0.3
1936 Cle-A	93	319	39	112	32	6	2	48	16	9	5	2	.351	.382	.508	.890	117	7	61	7.58	-8	C-72/3-5,1-3,0-1	11	0.4
1937 Cle-A	72	168	26	48	12	3	3	22	17	7	1	4	.286	.355	.446	.801	100	-2	26	5.34	-4	C-38/1-5,3-1	5	-0.4
1938 StL-A	111	375	35	104	16	1	7	49	20	10	8	5	.277	.316	.381	.697	74	-17	45	4.21	11	C-99/1-6	8	-0.1
1939 StL-A	118	332	53	96	17	5	5	50	34	18	3	3	.289	.362	.416	.778	96	-2	49	5.23	5	0-59(31-0-28),C-19/1-4	6	0.0
1940*Det-A	78	220	36	68	14	4	3	41	31	11	2	0	.309	.399	.450	.849	109	5	44	7.49	0	C-57/3-6	9	0.7
1941 Det-A	85	234	29	66	15	1	3	29	35	11	0	3	.282	.375	.393	.769	94	-2	36	5.48	-2	C-63	8	0.0
1942 Bro-N	43	101	11	27	2	1	1	14	12	6	1	....	.267	.345	.337	.682	98	0	13	4.42	-2	C-41	4	-0.1
1947 Pit-N	38	55	1	14	3	0	0	8	6	3	1	....	.255	.328	.309	.637	68	-2	6	3.72	0	C-12	1	-0.1
Total 12	962	2840	347	820	152	32	29	388	240	119	30	24	.289	.346	.395	.742	91	-41	397	5.03	-4	C-414,1-133,3-127/0-65,2-6	71	-3.0

• SULLIVAN, Chub John Frank Sullivan b: 1/12/1856, Boston, MA d: 9/12/1881, Boston, MA BR/TR, 6', 164 lbs. Deb: 9/24/1877

YEAR TM-L	G	AB	R	H	2B	3B	HR	RBI	BB	SO	SB	CS	AVG	OBP	SLG	OPS	OPS+	BR/A	RC	RC/G	FR	G/POS	WS	TPW
1877 Cin-N	8	32	4	8	0	0	0	4	1	0	....	....	.250	.273	.250	.523	74	-1	2	2.56	-1	/1-8	0	-0.1
1878 Cin-N	61	244	29	63	4	2	0	20	2	9	....	....	.258	.264	.291	.555	91	-2	19	2.92	7	*1-61	5	0.2
1880 Wor-N	43	166	22	43	6	3	0	0	4	6	....	....	.259	.276	.331	.608	96	-1	16	3.48	3	1-43	4	0.0
Total 3	112	442	55	114	10	5	0	24	7	15	....	....	.258	.269	.303	.573	92	-3	37	3.11	10	1-112	9	0.1

• SULLIVAN, Dan Daniel C. "Link" Sullivan b: 5/9/1857, Providence, RI d: 10/26/1893, Providence, RI TR, 5'11", 194 lbs. Deb: 5/2/1882 Career OF: 1-5-1

YEAR TM-L	G	AB	R	H	2B	3B	HR	RBI	BB	SO	SB	CS	AVG	OBP	SLG	OPS	OPS+	BR/A	RC	RC/G	FR	G/POS	WS	TPW
1882 Lou-a	67	286	44	78	8	2	0	....	9	....	....	....	.273	.295	.315	.610	112	4	27	3.66	2	C-54,3-10/0-4(0-3-1),S-1	10	1.0
1883 Lou-a	36	145	8	31	5	2	0	0	3	....	....	....	.214	.230	.276	.506	67	-5	9	2.31	-3	C-31/3-2,0-2(0-2-0),S-1	3	-0.5
1884 Lou-a	63	247	27	59	8	6	0	26	9	....	....	....	.239	.268	.320	.588	95	-1	22	3.18	-11	C-63/0-1	5	-0.6
1885 Lou-a	13	44	3	8	1	0	0	4	2	....	....	....	.182	.234	.205	.439	39	-3	2	1.62	-1	C-13	0	-0.3
StL-a	17	60	4	7	2	0	0	3	6	....	....	....	.117	.197	.150	.347	10	-6	2	.93	1	C-13/1-4	1	-0.4
Yr.	30	104	7	15	3	0	0	7	8	....	....	....	.144	.212	.173	.385	22	-9	4	1.21	0	C-26/1-4	1	-0.7
1886 Pit-a	1	4	0	0	0	0	0	0	0	....	0	....	.000	.000	.000	.000	-101	-1	0	.00	-1	/C-1	0	-0.1
Total 5	197	786	86	183	24	10	0	33	29	....	0	....	.233	.262	.289	.551	85	-12	62	2.87	-13	C-175/3-12,0-7,1-4,S-2	19	-0.9

• SULLIVAN, Denny Dennis William Sullivan b: 9/28/1882, Hillsboro, WI d: 6/2/1956, West Los Angeles, CA BL/TR, 5'10" Deb: 4/22/1905 Career OF: 1-235-11

YEAR TM-L	G	AB	R	H	2B	3B	HR	RBI	BB	SO	SB	CS	AVG	OBP	SLG	OPS	OPS+	BR/A	RC	RC/G	FR	G/POS	WS	TPW
1905 Was-A	3	11	0	0	0	0	0	0	1	....	0	....	.000	.083	.000	.083	-76	-2	0	.00	-0	/0-3(0-0-3)	0	-0.2
1907 Bos-A	144	551	73	135	18	0	1	26	44	....	16	....	.245	.315	.283	.598	92	-3	59	3.54	0	*0-143(0-143-0)	12	-1.1
1908 Bos-A	101	355	33	85	7	8	0	25	14	....	14	....	.239	.276	.304	.580	86	-6	34	3.07	5	0-97(0-92-5)	9	-0.7
Cle-A	4	6	0	0	0	0	0	0	0	....	0	....	.000	.000	.000	.000	-100	-1	0	.00	0	/0-2(1-0-1)	0	-0.2
Yr.	105	361	33	85	7	8	0	25	14	....	14	....	.235	.272	.299	.571	83	-8	34	3.01	5	0-99(1-92-6)	9	-0.9
1909 Cle-A	3	2	0	1	0	0	0	0	0	....	0	....	.500	.500	.500	1.000	207	0	0	12.79	0	/0-2(0-0-2)	0	0.0
Total 4	255	925	106	221	25	8	1	51	59	....	30	....	.239	.296	.286	.582	87	-13	93	3.29	4	0-247	21	-2.3

• SULLIVAN, Denny Dennis J. Sullivan b: 6/26/1858, Boston, MA d: 12/31/1925, Boston, MA TR, 5'9", 170 lbs. Deb: 8/25/1879

YEAR TM-L	G	AB	R	H	2B	3B	HR	RBI	BB	SO	SB	CS	AVG	OBP	SLG	OPS	OPS+	BR/A	RC	RC/G	FR	G/POS	WS	TPW
1879 Pro-N	5	19	5	5	2	0	0	2	1	1	....	....	.263	.300	.368	.668	121	0	2	4.31	-3	/3-4,0-1	0	-0.2
1880 Bos-N	1	4	1	1	0	0	0	1	0	1	....	....	.250	.250	.250	.500	72	-0	0	2.35	0	/C-1	0	0.0
Total 2	6	23	6	6	2	0	0	3	1	2	....	....	.261	.292	.348	.639	113	0	2	3.96	-3	/3-4,C-1,0-1	0	-0.3

• SULLIVAN, Haywood Haywood Cooper Sullivan b: 12/15/1930, Donaldsonville, GA d: 2/12/2003, Fort Myers, FL BR/TR, 6'4", 215 lbs. Deb: 9/20/1955 M

YEAR TM-L	G	AB	R	H	2B	3B	HR	RBI	BB	SO	SB	CS	AVG	OBP	SLG	OPS	OPS+	BR/A	RC	RC/G	FR	G/POS	WS	TPW
1955 Bos-A	2	6	1	0	0	0	0	0	0	1	0	0	.000	.000	.000	.000	-92	-2	0	.00	0	/C-2	0	-0.1
1957 Bos-A	2	1	0	0	0	0	0	0	0	0	0	0	.000	.000	.000	.000	-95	-0	0	.00	0	/C-1	0	0.0
1959 Bos-A	4	2	0	0	0	0	0	0	1	1	0	0	.000	.333	.000	.333		-0	0	1.17	0	/C-2	0	0.0
1960 Bos-A	52	124	9	20	1	0	3	10	16	24	0	0	.161	.257	.242	.499	35	-11	8	2.00	1	C-50	2	-0.8
1961 KC-A	117	331	42	80	16	2	6	40	46	45	1	0	.242	.334	.356	.691	84	-6	41	4.18	1	C-88,1-16/0-5(2-0-3)	8	-0.2
1962 KC-A	95	274	33	68	7	2	4	29	31	54	1	0	.248	.327	.332	.659	75	-9	31	3.78	-1	C-94/1-1	5	-0.5
1963 KC-A	40	113	9	24	6	1	0	8	15	15	0	0	.212	.305	.283	.588	63	-5	9	2.56	1	C-37	2	-0.2
Total 7	312	851	94	192	30	5	13	87	109	140	2	0	.226	.314	.318	.633	70	-34	89	3.44	2	C-274/1-17,0-5	17	-2.0

• SULLIVAN, Jackie Carl Mancel Sullivan b: 2/22/1918, Princeton, TX d: 10/15/1992, Dallas, TX BR/TR, 5'11", 172 lbs. Deb: 7/6/1944

YEAR TM-L	G	AB	R	H	2B	3B	HR	RBI	BB	SO	SB	CS	AVG	OBP	SLG	OPS	OPS+	BR/A	RC	RC/G	FR	G/POS	WS	TPW
1944 Det-A	1	1	0	0	0	0	0	0	0	0	0	0	.000	.000	.000	.000	-95	-0	0	.00	0	/2-1	0	-0.1

• SULLIVAN, Joe Joseph Daniel Sullivan b: 1/6/1870, Charlestown, MA d: 11/2/1897, Charlestown, MA, 5'10", 178 lbs. Deb: 4/27/1893 Career OF: 56-39-2

YEAR TM-L	G	AB	R	H	2B	3B	HR	RBI	BB	SO	SB	CS	AVG	OBP	SLG	OPS	OPS+	BR/A	RC	RC/G	FR	G/POS	WS	TPW
1893 Was-N	128	508	72	134	16	13	2	64	36	24	7	....	.264	.322	.358	.681	83	-14	62	4.43	-40	*S-128	7	-3.9
1894 Was-N	17	60	7	15	3	0	0	5	6	2	3	....	.250	.357	.300	.657	62	-3	8	4.44	-2	/2-8,S-6,3-1,0-1	1	-0.4
Phi-N	77	312	65	110	10	8	3	63	24	10	12	....	.353	.408	.465	.872	113	7	66	8.44	-10	S-75	9	0.0
Yr.	94	372	72	125	13	8	3	68	30	12	15	....	.336	.399	.438	.837	104	4	73	7.71	-13	S-81/2-8,3-1,0-1	10	-0.3
1895 Phi-N	94	373	75	126	7	3	2	50	24	20	15	....	.338	.395	.389	.783	102	2	66	6.94	-19	*S-89/0-6(3-2-1)	10	-1.0
1896 Phi-N	48	191	45	48	5	3	2	24	18	12	9	....	.251	.347	.340	.687	82	-4	26	4.87	-3	0-45(8-37-0)/3-2,S-2	4	-0.9
StL-N	51	212	25	62	4	2	2	21	9	12	5	....	.292	.351	.358	.709	91	-2	30	5.08	-3	0-45(45-0-0)/2-7	4	-0.8
Yr.	99	403	70	110	9	5	4	45	27	24	14	....	.273	.349	.350	.699	87	-7	56	4.98	-7	*0-90(53-37-0)/2-7,3-2,S-2	8	-1.7
Total 4	415	1656	289	495	45	29	11	227	117	80	51	....	.299	.362	.381	.743	93	-14	258	5.81	-79	S-300/0-97,2-15,3-3	35	-6.9

• SULLIVAN, John John Peter Sullivan b: 1/3/1941, Somerville, NJ BL/TR, 6', 195 lbs. Deb: 9/20/1963 C

YEAR TM-L	G	AB	R	H	2B	3B	HR	RBI	BB	SO	SB	CS	AVG	OBP	SLG	OPS	OPS+	BR/A	RC	RC/G	FR	G/POS	WS	TPW
1963 Det-A	3	5	0	0	0	0	0	0	2	1	0	0	.000	.286	.000	.286	-11	-1	0	.33	0	/C-2	0	-0.1
1964 Det-A	2	3	0	0	0	0	0	0	0	1	0	0	.000	.000	.000	.000	-99	-1	0	.00	0	/C-2	0	-0.1
1965 Det-A	34	86	5	23	0	0	2	11	9	13	0	0	.267	.344	.337	.681	93	-0	11	4.40	1	C-29	4	0.2
1967 NY-N	65	147	4	32	5	0	0	6	6	26	0	2	.218	.248	.252	.500	44	-12	9	1.90	0	C-57	1	-1.1
1968 Phi-N	12	18	0	4	0	0	0	1	2	4	0	0	.222	.300	.222	.522	59	-1	1	1.53	0	/C-8	0	-0.1
Total 5	116	259	9	59	5	0	2	18	19	45	0	2	.228	.283	.270	.553	59	-14	20	2.57	1	/C-98	5	-1.1

• SULLIVAN, John John Paul Sullivan b: 11/2/1920, Chicago, IL BR/TR, 5'10", 170 lbs. Deb: 6/7/1942

YEAR TM-L	G	AB	R	H	2B	3B	HR	RBI	BB	SO	SB	CS	AVG	OBP	SLG	OPS	OPS+	BR/A	RC	RC/G	FR	G/POS	WS	TPW
1942 Was-A	94	357	38	84	16	1	0	42	25	30	2	0	.235	.285	.286	.571	61	-18	31	2.93	-11	S-92	5	-2.3
1943 Was-A	134	456	49	95	12	2	1	55	57	59	6	2	.208	.298	.250	.548	63	-19	39	2.74	16	*S-133	10	0.9
1944 Was-A	138	471	49	118	12	1	0	30	52	43	3	3	.251	.325	.280	.605	77	-13	46	3.26	-10	*S-138	10	-1.2
1947 Was-A	49	133	13	34	0	1	0	5	22	14	0	2	.256	.361	.271	.632	79	-3	15	3.83	1	S-40/2-1	4	0.0
1948 Was-A	85	173	25	36	4	1	0	12	22	25	2	2	.208	.297	.243	.540	46	-13	14	2.69	-6	S-57/2-4	1	-1.5
1949 StL-A	105	243	29	55	8	3	0	18	38	35	5	2	.226	.331	.284	.615	61	-13	25	3.37	-8	S-71,3-23/2-6	4	-1.7
Total 6	605	1833	203	422	52	9	1	162	216	206	18	11	.230	.312	.270	.582	66	-78	169	3.06	-20	S-531/3-23,2-11	34	-5.8

• SULLIVAN, John John Lawrence Sullivan b: 3/21/1890, Williamsport, PA d: 4/1/1966, Milton, PA BR/TR, 5'11", 180 lbs. Deb: 4/18/1920 Career OF: 79-6-46

YEAR TM-L	G	AB	R	H	2B	3B	HR	RBI	BB	SO	SB	CS	AVG	OBP	SLG	OPS	OPS+	BR/A	RC	RC/G	FR	G/POS	WS	TPW
1920 Bos-N	81	250	36	74	14	4	1	28	29	29	3	2	.296	.374	.396	.770	126	10	39	5.47	0	0-66(16-5-45)/1-6	10	0.8
1921 Bos-N	5	5	0	0	0	0	0	0	0	0	0	0	.000	.000	.000	.000	-106	-1	0	.00	0	....	0	-0.1
Chi-N	76	240	28	79	14	4	4	41	19	26	3	5	.329	.381	.471	.852	124	8	42	6.32	-5	0-66(63-1-1)	8	-0.2
Yr.	81	245	28	79	14	4	4	41	19	26	3	5	.322	.374	.461	.835	120	6	42	6.14	-5	0-66(63-1-1)	8	-0.3
Total 2	162	495	64	153	28	8	5	69	48	55	6	7	.309	.374	.428	.802	123	17	80	5.80	-5	0-132/1-6	18	0.5

• SULLIVAN, John John Eugene Sullivan b: 2/16/1873, Chicago, IL d: 6/5/1924, St. Paul, MN BR/TR, 5'10", 170 lbs. Deb: 4/19/1905

YEAR TM-L	G	AB	R	H	2B	3B	HR	RBI	BB	SO	SB	CS	AVG	OBP	SLG	OPS	OPS+	BR/A	RC	RC/G	FR	G/POS	WS	TPW
1905 Det-A	13	32	4	5	0	0	0	4	4	....	0	....	.156	.250	.156	.406	30	-2	2	1.66	2	C-12	1	0.1
1908 Pit-N	1	1	0	0	0	0	0	0	0	....	0	....	.000	.000	.000	.000	-100	-0	0	.00	1	/C-1	0	0.0
Total 2	14	33	4	5	0	0	0	4	4	....	0	....	.152	.243	.152	.395	26	-3	2	1.61	3	/C-13	1	0.1

• SULLIVAN, Marc Marc Cooper Sullivan b: 7/25/1958, Quincy, MA BR/TR, 6'4", 205 lbs. Deb: 10/1/1982

YEAR TM-L	G	AB	R	H	2B	3B	HR	RBI	BB	SO	SB	CS	AVG	OBP	SLG	OPS	OPS+	BR/A	RC	RC/G	FR	G/POS	WS	TPW
1982 Bos-A	2	6	0	2	0	0	0	0	0	2	0	0	.333	.333	.333	.667	79	-0	1	4.50	0	/C-2	0	0.0
1984 Bos-A	2	6	1	3	0	0	0	1	1	0	0	0	.500	.571	.500	1.071	191	1	2	16.77	1	/C-2	1	0.2
1985 Bos-A	32	69	10	12	2	0	2	3	6	15	0	0	.174	.240	.290	.530	43	-6	5	2.42	0	C-32	1	-0.5
1986 Bos-A	41	119	15	23	4	0	1	14	7	32	0	0	.193	.262	.252	.514	40	-10	9	2.30	-1	C-41	2	-0.9

YEAR TM-L	G	AB	R	H	2B	3B	HR	RBI	BB	SO	SB	CS	AVG	OBP	SLG	OPS	OPS+	BR/A	RC	RC/G	FR	G/POS	WS	TPW
1987 Bos-A	60	160	11	27	5	0	2	10	4	43	0	0	.169	.199	.238	.436	15	-20	7	1.30	2	C-60	2	-1.5
Total 5	137	360	37	67	11	0	5	28	18	92	0	0	.186	.237	.258	.495	33	-35	23	2.03	2	C-137	6	-2.6

• SULLIVAN, Marty Martin C. Sullivan b: 10/20/1862, Lowell, MA d: 1/6/1894, Lowell, MA BR/TR Deb: 4/30/1887 U Career OF: 322-67-3

YEAR TM-L	G	AB	R	H	2B	3B	HR	RBI	BB	SO	SB	CS	AVG	OBP	SLG	OPS	OPS+	BR/A	RC	RC/G	FR	G/POS	WS	TPW
1887 Chi-N	115	508	98	170	13	16	7	77	36	53	35	....	.335	.340	.424	.764	98	-4	82	6.42	-4	*O-115(111-3-1)/P-1	12	-1.0
1888 Chi-N	75	314	40	74	12	6	7	39	15	32	9	....	.236	.273	.379	.652	99	-2	36	4.03	4	O-75(74-1-0)	7	-0.1
1889 Ind-N	69	256	45	73	11	3	4	35	50	31	15	....	.285	.404	.398	.802	122	10	48	7.01	-8	O-64(0-63-1)/1-5	9	0.0
1890 Bos-N	121	505	82	144	19	7	6	61	56	48	33	....	.285	.357	.386	.743	108	4	83	6.12	2	*O-120(120-0-0)/3-1	16	0.1
1891 Bos-N	17	67	15	15	1	0	2	7	5	3	7	....	.224	.288	.328	.616	71	-3	9	4.44	-1	O-17(17-0-0)	2	-0.4
Cle-N	1	4	0	1	0	0	0	1	0	1	0	....	.250	.250	.250	.500	44	-0	0	2.31	0	/O-1	0	0.0
Yr.	18	71	15	16	1	0	2	8	5	4	7	....	.225	.286	.324	.610	69	-3	9	4.32	-1	O-18(17-0-1)	2	-0.4
Total 5	398	1654	280	477	56	32	26	220	162	168	99	....	.288	.341	.395	.736	104	5	258	5.83	-7	O-392/1-5,3-1,P-1	46	-1.4

• SULLIVAN, Mike Michael Joseph Sullivan b: 6/10/1860, Webster, MA d: 6/16/1929, Webster, MA BR/TR, 5'8.5", 165 lbs. Deb: 4/26/1888

YEAR TM-L	G	AB	R	H	2B	3B	HR	RBI	BB	SO	SB	CS	AVG	OBP	SLG	OPS	OPS+	BR/A	RC	RC/G	FR	G/POS	WS	TPW
1888 Phi-a	28	112	20	31	5	6	1	19	3	....	10	....	.277	.296	.455	.751	140	4	18	6.16	-5	O-18(16-0-2),3-10	4	-0.1

• SULLIVAN, Pat Patrick J. Sullivan b: 12/22/1862, Milwaukee, WI TR, 5'11", 165 lbs. Deb: 8/30/1884

YEAR TM-L	G	AB	R	H	2B	3B	HR	RBI	BB	SO	SB	CS	AVG	OBP	SLG	OPS	OPS+	BR/A	RC	RC/G	FR	G/POS	WS	TPW
1884 KC-U	31	114	15	22	3	1	0	....	4	....	....	....	.193	.220	.237	.457	63	-3	6	1.86	-0	3-21/O-9(1-8-0),C-1,P-1	1	-0.8

• SULLIVAN, Russ Russell Guy Sullivan b: 2/19/1923, Fredericksburg, VA BL/TR, 6', 196 lbs. Deb: 9/8/1951 Career OF: 32-0-10

YEAR TM-L	G	AB	R	H	2B	3B	HR	RBI	BB	SO	SB	CS	AVG	OBP	SLG	OPS	OPS+	BR/A	RC	RC/G	FR	G/POS	WS	TPW
1951 Det-A	7	26	2	5	1	0	1	1	2	1	0	0	.192	.250	.346	.596	60	-2	2	3.13	0	/O-7(6-0-1)	0	-0.2
1952 Det-A	15	52	7	17	2	1	3	5	3	5	1	0	.327	.375	.577	.952	161	4	12	9.35	-1	O-14(6-0-9)	2	0.3
1953 Det-A	23	72	7	18	5	1	1	6	13	5	0	0	.250	.379	.389	.768	109	2	11	4.99	2	O-20(20-0-0)	2	0.2
Total 3	45	150	16	40	8	2	5	12	18	11	1	0	.267	.357	.447	.803	118	4	25	5.98	1	/O-41	4	0.3

• SULLIVAN, Sleeper Thomas Jefferson "Old Iron Hands" Sullivan b: 1859, Ireland d: 10/13/1909, St. Louis, MO BR/TR, 175 lbs. Deb: 5/3/1881 U Career OF: 0-3-6

YEAR TM-L	G	AB	R	H	2B	3B	HR	RBI	BB	SO	SB	CS	AVG	OBP	SLG	OPS	OPS+	BR/A	RC	RC/G	FR	G/POS	WS	TPW
1881 Buf-N	35	121	13	23	4	0	0	15	1	21	....	....	.190	.197	.223	.420	32	-9	5	1.50	-11	C-31/O-5(0-2-4)	0	-1.8
1882 StL-a	51	188	24	34	3	3	0	....	3	....	....	....	.181	.194	.229	.422	40	-12	9	1.55	-18	C-51	1	-2.4
1883 StL-a	8	27	2	6	0	1	0	0	0	....	....	....	.222	.222	.296	.519	62	-1	2	2.43	2	/C-6,O-2(0-1-1)	1	0.2
Lou-a	1	2	0	0	0	0	0	0	0	....	....	....	.000	.000	.000	.000	-108	-0	0	.00	0	/C-1	0	0.0
Yr.	9	29	2	6	0	1	0	0	0	....	....	....	.207	.207	.276	.483	50	-2	2	2.22	3	/C-7,O-2(0-1-1)	1	0.1
1884 StL-U	2	9	0	1	0	0	0	....	0	....	....	....	.111	.111	.111	.222	-24	-1	0	.40	0	/C-1,O-1,P-1	0	-0.2
Total 4	97	347	39	64	7	4	0	15	4	21	....	....	.184	.194	.228	.421	37	-24	16	1.56	-27	/C-90,O-8,P-1	2	-4.3

• SULLIVAN, Suter Suter G. Sullivan b: 10/14/1872, Baltimore, MD d: 4/19/1925, Baltimore, MD, 6', 170 lbs. Deb: 7/24/1898 Career OF: 1-0-30 ♦

YEAR TM-L	G	AB	R	H	2B	3B	HR	RBI	BB	SO	SB	CS	AVG	OBP	SLG	OPS	OPS+	BR/A	RC	RC/G	FR	G/POS	WS	TPW
1898 StL-N	42	144	10	32	3	0	0	12	13	....	1	....	.222	.300	.243	.543	55	-8	11	2.63	-12	S-23,O-10(0-0-10)/2-6,1-1,P	1	-1.5
1899 Cle-N	127	473	37	116	16	3	0	55	25	....	16	....	.245	.297	.292	.589	67	-21	48	3.48	-2	*3-101,O-20(1-0-20)/1-3,S,2	4	-2.1
Total 2	169	617	47	148	19	3	0	67	38	....	17	....	.240	.298	.280	.578	64	-29	59	3.28	-14	3-101/O-30,S-26,2-8,1-4,P-1	5	-3.6

• SULLIVAN, Ted Timothy Paul Sullivan b: 1851, County Clare, Ireland d: 7/5/1929, Washington, DC Deb: 7/16/1884 M

YEAR TM-L	G	AB	R	H	2B	3B	HR	RBI	BB	SO	SB	CS	AVG	OBP	SLG	OPS	OPS+	BR/A	RC	RC/G	FR	G/POS	WS	TPW
1884 KC-U	3	9	0	3	0	0	0	....	1	....	....	....	.333	.400	.333	.733	173	1	1	5.74	-1	/O-2(0-0-2),S-1	1	0.0

• SULLIVAN, Tom Thomas Brandon Sullivan b: 12/19/1906, Nome, AK d: 8/16/1944, Seattle, WA BR/TR, 6', 190 lbs. Deb: 6/14/1925

YEAR TM-L	G	AB	R	H	2B	3B	HR	RBI	BB	SO	SB	CS	AVG	OBP	SLG	OPS	OPS+	BR/A	RC	RC/G	FR	G/POS	WS	TPW
1925 Cin-N	1	1	0	0	0	0	0	0	0	0	0	0	.000	.000	.000	.000	-102	-0	0	.00	0	/C-1	0	0.0

• SUMMA, Homer Homer Wayne Summa b: 11/3/1898, Gentry, MO d: 1/29/1966, Los Angeles, CA BL/TR, 5'10.5", 170 lbs. Deb: 9/13/1920 Career OF: 40-13-730

YEAR TM-L	G	AB	R	H	2B	3B	HR	RBI	BB	SO	SB	CS	AVG	OBP	SLG	OPS	OPS+	BR/A	RC	RC/G	FR	G/POS	WS	TPW
1920 Pit-N	10	22	1	7	1	1	0	1	3	1	1	0	.318	.400	.455	.855	141	2	4	6.15	0	/O-6(1-5-0)	1	0.2
1922 Cle-A	12	46	9	16	3	3	1	6	1	1	1	2	.348	.400	.609	1.009	159	3	10	8.46	1	O-12(0-0-12)	2	0.4
1923 Cle-A	137	525	92	172	27	6	3	69	33	20	9	13	.328	.374	.419	.793	109	3	80	5.41	-11	*O-136(0-3-133)	14	-1.7
1924 Cle-A	111	390	55	113	21	6	2	38	11	16	4	2	.290	.311	.390	.701	79	-14	46	4.30	-4	O-95(0-3-92)	5	-2.3
1925 Cle-A	75	224	28	74	10	1	0	25	13	6	3	2	.330	.375	.384	.759	92	-2	33	5.46	-3	O-54(18-1-35)/3-2	5	-0.7
1926 Cle-A	154	581	74	179	31	6	4	76	47	9	15	8	.308	.368	.403	.771	100	1	88	5.47	7	*O-154(0-0-154)	20	-0.4
1927 Cle-A	145	574	72	164	41	7	4	74	32	18	6	5	.286	.331	.402	.734	89	-11	77	4.59	-9	*O-145(0-1-144)	12	-3.0
1928 Cle-A	134	504	60	143	26	3	3	57	20	15	4	2	.284	.319	.365	.684	78	-16	59	4.07	-2	*O-132(0-0-132)	7	-2.8
1929*Phi-A	37	81	12	22	4	0	0	10	2	1	1	1	.272	.298	.321	.619	57	-5	8	3.18	-2	O-24(18-0-16)	1	-0.9
1930 Phi-A	25	54	10	15	2	1	1	5	4	1	0	0	.278	.339	.407	.746	85	-1	8	4.85	0	O-15(3-0-12)	1	-0.3
Total 10	840	3001	413	905	166	34	18	361	166	88	44	35	.302	.346	.398	.743	92	-41	413	4.87	-22	O-773/3-2	68	-11.6

• SUMMERS, Champ John Junior Summers b: 6/15/1946, Bremerton, WA BL/TR, 6'2", 205 lbs. Deb: 5/4/1974 C Career OF: 103-0-160

YEAR TM-L	G	AB	R	H	2B	3B	HR	RBI	BB	SO	SB	CS	AVG	OBP	SLG	OPS	OPS+	BR/A	RC	RC/G	FR	G/POS	WS	TPW
1974 Oak-A	20	24	2	3	1	0	0	3	1	5	0	0	.125	.160	.167	.327	-6	-3	1	.88	-1	O-12(8-0-4)/D-2	0	-0.4
1975 Chi-N	76	91	14	21	5	1	1	16	10	13	0	0	.231	.314	.341	.654	78	-3	10	3.53	-1	O-18(15-0-3)	1	-0.4
1976 Chi-N	83	126	11	26	2	0	3	13	13	31	1	0	.206	.286	.294	.579	59	-6	11	2.81	-1	O-26(19-0-7),1-10/C-1	1	-0.9
1977 Cin-N	59	76	11	13	4	0	3	6	6	16	0	0	.171	.241	.342	.583	53	-5	6	2.29	0	O-16(3-0-13)/3-1	0	-0.6
1978 Cin-N	13	35	4	9	2	0	1	3	7	4	2	1	.257	.381	.400	.781	118	1	5	4.78	-1	O-12(0-0-12)	1	0.0
1979 Cin-N	27	60	10	12	2	1	1	11	13	15	0	1	.200	.351	.317	.668	83	-1	7	3.97	0	O-13(4-0-9)/1-6	1	-0.1
Det-A	90	246	47	77	12	1	20	51	40	33	7	6	.313	.415	.614	1.029	168	23	63	9.41	-4	O-69(2-0-67),D-10/1-4	15	1.7
1980 Det-A	120	347	61	103	19	1	17	60	52	52	4	3	.297	.396	.504	.900	142	21	69	7.17	-3	D-64,O-47(21-0-26)/1-1	15	1.5
1981 Det-A	64	165	16	42	8	0	3	21	19	35	1	1	.255	.342	.358	.700	98	0	22	4.68	0	D-37,O-18(0-0-18)	5	-0.2
1982 SF-N	70	125	15	31	5	0	4	19	16	17	0	1	.248	.347	.384	.731	104	1	17	4.42	-2	O-31(30-0-1)/1-3	4	-0.2
1983 SF-N	29	22	3	3	0	0	0	3	7	8	0	0	.136	.345	.136	.481	39	-1	1	1.46	-0	/O-1	0	-0.1
1984*SD-N	47	54	5	10	3	0	1	12	4	15	0	0	.185	.254	.296	.551	54	-3	4	2.20	-1	/1-8	0	-0.5
Total 11	698	1371	199	350	63	4	54	218	188	244	15	13	.255	.353	.425	.778	111	23	215	5.36	-12	O-263,D-113/1-32,3-1,C-1	43	-0.4

• SUMMERS, Kid William Summers b: Toronto, Canada d: 10/16/1895, Toronto, Canada TR, 5'10" Deb: 8/5/1893

YEAR TM-L	G	AB	R	H	2B	3B	HR	RBI	BB	SO	SB	CS	AVG	OBP	SLG	OPS	OPS+	BR/A	RC	RC/G	FR	G/POS	WS	TPW
1893 StL-N	2	1	1	0	0	0	0	0	0	0	0	....	.000	.500	.000	.500	37	0	0	.00	0	/C-1,O-1	0	0.0

• SUMNER, Carl Carl Ringdahl "Lefty" Sumner b: 9/28/1908, Cambridge, MA d: 2/8/1999, Chatham, MA BL/TL, 5'8", 170 lbs. Deb: 7/28/1928

YEAR TM-L	G	AB	R	H	2B	3B	HR	RBI	BB	SO	SB	CS	AVG	OBP	SLG	OPS	OPS+	BR/A	RC	RC/G	FR	G/POS	WS	TPW
1928 Bos-A	16	29	6	8	1	1	0	3	5	6	0	0	.276	.382	.379	.762	103	0	5	5.70	-1	O-10(5-4-1)	1	-0.1

• SUNDAY, Art Arthur Sunday b: 1/21/1862, Springfield, IL d: 10/2/1926, Reno, NV BL/TL, 5'9", 193 lbs. Deb: 5/5/1890

YEAR TM-L	G	AB	R	H	2B	3B	HR	RBI	BB	SO	SB	CS	AVG	OBP	SLG	OPS	OPS+	BR/A	RC	RC/G	FR	G/POS	WS	TPW
1890 Bro-P	24	83	26	22	5	1	0	13	15	9	0	....	.265	.419	.349	.768	100	1	12	5.51	-2	O-24(0-5-20)	3	-0.1

• SUNDAY, Billy William Ashley "Parson,The Evangelist" Sunday
b: 11/9/1862, Ames, IA d: 11/6/1935, Chicago, IL BL/TR, 5'10", 160 lbs. Deb: 5/22/1883 Career OF: 7-235-260

YEAR TM-L	G	AB	R	H	2B	3B	HR	RBI	BB	SO	SB	CS	AVG	OBP	SLG	OPS	OPS+	BR/A	RC	RC/G	FR	G/POS	WS	TPW
1883 Chi-N	14	54	6	13	4	0	0	5	1	18	....	....	.241	.255	.315	.569	66	-2	4	2.98	-2	O-14(1-0-13)	0	-0.4
1884 Chi-N	43	176	25	39	4	1	4	28	4	36	....	....	.222	.239	.324	.563	69	-7	14	2.80	-6	O-43(0-9-34)	1	-1.2
1885*Chi-N	46	172	36	44	3	3	2	20	12	33	....	....	.256	.304	.343	.647	95	-2	18	3.88	-3	O-46(1-4-43)	5	-0.5
1886 Chi-N	28	103	16	25	2	2	0	6	7	26	10	....	.243	.291	.301	.592	69	-4	12	4.23	1	O-28(1-0-27)	3	-0.3
1887 Chi-N	50	220	41	79	6	6	3	32	21	20	34	....	.359	.362	.427	.789	105	1	44	8.30	-7	O-50(2-23-25)	6	-0.6
1888 Pit-N	120	505	69	119	14	3	0	15	12	36	71	....	.236	.256	.275	.532	75	-14	55	3.86	11	*O-120(1-117-3)	13	-0.7
1889 Pit-N	81	321	62	77	10	6	2	25	27	33	47	....	.240	.307	.321	.628	85	-5	48	5.19	8	O-81(1-80)	8	0.2
1890 Pit-N	86	358	58	92	9	2	1	33	32	20	56	....	.257	.327	.302	.628	94	-0	55	5.47	5	O-86(0-51-35)/P-1	7	0.2
Phi-N	31	119	26	31	3	1	0	6	18	7	28	....	.261	.367	.303	.669	93	-0	24	7.25	2	O-31(0-31-0)	5	0.0
Yr.	117	477	84	123	12	3	1	39	50	27	84	....	.258	.337	.302	.639	94	-0	79	5.91	7	*O-117(0-82-35)/P-1	12	0.3
Total 8	499	2028	339	519	55	24	12	170	134	229	246	....	.256	.300	.317	.617	85	-34	275	4.87	10	O-499/P-1	48	-3.3

• SUNDBERG, Jim James Howard Sundberg b: 5/18/1951, Galesburg, IL BR/TR, 6', 195 lbs. Deb: 4/4/1974 Career OF: 3-0-0

YEAR TM-L	G	AB	R	H	2B	3B	HR	RBI	BB	SO	SB	CS	AVG	OBP	SLG	OPS	OPS+	BR/A	RC	RC/G	FR	G/POS	WS	TPW
1974 Tex-A★	132	368	45	91	13	3	3	36	62	61	2	4	.247	.356	.323	.679	99	1	43	3.70	5	*C-132	15	1.3
1975 Tex-A	155	472	45	94	9	0	6	36	51	77	3	1	.199	.283	.256	.539	54	-27	35	2.32	5	*C-155	7	-1.5
1976 Tex-A	140	448	33	102	24	2	3	34	37	61	0	0	.228	.287	.310	.597	73	-15	39	2.80	12	*C-140	12	0.4
1977 Tex-A	149	453	61	132	20	3	6	65	53	77	2	3	.291	.368	.389	.757	105	5	67	5.10	11	*C-149	22	2.3
1978 Tex-A★	149	518	54	144	23	6	6	58	64	70	2	5	.278	.361	.380	.741	108	6	69	4.62	8	*C-148/D-1	23	2.3

YEAR TM-L	G	AB	R	H	2B	3B	HR	RBI	BB	SO	SB	CS	AVG	OBP	SLG	OPS	OPS+	BR/A	RC	RC/G	FR	G/POS	WS	TPW
1979 Tex-A	150	495	50	136	23	4	5	64	51	51	3	3	.275	.348	.368	.716	95	-3	62	4.30	3	*C-150	18	0.7
1980 Tex-A	151	505	59	138	24	1	10	63	64	67	2	2	.273	.356	.384	.740	106	6	69	4.75	3	*C-151	18	1.6
1981 Tex-A	102	339	42	94	17	2	3	28	50	48	2	5	.277	.372	.366	.738	120	9	48	4.93	-1	C-98/O-2(2-0-0)	17	1.3
1982 Tex-A	139	470	37	118	22	5	10	47	49	57	2	6	.251	.323	.383	.706	98	-3	57	4.03	7	*C-132/O-1	15	1.0
1983 Tex-A	131	378	30	76	14	0	2	28	35	64	0	4	.201	.272	.254	.526	47	-29	26	2.20	-1	*C-131	7	-2.4
1984 Mil-A★	110	348	43	91	19	4	7	43	38	63	1	1	.261	.334	.399	.734	106	3	48	4.75	5	*C-109	15	1.4
1985*KC-A	115	367	38	90	12	4	10	35	33	67	0	2	.245	.309	.381	.691	88	-7	42	3.85	-2	*C-112	11	-0.4
1986 KC-A	140	429	41	91	9	1	12	42	57	91	1	1	.212	.305	.322	.626	69	-18	44	3.41	-2	*C-134	10	-1.4
1987 Chi-N	61	139	9	28	2	0	4	15	19	40	0	0	.201	.306	.302	.608	60	-8	13	3.17	3	C-57	3	-0.3
1988 Chi-N	24	54	8	13	1	0	2	9	8	15	0	0	.241	.339	.370	.709	99	0	7	4.30	0	C-20	2	0.1
Tex-A	38	91	13	26	4	0	4	13	5	17	0	0	.286	.323	.462	.784	114	1	13	5.07	1	C-36	2	0.4
1989 Tex-A	76	147	13	29	7	1	2	8	23	37	0	0	.197	.306	.299	.605	70	-5	15	3.12	-1	C-73/D-1	3	-0.3
Total 16	1962	6021	621	1493	243	36	95	624	699	963	20	37	.248	.328	.348	.676	89	-85	698	3.86	56	*C-1927/O-3,D-2	200	6.5

• SURHOFF, B.J. William James Surhoff b: 8/4/1964, Bronx, NY BL/TR, 6'1", 200 lbs. Deb: 4/8/1987 Career OF: 824-5-40

YEAR TM-L	G	AB	R	H	2B	3B	HR	RBI	BB	SO	SB	CS	AVG	OBP	SLG	OPS	OPS+	BR/A	RC	RC/G	FR	G/POS	WS	TPW
1987 Mil-A	115	395	50	118	22	3	7	68	36	30	11	10	.299	.357	.423	.780	103	-0	56	4.79	0	C-98,3-10/D-7,1-1	15	0.4
1988 Mil-A	139	493	47	121	21	0	5	38	31	49	21	6	.245	.294	.318	.613	71	-18	46	3.08	-1	*C-106,3-31/1-2,O-1,S-1	11	-1.2
1989 Mil-A	126	436	42	108	17	4	5	55	25	29	14	12	.248	.293	.339	.633	78	-16	41	3.07	0	*C-106,D-12/3-6	8	-1.0
1990 Mil-A	135	474	55	131	21	4	6	59	41	37	18	7	.276	.335	.376	.711	99	0	61	4.42	2	*C-125,3-11	15	1.0
1991 Mil-A	143	505	57	146	19	4	5	68	26	33	5	8	.289	.324	.372	.696	94	-7	54	3.55	4	*C-127/D-6,3-5,O-2(0-1-1),2	13	0.4
1992 Mil-A	139	480	63	121	19	1	4	62	46	41	14	8	.252	.320	.321	.641	82	-12	50	3.47	4	*C-109,1-17/D-9,O-7(5-1-1),3	16	-0.2
1993 Mil-A	148	552	66	151	38	3	7	79	36	47	12	9	.274	.320	.391	.712	92	-9	67	4.24	3	*3-121,O-24(12-0-14)/1-8,C,D	16	-0.5
1994 Mil-A	40	134	20	35	11	2	5	22	16	14	0	1	.261	.340	.485	.825	105	0	21	5.16	0	3-18,C-12/1-8,O-3(0-0-3),D	4	-0.1
1995 Mil-A	117	415	72	133	26	3	13	73	37	43	7	3	.320	.382	.492	.873	118	11	78	7.09	2	O-60(54-3-9),1-55,C-18/D-3	16	0.8
1996*Bal-A	143	537	74	157	27	6	21	82	47	79	0	1	.292	.353	.482	.835	109	6	92	6.32	-9	*3-106,D-10/O-3(27-0-0),1	17	-0.3
1997*Bal-A	147	528	80	150	30	4	18	88	49	60	1	1	.284	.351	.458	.809	112	9	86	5.79	8	O-27(133-0-0)/D-9,1-3,3-3	19	0.9
1998 Bal-A	162	573	79	160	34	1	22	92	49	81	9	7	.279	.337	.457	.794	106	2	85	5.16	0	*O-133(157-0-0)/1-1	13	-0.4
1999 Bal-A★	162	673	104	207	38	1	28	107	43	78	5	1	.308	.351	.492	.843	116	15	114	6.24	13	*O-157(148-0-0),D-13/3-2	17	1.8
2000 Bal-A	103	411	56	120	27	0	13	57	29	46	7	2	.292	.342	.453	.794	104	2	64	5.78	2	*O-148(102-0-0)/D-1	11	-0.1
*Atl-N	44	128	13	37	9	2	1	11	12	12	3	0	.289	.355	.414	.769	93	-1	19	5.11	-1	*O-102(32-0-0)	3	-0.3
2001*Atl-N	141	484	68	131	33	1	10	58	38	48	9	3	.271	.325	.405	.730	85	-10	65	4.77	-3	O-32(129-0-0)/D-3	12	-1.8
2002 Atl-N	25	75	5	22	5	0	0	9	9	5	1	3	.293	.369	.360	.729	92	-2	10	4.49	3	*O-129(0-0-9),1-11	2	0.0
2003 Bal-A	93	319	32	94	20	0	5	41	29	29	2	2	.295	.355	.404	.760	104	1	47	5.33	-5	D-39,O-27(24-0-3),1-22	9	-0.8
Total 17	2122	7612	983	2142	417	39	175	1069	599	761	139	84	.281	.336	.415	.752	98	-28	1054	4.84	21	O-855,C-704,3-316,1-130,D/2,S	217	-1.3

• SUSCE, George George Cyril Methodius "Good Kid" Susce b: 8/13/1907, Pittsburgh, PA d: 2/25/1986, Sarasota, FL BR/TR, 5'11.5", 200 lbs. Deb: 4/23/1929

YEAR TM-L	G	AB	R	H	2B	3B	HR	RBI	BB	SO	SB	CS	AVG	OBP	SLG	OPS	OPS+	BR/A	RC	RC/G	FR	G/POS	WS	TPW
1929 Phi-N	17	17	5	5	3	0	1	1	1	2	0	....	.294	.368	.647	1.015	137	1	4	8.55	-2	C-11	1	-0.1
1932 Det-A	2	0	0	0	0	0	0	0	0	0	0	0	....	....	....	....	-96	0	0	....	-1	/C-2	0	0.0
1939 Pit-N	31	75	8	17	3	1	1	4	12	5	0	....	.227	.333	.333	.667	81	-2	8	3.08	0	C-31	2	0.0
1940 StL-A	61	113	6	24	4	0	0	13	9	9	1	0	.212	.282	.248	.530	38	-10	7	1.93	-2	C-61	2	-0.8
1941 Cle-A	1	0	0	0	0	0	0	0	0	0	0	0	....	....	....	....	-105	0	0	....	0	/C-1	0	0.0
1942 Cle-A	2	1	1	1	0	0	0	0	1	0	0	0	1.000	1.000	1.000	2.000	492	1	1	∞	0	/C-2	0	0.1
1943 Cle-A	3	1	0	0	0	0	0	0	0	0	0	0	.000	.000	.000	.000	-107	-0	0	.00	0	/C-3	0	-0.1
1944 Cle-A	29	61	3	14	1	0	0	4	2	5	0	0	.230	.254	.246	.500	45	-4	4	2.08	-1	C-29	1	-0.4
Total 8	146	268	23	61	11	1	2	22	25	21	1	0	.228	.301	.299	.599	61	-15	24	2.63	-6	C-140	6	-1.4

• SUSKO, Pete Peter Jonathan Susko b: 7/2/1904, Laura, OH d: 5/22/1978, Jacksonville, FL BL/TL, 5'11", 172 lbs. Deb: 8/1/1934

YEAR TM-L	G	AB	R	H	2B	3B	HR	RBI	BB	SO	SB	CS	AVG	OBP	SLG	OPS	OPS+	BR/A	RC	RC/G	FR	G/POS	WS	TPW
1934 Was-A	58	224	25	64	5	3	2	25	18	10	3	4	.286	.342	.362	.703	85	-6	28	4.30	2	1-58	4	-0.9

• SUTCLIFFE, Butch Charles Inigo Sutcliffe b: 7/22/1915, Fall River, MA d: 3/2/1994, Fall River, MA BR/TR, 5'8.5", 165 lbs. Deb: 8/28/1938

YEAR TM-L	G	AB	R	H	2B	3B	HR	RBI	BB	SO	SB	CS	AVG	OBP	SLG	OPS	OPS+	BR/A	RC	RC/G	FR	G/POS	WS	TPW
1938 Bos-N	4	4	1	1	0	0	0	2	2	1	0	....	.250	.500	.250	.750	124	0	1	3.48	-1	/C-3	0	0.0

• SUTCLIFFE, Sy Elmer Ellsworth Sutcliffe b: 4/15/1862, Wheaton, IL d: 2/13/1893, Wheaton, IL BL/TL, 6'2", 170 lbs. Deb: 10/2/1884 U Career OF: 10-5-43

YEAR TM-L	G	AB	R	H	2B	3B	HR	RBI	BB	SO	SB	CS	AVG	OBP	SLG	OPS	OPS+	BR/A	RC	RC/G	FR	G/POS	WS	TPW
1884 Chi-N	4	15	4	3	1	0	0	2	2	4	....	....	.200	.294	.267	.561	72	-0	1	2.76	0	/C-4	0	0.0
1885 Chi-N	11	43	5	8	1	1	0	4	2	5	....	....	.186	.222	.256	.478	47	-3	3	1.93	-3	C-11/O-1	1	-0.5
StL-N	16	49	2	6	1	0	0	4	5	10	....	....	.122	.204	.143	.347	15	-4	1	.92	-3	C-14/O-2(0-0-2)	0	-0.6
Yr.	27	92	7	14	2	1	0	8	7	15	....	....	.152	.212	.196	.408	29	-7	4	1.37	-6	C-25/O-3(0-0-3)	1	-1.0
1888 Det-N	49	191	17	49	5	3	0	23	5	14	6	....	.257	.276	.314	.590	88	-3	19	3.54	9	S-24,C-14/1-5,O-4(0-0-4),2	5	0.7
1889 Cle-N	46	161	17	40	3	2	1	21	14	6	5	....	.248	.309	.311	.619	75	-5	17	3.81	5	C-37/1-8,O-1	4	0.2
1890 Cle-P	99	386	62	127	14	8	2	60	33	16	10	....	.329	.382	.422	.804	125	14	68	7.06	4	C-84,O-15(1-0-14)/S-4,3-2	12	2.0
1891 Was-a	53	201	29	71	8	3	2	33	17	17	8	....	.353	.409	.453	.862	153	14	42	8.46	-1	O-35(9-5-21),C-22/S-3,3-1	9	1.2
1892 Bal-N	66	276	41	77	10	7	1	27	14	15	12	....	.279	.316	.377	.693	106	0	38	5.10	-7	1-66	6	-0.7
Total 7	344	1322	177	381	43	24	6	174	92	87	41	....	.288	.336	.371	.707	107	13	188	5.36	4	C-186/1-79,O-58,S-31,3-3,2	37	2.4

• SUTHERLAND, Gary Gary Lynn Sutherland b: 9/27/1944, Glendale, CA BR/TR, 6', 185 lbs. Deb: 9/17/1966 Career OF: 31-0-6

YEAR TM-L	G	AB	R	H	2B	3B	HR	RBI	BB	SO	SB	CS	AVG	OBP	SLG	OPS	OPS+	BR/A	RC	RC/G	FR	G/POS	WS	TPW
1966 Phi-N	3	3	0	0	0	0	0	0	0	0	0	0	.000	.000	.000	.000	-100	-1	0	.00	0	/S-1	0	-0.1
1967 Phi-N	103	231	23	57	12	1	1	19	17	22	0	3	.247	.298	.320	.619	76	-8	20	2.96	-2	S-66,O-25(25-0-0)	4	-0.9
1968 Phi-N	67	138	16	38	7	0	0	15	8	15	0	0	.275	.315	.326	.641	93	-1	15	3.94	0	2-17,3-10,S-10/O-7(2-0-5)	5	0.0
1969 Mon-N	141	544	63	130	26	1	3	35	37	31	5	7	.239	.290	.307	.597	67	-26	46	2.80	-3	*2-139,S-15/O-1	6	-2.1
1970 Mon-N	116	359	37	74	10	0	3	26	31	22	2	2	.206	.273	.259	.532	43	-29	26	2.30	-5	2-97,S-15/3-1	3	-2.8
1971 Mon-N	111	304	25	78	7	2	4	26	18	12	3	4	.257	.302	.332	.635	79	-10	28	3.02	-5	2-56,S-46/O-4(4-0-0),3-2	5	-0.8
1972 Hou-N	5	8	0	1	0	0	0	1	0	0	0	0	.125	.125	.125	.250	-29	-1	0	.48	-1	/2-1,3-1	0	-0.2
1973 Hou-N	16	54	8	14	5	0	0	3	3	5	0	0	.259	.298	.352	.650	80	-2	5	3.30	-2	2-14/S-1	1	-0.2
1974 Det-A	149	619	60	157	20	1	5	49	26	37	1	3	.254	.284	.313	.597	69	-26	51	2.83	-19	*2-147,S-10/3-4	8	-3.6
1975 Det-A	129	503	51	130	12	3	6	39	45	41	0	2	.258	.323	.330	.653	81	-12	53	3.62	-14	*2-128	10	-1.8
1976 Det-A	42	117	10	24	5	2	0	6	7	12	0	1	.205	.250	.282	.532	53	-8	7	1.91	2	2-42	1	-0.3
Mil-A	59	115	9	25	2	0	1	9	8	7	0	2	.217	.274	.261	.535	58	-7	7	1.73	-5	2-45/D-8,1-2	1	-1.1
Yr.	101	232	19	49	7	2	1	15	15	19	0	3	.211	.262	.272	.534	56	-14	14	1.82	-4	2-87/D-8,1-2	2	-1.4
1977 SD-N	80	103	5	25	3	0	1	11	7	15	0	0	.243	.291	.301	.592	66	-5	9	2.84	-5	2-30,3-21/1-4	1	-0.9
1978 StL-N	10	6	1	1	0	0	0	0	0	0	0	0	.167	.167	.167	.333	-7	-1	0	.98	0	/2-1	0	-0.1
Total 13	1031	3104	308	754	109	10	24	239	207	219	11	24	.243	.292	.308	.600	69	-137	268	2.87	-60	2-717,S-164/3-39,O-37,D-8,1	45	-15.0

• SUTHERLAND, Leo Leonardo (Cantin) Sutherland b: 4/6/1958, Santiago de Cuba, Cuba BL/TL, 5'10", 165 lbs. Deb: 8/11/1980 Career OF: 20-11-0

YEAR TM-L	G	AB	R	H	2B	3B	HR	RBI	BB	SO	SB	CS	AVG	OBP	SLG	OPS	OPS+	BR/A	RC	RC/G	FR	G/POS	WS	TPW
1980 Chi-A	34	89	9	23	3	0	0	5	1	11	4	1	.258	.267	.292	.559	53	-5	7	2.53	-2	O-23(16-7-0)	0	-0.8
1981 Chi-A	11	12	6	2	0	0	0	0	3	1	2	1	.167	.333	.167	.500	49	-1	1	2.44	0	/O-7(4-4-0)	0	-0.1
Total 2	45	101	15	25	3	0	0	5	4	12	6	2	.248	.276	.277	.553	53	-6	8	2.52	-2	/O-30	0	-0.9

• SUTKO, Glenn Glenn Edward Sutko b: 5/9/1968, Atlanta, GA BR/TR, 6'3", 225 lbs. Deb: 10/3/1990

YEAR TM-L	G	AB	R	H	2B	3B	HR	RBI	BB	SO	SB	CS	AVG	OBP	SLG	OPS	OPS+	BR/A	RC	RC/G	FR	G/POS	WS	TPW
1990 Cin-N	1	1	0	0	0	0	0	0	0	1	0	0	.000	.000	.000	.000	-96	-0	0	.00	-0	/C-1	0	0.0
1991 Cin-N	10	10	0	1	0	0	0	1	2	6	0	0	.100	.250	.100	.350	2	-1	0	1.14	-1	/C-9	0	-0.2
Total 2	11	11	0	1	0	0	0	1	2	7	0	0	.091	.231	.091	.322	-5	-2	0	1.03	-1	/C-10	0	-0.2

• SUTTON, Ezra Ezra Ballou Sutton
b: 9/17/1850, Palmyra, NY d: 6/20/1907, Braintree, MA BR/TR, 5'8.5", 153 lbs. Deb: 5/4/1871 U NA OF: 0-1-2 Career OF: 29-7-30

YEAR TM-L	G	AB	R	H	2B	3B	HR	RBI	BB	SO	SB	CS	AVG	OBP	SLG	OPS	OPS+	BR/A	RC	RC/G	FR	G/POS	WS	TPW
1871 Cle-n	29	128	35	45	3	7	3	23	1	0	3	1	.352	.357	.555	.911	166	11	27	10.14	2	*3-29/O-2(0-1-1),C-1	....	0.8
1872 Cle-n	22	107	30	30	6	1	0	10	1	1	1	0	.280	.287	.355	.642	102	1	11	4.62	-3	3-22	....	-0.2
1873 Ath-n	51	242	51	81	7	6	0	33	2	2	1	3	.335	.340	.413	.753	114	1	35	6.55	4	*3-43/S-8,2-2	....	0.3
1874 Ath-n	55	243	54	71	10	3	0	28	0	2	6	4	.292	.292	.358	.650	99	-3	28	4.75	4	3-36,S-20	....	0.1
1875 Ath-n	75	358	83	116	11	7	1	59	1	3	13	10	.324	.326	.402	.728	136	9	52	6.14	11	*3-73/1-2,P-2,O-1,S-1	....	1.4
1876 Phi-N	54	239	45	70	12	7	1	31	3	2	....	....	.293	.305	.419	.725	140	10	31	5.23	-10	1-29,2-15/3-8,O-4(0-0-4)	5	-0.1

YEAR TM-L	G	AB	R	H	2B	3B	HR	RBI	BB	SO	SB	CS	AVG	OBP	SLG	OPS	OPS+	BR/A	RC	RC/G	FR	G/POS	WS	TPW
1877 Bos-N	58	253	43	74	10	6	0	39	4	10	....	....	.292	.304	.379	.683	110	2	30	4.59	-2	S-36,3-22	9	0.2
1878 Bos-N	60	239	31	54	9	3	1	29	2	14	....	....	.226	.232	.301	.534	69	-9	17	2.55	-2	*3-59/S-1	7	-0.8
1879 Bos-N	84	339	54	84	13	4	0	34	2	18	....	....	.248	.252	.310	.562	82	-7	27	2.98	-10	S-51,3-33	8	-1.2
1880 Bos-N	76	288	41	72	9	2	0	25	7	7	....	....	.250	.268	.295	.563	93	-2	23	2.97	-7	S-39,3-37	8	-0.6
1881 Bos-N	83	333	43	97	12	4	0	31	13	9	....	....	.291	.318	.351	.669	115	6	38	4.36	-1	*3-81/S-2	12	0.7
1882 Bos-N	81	319	44	80	8	1	2	38	24	25	....	....	.251	.303	.301	.604	94	-1	30	3.43	-1	*3-77/S-4	9	-0.1
1883 Bos-N	94	414	101	134	28	15	3	73	17	12	....	....	.324	.350	.486	.836	147	22	72	7.09	0	*3-93/O-1,S-1	21	2.1
1884 Bos-N	110	468	102	**162**	28	7	3	61	29	22	....	....	.346	.384	.455	.839	164	34	84	7.54	-3	*3-110	28	3.0
1885 Bos-N	110	457	78	143	23	8	4	47	17	25	....	....	.313	.338	.425	.762	151	24	67	5.77	-7	*3-91,S-16/2-2,1-1	22	1.9
1886 Bos-N	116	499	83	138	21	6	3	48	26	21	18	....	.277	.312	.361	.673	108	5	63	4.74	1	O-43(20-7-16),3-28,S-28,2-18	16	0.6
1887 Bos-N	77	339	58	112	14	9	3	46	13	6	17	....	.330	.342	.429	.771	116	7	55	6.43	17	S-37,O-18(9-0-9),2-13,3-11	11	2.1
1888 Bos-N	28	110	16	24	3	1	1	16	7	3	10	....	.218	.277	.291	.568	78	-3	12	3.75	-4	3-27/S-1	2	-0.6
Total 5 n	232	1078	253	343	37	24	4	153	5	8	24	18	.318	.321	.408	.729	123	19	154	6.19	18	3-203/S-29,O-3,1-2,2-P-2,C	....	2.4
Total 13	1031	4297	739	1244	190	73	21	518	164	174	45	....	.290	.315	.381	.696	119	88	550	4.92	-30	3-677,S-216/O-66,2-48,1-30	158	7.2
• SUTTON, Larry	Larry James Sutton b: 5/14/1970, West Covina, CA BL/TL, 5'11", 175 lbs. Deb: 8/17/1997 Career OF: 45-0-53																							
1997 KC-A	27	69	9	20	2	0	2	8	5	12	0	0	.290	.338	.406	.744	91	-1	10	5.37	-0	1-12/O-9(1-0-0),D-3	2	-0.2
1998 KC-A	111	310	29	76	14	2	5	42	29	46	3	3	.245	.316	.352	.667	71	-14	35	3.76	-1	/1-6,D-3,O-1	6	-1.8
1999 KC-A	43	102	14	23	6	0	2	15	13	17	1	0	.225	.313	.343	.656	66	-5	11	3.44	-3	O-79(0-0-1),1-30/D-5	1	-1.0
2000 StL-N	23	25	5	8	0	0	1	6	5	7	0	0	.320	.433	.440	.873	121	1	5	7.37	0	/1-6,O-1	1	0.1
2001 StL-N	33	42	3	5	1	0	1	3	1	10	0	0	.119	.140	.214	.354	-11	-7	1	.77	1	1-11/O-4(0-0-3)	0	-0.7
2002 Oak-A	7	19	3	2	0	0	1	3	1	8	0	0	.105	.150	.263	.413	7	-3	1	1.25	0	/1-6,O-3(2-0-1)	0	-0.3
Total 6	244	567	63	134	23	2	12	77	54	100	4	3	.236	.306	.347	.654	68	-28	63	3.69	-3	/O-97,1-71,D-11	10	-3.8
• SUZUKI, Ichiro	Ichiro Suzuki b: 10/22/1973, Kasugai, Japan BL/TR, 5'9", 160 lbs. Deb: 4/2/2001 Career OF: 0-3-461																							
2001*Sea-A★	157	692	127	**242**	34	8	8	69	30	53	**56**	14	**.350**	.384	.457	.840	128	32	127	7.22	4	/D-4,O-3(0-0-152)	36	2.7
2002 Sea-A★	157	647	111	208	27	8	8	51	68	62	31	15	.321	.390	.425	.815	121	22	109	6.26	4	*O-152(0-3-150)/D-4	25	1.6
2003 Sea-A★	159	679	111	212	29	8	13	62	36	69	34	8	.312	.352	.436	.788	110	13	109	6.10	4	*O-159(0-0-159)	23	0.8
Total 3	473	2018	349	662	90	24	29	182	134	184	121	37	.328	.375	.440	.815	120	67	345	6.52	13	O-314/D-8	84	5.2
• SVEUM, Dale	Dale Curtis Sveum b: 11/23/1963, Richmond, CA BB/TR, 6'2", 185 lbs. Deb: 5/12/1986 Career OF: 2-0-0																							
1986 Mil-A	91	317	35	78	13	2	7	35	32	63	4	3	.246	.317	.366	.683	83	-8	37	3.90	-5	3-65,2-13,S-13	7	-1.2
1987 Mil-A	153	535	86	135	27	3	25	95	40	133	2	6	.252	.306	.454	.760	95	-8	70	4.44	-9	*S-142,2-13	15	-0.1
1988 Mil-A	129	467	41	113	14	4	9	51	21	122	1	0	.242	.276	.347	.623	73	-18	45	3.29	-4	*S-127/2-1,D-1	10	-1.2
1990 Mil-A	48	117	15	23	7	0	1	12	12	30	0	1	.197	.282	.282	.564	59	-7	10	2.63	-3	3-22,2-16/1-5,S-5	2	-1.0
1991 Mil-A	90	266	33	64	19	1	4	43	32	78	2	4	.241	.324	.365	.689	93	-4	31	3.72	-8	S-51,3-38/D-3,2-2	7	-0.8
1992 Phi-N	54	135	13	24	4	0	2	16	16	39	0	0	.178	.265	.252	.517	47	-9	9	2.00	3	S-34/3-5,1-4	2	-0.4
Chi-A	40	114	15	25	9	0	2	12	12	29	1	1	.219	.294	.351	.645	81	-3	12	3.47	-2	S-37/1-2,3-2	2	-0.3
1993 Oak-A	30	79	12	14	2	1	2	6	16	21	0	0	.177	.316	.304	.620	72	-3	8	3.29	-3	1-14/3-7,2-4,D-2,O-1,S-1	1	-0.6
1994 Sea-A	10	27	3	5	0	0	1	2	2	10	0	0	.185	.241	.296	.538	37	-3	2	2.07	1	/D-4,3-3	0	-0.2
1996 Pit-N	12	34	9	12	5	0	1	5	6	6	0	0	.353	.450	.588	1.038	167	4	10	11.91	0	3-10	2	0.3
1997 Pit-N	126	306	30	80	20	1	12	47	27	81	0	3	.261	.321	.451	.772	98	-3	42	4.64	1	3-47,S-28,1-21/2-2	6	-0.1
1998 NY-A	30	58	6	9	0	0	0	3	4	16	0	0	.155	.210	.155	.365	-3	-9	2	.97	0	1-21/3-6,D-3	0	-1.0
1999 Pit-N	49	71	7	15	5	1	3	13	7	28	0	0	.211	.282	.437	.719	78	-3	9	4.30	0	*O-152(1-0-0),3-12/1-4,S-4,2	1	-0.2
Total 12	862	2526	305	597	125	13	69	340	227	656	10	18	.236	.301	.378	.679	82	-74	286	3.76	-30	S-442,3-217,O-153/1-71,2-53,D	55	-6.9
• SWACINA, Harry	Harry Joseph "Swats" Swacina b: 8/22/1881, St. Louis, MO d: 6/21/1944, Birmingham, AL BR/TR, 6'2", 190 lbs. Deb: 9/13/1907																							
1907 Pit-N	26	95	9	19	1	1	0	10	4	....	1	....	.200	.240	.232	.472	47	-6	6	1.97	-1	1-26	0	-0.8
1908 Pit-N	53	176	7	38	6	1	0	13	5	....	4	....	.216	.238	.261	.499	59	-9	12	2.12	-3	1-50	2	-1.5
1914 Bal-F	158	617	70	173	26	8	0	90	14	23	15	....	.280	.297	.348	.646	84	-16	66	3.63	10	*1-158	12	-0.9
1915 Bal-F	85	301	24	74	13	1	1	38	9	11	9	....	.246	.268	.306	.573	64	-15	26	2.85	4	1-75/2-1	2	-1.3
Total 4	322	1189	110	304	46	11	1	151	32	34	29	....	.256	.276	.315	.592	72	-45	109	3.05	10	1-309/2-1	16	-4.5
• SWAN, Andy	Andrew J. Swan b: 5/11/1845, Tewksbury, MA d: 8/27/1885, Lawrence, MA Deb: 7/23/1884																							
1884 Was-a	5	21	3	3	1	0	0	0	0	....	....	....	.143	.143	.190	.333	9	-2	1	.89	-2	/1-3,3-2	0	-0.4
Ric-a	3	10	2	5	0	0	0	0	0	....	....	....	.500	.500	.500	1.000	230	1	3	14.09	0	/1-3	1	0.1
Yr.	8	31	5	8	1	0	0	0	0	....	....	....	.258	.258	.290	.548	80	-1	3	3.76	-3	/1-6,3-2	1	-0.3
• SWANDELL, Marty	John Martin Swandell b: 7/1841, Baden, Germany d: 10/25/1906, Brooklyn, NY TL, 5'10.5", 146 lbs. Deb: 5/7/1872 U																							
1872 Eck-n	14	55	7	11	0	0	0	4	2	1	0	0	.200	.228	.200	.428	39	-2	3	1.81	-5	/3-8,O-4(0-4-0),1-1,2-1	....	-0.5
1873 Res-n	2	9	1	1	0	0	0	1	0	0	0	0	.111	.111	.111	.222	-37	-1	0	.43	0	/1-2	....	-0.1
Total 2 n	16	64	8	12	0	0	0	5	2	1	0	0	.188	.212	.188	.400	28	-4	3	1.60	-5	/3-8,O-4,1-3,2-1	....	-0.6
• SWANDER, Pinky	Edward O. Swander b: 7/4/1880, Portsmouth, OH d: 10/24/1944, Springfield, MA BL/TL, 5'9", 180 lbs. Deb: 9/18/1903																							
1903 StL-A	14	51	9	14	2	2	0	6	10	....	0	....	.275	.413	.392	.805	146	4	8	6.06	-1	O-14(0-0-14)	3	0.2
1904 StL-A	1	1	0	0	0	0	0	0	0	....	0	....	.000	.000	.000	.000	-107	-0	0	.00	0	....	0	0.0
Total 2	15	52	9	14	2	2	0	6	10	....	0	....	.269	.406	.385	.791	142	4	8	5.90	-1	/O-14	3	0.2
• SWANN, Pedro	Pedro Maurice Swann b: 10/27/1970, Wilmington, DE BL/TR, 6', 200 lbs. Deb: 9/9/2000 Career OF: 7-1-3																							
2000 Atl-N	4	2	0	0	0	0	0	0	0	2	0	0	.000	.000	.000	.000	-100	-1	0	.00	0	/O-1	0	-0.1
2002 Tor-A	13	12	3	1	0	0	0	1	1	6	0	0	.083	.154	.083	.237	-33	-2	0	.48	0	/D-3,O-3(0-0-1)	0	-0.2
2003 Bal-A	8	14	3	3	1	0	1	2	1	4	0	0	.214	.267	.500	.767	99	-0	1	3.27	0	/O-6(6-0-0),D-1	0	0.0
Total 3	25	28	6	4	1	0	1	3	2	12	0	0	.143	.200	.286	.486	29	-3	2	1.78	-1	/O-10,D-4	0	-0.4
• SWANSON, Bill	William Andrew Swanson b: 10/12/1888, New York, NY d: 10/14/1954, New York, NY BB/TR, 5'6", 156 lbs. Deb: 9/2/1914																							
1914 Bos-A	11	20	0	4	2	0	0	0	3	4	0	1	.200	.304	.300	.604	82	-1	2	2.44	-3	/2-6,3-3,S-1	0	-0.4
• SWANSON, Evar	Ernest Evar Swanson b: 10/15/1902, DeKalb, IL d: 7/17/1973, Galesburg, IL BR/TR, 5'9", 170 lbs. Deb: 4/18/1929 Career OF: 118-128-229																							
1929 Cin-N	148	574	100	172	35	12	4	43	41	47	33	....	.300	.353	.423	.776	96	-4	84	5.23	2	*O-142(91-51-0)	14	-1.0
1930 Cin-N	95	301	43	93	15	3	2	22	11	17	4	....	.309	.335	.399	.734	81	-10	39	4.61	-2	O-71(3-68-0)	5	-1.3
1932 Chi-A	14	52	9	16	3	1	0	8	8	3	3	1	.308	.400	.404	.804	116	2	9	6.35	-1	O-14(14-0-0)	2	0.0
1933 Chi-A	144	539	102	165	25	7	1	63	93	35	19	11	.306	.411	.384	.795	116	19	92	6.11	-6	*O-139(6-8-129)	18	0.4
1934 Chi-A	117	426	71	127	9	5	0	34	59	31	10	3	.298	.385	.343	.727	86	-5	61	5.25	-4	*O-105(4-1-100)	10	-1.4
Total 5	518	1892	325	573	87	28	7	170	212	133	69	15	.303	.376	.390	.766	98	2	285	5.42	-12	O-471	49	-3.3
• SWANSON, Karl	Karl Edward Swanson b: 12/17/1900, North Henderson, IL d: 4/3/2002, Rock Island, IL BL/TR, 5'10", 155 lbs. Deb: 8/12/1928																							
1928 Chi-A	22	64	2	9	1	0	0	6	4	7	3	0	.141	.191	.156	.347	-8	-9	3	1.15	-1	2-21	1	-1.0
1929 Chi-A	2	1	0	0	0	0	0	0	0	0	0	0	.000	.000	.000	.000	-101	-0	0	.00	0	....	0	0.0
Total 2	24	65	2	9	1	0	0	6	4	7	3	0	.138	.188	.154	.342	-9	-10	3	1.13	-1	/2-21	1	-1.0
• SWANSON, Stan	Stanley Lawrence Swanson b: 5/19/1944, Yuba City, CA BR/TR, 5'11", 168 lbs. Deb: 6/23/1971																							
1971 Mon-N	49	106	14	26	3	0	2	11	10	13	1	3	.245	.310	.330	.641	81	-4	11	3.31	0	O-38(24-16-2)	2	-0.5
• SWARTWOOD, Ed	Cyrus Edward Swartwood b: 1/12/1859, Rockford, IL d: 5/15/1924, Pittsburgh, PA BL/TR, 5'11", 198 lbs. Deb: 8/11/1881 Career OF: 47-89-502																							
1881 Buf-N	1	3	0	1	0	0	0	0	1	0	....	....	.333	.500	.333	.833	169	0	1	6.92	0	/O-1	0	0.0
1882 Pit-a	76	325	**86**	107	**18**	11	4	....	21	....	....	....	.329	.370	.489	.859	197	33	60	7.74	-10	*O-73(0-29-44)/1-4	16	1.9
1883 Pit-a	94	412	86	**147**	24	8	3	0	25	....	....	....	**.357**	**.394**	.476	**.869**	**187**	**40**	79	**8.35**	-3	1-60,O-37(0-31-6)/C-3	19	2.7
1884 Pit-a	102	399	74	115	19	6	0	0	33	....	....	....	.288	.365	.366	.731	137	18	55	5.28	-8	*O-79(0-2-77),1-22/3-1,P-1	16	0.4
1885 Bro-a	99	399	80	106	8	9	0	49	36	....	....	....	.266	.334	.331	.665	110	6	45	4.17	-8	*O-95(47-0-48)/1-4,C-1,S-1	13	-0.5
1886 Bro-a	122	471	95	132	13	10	3	58	**70**	....	37	....	.280	.377	.369	.746	133	21	82	6.49	6	*O-122(0-20-103)/C-1	21	2.2
1887 Bro-a	91	409	72	138	14	8	1	54	46	....	29	....	.337	.342	.344	.687	91	-4	54	5.38	2	*O-91(0-0-91)	8	-0.2

YEAR TM-L	G	AB	R	H	2B	3B	HR	RBI	BB	SO	SB	CS	AVG	OBP	SLG	OPS	OPS+	BR/A	RC	RC/G	FR	G/POS	WS	TPW
1890 Tol-a	126	462	106	151	23	11	3	64	80	....	53	....	.327	**.444**	.444	.887	157	38	117	10.00	7	*O-126(0-7-119)/P-1	23	3.9
1892 Pit-N	13	42	8	10	1	0	0	4	13	11	1	....	.238	.418	.262	.680	106	2	5	4.34	4	O-13(0-0-13)	2	0.4
Total 9	724	2922	607	907	120	63	14	229	325	11	120	....	.310	.379	.400	.778	143	155	498	6.72	-10	O-637/1-90,C-5,P-2,3-1,S-1	118	10.8

• SWEASY, Charlie Charles James Sweasy b: 11/2/1847, Newark, NJ d: 3/30/1908, Newark, NJ BR/TR, 5'9", 172 lbs. Deb: 5/19/1871 M/U NA OF: 0-0-2

YEAR TM-L	G	AB	R	H	2B	3B	HR	RBI	BB	SO	SB	CS	AVG	OBP	SLG	OPS	OPS+	BR/A	RC	RC/G	FR	G/POS	WS	TPW
1871 Oly-n	5	19	5	4	1	0	0	4	1	0	0	0	.211	.250	.263	.513	50	-1	1	2.69	-1	/2-5	....	-0.2
1872 Cle-n	12	57	8	16	0	0	0	6	2	1	1	0	.281	.305	.281	.586	86	-0	5	4.02	4	2-11/O-1	....	0.2
1873 Bos-n	1	4	0	1	0	0	0	0	0	0	0	0	.250	.250	.250	.500	45	-0	0	2.61	0	/2-1	....	0.0
1874 Bal-n	8	33	2	8	0	0	0	4	2	0	0	0	.242	.286	.242	.528	71	-1	2	2.81	-8	/2-8,O-1	....	-0.7
Atl-n	10	44	4	5	1	0	0	3	0	0	0	0	.114	.114	.136	.250	-23	-5	1	.54	6	2-10	....	0.0
Yr.	18	77	6	13	1	0	0	7	2	0	0	0	.169	.190	.182	.372	19	-6	3	1.43	-2	2-18/O-1	....	-0.7
1875 RS-n	19	76	7	13	1	0	0	4	3	1	2	4	.171	.203	.184	.387	39	-5	3	1.46	-6	2-19	....	-1.0
1876 Cin-N	56	227	18	46	5	2	0	10	2	5	....	....	.203	.211	.244	.456	60	-7	12	1.86	0	*2-55/O-1	0	-0.3
1878 Pro-N	55	212	23	37	3	0	0	8	7	23	....	....	.175	.201	.189	.390	29	-16	8	1.29	-16	*2-55	1	-2.7
Total 5 n	55	233	26	47	3	0	0	21	8	2	3	4	.202	.228	.215	.443	45	-13	13	2.12	-5	/2-54,O-2	....	-1.7
Total 2	111	439	41	83	8	2	0	18	9	28	....	....	.189	.206	.217	.424	45	-22	20	1.58	-15	2-110/O-1	1	-3.0

• SWEENEY, Bill William John Sweeney b: 3/6/1886, Covington, KY d: 5/26/1948, Cambridge, MA BR/TR, 5'11", 175 lbs. Deb: 6/14/1907

YEAR TM-L	G	AB	R	H	2B	3B	HR	RBI	BB	SO	SB	CS	AVG	OBP	SLG	OPS	OPS+	BR/A	RC	RC/G	FR	G/POS	WS	TPW
1907 Chi-N	3	10	1	1	0	0	0	1	1	....	1	....	.100	.182	.100	.282	-11	-1	0	1.21	-2	/S-3	0	-0.4
Bos-N	58	191	24	50	2	0	0	18	15	....	8	....	.262	.316	.272	.588	85	-3	19	3.58	-3	3-23,S-15,O-11(9-1-1)/2-5,1	4	-0.7
Yr.	61	201	25	51	2	0	0	19	16	....	9	....	.254	.309	.264	.572	79	-4	20	3.42	-5	3-23,S-18,O-11(9-1-1)/2-5,1	4	-1.1
1908 Bos-N	127	418	44	102	15	3	0	40	45	....	17	....	.244	.317	.294	.612	97	-0	45	3.52	5	*3-123/S-3,2-1	13	1.0
1909 Bos-N	138	493	44	120	19	3	1	36	37	....	25	....	.243	.296	.300	.596	81	-12	50	3.42	-3	*3-112,S-26	10	-1.1
1910 Bos-N	150	499	43	133	22	4	5	46	61	28	25	....	.267	.349	.357	.705	101	1	71	4.82	-21	*S-110,3-21,1-17	11	-1.6
1911 Bos-N	137	523	92	164	33	6	3	63	77	26	33	....	.314	.404	.417	.820	120	17	101	7.08	-4	*2-136	19	1.5
1912 Bos-N	153	593	84	204	31	13	1	100	68	34	27	....	.344	.416	.445	.861	133	29	123	7.40	20	*2-153	20	5.1
1913 Bos-N	139	502	65	129	17	6	0	47	66	50	18	....	.257	.347	.315	.662	88	-5	59	3.92	-8	*2-137	15	-1.1
1914 Chi-N	134	463	45	101	14	5	1	38	53	15	18	....	.218	.298	.276	.575	71	-15	44	2.96	25	*2-134	11	1.2
Total 8	1039	3692	442	1004	153	40	11	389	423	153	172	....	.272	.349	.344	.693	99	11	513	4.71	9	2-566,3-279,S-157/1-18,O-11	103	4.0

• SWEENEY, Bill William Joseph Sweeney b: 12/29/1904, Cleveland, OH d: 4/18/1957, San Diego, CA BR/TR, 5'11", 180 lbs. Deb: 4/13/1928 C

YEAR TM-L	G	AB	R	H	2B	3B	HR	RBI	BB	SO	SB	CS	AVG	OBP	SLG	OPS	OPS+	BR/A	RC	RC/G	FR	G/POS	WS	TPW
1928 Det-A	89	309	47	78	15	5	0	19	15	28	12	9	.252	.287	.333	.620	62	-19	28	3.06	1	1-75/O-3(3-0-0)	2	-2.2
1930 Bos-A	88	243	32	75	13	0	4	30	9	15	5	3	.309	.333	.412	.745	91	-4	32	4.94	2	1-56/3-1	4	-0.5
1931 Bos-A	131	498	48	147	30	3	1	58	20	30	5	12	.295	.322	.373	.696	87	-13	56	3.98	11	*1-124	8	-1.2
Total 3	308	1050	127	300	58	8	5	107	44	73	22	24	.286	.314	.370	.685	80	-35	117	3.91	14	1-255/O-3,3-1	14	-3.9

• SWEENEY, Buck Charles Francis Sweeney b: 4/15/1890, Pittsburgh, PA d: 3/13/1955, Pittsburgh, PA Deb: 9/28/1914

YEAR TM-L	G	AB	R	H	2B	3B	HR	RBI	BB	SO	SB	CS	AVG	OBP	SLG	OPS	OPS+	BR/A	RC	RC/G	FR	G/POS	WS	TPW
1914 Phi-A	1	1	0	0	0	0	0	0	0	1	0	....	.000	.000	.000	.000	-104	-0	0	.00	-0	/O-1	0	0.0

• SWEENEY, Charlie Charles J. Sweeney
b: 4/13/1863, San Francisco, CA d: 4/4/1902, San Francisco, CA BR/TR, 5'10.5", 181 lbs. Deb: 5/11/1882 U Career OF: 30-31-31 ♦

YEAR TM-L	G	AB	R	H	2B	3B	HR	RBI	BB	SO	SB	CS	AVG	OBP	SLG	OPS	OPS+	BR/A	RC	RC/G	FR	G/POS	WS	TPW
1882 Pro-N	1	4	0	0	0	0	0	0	0	1	....	....	.000	.000	.000	.000	-100	-1	0	.00	0	/O-1	0	-0.1
1883 Pro-N	22	87	9	19	3	0	0	15	2	10	....	....	.218	.236	.253	.489	47	-3	5	2.15	3	P-20/O-7(2-3-2)	9	-0.7
1884 Pro-N	41	168	24	50	9	0	1	19	11	17	....	....	.298	.341	.369	.710	126	9	22	5.05	0	P-27,O-17(0-5-13)/1-1	32	2.9
StL-U	45	171	31	54	14	2	1	....	10	....	....	....	.316	.354	.439	.792	160	12	27	6.51	6	P-33,O-13(13-0-0)/1-1	35	3.1
1885 StL-N	71	267	27	55	7	1	0	24	12	33	....	....	.206	.240	.240	.480	59	-6	16	2.01	-4	O-39(14-19-6),P-35	12	-5.1
1886 StL-N	17	64	4	16	2	0	0	7	3	10	0	....	.250	.284	.281	.565	77	1	5	2.94	0	P-11/O-4(0-4-0),S-2	3	-1.0
1887 Cle-a	36	154	22	51	4	4	0	19	21	....	11	....	.331	.331	.316	.647	83	-1	18	4.72	-5	1-20,O-10(1-0-9)/P-3,3-2,S	2	-1.4
Total 6	233	915	117	245	39	7	2	84	59	71	11	....	.268	.297	.317	.614	94	12	93	3.81	1	P-129/O-91,1-22,S-4,3-2	93	-2.2

• SWEENEY, Dan Daniel J. Sweeney b: 1/28/1868, Philadelphia, PA d: 7/13/1913, Louisville, KY, 5'5", 160 lbs. Deb: 4/18/1895

YEAR TM-L	G	AB	R	H	2B	3B	HR	RBI	BB	SO	SB	CS	AVG	OBP	SLG	OPS	OPS+	BR/A	RC	RC/G	FR	G/POS	WS	TPW
1895 Lou-N	22	90	18	24	5	0	1	16	17	2	2	....	.267	.389	.356	.744	99	1	14	5.54	-3	O-22(0-1-21)	2	-0.2

• SWEENEY, Ed Edward Francis "Ed" Sweeney b: 7/19/1888, Chicago, IL d: 7/4/1947, Chicago, IL BR/TR, 6'1", 200 lbs. Deb: 5/16/1908 Career OF: 0-1-1

YEAR TM-L	G	AB	R	H	2B	3B	HR	RBI	BB	SO	SB	CS	AVG	OBP	SLG	OPS	OPS+	BR/A	RC	RC/G	FR	G/POS	WS	TPW
1908 NY-A	32	82	4	12	2	0	0	2	5	....	0	....	.146	.195	.171	.366	19	-7	3	.99	-4	C-25/1-1,O-1	1	-1.0
1909 NY-A	67	176	18	47	3	0	0	21	16	....	3	....	.267	.328	.284	.612	93	-1	18	3.40	-2	C-62/1-3	6	0.3
1910 NY-A	78	215	25	43	4	4	0	13	17	....	12	....	.200	.271	.256	.527	62	-10	18	2.64	-7	C-77	5	-1.0
1911 NY-A	83	229	17	53	6	5	0	18	14	....	8	....	.231	.299	.301	.600	63	-12	24	3.25	-2	C-83	4	-0.8
1912 NY-A	110	351	37	94	12	1	0	30	27	....	6	....	.268	.325	.308	.633	77	-11	37	3.63	5	*C-108	7	0.3
1913 NY-A	117	351	35	93	10	2	2	40	37	41	11	....	.265	.348	.322	.670	96	-0	42	4.02	8	*C-112/1-1,O-1	12	1.7
1914 NY-A	87	258	25	55	8	1	1	22	35	30	19	6	.213	.316	.264	.580	75	-5	26	3.21	4	C-78	9	0.6
1915 NY-A	53	137	12	26	2	0	0	5	25	12	3	3	.190	.319	.204	.523	57	-7	11	2.36	-2	C-53	3	-0.5
1919 Pit-N	17	42	0	4	1	0	0	0	5	6	1	....	.095	.191	.119	.311	-5	-5	1	.69	-1	C-15	0	-0.6
Total 9	644	1841	173	427	48	13	3	151	181	89	63	9	.232	.310	.277	.587	72	-58	180	3.14	-1	C-613/1-5,O-2	47	-1.0

• SWEENEY, Hank Harry Leon Sweeney b: 12/28/1915, Franklin, TN d: 5/6/1980, Columbia, TN BL/TL, 6', 185 lbs. Deb: 10/1/1944

YEAR TM-L	G	AB	R	H	2B	3B	HR	RBI	BB	SO	SB	CS	AVG	OBP	SLG	OPS	OPS+	BR/A	RC	RC/G	FR	G/POS	WS	TPW
1944 Pit-N	1	2	0	0	0	0	0	0	0	1	0	....	.000	.000	.000	.000	-96	-1	0	.00	0	/1-1	0	0.0

• SWEENEY, Jerry Jeremiah H. Sweeney b: 1860, Boston, MA d: 8/25/1891, Boston, MA, 5'9.5", 157 lbs. Deb: 8/22/1884

YEAR TM-L	G	AB	R	H	2B	3B	HR	RBI	BB	SO	SB	CS	AVG	OBP	SLG	OPS	OPS+	BR/A	RC	RC/G	FR	G/POS	WS	TPW
1884 KC-U	31	129	16	34	3	0	0	....	4	....	....	....	.264	.286	.287	.573	108	2	11	3.19	2	1-31	3	0.1

• SWEENEY, Mark Mark Patrick Sweeney b: 10/26/1969, Framingham, MA BL/TL, 6'1", 195 lbs. Deb: 8/4/1995 Career OF: 89-1-83

YEAR TM-L	G	AB	R	H	2B	3B	HR	RBI	BB	SO	SB	CS	AVG	OBP	SLG	OPS	OPS+	BR/A	RC	RC/G	FR	G/POS	WS	TPW
1995 StL-N	37	77	5	21	2	0	2	13	10	15	1	1	.273	.356	.377	.733	94	-1	10	4.33	-1	1-19/O-1	1	-0.3
1996*StL-N	98	170	32	45	9	0	3	22	33	29	3	0	.265	.387	.371	.758	102	3	27	5.46	-2	1-15/O-1	7	-0.1
1997 StL-N	44	61	5	13	3	0	0	4	9	14	0	1	.213	.324	.262	.586	56	-4	5	2.70	-1	O-43(10-0-15)/1-4	0	-0.5
SD-N	71	103	11	33	4	0	2	19	11	18	2	2	.320	.386	.417	.803	121	3	17	6.17	-1	O-25(6-1-13)/1-7	5	0.1
Yr.	115	164	16	46	7	0	2	23	20	32	2	3	.280	.362	.360	.722	96	-1	22	4.72	-2	O-68(16-1-28),1-11	5	-0.5
1998*SD-N	122	192	17	45	8	3	2	15	26	37	1	2	.234	.329	.339	.667	82	-5	22	3.73	-4	1-21,O-20(5-0-29)/D-1	3	-1.2
1999 Cin-N	37	31	6	11	3	0	2	7	4	9	0	0	.355	.429	.645	1.074	162	3	8	9.47	0	O-34(1-0-0)/1-1	2	0.3
2000 Mil-N	71	73	9	16	6	0	1	6	12	18	0	0	.219	.337	.342	.680	74	-3	9	4.22	1	/D-4,1-2,O-1	1	-0.2
2001 Mil-N	48	89	9	23	3	1	3	11	12	23	2	1	.258	.347	.416	.762	98	-0	14	5.45	-1	/O-3(20-0-3),1-2	1	-0.2
2002 SD-N	48	65	3	11	3	0	1	4	4	19	0	0	.169	.217	.262	.479	28	-7	4	1.80	0	O-20(0-0-5),1-11/D-1	0	-0.8
2003 Col-N	67	97	13	25	9	0	2	14	9	27	0	1	.258	.321	.412	.733	78	-4	12	4.43	-2	O-17(7-0-11)/1-8,D-1	2	-0.7
Total 9	643	958	110	243	50	4	18	115	130	209	9	8	.254	.345	.371	.716	89	-15	128	4.54	-12	O-165/1-90,D-7	22	-3.6

• SWEENEY, Mike Michael John Sweeney b: 7/22/1973, Orange, CA BR/TR, 6'1", 195 lbs. Deb: 9/4/1995

YEAR TM-L	G	AB	R	H	2B	3B	HR	RBI	BB	SO	SB	CS	AVG	OBP	SLG	OPS	OPS+	BR/A	RC	RC/G	FR	G/POS	WS	TPW
1995 KC-A	4	4	1	1	0	0	0	0	0	0	0	0	.250	.250	.250	.500	30	-0	0	2.25	-1	/C-4	0	-0.1
1996 KC-A	50	165	23	46	10	0	4	24	18	21	1	2	.279	.364	.412	.776	96	-1	24	4.85	-1	C-26,D-22	4	-0.1
1997 KC-A	84	240	30	58	8	0	7	31	17	33	3	2	.242	.308	.363	.670	72	-10	26	3.55	1	C-76/D-3	5	-0.4
1998 KC-A	92	282	32	73	18	0	8	35	24	38	2	3	.259	.321	.408	.729	86	-7	36	4.32	-4	C-91	8	-0.5
1999 KC-A	150	575	101	185	44	2	22	102	54	48	6	1	.322	.390	.520	.910	127	24	113	7.35	-6	D-75,1-74/C-4	16	0.6
2000 KC-A★	159	618	105	206	30	0	29	144	71	67	8	3	.333	.415	.523	.937	131	32	136	8.27	0	*1-114,D-45	26	1.8
2001 KC-A★	147	559	97	170	46	0	29	99	64	64	10	3	.304	.378	.542	.920	128	23	113	7.43	-2	*1-108,D-38	18	0.9
2002 KC-A★	126	471	81	160	31	1	24	86	61	46	9	7	.340	.422	.563	.985	142	30	112	9.02	9	*1-102,D-24	19	2.7
2003 KC-A★	108	392	62	115	18	1	16	83	64	56	3	2	.293	.395	.467	.862	111	9	73	6.62	1	D-62,1-45	15	0.2
Total 9	920	3306	532	1014	205	4	139	604	373	373	42	23	.307	.385	.497	.882	119	99	632	6.95	-3	1-443,D-269,C-201	111	5.0

• SWEENEY, Pete Peter Jay Sweeney b: 12/31/1863, CA d: 8/22/1901, San Francisco, CA BR/TR Deb: 9/28/1888 Career OF: 3-5-3

YEAR TM-L	G	AB	R	H	2B	3B	HR	RBI	BB	SO	SB	CS	AVG	OBP	SLG	OPS	OPS+	BR/A	RC	RC/G	FR	G/POS	WS	TPW
1888 Was-N	11	44	3	8	0	1	0	5	0	4	0	....	.182	.182	.227	.409	31	-3	2	1.40	-1	/3-8,O-3(3-0-0)	0	-0.4
1889 Was-N	49	193	13	44	7	3	1	23	11	26	8	....	.228	.284	.311	.595	70	-8	20	3.52	-11	3-47/2-1,O-1	2	-1.6
StL-a	9	38	8	14	2	0	0	8	1	5	2	....	.368	.415	.421	.836	122	1	8	8.45	0	/3-8,O-1	2	0.1

YEAR TM-L	G	AB	R	H	2B	3B	HR	RBI	BB	SO	SB	CS	AVG	OBP	SLG	OPS	OPS+	BR/A	RC	RC/G	FR	G/POS	WS	TPW
1890 StL-a	49	190	23	34	3	2	0	10	17	....	8	....	.179	.271	.216	.487	38	-16	14	2.31	-6	2-23,3-21/1-3,O-2(0-0-2)	2	-1.8
Lou-a	2	7	1	1	1	0	0	1	1	....	1	....	.143	.250	.286	.536	59	-0	1	3.40	-1	/S-2	0	-0.1
Phi-a	14	49	5	8	1	1	0	0	7	....	0	....	.163	.281	.224	.505	50	-3	3	2.05	-5	/2-9,O-4(0-4-0),3-2	1	-0.7
Yr.	65	246	29	43	5	3	0	11	25	....	9	....	.175	.272	.220	.492	41	-19	18	2.29	-12	2-32,3-23/O-6(0-4-2),1-3,S	3	-2.6
Total 3	134	521	53	109	14	7	1	47	37	35	19	....	.209	.280	.269	.548	57	-29	47	3.01	-24	/3-86,2-33,O-11,1-3,S-2	7	-4.5
• SWEENEY, Rooney	John J. Sweeney b: 11/1/1858, New York, NY, 5'8", 155 lbs. Deb: 7/25/1883 Career OF: 1-7-13																							
1883 Bal-a	25	101	13	21	5	2	0	0	4	....	....	....	.208	.238	.297	.535	69	-4	7	2.56	4	C-23/O-3(0-0-3)	1	0.1
1884 Bal-U	48	186	37	42	7	1	0	....	15	....	....	....	.226	.284	.274	.558	81	-4	15	2.88	-5	C-33,O-16(0-6-10)/3-1	5	-0.5
1885 StL-N	3	11	1	1	0	0	0	0	0	4	....	....	.091	.091	.091	.182	-44	-2	0	.25	0	/O-2(1-1-0),C-1	0	-0.2
Total 3	76	298	51	64	12	3	0	0	19	4	....	....	.215	.262	.275	.537	73	-9	22	2.66	-1	/C-57,O-21,3-1	6	-0.6
• SWEET, Rick	Ricky Joe Sweet b: 9/7/1952, Longview, WA BB/TR, 6'1", 200 lbs. Deb: 4/8/1978 C																							
1978 SD-N	88	226	15	50	8	0	1	11	27	22	1	4	.221	.307	.270	.577	68	-11	19	2.69	-2	C-76	4	-1.0
1982 NY-N	3	3	0	1	0	0	0	0	0	1	0	0	.333	.333	.333	.667	88	-0	0	4.50	0	....	0	0.0
Sea-A	88	258	29	66	6	1	4	24	20	24	3	0	.256	.314	.333	.648	76	-8	29	3.91	-1	C-83	7	-0.5
1983 Sea-A	93	249	18	55	9	0	1	22	13	26	2	2	.221	.260	.269	.529	44	-20	15	1.94	2	C-85	3	-1.5
Total 3	272	736	62	172	23	1	6	57	60	73	6	6	.234	.294	.292	.586	63	-38	63	2.84	-1	C-244	14	-2.9
• SWEIGERT, Ham	Hampton Sweigert Deb: 10/12/1890																							
1890 Phi-a	1	1	0	0	0	0	0	0	1	....	1	....	.000	.500	.000	.500	49	0	1	13.58	1	/O-1	0	0.1
• SWENTOR, Augie	August William Swentor b: 11/21/1899, Seymour, CT d: 11/10/1969, Waterbury, CT BR/TR, 6', 185 lbs. Deb: 9/12/1922																							
1922 Chi-A	1	1	0	0	0	0	0	0	0	1	0	0	.000	.000	.000	.000	-101	-0	0	.00	0	....	0	0.0
• SWETT, Pop	William E. Swett b: 4/16/1870, San Francisco, CA d: 11/22/1934, San Francisco, CA, 6', 175 lbs. Deb: 5/3/1890																							
1890 Bos-P	37	94	16	18	4	3	1	12	16	26	4	....	.191	.321	.330	.651	69	-4	12	4.10	-6	C-34/O-3(0-0-3)	2	-0.7
• SWIFT, Bob	Robert Virgil Swift b: 3/6/1915, Salina, KS d: 10/17/1966, Detroit, MI BR/TR, 5'11.5", 180 lbs. Deb: 4/16/1940 M/C																							
1940 StL-A	130	398	37	97	20	1	0	39	28	39	1	0	.244	.295	.299	.594	53	-27	36	3.11	-3	*C-128	5	-2.2
1941 StL-A	63	170	13	44	7	0	0	21	22	11	2	0	.259	.344	.300	.644	69	-6	19	3.82	-1	C-58	4	-0.4
1942 StL-A	29	76	3	15	4	0	1	8	3	5	0	2	.197	.228	.289	.517	44	-7	5	1.85	0	C-28	1	-0.5
Phi-A	60	192	9	44	3	0	0	15	13	17	1	2	.229	.278	.245	.523	48	-14	13	2.27	1	C-60	2	-0.9
Yr.	89	268	12	59	7	0	1	23	16	22	1	4	.220	.264	.257	.522	47	-21	18	2.14	2	C-88	3	-1.4
1943 Phi-A	77	224	16	43	5	1	1	11	35	16	0	0	.192	.301	.237	.538	58	-10	17	2.35	1	C-77	3	-0.5
1944 Det-A	80	247	15	63	11	1	1	19	27	27	2	0	.255	.331	.320	.651	82	-5	27	3.64	4	C-76	9	0.4
1945*Det-A	95	279	19	65	5	0	0	24	26	22	1	0	.233	.298	.251	.549	56	-14	22	2.64	3	C-94	7	-0.7
1946 Det-A	42	107	13	25	2	0	2	10	14	7	0	0	.234	.322	.308	.631	72	-4	11	3.34	-2	C-42	3	-0.4
1947 Det-A	97	279	23	70	11	0	1	21	33	16	2	2	.251	.330	.301	.631	74	-9	29	3.43	0	C-97	8	-0.4
1948 Det-A	113	292	23	65	6	0	4	33	51	29	1	0	.223	.338	.284	.622	65	-13	32	3.44	-1	*C-112	8	-0.8
1949 Det-A	74	189	16	45	6	0	2	18	26	20	0	0	.238	.330	.302	.632	68	-8	21	3.87	-2	C-69	5	-0.8
1950 Det-A	67	132	14	30	4	0	2	9	25	6	0	0	.227	.350	.303	.653	66	-6	15	3.56	-2	C-66	4	-0.5
1951 Det-A	44	104	8	20	0	0	0	5	12	10	0	0	.192	.276	.192	.468	28	-10	7	2.10	0	C-43	1	-0.9
1952 Det-A	28	58	3	8	1	0	0	4	7	7	0	0	.138	.242	.155	.398	12	-7	2	.92	0	C-28	1	-0.6
1953 Det-A	2	3	0	1	1	0	0	1	2	1	0	0	.333	.600	.667	1.267	244	1	2	20.82	0	/C-2	0	0.1
Total 14	1001	2750	212	635	86	3	14	238	324	233	10	6	.231	.313	.280	.592	61	-138	256	3.07	-1	C-980	61	-9.1
• SWINDELLS, Charlie	Charles Jay "Swin" Swindells b: 10/26/1878, Rockford, IL d: 7/22/1940, Portland, OR BR/TR, 5'11.5", 180 lbs. Deb: 9/7/1904																							
1904 StL-N	3	8	0	1	0	0	0	0	0	....	0	....	.125	.125	.125	.250	-24	-1	0	.48	-1	/C-3	0	-0.2
• SWISHER, Steve	Steven Eugene Swisher b: 8/9/1951, Parkersburg, WV BR/TR, 6'2", 205 lbs. Deb: 6/14/1974 C																							
1974 Chi-N	90	280	21	60	5	0	5	27	37	63	0	3	.214	.310	.286	.596	65	-14	25	2.91	2	C-90	5	-0.8
1975 Chi-N	93	254	20	54	16	2	1	22	30	57	1	0	.213	.306	.303	.609	66	-11	22	2.64	0	C-93	3	-0.8
1976 Chi-N★	109	377	25	89	13	3	5	42	20	82	2	1	.236	.278	.326	.604	65	-18	33	2.82	-2	*C-107	5	-1.5
1977 Chi-N	74	205	21	39	7	0	5	15	9	47	0	0	.190	.231	.298	.529	37	-19	14	2.16	-2	C-72	3	-1.8
1978 StL-N	45	115	11	32	5	1	1	10	8	14	1	0	.278	.331	.365	.696	96	-1	13	3.84	-1	C-42	4	0.0
1979 StL-N	38	73	4	11	1	1	1	3	6	17	0	0	.151	.215	.233	.448	22	-8	4	1.49	-2	C-33	1	-0.9
1980 StL-N	18	24	2	6	1	0	0	2	1	7	0	0	.250	.280	.292	.572	58	-1	1	1.96	-1	/C-8	0	-0.2
1981 SD-N	16	28	2	4	0	0	0	0	2	11	0	0	.143	.200	.143	.343	-2	-4	1	.81	-1	C-10	0	-0.4
1982 SD-N	26	58	2	10	1	0	2	3	5	24	0	0	.172	.238	.293	.531	50	-4	4	2.43	-1	C-26	1	-0.5
Total 9	509	1414	108	305	49	7	20	124	118	322	4	4	.216	.281	.303	.584	60	-79	117	2.64	-9	C-481	22	-7.1
• SWOBODA, Ron	Ronald Alan "Rocky" Swoboda b: 6/30/1944, Baltimore, MD BR/TR, 6'2", 205 lbs. Deb: 4/12/1965 Career OF: 201-57-524																							
1965 NY-N	135	399	52	91	15	3	19	50	33	102	2	3	.228	.292	.424	.716	102	-1	47	3.91	1	*O-112(73-26-15)	9	-0.6
1966 NY-N	112	342	34	76	9	4	8	50	31	76	4	2	.222	.296	.342	.638	79	-9	34	3.30	3	O-97(88-0-10)	7	-1.1
1967 NY-N	134	449	47	126	17	3	13	53	41	96	3	1	.281	.342	.419	.761	118	11	65	5.26	-2	*O-108(0-0-108),1-20	15	0.1
1968 NY-N	132	450	46	109	14	6	11	59	52	113	8	1	.242	.326	.373	.699	109	8	55	4.18	4	*O-125(0-0-125)	14	0.3
1969*NY-N	109	327	38	77	10	2	9	52	43	90	1	1	.235	.328	.361	.689	91	-3	39	3.96	0	O-97(22-0-77)	10	-0.9
1970 NY-N	115	245	29	57	8	2	9	40	40	72	2	4	.233	.343	.392	.734	96	-2	33	4.40	-2	*O-100(1-0-100)	6	-0.7
1971 Mon-N	39	75	7	19	4	3	0	6	11	16	0	1	.253	.364	.387	.750	112	1	10	4.58	1	O-26(10-17-3)	3	0.2
NY-A	54	138	17	36	2	1	2	20	27	35	0	0	.261	.393	.333	.726	114	5	20	4.98	-2	O-47(7-1-39)	5	0.1
1972 NY-A	63	113	9	28	8	0	1	12	17	29	0	1	.248	.346	.345	.691	110	2	14	4.34	-1	O-35(0-5-35)/1-2	4	-0.1
1973 NY-A	35	43	6	5	0	0	1	2	4	18	0	0	.116	.191	.186	.378	7	-5	2	1.23	0	O-20(0-8-12)/D-4	0	-0.6
Total 9	928	2581	285	624	87	24	73	344	299	647	20	14	.242	.325	.379	.704	101	6	320	4.19	3	O-767/1-22,D-4	73	-3.3
• SYLVESTER, Lou	Louis J. Sylvester b: 2/14/1855, Springfield, IL d: 5/5/1936, Brooklyn, NY BR/TR, 5'6", 165 lbs. Deb: 4/18/1884 U Career OF: 73-62-38 ♦																							
1884 Cin-U	82	333	67	89	13	8	2	....	18	....	....	....	.267	.305	.372	.677	118	5	39	4.45	-3	*O-81(54-6-22)/P-6,S-2	13	-0.1
1886 Lou-a	45	154	41	35	5	3	0	17	29	....	3	....	.227	.350	.299	.648	98	1	18	3.99	1	O-45(0-45-0)	4	0.0
Cin-a	17	55	10	10	0	0	3	8	7	....	2	....	.182	.286	.345	.631	94	-0	6	3.69	1	O-17(7-7-3)	1	0.0
Yr.	62	209	51	45	5	3	3	25	36	....	5	....	.215	.333	.311	.644	97	0	24	3.90	2	O-62(7-52-3)	5	0.0
1887 StL-a	29	125	20	38	4	3	1	18	13	....	13	....	.304	.310	.339	.649	73	-5	16	5.02	2	O-29(12-4-13)/2-1	3	-0.3
Total 3	173	667	138	172	22	14	6	43	67	....	18	....	.258	.315	.347	.662	103	1	79	4.37	1	O-172/P-6,S-2,2-1	21	-0.3
• SZEKELY, Joe	Joseph Szekely b: 2/2/1925, Cleveland, OH BR/TR, 5'11", 180 lbs. Deb: 9/13/1953																							
1953 Cin-N	5	13	0	1	0	0	0	0	0	3	0	0	.077	.077	.077	.154	-59	-3	0	.00	1	/O-3(0-0-3)	0	-0.2
• SZOTKIEWICZ, Ken	Kenneth John Szotkiewicz b: 2/25/1947, Wilmington, DE BL/TR, 6', 165 lbs. Deb: 4/7/1970																							
1970 Det-A	47	84	9	9	1	0	3	9	12	29	0	0	.107	.219	.226	.445	23	-9	5	1.60	2	S-44	1	-0.4
• TABB, Jerry	Jerry Lynn Tabb b: 3/17/1952, Altus, OK BL/TR, 6'2", 195 lbs. Deb: 9/8/1976																							
1976 Chi-N	11	24	2	7	0	0	0	0	3	2	0	0	.292	.370	.292	.662	82	-0	3	4.58	0	/1-6	1	-0.1
1977 Oak-A	51	144	8	32	3	0	6	19	10	26	0	1	.222	.273	.368	.641	74	-6	13	2.90	-2	1-36/D-5	1	-1.0
1978 Oak-A	12	9	0	1	0	0	0	1	2	5	0	0	.111	.273	.111	.384	12	-1	0	1.16	0	/1-2,D-2	0	-0.1
Total 3	74	177	10	40	3	0	6	20	15	33	0	1	.226	.286	.345	.631	72	-7	16	3.00	-3	/1-44,D-7	2	-1.2
• TABLER, Pat	Patrick Sean Tabler b: 2/2/1958, Hamilton, OH BR/TR, 6'3", 200 lbs. Deb: 8/21/1981 Career OF: 204-0-80																							
1981 Chi-N	35	101	11	19	3	1	1	5	13	26	0	1	.188	.281	.267	.548	54	-6	7	2.21	1	2-35	1	-0.4
1982 Chi-N	25	85	9	20	4	2	1	7	6	20	0	0	.235	.293	.365	.658	81	-2	9	3.33	-4	3-25	2	-0.7
1983 Cle-A	124	430	56	125	23	5	6	65	56	63	2	4	.291	.374	.409	.783	111	7	63	5.14	-8	O-88(87-0-1),3-25/D-6,2-2	12	-0.5
1984 Cle-A	144	473	66	137	21	3	10	68	47	62	3	1	.290	.358	.410	.768	110	8	68	5.11	-7	1-67,O-43(43-0-0),3-36/2-1,D	13	-0.4
1985 Cle-A	117	404	47	111	18	3	5	59	27	55	0	6	.275	.323	.371	.695	90	-8	43	3.67	0	1-92,D-18/3-4,2-1	6	-1.4
1986 Cle-A	130	473	61	154	29	2	6	48	29	75	3	1	.326	.368	.433	.802	119	13	74	5.97	1	*1-107,D-18	16	0.7

YEAR TM-L	G	AB	R	H	2B	3B	HR	RBI	BB	SO	SB	CS	AVG	OBP	SLG	OPS	OPS+	BR/A	RC	RC/G	FR	G/POS	WS	TPW
1987 Cle-A★	151	553	66	170	34	3	11	86	51	84	5	2	.307	.372	.439	.812	113	12	93	6.31	6	1-82,D-66	15	1.0
1988 Cle-A	41	143	16	32	5	1	1	17	23	27	1	0	.224	.335	.294	.629	76	-4	15	3.63	0	D-29,1-10	3	-0.5
KC-A	89	301	37	93	17	2	1	49	23	41	2	3	.309	.362	.389	.751	109	3	42	5.11	-1	D-40,O-37(28-0-9)/1-7,3-1	10	-0.1
Yr.	130	444	53	125	22	3	2	66	46	68	3	3	.282	.353	.358	.711	98	-0	57	4.60	-2	D-69,O-37(28-0-9),1-17/3-1	13	-0.7
1989 KC-A	123	390	36	101	11	1	2	42	37	42	0	0	.259	.326	.308	.634	80	-9	39	3.38	3	O-55(26-0-28),D-39,1-20/2-3,3	5	-1.0
1990 KC-A	75	195	12	53	14	0	1	19	20	21	0	2	.272	.343	.359	.702	98	-1	22	3.89	-1	O-42(11-0-31),D-15/3-6,1-5	4	-0.4
NY-N	17	43	6	12	1	1	1	10	3	8	0	0	.279	.340	.419	.759	108	0	6	5.65	1	O-10(3-0-8)	2	0.1
1991*Tor-A	82	185	20	40	5	1	1	21	29	21	0	0	.216	.326	.270	.596	64	-8	18	3.16	1	D-57,1-20/O-1	2	-1.0
1992*Tor-A	49	135	11	34	5	0	0	16	11	14	0	0	.252	.308	.289	.597	65	-6	11	2.81	2	1-34/O-8(5-0-3),D-2,3-1	2	-0.7
Total 12	1202	3911	454	1101	190	25	47	512	375	559	16	20	.282	.348	.379	.727	99	-2	511	4.61	-7	1-444,D-291,O-284/3-99,2-42	93	-5.5

• TABOR, Greg Gregory Steven Tabor b: 5/21/1961, Castro Valley, CA BR/TR, 6', 165 lbs. Deb: 9/10/1987

YEAR TM-L	G	AB	R	H	2B	3B	HR	RBI	BB	SO	SB	CS	AVG	OBP	SLG	OPS	OPS+	BR/A	RC	RC/G	FR	G/POS	WS	TPW
1987 Tex-A	9	9	4	1	1	0	0	1	0	4	0	0	.111	.111	.222	.333	-15	-2	0	.75	-0	/2-4,D-1	0	-0.1

• TABOR, Jim James Reubin "Rawhide" Tabor b: 11/5/1916, New Hope, AL d: 8/22/1953, Sacramento, CA BR/TR, 6'2", 175 lbs. Deb: 8/2/1938

YEAR TM-L	G	AB	R	H	2B	3B	HR	RBI	BB	SO	SB	CS	AVG	OBP	SLG	OPS	OPS+	BR/A	RC	RC/G	FR	G/POS	WS	TPW
1938 Bos-A	19	57	8	18	3	2	1	8	1	6	0	1	.316	.328	.491	.819	98	-1	8	5.45	0	3-11/S-2	1	-0.1
1939 Bos-A	149	577	76	167	33	8	14	95	40	54	16	10	.289	.337	.447	.784	95	-8	82	5.01	-3	*3-148	16	-0.5
1940 Bos-A	120	459	73	131	28	6	21	81	42	58	14	10	.285	.345	.510	.855	114	6	81	6.33	0	*3-120	16	1.0
1941 Bos-A	126	498	65	139	29	3	16	101	36	48	17	9	.279	.328	.446	.773	100	-2	69	4.75	-5	*3-125	12	-0.2
1942 Bos-A	139	508	56	128	18	2	12	75	37	47	6	13	.252	.303	.366	.669	85	-16	53	3.46	-7	*3-138	8	-1.9
1943 Bos-A	137	537	57	130	26	3	13	85	43	54	7	7	.242	.299	.374	.674	95	-6	59	3.71	-10	*3-133/O-2(2-0-0)	12	-1.6
1944 Bos-A	116	438	58	125	25	3	13	72	31	38	4	4	.285	.334	.445	.779	123	10	63	4.96	-0	*3-114	16	1.2
1946 Phi-N	124	463	53	124	15	2	10	50	36	51	3	....	.268	.322	.374	.696	100	-2	56	4.19	-1	*3-124	13	-0.3
1947 Phi-N	75	251	27	59	14	0	4	31	20	21	2	....	.235	.297	.339	.635	71	-11	25	3.31	-8	3-67	3	-1.9
Total 9	1005	3788	473	1021	191	29	104	598	286	377	69	54	.270	.322	.418	.739	99	-29	496	4.51	-35	3-980/O-2,S-2	97	-4.3

• TACKETT, Jeff Jeffrey Wilson Tackett b: 12/1/1965, Fresno, CA BR/TR, 6'2", 200 lbs. Deb: 9/11/1991

YEAR TM-L	G	AB	R	H	2B	3B	HR	RBI	BB	SO	SB	CS	AVG	OBP	SLG	OPS	OPS+	BR/A	RC	RC/G	FR	G/POS	WS	TPW
1991 Bal-A	6	8	1	1	0	0	0	0	2	2	0	0	.125	.300	.125	.425	23	-1	1	1.88	0	/C-6	0	-0.1
1992 Bal-A	65	179	21	43	8	1	5	24	17	28	0	0	.240	.313	.380	.693	91	-2	19	3.28	-0	C-64/3-1	4	0.2
1993 Bal-A	39	87	8	15	3	0	0	9	13	28	0	0	.172	.280	.207	.487	32	-8	5	1.73	0	C-38/P-1	1	-0.6
1994 Bal-A	26	53	5	12	3	1	2	9	5	13	0	0	.226	.317	.434	.751	87	-1	6	3.72	1	C-26	1	0.0
Total 4	136	327	35	71	14	2	7	42	37	71	0	0	.217	.304	.336	.641	72	-12	31	2.88	0	C-134/3-1,P-1	6	-0.5

• TAGUCHI, So So Taguchi b: 7/2/1969, Hyogo Prefecture, Japan BR/TR, 5'10", 163 lbs. Deb: 6/10/2002 Career OF: 19-22-13

YEAR TM-L	G	AB	R	H	2B	3B	HR	RBI	BB	SO	SB	CS	AVG	OBP	SLG	OPS	OPS+	BR/A	RC	RC/G	FR	G/POS	WS	TPW
2002 StL-N	19	15	4	6	0	0	0	2	2	1	1	0	.400	.471	.400	.871	136	1	3	8.35	1	O-14(8-6-0)	1	0.3
2003 StL-N	43	54	9	14	3	1	3	13	4	11	0	0	.259	.310	.519	.829	116	1	8	4.99	1	O-38(11-16-13)/2-1	3	0.1
Total 2	62	69	13	20	3	1	3	15	6	12	1	0	.290	.347	.493	.839	121	2	11	5.67	2	/O-52,2-1	4	0.4

• TAITT, Doug Douglas John "Poco" Taitt b: 8/3/1902, Bay City, MI d: 12/12/1970, Portland, OR BL/TR, 6', 176 lbs. Deb: 4/10/1928 Career OF: 58-0-171

YEAR TM-L	G	AB	R	H	2B	3B	HR	RBI	BB	SO	SB	CS	AVG	OBP	SLG	OPS	OPS+	BR/A	RC	RC/G	FR	G/POS	WS	TPW
1928 Bos-A	143	482	51	144	28	14	3	61	36	32	13	6	.299	.350	.434	.784	107	5	74	5.41	9	*O-139(9-0-130)/P-1	13	0.0
1929 Bos-A	26	65	6	18	4	0	0	6	8	5	0	1	.277	.365	.338	.703	84	-1	8	4.47	1	O-21(11-0-11)	1	-0.2
Chi-A	47	124	11	21	7	0	0	12	8	13	0	0	.169	.220	.226	.446	15	-16	7	1.63	2	O-30(0-0-30)	1	-1.5
Yr.	73	189	17	39	11	0	0	18	16	18	0	1	.206	.272	.265	.536	40	-17	15	2.53	3	O-51(11-0-41)	2	-1.7
1931 Phi-N	38	151	13	34	4	2	1	15	4	14	0	....	.225	.245	.298	.543	42	-13	11	2.42	4	O-38(38-0-0)	1	-1.1
1932 Phi-N	4	2	0	0	0	0	0	1	2	0	0	....	.000	.500	.000	.500	43	0	0	3.21	0	....	0	0.0
Total 4	258	824	81	217	43	16	4	95	58	64	13	7	.263	.314	.369	.683	80	-25	100	4.14	16	O-228/P-1	16	-2.8

• TALBOT, Bob Robert Dale Talbot b: 6/6/1927, Visalia, CA BR/TR, 6', 170 lbs. Deb: 9/16/1953 Career OF: 0-118-0

YEAR TM-L	G	AB	R	H	2B	3B	HR	RBI	BB	SO	SB	CS	AVG	OBP	SLG	OPS	OPS+	BR/A	RC	RC/G	FR	G/POS	WS	TPW
1953 Chi-N	8	30	5	10	0	1	0	0	0	4	1	0	.333	.333	.400	.733	88	-0	3	3.90	2	/O-7(0-7-0)	1	0.1
1954 Chi-N	114	403	45	97	15	4	1	19	16	25	3	6	.241	.275	.305	.580	50	-32	32	2.69	-2	*O-111(0-111-0)	3	-3.8
Total 2	122	433	50	107	15	5	1	19	16	29	4	6	.247	.279	.312	.591	53	-32	36	2.77	0	O-118	4	-3.7

• TALTON, Tim Marion Lee Talton b: 1/14/1939, Pikeville, NC BL/TR, 6'3", 200 lbs. Deb: 7/8/1966

YEAR TM-L	G	AB	R	H	2B	3B	HR	RBI	BB	SO	SB	CS	AVG	OBP	SLG	OPS	OPS+	BR/A	RC	RC/G	FR	G/POS	WS	TPW
1966 KC-A	37	53	8	18	3	1	2	6	1	5	0	1	.340	.364	.547	.911	163	3	10	7.65	0	C-14/1-9	3	0.4
1967 KC-A	46	59	7	15	3	1	0	5	7	13	0	0	.254	.333	.339	.672	102	0	6	3.23	-1	C-22/1-1	1	0.0
Total 2	83	112	15	33	6	2	2	11	8	18	0	1	.295	.347	.438	.785	129	4	16	5.08	0	/C-36,1-10	4	0.4

• TAMARGO, John John Felix Tamargo b: 11/7/1951, Tampa, FL BB/TR, 5'10", 180 lbs. Deb: 9/3/1976 C

YEAR TM-L	G	AB	R	H	2B	3B	HR	RBI	BB	SO	SB	CS	AVG	OBP	SLG	OPS	OPS+	BR/A	RC	RC/G	FR	G/POS	WS	TPW
1976 StL-N	10	10	2	3	0	0	0	1	3	0	0	0	.300	.462	.300	.762	118	1	2	4.61	-0	/C-1	0	0.1
1977 StL-N	4	4	0	0	0	0	0	0	0	2	0	0	.000	.000	.000	.000	-102	-1	0	.00	0	/C-1	0	-0.1
1978 StL-N	6	6	0	0	0	0	0	0	0	2	0	0	.000	.000	.000	.000	-102	-2	0	.00	0	/C-1	0	-0.2
SF-N	36	92	6	22	4	1	1	8	18	7	1	1	.239	.364	.337	.701	101	1	12	4.41	-2	C-31	4	0.0
Yr.	42	98	6	22	4	1	1	8	18	9	1	1	.224	.345	.316	.661	91	-1	12	4.09	-2	C-32	4	-0.2
1979 SF-N	30	60	7	12	3	0	2	6	4	8	0	0	.200	.250	.350	.600	66	-3	6	2.98	1	C-17	1	-0.2
Mon-N	12	21	0	8	2	0	0	5	3	3	0	0	.381	.458	.476	.935	157	2	5	9.59	0	/C-4	2	0.2
Yr.	42	81	7	20	5	0	2	11	7	11	0	0	.247	.307	.383	.690	91	-1	11	4.41	1	C-21	3	0.0
1980 Mon-N	37	51	4	14	3	0	1	13	6	5	0	0	.275	.351	.392	.743	107	1	8	5.41	0	C-12	2	0.1
Total 5	135	244	19	59	12	1	4	33	34	27	1	1	.242	.335	.348	.683	93	-2	32	4.39	-2	/C-67	9	-0.1

• TANKERSLEY, Leo Lawrence William Tankersley b: 6/8/1901, Terrell, TX d: 9/18/1980, Dallas, TX BR/TR, 6', 176 lbs. Deb: 7/2/1925

YEAR TM-L	G	AB	R	H	2B	3B	HR	RBI	BB	SO	SB	CS	AVG	OBP	SLG	OPS	OPS+	BR/A	RC	RC/G	FR	G/POS	WS	TPW
1925 Chi-A	1	3	0	0	0	0	0	0	0	0	0	0	.000	.000	.000	.000	-106	-1	0	.00	0	/C-1	0	-0.1

• TANNEHILL, Jesse Jesse Niles "Tanny,Powder" Tannehill
b: 7/14/1874, Dayton, KY d: 9/22/1956, Dayton, KY BB/TL, 5'8", 150 lbs. Deb: 6/17/1894 C/U Career OF: 28-32-27 ♦

YEAR TM-L	G	AB	R	H	2B	3B	HR	RBI	BB	SO	SB	CS	AVG	OBP	SLG	OPS	OPS+	BR/A	RC	RC/G	FR	G/POS	WS	TPW
1894 Cin-N	5	11	0	0	0	0	0	1	1	2	0	....	.000	.083	.000	.083	-76	-2	0	.00	-1	/P-5	1	-0.6
1897 Pit-N	56	184	22	49	8	2	0	22	18	....	4	....	.266	.338	.332	.670	80	-1	23	4.42	4	O-33(4-27-2),P-21	14	0.0
1898 Pit-N	60	152	25	44	9	3	1	17	7	....	4	....	.289	.321	.408	.729	111	9	22	5.18	4	P-43/O-7(3-4-0)	34	2.9
1899 Pit-N	48	136	18	34	5	3	0	11	8	....	2	....	.250	.301	.331	.632	74	5	15	3.75	2	P-40/O-1	27	4.1
1900 Pit-N	34	110	19	37	7	0	0	17	5	....	2	....	.336	.365	.400	.765	110	8	18	6.05	1	P-29/O-4(0-0-4)	23	2.5
1901 Pit-N	42	135	19	33	3	3	1	12	6	....	0	....	.244	.277	.333	.610	74	2	13	3.31	-2	P-32,O-10(9-0-1)	22	3.0
1902 Pit-N	44	148	27	43	6	1	1	17	12	....	3	....	.291	.348	.365	.713	116	8	20	5.11	-2	P-26,O-16(5-0-11)	24	2.2
1903 NY-A	40	111	18	26	6	2	1	13	8	....	1	....	.234	.292	.351	.643	87	5	12	3.72	2	P-32/O-5(4-1-0)	15	0.3
1904 Bos-A	45	122	14	24	2	6	0	6	9	....	1	....	.197	.252	.311	.563	73	3	10	2.73	3	P-33/O-2(2-0-0)	25	2.4
1905 Bos-A	37	93	11	21	2	0	1	12	16	....	1	....	.226	.339	.280	.619	96	6	10	3.48	2	P-37	26	1.5
1906 Bos-A	31	79	12	22	2	2	0	4	6	....	1	....	.278	.329	.354	.684	114	6	10	4.53	0	P-27	13	-0.1
1907 Bos-A	21	51	2	10	3	1	0	6	2	....	0	....	.196	.241	.294	.535	71	1	4	2.40	0	P-18	7	-0.3
1908 Bos-A	1	2	0	1	0	0	0	0	0	....	0	....	.500	.500	.500	1.000	219	0	0	12.79	0	/P-1	0	0.0
Was-A	26	43	1	11	1	0	0	3	2	....	0	....	.256	.289	.279	.568	92	2	3	2.70	1	P-10	1	-1.1
Yr.	27	45	1	12	1	0	0	3	2	....	0	....	.267	.298	.289	.587	98	3	4	3.00	2	P-11	1	-1.2
1909 Was-A	16	36	2	6	1	0	0	1	5	....	0	....	.167	.286	.194	.480	55	-1	2	1.67	0	/O-9(0-0-9),P-3	1	-0.5
1911 Cin-N	1	1	0	0	0	0	0	0	0	1	0	....	.000	.000	.000	.000	-104	-0	0	.00	0	/P-1	0	-0.2
Total 15	507	1414	190	361	55	23	5	142	105	3	19	....	.255	.310	.337	.648	89	53	163	4.00	14	P-358/O-87	233	16.2

• TANNEHILL, Lee Lee Ford Tannehill b: 10/26/1880, Dayton, KY d: 2/16/1938, Live Oak, FL BR/TR, 5'11", 170 lbs. Deb: 4/22/1903

YEAR TM-L	G	AB	R	H	2B	3B	HR	RBI	BB	SO	SB	CS	AVG	OBP	SLG	OPS	OPS+	BR/A	RC	RC/G	FR	G/POS	WS	TPW
1903 Chi-A	138	503	48	113	14	3	2	50	25	....	10	....	.225	.263	.276	.539	65	-21	42	2.74	0	*S-138	8	-1.7
1904 Chi-A	153	547	50	125	31	5	0	61	20	....	14	....	.229	.260	.303	.563	81	-13	50	3.00	26	*3-153	17	2.0
1905 Chi-A	142	480	38	96	17	2	0	39	45	....	8	....	.200	.274	.244	.518	67	-16	38	2.48	23	*3-142	13	1.2
1906*Chi-A	116	378	26	69	8	3	0	33	31	....	7	....	.183	.254	.220	.473	50	-21	25	2.07	26	3-99,S-17	10	1.0
1907 Chi-A	33	108	9	26	2	0	0	11	8	....	3	....	.241	.293	.259	.552	79	-2	10	3.03	2	3-31/S-2	4	0.1
1908 Chi-A	141	482	44	104	15	3	0	35	25	....	6	....	.216	.257	.259	.517	69	-17	34	2.24	10	*3-136/S-5	13	-0.3
1909 Chi-A	155	531	39	118	21	5	0	47	31	....	12	....	.222	.269	.281	.550	77	-15	44	2.62	-1	3-91,S-64	14	-1.3

YEAR TM-L	G	AB	R	H	2B	3B	HR	RBI	BB	SO	SB	CS	AVG	OBP	SLG	OPS	OPS+	BR/A	RC	RC/G	FR	G/POS	WS	TPW
1910 Chi-A	67	230	17	51	10	0	1	21	11	....	3	....	.222	.263	.278	.542	73	-8	18	2.46	5	S-38,1-23/3-6	5	-0.2
1911 Chi-A	141	516	60	131	17	6	0	49	32	....	0	....	.254	.300	.310	.610	72	-20	49	3.12	37	*S-102,2-27/3-7,1-5	15	2.4
1912 Chi-A	4	3	0	0	0	0	0	0	1	....	0	....	.000	.400	.000	.400	18	-0	0	.00	-2	/3-3,S-1	0	-0.2
Total 10	**1090**	**3778**	**331**	**833**	**135**	**27**	**3**	**346**	**229**	**....**	**63**	**....**	**.220**	**.269**	**.273**	**.542**	**70**	**-134**	**310**	**2.63**	**128**	**3-668,S-367/1-28,2-27**	**99**	**3.0**

• TANNER, Chuck Charles William Tanner b: 7/4/1929, New Castle, PA BL/TL, 6', 185 lbs. Deb: 4/12/1955 M Career OF: 146-35-24

YEAR TM-L	G	AB	R	H	2B	3B	HR	RBI	BB	SO	SB	CS	AVG	OBP	SLG	OPS	OPS+	BR/A	RC	RC/G	FR	G/POS	WS	TPW
1955 Mil-N	97	243	27	60	9	3	6	27	27	32	0	0	.247	.322	.383	.705	91	-3	28	3.82	0	0-62(52-0-11)	5	-0.6
1956 Mil-N	60	63	6	15	2	0	1	4	10	10	0	0	.238	.342	.317	.660	84	-1	7	3.52	-1	/0-8(7-0-1)	1	-0.2
1957 Mil-N	22	69	5	17	3	0	2	6	5	4	0	0	.246	.297	.377	.674	86	-2	8	3.95	0	0-18(18-0-0)	2	-0.3
Chi-N	95	318	42	91	16	2	7	42	23	20	0	2	.286	.338	.415	.753	103	0	44	4.88	-2	0-82(59-25-0)	8	-0.7
Yr.	117	387	47	108	19	2	9	48	28	24	0	2	.279	.331	.408	.739	100	-1	51	4.71	-2	*0-100(77-25-0)	10	-1.0
1958 Chi-N	73	103	10	27	6	0	4	17	9	10	1	0	.262	.321	.437	.758	100	-0	14	4.97	-1	0-15(2-3-10)	2	-0.2
1959 Cle-A	14	48	6	12	2	0	1	5	2	9	0	0	.250	.280	.354	.634	76	-2	4	2.99	0	0-10(3-7-0)	1	-0.2
1960 Cle-A	21	25	2	7	1	0	0	4	4	6	1	0	.280	.379	.320	.699	94	0	3	4.54	0	/0-4(4-0-0)	1	0.0
1961 LA-A	7	8	0	1	0	0	0	0	2	2	0	0	.125	.300	.125	.425	16	-1	0	1.76	0	/0-1	0	-0.1
1962 LA-A	7	8	0	1	0	0	0	0	0	0	0	0	.125	.125	.125	.250	-34	-1	0	.00	0	/0-2(1-0-1)	0	-0.2
Total 8	**396**	**885**	**98**	**231**	**39**	**5**	**21**	**105**	**82**	**93**	**2**	**2**	**.261**	**.325**	**.388**	**.713**	**93**	**-9**	**109**	**4.21**	**-5**	**0-202**	**20**	**-2.4**

• TAPPAN, Walter Walter Van Dorn "Tap" Tappan b: 10/8/1890, Carlinville, IL d: 12/19/1967, Lynwood, CA BR/TR, 5'8", 158 lbs. Deb: 4/16/1914

YEAR TM-L	G	AB	R	H	2B	3B	HR	RBI	BB	SO	SB	CS	AVG	OBP	SLG	OPS	OPS+	BR/A	RC	RC/G	FR	G/POS	WS	TPW
1914 KC-F	18	39	1	8	1	0	1	3	1	0	1	....	.205	.225	.308	.533	53	-3	3	2.20	-2	/S-8,3-6,2-1	0	-0.4

• TAPPE, El Elvin Walter Tappe b: 5/21/1927, Quincy, IL d: 10/10/1998, Quincy, IL BR/TR, 5'11", 180 lbs. Deb: 4/24/1954 M/C

YEAR TM-L	G	AB	R	H	2B	3B	HR	RBI	BB	SO	SB	CS	AVG	OBP	SLG	OPS	OPS+	BR/A	RC	RC/G	FR	G/POS	WS	TPW
1954 Chi-N	46	119	5	22	3	0	0	4	10	9	0	0	.185	.248	.210	.458	20	-14	7	1.75	0	C-46	1	-1.2
1955 Chi-N	2	0	0	0	0	0	0	0	0	0	0	0	....	....	....	....	-100	0	0	....	0	/C-2	0	0.0
1956 Chi-N	3	1	0	0	0	0	0	0	1	0	0	0	.000	.500	.000	.500	51	0	0	3.51	0	/C-3	0	0.0
1958 Chi-N	17	28	2	6	0	0	0	4	3	1	0	0	.214	.290	.214	.505	37	-2	1	1.60	-1	C-16	0	-0.3
1960 Chi-N	51	103	11	24	7	0	0	3	11	12	0	1	.233	.313	.301	.614	70	-4	10	3.09	3	C-49	2	0.1
1962 Chi-N	26	53	3	11	0	0	0	6	4	3	0	0	.208	.288	.208	.496	34	-5	3	1.96	2	C-26	1	-0.2
Total 6	**145**	**304**	**21**	**63**	**10**	**0**	**0**	**17**	**29**	**25**	**0**	**1**	**.207**	**.283**	**.240**	**.523**	**42**	**-25**	**22**	**2.23**	**4**	**C-142**	**4**	**-1.6**

• TAPPE, Ted Theodore Nash Tappe b: 2/2/1931, Seattle, WA BL/TR, 6'3", 185 lbs. Deb: 9/14/1950

YEAR TM-L	G	AB	R	H	2B	3B	HR	RBI	BB	SO	SB	CS	AVG	OBP	SLG	OPS	OPS+	BR/A	RC	RC/G	FR	G/POS	WS	TPW
1950 Cin-N	7	5	1	1	0	0	1	1	1	1	0	....	.200	.333	.800	1.133	187	1	1	9.59	0	....	0	0.1
1951 Cin-N	4	3	0	1	0	0	0	0	0	0	0	0	.333	.333	.333	.667	79	-0	0	4.61	0	....	0	0.0
1955 Chi-N	23	50	12	13	2	0	4	10	11	11	0	0	.260	.413	.540	.953	151	4	12	8.91	1	0-15(0-0-15)	3	0.4
Total 3	**34**	**58**	**13**	**15**	**2**	**0**	**5**	**11**	**12**	**12**	**0**	**0**	**.259**	**.403**	**.552**	**.955**	**151**	**5**	**14**	**8.78**	**1**	**/0-15**	**3**	**0.5**

• TARASCO, Tony Anthony Giacinto Tarasco b: 12/9/1970, New York, NY BL/TR, 6', 205 lbs. Deb: 4/30/1993 Career OF: 79-12-245

YEAR TM-L	G	AB	R	H	2B	3B	HR	RBI	BB	SO	SB	CS	AVG	OBP	SLG	OPS	OPS+	BR/A	RC	RC/G	FR	G/POS	WS	TPW
1993★Atl-N	24	35	6	8	2	0	0	2	0	5	0	1	.229	.250	.286	.536	43	-3	2	1.84	0	0-12(4-0-8)	0	-0.4
1994 Atl-N	87	132	16	36	6	0	5	19	9	17	5	0	.273	.319	.432	.751	91	-1	18	4.56	0	0-45(26-0-22)	4	-0.2
1995 Mon-N	126	438	64	109	18	4	14	40	51	78	24	3	.249	.330	.404	.734	89	-3	64	5.12	0	*0-116(11-0-105)	12	-1.0
1996★Bal-A	31	84	14	20	3	0	1	9	7	15	5	3	.238	.297	.310	.606	54	-6	8	3.03	1	/D-6,0-5(0-1-22)	0	-0.6
1997 Bal-A	100	166	26	34	8	1	7	26	25	33	2	2	.205	.313	.392	.704	85	-4	21	4.07	2	0-23(7-8-68)/D-2	5	-0.5
1998 Cin-N	15	24	5	5	2	0	1	4	3	5	0	0	.208	.296	.417	.713	84	-1	3	4.36	0	0-81(4-1-2)	0	-0.1
1999 NY-A	14	31	5	5	2	0	0	3	3	5	1	0	.161	.235	.226	.461	19	-4	2	1.70	-1	/0-7(9-0-5)	0	-0.5
2002 NY-N	60	96	15	24	5	0	6	15	8	13	2	1	.250	.308	.490	.797	110	1	14	4.97	3	0-12(18-2-13)/1-7,D-2	2	0.3
Total 8	**457**	**1006**	**151**	**241**	**46**	**5**	**34**	**118**	**106**	**171**	**39**	**10**	**.240**	**.315**	**.397**	**.711**	**84**	**-22**	**131**	**4.41**	**5**	**0-301/D-10,1-7**	**23**	**-2.9**

• TARBERT, Arlie Wilbur Arlington Tarbert b: 9/10/1904, Cleveland, OH d: 11/27/1946, Cleveland, OH BR/TR, 6', 160 lbs. Deb: 6/18/1927 Career OF: 10-3-20

YEAR TM-L	G	AB	R	H	2B	3B	HR	RBI	BB	SO	SB	CS	AVG	OBP	SLG	OPS	OPS+	BR/A	RC	RC/G	FR	G/POS	WS	TPW
1927 Bos-A	33	69	5	13	1	0	0	5	3	12	0	0	.188	.253	.203	.456	20	-8	4	1.80	0	0-27(10-3-14)	0	-0.8
1928 Bos-A	6	17	1	3	1	0	0	2	1	1	1	0	.176	.222	.235	.458	21	-2	1	1.89	0	/0-6(0-0-6)	0	-0.2
Total 2	**39**	**86**	**6**	**16**	**2**	**0**	**0**	**7**	**4**	**13**	**1**	**0**	**.186**	**.247**	**.209**	**.457**	**20**	**-10**	**5**	**1.81**	**1**	**/0-33**	**0**	**-1.0**

• TARTABULL, Danny Danilo (Mora) Tartabull b: 10/30/1962, San Juan, Puerto Rico BR/TR, 6'1.5", 205 lbs. Deb: 9/7/1984 Career OF: 15-0-904

YEAR TM-L	G	AB	R	H	2B	3B	HR	RBI	BB	SO	SB	CS	AVG	OBP	SLG	OPS	OPS+	BR/A	RC	RC/G	FR	G/POS	WS	TPW
1984 Sea-A	10	20	3	6	1	0	2	7	2	3	0	0	.300	.391	.650	1.041	185	2	5	9.65	0	/S-8,2-1	2	0.3
1985 Sea-A	19	61	8	20	7	1	1	7	8	14	1	0	.328	.406	.525	.930	152	5	14	8.70	-1	S-16/3-4	3	0.5
1986 Sea-A	137	511	76	138	25	6	25	96	61	157	4	8	.270	.349	.489	.838	124	14	85	5.80	-5	*0-101(14-0-87),2-31/D-3,3	15	0.6
1987 KC-A	158	582	95	180	27	3	34	101	79	136	9	4	.309	.393	.541	.934	141	35	124	7.90	-7	*0-149(0-0-150)/D-6	24	2.0
1988 KC-A	146	507	80	139	38	3	26	102	76	119	8	5	.274	.373	.515	.888	145	31	99	6.88	-4	*0-130(0-0-130),D-13	22	2.3
1989 KC-A	133	441	54	118	22	0	18	62	69	123	4	2	.268	.370	.440	.810	128	18	74	5.86	-2	0-71(0-0-73),D-55	13	1.3
1990 KC-A	88	313	41	84	19	0	15	60	36	93	1	1	.268	.344	.473	.817	128	11	50	5.56	-3	0-52(0-0-52),D-32	10	0.6
1991 KC-A★	132	484	78	153	35	3	31	100	65	121	6	3	.316	.400	**.593**	.993	170	46	116	8.99	-11	*0-124(0-0-124)/D-6	28	3.2
1992 NY-A	123	421	72	112	19	0	25	85	103	115	2	2	.266	.410	.489	.900	152	34	91	7.64	-2	0-69(1-0-68),D-53	23	2.9
1993 NY-A	138	513	87	128	33	2	31	102	92	156	0	0	.250	.366	.503	.869	135	27	99	6.72	-1	D-88,0-50(0-0-50)	21	1.7
1994 NY-A	104	399	68	102	24	1	19	67	66	111	1	1	.256	.363	.464	.826	115	10	68	5.89	1	D-78,0-26(0-0-26)	10	0.4
1995 NY-A	59	192	25	43	12	0	6	28	33	54	0	0	.224	.341	.380	.721	88	-3	26	4.39	0	D-39,0-18(0-0-18)	3	-0.5
Oak-A	24	88	9	23	4	0	2	7	10	28	0	2	.261	.337	.375	.712	90	-2	10	3.92	-0	D-22/0-1	1	-0.3
Yr.	83	280	34	66	16	0	8	35	43	82	0	2	.236	.340	.379	.718	89	-5	36	4.24	0	D-61,0-19(0-0-19)	4	-0.9
1996 Chi-A	132	472	58	120	23	3	27	101	64	128	1	2	.254	.343	.487	.831	112	7	79	5.79	-2	0-29(0-0-122),D-10	13	-0.2
1997 Phi-N	3	7	2	0	0	0	0	0	4	4	0	0	.000	.364	.000	.364	5	-1	0	1.46	0	*0-122(0-0-3)	0	-0.1
Total 14	**1406**	**5011**	**756**	**1366**	**289**	**22**	**262**	**925**	**768**	**1362**	**37**	**30**	**.273**	**.371**	**.496**	**.867**	**133**	**236**	**940**	**6.62**	**-37**	**0-942,D-405/2-32,S-24,3-5**	**188**	**14.6**

• TARTABULL, Jose Jose Milages (Guzman) Tartabull b: 11/27/1938, Cienfuegos, Cuba BL/TL, 5'11", 165 lbs. Deb: 4/10/1962 Career OF: 129-342-88

YEAR TM-L	G	AB	R	H	2B	3B	HR	RBI	BB	SO	SB	CS	AVG	OBP	SLG	OPS	OPS+	BR/A	RC	RC/G	FR	G/POS	WS	TPW
1962 KC-A	107	310	49	86	6	5	0	22	20	19	19	5	.277	.323	.329	.652	74	-9	36	4.08	2	0-85(1-85-0)	7	-1.0
1963 KC-A	79	242	27	58	8	5	1	19	17	17	16	1	.240	.290	.326	.616	69	-7	26	3.64	-4	0-71(1-70-0)	5	-1.3
1964 KC-A	104	100	9	20	2	0	0	3	5	12	4	0	.200	.238	.220	.458	28	-9	6	2.03	1	0-59(44-13-5)	0	-1.0
1965 KC-A	68	218	28	68	11	4	1	19	18	20	11	5	.312	.364	.413	.777	122	6	33	5.39	2	0-54(26-27-8)	9	0.6
1966 KC-A	37	127	13	30	2	3	0	4	11	13	8	1	.236	.297	.299	.596	74	-3	13	3.53	-1	0-32(1-32-0)	4	-0.5
Bos-A	68	195	28	54	7	4	0	11	6	11	11	3	.277	.299	.354	.652	79	-5	20	3.58	-4	0-47(0-47-0)	4	-1.0
Yr.	105	322	41	84	9	7	0	15	17	24	19	4	.261	.298	.332	.630	77	-7	34	3.56	-5	0-79(1-79-0)	8	-1.5
1967★Bos-A	115	247	36	55	1	2	0	10	23	26	6	6	.223	.289	.243	.532	54	-15	18	2.31	-3	0-83(12-19-55)	1	-2.3
1968 Bos-A	72	139	24	39	6	0	0	6	6	5	2	3	.281	.310	.324	.634	87	-3	14	3.55	0	0-43(12-11-20)	3	-0.6
1969 Oak-A	75	266	28	71	11	1	0	11	9	11	3	4	.267	.291	.316	.607	73	-12	24	3.18	-1	0-63(28-36-0)	4	-1.6
1970 Oak-A	24	13	5	3	2	0	0	2	0	2	1	0	.231	.231	.385	.615	69	-0	1	3.18	0	/0-6(4-2-0)	0	-0.1
Total 9	**749**	**1857**	**247**	**484**	**56**	**24**	**2**	**107**	**115**	**136**	**81**	**28**	**.261**	**.304**	**.320**	**.624**	**75**	**-56**	**192**	**3.54**	**-9**	**0-543**	**37**	**-8.9**

• TARVER, La Schelle La Schelle Tarver b: 1/30/1959, Modesto, CA BL/TL, 5'11", 165 lbs. Deb: 7/12/1986

YEAR TM-L	G	AB	R	H	2B	3B	HR	RBI	BB	SO	SB	CS	AVG	OBP	SLG	OPS	OPS+	BR/A	RC	RC/G	FR	G/POS	WS	TPW
1986 Bos-A	13	25	3	3	0	0	0	1	1	4	0	1	.120	.154	.120	.274	-24	-5	0	.44	0	/0-9(3-7-0)	0	-0.5

• TASBY, Willie Willie Tasby b: 1/8/1933, Shreveport, LA BR/TR, 5'11", 175 lbs. Deb: 9/9/1958 Career OF: 65-460-48

YEAR TM-L	G	AB	R	H	2B	3B	HR	RBI	BB	SO	SB	CS	AVG	OBP	SLG	OPS	OPS+	BR/A	RC	RC/G	FR	G/POS	WS	TPW
1958 Bal-A	18	50	6	10	3	0	1	1	7	15	1	1	.200	.310	.320	.630	78	-2	5	3.59	-1	0-16(6-12-5)	1	-0.3
1959 Bal-A	142	505	69	126	16	5	13	48	34	80	3	5	.250	.305	.378	.683	88	-11	57	3.88	-1	*0-137(5-132-1)	12	-1.8
1960 Bal-A	39	85	9	18	2	1	0	3	9	12	1	0	.212	.295	.259	.554	52	-5	7	2.65	0	0-36(17-9-18)	1	-0.7
Bos-A	105	385	68	108	17	1	7	37	51	54	3	1	.281	.372	.384	.756	101	3	58	5.28	-5	*0-102(0-102-0)	11	-0.7
Yr.	144	470	77	126	19	2	7	40	60	66	4	1	.268	.358	.362	.720	93	-2	65	4.78	-5	*0-138(17-111-18)	12	-1.4
1961 Was-A	141	494	54	124	13	2	17	63	58	94	4	10	.251	.332	.389	.721	96	-6	60	4.05	-2	*0-139(0-138-1)	11	-1.2
1962 Was-A	11	34	4	7	0	0	0	0	2	6	0	0	.206	.250	.206	.456	24	-4	2	1.61	-1	0-10(7-3-0)	0	-0.5
Cle-A	75	199	25	48	7	0	4	17	25	41	0	2	.241	.326	.337	.663	81	-6	22	3.69	-1	0-66(12-57-10)/3-1	4	-0.9
Yr.	86	233	29	55	7	0	4	17	27	47	0	2	.236	.315	.318	.633	73	-9	23	3.38	-2	0-76(19-60-10)/3-1	4	-1.4
1963 Cle-A	52	116	11	26	3	1	4	5	15	25	0	1	.224	.318	.371	.689	93	-1	13	3.49	-2	0-37(18-7-13)/2-1	2	-0.6
Total 6	**583**	**1868**	**246**	**467**	**61**	**10**	**46**	**174**	**201**	**327**	**12**	**20**	**.250**	**.328**	**.367**	**.695**	**90**	**-31**	**224**	**4.05**	**-13**	**0-543/2-1,3-1**	**42**	**-6.6**

YEAR TM-L	G	AB	R	H	2B	3B	HR	RBI	BB	SO	SB	CS	AVG	OBP	SLG	OPS	OPS+	BR/A	RC	RC/G	FR	G/POS	WS	TPW
• TATE, Bennie	Henry Bennett Tate b: 12/3/1901, Whitwell, TN d: 10/27/1973, West Frankfort, IL BL/TR, 5'8", 165 lbs. Deb: 4/29/1924																							
1924*Was-A	21	43	2	13	2	0	0	7	1	2	0	0	.302	.318	.349	.667	74	-2	5	4.03	-3	C-14	1	-0.4
1925 Was-A	16	27	0	13	3	0	0	7	2	2	0	0	.481	.517	.593	1.110	184	4	8	14.44	0	C-14	2	0.4
1926 Was-A	59	142	17	38	5	2	1	13	15	1	0	0	.268	.338	.352	.690	82	-3	18	4.39	1	C-45	5	0.0
1927 Was-A	61	131	12	41	5	1	1	24	8	4	0	3	.313	.357	.389	.746	95	-2	17	4.70	-1	C-39	5	-0.1
1928 Was-A	57	122	10	30	6	0	0	15	10	4	0	4	.246	.303	.295	.598	58	-9	10	2.75	1	C-30	2	-0.6
1929 Was-A	81	265	26	78	12	3	0	30	16	8	2	5	.294	.335	.362	.697	79	-10	31	4.12	2	C-74	7	-0.3
1930 Was-A	14	20	1	5	0	0	0	2	0	1	0	0	.250	.250	.250	.500	27	-2	1	2.12	0	/C-9	0	-0.2
Chi-A	72	230	26	73	11	2	0	27	18	10	2	1	.317	.367	.383	.750	94	-1	33	5.34	-1	C-70	7	0.1
Yr.	86	250	27	78	11	2	0	29	18	11	2	1	.312	.358	.372	.730	89	-4	34	5.07	-1	C-79	7	-0.1
1931 Chi-A	89	273	27	73	12	3	0	22	26	10	1	1	.267	.331	.333	.664	80	-6	31	4.00	8	C-85	8	0.6
1932 Chi-A	4	10	1	1	0	0	0	0	1	0	0	0	.100	.182	.100	.282	-27	-2	0	.65	0	/C-4	0	-0.1
Bos-A	81	273	21	67	12	5	2	26	20	6	0	1	.245	.297	.348	.645	68	-13	28	3.58	5	C-76	3	-0.4
Yr.	85	283	22	68	12	5	2	26	21	6	0	1	.240	.293	.339	.632	65	-15	29	3.46	5	C-80	3	-0.5
1934 Chi-N	11	24	1	3	0	0	0	0	1	3	0	....	.125	.160	.125	.285	-23	-4	0	.31	0	/C-8	0	-0.4
Total 10	566	1560	144	435	68	16	4	173	118	51	5	15	.279	.330	.351	.681	78	-52	183	4.13	12	C-468	40	-1.3
• TATE, Hughie	Hugh Henry Tate b: 5/19/1880, Everett, PA d: 8/7/1956, Greenville, PA BR/TR, 5'11", 190 lbs. Deb: 9/21/1905																							
1905 Was-A	4	13	1	4	0	1	0	2	0	....	1	....	.308	.308	.462	.769	149	1	2	6.50	0	/O-3(3-0-0)	1	0.1
• TATE, Lee	Lee Willie "Skeeter" Tate b: 3/18/1932, Black Rock, AR BR/TR, 5'10", 165 lbs. Deb: 9/12/1958																							
1958 StL-N	10	35	4	7	2	0	0	1	4	3	0	0	.200	.282	.257	.539	42	-3	3	2.40	-2	/S-9	0	-0.4
1959 StL-N	41	50	5	7	1	1	1	4	5	7	0	0	.140	.232	.260	.492	29	-5	3	1.67	-4	S-39/2-2,3-2	1	-0.8
Total 2	51	85	9	14	3	1	1	5	9	10	0	0	.165	.253	.259	.511	34	-8	5	1.95	-6	/S-48,2-2,3-2	1	-1.2
• TATE, Pop	Edward Christopher "Dimples" Tate b: 12/22/1860, Richmond, VA d: 6/25/1932, Richmond, VA BR/TL, 5'10", 178 lbs. Deb: 9/26/1885 U Career OF: 0-0-9																							
1885 Bos-N	4	13	1	2	0	0	0	2	1	3	....	....	.154	.214	.154	.368	21	-1	0	1.08	2	/C-4	0	0.1
1886 Bos-N	31	106	13	24	3	1	0	3	7	17	0	....	.226	.274	.274	.548	69	-4	8	2.69	-3	C-31	2	-0.3
1887 Bos-N	60	239	34	68	5	3	0	27	8	9	7	....	.285	.296	.307	.604	70	-9	24	3.67	15	C-53/O-8(0-0-8)	5	0.8
1888 Bos-N	41	148	18	34	7	1	1	6	8	7	3	....	.230	.278	.311	.589	84	-3	14	3.31	-2	C-41/O-1	3	-0.1
1889 Bal-a	72	253	28	46	6	3	1	27	13	37	4	....	.182	.236	.241	.477	37	-21	16	2.01	-6	C-62,1-10	3	-2.0
1890 Bal-a	19	71	7	13	1	1	0	6	4	....	3	....	.183	.284	.225	.509	46	-5	6	2.53	1	C-11/1-8	1	-0.3
Total 6	227	830	101	187	22	9	2	71	41	73	17	....	.225	.269	.274	.543	59	-43	68	2.80	7	C-202/1-18,O-9	14	-1.8
• TATIS, Fernando	Fernando Tatis b: 1/1/1975, San Pedro de Macoris, Dominican Republic BR/TR, 6'1", 175 lbs. Deb: 7/26/1997																							
1997 Tex-A	60	223	29	57	9	0	8	29	14	42	3	0	.256	.300	.404	.703	77	-7	26	4.03	-9	3-60	3	-1.5
1998 Tex-A	95	330	41	89	17	2	3	32	12	66	6	2	.270	.303	.361	.664	69	-15	34	3.57	8	3-94	4	-0.6
StL-N	55	202	28	58	16	2	8	26	24	57	7	3	.287	.368	.505	.873	128	8	37	6.47	0	3-55/S-3	5	0.9
1999 StL-N	149	537	104	160	31	2	34	107	82	128	21	9	.298	.406	.553	.959	139	34	125	8.39	1	*3-147	23	3.6
2000*StL-N	96	324	59	82	21	1	18	64	57	94	2	3	.253	.381	.491	.872	118	9	60	6.24	-9	3-91/D-2,1-1	11	0.1
2001 Mon-N	41	145	20	37	9	0	2	11	16	43	0	0	.255	.345	.359	.704	81	-4	18	4.23	-11	3-41	2	-1.3
2002 Mon-N	114	381	43	87	18	1	15	55	35	90	2	2	.228	.307	.399	.706	81	-12	44	3.74	-9	3-99/D-4	5	-2.0
2003 Mon-N	53	175	15	34	6	0	2	15	18	40	2	1	.194	.281	.263	.543	36	-17	13	2.28	-1	3-49	1	-1.7
Total 7	663	2317	339	604	127	8	90	339	258	560	43	20	.261	.347	.439	.786	99	-3	357	5.26	-32	3-636/D-6,S-3,1-1	54	-2.6
• TATUM, Jarvis	Jarvis Tatum b: 10/11/1946, Fresno, CA d: 1/6/2003, Los Angeles, CA BR/TR, 6', 185 lbs. Deb: 9/7/1968 Career OF: 8-54-17																							
1968 Cal-A	17	51	7	9	1	0	0	2	0	9	0	0	.176	.176	.196	.373	13	-5	2	.98	0	O-11(0-11-0)	0	-0.7
1969 Cal-A	10	22	2	7	0	0	0	0	0	6	0	1	.318	.318	.318	.636	83	-1	2	2.53	0	/O-5(0-0-5)	0	-0.2
1970 Cal-A	75	181	28	43	7	0	0	6	17	35	1	0	.238	.303	.276	.579	63	-8	15	2.85	0	O-58(8-43-12)	3	-1.1
Total 3	102	254	37	59	8	0	0	8	17	50	1	1	.232	.280	.264	.544	55	-15	18	2.43	-1	/O-74	3	-2.0
• TATUM, Jim	James Ray Tatum b: 10/9/1967, San Diego, CA BR/TR, 6'2", 200 lbs. Deb: 9/18/1992 Career OF: 8-0-1																							
1992 Mil-A	5	8	0	1	0	0	0	0	1	2	0	0	.125	.222	.125	.347		-1	0	1.08	-1	/3-5	0	-0.2
1993 Col-N	92	98	7	20	5	0	1	12	5	27	0	0	.204	.250	.286	.536	37	-9	8	2.53	-1	1-12/3-6,O-3(2-0-1)	0	-1.1
1995 Col-N	34	34	4	8	1	1	0	4	1	7	0	0	.235	.257	.324	.581	40	-3	3	2.57	0	/O-2(2-0-0),C-1	0	-0.3
1996 Bos-A	2	8	1	1	0	0	0	0	0	2	0	0	.125	.125	.125	.250	-36	-2	0	.48	0	/3-2	0	-0.2
SD-N	5	3	0	0	0	0	0	0	0	1	0	0	.000	.000	.000	.000	-106	-1	0	.00	0	/3-1	0	-0.1
1998 NY-N	35	50	4	9	1	2	2	13	3	19	0	0	.180	.226	.400	.626	61	-3	5	2.89	0	/1-9,C-4,3-3,O-3(4-0-0),D-1	1	-0.4
Total 5	173	201	16	39	7	3	3	29	10	58	0	0	.194	.236	.303	.539	38	-19	15	2.44	-3	/1-21,3-17,O-8,C-5,D-1	1	-2.2
• TATUM, Tommy	V T Tatum b: 7/16/1919, Decatur, TX d: 11/7/1989, Oklahoma City, OK BR/TR, 6', 185 lbs. Deb: 8/1/1941 Career OF: 12-40-5																							
1941 Bro-N	8	12	1	2	1	0	0	1	1	3	0	....	.167	.231	.250	.481	34	-1	1	2.03	-0	/O-4(1-3-0)	0	-0.1
1947 Bro-N	4	6	0	0	0	0	0	0	0	1	0	....	.000	.000	.000	.000	-96	-2	0	.00	0	/O-3(2-0-1)	0	-0.2
Cin-N	69	176	19	48	5	2	1	16	16	16	7	....	.273	.333	.341	.674	80	-5	21	4.28	3	O-49(9-37-4)/2-1	4	-0.3
Yr.	73	182	19	48	5	2	1	16	16	17	7	....	.264	.323	.330	.653	75	-7	21	4.09	3	O-52(11-37-5)/2-1	4	-0.5
Total 2	81	194	20	50	6	2	1	17	17	20	7	....	.258	.318	.325	.642	72	-8	22	3.95	3	/O-56,2-1	4	-0.7
• TAUBENSEE, Eddie	Edward Kenneth Taubensee b: 10/31/1968, Beeville, TX BL/TR, 6'4", 205 lbs. Deb: 5/18/1991																							
1991 Cle-A	26	66	5	16	2	1	0	8	5	16	0	0	.242	.296	.303	.599	66	-3	6	3.08	-1	C-25	1	-0.3
1992 Hou-N	104	297	23	66	15	0	5	28	31	78	2	1	.222	.300	.323	.623	80	-8	30	3.41	3	*C-103	8	0.1
1993 Hou-N	94	288	26	72	11	1	9	42	21	44	1	0	.250	.301	.389	.690	86	-6	32	3.83	-1	C-90	7	-0.1
1994 Hou-N	5	10	0	1	0	0	0	0	0	3	0	0	.100	.100	.100	.200	-50	-2	0	.00	0	/C-5	0	-0.2
Cin-N	61	177	29	52	8	2	8	21	15	28	2	0	.294	.349	.497	.846	118	5	31	6.51	-4	C-61	6	0.4
Yr.	66	187	29	53	8	2	8	21	15	31	2	0	.283	.337	.476	.813	110	3	31	6.04	-4	C-66	6	0.2
1995*Cin-N	80	218	32	62	14	2	9	44	22	52	2	2	.284	.355	.491	.846	121	6	39	6.43	-4	C-65/1-3	9	0.6
1996 Cin-N	108	327	46	95	20	0	12	48	26	64	3	4	.291	.343	.462	.805	111	3	51	5.57	0	C-94	11	0.8
1997 Cin-N	108	254	26	68	18	0	10	34	22	66	0	1	.268	.329	.457	.785	101	-1	39	5.36	-2	C-64/1-7,O-4(6-0-5),D-3	7	0.0
1998 Cin-N	130	431	61	120	27	0	11	72	52	93	1	0	.278	.356	.418	.774	101	2	67	5.62	-3	*C-126	16	0.7
1999 Cin-N	126	424	58	132	22	2	21	87	30	67	0	2	.311	.358	.521	.879	116	8	75	6.49	-3	*C-124	15	1.2
2000 Cin-N	81	266	29	71	12	0	6	24	21	44	0	0	.267	.325	.380	.705	76	-10	32	4.26	-4	C-76	4	-0.8
2001 Cle-A	52	116	16	29	2	1	3	11	10	19	0	0	.250	.315	.362	.677	77	-4	13	3.87	-6	C-38/D-5	1	-0.7
Total 11	975	2874	351	784	151	9	94	419	255	574	11	10	.273	.334	.430	.764	99	-12	415	5.12	-25	C-871/1-10,D-8,O-4	85	1.5
• TAUBY, Fred	Frederick Joseph Tauby b: 3/27/1906, Canton, OH d: 11/23/1955, Concord, CA BR/TR, 5'9.5", 168 lbs. Deb: 9/1/1935 Career OF: 4-4-6																							
1935 Chi-A	13	32	5	4	1	0	0	2	2	3	0	0	.125	.176	.156	.333	-13	-5	1	.93	2	/O-7(1-1-5)	0	-0.4
1937 Phi-N	11	20	2	0	0	0	0	3	0	5	1	....	.000	.000	.000	.000	-92	-5	0	.00	0	/O-7(3-3-1)	0	-0.6
Total 2	24	52	7	4	1	0	0	5	2	8	1	0	.077	.111	.096	.207	-41	-11	1	.56	2	/O-14	0	-1.0
• TAUSSIG, Don	Donald Franklin Taussig b: 2/19/1932, New York, NY BR/TR, 6', 180 lbs. Deb: 4/23/1958 Career OF: 79-20-41																							
1958 SF-N	39	50	10	10	0	0	1	4	3	8	0	0	.200	.245	.260	.505	35	-5	3	2.24	0	O-36(27-0-11)	0	-0.6
1961 StL-N	98	188	27	54	14	5	2	25	16	34	2	2	.287	.343	.447	.790	98	-1	28	5.09	3	O-87(48-20-30)	6	-0.1
1962 Hou-N	16	25	1	5	0	0	1	1	2	11	0	0	.200	.259	.320	.579	59	-2	2	2.43	0	/O-4(4-0-0)	0	-0.1
Total 3	153	263	38	69	14	5	4	30	21	53	2	2	.262	.317	.399	.716	83	-7	33	4.27	3	O-127	6	-0.8
• TAVAREZ, Jesus	Jesus Rafael (Alcantaras) Tavarez b: 3/26/1971, Santo Domingo, Dominican Republic BB/TR, 6', 170 lbs. Deb: 5/23/1994 Career OF: 34-113-60																							
1994 Fla-N	17	39	4	7	0	0	0	4	1	5	1	1	.179	.200	.179	.379		-6	1	1.13	1	O-11(1-2-8)	1	-0.6
1995 Fla-N	63	190	31	55	6	2	2	13	16	27	7	5	.289	.348	.374	.722	90	-3	25	4.71	-2	O-61(4-47-32)	6	-0.6
1996 Fla-N	98	114	14	25	3	0	0	6	7	18	5	1	.219	.264	.246	.510	37	-10	8	2.26	-3	O-11(25-30-12)	1	-1.3
1997 Bos-A	42	69	12	12	3	1	0	9	4	9	0	0	.174	.219	.246	.466	21	-8	4	1.58	-1	O-65(4-29-4)/D-2	1	-0.9

YEAR TM-L	G	AB	R	H	2B	3B	HR	RBI	BB	SO	SB	CS	AVG	OBP	SLG	OPS	OPS+	BR/A	RC	RC/G	FR	G/POS	WS	TPW
1998 Bal-A	8	11	2	2	0	0	1	1	2	3	0	1	.182	.308	.455	.762	96	-1	1	3.44	-1	0-35(0-5-4)	0	-0.1
Total 5	228	423	63	101	12	3	3	33	30	62	13	8	.239	.291	.303	.593	57	-28	39	3.10	-4	0-183/D-2	9	-3.4

• TAVENER, Jackie John Adam "Rabbit" Tavener b: 12/27/1897, Celina, OH d: 9/14/1969, Fort Worth, TX BL/TR, 5'5", 138 lbs. Deb: 9/24/1921

YEAR TM-L	G	AB	R	H	2B	3B	HR	RBI	BB	SO	SB	CS	AVG	OBP	SLG	OPS	OPS+	BR/A	RC	RC/G	FR	G/POS	WS	TPW
1921 Det-A	2	4	0	0	0	0	0	0	0	1	0	0	.000	.000	.000	.000	-101	-1	0	.00	0	/S-2	0	-0.1
1925 Det-A	134	453	45	111	11	11	0	47	39	60	5	4	.245	.309	.318	.627	60	-27	47	3.34	-3	*S-134	8	-1.5
1926 Det-A	156	532	65	141	22	14	1	58	52	53	8	7	.265	.332	.365	.696	80	-16	66	4.12	9	*S-156	16	1.0
1927 Det-A	116	419	60	115	22	9	5	59	36	38	19	8	.274	.333	.406	.739	90	-6	58	4.65	-1	*S-114	13	0.5
1928 Det-A	132	473	59	123	24	15	5	52	33	51	13	8	.260	.314	.406	.720	86	-11	60	4.23	12	*S-131	13	1.5
1929 Cle-A	92	250	25	53	9	4	2	27	26	28	1	4	.212	.289	.304	.593	51	-20	23	2.80	9	S-89	5	-0.2
Total 6	632	2131	254	543	88	53	13	243	186	231	46	31	.255	.318	.364	.682	75	-82	254	3.90	28	S-626	55	1.2

• TAVERAS, Alex Alejandro Antonio (Betances) Taveras b: 10/9/1955, Santiago, Dominican Republic BR/TR, 5'10", 155 lbs. Deb: 9/9/1976

YEAR TM-L	G	AB	R	H	2B	3B	HR	RBI	BB	SO	SB	CS	AVG	OBP	SLG	OPS	OPS+	BR/A	RC	RC/G	FR	G/POS	WS	TPW
1976 Hou-N	14	46	3	10	0	0	0	2	2	1	1	2	.217	.250	.217	.467	37	-5	2	1.24	-1	/2-7,S-7	0	-0.4
1982 LA-N	11	3	1	1	1	0	0	2	0	1	0	0	.333	.333	.667	1.000	178	0	1	9.00	-1	/2-4,3-4,S-2	0	-0.1
1983 LA-N	10	4	0	0	0	0	0	0	0	1	0	0	.000	.000	.000	.000	-101	-1	0	.00	-2	/S-3,2-2,3-1	0	-0.3
Total 3	35	53	4	11	1	0	0	4	2	3	1	2	.208	.236	.226	.463	34	-5	3	1.47	-4	/2-13,S-12,3-5	0	-0.8

• TAVERAS, Frank Franklin Crisostomo (Fabian) Taveras b: 12/24/1949, Las Matas de Santa Cruz, Dominican Republic BR/TR, 6', 168 lbs. Deb: 9/25/1971

YEAR TM-L	G	AB	R	H	2B	3B	HR	RBI	BB	SO	SB	CS	AVG	OBP	SLG	OPS	OPS+	BR/A	RC	RC/G	FR	G/POS	WS	TPW
1971 Pit-N	1	0	0	0	0	0	0	0	0	0	0	0	....	....	....	....	-99	0	0	....	0	....	0	0.0
1972 Pit-N	4	3	0	0	0	0	0	0	1	1	0	0	.000	.250	.000	.250	-24	-0	0	.00	-1	/S-4	0	-0.1
1974*Pit-N	126	333	33	82	4	2	0	26	25	41	13	4	.246	.303	.270	.573	63	-15	29	2.87	-6	*S-124	6	-0.9
1975*Pit-N	134	378	44	80	9	4	0	23	37	42	17	6	.212	.285	.257	.542	52	-23	32	2.69	4	*S-132	7	-0.6
1976 Pit-N	144	519	76	134	8	6	0	24	44	79	58	11	.258	.321	.297	.618	75	-8	56	3.64	6	*S-141	16	1.5
1977 Pit-N	147	544	72	137	20	10	1	29	38	71	**70**	18	.252	.308	.331	.639	69	-16	61	3.69	4	*S-146	14	0.2
1978 Pit-N	157	654	81	182	31	9	0	38	29	60	46	25	.278	.314	.353	.667	82	-18	72	3.77	-17	*S-157	16	-1.9
1979 Pit-N	11	45	4	11	3	0	0	1	0	2	2	1	.244	.244	.311	.556	48	-3	3	1.95	-2	S-11	0	-0.4
NY-N	153	635	89	167	26	9	1	33	33	72	42	19	.263	.301	.337	.639	77	-21	63	3.36	-6	*S-153	12	-1.1
Yr.	164	680	93	178	29	9	1	34	33	74	44	20	.262	.298	.335	.633	75	-24	66	3.26	-8	*S-164	12	-1.5
1980 NY-N	141	562	65	157	27	0	0	25	23	64	32	18	.279	.309	.327	.636	80	-17	53	3.16	-18	*S-140	10	-2.2
1981 NY-N	84	283	30	65	11	3	0	11	12	36	16	4	.230	.266	.290	.556	58	-14	23	2.68	-13	S-79	3	-2.2
1982 Mon-N	48	87	9	14	5	1	0	4	7	6	4	0	.161	.223	.241	.465	29	-8	5	1.79	-1	S-26,2-19	1	-0.7
Total 11	1150	4043	503	1029	144	44	2	214	249	474	300	106	.255	.302	.313	.615	71	-144	395	3.27	-51	*S-1113/2-19	85	-8.5

• TAYLOR, Ben Benjamin Eugene Taylor b: 9/30/1927, Metropolis, IL d: 5/11/1999, Alma, OK BL/TL, 6', 185 lbs. Deb: 7/29/1951

YEAR TM-L	G	AB	R	H	2B	3B	HR	RBI	BB	SO	SB	CS	AVG	OBP	SLG	OPS	OPS+	BR/A	RC	RC/G	FR	G/POS	WS	TPW
1951 StL-A	33	93	14	24	2	1	3	6	9	22	1	1	.258	.337	.398	.734	95	-1	12	4.55	-2	1-25	2	-0.4
1952 Det-A	7	18	0	3	0	0	0	0	0	5	0	0	.167	.167	.167	.333	-7	-3	0	.58	0	/1-4	0	-0.3
1955 Mil-N	12	10	2	1	0	0	0	0	2	4	0	0	.100	.250	.100	.350	-3	-1	0	1.14	0	/1-1	0	-0.2
Total 3	52	121	16	28	2	1	3	6	11	31	1	1	.231	.306	.339	.645	73	-5	13	3.59	-2	/1-30	2	-0.8

• TAYLOR, Bill William Michael Taylor b: 12/30/1929, Alhambra, CA BL/TR, 6'3", 212 lbs. Deb: 4/14/1954 Career OF: 12-0-6

YEAR TM-L	G	AB	R	H	2B	3B	HR	RBI	BB	SO	SB	CS	AVG	OBP	SLG	OPS	OPS+	BR/A	RC	RC/G	FR	G/POS	WS	TPW
1954 NY-N	55	65	4	12	1	0	2	10	3	15	0	0	.185	.243	.292	.535	38	-6	5	2.47	0	/0-9(7-0-2)	0	-0.6
1955 NY-N	65	64	9	17	4	0	4	12	1	16	0	0	.266	.277	.516	.793	104	-0	8	4.06	0	/0-2(0-0-2)	1	0.0
1956 NY-N	1	4	0	1	1	0	0	0	0	1	0	0	.250	.250	.500	.750	96	-0	1	4.50	-0	/0-1	0	0.0
1957 NY-N	11	9	0	0	0	0	0	0	1	2	0	0	.000	.100	.000	.100	-70	-2	0	.08	0	....	0	-0.2
Det-A	9	23	4	8	2	0	1	3	0	3	0	0	.348	.348	.565	.913	142	1	5	8.14	-0	/0-5(5-0-0)	1	0.1
1958 Det-A	8	8	0	3	0	0	0	1	0	2	0	0	.375	.375	.375	.750	100	-0	1	6.08	0	/0-1	0	0.0
Total 5	149	173	17	41	8	0	7	26	5	39	0	0	.237	.267	.405	.671	73	-7	19	3.70	0	/0-18	2	-0.8

• TAYLOR, Billy William Henry "Bollicky Bill" Taylor
b: 1855, Washington, DC d: 5/14/1900, Jacksonville, FL BR/TR, 5'11.5", 204 lbs. Deb: 5/21/1881 Career OF: 24-15-38 ♦

YEAR TM-L	G	AB	R	H	2B	3B	HR	RBI	BB	SO	SB	CS	AVG	OBP	SLG	OPS	OPS+	BR/A	RC	RC/G	FR	G/POS	WS	TPW
1881 Wor-N	6	28	3	3	1	0	0	2	0	2	....	....	.107	.107	.143	.250	-21	-4	0	.47	1	/0-5(0-0-5),P-1	0	-0.7
Det-N	1	4	0	2	2	0	0	1	0	0	....	....	.500	.500	1.000	1.500	345	1	2	27.68	0	/3-1	0	0.1
Cle-N	24	103	6	25	1	0	0	12	0	8	....	....	.243	.243	.252	.495	59	-5	6	2.24	-2	0-23(23-0-0)/3-1,P-1	2	-0.6
Yr.	31	135	9	30	4	0	0	15	0	10	....	....	.222	.222	.252	.474	51	-7	9	2.30	-1	0-28(23-0-5)/3-2,P-2	2	-1.2
1882 Pit-a	70	299	40	84	16	13	3	....	7	....	....	....	.281	.297	.452	.749	156	17	41	5.36	-9	C-27,1-23,3-14/0-8(0-6-2),P	12	0.2
1883 Pit-a	83	369	43	96	13	7	2	0	9	....	....	....	.260	.278	.350	.627	105	5	37	3.77	-7	0-37(0-8-29),C-33,P-19/1-9	9	-2.4
1884 StL-U	43	186	44	68	23	1	3	....	7	....	....	....	.366	.389	.548	.937	206	21	41	9.64	1	P-33,1-10/0-4(1-1-2)	41	4.3
Phi-a	30	111	8	28	6	2	0	0	2	....	....	....	.252	.272	.342	.614	93	3	11	3.51	2	P-30	24	2.6
1885 Phi-a	6	21	0	4	0	0	0	2	0	....	....	....	.190	.190	.190	.381	19	-1	1	1.24	-1	/P-6	2	0.1
1886 Bal-a	10	39	4	12	0	1	0	8	1	....	1	....	.308	.325	.359	.684	117	2	5	5.00	-1	/P-8,1-1,C-1	2	-1.3
1887 Phi-a	1	4	0	1	0	0	0	1	0	....	0	....	.250	.250	.250	.500	40	-0	0	2.31	0	/P-1	1	0.1
Total 7	274	1164	148	323	62	24	8	26	26	10	1	....	.277	.294	.393	.686	126	39	144	4.77	-17	P-100/0-77,C-61,1-43,3-16	93	2.2

• TAYLOR, Billy William H. Taylor b: 12/1870, Pittsburgh, PA d: 9/12/1905, Cincinnati, OH TR, 5'10", 160 lbs. Deb: 9/19/1898

YEAR TM-L	G	AB	R	H	2B	3B	HR	RBI	BB	SO	SB	CS	AVG	OBP	SLG	OPS	OPS+	BR/A	RC	RC/G	FR	G/POS	WS	TPW
1898 Lou-N	9	24	2	6	1	0	0	2	1	....	1	....	.250	.308	.292	.599	73	-1	3	3.70	-1	/3-7,2-1	1	-0.1

• TAYLOR, Bob Robert Lee Taylor b: 3/20/1944, Leland, MS BL/TR, 5'9", 170 lbs. Deb: 4/9/1970

YEAR TM-L	G	AB	R	H	2B	3B	HR	RBI	BB	SO	SB	CS	AVG	OBP	SLG	OPS	OPS+	BR/A	RC	RC/G	FR	G/POS	WS	TPW
1970 SF-N	63	84	12	16	0	0	2	10	12	13	0	0	.190	.320	.262	.582	58	-4	8	2.88	0	0-26(22-0-5)/C-1	1	-0.5

• TAYLOR, Carl Carl Means Taylor b: 1/20/1944, Sarasota, FL BR/TR, 6'2", 207 lbs. Deb: 4/11/1968 Career OF: 27-0-79

YEAR TM-L	G	AB	R	H	2B	3B	HR	RBI	BB	SO	SB	CS	AVG	OBP	SLG	OPS	OPS+	BR/A	RC	RC/G	FR	G/POS	WS	TPW
1968 Pit-N	44	71	5	15	1	0	0	7	10	10	1	0	.211	.309	.225	.534	63	-2	5	2.14	-1	C-29/0-2(1-0-1)	0	-0.3
1969 Pit-N	104	221	30	77	10	1	4	33	31	36	0	1	.348	.435	.457	.892	153	17	45	7.74	-1	0-36(19-0-19),1-24	11	1.3
1970 StL-N	104	245	39	61	12	2	6	45	41	30	5	2	.249	.359	.388	.747	98	1	34	4.65	-1	0-46(0-0-46),1-15/3-1	6	-0.4
1971 KC-A	20	39	3	7	0	0	0	3	5	13	0	1	.179	.273	.179	.452	30	-4	2	1.52	0	0-12(6-0-6)	0	-0.5
Pit-N	7	12	1	2	0	1	0	0	0	5	0	0	.167	.167	.333	.500	38	-1	0	.82	0	/0-1	0	-0.1
1972 KC-A	63	113	17	30	2	1	0	11	17	16	4	1	.265	.366	.301	.667	101	2	14	4.12	-2	C-21/0-7(1-0-6),1-6,3-5	3	0.0
1973 KC-A	69	145	18	33	6	1	0	16	32	20	2	2	.228	.367	.283	.650	79	-2	17	3.77	-2	C-63/1-2,D-1	4	-0.2
Total 6	411	846	113	225	31	6	10	115	136	130	12	7	.266	.371	.352	.723	103	10	117	4.68	-6	C-113,0-104/1-47,3-6,D-1	24	-0.1

• TAYLOR, Chink C L Taylor b: 2/9/1898, Burnet, TX d: 7/7/1980, Temple, TX BR/TR, 5'9", 160 lbs. Deb: 4/18/1925

YEAR TM-L	G	AB	R	H	2B	3B	HR	RBI	BB	SO	SB	CS	AVG	OBP	SLG	OPS	OPS+	BR/A	RC	RC/G	FR	G/POS	WS	TPW
1925 Chi-N	8	6	2	0	0	0	0	0	0	0	0	0	.000	.000	.000	.000	-99	-2	0	.00	0	/0-2(1-0-1)	0	-0.2

• TAYLOR, Danny Daniel Turney Taylor b: 12/23/1900, Lash, PA d: 10/11/1972, Latrobe, PA BR/TR, 5'10", 190 lbs. Deb: 6/30/1926 Career OF: 310-235-18

YEAR TM-L	G	AB	R	H	2B	3B	HR	RBI	BB	SO	SB	CS	AVG	OBP	SLG	OPS	OPS+	BR/A	RC	RC/G	FR	G/POS	WS	TPW
1926 Was-A	21	50	10	15	0	1	1	5	5	7	1	2	.300	.364	.400	.764	101	-0	7	4.91	0	0-12(0-1-11)	1	-0.1
1929 Chi-N	2	3	0	0	0	0	0	0	1	1	0	....	.000	.250	.000	.250	-32	-1	0	.52	-0	/0-1	0	-0.1
1930 Chi-N	74	219	43	62	14	3	2	37	27	34	6	....	.283	.364	.402	.766	84	-5	32	5.15	-2	0-52(52-0-0)	5	-0.9
1931 Chi-N	88	270	48	81	13	6	5	41	31	46	4	....	.300	.372	.448	.820	117	7	47	6.36	2	0-67(39-22-4)	10	0.5
1932 Chi-N	6	22	3	5	2	0	0	3	3	1	1	....	.227	.320	.318	.638	73	-1	2	3.70	0	/0-6(0-4-2)	0	-0.1
Bro-N	105	395	84	128	22	7	11	48	33	41	13	....	.324	.378	.499	.876	136	20	76	7.21	4	0-96(0-96-0)	18	2.1
Yr.	111	417	87	133	24	7	11	51	36	42	14	....	.319	.374	.489	.864	133	19	78	7.00	4	*0-102(0-100-2)	18	2.0
1933 Bro-N	103	358	75	102	21	9	9	40	47	45	11	....	.285	.368	.469	.837	144	21	64	6.46	-7	0-91(0-91-0)	16	1.3
1934 Bro-N	120	405	62	121	24	6	7	57	63	47	12	....	.299	.396	.440	.835	130	20	74	6.68	0	*0-108(89-21-0)	15	1.5
1935 Bro-N	112	352	51	102	19	5	7	59	46	32	6	....	.290	.372	.432	.804	118	10	60	6.12	-3	0-99(99-0-0)	13	0.1
1936 Bro-N	43	116	12	34	6	0	2	15	11	14	2	....	.293	.359	.397	.756	102	1	16	5.18	0	0-31(31-0-0)	3	-0.1
Total 9	674	2190	388	650	121	37	44	305	267	268	56	2	.297	.374	.446	.821	122	72	379	6.28	-6	0-563	81	4.3

• TAYLOR, Dwight Dwight Bernard Taylor b: 3/24/1960, Los Angeles, CA BL/TL, 5'9", 166 lbs. Deb: 4/14/1986

YEAR TM-L	G	AB	R	H	2B	3B	HR	RBI	BB	SO	SB	CS	AVG	OBP	SLG	OPS	OPS+	BR/A	RC	RC/G	FR	G/POS	WS	TPW
1986 KC-A	4	2	1	0	0	0	0	0	0	0	0	0	.000	.000	.000	.000	-98	-1	0	.00	0	/D-2,0-1	0	-0.1

YEAR TM-L	G	AB	R	H	2B	3B	HR	RBI	BB	SO	SB	CS	AVG	OBP	SLG	OPS	OPS+	BR/A	RC	RC/G	FR	G/POS	WS	TPW
• TAYLOR, Ed	Edward James Taylor b: 11/17/1901, Chicago, IL d: 1/30/1992, Chula Vista, CA BR/TR, 5'6.5", 160 lbs. Deb: 4/14/1926																							
1926 Bos-N	92	272	37	73	8	2	0	33	38	26	4	....	.268	.368	.313	.681	93	-0	34	4.13	-2	3-62,S-33	8	0.4
• TAYLOR, Fred	Frederick Rankin Taylor b: 12/3/1924, Zanesville, OH d: 1/6/2002, Columbus, OH BL/TR, 6'3", 201 lbs. Deb: 9/12/1950																							
1950 Was-A	6	16	1	2	0	0	0	0	1	2	0	0	.125	.176	.125	.301	-23	-3	0	.79	0	/1-3	0	-0.3
1951 Was-A	6	12	1	2	1	0	0	0	0	4	0	0	.167	.167	.250	.417	12	-2	1	1.38	0	/1-2	0	-0.2
1952 Was-A	10	19	3	5	1	0	0	4	3	2	0	0	.263	.364	.316	.679	93	-0	3	4.86	1	/1-5	1	0.1
Total 3	**22**	**47**	**5**	**9**	**2**	**0**	**0**	**4**	**4**	**8**	**0**	**0**	**.191**	**.255**	**.234**	**.489**	**35**	**-5**	**3**	**2.44**	**1**	**/1-10**	**1**	**-0.3**
• TAYLOR, Harry	Harry Leonard Taylor b: 4/4/1866, Halsey Valley, NY d: 7/12/1955, Buffalo, NY BL, 6'2", 160 lbs. Deb: 4/18/1890																							
1890*Lou-a	134	553	115	169	7	7	0	53	68	....	45	....	.306	.383	.344	.726	117	14	92	6.36	14	*1-118,S-12/2-4,C-1	19	1.6
1891 Lou-a	91	348	80	103	7	3	2	35	55	30	15	....	.296	.400	.351	.750	116	11	56	6.07	5	1-92/2-1,3-1,C-1	12	0.7
1892 Lou-N	125	493	66	128	7	1	0	34	58	23	24	....	.260	.342	.278	.620	96	1	56	4.18	-2	0-73(23-0-50),1-34,2-14/3-5,S	13	-0.4
1893 Bal-N	88	360	50	102	9	1	1	54	32	11	24	....	.283	.347	.322	.669	77	-12	50	5.11	-3	*1-88	6	-1.2
Total 4	**438**	**1754**	**311**	**502**	**30**	**12**	**3**	**176**	**213**	**64**	**108**	**....**	**.286**	**.368**	**.322**	**.690**	**103**	**15**	**255**	**5.41**	**15**	**1-332/0-73,2-19,S-14,3-6,C**	**50**	**0.7**
• TAYLOR, Harry	Harry Warren Taylor b: 12/26/1907, McKeesport, PA d: 4/27/1969, Toledo, OH BL/TL, 6'1.5", 185 lbs. Deb: 4/14/1932																							
1932 Chi-N	10	8	1	1	0	0	0	0	1	1	0	....	.125	.222	.125	.347	-4	-1	0	1.01	0	/1-1	0	-0.1
• TAYLOR, Hawk	Robert Dale Taylor b: 4/3/1939, Metropolis, IL BR/TR, 6'1", 190 lbs. Deb: 6/9/1957 Career OF: 37-3-22																							
1957 Mil-N	7	1	2	0	0	0	0	0	0	0	0	0	.000	.000	.000	.000	-108	-0	0	.00	0	/C-1	0	-0.1
1958 Mil-N	4	8	1	1	1	0	0	0	0	3	0	0	.125	.125	.250	.375	-4	-1	0	.96	0	/0-4(4-0-0)	0	-0.1
1961 Mil-N	20	26	1	5	0	0	1	1	3	11	0	1	.192	.276	.308	.584	58	-2	2	2.60	0	/0-5(4-0-1),C-1	0	-0.2
1962 Mil-N	20	47	3	12	0	0	0	2	2	10	0	1	.255	.286	.255	.541	48	-4	3	2.49	1	0-11(7-0-4)	0	-0.4
1963 Mil-N	16	29	1	2	0	0	0	0	1	12	0	0	.069	.100	.069	.169	-51	-6	0	.15	-0	/0-8(4-3-1)	0	-0.6
1964 NY-N	92	225	20	54	8	0	4	23	8	33	0	0	.240	.272	.329	.601	70	-9	19	2.81	4	C-45,0-16(16-0-0)	3	-0.4
1965 NY-N	25	46	5	7	0	0	4	10	1	8	0	0	.152	.170	.413	.583	61	-3	2	1.59	0	C-15/1-1	0	-0.3
1966 NY-N	53	109	5	19	2	0	3	12	3	19	0	1	.174	.204	.275	.479	32	-11	4	1.22	2	C-29,1-13	1	-0.9
1967 NY-N	13	37	3	9	3	0	0	4	2	8	0	0	.243	.282	.324	.606	74	-1	3	3.33	0	C-12	1	-0.1
Cal-A	23	52	5	16	3	0	1	3	4	8	0	0	.308	.357	.423	.780	135	2	8	5.70	1	C-19	3	0.4
1969 KC-A	64	89	7	24	5	0	3	21	6	18	0	0	.270	.316	.427	.743	105	0	11	4.19	0	0-18(2-0-16)/C-6	2	0.0
1970 KC-A	57	55	3	9	3	0	0	6	6	16	0	0	.164	.258	.218	.476	33	-5	3	1.85	0	/C-3,1-1	0	-0.5
Total 11	**394**	**724**	**56**	**158**	**25**	**0**	**16**	**82**	**36**	**146**	**0**	**3**	**.218**	**.259**	**.319**	**.578**	**63**	**-39**	**57**	**2.58**	**6**	**C-131/0-62,1-15**	**10**	**-3.3**
• TAYLOR, Joe	Joe Cephus Taylor b: 3/2/1926, Chapman, AL d: 3/18/1993, Pittsburgh, PA BR/TR, 6'1", 185 lbs. Deb: 8/26/1954 Career OF: 35-6-42																							
1954 Phi-A	18	58	5	13	1	1	1	8	2	9	0	1	.224	.250	.328	.578	57	-4	4	2.20	-1	0-16(9-0-8)	0	-0.6
1957 Cin-N	33	107	14	28	7	0	4	9	6	24	0	1	.262	.301	.439	.740	89	-2	13	4.30	2	0-27(19-0-8)	2	-0.2
1958 StL-N	18	23	2	7	3	0	1	3	2	4	0	0	.304	.360	.565	.925	135	1	5	7.28	0	/0-5(2-2-1)	1	0.1
Bal-A	36	77	11	21	4	0	2	9	7	19	0	0	.273	.333	.403	.736	107	1	9	3.95	0	0-21(3-4-15)	2	0.0
1959 Bal-A	14	32	2	5	1	0	1	2	11	5	0	0	.156	.372	.281	.653	84	-0	4	4.41	0	0-12(2-0-10)	1	0.0
Total 4	**119**	**297**	**34**	**74**	**16**	**1**	**9**	**31**	**28**	**61**	**0**	**2**	**.249**	**.314**	**.401**	**.715**	**91**	**-5**	**35**	**4.02**	**1**	**/0-81**	**6**	**-0.7**
• TAYLOR, Leo	Leo Thomas "Chink" Taylor b: 5/13/1901, Walla Walla, WA d: 5/20/1982, Seattle, WA BR/TR, 5'10.5", 150 lbs. Deb: 5/3/1923																							
1923 Chi-A	1	0	0	0	0	0	0	0	0	0	0	0	....			....	-101	0	0	....	0	....	0	0.0
• TAYLOR, Live Oak	Edward S. Taylor d: 2/19/1888, San Francisco, CA Deb: 8/21/1877 Career OF: 2-41-0																							
1877 Har-N	2	8	0	3	0	0	0	0	0	2	....	....	.375	.375	.375	.750	153	0	1	6.34	0	/0-2(2-0-0)	0	0.0
1884 Pit-a	41	152	22	32	4	1	0	0	6	....	....	....	.211	.255	.250	.505	64	-6	10	2.27	-4	0-41(0-41-0)	1	-1.0
Total 2	**43**	**160**	**22**	**35**	**4**	**1**	**0**	**0**	**6**	**2**	**....**	**....**	**.219**	**.260**	**.256**	**.517**	**68**	**-5**	**11**	**2.44**	**-4**	**/0-43**	**1**	**-1.0**
• TAYLOR, Reggie	Reginald Tremain Taylor b: 1/12/1977, Newberry, SC BL/TR, 6'1", 178 lbs. Deb: 9/17/2000 Career OF: 47-122-9																							
2000 Phi-N	9	11	1	1	0	0	0	0	0	8	1	0	.091	.091	.091	.182	-54	-2	0	.37	-1	/0-8(0-3-0)	0	-0.3
2001 Phi-N	5	7	1	0	0	0	0	0	1	1	0	0	.000	.125	.000	.125	-65	-2	0	.13	0	/0-3(0-2-0)	0	-0.2
2002 Cin-N	135	287	41	73	15	4	9	38	14	79	11	8	.254	.294	.429	.722	85	-9	33	3.76	0	/0-2(34-68-6)	5	-0.9
2003 Cin-N	100	180	17	39	5	2	5	19	11	68	7	0	.217	.266	.350	.616	60	-10	17	3.15	0	0-60(13-49-3)	1	-1.0
Total 4	**249**	**485**	**60**	**113**	**20**	**6**	**14**	**57**	**26**	**156**	**19**	**8**	**.233**	**.276**	**.386**	**.662**	**70**	**-23**	**50**	**3.39**	**-1**	**/0-73**	**6**	**-2.4**
• TAYLOR, Sammy	Samuel Douglas Taylor b: 2/27/1933, Woodruff, SC BL/TR, 6'2", 185 lbs. Deb: 4/20/1958																							
1958 Chi-N	96	301	30	78	12	2	6	36	27	46	2	1	.259	.320	.372	.692	84	-7	35	3.98	-4	C-87	7	-0.7
1959 Chi-N	110	353	41	95	13	2	13	43	35	47	1	0	.269	.337	.428	.765	103	2	51	5.16	-8	*C-109	8	-0.2
1960 Chi-N	74	150	14	31	9	0	3	17	6	18	0	1	.207	.242	.327	.569	55	-10	10	2.22	2	C-43	1	-0.7
1961 Chi-N	89	235	26	56	8	2	8	23	23	39	0	0	.238	.317	.391	.708	85	-5	29	4.14	-1	C-75	5	-0.3
1962 Chi-N	7	15	0	2	1	0	0	1	3	3	0	0	.133	.278	.200	.478	30	-1	1	1.51	0	/C-6	0	-0.1
NY-N	68	158	12	35	4	2	3	20	23	17	0	0	.222	.328	.329	.657	76	-5	18	3.74	2	C-50	2	-0.1
Yr.	75	173	12	37	5	2	3	21	26	20	0	0	.214	.323	.318	.641	72	-6	19	3.52	2	C-56	2	-0.2
1963 NY-N	22	35	3	9	0	1	0	6	5	7	0	0	.257	.350	.314	.664	91	-0	3	3.03	0	C-13	1	0.1
Cin-N	3	6	0	0	0	0	0	0	0	2	0	0	.000	.000	.000	.000	-97	-1	0	.00	0	/C-2	0	-0.2
Yr.	25	41	3	9	0	1	0	6	5	9	0	0	.220	.304	.268	.573	67	-2	3	2.53	0	C-15	1	-0.1
Cle-A	4	10	1	3	0	0	0	1	0	2	0	0	.300	.300	.300	.600	69	-0	1	3.47	1	/C-2	0	0.0
Total 6	**473**	**1263**	**127**	**309**	**47**	**9**	**33**	**147**	**122**	**181**	**3**	**2**	**.245**	**.315**	**.375**	**.690**	**84**	**-29**	**147**	**3.98**	**-9**	**C-387**	**24**	**-2.2**
• TAYLOR, Sandy	James B. Taylor, 5'10.5", 175 lbs. Deb: 8/11/1879																							
1879 Tro-N	24	97	10	21	4	0	0	8	1	8	....	....	.216	.224	.258	.482	63	-3	6	2.12	-2	0-24(24-0-0)	0	-0.7
• TAYLOR, Tommy	Thomas Livingstone Carlton Taylor b: 9/17/1892, Mexia, TX d: 4/5/1956, Greenville, MS BR/TR, 5'8.5", 160 lbs. Deb: 7/9/1924																							
1924*Was-A	26	73	11	19	3	1	0	10	2	8	2	0	.260	.289	.329	.618	61	-4	7	3.48	-3	3-16/2-2,0-1	1	-0.6
• TAYLOR, Tony	Antonio Nemesio (Sanchez) Taylor b: 12/19/1935, Central Alara, Cuba BR/TR, 5'9", 179 lbs. Deb: 4/15/1958 C Career OF: 19-0-0																							
1958 Chi-N	140	497	63	117	15	3	6	27	40	93	21	6	.235	.301	.314	.615	64	-23	50	3.30	8	*2-137/3-1	8	-0.5
1959 Chi-N	150	624	96	175	30	8	8	38	45	86	23	9	.280	.335	.393	.727	94	-4	84	4.74	10	*2-149/S-2	19	1.7
1960 Chi-N	19	76	14	20	3	3	1	9	8	12	2	0	.263	.341	.421	.762	108	1	12	5.22	4	2-19	3	0.7
Phi-N★	127	505	66	145	22	4	4	35	33	86	24	11	.287	.333	.370	.704	92	-5	62	4.25	5	*2-123/3-4	13	1.0
Yr.	146	581	80	165	25	7	5	44	41	98	26	11	.284	.334	.377	.711	94	-3	73	4.38	9	*2-142/3-4	16	1.7
1961 Phi-N	106	400	47	100	17	3	2	26	29	59	11	5	.250	.304	.323	.626	67	-18	38	3.23	1	2-91/3-3	5	-0.9
1962 Phi-N	152	625	87	162	21	5	7	43	68	82	20	9	.259	.337	.342	.679	85	-11	76	4.21	-10	*2-150/S-2	16	-0.8
1963 Phi-N	157	640	102	180	20	10	5	49	42	99	23	9	.281	.332	.367	.700	102	4	79	4.35	-4	*2-149,3-13	23	1.3
1964 Phi-N	154	570	62	143	13	6	4	46	46	74	13	7	.251	.321	.316	.637	81	-12	60	3.57	-12	*2-150	15	-1.2
1965 Phi-N	106	323	41	74	14	3	3	27	22	58	5	4	.229	.303	.319	.621	76	-10	32	3.23	-8	2-86/3-5	6	-1.2
1966 Phi-N	125	434	47	105	14	8	5	40	31	56	8	4	.242	.294	.346	.640	77	-13	42	3.19	-4	2-68,3-52	9	-1.3
1967 Phi-N	132	462	55	110	16	6	2	34	42	74	10	9	.238	.308	.312	.620	77	-14	42	2.95	-4	1-58,3-44,2-42/S-3	7	-2.1
1968 Phi-N	145	547	59	137	20	2	3	38	39	60	22	5	.250	.304	.311	.615	85	-7	54	3.36	9	*3-138/2-5,1-1	17	0.3
1969 Phi-N	138	557	68	146	24	5	3	30	42	62	19	10	.262	.318	.339	.658	87	-10	60	3.67	1	3-71,2-57,1-10	12	-0.7
1970 Phi-N	124	439	74	132	26	9	9	55	50	67	9	11	.301	.376	.462	.838	127	14	71	5.75	7	2-59,3-38,0-18(18-0-0)/S-1	19	2.3
1971 Phi-N	36	107	9	25	2	1	1	5	9	10	2	2	.234	.293	.299	.592	68	-5	9	2.68	4	2-14,3-11/1-2	1	0.0
Det-A	55	181	27	52	10	2	3	19	12	11	5	1	.287	.335	.414	.749	107	2	25	4.97	2	2-51/3-3	7	0.7
1972*Det-A	78	228	33	69	12	4	1	20	14	34	5	1	.303	.348	.404	.752	119	6	31	4.87	-3	2-67/3-8,1-1	9	0.6
1973 Det-A	84	275	35	63	9	3	5	24	17	29	9	5	.229	.276	.338	.615	68	-12	24	2.78	-3	2-72/1-6,3-4,D-2,0-1	4	-1.2
1974 Phi-N	62	64	5	21	4	0	2	13	6	6	0	0	.328	.394	.484	.879	139	3	12	6.93	-3	/1-7,3-5,2-4	3	0.0
1975 Phi-N	79	103	13	25	5	1	1	17	17	18	3	3	.243	.355	.340	.695	90	-1	12	3.77	0	3-16/1-4,2-3	2	-0.1

YEAR TM-L	G	AB	R	H	2B	3B	HR	RBI	BB	SO	SB	CS	AVG	OBP	SLG	OPS	OPS+	BR/A	RC	RC/G	FR	G/POS	WS	TPW
1976 Phi-N	26	23	2	6	1	0	0	3	1	7	0	0	.261	.320	.304	.624	75	-1	2	3.71	-1	/2-2,3-1	0	-0.2
Total 19	2195	7680	1005	2007	298	86	75	598	613	1083	234	111	.261	.322	.352	.674	88	-117	876	3.89	-4	*2-1498,3-417/1-89,0-19,S-8,D	198	-1.6

• TAYLOR, Zachary Zachary H. Taylor Deb: 9/10/1874

YEAR TM-L	G	AB	R	H	2B	3B	HR	RBI	BB	SO	SB	CS	AVG	OBP	SLG	OPS	OPS+	BR/A	RC	RC/G	FR	G/POS	WS	TPW
1874 Bal-n	13	48	3	12	0	0	0	3	0	1	0	0	.250	.250	.250	.500	61	-2	3	2.56	-1	1-13	....	-0.2

• TAYLOR, Zack James Wren Taylor b: 7/27/1898, Yulee, FL d: 9/19/1974, Orlando, FL BR/TR, 5'11.5", 180 lbs. Deb: 6/15/1920 M/C

YEAR TM-L	G	AB	R	H	2B	3B	HR	RBI	BB	SO	SB	CS	AVG	OBP	SLG	OPS	OPS+	BR/A	RC	RC/G	FR	G/POS	WS	TPW
1920 Bro-N	9	13	3	5	2	0	0	5	0	2	0	1	.385	.385	.538	.923	158	0	2	6.09	-1	/C-9	0	0.0
1921 Bro-N	30	102	6	20	0	2	0	8	1	8	2	0	.196	.212	.235	.447	17	-11	5	1.66	1	C-30	2	-0.8
1922 Bro-N	7	14	0	3	0	0	0	2	1	1	0	0	.214	.267	.214	.481	26	-1	1	2.00	0	/C-6	0	-0.1
1923 Bro-N	96	337	29	97	11	6	0	46	9	13	2	5	.288	.312	.356	.668	78	-12	36	3.80	10	C-84	8	0.3
1924 Bro-N	99	345	36	100	9	4	1	39	14	14	0	1	.290	.319	.348	.667	81	-9	38	3.97	-5	C-93	13	-0.8
1925 Bro-N	109	352	33	109	16	4	3	44	17	19	0	0	.310	.343	.403	.747	92	-4	48	5.20	2	C-96	12	0.3
1926 Bos-N	125	432	36	110	22	3	0	42	28	27	1	....	.255	.303	.319	.622	74	-16	41	3.26	11	*C-123	12	0.3
1927 Bos-N	30	96	8	23	2	1	1	14	8	5	0	....	.240	.298	.313	.611	69	-4	9	3.14	12	C-27	3	0.9
NY-N	83	258	18	60	7	3	0	21	17	20	2	....	.233	.283	.283	.566	52	-18	21	2.63	-3	C-81	3	-1.6
Yr.	113	354	26	83	9	4	1	35	25	25	2	....	.234	.287	.291	.578	56	-22	30	2.77	8	*C-108	6	-0.7
1928 Bos-N	125	399	36	100	15	1	2	30	33	29	2	....	.251	.313	.308	.621	66	-19	39	3.30	0	*C-124	6	-1.2
1929 Bos-N	34	101	8	25	7	0	0	10	7	9	0	....	.248	.303	.317	.620	56	-7	10	3.14	5	C-31	1	0.0
*Chi-N	64	215	29	59	16	3	1	31	19	18	0	....	.274	.336	.391	.727	79	-7	28	4.57	-2	C-64	7	-0.5
Yr.	98	316	37	84	23	3	1	41	26	27	0	....	.266	.326	.367	.693	72	-14	38	4.09	3	C-95	8	-0.5
1930 Chi-N	32	95	12	22	2	1	1	11	2	12	0	....	.232	.255	.305	.560	34	-10	7	2.43	1	C-28	2	-0.7
1931 Chi-N	8	4	0	1	0	0	0	0	2	1	0	....	.250	.500	.250	.750	106	0	1	4.79	0	/C-5	0	0.0
1932 Chi-N	21	30	2	6	1	0	0	3	1	4	0	....	.200	.226	.233	.459	24	-3	2	1.72	0	C-14	1	-0.2
1933 Chi-N	16	11	0	0	0	0	0	0	0	1	0	....	.000	.000	.000	.000	-100	-3	0	.00	-3	C-12	0	-0.6
1934 NY-A	4	7	0	1	0	0	0	0	0	1	0	0	.143	.143	.143	.286	-28	-1	0	.61	0	/C-3	0	-0.1
1935 Bro-N	26	54	2	7	3	0	0	5	2	8	0	....	.130	.175	.185	.361	-3	-8	1	.61	2	C-26	1	-0.5
Total 16	918	2865	258	748	113	28	9	311	161	192	9	7	.261	.304	.329	.634	68	-133	289	3.47	29	C-856	71	-5.2

• TEBBETTS, Birdie George Robert Tebbetts b: 11/10/1912, Burlington, VT d: 3/24/1999, Manatee, FL BR/TR, 5'11.5", 170 lbs. Deb: 9/16/1936 M

YEAR TM-L	G	AB	R	H	2B	3B	HR	RBI	BB	SO	SB	CS	AVG	OBP	SLG	OPS	OPS+	BR/A	RC	RC/G	FR	G/POS	WS	TPW
1936 Det-A	10	33	7	10	1	2	1	4	5	3	0	0	.303	.395	.545	.940	129	1	7	8.43	1	C-10	2	0.2
1937 Det-A	50	162	15	31	4	3	2	16	10	13	0	0	.191	.238	.290	.528	32	-18	12	2.28	-2	C-48	2	-1.6
1938 Det-A	53	143	16	42	6	2	1	25	12	13	1	2	.294	.348	.385	.733	79	-5	19	4.76	0	C-53	4	-0.4
1939 Det-A	106	341	37	89	22	2	4	53	25	20	2	1	.261	.315	.372	.688	70	-16	40	3.98	1	*C-100	7	-0.9
1940*Det-A	111	379	46	112	24	4	4	46	35	14	4	5	.296	.357	.412	.768	90	-6	55	5.28	6	*C-107	13	0.6
1941 Det-A★	110	359	28	102	19	4	2	47	38	29	1	2	.284	.354	.376	.730	85	-8	50	4.99	5	C-98	11	0.3
1942 Det-A★	99	308	24	76	11	0	1	27	39	17	4	0	.247	.335	.292	.627	71	-9	33	3.62	0	C-97	9	-0.3
1946 Det-A	87	280	20	68	11	2	1	34	28	23	1	3	.243	.312	.307	.619	69	-12	26	3.07	-2	C-87	7	-1.0
1947 Det-A	20	53	1	5	1	0	0	2	3	3	0	1	.094	.143	.113	.256	-28	-10	1	.35	2	C-20	2	-0.7
Bos-A	90	291	22	87	10	0	1	28	21	30	2	4	.299	.346	.344	.690	86	-6	34	4.14	-1	C-89	7	-0.3
Yr.	110	344	23	92	11	0	1	30	24	33	2	5	.267	.315	.308	.623	68	-16	34	3.41	1	*C-109	9	-1.0
1948 Bos-A★	128	446	54	125	26	2	5	68	62	32	5	2	.280	.371	.381	.752	95	-1	63	4.87	-10	*C-126	14	-0.4
1949 Bos-A★	122	403	42	109	14	0	5	48	62	22	8	1	.270	.369	.342	.712	83	-7	55	4.71	-7	*C-118	11	-0.7
1950 Bos-A	79	268	33	83	10	1	8	45	29	26	1	1	.310	.377	.444	.821	100	-0	43	5.77	0	C-74	10	0.3
1951 Cle-A	55	137	8	36	6	0	2	18	8	7	0	0	.263	.308	.350	.659	82	-4	14	3.72	1	C-44	4	-0.1
1952 Cle-A	42	101	4	25	4	0	1	8	12	9	0	1	.248	.339	.317	.656	89	-1	11	3.40	-1	C-37	3	-0.1
Total 14	1162	3704	357	1000	169	22	38	469	389	261	29	23	.270	.341	.358	.700	80	-102	461	4.31	-8	*C-1108	106	-5.0

• TEBEAU, George George E. "White Wings" Tebeau b: 12/26/1861, St. Louis, MO d: 2/4/1923, Denver, CO BR/TR, 5'9", 175 lbs. Deb: 4/16/1887 Career OF: 349-170-51

YEAR TM-L	G	AB	R	H	2B	3B	HR	RBI	BB	SO	SB	CS	AVG	OBP	SLG	OPS	OPS+	BR/A	RC	RC/G	FR	G/POS	WS	TPW
1887 Cin-a	85	349	57	125	12	5	4	33	31	....	37	....	.358	.364	.403	.766	111	5	62	7.41	2	*0-84(80-1-3)/P-1	11	-0.4
1888 Cin-a	121	411	72	94	12	12	3	51	61	....	37	....	.229	.338	.338	.676	111	7	61	5.20	4	*0-121(121-0-0)	15	0.7
1889 Cin-a	135	496	110	125	21	11	7	70	69	62	61	....	.252	.350	.381	.731	105	4	90	6.41	-7	*0-134(134-0-0)/1-1	14	-0.7
1890 Tol-a	94	381	71	102	16	10	1	36	51	....	55	....	.268	.359	.370	.729	112	6	72	6.84	1	*0-94(1-93-0)/P-1	12	0.0
1894 Was-N	61	222	41	50	10	6	0	28	37	20	17	....	.225	.341	.324	.665	63	-12	31	4.70	-6	0-61(8-53-0)	2	-1.7
Cle-N	40	150	32	47	9	4	0	25	25	18	9	....	.313	.411	.427	.838	99	0	31	7.77	-3	0-27(4-23-0),1-12/3-1	4	-0.4
Yr.	101	372	73	97	19	10	0	53	62	38	26	....	.261	.369	.366	.735	77	-12	62	5.85	-9	*0-88(12-76-0),1-12/3-1	6	-2.1
1895 Cle-N	92	341	58	111	16	6	0	68	50	29	12	....	.326	.413	.408	.821	106	5	64	7.51	-4	0-49(1-0-48),1-42	13	-0.1
Total 6	628	2350	441	654	96	54	15	311	324	129	228	....	.278	.364	.376	.740	104	14	410	6.45	-13	0-570/1-55,P-2,3-1	71	-2.5

• TEBEAU, Patsy Oliver Wendell Tebeau b: 12/5/1864, St. Louis, MO d: 5/15/1918, St. Louis, MO BR/TR, 5'8", 163 lbs. Deb: 9/20/1887 M

YEAR TM-L	G	AB	R	H	2B	3B	HR	RBI	BB	SO	SB	CS	AVG	OBP	SLG	OPS	OPS+	BR/A	RC	RC/G	FR	G/POS	WS	TPW
1887 Chi-N	20	72	8	15	3	0	0	10	4	4	8	....	.208	.208	.206	.414	14	-8	5	2.18	-3	3-20	1	-0.9
1889 Cle-N	136	521	72	147	20	6	8	76	37	41	26	....	.282	.332	.390	.722	103	1	78	5.52	0	*3-136	15	0.3
1890 Cle-P	110	450	86	134	26	6	5	74	34	20	14	....	.298	.351	.416	.767	114	9	72	6.18	9	*3-110	13	1.6
1891 Cle-N	61	249	38	65	8	3	1	41	16	13	12	....	.261	.313	.329	.643	84	-6	30	4.43	3	3-61/0-1	6	-0.2
1892*Cle-N	86	340	47	83	13	3	2	49	23	34	6	....	.244	.307	.318	.625	85	-7	36	3.77	1	3-74/2-5,1-4,S-3	10	-0.4
1893 Cle-N	116	486	90	160	32	8	2	102	32	11	19	....	.329	.375	.440	.816	110	4	90	7.29	3	1-57,3-56/2-3	15	0.6
1894 Cle-N	125	523	82	158	23	7	3	89	35	35	30	....	.302	.347	.390	.737	75	-24	83	5.93	5	*1-115,2-10/3-2,S-1	8	-1.4
1895*Cle-N	63	264	50	84	13	2	2	52	16	18	8	....	.318	.362	.405	.767	92	-4	43	6.40	7	1-49/2-9,3-6	9	0.3
1896*Cle-N	132	543	56	146	22	6	2	94	21	22	20	....	.269	.300	.343	.642	65	-30	65	4.18	14	*1-122/3-7,2-5,P-1,S-1	7	-1.4
1897 Cle-N	109	412	62	110	15	9	0	59	30	....	11	....	.267	.323	.347	.670	73	-17	52	4.44	13	*1-92,2-18/3-2,S-1	6	-0.3
1898 Cle-N	131	477	53	123	11	4	1	63	53	....	5	....	.258	.341	.304	.645	86	-6	54	3.93	4	1-91,2-34/S-7,3-3	12	-0.1
1899 StL-N	77	281	27	69	10	3	1	26	18	....	5	....	.246	.303	.313	.616	67	-13	29	3.61	-3	1-65,S-11/2-1,3-1	3	-1.4
1900 StL-N	1	4	0	0	0	0	0	0	0	....	0	....	.000	.000	.000	.000	-101	-1	0	.00	-1	/S-1	0	-0.1
Total 13	1167	4622	671	1294	196	57	27	735	319	198	164	....	.280	.332	.364	.696	86	-104	636	5.03	53	1-595,3-478/2-85,S-25,0-1,P	105	-3.5

• TEBEAU, Pussy Charles Alston Tebeau b: 2/22/1870, Worcester, MA d: 3/25/1950, Pittsfield, MA BR/TR, 5'10", 175 lbs. Deb: 7/22/1895

YEAR TM-L	G	AB	R	H	2B	3B	HR	RBI	BB	SO	SB	CS	AVG	OBP	SLG	OPS	OPS+	BR/A	RC	RC/G	FR	G/POS	WS	TPW
1895 Cle-N	2	6	3	3	0	0	0	1	2	1	1	....	.500	.625	.500	1.125	182	1	3	23.06	1	/0-2(0-0-2)	1	0.1

• TEED, Dick Richard Leroy Teed b: 3/8/1926, Springfield, MA BB/TR, 5'11", 180 lbs. Deb: 7/24/1953

YEAR TM-L	G	AB	R	H	2B	3B	HR	RBI	BB	SO	SB	CS	AVG	OBP	SLG	OPS	OPS+	BR/A	RC	RC/G	FR	G/POS	WS	TPW
1953 Bro-N	1	1	0	0	0	0	0	0	0	1	0	0	.000	.000	.000	.000	-98	-0	0	.00	0	....	0	0.0

• TEIXEIRA, Mark Mark Charles Teixeira b: 4/11/1981, Annapolis, MD BB/TR, 6'3", 215 lbs. Deb: 4/1/2003

YEAR TM-L	G	AB	R	H	2B	3B	HR	RBI	BB	SO	SB	CS	AVG	OBP	SLG	OPS	OPS+	BR/A	RC	RC/G	FR	G/POS	WS	TPW
2003 Tex-A	146	529	66	137	29	5	26	84	44	120	1	2	.259	.332	.480	.812	102	-0	82	5.39	-8	*1-116,0-25(14-0-11),3-15/D	13	-1.8

• TEJADA, Miguel Miguel Odalis (Martinez) Tejada b: 5/25/1976, Bani, Dominican Republic BR/TR, 5'10", 170 lbs. Deb: 8/27/1997

YEAR TM-L	G	AB	R	H	2B	3B	HR	RBI	BB	SO	SB	CS	AVG	OBP	SLG	OPS	OPS+	BR/A	RC	RC/G	FR	G/POS	WS	TPW
1997 Oak-A	26	99	10	20	3	2	2	10	2	22	2	0	.202	.240	.333	.574	49	-7	7	2.46	-4	S-26	1	-0.9
1998 Oak-A	105	365	53	85	20	1	11	45	28	86	5	6	.233	.300	.384	.684	78	-14	40	3.63	2	*S-104	7	-0.3
1999 Oak-A	159	593	93	149	33	4	21	84	57	94	8	7	.251	.327	.427	.754	94	-8	83	4.68	10	*S-159/D-1	20	1.4
2000*Oak-A	160	607	105	167	32	1	30	115	66	102	6	0	.275	.350	.479	.829	110	9	102	6.00	-5	*S-160	23	1.6
2001*Oak-A	162	622	107	166	31	3	31	113	43	89	11	5	.267	.327	.476	.803	108	5	94	5.31	2	*S-162	25	2.0
2002*Oak-A★	162	662	108	204	30	0	34	131	38	84	7	2	.308	.356	.508	.863	126	23	114	6.33	-5	*S-162	32	3.0
2003*Oak-A	162	636	98	177	42	0	27	106	53	65	10	0	.278	.340	.472	.811	110	10	103	5.80	-1	*S-162	26	2.2
Total 7	936	3584	574	968	191	11	156	604	287	542	49	20	.270	.334	.460	.794	105	19	544	5.31	-1	S-935/D-1	134	9.1

• TEJADA, Wilfredo Wilfredo Aristides (Andujar) Tejada b: 11/12/1962, Santo Domingo, Dominican Republic BR/TR, 6', 175 lbs. Deb: 9/9/1986

YEAR TM-L	G	AB	R	H	2B	3B	HR	RBI	BB	SO	SB	CS	AVG	OBP	SLG	OPS	OPS+	BR/A	RC	RC/G	FR	G/POS	WS	TPW
1986 Mon-N	10	25	1	6	1	0	0	2	2	8	0	0	.240	.296	.280	.576	60	-1	2	2.54	1	C-10	0	0.0
1988 Mon-N	8	15	1	4	2	0	0	2	0	4	0	0	.267	.267	.400	.667	85	-0	2	3.67	0	/C-7	1	0.0
Total 2	18	40	2	10	3	0	0	4	2	12	0	0	.250	.286	.325	.611	70	-2	4	2.96	1	/C-17	1	0.0

• TEMPLE, Johnny John Ellis Temple b: 8/8/1927, Lexington, NC d: 1/9/1994, White Rock, SC BR/TR, 5'11", 175 lbs. Deb: 4/15/1952 C

YEAR TM-L	G	AB	R	H	2B	3B	HR	RBI	BB	SO	SB	CS	AVG	OBP	SLG	OPS	OPS+	BR/A	RC	RC/G	FR	G/POS	WS	TPW
1952 Cin-N	30	97	8	19	3	0	1	5	5	1	2	1	.196	.235	.258	.493	37	-8	5	1.81	0	2-22	1	-0.8

YEAR TM-L	G	AB	R	H	2B	3B	HR	RBI	BB	SO	SB	CS	AVG	OBP	SLG	OPS	OPS+	BR/A	RC	RC/G	FR	G/POS	WS	TPW
1953 Cin-N	63	110	14	29	4	0	1	9	7	12	1	0	.264	.314	.327	.641	67	-5	12	4.07	3	2-44	2	0.1
1954 Cin-N	146	505	60	155	14	8	0	44	62	24	21	7	.307	.385	.366	.751	94	1	77	5.60	2	*2-144	19	1.3
1955 Cin-N	150	588	94	165	20	3	0	50	80	32	19	4	.281	.368	.325	.693	81	-9	79	4.78	3	*2-149/S-1	16	0.5
1956 Cin-N★	154	632	88	180	18	3	2	41	58	40	14	4	.285	.346	.332	.678	78	-15	76	4.21	-6	*2-154/0-1	16	-1.0
1957 Cin-N★	145	557	85	158	24	4	0	37	**94**	34	19	5	.284	.391	.341	.732	92	2	86	5.42	-3	*2-145	19	1.0
1958 Cin-N	141	542	82	166	31	6	3	47	91	41	15	8	.306	.406	.402	.808	109	12	96	6.30	-2	*2-141/1-1	21	2.1
1959 Cin-N★	149	598	102	186	35	6	8	67	72	40	14	3	.311	.387	.430	.817	114	16	104	6.27	-17	*2-149	22	1.1
1960 Cle-A	98	381	50	102	13	1	2	19	32	20	11	5	.268	.326	.323	.649	79	-11	41	3.66	-15	2-77,3-17	8	-2.0
1961 Cle-A★	129	518	73	143	22	3	3	30	61	36	9	5	.276	.352	.347	.700	90	-6	65	4.39	-14	*2-129	12	-0.9
1962 Bal-A	78	270	28	71	8	1	1	17	36	22	7	4	.263	.352	.311	.663	84	-5	33	4.10	1	2-71	8	0.2
Hou-N	31	95	14	25	4	0	0	12	7	11	1	0	.263	.314	.305	.619	72	-3	10	3.34	-4	2-26/3-1	1	-0.6
1963 Hou-N	100	322	22	85	12	1	1	17	41	24	7	2	.264	.347	.317	.664	99	2	40	4.18	-10	2-61,3-29	12	-0.3
1964 Cin-N	6	3	0	0	0	0	0	0	2	1	0	0	.000	.400	.000	.400	23	-0	0	.94	0	....	0	0.0
Total 13	1420	5218	720	1484	208	36	22	395	648	338	140	48	.284	.365	.351	.716	91	-30	725	4.87	-62	*2-1312/3-47,1-1,0-1,S-1	157	0.8

• TEMPLETON, Garry   Garry Lewis Templeton   b: 3/24/1956, Lockney, TX   BB/TR, 5'11", 190 lbs.   Deb: 8/9/1976

YEAR TM-L	G	AB	R	H	2B	3B	HR	RBI	BB	SO	SB	CS	AVG	OBP	SLG	OPS	OPS+	BR/A	RC	RC/G	FR	G/POS	WS	TPW
1976 StL-N	53	213	32	62	8	2	1	17	7	33	11	7	.291	.317	.362	.678	91	-4	24	3.97	-1	S-53	5	0.2
1977 StL-N★	153	621	94	200	19	**18**	8	79	15	70	28	24	.322	.339	.449	.788	111	3	85	5.00	5	*S-151	24	2.4
1978 StL-N	155	647	82	181	31	**13**	2	47	22	87	34	11	.280	.304	.377	.682	91	-8	74	4.10	19	*S-155	21	2.9
1979 StL-N★	154	672	105	**211**	32	**19**	9	62	18	91	26	10	.314	.333	.458	.791	113	10	100	5.57	21	*S-150	25	4.8
1980 StL-N	118	504	83	161	19	9	4	43	18	43	31	15	.319	.343	.417	.760	108	4	66	4.80	27	*S-115	17	4.5
1981 StL-N	80	333	47	96	16	8	1	33	14	55	8	12	.288	.317	.393	.710	98	-6	37	3.95	7	S-76	10	1.1
1982 SD-N	141	563	76	139	25	8	6	64	26	82	27	16	.247	.281	.352	.633	80	-18	49	2.79	-2	*S-136	11	-0.6
1983 SD-N	126	460	39	121	20	2	3	40	21	57	16	6	.263	.295	.335	.630	77	-15	42	3.05	-2	*S-123	10	-0.3
1984*SD-N	148	493	40	127	19	3	2	35	39	81	8	3	.258	.313	.320	.634	79	-14	48	3.42	6	*S-146	16	0.8
1985 SD-N★	148	546	63	154	30	2	6	55	41	88	16	6	.282	.333	.377	.711	100	-0	69	4.55	13	*S-148	21	3.0
1986 SD-N	147	510	42	126	21	2	2	44	35	86	10	5	.247	.297	.308	.605	68	-23	44	2.96	-9	*S-144	8	-1.8
1987 SD-N	148	510	42	113	13	5	5	48	42	92	14	3	.222	.282	.296	.578	55	-32	42	2.68	8	*S-146	6	-0.9
1988 SD-N	110	362	35	90	15	7	3	36	20	50	8	2	.249	.288	.354	.642	85	-8	36	3.39	1	*S-105/3-2	12	0.2
1989 SD-N	142	506	43	129	26	3	6	40	23	80	1	3	.255	.287	.354	.641	82	-15	47	3.12	5	*S-140	11	0.1
1990 SD-N	144	505	45	125	25	3	9	59	24	59	1	4	.248	.282	.362	.644	75	-21	46	3.00	-8	*S-135	10	-1.8
1991 SD-N	32	57	5	11	1	1	1	6	1	9	0	1	.193	.207	.298	.505	39	-5	2	1.28	1	3-15/S-1	0	-0.5
NY-N	80	219	20	50	9	1	2	20	9	29	3	1	.228	.259	.306	.565	59	-12	16	2.36	2	S-40,1-25/3-2,0-2(0-0-2)	2	-0.9
Yr.	112	276	25	61	10	2	3	26	10	38	3	2	.221	.248	.304	.553	55	-18	18	2.12	3	S-41,1-25,3-17/0-2(0-0-2)	2	-1.4
Total 16	2079	7721	893	2096	329	106	70	728	375	1092	242	129	.271	.306	.369	.675	87	-164	829	3.71	93	*S-1964/1-25,3-19,0-2	209	13.0

• TENACE, Gene   Fury Gene Tenace   b: 10/10/1946, Russellton, PA   BR/TR, 6', 190 lbs.   Deb: 5/29/1969   M/C   Career OF: 1-0-10

YEAR TM-L	G	AB	R	H	2B	3B	HR	RBI	BB	SO	SB	CS	AVG	OBP	SLG	OPS	OPS+	BR/A	RC	RC/G	FR	G/POS	WS	TPW
1969 Oak-A	16	38	1	6	0	0	1	2	1	15	0	0	.158	.200	.237	.437	23	-4	2	1.61	0	C-13	0	-0.4
1970 Oak-A	38	105	19	32	6	0	7	20	23	30	0	2	.305	.430	.562	.992	178	11	26	9.01	3	C-30	8	1.7
1971*Oak-A	65	179	26	49	7	0	7	25	29	34	2	1	.274	.381	.430	.811	132	9	31	6.24	-4	C-52/0-1	10	0.7
1972*Oak-A	82	227	22	51	5	3	5	32	24	42	0	0	.225	.307	.339	.646	97	-1	24	3.63	-5	C-49/0-9(0-0-9),1-7,2-2,3	7	-0.4
1973*Oak-A	160	510	83	132	18	2	24	84	101	94	2	2	.259	.391	.443	.834	142	33	94	6.21	-3	*1-134,C-33/D-3,2-1	26	2.2
1974*Oak-A	158	484	71	102	17	1	26	73	**110**	105	2	9	.211	.370	.411	.781	133	23	78	5.18	-3	*1-106,C-79/2-3	22	1.7
1975*Oak-A★	158	498	83	127	17	0	29	87	106	127	7	4	.255	.398	.464	.862	146	36	100	6.95	1	*C-125,1-68/D-1	32	4.0
1976 Oak-A	128	417	64	104	19	1	22	66	81	91	5	4	.249	.376	.458	.835	150	28	76	6.26	-2	1-70,C-65/D-2	22	2.6
1977 SD-N	147	437	66	102	24	4	15	61	**125**	119	5	3	.233	.417	.410	.827	137	33	87	6.73	1	C-99,1-36,3-14	25	3.7
1978 SD-N	142	401	60	90	18	4	16	61	101	98	6	5	.224	.394	.409	.803	135	24	73	6.08	1	1-80,C-71/3-1	22	2.6
1979 SD-N	151	463	61	122	16	4	20	67	105	106	2	6	.263	.407	.445	.852	141	30	91	6.78	-1	C-94,1-72	24	3.0
1980 SD-N	133	316	46	70	11	1	17	50	92	63	4	4	.222	.403	.424	.827	139	22	58	5.93	-2	*C-104,1-19	15	2.4
1981 StL-N	58	129	26	30	7	0	5	22	38	26	0	0	.233	.421	.403	.824	131	8	26	6.84	-1	C-38/1-7	8	0.9
1982*StL-N	66	124	18	32	9	0	7	18	36	31	1	1	.258	.439	.500	.939	160	13	31	8.82	-1	C-37/1-7	9	1.4
1983 Pit-N	53	62	7	11	5	0	0	6	12	17	0	1	.177	.346	.258	.604	68	-2	7	3.49	-2	1-19/C-3,0-1	1	-0.5
Total 15	1555	4390	653	1060	179	20	201	674	984	998	36	42	.241	.391	.429	.819	137	264	805	6.19	-16	C-892,1-625/3-17,0-11,2-6,D	231	25.7

• TENER, John   John Kinley Tener   b: 7/25/1863, County Tyrone, Ireland   d: 5/19/1946, Pittsburgh, PA   BR/TR, 6'4", 180 lbs.   Deb: 6/8/1885   U   Career OF: 4-0-6   ♦

YEAR TM-L	G	AB	R	H	2B	3B	HR	RBI	BB	SO	SB	CS	AVG	OBP	SLG	OPS	OPS+	BR/A	RC	RC/G	FR	G/POS	WS	TPW
1885 Bal-a	1	4	0	0	0	0	0	0	0	....	....	....	.000	.000	.000	.000	-102	-1	0	.00	-1	/0-1	0	-0.2
1888 Chi-N	12	46	4	9	1	0	0	1	1	15	1	....	.196	.229	.217	.447	40	-0	3	1.89	1	P-12/0-1	6	0.1
1889 Chi-N	42	150	18	41	4	2	1	19	7	22	2	....	.273	.306	.347	.652	78	4	17	4.11	3	P-35/0-6(1-0-5),1-2	18	1.6
1890 Pit-P	18	63	7	12	0	0	2	5	7	10	1	....	.190	.301	.286	.587	62	1	6	3.11	3	P-14/3-2,0-2(2-0-0)	0	-3.2
Total 4	73	263	29	62	5	2	3	25	15	47	4	....	.236	.287	.304	.591	65	4	25	3.37	5	/P-61,0-10,1-2,3-2	24	-1.7

• TENNANT, Tom   Thomas Francis Tennant   b: 7/3/1882, Monroe, WI   d: 2/15/1955, San Carlos, CA   BL/TL, 5'11", 165 lbs.   Deb: 4/18/1912

YEAR TM-L	G	AB	R	H	2B	3B	HR	RBI	BB	SO	SB	CS	AVG	OBP	SLG	OPS	OPS+	BR/A	RC	RC/G	FR	G/POS	WS	TPW
1912 StL-A	2	2	1	0	0	0	0	0	0	....	0	....	.000	.000	.000	.000	-104	-1	0	.00	0	....	0	-0.1

• TENNEY, Fred   Frederick Tenney   b: 11/26/1871, Georgetown, MA   d: 7/3/1952, Boston, MA   BL/TL, 5'9", 155 lbs.   Deb: 6/16/1894   M   Career OF: 35-7-62

YEAR TM-L	G	AB	R	H	2B	3B	HR	RBI	BB	SO	SB	CS	AVG	OBP	SLG	OPS	OPS+	BR/A	RC	RC/G	FR	G/POS	WS	TPW
1894 Bos-N	27	86	23	34	7	1	2	21	12	9	6	....	.395	.469	.570	1.039	133	5	26	13.23	1	C-20/0-6(3-2-1),1-1	4	0.5
1895 Bos-N	49	173	35	47	9	1	1	21	24	5	6	....	.272	.360	.353	.713	80	-5	25	5.27	1	0-28(25-3-0),C-21	4	-0.4
1896 Bos-N	88	348	64	117	14	3	2	49	36	12	18	....	.336	.400	.411	.811	108	4	69	7.21	1	0-60(7-0-53),C-27	12	0.4
1897*Bos-N	132	566	125	180	24	3	1	85	49	....	34	....	.318	.376	.376	.753	93	-5	99	6.33	1	*1-128/0-4(0-0-4)	15	-0.4
1898 Bos-N	117	488	106	160	25	5	0	62	33	....	23	....	.328	.370	.400	.770	114	8	85	6.53	-1	*1-117/C-1	17	0.6
1899 Bos-N	150	603	115	209	19	17	1	67	63	....	28	....	.347	.411	.439	.851	121	19	126	8.03	7	*1-150	25	2.3
1900 Bos-N	112	437	77	122	13	5	1	56	39	....	17	....	.279	.346	.339	.685	80	-12	60	4.89	6	*1-111	7	-0.6
1901 Bos-N	115	451	66	127	13	1	1	22	37	....	15	....	.282	.340	.322	.662	85	-8	58	4.52	8	*1-113/C-2	9	-0.2
1902 Bos-N	134	489	88	154	18	3	2	30	73	....	21	....	.315	.409	.376	.785	141	29	90	6.57	6	*1-134	25	3.4
1903 Bos-N	122	447	79	140	22	3	3	41	70	....	21	....	.313	.415	.396	.811	137	27	87	7.11	4	*1-122	21	2.8
1904 Bos-N	147	533	76	144	17	9	1	37	57	....	17	....	.270	.351	.341	.692	118	14	75	4.72	7	*1-144/0-4(0-1-3)	19	1.9
1905 Bos-N	149	549	84	158	18	3	0	28	67	....	17	....	.288	.368	.332	.700	111	11	77	4.96	25	*1-148/P-1	17	3.5
1906 Bos-N	143	544	61	154	12	8	1	28	58	....	17	....	.283	.357	.340	.698	121	15	76	4.88	7	*1-143	17	2.1
1907 Bos-N	150	554	83	151	18	8	0	26	82	....	15	....	.273	.371	.334	.705	122	18	79	4.87	6	*1-149	22	2.4
1908 NY-N	156	583	**101**	149	20	1	2	49	72	....	17	....	.256	.344	.304	.648	102	5	68	3.88	10	*1-156	19	1.4
1909 NY-N	101	375	43	88	8	2	3	30	52	....	8	....	.235	.333	.291	.623	92	-1	39	3.44	10	1-98	9	0.8
1911 Bos-N	102	369	52	97	13	4	1	36	50	17	5	....	.263	.352	.328	.680	84	-7	45	4.12	0	1-96/0-2(0-1-1)	7	-0.8
Total 17	1994	7595	1278	2231	270	77	22	688	874	43	285	....	.294	.371	.358	.730	110	116	1184	5.52	99	*1-1810,0-104/C-71,P-1	249	19.6

• TENNEY, Fred   Fred Clay Tenney   b: 7/9/1859, Marlborough, NH   d: 6/15/1919, Fall River, MA   Deb: 4/28/1884

YEAR TM-L	G	AB	R	H	2B	3B	HR	RBI	BB	SO	SB	CS	AVG	OBP	SLG	OPS	OPS+	BR/A	RC	RC/G	FR	G/POS	WS	TPW
1884 Was-U	32	119	17	28	3	1	0	....	6	....	....	....	.235	.272	.277	.549	89	-1	9	2.83	-2	0-27(0-1-26)/1-6	3	-0.3
Bos-U	4	17	1	2	0	0	0	....	0	....	....	....	.118	.118	.118	.235	-21	-2	0	.45	-1	/P-4	2	0.0
Wil-U	1	3	0	0	0	0	0	....	0	....	....	....	.000	.000	.000	.000	-97	-1	0	.00	0	/P-1	0	0.1
Yr.	37	139	18	30	3	1	0	....	6	....	....	....	.216	.248	.252	.500	72	-3	9	2.43	-3	0-27(0-1-26)/1-6,P-5	5	-0.2

• TEPEDINO, Frank   Frank Ronald Tepedino   b: 11/23/1947, Brooklyn, NY   BL/TL, 5'11", 192 lbs.   Deb: 5/12/1967   Career OF: 2-0-13

YEAR TM-L	G	AB	R	H	2B	3B	HR	RBI	BB	SO	SB	CS	AVG	OBP	SLG	OPS	OPS+	BR/A	RC	RC/G	FR	G/POS	WS	TPW
1967 NY-A	9	5	0	2	0	0	0	0	1	1	0	0	.400	.500	.400	.900	175	1	1	10.17	0	/1-1	0	0.0
1969 NY-A	13	39	6	9	0	0	0	4	4	4	1	0	.231	.302	.231	.533	53	-2	3	2.28	-1	0-13(0-0-13)	0	-0.4
1970 NY-A	16	19	2	6	2	0	0	2	1	2	0	1	.316	.350	.421	.771	118	-0	2	3.72	0	/1-1,0-1	0	-0.1
1971 NY-A	6	6	0	0	0	0	0	0	0	0	0	0	.000	.000	.000	.000	-107	-2	0	.00	-0	/0-1	0	-0.2
Mil-A	53	106	11	21	1	0	2	7	4	17	2	2	.198	.234	.264	.498	41	-9	6	1.92	3	1-28	0	-0.8
Yr.	59	112	11	21	1	0	2	7	4	17	2	2	.188	.222	.250	.472	34	-10	6	1.78	3	1-28/0-1	0	-1.0
1972 NY-A	8	8	0	0	0	0	0	0	0	1	0	0	.000	.000	.000	.000	-103	-2	0	.00	0	....	0	-0.2
1973 Atl-N	74	148	20	45	5	0	4	29	13	21	0	0	.304	.360	.419	.779	107	2	21	5.02	2	1-58	3	0.1
1974 Atl-N	78	169	11	39	5	1	0	16	9	13	1	2	.231	.274	.272	.546	51	-12	11	2.17	2	1-46	0	-1.3

YEAR TM-L	G	AB	R	H	2B	3B	HR	RBI	BB	SO	SB	CS	AVG	OBP	SLG	OPS	OPS+	BR/A	RC	RC/G	FR	G/POS	WS	TPW
1975 Atl-N	8	7	0	0	0	0	0	0	1	2	0	0	.000	.125	.000	.125	-61	-1	0	.00	0	....	0	-0.2
Total 8	**265**	**507**	**50**	**122**	**13**	**1**	**6**	**58**	**33**	**61**	**4**	**5**	**.241**	**.290**	**.306**	**.595**	**64**	**-26**	**44**	**2.89**	**5**	**1-134/0-15**	**3**	**-3.0**
• TEPSIC, Joe	Joseph John Tepsic b: 9/18/1923, Slovan, PA BR/TR, 5'9", 170 lbs. Deb: 7/12/1946																							
1946 Bro-N	15	5	2	0	0	0	0	0	1	1	0	....	.000	.167	.000	.167	-50	-1	0	.23	-0	/0-1	0	-0.1
• TERRELL, Jerry	Jerry Wayne Terrell b: 7/13/1946, Waseca, MN BR/TR, 5'11", 170 lbs. Deb: 4/14/1973 Career OF: 12-1-11																							
1973 Min-A	124	438	43	116	15	2	1	32	21	56	13	7	.265	.300	.315	.615	71	-17	42	3.28	-4	S-81,3-30,2-14/D-1,0-1	7	-1.2
1974 Min-A	116	229	43	56	4	6	0	19	11	27	3	2	.245	.279	.314	.594	68	-10	19	2.73	2	S-34,2-26,3-21,D-12/0-3(3-0-0),1	3	-0.4
1975 Min-A	108	385	48	110	16	2	1	36	19	27	4	4	.286	.324	.345	.670	87	-7	41	3.64	0	S-41,2-39,1-15,3-12/0-6(0-0-6),D	7	-0.3
1976 Min-A	89	171	29	42	3	1	0	8	9	15	11	2	.246	.287	.275	.562	63	-6	14	2.76	-1	2-31,3-26,S-16,D-12/0-6(3-1-2)	3	-0.5
1977 Min-A	93	214	32	48	6	0	1	20	11	21	10	4	.224	.265	.266	.532	46	-15	13	1.90	-1	3-59,2-14/D-9,S-7,1-1,0-1	2	-1.5
1978 KC-A	73	133	14	27	1	0	0	8	4	13	8	4	.203	.226	.211	.437	23	-14	6	1.31	4	2-31,3-25,S-11/1-5	2	-0.9
1979 KC-A	31	40	5	12	3	0	1	2	1	1	1	0	.300	.317	.450	.767	102	0	5	4.40	2	3-19/2-7,D-1,P-1,S-1	1	0.2
1980 KC-A	23	16	4	1	0	0	0	0	0	0	0	0	.063	.063	.063	.125	-65	-4	0	.11	1	/0-7(6-0-1),1-3,2-3,D-1,P-1	0	-0.3
Total 8	**657**	**1626**	**218**	**412**	**48**	**11**	**4**	**125**	**76**	**160**	**50**	**23**	**.253**	**.289**	**.304**	**.593**	**66**	**-73**	**141**	**2.84**	**3**	**3-192,S-191,2-165/D-38,1,0,P**	**25**	**-4.9**
• TERRELL, Tom	John Thomas Terrell b: 6/29/1867, Louisville, KY d: 7/9/1893, Louisville, KY Deb: 10/5/1886																							
1886 Lou-a	1	4	0	1	0	0	0	0	0	....	0	....	.250	.250	.250	.500	54	-0	0	2.31	-1	/C-1,0-1	0	-0.1
• TERRERO, Luis	Luis Enrique Terrero b: 5/18/1980, Barahona, Dominican Republic BR/TR, 6'2", 206 lbs. Deb: 7/10/2003																							
2003 Ari-N	5	4	0	1	0	0	0	0	0	1	0	0	.250	.400	.250	.650	68	-0	1	4.54	0	/0-3(0-2-1)	0	0.0
• TERRY,	Wallace W. Terry b: 10/1850, Attleboro, PA d: 1/21/1916, Philadelphia, PA Deb: 4/26/1875																							
1875 Was-n	6	22	0	4	0	1	0	2	0	1	0	0	.182	.182	.273	.455	58	-1	1	1.83	-3	/1-4,0-3(0-1-2)	....	-0.3
• TERRY, Adonis	William H Terry b: 8/7/1864, Westfield, MA d: 2/24/1915, Milwaukee, WI BR/TR, 5'11.5", 168 lbs. Deb: 5/1/1884 U Career OF: 94-43-79 ♦																							
1884 Bro-a	67	236	15	55	10	3	0	0	8	....	....	....	.233	.258	.301	.559	81	2	19	2.85	-3	P-56,0-13(2-7-4)	29	0.1
1885 Bro-a	71	264	23	45	1	3	1	20	10	....	....	....	.170	.201	.208	.409	29	-17	11	1.40	2	0-47(26-11-10),P-25/3-1	9	-3.4
1886 Bro-a	75	299	34	71	8	9	2	39	10	....	17	....	.237	.265	.344	.609	89	-1	33	3.85	3	P-34,0-32(10-11-11),S-13	26	1.1
1887 Bro-a	86	368	56	119	6	10	3	65	16	....	27	....	.323	.323	.392	.715	98	4	55	5.93	3	0-49(12-4-33),P-40/S-2	27	0.9
1888 Bro-a	30	115	13	29	6	0	0	8	5	....	7	....	.252	.283	.304	.588	88	2	12	3.83	2	P-23/0-7(2-4-1),1-2	21	2.2
1889*Bro-a	49	160	29	48	6	6	2	26	14	14	8	....	.300	.356	.450	.806	128	12	29	6.91	6	P-41,1-10	30	2.3
1890*Bro-N	99	363	63	101	17	9	4	59	40	34	32	....	.278	.356	.408	.764	122	18	66	6.65	-2	0-54(42-5-7),P-46/1-1	41	3.0
1891 Bro-N	30	91	10	19	7	1	0	6	9	26	4	....	.209	.301	.308	.609	78	3	10	3.70	-1	P-25/0-5(0-0-5)	9	-1.1
1892 Bal-N	1	4	0	0	0	0	0	0	0	1	0	....	.000	.000	.000	.000	-97	-1	0	.00	0	/P-1	0	-0.1
Pit-N	31	100	10	16	0	4	2	11	10	11	2	....	.160	.236	.300	.536	62	1	8	2.49	0	P-30/0-1	20	1.3
Yr.	32	104	10	16	0	4	2	11	10	12	2	....	.154	.228	.288	.517	56	0	8	2.38	0	P-31/0-1	20	1.2
1893 Pit-N	26	71	9	18	4	3	0	11	3	12	1	....	.254	.293	.394	.688	84	2	9	4.36	0	P-26	13	0.0
1894 Pit-N	1	0	0	0	0	0	0	0	0	0	0	....	....	....	....	....	-101	0	0	....	-0	/P-1	0	-0.4
Chi-N	30	95	19	33	4	2	0	17	11	12	3	....	.347	.415	.432	.847	99	5	19	7.85	-1	P-23/0-7(0-0-7),1-2	8	0.3
Yr.	31	95	19	33	4	2	0	17	11	12	3	....	.347	.415	.432	.847	99	5	19	7.85	-1	P-24/0-7(0-0-7),1-2	8	0.0
1895 Chi-N	40	137	18	30	3	2	1	10	2	17	1	....	.219	.236	.292	.528	33	-7	10	2.51	2	P-38/0-1,S-1	22	0.3
1896 Chi-N	30	99	14	26	4	2	0	15	8	12	4	....	.263	.324	.343	.668	73	3	13	4.53	-2	P-30	18	0.2
1897 Chi-N	1	3	1	0	0	0	0	0	0	....	0	....	.000	.000	.000	.000	-96	-1	0	.00	0	/P-1	0	-0.5
Total 14	**667**	**2405**	**314**	**610**	**76**	**54**	**15**	**287**	**146**	**139**	**106**	**....**	**.254**	**.295**	**.344**	**.639**	**85**	**27**	**293**	**4.35**	**9**	**P-440,0-216/S-16,1-15,3-1**	**273**	**6.4**
• TERRY, Bill	William Harold "Memphis Bill" Terry b: 10/30/1896, Atlanta, GA d: 1/9/1989, Jacksonville, FL BL/TL, 6'1", 200 lbs. Deb: 9/24/1923 M HOF: 1954 Career OF: 2-0-13																							
1923 NY-N	3	7	1	1	0	0	0	0	2	2	0	0	.143	.333	.143	.476	30	-1	0	2.15	0	/1-2	0	-0.1
1924*NY-N	77	163	26	39	7	2	5	24	17	18	1	1	.239	.311	.399	.710	91	-2	21	4.35	-1	1-35	4	-0.5
1925 NY-N	133	489	75	156	31	6	11	70	42	52	4	5	.319	.374	.474	.848	120	14	86	6.66	7	*1-126	18	1.2
1926 NY-N	98	225	26	65	12	5	5	43	22	17	3	....	.289	.352	.453	.806	117	5	35	5.47	5	1-38,0-14(1-0-13)	8	0.6
1927 NY-N	150	580	101	189	32	13	20	121	46	53	1	....	.326	.377	.529	.907	141	31	112	7.09	9	*1-150	27	2.9
1928 NY-N	149	568	100	185	36	11	17	101	64	36	7	....	.326	.394	.518	.912	136	29	114	7.39	-2	*1-149	24	1.7
1929 NY-N	150	607	103	226	39	5	14	117	48	35	10	....	.372	.418	.522	.941	132	30	128	8.33	6	*1-149/0-1	24	2.4
1930 NY-N	154	633	139	**254**	39	15	23	129	57	33	8	....	**.401**	.452	.619	1.071	159	61	170	11.10	12	*1-154	32	5.5
1931 NY-N	153	611	**121**	213	43	**20**	9	112	47	36	8	....	.349	.397	.529	.926	150	**42**	130	8.43	6	*1-153	29	3.4
1932 NY-N	154	643	124	225	42	11	28	117	32	23	4	....	.350	.382	.580	.962	158	49	142	8.79	13	*1-154	32	4.7
1933*NY-N★	123	475	68	153	20	5	6	58	40	23	3	....	.322	.375	.423	.798	129	19	77	6.11	0	*1-117	21	0.8
1934 NY-N★	153	602	109	213	30	6	8	83	60	47	0	....	.354	.414	.463	.878	138	34	122	7.92	5	*1-153	29	2.4
1935 NY-N★	145	596	91	203	32	8	6	64	41	55	7	....	.341	.383	.451	.834	126	21	104	6.67	10	*1-143	23	1.8
1936*NY-N	79	229	36	71	10	5	2	39	19	19	0	....	.310	.363	.424	.786	112	4	35	5.57	1	1-56	7	0.0
Total 14	**1721**	**6428**	**1120**	**2193**	**373**	**112**	**154**	**1078**	**537**	**449**	**56**	**6**	**.341**	**.393**	**.506**	**.899**	**136**	**337**	**1275**	**7.60**	**71**	***1-1579/0-15**	**278**	**26.9**
• TERRY, Zeb	Zebulon Alexander Terry b: 6/17/1891, Denison, TX d: 3/14/1988, Los Angeles, CA BR/TR, 5'8", 129 lbs. Deb: 4/12/1916																							
1916 Chi-A	94	269	20	51	8	4	0	17	33	36	4	....	.190	.292	.249	.541	62	-12	23	2.59	-3	S-93	6	-1.0
1917 Chi-A	2	1	0	0	0	0	0	0	2	0	0	....	.000	.667	.000	.667	102	0	0	.00	0	/S-1	0	0.0
1918 Bos-N	28	105	17	32	2	2	0	8	8	14	1	....	.305	.360	.362	.722	125	3	14	4.70	6	S-27	5	1.3
1919 Pit-N	129	472	46	107	12	6	0	27	31	26	12	....	.227	.280	.278	.558	65	-20	39	2.67	-6	*S-127	10	-1.8
1920 Chi-N	133	496	56	139	26	9	0	52	44	22	12	16	.280	.341	.369	.710	102	-0	61	4.01	6	S-70,2-63	17	1.2
1921 Chi-N	123	488	59	134	18	1	2	45	27	19	1	13	.275	.318	.328	.646	71	-23	49	3.24	1	*2-122	7	-1.9
1922 Chi-N	131	496	56	142	24	2	0	67	34	16	2	11	.286	.335	.343	.677	74	-22	56	3.69	8	*2-125/S-4,3-3	10	-1.0
Total 7	**640**	**2327**	**254**	**605**	**90**	**24**	**2**	**216**	**179**	**133**	**32**	**40**	**.260**	**.318**	**.322**	**.640**	**78**	**-73**	**243**	**3.37**	**12**	**S-322,2-310/3-3**	**55**	**-3.1**
• TERWILLIGER, Wayne	Willard Wayne "Twig" Terwilliger b: 6/27/1925, Clare, MI BR/TR, 5'11", 170 lbs. Deb: 8/6/1949 C																							
1949 Chi-N	36	112	11	25	2	1	2	10	16	22	0	....	.223	.326	.313	.638	74	-4	13	3.82	-2	2-34	3	-0.4
1950 Chi-N	133	480	63	116	22	3	10	32	43	63	13	....	.242	.311	.363	.673	77	-16	56	3.94	-22	*2-126/1-1,3-1,0-1	9	-3.1
1951 Chi-N	50	192	26	41	6	0	0	10	29	21	3	1	.214	.317	.245	.562	52	-12	17	2.84	-3	2-49	2	-1.2
Bro-N	37	50	11	14	1	0	0	4	8	7	1	0	.280	.390	.300	.690	86	-0	7	4.96	1	2-24/3-1	2	0.2
Yr.	87	242	37	55	7	0	0	14	37	28	4	1	.227	.332	.256	.588	59	-12	24	3.24	-2	2-73/3-1	4	-1.0
1953 Was-A	134	464	62	117	24	4	4	46	64	65	7	4	.252	.343	.347	.690	89	-6	58	4.17	14	*2-133	15	1.9
1954 Was-A	106	337	42	70	10	1	3	24	32	40	3	3	.208	.282	.270	.552	55	-21	27	2.50	1	2-90,3-10/S-3	4	-1.4
1955 NY-N	80	257	29	66	16	1	1	18	36	42	2	4	.257	.350	.339	.689	84	-6	30	3.74	8	2-78/3-1,S-1	8	0.9
1956 NY-N	14	18	0	4	1	0	0	0	0	5	0	0	.222	.222	.278	.500	34	-2	1	2.14	-1	/2-6	0	-0.3
1959 KC-A	74	180	27	48	11	0	2	18	19	31	2	2	.267	.337	.361	.698	90	-3	23	4.35	0	2-63/S-2,3-1	5	0.2
1960 KC-A	2	1	0	0	0	0	0	0	0	0	0	0	.000	.000	.000	.000	-99	-0	0	.00	0	/2-2	0	-0.1
Total 9	**666**	**2091**	**271**	**501**	**93**	**10**	**22**	**162**	**247**	**296**	**31**	**14**	**.240**	**.323**	**.325**	**.648**	**75**	**-69**	**230**	**3.65**	**-5**	**2-605/3-14,S-6,1-1,0-1**	**48**	**-3.3**
• TESCH, Al	Albert John "Tiny" Tesch b: 1/27/1891, Jersey City, NJ d: 8/3/1947, Jersey City, NJ BB/TR, 5'10", 155 lbs. Deb: 8/21/1915																							
1915 Bro-F	8	7	2	2	1	0	0	2	0	0	0	....	.286	.286	.429	.714	111	0	1	4.15	0	/2-3	0	0.0
• TESTA, Nick	Nicholas Testa b: 6/29/1928, New York, NY BR/TR, 5'8", 180 lbs. Deb: 4/23/1958 C																							
1958 SF-N	1	0	0	0	0	0	0	0	0	0	0	0	....	....	....	....	-102	0	0	....	-1	/C-1	0	-0.1
• TETTELBACH, Dick	Richard Morley "Tut" Tettelbach b: 6/26/1929, New Haven, CT d: 1/26/1995, East Harwich, MA BR/TR, 6', 195 lbs. Deb: 9/25/1955 Career OF: 22-2-0																							
1955 NY-A	2	5	0	0	0	0	0	0	0	0	0	0	.000	.000	.000	.000	-102	-1	0	.00	0	/0-2(2-0-0)	0	-0.1
1956 Was-A	18	64	10	10	1	2	1	9	14	15	0	1	.156	.308	.281	.589	56	-4	7	3.04	0	0-18(18-0-0)	1	-0.5
1957 Was-A	9	11	2	2	0	0	0	1	4	2	0	0	.182	.400	.182	.582	65	-0	1	3.60	0	/0-3(2-2-0)	0	-0.1
Total 3	**29**	**80**	**12**	**12**	**1**	**2**	**1**	**10**	**18**	**17**	**0**	**1**	**.150**	**.306**	**.250**	**.556**	**50**	**-6**	**8**	**2.91**	**1**	**/0-23**	**1**	**-0.7**

YEAR TM-L	G	AB	R	H	2B	3B	HR	RBI	BB	SO	SB	CS	AVG	OBP	SLG	OPS	OPS+	BR/A	RC	RC/G	FR	G/POS	WS	TPW
• TETTLETON, Mickey	Mickey Lee Tettleton b: 9/16/1960, Oklahoma City, OK BB/TR, 6'2", 212 lbs. Deb: 6/30/1984 Career OF: 24-0-120																							
1984 Oak-A	33	76	10	20	2	1	1	5	11	21	0	0	.263	.356	.355	.712	105	1	10	4.35	1	C-32	3	0.3
1985 Oak-A	78	211	23	53	12	0	3	15	28	59	2	2	.251	.344	.351	.695	98	-0	26	4.11	1	C-76/D-1	7	0.4
1986 Oak-A	90	211	26	43	9	0	10	35	39	51	7	1	.204	.331	.389	.719	103	3	31	4.53	-3	C-89	8	0.4
1987 Oak-A	82	211	19	41	3	0	8	26	30	65	1	1	.194	.295	.322	.617	68	-10	22	3.22	-1	C-80/1-1,D-1	4	-0.7
1988 Bal-A	86	283	31	74	11	1	11	37	28	70	0	1	.261	.332	.424	.756	113	4	38	4.66	-2	C-80	9	0.7
1989 Bal-A★	117	411	72	106	21	2	26	65	73	117	3	2	.258	.371	.509	.880	150	28	80	6.79	-0	C-75,D-43	20	3.2
1990 Bal-A	135	444	68	99	21	2	15	51	106	160	2	4	.223	.378	.381	.759	117	14	71	5.35	-4	C-90,D-40/1-5,0-1	16	1.5
1991 Det-A	154	501	85	132	17	2	31	89	101	131	3	3	.263	.389	.491	.880	140	30	99	6.90	0	*C-125,D-24/0-3(2-0-1),1-1	27	3.7
1992 Det-A	157	525	82	125	25	0	32	83	**122**	137	0	6	.238	.383	.469	.851	137	28	100	6.49	1	*C-113,D-40/1-3,0-2(1-0-1)	24	3.4
1993 Det-A	152	522	79	128	25	4	32	110	109	139	3	7	.245	.376	.492	.868	132	24	101	6.64	-3	1-59,C-56,0-55(18-0-39)/D-4	24	1.8
1994 Det-A★	107	339	57	84	18	2	17	51	97	98	0	1	.248	.422	.463	.885	127	19	74	7.64	0	C-53,1-24,D-22,0-18(1-0-17)	14	1.8
1995 Tex-A	134	429	76	102	19	1	32	78	107	110	0	0	.238	.398	.510	.908	131	24	95	7.55	0	0-63(2-0-61),D-58/1-9,C-3	17	1.6
1996*Tex-A	143	491	78	121	26	1	24	83	95	137	2	1	.246	.372	.450	.822	101	3	86	5.92	-1	*D-115,1-23	11	-0.7
1997 Tex-A	17	44	5	4	1	0	3	4	3	12	0	0	.091	.167	.318	.485	22	-5	2	1.42	0	D-13	0	-0.6
Total 14	**1485**	**4698**	**711**	**1132**	**210**	**16**	**245**	**732**	**949**	**1307**	**23**	**29**	**.241**	**.372**	**.449**	**.821**	**122**	**163**	**836**	**6.02**	**-12**	**C-872,D-361,0-142,1-125**	**184**	**16.8**
• TEUFEL, Tim	Timothy Shawn Teufel b: 7/7/1958, Greenwich, CT BR/TR, 6', 175 lbs. Deb: 9/3/1983																							
1983 Min-A	21	78	11	24	7	1	3	6	2	8	0	0	.308	.325	.538	.863	128	2	13	6.29	1	2-18/D-1,S-1	3	0.5
1984 Min-A	157	568	76	149	30	3	14	61	76	73	1	3	.262	.351	.400	.751	103	3	79	4.76	6	*2-157	19	1.8
1985 Min-A	138	434	58	113	24	3	10	50	48	70	4	2	.260	.338	.399	.737	95	-2	58	4.48	-19	*2-137/D-1	11	-1.5
1986*NY-N	93	279	35	69	20	1	4	31	32	42	1	2	.247	.327	.369	.696	94	-3	34	4.10	-9	2-84/1-3,3-1	8	-0.9
1987 NY-N	97	299	55	92	29	0	14	61	44	53	3	2	.308	.400	.545	.945	156	24	66	8.04	-10	2-92/1-1	15	1.8
1988*NY-N	90	273	35	64	20	0	4	31	29	41	0	1	.234	.310	.352	.662	94	-3	30	3.65	1	2-84/1-3	8	0.0
1989 NY-N	83	219	27	56	7	2	2	15	32	50	1	3	.256	.353	.333	.687	102	1	27	4.20	1	2-40,1-33	6	0.0
1990 NY-N	80	175	28	43	11	0	10	24	15	33	0	0	.246	.305	.480	.785	113	2	24	4.75	-3	1-24,2-24,3-10	4	-0.2
1991 NY-N	20	34	2	4	0	0	1	2	2	8	1	1	.118	.167	.206	.373	4	-5	1	.97	-1	/1-6,3-5,2-1	0	-0.6
SD-N	97	307	39	70	16	0	11	42	49	69	8	2	.228	.336	.388	.724	100	2	42	4.47	-3	2-65,3-48	11	0.1
Yr.	117	341	41	74	16	0	12	44	51	77	9	3	.217	.321	.370	.690	91	-3	43	4.09	-4	2-66,3-53/1-6	11	-0.5
1992 SD-N	101	246	23	55	10	0	6	25	31	45	2	1	.224	.313	.337	.650	83	-5	26	3.52	-3	2-52,3-26/1-5	5	-0.7
1993 SD-N	96	200	26	50	11	2	7	31	27	39	2	2	.250	.339	.430	.769	102	0	27	4.49	2	2-52/3-9,1-8	6	0.4
Total 11	**1073**	**3112**	**415**	**789**	**185**	**12**	**86**	**379**	**387**	**531**	**23**	**19**	**.254**	**.338**	**.404**	**.742**	**104**	**17**	**427**	**4.66**	**-37**	**2-806/3-99,1-83,D-2,S-1**	**96**	**0.7**
• TEXTOR, George	George Bernhardt Textor b: 12/27/1888, Newport, KY d: 3/10/1954, Massillon, OH BB/TR, 5'10.5", 174 lbs. Deb: 4/19/1914																							
1914 Ind-F	22	57	2	10	0	0	0	4	2	9	0	....	.175	.230	.175	.405	14	-6	2	1.14	3	C-21	1	-0.3
1915 New-F	3	6	1	2	0	0	0	0	0	0	0	....	.333	.333	.333	.667	102	-0	1	4.07	0	/C-3	0	0.0
Total 2	**25**	**63**	**3**	**12**	**0**	**0**	**0**	**4**	**2**	**9**	**0**	**....**	**.190**	**.239**	**.190**	**.429**	**22**	**-6**	**3**	**1.37**	**2**	**/C-24**	**1**	**-0.3**
• THACKER, Moe	Morris Benton Thacker b: 5/21/1934, Louisville, KY d: 11/13/1997, Louisville, KY BR/TR, 6'3", 210 lbs. Deb: 8/3/1958																							
1958 Chi-N	11	24	4	6	1	0	2	3	1	7	0	0	.250	.280	.542	.822	113	0	3	4.21	0	/C-9	1	0.1
1960 Chi-N	54	90	5	14	1	0	0	6	14	20	1	1	.156	.269	.167	.436	23	-9	4	1.39	2	C-50	1	-0.6
1961 Chi-N	25	35	3	6	0	0	0	2	11	11	0	0	.171	.383	.171	.554	53	-2	3	2.88	-1	C-25	0	-0.2
1962 Chi-N	65	107	8	20	5	0	0	9	14	40	0	1	.187	.287	.234	.521	40	-9	8	2.25	4	C-65	2	-0.3
1963 StL-N	3	4	0	0	0	0	0	0	0	3	0	0	.000	.000	.000	.000	-91	-1	0	.00	0	/C-3	0	-0.1
Total 5	**158**	**260**	**20**	**46**	**7**	**0**	**2**	**20**	**40**	**81**	**1**	**2**	**.177**	**.291**	**.227**	**.518**	**41**	**-21**	**18**	**2.16**	**5**	**C-152**	**4**	**-1.2**
• THAKE, Al	Albert Thake b: 9/21/1849, Wymondham, England d: 9/1/1872, Fort Hamilton, NY, 6' Deb: 6/13/1872																							
1872 Atl-n	18	78	14	23	2	2	0	15	0	2	2	0	.295	.295	.372	.667	89	-2	9	5.28	-1	0-18(18-0-0)/2-1	....	-0.2
• THAMES, Marcus	Marcus Markley Thames b: 3/6/1977, Louisville, MS BR/TR, 6'2", 205 lbs. Deb: 6/10/2002 Career OF: 7-0-24																							
2002 NY-A	7	13	2	3	1	0	1	2	0	4	0	0	.231	.231	.538	.769	97	-0	2	4.36	0	/0-7(3-0-4)	0	0.0
2003 Tex-A	30	73	12	15	2	0	1	4	8	18	0	1	.205	.301	.274	.575	49	-6	6	2.64	-1	0-24(4-0-20)/D-4	0	-0.7
Total 2	**37**	**86**	**14**	**18**	**3**	**0**	**2**	**6**	**8**	**22**	**0**	**1**	**.209**	**.292**	**.314**	**.606**	**55**	**-6**	**8**	**2.88**	**-1**	**/0-31,D-4**	**0**	**-0.8**
• THEOBALD, Ron	Ronald Merrill Theobald b: 7/28/1943, Oakland, CA BR/TR, 5'8", 165 lbs. Deb: 4/12/1971																							
1971 Mil-A	126	388	50	107	12	2	1	23	38	39	11	8	.276	.345	.325	.670	92	-4	46	3.97	11	*2-111/3-1,S-1	11	1.5
1972 Mil-A	125	391	45	86	11	0	1	19	68	38	0	7	.220	.343	.256	.598	81	-8	37	2.98	8	*2-113	10	0.8
Total 2	**251**	**779**	**95**	**193**	**23**	**2**	**2**	**42**	**106**	**77**	**11**	**15**	**.248**	**.344**	**.290**	**.634**	**86**	**-12**	**83**	**3.46**	**19**	**2-224/3-1,S-1**	**21**	**2.3**
• THEODORE, George	George Basil Theodore b: 11/13/1946, Salt Lake City, UT BR/TR, 6'4", 190 lbs. Deb: 4/14/1973 Career OF: 36-4-5																							
1973*NY-N	45	116	14	30	4	0	1	15	10	13	1	0	.259	.323	.319	.642	80	-3	11	3.02	0	0-33(28-4-1)/1-4	2	-0.5
1974 NY-N	60	76	7	12	1	0	1	1	8	14	0	0	.158	.247	.211	.458	29	-7	3	1.16	-3	1-14,0-12(8-0-4)	0	-1.1
Total 2	**105**	**192**	**21**	**42**	**5**	**0**	**2**	**16**	**18**	**27**	**1**	**0**	**.219**	**.292**	**.276**	**.568**	**60**	**-10**	**14**	**2.22**	**-2**	**/0-45,1-18**	**2**	**-1.6**
• THEVENOW, Tommy	Thomas Joseph Thevenow b: 9/6/1903, Madison, IN d: 7/29/1957, Madison, IN BR/TR, 5'10", 155 lbs. Deb: 9/4/1924																							
1924 StL-N	23	89	4	18	4	1	0	7	1	6	1	3	.202	.211	.270	.481	28	-10	4	1.49	9	S-23	2	0.1
1925 StL-N	50	175	17	47	7	2	0	17	7	12	3	0	.269	.301	.331	.632	60	-10	18	3.61	-0	S-50	4	-0.4
1926*StL-N	156	563	64	144	15	5	2	63	27	26	8	....	.256	.291	.311	.602	60	-33	50	2.98	41	*S-156	15	2.5
1927 StL-N	59	191	23	37	6	1	0	4	14	8	2	....	.194	.249	.236	.484	29	-19	11	1.89	4	S-59	3	-0.9
1928*StL-N	69	171	11	35	8	3	0	13	20	12	0	....	.205	.288	.287	.575	50	-13	15	2.72	1	S-64/3-3,1-1	3	-0.5
1929 Phi-N	90	317	30	72	11	0	0	35	25	25	3	....	.227	.288	.262	.550	35	-33	25	2.50	-20	S-90	1	-3.9
1930 Phi-N	156	573	57	164	21	1	0	78	23	26	1	....	.286	.316	.326	.642	52	-45	58	3.46	-27	*S-156	3	-4.9
1931 Pit-N	120	404	35	86	12	1	0	38	28	22	0	....	.213	.266	.248	.513	39	-34	28	2.26	18	*S-120	8	-0.8
1932 Pit-N	59	194	12	46	3	3	0	26	7	12	0	....	.237	.264	.284	.547	48	-14	15	2.54	4	S-29,3-22	2	-0.7
1933 Pit-N	73	253	20	79	5	1	0	34	3	5	2	....	.312	.320	.340	.660	89	-4	25	3.59	1	2-61/S-3,3-1	5	0.1
1934 Pit-N	122	446	37	121	16	2	0	54	20	20	0	....	.271	.306	.316	.622	65	-22	41	3.24	-2	2-75,3-44/S-1	6	-1.7
1935 Pit-N	110	408	38	97	9	9	0	47	12	23	1	....	.238	.261	.304	.565	50	-30	30	2.49	9	3-82,S-13/2-8	5	-1.6
1936 Cin-N	106	321	25	75	7	2	0	36	15	23	2	....	.234	.268	.268	.536	48	-24	21	2.16	-2	S-68,2-33,3-12	3	-2.0
1937 Bos-N	21	34	5	4	0	1	0	2	4	2	0	....	.118	.211	.176	.387	7	-4	2	1.38	0	S-12/3-6,2-2	0	-0.4
1938 Pit-N	15	25	2	5	0	0	0	2	4	0	0	....	.200	.333	.200	.533	49	-1	2	2.84	0	/2-9,S-4,3-1	0	-0.1
Total 15	**1229**	**4164**	**380**	**1030**	**124**	**32**	**2**	**456**	**210**	**222**	**23**	**3**	**.247**	**.285**	**.294**	**.579**	**52**	**-295**	**346**	**2.77**	**36**	**S-848,2-188,3-171/1-1**	**60**	**-15.1**
• THIELMAN, Henry	Henry Joseph Thielman b: 10/3/1880, St. Cloud, MN d: 9/2/1942, New York, NY BR/TR, 5'11", 175 lbs. Deb: 4/17/1902 Career OF: 3-6-1 ♦																							
1902 NY-N	6	9	0	1	0	0	0	0	2	....	1	....	.111	.273	.111	.384	19	-1	1	1.85	1	/0-3(0-2-1),P-2	0	0.0
Cin-N	28	91	6	12	0	2	0	4	5	....	0	....	.132	.177	.176	.353	8	-5	3	1.02	-2	P-25/0-3(3-0-0)	8	-1.6
Yr.	34	100	6	13	0	2	0	4	7	....	1	....	.130	.187	.170	.357	9	-5	4	1.09	-1	P-27/0-6(3-2-1)	8	-1.6
1903 Bro-N	9	23	3	5	1	0	1	2	5	....	0	....	.217	.357	.391	.748	117	2	3	4.85	-1	/0-5(0-4-0),P-4	1	-0.1
Total 2	**43**	**123**	**9**	**18**	**1**	**2**	**1**	**6**	**12**	**....**	**1**	**....**	**.146**	**.222**	**.211**	**.434**	**31**	**-4**	**7**	**1.72**	**-2**	**/P-31,0-11**	**9**	**-1.7**
• THOMAS, Andres	Andres Perez Thomas b: 11/10/1963, Boca Chica, Dominican Republic BR/TR, 6'1", 185 lbs. Deb: 9/3/1985																							
1985 Atl-N	15	18	6	5	0	0	0	2	0	2	0	0	.278	.278	.278	.556	53	-1	1	2.09	-1	S-10	0	-0.2
1986 Atl-N	102	323	26	81	17	2	6	32	8	49	4	6	.251	.269	.372	.640	71	-16	26	2.63	1	S-97	4	-0.7
1987 Atl-N	82	324	29	75	11	0	5	39	14	50	6	5	.231	.268	.312	.579	50	-25	25	2.59	-1	S-81	3	-1.7
1988 Atl-N	153	606	54	153	22	2	13	68	14	95	7	3	.252	.271	.360	.630	76	-22	54	3.02	-11	*S-150	9	-2.3
1989 Atl-N	141	554	41	118	18	0	13	57	12	62	3	3	.213	.230	.316	.546	53	-37	35	2.05	-1	*S-138	5	-2.8
1990 Atl-N	84	278	26	61	8	0	5	30	11	43	2	1	.219	.249	.302	.551	48	-21	18	2.18	-5	S-72/3-5	2	-2.1
Total 6	**577**	**2103**	**182**	**493**	**76**	**4**	**42**	**228**	**59**	**301**	**22**	**18**	**.234**	**.256**	**.334**	**.591**	**61**	**-121**	**159**	**2.51**	**-18**	**S-548/3-5**	**23**	**-9.7**
• THOMAS, Bill	William Miskey Thomas b: 12/8/1877, Norristown, PA d: 1/14/1950, Evansburg, PA BR/TR, 5'10", 190 lbs. Deb: 5/1/1902																							
1902 Phi-N	6	17	1	2	0	0	0	0	1	....	0	....	.118	.167	.118	.284	-12	-2	0	.60	0	/0-3(2-0-1),1-1,2-1	0	-0.3

• THOMAS, Bud John Tillman Thomas b: 3/10/1929, Sedalia, MO BR/TR, 6', 180 lbs. Deb: 9/2/1951

YEAR TM-L	G	AB	R	H	2B	3B	HR	RBI	BB	SO	SB	CS	AVG	OBP	SLG	OPS	OPS+	BR/A	RC	RC/G	FR	G/POS	WS	TPW
1951 StL-A	14	20	3	7	0	0	1	1	0	3	2	0	.350	.350	.500	.850	124	1	4	8.21	0	S-14	1	0.1

• THOMAS, Dan Danny Lee Thomas b: 5/9/1951, Birmingham, AL d: 7/3/1980, Mobile, AL BR/TR, 6'2", 190 lbs. Deb: 9/2/1976 Career OF: 41-0-0

YEAR TM-L	G	AB	R	H	2B	3B	HR	RBI	BB	SO	SB	CS	AVG	OBP	SLG	OPS	OPS+	BR/A	RC	RC/G	FR	G/POS	WS	TPW
1976 Mil-A	32	105	13	29	5	1	4	15	14	28	1	2	.276	.372	.457	.829	145	6	18	6.22	0	O-32(32-0-0)	5	0.4
1977 Mil-A	22	70	11	19	3	2	2	11	8	11	0	2	.271	.354	.457	.812	119	1	11	5.27	0	/D-9,O-9(9-0-0)	2	0.1
Total 2	54	175	24	48	8	3	6	26	22	39	1	4	.274	.365	.457	.822	135	7	29	5.83	0	/O-41,D-9	7	0.4

• THOMAS, Derrel Derrel Osborn Thomas b: 1/14/1951, Los Angeles, CA BB/TR, 6', 160 lbs. Deb: 9/14/1971 Career OF: 93-394-65

YEAR TM-L	G	AB	R	H	2B	3B	HR	RBI	BB	SO	SB	CS	AVG	OBP	SLG	OPS	OPS+	BR/A	RC	RC/G	FR	G/POS	WS	TPW
1971 Hou-N	5	5	0	0	0	0	0	0	0	2	0	1	.000	.000	.000	.000	-103	-2	0	.00	-0	/2-1	0	-0.2
1972 SD-N	130	500	48	115	15	5	5	36	41	73	9	9	.230	.291	.310	.601	76	-18	45	3.01	-7	2-83,S-49/O-3(0-2-1)	9	-1.5
1973 SD-N	113	404	41	96	7	1	0	22	34	52	15	5	.238	.300	.260	.560	61	-19	35	2.92	-12	S-74,2-47	6	-2.0
1974 SD-N	141	523	48	129	24	6	3	41	51	58	7	8	.247	.315	.333	.647	85	-13	54	3.47	-11	*2-104,3-22,O-20(1-19-0)/S	12	-1.8
1975 SF-N	144	540	99	149	21	9	6	48	57	56	28	13	.276	.348	.381	.730	98	-0	75	4.79	-2	*2-141/O-1	17	0.7
1976 SF-N	81	272	38	63	5	4	2	19	29	26	10	11	.232	.315	.301	.616	73	-12	26	2.96	-2	2-69/O-2(0-1-1),3-1,S-1	5	-0.9
1977 SF-N	148	506	75	135	13	10	8	44	46	70	15	13	.267	.330	.379	.710	90	-9	63	4.16	2	O-78(4-74-0),2-27,S-26/3-6,1	13	-0.6
1978 SD-N	128	352	36	80	10	2	3	26	35	37	11	6	.227	.303	.293	.595	73	-13	34	3.14	-3	O-77(12-67-0),2-40,3-26,1-14	7	-1.7
1979 LA-N	141	406	47	104	15	4	5	44	41	49	18	5	.256	.332	.350	.682	87	-5	49	4.08	-2	*O-119(0-119-0),3-18/2-5,S,1	10	-0.8
1980 LA-N	117	297	32	79	18	3	1	22	26	48	7	9	.266	.327	.357	.684	93	-6	33	3.74	-3	O-52(4-40-8),S-49,2-18/C-5,3	8	-0.4
1981★LA-N	80	218	25	54	4	0	4	24	25	23	7	2	.248	.325	.321	.646	87	-3	25	3.83	-4	2-30,S-26,O-18(3-10-6),3-10	7	-0.3
1982 LA-N	66	98	13	26	2	1	0	2	10	12	2	3	.265	.333	.306	.639	82	-3	10	3.34	-6	O-28(6-16-6),2-18,3-14/S-6	2	-0.8
1983★LA-N	118	192	38	48	6	6	2	8	27	36	9	3	.250	.348	.375	.723	101	2	27	4.60	-2	O-82(15-42-29),S-13/2-9,3	7	0.0
1984 Mon-N	108	243	26	62	12	2	0	20	20	33	0	4	.255	.312	.321	.633	82	-8	23	3.10	-8	S-62,O-48(41-0-7),2-15/3-4,1	4	-1.2
Cal-A	14	29	3	4	0	1	0	2	3	4	0	0	.138	.219	.207	.426	19	-3	1	1.33	-2	/O-7(2-2-4),S-4,3-3	0	-0.6
1985 Phi-N	63	92	16	19	2	0	4	12	11	14	2	0	.207	.291	.359	.650	79	-2	10	3.41	-4	S-21/O-7(5-2-0),2-1,3-1,C	2	-0.6
Total 15	1597	4677	585	1163	154	54	43	370	456	593	140	92	.249	.319	.332	.651	83	-114	509	3.63	-66	2-608,O-542,S-339,3-116/1,C	109	-12.8

• THOMAS, Frank Frank Edward "Big Hurt" Thomas b: 5/27/1968, Columbus, GA BR/TR, 6'5", 257 lbs. Deb: 8/2/1990

YEAR TM-L	G	AB	R	H	2B	3B	HR	RBI	BB	SO	SB	CS	AVG	OBP	SLG	OPS	OPS+	BR/A	RC	RC/G	FR	G/POS	WS	TPW
1990 Chi-A	60	191	39	63	11	3	7	31	44	54	0	1	.330	.460	.529	.989	180	23	49	9.69	-3	1-51/D-8	13	1.7
1991 Chi-A	158	559	104	178	31	2	32	109	**138**	112	1	2	.318	**.454**	.553	**1.007**	**181**	**70**	145	**9.65**	-3	*D-101,1-56	**34**	6.0
1992 Chi-A	160	573	108	185	**46**	2	24	115	**122**	88	6	3	.323	**.446**	.536	**.981**	176	**66**	142	**9.08**	-8	*1-158/D-2	33	4.6
1993★Chi-A★	153	549	106	174	36	0	41	128	112	54	4	2	.317	.434	.607	1.041	180	67	149	10.07	-6	*1-150/D-4	32	4.6
1994 Chi-A★	113	399	**106**	141	34	1	38	101	**109**	61	2	3	.353	**.494**	**.729**	**1.223**	**214**	**74**	145	**13.88**	-5	1-99,D-13	**25**	**5.5**
1995 Chi-A★	145	493	102	152	27	0	40	111	**136**	74	3	2	.308	.463	.606	1.069	184	70	144	10.57	-10	1-90,D-54	28	4.5
1996 Chi-A★	141	527	110	184	26	0	40	134	109	70	1	1	.349	.465	.626	1.091	181	71	150	10.73	-2	*1-139	28	5.1
1997 Chi-A★	146	530	110	184	35	0	35	125	109	69	1	1	**.347**	**.461**	.611	**1.072**	**184**	**71**	153	**11.20**	-2	1-97,D-49	**39**	5.4
1998 Chi-A	160	585	109	155	35	2	29	109	110	93	7	0	.265	.387	.480	.867	127	29	116	6.85	-1	*D-146,1-14	25	1.6
1999 Chi-A	135	486	74	148	36	0	15	77	87	66	3	3	.305	.419	.471	.890	126	23	99	7.33	-5	D-83,1-49	16	0.8
2000★Chi-A	159	582	115	191	44	0	43	143	112	94	1	3	.328	.441	.625	1.066	163	59	163	10.60	-1	*D-127,1-30	34	4.3
2001 Chi-A	20	68	8	15	3	0	4	10	10	12	0	0	.221	.321	.441	.762	95	-1	10	5.16	0	D-16/1-3	1	-0.2
2002 Chi-A	148	523	77	132	29	1	28	92	88	115	3	0	.252	.367	.472	.840	118	16	96	6.31	0	*D-140/1-4	16	0.7
2003 Chi-A	153	546	87	146	35	0	42	105	100	115	0	0	.267	.392	.562	.954	148	41	126	8.18	-3	*D-124,1-27	23	2.7
Total 14	1851	6611	1255	2048	428	11	418	1390	1386	1077	32	21	.310	.434	.568	1.002	165	680	1687	9.34	-50	1-967,D-867	347	47.4

• THOMAS, Frank Frank Joseph Thomas b: 6/11/1929, Pittsburgh, PA BR/TR, 6'3", 205 lbs. Deb: 8/17/1951 Career OF: 709-308-48

YEAR TM-L	G	AB	R	H	2B	3B	HR	RBI	BB	SO	SB	CS	AVG	OBP	SLG	OPS	OPS+	BR/A	RC	RC/G	FR	G/POS	WS	TPW
1951 Pit-N	39	148	21	39	9	2	2	16	9	15	0	2	.264	.306	.392	.698	84	-5	16	3.76	1	O-37(0-37-0)	3	-0.5
1952 Pit-N	6	21	1	2	0	0	0	0	1	1	0	0	.095	.136	.095	.232	-34	-4	0	.14	0	/O-5(0-5-0)	0	-0.4
1953 Pit-N	128	455	68	116	22	1	30	102	50	93	1	2	.255	.331	.505	.837	115	8	76	5.76	8	*O-118(6-96-16)	14	1.0
1954 Pit-N★	153	577	81	172	32	7	23	94	51	74	3	2	.298	.365	.497	.863	124	19	106	6.60	4	*O-153(48-109-0)	26	1.5
1955 Pit-N★	142	510	72	125	16	2	25	72	60	76	2	0	.245	.327	.431	.758	100	1	72	4.75	-2	*O-139(86-59-0)	15	-0.9
1956 Pit-N	157	588	69	166	24	3	25	80	36	61	0	5	.282	.329	.461	.790	112	6	80	4.75	-11	*3-111,O-56(56-0-0)/2-4	16	-0.8
1957 Pit-N	151	594	72	172	30	1	23	89	44	66	3	1	.290	.342	.460	.801	116	13	90	5.33	2	1-71,O-59(46-2-19),3-31	16	0.8
1958 Pit-N★	149	562	89	158	26	4	35	109	42	79	0	1	.281	.339	.528	.867	129	20	95	5.90	-30	*3-139/O-8(5-0-3),1-2	20	-1.1
1959 Cin-N	108	374	41	84	18	2	12	47	27	56	0	2	.225	.282	.380	.662	72	-17	37	3.16	-1	3-64,O-33(33-0-0),1-14	4	-2.0
1960 Chi-N	135	479	54	114	12	1	21	64	28	74	1	0	.238	.280	.399	.679	84	-12	51	3.62	-8	1-50,O-49(44-0-6),3-33	8	-2.6
1961 Chi-N	15	50	7	13	2	0	2	6	2	8	0	0	.260	.288	.420	.708	84	-1	5	3.35	0	O-10(10-0-0)/1-6	1	-0.2
Mil-N	124	423	58	120	13	3	25	67	29	70	2	4	.284	.338	.506	.844	128	14	66	5.38	-4	*O-109(109-0-0),1-11	15	0.4
Yr.	139	473	65	133	15	3	27	73	31	78	2	4	.281	.333	.497	.830	123	13	71	5.16	-3	*O-119(119-0-0),1-17	16	0.2
1962 NY-N	156	571	69	152	23	3	34	94	48	95	2	1	.266	.332	.496	.827	117	12	91	5.58	5	*O-126(126-0-0),1-11,3-10	12	0.9
1963 NY-N	126	420	34	109	9	1	15	60	33	48	0	0	.260	.318	.393	.711	102	1	46	3.73	4	O-96(96-0-0),1-15/3-1	10	-0.1
1964 NY-N	60	197	19	50	6	1	3	19	10	29	1	1	.254	.297	.340	.637	81	-5	19	3.40	5	O-31(31-0-0),1-19/3-2	3	-0.3
Phi-N	39	143	20	42	11	0	7	26	5	12	0	1	.294	.318	.517	.835	132	5	22	5.29	2	1-36	5	0.5
Yr.	99	340	39	92	17	1	10	45	15	41	1	2	.271	.305	.415	.720	103	-0	41	4.19	6	1-55,O-31(31-0-0)/3-2	8	0.2
1965 Phi-N	35	77	7	20	4	0	1	7	4	10	0	0	.260	.296	.351	.647	83	-2	7	3.20	-1	O-12(9-0-4),1-11/3-1	1	-0.4
Hou-N	23	58	7	10	2	0	3	9	3	15	0	0	.172	.213	.362	.575	63	-3	5	2.58	-2	1-16/3-2,O-1	0	-0.6
Mil-N	15	33	3	7	3	0	0	1	2	11	0	0	.212	.257	.303	.560	57	-2	3	2.76	0	/1-6,O-3(3-0-0)	0	-0.3
Yr.	73	168	17	37	9	0	4	17	9	36	0	0	.220	.260	.345	.605	71	-7	15	2.89	-3	1-33,O-16(13-0-4)/3-3	1	-1.3
1966 Chi-N	5	5	0	0	0	0	0	0	0	1	0	0	.000	.000	.000	.000	-99	-1	0	.00	0	....	0	-0.1
Total 16	1766	6285	792	1671	262	31	286	962	484	894	15	22	.266	.323	.454	.777	108	48	886	4.86	-29	*O-1045,3-394,1-268/2-4	169	-5.2

• THOMAS, Fred Frederick Harvey "Tommy" Thomas b: 12/19/1892, Milwaukee, WI d: 1/15/1986, Rice Lake, WI BR/TR, 5'10", 160 lbs. Deb: 4/22/1918

YEAR TM-L	G	AB	R	H	2B	3B	HR	RBI	BB	SO	SB	CS	AVG	OBP	SLG	OPS	OPS+	BR/A	RC	RC/G	FR	G/POS	WS	TPW
1918★Bos-A	44	144	19	37	2	1	1	11	15	20	4	....	.257	.331	.306	.637	94	-1	16	3.57	4	3-41/S-1	6	0.5
1919 Phi-A	124	453	42	96	11	10	2	23	43	52	12	....	.212	.283	.294	.577	61	-24	41	2.81	-17	*3-124	3	-3.8
1920 Phi-A	76	255	27	59	6	3	1	11	26	17	8	4	.231	.307	.290	.598	58	-14	25	3.09	-6	3-61,S-12	4	-1.7
Was-A	3	7	0	1	0	0	0	0	0	1	0	1	.143	.143	.143	.286	-25	-2	0	.00	1	/3-2	0	0.0
Yr.	79	262	27	60	6	3	1	11	26	18	8	5	.229	.303	.286	.590	56	-16	25	2.99	-5	3-63,S-12	4	-1.8
Total 3	247	859	88	193	19	14	4	45	84	90	24	5	.225	.297	.293	.591	65	-40	81	2.99	-18	3-228/S-13	13	-5.2

• THOMAS, George George Edward Thomas b: 11/29/1937, Minneapolis, MN BR/TR, 6'3.5", 190 lbs. Deb: 9/11/1957 C Career OF: 136-170-186

YEAR TM-L	G	AB	R	H	2B	3B	HR	RBI	BB	SO	SB	CS	AVG	OBP	SLG	OPS	OPS+	BR/A	RC	RC/G	FR	G/POS	WS	TPW
1957 Det-A	1	1	0	0	0	0	0	0	0	1	0	0	.000	.000	.000	.000	-98	-0	0	.00	-1	/3-1	0	-0.1
1958 Det-A	1	0	0	0	0	0	0	0	0	0	0	0	....	....	....	....	-93	0	0	....	0	/O-1	0	0.0
1961 Det-A	17	6	2	0	0	0	0	0	0	4	0	0	.000	.000	.000	.000	-97	-2	0	.00	0	/O-2(0-0-2),S-1	0	-0.2
LA-A	79	282	39	79	12	1	13	59	21	66	3	6	.280	.337	.468	.805	101	-2	43	5.35	-7	O-45(24-17-4),3-38	6	-1.1
Yr.	96	288	41	79	12	1	13	59	21	70	3	6	.274	.330	.458	.788	97	-4	43	5.20	-8	O-47(24-17-6),3-38/S-1	6	-1.3
1962 LA-A	56	181	13	43	10	2	4	12	21	37	0	0	.238	.320	.381	.701	91	-2	23	4.37	0	O-51(3-8-45)	5	-0.6
1963 LA-A	53	167	14	35	7	1	4	15	9	32	0	0	.210	.254	.335	.590	68	-8	14	2.67	-1	O-39(3-1-35),3-10/1-4	2	-1.2
Det-A	49	109	13	26	4	1	1	11	11	22	2	1	.239	.314	.321	.635	76	-3	12	3.63	-1	O-40(2-30-9)/2-1	2	-0.6
Yr.	102	276	27	61	11	2	5	26	20	54	2	1	.221	.279	.330	.608	71	-11	25	3.05	-3	O-79(5-31-44),3-10/1-4,2-1	4	-1.9
1964 Det-A	105	308	39	88	15	2	12	44	18	53	4	1	.286	.331	.464	.796	117	7	47	5.46	-3	O-90(17-57-19)/3-1	11	0.0
1965 Det-A	79	169	19	36	5	1	3	10	12	39	2	3	.213	.273	.308	.581	64	-9	13	2.52	-2	O-59(5-26-28)/2-1	1	-1.5
1966 Bos-A	69	173	25	41	4	0	5	20	23	33	1	0	.237	.333	.347	.680	87	-2	20	3.83	-1	O-48(10-25-15)/3-6,1-2,C-2	4	-0.5
1967★Bos-A	65	89	10	19	2	0	1	6	3	23	0	1	.213	.255	.270	.525	51	-6	6	2.34	-1	O-43(20-3-20)/1-3,C-1	1	-0.9
1968 Bos-A	12	10	3	2	0	0	1	1	1	3	1	0	.200	.273	.500	.773	122	0	2	5.32	-0	/O-9(5-2-2)	1	0.0
1969 Bos-A	29	51	9	18	3	1	0	8	3	11	0	0	.353	.400	.451	.851	131	2	10	7.66	-1	O-12(8-1-3),1-10/3-1,C-1	2	0.1
1970 Bos-A	38	99	13	34	8	0	2	13	11	12	0	0	.343	.420	.485	.904	139	6	20	8.01	-3	O-26(25-0-1)/3-6	4	0.2
1971 Bos-A	9	13	0	1	0	0	0	1	1	4	0	0	.077	.143	.077	.220	-34	-2	0	.41	0	/O-5(3-0-2)	0	-0.3
Min-A	23	30	4	8	1	0	0	2	4	3	0	0	.267	.353	.300	.653	84	-0	4	4.35	-2	O-11(11-0-0)/1-1,3-1	1	-0.2
Yr.	32	43	4	9	1	0	0	3	5	7	0	0	.209	.292	.233	.524	49	-3	4	2.96	-2	O-16(14-0-2)/1-1,3-1	1	-0.5
Total 13	685	1688	203	430	71	9	46	202	138	343	13	12	.255	.318	.389	.707	91	-22	213	4.35	-24	O-481/3-64,1-20,C-4,2-2,S-1	40	-7.1

YEAR TM-L	G	AB	R	H	2B	3B	HR	RBI	BB	SO	SB	CS	AVG	OBP	SLG	OPS	OPS+	BR/A	RC	RC/G	FR	G/POS	WS	TPW
• THOMAS, Gorman	James Gorman Thomas b: 12/12/1950, Charleston, SC BR/TR, 6'2", 210 lbs. Deb: 4/6/1973 Career OF: 66-967-133																							
1973 Mil-A	59	155	16	29	7	1	2	11	14	61	5	5	.187	.254	.284	.538	53	-11	11	2.14	-2	O-50(4-1-46)/D-3,3-1	1	-1.6
1974 Mil-A	17	46	10	12	4	0	2	11	8	15	4	0	.261	.370	.478	.849	143	4	9	6.06	0	O-13(4-1-8)/D-2	2	0.3
1975 Mil-A	121	240	34	43	12	2	10	28	31	84	4	2	.179	.273	.371	.644	80	-7	25	3.21	-7	*O-113(23-92-1)/D-6	4	-1.7
1976 Mil-A	99	227	27	45	9	2	8	36	31	67	2	3	.198	.297	.361	.659	94	-3	24	3.23	-2	O-94(1-66-29)/3-1,D-1	5	-0.8
1978 Mil-A	137	452	70	111	24	1	32	86	73	133	3	4	.246	.353	.515	.868	141	24	85	6.35	-6	*O-137(0-137-0)	21	1.6
1979 Mil-A	156	557	97	136	29	0	**45**	123	98	175	1	5	.244	.359	.539	.898	138	29	110	6.70	-5	*O-152(0-152-0)/D-4	26	2.1
1980 Mil-A	162	628	78	150	26	3	38	105	58	170	8	5	.239	.305	.471	.777	113	8	91	4.91	-8	*O-160(0-160-0)/D-2	19	-0.2
1981*Mil-A★	103	363	54	94	22	0	21	65	50	85	4	5	.259	.352	.493	.845	149	22	63	5.94	2	O-97(0-49-49)/D-6	20	2.1
1982*Mil-A	158	567	96	139	29	1	**39**	112	84	143	3	7	.245	.347	.506	.853	139	29	100	5.90	2	*O-157(0-157-0)	25	2.8
1983 Mil-A	46	164	21	30	6	1	5	18	23	50	2	1	.183	.287	.323	.610	73	-6	15	2.84	-2	O-46(0-46-0)	2	-0.9
Cle-A	106	371	51	82	17	0	17	51	57	98	8	3	.221	.326	.404	.731	96	-1	51	4.52	2	*O-106(0-106-0)	10	0.0
Yr.	152	535	72	112	23	1	22	69	80	148	10	4	.209	.314	.379	.694	89	-7	67	3.98	0	*O-152(0-152-0)	12	-0.9
1984 Sea-A	35	108	6	17	3	0	1	13	28	27	0	3	.157	.336	.213	.549	56	-6	9	2.47	1	O-34(34-0-0)/D-1	0	-0.6
1985 Sea-A	135	484	76	104	16	1	32	87	84	126	3	2	.215	.332	.450	.783	111	8	74	5.05	0	*D-133	13	0.3
1986 Sea-A	57	170	24	33	4	0	10	26	27	55	1	2	.194	.308	.394	.702	89	-3	21	4.06	0	D-52	2	-0.5
Mil-A	44	145	21	26	4	1	6	10	31	50	2	2	.179	.324	.345	.669	80	-4	17	3.75	-1	D-36/1-6	2	-0.6
Yr.	101	315	45	59	8	1	16	36	58	105	3	4	.187	.316	.371	.687	84	-7	39	3.91	-1	D-88/1-6	4	-1.0
Total 13	1435	4677	681	1051	212	13	268	782	697	1339	50	49	.225	.328	.448	.775	114	83	706	4.95	-28	*O-1159,D-246/1-6,3-2	152	2.4
• THOMAS, Herb	Herbert Mark Thomas b: 5/26/1902, Sampson City, FL d: 12/4/1991, Starke, FL BR/TR, 5'4.5", 157 lbs. Deb: 8/28/1924 Career OF: 1-32-2																							
1924 Bos-N	32	127	12	28	4	1	1	8	9	8	5	2	.220	.288	.291	.579	58	-7	11	2.94	6	O-32(0-32-0)	2	-0.2
1925 Bos-N	5	17	2	4	0	1	0	0	2	0	0	1	.235	.350	.353	.703	88	-1	2	3.70	-1	/2-5	0	-0.2
1927 Bos-N	24	74	11	17	6	1	0	6	3	9	2	....	.230	.269	.338	.607	67	-4	7	2.83	-1	2-17/S-2	1	-0.4
NY-N	13	17	2	3	1	1	0	1	1	1	0	....	.176	.263	.353	.616	64	-1	2	2.96	0	/O-3(1-0-2),S-1	0	-0.1
Yr.	37	91	13	20	7	2	0	7	4	10	2	....	.220	.268	.341	.609	66	-5	8	2.86	-1	2-17/O-3(1-0-2),S-3	1	-0.6
Total 3	74	235	27	52	11	4	1	15	15	18	7	3	.221	.285	.315	.600	64	-12	21	2.96	3	/O-35,2-22,S-3	3	-0.9
• THOMAS, Ira	Ira Felix Thomas b: 1/22/1881, Ballston Spa, NY d: 10/11/1958, Philadelphia, PA BR/TR, 6'2", 200 lbs. Deb: 5/18/1906 C																							
1906 NY-A	44	115	12	23	1	2	0	15	8	....	2	....	.200	.258	.243	.502	52	-6	8	2.31	-4	C-42	1	-0.7
1907 NY-A	80	208	20	40	5	4	1	24	10	....	5	....	.192	.240	.269	.509	58	-10	15	2.38	4	C-61/1-2	3	0.0
1908*Det-A	40	101	6	31	1	0	0	8	5	....	0	....	.307	.346	.317	.663	111	1	11	3.98	-2	C-29	4	0.2
1909 Phi-A	84	256	22	57	9	3	0	31	18	....	4	....	.223	.292	.281	.573	79	-6	22	2.80	6	C-84	9	0.9
1910*Phi-A	60	180	14	50	8	2	1	19	6	....	2	....	.278	.301	.361	.662	108	1	20	3.84	1	C-60	8	0.7
1911*Phi-A	103	297	33	81	14	3	0	39	23	....	4	....	.273	.341	.340	.682	92	-3	36	4.16	3	*C-103	13	0.7
1912 Phi-A	48	139	14	30	4	2	1	13	8	....	3	....	.216	.268	.295	.563	63	-7	12	2.69	-2	C-48	3	-0.5
1913 Phi-A	22	53	3	15	4	1	0	6	4	8	0	....	.283	.333	.396	.730	116	1	7	4.42	-1	C-21	3	0.1
1914 Phi-A	2	3	0	0	0	0	0	0	0	0	0	....	.000	.000	.000	.000	-104	-1	0	.00	0	/C-1	0	-0.1
1915 Phi-A	1	0	0	0	0	0	0	0	0	0	0	....	....	....	....	....	-104	0	0	....	0	/C-1	0	0.0
Total 10	484	1352	124	327	46	17	3	155	82	8	20	....	.242	.296	.308	.604	82	-31	131	3.23	5	C-450/1-2	44	1.3
• THOMAS, Kite	Keith Marshall Thomas b: 4/27/1923, Kansas City, KS d: 1/7/1995, Rocky Mount, NC BR/TR, 6'1.5", 195 lbs. Deb: 4/19/1952 Career OF: 21-0-31																							
1952 Phi-A	75	116	24	29	6	1	6	18	20	27	0	1	.250	.365	.474	.839	124	4	20	5.96	-1	O-29(12-0-17)	5	0.2
1953 Phi-A	24	49	1	6	0	0	0	2	3	6	0	0	.122	.173	.122	.296	-18	-8	1	.56	-1	O-15(6-0-9)	0	-0.9
Was-A	38	58	10	17	3	2	1	12	11	7	0	0	.293	.414	.466	.880	140	4	11	6.20	-1	/O-8(3-0-5),C-1	2	0.3
Yr.	62	107	11	23	3	2	1	14	14	13	0	0	.215	.311	.308	.620	73	-4	11	3.41	-2	O-23(9-0-14)/C-1	2	-0.7
Total 2	137	223	35	52	9	3	7	32	34	40	0	1	.233	.340	.395	.734	100	-0	32	4.69	-3	/O-52,C-1	7	-0.5
• THOMAS, Lee	James Leroy Thomas b: 2/5/1936, Peoria, IL BL/TR, 6'2", 198 lbs. Deb: 4/22/1961 C Career OF: 83-20-392																							
1961 NY-A	2	2	0	1	0	0	0	0	0	0	0	0	.500	.500	.500	1.000	177	0	1	13.50	0	....	0	0.0
LA-A	130	450	77	128	11	5	24	70	47	74	0	5	.284	.355	.491	.846	111	4	75	5.88	-3	O-86(26-0-65),1-34	12	-0.6
Yr.	132	452	77	129	11	5	24	70	47	74	0	5	.285	.355	.491	.846	111	5	75	5.90	-3	O-86(26-0-65),1-34	12	-0.6
1962 LA-A★	160	583	88	169	21	2	26	104	55	74	6	1	.290	.357	.467	.824	124	20	96	5.91	-8	1-90,O-74(17-18-42)	22	0.3
1963 LA-A	149	528	52	116	12	6	9	55	53	82	6	0	.220	.302	.316	.618	78	-13	52	3.27	5	*1-104,O-43(2-0-41)	9	-1.9
1964 LA-A	47	172	14	47	8	1	2	24	18	22	1	0	.273	.342	.366	.708	108	2	23	4.69	0	O-47(1-0-46)/1-1	6	-0.2
Bos-A	107	401	44	103	19	2	13	42	34	29	2	1	.257	.321	.411	.733	97	-2	50	4.30	-2	*O-107(0-0-107)/1-1	9	-1.1
Yr.	154	573	58	150	27	3	15	66	52	51	3	1	.262	.328	.398	.725	100	1	73	4.41	-2	*O-154(1-0-153)/1-2	15	-1.3
1965 Bos-A	151	521	74	141	27	4	22	75	72	42	6	2	.271	.362	.464	.827	126	19	87	5.83	0	*1-127,O-20(14-0-6)	15	1.1
1966 Atl-N	39	126	11	25	1	1	6	15	10	15	1	1	.198	.263	.365	.628	71	-5	13	3.28	3	1-36	2	-0.5
Chi-N	75	149	15	36	4	0	1	9	14	15	0	0	.242	.319	.289	.608	70	-5	14	3.29	2	1-20,O-17(16-1-0)	2	-0.7
Yr.	114	275	26	61	5	1	7	24	24	30	1	1	.222	.294	.324	.617	70	-11	27	3.29	3	1-56,O-17(16-1-0)	4	-1.2
1967 Chi-N	77	191	16	42	4	1	2	23	15	22	1	0	.220	.287	.283	.570	61	-9	16	2.78	-1	O-43(0-1-43),1-10	2	-1.4
1968 Hou-N	90	201	14	39	4	0	1	11	14	22	2	1	.194	.250	.229	.479	45	-13	11	1.73	-1	O-48(7-0-42)/1-2	1	-1.9
Total 8	1027	3324	405	847	111	22	106	428	332	397	25	11	.255	.328	.397	.725	98	-2	438	4.52	-7	O-485,1-425	80	-6.8
• THOMAS, Leo	Leo Raymond "Tommy" Thomas b: 7/26/1923, Turlock, CA d: 3/5/2001, Concord, CA BR/TR, 5'11.5", 178 lbs. Deb: 4/29/1950																							
1950 StL-A	35	121	19	24	6	0	1	9	20	14	0	1	.198	.312	.273	.585	49	-10	11	2.78	-2	3-35	1	-1.1
1952 StL-A	41	124	12	29	5	1	0	12	17	7	2	0	.234	.336	.290	.626	73	-3	13	3.55	3	3-37/S-3,2-1	3	-0.1
Chi-A	19	24	1	4	0	0	0	6	6	4	0	0	.167	.333	.167	.500	42	-1	2	2.21	1	/3-9	0	-0.1
Yr.	60	148	13	33	5	1	0	18	23	11	2	0	.223	.335	.270	.606	67	-5	15	3.28	4	3-46/S-3,2-1	3	-0.1
Total 2	95	269	32	57	11	1	1	27	43	25	2	1	.212	.325	.271	.596	59	-14	27	3.05	1	/3-81,S-3,2-1	4	-1.2
• THOMAS, Pinch	Chester David Thomas b: 1/24/1888, Camp Point, IL d: 12/24/1953, Modesto, CA BL/TR, 5'9.5", 173 lbs. Deb: 4/24/1912																							
1912 Bos-A	13	30	0	6	0	0	0	5	2	....	1	....	.200	.250	.200	.450	28	-3	2	1.85	0	/C-8	1	-0.2
1913 Bos-A	38	91	6	26	1	2	1	15	2	11	1	....	.286	.309	.374	.682	97	-1	10	3.94	1	C-31	3	0.2
1914 Bos-A	66	130	9	25	1	0	0	5	18	17	1	....	.192	.291	.200	.491	48	-8	8	2.03	-5	C-64/1-1	3	-1.0
1915*Bos-A	86	203	21	48	4	4	0	21	13	20	3	2	.236	.286	.296	.581	76	-7	18	2.96	1	C-82	7	-0.1
1916*Bos-A	99	216	21	57	10	1	1	21	33	13	4	....	.264	.364	.333	.697	109	4	30	4.52	-4	C-90	11	0.5
1917 Bos-A	83	202	24	48	7	0	0	24	27	9	2	....	.238	.333	.272	.606	86	-2	19	3.10	-5	C-77	7	-0.1
1918 Cle-A	32	73	2	18	0	1	0	5	6	6	0	....	.247	.304	.274	.578	68	-3	6	2.73	-3	C-24	2	-0.4
1919 Cle-A	34	46	2	5	0	0	0	2	4	3	0	....	.109	.180	.109	.289	-17	-7	1	.63	-1	C-21	0	-0.8
1920*Cle-A	9	9	2	3	1	0	0	0	3	1	0	0	.333	.500	.444	.944	147	1	2	10.13	0	/C-7	1	0.1
1921 Cle-A	21	35	1	9	3	0	0	4	10	2	0	2	.257	.422	.343	.765	96	1	6	5.88	-2	C-19	1	-0.1
Total 10	481	1035	88	245	27	8	2	102	118	82	12	2	.237	.318	.284	.602	79	-25	104	3.25	-19	C-423/1-1	36	-1.9
• THOMAS, Ray	Raymond Joseph Thomas b: 7/9/1910, Dover, NH d: 12/6/1993, Wilson, NC BR/TR, 5'10.5", 175 lbs. Deb: 7/22/1938																							
1938 Bro-N	1	3	1	1	0	0	0	0	0	0	0	....	.333	.333	.333	.667	82	-0	0	4.61	-0	/C-1	0	0.0
• THOMAS, Red	Robert William Thomas b: 4/25/1898, Hargrove, AL d: 3/22/1962, Fremont, OH BR/TR, 5'11", 165 lbs. Deb: 9/13/1921																							
1921 Chi-N	8	30	5	8	3	0	1	5	4	5	0	1	.267	.371	.467	.838	120	1	5	5.59	0	/O-8(0-8-0)	1	0.1
• THOMAS, Roy	Roy Allen Thomas b: 3/24/1874, Norristown, PA d: 11/20/1959, Norristown, PA BL/TL, 5'11", 150 lbs. Deb: 4/14/1899 C Career OF: 75-1349-11																							
1899 Phi-N	150	547	137	178	12	4	0	47	115	....	42	....	.325	.457	.362	.819	130	36	116	7.86	0	*O-135(0-135-0),1-14	30	2.5
1900 Phi-N	140	531	**132**	168	4	3	0	33	**115**	....	37	....	.316	.451	.335	.786	119	27	102	7.16	-7	*O-139(0-139-0)/P-1	25	1.0
1901 Phi-N	129	479	102	148	5	2	1	28	**100**	....	27	....	.309	.437	.334	.771	123	24	86	6.62	-4	*O-129(0-129-0)	24	1.3
1902 Phi-N	138	500	89	143	4	7	0	24	**107**	....	17	....	.286	**.414**	.322	.736	127	26	79	5.57	1	*O-138(0-138-0)	25	2.1
1903 Phi-N	130	477	88	156	11	2	1	27	**107**	....	17	....	.327	**.453**	.365	.818	139	35	92	7.18	7	*O-130(0-130-0)	23	3.4
1904 Phi-N	139	496	92	144	6	6	3	29	**102**	....	28	....	.290	.416	.345	.761	141	33	86	6.24	7	*O-139(0-139-0)	28	3.6
1905 Phi-N	147	562	118	178	11	6	0	31	93	....	23	....	.317	.417	.358	.775	137	33	98	6.40	8	*O-147(0-147-0)	31	3.5
1906 Phi-N	142	493	81	125	10	7	0	16	**107**	....	22	....	.254	.393	.302	.695	117	18	71	4.85	-2	*O-142(0-142-0)	26	1.1

YEAR TM-L	G	AB	R	H	2B	3B	HR	RBI	BB	SO	SB	CS	AVG	OBP	SLG	OPS	OPS+	BR/A	RC	RC/G	FR	G/POS	WS	TPW
1907 Phi-N	121	419	70	102	15	3	1	23	**83**	....	11	....	.243	.374	.301	.674	113	12	55	4.31	-1	*O-121(0-121-0)	21	0.7
1908 Phi-N	6	24	2	4	0	0	0	0	2	....	0	....	.167	.231	.167	.397	26	-2	1	1.13	-1	/O-6(0-6-0)	0	-0.3
Pit-N	102	386	52	99	11	10	1	24	49	....	11	....	.256	.348	.345	.692	121	11	50	4.39	-3	*O-101(0-101-0)	19	0.3
Yr.	108	410	54	103	11	10	1	24	51	....	11	....	.251	.341	.334	.675	116	9	51	4.18	-4	*O-107(0-107-0)	19	0.0
1909 Bos-N	82	281	36	74	9	1	0	11	47	....	5	....	.263	.369	.302	.671	104	4	34	4.08	1	O-76(75-2-0)	8	0.0
1910 Phi-N	23	71	7	13	0	2	0	4	7	5	4	....	.183	.266	.239	.505	46	-5	6	2.41	-1	O-20(0-20-0)	0	-0.7
1911 Phi-N	21	30	5	5	2	0	0	2	8	6	0	....	.167	.342	.233	.575	61	-1	3	2.69	1	O-11(0-0-11)	0	-0.1
Total 13	**1470**	**5296**	**1011**	**1537**	**100**	**53**	**7**	**299**	**1042**	**11**	**244**	**....**	**.290**	**.413**	**.333**	**.747**	**124**	**252**	**880**	**5.89**	**6**	***O-1434/1-14,P-1**	**260**	**18.4**
• THOMAS, Valmy	Valmy Thomas b: 10/21/1928, Santurce, Puerto Rico BR/TR, 5'9", 165 lbs. Deb: 4/16/1957																							
1957 NY-N	88	241	30	60	10	3	6	31	16	29	0	0	.249	.298	.390	.688	83	-6	28	3.91	0	C-88	6	-0.2
1958 SF-N	63	143	14	37	5	0	3	16	13	24	1	0	.259	.325	.357	.681	82	-3	17	4.00	0	C-61	4	-0.1
1959 Phi-N	66	140	5	28	2	0	1	7	9	19	1	0	.200	.253	.236	.489	31	-14	7	1.67	0	C-65/3-1	1	-1.1
1960 Bal-A	8	16	0	1	0	0	0	0	1	0	0	1	.063	.118	.063	.180	-50	-4	0	.00	0	/C-8	0	-0.3
1961 Cle-A	27	86	7	18	3	0	2	6	6	7	0	0	.209	.261	.314	.575	54	-6	5	1.90	3	C-27	2	-0.2
Total 5	**252**	**626**	**56**	**144**	**20**	**3**	**12**	**60**	**45**	**79**	**2**	**1**	**.230**	**.285**	**.329**	**.614**	**64**	**-33**	**57**	**2.97**	**3**	**C-249/3-1**	**13**	**-1.9**
• THOMAS, Walt	William Walter "Tommy" Thomas b: 4/28/1884, Altoona, PA d: 6/6/1950, Altoona, PA BR/TR, 5'8", 156 lbs. Deb: 9/18/1908																							
1908 Bos-N	5	13	2	2	0	0	0	1	3	....	2	....	.154	.313	.154	.466	51	-0	1	2.93	-1	/S-5	0	-0.1
• THOMASON, Art	Arthur Wilson Thomason b: 2/12/1889, Liberty, MO d: 5/2/1944, Kansas City, MO BL/TL, 5'8", 150 lbs. Deb: 8/10/1910																							
1910 Cle-A	20	70	4	12	0	1	0	2	5	....	3	....	.171	.227	.200	.427	33	-5	4	1.64	2	O-20(0-1-19)	0	-0.5
• THOMASSON, Gary	Gary Leah Thomasson b: 7/29/1951, San Diego, CA BL/TL, 6'1", 180 lbs. Deb: 9/5/1972 Career OF: 182-247-206																							
1972 SF-N	10	27	5	9	1	1	0	1	1	7	0	0	.333	.357	.444	.802	125	1	4	5.60	-1	/1-7,O-2(2-0-0)	1	-0.1
1973 SF-N	112	235	35	67	10	4	4	30	22	43	2	0	.285	.346	.413	.759	105	2	36	5.54	-3	1-47,O-43(23-11-9)	8	-0.5
1974 SF-N	120	315	41	77	14	3	2	29	38	56	7	1	.244	.326	.327	.653	79	-7	35	3.72	2	O-76(20-32-26),1-15	6	-0.9
1975 SF-N	114	326	44	74	12	3	7	32	37	48	9	3	.227	.308	.347	.654	78	-9	38	3.93	2	O-74(27-34-18),1-17	8	-1.3
1976 SF-N	103	328	45	85	20	5	8	38	30	45	8	3	.259	.323	.424	.747	107	3	45	4.87	-5	O-54(5-35-19),1-39	10	-0.7
1977 SF-N	145	446	63	114	24	6	17	71	75	102	16	4	.256	.364	.451	.815	117	15	78	5.95	-4	*O-113(62-49-20),1-31	16	0.5
1978 Oak-A	47	154	17	31	4	1	5	16	15	44	4	1	.201	.272	.338	.610	74	-5	14	3.01	1	O-44(0-0-44)/1-5	2	-0.6
*NY-A	55	116	20	32	4	1	3	20	13	22	0	2	.276	.349	.405	.754	114	1	17	5.23	1	O-50(24-16-12)/D-1	5	0.0
Yr.	102	270	37	63	8	2	8	36	28	66	4	3	.233	.305	.367	.672	92	-3	31	3.90	2	O-94(24-16-56)/1-5,D-1	7	-0.6
1979 LA-N	115	315	39	78	11	1	14	45	43	70	4	2	.248	.340	.422	.762	108	4	47	5.11	-4	*O-100(10-61-43)/1-1	10	-0.2
1980 LA-N	80	111	6	24	3	0	1	12	17	26	0	0	.216	.326	.270	.596	69	-4	10	3.07	0	O-31(9-9-15)/1-1	1	-0.5
Total 9	**901**	**2373**	**315**	**591**	**103**	**25**	**61**	**294**	**291**	**463**	**50**	**16**	**.249**	**.332**	**.391**	**.723**	**98**	**0**	**324**	**4.69**	**-13**	**O-587,1-163/D-1**	**67**	**-4.4**
• THOME, Jim	James Howard Thome b: 8/27/1970, Peoria, IL BL/TR, 6'3", 220 lbs. Deb: 9/4/1991																							
1991 Cle-A	27	98	7	25	4	2	1	9	5	16	1	1	.255	.298	.367	.665	83	-3	9	3.27	1	3-27	1	-0.2
1992 Cle-A	40	117	8	24	3	1	2	12	10	34	2	0	.205	.279	.299	.578	63	-5	10	2.75	-5	3-40	1	-1.0
1993 Cle-A	47	154	28	41	11	0	7	22	29	36	2	1	.266	.396	.474	.870	133	9	31	6.86	0	3-47	6	0.9
1994 Cle-A	98	321	58	86	20	1	20	52	46	84	3	3	.268	.360	.523	.883	124	10	58	6.24	-3	3-94	10	0.8
1995*Cle-A	137	452	92	142	29	3	25	73	97	113	4	3	.314	.440	.558	.998	155	41	118	9.81	-15	*3-134/D-1	24	2.6
1996*Cle-A	151	505	122	157	28	5	38	116	123	141	2	2	.311	.451	.612	1.063	166	57	146	10.80	-11	*3-150/D-1	28	4.4
1997*Cle-A★	147	496	104	142	25	0	40	102	**120**	146	1	1	.286	.428	.579	1.007	154	45	131	9.48	-2	*1-145	26	2.8
1998*Cle-A★	123	440	89	129	34	2	30	85	89	141	1	0	.293	.417	.584	1.001	151	37	113	9.46	-2	*1-117/D-6	19	2.2
1999*Cle-A★	146	494	101	137	27	2	33	108	**127**	171	0	0	.277	.429	.540	.969	139	35	125	9.19	8	*1-111,D-36	26	2.9
2000 Cle-A	158	557	106	150	33	1	37	106	118	171	1	0	.269	.401	.531	.932	131	30	127	8.18	4	*1-106,D-48	20	2.0
2001*Cle-A	156	526	101	153	26	1	49	124	111	185	0	1	.291	.418	.624	1.042	167	55	143	9.97	-8	*1-148/D-6	31	3.2
2002 Cle-A	147	480	101	146	19	2	52	118	**122**	139	1	2	.304	.450	**.677**	**1.127**	**197**	**73**	155	**12.05**	-3	*1-128,D-18	34	5.5
2003 Phi-N	159	578	111	154	30	3	**47**	131	111	182	0	3	.266	.388	.573	.961	156	48	135	8.33	-3	*1-156/D-2	30	3.0
Total 13	**1536**	**5218**	**1028**	**1486**	**289**	**23**	**381**	**1058**	**1108**	**1559**	**18**	**17**	**.285**	**.414**	**.568**	**.982**	**151**	**431**	**1300**	**9.03**	**-38**	**1-911,3-492,D-118**	**256**	**29.2**
• THOMPSON, Andrew	Andrew M. Thompson b: 1846, IL Deb: 4/26/1875																							
1875 Was-n	11	41	3	4	0	1	0	3	0	1	0	0	.098	.098	.146	.244	-17	-4	1	.48	-6	C-11/O-1	....	-0.9
• THOMPSON, Andy	Andrew John Thompson b: 10/8/1975, Oconomowoc, WI BR/TR, 6'3", 215 lbs. Deb: 5/2/2000																							
2000 Tor-A	2	6	2	1	0	0	0	1	3	2	0	0	.167	.444	.167	.611	62	-0	1	4.27	-1	*O-103(2-0-0)	0	-0.1
• THOMPSON, Bobby	Bobby La Rue Thompson b: 11/3/1953, Charlotte, NC BB/TR, 5'11", 175 lbs. Deb: 4/16/1978																							
1978 Tex-A	64	120	23	27	3	3	2	12	9	26	7	2	.225	.290	.350	.640	79	-3	13	3.63	-1	O-52(8-37-10)/D-3	3	-0.5
• THOMPSON, Danny	Danny Leon Thompson b: 2/1/1947, Wichita, KS d: 12/10/1976, Rochester, MN BR/TR, 6', 183 lbs. Deb: 6/25/1970																							
1970*Min-A	96	302	25	66	9	0	0	22	7	39	0	0	.219	.236	.248	.485	33	-28	17	1.85	-5	2-81,3-37/S-6	3	-2.8
1971 Min-A	48	57	10	15	2	0	0	7	7	12	0	0	.263	.344	.298	.642	81	-1	5	2.77	-3	3-17/2-3,S-1	0	-0.5
1972 Min-A	144	573	54	158	22	6	4	48	34	57	3	4	.276	.319	.356	.675	96	-4	63	3.78	-5	*S-144	15	0.9
1973 Min-A	99	347	29	78	13	2	1	36	16	41	1	0	.225	.263	.282	.545	52	-22	24	2.27	-5	S-95/3-1,D-1	3	-1.6
1974 Min-A	97	264	25	66	6	1	4	25	22	29	1	1	.250	.313	.326	.638	81	-6	24	2.95	-8	S-88/3-5,D-1	3	-0.6
1975 Min-A	112	355	25	96	11	2	5	37	18	30	0	3	.270	.306	.355	.661	84	-9	37	3.55	-17	*S-100/3-7,D-3,2-1	5	-1.6
1976 Min-A	34	124	9	29	4	0	0	6	3	8	1	1	.234	.258	.266	.524	52	-8	9	2.31	4	S-34	2	0.0
Tex-A	64	196	12	42	3	0	1	13	13	19	2	2	.214	.267	.245	.512	49	-13	13	2.05	0	3-39,2-14,S-10/D-1	1	-1.2
Yr.	98	320	21	71	7	0	1	19	16	27	3	3	.222	.263	.253	.516	50	-21	21	2.14	3	S-44,3-39,2-14/D-1	3	-1.3
Total 7	**694**	**2218**	**189**	**550**	**70**	**11**	**15**	**194**	**120**	**235**	**8**	**11**	**.248**	**.289**	**.310**	**.599**	**70**	**-92**	**192**	**2.86**	**-39**	**S-478,3-106/2-99,D-6**	**32**	**-7.4**
• THOMPSON, Don	Donald Newlin Thompson b: 12/28/1923, Swepsonville, NC BL/TL, 6', 185 lbs. Deb: 4/24/1949 Career OF: 134-16-27																							
1949 Bos-N	7	11	0	2	0	0	0	0	0	2	0	....	.182	.182	.182	.364	-2	-2	0	1.09	0	/O-2(0-0-2)	0	-0.2
1951 Bro-N	80	118	25	27	3	0	0	6	12	12	2	8	.229	.305	.254	.560	51	-11	8	2.24	0	O-61(56-6-0)	1	-1.3
1953*Bro-N	96	153	25	37	5	0	1	12	14	13	2	3	.242	.310	.294	.604	57	-10	13	2.81	2	O-81(51-8-25)	1	-1.1
1954 Bro-N	34	25	2	1	0	0	0	1	5	5	0	0	.040	.226	.040	.266	-25	-5	1	.65	-1	O-29(27-2-0)	0	-0.6
Total 4	**217**	**307**	**52**	**67**	**8**	**0**	**1**	**19**	**31**	**32**	**4**	**11**	**.218**	**.296**	**.254**	**.550**	**46**	**-27**	**22**	**2.33**	**0**	**O-173**	**2**	**-3.2**
• THOMPSON, Frank	Frank E. Thompson b: 7/2/1895, Springfield, MO d: 6/27/1940, Jasper County, MO BR/TR, 5'8", 155 lbs. Deb: 5/6/1920																							
1920 StL-A	22	53	7	9	0	0	0	5	13	10	1	1	.170	.343	.170	.513	38	-4	4	2.44	-3	3-14/2-2	0	-0.7
• THOMPSON, Frank	Frank Thompson Deb: 9/11/1875																							
1875 Atl-n	1	5	1	2	0	0	0	1	0	0	0	0	.400	.400	.400	.800	205	1	1	8.06	-1	/O-1	....	0.0
• THOMPSON, Fresco	Lafayette Fresco "Tommy" Thompson b: 6/6/1902, Centreville, AL d: 11/20/1968, Fullerton, CA BR/TR, 5'8", 150 lbs. Deb: 9/5/1925																							
1925 Pit-N	14	37	4	9	2	1	0	8	4	1	2	1	.243	.317	.351	.668	66	-2	4	3.87	1	2-12	0	-0.1
1926 NY-N	2	8	1	5	0	0	0	1	2	0	1	....	.625	.700	.625	1.325	262	2	4	31.14	0	/2-2	1	0.3
1927 Phi-N	153	597	78	181	32	14	1	70	34	36	19	....	.303	.343	.409	.752	99	-2	81	4.86	-16	*2-153	14	-1.3
1928 Phi-N	152	634	99	182	34	11	3	50	42	27	19	....	.287	.332	.390	.722	85	-15	80	4.40	-14	*2-152	10	-2.4
1929 Phi-N	148	623	115	202	41	3	4	53	75	34	16	....	.324	.398	.419	.817	96	-1	104	6.20	-9	*2-148	16	-0.5
1930 Phi-N	122	478	77	135	34	4	4	46	35	29	7	....	.282	.331	.395	.727	70	-24	61	4.45	-19	*2-112	5	-3.5
1931 Bro-N	74	181	26	48	6	1	1	21	23	16	5	....	.265	.351	.326	.677	84	-3	22	4.29	-3	2-43,S-10/3-5	5	-0.4
1932 Bro-N	3	1	0	0	0	0	0	0	0	0	0	....	.000	.000	.000	.000	-102	-0	0	.00	0	....	0	0.0
1934 NY-N	1	1	0	0	0	0	0	0	0	0	0	....	.000	.000	.000	.000	-102	-0	0	.00	0	....	0	0.0
Total 9	**669**	**2560**	**400**	**762**	**149**	**34**	**13**	**249**	**215**	**143**	**69**	**1**	**.298**	**.353**	**.398**	**.751**	**88**	**-45**	**357**	**4.96**	**-59**	**2-622/S-10,3-5**	**51**	**-8.0**
• THOMPSON, Hank	Henry Curtis Thompson b: 12/8/1925, Oklahoma City, OK d: 9/30/1969, Fresno, CA BL/TR, 5'9", 174 lbs. Deb: 7/17/1947 Career OF: 30-53-21																							
1947 StL-A	27	78	10	20	1	1	0	5	10	7	2	1	.256	.341	.295	.636	76	-2	8	3.66	-1	2-19	2	-0.2
1949 NY-N	75	275	51	77	10	4	9	34	42	30	5	....	.280	.377	.444	.821	120	9	50	6.70	-2	2-69/3-1	10	1.0

YEAR TM-L	G	AB	R	H	2B	3B	HR	RBI	BB	SO	SB	CS	AVG	OBP	SLG	OPS	OPS+	BR/A	RC	RC/G	FR	G/POS	WS	TPW
1950 NY-N	148	512	82	148	17	6	20	91	83	60	8	....	.289	.391	.463	.854	123	20	97	6.92	10	*3-138,0-10(0-2-9)	23	2.8
1951*NY-N	87	264	37	62	8	4	8	33	43	23	1	2	.235	.342	.386	.728	95	-2	36	4.64	-10	3-71	7	-1.2
1952 NY-N	128	423	67	110	13	9	17	67	50	38	4	4	.260	.344	.454	.798	119	10	68	5.58	-1	0-72(20-51-1),3-46/2-4	18	0.6
1953 NY-N	114	388	80	117	15	8	24	74	60	39	6	5	.302	.400	.567	.967	146	27	93	8.85	-1	*3-101/0-9(1-0-8),2-1	18	2.4
1954*NY-N	136	448	76	118	18	1	26	86	90	58	3	0	.263	.392	.482	.874	126	21	92	7.10	4	*3-130/2-2,0-1	21	2.4
1955 NY-N	135	432	65	106	13	1	17	63	84	56	2	2	.245	.373	.398	.771	104	6	71	5.52	2	*3-124/2-7,S-1	18	0.9
1956 NY-N	83	183	24	43	9	0	8	29	31	26	2	1	.235	.349	.415	.764	105	2	29	5.25	1	3-44,0-10(8-0-3)/S-1	6	0.3
Total 9	933	3003	492	801	104	34	129	482	493	337	33	15	.267	.374	.453	.827	118	90	545	6.36	2	3-655,2-102,0-102/S-2	123	9.0

• THOMPSON, Homer Homer Thomas Thompson b: 6/1/1891, Spring City, TN d: 9/12/1957, Atlanta, GA BR/TR, 5'9", 160 lbs. Deb: 10/5/1912

YEAR TM-L	G	AB	R	H	2B	3B	HR	RBI	BB	SO	SB	CS	AVG	OBP	SLG	OPS	OPS+	BR/A	RC	RC/G	FR	G/POS	WS	TPW
1912 NY-A	1	0	0	0	0	0	0	0	0	....	0	....	....	....	....	....	-94	0	0	....	-1	/C-1	0	-0.1

• THOMPSON, Jason Jason Michael Thompson b: 6/13/1971, Orlando, FL BL/TL, 6'4", 200 lbs. Deb: 6/9/1996

YEAR TM-L	G	AB	R	H	2B	3B	HR	RBI	BB	SO	SB	CS	AVG	OBP	SLG	OPS	OPS+	BR/A	RC	RC/G	FR	G/POS	WS	TPW
1996 SD-N	13	49	4	11	4	0	2	6	1	14	0	0	.224	.240	.429	.669	76	-2	5	3.55	1	1-13	1	-0.2

• THOMPSON, Jason Jason Dolph Thompson b: 7/6/1954, Hollywood, CA BL/TL, 6'4", 210 lbs. Deb: 4/23/1976

YEAR TM-L	G	AB	R	H	2B	3B	HR	RBI	BB	SO	SB	CS	AVG	OBP	SLG	OPS	OPS+	BR/A	RC	RC/G	FR	G/POS	WS	TPW
1976 Det-A	123	412	45	90	12	1	17	54	68	72	2	4	.218	.331	.376	.707	103	2	53	4.22	-1	*1-117	12	-0.9
1977 Det-A★	158	585	87	158	24	5	31	105	73	91	0	1	.270	.352	.487	.839	120	16	100	5.96	-3	*1-158	18	0.3
1978 Det-A★	153	589	79	169	25	3	26	96	74	96	0	0	.287	.367	.472	.839	130	25	104	6.42	1	*1-151	22	1.7
1979 Det-A	145	492	58	121	16	1	20	79	70	90	2	0	.246	.341	.404	.746	97	-0	68	4.70	3	*1-140/D-2	13	-0.5
1980 Det-A	36	126	10	27	5	0	4	20	13	26	0	1	.214	.293	.349	.642	73	-5	12	3.13	4	1-36	1	-0.3
Cal-A	102	312	59	99	14	0	17	70	70	60	2	0	.317	.442	.526	.968	168	34	76	9.12	-1	1-47,D-45	18	2.9
Yr.	138	438	69	126	19	0	21	90	83	86	2	1	.288	.402	.475	.877	143	29	89	7.21	3	1-83,D-45	19	2.6
1981 Pit-N	86	223	36	54	13	0	15	42	59	49	0	0	.242	.401	.502	.903	150	17	48	7.33	-1	1-78	11	1.3
1982 Pit-N★	156	550	87	156	32	0	31	101	101	107	1	0	.284	.397	.511	.908	148	39	117	7.60	-6	*1-155	27	2.4
1983 Pit-N	152	517	70	134	20	1	18	76	99	128	1	0	.259	.379	.406	.785	115	15	84	5.63	-7	*1-151	17	-0.1
1984 Pit-N	154	543	61	138	22	0	17	74	87	73	0	0	.254	.359	.389	.748	110	10	78	5.01	-9	*1-152	14	-0.9
1985 Pit-N	123	402	42	97	17	1	12	61	84	58	0	0	.241	.372	.378	.751	111	10	61	5.21	1	*1-114	11	0.4
1986 Mon-N	30	51	6	10	4	0	0	4	18	12	0	1	.196	.406	.275	.680	92	0	7	4.57	-3	1-15	1	-0.3
Total 11	1418	4802	640	1253	204	12	208	782	816	862	8	7	.261	.369	.438	.808	121	162	809	5.86	-22	*1-1314/D-47	165	5.9

• THOMPSON, Milt Milton Bernard Thompson b: 1/5/1959, Washington, DC BL/TR, 5'11", 170 lbs. Deb: 9/4/1984 Career OF: 398-518-182

YEAR TM-L	G	AB	R	H	2B	3B	HR	RBI	BB	SO	SB	CS	AVG	OBP	SLG	OPS	OPS+	BR/A	RC	RC/G	FR	G/POS	WS	TPW
1984 Atl-N	25	99	16	30	1	0	2	4	11	11	14	2	.303	.373	.374	.746	103	3	16	6.00	3	0-25(25-0-0)	4	0.5
1985 Atl-N	73	182	17	55	7	2	0	6	7	36	9	4	.302	.339	.363	.701	91	-2	23	4.66	-3	0-49(23-5-27)	4	-0.7
1986 Phi-N	96	299	38	75	7	1	6	23	26	62	19	4	.251	.313	.341	.654	78	-7	34	3.91	-3	0-89(0-89-0)	7	-1.2
1987 Phi-N	150	527	86	159	26	9	7	43	42	87	46	10	.302	.353	.425	.778	102	6	85	5.87	1	*0-146(1-145-1)	19	0.5
1988 Phi-N	122	378	53	109	16	2	2	33	39	59	17	9	.288	.356	.357	.714	103	2	48	4.50	1	*0-112(0-112-5)	12	0.2
1989 StL-N	155	545	60	158	28	8	4	68	39	91	27	8	.290	.342	.393	.734	106	6	73	4.83	-1	*0-147(23-123-3)	19	0.2
1990 StL-N	135	418	42	91	14	7	6	30	39	60	25	5	.218	.292	.328	.620	70	-14	44	3.50	-4	*0-116(12-14-96)	6	-2.2
1991 StL-N	115	326	55	100	16	5	6	34	32	53	16	9	.307	.369	.442	.810	126	11	53	5.90	2	0-91(72-12-12)	11	1.1
1992 StL-N	109	208	31	61	9	1	4	17	16	39	18	6	.293	.350	.404	.753	116	6	30	5.21	-1	0-45(35-1-11)	6	0.3
1993*Phi-N	129	340	42	89	14	2	4	44	40	57	9	4	.262	.343	.350	.693	87	-5	41	4.18	-3	*0-106(102-4-0)	8	-1.2
1994 Phi-N	87	220	29	60	7	0	3	30	23	28	7	2	.273	.350	.345	.695	80	-5	28	4.40	-4	0-79(72-12-0)	7	-1.1
Hou-N	9	21	5	6	0	0	1	3	1	2	2	0	.286	.318	.429	.747	97	0	3	4.74	0	/0-6(0-0-6)	0	0.1
Yr.	96	241	34	66	7	0	4	33	24	30	9	2	.274	.347	.353	.700	82	-5	30	4.43	-3	0-85(72-12-6)	7	-1.0
1995 Hou-N	92	132	14	29	9	0	2	19	14	37	4	2	.220	.299	.333	.633	71	-6	13	3.21	1	0-34(15-1-21)	3	-0.6
1996 LA-N	48	51	2	6	1	0	0	1	6	10	1	1	.118	.211	.137	.348	-6	-8	2	.92	0	/0-2(17-0-0)	0	-0.8
Col-N	14	15	1	1	1	0	0	2	1	3	0	0	.067	.125	.133	.258	-26	-3	0	.54	0	0-17(1-0-0)	0	-0.3
Yr.	62	66	3	7	2	0	0	3	7	13	1	1	.106	.192	.136	.328	-11	-11	2	.83	0	0-19(18-0-0)	0	-1.1
Total 13	1359	3761	491	1029	156	37	47	357	336	635	214	66	.274	.337	.372	.709	94	-16	494	4.61	-12	*0-1064	106	-5.3

• THOMPSON, Robby Robert Randall Thompson b: 5/10/1962, West Palm Beach, FL BR/TR, 5'11", 170 lbs. Deb: 4/8/1986 C

YEAR TM-L	G	AB	R	H	2B	3B	HR	RBI	BB	SO	SB	CS	AVG	OBP	SLG	OPS	OPS+	BR/A	RC	RC/G	FR	G/POS	WS	TPW
1986 SF-N	149	549	73	149	27	3	7	47	42	112	12	15	.271	.329	.370	.699	97	-7	64	3.88	5	*2-149/S-1	15	0.6
1987*SF-N	132	420	62	110	26	5	10	44	40	91	16	11	.262	.338	.419	.757	104	0	58	4.71	-2	*2-126	14	0.5
1988 SF-N★	138	477	66	126	24	6	7	48	40	111	14	5	.264	.326	.384	.710	108	5	62	4.38	-4	*2-134	16	0.4
1989*SF-N	148	547	91	132	26	**11**	13	50	51	133	12	2	.241	.321	.400	.721	108	7	75	4.67	14	*2-148	19	2.6
1990 SF-N	144	498	67	122	22	3	15	56	34	96	14	4	.245	.301	.392	.693	92	-6	59	4.00	12	*2-142	15	1.0
1991 SF-N	144	492	74	129	24	5	19	48	63	95	14	7	.262	.353	.447	.800	128	19	81	5.68	3	*2-144	22	2.6
1992 SF-N	128	443	54	115	25	1	14	49	43	75	5	9	.260	.336	.415	.751	118	7	61	4.59	19	*2-120	16	3.2
1993 SF-N★	128	494	85	154	30	2	19	65	45	97	10	4	.312	.377	.496	.873	136	25	94	7.00	22	*2-128	26	5.3
1994 SF-N	35	129	13	27	8	2	2	7	15	32	3	1	.209	.292	.349	.641	69	-6	14	3.39	5	2-35	1	0.1
1995 SF-N	95	336	51	75	15	0	8	23	42	76	1	2	.223	.317	.339	.656	75	-12	39	3.81	-4	2-91	8	-1.2
1996 SF-N	63	227	35	48	11	1	5	21	24	69	2	2	.211	.301	.335	.636	70	-10	23	3.26	2	2-62	3	-0.6
Total 11	1304	4612	671	1187	238	39	119	458	439	987	103	62	.257	.331	.403	.734	105	21	630	4.63	72	*2-1279/S-1	155	14.7

• THOMPSON, Ryan Ryan Orlando Thompson b: 11/4/1967, Chestertown, MD BR/TR, 6'3", 200 lbs. Deb: 9/1/1992 Career OF: 68-269-76

YEAR TM-L	G	AB	R	H	2B	3B	HR	RBI	BB	SO	SB	CS	AVG	OBP	SLG	OPS	OPS+	BR/A	RC	RC/G	FR	G/POS	WS	TPW
1992 NY-N	30	108	15	24	7	1	3	10	8	24	2	2	.222	.276	.389	.665	87	-3	11	3.31	-1	0-29(0-26-10)	2	-0.4
1993 NY-N	80	288	34	72	19	2	11	26	19	81	2	7	.250	.303	.444	.748	98	-5	36	4.10	3	0-76(0-76-0)	5	-0.1
1994 NY-N	98	334	39	75	14	1	18	59	28	94	1	1	.225	.304	.434	.738	90	-6	43	4.24	4	0-98(0-98-0)	10	-0.1
1995 NY-N	75	267	39	67	13	0	7	31	19	77	3	1	.251	.310	.378	.689	83	-7	29	3.60	3	0-74(11-38-31)	5	-0.5
1996 Cle-A	8	22	2	7	0	0	1	5	1	6	0	0	.318	.348	.455	.802	101	-0	4	6.42	0	/0-1	1	0.0
1999 Hou-N	12	20	2	4	1	0	1	5	2	7	0	0	.200	.273	.400	.673	68	-1	2	3.08	0	/0-8(2-5-3)	0	-0.1
2000 NY-A	33	50	12	13	3	0	3	14	5	12	0	1	.260	.339	.500	.839	110	0	9	6.07	-1	0-10(20-9-6)	2	-0.1
2001 Fla-N	18	31	6	9	5	0	0	2	1	8	0	0	.290	.313	.452	.764	97	-0	4	4.01	-1	0-31(1-4-12)	0	-0.2
2002 Mil-N	62	137	16	34	9	2	8	24	7	38	1	0	.248	.295	.518	.813	110	1	18	4.47	-1	0-16(34-5-14)	2	-0.1
Total 9	416	1257	165	305	71	6	52	176	90	347	9	12	.243	.304	.433	.736	93	-21	154	4.09	7	0-343	27	-1.7

• THOMPSON, Sam Samuel Luther "Big Sam" Thompson
b: 3/5/1860, Danville, IN d: 11/7/1922, Detroit, MI BL/TL, 6'2", 207 lbs. Deb: 7/2/1885 HOF: 1974 Career OF: 3-2-1401

YEAR TM-L	G	AB	R	H	2B	3B	HR	RBI	BB	SO	SB	CS	AVG	OBP	SLG	OPS	OPS+	BR/A	RC	RC/G	FR	G/POS	WS	TPW
1885 Det-N	63	254	58	77	11	9	7	44	16	22	....	....	.303	.344	.500	.844	170	19	45	6.84	6	0-63(0-0-63)/3-1	10	2.2
1886 Det-N	122	503	101	156	18	13	8	89	35	31	13	....	.310	.355	.445	.800	138	22	86	6.71	6	*0-122(0-0-122)	21	2.4
1887*Det-N	127	577	118	235	29	**23**	10	**166**	32	19	22	....	.407	.416	**.571**	.987	166	47	142	11.01	2	*0-127(0-0-127)	**29**	**4.0**
1888 Det-N	56	238	51	67	10	8	6	40	23	10	5	....	.282	.352	.466	.819	159	16	42	6.61	-7	0-56(0-0-56)	10	0.8
1889 Phi-N	128	533	103	158	36	4	**20**	111	36	22	24	....	.296	.348	.492	.839	123	11	102	7.21	-13	*0-128(0-0-128)	17	-0.3
1890 Phi-N	132	549	116	**172**	**41**	9	4	102	42	29	25	....	.313	.371	.443	.813	133	21	102	7.16	-0	*0-132(0-0-132)	19	1.7
1891 Phi-N	133	554	108	163	23	10	7	90	52	20	29	....	.294	.363	.410	.773	122	15	95	6.58	16	*0-133(0-2-131)	22	2.6
1892 Phi-N	153	609	109	186	28	11	9	104	59	19	28	....	.305	.377	.432	.809	145	33	112	7.18	-1	*0-153(3-0-150)	22	2.1
1893 Phi-N	131	600	130	**222**	**37**	13	11	126	50	17	18	....	.370	.424	.530	.954	153	44	146	10.23	-10	*0-131(0-0-131)/1-1	22	2.2
1894 Phi-N	102	451	114	187	32	28	13	**147**	41	13	27	....	.415	.465	**.696**	1.161	**182**	57	162	15.99	-7	*0-99(0-0-99)	20	3.4
1895 Phi-N	119	538	131	211	45	21	**18**	**165**	31	11	27	....	.392	.430	**.654**	1.085	176	56	167	13.72	12	*0-118(0-0-118)	28	5.0
1896 Phi-N	119	517	103	154	28	7	12	100	28	13	12	....	.298	.341	.449	.790	108	3	86	6.20	13	*0-119(0-0-119)	13	0.8
1897 Phi-N	3	13	2	3	0	1	0	3	1	....	0	....	.231	.286	.385	.670	78	-0	1	3.88	-0	/0-3(0-0-3)	0	-0.1
1898 Phi-N	14	63	14	22	5	3	1	15	4	....	2	....	.349	.388	.571	.959	182	6	15	9.77	3	0-14(0-0-14)	3	0.8
1906 Det-A	8	31	4	7	0	1	0	3	1	....	0	....	.226	.250	.290	.540	67	-1	2	2.55	-1	/0-8(0-0-8)	0	-0.3
Total 15	1410	6030	1262	2020	343	161	126	1305	451	226	232	....	.335	.384	.506	.890	146	348	1307	8.67	19	*0-1406/1-1,3-1	236	27.3

• THOMPSON, Scot Vernon Scot Thompson b: 12/7/1955, Grove City, PA BL/TL, 6'3", 195 lbs. Deb: 9/3/1978 Career OF: 61-66-150

YEAR TM-L	G	AB	R	H	2B	3B	HR	RBI	BB	SO	SB	CS	AVG	OBP	SLG	OPS	OPS+	BR/A	RC	RC/G	FR	G/POS	WS	TPW
1978 Chi-N	19	36	7	15	3	0	0	2	2	4	0	0	.417	.447	.500	.947	147	2	8	10.19	0	/0-5(0-5-1),1-2	2	0.2
1979 Chi-N	128	346	36	100	13	5	2	29	17	37	4	3	.289	.324	.373	.697	82	-9	40	4.14	-1	*0-100(12-26-72)	7	-1.4
1980 Chi-N	102	226	26	48	10	1	2	13	28	31	6	6	.212	.302	.292	.594	62	-12	19	2.74	0	0-66(1-14-52),1-12	2	-1.6

YEAR TM-L	G	AB	R	H	2B	3B	HR	RBI	BB	SO	SB	CS	AVG	OBP	SLG	OPS	OPS+	BR/A	RC	RC/G	FR	G/POS	WS	TPW
1981 Chi-N	57	115	8	19	5	0	0	8	7	8	2	0	.165	.213	.209	.422	19	-12	6	1.45	-3	0-30(3-20-8)/1-3	0	-1.6
1982 Chi-N	49	74	11	27	5	1	0	7	5	4	0	1	.365	.405	.459	.865	138	3	13	7.00	2	0-23(20-1-4)/1-4	3	0.5
1983 Chi-N	53	88	4	17	3	1	0	10	3	14	0	0	.193	.220	.250	.470	28	-9	4	1.44	-1	0-29(23-0-6)/1-1	0	-1.1
1984 SF-N	120	245	30	75	7	1	1	31	30	26	5	3	.306	.382	.355	.737	112	5	32	4.58	-3	1-87/0-6(2-0-4)	7	-0.2
1985 SF-N	64	111	8	23	5	0	0	6	2	10	0	0	.207	.221	.252	.473	34	-10	5	1.46	2	1-24	0	-1.0
Mon-N	34	32	2	9	1	0	0	4	3	7	0	0	.281	.343	.313	.655	90	-0	3	3.73	1	/1-3,0-3(0-0-3)	1	0.0
Yr.	98	143	10	32	6	0	0	10	5	17	0	0	.224	.250	.266	.516	47	-11	9	1.94	2	1-27/0-3(0-0-3)	1	-1.0
Total 8	626	1273	132	333	52	9	5	110	97	141	17	13	.262	.315	.328	.643	76	-42	131	3.49	-3	0-262,1-136	22	-6.2

• THOMPSON, Shag James Alfred Thompson b: 4/29/1893, Haw River, NC d: 1/7/1990, Black Mountain, NC BL/TR, 5'8.5", 165 lbs. Deb: 6/8/1914 Career OF: 3-19-1

YEAR TM-L	G	AB	R	H	2B	3B	HR	RBI	BB	SO	SB	CS	AVG	OBP	SLG	OPS	OPS+	BR/A	RC	RC/G	FR	G/POS	WS	TPW
1914 Phi-A	16	29	3	5	0	1	0	2	7	8	1	....	.172	.351	.241	.593	82	-0	3	3.15	1	/0-8(2-6-0)	1	0.1
1915 Phi-A	17	33	5	11	2	0	0	2	4	6	0	1	.333	.405	.394	.799	144	1	5	5.67	1	/0-7(0-7-0)	2	0.3
1916 Phi-A	15	17	4	0	0	0	0	0	7	6	1	....	.000	.292	.000	.292	-12	-2	0	.38	0	/0-8(1-6-1)	0	-0.3
Total 3	48	79	12	16	2	1	0	4	18	20	2	1	.203	.357	.253	.610	82	-0	8	3.32	2	/0-23	3	0.1

• THOMPSON, Tim Charles Lemoine Thompson b: 3/1/1924, Coalport, PA BL/TR, 5'11", 190 lbs. Deb: 4/28/1954 C

YEAR TM-L	G	AB	R	H	2B	3B	HR	RBI	BB	SO	SB	CS	AVG	OBP	SLG	OPS	OPS+	BR/A	RC	RC/G	FR	G/POS	WS	TPW
1954 Bro-N	10	13	2	2	1	0	0	1	1	1	0	0	.154	.214	.231	.445	15	-2	1	1.71	-1	/C-2,0-1	0	-0.2
1956 KC-A	92	268	21	73	13	2	1	27	17	23	2	4	.272	.321	.347	.668	76	-11	29	3.83	4	C-68	5	-0.3
1957 KC-A	81	230	25	47	10	0	7	19	18	26	0	0	.204	.262	.339	.601	62	-13	20	2.94	1	C-62	3	-0.9
1958 Det-A	4	6	1	1	0	0	0	0	3	2	0	0	.167	.444	.167	.611	70	0	1	4.27	0	/C-4	0	0.0
Total 4	187	517	49	123	24	2	8	47	39	52	2	4	.238	.294	.338	.632	68	-25	51	3.37	5	C-136/0-1	8	-1.4

• THOMPSON, Tommy Rupert Lockhart Thompson b: 5/19/1910, Elkhart, IL d: 5/24/1971, Auburn, CA BL/TR, 5'9.5", 155 lbs. Deb: 9/3/1933 Career OF: 29-48-177

YEAR TM-L	G	AB	R	H	2B	3B	HR	RBI	BB	SO	SB	CS	AVG	OBP	SLG	OPS	OPS+	BR/A	RC	RC/G	FR	G/POS	WS	TPW
1933 Bos-N	24	97	6	18	1	0	0	6	4	6	0	....	.186	.218	.196	.414	20	-10	4	1.11	2	0-24(1-13-10)	1	-1.0
1934 Bos-N	105	343	40	91	12	3	0	37	13	19	2	....	.265	.300	.318	.618	71	-14	34	3.42	9	0-82(6-1-75)	6	-1.0
1935 Bos-N	112	297	34	81	7	1	4	30	36	17	2	....	.273	.353	.343	.697	96	-0	36	4.13	2	0-85(12-12-62)	5	-0.3
1936 Bos-N	106	266	37	76	9	0	4	36	31	12	3	....	.286	.362	.365	.727	103	2	38	5.05	0	0-39(10-22-7),1-25	7	-0.2
1938 Chi-A	19	18	2	2	0	0	0	2	1	2	0	0	.111	.158	.111	.269	-31	-4	0	.57	0	/1-1	0	-0.3
1939 Chi-A	1	0	0	0	0	0	0	1	0	0	0	0	....	....	....	....	-97	0	0	.00	0	....	0	0.0
StL-A	30	86	23	26	5	0	1	7	23	7	0	0	.302	.455	.395	.850	117	4	18	7.93	0	0-23(0-0-23)	3	0.2
Yr.	31	86	23	26	5	0	1	8	23	7	0	0	.302	.455	.395	.850	115	4	18	7.80	0	0-23(0-0-23)	3	0.2
Total 6	397	1107	142	294	34	4	9	119	108	63	7	0	.266	.335	.328	.663	84	-22	130	4.03	12	0-253/1-26	22	-2.6

• THOMPSON, Tug John P. Thompson b: London, Canada BL/TR, 5'8", 160 lbs. Deb: 8/31/1882 Career OF: 0-8-5

YEAR TM-L	G	AB	R	H	2B	3B	HR	RBI	BB	SO	SB	CS	AVG	OBP	SLG	OPS	OPS+	BR/A	RC	RC/G	FR	G/POS	WS	TPW
1882 Cin-a	1	5	0	1	0	0	0	....	0	....	....	....	.200	.200	.200	.400	33	-0	0	1.44	0	/0-1	0	-0.1
1884 Ind-a	24	97	10	20	3	0	0	0	2	....	....	....	.206	.222	.237	.459	51	-5	5	1.87	-6	C-12,0-12(0-7-5)	0	-1.0
Total 2	25	102	10	21	3	0	0	0	2	....	....	....	.206	.221	.235	.456	50	-5	5	1.85	-7	/0-13,C-12	0	-1.0

• THOMSON, Bobby Robert Brown "Flying Scot,The Staten Island Scot" Thomson b: 10/25/1923, Glasgow, Scotland BR/TR, 6'2", 185 lbs. Deb: 9/9/1946 Career OF: 511-982-59

YEAR TM-L	G	AB	R	H	2B	3B	HR	RBI	BB	SO	SB	CS	AVG	OBP	SLG	OPS	OPS+	BR/A	RC	RC/G	FR	G/POS	WS	TPW
1946 NY-N	18	54	8	17	4	1	2	9	4	5	0	....	.315	.362	.537	.899	152	3	10	7.36	-1	3-16	2	0.3
1947 NY-N	138	545	105	154	26	5	29	85	40	78	1	....	.283	.336	.508	.844	121	12	92	6.12	-1	*0-127(0-127-0)/2-9	20	0.8
1948 NY-N★	138	471	75	117	20	2	16	63	30	77	2	....	.248	.296	.401	.697	87	-11	53	3.82	0	*0-125(64-57-4)	9	-1.8
1949 NY-N★	156	641	99	198	35	9	27	109	44	45	10	....	.309	.355	.518	.873	131	25	115	6.73	5	*0-156(0-156-0)	26	2.6
1950 NY-N	149	563	79	142	22	7	25	85	55	45	3	....	.252	.324	.449	.774	101	-1	81	5.01	6	*0-149(0-149-0)	18	0.1
1951*NY-N	148	518	89	152	27	8	32	101	73	57	5	5	.293	.385	.562	.947	150	36	113	7.80	-9	0-77(33-43-3),3-69	26	2.3
1952 NY-N★	153	608	89	164	29	**14**	24	108	52	74	5	2	.270	.331	.482	.813	122	16	97	5.62	-3	3-91,0-63(0-63-0)	25	1.2
1953 NY-N	154	608	80	175	22	6	26	106	43	57	4	2	.288	.338	.472	.810	106	4	95	5.62	-4	*0-154(0-153-1)	17	-0.7
1954 Mil-N	43	99	7	23	3	0	2	15	12	29	0	0	.232	.315	.323	.639	71	-4	10	3.41	2	0-26(26-0-0)	1	-0.4
1955 Mil-N	101	343	40	88	12	3	12	56	34	52	2	1	.257	.324	.414	.738	99	-1	45	4.43	-2	0-91(88-3-0)	9	-0.8
1956 Mil-N	142	451	59	106	10	4	20	74	43	75	2	4	.235	.304	.408	.712	95	-5	55	4.03	0	*0-136(128-18-0)/3-3	12	-1.4
1957 Mil-N	41	148	15	35	5	3	4	23	8	27	2	1	.236	.285	.392	.677	86	-3	17	3.89	0	0-38(36-5-1)	3	-0.6
NY-N	81	215	24	52	7	4	8	38	19	39	1	2	.242	.303	.423	.727	93	-3	28	4.38	-3	0-71(54-3-17)/3-1	5	-1.0
Yr.	122	363	39	87	12	7	12	61	27	66	3	3	.240	.296	.410	.706	90	-7	44	4.18	-3	*0-109(90-8-18)/3-1	8	-1.6
1958 Chi-N	152	547	67	155	27	5	21	82	56	76	0	2	.283	.354	.466	.820	117	12	87	5.65	-2	*0-148(7-143-1)/3-4	19	0.2
1959 Chi-N	122	374	55	97	15	2	11	52	35	50	1	0	.259	.326	.398	.724	92	-4	48	4.44	5	*0-116(62-49-29)	10	-0.4
1960 Bos-A	40	114	12	30	3	1	5	20	11	15	0	1	.263	.328	.439	.767	102	-0	15	4.53	-1	0-27(12-13-2)/1-1	3	-0.3
Bal-A	3	6	0	0	0	0	0	0	0	3	0	0	.000	.000	.000	.000	-101	-2	0	.00	0	/0-2(1-0-1)	0	-0.2
Yr.	43	120	12	30	3	1	5	20	11	18	0	1	.250	.313	.417	.730	93	-2	15	4.21	-1	0-29(13-13-3)/1-1	3	-0.5
Total 15	1779	6305	903	1705	267	74	264	1026	559	804	38	20	.270	.333	.462	.795	111	74	960	5.36	-9	*0-1506,3-184/2-9,1-1	205	-0.1

• THON, Dickie Richard William Thon b: 6/20/1958, South Bend, IN BR/TR, 5'11", 175 lbs. Deb: 5/22/1979

YEAR TM-L	G	AB	R	H	2B	3B	HR	RBI	BB	SO	SB	CS	AVG	OBP	SLG	OPS	OPS+	BR/A	RC	RC/G	FR	G/POS	WS	TPW
1979*Cal-A	35	56	6	19	3	0	0	8	5	10	0	0	.339	.393	.393	.786	117	2	8	5.71	-1	2-24/S-8,3-1,D-1	2	0.1
1980 Cal-A	80	267	32	68	12	2	0	15	10	28	7	5	.255	.284	.315	.599	65	-14	23	2.85	2	S-22,2-21,D-15,3-10/1-1	3	-1.0
1981*Hou-N	49	95	13	26	6	0	0	3	9	13	6	1	.274	.337	.337	.673	96	1	11	4.06	-4	2-28,S-13/3-5	3	-0.2
1982 Hou-N	136	496	73	137	31	**10**	3	36	37	48	37	8	.276	.328	.397	.725	110	10	69	4.94	11	*S-119/3-8,2-1	22	3.5
1983 Hou-N★	154	619	81	177	28	9	20	79	54	73	34	16	.286	.345	.457	.802	128	22	95	5.34	26	*S-154	30	**6.8**
1984 Hou-N	5	17	3	6	0	1	0	1	0	4	0	1	.353	.389	.471	.859	151	1	2	4.77	0	/S-5	1	0.1
1985 Hou-N	84	251	26	63	6	1	6	29	18	50	8	3	.251	.301	.355	.656	85	-5	27	3.79	7	S-79	9	0.9
1986*Hou-N	106	278	24	69	13	1	3	21	29	49	6	5	.248	.319	.335	.654	83	-7	28	3.43	3	*S-104	8	0.5
1987 Hou-N	32	66	6	14	1	0	1	3	16	13	3	0	.212	.366	.273	.639	75	-1	8	4.10	-3	S-31	2	-0.1
1988 SD-N	95	258	36	68	12	2	1	18	33	49	19	4	.264	.349	.337	.687	100	3	34	4.58	-2	S-70/2-2,3-1	9	0.6
1989 Phi-N	136	435	45	118	18	4	15	60	33	81	6	3	.271	.323	.434	.757	114	7	61	4.95	1	*S-129	20	1.9
1990 Phi-N	149	552	54	141	20	4	8	48	37	77	12	5	.255	.306	.350	.655	80	-16	57	3.54	2	*S-148	10	-0.2
1991 Phi-N	146	539	44	136	18	4	9	44	25	84	11	5	.252	.285	.351	.636	79	-17	52	3.34	3	*S-146	12	-0.2
1992 Tex-A	95	275	30	68	15	3	4	37	20	40	12	2	.247	.298	.367	.666	89	-3	32	3.98	-4	S-87	9	-0.1
1993 Mil-A	85	245	23	66	10	1	1	33	22	39	6	5	.269	.330	.331	.660	79	-8	27	3.69	-2	S-28,3-25,2-22,D-14	7	-0.7
Total 15	1387	4449	496	1176	193	42	71	435	348	658	167	63	.264	.319	.374	.693	96	-26	536	4.16	40	*S-1143/2-98,3-50,D-30,1-1	147	11.9

• THONEY, Jack John "Bullet Jack" Thoney b: 12/8/1879, Fort Thomas, KY d: 10/24/1948, Covington, KY BR/TR, 5'10", 175 lbs. Deb: 4/26/1902 Career OF: 97-52-15

YEAR TM-L	G	AB	R	H	2B	3B	HR	RBI	BB	SO	SB	CS	AVG	OBP	SLG	OPS	OPS+	BR/A	RC	RC/G	FR	G/POS	WS	TPW
1902 Cle-A	28	105	14	30	7	1	0	11	9	....	4	....	.286	.342	.371	.714	102	0	15	5.30	-9	2-14,S-11/0-2(0-0-2)	3	-0.8
Bal-A	3	11	1	0	0	0	0	0	1	....	1	....	.000	.083	.000	.083	-72	-3	0	.21	-1	/3-3	0	-0.3
Yr.	31	116	15	30	7	1	0	11	10	....	5	....	.259	.317	.336	.654	85	-2	15	4.66	-11	2-14,S-11/3-3,0-2(0-0-2)	3	-1.2
1903 Cle-A	32	122	10	25	3	0	1	9	2	....	7	....	.205	.218	.254	.472	42	-9	8	2.32	1	0-24(0-23-1)/2-5,3-2	1	-1.0
1904 Was-A	17	70	6	21	3	0	0	6	1	....	2	....	.300	.310	.343	.653	108	0	8	4.47	1	0-17(0-8-9)	2	0.1
NY-A	36	128	17	24	4	2	0	12	8	....	9	....	.188	.241	.250	.491	53	-7	10	2.58	-2	3-26,0-10(0-10-0)	1	-1.0
Yr.	53	198	23	45	7	2	0	18	9	....	11	....	.227	.264	.283	.547	71	-7	19	3.18	-1	0-27(0-18-9),3-26	3	-0.9
1908 Bos-A	109	416	58	106	5	9	2	30	13	....	16	....	.255	.282	.325	.607	94	-4	42	3.39	8	*0-101(87-11-3)	11	-0.2
1909 Bos-A	13	40	1	5	1	0	0	3	2	....	2	....	.125	.167	.150	.317		-5	1	.93	1	0-10(10-0-0)	0	-0.4
1911 Bos-A	26	20	5	5	0	0	0	2	0	....	1	....	.250	.250	.250	.500	40	-1	1	2.45	0	....	0	-0.1
Total 6	264	912	112	216	23	12	3	73	36	....	42	....	.237	.269	.298	.567	76	-28	87	3.21	-2	0-164/3-31,2-19,S-11	18	-3.9

• THORNTON, Andre Andre Thornton b: 8/13/1949, Tuskegee, AL BR/TR, 6'3", 205 lbs. Deb: 7/28/1973

YEAR TM-L	G	AB	R	H	2B	3B	HR	RBI	BB	SO	SB	CS	AVG	OBP	SLG	OPS	OPS+	BR/A	RC	RC/G	FR	G/POS	WS	TPW
1973 Chi-N	17	35	3	7	3	0	0	2	7	9	0	0	.200	.333	.286	.619	68	-1	4	3.41	1	/1-9	1	-0.1
1974 Chi-N	107	303	41	79	16	4	10	46	48	50	2	1	.261	.369	.439	.808	120	9	51	5.94	7	1-90/3-1	12	1.0
1975 Chi-N	120	372	70	109	21	4	18	60	88	63	3	2	.293	.433	.516	.949	156	33	89	8.62	-2	*1-113/3-2	23	2.4
1976 Chi-N	27	85	8	17	6	0	2	14	20	14	2	0	.200	.364	.341	.706	93	1	13	5.09	2	1-25	3	0.1
Mon-N	69	183	20	35	5	2	9	24	28	32	2	1	.191	.308	.388	.696	93	-2	24	4.23	0	1-43,0-11(0-0-11)	4	-0.6
Yr.	96	268	28	52	11	2	11	38	48	46	4	1	.194	.327	.373	.700	93	-1	37	4.50	1	1-68,0-11(0-0-11)	7	-0.5
1977 Cle-A	131	433	77	114	20	5	28	70	70	82	3	4	.263	.379	.527	.906	149	30	89	7.15	0	*1-117/D-9	20	2.3

YEAR TM-L	G	AB	R	H	2B	3B	HR	RBI	BB	SO	SB	CS	AVG	OBP	SLG	OPS	OPS+	BR/A	RC	RC/G	FR	G/POS	WS	TPW
1978 Cle-A	145	508	97	133	22	4	33	105	93	72	4	7	.262	.382	.516	.898	152	36	99	6.54	5	*1-145	25	3.3
1979 Cle-A	143	515	89	120	31	1	26	93	90	93	5	4	.233	.351	.449	.800	114	11	86	5.57	1	*1-130,D-13	19	0.4
1981 Cle-A	69	226	22	54	12	0	6	30	23	37	3	1	.239	.309	.372	.681	97	-1	23	3.13	0	D-53,1-11	3	-0.3
1982 Cle-A★	161	589	90	161	26	1	32	116	109	81	6	7	.273	.389	.484	.872	139	34	109	6.35	0	*D-152/1-8	20	2.8
1983 Cle-A	141	508	78	143	27	1	17	77	87	72	4	2	.281	.389	.439	.828	123	20	90	6.34	1	*D-114,1-27	18	1.5
1984 Cle-A★	155	587	91	159	26	0	33	99	91	79	6	5	.271	.371	.484	.854	132	27	108	6.48	0	*D-144,1-11	21	2.1
1985 Cle-A	124	461	49	109	13	0	22	88	47	75	3	2	.236	.307	.408	.715	94	-4	56	4.02	0	*D-122	8	-0.9
1986 Cle-A	120	401	49	92	14	0	17	66	65	67	4	1	.229	.338	.392	.730	100	2	55	4.55	0	*D-110	9	-0.2
1987 Cle-A	36	85	8	10	2	0	0	5	10	25	1	0	.118	.211	.141	.352	-4	-13	3	1.10	0	D-21	0	-1.2
Total 14	1565	5291	792	1342	244	22	253	895	876	851	48	37	.254	.364	.452	.815	123	181	900	5.78	14	D-738,1-729/0-11,3-3	186	12.5

• THORNTON, Lou Louis Thornton b: 4/26/1963, Montgomery, AL BL/TR, 6'2", 185 lbs. Deb: 4/8/1985 Career OF: 32-2-24

YEAR TM-L	G	AB	R	H	2B	3B	HR	RBI	BB	SO	SB	CS	AVG	OBP	SLG	OPS	OPS+	BR/A	RC	RC/G	FR	G/POS	WS	TPW
1985*Tor-A	56	72	18	17	1	1	1	8	2	24	1	0	.236	.267	.319	.586	58	-4	6	2.76	-1	0-35(16-0-20),D-16	1	-0.6
1987 Tor-A	12	2	5	1	0	0	0	0	1	0	0	1	.500	.667	.500	1.167	212	0	0	.00	-1	/D-6,0-4(4-0-0)	0	-0.1
1988 Tor-A	11	2	1	0	0	0	0	0	0	0	0	0	.000	.000	.000	.000	-100	-1	0	.00	-1	0-10(9-0-1)/D-1	0	-0.2
1989 NY-N	13	13	5	4	1	0	0	1	0	1	2	0	.308	.308	.385	.692	102	0	2	5.58	0	/0-6(3-1-2)	0	0.0
1990 NY-N	3	0	0	0	0	0	0	0	0	0	0	0	....	....	....	....	-100	0	0	....	0	/0-2(0-1-1)	0	0.0
Total 5	95	89	29	22	2	1	1	9	3	25	3	1	.247	.280	.326	.605	66	-4	8	2.92	-3	/0-57,D-23	1	-0.9

• THORNTON, Otis Otis Benjamin Thornton b: 6/30/1945, Docena, AL BR/TR, 6'1", 186 lbs. Deb: 7/6/1973

YEAR TM-L	G	AB	R	H	2B	3B	HR	RBI	BB	SO	SB	CS	AVG	OBP	SLG	OPS	OPS+	BR/A	RC	RC/G	FR	G/POS	WS	TPW
1973 Hou-N	2	3	0	0	0	0	0	1	0	2	0	0	.000	.000	.000	.000	-100	-1	0	.00	0	/C-2	0	-0.1

• THORNTON, Walter Walter Miller Thornton b: 2/18/1875, Lewiston, ME d: 7/14/1960, Los Angeles, CA BL/TL, 6'1", 180 lbs. Deb: 7/1/1895 Career OF: 50-36-10 ♦

YEAR TM-L	G	AB	R	H	2B	3B	HR	RBI	BB	SO	SB	CS	AVG	OBP	SLG	OPS	OPS+	BR/A	RC	RC/G	FR	G/POS	WS	TPW
1895 Chi-N	8	22	4	7	1	0	1	7	3	1	0	....	.318	.400	.500	.900	123	2	5	8.12	-1	/P-7,1-1	1	-0.2
1896 Chi-N	9	22	6	8	0	1	0	1	5	2	2	....	.364	.481	.455	.936	142	2	6	11.21	-1	/P-5,0-3(0-2-1)	2	-0.1
1897 Chi-N	75	265	39	85	9	6	0	55	30	....	13	....	.321	.402	.400	.802	108	8	50	7.14	-8	0-59(48-8-3),P-16	14	-0.6
1898 Chi-N	62	210	34	62	5	2	0	14	22	....	8	....	.295	.362	.338	.700	101	6	30	5.22	-2	0-34(2-26-6),P-28	19	0.8
Total 4	154	519	83	162	15	9	1	77	60	3	23	....	.312	.390	.382	.771	107	18	90	6.54	-12	/0-96,P-56,1-1	36	-0.1

• THORPE, Bob Benjamin Robert Thorpe b: 11/19/1926, Caryville, FL d: 10/30/1996, Waveland, MS BR/TR, 6'1.5", 190 lbs. Deb: 4/19/1951 Career OF: 18-0-78

YEAR TM-L	G	AB	R	H	2B	3B	HR	RBI	BB	SO	SB	CS	AVG	OBP	SLG	OPS	OPS+	BR/A	RC	RC/G	FR	G/POS	WS	TPW
1951 Bos-N	2	2	1	1	0	1	0	1	0	0	0	0	.500	.500	1.500	2.000	448	1	2	41.51	0	....	0	0.1
1952 Bos-N	81	292	20	76	8	2	3	26	5	42	3	1	.260	.275	.332	.607	70	-12	26	3.04	-1	0-72(8-0-70)	4	-1.7
1953 Mil-N	27	37	1	6	1	0	0	5	1	6	0	1	.162	.184	.189	.373	-3	-6	1	1.00	0	0-18(10-0-8)	0	-0.6
Total 3	110	331	22	83	9	3	3	32	6	48	3	2	.251	.266	.323	.590	64	-18	28	2.93	-1	/0-90	4	-2.2

• THORPE, Jim James Francis Thorpe b: 5/28/1887, Prague, OK d: 3/28/1953, Long Beach, CA BR/TR, 6'1", 185 lbs. Deb: 4/14/1913 Career OF: 72-69-69

YEAR TM-L	G	AB	R	H	2B	3B	HR	RBI	BB	SO	SB	CS	AVG	OBP	SLG	OPS	OPS+	BR/A	RC	RC/G	FR	G/POS	WS	TPW
1913 NY-N	19	35	6	5	0	0	1	2	1	9	2	....	.143	.167	.229	.395	12	-4	1	1.21	0	/0-9(3-7-0)	0	-0.4
1914 NY-N	30	31	5	6	1	0	0	2	0	4	1	....	.194	.194	.226	.419	25	-3	1	1.42	-1	/0-4(0-2-2)	0	-0.4
1915 NY-N	17	52	8	12	3	1	0	1	2	16	4	2	.231	.259	.327	.586	82	-1	5	2.86	-1	0-15(0-13-2)	1	-0.4
1917 Cin-N	77	251	29	62	2	8	4	36	6	35	11	....	.247	.267	.367	.634	98	-2	26	3.42	0	0-69(38-0-33)	6	-0.6
*NY-N	26	57	12	11	3	2	0	4	8	10	1	....	.193	.303	.316	.619	93	-0	6	3.09	-1	0-18(6-1-13)	1	-0.2
Yr.	103	308	41	73	5	10	4	40	14	45	12	....	.237	.275	.357	.632	97	-3	32	3.36	-1	0-87(44-1-46)	7	-0.9
1918 NY-N	58	113	15	28	4	4	1	11	4	18	3	....	.248	.286	.381	.666	104	-0	12	3.72	-6	0-44(2-33-12)	4	-0.9
1919 NY-N	2	3	0	1	0	0	0	1	0	0	0	....	.333	.333	.333	.667	102	-0	0	3.77	-0	/0-2(1-1-0)	0	0.0
Bos-N	60	156	16	51	7	3	1	25	6	30	7	....	.327	.360	.429	.789	142	7	25	6.06	-5	0-38(22-12-7)/1-2	6	0.0
Yr.	62	159	16	52	7	3	1	26	6	30	7	....	.327	.359	.428	.787	141	7	26	6.00	-5	0-40(23-13-7)/1-2	6	0.0
Total 6	289	698	91	176	20	18	7	82	27	122	29	2	.252	.286	.362	.648	100	-4	77	3.71	-14	0-199/1-2	18	-2.9

• THRASHER, Buck Frank Edward Thrasher b: 8/6/1889, Watkinsville, GA d: 6/12/1938, Cleveland, OH BL/TR, 5'11", 182 lbs. Deb: 9/27/1916 Career OF: 0-0-29

YEAR TM-L	G	AB	R	H	2B	3B	HR	RBI	BB	SO	SB	CS	AVG	OBP	SLG	OPS	OPS+	BR/A	RC	RC/G	FR	G/POS	WS	TPW
1916 Phi-A	7	29	4	9	2	1	0	4	2	1	0	....	.310	.355	.448	.803	148	1	5	5.89	0	/0-7(0-0-7)	1	0.1
1917 Phi-A	23	77	5	18	2	1	0	2	3	12	0	....	.234	.272	.286	.557	71	-3	6	2.54	-3	0-22(0-0-22)	1	-0.7
Total 2	30	106	9	27	4	2	0	6	5	13	0	....	.255	.295	.330	.625	92	-2	11	3.37	-3	/0-29	2	-0.6

• THRONEBERRY, Faye Maynard Faye Throneberry b: 6/22/1931, Fisherville, TN d: 4/26/1999, Memphis, TN BL/TR, 5'11", 190 lbs. Deb: 4/15/1952 Career OF: 101-75-177

YEAR TM-L	G	AB	R	H	2B	3B	HR	RBI	BB	SO	SB	CS	AVG	OBP	SLG	OPS	OPS+	BR/A	RC	RC/G	FR	G/POS	WS	TPW
1952 Bos-A	98	310	38	80	11	3	5	23	33	67	16	7	.258	.331	.361	.693	86	-5	41	4.61	5	0-86(11-4-71)	8	-0.3
1955 Bos-A	60	144	20	37	7	3	6	27	14	31	0	0	.257	.327	.472	.799	103	0	23	5.49	0	0-34(32-0-3)	4	-0.2
1956 Bos-A	24	50	6	11	2	0	1	3	3	16	0	0	.220	.264	.320	.584	48	-4	4	2.74	-1	0-13(8-2-3)	0	-0.6
1957 Bos-A	1	1	0	0	0	0	0	0	0	1	0	0	.000	.000	.000	.000	-95	-0	0	.00	0	....	0	0.0
Was-A	68	195	21	36	8	2	2	12	17	37	0	1	.185	.254	.277	.530	45	-15	14	2.27	-2	0-58(14-48-2)	1	-2.1
Yr.	69	196	21	36	8	2	2	12	17	38	0	1	.184	.252	.276	.528	45	-15	14	2.26	-2	0-58(14-48-2)	1	-2.1
1958 Was-A	44	87	12	16	1	1	4	7	4	28	0	1	.184	.245	.356	.601	64	-5	8	2.88	0	0-26(5-13-8)	1	-0.6
1959 Was-A	117	327	36	82	11	2	10	42	33	61	6	4	.251	.325	.388	.713	95	-2	42	4.43	-1	0-86(16-1-71)	8	-0.7
1960 Was-A	85	157	18	39	7	1	1	23	18	33	1	1	.248	.330	.325	.654	77	-5	17	3.71	0	0-34(12-7-17)	2	-0.6
1961 LA-A	24	31	1	6	1	0	0	0	5	10	0	0	.194	.306	.226	.531	40	-3	2	2.38	1	/0-5(3-0-2)	0	-0.2
Total 8	521	1302	152	307	48	12	29	137	127	284	23	14	.236	.309	.358	.666	79	-39	151	3.92	1	0-342	24	-5.3

• THRONEBERRY, Marv Marvin Eugene "Marvelous Marv" Throneberry
b: 9/2/1933, Collierville, TN d: 6/23/1994, Fisherville, TN BL/TL, 6'1", 197 lbs. Deb: 9/25/1955 Career OF: 1-0-44

YEAR TM-L	G	AB	R	H	2B	3B	HR	RBI	BB	SO	SB	CS	AVG	OBP	SLG	OPS	OPS+	BR/A	RC	RC/G	FR	G/POS	WS	TPW
1955 NY-A	1	2	1	2	1	0	0	3	0	0	1	0	1.000	1.000	1.500	2.500	573	1	3	72.72	0	/1-1	1	0.2
1958*NY-A	60	150	30	34	5	2	7	19	19	40	1	1	.227	.318	.427	.744	107	1	21	4.68	-1	1-40/0-5(0-0-5)	4	-0.3
1959 NY-A	80	192	27	46	5	0	8	22	18	51	0	0	.240	.305	.391	.695	93	-2	24	4.19	1	1-54,0-13(1-0-12)	4	-0.3
1960 KC-A	104	236	29	59	9	2	11	41	23	60	0	0	.250	.317	.445	.762	103	0	32	4.68	5	1-71	6	0.2
1961 KC-A	40	130	17	31	2	1	6	24	19	30	0	0	.238	.336	.408	.743	97	-0	18	4.63	0	1-30,0-10(0-0-10)	3	-0.2
Bal-A	56	96	9	20	3	0	5	11	12	20	0	0	.208	.296	.396	.692	85	-2	11	3.95	1	0-15(0-0-15),1-11	2	-0.2
Yr.	96	226	26	51	5	1	11	35	31	50	0	0	.226	.319	.403	.722	92	-3	29	4.34	2	1-41,0-25(0-0-25)	5	-0.4
1962 Bal-A	9	9	1	0	0	0	0	0	4	6	0	0	.000	.308	.000	.308	-9	-1	0	.96	0	/0-2(0-0-2)	0	-0.1
NY-N	116	357	29	87	11	3	16	49	34	83	1	3	.244	.309	.426	.735	94	-5	46	4.33	1	1-97	5	-1.0
1963 NY-N	14	14	0	2	1	0	0	1	1	5	0	0	.143	.200	.214	.414	19	-1	1	1.47	0	/1-3	0	-0.2
Total 7	480	1186	143	281	37	8	53	170	130	295	3	4	.237	.313	.416	.729	96	-10	155	4.43	7	1-307/0-45	25	-2.0

• THURMAN, Bob Robert Burns Thurman b: 5/14/1917, Wichita, KS d: 10/31/1998, Wichita, KS BL/TL, 6'1", 205 lbs. Deb: 4/14/1955 Career OF: 107-0-43

YEAR TM-L	G	AB	R	H	2B	3B	HR	RBI	BB	SO	SB	CS	AVG	OBP	SLG	OPS	OPS+	BR/A	RC	RC/G	FR	G/POS	WS	TPW
1955 Cin-N	82	152	19	33	2	3	7	22	17	26	0	2	.217	.296	.408	.704	80	-6	16	3.46	0	0-36(36-0-0)	2	-0.7
1956 Cin-N	80	139	25	41	5	2	8	22	10	14	0	0	.295	.342	.532	.875	123	4	25	6.49	0	0-29(9-0-20)	5	0.3
1957 Cin-N	74	190	38	47	4	2	16	40	15	33	0	0	.247	.306	.542	.848	114	3	31	5.77	2	0-44(29-0-15)	6	0.3
1958 Cin-N	94	178	23	41	7	4	4	20	20	38	1	2	.230	.322	.382	.704	81	-5	21	3.99	-0	0-41(33-0-8)	3	-0.8
1959 Cin-N	4	4	1	1	0	0	0	2	0	1	0	0	.250	.250	.250	.500	33	-0	0	2.25	0	....	0	0.0
Total 5	334	663	106	163	18	11	35	106	62	112	1	4	.246	.315	.465	.780	98	-4	94	4.83	2	0-150	16	-0.8

• THURMAN, Gary Gary Montez Thurman b: 11/12/1964, Indianapolis, IN BR/TR, 5'10", 175 lbs. Deb: 8/30/1987 Career OF: 132-84-147

YEAR TM-L	G	AB	R	H	2B	3B	HR	RBI	BB	SO	SB	CS	AVG	OBP	SLG	OPS	OPS+	BR/A	RC	RC/G	FR	G/POS	WS	TPW
1987 KC-A	27	81	12	24	2	0	0	5	8	20	7	2	.296	.360	.321	.681	81	-1	10	4.60	4	0-27(22-6-0)	3	0.1
1988 KC-A	35	66	6	11	1	0	0	2	4	20	5	1	.167	.214	.182	.396	12	-7	3	1.51	-1	0-32(22-11-0)/D-1	0	-0.8
1989 KC-A	72	87	24	17	2	1	0	5	15	26	16	0	.195	.314	.241	.555	59	-1	11	3.92	-1	0-60(12-28-24)/D-4	2	-0.2
1990 KC-A	23	60	5	14	3	0	0	3	2	12	1	1	.233	.258	.283	.541	52	-4	4	2.07	-1	0-21(5-2-15)	0	-0.6
1991 KC-A	80	184	24	51	9	0	2	13	11	42	15	5	.277	.321	.359	.680	87	-2	21	3.94	-5	0-72(39-9-29)	4	-0.9
1992 KC-A	88	200	25	49	6	3	0	20	9	34	9	6	.245	.281	.305	.586	62	-11	17	2.69	1	0-67(7-2-59)/D-9	4	-1.3
1993 Det-A	75	89	22	19	2	2	0	13	11	30	7	0	.213	.300	.281	.581	57	-4	9	3.26	1	0-53(17-21-15)/D-9	2	-0.4
1995 Sea-A	13	25	3	8	2	0	0	3	1	3	5	2	.320	.346	.400	.746	93	-0	3	4.68	0	/0-9(5-1-4)	1	-0.1
1997 NY-N	11	6	0	1	0	0	0	0	0	0	0	1	.167	.167	.167	.333	-13	-1	0	.00	0	0-51(3-4-1)	0	-0.2
Total 9	424	798	121	194	27	6	2	64	61	187	65	18	.243	.298	.299	.598	65	-32	78	3.23	-3	0-392/D-23	16	-4.3

YEAR TM-L	G	AB	R	H	2B	3B	HR	RBI	BB	SO	SB	CS	AVG	OBP	SLG	OPS	OPS+	BR/A	RC	RC/G	FR	G/POS	WS	TPW
• THURSTON, Joe	Joseph William Thurston b: 9/29/1979, Fairfield, CA BL/TR, 5'11", 175 lbs. Deb: 9/2/2002																							
2002 LA-N	8	13	1	6	1	0	0	1	0	1	0	0	.462	.462	.538	1.000	174	1	3	9.65	0	/2-4	1	0.2
2003 LA-N	12	10	2	2	0	0	0	0	1	1	0	0	.200	.273	.200	.473	28	-1	1	2.08	1	/2-3	0	0.0
Total 2	20	23	3	8	1	0	0	1	1	2	0	0	.348	.375	.391	.766	112	0	4	6.09	1	/2-7	1	0.2
• TIEMEYER, Eddie	Edward Carl Tiemeyer b: 5/9/1885, Cincinnati, OH d: 9/27/1946, Cincinnati, OH BR/TR, 5'11.5", 185 lbs. Deb: 8/19/1906																							
1906 Cin-N	5	11	3	2	0	0	0	0	1	....	0	....	.182	.250	.182	.432	33	-1	1	1.48	1	/3-3,P-1	0	0.0
1907 Cin-N	1	0	1	0	0	0	0	0	1	....	0	....	....	1.000	....	1.000	206	0	0	....	0	....	0	0.0
1909 NY-A	3	8	1	3	1	0	0	0	1	....	0	....	.375	.444	.500	.944	197	1	2	9.10	-1	/1-3	1	0.0
Total 3	9	19	5	5	1	0	0	0	3	....	0	....	.263	.364	.316	.679	108	0	2	4.20	-0	/1-3,3-3,P-1	1	0.1
• TIERNAN, Mike	Michael Joseph "Silent Mike" Tiernan b: 1/21/1867, Trenton, NJ d: 11/9/1918, New York, NY BL/TL, 5'11", 165 lbs. Deb: 4/30/1887 U Career OF: 170-148-1158																							
1887 NY-N	103	439	82	149	13	12	10	62	32	31	28	....	.339	.344	.452	.796	125	14	75	6.83	-6	*O-103(34-11-58)/P-5	12	-0.4
1888*NY-N	113	443	75	130	16	8	9	52	42	42	52	....	.293	.364	.427	.790	153	28	90	7.75	2	*O-113(0-1-112)	26	2.7
1889*NY-N	122	499	**147**	167	23	14	10	73	**96**	32	33	....	.335	.447	.497	.944	163	**48**	129	10.27	-4	*O-122(0-1-122)	**28**	3.6
1890 NY-N	133	553	132	168	25	21	**13**	59	68	53	56	....	.304	.385	**.495**	**.880**	**156**	**38**	130	8.96	-10	*O-133(2-131-1)	26	2.1
1891 NY-N	134	542	111	166	30	12	**16**	73	69	32	53	....	.306	.388	.494	**.882**	**163**	**43**	128	9.16	-5	*O-134(0-4-130)	26	3.2
1892 NY-N	116	450	79	129	16	10	5	66	57	46	20	....	.287	.369	.400	.769	135	20	76	6.37	-2	*O-116(0-0-116)	18	1.1
1893 NY-N	125	511	114	158	19	12	14	102	72	24	26	....	.309	.399	.476	.874	131	23	110	8.25	-6	*O-125(0-0-125)	16	0.8
1894*NY-N	113	429	87	120	20	13	5	78	55	21	28	....	.280	.363	.422	.785	90	-8	78	6.54	-7	*O-111(0-0-111)	11	-1.6
1895 NY-N	120	476	127	165	23	21	7	70	66	19	36	....	.347	.427	.527	.955	149	36	126	10.78	-1	*O-119(0-0-119)	22	2.3
1896 NY-N	133	521	132	192	24	16	7	89	77	18	35	....	.369	.452	.516	.968	159	48	141	11.21	-2	*O-133(0-0-133)	25	3.3
1897 NY-N	128	532	123	174	29	10	5	72	61	....	40	....	.327	.397	.447	.845	126	21	113	8.36	-7	*O-127(38-0-89)	23	0.5
1898 NY-N	103	415	90	116	15	11	5	49	43	....	19	....	.280	.357	.405	.762	122	12	70	5.97	-4	*O-103(96-0-7)	16	0.0
1899 NY-N	35	137	17	35	4	2	0	7	10	....	2	....	.255	.306	.314	.620	73	-5	14	3.67	-2	O-35(0-0-35)	2	-0.8
Total 13	1478	5947	1316	1869	257	162	106	852	748	318	428	....	.314	.392	.463	.854	139	318	1279	8.31	-55	*O-1474/P-5	251	16.8
• TIERNEY, Bill	William J. Tierney b: 5/14/1858, Boston, MA d: 9/21/1898, Boston, MA Deb: 5/2/1882																							
1882 Cin-a	1	5	1	0	0	0	0	....	0	....	....	....	.000	.000	.000	.000	-95	-1	0	.00	0	/1-1	0	-0.1
1884 Bal-U	1	3	0	1	0	0	0	....	1	....	....	....	.333	.500	.333	.833	169	0	1	7.18	0	/O-1	0	0.0
Total 2	2	8	1	1	0	0	0	....	1	....	....	....	.125	.222	.125	.347	23	-1	1	2.05	0	/1-1,O-1	0	-0.1
• TIERNEY, Cotton	James Arthur Tierney b: 2/10/1894, Kansas City, KS d: 4/18/1953, Kansas City, MO BR/TR, 5'8", 175 lbs. Deb: 9/23/1920 Career OF: 3-0-10																							
1920 Pit-N	12	46	4	11	5	0	0	8	3	4	1	1	.239	.286	.348	.634	79	-1	5	3.07	1	2-10/S-2	1	-0.1
1921 Pit-N	117	442	49	132	22	8	3	52	24	31	4	6	.299	.338	.405	.743	93	-5	59	4.69	-16	2-72,3-32/O-4(0-0-4),S-3	12	-1.6
1922 Pit-N	122	441	58	152	26	14	7	86	22	40	7	8	.345	.378	.515	.893	127	15	82	6.80	-26	*2-105/O-2(0-0-2),3-1,S-1	15	-0.8
1923 Pit-N	29	120	22	35	5	2	2	23	2	10	2	1	.292	.309	.417	.726	88	-2	15	4.43	-2	2-29	3	-0.3
Phi-N	121	480	68	152	31	1	11	65	24	42	3	4	.317	.352	.454	.806	100	-1	75	5.85	13	*2-115/O-7(3-0-4),3-2	13	1.4
Yr.	150	600	90	187	36	3	13	88	26	52	5	5	.312	.343	.447	.790	97	-4	90	5.55	11	*2-144/O-7(3-0-4),3-2	16	1.0
1924 Bos-N	136	505	38	131	16	1	6	58	22	37	11	8	.259	.296	.331	.626	71	-21	49	3.31	-16	*2-115,3-22	8	-3.2
1925 Bro-N	93	265	27	68	14	4	2	39	12	23	0	3	.257	.294	.362	.656	68	-14	27	3.53	-8	3-61/1-1,2-1	3	-1.7
Total 6	630	2299	266	681	119	30	31	331	109	187	28	31	.296	.332	.415	.746	93	-30	312	4.81	-53	2-447,3-118/O-13,S-6,1-1	55	-6.2
• TILLEY, John	John C. Tilley b: New York, NY BR, 5'7", 154 lbs. Deb: 8/23/1882 Career OF: 40-1-0																							
1882 Cle-N	15	56	2	5	1	1	0	4	2	11	....	....	.089	.121	.143	.264	-16	-7	1	.53	2	O-15(14-1-0)	0	-0.5
1884 Tol-a	17	56	5	10	2	0	0	0	4	....	....	....	.179	.246	.214	.460	50	-3	3	1.81	-3	O-17(17-0-0)	0	-0.6
StP-U	9	26	2	4	1	0	0	....	3	....	....	....	.154	.241	.192	.434	48	-1	1	1.57	1	/O-9(9-0-0)	0	-0.1
Total 2	41	138	9	19	4	1	0	4	9	11	....	....	.138	.196	.181	.377	23	-11	5	1.22	0	/O-41	0	-1.1
• TILLMAN, Bob	John Robert Tillman b: 3/24/1937, Nashville, TN d: 6/23/2000, Gallatin, TN BR/TR, 6'4", 205 lbs. Deb: 4/15/1962																							
1962 Bos-A	81	249	28	57	6	4	14	38	19	65	0	0	.229	.286	.454	.740	92	-4	31	4.12	-5	C-66	5	-0.6
1963 Bos-A	96	307	24	69	10	2	8	32	34	64	0	0	.225	.304	.349	.653	80	-8	33	3.66	-4	C-95	7	-0.7
1964 Bos-A	131	425	43	118	18	1	17	61	49	74	0	0	.278	.352	.445	.797	114	9	65	5.43	-3	*C-131	16	1.3
1965 Bos-A	111	368	20	79	10	3	6	35	40	69	0	0	.215	.292	.307	.599	66	-16	32	2.83	-2	*C-106	3	-1.3
1966 Bos-A	78	204	12	47	8	0	3	24	22	35	0	0	.230	.305	.314	.619	71	-7	20	3.22	0	C-72	5	-0.5
1967 Bos-A	30	64	4	12	1	0	1	4	3	18	0	0	.188	.224	.250	.474	37	-5	3	1.63	-1	C-26	1	-0.5
NY-A	22	63	5	16	1	0	2	9	7	17	0	0	.254	.329	.365	.694	109	1	7	4.01	1	C-15	2	0.3
Yr.	52	127	9	28	2	0	3	13	10	35	0	0	.220	.277	.307	.584	74	-4	11	2.77	1	C-41	3	-0.2
1968 Atl-N	86	236	16	52	4	0	5	20	16	55	1	0	.220	.278	.301	.579	74	-7	19	2.63	-3	C-75	4	-0.7
1969*Atl-N	69	190	18	37	5	0	12	29	18	47	0	0	.195	.264	.411	.675	86	-4	19	3.28	-5	C-69	5	-0.7
1970 Atl-N	71	223	19	53	5	0	11	30	20	66	0	0	.238	.300	.408	.708	83	-6	28	4.33	-5	C-70	5	-0.8
Total 9	775	2329	189	540	68	10	79	282	228	510	1	0	.232	.302	.371	.673	84	-48	258	3.71	-25	C-725	53	-4.2
• TILLMAN, Rusty	Kerry Jerome Tillman b: 8/29/1960, Jacksonville, FL BR/TR, 6', 185 lbs. Deb: 6/6/1982 Career OF: 9-0-13																							
1982 NY-N	12	13	4	2	1	0	0	0	0	4	1	0	.154	.154	.231	.385	6	-1	1	1.33	0	/O-3(0-0-3)	0	-0.2
1986 Oak-A	22	39	6	10	1	0	1	6	3	11	2	0	.256	.310	.359	.668	88	-0	5	4.56	-1	O-17(8-0-10)	1	-0.1
1988 SF-N	4	4	1	1	0	0	1	3	2	1	0	0	.250	.500	1.000	1.500	335	1	2	20.34	-0	/O-1	1	0.1
Total 3	38	56	11	13	2	0	2	9	5	16	3	0	.232	.295	.375	.670	95	-0	8	4.83	-1	/O-21	2	-0.1
• TIMMONS, Ozzie	Osborne Llewellyn Timmons b: 9/18/1970, Tampa, FL BR/TR, 6'2", 205 lbs. Deb: 4/26/1995 Career OF: 89-0-40																							
1995 Chi-N	77	171	30	45	10	1	8	28	13	32	3	0	.263	.315	.474	.789	107	1	23	4.65	-1	O-55(49-0-6)	5	-0.1
1996 Chi-N	65	140	18	28	4	0	7	16	15	30	1	0	.200	.282	.379	.661	70	-6	16	3.78	1	/O-7(25-0-22)	2	-0.7
1997 Cin-N	6	9	1	3	1	0	0	0	0	1	0	0	.333	.333	.444	.778	100	-0	1	6.00	0	O-47(1-0-0)	0	0.0
1999 Sea-A	26	44	4	5	2	0	1	3	4	12	0	1	.114	.188	.227	.415	5	-7	2	1.24	-1	/D-5,1-1,O-1	0	-0.7
2000 TB-A	12	41	9	14	3	0	4	13	1	7	0	0	.341	.357	.707	1.064	162	3	9	8.43	-2	O-17(2-0-7)/D-1	1	0.1
Total 5	186	405	62	95	20	1	20	60	33	82	4	1	.235	.294	.437	.731	88	-9	51	4.28	-3	O-127/D-6,1-1	8	-1.5
• TINGLEY, Ron	Ronald Irvin Tingley b: 5/27/1959, Presque Isle, ME BR/TR, 6'2", 194 lbs. Deb: 9/25/1982																							
1982 SD-N	8	20	0	2	0	0	0	0	0	7	0	0	.100	.100	.100	.200	-46	-4	0	.34	-1	/C-8	0	-0.4
1988 Cle-A	9	24	1	4	0	0	1	2	2	8	0	0	.167	.231	.292	.522	44	-2	1	1.86	1	/C-9	0	0.0
1989 Cal-A	4	3	0	1	0	0	0	0	1	0	0	0	.333	.500	.333	.833	142	0	1	8.51	0	/C-4	0	0.0
1990 Cal-A	5	3	0	0	0	0	0	0	1	1	0	0	.000	.250	.000	.250	-25	-0	0	.00	0	/C-5	0	-0.1
1991 Cal-A	45	115	11	23	7	0	1	13	8	34	1	1	.200	.258	.287	.545	51	-8	9	2.45	3	C-45	2	-0.2
1992 Cal-A	71	127	15	25	2	1	3	8	13	35	0	1	.197	.282	.299	.581	62	-7	11	2.55	3	C-69	3	-0.1
1993 Cal-A	58	90	7	18	7	0	0	12	9	22	1	2	.200	.280	.278	.558	49	-7	6	2.10	1	C-58	1	-0.4
1994 Fla-N	19	52	4	9	3	1	1	2	5	18	0	0	.173	.246	.327	.573	46	-4	4	2.31	0	C-18	1	-0.3
Chi-A	5	5	0	0	0	0	0	0	0	2	0	0	.000	.000	.000	.000	-102	-1	0	.00	0	/C-5	0	-0.1
1995 Det-A	54	124	14	28	8	1	4	18	15	38	0	1	.226	.309	.403	.713	84	-4	16	4.19	0	C-53/1-1	3	-0.1
Total 9	278	563	52	110	27	3	10	55	54	165	2	5	.195	.271	.307	.578	56	-37	48	2.64	6	C-274/1-1	10	-1.7
• TINKER, Joe	Joseph Bert Tinker b: 7/27/1880, Muscotah, KS d: 7/27/1948, Orlando, FL BR/TR, 5'9", 175 lbs. Deb: 4/17/1902 M HOF: 1946																							
1902 Chi-N	133	501	55	132	19	5	2	55	26	....	27	....	.263	.300	.333	.633	98	-3	62	4.22	5	*S-124/3-8	17	0.7
1903 Chi-N	124	460	67	134	21	7	2	70	37	....	27	....	.291	.345	.380	.726	110	5	73	5.70	18	*S-107,3-19	21	2.6
1904 Chi-N	141	488	55	108	12	13	3	41	29	....	41	....	.221	.268	.318	.585	80	-13	55	3.64	22	*S-140/O-1	20	1.5
1905 Chi-N	149	547	70	135	18	8	2	66	34	....	31	....	.247	.292	.320	.612	79	-15	65	3.82	33	*S-149	18	2.3
1906*Chi-N	148	523	75	122	18	4	1	64	43	....	30	....	.233	.293	.289	.581	77	-14	59	3.48	18	*S-147/3-1	17	1.0
1907*Chi-N	117	402	36	89	11	3	1	36	25	....	20	....	.221	.269	.271	.540	65	-17	37	2.95	15	*S-113	11	0.2
1908*Chi-N	157	548	67	146	22	14	6	68	32	....	30	....	.266	.307	.391	.697	117	8	75	4.50	34	*S-157	32	5.5
1909 Chi-N	143	516	56	132	26	11	4	57	17	....	23	....	.256	.280	.372	.652	100	-4	59	3.79	25	*S-143	24	2.8

YEAR TM-L	G	AB	R	H	2B	3B	HR	RBI	BB	SO	SB	CS	AVG	OBP	SLG	OPS	OPS+	BR/A	RC	RC/G	FR	G/POS	WS	TPW
1910*Chi-N	134	473	48	136	25	9	3	69	24	35	20	....	.288	.322	.397	.719	110	3	66	4.85	17	*S-132	22	2.6
1911 Chi-N	144	536	61	149	24	12	4	69	39	31	30	....	.278	.327	.390	.717	100	-3	77	4.96	24	*S-143	21	3.2
1912 Chi-N	142	550	80	155	24	7	0	75	38	21	25	....	.282	.331	.351	.681	87	-11	73	4.36	27	*S-142	19	2.6
1913 Cin-N	110	382	47	121	20	13	1	57	20	26	10	....	.317	.352	.445	.797	127	12	61	5.68	13	*S-101/3-9	17	3.3
1914 Chi-F	126	438	50	112	21	7	2	46	38	30	19	....	.256	.317	.349	.666	95	-3	54	3.92	22	*S-125	16	2.9
1915 Chi-F	31	67	7	18	2	1	0	9	13	5	3	....	.269	.388	.328	.716	118	2	9	4.84	0	S-16/2-5,3-4	3	0.4
1916 Chi-N	7	10	0	1	0	0	0	1	1	1	0	....	.100	.182	.100	.282	-11	-1	0	.80	0	/S-4,3-2	0	-0.2
Total 15	1806	6441	774	1690	263	114	31	783	416	149	336	....	.262	.308	.353	.661	95	-54	826	4.26	274	*S-1743/3-43,2-5,0-1	258	31.5
• TINSLEY, Lee	Lee Owen Tinsley b: 3/4/1969, Shelbyville, KY BB/TR, 5'11", 185 lbs. Deb: 4/6/1993 Career OF: 88-216-14																							
1993 Sea-A	11	19	2	3	1	0	1	2	2	9	0	0	.158	.238	.368	.607	60	-1	1	2.27	-1	/O-6(5-1-1),D-2	0	-0.2
1994 Bos-A	78	144	27	32	4	0	2	14	19	36	13	0	.222	.317	.292	.609	56	-7	17	3.80	-2	O-60(27-26-11),D-10	3	-0.9
1995*Bos-A	100	341	61	97	17	1	7	41	39	74	18	8	.284	.360	.402	.761	95	-2	50	5.00	-1	O-97(0-97-0)	10	-0.2
1996 Phi-N	31	52	1	7	0	0	0	2	4	22	2	4	.135	.196	.135	.331	-11	-10	1	.53	-2	/O-9(18-7-0)	0	-1.2
Bos-A	92	192	28	47	6	1	3	14	13	56	6	8	.245	.300	.333	.633	59	-15	17	2.85	2	O-22(4-79-0)	2	-1.1
1997 Sea-A	49	122	12	24	6	2	0	6	11	34	2	0	.197	.263	.279	.542	42	-10	9	2.34	0	O-83(34-6-2)/D-5	1	-1.1
Total 5	361	870	131	210	34	4	13	79	88	231	41	20	.241	.314	.334	.648	66	-44	95	3.57	-3	O-277/D-17	16	-4.7
• TIPPER, Jim	James Tipper b: 6/18/1849, Middletown, CT d: 4/21/1895, New Haven, CT, 5'5.5", 148 lbs. Deb: 4/26/1872 NA OF: 72-32-3																							
1872 Man-n	24	112	23	31	5	1	0	15	0	0	0	0	.277	.277	.339	.616	94	-0	11	4.13	-3	O-19(19-0-0)/3-5	....	-0.2
1874 Har-n	45	197	36	60	8	0	0	19	1	7	0	1	.305	.308	.345	.653	104	-1	21	4.67	-3	*O-45(45-0-0)	....	-0.2
1875 NH-n	41	159	10	25	1	0	0	4	1	6	1	0	.157	.163	.164	.326	16	-11	4	.99	-1	O-41(8-32-3)	....	-1.0
Total 3 n	110	468	69	116	14	1	0	38	2	13	1	1	.248	.251	.282	.533	71	-11	37	3.15	-7	O-105/3-5	....	-1.4
• TIPTON, Eric	Eric Gordon "Dukie,Blue Devil" Tipton b: 4/20/1915, Petersburg, VA d: 8/29/2001, Newport News, VA BR/TR, 5'11", 190 lbs. Deb: 6/9/1939 Career OF: 435-20-3																							
1939 Phi-A	47	104	12	24	4	2	1	14	13	7	2	0	.231	.316	.337	.653	68	-4	11	3.47	-2	O-34(33-0-2)	1	-0.7
1940 Phi-A	2	8	2	1	0	1	0	0	1	1	0	0	.125	.222	.375	.597	53	-1	1	2.86	-0	/O-2(2-0-0)	0	-0.1
1941 Phi-A	1	4	0	2	0	0	0	0	0	0	0	0	.500	.500	.500	1.000	169	0	1	13.84	-0	/O-1	0	0.0
1942 Cin-N	63	207	22	46	5	5	4	18	25	14	1	....	.222	.309	.353	.662	94	-2	22	3.41	-2	O-58(38-20-1)	5	-0.6
1943 Cin-N	140	493	82	142	26	7	9	49	85	36	1	....	.288	.395	.424	.819	138	28	88	6.52	-1	*O-139(139-0-0)	27	2.0
1944 Cin-N	140	479	62	144	28	3	3	36	59	32	5	....	.301	.380	.390	.770	121	16	71	5.29	4	*O-139(139-0-0)	21	1.2
1945 Cin-N	108	331	32	80	17	1	5	34	40	37	11	....	.242	.327	.344	.671	89	-5	40	4.04	-2	O-83(83-0-0)	7	-1.2
Total 7	501	1626	212	439	80	19	22	151	223	127	20	0	.270	.360	.383	.744	113	32	234	5.00	-2	O-456	61	0.5
• TIPTON, Joe	Joe Hicks Tipton b: 2/18/1922, McCaysville, GA d: 3/1/1994, Birmingham, AL BR/TR, 5'11", 185 lbs. Deb: 5/2/1948																							
1948*Cle-A	47	90	11	26	3	0	1	13	4	10	0	0	.289	.333	.356	.689	85	-2	12	4.78	2	C-40	3	0.1
1949 Chi-A	67	191	20	39	5	3	3	19	27	17	1	1	.204	.306	.309	.615	65	-10	19	3.25	2	C-53	3	-0.5
1950 Phi-A	64	184	15	49	5	1	6	20	19	16	0	0	.266	.335	.402	.737	90	-3	26	5.00	0	C-59	5	-0.1
1951 Phi-A	72	213	23	51	9	0	3	20	51	25	1	1	.239	.389	.324	.713	92	1	32	5.21	5	C-72	8	1.0
1952 Phi-A	23	68	6	13	4	0	3	8	15	10	0	0	.191	.337	.382	.720	94	-0	10	4.67	2	C-23	3	0.2
Cle-A	43	105	15	26	2	0	6	22	21	21	1	0	.248	.383	.438	.821	137	6	19	6.07	-1	C-35	6	0.7
Yr.	66	173	21	39	6	0	9	30	36	31	1	0	.225	.365	.416	.781	120	6	29	5.50	1	C-58	9	1.0
1953 Cle-A	47	109	17	25	2	0	6	13	19	13	0	0	.229	.359	.413	.772	111	2	16	4.70	0	C-46	4	0.4
1954 Was-A	54	157	9	35	6	1	1	10	30	30	0	1	.223	.354	.293	.647	83	-2	18	3.84	0	C-52	3	0.1
Total 7	417	1117	116	264	36	5	29	125	186	142	3	3	.236	.351	.355	.706	92	-8	152	4.59	10	C-380	35	2.0
• TISCHINSKI, Tom	Thomas Arthur Tischinski b: 7/12/1944, Kansas City, MO BR/TR, 5'10", 190 lbs. Deb: 4/11/1969																							
1969 Min-A	37	47	2	9	0	0	0	2	8	8	0	0	.191	.309	.191	.501	42	-3	4	2.44	1	C-32	1	-0.2
1970 Min-A	24	46	6	9	0	0	1	2	9	6	0	0	.196	.327	.261	.588	63	-2	4	3.07	0	C-22	2	-0.1
1971 Min-A	21	23	0	3	2	0	0	2	1	4	0	0	.130	.200	.217	.417	18	-3	1	.81	1	C-21	1	-0.1
Total 3	82	116	8	21	2	0	1	6	18	18	0	0	.181	.296	.224	.520	46	-8	9	2.33	2	/C-75	4	-0.5
• TITUS, John	John Franklin "Silent John" Titus b: 2/21/1876, St. Clair, PA d: 1/8/1943, St. Clair, PA BL/TL, 5'9", 156 lbs. Deb: 6/8/1903 Career OF: 142-12-1204																							
1903 Phi-N	72	280	38	80	15	6	2	34	19	....	5	....	.286	.340	.404	.744	115	5	42	5.33	2	O-72(34-2-36)	7	0.3
1904 Phi-N	146	504	60	148	25	5	4	55	46	....	15	....	.294	.362	.387	.749	136	22	79	5.65	3	*O-140(105-2-33)	21	1.9
1905 Phi-N	147	548	99	169	36	14	2	89	69	....	11	....	.308	.397	.436	.834	154	39	103	6.93	1	*O-147(0-0-147)	29	3.5
1906 Phi-N	145	484	67	129	22	5	1	57	78	....	12	....	.267	.378	.339	.717	124	18	71	4.96	-1	*O-142(8-0-134)	23	1.2
1907 Phi-N	145	523	72	144	23	12	3	63	47	....	9	....	.275	.345	.382	.728	130	18	75	5.03	-7	*O-142(0-0-142)	22	0.5
1908 Phi-N	149	539	75	154	24	5	2	48	53	....	27	....	.286	.365	.360	.725	127	19	82	5.15	-3	*O-149(0-0-149)	23	1.1
1909 Phi-N	151	540	69	146	22	6	3	46	66	....	23	....	.270	.367	.350	.717	121	17	79	4.92	6	*O-149(0-0-149)	20	1.7
1910 Phi-N	143	535	91	129	26	5	3	35	93	44	20	....	.241	.358	.325	.683	96	1	70	4.32	-1	*O-142(1-0-142)	17	-0.7
1911 Phi-N	76	236	35	67	14	1	8	26	32	16	3	....	.284	.372	.453	.825	129	9	40	6.07	0	O-60(1-0-59)	9	0.6
1912 Phi-N	45	157	43	43	9	5	3	22	33	14	6	....	.274	.403	.452	.855	125	7	31	6.74	-5	O-42(0-0-42)	6	0.0
Bos-N	96	345	56	112	23	6	2	48	49	20	5	....	.325	.422	.443	.865	134	19	67	6.99	-6	O-96(1-0-96)	11	0.8
Yr.	141	502	99	155	32	11	5	70	82	34	11	....	.309	.416	.446	.862	132	26	98	6.91	-11	*O-138(1-0-138)	17	0.8
1913 Bos-N	87	269	33	80	14	2	5	38	35	22	4	....	.297	.392	.420	.812	129	12	45	5.85	-4	O-75(0-0-75)	13	0.5
Total 11	1402	4960	738	1401	253	72	38	561	620	116	140	....	.282	.373	.385	.758	127	186	784	5.49	-13	*O-1356	201	11.4
• TOBIN, Bill	William F. Tobin b: 10/10/1854, Hartford, CT d: 10/10/1912, Hartford, CT BL Deb: 7/21/1880																							
1880 Wor-N	5	16	1	2	0	0	0	3	0	5	....	....	.125	.125	.125	.250	-14	-2	0	.50	0	/1-5	0	-0.2
Tro-N	33	136	14	22	1	1	0	8	4	20	....	....	.162	.186	.184	.370	24	-11	5	1.15	-3	1-33	0	-1.5
Yr.	38	152	15	24	1	1	0	11	4	25	....	....	.158	.179	.178	.357	20	-13	5	1.08	-3	1-38	0	-1.7
• TOBIN, Jack	John Thomas Tobin b: 5/4/1892, St. Louis, MO d: 12/10/1969, St. Louis, MO BL/TL, 5'8", 142 lbs. Deb: 4/16/1914 C Career OF: 220-137-1139																							
1914 StL-F	139	529	81	143	24	10	7	35	51	53	20	....	.270	.340	.393	.733	102	1	75	4.75	4	*O-132(12-7-113)	15	-0.1
1915 StL-F	158	625	92	**184**	26	13	6	51	68	42	31	....	.294	.366	.406	.773	121	17	101	5.68	1	*O-158(0-31-128)	23	1.0
1916 StL-A	77	150	16	32	4	1	0	10	12	13	7	....	.213	.272	.253	.525	61	-7	13	2.68	-6	O-41(0-6-35)	1	-1.6
1918 StL-A	122	480	59	133	19	5	0	36	48	26	13	....	.277	.349	.338	.686	110	7	60	4.21	-1	*O-122(43-78-1)	15	-0.1
1919 StL-A	127	486	54	159	22	7	6	57	36	24	8	....	.327	.376	.438	.814	125	15	82	6.11	1	*O-123(123-0-0)	18	1.2
1920 StL-A	147	593	94	202	34	10	4	62	39	23	21	13	.341	.383	.452	.835	117	15	101	6.35	-1	*O-147(34-0-113)	18	0.6
1921 StL-A	150	671	132	236	31	**18**	8	59	45	22	7	12	.352	.395	.487	.882	117	14	125	7.20	4	*O-150(0-8-143)	25	0.5
1922 StL-A	146	625	122	207	34	8	13	66	56	22	7	9	.331	.388	.474	.862	119	16	113	6.79	-9	*O-145(0-1-144)	19	-0.4
1923 StL-A	151	637	91	202	32	15	13	73	42	13	8	7	.317	.363	.476	.839	113	10	108	6.31	-18	*O-151(0-0-151)	18	-2.0
1924 StL-A	136	569	87	170	30	8	2	48	50	12	6	10	.299	.357	.390	.748	87	-13	79	4.99	-4	*O-132(1-1-130)	12	-2.6
1925 StL-A	77	193	25	58	11	0	2	27	9	5	8	2	.301	.335	.389	.724	79	-5	26	4.87	-1	O-39(1-1-38)/1-3	4	-0.8
1926 Was-A	27	33	5	7	0	1	0	3	0	0	0	0	.212	.212	.273	.485	26	-4	2	1.82	0	/O-7(0-4-3)	0	-0.4
Bos-A	51	209	26	57	9	0	1	14	16	3	6	5	.273	.324	.330	.655	73	-9	22	3.66	-2	O-51(0-51)	2	-1.4
Yr.	78	242	31	64	9	1	1	17	16	3	6	5	.264	.310	.322	.632	67	-12	24	3.39	-2	O-58(1-4-54)	2	-1.8
1927 Bos-A	111	374	52	116	18	3	2	40	36	9	5	4	.310	.371	.390	.761	100	0	55	5.39	-2	O-93(5-0-89)	9	-0.9
Total 13	1619	6174	936	1906	294	99	64	581	508	267	147	62	.309	.364	.420	.784	108	57	961	5.62	-34	*O-1491/1-3	179	-7.0
• TOBIN, Johnny	John Martin "Tip" Tobin b: 9/15/1906, Jamaica Plain, MA d: 8/6/1983, Rhinebeck, NY BR/TR, 6'3", 187 lbs. Deb: 9/22/1932																							
1932 NY-N	1	1	0	0	0	0	0	0	0	0	0	....	.000	.000	.000	.000	-102	-0	0	.00	0	....	0	0.0
• TOBIN, Johnny	John Patrick "Jackie" Tobin b: 1/8/1921, Oakland, CA d: 1/18/1982, Oakland, CA BL/TR, 6', 165 lbs. Deb: 4/20/1945																							
1945 Bos-A	84	278	25	70	6	2	0	21	26	24	2	6	.252	.320	.288	.608	75	-10	26	3.08	-3	3-72/2-5,0-1	5	-1.2
• TOCA, Jorge	Jorge Luis (Gomez) Toca b: 1/7/1975, Remedios, Cuba BR/TR, 6'3", 220 lbs. Deb: 9/12/1999 Career OF: 3-0-0																							
1999 NY-N	4	3	0	1	0	0	0	0	0	2	0	0	.333	.333	.333	.667	72	-0	0	4.50	0	/1-1	0	0.0
2000 NY-N	8	7	1	3	1	0	0	4	0	1	0	0	.429	.429	.571	1.000	156	1	2	11.57	0	O-41(1-0-0)/1-5	0	0.0

YEAR TM-L	G	AB	R	H	2B	3B	HR	RBI	BB	SO	SB	CS	AVG	OBP	SLG	OPS	OPS+	BR/A	RC	RC/G	FR	G/POS	WS	TPW
2001 NY-N	13	17	3	3	0	0	0	1	0	8	0	0	.176	.176	.176	.353	-9	-3	1	1.02	0	/1-3,0-1	0	-0.3
Total 3	25	27	4	7	1	0	0	5	0	11	0	0	.259	.259	.296	.556	43	-2	3	3.48	0	/0-42,1-9	0	-0.3

• TODD, Al Alfred Chester Todd b: 1/7/1902, Troy, NY d: 3/8/1985, Elmira, NY BR/TR, 6'1", 198 lbs. Deb: 4/25/1932

YEAR TM-L	G	AB	R	H	2B	3B	HR	RBI	BB	SO	SB	CS	AVG	OBP	SLG	OPS	OPS+	BR/A	RC	RC/G	FR	G/POS	WS	TPW
1932 Phi-N	33	70	8	16	5	0	0	9	1	9	1	....	.229	.260	.300	.560	45	-6	6	2.61	-4	C-25	0	-0.8
1933 Phi-N	73	136	13	28	4	0	0	10	4	18	1	....	.206	.239	.235	.475	32	-12	8	1.82	1	C-34/0-2(2-0-0)	1	-0.9
1934 Phi-N	91	302	33	96	22	2	4	41	10	39	3	....	.318	.344	.444	.788	96	-2	44	5.56	0	C-82	7	0.2
1935 Phi-N	107	328	40	95	18	3	3	42	19	35	3	....	.290	.334	.390	.725	85	-7	42	4.67	-4	C-87	7	-0.6
1936 Pit-N	76	267	28	73	10	5	2	28	11	24	4	....	.273	.307	.371	.678	80	-8	31	4.19	-1	C-70	7	-0.4
1937 Pit-N	133	514	51	158	18	10	8	86	16	36	2	....	.307	.330	.428	.758	104	1	69	4.96	-1	*C-128	17	0.7
1938 Pit-N	133	491	52	130	19	7	7	75	18	31	2	....	.265	.296	.375	.671	83	-13	48	3.32	7	*C-132	13	0.2
1939 Bro-N	86	245	28	68	10	0	5	32	13	16	1	....	.278	.317	.380	.696	83	-6	28	3.94	2	C-73	7	0.0
1940 Chi-N	104	381	31	97	13	2	6	42	11	29	1	....	.255	.283	.346	.629	74	-15	36	3.22	-6	*C-104	6	-1.4
1941 Chi-N	6	6	1	1	0	0	0	0	0	1	0	....	.167	.167	.167	.333	-6	-1	0	.90	0	....	0	-0.1
1943 Chi-N	21	45	1	6	0	0	0	1	1	5	0	....	.133	.152	.133	.286	-17	-7	1	.55	-1	C-17	1	-0.8
Total 11	863	2785	286	768	119	29	35	366	104	243	18	....	.276	.307	.377	.684	82	-76	312	3.96	-7	C-752/0-2	66	-3.9

• TODT, Phil Philip Julius "Hook" Todt b: 8/9/1901, St. Louis, MO d: 11/15/1973, St. Louis, MO BL/TL, 6', 175 lbs. Deb: 4/25/1924

YEAR TM-L	G	AB	R	H	2B	3B	HR	RBI	BB	SO	SB	CS	AVG	OBP	SLG	OPS	OPS+	BR/A	RC	RC/G	FR	G/POS	WS	TPW
1924 Bos-A	52	103	17	27	8	2	1	14	6	9	0	1	.262	.309	.408	.717	84	-3	13	4.30	-1	1-18/0-4(0-2-2)	2	-0.5
1925 Bos-A	141	544	62	151	29	13	11	75	44	29	3	2	.278	.343	.439	.782	97	-3	83	5.47	1	*1-140	11	-1.0
1926 Bos-A	154	599	56	153	19	12	7	69	40	38	3	2	.255	.306	.362	.669	76	-22	68	3.85	11	*1-154	8	-2.0
1927 Bos-A	140	516	55	122	22	6	6	52	28	23	6	2	.236	.280	.337	.617	61	-31	50	3.16	9	*1-139	5	-2.9
1928 Bos-A	144	539	61	136	31	8	12	73	26	47	6	5	.252	.290	.406	.697	83	-17	63	3.80	4	*1-144	9	-2.1
1929 Bos-A	153	534	49	140	38	10	4	64	31	28	6	7	.262	.305	.393	.698	80	-18	63	3.92	7	*1-153	8	-2.0
1930 Bos-A	111	383	49	103	22	5	11	62	24	33	4	1	.269	.312	.439	.751	92	-6	53	4.79	7	*1-104	7	-0.5
1931*Phi-A	62	197	23	48	14	2	5	44	8	22	1	1	.244	.273	.411	.684	73	-8	22	3.76	-3	1-52	3	-1.5
Total 8	957	3415	372	880	183	58	57	453	207	229	29	21	.258	.305	.395	.700	81	-108	414	4.10	35	1-904/0-4	53	-12.6

• TOLAN, Bobby Robert Tolan b: 11/19/1945, Los Angeles, CA BL/TL, 5'11", 170 lbs. Deb: 9/3/1965 C Career OF: 131-561-348

YEAR TM-L	G	AB	R	H	2B	3B	HR	RBI	BB	SO	SB	CS	AVG	OBP	SLG	OPS	OPS+	BR/A	RC	RC/G	FR	G/POS	WS	TPW
1965 StL-N	17	69	8	13	2	0	0	6	0	4	2	1	.188	.200	.217	.417	16	-8	3	1.30	-1	0-17(0-0-17)	0	-1.0
1966 StL-N	43	93	10	16	5	1	1	6	6	15	1	2	.172	.238	.280	.517	43	-8	6	1.95	-1	0-26(10-0-16)/1-1	0	-1.0
1967*StL-N	110	265	35	67	7	3	6	32	19	43	12	7	.253	.313	.370	.682	96	-2	30	3.69	2	0-80(6-54-25),1-13	8	-0.3
1968*StL-N	92	278	28	64	12	1	5	17	13	42	9	5	.230	.272	.335	.607	82	-7	23	2.72	-1	0-67(2-9-57)/1-9	5	-1.3
1969 Cin-N	152	637	104	194	25	10	21	93	27	92	26	12	.305	.348	.474	.822	122	17	103	5.86	-2	*0-150(0-88-62)	27	1.0
1970*Cin-N	152	589	112	186	34	6	16	80	62	94	**57**	20	.316	.388	.475	.864	125	25	113	6.80	3	*0-150(0-150-0)	29	2.4
1972*Cin-N	149	604	88	171	28	5	8	82	44	88	42	15	.283	.338	.386	.724	112	11	78	4.44	6	*0-149(0-149-0)	22	1.5
1973 Cin-N	129	457	42	94	14	2	9	51	27	68	15	10	.206	.255	.304	.559	57	-29	33	2.25	-3	*0-120(0-76-65)	3	-3.8
1974 SD-N	95	357	45	95	16	1	8	40	20	41	7	9	.266	.321	.384	.705	101	-3	42	4.02	-4	0-88(1-9-81)	10	-1.2
1975 SD-N	147	506	58	129	19	4	5	43	28	45	11	13	.255	.307	.338	.645	84	-16	48	3.09	-1	*0-120(90-16-19),1-27	8	-2.5
1976*Phi-N	110	272	32	71	7	0	5	35	7	39	10	5	.261	.290	.342	.632	76	-9	25	3.02	-8	1-50,0-35(20-10-5)	3	-2.3
1977 Phi-N	15	16	1	2	0	0	0	1	1	4	0	0	.125	.176	.125	.301	-17	-3	0	.77	0	/1-5	0	-0.3
Pit-N	49	74	7	15	4	0	2	9	4	10	1	1	.203	.244	.338	.581	53	-5	6	2.51	0	1-20/0-2(2-0-0)	0	-0.7
Yr.	64	90	8	17	4	0	2	10	5	14	1	1	.189	.232	.300	.532	40	-8	6	2.20	0	1-25/0-2(2-0-0)	0	-1.0
1979 SD-N	22	21	2	4	0	1	0	2	0	2	0	0	.190	.190	.286	.476	30	-2	1	.76	0	/1-5,0-1	0	-0.2
Total 13	1282	4238	572	1121	173	34	86	497	258	587	193	100	.265	.317	.382	.699	95	-37	511	4.05	-10	*0-1005,1-130	115	-9.8

• TOLENTINO, Jose Jose (Franco) Tolentino b: 6/3/1961, Mexico City, Mexico BL/TL, 6'1", 195 lbs. Deb: 7/28/1991

YEAR TM-L	G	AB	R	H	2B	3B	HR	RBI	BB	SO	SB	CS	AVG	OBP	SLG	OPS	OPS+	BR/A	RC	RC/G	FR	G/POS	WS	TPW
1991 Hou-N	44	54	6	14	4	0	1	6	4	9	0	0	.259	.310	.389	.699	101	-0	6	3.84	1	1-10/0-1	2	0.0

• TOLLESON, Wayne Jimmy Wayne Tolleson b: 11/22/1955, Spartanburg, SC BB/TR, 5'9", 160 lbs. Deb: 9/1/1981 Career OF: 1-2-0

YEAR TM-L	G	AB	R	H	2B	3B	HR	RBI	BB	SO	SB	CS	AVG	OBP	SLG	OPS	OPS+	BR/A	RC	RC/G	FR	G/POS	WS	TPW
1981 Tex-A	14	24	6	4	0	0	0	1	1	5	2	0	.167	.200	.167	.367	7	-2	1	1.43	-1	/3-6,S-2	0	-0.3
1982 Tex-A	38	70	6	8	1	0	0	2	5	14	1	1	.114	.173	.129	.302	-16	-11	2	.70	-5	S-26/3-4,2-1	1	-1.4
1983 Tex-A	134	470	64	122	13	2	3	20	40	68	33	10	.260	.320	.315	.635	77	-11	51	3.65	-11	*2-112,S-26/D-1	10	-1.5
1984 Tex-A	118	338	35	72	9	2	0	9	27	47	22	4	.213	.277	.251	.529	46	-21	25	2.30	-11	*2-109/S-7,3-5,D-1,0-1	3	-2.7
1985 Tex-A	123	323	45	101	9	5	1	18	21	46	21	12	.313	.355	.381	.735	100	-1	43	4.57	-10	S-81,2-29,3-12/D-6	8	-0.3
1986 Chi-A	81	260	39	65	7	3	3	29	38	43	13	6	.250	.346	.335	.680	84	-5	33	4.16	0	3-65,S-18/D-2,0-2(1-1-0)	6	-0.4
NY-A	60	215	22	61	9	2	0	14	14	33	4	4	.284	.333	.344	.678	86	-5	25	4.00	8	S-56/3-7,2-3	6	0.9
Yr.	141	475	61	126	16	5	3	43	52	76	17	10	.265	.340	.339	.679	84	-9	58	4.09	8	S-74,3-72/2-3,D-2,0-2(1-1-0)	12	0.5
1987 NY-A	121	349	48	77	4	0	1	22	43	72	5	3	.221	.306	.241	.547	48	-25	29	2.75	2	*S-119/3-3	6	-1.1
1988 NY-A	21	59	8	15	2	0	0	5	8	12	1	0	.254	.343	.288	.631	79	-1	7	3.78	2	2-12,3-10/S-1	2	0.1
1989 NY-A	80	140	16	23	5	2	1	9	16	23	5	1	.164	.255	.250	.505	43	-10	10	2.14	-1	3-28,S-28,2-13,D-10	1	-0.9
1990 NY-A	73	74	12	11	1	1	0	4	6	21	1	0	.149	.213	.189	.402	13	-8	4	1.48	3	S-45,2-13/D-5,3-3	2	-0.3
Total 10	863	2322	301	559	60	17	9	133	219	384	108	41	.241	.308	.293	.601	65	-100	228	3.22	-25	S-409,2-292,3-143/D-25,0-3	45	-8.0

• TOLMAN, Tim Timothy Lee Tolman b: 4/20/1956, Santa Monica, CA BR/TR, 6', 195 lbs. Deb: 9/9/1981 Career OF: 19-0-16

YEAR TM-L	G	AB	R	H	2B	3B	HR	RBI	BB	SO	SB	CS	AVG	OBP	SLG	OPS	OPS+	BR/A	RC	RC/G	FR	G/POS	WS	TPW
1981 Hou-N	4	8	0	1	0	0	0	0	0	0	0	0	.125	.125	.125	.250	-30	-1	0	.48	0	/0-3(3-0-1)	0	-0.2
1982 Hou-N	15	26	4	5	2	0	1	3	4	3	0	0	.192	.300	.385	.685	98	-0	3	3.61	0	/0-5(4-0-1),1-1	1	0.0
1983 Hou-N	43	56	4	11	4	0	2	10	6	9	0	1	.196	.274	.375	.649	83	-2	5	3.09	-1	/1-7,0-3(3-0-0)	1	-0.3
1984 Hou-N	14	17	2	3	1	0	0	0	0	3	0	0	.176	.176	.235	.412	16	-2	1	1.36	0	/0-3(1-0-2),1-1	0	-0.2
1985 Hou-N	31	43	4	6	1	0	2	8	1	10	0	1	.140	.178	.302	.480	33	-5	2	1.48	0	/0-9(6-0-3),1-6	0	-0.5
1986 Det-A	16	34	4	6	1	0	0	2	6	4	1	1	.176	.300	.206	.506	41	-3	3	2.30	-1	/D-9,0-4(0-0-4),1-3	0	-0.4
1987 Det-A	9	12	3	1	1	0	0	1	7	2	0	0	.083	.450	.167	.617	76	0	2	3.43	0	/0-7(2-0-5),D-2	0	0.0
Total 7	132	196	21	33	10	0	5	24	24	31	1	3	.168	.266	.296	.562	57	-12	16	2.43	-2	/0-34,1-18,D-11	2	-1.6

• TOLSON, Chick Charles Julius "Toby,Slug" Tolson b: 5/3/1895, Washington, DC d: 4/16/1965, Washington, DC BR/TR, 6', 185 lbs. Deb: 7/3/1925

YEAR TM-L	G	AB	R	H	2B	3B	HR	RBI	BB	SO	SB	CS	AVG	OBP	SLG	OPS	OPS+	BR/A	RC	RC/G	FR	G/POS	WS	TPW
1925 Cle-A	3	12	0	3	0	0	0	0	2	1	0	0	.250	.357	.250	.607	56	-1	1	3.55	-0	/1-3	0	-0.1
1926 Chi-N	57	80	4	25	6	1	1	8	5	8	0	....	.313	.353	.450	.803	113	1	12	5.50	0	1-13	2	0.1
1927 Chi-N	39	54	6	16	4	0	2	17	4	9	0	....	.296	.345	.481	.826	119	1	9	5.50	-0	/1-8	2	0.1
1929*Chi-N	32	109	13	28	5	0	1	19	9	16	0	....	.257	.325	.330	.655	63	-6	12	3.67	-2	1-31	1	-0.9
1930 Chi-N	13	20	0	6	1	0	0	1	6	5	1	....	.300	.462	.350	.812	99	1	4	6.82	0	/1-5	1	0.1
Total 5	144	275	23	78	16	1	4	45	26	39	1	0	.284	.350	.393	.743	91	-4	38	4.76	-1	/1-60	6	-0.8

• TOMBERLIN, Andy Andy Lee Tomberlin b: 11/7/1966, Monroe, NC BL/TL, 5'11", 160 lbs. Deb: 8/12/1993 Career OF: 30-18-37

YEAR TM-L	G	AB	R	H	2B	3B	HR	RBI	BB	SO	SB	CS	AVG	OBP	SLG	OPS	OPS+	BR/A	RC	RC/G	FR	G/POS	WS	TPW
1993 Pit-N	27	42	4	12	0	1	1	5	2	14	0	0	.286	.333	.405	.738	97	-0	6	5.33	0	/0-7(6-0-1)	1	0.0
1994 Bos-A	18	36	1	7	0	1	1	1	6	12	1	0	.194	.310	.333	.643	63	-2	4	4.06	1	0-11(5-0-6)/D-5,P-1	0	0.0
1995 Oak-A	46	85	15	18	0	0	4	10	5	22	4	1	.212	.256	.353	.608	60	-5	7	2.81	-1	0-42(5-18-20)/D-2	0	-0.6
1996 NY-N	63	66	12	17	4	0	3	10	9	27	0	0	.258	.355	.455	.810	117	2	12	6.38	0	/0-2(9-0-8),1-1	1	0.1
1997 NY-N	6	7	0	2	0	0	0	0	1	3	0	0	.286	.375	.286	.661	79	-0	1	4.58	0	0-17(1-0-1)	0	0.0
1998 Det-A	32	69	8	15	2	0	2	12	3	25	1	0	.217	.280	.333	.613	58	-4	6	2.82	0	D-22/0-2(4-0-1)	1	-0.5
Total 6	192	305	40	71	6	2	11	38	26	103	6	1	.233	.304	.374	.677	78	-9	36	4.03	0	/0-81,D-29,1-1,P-1	3	-1.0

• TOMER, George George Clarence Tomer b: 11/26/1895, Perry, IA d: 12/15/1984, Perry, IA BL/TR, 6', 180 lbs. Deb: 9/17/1913

YEAR TM-L	G	AB	R	H	2B	3B	HR	RBI	BB	SO	SB	CS	AVG	OBP	SLG	OPS	OPS+	BR/A	RC	RC/G	FR	G/POS	WS	TPW
1913 StL-A	1	1	0	0	0	0	0	0	0	1	0	....	.000	.000	.000	.000	-103	-0	0	.00	0	....	0	0.0

• TOMNEY, Phil Philip Howard "Buster" Tomney b: 6/17/1863, Reading, PA d: 3/18/1892, Reading, PA BR/TR, 5'7", 155 lbs. Deb: 9/7/1888

YEAR TM-L	G	AB	R	H	2B	3B	HR	RBI	BB	SO	SB	CS	AVG	OBP	SLG	OPS	OPS+	BR/A	RC	RC/G	FR	G/POS	WS	TPW
1888 Lou-a	34	120	15	18	3	0	0	4	7	....	11	....	.150	.197	.175	.372	20	-11	6	1.71	3	S-34	2	-0.6
1889 Lou-a	112	376	61	80	8	5	4	38	46	47	26	....	.213	.304	.293	.596	71	-13	42	3.79	-2	*S-112	6	-1.0
1890*Lou-a	108	386	72	107	21	7	1	58	43	....	27	....	.277	.357	.376	.733	119	9	63	5.98	21	*S-108	18	3.0
Total 3	254	882	148	205	32	12	5	100	96	47	64	....	.232	.313	.313	.626	85	-14	112	4.38	22	S-254	26	1.4

YEAR TM-L	G	AB	R	H	2B	3B	HR	RBI	BB	SO	SB	CS	AVG	OBP	SLG	OPS	OPS+	BR/A	RC	RC/G	FR	G/POS	WS	TPW
• TONNEMAN, Tony	Charles Richard Tonneman b: 9/10/1881, Chicago, IL d: 8/7/1951, Prescott, AZ BR/TR, 5'10.5", 175 lbs. Deb: 9/19/1911																							
1911 Bos-A	2	5	0	1	1	0	0	3	1	....	0	....	.200	.333	.400	.733	105	0	1	3.95	0	/C-2	0	0.0
• TOOLEY, Bert	Albert R. Tooley b: 8/30/1886, Howell, MI d: 8/17/1976, Marshall, MI BR/TR, 5'10", 155 lbs. Deb: 4/12/1911																							
1911 Bro-N	119	433	55	89	11	3	1	29	53	63	18	....	.206	.295	.252	.547	56	-24	37	2.74	-3	*S-114	7	-2.0
1912 Bro-N	77	265	34	62	6	5	2	37	19	21	12	....	.234	.285	.317	.602	67	-13	28	3.25	-18	S-76	2	-2.5
Total 2	**196**	**698**	**89**	**151**	**17**	**8**	**3**	**66**	**72**	**84**	**30**	**....**	**.216**	**.291**	**.277**	**.568**	**60**	**-37**	**64**	**2.93**	**-21**	**S-190**	**9**	**-4.5**
• TOPORCER, Specs	George Toporcer b: 2/9/1899, New York, NY d: 5/17/1989, Huntington Station, NY BL/TR, 5'10.5", 165 lbs. Deb: 4/13/1921																							
1921 StL-N	22	53	4	14	1	0	0	2	3	4	1	0	.264	.304	.283	.587	57	-3	5	3.19	0	2-12/S-2	1	-0.2
1922 StL-N	116	352	56	114	25	6	3	36	24	18	2	1	.324	.370	.455	.825	117	9	60	6.26	-5	S-91/3-6,2-1,0-1	14	1.2
1923 StL-N	97	303	45	77	11	3	3	35	41	14	4	3	.254	.349	.340	.689	84	-5	38	4.31	-0	2-52,S-33/1-1,3-1	7	-0.1
1924 StL-N	70	198	30	62	10	3	1	24	11	14	2	3	.313	.362	.409	.771	108	2	29	5.37	-4	3-33,S-25/2-3	5	0.1
1925 StL-N	83	268	38	76	13	4	2	26	36	15	7	2	.284	.373	.384	.757	92	-1	41	5.46	3	S-66/2-7	9	0.9
1926*StL-N	64	88	13	22	3	2	0	9	8	9	1	....	.250	.327	.330	.656	74	-3	10	3.55	-3	2-27/S-5,3-1	1	-0.5
1927 StL-N	86	290	37	72	13	4	0	19	27	16	5	....	.248	.314	.321	.635	68	-13	30	3.38	-4	3-54,S-27/2-2,1-1	6	-1.1
1928 StL-N	8	14	0	0	0	0	0	0	0	3	0	....	.000	.000	.000	.000	-98	-4	0	.00	0	/1-1,2-1	0	-0.4
Total 8	**546**	**1566**	**223**	**437**	**76**	**22**	**9**	**151**	**150**	**93**	**22**	**9**	**.279**	**.347**	**.373**	**.720**	**90**	**-17**	**212**	**4.73**	**-12**	**S-249,2-105/3-95,1-3,0-1**	**43**	**0.0**
• TORBORG, Jeff	Jeffrey Allen Torborg b: 11/26/1941, Plainfield, NJ BR/TR, 6'.5", 195 lbs. Deb: 5/10/1964 M/C																							
1964 LA-N	28	43	4	10	1	1	0	4	3	8	0	0	.233	.298	.302	.600	75	-1	4	3.27	-1	C-27	1	-0.2
1965 LA-N	56	150	8	36	5	1	3	13	10	26	0	0	.240	.292	.347	.639	85	-3	14	3.17	-2	C-53	5	-0.4
1966 LA-N	46	120	4	27	3	0	1	13	10	23	0	0	.225	.285	.275	.560	61	-6	9	2.34	-1	C-45	2	-0.6
1967 LA-N	76	196	11	42	4	1	2	12	13	31	1	3	.214	.267	.276	.542	60	-11	13	2.12	0	C-75	2	-0.9
1968 LA-N	37	93	2	15	2	0	0	4	6	10	0	0	.161	.212	.183	.395	21	-9	4	1.18	2	C-37	2	-0.6
1969 LA-N	51	124	7	23	4	0	0	7	9	17	1	0	.185	.241	.218	.458	31	-11	7	1.84	2	C-50	2	-0.7
1970 LA-N	64	134	11	31	8	0	1	17	14	15	1	1	.231	.304	.313	.617	69	-6	13	3.19	-1	C-63	3	-0.5
1971 Cal-A	55	123	6	25	5	0	0	5	3	6	0	0	.203	.222	.244	.466	34	-11	6	1.61	1	C-49	2	-0.9
1972 Cal-A	59	153	5	32	3	0	0	8	14	21	0	0	.209	.280	.229	.509	56	-8	9	1.96	2	C-58	3	-0.4
1973 Cal-A	102	255	20	56	7	0	1	18	21	32	0	2	.220	.279	.259	.538	57	-15	18	2.26	-5	*C-102	3	-1.6
Total 10	**574**	**1391**	**78**	**297**	**42**	**3**	**8**	**101**	**103**	**189**	**3**	**6**	**.214**	**.270**	**.265**	**.535**	**56**	**-82**	**97**	**2.25**	**-5**	**C-559**	**25**	**-6.7**
• TORCATO, Tony	Anthony Dale Torcato b: 10/25/1979, Woodland, CA BL/TR, 6'1", 195 lbs. Deb: 7/26/2002 Career OF: 4-0-5																							
2002 SF-N	5	11	0	3	1	0	0	0	0	2	0	0	.273	.273	.364	.636	69	-1	1	3.68	-1	/0-3(0-0-3)	0	-0.1
2003 SF-N	14	16	0	3	1	0	0	1	0	4	0	0	.188	.235	.250	.485	27	-2	1	2.05	0	/0-6(4-0-2)	0	-0.2
Total 2	**19**	**27**	**0**	**6**	**2**	**0**	**0**	**1**	**0**	**6**	**0**	**0**	**.222**	**.250**	**.296**	**.546**	**43**	**-2**	**2**	**2.64**	**-1**	**/0-9**	**0**	**-0.4**
• TORGESON, Earl	Clifford Earl "The Earl Of Snohomish" Torgeson b: 1/1/1924, Snohomish, WA d: 11/8/1990, Everett, WA BL/TL, 6'3", 180 lbs. Deb: 4/15/1947 C Career OF: 2-0-4																							
1947 Bos-N	128	399	73	112	20	6	16	78	82	59	11	....	.281	.403	.481	.885	137	24	83	7.61	5	*1-117	18	2.5
1948*Bos-N	134	438	70	111	23	5	10	67	81	54	19	....	.253	.372	.397	.770	110	9	71	5.55	3	*1-129	14	0.9
1949 Bos-N	25	100	17	26	5	1	4	19	13	4	4	....	.260	.345	.450	.795	118	2	15	5.40	-4	1-25	3	-0.2
1950 Bos-N	156	576	**120**	167	30	3	23	87	119	69	15	....	.290	.412	.472	.885	141	40	121	7.65	6	*1-156	**32**	4.0
1951 Bos-N	155	581	99	153	21	4	24	92	102	70	20	11	.263	.375	.437	.812	127	25	99	5.80	1	*1-155	20	2.1
1952 Bos-N	122	382	49	88	17	0	5	34	81	38	11	7	.230	.366	.314	.681	94	1	51	4.32	-0	*1-105/0-5(2-0-3)	11	-0.3
1953 Phi-N	111	379	58	104	25	8	11	64	53	57	7	1	.274	.366	.470	.836	117	11	70	6.59	3	*1-105	14	0.8
1954 Phi-N	135	490	63	133	22	6	5	54	75	52	7	1	.271	.368	.371	.740	93	-1	71	4.96	-2	*1-133	10	-1.1
1955 Phi-N	47	150	29	40	5	3	1	17	32	20	2	3	.267	.396	.360	.756	104	2	22	5.02	2	1-43	4	0.2
Det-A	89	300	58	85	10	1	9	50	61	29	9	0	.283	.404	.413	.818	123	15	56	6.63	3	1-83	12	1.3
1956 Det-A	117	318	61	84	9	3	12	42	78	47	6	4	.264	.409	.425	.834	120	13	61	6.71	-4	1-83	12	0.5
1957 Det-A	30	50	5	12	2	1	1	5	12	10	0	0	.240	.387	.380	.767	107	1	8	5.68	0	1-17	2	0.1
Chi-A	86	251	53	74	11	2	7	46	49	44	7	3	.295	.410	.438	.848	131	14	47	6.57	-5	1-70/0-1	11	0.5
Yr.	116	301	58	86	13	3	8	51	61	54	7	3	.286	.406	.429	.835	127	15	56	6.42	-4	1-87/0-1	13	0.6
1958 Chi-A	96	188	37	50	8	0	10	30	48	29	7	2	.266	.415	.468	.883	145	15	39	7.19	-2	1-73	10	1.0
1959*Chi-A	127	277	40	61	5	3	9	45	62	55	7	6	.220	.363	.357	.720	100	2	39	4.47	-8	*1-103	8	-1.1
1960 Chi-A	68	57	12	15	2	0	2	9	21	8	1	0	.263	.462	.404	.865	137	5	13	8.44	0	1-10	3	0.5
1961 Chi-A	20	15	1	1	0	0	0	1	3	5	0	0	.067	.222	.067	.289	-19	-3	0	.61	0	/1-1	0	-0.3
NY-A	22	18	3	2	0	0	0	0	8	3	0	1	.111	.385	.111	.496	42	-1	1	1.88	0	/1-8	0	-0.2
Yr.	42	33	4	3	0	0	0	1	11	8	0	1	.091	.318	.091	.409	16	-4	2	1.29	-1	/1-9	0	-0.5
Total 15	**1668**	**4969**	**848**	**1318**	**215**	**46**	**149**	**740**	**980**	**653**	**133**	**39**	**.265**	**.387**	**.417**	**.804**	**118**	**175**	**870**	**6.05**	**-2**	***1-1416/0-6**	**184**	**11.1**
• TORPHY, Red	Walter Anthony Torphy b: 11/6/1891, Fall River, MA d: 2/11/1980, Fall River, MA BR/TR, 5'11", 169 lbs. Deb: 9/25/1920																							
1920 Bos-N	3	15	1	3	2	0	0	2	0	1	0	0	.200	.200	.333	.533	54	-1	1	2.12	-1	/1-3	0	-0.2
• TORRE, Frank	Frank Joseph Torre b: 12/30/1931, Brooklyn, NY BL/TL, 6'4", 205 lbs. Deb: 4/20/1956																							
1956 Mil-N	111	159	17	41	6	0	0	16	11	4	1	0	.258	.306	.296	.601	67	-7	14	2.97	5	1-89	2	-0.5
1957*Mil-N	129	364	46	99	19	5	5	40	29	19	0	0	.272	.341	.393	.734	104	2	49	4.62	0	*1-117	10	-0.3
1958*Mil-N	138	372	41	115	22	5	6	55	42	14	2	0	.309	.390	.444	.833	131	18	63	6.11	7	*1-122	16	1.9
1959 Mil-N	115	263	23	60	15	1	1	33	35	12	0	0	.228	.326	.304	.630	75	-8	28	3.49	2	1-87	5	-1.0
1960 Mil-N	21	44	2	9	1	0	0	5	3	2	0	0	.205	.255	.227	.483	36	-4	3	1.84	-1	1-17	0	-0.5
1962 Phi-N	108	168	13	52	8	2	0	20	24	6	1	1	.310	.408	.381	.789	117	5	26	5.47	0	1-76	6	0.3
1963 Phi-N	92	112	8	28	7	2	1	10	11	7	0	0	.250	.333	.375	.708	105	1	15	4.52	2	1-56	3	0.2
Total 7	**714**	**1482**	**150**	**404**	**78**	**15**	**13**	**179**	**155**	**64**	**4**	**1**	**.273**	**.352**	**.372**	**.724**	**101**	**8**	**197**	**4.58**	**16**	**1-564**	**42**	**0.1**
• TORRE, Joe	Joseph Paul Torre b: 7/18/1940, Brooklyn, NY BR/TR, 6'2", 212 lbs. Deb: 9/25/1960 M																							
1960 Mil-N	2	2	0	1	0	0	0	0	0	1	0	0	.500	.500	.500	1.000	189	0	1	13.50	0	....	0	0.0
1961 Mil-N	113	406	40	113	21	4	10	42	28	60	3	5	.278	.331	.424	.755	105	1	54	4.67	-3	*C-112	13	0.3
1962 Mil-N	80	220	23	62	8	1	5	26	24	24	1	0	.282	.358	.395	.753	105	2	31	5.10	2	C-63	9	0.7
1963 Mil-N★	142	501	57	147	19	4	14	71	42	79	1	5	.293	.354	.431	.785	126	15	71	4.96	0	*C-105,1-37/0-2(2-0-0)	20	2.0
1964 Mil-N★	154	601	87	193	36	5	20	109	36	67	2	4	.321	.366	.498	.864	140	30	99	6.09	-1	C-96,1-70	28	3.1
1965 Mil-N★	148	523	68	152	21	1	27	80	61	79	0	1	.291	.373	.489	.863	140	29	91	6.21	-2	*C-100,1-49	23	3.0
1966 Atl-N★	148	546	83	172	20	3	36	101	60	61	0	4	.315	.385	.560	.945	156	41	112	7.49	8	*C-114,1-36	29	5.4
1967 Atl-N★	135	477	67	132	18	1	20	68	49	75	2	2	.277	.348	.444	.792	127	17	68	4.92	8	*C-114,1-23	18	3.1
1968 Atl-N	115	424	45	115	11	2	10	55	34	72	1	0	.271	.333	.377	.710	112	7	51	4.21	-4	C-92,1-29	15	0.7
1969 StL-N	159	602	72	174	29	6	18	101	66	85	0	0	.289	.364	.447	.811	126	21	99	6.06	1	*1-144,C-17	23	1.2
1970 StL-N★	161	624	89	203	27	9	21	100	70	91	2	2	.325	.399	.498	.898	136	33	120	7.21	-12	C-90,3-73/1-1	25	2.5
1971 StL-N★	161	634	97	**230**	34	8	24	**137**	63	70	4	1	**.363**	.424	.555	.979	168	58	145	9.14	-20	*3-161	**41**	4.1
1972 StL-N★	149	544	71	157	26	6	11	81	54	64	3	0	.289	.361	.419	.781	123	18	80	5.25	-16	*3-117,1-27	18	-0.1
1973 StL-N★	141	519	67	149	17	2	13	69	65	78	2	0	.287	.377	.403	.780	116	15	78	5.35	-5	*1-114,3-58	19	0.2
1974 StL-N	147	529	59	149	28	1	11	70	69	88	1	2	.282	.373	.401	.774	117	14	80	5.36	2	*1-139,3-18	16	0.5
1975 NY-N	114	361	33	89	16	3	6	35	35	55	0	0	.247	.317	.357	.674	91	-5	36	3.29	4	3-83,1-24	8	-0.3
1976 NY-N	114	310	36	95	10	3	5	31	21	35	1	3	.306	.360	.406	.767	124	8	41	4.60	3	1-78/3-4	10	0.6
1977 NY-N	26	51	2	9	3	0	1	9	2	10	0	0	.176	.208	.294	.502	34	-5	2	1.37	-1	1-16/3-1	0	-0.7
Total 18	**2209**	**7874**	**996**	**2342**	**344**	**59**	**252**	**1185**	**779**	**1094**	**23**	**29**	**.297**	**.367**	**.452**	**.819**	**128**	**298**	**1258**	**5.75**	**-36**	**C-903,1-787,3-515/0-2**	**315**	**26.5**
• TORREALBA, Steve	Steven Alexander Torrealba b: 2/24/1978, Barquisimeto, Venezuela BR/TR, 6', 175 lbs. Deb: 10/6/2001																							
2001*Atl-N	2	2	0	1	0	0	0	0	0	0	0	0	.500	.500	.500	1.000	157	0	0	.00	0	/C-2	0	0.0
2002 Atl-N	13	17	1	1	0	0	0	1	3	4	0	0	.059	.200	.059	.259	-27	-3	0	.70	-1	C-12	0	-0.4
Total 2	**15**	**19**	**1**	**2**	**0**	**0**	**0**	**1**	**3**	**4**	**0**	**0**	**.105**	**.227**	**.105**	**.333**	**-11**	**-3**	**0**	**.62**	**-1**	**/C-14**	**0**	**-0.4**

• TORREALBA, Yorvit — Yorvit Adolfo Torrealba b: 7/19/1978, Caracas, Venezuela BR/TR, 5'11", 190 lbs. Deb: 9/5/2001

YEAR TM-L	G	AB	R	H	2B	3B	HR	RBI	BB	SO	SB	CS	AVG	OBP	SLG	OPS	OPS+	BR/A	RC	RC/G	FR	G/POS	WS	TPW
2001 SF-N	3	4	0	2	0	1	0	2	0	0	0	0	.500	.500	1.000	1.500	295	1	2	27.00	-1	/C-3	1	0.1
2002 SF-N	53	136	17	38	10	0	2	14	14	20	0	0	.279	.355	.397	.752	102	1	16	3.96	2	C-53	4	0.5
2003*SF-N	66	200	22	52	10	2	4	29	14	39	1	0	.260	.315	.390	.705	85	-5	25	4.33	3	C-66/O-1	7	0.3
Total 3	122	340	39	92	20	3	6	45	28	59	1	0	.271	.333	.400	.733	94	-3	43	4.34	4	C-122/O-1	12	0.8

• TORRES, Andres — Andres Vungo (Feliciano) Torres b: 1/26/1978, Aguadilla, Puerto Rico BB/TR, 5'10", 175 lbs. Deb: 4/7/2002 Career OF: 1-55-16

YEAR TM-L	G	AB	R	H	2B	3B	HR	RBI	BB	SO	SB	CS	AVG	OBP	SLG	OPS	OPS+	BR/A	RC	RC/G	FR	G/POS	WS	TPW
2002 Det-A	19	70	7	14	1	1	0	3	6	16	2	2	.200	.273	.243	.516	41	-6	4	1.96	-1	O-19(O-19-0)	0	-0.7
2003 Det-A	59	168	23	37	4	3	1	9	10	35	5	5	.220	.264	.298	.562	52	-13	12	2.15	0	O-50(1-36-16)/D-3	0	-1.3
Total 2	78	238	30	51	5	4	1	12	16	51	7	7	.214	.267	.282	.548	49	-19	16	2.09	-1	/O-69,D-3	0	-2.0

• TORRES, Felix — Felix (Sanchez) Torres b: 5/1/1932, Ponce, Puerto Rico BR/TR, 5'11", 165 lbs. Deb: 4/10/1962

YEAR TM-L	G	AB	R	H	2B	3B	HR	RBI	BB	SO	SB	CS	AVG	OBP	SLG	OPS	OPS+	BR/A	RC	RC/G	FR	G/POS	WS	TPW
1962 LA-A	127	451	44	117	19	4	11	74	28	73	0	0	.259	.308	.392	.701	90	-8	50	3.73	-3	*3-123	9	-1.0
1963 LA-A	138	463	40	121	32	1	4	51	30	73	1	0	.261	.310	.361	.671	93	-5	48	3.48	-8	*3-122/1-2	10	-1.4
1964 LA-A	100	277	25	64	10	0	12	28	13	56	1	3	.231	.268	.397	.665	91	-6	25	2.91	-7	3-72/1-3	4	-1.3
Total 3	365	1191	109	302	61	5	27	153	71	202	2	3	.254	.300	.381	.681	91	-18	123	3.44	-17	3-317/1-5	23	-3.8

• TORRES, Gil — Don Gilberto (Nunez) Torres b: 8/23/1915, Regla, Cuba d: 1/10/1983, Regla, Cuba BR/TR, 6', 155 lbs. Deb: 4/25/1940

YEAR TM-L	G	AB	R	H	2B	3B	HR	RBI	BB	SO	SB	CS	AVG	OBP	SLG	OPS	OPS+	BR/A	RC	RC/G	FR	G/POS	WS	TPW
1940 Was-A	2	0	0	0	0	0	0	0	0	0	0	0	....	....	....	....	-107	0	0	....	0	/P-2	0	0.1
1944 Was-A	134	524	42	140	20	6	0	58	21	24	10	7	.267	.297	.328	.625	82	-15	47	2.99	10	*3-123,2-10/1-4	10	-0.3
1945 Was-A	147	562	39	133	12	5	0	48	21	29	7	4	.237	.264	.276	.540	62	-29	40	2.34	-11	*S-145/3-2	7	-3.0
1946 Was-A	63	185	18	47	8	0	0	13	11	12	3	2	.254	.296	.297	.593	70	-7	16	2.83	-3	S-31,3-18/2-7,P-3	3	-1.2
Total 4	346	1271	99	320	40	11	0	119	53	65	20	13	.252	.282	.301	.583	71	-51	102	2.67	-4	S-176,3-143/2-17,P-5,1-4	20	-4.3

• TORRES, Hector — Hector Epitacio (Marroquin) Torres b: 9/16/1945, Monterrey, Mexico BR/TR, 6', 175 lbs. Deb: 4/10/1968 C

YEAR TM-L	G	AB	R	H	2B	3B	HR	RBI	BB	SO	SB	CS	AVG	OBP	SLG	OPS	OPS+	BR/A	RC	RC/G	FR	G/POS	WS	TPW
1968 Hou-N	128	466	44	104	11	1	1	24	18	64	2	3	.223	.252	.258	.510	54	-27	29	2.02	-7	*S-127/2-1	5	-2.7
1969 Hou-N	34	69	5	11	1	0	1	8	2	12	0	0	.159	.183	.217	.400	12	-8	2	.97	-5	S-22	0	-1.1
1970 Hou-N	31	65	6	16	1	2	0	5	6	8	0	0	.246	.310	.323	.633	73	-3	6	3.36	-4	S-22/2-6	1	-0.5
1971 Chi-N	31	58	4	13	3	0	0	2	4	10	0	0	.224	.274	.276	.550	49	-4	4	1.97	0	S-18/2-4	1	-0.2
1972 Mon-N	83	181	14	28	4	1	2	7	13	26	0	2	.155	.215	.221	.436	24	-19	8	1.36	-1	2-60,S-16/O-2(1-0-1),3-1,P	2	-1.9
1973 Hou-N	38	66	3	6	1	0	0	2	7	13	0	1	.091	.189	.106	.295	-16	-11	1	.49	-1	S-22,2-13	1	-0.9
1975 SD-N	112	352	31	91	12	0	5	26	22	32	2	3	.259	.302	.335	.637	82	-11	34	3.26	7	S-75,3-42,2-16	10	0.5
1976 SD-N	74	215	8	42	6	0	4	15	16	31	2	1	.195	.254	.279	.533	56	-13	14	2.06	-5	S-63/3-4,2-3	1	-1.3
1977 Tor-A	91	266	33	64	7	3	5	26	16	33	1	1	.241	.286	.346	.632	70	-11	24	2.96	-4	S-68,2-23/3-2	3	-0.8
Total 9	622	1738	148	375	46	7	18	115	104	229	7	11	.216	.262	.281	.543	55	-106	123	2.26	-20	S-433,2-126/3-49,O-2,P-1	24	-9.0

• TORRES, Ricardo — Ricardo J. (Martinez) Torres b: 4/16/1891, Regla, Cuba d: 4/17/1960, Regla, Cuba BR/TR, 5'11", 160 lbs. Deb: 5/18/1920

YEAR TM-L	G	AB	R	H	2B	3B	HR	RBI	BB	SO	SB	CS	AVG	OBP	SLG	OPS	OPS+	BR/A	RC	RC/G	FR	G/POS	WS	TPW
1920 Was-A	16	30	8	10	1	0	0	3	1	4	0	0	.333	.355	.367	.722	94	-0	4	5.08	-1	/1-7,C-5	1	-0.1
1921 Was-A	2	3	1	1	0	0	0	0	1	1	0	0	.333	.500	.333	.833	122	0	1	8.01	-1	/C-2	0	0.0
1922 Was-A	4	4	0	0	0	0	0	0	0	1	0	0	.000	.000	.000	.000	-105	-1	0	.00	0	/C-3	0	-0.1
Total 3	22	37	9	11	1	0	0	3	2	6	0	0	.297	.333	.324	.658	76	-1	4	4.53	-1	/C-10,1-7	1	-0.1

• TORRES, Rusty — Rosendo (Hernandez) Torres b: 9/30/1948, Aguadilla, Puerto Rico BB/TR, 5'10", 180 lbs. Deb: 9/20/1971 Career OF: 96-251-240

YEAR TM-L	G	AB	R	H	2B	3B	HR	RBI	BB	SO	SB	CS	AVG	OBP	SLG	OPS	OPS+	BR/A	RC	RC/G	FR	G/POS	WS	TPW
1971 NY-A	9	26	5	10	3	0	2	3	0	8	0	1	.385	.385	.731	1.115	223	3	7	10.45	0	/O-5(0-1-4)	2	0.4
1972 NY-A	80	199	15	42	7	0	3	13	18	44	0	4	.211	.280	.291	.571	72	-8	16	2.59	-1	O-62(1-1-60)	2	-1.4
1973 Cle-A	122	312	31	64	8	1	7	28	50	62	6	5	.205	.321	.304	.625	76	-9	32	3.24	-2	*O-114(1-37-77)	5	-1.6
1974 Cle-A	108	150	19	28	2	0	3	12	13	24	2	1	.187	.252	.260	.512	48	-10	10	2.14	1	O-94(35-38-24)/D-1	1	-1.1
1976 Cal-A	120	264	37	54	16	3	6	27	36	39	4	4	.205	.300	.356	.656	98	-2	29	3.45	-1	*O-105(0-104-1)/D-6,3-1	8	-0.6
1977 Cal-A	58	77	9	12	1	1	3	10	10	18	0	1	.156	.253	.312	.565	55	-5	6	2.28	-2	O-54(4-40-10)	1	-0.8
1978 Chi-A	16	44	7	14	3	0	3	6	6	7	0	1	.318	.400	.591	.991	174	4	10	8.83	-1	O-14(4-5-8)	3	0.3
1979 Chi-A	90	170	26	43	5	0	8	24	23	37	0	0	.253	.349	.424	.772	107	2	26	5.05	1	O-85(36-17-35)	5	0.1
1980 KC-A	51	72	10	12	0	0	0	3	8	7	1	3	.167	.250	.167	.417	16	-9	3	1.23	0	O-40(15-8-21)/D-1	1	-1.0
Total 9	654	1314	159	279	45	5	35	126	164	246	13	20	.212	.303	.334	.637	82	-34	139	3.38	-6	O-573/D-8,3-1	28	-5.9

• TORVE, Kelvin — Kelvin Curtis Torve b: 1/10/1960, Rapid City, SD BL/TR, 6'3", 205 lbs. Deb: 6/25/1988

YEAR TM-L	G	AB	R	H	2B	3B	HR	RBI	BB	SO	SB	CS	AVG	OBP	SLG	OPS	OPS+	BR/A	RC	RC/G	FR	G/POS	WS	TPW
1988 Min-A	12	16	1	3	0	0	1	2	1	2	0	1	.188	.235	.375	.610	66	-1	1	2.13	0	/1-4,D-1	0	-0.1
1990 NY-N	20	38	0	11	4	0	0	2	4	9	0	0	.289	.386	.395	.781	116	1	6	5.81	-2	/1-9,O-1	2	-0.2
1991 NY-N	10	8	0	0	0	0	0	0	0	1	0	0	.000	.000	.000	.000	-101	-2	0	.00	1	/1-1	0	-0.2
Total 3	42	62	1	14	4	0	1	4	5	12	0	1	.226	.304	.339	.643	78	-2	7	3.77	-1	/1-14,D-1,O-1	2	-0.5

• TOVAR, Cesar — Cesar Leonardo "Pepito" Tovar
b: 7/3/1940, Caracas, Venezuela d: 7/14/1994, Caracas, Venezuela BR/TR, 5'9", 155 lbs. Deb: 4/12/1965 Career OF: 378-471-205

YEAR TM-L	G	AB	R	H	2B	3B	HR	RBI	BB	SO	SB	CS	AVG	OBP	SLG	OPS	OPS+	BR/A	RC	RC/G	FR	G/POS	WS	TPW
1965 Min-A	18	25	3	5	1	0	0	2	2	3	2	0	.200	.259	.240	.499	41	-2	2	2.65	0	/2-4,3-2,O-2(0-2-0),S-1	0	-0.1
1966 Min-A	134	465	57	121	19	5	2	41	44	50	16	6	.260	.329	.335	.665	86	-6	54	3.96	-1	2-76,S-31,O-24(4-20-0)	14	0.1
1967 Min-A	164	649	98	173	32	7	6	47	46	51	19	11	.267	.328	.365	.693	97	-2	80	4.19	-8	O-74(10-64-5),3-70,2-36/S-9	21	-1.1
1968 Min-A	157	613	89	167	31	6	6	47	34	41	35	13	.272	.328	.372	.700	107	7	80	4.58	-1	O-78(39-34-10),3-75,S-35,2/1,C,P	22	0.6
1969*Min-A	158	535	99	154	25	5	11	52	37	37	45	12	.288	.344	.415	.759	109	10	80	5.28	0	*O-113(39-70-8),2-41,3-20	19	0.8
1970*Min-A	161	650	120	195	**36**	**13**	10	54	52	47	30	15	.300	.359	.442	.801	118	16	103	5.64	-5	*O-151(39-134-2)/2-8,3-4	28	0.6
1971 Min-A	157	657	94	**204**	29	3	1	45	45	39	18	14	.311	.357	.368	.726	103	1	87	4.87	-1	*O-154(98-44-47)/3-7,2-2	21	-0.9
1972 Min-A	141	548	86	145	20	6	2	31	39	39	21	10	.265	.329	.334	.663	93	-3	63	3.99	5	*O-139(38-5-101)	17	-0.6
1973 Phi-N	97	328	49	88	18	4	1	21	29	35	6	4	.268	.337	.357	.694	90	-4	41	4.44	1	3-46,O-24(6-3-16),2-22	8	-0.3
1974 Tex-A	138	562	78	164	24	6	4	58	47	33	13	9	.292	.356	.377	.733	114	10	79	5.07	2	*O-135(66-87-11)/D-3	22	0.7
1975 Tex-A	102	427	53	110	16	0	3	28	27	25	16	11	.258	.306	.316	.623	77	-14	40	3.18	-2	D-66,O-31(25-6-1)/2-1	5	-2.0
*Oak-A	19	26	5	6	1	0	0	3	3	3	4	0	.231	.310	.269	.580	67	-0	3	4.13	-2	/D-7,2-4,3-3,S-1	1	-0.2
Yr.	121	453	58	116	17	0	3	31	30	28	20	11	.256	.307	.313	.620	76	-14	43	3.23	-4	D-73,O-31(25-6-1)/2-5,3-3,S	6	-2.2
1976 Oak-A	29	45	1	8	0	0	0	4	4	4	1	2	.178	.275	.178	.452	36	-4	2	1.65	0	O-20(14-2-4)/D-4	0	-0.6
NY-A	13	39	2	6	1	0	0	2	4	3	0	1	.154	.250	.179	.429	27	-4	2	1.47	1	D-10/2-3	0	-0.3
Yr.	42	84	3	14	1	0	0	6	8	7	1	3	.167	.263	.179	.442	32	-8	4	1.57	0	O-20(14-2-4),D-14/2-3	0	-1.0
Total 12	1488	5569	834	1546	253	55	46	435	413	410	226	108	.278	.337	.368	.705	99	4	717	4.51	-10	O-945,3-227,2-215/D,S,1,C,P	178	-3.3

• TOWNE, Babe — Jay King Towne b: 3/12/1880, Coon Rapids, IA d: 10/29/1938, Des Moines, IA BR/TR, 5'10", 180 lbs. Deb: 8/1/1906

YEAR TM-L	G	AB	R	H	2B	3B	HR	RBI	BB	SO	SB	CS	AVG	OBP	SLG	OPS	OPS+	BR/A	RC	RC/G	FR	G/POS	WS	TPW
1906*Chi-A	14	36	3	10	0	0	0	6	7	....	0	....	.278	.395	.278	.673	115	1	4	4.13	-3	C-13	2	-0.1

• TOWNSEND, George — George Hodgson "Sleepy" Townsend
b: 6/4/1867, Hartsdale, NY d: 3/15/1930, New Haven, CT BR/TR, 5'7.5", 180 lbs. Deb: 6/25/1887 U Career OF: 1-1-4

YEAR TM-L	G	AB	R	H	2B	3B	HR	RBI	BB	SO	SB	CS	AVG	OBP	SLG	OPS	OPS+	BR/A	RC	RC/G	FR	G/POS	WS	TPW
1887 Phi-a	31	112	12	24	3	0	0	14	3	....	8	....	.214	.214	.220	.434	21	-12	7	2.16	-1	C-28/O-3(1-0-2)	1	-0.9
1888 Phi-a	42	161	13	25	6	0	0	12	4	....	2	....	.155	.181	.193	.373	20	-15	6	1.21	1	C-42	2	-0.9
1890 Bal-a	18	67	6	16	4	1	0	9	4	....	3	....	.239	.282	.328	.610	73	-3	7	3.75	3	C-18	1	0.2
1891 Bal-a	61	204	29	39	5	4	0	18	20	21	3	....	.191	.279	.255	.534	52	-13	16	2.53	0	C-58/O-3(0-1-2)	2	-0.7
Total 4	152	544	60	104	18	5	0	53	31	21	16	....	.191	.239	.238	.477	39	-42	36	2.19	4	C-146/O-6	6	-2.4

• TOY, Jim — James Madison Toy b: 2/20/1858, Beaver Falls, PA d: 3/13/1919, Cresson, PA BR, 5'6", 160 lbs. Deb: 4/20/1887

YEAR TM-L	G	AB	R	H	2B	3B	HR	RBI	BB	SO	SB	CS	AVG	OBP	SLG	OPS	OPS+	BR/A	RC	RC/G	FR	G/POS	WS	TPW
1887 Cle-a	109	440	56	111	20	5	1	56	17	....	8	....	.252	.256	.300	.556	56	-26	35	2.90	-3	1-82,O-11(2-2-7),C-10/3-8,S	3	-2.8
1890 Bro-a	44	160	11	29	3	0	0	7	11	....	2	....	.181	.238	.200	.438	30	-14	8	1.68	4	C-44	1	-0.5
Total 2	153	600	67	140	23	5	1	63	28	....	10	....	.233	.251	.273	.524	49	-39	44	2.56	2	/1-82,C-54,O-11,3-8,S-3	4	-3.3

• TRABER, Jim — James Joseph Traber b: 12/26/1961, Columbus, OH BL/TL, 6', 194 lbs. Deb: 9/21/1984 Career OF: 9-0-9

YEAR TM-L	G	AB	R	H	2B	3B	HR	RBI	BB	SO	SB	CS	AVG	OBP	SLG	OPS	OPS+	BR/A	RC	RC/G	FR	G/POS	WS	TPW
1984 Bal-A	10	21	3	5	0	0	0	2	2	4	0	0	.238	.304	.238	.542	54	-1	2	2.27	0	/D-9	0	-0.1
1986 Bal-A	65	212	28	54	7	0	13	44	18	31	0	0	.255	.328	.472	.799	116	4	32	5.11	2	1-29,D-21/O-8(7-0-1)	6	0.3
1988 Bal-A	103	352	25	78	6	0	10	45	19	42	1	2	.222	.263	.324	.587	65	-18	28	2.66	4	1-57,D-30,O-11(2-0-8)	3	-1.9

YEAR TM-L	G	AB	R	H	2B	3B	HR	RBI	BB	SO	SB	CS	AVG	OBP	SLG	OPS	OPS+	BR/A	RC	RC/G	FR	G/POS	WS	TPW
1989 Bal-A	86	234	14	49	8	0	4	26	19	41	4	3	.209	.269	.295	.564	61	-13	18	2.38	3	1-69/D-5	2	-1.4
Total 4	264	819	70	186	21	0	27	117	58	118	5	5	.227	.283	.352	.635	77	-28	79	3.18	9	1-155/D-65,0-19	11	-3.2
• TRACEWSKI, Dick	Richard Joseph Tracewski b: 2/3/1935, Eynon, PA BR/TR, 5'11", 167 lbs. Deb: 4/12/1962 M/C																							
1962 LA-N	15	2	3	0	0	0	0	0	2	0	0	0	.000	.500	.000	.500	50	0	0	3.51	0	/S-4	0	0.0
1963*LA-N	104	217	23	49	2	1	1	10	19	39	2	3	.226	.288	.258	.546	63	-11	16	2.50	2	S-81,2-23	5	-0.3
1964 LA-N	106	304	31	75	13	4	1	26	31	61	3	3	.247	.316	.326	.642	87	-5	33	3.68	-3	2-56,3-30,S-19	8	-0.3
1965*LA-N	78	186	17	40	6	0	1	20	25	30	2	6	.215	.315	.263	.578	69	-9	15	2.64	1	3-53,2-14/S-7	3	-0.8
1966 Det-A	81	124	15	24	1	1	0	7	10	32	1	1	.194	.254	.218	.471	36	-10	7	1.90	0	2-70/S-3	1	-0.8
1967 Det-A	74	107	19	30	4	2	1	9	8	20	1	1	.280	.330	.383	.714	107	1	14	4.54	3	S-44,2-12,3-10	4	0.6
1968*Det-A	90	212	30	33	3	1	4	15	24	51	3	0	.156	.242	.236	.477	44	-13	13	1.86	3	S-51,3-16,2-14	3	-0.8
1969 Det-A	66	79	10	11	2	0	0	4	15	20	3	0	.139	.277	.165	.441	25	-7	5	1.70	1	S-41,2-13/3-6	1	-0.3
Total 8	614	1231	148	262	31	9	8	91	134	253	15	14	.213	.291	.272	.563	65	-54	104	2.73	5	S-250,2-202,3-115	25	-2.5
• TRACY, Andy	Andrew Michael Tracy b: 12/11/1973, Bowling Green, OH BL/TR, 6'3", 220 lbs. Deb: 4/25/2000																							
2000 Mon-N	83	192	29	50	8	1	11	32	22	61	1	0	.260	.343	.484	.827	103	1	33	6.01	-7	3-34,1-27	5	-0.7
2001 Mon-N	38	55	4	6	1	0	2	8	6	26	0	0	.109	.197	.236	.433	11	-8	3	1.41	-1	3-11/1-3,D-2	0	-0.9
Total 2	121	247	33	56	9	1	13	40	28	87	1	0	.227	.310	.429	.740	82	-7	35	4.81	-8	/3-45,1-30,D-2	5	-1.6
• TRACY, Jim	James Edwin Tracy b: 12/31/1955, Hamilton, OH BL/TR, 6', 185 lbs. Deb: 7/20/1980 M/C Career OF: 32-0-15																							
1980 Chi-N	42	122	12	31	3	3	3	9	13	37	2	2	.254	.326	.402	.728	95	-1	16	4.56	-1	0-31(22-0-14)/1-1	3	-0.3
1981 Chi-N	45	63	6	15	2	1	0	5	12	14	1	0	.238	.360	.302	.662	85	-0	8	4.03	0	0-11(10-0-1)	1	-0.1
Total 2	87	185	18	46	5	4	3	14	25	51	3	2	.249	.338	.368	.706	92	-2	24	4.38	-1	/0-42,1-1	4	-0.4
• TRAFFLEY, Bill	William Franklin Traffley b: 12/21/1859, Staten Island, NY d: 6/23/1908, Des Moines, IA BR/TR, 5'11.5", 185 lbs. Deb: 7/27/1878 U Career OF: 0-5-11																							
1878 Chi-N	2	9	1	1	0	0	0	1	0	1	....	....	.111	.111	.111	.222	-25	-1	0	.39	0	/C-2	0	-0.1
1883 Cin-a	30	105	17	21	5	0	0	8	4	....	....	....	.200	.229	.248	.477	51	-6	6	2.04	-3	C-29/S-2	2	-0.6
1884 Bal-a	53	210	25	37	4	6	0	0	3	....	....	....	.176	.192	.252	.444	42	-14	10	1.65	-7	C-47/0-6(0-0-6),1-1	3	-1.6
1885 Bal-a	69	254	27	39	4	5	1	20	17	....	....	....	.154	.215	.220	.436	38	-17	12	1.55	1	C-61,0-10(0-5-5)/2-3	3	-1.0
1886 Bal-a	25	85	15	18	0	1	0	7	10	....	8	....	.212	.295	.235	.530	69	-3	8	3.41	-2	C-25	3	-0.2
Total 5	179	663	85	116	13	12	1	36	34	1	8	....	.175	.220	.235	.455	45	-41	37	1.87	-12	C-164/0-16,2-3,S-2,1-1	11	-3.5
• TRAFFLEY, John	John M. Traffley b: 1862, Chicago, IL d: 5/15/1900, Baltimore, MD, 5'9", 180 lbs. Deb: 6/15/1889																							
1889 Lou-a	1	2	0	1	0	0	0	0	0	0	0	....	.500	.500	.500	1.000	188	0	1	13.58	0	/0-1	0	0.0
• TRAGESSER, Walt	Walter Joseph Tragesser b: 6/14/1887, Lafayette, IN d: 12/14/1970, Lafayette, IN BR/TR, 6', 175 lbs. Deb: 7/30/1913																							
1913 Bos-N	2	0	0	0	0	0	0	0	0	0	0	....	....	....	....	....	-98	0	0	....	-1	/C-2	0	-0.1
1915 Bos-N	7	7	1	0	0	0	0	0	0	2	0	....	.000	.000	.000	.000	-102	-2	0	.00	0	/C-7	0	-0.2
1916 Bos-N	41	54	3	11	1	0	0	4	5	10	0	....	.204	.283	.222	.506	59	-2	4	2.12	0	C-29	2	-0.1
1917 Bos-N	98	297	23	66	10	2	0	25	15	36	5	....	.222	.264	.269	.534	68	-12	22	2.38	0	C-94	6	-0.5
1918 Bos-N	7	1	0	0	0	0	0	0	0	0	0	....	.000	.000	.000	.000	-104	-0	0	.00	-2	/C-7	0	-0.2
1919 Bos-N	20	40	3	7	2	0	0	3	2	10	1	....	.175	.233	.225	.458	39	-3	2	1.71	1	C-14	0	-0.1
Phi-N	35	114	7	27	7	0	0	8	9	31	4	....	.237	.298	.298	.597	74	-3	10	3.13	5	C-34	2	0.5
Yr.	55	154	10	34	9	0	0	11	11	41	5	....	.221	.281	.279	.561	65	-6	13	2.73	6	C-48	2	0.4
1920 Phi-N	62	176	17	37	11	1	6	26	4	36	4	0	.210	.236	.386	.623	73	-5	16	3.08	-3	C-52	3	-0.5
Total 7	272	689	54	148	31	3	6	66	35	125	14	0	.215	.260	.295	.555	66	-28	54	2.58	0	C-239	13	-1.3
• TRAMBACK, Red	Stephen Joseph Tramback b: 10/1/1915, Iselin, PA d: 12/28/1979, Buffalo, NY BL/TL, 6', 175 lbs. Deb: 9/15/1940																							
1940 NY-N	2	4	0	1	0	0	0	0	1	1	1	....	.250	.400	.250	.650	82	-0	1	4.54	0	/0-1	0	0.0
• TRAMMELL, Alan	Alan Stuart Trammell b: 2/21/1958, Garden Grove, CA BR/TR, 6', 175 lbs. Deb: 9/9/1977 M/C Career OF: 5-4-0																							
1977 Det-A	19	43	6	8	0	0	0	0	4	12	0	0	.186	.255	.186	.441	21	-5	2	1.60	0	S-19	0	-0.4
1978 Det-A	139	448	49	120	14	6	2	34	45	56	3	1	.268	.337	.339	.677	88	-5	52	4.02	3	*S-139	14	1.3
1979 Det-A	142	460	68	127	11	4	6	50	43	55	17	14	.276	.338	.357	.694	85	-11	56	4.06	-10	*S-142	13	-0.7
1980 Det-A★	146	560	107	168	21	5	9	65	69	63	12	12	.300	.380	.404	.783	112	9	87	5.43	-11	*S-144	21	1.4
1981 Det-A	105	392	52	101	15	3	2	31	49	31	10	3	.258	.345	.327	.671	91	-1	47	3.95	13	*S-105	14	2.4
1982 Det-A	157	489	66	126	34	3	9	57	52	47	19	8	.258	.329	.395	.724	97	-1	67	4.59	0	*S-157	16	1.5
1983 Det-A	142	505	83	161	31	2	14	66	57	64	30	10	.319	.388	.471	.859	139	30	96	6.83	4	*S-140	26	4.8
1984*Det-A★	139	555	85	174	34	5	14	69	60	63	19	13	.314	.383	.468	.852	135	26	100	6.59	8	*S-114,D-22	29	4.5
1985 Det-A★	149	605	79	156	21	7	13	57	50	71	14	5	.258	.317	.380	.697	90	-8	76	4.26	-6	*S-149	16	0.3
1986 Det-A	151	574	107	159	33	7	21	75	59	57	25	12	.277	.350	.469	.818	121	16	95	5.74	13	*S-149/D-2	26	4.5
1987*Det-A★	151	597	109	205	34	3	28	105	60	47	21	2	.343	.406	.551	.957	157	53	137	8.94	-1	*S-149	**35**	**6.4**
1988 Det-A★	128	466	73	145	24	1	15	69	46	46	7	4	.311	.378	.464	.841	140	24	79	6.19	6	*S-125	23	4.1
1989 Det-A	121	449	54	109	20	3	5	43	45	45	10	2	.243	.317	.334	.651	86	-7	50	3.75	3	*S-117/D-2	13	0.6
1990 Det-A★	146	559	71	170	37	1	14	89	68	55	12	10	.304	.381	.449	.830	130	22	95	6.13	-1	*S-142/D-3	29	3.2
1991 Det-A	101	375	57	93	20	0	9	55	37	39	11	2	.248	.320	.373	.694	90	-4	47	4.26	6	S-92/D-6	12	0.9
1992 Det-A	29	102	11	28	7	1	1	11	15	4	2	2	.275	.373	.392	.765	114	2	14	4.46	-1	S-27/D-1	4	0.3
1993 Det-A	112	401	72	132	25	3	12	60	38	38	12	8	.329	.390	.496	.886	137	20	77	7.14	-6	S-63,3-35/0-8(4-4-0),D-6	17	1.8
1994 Det-A	76	292	38	78	17	1	8	28	16	35	3	0	.267	.307	.414	.722	84	-8	36	4.31	-6	S-63,D-11	3	-0.8
1995 Det-A	74	223	28	60	12	0	2	23	27	19	3	1	.269	.348	.350	.698	83	-5	27	4.11	-5	S-60/D-6	6	-0.5
1996 Det-A	66	193	16	45	2	0	1	16	10	27	6	0	.233	.271	.259	.530	35	-18	15	2.53	-5	S-43,2-11/3-8,0-5(1-0-0)	1	-1.8
Total 20	2293	8288	1231	2365	412	55	185	1003	850	874	236	109	.285	.354	.415	.770	110	132	1254	5.30	2	*S-2139/D-59,3-43,0-13,2-11	318	33.7
• TRAMMELL, Bubba	Thomas Bubba Trammell b: 11/6/1971, Knoxville, TN BR/TR, 6'3", 205 lbs. Deb: 4/1/1997 Career OF: 194-0-297																							
1997 Det-A	44	123	14	28	5	0	4	13	15	35	3	1	.228	.312	.366	.677	77	-4	15	3.97	0	D-15/0-1	2	-0.5
1998 TB-A	59	199	28	57	18	1	12	35	16	45	0	2	.286	.340	.568	.907	128	6	37	6.61	2	0-28(23-0-16),D-19	4	0.5
1999 TB-A	82	283	49	82	19	0	14	39	43	37	0	2	.290	.385	.505	.891	123	10	55	7.06	0	0-37(61-0-20)/D-7	9	0.5
2000 TB-A	66	189	19	52	11	2	7	33	21	30	3	0	.275	.354	.466	.819	106	2	32	5.96	-2	0-74(26-0-24)/D-9	6	-0.2
*NY-N	36	56	9	13	2	0	3	12	8	19	1	0	.232	.328	.429	.757	93	-0	8	4.31	0	0-48(11-0-16)	2	-0.1
2001 SD-N	142	490	66	128	20	3	25	92	48	78	2	2	.261	.332	.467	.799	113	8	75	5.39	-1	0-25(34-0-102)/D-2	17	0.0
2002 SD-N	133	403	54	98	16	1	17	56	53	71	1	3	.243	.336	.414	.750	106	2	58	4.86	-7	*0-132(23-0-104)/D-2	11	-1.0
2003 NY-A	22	55	4	11	5	0	0	5	6	10	0	0	.200	.279	.291	.570	52	-4	5	2.76	1	D-14/0-3(3-0-0)	0	-0.4
Total 7	584	1798	243	469	96	7	82	285	210	325	10	10	.261	.341	.459	.800	109	20	283	5.49	-8	0-348/D-68	51	-1.2
• TRAVIS, Cecil	Cecil Howell Travis b: 8/8/1913, Riverdale, GA BL/TR, 6'1.5", 185 lbs. Deb: 5/16/1933 Career OF: 17-0-52																							
1933 Was-A	18	43	7	13	1	0	0	2	2	5	0	0	.302	.348	.326	.673	80	-1	5	4.36	1	3-15	1	0.0
1934 Was-A	109	392	48	125	22	4	1	53	24	37	1	5	.319	.361	.403	.764	101	-2	56	5.25	6	3-99	10	0.7
1935 Was-A	138	534	85	170	27	8	0	61	41	28	4	2	.318	.377	.399	.776	104	4	82	5.84	18	*3-114,0-16(16-0-0)	20	2.5
1936 Was-A	138	517	77	164	34	10	2	92	39	21	4	4	.317	.366	.433	.800	102	0	82	5.99	-4	S-71,0-53(1-0-52)/2-4,3-2	15	-0.1
1937 Was-A	135	526	72	181	27	7	3	66	39	34	3	2	.344	.395	.439	.834	115	13	92	6.86	2	*S-129	22	2.2
1938 Was-A★	146	567	96	190	30	5	5	67	58	22	6	5	.335	.401	.432	.833	117	16	100	6.72	3	*S-143	20	2.6
1939 Was-A	130	476	55	139	20	9	5	63	34	25	0	3	.292	.342	.403	.745	97	-4	65	4.85	-6	*S-118	13	-0.2
1940 Was-A★	136	528	60	170	37	11	2	76	48	23	0	1	.322	.381	.445	.826	121	17	94	6.87	5	*3-113,S-23	22	2.6
1941 Was-A★	152	608	106	**218**	39	19	7	101	52	25	2	2	.359	.410	.520	.930	151	43	131	8.70	-8	*S-136,3-16	34	4.5
1945 Was-A	15	54	4	13	2	1	0	10	4	5	0	1	.241	.293	.315	.608	83	-2	4	2.43	1	3-14	1	-0.1
1946 Was-A	137	465	45	117	22	3	1	56	45	47	2	4	.252	.323	.318	.641	85	-10	47	3.39	-9	S-75,3-56	10	-1.5
1947 Was-A	74	204	10	44	4	1	1	10	16	19	1	3	.216	.273	.260	.533	50	-15	14	2.29	-2	3-39,S-15	1	-1.7
Total 12	1328	4914	665	1544	265	78	27	657	402	291	23	32	.314	.370	.416	.786	109	59	772	5.86	8	S-710,3-468/0-69,2-4	169	11.6

YEAR TM-L	G	AB	R	H	2B	3B	HR	RBI	BB	SO	SB	CS	AVG	OBP	SLG	OPS	OPS+	BR/A	RC	RC/G	FR	G/POS	WS	TPW
• TRAXLER, Brian	Brian Lee Traxler b: 9/26/1967, Waukegan, IL BL/TL, 5'10", 200 lbs. Deb: 4/24/1990																							
1990 LA-N	9	11	0	1	1	0	0	0	0	4	0	0	.091	.091	.182	.273	-28	-2	0	.49	0	/1-3	0	-0.2
• TRAY, Jim	James Tray b: 2/14/1860, Jackson, MI d: 7/28/1905, Jackson, MI, 5'11", 180 lbs. Deb: 9/6/1884																							
1884 Ind-a	6	21	2	6	0	0	0	0	2	....	....	....	.286	.348	.286	.634	112	0	2	3.92	-2	/C-4,1-2	1	-0.1
• TRAYNOR, Pie	Harold Joseph Traynor b: 11/11/1899, Framingham, MA d: 3/16/1972, Pittsburgh, PA BR/TR, 6', 170 lbs. Deb: 9/15/1920 M HOF: 1948																							
1920 Pit-N	17	52	6	11	3	1	0	2	3	6	1	3	.212	.268	.308	.576	63	-3	4	2.17	-8	S-17	0	-1.1
1921 Pit-N	7	19	0	5	0	0	0	2	1	2	0	0	.263	.300	.263	.563	49	-1	2	2.87	0	/3-3,S-1	1	-0.1
1922 Pit-N	142	571	89	161	17	12	4	81	27	28	17	3	.282	.319	.375	.694	77	-16	70	4.36	-2	*3-124,S-18	13	-0.7
1923 Pit-N	153	616	108	208	19	**19**	12	101	34	19	28	13	.338	.377	.489	.866	124	22	112	6.93	10	*3-152/S-1	28	4.0
1924 Pit-N	142	545	86	160	26	13	5	82	37	26	24	18	.294	.340	.417	.756	100	-2	74	4.72	12	*3-141	17	1.9
1925*Pit-N	150	591	114	189	39	14	6	106	52	19	15	9	.320	.377	.464	.840	106	6	103	6.45	27	*3-150/S-1	26	4.0
1926 Pit-N	152	574	83	182	25	17	3	92	38	14	8	....	.317	.361	.436	.796	108	5	88	5.44	12	*3-148/S-3	22	2.6
1927*Pit-N	149	573	93	196	32	9	5	106	22	11	11	....	.342	.370	.455	.825	112	9	92	5.81	24	*3-143/S-9	26	4.2
1928 Pit-N	144	569	91	192	38	12	3	124	28	10	12	....	.337	.370	.462	.832	112	8	93	5.78	10	*3-144	22	2.7
1929 Pit-N	130	540	94	192	27	12	4	108	30	7	13	....	.356	.393	.472	.865	111	9	96	6.73	6	*3-130	21	2.1
1930 Pit-N	130	497	90	182	22	11	9	119	48	19	7	....	.366	.423	.509	.932	124	21	104	8.03	7	*3-130	22	3.2
1931 Pit-N	155	615	81	183	37	15	2	103	54	28	6	....	.298	.354	.416	.771	107	6	93	5.51	0	*3-155	20	1.2
1932 Pit-N	135	513	74	169	27	10	2	68	32	20	6	....	.329	.373	.433	.806	118	13	84	6.24	10	*3-127	21	2.8
1933 Pit-N★	154	624	85	190	27	6	1	82	35	24	5	....	.304	.342	.372	.714	104	3	80	4.66	8	*3-154	20	1.8
1934 Pit-N★	119	444	62	137	22	10	1	61	21	27	3	....	.309	.341	.410	.751	98	-2	56	4.57	-1	*3-110	11	0.1
1935 Pit-N	57	204	24	57	10	3	1	36	10	17	2	....	.279	.323	.373	.695	84	-5	23	3.90	-2	3-49/1-1	4	-0.4
1937 Pit-N	5	12	3	2	0	0	0	0	0	1	0	....	.167	.167	.167	.333	-9	-2	0	.42	1	/3-3	0	-0.1
Total 17	1941	7559	1183	2416	371	164	58	1273	472	278	158	46	.320	.362	.435	.797	107	71	1174	5.65	114	*3-1863/S-50,1-1	274	28.2
• TREACEY, Fred	Frederick S. Treacey b: 1847, Brooklyn, NY, 5'9.5", 145 lbs. Deb: 5/16/1871 U NA OF: 81-110-24																							
1871 Chi-n	25	124	39	42	7	5	**4**	33	2	5	13	5	.339	.349	.573	.922	144	5	30	10.89	8	*O-25(25-0-0)	....	0.9
1872 Ath-n	47	236	53	65	7	3	2	29	5	10	7	5	.275	.290	.356	.646	97	-2	27	4.77	-2	*O-47(0-47-0)	....	-0.2
1873 Phi-n	51	243	49	62	7	2	1	32	5	6	2	3	.255	.270	.313	.583	70	-10	22	3.58	2	*O-51(1-51-0)	....	-0.6
1874 Chi-n	35	148	18	28	5	0	0	12	2	6	4	4	.189	.200	.223	.423	35	-11	8	1.84	7	O-35(2-11-24)	....	-0.2
1875 Cen-n	11	46	9	12	3	0	0	2	2	0	1	0	.261	.292	.326	.618	124	2	5	4.15	1	O-11(11-0-0)	....	0.2
Phi-n	43	179	23	38	3	3	0	15	1	3	6	3	.212	.217	.263	.479	63	-7	12	2.41	1	O-43(42-1-0)	....	-0.4
Yr.	54	225	32	50	6	3	0	17	3	3	7	3	.222	.232	.276	.508	76	-5	17	2.74	2	*O-54(53-1-0)	....	-0.2
1876 NY-N	57	257	47	54	5	1	0	18	1	5	....	....	.210	.214	.238	.452	58	-9	13	1.85	10	*O-57(52-0-5)	3	-0.2
Total 5 n	212	976	191	247	32	13	7	123	17	30	33	20	.253	.266	.334	.600	82	-23	103	4.22	18	O-212	....	-0.3
• TREACEY, Pete	Peter Treacey b: 1852, Brooklyn, NY Deb: 8/5/1876																							
1876 NY-N	2	6	1	0	0	0	0	0	1	0	....	....	.000	.167	.000	.167	-46	-1	0	.00	-2	/S-2	0	-0.2
• TREADAWAY, Ray	Edgar Raymond Treadaway b: 10/31/1907, Ragland, AL d: 10/12/1935, Chattanooga, TN BL/TR, 5'7", 150 lbs. Deb: 9/17/1930																							
1930 Was-A	6	19	1	4	2	0	0	1	0	3	0	0	.211	.211	.316	.526	31	-2	1	2.14	-1	/3-4	0	-0.3
• TREADWAY, George	George B. Treadway b: 11/11/1866, Greenup County, KY d: 11/5/1928, Riverside, CA BL, 6', 185 lbs. Deb: 4/27/1893 Career OF: 121-0-203																							
1893 Bal-N	115	458	78	119	16	17	1	67	58	50	24	....	.260	.348	.376	.724	91	-7	70	5.47	5	*O-115(1-0-114)	10	-0.6
1894 Bro-N	124	482	125	157	28	26	4	102	73	43	27	....	.326	.417	.517	.933	134	29	118	9.43	-5	*O-122(120-0-2)/1-1	19	1.0
1895 Bro-N	87	343	56	89	14	3	8	54	33	22	9	....	.259	.328	.388	.716	92	-4	48	5.06	-8	*O-86(0-0-86)	8	-1.3
1896 Lou-N	2	7	0	1	0	0	0	1	1	0	0	....	.143	.250	.143	.393	5	-1	0	1.13	-1	/1-1,O-1	0	-0.2
Total 4	328	1290	259	366	58	46	13	224	165	115	60	....	.284	.368	.430	.799	107	17	236	6.72	-9	O-324/1-2	37	-1.1
• TREADWAY, Jeff	Hugh Jeffery Treadway b: 1/22/1963, Columbus, GA BL/TR, 5'10", 170 lbs. Deb: 9/4/1987																							
1987 Cin-N	23	84	9	28	4	0	2	4	2	6	1	0	.333	.356	.452	.809	108	1	14	6.13	1	2-21	3	0.3
1988 Cin-N	103	301	30	76	19	4	2	23	27	30	2	0	.252	.320	.362	.682	92	-3	36	4.10	1	2-97/3-2	10	0.1
1989 Atl-N	134	473	58	131	18	3	8	40	30	38	3	2	.277	.320	.378	.699	96	-3	56	4.18	-5	*2-123/3-6	11	-0.5
1990 Atl-N	128	474	56	134	20	2	11	59	25	42	3	4	.283	.323	.403	.726	93	-7	59	4.40	7	*2-122	15	0.3
1991*Atl-N	106	306	41	98	17	2	3	32	23	19	2	2	.320	.372	.418	.790	115	6	46	5.61	-6	2-93	11	0.2
1992*Atl-N	61	126	5	28	6	1	0	5	9	16	1	2	.222	.274	.286	.560	55	-8	9	2.34	2	2-45/3-1	1	-0.6
1993 Cle-A	97	221	25	67	14	1	2	27	14	21	1	1	.303	.350	.403	.753	102	0	30	4.94	0	3-42,2-19/D-4	7	0.1
1994 LA-N	52	67	14	20	3	0	0	5	5	8	1	1	.299	.356	.343	.699	89	-1	9	4.26	-1	2-24/3-3	1	-0.1
1995 LA-N	17	17	2	2	0	1	0	3	0	2	0	0	.118	.118	.235	.353	-11	-3	0	.85	0	/3-2,2-1	0	-0.3
Mon-N	41	50	4	12	2	0	0	10	5	2	0	1	.240	.309	.280	.589	55	-4	4	3.03	0	2-11/3-1	1	-0.3
Yr.	58	67	6	14	2	1	0	13	5	4	0	1	.209	.264	.269	.533	39	-6	5	2.42	0	2-12/3-3	1	-0.6
Total 9	762	2119	244	596	103	14	28	208	140	184	14	13	.281	.329	.383	.712	94	-22	264	4.39	-1	2-556/3-57,D-4	60	-0.8
• TREADWAY, Red	Thadford Leon Treadway b: 4/28/1920, Athalone, NC d: 5/26/1994, Atlanta, GA BL/TR, 5'10", 175 lbs. Deb: 7/25/1944 Career OF: 37-20-45																							
1944 NY-N	50	170	23	51	5	2	0	5	13	11	2	....	.300	.350	.353	.703	98	-0	22	4.77	0	O-38(10-2-27)	4	-0.3
1945 NY-N	88	224	31	54	4	2	4	23	20	13	3	....	.241	.303	.330	.634	75	-8	24	3.75	-4	O-60(27-18-18)	3	-1.4
Total 2	138	394	54	105	9	4	4	28	33	24	5	....	.266	.323	.340	.663	85	-8	46	4.17	-3	/O-98	7	-1.7
• TRECHOCK, Frank	Frank Adam Trechock b: 12/24/1915, Windber, PA d: 1/16/1989, Minneapolis, MN BR/TR, 5'10", 175 lbs. Deb: 9/19/1937																							
1937 Was-A	1	4	0	2	0	0	0	0	0	1	0	0	.500	.500	.500	1.000	160	0	1	12.72	0	/S-1	0	0.1
• TREMARK, Nick	Nicholas Joseph Tremark b: 10/15/1912, Yonkers, NY d: 9/7/2000, Tomball, TX BL/TL, 5'5", 150 lbs. Deb: 8/9/1934 Career OF: 8-3-10																							
1934 Bro-N	17	28	3	7	1	0	0	6	2	2	0	....	.250	.300	.286	.586	61	-2	2	2.85	0	/O-9(8-1-0)	0	-0.2
1935 Bro-N	10	13	1	3	1	0	0	3	1	1	0	....	.231	.286	.308	.593	61	-1	1	3.36	-0	/O-4(0-0-4)	0	-0.1
1936 Bro-N	8	32	6	8	2	0	0	1	3	2	0	....	.250	.333	.313	.646	74	-1	3	3.73	1	/O-8(0-2-6)	1	-0.1
Total 3	35	73	10	18	4	0	0	10	6	5	0	....	.247	.313	.301	.614	67	-3	7	3.33	1	/O-21	1	-0.4
• TREMIE, Chris	Christopher James Tremie b: 10/17/1969, Houston, TX BR/TR, 6', 200 lbs. Deb: 7/1/1995																							
1995 Chi-A	10	24	0	4	0	0	0	0	1	2	0	0	.167	.200	.167	.367	-3	-4	1	1.18	0	/C-9,D-1	0	-0.3
1998 Tex-A	2	3	2	1	1	0	0	0	1	1	0	0	.333	.500	.667	1.167	192	0	1	15.26	0	/D-2	0	0.0
1999 Pit-N	9	14	1	1	0	0	0	1	2	4	0	0	.071	.188	.071	.259	-31	-3	0	.59	-0	/C-8	0	-0.2
Total 3	21	41	3	6	1	0	0	1	4	7	0	0	.146	.222	.171	.393	4	-6	2	1.75	0	/C-17,D-3	0	-0.5
• TREMPER, Overton	Carlton Overton Tremper b: 3/22/1906, Brooklyn, NY d: 1/9/1996, Clearwater, FL BR/TR, 5'10", 163 lbs. Deb: 6/16/1927 Career OF: 25-1-1																							
1927 Bro-N	26	60	4	14	0	0	0	4	0	2	0	....	.233	.246	.233	.479	29	-6	3	1.83	0	O-18(18-0-0)	0	-0.7
1928 Bro-N	10	31	1	6	2	1	0	1	0	1	0	....	.194	.194	.323	.516	33	-3	2	1.82	1	/O-9(7-1-1)	0	-0.3
Total 2	36	91	5	20	2	1	0	5	0	3	0	....	.220	.228	.264	.492	30	-9	5	1.83	0	/O-27	0	-1.0
• TRENWITH, George	George W. Trenwith b: 1851, Philadelphia, PA d: 2/1/1890, Philadelphia, PA Deb: 4/30/1875																							
1875 Cen-n	10	45	5	8	2	0	0	4	1	2	0	0	.178	.196	.222	.418	49	-2	2	1.60	-6	3-10	....	-0.7
NH-n	6	25	1	6	2	0	0	3	0	1	0	0	.240	.240	.320	.560	106	0	2	3.06	-2	/3-6	....	-0.1
Yr.	16	70	6	14	4	0	0	7	1	3	0	0	.200	.211	.257	.468	69	-1	4	2.09	-8	3-16	....	-0.8
• TRESH, Mike	Michael Tresh b: 2/23/1914, Hazleton, PA d: 10/4/1966, Detroit, MI BR/TR, 5'11", 170 lbs. Deb: 9/4/1938																							
1938 Chi-A	10	29	3	7	2	0	0	2	8	4	0	0	.241	.405	.310	.716	80	-0	4	5.06	1	C-10	1	0.1
1939 Chi-A	119	352	49	91	5	2	0	38	64	30	3	2	.259	.377	.284	.661	70	-12	43	4.11	-1	*C-119	10	-0.6
1940 Chi-A	135	480	62	135	15	5	1	64	49	40	3	10	.281	.349	.340	.689	78	-17	56	4.05	0	*C-135	12	-0.8
1941 Chi-A	115	390	38	98	10	1	0	33	38	27	1	0	.251	.319	.282	.601	61	-20	36	3.14	5	*C-115	9	-0.8
1942 Chi-A	72	233	21	54	8	1	0	15	28	24	2	0	.232	.314	.275	.589	68	-8	22	3.11	-4	C-72	4	-0.8
1943 Chi-A	86	279	20	60	3	0	0	20	37	20	2	1	.215	.307	.226	.533	57	-13	22	2.51	-2	C-85	6	-1.1

YEAR TM-L	G	AB	R	H	2B	3B	HR	RBI	BB	SO	SB	CS	AVG	OBP	SLG	OPS	OPS+	BR/A	RC	RC/G	FR	G/POS	WS	TPW
1944 Chi-A	93	312	22	81	8	1	0	25	37	15	0	3	.260	.342	.292	.634	83	-6	32	3.53	-1	C-93	9	-0.2
1945 Chi-A★	150	458	50	114	12	0	0	47	65	37	6	3	.249	.342	.275	.617	82	-7	48	3.57	2	*C-150	15	0.5
1946 Chi-A	80	217	28	47	5	2	0	21	36	24	0	2	.217	.336	.258	.594	70	-7	21	3.15	6	C-79	8	0.3
1947 Chi-A	90	274	19	66	6	2	0	20	26	26	2	0	.241	.311	.277	.589	67	-11	24	3.01	-2	C-89	4	-0.9
1948 Chi-A	39	108	10	27	1	0	1	11	9	9	0	0	.250	.308	.287	.595	61	-6	10	3.31	-1	C-34	1	-0.5
1949 Cle-A	38	37	4	8	0	0	0	1	5	7	0	0	.216	.310	.216	.526	41	-3	3	2.73	1	C-38	1	-0.1
Total 12	1027	3169	326	788	75	14	2	297	402	263	19	21	.249	.335	.283	.619	71	-113	322	3.43	5	*C-1019	80	-4.9

• TRESH, Tom Thomas Michael Tresh b: 9/20/1937, Detroit, MI BB/TR, 6'1", 191 lbs. Deb: 9/3/1961 Career OF: 516-293-28

YEAR TM-L	G	AB	R	H	2B	3B	HR	RBI	BB	SO	SB	CS	AVG	OBP	SLG	OPS	OPS+	BR/A	RC	RC/G	FR	G/POS	WS	TPW
1961 NY-A	9	8	1	2	0	0	0	0	0	1	0	0	.250	.250	.250	.500	36	-1	0	.96	0	/S-3	0	0.0
1962*NY-A★	157	622	94	178	26	5	20	93	67	74	4	8	.286	.363	.441	.803	119	14	103	5.91	-10	*S-111,O-43(43-0-0)	25	1.2
1963*NY-A★	145	520	91	140	28	5	25	71	83	79	3	3	.269	.374	.487	.861	140	29	100	6.86	-2	*O-144(46-101-0)	**29**	2.2
1964*NY-A	153	533	75	131	25	5	16	73	73	110	13	0	.246	.344	.402	.746	105	8	78	5.03	-1	*O-146(106-69-6)	20	0.0
1965 NY-A	156	602	94	168	29	6	26	74	59	92	5	2	.279	.348	.477	.825	133	25	101	6.08	0	*O-154(100-105-18)	25	2.0
1966 NY-A	151	537	76	125	12	4	27	68	86	89	5	4	.233	.345	.421	.766	123	18	81	5.06	21	O-84(69-18-0),3-64	22	3.7
1967 NY-A	130	448	45	98	23	3	14	53	50	86	1	0	.219	.303	.377	.680	104	3	51	3.77	0	*O-118(118-0-0)	13	-0.5
1968 NY-A	152	507	60	99	18	3	11	52	76	97	10	5	.195	.305	.308	.613	89	-5	51	3.25	-8	*S-119,O-27(27-0-0)	15	-0.4
1969 NY-A	45	143	13	26	5	2	1	9	17	23	2	1	.182	.269	.266	.534	52	-9	11	2.41	-1	S-41	2	-0.6
Det-A	94	331	46	74	13	1	13	37	39	47	2	2	.224	.309	.387	.696	90	-5	41	4.09	-1	S-77,O-11(7-0-4)/3-1	9	0.1
Yr.	139	474	59	100	18	3	14	46	56	70	4	3	.211	.297	.350	.647	78	-15	52	3.57	-2	*S-118,O-11(7-0-4)/3-1	11	-0.4
Total 9	1192	4251	595	1041	179	34	153	530	550	698	45	25	.245	.337	.411	.748	112	78	618	4.97	-2	O-727,S-351/3-65	160	7.8

• TREVINO, Alex Alejandro (Castro) Trevino b: 8/26/1957, Monterrey, Mexico BR/TR, 5'10", 170 lbs. Deb: 9/11/1978 Career OF: 4-0-2

YEAR TM-L	G	AB	R	H	2B	3B	HR	RBI	BB	SO	SB	CS	AVG	OBP	SLG	OPS	OPS+	BR/A	RC	RC/G	FR	G/POS	WS	TPW
1978 NY-N	6	12	3	3	0	0	0	0	1	2	0	0	.250	.308	.250	.558	60	-1	1	2.03	1	/C-5,3-1	0	0.0
1979 NY-N	79	207	24	56	11	1	0	20	20	27	2	2	.271	.338	.333	.671	87	-4	22	3.64	5	C-36,3-27/2-8	5	0.3
1980 NY-N	106	355	26	91	11	2	0	37	13	41	0	3	.256	.285	.299	.583	65	-19	27	2.59	2	C-86,3-14/2-1	5	-1.4
1981 NY-N	56	149	17	39	2	0	0	10	13	19	3	0	.262	.325	.275	.600	73	-4	14	3.27	-4	C-45/2-4,O-2(2-0-1),3-1	2	-0.6
1982 Cin-N	120	355	24	89	10	3	1	33	34	34	3	1	.251	.321	.304	.626	74	-11	33	3.04	-2	*C-116/3-2	5	-0.8
1983 Cin-N	74	167	14	36	8	1	1	13	17	20	0	0	.216	.288	.293	.581	59	-9	14	2.81	-1	C-63/3-4,2-1	4	-0.7
1984 Cin-N	6	6	0	1	0	0	0	0	0	2	0	0	.167	.167	.167	.333	-6	-1	0	.90	-1	/C-4	0	-0.2
Atl-N	79	266	36	65	16	0	3	28	16	27	5	2	.244	.290	.338	.628	71	-11	26	3.33	4	C-79	8	-0.3
Yr.	85	272	36	66	16	0	3	28	16	29	5	2	.243	.287	.335	.622	69	-12	26	3.27	4	C-83	8	-0.4
1985 SF-N	57	157	17	34	10	1	6	19	20	24	0	0	.217	.305	.408	.713	103	0	19	3.99	-3	C-55/3-1	4	-0.1
1986 LA-N	89	202	31	53	13	0	4	26	27	35	0	0	.262	.352	.386	.738	111	4	28	4.75	2	C-63/1-1	7	0.8
1987 LA-N	72	144	16	32	7	1	3	16	6	28	1	0	.222	.273	.347	.620	65	-8	12	2.69	1	C-45/O-2(1-0-1),3-1	2	-0.5
1988 Hou-N	78	193	19	48	17	0	2	13	24	29	5	2	.249	.341	.368	.709	108	3	24	4.04	-2	C-74/O-1	5	0.4
1989 Hou-N	59	131	15	38	7	1	2	16	7	18	0	0	.290	.331	.405	.736	113	2	17	4.72	-1	C-32/1-2,3-2	4	0.2
1990 Hou-N	42	69	3	13	3	0	1	10	6	11	0	1	.188	.273	.275	.548	53	-5	5	2.19	0	C-30/1-1	1	-0.4
NY-N	9	10	0	3	1	0	0	2	1	0	0	0	.300	.364	.400	.764	110	0	2	5.38	-1	/C-7	0	-0.1
Cin-N	7	7	0	3	1	0	0	1	0	0	0	0	.429	.500	.571	1.071	186	1	2	14.38	0	/C-2	1	0.1
Yr.	58	86	3	19	5	0	1	13	7	11	0	1	.221	.302	.314	.616	70	-4	9	3.20	-1	C-39/1-1	2	-0.4
Total 13	939	2430	245	604	117	10	23	244	205	317	19	11	.249	.312	.333	.645	81	-63	247	3.39	-1	C-742/3-53,2-14,O-5,1-4	53	-3.2

• TREVINO, Bobby Carlos (Castro) Trevino b: 8/15/1943, Monterrey, Mexico BR/TR, 6'2", 185 lbs. Deb: 5/22/1968

YEAR TM-L	G	AB	R	H	2B	3B	HR	RBI	BB	SO	SB	CS	AVG	OBP	SLG	OPS	OPS+	BR/A	RC	RC/G	FR	G/POS	WS	TPW
1968 Cal-A	17	40	1	9	1	0	0	1	2	9	0	1	.225	.262	.250	.512	58	-3	3	2.11	0	O-11(1-7-5)	0	-0.4

• TRIANDOS, Gus Gus Triandos b: 7/30/1930, San Francisco, CA BR/TR, 6'3", 215 lbs. Deb: 8/13/1953

YEAR TM-L	G	AB	R	H	2B	3B	HR	RBI	BB	SO	SB	CS	AVG	OBP	SLG	OPS	OPS+	BR/A	RC	RC/G	FR	G/POS	WS	TPW
1953 NY-A	18	51	5	8	2	0	1	6	3	9	0	0	.157	.204	.255	.459	24	-6	3	1.79	-1	1-12/C-5	0	-0.7
1954 NY-A	2	1	0	0	0	0	0	0	0	1	0	0	.000	.000	.000	.000	-104	-0	0	.00	0	/C-1	0	-0.1
1955 Bal-A	140	481	47	133	17	3	12	65	40	55	0	0	.277	.335	.399	.734	104	1	64	4.78	2	*1-103,C-36/3-1	14	0.0
1956 Bal-A	131	452	47	126	18	1	21	88	48	73	0	0	.279	.351	.462	.813	122	13	68	5.22	11	C-89,1-52	19	2.5
1957 Bal-A★	129	418	44	106	21	1	19	72	38	73	0	0	.254	.320	.445	.765	114	7	58	4.68	1	*C-120	14	1.4
1958 Bal-A★	137	474	59	116	10	0	30	79	60	65	1	0	.245	.331	.456	.787	120	13	67	4.67	2	*C-132	18	2.3
1959 Bal-A★	126	393	43	85	7	1	25	73	65	56	0	0	.216	.332	.430	.762	110	6	57	4.70	0	*C-125	13	1.2
1960 Bal-A	109	364	36	98	18	0	12	54	41	62	0	0	.269	.345	.418	.762	106	3	52	4.91	-2	*C-105	13	0.6
1961 Bal-A	115	397	35	97	21	0	17	63	44	60	0	0	.244	.321	.426	.747	100	-1	52	4.47	0	*C-114	14	0.5
1962 Bal-A	66	207	20	33	7	0	6	23	29	43	0	0	.159	.263	.280	.543	48	-15	15	2.31	-2	C-63	2	-1.4
1963 Det-A	106	327	28	78	13	0	14	41	32	67	0	0	.239	.318	.407	.725	98	-1	41	4.24	-2	C-90	11	0.2
1964 Phi-N	73	188	17	47	9	0	8	33	26	41	0	0	.250	.344	.426	.770	117	5	27	4.75	-1	C-64/1-1	8	0.7
1965 Phi-N	30	82	3	14	2	0	0	4	9	17	0	0	.171	.253	.195	.448	29	-8	4	1.51	-1	C-28	1	-0.8
Hou-N	24	72	5	13	2	0	2	7	5	14	0	0	.181	.244	.292	.535	54	-4	5	2.18	-3	C-20	0	-0.6
Yr.	54	154	8	27	4	0	2	11	14	31	0	0	.175	.249	.240	.489	40	-12	9	1.82	-3	C-48	1	-1.4
Total 13	1206	3907	389	954	147	6	167	608	440	636	1	0	.244	.324	.413	.737	103	14	514	4.42	5	C-992,1-168/3-1	127	5.7

• TRILLO, Manny Jesus Manuel Marcano Trillo b: 12/25/1950, Caripito, Venezuela BR/TR, 6'1", 164 lbs. Deb: 6/28/1973

YEAR TM-L	G	AB	R	H	2B	3B	HR	RBI	BB	SO	SB	CS	AVG	OBP	SLG	OPS	OPS+	BR/A	RC	RC/G	FR	G/POS	WS	TPW
1973 Oak-A	17	12	0	3	2	0	0	3	0	4	0	0	.250	.250	.417	.667	90	-0	1	2.25	0	2-16	0	0.0
1974*Oak-A	21	33	3	5	0	0	0	2	2	8	0	0	.152	.222	.152	.374	10	-4	1	1.27	1	2-21	1	-0.2
1975 Chi-N	154	545	55	135	12	2	7	70	45	78	1	7	.248	.309	.316	.624	70	-25	53	3.18	-5	*2-153/S-1	11	-2.0
1976 Chi-N	158	582	42	139	24	3	4	59	53	70	17	6	.239	.306	.311	.617	69	-22	55	3.14	10	*2-156/S-1	14	-0.2
1977 Chi-N★	152	504	51	141	18	5	7	57	44	58	3	5	.280	.344	.377	.721	84	-12	62	4.23	5	*2-149	14	0.1
1978 Chi-N	152	552	53	144	17	5	4	55	50	67	0	7	.261	.325	.332	.656	75	-21	59	3.63	11	*2-149	15	-0.2
1979 Phi-N	118	431	40	112	22	1	6	42	20	59	4	7	.260	.299	.357	.656	76	-17	42	3.21	6	*2-118	8	-0.5
1980*Phi-N	141	531	68	155	25	9	7	43	32	46	8	3	.292	.336	.412	.748	102	1	70	4.69	16	*2-140	19	2.7
1981*Phi-N★	94	349	37	100	14	3	6	36	26	37	10	4	.287	.341	.395	.737	104	2	48	4.79	2	2-94	12	0.9
1982 Phi-N★	149	549	52	149	24	1	0	39	33	53	8	10	.271	.316	.319	.635	76	-20	52	3.25	0	*2-149	14	-1.2
1983 Cle-A★	88	320	33	87	13	1	1	29	21	46	1	3	.272	.317	.328	.645	75	-12	30	3.19	13	2-87	6	0.6
Mon-N	31	121	16	32	8	0	2	16	10	18	0	0	.264	.331	.380	.711	97	-1	16	4.50	3	2-31	4	0.4
1984 SF-N	98	401	45	102	21	1	4	36	25	55	0	0	.254	.303	.342	.645	84	-10	41	3.55	1	2-96/3-4	9	-0.4
1985 SF-N	125	451	36	101	16	2	3	25	40	44	2	0	.224	.289	.288	.577	65	-21	40	2.93	-1	*2-120/3-1	8	-1.7
1986 Chi-N	81	152	22	45	10	0	1	19	16	21	0	2	.296	.363	.382	.745	98	-1	21	5.00	-5	3-53,1-11/2-6	4	-0.7
1987 Chi-N	108	214	27	63	8	0	8	26	25	37	0	3	.294	.368	.444	.812	110	2	34	5.52	-6	1-47,3-35,2-10/S-6	5	-0.6
1988 Chi-N	76	164	15	41	5	0	1	14	8	32	2	0	.250	.285	.299	.584	65	-7	15	3.02	-1	1-24,3-17,2-13/S-7	2	-1.0
1989 Cin-N	17	39	3	8	0	0	0	0	2	9	0	0	.205	.262	.205	.467	34	-3	2	2.00	-2	2-10/1-3,S-1	0	-0.5
Total 17	1780	5950	598	1562	239	33	61	571	452	742	56	57	.263	.318	.345	.663	80	-170	641	3.66	49	*2-1518,3-110/1-85,S-16	146	-4.3

• TRIPLETT, Coaker Herman Coaker Triplett b: 12/18/1911, Boone, NC d: 1/30/1992, Boone, NC BR/TR, 5'11", 185 lbs. Deb: 4/19/1938 Career OF: 314-3-18

YEAR TM-L	G	AB	R	H	2B	3B	HR	RBI	BB	SO	SB	CS	AVG	OBP	SLG	OPS	OPS+	BR/A	RC	RC/G	FR	G/POS	WS	TPW
1938 Chi-N	12	36	4	9	2	1	0	2	0	1	0	....	.250	.250	.361	.611	64	-2	3	2.41	0	/O-9(6-2-1)	0	-0.2
1941 StL-N	76	185	29	53	6	3	3	21	18	27	0	....	.286	.350	.400	.750	104	1	25	4.85	1	O-46(38-0-8)	5	0.0
1942 StL-N	64	154	18	42	7	4	1	23	17	15	1	....	.273	.345	.390	.735	107	1	20	4.69	1	O-46(45-0-1)	5	0.1
1943 StL-N	9	25	1	2	0	0	1	4	1	6	0	....	.080	.115	.200	.315	-9	-4	0	.46	0	/O-6(2-0-4)	0	-0.5
Phi-N	105	360	45	98	16	4	14	52	28	28	2	....	.272	.325	.456	.780	129	11	52	5.13	-1	O-90(90-0-0)	13	0.5
Yr.	114	385	46	100	16	4	15	56	29	34	2	....	.260	.312	.439	.751	121	7	52	4.75	-2	O-96(92-0-4)	13	0.0
1944 Phi-N	84	184	15	43	5	1	1	25	19	10	1	....	.234	.305	.288	.593	70	-7	15	2.72	0	O-44(41-1-2)	1	-1.0
1945 Phi-N	120	363	36	87	11	1	7	46	40	27	6	....	.240	.315	.333	.648	83	-8	39	3.73	-6	O-92(92-0-2)	6	-2.0
Total 6	470	1307	148	334	47	14	27	173	123	114	10	....	.256	.320	.375	.694	97	-8	155	4.11	-4	O-333	30	-3.1

• TROSKY, Hal Harold Arthur Trosky, Sr. b: 11/11/1912, Norway, IA d: 6/18/1979, Cedar Rapids, IA BL/TR, 6'2", 207 lbs. Deb: 9/11/1933

YEAR TM-L	G	AB	R	H	2B	3B	HR	RBI	BB	SO	SB	CS	AVG	OBP	SLG	OPS	OPS+	BR/A	RC	RC/G	FR	G/POS	WS	TPW
1933 Cle-A	11	44	6	13	1	2	1	8	2	12	0	0	.295	.340	.477	.818	110	0	7	6.08	0	1-11	1	-0.1
1934 Cle-A	154	625	117	206	45	9	35	142	58	49	2	2	.330	.388	.598	.987	149	41	145	9.10	0	*1-154	28	2.5
1935 Cle-A	154	632	84	171	33	7	26	113	46	60	1	2	.271	.321	.468	.789	100	-4	94	5.39	1	*1-153	15	-1.6

YEAR TM-L	G	AB	R	H	2B	3B	HR	RBI	BB	SO	SB	CS	AVG	OBP	SLG	OPS	OPS+	BR/A	RC	RC/G	FR	G/POS	WS	TPW
1936 Cle-A	151	629	124	216	45	9	42	**162**	36	58	6	5	.343	.382	.644	1.026	148	40	150	9.45	-4	*1-151/2-1	21	1.9
1937 Cle-A	153	601	104	179	36	9	32	128	65	60	3	1	.298	.367	.547	.915	127	22	122	7.60	-5	*1-152	24	0.3
1938 Cle-A	150	554	106	185	40	9	19	110	67	40	5	1	.334	.407	.542	.948	138	33	125	8.83	-0	*1-148	25	1.7
1939 Cle-A	122	448	89	150	31	4	25	104	52	28	2	3	.335	.405	.589	.994	157	36	108	9.18	13	*1-118	23	3.5
1940 Cle-A	140	522	85	154	39	4	25	93	79	45	1	2	.295	.392	.529	.920	140	32	116	8.28	-6	*1-139	27	1.2
1941 Cle-A	89	310	43	91	17	0	11	51	44	21	1	2	.294	.383	.455	.838	127	12	57	6.72	-4	1-85	11	0.1
1944 Chi-A	135	497	55	120	32	2	10	70	62	30	3	2	.241	.327	.374	.701	101	1	62	4.24	-5	*1-130	14	-1.1
1946 Chi-A	88	299	22	76	12	3	2	31	34	37	4	3	.254	.330	.334	.665	89	-4	33	3.72	-5	1-80	6	-1.2
Total 11	1347	5161	835	1561	331	58	228	1012	545	440	28	23	.302	.371	.522	.892	129	210	1018	7.36	-15	*1-1321/2-1	195	7.1
• TROST, Mike	Michael J. Trost b: 1866, Philadelphia, PA d: 3/24/1901, Philadelphia, PA TR, 6'.5", 180 lbs. Deb: 8/21/1890																							
1890 StL-a	17	51	10	13	2	0	1	7	6	....	4	....	.255	.345	.353	.698	92	-1	8	5.42	-1	C-13/O-4(0-3-1)	2	-0.1
1895 Lou-N	3	12	1	1	0	0	0	1	0	1	1	....	.083	.083	.083	.167	-61	-3	0	.42	0	/1-3	0	-0.3
Total 2	20	63	11	14	2	0	1	8	6	1	5	....	.222	.300	.302	.602	66	-4	8	4.30	-2	/C-13,O-4,1-3	2	-0.4
• TROTT, Sam	Samuel W. Trott b: 3/1859, MD d: 6/5/1925, Catonsville, MD BL/TL, 5'9", 190 lbs. Deb: 5/29/1880 M Career OF: 8-5-14																							
1880 Bos-N	39	125	14	26	4	1	0	9	3	5	....	....	.208	.227	.256	.483	65	-4	7	2.06	5	C-36/O-4(1-3-0)	3	0.2
1881 Det-N	6	25	3	5	2	1	0	2	1	3	....	....	.200	.231	.360	.591	79	-1	2	2.87	-1	/C-6	1	-0.1
1882 Det-N	32	129	11	31	7	1	0	12	0	13	....	....	.240	.240	.310	.550	75	-4	10	2.76	4	C-23/1-3,2-3,S-3,O-2(2-0-0),3	3	0.2
1883 Det-N	75	295	27	72	14	1	0	29	10	23	....	....	.244	.269	.298	.567	76	-8	24	2.99	-14	2-42,C-34/O-6(0-1-5),1-1	5	-1.5
1884 Bal-a	71	284	36	73	17	9	3	0	4	....	....	....	.257	.272	.412	.684	116	3	33	4.26	-2	C-60/2-6,O-5(1-1-3)	12	0.6
1885 Bal-a	21	88	12	24	2	2	0	12	5	....	....	....	.273	.312	.341	.653	108	1	10	4.05	-3	C-17/O-4(0-0-4),2-2,S-1	2	-0.1
1887 Bal-a	85	327	44	104	16	3	0	37	27	....	8	....	.318	.322	.330	.652	87	-4	35	4.28	-7	C-69,2-11/O-3(3-0-0),1-2,S	9	-0.4
1888 Bal-a	31	108	19	30	11	4	0	22	4	....	1	....	.278	.304	.454	.757	145	5	16	5.39	-6	C-27/O-3(1-0-2),1-1,2-1	4	0.1
Total 8	360	1381	166	365	73	22	3	123	54	44	9	....	.264	.280	.343	.623	93	-11	137	3.67	-23	C-272/2-65,O-27,1-7,S-5,3-1	39	-0.9
• TROUPPE, Quincy	Quincy Thomas Trouppe b: 12/25/1912, Dublin, GA d: 8/10/1993, Creve Coeur, MO BB/TR, 6'2.5", 225 lbs. Deb: 4/30/1952																							
1952 Cle-A	6	10	1	1	0	0	0	0	1	3	0	0	.100	.182	.100	.282	-22	-2	0	.32	0	/C-6	0	-0.1
• TROY, Dasher	John Joseph Troy b: 5/8/1856, New York, NY d: 3/30/1938, Ozone Park, NY BR/TR, 5'5", 154 lbs. Deb: 8/23/1881																							
1881 Det-N	11	44	2	15	3	0	0	4	3	8	....	....	.341	.383	.409	.792	143	2	7	6.58	-1	/3-7,2-4	2	0.1
1882 Det-N	40	152	22	37	7	2	0	14	5	10	....	....	.243	.268	.316	.583	86	-2	13	3.15	-16	2-31,S-11	3	-1.5
Pro-N	4	17	1	4	0	0	0	1	0	1	....	....	.235	.235	.235	.471	52	-1	1	2.04	-1	/S-4	0	-0.2
Yr.	44	169	23	41	7	2	0	15	5	11	....	....	.243	.264	.308	.572	83	-3	14	3.03	-17	2-31,S-15	3	-1.7
1883 NY-N	85	316	37	68	7	5	0	20	9	33	....	....	.215	.237	.269	.506	54	-17	21	2.29	-5	*2-73,S-12	3	-1.7
1884*NY-a	107	421	80	111	22	10	2	0	19	....	....	....	.264	.300	.378	.678	123	10	49	4.34	-13	*2-107	14	0.1
1885 NY-a	45	177	24	39	3	3	2	12	5	....	....	....	.220	.258	.305	.563	84	-3	14	2.79	-17	2-42/O-2(0-0-2),S-1	3	-1.6
Total 5	292	1127	166	274	42	20	4	51	41	52	....	....	.243	.274	.327	.601	92	-10	105	3.37	-53	2-257/S-28,3-7,O-2	25	-4.7
• TRUAX, Fred	Frederick W. Truax b: 1868, d: 12/18/1899, Omaha, NE Deb: 8/18/1890																							
1890 Pit-N	1	3	0	1	0	0	0	1	1	1	0	....	.333	.500	.333	.833	163	0	1	6.79	-0	/O-1	0	0.0
• TRUBY, Chris	Christopher John Truby b: 12/9/1973, Palm Springs, CA BR/TR, 6'2", 190 lbs. Deb: 6/16/2000																							
2000 Hou-N	78	258	28	67	15	4	11	59	10	56	2	1	.260	.300	.477	.777	87	-7	36	4.83	1	3-74	7	-0.5
2001*Hou-N	48	136	11	28	6	1	8	23	13	38	1	2	.206	.280	.441	.721	78	-6	17	3.97	-5	3-35/1-1	3	-1.0
2002 Mon-N	35	105	12	27	5	2	2	7	5	27	1	1	.257	.297	.400	.697	79	-4	12	3.91	-6	*O-122(1-0-0),3-31/1-2	1	-0.9
Det-A	89	277	23	55	13	2	2	15	5	71	1	1	.199	.218	.282	.500	33	-27	16	1.85	7	3-89	2	-1.8
2003 TB-A	13	43	4	12	3	0	0	3	5	13	0	0	.279	.354	.349	.703	88	-1	5	4.49	4	3-13	1	0.3
Total 4	263	819	78	189	42	9	23	107	38	205	5	5	.231	.273	.388	.661	67	-44	86	3.50	1	3-242,O-122/1-3	14	-3.8
• TRUBY, Harry	Harry Garvin "Bird Eye" Truby b: 5/12/1870, Ironton, OH d: 3/21/1953, Ironton, OH TR, 5'11", 185 lbs. Deb: 8/21/1895 U																							
1895 Chi-N	33	119	17	40	3	0	0	16	10	7	7	....	.336	.402	.361	.763	92	-1	21	6.92	-2	2-33	4	-0.1
1896 Chi-N	29	109	13	28	2	2	2	31	6	5	4	....	.257	.314	.367	.681	76	-4	14	4.63	0	2-28	2	-0.2
Pit-N	8	32	1	5	0	0	0	3	2	4	1	....	.156	.206	.156	.362	-4	-5	1	1.31	-1	/2-8	0	-0.4
Yr.	37	141	14	33	2	2	2	34	8	9	5	....	.234	.289	.319	.609	58	-9	16	3.77	-1	2-36	2	-0.7
Total 2	70	260	31	73	5	2	2	50	18	16	12	....	.281	.342	.338	.680	74	-10	37	5.12	-2	/2-69	6	-0.8
• TRUESDALE, Frank	Frank Day Truesdale b: 3/31/1884, St. Louis, MO d: 8/27/1943, Albuquerque, NM BB/TR, 5'8", 145 lbs. Deb: 4/27/1910																							
1910 StL-A	123	415	39	91	7	2	1	25	48	....	29	....	.219	.303	.253	.556	79	-8	40	3.15	-11	*2-122	9	-2.0
1911 StL-A	1	0	1	0	0	0	0	0	0	....	0	....	....	....	....	....	-104	0	0	....	0	....	0	0.0
1914 NY-A	77	217	22	46	4	0	0	13	39	35	11	11	.212	.340	.230	.570	72	-7	18	2.62	1	2-67/3-4	5	-0.6
1918 Bos-A	15	36	6	10	1	0	0	2	4	5	1	....	.278	.350	.306	.656	99	0	4	3.90	-2	2-10	1	-0.1
Total 4	216	668	68	147	12	2	1	40	91	40	41	11	.220	.318	.249	.567	78	-15	63	3.01	-12	2-199/3-4	15	-2.8
• TRUMBULL, Ed	Edward J. Trumbull b: 11/3/1860, Chicopee, MA d: 1/14/1937, Kingston, PA Deb: 5/10/1884 ♦																							
1884 Was-a	25	86	5	10	2	0	0	0	2	....	....	....	.116	.136	.140	.276	-11	-8	2	.61	-1	O-15(2-8-5),P-10	0	-1.7
• TUBBS, Greg	Gregory Alan Tubbs b: 8/31/1962, Smithville, TN BR/TR, 5'9", 185 lbs. Deb: 8/1/1993																							
1993 Cin-N	35	59	10	11	0	0	1	2	14	10	3	1	.186	.351	.237	.589	61	-2	7	3.62	-1	O-21(11-14-2)	1	-0.3
• TUCKER, Eddie	Eddie Jack "Scooter" Tucker b: 11/18/1966, Greenville, MS BR/TR, 6'2", 205 lbs. Deb: 6/14/1992																							
1992 Hou-N	20	50	5	6	1	0	0	3	3	13	1	1	.120	.200	.140	.340	-2	-7	1	.75	-1	C-19	0	-0.7
1993 Hou-N	9	26	1	5	1	0	0	3	2	3	0	0	.192	.250	.231	.481	31	-3	2	2.10	0	/C-8	0	-0.2
1995 Hou-N	5	7	1	2	0	0	1	1	0	0	0	0	.286	.286	.714	1.000	164	1	1	7.71	0	/C-3	0	0.1
Cle-A	17	20	2	0	0	0	0	0	5	4	0	0	.000	.231	.000	.231	-33	-4	0	.59	0	C-17	0	-0.4
Total 3	51	103	9	13	2	0	1	7	10	20	1	1	.126	.224	.175	.399	8	-13	5	1.38	-1	/C-47	0	-1.2
• TUCKER, Michael	Michael Anthony Tucker b: 6/25/1971, South Boston, VA BL/TR, 6'2", 185 lbs. Deb: 4/26/1995 Career OF: 281-162-611																							
1995 KC-A	62	177	23	46	10	0	4	17	18	51	2	3	.260	.332	.384	.716	84	-5	22	4.31	1	O-36(30-1-5),D-22	3	-0.7
1996 KC-A	108	339	55	88	18	4	12	53	40	69	10	4	.260	.350	.442	.792	99	-0	54	5.41	2	/1-9,D-5,O-1	9	-0.3
1997*Atl-N	138	499	80	141	25	7	14	56	44	116	12	7	.283	.348	.445	.793	104	2	78	5.58	1	O-98(53-0-102)	15	-0.3
1998*Atl-N	130	414	54	101	27	3	13	46	49	112	8	3	.244	.328	.418	.746	94	-3	59	4.93	4	*O-129(0-0-118)	11	-0.4
1999 Cin-N	133	296	55	75	8	5	11	44	37	81	11	4	.253	.342	.426	.768	90	-4	45	5.16	4	*O-118(0-13-107)	10	-0.3
2000 Cin-N	148	270	55	72	13	4	15	36	44	64	13	6	.267	.383	.511	.894	121	9	55	6.95	-1	*O-114(41-28-67)/2-1	7	0.6
2001 Cin-N	86	231	31	56	10	1	7	30	23	55	12	5	.242	.314	.385	.699	76	-8	29	3.97	2	*O-120(37-32-19)	4	-0.7
Chi-N	63	205	31	54	9	7	5	31	23	47	4	3	.263	.341	.449	.789	107	2	31	5.11	0	O-70(38-44-6)/1-4	6	0.1
Yr.	149	436	62	110	19	8	12	61	46	102	16	8	.252	.326	.415	.742	91	-6	60	4.49	2	*O-190(75-76-25)/1-4	10	-0.6
2002 KC-A	144	475	65	118	27	6	12	56	56	105	23	9	.248	.331	.406	.738	85	-9	67	4.79	4	O-57(33-14-67),D-23/1-5,2	8	-1.1
2003 KC-A	104	389	61	102	20	5	13	55	39	88	8	10	.262	.333	.440	.772	89	-9	54	4.66	-3	O-85(21-30-47),D-15	10	-1.5
Total 9	1116	3295	510	853	167	42	106	424	373	788	103	54	.259	.340	.432	.772	95	-26	493	5.11	15	O-828/D-65,1-18,2-3	83	-4.6
• TUCKER, Ollie	Oliver Dinwiddie Tucker b: 1/27/1902, Radiant, VA d: 7/13/1940, Radiant, VA BL/TR, 5'11", 180 lbs. Deb: 4/17/1927 Career OF: 0-0-19																							
1927 Was-A	20	24	1	5	2	0	0	8	4	2	0	0	.208	.321	.292	.613	61	-1	3	3.21	0	/O-5(0-0-5)	0	-0.2
1928 Cle-A	14	47	5	6	0	0	1	2	7	3	0	2	.128	.255	.191	.446	19	-6	2	1.44	1	O-14(0-0-14)	0	-0.6
Total 2	34	71	6	11	2	0	1	10	11	5	0	2	.155	.277	.225	.502	34	-8	5	2.03	1	/O-19	0	-0.8
• TUCKER, Thurman	Thurman Lowell "Joe E." Tucker b: 9/26/1917, Gordon, TX d: 5/7/1993, Oklahoma City, OK BL/TR, 5'10.5", 170 lbs. Deb: 4/14/1942 Career OF: 19-552-4																							
1942 Chi-A	7	24	2	3	0	1	0	1	0	4	0	0	.125	.125	.208	.333	-7	-3	1	.82	0	/O-5(0-5-0)	0	-0.4
1943 Chi-A	139	528	81	124	15	6	3	39	79	72	29	17	.235	.336	.303	.639	87	-6	60	3.75	9	*O-132(0-132-0)	16	0.0
1944 Chi-A★	124	446	59	128	15	6	2	46	57	40	13	12	.287	.368	.361	.729	110	6	63	5.06	13	*O-120(0-120-0)	20	1.6

YEAR TM-L	G	AB	R	H	2B	3B	HR	RBI	BB	SO	SB	CS	AVG	OBP	SLG	OPS	OPS+	BR/A	RC	RC/G	FR	G/POS	WS	TPW
1946 Chi-A	121	438	62	126	20	3	1	36	54	45	9	10	.288	.367	.354	.721	106	3	61	5.04	3	*0-110(0-110-0)	16	0.4
1947 Chi-A	89	254	28	60	9	4	1	17	38	25	10	4	.236	.336	.315	.651	85	-4	31	4.25	1	0-65(0-65-0)	7	-0.4
1948*Cle-A	83	242	52	63	13	2	1	19	31	17	11	2	.260	.347	.343	.690	86	-3	33	4.78	3	0-66(0-66-0)	8	-0.1
1949 Cle-A	80	197	28	48	5	2	0	14	18	19	4	2	.244	.307	.289	.596	59	-12	19	3.22	2	0-42(4-38-0)	3	-1.1
1950 Cle-A	57	101	13	18	2	0	1	7	14	14	1	0	.178	.284	.228	.512	34	-10	8	2.59	-1	0-34(15-16-4)	1	-1.1
1951 Cle-A	1	1	0	0	0	0	0	0	0	1	0	0	.000	.000	.000	.000	-106	-0	0	.00	0	....	0	0.0
Total 9	701	2231	325	570	79	24	9	179	291	237	77	47	.255	.342	.325	.667	89	-28	275	4.27	30	0-574	71	-1.2

• TUCKER, Tommy

Thomas Joseph "Foghorn" Tucker
b: 10/28/1863, Holyoke, MA d: 10/22/1935, Montague, MA BB/TR, 5'11", 165 lbs. Deb: 4/16/1887 Career OF: 2-12-6

YEAR TM-L	G	AB	R	H	2B	3B	HR	RBI	BB	SO	SB	CS	AVG	OBP	SLG	OPS	OPS+	BR/A	RC	RC/G	FR	G/POS	WS	TPW
1887 Bal-a	136	553	114	173	15	9	6	84	29	....	85	....	.313	.347	.372	.719	107	7	100	7.08	10	*1-136	16	0.5
1888 Bal-a	136	520	74	149	17	12	6	61	16	....	43	....	.287	.330	.400	.730	137	20	85	6.18	4	*1-129/0-7(2-0-5),P-1	20	1.2
1889 Bal-a	134	527	103	**196**	22	11	5	99	42	26	63	....	**.372**	**.450**	.484	**.934**	**169**	**51**	147	**11.75**	-1	*1-123,0-12(0-11-1)	**30**	3.3
1890 Bos-N	132	539	104	159	17	8	1	62	56	22	43	....	.295	.387	.362	.749	110	9	94	6.59	5	*1-132	17	0.2
1891 Bos-N	140	548	103	148	16	5	2	69	37	30	26	....	.270	.349	.328	.677	87	-9	74	4.97	-3	*1-140/P-1	12	-2.2
1892*Bos-N	149	542	85	153	15	7	1	62	45	35	22	....	.282	.365	.341	.707	104	4	78	5.38	-14	*1-149	17	-1.0
1893 Bos-N	121	486	83	138	13	2	7	91	27	31	8	....	.284	.347	.362	.709	82	-15	65	4.98	-7	*1-121	11	-1.8
1894 Bos-N	123	500	112	165	24	6	3	100	53	21	18	....	.330	.412	.420	.832	90	-8	96	7.48	-1	*1-123/0-1	13	-0.8
1895 Bos-N	126	465	87	115	19	6	3	73	63	29	15	....	.247	.360	.333	.693	75	-16	64	4.79	2	*1-125	9	-1.3
1896 Bos-N	122	474	74	144	27	5	2	72	30	29	6	....	.304	.363	.395	.757	94	-5	73	5.71	-4	*1-122	10	-0.9
1897 Bos-N	4	14	0	3	2	0	0	4	2	....	0	....	.214	.313	.357	.670	72	-1	2	3.86	0	/1-4	0	0.0
Was-N	93	352	52	119	18	5	5	61	27	....	18	....	.338	.403	.460	.863	128	15	75	8.38	-11	*1-93	11	0.3
Yr.	97	366	52	122	20	5	5	65	29	....	18	....	.333	.399	.456	.855	126	14	76	8.18	-10	*1-97	11	0.3
1898 Bro-N	73	283	35	79	9	4	1	34	12	....	1	....	.279	.325	.350	.674	93	-3	34	4.30	11	1-73	6	0.7
StL-N	72	252	18	60	7	2	0	20	18	....	1	....	.238	.319	.282	.601	71	-9	24	3.26	4	1-72	2	-0.5
Yr.	145	535	53	139	16	6	1	54	30	....	2	....	.260	.322	.318	.640	83	-12	58	3.80	15	*1-145	8	0.2
1899 Cle-N	127	456	40	110	19	3	0	40	24	....	3	....	.241	.297	.296	.593	68	-20	43	3.22	-2	*1-127	2	-2.0
Total 13	1688	6511	1084	1911	240	85	42	932	481	223	352	....	.294	.364	.373	.737	103	20	1052	6.05	-9	*1-1669/0-20,P-2	176	-4.5

• TURANG, Brian

Brian Craig Turang b: 6/14/1967, Long Beach, CA BR/TR, 5'10", 170 lbs. Deb: 8/13/1993 Career OF: 46-26-1

YEAR TM-L	G	AB	R	H	2B	3B	HR	RBI	BB	SO	SB	CS	AVG	OBP	SLG	OPS	OPS+	BR/A	RC	RC/G	FR	G/POS	WS	TPW
1993 Sea-A	40	140	22	35	11	1	0	7	17	20	6	2	.250	.340	.343	.682	83	-2	17	4.21	-2	0-38(26-14-1)/3-2,2-1,D-1	3	-0.5
1994 Sea-A	38	112	9	21	5	1	1	8	7	25	3	1	.188	.242	.277	.518	33	-11	8	2.34	-1	0-30(20-12-0)/2-5,D-4	1	-1.2
Total 2	78	252	31	56	16	2	1	15	24	45	9	3	.222	.297	.313	.611	61	-14	26	3.35	-3	/0-68,2-6,D-5,3-2	4	-1.7

• TURBIDY, Jerry

Jeremiah Turbidy b: 7/4/1852, Dudley, MA d: 9/5/1920, Webster, MA BR, 5'8", 165 lbs. Deb: 7/27/1884

YEAR TM-L	G	AB	R	H	2B	3B	HR	RBI	BB	SO	SB	CS	AVG	OBP	SLG	OPS	OPS+	BR/A	RC	RC/G	FR	G/POS	WS	TPW
1884 KC-U	13	49	5	11	4	0	0	....	3	....	....	....	.224	.269	.306	.575	108	1	4	3.05	5	S-13	1	0.5

• TURCHIN, Eddie

Edward Lawrence "Smiley" Turchin b: 2/10/1917, New York, NY d: 2/8/1982, Brookhaven, NY BR/TR, 5'10", 165 lbs. Deb: 5/9/1943

YEAR TM-L	G	AB	R	H	2B	3B	HR	RBI	BB	SO	SB	CS	AVG	OBP	SLG	OPS	OPS+	BR/A	RC	RC/G	FR	G/POS	WS	TPW
1943 Cle-A	11	13	4	3	0	0	0	1	3	1	0	0	.231	.375	.231	.606	84	0	1	2.96	0	/3-4,S-2	0	0.0

• TURGEON, Pete

Eugene Joseph Turgeon b: 1/3/1897, Minneapolis, MN d: 1/24/1977, Wichita Falls, TX BR/TR, 5'6", 145 lbs. Deb: 9/20/1923

YEAR TM-L	G	AB	R	H	2B	3B	HR	RBI	BB	SO	SB	CS	AVG	OBP	SLG	OPS	OPS+	BR/A	RC	RC/G	FR	G/POS	WS	TPW
1923 Chi-N	3	6	1	1	0	0	0	0	0	0	0	0	.167	.167	.167	.333	-12	-1	0	.85	0	/S-2	0	-0.1

• TURNER, Chris

Christopher Wan Turner b: 3/23/1969, Bowling Green, KY BR/TR, 6'2", 190 lbs. Deb: 8/27/1993 Career OF: 1-0-1

YEAR TM-L	G	AB	R	H	2B	3B	HR	RBI	BB	SO	SB	CS	AVG	OBP	SLG	OPS	OPS+	BR/A	RC	RC/G	FR	G/POS	WS	TPW
1993 Cal-A	25	75	9	21	5	0	1	13	9	16	1	1	.280	.365	.387	.751	99	-0	11	5.21	0	C-25	3	0.2
1994 Cal-A	58	149	23	36	7	1	1	12	10	29	3	0	.242	.294	.322	.616	58	-9	15	3.41	4	C-57	2	-0.2
1995 Cal-A	5	10	0	1	0	0	0	1	0	3	0	0	.100	.100	.100	.200	-48	-2	0	.30	0	/C-4,D-1	0	-0.2
1996 Cal-A	4	3	1	1	0	0	0	1	1	0	0	0	.333	.500	.333	.833	119	0	1	6.41	0	*0-108(1-0-0)/C-3	0	0.0
1997 Ana-A	13	23	4	6	1	1	1	2	5	8	0	0	.261	.393	.522	.915	134	1	5	7.86	0	/C-8,1-2,D-1,0-1	1	0.1
1998 KC-A	4	9	0	0	0	0	0	0	0	4	0	0	.000	.100	.000	.100	-69	-2	0	.00	0	/C-4	0	-0.2
1999 Cle-A	12	21	3	4	0	0	0	0	1	8	1	0	.190	.227	.190	.418	8	-3	1	1.73	-1	C-12	0	-0.3
2000 NY-A	37	89	9	21	3	0	1	7	10	21	0	1	.236	.320	.303	.623	60	-6	9	3.25	-2	C-36/1-1	1	-0.6
Total 8	158	379	49	90	16	2	4	36	36	89	5	2	.237	.310	.322	.632	64	-20	42	3.70	1	C-149,0-109/1-3,D-2	7	-1.1

• TURNER, Earl

Earl Edwin Turner b: 5/6/1923, Pittsfield, MA d: 10/20/1999, Lee, MA BR/TR, 5'9", 170 lbs. Deb: 9/25/1948

YEAR TM-L	G	AB	R	H	2B	3B	HR	RBI	BB	SO	SB	CS	AVG	OBP	SLG	OPS	OPS+	BR/A	RC	RC/G	FR	G/POS	WS	TPW
1948 Pit-N	2	1	0	0	0	0	0	0	0	0	0	....	.000	.000	.000	.000	-98	-0	0	.00	0	/C-1	0	-0.1
1950 Pit-N	40	74	10	18	0	0	3	5	4	13	1	....	.243	.282	.365	.647	66	-4	7	3.13	0	C-34	1	-0.2
Total 2	42	75	10	18	0	0	3	5	4	13	1	....	.240	.278	.360	.638	64	-4	7	3.07	0	/C-35	1	-0.3

• TURNER, Jerry

John Webber Turner b: 1/17/1954, Texarkana, AR BL/TL, 5'9", 180 lbs. Deb: 9/2/1974 Career OF: 305-21-76

YEAR TM-L	G	AB	R	H	2B	3B	HR	RBI	BB	SO	SB	CS	AVG	OBP	SLG	OPS	OPS+	BR/A	RC	RC/G	FR	G/POS	WS	TPW
1974 SD-N	17	48	4	14	1	0	0	2	3	5	2	1	.292	.333	.313	.646	85	-1	5	4.07	1	0-13(13-0-0)	1	-0.1
1975 SD-N	11	22	1	6	0	0	0	0	2	1	0	0	.273	.333	.273	.606	74	-1	2	2.90	0	/0-4(4-0-0)	0	-0.1
1976 SD-N	105	281	41	75	16	5	5	37	32	38	12	6	.267	.342	.413	.755	123	8	41	4.97	1	0-74(74-0-0)	11	0.6
1977 SD-N	118	289	43	71	16	1	10	48	31	43	12	4	.246	.319	.412	.731	105	3	38	4.48	4	0-69(65-4-2)	9	0.4
1978 SD-N	106	225	28	63	9	1	8	37	21	32	6	4	.280	.349	.436	.785	128	7	34	5.32	0	0-58(28-17-24)	8	0.6
1979 SD-N	138	448	55	111	23	2	9	61	34	58	4	2	.248	.304	.368	.672	88	-9	50	3.84	3	*0-115(114-0-2)	9	-1.1
1980 SD-N	85	153	22	44	5	0	3	18	10	18	8	3	.288	.339	.379	.718	106	2	20	4.74	0	0-34(5-0-30)	4	0.0
1981 SD-N	33	31	5	7	0	0	2	6	4	3	0	1	.226	.314	.419	.734	115	0	4	3.58	0	/0-4(0-0-4)	0	0.0
Chi-A	10	12	1	2	0	0	0	2	1	2	0	0	.167	.231	.167	.397	16	-1	1	1.41	0	/0-1	0	-0.1
1982 Det-A	85	210	21	52	3	0	8	27	20	37	1	3	.248	.313	.376	.689	88	-5	25	4.04	-1	D-50,0-13(2-0-12)	3	-0.7
1983 SD-N	25	23	1	3	0	0	0	0	1	8	0	0	.130	.167	.130	.297	-17	-4	0	.48	0	/0-1	0	-0.4
Total 10	733	1742	222	448	73	9	45	238	159	245	45	24	.257	.322	.387	.709	102	0	220	4.34	7	0-386/D-50	45	-0.9

• TURNER, Shane

Shane Lee Turner b: 1/8/1963, Los Angeles, CA BL/TR, 5'10", 180 lbs. Deb: 8/19/1988

YEAR TM-L	G	AB	R	H	2B	3B	HR	RBI	BB	SO	SB	CS	AVG	OBP	SLG	OPS	OPS+	BR/A	RC	RC/G	FR	G/POS	WS	TPW
1988 Phi-N	18	35	1	6	0	0	0	1	5	9	0	0	.171	.275	.171	.446	30	-3	2	1.64	-1	/3-8,S-5	0	-0.4
1991 Bal-A	4	1	0	0	0	0	0	0	0	0	0	0	.000	.000	.000	.000	-104	-0	0	.00	0	/2-1,D-1	0	0.0
1992 Sea-A	34	74	8	20	5	0	0	5	9	15	2	1	.270	.349	.338	.687	93	-0	8	3.60	0	3-18,0-15(15-0-1)	1	-0.1
Total 3	56	110	9	26	5	0	0	6	14	24	2	1	.236	.323	.282	.604	72	-4	10	2.94	-1	/3-26,0-15,S-5,2-1,D-1	1	-0.5

• TURNER, Terry

Terrence Lamont "Cotton Top" Turner b: 2/28/1881, Sandy Lake, PA d: 7/18/1960, Cleveland, OH BR/TR, 5'8", 149 lbs. Deb: 8/25/1901 C

YEAR TM-L	G	AB	R	H	2B	3B	HR	RBI	BB	SO	SB	CS	AVG	OBP	SLG	OPS	OPS+	BR/A	RC	RC/G	FR	G/POS	WS	TPW
1901 Pit-N	2	7	0	3	0	0	0	1	0	....	0	....	.429	.429	.429	.857	145	0	1	8.73	1	/3-2	1	0.1
1904 Cle-A	111	404	41	95	9	6	1	45	11	....	5	....	.235	.255	.295	.550	74	-13	35	2.79	2	*S-111	8	-0.8
1905 Cle-A	155	586	49	155	16	14	4	72	14	....	17	....	.265	.289	.360	.649	104	-1	69	4.10	-20	*S-155	16	-1.7
1906 Cle-A	147	584	85	170	27	7	2	62	35	....	27	....	.291	.338	.372	.709	123	15	87	5.31	32	*S-147	28	5.7
1907 Cle-A	140	524	57	127	20	7	0	46	19	....	27	....	.242	.272	.307	.579	84	-11	54	3.47	-10	*S-139	17	-1.8
1908 Cle-A	60	201	21	48	11	1	0	19	15	....	18	....	.239	.298	.303	.602	95	-1	23	3.79	-3	0-36(0-2-34),S-17	6	-0.6
1909 Cle-A	53	208	25	52	7	4	0	16	14	....	14	....	.250	.304	.322	.626	94	-2	24	3.93	8	2-26,S-26	7	0.8
1910 Cle-A	150	574	71	132	14	6	0	33	53	....	31	....	.230	.301	.275	.576	79	-13	57	3.22	6	S-94,3-46/2-9	14	-0.2
1911 Cle-A	117	417	59	105	16	9	0	28	34	....	29	....	.252	.310	.333	.643	78	-13	52	4.10	1	3-94,2-14,S-10	11	-0.8
1912 Cle-A	103	370	54	114	14	4	0	33	31	....	19	....	.308	.363	.368	.731	106	3	57	5.41	5	*3-103	13	1.0
1913 Cle-A	120	388	60	96	13	4	0	44	55	35	13	....	.247	.348	.302	.650	88	-4	48	3.77	19	3-71,2-25,S-21	13	2.1
1914 Cle-A	121	428	43	105	14	9	1	33	44	36	17	13	.245	.319	.327	.646	91	-7	50	3.57	15	*3-104,2-17	11	1.3
1915 Cle-A	75	262	35	66	14	1	0	14	29	13	12	11	.252	.329	.313	.642	90	-5	29	3.47	-7	2-51,3-20	4	-1.1
1916 Cle-A	124	428	52	112	15	3	0	38	40	29	15	....	.262	.325	.311	.636	86	-7	52	3.93	2	3-77,2-42	13	-0.3
1917 Cle-A	69	180	16	37	7	0	0	15	14	19	4	....	.206	.263	.244	.507	51	-11	13	2.19	-1	3-40,2-23/S-1	2	-1.2
1918 Cle-A	74	233	24	58	7	2	0	23	22	15	6	....	.249	.316	.296	.613	77	-6	24	3.28	0	3-46,2-26/S-1	6	-0.5
1919 Phi-A	38	127	7	24	3	0	0	6	5	9	2	....	.189	.220	.213	.432	21	-14	6	1.52	0	S-19,2-17/3-1	1	-1.3
Total 17	1659	5921	699	1499	207	77	8	528	435	156	256	24	.253	.308	.318	.626	89	-89	681	3.78	51	S-741,3-604,2-250/0-36	171	0.7

• TURNER, Tom

Thomas Richard Turner b: 9/8/1916, Custer, OK d: 5/14/1986, Kennewick, WA BR/TR, 6'2", 195 lbs. Deb: 4/25/1940

YEAR TM-L	G	AB	R	H	2B	3B	HR	RBI	BB	SO	SB	CS	AVG	OBP	SLG	OPS	OPS+	BR/A	RC	RC/G	FR	G/POS	WS	TPW
1940 Chi-A	37	96	11	20	1	2	0	6	3	12	1	0	.208	.240	.260	.500	29	-10	6	2.06	-1	C-29	1	-0.9

YEAR TM-L	G	AB	R	H	2B	3B	HR	RBI	BB	SO	SB	CS	AVG	OBP	SLG	OPS	OPS+	BR/A	RC	RC/G	FR	G/POS	WS	TPW
1941 Chi-A	38	126	7	30	5	0	0	8	9	15	2	0	.238	.289	.278	.567	51	-8	10	2.85	2	C-35	2	-0.4
1942 Chi-A	56	182	18	44	9	1	3	21	19	15	0	1	.242	.313	.352	.665	89	-3	21	3.76	-2	C-54	5	-0.1
1943 Chi-A	51	154	16	37	7	1	2	11	13	21	1	0	.240	.299	.338	.637	86	-3	15	3.21	-2	C-49	4	-0.1
1944 Chi-A	36	113	9	26	6	0	2	13	5	16	0	1	.230	.263	.336	.599	71	-5	8	2.23	-2	C-36	1	-0.5
*StL-A	15	25	2	8	1	0	0	4	2	5	0	0	.320	.370	.360	.730	103	0	3	4.69	-1	C-11	1	0.0
Yr.	51	138	11	34	7	0	2	17	7	21	0	1	.246	.283	.341	.623	77	-5	11	2.64	-2	C-47	2	-0.5
Total 5	233	696	63	165	29	4	7	63	51	84	4	2	.237	.290	.320	.611	71	-29	63	3.01	-5	C-214	14	-2.1

• TURNER, Tuck George A. Turner b: 2/13/1873, West New Brighton, NY d: 7/16/1945, Staten Island, NY BB/TL, 5'6.5", 155 lbs. Deb: 8/18/1893 Career OF: 87-54-224

YEAR TM-L	G	AB	R	H	2B	3B	HR	RBI	BB	SO	SB	CS	AVG	OBP	SLG	OPS	OPS+	BR/A	RC	RC/G	FR	G/POS	WS	TPW
1893 Phi-N	36	155	32	50	4	3	1	13	9	19	7	....	.323	.364	.406	.770	105	1	26	6.58	-2	O-36(1-35-0)	4	-0.3
1894 Phi-N	82	347	95	145	21	9	1	84	24	13	11	....	.418	.458	.539	.997	143	24	91	11.91	-5	O-78(54-3-22)/P-1	12	1.0
1895 Phi-N	59	210	51	81	8	6	2	43	25	11	14	....	.386	.453	.510	.963	147	16	57	11.56	-4	O-55(31-9-15)	9	0.7
1896 Phi-N	13	32	12	7	2	0	0	0	8	5	6	....	.219	.375	.281	.656	75	-1	6	6.11	1	/O-8(1-7-0)	1	0.0
StL-N	51	203	30	50	7	8	1	27	14	21	6	....	.246	.298	.374	.673	80	-7	25	4.33	-3	O-51(0-0-51)	2	-1.0
Yr.	64	235	42	57	9	8	1	27	22	26	12	....	.243	.310	.362	.672	79	-7	31	4.58	-1	O-59(1-7-51)	3	-1.0
1897 StL-N	103	416	58	121	17	12	2	41	35	....	8	....	.291	.350	.404	.754	101	-0	64	5.62	-3	*O-102(0-0-102)	8	-0.7
1898 StL-N	35	141	20	28	8	0	0	7	14	....	1	....	.199	.280	.255	.536	52	-9	11	2.54	-3	O-34(0-0-34)	0	-1.3
Total 6	379	1504	298	482	67	38	7	215	129	69	53	....	.320	.378	.430	.807	109	25	280	7.15	-19	O-364/P-1	36	-1.7

• TUTTLE, Bill William Robert Tuttle b: 7/4/1929, Elwood, IL d: 7/27/1998, Anoka, MN BR/TR, 6', 190 lbs. Deb: 9/10/1952 Career OF: 4-1139-67

YEAR TM-L	G	AB	R	H	2B	3B	HR	RBI	BB	SO	SB	CS	AVG	OBP	SLG	OPS	OPS+	BR/A	RC	RC/G	FR	G/POS	WS	TPW
1952 Det-A	7	25	2	6	0	0	0	2	0	1	0	0	.240	.240	.240	.480	34	-2	1	1.27	1	/O-6(3-3-0)	0	-0.2
1954 Det-A	147	530	64	141	20	11	7	58	62	60	5	8	.266	.345	.385	.730	102	-1	69	4.42	-3	*O-145(1-144-0)	15	-1.1
1955 Det-A	154	603	102	168	23	4	14	78	76	54	6	3	.279	.360	.400	.760	106	7	85	4.76	1	*O-154(0-154-0)	18	0.0
1956 Det-A	140	546	61	138	22	4	9	65	38	48	5	4	.253	.303	.357	.660	73	-23	55	3.42	-1	*O-137(0-137-0)	7	-3.0
1957 Det-A	133	451	49	113	12	4	5	47	44	41	2	6	.251	.319	.328	.647	75	-17	45	3.31	-4	*O-128(0-128-0)	8	-2.8
1958 KC-A	148	511	77	118	14	9	11	51	74	58	7	9	.231	.329	.358	.687	88	-9	59	3.73	-3	*O-145(0-107-46)	12	-1.9
1959 KC-A	126	463	74	139	19	6	7	43	48	38	10	6	.300	.371	.413	.783	113	9	71	5.47	7	*O-121(0-121-0)	16	1.1
1960 KC-A	151	559	75	143	21	3	8	40	66	52	1	5	.256	.337	.347	.684	85	-13	64	3.83	6	*O-148(0-148-0)	12	-1.4
1961 KC-A	25	84	15	22	2	2	0	8	9	9	0	0	.262	.333	.333	.667	78	-2	10	3.92	-2	O-25(0-25-0)	2	-0.5
Min-A	113	370	38	91	12	3	5	38	43	41	1	3	.246	.324	.335	.660	73	-15	39	3.44	-2	3-85,O-64(0-63-6)/2-2	5	-1.8
Yr.	138	454	53	113	14	5	5	46	52	50	1	3	.249	.326	.335	.661	74	-17	49	3.53	-4	O-89(0-88-6),3-85/2-2	7	-2.3
1962 Min-A	110	123	21	26	4	1	1	13	19	14	1	0	.211	.322	.285	.606	62	-6	12	3.11	-3	*O-104(0-95-15)	2	-1.1
1963 Min-A	16	3	0	0	0	0	0	0	1	0	0	0	.000	.250	.000	.250	-22	-0	0	.00	0	O-14(0-14-0)	0	-0.1
Total 11	1270	4268	578	1105	149	47	67	443	480	416	38	44	.259	.336	.363	.699	89	-73	509	4.00	-3	*O-1191/3-85,2-2	97	-12.7

• TUTWILER, Guy Guy Isbel "King Tut" Tutwiler b: 7/17/1888, Coalburg, AL d: 8/15/1930, Birmingham, AL BL/TR, 6', 175 lbs. Deb: 8/29/1911

YEAR TM-L	G	AB	R	H	2B	3B	HR	RBI	BB	SO	SB	CS	AVG	OBP	SLG	OPS	OPS+	BR/A	RC	RC/G	FR	G/POS	WS	TPW
1911 Det-A	13	32	3	6	2	0	0	3	2	....	0	....	.188	.235	.250	.485	34	-3	2	1.81	-3	/2-6,O-3(3-0-0)	0	-0.5
1913 Det-A	14	47	4	10	0	1	0	7	4	12	2	....	.213	.275	.255	.530	56	-3	4	2.42	2	1-14	0	-0.1
Total 2	27	79	7	16	2	1	0	10	6	12	2	....	.203	.259	.253	.512	47	-6	5	2.16	-1	/1-14,2-6,O-3	0	-0.7

• TWINEHAM, Art Arthur W. "Old Hoss" Twineham b: 11/26/1866, Galesburg, IL BL/TL, 6'1.5", 190 lbs. Deb: 9/11/1893

YEAR TM-L	G	AB	R	H	2B	3B	HR	RBI	BB	SO	SB	CS	AVG	OBP	SLG	OPS	OPS+	BR/A	RC	RC/G	FR	G/POS	WS	TPW
1893 StL-N	14	48	8	15	2	0	0	11	1	2	0	....	.313	.340	.354	.694	84	-1	6	4.76	0	C-14	1	0.0
1894 StL-N	38	127	22	40	4	1	1	16	9	11	2	....	.315	.387	.386	.773	87	-2	20	6.05	0	C-38	4	0.1
Total 2	52	175	30	55	6	1	1	27	10	13	2	....	.314	.375	.377	.752	86	-3	26	5.70	0	/C-52	5	0.1

• TWITCHELL, Larry Lawrence Grant Twitchell b: 2/18/1864, Cleveland, OH d: 4/23/1930, Cleveland, OH BR/TR, 6', 185 lbs. Deb: 4/30/1886 U Career OF: 511-10-88 ♦

YEAR TM-L	G	AB	R	H	2B	3B	HR	RBI	BB	SO	SB	CS	AVG	OBP	SLG	OPS	OPS+	BR/A	RC	RC/G	FR	G/POS	WS	TPW
1886 Det-N	4	16	0	1	0	0	0	0	0	2	0	....	.063	.063	.063	.125	-60	-2	0	.12	0	/P-4,O-2(1-1-0)	0	-1.0
1887*Det-N	65	272	44	96	14	6	0	51	8	19	12	....	.353	.358	.432	.789	114	7	46	6.96	-7	O-53(44-9-0),P-15	15	-0.4
1888 Det-N	131	524	71	128	19	4	5	67	28	45	14	....	.244	.286	.324	.611	94	-3	54	3.68	-9	*O-131(131-0-0)/P-2	10	-1.8
1889 Cle-N	134	549	73	151	16	11	4	95	29	37	17	....	.275	.315	.366	.681	92	-8	70	4.69	-7	*O-134(134-0-0)/P-1	11	-1.6
1890 Cle-P	56	233	33	52	6	3	2	36	17	17	4	....	.223	.279	.300	.579	60	-13	21	3.16	-7	O-56(1-0-56)	1	-1.6
Buf-P	44	172	24	38	3	1	2	17	23	12	4	....	.221	.316	.285	.601	67	-3	17	3.46	2	O-32(4-0-28),P-13/1-3	4	-0.6
Yr.	100	405	57	90	9	4	4	53	40	29	8	....	.222	.295	.294	.589	63	-16	38	3.29	-5	O-88(5-0-84),P-13/1-3	5	-2.2
1891 Col-a	57	224	32	62	9	4	2	35	20	28	10	....	.277	.341	.379	.721	113	4	33	5.44	-6	O-56(56-0-0)/P-6	8	-0.6
1892 Was-N	51	192	20	42	9	5	0	20	11	31	8	....	.219	.275	.318	.593	82	-5	19	3.51	-3	O-48(46-0-2)/S-3,3-1	3	-1.1
1893 Lou-N	45	187	37	58	11	3	2	31	17	20	7	....	.310	.377	.433	.810	125	7	34	6.98	-3	O-45(43-0-2)	6	-0.1
1894 Lou-N	52	210	28	56	16	3	2	32	15	20	8	....	.267	.316	.400	.716	77	-8	30	5.02	7	O-51(51-0-0)/P-1	2	-0.5
Total 9	639	2579	362	684	103	40	19	384	168	231	84	....	.265	.313	.356	.669	91	-24	325	4.57	-34	O-608/P-42,1-3,S-3,3-1	60	-9.3

• TWOMBLY, Babe Clarence Edward Twombly
b: 1/18/1896, Jamaica Plain, MA d: 11/23/1974, San Clemente, CA BL/TR, 5'10", 165 lbs. Deb: 4/14/1920 Career OF: 15-44-31

YEAR TM-L	G	AB	R	H	2B	3B	HR	RBI	BB	SO	SB	CS	AVG	OBP	SLG	OPS	OPS+	BR/A	RC	RC/G	FR	G/POS	WS	TPW
1920 Chi-N	78	183	25	43	1	1	2	14	17	20	5	9	.235	.303	.284	.588	68	-9	15	2.58	-1	O-45(5-15-25)/2-2	2	-1.3
1921 Chi-N	87	175	22	66	8	1	1	18	11	10	4	6	.377	.414	.451	.865	129	6	31	6.87	3	O-45(10-29-6)	6	0.7
Total 2	165	358	47	109	9	2	3	32	28	30	9	15	.304	.357	.366	.723	97	-3	46	4.46	2	/O-90,2-2	8	-0.7

• TWOMBLY, George George Frederick "Silent George" Twombly
b: 6/4/1892, Boston, MA d: 2/17/1975, Lexington, MA BR/TR, 5'9", 165 lbs. Deb: 7/9/1914 Career OF: 81-34-9

YEAR TM-L	G	AB	R	H	2B	3B	HR	RBI	BB	SO	SB	CS	AVG	OBP	SLG	OPS	OPS+	BR/A	RC	RC/G	FR	G/POS	WS	TPW
1914 Cin-N	68	240	22	56	0	5	0	19	14	27	12	....	.233	.284	.275	.559	64	-11	21	2.90	3	O-68(68-0-1)	3	-1.1
1915 Cin-N	46	66	5	13	0	1	0	5	8	8	5	3	.197	.293	.227	.521	57	-3	5	2.34	1	O-24(10-13-1)	0	-0.4
1916 Cin-N	3	5	0	0	0	0	0	0	1	1	0	....	.000	.167	.000	.167	-48	-1	0	.00	0	/O-1	0	-0.1
1917 Bos-N	32	102	8	19	1	1	0	9	18	5	4	....	.186	.314	.216	.530	68	-3	9	2.52	-4	O-29(1-21-7)/1-1	1	-1.0
1919 Was-A	1	4	0	0	0	0	0	0	0	0	0	....	.000	.000	.000	.000	-101	-1	0	.00	0	/O-1	0	-0.1
Total 5	150	417	35	88	1	7	0	33	41	41	21	3	.211	.289	.247	.536	61	-19	35	2.63	0	O-123/1-1	4	-2.6

• TYACK, Jim James Frederick Tyack b: 1/9/1911, Florence, MT d: 1/3/1995, Bakersfield, CA BL/TR, 6'2", 195 lbs. Deb: 4/20/1943

YEAR TM-L	G	AB	R	H	2B	3B	HR	RBI	BB	SO	SB	CS	AVG	OBP	SLG	OPS	OPS+	BR/A	RC	RC/G	FR	G/POS	WS	TPW
1943 Phi-A	54	155	11	40	8	1	0	23	14	9	1	1	.258	.320	.323	.642	88	-2	17	3.68	-1	O-38(9-2-27)	4	-0.6

• TYLER, Fred Frederick Franklin "Clancy" Tyler b: 12/16/1891, Derry, NH d: 10/14/1945, East Derry, NH BR/TR, 5'10.5", 180 lbs. Deb: 10/3/1914

YEAR TM-L	G	AB	R	H	2B	3B	HR	RBI	BB	SO	SB	CS	AVG	OBP	SLG	OPS	OPS+	BR/A	RC	RC/G	FR	G/POS	WS	TPW
1914 Bos-N	6	19	2	2	0	0	0	2	1	5	0	....	.105	.150	.105	.255	-24	-3	0	.51	1	/C-6	0	-0.2

• TYLER, Johnnie John Anthony "Ty Ty,Katz" Tyler
b: 7/30/1906, Mount Pleasant, PA d: 7/11/1972, Mount Pleasant, PA BB/TR, 6', 175 lbs. Deb: 9/16/1934 Career OF: 11-1-0

YEAR TM-L	G	AB	R	H	2B	3B	HR	RBI	BB	SO	SB	CS	AVG	OBP	SLG	OPS	OPS+	BR/A	RC	RC/G	FR	G/POS	WS	TPW
1934 Bos-N	3	6	0	1	0	0	0	1	0	3	0	....	.167	.167	.167	.333	-11	-1	0	.92	1	/O-1	0	0.0
1935 Bos-N	13	47	7	16	2	1	2	11	4	3	0	....	.340	.404	.553	.957	168	4	11	9.52	0	O-11(11-0-0)	2	0.3
Total 2	16	53	7	17	2	1	2	12	4	6	0	....	.321	.379	.509	.889	150	4	11	8.36	0	/O-12	2	0.3

• TYNER, Jason Jason Renyt Tyner b: 4/23/1977, Bedford, TX BL/TL, 6'1", 170 lbs. Deb: 6/5/2000 Career OF: 146-56-26

YEAR TM-L	G	AB	R	H	2B	3B	HR	RBI	BB	SO	SB	CS	AVG	OBP	SLG	OPS	OPS+	BR/A	RC	RC/G	FR	G/POS	WS	TPW
2000 NY-N	13	41	3	8	2	0	0	5	1	4	1	1	.195	.233	.244	.476	21	-5	2	1.53	1	/O-1	0	-0.4
TB-A	37	83	6	20	2	0	0	8	4	12	6	1	.241	.284	.265	.549	41	-7	7	2.75	3	O-12(27-4-0)/D-1	1	-0.4
2001 TB-A	105	396	51	111	8	5	0	21	15	42	31	6	.280	.312	.326	.637	69	-14	43	3.80	1	O-31(57-47-3)	6	-1.4
2002 TB-A	44	168	17	36	2	1	0	9	7	19	7	1	.214	.250	.238	.488	31	-15	11	2.18	1	*O-100(41-1-0)/D-1	1	-1.6
2003 TB-A	46	90	12	25	7	0	0	6	10	12	2	1	.278	.350	.356	.706	88	-1	12	4.64	-1	O-32(9-2-23)/D-4	2	-0.3
Total 4	245	778	89	200	21	6	0	49	37	89	47	10	.257	.296	.299	.595	58	-42	75	3.27	6	O-176/D-6	10	-4.1

• TYREE, Earl Earl Carlton "Ty" Tyree b: 3/4/1890, Huntsville, IL d: 5/17/1954, Rushville, IL BR/TR, 5'8", 160 lbs. Deb: 10/5/1914

YEAR TM-L	G	AB	R	H	2B	3B	HR	RBI	BB	SO	SB	CS	AVG	OBP	SLG	OPS	OPS+	BR/A	RC	RC/G	FR	G/POS	WS	TPW
1914 Chi-N	1	4	1	0	0	0	0	0	0	0	0	....	.000	.000	.000	.000	-100	-1	0	.00	0	/C-1	0	-0.1

• TYRONE, Jim James Vernon Tyrone b: 1/29/1949, Alice, TX BR/TR, 6'1", 185 lbs. Deb: 8/27/1972 Career OF: 42-5-83

YEAR TM-L	G	AB	R	H	2B	3B	HR	RBI	BB	SO	SB	CS	AVG	OBP	SLG	OPS	OPS+	BR/A	RC	RC/G	FR	G/POS	WS	TPW
1972 Chi-N	13	8	1	0	0	0	0	0	0	3	1	0	.000	.000	.000	.000	-90	-2	0	.00	0	/O-4(3-0-1)	0	-0.2
1974 Chi-N	57	81	19	15	0	1	3	3	6	8	1	1	.185	.241	.321	.562	54	-6	6	2.27	-1	O-32(21-1-12)/3-1	0	-0.7
1975 Chi-N	11	22	0	5	0	1	0	3	1	4	1	1	.227	.261	.318	.579	57	-2	2	2.46	1	/O-8(8-0-0)	0	-0.1

YEAR TM-L	G	AB	R	H	2B	3B	HR	RBI	BB	SO	SB	CS	AVG	OBP	SLG	OPS	OPS+	BR/A	RC	RC/G	FR	G/POS	WS	TPW
1977 Oak-A	96	294	32	72	11	1	5	26	25	62	3	1	.245	.304	.340	.644	76	-9	31	3.55	-1	0-81(10-4-70)/D-4,1-1,S-1	5	-1.3
Total 4	**177**	**405**	**52**	**92**	**11**	**3**	**8**	**32**	**32**	**77**	**6**	**3**	**.227**	**.284**	**.328**	**.612**	**68**	**-18**	**39**	**3.14**	**0**	**0-125/D-4,1-1,3-1,S-1**	**5**	**-2.4**
• TYRONE, Wayne	Oscar Wayne Tyrone b: 8/1/1950, Alice, TX BR/TR, 6'1", 185 lbs. Deb: 7/15/1976																							
1976 Chi-N	30	57	3	13	1	0	1	8	3	21	0	0	.228	.267	.298	.565	55	-3	5	2.77	-1	/O-7(6-0-1),1-5,3-5	0	-0.5
• TYSON, Mike	Michael Ray Tyson b: 1/13/1950, Rocky Mount, NC BR/TR, 5'9", 170 lbs. Deb: 9/5/1972																							
1972 StL-N	13	37	1	7	1	0	0	0	1	9	0	1	.189	.211	.216	.427	22	-4	2	1.33	0	2-11/S-2	1	-0.4
1973 StL-N	144	469	48	114	15	4	1	33	23	66	2	5	.243	.281	.299	.580	61	-27	37	2.65	0	*S-128,2-16	8	-1.2
1974 StL-N	151	422	35	94	14	5	1	37	22	70	4	2	.223	.266	.287	.553	55	-26	29	2.25	12	*S-143,2-12	8	0.2
1975 StL-N	122	368	45	98	16	3	2	37	24	39	5	2	.266	.316	.342	.659	80	-10	40	3.77	3	S-95,2-24/3-5	11	0.3
1976 StL-N	76	245	26	70	12	9	3	28	16	34	3	1	.286	.330	.445	.774	117	5	34	5.02	5	2-74	8	1.5
1977 StL-N	138	418	42	103	15	2	7	57	30	48	3	4	.246	.300	.342	.642	73	-17	41	3.31	26	*2-135	12	1.5
1978 StL-N	125	377	26	88	16	0	3	26	24	41	2	0	.233	.279	.300	.579	63	-19	29	2.57	-2	*2-124	5	-1.6
1979 StL-N	75	190	18	42	8	2	5	20	13	28	2	1	.221	.275	.363	.638	72	-8	18	3.06	2	2-71	4	-0.3
1980 Chi-N	123	341	34	81	19	3	3	23	15	61	1	2	.238	.274	.337	.611	65	-18	31	3.03	-5	*2-117	5	-1.8
1981 Chi-N	50	92	6	17	2	0	2	8	7	15	1	0	.185	.250	.272	.522	46	-6	7	2.43	-2	2-36/S-1	1	-0.8
Total 10	**1017**	**2959**	**281**	**714**	**118**	**28**	**27**	**269**	**175**	**411**	**23**	**18**	**.241**	**.287**	**.327**	**.614**	**69**	**-132**	**268**	**3.04**	**38**	**2-620,S-369/3-5**	**63**	**-2.5**
• TYSON, Turkey	Cecil Washington "Slim" Tyson b: 12/6/1914, Elm City, NC d: 2/17/2000, Elm City, NC BL/TR, 6'5.5", 225 lbs. Deb: 4/23/1944																							
1944 Phi-N	1	1	0	0	0	0	0	0	0	0	0	....	.000	.000	.000	.000	-103	-0	0	.00	0	....	0	0.0
• TYSON, Ty	Albert Thomas Tyson b: 6/1/1892, Wilkes-Barre, PA d: 8/16/1953, Buffalo, NY BR/TR, 5'11", 169 lbs. Deb: 4/13/1926 Career OF: 53-125-16																							
1926 NY-N	97	335	40	98	16	1	3	35	15	28	6	....	.293	.329	.373	.702	90	-5	40	4.29	1	O-92(12-83-0)	9	-0.8
1927 NY-N	43	159	24	42	7	2	1	17	10	19	5	....	.264	.308	.352	.660	76	-6	17	3.61	0	O-41(40-1-2)	2	-0.9
1928 Bro-N	59	210	25	57	11	1	1	21	10	14	3	....	.271	.317	.348	.665	75	-8	23	3.75	-1	O-55(1-41-14)	4	-1.1
Total 3	**199**	**704**	**89**	**197**	**34**	**4**	**5**	**73**	**35**	**61**	**14**	**....**	**.280**	**.320**	**.361**	**.681**	**82**	**-19**	**79**	**3.96**	**0**	**O-188**	**15**	**-2.8**
• UECKER, Bob	Robert George Uecker b: 1/26/1935, Milwaukee, WI BR/TR, 6'1", 190 lbs. Deb: 4/13/1962																							
1962 Mil-N	33	64	5	16	2	0	1	8	7	15	0	0	.250	.324	.328	.652	78	-2	6	3.40	0	C-24	2	-0.1
1963 Mil-N	13	16	3	4	2	0	0	0	2	5	0	0	.250	.333	.375	.708	105	0	2	3.76	0	/C-6	1	0.0
1964 StL-N	40	106	8	21	1	0	1	6	17	24	0	1	.198	.315	.236	.550	53	-6	9	2.75	-1	C-40	2	-0.5
1965 StL-N	53	145	17	33	7	0	2	10	24	27	0	1	.228	.345	.317	.662	80	-3	18	4.13	0	C-49	5	-0.1
1966 Phi-N	78	207	15	43	6	0	7	30	22	36	0	0	.208	.284	.338	.622	72	-8	19	2.83	-1	C-76	5	-0.6
1967 Phi-N	18	35	3	6	2	0	0	7	5	9	0	0	.171	.275	.229	.504	45	-2	2	2.03	-1	C-17	0	-0.3
Atl-N	62	158	14	23	2	0	3	13	19	51	0	1	.146	.237	.215	.452	31	-14	8	1.58	-2	C-59	1	-1.5
Yr.	80	193	17	29	4	0	3	20	24	60	0	1	.150	.244	.218	.462	33	-17	11	1.66	-3	C-76	1	-1.7
Total 6	**297**	**731**	**65**	**146**	**22**	**0**	**14**	**74**	**96**	**167**	**0**	**3**	**.200**	**.295**	**.287**	**.582**	**62**	**-35**	**64**	**2.80**	**-5**	**C-271**	**16**	**-3.1**
• UGUETO, Luis	Luis Enrique Ugueto b: 2/15/1979, Caracas, Venezuela BB/TR, 5'11", 170 lbs. Deb: 4/3/2002																							
2002 Sea-A	62	23	19	5	0	0	1	1	2	8	8	4	.217	.280	.348	.628	68	-1	2	1.87	2	D-14,2-11/S-8,3-1	0	0.1
2003 Sea-A	12	5	4	1	0	0	0	1	1	0	2	0	.200	.333	.200	.533	47	0	1	5.18	0	/2-4,D-3,3-1,S-1	0	0.0
Total 2	**74**	**28**	**23**	**6**	**0**	**0**	**1**	**2**	**3**	**8**	**10**	**4**	**.214**	**.290**	**.321**	**.612**	**64**	**-1**	**2**	**2.38**	**2**	**/D-17,2-15,S-9,3-2**	**0**	**0.1**
• UHALT, Frenchy	Bernard Bartholomew Uhalt b: 4/27/1910, Bakersfield, CA BL/TR, 5'10", 180 lbs. Deb: 4/17/1934																							
1934 Chi-A	57	165	28	40	5	1	0	16	29	12	6	5	.242	.359	.285	.644	66	-8	19	3.72	-3	O-40(4-14-22)	2	-1.2
• UHLAENDER, Ted	Theodore Otto Uhlaender b: 10/21/1940, Chicago Heights, IL BL/TR, 6'2", 190 lbs. Deb: 9/4/1965 C Career OF: 166-602-45																							
1965 Min-A	13	22	1	4	0	0	0	1	0	2	1	0	.182	.182	.182	.364	3	-3	1	1.23	1	/O-4(4-0-0)	0	-0.2
1966 Min-A	105	367	39	83	12	2	2	22	27	33	10	2	.226	.281	.286	.567	60	-18	32	2.87	1	*O-100(4-96-0)	7	-2.1
1967 Min-A	133	415	41	107	19	7	6	49	13	45	4	4	.258	.285	.381	.666	88	-8	44	3.70	2	*O-118(0-118-0)	11	-1.1
1968 Min-A	140	488	52	138	21	5	7	52	28	46	16	7	.283	.326	.389	.715	110	6	63	4.64	-7	*O-129(0-129-0)	18	-0.6
1969*Min-A	152	554	93	151	18	2	8	62	44	52	15	9	.273	.331	.356	.686	90	-8	68	4.31	-2	*O-150(44-108-1)	14	-1.5
1970 Cle-A	141	473	56	127	21	2	11	46	39	44	3	6	.268	.326	.391	.717	92	-7	60	4.37	-6	*O-134(24-116-8)	9	-1.7
1971 Cle-A	141	500	52	144	20	3	2	47	38	44	3	6	.288	.338	.352	.690	88	-9	59	4.26	-1	*O-131(87-33-13)	11	-1.8
1972*Cin-N	73	113	9	18	3	0	0	6	13	11	0	1	.159	.246	.186	.432	26	-11	5	1.20	0	O-27(3-2-23)	0	-1.3
Total 8	**898**	**2932**	**343**	**772**	**114**	**21**	**36**	**285**	**202**	**277**	**52**	**35**	**.263**	**.313**	**.353**	**.667**	**86**	**-58**	**330**	**3.92**	**-12**	**O-793**	**70**	**-10.3**
• UHLER, Maury	Maurice William Uhler b: 12/14/1886, Pikesville, MD d: 5/4/1918, Baltimore, MD BR/TR, 5'11", 165 lbs. Deb: 4/14/1914																							
1914 Cin-N	46	56	12	12	2	0	0	3	5	11	4	....	.214	.279	.250	.529	56	-3	5	2.68	-2	O-36(22-11-3)	1	-0.7
• UHLIR, Charlie	Charles Karel Uhlir b: 7/30/1912, Chicago, IL d: 7/9/1984, Spirit Lake, IA BL/TL, 5'7.5", 150 lbs. Deb: 8/3/1934																							
1934 Chi-A	14	27	3	4	0	0	0	3	2	6	0	0	.148	.207	.148	.355	-7	-4	1	1.07	0	/O-6(6-0-0)	0	-0.4
• ULISNEY, Mike	Michael Edward "Slugs" Ulisney b: 9/28/1917, Greenwald, PA BR/TR, 5'9", 165 lbs. Deb: 5/5/1945																							
1945 Bos-N	11	18	4	7	1	0	1	4	1	0	0	....	.389	.421	.611	1.032	184	2	5	11.64	-1	/C-4	1	0.1
• ULLGER, Scott	Scott Matthew Ullger b: 6/10/1956, New York, NY BR/TR, 6'2", 186 lbs. Deb: 4/17/1983 C																							
1983 Min-A	35	79	8	15	4	0	0	5	5	21	0	2	.190	.247	.241	.488	34	-8	3	1.18	-3	1-30/3-3,D-1	0	-1.2
• ULRICH, George	George T. Ulrich b: 6/5/1869, Philadelphia, PA Deb: 5/1/1892 Career OF: 11-1-0																							
1892 Was-N	6	24	1	7	1	0	0	0	0	4	2	....	.292	.292	.333	.625	91	-0	3	4.75	-0	/3-3,C-2,S-2	0	0.0
1893 Cin-N	1	3	0	0	0	0	0	0	0	0	1	....	.000	.250	.000	.250	-31	-1	0	2.26	-0	/O-1	0	0.0
1896 NY-N	14	45	4	8	1	0	0	1	1	1	0	....	.178	.229	.200	.429	14	-6	2	1.60	0	O-11(11-0-0)/3-3	0	-0.6
Total 3	**21**	**72**	**5**	**15**	**2**	**0**	**0**	**1**	**1**	**5**	**3**	**....**	**.208**	**.250**	**.236**	**.486**	**36**	**-7**	**6**	**2.54**	**0**	**/O-12,3-6,C-2,S-2**	**0**	**-0.7**
• UMPHLETT, Tom	Thomas Mullen Umphlett b: 5/12/1930, Scotland Neck, NC BR/TR, 6'2", 180 lbs. Deb: 4/16/1953 Career OF: 30-202-109																							
1953 Bos-A	137	495	53	140	27	5	3	59	34	30	4	2	.283	.331	.376	.707	86	-10	62	4.49	1	*O-136(0-136-0)	14	-1.6
1954 Was-A	114	342	21	75	8	3	1	33	17	42	1	2	.219	.256	.269	.525	46	-26	21	1.98	2	*O-101(12-4-86)	2	-2.8
1955 Was-A	110	323	34	70	10	0	2	19	24	35	2	1	.217	.271	.266	.537	47	-24	24	2.45	0	*O-103(18-62-23)	1	-2.9
Total 3	**361**	**1160**	**108**	**285**	**45**	**8**	**6**	**111**	**75**	**107**	**7**	**5**	**.246**	**.293**	**.314**	**.606**	**64**	**-60**	**107**	**3.13**	**3**	**O-340**	**17**	**-7.3**
• UNGLAUB, Bob	Robert Alexander Unglaub b: 7/31/1881, Baltimore, MD d: 11/29/1916, Baltimore, MD BR/TR, 5'11", 178 lbs. Deb: 4/15/1904 M																							
1904 NY-A	6	19	2	4	0	0	0	2	0	....	0	....	.211	.211	.211	.421	32	-1	1	1.52	-1	/3-4,S-1	0	-0.3
Bos-A	9	13	1	2	1	0	0	2	1	....	0	....	.154	.214	.231	.445	39	-1	1	1.59	-2	/2-3,3-2,S-1	0	-0.3
Yr.	15	32	3	6	1	0	0	4	1	....	0	....	.188	.212	.219	.431	35	-2	2	1.55	-3	/3-6,2-3,S-2	0	-0.6
1905 Bos-A	43	121	18	27	5	1	0	11	6	....	2	....	.223	.260	.281	.541	71	-4	10	2.72	0	3-21/2-7,1-2	2	-0.4
1907 Bos-A	139	544	49	138	17	13	1	62	23	....	14	....	.254	.284	.338	.622	99	-3	59	3.73	2	*1-139	10	-0.4
1908 Bos-A	72	266	23	70	11	3	1	25	7	....	6	....	.263	.287	.338	.626	100	-1	27	3.46	-1	1-72	6	-0.4
Was-A	72	276	23	85	10	5	0	29	8	....	8	....	.308	.327	.380	.708	142	11	36	4.79	7	3-39,2-27/1-4	12	2.2
Yr.	144	542	46	155	21	8	1	54	15	....	14	....	.286	.308	.360	.667	121	9	64	4.11	6	1-76,3-39,2-27	18	1.8
1909 Was-A	130	480	43	127	14	9	3	41	22	....	15	....	.265	.301	.350	.651	111	4	54	3.85	-2	1-57,O-42(8-0-34),2-25/3-4	12	-0.1
1910 Was-A	124	431	29	101	9	4	0	44	21	....	21	....	.234	.270	.274	.544	74	-14	37	2.81	5	*1-124	5	-1.3
Total 6	**595**	**2150**	**188**	**554**	**67**	**35**	**5**	**216**	**88**	**....**	**66**	**....**	**.258**	**.288**	**.328**	**.617**	**100**	**-11**	**226**	**3.56**	**8**	**1-398/3-70,2-62,O-42,S-2**	**47**	**-1.0**
• UNROE, Tim	Timothy Brian Unroe b: 10/7/1970, Round Lake Beach, IL BR/TR, 6'3", 200 lbs. Deb: 5/30/1995 Career OF: 7-0-9																							
1995 Mil-A	2	4	0	1	0	0	0	0	0	0	0	0	.250	.250	.250	.500	29	-0	0	2.25	0	/1-2	0	-0.1
1996 Mil-A	14	16	5	3	0	0	0	0	4	5	0	1	.188	.350	.188	.538	40	-2	1	2.34	0	O-42(1-0-0),1-11/3-3,D-1	0	-0.2
1997 Mil-A	32	16	3	4	1	0	2	5	2	9	2	0	.250	.333	.688	1.021	156	2	4	9.42	0	1-23/3-2,2-1,O-1	1	0.1
1999 Ana-A	27	54	5	13	2	0	1	6	4	16	0	0	.241	.305	.333	.638	63	-3	6	3.88	0	/D-9,3-3,O-2(4-0-8),2-1	1	-0.4

YEAR TM-L	G	AB	R	H	2B	3B	HR	RBI	BB	SO	SB	CS	AVG	OBP	SLG	OPS	OPS+	BR/A	RC	RC/G	FR	G/POS	WS	TPW
2000 Atl-N	4	5	0	0	0	0	0	0	1	2	0	0	.000	.167	.000	.167	-53	-1	0	.50	0	0-12(1-0-0)/1-2	0	-0.1
Total 5	79	95	13	21	3	0	3	11	11	32	2	1	.221	.308	.347	.656	66	-5	12	4.14	-1	/0-57,1-38,D-10,3-8,2-2	2	-0.7

• UNSER, Al — Albert Bernard Unser b: 10/12/1912, Morrisonville, IL d: 7/5/1995, Decatur, IL BR/TR, 6'1", 175 lbs. Deb: 9/14/1942

YEAR TM-L	G	AB	R	H	2B	3B	HR	RBI	BB	SO	SB	CS	AVG	OBP	SLG	OPS	OPS+	BR/A	RC	RC/G	FR	G/POS	WS	TPW
1942 Det-A	4	8	2	3	0	0	0	0	0	2	0	0	.375	.375	.375	.750	103	0	1	3.08	0	/C-4	0	0.0
1943 Det-A	38	101	14	25	5	0	0	4	15	15	0	1	.248	.350	.297	.647	84	-2	11	3.70	2	C-37	3	0.2
1944 Det-A	11	25	2	3	0	1	1	5	3	2	0	0	.120	.214	.320	.534	49	-2	2	2.36	-2	/2-5,C-1	0	-0.4
1945 Cin-N	67	204	23	54	10	3	3	21	14	24	0	....	.265	.318	.387	.705	98	-1	25	4.35	-2	C-61	6	0.0
Total 4	120	338	41	85	15	4	4	30	32	43	0	1	.251	.322	.355	.677	90	-5	39	3.96	-2	C-103/2-5	9	-0.1

• UNSER, Del — Delbert Bernard Unser b: 12/9/1944, Decatur, IL BL/TL, 6'1", 180 lbs. Deb: 4/10/1968 C Career OF: 118-1112-226

YEAR TM-L	G	AB	R	H	2B	3B	HR	RBI	BB	SO	SB	CS	AVG	OBP	SLG	OPS	OPS+	BR/A	RC	RC/G	FR	G/POS	WS	TPW
1968 Was-A	156	635	66	146	13	7	1	30	46	66	11	6	.230	.284	.277	.561	73	-21	52	2.79	9	*0-156(0-156-0)/1-1	12	-1.9
1969 Was-A	153	581	69	166	19	**8**	7	57	58	54	8	10	.286	.351	.382	.733	110	5	79	4.85	1	*0-149(0-149-0)	20	0.2
1970 Was-A	119	322	37	83	5	1	5	30	30	29	1	1	.258	.321	.326	.647	83	-7	35	3.77	2	*0-103(11-43-50)	6	-1.0
1971 Was-A	153	581	63	148	19	6	9	41	59	68	11	6	.255	.326	.355	.680	98	-1	70	4.21	1	*0-151(8-105-68)	17	-0.7
1972 Cle-A	132	383	29	91	12	0	1	17	28	46	5	9	.238	.291	.277	.568	67	-18	31	2.61	2	*0-119(14-85-23)	6	-2.3
1973 Phi-N	136	440	64	127	20	4	11	52	47	55	5	8	.289	.359	.427	.786	114	6	68	5.50	14	*0-132(0-132-0)	16	1.7
1974 Phi-N	142	454	72	120	18	5	11	61	50	62	6	4	.264	.339	.399	.737	101	0	62	4.72	2	*0-135(0-135-0)	15	-0.1
1975 NY-N	147	531	65	156	18	2	10	53	37	76	4	3	.294	.340	.392	.732	107	3	70	4.78	7	*0-144(0-144-0)	19	0.6
1976 NY-N	77	276	28	63	13	2	5	25	18	40	4	4	.228	.278	.344	.622	80	-9	26	3.05	-2	0-77(2-75-0)	6	-1.4
Mon-N	69	220	29	50	6	2	7	15	11	44	3	3	.227	.264	.368	.632	75	-9	21	3.00	2	0-65(29-13-34)	3	-1.0
Yr.	146	496	57	113	19	4	12	40	29	84	7	7	.228	.272	.355	.627	78	-18	46	3.03	0	*0-142(31-88-34)	9	-2.4
1977 Mon-N	113	289	33	79	14	1	12	40	33	41	2	5	.273	.348	.453	.801	116	5	45	5.29	-2	0-72(11-34-27),1-27	8	0.0
1978 Mon-N	130	179	16	35	5	0	2	15	24	29	2	0	.196	.294	.257	.551	56	-10	15	2.67	0	1-64,0-33(7-12-14)	2	-1.3
1979 Phi-N	95	141	26	42	8	0	6	29	14	33	2	0	.298	.361	.482	.844	124	5	24	6.13	-2	0-30(16-11-3),1-22	5	0.2
1980*Phi-N	96	110	15	29	6	4	0	10	10	21	0	1	.264	.325	.391	.716	94	-1	14	4.26	1	1-31,0-23(13-12-1)	3	-0.2
1981 Phi-N	62	59	5	9	3	0	0	6	13	9	0	0	.153	.306	.203	.509	45	-4	4	2.34	0	1-18,0-16(7-6-4)	0	-0.5
1982 Phi-N	19	14	0	0	0	0	0	0	3	2	0	0	.000	.176	.000	.176	-46	-3	0	.11	0	/1-5,0-2(0-0-2)	0	-0.3
Total 15	1799	5215	617	1344	179	42	87	481	481	675	64	60	.258	.321	.358	.680	93	-58	616	4.06	33	*0-1407,1-168	138	-7.9

• UPRIGHT, Dixie — Roy T. Upright b: 5/30/1926, Kannapolis, NC d: 11/13/1986, Concord, NC BL/TL, 6', 175 lbs. Deb: 4/18/1953

YEAR TM-L	G	AB	R	H	2B	3B	HR	RBI	BB	SO	SB	CS	AVG	OBP	SLG	OPS	OPS+	BR/A	RC	RC/G	FR	G/POS	WS	TPW
1953 StL-A	9	8	3	2	0	0	1	1	1	3	0	0	.250	.333	.625	.958	151	1	2	8.08	0	....	0	0.1

• UPSHAW, Willie — Willie Clay Upshaw b: 4/27/1957, Blanco, TX BL/TL, 6', 185 lbs. Deb: 4/9/1978 C Career OF: 53-6-9

YEAR TM-L	G	AB	R	H	2B	3B	HR	RBI	BB	SO	SB	CS	AVG	OBP	SLG	OPS	OPS+	BR/A	RC	RC/G	FR	G/POS	WS	TPW
1978 Tor-A	95	224	26	53	8	2	1	17	21	35	4	6	.237	.302	.304	.606	69	-10	20	2.90	-3	0-52(46-6-1),D-18,1-10	2	-1.6
1980 Tor-A	34	61	10	13	3	1	1	5	6	14	1	0	.213	.284	.344	.628	68	-3	7	3.59	1	1-14,D-12/0-1	1	-0.2
1981 Tor-A	61	111	15	19	3	1	4	10	11	16	2	1	.171	.252	.324	.576	61	-6	9	2.72	1	D-15,1-14,0-14(6-0-8)	1	-0.6
1982 Tor-A	160	580	77	155	25	7	21	75	52	91	8	8	.267	.329	.443	.772	100	-2	82	4.83	3	*1-155/D-5	14	-0.8
1983 Tor-A	160	579	99	177	26	7	27	104	61	98	10	7	.306	.377	.515	.891	134	27	113	7.12	5	*1-159/D-1	22	2.2
1984 Tor-A	152	569	79	158	31	9	19	84	55	86	10	4	.278	.347	.464	.811	118	14	92	5.80	-1	*1-151/D-1	17	0.4
1985*Tor-A	148	501	79	138	31	5	15	65	48	71	8	8	.275	.344	.447	.791	112	6	76	5.42	5	*1-147/D-1	14	0.3
1986 Tor-A	155	573	85	144	28	6	9	60	78	87	23	5	.251	.343	.368	.711	91	-2	80	4.83	8	*1-154/D-1	15	-0.4
1987 Tor-A	150	512	68	125	22	4	15	58	58	78	10	11	.244	.325	.391	.715	87	-12	65	4.27	10	*1-146	11	-1.1
1988 Cle-A	149	493	58	121	22	3	11	50	62	66	12	9	.245	.332	.369	.701	94	-5	61	4.14	4	*1-144	10	-1.0
Total 10	1264	4203	596	1103	199	45	123	528	452	642	88	59	.262	.337	.419	.756	102	8	605	4.98	33	*1-1094/0-67,D-54	107	-2.8

• UPTON, Tom — Thomas Herbert "Muscles" Upton b: 12/29/1926, Esther, MO BR/TR, 6', 160 lbs. Deb: 4/19/1950

YEAR TM-L	G	AB	R	H	2B	3B	HR	RBI	BB	SO	SB	CS	AVG	OBP	SLG	OPS	OPS+	BR/A	RC	RC/G	FR	G/POS	WS	TPW
1950 StL-A	124	389	50	92	5	6	2	30	52	45	7	2	.237	.328	.296	.624	58	-23	42	3.59	-4	*S-115/2-2,3-1	6	-1.9
1951 StL-A	52	131	9	26	4	3	0	12	12	22	1	1	.198	.271	.275	.546	46	-10	10	2.24	-4	S-47	1	-1.2
1952 Was-A	5	5	1	0	0	0	0	0	1	0	0	0	.000	.167	.000	.167	-53	-1	0	.50	0	/S-3	0	-0.1
Total 3	181	525	60	118	9	9	2	42	65	67	8	3	.225	.313	.288	.600	54	-34	51	3.19	-8	S-165/2-2,3-1	7	-3.1

• URBAN, Luke — Louis John Urban b: 3/22/1898, Fall River, MA d: 12/7/1980, Somerset, MA BR/TR, 5'8", 168 lbs. Deb: 7/19/1927

YEAR TM-L	G	AB	R	H	2B	3B	HR	RBI	BB	SO	SB	CS	AVG	OBP	SLG	OPS	OPS+	BR/A	RC	RC/G	FR	G/POS	WS	TPW
1927 Bos-N	35	111	11	32	5	0	0	10	3	6	1	....	.288	.313	.333	.646	79	-3	11	3.61	-1	C-34	2	-0.2
1928 Bos-N	15	17	0	3	0	0	0	2	0	1	0	....	.176	.222	.176	.399	6	-2	1	1.26	0	C-10	0	-0.2
Total 2	50	128	11	35	5	0	0	12	3	7	1	....	.273	.301	.313	.613	69	-6	12	3.24	0	/C-44	2	-0.4

• URBANSKI, Billy — William Michael Urbanski b: 6/5/1903, Linoleumville, NY d: 7/12/1973, Perth Amboy, NJ BR/TR, 5'8", 165 lbs. Deb: 7/4/1931

YEAR TM-L	G	AB	R	H	2B	3B	HR	RBI	BB	SO	SB	CS	AVG	OBP	SLG	OPS	OPS+	BR/A	RC	RC/G	FR	G/POS	WS	TPW
1931 Bos-N	82	303	22	72	13	4	0	17	10	32	3	....	.238	.274	.307	.581	58	-18	27	2.81	6	3-68,S-19	4	-0.8
1932 Bos-N	136	563	80	153	25	8	8	46	28	60	8	....	.272	.307	.387	.695	89	-10	68	4.11	6	*S-136	17	0.6
1933 Bos-N	144	566	65	142	21	4	0	35	33	48	4	....	.251	.298	.302	.600	78	-16	52	3.11	1	*S-143	15	-0.4
1934 Bos-N	146	605	104	177	30	6	7	53	56	37	4	....	.293	.357	.397	.754	110	10	90	5.42	-7	*S-146	25	1.3
1935 Bos-N	132	514	53	118	17	0	4	30	40	32	3	....	.230	.286	.286	.572	59	-29	42	2.69	-29	*S-129	1	-4.7
1936 Bos-N	122	494	55	129	17	5	0	26	31	42	2	....	.261	.310	.316	.626	74	-18	48	3.38	-23	S-80,3-38	8	-3.3
1937 Bos-N	1	1	0	0	0	0	0	0	0	1	0	....	.000	.000	.000	.000	-110	-0	0	.00	0	....	0	0.0
Total 7	763	3046	379	791	123	27	19	207	198	252	24	....	.260	.309	.337	.646	80	-82	327	3.66	-46	S-653,3-106	70	-7.5

• URIBE, Jose — Jose Altagracia Uribe b: 1/21/1959, San Cristobal, Dominican Republic BB/TR, 5'10", 165 lbs. Deb: 9/13/1984

YEAR TM-L	G	AB	R	H	2B	3B	HR	RBI	BB	SO	SB	CS	AVG	OBP	SLG	OPS	OPS+	BR/A	RC	RC/G	FR	G/POS	WS	TPW
1984 StL-N	8	19	4	4	0	0	0	3	0	2	1	0	.211	.211	.211	.421	19	-2	1	1.20	0	/S-5,2-1	0	-0.1
1985 SF-N	147	476	46	113	20	4	3	26	30	57	8	2	.237	.285	.315	.601	71	-19	44	3.16	-4	*S-145/2-1	10	-0.8
1986 SF-N	157	453	46	101	15	1	3	43	61	76	22	11	.223	.315	.280	.596	69	-18	43	3.19	16	*S-156	13	1.5
1987*SF-N	95	309	44	90	16	5	5	30	24	35	12	2	.291	.344	.424	.768	107	4	48	5.64	12	S-95	14	2.5
1988 SF-N	141	493	47	124	10	7	3	35	36	69	14	10	.252	.302	.318	.621	82	-14	48	3.33	1	*S-140	12	-0.3
1989*SF-N	151	453	34	100	12	6	1	30	34	74	6	6	.221	.275	.280	.556	61	-25	34	2.47	23	*S-150	11	1.0
1990 SF-N	138	415	35	103	8	6	1	24	29	49	5	9	.248	.297	.304	.601	68	-22	35	2.81	3	*S-134	6	-1.0
1991 SF-N	90	231	23	51	8	4	1	12	20	33	3	4	.221	.283	.303	.586	67	-11	20	2.82	4	S-87	5	-0.2
1992 SF-N	66	162	24	39	9	1	2	13	14	25	2	2	.241	.301	.346	.647	88	-3	17	3.36	3	S-62	6	0.4
1993 Hou-N	45	53	4	13	1	0	0	3	8	5	1	0	.245	.355	.264	.619	71	-1	6	3.42	-3	S-41	1	-0.3
Total 10	1038	3064	307	738	99	34	19	219	256	425	74	46	.241	.300	.314	.614	75	-111	294	3.24	54	*S-1015/2-2	78	2.7

• URIBE, Juan — Juan C. (Tena) Uribe b: 7/22/1979, Bani, Dominican Republic BR/TR, 5'11", 173 lbs. Deb: 4/8/2001

YEAR TM-L	G	AB	R	H	2B	3B	HR	RBI	BB	SO	SB	CS	AVG	OBP	SLG	OPS	OPS+	BR/A	RC	RC/G	FR	G/POS	WS	TPW
2001 Col-N	72	273	32	82	15	11	8	53	8	55	3	0	.300	.325	.524	.849	93	-3	45	6.12	-6	S-69	7	-0.3
2002 Col-N	155	566	69	136	25	7	6	49	34	120	9	2	.240	.289	.341	.630	56	-36	54	3.16	29	*S-155	10	0.6
2003 Col-N	87	316	45	80	19	3	10	33	17	60	7	2	.253	.298	.427	.725	76	-12	41	4.45	22	S-74,2-11/0-1	9	1.6
Total 3	314	1155	146	298	59	21	24	135	59	235	19	4	.258	.300	.408	.708	70	-50	140	4.16	45	S-298/2-11,0-1	26	1.9

• URY, Lon — Louis Newton "Old Sleep" Ury b: 4/1877, Fort Scott, KS d: 3/4/1918, Kansas City, MO TR, 6' Deb: 9/9/1903

YEAR TM-L	G	AB	R	H	2B	3B	HR	RBI	BB	SO	SB	CS	AVG	OBP	SLG	OPS	OPS+	BR/A	RC	RC/G	FR	G/POS	WS	TPW
1903 StL-N	2	7	0	1	0	0	0	0	0				.143	.143	.143	.286	-19	-1	0	.65	0	/1-2	0	-0.1

• USHER, Bob — Robert Royce Usher b: 3/1/1925, San Diego, CA BR/TR, 6'1.5", 180 lbs. Deb: 4/16/1946 Career OF: 46-295-41

YEAR TM-L	G	AB	R	H	2B	3B	HR	RBI	BB	SO	SB	CS	AVG	OBP	SLG	OPS	OPS+	BR/A	RC	RC/G	FR	G/POS	WS	TPW
1946 Cin-N	92	152	16	31	5	1	1	14	13	27	2	....	.204	.271	.270	.541	56	-9	12	2.53	2	0-80(23-32-25)/3-1	1	-1.0
1947 Cin-N	9	22	2	4	0	0	1	1	2	2	0	....	.182	.250	.318	.568	50	-2	2	2.23	0	/0-8(3-5-0)	0	-0.1
1950 Cin-N	106	321	51	83	17	0	6	35	27	38	3	....	.259	.316	.368	.684	79	-10	37	3.91	-6	0-93(4-80-12)	6	-1.8
1951 Cin-N	114	303	27	63	12	2	5	25	19	36	4	5	.208	.257	.310	.567	51	-23	23	2.35	2	0-98(14-82-2)	3	-2.4
1952 Chi-N	1	0	0	0	0	0	0	0	1	0	0	0	....	1.000	....	1.000	197	0	0	∞	0	....	0	0.0
1957 Cle-A	10	8	1	1	0	0	0	0	1	3	0	0	.125	.222	.125	.347	-3	-1	0	1.20	-1	/0-4(1-3-0),3-1	0	-0.2
Was-A	96	295	36	77	7	1	5	27	27	30	0	0	.261	.327	.342	.670	84	-6	34	3.95	-3	0-95(1-93-2)	6	-1.3
Yr.	106	303	37	78	7	1	5	27	28	33	0	0	.257	.324	.337	.661	82	-7	34	3.86	-3	0-99(2-96-2)/3-1	6	-1.5
Total 6	428	1101	133	259	41	4	18	102	90	136	9	5	.235	.295	.329	.624	68	-51	107	3.21	-5	0-378/3-2	16	-6.8

YEAR TM-L	G	AB	R	H	2B	3B	HR	RBI	BB	SO	SB	CS	AVG	OBP	SLG	OPS	OPS+	BR/A	RC	RC/G	FR	G/POS	WS	TPW
• USSAT, Dutch	William August Ussat b: 4/11/1904, Dayton, OH d: 5/29/1959, Dayton, OH BR/TR, 6'1", 170 lbs. Deb: 9/13/1925																							
1925 Cle-A	1	1	0	0	0	0	0	0	0	0	0	0	.000	.000	.000	.000	-99	-0	0	.00	0	/2-1	0	0.0
1927 Cle-A	4	16	4	3	0	1	0	2	0	1	0	0	.188	.278	.313	.590	53	-1	1	3.00	0	/3-4	0	-0.1
Total 2	**5**	**17**	**4**	**3**	**0**	**1**	**0**	**2**	**0**	**1**	**0**	**0**	**.176**	**.263**	**.294**	**.557**	**45**	**-1**	**1**	**2.79**	**0**	**/3-4,2-1**	**0**	**-0.1**
• UTLEY, Chase	Chase Cameron Utley b: 12/17/1978, Pasadena, CA BL/TR, 6'1", 170 lbs. Deb: 4/4/2003																							
2003 Phi-N	43	134	13	32	10	1	2	21	11	22	2	0	.239	.325	.373	.698	87	-2	17	4.32	4	2-37	5	0.3
• VACHE, Tex	Ernest Lewis Vache b: 11/17/1889, Santa Monica, CA d: 6/11/1953, Los Angeles, CA BR/TR, 6'1", 200 lbs. Deb: 4/16/1925																							
1925 Bos-A	110	252	41	79	15	7	3	48	21	33	2	2	.313	.382	.464	.846	114	5	45	6.73	-5	O-53(57-0-1)	7	-0.3
• VADEBONCOEUR, Gene	Onesime Eugene Vadeboncoeur b: 7/15/1858, Louiseville, Canada d: 10/16/1935, Haverhill, MA BR/TR, 5'6", 150 lbs. Deb: 7/11/1884																							
1884 Phi-N	4	14	1	3	0	0	0	3	1	2	....	....	.214	.267	.214	.481	56	-1	1	2.05	1	/C-4	0	0.0
• VAHRENHORST, Harry	Harry Henry "Van" Vahrenhorst b: 2/13/1885, St. Louis, MO d: 10/10/1943, St. Louis, MO BR/TR, 6'1", 175 lbs. Deb: 9/21/1904																							
1904 StL-A	1	1	0	0	0	0	0	0	0	....	0	....	.000	.000	.000	.000	-107	-0	0	.00	0	....	0	0.0
• VAIL, Mike	Michael Lewis Vail b: 11/10/1951, San Francisco, CA BR/TR, 6'1", 185 lbs. Deb: 8/18/1975 Career OF: 124-1-278																							
1975 NY-N	38	162	17	49	8	1	3	17	9	37	0	0	.302	.339	.420	.759	115	2	23	5.25	9	O-36(35-1-0)	6	1.0
1976 NY-N	53	143	8	31	5	1	0	9	6	19	0	1	.217	.248	.266	.514	49	-10	9	1.95	-1	O-35(2-0-33)	1	-1.4
1977 NY-N	108	279	29	73	12	1	8	35	19	58	0	7	.262	.313	.398	.711	94	-6	30	3.65	-2	O-85(2-0-83)	4	-1.2
1978 Cle-A	14	34	2	8	2	1	0	2	1	9	1	1	.235	.257	.353	.610	71	-2	3	2.73	0	/O-9(2-0-7),D-1	0	-0.2
Chi-N	74	180	15	60	6	2	4	33	3	24	0	1	.333	.344	.456	.800	109	1	25	5.31	-2	O-45(7-0-39)/3-1	5	-0.3
1979 Chi-N	87	179	28	60	8	2	7	35	14	27	0	2	.335	.383	.520	.903	131	7	34	7.22	-1	O-39(1-0-38)/3-2	7	0.4
1980 Chi-N	114	312	30	93	17	2	6	47	14	77	2	5	.298	.330	.423	.753	101	-2	40	4.60	1	O-77(19-0-61)	7	-0.4
1981 Cin-N	31	31	1	5	0	0	0	3	0	9	0	0	.161	.161	.161	.323	-8	-4	1	.65	0	/O-3(0-0-3)	0	-0.5
1982 Cin-N	78	189	9	48	10	1	4	29	6	33	0	0	.254	.277	.381	.658	81	-6	18	3.19	2	O-52(50-0-2)	2	-0.6
1983 SF-N	18	26	1	4	1	0	0	3	0	7	0	0	.154	.185	.192	.377	5	-3	1	1.20	-1	/1-4,O-2(2-0-0)	0	-0.4
Mon-N	34	53	5	15	2	0	2	4	8	10	0	0	.283	.387	.434	.821	128	2	9	6.51	2	O-15(3-0-12)/1-1,3-1	2	0.4
Yr.	52	79	6	19	3	0	2	7	8	17	0	0	.241	.326	.354	.680	90	-1	10	4.59	1	O-17(5-0-12)/1-5,3-1	2	-0.1
1984 LA-N	16	16	1	1	0	0	0	2	1	7	0	0	.063	.118	.063	.180	-49	-3	0	.27	0	/O-1	0	-0.3
Total 10	**665**	**1604**	**146**	**447**	**71**	**11**	**34**	**219**	**81**	**317**	**3**	**17**	**.279**	**.315**	**.400**	**.716**	**94**	**-25**	**192**	**4.22**	**7**	**O-399/1-5,3-4,D-1**	**34**	**-3.7**
• VALDERRAMA, Carlos	Carlos Alberto Valderrama b: 11/30/1977, Bachaquero, Venezuela BR/TR, 6', 175 lbs. Deb: 6/21/2003																							
2003 SF-N	7	7	0	1	0	0	0	0	0	3	1	0	.143	.143	.143	.286	-26	-1	0	.98	0	/O-5(4-2-0)	0	-0.1
• VALDES, Pedro	Pedro Jose (Manzo) Valdes b: 6/29/1973, Fajardo, Puerto Rico BL/TL, 6'1", 180 lbs. Deb: 5/15/1996 Career OF: 7-0-16																							
1996 Chi-N	9	8	2	1	1	0	0	1	1	5	0	0	.125	.222	.250	.472	24	-1	1	1.94	0	/O-1	0	-0.1
1998 Chi-N	14	23	1	5	1	1	0	2	1	3	0	1	.217	.250	.348	.598	53	-2	1	1.86	0	/O-2(6-0-1)	0	-0.2
2000 Tex-A	30	54	4	15	5	0	1	5	6	7	0	0	.278	.350	.426	.776	94	-1	9	5.95	-1	/O-7(1-0-13),D-4	1	-0.2
Total 3	**53**	**85**	**7**	**21**	**7**	**1**	**1**	**8**	**8**	**15**	**0**	**1**	**.247**	**.312**	**.388**	**.700**	**77**	**-4**	**10**	**4.29**	**-1**	**/O-10,D-4**	**1**	**-0.5**
• VALDES, Roy	Rogelio Lazaro (Rojas) Valdes b: 2/23/1920, Havana, Cuba BR/TR, 5'11", 185 lbs. Deb: 5/3/1944																							
1944 Was-A	1	1	0	0	0	0	0	0	0	0	0	0	.000	.000	.000	.000	-105	-0	0	.00	0	....	0	0.0
• VALDESPINO, Sandy	Hilario (Borroto) Valdespino b: 1/24/1939, San Jose de las Lajas, Cuba BL/TL, 5'8", 170 lbs. Deb: 4/12/1965 Career OF: 199-1-20																							
1965*Min-A	108	245	38	64	8	2	1	22	20	28	7	4	.261	.322	.322	.645	80	-6	26	3.52	3	O-57(43-0-17)	6	-0.6
1966 Min-A	52	108	11	19	1	1	2	9	4	24	2	2	.176	.212	.259	.472	33	-10	5	1.28	-1	O-23(22-1-0)	0	-1.3
1967 Min-A	99	97	9	16	2	0	1	3	5	22	3	1	.165	.206	.216	.422	23	-9	4	1.43	0	O-65(64-0-1)	0	-1.2
1968 Atl-N	36	86	8	20	1	0	1	4	10	20	0	0	.233	.320	.279	.599	81	-1	8	3.34	0	O-20(20-0-0)	2	-0.3
1969 Hou-N	41	119	17	29	4	0	0	12	15	19	2	2	.244	.328	.277	.606	73	-4	12	3.32	1	O-29(29-0-0)	2	-0.5
Sea-A	20	38	3	8	1	0	0	2	1	7	0	1	.211	.250	.237	.487	37	-4	2	1.87	2	/O-7(7-0-0)	0	-0.3
1970 Mil-A	8	9	0	0	0	0	0	0	0	4	0	0	.000	.000	.000	.000	-99	-2	0	.00	0	/O-1	0	-0.3
1971 KC-A	18	63	10	20	6	0	2	15	2	5	0	0	.317	.338	.508	.846	138	3	10	6.00	0	O-15(13-0-2)	3	0.2
Total 7	**382**	**765**	**96**	**176**	**23**	**3**	**7**	**67**	**57**	**129**	**14**	**10**	**.230**	**.288**	**.295**	**.583**	**66**	**-34**	**67**	**2.88**	**4**	**O-217**	**13**	**-4.3**
• VALDEZ, Julio	Julio Julian Valdez b: 6/3/1956, San Cristobal, Dominican Republic BB/TR, 6'2", 160 lbs. Deb: 9/2/1980																							
1980 Bos-A	8	19	4	5	1	0	1	4	0	5	2	0	.263	.300	.474	.774	103	0	3	5.56	0	/S-8	1	0.2
1981 Bos-A	17	23	1	5	0	0	0	3	0	2	0	1	.217	.217	.217	.435	24	-3	1	1.24	0	S-17	0	-0.2
1982 Bos-A	28	20	3	5	1	0	0	1	0	7	1	0	.250	.250	.300	.550	47	-1	2	2.63	0	S-22/D-3	1	0.0
1983 Bos-A	12	25	3	3	0	0	0	0	1	4	0	0	.120	.185	.120	.305	-13	-4	1	.80	-3	/2-9,S-2,D-1	0	-0.7
Total 4	**65**	**87**	**11**	**18**	**2**	**0**	**1**	**8**	**1**	**18**	**3**	**1**	**.207**	**.233**	**.264**	**.498**	**37**	**-7**	**6**	**2.30**	**-3**	**/S-49,2-9,D-4**	**2**	**-0.8**
• VALDEZ, Mario	Mario A. Valdez b: 11/19/1974, Obregon, Mexico BL/TL, 6'2", 190 lbs. Deb: 6/15/1997																							
1997 Chi-A	54	115	11	28	7	0	1	13	17	39	1	0	.243	.356	.330	.686	84	-2	15	4.31	-2	1-47/D-2,3-1	1	-0.6
2000 Oak-A	5	12	0	0	0	0	0	0	0	3	0	0	.000	.000	.000	.000	-102	-4	0	.00	0	/1-4	0	-0.4
2001 Oak-A	32	54	7	15	1	0	1	8	12	18	0	0	.278	.418	.352	.770	106	1	9	6.40	1	O-14(7-0-0),D-12/1-6	2	0.1
Total 3	**91**	**181**	**18**	**43**	**8**	**0**	**2**	**21**	**29**	**60**	**1**	**0**	**.238**	**.355**	**.315**	**.670**	**80**	**-4**	**24**	**4.52**	**-1**	**/1-57,D-14,O-14,3-1**	**3**	**-0.9**
• VALDIVIELSO, Jose	Jose (Lopez) Valdivielso b: 5/22/1934, Matanzas, Cuba BR/TR, 6'1", 175 lbs. Deb: 6/21/1955																							
1955 Was-A	94	294	32	65	12	5	2	28	21	38	1	2	.221	.280	.316	.596	63	-17	26	2.84	11	S-94	6	0.2
1956 Was-A	90	246	18	58	8	2	4	29	29	36	3	1	.236	.319	.333	.652	72	-9	26	3.54	-7	S-90	4	-0.9
1959 Was-A	24	14	1	4	0	0	0	0	1	3	0	0	.286	.333	.286	.619	72	-1	1	3.60	-2	S-21	0	-0.2
1960 Was-A	117	268	23	57	1	1	2	19	20	36	1	2	.213	.277	.246	.524	42	-22	19	2.18	1	*S-115/3-1	4	-1.4
1961 Min-A	76	149	15	29	5	0	1	9	8	19	1	1	.195	.236	.248	.484	28	-16	8	1.61	-2	S-43,2-15,3-14	2	-1.5
Total 5	**401**	**971**	**89**	**213**	**26**	**8**	**9**	**85**	**79**	**132**	**6**	**6**	**.219**	**.284**	**.290**	**.574**	**55**	**-64**	**80**	**2.64**	**1**	**S-363/2-15,3-15**	**16**	**-3.7**
• VALENT, Eric	Eric Christian Valent b: 4/4/1977, La Mirada, CA BL/TL, 6', 191 lbs. Deb: 6/8/2001 Career OF: 7-0-11																							
2001 Phi-N	22	41	3	4	2	0	0	1	4	11	0	0	.098	.196	.146	.342	-10	-7	1	1.04	3	/O-7(7-0-1),D-4	1	-0.4
2002 Phi-N	7	10	1	2	0	0	0	0	0	3	0	0	.200	.200	.200	.400	6	-1	0	.60	-1	/O-8(0-0-2),1-1	0	-0.2
2003 Cin-N	18	42	3	9	0	0	0	1	2	9	0	0	.214	.250	.214	.464	23	-5	2	1.95	1	/O-8(0-0-8)	0	-0.4
Total 3	**47**	**93**	**7**	**15**	**2**	**0**	**0**	**2**	**6**	**23**	**0**	**0**	**.161**	**.220**	**.183**	**.403**	**6**	**-13**	**4**	**1.37**	**3**	**/O-23,D-4,1-1**	**1**	**-1.0**
• VALENTIN, Javier	Jose Javier (Rosario) Valentin b: 9/19/1975, Manati, Puerto Rico BB/TR, 5'10", 198 lbs. Deb: 9/13/1997																							
1997 Min-A	4	7	1	2	0	0	0	0	0	3	0	0	.286	.286	.286	.571	49	-1	1	3.09	0	/C-4	0	0.0
1998 Min-A	55	162	11	32	7	1	3	18	11	30	0	0	.198	.249	.309	.557	43	-14	11	2.13	-4	C-53/D-1	2	-1.4
1999 Min-A	78	218	22	54	12	1	5	28	22	39	0	0	.248	.320	.381	.700	75	-8	28	4.39	-3	C-76	5	-0.6
2002 Min-A	4	4	0	2	0	0	0	0	0	0	0	0	.500	.500	.500	1.000	165	0	1	13.50	1	/C-4	0	0.2
2003 TB-A	49	135	13	30	7	1	3	15	5	31	0	0	.222	.255	.356	.611	60	-8	10	2.44	3	C-42/D-5	2	-0.3
Total 5	**190**	**526**	**47**	**120**	**26**	**3**	**11**	**61**	**38**	**103**	**0**	**0**	**.228**	**.283**	**.352**	**.634**	**62**	**-31**	**51**	**3.17**	**-2**	**C-179/D-6**	**9**	**-2.1**
• VALENTIN, John	John William Valentin b: 2/18/1967, Mineola, NY BR/TR, 6', 185 lbs. Deb: 7/27/1992																							
1992 Bos-A	58	185	21	51	13	0	5	25	20	17	1	0	.276	.353	.427	.780	110	3	28	5.28	0	S-58	7	0.8
1993 Bos-A	144	468	50	130	40	3	11	66	49	77	3	4	.278	.349	.447	.795	106	3	73	5.30	10	*S-144	16	2.4
1994 Bos-A	84	301	53	95	26	2	9	49	42	38	3	1	.316	.405	.505	.910	127	13	65	8.01	-2	S-83/D-1	14	1.7
1995*Bos-A	135	520	108	155	37	2	27	102	81	67	20	5	.298	.403	.533	.935	136	32	119	8.30	1	*S-135	29	4.1
1996 Bos-A	131	527	84	156	29	3	13	59	63	59	9	10	.296	.379	.436	.815	103	2	85	5.70	-1	*S-118,3-12/D-1	17	0.9
1997 Bos-A	143	575	95	176	**47**	5	18	77	58	66	7	4	.306	.375	.499	.874	123	19	103	6.44	13	2-79,3-64	21	3.5
1998*Bos-A	153	588	113	145	44	1	23	73	77	82	4	5	.247	.343	.442	.785	100	-1	92	5.33	20	*3-153/2-1	19	2.0
1999*Bos-A	113	450	58	114	27	1	12	70	40	68	0	1	.253	.320	.398	.718	79	-15	56	4.27	13	*3-111/D-2	12	-0.1
2000 Bos-A	10	35	6	9	1	0	2	2	2	5	0	1	.257	.297	.457	.754	85	-1	4	3.76	-3	3-10	0	-0.4

YEAR	TM-L	G	AB	R	H	2B	3B	HR	RBI	BB	SO	SB	CS	AVG	OBP	SLG	OPS	OPS+	BR/A	RC	RC/G	FR	G/POS	WS	TPW
2001	Bos-A	20	60	8	12	2	0	1	5	9	8	0	0	.200	.314	.283	.598	59	-3	5	2.62	-1	S-18/3-3	1	-0.3
2002	NY-N	114	208	18	50	15	0	3	30	22	37	0	0	.240	.342	.356	.697	88	-3	26	4.26	0	S-24,1-22,3-18/2-3,D-2	7	-0.2
Total	**11**	**1105**	**3917**	**614**	**1093**	**281**	**17**	**124**	**558**	**463**	**524**	**47**	**31**	**.279**	**.363**	**.454**	**.817**	**108**	**48**	**656**	**5.86**	**51**	**S-580,3-371/2-83,1-22,D-6**	**143**	**14.5**

• VALENTIN, Jose Jose Antonio Valentin b: 10/12/1969, Manati, Puerto Rico BB/TR, 5'10", 175 lbs. Deb: 9/17/1992 Career OF: 0-24-1

YEAR	TM-L	G	AB	R	H	2B	3B	HR	RBI	BB	SO	SB	CS	AVG	OBP	SLG	OPS	OPS+	BR/A	RC	RC/G	FR	G/POS	WS	TPW
1992	Mil-A	4	3	1	0	0	0	0	1	0	0	0	0	.000	.000	.000	.000	-102	-1	0	.00	-1	/2-1,S-1	0	-0.2
1993	Mil-A	19	53	10	13	1	2	1	7	7	16	1	0	.245	.344	.396	.740	100	0	8	4.86	-1	S-19	2	0.1
1994	Mil-A	97	285	47	68	19	0	11	46	38	75	12	3	.239	.332	.421	.753	89	-4	44	5.21	18	S-83,2-18/3-1	12	2.0
1995	Mil-A	112	338	62	74	23	3	11	49	37	83	16	8	.219	.296	.402	.698	75	-14	43	4.06	4	*S-104/D-4,3-1	8	-0.2
1996	Mil-A	154	552	90	143	33	7	24	95	66	145	17	4	.259	.338	.475	.813	99	-1	93	5.89	4	*S-151	20	1.5
1997	Mil-A	136	494	58	125	23	1	17	58	39	109	19	8	.253	.313	.407	.720	85	-11	64	4.42	3	*S-134/D-1	13	0.3
1998	Mil-N	151	428	65	96	24	0	16	49	63	105	10	7	.224	.325	.393	.718	88	-8	58	4.51	-1	*S-139/D-1	15	0.1
1999	Mil-N	89	256	45	58	9	5	10	38	48	52	3	2	.227	.353	.418	.771	95	-2	41	5.22	-13	S-85	8	-0.8
2000*	Chi-A	144	568	107	155	37	6	25	92	59	106	19	2	.273	.345	.491	.837	107	8	99	6.05	21	*S-141/0-2(0-0-1)	24	3.7
2001	Chi-A	124	438	74	113	22	2	28	68	50	114	9	6	.258	.338	.509	.847	115	8	75	5.82	12	3-66,S-43/0-1	15	2.2
2002	Chi-A	135	474	70	118	26	4	25	75	43	99	3	3	.249	.314	.479	.793	104	1	70	5.02	7	3-83,S-50/D-1	16	1.2
2003	Chi-A	144	503	79	119	26	2	28	74	54	114	8	3	.237	.314	.463	.778	102	1	75	5.04	15	*S-143	18	2.5
Total	**12**	**1309**	**4392**	**708**	**1082**	**243**	**32**	**196**	**652**	**504**	**1018**	**117**	**46**	**.246**	**.327**	**.450**	**.777**	**97**	**-23**	**669**	**5.16**	**67**	***S-1093,3-151/2-19,D-7,0-3**	**151**	**12.4**

• VALENTINE, Bob Robert Valentine Deb: 5/20/1876

YEAR	TM-L	G	AB	R	H	2B	3B	HR	RBI	BB	SO	SB	CS	AVG	OBP	SLG	OPS	OPS+	BR/A	RC	RC/G	FR	G/POS	WS	TPW
1876	NY-N	1	3	0	0	0	0	0	0	0	0	....	....	.000	.000	.000	.000	-115	-1	0	.00	-1	/C-1	0	-0.1

• VALENTINE, Bobby Robert John Valentine b: 5/13/1950, Stamford, CT BR/TR, 5'10", 189 lbs. Deb: 9/2/1969 M/C Career OF: 87-18-26

YEAR	TM-L	G	AB	R	H	2B	3B	HR	RBI	BB	SO	SB	CS	AVG	OBP	SLG	OPS	OPS+	BR/A	RC	RC/G	FR	G/POS	WS	TPW
1969	LA-N	5	0	3	0	0	0	0	0	0	0	0	0	....	....	....	....	-108	0	0	....	0	....	0	0.0
1971	LA-N	101	281	32	70	10	2	1	25	15	20	5	3	.249	.292	.310	.602	75	-10	24	2.81	-4	S-37,3-23,2-21,0-11(0-3-8)	5	-1.1
1972	LA-N	119	391	42	107	11	2	3	32	27	33	5	5	.274	.324	.335	.659	90	-6	41	3.52	-3	2-49,3-39,0-16(5-8-4),S-10	9	-0.6
1973	Cal-A	32	126	12	38	5	2	1	13	5	9	6	1	.302	.328	.397	.725	112	2	17	4.89	2	S-25/0-8(1-7-0)	5	0.7
1974	Cal-A	117	371	39	97	10	3	3	39	25	25	8	5	.261	.313	.329	.642	90	-5	39	3.46	-6	0-62(62-0-0),S-36,3-15/D-4,2	7	-1.2
1975	Cal-A	26	57	5	16	2	0	0	5	4	3	0	2	.281	.339	.316	.654	92	-1	6	3.28	-2	D-13/1-3,3-2,0-2(1-0-1)	1	-0.4
	SD-N	7	15	1	2	0	0	1	1	4	0	1	0	.133	.316	.333	.649	85	0	2	4.10	0	/0-4(4-0-0)	0	0.0
1976	SD-N	15	49	3	18	4	0	0	4	6	2	0	1	.367	.436	.449	.885	165	4	9	6.80	2	0-10(7-0-5)/1-4	3	0.6
1977	SD-N	44	67	5	12	3	0	1	10	7	10	0	0	.179	.257	.269	.525	46	-5	4	1.96	0	3-10,S-10/1-1	0	-0.5
	NY-N	42	83	8	11	1	0	1	3	6	9	0	0	.133	.191	.181	.372		-12	2	.87	1	1-15,S-14/3-4	1	-1.1
	Yr.	86	150	13	23	4	0	2	13	13	19	0	0	.153	.221	.220	.441	21	-17	7	1.34	1	S-24,1-16,3-14	1	-1.6
1978	NY-N	69	160	17	43	7	0	1	18	19	18	1	1	.269	.350	.331	.681	95	-1	18	3.72	-1	2-45/3-9	4	-0.1
1979	Sea-A	62	98	9	27	6	0	0	7	22	5	1	2	.276	.408	.337	.745	102	1	14	4.82	-6	S-29,0-15(7-0-8)/2-4,3-4,C,D	3	-0.4
Total	**10**	**639**	**1698**	**176**	**441**	**59**	**9**	**12**	**157**	**140**	**134**	**27**	**20**	**.260**	**.319**	**.326**	**.646**	**87**	**-33**	**177**	**3.44**	**-17**	**S-161,0-128,2-120,3-106/1,D,C**	**38**	**-4.1**

• VALENTINE, Ellis Ellis Clarence Valentine b: 7/30/1954, Helena, AR BR/TR, 6'4", 207 lbs. Deb: 9/3/1975 Career OF: 27-62-777

YEAR	TM-L	G	AB	R	H	2B	3B	HR	RBI	BB	SO	SB	CS	AVG	OBP	SLG	OPS	OPS+	BR/A	RC	RC/G	FR	G/POS	WS	TPW
1975	Mon-N	12	33	2	12	4	0	1	3	2	4	0	0	.364	.400	.576	.976	161	3	7	8.90	0	0-11(0-0-11)	2	0.2
1976	Mon-N	94	305	36	85	15	2	7	39	30	51	14	1	.279	.343	.410	.753	108	6	46	5.33	3	0-88(2-55-31)	10	0.7
1977	Mon-N★	127	508	63	149	28	2	25	76	30	58	13	5	.293	.333	.504	.837	124	15	78	5.49	-4	*0-126(0-0-126)	15	0.5
1978	Mon-N	151	570	75	165	35	2	25	76	35	88	13	8	.289	.333	.489	.822	129	18	90	5.68	10	*0-146(0-3-145)	22	2.1
1979	Mon-N	146	548	73	151	29	3	21	82	22	74	11	9	.276	.305	.454	.759	105	-1	65	4.03	-5	*0-144(0-0-144)	14	-1.4
1980	Mon-N	86	311	40	98	22	2	13	67	25	44	5	5	.315	.372	.524	.896	147	17	60	7.22	-5	0-83(0-0-83)	15	0.9
1981	Mon-N	22	76	8	16	3	0	3	15	6	11	0	1	.211	.268	.368	.637	78	-3	7	2.85	-1	0-21(0-0-21)	1	-0.5
	NY-N	48	169	15	35	8	1	5	21	5	38	0	3	.207	.230	.355	.585	65	-10	12	2.37	1	0-47(0-0-47)	1	-1.3
	Yr.	70	245	23	51	11	1	8	36	11	49	0	4	.208	.242	.359	.601	69	-13	19	2.52	0	0-68(0-0-68)	2	-1.8
1982	NY-N	111	337	33	97	14	1	8	48	5	38	1	3	.288	.300	.407	.707	97	-5	36	3.75	0	0-98(14-4-82)	7	-1.0
1983	Cal-A	86	271	30	65	10	2	13	43	18	48	2	1	.240	.287	.435	.723	97	-2	33	4.04	-2	0-85(11-0-80)	5	-0.9
1985	Tex-A	11	38	5	8	1	0	2	4	2	8	0	1	.211	.250	.395	.645	72	-2	3	2.62	0	/0-7(0-0-7),D-4	0	-0.3
Total	**10**	**894**	**3166**	**380**	**881**	**169**	**15**	**123**	**474**	**180**	**462**	**59**	**37**	**.278**	**.319**	**.458**	**.776**	**113**	**36**	**437**	**4.84**	**-5**	**0-856/D-4**	**92**	**-0.9**

• VALENTINE, Fred Fred Lee "Squeaky" Valentine b: 1/19/1935, Clarksdale, MS BB/TR, 6'1", 190 lbs. Deb: 9/7/1959 Career OF: 95-160-204

YEAR	TM-L	G	AB	R	H	2B	3B	HR	RBI	BB	SO	SB	CS	AVG	OBP	SLG	OPS	OPS+	BR/A	RC	RC/G	FR	G/POS	WS	TPW
1959	Bal-A	12	19	0	6	0	0	0	1	3	4	0	1	.316	.409	.316	.725	104	-0	2	4.75	0	/0-8(3-0-6)	0	0.0
1963	Bal-A	26	41	5	11	1	0	0	1	8	5	0	0	.268	.388	.293	.680	96	0	5	4.12	0	0-10(1-0-10)	1	0.0
1964	Was-A	102	212	20	48	5	0	4	20	21	44	4	2	.226	.305	.307	.612	71	-8	20	3.08	0	0-57(22-14-22)	3	-1.0
1965	Was-A	12	29	6	7	0	0	0	1	4	5	3	0	.241	.353	.241	.594	73	-0	3	3.74	0	0-11(5-6-1)	1	-0.1
1966	Was-A	146	508	77	140	29	7	16	59	51	63	22	10	.276	.353	.455	.808	132	22	81	5.51	0	*0-138(32-63-70)/1-2	24	1.6
1967	Was-A	151	457	52	107	16	1	11	44	56	76	17	3	.234	.331	.346	.677	104	7	58	4.34	-4	*0-136(26-70-55)	18	-0.4
1968	Was-A	37	101	11	24	2	0	3	7	6	11	1	0	.238	.294	.347	.640	96	-0	9	3.04	0	0-27(0-1-26)	2	-0.2
	Bal-A	47	91	9	17	3	2	2	5	7	20	0	0	.187	.253	.330	.582	75	-3	8	2.80	1	0-26(6-6-14)	1	-0.4
	Yr.	84	192	20	41	5	2	5	12	13	31	1	0	.214	.274	.339	.613	86	-3	17	2.93	1	0-53(6-7-40)	3	-0.6
Total	**7**	**533**	**1458**	**180**	**360**	**56**	**10**	**36**	**138**	**156**	**228**	**47**	**16**	**.247**	**.331**	**.373**	**.704**	**106**	**18**	**187**	**4.35**	**-3**	**0-413/1-2**	**50**	**-0.6**

• VALENZUELA, Benny Benjamin Beltran "Papelero" Valenzuela b: 6/2/1933, Los Mochis, Mexico BR/TR, 5'10", 175 lbs. Deb: 4/27/1958

YEAR	TM-L	G	AB	R	H	2B	3B	HR	RBI	BB	SO	SB	CS	AVG	OBP	SLG	OPS	OPS+	BR/A	RC	RC/G	FR	G/POS	WS	TPW
1958	StL-N	10	14	0	3	1	0	0	0	1	0	0	0	.214	.267	.286	.552	44	-1	1	2.79	0	/3-3	0	-0.2

• VALERA, Yohanny Yohanny Valera b: 8/17/1976, Santo Domingo, Dominican Republic BR/TR, 6'1", 196 lbs. Deb: 9/13/2000

YEAR	TM-L	G	AB	R	H	2B	3B	HR	RBI	BB	SO	SB	CS	AVG	OBP	SLG	OPS	OPS+	BR/A	RC	RC/G	FR	G/POS	WS	TPW
2000	Mon-N	7	10	1	0	0	0	0	1	1	5	0	0	.000	.167	.000	.167	-52	-2	0	.39	1	/C-7	0	-0.1

• VALLE, Dave David Valle b: 10/30/1960, Bayside, NY BR/TR, 6'2", 200 lbs. Deb: 9/7/1984

YEAR	TM-L	G	AB	R	H	2B	3B	HR	RBI	BB	SO	SB	CS	AVG	OBP	SLG	OPS	OPS+	BR/A	RC	RC/G	FR	G/POS	WS	TPW
1984	Sea-A	13	27	4	8	1	0	1	4	1	5	0	0	.296	.321	.444	.766	111	0	4	5.60	0	C-13	1	0.1
1985	Sea-A	31	70	2	11	1	0	0	4	1	17	0	0	.157	.181	.171	.352	-3	-10	2	.95	-1	C-31	1	-1.0
1986	Sea-A	22	53	10	18	3	0	5	15	7	7	0	0	.340	.417	.679	1.096	191	7	14	10.58	-2	C-12/1-4	3	0.5
1987	Sea-A	95	324	40	83	16	3	12	53	15	46	2	0	.256	.295	.435	.731	86	-7	38	3.95	-1	C-75,D-14/1-2,0-1	8	-0.5
1988	Sea-A	93	290	29	67	15	2	10	50	18	38	0	1	.231	.297	.400	.697	89	-5	31	3.48	5	C-84/D-3,1-1	9	0.5
1989	Sea-A	94	316	32	75	10	3	7	34	29	32	0	0	.237	.313	.354	.668	85	-6	34	3.51	4	C-93	9	0.3
1990	Sea-A	107	308	37	66	15	0	7	33	45	48	1	2	.214	.328	.331	.659	84	-6	34	3.55	0	*C-104/1-1	8	0.0
1991	Sea-A	132	324	38	63	8	1	8	32	34	49	0	2	.194	.289	.299	.588	63	-17	26	2.37	-2	*C-129/1-2	6	-1.2
1992	Sea-A	124	367	39	88	16	1	9	30	27	58	0	0	.240	.306	.362	.668	86	-7	41	3.79	0	*C-122	5	0.0
1993	Sea-A	135	423	48	109	19	0	13	63	48	56	1	0	.258	.357	.395	.751	100	2	59	4.64	5	*C-135	17	1.6
1994	Bos-A	30	76	6	12	2	1	1	5	9	18	0	1	.158	.256	.250	.506	30	-9	5	1.89	-2	C-28/1-2	1	-0.9
	Mil-A	16	36	8	14	6	0	1	5	9	4	0	1	.389	.522	.639	1.161	189	5	12	13.63	-1	C-12/D-2	2	0.5
	Yr.	46	112	14	26	8	1	2	10	18	22	0	2	.232	.348	.375	.723	84	-3	17	4.92	-3	C-40/1-2,D-2	3	-0.4
1995	Tex-A	36	75	7	18	3	0	0	5	6	18	1	0	.240	.305	.280	.585	52	-5	7	2.98	-0	C-29/1-7	2	-0.3
1996	Tex-A	42	86	14	26	6	1	3	17	9	17	0	0	.302	.368	.500	.868	111	1	15	6.55	1	C-35/1-5,D-1	6	0.4
Total	**13**	**970**	**2775**	**314**	**658**	**121**	**12**	**77**	**350**	**258**	**413**	**5**	**7**	**.237**	**.316**	**.373**	**.689**	**85**	**-57**	**322**	**3.81**	**7**	**C-902/1-24,D-20,0-1**	**78**	**0.0**

• VALLE, Hector Hector Jose Valle b: 10/27/1940, Vaga Baja, Puerto Rico BR/TR, 5'9", 180 lbs. Deb: 6/6/1965

YEAR	TM-L	G	AB	R	H	2B	3B	HR	RBI	BB	SO	SB	CS	AVG	OBP	SLG	OPS	OPS+	BR/A	RC	RC/G	FR	G/POS	WS	TPW
1965	LA-N	9	13	1	4	0	0	0	2	2	3	0	0	.308	.400	.308	.708	110	0	2	5.42	0	/C-6	1	0.0

• VALO, Elmer Elmer William Valo b: 3/5/1921, Ribnik, Czechoslovakia d: 7/19/1998, Palmerton, PA BL/TR, 5'11", 190 lbs. Deb: 9/22/1940 C Career OF: 352-38-952

YEAR	TM-L	G	AB	R	H	2B	3B	HR	RBI	BB	SO	SB	CS	AVG	OBP	SLG	OPS	OPS+	BR/A	RC	RC/G	FR	G/POS	WS	TPW
1940	Phi-A	6	23	6	8	0	0	0	0	3	0	2	0	.348	.423	.348	.771	104	1	4	7.63	0	/0-6(6-0-0)	1	0.1
1941	Phi-A	15	50	13	21	0	1	2	6	4	2	0	0	.420	.463	.580	1.043	179	6	14	12.31	0	0-10(10-0-0)	3	0.5
1942	Phi-A	133	459	64	115	13	10	2	40	70	21	13	8	.251	.355	.336	.690	95	-0	58	4.18	-3	*0-122(1-1-120)	12	-1.2
1943	Phi-A	77	249	31	55	6	2	3	18	35	13	2	6	.221	.319	.297	.616	81	-7	24	3.12	-3	0-63(9-0-54)	4	-1.5
1946	Phi-A	108	348	59	107	21	6	1	31	60	18	9	8	.307	.411	.411	.822	131	16	64	6.83	-3	0-90(5-0-85)	12	1.1
1947	Phi-A	112	370	60	111	12	6	5	36	64	21	11	3	.300	.406	.405	.811	123	16	69	6.70	1	*0-104(0-0-104)	17	1.5
1948	Phi-A	113	383	72	117	17	4	3	46	81	13	10	6	.305	.432	.394	.826	120	17	72	6.73	-6	*0-109(0-0-109)	17	0.7
1949	Phi-A	150	547	86	155	27	12	5	85	119	32	14	11	.283	.413	.404	.817	121	21	101	6.43	7	*0-150(150-0-0)	24	1.6

YEAR	TM-L	G	AB	R	H	2B	3B	HR	RBI	BB	SO	SB	CS	AVG	OBP	SLG	OPS	OPS+	BR/A	RC	RC/G	FR	G/POS	WS	TPW
1950	Phi-A	129	446	62	125	16	5	10	46	82	22	12	7	.280	.400	.406	.806	109	9	81	6.37	1	*O-117(33-0-85)	13	0.5
1951	Phi-A	123	444	75	134	27	8	7	55	75	20	11	6	.302	.412	.446	.858	129	22	87	7.10	0	*O-116(1-22-95)	17	1.8
1952	Phi-A	129	388	69	109	26	4	5	47	101	16	12	11	.281	.432	.407	.839	126	19	76	6.75	-4	*O-121(2-11-108)	19	1.2
1953	Phi-A	50	85	15	19	3	0	0	9	22	7	0	1	.224	.383	.259	.642	73	-2	10	3.93	0	O-25(10-0-15)	1	-0.3
1954	Phi-A	95	224	28	48	11	6	1	33	51	18	2	1	.214	.360	.330	.690	90	-1	31	4.56	-1	O-62(34-0-30)	7	-0.5
1955	KC-A	112	283	50	103	17	4	3	37	52	18	5	3	.364	.463	.484	.947	153	25	67	9.48	2	O-72(46-4-23)	18	2.3
1956	KC-A	9	9	1	2	0	0	0	2	1	1	0	0	.222	.300	.222	.522	40	-1	1	2.56	0	/O-1	0	-0.1
	Phi-N	98	291	40	84	13	3	5	37	48	21	7	6	.289	.395	.405	.800	118	9	48	5.78	-6	O-87(0-0-87)	12	0.0
1957	Bro-N	81	161	14	44	10	1	4	26	25	16	0	1	.273	.374	.422	.797	104	1	24	5.13	-1	O-36(26-0-14)	5	-0.1
1958	LA-N	65	101	9	25	2	1	1	14	12	11	0	1	.248	.327	.317	.644	69	-5	11	3.56	-1	O-26(16-0-13)	1	-0.6
1959	Cle-A	34	24	3	7	0	0	0	5	7	0	0	0	.292	.452	.292	.743	113	1	3	4.49	0	/O-2(0-0-2)	1	0.1
1960	NY-A	8	5	1	0	0	0	0	0	2	1	0	0	.000	.286	.000	.286	-17	-1	0	.80	0	/O-2(0-0-2)	0	-0.1
	Was-A	76	64	6	18	3	0	0	16	17	4	0	0	.281	.439	.328	.767	110	2	11	5.77	1	/O-6(1-0-5)	2	0.3
	Yr.	84	69	7	18	3	0	0	16	19	5	0	0	.261	.427	.304	.731	100	2	11	5.33	0	/O-8(1-0-7)	2	0.2
1961	Min-A	33	32	0	5	2	0	0	4	3	3	0	0	.156	.250	.219	.469	25	-3	2	1.41	0	/O-1	0	-0.3
	Phi-N	50	43	4	8	2	0	1	8	8	6	0	0	.186	.327	.302	.629	69	-2	5	3.87	0	/O-1	1	-0.2
Total	**20**	**1806**	**5029**	**768**	**1420**	**228**	**73**	**58**	**601**	**942**	**284**	**110**	**79**	**.282**	**.399**	**.391**	**.791**	**114**	**145**	**864**	**6.01**	**-17**	***O-1329**	**187**	**6.8**

• VAN BUREN, Deacon

Edward Eugene Van Buren b: 12/14/1870, LaSalle County, IL d: 6/29/1957, Portland, OR BL/TR, 5'10", 175 lbs. Deb: 4/21/1904

YEAR	TM-L	G	AB	R	H	2B	3B	HR	RBI	BB	SO	SB	CS	AVG	OBP	SLG	OPS	OPS+	BR/A	RC	RC/G	FR	G/POS	WS	TPW
1904	Bro-N	1	1	0	1	0	0	0	0	0	....	0	....	1.000	1.000	1.000	2.000	531	0	1	∞	0	....	0	0.1
	Phi-N	12	43	2	10	2	0	0	3	3	....	2	....	.233	.283	.279	.562	76	-1	4	3.19	1	O-12(12-0-0)	1	-0.1
	Yr.	13	44	2	11	2	0	0	3	3	....	2	....	.250	.298	.295	.593	86	-1	5	3.19	1	O-12(12-0-0)	1	-0.1

• VAN BURKLEO, Ty

Tyler Lee Van Burkleo b: 10/7/1963, Oakland, CA BL/TL, 6'5", 225 lbs. Deb: 7/28/1993

YEAR	TM-L	G	AB	R	H	2B	3B	HR	RBI	BB	SO	SB	CS	AVG	OBP	SLG	OPS	OPS+	BR/A	RC	RC/G	FR	G/POS	WS	TPW
1993	Cal-A	12	33	2	5	3	0	1	1	6	9	1	0	.152	.282	.333	.615	63	-2	4	3.56	-2	1-12	0	-0.4
1994	Col-N	2	5	0	0	0	0	0	0	0	1	0	0	.000	.000	.000	.000	-86	-1	0	.00	0	/1-2	0	-0.1
Total	**2**	**14**	**38**	**2**	**5**	**3**	**0**	**1**	**1**	**6**	**10**	**1**	**0**	**.132**	**.250**	**.289**	**.539**	**46**	**-3**	**4**	**3.02**	**-2**	**/1-14**	**0**	**-0.6**

• VAN CAMP, Al

Albert Joseph Van Camp b: 9/7/1903, Moline, IL d: 2/2/1981, Bensenville, IL BR/TR, 5'11.5", 175 lbs. Deb: 9/11/1928

YEAR	TM-L	G	AB	R	H	2B	3B	HR	RBI	BB	SO	SB	CS	AVG	OBP	SLG	OPS	OPS+	BR/A	RC	RC/G	FR	G/POS	WS	TPW
1928	Cle-A	5	17	0	4	1	0	0	2	0	1	1	0	.235	.235	.294	.529	38	-1	1	2.43	-1	/1-5	0	-0.3
1931	Bos-A	101	324	34	89	15	4	0	33	20	24	3	2	.275	.319	.346	.665	79	-9	36	3.97	1	O-59(58-3-2),1-25	5	-1.2
1932	Bos-A	34	103	10	23	4	2	0	6	4	17	0	0	.223	.252	.301	.553	44	-9	8	2.51	1	1-25	0	-1.0
Total	**3**	**140**	**444**	**44**	**116**	**20**	**6**	**0**	**41**	**24**	**42**	**4**	**2**	**.261**	**.301**	**.333**	**.634**	**69**	**-19**	**45**	**3.54**	**1**	**/O-59,1-55**	**5**	**-2.4**

• VAN DUSEN, Fred

Frederick William Van Dusen b: 7/31/1937, Jackson Heights, NY BL/TL, 6'3", 180 lbs. Deb: 9/11/1955

YEAR	TM-L	G	AB	R	H	2B	3B	HR	RBI	BB	SO	SB	CS	AVG	OBP	SLG	OPS	OPS+	BR/A	RC	RC/G	FR	G/POS	WS	TPW
1955	Phi-N	1	0	0	0	0	0	0	0	0	0	0	0	....	1.000	....	1.000	198	0	0	∞	0	....	0	0.0

• VAN DYKE, Bill

William Jennings Van Dyke b: 12/15/1863, Paris, IL d: 5/5/1933, El Paso, TX BR/TR, 5'8", 170 lbs. Deb: 4/17/1890 Career OF: 112-5-0

YEAR	TM-L	G	AB	R	H	2B	3B	HR	RBI	BB	SO	SB	CS	AVG	OBP	SLG	OPS	OPS+	BR/A	RC	RC/G	FR	G/POS	WS	TPW
1890	Tol-a	129	502	74	129	14	11	2	54	25	....	73	....	.257	.296	.341	.637	85	-13	74	5.26	-6	*O-110(109-1-0),3-18/2-2,C	10	-2.0
1892	StL-N	4	16	2	2	0	0	0	1	0	1	0	....	.125	.125	.125	.250	-26	-2	0	.49	-1	/O-4(0-4-0)	0	-0.3
1893	Bos-N	3	12	2	3	1	0	0	1	0	1	1	....	.250	.250	.333	.583	50	-1	1	3.77	0	/O-3(3-0-0)	0	-0.1
Total	**3**	**136**	**530**	**78**	**134**	**15**	**11**	**2**	**56**	**25**	**2**	**74**	**....**	**.253**	**.290**	**.334**	**.624**	**81**	**-16**	**76**	**5.06**	**-7**	**O-117/3-18,2-2,C-1**	**10**	**-2.4**

• VAN GORDER, Dave

David Thomas Van Gorder b: 3/27/1957, Los Angeles, CA BR/TR, 6'2", 205 lbs. Deb: 6/15/1982

YEAR	TM-L	G	AB	R	H	2B	3B	HR	RBI	BB	SO	SB	CS	AVG	OBP	SLG	OPS	OPS+	BR/A	RC	RC/G	FR	G/POS	WS	TPW
1982	Cin-N	51	137	4	25	3	1	0	7	14	19	1	0	.182	.263	.219	.482	35	-11	8	1.87	0	C-51	1	-1.0
1984	Cin-N	38	101	10	23	2	0	0	6	12	17	0	0	.228	.310	.248	.557	56	-6	8	2.72	1	C-36/1-1	2	-0.3
1985	Cin-N	73	151	12	36	7	0	2	24	9	19	0	0	.238	.286	.325	.610	67	-7	13	2.77	-1	C-70	2	-0.7
1986	Cin-N	9	10	0	0	0	0	0	0	1	2	0	0	.000	.091	.000	.091	-70	-2	0	.00	0	/C-7	0	-0.3
1987	Bal-A	12	21	4	5	0	0	1	1	3	6	0	0	.238	.333	.381	.714	91	-0	3	4.07	-1	C-12	1	-0.1
Total	**5**	**183**	**420**	**30**	**89**	**12**	**1**	**3**	**38**	**39**	**63**	**1**	**0**	**.212**	**.282**	**.267**	**.549**	**52**	**-27**	**32**	**2.43**	**-2**	**C-176/1-1**	**6**	**-2.4**

• VAN HALTREN, George

George Edward Martin "Rip" Van Haltren
b: 3/30/1866, St. Louis, MO d: 9/29/1945, Oakland, CA BL/TL, 5'11", 170 lbs. Deb: 6/27/1887 M Career OF: 313-1372-147 ♦

YEAR	TM-L	G	AB	R	H	2B	3B	HR	RBI	BB	SO	SB	CS	AVG	OBP	SLG	OPS	OPS+	BR/A	RC	RC/G	FR	G/POS	WS	TPW
1887	Chi-N	45	187	30	50	4	0	3	17	15	15	12	....	.267	.271	.279	.550	47	-9	17	3.23	-2	O-27(4-0-23),P-20	13	0.0
1888	Chi-N	81	318	46	90	9	14	4	34	22	34	21	....	.283	.329	.437	.767	133	17	54	6.40	2	O-57(47-4-7),P-30	24	-0.4
1889	Chi-N	134	543	126	168	20	10	9	81	82	41	28	....	.309	.405	.433	.838	128	23	109	7.71	-1	*O-130(115-15-0)/S-3,2-1	21	1.5
1890	Bro-P	92	376	84	126	8	9	5	54	41	23	35	....	.335	.405	.444	.849	119	16	84	9.05	4	O-67(6-12-49),P-28/S-3	30	1.5
1891	Bal-a	139	566	136	180	14	15	9	83	71	46	75	....	.318	.398	.443	.841	139	29	133	9.13	-10	O-81(79-0-2),S-59/P-6,2-2	26	1.4
1892	Bal-N	135	556	105	168	20	12	7	57	70	34	49	....	.302	.382	.419	.801	138	27	110	7.69	-5	*O-129(16-62-53)/P-4,3-3,1,S	19	0.5
	Pit-N	13	55	10	11	2	2	0	5	6	0	6	....	.200	.279	.309	.588	77	-2	7	4.03	-1	O-13(0-13-0)	1	-0.3
	Yr.	148	611	115	179	22	14	7	62	76	34	55	....	.293	.373	.409	.782	133	25	117	7.31	-6	*O-142(16-75-53)/P-4,3-3,1,S	20	0.1
1893	Pit-N	124	529	129	179	14	11	3	79	75	25	37	....	.338	.422	.423	.846	127	24	113	8.56	-5	*O-111(0-111-0),S-12/2-2	20	1.0
1894*	NY-N	139	528	109	175	22	4	7	104	55	23	43	....	.331	.399	.428	.827	104	5	112	8.48	0	*O-137(0-137-0)	21	-0.3
1895	NY-N	131	521	113	177	23	19	8	103	57	29	32	....	.340	.408	.503	.911	137	29	123	9.53	1	*O-131(0-131-0)/P-1	22	1.4
1896	NY-N	133	562	136	197	18	**21**	5	74	55	36	39	....	.351	.410	.484	.894	139	32	131	9.42	3	*O-133(0-133-0)/P-2	23	2.4
1897	NY-N	130	566	119	186	22	9	3	64	42	....	50	....	.329	.376	.415	.791	112	9	110	7.58	12	*O-129(0-129-0)	24	1.1
1898	NY-N	156	654	129	204	28	16	2	68	59	....	36	....	.312	.372	.413	.785	129	24	117	6.84	3	*O-156(17-138-3)	29	1.5
1899	NY-N	152	607	118	183	22	3	2	58	75	....	31	....	.301	.379	.357	.737	106	9	97	6.00	10	*O-151(23-128-0)	18	0.8
1900	NY-N	141	571	114	180	30	7	1	51	50	....	**45**	....	.315	.371	.398	.769	118	14	105	6.89	12	*O-141(0-141-0)/P-1	21	1.7
1901	NY-N	135	543	82	182	23	6	1	47	51	....	24	....	.335	.396	.405	.801	138	28	100	7.20	8	*O-135(0-135-0)/P-1	23	2.9
1902	NY-N	26	96	14	24	1	2	0	7	17	....	6	....	.250	.363	.302	.665	106	2	13	4.79	2	O-24(3-13-8)	3	0.2
1903	NY-N	84	280	42	72	6	1	0	28	28	....	14	....	.257	.327	.286	.613	72	-9	32	4.00	-4	O-75(3-70-2)	6	-1.7
Total	**17**	**1990**	**8058**	**1642**	**2552**	**286**	**161**	**69**	**1014**	**871**	**306**	**583**	**....**	**.317**	**.385**	**.417**	**.802**	**122**	**270**	**1568**	**7.52**	**28**	***O-1827/P-93,S-79,2-5,3-3,1**	**344**	**15.3**

• VAN NOY, Jay

Jay Lowell Van Noy b: 11/4/1928, Garland, UT BL/TR, 6'1", 200 lbs. Deb: 6/18/1951

YEAR	TM-L	G	AB	R	H	2B	3B	HR	RBI	BB	SO	SB	CS	AVG	OBP	SLG	OPS	OPS+	BR/A	RC	RC/G	FR	G/POS	WS	TPW
1951	StL-N	6	7	1	0	0	0	0	0	1	6	0	0	.000	.125	.000	.125	-63	-2	0	.13	-0	/O-1	0	-0.2

• VAN ROBAYS, Maurice

Maurice Rene "Bomber" Van Robays b: 11/15/1914, Detroit, MI d: 3/1/1965, Detroit, MI BR/TR, 6'.5", 190 lbs. Deb: 9/7/1939 Career OF: 403-3-64

YEAR	TM-L	G	AB	R	H	2B	3B	HR	RBI	BB	SO	SB	CS	AVG	OBP	SLG	OPS	OPS+	BR/A	RC	RC/G	FR	G/POS	WS	TPW
1939	Pit-N	27	105	13	33	9	0	2	16	6	10	0	....	.314	.351	.457	.808	118	2	16	5.72	-2	O-25(25-0-0)/3-1	3	-0.1
1940	Pit-N	145	572	82	156	27	7	11	116	33	58	2	....	.273	.316	.402	.718	98	-4	69	4.32	-6	*O-143(137-0-6)/1-1	13	-1.8
1941	Pit-N	129	457	62	129	23	5	4	78	41	29	0	....	.282	.343	.381	.723	104	2	57	4.38	3	*O-121(121-0-0)	13	-0.2
1942	Pit-N	100	328	29	76	13	5	1	46	30	24	0	....	.232	.298	.311	.609	76	-10	30	3.05	1	O-84(84-0-0)	5	-1.5
1943	Pit-N	69	236	32	68	17	7	1	35	18	19	0	....	.288	.344	.432	.776	119	5	34	5.11	-4	O-60(15-0-45)	7	-0.3
1946	Pit-N	59	146	14	31	5	3	1	12	11	15	0	....	.212	.272	.308	.580	63	-8	11	2.48	-2	O-37(21-3-13)/1-2	1	-1.2
Total	**6**	**529**	**1844**	**232**	**493**	**94**	**27**	**20**	**303**	**139**	**155**	**2**	**....**	**.267**	**.321**	**.380**	**.702**	**97**	**-12**	**218**	**4.11**	**-10**	**O-470/1-3,3-1**	**42**	**-5.0**

• VAN SLYKE, Andy

Andrew James Van Slyke b: 12/21/1960, Utica, NY BL/TR, 6'1", 192 lbs. Deb: 6/17/1983 Career OF: 89-1119-316

YEAR	TM-L	G	AB	R	H	2B	3B	HR	RBI	BB	SO	SB	CS	AVG	OBP	SLG	OPS	OPS+	BR/A	RC	RC/G	FR	G/POS	WS	TPW
1983	StL-N	101	309	51	81	15	5	8	38	46	64	21	7	.262	.360	.421	.780	115	9	50	5.54	0	O-69(50-7-23),3-30/1-9	11	0.6
1984	StL-N	137	361	45	88	16	4	7	50	63	71	28	5	.244	.356	.368	.725	107	9	54	5.10	-1	O-81(34-15-35),3-32,1-30	14	0.5
1985*	StL-N	146	424	61	110	25	6	13	55	47	54	34	6	.259	.336	.439	.775	116	13	66	5.45	6	*O-142(4-10-133)/1-2	18	1.4
1986	StL-N	137	418	48	113	23	7	13	61	47	85	21	8	.270	.345	.452	.798	119	11	68	5.80	8	*O-110(1-27-87),1-38	17	1.5
1987	Pit-N	157	564	93	165	36	11	21	82	56	122	34	8	.293	.361	.507	.868	126	23	108	6.94	6	*O-150(0-114-37)/1-1	25	2.6
1988	Pit-N★	154	587	101	169	23	**15**	25	100	57	126	30	9	.288	.352	.506	.858	146	35	107	6.41	9	*O-152(0-152-0)	28	4.5
1989	Pit-N	130	476	64	113	18	9	9	53	47	100	16	4	.237	.310	.370	.680	97	-1	55	3.84	4	*O-123(0-123-0)/1-2	14	0.1
1990*	Pit-N	136	493	67	140	26	6	17	77	66	89	14	4	.284	.370	.465	.834	133	24	89	6.51	-5	*O-133(0-133-0)	23	1.7
1991*	Pit-N	138	491	87	130	24	7	17	83	71	85	10	3	.265	.362	.446	.808	128	21	85	6.04	-1	*O-135(0-135-0)	22	1.8
1992*	Pit-N★	154	614	103	**199**	**45**	12	14	89	58	99	12	3	.324	.386	.505	.891	152	43	122	7.56	6	*O-154(0-154-0)	35	5.0
1993	Pit-N★	83	323	42	100	13	4	8	50	24	40	11	2	.310	.361	.449	.810	116	8	50	5.55	-4	O-78(0-78-0)	12	0.5
1994	Pit-N	105	374	41	92	18	3	6	30	52	72	7	0	.246	.341	.358	.699	82	-7	48	4.43	5	O-99(0-99-0)	8	-0.1
1995	Bal-A	17	63	6	10	1	0	3	8	5	15	0	0	.159	.221	.317	.538	37	-6	4	2.17	1	O-17(0-16-1)	1	-0.5

YEAR TM-L	G	AB	R	H	2B	3B	HR	RBI	BB	SO	SB	CS	AVG	OBP	SLG	OPS	OPS+	BR/A	RC	RC/G	FR	G/POS	WS	TPW
Phi-N	63	214	26	52	10	2	3	16	28	41	7	0	.243	.336	.350	.687	81	-4	27	4.28	0	0-56(0-56-0)	3	-0.4
Total 13	1658	5711	835	1562	293	91	164	792	667	1063	245	59	.274	.352	.443	.795	120	178	933	5.76	34	*0-1499/1-82,3-62	231	19.2

• VAN ZANDT, Ike Charles Isaac Van Zandt b: 2/1876, Brooklyn, NY d: 9/14/1908, Nashua, NH BL/TL Deb: 8/5/1901 Career OF: 1-29-46 ♦

YEAR TM-L	G	AB	R	H	2B	3B	HR	RBI	BB	SO	SB	CS	AVG	OBP	SLG	OPS	OPS+	BR/A	RC	RC/G	FR	G/POS	WS	TPW
1901 NY-N	3	6	1	1	0	0	0	0	0	....	0	....	.167	.167	.167	.333	-3	-0	0	.91	-1	/P-2,0-1	0	-0.6
1904 Chi-N	3	11	0	0	0	0	0	0	0	....	0	....	.000	.000	.000	.000	-100	-3	0	.00	0	/0-3(0-0-1)	0	-0.3
1905 StL-A	94	322	31	75	15	1	1	20	7	....	7	....	.233	.252	.295	.547	77	-9	27	2.82	-8	0-75(0-29-45)/1-1,P-1	4	-2.0
Total 3	100	339	32	76	15	1	1	20	7	....	7	....	.224	.242	.283	.525	70	-12	27	2.67	-9	/0-79,P-3,1-1	4	-2.9

• VAN ZANT, Dick Richard "Foghorn Dick" Van Zant b: 11/1864, Richmond, IN d: 8/6/1912, Richmond, IN, 6' Deb: 10/4/1888

YEAR TM-L	G	AB	R	H	2B	3B	HR	RBI	BB	SO	SB	CS	AVG	OBP	SLG	OPS	OPS+	BR/A	RC	RC/G	FR	G/POS	WS	TPW
1888 Cle-a	10	31	1	8	1	0	0	1	1	....	1	....	.258	.303	.290	.593	93	-0	3	3.65	-1	3-10	1	-0.1

• VANDAGRIFT, Carl Carl William Vandagrift b: 4/22/1883, Cantrall, IL d: 10/9/1920, Fort Wayne, IN BR/TR, 5'8", 155 lbs. Deb: 5/19/1914

YEAR TM-L	G	AB	R	H	2B	3B	HR	RBI	BB	SO	SB	CS	AVG	OBP	SLG	OPS	OPS+	BR/A	RC	RC/G	FR	G/POS	WS	TPW
1914 Ind-F	43	136	25	34	4	0	0	9	9	15	7	....	.250	.301	.279	.581	59	-7	15	3.17	-3	2-28,3-12/S-5	2	-1.0

• VANDER WAL, John John Henry Vander Wal b: 4/29/1966, Grand Rapids, MI BL/TL, 6'1", 197 lbs. Deb: 9/6/1991 Career OF: 238-2-347

YEAR TM-L	G	AB	R	H	2B	3B	HR	RBI	BB	SO	SB	CS	AVG	OBP	SLG	OPS	OPS+	BR/A	RC	RC/G	FR	G/POS	WS	TPW
1991 Mon-N	21	61	4	13	4	1	1	8	1	18	0	0	.213	.226	.361	.586	63	-3	4	2.30	0	0-17(17-0-0)	0	-0.4
1992 Mon-N	105	213	21	51	8	2	4	20	24	36	3	0	.239	.316	.352	.669	90	-2	25	4.17	1	0-57(55-0-4)/1-7	5	-0.4
1993 Mon-N	106	215	34	50	7	4	5	30	27	30	6	3	.233	.321	.372	.693	81	-6	26	4.11	-2	1-42,0-38(27-2-10)	6	-1.1
1994 Col-N	91	110	12	27	3	1	5	15	16	31	2	1	.245	.341	.427	.769	85	-2	16	4.79	-1	1-14/0-7(5-0-2)	3	-0.5
1995*Col-N	105	101	15	35	8	1	5	21	16	23	1	1	.347	.436	.594	1.030	131	5	26	10.03	0	1-10,0-10(7-0-3)	4	0.4
1996 Col-N	104	151	20	38	6	2	5	31	19	38	2	2	.252	.339	.417	.756	79	-5	22	5.07	-1	0-24(25-0-1),1-10	4	-0.7
1997 Col-N	76	92	7	16	2	0	1	11	10	33	1	1	.174	.255	.228	.483	23	-11	5	1.86	-2	0-25(2-0-8)/1-5,D-2	0	-1.3
1998 Col-N	89	104	18	30	10	1	5	20	16	29	0	0	.288	.383	.548	.931	116	3	23	8.15	1	0-10(3-0-22)/1-2	3	0.3
*SD-N	20	25	3	6	3	0	0	0	6	5	0	0	.240	.387	.360	.747	106	1	4	5.06	1	0-25(2-0-3)/1-3,D-3	1	0.1
Yr.	109	129	21	36	13	1	5	20	22	34	0	0	.279	.384	.512	.896	114	3	27	7.51	2	0-35(5-0-25)/1-5,D-3	4	0.4
1999 SD-N	132	246	26	67	18	0	6	41	37	59	2	1	.272	.372	.419	.791	108	4	40	5.76	-1	1-28/0-5(45-0-3),D-1	8	0.0
2000 Pit-N	134	384	74	115	29	0	24	94	72	92	11	2	.299	.413	.563	.975	144	30	94	9.05	-5	0-48(13-0-65),1-33/D-3	19	1.8
2001 Pit-N	97	313	39	87	22	3	11	50	42	84	7	4	.278	.365	.473	.838	112	6	54	6.05	-8	0-78(20-0-56),1-13/D-7	10	-0.7
SF-N	49	139	19	35	6	1	3	20	26	38	1	2	.252	.370	.374	.744	101	0	20	4.86	1	0-73(3-0-38)/1-1	3	0.0
Yr.	146	452	58	122	28	4	14	70	68	122	8	6	.270	.367	.442	.809	108	6	74	5.67	-7	*0-151(23-0-94),1-14/D-7	13	-0.7
2002*NY-A	84	219	30	57	17	1	6	20	23	58	1	1	.260	.331	.429	.760	101	-0	30	4.65	-4	0-41(8-0-49),D-14/1-6	2	-0.7
2003 Mil-N	117	327	50	84	25	1	14	45	46	104	1	2	.257	.350	.468	.818	113	6	55	5.91	-1	0-89(6-0-83)	8	0.1
Total 13	1330	2700	372	711	168	18	95	426	381	678	38	20	.263	.356	.444	.801	105	25	445	5.76	-21	0-547,1-174/D-30	76	-3.1

• VANN, John John Silas Vann b: 6/7/1893, Fairfield, OK d: 6/10/1958, Shreveport, LA BR/TR Deb: 6/11/1913

YEAR TM-L	G	AB	R	H	2B	3B	HR	RBI	BB	SO	SB	CS	AVG	OBP	SLG	OPS	OPS+	BR/A	RC	RC/G	FR	G/POS	WS	TPW
1913 StL-N	1	1	0	0	0	0	0	0	0	1	0	....	.000	.000	.000	.000	-101	-0	0	.00	0	....	0	0.0

• VARGAS, Eddie Hediberto (Rodriguez) Vargas b: 2/23/1959, Guanica, Puerto Rico BR/TR, 6'4", 205 lbs. Deb: 9/8/1982

YEAR TM-L	G	AB	R	H	2B	3B	HR	RBI	BB	SO	SB	CS	AVG	OBP	SLG	OPS	OPS+	BR/A	RC	RC/G	FR	G/POS	WS	TPW
1982 Pit-N	8	8	1	3	1	0	0	3	0	2	0	0	.375	.375	.500	.875	139	0	2	6.78	0	/1-5	0	0.0
1984 Pit-N	18	31	3	7	2	0	0	2	3	5	0	0	.226	.294	.290	.584	65	-1	3	3.24	0	1-13	0	-0.2
Total 2	26	39	4	10	3	0	0	5	3	7	0	0	.256	.310	.333	.643	80	-1	4	3.94	0	/1-18	0	-0.2

• VARITEK, Jason Jason Andrew Varitek b: 4/11/1972, Rochester, MN BB/TR, 6'2", 210 lbs. Deb: 9/24/1997

YEAR TM-L	G	AB	R	H	2B	3B	HR	RBI	BB	SO	SB	CS	AVG	OBP	SLG	OPS	OPS+	BR/A	RC	RC/G	FR	G/POS	WS	TPW
1997 Bos-A	1	1	0	1	0	0	0	0	0	0	0	0	1.000	1.000	1.000	2.000	416	0	1	∞	0	/C-1	0	0.0
1998*Bos-A	86	221	31	56	13	0	7	33	17	45	2	2	.253	.313	.407	.720	84	-6	26	3.88	-1	C-75/D-3	5	-0.3
1999*Bos-A	144	483	70	130	39	2	20	76	46	85	1	2	.269	.335	.482	.818	102	-1	76	5.40	0	*C-140/D-2	12	0.8
2000 Bos-A	139	448	55	111	31	1	10	65	60	84	1	1	.248	.344	.388	.733	83	-11	60	4.49	-2	*C-128/D-1	7	-0.4
2001 Bos-A	51	174	19	51	11	1	7	25	21	35	0	0	.293	.372	.489	.861	123	6	31	6.35	12	C-50	8	2.1
2002 Bos-A	132	467	58	124	27	1	10	61	41	95	4	3	.266	.334	.392	.726	90	-7	60	4.45	7	*C-127/D-1	12	0.9
2003*Bos-A★	142	451	63	123	31	1	25	85	51	106	3	2	.273	.356	.512	.868	122	14	82	6.27	-7	*C-137/D-4	17	1.5
Total 7	695	2245	296	596	152	6	79	345	236	450	11	10	.265	.342	.444	.786	100	-4	335	5.10	9	C-658/D-11	61	4.6

• VARNER, Buck Glen Gann Varner b: 8/17/1930, Hixson, TN BL/TR, 5'10", 170 lbs. Deb: 9/19/1952

YEAR TM-L	G	AB	R	H	2B	3B	HR	RBI	BB	SO	SB	CS	AVG	OBP	SLG	OPS	OPS+	BR/A	RC	RC/G	FR	G/POS	WS	TPW
1952 Was-A	2	4	0	0	0	0	0	0	1	1	0	0	.000	.200	.000	.200	-43	-1	0	.00	-0	/0-1	0	-0.1

• VARNEY, Pete Richard Fred Varney b: 4/10/1949, Roxbury, MA BR/TR, 6'3", 235 lbs. Deb: 8/26/1973

YEAR TM-L	G	AB	R	H	2B	3B	HR	RBI	BB	SO	SB	CS	AVG	OBP	SLG	OPS	OPS+	BR/A	RC	RC/G	FR	G/POS	WS	TPW
1973 Chi-A	5	4	0	0	0	0	0	0	1	0	0	0	.000	.200	.000	.200	-38	-1	0	.35	0	/C-5	0	-0.1
1974 Chi-A	9	28	1	7	0	0	0	2	1	8	0	0	.250	.276	.250	.526	51	-2	2	2.55	0	/C-9	0	-0.1
1975 Chi-A	36	107	12	29	5	1	2	8	6	28	2	0	.271	.316	.393	.708	98	-0	14	4.68	0	C-34/D-2	4	0.1
1976 Chi-A	14	41	5	10	2	0	3	5	2	9	0	0	.244	.279	.512	.791	127	1	5	4.09	-1	C-14	1	0.1
Atl-N	5	10	0	1	0	0	0	0	0	2	0	0	.100	.100	.100	.200	-41	-2	0	.00	0	/C-5	0	-0.1
Total 4	69	190	18	47	7	1	5	15	10	47	2	0	.247	.289	.374	.662	87	-3	21	3.80	-1	/C-67,D-2	5	-0.2

• VARSHO, Gary Gary Andrew Varsho b: 6/20/1961, Marshfield, WI BL/TR, 5'11", 190 lbs. Deb: 7/6/1988 C Career OF: 88-9-129

YEAR TM-L	G	AB	R	H	2B	3B	HR	RBI	BB	SO	SB	CS	AVG	OBP	SLG	OPS	OPS+	BR/A	RC	RC/G	FR	G/POS	WS	TPW
1988 Chi-N	46	73	6	20	3	0	0	5	1	6	5	0	.274	.284	.315	.599	69	-2	7	3.69	-2	0-18(10-0-8)	2	-0.5
1989 Chi-N	61	87	10	16	4	2	0	6	4	13	3	0	.184	.220	.276	.496	38	-7	6	2.20	0	0-21(17-0-4)	0	-0.8
1990 Chi-N	46	48	10	12	4	0	0	1	1	6	2	0	.250	.265	.333	.599	59	-2	4	3.05	0	/0-3(2-0-1)	0	-0.3
1991*Pit-N	99	187	23	51	11	2	4	23	19	34	9	2	.273	.346	.417	.763	115	5	29	5.46	0	0-54(5-5-45)/1-3	7	0.4
1992*Pit-N	103	162	22	36	6	3	4	22	10	32	5	2	.222	.267	.370	.638	80	-5	16	3.28	-1	0-44(14-2-28)	3	-0.7
1993 Cin-N	77	95	8	22	6	0	2	11	9	19	1	0	.232	.305	.358	.663	76	-3	11	3.86	1	0-22(13-0-9)	2	-0.3
1994 Pit-N	67	82	15	21	6	3	0	5	4	19	0	1	.256	.307	.402	.709	82	-3	10	4.08	-2	0-36(18-2-18)/1-1	1	-0.5
1995 Phi-N	72	103	7	26	1	1	0	11	7	17	2	0	.252	.313	.282	.594	58	-6	10	3.36	-1	0-25(9-0-16)	1	-0.8
Total 8	571	837	101	204	41	11	10	84	55	146	27	5	.244	.296	.355	.651	79	-23	93	3.81	-5	0-223/1-4	16	-3.4

• VATCHER, Jim James Ernest Vatcher b: 5/27/1965, Santa Monica, CA BR/TR, 5'9", 165 lbs. Deb: 5/30/1990 Career OF: 16-1-37

YEAR TM-L	G	AB	R	H	2B	3B	HR	RBI	BB	SO	SB	CS	AVG	OBP	SLG	OPS	OPS+	BR/A	RC	RC/G	FR	G/POS	WS	TPW
1990 Phi-N	36	46	5	12	1	0	1	4	4	6	0	0	.261	.320	.348	.668	84	-1	5	3.94	-1	0-24(12-0-12)	2	-0.2
Atl-N	21	27	2	7	1	1	0	3	1	9	0	0	.259	.286	.370	.656	75	-1	3	3.96	-0	/0-6(2-0-4)	0	-0.1
Yr.	57	73	7	19	2	1	1	7	5	15	0	0	.260	.308	.356	.664	81	-2	8	3.95	-1	0-30(14-0-16)	2	-0.3
1991 SD-N	17	20	3	4	0	0	0	2	4	6	1	0	.200	.333	.200	.533	52	-1	2	3.13	-0	0-11(2-0-9)	1	-0.1
1992 SD-N	13	16	1	4	1	0	0	2	3	6	0	0	.250	.368	.313	.681	93	0	2	4.58	1	0-13(0-1-12)	1	0.0
Total 3	87	109	11	27	3	1	1	11	12	27	1	0	.248	.322	.321	.643	77	-3	12	3.89	0	/0-54	4	-0.4

• VAUGHAN, Arky Joseph Floyd Vaughan b: 3/9/1912, Clifty, AR d: 8/30/1952, Eagleville, CA BL/TR, 5'10.5", 175 lbs. Deb: 4/17/1932 HOF: 1985 Career OF: 60-0-0

YEAR TM-L	G	AB	R	H	2B	3B	HR	RBI	BB	SO	SB	CS	AVG	OBP	SLG	OPS	OPS+	BR/A	RC	RC/G	FR	G/POS	WS	TPW
1932 Pit-N	129	497	71	158	15	10	4	61	39	26	10	....	.318	.375	.412	.787	113	11	79	5.87	8	*S-128	21	2.8
1933 Pit-N	152	573	85	180	29	**19**	9	97	64	23	3	....	.314	.388	.478	.866	146	36	112	7.28	7	*S-152	34	**5.7**
1934 Pit-N★	149	558	115	186	41	11	12	94	**94**	38	10	....	.333	**.431**	.511	.942	148	43	135	9.59	20	*S-149	36	**7.2**
1935 Pit-N★	137	499	108	192	34	10	19	99	**97**	18	4	....	**.385**	**.491**	**.607**	**1.098**	**187**	**69**	163	**13.78**	-1	*S-137	**39**	**7.6**
1936 Pit-N★	156	568	**122**	190	30	11	9	78	**118**	21	6	....	.335	**.453**	.474	.927	146	46	137	9.34	8	*S-156	35	**6.4**
1937 Pit-N★	126	469	71	151	17	**17**	5	72	54	22	7	....	.322	.394	.463	.857	132	22	91	7.44	9	*S-108,0-12(12-0-0)	25	3.7
1938 Pit-N★	148	541	88	174	35	5	7	68	104	21	14	....	.322	.433	.444	.876	140	37	115	8.22	9	*S-147	34	5.7
1939 Pit-N★	152	595	94	182	30	11	6	62	70	20	12	....	.306	.385	.424	.808	119	18	103	6.34	-3	*S-152	25	2.6
1940 Pit-N★	156	594	**113**	178	40	**15**	7	95	88	25	12	....	.300	.393	.453	.846	134	30	113	7.17	-10	*S-155/3-2	31	3.2
1941 Pit-N★	106	374	69	118	20	7	6	38	50	13	8	....	.316	.399	.455	.854	141	22	72	7.23	-7	S-97/3-3	19	2.2
1942 Bro-N★	128	495	82	137	18	4	2	49	51	17	8	....	.277	.348	.341	.689	100	1	63	4.58	-5	*3-119/S-5,2-1	19	0.2
1943 Bro-N	149	610	**112**	186	39	6	5	66	60	13	**20**	....	.305	.370	.413	.783	126	20	96	5.84	-3	S-99,3-55	28	2.8
1947*Bro-N	64	126	24	41	5	2	2	25	27	11	4	....	.325	.444	.444	.889	132	8	27	8.44	2	0-22(22-0-0),3-10	7	0.8
1948 Bro-N	65	123	19	30	3	0	3	22	21	8	0	....	.244	.354	.341	.696	86	-2	15	4.31	2	0-26(26-0-0)/3-8	3	-0.1
Total 14	1817	6622	1173	2103	356	128	96	926	937	276	118	....	.318	.406	.453	.859	135	361	1323	7.57	36	*S-1485,3-197/0-60,2-1	356	50.7

YEAR TM-L	G	AB	R	H	2B	3B	HR	RBI	BB	SO	SB	CS	AVG	OBP	SLG	OPS	OPS+	BR/A	RC	RC/G	FR	G/POS	WS	TPW
• VAUGHAN, Glenn	Glenn Edward "Sparky" Vaughan b: 2/15/1944, Compton, CA BB/TR, 5'11", 170 lbs. Deb: 9/20/1963																							
1963 Hou-N	9	30	1	5	0	0	0	0	2	5	1	0	.167	.219	.167	.385	13	-3	1	1.18	-1	/S-9,3-1	0	-0.4
• VAUGHN, Bobby	Robert Vaughn b: 6/4/1885, Stamford, NY d: 4/11/1965, Seattle, WA BR/TR, 5'9", 150 lbs. Deb: 6/12/1909																							
1909 NY-A	5	14	1	2	0	0	0	0	1	....	1	....	.143	.200	.143	.343	8	-1	1	1.21	-3	/2-4,S-1	0	-0.5
1915 StL-F	144	521	69	146	19	9	0	32	58	38	24	....	.280	.356	.351	.707	103	4	75	4.70	-3	*2-127,S-12/3-8	17	0.4
Total 2	149	535	70	148	19	9	0	32	59	38	25	....	.277	.352	.346	.698	101	2	76	4.60	-6	2-131/S-13,3-8	17	-0.2
• VAUGHN, Farmer	Harry Francis Vaughn b: 3/1/1864, Ruraldale, OH d: 2/21/1914, Cincinnati, OH BR/TR, 6'3", 177 lbs. Deb: 10/7/1886 U Career OF: 59-14-35																							
1886 Cin-a	1	3	0	0	0	0	0	0	0	....	0	....	.000	.250	.000	.250	-19	-0	0	.00	0	/C-1	0	0.0
1888 Lou-a	51	189	15	37	4	2	1	21	4	....	4	....	.196	.216	.254	.470	51	-11	12	2.05	-1	0-28(22-1-5),C-25	2	-1.0
1889 Lou-a	90	360	39	86	11	5	3	45	7	41	13	....	.239	.253	.322	.576	64	-19	34	3.24	5	C-54,0-20(5-9-4),1-18/3-3	2	-1.0
1890 NY-P	44	166	27	44	7	0	1	22	10	9	6	....	.265	.307	.325	.632	63	-10	19	4.18	-4	C-30,0-12(8-1-3)/2-1,3-1	3	-1.0
1891 Cin-a	51	175	21	45	7	1	1	14	14	15	7	....	.257	.316	.326	.642	77	-6	21	4.22	3	C-44/0-6(3-1-2),1-2,3-2,P	5	0.0
Mil-a	25	99	13	33	7	0	0	9	4	5	1	....	.333	.359	.404	.763	98	-1	15	6.06	-2	C-20/1-4,0-1	3	-0.2
Yr.	76	274	34	78	14	1	1	23	18	20	8	....	.285	.331	.354	.685	84	-7	36	4.84	1	C-64/0-7(4-1-2),1-6,3-2,P	8	-0.2
1892 Cin-N	91	346	45	88	10	5	2	50	16	13	10	....	.254	.295	.329	.625	90	-6	38	3.92	-8	C-67,1-14,0-11(4-0-7)/3-6	8	-0.7
1893 Cin-N	121	483	68	135	17	12	1	108	35	17	16	....	.280	.332	.371	.703	85	-13	66	5.05	-2	C-80,0-23(12-1-10),1-21	12	-0.7
1894 Cin-N	72	284	50	88	15	5	8	64	12	11	5	....	.310	.338	.482	.820	93	-6	49	6.52	-2	C-43,1-27/0-8(4-1-3),S-3	7	-0.4
1895 Cin-N	92	334	60	102	23	5	1	48	17	10	15	....	.305	.339	.413	.752	90	-7	54	6.13	2	C-77,1-15/2-1,3-1	9	0.2
1896 Cin-N	114	433	71	127	20	9	2	66	16	7	7	....	.293	.320	.395	.715	82	-14	59	5.01	0	1-57,C-57	10	-0.8
1897 Cin-N	54	199	21	58	13	5	0	30	2	....	2	....	.291	.299	.407	.706	80	-8	26	4.71	-3	1-35,C-15	4	-0.8
1898 Cin-N	78	275	35	84	12	4	1	46	11	....	4	....	.305	.339	.389	.728	101	-1	39	5.29	-3	1-39,C-33	9	-0.1
1899 Cin-N	31	108	9	19	1	0	0	2	3	....	2	....	.176	.198	.185	.383	5	-14	5	1.38	1	1-21/C-7,0-1	1	-1.1
Total 13	915	3454	474	946	147	53	21	525	151	128	92	....	.274	.307	.365	.672	80	-116	435	4.57	-13	C-553,1-253,0-110/3-13,S,2,P	75	-7.4
• VAUGHN, Fred	Frederick Thomas "Muscles" Vaughn b: 10/18/1918, Coalinga, CA d: 3/2/1964, Lake Wales, FL BR/TR, 5'10", 185 lbs. Deb: 8/20/1944																							
1944 Was-A	30	109	10	28	2	1	1	21	9	24	2	2	.257	.319	.321	.640	87	-2	11	3.56	-2	2-26/3-3	2	-0.3
1945 Was-A	80	268	28	63	7	4	1	25	23	48	0	3	.235	.298	.302	.600	81	-8	25	3.13	-9	2-76/S-1	5	-1.4
Total 2	110	377	38	91	9	5	2	46	32	72	2	5	.241	.304	.308	.612	83	-10	36	3.25	-12	2-102/3-3,S-1	7	-1.7
• VAUGHN, Greg	Gregory Lamont Vaughn b: 7/3/1965, Sacramento, CA BR/TR, 6', 193 lbs. Deb: 8/10/1989 Career OF: 1261-4-3																							
1989 Mil-A	38	113	18	30	3	0	5	23	13	23	4	1	.265	.341	.425	.766	116	3	18	5.61	-1	0-24(23-0-0),D-13	6	0.1
1990 Mil-A	120	382	51	84	26	2	17	61	33	91	7	4	.220	.284	.432	.716	98	-3	44	3.66	0	*0-106(106-0-0)/D-8	10	-0.7
1991 Mil-A	145	542	81	132	24	5	27	98	62	125	2	2	.244	.322	.456	.778	116	10	82	5.21	3	*0-135(134-0-1),D-10	20	0.8
1992 Mil-A	141	501	77	114	18	2	23	78	60	123	15	15	.228	.316	.409	.725	104	-1	63	4.11	-2	*0-131(131-0-1)/D-7	16	-0.9
1993 Mil-A★	154	569	97	152	28	2	30	97	89	118	10	7	.267	.371	.482	.853	129	24	106	6.56	-3	0-94(94-0-0),D-58	22	1.3
1994 Mil-A	95	370	59	94	24	1	19	55	51	93	9	5	.254	.346	.478	.824	105	2	62	5.81	2	0-81(81-1-0),D-14	9	0.0
1995 Mil-A	108	392	67	88	19	1	17	59	55	89	10	4	.224	.320	.408	.728	83	-10	52	4.34	0	*D-104	5	-1.6
1996 Mil-A★	102	375	78	105	16	0	31	95	58	99	5	2	.280	.382	.571	.953	132	18	84	8.04	-3	0-57(98-3-0)/D-1	14	1.1
*SD-N	43	141	20	29	3	1	10	22	24	31	4	1	.206	.329	.454	.783	111	3	23	5.44	1	*0-100(39-0-0)	3	0.2
1997 SD-N	120	361	60	78	10	0	18	57	56	110	7	4	.216	.325	.393	.718	95	-3	48	4.36	3	0-39(94-0-0)/D-3	7	-0.4
1998*SD-N★	158	573	112	156	28	4	50	119	79	121	11	4	.272	.365	.597	.962	159	48	128	8.01	3	0-94(151-0-0)/D-4	30	4.3
1999 Cin-N	153	550	104	135	20	2	45	118	85	137	15	2	.245	.350	.535	.884	116	14	108	6.74	2	*0-151(144-0-0)/D-6	24	1.0
2000 TB-A	127	461	83	117	27	1	28	74	80	128	8	1	.254	.366	.499	.865	117	14	88	6.67	4	*0-144(72-0-0),D-52	16	1.1
2001 TB-A★	136	485	74	113	25	0	24	82	71	130	11	5	.233	.335	.433	.768	102	2	72	4.97	4	D-76,0-72(57-0-0)	15	-0.1
2002 TB-A	69	251	28	41	10	2	8	29	41	82	3	2	.163	.288	.315	.603	61	-14	24	3.00	2	0-57(31-0-0),D-38	1	-1.5
2003 Col-N	22	37	8	7	3	0	3	5	8	13	0	0	.189	.333	.514	.847	102	0	7	6.13	0	/0-7(6-0-1),D-3	1	0.0
Total 15	1731	6103	1017	1475	284	23	355	1072	865	1513	121	59	.242	.339	.470	.810	113	106	1009	5.62	17	*0-1292,D-397	199	4.7
• VAUGHN, Mo	Maurice Samuel "Hit Dog" Vaughn b: 12/15/1967, Norwalk, CT BL/TR, 6'1", 230 lbs. Deb: 6/27/1991																							
1991 Bos-A	74	219	21	57	12	0	4	32	26	43	2	1	.260	.344	.370	.714	93	-1	28	4.33	-3	1-49,D-16	6	-0.8
1992 Bos-A	113	355	42	83	16	2	13	57	47	67	3	3	.234	.328	.400	.728	97	-2	47	4.41	-5	1-85,D-20	7	-1.4
1993 Bos-A	152	539	86	160	34	1	29	101	79	130	4	3	.297	.395	.525	.920	136	29	111	7.43	-7	*1-131,D-19	19	1.0
1994 Bos-A	111	394	65	122	25	1	26	82	57	112	4	4	.310	.410	.576	.986	144	26	93	8.83	-9	*1-106/D-1	17	0.7
1995*Bos-A★	140	550	98	165	28	3	39	**126**	68	150	11	4	.300	.391	.575	.965	143	35	121	7.97	-5	*1-138/D-2	24	1.7
1996 Bos-A★	161	635	118	207	29	1	44	143	95	154	2	0	.326	.425	.583	1.007	148	50	158	9.45	-13	*1-146,D-15	29	2.1
1997 Bos-A	141	527	91	166	24	0	35	96	86	154	2	2	.315	.422	.560	.982	151	42	128	9.18	-7	*1-131/D-9	22	2.2
1998*Bos-A★	154	609	107	205	31	2	40	115	61	144	0	0	.337	.404	.591	.995	151	46	144	9.27	-1	*1-142,D-12	25	3.0
1999 Ana-A	139	524	63	147	20	0	33	108	54	127	0	0	.281	.360	.508	.868	119	14	96	6.63	0	1-72,D-70	19	0.3
2000 Ana-A	161	614	93	167	31	0	36	117	79	181	2	0	.272	.368	.498	.866	113	13	114	6.63	-13	*1-147,0-31(0-1-0),D-14	17	-1.3
2002 NY-N	139	487	67	126	18	0	26	72	59	145	0	1	.259	.351	.456	.807	115	10	77	5.47	-12	*1-134	14	-1.4
2003 NY-N	27	79	10	15	2	0	3	15	14	22	0	0	.190	.326	.329	.655	74	-3	9	3.67	-3	1-24	1	-0.7
Total 12	1512	5532	861	1620	270	10	328	1064	725	1429	30	18	.293	.385	.523	.909	131	261	1127	7.40	-77	*1-1305,D-178/0-31	200	5.5
• VAZQUEZ, Ramon	Ramon Luis Vazquez b: 8/21/1976, Aibonito, Puerto Rico BL/TR, 5'11", 170 lbs. Deb: 9/7/2001																							
2001*Sea-A	17	35	5	8	0	0	0	4	0	3	0	0	.229	.229	.229	.457	22	-4	2	1.82	-3	S-10/2-6,3-2,D-1	0	-0.6
2002 SD-N	128	423	50	116	21	5	2	32	45	79	7	2	.274	.345	.362	.707	95	-2	55	4.67	3	2-81,S-41,3-20	14	0.7
2003 SD-N	116	422	56	110	17	4	3	30	52	88	10	3	.261	.345	.341	.686	88	-5	54	4.47	-11	*S-108/3-4,2-3	10	-0.8
Total 3	261	880	111	234	38	9	5	66	97	170	17	5	.266	.341	.347	.687	89	-11	111	4.45	-11	S-159/2-90,3-26,D-1	24	-0.7
• VEACH, Bobby	Robert Hayes Veach b: 6/29/1888, Island, KY d: 8/7/1945, Detroit, MI BL/TR, 5'11", 160 lbs. Deb: 9/6/1912 Career OF: 1671-14-65																							
1912 Det-A	23	79	8	27	5	1	0	15	5	....	2	....	.342	.388	.430	.819	138	4	14	6.61	3	0-22(22-0-0)	3	0.5
1913 Det-A	137	491	54	132	22	10	0	64	53	31	22	....	.269	.346	.354	.700	107	5	66	4.48	-4	*0-135(135-0-0)	13	-0.5
1914 Det-A	149	531	56	146	19	14	1	72	50	29	20	20	.275	.341	.369	.710	110	1	68	4.25	10	*0-145(145-0-0)	18	0.6
1915 Det-A	152	569	81	178	**40**	10	3	**112**	68	43	16	19	.313	.390	.434	.824	140	23	97	5.99	6	*0-152(152-0-0)	30	2.4
1916 Det-A	150	566	92	173	33	15	3	91	52	41	24	15	.306	.367	.433	.800	135	21	94	5.68	1	*0-150(150-0-0)	27	1.8
1917 Det-A	154	571	79	182	31	12	8	**103**	61	44	21	....	.319	.393	.457	.850	160	41	108	6.81	2	*0-154(154-0-0)	31	4.0
1918 Det-A	127	499	59	139	21	13	3	**78**	35	23	21	....	.279	.331	.391	.722	123	11	69	4.65	-3	*0-127(124-1-2)/P-1	17	0.3
1919 Det-A	139	538	87	**191**	**45**	**17**	3	101	33	33	19	....	.355	.398	.519	.916	160	40	115	8.07	7	*0-138(138-0-0)	32	4.3
1920 Det-A	154	612	92	188	39	15	11	113	36	22	11	7	.307	.353	.474	.827	121	16	101	6.00	18	*0-154(154-0-0)	25	2.7
1921 Det-A	150	612	110	207	43	13	16	128	48	31	14	10	.338	.387	.529	.917	133	28	123	7.36	11	*0-149(149-0-0)	22	2.5
1922 Det-A	155	618	96	202	34	13	9	126	42	27	9	1	.327	.377	.468	.845	123	22	111	6.51	10	*0-154(154-0-0)	22	2.0
1923 Det-A	114	293	45	94	13	3	2	39	29	21	10	3	.321	.388	.406	.794	111	7	49	5.96	-4	0-85(46-13-26)	9	-0.2
1924 Bos-A	142	519	77	153	35	9	5	99	47	18	5	5	.295	.359	.426	.785	102	0	81	5.35	-3	*0-130(130-0-0)	13	-1.2
1925 Bos-A	1	5	0	1	0	0	0	2	1	1	0	0	.200	.333	.200	.533	38	-0	0	2.67	0	/0-1	0	0.0
NY-A	56	116	13	41	10	2	0	15	8	0	1	4	.353	.400	.474	.874	123	3	20	6.70	2	0-33(13-0-30)	3	0.3
*Was-A	18	37	4	9	3	0	0	8	3	3	0	0	.243	.300	.324	.624	59	-2	4	3.28	0	0-11(4-0-7)	0	-0.3
Yr.	75	158	17	51	13	2	0	25	12	4	1	4	.323	.374	.430	.805	105	-0	25	5.64	2	0-45(18-0-37)	3	-0.1
Total 14	1821	6656	953	2063	393	147	64	1166	571	367	195	84	.310	.370	.442	.812	128	220	1120	5.94	55	*0-1740/P-1	265	19.2
• VEACH, Peek-A-Boo	William Walter Veach b: 6/15/1862, Indianapolis, IN d: 11/12/1937, Indianapolis, IN, 6', 175 lbs. Deb: 8/24/1884 ♦																							
1884 KC-U	27	82	9	11	1	0	1	....	9	....	....	....	.134	.220	.183	.403	43	-2	3	1.33	1	0-14(11-2-1),P-12/1-1,2-1	2	0.1
1887 Lou-a	1	4	0	1	0	0	0	0	1	....	0	....	.250	.250	.000	.250	-26	-0	0	.00	0	/P-1	1	0.0
1890 Cle-N	64	238	24	56	10	5	0	32	33	28	9	....	.235	.336	.319	.655	93	-1	29	4.26	7	1-64	5	0.0
Pit-N	8	30	6	9	1	1	2	5	8	3	0	....	.300	.447	.600	1.047	231	6	8	10.42	0	/1-8	2	0.4
Yr.	72	268	30	65	11	6	2	37	41	31	9	....	.243	.349	.351	.700	110	4	38	4.90	7	1-72	7	0.4
Total 3	100	354	39	77	12	6	3	37	51	31	9	....	.218	.319	.309	.628	94	2	41	3.93	7	/1-73,0-14,P-13,2-1	10	0.6

YEAR TM-L	G	AB	R	H	2B	3B	HR	RBI	BB	SO	SB	CS	AVG	OBP	SLG	OPS	OPS+	BR/A	RC	RC/G	FR	G/POS	WS	TPW
• VEAL, Coot	Orville Inman Veal b: 7/9/1932, Sandersville, GA BR/TR, 6'1", 165 lbs. Deb: 7/30/1958																							
1958 Det-A	58	207	29	53	10	2	0	16	14	21	1	1	.256	.306	.324	.630	68	-9	19	2.99	-3	S-58	3	-0.7
1959 Det-A	77	89	12	18	1	0	1	15	8	7	0	0	.202	.276	.247	.523	42	-7	7	2.48	3	S-72	2	-0.2
1960 Det-A	27	64	8	19	5	1	0	8	11	7	0	0	.297	.400	.406	.806	112	2	11	5.57	3	S-22/3-3,2-1	3	0.6
1961 Was-A	69	218	21	44	10	0	0	8	19	29	1	8	.202	.275	.248	.523	43	-21	15	1.99	-1	S-63	2	-1.6
1962 Pit-N	1	1	0	0	0	0	0	0	0	1	0	0	.000	.000	.000	.000	-100	-0	0	.00	0	....	0	0.0
1963 Det-A	15	32	5	7	0	0	0	4	4	4	0	0	.219	.306	.219	.524	48	-2	2	1.46	0	S-12	1	-0.1
Total 6	247	611	75	141	26	3	1	51	56	69	2	9	.231	.301	.288	.589	59	-37	53	2.70	2	S-227/3-3,2-1	11	-2.1
• VEGA, Jesus	Jesus Anthony (Morales) Vega b: 10/14/1955, Bayamon, Puerto Rico BR/TR, 6'1", 176 lbs. Deb: 9/5/1979																							
1979 Min-A	4	7	0	0	0	0	0	0	0	2	0	0	.000	.000	.000	.000	-96	-2	0	.00	0	/D-3	0	-0.2
1980 Min-A	12	30	3	5	0	0	0	4	3	7	1	0	.167	.242	.167	.409	13	-3	1	1.40	0	/D-9,1-2	0	-0.3
1982 Min-A	71	199	23	53	6	0	5	29	8	19	6	1	.266	.295	.372	.667	80	-5	21	3.64	0	D-39,1-18/O-1	2	-0.7
Total 3	87	236	26	58	6	0	5	33	11	28	7	1	.246	.279	.335	.614	66	-10	23	3.19	0	/D-51,1-20,O-1	2	-1.3
• VELANDIA, Jorge	Jorge Luis (Macias) Velandia b: 1/12/1975, Caracas, Venezuela BR/TR, 5'9", 160 lbs. Deb: 6/20/1997																							
1997 SD-N	14	29	0	3	2	0	0	0	1	7	0	0	.103	.133	.172	.306	-23	-5	1	.73	-1	/S-6,2-5,3-3	0	-0.6
1998 Oak-A	8	4	0	1	0	0	0	0	0	1	0	0	.250	.250	.250	.500	31	-0	0	2.25	0	/S-7,2-1	0	-0.1
1999 Oak-A	63	48	4	9	1	0	0	2	2	13	2	0	.188	.235	.208	.444	15	-6	3	1.93	1	2-52/S-8,3-2,D-1	1	-0.3
2000 Oak-A	18	24	1	3	1	0	0	2	0	6	0	0	.125	.160	.167	.327	-17	-4	1	.88	1	2-14/S-4	0	-0.3
NY-N	15	7	1	0	0	0	0	0	2	2	0	0	.000	.222	.000	.222	-39	-1	0	.45	-2	/2-7,S-7,3-3	0	-0.3
2001 NY-N	9	9	1	0	0	0	0	0	2	1	0	0	.000	.182	.000	.182	-49	-2	0	.28	-2	/S-8,3-1	0	-0.3
2003 NY-N	23	58	6	11	3	1	0	8	10	15	0	0	.190	.309	.276	.585	56	-4	6	2.95	4	S-23	2	0.2
Total 6	150	179	13	27	7	1	0	12	17	45	2	0	.151	.232	.201	.433	14	-23	10	1.77	1	/2-79,S-63,3-9,D-1	3	-1.6
• VELARDE, Randy	Randy Lee Velarde b: 11/24/1962, Midland, TX BR/TR, 6', 190 lbs. Deb: 8/20/1987 Career OF: 97-4-12																							
1987 NY-A	8	22	1	4	0	0	0	1	0	6	0	0	.182	.182	.182	.364	-3	-3	1	.78	0	/S-8	0	-0.3
1988 NY-A	48	115	18	20	6	0	5	12	8	24	1	1	.174	.240	.357	.597	65	-6	9	2.50	1	2-24,S-14,3-11	2	-0.4
1989 NY-A	33	100	12	34	4	2	2	11	7	14	0	3	.340	.389	.480	.869	145	4	18	6.80	0	3-27/S-9	5	0.5
1990 NY-A	95	229	21	48	6	2	5	19	20	53	0	3	.210	.276	.319	.595	66	-12	19	2.65	-5	3-74,S-15/O-5(5-0-0),2-3,D	2	-1.6
1991 NY-A	80	184	19	45	11	1	1	15	18	43	3	1	.245	.322	.332	.653	81	-4	20	3.55	-2	3-50,S-31/O-2(2-0-0)	3	-0.4
1992 NY-A	121	412	57	112	24	1	7	46	38	78	7	2	.272	.336	.386	.722	103	2	53	4.39	1	S-75,3-26,O-23(14-2-7)/2-3	13	0.8
1993 NY-A	85	226	28	68	13	2	7	24	18	39	2	2	.301	.363	.469	.832	126	8	34	5.26	0	O-50(48-2-0),S-26,3-16/D-1	7	0.7
1994 NY-A	77	280	47	78	16	1	9	34	22	61	4	2	.279	.340	.439	.779	103	1	41	5.15	2	S-49,3-27/O-7(6-0-1),2-5	8	0.5
1995*NY-A	111	367	60	102	19	1	7	46	55	64	5	1	.278	.378	.392	.770	102	4	58	5.54	3	2-62,S-28,O-20(20-0-1),3-19	13	1.0
1996 Cal-A	136	530	82	151	27	3	14	54	70	118	7	7	.285	.374	.426	.800	104	3	88	5.92	-21	*2-114,3-28/S-7	17	-1.1
1997 Ana-A	1	0	0	0	0	0	0	0	0	0	0	0	....	....	....	....	-99	0	0	....	0	....	0	0.0
1998 Ana-A	51	188	29	49	13	1	4	26	34	42	7	2	.261	.377	.404	.781	103	3	29	5.31	2	2-51	8	0.6
1999 Ana-A	95	376	57	115	15	4	9	48	43	56	13	4	.306	.383	.439	.822	110	8	65	6.40	2	2-95	14	1.4
Oak-A	61	255	48	85	10	3	7	28	27	42	11	4	.333	.401	.478	.880	129	12	47	6.80	2	2-61	10	1.6
Yr.	156	631	105	200	25	7	16	76	70	98	24	8	.317	.390	.455	.845	117	20	112	6.56	5	*2-156	24	3.0
2000*Oak-A	122	485	82	135	23	0	12	41	54	95	9	3	.278	.354	.400	.754	93	-4	69	4.99	19	*2-122	14	1.9
2001 Tex-A	78	296	46	88	16	2	9	31	29	73	4	2	.297	.370	.456	.826	112	6	50	6.04	-3	2-52/1-9,3-7,D-6,O-2(0-0-2)	7	0.4
*NY-A	15	46	4	7	3	0	0	1	5	13	2	0	.152	.278	.217	.495	33	-4	4	2.51	3	/3-7,D-4,O-3(2-0-1),1-1	0	-0.2
Yr.	93	342	50	95	19	2	9	32	34	86	6	2	.278	.357	.424	.781	101	2	53	5.50	-0	2-52,3-14,1-10,D-10/O-5(2-0-3)	7	0.2
2002*Oak-A	56	133	22	30	8	0	2	8	15	32	3	0	.226	.327	.331	.658	75	-4	15	3.79	0	2-38/1-5,D-4,3-1	3	-0.2
Total 16	1273	4244	633	1171	214	23	100	445	463	853	78	37	.276	.354	.408	.762	101	12	619	5.09	3	2-630,3-293,S-262,O-112/D,1	126	5.2
• VELASQUEZ, Guillermo	Guillermo (Burgara) Velasquez b: 4/23/1968, Mexicali, Mexico BL/TR, 6'3", 220 lbs. Deb: 9/14/1992 Career OF: 6-0-2																							
1992 SD-N	15	23	1	7	0	0	1	5	1	7	0	0	.304	.333	.435	.768	114	0	3	5.77	0	/1-3,O-2(2-0-0)	1	0.0
1993 SD-N	79	143	7	30	2	0	3	20	13	35	0	0	.210	.276	.287	.562	50	-10	11	2.61	0	1-38/O-6(4-0-2)	1	-1.3
Total 2	94	166	8	37	2	0	4	25	14	42	0	0	.223	.283	.307	.591	58	-10	15	2.99	0	/1-41,O-8	2	-1.3
• VELAZQUEZ, Freddie	Federico Antonio (Velasquez) Velazquez b: 12/6/1937, Santo Domingo, Dominican Republic BR/TR, 6'1", 185 lbs. Deb: 4/20/1969																							
1969 Sea-A	6	16	1	2	2	0	0	2	1	3	0	0	.125	.176	.250	.426	18	-2	0	.42	0	/C-5	0	-0.2
1973 Atl-N	15	23	2	8	1	0	0	3	1	3	0	0	.348	.375	.391	.766	105	0	3	6.25	0	C-11	1	0.0
Total 2	21	39	3	10	3	0	0	5	2	6	0	0	.256	.293	.333	.626	69	-2	4	3.24	-1	/C-16	1	-0.2
• VELEZ, Otto	Otoniel (Franceschi) Velez b: 11/29/1950, Ponce, Puerto Rico BR/TR, 6', 195 lbs. Deb: 9/4/1973 Career OF: 88-0-197																							
1973 NY-A	23	77	9	15	4	0	2	7	15	24	0	1	.195	.326	.325	.651	87	-1	9	3.90	0	O-23(0-0-23)	2	-0.2
1974 NY-A	27	67	9	14	1	1	2	10	15	24	0	0	.209	.354	.343	.697	104	1	9	4.45	-3	1-21/O-3(0-0-3),3-2	2	-0.3
1975 NY-A	6	8	0	2	0	0	0	1	2	0	0	0	.250	.400	.250	.650	90	0	1	4.54	0	/1-1,D-1	0	0.0
1976*NY-A	49	94	11	25	6	0	2	10	23	26	0	0	.266	.410	.394	.804	138	6	17	6.62	-2	O-24(6-0-19)/1-8,D-5,3-1	5	0.3
1977 Tor-A	120	360	50	92	19	3	16	62	65	87	4	2	.256	.371	.458	.829	123	14	64	6.00	0	O-79(0-0-79),D-28	11	1.0
1978 Tor-A	91	248	29	66	14	2	9	38	45	41	1	3	.266	.383	.448	.831	130	11	43	5.85	5	O-74(39-0-39)/D-9,1-1	10	1.2
1979 Tor-A	99	274	45	79	21	0	15	48	46	45	0	1	.288	.396	.529	.925	145	19	58	7.60	-2	O-73(43-0-34)/D-9,1-6	11	1.3
1980 Tor-A	104	357	54	96	12	3	20	62	54	86	0	0	.269	.368	.487	.855	126	14	65	6.44	0	D-97/1-3	12	1.1
1981 Tor-A	80	240	32	51	9	2	11	28	55	60	0	3	.213	.366	.404	.770	114	6	38	5.09	0	D-74/1-1	6	0.4
1982 Tor-A	28	52	4	10	1	0	1	5	13	15	1	0	.192	.354	.269	.623	68	-1	6	3.80	0	D-24	1	-0.2
1983 Cle-A	10	25	1	2	0	0	0	1	3	6	0	0	.080	.179	.080	.259	-25	-4	0	.58	0	/D-8	0	-0.4
Total 11	637	1802	244	452	87	11	78	272	336	414	6	10	.251	.372	.441	.813	122	63	311	5.88	-1	O-276,D-255/1-41,3-3	60	4.1
• VELTMAN, Pat	Arthur Patrick Veltman b: 3/24/1906, Mobile, AL d: 10/1/1980, San Antonio, TX BR/TR, 6', 175 lbs. Deb: 4/17/1926																							
1926 Chi-A	5	4	1	1	0	0	0	0	1	1	0	0	.250	.400	.250	.650	75	-0	0	4.27	0	/S-1	0	0.0
1928 NY-N	1	3	1	1	0	1	0	0	1	0	0	....	.333	.500	1.000	1.500	282	1	2	19.71	-0	/O-1	0	0.1
1929 NY-N	2	1	1	0	0	0	0	0	2	0	0	....	.000	.667	.000	.667	81	0	0	8.38	0	/C-1	0	0.0
1931 Bos-N	1	1	0	0	0	0	0	0	0	0	0	....	.000	.000	.000	.000	-104	-0	0	.00	0	....	0	0.0
1932 NY-N	2	1	0	0	0	0	0	0	0	1	0	....	.000	.000	.000	.000	-102	-0	0	.00	0	....	0	0.0
1934 Pit-N	12	28	1	3	0	0	0	2	0	1	0	....	.107	.107	.107	.214	-41	-6	0	.36	0	C-11	0	-0.5
Total 6	23	38	4	5	0	1	0	2	4	3	0	0	.132	.214	.184	.398	9	-5	3	2.11	-1	/C-12,O-1,S-1	0	-0.5
• VENABLE, Max	William McKinley Venable b: 6/6/1957, Phoenix, AZ BL/TR, 5'10", 185 lbs. Deb: 4/8/1979 Career OF: 247-141-113																							
1979 SF-N	55	85	12	14	1	1	0	3	10	18	3	3	.165	.260	.200	.460	29	-9	5	1.77	-1	O-25(6-2-21)	0	-1.1
1980 SF-N	64	138	13	37	5	0	0	10	15	22	8	2	.268	.340	.304	.644	83	-2	16	3.83	-1	O-40(16-14-11)	3	-0.4
1981 SF-N	18	32	2	6	0	2	0	1	4	3	3	1	.188	.278	.313	.590	68	-1	3	3.15	0	/O-5(0-2-3)	1	-0.2
1982 SF-N	71	125	17	28	2	1	1	7	7	16	9	3	.224	.265	.280	.545	53	-7	9	2.50	2	O-53(33-12-8)	1	-0.7
1983 SF-N	94	228	28	50	7	4	6	27	22	34	15	2	.219	.296	.364	.660	85	-3	27	3.91	2	O-66(32-25-14)	6	-0.4
1984 Mon-N	38	71	7	17	2	0	2	7	3	7	1	0	.239	.280	.352	.632	80	-2	7	3.64	-1	O-27(23-3-3)	1	-0.4
1985 Cin-N	77	135	21	39	12	3	0	10	6	17	11	3	.289	.319	.422	.741	101	1	18	4.67	1	O-39(31-7-3)	5	0.1
1986 Cin-N	108	147	17	31	7	1	2	15	17	24	7	2	.211	.293	.313	.606	64	-7	15	3.37	-1	O-57(49-8-3)	2	-0.9
1987 Cin-N	7	7	2	1	0	0	0	2	0	0	0	0	.143	.143	.143	.286	-23	-1	0	.64	0	/O-4(0-4-0)	0	-0.1
1989 Cal-A	20	53	7	19	4	0	0	4	1	16	0	0	.358	.370	.434	.804	128	2	9	6.36	0	O-13(4-4-7)	2	0.1
1990 Cal-A	93	189	26	49	9	3	4	21	24	31	5	1	.259	.343	.402	.745	110	3	28	4.88	0	O-77(40-33-10)/D-1	5	0.2
1991 Cal-A	82	187	24	46	8	2	3	21	11	30	2	1	.246	.295	.358	.653	80	-5	19	3.36	-1	O-65(13-27-30)/D-3	3	-0.8
Total 12	727	1397	176	337	57	17	18	128	120	218	64	18	.241	.304	.345	.649	81	-31	157	3.73	0	O-471/D-4	29	-4.5
• VENTURA, Robin	Robin Mark Ventura b: 7/14/1967, Santa Maria, CA BL/TR, 6'1", 198 lbs. Deb: 9/12/1989																							
1989 Chi-A	16	45	5	8	3	0	0	7	8	6	0	0	.178	.315	.244	.559	61	-2	4	2.73	1	3-16	1	0.0
1990 Chi-A	150	493	48	123	17	1	5	54	55	53	1	4	.249	.326	.318	.645	83	-12	54	3.70	7	*3-147/1-1	15	-0.4
1991 Chi-A	157	606	92	172	25	1	23	100	80	67	2	4	.284	.371	.442	.813	127	23	97	5.52	13	*3-151,1-31	25	3.6

YEAR TM-L	G	AB	R	H	2B	3B	HR	RBI	BB	SO	SB	CS	AVG	OBP	SLG	OPS	OPS+	BR/A	RC	RC/G	FR	G/POS	WS	TPW
1992 Chi-A★	157	592	85	167	38	1	16	93	93	71	2	4	.282	.380	.431	.810	128	24	99	5.89	26	*3-157/1-2	30	**5.2**
1993*Chi-A	157	554	85	145	27	1	22	94	105	82	1	6	.262	.382	.433	.815	121	18	92	5.63	1	*3-155/1-4	21	2.1
1994 Chi-A	109	401	57	113	15	1	18	78	61	69	3	1	.282	.379	.459	.838	117	12	72	6.30	9	*3-108/1-3,S-1	16	2.0
1995 Chi-A	135	492	79	145	22	0	26	93	75	98	4	3	.295	.389	.498	.887	135	26	98	7.19	1	*3-121,1-18/D-1	17	2.6
1996 Chi-A	158	586	96	168	31	2	34	105	78	81	1	3	.287	.372	.520	.893	129	24	110	6.67	9	*3-150,1-14	20	3.2
1997 Chi-A	54	183	27	48	10	1	6	26	34	21	0	0	.262	.378	.426	.804	114	5	31	5.99	6	3-54	8	1.1
1998 Chi-A	161	590	84	155	31	4	21	91	79	111	1	1	.263	.351	.436	.786	106	5	92	5.51	22	*3-161	21	2.8
1999*NY-N	161	588	88	177	38	0	32	120	74	109	1	1	.301	.382	.529	.911	131	27	118	7.39	25	*3-160/1-1	30	**5.2**
2000*NY-N	141	469	61	109	23	1	24	84	75	91	3	5	.232	.341	.439	.780	99	-2	69	4.84	17	*3-137/1-1	15	1.6
2001 NY-N	142	456	70	108	20	0	21	61	88	101	2	5	.237	.361	.419	.780	106	5	70	5.11	15	*3-139	17	2.1
2002*NY-A★	141	465	68	115	17	0	27	93	90	101	3	1	.247	.372	.458	.830	120	16	82	5.95	18	*3-137/1-5	20	3.4
2003 NY-A	89	283	31	71	13	0	9	42	40	62	0	0	.251	.344	.392	.736	95	-1	39	4.68	2	3-80/D-3,2-1	9	0.1
LA-N	49	109	11	24	5	1	5	13	18	25	0	0	.220	.331	.422	.753	100	0	15	4.73	-3	1-42/3-3	1	-0.5
Total 15	1977	6912	987	1848	335	14	289	1154	1053	1148	24	38	.267	.366	.445	.811	116	169	1142	5.73	169	*3-1876,1-122/D-4,2-1,S-1	266	34.1
• VENTURA, Vince	Vincent Ventura b: 4/18/1917, New York, NY d: 9/11/2001, Lake Worth, FL BR/TR, 6'1.5", 190 lbs. Deb: 5/8/1945																							
1945 Was-A	18	58	4	12	0	0	0	2	4	4	0	0	.207	.258	.207	.465	39	-4	3	1.54	-1	0-15(15-0-0)	0	-0.7
• VERAS, Quilvio	Quilvio Alberto (Perez) Veras b: 4/3/1971, Santo Domingo, Dominican Republic BB/TR, 5'9", 170 lbs. Deb: 4/25/1995																							
1995 Fla-N	124	440	86	115	20	7	5	32	80	68	**56**	21	.261	.386	.373	.758	101	7	72	5.39	16	*2-122/0-2(0-1-1)	15	2.9
1996 Fla-N	73	253	40	64	8	1	4	14	51	42	8	8	.253	.382	.340	.722	96	-1	36	4.82	6	2-67	7	0.9
1997 SD-N	145	539	74	143	23	1	3	45	72	84	33	12	.265	.359	.328	.688	89	-3	71	4.43	-14	*2-142	15	-1.0
1998*SD-N	138	517	79	138	24	2	6	45	84	78	24	9	.267	.376	.356	.732	101	6	77	5.23	20	*2-131	23	3.2
1999 SD-N	132	475	95	133	25	2	6	41	65	88	30	17	.280	.369	.379	.748	97	-1	69	5.07	9	*2-118	16	1.3
2000 Atl-N	84	298	56	92	15	0	5	37	51	50	25	12	.309	.418	.409	.827	110	8	54	6.23	-4	2-82	13	0.7
2001 Atl-N	71	258	39	65	14	2	3	25	24	52	7	4	.252	.332	.357	.689	77	-9	32	4.15	6	2-67	6	0.0
Total 7	767	2780	469	750	129	15	32	239	427	462	183	83	.270	.374	.362	.736	96	7	412	5.04	40	2-729/0-2	95	7.9
• VERAS, Wilton	Wilton Andres Veras b: 1/19/1978, Monte Cristi, Dominican Republic BR/TR, 6'2", 198 lbs. Deb: 7/1/1999																							
1999 Bos-A	36	118	14	34	5	1	2	13	5	14	0	2	.288	.328	.398	.726	82	-4	13	3.88	3	3-35	1	-0.1
2000 Bos-A	49	164	21	40	7	1	0	14	7	20	0	0	.244	.283	.299	.582	46	-14	14	2.92	4	3-49	2	-0.8
Total 2	85	282	35	74	12	2	2	27	12	34	0	2	.262	.302	.340	.642	61	-18	28	3.32	7	/3-84	3	-0.9
• VERBAN, Emil	Emil Matthew "Dutch,Antelope" Verban b: 8/27/1915, Lincoln, IL d: 6/8/1989, Quincy, IL BR/TR, 5'11", 165 lbs. Deb: 4/18/1944																							
1944*StL-N	146	498	51	128	14	2	0	43	19	14	0	....	.257	.287	.293	.580	62	-26	43	2.96	16	*2-146	9	-0.2
1945 StL-N★	155	597	59	166	22	8	0	72	19	15	4	....	.278	.304	.342	.645	77	-20	61	3.64	6	*2-155	14	-0.6
1946 StL-N	1	1	0	0	0	0	0	0	0	0	0	....	.000	.000	.000	.000	-96	-0	0	.00	0	....	0	0.0
Phi-N★	138	473	44	130	17	5	0	34	21	18	5	....	.275	.306	.332	.638	83	-12	48	3.57	-4	*2-138	11	-0.9
Yr.	139	474	44	130	17	5	0	34	21	18	5	....	.274	.305	.331	.636	83	-13	48	3.57	-4	*2-138	11	-0.9
1947 Phi-N★	155	540	50	154	14	8	0	42	23	8	5	....	.285	.316	.341	.656	77	-19	56	3.71	20	*2-155	13	0.9
1948 Phi-N	55	169	14	39	5	1	0	11	11	5	0	....	.231	.282	.272	.554	51	-12	14	2.57	2	2-54	1	-0.7
Chi-N	56	248	37	73	15	1	1	16	4	7	4	....	.294	.308	.375	.683	88	-6	28	4.16	-4	2-56	5	-0.7
Yr.	111	417	51	112	20	2	1	27	15	12	4	....	.269	.297	.333	.631	72	-17	41	3.45	-2	*2-110	6	-1.4
1949 Chi-N	98	343	38	99	11	1	0	22	8	2	3	....	.289	.309	.327	.635	72	-14	34	3.58	-6	2-88	6	-1.6
1950 Chi-N	45	37	7	4	1	0	0	1	3	5	0	....	.108	.175	.135	.310	-17	-6	1	.90	-2	/2-8,S-3,3-1,0-1	0	-0.8
Bos-N	4	5	1	0	0	0	0	0	0	0	0	....	.000	.000	.000	.000	-107	-1	0	.00	-1	/2-2	0	-0.2
Yr.	49	42	8	4	1	0	0	1	3	5	0	....	.095	.156	.119	.275	-27	-8	1	.79	-3	2-10/S-3,3-1,0-1	0	-1.0
Total 7	853	2911	301	793	99	26	1	241	108	74	21	....	.272	.301	.325	.626	73	-117	286	3.44	26	2-802/S-3,3-1,0-1	59	-4.8
• VERBLE, Gene	Gene Kermit "Satchel" Verble b: 6/29/1928, Concord, NC BR/TR, 5'10", 163 lbs. Deb: 4/17/1951																							
1951 Was-A	68	177	16	36	3	2	0	15	18	10	1	1	.203	.277	.243	.520	42	-14	12	2.11	0	S-28,2-19/3-1	1	-1.2
1953 Was-A	13	21	4	4	0	0	0	2	2	1	0	0	.190	.261	.190	.451	24	-2	1	1.52	0	/S-8	0	-0.1
Total 2	81	198	20	40	3	2	0	17	20	11	1	1	.202	.275	.237	.513	40	-16	13	2.04	0	/S-36,2-19,3-1	1	-1.3
• VERDI, Frank	Frank Michael Verdi b: 6/2/1926, Brooklyn, NY BR/TR, 5'10.5", 170 lbs. Deb: 5/10/1953																							
1953 NY-A	1	0	0	0	0	0	0	0	0	0	0	0	....	....	....	....	-104	0	0	....	-1	/S-1	0	-0.1
• VERGEZ, Johnny	John Louis Vergez b: 7/9/1906, Oakland, CA d: 7/15/1991, Davis, CA BR/TR, 5'8", 165 lbs. Deb: 4/14/1931																							
1931 NY-N	152	565	67	157	24	2	13	81	29	65	11	....	.278	.320	.396	.716	94	-6	73	4.57	-1	*3-152	14	-0.2
1932 NY-N	118	376	42	98	21	3	6	43	25	36	1	....	.261	.310	.380	.690	86	-8	45	4.19	0	*3-111/S-1	9	-0.3
1933 NY-N	123	458	57	124	21	6	16	72	39	66	1	....	.271	.332	.448	.780	123	13	66	5.03	-20	*3-123	17	-0.3
1934 NY-N	108	320	31	64	18	1	7	27	28	55	1	....	.200	.269	.328	.597	60	-18	29	3.02	5	*3-104	6	-1.0
1935 Phi-N	148	546	56	136	27	4	9	63	46	67	8	....	.249	.312	.363	.675	73	-21	64	4.07	-9	*3-148/S-2	10	-2.4
1936 Phi-N	15	40	4	11	2	0	1	5	3	11	0	....	.275	.326	.400	.726	86	-1	6	5.07	0	3-12	1	0.0
StL-N	8	18	1	3	1	0	0	1	1	3	0	....	.167	.211	.222	.433	17	-2	1	1.65	0	/3-8	0	-0.2
Yr.	23	58	5	14	3	0	1	6	4	14	0	....	.241	.290	.345	.635	65	-3	7	3.93	0	3-20	1	-0.2
Total 6	672	2323	258	593	114	16	52	292	171	303	22	....	.255	.311	.385	.696	88	-43	285	4.24	-24	3-658/S-3	57	-4.4
• VERNON, Mickey	James Barton Vernon b: 4/22/1918, Marcus Hook, PA BL/TL, 6'2", 180 lbs. Deb: 7/8/1939 M/C																							
1939 Was-A	76	276	23	71	15	4	1	30	24	28	1	1	.257	.317	.351	.668	76	-10	31	3.83	-3	1-75	3	-1.9
1940 Was-A	5	19	0	3	0	0	0	0	0	3	0	0	.158	.158	.158	.316	-19	-3	0	.51	0	/1-4	0	-0.4
1941 Was-A	138	531	73	159	27	11	9	93	43	51	9	3	.299	.352	.443	.794	114	10	84	5.74	-10	*1-132	16	-1.2
1942 Was-A	151	621	76	168	34	6	9	86	59	63	25	6	.271	.337	.388	.725	104	6	87	5.03	-5	*1-151	20	-1.3
1943 Was-A	145	553	89	148	29	8	7	70	67	55	24	8	.268	.357	.387	.744	122	19	83	5.20	-8	*1-143	21	0.3
1946 Was-A★	148	587	88	207	**51**	8	8	85	49	64	14	10	**.353**	.403	.508	.910	163	46	120	8.00	2	*1-147	33	4.6
1947 Was-A	154	600	77	159	29	12	7	85	49	42	12	12	.265	.320	.388	.709	99	-5	73	4.22	-7	*1-154	15	-1.8
1948 Was-A★	150	558	78	135	27	7	3	48	54	43	15	11	.242	.310	.332	.641	73	-24	56	3.32	9	*1-150	7	-1.9
1949 Cle-A	153	584	72	170	27	4	18	83	58	51	9	7	.291	.357	.443	.801	113	8	96	5.82	19	*1-153	21	2.1
1950 Cle-A	28	90	8	17	0	0	0	10	12	10	2	0	.189	.284	.189	.473	24	-9	6	2.27	2	1-25	0	-0.8
Was-A	90	327	47	100	17	3	9	65	50	29	6	1	.306	.404	.459	.863	127	16	67	7.77	2	1-85	13	1.3
Yr.	118	417	55	117	17	3	9	75	62	39	8	1	.281	.379	.400	.779	104	6	74	6.42	4	*1-110	13	0.6
1951 Was-A	141	546	69	160	30	7	9	87	53	45	7	6	.293	.358	.423	.781	112	8	84	5.61	4	*1-137	18	0.7
1952 Was-A	154	569	71	143	33	9	10	80	89	66	7	7	.251	.353	.394	.746	111	9	84	5.03	6	*1-153	20	1.0
1953 Was-A★	152	608	101	205	**43**	11	15	115	63	57	4	6	**.337**	.403	.518	.921	151	42	127	8.03	6	*1-152	29	3.8
1954 Was-A★	151	597	90	173	**33**	14	20	97	61	61	1	4	.290	.360	.492	.853	139	29	106	6.38	-5	*1-148	24	1.5
1955 Was-A★	150	538	74	162	23	8	14	85	74	50	0	4	.301	.389	.452	.840	132	24	93	6.13	-10	*1-144	21	0.6
1956 Bos-A★	119	403	67	125	28	4	15	84	57	40	1	0	.310	.405	.511	.916	125	16	84	7.72	-3	*1-108	15	0.7
1957 Bos-A	102	270	36	65	18	1	7	38	41	35	0	0	.241	.351	.393	.744	97	0	38	4.75	2	1-70	6	-0.1
1958 Cle-A★	119	355	49	104	22	3	8	55	44	56	0	4	.293	.374	.439	.814	126	12	58	5.85	-2	1-96	13	0.5
1959 Mil-N	74	91	8	20	4	0	3	14	7	20	0	0	.220	.283	.363	.645	77	-3	9	3.38	0	1-10/0-4(2-0-2)	1	-0.4
1960 Pit-N	9	8	0	1	0	0	0	1	1	0	0	0	.125	.222	.125	.347	-2	-1	0	.86	0	....	0	-0.1
Total 20	2409	8731	1196	2495	490	120	172	1311	955	869	137	90	.286	.359	.428	.788	117	189	1387	5.67	0	*1-2237/0-4	296	7.6
• VERSALLES, Zoilo	Zoilo Casanova (Rodriguez) "Zorro" Versalles b: 12/18/1939, Havana, Cuba d: 6/9/1995, Bloomington, MN BR/TR, 5'10", 150 lbs. Deb: 8/1/1959																							
1959 Was-A	29	59	4	9	0	0	1	1	4	15	1	0	.153	.219	.203	.422	17	-7	3	1.63	-2	S-29	1	-0.7
1960 Was-A	15	45	2	6	2	2	0	4	2	5	0	0	.133	.170	.267	.437	16	-6	2	1.48	-2	S-15	1	-0.7
1961 Min-A	129	510	65	143	25	5	7	53	25	61	16	9	.280	.315	.390	.705	83	-14	61	4.21	1	*S-129	13	-0.2
1962 Min-A	160	568	69	137	18	3	17	67	37	71	5	5	.241	.290	.373	.663	74	-23	59	3.40	25	*S-160	16	1.6
1963 Min-A★	159	621	74	162	31	**13**	10	54	33	66	7	4	.261	.303	.401	.704	94	-7	74	4.14	10	*S-159	19	1.8
1964 Min-A	160	659	94	171	33	**10**	20	64	42	88	14	4	.259	.312	.431	.743	103	3	91	4.86	-7	*S-160	18	1.0
1965*Min-A★	160	666	**126**	182	**45**	**12**	19	77	41	122	27	5	.273	.322	.462	.785	115	15	102	5.41	5	*S-160	32	3.6

YEAR TM-L	G	AB	R	H	2B	3B	HR	RBI	BB	SO	SB	CS	AVG	OBP	SLG	OPS	OPS+	BR/A	RC	RC/G	FR	G/POS	WS	TPW
1966 Min-A	137	543	73	135	20	6	7	36	40	85	10	12	.249	.308	.346	.655	83	-15	55	3.43	-7	*S-135	12	-1.1
1967 Min-A	160	581	63	116	16	7	6	50	33	113	5	3	.200	.250	.282	.532	53	-35	39	2.17	12	*S-159	9	-1.0
1968 LA-N	122	403	29	79	16	3	2	24	26	84	6	4	.196	.245	.266	.510	57	-22	26	2.03	0	*S-119	5	-1.3
1969 Cle-A	72	217	21	49	11	1	1	13	21	47	3	1	.226	.300	.300	.600	66	-10	19	2.94	1	2-46,3-30/S-3	4	-0.7
Was-A	31	75	9	20	2	1	0	6	3	13	1	0	.267	.304	.320	.624	79	-2	7	3.59	0	S-13/2-6,3-5	2	-0.1
Yr.	103	292	30	69	13	2	1	19	24	60	4	1	.236	.301	.305	.606	69	-12	27	3.10	1	2-52,3-35,S-16	6	-0.8
1971 Atl-N	66	194	21	37	11	0	5	22	11	40	2	1	.191	.234	.325	.559	53	-13	13	2.09	-6	3-30,S-24/2-1	2	-1.7
Total 12	1400	5141	650	1246	230	63	95	471	318	810	97	48	.242	.292	.367	.659	81	-135	552	3.62	30	*S-1265/3-65,2-53	134	0.5

• VERYZER, Tom Thomas Martin Veryzer b: 2/11/1953, Port Jefferson, NY BR/TR, 6'1.5", 185 lbs. Deb: 8/14/1973

YEAR TM-L	G	AB	R	H	2B	3B	HR	RBI	BB	SO	SB	CS	AVG	OBP	SLG	OPS	OPS+	BR/A	RC	RC/G	FR	G/POS	WS	TPW
1973 Det-A	18	20	1	6	0	1	0	2	2	4	0	0	.300	.364	.400	.764	108	0	3	5.98	-5	S-18	1	-0.4
1974 Det-A	22	55	4	13	2	0	2	9	5	8	1	0	.236	.300	.382	.682	92	-0	7	4.40	-2	S-20	2	-0.1
1975 Det-A	128	404	37	102	13	1	5	48	23	76	2	6	.252	.301	.327	.628	74	-16	38	3.21	-16	*S-128	6	-1.7
1976 Det-A	97	354	31	83	8	2	1	25	21	44	1	4	.234	.289	.277	.566	64	-17	27	2.45	-5	S-97	4	-1.2
1977 Det-A	125	350	31	69	12	1	2	28	16	44	0	1	.197	.232	.254	.487	31	-34	21	1.88	-3	*S-124	5	-2.5
1978 Cle-A	130	421	48	114	18	4	1	32	13	36	1	2	.271	.301	.340	.640	81	-12	42	3.42	-9	*S-129	8	-0.9
1979 Cle-A	149	449	41	99	9	3	0	34	34	54	2	5	.220	.281	.254	.535	45	-35	32	2.29	12	*S-148	9	-0.8
1980 Cle-A	109	358	28	97	12	0	2	28	10	25	0	5	.271	.306	.321	.627	72	-16	32	3.02	10	*S-108	7	0.4
1981 Cle-A	75	221	13	54	4	0	0	14	10	10	1	0	.244	.280	.262	.543	58	-12	16	2.40	-4	S-75	3	-0.9
1982 NY-N	40	54	6	18	2	0	0	4	3	4	1	0	.333	.368	.370	.739	108	1	7	5.22	-4	2-26,S-16	2	-0.2
1983 Chi-N	59	88	5	18	3	0	1	3	3	13	0	0	.205	.231	.273	.503	37	-8	5	2.04	-1	S-28,3-17	1	-0.7
1984*Chi-N	44	74	5	14	1	0	0	4	3	11	0	0	.189	.259	.203	.462	29	-7	4	1.59	-4	S-36/3-5,2-4	1	-0.9
Total 12	996	2848	250	687	84	12	14	231	143	329	9	23	.241	.285	.294	.579	61	-157	235	2.73	-32	S-927/2-30,3-22	49	-9.9

• VICK, Ernie Henry Arthur Vick b: 7/2/1900, Toledo, OH d: 7/16/1980, Ann Arbor, MI BR/TR, 5'9.5", 185 lbs. Deb: 6/29/1922

YEAR TM-L	G	AB	R	H	2B	3B	HR	RBI	BB	SO	SB	CS	AVG	OBP	SLG	OPS	OPS+	BR/A	RC	RC/G	FR	G/POS	WS	TPW
1922 StL-N	3	6	1	2	2	0	0	0	0	0	0	0	.333	.333	.667	1.000	159	0	1	8.48	0	/C-3	0	0.0
1924 StL-N	16	23	2	8	1	0	0	0	3	3	0	0	.348	.423	.391	.814	122	1	4	7.02	1	C-16	1	0.3
1925 StL-N	14	32	3	6	2	1	0	3	3	1	0	0	.188	.257	.313	.570	44	-3	3	2.66	-1	/C-9	0	-0.3
1926 StL-N	24	51	6	10	2	0	0	4	3	4	0	....	.196	.241	.235	.476	27	-5	3	1.79	0	C-23	1	-0.4
Total 4	57	112	12	26	7	1	0	7	9	8	0	0	.232	.289	.313	.602	58	-7	11	3.23	0	/C-51	2	-0.5

• VICK, Sammy Samuel Bruce Vick b: 4/12/1895, Batesville, MS d: 8/17/1986, Memphis, TN BR/TR, 5'10.5", 163 lbs. Deb: 9/20/1917 Career OF: 4-1-153

YEAR TM-L	G	AB	R	H	2B	3B	HR	RBI	BB	SO	SB	CS	AVG	OBP	SLG	OPS	OPS+	BR/A	RC	RC/G	FR	G/POS	WS	TPW
1917 NY-A	10	36	4	10	3	0	0	2	1	6	2	....	.278	.297	.361	.658	100	-0	4	4.05	-1	0-10(0-0-10)	1	-0.1
1918 NY-A	2	3	1	2	0	0	0	1	0	0	0	....	.667	.667	.667	1.333	296	1	1	32.98	0	/0-1	0	0.1
1919 NY-A	106	407	59	101	15	9	2	27	35	55	9	....	.248	.308	.344	.652	82	-10	44	3.63	-1	*0-100(0-0-100)	9	-1.7
1920 NY-A	51	118	21	26	7	1	0	11	14	20	1	1	.220	.313	.297	.610	60	-6	12	3.30	-2	0-33(4-1-28)	2	-0.9
1921 Bos-A	44	77	5	20	3	1	0	9	1	10	0	1	.260	.269	.325	.594	52	-6	6	2.79	-0	0-14(0-0-14)	0	-0.7
Total 5	213	641	90	159	28	11	2	50	51	91	12	2	.248	.305	.335	.641	76	-22	67	3.55	-3	0-158	12	-3.4

• VICO, George George Steve "Sam" Vico b: 8/9/1923, San Fernando, CA d: 1/14/1994, Redondo Beach, CA BL/TR, 6'4", 200 lbs. Deb: 4/20/1948

YEAR TM-L	G	AB	R	H	2B	3B	HR	RBI	BB	SO	SB	CS	AVG	OBP	SLG	OPS	OPS+	BR/A	RC	RC/G	FR	G/POS	WS	TPW
1948 Det-A	144	521	50	139	23	9	8	58	39	39	2	2	.267	.326	.392	.718	88	-11	63	4.03	1	*1-142	9	-1.5
1949 Det-A	67	142	15	27	5	2	4	18	21	17	0	0	.190	.311	.338	.649	72	-6	16	3.56	2	1-53	2	-0.5
Total 2	211	663	65	166	28	11	12	76	60	56	2	2	.250	.323	.380	.703	84	-17	79	3.92	2	1-195	11	-2.0

• VICTORINO, Shane Shane Patrick Victorino b: 11/30/1980, Wailuku, HI BB/TR, 5'9", 160 lbs. Deb: 4/2/2003

YEAR TM-L	G	AB	R	H	2B	3B	HR	RBI	BB	SO	SB	CS	AVG	OBP	SLG	OPS	OPS+	BR/A	RC	RC/G	FR	G/POS	WS	TPW
2003 SD-N	36	73	8	11	2	0	0	4	7	17	7	2	.151	.235	.178	.413	11	-9	3	1.09	0	0-32(15-17-3)	0	-0.9

• VIDAL, Jose Jose (Nicolas) "Papito" Vidal b: 4/3/1940, Batey Lechugas, Dominican Republic BR/TR, 6', 190 lbs. Deb: 9/5/1966 Career OF: 20-9-29

YEAR TM-L	G	AB	R	H	2B	3B	HR	RBI	BB	SO	SB	CS	AVG	OBP	SLG	OPS	OPS+	BR/A	RC	RC/G	FR	G/POS	WS	TPW
1966 Cle-A	17	32	4	6	1	1	0	3	5	11	0	1	.188	.297	.281	.579	67	-2	3	2.78	0	0-11(0-3-8)	1	-0.3
1967 Cle-A	16	34	4	4	0	0	0	0	7	12	0	1	.118	.268	.118	.386	17	-4	1	.93	0	0-10(8-6-1)	0	-0.4
1968 Cle-A	37	54	5	9	0	0	2	5	2	15	3	0	.167	.196	.278	.474	43	-3	3	2.01	0	0-26(11-0-15)/1-1	0	-0.4
1969 Sea-A	18	26	7	5	0	1	1	2	4	8	1	1	.192	.323	.385	.707	99	-0	3	4.21	-1	/0-6(1-0-5)	0	-0.1
Total 4	88	146	20	24	1	2	3	10	18	46	4	3	.164	.261	.260	.521	53	-9	11	2.28	-1	/0-53,1-1	1	-1.2

• VIDRO, Jose Jose Angel (Cetty) Vidro b: 8/27/1974, Mayaguez, Puerto Rico BB/TR, 5'11", 175 lbs. Deb: 6/8/1997

YEAR TM-L	G	AB	R	H	2B	3B	HR	RBI	BB	SO	SB	CS	AVG	OBP	SLG	OPS	OPS+	BR/A	RC	RC/G	FR	G/POS	WS	TPW
1997 Mon-N	67	169	19	42	12	1	2	17	11	20	1	0	.249	.302	.367	.669	74	-6	20	4.06	0	3-36/2-5,D-5	3	-0.6
1998 Mon-N	83	205	24	45	12	0	0	18	27	33	2	2	.220	.322	.278	.600	61	-11	20	3.06	-6	2-56/3-7	2	-1.5
1999 Mon-N	140	494	67	150	45	2	12	59	29	51	0	4	.304	.347	.476	.823	108	2	77	5.72	-11	*2-121,1-14/0-3(3-0-0),3-2	11	-0.4
2000 Mon-N★	153	606	101	200	51	2	24	97	49	69	5	4	.330	.382	.540	.922	126	22	120	7.46	-10	*2-153	25	1.8
2001 Mon-N	124	486	82	155	34	1	15	59	31	49	4	1	.319	.372	.486	.858	117	13	83	6.36	-14	*2-121/D-2	18	0.4
2002 Mon-N★	152	604	103	190	43	3	19	96	60	70	2	1	.315	.379	.490	.869	123	20	113	6.91	-2	*2-152	29	2.5
2003 Mon-N★	144	509	77	158	36	0	15	65	69	50	3	2	.310	.400	.470	.870	107	8	96	6.87	-16	*2-137	17	-0.2
Total 7	863	3073	473	940	233	9	87	411	276	342	17	14	.306	.369	.473	.842	110	48	528	6.27	-60	2-745/3-45,1-14,D-7,0-3	105	2.1

• VILLANUEVA, Hector Hector (Balasquide) Villanueva b: 10/2/1964, Rio Piedras, Puerto Rico BR/TR, 6'1", 220 lbs. Deb: 6/1/1990

YEAR TM-L	G	AB	R	H	2B	3B	HR	RBI	BB	SO	SB	CS	AVG	OBP	SLG	OPS	OPS+	BR/A	RC	RC/G	FR	G/POS	WS	TPW
1990 Chi-N	52	114	14	31	4	1	7	18	4	27	1	0	.272	.308	.509	.817	112	1	17	5.30	-2	C-23,1-14	5	0.0
1991 Chi-N	71	192	23	53	10	1	13	32	21	30	0	0	.276	.347	.542	.889	140	10	36	6.87	0	C-55/1-6	9	1.2
1992 Chi-N	51	112	9	17	6	0	2	13	11	24	0	0	.152	.228	.259	.487	37	-10	6	1.58	1	C-28/1-6	2	-0.7
1993 StL-N	17	55	7	8	1	0	3	9	4	17	0	0	.145	.203	.327	.531	40	-5	3	1.55	-1	C-17	1	-0.5
Total 4	191	473	53	109	21	2	25	72	40	98	1	0	.230	.293	.442	.735	97	-4	62	4.42	-2	C-123/1-26	17	0.1

• VINA, Fernando Fernando Vina b: 4/16/1969, Sacramento, CA BL/TR, 5'9", 170 lbs. Deb: 4/10/1993

YEAR TM-L	G	AB	R	H	2B	3B	HR	RBI	BB	SO	SB	CS	AVG	OBP	SLG	OPS	OPS+	BR/A	RC	RC/G	FR	G/POS	WS	TPW
1993 Sea-A	24	45	5	10	2	0	0	2	4	3	6	0	.222	.327	.267	.594	61	-1	6	4.20	0	2-16/S-4,D-2	1	0.0
1994 NY-N	79	124	20	31	6	0	0	6	12	11	3	1	.250	.372	.298	.670	78	-2	15	4.13	-1	2-13,3-12/S-9,0-6(6-0-0)	3	-0.2
1995 Mil-A	113	288	46	74	7	7	3	29	22	28	6	3	.257	.329	.361	.690	75	-11	35	4.12	1	2-99/S-6,3-2	8	-0.5
1996 Mil-A	140	554	94	157	19	10	7	46	38	35	16	7	.283	.344	.392	.735	82	-15	73	4.63	17	*2-137	13	0.8
1997 Mil-A	79	324	37	89	12	2	4	28	12	23	8	7	.275	.315	.361	.676	75	-13	36	3.85	9	2-77/D-1	7	-0.1
1998 Mil-N★	159	637	101	198	39	7	7	45	54	46	22	16	.311	.387	.427	.814	114	13	108	6.22	18	*2-158	30	3.8
1999 Mil-N	37	154	17	41	7	0	1	16	14	6	5	2	.266	.343	.331	.674	72	-6	19	4.30	2	2-37	4	-0.2
2000*StL-N	123	487	81	146	24	6	4	31	36	36	10	8	.300	.381	.398	.779	97	-2	77	5.85	24	*2-122	18	2.6
2001*StL-N	154	631	95	191	30	8	9	56	32	35	17	7	.303	.358	.418	.776	101	2	97	5.69	-3	*2-151	22	0.6
2002*StL-N	150	622	75	168	29	5	1	54	44	36	17	11	.270	.336	.338	.674	80	-18	72	4.00	-5	*2-150	16	-1.6
2003 StL-N	61	259	35	65	14	4	4	23	11	24	4	4	.251	.310	.382	.692	82	-8	30	3.89	0	2-60	4	-0.5
Total 11	1119	4125	606	1170	189	49	40	336	279	283	114	66	.284	.351	.382	.734	90	-62	568	4.88	63	*2-1020/S-19,3-14,0-6,D-3	126	4.7

• VINSON, Charlie Charles Anthony "Chuck" Vinson b: 1/5/1944, Washington, DC BL/TL, 6'3", 207 lbs. Deb: 9/19/1966

YEAR TM-L	G	AB	R	H	2B	3B	HR	RBI	BB	SO	SB	CS	AVG	OBP	SLG	OPS	OPS+	BR/A	RC	RC/G	FR	G/POS	WS	TPW
1966 Cal-A	13	22	3	4	2	0	1	6	5	9	0	0	.182	.357	.409	.766	123	1	4	5.66	-1	1-11	1	-0.1

• VINSON, Rube Ernest Augustus Vinson b: 3/20/1879, Dover, DE d: 10/12/1951, Chester, PA BL, 5'9", 168 lbs. Deb: 9/27/1904 Career OF: 49-9-0

YEAR TM-L	G	AB	R	H	2B	3B	HR	RBI	BB	SO	SB	CS	AVG	OBP	SLG	OPS	OPS+	BR/A	RC	RC/G	FR	G/POS	WS	TPW
1904 Cle-A	15	49	12	15	1	0	0	2	10	....	2	....	.306	.433	.327	.760	143	3	8	6.23	3	0-15(15-0-0)	3	0.6
1905 Cle-A	39	134	12	26	3	1	0	9	7	....	4	....	.194	.245	.231	.476	50	-8	9	2.20	-2	0-36(27-9-0)	0	-1.3
1906 Chi-A	10	24	2	6	0	0	0	3	2	....	1	....	.250	.308	.250	.558	77	-1	2	3.28	-2	/0-7(7-0-0)	1	-0.4
Total 3	64	207	26	47	4	1	0	14	19	....	7	....	.227	.301	.256	.557	77	-5	20	3.15	-1	/0-58	4	-1.0

• VIOX, Jim James Harry Viox b: 12/30/1890, Lockland, OH d: 1/6/1969, Erlanger, KY BR/TR, 5'7", 150 lbs. Deb: 5/9/1912 Career OF: 0-2-5

YEAR TM-L	G	AB	R	H	2B	3B	HR	RBI	BB	SO	SB	CS	AVG	OBP	SLG	OPS	OPS+	BR/A	RC	RC/G	FR	G/POS	WS	TPW
1912 Pit-N	33	70	8	13	2	3	1	7	3	9	2	....	.186	.219	.343	.562	53	-5	6	2.36	-6	3-10/S-8,0-3(0-0-3),2-1	1	-1.1
1913 Pit-N	137	492	86	156	32	8	2	65	64	28	14	....	.317	.399	.427	.826	142	29	88	6.31	-30	*2-124,S-10	23	0.2
1914 Pit-N	143	506	52	134	18	5	1	57	63	33	9	....	.265	.351	.326	.677	106	6	60	4.04	-18	*2-138/0-2(0-0-2),S-2	16	-1.0
1915 Pit-N	150	503	56	129	17	8	2	45	75	31	12	8	.256	.357	.334	.691	111	10	63	4.26	-13	*2-134,3-13/0-2(0-2-0)	18	-0.1

YEAR TM-L	G	AB	R	H	2B	3B	HR	RBI	BB	SO	SB	CS	AVG	OBP	SLG	OPS	OPS+	BR/A	RC	RC/G	FR	G/POS	WS	TPW
1916 Pit-N	43	132	12	33	7	0	1	17	17	11	2	....	.250	.340	.326	.666	104	1	16	4.03	-3	2-25,3-11	3	-0.1
Total 5	506	1703	214	465	76	24	7	191	222	112	39	8	.273	.361	.358	.719	116	41	233	4.65	-71	2-422/3-34,S-20,0-7	61	-2.1

• VIRDON, Bill

William Charles Virdon b: 6/9/1931, Hazel Park, MI BL/TR, 6', 175 lbs. Deb: 4/12/1955 M/C Career OF: 3-1504-37

YEAR TM-L	G	AB	R	H	2B	3B	HR	RBI	BB	SO	SB	CS	AVG	OBP	SLG	OPS	OPS+	BR/A	RC	RC/G	FR	G/POS	WS	TPW
1955 StL-N	144	534	58	150	18	6	17	68	36	64	2	4	.281	.327	.433	.760	100	-2	73	4.80	-7	*0-142(1-109-34)	14	-1.6
1956 StL-N	24	71	10	15	2	0	2	9	5	8	0	1	.211	.273	.324	.597	60	-5	6	2.88	-1	0-24(0-24-0)	1	-0.7
Pit-N	133	509	67	170	21	10	8	37	33	63	6	6	.334	.376	.462	.837	126	17	84	6.29	0	*0-130(0-130-0)	20	1.1
Yr.	157	580	77	185	23	10	10	46	38	71	6	7	.319	.363	.445	.808	118	13	90	5.80	-1	*0-154(0-154-0)	21	0.4
1957 Pit-N	144	561	59	141	28	11	8	50	33	69	3	3	.251	.293	.383	.676	82	-16	62	3.78	6	*0-141(0-141-0)	12	-1.7
1958 Pit-N	144	604	75	161	24	11	9	46	52	70	5	3	.267	.326	.387	.713	90	-9	78	4.64	3	*0-143(0-143-0)	20	-1.3
1959 Pit-N	144	519	67	132	24	2	8	41	55	65	7	4	.254	.328	.355	.683	82	-12	62	4.14	16	*0-144(0-144-0)	15	-0.3
1960*Pit-N	120	409	60	108	16	9	8	40	40	44	8	2	.264	.330	.406	.735	99	1	57	4.94	3	*0-109(0-109-0)	14	-0.2
1961 Pit-N	146	599	81	156	22	8	9	58	49	45	5	8	.260	.316	.369	.685	81	-19	71	4.10	2	*0-145(0-145-0)	14	-2.1
1962 Pit-N	156	663	82	164	27	**10**	6	47	36	65	5	13	.247	.287	.345	.633	69	-35	62	3.15	3	*0-156(0-156-0)	12	-3.7
1963 Pit-N	142	554	58	149	22	6	8	53	43	55	1	2	.269	.322	.374	.695	99	-1	68	4.31	3	*0-142(0-142-0)	16	-0.2
1964 Pit-N	145	473	59	115	11	3	3	27	30	48	1	5	.243	.288	.298	.586	66	-23	38	2.71	-5	*0-134(0-134-0)	5	-3.3
1965 Pit-N	135	481	58	134	22	5	4	24	30	49	4	3	.279	.322	.370	.692	94	-4	58	4.29	-4	*0-128(1-127-0)	14	-1.4
1968 Pit-N	6	3	1	1	0	0	1	2	0	2	0	0	.333	.333	1.333	1.667	388	1	1	18.00	0	/0-4(1-0-3)	0	0.1
Total 12	1583	5980	735	1596	237	81	91	502	442	647	47	54	.267	.318	.379	.697	89	-108	721	4.22	20	*0-1542	157	-15.3

• VIRGIL, Ozzie

Osvaldo Jose (Pichardo) Virgil b: 5/17/1933, Monte Cristi, Dominican Republic BR/TR, 6'1", 175 lbs. Deb: 9/23/1956 C Career OF: 8-0-18

YEAR TM-L	G	AB	R	H	2B	3B	HR	RBI	BB	SO	SB	CS	AVG	OBP	SLG	OPS	OPS+	BR/A	RC	RC/G	FR	G/POS	WS	TPW
1956 NY-N	3	12	2	5	1	1	0	2	0	0	1	0	.417	.417	.667	1.083	186	2	4	13.69	0	/3-3	1	0.1
1957 NY-N	96	226	26	53	0	2	4	24	14	27	2	3	.235	.279	.305	.584	57	-15	17	2.51	1	3-62,0-24(8-0-16)/S-1	2	-1.5
1958 Det-A	49	193	19	47	10	2	3	19	8	20	1	0	.244	.274	.363	.636	68	-8	18	3.20	3	3-49	3	-0.5
1960 Det-A	62	132	16	30	4	2	3	13	4	14	1	1	.227	.250	.356	.606	58	-9	11	2.76	1	3-42/2-8,S-5,C-1	2	-0.7
1961 Det-A	20	30	1	4	0	0	1	1	1	5	0	0	.133	.161	.233	.395	4	-4	1	.68	-2	/3-9,C-3,2-1,S-1	0	-0.6
KC-A	11	21	1	3	0	0	0	0	0	3	0	0	.143	.143	.143	.286	-23	-4	0	.00	0	/3-4,C-3	0	-0.4
Yr.	31	51	2	7	0	0	1	1	1	8	0	0	.137	.154	.196	.350	-7	-8	1	.37	-2	3-13/C-6,2-1,S-1	0	-1.0
1962 Bal-A	1	0	0	0	0	0	0	0	1	0	0	0	....	1.000	....	1.000	206	0	0	....	0	....	0	0.0
1965 Pit-N	39	49	3	13	2	0	1	5	2	10	0	0	.265	.294	.367	.661	85	-1	5	3.58	0	C-15/3-7,2-5	1	-0.1
1966 SF-N	42	89	7	19	2	0	2	9	4	12	1	1	.213	.247	.303	.551	51	-6	6	2.08	-2	3-13,C-13/1-5,2-2,0-2(0-0-2)	1	-0.9
1969 SF-N	1	1	0	0	0	0	0	0	0	0	0	0	.000	.000	.000	.000	-102	-0	0	.00	0	....	0	0.0
Total 9	324	753	75	174	19	7	14	73	34	91	6	5	.231	.264	.331	.595	59	-45	62	2.69	0	3-189/C-35,0-26,2-16,S-7,1	10	-4.6

• VIRGIL, Ozzie

Osvaldo Jose (Lopez) Virgil b: 12/7/1956, Mayaguez, Puerto Rico BR/TR, 6'1", 205 lbs. Deb: 10/5/1980

YEAR TM-L	G	AB	R	H	2B	3B	HR	RBI	BB	SO	SB	CS	AVG	OBP	SLG	OPS	OPS+	BR/A	RC	RC/G	FR	G/POS	WS	TPW
1980 Phi-N	1	5	1	1	1	0	0	0	0	1	0	0	.200	.200	.400	.600	60	-0	0	2.70	0	/C-1	0	0.0
1981 Phi-N	6	6	0	0	0	0	0	0	0	2	0	0	.000	.000	.000	.000	-96	-2	0	.00	0	/C-1	0	-0.2
1982 Phi-N	49	101	11	24	6	0	3	8	10	26	0	1	.238	.306	.386	.692	90	-2	11	3.75	-3	C-35	3	-0.3
1983*Phi-N	55	140	11	30	7	0	6	23	8	34	0	2	.214	.272	.393	.664	83	-5	12	2.67	-1	C-51	3	-0.5
1984 Phi-N	141	456	61	119	21	2	18	68	45	91	1	1	.261	.334	.434	.768	112	7	62	4.62	-3	*C-137	14	1.0
1985 Phi-N★	131	426	47	105	16	3	19	55	49	85	0	0	.246	.331	.432	.763	109	5	59	4.75	-1	*C-120	16	1.0
1986 Atl-N	114	359	45	80	9	0	15	48	63	73	1	0	.223	.345	.373	.718	93	-2	49	4.52	8	*C-111	14	1.2
1987 Atl-N★	123	429	57	106	13	1	27	72	47	81	0	1	.247	.331	.471	.802	104	1	63	4.92	3	*C-122	13	1.0
1988 Atl-N	107	320	23	82	10	0	9	31	22	54	2	0	.256	.314	.372	.686	92	-3	36	3.91	1	C-96	8	0.3
1989 Tor-A	9	11	2	2	1	0	1	2	4	3	0	0	.182	.400	.545	.945	174	1	3	8.45	0	/D-6,C-1	1	0.1
1990 Tor-A	3	5	0	0	0	0	0	0	0	3	0	0	.000	.000	.000	.000	-95	-1	0	.00	-1	/C-2,D-1	0	-0.2
Total 11	739	2258	258	549	84	6	98	307	248	453	4	5	.243	.326	.416	.742	101	-1	296	4.40	3	C-677/D-7	72	3.5

• VIRTUE, Jake

Jacob Kitchline "Guesses" Virtue b: 3/2/1865, Philadelphia, PA d: 2/3/1943, Camden, NJ BB/TL, 5'9.5", 165 lbs. Deb: 7/21/1890 Career OF: 0-25-9

YEAR TM-L	G	AB	R	H	2B	3B	HR	RBI	BB	SO	SB	CS	AVG	OBP	SLG	OPS	OPS+	BR/A	RC	RC/G	FR	G/POS	WS	TPW
1890 Cle-N	62	223	39	68	6	5	2	25	49	15	9	....	.305	.432	.404	.836	147	17	44	7.50	1	1-62	10	1.1
1891 Cle-N	139	517	82	135	19	14	2	72	75	40	15	....	.261	.363	.364	.727	107	7	76	5.34	-4	*1-139	15	-0.9
1892*Cle-N	147	557	98	157	15	20	2	89	84	68	14	....	.282	.380	.391	.771	128	21	90	6.10	10	*1-147	22	2.8
1893 Cle-N	97	378	87	100	16	10	1	60	54	14	11	....	.265	.358	.368	.726	88	-7	55	5.25	0	1-73,0-13(0-9-4)/3-5,S-5,P	9	-0.5
1894 Cle-N	29	89	15	23	4	1	0	10	13	3	1	....	.258	.359	.326	.685	64	-5	11	4.35	-1	0-21(0-16-5)/2-3,1-2,P-1	1	-0.5
Total 5	474	1764	321	483	60	50	7	256	275	140	50	....	.274	.376	.376	.753	113	33	276	5.77	6	1-423/0-34,3-5,S-5,2-3,P-2	57	2.0

• VISNER, Joe

Joseph Paul Visner b: 9/27/1859, Minneapolis, MN d: 6/17/1945, Fosston, MN BL/TR, 5'11", 180 lbs. Deb: 7/4/1885 Career OF: 2-2-179

YEAR TM-L	G	AB	R	H	2B	3B	HR	RBI	BB	SO	SB	CS	AVG	OBP	SLG	OPS	OPS+	BR/A	RC	RC/G	FR	G/POS	WS	TPW
1885 Bal-a	4	13	2	3	0	0	0	2	2	....	....	....	.231	.333	.231	.564	82	-0	1	2.77	-1	/0-4(0-2-2)	0	-0.1
1889*Bro-a	80	295	56	76	12	10	8	68	36	36	13	....	.258	.346	.447	.794	125	9	51	6.23	-7	C-53,0-29(2-0-27)	14	0.4
1890 Pit-P	127	521	110	139	15	**22**	3	71	76	44	18	....	.267	.369	.397	.766	114	14	85	6.01	-7	*0-127(0-0-127)	14	0.4
1891 Was-a	18	68	13	19	2	3	1	7	8	7	2	....	.279	.355	.441	.796	134	3	12	6.30	-3	0-17(0-0-17)/3-1,C-1	2	0.0
StL-a	6	27	2	4	0	1	0	1	0	3	0	....	.148	.148	.222	.370	5	-4	1	1.05	1	/0-6(0-0-6)	0	-0.3
Yr.	24	95	15	23	2	4	1	8	8	10	2	....	.242	.301	.379	.680	100	-1	13	4.62	-2	0-23(0-0-23)/3-1,C-1	2	-0.3
Total 4	235	924	183	241	29	36	12	149	122	90	33	....	.261	.354	.409	.764	115	22	150	5.89	-18	0-183/C-54,3-1	30	0.4

• VITIELLO, Joe

Joseph David Vitiello b: 4/11/1970, Cambridge, MA BR/TR, 6'2", 215 lbs. Deb: 4/29/1995 Career OF: 27-0-18

YEAR TM-L	G	AB	R	H	2B	3B	HR	RBI	BB	SO	SB	CS	AVG	OBP	SLG	OPS	OPS+	BR/A	RC	RC/G	FR	G/POS	WS	TPW
1995 KC-A	53	130	13	33	4	0	7	21	8	25	0	0	.254	.317	.446	.763	95	-2	18	4.72	-1	D-38/1-8	2	-0.4
1996 KC-A	85	257	29	62	15	1	8	40	38	69	2	0	.241	.346	.401	.746	88	-4	35	4.50	1	D-70/1-9,0-1	4	-0.7
1997 KC-A	51	130	11	31	6	0	5	18	14	37	0	0	.238	.322	.400	.722	85	-3	17	4.61	-1	0-28(12-0-16),D-12/1-1	2	-0.5
1998 KC-A	3	7	0	1	0	0	0	0	1	2	0	0	.143	.250	.143	.393	6	-1	0	1.42	0	/D-2	0	-0.1
1999 KC-A	13	41	4	6	1	0	1	4	2	9	0	0	.146	.222	.244	.466	18	-5	2	1.43	1	1-10/D-2	0	-0.5
2000 SD-N	39	52	7	13	3	0	2	8	10	9	0	0	.250	.371	.423	.794	107	1	9	5.78	-1	1-17/0-1	1	-0.1
2003 Mon-N	38	76	12	26	6	0	3	13	7	14	0	0	.342	.412	.539	.951	123	3	17	9.00	0	0-15(15-0-0),1-12/D-1	2	0.2
Total 7	282	693	76	172	35	1	26	104	80	165	2	0	.248	.337	.414	.751	89	-11	98	4.84	-1	D-125/1-57,0-45	11	-2.1

• VITT, Ossie

Oscar Joseph Vitt b: 1/4/1890, San Francisco, CA d: 1/31/1963, Oakland, CA BR/TR, 5'10", 150 lbs. Deb: 4/11/1912 M Career OF: 30-6-1

YEAR TM-L	G	AB	R	H	2B	3B	HR	RBI	BB	SO	SB	CS	AVG	OBP	SLG	OPS	OPS+	BR/A	RC	RC/G	FR	G/POS	WS	TPW
1912 Det-A	76	273	39	67	4	4	0	19	18	....	17	....	.245	.297	.289	.586	70	-11	28	3.44	-1	0-28(25-1-1),3-24,2-15	4	-1.2
1913 Det-A	99	359	45	86	11	3	2	33	31	18	5	....	.240	.304	.304	.607	79	-10	36	3.08	-1	2-78,3-17/0-2(0-2-0)	6	-1.0
1914 Det-A	66	195	35	49	7	0	0	8	31	8	10	8	.251	.354	.287	.641	90	-2	24	3.63	-1	2-36,3-16/0-2(2-0-0),S-1	5	-0.2
1915 Det-A	152	560	116	140	18	13	1	48	80	22	26	18	.250	.348	.334	.682	99	-1	74	4.06	11	*3-151/2-2	23	1.6
1916 Det-A	153	597	88	135	17	12	0	42	75	28	18	....	.226	.314	.295	.608	80	-14	65	3.44	30	*3-151/S-2	21	2.4
1917 Det-A	140	512	65	130	13	6	0	47	56	15	18	....	.254	.329	.303	.631	93	-3	58	3.65	-13	*3-140	14	-1.4
1918 Det-A	81	267	29	64	5	2	0	17	32	6	5	....	.240	.321	.273	.594	83	-5	27	3.06	5	3-66/2-9,0-3(0-3-0)	7	0.2
1919 Bos-A	133	469	64	114	10	3	0	40	44	11	9	....	.243	.309	.277	.587	69	-18	47	3.06	14	*3-133	9	-0.1
1920 Bos-A	87	296	50	65	10	4	1	28	43	10	5	4	.220	.321	.291	.611	65	-13	31	3.17	-1	3-64,2-21	6	-1.1
1921 Bos-A	78	232	29	44	11	1	0	13	45	13	1	2	.190	.321	.246	.567	48	-17	22	2.85	-4	3-71/0-3(3-0-0),1-2	4	-1.6
Total 10	1065	3760	560	894	106	48	4	295	455	131	114	32	.238	.322	.295	.617	80	-94	412	3.40	40	3-833,2-161/0-38,S-3,1-2	99	-2.3

• VIZCAINO, Jose

Jose Luis (Pimental) Vizcaino b: 3/26/1968, San Cristobal, Dominican Republic BB/TR, 6'1", 180 lbs. Deb: 9/10/1989

YEAR TM-L	G	AB	R	H	2B	3B	HR	RBI	BB	SO	SB	CS	AVG	OBP	SLG	OPS	OPS+	BR/A	RC	RC/G	FR	G/POS	WS	TPW
1989 LA-N	7	10	2	2	0	0	0	0	0	1	0	0	.200	.200	.200	.400	15	-1	0	1.37	-1	/S-5	0	-0.2
1990 LA-N	37	51	3	14	1	1	0	2	4	8	1	1	.275	.327	.333	.661	85	-1	5	3.69	-1	S-11/2-6	1	-0.1
1991 Chi-N	93	145	7	38	5	0	0	10	5	18	2	1	.262	.287	.297	.583	61	-8	13	3.02	-6	3-57,S-33/2-9	2	-1.2
1992 Chi-N	86	285	25	64	10	4	1	17	14	35	3	0	.225	.261	.298	.559	57	-16	23	2.63	-2	S-50,3-29/2-5	4	-1.6
1993 Chi-N	151	551	74	158	19	4	4	54	46	71	12	9	.287	.345	.358	.703	90	-9	69	4.33	5	S-81,3-44,2-34	15	0.4
1994 NY-N	103	410	47	105	13	3	3	33	33	62	1	11	.256	.315	.324	.639	68	-24	40	3.26	-4	*S-102	7	-2.0
1995 NY-N	135	509	66	146	21	5	3	56	35	76	8	3	.287	.334	.365	.699	87	-10	61	4.15	11	*S-134/2-1	16	1.2
1996 NY-N	96	363	47	110	12	6	1	32	28	58	9	5	.303	.358	.377	.735	99	-1	50	4.94	4	2-93	10	0.7
*Cle-A	48	179	23	51	5	2	0	13	7	24	6	2	.285	.312	.335	.647	64	-10	19	3.76	0	2-45/S-4,D-1	4	-0.7
1997*SF-N	151	568	77	151	19	7	5	50	48	87	8	8	.266	.323	.350	.673	79	-20	63	3.76	11	*S-147/2-5	17	0.2
1998 LA-N	67	237	30	62	9	0	3	29	17	35	7	3	.262	.314	.338	.651	76	-8	26	3.60	1	S-66	8	-0.2

YEAR TM-L	G	AB	R	H	2B	3B	HR	RBI	BB	SO	SB	CS	AVG	OBP	SLG	OPS	OPS+	BR/A	RC	RC/G	FR	G/POS	WS	TPW
1999 LA-N	94	266	27	67	9	0	1	29	20	23	2	1	.252	.307	.297	.604	57	-18	24	2.93	-1	S-44,2-30/3-9,0-1	4	-1.4
2000 LA-N	40	93	9	19	2	1	0	4	10	15	1	0	.204	.288	.247	.536	39	-8	7	2.32	-1	S-19,3-12/2-3,1-1,D-1	1	-0.7
*NY-A	73	174	23	48	8	1	0	10	12	28	5	7	.276	.323	.333	.656	67	-11	17	3.32	3	2-62/3-6,D-4,S-2	2	-0.5
2001*Hou-N	107	256	38	71	8	3	1	14	15	33	3	2	.277	.322	.344	.666	69	-12	28	3.74	-6	S-53,2-18/3-7	4	-1.3
2002 Hou-N	125	406	53	123	19	2	5	37	24	40	3	5	.303	.343	.397	.740	90	-8	54	4.88	-4	S-58,3-30,2-25/1-5	11	-0.6
2003 Hou-N	91	189	14	47	7	3	3	26	8	22	0	1	.249	.283	.365	.648	64	-11	18	3.18	-1	S-32,2-20/3-2,1-1	4	-1.0
Total 15	1504	4692	565	1276	167	42	30	416	326	636	71	59	.272	.321	.345	.666	76	-174	516	3.77	8	S-841,2-356,3-196/1-7,D-6,0	110	-8.9

• VIZQUEL, Omar Omar Enrique (Gonzalez) Vizquel b: 4/24/1967, Caracas, Venezuela BB/TR, 5'9", 165 lbs. Deb: 4/3/1989

YEAR TM-L	G	AB	R	H	2B	3B	HR	RBI	BB	SO	SB	CS	AVG	OBP	SLG	OPS	OPS+	BR/A	RC	RC/G	FR	G/POS	WS	TPW
1989 Sea-A	143	387	45	85	7	3	1	20	28	40	1	4	.220	.274	.261	.535	50	-27	28	2.33	-9	*S-143	3	-2.6
1990 Sea-A	81	255	19	63	3	2	2	18	18	22	4	1	.247	.297	.298	.595	66	-11	23	2.90	1	S-81	3	-0.4
1991 Sea-A	142	426	42	98	16	4	1	41	45	37	7	2	.230	.304	.293	.597	66	-18	40	3.12	16	*S-138/2-1	14	0.9
1992 Sea-A	136	483	49	142	20	4	0	21	32	38	15	13	.294	.340	.352	.692	94	-6	54	3.87	3	*S-136	12	0.7
1993 Sea-A	158	560	68	143	14	2	2	31	50	71	12	14	.255	.321	.298	.619	67	-29	54	3.24	15	*S-155/D-2	12	-0.1
1994 Cle-A	69	286	39	78	10	1	1	33	23	23	13	4	.273	.327	.325	.652	69	-12	32	3.83	-2	S-69	7	-0.8
1995*Cle-A	136	542	87	144	28	0	6	56	59	59	29	11	.266	.339	.351	.689	79	-15	70	4.38	-5	*S-136	17	-0.8
1996*Cle-A	151	542	98	161	36	1	9	64	56	42	35	9	.297	.367	.417	.784	98	3	88	5.63	-9	*S-150	16	0.6
1997*Cle-A	153	565	89	158	23	6	5	49	57	58	43	12	.280	.348	.368	.716	84	-8	75	4.47	-4	*S-152	14	0.0
1998*Cle-A★	151	576	86	166	30	6	2	50	62	64	37	12	.288	.361	.372	.733	88	-5	83	4.95	3	*S-151	18	0.9
1999*Cle-A★	144	574	112	191	36	4	5	66	65	50	42	9	.333	.402	.436	.837	109	15	109	6.94	-14	*S-143/0-1	22	1.2
2000 Cle-A	156	613	101	176	27	3	7	66	87	72	22	10	.287	.380	.375	.755	90	-5	93	5.31	-16	*S-156	16	-0.8
2001*Cle-A	155	611	84	156	26	8	2	50	61	72	13	9	.255	.325	.334	.659	73	-24	67	3.64	-5	*S-154	12	-1.6
2002 Cle-A★	151	582	85	160	31	5	14	72	56	64	18	10	.275	.347	.418	.764	104	3	87	5.12	-5	*S-150	21	1.0
2003 Cle-A	64	250	43	61	13	2	2	19	29	20	8	3	.244	.323	.336	.659	77	-8	26	3.40	13	S-64	5	1.0
Total 15	1990	7252	1047	1982	320	51	59	656	728	732	299	123	.273	.342	.356	.698	83	-148	930	4.36	-19	*S-1978/D-2,2-1,0-1	192	-0.9

• VOGEL, Otto Otto Henry Vogel b: 10/26/1899, Mendota, IL d: 7/19/1969, Iowa City, IA BR/TR, 6', 195 lbs. Deb: 6/5/1923 Career OF: 15-1-61

YEAR TM-L	G	AB	R	H	2B	3B	HR	RBI	BB	SO	SB	CS	AVG	OBP	SLG	OPS	OPS+	BR/A	RC	RC/G	FR	G/POS	WS	TPW
1923 Chi-N	41	81	10	17	0	1	1	6	7	11	2	3	.210	.297	.272	.568	51	-6	7	2.55	0	0-24(3-0-21)/3-1	0	-0.7
1924 Chi-N	70	172	28	46	11	2	1	24	10	26	4	4	.267	.319	.372	.691	84	-4	20	3.88	1	0-53(12-1-40)/3-2	4	-0.7
Total 2	111	253	38	63	11	3	2	30	17	37	6	7	.249	.312	.340	.652	73	-11	27	3.44	1	/0-77,3-3	4	-1.4

• VOIGT, Jack John David Voigt b: 5/17/1966, Sarasota, FL BR/TR, 6'1", 175 lbs. Deb: 8/3/1992 Career OF: 93-13-85

YEAR TM-L	G	AB	R	H	2B	3B	HR	RBI	BB	SO	SB	CS	AVG	OBP	SLG	OPS	OPS+	BR/A	RC	RC/G	FR	G/POS	WS	TPW
1992 Bal-A	1	0	0	0	0	0	0	0	0	0	0	0	....	....	....	....	-98	0	0	....	0	....	0	0.0
1993 Bal-A	64	152	32	45	11	1	6	23	25	33	1	0	.296	.395	.500	.895	133	8	31	7.71	1	0-43(22-0-23)/D-9,1-5,3-3	6	0.6
1994 Bal-A	59	141	15	34	5	0	3	20	18	25	0	0	.241	.331	.340	.672	70	-6	18	4.33	0	0-54(17-1-37)/1-6,D-2	3	-0.8
1995 Bal-A	3	1	1	1	0	0	0	0	0	0	0	0	1.000	1.000	1.000	2.000	416	0	1	∞	0	/1-1,D-1	0	0.1
Tex-A	33	62	8	10	3	0	2	8	10	14	0	0	.161	.278	.306	.584	51	-5	5	2.68	0	0-25(8-0-17)/1-5,D-2	0	-0.6
Yr.	36	63	9	11	3	0	2	8	10	14	0	0	.175	.288	.317	.605	56	-4	6	2.68	0	0-25(8-0-17)/1-6,D-3	0	-0.5
1996 Tex-A	5	9	1	1	0	0	0	0	0	2	0	0	.111	.111	.111	.222	-41	-2	0	.38	0	/0-3(2-0-1),3-1	0	-0.2
1997 Mil-A	72	151	20	37	9	2	8	22	19	36	1	2	.245	.333	.490	.823	110	1	23	5.05	0	0-40(35-2-5),1-19/3-6,D-1	5	-0.1
1998 Oak-A	57	72	7	10	4	0	1	10	6	19	5	1	.139	.205	.236	.441	15	-9	4	1.60	0	1-27,0-20(9-10-2)/D-3,3-2	0	-1.0
Total 7	294	588	84	138	32	3	20	83	78	129	7	3	.235	.326	.401	.728	88	-11	83	4.67	0	0-185/1-63,D-18,3-12	14	-1.9

• VOLLMER, Clyde Clyde Frederick Vollmer b: 9/24/1921, Cincinnati, OH BR/TR, 6'1", 190 lbs. Deb: 5/31/1942 Career OF: 197-191-169

YEAR TM-L	G	AB	R	H	2B	3B	HR	RBI	BB	SO	SB	CS	AVG	OBP	SLG	OPS	OPS+	BR/A	RC	RC/G	FR	G/POS	WS	TPW
1942 Cin-N	12	43	2	4	0	0	1	4	1	5	0	....	.093	.114	.163	.276	-20	-7	1	.57	1	0-11(10-1-0)	1	-0.7
1946 Cin-N	9	22	1	4	0	0	0	1	1	3	2	....	.182	.217	.182	.399	14	-2	1	1.42	0	/0-7(5-3-1)	0	-0.3
1947 Cin-N	78	155	19	34	10	0	1	13	9	18	0	....	.219	.267	.303	.570	51	-11	13	2.74	-1	0-66(8-58-0)	1	-1.3
1948 Cin-N	7	9	0	1	0	0	0	0	1	1	0	....	.111	.200	.111	.311	-14	-1	0	.38	0	/0-2(0-1-1)	0	-0.2
Was-A	1	5	1	2	0	0	0	0	0	1	0	0	.400	.400	.400	.800	116	0	1	7.38	0	/0-1	0	0.0
1949 Was-A	129	443	58	112	17	1	14	59	53	62	1	2	.253	.335	.391	.726	94	-6	59	4.57	-2	*0-114(0-99-15)	11	-1.0
1950 Was-A	6	14	4	4	0	0	0	1	2	3	1	0	.286	.375	.286	.661	75	-0	2	5.20	1	/0-3(3-0-0)	0	0.0
Bos-A	57	169	35	48	10	0	7	37	21	35	1	0	.284	.363	.467	.831	102	0	29	6.28	-2	0-39(17-11-11)	5	-0.3
Yr.	63	183	39	52	10	0	7	38	23	38	2	0	.284	.364	.454	.818	99	0	31	6.20	-1	0-42(20-11-11)	5	-0.3
1951 Bos-A	115	386	66	97	9	2	22	85	55	66	0	0	.251	.346	.456	.802	105	2	59	5.08	-2	*0-106(2-8-97)	10	-0.3
1952 Bos-A	90	250	35	66	12	4	11	50	39	47	2	2	.264	.370	.476	.846	125	9	42	5.67	1	0-70(43-9-21)	9	0.6
1953 Bos-A	1	0	0	0	0	0	0	0	1	0	0	0	....	1.000	....	1.000	180	0	0	∞	0	....	0	0.0
Was-A	118	408	54	106	15	3	11	74	48	59	0	2	.260	.342	.392	.734	100	-0	58	5.00	1	*0-106(104-0-2)	12	-0.6
Yr.	119	408	54	106	15	3	11	74	49	59	0	2	.260	.343	.392	.736	100	0	58	5.00	1	*0-106(104-0-2)	12	-0.6
1954 Was-A	62	117	8	30	4	0	2	15	12	28	0	0	.256	.331	.342	.673	89	-2	13	4.00	0	0-26(5-0-21)	2	-0.2
Total 10	685	2021	283	508	77	10	69	339	243	328	7	6	.251	.335	.402	.737	95	-18	278	4.70	-3	0-551	51	-4.2

• VON KOLNITZ, Fritz Alfred Holmes Von Kolnitz b: 5/20/1893, Charleston, SC d: 3/18/1948, Mount Pleasant, SC BR/TR, 5'10.5", 175 lbs. Deb: 4/18/1914 Career OF: 2-7-3

YEAR TM-L	G	AB	R	H	2B	3B	HR	RBI	BB	SO	SB	CS	AVG	OBP	SLG	OPS	OPS+	BR/A	RC	RC/G	FR	G/POS	WS	TPW
1914 Cin-N	41	104	8	23	2	0	0	6	6	16	4	....	.221	.270	.240	.511	51	-6	7	2.31	-2	3-20,0-11(2-7-2)/C-2,1-1	1	-0.8
1915 Cin-N	50	78	6	15	4	1	0	6	7	11	1	3	.192	.259	.269	.528	59	-5	5	1.98	-5	3-18/S-6,1-3,C-2,0-1	0	-1.0
1916 Chi-A	24	44	1	10	3	0	0	7	2	6	0	....	.227	.261	.295	.556	66	-2	3	2.59	-2	3-13	0	-0.4
Total 3	115	226	15	48	9	1	0	19	15	33	5	3	.212	.264	.261	.526	56	-13	16	2.24	-8	/3-51,0-12,S-6,1-4,C-4	1	-2.3

• VOSMIK, Joe Joseph Franklin Vosmik b: 4/4/1910, Cleveland, OH d: 1/27/1962, Cleveland, OH BR/TR, 6', 185 lbs. Deb: 9/13/1930 Career OF: 1283-15-75

YEAR TM-L	G	AB	R	H	2B	3B	HR	RBI	BB	SO	SB	CS	AVG	OBP	SLG	OPS	OPS+	BR/A	RC	RC/G	FR	G/POS	WS	TPW
1930 Cle-A	9	26	1	6	2	0	0	4	1	1	0	0	.231	.259	.308	.567	41	-2	2	2.72	1	/0-5(1-4-0)	0	-0.2
1931 Cle-A	149	591	80	189	36	14	7	117	38	30	7	7	.320	.363	.464	.827	110	8	97	6.18	6	*0-147(147-1-0)	18	0.5
1932 Cle-A	153	621	106	194	39	12	10	97	58	42	2	3	.312	.376	.462	.838	109	8	109	6.61	20	*0-153(153-0-0)	24	1.7
1933 Cle-A	119	438	53	115	20	10	4	56	42	13	0	2	.263	.331	.381	.713	85	-10	56	4.56	5	*0-113(113-0-0)	12	-1.1
1934 Cle-A	104	405	71	138	33	2	6	78	35	10	1	1	.341	.393	.477	.870	122	13	76	7.29	-3	*0-104(104-0-0)	15	0.3
1935 Cle-A★	152	620	93	**216**	**47**	**20**	10	110	59	30	2	1	.348	.408	.537	.946	140	37	137	8.85	5	*0-150(150-0-0)	28	3.1
1936 Cle-A	138	506	76	145	29	7	7	94	79	21	5	1	.287	.383	.413	.796	96	-1	85	6.14	-1	*0-136(136-0-1)	11	-0.9
1937 StL-A	144	594	81	193	47	9	4	93	49	38	2	3	.325	.377	.455	.832	108	6	102	6.51	7	*0-143(143-0-0)	12	0.4
1938 Bos-A	146	621	121	**201**	37	6	9	86	59	26	0	3	.324	.384	.446	.830	103	2	107	6.59	4	*0-146(146-1-0)	19	-0.3
1939 Bos-A	145	554	89	153	29	6	7	84	66	33	4	3	.276	.356	.388	.744	87	-10	73	4.41	-4	*0-144(144-0-0)	11	-2.1
1940 Bro-N	116	404	45	114	14	6	1	42	22	21	0	....	.282	.321	.354	.675	81	-11	45	4.04	-1	0-99(39-9-51)	9	-1.7
1941 Bro-N	25	56	0	11	0	0	0	4	4	4	0	....	.196	.250	.196	.446	26	-5	3	1.51	0	0-18(2-0-16)	0	-0.6
1944 Was-A	14	36	2	7	2	0	0	9	2	3	0	0	.194	.237	.250	.487	41	-3	2	1.85	0	0-12(5-0-7)	0	-0.4
Total 13	1414	5472	818	1682	335	92	65	874	514	272	23	24	.307	.369	.438	.807	104	30	895	6.05	37	*0-1370	159	-1.2

• VOSS, Alex Alexander Voss b: 5/16/1858, Roswell, GA d: 8/31/1906, Cincinnati, OH BR/TR, 6'1", 180 lbs. Deb: 4/17/1884 ♦

YEAR TM-L	G	AB	R	H	2B	3B	HR	RBI	BB	SO	SB	CS	AVG	OBP	SLG	OPS	OPS+	BR/A	RC	RC/G	FR	G/POS	WS	TPW
1884 Was-U	63	245	33	47	9	0	0	....	5	....	....	....	.192	.208	.229	.437	49	-11	12	1.69	4	P-27,3-16,1-15,0-13(0-7-6)/S	10	-1.4
KC-U	14	45	1	4	0	0	0	....	0	....	....	....	.089	.089	.089	.178	-46	-6	0	.25	1	/0-8(5-3-0),P-7	0	-1.2
Yr.	77	290	34	51	9	0	0	....	5	....	....	....	.176	.190	.207	.397	35	-16	12	1.44	5	P-34,0-21(5-10-6),3-16,1-15/S	10	-2.6

• VOSS, Bill William Edward Voss b: 10/31/1943, Glendale, CA BL/TL, 6'2", 160 lbs. Deb: 9/14/1965 Career OF: 21-36-328

YEAR TM-L	G	AB	R	H	2B	3B	HR	RBI	BB	SO	SB	CS	AVG	OBP	SLG	OPS	OPS+	BR/A	RC	RC/G	FR	G/POS	WS	TPW
1965 Chi-A	11	33	4	6	0	1	1	3	3	5	0	0	.182	.250	.333	.583	68	-1	3	2.82	-1	0-10(0-0-10)	1	-0.3
1966 Chi-A	2	2	0	0	0	0	0	0	0	2	0	0	.000	.000	.000	.000	-107	-1	0	.00	-0	/0-1	0	-0.1
1967 Chi-A	13	22	4	2	0	0	0	0	0	1	1	1	.091	.091	.091	.182	-48	-4	0	.00	0	0-11(1-2-9)	0	-0.5
1968 Chi-A	61	167	14	26	2	1	2	15	16	34	5	3	.156	.238	.216	.453	38	-12	9	1.73	2	0-55(5-2-53)	1	-1.6
1969 Cal-A	133	349	33	91	11	4	2	40	35	40	5	3	.261	.328	.332	.661	90	-5	38	3.72	6	*0-111(6-4-104)/1-2	9	-0.4
1970 Cal-A	80	181	21	44	4	3	3	30	23	18	2	1	.243	.335	.348	.683	92	-1	22	4.12	4	0-55(0-0-55)	6	0.0
1971 Mil-A	97	275	31	69	4	0	10	30	24	45	2	2	.251	.313	.375	.688	95	-2	33	4.14	0	0-79(4-13-67)	7	-0.7
1972 Mil-A	27	36	1	3	1	0	0	1	5	4	0	1	.083	.195	.111	.306	-7	-5	1	.39	-1	0-11(3-0-9)	0	-0.7
Oak-A	40	97	10	22	5	1	1	5	9	16	0	0	.227	.299	.330	.629	92	-1	10	3.28	1	0-34(1-13-21)	3	-0.1
Yr.	67	133	11	25	6	1	1	6	14	20	0	1	.188	.270	.271	.541	64	-6	10	2.34	0	0-45(4-13-30)	3	-0.8

YEAR TM-L	G	AB	R	H	2B	3B	HR	RBI	BB	SO	SB	CS	AVG	OBP	SLG	OPS	OPS+	BR/A	RC	RC/G	FR	G/POS	WS	TPW
StL-N	11	15	1	4	2	0	0	3	2	2	0	0	.267	.353	.400	.753	115	0	2	4.06	0	/O-2(0-2-0)	0	0.0
Total 8	475	1177	119	267	29	10	19	127	117	167	15	11	.227	.300	.317	.617	78	-33	117	3.29	11	O-369/1-2	27	-4.3

• VOYLES, Phil Philip Vance Voyles b: 5/12/1900, Murphy, NC d: 11/3/1972, Marlboro, MA BL/TR, 5'11.5", 175 lbs. Deb: 9/4/1929

YEAR TM-L	G	AB	R	H	2B	3B	HR	RBI	BB	SO	SB	CS	AVG	OBP	SLG	OPS	OPS+	BR/A	RC	RC/G	FR	G/POS	WS	TPW
1929 Bos-N	20	68	9	16	0	2	0	14	6	8	0	....	.235	.297	.294	.591	49	-5	6	2.82	-1	O-20(1-19-0)	0	-0.6

• VUKOVICH, George George Stephen Vukovich b: 6/24/1956, Chicago, IL BL/TR, 6', 198 lbs. Deb: 4/13/1980 Career OF: 77-4-482

YEAR TM-L	G	AB	R	H	2B	3B	HR	RBI	BB	SO	SB	CS	AVG	OBP	SLG	OPS	OPS+	BR/A	RC	RC/G	FR	G/POS	WS	TPW
1980*Phi-N	78	58	6	13	1	1	0	8	6	9	0	0	.224	.297	.276	.573	58	-3	5	2.90	-1	O-28(13-0-15)	0	-0.5
1981*Phi-N	20	26	5	10	0	0	1	4	1	0	1	0	.385	.407	.500	.907	150	2	6	9.47	0	/O-9(3-1-5)	2	0.2
1982 Phi-N	123	335	41	91	18	2	6	42	32	47	2	9	.272	.335	.391	.726	100	-4	41	4.28	2	*O-102(15-0-100)	9	-0.6
1983 Cle-A	124	312	31	77	13	2	3	44	24	37	3	4	.247	.305	.330	.635	72	-13	30	3.19	-2	*O-122(20-3-107)	3	-1.9
1984 Cle-A	134	437	38	133	22	5	9	60	34	61	1	4	.304	.356	.439	.795	117	8	66	5.53	14	*O-130(16-0-124)	15	1.6
1985 Cle-A	149	434	43	106	22	0	8	45	30	75	2	2	.244	.295	.350	.645	76	-15	43	3.41	0	*O-137(10-0-131)	6	-2.0
Total 6	628	1602	164	430	76	10	27	203	127	229	9	19	.268	.324	.379	.703	92	-25	191	4.16	12	O-528	35	-3.3

• VUKOVICH, John John Christopher Vukovich b: 7/31/1947, Sacramento, CA BR/TR, 6'1", 190 lbs. Deb: 9/11/1970 M/C

YEAR TM-L	G	AB	R	H	2B	3B	HR	RBI	BB	SO	SB	CS	AVG	OBP	SLG	OPS	OPS+	BR/A	RC	RC/G	FR	G/POS	WS	TPW
1970 Phi-N	3	8	1	1	0	0	0	0	1	0	0	0	.125	.222	.125	.347	-5	-1	0	1.08	0	/S-2,3-1	0	-0.1
1971 Phi-N	74	217	11	36	5	0	0	14	12	34	2	1	.166	.213	.189	.402	15	-24	9	1.26	1	3-74	2	-2.6
1973 Mil-A	55	128	10	16	3	0	2	9	9	40	0	2	.125	.182	.195	.378	7	-17	5	1.04	-4	3-40,1-13/S-1	1	-2.2
1974 Mil-A	38	80	5	15	1	0	3	11	1	16	2	1	.188	.198	.313	.510	45	-6	4	1.63	-2	3-12,S-12,2-11/1-4	1	-0.7
1975 Cin-N	31	38	4	8	3	0	0	2	4	5	0	0	.211	.286	.289	.575	59	-2	4	2.87	-1	3-31	0	-0.3
1976 Phi-N	4	8	2	1	0	0	1	2	0	2	0	0	.125	.125	.500	.625	69	-0	1	1.93	0	/3-4,1-1	0	-0.1
1977 Phi-N	2	2	0	0	0	0	0	0	0	1	0	0	.000	.000	.000	.000	-96	-1	0	.00	0	....	0	-0.1
1979 Phi-N	10	15	0	3	1	0	0	1	0	3	0	0	.200	.200	.267	.467	25	-2	1	1.80	1	/3-7,2-3	0	0.0
1980 Phi-N	49	62	4	10	1	1	0	5	2	7	0	1	.161	.200	.210	.410	14	-8	2	1.03	-6	3-34/2-9,S-5,1-1	1	-1.4
1981 Phi-N	11	1	0	0	0	0	0	0	0	1	0	0	.000	.000	.000	.000	-96	-0	0	.00	-2	/3-9,1-1,2-1	0	-0.3
Total 10	277	559	37	90	14	1	6	44	29	109	4	5	.161	.205	.222	.427	20	-61	25	1.35	-14	3-212/2-24,1-20,S-20	5	-7.8

• WADDEY, Frank Frank Orum Waddey b: 8/21/1905, Memphis, TN d: 10/21/1990, Knoxville, TN BL/TL, 5'10.5", 185 lbs. Deb: 4/16/1931

YEAR TM-L	G	AB	R	H	2B	3B	HR	RBI	BB	SO	SB	CS	AVG	OBP	SLG	OPS	OPS+	BR/A	RC	RC/G	FR	G/POS	WS	TPW
1931 StL-A	14	22	3	6	1	0	0	2	2	3	0	0	.273	.333	.318	.652	70	-1	2	3.99	0	/O-7(1-5-1)	0	-0.1

• WADE, Gale Galeard Lee Wade b: 1/20/1929, Hollister, MO BL/TR, 6'1.5", 185 lbs. Deb: 4/11/1955 Career OF: 0-12-0

YEAR TM-L	G	AB	R	H	2B	3B	HR	RBI	BB	SO	SB	CS	AVG	OBP	SLG	OPS	OPS+	BR/A	RC	RC/G	FR	G/POS	WS	TPW
1955 Chi-N	9	33	5	6	1	0	1	1	4	3	0	0	.182	.270	.303	.573	52	-2	3	2.55	0	/O-9(0-9-0)	0	-0.3
1956 Chi-N	10	12	0	0	0	0	0	0	1	0	0	0	.000	.077	.000	.077	-78	-3	0	.00	-1	/O-3(0-3-0)	0	-0.4
Total 2	19	45	5	6	1	0	1	1	5	3	0	0	.133	.220	.222	.442	19	-5	3	1.72	-1	/O-12	0	-0.7

• WADE, Ham Abraham Lincoln Wade b: 12/20/1880, Spring City, PA d: 7/21/1968, Riverside, NJ BR/TR, 5'8", 155 lbs. Deb: 9/9/1907

YEAR TM-L	G	AB	R	H	2B	3B	HR	RBI	BB	SO	SB	CS	AVG	OBP	SLG	OPS	OPS+	BR/A	RC	RC/G	FR	G/POS	WS	TPW
1907 NY-N	1	0	0	0	0	0	0	0	0	....	0	....	....	1.000	....	1.000	208	0	0	....	0	/O-1	0	0.0

• WADE, Rip Richard Frank Wade b: 1/12/1898, Duluth, MN d: 6/15/1957, Duluth, MN BL/TR, 5'11", 174 lbs. Deb: 4/19/1923

YEAR TM-L	G	AB	R	H	2B	3B	HR	RBI	BB	SO	SB	CS	AVG	OBP	SLG	OPS	OPS+	BR/A	RC	RC/G	FR	G/POS	WS	TPW
1923 Was-A	33	69	8	16	2	2	2	14	5	10	0	0	.232	.284	.406	.690	84	-2	8	3.82	1	O-19(5-12-2)	1	-0.1

• WAGENHORST, Woody Ellwood Otto Wagenhorst b: 6/3/1863, Kutztown, PA d: 2/12/1946, Washington, DC, 5'11", 165 lbs. Deb: 6/25/1888

YEAR TM-L	G	AB	R	H	2B	3B	HR	RBI	BB	SO	SB	CS	AVG	OBP	SLG	OPS	OPS+	BR/A	RC	RC/G	FR	G/POS	WS	TPW
1888 Phi-N	2	8	2	1	0	0	0	0	0	1	0	....	.125	.125	.125	.250	-19	-1	0	.49	-1	/3-2	0	-0.2

• WAGNER, Bill William Joseph Wagner b: 1/2/1894, Jessup, IA d: 1/11/1951, Waterloo, IA BR/TR, 6', 187 lbs. Deb: 7/16/1914

YEAR TM-L	G	AB	R	H	2B	3B	HR	RBI	BB	SO	SB	CS	AVG	OBP	SLG	OPS	OPS+	BR/A	RC	RC/G	FR	G/POS	WS	TPW
1914 Pit-N	3	1	0	0	0	0	0	0	0	0	0	....	.000	.000	.000	.000	-105	-0	0	.00	-1	/C-3	0	-0.1
1915 Pit-N	5	5	0	0	0	0	0	0	1	2	0	....	.000	.167	.000	.167	-48	-1	0	.00	1	/C-3	0	0.0
1916 Pit-N	19	38	2	9	0	2	0	2	5	8	0	....	.237	.326	.342	.668	104	0	4	3.79	0	C-15	1	0.1
1917 Pit-N	53	151	15	31	7	2	0	9	11	22	1	....	.205	.264	.278	.542	64	-6	11	2.35	-2	C-37,1-12	2	-0.7
1918 Bos-N	13	47	2	10	0	0	1	7	4	5	0	....	.213	.275	.277	.551	71	-2	3	2.38	-2	C-13	1	-0.3
Total 5	93	242	19	50	7	4	1	18	21	37	1	....	.207	.273	.281	.554	69	-9	19	2.49	-5	/C-71,1-12	4	-1.0

• WAGNER, Butts Albert Wagner b: 9/17/1871, Chartiers, PA d: 11/26/1928, Pittsburgh, PA BR/TR, 5'10", 170 lbs. Deb: 4/27/1898

YEAR TM-L	G	AB	R	H	2B	3B	HR	RBI	BB	SO	SB	CS	AVG	OBP	SLG	OPS	OPS+	BR/A	RC	RC/G	FR	G/POS	WS	TPW
1898 Was-N	63	223	20	50	11	2	1	31	14	....	4	....	.224	.279	.305	.584	67	-10	21	3.16	-12	3-39,O-10(1-9-0)/S-8,2-5	1	-2.0
Bro-N	11	38	2	9	1	1	0	3	2	....	0	....	.237	.275	.316	.591	69	-2	4	3.09	-2	3-11	1	-0.3
Yr.	74	261	22	59	12	3	1	34	16	....	4	....	.226	.279	.307	.585	68	-12	24	3.15	-14	3-50,O-10(1-9-0)/S-8,2-5	2	-2.3

• WAGNER, Hal Harold Edward Wagner b: 7/2/1915, East Riverton, NJ d: 8/4/1979, Riverside, NJ BL/TR, 6', 165 lbs. Deb: 10/3/1937

YEAR TM-L	G	AB	R	H	2B	3B	HR	RBI	BB	SO	SB	CS	AVG	OBP	SLG	OPS	OPS+	BR/A	RC	RC/G	FR	G/POS	WS	TPW
1937 Phi-A	1	0	0	0	0	0	0	0	0	0	0	0	....	....	....	....	-102	0	0	....	0	/C-1	0	0.0
1938 Phi-A	33	88	10	20	2	1	0	8	8	9	0	0	.227	.299	.273	.572	45	-7	8	2.90	-1	C-30	1	-0.6
1939 Phi-A	5	8	0	1	0	0	0	0	0	3	0	0	.125	.125	.125	.250	-37	-2	0	.48	0	/C-5	0	-0.1
1940 Phi-A	34	75	9	19	5	1	0	10	11	6	0	0	.253	.356	.347	.703	85	-1	10	4.52	2	C-28	2	0.2
1941 Phi-A	46	131	18	29	8	2	1	15	19	9	1	0	.221	.320	.336	.656	75	-4	16	4.15	0	C-42	3	-0.1
1942 Phi-A★	104	288	26	68	17	1	1	30	24	29	1	0	.236	.304	.313	.616	74	-10	28	3.32	2	C-94	6	-0.2
1943 Phi-A	111	289	22	69	17	1	1	26	36	17	3	3	.239	.327	.315	.642	89	-4	31	3.52	-1	C-99	7	0.0
1944 Phi-A	5	4	0	1	0	0	0	0	0	0	0	0	.250	.250	.250	.500	44	-0	0	2.31	0	/C-1	0	0.0
Bos-A	66	223	21	74	13	4	1	38	29	14	1	1	.332	.418	.439	.857	147	15	45	7.82	1	C-64	13	2.1
Yr.	71	227	21	75	13	4	1	38	29	14	1	1	.330	.415	.436	.852	145	15	45	7.71	1	C-65	13	2.1
1946*Bos-A★	117	370	39	85	12	2	6	52	69	32	3	1	.230	.354	.322	.675	85	-4	48	4.36	-14	*C-116	12	-1.2
1947 Bos-A	21	65	5	15	3	0	0	6	9	5	0	0	.231	.324	.277	.601	63	-3	7	3.39	-1	C-21	1	-0.3
Det-A	71	191	19	55	10	0	5	33	28	16	0	1	.288	.382	.419	.801	119	5	33	6.33	-1	C-71	10	0.7
Yr.	92	256	24	70	13	0	5	39	37	21	0	1	.273	.367	.383	.750	105	3	40	5.54	-2	C-92	11	0.5
1948 Det-A	54	109	10	22	3	0	0	10	20	11	1	0	.202	.326	.229	.555	48	-7	10	2.93	-1	C-52	2	-0.7
Phi-N	3	4	0	0	0	0	0	0	0	0	0	....	.000	.000	.000	.000	-102	-1	0	.00	0	/C-1	0	-0.1
1949 Phi-N	1	4	0	0	0	0	0	0	0	1	0	....	.000	.000	.000	.000	-103	-1	0	.00	0	/C-1	0	-0.2
Total 12	672	1849	179	458	90	12	15	228	253	152	10	6	.248	.343	.334	.677	88	-23	235	4.36	-14	C-626	57	-0.3

• WAGNER, Heinie Charles F. Wagner b: 9/23/1880, New York, NY d: 3/20/1943, New Rochelle, NY BR/TR, 5'9", 183 lbs. Deb: 7/1/1902 M/C

YEAR TM-L	G	AB	R	H	2B	3B	HR	RBI	BB	SO	SB	CS	AVG	OBP	SLG	OPS	OPS+	BR/A	RC	RC/G	FR	G/POS	WS	TPW
1902 NY-N	17	56	4	12	1	0	0	2	0	....	3	....	.214	.214	.232	.446	38	-4	4	2.13	-6	S-17	0	-1.0
1906 Bos-A	9	32	1	9	0	0	0	4	1	....	2	....	.281	.303	.281	.584	83	-1	4	3.87	1	/2-9	1	0.1
1907 Bos-A	111	385	29	82	10	4	2	21	31	....	20	....	.213	.275	.275	.550	76	-10	37	3.11	12	*S-109/2-1,3-1	9	0.7
1908 Bos-A	153	526	62	130	11	5	1	46	27	....	20	....	.247	.288	.293	.581	86	-9	50	3.14	28	*S-153	18	2.8
1909 Bos-A	124	430	53	110	16	7	1	49	35	....	18	....	.256	.316	.333	.649	103	1	50	3.97	10	*S-123/2-1	17	1.8
1910 Bos-A	142	491	61	134	26	7	1	52	44	....	26	....	.273	.335	.360	.696	115	8	68	4.70	-3	*S-140	18	1.1
1911 Bos-A	80	261	34	67	13	8	1	38	29	....	15	....	.257	.340	.379	.719	101	1	38	4.98	-5	2-40,S-32	8	-0.1
1912*Bos-A	144	504	75	138	25	6	2	68	62	....	21	....	.274	.358	.359	.717	100	1	72	4.94	-2	*S-144	20	1.0
1913 Bos-A	110	365	43	83	14	8	2	34	40	29	9	....	.227	.316	.326	.642	86	-7	38	3.42	5	*S-103/2-5,3-1	11	0.7
1915 Bos-A	84	267	38	64	11	2	0	29	37	34	8	4	.240	.339	.296	.635	93	-1	30	3.65	-9	2-79/3-1,O-1	9	-0.9
1916 Bos-A	6	8	2	4	1	0	0	0	3	0	2	....	.500	.636	.625	1.261	278	2	4	27.71	0	/3-4,2-1,S-1	1	0.3
1918 Bos-A	3	8	0	1	0	0	0	0	1	0	0	....	.125	.222	.125	.347	5	-1	0	.74	0	/2-2,3-1	0	-0.1
Total 12	983	3333	402	834	128	47	10	343	310	63	144	4	.250	.319	.326	.645	95	-19	396	3.96	33	S-822,2-138/3-8,O-1	112	6.2

• WAGNER, Honus John Peter "The Flying Dutchman" Wagner
b: 2/24/1874, Chartiers, PA d: 12/6/1955, Carnegie, PA BR/TR, 5'11", 200 lbs. Deb: 7/19/1897 M/C HOF: 1936 Career OF: 35-66-272

YEAR TM-L	G	AB	R	H	2B	3B	HR	RBI	BB	SO	SB	CS	AVG	OBP	SLG	OPS	OPS+	BR/A	RC	RC/G	FR	G/POS	WS	TPW
1897 Lou-N	62	242	38	81	18	4	2	39	15	....	20	....	.335	.376	.467	.843	126	8	51	8.19	3	O-52(1-52-0)/2-9	9	0.7
1898 Lou-N	151	588	80	176	29	3	10	105	31	....	27	....	.299	.341	.410	.751	117	10	95	5.94	6	1-75,3-65,2-10	22	1.5
1899 Lou-N	148	575	100	196	45	13	7	114	40	....	37	....	.341	.395	.501	.895	145	34	132	9.12	5	3-75,O-61(3-0-58)/2-7,1-4	26	3.3
1900*Pit-N	135	527	107	201	**45**	**22**	4	100	41	....	38	....	**.381**	.434	**.573**	**1.007**	**175**	53	152	**12.17**	-1	*O-118(0-0-118)/3-9,2-7,1,P	**34**	4.3
1901 Pit-N	140	549	101	194	37	11	6	**126**	53	....	**49**	....	.353	.417	.494	.911	159	42	138	10.00	15	S-61,O-54(1-0-53),3-24/2-1	37	5.6
1902 Pit-N	136	534	**105**	176	**30**	16	3	**91**	43	....	**42**	....	.330	.394	**.463**	**.857**	**159**	**37**	118	**8.51**	10	O-61(20-11-30),S-44,1-32/2,P	**35**	**4.9**

YEAR	TM-L	G	AB	R	H	2B	3B	HR	RBI	BB	SO	SB	CS	AVG	OBP	SLG	OPS	OPS+	BR/A	RC	RC/G	FR	G/POS	WS	TPW
1903*	Pit-N	129	512	97	182	30	**19**	5	101	44	....	46	....	**.355**	.414	.518	.931	160	39	133	10.39	28	*S-111,0-12(1-0-11)/1-6	**35**	**6.7**
1904	Pit-N	132	490	97	171	**44**	14	4	75	59	....	**53**	....	**.349**	**.423**	**.520**	**.944**	**186**	**50**	134	**10.75**	-7	*S-121/0-8(6-2-0),1-3,2-2	**43**	**5.0**
1905	Pit-N	147	548	114	199	32	14	6	101	54	....	57	....	.363	.427	.505	.932	173	50	147	**10.72**	22	*S-145/0-2(2-0-0)	**46**	**7.9**
1906	Pit-N	142	516	**103**	175	**38**	9	2	71	58	....	53	....	**.339**	.416	.459	**.875**	166	41	124	**9.31**	22	*S-137/0-2(0-0-2),3-1	**46**	**7.5**
1907	Pit-N	142	515	98	180	**38**	14	6	82	46	....	**61**	....	**.350**	**.408**	**.513**	**.921**	**186**	**49**	137	**10.20**	11	*S-138/1-4	**44**	**7.4**
1908	Pit-N	151	568	100	**201**	**39**	**19**	10	**109**	54	....	**53**	....	**.354**	**.415**	**.542**	**.957**	**205**	**66**	148	**10.07**	17	*S-151	**59**	**10.2**
1909*	Pit-N	137	495	92	168	**39**	10	5	**100**	66	....	35	....	**.339**	**.420**	**.489**	**.909**	**173**	**44**	117	**8.58**	22	*S-136/0-1	**42**	**7.8**
1910	Pit-N	150	556	90	**178**	34	8	4	81	59	47	24	....	.320	.390	.432	.822	131	23	103	6.73	18	*S-138,1-11/2-2	30	**4.8**
1911	Pit-N	130	473	87	158	23	16	9	89	67	34	20	....	**.334**	.423	.507	**.930**	154	36	109	**8.70**	12	*S-101,1-28/0-1	30	**5.5**
1912	Pit-N	145	558	91	181	35	20	7	**102**	59	38	26	....	.324	.395	.496	.891	145	34	118	7.76	40	*S-143	**35**	**8.3**
1913	Pit-N	114	413	51	124	18	4	3	56	26	40	21	....	.300	.349	.385	.734	114	7	60	5.11	23	*S-105	18	3.9
1914	Pit-N	150	552	60	139	15	9	1	50	51	51	23	....	.252	.317	.317	.634	93	-5	60	3.67	14	*S-132,3-17/1-1	19	2.1
1915	Pit-N	156	566	68	155	32	17	6	78	39	64	22	15	.274	.325	.422	.747	127	14	79	4.76	10	*S-131,2-12,1-10	23	3.7
1916	Pit-N	123	432	45	124	15	9	1	39	34	36	11	....	.287	.350	.370	.721	120	11	61	4.99	-1	S-92,1-24/2-4	17	1.9
1917	Pit-N	74	230	15	61	7	1	0	24	24	17	5	....	.265	.337	.304	.642	94	-1	25	3.69	-3	1-47,3-18/2-2,S-1	5	-0.4
Total	21	2794	10439	1739	3420	643	252	101	1733	963	327	723	15	.328	.391	.467	.858	151	642	2239	8.07	266	*S-1887,0-372,1-248,3-209/2,P	655	102.7

• WAGNER, Joe Joseph Bernard Wagner b: 4/24/1889, New York, NY d: 11/15/1948, Bronx, NY BR/TR, 5'11", 165 lbs. Deb: 4/25/1915

YEAR	TM-L	G	AB	R	H	2B	3B	HR	RBI	BB	SO	SB	CS	AVG	OBP	SLG	OPS	OPS+	BR/A	RC	RC/G	FR	G/POS	WS	TPW
1915	Cin-N	75	197	17	35	5	2	0	13	8	35	4	6	.178	.210	.223	.433	31	-19	9	1.39	3	2-46,S-12/3-2	2	-1.6

• WAGNER, Leon Leon Lamar "Daddy Wags" Wagner b: 5/13/1934, Chattanooga, TN BL/TR, 6'1", 195 lbs. Deb: 6/22/1958 Career OF: 1026-1-126

YEAR	TM-L	G	AB	R	H	2B	3B	HR	RBI	BB	SO	SB	CS	AVG	OBP	SLG	OPS	OPS+	BR/A	RC	RC/G	FR	G/POS	WS	TPW
1958	SF-N	74	221	31	70	9	0	13	35	18	34	1	0	.317	.371	.534	.905	139	12	45	7.99	0	0-57(57-0-0)	10	1.0
1959	SF-N	87	129	20	29	4	3	5	22	25	24	0	0	.225	.363	.419	.782	110	3	20	5.20	-2	0-28(28-0-0)	4	-0.1
1960	StL-N	39	98	12	21	2	0	4	11	17	17	0	1	.214	.336	.357	.693	83	-2	12	4.21	0	0-32(29-0-4)	2	-0.4
1961	LA-A	133	453	74	127	19	2	28	79	48	65	5	1	.280	.353	.517	.870	116	10	85	6.78	4	*0-116(104-0-14)	14	0.7
1962	LA-A★	160	612	96	164	21	5	37	107	50	87	7	5	.268	.328	.500	.828	123	16	101	5.83	-4	*0-156(102-0-62)	24	0.3
1963	LA-A★	149	550	73	160	11	1	26	90	49	73	5	7	.291	.356	.456	.813	134	22	90	5.93	0	*0-141(136-0-7)	22	1.5
1964	Cle-A	163	641	94	162	19	2	31	100	56	121	14	2	.253	.319	.434	.752	108	8	89	4.79	-7	*0-163(163-0-0)	18	-0.9
1965	Cle-A	144	517	91	152	18	1	28	79	60	52	12	2	.294	.371	.495	.866	143	31	99	7.09	-13	*0-134(134-0-0)	24	1.2
1966	Cle-A	150	549	70	153	20	0	23	66	46	69	5	2	.279	.336	.441	.776	121	15	80	5.20	-5	*0-139(139-0-0)	19	0.3
1967	Cle-A	135	433	56	105	15	1	15	54	37	76	3	3	.242	.320	.386	.705	106	3	55	4.32	-2	*0-117(117-0-0)	12	-0.4
1968	Cle-A	38	49	5	9	4	0	0	6	6	6	0	0	.184	.273	.265	.538	65	-2	3	2.21	-1	0-10(7-0-3)	0	-0.4
	Chi-A	69	162	14	46	8	0	1	18	21	31	2	1	.284	.366	.352	.718	117	4	22	5.00	-2	0-46(9-1-36)	5	0.0
	Yr.	107	211	19	55	12	0	1	24	27	37	2	1	.261	.345	.332	.676	105	2	25	4.27	-3	0-56(16-1-39)	5	-0.4
1969	SF-N	11	12	0	4	0	0	0	2	2	1	0	0	.333	.467	.333	.800	130	1	2	7.12	0	/0-1	1	0.1
Total	12	1352	4426	636	1202	150	15	211	669	435	656	54	24	.272	.343	.455	.798	120	121	703	5.66	-32	*0-1140	155	2.9

• WAGNER, Mark Mark Duane Wagner b: 3/4/1954, Conneaut, OH BR/TR, 6', 175 lbs. Deb: 8/20/1976

YEAR	TM-L	G	AB	R	H	2B	3B	HR	RBI	BB	SO	SB	CS	AVG	OBP	SLG	OPS	OPS+	BR/A	RC	RC/G	FR	G/POS	WS	TPW
1976	Det-A	39	115	9	30	2	3	0	12	6	18	0	2	.261	.298	.330	.628	80	-4	11	3.25	-2	S-39	3	-0.2
1977	Det-A	22	48	4	7	0	1	1	3	4	12	0	1	.146	.226	.250	.476	28	-5	3	1.75	-1	S-21/2-1	1	-0.4
1978	Det-A	39	109	10	26	1	2	0	6	3	11	1	0	.239	.272	.284	.556	55	-6	8	2.50	-3	S-35/2-4	2	-0.7
1979	Det-A	75	146	16	40	3	0	1	13	16	25	3	2	.274	.346	.315	.661	77	-4	17	3.89	0	S-41,2-29/3-2,D-1	4	-0.1
1980	Det-A	45	72	5	17	1	0	0	3	7	11	0	1	.236	.304	.250	.554	52	-5	6	2.76	-7	S-28/3-9,2-6	1	-1.0
1981	Tex-A	50	85	15	22	4	1	1	14	8	13	1	1	.259	.323	.365	.687	103	0	10	3.91	-2	S-43/2-4,3-2	3	0.1
1982	Tex-A	60	179	14	43	4	1	0	8	10	28	1	0	.240	.280	.274	.554	56	-11	13	2.42	-6	S-60	2	-1.0
1983	Tex-A	2	2	0	0	0	0	0	0	0	1	0	0	.000	.000	.000	.000	-102	-1	0	.00	0	/S-2	0	-0.1
1984	Oak-A	82	87	8	20	5	1	0	12	7	11	2	0	.230	.287	.310	.598	70	-3	7	2.51	-1	S-57,3-15/2-8,D-3,P-1	2	-0.1
Total	9	414	843	81	205	20	9	3	71	61	130	8	7	.243	.297	.299	.596	67	-38	76	2.92	-23	S-326/2-52,3-28,D-4,P-1	18	-3.4

• WAHL, Kermit Kermit Emerson Wahl b: 11/18/1922, Columbia, SD d: 9/16/1987, Tucson, AZ BR/TR, 5'11", 170 lbs. Deb: 6/23/1944

YEAR	TM-L	G	AB	R	H	2B	3B	HR	RBI	BB	SO	SB	CS	AVG	OBP	SLG	OPS	OPS+	BR/A	RC	RC/G	FR	G/POS	WS	TPW
1944	Cin-N	4	1	0	0	0	0	0	0	0	0	0	....	.000	.000	.000	.000	-104	-0	0	.00	0	/3-1	0	-0.1
1945	Cin-N	71	194	18	39	8	2	0	10	23	22	2	....	.201	.286	.263	.549	54	-12	16	2.62	-7	2-32,S-31/3-7	3	-1.5
1947	Cin-N	39	81	8	14	0	0	1	4	6	12	0	....	.173	.239	.210	.449	20	-9	4	1.70	-1	3-20/S-9,2-2	1	-1.0
1950	Phi-A	89	280	26	72	12	3	2	27	30	30	1	1	.257	.331	.343	.674	74	-11	32	3.88	-1	3-61,S-18/2-2	4	-1.0
1951	Phi-A	20	59	4	11	2	0	0	6	9	5	0	0	.186	.294	.220	.514	40	-5	4	2.23	1	3-18	1	-0.3
	StL-A	8	27	2	9	1	1	0	3	0	3	0	0	.333	.333	.444	.778	106	0	4	5.18	1	/3-6	1	0.1
	Yr.	28	86	6	20	3	1	0	9	9	8	0	0	.233	.305	.291	.596	58	-5	8	3.02	2	3-24	2	-0.3
Total	5	231	642	58	145	23	6	3	50	68	72	3	1	.226	.302	.294	.596	59	-37	60	3.09	-8	3-113/S-58,2-36	10	-3.9

• WAITKUS, Eddie Edward Stephen Waitkus b: 9/4/1919, Cambridge, MA d: 9/16/1972, Jamaica Plain, MA BL/TL, 6', 175 lbs. Deb: 4/15/1941

YEAR	TM-L	G	AB	R	H	2B	3B	HR	RBI	BB	SO	SB	CS	AVG	OBP	SLG	OPS	OPS+	BR/A	RC	RC/G	FR	G/POS	WS	TPW
1941	Chi-N	12	28	1	5	0	0	0	0	0	3	0	....	.179	.207	.179	.385	10	-3	1	1.02	-1	/1-9	0	-0.5
1946	Chi-N	113	441	50	134	24	5	4	55	23	14	3	....	.304	.340	.408	.748	114	6	60	5.06	3	*1-106	15	0.5
1947	Chi-N	130	514	60	150	28	6	2	35	32	17	3	....	.292	.336	.381	.717	94	-6	66	4.72	3	*1-126	12	-0.6
1948	Chi-N★	139	562	87	166	27	10	7	44	43	19	11	....	.295	.348	.416	.764	110	7	81	5.26	4	*1-116,0-20(20-0-0)	15	0.5
1949	Phi-N★	54	209	41	64	16	3	1	28	33	12	3	....	.306	.403	.426	.829	126	9	38	6.86	1	1-54	8	0.8
1950*	Phi-N	154	641	102	182	32	5	2	44	55	29	3	....	.284	.341	.359	.700	86	-13	79	4.48	2	*1-154	15	-1.6
1951	Phi-N	145	610	65	157	27	4	1	46	53	22	0	3	.257	.317	.320	.636	73	-24	64	3.73	0	*1-144	9	-2.9
1952	Phi-N	146	499	51	144	29	4	2	49	64	23	2	2	.289	.371	.375	.745	108	8	75	5.51	-2	*1-146	16	0.1
1953	Phi-N	81	247	24	72	9	2	1	16	13	23	1	1	.291	.330	.356	.686	79	-8	30	4.45	3	1-59	5	-0.8
1954	Bal-A	95	311	35	88	17	4	2	33	28	25	0	1	.283	.344	.383	.727	107	2	41	4.55	2	1-78	7	0.0
1955	Bal-A	38	85	2	22	1	1	0	9	11	10	2	0	.259	.344	.294	.638	78	-2	9	3.95	-2	1-26	2	-0.5
	Phi-N	33	107	10	30	5	0	2	14	17	7	0	1	.280	.379	.383	.762	105	1	15	5.04	2	1-31	3	0.2
Total	11	1140	4254	528	1214	215	44	24	373	372	204	28	8	.285	.344	.374	.718	97	-22	560	4.77	14	*1-1049/0-20	107	-4.8

• WAITT, Charlie Charles C. Waitt b: 10/14/1853, Hallowell, ME d: 10/21/1912, San Francisco, CA TR, 5'11", 165 lbs. Deb: 5/25/1875 Career OF: 60-1-22

YEAR	TM-L	G	AB	R	H	2B	3B	HR	RBI	BB	SO	SB	CS	AVG	OBP	SLG	OPS	OPS+	BR/A	RC	RC/G	FR	G/POS	WS	TPW
1875	StL-n	30	113	14	23	10	0	0	12	2	7	3	2	.204	.217	.292	.509	83	-1	8	2.57	-2	0-28(2-7-23)/1-4	....	-0.1
1877	Chi-N	10	41	2	4	0	0	0	2	0	3	....	....	.098	.098	.098	.195	-34	-6	0	.30	2	0-10(0-0-10)	0	-0.4
1882	Bal-a	72	250	19	39	4	0	0	....	13		....	....	.156	.198	.172	.370	28	-17	9	1.16	-3	*0-72(60-0-12)	1	-2.0
1883	Phi-N	1	3	0	1	0	0	0	0	0	1	....	....	.333	.333	.333	.667	114	0	0	4.70	-1	/0-1	0	-0.1
Total	3	83	294	21	44	4	0	0	2	13	4	....	....	.150	.186	.163	.349	20	-23	9	1.06	-2	/0-83	1	-2.5

• WAKAMATSU, Don Wilbur Donald Wakamatsu b: 2/22/1963, Hood River, OR BR/TR, 6'2", 200 lbs. Deb: 5/22/1991 C

YEAR	TM-L	G	AB	R	H	2B	3B	HR	RBI	BB	SO	SB	CS	AVG	OBP	SLG	OPS	OPS+	BR/A	RC	RC/G	FR	G/POS	WS	TPW
1991	Chi-A	18	31	2	7	0	0	0	0	1	6	0	0	.226	.250	.226	.476	33	-3	2	2.04	0	C-18	1	-0.2

• WAKEFIELD, Dick Richard Cummings Wakefield b: 5/6/1921, Chicago, IL d: 8/26/1985, Redford, MI BL/TR, 6'4", 210 lbs. Deb: 6/26/1941 Career OF: 541-0-16

YEAR	TM-L	G	AB	R	H	2B	3B	HR	RBI	BB	SO	SB	CS	AVG	OBP	SLG	OPS	OPS+	BR/A	RC	RC/G	FR	G/POS	WS	TPW
1941	Det-A	7	7	0	1	0	0	0	0	0	1	0	0	.143	.143	.143	.286	-22	-1	0	.66	-0	/0-1	0	-0.1
1943	Det-A★	155	633	91	**200**	**38**	8	7	79	62	60	4	5	.316	.377	.434	.811	127	21	101	5.90	-4	*0-155(140-0-15)	24	0.8
1944	Det-A	78	276	53	98	15	5	12	53	55	29	2	2	.355	.464	.576	1.040	186	34	80	11.82	-3	0-78(78-0-0)	22	2.7
1946	Det-A	111	396	64	106	11	5	12	59	59	55	3	5	.268	.364	.412	.776	110	5	63	5.64	0	*0-104(104-0-0)	15	-0.2
1947	Det-A	112	368	59	104	15	5	8	51	80	44	1	4	.283	.412	.416	.828	127	17	69	6.65	-2	*0-101(101-0-0)	16	0.7
1948	Det-A	110	322	50	89	20	5	11	53	70	55	0	1	.276	.406	.472	.878	129	15	67	7.56	-2	0-86(86-0-0)	14	0.7
1949	Det-A	59	126	17	26	3	1	6	19	32	24	0	0	.206	.367	.389	.756	100	1	20	5.16	2	0-32(32-0-0)	4	0.1
1950	NY-A	3	2	0	1	0	0	0	1	1	1	0	0	.500	.667	.500	1.167	208	1	1	23.13	0	....	0	0.0
1952	NY-N	3	2	0	0	0	0	0	0	1	1	0	0	.000	.333	.000	.333		-0	0	.00	0	....	0	0.0
Total	9	638	2132	334	625	102	29	56	315	360	270	10	17	.293	.396	.447	.843	130	93	402	6.85	-9	0-557	95	4.6

• WAKEFIELD, Howard Howard John Wakefield b: 4/2/1884, Bucyrus, OH d: 4/16/1941, Chicago, IL BR/TR, 6'1", 185 lbs. Deb: 9/18/1905

YEAR	TM-L	G	AB	R	H	2B	3B	HR	RBI	BB	SO	SB	CS	AVG	OBP	SLG	OPS	OPS+	BR/A	RC	RC/G	FR	G/POS	WS	TPW
1905	Cle-A	10	26	3	4	0	0	0	1	0	....	0	....	.154	.185	.154	.339	8	-3	1	.91	0	/C-8	0	-0.3
1906	Was-A	77	211	17	59	9	2	1	21	7	....	6	....	.280	.303	.355	.658	111	2	25	4.36	-3	C-60	7	0.4

YEAR TM-L	G	AB	R	H	2B	3B	HR	RBI	BB	SO	SB	CS	AVG	OBP	SLG	OPS	OPS+	BR/A	RC	RC/G	FR	G/POS	WS	TPW
1907 Cle-A	26	37	4	5	2	0	0	3	3	....	0	....	.135	.200	.189	.389	24	-3	1	1.19	-2	C-11	0	-0.5
Total 3	113	274	24	68	11	2	1	25	10	....	6	....	.248	.277	.314	.591	89	-4	28	3.51	-6	/C-79	7	-0.4

• WAKELAND, Chris — Christopher Robert Wakeland b: 6/15/1974, Huntington Beach, CA BL/TL, 6', 185 lbs. Deb: 9/4/2001

YEAR TM-L	G	AB	R	H	2B	3B	HR	RBI	BB	SO	SB	CS	AVG	OBP	SLG	OPS	OPS+	BR/A	RC	RC/G	FR	G/POS	WS	TPW
2001 Det-A	10	36	5	9	2	0	2	6	0	13	0	0	.250	.250	.472	.722	88	-1	4	4.25	2	0-10(0-0-10)	1	0.0

• WALBECK, Matt — Matthew Lovick Walbeck b: 10/2/1969, Sacramento, CA BB/TR, 5'11", 190 lbs. Deb: 4/7/1993

YEAR TM-L	G	AB	R	H	2B	3B	HR	RBI	BB	SO	SB	CS	AVG	OBP	SLG	OPS	OPS+	BR/A	RC	RC/G	FR	G/POS	WS	TPW
1993 Chi-N	11	30	2	6	2	0	1	6	1	6	0	0	.200	.226	.367	.592	56	-2	3	2.86	0	C-11	1	-0.2
1994 Min-A	97	338	31	69	12	0	5	35	17	37	1	1	.204	.246	.284	.531	36	-33	23	2.20	-1	C-95/D-1	5	-2.5
1995 Min-A	115	393	40	101	18	1	1	44	25	71	3	1	.257	.303	.316	.619	61	-23	36	3.20	-6	*C-113	5	-2.0
1996 Min-A	63	215	25	48	10	0	2	24	9	34	3	1	.223	.254	.298	.552	38	-21	15	2.33	-1	C-61	3	-1.6
1997 Det-A	47	137	18	38	3	0	3	10	12	19	3	3	.277	.336	.365	.701	84	-4	16	3.97	-1	C-44	2	-0.2
1998 Ana-A	108	338	41	87	15	2	6	46	30	68	1	1	.257	.322	.367	.688	78	-11	40	3.94	-1	*C-104/D-2	9	-0.5
1999 Ana-A	107	288	26	69	8	1	3	22	26	46	2	3	.240	.309	.306	.615	58	-19	25	2.89	0	C-97/D-1	4	-1.3
2000 Ana-A	47	146	17	29	5	0	6	12	7	22	0	1	.199	.240	.356	.596	47	-13	12	2.67	-2	C-44/1-2,D-1	2	-1.2
2001 Phi-N	1	1	0	1	0	0	0	0	0	0	0	0	1.000	1.000	1.000	2.000	431	0	1	∞	0	....	0	0.0
2002 Det-A	27	85	4	20	2	0	0	3	3	14	0	0	.235	.261	.259	.520	41	-7	5	2.18	-2	C-27	1	-0.7
2003 Det-A	59	138	11	24	4	1	1	6	3	26	0	1	.174	.197	.239	.436	16	-17	6	1.32	-5	C-55	0	-1.8
Total 11	682	2109	215	492	79	5	28	208	133	343	13	12	.233	.282	.315	.597	54	-150	182	2.86	-20	C-651/D-5,1-2	32	-12.0

• WALCZAK, Ed — Edwin Joseph "Husky" Walczak b: 9/21/1918, Arctic, RI d: 3/10/1998, Norwich, CT BR/TR, 5'11", 180 lbs. Deb: 9/3/1945

YEAR TM-L	G	AB	R	H	2B	3B	HR	RBI	BB	SO	SB	CS	AVG	OBP	SLG	OPS	OPS+	BR/A	RC	RC/G	FR	G/POS	WS	TPW
1945 Phi-N	20	57	6	12	3	0	0	2	6	9	0	....	.211	.286	.263	.549	55	-3	4	2.42	-2	2-17/S-2	0	-0.5

• WALDEN, Fred — Thomas Fred Walden b: 6/25/1890, Fayette, MO d: 9/27/1955, Jefferson Barracks, MO BR/TR Deb: 6/3/1912

YEAR TM-L	G	AB	R	H	2B	3B	HR	RBI	BB	SO	SB	CS	AVG	OBP	SLG	OPS	OPS+	BR/A	RC	RC/G	FR	G/POS	WS	TPW
1912 StL-A	1	0	0	0	0	0	0	0	0	....	0	....	....	....	....	....	-104	0	0	....	-1	/C-1	0	-0.1

• WALDRON, Irv — Irving J. Waldron b: 1/21/1876, Hillside, NY d: 7/22/1944, Worcester, MA BR/TR, 5'5.5" Deb: 4/25/1901

YEAR TM-L	G	AB	R	H	2B	3B	HR	RBI	BB	SO	SB	CS	AVG	OBP	SLG	OPS	OPS+	BR/A	RC	RC/G	FR	G/POS	WS	TPW
1901 Mil-A	62	266	48	79	8	6	0	29	16	....	12	....	.297	.342	.372	.714	103	1	39	5.44	-2	0-62(0-0-62)	6	-0.3
Was-A	79	332	54	107	14	3	0	23	22	....	8	....	.322	.368	.383	.751	110	5	52	5.93	-6	0-78(0-69-9)	9	-0.4
Yr.	141	598	102	186	22	9	0	52	38	....	20	....	.311	.356	.378	.734	107	6	91	5.71	-8	*0-140(0-69-71)	15	-0.7

• WALEWANDER, Jim — James Walewander b: 5/2/1962, Chicago, IL BB/TR, 5'10", 160 lbs. Deb: 5/31/1987

YEAR TM-L	G	AB	R	H	2B	3B	HR	RBI	BB	SO	SB	CS	AVG	OBP	SLG	OPS	OPS+	BR/A	RC	RC/G	FR	G/POS	WS	TPW
1987 Det-A	53	54	24	13	3	1	1	4	7	6	2	1	.241	.328	.389	.717	93	-0	7	3.94	3	2-24,3-17/D-8,S-3	2	0.3
1988 Det-A	88	175	23	37	5	0	0	6	12	26	11	4	.211	.262	.240	.502	43	-13	13	2.20	0	2-61/D-9,S-8,3-3	2	-1.1
1990 NY-A	9	5	1	1	1	0	0	1	0	0	1	1	.200	.200	.400	.600	63	-1	0	.00	0	/2-2,3-2,D-2,S-1	0	-0.1
1993 Cal-A	12	8	2	1	0	0	0	3	5	1	1	1	.125	.462	.125	.587	64	-0	1	3.58	0	/S-6,D-3,2-2	1	0.1
Total 4	162	242	50	52	9	1	1	14	24	33	15	7	.215	.286	.273	.558	56	-14	20	2.58	3	/2-89,3-22,D-22,S-18	5	-0.8

• WALKER, Chico — Cleotha Walker b: 11/25/1958, Jackson, MS BB/TR, 5'9", 179 lbs. Deb: 9/2/1980 Career OF: 87-66-42

YEAR TM-L	G	AB	R	H	2B	3B	HR	RBI	BB	SO	SB	CS	AVG	OBP	SLG	OPS	OPS+	BR/A	RC	RC/G	FR	G/POS	WS	TPW
1980 Bos-A	19	57	3	12	0	0	1	5	6	10	3	2	.211	.297	.263	.560	52	-4	5	2.51	0	2-11/D-7	0	-0.4
1981 Bos-A	6	17	3	6	0	0	0	2	1	2	0	2	.353	.389	.353	.742	108	-1	2	3.61	0	/2-5	0	0.0
1983 Bos-A	4	5	2	2	0	2	0	1	0	0	0	0	.400	.400	1.200	1.600	299	1	2	21.60	1	/0-3(3-0-0)	1	0.2
1984 Bos-A	3	2	0	0	0	0	0	1	0	1	0	0	.000	.000	.000	.000	-96	-1	0	.00	0	/2-1	0	-0.1
1985 Chi-N	21	12	3	1	0	0	0	0	0	5	1	0	.083	.083	.083	.167	-48	-2	0	.31	-1	/0-6(3-0-3),2-2	0	-0.4
1986 Chi-N	28	101	21	28	3	2	1	7	10	20	15	4	.277	.342	.376	.719	91	0	14	4.51	-2	0-26(1-11-22)	2	-0.3
1987 Chi-N	47	105	15	21	4	0	0	7	12	23	11	4	.200	.282	.238	.520	38	-9	8	2.40	-2	0-33(25-3-5)/3-2	0	-1.2
1988 Cal-A	33	78	8	12	1	0	0	2	6	15	2	1	.154	.214	.167	.381	8	-9	3	1.10	0	0-17(5-12-0)/2-7,3-2	0	-1.0
1991 Chi-N	124	374	51	96	10	1	6	34	33	57	13	5	.257	.317	.337	.654	80	-9	42	3.92	-6	3-57,0-53(20-36-8)/2-6	9	-1.6
1992 Chi-N	19	26	2	3	0	0	0	2	3	4	1	0	.115	.207	.115	.322	-6	-3	1	1.08	-1	/0-6(6-0-1),2-2,3-2	0	-0.4
NY-N	107	227	24	70	12	1	4	36	24	46	14	1	.308	.375	.423	.797	127	11	37	5.76	-3	3-36,2-16,0-15(9-4-2)	10	0.9
Yr.	126	253	26	73	12	1	4	38	27	50	15	1	.289	.357	.391	.748	113	8	37	5.19	-3	3-38,0-21(15-4-3),2-18	10	0.4
1993 NY-N	115	213	18	48	7	1	5	19	14	29	7	0	.225	.273	.338	.611	63	-10	21	3.29	-2	2-24,3-23,0-15(15-0-1)	2	-1.1
Total 11	526	1217	150	299	37	7	17	116	109	212	67	19	.246	.308	.329	.638	75	-35	134	3.69	-16	0-174,3-122/2-74,D-7	24	-5.4

• WALKER, Curt — William Curtis Walker b: 7/3/1896, Beeville, TX d: 12/9/1955, Beeville, TX BL/TR, 5'9.5", 170 lbs. Deb: 9/17/1919 Career OF: 105-95-1120

YEAR TM-L	G	AB	R	H	2B	3B	HR	RBI	BB	SO	SB	CS	AVG	OBP	SLG	OPS	OPS+	BR/A	RC	RC/G	FR	G/POS	WS	TPW
1919 NY-A	1	1	0	0	0	0	0	0	0	0	0	....	.000	.000	.000	.000	-99	-0	0	.00	0	....	0	0.0
1920 NY-N	8	14	0	1	0	0	0	0	1	3	0	0	.071	.133	.071	.205	-41	-2	0	.33	-1	/0-4(1-2-1)	0	-0.3
1921 NY-N	64	192	30	55	13	5	3	35	15	8	4	3	.286	.338	.453	.791	107	2	29	5.23	3	0-58(0-46-13)	7	0.2
Phi-N	21	77	11	26	2	1	0	8	5	5	0	2	.338	.378	.390	.768	96	-1	11	5.09	0	0-21(7-7-10)	2	-0.2
Yr.	85	269	41	81	15	6	3	43	20	13	4	5	.301	.349	.435	.784	104	1	40	5.19	2	0-79(7-53-23)	9	0.0
1922 Phi-N	148	581	102	196	36	11	12	89	56	46	11	4	.337	.399	.499	.899	119	19	118	7.73	11	*0-147(0-0-147)	16	1.8
1923 Phi-N	140	527	66	148	26	5	5	66	45	31	12	12	.281	.337	.378	.715	79	-17	66	4.40	-3	*0-137(12-0-125)/1-1	6	-3.0
1924 Phi-N	24	71	11	21	6	1	1	8	7	4	0	1	.296	.359	.451	.810	103	0	11	5.64	-1	0-20(0-0-20)	2	-0.2
Cin-N	109	397	55	119	21	10	4	46	44	15	7	5	.300	.371	.433	.804	117	11	65	5.88	6	*0-109(3-23-86)	15	0.9
Yr.	133	468	66	140	27	11	5	54	51	19	7	6	.299	.369	.436	.805	114	11	76	5.84	5	*0-129(3-23-106)	17	0.7
1925 Cin-N	145	509	86	162	22	16	6	71	57	31	14	11	.318	.387	.460	.847	118	14	91	6.48	5	*0-141(4-15-124)	21	0.8
1926 Cin-N	155	571	83	175	24	20	6	78	60	31	3	....	.306	.372	.450	.823	124	19	95	5.78	6	*0-152(1-0-151)	22	1.3
1927 Cin-N	146	527	60	154	16	10	6	80	47	19	5	....	.292	.350	.395	.745	102	2	72	4.70	5	*0-141(0-0-141)	16	-0.4
1928 Cin-N	123	427	64	119	15	12	6	73	49	14	19	....	.279	.354	.412	.766	101	1	63	4.90	-1	*0-122(0-0-122)	14	-1.0
1929 Cin-N	141	492	76	154	28	15	7	83	85	17	17	....	.313	.416	.474	.890	126	24	99	7.16	-3	*0-138(0-0-138)	19	1.0
1930 Cin-N	134	472	74	145	26	11	8	51	64	30	4	....	.307	.391	.460	.851	110	10	85	6.57	-5	*0-120(77-2-42)	13	-0.4
Total 12	1359	4858	718	1475	235	117	64	688	535	254	96	38	.304	.374	.440	.813	110	81	805	5.88	22	*0-1310/1-1	153	0.4

• WALKER, Dixie — Fred "The Peoples Cherce" Walker
b: 9/24/1910, Villa Rica, GA d: 5/17/1982, Birmingham, AL BL/TR, 6'1", 175 lbs. Deb: 4/28/1931 Career OF: 249-312-1204

YEAR TM-L	G	AB	R	H	2B	3B	HR	RBI	BB	SO	SB	CS	AVG	OBP	SLG	OPS	OPS+	BR/A	RC	RC/G	FR	G/POS	WS	TPW
1931 NY-A	2	10	1	3	2	0	0	1	0	4	0	0	.300	.300	.500	.800	113	0	1	5.45	-0	/0-2(1-0-1)	0	0.0
1933 NY-A	98	328	68	90	15	7	15	51	26	28	2	2	.274	.330	.500	.830	125	9	54	5.82	-0	0-77(15-60-3)	11	0.7
1934 NY-A	17	17	2	2	0	0	0	0	1	3	0	0	.118	.167	.118	.284	-27	-3	0	.70	-0	/0-1	0	-0.3
1935 NY-A	8	13	1	2	1	0	0	1	0	1	0	0	.154	.154	.231	.385	-2	-2	0	1.07	0	/0-2(2-0-0)	0	-0.2
1936 NY-A	6	20	3	7	0	2	1	5	1	3	1	1	.350	.381	.700	1.081	167	2	5	8.95	0	/0-5(0-5-0)	1	0.1
Chi-A	26	70	12	19	2	0	0	11	14	6	1	0	.271	.400	.300	.700	73	-2	10	5.07	1	0-17(0-16-1)	2	-0.1
Yr.	32	90	15	26	2	2	1	16	15	9	2	1	.289	.396	.389	.785	91	-0	14	5.91	1	0-22(0-21-1)	3	0.0
1937 Chi-A	154	593	105	179	28	**16**	9	95	78	26	1	2	.302	.383	.449	.832	109	9	105	6.44	-6	*0-154(0-0-154)	20	-0.6
1938 Det-A	127	454	84	140	27	6	6	43	65	32	5	4	.308	.396	.434	.830	102	3	81	6.63	1	*0-114(94-26-0)	14	-0.1
1939 Det-A	43	154	30	47	4	5	4	19	15	8	4	1	.305	.367	.474	.841	105	1	26	5.87	3	0-37(23-4-11)	5	0.2
Bro-N	61	225	27	63	6	4	2	38	20	10	1	....	.280	.339	.369	.708	87	-4	28	4.33	0	0-59(0-59-0)	6	-0.5
1940 Bro-N	143	556	75	171	37	8	6	66	42	21	3	....	.308	.357	.435	.793	111	8	88	5.95	-9	*0-136(14-112-20)	22	-0.6
1941*Bro-N	148	531	88	165	32	8	9	71	70	18	4	....	.311	.391	.452	.843	131	24	99	7.06	10	*0-146(22-22-105)	26	2.6
1942 Bro-N	118	393	57	114	28	1	6	54	47	15	1	....	.290	.367	.412	.780	126	13	64	5.91	1	*0-110(0-7-104)	19	0.9
1943 Bro-N★	138	540	83	163	32	6	5	71	49	24	3	....	.302	.363	.411	.774	123	16	82	5.64	-1	*0-136(57-0-82)	22	0.7
1944 Bro-N★	147	535	77	191	37	8	13	91	72	27	6	....	**.357**	.434	.529	.963	173	54	128	9.80	-6	*0-140(19-0-125)	33	4.0
1945 Bro-N★	154	607	102	182	42	9	8	**124**	75	16	6	....	.300	.381	.438	.820	128	24	105	6.52	8	*0-153(0-0-153)	28	2.1
1946 Bro-N★	150	576	80	184	29	9	9	116	67	28	14	....	.319	.391	.448	.839	136	28	104	6.97	-8	*0-149(0-0-149)	27	1.7
1947*Bro-N★	148	529	77	162	31	3	9	94	97	26	6	....	.306	.415	.427	.842	119	20	101	7.07	-8	*0-147(0-0-147)	23	0.7
1948 Pit-N	129	408	39	129	19	3	2	54	52	18	1	....	.316	.393	.392	.786	111	8	66	6.11	-3	*0-112(1-1-110)	15	0.3
1949 Pit-N	88	181	26	51	4	1	1	18	26	11	0	....	.282	.372	.331	.703	88	-2	24	4.66	-1	0-39(0-0-39)/1-3	4	-0.3
Total 18	1905	6740	1037	2064	376	96	105	1023	817	325	59	10	.306	.383	.437	.820	121	206	1171	6.48	-17	*0-1736/1-3	278	11.2

• WALKER, Duane — Duane Allen Walker b: 3/13/1957, Pasadena, TX BL/TL, 6', 185 lbs. Deb: 5/25/1982 Career OF: 148-15-93

YEAR TM-L	G	AB	R	H	2B	3B	HR	RBI	BB	SO	SB	CS	AVG	OBP	SLG	OPS	OPS+	BR/A	RC	RC/G	FR	G/POS	WS	TPW
1982 Cin-N	86	239	26	52	10	0	5	22	27	58	9	3	.218	.302	.322	.624	73	-8	26	3.55	2	0-69(40-2-31)	4	-0.9
1983 Cin-N	109	225	14	53	12	1	2	29	20	43	6	3	.236	.298	.324	.622	70	-9	23	3.52	-1	0-60(35-0-26)	4	-1.4

YEAR TM-L	G	AB	R	H	2B	3B	HR	RBI	BB	SO	SB	CS	AVG	OBP	SLG	OPS	OPS+	BR/A	RC	RC/G	FR	G/POS	WS	TPW
1984 Cin-N	83	195	35	57	10	3	10	28	33	35	7	3	.292	.395	.528	.923	150	14	43	8.06	-4	0-68(51-13-9)	11	0.8
1985 Cin-N	37	48	5	8	2	1	2	6	6	18	1	0	.167	.259	.375	.634	72	-2	5	3.14	-1	0-10(8-0-2)	1	-0.3
Tex-A	53	132	14	23	2	0	5	11	15	29	2	1	.174	.264	.303	.567	54	-8	11	2.65	2	0-32(12-0-23),D-10	1	-0.8
1988 StL-N	24	22	1	4	1	0	0	3	2	7	0	0	.182	.250	.227	.477	37	-2	1	1.63	-1	/0-4(2-0-2),1-1	0	-0.3
Total 5	**392**	**861**	**95**	**197**	**37**	**5**	**24**	**99**	**103**	**190**	**25**	**10**	**.229**	**.313**	**.367**	**.680**	**87**	**-15**	**109**	**4.26**	**-3**	**0-243/D-10,1-1**	**21**	**-2.9**

• WALKER, Ernie Ernest Robert Walker b: 9/17/1890, Blossburg, AL d: 4/1/1965, Pell City, AL BL/TR, 6', 165 lbs. Deb: 4/13/1913 Career OF: 22-14-36

YEAR TM-L	G	AB	R	H	2B	3B	HR	RBI	BB	SO	SB	CS	AVG	OBP	SLG	OPS	OPS+	BR/A	RC	RC/G	FR	G/POS	WS	TPW
1913 StL-A	7	14	0	3	0	0	0	2	0	5	0	....	.214	.214	.214	.429	26	-1	1	1.35	0	/0-2(0-2-0)	0	-0.2
1914 StL-A	74	131	19	39	5	3	1	14	13	26	6	4	.298	.366	.405	.770	137	5	20	5.39	0	0-38(19-9-9)	6	0.4
1915 StL-A	50	109	15	23	4	2	0	9	23	32	5	8	.211	.348	.284	.633	93	-2	10	2.88	-2	0-33(3-3-27)	2	-0.6
Total 3	**131**	**254**	**34**	**65**	**9**	**5**	**1**	**25**	**36**	**63**	**11**	**12**	**.256**	**.351**	**.343**	**.693**	**112**	**2**	**31**	**4.00**	**-3**	**/0-73**	**8**	**-0.4**

• WALKER, Fleet Moses Fleetwood Walker b: 10/7/1856, Mount Pleasant, OH d: 5/11/1924, Cleveland, OH BR/TR, 159 lbs. Deb: 5/1/1884

YEAR TM-L	G	AB	R	H	2B	3B	HR	RBI	BB	SO	SB	CS	AVG	OBP	SLG	OPS	OPS+	BR/A	RC	RC/G	FR	G/POS	WS	TPW
1884 Tol-a	42	152	23	40	2	3	0	0	8	....	....	....	.263	.325	.316	.641	106	1	16	3.93	-1	C-41/0-1	4	0.3

• WALKER, Frank Charles Franklin Walker b: 9/22/1894, Enoree, SC d: 9/16/1974, Bristol, TN BR/TR, 5'11", 165 lbs. Deb: 9/6/1917 Career OF: 6-95-10

YEAR TM-L	G	AB	R	H	2B	3B	HR	RBI	BB	SO	SB	CS	AVG	OBP	SLG	OPS	OPS+	BR/A	RC	RC/G	FR	G/POS	WS	TPW
1917 Det-A	2	2	0	0	0	0	0	0	0	1	0	....	.000	.000	.000	.000	-100	-0	0	.00	0	....	0	-0.1
1918 Det-A	55	167	10	33	10	3	1	20	7	29	3	....	.198	.234	.311	.546	67	-8	12	2.25	-5	0-45(3-34-9)	1	-1.8
1920 Phi-A	24	91	10	21	2	2	0	10	5	14	0	2	.231	.286	.297	.582	54	-7	7	2.67	-1	0-24(0-24-0)	0	-0.9
1921 Phi-A	19	66	6	15	3	0	1	6	8	11	1	0	.227	.311	.318	.629	60	-4	7	3.57	0	0-19(3-16-0)	1	-0.4
1925 NY-N	39	81	12	18	1	0	1	5	9	11	1	1	.222	.308	.272	.579	51	-6	7	2.92	0	0-21(0-21-1)	0	-0.6
Total 5	**139**	**407**	**38**	**87**	**16**	**5**	**3**	**41**	**29**	**66**	**5**	**3**	**.214**	**.273**	**.300**	**.572**	**59**	**-24**	**34**	**2.67**	**-7**	**0-109**	**2**	**-3.9**

• WALKER, Gee Gerald Holmes Walker b: 3/19/1908, Gulfport, MS d: 3/20/1981, Jackson, MS BR/TR, 5'11", 188 lbs. Deb: 4/14/1931 C Career OF: 742-463-420

YEAR TM-L	G	AB	R	H	2B	3B	HR	RBI	BB	SO	SB	CS	AVG	OBP	SLG	OPS	OPS+	BR/A	RC	RC/G	FR	G/POS	WS	TPW
1931 Det-A	59	189	20	56	17	2	1	28	14	21	10	7	.296	.345	.423	.768	98	-1	26	4.98	-4	0-44(1-41-1)	4	-0.6
1932 Det-A	127	480	71	155	32	6	8	78	13	38	30	6	.323	.345	.465	.809	104	5	78	6.12	-1	*0-116(39-79-0)	17	-0.1
1933 Det-A	127	483	68	135	29	7	9	64	15	49	26	9	.280	.304	.424	.728	89	-8	61	4.48	-3	*0-113(92-8-13)	10	-1.6
1934*Det-A	98	347	54	104	19	2	6	39	19	20	20	9	.300	.340	.418	.758	94	-4	49	5.03	0	0-80(9-48-23)	10	-0.6
1935*Det-A	98	362	52	109	22	6	7	53	15	21	6	4	.301	.329	.453	.782	104	-0	52	5.24	-4	0-85(29-45-11)	10	-0.7
1936 Det-A	134	550	105	194	55	5	12	93	23	30	17	8	.353	.387	.536	.924	125	19	112	7.96	3	*0-125(2-21-103)	20	1.3
1937 Det-A★	151	635	105	213	42	4	18	113	41	74	23	7	.335	.380	.499	.880	117	17	121	7.45	-5	*0-151(88-11-54)	22	0.4
1938 Chi-A	120	442	69	135	23	6	16	87	38	32	9	4	.305	.360	.493	.854	109	5	79	6.68	-3	*0-107(50-0-57)	12	-0.4
1939 Chi-A	149	598	95	174	30	11	13	111	28	43	17	6	.291	.330	.443	.773	94	-8	84	4.94	6	*0-147(147-0-0)	16	-0.9
1940 Was-A	140	595	87	175	29	7	13	96	24	58	21	4	.294	.325	.432	.757	101	2	84	5.21	-2	*0-140(140-0-0)	14	-0.8
1941 Cle-A	121	445	56	126	26	11	6	48	18	46	12	6	.283	.313	.431	.744	100	-3	56	4.32	6	*0-105(103-2-0)	10	-0.3
1942 Cin-N	119	422	40	97	20	2	5	50	31	44	11	....	.230	.290	.322	.613	79	-12	40	3.28	1	*0-110(20-74-19)	10	-1.7
1943 Cin-N	114	429	48	105	23	2	3	54	12	38	6	....	.245	.270	.329	.599	74	-17	35	2.79	-3	*0-106(15-75-17)	6	-2.5
1944 Cin-N	121	478	56	133	21	3	5	62	23	48	7	....	.278	.318	.366	.684	96	-4	53	3.91	-4	*0-117(1-59-61)	13	-1.4
1945 Cin-N	106	316	28	80	11	2	2	21	16	38	8	....	.253	.289	.320	.609	71	-13	29	3.21	-4	0-67(6-0-61)/3-3	4	-2.1
Total 15	**1784**	**6771**	**954**	**1991**	**399**	**76**	**124**	**997**	**330**	**600**	**223**	**70**	**.294**	**.331**	**.430**	**.761**	**99**	**-23**	**959**	**5.12**	**-16**	***0-1613/3-3**	**178**	**-12.0**

• WALKER, Greg Gregory Lee Walker b: 10/6/1959, Douglas, GA BL/TR, 6'3", 210 lbs. Deb: 9/18/1982 C

YEAR TM-L	G	AB	R	H	2B	3B	HR	RBI	BB	SO	SB	CS	AVG	OBP	SLG	OPS	OPS+	BR/A	RC	RC/G	FR	G/POS	WS	TPW
1982 Chi-A	11	17	3	7	2	1	2	7	2	3	0	0	.412	.474	1.000	1.474	292	4	8	22.41	0	/D-4	2	0.4
1983*Chi-A	118	307	32	83	16	3	10	55	28	57	2	1	.270	.335	.440	.775	107	3	46	5.42	-4	1-59,D-21	10	-0.4
1984 Chi-A	136	442	62	130	29	2	24	75	35	66	8	5	.294	.349	.532	.880	134	19	79	6.50	0	*1-101,D-21	15	1.3
1985 Chi-A	163	601	77	155	38	4	24	92	44	100	5	2	.258	.311	.454	.765	102	0	81	4.68	-7	*1-151/D-7	17	-1.6
1986 Chi-A	78	282	37	78	10	6	13	51	29	44	1	2	.277	.348	.493	.841	122	8	48	6.12	-0	1-77/D-1	10	0.3
1987 Chi-A	157	566	85	145	33	2	27	94	75	112	2	1	.256	.348	.465	.813	110	9	93	5.71	-9	*1-154/D-3	15	-1.0
1988 Chi-A	99	377	45	93	22	1	8	42	29	77	0	1	.247	.306	.374	.680	90	-6	43	3.90	-16	1-98	8	-2.9
1989 Chi-A	77	233	25	49	14	0	5	26	23	50	0	0	.210	.290	.335	.624	77	-7	22	3.03	-5	1-48,D-23	2	-1.6
1990 Chi-A	2	5	0	1	0	0	0	0	0	2	0	0	.200	.200	.200	.400	12	-1	0	1.35	0	/1-1,D-1	0	-0.1
Bal-A	14	34	2	5	0	0	0	2	3	9	1	0	.147	.237	.147	.384	10	-4	1	1.05	0	D-11	0	-0.4
Yr.	16	39	2	6	0	0	0	2	3	11	1	0	.154	.233	.154	.386	10	-4	1	1.09	0	D-12/1-1	0	-0.5
Total 9	**855**	**2864**	**368**	**746**	**164**	**19**	**113**	**444**	**268**	**520**	**19**	**12**	**.260**	**.328**	**.449**	**.777**	**107**	**25**	**422**	**5.14**	**-41**	**1-689/D-92**	**79**	**-6.0**

• WALKER, Harry Harry William "Harry The Hat" Walker
b: 10/22/1916, Pascagoula, MS d: 8/8/1999, Birmingham, AL BL/TR, 6'2", 190 lbs. Deb: 9/25/1940 M/C Career OF: 116-522-53

YEAR TM-L	G	AB	R	H	2B	3B	HR	RBI	BB	SO	SB	CS	AVG	OBP	SLG	OPS	OPS+	BR/A	RC	RC/G	FR	G/POS	WS	TPW
1940 StL-N	7	27	2	5	2	0	0	6	0	2	0	....	.185	.185	.259	.444	20	-3	1	1.58	1	/0-7(2-5-1)	0	-0.2
1941 StL-N	7	15	3	4	1	0	0	1	2	1	0	....	.267	.353	.333	.686	88	-0	2	4.78	0	/0-5(5-0-0)	0	-0.1
1942*StL-N	74	191	38	60	12	2	0	16	11	14	2	....	.314	.355	.398	.753	112	2	28	5.47	-2	0-56(12-43-3)/2-2	8	-0.1
1943*StL-N★	148	564	76	166	28	6	2	53	40	24	5	....	.294	.341	.376	.717	102	1	76	4.66	-5	*0-144(0-143-1)/2-1	17	-0.8
1946*StL-N	112	346	53	82	14	6	3	27	30	29	12	....	.237	.300	.338	.638	77	-11	37	3.62	1	0-92(13-79-0)/1-8	8	-1.3
1947 StL-N	10	25	2	5	1	0	0	0	4	2	0	....	.200	.310	.240	.550	46	-2	2	2.50	-1	0-10(2-7-0)	0	-0.3
Phi-N★	130	488	79	181	28	16	1	41	59	37	13	....	.371	.443	.500	.943	155	41	111	9.01	5	*0-127(0-127-0)/1-4	24	4.2
Yr.	140	513	81	186	29	**16**	1	41	63	39	13	....	**.363**	.436	.487	.924	150	39	113	8.62	4	*0-137(2-134-0)/1-4	24	3.9
1948 Phi-N	112	332	34	97	11	2	2	23	33	30	4	....	.292	.358	.355	.713	95	-1	44	5.00	1	0-81(21-58-3)/1-4,3-1	9	-0.4
1949 Chi-N	42	159	20	42	6	3	1	14	11	6	2	....	.264	.312	.358	.670	81	-5	18	4.03	-1	0-39(27-0-13)	3	-0.7
Cin-N	86	314	53	100	15	2	1	23	34	17	4	....	.318	.385	.389	.774	107	4	48	5.81	-1	0-77(22-26-29)/1-1	10	0.0
Yr.	128	473	73	142	21	5	2	37	45	23	6	....	.300	.361	.378	.739	98	-0	66	5.18	-2	*0-116(49-26-42)/1-1	13	-0.7
1950 StL-N	60	150	17	31	5	0	0	7	18	12	0	....	.207	.292	.240	.532	40	-13	11	2.54	-1	0-46(9-30-3)/1-2	1	-1.5
1951 StL-N	8	26	6	8	1	0	0	2	2	1	0	0	.308	.357	.346	.703	89	-0	3	5.22	0	/0-6(2-4-0),1-1	0	-0.1
1955 StL-N	11	14	2	5	2	0	0	1	1	0	0	0	.357	.400	.500	.900	137	1	3	8.71	1	/0-1	1	0.2
Total 11	**807**	**2651**	**385**	**786**	**126**	**37**	**10**	**214**	**245**	**175**	**42**	**0**	**.296**	**.358**	**.383**	**.741**	**103**	**14**	**386**	**5.28**	**-2**	**0-691/1-20,2-3,3-1**	**82**	**-1.1**

• WALKER, Hub Harvey Willos Walker b: 8/17/1906, Gulfport, MS d: 11/26/1982, San Jose, CA BL/TR, 5'10.5", 175 lbs. Deb: 4/15/1931 Career OF: 51-154-7

YEAR TM-L	G	AB	R	H	2B	3B	HR	RBI	BB	SO	SB	CS	AVG	OBP	SLG	OPS	OPS+	BR/A	RC	RC/G	FR	G/POS	WS	TPW
1931 Det-A	90	252	27	72	13	1	0	16	23	25	10	1	.286	.355	.345	.700	82	-3	34	4.82	-3	0-66(4-60-2)	5	-0.7
1935 Det-A	9	25	4	4	3	0	0	1	3	4	0	0	.160	.250	.280	.530	38	-2	2	2.32	0	/0-7(0-7-0)	0	-0.3
1936 Cin-N	92	258	49	71	18	1	4	23	35	32	8	....	.275	.366	.399	.765	113	6	41	5.72	-2	0-73(25-47-2)/1-1,C-1	9	0.2
1937 Cin-N	78	221	33	55	9	4	1	19	34	24	7	....	.249	.349	.339	.688	92	-1	28	4.33	0	0-58(17-40-1)/2-3	5	-0.3
1945*Det-A	28	23	4	3	0	0	0	1	9	4	1	0	.130	.375	.130	.505	46	-1	2	2.62	0	/0-7(5-0-2)	0	-0.1
Total 5	**297**	**779**	**117**	**205**	**43**	**6**	**5**	**60**	**104**	**89**	**26**	**1**	**.263**	**.354**	**.353**	**.707**	**92**	**-1**	**106**	**4.80**	**-5**	**0-211/2-3,1-1,C-1**	**19**	**-1.2**

• WALKER, Johnny John Miles Walker b: 12/11/1896, Toulon, IL d: 8/19/1976, Hollywood, FL BR/TR, 6', 175 lbs. Deb: 9/19/1919

YEAR TM-L	G	AB	R	H	2B	3B	HR	RBI	BB	SO	SB	CS	AVG	OBP	SLG	OPS	OPS+	BR/A	RC	RC/G	FR	G/POS	WS	TPW
1919 Phi-A	3	9	0	0	0	0	0	0	0	2	0	....	.000	.000	.000	.000	-99	-2	0	.00	-1	/C-3	0	-0.3
1920 Phi-A	9	22	0	5	1	0	0	5	0	1	0	0	.227	.227	.273	.500	32	-2	1	1.96	0	/C-6	0	-0.2
1921 Phi-A	113	423	41	109	14	5	2	46	9	29	5	0	.258	.278	.329	.607	54	-29	39	3.21	-3	1-99/C-7	1	-3.5
Total 3	**125**	**454**	**41**	**114**	**15**	**5**	**2**	**51**	**9**	**32**	**5**	**0**	**.251**	**.270**	**.319**	**.590**	**50**	**-33**	**40**	**3.06**	**-3**	**/1-99,C-16**	**1**	**-4.0**

• WALKER, Larry Larry Kenneth Robert Walker b: 12/1/1966, Maple Ridge, Canada BL/TR, 6'2", 215 lbs. Deb: 8/16/1989 Career OF: 33-68-1558

YEAR TM-L	G	AB	R	H	2B	3B	HR	RBI	BB	SO	SB	CS	AVG	OBP	SLG	OPS	OPS+	BR/A	RC	RC/G	FR	G/POS	WS	TPW
1989 Mon-N	20	47	4	8	0	0	0	4	5	13	1	1	.170	.264	.170	.434	26	-5	3	1.70	2	0-15(2-0-13)	0	-0.3
1990 Mon-N	133	419	59	101	18	3	19	51	49	112	21	7	.241	.328	.434	.762	112	8	61	4.87	8	*0-124(0-0-123)	12	1.3
1991 Mon-N	137	487	59	141	30	2	16	64	42	102	14	9	.290	.352	.458	.810	128	16	78	5.74	6	*0-102(0-5-99),1-39	20	1.7
1992 Mon-N★	143	528	85	159	31	4	23	93	41	97	18	6	.301	.358	.506	.864	143	30	95	6.55	7	*0-139(0-0-139)	26	3.5
1993 Mon-N	138	490	85	130	24	5	22	86	80	76	29	7	.265	.375	.469	.844	119	18	92	6.49	7	*0-132(0-0-132)/1-4	24	1.8
1994 Mon-N	103	395	76	127	**44**	2	19	86	47	74	15	5	.322	.399	.587	.986	151	31	93	8.75	0	0-68(0-0-68),1-35	21	2.4
1995*Col-N	131	494	96	151	31	5	36	101	49	72	16	3	.306	.384	.607	.991	122	17	114	8.47	1	*0-129(0-4-129)	18	1.2
1996 Col-N	83	272	58	75	18	4	18	58	20	58	18	2	.276	.346	.570	.915	110	5	54	6.98	-1	0-83(0-54-33)	10	0.3
1997 Col-N★	153	568	143	208	46	4	**49**	130	78	90	33	8	.366	**.455**	**.720**	**1.175**	164	60	187	**13.05**	-5	*0-151(0-2-150)/1-3,D-1	32	4.6
1998 Col-N★	130	454	113	165	46	3	23	67	64	61	14	4	**.363**	.446	.630	1.076	147	36	130	11.43	-1	*0-123(0-3-123)/2-1,3-1,D	17	2.8
1999 Col-N★	127	438	108	166	26	4	37	115	57	52	11	4	**.379**	**.464**	**.710**	**1.174**	151	38	143	**13.16**	4	*0-114(0-0-114)/D-1	24	3.4

YEAR	TM-L	G	AB	R	H	2B	3B	HR	RBI	BB	SO	SB	CS	AVG	OBP	SLG	OPS	OPS+	BR/A	RC	RC/G	FR	G/POS	WS	TPW
2000	Col-N	87	314	64	97	21	7	9	51	46	40	5	5	.309	.412	.506	.918	104	3	64	7.29	9	O-83(31-0-52)/D-3	11	0.7
2001	Col-N★	142	497	107	174	35	3	38	123	82	103	14	5	**.350**	.455	.662	1.117	150	43	155	12.13	-1	*O-129(0-0-129)/D-5	25	3.4
2002	Col-N	136	477	95	161	40	4	26	104	65	73	6	5	.338	.424	.602	1.026	144	32	123	9.98	1	*O-123(0-0-123)/D-7	26	2.6
2003	Col-N	143	454	86	129	25	7	16	79	98	87	7	4	.284	.423	.476	.899	117	17	98	7.78	-8	*O-131(0-0-131)/D-2	18	0.2
Total	15	1806	6334	1238	1992	435	57	351	1212	823	1110	222	75	.314	.403	.567	.971	134	349	1489	8.70	29	*O-1646/1-81,D-20,2-1,3-1	284	29.7

• WALKER, Oscar

Oscar Walker b: 3/18/1854, Brooklyn, NY d: 5/20/1889, Brooklyn, NY BL/TL, 5'10", 166 lbs. Deb: 9/17/1875 Career OF: 20-124-5

YEAR	TM-L	G	AB	R	H	2B	3B	HR	RBI	BB	SO	SB	CS	AVG	OBP	SLG	OPS	OPS+	BR/A	RC	RC/G	FR	G/POS	WS	TPW
1875	Atl-n	1	2	0	0	0	0	0	0	1	0	0	0	.000	.333	.000	.333	30	0	0	.00	0	/1-1,O-1	....	0.0
1879	Buf-N	72	287	35	79	15	6	1	35	8	38	....	....	.275	.295	.380	.675	118	5	33	4.44	6	*1-72	8	0.6
1880	Buf-N	34	126	12	29	4	2	1	15	6	18	....	....	.230	.265	.317	.583	94	-1	11	3.08	-2	1-24,O-11(3-7-1)	3	-0.4
1882	StL-a	76	318	48	76	15	7	**7**	....	10	....	....	....	.239	.262	.396	.658	115	4	34	3.92	3	*O-75(1-74-0)/1-1,2-1	12	0.4
1884	Bro-a	95	382	59	103	12	8	2	0	9	....	....	....	.270	.292	.359	.651	110	3	41	4.04	1	O-59(16-43-0),1-36	10	-0.1
1885	Bal-a	4	13	1	0	0	0	0	1	0	....	....	....	.000	.000	.000	.000	-102	-3	0	.00	-1	/O-4(0-0-4)	0	-0.4
Total	5	281	1126	155	287	46	23	11	51	33	56	....	....	.255	.278	.366	.644	109	9	119	3.93	7	O-149,1-133/2-1	33	0.2

• WALKER, Rube

Albert Bluford Walker b: 5/16/1926, Lenoir, NC d: 12/12/1992, Morganton, NC BL/TR, 6', 185 lbs. Deb: 4/20/1948 C

YEAR	TM-L	G	AB	R	H	2B	3B	HR	RBI	BB	SO	SB	CS	AVG	OBP	SLG	OPS	OPS+	BR/A	RC	RC/G	FR	G/POS	WS	TPW
1948	Chi-N	79	171	17	47	8	0	5	26	24	17	0	....	.275	.371	.409	.780	115	4	25	5.18	-1	C-44	5	0.6
1949	Chi-N	56	172	11	42	4	1	3	22	9	18	0	....	.244	.282	.331	.613	66	-9	15	3.10	-1	C-43	2	-0.8
1950	Chi-N	74	213	19	49	7	1	6	16	18	34	0	....	.230	.290	.357	.647	70	-10	22	3.61	1	C-62	4	-0.5
1951	Chi-N	37	107	9	25	4	0	2	5	12	13	0	0	.234	.311	.327	.638	70	-4	11	3.40	0	C-31	2	-0.3
	Bro-N	36	74	6	18	4	0	2	9	6	14	0	0	.243	.300	.378	.678	80	-2	8	3.59	0	C-23	2	-0.2
	Yr.	73	181	15	43	8	0	4	14	18	27	0	0	.238	.307	.348	.655	74	-7	19	3.48	0	C-54	4	-0.5
1952	Bro-N	46	139	9	36	8	0	1	19	8	17	0	0	.259	.304	.338	.642	77	-4	14	3.61	-2	C-40	4	-0.4
1953	Bro-N	43	95	5	23	6	0	3	9	7	11	0	0	.242	.301	.400	.701	79	-3	12	4.42	0	C-28	3	-0.2
1954	Bro-N	50	155	12	28	7	0	5	23	24	17	0	0	.181	.294	.323	.617	59	-9	15	3.05	0	C-47	3	-0.7
1955	Bro-N	48	103	6	26	5	0	2	13	15	11	1	0	.252	.347	.359	.707	86	-1	11	3.53	-1	C-35	3	-0.1
1956*	Bro-N	54	146	5	31	6	1	3	20	7	18	0	1	.212	.248	.329	.577	49	-11	11	2.45	0	C-43	2	-0.9
1957	Bro-N	60	166	12	30	8	0	2	23	15	33	2	0	.181	.249	.265	.514	35	-15	10	1.88	1	C-50	3	-1.2
1958	LA-N	25	44	3	5	2	0	1	7	5	10	0	0	.114	.204	.227	.431	14	-6	2	1.16	0	C-20	0	-0.5
Total	11	608	1585	114	360	69	3	35	192	150	213	3	1	.227	.296	.341	.637	69	-71	158	3.30	-2	C-466	33	-5.2

• WALKER, Speed

Joseph Richard Walker b: 1/23/1898, Munhall, PA d: 1/20/1959, West Mifflin, PA BR/TR, 6', 170 lbs. Deb: 9/15/1923

YEAR	TM-L	G	AB	R	H	2B	3B	HR	RBI	BB	SO	SB	CS	AVG	OBP	SLG	OPS	OPS+	BR/A	RC	RC/G	FR	G/POS	WS	TPW
1923	StL-N	2	7	1	2	0	0	0	0	0	1	0	0	.286	.286	.286	.571	52	-0	1	2.91	0	/1-2	0	-0.1

• WALKER, Tilly

Clarence William Walker b: 9/4/1887, Telford, TN d: 9/21/1959, Unicoi, TN BR/TR, 5'11", 165 lbs. Deb: 6/10/1911 Career OF: 725-577-43

YEAR	TM-L	G	AB	R	H	2B	3B	HR	RBI	BB	SO	SB	CS	AVG	OBP	SLG	OPS	OPS+	BR/A	RC	RC/G	FR	G/POS	WS	TPW
1911	Was-A	95	356	44	99	6	4	2	39	15	....	12	....	.278	.311	.334	.645	82	-10	41	3.91	0	O-94(94-0-0)	6	-1.3
1912	Was-A	39	110	22	30	2	1	0	9	8	....	11	....	.273	.333	.309	.642	83	-2	15	4.72	-1	O-34(3-6-22)/2-1	3	-0.5
1913	StL-A	23	85	7	25	4	1	0	11	2	9	5	....	.294	.310	.365	.675	100	-1	11	4.26	-1	O-23(23-0-0)	2	-0.3
1914	StL-A	151	517	67	154	24	16	6	78	51	72	29	17	.298	.365	.441	.806	148	27	87	5.82	11	*O-145(145-0-0)	28	3.6
1915	StL-A	144	510	53	137	20	7	5	49	36	77	20	17	.269	.323	.365	.688	110	1	62	4.01	8	*O-139(1-119-19)	16	0.0
1916*	Bos-A	128	467	68	124	29	11	3	46	23	45	14	....	.266	.303	.394	.697	109	1	61	4.46	-7	*O-128(3-125-0)	18	-1.5
1917	Bos-A	106	337	41	83	18	7	2	37	25	38	6	....	.246	.300	.359	.659	102	-1	38	3.62	7	O-96(0-96-0)	12	0.0
1918	Phi-A	114	414	56	122	20	0	**11**	48	41	44	8	....	.295	.360	.423	.782	134	16	64	5.37	4	*O-109(0-109-0)	17	1.4
1919	Phi-A	125	456	47	133	30	6	10	64	26	41	8	....	.292	.330	.450	.779	116	7	68	5.21	-4	*O-115(28-85-2)	10	-0.3
1920	Phi-A	149	585	79	157	23	7	17	82	41	59	8	3	.268	.321	.419	.739	94	-5	80	4.70	7	*O-149(123-26-0)	11	-0.5
1921	Phi-A	142	556	89	169	32	5	23	101	73	41	3	5	.304	.389	.504	.892	125	21	110	7.33	6	*O-142(142-0-0)	16	1.5
1922	Phi-A	153	565	111	160	31	4	37	99	61	67	4	3	.283	.357	.549	.906	130	22	111	6.97	-4	*O-148(137-11-0)	22	0.7
1923	Phi-A	52	109	12	30	5	2	2	16	14	11	1	2	.275	.368	.413	.781	104	0	17	5.28	-1	O-26(26-0-0)	3	-0.2
Total	13	1421	5067	696	1423	244	71	118	679	416	504	129	47	.281	.339	.427	.766	115	76	763	5.21	26	*O-1348/2-1	164	2.5

• WALKER, Todd

Todd Arthur Walker b: 5/25/1973, Bakersfield, CA BL/TR, 6', 180 lbs. Deb: 8/30/1996

YEAR	TM-L	G	AB	R	H	2B	3B	HR	RBI	BB	SO	SB	CS	AVG	OBP	SLG	OPS	OPS+	BR/A	RC	RC/G	FR	G/POS	WS	TPW
1996	Min-A	25	82	8	21	6	0	0	6	4	13	2	0	.256	.291	.329	.620	55	-5	7	2.87	1	3-20/2-4,D-1	1	-0.3
1997	Min-A	52	156	15	37	7	1	3	16	11	30	7	0	.237	.292	.353	.644	66	-6	16	3.45	-2	3-40/2-8,D-2	2	-0.7
1998	Min-A	143	528	85	167	41	3	12	62	47	65	19	7	.316	.374	.473	.848	117	14	92	6.44	-7	*2-140/D-1	19	1.3
1999	Min-A	143	531	62	148	37	4	6	46	52	83	18	10	.279	.344	.397	.742	85	-12	70	4.63	-6	*2-103,D-40	9	-1.5
2000	Min-A	23	77	14	18	1	0	2	8	7	10	3	0	.234	.298	.325	.622	55	-5	8	3.14	-4	2-19/D-2	0	-0.7
	Col-N	57	171	28	54	10	4	7	36	20	19	4	1	.316	.391	.544	.934	106	2	38	8.21	-10	2-52	5	-0.5
2001	Col-N	85	290	52	86	18	2	12	43	25	40	1	3	.297	.352	.497	.849	95	-3	48	5.86	0	2-77	6	0.0
	Cin-N	66	261	41	77	17	0	5	32	26	42	0	5	.295	.361	.418	.779	96	-3	38	5.17	-6	2-65/S-1	6	-0.6
	Yr.	151	551	93	163	35	2	17	75	51	82	1	8	.296	.357	.459	.816	96	-6	85	5.53	-6	*2-142/S-1	12	-0.5
2002	Cin-N	155	612	79	183	42	3	11	64	50	81	8	5	.299	.355	.431	.786	103	2	94	5.59	-3	*2-154	21	0.6
2003*	Bos-A	144	587	92	166	38	4	13	85	48	54	1	1	.283	.338	.428	.766	98	-2	82	4.93	-11	*2-139/D-2	14	-0.6
Total	8	893	3295	476	957	217	21	71	398	290	437	63	32	.290	.350	.434	.783	96	-19	492	5.32	-47	2-761/3-60,D-48,S-1	83	-3.1

• WALKER, Tony

Anthony Bruce Walker b: 7/1/1959, San Diego, CA BR/TR, 6'2", 205 lbs. Deb: 4/8/1986

YEAR	TM-L	G	AB	R	H	2B	3B	HR	RBI	BB	SO	SB	CS	AVG	OBP	SLG	OPS	OPS+	BR/A	RC	RC/G	FR	G/POS	WS	TPW
1986	Hou-N	84	90	19	20	7	0	2	10	11	15	11	3	.222	.307	.367	.674	87	-1	10	3.61	-3	O-68(0-69-0)	3	-0.4

• WALKER, Walt

Walter S. Walker b: 3/12/1860, Berlin, MI d: 2/28/1922, Pontiac, MI TR, 5'10.5", 162 lbs. Deb: 5/8/1884

YEAR	TM-L	G	AB	R	H	2B	3B	HR	RBI	BB	SO	SB	CS	AVG	OBP	SLG	OPS	OPS+	BR/A	RC	RC/G	FR	G/POS	WS	TPW
1884	Det-N	1	4	1	1	0	0	0	0	0	0	....	....	.250	.250	.250	.500	61	-0	0	2.35	0	/C-1	0	0.0

• WALKER, Welday

Welday Wilberforce Walker b: 7/27/1860, Steubenville, OH d: 11/23/1937, Steubenville, OH Deb: 7/15/1884

YEAR	TM-L	G	AB	R	H	2B	3B	HR	RBI	BB	SO	SB	CS	AVG	OBP	SLG	OPS	OPS+	BR/A	RC	RC/G	FR	G/POS	WS	TPW
1884	Tol-a	5	18	1	4	1	0	0	2	0	....	....	....	.222	.222	.278	.500	60	-1	1	2.24	-1	/O-5(4-1-0)	1	-0.2

• WALL, Howard

Howard Cornelius Wall b: 12/1854, Washington, DC Deb: 9/13/1873

YEAR	TM-L	G	AB	R	H	2B	3B	HR	RBI	BB	SO	SB	CS	AVG	OBP	SLG	OPS	OPS+	BR/A	RC	RC/G	FR	G/POS	WS	TPW
1873	Was-n	1	4	1	1	0	0	0	0	0	0	0	0	.250	.250	.250	.500	51	-0	0	2.61	-1	/S-1	....	-0.1

• WALL, Joe

Joseph Francis "Gummy" Wall b: 7/24/1873, Brooklyn, NY d: 7/17/1936, Brooklyn, NY BL/TL Deb: 9/22/1901 U Career OF: 0-0-4

YEAR	TM-L	G	AB	R	H	2B	3B	HR	RBI	BB	SO	SB	CS	AVG	OBP	SLG	OPS	OPS+	BR/A	RC	RC/G	FR	G/POS	WS	TPW
1901	NY-N	4	8	0	4	0	0	0	1	0	....	0	....	.500	.500	.500	1.000	198	1	2	13.58	-1	/C-2,O-1	1	0.0
1902	NY-N	6	14	2	5	2	0	0	0	2	....	0	....	.357	.438	.500	.938	191	2	3	9.24	0	/O-3(0-0-3)	1	0.2
	Bro-N	5	18	0	3	0	0	0	0	3	....	0	....	.167	.318	.167	.485	50	-1	1	1.73	-2	/C-5	0	-0.3
	Yr.	11	32	2	8	2	0	0	0	5	....	0	....	.250	.368	.313	.681	109	1	4	4.55	-2	/C-5,O-3(0-0-3)	1	-0.1
Total	2	15	40	2	12	2	0	0	1	5	....	0	....	.300	.391	.350	.741	125	2	6	5.84	-2	/C-7,O-4	2	0.0

• WALLACE, Bobby

Rhoderick John Wallace
b: 11/4/1873, Pittsburgh, PA d: 11/3/1960, Torrance, CA BR/TR, 5'8", 170 lbs. Deb: 9/15/1894 M/C/U HOF: 1953 Career OF: 4-6-16 ♦

YEAR	TM-L	G	AB	R	H	2B	3B	HR	RBI	BB	SO	SB	CS	AVG	OBP	SLG	OPS	OPS+	BR/A	RC	RC/G	FR	G/POS	WS	TPW
1894	Cle-N	4	13	0	2	1	0	0	1	0	1	0	....	.154	.154	.231	.385	-8	-1	0	1.12	1	/P-4	2	0.0
1895	Cle-N	30	98	16	21	2	3	0	10	6	17	0	....	.214	.274	.296	.570	44	-3	9	2.88	3	P-30	14	1.6
1896*	Cle-N	45	149	19	35	6	3	1	17	11	21	2	....	.235	.288	.336	.623	60	-5	16	3.55	-1	O-23(3-6-15),P-22/1-1	15	1.1
1897	Cle-N	130	516	99	173	33	21	4	112	48	....	14	....	.335	.394	.504	.898	129	20	112	8.32	18	*3-130/O-1	21	3.4
1898	Cle-N	154	593	81	160	25	13	3	99	63	....	7	....	.270	.344	.371	.715	106	5	82	4.86	13	*3-141,2-13	25	2.0
1899	StL-N	151	577	91	170	28	14	12	108	54	....	17	....	.295	.357	.454	.811	119	13	103	6.60	20	*S-100,3-52	25	3.6
1900	StL-N	126	485	70	130	25	9	4	70	40	....	7	....	.268	.328	.381	.709	96	-4	65	4.80	6	*S-126/3-1	13	0.8
1901	StL-N	134	550	69	178	34	15	2	91	20	....	15	....	.324	.351	.451	.802	138	24	96	6.63	27	*S-134	26	5.4
1902	StL-A	133	494	71	141	32	9	1	63	45	....	18	....	.285	.350	.393	.743	107	5	77	5.67	15	*S-131/O-1,P-1	22	2.4
1903	StL-A	135	511	63	136	21	7	1	54	28	....	10	....	.266	.309	.341	.650	97	-2	59	4.10	13	*S-135	20	1.6
1904	StL-A	139	541	57	149	29	4	2	69	42	....	20	....	.275	.330	.355	.685	124	15	73	4.81	4	*S-139	23	2.6
1905	StL-A	156	587	67	159	25	9	1	59	45	....	13	....	.271	.324	.349	.673	120	13	73	4.46	0	*S-156	21	2.0
1906	StL-A	139	476	64	123	21	7	2	67	58	....	24	....	.258	.344	.345	.688	121	14	68	4.92	12	*S-138	23	3.3
1907	StL-A	147	538	56	138	20	7	0	70	54	....	16	....	.257	.328	.320	.647	107	6	64	4.17	13	*S-147	20	2.6
1908	StL-A	137	487	59	123	24	4	1	60	52	....	5	....	.253	.327	.324	.652	111	7	54	3.68	20	*S-137	21	3.7
1909	StL-A	116	403	36	96	12	2	0	35	38	....	7	....	.238	.310	.278	.588	92	-2	36	3.03	5	S-87,3-29	13	0.7

YEAR TM-L	G	AB	R	H	2B	3B	HR	RBI	BB	SO	SB	CS	AVG	OBP	SLG	OPS	OPS+	BR/A	RC	RC/G	FR	G/POS	WS	TPW
1910 StL-A	138	508	47	131	19	7	0	37	49	....	12	....	.258	.324	.323	.647	110	6	57	3.80	12	S-99,3-39	20	2.5
1911 StL-A	125	410	35	95	12	2	0	31	46	....	8	....	.232	.312	.271	.583	66	-17	37	2.98	1	*S-124/2-1	7	-0.7
1912 StL-A	100	323	39	78	14	5	0	31	43	....	3	....	.241	.332	.316	.648	89	-4	35	3.60	7	S-87,3-10/2-2	8	1.0
1913 StL-A	55	147	11	31	5	0	0	21	14	16	1	....	.211	.293	.245	.538	59	-7	11	2.35	-1	S-39/3-7	2	-0.6
1914 StL-A	26	73	3	16	2	1	0	5	5	13	1	1	.219	.269	.274	.543	66	-3	6	2.53	-2	S-19/3-2	1	-0.5
1915 StL-A	9	13	1	3	0	1	0	4	5	0	0	1	.231	.444	.385	.829	154	1	2	4.68	-1	/S-9	1	0.1
1916 StL-A	14	18	0	5	0	0	0	1	2	1	0	....	.278	.350	.278	.628	93	-0	2	3.70	1	/3-9,S-5	1	0.1
1917 StL-N	8	10	0	1	0	0	0	2	0	1	0	....	.100	.100	.100	.200	-40	-2	0	.43	-2	/3-5,S-2	0	-0.4
1918 StL-N	32	98	3	15	1	0	0	4	6	9	1	....	.153	.202	.163	.365	12	-10	4	1.07	-4	2-17,S-12/3-1	1	-1.4
Total 25	2383	8618	1057	2309	391	143	34	1121	774	79	201	2	.268	.332	.358	.690	105	68	1140	4.64	180	*S-1826,3-426/P-57,2-33,0,1	345	36.7

• WALLACE, Doc Frederick Renshaw "Jesse" Wallace b: 9/30/1893, Church Hill, MD d: 12/31/1964, Haverford, PA BR/TR, 5'6.5", 135 lbs. Deb: 5/2/1919

YEAR TM-L	G	AB	R	H	2B	3B	HR	RBI	BB	SO	SB	CS	AVG	OBP	SLG	OPS	OPS+	BR/A	RC	RC/G	FR	G/POS	WS	TPW
1919 Phi-N	2	4	0	1	0	0	0	0	0	1	0	....	.250	.250	.250	.500	47	-0	0	1.99	-1	/S-2	0	-0.1

• WALLACE, Don Donald Allen Wallace b: 8/25/1940, Sapulpa, OK BL/TR, 5'8", 165 lbs. Deb: 4/12/1967

YEAR TM-L	G	AB	R	H	2B	3B	HR	RBI	BB	SO	SB	CS	AVG	OBP	SLG	OPS	OPS+	BR/A	RC	RC/G	FR	G/POS	WS	TPW
1967 Cal-A	23	6	2	0	0	0	0	0	3	2	0	1	.000	.333	.000	.333	6	-1	0	.88	0	/2-4,1-1,3-1	0	-0.1

• WALLACE, Jack Clarence Eugene Wallace b: 8/6/1890, Winnfield, LA d: 10/15/1960, Winnfield, LA BR/TR, 5'10.5", 175 lbs. Deb: 9/27/1915

YEAR TM-L	G	AB	R	H	2B	3B	HR	RBI	BB	SO	SB	CS	AVG	OBP	SLG	OPS	OPS+	BR/A	RC	RC/G	FR	G/POS	WS	TPW
1915 Chi-N	2	7	1	2	0	0	0	1	0	2	0	....	.286	.375	.286	.661	101	0	1	3.98	2	/C-2	0	0.2

• WALLACE, Jim James L. Wallace b: 11/14/1881, Boston, MA d: 5/16/1953, Revere, MA BL/TL, 5'9", 150 lbs. Deb: 8/24/1905

YEAR TM-L	G	AB	R	H	2B	3B	HR	RBI	BB	SO	SB	CS	AVG	OBP	SLG	OPS	OPS+	BR/A	RC	RC/G	FR	G/POS	WS	TPW
1905 Pit-N	7	29	3	6	1	0	0	3	3	....	2	....	.207	.281	.241	.523	55	-2	3	2.95	1	/O-7(0-0-7)	1	-0.1

• WALLACH, Tim Timothy Charles Wallach b: 9/14/1957, Huntington Beach, CA BR/TR, 6'3", 200 lbs. Deb: 9/6/1980 Career OF: 4-0-36

YEAR TM-L	G	AB	R	H	2B	3B	HR	RBI	BB	SO	SB	CS	AVG	OBP	SLG	OPS	OPS+	BR/A	RC	RC/G	FR	G/POS	WS	TPW
1980 Mon-N	5	11	1	2	0	0	1	2	1	5	0	0	.182	.250	.455	.705	93	-0	1	3.95	0	/O-3(2-0-1),1-1	0	-0.1
1981*Mon-N	71	212	19	50	9	1	4	13	15	37	0	1	.236	.299	.344	.643	81	-6	22	3.54	-3	O-35(1-0-34),1-16,3-15	4	-1.2
1982 Mon-N	158	596	89	160	31	3	28	97	36	81	6	4	.268	.314	.471	.786	115	8	84	4.87	7	*3-156/O-2(1-0-1),1-1	20	1.4
1983 Mon-N	156	581	54	156	33	3	19	70	55	97	0	3	.269	.338	.434	.772	113	8	85	5.19	3	*3-156	19	0.9
1984 Mon-N★	160	582	55	143	25	4	18	72	50	101	3	7	.246	.313	.395	.708	102	-2	70	4.06	28	*3-160/S-1	18	2.5
1985 Mon-N★	155	569	70	148	36	3	22	81	38	79	9	9	.260	.312	.450	.762	117	8	73	4.35	36	*3-154	23	4.4
1986 Mon-N	134	480	50	112	22	1	18	71	44	72	8	4	.233	.311	.396	.707	94	-5	57	3.88	15	*3-132	14	0.9
1987 Mon-N★	153	593	89	177	**42**	4	26	123	37	98	9	5	.298	.347	.514	.861	121	15	105	6.56	6	*3-150/P-1	28	2.0
1988 Mon-N	159	592	52	152	32	5	12	69	38	88	2	6	.257	.305	.389	.693	94	-9	64	3.66	18	*3-153/2-1	16	1.1
1989 Mon-N★	154	573	76	159	**42**	0	13	77	58	81	3	7	.277	.345	.419	.764	116	9	77	4.61	-4	*3-153/P-1	20	0.6
1990 Mon-N★	161	626	69	185	37	5	21	98	42	80	6	9	.296	.343	.471	.814	126	16	96	5.51	11	*3-161	26	2.9
1991 Mon-N	151	577	60	130	22	1	13	73	50	100	2	4	.225	.294	.334	.628	77	-19	56	3.22	5	*3-149	11	-1.4
1992 Mon-N	150	537	53	120	29	1	9	59	50	90	2	2	.223	.299	.331	.631	79	-15	54	3.37	15	3-85,1-71	12	-0.6
1993 LA-N	133	477	42	106	19	1	12	62	32	70	0	2	.222	.275	.342	.617	68	-24	44	3.00	-7	*3-130/1-1	6	-2.9
1994 LA-N	113	414	68	116	21	1	23	78	46	80	0	2	.280	.358	.502	.860	130	16	72	6.21	-13	*3-113	18	0.5
1995*LA-N	97	327	24	87	22	2	9	38	27	69	0	0	.266	.330	.428	.758	107	2	44	4.67	-3	3-96/1-1	9	0.1
1996 Cal-A	57	190	23	45	7	0	8	20	18	47	1	0	.237	.306	.400	.706	78	-7	24	4.31	5	3-46/D-8,1-3	2	-0.2
*LA-N	45	162	14	37	3	1	4	22	12	32	0	1	.228	.286	.333	.619	68	-8	15	3.06	-7	3-45	2	-1.4
Total 17	2212	8099	908	2085	432	36	260	1125	649	1307	51	66	.257	.319	.416	.735	103	-13	1041	4.42	112	*3-2054/1-94,O-40,D-8,P-2,2,S	248	9.6

• WALLAESA, Jack John Wallaesa b: 8/31/1919, Easton, PA d: 12/27/1986, Easton, PA BB/TR, 6'3", 191 lbs. Deb: 9/22/1940 Career OF: 23-0-0

YEAR TM-L	G	AB	R	H	2B	3B	HR	RBI	BB	SO	SB	CS	AVG	OBP	SLG	OPS	OPS+	BR/A	RC	RC/G	FR	G/POS	WS	TPW
1940 Phi-A	6	20	0	3	0	0	0	2	0	2	0	0	.150	.150	.150	.300	-22	-4	0	.73	0	/S-6	0	-0.3
1942 Phi-A	36	117	13	30	4	1	2	13	8	26	0	1	.256	.315	.359	.674	90	-2	14	4.14	-5	S-36	3	-0.5
1946 Phi-A	63	194	16	38	4	2	5	11	14	47	1	0	.196	.250	.314	.564	57	-11	16	2.72	-10	S-59	1	-1.9
1947 Chi-A	81	205	25	40	9	1	7	32	23	51	2	2	.195	.279	.351	.631	77	-7	20	3.17	6	S-27,O-22(22-0-0)/3-1	4	-0.2
1948 Chi-A	33	48	2	9	0	0	1	3	1	12	0	0	.188	.204	.250	.454	21	-6	2	1.35	0	/S-5,O-1	0	-0.5
Total 5	219	584	56	120	17	4	15	61	46	138	3	3	.205	.267	.325	.592	66	-30	52	2.96	-10	S-133/O-23,3-1	8	-3.4

• WALLEN, Norm Norman Edward Wallen b: 2/13/1917, Milwaukee, WI d: 6/20/1994, Milwaukee, WI BR/TR, 5'11.5", 175 lbs. Deb: 4/20/1945

YEAR TM-L	G	AB	R	H	2B	3B	HR	RBI	BB	SO	SB	CS	AVG	OBP	SLG	OPS	OPS+	BR/A	RC	RC/G	FR	G/POS	WS	TPW
1945 Bos-N	4	15	1	2	0	1	0	1	1	1	0	....	.133	.188	.267	.454	25	-2	1	1.66	-1	/3-4	0	-0.3

• WALLER, Ty Elliott Tyrone Waller b: 3/14/1957, Fresno, CA BR/TR, 6', 180 lbs. Deb: 9/6/1980 C Career OF: 2-10-1

YEAR TM-L	G	AB	R	H	2B	3B	HR	RBI	BB	SO	SB	CS	AVG	OBP	SLG	OPS	OPS+	BR/A	RC	RC/G	FR	G/POS	WS	TPW
1980 StL-N	5	12	3	1	0	0	0	0	1	5	0	0	.083	.154	.083	.237	-31	-2	0	.48	-1	/3-5	0	-0.3
1981 Chi-N	30	71	10	19	2	1	3	13	4	18	2	0	.268	.307	.451	.757	108	1	10	5.21	-1	3-22/2-3,O-3(0-3-0)	2	0.0
1982 Chi-N	17	21	4	5	0	0	0	1	2	5	0	0	.238	.304	.238	.542	52	-1	2	2.80	-1	/O-7(1-5-1),3-1	0	-0.2
1987 Hou-N	11	6	1	1	1	0	0	0	0	3	0	0	.167	.167	.333	.500	30	-1	0	1.80	0	/O-3(1-2-0)	0	-0.1
Total 4	63	110	18	26	3	1	3	14	7	31	2	0	.236	.282	.364	.646	78	-3	13	3.94	-3	/3-28,O-13,2-3	2	-0.7

• WALLING, Denny Dennis Martin Walling b: 4/17/1954, Neptune, NJ BL/TR, 6', 185 lbs. Deb: 9/7/1975 C Career OF: 131-27-135

YEAR TM-L	G	AB	R	H	2B	3B	HR	RBI	BB	SO	SB	CS	AVG	OBP	SLG	OPS	OPS+	BR/A	RC	RC/G	FR	G/POS	WS	TPW
1975 Oak-A	6	8	0	1	1	0	0	2	0	4	0	0	.125	.125	.250	.375	4	-1	0	.96	0	/O-3(1-2-0)	0	-0.1
1976 Oak-A	3	11	1	3	0	0	0	0	0	3	0	0	.273	.273	.273	.545	63	-1	1	2.76	-1	/O-3(2-2-0)	0	-0.1
1977 Hou-N	6	21	1	6	0	1	0	6	2	4	0	1	.286	.348	.381	.729	105	-0	3	4.38	0	/O-5(2-1-2)	1	0.0
1978 Hou-N	120	247	30	62	11	3	3	36	30	24	9	2	.251	.335	.356	.691	101	2	32	4.54	-1	O-78(66-7-4)	8	-0.2
1979 Hou-N	82	147	21	48	8	4	3	31	17	21	3	2	.327	.396	.497	.893	151	10	29	7.58	-1	O-42(7-0-35)	9	0.7
1980*Hou-N	100	284	30	85	6	5	3	29	35	26	4	3	.299	.376	.387	.764	123	9	43	5.69	-1	1-63,O-19(1-0-18)	11	0.5
1981*Hou-N	65	158	23	37	6	0	5	23	28	17	2	1	.234	.349	.367	.717	109	3	22	4.60	-1	1-27,O-27(5-1-21)	5	0.0
1982 Hou-N	85	146	22	30	4	1	1	14	23	19	4	2	.205	.314	.267	.581	69	-5	12	2.68	1	O-32(4-11-18),1-20	2	-0.6
1983 Hou-N	100	135	24	40	5	3	3	19	15	16	2	2	.296	.367	.444	.811	132	5	22	6.07	-2	1-42,3-13,O-13(2-0-12)	6	0.2
1984 Hou-N	87	249	37	70	11	5	3	31	16	28	7	1	.281	.327	.402	.729	112	4	33	4.82	3	3-52,1-16/O-6(3-3-0)	8	0.6
1985 Hou-N	119	345	44	93	20	1	7	45	25	26	5	2	.270	.319	.394	.713	101	-0	42	4.30	-2	3-51,1-46,O-13(6-0-7)	10	-0.5
1986*Hou-N	130	382	54	119	23	1	13	58	36	31	1	1	.312	.371	.479	.850	136	18	67	6.55	12	*3-102,O-11(6-0-5)/1-4	18	2.9
1987 Hou-N	110	325	45	92	21	4	5	33	39	37	5	1	.283	.360	.418	.778	109	5	50	5.38	3	3-79,1-16/O-7(6-0-2)	11	0.6
1988 Hou-N	65	176	19	43	10	2	1	20	15	18	1	0	.244	.304	.341	.645	88	-3	19	3.72	2	3-51/1-3,O-1	6	-0.1
StL-N	19	58	3	13	3	0	0	1	2	7	1	0	.224	.250	.276	.526	50	-4	4	2.33	0	O-11(10-0-1)/3-5,1-1	0	-0.4
Yr.	84	234	22	56	13	2	1	21	17	25	2	0	.239	.291	.325	.616	79	-6	23	3.37	2	3-56,O-12(11-0-1)/1-4	6	-0.5
1989 StL-N	69	79	9	24	7	0	1	11	14	12	0	0	.304	.409	.430	.839	136	4	15	7.12	-2	1-20/3-9,O-6(3-0-3)	3	0.2
1990 StL-N	78	127	7	28	5	0	1	19	8	15	0	0	.220	.267	.283	.550	51	-9	9	2.25	2	1-15,3-11/O-8(3-0-5)	1	-0.8
1991 Tex-A	24	44	1	4	1	0	0	2	3	8	0	0	.091	.184	.114	.297	-16	-7	1	.48	-1	3-14/O-5(3-0-2)	0	-0.8
1992 Hou-N	3	3	1	1	0	0	0	0	0	0	0	0	.333	.333	.333	.667	94	-0	0	4.50	0	....	0	0.0
Total 18	1271	2945	372	799	142	30	49	380	308	316	44	18	.271	.341	.390	.731	107	31	405	4.85	12	3-387,O-290,1-273	99	2.0

• WALLIS, Joe Harold Joseph Wallis b: 1/9/1952, East St. Louis, IL BB/TR, 5'11", 195 lbs. Deb: 9/2/1975 Career OF: 15-198-63

YEAR TM-L	G	AB	R	H	2B	3B	HR	RBI	BB	SO	SB	CS	AVG	OBP	SLG	OPS	OPS+	BR/A	RC	RC/G	FR	G/POS	WS	TPW
1975 Chi-N	16	56	9	16	2	2	1	4	5	14	2	0	.286	.344	.446	.791	113	1	9	5.90	0	O-15(0-14-1)	2	0.1
1976 Chi-N	121	338	51	86	11	5	5	21	33	62	3	9	.254	.323	.361	.684	86	-9	39	3.96	3	O-90(10-68-16)	8	-1.0
1977 Chi-N	56	80	14	20	3	0	2	8	16	25	0	1	.250	.375	.363	.738	89	-1	12	5.07	0	O-35(0-35-0)	2	-0.1
1978 Chi-N	28	55	7	17	2	1	1	6	5	13	0	2	.309	.367	.436	.803	110	-0	8	5.63	0	O-25(0-25-0)	2	0.0
Oak-A	85	279	28	66	16	1	6	26	26	42	1	4	.237	.302	.366	.667	91	-5	31	3.72	0	O-80(5-55-23)/D-1	7	-0.8
1979 Oak-A	23	78	6	11	2	0	1	3	10	18	1	0	.141	.247	.205	.452	25	-8	5	1.79	0	O-23(0-1-23)	0	-0.8
Total 5	329	886	115	216	36	9	16	68	95	174	7	16	.244	.318	.359	.677	85	-22	104	3.97	3	O-268/D-1	21	-2.6

• WALLS, Lee Ray Lee Walls b: 1/6/1933, San Diego, CA d: 10/11/1993, Los Angeles, CA BR/TR, 6'3", 205 lbs. Deb: 4/21/1952 C Career OF: 208-58-352

YEAR TM-L	G	AB	R	H	2B	3B	HR	RBI	BB	SO	SB	CS	AVG	OBP	SLG	OPS	OPS+	BR/A	RC	RC/G	FR	G/POS	WS	TPW
1952 Pit-N	32	80	6	15	0	1	2	5	8	22	0	0	.188	.261	.288	.549	51	-5	6	2.62	0	O-19(1-18-0)	1	-0.6
1956 Pit-N	143	474	72	130	20	11	11	54	50	83	3	5	.274	.346	.432	.778	110	6	70	5.08	0	*O-133(74-10-56)/3-1	14	-0.2
1957 Pit-N	8	22	3	4	1	0	0	0	2	5	1	0	.182	.250	.227	.477	30	-2	2	2.27	0	/O-7(7-0-0)	0	-0.2
Chi-N	117	366	42	88	10	5	6	33	27	67	5	3	.240	.294	.344	.639	72	-15	36	3.28	-3	O-94(67-29-6)/3-1	4	-2.3
Yr.	125	388	45	92	11	5	6	33	29	72	6	3	.237	.292	.338	.629	70	-17	38	3.22	-3	O-101(74-29-6)/3-1	4	-2.5
1958 Chi-N★	136	513	80	156	19	3	24	72	47	62	4	4	.304	.371	.493	.865	128	20	94	6.66	0	*O-132(0-0-132)	20	1.5

YEAR TM-L	G	AB	R	H	2B	3B	HR	RBI	BB	SO	SB	CS	AVG	OBP	SLG	OPS	OPS+	BR/A	RC	RC/G	FR	G/POS	WS	TPW
1959 Chi-N	120	354	43	91	18	3	8	33	42	73	0	2	.257	.344	.393	.737	97	-2	49	4.77	-4	*O-119(0-0-119)	10	-1.0
1960 Cin-N	29	84	12	23	3	2	1	7	17	20	2	0	.274	.396	.393	.789	115	3	14	5.53	-1	O-24(12-0-12)/1-2	2	0.1
Phi-N	65	181	19	36	6	1	3	19	14	32	3	2	.199	.256	.293	.549	50	-13	13	2.31	-2	3-34,O-13(8-0-5)/1-7	1	-1.6
Yr.	94	265	31	59	9	3	4	26	31	52	5	2	.223	.304	.325	.629	72	-10	27	3.28	-3	O-37(20-0-17),3-34/1-9	3	-1.5
1961 Phi-N	91	261	32	73	6	4	8	30	19	48	2	2	.280	.329	.425	.754	99	-1	34	4.49	-2	1-28,3-26,O-17(11-1-8)	5	-0.5
1962 LA-N	60	109	9	29	3	1	0	17	10	21	1	0	.266	.328	.312	.640	77	-3	12	3.75	0	O-17(15-0-3),1-11/3-4	2	-0.5
1963 LA-N	64	86	12	20	1	0	3	11	7	25	0	0	.233	.290	.349	.639	89	-1	8	2.98	2	O-18(10-0-8)/1-5,3-2	2	0.0
1964 LA-N	37	28	1	5	1	0	0	3	2	12	0	0	.179	.233	.214	.448	29	-3	1	1.47	-1	/O-6(3-0-3),C-1	0	-0.4
Total 10	902	2558	331	670	88	31	66	284	245	470	21	18	.262	.330	.398	.728	96	-16	338	4.53	-12	O-599/3-68,1-53,C-1	61	-5.6

• WALSH, Austin Austin Edward Walsh b: 9/1/1891, Cambridge, MA d: 1/26/1955, Glendale, CA BL/TL, 5'11", 175 lbs. Deb: 4/19/1914

YEAR TM-L	G	AB	R	H	2B	3B	HR	RBI	BB	SO	SB	CS	AVG	OBP	SLG	OPS	OPS+	BR/A	RC	RC/G	FR	G/POS	WS	TPW
1914 Chi-F	57	121	14	29	6	1	1	10	4	25	0	....	.240	.264	.331	.595	73	-5	10	2.72	1	O-30(21-1-8)	2	-0.5

• WALSH, Dee Leo Thomas Walsh b: 3/28/1890, St. Louis, MO d: 7/14/1971, St. Louis, MO BB/TR, 5'9.5", 165 lbs. Deb: 4/10/1913

YEAR TM-L	G	AB	R	H	2B	3B	HR	RBI	BB	SO	SB	CS	AVG	OBP	SLG	OPS	OPS+	BR/A	RC	RC/G	FR	G/POS	WS	TPW
1913 StL-A	23	53	8	9	0	1	0	5	6	11	3	....	.170	.302	.208	.509	51	-3	4	2.33	-2	S-22/3-1	1	-0.4
1914 StL-A	7	23	1	2	0	0	0	1	2	4	1	1	.087	.160	.087	.247	-27	-4	0	.41	0	/S-7	0	-0.4
1915 StL-A	59	150	13	33	5	0	0	6	14	25	6	6	.220	.308	.253	.561	71	-6	12	2.58	3	O-45(0-21-24)/3-2,2-1,P-1,S	2	-0.8
Total 3	89	226	22	44	5	1	0	12	22	40	10	7	.195	.292	.226	.517	56	-13	17	2.28	1	/O-45,S-30,3-3,2-1,P-1	3	-1.6

• WALSH, Jimmy Michael Timothy "Runt" Walsh b: 3/25/1886, Lima, OH d: 1/21/1947, Baltimore, MD BR/TR, 5'9", 174 lbs. Deb: 4/25/1910 Career OF: 29-16-33

YEAR TM-L	G	AB	R	H	2B	3B	HR	RBI	BB	SO	SB	CS	AVG	OBP	SLG	OPS	OPS+	BR/A	RC	RC/G	FR	G/POS	WS	TPW
1910 Phi-N	88	242	28	60	8	3	3	31	25	38	5	....	.248	.323	.343	.666	91	-3	29	3.89	-4	2-26,O-26(7-14-6)/S-9,3-5	7	-0.8
1911 Phi-N	94	289	29	78	20	3	1	31	21	30	5	....	.270	.324	.370	.694	93	-4	36	4.24	-4	O-48(22-2-25),2-14/S-9,3-7,C,1,P	7	-1.1
1912 Phi-N	51	150	16	40	6	3	2	19	8	20	3	....	.267	.304	.387	.690	83	-4	18	4.03	-0	2-31,3-12/C-5	3	-0.4
1913 Phi-N	26	30	3	10	4	0	0	5	1	5	1	....	.333	.355	.467	.822	128	1	5	6.20	-2	/2-6,S-3,3-1,O-1	1	-0.1
1914 Bal-F	120	428	54	132	25	4	10	65	22	56	18	....	.308	.345	.456	.801	128	13	69	5.85	-7	*3-113/2-1,O-1,S-1	19	1.0
1915 Bal-F	106	401	43	121	20	1	9	60	21	44	12	....	.302	.340	.424	.764	116	6	60	5.27	-11	*3-106	11	-0.1
StL-F	17	31	5	6	1	0	0	1	3	4	1	....	.194	.306	.226	.531	54	-2	2	2.35	0	/3-9	0	-0.1
Yr.	123	432	48	127	21	1	9	61	24	48	13	....	.294	.337	.410	.747	111	5	62	5.04	-11	*3-115	11	-0.3
Total 6	502	1571	178	447	84	14	25	212	101	197	45	....	.285	.332	.404	.735	107	7	220	4.83	-26	3-253/2-78,O-76,S-22,C-9,1,P	48	-1.6

• WALSH, Jimmy James Charles Walsh b: 9/22/1885, Kallila, Ireland d: 7/3/1962, Syracuse, NY BL/TR, 5'10.5", 170 lbs. Deb: 8/26/1912 Career OF: 162-169-165

YEAR TM-L	G	AB	R	H	2B	3B	HR	RBI	BB	SO	SB	CS	AVG	OBP	SLG	OPS	OPS+	BR/A	RC	RC/G	FR	G/POS	WS	TPW
1912 Phi-A	31	107	11	27	8	2	0	15	12	....	7	....	.252	.328	.364	.692	102	0	15	4.70	0	O-30(30-0-0)	3	-0.1
1913 Phi-A	97	303	56	77	16	5	0	27	38	40	15	....	.254	.341	.340	.681	102	1	39	4.22	-1	O-90(38-43-12)	11	-0.4
1914 NY-A	43	136	13	26	1	3	1	11	29	21	6	9	.191	.333	.265	.598	80	-5	12	2.57	-1	O-41(37-4-0)	3	-0.8
*Phi-A	68	216	35	51	11	6	3	36	30	27	6	12	.236	.340	.384	.724	123	2	29	3.81	0	O-56(25-26-6)/1-3,3-3,S-1	8	-0.1
Yr.	111	352	48	77	12	9	4	47	59	48	12	21	.219	.337	.338	.675	107	-3	40	3.35	-1	O-97(62-30-6)/1-3,3-3,S-1	11	-0.9
1915 Phi-A	117	417	48	86	15	6	1	20	57	64	22	12	.206	.306	.278	.584	78	-11	40	2.96	5	*O-109(29-44-36)/3-2,1-1	6	-1.3
1916 Phi-A	114	390	42	91	13	6	1	27	54	36	27	14	.233	.330	.305	.635	95	-1	45	3.54	1	*O-113(0-6-107)/1-1	7	-0.7
*Bos-A	14	17	5	3	1	0	0	2	4	2	3	2	.176	.333	.235	.569	71	-1	2	2.59	-1	/O-6(1-3-2),3-2	0	-0.1
Yr.	128	407	47	94	14	6	1	29	58	38	30	16	.231	.330	.302	.632	94	-2	47	3.49	0	*O-119(1-9-109)/3-2,1-1	7	-0.9
1917 Bos-A	57	185	25	49	6	3	0	12	25	14	6	....	.265	.352	.330	.682	109	3	22	4.24	0	O-47(2-43-2)	8	0.0
Total 6	541	1771	235	410	71	31	6	150	249	204	92	49	.232	.330	.317	.647	96	-11	203	3.59	3	O-492/3-7,1-5,S-1	46	-3.6

• WALSH, Joe Joseph Patrick "Tweet" Walsh b: 3/13/1917, Boston, MA d: 10/5/1996, Boston, MA BR/TR, 5'10", 155 lbs. Deb: 7/1/1938

YEAR TM-L	G	AB	R	H	2B	3B	HR	RBI	BB	SO	SB	CS	AVG	OBP	SLG	OPS	OPS+	BR/A	RC	RC/G	FR	G/POS	WS	TPW
1938 Bos-N	4	8	0	0	0	0	0	0	0	2	0	....	.000	.000	.000	.000	-111	-2	0	.00	-1	/S-4	0	-0.3

• WALSH, Joe Joseph Francis Walsh b: 10/14/1886, Minersville, PA d: 1/6/1967, Buffalo, NY BR/TR, 6'2", 170 lbs. Deb: 10/8/1910

YEAR TM-L	G	AB	R	H	2B	3B	HR	RBI	BB	SO	SB	CS	AVG	OBP	SLG	OPS	OPS+	BR/A	RC	RC/G	FR	G/POS	WS	TPW
1910 NY-A	1	4	0	2	1	0	0	2	0	....	0	....	.500	.500	.750	1.250	275	1	1	19.19	0	/C-1	0	0.1
1911 NY-A	4	9	2	2	1	0	0	0	0	....	0	....	.222	.222	.333	.556	51	-1	1	2.31	-1	/C-4	0	-0.2
Total 2	5	13	2	4	2	0	0	2	0	....	0	....	.308	.308	.462	.769	120	0	2	6.06	-1	/C-5	0	-0.1

• WALSH, Joe Joseph R. "Reddy" Walsh b: 11/5/1864, Chicago, IL d: 8/8/1911, Omaha, NE BL/TR Deb: 9/3/1891

YEAR TM-L	G	AB	R	H	2B	3B	HR	RBI	BB	SO	SB	CS	AVG	OBP	SLG	OPS	OPS+	BR/A	RC	RC/G	FR	G/POS	WS	TPW
1891 Bal-a	26	100	14	21	0	1	1	10	6	18	4	....	.210	.255	.260	.515	47	-7	8	2.63	2	2-13,S-13	1	-0.4

• WALSH, John John Gabriel Walsh b: 3/25/1879, Wilkes-Barre, PA d: 4/25/1947, Jamaica, NY BR/TR, 5'8.5", 162 lbs. Deb: 6/22/1903

YEAR TM-L	G	AB	R	H	2B	3B	HR	RBI	BB	SO	SB	CS	AVG	OBP	SLG	OPS	OPS+	BR/A	RC	RC/G	FR	G/POS	WS	TPW
1903 Phi-N	1	3	0	0	0	0	0	0	0	....	0	....	.000	.000	.000	.000	-103	-1	0	.00	0	/3-1	0	0.0

• WALSH, Tom Thomas Joseph Walsh b: 2/28/1885, Davenport, IA d: 3/16/1963, Naples, FL BR/TR, 5'11", 170 lbs. Deb: 8/15/1906

YEAR TM-L	G	AB	R	H	2B	3B	HR	RBI	BB	SO	SB	CS	AVG	OBP	SLG	OPS	OPS+	BR/A	RC	RC/G	FR	G/POS	WS	TPW
1906 Chi-N	2	1	0	0	0	0	0	0	0	....	0	....	.000	.000	.000	.000	-95	-0	0	.00	-1	/C-2	0	-0.1

• WALSH, Walt Walter William Walsh b: 4/30/1897, Newark, NJ d: 1/15/1966, Avon-by-the-Sea, NJ BR/TR, 5'11", 170 lbs. Deb: 5/4/1920

YEAR TM-L	G	AB	R	H	2B	3B	HR	RBI	BB	SO	SB	CS	AVG	OBP	SLG	OPS	OPS+	BR/A	RC	RC/G	FR	G/POS	WS	TPW
1920 Phi-N	2	0	0	0	0	0	0	0	0	0	0	0	....	....	....	....	-96	0	0	....	0	....	0	0.0

• WALTERS, Bucky William Henry Walters b: 4/19/1909, Philadelphia, PA d: 4/20/1991, Abington, PA BR/TR, 6'1", 180 lbs. Deb: 9/18/1931 M/C/U Career OF: 6-0-0 ♦

YEAR TM-L	G	AB	R	H	2B	3B	HR	RBI	BB	SO	SB	CS	AVG	OBP	SLG	OPS	OPS+	BR/A	RC	RC/G	FR	G/POS	WS	TPW
1931 Bos-N	9	38	2	8	2	0	0	0	0	3	0	....	.211	.211	.263	.474	28	-4	2	1.78	1	/3-6,2-3	0	-0.3
1932 Bos-N	22	75	8	14	3	1	0	4	2	18	0	....	.187	.208	.253	.461	24	-8	4	1.64	0	3-22	1	-0.7
1933 Bos-A	52	195	27	50	8	3	4	28	19	24	1	1	.256	.326	.390	.715	90	-3	26	4.35	1	3-43/2-7	4	0.0
1934 Bos-A	23	88	10	19	4	4	4	18	3	12	0	0	.216	.242	.489	.730	79	-4	10	3.90	4	3-23	2	0.0
Phi-N	83	300	36	78	20	3	4	38	19	54	1	....	.260	.308	.387	.695	75	-11	34	3.91	-6	3-80/2-3,P-2	5	-1.2
1935 Phi-N	49	96	14	24	2	1	0	6	9	12	0	....	.250	.314	.292	.606	58	2	9	3.30	2	P-24/O-5(5-0-0),2-2,3-1	11	1.0
1936 Phi-N	64	121	12	29	10	1	1	16	7	15	0	....	.240	.281	.364	.645	66	5	12	3.36	8	P-40/2-1,3-1	14	2.1
1937 Phi-N★	56	137	15	38	6	0	1	16	5	16	1	....	.277	.303	.343	.646	69	5	14	3.64	4	P-37/3-8	14	-0.2
1938 Phi-N	15	35	6	10	2	0	1	3	1	5	1	....	.286	.306	.429	.734	100	3	4	4.51	0	P-12	3	-0.6
Cin-N	36	64	10	9	1	0	0	5	7	18	0	....	.141	.236	.156	.392	10	-0	3	1.35	2	P-27	9	-0.4
Yr.	51	99	16	19	3	0	1	8	8	23	1	....	.192	.259	.253	.512	39	3	7	2.33	3	P-39	12	-0.9
1939*Cin-N★	40	120	16	39	8	1	1	16	5	12	1	....	.325	.357	.433	.790	111	13	18	5.66	5	P-39	38	5.9
1940*Cin-N★	37	117	11	24	3	0	1	18	4	14	2	....	.205	.231	.256	.488	34	2	7	1.96	-0	P-36	32	3.6
1941 Cin-N★	39	106	6	20	6	0	0	9	7	13	0	....	.189	.239	.245	.484	36	2	6	1.78	2	P-37	27	2.9
1942 Cin-N★	40	99	13	24	6	1	2	13	3	13	0	....	.242	.265	.384	.649	89	7	10	3.27	2	P-34/O-1	20	2.5
1943 Cin-N	37	90	11	24	7	1	1	12	6	15	1	....	.267	.313	.400	.713	107	8	12	4.32	1	P-34	15	-0.5
1944 Cin-N★	37	107	9	30	4	0	0	13	8	18	0	....	.280	.330	.318	.648	86	8	12	4.03	1	P-34	32	3.7
1945 Cin-N	24	61	11	14	3	0	3	8	3	14	2	....	.230	.266	.426	.692	93	5	6	3.29	0	P-22	16	2.6
1946 Cin-N	24	55	6	7	2	0	0	5	4	12	2	....	.127	.186	.164	.350		-1	2	.98	2	P-22	11	0.8
1947 Cin-N	20	45	3	12	2	0	0	4	2	13	0	....	.267	.298	.311	.609	62	3	4	3.43	-1	P-20	3	-1.8
1948 Cin-N	7	15	1	4	0	0	0	2	0	2	0	....	.267	.267	.267	.533	46	1	1	1.80	1	/P-7	1	-0.2
1950 Bos-N	1	2	0	0	0	0	0	0	0	0	0	....	.000	.000	.000	.000	-107	-0	0	.00	0	/P-1	0	-0.1
Total 19	715	1966	227	477	99	16	23	234	114	303	12	1	.243	.286	.344	.630	68	31	198	3.35	28	P-428,3-184/2-16,O-6	258	19.3

• WALTERS, Dan Daniel Gene Walters b: 8/15/1966, Brunswick, ME BR/TR, 6'4", 225 lbs. Deb: 6/1/1992

YEAR TM-L	G	AB	R	H	2B	3B	HR	RBI	BB	SO	SB	CS	AVG	OBP	SLG	OPS	OPS+	BR/A	RC	RC/G	FR	G/POS	WS	TPW
1992 SD-N	57	179	14	45	11	1	4	22	10	28	1	0	.251	.298	.391	.689	92	-2	21	4.04	0	C-55	4	0.1
1993 SD-N	27	94	6	19	3	0	1	10	7	13	0	0	.202	.257	.266	.523	40	-8	6	2.18	1	C-26	1	-0.6
Total 2	84	273	20	64	14	1	5	32	17	41	1	0	.234	.284	.348	.632	74	-10	27	3.37	1	/C-81	5	-0.4

• WALTERS, Fred Fred James "Whale" Walters b: 9/4/1912, Laurel, MS d: 2/1/1980, Laurel, MS BR/TR, 6'1", 210 lbs. Deb: 4/17/1945

YEAR TM-L	G	AB	R	H	2B	3B	HR	RBI	BB	SO	SB	CS	AVG	OBP	SLG	OPS	OPS+	BR/A	RC	RC/G	FR	G/POS	WS	TPW
1945 Bos-A	40	93	2	16	2	0	0	5	10	9	1	1	.172	.252	.194	.446	29	-8	4	1.45	3	C-38	2	-0.4

• WALTERS, Ken Kenneth Rogers Walters b: 11/11/1933, Fresno, CA BR/TR, 6'1", 180 lbs. Deb: 4/12/1960 Career OF: 16-6-179

YEAR TM-L	G	AB	R	H	2B	3B	HR	RBI	BB	SO	SB	CS	AVG	OBP	SLG	OPS	OPS+	BR/A	RC	RC/G	FR	G/POS	WS	TPW
1960 Phi-N	124	426	42	102	10	0	8	37	16	50	4	3	.239	.269	.319	.588	60	-25	34	2.65	9	*O-119(5-2-116)	3	-2.0
1961 Phi-N	86	180	23	41	8	2	2	14	5	25	2	2	.228	.253	.328	.580	53	-13	13	2.34	0	O-56(0-4-53)/1-5,3-1	1	-1.5
1963 Cin-N	49	75	6	14	2	0	1	7	4	14	0	2	.187	.238	.253	.491	40	-7	4	1.83	-2	O-21(11-0-10)/1-1	0	-1.0
Total 3	259	681	71	157	20	2	11	58	25	89	6	7	.231	.261	.314	.575	56	-44	51	2.47	8	O-196/1-6,3-1	4	-4.5

YEAR TM-L	G	AB	R	H	2B	3B	HR	RBI	BB	SO	SB	CS	AVG	OBP	SLG	OPS	OPS+	BR/A	RC	RC/G	FR	G/POS	WS	TPW
• WALTERS, Roxy	Alfred John Walters b: 11/5/1892, San Francisco, CA d: 6/3/1956, Alameda, CA BR/TR, 5'8.5", 160 lbs. Deb: 9/16/1915																							
1915 NY-A	2	3	0	1	0	0	0	0	0	0	0	....	.333	.333	.333	.667	100	-0	0	4.42	0	/C-2	0	0.1
1916 NY-A	66	203	13	54	9	3	0	23	14	42	2	....	.266	.320	.340	.660	96	-2	24	3.96	8	C-65	8	1.3
1917 NY-A	61	171	16	45	2	0	0	14	9	22	2	....	.263	.304	.275	.579	76	-5	15	2.92	1	C-57	5	0.0
1918 NY-A	64	191	18	38	5	1	0	12	9	18	3	....	.199	.239	.236	.474	42	-14	11	1.78	-3	C-50/O-9(0-0-9)	2	-1.5
1919 Bos-A	48	135	7	26	2	0	0	9	7	15	1	....	.193	.259	.207	.466	33	-12	8	1.79	1	C-47	2	-0.7
1920 Bos-A	88	258	25	51	11	1	0	28	30	21	2	2	.198	.303	.248	.551	49	-17	22	2.67	6	C-85/1-2	5	-0.4
1921 Bos-A	54	169	17	34	4	1	0	14	10	11	3	0	.201	.254	.237	.491	26	-18	11	2.12	7	C-54	4	-0.7
1922 Bos-A	38	98	4	19	2	0	0	6	6	8	0	0	.194	.240	.214	.455	19	-11	6	1.74	1	C-36	2	-0.8
1923 Bos-A	40	104	9	26	4	0	0	5	2	6	0	2	.250	.264	.288	.553	45	-9	8	2.24	2	C-36/2-1	2	-0.5
1924 Cle-A	32	74	10	19	2	0	0	5	10	6	0	1	.257	.345	.284	.629	63	-4	8	3.49	1	C-25/2-7	2	-0.2
1925 Cle-A	5	20	0	4	0	0	0	0	0	2	0	0	.200	.200	.200	.400	2	-3	1	1.27	1	/C-5	0	-0.2
Total 11	498	1426	119	317	41	6	0	116	97	151	13	5	.222	.281	.259	.541	52	-95	113	2.52	25	C-462/O-9,2-8,1-2	32	-3.5
• WALTON, Danny	Daniel James "Mickey" Walton b: 7/14/1947, Los Angeles, CA BR/TR, 6', 200 lbs. Deb: 4/20/1968 Career OF: 172-1-6																							
1968 Hou-N	2	2	0	0	0	0	0	0	0	1	0	0	.000	.000	.000	.000	-102	-0	0	.00	0	....	0	-0.1
1969 Sea-A	23	92	12	20	1	2	3	10	5	26	2	0	.217	.280	.370	.650	82	-2	9	2.94	-2	O-23(23-0-0)	1	-0.5
1970 Mil-A	117	397	32	102	20	1	17	66	51	126	2	3	.257	.350	.441	.791	116	8	63	5.55	-5	*O-114(114-0-0)	13	-0.2
1971 Mil-A	30	69	5	14	3	0	2	9	7	22	0	0	.203	.286	.333	.619	76	-2	6	2.88	-2	O-19(19-1-0)/3-1	1	-0.5
NY-A	5	14	1	2	0	0	1	2	0	7	0	0	.143	.143	.357	.500	40	-1	1	1.61	0	/O-4(1-0-3)	0	-0.1
Yr.	35	83	6	16	3	0	3	11	7	29	0	0	.193	.264	.337	.601	70	-3	7	2.66	-2	O-23(20-1-3)/3-1	1	-0.6
1973 Min-A	37	96	13	17	1	1	4	8	17	28	0	0	.177	.301	.333	.634	75	-3	10	3.29	-0	O-18(15-0-3),D-11/3-1	1	-0.4
1975 Min-A	42	63	4	11	2	0	1	8	4	18	0	0	.175	.224	.254	.478	34	-6	3	1.45	-1	/1-7,D-6,C-2	0	-0.7
1976 LA-N	18	15	0	2	0	0	0	2	1	2	0	0	.133	.188	.133	.321	-8	-2	0	.95	0	....	0	-0.2
1977 Hou-N	13	21	0	4	0	0	0	1	0	5	0	0	.190	.190	.190	.381	3	-3	1	1.21	-1	/1-5	0	-0.4
1980 Tex-A	10	10	2	2	0	0	0	1	3	5	0	0	.200	.385	.200	.585	67	-0	1	3.61	0	/D-1	0	0.0
Total 9	297	779	69	174	27	4	28	107	88	240	4	3	.223	.310	.376	.686	90	-11	94	3.99	-9	O-178/D-18,1-12,3-2,C-2	16	-3.1
• WALTON, Jerome	Jerome O'Terrell Walton b: 7/8/1965, Newnan, GA BR/TR, 6'1", 175 lbs. Deb: 4/4/1989 Career OF: 111-373-36																							
1989*Chi-N	116	475	64	139	23	3	5	46	27	77	24	7	.293	.339	.385	.724	99	1	64	4.86	-4	*O-115(0-115-0)	17	-0.5
1990 Chi-N	101	392	63	103	16	2	2	21	50	70	14	7	.263	.352	.329	.681	82	-8	49	4.39	-6	O-98(0-99-0)	9	-1.6
1991 Chi-N	123	270	42	59	13	1	5	17	19	55	7	3	.219	.277	.330	.607	67	-12	24	2.88	-6	*O-101(0-100-1)	2	-2.1
1992 Chi-N	30	55	7	7	0	1	0	1	9	13	1	2	.127	.273	.164	.436	26	-6	3	1.52	-1	O-24(22-1-1)	0	-0.8
1993 Cal-A	5	2	2	0	0	0	0	0	1	2	1	0	.000	.333	.000	.333	-2	-0	0	3.51	-0	/D-4,O-1	0	0.0
1994 Cin-N	46	68	10	21	4	0	1	9	4	12	1	3	.309	.347	.412	.759	98	-1	8	4.20	-1	O-26(16-5-6)/1-7	1	-0.3
1995*Cin-N	102	162	32	47	12	1	8	22	17	25	10	7	.290	.372	.525	.896	134	7	32	6.78	0	O-89(36-50-8)/1-3	7	0.5
1996 Atl-N	37	47	9	16	5	0	1	4	5	10	0	0	.340	.404	.511	.914	132	2	10	7.53	0	O-28(23-1-5)	2	0.1
1997*Bal-A	26	68	8	20	1	0	3	9	4	10	0	0	.294	.333	.441	.775	103	0	9	4.64	0	O-19(9-2-11)/1-5,D-2	2	-0.1
1998 TB-A	12	34	4	11	3	0	0	3	2	6	0	0	.324	.361	.412	.773	99	-0	5	5.45	2	/O-8(4-0-4),D-3	0	0.1
Total 10	598	1573	241	423	77	8	25	132	138	280	58	29	.269	.335	.376	.711	91	-17	205	4.48	-18	O-509/1-15,D-9	40	-4.6
• WALTON, Reggie	Reginald Sherard Walton b: 10/24/1952, Kansas City, MO BR/TR, 6'3", 205 lbs. Deb: 6/13/1980 Career OF: 11-0-12																							
1980 Sea-A	31	83	8	23	6	0	2	9	3	10	2	2	.277	.310	.422	.732	98	-1	10	4.33	-1	O-17(6-0-11),D-11	2	-0.3
1981 Sea-A	12	6	1	0	0	0	0	0	1	2	0	0	.000	.143	.000	.143	-54	-1	0	.17	-1	/O-4(3-0-1),D-1	0	-0.2
1982 Pit-N	13	15	1	3	1	0	0	0	1	1	0	0	.200	.294	.267	.561	56	-1	1	2.99	0	/O-2(2-0-0)	0	-0.1
Total 3	56	104	10	26	7	0	2	9	5	13	2	2	.250	.297	.375	.672	82	-3	12	3.83	-2	/O-23,D-12	2	-0.7
• WAMBSGANSS, Bill	William Adolph Wambsganss b: 3/19/1894, Cleveland, OH d: 12/8/1985, Lakewood, OH BR/TR, 5'11", 175 lbs. Deb: 8/4/1914																							
1914 Cle-A	43	143	12	31	6	2	0	12	8	24	2	7	.217	.277	.287	.564	67	-9	10	2.25	-6	S-36/2-4	1	-1.3
1915 Cle-A	121	375	30	73	4	4	0	21	36	50	8	9	.195	.272	.227	.499	48	-26	24	2.01	-13	2-78,3-35	2	-3.9
1916 Cle-A	136	475	57	117	14	4	0	45	41	40	13	....	.246	.313	.293	.605	77	-13	52	3.48	-17	*S-106,2-24/3-5	10	-2.4
1917 Cle-A	141	499	52	127	17	6	0	43	37	42	16	....	.255	.315	.313	.628	85	-9	54	3.54	10	*2-137/1-3	13	0.3
1918 Cle-A	87	315	34	93	15	2	0	40	21	21	16	....	.295	.345	.356	.701	102	0	44	4.65	-8	2-87	10	-0.6
1919 Cle-A	139	526	60	146	17	6	2	60	32	24	18	....	.278	.323	.344	.667	82	-13	63	4.06	11	*2-139	14	0.0
1920*Cle-A	153	565	83	138	16	11	1	55	54	26	9	18	.244	.316	.317	.633	66	-31	57	3.10	13	*2-153	9	-1.5
1921 Cle-A	107	410	80	117	28	5	2	47	44	27	13	7	.285	.359	.393	.752	90	-5	61	4.70	-7	*2-103/3-2	10	-0.9
1922 Cle-A	142	538	89	141	22	6	0	47	60	26	17	10	.262	.341	.325	.666	74	-19	64	3.80	-10	*2-125,S-16	10	-2.3
1923 Cle-A	101	345	59	100	20	4	1	59	43	15	10	9	.290	.373	.380	.753	99	-0	51	4.80	-1	2-88/3-4,S-2	10	0.1
1924 Bos-A	156	636	93	174	41	5	0	49	54	33	14	8	.274	.334	.354	.688	77	-21	78	4.09	8	*2-156	11	-0.8
1925 Bos-A	111	360	50	83	12	4	1	41	52	21	3	5	.231	.329	.294	.624	59	-22	38	3.36	-2	*2-103/1-6	4	-2.0
1926 Phi-A	54	54	11	19	3	0	0	1	8	8	1	1	.352	.444	.407	.852	117	2	10	7.04	-2	S-17/2-8	2	0.1
Total 13	1491	5241	710	1359	215	59	7	520	490	357	140	74	.259	.328	.327	.655	78	-166	608	3.73	-24	*2-1205,S-177/3-46,1-9	106	-15.2
• WANER, Lloyd	Lloyd James "Little Poison" Waner b: 3/16/1906, Harrah, OK d: 7/22/1982, Oklahoma City, OK BL/TR, 5'9", 150 lbs. Deb: 4/12/1927 HOF: 1967 Career OF: 124-1663-33																							
1927*Pit-N	150	629	**133**	223	17	6	2	27	37	23	14	....	.355	.396	.410	.806	108	9	99	6.19	-10	*O-150(42-109-0)/2-1	25	-0.8
1928 Pit-N	152	659	121	221	22	14	5	61	40	13	8	....	.335	.377	.434	.811	107	7	104	5.97	-4	*O-152(10-143-0)	26	-0.4
1929 Pit-N	151	662	134	234	28	**20**	5	74	37	20	6	....	.353	.395	.479	.874	113	13	121	7.05	5	*O-151(0-151-0)	27	1.1
1930 Pit-N	68	260	32	94	8	3	1	36	5	5	3	....	.362	.376	.427	.803	93	-3	39	5.90	1	O-65(0-65-0)	8	-0.3
1931 Pit-N	154	681	90	**214**	25	13	4	57	39	16	7	....	.314	.352	.407	.759	105	4	99	5.44	7	*O-153(0-153-0)/2-1	24	0.7
1932 Pit-N	134	565	90	188	27	11	2	38	31	11	6	....	.333	.367	.430	.798	116	12	90	6.15	0	*O-131(0-131-0)	23	0.9
1933 Pit-N	121	500	59	138	14	5	0	26	22	8	3	....	.276	.307	.324	.631	80	-13	52	3.76	-2	*O-114(65-49-0)	10	-2.1
1934 Pit-N	140	611	95	173	27	6	1	48	38	12	6	....	.283	.326	.352	.678	80	-17	73	4.47	-2	*O-139(0-139-0)	14	-2.2
1935 Pit-N	122	537	83	166	22	14	0	46	22	10	1	....	.309	.336	.402	.739	94	-5	73	5.18	1	*O-121(0-121-0)	16	-0.7
1936 Pit-N	106	414	67	133	13	8	1	31	31	5	1	....	.321	.369	.399	.767	104	3	62	5.79	-7	O-92(0-92-0)	14	-0.6
1937 Pit-N	129	537	80	177	23	4	1	45	34	12	3	....	.330	.370	.393	.762	107	6	81	5.78	-1	*O-123(0-123-0)	19	0.2
1938 Pit-N★	147	619	79	194	25	7	5	57	28	11	5	....	.313	.343	.401	.744	103	1	85	5.14	4	*O-144(0-144-0)	19	0.1
1939 Pit-N	112	379	49	108	15	3	0	24	17	13	0	....	.285	.321	.340	.661	79	-12	42	3.95	5	O-92(0-92-0)/3-1	7	-0.8
1940 Pit-N	72	166	30	43	3	0	0	3	5	5	2	....	.259	.285	.277	.562	56	-10	13	2.89	0	O-42(1-41-0)	2	-1.1
1941 Pit-N	3	4	2	1	0	0	0	1	2	0	0	....	.250	.500	.250	.750	116	0	1	6.84	0	/O-1	0	0.1
Bos-N	19	51	7	21	1	0	0	4	2	0	1	....	.412	.434	.431	.865	151	3	10	8.80	0	O-15(3-11-1)	3	0.3
Cin-N	55	164	17	42	4	1	0	6	8	0	0	....	.256	.291	.293	.583	64	-8	14	2.93	0	O-44(0-13-31)	3	-1.0
Yr.	77	219	26	64	5	1	0	11	12	0	1	....	.292	.329	.324	.653	85	-4	24	4.09	0	O-60(3-25-32)	6	-0.6
1942 Phi-N	101	287	23	75	7	3	0	10	16	6	1	....	.261	.300	.307	.607	82	-7	27	3.35	-3	O-75(0-75-0)	4	-1.3
1944 Bro-N	15	14	3	4	0	0	0	1	3	0	0	....	.286	.412	.286	.697	101	0	2	4.14	0	/O-4(0-4-0)	0	0.0
Pit-N	19	14	2	5	0	0	0	2	2	0	0	....	.357	.438	.357	.795	120	1	2	7.25	0	/O-7(1-6-0)	1	0.0
Yr.	34	28	5	9	0	0	0	3	5	0	0	....	.321	.424	.321	.746	110	1	4	5.54	-1	O-11(1-10-0)	1	0.0
1945 Pit-N	23	19	5	5	0	0	0	1	1	3	0	....	.263	.300	.263	.563	55	-1	2	3.04	1	/O-3(2-0-1)	0	-0.1
Total 18	1993	7772	1201	2459	281	118	27	598	420	173	67	....	.316	.353	.393	.747	98	-18	1092	5.28	-5	*O-1818/2-2,3-1	245	-8.1
• WANER, Paul	Paul Glee "Big Poison" Waner b: 4/16/1903, Harrah, OK d: 8/29/1965, Sarasota, FL BL/TL, 5'8.5", 153 lbs. Deb: 4/13/1926 C HOF: 1952 Career OF: 18-18-2256																							
1926 Pit-N	144	536	101	180	35	**22**	8	79	66	19	11	....	.336	**.413**	.528	.941	144	34	115	**8.15**	1	*O-139(6-0-133)	**28**	2.4
1927*Pit-N	155	623	114	**237**	42	**18**	9	**131**	60	14	5	....	**.380**	.437	.549	.986	152	47	145	9.23	0	*O-143(0-0-143),1-14	36	3.4
1928 Pit-N	152	602	**142**	223	**50**	19	6	86	77	16	6	....	.370	.446	.547	.992	152	49	145	9.62	0	*O-131(0-0-131),1-24	**34**	3.6
1929 Pit-N	151	596	131	200	43	15	15	100	89	24	15	....	.336	.424	.534	.958	132	33	135	8.52	-1	*O-143(0-0-143)/1-7	30	1.8
1930 Pit-N	145	589	117	217	32	18	8	77	57	18	18	....	.368	.428	.525	.952	128	29	129	8.67	-7	*O-143(0-5-138)	26	0.9
1931 Pit-N	150	559	88	180	35	10	6	70	73	21	6	....	.322	.404	.453	.857	131	28	108	7.19	10	*O-138(0-0-138),1-10	26	2.8
1932 Pit-N	154	630	107	215	**62**	10	8	82	56	24	13	....	.341	.397	.510	.906	144	40	130	7.96	-8	*O-154(0-9-145)	32	2.2
1933 Pit-N★	154	618	101	191	38	16	7	70	60	20	3	....	.309	.372	.456	.828	136	29	109	6.55	-3	*O-154(0-0-154)	28	1.8

YEAR TM-L	G	AB	R	H	2B	3B	HR	RBI	BB	SO	SB	CS	AVG	OBP	SLG	OPS	OPS+	BR/A	RC	RC/G	FR	G/POS	WS	TPW
1934 Pit-N★	146	599	**122**	**217**	32	16	14	90	68	24	8	....	**.362**	.429	.539	.968	154	48	142	9.47	-2	*0-145(0-0-145)	30	3.6
1935 Pit-N★	139	549	98	176	29	12	11	78	61	22	2	....	.321	.392	.477	.869	128	23	105	7.11	-2	*0-136(0-0-136)	22	1.3
1936 Pit-N	148	585	107	218	53	9	5	94	74	29	7	....	**.373**	.446	.520	.965	155	49	140	9.81	4	*0-145(0-0-145)	32	4.3
1937 Pit-N★	154	619	94	219	30	9	2	74	63	34	4	....	.354	.413	.441	.855	132	30	118	7.60	0	*0-150(0-0-150)/1-3	28	2.0
1938 Pit-N	148	625	77	175	31	6	6	69	47	28	2	....	.280	.331	.378	.709	94	-6	79	4.48	-1	*0-147(0-1-148)	15	-1.6
1939 Pit-N	125	461	62	151	30	6	3	45	35	18	0	....	.328	.375	.438	.813	120	12	74	6.05	0	*0-106(0-0-106)	14	0.6
1940 Pit-N	89	238	32	69	16	1	1	32	23	14	0	....	.290	.352	.378	.731	102	1	32	5.05	1	0-45(0-0-45)/1-8	7	0.0
1941 Bro-N	11	35	5	6	0	0	0	4	8	0	0	....	.171	.326	.171	.497	41	-2	2	1.98	-1	/0-9(0-0-9)	0	-0.3
Bos-N	95	294	40	82	10	2	2	46	47	14	1	....	.279	.378	.347	.725	110	6	41	4.97	2	0-77(10-3-66)/1-7	9	0.4
Yr.	106	329	45	88	10	2	2	50	55	14	1	....	.267	.372	.328	.701	102	4	43	4.59	1	0-86(10-3-75)/1-7	9	0.1
1942 Bos-N	114	333	43	86	17	1	1	39	62	20	2	....	.258	.376	.324	.701	108	7	45	4.66	-5	0-94(0-0-94)	11	-0.4
1943 Bro-N	82	225	29	70	16	0	1	26	35	9	0	....	.311	.406	.396	.802	132	11	37	5.86	-3	0-57(1-0-56)	10	0.5
1944 Bro-N	83	136	16	39	4	1	0	16	27	7	0	....	.287	.405	.331	.736	111	4	20	5.40	-1	0-32(1-0-31)	5	0.1
NY-A	9	7	1	1	0	0	0	1	2	1	1	0	.143	.333	.143	.476	37	-0	1	3.10	0	....	0	0.0
1945 NY-A	1	0	0	0	0	0	0	0	1	0	0	0	....	1.000	....	1.000	191	0	0	∞	0	....	0	0.0
Total 20	2549	9459	1627	3152	605	191	113	1309	1091	376	104	0	.333	.404	.473	.878	133	473	1853	7.43	-15	*0-2288/1-73	423	29.5

• WANNER, Jack

Clarence Curtis "Johnny" Wanner b: 11/29/1885, Geneseo, IL d: 5/28/1919, Geneseo, IL BR/TR, 5'11.5", 190 lbs. Deb: 9/28/1909

YEAR TM-L	G	AB	R	H	2B	3B	HR	RBI	BB	SO	SB	CS	AVG	OBP	SLG	OPS	OPS+	BR/A	RC	RC/G	FR	G/POS	WS	TPW
1909 NY-A	3	8	0	1	0	0	0	0	2	....	1	....	.125	.300	.125	.425	35	-0	1	2.16	-1	/S-2	0	-0.2

• WANNINGER, Pee-Wee

Paul Louis Wanninger b: 12/12/1902, Birmingham, AL d: 3/7/1981, North Augusta, SC BL/TR, 5'7", 150 lbs. Deb: 4/22/1925

YEAR TM-L	G	AB	R	H	2B	3B	HR	RBI	BB	SO	SB	CS	AVG	OBP	SLG	OPS	OPS+	BR/A	RC	RC/G	FR	G/POS	WS	TPW
1925 NY-A	117	403	35	95	13	6	1	22	11	34	3	5	.236	.256	.305	.561	43	-37	30	2.47	-2	*S-111/3-3,2-1	5	-2.6
1927 Bos-A	18	60	4	12	0	0	0	1	6	2	2	4	.200	.284	.200	.484	28	-7	3	1.63	-1	S-15	1	-0.7
Cin-N	28	93	14	23	2	2	0	8	6	7	0	....	.247	.293	.312	.605	64	-5	9	2.95	3	S-28	2	0.1
Total 2	163	556	53	130	15	8	1	31	23	43	5	9	.234	.266	.295	.560	45	-50	42	2.46	0	S-154/3-3,2-1	8	-3.1

• WARD, Aaron

Aaron Lee Ward b: 8/28/1896, Bonneville, AR d: 1/30/1961, New Orleans, LA BR/TR, 5'10.5", 160 lbs. Deb: 8/14/1917

YEAR TM-L	G	AB	R	H	2B	3B	HR	RBI	BB	SO	SB	CS	AVG	OBP	SLG	OPS	OPS+	BR/A	RC	RC/G	FR	G/POS	WS	TPW
1917 NY-A	8	26	0	3	0	0	0	1	1	5	0	....	.115	.148	.115	.264	-19	-4	0	.44	-4	/S-7	0	-0.8
1918 NY-A	20	32	2	4	1	0	0	1	2	7	1	....	.125	.176	.156	.333		-4	1	.96	0	S-12/0-4(0-4-0),2-3	1	-0.5
1919 NY-A	27	34	5	7	2	0	0	2	5	6	0	....	.206	.308	.265	.572	61	-2	3	2.59	0	/1-5,3-3,S-2,2-1	1	-0.1
1920 NY-A	127	496	62	127	18	7	11	54	33	84	7	5	.256	.304	.387	.691	79	-16	58	3.95	19	*3-114,S-12	16	0.7
1921★NY-A	153	556	77	170	30	10	5	75	42	68	6	8	.306	.363	.423	.786	98	-3	85	5.34	15	*2-124,3-33	20	1.6
1922★NY-A	154	558	69	149	19	5	7	68	45	64	6	4	.267	.328	.357	.685	77	-19	68	4.05	10	*2-152/3-2	14	-0.4
1923★NY-A	152	567	79	161	26	11	10	82	56	65	8	8	.284	.351	.422	.773	101	-1	84	5.23	26	*2-152	22	2.8
1924 NY-A	120	400	42	101	13	10	8	66	40	45	1	4	.253	.324	.395	.719	85	-11	52	4.23	12	*2-120/S-1	12	0.3
1925 NY-A	125	439	41	108	22	3	4	38	49	49	1	4	.246	.326	.337	.663	70	-21	50	3.84	-9	*2-113,3-10	8	-2.4
1926 NY-A	22	31	5	10	2	0	0	3	2	6	0	0	.323	.364	.387	.751	97	-0	4	5.32	-1	/2-4,3-1	1	-0.1
1927 Chi-A	145	463	75	125	25	8	5	56	63	56	6	5	.270	.360	.391	.751	97	-1	69	4.96	-13	*2-139/3-6	12	-0.9
1928 Cle-A	6	9	0	1	0	0	0	0	1	2	0	0	.111	.200	.111	.311	-16	-2	0	.91	-1	/3-3,S-2,2-1	0	-0.2
Total 12	1059	3611	457	966	158	54	50	446	339	457	36	38	.268	.335	.383	.717	85	-82	475	4.44	52	2-809,3-172/S-36,1-5,0-4	107	0.0

• WARD, Chris

Chris Gilbert Ward b: 5/18/1949, Oakland, CA BL/TL, 6', 180 lbs. Deb: 9/10/1972

YEAR TM-L	G	AB	R	H	2B	3B	HR	RBI	BB	SO	SB	CS	AVG	OBP	SLG	OPS	OPS+	BR/A	RC	RC/G	FR	G/POS	WS	TPW
1972 Chi-N	1	1	0	0	0	0	0	0	0	0	0	0	.000	.000	.000	.000	-90	-0	0	.00	0	....	0	0.0
1974 Chi-N	92	137	8	28	4	0	1	15	18	13	0	2	.204	.297	.255	.552	53	-9	10	2.42	0	0-22(21-0-1)/1-6	0	-1.1
Total 2	93	138	8	28	4	0	1	15	18	13	0	2	.203	.295	.254	.548	52	-9	10	2.40	0	/0-22,1-6	0	-1.1

• WARD, Chuck

Charles William Ward b: 7/30/1894, St. Louis, MO d: 4/4/1969, Indian Rocks, FL BR/TR, 5'11.5", 170 lbs. Deb: 4/11/1917

YEAR TM-L	G	AB	R	H	2B	3B	HR	RBI	BB	SO	SB	CS	AVG	OBP	SLG	OPS	OPS+	BR/A	RC	RC/G	FR	G/POS	WS	TPW
1917 Pit-N	125	423	25	100	12	3	0	43	32	43	5	....	.236	.302	.279	.581	76	-11	38	2.87	-18	*S-112/2-8,3-5	7	-2.3
1918 Bro-N	2	6	0	2	0	0	0	3	0	0	0	....	.333	.333	.333	.667	104	-0	1	3.98	0	/3-2	0	0.0
1919 Bro-N	45	150	7	35	1	2	0	8	7	11	0	....	.233	.277	.267	.543	62	-7	11	2.42	-7	3-45	2	-1.4
1920 Bro-N	19	71	7	11	1	0	0	4	3	3	1	0	.155	.200	.169	.369	6	-8	3	1.19	-4	S-19	1	-1.2
1921 Bro-N	12	28	1	2	1	0	0	0	4	2	0	0	.071	.188	.107	.295	-19	-5	1	.81	0	S-12	0	-0.4
1922 Bro-N	33	91	12	25	5	1	0	14	5	8	1	1	.275	.320	.352	.671	74	-4	10	3.77	-9	S-31/3-2	2	-0.9
Total 6	236	769	52	175	20	6	0	72	51	67	7	1	.228	.286	.269	.555	63	-34	64	2.63	-38	S-174/3-54,2-8	12	-6.1

• WARD, Daryle

Daryle Lamar Ward b: 6/27/1975, Lynwood, CA BL/TL, 6'2", 230 lbs. Deb: 5/14/1998 Career OF: 234-0-19

YEAR TM-L	G	AB	R	H	2B	3B	HR	RBI	BB	SO	SB	CS	AVG	OBP	SLG	OPS	OPS+	BR/A	RC	RC/G	FR	G/POS	WS	TPW
1998 Hou-N	4	3	1	1	0	0	0	0	1	2	0	0	.333	.500	.333	.833	128	0	1	8.51	0	....	0	0.0
1999★Hou-N	64	150	11	41	6	0	8	30	9	31	0	0	.273	.314	.473	.788	97	-2	22	5.14	0	0-31(31-0-0),1-10/D-3	3	-0.3
2000 Hou-N	119	264	36	68	10	2	20	47	15	61	0	0	.258	.297	.538	.835	100	-2	40	5.31	-4	0-47(43-0-4),1-19/D-4	3	-0.8
2001★Hou-N	95	213	21	56	15	0	9	39	19	48	0	0	.263	.326	.460	.786	95	-2	32	5.34	-2	0-42(27-0-15)/1-9,D-3	5	-0.6
2002 Hou-N	136	453	41	125	31	0	12	72	33	82	1	3	.276	.326	.424	.750	92	-8	61	4.75	-4	*0-122(122-0-0)/D-1	10	-1.6
2003 LA-N	52	109	6	20	1	0	0	9	3	19	0	0	.183	.212	.193	.405	7	-15	4	1.14	-0	1-13,0-11(11-0-0)	0	-1.6
Total 6	470	1192	116	311	63	2	49	197	80	243	1	3	.261	.309	.440	.749	87	-28	159	4.67	-10	0-253/1-51,D-11	21	-4.9

• WARD, Gary

Gary Lamell Ward b: 12/6/1953, Los Angeles, CA BR/TR, 6'2", 202 lbs. Deb: 9/3/1979 C Career OF: 848-181-111

YEAR TM-L	G	AB	R	H	2B	3B	HR	RBI	BB	SO	SB	CS	AVG	OBP	SLG	OPS	OPS+	BR/A	RC	RC/G	FR	G/POS	WS	TPW
1979 Min-A	10	14	2	4	0	0	0	1	3	3	0	1	.286	.412	.286	.697	89	-0	2	4.14	0	/0-5(1-0-4),D-3	0	-0.1
1980 Min-A	13	41	11	19	6	2	1	10	3	6	0	0	.463	.500	.780	1.280	228	7	16	18.06	0	0-12(12-0-0)	4	0.7
1981 Min-A	85	295	42	78	7	6	3	29	28	48	5	2	.264	.328	.359	.687	92	-2	34	3.91	1	0-80(61-19-1)/D-2	7	-0.5
1982 Min-A	152	570	85	165	33	7	28	91	37	105	13	1	.289	.334	.519	.853	127	21	95	5.99	-1	*0-150(127-4-25)/D-2	20	1.3
1983 Min-A★	157	623	76	173	34	5	19	88	44	98	8	1	.278	.328	.440	.768	105	5	85	4.74	14	*0-152(152-0-0)/D-2	17	1.1
1984 Tex-A	155	602	97	171	21	7	21	79	55	95	7	5	.284	.344	.447	.791	113	10	87	5.09	-1	*0-148(58-59-36)/D-5	20	0.3
1985 Tex-A★	154	593	77	170	28	7	15	70	39	97	26	7	.287	.332	.433	.765	106	6	82	4.85	-6	*0-153(139-21-1)/D-1	12	-0.6
1986 Tex-A	105	380	54	120	15	2	5	51	31	72	12	8	.316	.373	.405	.779	109	5	56	5.36	6	*0-104(102-4-0)/D-1	14	0.6
1987 NY-A	146	529	65	131	22	1	16	78	33	101	9	1	.248	.293	.384	.677	78	-16	55	3.52	-2	0-94(69-30-5),D-36,1-15	7	-2.2
1988 NY-A	91	231	26	52	8	0	4	24	24	41	0	1	.225	.304	.312	.615	73	-8	21	2.96	-3	0-54(17-39-3),1-11/D-9,3-2	3	-1.4
1989 NY-A	8	17	3	5	1	0	0	1	3	5	0	0	.294	.400	.353	.753	115	1	2	4.74	0	/0-6(0-0-6),D-1	0	0.0
Det-A	105	275	24	69	10	2	9	29	21	54	1	3	.251	.304	.400	.704	99	-2	30	3.65	1	0-51(35-5-14),1-26,D-26	2	-0.5
Yr.	113	292	27	74	11	2	9	30	24	59	1	3	.253	.310	.397	.707	100	-2	33	3.71	1	0-57(35-5-20),D-27,1-26	2	-0.5
1990 Det-A	106	309	32	79	11	2	9	46	30	50	2	0	.256	.324	.392	.715	98	-0	38	4.13	1	0-85(75-0-16),D-13/1-2	8	-0.3
Total 12	1287	4479	594	1236	196	41	130	597	351	775	83	30	.276	.330	.425	.755	104	24	602	4.68	10	*0-1094,D-101/1-54,3-2	114	-1.6

• WARD, Hap

Joseph Nichols Ward b: 11/15/1885, Leesburg, NJ d: 9/13/1979, Elmer, NJ BR Deb: 5/18/1912

YEAR TM-L	G	AB	R	H	2B	3B	HR	RBI	BB	SO	SB	CS	AVG	OBP	SLG	OPS	OPS+	BR/A	RC	RC/G	FR	G/POS	WS	TPW
1912 Det-A	1	2	0	0	0	0	0	0	0	....	0	....	.000	.000	.000	.000	-103	-1	0	.00	0	/0-1	0	-0.1

• WARD, Jay

John Francis Ward b: 9/9/1938, Brookfield, MO BR/TR, 6'1", 185 lbs. Deb: 5/6/1963 C Career OF: 4-0-0

YEAR TM-L	G	AB	R	H	2B	3B	HR	RBI	BB	SO	SB	CS	AVG	OBP	SLG	OPS	OPS+	BR/A	RC	RC/G	FR	G/POS	WS	TPW
1963 Min-A	9	15	0	1	1	0	0	2	1	5	0	0	.067	.125	.133	.258	-27	-3	0	.54	0	/3-4,0-1	0	-0.3
1964 Min-A	12	31	4	7	2	0	0	2	6	13	0	0	.226	.351	.290	.642	80	-1	4	4.07	-1	/2-9,0-3(3-0-0)	1	-0.1
1970 Cin-N	6	3	0	0	0	0	0	0	2	1	0	0	.000	.400	.000	.400	16	-0	0	1.87	-1	/3-2,1-1,2-1	0	-0.1
Total 3	27	49	4	8	3	0	0	4	9	19	0	0	.163	.293	.224	.518	45	-3	4	2.71	-2	/2-10,3-6,0-4,1-1	1	-0.5

• WARD, Jim

James H. H. Ward b: 3/2/1855, Boston, MA d: 6/4/1886, Boston, MA Deb: 8/3/1876

YEAR TM-L	G	AB	R	H	2B	3B	HR	RBI	BB	SO	SB	CS	AVG	OBP	SLG	OPS	OPS+	BR/A	RC	RC/G	FR	G/POS	WS	TPW
1876 Phi-N	1	4	1	2	0	0	0	1	0	1	....	....	.500	.500	.500	1.000	236	1	1	14.35	0	/C-1	0	0.0

• WARD, Joe

Joseph A. Ward b: 9/2/1884, Philadelphia, PA d: 8/11/1934, Philadelphia, PA TR Deb: 4/24/1906

YEAR TM-L	G	AB	R	H	2B	3B	HR	RBI	BB	SO	SB	CS	AVG	OBP	SLG	OPS	OPS+	BR/A	RC	RC/G	FR	G/POS	WS	TPW
1906 Phi-N	35	129	12	38	8	6	0	11	5	....	2	....	.295	.321	.450	.771	140	5	20	5.57	-3	3-27/2-3,S-1	6	0.3
1909 NY-A	9	28	3	5	0	0	0	0	1	....	2	....	.179	.233	.179	.412	30	-2	2	1.84	-4	/2-7,1-1	0	-0.7
Phi-N	74	184	21	49	8	2	0	23	9	....	7	....	.266	.304	.332	.636	96	-1	21	3.78	-9	2-48/S-8,1-5,0-2(1-1-0)	4	-1.2
1910 Phi-N	48	124	11	18	2	1	0	13	3	11	1	....	.145	.178	.177	.356	4	-16	5	1.03	1	1-32/3-1,S-1	0	-1.6
Total 3	166	465	47	110	18	9	0	47	18	11	12	....	.237	.271	.314	.585	78	-15	47	3.24	-15	/2-58,1-38,3-28,S-10,0-2	10	-3.2

YEAR TM-L	G	AB	R	H	2B	3B	HR	RBI	BB	SO	SB	CS	AVG	OBP	SLG	OPS	OPS+	BR/A	RC	RC/G	FR	G/POS	WS	TPW
• WARD, John					John E. Ward b: Washington, DC Deb: 5/23/1884																			
1884 Was-U	1	4	0	1	0	0	0	....	0	....	....	....	.250	.250	.250	.500	72	-0	0	2.39	0	/0-1	0	0.0
• WARD, John					John Montgomery "Monte" Ward b: 3/3/1860, Bellefonte, PA d: 3/4/1925, Augusta, GA BL/TR, 5'9", 165 lbs. Deb: 7/15/1878 M/U HOF: 1964 Career OF: 4-110-101 ♦																			
1878 Pro-N	37	138	14	27	5	4	1	15	2	13	....	....	.196	.207	.312	.519	69	1	9	2.26	2	P-37	24	2.2
1879 Pro-N	83	364	71	104	9	4	2	41	7	14	....	....	.286	.299	.349	.648	115	15	39	4.19	3	*P-70,3-16/0-8(4-0-4)	51	2.2
1880 Pro-N	86	356	53	81	12	2	0	27	6	16	....	....	.228	.240	.272	.513	76	-3	24	2.39	16	*P-70,3-25/0-2(0-0-2)	51	2.6
1881 Pro-N	85	357	56	87	18	6	0	53	5	10	....	....	.244	.254	.328	.582	83	-2	30	3.05	5	0-40(0-4-36),P-39,S-13	27	2.7
1882 Pro-N	83	355	58	87	10	3	1	39	13	22	....	....	.245	.272	.299	.570	83	-4	30	3.03	11	0-50(0-2-48),P-33/S-4	31	0.5
1883 NY-N	88	380	76	97	18	7	7	54	8	25	....	....	.255	.271	.395	.665	100	5	42	4.04	15	0-56(0-45-11),P-34/3-5,S-2,2	28	2.3
1884 NY-N	113	482	98	122	11	8	2	51	28	47	....	....	.253	.294	.322	.616	91	-4	47	3.57	8	0-59(0-59-0),2-47/P-9	16	0.0
1885 NY-N	111	446	72	101	8	9	0	37	17	39	....	....	.226	.255	.285	.540	75	-12	33	2.60	17	*S-111	12	0.8
1886 NY-N	122	491	82	134	17	5	2	81	19	46	36	....	.273	.300	.340	.640	93	-5	62	4.72	-8	*S-122	21	-0.8
1887 NY-N	129	574	114	213	16	5	1	53	29	12	**111**	....	.371	.375	.391	.766	118	15	125	9.15	23	*S-129	25	3.6
1888*NY-N	122	510	70	128	14	5	2	49	9	13	38	....	.251	.265	.310	.575	84	-10	53	3.77	1	*S-122	15	-0.5
1889*NY-N	114	479	87	143	13	4	1	67	27	7	62	....	.299	.339	.349	.687	92	-6	79	6.27	12	*S-108/2-7	17	0.8
1890 Bro-P	128	561	134	188	15	12	4	60	51	22	63	....	.335	.393	.426	.819	112	8	122	8.79	20	*S-128	**27**	2.5
1891 Bro-N	105	441	85	122	13	5	0	39	36	10	57	....	.277	.335	.329	.664	94	-3	69	5.88	12	S-87,2-18	15	1.1
1892 Bro-N	148	614	109	163	13	3	1	47	82	19	**88**	....	.265	.355	.301	.656	102	6	99	5.94	7	*2-148	23	1.8
1893 NY-N	135	588	129	193	27	9	2	77	47	5	46	....	.328	.379	.415	.794	110	8	113	7.56	5	*2-134	17	1.5
1894*NY-N	138	549	102	146	12	5	0	77	35	6	39	....	.266	.311	.306	.617	50	-45	66	4.29	12	*2-136	9	-2.0
Total 17	1827	7685	1410	2136	231	96	26	867	421	326	540	....	.278	.314	.341	.655	93	-37	1042	5.05	161	S-826,2-491,P-292,0-215/3-46	409	21.3
• WARD, Kevin					Kevin Michael Ward b: 9/28/1961, Lansdale, PA BR/TR, 6'1", 195 lbs. Deb: 5/10/1991 Career OF: 67-9-10																			
1991 SD-N	44	107	13	26	7	2	2	8	9	27	1	4	.243	.308	.402	.710	95	-2	11	3.48	-1	0-33(31-0-2)	1	-0.5
1992 SD-N	81	147	12	29	5	0	3	12	14	38	2	3	.197	.276	.293	.569	60	-9	10	2.09	-1	0-51(36-9-8)	1	-1.1
Total 2	125	254	25	55	12	2	5	20	23	65	3	7	.217	.289	.339	.628	75	-11	22	2.65	-2	/0-84	2	-1.6
• WARD, Pete					Peter Thomas Ward b: 7/26/1939, Montreal, Canada BL/TR, 6'1", 200 lbs. Deb: 9/21/1962 C Career OF: 139-0-54																			
1962 Bal-A	8	21	1	3	2	0	0	2	4	5	0	0	.143	.280	.238	.518	43	-2	2	2.54	0	/0-6(2-0-4)	0	-0.2
1963 Chi-A	157	600	80	177	34	6	22	84	52	77	7	6	.295	.356	.482	.838	135	26	104	6.31	-10	*3-154/2-1,S-1	25	1.7
1964 Chi-A	144	539	61	152	28	3	23	94	56	76	1	1	.282	.352	.473	.825	131	22	91	6.06	12	*3-138	27	3.5
1965 Chi-A	138	507	62	125	25	3	10	57	56	83	2	4	.247	.329	.367	.696	104	2	61	4.12	-3	*3-134/2-1	17	-0.1
1966 Chi-A	84	251	22	55	7	1	3	28	24	49	3	1	.219	.295	.291	.586	74	-8	23	2.94	4	0-59(44-0-18),3-16/1-5	5	-0.8
1967 Chi-A	146	467	49	109	16	2	18	62	61	109	3	2	.233	.336	.392	.728	119	13	65	4.77	-1	0-89(74-0-19),1-39,3-22	20	0.6
1968 Chi-A	125	399	43	86	15	0	15	50	76	85	4	3	.216	.355	.366	.721	117	12	58	4.86	-2	3-77,1-31,0-22(16-0-7)	15	0.9
1969 Chi-A	105	199	22	49	7	0	6	32	33	38	0	0	.246	.362	.372	.734	100	1	30	5.14	-1	1-25,3-21/0-9(3-0-6)	6	-0.2
1970 NY-A	66	77	5	20	2	2	1	18	9	17	0	0	.260	.337	.377	.714	102	0	10	4.69	-1	1-13	2	-0.1
Total 9	973	3060	345	776	136	17	98	427	371	539	20	17	.254	.342	.405	.747	115	66	443	5.02	-2	3-562,0-185,1-113/2-2,S-1	117	5.3
• WARD, Piggy					Frank Gray Ward b: 4/16/1867, Chambersburg, PA d: 10/24/1912, Altoona, PA BB/TR, 5'9.5", 196 lbs. Deb: 6/12/1883 Career OF: 21-4-85																			
1883 Phi-N	1	5	0	0	0	0	0	0	0	2	....	....	.000	.000	.000	.000	-110	-1	0	.00	0	/3-1	0	-0.1
1889 Phi-N	7	25	0	4	1	0	0	4	0	7	1	....	.160	.160	.200	.360		-4	1	1.24	-3	/2-6,0-1	0	-0.6
1891 Pit-N	6	18	3	6	0	0	0	2	3	3	3	....	.333	.455	.333	.788	134	1	4	9.43	-1	/0-5(5-0-0)	1	0.0
1892 Bal-N	56	186	28	54	6	5	1	33	31	18	10	....	.290	.403	.392	.795	137	10	34	7.01	1	0-43(0-0-43)/2-7,S-5,C-1	6	0.8
1893 Bal-N	11	49	11	12	1	3	0	5	5	2	4	....	.245	.327	.388	.715	88	-1	8	5.53	-1	/0-9(9-0-0),1-2	1	-0.3
Cin-N	42	150	44	42	4	1	0	10	37	10	27	....	.280	.440	.320	.760	101	4	34	8.31	-1	0-40(1-0-39)/1-1	6	0.1
Yr.	53	199	55	54	5	4	0	15	42	12	31	....	.271	.415	.337	.752	98	3	42	7.60	-2	0-49(10-0-39)/1-3	7	-0.2
1894 Was-N	98	347	86	105	11	7	0	36	80	31	41	....	.303	.447	.375	.822	103	10	78	8.43	-16	2-79,0-12(6-3-3)/S-3,3-1	9	-0.2
Total 6	221	780	172	223	23	16	1	90	156	73	86	....	.286	.419	.360	.779	107	19	159	7.55	-20	0-110/2-92,S-8,1-3,3-2,C-1	23	-0.2
• WARD, Preston					Preston Meyer Ward b: 7/24/1927, Columbia, MO BL/TR, 6'4", 198 lbs. Deb: 4/20/1948 Career OF: 17-27-51																			
1948 Bro-N	42	146	9	38	9	2	1	21	15	23	0	....	.260	.329	.370	.699	86	-3	19	4.73	-1	1-38	3	-0.5
1950 Chi-N	80	285	31	72	11	2	6	33	27	42	3	....	.253	.317	.368	.686	81	-8	34	4.03	7	1-76	5	-0.4
1953 Chi-N	33	100	10	23	5	0	4	12	18	21	3	1	.230	.347	.400	.747	92	-1	15	4.89	-3	0-27(0-27-0)/1-7	2	-0.5
Pit-N	88	281	35	59	7	1	8	27	44	39	1	3	.210	.319	.327	.646	69	-13	31	3.58	0	1-78	3	-1.7
Yr.	121	381	45	82	12	1	12	39	62	60	4	4	.215	.327	.346	.673	75	-13	46	3.92	-3	1-85,0-27(0-27-0)	5	-2.1
1954 Pit-N	117	360	37	97	16	2	7	48	39	61	0	0	.269	.341	.383	.724	90	-5	49	4.81	5	1-48,0-42(0-0-42),3-11	9	-0.4
1955 Pit-N	84	179	16	38	7	4	5	25	22	28	0	0	.212	.299	.380	.678	80	-5	21	3.74	-1	1-48/0-1	3	-0.8
1956 Pit-N	16	30	3	10	0	1	1	11	6	4	0	0	.333	.444	.500	.944	157	3	7	9.50	-1	/3-5,0-5(0-0-5)	2	0.2
Cle-A	87	150	18	38	10	0	6	21	16	20	0	0	.253	.325	.440	.765	98	-1	23	5.34	2	1-60,0-17(14-0-3)	5	-0.2
1957 Cle-A	10	11	2	2	1	0	0	0	0	2	0	0	.182	.182	.273	.455	23	-1	1	1.64	0	/1-1	0	-0.1
1958 Cle-A	48	148	22	50	3	1	4	21	10	27	0	1	.338	.384	.453	.836	133	6	26	6.79	2	3-24,1-21	6	0.7
KC-A	81	268	28	68	10	1	6	24	27	36	0	1	.254	.322	.366	.688	87	-5	33	4.17	-6	1-39,3-34/0-2(2-0-0)	6	-1.4
Yr.	129	416	50	118	13	2	10	45	37	63	0	2	.284	.344	.397	.740	103	1	59	5.03	-4	1-60,3-58/0-2(2-0-0)	12	-0.7
1959 KC-A	58	109	8	27	4	1	2	19	7	12	0	0	.248	.293	.358	.651	76	-4	11	3.37	-3	1-22/0-1	1	-0.8
Total 9	744	2067	219	522	83	15	50	262	231	315	7	6	.253	.328	.380	.708	88	-37	269	4.47	0	1-438/0-95,3-74	45	-5.8
• WARD, Rube					John Andrew Ward b: 2/6/1879, New Lexington, OH d: 1/17/1945, Akron, OH Deb: 4/28/1902																			
1902 Bro-N	13	31	4	9	1	0	0	2	2	....	0	....	.290	.333	.323	.656	102	0	3	4.12	-1	0-11(6-1-4)	1	-0.1
• WARD, Turner					Turner Max Ward b: 4/11/1965, Orlando, FL BB/TR, 6'2", 200 lbs. Deb: 9/10/1990 Career OF: 169-182-220																			
1990 Cle-A	14	46	10	16	2	1	1	10	3	8	3	0	.348	.388	.500	.888	147	3	9	8.11	0	0-13(0-0-13)/D-1	3	0.3
1991 Cle-A	40	100	11	23	7	0	0	5	10	16	0	0	.230	.300	.300	.600	66	-4	10	3.21	0	0-38(0-2-36)	1	-0.5
Tor-A	8	13	1	4	0	0	0	2	1	2	0	0	.308	.357	.308	.665	83	-0	1	3.29	0	/0-6(1-0-5)	0	-0.1
Yr.	48	113	12	27	7	0	0	7	11	18	0	0	.239	.306	.301	.607	68	-5	11	3.21	0	0-44(1-2-41)	1	-0.6
1992 Tor-A	18	29	7	10	3	0	1	3	4	4	0	1	.345	.424	.552	.976	164	2	6	7.97	0	0-12(2-4-6)	1	0.2
1993 Tor-A	72	167	20	32	4	2	4	28	23	26	3	3	.192	.293	.311	.605	62	-9	15	2.60	-2	0-65(33-10-22)/1-1	2	-1.3
1994 Mil-A	102	367	55	85	15	2	9	45	52	68	6	2	.232	.332	.357	.689	74	-13	45	4.11	2	0-99(35-52-25)/3-1	9	-1.3
1995 Mil-A	44	129	19	34	3	1	4	16	14	21	6	1	.264	.340	.395	.736	86	-2	19	5.00	3	0-40(26-7-19)/D-1	3	0.0
1996 Mil-A	43	67	7	12	2	1	2	10	13	17	3	0	.179	.313	.328	.641	60	-3	8	3.38	0	0-32(15-3-18)/D-1	1	-0.4
1997 Pit-N	71	167	33	59	16	1	7	33	18	17	4	1	.353	.422	.587	1.009	158	15	43	10.20	-1	0-54(11-31-23)	9	1.3
1998 Pit-N	123	282	33	74	13	3	9	46	27	40	5	4	.262	.335	.426	.761	97	-2	41	4.85	1	0-97(41-48-22)/D-1	9	-0.3
1999 Pit-N	49	91	2	19	2	0	0	8	13	9	2	2	.209	.314	.231	.545	41	-8	7	2.49	-1	0-34(5-22-13)	0	-1.0
*Ari-N	10	23	6	8	1	0	2	7	2	6	0	0	.348	.400	.652	1.052	159	2	6	10.41	0	/0-5(0-2-4)	2	0.2
Yr.	59	114	8	27	3	0	2	15	15	15	2	2	.237	.331	.316	.647	64	-6	14	3.81	-1	0-39(5-24-17)	2	-0.7
2000 Ari-N	15	52	5	9	4	0	0	4	5	7	1	1	.173	.246	.250	.496	25	-6	3	1.48	0	0-15(0-1-14)	1	-0.6
2001 Phi-N	17	15	1	4	1	0	0	2	1	6	0	0	.267	.353	.333	.686	81	-0	2	3.48	0	....	0	0.0
Total 12	626	1548	210	389	73	11	39	219	186	247	33	15	.251	.337	.388	.725	87	-27	214	4.62	1	0-510/D-4,1-1,3-1	41	-3.4
• WARES, Buzzy					Clyde Ellsworth Wares b: 5/23/1886, Vandalia, MI d: 5/26/1964, South Bend, IN BR/TR, 5'10", 150 lbs. Deb: 9/15/1913 C																			
1913 StL-A	11	35	5	10	2	0	0	1	1	3	2	....	.286	.306	.343	.648	92	-1	4	3.97	-2	/2-9	1	-0.2
1914 StL-A	81	215	20	45	10	1	0	23	28	35	10	10	.209	.300	.265	.566	73	-9	19	2.59	-5	S-68/2-8	4	-1.0
Total 2	92	250	25	55	12	1	0	24	29	38	12	10	.220	.301	.276	.577	75	-9	23	2.75	-7	/S-68,2-17	5	-1.3
• WARNER, Fred					Frederick John Rodney Warner b: 1855, Philadelphia, PA d: 2/13/1886, Philadelphia, PA, 5'7", 155 lbs. Deb: 4/30/1875 Career OF: 15-8-2																			
1875 Cen-n	14	57	11	14	4	0	0	2	1	2	0	0	.246	.259	.316	.574	107	1	5	3.27	-1	0-14(0-14-0)	....	0.0
1876 Phi-N	1	3	0	0	0	0	0	0	0	0	....	....	.000	.000	.000	.000	-101	-1	0	.00	0	/0-1	0	-0.1
1878 Ind-N	43	165	19	41	4	0	0	10	2	15	....	....	.248	.257	.273	.530	86	-1	12	2.63	-1	S-41/0-2(2-0-0)	4	-0.1

YEAR TM-L	G	AB	R	H	2B	3B	HR	RBI	BB	SO	SB	CS	AVG	OBP	SLG	OPS	OPS+	BR/A	RC	RC/G	FR	G/POS	WS	TPW
1879 Cle-N	76	316	32	77	11	4	0	22	2	20	....	....	.244	.248	.304	.552	82	-6	24	2.86	0	3-54,0-21(13-7-1)/1-1	5	-0.5
1883 Phi-N	39	141	13	32	6	1	0	13	5	21	....	....	.227	.253	.284	.537	69	-4	10	2.62	-10	3-38/0-1	1	-1.2
1884 Bro-a	84	352	40	78	4	0	1	0	17	....	....	....	.222	.259	.241	.501	64	-14	23	2.27	-7	*3-84	5	-1.7
Total 5	243	977	104	228	25	5	1	45	26	56	....	....	.233	.254	.272	.526	73	-26	69	2.56	-18	3-176/S-41,0-25,1-1	15	-3.6
• WARNER, Hooks	Hoke Hayden Warner b: 5/22/1894, Del Rio, TX d: 2/19/1947, San Francisco, CA BL/TR, 5'10.5", 170 lbs. Deb: 8/21/1916																							
1916 Pit-N	44	168	12	40	1	1	2	14	6	19	6	....	.238	.264	.292	.556	70	-6	15	2.92	-5	3-42/2-1	2	-1.2
1917 Pit-N	3	5	0	1	0	0	0	0	0	1	0	....	.200	.200	.200	.400	22	-0	0	1.17	1	/3-1	0	0.0
1919 Pit-N	6	8	0	1	0	0	0	2	3	1	0	....	.125	.364	.125	.489	48	-0	0	1.30	0	/3-3	0	0.0
1921 Chi-N	14	38	4	8	1	0	0	3	2	1	1	1	.211	.268	.237	.505	35	-4	2	2.06	1	3-10	0	-0.2
Total 4	67	219	16	50	2	1	2	19	11	22	7	1	.228	.268	.274	.542	62	-11	18	2.66	-4	/3-56,2-1	2	-1.4
• WARNER, Jack	John Ralph Warner b: 8/29/1903, Evansville, IN d: 3/13/1986, Mount Vernon, IL BR/TR, 5'9.5", 165 lbs. Deb: 9/24/1925																							
1925 Det-A	10	39	7	13	0	0	0	2	3	6	0	0	.333	.381	.333	.714	84	-1	5	5.14	2	3-10	1	0.1
1926 Det-A	100	311	41	78	8	6	0	34	38	24	8	4	.251	.342	.315	.657	71	-12	37	3.86	2	3-95/S-3	7	-0.4
1927 Det-A	139	559	78	149	22	9	1	45	47	45	14	4	.267	.330	.343	.674	74	-19	67	4.12	-6	*3-138	12	-1.5
1928 Det-A	75	206	33	44	4	4	0	13	16	15	4	4	.214	.274	.272	.545	43	-18	16	2.41	2	3-52/S-7	2	-1.2
1929 Bro-N	17	62	3	17	2	0	0	4	7	6	3	....	.274	.348	.306	.654	65	-3	7	3.78	-1	S-17	1	-0.2
1930 Bro-N	21	25	4	8	1	0	0	0	2	7	1	....	.320	.370	.360	.730	79	-1	3	4.79	1	/3-8	0	0.0
1931 Bro-N	9	4	2	2	0	0	0	0	1	1	0	....	.500	.600	.500	1.100	200	1	1	17.12	0	/S-2,3-1	0	0.1
1933 Phi-N	107	340	31	76	15	1	0	22	28	33	1	....	.224	.285	.274	.558	53	-20	26	2.46	-5	2-71,3-30/S-1	3	-2.1
Total 8	478	1546	199	387	52	20	1	120	142	137	31	12	.250	.319	.312	.630	65	-73	162	3.48	-5	3-334/2-71,S-30	26	-5.1
• WARNER, Jackie	John Joseph Warner b: 8/1/1943, Monrovia, CA BR/TR, 6', 180 lbs. Deb: 4/12/1966																							
1966 Cal-A	45	123	22	26	4	1	7	16	9	55	0	0	.211	.265	.431	.696	99	-1	14	3.74	-1	0-37(0-0-37)	3	-0.4
• WARNER, John	John Joseph "Jack" Warner b: 8/15/1872, New York, NY d: 12/21/1943, Queens, NY BL/TR, 5'11", 165 lbs. Deb: 4/23/1895 U																							
1895 Bos-N	3	7	2	1	0	0	0	1	1	0	0	....	.143	.333	.143	.476	24	-1	0	1.54	1	/C-3	0	0.0
Lou-N	67	232	20	62	4	2	1	20	11	16	10	....	.267	.320	.315	.635	68	-10	28	4.31	-4	C-64/1-3,2-1	3	-0.7
Yr.	70	239	22	63	4	2	1	21	12	16	10	....	.264	.320	.310	.630	67	-11	28	4.22	-3	C-67/1-3,2-1	3	-0.7
1896 Lou-N	33	110	9	25	1	1	0	10	10	10	3	....	.227	.303	.255	.558	50	-8	10	3.02	2	C-32/1-1	1	-0.2
NY-N	19	54	9	14	1	0	0	3	3	7	1	....	.259	.310	.278	.588	57	-3	6	3.39	-2	C-19	1	-0.3
Yr.	52	164	18	39	2	1	0	13	13	17	4	....	.238	.306	.262	.568	52	-11	16	3.15	0	C-51/1-1	2	-0.5
1897 NY-N	111	400	50	109	6	3	2	51	26	....	8	....	.273	.342	.318	.659	77	-12	48	4.30	5	*C-110	13	0.3
1898 NY-N	110	373	40	96	14	5	0	42	22	....	9	....	.257	.316	.322	.638	85	-7	42	3.99	8	*C-109/0-1	13	1.1
1899 NY-N	88	293	38	78	8	1	0	19	15	....	15	....	.266	.315	.300	.616	72	-11	34	4.10	7	C-82/1-3	7	0.3
1900 NY-N	34	108	15	27	4	0	0	13	8	....	1	....	.250	.319	.287	.606	71	-4	11	3.45	4	C-31	2	0.3
1901 NY-N	87	291	19	70	6	1	0	20	3	....	3	....	.241	.268	.268	.536	58	-16	23	2.68	7	C-84	4	-0.2
1902 Bos-A	65	222	19	52	5	7	0	12	13	....	0	....	.234	.286	.320	.606	66	-11	21	3.24	5	C-64	6	0.0
1903 NY-N	89	285	38	81	8	5	0	34	7	....	5	....	.284	.322	.347	.670	87	-5	35	4.42	4	C-85	11	0.6
1904 NY-N	86	287	29	57	5	1	1	15	14	....	7	....	.199	.253	.233	.487	48	-17	20	2.20	-2	C-86	5	-1.2
1905 StL-N	41	137	9	35	2	2	1	12	6	....	2	....	.255	.301	.321	.623	88	-2	14	3.62	2	C-41	3	0.5
Det-A	36	119	12	24	2	3	0	7	8	....	2	....	.202	.252	.269	.521	65	-5	9	2.46	-1	C-36	3	-0.2
1906 Det-A	50	153	15	37	4	2	0	10	12	....	4	....	.242	.326	.294	.620	92	-1	17	3.74	9	C-49	7	1.4
Was-A	32	103	5	21	4	1	1	9	2	....	3	....	.204	.226	.291	.518	65	-5	8	2.48	6	C-32	2	0.6
Yr.	82	256	20	58	8	3	1	19	14	....	7	....	.227	.288	.293	.581	82	-5	24	3.22	15	C-81	9	2.0
1907 Was-A	72	207	11	53	5	0	0	17	12	....	3	....	.256	.306	.280	.586	95	-1	19	3.30	-3	C-64	4	0.2
1908 Was-A	51	116	8	28	2	1	0	8	8	....	7	....	.241	.313	.276	.588	100	0	12	3.46	0	C-41/1-1	4	0.4
Total 14	1074	3497	348	870	81	35	6	303	181	33	83	....	.249	.303	.297	.600	74	-118	357	3.52	47	*C-1032/1-8,2-1,0-1	89	2.8
• WARNOCK, Hal	Harold Charles Warnock b: 1/6/1912, New York, NY d: 2/8/1997, Tucson, AZ BL/TR, 6'2", 180 lbs. Deb: 9/2/1935																							
1935 StL-A	6	7	1	2	2	0	0	0	0	3	0	0	.286	.286	.571	.857	112	0	1	5.81	0	/0-2(1-1-0)	0	0.0
• WARREN, Bennie	Bennie Louis Warren b: 3/2/1912, Elk City, OK d: 5/11/1994, Oklahoma City, OK BR/TR, 6'1", 184 lbs. Deb: 9/13/1939																							
1939 Phi-N	18	56	4	13	0	0	1	7	7	7	0	....	.232	.317	.286	.603	66	-2	6	3.24	0	C-17	1	-0.2
1940 Phi-N	106	289	33	71	6	1	12	34	40	46	1	....	.246	.339	.398	.737	107	3	39	4.65	4	C-97/1-1	8	1.3
1941 Phi-N	121	345	34	74	13	2	9	35	44	66	0	....	.214	.309	.342	.651	86	-6	36	3.36	8	*C-110	6	0.8
1942 Phi-N	90	225	19	47	6	3	7	20	24	36	0	....	.209	.288	.356	.644	92	-3	22	3.15	2	C-78/1-1	4	0.3
1946 NY-N	39	69	7	11	1	1	4	8	14	21	0	....	.159	.301	.377	.678	91	-1	9	4.06	-2	C-30	2	-0.2
1947 NY-N	3	5	0	1	0	0	0	0	0	1	0	....	.200	.200	.200	.400	6	-1	0	.00	-1	/C-3	0	-0.1
Total 6	377	989	97	217	26	7	33	104	129	177	1	....	.219	.313	.360	.673	93	-9	111	3.70	11	C-335/1-2	21	2.0
• WARREN, Bill	William Hackney "Hack" Warren b: 2/11/1887, Cairo, IL d: 1/28/1960, Whiteville, TN BR/TR, 5'8", 165 lbs. Deb: 4/30/1914																							
1914 Ind-F	26	50	5	12	2	0	0	5	5	7	2	....	.240	.309	.280	.589	61	-2	5	3.09	-2	C-23	1	-0.3
1915 New-F	5	3	0	1	0	0	0	1	0	0	0	....	.333	.333	.333	.667	102	-0	0	4.07	0	/1-1,C-1	0	0.0
Total 2	31	53	5	13	2	0	0	6	5	7	2	....	.245	.310	.283	.593	64	-2	5	3.14	-2	/C-24,1-1	1	-0.3
• WARSTLER, Rabbit	Harold Burton Warstler b: 9/13/1903, North Canton, OH d: 5/31/1964, North Canton, OH BR/TR, 5'7.5", 150 lbs. Deb: 7/24/1930																							
1930 Bos-A	54	162	16	30	2	3	1	13	20	21	0	2	.185	.275	.253	.528	36	-16	12	2.29	1	S-54	2	-0.9
1931 Bos-A	66	181	20	44	5	3	0	10	15	27	2	3	.243	.308	.304	.612	65	-9	17	3.18	-8	2-42,S-19/3-1	2	-1.3
1932 Bos-A	115	388	26	82	15	5	0	34	22	43	9	6	.211	.259	.276	.535	40	-35	28	2.33	6	*S-107	5	-2.0
1933 Bos-A	92	322	44	70	13	1	1	17	42	36	2	4	.217	.308	.273	.581	55	-21	29	2.92	-2	S-87	4	-1.6
1934 Phi-A	117	419	56	99	19	3	1	36	51	30	9	3	.236	.321	.303	.624	64	-21	45	3.51	12	*2-107/S-2	6	-0.2
1935 Phi-A	138	496	62	124	20	7	3	59	56	53	8	4	.250	.326	.337	.663	72	-20	58	3.90	5	*2-136/3-2	7	-0.5
1936 Phi-A	66	236	27	59	8	6	1	24	36	16	0	0	.250	.354	.347	.701	75	-8	32	4.40	12	2-66	5	0.7
Bos-N	74	304	27	64	6	0	0	17	22	33	2	....	.211	.266	.230	.496	37	-26	19	2.11	8	S-74	3	-1.3
1937 Bos-N	149	555	57	124	20	0	3	36	51	62	4	....	.223	.291	.276	.567	60	-30	48	2.77	-1	*S-149	10	-2.0
1938 Bos-N	142	467	37	108	10	4	0	40	48	38	3	....	.231	.303	.270	.573	65	-21	39	2.79	2	*S-135/2-7	9	-0.9
1939 Bos-N	114	342	34	83	11	3	0	24	24	31	2	....	.243	.292	.292	.585	62	-18	29	2.93	1	S-49,2-43,3-21	6	-1.1
1940 Bos-N	33	57	6	12	0	0	0	4	10	5	0	....	.211	.328	.211	.539	54	-3	4	2.16	0	2-24/3-2,S-1	0	-0.2
Chi-N	45	159	19	36	4	1	1	18	8	19	1	....	.226	.263	.283	.546	52	-11	12	2.47	-3	S-28,2-17	2	-1.1
Yr.	78	216	25	48	4	1	1	22	18	24	1	....	.222	.282	.264	.546	53	-14	16	2.38	-3	2-41,S-29/3-2	2	-1.3
Total 11	1205	4088	431	935	133	36	11	332	405	414	42	22	.229	.300	.287	.587	59	-238	372	2.98	32	S-705,2-442/3-26	61	-12.3
• WARWICK, Bill	Firmin Newton Warwick b: 11/26/1897, Philadelphia, PA d: 12/19/1984, San Antonio, TX BR/TR, 6'.5", 180 lbs. Deb: 7/18/1921																							
1921 Pit-N	1	1	0	0	0	0	0	0	0	0	0	0	.000	.000	.000	.000	-98	-0	0	.00	0	/C-1	0	-0.1
1925 StL-N	13	41	8	12	1	2	1	6	5	5	0	1	.293	.370	.488	.857	114	1	7	6.09	0	C-13	1	0.1
1926 StL-N	9	14	0	5	0	0	0	2	0	2	0	....	.357	.357	.357	.714	89	-0	2	4.40	0	/C-9	1	0.0
Total 3	23	56	8	17	1	2	1	8	5	7	0	1	.304	.361	.446	.807	105	0	9	5.55	-1	/C-23	2	0.0
• WARWICK, Carl	Carl Wayne Warwick b: 2/27/1937, Dallas, TX BR/TL, 5'10", 170 lbs. Deb: 4/11/1961 Career OF: 79-175-201																							
1961 LA-N	19	11	2	1	0	0	0	1	2	3	0	0	.091	.231	.091	.322	-9	-2	0	.57	-1	0-12(6-5-1)	0	-0.3
StL-N	55	152	27	38	6	2	4	16	18	33	3	0	.250	.329	.395	.724	83	-3	21	4.68	0	0-48(15-34-10)	4	-0.5
Yr.	74	163	29	39	6	2	4	17	20	36	3	0	.239	.322	.374	.697	77	-5	22	4.34	-2	0-60(21-39-11)	4	-0.8
1962 StL-N	13	23	4	8	0	0	1	4	2	2	2	0	.348	.400	.478	.878	123	1	4	5.00	0	0-10(1-0-9)	0	0.1
Hou-N	130	477	63	124	17	1	16	60	38	77	2	3	.260	.315	.400	.715	98	-4	59	4.30	0	*0-128(15-116-9)	11	-0.9
Yr.	143	500	67	132	17	1	17	64	40	79	4	3	.264	.319	.404	.723	99	-3	63	4.33	0	*0-138(16-116-18)	12	-0.8
1963 Hou-N	150	528	49	134	19	5	7	47	49	70	3	3	.254	.320	.348	.668	98	-1	58	3.75	-4	*0-141(23-11-114)/1-2	15	-1.5
1964*StL-N	88	158	14	41	7	1	3	15	11	30	2	0	.259	.308	.373	.681	83	-3	19	4.13	-1	0-49(11-0-41)	3	-0.6
1965 StL-N	50	77	3	12	2	1	0	6	4	18	1	0	.156	.198	.208	.405	13	-9	3	1.22	-1	0-21(4-2-15)/1-4	0	-1.1
Bal-A	9	14	3	0	0	0	0	0	3	2	0	0	.000	.176	.000	.176	-44	-3	0	.27	0	/0-3(1-0-2)	0	-0.3

YEAR TM-L	G	AB	R	H	2B	3B	HR	RBI	BB	SO	SB	CS	AVG	OBP	SLG	OPS	OPS+	BR/A	RC	RC/G	FR	G/POS	WS	TPW
1966 Chi-N	16	22	3	5	0	0	0	0	0	6	0	0	.227	.227	.227	.455	26	-2	1	1.80	1	0-10(3-7-0)	0	-0.2
Total 6	**530**	**1462**	**168**	**363**	**51**	**10**	**31**	**149**	**127**	**241**	**13**	**6**	**.248**	**.309**	**.360**	**.670**	**88**	**-25**	**165**	**3.84**	**-7**	**0-422/1-6**	**34**	**-5.3**
• WASDELL, Jimmy	James Charles Wasdell b: 5/15/1914, Cleveland, OH d: 8/6/1983, New Port Richey, FL BL/TL, 5'11", 185 lbs. Deb: 9/3/1937 Career OF: 227-43-210																							
1937 Was-A	32	110	13	28	4	4	2	12	7	13	0	1	.255	.299	.418	.717	82	-4	13	4.22	1	1-21/0-7(3-0-4)	2	-0.5
1938 Was-A	53	140	19	33	2	1	2	16	12	12	5	2	.236	.296	.307	.603	55	-10	13	3.18	-1	1-26/0-6(0-0-6)	1	-1.2
1939 Was-A	29	109	12	33	5	1	0	13	9	16	3	1	.303	.361	.367	.728	94	-1	15	5.17	-2	1-28	2	-0.5
1940 Was-A	10	35	3	3	1	0	0	0	2	7	0	0	.086	.135	.114	.249	-37	-7	1	.53	-1	/1-8	0	-0.9
Bro-N	77	230	35	64	14	4	3	37	18	24	4	....	.278	.333	.413	.746	99	-1	32	4.94	-8	0-42(1-1-40),1-17	6	-1.3
1941*Bro-N	94	265	39	79	14	3	4	48	16	15	2	....	.298	.345	.419	.764	110	3	40	5.64	-2	0-54(8-0-46),1-15	9	-0.3
1942 Pit-N	122	409	44	106	11	2	3	38	47	22	1	....	.259	.337	.318	.655	90	-4	46	3.87	-2	0-97(36-2-61)/1-7	10	-1.3
1943 Pit-N	4	2	0	1	0	0	0	1	2	0	0	....	.500	.750	.500	1.250	256	1	1	30.78	0	....	0	0.1
Phi-N	141	522	54	136	19	6	4	67	46	22	6	....	.261	.323	.343	.666	96	-3	58	3.86	3	1-82,0-56(39-22-5)	12	-0.7
Yr.	145	524	54	137	19	6	4	68	48	22	6	....	.261	.326	.344	.669	97	-2	59	3.93	3	1-82,0-56(39-22-5)	12	-0.6
1944 Phi-N	133	451	47	125	20	3	3	40	45	17	0	....	.277	.344	.355	.699	100	1	55	4.22	-4	*0-121(118-5-3)/1-4	9	-1.1
1945 Phi-N	134	500	65	150	19	8	7	60	32	11	7	....	.300	.346	.412	.758	113	7	72	5.35	-7	0-65(17-13-37),1-63	15	-0.7
1946 Phi-N	26	51	7	13	0	2	1	5	3	2	0	....	.255	.309	.392	.701	101	-0	6	3.87	-1	0-11(4-0-6)/1-2	1	-0.1
Cle-A	32	41	1	11	0	0	0	4	4	4	1	0	.268	.333	.268	.602	74	-1	4	3.13	-1	/1-4,0-3(1-0-2)	0	-0.2
1947 Cle-A	1	1	0	0	0	0	0	0	0	0	0	0	.000	.000	.000	.000	-103	-0	0	.00	0	....	0	0.0
Total 11	**888**	**2866**	**339**	**782**	**109**	**34**	**29**	**341**	**243**	**165**	**29**	**4**	**.273**	**.332**	**.365**	**.697**	**96**	**-19**	**355**	**4.39**	**-25**	**0-462,1-277**	**67**	**-8.6**
• WASEM, Link	Lincoln William Wasem b: 1/30/1911, Birmingham, OH d: 3/6/1979, South Laguna, CA BR/TR, 5'9.5", 180 lbs. Deb: 5/5/1937																							
1937 Bos-N	2	1	0	0	0	0	0	0	0	0	0	....	.000	.000	.000	.000	-110	-0	0	.00	0	/C-2	0	0.0
• WASHBURN, Libe	Libeus Washburn b: 6/16/1874, Lynn, NH d: 3/22/1940, Malone, NY BB/TL, 5'10", 180 lbs. Deb: 5/30/1902 Career OF: 1-2-1 ♦																							
1902 NY-N	6	9	1	4	0	0	0	0	2	....	1	....	.444	.615	.444	1.060	229	2	3	16.72	0	/0-3(0-2-1)	1	0.2
1903 Phi-N	8	18	1	3	0	0	0	1	1	....	0	....	.167	.211	.167	.377	8	-1	1	1.14	-1	/P-4,0-2(1-0-0)	0	-0.6
Total 2	**14**	**27**	**2**	**7**	**0**	**0**	**0**	**1**	**3**	**....**	**1**	**....**	**.259**	**.375**	**.259**	**.634**	**98**	**1**	**4**	**5.04**	**-1**	**/0-5,P-4**	**1**	**-0.4**
• WASHINGTON, Claudell	Claudell Washington b: 8/31/1954, Los Angeles, CA BL/TL, 6', 190 lbs. Deb: 7/5/1974 Career OF: 324-320-1101																							
1974*Oak-A	73	221	16	63	10	5	0	19	13	44	6	8	.285	.328	.376	.703	109	-0	24	3.73	0	D-38,0-32(14-10-10)	5	-0.2
1975*Oak-A★	148	590	86	182	24	7	10	77	32	80	40	15	.308	.349	.424	.773	120	17	85	5.20	-6	*0-148(112-35-11)	22	0.3
1976 Oak-A	134	490	65	126	20	6	5	53	30	90	37	20	.257	.304	.353	.657	96	-5	49	3.24	-4	*0-126(0-30-105)/D-4	10	-1.5
1977 Tex-A	129	521	63	148	31	2	12	68	25	112	21	8	.284	.321	.420	.741	99	-0	68	4.62	2	*0-127(93-41-4)/D-1	13	-0.3
1978 Tex-A	12	42	1	7	0	0	0	2	1	12	0	1	.167	.186	.167	.353		-6	1	.74	-1	/0-7(1-0-6),D-4	0	-0.7
Chi-A	86	314	33	83	16	5	6	31	12	57	5	5	.264	.294	.404	.698	94	-5	34	3.71	-4	0-82(15-8-63)/D-1	7	-1.3
Yr.	98	356	34	90	16	5	6	33	13	69	5	6	.253	.281	.376	.657	83	-11	35	3.32	-4	0-89(16-8-69)/D-5	7	-2.0
1979 Chi-A	131	471	79	132	33	5	13	66	28	93	19	11	.280	.325	.454	.779	108	3	65	4.81	0	*0-122(0-1-121)/D-3	13	-0.3
1980 Chi-A	32	90	15	26	4	2	1	12	5	19	4	2	.289	.333	.411	.744	103	0	11	3.98	0	0-23(21-0-3)/D-2	2	-0.1
NY-N	79	284	38	78	16	4	10	42	20	63	17	5	.275	.325	.465	.789	121	8	42	5.27	5	0-70(23-1-58)	10	1.1
1981 Atl-N	85	320	37	93	22	3	5	37	15	47	12	6	.291	.330	.425	.755	110	3	44	4.73	-2	0-79(0-0-79)	10	-0.3
1982*Atl-N	150	563	94	150	24	6	16	80	50	107	33	10	.266	.333	.416	.748	104	5	80	4.91	-8	*0-139(0-0-139)	18	-1.1
1983 Atl-N	134	496	75	138	24	8	9	44	35	103	31	9	.278	.326	.413	.739	96	-1	67	4.76	1	*0-128(0-0-128)	13	-0.7
1984 Atl-N★	120	416	62	119	21	2	17	61	59	77	21	9	.286	.376	.469	.845	127	17	73	6.19	-5	*0-107(0-0-107)	17	0.7
1985 Atl-N	122	398	62	110	14	6	15	43	40	66	14	4	.276	.344	.455	.799	115	8	61	5.38	-5	0-99(0-0-99)	12	-0.1
1986 Atl-N	40	137	17	37	11	0	5	14	14	26	4	7	.270	.338	.460	.798	112	-0	18	4.36	-1	0-38(0-0-38)	3	-0.2
NY-A	54	135	19	32	5	0	6	16	7	33	6	1	.237	.285	.407	.692	87	-2	16	3.92	-1	0-39(11-20-9)	2	-0.4
1987 NY-A	102	312	42	87	17	0	9	44	27	54	10	1	.279	.336	.420	.756	100	1	46	5.46	1	0-72(2-69-1),D-13	10	0.1
1988 NY-A	126	455	62	140	22	3	11	64	24	74	15	6	.308	.345	.442	.787	120	11	68	5.57	-2	*0-117(13-103-8)	15	0.7
1989 Cal-A	110	418	53	114	18	4	13	42	27	84	13	5	.273	.320	.428	.748	111	5	57	4.77	-1	*0-100(0-2-99)/D-7	12	0.1
1990 Cal-A	12	34	3	6	1	0	1	3	2	8	1	0	.176	.222	.294	.516	44	-2	2	2.00	1	/0-9(0-0-9)	0	-0.2
NY-A	33	80	4	13	1	1	0	6	2	17	3	1	.163	.183	.200	.383	7	-10	3	1.11	0	0-21(19-0-4)/D-2	0	-1.1
Yr.	45	114	7	19	2	1	1	9	4	25	4	1	.167	.195	.228	.423	18	-12	5	1.37	1	0-30(19-0-13)/D-2	0	-1.3
Total 17	**1912**	**6787**	**926**	**1884**	**334**	**69**	**164**	**824**	**468**	**1266**	**312**	**134**	**.278**	**.328**	**.420**	**.747**	**106**	**47**	**914**	**4.70**	**-30**	***0-1685/D-75**	**194**	**-5.6**
• WASHINGTON, George	Sloan Vernon "Vern" Washington b: 6/4/1907, Linden, TX d: 2/17/1985, Linden, TX BL/TR, 5'11.5", 190 lbs. Deb: 4/17/1935 Career OF: 0-0-91																							
1935 Chi-A	108	339	40	96	22	3	8	47	10	18	1	0	.283	.310	.437	.746	89	-7	45	4.87	5	0-79(0-0-79)	7	-0.7
1936 Chi-A	20	49	6	8	2	0	1	5	1	4	0	0	.163	.180	.265	.445	8	-7	2	1.48	0	0-12(0-0-12)	0	-0.7
Total 2	**128**	**388**	**46**	**104**	**24**	**3**	**9**	**52**	**11**	**22**	**1**	**0**	**.268**	**.294**	**.415**	**.708**	**79**	**-15**	**48**	**4.39**	**5**	**/0-91**	**7**	**-1.3**
• WASHINGTON, Herb	Herbert Lee Washington b: 11/16/1951, Belzonia, MS BR/TR, 6', 170 lbs. Deb: 4/4/1974																							
1974*Oak-A	92	0	29	0	0	0	0	0	0	0	29	16	....	....	....	....	-107	-1	0	.00	0	D-28	0	-0.1
1975 Oak-A	13	0	4	0	0	0	0	0	0	0	2	1	....	....	....	....	-102	-0	0	.00	0	/D-3	0	0.0
Total 2	**105**	**0**	**33**	**0**	**0**	**0**	**0**	**0**	**0**	**0**	**31**	**17**	**....**	**....**	**....**	**....**	**....**	**-1**	**0**	**.00**	**0**	**/D-31**	**0**	**-0.1**
• WASHINGTON, La Rue	LaRue Washington b: 9/7/1953, Long Beach, CA BR/TR, 6', 170 lbs. Deb: 9/7/1978																							
1978 Tex-A	3	3	0	0	0	0	0	0	0	1	0	0	.000	.000	.000	.000	-100	-1	0	.00	1	/2-2,D-1	0	0.0
1979 Tex-A	25	18	5	5	0	0	0	2	4	0	2	1	.278	.409	.278	.687	90	0	3	4.97	0	0-13(0-12-1)/3-1,D-1	1	0.0
Total 2	**28**	**21**	**5**	**5**	**0**	**0**	**0**	**2**	**4**	**1**	**2**	**1**	**.238**	**.360**	**.238**	**.598**	**68**	**-1**	**3**	**4.09**	**1**	**/0-13,2-2,D-2,3-1**	**1**	**0.0**
• WASHINGTON, Ron	Ronald Washington b: 4/29/1952, New Orleans, LA BR/TR, 5'11", 163 lbs. Deb: 9/10/1977 C Career OF: 2-2-0																							
1977 LA-N	10	19	4	7	0	0	0	1	0	2	1	1	.368	.400	.368	.768	108	0	2	4.50	-1	S-10	0	0.0
1981 Min-A	28	84	8	19	3	1	0	5	4	14	4	1	.226	.270	.286	.555	56	-4	7	2.71	-1	S-26/0-2(0-2-0)	1	-0.3
1982 Min-A	119	451	48	122	17	6	5	39	14	79	3	3	.271	.292	.368	.661	78	-15	45	3.50	-9	S-91,2-37/3-1	8	-1.5
1983 Min-A	99	317	28	78	7	3	4	26	22	50	10	5	.246	.297	.325	.622	69	-14	30	3.18	-14	S-81,2-14/3-1,D-1	4	-1.9
1984 Min-A	88	197	25	58	11	5	3	23	4	31	1	1	.294	.312	.447	.759	102	-0	26	4.72	-2	S-71/2-9,D-4,3-2	6	0.3
1985 Min-A	70	135	24	37	6	4	1	14	8	15	5	1	.274	.315	.400	.715	89	-2	17	4.25	-5	S-31,2-24/3-7,D-7,1-1	3	-0.4
1986 Min-A	48	74	15	19	3	0	4	11	3	21	1	2	.257	.286	.459	.745	96	-1	9	4.09	-4	2-16,D-15/S-7,3-3	1	-0.5
1987 Bal-A	26	79	7	16	3	1	1	6	1	15	0	1	.203	.213	.304	.516	36	-8	4	1.73	2	3-20/2-3,D-2,0-2(2-0-0),S	1	-0.6
1988 Cle-A	69	223	30	57	14	2	2	21	9	35	3	3	.256	.300	.363	.663	82	-6	24	3.73	-13	S-54/3-8,2-7,D-1	4	-1.6
1989 Hou-N	7	7	1	1	1	0	0	0	0	4	0	0	.143	.143	.286	.429	20	-1	0	1.29	0	/2-1,3-1	0	-0.1
Total 10	**564**	**1586**	**190**	**414**	**65**	**22**	**20**	**146**	**65**	**266**	**28**	**18**	**.261**	**.294**	**.368**	**.662**	**78**	**-52**	**165**	**3.57**	**-47**	**S-372,2-111/3-43,D-30,0-4,1**	**28**	**-6.6**
• WASHINGTON, U L	U L Washington b: 10/27/1953, Stringtown, OK BB/TR, 5'11", 175 lbs. Deb: 9/6/1977																							
1977 KC-A	10	20	0	4	1	1	0	1	5	4	1	0	.200	.360	.350	.710	94	0	3	5.13	-2	/S-9	1	-0.1
1978 KC-A	69	129	10	34	2	1	0	9	10	20	12	6	.264	.317	.295	.611	71	-5	12	3.13	-3	S-49,2-19/D-1	2	-0.5
1979 KC-A	101	268	32	68	12	5	2	25	20	44	10	7	.254	.306	.358	.664	77	-10	30	3.68	-1	S-50,2-46/D-3,3-1	5	-0.4
1980*KC-A	153	549	79	150	16	11	6	53	53	78	20	7	.273	.337	.375	.712	94	-2	70	4.41	-9	*S-152	16	0.5
1981*KC-A	98	339	40	77	19	1	2	29	41	43	10	10	.227	.311	.307	.617	79	-10	32	3.09	-4	S-98	8	-0.4
1982 KC-A	119	437	64	125	19	3	10	60	38	48	23	7	.286	.343	.412	.755	106	6	65	5.23	4	*S-117/D-1	18	2.2
1983 KC-A	144	547	76	129	19	6	5	41	48	78	40	7	.236	.299	.320	.619	70	-16	59	3.66	-2	*S-140/D-1	13	-0.4
1984*KC-A	63	170	18	38	6	0	1	10	14	31	4	6	.224	.283	.276	.559	55	-12	13	2.47	-1	S-61	2	-0.7
1985 Mon-N	68	193	24	48	9	4	1	17	15	33	6	3	.249	.303	.352	.655	88	-4	21	3.74	-1	2-43/S-9,3-3	5	-0.2
1986 Pit-N	72	135	14	27	0	4	0	10	15	27	6	0	.200	.280	.259	.539	49	-8	12	2.76	0	S-51/2-3	1	-0.5
1987 Pit-N	10	10	1	3	0	0	0	0	2	3	0	0	.300	.417	.300	.717	93	0	2	4.61	0	/3-1,S-1	0	0.0
Total 11	**907**	**2797**	**358**	**703**	**103**	**36**	**27**	**255**	**261**	**409**	**132**	**53**	**.251**	**.315**	**.343**	**.658**	**82**	**-61**	**320**	**3.84**	**-19**	**S-737,2-111/D-6,3-5**	**71**	**-0.5**
• WASINGER, Mark	Mark Thomas Wasinger b: 8/4/1961, Monterey, CA BR/TR, 6', 165 lbs. Deb: 5/27/1986																							
1986 SD-N	3	8	0	0	0	0	0	1	0	2	0	0	.000	.000	.000	.000	-102	-2	0	.00	-2	/3-3,2-1	0	-0.4
1987 SF-N	44	80	16	22	3	0	1	3	8	14	2	0	.275	.341	.350	.691	88	-1	10	4.13	1	3-21,2-10/S-2	2	0.1

YEAR TM-L	G	AB	R	H	2B	3B	HR	RBI	BB	SO	SB	CS	AVG	OBP	SLG	OPS	OPS+	BR/A	RC	RC/G	FR	G/POS	WS	TPW
1988 SF-N	3	2	1	0	0	0	0	0	0	0	0	0	.000	.000	.000	.000	-105	-1	0	.00	0	/3-1	0	-0.1
Total 3	50	90	17	22	3	0	1	4	8	16	2	0	.244	.306	.311	.617	67	-4	10	3.52	0	/3-25,2-11,S-2	2	-0.4
• WASZGIS, B.J.	Robert Michael Waszgis b: 8/24/1970, Omaha, NE BR/TR, 6'2", 215 lbs. Deb: 7/29/2000																							
2000 Tex-A	24	45	6	10	1	0	0	4	4	10	0	0	.222	.300	.244	.544	40	-4	4	2.57	-4	C-23/1-3	0	-0.7
• WATERMAN, Fred	Frederick A. Waterman b: 1845, New York, NY d: 12/16/1899, Cincinnati, OH, 5'7.5", 148 lbs. Deb: 5/5/1871 U																							
1871 Oly-n	32	158	46	50	7	4	0	17	10	0	11	3	.316	.357	.411	.769	127	7	28	7.90	3	*3-28/C-6	....	0.7
1872 Oly-n	9	45	13	17	1	2	0	6	0	0	0	0	.378	.378	.489	.867	174	4	9	9.43	3	/3-7,C-2	....	0.5
1873 Was-n	15	80	20	28	1	1	0	12	1	1	0	0	.350	.358	.388	.746	125	3	11	6.67	-6	/S-9,0-4(0-3-1),3-2	....	-0.3
1875 Chi-n	5	20	2	6	0	0	0	3	0	2	0	1	.300	.300	.300	.600	108	-0	2	3.63	-3	/3-5	....	-0.3
Total 4 n	61	303	81	101	9	7	0	38	11	3	11	4	.333	.357	.409	.766	132	13	50	7.48	-3	/3-42,S-9,C-8,0-4	....	0.6
• WATHAN, Dusty	Dustin James Wathan b: 8/22/1973, Jacksonville, FL BR/TR, 6'4", 215 lbs. Deb: 9/24/2002																							
2002 KC-A	3	5	1	3	1	0	0	1	0	1	0	0	.600	.667	.800	1.467	258	1	3	38.34	1	/C-3	1	0.2
• WATHAN, John	John David Wathan b: 10/4/1949, Cedar Rapids, IA BR/TR, 6'2", 205 lbs. Deb: 5/26/1976 M/C Career OF: 28-0-37																							
1976*KC-A	27	42	5	12	1	0	0	5	2	5	0	2	.286	.333	.310	.643	88	-1	4	2.96	-1	C-23/1-3	1	-0.2
1977*KC-A	55	119	18	39	5	3	2	21	5	8	2	0	.328	.355	.471	.825	122	4	20	6.49	-2	C-35/1-5,D-2	5	0.3
1978*KC-A	67	190	19	57	10	1	2	28	3	12	2	1	.300	.325	.395	.720	99	-1	23	4.29	0	1-47,C-21	5	-0.2
1979 KC-A	90	199	26	41	7	3	2	28	7	24	2	1	.206	.233	.302	.535	42	-17	13	1.93	-1	1-49,C-23,D-11/0-3(2-0-1)	1	-1.8
1980*KC-A	126	453	57	138	14	7	6	58	50	42	17	3	.305	.377	.406	.784	114	13	69	5.43	-4	C-77,0-35(19-0-17),1-12	17	1.0
1981*KC-A	89	301	24	76	9	3	1	19	19	23	11	6	.252	.301	.312	.614	78	-9	27	2.95	-3	C-73,0-16(3-0-13)/1-1	4	-0.9
1982 KC-A	121	448	79	121	11	3	3	51	48	46	36	9	.270	.343	.328	.671	85	-3	49	3.61	-8	*C-120/1-3	9	-0.6
1983 KC-A	128	437	49	107	18	3	2	32	27	56	28	7	.245	.290	.314	.604	66	-17	40	3.08	-0	C-92,1-37/0-9(3-0-6)	6	-1.5
1984*KC-A	97	171	17	31	7	1	2	10	21	34	6	6	.181	.271	.269	.540	50	-13	12	2.00	-2	C-59,1-33/D-4,0-1	2	-1.3
1985*KC-A	60	145	11	34	8	1	1	9	17	15	1	1	.234	.319	.324	.643	76	-5	15	3.47	0	C-49/1-6,D-2	5	-0.2
Total 10	860	2505	305	656	90	25	21	261	199	265	105	36	.262	.320	.343	.663	83	-49	271	3.62	-20	C-572,1-196/0-64,D-19	55	-5.4
• WATKINS, Bill	William Henry Watkins b: 5/5/1858, Brantford, Canada d: 6/9/1937, Port Huron, MI, 5'10", 156 lbs. Deb: 8/1/1884 M																							
1884 Ind-a	34	127	16	26	4	0	0	0	5	....	....	....	.205	.241	.236	.477	58	-6	7	2.01	-5	3-23/2-9,S-2	1	-0.9
• WATKINS, Dave	David Roger Watkins b: 3/15/1944, Owensboro, KY BR/TR, 5'10", 185 lbs. Deb: 4/9/1969																							
1969 Phi-N	69	148	17	26	2	1	4	12	22	53	2	3	.176	.291	.284	.574	63	-8	13	2.72	-1	C-54/0-5(5-0-1),3-1	2	-0.7
• WATKINS, Ed	James Edward Watkins b: 6/21/1877, Philadelphia, PA d: 3/29/1933, Kelvin, AZ Deb: 9/6/1902																							
1902 Phi-N	1	3	0	0	0	0	0	0	1	....	0	....	.000	.250	.000	.250	-22	-0	0	.00	0	/0-1	0	-0.1
• WATKINS, George	George Archibald Watkins b: 6/4/1900, Freestone County, TX d: 6/1/1970, Houston, TX BL/TR, 6', 175 lbs. Deb: 4/15/1930 Career OF: 266-118-434																							
1930*StL-N	119	391	85	146	32	7	17	87	24	49	5	....	.373	.415	.621	1.037	141	25	96	10.03	-3	0-89(3-1-85),1-13/2-1	17	1.3
1931*StL-N	131	503	93	145	30	13	13	51	31	66	15	....	.288	.336	.477	.813	112	6	81	5.89	-3	*0-129(0-9-121)	17	-0.4
1932 StL-N	127	458	67	143	35	3	9	63	45	46	18	....	.312	.384	.461	.844	122	16	84	6.92	-2	*0-120(38-19-62)	16	0.7
1933 StL-N	138	525	66	146	24	5	5	62	39	62	11	....	.278	.342	.371	.713	98	0	71	4.84	0	*0-135(0-0-135)	15	-0.8
1934 NY-N	105	296	38	73	18	3	6	33	24	34	2	....	.247	.316	.389	.704	90	-4	40	4.77	-4	0-81(8-68-5)	8	-1.0
1935 Phi-N	150	600	80	162	25	5	17	76	40	78	3	....	.270	.320	.413	.733	87	-12	82	4.85	1	*0-148(128-20-1)	12	-1.8
1936 Phi-N	19	70	7	17	4	0	2	5	5	13	2	....	.243	.293	.386	.679	74	-3	8	4.06	-1	0-17(17-0-0)	1	-0.5
Bro-N	105	364	54	93	24	6	4	43	38	34	5	....	.255	.334	.387	.722	93	-3	51	5.01	-5	0-98(72-1-25)	9	-1.3
Yr.	124	434	61	110	28	6	6	48	43	47	7	....	.253	.328	.387	.715	90	-6	59	4.86	-6	*0-115(89-1-25)	10	-1.8
Total 7	894	3207	490	925	192	42	73	420	246	382	61	....	.288	.347	.443	.790	105	25	513	5.84	-16	0-817/1-13,2-1	95	-3.8
• WATKINS, Pat	William Patrick Watkins b: 9/2/1972, Raleigh, NC BR/TR, 6'2", 185 lbs. Deb: 9/9/1997 Career OF: 17-55-33																							
1997 Cin-N	17	29	2	6	2	0	0	0	0	5	1	0	.207	.207	.276	.483	25	-3	2	1.63	0	0-15(0-15-0)	0	-0.3
1998 Cin-N	83	147	11	39	8	1	2	15	8	26	1	3	.265	.308	.374	.682	77	-6	16	3.56	-3	0-77(13-39-28)	2	-1.0
1999 Col-N	16	19	2	1	0	0	0	0	2	5	0	0	.053	.143	.053	.195	-38	-4	0	.25	0	0-10(4-1-5)	0	-0.4
Total 3	116	195	15	46	10	1	2	15	10	36	2	3	.236	.277	.328	.605	58	-14	18	2.86	-2	0-102	2	-1.7
• WATLINGTON, Neal	Julius Neal Watlington b: 12/25/1922, Yanceyville, NC BL/TR, 6', 195 lbs. Deb: 7/10/1953																							
1953 Phi-A	21	44	4	7	1	0	0	3	3	8	0	1	.159	.213	.182	.395	7	-6	2	1.06	1	/C-9	1	-0.4
• WATSON, Art	Arthur Stanhope "Watty" Watson b: 1/11/1884, Jeffersonville, IN d: 5/9/1950, Buffalo, NY BL/TR, 5'10", 175 lbs. Deb: 5/19/1914																							
1914 Bro-F	22	46	7	13	4	1	1	3	1	6	0	....	.283	.298	.478	.776	118	1	6	4.73	-1	C-18	2	0.1
1915 Bro-F	9	19	4	5	0	3	0	1	3	4	0	....	.263	.364	.579	.943	179	2	4	7.08	0	/C-7	1	0.2
Buf-F	22	30	6	14	1	0	1	13	0	4	0	....	.467	.467	.600	1.067	213	4	8	12.46	-1	/C-6,0-1	2	0.3
Yr.	31	49	10	19	1	3	1	14	3	8	0	....	.388	.423	.592	1.015	199	6	12	10.03	-2	C-13/0-1	3	0.5
Total 2	53	95	17	32	5	4	2	17	4	14	0	....	.337	.364	.537	.900	161	6	18	7.30	-2	/C-31,0-1	5	0.6
• WATSON, Bob	Robert Jose "Bull" Watson b: 4/10/1946, Los Angeles, CA BR/TR, 6'.5", 205 lbs. Deb: 9/9/1966 C Career OF: 570-0-1																							
1966 Hou-N	1	1	0	0	0	0	0	0	0	0	0	0	.000	.000	.000	.000	-107	-0	0	.00	0	....	0	0.0
1967 Hou-N	6	14	1	3	0	0	1	2	0	3	0	0	.214	.214	.429	.643	82	-0	1	1.93	0	/1-3	0	-0.1
1968 Hou-N	45	140	13	32	7	0	2	8	13	32	1	0	.229	.299	.321	.620	88	-2	13	2.99	-7	0-40(40-0-1)	2	-1.2
1969 Hou-N	20	40	3	11	3	0	0	3	6	5	0	0	.275	.396	.350	.746	113	1	6	5.93	0	/0-6(6-0-0),1-5,C-1	2	0.1
1970 Hou-N	97	327	48	89	19	2	11	61	24	59	1	1	.272	.330	.443	.773	110	3	46	4.82	-8	1-83/C-6,0-1	9	-1.1
1971 Hou-N	129	468	49	135	17	3	9	67	41	56	0	3	.288	.348	.395	.744	113	7	62	4.71	-4	0-87(87-0-0),1-45	15	-0.5
1972 Hou-N	147	548	74	171	27	4	16	86	53	83	1	1	.312	.381	.464	.844	142	30	100	6.88	-10	*0-143(143-0-0)/1-2	26	1.3
1973 Hou-N★	158	573	97	179	24	3	16	94	85	73	1	4	.312	.405	.449	.853	137	31	104	6.66	-5	*0-142(142-0-0),1-26/C-3	28	1.8
1974 Hou-N	150	524	69	156	19	4	11	67	60	61	3	4	.298	.373	.412	.785	125	17	80	5.48	2	*0-140(140-0-0),1-35	18	1.2
1975 Hou-N★	132	485	67	157	27	1	18	85	40	50	3	5	.324	.379	.495	.874	152	30	87	6.75	-1	*1-118/0-9(9-0-0)	20	2.0
1976 Hou-N	157	585	76	183	31	3	16	102	62	64	3	3	.313	.382	.458	.841	151	38	102	6.46	1	*1-155	31	2.9
1977 Hou-N	151	554	77	160	38	6	22	110	57	69	5	0	.289	.362	.498	.861	141	32	102	6.78	15	*1-146	23	3.9
1978 Hou-N	139	461	51	133	25	4	14	79	51	57	3	1	.289	.364	.451	.816	137	23	72	5.45	13	*1-128	17	3.0
1979 Hou-N	49	163	15	39	4	0	3	18	16	23	0	0	.239	.307	.319	.626	75	-5	16	3.41	6	1-44	3	-0.2
Bos-A	84	312	48	105	19	4	13	53	29	33	3	2	.337	.402	.548	.950	145	20	66	8.09	2	1-58,D-26	13	1.8
1980*NY-A	130	469	62	144	25	3	13	68	48	56	2	1	.307	.373	.456	.829	128	18	75	5.77	-1	*1-104,D-21	17	1.1
1981*NY-A	59	156	15	33	3	3	6	12	24	17	0	0	.212	.317	.385	.701	103	1	17	3.48	-2	1-50/D-6	3	-0.4
1982 NY-A	7	17	3	4	3	0	0	3	3	0	0	0	.235	.350	.412	.762	110	0	2	4.50	-1	/1-6,D-1	0	-0.1
Atl-N	57	114	16	28	3	1	5	22	14	20	1	1	.246	.328	.421	.749	104	0	15	4.35	-3	1-27/0-2(2-0-0)	3	-0.4
1983 Atl-N	65	149	14	46	9	0	6	37	18	23	0	2	.309	.383	.490	.873	131	6	26	6.29	-3	1-34	5	0.1
1984 Atl-N	49	85	4	18	4	0	2	12	9	12	0	0	.212	.287	.329	.617	68	-4	8	3.10	1	1-19	1	-0.4
Total 19	1832	6185	802	1826	307	41	184	989	653	796	27	28	.295	.367	.447	.814	130	246	1001	5.83	-5	*1-1088,0-570/D-54,C-10	236	14.6
• WATSON, Johnny	John Thomas Watson b: 1/16/1908, Tazewell, VA d: 4/29/1965, Huntington, WV BL/TR, 6', 175 lbs. Deb: 9/26/1930																							
1930 Det-A	4	12	1	3	2	0	0	3	1	2	0	0	.250	.308	.417	.724	80	-0	2	4.19	0	/S-4	0	0.0
• WATSON, Matt	Matthew Kyle Watson b: 9/5/1978, Lancaster, PA BL/TR, 5'11", 200 lbs. Deb: 9/12/2003																							
2003 NY-N	15	23	0	4	2	0	0	2	1	5	0	0	.174	.208	.261	.469	22	-3	1	1.39	0	/0-5(5-0-0)	0	-0.2
• WATSON, Mother	Walter L. Watson b: 1/27/1865, Middleport, OH d: 11/23/1898, Middleport, OH, 5'9", 145 lbs. Deb: 5/19/1887 ♦																							
1887 Cin-a	2	9	1	2	0	0	0	0	1	....	0	....	.222	.300	.125	.425	20	-0	0	1.19	-1	/P-2,0-1	0	-0.3
• WATT, Allie	Albert Bailey Watt b: 12/12/1899, Philadelphia, PA d: 3/15/1968, Norfolk, VA BR/TR, 5'8", 154 lbs. Deb: 10/3/1920																							
1920 Was-A	1	1	0	1	1	0	0	1	0	0	0	0	1.000	1.000	2.000	3.000	700	1	2	∞	0	/2-1	0	0.1

• WATWOOD, Johnny

John Clifford "Lefty" Watwood b: 8/17/1905, Alexander City, AL d: 3/1/1980, Goodwater, AL BL/TL, 6'1", 186 lbs. Deb: 4/16/1929 Career OF: 22-191-90

YEAR TM-L	G	AB	R	H	2B	3B	HR	RBI	BB	SO	SB	CS	AVG	OBP	SLG	OPS	OPS+	BR/A	RC	RC/G	FR	G/POS	WS	TPW
1929 Chi-A	85	278	33	84	12	6	2	28	22	21	6	3	.302	.355	.410	.766	98	-1	41	5.33	-1	0-77(1-53-23)	7	-0.5
1930 Chi-A	133	427	75	129	25	4	2	51	52	35	5	7	.302	.382	.393	.775	100	1	66	5.46	5	1-62,0-52(1-36-14)	11	-0.1
1931 Chi-A	128	367	51	104	16	6	1	47	56	30	9	3	.283	.380	.368	.748	103	7	56	5.36	2	*0-102(4-76-24)/1-4	12	0.5
1932 Chi-A	13	49	5	15	2	0	0	0	1	3	0	0	.306	.333	.347	.680	82	-1	6	4.21	0	0-13(4-1-11)	1	-0.2
Bos-A	95	266	26	66	11	0	0	30	20	11	7	4	.248	.301	.289	.590	55	-17	24	3.03	0	0-46(7-25-14),1-18	1	-1.9
Yr.	108	315	31	81	13	0	0	30	21	14	7	4	.257	.306	.298	.604	59	-19	30	3.21	0	0-59(11-26-25),1-18	2	-2.1
1933 Bos-A	13	30	2	4	0	0	0	2	3	3	0	0	.133	.212	.133	.345	-7	-5	1	.99	-1	/0-9(5-0-4)	0	-0.5
1939 Phi-N	2	6	0	1	0	0	0	0	0	0	0	....	.167	.167	.167	.333	-11	-1	0	.90	-1	/1-2	0	-0.2
Total 6	**469**	**1423**	**192**	**403**	**66**	**16**	**5**	**158**	**154**	**103**	**27**	**17**	**.283**	**.356**	**.363**	**.718**	**89**	**-17**	**193**	**4.77**	**4**	**0-299/1-86**	**32**	**-3.0**

• WAY, Bob

Robert Clinton Way b: 4/2/1906, Emlenton, PA d: 6/20/1974, Pittsburgh, PA BR/TR, 5'10.5", 168 lbs. Deb: 4/12/1927

YEAR TM-L	G	AB	R	H	2B	3B	HR	RBI	BB	SO	SB	CS	AVG	OBP	SLG	OPS	OPS+	BR/A	RC	RC/G	FR	G/POS	WS	TPW
1927 Chi-A	5	3	3	1	0	0	0	1	0	0	0	0	.333	.333	.333	.667	75	-0	0	4.24	0	/2-1	0	0.0

• WEATHERLY, Roy

Cyril Roy "Stormy" Weatherly b: 2/25/1915, Warren, TX d: 1/19/1991, Woodville, TX BL/TR, 5'6.5", 170 lbs. Deb: 6/27/1936 Career OF: 65-480-137

YEAR TM-L	G	AB	R	H	2B	3B	HR	RBI	BB	SO	SB	CS	AVG	OBP	SLG	OPS	OPS+	BR/A	RC	RC/G	FR	G/POS	WS	TPW
1936 Cle-A	84	349	64	117	28	6	8	53	16	29	3	8	.335	.364	.519	.883	115	3	61	6.75	5	0-84(3-5-80)	9	0.3
1937 Cle-A	53	134	19	27	4	0	5	13	6	14	1	1	.201	.246	.343	.590	47	-12	11	2.70	2	0-38(7-0-32)/3-1	0	-1.1
1938 Cle-A	83	210	32	55	14	3	2	18	14	14	8	5	.262	.308	.386	.694	74	-10	24	3.96	2	0-55(6-41-8)	4	-0.8
1939 Cle-A	95	323	43	100	16	6	1	32	19	23	7	2	.310	.348	.406	.754	95	-2	47	5.54	-3	0-76(36-27-14)	9	-0.8
1940 Cle-A	135	578	90	175	35	11	12	59	27	26	9	8	.303	.335	.464	.799	108	3	88	5.55	0	*0-135(1-134-0)	20	0.0
1941 Cle-A	102	363	59	105	21	5	3	37	32	20	2	5	.289	.350	.399	.750	103	-0	52	5.08	-7	0-88(0-87-1)	9	-1.0
1942 Cle-A	128	473	61	122	23	7	5	39	35	25	8	13	.258	.310	.368	.678	96	-8	54	3.90	4	*0-117(0-117-0)	13	-0.6
1943*NY-A	77	280	37	74	8	3	7	28	18	9	4	7	.264	.311	.389	.700	104	-2	34	4.07	-2	0-68(0-68-0)	9	-0.6
1946 NY-A	2	2	0	1	0	0	0	0	0	0	0	0	.500	.500	.500	1.000	178	0	1	13.84	0	....	0	0.0
1950 NY-N	52	69	10	18	3	3	0	11	13	10	0	....	.261	.378	.391	.769	102	1	10	5.12	1	0-15(12-1-2)	2	0.1
Total 10	**811**	**2781**	**415**	**794**	**152**	**44**	**43**	**290**	**180**	**170**	**42**	**49**	**.286**	**.331**	**.418**	**.749**	**98**	**-28**	**382**	**4.89**	**3**	**0-676/3-1**	**75**	**-4.5**

• WEAVER, Art

Arthur Coggshall "Six O'Clock" Weaver b: 4/7/1879, Wichita, KS d: 3/23/1917, Denver, CO TR, 6'1", 160 lbs. Deb: 9/14/1902

YEAR TM-L	G	AB	R	H	2B	3B	HR	RBI	BB	SO	SB	CS	AVG	OBP	SLG	OPS	OPS+	BR/A	RC	RC/G	FR	G/POS	WS	TPW
1902 StL-N	11	33	2	6	2	0	0	3	1	....	0	....	.182	.206	.242	.448	40	-2	2	1.66	1	C-11	0	0.0
1903 StL-N	16	49	4	12	0	0	0	5	4	....	1	....	.245	.302	.245	.547	58	-3	4	2.91	1	C-16	1	0.1
Pit-N	16	48	8	11	0	1	0	3	2	....	0	....	.229	.260	.271	.531	50	-3	3	2.48	-1	C-11/1-5	1	-0.3
Yr.	32	97	12	23	0	1	0	8	6	....	1	....	.237	.282	.258	.539	54	-6	8	2.70	0	C-27/1-5	2	-0.3
1905 StL-A	28	92	5	11	2	1	0	3	1	....	0	....	.120	.129	.163	.292	-8	-11	2	.68	2	C-28	1	-0.7
1908 Chi-A	15	35	1	7	1	0	0	1	1	....	0	....	.200	.222	.229	.451	47	-2	2	1.58	-1	C-15	0	-0.3
Total 4	**86**	**257**	**20**	**47**	**5**	**2**	**0**	**15**	**9**	**....**	**1**	**....**	**.183**	**.211**	**.218**	**.428**	**30**	**-22**	**13**	**1.63**	**2**	**/C-81,1-5**	**3**	**-1.4**

• WEAVER, Buck

George Daniel Weaver b: 8/18/1890, Pottstown, PA d: 1/31/1956, Chicago, IL BB/TR, 5'11", 170 lbs. Deb: 4/11/1912

YEAR TM-L	G	AB	R	H	2B	3B	HR	RBI	BB	SO	SB	CS	AVG	OBP	SLG	OPS	OPS+	BR/A	RC	RC/G	FR	G/POS	WS	TPW
1912 Chi-A	147	523	55	117	21	8	1	43	9	....	12	....	.224	.245	.300	.546	58	-32	41	2.50	-8	*S-147	8	-2.9
1913 Chi-A	151	533	51	145	17	8	4	52	15	60	20	....	.272	.302	.356	.659	93	-8	61	3.83	34	*S-151	23	4.0
1914 Chi-A	136	541	64	133	20	9	2	28	20	40	14	20	.246	.279	.327	.606	83	-20	47	2.86	-9	*S-134	8	-2.2
1915 Chi-A	148	563	83	151	18	11	3	49	32	58	24	20	.268	.316	.355	.671	98	-8	68	3.78	6	*S-148	21	0.9
1916 Chi-A	151	582	78	132	27	6	3	38	30	48	22	13	.227	.280	.309	.589	76	-20	57	2.93	18	3-85,S-66	14	0.5
1917*Chi-A	118	447	64	127	16	5	3	32	27	29	19	....	.284	.332	.362	.694	109	4	61	4.45	21	*3-107,S-10	21	3.2
1918 Chi-A	112	420	37	126	12	5	0	29	11	24	20	....	.300	.323	.352	.675	103	-1	53	4.29	7	S-98,3-11/2-1	15	1.5
1919*Chi-A	140	571	89	169	33	9	3	75	11	21	22	....	.296	.315	.401	.716	100	-4	77	4.61	8	3-97,S-43	20	1.0
1920 Chi-A	151	629	102	208	34	8	2	74	28	23	19	17	.331	.365	.420	.785	107	4	93	5.29	-2	*3-127,S-25	22	0.7
Total 9	**1254**	**4809**	**623**	**1308**	**198**	**69**	**21**	**420**	**183**	**303**	**172**	**70**	**.272**	**.307**	**.355**	**.662**	**92**	**-85**	**557**	**3.81**	**74**	**S-822,3-427/2-1**	**152**	**6.7**

• WEAVER, Farmer

William B. Weaver b: 3/23/1865, Parkersburg, WV d: 1/23/1943, Akron, OH BL, 5'10" Deb: 9/16/1888 U Career OF: 132-408-111

YEAR TM-L	G	AB	R	H	2B	3B	HR	RBI	BB	SO	SB	CS	AVG	OBP	SLG	OPS	OPS+	BR/A	RC	RC/G	FR	G/POS	WS	TPW
1888 Lou-a	26	112	12	28	1	1	0	8	3	....	12	....	.250	.276	.277	.553	79	-3	12	3.91	-1	0-26(0-26-0)	2	-0.4
1889 Lou-a	124	499	62	145	17	6	0	60	40	22	21	....	.291	.352	.349	.700	101	2	70	5.26	5	*0-123(0-123-0)/C-2,2-1,3	8	0.3
1890*Lou-a	130	557	101	161	27	9	3	67	29	....	45	....	.289	.333	.386	.719	114	7	89	5.94	-2	*0-127(0-126-1)/S-2,3-1	18	0.1
1891 Lou-a	133	556	74	157	25	7	1	53	33	23	30	....	.282	.335	.358	.693	99	-2	79	5.22	10	*0-132(0-132-0)/C-4	14	0.3
1892 Lou-N	138	551	58	140	15	4	0	57	40	17	30	....	.254	.315	.296	.611	92	-4	62	4.09	-6	*0-122(109-1-12),C-15/1-1	13	-1.7
1893 Lou-N	106	439	79	128	17	7	2	49	27	12	17	....	.292	.348	.376	.724	100	0	65	5.53	2	*0-85(20-0-65),C-21	11	-0.1
1894 Lou-N	64	244	19	54	5	2	3	24	7	11	3	....	.221	.249	.295	.544	33	-27	19	2.62	1	0-35(2-0-33),C-17,1-10/2-1	1	-2.0
Pit-N	30	115	16	40	7	2	0	24	6	1	4	....	.348	.405	.443	.848	106	1	23	7.91	-4	C-14,S-12/3-5,0-1	4	-0.1
Yr.	94	359	35	94	12	4	3	48	13	12	7	....	.262	.301	.343	.643	57	-26	42	4.12	-3	0-36(3-0-33),C-31,S-12,1-10/3,2	5	-2.1
Total 7	**751**	**3073**	**421**	**853**	**114**	**38**	**9**	**342**	**185**	**86**	**162**	**....**	**.278**	**.330**	**.348**	**.678**	**96**	**-25**	**419**	**5.01**	**7**	**0-651/C-73,S-14,1-11,3-7,2**	**71**	**-3.6**

• WEAVER, Jim

James Francis Weaver b: 10/10/1959, Kingston, NY BL/TL, 6'3", 190 lbs. Deb: 4/10/1985 Career OF: 2-5-10

YEAR TM-L	G	AB	R	H	2B	3B	HR	RBI	BB	SO	SB	CS	AVG	OBP	SLG	OPS	OPS+	BR/A	RC	RC/G	FR	G/POS	WS	TPW
1985 Det-A	12	7	2	1	1	0	0	0	1	4	0	1	.143	.250	.286	.536	47	-1	0	1.09	-1	/D-4,0-4(0-3-1)	0	-0.2
1987 Sea-A	7	4	2	0	0	0	0	0	2	3	1	1	.000	.333	.000	.333	-1	-1	0	.94	0	/0-4(1-2-2)	0	0.0
1989 SF-N	12	20	2	4	3	0	0	2	0	7	1	0	.200	.200	.350	.550	56	-1	2	2.54	0	/0-8(1-0-7)	0	-0.1
Total 3	**31**	**31**	**6**	**5**	**4**	**0**	**0**	**2**	**3**	**14**	**2**	**2**	**.161**	**.235**	**.290**	**.526**	**44**	**-3**	**2**	**1.89**	**0**	**/0-16,D-4**	**0**	**-0.3**

• WEBB, Bill

William Joseph Webb b: 6/25/1895, Chicago, IL d: 1/12/1943, Chicago, IL BR/TR, 5'10", 161 lbs. Deb: 9/17/1917 C

YEAR TM-L	G	AB	R	H	2B	3B	HR	RBI	BB	SO	SB	CS	AVG	OBP	SLG	OPS	OPS+	BR/A	RC	RC/G	FR	G/POS	WS	TPW
1917 Pit-N	5	15	1	3	0	0	0	0	2	3	0	....	.200	.294	.200	.494	51	-1	1	1.80	1	/2-4,S-1	0	0.0

• WEBB, Earl

William Earl Webb b: 9/17/1897, Bon Air, TN d: 5/23/1965, Jamestown, TN BL/TR, 6'1", 185 lbs. Deb: 8/13/1925 Career OF: 13-0-524

YEAR TM-L	G	AB	R	H	2B	3B	HR	RBI	BB	SO	SB	CS	AVG	OBP	SLG	OPS	OPS+	BR/A	RC	RC/G	FR	G/POS	WS	TPW
1925 NY-N	4	3	0	0	0	0	0	0	1	1	0	0	.000	.250	.000	.250	-31	-1	0	.55	0	....	0	0.0
1927 Chi-N	102	332	58	100	18	4	14	52	48	31	3	....	.301	.391	.506	.897	138	19	66	6.94	4	0-86(8-0-78)	15	1.5
1928 Chi-N	62	140	22	35	7	3	3	23	14	17	0	....	.250	.318	.407	.725	90	-3	18	4.26	1	0-31(0-0-31)	3	-0.4
1930 Bos-A	127	449	61	145	30	6	16	66	44	56	2	1	.323	.385	.523	.908	133	22	91	7.61	-6	*0-116(0-0-116)	14	0.7
1931 Bos-A	151	589	96	196	**67**	3	14	103	70	51	2	2	.333	.404	.528	.932	151	46	127	8.50	1	*0-151(0-0-151)	25	3.5
1932 Bos-A	52	192	23	54	9	1	5	27	25	15	0	0	.281	.364	.417	.781	105	2	30	5.74	-1	0-50(0-0-50)/1-2	4	-0.2
Det-A	88	338	49	97	19	8	3	51	39	18	1	1	.287	.361	.417	.778	97	-1	52	5.69	0	0-85(0-0-85)	10	-0.5
Yr.	140	530	72	151	28	9	8	78	64	33	1	1	.285	.362	.417	.779	100	1	82	5.71	0	*0-135(0-0-135)/1-2	14	-0.7
1933 Det-A	6	11	1	3	0	0	0	3	3	0	0	0	.273	.429	.273	.701	87	0	2	5.15	0	/0-2(0-0-2)	0	0.0
Chi-A	58	107	16	31	5	0	1	8	16	13	0	0	.290	.382	.364	.747	103	1	16	5.42	-2	0-16(5-0-11),1-10	3	-0.2
Yr.	64	118	17	34	5	0	1	11	19	13	0	0	.288	.387	.356	.743	101	1	18	5.40	-2	0-18(5-0-13),1-10	3	-0.2
Total 7	**650**	**2161**	**326**	**661**	**155**	**25**	**56**	**333**	**260**	**202**	**8**	**4**	**.306**	**.381**	**.478**	**.859**	**126**	**87**	**402**	**6.88**	**-2**	**0-537/1-12**	**74**	**4.4**

• WEBB, Skeeter

James Laverne Webb b: 11/4/1909, Meridian, MS d: 7/8/1986, Meridian, MS BR/TR, 5'9.5", 150 lbs. Deb: 7/20/1932

YEAR TM-L	G	AB	R	H	2B	3B	HR	RBI	BB	SO	SB	CS	AVG	OBP	SLG	OPS	OPS+	BR/A	RC	RC/G	FR	G/POS	WS	TPW
1932 StL-N	1	0	0	0	0	0	0	0	0	0	0	....	....	....	....	....	-97	0	0	....	-1	/S-1	0	-0.1
1938 Cle-A	20	58	11	16	2	0	0	2	8	7	1	0	.276	.364	.310	.674	72	-2	7	4.54	-2	S-13/3-3,2-2	2	-0.2
1939 Cle-A	81	269	28	71	14	1	2	26	15	24	1	1	.264	.305	.346	.651	68	-13	28	3.66	-5	S-81	6	-1.2
1940 Chi-A	84	334	33	79	11	2	1	29	30	33	3	6	.237	.299	.290	.590	53	-25	30	2.99	3	2-74/S-7,3-1	4	-1.6
1941 Chi-A	29	84	7	16	2	0	0	6	3	9	1	0	.190	.227	.214	.442	18	-10	4	1.69	-3	2-18/S-5,3-3	1	-1.1
1942 Chi-A	32	94	5	16	2	1	0	4	4	13	1	2	.170	.204	.213	.417	18	-11	4	1.28	0	2-29	1	-1.0
1943 Chi-A	58	213	15	50	5	2	0	22	6	19	5	4	.235	.256	.277	.533	56	-13	14	2.22	0	2-54	2	-1.1
1944 Chi-A	139	513	44	108	19	6	0	30	20	39	7	3	.211	.242	.271	.513	47	-36	33	2.12	3	*S-135/2-5	7	-2.4
1945*Det-A	118	407	43	81	12	2	0	21	30	35	8	7	.199	.254	.238	.492	41	-32	25	1.90	7	*S-104,2-11	6	-1.7
1946 Det-A	64	169	12	37	1	1	0	17	9	18	3	3	.219	.258	.237	.495	37	-15	10	1.84	0	2-50/S-8	3	-1.2
1947 Det-A	50	79	13	16	3	0	0	6	7	9	3	0	.203	.267	.241	.508	41	-6	6	2.58	-4	2-30/S-6	1	-0.9
1948 Phi-A	23	54	5	8	2	0	0	3	0	9	0	0	.148	.148	.185	.333	-12	-9	1	.65	2	/2-9,S-8	1	-0.6
Total 12	**699**	**2274**	**216**	**498**	**73**	**15**	**3**	**166**	**132**	**215**	**33**	**26**	**.219**	**.263**	**.268**	**.531**	**46**	**-172**	**164**	**2.34**	**0**	**S-368,2-282/3-7**	**34**	**-13.1**

• WEBER, Harry

Henry J. Weber b: 3/1862, NY d: 12/22/1926, Indianapolis, IN Deb: 7/22/1884

YEAR TM-L	G	AB	R	H	2B	3B	HR	RBI	BB	SO	SB	CS	AVG	OBP	SLG	OPS	OPS+	BR/A	RC	RC/G	FR	G/POS	WS	TPW
1884 Ind-a	3	8	0	0	0	0	0	0	0	....	....	....	.000	.111	.000	.111	-62	-1	0	.00	0	/C-3	0	-0.1

YEAR TM-L	G	AB	R	H	2B	3B	HR	RBI	BB	SO	SB	CS	AVG	OBP	SLG	OPS	OPS+	BR/A	RC	RC/G	FR	G/POS	WS	TPW
• WEBER, Joe	Joseph Edward Weber b: 2/15/1862, Hamilton, Canada d: 12/15/1921, Hamilton, Canada Deb: 5/30/1884																							
1884 Det-N	2	8	0	0	0	0	0	0	0	2	....	....	.000	.000	.000	.000	-106	-2	0	.00	0	/0-2(1-0-1)	0	-0.1
• WEBSTER, Lenny	Leonard Irell Webster b: 2/10/1965, New Orleans, LA BR/TR, 5'9", 191 lbs. Deb: 9/1/1989																							
1989 Min-A	14	20	3	6	2	0	0	1	3	2	0	0	.300	.391	.400	.791	116	1	3	6.63	0	C-14	1	0.0
1990 Min-A	2	6	1	2	1	0	0	0	1	1	0	0	.333	.429	.500	.929	149	0	1	9.43	0	/C-2	0	0.0
1991 Min-A	18	34	7	10	1	0	3	8	6	10	0	0	.294	.400	.588	.988	162	3	8	7.54	0	C-17	2	0.4
1992 Min-A	53	118	10	33	10	1	1	13	9	11	0	2	.280	.331	.407	.737	102	-1	15	4.32	-2	C-49/D-1	2	0.0
1993 Min-A	49	106	14	21	2	0	1	8	11	8	1	0	.198	.274	.245	.519	40	-9	8	2.42	0	C-45/D-1	1	-0.6
1994 Mon-N	57	143	13	39	10	0	5	23	16	24	0	0	.273	.370	.448	.817	111	3	23	5.49	-1	C-46	5	0.4
1995 Phi-N	49	150	18	40	9	0	4	14	16	27	0	0	.267	.337	.407	.744	94	-1	20	4.80	-2	C-43	3	-0.1
1996 Mon-N	78	174	18	40	10	0	2	17	25	21	0	0	.230	.333	.322	.655	72	-7	18	3.30	2	C-63	2	-0.1
1997*Bal-A	98	259	29	66	8	1	7	37	22	46	0	1	.255	.318	.375	.693	82	-7	29	3.76	0	C-97/D-1	7	-0.2
1998 Bal-A	108	309	37	88	16	0	10	46	15	38	0	0	.285	.318	.434	.752	94	-4	40	4.56	1	*C-102/D-4	7	0.2
1999 Bal-A	16	36	1	6	1	0	0	3	8	5	0	0	.167	.333	.194	.528	41	-3	3	2.53	0	C-12/D-2	0	-0.2
Bos-A	6	14	0	0	0	0	0	1	2	2	0	0	.000	.176	.000	.176	-48	-3	0	.27	0	/C-6	0	-0.2
Yr.	22	50	1	6	1	0	0	4	10	7	0	0	.120	.290	.140	.430	16	-6	3	1.83	1	C-18/D-2	0	-0.4
2000 Mon-N	39	81	6	17	3	0	0	5	6	14	0	0	.210	.264	.247	.511	29	-9	4	1.72	-3	C-32	1	-1.0
Total 12	**587**	**1450**	**157**	**368**	**73**	**2**	**33**	**176**	**140**	**209**	**1**	**3**	**.254**	**.325**	**.375**	**.700**	**84**	**-36**	**172**	**4.03**	**-6**	**C-528/D-9**	**31**	**-1.3**
• WEBSTER, Mitch	Mitchell Dean Webster b: 5/16/1959, Larned, KS BB/TL, 6'.5", 185 lbs. Deb: 9/2/1983 Career OF: 275-425-393																							
1983 Tor-A	11	11	2	2	0	0	0	0	1	1	0	0	.182	.250	.182	.432	20	-1	1	1.70	-1	/0-7(0-7-0),D-2	0	-0.2
1984 Tor-A	26	22	9	5	2	1	0	4	1	7	0	0	.227	.261	.409	.670	79	-1	2	3.02	-1	0-10(3-7-0)/D-9,1-1	0	-0.2
1985 Tor-A	4	1	0	0	0	0	0	0	0	0	0	1	.000	.000	.000	.000	-98	-1	0	.00	0	/D-2,0-2(2-0-0)	0	-0.1
Mon-N	74	212	32	58	8	2	11	30	20	33	15	9	.274	.336	.486	.822	135	8	33	5.27	0	0-64(4-52-20)	9	0.7
1986 Mon-N	151	576	89	167	31	**13**	8	49	57	78	36	15	.290	.358	.431	.788	117	15	90	5.53	-2	*0-146(8-118-44)	22	0.9
1987 Mon-N	156	588	101	165	30	8	15	63	70	95	33	10	.281	.363	.435	.798	107	9	99	5.94	-6	*0-153(0-0-153)	23	-0.4
1988 Mon-N	81	259	33	66	5	2	2	13	36	37	12	10	.255	.357	.313	.669	90	-4	31	3.93	-3	0-71(12-53-12)	7	-0.9
Chi-N	70	264	36	70	11	6	4	26	19	50	10	4	.265	.322	.398	.719	101	0	35	4.65	-3	0-65(8-52-10)	10	-0.4
Yr.	151	523	69	136	16	8	6	39	55	87	22	14	.260	.340	.356	.695	95	-3	66	4.28	-6	*0-136(20-105-22)	17	-1.3
1989*Chi-N	98	272	40	70	12	4	3	19	30	55	14	2	.257	.333	.364	.697	92	-0	36	4.59	-1	0-74(52-13-21)	7	-0.4
1990 Cle-A	128	437	58	110	20	6	12	55	20	61	22	6	.252	.289	.407	.696	93	-4	52	3.97	-2	*0-118(25-95-0)/1-3,D-3	13	-0.9
1991 Cle-A	13	32	2	4	0	0	0	0	3	9	2	2	.125	.200	.125	.325	-8	-5	1	.77	0	0-10(6-1-6)	0	-0.6
Pit-N	36	97	9	17	3	4	1	9	9	31	0	0	.175	.245	.320	.565	59	-6	7	2.33	0	0-29(2-9-20)	1	-0.7
LA-N	58	74	12	21	5	1	1	10	9	21	0	1	.284	.361	.419	.780	121	2	12	5.74	-1	0-36(29-4-7)/1-1	3	0.1
Yr.	94	171	21	38	8	5	2	19	18	52	0	1	.222	.296	.363	.659	86	-4	19	3.69	-1	0-65(31-13-27)/1-1	4	-0.7
1992 LA-N	135	262	33	70	12	5	6	35	27	49	11	5	.267	.340	.420	.760	116	6	40	5.06	-4	0-90(36-8-56)	7	-0.1
1993 LA-N	88	172	26	42	6	2	2	14	11	24	4	6	.244	.297	.337	.635	74	-9	16	2.95	-2	0-56(32-2-27)	2	-1.3
1994 LA-N	82	84	16	23	4	0	4	12	8	13	1	2	.274	.344	.464	.808	116	1	13	5.20	-2	0-48(45-0-6)	1	-0.1
1995*LA-N	54	56	6	10	1	1	1	3	4	14	0	0	.179	.246	.286	.532	43	-5	4	2.21	-1	0-25(11-4-11)	0	-0.6
Total 13	**1265**	**3419**	**504**	**900**	**150**	**55**	**70**	**342**	**325**	**578**	**160**	**73**	**.263**	**.332**	**.401**	**.733**	**101**	**7**	**471**	**4.69**	**-30**	***0-1004/D-16,1-5**	**105**	**-5.2**
• WEBSTER, Ray	Ramon Alberto Webster b: 8/31/1942, Colon, Panama BL/TL, 6', 185 lbs. Deb: 4/11/1967 Career OF: 15-0-2																							
1967 KC-A	122	360	41	92	15	4	11	51	32	44	5	3	.256	.320	.411	.731	118	8	46	4.37	-1	1-83,0-15(14-0-2)	11	0.2
1968 Oak-A	66	196	17	42	11	1	3	23	12	24	3	0	.214	.260	.327	.586	81	-5	16	2.66	-1	1-55	3	-1.0
1969 Oak-A	64	77	5	20	0	1	1	13	12	8	0	0	.260	.367	.325	.691	99	1	9	3.99	1	1-13	2	0.1
1970 SD-N	95	116	12	30	3	0	2	11	11	12	1	1	.259	.323	.336	.659	80	-3	13	3.85	-1	1-15/0-1	2	-0.5
1971 SD-N	10	8	0	1	0	0	0	0	2	1	0	0	.125	.300	.125	.425	26	-1	0	1.76	0	....	0	-0.1
Oak-A	7	5	0	0	0	0	0	0	0	2	0	0	.000	.000	.000	.000	-102	-1	0	.00	0	/1-1	0	-0.2
Chi-N	16	16	1	5	2	0	0	0	1	3	0	0	.313	.353	.438	.790	107	0	3	6.29	0	/1-1	0	0.0
Yr.	26	24	1	6	2	0	0	0	3	4	0	0	.250	.333	.333	.667	77	-0	3	4.53	0	/1-1	0	0.0
Total 5	**380**	**778**	**76**	**190**	**31**	**6**	**17**	**98**	**70**	**94**	**9**	**4**	**.244**	**.309**	**.365**	**.674**	**99**	**-2**	**87**	**3.78**	**-1**	**1-168/0-16**	**18**	**-1.4**
• WEBSTER, Ray	Raymond George Webster b: 11/15/1937, Grass Valley, CA BR/TR, 6', 175 lbs. Deb: 4/17/1959																							
1959 Cle-A	40	74	10	15	2	1	2	10	5	7	1	0	.203	.253	.338	.591	63	-4	6	2.68	-1	2-24/3-4	1	-0.4
1960 Bos-A	7	3	1	0	0	0	0	1	1	0	0	0	.000	.250	.000	.250	-25	-1	0	1.05	0	/2-1	0	0.0
Total 2	**47**	**77**	**11**	**15**	**2**	**1**	**2**	**11**	**6**	**7**	**1**	**0**	**.195**	**.253**	**.325**	**.578**	**58**	**-4**	**6**	**2.58**	**-1**	**/2-25,3-4**	**1**	**-0.4**
• WECKBECKER, Pete	Peter Weckbecker b: 8/30/1864, Butler, PA d: 5/16/1935, Hampton, VA, 5'7", 150 lbs. Deb: 10/5/1889																							
1889 Ind-N	1	1	0	0	0	0	0	2	0	0	0	....	.000	.000	.000	.000	-98	-0	0	.00	0	/C-1	0	0.0
1890*Lou-a	32	101	17	24	1	0	0	11	8	....	7	....	.238	.300	.248	.548	63	-5	10	3.39	-4	C-32	2	-0.5
Total 2	**33**	**102**	**17**	**24**	**1**	**0**	**0**	**13**	**8**	**0**	**7**	**....**	**.235**	**.297**	**.245**	**.542**	**61**	**-5**	**10**	**3.34**	**-4**	**/C-33**	**2**	**-0.6**
• WEDGE, Eric	Eric Michael Wedge b: 1/27/1968, Fort Wayne, IN BR/TR, 6'3", 215 lbs. Deb: 10/5/1991 M																							
1991 Bos-A	1	1	0	1	0	0	0	0	0	0	0	0	1.000	1.000	1.000	2.000	434	0	1	∞	0	/D-1	0	0.0
1992 Bos-A	27	68	11	17	2	0	5	11	13	18	0	0	.250	.370	.500	.870	133	3	14	7.33	0	D-20/C-5	4	0.3
1993 Col-N	9	11	2	2	0	0	0	1	0	4	0	0	.182	.182	.182	.364	-2	-2	0	1.09	0	/C-1	0	-0.1
1994 Bos-A	2	6	0	0	0	0	0	0	1	3	0	0	.000	.143	.000	.143	-56	-1	0	.17	0	/D-2	0	-0.1
Total 4	**39**	**86**	**13**	**20**	**2**	**0**	**5**	**12**	**14**	**25**	**0**	**0**	**.233**	**.340**	**.430**	**.770**	**108**	**1**	**15**	**5.83**	**0**	**/D-23,C-6**	**4**	**0.1**
• WEEDEN, Bert	Charles Albert Weeden b: 12/21/1882, Northwood, NH d: 1/7/1939, Northwood, NH BL/TL, 6', 200 lbs. Deb: 6/4/1911																							
1911 Bos-N	1	1	0	0	0	0	0	0	0	0	0	....	.000	.000	.000	.000	-93	-0	0	.00	0	....	0	0.0
• WEEKLY, Johnny	John Weekly b: 6/14/1937, Waterproof, LA d: 11/24/1974, Walnut Creek, CA BR/TR, 6', 200 lbs. Deb: 4/13/1962 Career OF: 19-0-17																							
1962 Hou-N	13	26	3	5	1	0	2	2	7	4	0	0	.192	.364	.462	.825	129	1	5	6.46	0	/0-7(4-0-4)	1	0.1
1963 Hou-N	34	80	4	18	3	0	3	14	7	14	0	0	.225	.295	.375	.670	98	-0	9	3.58	0	0-23(15-0-8)	2	-0.1
1964 Hou-N	6	15	0	2	0	0	0	3	1	3	0	0	.133	.188	.133	.321	-8	-2	0	.62	0	/0-5(0-0-5)	0	-0.2
Total 3	**53**	**121**	**7**	**25**	**4**	**0**	**5**	**19**	**15**	**21**	**0**	**0**	**.207**	**.299**	**.364**	**.663**	**92**	**-1**	**14**	**3.70**	**1**	**/0-35**	**3**	**-0.3**
• WEEKS, Rickie	Rickie Darnell Weeks b: 9/13/1982, Altamonte Springs, FL BR/TR, 6', 195 lbs. Deb: 9/15/2003																							
2003 Mil-N	7	12	1	2	1	0	0	0	1	6	0	0	.167	.286	.250	.536	42	-1	1	2.72	-4	/2-4	0	-0.4
• WEHNER, John	John Paul Wehner b: 6/29/1967, Pittsburgh, PA BR/TR, 6'3", 205 lbs. Deb: 7/17/1991 Career OF: 69-29-54																							
1991 Pit-N	37	106	15	36	7	0	0	7	7	17	3	0	.340	.381	.406	.786	123	4	18	6.81	2	3-36	5	0.6
1992*Pit-N	55	123	11	22	6	0	0	4	12	22	3	0	.179	.252	.228	.479	37	-9	7	1.83	-1	3-34,1-13/2-5	1	-1.2
1993 Pit-N	29	35	3	5	0	0	0	0	6	10	0	0	.143	.268	.143	.411	14	-4	2	1.58	1	0-13(4-8-2)/2-3,3-3	0	-0.3
1994 Pit-N	2	4	1	1	1	0	0	3	0	1	0	0	.250	.250	.500	.750	88	-0	1	4.50	0	/3-1	0	0.0
1995 Pit-N	52	107	13	33	0	3	0	5	10	17	3	1	.308	.368	.364	.732	92	-1	15	4.87	1	0-23(18-2-3),3-19/C-1,S-1	2	0.1
1996 Pit-N	86	139	19	36	9	1	2	13	8	22	1	5	.259	.299	.381	.681	76	-7	14	3.25	-1	0-29(9-13-8),3-24,2-12/C-1	1	-0.8
1997*Fla-N	44	36	8	10	2	0	0	2	2	5	1	0	.278	.333	.333	.667	79	-1	4	3.54	-2	0-27(10-1-19)/3-6	0	-0.4
1998 Fla-N	53	88	10	20	2	0	0	5	7	12	1	0	.227	.284	.250	.534	44	-7	6	2.33	1	0-23(12-2-11)/3-8	0	-0.7
1999 Pit-N	39	65	6	12	2	0	1	4	7	12	1	0	.185	.264	.262	.525	34	-7	5	2.38	-1	0-17(12-2-6)/3-2,S-2,2-1	0	-0.8
2000 Pit-N	21	50	10	15	3	0	1	9	4	6	0	0	.300	.352	.420	.772	95	-0	7	5.39	0	3-16/0-1	1	0.0
2001 Pit-N	43	51	3	10	1	0	0	2	10	12	2	1	.196	.328	.216	.544	44	-4	4	2.49	0	1-11/0-8(3-1-5),3-6,2-1,C	0	-0.4
Total 11	**461**	**804**	**99**	**200**	**33**	**4**	**4**	**54**	**73**	**136**	**15**	**7**	**.249**	**.312**	**.315**	**.627**	**67**	**-37**	**82**	**3.44**	**-1**	**3-155,0-141/1-24,2-22,C-3,S**	**10**	**-3.9**
• WEIGEL, Ralph	Ralph Richard "Wig" Weigel b: 10/2/1921, Coldwater, OH d: 4/15/1992, Memphis, TN BR/TR, 6'1", 180 lbs. Deb: 9/18/1946																							
1946 Cle-A	6	12	0	2	0	0	0	0	0	2	1	0	.167	.167	.167	.333	-7	-1	0	1.16	0	/C-6	0	-0.2
1948 Chi-A	66	163	8	38	7	3	0	26	13	18	1	2	.233	.294	.313	.607	63	-10	14	2.91	-1	C-39/0-2(2-0-0)	1	-0.8

YEAR TM-L	G	AB	R	H	2B	3B	HR	RBI	BB	SO	SB	CS	AVG	OBP	SLG	OPS	OPS+	BR/A	RC	RC/G	FR	G/POS	WS	TPW
1949 Was-A	34	60	4	14	2	0	0	4	8	6	0	1	.233	.324	.267	.590	58	-4	5	2.64	0	C-21	1	-0.3
Total 3	106	235	12	54	9	3	0	30	21	26	2	3	.230	.296	.294	.589	59	-15	20	2.75	-1	/C-66,0-2	2	-1.3

• WEIHE, Podge John Garibaldi Weihe b: 11/13/1862, Cincinnati, OH d: 4/15/1914, Cincinnati, OH BR/TR, 5'11", 175 lbs. Deb: 8/6/1883 Career OF: 1-24-35

YEAR TM-L	G	AB	R	H	2B	3B	HR	RBI	BB	SO	SB	CS	AVG	OBP	SLG	OPS	OPS+	BR/A	RC	RC/G	FR	G/POS	WS	TPW
1883 Cin-a	1	4	1	1	0	0	0	0	0	....	....	....	.250	.250	.250	.500	58	-0	0	2.39	0	/0-1	0	0.0
1884 Ind-a	63	256	29	65	13	2	4	0	9	....	....	....	.254	.279	.367	.646	112	3	27	3.87	-2	0-58(1-23-35)/2-4,1-3	6	0.0
Total 2	64	260	30	66	13	2	4	0	9	....	....	....	.254	.279	.365	.644	111	3	27	3.85	-2	/0-59,2-4,1-3	6	0.0

• WEINGARTNER, Elmer Elmer William "Dutch" Weingartner b: 8/13/1918, Cleveland, OH BR/TR, 5'11", 178 lbs. Deb: 4/19/1945

YEAR TM-L	G	AB	R	H	2B	3B	HR	RBI	BB	SO	SB	CS	AVG	OBP	SLG	OPS	OPS+	BR/A	RC	RC/G	FR	G/POS	WS	TPW
1945 Cle-A	20	39	5	9	1	0	0	1	4	11	0	0	.231	.302	.256	.559	66	-2	3	3.04	-3	S-20	1	-0.4

• WEINTRAUB, Phil Philip "Mickey" Weintraub b: 10/12/1907, Chicago, IL d: 6/21/1987, Palm Springs, CA BL/TL, 6'1", 195 lbs. Deb: 9/5/1933 Career OF: 59-9-14

YEAR TM-L	G	AB	R	H	2B	3B	HR	RBI	BB	SO	SB	CS	AVG	OBP	SLG	OPS	OPS+	BR/A	RC	RC/G	FR	G/POS	WS	TPW
1933 NY-N	8	15	3	3	0	0	1	1	3	2	0	....	.200	.333	.400	.733	110	0	2	5.20	-1	/0-6(0-0-6)	0	-0.1
1934 NY-N	31	74	13	26	2	0	0	15	15	10	0	....	.351	.461	.378	.839	130	5	15	8.31	-1	0-20(12-9-0)	4	0.3
1935 NY-N	64	112	18	27	3	3	1	6	17	13	0	....	.241	.341	.348	.689	87	-1	14	4.33	0	1-19/0-7(1-0-6)	2	-0.3
1937 Cin-N	49	177	27	48	10	4	3	20	19	25	1	....	.271	.345	.424	.769	113	3	25	5.01	-2	0-47(45-0-2)	4	-0.2
NY-N	6	9	3	3	2	0	0	1	1	1	0	....	.333	.400	.556	.956	155	1	2	9.69	-0	/0-1	1	0.1
Yr.	55	186	30	51	12	4	3	21	20	26	1	....	.274	.348	.430	.778	115	4	28	5.21	-2	0-48(46-0-2)	5	-0.1
1938 Phi-N	100	351	51	109	23	2	4	45	64	43	1	....	.311	.422	.422	.844	132	20	68	7.19	0	1-98	15	1.0
1944 NY-N	104	361	55	114	18	9	13	77	59	59	0	....	.316	.412	.524	.935	163	31	82	8.66	2	1-99	20	2.9
1945 NY-N	82	283	45	77	9	1	10	42	54	29	2	....	.272	.389	.417	.806	122	11	48	5.84	1	1-77	10	0.8
Total 7	444	1382	215	407	67	19	32	207	232	182	4	....	.295	.398	.440	.838	132	69	256	6.77	-1	1-293/0-81	56	4.5

• WEIS, Al Albert John Weis b: 4/2/1938, Franklin Square, NY BB/TR, 6', 170 lbs. Deb: 9/15/1962 Career OF: 0-4-0

YEAR TM-L	G	AB	R	H	2B	3B	HR	RBI	BB	SO	SB	CS	AVG	OBP	SLG	OPS	OPS+	BR/A	RC	RC/G	FR	G/POS	WS	TPW
1962 Chi-A	7	12	2	1	0	0	0	0	2	3	1	0	.083	.267	.083	.350	-1	-1	1	1.51	-1	/S-4,2-1,3-1	0	-0.2
1963 Chi-A	99	210	41	57	9	0	0	18	18	37	15	1	.271	.335	.314	.649	85	-1	26	4.31	0	2-48,S-27/3-1	8	0.5
1964 Chi-A	133	328	36	81	4	4	2	23	22	41	22	7	.247	.300	.302	.602	70	-11	32	3.13	-1	*2-116/S-9,0-2(0-2-0)	8	-0.5
1965 Chi-A	103	135	29	40	4	3	1	12	12	22	4	1	.296	.362	.393	.755	122	4	20	5.18	0	2-74/S-7,3-2,0-2(0-2-0)	8	0.9
1966 Chi-A	129	187	20	29	4	1	0	9	17	50	3	5	.155	.233	.187	.420	24	-20	8	1.30	0	2-96,S-18	3	-1.4
1967 Chi-A	50	53	9	13	2	0	0	4	1	7	3	3	.245	.273	.283	.556	67	-3	3	1.86	1	2-32,S-13	1	-0.1
1968 NY-N	90	274	15	47	6	0	1	14	21	63	3	1	.172	.236	.204	.440	33	-22	14	1.63	1	S-59,2-29/3-2	3	-1.5
1969*NY-N	103	247	20	53	9	2	2	23	15	51	3	3	.215	.260	.291	.551	53	-16	19	2.43	8	S-52,2-43/3-1	4	-0.1
1970 NY-N	75	121	20	25	7	1	1	11	7	21	1	1	.207	.256	.306	.562	50	-9	8	2.17	-3	2-44,S-15	1	-0.9
1971 NY-N	11	11	3	0	0	0	0	1	2	4	0	0	.000	.154	.000	.154	-54	-2	0	.25	0	/2-5,3-2	0	-0.2
Total 10	800	1578	195	346	45	11	7	115	117	299	55	22	.219	.279	.275	.554	59	-81	132	2.67	5	2-488,S-204/3-9,0-4	36	-3.6

• WEIS, Butch Arthur John Weis b: 3/2/1901, St. Louis, MO d: 5/4/1997, St. Louis, MO BL/TL, 5'11", 180 lbs. Deb: 4/15/1922 Career OF: 63-0-26

YEAR TM-L	G	AB	R	H	2B	3B	HR	RBI	BB	SO	SB	CS	AVG	OBP	SLG	OPS	OPS+	BR/A	RC	RC/G	FR	G/POS	WS	TPW
1922 Chi-N	2	2	2	1	0	0	0	0	0	0	0	0	.500	.500	.500	1.000	156	0	0	12.72	0	....	0	0.0
1923 Chi-N	22	26	2	6	1	0	0	2	5	8	0	1	.231	.355	.269	.624	67	-1	3	3.24	0	/0-6(4-0-2)	0	-0.2
1924 Chi-N	37	133	19	37	8	1	0	23	15	14	4	5	.278	.356	.353	.709	90	-2	17	4.20	5	0-36(14-0-22)	4	0.0
1925 Chi-N	67	180	16	48	5	3	2	25	23	22	2	4	.267	.350	.361	.711	81	-6	23	4.38	-2	0-47(45-0-2)	3	-1.0
Total 4	128	341	39	92	14	4	2	50	43	44	6	10	.270	.353	.352	.705	84	-9	43	4.25	3	/0-89	7	-1.1

• WEISER, Bud Harry Budson Weiser b: 1/8/1891, Shamokin, PA d: 7/31/1961, Shamokin, PA BR/TR, 5'11", 165 lbs. Deb: 4/29/1915 Career OF: 8-16-0

YEAR TM-L	G	AB	R	H	2B	3B	HR	RBI	BB	SO	SB	CS	AVG	OBP	SLG	OPS	OPS+	BR/A	RC	RC/G	FR	G/POS	WS	TPW
1915 Phi-N	37	64	6	9	2	0	0	8	7	12	2	2	.141	.236	.172	.408	24	-6	3	1.41	-3	0-20(4-16-0)	0	-1.1
1916 Phi-N	4	10	1	3	1	0	0	1	0	3	0	....	.300	.300	.400	.700	110	0	1	4.46	0	/0-4(4-0-0)	0	0.0
Total 2	41	74	7	12	3	0	0	9	7	15	2	2	.162	.244	.203	.447	34	-6	5	1.72	-3	/0-24	0	-1.1

• WEISS, Gary Gary Lee Weiss b: 12/27/1955, Brenham, TX BB/TR, 5'10", 170 lbs. Deb: 9/13/1980

YEAR TM-L	G	AB	R	H	2B	3B	HR	RBI	BB	SO	SB	CS	AVG	OBP	SLG	OPS	OPS+	BR/A	RC	RC/G	FR	G/POS	WS	TPW
1980 LA-N	8	0	2	0	0	0	0	0	0	0	0	0	....	....	....	....	-102	0	0	....	0	....	0	0.0
1981 LA-N	14	19	2	2	0	0	0	1	1	4	0	0	.105	.150	.105	.255	-28	-3	0	.60	0	S-13	0	-0.3
Total 2	22	19	4	2	0	0	0	1	1	4	0	0	.105	.150	.105	.255	-28	-3	0	.60	0	/S-13	0	-0.3

• WEISS, Joe Joseph Harold Weiss b: 1/27/1894, Chicago, IL d: 7/7/1967, Cedar Rapids, IA BR/TR, 6', 165 lbs. Deb: 8/29/1915

YEAR TM-L	G	AB	R	H	2B	3B	HR	RBI	BB	SO	SB	CS	AVG	OBP	SLG	OPS	OPS+	BR/A	RC	RC/G	FR	G/POS	WS	TPW
1915 Chi-F	29	85	6	19	1	2	0	11	3	24	0	....	.224	.250	.282	.532	60	-5	6	2.20	0	1-29	1	-0.6

• WEISS, Walt Walter William Weiss b: 11/28/1963, Tuxedo, NY BB/TR, 6', 175 lbs. Deb: 7/12/1987

YEAR TM-L	G	AB	R	H	2B	3B	HR	RBI	BB	SO	SB	CS	AVG	OBP	SLG	OPS	OPS+	BR/A	RC	RC/G	FR	G/POS	WS	TPW
1987 Oak-A	16	26	3	12	4	0	0	1	2	2	1	2	.462	.500	.615	1.115	208	3	7	11.54	2	S-11/D-2	2	0.6
1988*Oak-A	147	452	44	113	17	3	3	39	35	56	4	4	.250	.317	.321	.637	82	-11	47	3.44	21	*S-147	15	2.1
1989*Oak-A	84	236	30	55	11	0	3	21	21	39	6	1	.233	.298	.318	.616	76	-6	23	3.28	4	S-84	7	0.3
1990*Oak-A	138	445	50	118	17	1	2	35	46	53	9	3	.265	.339	.321	.661	89	-4	51	4.01	4	*S-137	15	1.0
1991 Oak-A	40	133	15	30	6	1	0	13	12	14	6	0	.226	.290	.286	.575	63	-5	12	2.99	-3	S-40	2	-0.5
1992*Oak-A	103	316	36	67	5	2	0	21	43	39	6	3	.212	.308	.241	.549	59	-16	26	2.50	1	*S-103	5	-0.8
1993 Fla-N	158	500	50	133	14	2	1	39	79	73	7	3	.266	.369	.308	.677	79	-10	63	4.44	-18	*S-153	13	-1.6
1994 Col-N	110	423	58	106	11	4	1	32	56	58	12	7	.251	.338	.303	.641	59	-24	47	3.74	-1	*S-110	7	-1.6
1995*Col-N	137	427	65	111	17	3	1	25	98	57	15	3	.260	.404	.321	.725	73	-10	66	5.33	-2	*S-136	12	-0.1
1996 Col-N	155	517	89	146	20	2	8	48	80	78	10	2	.282	.385	.375	.760	82	-9	82	5.50	-31	*S-155	8	-2.7
1997 Col-N	121	393	52	106	23	5	4	38	66	56	5	2	.270	.377	.384	.762	81	-8	61	5.46	4	*S-119	13	0.5
1998*Atl-N★	96	347	64	97	18	2	0	27	59	53	7	1	.280	.389	.343	.732	94	2	53	5.32	-1	S-96	12	0.8
1999*Atl-N	110	279	38	63	13	4	2	29	35	48	7	3	.226	.319	.323	.641	63	-16	32	3.78	-6	*S-102	7	-1.4
2000*Atl-N	80	192	29	50	6	2	0	18	26	32	1	1	.260	.357	.313	.670	71	-8	24	4.25	5	S-69	5	0.2
Total 14	1495	4686	623	1207	182	31	25	386	658	658	96	35	.258	.354	.326	.679	77	-122	595	4.32	-20	*S-1462/D-2	123	-3.0

• WELAJ, Johnny John Ludwig Welaj b: 5/27/1914, Moss Creek, PA d: 9/13/2003, Arlington, TX BR/TR, 6', 164 lbs. Deb: 5/2/1939 Career OF: 56-82-64

YEAR TM-L	G	AB	R	H	2B	3B	HR	RBI	BB	SO	SB	CS	AVG	OBP	SLG	OPS	OPS+	BR/A	RC	RC/G	FR	G/POS	WS	TPW
1939 Was-A	63	201	23	55	11	2	1	33	13	20	13	2	.274	.318	.363	.681	80	-4	25	4.36	0	0-55(13-17-26)	4	-0.6
1940 Was-A	88	215	31	55	9	0	3	21	19	20	8	7	.256	.322	.340	.662	77	-8	23	3.63	-2	0-53(15-35-3)	3	-1.1
1941 Was-A	49	96	16	20	4	0	0	5	6	16	3	1	.208	.255	.250	.505	36	-9	6	1.90	-1	0-19(13-3-3)	0	-1.0
1943 Phi-A	93	281	45	68	16	1	0	15	15	17	12	5	.242	.280	.306	.586	72	-10	24	2.91	-4	0-72(15-27-32)	4	-1.9
Total 4	293	793	115	198	40	3	4	74	53	73	36	15	.250	.298	.323	.621	71	-32	79	3.33	-6	0-199	11	-4.6

• WELCH, Curt Curtis Benton Welch b: 2/10/1862, Williamsport, OH d: 8/29/1896, East Liverpool, OH BR/TR, 5'10", 175 lbs. Deb: 5/1/1884 Career OF: 17-1059-0

YEAR TM-L	G	AB	R	H	2B	3B	HR	RBI	BB	SO	SB	CS	AVG	OBP	SLG	OPS	OPS+	BR/A	RC	RC/G	FR	G/POS	WS	TPW
1884 Tol-a	109	425	61	95	24	5	0	0	10	....	....	....	.224	.248	.304	.552	76	-12	33	2.74	17	*0-107(1-106-0)/2-2,C-2,1	9	0.1
1885*StL-a	112	432	84	117	18	8	3	69	23	....	....	....	.271	.318	.370	.689	112	5	52	4.47	13	*0-112(0-112-0)	22	1.3
1886*StL-a	138	563	114	158	31	13	2	95	29	....	59	....	.281	.332	.393	.724	121	11	95	6.35	7	*0-138(0-138-0)/2-2	21	1.2
1887*StL-a	131	569	98	176	32	7	3	108	25	....	89	....	.309	.322	.379	.701	86	-15	97	6.70	13	*0-123(0-123-0)/2-8,1-1	18	-0.5
1888 Phi-a	136	549	125	155	22	8	1	61	33	....	95	....	.282	.355	.357	.712	129	20	106	7.26	2	*0-135(0-135-0)/2-3	25	1.6
1889 Phi-a	125	516	134	140	**39**	6	0	39	67	30	66	....	.271	.375	.370	.746	114	13	99	6.97	6	*0-125(0-125-0)	20	1.2
1890 Phi-a	103	396	100	106	21	4	2	40	49	....	64	....	.268	.392	.356	.748	123	16	82	7.53	6	*0-103(0-103-0)/P-1	17	1.1
Bal-a	19	68	16	9	4	0	0	5	9	....	8	....	.132	.253	.191	.444	28	-6	5	2.45	1	0-17(0-17-0)/1-2	1	-0.6
Yr.	122	464	116	115	25	4	2	45	58	....	72	....	.248	.372	.332	.704	110	10	88	6.67	7	*0-120(0-120-0)/1-2,P-1	18	0.6
1891 Bal-a	132	514	122	138	22	10	3	55	77	42	50	....	.268	.400	.368	.768	119	18	98	6.91	12	*0-113(1-112-0),2-21/S-2	24	2.3
1892 Bal-N	63	237	42	56	1	3	1	22	36	9	14	....	.236	.363	.278	.641	92	0	30	4.44	-5	0-63(0-63-0)	5	-0.8
Cin-N	25	94	14	19	0	2	1	7	7	8	7	....	.202	.299	.277	.576	75	-3	10	3.64	-1	0-25(1-25-0)	2	-0.5
Yr.	88	331	56	75	1	5	2	29	43	17	21	....	.227	.345	.278	.623	87	-2	40	4.20	-6	0-88(1-88-0)	7	-1.3
1893 Lou-N	14	47	5	8	1	0	0	2	16	4	1	....	.170	.400	.191	.591	64	-1	4	2.79	-1	0-14(14-0-0)	1	-0.2
Total 10	1107	4410	915	1177	215	66	16	503	381	93	453	....	.267	.345	.353	.698	107	48	712	5.91	70	*0-1075/2-36,1-4,C-2,S-2,P	165	6.3

• WELCH, Frank Frank Tiguer "Bugger" Welch
b: 8/10/1897, Birmingham, AL d: 7/25/1957, Birmingham, AL BR/TR, 5'9", 175 lbs. Deb: 9/9/1919 Career OF: 35-203-390

YEAR TM-L	G	AB	R	H	2B	3B	HR	RBI	BB	SO	SB	CS	AVG	OBP	SLG	OPS	OPS+	BR/A	RC	RC/G	FR	G/POS	WS	TPW
1919 Phi-A	15	54	5	9	1	1	2	7	7	10	0	....	.167	.262	.333	.596	66	-3	5	2.56	0	0-15(0-15-0)	0	-0.4
1920 Phi-A	100	360	43	93	17	5	4	40	26	41	2	9	.258	.312	.367	.679	78	-14	39	3.66	-5	0-97(0-84-16)	4	-2.5

YEAR TM-L	G	AB	R	H	2B	3B	HR	RBI	BB	SO	SB	CS	AVG	OBP	SLG	OPS	OPS+	BR/A	RC	RC/G	FR	G/POS	WS	TPW
1921 Phi-A	115	403	48	115	18	6	7	45	34	43	6	0	.285	.347	.412	.759	92	-3	60	5.27	-2	*O-104(3-93-8)	7	-0.9
1922 Phi-A	114	375	43	97	17	3	11	49	40	40	3	4	.259	.335	.408	.743	90	-6	52	4.68	1	*O-104(4-6-94)	9	-1.3
1923 Phi-A	125	421	56	125	19	9	4	55	48	40	1	4	.297	.374	.413	.788	106	4	67	5.57	5	*O-117(0-0-117)	14	0.0
1924 Phi-A	94	293	47	85	13	2	5	31	35	27	2	3	.290	.372	.399	.771	98	-1	45	5.31	2	O-74(0-2-72)	8	-0.4
1925 Phi-A	85	202	40	56	5	4	4	41	29	14	2	1	.277	.373	.401	.774	90	-2	33	5.24	0	O-57(0-0-57)	5	-0.6
1926 Phi-A	75	174	26	49	8	1	4	23	26	9	2	5	.282	.381	.408	.789	100	-1	28	5.18	0	O-49(28-3-20)	5	-0.3
1927 Bos-A	15	28	2	5	2	0	0	4	5	1	0	2	.179	.303	.250	.553	46	-3	2	2.03	2	/O-6(0-0-6)	0	-0.2
Total 9	**738**	**2310**	**310**	**634**	**100**	**31**	**41**	**295**	**250**	**225**	**18**	**28**	**.274**	**.350**	**.398**	**.748**	**92**	**-29**	**330**	**4.85**	**2**	**O-623**	**52**	**-6.6**
• WELCH, Herb	Herbert M. "Dutch" Welch b: 10/19/1898, Ro Ellen, TN d: 4/13/1967, Memphis, TN BL/TR, 5'6", 154 lbs. Deb: 9/15/1925																							
1925 Bos-A	13	38	2	11	0	1	0	2	0	6	0	0	.289	.289	.342	.632	60	-2	4	3.55	-1	S-13	1	-0.2
• WELCH, Milt	Milton Edward Welch b: 7/26/1924, Farmersville, IL BR/TR, 5'10", 175 lbs. Deb: 6/5/1945																							
1945 Det-A	1	2	0	0	0	0	0	0	0	1	0	0	.000	.000	.000	.000	-94	-0	0	.00	0	/C-1	0	0.0
• WELCH, Tub	James T. Welch b: 7/3/1866, St. Louis, MO TR, 5'11", 230 lbs. Deb: 6/12/1890																							
1890 Tol-a	35	108	15	31	3	1	1	14	8	....	7	....	.287	.358	.361	.719	109	1	17	5.81	-1	C-25,1-10	4	0.1
1895 Lou-N	47	153	18	37	4	1	1	8	13	7	2	....	.242	.310	.301	.610	62	-8	15	3.55	-1	C-28,1-20	1	-0.5
Total 2	**82**	**261**	**33**	**68**	**7**	**2**	**2**	**22**	**21**	**7**	**9**	**....**	**.261**	**.330**	**.326**	**.656**	**81**	**-7**	**32**	**4.45**	**-2**	**/C-53,1-30**	**5**	**-0.4**
• WELCHONCE, Harry	Harry Monroe "Welch" Welchonce b: 11/20/1883, North Point, PA d: 2/26/1977, Arcadia, CA BL/TR, 6', 170 lbs. Deb: 4/17/1911																							
1911 Phi-N	26	66	9	14	4	0	0	6	7	8	0	....	.212	.288	.273	.560	56	-4	5	2.50	-2	O-17(1-6-11)	1	-0.6
• WELDAY, Mike	Lyndon Earl Welday b: 12/19/1879, Conway, IA d: 5/28/1942, Leavenworth, KS BL/TL, 5'8", 165 lbs. Deb: 4/21/1907 Career OF: 11-18-6																							
1907 Chi-A	24	35	2	8	1	1	0	0	6	....	0	....	.229	.341	.314	.656	113	1	4	3.80	0	O-15(4-8-3)	1	0.1
1909 Chi-A	29	74	3	14	0	0	0	5	4	....	2	....	.189	.231	.189	.420	34	-6	4	1.57	1	O-20(7-10-3)	1	-0.6
Total 2	**53**	**109**	**5**	**22**	**1**	**1**	**0**	**5**	**10**	**....**	**2**	**....**	**.202**	**.269**	**.229**	**.498**	**62**	**-5**	**8**	**2.29**	**2**	**/O-35**	**2**	**-0.5**
• WELF, Ollie	Oliver Henry Welf b: 1/17/1889, Cleveland, OH d: 6/15/1967, Cleveland, OH BR/TL, 5'9", 160 lbs. Deb: 8/30/1916																							
1916 Cle-A	1	0	0	0	0	0	0	0	0	0	0	....	....	....	....	....	-94	0	0	....	0	....	0	0.0
• WELLMAN, Bob	Robert Joseph Wellman b: 7/15/1925, Norwood, OH d: 12/20/1994, Villa Hills, KY BR/TR, 6'4", 210 lbs. Deb: 9/23/1948 Career OF: 0-0-3																							
1948 Phi-A	4	10	1	2	0	1	0	0	3	2	0	0	.200	.385	.400	.785	109	0	2	6.33	0	/1-2,O-1	1	0.0
1950 Phi-A	11	15	1	5	0	0	1	1	0	3	0	0	.333	.333	.533	.867	121	0	3	7.38	-0	/O-2(0-0-2)	0	0.0
Total 2	**15**	**25**	**2**	**7**	**0**	**1**	**1**	**1**	**3**	**5**	**0**	**0**	**.280**	**.357**	**.480**	**.837**	**115**	**1**	**5**	**6.92**	**0**	**/O-3,1-2**	**1**	**0.0**
• WELLMAN, Brad	Brad Eugene Wellman b: 8/17/1959, Lodi, CA BR/TR, 6', 170 lbs. Deb: 9/4/1982																							
1982 SF-N	6	4	1	1	0	0	0	0	0	1	0	0	.250	.250	.250	.500	40	-0	0	2.25	-1	/2-2	0	-0.1
1983 SF-N	82	182	15	39	3	0	1	16	22	39	5	3	.214	.299	.247	.546	55	-11	14	2.45	-7	2-74/S-2	1	-1.5
1984 SF-N	93	265	23	60	9	1	2	25	19	41	10	5	.226	.278	.291	.569	62	-14	21	2.47	0	2-54,S-34/3-9	4	-0.9
1985 SF-N	71	174	16	41	11	1	0	16	4	33	5	2	.236	.269	.310	.580	65	-9	14	2.70	-3	2-36,3-25/S-3	3	-1.1
1986 SF-N	12	13	0	2	0	0	0	1	1	2	0	0	.154	.214	.154	.368	3	-2	0	1.19	-1	/S-8,2-1,3-1	0	-0.2
1987 LA-N	3	4	1	1	0	0	0	1	0	1	0	0	.250	.250	.250	.500	34	-0	0	2.25	0	/2-1,3-1,S-1	0	-0.1
1988 KC-A	71	107	11	29	3	0	1	6	6	23	1	2	.271	.322	.327	.649	81	-3	11	3.68	0	2-46,S-15/3-4,D-3	2	-0.2
1989 KC-A	103	178	30	41	4	0	2	12	7	36	5	3	.230	.263	.287	.550	55	-11	12	2.13	2	2-64,S-34/3-3,D-1	3	-0.6
Total 8	**441**	**927**	**97**	**214**	**30**	**2**	**6**	**77**	**59**	**176**	**26**	**15**	**.231**	**.282**	**.287**	**.569**	**61**	**-50**	**73**	**2.55**	**-10**	**2-278/S-97,3-43,D-4**	**13**	**-4.8**
• WELLS, Greg	Gregory DeWayne Wells b: 4/25/1954, McIntosh, AL BR/TR, 6'5", 218 lbs. Deb: 8/10/1981																							
1981 Tor-A	32	73	7	18	5	0	0	5	5	12	0	2	.247	.295	.315	.610	71	-4	6	2.71	0	1-22/D-3	0	-0.5
1982 Min-A	15	54	5	11	1	2	0	3	1	8	0	0	.204	.218	.296	.514	39	-5	4	2.19	-2	1-10/D-5	0	-0.7
Total 2	**47**	**127**	**12**	**29**	**6**	**2**	**0**	**8**	**6**	**20**	**0**	**2**	**.228**	**.263**	**.307**	**.570**	**57**	**-8**	**10**	**2.48**	**-1**	**/1-32,D-8**	**0**	**-1.1**
• WELLS, Jake	Jacob Wells b: 8/9/1863, Memphis, TN d: 3/16/1927, Hendersonville, NC BR/TR, 5'11", 167 lbs. Deb: 8/10/1888																							
1888 Det-N	16	57	5	9	1	0	0	2	0	5	0	....	.158	.158	.175	.333	6	-6	2	.91	0	C-16	1	-0.4
1890 StL-a	30	105	17	25	3	0	0	12	10	....	1	....	.238	.333	.267	.600	67	-4	10	3.28	1	C-28/O-3(3-0-0)	3	-0.1
Total 2	**46**	**162**	**22**	**34**	**4**	**0**	**0**	**14**	**10**	**5**	**1**	**....**	**.210**	**.277**	**.235**	**.511**	**48**	**-10**	**12**	**2.39**	**1**	**/C-44,O-3**	**4**	**-0.5**
• WELLS, Leo	Leo Donald Wells b: 7/18/1917, Kansas City, KS BR/TR, 5'9", 170 lbs. Deb: 4/16/1942																							
1942 Chi-A	35	62	8	12	2	0	1	4	4	5	1	0	.194	.242	.274	.517	46	-4	4	2.27	4	S-12/3-6	1	0.1
1946 Chi-A	45	127	11	24	4	1	1	11	12	34	3	4	.189	.259	.260	.519	47	-10	8	1.96	1	3-38/S-2	1	-1.0
Total 2	**80**	**189**	**19**	**36**	**6**	**1**	**2**	**15**	**16**	**39**	**4**	**4**	**.190**	**.254**	**.265**	**.518**	**47**	**-14**	**13**	**2.05**	**5**	**/3-44,S-14**	**2**	**-0.9**
• WELLS, Vernon	Vernon M. Wells b: 12/8/1978, Shreveport, LA BR/TR, 6'1", 210 lbs. Deb: 8/30/1999 Career OF: 0-361-16																							
1999 Tor-A	24	88	8	23	5	0	1	8	4	18	1	1	.261	.293	.352	.646	63	-5	7	2.65	2	O-24(0-24-0)	1	-0.3
2000 Tor-A	3	2	0	0	0	0	0	0	0	0	0	0	.000	.000	.000	.000	-97	-1	0	.00	0	/O-3(0-3-0)	0	-0.1
2001 Tor-A	30	96	14	30	8	0	1	6	5	15	5	0	.313	.353	.427	.780	102	1	16	6.43	1	O-30(0-27-3)	3	0.2
2002 Tor-A	159	608	87	167	34	4	23	100	27	85	9	4	.275	.309	.457	.766	96	-5	81	4.67	-4	*O-159(0-146-13)	17	-0.8
2003 Tor-A★	161	678	118	**215**	**49**	5	33	117	42	80	4	1	.317	.363	.550	.913	134	32	129	7.06	-9	*O-161(0-161-0)	26	2.3
Total 5	**377**	**1472**	**227**	**435**	**96**	**9**	**58**	**231**	**78**	**198**	**19**	**6**	**.296**	**.336**	**.491**	**.827**	**112**	**22**	**233**	**5.70**	**-9**	**O-377**	**47**	**1.4**
• WELSH, Jimmy	James Daniel Welsh b: 10/9/1902, Denver, CO d: 10/30/1970, Oakland, CA BL/TR, 6'1", 174 lbs. Deb: 4/14/1925 Career OF: 45-398-252																							
1925 Bos-N	122	484	69	151	25	8	7	63	20	24	7	4	.312	.350	.440	.790	110	7	74	5.64	3	*O-116(7-1-109)/2-3	15	0.0
1926 Bos-N	134	490	69	136	18	11	3	57	33	28	6	....	.278	.333	.378	.711	100	-0	62	4.14	7	*O-129(0-0-129)	12	-0.4
1927 Bos-N	131	497	72	143	26	7	9	54	23	27	11	....	.288	.330	.423	.752	109	4	67	4.57	5	*O-129(1-121-11)/1-1	13	0.3
1928 NY-N	124	476	77	146	22	5	9	54	29	30	4	....	.307	.357	.431	.787	104	2	71	5.41	2	*O-117(6-110-1)	15	0.0
1929 NY-N	38	129	25	32	7	0	2	8	9	3	3	....	.248	.331	.349	.680	69	-6	15	3.90	-1	O-35(30-7-0)	2	-0.8
Bos-N	53	186	24	54	8	7	2	16	13	9	1	....	.290	.350	.441	.791	98	-1	28	5.20	6	O-51(1-49-2)	6	0.2
Yr.	91	315	49	86	15	7	4	24	22	12	4	....	.273	.342	.403	.745	86	-7	44	4.66	5	O-86(31-56-2)	8	-0.5
1930 Bos-N	113	422	51	116	21	9	3	36	29	23	5	....	.275	.327	.389	.716	75	-18	53	4.34	4	*O-110(0-110-0)	11	-1.6
Total 6	**715**	**2684**	**387**	**778**	**127**	**47**	**35**	**288**	**156**	**144**	**37**	**4**	**.290**	**.340**	**.411**	**.751**	**98**	**-12**	**370**	**4.79**	**26**	**O-687/2-3,1-1**	**74**	**-2.2**
• WENDELL, Lew	Lewis Charles Wendell b: 3/22/1892, New York, NY d: 7/11/1953, Brooklyn, NY BR/TR, 5'11", 178 lbs. Deb: 6/10/1915																							
1915 NY-N	20	36	0	8	1	1	0	5	2	7	0	....	.222	.263	.306	.569	76	-1	3	2.78	-1	C-18	1	-0.1
1916 NY-N	2	2	0	0	0	0	0	0	0	2	0	....	.000	.000	.000	.000	-106	-0	0	.00	0	....	0	-0.1
1924 Phi-N	21	32	3	8	1	0	0	2	3	5	0	0	.250	.314	.281	.596	54	-2	3	3.26	0	C-17	0	-0.1
1925 Phi-N	18	26	0	2	0	0	0	3	1	3	0	0	.077	.111	.077	.188	-47	-6	0	.36	-1	/C-9	0	-0.6
1926 Phi-N	1	4	0	0	0	0	0	0	0	0	0	....	.000	.000	.000	.000	-95	-1	0	.00	-1	/C-1	0	-0.2
Total 5	**62**	**100**	**3**	**18**	**2**	**1**	**0**	**10**	**6**	**17**	**0**	**0**	**.180**	**.226**	**.220**	**.446**	**26**	**-10**	**6**	**1.96**	**-2**	**/C-45**	**1**	**-1.1**
• WENTZ, Jack	John George Wentz b: 3/4/1863, Louisville, KY d: 9/14/1907, Louisville, KY BR/TR, 5'10.5", 175 lbs. Deb: 4/15/1891																							
1891 Lou-a	1	4	0	1	0	0	0	0	0	0	0	....	.250	.250	.250	.500	44	-0	0	2.26	-1	/2-1	0	-0.1
• WENTZEL, Stan	Stanley Aaron Wentzel b: 1/13/1917, Lorane, PA d: 11/28/1991, St. Lawrence, PA BR/TR, 6'1", 200 lbs. Deb: 9/23/1945																							
1945 Bos-N	4	19	3	4	0	1	0	6	0	3	1	....	.211	.211	.316	.526	45	-2	1	2.27	0	/O-4(0-4-0)	0	-0.2
• WERA, Julie	Julian Valentine Wera b: 2/9/1902, Winona, MN d: 12/12/1975, Rochester, MN BR/TR, 5'8", 164 lbs. Deb: 4/14/1927																							
1927 NY-A	38	42	7	10	3	0	1	8	1	5	0	0	.238	.273	.381	.654	70	-2	4	3.58	-2	3-19	1	-0.3
1929 NY-A	5	12	1	5	0	0	0	2	1	1	0	0	.417	.462	.417	.878	137	1	2	7.86	0	/3-4	0	0.1
Total 2	**43**	**54**	**8**	**15**	**3**	**0**	**1**	**10**	**2**	**6**	**0**	**0**	**.278**	**.316**	**.389**	**.705**	**86**	**-1**	**7**	**4.44**	**-2**	**/3-23**	**1**	**-0.2**
• WERBER, Billy	William Murray Werber b: 6/20/1908, Berwyn, MD BR/TR, 5'10", 170 lbs. Deb: 6/25/1930 Career OF: 39-2-7																							
1930 NY-A	4	14	5	4	0	0	0	2	3	1	0	0	.286	.412	.286	.697	84	-0	2	5.01	1	/S-3,3-1	0	0.1

YEAR TM-L	G	AB	R	H	2B	3B	HR	RBI	BB	SO	SB	CS	AVG	OBP	SLG	OPS	OPS+	BR/A	RC	RC/G	FR	G/POS	WS	TPW
1933 NY-A	3	2	0	0	0	0	0	0	0	0	0	0	.000	.000	.000	.000	-106	-1	0	.00	0	/3-1	0	-0.1
Bos-A	108	425	64	110	30	6	3	39	33	39	15	5	.259	.312	.379	.691	83	-10	52	4.12	-12	S-71,3-38/2-2	8	-1.5
Yr.	111	427	64	110	30	6	3	39	33	39	15	5	.258	.311	.377	.688	82	-10	52	4.10	-12	S-71,3-39/2-2	8	-1.6
1934 Bos-A	152	623	129	200	41	10	11	67	77	37	**40**	15	.321	.397	.472	.868	115	17	121	7.07	19	*3-130,S-22	26	4.0
1935 Bos-A	124	462	84	118	30	3	14	61	69	41	**29**	7	.255	.357	.424	.781	95	0	76	5.54	14	*3-123	14	1.8
1936 Bos-A	145	535	89	147	29	6	10	67	89	37	23	13	.275	.382	.407	.790	90	-7	89	5.70	-5	*3-101,0-45(38-0-7)/2-1	13	-1.0
1937 Phi-A	128	493	85	144	31	4	7	70	74	39	**35**	13	.292	.386	.414	.799	103	7	84	6.05	9	*3-125/0-3(1-2-0)	14	1.8
1938 Phi-A	134	499	92	129	22	7	11	69	93	37	19	15	.259	.377	.397	.774	97	-2	79	5.35	5	*3-134	13	0.7
1939*Cin-N	147	599	**115**	173	35	5	5	57	91	46	15	....	.289	.388	.389	.777	109	12	96	5.79	13	*3-147	25	3.0
1940*Cin-N	143	584	105	162	35	5	12	48	68	40	16	....	.277	.361	.416	.777	112	11	92	5.76	11	*3-143	27	2.8
1941 Cin-N	109	418	56	100	9	2	4	46	53	24	14	....	.239	.328	.299	.627	77	-11	43	3.53	13	*3-107	15	0.6
1942 NY-N	98	370	51	76	9	2	1	13	51	22	9	....	.205	.308	.249	.557	64	-15	30	2.65	14	3-93	7	0.2
Total 11	**1295**	**5024**	**875**	**1363**	**271**	**50**	**78**	**539**	**701**	**363**	**215**	**68**	**.271**	**.364**	**.392**	**.756**	**97**	**1**	**765**	**5.29**	**81**	***3-1143/S-96,0-48,2-3**	**162**	**12.4**

• WERDEN, Perry

Percival Wheritt "Moose" Werden
b: 7/21/1865, St. Louis, MO d: 1/9/1934, Minneapolis, MN BR/TR, 6'2", 220 lbs. Deb: 4/24/1884 Career OF: 7-5-3 ♦

YEAR TM-L	G	AB	R	H	2B	3B	HR	RBI	BB	SO	SB	CS	AVG	OBP	SLG	OPS	OPS+	BR/A	RC	RC/G	FR	G/POS	WS	TPW
1884 StL-U	18	76	7	18	2	0	0	....	2	....	....	....	.237	.256	.263	.520	73	-1	5	2.54	1	P-16/0-6(4-1-1)	15	0.7
1888 Was-N	3	10	0	3	0	0	0	2	1	4	0	....	.300	.364	.300	.664	120	0	1	4.31	0	/0-3(3-0-0)	0	0.0
1890 Tol-a	128	498	113	147	22	**20**	6	72	78	....	59	....	.295	.404	.456	.860	149	32	118	8.94	3	*1-124/0-5(0-4-1)	20	2.2
1891 Bal-a	139	552	102	160	20	18	6	104	52	59	46	....	.290	.363	.424	.787	123	15	104	7.04	8	*1-139	19	1.0
1892 StL-N	149	598	73	154	22	6	8	84	59	52	20	....	.258	.328	.355	.683	112	9	78	4.75	14	*1-149	17	2.1
1893 StL-N	125	500	73	138	22	**29**	1	94	49	25	11	....	.276	.349	.442	.791	109	4	83	6.07	9	*1-124/0-1	11	1.0
1897 Lou-N	133	512	76	154	21	14	5	83	41	....	15	....	.301	.365	.426	.791	112	9	88	6.41	17	*1-131	15	2.1
Total 7	**695**	**2746**	**444**	**774**	**109**	**87**	**26**	**439**	**282**	**140**	**151**	**....**	**.282**	**.358**	**.413**	**.772**	**120**	**68**	**478**	**6.43**	**52**	**1-667/P-16,0-15**	**97**	**9.1**

• WERHAS, Johnny

John Charles "Peaches" Werhas b: 2/7/1938, Highland Park, MI BR/TR, 6'2", 200 lbs. Deb: 4/14/1964

YEAR TM-L	G	AB	R	H	2B	3B	HR	RBI	BB	SO	SB	CS	AVG	OBP	SLG	OPS	OPS+	BR/A	RC	RC/G	FR	G/POS	WS	TPW
1964 LA-N	29	83	6	16	2	1	0	8	13	12	0	0	.193	.302	.241	.543	59	-4	6	2.43	0	3-28	1	-0.4
1965 LA-N	4	3	1	0	0	0	0	0	1	2	0	0	.000	.250	.000	.250	-24	-0	0	.00	0	/1-1	0	-0.1
1967 LA-N	7	7	0	1	0	0	0	0	0	3	0	0	.143	.143	.143	.286	-20	-1	0	.64	0	....	0	-0.1
Cal-A	49	75	8	12	1	1	2	6	10	22	0	0	.160	.267	.280	.547	64	-3	5	2.09	-1	3-30/1-4,0-1	1	-0.4
Total 3	**89**	**168**	**15**	**29**	**3**	**2**	**2**	**14**	**24**	**39**	**0**	**0**	**.173**	**.280**	**.250**	**.530**	**57**	**-8**	**12**	**2.14**	**-1**	**/3-58,1-5,0-1**	**2**	**-1.0**

• WERNER, Don

Donald Paul Werner b: 3/8/1953, Appleton, WI BR/TR, 6'1", 185 lbs. Deb: 9/2/1975

YEAR TM-L	G	AB	R	H	2B	3B	HR	RBI	BB	SO	SB	CS	AVG	OBP	SLG	OPS	OPS+	BR/A	RC	RC/G	FR	G/POS	WS	TPW
1975 Cin-N	7	8	0	1	0	0	0	0	0	2	0	0	.125	.222	.125	.347	-2	-1	0	1.08	0	/C-7	0	-0.1
1976 Cin-N	3	4	0	2	1	0	0	1	1	1	0	0	.500	.600	.750	1.350	275	1	2	26.41	0	/C-3	0	0.2
1977 Cin-N	10	23	3	4	0	0	2	4	2	3	0	1	.174	.240	.435	.675	75	-1	2	2.04	0	C-10	1	-0.1
1978 Cin-N	50	113	7	17	2	1	0	11	14	30	1	0	.150	.250	.186	.436	23	-11	6	1.69	1	C-49	2	-0.8
1980 Cin-N	24	64	2	11	2	0	0	5	7	10	1	0	.172	.264	.203	.467	32	-5	4	1.81	-3	C-24	0	-0.8
1981 Tex-A	2	8	1	2	0	0	0	0	0	2	0	1	.250	.250	.250	.500	47	-1	0	.96	0	/D-2	0	-0.1
1982 Tex-A	22	59	4	12	2	0	0	3	3	7	0	0	.203	.242	.237	.479	34	-5	4	1.86	0	C-22	1	-0.5
Total 7	**118**	**279**	**17**	**49**	**7**	**1**	**2**	**24**	**27**	**53**	**2**	**2**	**.176**	**.256**	**.229**	**.485**	**36**	**-24**	**18**	**1.95**	**-2**	**C-115/D-2**	**4**	**-2.3**

• WERRICK, Joe

Joseph Abraham Werrick b: 10/25/1861, St. Paul, MN d: 5/10/1943, St. Peter, MN BR/TR, 5'9", 151 lbs. Deb: 9/27/1884

YEAR TM-L	G	AB	R	H	2B	3B	HR	RBI	BB	SO	SB	CS	AVG	OBP	SLG	OPS	OPS+	BR/A	RC	RC/G	FR	G/POS	WS	TPW
1884 StP-U	9	27	3	2	0	0	0	....	1	....	....	....	.074	.107	.074	.181	-38	-4	0	.25	-1	/S-9	0	-0.4
1886 Lou-a	136	561	75	140	20	14	3	62	33	....	19	....	.250	.294	.351	.645	96	-6	65	4.17	-6	*3-136	11	-0.8
1887 Lou-a	136	571	90	190	21	13	7	99	38	....	49	....	.333	.336	.413	.749	106	2	93	6.57	0	*3-136	14	0.4
1888 Lou-a	111	413	49	89	12	7	0	51	30	....	15	....	.215	.274	.278	.552	79	-9	36	3.04	-17	3-89,S-11/2-8,0-3(3-0-0)	7	-2.2
Total 4	**392**	**1572**	**217**	**421**	**53**	**34**	**10**	**212**	**102**	**....**	**83**	**....**	**.268**	**.300**	**.348**	**.648**	**93**	**-17**	**194**	**4.56**	**-24**	**3-361/S-20,2-8,0-3**	**32**	**-3.0**

• WERT, Don

Donald Ralph Wert b: 7/29/1938, Strasburg, PA BR/TR, 5'10", 165 lbs. Deb: 5/11/1963

YEAR TM-L	G	AB	R	H	2B	3B	HR	RBI	BB	SO	SB	CS	AVG	OBP	SLG	OPS	OPS+	BR/A	RC	RC/G	FR	G/POS	WS	TPW
1963 Det-A	78	251	31	65	6	2	7	25	24	51	3	3	.259	.329	.382	.711	95	-2	31	4.16	4	3-47,2-21/S-8	7	0.4
1964 Det-A	148	525	63	135	18	5	9	55	50	74	3	4	.257	.329	.362	.691	91	-7	63	4.05	7	*3-142/S-4	15	0.0
1965 Det-A	162	609	81	159	22	2	12	54	73	71	5	6	.261	.343	.363	.706	100	-0	76	4.27	12	*3-161/S-3,2-1	21	1.3
1966 Det-A	150	559	56	150	20	2	11	70	64	69	6	3	.268	.346	.370	.716	103	4	71	4.25	-14	*3-150	17	-1.1
1967 Det-A	142	534	60	137	23	2	6	40	44	59	1	1	.257	.321	.341	.662	93	-4	58	3.65	-1	*3-140/S-1	14	-0.6
1968*Det-A★	150	536	44	107	15	1	12	37	37	79	0	3	.200	.258	.299	.556	66	-24	40	2.36	2	*3-150/S-2	7	-2.5
1969 Det-A	132	423	46	95	11	1	14	50	49	60	3	1	.225	.307	.355	.661	81	-11	45	3.49	3	*3-129	10	-0.8
1970 Det-A	128	363	34	79	13	0	6	33	44	56	1	3	.218	.309	.303	.612	69	-15	33	2.91	-4	*3-117/2-2	5	-2.0
1971 Was-A	20	40	2	2	1	0	0	2	4	10	0	0	.050	.156	.075	.231	-35	-7	0	.33	-1	/3-7,S-7,2-1	0	-0.8
Total 9	**1110**	**3840**	**417**	**929**	**129**	**15**	**77**	**366**	**389**	**529**	**22**	**24**	**.242**	**.317**	**.343**	**.660**	**87**	**-65**	**417**	**3.60**	**8**	***3-1043/2-25,S-25**	**96**	**-6.0**

• WERTH, Dennis

Dennis Dean Werth b: 12/29/1952, Lincoln, IL BR/TR, 6'1", 200 lbs. Deb: 9/17/1979 Career OF: 7-0-9

YEAR TM-L	G	AB	R	H	2B	3B	HR	RBI	BB	SO	SB	CS	AVG	OBP	SLG	OPS	OPS+	BR/A	RC	RC/G	FR	G/POS	WS	TPW
1979 NY-A	3	4	1	1	0	0	0	0	0	0	0	0	.250	.250	.250	.500	36	-0	0	2.25	0	/1-1	0	0.0
1980 NY-A	39	65	15	20	3	0	3	12	12	19	0	1	.308	.416	.492	.908	150	5	13	6.91	-2	1-12/D-8,0-8(3-0-5),3-1,C	3	0.2
1981 NY-A	34	55	7	6	1	0	0	1	12	12	1	0	.109	.269	.127	.396	18	-5	2	1.14	1	1-19/0-8(4-0-4),D-4,C-3	1	-0.5
1982 KC-A	41	15	5	2	0	0	0	2	4	2	0	0	.133	.316	.133	.449	29	-1	1	1.54	0	1-35/C-2	0	-0.2
Total 4	**117**	**139**	**28**	**29**	**4**	**0**	**3**	**15**	**28**	**33**	**1**	**1**	**.209**	**.341**	**.302**	**.643**	**79**	**-2**	**16**	**3.54**	**-1**	**/1-67,0-16,D-12,C-6,3-1**	**4**	**-0.6**

• WERTH, Jayson

Jayson Richard Gowan Werth b: 5/20/1979, Springfield, IL BR/TR, 6'5", 190 lbs. Deb: 9/1/2002 Career OF: 4-2-29

YEAR TM-L	G	AB	R	H	2B	3B	HR	RBI	BB	SO	SB	CS	AVG	OBP	SLG	OPS	OPS+	BR/A	RC	RC/G	FR	G/POS	WS	TPW
2002 Tor-A	15	46	4	12	2	1	0	6	6	11	1	0	.261	.346	.348	.694	82	-1	5	3.40	1	0-15(4-1-10)	1	0.0
2003 Tor-A	26	48	7	10	4	0	2	10	3	22	1	0	.208	.255	.417	.672	72	-2	5	3.86	1	0-20(0-1-19)/D-2	1	-0.2
Total 2	**41**	**94**	**11**	**22**	**6**	**1**	**2**	**16**	**9**	**33**	**2**	**0**	**.234**	**.301**	**.383**	**.684**	**77**	**-3**	**10**	**3.63**	**2**	**/0-35,D-2**	**2**	**-0.2**

• WERTZ, Del

Dwight Lyman Moody Wertz b: 10/11/1888, Canton, OH d: 5/26/1958, Sarasota, FL BR/TR, 5'10", 160 lbs. Deb: 5/23/1914

YEAR TM-L	G	AB	R	H	2B	3B	HR	RBI	BB	SO	SB	CS	AVG	OBP	SLG	OPS	OPS+	BR/A	RC	RC/G	FR	G/POS	WS	TPW
1914 Buf-F	3	0	1	0	0	0	0	0	0	0	0	....	....	....	....	....	-96	0	0	....	0	/S-1	0	0.0

• WERTZ, Vic

Victor Woodrow Wertz b: 2/9/1925, York, PA d: 7/7/1983, Detroit, MI BL/TR, 6', 186 lbs. Deb: 4/15/1947 Career OF: 105-4-783

YEAR TM-L	G	AB	R	H	2B	3B	HR	RBI	BB	SO	SB	CS	AVG	OBP	SLG	OPS	OPS+	BR/A	RC	RC/G	FR	G/POS	WS	TPW
1947 Det-A	102	333	60	96	22	4	6	44	47	66	2	0	.288	.376	.432	.809	121	11	56	6.04	-1	0-83(38-2-43)	12	0.6
1948 Det-A	119	391	49	97	19	9	7	67	48	70	0	0	.248	.335	.396	.731	91	-5	56	4.95	1	0-98(64-1-36)	9	-1.0
1949 Det-A★	155	608	96	185	26	6	20	133	80	61	2	3	.304	.385	.465	.851	124	20	110	6.59	0	*0-155(0-0-155)	23	1.5
1950 Det-A	149	559	99	172	37	4	27	123	91	55	0	1	.308	.408	.533	.941	135	30	128	8.54	-4	*0-145(0-0-145)	26	2.0
1951 Det-A★	138	501	86	143	24	4	27	94	78	61	0	3	.285	.383	.511	.894	139	27	101	7.24	5	*0-131(0-0-131)	22	2.7
1952 Det-A★	85	285	46	70	15	3	17	51	46	44	1	0	.246	.352	.498	.851	134	13	53	6.47	5	0-79(0-0-79)	10	1.6
StL-A	37	130	22	45	5	0	6	19	23	20	0	0	.346	.444	.523	.968	164	12	33	10.02	-3	0-36(0-0-36)	7	0.9
Yr.	122	415	68	115	20	3	23	70	69	64	1	0	.277	.381	.506	.887	143	26	86	7.48	2	*0-115(0-0-115)	17	2.5
1953 StL-A	128	440	61	118	18	6	19	70	72	44	1	4	.268	.376	.466	.842	124	15	79	6.26	2	*0-121(0-1-120)	12	1.3
1954 Bal-A	29	94	5	19	1	0	1	13	11	17	0	0	.202	.286	.245	.530	50	-6	7	2.53	2	0-27(0-0-27)	1	-0.5
*Cle-A	94	295	33	81	14	2	14	48	34	40	0	2	.275	.350	.478	.828	123	8	50	5.95	5	1-83/0-5(2-0-3)	12	0.9
Yr.	123	389	38	100	15	2	15	61	45	57	0	2	.257	.334	.422	.756	105	2	57	5.08	8	1-83,0-32(2-0-30)	13	0.4
1955 Cle-A	74	257	30	65	11	2	14	55	32	33	1	1	.253	.338	.475	.813	112	3	41	5.43	-1	1-63/0-9(1-0-8)	8	-0.1
1956 Cle-A	136	481	65	127	22	0	32	106	75	87	0	0	.264	.369	.509	.878	127	19	93	6.84	4	*1-133	21	1.5
1957 Cle-A★	144	515	84	145	21	0	28	105	78	88	2	3	.282	.378	.485	.864	135	26	97	6.66	-5	*1-139	24	1.4
1958 Cle-A	25	43	5	12	1	0	3	12	5	7	0	0	.279	.354	.512	.866	139	2	7	5.96	1	/1-8	2	0.3
1959 Bos-A	94	247	38	68	13	0	7	49	22	32	0	0	.275	.339	.413	.752	101	0	34	5.00	2	1-64	6	-0.1
1960 Bos-A	131	443	45	125	22	0	19	103	37	54	0	2	.282	.339	.460	.799	110	4	66	5.23	1	*1-117	11	-0.1
1961 Bos-A	99	317	33	83	16	2	11	60	38	43	0	0	.262	.345	.429	.774	103	1	46	4.94	4	1-86	9	0.1
Det-A	8	6	0	1	0	0	0	1	0	1	0	0	.167	.167	.167	.333	-10	-1	0	.90	0	....	0	-0.1
Yr.	107	323	33	84	16	2	11	61	38	44	0	0	.260	.342	.424	.766	101	0	46	4.86	4	1-86	9	0.0
1962 Det-A	74	105	7	34	2	0	5	18	5	13	0	0	.324	.360	.486	.846	121	3	18	6.84	1	1-16	4	0.3
1963 Det-A	6	5	0	0	0	0	0	0	0	1	0	0	.000	.000	.000	.000	-97	-1	0	.00	0	....	0	-0.1

YEAR TM-L	G	AB	R	H	2B	3B	HR	RBI	BB	SO	SB	CS	AVG	OBP	SLG	OPS	OPS+	BR/A	RC	RC/G	FR	G/POS	WS	TPW
Min-A	35	44	3	6	0	0	3	7	6	5	0	0	.136	.240	.341	.581	59	-3	4	2.44	1	/1-6	0	-0.2
Yr.	41	49	3	6	0	0	3	7	6	6	0	0	.122	.218	.306	.524	45	-4	4	2.17	1	/1-6	0	-0.3
Total 17	1862	6099	867	1692	289	42	266	1178	828	842	9	19	.277	.366	.469	.836	121	179	1079	6.28	20	0-889,1-715	219	13.0
• WESSINGER, Jim	James Michael Wessinger b: 9/25/1955, Utica, NY BR/TR, 5'10", 165 lbs. Deb: 8/4/1979																							
1979 Atl-N	10	7	2	0	0	0	0	0	1	4	0	0	.000	.125	.000	.125	-59	-2	0	.13	-1	/2-2	0	-0.2
• WESSON, Barry	Barry Jarvis Wesson b: 4/6/1977, Tupelo, MS BR/TR, 6'2", 212 lbs. Deb: 7/15/2002 Career OF: 8-9-7																							
2002 Hou-N	15	20	1	4	0	1	0	1	1	5	0	0	.200	.238	.300	.538	39	-2	1	1.34	-1	0-15(3-9-3)	0	-0.3
2003 Ana-A	10	11	2	2	0	0	1	3	0	4	1	0	.182	.182	.455	.636	62	-0	1	3.01	0	/0-9(5-0-4)	0	0.0
Total 2	25	31	3	6	0	1	1	4	1	9	1	0	.194	.219	.355	.574	47	-2	2	1.90	-1	/0-24	0	-0.3
• WEST, Billy	William O. West b: 8/15/1853, Williamsburg, NY d: 10/27/1928, Richmond Hill, NY Deb: 5/22/1874																							
1874 Atl-n	9	35	4	8	1	0	0	2	1	2	0	0	.229	.250	.257	.507	71	-1	2	2.56	-2	/2-9,C-1,S-1	....	-0.2
1876 NY-N	1	4	0	0	0	0	0	0	0	0	....	....	.000	.000	.000	.000	-115	-1	0	.00	-0	/2-1	0	-0.1
• WEST, Buck	Milton Douglas West b: 8/29/1860, Spring Mill, OH d: 1/13/1929, Mansfield, OH BL/TR, 5'10", 200 lbs. Deb: 8/24/1884 Career OF: 0-37-33																							
1884 Cin-a	33	131	20	32	2	8	1	15	2	....	....	....	.244	.256	.405	.660	107	0	14	3.86	-5	0-33(0-33-0)	3	-0.6
1890 Cle-N	37	151	20	37	6	1	2	29	7	11	4	....	.245	.283	.338	.621	82	-4	16	3.71	-1	0-37(0-4-33)	2	-0.5
Total 2	70	282	40	69	8	9	3	44	9	11	4	....	.245	.271	.369	.639	93	-4	30	3.78	-6	/0-70	5	-1.1
• WEST, Dick	Richard Thomas West b: 11/24/1915, Louisville, KY d: 3/13/1996, Fort Wayne, IN BR/TR, 6'2", 180 lbs. Deb: 9/28/1938 Career OF: 11-0-0																							
1938 Cin-N	1	1	0	0	0	0	0	0	0	0	0	....	.000	.000	.000	.000	-103	-0	0	.00	0	....	0	0.0
1939 Cin-N	8	19	1	4	0	0	0	4	1	4	0	....	.211	.250	.211	.461	25	-2	1	1.92	0	/0-5(5-0-0),C-1	0	-0.3
1940 Cin-N	7	28	4	11	2	0	1	6	0	2	1	....	.393	.393	.571	.964	161	2	6	9.98	0	/C-7	2	0.2
1941 Cin-N	67	172	15	37	5	2	1	17	6	23	4	....	.215	.246	.285	.531	49	-12	12	2.27	-5	C-64	2	-1.5
1942 Cin-N	33	79	9	14	3	0	1	8	5	13	1	....	.177	.226	.253	.479	40	-6	5	2.00	-1	C-17/0-6(6-0-0)	1	-0.6
1943 Cin-N	3	0	1	0	0	0	0	0	0	0	0	....	....	....	....	....	-101	0	0		0	....	0	0.0
Total 6	119	299	30	66	10	2	3	35	12	42	6	....	.221	.253	.298	.551	54	-19	24	2.71	-6	/C-89,0-11	5	-2.2
• WEST, Max	Max Edward West b: 11/28/1916, Dexter, MO d: 12/31/2003, Sierra Madre, CA BL/TR, 6'1.5", 182 lbs. Deb: 4/19/1938 Career OF: 342-115-171																							
1938 Bos-N	123	418	47	98	16	5	10	63	38	38	5	....	.234	.300	.368	.668	92	-5	46	3.76	-4	*0-109(75-0-36)/1-7	11	-1.6
1939 Bos-N	130	449	67	128	26	6	19	82	51	55	1	....	.285	.364	.497	.861	139	24	82	6.59	2	*0-124(44-46-54)	20	2.0
1940 Bos-N★	139	524	72	137	27	5	7	72	65	54	2	....	.261	.344	.372	.716	103	4	72	4.94	4	*0-102(4-59-49),1-36	17	0.0
1941 Bos-N	138	484	63	134	28	4	12	68	72	68	5	....	.277	.373	.426	.798	130	21	80	5.92	5	*0-132(126-5-5)	20	1.9
1942 Bos-N	134	452	54	115	22	0	16	56	68	59	4	....	.254	.354	.409	.764	126	16	71	5.54	1	1-85,0-50(36-2-13)	19	0.7
1946 Bos-N	1	1	0	0	0	0	0	0	0	1	0	....	.000	.000	.000	.000	-99	-0	0	.00	0	/1-1	0	0.0
Cin-N	72	202	16	43	13	0	5	18	32	36	1	....	.213	.323	.351	.675	95	-1	24	3.96	-1	0-58(54-3-1)	4	-0.7
Yr.	73	203	16	43	13	0	5	18	32	37	1	....	.212	.322	.350	.672	94	-1	24	3.93	-1	0-58(54-3-1)/1-1	4	-0.7
1948 Pit-N	87	146	19	26	4	0	8	21	27	29	1	....	.178	.310	.370	.680	82	-4	18	3.83	1	1-32,0-16(3-0-13)	3	-0.3
Total 7	824	2676	338	681	136	20	77	380	353	340	19	....	.254	.344	.407	.751	114	54	392	5.15	9	0-591,1-161	94	2.0
• WEST, Max	Walter Maxwell West b: 7/14/1904, Sunset, TX d: 4/25/1971, Houston, TX BR/TR, 5'11", 165 lbs. Deb: 9/18/1928 Career OF: 2-5-1																							
1928 Bro-N	7	21	4	6	1	1	0	1	4	1	0	....	.286	.400	.429	.829	118	1	4	6.10	1	/0-6(1-4-1)	1	0.2
1929 Bro-N	5	8	1	2	1	0	0	1	1	0	0	....	.250	.333	.375	.708	77	-0	1	3.85	-0	/0-2(1-1-0)	0	0.0
Total 2	12	29	5	8	2	1	0	2	5	1	0	....	.276	.382	.414	.796	107	0	5	5.42	1	/0-8	1	0.2
• WEST, Sam	Samuel Filmore West b: 10/5/1904, Longview, TX d: 11/23/1985, Lubbock, TX BL/TL, 5'11", 165 lbs. Deb: 4/17/1927 C Career OF: 92-1454-31																							
1927 Was-A	38	67	9	16	4	1	0	6	8	8	1	0	.239	.320	.328	.648	69	-3	8	3.93	0	0-18(5-8-5)	1	-0.3
1928 Was-A	125	378	59	114	30	7	3	40	20	23	5	6	.302	.338	.442	.780	104	-0	54	5.23	0	*0-116(53-60-6)	10	-0.6
1929 Was-A	142	510	60	136	16	8	3	75	45	41	9	8	.267	.326	.347	.673	73	-21	59	3.86	14	*0-139(4-136-0)	11	-1.2
1930 Was-A	120	411	75	135	22	10	6	67	37	34	5	5	.328	.385	.474	.860	116	10	75	6.82	3	*0-118(1-117-0)	18	0.7
1931 Was-A	132	526	77	175	43	13	3	91	30	37	6	8	.333	.369	.481	.850	121	14	90	6.57	12	*0-127(0-127-0)	24	2.1
1932 Was-A	146	554	88	159	27	12	6	83	48	57	4	5	.287	.345	.412	.756	96	-4	79	5.11	12	*0-143(0-143-0)	19	0.4
1933 StL-A★	133	517	93	155	25	12	11	48	59	49	10	8	.300	.373	.458	.831	112	8	89	6.28	6	*0-127(0-127-0)	14	1.0
1934 StL-A★	122	482	90	157	22	10	9	55	62	55	3	5	.326	.403	.469	.871	115	10	92	7.19	4	*0-120(0-120-0)	18	1.0
1935 StL-A★	138	527	93	158	37	4	10	70	75	46	1	6	.300	.388	.442	.830	109	7	92	6.32	8	*0-135(0-135-0)	18	1.1
1936 StL-A	152	533	78	148	26	4	7	70	94	70	2	0	.278	.386	.381	.767	87	-7	85	5.72	-2	*0-148(0-148-0)	12	-1.1
1937 StL-A★	122	457	68	150	37	4	7	58	46	28	1	1	.328	.390	.473	.862	115	11	85	7.25	9	*0-105(0-105-0)	12	1.6
1938 StL-A	44	165	17	51	8	2	1	27	14	9	1	0	.309	.363	.400	.763	91	-2	25	5.61	-6	0-41(0-41-0)	3	-0.8
Was-A	92	344	51	104	19	5	5	47	33	21	1	1	.302	.363	.430	.794	105	2	55	5.80	-2	0-85(1-84-0)	10	-0.2
Yr.	136	509	68	155	27	7	6	74	47	30	2	1	.305	.363	.420	.784	101	0	79	5.74	-8	*0-126(1-125-0)	13	-0.9
1939 Was-A	115	390	52	110	20	8	3	52	67	29	1	1	.282	.387	.397	.785	109	8	65	5.89	3	0-89(23-55-11),1-17	13	0.6
1940 Was-A	57	99	7	25	6	1	1	18	16	13	0	2	.253	.357	.364	.720	93	-1	14	4.86	0	1-12/0-9(0-3-6)	2	-0.3
1941 Was-A	26	37	3	10	0	0	0	6	11	2	1	0	.270	.438	.270	.708	95	1	6	5.85	-0	/0-8(4-1-3)	2	0.1
1942 Chi-A	49	151	14	35	5	0	0	25	31	18	2	0	.232	.363	.265	.628	80	-1	18	4.04	-1	0-45(1-44-0)	5	-0.3
Total 16	1753	6148	934	1838	347	101	75	838	696	540	53	56	.299	.371	.425	.796	103	32	991	5.86	58	*0-1573/1-29	192	3.8
• WESTERBERG, Oscar	Oscar William Westerberg b: 7/8/1882, Alameda, CA d: 4/17/1909, Alameda, CA BB/TR, 6', 186 lbs. Deb: 9/5/1907																							
1907 Bos-N	2	6	0	2	0	0	0	1	1	....	0	....	.333	.429	.333	.762	139	0	1	5.71	0	/S-2	0	0.1
• WESTLAKE, Jim	James Patrick Westlake b: 7/3/1930, Sacramento, CA d: 1/3/2003, Sacramento, CA BL/TL, 6'1", 190 lbs. Deb: 4/16/1955																							
1955 Phi-N	1	1	0	0	0	0	0	0	0	1	0	0	.000	.000	.000	.000	-102	-0	0	.00	0	....	0	0.0
• WESTLAKE, Wally	Waldon Thomas Westlake b: 11/8/1920, Gridley, CA BR/TR, 6', 186 lbs. Deb: 4/15/1947 Career OF: 137-344-385																							
1947 Pit-N	112	407	59	111	17	4	17	69	27	63	5	....	.273	.324	.459	.784	103	-0	56	4.79	-2	*0-109(0-12-97)	9	-0.6
1948 Pit-N	132	428	78	122	10	6	17	65	46	40	2	....	.285	.360	.456	.815	117	10	71	6.01	-4	*0-125(1-67-57)	17	0.2
1949 Pit-N	147	525	77	148	24	8	23	104	45	69	6	....	.282	.345	.490	.835	118	12	86	5.93	0	*0-143(0-51-92)	17	0.7
1950 Pit-N	139	477	69	136	15	6	24	95	48	78	1	....	.285	.359	.493	.852	118	11	83	6.22	-1	*0-123(5-97-26)	14	0.7
1951 Pit-N	50	181	28	51	4	0	16	45	9	26	0	1	.282	.323	.569	.892	131	6	32	6.44	2	3-34,0-11(10-1-0)	7	0.7
StL-N★	73	267	36	68	8	5	6	39	24	42	1	2	.255	.325	.390	.715	91	-4	34	4.32	2	0-68(11-29-28)	6	-0.5
Yr.	123	448	64	119	12	5	22	84	33	68	1	3	.266	.324	.462	.786	107	-2	66	5.14	3	0-79(21-30-28),3-34	13	0.2
1952 StL-N	21	74	7	16	3	0	0	10	8	11	1	1	.216	.293	.257	.549	53	-5	5	2.33	6	0-15(0-15-0)	2	0.1
Cin-N	59	183	29	37	4	0	3	14	31	29	0	2	.202	.324	.273	.597	67	-8	16	2.74	-4	0-56(5-43-10)	2	-1.3
Yr.	80	257	36	53	7	0	3	24	39	40	1	3	.206	.315	.268	.584	63	-12	22	2.62	2	0-71(5-58-10)	4	-1.2
Cle-A	29	69	11	16	4	1	1	9	8	16	1	0	.232	.312	.362	.674	93	-0	8	3.81	2	0-28(12-4-20)	2	0.1
1953 Cle-A	82	218	42	72	7	1	9	46	35	29	2	0	.330	.427	.495	.923	152	18	49	8.50	-2	0-72(38-12-36)	12	1.3
1954*Cle-A	85	240	36	63	9	2	11	42	26	37	0	1	.263	.340	.454	.794	114	4	36	5.02	-4	0-70(49-10-14)	9	-0.4
1955 Cle-A	16	20	2	5	1	0	0	1	3	5	0	0	.250	.348	.300	.648	73	-1	2	3.35	0	/0-7(4-3-0)	0	-0.1
Bal-A	8	24	0	3	1	0	0	0	6	5	0	0	.125	.300	.167	.467	30	-2	1	1.82	0	/0-7(2-0-5)	0	-0.2
Yr.	24	44	2	8	2	0	0	1	9	10	0	0	.182	.321	.227	.548	49	-3	3	2.46	0	0-14(6-3-5)	0	-0.3
1956 Phi-N	5	4	0	0	0	0	0	0	1	3	0	0	.000	.200	.000	.200	-41	-1	0	.35	0	....	0	-0.1
Total 10	958	3117	474	848	107	33	127	539	317	453	19	7	.272	.346	.450	.795	110	40	480	5.39	-6	0-834/3-34	97	0.6
• WESTON, Al	Alfred John Weston b: 12/11/1905, Lynn, MA d: 11/13/1997, San Diego, CA BR/TR, 6', 195 lbs. Deb: 7/7/1929																							
1929 Bos-N	3	3	0	0	0	0	0	0	0	2	0	....	.000	.000	.000	.000	-104	-1	0	.00	0	....	0	-0.1
• WESTRUM, Wes	Wesley Noreen Westrum b: 11/28/1922, Clearbrook, MN d: 5/28/2002, Clearbrook, MN BR/TR, 5'11", 185 lbs. Deb: 9/17/1947 M/C																							
1947 NY-N	6	12	1	5	1	0	0	2	0	2	0	....	.417	.417	.500	.917	141	1	3	9.64	0	/C-2	1	0.1
1948 NY-N	66	125	14	20	3	1	4	16	20	36	3	....	.160	.276	.296	.572	54	-8	11	2.89	1	C-63	3	-0.5
1949 NY-N	64	169	23	41	4	1	7	28	37	39	1	....	.243	.385	.402	.787	111	4	28	5.69	-2	C-62	7	0.5

YEAR TM-L	G	AB	R	H	2B	3B	HR	RBI	BB	SO	SB	CS	AVG	OBP	SLG	OPS	OPS+	BR/A	RC	RC/G	FR	G/POS	WS	TPW
1950 NY-N	140	437	68	103	13	3	23	71	92	73	2	....	.236	.371	.437	.808	111	10	74	5.75	6	*C-139	22	2.2
1951*NY-N	124	361	59	79	12	0	20	70	104	93	1	0	.219	.400	.418	.818	119	16	70	6.36	-2	*C-122	20	2.1
1952 NY-N★	114	322	47	71	11	0	14	43	76	68	1	2	.220	.374	.385	.759	110	8	53	5.50	0	*C-112	18	1.4
1953 NY-N★	107	290	40	65	5	0	12	30	56	73	2	0	.224	.352	.366	.717	86	-4	41	4.74	3	*C-106/3-1	9	0.4
1954*NY-N	98	246	25	46	3	1	8	27	45	60	0	1	.187	.320	.305	.625	63	-13	27	3.56	-2	C-98	6	-1.0
1955 NY-N	69	137	11	29	1	0	4	18	24	18	0	1	.212	.333	.307	.640	71	-5	14	3.01	-1	C-68	3	-0.3
1956 NY-N	68	132	10	29	5	2	3	8	25	28	0	0	.220	.348	.356	.704	90	-1	16	4.01	1	C-67	5	0.3
1957 NY-N	63	91	4	15	1	0	1	2	10	24	0	1	.165	.255	.209	.464	26	-10	5	1.76	-0	C-63	1	-0.8
Total 11	**919**	**2322**	**302**	**503**	**59**	**8**	**96**	**315**	**489**	**514**	**10**	**5**	**.217**	**.357**	**.373**	**.730**	**95**	**-1**	**342**	**4.86**	**4**	**C-902/3-1**	**95**	**4.4**

• WETHERBY, Jeff Jeffrey Barret Wetherby b: 10/18/1963, Granada Hills, CA BL/TL, 6'2", 195 lbs. Deb: 6/7/1989

YEAR TM-L	G	AB	R	H	2B	3B	HR	RBI	BB	SO	SB	CS	AVG	OBP	SLG	OPS	OPS+	BR/A	RC	RC/G	FR	G/POS	WS	TPW
1989 Atl-N	52	48	5	10	2	1	1	7	4	6	1	0	.208	.269	.354	.623	75	-1	4	2.76	-0	/O-9(7-0-2)	1	-0.2

• WETZEL, Dutch Franklin Burton Wetzel b: 7/7/1893, Columbus, IN d: 3/5/1942, Hollywood, CA BR/TR, 5'9.5", 177 lbs. Deb: 9/15/1920 Career OF: 17-5-11

YEAR TM-L	G	AB	R	H	2B	3B	HR	RBI	BB	SO	SB	CS	AVG	OBP	SLG	OPS	OPS+	BR/A	RC	RC/G	FR	G/POS	WS	TPW
1920 StL-A	7	21	5	9	1	1	0	5	4	1	0	1	.429	.520	.571	1.091	183	2	6	11.36	0	/O-6(5-1-0)	1	0.2
1921 StL-A	61	119	16	25	2	0	2	10	9	20	0	0	.210	.271	.277	.549	38	-11	9	2.61	-1	O-27(12-4-11)	1	-1.3
Total 2	**68**	**140**	**21**	**34**	**3**	**1**	**2**	**15**	**13**	**21**	**0**	**1**	**.243**	**.312**	**.321**	**.633**	**62**	**-9**	**15**	**3.75**	**-1**	**/O-33**	**2**	**-1.1**

• WHALEY, Bill William Carl Whaley b: 2/10/1899, Indianapolis, IN d: 3/3/1943, Indianapolis, IN BR/TR, 5'11", 178 lbs. Deb: 4/18/1923

YEAR TM-L	G	AB	R	H	2B	3B	HR	RBI	BB	SO	SB	CS	AVG	OBP	SLG	OPS	OPS+	BR/A	RC	RC/G	FR	G/POS	WS	TPW
1923 StL-A	23	50	5	12	2	1	0	1	4	2	0	0	.240	.309	.320	.629	62	-3	5	3.53	0	O-13(4-9-0)	1	-0.3

• WHALING, Bert Albert James Whaling b: 6/22/1888, Los Angeles, CA d: 1/21/1965, Sawtelle, CA BR/TR, 6', 185 lbs. Deb: 4/22/1913

YEAR TM-L	G	AB	R	H	2B	3B	HR	RBI	BB	SO	SB	CS	AVG	OBP	SLG	OPS	OPS+	BR/A	RC	RC/G	FR	G/POS	WS	TPW
1913 Bos-N	79	211	22	51	8	2	0	25	10	32	3	....	.242	.283	.299	.581	65	-10	19	2.80	-1	C-77	5	-0.6
1914 Bos-N	60	172	18	36	7	0	0	12	21	28	2	....	.209	.303	.250	.553	65	-7	13	2.49	3	C-59	5	0.1
1915 Bos-N	72	190	10	42	6	2	0	13	8	38	0	1	.221	.264	.274	.537	64	-9	14	2.43	-1	C-69	4	-0.6
Total 3	**211**	**573**	**50**	**129**	**21**	**4**	**0**	**50**	**39**	**98**	**5**	**1**	**.225**	**.283**	**.276**	**.558**	**65**	**-26**	**46**	**2.59**	**1**	**C-205**	**14**	**-1.1**

• WHEAT, Mack McKinley Davis Wheat b: 6/9/1893, Polo, MO d: 8/14/1979, Los Banos, CA BR/TR, 5'11.5", 167 lbs. Deb: 4/14/1915 Career OF: 10-2-4

YEAR TM-L	G	AB	R	H	2B	3B	HR	RBI	BB	SO	SB	CS	AVG	OBP	SLG	OPS	OPS+	BR/A	RC	RC/G	FR	G/POS	WS	TPW
1915 Bro-N	8	14	0	1	0	0	0	0	0	5	0	....	.071	.071	.071	.143	-56	-3	0	.15	-1	/C-8	0	-0.3
1916 Bro-N	2	2	0	0	0	0	0	0	0	1	0	....	.000	.000	.000	.000	-97	-0	0	.00	0	/C-2	0	-0.1
1917 Bro-N	29	60	2	8	1	0	0	0	1	12	1	....	.133	.161	.150	.311	-4	-7	1	.73	1	C-18/O-9(9-1-0)	1	-0.6
1918 Bro-N	57	157	11	34	7	1	1	3	8	24	2	....	.217	.255	.293	.548	67	-7	12	2.41	0	C-38/O-7(1-1-4)	2	-0.5
1919 Bro-N	41	112	5	23	3	0	0	8	2	22	1	....	.205	.246	.232	.478	43	-8	7	1.84	-1	C-38	1	-0.7
1920 Phi-N	78	230	15	52	10	3	3	20	8	35	3	1	.226	.261	.335	.596	67	-9	20	2.95	3	C-74	4	0.0
1921 Phi-N	10	27	1	5	2	1	0	4	0	3	0	0	.185	.241	.333	.575	47	-2	2	2.66	2	/C-9	0	0.1
Total 7	**225**	**602**	**34**	**123**	**23**	**5**	**4**	**35**	**19**	**102**	**7**	**1**	**.204**	**.241**	**.279**	**.520**	**51**	**-36**	**42**	**2.26**	**5**	**C-187/O-16**	**8**	**-2.1**

• WHEAT, Zack Zachary Davis "Buck" Wheat
b: 5/23/1888, Hamilton, MO d: 3/11/1972, Sedalia, MO BL/TR, 5'10", 170 lbs. Deb: 9/11/1909 HOF: 1959 Career OF: 2328-5-5

YEAR TM-L	G	AB	R	H	2B	3B	HR	RBI	BB	SO	SB	CS	AVG	OBP	SLG	OPS	OPS+	BR/A	RC	RC/G	FR	G/POS	WS	TPW
1909 Bro-N	26	102	15	31	7	3	0	4	6	....	1	....	.304	.343	.431	.774	145	5	15	5.28	1	O-26(25-1-0)	4	0.5
1910 Bro-N	156	606	78	172	36	15	2	55	47	80	16	....	.284	.341	.403	.744	120	13	87	5.10	1	*O-156(156-0-0)	21	0.5
1911 Bro-N	140	534	55	153	26	13	5	76	29	58	21	....	.287	.332	.412	.744	112	6	79	5.15	-6	*O-136(135-1-0)	16	-0.6
1912 Bro-N	123	453	70	138	28	7	8	65	39	40	16	....	.305	.367	.450	.818	128	16	79	6.29	-1	*O-120(120-0-0)	16	1.0
1913 Bro-N	138	535	64	161	28	10	7	58	25	45	19	....	.301	.335	.430	.764	114	7	79	5.24	5	*O-135(135-0-0)	16	0.7
1914 Bro-N	145	533	66	170	26	9	9	89	47	50	20	....	.319	.377	.452	.830	143	27	95	6.49	12	*O-144(144-0-0)	26	3.6
1915 Bro-N	146	528	64	136	15	12	5	66	52	42	21	14	.258	.330	.360	.690	107	3	65	4.15	8	*O-144(144-0-0)	24	0.5
1916*Bro-N	149	568	76	177	32	13	9	73	43	49	19	....	.312	.366	**.461**	.828	149	**32**	103	**6.71**	3	*O-149(149-1-0)	**32**	3.3
1917 Bro-N	109	362	38	113	15	11	1	41	20	18	5	....	.312	.352	.423	.774	133	13	53	5.44	5	O-98(98-0-0)	16	1.6
1918 Bro-N	105	409	39	137	15	3	0	51	16	17	9	....	**.335**	.369	.386	.755	131	14	59	5.52	2	*O-105(105-0-0)	16	1.3
1919 Bro-N	137	536	70	159	23	11	5	62	33	27	15	....	.297	.344	.409	.753	123	14	76	5.18	-4	*O-137(137-0-0)	21	0.6
1920*Bro-N	148	583	89	191	26	13	9	73	48	21	8	10	.328	.385	.463	.848	138	29	102	6.64	-3	*O-148(148-0-0)	28	2.2
1921 Bro-N	148	568	91	182	31	10	14	85	44	19	11	8	.320	.372	.484	.857	120	18	101	6.65	2	*O-148(148-0-0)	23	0.8
1922 Bro-N	152	600	92	201	29	12	16	112	45	22	9	6	.335	.388	.503	.891	129	26	116	7.47	0	*O-152(152-0-0)	27	1.3
1923 Bro-N	98	349	63	131	13	5	8	65	23	12	3	3	.375	.417	.510	.927	147	24	73	8.61	-5	O-87(85-0-2)	15	1.2
1924 Bro-N	141	566	92	212	41	8	14	97	49	18	3	4	.375	.428	.549	.978	165	53	132	9.64	3	*O-139(139-0-0)	35	4.5
1925 Bro-N	150	616	125	221	42	14	14	103	45	22	3	1	.359	.403	.541	.944	143	40	134	8.76	-2	*O-149(149-0-0)	27	2.5
1926 Bro-N	111	411	68	119	31	2	5	35	21	14	4	....	.290	.326	.411	.737	99	-2	53	4.54	1	*O-102(102-0-0)	10	-0.8
1927 Phi-A	88	247	34	80	12	1	1	38	18	5	2	3	.324	.379	.393	.772	95	-2	37	5.53	-2	O-62(57-2-3)	7	-0.7
Total 19	**2410**	**9106**	**1289**	**2884**	**476**	**172**	**132**	**1248**	**650**	**559**	**205**	**49**	**.317**	**.367**	**.450**	**.817**	**129**	**336**	**1540**	**6.27**	**21**	***O-2337**	**380**	**24.0**

• WHEATON, Woody Elwood Pierce Wheaton b: 10/3/1914, Philadelphia, PA d: 12/11/1995, Lancaster, PA BL/TL, 5'8.5", 160 lbs. Deb: 9/28/1943 Career OF: 0-15-0 ♦

YEAR TM-L	G	AB	R	H	2B	3B	HR	RBI	BB	SO	SB	CS	AVG	OBP	SLG	OPS	OPS+	BR/A	RC	RC/G	FR	G/POS	WS	TPW
1943 Phi-A	7	30	2	6	2	0	0	2	3	2	0	0	.200	.294	.267	.561	65	-1	2	2.64	0	/O-7(0-7-0)	1	-0.1
1944 Phi-A	30	59	1	11	2	0	0	5	5	3	1	2	.186	.250	.220	.470	35	-4	3	1.33	1	P-11/O-8(0-8-0)	2	-0.2
Total 2	**37**	**89**	**3**	**17**	**4**	**0**	**0**	**7**	**8**	**5**	**1**	**2**	**.191**	**.265**	**.236**	**.501**	**45**	**-5**	**5**	**1.74**	**2**	**/O-15,P-11**	**3**	**-0.3**

• WHEELER, Dick Richard Wheeler b: 1/14/1898, Keene, NH d: 2/12/1962, Lexington, MA BR/TR, 5'11", 185 lbs. Deb: 6/17/1918

YEAR TM-L	G	AB	R	H	2B	3B	HR	RBI	BB	SO	SB	CS	AVG	OBP	SLG	OPS	OPS+	BR/A	RC	RC/G	FR	G/POS	WS	TPW
1918 StL-N	3	6	0	0	0	0	0	0	0	3	0	....	.000	.000	.000	.000	-104	-1	0	.00	-1	/O-2(0-0-2)	0	-0.3

• WHEELER, Don Donald Wesley "Scott" Wheeler b: 9/29/1922, Minneapolis, MN d: 12/10/2003, Minneapolis, MN BR/TR, 5'10", 175 lbs. Deb: 4/23/1949

YEAR TM-L	G	AB	R	H	2B	3B	HR	RBI	BB	SO	SB	CS	AVG	OBP	SLG	OPS	OPS+	BR/A	RC	RC/G	FR	G/POS	WS	TPW
1949 Chi-A	67	192	17	46	9	2	1	22	27	19	2	0	.240	.333	.323	.656	76	-6	22	3.96	1	C-58	5	-0.1

• WHEELER, Ed Edward Raymond Wheeler b: 5/24/1915, Los Angeles, CA d: 8/4/1983, Centralia, WA BR/TR, 5'9", 160 lbs. Deb: 4/19/1945

YEAR TM-L	G	AB	R	H	2B	3B	HR	RBI	BB	SO	SB	CS	AVG	OBP	SLG	OPS	OPS+	BR/A	RC	RC/G	FR	G/POS	WS	TPW
1945 Cle-A	46	72	12	14	2	0	0	1	8	13	1	1	.194	.275	.222	.497	47	-5	5	2.28	-5	3-14,S-11/2-3	0	-1.0

• WHEELER, Ed Edward L. Wheeler b: 6/15/1878, Sherman, MI d: 8/15/1960, Fort Worth, TX BB/TR, 5'10", 160 lbs. Deb: 5/10/1902

YEAR TM-L	G	AB	R	H	2B	3B	HR	RBI	BB	SO	SB	CS	AVG	OBP	SLG	OPS	OPS+	BR/A	RC	RC/G	FR	G/POS	WS	TPW
1902 Bro-N	30	96	4	12	0	0	0	5	3	....	1	....	.125	.152	.125	.277	-15	-13	2	.68	-3	3-11,2-10/S-5	1	-1.7

• WHEELER, George George Harrison "Heavy" Wheeler b: 11/10/1881, Shelburn, IN d: 6/13/1918, Clinton, IN BL/TR, 5'9.5", 180 lbs. Deb: 7/27/1910

YEAR TM-L	G	AB	R	H	2B	3B	HR	RBI	BB	SO	SB	CS	AVG	OBP	SLG	OPS	OPS+	BR/A	RC	RC/G	FR	G/POS	WS	TPW
1910 Cin-N	3	3	0	0	0	0	0	0	0	2	0	....	.000	.000	.000	.000	-105	-1	0	.00	0	....	0	-0.1

• WHEELER, Harry Harry Eugene Wheeler
b: 3/3/1858, Versailles, IN d: 10/9/1900, Cincinnati, OH BR/TR, 5'11", 165 lbs. Deb: 6/19/1878 M/U Career OF: 115-40-82 ♦

YEAR TM-L	G	AB	R	H	2B	3B	HR	RBI	BB	SO	SB	CS	AVG	OBP	SLG	OPS	OPS+	BR/A	RC	RC/G	FR	G/POS	WS	TPW
1878 Pro-N	7	27	7	4	0	0	0	1	2	15	....	....	.148	.207	.148	.355	18	-1	1	1.01	-2	/P-7	3	-1.0
1879 Cin-N	1	3	0	0	0	0	0	0	0	2	....	....	.000	.000	.000	.000	-105	-1	0	.00	0	/O-1,P-1	0	-0.9
1880 Cle-N	1	4	0	1	0	0	0	0	0	0	....	....	.250	.250	.250	.500	71	-0	0	2.35	0	/O-1	0	0.0
Cin-N	17	65	1	6	2	0	0	2	0	15	....	....	.092	.092	.123	.215	-28	-8	1	.35	0	O-17(16-1-0)	0	-0.9
Yr.	18	69	1	7	2	0	0	2	0	15	....	....	.101	.101	.130	.232	-22	-8	1	.45	0	O-18(17-1-0)	0	-0.9
1882 Cin-a	76	344	59	86	11	11	1	29	7	....	....	....	.250	.265	.355	.620	101	-0	33	3.60	-8	*O-64(0-0-64),1-12/P-4	9	-1.6
1883 Col-a	82	371	42	84	6	7	0	0	6	....	....	....	.226	.239	.280	.519	72	-10	25	2.48	-2	*O-82(82-0-0)/2-1,P-1	4	-1.5
1884 StL-a	5	19	0	5	2	0	0	0	1	....	....	....	.263	.300	.368	.668	113	0	2	4.23	-1	/O-5(4-1-0)	1	-0.1
KC-U	14	62	11	16	1	0	0	....	3	....	....	....	.258	.292	.274	.567	106	1	5	3.10	0	O-13(12-0-1)/P-1	2	0.2
CP-U	37	158	29	36	5	3	1	....	4	....	....	....	.228	.247	.316	.563	95	-0	13	2.90	-6	O-37(0-37-0)	3	-0.7
Bal-U	17	69	3	18	2	0	0	....	0	....	....	....	.261	.261	.290	.551	78	-2	5	2.94	0	O-17(0-1-16)	2	-0.2
Yr.	68	289	43	70	8	3	1	....	7	....	....	....	.242	.260	.301	.561	94	-1	23	2.95	-6	O-67(12-38-17)/P-1	7	-0.7
Total 6	**257**	**1122**	**152**	**256**	**29**	**21**	**2**	**32**	**23**	**32**	**....**	**....**	**.228**	**.244**	**.297**	**.540**	**80**	**-21**	**86**	**2.77**	**-20**	**O-237/P-14,1-12,2-1**	**24**	**-6.7**

• WHEELOCK, Bobby Warren H. Wheelock b: 8/6/1864, Charlestown, MA d: 3/13/1928, Boston, MA BR/TR, 5'8", 160 lbs. Deb: 5/19/1887

YEAR TM-L	G	AB	R	H	2B	3B	HR	RBI	BB	SO	SB	CS	AVG	OBP	SLG	OPS	OPS+	BR/A	RC	RC/G	FR	G/POS	WS	TPW
1887 Bos-N	48	181	32	57	4	2	2	15	15	15	20	....	.315	.315	.337	.652	83	-3	25	5.24	-3	O-28(9-1-18),S-20/2-4	4	-0.5
1890 Col-a	52	190	24	45	6	1	1	16	25	....	34	....	.237	.326	.295	.620	89	-2	30	5.49	2	S-52	6	0.2
1891 Col-a	136	498	82	114	15	1	0	39	78	55	52	....	.229	.336	.263	.599	76	-11	63	4.34	12	*S-136	17	0.5
Total 3	**236**	**869**	**138**	**216**	**25**	**4**	**3**	**70**	**118**	**70**	**106**	**....**	**.249**	**.330**	**.285**	**.614**	**80**	**-16**	**118**	**4.77**	**12**	**S-208/O-28,2-4**	**27**	**0.2**

YEAR TM-L	G	AB	R	H	2B	3B	HR	RBI	BB	SO	SB	CS	AVG	OBP	SLG	OPS	OPS+	BR/A	RC	RC/G	FR	G/POS	WS	TPW
• WHELAN, Jimmy	James Francis Whelan b: 5/11/1890, Kansas City, MO d: 11/29/1929, Dayton, OH BR/TR, 5'8.5", 165 lbs. Deb: 4/24/1913																							
1913 StL-N	1	1	0	0	0	0	0	0	0	0	0	....	.000	.000	.000	.000	-101	-0	0	.00	0	....	0	0.0
• WHELAN, Tom	Thomas Joseph Whelan b: 1/3/1894, Lynn, MA d: 6/26/1957, Boston, MA BR/TR, 5'11", 175 lbs. Deb: 8/13/1920																							
1920 Bos-N	1	1	0	0	0	0	0	0	1	1	0	0	.000	.500	.000	.500	54	0	0	3.31	0	/1-1	0	0.0
• WHISENANT, Pete	Thomas Peter Whisenant b: 12/14/1929, Asheville, NC d: 3/22/1996, Port Charlotte, FL BR/TR, 6'2", 200 lbs. Deb: 4/16/1952 C Career OF: 122-142-92																							
1952 Bos-N	24	52	3	10	2	0	0	7	4	13	1	1	.192	.250	.231	.481	35	-5	3	1.63	2	0-14(9-5-0)	0	-0.4
1955 StL-N	58	115	10	22	5	1	2	9	5	29	2	0	.191	.225	.304	.529	39	-10	8	2.19	-0	0-40(12-11-19)	1	-1.2
1956 Chi-N	103	314	37	75	16	3	11	46	24	53	8	2	.239	.295	.414	.709	89	-5	38	4.06	-1	0-93(6-84-0)	8	-1.0
1957 Cin-N	67	90	18	19	3	2	5	11	5	24	0	1	.211	.253	.456	.708	80	-3	10	3.50	-1	0-43(24-9-12)	2	-0.6
1958 Cin-N	85	203	33	48	9	2	11	40	18	37	3	0	.236	.299	.463	.762	93	-2	28	4.57	-1	0-66(26-2-42)/2-1	5	-0.6
1959 Cin-N	36	71	13	17	2	0	5	11	8	18	0	0	.239	.316	.479	.795	105	0	11	5.38	0	0-21(5-0-16)	2	-0.1
1960 Cin-N	1	1	0	0	0	0	0	0	0	0	0	0	.000	.000	.000	.000	-98	-0	0	.00	0	....	0	0.0
Cle-A	7	6	0	1	0	0	0	0	0	2	0	0	.167	.167	.167	.333	-10	-1	0	.90	0	/0-2(2-0-0)	0	-0.1
Was-A	58	115	19	26	9	0	3	9	19	14	2	1	.226	.336	.383	.718	93	-1	15	4.44	0	0-47(23-31-1)	3	-0.3
Yr.	65	121	19	27	9	0	3	9	19	16	2	1	.223	.329	.372	.700	89	-2	15	4.26	-1	0-49(25-31-1)	3	-0.4
1961 Min-A	10	6	1	0	0	0	0	0	1	2	0	0	.000	.143	.000	.143	-55	-1	0	.17	0	/0-5(5-0-0)	0	-0.2
Cin-N	26	15	6	3	0	0	0	1	2	4	1	0	.200	.294	.200	.494	34	-1	1	1.97	-1	0-12(10-0-2)/3-1,C-1	0	-0.3
Total 8	475	988	140	221	46	8	37	134	86	196	17	5	.224	.287	.399	.685	80	-29	114	3.80	-3	0-343/2-1,3-1,C-1	21	-4.6
• WHISENTON, Larry	Larry Whisenton b: 7/3/1956, St. Louis, MO BL/TL, 6'1", 190 lbs. Deb: 9/17/1977 Career OF: 39-0-14																							
1977 Atl-N	4	4	1	1	0	0	0	1	0	3	0	0	.250	.250	.250	.500	31	-0	0	2.25	0	....	0	0.0
1978 Atl-N	6	16	1	3	1	0	0	2	1	2	0	0	.188	.235	.250	.485	32	-1	1	2.08	0	/0-4(0-0-4)	0	-0.2
1979 Atl-N	13	37	3	9	2	1	0	1	3	3	1	0	.243	.300	.351	.651	72	-1	4	3.58	2	0-13(9-0-4)	1	0.0
1981 Atl-N	9	5	1	1	0	0	0	0	2	1	0	0	.200	.429	.200	.629	81	0	1	4.40	-1	/0-2(1-0-1)	0	-0.1
1982*Atl-N	84	143	21	34	7	2	4	17	23	33	2	2	.238	.343	.399	.742	103	1	20	4.63	-1	0-34(29-0-5)	4	-0.2
Total 5	116	205	27	48	10	3	4	21	29	42	3	2	.234	.329	.371	.700	90	-3	26	4.19	0	/0-53	5	-0.5
• WHISTLER, Lew	Lewis W. Whistler b: 3/10/1868, St. Louis, MO d: 12/30/1959, St. Louis, MO TR, 5'10.5", 178 lbs. Deb: 8/7/1890 U Career OF: 15-5-12																							
1890 NY-N	45	170	27	49	9	7	2	29	20	37	8	....	.288	.366	.459	.825	140	8	32	7.08	-1	1-45	6	0.3
1891 NY-N	72	265	39	65	8	7	3	38	24	45	4	....	.245	.315	.362	.677	101	0	32	4.36	-13	S-33,0-22(14-5-3)/1-7,2-6,3	6	-1.1
1892 Bal-N	52	209	32	47	6	6	2	21	18	22	12	....	.225	.296	.340	.635	90	-3	25	4.19	-1	1-51/0-1	3	-0.5
Lou-N	80	285	42	67	4	7	5	34	30	45	14	....	.235	.312	.351	.663	109	4	36	4.52	0	1-72,2-10	8	0.3
Yr.	132	494	74	114	10	13	7	55	48	67	26	....	.231	.305	.346	.651	101	0	62	4.38	-2	*1-123,2-10/0-1	11	-0.2
1893 Lou-N	13	47	5	10	1	1	0	9	5	5	1	....	.213	.302	.277	.578	59	-3	4	3.10	-1	1-13	1	-0.3
StL-N	10	38	5	9	1	0	0	2	3	2	0	....	.237	.293	.263	.556	48	-3	3	2.74	-1	/0-9(0-0-9),1-1	0	-0.3
Yr.	23	85	10	19	2	1	0	11	8	7	1	....	.224	.298	.271	.568	54	-5	7	2.94	-1	1-14/0-9(0-0-9)	1	-0.6
Total 4	272	1014	150	247	29	28	12	133	100	156	39	....	.244	.318	.363	.681	104	3	134	4.68	-16	1-189/S-33,0-32,2-16,3-5	24	-1.5
• WHITAKER, Lou	Louis Rodman Whitaker b: 5/12/1957, Brooklyn, NY BL/TR, 5'11", 160 lbs. Deb: 9/9/1977																							
1977 Det-A	11	32	5	8	1	0	0	2	4	6	2	2	.250	.333	.281	.615	66	-2	3	3.14	-1	/2-9	0	-0.2
1978 Det-A	139	484	71	138	12	7	3	58	61	65	7	7	.285	.366	.357	.724	101	2	66	4.66	26	*2-136/D-2	17	3.6
1979 Det-A	127	423	75	121	14	8	3	42	78	66	20	10	.286	.398	.378	.777	107	9	69	5.49	17	*2-126	20	3.1
1980 Det-A	145	477	68	111	19	1	1	45	73	79	8	4	.233	.335	.283	.618	69	-17	50	3.43	7	*2-143	11	-0.2
1981 Det-A	109	335	48	88	14	4	5	36	40	42	5	3	.263	.343	.373	.716	103	2	45	4.61	11	*2-108	13	2.0
1982 Det-A	152	560	76	160	22	8	15	65	48	58	11	3	.286	.343	.434	.777	111	10	85	5.45	18	*2-149/D-1	22	3.6
1983 Det-A★	161	643	94	206	40	6	12	72	67	70	17	10	.320	.385	.457	.842	134	30	114	6.61	7	*2-160	29	4.5
1984*Det-A★	143	558	90	161	25	1	13	56	62	63	6	5	.289	.360	.407	.766	112	10	83	5.33	10	*2-142	22	2.8
1985 Det-A★	152	609	102	170	29	8	21	73	80	56	6	4	.279	.365	.456	.821	124	21	107	6.32	1	*2-150	24	3.0
1986 Det-A★	144	584	95	157	26	6	20	73	63	70	13	8	.269	.340	.437	.777	110	7	82	4.84	9	*2-141	19	2.3
1987*Det-A★	149	604	110	160	38	6	16	59	71	108	13	5	.265	.343	.427	.770	107	7	93	5.45	-1	*2-148	20	1.4
1988 Det-A	115	403	54	111	18	2	12	55	66	61	2	0	.275	.377	.419	.797	128	18	67	5.90	1	*2-110	20	2.1
1989 Det-A	148	509	77	128	21	1	28	85	89	59	6	3	.251	.366	.462	.828	135	26	91	6.15	1	*2-146/D-2	25	3.1
1990 Det-A	132	472	75	112	22	2	18	60	74	71	8	2	.237	.341	.407	.747	107	7	68	4.88	9	*2-130/D-1	19	2.0
1991 Det-A	138	470	94	131	26	2	23	78	90	45	4	2	.279	.397	.489	.886	142	30	99	7.55	-4	*2-135/D-3	26	2.9
1992 Det-A	130	453	77	126	26	0	19	71	81	46	6	4	.278	.389	.461	.850	136	25	85	6.57	-8	*2-119,D-10	24	1.9
1993 Det-A	119	383	72	111	32	1	9	67	78	46	3	3	.290	.415	.449	.864	133	22	78	7.20	13	*2-110	19	3.9
1994 Det-A	92	322	67	97	21	2	12	43	41	47	2	0	.301	.382	.491	.873	122	12	61	6.83	2	2-83/D-5	10	1.5
1995 Det-A	84	249	36	73	14	0	14	44	31	41	4	0	.293	.376	.518	.894	130	12	49	7.18	-3	2-63/D-8	11	1.0
Total 19	2390	8570	1386	2369	420	65	244	1084	1197	1099	143	75	.276	.366	.426	.792	117	230	1396	5.71	115	*2-2308/D-32	351	44.3
• WHITAKER, Steve	Stephen Edward Whitaker b: 5/7/1943, Tacoma, WA BL/TR, 6', 187 lbs. Deb: 8/23/1966 Career OF: 67-39-108																							
1966 NY-A	31	114	15	28	3	2	7	15	9	24	0	0	.246	.306	.491	.798	130	4	18	5.64	0	0-31(4-20-10)	4	0.3
1967 NY-A	122	441	37	107	12	3	11	50	23	89	2	5	.243	.285	.358	.643	92	-7	43	3.35	6	*0-114(26-12-78)	10	-1.0
1968 NY-A	28	60	3	7	2	0	0	3	8	18	0	1	.117	.221	.150	.371	14	-6	2	1.14	0	0-14(6-7-2)	0	-0.8
1969 Sea-A	69	116	15	29	2	1	6	13	12	29	2	0	.250	.326	.440	.765	114	2	18	5.33	1	0-39(22-0-18)	4	0.2
1970 SF-N	16	27	3	3	1	0	0	4	2	14	0	0	.111	.172	.148	.321	-13	-4	1	.70	-1	/0-9(9-0-0)	0	-0.5
Total 5	266	758	73	174	20	6	24	85	54	174	4	6	.230	.285	.367	.652	91	-12	82	3.65	6	0-207	18	-1.9
• WHITE, Barney	William Barney "Bear" White b: 6/25/1923, Paris, TX d: 7/24/2002, Tyler, TX BR/TR, 5'11", 186 lbs. Deb: 6/5/1945																							
1945 Bro-N	4	1	2	0	0	0	0	0	1	1	0	....	.000	.500	.000	.500	46	0	0	3.51	0	/3-1,S-1	0	0.0
• WHITE, Bill	William Dighton White b: 5/1/1860, Bridgeport, OH d: 12/29/1924, Bellaire, OH TR Deb: 5/3/1884																							
1884 Pit-a	74	291	25	66	7	10	0	0	13	....	....	....	.227	.262	.320	.582	87	-4	25	3.06	-12	S-60,3-10/0-4(0-0-4)	5	-1.3
1886 Lou-a	135	557	96	143	17	10	1	66	37	....	14	....	.257	.304	.329	.633	93	-7	61	4.01	5	*S-135/P-1	13	0.1
1887 Lou-a	132	559	85	176	7	9	2	79	47	....	41	....	.315	.315	.313	.627	74	-18	65	4.57	13	*S-132	13	0.0
1888 Lou-a	49	198	35	55	6	5	1	30	7	....	15	....	.278	.313	.374	.686	122	4	29	5.38	-1	S-38,3-11	6	0.4
*StL-a	76	275	31	48	2	3	2	30	21	....	6	....	.175	.238	.225	.464	44	-18	17	1.98	6	S-74/2-2	4	-0.9
Yr.	125	473	66	103	8	8	3	60	28	....	21	....	.218	.269	.288	.556	76	-14	45	3.29	5	*S-112,3-11/2-2	10	-0.5
Total 4	466	1880	272	488	39	37	6	205	125	....	76	....	.260	.292	.312	.604	82	-44	196	3.82	11	S-439/3-21,0-4,2-2,P-1	41	-1.7
• WHITE, Bill	William DeKova White b: 1/28/1934, Lakewood, FL BL/TL, 6', 195 lbs. Deb: 5/7/1956 Career OF: 99-37-21																							
1956 NY-N	138	508	63	130	23	7	22	59	47	72	15	8	.256	.324	.459	.782	108	5	76	5.11	7	*1-138/0-2(1-0-1)	16	0.4
1958 SF-N	26	29	5	7	1	0	1	4	7	5	1	0	.241	.389	.379	.768	107	1	5	6.24	0	/1-3,0-2(1-0-1)	1	0.1
1959 StL-N★	138	517	77	156	33	9	12	72	34	61	15	10	.302	.347	.470	.817	108	4	83	5.86	-5	0-92(86-9-0),1-71	14	-0.8
1960 StL-N★	144	554	81	157	27	10	16	79	42	83	12	6	.283	.336	.455	.791	105	3	84	5.40	-7	*1-123,0-29(3-28-0)	18	-1.2
1961 StL-N★	153	591	89	169	28	11	20	90	64	84	8	11	.286	.357	.472	.829	107	4	96	5.71	-2	*1-151	16	-0.7
1962 StL-N	159	614	93	199	31	3	20	102	58	69	9	7	.324	.388	.482	.870	120	18	114	7.05	3	*1-146,0-27(8-0-19)	22	1.1
1963 StL-N★	162	658	106	200	26	8	27	109	59	100	10	9	.304	.361	.491	.852	131	25	117	6.55	0	*1-162	27	1.6
1964*StL-N★	160	631	92	191	37	4	21	102	52	103	7	6	.303	.357	.474	.831	121	17	107	6.26	3	*1-160	26	1.1
1965 StL-N	148	543	82	157	26	3	24	73	63	86	3	3	.289	.367	.481	.848	125	19	97	6.51	6	*1-144	22	1.7
1966 Phi-N	159	577	85	159	23	6	22	103	68	109	16	6	.276	.355	.451	.806	122	20	96	5.86	5	*1-158	24	1.6
1967 Phi-N	110	308	29	77	6	2	8	33	52	61	6	1	.250	.364	.360	.724	107	6	44	4.96	-1	1-95	11	0.0
1968 Phi-N	127	385	34	92	16	2	9	40	39	79	0	1	.239	.312	.361	.673	102	1	44	3.86	1	*1-111	12	-0.6
1969 StL-N	49	57	7	12	1	0	0	4	11	15	1	0	.211	.338	.228	.566	61	-2	5	2.71	1	1-15	0	-0.2
Total 13	1673	5972	843	1706	278	65	202	870	596	927	103	68	.286	.353	.455	.809	115	121	968	5.81	11	*1-1477,0-152	209	4.2

YEAR TM-L	G	AB	R	H	2B	3B	HR	RBI	BB	SO	SB	CS	AVG	OBP	SLG	OPS	OPS+	BR/A	RC	RC/G	FR	G/POS	WS	TPW
• WHITE, Bill	William Edward White b: 1860, Milner, GA Deb: 6/21/1879																							
1879 Pro-N	1	4	1	1	0	0	0	0	0	1	....	....	.250	.250	.250	.500	66	-0	0	2.39	0	/1-1	0	0.0
• WHITE, C.B.	C. B. White b: Wakeman, OH Deb: 6/1/1883																							
1883 Phi-N	1	1	0	0	0	0	0	0	0	0	....	....	.000	.000	.000	.000	-110	-0	0	.00	-1	/3-1,S-1	0	-0.1
• WHITE, Charlie	Charles White b: 8/12/1927, Kingston, NC d: 5/26/1998, Sea-Tac, WA BL/TR, 5'11", 192 lbs. Deb: 4/18/1954																							
1954 Mil-N	50	93	14	22	4	0	1	8	9	8	0	0	.237	.304	.312	.616	65	-5	8	2.84	-1	C-28	1	-0.5
1955 Mil-N	12	30	3	7	1	0	0	4	5	7	0	0	.233	.361	.267	.628	74	-1	3	3.59	0	C-10	1	-0.1
Total 2	62	123	17	29	5	0	1	12	14	15	0	0	.236	.319	.301	.620	67	-5	11	3.02	-2	/C-38	2	-0.6
• WHITE, Deacon	James Laurie White b: 12/7/1847, Caton, NY d: 7/7/1939, Aurora, IL BL/TR, 5'11", 175 lbs. Deb: 5/4/1871 M/U NA OF: 2-1-48 Career OF: 8-5-101																							
1871 Cle-n	29	146	40	47	6	5	1	21	4	1	2	2	.322	.340	.452	.792	132	6	24	7.39	-3	*C-29/S-2,2-1,3-1,0-1	....	0.2
1872 Cle-n	22	109	21	37	2	2	0	22	4	1	0	0	.339	.363	.394	.757	141	6	16	6.89	1	C-14/2-7,0-5(2-1-3)	....	0.5
1873 Bos-n	60	310	79	121	15	6	0	**66**	0	2	6	2	.390	.390	.477	.868	144	15	62	9.84	-3	*C-56/0-9(0-0-9)	....	0.9
1874 Bos-n	70	352	75	106	5	7	3	52	4	0	1	1	.301	.309	.381	.690	113	3	43	5.19	-5	*C-58,0-21(0-0-21)/1-1	....	0.0
1875 Bos-n	80	371	76	136	23	3	1	60	3	2	2	3	**.367**	.372	.453	.824	178	26	65	8.03	11	*C-75,0-14(0-0-14)/1-1	....	3.3
1876 Chi-N	66	310	66	104	18	1	1	**60**	7	3	....	....	.335	.358	.419	.777	141	12	47	6.56	4	*C-63/1-3,0-3(3-0-0),3-1,P	13	1.5
1877 Bos-N	59	266	51	**103**	14	**11**	2	**49**	8	3	....	....	**.387**	.405	**.545**	**.950**	**190**	**26**	60	**10.16**	0	1-35,0-19(0-0-19)/C-7	16	2.1
1878 Cin-N	61	258	41	81	4	1	0	29	10	5	....	....	.314	.340	.337	.677	136	11	30	4.70	-1	*C-48,0-16(0-0-16)/3-1	11	1.0
1879 Cin-N	78	333	55	110	16	6	1	52	6	9	....	....	.330	.342	.423	.766	159	21	49	6.21	4	*C-59,0-21(0-4-18)/1-2	17	2.4
1880 Cin-N	35	141	21	42	4	2	0	7	9	7	....	....	.298	.340	.355	.695	137	6	17	4.84	-6	0-33(0-1-33)/1-3,2-1	4	-0.1
1881 Buf-N	78	319	58	99	24	4	0	53	9	8	....	....	.310	.329	.411	.740	133	11	44	5.43	-10	1-26,2-25,0-17(2-0-15)/3-7,C	12	0.1
1882 Buf-N	83	337	51	95	17	0	1	33	15	16	....	....	.282	.313	.341	.654	108	3	37	4.19	-12	*3-63,C-20	10	-0.5
1883 Buf-N	94	391	62	114	14	5	0	47	23	18	....	....	.292	.331	.353	.684	106	3	47	4.65	-11	*3-77,C-22	12	-0.4
1884 Buf-N	110	452	82	147	16	11	5	74	32	13	....	....	.325	.370	.442	.812	149	25	76	6.84	-6	*3-108/C-3	21	1.9
1885 Buf-N	98	404	54	118	6	6	0	57	12	11	....	....	.292	.313	.337	.649	106	2	44	4.11	-2	*3-98	12	0.1
1886 Det-N	124	491	65	142	19	5	1	76	31	35	9	....	.289	.331	.354	.686	105	3	62	4.81	-2	*3-124	15	0.3
1887*Det-N	111	475	71	162	20	11	3	75	26	15	20	....	.341	.353	.416	.770	109	5	75	6.35	2	*3-106/0-3(3-0-0),1-2	15	0.8
1888 Det-N	125	527	75	157	22	5	4	71	21	24	12	....	.298	.336	.381	.717	128	16	73	5.35	-2	*3-125	18	1.7
1889 Pit-N	55	225	35	57	10	1	0	26	16	18	2	....	.253	.314	.307	.621	82	-5	23	3.61	-6	3-52/1-3	4	-0.8
1890 Buf-P	122	439	62	114	13	4	0	47	67	30	3	....	.260	.381	.308	.688	93	3	54	4.48	7	3-64,1-57/P-1,S-1	10	0.3
Total 5 n	261	1288	291	447	51	23	5	221	15	6	11	8	.347	.355	.434	.789	144	56	209	7.44	1	C-232/0-50,2-8,1-2,S-2,3-1	....	5.0
Total 15	1299	5368	849	1645	217	73	18	756	292	215	46	....	.306	.344	.382	.726	123	141	738	5.41	-42	3-826,C-226,1-131,0-112/2,P,S	190	10.5
• WHITE, Derrick	Derrick Ramon White b: 10/12/1969, San Rafael, CA BR/TR, 6'1", 220 lbs. Deb: 7/22/1993 Career OF: 7-0-5																							
1993 Mon-N	17	49	6	11	3	0	2	4	2	12	2	0	.224	.269	.408	.677	75	-2	5	3.73	0	1-17	0	-0.3
1995 Det-A	39	48	3	9	2	0	0	2	0	7	1	0	.188	.188	.229	.417	8	-6	2	1.30	0	1-16,D-11/0-9(4-0-5)	0	-0.7
1998 Chi-N	11	10	1	1	0	0	1	2	0	5	0	0	.100	.100	.400	.500	23	-1	0	1.20	0	/0-1	0	-0.1
Col-N	9	9	0	0	0	0	0	0	0	4	0	0	.000	.000	.000	.000	-82	-2	0	.00	0	/0-2(2-0-0),D-1	0	-0.3
Yr.	20	19	1	1	0	0	1	2	0	9	0	0	.053	.053	.211	.263	-27	-4	0	.60	0	/0-3(3-0-0),D-1	0	-0.4
Total 3	76	116	10	21	5	0	3	8	2	28	3	0	.181	.202	.302	.503	32	-12	8	2.15	-1	/1-33,D-12,0-12	0	-1.4
• WHITE, Devon	Devon Markes White b: 12/29/1962, Kingston, Jamaica BB/TR, 6'1", 182 lbs. Deb: 9/2/1985 Career OF: 50-1723-130																							
1985 Cal-A	21	7	7	1	0	0	0	0	1	3	3	1	.143	.333	.143	.476	37	-0	1	2.64	0	0-16(14-1-3)	0	-0.1
1986*Cal-A	29	51	8	12	1	1	1	3	6	8	6	0	.235	.316	.353	.669	83	0	7	4.96	-1	0-28(17-7-5)	2	-0.1
1987 Cal-A	159	639	103	168	33	5	24	87	39	135	32	11	.263	.307	.443	.750	99	-1	87	4.63	8	*0-159(6-64-120)	17	0.0
1988 Cal-A	122	455	76	118	22	2	11	51	23	84	17	8	.259	.298	.389	.687	93	-6	52	3.96	8	*0-116(0-116-0)	11	0.1
1989 Cal-A★	156	636	86	156	18	13	12	56	31	129	44	16	.245	.283	.371	.654	84	-13	64	3.37	14	*0-154(0-154-0)/D-1	14	-0.2
1990 Cal-A	125	443	57	96	17	3	11	44	44	116	21	6	.217	.292	.343	.635	79	-11	47	3.41	6	*0-122(0-122-0)	7	-0.7
1991*Tor-A	156	642	110	181	40	10	17	60	55	135	33	10	.282	.345	.455	.800	115	15	105	5.77	6	*0-156(0-156-0)	24	1.9
1992*Tor-A	153	641	98	159	26	7	17	60	47	133	37	4	.248	.304	.390	.694	89	-5	81	4.39	4	*0-152(0-152-0)/D-1	19	-0.3
1993*Tor-A★	146	598	116	163	42	6	15	52	57	127	34	4	.273	.343	.438	.781	108	12	99	5.94	-1	*0-145(0-145-0)	20	1.2
1994 Tor-A	100	403	67	109	24	6	13	49	21	80	11	3	.270	.315	.457	.771	95	-4	59	5.15	-1	0-98(0-98-0)	11	-0.4
1995 Tor-A	101	427	61	121	23	5	10	53	29	97	11	2	.283	.336	.431	.767	99	-0	64	5.43	-1	0-99(0-99-0)	12	-0.1
1996 Fla-N	146	552	77	151	37	6	17	84	38	99	22	6	.274	.329	.455	.784	108	6	84	5.28	-5	*0-139(0-139-0)	18	0.2
1997*Fla-N	74	265	37	65	13	1	6	34	32	65	13	5	.245	.342	.370	.712	90	-2	36	4.62	0	0-72(0-72-0)	9	-0.2
1998 Ari-N★	146	563	84	157	32	1	22	85	42	102	22	8	.279	.339	.456	.795	107	6	88	5.42	-3	*0-144(0-144-0)	18	0.4
1999 LA-N	134	474	60	127	20	2	14	68	39	88	19	5	.268	.338	.407	.745	93	-4	67	4.94	-4	*0-128(0-128-0)/D-1	12	-0.7
2000 LA-N	47	158	26	42	5	1	4	13	9	30	3	6	.266	.310	.386	.696	79	-8	17	3.60	-2	0-40(0-40-0)	2	-0.9
2001 Mil-N	126	390	52	108	25	2	14	47	28	95	18	3	.277	.344	.459	.803	108	7	64	5.92	-5	*0-100(13-86-2)	11	0.2
Total 17	1941	7344	1125	1934	378	71	208	846	541	1526	346	98	.263	.321	.419	.740	98	-8	1020	4.82	23	*0-1868/D-3	207	0.3
• WHITE, Doc	Guy Harris White b: 4/9/1879, Washington, DC d: 2/19/1969, Silver Spring, MD BL/TL, 6'1", 150 lbs. Deb: 4/22/1901 U Career OF: 20-51-14 ♦																							
1901 Phi-N	31	98	15	27	3	1	1	10	2	....	1	....	.276	.297	.357	.654	87	5	12	3.98	2	P-31/0-1	16	1.0
1902 Phi-N	61	179	17	47	3	1	1	15	11	....	5	....	.263	.305	.307	.613	89	5	20	3.74	-1	P-36,0-19(17-0-2)	27	2.0
1903 Chi-A	38	99	10	20	3	0	0	5	19	....	1	....	.202	.331	.232	.563	74	6	8	2.78	3	P-37/0-1	23	3.5
1904 Chi-A	33	76	7	12	2	0	0	2	10	....	3	....	.158	.256	.184	.440	42	0	5	1.90	1	P-30/0-2(0-2-0)	17	1.4
1905 Chi-A	37	90	7	15	4	1	0	7	4	....	3	....	.167	.202	.233	.435	40	-0	5	1.79	2	P-36/0-1	22	1.5
1906*Chi-A	29	65	11	12	1	1	0	3	13	....	3	....	.185	.321	.231	.551	75	3	7	3.08	3	P-28/0-1	25	2.8
1907 Chi-A	48	90	12	20	1	0	0	2	12	....	2	....	.222	.314	.233	.547	78	4	9	2.96	4	P-46/0-2(0-0-2),2-1	25	1.1
1908 Chi-A	51	109	12	25	1	0	0	10	12	....	4	....	.229	.306	.239	.544	79	5	10	2.81	7	P-41/0-3(0-2-1)	20	0.0
1909 Chi-A	72	192	24	45	1	5	0	7	33	....	7	....	.234	.347	.292	.638	106	8	23	3.76	-3	0-40(1-35-4),P-24	20	1.9
1910 Chi-A	56	126	14	25	1	2	0	8	14	....	2	....	.198	.279	.238	.517	65	2	10	2.31	3	P-33,0-14(0-10-4)	15	-0.4
1911 Chi-A	39	78	12	20	1	1	0	6	7	....	1	....	.256	.318	.295	.613	73	3	8	3.31	-1	P-34/1-2,0-1	14	0.9
1912 Chi-A	32	56	5	7	1	1	0	0	7	....	0	....	.125	.222	.179	.401	15	-1	2	1.19	-1	P-32	9	0.1
1913 Chi-A	21	25	1	3	0	0	0	0	3	1	0	....	.120	.214	.120	.334	-2	-1	1	.92	2	P-19/1-1	2	-0.8
Total 13	548	1283	147	278	22	13	2	75	147	1	32	....	.217	.298	.259	.556	74	37	121	2.91	21	P-427/0-85,1-3,2-1	235	15.0
• WHITE, Don	Donald William White b: 1/8/1919, Everett, WA d: 6/15/1987, Carlsbad, CA BR/TR, 6'1", 195 lbs. Deb: 4/19/1948 Career OF: 39-7-60																							
1948 Phi-A	86	253	29	62	14	2	1	28	19	16	0	1	.245	.303	.328	.631	68	-13	25	3.36	-2	0-54(33-7-17),3-17	4	-1.7
1949 Phi-A	57	169	12	36	6	0	0	10	14	12	2	0	.213	.273	.249	.522	40	-14	12	2.35	0	0-48(6-0-43)/3-4	1	-1.6
Total 2	143	422	41	98	20	2	1	38	33	28	2	1	.232	.291	.296	.587	56	-27	38	2.95	-3	0-102/3-21	5	-3.3
• WHITE, Ed	Edward Perry White b: 4/6/1926, Anniston, AL d: 9/28/1982, Lakeland, FL BR/TR, 6'2", 200 lbs. Deb: 9/16/1955																							
1955 Chi-A	3	4	0	2	0	0	0	0	1	1	0	0	.500	.600	.500	1.100	193	1	1	18.31	-0	/0-2(0-0-2)	0	0.1
• WHITE, Elder	Elder Lafayette White b: 12/23/1934, Colerain, NC BR/TR, 5'11", 165 lbs. Deb: 4/10/1962																							
1962 Chi-N	23	53	4	8	2	0	0	1	8	11	3	0	.151	.274	.189	.463	26	-5	4	1.93	0	S-15/3-1	1	-0.4
• WHITE, Elmer	Elmer White b: 12/7/1850, Caton, NY d: 3/17/1872, Caton, NY Deb: 5/4/1871																							
1871 Cle-n	15	70	13	18	2	0	0	9	1	6	0	1	.257	.268	.286	.553	62	-4	5	3.26	-1	0-15(0-0-15)/C-3	....	-0.2
• WHITE, Frank	Frank White b: 9/4/1950, Greenville, MS BR/TR, 5'11", 170 lbs. Deb: 6/12/1973 C Career OF: 0-1-1																							
1973 KC-A	51	139	20	31	6	1	0	5	8	23	3	1	.223	.265	.281	.546	50	-9	11	2.60	1	S-37,2-11	2	-0.4
1974 KC-A	99	204	19	45	6	3	1	18	5	33	3	4	.221	.239	.294	.533	50	-15	13	2.02	-5	2-50,S-29,3-16/D-3	3	-1.5
1975 KC-A	111	304	43	76	10	2	7	36	20	39	11	3	.250	.298	.365	.664	84	-6	34	3.84	0	2-67,S-42/3-4,C-1,D-1	9	0.2
1976*KC-A	152	446	39	102	17	6	2	46	19	42	20	11	.229	.265	.307	.572	67	-20	37	2.60	11	*2-130,S-37	9	0.2
1977*KC-A	152	474	59	116	21	5	5	50	25	67	23	5	.245	.285	.342	.627	70	-17	49	3.48	3	*2-152/S-4	13	-0.7
1978*KC-A★	143	461	66	127	24	6	7	50	26	59	13	10	.275	.318	.399	.717	98	-4	59	4.43	5	*2-140	16	0.9
1979 KC-A★	127	467	73	124	26	4	10	48	25	54	28	8	.266	.304	.403	.707	87	-7	56	4.04	2	*2-125	11	0.1

YEAR TM-L	G	AB	R	H	2B	3B	HR	RBI	BB	SO	SB	CS	AVG	OBP	SLG	OPS	OPS+	BR/A	RC	RC/G	FR	G/POS	WS	TPW
1980*KC-A	154	560	70	148	23	4	7	60	19	69	19	6	.264	.291	.357	.648	76	-18	57	3.47	8	*2-153	13	-0.2
1981*KC-A★	94	364	35	91	17	1	9	38	19	50	4	2	.250	.287	.376	.664	91	-5	37	3.43	0	2-93	7	0.0
1982 KC-A★	145	524	71	156	45	6	11	56	16	65	10	7	.298	.321	.469	.790	114	7	73	4.96	0	*2-144	18	1.4
1983 KC-A	146	549	52	143	35	6	11	77	20	51	13	5	.260	.286	.406	.693	88	-11	58	3.56	15	*2-145	15	1.2
1984*KC-A	129	479	58	130	22	5	17	56	27	72	5	5	.271	.313	.445	.758	106	1	63	4.55	10	*2-129	18	1.9
1985*KC-A	149	563	62	140	25	1	22	69	28	86	10	4	.249	.285	.414	.699	88	-11	65	3.98	-1	*2-149	16	-0.4
1986 KC-A★	151	566	76	154	37	3	22	84	43	88	4	4	.272	.326	.465	.790	110	5	84	5.19	0	*2-151/3-1,S-1	20	1.3
1987 KC-A	154	563	67	138	32	2	17	78	51	86	1	3	.245	.310	.400	.710	84	-15	67	3.99	-8	*2-152/D-1	14	-1.4
1988 KC-A	150	537	48	126	25	1	8	58	21	67	7	3	.235	.269	.330	.598	66	-26	44	2.70	10	*2-148/D-3	9	-1.2
1989 KC-A	135	418	34	107	22	1	2	36	30	52	3	2	.256	.309	.328	.637	80	-12	43	3.53	10	*2-132/0-1	14	0.2
1990 KC-A	82	241	20	52	14	1	2	21	10	32	1	0	.216	.256	.307	.563	58	-14	18	2.43	3	2-79/0-1	4	-1.0
Total 18	**2324**	**7859**	**912**	**2006**	**407**	**58**	**160**	**886**	**412**	**1035**	**178**	**83**	**.255**	**.295**	**.383**	**.678**	**85**	**-176**	**866**	**3.74**	**64**	***2-2150,S-150/3-21,D-8,0-2,C**	**211**	**0.6**

• WHITE, Fuzz Albert Eugene White b: 6/27/1918, Springfield, MO BL/TR, 6', 175 lbs. Deb: 9/17/1940

YEAR TM-L	G	AB	R	H	2B	3B	HR	RBI	BB	SO	SB	CS	AVG	OBP	SLG	OPS	OPS+	BR/A	RC	RC/G	FR	G/POS	WS	TPW
1940 StL-A	2	2	0	0	0	0	0	0	0	0	0	0	.000	.000	.000	.000	-98	-1	0	.00	0	....	0	-0.1
1947 NY-N	7	13	3	3	0	0	0	0	0	0	0	....	.231	.231	.231	.462	23	-1	0	1.13	0	/0-5(0-0-5)	0	-0.2
Total 2	**9**	**15**	**3**	**3**	**0**	**0**	**0**	**0**	**0**	**0**	**0**	**0**	**.200**	**.200**	**.200**	**.400**	**7**	**-2**	**0**	**.96**	**0**	**/0-5**	**0**	**-0.2**

• WHITE, Jack John Wallace White b: 1/19/1878, Traders Point, IN d: 9/30/1963, Indianapolis, IN BR/TR, 5'6" Deb: 6/26/1904

YEAR TM-L	G	AB	R	H	2B	3B	HR	RBI	BB	SO	SB	CS	AVG	OBP	SLG	OPS	OPS+	BR/A	RC	RC/G	FR	G/POS	WS	TPW
1904 Bos-N	1	5	1	0	0	0	0	0	0	....	0	....	.000	.000	.000	.000	-104	-1	0	.00	1	/0-1	0	0.0

• WHITE, Jack John Peter White b: 8/31/1905, New York, NY d: 6/19/1971, Flushing, NY BB/TR, 5'7.5", 150 lbs. Deb: 6/22/1927

YEAR TM-L	G	AB	R	H	2B	3B	HR	RBI	BB	SO	SB	CS	AVG	OBP	SLG	OPS	OPS+	BR/A	RC	RC/G	FR	G/POS	WS	TPW
1927 Cin-N	5	4	1	0	0	0	0	0	0	0	0	....	.000	.000	.000	.000	-103	-1	0	.00	-1	/2-3,S-2	0	-0.2
1928 Cin-N	1	3	0	0	0	0	0	0	0	1	0	....	.000	.000	.000	.000	-102	-1	0	.00	-1	/2-1	0	-0.2
Total 2	**6**	**7**	**1**	**0**	**0**	**0**	**0**	**0**	**0**	**1**	**0**	**....**	**.000**	**.000**	**.000**	**.000**	**-103**	**-2**	**0**	**.00**	**-2**	**/2-4,S-2**	**0**	**-0.4**

• WHITE, Jerry Jerome Cardell White b: 8/23/1952, Shirley, MA BB/TR, 5'10", 165 lbs. Deb: 9/16/1974 C Career OF: 148-194-78

YEAR TM-L	G	AB	R	H	2B	3B	HR	RBI	BB	SO	SB	CS	AVG	OBP	SLG	OPS	OPS+	BR/A	RC	RC/G	FR	G/POS	WS	TPW
1974 Mon-N	9	10	0	4	1	1	0	2	0	0	3	0	.400	.400	.700	1.100	193	2	3	15.41	-0	/0-7(5-2-0)	1	0.2
1975 Mon-N	39	97	14	29	4	1	2	7	10	7	5	2	.299	.364	.423	.787	113	2	16	6.13	1	0-30(7-24-0)	4	0.2
1976 Mon-N	114	278	32	68	11	1	2	21	27	31	15	7	.245	.316	.313	.629	76	-8	29	3.47	-2	0-92(27-67-0)	5	-1.3
1977 Mon-N	16	21	4	4	0	0	0	1	1	3	1	0	.190	.227	.190	.418	14	-2	1	1.30	0	/0-8(7-0-1)	0	-0.3
1978 Mon-N	18	10	2	2	0	0	0	0	1	3	1	0	.200	.273	.200	.473	34	-1	1	2.56	0	/0-3(1-0-2)	0	-0.1
Chi-N	59	136	22	37	6	0	1	10	23	16	4	3	.272	.377	.338	.716	90	-1	18	4.61	-0	0-54(0-54-0)	5	-0.2
Yr.	77	146	24	39	6	0	1	10	24	19	5	3	.267	.371	.329	.699	87	-2	19	4.47	-1	0-57(1-54-2)	5	-0.3
1979 Mon-N	88	138	30	41	7	1	3	18	21	23	8	4	.297	.394	.428	.821	125	6	25	6.50	-1	0-43(6-13-26)	6	0.4
1980 Mon-N	110	214	22	56	9	3	7	23	30	37	8	7	.262	.355	.430	.785	118	4	34	5.36	-2	0-84(62-7-18)	8	-0.1
1981*Mon-N	59	119	11	26	5	1	3	11	13	17	5	2	.218	.295	.353	.648	82	-3	14	3.74	-2	0-39(7-13-20)	3	-0.6
1982 Mon-N	69	115	13	28	6	1	2	13	8	26	3	3	.243	.304	.365	.669	85	-3	12	3.56	-1	0-30(21-9-2)	2	-0.5
1983 Mon-N	40	34	4	5	1	0	0	0	12	8	4	0	.147	.383	.176	.559	60	0	4	4.09	0	0-13(2-5-6)	1	0.0
1986 StL-N	25	24	1	3	0	0	1	3	2	3	0	0	.125	.192	.250	.442	21	-3	1	1.20	0	/0-6(3-0-3)	0	-0.3
Total 11	**646**	**1196**	**155**	**303**	**50**	**9**	**21**	**109**	**148**	**174**	**57**	**28**	**.253**	**.339**	**.363**	**.702**	**93**	**-7**	**158**	**4.48**	**-8**	**0-409**	**35**	**-2.7**

• WHITE, Jo-Jo Joyner Clifford White b: 6/1/1909, Red Oak, GA d: 10/9/1986, Tacoma, WA BL/TR, 5'11", 165 lbs. Deb: 4/15/1932 M/C Career OF: 73-522-97

YEAR TM-L	G	AB	R	H	2B	3B	HR	RBI	BB	SO	SB	CS	AVG	OBP	SLG	OPS	OPS+	BR/A	RC	RC/G	FR	G/POS	WS	TPW
1932 Det-A	80	208	25	54	6	3	2	21	22	19	6	8	.260	.330	.346	.677	73	-10	23	3.75	2	0-48(16-17-16)	3	-0.9
1933 Det-A	91	234	43	59	9	5	2	34	27	26	5	5	.252	.337	.359	.696	83	-6	29	4.13	0	0-54(16-32-6)	5	-0.8
1934*Det-A	115	384	97	120	18	5	0	44	69	39	28	6	.313	.419	.385	.804	108	13	71	6.78	1	*0-100(1-93-6)	16	1.0
1935*Det-A	114	412	82	99	13	12	2	32	68	42	19	10	.240	.348	.345	.693	82	-9	53	4.34	-4	0-98(0-98-0)	9	-1.4
1936 Det-A	58	51	11	14	3	0	0	6	9	10	2	0	.275	.383	.333	.717	78	-1	7	5.37	-1	0-18(0-18-1)	1	-0.1
1937 Det-A	94	305	50	75	5	7	0	21	50	40	12	7	.246	.354	.308	.662	67	-14	37	4.05	-7	0-82(3-79-0)	6	-2.1
1938 Det-A	78	206	40	54	6	1	0	15	30	15	3	4	.262	.359	.301	.660	63	-12	24	3.95	-2	0-55(21-34-1)	3	-1.4
1943 Phi-A	139	500	69	124	17	7	1	30	61	51	12	4	.248	.335	.316	.651	91	-2	59	3.99	-4	*0-133(2-131-0)	13	-1.0
1944 Phi-A	85	267	30	59	4	2	1	21	40	27	5	4	.221	.329	.262	.591	71	-9	27	3.33	-2	0-74(10-9-57)/S-1	5	-1.6
Cin-N	24	85	9	20	2	0	0	5	10	7	0	....	.235	.316	.259	.575	65	-4	8	3.23	2	0-23(4-11-10)	2	-0.3
Total 9	**878**	**2652**	**456**	**678**	**83**	**42**	**8**	**229**	**386**	**276**	**92**	**48**	**.256**	**.353**	**.328**	**.681**	**82**	**-54**	**337**	**4.35**	**-13**	**0-685/S-1**	**63**	**-8.6**

• WHITE, Mike Joyner Michael White b: 12/18/1938, Detroit, MI BR/TR, 5'8", 160 lbs. Deb: 9/21/1963

YEAR TM-L	G	AB	R	H	2B	3B	HR	RBI	BB	SO	SB	CS	AVG	OBP	SLG	OPS	OPS+	BR/A	RC	RC/G	FR	G/POS	WS	TPW
1963 Hou-N	3	7	0	2	0	0	0	0	0	0	0	0	.286	.286	.286	.571	69	-0	1	3.09	-0	/2-2	0	0.0
1964 Hou-N	89	280	30	76	11	3	0	27	20	47	1	1	.271	.320	.332	.652	89	-4	28	3.54	-1	0-72(9-55-8),2-10/3-3	7	-0.7
1965 Hou-N	8	9	0	0	0	0	0	0	1	2	0	0	.000	.100	.000	.100	-74	-2	0	.08	0	/3-1	0	-0.2
Total 3	**100**	**296**	**30**	**78**	**11**	**3**	**0**	**27**	**21**	**49**	**1**	**1**	**.264**	**.312**	**.321**	**.633**	**84**	**-6**	**29**	**3.40**	**-1**	**/0-72,2-12,3-4**	**7**	**-1.0**

• WHITE, Myron Myron Alan White b: 8/1/1957, Long Beach, CA BL/TL, 5'11", 180 lbs. Deb: 9/4/1978

YEAR TM-L	G	AB	R	H	2B	3B	HR	RBI	BB	SO	SB	CS	AVG	OBP	SLG	OPS	OPS+	BR/A	RC	RC/G	FR	G/POS	WS	TPW
1978 LA-N	7	4	1	2	0	0	0	1	0	1	0	1	.500	.500	.500	1.000	181	-0	1	3.40	0	/0-4(1-0-3)	0	0.0

• WHITE, Rondell Rondell Bernard White b: 2/23/1972, Milledgeville, GA BR/TR, 6'1", 205 lbs. Deb: 9/1/1993 Career OF: 585-513-0

YEAR TM-L	G	AB	R	H	2B	3B	HR	RBI	BB	SO	SB	CS	AVG	OBP	SLG	OPS	OPS+	BR/A	RC	RC/G	FR	G/POS	WS	TPW
1993 Mon-N	23	73	9	19	3	1	2	15	7	16	1	2	.260	.325	.411	.736	92	-2	9	3.98	-1	0-21(19-5-0)	3	-0.3
1994 Mon-N	40	97	16	27	10	1	2	13	9	18	1	1	.278	.358	.464	.822	111	1	17	6.19	-1	0-29(25-4-0)	4	0.0
1995 Mon-N	130	474	87	140	33	4	13	57	41	87	25	5	.295	.359	.464	.823	111	10	80	6.14	-2	*0-119(8-111-0)	14	0.9
1996 Mon-N	88	334	35	98	19	4	6	41	22	53	14	6	.293	.341	.428	.769	99	-1	46	4.88	5	0-86(0-86-0)	10	0.5
1997 Mon-N	151	592	84	160	29	5	28	82	31	111	16	8	.270	.318	.478	.796	105	1	83	4.86	6	*0-151(0-151-0)	17	0.8
1998 Mon-N	97	357	54	107	21	2	17	58	30	57	16	7	.300	.365	.513	.878	130	15	66	6.69	8	0-96(15-82-0)/D-1	16	2.3
1999 Mon-N	138	539	83	168	26	6	22	64	32	85	10	6	.312	.363	.505	.867	120	14	93	6.28	0	*0-135(102-73-0)	15	1.0
2000 Mon-N	75	290	52	89	24	0	11	54	28	67	5	1	.307	.372	.503	.875	115	7	56	7.24	7	0-74(74-0-0)	12	1.0
Chi-N	19	67	7	22	2	0	2	7	5	12	0	2	.328	.392	.448	.840	114	1	12	6.67	2	0-18(18-0-0)	2	0.1
Yr.	94	357	59	111	26	0	13	61	33	79	5	3	.311	.376	.493	.869	115	8	67	7.13	8	0-92(92-0-0)	14	1.1
2001 Chi-N	95	323	43	99	19	1	17	50	26	56	1	0	.307	.371	.529	.900	136	17	59	6.71	-1	0-90(90-0-0)	12	1.2
2002*NY-A	126	455	59	109	21	0	14	62	25	86	1	2	.240	.291	.378	.669	77	-17	48	3.55	3	*0-113(113-1-0),D-11	6	-1.9
2003 SD-N★	115	413	49	115	17	3	18	66	25	71	1	4	.278	.332	.465	.797	115	6	60	5.12	0	*0-104(104-0-0)/D-3	11	0.2
KC-A	22	75	13	26	6	1	4	21	6	8	0	0	.347	.410	.613	1.023	145	5	18	9.42	2	0-17(17-0-0)/D-4	4	0.6
Total 11	**1119**	**4089**	**591**	**1179**	**230**	**28**	**156**	**590**	**287**	**727**	**91**	**44**	**.288**	**.345**	**.473**	**.818**	**111**	**58**	**648**	**5.64**	**27**	***0-1053/D-19**	**126**	**6.3**

• WHITE, Roy Roy Hilton White b: 12/27/1943, Los Angeles, CA BB/TR, 5'10", 172 lbs. Deb: 9/7/1965 C Career OF: 1520-63-56

YEAR TM-L	G	AB	R	H	2B	3B	HR	RBI	BB	SO	SB	CS	AVG	OBP	SLG	OPS	OPS+	BR/A	RC	RC/G	FR	G/POS	WS	TPW
1965 NY-A	14	42	7	14	2	0	0	3	4	7	2	1	.333	.404	.381	.785	125	2	7	6.54	0	0-10(0-1-9)/2-1	2	0.1
1966 NY-A	115	316	39	71	13	2	7	20	37	43	14	7	.225	.308	.345	.653	91	-3	35	3.66	-2	0-82(72-12-0)/2-2	7	-1.0
1967 NY-A	70	214	22	48	8	0	2	18	19	25	10	4	.224	.291	.290	.580	75	-6	20	3.04	-5	0-36(5-0-31),3-17	4	-1.5
1968 NY-A	159	577	89	154	20	7	17	62	73	50	20	11	.267	.352	.414	.766	136	26	86	5.14	5	*0-154(119-25-12)	29	2.5
1969 NY-A★	130	448	55	130	30	5	7	74	81	51	18	10	.290	.400	.426	.826	136	25	81	6.24	5	*0-126(126-0-0)	22	2.3
1970 NY-A★	162	609	109	180	30	6	22	94	95	66	24	10	.296	.391	.473	.864	144	40	116	6.78	1	*0-161(161-0-1)	34	3.3
1971 NY-A	147	524	86	153	22	7	19	84	86	66	14	7	.292	.399	.469	.868	154	41	103	6.85	8	*0-145(145-0-0)	29	4.3
1972 NY-A	155	556	76	150	29	0	10	54	**99**	59	23	7	.270	.385	.376	.761	131	29	88	5.53	3	*0-155(155-0-0)	26	2.6
1973 NY-A	162	639	88	157	22	3	18	60	78	81	16	9	.246	.330	.374	.704	101	2	80	4.23	1	*0-162(162-0-0)	15	-0.7
1974 NY-A	136	473	68	130	19	8	7	43	67	44	15	6	.275	.369	.393	.763	123	18	73	5.40	1	0-67(67-0-0),D-53	19	1.4
1975 NY-A	148	556	81	161	32	5	12	59	72	50	16	15	.290	.373	.430	.803	130	21	91	5.84	1	*0-135(135-0-0)/1-7,D-2	21	1.3
1976*NY-A	156	626	**104**	179	29	3	14	65	83	52	31	13	.286	.370	.409	.778	129	26	98	5.40	1	*0-156(140-21-1)	26	2.0
1977*NY-A	143	519	72	139	25	2	14	52	75	58	18	11	.268	.360	.405	.765	109	8	77	5.02	1	*0-135(133-1-2)/D-4	17	0.2
1978*NY-A	103	346	44	93	13	3	8	43	42	35	10	4	.269	.351	.393	.744	112	7	48	4.80	-2	0-74(73-3-0),D-23	11	0.1
1979 NY-A	81	205	24	44	6	0	3	27	23	21	2	2	.215	.294	.288	.582	59	-12	17	2.67	2	D-29,0-27(27-0-0)	1	-1.2
Total 15	**1881**	**6650**	**964**	**1803**	**300**	**51**	**160**	**758**	**934**	**708**	**233**	**117**	**.271**	**.363**	**.404**	**.767**	**123**	**223**	**1020**	**5.29**	**19**	***0-1625,D-111/3-17,1-7,2-3**	**263**	**15.6**

YEAR	TM-L	G	AB	R	H	2B	3B	HR	RBI	BB	SO	SB	CS	AVG	OBP	SLG	OPS	OPS+	BR/A	RC	RC/G	FR	G/POS	WS	TPW
• WHITE, Sam	Samuel Lambeth White b: 8/23/1892, Preston, England d: 11/11/1929, Philadelphia, PA BL/TR, 6', 185 lbs. Deb: 9/8/1919																								
1919	Bos-N	1	1	0	0	0	0	0	0	0	0	0	....	.000	.000	.000	.000	-104	-0	0	.00	1	/C-1	0	0.1
• WHITE, Sammy	Samuel Charles White b: 7/7/1927, Wenatchee, WA d: 8/5/1991, Princeville, HI BR/TR, 6'3", 195 lbs. Deb: 9/26/1951																								
1951	Bos-A	4	11	0	2	0	0	0	0	0	3	0	0	.182	.182	.182	.364	-1	-2	0	1.12	0	/C-4	0	-0.1
1952	Bos-A	115	381	35	107	20	2	10	49	16	43	2	3	.281	.310	.423	.732	95	-5	46	4.25	1	*C-110	12	0.1
1953	Bos-A★	136	476	59	130	34	2	13	64	29	48	3	2	.273	.318	.435	.752	96	-4	63	4.60	1	*C-131	16	0.3
1954	Bos-A	137	493	46	139	25	2	14	75	21	50	1	3	.282	.311	.426	.737	90	-9	60	4.18	2	*C-133	11	-0.1
1955	Bos-A	143	544	65	142	30	4	11	64	44	58	1	2	.261	.324	.392	.716	84	-14	64	3.98	-4	*C-143	12	-1.1
1956	Bos-A	114	392	28	96	15	2	5	44	35	40	2	1	.245	.307	.332	.638	61	-22	37	3.08	-5	*C-114	6	-2.1
1957	Bos-A	111	340	24	73	10	1	3	31	25	38	0	1	.215	.268	.276	.545	46	-25	22	2.04	-5	*C-111	5	-2.6
1958	Bos-A	102	328	25	85	15	3	6	35	21	37	1	1	.259	.306	.378	.684	81	-9	37	3.92	-3	*C-102	7	-0.8
1959	Bos-A	119	377	34	107	13	4	1	42	23	39	4	2	.284	.327	.347	.674	81	-10	40	3.70	3	*C-119	10	-0.2
1961	Mil-N	21	63	1	14	1	0	1	5	2	9	0	0	.222	.246	.286	.532	43	-5	4	2.26	0	C-20	1	-0.4
1962	Phi-N	41	97	7	21	4	0	2	12	2	16	0	0	.216	.240	.320	.560	50	-7	6	1.85	0	C-40	1	-0.6
Total	11	1043	3502	324	916	167	20	66	421	218	381	14	15	.262	.307	.377	.684	79	-113	379	3.67	-10	*C-1027	81	-7.4
• WHITE, Warren	William Warren White b: 1844, Washington, DC, 5'10.5", 170 lbs. Deb: 6/17/1871 M/U																								
1871	Oly-n	1	4	0	0	0	0	0	0	0	0	0	0	.000	.000	.000	.000	-106	-1	0	.00	0	/2-1	....	-0.1
1872	Nat-n	10	45	7	13	0	0	0	4	0	0	0	0	.289	.289	.289	.578	67	-2	4	3.73	7	/3-9,S-1	....	0.3
1873	Was-n	39	160	29	43	3	4	0	21	0	1	1	1	.269	.269	.338	.606	82	-3	15	3.92	1	*3-37/S-3	....	-0.2
1874	Bal-n	45	211	21	57	1	0	0	17	2	2	2	0	.270	.277	.275	.552	77	-5	17	3.22	19	*3-45/C-3	....	1.1
1875	Chi-n	69	287	37	71	9	0	0	23	0	3	3	10	.247	.247	.279	.526	82	-9	22	2.81	5	*3-59/0-5(0-5-0),S-5,2-2	....	-0.4
1884	Was-U	4	18	2	1	0	0	0	....	0	....	....	....	.056	.056	.056	.111	-65	-3	0	.09	-1	/3-2,2-1,S-1	0	-0.3
Total	5 n	164	707	94	184	13	4	0	65	2	6	6	11	.260	.262	.290	.552	78	-21	57	3.21	33	3-150/S-9,0-5,2-3,C-3	....	0.8
• WHITED, Ed	Edward Morris Whited b: 2/9/1964, Bristol, PA BR/TR, 6'3", 195 lbs. Deb: 7/5/1989																								
1989	Atl-N	36	74	5	12	3	0	1	4	6	15	1	0	.162	.225	.243	.468	33	-6	4	1.64	-3	3-29/1-3	0	-1.0
• WHITEHEAD, Burgess	Burgess Urquhart "Whitey" Whitehead b: 6/29/1910, Tarboro, NC d: 11/25/1993, Windsor, NC BR/TR, 5'10.5", 160 lbs. Deb: 4/30/1933																								
1933	StL-N	12	7	2	2	0	0	0	1	0	1	0	....	.286	.286	.286	.571	60	-0	0	1.24	-3	/S-9,2-3	0	-0.3
1934*	StL-N	100	332	55	92	13	5	1	24	12	19	5	....	.277	.310	.355	.666	73	-13	38	4.09	6	2-48,S-29,3-28	8	-0.3
1935	StL-N★	107	338	45	89	10	2	0	33	11	14	5	....	.263	.289	.305	.593	57	-21	30	3.12	9	2-80/3-8,S-6	6	-0.6
1936*	NY-N	154	632	99	176	31	3	4	47	29	32	14	....	.278	.317	.356	.673	82	-17	70	3.88	7	*2-153	17	0.0
1937*	NY-N★	152	574	64	164	15	6	5	52	28	20	7	....	.286	.323	.359	.682	84	-13	67	4.25	9	*2-152	19	0.6
1939	NY-N	95	335	31	80	6	3	2	24	24	19	1	....	.239	.299	.293	.592	59	-19	28	2.70	7	2-91/S-4,3-1	5	-0.6
1940	NY-N	133	568	68	160	9	6	4	36	26	17	9	....	.282	.319	.340	.659	81	-15	59	3.70	3	3-74,2-57/S-4	12	-0.5
1941	NY-N	116	403	41	92	15	4	1	23	14	10	7	....	.228	.258	.293	.551	54	-26	27	2.13	1	*2-104/3-1	3	-1.9
1946	Pit-N	55	127	10	28	1	2	0	5	6	6	3	....	.220	.261	.260	.521	47	-9	8	2.19	-3	2-30/3-4,S-1	1	-1.1
Total	9	924	3316	415	883	100	31	17	245	150	138	51	....	.266	.304	.331	.634	72	-133	328	3.42	36	2-718,3-116/S-53	71	-4.9
• WHITEHEAD, Milt	Milton P. Whitehead b: 1862, Canada d: 8/15/1901, Highland, CA BB/TR Deb: 4/20/1884																								
1884	StL-U	99	393	61	83	15	1	1	....	8	....	....	....	.211	.227	.262	.489	62	-16	24	2.16	-2	*S-94/0-2(0-2-0),2-1,3-1,P	8	-1.8
	KC-U	5	22	2	3	0	0	0	....	0	....	....	....	.136	.136	.136	.273	-9	-2	0	.62	1	/2-3,3-1,C-1,S-1	0	-0.1
	Yr.	104	415	63	86	15	1	1	....	8	....	....	....	.207	.222	.255	.478	59	-18	24	2.07	-1	*S-95/2-4,3-2,0-2(0-2-0),C,P	8	-1.9
• WHITEHOUSE, Gil	Gilbert Arthur Whitehouse b: 10/15/1893, Somerville, MA d: 2/14/1926, Brewer, ME BB/TR, 5'10", 170 lbs. Deb: 6/20/1912																								
1912	Bos-N	2	3	0	0	0	0	0	0	0	3	0	....	.000	.000	.000	.000	-98	-1	0	.00	-1	/C-2	0	-0.2
1915	New-F	35	120	16	27	6	2	0	9	6	16	3	....	.225	.268	.308	.576	73	-4	10	2.77	-1	0-28(0-2-26)/C-1,P-1	2	-0.7
Total	2	37	123	16	27	6	2	0	9	6	19	3	....	.220	.262	.301	.562	69	-5	10	2.68	-2	/0-28,C-3,P-1	2	-0.9
• WHITELEY, Gurdon	Gurdon W. Whiteley b: 10/5/1859, Ashaway, RI d: 11/24/1924, Cranston, RI, 5'11", 190 lbs. Deb: 8/7/1884 Career OF: 12-3-25																								
1884	Cle-N	8	34	4	5	0	0	0	0	1	8	....	....	.147	.171	.147	.318	1	-4	1	.83	1	/0-8(4-3-1)	0	-0.3
1885	Bos-N	33	135	14	25	2	2	1	7	1	25	....	....	.185	.191	.252	.443	44	-8	7	1.64	-2	0-32(8-0-24)/C-1	0	-1.0
Total	2	41	169	18	30	2	2	1	7	2	33	....	....	.178	.187	.231	.418	35	-12	8	1.47	-1	/0-40,C-1	0	-1.3
• WHITEMAN, George	George "Lucky" Whiteman b: 12/23/1882, Peoria, IL d: 2/10/1947, Houston, TX BR/TR, 5'7", 160 lbs. Deb: 9/13/1907 Career OF: 71-4-7																								
1907	Bos-A	4	12	0	2	0	0	0	1	0	....	0	....	.167	.167	.167	.333	6	-1	0	.91	0	/0-2(2-0-0)	0	-0.2
1913	NY-A	11	32	8	11	3	1	0	2	7	2	2	....	.344	.462	.500	.962	181	4	8	9.11	1	0-11(4-4-3)	2	0.4
1918*	Bos-A	71	214	24	57	14	0	1	28	20	9	9	....	.266	.335	.346	.681	107	2	28	4.18	-5	0-69(65-0-4)	8	-0.7
Total	3	86	258	32	70	17	1	1	31	27	11	11	....	.271	.345	.357	.702	113	4	36	4.58	-5	/0-82	10	-0.4
• WHITEN, Mark	Mark Anthony Whiten b: 11/25/1966, Pensacola, FL BB/TR, 6'3", 215 lbs. Deb: 7/12/1990 Career OF: 131-67-696																								
1990	Tor-A	33	88	12	24	1	1	2	7	7	14	2	0	.273	.326	.375	.701	90	-1	11	4.43	0	0-30(3-0-27)/D-2	2	-0.2
1991	Tor-A	46	149	12	33	4	3	2	19	11	35	0	1	.221	.280	.329	.608	65	-8	13	2.74	-1	0-42(0-0-42)	2	-1.0
	Cle-A	70	258	34	66	14	4	7	26	19	50	4	2	.256	.312	.422	.734	101	-1	32	4.25	4	0-67(0-8-63)/D-3	5	0.1
	Yr.	116	407	46	99	18	7	9	45	30	85	4	3	.243	.300	.388	.688	88	-8	45	3.68	3	*0-109(0-8-105)/D-3	7	-0.9
1992	Cle-A	148	508	73	129	19	4	9	43	72	102	16	12	.254	.349	.360	.709	101	1	64	4.24	3	*0-144(0-0-144)/D-2	11	-0.1
1993	StL-N	152	562	81	142	13	4	25	99	58	110	15	8	.253	.325	.423	.748	100	-1	76	4.65	0	*0-148(0-22-138)	17	-0.8
1994	StL-N	92	334	57	98	18	2	14	53	37	75	10	5	.293	.366	.485	.851	122	10	58	6.22	8	0-90(0-0-90)	12	1.3
1995	Bos-A	32	108	13	20	3	0	1	10	8	23	1	0	.185	.241	.241	.482	25	-12	6	1.64	3	0-31(0-0-31)/D-1	1	-1.0
	Phi-N	60	212	38	57	10	1	11	37	31	63	7	0	.269	.365	.481	.846	120	8	40	6.73	-1	0-55(0-0-55)	9	0.4
1996	Phi-N	60	182	33	43	8	0	7	21	33	62	13	3	.236	.356	.396	.752	97	1	26	4.69	1	0-51(0-8-44)	3	0.1
	Atl-N	36	90	12	23	5	1	3	17	16	25	2	5	.256	.368	.433	.801	105	-1	13	4.81	1	0-29(0-0-29)	4	-0.1
	Yr.	96	272	45	66	13	1	10	38	49	87	15	8	.243	.360	.408	.768	100	1	40	4.73	2	0-80(0-8-73)	7	0.0
	Sea-A	40	140	31	42	7	0	12	33	21	40	2	1	.300	.399	.607	1.006	149	11	35	9.49	2	0-39(36-0-4)	7	1.0
1997	NY-A	69	215	34	57	11	0	5	24	30	47	4	2	.265	.360	.386	.746	96	-0	30	4.89	-4	0-57(44-0-16)/D-6	5	-0.7
1998*	Cle-A	88	226	31	64	14	0	6	29	29	60	2	1	.283	.372	.425	.797	103	2	36	5.68	2	0-72(43-22-13)/D-5,P-1	6	0.2
1999	Cle-A	8	25	2	4	1	0	1	4	3	4	0	0	.160	.250	.320	.570	42	-2	2	2.31	1	/0-7(5-2-0)	0	-0.2
2000	Cle-A	6	7	2	2	1	0	0	1	3	2	0	0	.286	.500	.429	.929	136	1	2	10.21	0	/0-5(0-5-0)	0	0.0
Total	11	940	3104	465	804	129	20	105	423	378	712	78	40	.259	.343	.415	.758	101	8	444	4.91	18	0-867/D-19,P-1	84	-1.0
• WHITFIELD, Fred	Fred Dwight Whitfield b: 1/7/1938, Vandiver, AL BL/TL, 6'1", 190 lbs. Deb: 5/27/1962																								
1962	StL-N	73	158	20	42	7	1	8	34	7	30	1	0	.266	.301	.475	.776	95	-2	21	4.50	1	1-38	3	-0.2
1963	Cle-A	109	346	44	87	17	3	21	54	24	61	0	1	.251	.307	.500	.807	123	8	54	5.42	0	1-92	13	0.3
1964	Cle-A	101	293	29	79	13	1	10	29	12	58	0	5	.270	.303	.423	.726	100	-3	34	4.08	-3	1-79	7	-1.2
1965	Cle-A	132	468	49	137	23	1	26	90	16	42	2	2	.293	.319	.513	.832	131	15	71	5.45	4	*1-122	17	1.3
1966	Cle-A	137	502	59	121	15	2	27	78	27	76	1	2	.241	.285	.440	.725	105	1	61	4.18	-0	*1-132	13	-0.8
1967	Cle-A	100	257	24	56	10	0	9	31	25	45	3	3	.218	.290	.362	.652	91	-4	26	3.40	5	1-66	5	-0.3
1968	Cin-N	87	171	15	44	8	0	6	32	9	29	0	3	.257	.302	.409	.712	105	-0	20	3.97	0	1-41	4	-0.3
1969	Cin-N	74	74	2	11	0	0	1	8	18	27	0	0	.149	.315	.189	.504	42	-5	6	2.52	1	1-14	0	-0.4
1970	Mon-N	4	15	0	1	0	0	0	0	1	3	0	0	.067	.125	.067	.192	-47	-3	0	.14	2	/1-4	0	-0.2
Total	9	817	2284	242	578	93	8	108	356	139	371	7	16	.253	.301	.443	.743	107	8	293	4.42	10	1-588	62	-1.6
• WHITFIELD, Terry	Terry Bertland Whitfield b: 1/12/1953, Blythe, CA BL/TR, 6'1.5", 197 lbs. Deb: 9/29/1974 Career OF: 408-32-116																								
1974	NY-A	2	5	0	1	0	0	0	0	0	1	0	0	.200	.200	.200	.400	16	-1	0	1.35	0	/0-1	0	-0.1
1975	NY-A	28	81	9	22	1	1	0	7	1	17	1	0	.272	.280	.309	.589	68	-3	7	2.87	0	0-25(2-0-23)/D-1	1	-0.4
1976	NY-A	1	0	0	0	0	0	0	0	0	0	0	0	....	....	....	....	-101	0	0	....	0	/0-1	0	0.0
1977	SF-N	114	326	41	93	21	3	7	36	20	46	2	3	.285	.330	.433	.763	103	-0	46	5.08	-1	0-84(22-22-49)	9	-0.5
1978	SF-N	149	488	70	141	20	2	10	32	33	69	5	11	.289	.337	.400	.736	109	1	62	4.33	-6	*0-140(138-5-0)	14	-1.2
1979	SF-N	133	394	52	113	20	4	5	44	36	47	5	4	.287	.353	.396	.748	111	6	52	4.53	-3	*0-106(105-1-0)	12	-0.2

YEAR TM-L	G	AB	R	H	2B	3B	HR	RBI	BB	SO	SB	CS	AVG	OBP	SLG	OPS	OPS+	BR/A	RC	RC/G	FR	G/POS	WS	TPW
1980 SF-N	118	321	38	95	16	2	4	26	20	44	4	2	.296	.339	.396	.735	107	2	42	4.78	3	0-95(95-0-0)	11	0.2
1984 LA-N	87	180	15	44	8	0	4	18	17	35	1	4	.244	.313	.356	.669	88	-5	18	3.39	2	0-58(23-2-37)	3	-0.5
1985*LA-N	79	104	8	27	7	0	3	16	6	27	0	0	.260	.300	.413	.713	101	-0	12	4.27	1	0-28(21-1-7)	3	-0.1
1986 LA-N	19	14	0	1	0	0	0	0	5	2	0	0	.071	.316	.071	.387	14	-1	0	.90	-0	/0-1	0	-0.1
Total 10	730	1913	233	537	93	12	33	179	138	288	18	24	.281	.332	.394	.726	103	-2	241	4.37	-5	0-539/D-1	53	-3.0

• WHITING, Ed Edward C. Whiting b: 1860, Philadelphia, PA BL/TR, 188 lbs. Deb: 5/2/1882 Career OF: 5-3-2

YEAR TM-L	G	AB	R	H	2B	3B	HR	RBI	BB	SO	SB	CS	AVG	OBP	SLG	OPS	OPS+	BR/A	RC	RC/G	FR	G/POS	WS	TPW
1882 Bal-a	74	308	43	80	14	5	0	....	7	....	....	....	.260	.276	.338	.614	115	5	29	3.62	2	*C-72/1-3,0-2(1-0-1)	10	1.2
1883 Lou-a	58	240	35	70	16	4	2	0	9	....	....	....	.292	.317	.417	.734	145	12	33	5.36	-5	C-50/0-6(3-3-0),2-2,1-1,3	12	1.0
1884 Lou-a	42	157	16	35	7	3	0	18	9	....	....	....	.223	.274	.306	.580	93	-1	13	3.04	-3	C-40/1-2,0-2(1-0-1)	4	-0.1
1886 Was-N	6	21	0	0	0	0	0	0	1	12	0	....	.000	.045	.000	.045	-90	-5	0	.00	1	/C-6	0	-0.3
Total 4	180	726	94	185	37	12	2	18	26	12	0	....	.255	.282	.347	.630	114	12	75	3.89	-5	C-168/0-10,1-6,2-2,3-1	26	1.9

• WHITMAN, Dick Dick Corwin Whitman b: 11/9/1920, Woodburn, OR d: 2/12/2003, Peoria, AZ BL/TR, 5'11", 170 lbs. Deb: 4/16/1946 Career OF: 66-72-52

YEAR TM-L	G	AB	R	H	2B	3B	HR	RBI	BB	SO	SB	CS	AVG	OBP	SLG	OPS	OPS+	BR/A	RC	RC/G	FR	G/POS	WS	TPW
1946 Bro-N	104	265	39	69	15	3	2	31	22	19	5	....	.260	.317	.362	.679	91	-4	30	3.97	3	0-85(30-54-1)	8	-0.4
1947 Bro-N	4	10	1	4	0	0	0	2	1	0	0	....	.400	.455	.400	.855	124	0	2	7.68	0	/0-3(2-0-1)	1	0.0
1948 Bro-N	60	165	24	48	13	0	0	20	14	12	4	....	.291	.346	.370	.716	91	-2	22	4.68	1	0-48(12-4-34)	5	-0.3
1949*Bro-N	23	49	8	9	2	0	0	2	4	4	0	....	.184	.245	.224	.470	26	-5	2	1.61	-2	0-11(10-0-1)	0	-0.8
1950*Phi-N	75	132	21	33	7	0	0	12	10	10	1	....	.250	.317	.303	.620	65	-6	13	3.29	0	0-32(7-13-15)	2	-0.7
1951 Phi-N	19	17	0	2	0	0	0	0	0	1	0	0	.118	.118	.118	.235	-37	-3	0	.43	-1	/0-6(5-1-0)	0	-0.5
Total 6	285	638	93	165	37	3	2	67	51	46	10	0	.259	.316	.335	.652	78	-20	69	3.76	1	0-185	16	-2.6

• WHITMAN, Frank Walter Franklin "Hooker" Whitman b: 8/15/1924, Marengo, IN d: 2/6/1994, Maryville, IL BR/TR, 6'2", 175 lbs. Deb: 6/30/1946

YEAR TM-L	G	AB	R	H	2B	3B	HR	RBI	BB	SO	SB	CS	AVG	OBP	SLG	OPS	OPS+	BR/A	RC	RC/G	FR	G/POS	WS	TPW
1946 Chi-A	17	16	7	1	0	0	0	1	2	6	0	1	.063	.211	.063	.273	-22	-3	0	.48	-1	/S-6,1-1,2-1	0	-0.4
1948 Chi-A	3	6	0	0	0	0	0	0	0	3	0	0	.000	.000	.000	.000	-104	-2	0	.00	-1	/S-1	0	-0.3
Total 2	20	22	7	1	0	0	0	1	2	9	0	1	.045	.160	.045	.205	-42	-5	0	.35	-2	/S-7,1-1,2-1	0	-0.7

• WHITMER, Dan Daniel Charles Whitmer b: 11/23/1955, Redlands, CA BR/TR, 6'3", 195 lbs. Deb: 7/20/1980 C

YEAR TM-L	G	AB	R	H	2B	3B	HR	RBI	BB	SO	SB	CS	AVG	OBP	SLG	OPS	OPS+	BR/A	RC	RC/G	FR	G/POS	WS	TPW
1980 Cal-A	48	87	8	21	3	0	0	7	4	21	1	0	.241	.275	.276	.551	53	-5	7	2.28	-1	C-48	1	-0.4
1981 Tor-A	7	9	0	1	1	0	0	0	1	2	0	0	.111	.200	.222	.422	20	-1	0	.68	1	/C-7	0	0.0
Total 2	55	96	8	22	4	0	0	7	5	23	1	0	.229	.267	.271	.538	50	-6	7	2.12	0	/C-55	1	-0.4

• WHITMORE, Darrell Darrell Lamont Whitmore b: 11/18/1968, Front Royal, VA BL/TR, 6'1", 210 lbs. Deb: 6/25/1993 Career OF: 6-14-73

YEAR TM-L	G	AB	R	H	2B	3B	HR	RBI	BB	SO	SB	CS	AVG	OBP	SLG	OPS	OPS+	BR/A	RC	RC/G	FR	G/POS	WS	TPW
1993 Fla-N	76	250	24	51	8	2	4	19	10	72	4	2	.204	.249	.300	.549	44	-21	17	2.20	-3	0-69(1-0-69)	2	-2.7
1994 Fla-N	9	22	1	5	1	0	0	0	3	5	0	1	.227	.320	.273	.593	55	-2	2	2.85	0	/0-6(5-0-1)	0	-0.2
1995 Fla-N	27	58	6	11	2	0	1	2	5	15	0	0	.190	.254	.276	.530	40	-5	4	2.29	-1	0-16(0-14-3)	0	-0.6
Total 3	112	330	31	67	11	2	5	21	18	92	4	3	.203	.255	.294	.549	44	-28	23	2.26	-4	/0-91	2	-3.5

• WHITNEY, Art Arthur Wilson Whitney b: 1/16/1858, Brockton, MA d: 8/15/1943, Lowell, MA BR/TR, 5'8", 155 lbs. Deb: 5/1/1880 Career OF: 3-1-0

YEAR TM-L	G	AB	R	H	2B	3B	HR	RBI	BB	SO	SB	CS	AVG	OBP	SLG	OPS	OPS+	BR/A	RC	RC/G	FR	G/POS	WS	TPW
1880 Wor-N	76	302	38	67	13	5	1	36	9	15	....	....	.222	.244	.308	.552	79	-7	23	2.73	-2	*3-76	7	-0.6
1881 Det-N	58	214	23	39	7	5	0	9	7	15	....	....	.182	.208	.262	.470	45	-14	12	1.84	7	*3-58	3	-0.5
1882 Pro-N	11	40	2	3	0	0	0	1	2	11	....	....	.075	.119	.075	.194	-36	-6	0	.27	-3	S-11	0	-0.8
Det-N	31	115	10	21	0	0	0	4	1	12	....	....	.183	.190	.183	.372	20	-10	4	1.19	4	3-22/S-8,P-3	2	-0.9
Yr.	42	155	12	24	0	0	0	5	3	23	....	....	.155	.171	.155	.326	5	-16	4	.93	1	3-22,S-19/P-3	2	-1.7
1884 Pit-a	23	94	10	28	4	0	0	0	1	....	....	....	.298	.305	.340	.646	108	1	10	4.17	3	3-21/0-1,S-1	3	0.4
1885 Pit-a	90	373	53	87	10	4	0	28	16	....	....	....	.233	.267	.282	.548	74	-11	29	2.71	-9	*S-75/3-8,2-4,0-3(3-0-0)	6	-1.5
1886 Pit-a	136	511	70	122	13	4	0	55	51	....	15	....	.239	.315	.280	.595	87	-5	51	3.54	18	*3-95,S-42/P-1	19	1.5
1887 Pit-N	119	486	57	167	11	4	0	51	55	18	10	....	.344	.346	.304	.650	87	-3	50	4.16	2	*3-119	14	0.1
1888*NY-N	90	328	28	72	1	4	1	28	8	22	7	....	.220	.240	.256	.496	59	-15	22	2.36	7	3-90	5	-0.6
1889*NY-N	129	473	71	103	12	2	1	59	56	39	19	....	.218	.303	.258	.561	57	-25	44	3.14	2	*3-129/P-1	9	-1.7
1890 NY-P	119	442	71	97	12	3	0	45	64	19	8	....	.219	.322	.260	.582	52	-31	41	3.18	-11	3-88,S-31	6	-3.1
1891 Cin-a	93	347	42	69	6	1	3	33	31	20	8	....	.199	.270	.248	.518	44	-27	26	2.48	-5	*3-93	3	-2.6
StL-a	3	11	0	0	0	0	0	0	1	2	0	....	.000	.083	.000	.083	-66	-3	0	.00	2	/3-3	0	-0.1
Yr.	96	358	42	69	6	1	3	33	32	22	8	....	.193	.265	.240	.505	41	-30	26	2.39	-3	*3-96	3	-2.7
Total 11	978	3736	475	875	89	32	6	349	302	173	67	....	.234	.285	.269	.554	65	-158	312	2.93	17	3-802,S-168/P-5,2-4,0-4	77	-10.4

• WHITNEY, Frank Frank Thomas "Jumbo" Whitney b: 2/18/1856, Brockton, MA d: 10/30/1943, Baltimore, MD BR/TR, 5'7.5", 152 lbs. Deb: 5/17/1876

YEAR TM-L	G	AB	R	H	2B	3B	HR	RBI	BB	SO	SB	CS	AVG	OBP	SLG	OPS	OPS+	BR/A	RC	RC/G	FR	G/POS	WS	TPW
1876 Bos-N	34	140	27	33	7	1	0	15	1	3	....	....	.236	.243	.302	.545	79	-3	10	2.76	3	0-34(24-0-10)/2-1	3	-0.2

• WHITNEY, Jim James Evans "Grasshopper Jim" Whitney
b: 11/10/1857, Conklin, NY d: 5/21/1891, Binghamton, NY BL/TR, 6'2", 172 lbs. Deb: 5/2/1881 U Career OF: 5-85-41 ♦

YEAR TM-L	G	AB	R	H	2B	3B	HR	RBI	BB	SO	SB	CS	AVG	OBP	SLG	OPS	OPS+	BR/A	RC	RC/G	FR	G/POS	WS	TPW
1881 Bos-N	75	282	37	72	17	3	0	32	19	18	....	....	.255	.302	.337	.639	105	12	29	3.79	-5	*P-66,0-15(0-0-15)/1-2	**42**	2.2
1882 Bos-N	61	251	49	81	18	7	5	48	24	13	....	....	.323	.382	.510	.892	182	27	50	8.10	-2	P-49/0-9(0-1-9),1-6	40	**3.8**
1883 Bos-N	96	409	78	115	27	10	5	57	25	29	....	....	.281	.323	.433	.755	124	22	59	5.47	-2	P-62,0-40(0-40-0)/1-2	57	**6.4**
1884 Bos-N	66	270	41	70	17	5	3	40	16	38	....	....	.259	.301	.393	.693	117	12	33	4.49	0	P-38,1-15,0-15(0-15-0)/3-1	37	2.9
1885 Bos-N	72	290	35	68	8	4	0	36	17	24	....	....	.234	.277	.290	.567	86	5	24	2.90	3	P-51,0-17(2-13-2)/1-5	24	0.7
1886 KC-N	67	247	25	59	13	3	2	23	29	39	5	....	.239	.319	.340	.659	94	9	29	4.18	6	P-46,0-22(2-9-11)/3-1	21	-1.0
1887 Was-N	54	219	29	71	9	6	2	22	18	24	10	....	.324	.324	.398	.722	105	12	30	5.36	3	P-47/0-7(1-6-0)	34	4.8
1888 Was-N	42	141	13	24	0	0	1	17	7	20	3	....	.170	.209	.191	.401	30	-1	6	1.49	-2	P-39/0-3(0-0-3),1-1	17	-0.9
1889 Ind-N	10	32	6	12	4	1	0	4	5	6	2	....	.375	.474	.563	1.036	185	6	10	12.87	-1	/P-9,0-1	2	-1.3
1890 Phi-a	7	21	3	5	0	0	0	1	1	....	0	....	.238	.273	.238	.511	52	-0	1	2.31	-1	/P-6,0-1	1	-0.3
Total 10	550	2162	316	577	113	39	18	280	161	211	20	....	.267	.313	.375	.688	111	103	271	4.65	0	P-413,0-130/1-31,3-2	275	17.3

• WHITNEY, Pinky Arthur Carter Whitney b: 1/2/1905, San Antonio, TX d: 9/1/1987, Center, TX BR/TR, 5'10", 165 lbs. Deb: 4/11/1928

YEAR TM-L	G	AB	R	H	2B	3B	HR	RBI	BB	SO	SB	CS	AVG	OBP	SLG	OPS	OPS+	BR/A	RC	RC/G	FR	G/POS	WS	TPW
1928 Phi-N	151	585	73	176	35	4	10	103	36	30	3	....	.301	.342	.426	.768	96	-5	83	5.07	-7	*3-149	13	-0.2
1929 Phi-N	154	612	89	200	43	14	8	115	61	35	7	....	.327	.390	.482	.872	108	8	113	6.76	12	*3-154	21	2.7
1930 Phi-N	149	606	87	207	41	5	8	117	40	41	3	....	.342	.383	.465	.849	97	-3	104	6.55	9	*3-148	16	1.4
1931 Phi-N	130	501	64	144	36	5	9	74	30	38	6	....	.287	.331	.433	.765	96	-4	73	5.21	-10	*3-128	12	-0.9
1932 Phi-N	154	624	93	186	33	11	13	124	35	66	6	....	.298	.335	.449	.784	97	-3	95	5.39	9	*3-151/2-5	17	1.1
1933 Phi-N	31	121	12	32	4	0	3	19	8	8	1	....	.264	.310	.372	.682	83	-3	12	3.26	0	3-30	1	-0.2
Bos-N	100	382	42	94	17	2	8	49	25	23	2	....	.246	.296	.364	.660	95	-3	40	3.54	6	3-85,2-18	12	0.7
Yr.	131	503	54	126	21	2	11	68	33	31	3	....	.250	.299	.366	.665	92	-6	52	3.47	6	*3-115,2-18	13	0.6
1934 Bos-N	146	563	58	146	26	2	12	79	25	54	7	....	.259	.294	.377	.671	85	-14	61	3.77	4	*3-111,2-36/S-2	15	-0.4
1935 Bos-N	126	458	41	125	23	4	4	60	24	36	2	....	.273	.312	.367	.679	89	-8	51	3.93	-7	3-74,2-49	9	-0.9
1936 Bos-N	10	40	1	7	0	0	0	5	2	4	0	....	.175	.233	.175	.408	12	-5	1	1.14	1	3-10	1	-0.3
Phi-N★	114	411	44	121	17	3	6	59	37	33	2	....	.294	.354	.394	.748	92	-4	58	4.96	7	*3-111/2-1	10	0.7
Yr.	124	451	45	128	17	3	6	64	39	37	2	....	.284	.343	.375	.718	85	-9	60	4.58	9	*3-121/2-1	11	0.4
1937 Phi-N	138	487	56	166	19	4	8	79	43	44	6	....	.341	.395	.446	.841	118	14	84	6.49	-2	*3-130	16	1.6
1938 Phi-N	102	300	27	83	9	1	3	38	27	22	0	....	.277	.336	.343	.680	87	-5	34	3.98	-7	3-75/1-4,2-2	6	-1.0
1939 Phi-N	34	75	9	14	0	1	1	6	7	4	0	....	.187	.256	.253	.509	39	-6	5	1.89	2	1-12/2-8,3-2	0	-0.5
Total 12	1539	5765	696	1701	303	56	93	927	400	438	45	....	.295	.343	.415	.758	95	-41	815	5.02	17	*3-1358,2-119/1-16,S-2	149	4.0

• WHITT, Ernie Leo Ernest Whitt b: 6/13/1952, Detroit, MI BL/TR, 6'2", 200 lbs. Deb: 9/12/1976

YEAR TM-L	G	AB	R	H	2B	3B	HR	RBI	BB	SO	SB	CS	AVG	OBP	SLG	OPS	OPS+	BR/A	RC	RC/G	FR	G/POS	WS	TPW
1976 Bos-A	8	18	4	4	2	0	1	3	2	2	0	0	.222	.300	.500	.800	117	0	3	5.51	-1	/C-8	1	0.0
1977 Tor-A	23	41	4	7	3	0	0	6	2	12	0	0	.171	.209	.244	.453	23	-4	2	1.50	0	C-14	0	-0.4
1978 Tor-A	2	4	0	0	0	0	0	0	1	1	0	0	.000	.200	.000	.200	-38	-1	0	.35	1	/C-1	0	0.0
1980 Tor-A	106	295	23	70	12	2	6	34	22	30	1	3	.237	.290	.353	.643	72	-13	27	3.00	4	*C-105	6	-0.4
1981 Tor-A	74	195	16	46	9	0	1	16	20	30	5	2	.236	.307	.297	.604	70	-7	19	3.24	7	C-72	6	0.4
1982 Tor-A	105	284	28	74	14	2	11	42	26	34	3	1	.261	.323	.440	.763	98	-1	40	4.89	-4	C-98/D-1	9	-0.1
1983 Tor-A	123	344	53	88	15	2	17	56	50	55	1	1	.256	.350	.459	.810	114	7	55	5.51	1	*C-119	15	1.3

YEAR TM-L	G	AB	R	H	2B	3B	HR	RBI	BB	SO	SB	CS	AVG	OBP	SLG	OPS	OPS+	BR/A	RC	RC/G	FR	G/POS	WS	TPW
1984 Tor-A	124	315	35	75	12	1	15	46	43	49	0	3	.238	.331	.425	.757	104	1	44	4.64	2	*C-118	12	0.8
1985*Tor-A★	139	412	55	101	21	2	19	64	47	59	3	6	.245	.324	.444	.768	105	1	58	4.74	-4	*C-134	15	0.2
1986 Tor-A	131	395	48	106	19	2	16	56	35	39	0	1	.268	.328	.448	.776	106	2	56	4.94	-5	*C-129	13	0.2
1987 Tor-A	135	446	57	120	24	1	19	75	44	50	0	1	.269	.336	.455	.791	105	2	64	4.98	6	*C-131	16	1.3
1988 Tor-A	127	398	63	100	11	2	16	70	61	38	4	2	.251	.352	.410	.762	112	8	59	5.07	-1	*C-123	16	1.5
1989*Tor-A	129	385	42	101	24	1	11	53	52	53	5	4	.262	.350	.416	.766	122	11	56	5.07	0	*C-115/D-8	16	1.7
1990 Atl-N	67	180	14	31	8	0	2	10	23	27	0	2	.172	.266	.250	.516	40	-16	12	1.97	2	C-59	1	-1.1
1991 Bal-A	35	62	5	15	2	0	0	3	8	12	0	0	.242	.329	.274	.603	72	-2	5	2.94	0	C-20/D-2	0	-0.1
Total 15	1328	3774	447	938	176	15	134	534	436	491	22	26	.249	.327	.410	.737	99	-11	501	4.49	6	*C-1246/D-11	126	5.3

• WHITTED, Possum George Bostic Whitted b: 2/4/1890, Durham, NC d: 10/16/1962, Wilmington, NC BR/TR, 5'8.5", 168 lbs. Deb: 9/16/1912 Career OF: 438-107-107

YEAR TM-L	G	AB	R	H	2B	3B	HR	RBI	BB	SO	SB	CS	AVG	OBP	SLG	OPS	OPS+	BR/A	RC	RC/G	FR	G/POS	WS	TPW
1912 StL-N	12	46	7	12	3	0	0	7	3	5	1	....	.261	.306	.326	.632	75	-2	5	3.50	-3	3-12	1	-0.5
1913 StL-N	123	404	44	89	10	5	0	38	31	44	9	....	.220	.282	.270	.552	59	-21	32	2.54	0	0-41(20-3-18),S-38,3-22/2-7,1	4	-2.1
1914 StL-N	20	31	3	4	1	0	0	1	0	3	1	....	.129	.129	.161	.290	-14	-4	1	.69	-2	/3-5,0-3(2-0-2),2-1	0	-0.6
*Bos-N	66	218	36	57	11	4	2	31	18	18	10	....	.261	.326	.376	.703	109	2	30	4.40	3	0-38(0-38-0),2-15/1-4,3-4,S	8	0.3
Yr.	86	249	39	61	12	4	2	32	18	21	11	....	.245	.304	.349	.653	95	-2	31	3.88	1	0-41(2-38-2),2-16/3-9,1-4,S	8	-0.3
1915*Phi-N	128	448	46	126	17	3	1	43	29	47	24	15	.281	.328	.339	.667	101	-1	55	3.99	2	*0-119(53-66-0)/1-7	15	-0.6
1916 Phi-N	147	526	68	148	20	12	6	68	19	46	29	17	.281	.309	.399	.708	113	4	69	4.19	4	*0-136(136-0-0),1-16	20	0.3
1917 Phi-N	149	553	69	155	24	9	3	70	30	56	10	....	.280	.317	.373	.690	107	3	68	4.14	6	*0-141(141-0-0),1-10/3-7,2	18	0.4
1918 Phi-N	24	86	7	21	4	0	0	3	4	10	4	....	.244	.278	.291	.568	69	-3	7	2.94	2	0-22(22-0-0)/1-1	1	-0.3
1919 Phi-N	78	289	32	72	14	1	3	32	14	20	5	....	.249	.284	.336	.619	80	-8	28	3.22	-3	0-47(47-0-0),2-26/1-2	4	-1.4
Pit-N	35	131	15	51	7	7	0	21	6	4	7	....	.389	.420	.550	.970	183	13	32	9.74	6	1-33/3-2,0-1	9	2.0
Yr.	113	420	47	123	21	8	3	53	20	24	12	....	.293	.327	.402	.729	113	5	59	5.02	3	0-48(48-0-0),1-35,2-26/3-2	13	0.6
1920 Pit-N	134	494	53	129	11	12	1	74	35	36	11	11	.261	.314	.338	.652	85	-10	52	3.48	5	*3-125,1-10/0-1	14	-0.1
1921 Pit-N	108	403	60	114	23	7	7	63	26	21	5	10	.283	.328	.427	.755	96	-5	54	4.38	3	*0-102(15-0-87)/1-7	11	-1.1
1922 Bro-N	1	1	0	0	0	0	0	0	0	0	0	0	.000	.000	.000	.000	-101	-0	0	.00	0	....	0	0.0
Total 11	1025	3630	440	978	145	60	23	451	215	310	116	53	.269	.313	.361	.675	96	-33	433	3.92	24	0-651,3-177/1-92,2-50,S-41	105	-3.6

• WICKER, Floyd Floyd Euliss Wicker b: 9/12/1943, Burlington, NC BL/TR, 6'2", 175 lbs. Deb: 6/23/1968 Career OF: 17-7-6

YEAR TM-L	G	AB	R	H	2B	3B	HR	RBI	BB	SO	SB	CS	AVG	OBP	SLG	OPS	OPS+	BR/A	RC	RC/G	FR	G/POS	WS	TPW
1968 StL-N	5	4	2	2	0	0	0	0	0	0	0	0	.500	.500	.500	1.000	204	0	1	13.50	0	....	0	0.1
1969 Mon-N	41	39	2	4	0	0	0	2	2	20	0	0	.103	.146	.103	.249	-29	-7	1	.51	0	0-11(2-7-2)	0	-0.7
1970 Mil-A	15	41	3	8	1	0	1	3	1	8	0	0	.195	.214	.293	.507	38	-4	2	1.58	0	0-12(8-0-4)	0	-0.5
1971 Mil-A	11	8	0	1	0	0	0	0	2	0	0	0	.125	.300	.125	.425	24	-1	0	.46	0	....	0	-0.1
SF-N	9	21	3	3	0	0	0	1	2	5	0	0	.143	.250	.143	.393	14	-2	1	1.12	0	/0-7(7-0-0)	0	-0.3
Total 4	81	113	10	18	1	0	1	6	7	33	0	0	.159	.215	.195	.410	15	-13	5	1.25	0	/0-30	0	-1.5

• WICKLAND, Al Albert Wickland b: 1/27/1888, Chicago, IL d: 3/14/1980, Port Washington, WI BL/TL, 5'7", 155 lbs. Deb: 8/21/1913 Career OF: 145-25-259

YEAR TM-L	G	AB	R	H	2B	3B	HR	RBI	BB	SO	SB	CS	AVG	OBP	SLG	OPS	OPS+	BR/A	RC	RC/G	FR	G/POS	WS	TPW
1913 Cin-N	26	79	7	17	5	5	0	8	6	19	3	....	.215	.279	.405	.684	94	-1	9	3.69	0	0-24(0-24-0)	2	-0.3
1914 Chi-F	157	536	74	148	31	10	6	68	**81**	58	17	....	.276	.375	.405	.780	129	23	87	5.36	1	*0-157(30-1-129)	22	1.7
1915 Chi-F	30	86	11	21	2	2	1	5	13	11	3	....	.244	.343	.349	.692	110	1	11	4.25	0	0-24(5-0-20)	3	0.1
Pit-F	110	389	63	117	12	8	1	30	52	47	23	....	.301	.386	.380	.766	121	12	67	5.74	-1	*0-109(109-0-1)	17	0.7
Yr.	140	475	74	138	14	10	2	35	65	58	26	....	.291	.378	.375	.753	119	14	77	5.47	-1	*0-133(114-0-21)	20	0.8
1918 Bos-N	95	332	55	87	7	13	4	32	53	39	12	....	.262	.367	.398	.765	139	18	52	5.23	1	0-95(1-0-94)	15	1.5
1919 NY-A	26	46	2	7	1	0	0	1	2	10	0	....	.152	.188	.174	.361	2	-6	1	.95	0	0-15(0-0-15)	0	-0.7
Total 5	444	1468	212	397	58	38	12	144	207	184	58	....	.270	.364	.386	.750	123	48	227	5.12	1	0-424	59	3.0

• WIDGER, Chris Christopher Jon Widger b: 5/21/1971, Wilmington, DE BR/TR, 6'3", 195 lbs. Deb: 6/23/1995 Career OF: 2-0-3

YEAR TM-L	G	AB	R	H	2B	3B	HR	RBI	BB	SO	SB	CS	AVG	OBP	SLG	OPS	OPS+	BR/A	RC	RC/G	FR	G/POS	WS	TPW
1995*Sea-A	23	45	2	9	0	0	1	2	3	11	0	0	.200	.250	.267	.517	34	-4	3	2.38	0	C-19/0-3(2-0-1),D-1	0	-0.4
1996 Sea-A	8	11	1	2	0	0	0	0	0	5	0	0	.182	.250	.182	.432	12	-1	1	1.70	-1	/C-7	0	-0.2
1997 Mon-N	91	278	30	65	20	3	7	37	22	59	2	0	.234	.292	.403	.695	80	-9	32	3.87	-6	C-85	5	-0.9
1998 Mon-N	125	417	36	97	18	1	15	53	29	85	6	1	.233	.283	.388	.671	75	-16	46	3.82	-1	*C-123	10	-0.8
1999 Mon-N	124	383	42	101	24	1	14	56	28	86	1	4	.264	.325	.441	.767	94	-7	54	5.02	1	*C-118	8	0.2
2000 Mon-N	86	281	31	67	17	2	12	34	29	61	1	2	.238	.312	.441	.753	85	-8	38	4.63	2	C-85	4	-0.1
Sea-A	10	11	1	1	0	0	1	1	1	2	0	0	.091	.167	.364	.530	31	-1	1	1.92	-1	/C-6,1-2,D-2,0-1	0	-0.2
2002 NY-A	21	64	4	19	5	0	0	5	2	9	0	0	.297	.338	.375	.713	90	-1	8	5.08	-4	C-21	2	-0.4
2003 StL-N	44	102	9	24	9	0	0	14	6	20	0	0	.235	.284	.324	.608	61	-6	8	2.63	-1	C-41/1-1,0-1	2	-0.5
Total 8	532	1592	156	385	93	7	50	202	120	338	10	7	.242	.300	.403	.704	80	-54	192	4.14	-11	C-505/0-5,1-3,D-3	31	-3.3

• WIEDENBAUER, Tom Thomas John Wiedenbauer b: 11/5/1958, Menomonie, WI BR/TR, 6'1", 180 lbs. Deb: 9/14/1979

YEAR TM-L	G	AB	R	H	2B	3B	HR	RBI	BB	SO	SB	CS	AVG	OBP	SLG	OPS	OPS+	BR/A	RC	RC/G	FR	G/POS	WS	TPW
1979 Hou-N	4	6	0	4	1	0	0	2	0	2	0	0	.667	.667	.833	1.500	325	2	3	45.00	-0	/0-3(1-1-1)	1	0.2

• WIEDMAN, Stump George Edward Wiedman
b: 2/17/1861, Rochester, NY d: 3/3/1905, New York, NY BR/TR, 5'7.5", 165 lbs. Deb: 8/26/1880 U Career OF: 13-21-87 ♦

YEAR TM-L	G	AB	R	H	2B	3B	HR	RBI	BB	SO	SB	CS	AVG	OBP	SLG	OPS	OPS+	BR/A	RC	RC/G	FR	G/POS	WS	TPW
1880 Buf-N	23	78	8	8	1	0	0	3	2	11	....	....	.103	.125	.115	.240	-18	-8	1	.45	-2	P-17,0-13(1-11-1)	2	-1.4
1881 Det-N	13	47	8	12	1	0	0	5	2	2	....	....	.255	.286	.277	.562	74	0	4	2.94	-1	P-13	10	1.3
1882 Det-N	50	193	20	42	7	1	0	20	2	19	....	....	.218	.226	.264	.490	57	-6	12	2.15	0	P-46/0-6(1-2-2),S-1	35	1.5
1883 Det-N	79	313	34	58	6	1	1	24	4	38	....	....	.185	.196	.220	.416	27	-18	14	1.49	-4	P-52,0-35(1-5-29)/2-4	17	-2.9
1884 Det-N	81	300	24	49	6	0	0	26	13	41	....	....	.163	.198	.183	.381	22	-21	11	1.22	-7	0-53(0-0-53),P-26/2-1,S-1	5	-3.5
1885 Det-N	44	153	7	24	2	1	1	14	8	32	....	....	.157	.199	.203	.401	30	-5	6	1.32	-6	P-38/0-7(6-1-0),2-1	14	-1.2
1886 KC-N	51	179	13	30	2	0	0	7	5	46	3	....	.168	.190	.179	.369	12	-8	7	1.24	2	P-51/0-3(1-2-0)	17	-2.9
1887 Det-N	21	85	12	20	2	0	1	11	3	3	6	....	.235	.235	.232	.467	29	-3	6	2.46	-1	P-21/0-2(2-0-0)	8	-2.7
NY-a	14	50	5	11	1	1	0	1	4	....	2	....	.220	.220	.217	.437	23	-3	3	1.87	2	P-12/0-3(1-0-2)	3	-0.2
NY-N	1	3	0	1	0	0	0	0	0	0	0	....	.333	.333	.333	.667	90	0	0	4.53	0	/P-1	1	0.2
Yr.	22	88	12	21	2	0	1	11	3	3	6	....	.239	.239	.235	.474	31	-3	6	2.52	-1	P-22/0-2(2-0-0)	9	-2.5
1888 NY-N	2	7	1	0	0	0	0	1	2	1	0	....	.000	.222	.000	.222	-25	-0	0	.00	0	/P-2	0	-0.2
Total 9	379	1408	132	255	28	4	3	112	45	193	11	....	.181	.203	.207	.410	27	-72	64	1.51	-17	P-279,0-122/2-6,S-2	112	-12.0

• WIEGHAUS, Tom Thomas Robert Wieghaus b: 2/1/1957, Chicago Heights, IL BR/TR, 6', 195 lbs. Deb: 10/4/1981

YEAR TM-L	G	AB	R	H	2B	3B	HR	RBI	BB	SO	SB	CS	AVG	OBP	SLG	OPS	OPS+	BR/A	RC	RC/G	FR	G/POS	WS	TPW
1981 Mon-N	1	1	0	0	0	0	0	0	0	0	0	0	.000	.000	.000	.000	-99	-0	0	.00	-0	/C-1	0	0.0
1983 Mon-N	1	0	0	0	0	0	0	0	0	0	0	0	....	....	....	....	-101	0	0	....	0	/C-1	0	0.0
1984 Hou-N	6	10	0	0	0	0	0	1	1	3	0	0	.000	.091	.000	.091	-78	-2	0	.00	0	/C-6	0	-0.3
Total 3	8	11	0	0	0	0	0	1	1	3	0	0	.000	.083	.000	.083	-80	-3	0	.00	-1	/C-8	0	-0.3

• WIETELMANN, Whitey William Frederick Wietelmann b: 3/15/1919, Zanesville, OH d: 3/26/2002, San Diego, CA BB/TR, 6', 170 lbs. Deb: 9/6/1939 C

YEAR TM-L	G	AB	R	H	2B	3B	HR	RBI	BB	SO	SB	CS	AVG	OBP	SLG	OPS	OPS+	BR/A	RC	RC/G	FR	G/POS	WS	TPW
1939 Bos-N	23	69	2	14	1	0	0	5	2	9	1	....	.203	.225	.217	.443	21	-8	3	1.20	0	S-22/2-1	1	-0.6
1940 Bos-N	35	41	3	8	1	0	0	1	5	5	0	....	.195	.283	.220	.502	42	-3	3	2.13	-1	2-15/3-9,S-3	0	-0.3
1941 Bos-N	16	33	1	3	0	0	0	0	1	2	0	....	.091	.118	.091	.209	-43	-6	0	.40	0	2-10/S-5,3-2	0	-0.6
1942 Bos-N	13	34	4	7	2	0	0	0	4	5	0	....	.206	.289	.265	.554	64	-1	2	2.21	-2	S-11/2-1	0	-0.2
1943 Bos-N	153	534	33	115	14	1	0	39	46	40	9	....	.215	.281	.245	.527	54	-31	39	2.40	11	*S-153	9	-0.8
1944 Bos-N	125	417	46	100	18	1	2	32	33	25	0	....	.240	.300	.302	.602	67	-18	40	3.23	-8	*S-103,2-23/3-1	8	-1.8
1945 Bos-N	123	428	53	116	15	3	4	33	39	27	4	....	.271	.335	.348	.683	90	-6	53	4.56	-4	2-87,S-39/3-2,P-1	10	-0.8
1946 Bos-N	44	78	7	16	0	0	0	5	14	8	0	....	.205	.326	.205	.531	52	-4	6	2.65	-2	S-16/3-8,2-4,P-3	1	-0.9
1947 Pit-N	48	128	21	30	4	1	1	7	12	10	0	....	.234	.300	.305	.605	59	-8	11	2.81	-8	S-22,2-14/3-6,1-1	1	-1.3
Total 9	580	1762	170	409	55	6	7	122	156	131	14	....	.232	.298	.282	.580	63	-85	157	3.02	-13	S-374,2-155/3-28,P-4,1-1	30	-7.4

• WIGGINS, Alan Alan Anthony Wiggins b: 2/17/1958, Los Angeles, CA d: 1/6/1991, Los Angeles, CA BB/TR, 6'2", 160 lbs. Deb: 9/4/1981 Career OF: 123-67-20

YEAR TM-L	G	AB	R	H	2B	3B	HR	RBI	BB	SO	SB	CS	AVG	OBP	SLG	OPS	OPS+	BR/A	RC	RC/G	FR	G/POS	WS	TPW
1981 SD-N	15	14	4	5	0	0	0	0	1	0	2	0	.357	.400	.357	.757	125	1	3	7.56	-1	/0-4(4-0-0)	0	0.0
1982 SD-N	72	254	40	65	3	3	1	15	13	19	33	6	.256	.295	.303	.598	71	-5	25	3.35	1	0-68(51-19-6)/2-1	6	-0.7
1983 SD-N	144	503	83	139	20	2	0	22	65	43	66	13	.276	.360	.324	.684	94	8	72	4.89	0	*0-105(63-48-14),1-45	20	0.1
1984*SD-N	158	596	106	154	19	7	3	34	75	57	70	21	.258	.344	.329	.673	90	0	79	4.42	5	*2-157	23	1.4

YEAR TM-L	G	AB	R	H	2B	3B	HR	RBI	BB	SO	SB	CS	AVG	OBP	SLG	OPS	OPS+	BR/A	RC	RC/G	FR	G/POS	WS	TPW
1985 SD-N	10	37	3	2	1	0	0	0	2	4	0	1	.054	.103	.081	.184	-49	-8	0	.14	-0	/2-9	0	-0.8
Bal-A	76	298	43	85	11	4	0	21	29	16	30	13	.285	.353	.349	.702	96	-0	39	4.55	-12	2-76	8	-0.9
1986 Bal-A	71	239	30	60	3	1	0	11	22	20	21	7	.251	.314	.272	.586	62	-10	24	3.32	-3	2-66/D-1	4	-1.0
1987 Bal-A	85	306	37	71	4	2	1	15	28	34	20	7	.232	.299	.268	.566	53	-19	26	2.79	-1	D-44,2-33/O-5(5-0-0)	2	-1.9
Total 7	631	2247	346	581	61	19	5	118	235	193	242	68	.259	.331	.309	.640	80	-33	269	4.00	-13	2-342,O-182/1-45,D-45	63	-3.8
• WIGGINTON, Ty	Ty Allen Wigginton b: 10/11/1977, San Diego, CA BR/TR, 6', 200 lbs. Deb: 5/16/2002																							
2002 NY-N	46	116	18	35	8	0	6	18	8	19	2	1	.302	.357	.526	.883	134	5	21	6.37	2	3-14,1-13,2-12/O-2(1-0-1)	4	0.8
2003 NY-N	156	573	73	146	36	6	11	71	46	124	12	2	.255	.320	.396	.716	88	-9	73	4.36	-1	*3-155	15	-0.7
Total 2	202	689	91	181	44	6	17	89	54	143	14	3	.263	.326	.418	.744	96	-4	93	4.69	2	3-169/1-13,2-12,O-2	19	0.0
• WILBER, Del	Delbert Quentin "Babe" Wilber b: 2/24/1919, Lincoln Park, MI d: 7/18/2002, St. Petersburg, FL BR/TR, 6'3", 200 lbs. Deb: 4/21/1946 M/C																							
1946 StL-N	4	4	0	0	0	0	0	0	1	0	0	....	.000	.200	.000	.200	-39	-1	0	.35	0	/C-4	0	-0.1
1947 StL-N	51	99	7	23	8	1	0	12	5	13	0	....	.232	.269	.333	.603	57	-7	8	2.53	-1	C-34	1	-0.6
1948 StL-N	27	58	5	11	2	0	0	10	4	9	0	....	.190	.242	.224	.466	25	-6	3	1.47	-1	C-26	1	-0.7
1949 StL-N	2	4	0	1	0	0	0	0	0	0	0	....	.250	.250	.250	.500	33	-0	0	2.25	0	/C-2	0	0.0
1951 Phi-N	84	245	30	68	7	3	8	34	17	26	0	1	.278	.324	.429	.753	102	-0	33	4.87	-2	C-73	8	0.1
1952 Phi-N	2	2	0	0	0	0	0	0	0	1	0	0	.000	.000	.000	.000	-101	-1	0	.00	0	....	0	-0.1
Bos-A	47	135	7	36	10	1	3	23	7	20	1	0	.267	.308	.422	.730	94	-1	17	4.47	1	C-39	5	0.2
1953 Bos-A	58	112	16	27	6	1	7	29	6	21	0	0	.241	.286	.500	.786	103	-0	14	4.28	-2	C-28/1-2	3	-0.1
1954 Bos-A	24	61	2	8	2	1	1	7	4	6	0	0	.131	.185	.246	.431	15	-7	3	1.35	0	C-18	0	-0.7
Total 8	299	720	67	174	35	7	19	115	44	96	1	1	.242	.287	.389	.676	79	-24	78	3.66	-5	C-224/1-2	18	-1.9
• WILBORN, Claude	Claude Edward Wilborn b: 9/1/1912, Woodsdale, NC d: 11/13/1992, Roxboro, NC BL/TR, 6'1" Deb: 9/8/1940																							
1940 Bos-N	5	7	0	0	0	0	0	0	0	1	0	....	.000	.000	.000	.000	-106	-2	0	.00	0	/O-3(0-0-3)	0	-0.2
• WILBORN, Ted	Thaddeaus Inglehart Wilborn b: 12/16/1958, Waco, TX BB/TR, 6' Deb: 4/5/1979 Career OF: 5-2-3																							
1979 Tor-A	22	12	3	0	0	0	0	0	1	7	0	1	.000	.077	.000	.077	-76	-3	0	.00	0	/O-7(4-1-2),D-4	0	-0.4
1980 NY-A	8	8	2	2	0	0	0	1	0	1	0	0	.250	.250	.250	.500	38	-1	1	2.25	1	/O-3(1-1-1)	0	0.0
Total 2	30	20	5	2	0	0	0	1	1	8	0	1	.100	.143	.100	.243	-35	-4	1	.68	0	/O-10,D-4	0	-0.4
• WILEY,	John Wiley Deb: 6/23/1884																							
1884 Was-U	1	4	0	0	0	0	0	....	0	....	....	....	.000	.000	.000	.000	-103	-1	0	.00	-1	/3-1	0	-0.1
• WILFONG, Rob	Robert Daniel Wilfong b: 9/1/1953, Pasadena, CA BL/TR, 6'1", 185 lbs. Deb: 4/10/1977 Career OF: 2-9-1																							
1977 Min-A	73	171	22	42	1	1	1	13	17	26	10	4	.246	.321	.281	.602	67	-7	17	3.41	-2	2-66/D-1	3	-0.6
1978 Min-A	92	199	23	53	8	0	1	11	19	27	8	4	.266	.336	.322	.658	84	-3	24	3.88	-1	2-80/D-5	5	-0.1
1979 Min-A	140	419	71	131	22	6	9	59	29	54	11	4	.313	.360	.458	.818	115	9	72	5.89	0	*2-133/O-3(1-1-1)	18	1.5
1980 Min-A	131	416	55	103	16	5	8	45	34	61	10	6	.248	.309	.368	.677	79	-13	47	3.73	-11	*2-120/O-6(0-6-0)	11	-1.8
1981 Min-A	93	305	32	75	11	3	3	19	29	43	2	4	.246	.311	.331	.643	80	-9	33	3.68	2	2-93	8	-0.3
1982 Min-A	25	81	7	13	1	0	0	5	7	13	0	2	.160	.236	.173	.409	14	-10	3	1.00	3	2-22	1	-0.6
*Cal-A	55	102	17	25	4	2	1	11	7	17	4	0	.245	.294	.353	.647	77	-2	11	3.83	3	2-28/3-5,O-3(1-2-0),S-2,D	2	0.1
Yr.	80	183	24	38	5	2	1	16	14	30	4	2	.208	.268	.273	.541	49	-13	14	2.46	6	2-50/3-5,O-3(1-2-0),S-2,D	3	-0.5
1983 Cal-A	65	177	17	45	7	1	2	17	10	25	0	2	.254	.294	.339	.633	74	-7	17	3.33	0	2-39,3-13/S-6,D-1	3	-0.6
1984 Cal-A	108	307	31	76	13	2	6	33	20	53	3	2	.248	.298	.362	.659	82	-8	34	3.79	2	2-97/S-4,D-1	9	-0.2
1985 Cal-A	83	217	16	41	3	0	4	13	16	32	4	1	.189	.245	.258	.503	38	-18	15	2.24	10	2-69/D-2	4	-0.5
1986*Cal-A	92	288	25	63	11	3	3	33	16	34	1	4	.219	.265	.309	.574	56	-20	23	2.54	1	2-90	4	-1.4
1987 SF-N	2	8	2	1	0	0	1	2	1	2	1	0	.125	.222	.500	.722	89	0	1	4.10	0	/2-2	0	0.0
Total 11	959	2690	318	668	97	23	39	261	205	387	54	33	.248	.305	.345	.650	77	-88	297	3.67	5	2-839/3-18,O-12,S-12,D-11	68	-4.5
• WILHELM, Jim	James Webster Wilhelm b: 9/20/1952, San Rafael, CA BR/TR, 6'3", 190 lbs. Deb: 9/4/1978 Career OF: 7-32-1																							
1978 SD-N	10	19	2	7	2	0	0	4	0	2	1	0	.368	.400	.474	.874	155	2	4	7.59	0	O-10(3-7-0)	1	0.1
1979 SD-N	39	103	8	25	4	3	0	8	2	12	1	1	.243	.257	.340	.597	65	-6	9	2.98	-1	O-30(4-25-1)	1	-0.7
Total 2	49	122	10	32	6	3	0	12	2	14	2	1	.262	.280	.361	.641	81	-4	13	3.65	-1	/O-40	2	-0.6
• WILHELM, Spider	Charles Ernest Wilhelm b: 5/23/1929, Baltimore, MD d: 10/20/1992, Venice, FL BR/TR, 5'9", 170 lbs. Deb: 9/6/1953																							
1953 Phi-A	7	7	1	2	1	0	0	0	0	3	0	0	.286	.286	.429	.714	87	-0	1	4.74	-1	/S-6	0	-0.1
• WILHOIT, Joe	Joseph William Wilhoit b: 12/20/1885, Hiawatha, KS d: 9/25/1930, Santa Barbara, CA BL/TR, 6'2", 175 lbs. Deb: 4/12/1916 Career OF: 5-37-190																							
1916 Bos-N	116	383	44	88	13	4	2	38	27	45	18	....	.230	.282	.300	.582	83	-8	39	3.27	5	*O-108(1-1-106)	10	-0.9
1917 Bos-N	54	186	20	51	5	0	1	10	17	15	5	....	.274	.335	.317	.652	107	2	21	3.88	-3	O-52(0-0-52)	5	-0.5
Pit-N	9	10	0	2	0	0	0	0	1	1	0	....	.200	.273	.200	.473	44	-1	1	1.65	0	/O-3(1-0-2),1-1	0	0.0
*NY-N	34	50	9	17	2	2	0	8	8	5	0	....	.340	.431	.460	.891	179	5	10	7.42	0	O-11(0-2-10)	4	0.6
Yr.	97	246	29	70	7	2	1	18	26	21	5	....	.285	.353	.341	.694	119	6	32	4.43	-3	O-66(1-2-64)/1-1	9	0.0
1918 NY-N	64	135	13	37	3	3	0	15	17	14	4	....	.274	.355	.341	.696	115	3	17	4.43	-5	O-55(3-34-15)	6	-0.4
1919 Bos-A	6	18	7	6	0	0	0	2	5	2	1	....	.333	.478	.333	.812	138	1	3	6.87	-1	/O-5(0-0-5)	1	0.0
Total 4	283	782	93	201	23	9	3	73	75	82	28	....	.257	.323	.321	.644	102	3	91	3.89	-3	O-234/1-1	26	-1.2
• WILIE, Denney	Dennis Ernest Wilie b: 9/22/1890, Mount Calm, TX d: 6/20/1966, Hayward, CA BL/TL, 5'8", 155 lbs. Deb: 7/27/1911 Career OF: 25-28-14																							
1911 StL-N	28	51	10	12	3	1	0	3	8	11	3	....	.235	.361	.333	.694	97	0	7	4.70	1	O-15(11-3-2)	2	0.1
1912 StL-N	30	48	2	11	0	1	0	6	7	9	0	....	.229	.351	.271	.622	73	-1	5	3.13	-1	O-16(3-1-12)	1	-0.3
1915 Cle-A	45	131	14	33	4	1	2	10	26	18	2	6	.252	.384	.344	.727	116	2	17	4.13	-3	O-35(11-24-0)	3	-0.4
Total 3	103	230	26	56	7	3	2	19	41	38	5	6	.243	.372	.326	.698	103	1	28	4.04	-3	/O-66	6	-0.6
• WILKE, Harry	Henry Joseph Wilke b: 12/14/1900, Cincinnati, OH d: 6/21/1991, Hamilton, OH BR/TR, 5'10.5", 171 lbs. Deb: 5/12/1927																							
1927 Chi-N	3	9	0	0	0	0	0	0	0	1	0	....	.000	.000	.000	.000	-100	-3	0	.00	0	/3-3	0	-0.2
• WILKERSON, Brad	Stephen Bradley Wilkerson b: 6/1/1977, Owensboro, KY BL/TL, 6', 200 lbs. Deb: 7/12/2001 Career OF: 205-115-19																							
2001 Mon-N	47	117	11	24	7	2	1	5	17	41	2	1	.205	.306	.325	.631	62	-6	12	3.41	-1	O-38(38-0-0)	1	-0.8
2002 Mon-N	153	507	92	135	27	8	20	59	81	161	7	8	.266	.373	.469	.842	116	12	92	6.30	2	*O-129(72-73-3),1-23	17	1.0
2003 Mon-N	146	504	78	135	34	4	19	77	89	155	13	10	.268	.382	.464	.846	101	2	95	6.57	5	*O-135(95-42-16),1-27	17	0.1
Total 3	346	1128	181	294	68	14	40	141	187	357	22	19	.261	.370	.452	.822	104	7	199	6.10	6	O-302/1-50	35	0.3
• WILKERSON, Curtis	Curtis Vernon Wilkerson b: 4/26/1961, Petersburg, VA BB/TR, 5'9", 158 lbs. Deb: 9/10/1983 Career OF: 2-0-0																							
1983 Tex-A	16	35	7	6	0	1	0	1	2	5	3	0	.171	.216	.229	.445	23	-3	2	2.03	-1	/S-9,2-2,3-2	0	-0.3
1984 Tex-A	153	484	47	120	12	0	1	26	22	72	12	10	.248	.283	.279	.562	55	-31	38	2.57	-8	*S-116,2-47	5	-2.7
1985 Tex-A	129	360	35	88	11	6	0	22	22	63	14	7	.244	.295	.308	.604	65	-18	33	3.01	-12	*S-110,2-19/D-2	4	-1.8
1986 Tex-A	110	236	27	56	10	3	0	15	11	42	9	7	.237	.274	.305	.579	56	-16	19	2.70	-5	2-60,S-56/D-2	3	-1.4
1987 Tex-A	85	138	28	37	5	3	2	14	6	16	6	3	.268	.308	.391	.700	84	-4	16	4.13	-5	S-33,2-28,3-18/D-4	4	-0.5
1988 Tex-A	117	338	41	99	12	5	0	28	26	43	9	4	.293	.347	.358	.705	95	-1	42	4.46	-10	2-87,S-24,3-11/D-1	9	-0.8
1989*Chi-N	77	160	18	39	4	2	1	10	8	33	4	2	.244	.280	.313	.592	64	-8	14	2.88	-7	3-26,2-15/S-7,O-1	1	-1.5
1990 Chi-N	77	186	21	41	5	1	0	16	7	36	2	2	.220	.249	.258	.507	37	-17	11	1.95	-16	3-52,2-14/O-1,S-1	1	-3.3
1991*Pit-N	85	191	20	36	9	1	2	18	15	40	2	1	.188	.248	.277	.525	48	-13	14	2.29	6	2-30,S-15,3-14	2	-0.7
1992 KC-A	111	296	27	74	10	1	2	29	18	47	18	7	.250	.295	.311	.606	68	-12	28	3.10	-5	S-69,2-39/3-5,D-1	5	-1.2
1993 KC-A	12	28	1	4	0	0	0	0	1	6	2	0	.143	.172	.143	.315	-13	-4	1	.79	1	2-10/S-5	0	-0.3
Total 11	972	2452	272	600	78	23	8	179	138	403	81	43	.245	.288	.305	.593	63	-127	217	2.96	-62	S-444,2-351,3-128/D-10,O-2	34	-14.6
• WILKINS, Bobby	Robert Linwood Wilkins b: 8/11/1922, Denton, NC BR/TR, 5'9", 165 lbs. Deb: 4/18/1944																							
1944 Phi-A	24	25	7	6	0	0	0	3	1	4	0	0	.240	.296	.240	.536	55	-1	2	2.31	0	/S-9	0	-0.1
1945 Phi-A	62	154	22	40	6	0	0	4	10	17	2	4	.260	.305	.299	.604	76	-6	13	2.78	-6	S-40/O-4(4-0-0)	2	-1.0
Total 2	86	179	29	46	6	0	0	7	11	21	2	4	.257	.304	.291	.594	73	-7	15	2.71	-7	/S-49,O-4	2	-1.1

• WILKINS, Rick Richard David Wilkins b: 6/4/1967, Jacksonville, FL BL/TR, 6'2", 210 lbs. Deb: 6/6/1991

YEAR TM-L	G	AB	R	H	2B	3B	HR	RBI	BB	SO	SB	CS	AVG	OBP	SLG	OPS	OPS+	BR/A	RC	RC/G	FR	G/POS	WS	TPW
1991 Chi-N	86	203	21	45	9	0	6	22	19	56	3	3	.222	.307	.355	.662	82	-6	23	3.58	4	C-82	5	0.2
1992 Chi-N	83	244	20	66	9	1	8	22	28	53	0	2	.270	.346	.414	.760	111	3	34	4.85	4	C-73	10	1.2
1993 Chi-N	136	446	78	135	23	1	30	73	50	99	2	1	.303	.377	.561	.937	149	30	95	8.03	7	*C-133	28	4.7
1994 Chi-N	100	313	44	71	25	2	7	39	40	86	4	3	.227	.318	.387	.705	84	-8	40	4.32	2	C-95/1-2	9	0.0
1995 Chi-N	50	162	24	31	2	0	6	14	36	51	0	0	.191	.342	.315	.657	76	-4	18	3.52	1	C-49/1-2	3	-0.1
Hou-N	15	40	6	10	1	0	1	5	10	10	0	0	.250	.400	.350	.750	107	1	6	5.30	0	C-13	2	0.2
Yr.	65	202	30	41	3	0	7	19	46	61	0	0	.203	.353	.322	.675	82	-3	25	3.85	1	C-62/1-2	5	0.1
1996 Hou-N	84	254	34	54	8	2	6	23	46	81	0	1	.213	.336	.331	.666	83	-6	31	4.06	-1	C-82	7	-0.1
SF-N	52	157	19	46	10	0	8	36	21	40	0	2	.293	.376	.510	.886	137	7	29	6.44	4	C-42/1-7	7	1.3
Yr.	136	411	53	100	18	2	14	59	67	121	0	3	.243	.351	.399	.750	103	2	60	4.94	3	*C-124/1-7	14	1.2
1997 SF-N	66	190	18	37	5	0	6	23	17	65	0	0	.195	.261	.316	.577	52	-14	17	2.94	2	C-57	4	-0.9
*Sea-A	5	12	2	3	1	0	1	4	1	2	0	0	.250	.308	.583	.891	127	0	2	6.00	0	/C-3,D-2	0	0.0
1998 Sea-A	19	41	5	8	1	1	1	4	4	14	0	0	.195	.267	.341	.608	57	-3	4	2.87	0	/1-6,C-6,D-2	0	-0.3
NY-N	5	15	3	2	0	0	0	1	2	2	0	0	.133	.235	.133	.369		-2	1	1.23	0	/C-4	0	-0.2
1999 LA-N	3	4	0	0	0	0	0	0	0	2	0	0	.000	.000	.000	.000	-106	-1	0	.00	0	/C-1	0	-0.1
2000*StL-N	4	11	3	3	0	0	0	1	2	2	0	0	.273	.385	.273	.657	70	-0	1	4.57	2	/C-3	0	0.2
2001 SD-N	12	22	3	4	1	0	1	8	2	8	0	0	.182	.250	.364	.614	61	-1	2	2.52	1	/C-7,1-1	1	0.0
Total 11	720	2114	280	515	95	7	81	275	278	571	9	12	.244	.335	.410	.745	100	-3	303	4.88	25	C-650/1-18,D-4	76	6.2

• WILKINSON, Ed Edward Henry Wilkinson b: 6/20/1890, Jacksonville, OR d: 4/9/1918, Tucson, AZ BR/TR, 6', 170 lbs. Deb: 7/4/1911

YEAR TM-L	G	AB	R	H	2B	3B	HR	RBI	BB	SO	SB	CS	AVG	OBP	SLG	OPS	OPS+	BR/A	RC	RC/G	FR	G/POS	WS	TPW
1911 NY-A	10	13	2	3	0	0	0	1	0	....	0	....	.231	.231	.231	.462	27	-1	1	1.69	-1	/O-3(3-0-0),2-1	0	-0.2

• WILL, Bob Robert Lee "Butch" Will b: 7/15/1931, Berwyn, IL BL/TL, 5'10.5", 175 lbs. Deb: 4/16/1957 Career OF: 13-30-148

YEAR TM-L	G	AB	R	H	2B	3B	HR	RBI	BB	SO	SB	CS	AVG	OBP	SLG	OPS	OPS+	BR/A	RC	RC/G	FR	G/POS	WS	TPW
1957 Chi-N	70	112	13	25	3	0	1	10	5	21	1	0	.223	.256	.277	.533	44	-9	8	2.33	-3	O-30(0-30-0)	0	-1.3
1958 Chi-N	6	4	1	1	0	0	0	0	2	0	0	0	.250	.500	.250	.750	108	0	1	6.84	0	/O-1	0	0.0
1960 Chi-N	138	475	58	121	20	9	6	53	47	54	1	5	.255	.323	.373	.696	91	-8	56	3.99	2	*O-121(4-0-117)	10	-1.0
1961 Chi-N	86	113	9	29	9	0	0	8	15	19	0	1	.257	.344	.336	.680	80	-3	14	4.26	-1	O-30(9-0-22)/1-1	2	-0.6
1962 Chi-N	87	92	6	22	3	0	2	15	13	22	0	0	.239	.333	.337	.670	78	-3	11	4.07	0	/O-9(0-0-9)	1	-0.3
1963 Chi-N	23	23	0	4	0	0	0	1	1	3	0	0	.174	.208	.174	.382	11	-3	1	1.26	0	/1-1	0	-0.3
Total 6	410	819	87	202	35	9	9	87	83	119	2	6	.247	.317	.344	.661	80	-24	91	3.73	-3	O-191/1-2	13	-3.5

• WILLARD, Jerry Gerald Duane Willard b: 3/14/1960, Oxnard, CA BL/TR, 6'2", 195 lbs. Deb: 4/11/1984

YEAR TM-L	G	AB	R	H	2B	3B	HR	RBI	BB	SO	SB	CS	AVG	OBP	SLG	OPS	OPS+	BR/A	RC	RC/G	FR	G/POS	WS	TPW
1984 Cle-A	87	246	21	55	8	1	10	37	26	55	1	0	.224	.298	.386	.684	86	-5	28	3.82	-1	C-76/D-1	6	-0.2
1985 Cle-A	104	300	39	81	13	0	7	36	28	59	0	0	.270	.334	.383	.718	97	-1	40	4.76	6	C-96/D-1	10	0.9
1986 Oak-A	75	161	17	43	7	0	4	26	22	28	0	1	.267	.362	.385	.747	112	3	23	4.79	-2	C-71/D-1	6	0.3
1987 Oak-A	7	6	1	1	0	0	0	0	2	1	0	0	.167	.375	.167	.542	55	-0	1	3.08	0	/D-3,1-1,3-1	0	-0.1
1990 Chi-A	3	3	0	0	0	0	0	0	0	2	0	0	.000	.000	.000	.000	-102	-1	0	.00	0	/C-1	0	-0.1
1991*Atl-N	17	14	1	3	0	0	1	4	2	5	0	0	.214	.313	.429	.741	100	-0	2	5.00	0	/C-1	0	0.0
1992 Atl-N	26	23	2	8	1	0	2	7	1	3	0	0	.348	.375	.652	1.027	175	2	4	5.63	0	/C-1	1	0.2
Mon-N	21	25	0	3	0	0	0	1	1	7	0	0	.120	.154	.120	.274	-22	-4	0	.28	0	/1-5	0	-0.4
Yr.	47	48	2	11	1	0	2	8	2	10	0	0	.229	.260	.375	.635	73	-2	4	2.57	0	/1-5,C-1	1	-0.2
1994 Sea-A	6	5	1	1	0	0	1	3	1	1	0	0	.200	.333	.800	1.133	177	1	1	9.59	-1	/C-1,D-1	0	0.0
Total 8	346	783	82	195	29	1	25	114	83	161	1	1	.249	.323	.384	.708	95	-5	100	4.32	1	C-247/D-7,1-6,3-1	23	0.6

• WILLIAMS, Art Arthur Franklin Williams b: 8/26/1877, Somerville, MA d: 5/16/1941, Arlington, VA TR Deb: 5/7/1902

YEAR TM-L	G	AB	R	H	2B	3B	HR	RBI	BB	SO	SB	CS	AVG	OBP	SLG	OPS	OPS+	BR/A	RC	RC/G	FR	G/POS	WS	TPW
1902 Chi-N	49	167	20	38	3	0	0	14	17	....	9	....	.228	.310	.246	.556	74	-4	16	3.28	-3	O-24(4-0-22),1-19	3	-0.9

• WILLIAMS, Bernie Bernard Williams b: 10/8/1948, Alameda, CA BR/TR, 6'1", 175 lbs. Deb: 9/7/1970 Career OF: 43-3-5

YEAR TM-L	G	AB	R	H	2B	3B	HR	RBI	BB	SO	SB	CS	AVG	OBP	SLG	OPS	OPS+	BR/A	RC	RC/G	FR	G/POS	WS	TPW
1970 SF-N	7	16	2	5	2	0	0	1	2	1	1	1	.313	.389	.438	.826	122	0	2	4.64	1	/O-6(6-0-0)	0	0.1
1971 SF-N	35	73	8	13	1	0	1	5	12	24	1	1	.178	.294	.233	.527	52	-4	6	2.37	-2	O-27(22-0-5)	0	-0.7
1972 SF-N	46	68	12	13	3	1	3	9	7	22	0	0	.191	.267	.397	.664	85	-2	7	3.28	0	O-15(14-1-0)	1	-0.2
1974 SD-N	14	15	1	2	0	0	0	0	0	6	0	0	.133	.133	.133	.267	-26	-3	0	.55	0	/O-3(1-2-0)	0	-0.3
Total 4	102	172	23	33	6	1	4	15	21	53	2	2	.192	.280	.308	.588	65	-8	15	2.76	0	/O-51	1	-1.2

• WILLIAMS, Bernie Bernabe (Figueroa) Williams b: 9/13/1968, San Juan, Puerto Rico BB/TR, 6'2", 205 lbs. Deb: 7/7/1991 Career OF: 4-1619-4

YEAR TM-L	G	AB	R	H	2B	3B	HR	RBI	BB	SO	SB	CS	AVG	OBP	SLG	OPS	OPS+	BR/A	RC	RC/G	FR	G/POS	WS	TPW
1991 NY-A	85	320	43	76	19	4	3	34	48	57	10	5	.238	.339	.350	.689	91	-3	41	4.30	-1	O-85(0-85-0)	10	-0.5
1992 NY-A	62	261	39	73	14	2	5	26	29	36	7	6	.280	.354	.406	.760	113	4	37	4.99	4	O-62(4-55-4)	7	0.6
1993 NY-A	139	567	67	152	31	4	12	68	53	106	9	9	.268	.335	.400	.735	100	-2	72	4.38	3	*O-139(0-139-0)	15	0.2
1994 NY-A	108	408	80	118	29	1	12	57	61	54	16	9	.289	.386	.453	.839	120	13	72	6.21	4	*O-107(0-107-0)	14	1.7
1995*NY-A	144	563	93	173	29	9	18	82	75	98	8	6	.307	.393	.487	.880	129	24	109	7.14	3	*O-144(0-144-0)	27	2.6
1996*NY-A	143	551	108	168	26	7	29	102	82	72	17	4	.305	.395	.535	.930	132	30	118	7.77	0	*O-140(0-140-0)/D-2	26	2.8
1997*NY-A★	129	509	107	167	35	6	21	100	73	80	15	8	.328	.413	.544	.958	148	38	116	8.48	-6	*O-128(0-128-0)	24	3.1
1998*NY-A★	128	499	101	169	30	5	26	97	74	81	15	9	**.339**	.425	.575	1.000	163	47	117	8.75	-4	*O-123(0-123-0)/D-5	27	4.1
1999*NY-A★	158	591	116	202	28	6	25	115	100	95	9	10	.342	.438	.536	.974	149	45	140	9.11	-2	*O-155(0-155-0)/D-2	33	4.1
2000*NY-A★	141	537	108	165	37	6	30	121	71	84	13	5	.307	.393	.566	.959	140	34	118	8.07	-7	*O-137(0-137-0)/D-4	26	2.5
2001*NY-A★	146	540	102	166	38	0	26	94	78	67	11	5	.307	.401	.522	.923	139	33	113	7.58	-4	*O-145(0-144-0)/D-1	24	2.8
2002*NY-A	154	612	102	204	37	2	19	102	83	97	8	4	.333	.415	.493	.909	142	40	125	7.81	-15	*O-147(0-147-0)/D-7	30	2.4
2003*NY-A	119	445	77	117	19	1	15	64	71	61	5	0	.263	.368	.411	.779	107	8	66	5.12	-4	*O-115(0-115-0)/D-4	13	0.5
Total 13	1656	6403	1143	1950	372	53	241	1062	898	988	143	80	.305	.393	.492	.885	131	311	1245	7.05	-31	*O-1627/D-25	276	27.0

• WILLIAMS, Billy Billy Leo "Sweet Swingin' Billy from Whistler" Williams
b: 6/15/1938, Whistler, AL BL/TR, 6'1", 175 lbs. Deb: 8/6/1959 C HOF: 1987 Career OF: 1738-30-384

YEAR TM-L	G	AB	R	H	2B	3B	HR	RBI	BB	SO	SB	CS	AVG	OBP	SLG	OPS	OPS+	BR/A	RC	RC/G	FR	G/POS	WS	TPW
1959 Chi-N	18	33	0	5	0	1	0	2	1	7	0	0	.152	.176	.212	.389	3	-5	1	.77	0	O-10(10-0-0)	0	-0.5
1960 Chi-N	12	47	4	13	0	2	2	7	5	12	0	0	.277	.346	.489	.836	127	2	8	6.13	-1	O-12(12-0-0)	2	0.0
1961 Chi-N	146	529	75	147	20	7	25	86	45	70	6	0	.278	.340	.484	.824	114	11	87	5.87	-6	*O-135(110-0-27)	15	-0.3
1962 Chi-N★	159	618	94	184	22	8	22	91	70	72	9	9	.298	.373	.466	.839	119	16	107	6.28	5	*O-159(158-0-1)	18	1.1
1963 Chi-N	161	612	87	175	36	9	25	95	68	78	7	6	.286	.359	.497	.856	136	29	108	6.32	10	*O-160(160-0-0)	28	3.1
1964 Chi-N★	162	645	100	201	39	2	33	98	59	84	10	7	.312	.371	.532	.903	145	38	125	7.26	-3	*O-162(162-2-0)	28	2.7
1965 Chi-N★	164	645	115	203	39	6	34	108	65	76	10	1	.315	.380	.552	.932	155	49	132	7.61	-1	*O-164(34-28-106)	33	3.9
1966 Chi-N	162	648	100	179	23	5	29	91	69	61	6	3	.276	.350	.461	.811	122	20	104	5.75	4	*O-162(11-0-152)	21	1.3
1967 Chi-N	162	634	92	176	21	12	28	84	68	67	6	3	.278	.349	.481	.831	129	25	106	5.94	-6	*O-162(161-0-6)	28	1.0
1968 Chi-N★	163	642	91	185	30	8	30	98	48	53	4	1	.288	.340	.500	.840	140	31	107	6.02	-8	*O-163(137-0-47)	30	1.5
1969 Chi-N	163	642	103	188	33	10	21	95	59	70	3	2	.293	.356	.474	.830	116	14	106	6.02	3	*O-159(153-0-28)	24	0.7
1970 Chi-N	161	636	**137**	**205**	34	4	42	129	72	65	7	1	.322	.393	.586	.979	142	38	147	8.83	6	*O-160(155-0-9)	29	3.5
1971 Chi-N	157	594	86	179	27	5	28	93	77	44	7	5	.301	.384	.505	.889	131	26	112	6.90	1	*O-154(151-0-4)	26	1.9
1972 Chi-N★	150	574	95	191	34	6	37	122	62	59	3	1	**.333**	.403	**.606**	**1.010**	166	50	137	**9.14**	-1	*O-144(144-0-0)/1-5	32	4.4
1973 Chi-N★	156	576	72	166	22	2	20	86	76	72	4	3	.288	.372	.438	.810	115	13	94	5.89	14	*O-138(138-0-0),1-19	20	1.9
1974 Chi-N	117	404	55	113	22	0	16	68	67	44	4	5	.280	.383	.453	.836	128	16	71	6.22	5	1-65,O-43(41-0-4)	16	1.4
1975*Oak-A	155	520	68	127	20	1	23	81	76	68	0	0	.244	.343	.419	.762	117	13	78	5.16	0	*D-145/1-7	17	0.9
1976 Oak-A	120	351	36	74	12	0	11	41	58	44	4	2	.211	.323	.339	.662	98	1	41	3.86	0	*D-106/O-1	7	-0.2
Total 18	2488	9350	1410	2711	434	88	426	1475	1045	1046	90	49	.290	.364	.492	.856	130	385	1671	6.47	23	*O-2088,D-251/1-96	374	28.2

• WILLIAMS, Billy William Williams b: 6/13/1933, Newberry, SC BL/TR, 6'3", 195 lbs. Deb: 8/15/1969

YEAR TM-L	G	AB	R	H	2B	3B	HR	RBI	BB	SO	SB	CS	AVG	OBP	SLG	OPS	OPS+	BR/A	RC	RC/G	FR	G/POS	WS	TPW
1969 Sea-A	4	10	1	0	0	0	0	0	1	3	0	0	.000	.167	.000	.167	-51	-2	0	.11	1	/O-3(0-0-3)	0	-0.1

• WILLIAMS, Bob Robert Elias Williams b: 4/27/1884, Monday, OH d: 8/6/1962, Nelsonville, OH BR/TR, 6', 190 lbs. Deb: 7/3/1911

YEAR TM-L	G	AB	R	H	2B	3B	HR	RBI	BB	SO	SB	CS	AVG	OBP	SLG	OPS	OPS+	BR/A	RC	RC/G	FR	G/POS	WS	TPW
1911 NY-A	20	47	3	9	2	0	0	8	5	....	1	....	.191	.269	.234	.503	38	-4	3	2.11	-1	C-20	1	-0.4
1912 NY-A	20	44	7	6	1	0	0	3	9	....	0	....	.136	.283	.159	.442	26	-4	2	1.45	-3	C-20	0	-0.6

YEAR TM-L	G	AB	R	H	2B	3B	HR	RBI	BB	SO	SB	CS	AVG	OBP	SLG	OPS	OPS+	BR/A	RC	RC/G	FR	G/POS	WS	TPW
1913 NY-A	6	19	0	3	0	0	0	0	1	3	0	....	.158	.200	.158	.358	5	-2	1	.87	0	/C-6	0	-0.2
Total 3	**46**	**110**	**10**	**18**	**3**	**0**	**0**	**11**	**15**	**3**	**1**	**....**	**.164**	**.264**	**.191**	**.455**	**28**	**-10**	**6**	**1.62**	**-4**	**/C-46**	**1**	**-1.1**
• WILLIAMS, Cy	Fred Williams b: 12/21/1887, Wadena, IN d: 4/23/1974, Eagle River, WI BL/TL, 6'2", 180 lbs. Deb: 7/18/1912 Career OF: 85-1374-362																							
1912 Chi-N	28	62	3	15	1	1	0	1	6	14	2	....	.242	.309	.290	.599	64	-3	6	3.23	0	0-22(5-17-0)	1	-0.4
1913 Chi-N	49	156	17	35	3	3	4	32	5	26	5	....	.224	.262	.359	.621	76	-6	15	3.08	-1	0-44(36-9-0)	3	-0.9
1914 Chi-N	55	94	12	19	2	2	0	5	13	13	2	....	.202	.312	.266	.578	73	-3	8	2.77	-2	0-27(22-7-0)	2	-0.6
1915 Chi-N	151	518	59	133	22	6	13	64	26	49	15	10	.257	.305	.398	.703	112	4	64	4.19	3	*0-149(0-149-0)	19	-0.2
1916 Chi-N	118	405	55	113	19	9	**12**	66	51	64	6	....	.279	.372	.459	**.831**	140	21	74	6.19	-4	*0-116(0-115-1)	18	1.1
1917 Chi-N	138	468	53	113	22	4	5	42	38	78	8	....	.241	.308	.338	.646	91	-5	52	3.52	9	*0-136(0-136-0)	16	-0.4
1918 Phi-N	94	351	49	97	14	1	6	39	27	30	10	....	.276	.337	.373	.710	109	4	47	4.51	3	0-91(0-91-0)	12	0.2
1919 Phi-N	109	435	54	121	21	1	9	39	30	43	9	....	.278	.335	.393	.728	110	6	58	4.65	-1	*0-108(0-108-0)	12	-0.2
1920 Phi-N	148	590	88	192	36	10	**15**	72	32	45	18	12	.325	.364	.497	.861	139	29	103	6.41	9	*0-147(0-147-0)	24	3.1
1921 Phi-N	146	562	67	180	28	6	18	75	30	32	5	15	.320	.357	.488	.844	112	6	91	5.93	12	*0-146(0-146-0)	17	1.1
1922 Phi-N	151	584	98	180	30	6	26	92	74	49	11	14	.308	.392	.514	.905	120	16	116	7.16	3	*0-150(0-150-0)	17	1.2
1923 Phi-N	136	535	98	157	22	3	**41**	114	59	57	11	10	.293	.371	.576	.947	131	22	112	7.62	-11	*0-135(0-135-0)	17	0.5
1924 Phi-N	148	558	101	183	31	11	24	93	67	49	7	12	.328	.403	.552	.955	137	28	121	8.15	-8	*0-145(0-145-0)	21	1.5
1925 Phi-N	107	314	78	104	11	5	13	60	53	34	4	9	.331	.435	.522	.958	132	15	72	8.54	0	0-96(0-0-96)	12	0.9
1926 Phi-N	107	336	63	116	13	4	18	53	38	35	2	....	.345	.418	**.568**	.986	155	27	78	9.01	-3	0-93(0-0-93)	17	1.7
1927 Phi-N	131	492	86	135	18	2	**30**	98	61	57	0	....	.274	.365	.502	.867	128	19	90	6.41	-4	*0-130(0-0-130)	16	0.6
1928 Phi-N	99	238	31	61	9	0	12	37	54	34	0	....	.256	.400	.445	.845	117	8	45	6.34	2	0-69(20-9-40)	7	0.5
1929 Phi-N	66	65	11	19	2	0	5	21	22	9	0	....	.292	.471	.554	1.025	144	6	18	9.90	0	0-11(1-9-1)	3	0.4
1930 Phi-N	21	17	1	8	2	0	0	2	4	3	0	....	.471	.571	.588	1.160	169	2	6	16.95	0	/0-3(1-1-1)	1	0.2
Total 19	**2002**	**6780**	**1024**	**1981**	**306**	**74**	**251**	**1005**	**690**	**721**	**115**	**82**	**.292**	**.365**	**.470**	**.835**	**122**	**196**	**1177**	**6.13**	**5**	***0-1818**	**235**	**10.2**
• WILLIAMS, Dallas	Dallas McKinley Williams b: 2/28/1958, Brooklyn, NY BL/TL, 5'11", 165 lbs. Deb: 9/19/1981 C Career OF: 7-3-3																							
1981 Bal-A	2	2	0	1	0	0	0	0	0	0	0	0	.500	.500	.500	1.000	189	0	1	13.50	-0	/0-1	0	0.0
1983 Cin-N	18	36	2	2	0	0	0	1	3	6	0	0	.056	.128	.056	.184	-46	-7	0	.35	0	0-12(6-3-3)	0	-0.8
Total 2	**20**	**38**	**2**	**3**	**0**	**0**	**0**	**1**	**3**	**6**	**0**	**0**	**.079**	**.146**	**.079**	**.225**	**-35**	**-7**	**1**	**.70**	**0**	**/0-13**	**0**	**-0.8**
• WILLIAMS, Dana	Dana Lamont Williams b: 3/20/1963, Weirton, WV BR/TR, 5'10", 170 lbs. Deb: 6/21/1989 C																							
1989 Bos-A	8	5	1	1	1	0	0	0	0	1	0	0	.200	.333	.400	.733	100	0	1	5.09	1	/D-2,0-1	0	0.1
• WILLIAMS, Davey	David Carlous Williams b: 11/2/1927, Dallas, TX BR/TR, 5'10", 160 lbs. Deb: 9/16/1949 C																							
1949 NY-N	13	50	7	12	1	1	1	5	7	4	0	....	.240	.333	.360	.693	86	-1	7	4.61	-0	2-13	1	0.0
1951★NY-N	30	64	17	17	1	0	2	8	5	8	1	1	.266	.319	.375	.694	85	-2	7	3.60	1	2-22	2	0.0
1952 NY-N	138	540	70	137	26	3	13	55	48	63	2	3	.254	.324	.385	.709	95	-4	71	4.55	-10	*2-138	19	-0.7
1953 NY-N★	112	340	51	101	11	2	3	34	44	19	2	5	.297	.382	.368	.750	95	-2	50	5.36	-1	2-95	10	0.4
1954★NY-N	142	544	65	121	18	3	9	46	43	33	1	1	.222	.285	.316	.602	56	-36	48	2.91	4	*2-142	10	-2.0
1955 NY-N	82	247	25	62	4	1	4	15	17	17	0	2	.251	.305	.324	.628	67	-12	24	3.40	0	2-71	5	-0.9
Total 6	**517**	**1785**	**235**	**450**	**61**	**10**	**32**	**163**	**164**	**144**	**6**	**12**	**.252**	**.321**	**.351**	**.673**	**79**	**-57**	**207**	**3.98**	**-6**	**2-481**	**47**	**-3.3**
• WILLIAMS, Denny	Evon Daniel Williams b: 12/13/1899, Portland, OR d: 3/23/1929, San Clemente, CA BL/TR, 5'8.5", 150 lbs. Deb: 4/15/1921 Career OF: 62-16-1																							
1921 Cin-N	10	7	0	0	0	0	0	0	0	2	0	1	.000	.000	.000	.000	-105	-2	0	.00	-0	/0-1	0	-0.2
1924 Bos-A	25	85	17	31	3	0	0	4	10	5	3	3	.365	.438	.400	.838	117	2	15	6.96	0	0-19(19-0-0)	3	0.1
1925 Bos-A	69	218	28	50	1	3	0	13	17	11	2	6	.229	.285	.261	.547	39	-22	16	2.35	-2	0-52(42-11-0)	1	-2.5
1928 Bos-A	16	18	1	4	0	0	0	1	1	1	0	0	.222	.263	.222	.485	29	-2	1	2.04	0	/0-6(0-5-1)	0	-0.2
Total 4	**120**	**328**	**46**	**85**	**4**	**3**	**0**	**18**	**28**	**19**	**5**	**10**	**.259**	**.319**	**.290**	**.609**	**57**	**-24**	**32**	**3.28**	**-3**	**/0-78**	**4**	**-2.9**
• WILLIAMS, Dewey	Dewey Edgar "Dee" Williams b: 2/5/1916, Durham, NC d: 3/19/2000, Williston, ND BR/TR, 6', 160 lbs. Deb: 6/28/1944																							
1944 Chi-N	79	262	23	63	7	2	0	27	23	18	2	....	.240	.302	.282	.584	65	-12	22	2.74	1	C-77	5	-0.6
1945★Chi-N	59	100	16	28	2	2	2	5	13	13	0	....	.280	.363	.400	.763	114	2	14	4.75	-1	C-54	4	0.3
1946 Chi-N	4	5	0	1	0	0	0	0	0	2	0	....	.200	.200	.200	.400	14	-1	0	1.35	0	/C-2	0	0.0
1947 Chi-N	3	2	0	0	0	0	0	0	0	1	0	....	.000	.000	.000	.000	-104	-1	0	.00	0	/C-1	0	-0.1
1948 Cin-N	48	95	9	16	2	0	1	5	10	18	0	....	.168	.248	.221	.469	29	-9	6	1.89	-3	C-47	1	-1.0
Total 5	**193**	**464**	**48**	**108**	**11**	**4**	**3**	**37**	**46**	**52**	**2**	**....**	**.233**	**.302**	**.293**	**.595**	**67**	**-20**	**41**	**2.94**	**-3**	**C-181**	**10**	**-1.5**
• WILLIAMS, Dib	Edwin Dibrell Williams b: 1/19/1910, Greenbriar, AR d: 4/2/1992, Searcy, AR BR/TR, 5'11.5", 175 lbs. Deb: 4/27/1930																							
1930 Phi-A	67	191	24	50	10	3	3	22	15	19	2	1	.262	.322	.393	.715	77	-7	25	4.43	-1	2-39,S-19/3-1	5	-0.5
1931★Phi-A	86	294	41	79	12	2	6	40	19	21	2	0	.269	.313	.384	.697	78	-9	36	4.38	13	S-72,2-10/0-1	9	1.0
1932 Phi-A	62	215	30	54	10	1	4	24	22	23	0	1	.251	.329	.363	.692	76	-8	26	4.29	-3	2-53/S-3	5	-0.7
1933 Phi-A	115	408	52	118	20	5	11	73	32	35	1	0	.289	.342	.444	.786	106	3	63	5.66	-14	S-84,2-29/1-2	13	-0.4
1934 Phi-A	66	205	25	56	10	1	2	17	21	18	0	1	.273	.341	.361	.702	84	-5	26	4.30	1	2-53/S-2	4	-0.1
1935 Phi-A	4	10	0	1	0	0	0	0	0	1	0	0	.100	.100	.100	.200	-49	-2	0	.28	0	/2-2	0	-0.2
Bos-A	75	251	26	63	12	0	3	25	24	23	2	0	.251	.319	.335	.654	65	-13	28	3.86	-3	3-30,2-29,S-15/1-1	4	-1.1
Yr.	79	261	26	64	12	0	3	25	24	24	2	0	.245	.311	.326	.637	61	-15	29	3.70	-2	2-31,3-30,S-15/1-1	4	-1.3
Total 6	**475**	**1574**	**198**	**421**	**74**	**12**	**29**	**201**	**133**	**140**	**7**	**3**	**.267**	**.327**	**.385**	**.712**	**83**	**-40**	**204**	**4.56**	**-6**	**2-215,S-195/3-31,1-3,0-1**	**40**	**-1.9**
• WILLIAMS, Dick	Richard Hirschfeld Williams b: 5/7/1929, St. Louis, MO BR/TR, 6', 190 lbs. Deb: 6/10/1951 M/C Career OF: 283-156-64																							
1951 Bro-N	23	60	5	12	3	1	1	5	4	10	0	0	.200	.250	.333	.583	54	-4	5	3.03	0	0-15(15-0-0)	1	-0.5
1952 Bro-N	36	68	13	21	4	1	0	11	2	10	0	0	.309	.329	.397	.726	99	-0	8	3.99	0	0-25(19-6-0)/1-1,3-1	2	-0.2
1953★Bro-N	30	55	4	12	2	0	2	5	3	10	0	0	.218	.271	.364	.635	62	-3	6	3.31	-1	0-24(17-2-9)	0	-0.5
1954 Bro-N	16	34	5	5	0	0	1	2	2	7	0	0	.147	.194	.235	.430	11	-5	1	1.28	0	0-14(13-2-0)	0	-0.5
1956 Bro-N	7	7	0	2	0	0	0	0	0	1	0	0	.286	.286	.286	.571	50	-0	1	3.09	0	....	0	0.0
Bal-A	87	353	45	101	18	4	11	37	30	40	5	5	.286	.342	.453	.795	117	6	52	5.09	-4	0-81(9-66-19),1-10,2-10/3-4	12	-0.2
1957 Bal-A	47	167	16	39	10	2	1	17	14	21	0	1	.234	.293	.335	.628	76	-6	15	2.96	3	0-26(15-14-2),3-15,1-12	2	-0.5
Cle-A	67	205	33	58	7	0	6	17	12	19	3	4	.283	.326	.405	.731	99	-2	24	4.10	-3	0-37(18-20-0),3-19	5	-0.6
Yr.	114	372	49	97	17	2	7	34	26	40	3	5	.261	.311	.374	.684	89	-8	39	3.57	0	0-63(33-34-2),3-34,1-12	7	-1.1
1958 Bal-A	128	409	36	113	17	0	4	32	37	47	0	6	.276	.339	.347	.686	94	-5	44	3.59	-1	0-70(34-41-15),3-45,1-26/2	9	-1.1
1959 KC-A	130	488	72	130	33	1	16	75	28	60	4	1	.266	.313	.436	.749	102	-0	64	4.46	-2	3-80,1-32,0-23(13-2-8)/2-3	12	-0.5
1960 KC-A	127	420	47	121	31	0	12	65	39	68	0	0	.288	.350	.448	.798	113	7	62	5.25	3	3-57,1-34,0-25(25-0-0)	14	0.7
1961 Bal-A	103	310	37	64	15	2	8	24	20	38	0	4	.206	.255	.345	.600	60	-21	25	2.55	1	0-75(73-2-2),1-20/3-2	2	-2.4
1962 Bal-A	82	178	20	44	7	1	1	18	14	26	0	0	.247	.306	.315	.620	71	-7	16	2.97	-1	0-29(21-0-9),1-21/3-4	2	-1.0
1963 Bos-A	79	136	15	35	8	0	2	12	15	25	0	0	.257	.331	.360	.691	91	-1	17	4.25	-1	3-17,1-11/0-7(7-0-0)	3	-0.3
1964 Bos-A	61	69	10	11	2	0	5	11	7	10	0	0	.159	.247	.406	.653	74	-3	6	2.55	1	1-21,3-13/0-5(4-1-0)	1	-0.3
Total 13	**1023**	**2959**	**358**	**768**	**157**	**12**	**70**	**331**	**227**	**392**	**12**	**21**	**.260**	**.315**	**.392**	**.707**	**92**	**-45**	**346**	**3.94**	**-7**	**0-456,3-257,1-188/2-20**	**65**	**-8.0**
• WILLIAMS, Earl	Earl Baxter Williams b: 1/27/1903, Cumberland Gap, TN d: 3/10/1958, Knoxville, TN BR/TR, 6'.5", 185 lbs. Deb: 5/27/1928																							
1928 Bos-N	3	2	0	0	0	0	0	0	0	1	0	....	.000	.000	.000	.000	-106	-1	0	.00	0	/C-1	0	-0.1
• WILLIAMS, Earl	Earl Craig Williams b: 7/14/1948, Newark, NJ BR/TR, 6'3", 220 lbs. Deb: 9/13/1970																							
1970 Atl-N	10	19	4	7	4	0	0	5	3	4	0	0	.368	.455	.579	1.033	165	2	5	8.65	1	/1-4,3-3	1	0.3
1971 Atl-N	145	497	64	129	14	1	33	87	42	80	0	1	.260	.326	.491	.817	121	12	78	5.46	-2	C-72,3-42,1-31	19	1.2
1972 Atl-N	151	565	72	146	24	2	28	87	62	118	0	0	.258	.338	.457	.795	113	10	85	5.24	-12	*C-116,3-21,1-20	18	0.3
1973★Bal-A	132	459	58	109	18	1	22	83	66	107	0	2	.237	.337	.425	.762	114	9	65	4.73	-7	C-95,1-42/D-2	15	0.3
1974★Bal-A	118	413	47	105	16	0	14	52	40	79	0	2	.254	.330	.395	.725	111	6	54	4.37	-9	C-75,1-47/D-1	14	-0.3
1975 Atl-N	111	383	42	92	13	0	11	50	34	63	0	0	.240	.307	.360	.667	82	-10	40	3.45	-3	1-90,C-11	6	-2.0
1976 Atl-N	61	184	18	39	3	0	9	26	19	33	0	0	.212	.289	.375	.664	82	-5	19	3.19	-1	C-38,1-17	3	-0.6
Mon-N	61	190	17	45	10	2	8	29	14	32	0	0	.237	.289	.437	.726	100	-1	22	3.74	4	1-47,C-13	4	-0.1
Yr.	122	374	35	84	13	2	17	55	33	65	0	0	.225	.289	.406	.696	91	-6	40	3.47	3	1-64,C-51	7	-0.6

YEAR TM-L	G	AB	R	H	2B	3B	HR	RBI	BB	SO	SB	CS	AVG	OBP	SLG	OPS	OPS+	BR/A	RC	RC/G	FR	G/POS	WS	TPW
1977 Oak-A	100	348	39	84	13	0	13	38	18	58	2	0	.241	.288	.391	.679	84	-8	34	3.19	-1	D-45,C-36,1-29	5	-1.0
Total 8	889	3058	361	756	115	6	138	457	298	574	2	5	.247	.321	.424	.745	105	14	401	4.41	-30	C-456,1-327/3-66,D-48	85	-1.8
• WILLIAMS, Eddie	Edward Laquan Williams b: 11/1/1964, Shreveport, LA BR/TR, 6', 185 lbs. Deb: 4/18/1986 Career OF: 4-0-2																							
1986 Cle-A	5	7	2	1	0	0	0	1	0	3	0	0	.143	.143	.143	.286	-22	-1	0	.64	-1	/0-4(4-0-0)	0	-0.2
1987 Cle-A	22	64	9	11	4	0	1	4	9	19	0	0	.172	.284	.281	.565	50	-5	5	2.58	2	3-22	1	-0.3
1988 Cle-A	10	21	3	4	0	0	0	1	0	3	0	0	.190	.227	.190	.418	18	-2	1	1.18	1	3-10	0	-0.2
1989 Chi-A	66	201	25	55	8	0	3	10	18	31	1	2	.274	.345	.358	.704	101	-0	25	4.27	2	3-65	3	0.2
1990 SD-N	14	42	5	12	3	0	3	4	5	6	0	1	.286	.362	.571	.933	151	2	8	6.67	0	3-13	1	0.2
1994 SD-N	49	175	32	58	11	1	11	42	15	26	0	1	.331	.394	.594	.988	158	14	36	7.52	-1	1-46/3-1	7	0.9
1995 SD-N	97	296	35	77	11	1	12	47	23	47	0	0	.260	.322	.426	.748	99	-1	34	3.82	-2	1-81	3	-1.0
1996 Det-A	77	215	22	43	5	0	6	26	18	50	0	2	.200	.268	.307	.575	45	-20	16	2.38	-1	D-52/1-7,3-3,0-2(0-0-2)	0	-2.1
1997 LA-N	8	7	0	1	0	0	0	1	1	1	0	0	.143	.250	.143	.393	7	-1	0	1.13	0	....	0	-0.1
Pit-N	30	89	12	22	5	0	3	11	10	24	1	0	.247	.337	.404	.741	91	-1	13	4.78	-3	1-26	1	-0.6
Yr.	38	96	12	23	5	0	3	12	11	25	1	0	.240	.330	.385	.716	85	-2	13	4.49	-3	1-26	1	-0.6
1998 SD-N	17	28	1	4	0	0	0	3	2	6	0	0	.143	.200	.143	.343	-8	-4	1	.84	0	/1-7	0	-0.5
Total 10	395	1145	146	288	47	2	39	150	101	216	2	6	.252	.321	.398	.720	92	-19	140	4.05	-4	1-167,3-114/D-52,0-6	16	-3.6
• WILLIAMS, George	George Williams b: 10/23/1939, Detroit, MI BR/TR, 5'11", 165 lbs. Deb: 7/16/1961																							
1961 Phi-N	17	36	4	9	0	0	0	1	4	4	0	0	.250	.325	.250	.575	56	-2	3	3.23	1	2-15	0	-0.1
1962 Hou-N	5	8	1	3	1	0	0	2	0	1	0	0	.375	.375	.500	.875	143	0	2	8.10	0	/2-3	0	0.1
1964 KC-A	37	91	10	19	6	0	0	2	6	12	0	0	.209	.265	.275	.540	49	-6	7	2.33	0	2-20/3-2,0-2(2-0-0),S-2	1	-0.5
Total 3	59	135	15	31	7	0	0	5	10	17	0	0	.230	.288	.281	.569	56	-8	11	2.83	1	/2-38,3-2,0-2,S-2	1	-0.4
• WILLIAMS, George	George Erik Williams b: 4/22/1969, La Crosse, WI BB/TR, 5'10", 190 lbs. Deb: 7/14/1995																							
1995 Oak-A	29	79	13	23	5	1	3	14	11	21	0	0	.291	.391	.494	.885	137	5	16	7.31	-1	C-13,D-10	4	0.4
1996 Oak-A	56	132	17	20	5	0	3	10	28	32	0	0	.152	.313	.258	.570	48	-10	13	2.87	-2	C-43,D-11	1	-0.9
1997 Oak-A	76	201	30	58	9	1	3	22	35	46	0	1	.289	.399	.388	.787	109	4	34	6.17	-2	C-67/D-1	7	0.6
2000 SD-N	11	16	2	3	0	0	1	2	0	4	0	0	.188	.235	.375	.610	54	-1	1	3.06	-1	/C-6	0	-0.1
Total 4	172	428	62	104	19	2	10	48	74	103	0	1	.243	.365	.367	.732	93	-2	64	5.10	-4	C-129/D-22	12	0.0
• WILLIAMS, Gerald	Gerald Floyd Williams b: 8/10/1966, New Orleans, LA BR/TR, 6'2", 190 lbs. Deb: 9/15/1992 Career OF: 415-423-198																							
1992 NY-A	15	27	7	8	2	0	3	6	0	3	2	0	.296	.296	.704	1.000	174	3	6	8.44	-1	0-12(0-0-12)	1	0.2
1993 NY-A	42	67	11	10	2	3	0	6	1	14	2	0	.149	.186	.269	.454	21	-7	3	1.42	0	0-37(10-17-12)/D-1	0	-0.8
1994 NY-A	57	86	19	25	8	0	4	13	4	17	1	3	.291	.322	.523	.845	118	0	10	3.93	0	0-43(26-8-12)/D-2	0	0.0
1995*NY-A	100	182	33	45	18	2	6	28	22	34	4	2	.247	.332	.467	.799	106	1	28	5.20	2	0-92(70-2-26)/D-2	7	0.0
1996 NY-A	99	233	37	63	15	4	5	30	15	39	7	8	.270	.325	.433	.759	90	-6	29	4.12	-5	0-93(70-14-10)/D-2	4	-1.3
Mil-A	26	92	6	19	4	0	0	4	4	18	3	1	.207	.247	.250	.497	25	-11	6	2.08	1	0-26(0-25-1)	1	-0.8
Yr.	125	325	43	82	19	4	5	34	19	57	10	9	.252	.304	.382	.685	72	-17	35	3.53	-3	*0-119(70-39-11)/D-2	5	-2.1
1997 Mil-A	155	566	73	143	32	2	10	41	19	90	23	9	.253	.284	.369	.654	68	-27	58	3.47	3	*0-154(39-129-0)/D-1	9	-2.3
1998*Atl-N	129	266	46	81	19	2	10	44	17	48	11	5	.305	.353	.504	.857	122	8	46	6.28	-1	*0-120(56-11-61)	12	0.3
1999*Atl-N	143	422	76	116	24	1	17	68	33	67	19	11	.275	.336	.457	.794	98	-3	63	5.13	-1	*0-139(120-1-32)	13	-0.9
2000 TB-A	146	632	87	173	30	2	21	89	34	103	12	12	.274	.314	.427	.741	86	-19	82	4.54	2	*0-138(0-138-0)/D-7	14	-1.5
2001 TB-A	62	232	30	48	17	0	4	17	13	42	10	4	.207	.261	.332	.593	56	-15	19	2.52	7	0-59(0-59-0)	2	-0.8
NY-A	38	47	12	8	1	0	0	2	5	13	3	1	.170	.264	.191	.456	23	-5	3	1.81	-0	0-26(6-11-12)/D-6	0	-0.5
Yr.	100	279	42	56	18	0	4	19	18	55	13	5	.201	.262	.308	.570	50	-20	21	2.39	7	0-85(6-70-12)/D-6	2	-1.3
2002 NY-A	33	17	6	0	0	0	0	0	2	4	2	0	.000	.105	.000	.105	-69	-4	0	.12	-1	0-30(7-6-17)/D-1	0	-0.4
2003 Fla-N	27	31	5	4	1	0	0	3	2	5	3	0	.129	.182	.161	.343	-10	-4	1	1.30	0	0-16(11-2-3)	0	-0.5
Total 12	1072	2900	448	743	173	16	80	351	171	497	102	56	.256	.305	.410	.714	82	-89	355	4.12	7	0-985/D-22	63	-9.3
• WILLIAMS, Gus	August Joseph "Gloomy Gus" Williams b: 5/7/1888, Omaha, NE d: 4/16/1964, Sterling, IL BL/TL, 6', 185 lbs. Deb: 4/12/1911 Career OF: 7-0-381																							
1911 StL-A	9	26	1	7	3	0	0	4	0	....	0	....	.269	.296	.385	.681	93	-0	3	3.89	-1	/0-7(7-0-0)	0	-0.2
1912 StL-A	64	216	32	63	13	7	2	32	27	....	18	....	.292	.370	.444	.815	138	10	41	6.91	-1	0-62(0-0-62)	8	0.6
1913 StL-A	148	538	72	147	21	16	5	53	57	87	31	....	.273	.346	.400	.746	121	14	80	5.14	3	*0-143(0-0-143)	16	1.0
1914 StL-A	144	499	51	126	19	6	4	47	36	120	35	20	.253	.308	.339	.647	98	-4	56	3.62	-1	*0-142(0-0-141)	13	-1.4
1915 StL-A	45	119	15	24	2	2	1	11	6	16	11	1	.202	.246	.277	.523	59	-5	10	2.80	-2	0-35(0-0-35)	1	-0.8
Total 5	410	1398	171	367	58	31	12	147	126	223	95	21	.263	.327	.374	.702	110	15	191	4.59	-2	0-389	38	-0.8
• WILLIAMS, Harry	Harry Peter Williams b: 6/23/1890, Omaha, NE d: 12/21/1963, Huntington Park, CA BR/TR, 6'1.5", 200 lbs. Deb: 8/7/1913																							
1913 NY-A	27	82	18	21	3	1	1	12	15	10	6	....	.256	.378	.354	.731	114	2	13	5.07	-2	1-27	3	0.0
1914 NY-A	59	178	9	29	5	2	1	17	26	26	3	6	.163	.287	.230	.517	56	-11	12	1.97	-7	1-58	1	-2.0
Total 2	86	260	27	50	8	3	2	29	41	36	9	6	.192	.316	.269	.585	75	-9	25	2.89	-8	/1-85	4	-2.0
• WILLIAMS, Jim	James Alfred Williams b: 4/29/1947, Zachary, LA BR/TR, 6'2", 190 lbs. Deb: 9/8/1969 Career OF: 7-0-5																							
1969 SD-N	13	25	4	7	1	0	0	2	3	11	0	0	.280	.357	.320	.677	95	-0	3	4.56	0	/0-6(6-0-0)	1	-0.1
1970 SD-N	11	14	4	4	0	0	0	0	1	3	1	0	.286	.333	.286	.619	70	-0	2	4.30	0	/0-6(1-0-5)	0	-0.1
Total 2	24	39	8	11	1	0	0	2	4	14	1	0	.282	.349	.308	.657	86	-0	5	4.47	-1	/0-12	1	-0.1
• WILLIAMS, Jimmy	James Thomas Williams b: 12/20/1876, St. Louis, MO d: 1/16/1965, St. Petersburg, FL BR/TR, 5'9", 175 lbs. Deb: 4/15/1899																							
1899 Pit-N	153	621	126	220	28	**27**	9	116	60	....	26	....	.354	.416	.530	.946	159	49	152	9.90	8	*3-152	32	5.5
1900*Pit-N	106	416	73	110	15	11	5	68	32	....	18	....	.264	.323	.389	.712	95	-4	60	5.14	10	*3-103/S-4	15	0.7
1901 Bal-A	130	501	113	159	26	**21**	7	96	56	....	21	....	.317	.388	.495	.883	138	25	108	8.15	18	*2-130	22	4.0
1902 Bal-A	125	498	83	156	27	**21**	8	83	36	....	14	....	.313	.361	.500	.861	131	19	98	7.39	-4	*2-104,3-19/1-1	19	1.5
1903 NY-A	132	502	60	134	30	12	3	82	39	....	9	....	.267	.326	.392	.718	108	5	70	4.92	16	*2-132	22	2.3
1904 NY-A	146	559	62	147	31	7	2	74	38	....	14	....	.263	.314	.354	.669	106	4	70	4.36	11	*2-146	20	1.8
1905 NY-A	129	470	54	107	20	8	6	62	50	....	14	....	.228	.306	.343	.648	95	-3	56	3.99	13	*2-129	16	1.3
1906 NY-A	139	501	61	139	25	7	3	77	44	....	8	....	.277	.342	.373	.715	112	8	71	4.91	15	*2-139	20	2.6
1907 NY-A	139	504	53	136	17	11	2	63	35	....	14	....	.270	.319	.359	.678	107	3	65	4.54	-5	*2-139	19	-0.1
1908 StL-A	148	539	63	127	20	7	4	53	55	....	7	....	.236	.310	.321	.631	104	4	57	3.39	9	*2-148	18	1.6
1909 StL-A	110	374	32	73	3	6	0	22	29	....	6	....	.195	.257	.235	.492	60	-17	24	2.02	-7	*2-109	4	-2.6
Total 11	1457	5485	780	1508	242	138	49	796	474	....	151	....	.275	.337	.396	.733	113	93	830	5.36	83	*2-1176,3-274/S-4,1-1	207	18.6
• WILLIAMS, Jimy	James Francis Williams b: 10/4/1943, Santa Maria, CA BR/TR, 5'10", 170 lbs. Deb: 4/26/1966 M/C																							
1966 StL-N	13	11	1	3	0	0	0	1	1	5	0	0	.273	.333	.273	.606	71	-0	1	2.45	-3	/S-7,2-3	0	-0.3
1967 StL-N	1	2	0	0	0	0	0	0	0	1	0	0	.000	.000	.000	.000	-102	-1	0	.00	-0	/S-1	0	-0.1
Total 2	14	13	1	3	0	0	0	1	1	6	0	0	.231	.286	.231	.516	46	-1	1	1.83	-3	/S-8,2-3	0	-0.4
• WILLIAMS, Keith	David Keith Williams b: 4/21/1972, Bedford, PA BR/TR, 6', 190 lbs. Deb: 6/7/1996																							
1996 SF-N	9	20	0	5	0	0	0	0	0	6	0	0	.250	.250	.250	.500	34	-2	1	2.25	0	/0-4(1-0-3)	0	-0.2
• WILLIAMS, Ken	Kenneth Roy Williams b: 6/28/1890, Grants Pass, OR d: 1/22/1959, Grants Pass, OR BL/TR, 6', 170 lbs. Deb: 7/14/1915 Career OF: 1132-158-10																							
1915 Cin-N	71	219	22	53	10	4	0	16	15	20	4	3	.242	.297	.324	.621	86	-4	22	3.34	4	0-62(54-8-0)	4	-0.4
1916 Cin-N	10	27	1	3	0	0	0	1	2	5	1	....	.111	.172	.111	.284	-12	-4	1	.72	1	0-10(8-1-0)	0	-0.3
1918 StL-A	2	1	0	0	0	0	0	1	1	0	0	....	.000	.500	.000	.500	52	0	0	.00	0	....	0	0.0
1919 StL-A	65	227	32	68	10	5	6	35	26	25	7	....	.300	.376	.467	.843	133	10	42	6.38	1	0-63(0-63-0)	10	0.7
1920 StL-A	141	521	90	160	34	13	10	72	41	26	18	8	.307	.362	.480	.842	118	14	91	6.09	2	*0-138(104-34-0)	17	0.9
1921 StL-A	146	547	115	190	31	7	24	117	74	42	20	17	.347	.429	.561	.990	142	34	130	8.71	1	*0-145(145-0-0)	27	2.2
1922 StL-A	153	585	128	194	34	11	**39**	**155**	74	31	37	20	.332	.413	.627	1.040	162	52	149	9.34	4	*0-153(137-17-0)	**30**	4.3
1923 StL-A	147	555	106	198	37	12	29	91	79	32	18	17	.357	.439	.623	1.062	168	52	148	10.25	3	*0-145(145-0-0)	29	4.2
1924 StL-A	114	398	78	129	21	4	18	84	69	17	20	11	.324	.425	.533	.958	137	24	93	8.44	1	*0-109(109-0-0)	18	1.6

YEAR TM-L	G	AB	R	H	2B	3B	HR	RBI	BB	SO	SB	CS	AVG	OBP	SLG	OPS	OPS+	BR/A	RC	RC/G	FR	G/POS	WS	TPW
1925 StL-A	102	411	83	136	31	5	25	105	37	14	10	5	.331	.390	**.613**	1.003	144	25	97	8.84	3	*0-102(102-0-0)	20	1.9
1926 StL-A	108	347	55	97	15	7	17	74	39	23	5	4	.280	.354	.510	.864	118	7	63	6.21	2	0-92(91-1-0)/2-1	12	0.2
1927 StL-A	131	423	70	136	23	6	17	74	57	30	9	7	.322	.403	.525	.928	135	21	90	7.74	4	*0-113(110-4-0)	18	1.6
1928 Bos-A	133	462	59	140	25	1	8	67	37	15	4	9	.303	.356	.413	.769	103	-1	66	5.08	-3	*0-127(127-0-0)	12	-1.3
1929 Bos-A	74	139	21	48	14	2	3	21	15	7	1	5	.345	.409	.540	.949	146	8	29	7.38	0	0-39(0-30-10)/1-2	5	0.6
Total 14	1397	4862	860	1552	285	77	196	913	566	287	154	106	.319	.393	.530	.924	135	240	1021	7.56	23	*0-1298/1-2,2-1	202	16.4

• WILLIAMS, Kenny

Kenneth Royal Williams b: 4/6/1964, Berkeley, CA BR/TR, 6'2", 187 lbs. Deb: 9/2/1986 Career OF: 71-189-111

YEAR TM-L	G	AB	R	H	2B	3B	HR	RBI	BB	SO	SB	CS	AVG	OBP	SLG	OPS	OPS+	BR/A	RC	RC/G	FR	G/POS	WS	TPW
1986 Chi-A	15	31	2	4	0	0	1	1	1	11	1	1	.129	.182	.226	.408	10	-4	1	.91	1	0-10(1-4-5)/D-1	0	-0.4
1987 Chi-A	116	391	48	110	18	2	11	50	10	83	21	10	.281	.315	.422	.737	91	-6	50	4.53	3	*0-115(0-111-4)	11	-0.5
1988 Chi-A	73	220	18	35	4	2	8	28	10	64	6	5	.159	.223	.305	.527	46	-18	15	2.01	-2	0-38(0-12-29),3-32/D-3	1	-2.0
1989 Det-A	94	258	29	53	5	1	6	23	18	63	9	4	.205	.270	.302	.573	63	-13	21	2.59	3	0-87(28-35-27)/1-1,D-1	3	-1.2
1990 Det-A	57	83	10	11	2	0	0	5	3	24	2	2	.133	.172	.157	.329	-7	-12	2	.83	4	0-47(17-13-19)/D-6	1	-1.0
Tor-A	49	72	13	14	6	1	0	8	7	18	7	2	.194	.275	.306	.581	59	-3	7	2.88	-1	0-30(15-9-8)/D-9	1	-0.5
Yr.	106	155	23	25	8	1	0	13	10	42	9	4	.161	.222	.226	.447	24	-16	9	1.76	3	0-77(32-22-27),D-15	2	-1.5
1991 Tor-A	13	29	5	6	2	0	1	3	4	5	1	0	.207	.324	.379	.703	90	-0	4	4.12	0	/0-9(1-1-8),D-2	1	0.0
Mon-N	34	70	11	19	5	2	0	1	3	22	2	1	.271	.311	.400	.711	100	-0	9	4.35	1	0-24(9-4-11)	1	0.1
Total 6	451	1154	136	252	42	8	27	119	56	290	49	25	.218	.271	.339	.610	65	-57	108	3.05	10	0-360/3-32,D-22,1-1	19	-5.5

• WILLIAMS, Mark

Mark Westley Williams b: 7/28/1953, Elmira, NY BL/TL, 6', 180 lbs. Deb: 5/20/1977

YEAR TM-L	G	AB	R	H	2B	3B	HR	RBI	BB	SO	SB	CS	AVG	OBP	SLG	OPS	OPS+	BR/A	RC	RC/G	FR	G/POS	WS	TPW
1977 Oak-A	3	2	0	0	0	0	0	1	1	1	0	0	.000	.333	.000	.333		-0	0	1.17	0	/0-1	0	0.0

• WILLIAMS, Matt

Matthew Derrick Williams b: 11/28/1965, Bishop, CA BR/TR, 6'2", 210 lbs. Deb: 4/11/1987

YEAR TM-L	G	AB	R	H	2B	3B	HR	RBI	BB	SO	SB	CS	AVG	OBP	SLG	OPS	OPS+	BR/A	RC	RC/G	FR	G/POS	WS	TPW
1987 SF-N	84	245	28	46	9	2	8	21	16	68	4	3	.188	.240	.339	.579	54	-18	19	2.40	11	S-70,3-17	5	0.0
1988 SF-N	52	156	17	32	6	1	8	19	8	41	0	1	.205	.253	.410	.663	91	-3	14	2.73	3	3-43,S-14	2	0.1
1989*SF-N	84	292	31	59	18	1	18	50	14	72	1	2	.202	.244	.455	.699	98	-4	30	3.38	4	3-73,S-30	7	0.2
1990 SF-N★	159	617	87	171	27	2	33	**122**	33	138	7	4	.277	.321	.488	.809	124	15	92	5.31	-2	*3-159	28	1.5
1991 SF-N	157	589	72	158	24	5	34	98	33	128	5	5	.268	.314	.499	.813	129	18	88	5.24	9	*3-155/S-4	22	2.9
1992 SF-N	146	529	58	120	13	5	20	66	39	109	7	7	.227	.287	.384	.671	94	-8	54	3.35	5	*3-144	11	-0.2
1993 SF-N	145	579	105	170	33	4	38	110	27	80	1	3	.294	.330	.561	.891	137	25	101	6.32	9	*3-144	28	3.6
1994 SF-N★	112	445	74	119	16	3	**43**	96	33	87	1	0	.267	.321	.607	.928	141	23	83	6.57	13	*3-110	18	3.7
1995 SF-N★	76	283	53	95	17	1	23	65	30	58	2	0	.336	.403	.647	1.050	177	31	72	9.74	9	3-74	20	4.1
1996 SF-N★	105	404	69	122	16	1	22	85	39	91	1	2	.302	.372	.510	.882	135	19	75	6.71	7	3-92,1-13/S-1	18	2.6
1997*Cle-A	151	596	86	157	32	3	32	105	34	108	12	4	.263	.308	.488	.796	100	-2	85	5.03	-1	*3-151	18	-0.2
1998 Ari-N	135	510	72	136	26	1	20	71	43	102	5	1	.267	.327	.439	.767	100	-1	69	4.71	15	*3-134	12	1.5
1999*Ari-N★	154	627	98	190	37	2	35	142	41	93	2	0	.303	.348	.536	.884	118	15	112	6.52	15	*3-153	26	3.0
2000 Ari-N	96	371	43	102	18	2	12	47	20	51	1	2	.275	.317	.431	.749	84	-11	47	4.48	7	3-94/D-1	7	-0.3
2001*Ari-N	106	408	58	112	30	0	16	65	22	70	1	0	.275	.316	.466	.782	93	-5	55	4.76	6	*3-102/S-2	10	0.2
2002*Ari-N	60	215	29	56	7	2	12	40	21	41	3	1	.260	.326	.479	.805	100	-0	32	5.03	-1	3-56	6	-0.1
2003 Ari-N	44	134	17	33	9	0	4	16	16	26	0	0	.246	.336	.403	.739	83	-3	19	4.94	-1	3-42	3	-0.3
Total 17	1866	7000	997	1878	338	35	378	1218	469	1363	53	35	.268	.319	.489	.808	113	89	1047	5.23	106	*3-1743,S-121/1-13,D-1	241	22.1

• WILLIAMS, Otto

Otto George Williams b: 11/2/1877, Newark, NJ d: 3/19/1937, Omaha, NE BR/TR, 5'8", 165 lbs. Deb: 10/5/1902 C

YEAR TM-L	G	AB	R	H	2B	3B	HR	RBI	BB	SO	SB	CS	AVG	OBP	SLG	OPS	OPS+	BR/A	RC	RC/G	FR	G/POS	WS	TPW
1902 StL-N	2	5	0	2	0	0	0	2	1	....	1	....	.400	.500	.400	.900	185	1	2	13.58	0	/S-2	0	0.0
1903 StL-N	53	187	10	38	4	2	0	9	9	....	6	....	.203	.240	.246	.486	40	-15	13	2.30	-7	S-52/2-1	1	-2.0
Chi-N	38	130	14	29	5	0	0	13	4	....	8	....	.223	.246	.262	.508	46	-9	11	2.78	6	S-26/2-7,1-3,3-1	2	-0.2
Yr.	91	317	24	67	9	2	0	22	13	....	14	....	.211	.242	.252	.495	42	-24	24	2.49	-1	S-78/2-8,1-3,3-1	3	-2.2
1904 Chi-N	57	185	21	37	4	1	0	8	13	....	9	....	.200	.256	.232	.489	51	-10	14	2.43	2	0-21(0-0-21),1-11,S-10/2-6,3	3	-0.9
1906 Was-A	20	51	3	7	0	0	0	2	2	....	0	....	.137	.185	.137	.322	1	-6	2	.89	-1	/S-8,2-6,1-2,3-1	0	-0.7
Total 4	170	558	48	113	13	3	0	34	29	....	24	....	.203	.244	.237	.481	43	-40	42	2.38	0	/S-98,0-21,2-20,1-16,3-8	6	-3.8

• WILLIAMS, Papa

Fred Williams b: 7/17/1913, Meridian, MS d: 11/2/1993, Meridian, MS BR/TR, 6'1", 200 lbs. Deb: 4/19/1945

YEAR TM-L	G	AB	R	H	2B	3B	HR	RBI	BB	SO	SB	CS	AVG	OBP	SLG	OPS	OPS+	BR/A	RC	RC/G	FR	G/POS	WS	TPW
1945 Cle-A	16	19	0	4	0	0	0	0	1	2	0	0	.211	.250	.211	.461	36	-2	1	1.96	0	/1-3	0	-0.1

• WILLIAMS, Reggie

Reginald Dewayne Williams b: 8/29/1960, Memphis, TN BR/TR, 5'11", 185 lbs. Deb: 9/2/1985 Career OF: 64-87-48

YEAR TM-L	G	AB	R	H	2B	3B	HR	RBI	BB	SO	SB	CS	AVG	OBP	SLG	OPS	OPS+	BR/A	RC	RC/G	FR	G/POS	WS	TPW
1985 LA-N	22	9	4	3	0	0	0	0	0	4	1	0	.333	.333	.333	.667	90	0	1	5.28	0	0-15(12-2-1)	0	0.0
1986 LA-N	128	303	35	84	14	2	4	32	23	57	9	3	.277	.332	.376	.709	102	1	37	4.18	-2	*0-124(26-79-35)	8	-0.3
1987 LA-N	39	36	6	4	0	0	0	4	5	9	1	1	.111	.220	.111	.331	-9	-6	1	.68	-1	0-30(16-6-9)	0	-0.8
1988 Cle-A	11	31	7	7	2	0	1	3	0	6	0	0	.226	.226	.387	.613	66	-2	2	2.01	0	0-11(10-0-3)	0	-0.1
Total 4	200	379	52	98	16	2	5	39	28	76	11	4	.259	.313	.351	.664	88	-6	41	3.61	-3	0-180	8	-1.3

• WILLIAMS, Reggie

Reginald Bernard Williams b: 5/5/1966, Laurens, SC BB/TR, 6'1", 180 lbs. Deb: 9/8/1992 Career OF: 33-21-24

YEAR TM-L	G	AB	R	H	2B	3B	HR	RBI	BB	SO	SB	CS	AVG	OBP	SLG	OPS	OPS+	BR/A	RC	RC/G	FR	G/POS	WS	TPW
1992 Cal-A	14	26	5	6	1	1	0	2	1	10	0	2	.231	.259	.346	.605	68	-2	2	2.10	0	0-12(0-12-0)/D-2	0	-0.2
1995 LA-N	15	11	2	1	0	0	0	1	2	3	0	0	.091	.231	.091	.322	-12	-2	0	.95	-1	0-15(10-1-4)	0	-0.3
1998 Ana-A	29	36	7	13	1	0	1	5	7	11	3	3	.361	.477	.472	.949	147	3	8	8.46	-1	0-24(19-5-2)/D-2	2	0.1
1999 Ana-A	30	63	8	14	1	2	1	6	5	21	2	1	.222	.290	.349	.639	62	-4	6	2.84	1	0-24(4-3-18)/D-4	1	-0.3
Total 4	88	136	22	34	3	3	2	14	15	45	5	6	.250	.333	.360	.694	82	-5	16	3.86	0	/0-75,D-8	3	-0.7

• WILLIAMS, Rinaldo

Rinaldo Lewis Williams b: 12/18/1893, Santa Cruz, CA d: 4/24/1966, Cottonwood, AZ BL/TR Deb: 10/8/1914

YEAR TM-L	G	AB	R	H	2B	3B	HR	RBI	BB	SO	SB	CS	AVG	OBP	SLG	OPS	OPS+	BR/A	RC	RC/G	FR	G/POS	WS	TPW
1914 Bro-F	4	15	1	4	2	0	0	0	0	0	0	....	.267	.267	.400	.667	88	-0	2	3.37	0	/3-4	1	0.0

• WILLIAMS, Rip

Alva Mitchell "Buff" Williams b: 1/31/1882, Carthage, IL d: 7/23/1933, Keokuk, IA BR/TR, 5'11.5", 187 lbs. Deb: 4/12/1911 Career OF: 0-1-5

YEAR TM-L	G	AB	R	H	2B	3B	HR	RBI	BB	SO	SB	CS	AVG	OBP	SLG	OPS	OPS+	BR/A	RC	RC/G	FR	G/POS	WS	TPW
1911 Bos-A	95	284	36	68	8	5	0	31	24	....	9	....	.239	.314	.303	.617	73	-10	31	3.46	-5	1-57,C-38	5	-1.3
1912 Was-A	60	157	14	50	11	4	0	22	7	....	2	....	.318	.352	.439	.791	125	4	24	5.79	4	C-48	9	1.2
1913 Was-A	66	106	9	30	6	2	1	12	9	16	3	....	.283	.339	.406	.745	115	2	15	4.87	1	C-18/1-9,0-5(0-1-4)	5	0.4
1914 Was-A	81	169	17	47	6	4	1	22	13	19	2	2	.278	.341	.379	.719	112	2	22	4.62	1	C-44/1-8,0-1	7	0.5
1915 Was-A	91	197	14	48	8	4	0	31	18	20	4	3	.244	.320	.325	.645	91	-3	23	3.64	2	C-40,1-15/3-1	6	0.2
1916 Was-A	76	202	16	54	10	2	0	20	15	19	5	....	.267	.324	.337	.661	99	-1	25	4.12	-5	1-34,C-23/3-1	6	-0.5
1918 Cle-A	28	71	5	17	2	2	0	7	9	6	2	....	.239	.325	.324	.649	87	-1	9	3.62	-2	1-21/C-1	1	-0.4
Total 7	497	1186	111	314	51	23	2	145	95	80	27	5	.265	.328	.352	.680	97	-7	149	4.17	-4	C-212,1-144/0-6,3-2	39	0.1

• WILLIAMS, Ted

Theodore Samuel "The Kid,The Thumper,The Splendid Splinter,Teddy Ballgame" Williams
b: 8/30/1918, San Diego, CA d: 7/5/2002, Inverness, FL BL/TR, 6'3", 205 lbs. Deb: 4/20/1939 M HOF: 1966 Career OF: 1984-0-169

YEAR TM-L	G	AB	R	H	2B	3B	HR	RBI	BB	SO	SB	CS	AVG	OBP	SLG	OPS	OPS+	BR/A	RC	RC/G	FR	G/POS	WS	TPW
1939 Bos-A	149	565	131	185	44	11	31	**145**	107	64	2	1	.327	.436	.609	1.045	158	52	157	10.74	4	*0-149(0-0-149)	32	4.4
1940 Bos-A★	144	561	**134**	193	43	14	23	113	96	54	4	4	.344	**.442**	.594	1.036	159	53	154	10.76	1	*0-143(128-0-16)/P-1	30	4.2
1941 Bos-A★	143	456	**135**	185	33	3	**37**	120	**147**	27	2	4	**.406**	**.553**	**.735**	**1.287**	**232**	**100**	203	**19.24**	-2	*0-133(130-0-4)	**42**	**8.8**
1942 Bos-A★	150	522	**141**	186	34	5	**36**	**137**	**145**	51	3	2	**.356**	**.499**	**.648**	**1.147**	**214**	**90**	185	**14.27**	7	*0-150(150-0-0)	**46**	**9.0**
1946*Bos-A★	150	514	**142**	176	37	8	38	123	**156**	44	0	0	.342	**.497**	**.667**	**1.164**	**211**	**89**	188	**14.51**	3	*0-150(150-0-0)	**49**	**8.4**
1947 Bos-A★	156	528	**125**	181	40	9	**32**	**114**	**162**	47	0	1	**.343**	**.499**	**.634**	**1.133**	**199**	**83**	186	**14.01**	-1	*0-156(156-0-0)	**44**	**7.3**
1948 Bos-A★	137	509	124	188	**44**	3	25	127	**126**	41	4	0	**.369**	**.497**	**.615**	**1.112**	**185**	**72**	172	**13.99**	1	*0-134(134-0-0)	**39**	6.1
1949 Bos-A★	155	566	**150**	194	**39**	3	**43**	**159**	**162**	48	1	1	.343	**.490**	**.650**	**1.141**	**187**	**80**	193	**13.19**	-1	*0-155(155-0-0)	**40**	**6.6**
1950 Bos-A★	89	334	82	106	24	1	28	97	82	21	3	0	.317	.452	.647	1.099	163	35	103	11.63	-5	0-86(86-0-0)	19	2.2
1951 Bos-A★	148	531	109	169	28	4	30	126	**144**	45	1	1	.318	**.464**	**.556**	**1.019**	159	**53**	152	**11.02**	5	*0-147(147-0-0)	**34**	**4.6**
1952 Bos-A	6	10	2	4	0	1	1	3	2	2	0	0	.400	.500	.900	1.400	264	2	5	21.93	-0	/0-2(2-0-0)	1	0.2
1953 Bos-A★	37	91	17	37	6	0	13	34	19	10	0	1	.407	.509	.901	1.410	260	21	44	21.06	0	0-26(26-0-0)	9	1.9
1954 Bos-A★	117	386	93	133	23	1	29	89	**136**	32	0	0	.345	**.516**	**.635**	**1.151**	**193**	**62**	139	**14.16**	-1	*0-115(115-0-0)	29	5.6
1955 Bos-A★	98	320	77	114	21	3	28	83	91	24	2	0	.356	.501	.703	1.204	203	53	118	14.65	0	0-93(93-0-0)	23	4.8
1956 Bos-A★	136	400	71	138	28	2	24	82	102	39	0	0	.345	**.479**	.605	1.084	164	44	121	11.83	-1	*0-110(110-0-0)	25	3.6
1957 Bos-A★	132	420	96	163	28	1	38	87	119	43	0	1	**.388**	**.528**	**.731**	**1.259**	**227**	84	167	**16.64**	-2	*0-125(125-0-0)	38	7.8
1958 Bos-A★	129	411	81	135	23	2	26	85	98	49	1	0	**.328**	**.462**	.584	**1.046**	174	49	112	10.13	-6	*0-114(114-0-0)	25	3.9
1959 Bos-A★	103	272	32	69	15	0	10	43	52	27	0	0	.254	.377	.419	.796	113	7	45	5.68	-1	0-76(76-0-0)	9	0.3

YEAR TM-L	G	AB	R	H	2B	3B	HR	RBI	BB	SO	SB	CS	AVG	OBP	SLG	OPS	OPS+	BR/A	RC	RC/G	FR	G/POS	WS	TPW
1960 Bos-A★	113	310	56	98	15	0	29	72	75	41	1	1	.316	.454	.645	1.099	187	41	95	11.53	0	0-87(87-0-0)	21	3.7
Total 19	2292	7706	1798	2654	525	71	521	1839	2021	709	24	17	.344	.483	.634	1.116	187	1069	2539	12.96	1	*0-2151/P-1	555	93.5

• WILLIAMS, Walt Walter Allen "No Neck" Williams b: 12/19/1943, Brownwood, TX BR/TR, 5'6", 185 lbs. Deb: 4/21/1964 C Career OF: 242-13-338

YEAR TM-L	G	AB	R	H	2B	3B	HR	RBI	BB	SO	SB	CS	AVG	OBP	SLG	OPS	OPS+	BR/A	RC	RC/G	FR	G/POS	WS	TPW
1964 Hou-N	10	9	1	0	0	0	0	0	0	2	1	0	.000	.000	.000	.000	-106	-2	0	.00	0	/0-5(5-0-0)	0	-0.3
1967 Chi-A	104	275	35	66	16	3	3	15	17	20	3	2	.240	.289	.353	.642	92	-3	27	3.29	2	0-73(59-0-21)	7	-0.7
1968 Chi-A	63	133	6	32	6	0	1	8	4	17	0	1	.241	.273	.308	.582	75	-5	10	2.52	1	0-34(9-0-28)	1	-0.7
1969 Chi-A	135	471	59	143	22	1	3	32	26	33	6	2	.304	.344	.374	.718	96	-2	62	4.88	5	*0-111(34-0-83)	12	-0.3
1970 Chi-A	110	315	43	79	18	1	3	15	19	30	3	3	.251	.298	.343	.640	73	-12	32	3.45	2	0-79(13-3-64)	4	-1.5
1971 Chi-A	114	361	43	106	17	3	8	35	24	27	5	5	.294	.346	.424	.770	114	5	52	5.14	2	0-90(35-0-62)/3-1	11	0.2
1972 Chi-A	77	221	22	55	7	1	2	11	13	20	6	1	.249	.291	.317	.607	79	-5	21	3.29	1	0-57(5-0-53)/3-1	5	-0.8
1973 Cle-A	104	350	43	101	15	1	8	38	14	29	9	4	.289	.318	.406	.724	101	-1	43	4.34	3	0-61(61-0-0),D-26	9	-0.2
1974 NY-A	43	53	5	6	0	0	0	3	1	10	1	0	.113	.130	.113	.243	-31	-9	1	.29	0	0-24(13-0-13)/D-3	0	-0.9
1975 NY-A	82	185	27	52	5	1	5	16	8	23	0	1	.281	.321	.400	.721	106	0	23	4.34	-2	0-31(8-10-14),D-17/2-6	4	-0.3
Total 10	842	2373	284	640	106	11	33	173	126	211	34	19	.270	.311	.365	.677	90	-34	270	3.97	13	0-565/D-46,2-6,3-2	53	-5.4

• WILLIAMS, Wash Washington J. Williams b: Philadelphia, PA d: 8/9/1892, Philadelphia, PA, 5'11", 180 lbs. Deb: 8/5/1884 U Career OF: 0-0-3

YEAR TM-L	G	AB	R	H	2B	3B	HR	RBI	BB	SO	SB	CS	AVG	OBP	SLG	OPS	OPS+	BR/A	RC	RC/G	FR	G/POS	WS	TPW
1884 Ric-a	2	8	0	2	0	0	0	0	0	....	....	....	.250	.250	.250	.500	64	-0	1	2.35	-1	/0-2(0-0-2)	0	-0.1
1885 Chi-N	1	4	0	1	0	0	0	0	0	0	....	....	.250	.250	.250	.500	54	-0	0	2.31	0	/0-1,P-1	0	-0.3
Total 2	3	12	0	3	0	0	0	0	0	0	....	....	.250	.250	.250	.500	61	-1	1	2.33	-1	/0-3,P-1	0	-0.4

• WILLIAMS, Woody Woodrow Wilson Williams b: 8/21/1912, Pamplin, VA d: 2/24/1995, Appomattox, VA BR/TR, 5'11", 175 lbs. Deb: 9/5/1938

YEAR TM-L	G	AB	R	H	2B	3B	HR	RBI	BB	SO	SB	CS	AVG	OBP	SLG	OPS	OPS+	BR/A	RC	RC/G	FR	G/POS	WS	TPW
1938 Bro-N	20	51	6	17	1	1	0	6	4	1	1	....	.333	.382	.392	.774	111	1	8	6.38	-3	S-18/3-1	2	-0.1
1943 Cin-N	30	69	8	26	2	1	0	11	1	3	0	....	.377	.386	.435	.820	139	3	11	6.24	-3	2-12/3-7,S-5	4	0.1
1944 Cin-N	155	653	73	157	23	3	1	35	44	24	7	....	.240	.290	.289	.580	66	-30	56	2.96	19	*2-155	15	-0.2
1945 Cin-N	133	482	46	114	14	0	0	27	39	24	6	....	.237	.296	.266	.562	58	-27	40	2.80	-4	*2-133	7	-2.4
Total 4	338	1255	133	314	40	5	1	79	88	52	14	....	.250	.301	.292	.594	69	-53	115	3.18	10	2-300/S-23,3-8	28	-2.6

• WILLIAMSON, Antone Anthony Joseph Williamson b: 7/18/1973, Harbor City, CA BR/TR, 6'1", 195 lbs. Deb: 5/31/1997

YEAR TM-L	G	AB	R	H	2B	3B	HR	RBI	BB	SO	SB	CS	AVG	OBP	SLG	OPS	OPS+	BR/A	RC	RC/G	FR	G/POS	WS	TPW
1997 Mil-A	24	54	2	11	3	0	0	6	4	8	0	1	.204	.259	.259	.518	35	-6	3	1.81	-1	1-14/D-4	0	-0.8

• WILLIAMSON, Howie Nathaniel Howard Williamson b: 12/23/1904, Little Rock, AR d: 8/15/1969, Texarkana, AR BL/TL, 6', 170 lbs. Deb: 7/7/1928

YEAR TM-L	G	AB	R	H	2B	3B	HR	RBI	BB	SO	SB	CS	AVG	OBP	SLG	OPS	OPS+	BR/A	RC	RC/G	FR	G/POS	WS	TPW
1928 StL-N	10	9	0	2	0	0	0	0	1	4	0	....	.222	.300	.222	.522	38	-1	1	2.34	0	....	0	-0.1

• WILLIAMSON, Ned Edward Nagle Williamson b: 10/24/1857, Philadelphia, PA d: 3/3/1894, Mountain Valley Springs, AR BR/TR, 5'11", 210 lbs. Deb: 5/1/1878 U

YEAR TM-L	G	AB	R	H	2B	3B	HR	RBI	BB	SO	SB	CS	AVG	OBP	SLG	OPS	OPS+	BR/A	RC	RC/G	FR	G/POS	WS	TPW
1878 Ind-N	63	250	31	58	10	2	1	19	5	15	....	....	.232	.247	.300	.547	91	-1	19	2.72	-3	*3-63	6	-0.1
1879 Chi-N	80	320	66	94	20	13	1	36	24	31	....	....	.294	.343	.447	.790	149	17	50	6.23	16	*3-70/1-6,C-4	17	3.2
1880 Chi-N	75	311	65	78	20	2	0	31	15	26	....	....	.251	.285	.328	.613	101	0	30	3.52	13	*3-63,C-11/2-3	12	1.4
1881 Chi-N	82	343	56	92	12	6	1	48	19	19	....	....	.268	.307	.347	.654	98	-1	37	4.02	19	*3-76/2-4,P-3,S-2,C-1	14	2.1
1882 Chi-N	83	348	66	98	27	4	3	60	27	21	....	....	.282	.333	.408	.741	135	14	49	5.34	19	*3-83/P-1	16	3.1
1883 Chi-N	98	402	83	111	**49**	5	2	59	22	48	....	....	.276	.314	.438	.751	116	6	57	5.35	12	*3-97/C-3,P-1	16	1.8
1884 Chi-N	107	417	84	116	18	8	**27**	84	42	56	....	....	.278	.344	.554	.898	164	29	82	7.45	16	*3-99,C-10/P-2	19	4.0
1885*Chi-N	113	407	87	97	16	5	3	65	**75**	60	....	....	.238	.357	.324	.681	106	5	48	4.21	6	*3-113/P-2,C-1	21	1.5
1886*Chi-N	121	430	69	93	17	8	6	58	80	71	13	....	.216	.339	.335	.674	92	-3	55	4.37	-6	*S-121/C-4,P-2	14	-0.4
1887 Chi-N	127	512	77	190	20	14	9	78	73	57	45	....	.371	.377	.437	.815	111	7	92	7.54	-41	*S-127/P-1	13	-2.6
1888 Chi-N	132	452	75	113	9	14	8	73	65	71	25	....	.250	.352	.385	.737	126	15	72	5.72	-25	*S-132	20	-0.5
1889 Chi-N	47	173	16	41	3	1	1	30	23	22	2	....	.237	.340	.283	.623	71	-6	18	3.57	-18	S-47	3	-1.9
1890 Chi-P	73	261	34	51	7	3	2	26	36	35	3	....	.195	.311	.268	.580	53	-17	23	3.00	-14	3-52,S-21	2	-2.4
Total 13	1201	4626	809	1232	228	85	64	667	506	532	88	....	.266	.332	.384	.716	112	66	630	5.05	-5	3-716,S-450/C-34,P-12,2-7,1	173	9.1

• WILLIGROD, Julius Julius Willigrod b: 1857, Marshalltown, IA d: 9/27/1906, San Francisco, CA BL Deb: 7/15/1882

YEAR TM-L	G	AB	R	H	2B	3B	HR	RBI	BB	SO	SB	CS	AVG	OBP	SLG	OPS	OPS+	BR/A	RC	RC/G	FR	G/POS	WS	TPW
1882 Det-N	1	3	0	1	0	0	0	1	0	1	....	....	.333	.333	.333	.667	115	0	0	4.70	0	/S-1	0	0.0
Cle-N	9	36	5	5	1	1	0	2	3	7	....	....	.139	.205	.222	.427	38	-2	2	1.49	-1	/0-9(0-9-1)	0	-0.4
Yr.	10	39	5	6	1	1	0	3	3	8	....	....	.154	.214	.231	.445	44	-2	2	1.69	-1	/0-9(0-9-1),S-1	0	-0.3

• WILLINGHAM, Hugh Thomas Hugh Willingham b: 5/30/1906, Dalhart, TX d: 6/15/1988, El Reno, OK BR/TR, 6', 180 lbs. Deb: 9/13/1930

YEAR TM-L	G	AB	R	H	2B	3B	HR	RBI	BB	SO	SB	CS	AVG	OBP	SLG	OPS	OPS+	BR/A	RC	RC/G	FR	G/POS	WS	TPW
1930 Chi-A	3	4	2	1	0	0	0	0	2	1	0	0	.250	.500	.250	.750	100	0	1	6.44	-0	/2-1	0	0.0
1931 Phi-N	23	35	5	9	2	1	1	3	2	9	0	....	.257	.297	.457	.754	93	-1	5	4.78	-4	/S-8,3-2,0-1	0	-0.4
1932 Phi-N	4	2	0	0	0	0	0	0	0	0	0	....	.000	.000	.000	.000	-89	-1	0	.00	0	....	0	-0.1
1933 Phi-N	1	1	0	0	0	0	0	0	0	0	0	....	.000	.000	.000	.000	-89	-0	0	.00	0	....	0	0.0
Total 4	31	42	7	10	2	1	1	3	4	10	0	0	.238	.304	.405	.709	82	-1	6	4.49	-4	/S-8,3-2,2-1,0-1	0	-0.5

• WILLS, Wills Deb: 5/14/1884

YEAR TM-L	G	AB	R	H	2B	3B	HR	RBI	BB	SO	SB	CS	AVG	OBP	SLG	OPS	OPS+	BR/A	RC	RC/G	FR	G/POS	WS	TPW
1884 Was-a	4	15	1	2	2	0	0	0	0	....	....	....	.133	.133	.267	.400	31	-1	1	1.16	2	/0-4(1-3-0)	0	0.0
KC-U	5	21	2	3	1	0	0	....	0	....	....	....	.143	.143	.190	.333	13	-2	1	.91	1	/0-5(0-5-0)	0	-0.1

• WILLS, Bump Elliott Taylor Wills b: 7/27/1952, Washington, DC BB/TR, 5'9", 177 lbs. Deb: 4/7/1977

YEAR TM-L	G	AB	R	H	2B	3B	HR	RBI	BB	SO	SB	CS	AVG	OBP	SLG	OPS	OPS+	BR/A	RC	RC/G	FR	G/POS	WS	TPW
1977 Tex-A	152	541	87	155	28	6	9	62	65	96	28	12	.287	.363	.410	.773	109	10	83	5.32	9	*2-150/S-2,1-1,D-1	22	2.6
1978 Tex-A	157	539	78	135	17	4	9	57	63	91	52	14	.250	.333	.347	.680	91	1	68	4.15	9	*2-156	19	1.8
1979 Tex-A	146	543	90	148	21	3	5	46	53	58	35	11	.273	.342	.350	.692	88	-5	68	4.23	7	*2-146	15	1.0
1980 Tex-A	146	578	102	152	31	5	5	58	51	71	34	9	.263	.326	.360	.686	90	-4	73	4.20	3	*2-144	16	0.7
1981 Tex-A	102	410	51	103	13	2	2	41	32	49	12	9	.251	.307	.307	.614	82	-11	38	3.08	-4	*2-101/D-1	9	-0.9
1982 Chi-N	128	419	64	114	18	4	6	38	46	76	35	10	.272	.351	.377	.728	101	5	61	5.04	-6	*2-103	13	0.4
Total 6	831	3030	472	807	128	24	36	302	310	441	196	65	.266	.338	.360	.698	94	-3	390	4.35	18	2-800/D-2,S-2,1-1	94	5.7

• WILLS, Dave Davis Bowles Wills b: 1/26/1877, Charlottesville, VA d: 10/12/1959, Washington, DC BL/TL Deb: 6/8/1899

YEAR TM-L	G	AB	R	H	2B	3B	HR	RBI	BB	SO	SB	CS	AVG	OBP	SLG	OPS	OPS+	BR/A	RC	RC/G	FR	G/POS	WS	TPW
1899 Lou-N	24	94	15	21	3	1	0	12	2	....	1	....	.223	.240	.277	.516	41	-8	7	2.41	-2	1-24	0	-0.9

• WILLS, Maury Maurice Morning Wills b: 10/2/1932, Washington, DC BB/TR, 5'11", 170 lbs. Deb: 6/6/1959 M

YEAR TM-L	G	AB	R	H	2B	3B	HR	RBI	BB	SO	SB	CS	AVG	OBP	SLG	OPS	OPS+	BR/A	RC	RC/G	FR	G/POS	WS	TPW
1959*LA-N	83	242	27	63	5	2	0	7	13	27	7	3	.260	.298	.298	.596	55	-15	22	3.09	-1	S-82	5	-1.0
1960 LA-N	148	516	75	152	15	2	0	27	35	47	**50**	12	.295	.343	.331	.674	80	-7	62	4.27	15	*S-145	16	2.0
1961 LA-N★	148	613	105	173	12	10	1	31	59	50	**35**	15	.282	.346	.339	.686	76	-18	77	4.36	10	*S-148	21	0.5
1962 LA-N★	165	695	130	208	13	**10**	6	48	51	57	**104**	13	.299	.349	.373	.722	100	18	106	5.50	2	*S-165	32	3.5
1963*LA-N★	134	527	83	159	19	3	0	34	44	48	**40**	19	.302	.357	.349	.706	112	10	69	4.70	4	*S-109,3-33	27	2.5
1964 LA-N	158	630	81	173	15	5	2	34	41	73	**53**	17	.275	.319	.324	.643	88	-5	70	3.80	8	*S-149/3-6	20	1.7
1965*LA-N★	158	650	92	186	14	7	0	33	40	64	**94**	31	.286	.331	.329	.661	93	2	77	4.01	27	*S-155	28	4.5
1966*LA-N★	143	594	60	162	14	2	1	39	34	60	38	24	.273	.314	.308	.622	80	-18	57	3.25	7	*S-139/3-4	16	0.1
1967 Pit-N	149	616	92	186	12	9	3	45	31	44	29	10	.302	.336	.365	.702	100	2	78	4.56	4	*3-144/S-2	20	0.7
1968 Pit-N	153	627	76	174	12	6	0	31	45	57	52	21	.278	.327	.316	.643	95	-1	67	3.65	-14	*3-141,S-10	16	-1.6
1969 Mon-N	47	189	23	42	3	0	0	8	20	21	15	6	.222	.297	.238	.535	51	-11	15	2.53	1	S-46/2-1	2	-0.5
LA-N	104	434	57	129	7	8	4	39	39	40	25	15	.297	.357	.378	.734	114	7	59	4.87	6	*S-104	17	2.7
Yr.	151	623	80	171	10	8	4	47	59	61	40	21	.274	.338	.335	.674	95	-4	74	4.11	7	*S-150/2-1	19	2.2
1970 LA-N	132	522	77	141	19	3	0	34	50	34	28	13	.270	.334	.318	.652	79	-14	57	3.75	-10	*S-126/3-4	13	-0.9
1971 LA-N	149	601	73	169	14	3	3	44	40	44	15	8	.281	.326	.329	.656	91	-7	66	3.84	4	*S-144/3-4	19	1.4
1972 LA-N	71	132	16	17	3	1	0	4	10	18	1	1	.129	.190	.167	.357	2	-17	5	.96	1	S-31,3-26	1	-1.5
Total 14	1942	7588	1067	2134	177	71	20	458	552	684	586	208	.281	.331	.331	.662	88	-74	885	4.05	64	*S-1555,3-362/2-1	253	14.0

• WILLSON, Kid Frank Hoxie Willson b: 11/3/1895, Bloomington, NE d: 4/17/1964, Union Gap, WA BL/TL, 6'1", 190 lbs. Deb: 7/2/1918

YEAR TM-L	G	AB	R	H	2B	3B	HR	RBI	BB	SO	SB	CS	AVG	OBP	SLG	OPS	OPS+	BR/A	RC	RC/G	FR	G/POS	WS	TPW
1918 Chi-A	4	1	2	0	0	0	0	0	1	1	0	....	.000	.500	.000	.500	50	0	0	3.54	0	....	0	0.0
1927 Chi-A	7	10	1	1	0	0	0	1	0	2	0	0	.100	.100	.100	.200	-49	-2	0	.28	0	/0-2(1-1-0)	0	-0.2
Total 2	11	11	3	1	0	0	0	1	1	3	0	0	.091	.167	.091	.258	-26	-2	0	.87	0	/0-2	0	-0.2

• WILMOT, Walt Walter Robert Wilmot b: 10/18/1863, Plover, WI d: 2/1/1929, Chicago, IL BB/TR, 5'9" Deb: 4/20/1888 U Career OF: 743-184-32

YEAR TM-L	G	AB	R	H	2B	3B	HR	RBI	BB	SO	SB	CS	AVG	OBP	SLG	OPS	OPS+	BR/A	RC	RC/G	FR	G/POS	WS	TPW
1888 Was-N	119	473	61	106	16	9	4	43	23	55	46	....	.224	.263	.321	.584	90	-5	53	3.93	7	*O-119(119-0-0)	12	-0.2
1889 Was-N	108	432	88	125	19	**19**	9	57	51	32	40	....	.289	.367	.484	.851	146	26	94	8.09	11	*O-108(107-1-0)	17	2.9
1890 Chi-N	139	571	114	159	15	13	**13**	99	64	44	76	....	.278	.353	.419	.772	120	13	114	7.34	11	*O-139(27-112-0)	26	1.6
1891 Chi-N	121	498	102	137	14	10	11	71	55	21	42	....	.275	.353	.410	.763	122	13	89	6.66	0	*O-121(62-60-0)	21	0.8
1892 Chi-N	92	380	47	82	7	7	2	35	40	20	31	....	.216	.297	.287	.584	76	-11	43	3.86	1	O-92(92-0-0)	8	-1.7
1893 Chi-N	94	392	69	118	14	14	3	61	40	8	39	....	.301	.367	.431	.798	113	7	78	7.57	-3	*O-93(84-10-0)	11	-0.4
1894 Chi-N	135	604	136	199	45	12	5	130	36	27	76	....	.329	.368	.469	.837	96	-8	135	8.70	-10	*O-133(133-0-0)	13	-2.3
1895 Chi-N	108	466	86	132	16	6	8	72	30	19	28	....	.283	.327	.395	.721	80	-17	72	5.65	1	*O-108(108-0-0)	10	-2.1
1897 NY-N	11	34	8	9	2	0	1	4	2	....	1	....	.265	.306	.412	.717	91	-1	5	4.89	0	/O-9(5-1-3)	1	-0.1
1898 NY-N	35	138	16	33	4	2	2	22	9	....	4	....	.239	.286	.341	.626	82	-4	15	3.75	-1	O-34(6-0-29)	3	-0.7
Total 10	962	3988	727	1100	152	92	58	594	350	226	383	....	.276	.337	.404	.741	105	13	698	6.40	18	O-956	122	-2.0

• WILSON, Archie Archie Clifton Wilson b: 11/25/1923, Los Angeles, CA BR/TR, 5'11", 175 lbs. Deb: 9/18/1951 Career OF: 16-12-11

YEAR TM-L	G	AB	R	H	2B	3B	HR	RBI	BB	SO	SB	CS	AVG	OBP	SLG	OPS	OPS+	BR/A	RC	RC/G	FR	G/POS	WS	TPW
1951 NY-A	4	4	0	0	0	0	0	0	0	0	0	0	.000	.200	.000	.200	-44	-1	0	.00	0	/O-2(0-0-2)	0	-0.1
1952 NY-A	3	2	0	1	0	0	0	1	0	0	0	0	.500	.500	.500	1.000	190	0	1	13.84	0	....	0	0.0
Was-A	26	96	8	20	2	3	0	14	5	11	0	0	.208	.255	.292	.547	54	-6	5	1.72	-1	O-24(14-10-0)	1	-0.9
Bos-A	18	38	1	10	3	0	0	2	2	3	0	0	.263	.300	.342	.642	73	-1	4	3.05	1	O-13(2-2-9)	0	-0.1
Yr.	47	136	9	31	5	3	0	17	7	14	0	0	.228	.271	.309	.580	61	-7	9	2.18	-1	O-37(16-12-9)	1	-1.0
Total 2	51	140	9	31	5	3	0	17	7	14	0	0	.221	.268	.300	.568	57	-8	9	2.09	-1	/O-39	1	-1.1

• WILSON, Art Arthur Earl "Dutch" Wilson b: 12/11/1885, Macon, IL d: 6/12/1960, Chicago, IL BR/TR, 5'8", 170 lbs. Deb: 9/29/1908

YEAR TM-L	G	AB	R	H	2B	3B	HR	RBI	BB	SO	SB	CS	AVG	OBP	SLG	OPS	OPS+	BR/A	RC	RC/G	FR	G/POS	WS	TPW
1908 NY-N	1	0	0	0	0	0	0	0	0	....	0	....	....	....	....	....	-95	0	0	....	0	....	0	0.0
1909 NY-N	19	42	4	10	2	1	0	5	4	....	0	....	.238	.304	.333	.638	96	-0	4	3.34	0	C-19	1	0.1
1910 NY-N	26	52	10	14	4	1	0	5	9	6	2	....	.269	.387	.385	.772	125	2	9	5.56	0	C-25/1-1	3	0.4
1911*NY-N	66	109	17	33	9	1	1	17	19	12	6	....	.303	.411	.431	.842	132	6	22	7.07	-5	C-64	6	0.3
1912*NY-N	65	121	17	35	6	0	3	19	13	14	2	....	.289	.358	.413	.771	107	1	19	5.22	-7	C-61	5	-0.3
1913*NY-N	54	79	5	15	0	1	0	8	11	11	1	....	.190	.289	.215	.504	45	-5	5	1.97	0	C-49	1	-0.3
1914 Chi-F	137	440	78	128	31	8	10	64	70	80	13	....	.291	.394	.466	.860	153	33	84	6.54	5	*C-132	27	5.1
1915 Chi-F	96	269	44	82	11	2	7	31	65	38	8	....	.305	.442	.439	.880	169	28	56	7.20	-10	C-87	19	2.7
1916 Pit-N	53	128	11	33	5	2	1	12	13	27	4	....	.258	.331	.352	.683	109	2	17	4.37	-0	C-39	5	0.5
Chi-N	36	114	5	22	3	1	0	5	6	14	1	....	.193	.233	.237	.470	40	-8	7	1.89	-3	C-34	1	-0.9
Yr.	89	242	16	55	8	3	1	17	19	41	5	....	.227	.286	.298	.584	78	-7	24	3.18	-3	C-73	6	-0.4
1917 Chi-N	81	211	17	45	9	2	2	25	32	36	6	....	.213	.322	.303	.626	86	-2	22	3.35	2	C-75	8	0.6
1918 Bos-N	89	280	15	69	8	2	0	19	24	31	5	....	.246	.310	.289	.600	87	-4	26	3.10	-3	C-85	7	-0.1
1919 Bos-N	71	191	14	49	8	1	0	16	25	19	2	....	.257	.346	.309	.655	102	2	22	3.71	2	C-64/1-1	7	1.0
1920 Bos-N	16	19	0	1	0	0	0	0	1	1	0	0	.053	.143	.053	.195	-44	-3	0	.31	-2	/3-6,C-2	0	-0.6
1921 Cle-A	2	1	0	0	0	0	0	0	0	0	0	0	.000	.000	.000	.000	-98	-0	0	.00	0	/C-2	0	0.0
Total 14	812	2056	237	536	96	22	24	226	292	289	50	0	.261	.357	.364	.721	115	50	293	4.73	-21	C-738/3-6,1-2	90	8.4

• WILSON, Artie Arthur Lee Wilson b: 10/28/1920, Jefferson County, AL BL/TR, 5'10", 162 lbs. Deb: 4/18/1951

YEAR TM-L	G	AB	R	H	2B	3B	HR	RBI	BB	SO	SB	CS	AVG	OBP	SLG	OPS	OPS+	BR/A	RC	RC/G	FR	G/POS	WS	TPW
1951 NY-N	19	22	2	4	0	0	0	1	2	1	2	0	.182	.250	.182	.432	18	-2	1	2.12	0	/2-3,S-3,1-2	0	-0.2

• WILSON, Bill William G. Wilson b: 10/28/1867, Hannibal, MO d: 5/9/1924, St. Paul, MN TR Deb: 4/30/1890 U

YEAR TM-L	G	AB	R	H	2B	3B	HR	RBI	BB	SO	SB	CS	AVG	OBP	SLG	OPS	OPS+	BR/A	RC	RC/G	FR	G/POS	WS	TPW
1890 Pit-N	83	304	30	65	11	3	0	21	22	50	5	....	.214	.271	.270	.541	65	-12	24	2.68	6	C-38,O-25(4-8-13),1-18/S-1	1	-0.5
1897 Lou-N	107	389	44	83	12	4	1	41	18	....	9	....	.213	.257	.272	.530	41	-34	32	2.64	1	*C-103/3-1	3	-2.0
1898 Lou-N	29	102	5	17	1	2	1	13	5	....	3	....	.167	.213	.245	.458	32	-9	6	1.92	-1	C-28/1-1	1	-0.8
Total 3	219	795	79	165	24	9	2	75	45	50	17	....	.208	.257	.268	.525	49	-55	62	2.56	5	C-169/O-25,1-19,3-1,S-1	5	-3.2

• WILSON, Bill William Donald Wilson b: 11/6/1928, Central City, NE BR/TR, 6'2", 200 lbs. Deb: 9/24/1950 Career OF: 38-153-8

YEAR TM-L	G	AB	R	H	2B	3B	HR	RBI	BB	SO	SB	CS	AVG	OBP	SLG	OPS	OPS+	BR/A	RC	RC/G	FR	G/POS	WS	TPW
1950 Chi-A	3	6	0	0	0	0	0	0	2	2	0	0	.000	.250	.000	.250	-33	-1	0	.59	-0	/O-2(0-2-0)	0	-0.1
1953 Chi-A	9	17	1	1	0	0	0	1	0	7	0	0	.059	.111	.059	.170	-51	-4	0	.11	0	/O-3(0-3-0)	0	-0.4
1954 Chi-A	20	35	4	6	1	0	2	5	7	5	0	1	.171	.310	.371	.681	83	-1	3	2.55	-1	O-19(15-0-4)	0	-0.3
Phi-A	94	323	43	77	10	1	15	33	39	59	1	2	.238	.335	.415	.750	104	1	47	5.00	0	O-91(0-91-0)	11	-0.4
Yr.	114	358	47	83	11	1	17	38	46	64	1	3	.232	.333	.411	.743	102	0	50	4.71	-1	*O-110(15-91-4)	11	-0.7
1955 KC-A	98	273	39	61	12	0	15	38	24	63	1	1	.223	.289	.432	.721	91	-6	32	3.92	-4	O-82(23-57-4)/P-1	6	-1.2
Total 4	224	654	87	145	23	1	32	77	72	136	2	4	.222	.308	.407	.715	92	-10	83	4.18	-5	O-197/P-1	17	-2.4

• WILSON, Bob Robert Wilson b: 2/22/1925, Dallas, TX d: 4/23/1985, Dallas, TX BR/TR, 5'11", 197 lbs. Deb: 5/17/1958

YEAR TM-L	G	AB	R	H	2B	3B	HR	RBI	BB	SO	SB	CS	AVG	OBP	SLG	OPS	OPS+	BR/A	RC	RC/G	FR	G/POS	WS	TPW
1958 LA-N	3	5	0	1	0	0	0	0	0	1	0	0	.200	.200	.200	.400	6	-1	0	1.35	-0	/O-1	0	-0.1

• WILSON, Charlie Charles Woodrow "Swamp Baby" Wilson b: 1/13/1905, Clinton, SC d: 12/19/1970, Rochester, NY BB/TR, 5'10.5", 178 lbs. Deb: 4/14/1931

YEAR TM-L	G	AB	R	H	2B	3B	HR	RBI	BB	SO	SB	CS	AVG	OBP	SLG	OPS	OPS+	BR/A	RC	RC/G	FR	G/POS	WS	TPW
1931 Bos-N	16	58	7	11	4	0	1	11	3	5	0	....	.190	.230	.310	.540	45	-5	4	2.29	-1	3-14	0	-0.5
1932 StL-N	24	96	7	19	3	3	1	2	3	8	0	....	.198	.222	.323	.545	43	-8	7	2.30	-4	S-24	1	-1.0
1933 StL-N	1	1	0	0	0	0	0	0	0	1	0	....	.000	.000	.000	.000	-95	-0	0	.00	-1	/S-1	0	-0.1
1935 StL-N	16	31	1	10	0	0	0	1	2	2	0	....	.323	.364	.323	.686	83	-1	3	3.83	0	/3-8	1	0.0
Total 4	57	186	15	40	7	3	2	14	8	16	0	....	.215	.247	.317	.565	50	-14	14	2.52	-5	/S-25,3-22	2	-1.7

• WILSON, Chief John Owen Wilson b: 8/21/1883, Austin, TX d: 2/22/1954, Bertram, TX BL/TR, 6'2", 185 lbs. Deb: 4/15/1908 Career OF: 5-270-1010

YEAR TM-L	G	AB	R	H	2B	3B	HR	RBI	BB	SO	SB	CS	AVG	OBP	SLG	OPS	OPS+	BR/A	RC	RC/G	FR	G/POS	WS	TPW
1908 Pit-N	144	529	47	120	8	7	3	43	22	....	12	....	.227	.260	.285	.546	74	-17	42	2.57	-4	*O-144(1-34-109)	9	-3.2
1909*Pit-N	154	569	64	155	22	12	4	59	19	....	17	....	.272	.303	.374	.677	105	-0	69	4.13	4	*O-154(0-0-154)	19	-0.4
1910 Pit-N	146	536	59	148	14	13	4	50	21	68	8	....	.276	.312	.373	.685	94	-7	64	4.13	-1	*O-146(1-7-138)	14	-1.5
1911 Pit-N	148	544	72	163	34	12	12	**107**	41	55	10	....	.300	.353	.472	.826	126	15	93	6.11	3	*O-146(0-2-145)	22	1.0
1912 Pit-N	152	583	80	175	19	**36**	11	95	35	67	16	....	.300	.342	.513	.855	134	22	106	6.27	-2	*O-152(0-87-69)	24	1.1
1913 Pit-N	155	580	71	154	12	14	10	73	32	62	9	....	.266	.307	.386	.694	102	-1	68	3.98	-2	*O-155(0-3-153)	15	-1.2
1914 StL-N	154	580	64	150	27	12	9	73	32	66	14	....	.259	.302	.393	.695	107	2	69	4.09	14	*O-154(0-9-148)	18	0.7
1915 StL-N	107	348	33	96	13	6	3	39	19	43	8	15	.276	.321	.374	.694	110	-2	41	3.78	8	*O-105(3-70-33)	11	0.0
1916 StL-N	120	355	30	85	8	2	3	32	20	46	4	....	.239	.289	.299	.588	81	-8	33	3.08	-4	*O-113(0-58-61)	6	-2.0
Total 9	1280	4624	520	1246	157	114	59	571	241	407	98	15	.269	.311	.391	.702	105	3	585	4.29	15	*O-1269	138	-5.6

• WILSON, Craig Craig Alan Wilson b: 11/30/1976, Fountain Valley, CA BR/TR, 6'2", 217 lbs. Deb: 4/22/2001 Career OF: 9-0-127

YEAR TM-L	G	AB	R	H	2B	3B	HR	RBI	BB	SO	SB	CS	AVG	OBP	SLG	OPS	OPS+	BR/A	RC	RC/G	FR	G/POS	WS	TPW
2001 Pit-N	88	158	27	49	3	1	13	32	15	53	3	1	.310	.394	.589	.983	146	11	37	8.45	-2	1-26,O-14(1-0-13),C-10/D-2	8	0.7
2002 Pit-N	131	368	48	97	16	1	16	57	32	116	2	3	.264	.356	.443	.799	108	4	58	5.45	0	O-75(1-0-74),1-42/C-5,D-3	10	-0.2
2003 Pit-N	116	309	49	81	15	4	18	48	35	89	3	1	.262	.361	.511	.873	122	10	58	6.69	3	O-46(7-0-40),1-36,C-21/D-3	10	1.0
Total 3	335	835	124	227	34	6	47	137	82	258	8	5	.272	.365	.496	.861	121	26	153	6.46	2	O-135,1-104/C-36,D-8	28	1.6

• WILSON, Craig Craig Wilson b: 11/28/1964, Annapolis, MD BR/TR, 5'11", 175 lbs. Deb: 9/6/1989 Career OF: 13-0-10

YEAR TM-L	G	AB	R	H	2B	3B	HR	RBI	BB	SO	SB	CS	AVG	OBP	SLG	OPS	OPS+	BR/A	RC	RC/G	FR	G/POS	WS	TPW
1989 StL-N	6	4	1	1	0	0	0	1	1	2	0	0	.250	.400	.250	.650	87	0	1	4.54	-1	/3-2	0	-0.1
1990 StL-N	55	121	13	30	2	0	0	7	8	14	0	2	.248	.295	.264	.559	55	-8	8	2.06	1	3-13,O-13(7-0-7)/2-9,1-1	1	-0.8
1991 StL-N	60	82	5	14	2	0	0	13	6	10	0	0	.171	.227	.195	.422	20	-9	4	1.36	-1	3-12/O-5(5-0-0),1-4,2-3	0	-1.1
1992 StL-N	61	106	6	33	6	0	0	13	10	18	1	2	.311	.371	.368	.739	113	1	13	4.42	-1	3-18,2-11/O-3(0-0-3)	3	0.1
1993 KC-A	21	49	6	13	1	0	1	3	7	6	1	1	.265	.357	.347	.704	85	-1	7	4.70	1	3-15/2-1,O-1	2	0.0
Total 5	203	362	31	91	11	0	1	37	32	50	2	5	.251	.312	.290	.602	69	-17	32	2.90	-1	/3-60,2-24,O-22,1-5	6	-1.9

• WILSON, Craig Craig Franklin Wilson b: 9/3/1970, Chicago, IL BR/TR, 6', 185 lbs. Deb: 9/5/1998

YEAR TM-L	G	AB	R	H	2B	3B	HR	RBI	BB	SO	SB	CS	AVG	OBP	SLG	OPS	OPS+	BR/A	RC	RC/G	FR	G/POS	WS	TPW
1998 Chi-A	13	47	14	22	5	0	3	10	3	6	1	0	.468	.500	.766	1.266	229	9	18	17.68	0	/S-8,2-4,3-2	5	0.9
1999 Chi-A	98	252	28	60	8	1	4	26	23	22	1	1	.238	.302	.325	.627	60	-16	25	3.31	6	3-72,S-22/2-7,1-1	6	-0.7
2000 Chi-A	28	73	12	19	3	0	0	4	5	11	1	0	.260	.316	.301	.618	57	-5	6	2.70	6	3-15,S-10/2-4	1	0.2
Total 3	139	372	54	101	16	1	7	40	31	39	3	1	.272	.329	.376	.706	81	-11	50	4.54	12	/3-89,S-40,2-15,1-1	12	0.5

• WILSON, Dan

Daniel Allen Wilson b: 3/25/1969, Arlington Heights, IL BR/TR, 6'3", 190 lbs. Deb: 9/7/1992

YEAR TM-L	G	AB	R	H	2B	3B	HR	RBI	BB	SO	SB	CS	AVG	OBP	SLG	OPS	OPS+	BR/A	RC	RC/G	FR	G/POS	WS	TPW
1992 Cin-N	12	25	2	9	1	0	0	3	3	8	0	0	.360	.429	.400	.829	132	1	4	5.78	0	/C-9	1	0.2
1993 Cin-N	36	76	6	17	3	0	0	8	9	16	0	0	.224	.306	.263	.569	54	-5	6	2.63	0	C-35	1	-0.3
1994 Sea-A	91	282	24	61	14	2	3	27	10	57	1	2	.216	.246	.312	.558	42	-26	19	2.08	3	C-91	4	-1.5
1995*Sea-A	119	399	40	111	22	3	9	51	33	63	2	1	.278	.336	.416	.752	94	-5	54	4.76	1	*C-119	16	0.5
1996 Sea-A★	138	491	51	140	24	0	18	83	32	88	1	2	.285	.333	.444	.777	94	-7	69	4.85	3	*C-135	15	0.5
1997*Sea-A	146	508	66	137	31	1	15	74	39	72	7	2	.270	.328	.423	.751	95	-4	70	4.76	7	*C-144	21	1.2
1998 Sea-A	96	325	39	82	17	1	9	44	24	56	2	1	.252	.314	.394	.707	82	-9	41	4.16	-1	C-94	7	-0.3
1999 Sea-A	123	414	46	110	23	2	7	38	29	83	5	0	.266	.317	.382	.698	75	-15	50	4.13	1	*C-121/1-5	9	-0.5
2000*Sea-A	90	268	31	63	12	0	5	27	22	51	1	2	.235	.293	.336	.629	62	-16	25	3.02	-3	C-88/1-1,3-1	4	-1.3
2001*Sea-A	123	377	44	100	20	1	10	42	20	69	3	2	.265	.306	.403	.709	90	-7	46	4.21	-5	*C-122/1-2	14	-0.4
2002 Sea-A	115	359	35	106	16	1	6	44	18	81	1	0	.295	.332	.396	.728	96	-2	46	4.55	-6	*C-113/1-4	12	-0.1
2003 Sea-A	96	316	32	76	15	2	4	43	15	52	0	0	.241	.275	.339	.614	63	-18	28	2.99	-8	C-96	7	-1.8
Total 12	**1185**	**3840**	**416**	**1012**	**198**	**13**	**86**	**484**	**254**	**696**	**23**	**12**	**.264**	**.313**	**.389**	**.702**	**82**	**-112**	**458**	**4.05**	**-7**	***C-1167/1-12,3-1**	**111**	**-3.8**

• WILSON, Desi

Desi Bernard Wilson b: 5/9/1969, Glen Cove, NY BL/TL, 6'7", 230 lbs. Deb: 8/7/1996

YEAR TM-L	G	AB	R	H	2B	3B	HR	RBI	BB	SO	SB	CS	AVG	OBP	SLG	OPS	OPS+	BR/A	RC	RC/G	FR	G/POS	WS	TPW
1996 SF-N	41	118	10	32	2	0	2	12	12	27	0	2	.271	.338	.339	.677	83	-4	13	3.93	-1	1-33	2	-0.8

• WILSON, Eddie

Edward Francis Wilson b: 9/7/1909, Hamden, CT d: 4/11/1979, Hamden, CT BL/TL, 5'11", 165 lbs. Deb: 6/21/1936 Career OF: 0-1-67

YEAR TM-L	G	AB	R	H	2B	3B	HR	RBI	BB	SO	SB	CS	AVG	OBP	SLG	OPS	OPS+	BR/A	RC	RC/G	FR	G/POS	WS	TPW
1936 Bro-N	52	173	28	60	8	1	3	25	14	25	3	....	.347	.402	.457	.859	129	7	34	7.94	-4	0-47(0-0-47)	6	0.1
1937 Bro-N	36	54	11	12	4	1	1	8	17	14	1	....	.222	.408	.389	.797	116	2	11	6.69	-1	0-21(0-1-20)	2	0.0
Total 2	**88**	**227**	**39**	**72**	**12**	**2**	**4**	**33**	**31**	**39**	**4**	**....**	**.317**	**.404**	**.441**	**.844**	**126**	**10**	**44**	**7.60**	**-5**	**/0-68**	**8**	**0.1**

• WILSON, Enrique

Enrique (Martes) Wilson b: 7/27/1973, Santo Domingo, Dominican Republic BB/TR, 5'11", 160 lbs. Deb: 9/24/1997

YEAR TM-L	G	AB	R	H	2B	3B	HR	RBI	BB	SO	SB	CS	AVG	OBP	SLG	OPS	OPS+	BR/A	RC	RC/G	FR	G/POS	WS	TPW
1997 Cle-A	5	15	2	5	0	0	0	1	0	2	0	0	.333	.333	.333	.667	72	-1	2	4.50	0	/S-4,2-1	1	0.0
1998*Cle-A	32	90	13	29	6	0	2	12	4	8	2	4	.322	.358	.456	.813	106	-1	13	5.27	0	2-22,S-10/3-2	3	0.0
1999*Cle-A	113	332	41	87	22	1	2	24	25	41	5	4	.262	.316	.352	.668	67	-17	35	3.45	-7	3-61,S-35,2-21/D-1	3	-2.0
2000 Cle-A	40	117	16	38	9	0	2	12	7	11	2	1	.325	.363	.453	.816	103	0	19	6.03	-5	3-12/D-8,2-7,S-7	3	-0.4
Pit-N	40	122	11	32	6	1	3	15	11	13	0	1	.262	.323	.402	.725	82	-4	15	4.07	-4	3-16,2-11/S-8	2	-0.6
2001 Pit-N	46	129	7	24	3	0	1	8	3	23	0	3	.186	.205	.233	.437	12	-18	4	.93	2	S-28,2-10/3-2	1	-1.4
*NY-A	48	99	10	24	5	1	1	12	6	14	0	2	.242	.286	.343	.629	64	-6	9	2.80	5	S-20,3-19/2-7,D-1	2	-0.1
2002*NY-A	60	105	17	19	2	2	2	11	8	22	1	1	.181	.239	.295	.534	41	-9	7	2.10	2	3-26,S-14/2-7,D-1,0-1	1	-0.6
2003*NY-A	63	135	18	31	9	0	3	15	7	14	3	1	.230	.278	.363	.641	69	-6	13	3.24	-4	S-33,3-17,2-10/D-1	2	-0.7
Total 7	**447**	**1144**	**135**	**289**	**62**	**5**	**16**	**110**	**71**	**148**	**13**	**17**	**.253**	**.299**	**.358**	**.656**	**67**	**-63**	**117**	**3.36**	**-12**	**S-159,3-155/2-96,D-12,0-1**	**18**	**-5.8**

• WILSON, Frank

Francis Edward "Squash" Wilson b: 4/20/1901, Malden, MA d: 11/25/1974, Leicester, MA BL/TR, 6', 185 lbs. Deb: 6/20/1924 Career OF: 94-21-8

YEAR TM-L	G	AB	R	H	2B	3B	HR	RBI	BB	SO	SB	CS	AVG	OBP	SLG	OPS	OPS+	BR/A	RC	RC/G	FR	G/POS	WS	TPW
1924 Bos-N	61	215	20	51	7	0	1	15	23	22	3	4	.237	.311	.284	.595	63	-11	20	3.03	1	0-55(35-20-0)	3	-1.3
1925 Bos-N	12	31	3	13	1	1	0	0	4	1	2	1	.419	.486	.516	1.002	171	4	8	10.50	1	0-10(9-0-1)	2	0.3
1926 Bos-N	87	236	22	56	11	3	0	23	20	21	3	....	.237	.300	.309	.609	70	-10	22	3.07	1	0-56(50-1-6)	3	-1.3
1928 Cle-A	2	1	0	0	0	0	0	0	1	0	0	0	.000	.500	.000	.500	41	0	0	3.31	0	....	0	0.0
StL-A	6	5	1	0	0	0	0	0	0	0	0	0	.000	.000	.000	.000	-97	-1	0	.00	0	/0-1	0	-0.2
Yr.	8	6	1	0	0	0	0	0	1	0	0	0	.000	.143	.000	.143	-58	-1	0	.55	0	/0-1	0	-0.2
Total 4	**168**	**488**	**46**	**120**	**19**	**4**	**1**	**38**	**48**	**44**	**8**	**5**	**.246**	**.315**	**.307**	**.622**	**72**	**-18**	**50**	**3.40**	**3**	**0-122**	**8**	**-2.4**

• WILSON, Gary

James Garrett Wilson b: 1/12/1877, Baltimore, MD d: 5/1/1969, Randallstown, MD BR/TR, 5'7", 168 lbs. Deb: 9/27/1902

YEAR TM-L	G	AB	R	H	2B	3B	HR	RBI	BB	SO	SB	CS	AVG	OBP	SLG	OPS	OPS+	BR/A	RC	RC/G	FR	G/POS	WS	TPW
1902 Bos-A	2	8	0	1	0	0	0	1	0	....	0	....	.125	.125	.125	.250	-30	-1	0	.49	0	/2-2	0	-0.1

• WILSON, George

George Washington "Teddy" Wilson
b: 8/30/1925, Cherryville, NC d: 10/29/1974, Gastonia, NC BL/TR, 6'1.5", 185 lbs. Deb: 4/15/1952 Career OF: 19-1-16

YEAR TM-L	G	AB	R	H	2B	3B	HR	RBI	BB	SO	SB	CS	AVG	OBP	SLG	OPS	OPS+	BR/A	RC	RC/G	FR	G/POS	WS	TPW
1952 Chi-A	8	9	0	1	0	0	0	1	1	2	0	0	.111	.200	.111	.311	-12	-1	0	.87	-0	/0-1	0	-0.1
NY-N	62	112	9	27	7	0	2	16	3	14	0	0	.241	.261	.357	.618	69	-5	11	3.43	-2	0-21(16-1-4)/1-2	2	-0.9
1953 NY-N	11	8	0	1	0	0	0	0	2	2	0	0	.125	.364	.125	.489	34	-0	1	2.53	0	....	0	0.0
1956 NY-N	53	68	5	9	1	0	1	2	5	14	0	0	.132	.192	.191	.383	3	-9	3	1.13	0	/0-8(2-0-6)	0	-1.0
*NY-A	11	12	1	2	0	0	0	0	3	0	0	0	.167	.333	.167	.500	37	-1	1	2.50	-1	/0-6(1-0-5)	0	-0.2
Total 3	**145**	**209**	**15**	**40**	**8**	**0**	**3**	**19**	**14**	**32**	**0**	**0**	**.191**	**.246**	**.273**	**.518**	**40**	**-17**	**15**	**2.41**	**-3**	**/0-36,1-2**	**2**	**-2.2**

• WILSON, Glenn

Glenn Dwight Wilson b: 12/22/1958, Baytown, TX BR/TR, 6'1", 190 lbs. Deb: 4/15/1982 Career OF: 118-90-941

YEAR TM-L	G	AB	R	H	2B	3B	HR	RBI	BB	SO	SB	CS	AVG	OBP	SLG	OPS	OPS+	BR/A	RC	RC/G	FR	G/POS	WS	TPW
1982 Det-A	84	322	39	94	15	1	12	34	15	51	2	3	.292	.323	.457	.780	111	3	44	4.90	3	0-80(2-71-8)/D-4	10	0.4
1983 Det-A	144	503	55	135	25	6	11	65	25	79	1	1	.268	.307	.408	.715	97	-4	61	4.36	-5	*0-143(0-8-140)	12	-1.5
1984 Phi-N	132	341	28	82	21	3	6	31	17	56	7	1	.240	.279	.372	.651	80	-9	33	3.22	-3	*0-109(92-3-18)/3-4	4	-1.7
1985 Phi-N★	161	608	73	167	39	5	14	102	35	117	7	4	.275	.314	.424	.738	102	-1	73	4.16	15	*0-158(2-0-157)	15	0.6
1986 Phi-N	155	584	70	158	30	4	15	84	42	91	5	1	.271	.324	.413	.736	98	-2	76	4.58	10	*0-154(1-0-153)	17	0.0
1987 Phi-N	154	569	55	150	21	2	14	54	38	82	3	6	.264	.311	.381	.692	80	-20	62	3.74	4	*0-154(0-0-154)/P-1	10	-2.3
1988 Sea-A	78	284	28	71	10	1	3	17	15	52	1	1	.250	.288	.324	.612	68	-13	23	2.74	-2	0-75(0-0-75)/D-2	1	-1.7
Pit-N	37	126	11	34	8	0	2	15	3	18	0	0	.270	.292	.381	.673	93	-2	13	3.48	-1	0-35(0-4-32)	2	-0.4
1989 Pit-N	100	330	42	93	20	4	9	49	32	39	1	4	.282	.347	.448	.796	130	11	49	5.22	-3	0-85(0-1-85),1-10	14	0.5
Hou-N	28	102	8	22	6	0	2	15	5	14	0	1	.216	.252	.333	.586	68	-5	8	2.42	3	0-25(0-0-25)	2	-0.3
Yr.	128	432	50	115	26	4	11	64	37	53	1	5	.266	.326	.421	.747	116	6	57	4.52	-1	*0-110(0-1-110),1-10	16	0.2
1990 Hou-N	118	368	42	90	14	0	10	55	26	64	0	3	.245	.296	.364	.660	83	-11	35	3.15	6	*0-108(21-0-92)/1-1	7	-0.8
1993 Pit-N	10	14	0	2	0	0	0	0	0	9	0	0	.143	.143	.143	.286	-23	-2	0	.70	1	/0-5(0-3-2)	0	-0.2
Total 10	**1201**	**4151**	**451**	**1098**	**209**	**26**	**98**	**521**	**253**	**672**	**27**	**25**	**.265**	**.309**	**.398**	**.707**	**94**	**-57**	**479**	**3.97**	**27**	***0-1131/1-11,D-6,3-4,P-1**	**94**	**-7.5**

• WILSON, Grady

Grady Herbert Wilson b: 11/23/1922, Columbus, GA BR/TR, 6'.5", 170 lbs. Deb: 5/15/1948

YEAR TM-L	G	AB	R	H	2B	3B	HR	RBI	BB	SO	SB	CS	AVG	OBP	SLG	OPS	OPS+	BR/A	RC	RC/G	FR	G/POS	WS	TPW
1948 Pit-N	12	10	1	1	1	0	0	1	0	3	0	....	.100	.100	.200	.300	-20	-2	0	.60	-1	/S-7	0	-0.3

• WILSON, Hack

Lewis Robert Wilson
b: 4/26/1900, Ellwood City, PA d: 11/23/1948, Baltimore, MD BR/TR, 5'6", 190 lbs. Deb: 9/29/1923 HOF: 1979 Career OF: 190-925-148

YEAR TM-L	G	AB	R	H	2B	3B	HR	RBI	BB	SO	SB	CS	AVG	OBP	SLG	OPS	OPS+	BR/A	RC	RC/G	FR	G/POS	WS	TPW
1923 NY-N	3	10	0	2	0	0	0	0	0	1	0	0	.200	.200	.200	.400	6	-1	0	1.27	-1	/0-3(1-2-0)	0	-0.2
1924*NY-N	107	383	62	113	19	12	10	57	44	46	4	3	.295	.369	.486	.855	131	17	70	6.60	-5	*0-103(14-90-1)	16	0.8
1925 NY-N	62	180	28	43	7	4	6	30	21	33	5	2	.239	.322	.422	.744	92	-2	25	4.70	-3	0-50(27-23-4)	4	-0.6
1926 Chi-N	142	529	97	170	36	8	**21**	109	**69**	61	10	....	.321	.406	.539	**.944**	**150**	**38**	115	8.11	-1	*0-140(0-140-0)	26	**3.1**
1927 Chi-N	146	551	119	175	30	12	**30**	129	71	70	13	....	.318	.401	.579	.980	159	46	126	8.31	-2	*0-146(0-146-0)	31	3.7
1928 Chi-N	145	520	89	163	32	9	**31**	120	77	94	4	....	.313	.404	.588	.992	159	44	122	8.32	-7	*0-143(0-143-0)	28	3.1
1929*Chi-N	150	574	135	198	30	5	39	**159**	78	83	3	....	.345	.425	.618	1.044	155	49	148	9.81	0	*0-150(0-150-0)	32	4.0
1930 Chi-N	155	585	146	208	35	6	**56**	**191**	**105**	84	3	....	.356	.454	**.723**	**1.177**	**177**	**75**	189	**12.44**	-13	*0-155(0-155-0)	**35**	4.9
1931 Chi-N	112	395	66	103	22	4	13	61	63	69	1	....	.261	.362	.435	.798	112	8	66	5.91	-2	*0-103(40-60-3)	13	0.2
1932 Bro-N	135	481	77	143	37	5	23	123	51	85	2	....	.297	.366	.538	.904	142	28	97	7.33	0	*0-125(1-8-116)	21	2.1
1933 Bro-N	117	360	41	96	13	2	9	54	52	50	7	....	.267	.359	.389	.748	119	11	53	5.28	-6	0-90(75-8-7)/2-5	12	0.0
1934 Bro-N	67	172	24	45	5	0	6	27	40	33	0	....	.262	.401	.395	.796	120	7	30	6.18	1	0-43(27-0-16)	6	0.6
Phi-N	7	20	0	2	0	0	0	3	3	4	0	....	.100	.217	.100	.317	-11	-3	0	.50	0	/0-6(5-0-1)	0	-0.4
Yr.	74	192	24	47	5	0	6	30	43	37	0	....	.245	.383	.365	.748	107	4	31	5.43	1	0-49(32-0-17)	6	0.2
Total 12	**1348**	**4760**	**884**	**1461**	**266**	**67**	**244**	**1063**	**674**	**713**	**52**	**5**	**.307**	**.395**	**.545**	**.940**	**144**	**318**	**1042**	**7.96**	**-39**	***0-1257/2-5**	**224**	**21.4**

• WILSON, Henry

Henry C. Wilson b: 4/9/1877, Baltimore, MD Deb: 10/12/1898

YEAR TM-L	G	AB	R	H	2B	3B	HR	RBI	BB	SO	SB	CS	AVG	OBP	SLG	OPS	OPS+	BR/A	RC	RC/G	FR	G/POS	WS	TPW
1898 Bal-N	1	2	0	0	0	0	0	0	1	....	0	....	.000	.333	.000	.333	-2	-0	0	.00	0	/C-1	0	0.0

• WILSON, Icehouse

George Peacock Wilson b: 9/14/1912, Maricopa, CA d: 10/13/1973, Moraga, CA BR/TR, 6', 186 lbs. Deb: 5/31/1934

YEAR TM-L	G	AB	R	H	2B	3B	HR	RBI	BB	SO	SB	CS	AVG	OBP	SLG	OPS	OPS+	BR/A	RC	RC/G	FR	G/POS	WS	TPW
1934 Det-A	1	1	0	0	0	0	0	0	0	0	0	0	.000	.000	.000	.000	-100	-0	0	.00	0	....	0	0.0

• WILSON, Jack

Jack Eugene Wilson b: 12/29/1977, Westlake Village, CA BR/TR, 6', 170 lbs. Deb: 4/3/2001

YEAR TM-L	G	AB	R	H	2B	3B	HR	RBI	BB	SO	SB	CS	AVG	OBP	SLG	OPS	OPS+	BR/A	RC	RC/G	FR	G/POS	WS	TPW
2001 Pit-N	108	390	44	87	17	1	3	25	16	70	1	3	.223	.256	.295	.550	41	-36	29	2.42	0	*S-107	5	-2.7

YEAR TM-L	G	AB	R	H	2B	3B	HR	RBI	BB	SO	SB	CS	AVG	OBP	SLG	OPS	OPS+	BR/A	RC	RC/G	FR	G/POS	WS	TPW
2002 Pit-N	147	527	77	133	22	4	4	47	37	74	5	2	.252	.306	.332	.638	68	-25	55	3.56	-2	*S-143	12	-1.5
2003 Pit-N	150	558	58	143	21	3	9	62	36	74	5	5	.256	.306	.353	.659	70	-26	59	3.57	-6	*S-149	12	-2.0
Total 3	405	1475	179	363	60	8	16	134	89	218	11	10	.246	.293	.330	.623	62	-87	144	3.25	-8	S-399	29	-6.2

• WILSON, Jim James George Wilson b: 12/29/1960, Corvallis, OR BR/TR, 6'3", 230 lbs. Deb: 9/13/1985

YEAR TM-L	G	AB	R	H	2B	3B	HR	RBI	BB	SO	SB	CS	AVG	OBP	SLG	OPS	OPS+	BR/A	RC	RC/G	FR	G/POS	WS	TPW
1985 Cle-A	4	14	2	5	0	0	0	4	1	3	0	0	.357	.400	.357	.757	110	0	2	6.31	-1	/1-2,D-2	0	-0.1
1989 Sea-A	5	8	0	0	0	0	0	0	0	3	0	0	.000	.000	.000	.000	-97	-2	0	.00	0	/D-5	0	-0.2
Total 2	9	22	2	5	0	0	0	4	1	6	0	0	.227	.261	.227	.488	38	-2	2	3.34	-1	/D-7,1-2	0	-0.3

• WILSON, Jimmie James "Ace" Wilson b: 7/23/1900, Philadelphia, PA d: 5/31/1947, Bradenton, FL BR/TR, 6'1.5", 200 lbs. Deb: 4/17/1923 M/C/U Career OF: 2-1-1

YEAR TM-L	G	AB	R	H	2B	3B	HR	RBI	BB	SO	SB	CS	AVG	OBP	SLG	OPS	OPS+	BR/A	RC	RC/G	FR	G/POS	WS	TPW
1923 Phi-N	85	252	27	66	9	0	1	25	4	17	4	2	.262	.276	.310	.586	49	-19	21	2.88	-6	C-69/O-2(1-1-0)	1	-1.9
1924 Phi-N	95	280	32	78	16	3	6	39	17	12	5	4	.279	.322	.421	.744	87	-6	37	4.66	6	C-82/1-2,O-1	8	0.6
1925 Phi-N	108	335	42	110	19	3	3	54	32	25	5	3	.328	.390	.430	.820	100	2	57	6.48	-4	C-89/O-1	10	0.3
1926 Phi-N	90	279	40	85	10	2	4	32	25	20	3	....	.305	.362	.398	.760	99	0	40	5.09	3	C-79	9	0.8
1927 Phi-N	128	443	50	122	15	2	2	45	34	15	13	....	.275	.330	.332	.662	77	-14	48	3.80	-6	*C-124	8	-1.2
1928 Phi-N	21	70	11	21	4	1	0	13	9	8	3	....	.300	.380	.386	.765	97	0	10	5.31	4	C-20	2	0.5
*StL-N	120	411	45	106	26	2	2	50	45	24	9	....	.258	.333	.345	.678	76	-14	48	3.92	-6	*C-120	13	-1.1
Yr.	141	481	56	127	30	3	2	63	54	32	12	....	.264	.340	.351	.691	79	-14	59	4.12	-2	*C-140	15	-0.6
1929 StL-N	120	394	59	128	27	8	4	71	43	19	4	....	.325	.394	.464	.859	111	7	71	6.73	3	*C-119	16	1.6
1930*StL-N	107	362	54	115	25	7	1	58	28	17	8	....	.318	.368	.434	.802	90	-6	57	5.67	4	C-99	13	0.4
1931*StL-N	115	383	45	105	20	2	0	51	28	15	5	....	.274	.332	.337	.669	77	-12	45	4.12	6	*C-110	14	0.1
1932 StL-N	92	274	36	68	16	2	2	28	15	18	9	....	.248	.290	.343	.633	67	-13	28	3.47	4	C-75/1-3,2-1	6	-0.4
1933 StL-N★	113	369	34	94	17	0	1	45	23	33	6	....	.255	.300	.309	.609	70	-14	34	3.18	-2	*C-107	8	-1.0
1934 Phi-N	91	277	25	81	11	0	3	35	14	10	1	....	.292	.326	.365	.691	75	-10	31	3.98	3	C-77/1-1,2-1	5	-0.2
1935 Phi-N★	93	290	38	81	20	0	1	37	19	19	4	....	.279	.326	.359	.684	76	-10	35	4.33	2	C-78/2-1	7	-0.2
1936 Phi-N	85	230	25	64	12	0	1	27	12	21	5	....	.278	.314	.343	.658	70	-10	24	3.70	-3	C-63/1-1	2	-1.0
1937 Phi-N	39	87	15	24	3	0	1	8	6	4	1	....	.276	.323	.345	.667	75	-3	9	3.64	-1	C-22/1-2	1	-0.3
1938 Phi-N	3	2	0	0	0	0	0	0	0	1	0	....	.000	.000	.000	.000	-100	-1	0	.00	0	/C-1	0	0.0
1939 Cin-N	4	3	0	1	0	0	0	0	0	1	0	....	.333	.333	.333	.667	79	-0	0	3.42	-1	/C-1	0	-0.1
1940*Cin-N	16	37	2	9	2	0	0	3	2	1	1	....	.243	.282	.297	.579	59	-2	3	3.03	0	C-16	1	-0.2
Total 18	1525	4778	580	1358	252	32	32	621	356	280	86	9	.284	.336	.370	.707	81	-122	600	4.43	7	*C-1351/1-9,O-4,2-3	124	-3.4

• WILSON, Les Lester Wilbur "Tug" Wilson b: 7/17/1885, St. Louis, MI d: 4/4/1969, Edmonds, WA BL/TR, 5'11", 170 lbs. Deb: 7/15/1911

YEAR TM-L	G	AB	R	H	2B	3B	HR	RBI	BB	SO	SB	CS	AVG	OBP	SLG	OPS	OPS+	BR/A	RC	RC/G	FR	G/POS	WS	TPW
1911 Bos-A	5	7	0	0	0	0	0	0	2	....	0	....	.000	.222	.000	.222	-36	-1	0	.45	0	/O-3(2-0-1)	0	-0.1

• WILSON, Mike Samuel Marshall Wilson b: 12/2/1896, Edge Hill, PA d: 5/16/1978, Boynton Beach, FL BR/TR, 5'10.5", 160 lbs. Deb: 6/4/1921

YEAR TM-L	G	AB	R	H	2B	3B	HR	RBI	BB	SO	SB	CS	AVG	OBP	SLG	OPS	OPS+	BR/A	RC	RC/G	FR	G/POS	WS	TPW
1921 Pit-N	5	4	0	0	0	0	0	0	0	0	0	0	.000	.000	.000	.000	-98	-1	0	.00	-1	/C-5	0	-0.2

• WILSON, Mookie William Hayward Wilson b: 2/9/1956, Bamberg, SC BB/TR, 5'10", 170 lbs. Deb: 9/2/1980 C Career OF: 198-1067-90

YEAR TM-L	G	AB	R	H	2B	3B	HR	RBI	BB	SO	SB	CS	AVG	OBP	SLG	OPS	OPS+	BR/A	RC	RC/G	FR	G/POS	WS	TPW
1980 NY-N	27	105	16	26	5	3	0	4	12	19	7	7	.248	.325	.352	.677	91	-3	12	3.58	-2	O-26(1-26-0)	2	-0.6
1981 NY-N	92	328	49	89	8	8	3	14	20	59	24	12	.271	.317	.372	.689	96	-2	38	4.06	0	O-80(6-68-10)	9	-0.5
1982 NY-N	159	639	90	178	25	9	5	55	32	102	58	16	.279	.315	.369	.684	91	-3	78	4.33	5	*O-156(0-156-0)	19	-0.1
1983 NY-N	152	638	91	176	25	6	7	51	18	103	54	16	.276	.300	.367	.667	85	-11	71	3.95	1	*O-148(0-148-0)	17	-1.3
1984 NY-N	154	587	88	162	28	10	10	54	26	90	46	9	.276	.309	.409	.718	102	4	78	4.73	5	*O-146(0-146-0)	23	0.8
1985 NY-N	93	337	56	93	16	8	6	26	28	52	24	9	.276	.332	.424	.756	113	6	46	4.66	-3	O-83(4-83-0)	12	0.1
1986*NY-N	123	381	61	110	17	5	9	45	32	72	25	7	.289	.345	.430	.776	116	10	58	5.55	5	*O-114(78-65-3)	16	1.2
1987 NY-N	124	385	58	115	19	7	9	34	35	85	21	6	.299	.360	.455	.815	120	13	66	6.35	-1	*O-109(20-88-14)	15	1.0
1988*NY-N	112	378	61	112	17	5	8	41	27	63	15	4	.296	.346	.431	.778	128	14	55	5.18	1	*O-104(16-83-18)	17	1.4
1989 NY-N	80	249	22	51	10	1	3	18	10	47	7	4	.205	.238	.289	.528	53	-16	17	2.31	-1	O-71(13-44-25)	2	-2.0
*Tor-A	54	238	32	71	9	1	2	17	3	37	12	1	.298	.313	.370	.683	97	0	28	4.22	-1	O-54(16-22-20)	4	-0.2
1990 Tor-A	147	588	81	156	36	4	3	51	31	102	23	4	.265	.302	.355	.658	79	-15	64	3.81	-2	*O-141(8-133-0)/D-6	11	-2.0
1991*Tor-A	86	241	26	58	12	4	2	28	8	35	11	3	.241	.280	.349	.628	70	-9	24	3.29	-1	O-41(36-5-0),D-34	4	-1.3
Total 12	1403	5094	731	1397	227	71	67	438	282	866	327	98	.274	.315	.386	.701	96	-13	634	4.39	5	*O-1273/D-40	151	-3.4

• WILSON, Neil Samuel O'Neil Wilson b: 6/14/1935, Lexington, TN BL/TR, 6'1", 175 lbs. Deb: 4/17/1960

YEAR TM-L	G	AB	R	H	2B	3B	HR	RBI	BB	SO	SB	CS	AVG	OBP	SLG	OPS	OPS+	BR/A	RC	RC/G	FR	G/POS	WS	TPW
1960 SF-N	6	10	0	0	0	0	0	0	1	2	0	0	.000	.091	.000	.091	-77	-2	0	.00	-1	/C-6	0	-0.3

• WILSON, Nigel Nigel Edward Wilson b: 1/12/1970, Oshawa, Canada BL/TL, 6'1", 185 lbs. Deb: 9/8/1993 Career OF: 6-0-0

YEAR TM-L	G	AB	R	H	2B	3B	HR	RBI	BB	SO	SB	CS	AVG	OBP	SLG	OPS	OPS+	BR/A	RC	RC/G	FR	G/POS	WS	TPW
1993 Fla-N	7	16	0	0	0	0	0	0	0	11	0	0	.000	.000	.000	.000	-95	-4	0	.00	0	/O-3(3-0-0)	0	-0.5
1995 Cin-N	5	7	0	0	0	0	0	0	0	4	0	0	.000	.000	.000	.000	-101	-2	0	.00	-0	/O-2(2-0-0)	0	-0.2
1996*Cle-A	10	12	2	3	0	0	2	5	1	6	0	0	.250	.308	.750	1.058	157	1	3	8.55	0	/D-3,O-1	1	0.1
Total 3	22	35	2	3	0	0	2	5	1	21	0	0	.086	.111	.257	.368	-5	-6	3	2.40	0	/O-6,D-3	1	-0.6

• WILSON, Parke Parke Asel Wilson b: 10/26/1867, Keithsburg, IL d: 12/20/1934, Hermosa Beach, CA BR/TR, 5'11", 166 lbs. Deb: 7/19/1893 U Career OF: 4-4-3

YEAR TM-L	G	AB	R	H	2B	3B	HR	RBI	BB	SO	SB	CS	AVG	OBP	SLG	OPS	OPS+	BR/A	RC	RC/G	FR	G/POS	WS	TPW
1893 NY-N	31	114	16	28	4	1	2	21	7	9	5	....	.246	.289	.351	.640	69	-6	13	4.31	-2	C-31	2	-0.4
1894 NY-N	51	181	35	59	5	5	1	32	15	6	9	....	.326	.384	.425	.809	96	-1	34	7.21	-6	C-34,1-15	6	-0.3
1895 NY-N	67	238	32	56	9	0	0	30	14	16	11	....	.235	.281	.273	.554	44	-20	22	3.24	0	C-53,1-11/3-3	3	-1.3
1896 NY-N	75	253	33	60	2	0	0	23	13	14	9	....	.237	.277	.245	.522	39	-22	21	2.80	-4	C-71/1-2	2	-1.7
1897 NY-N	47	158	29	47	9	3	0	23	15	....	6	....	.297	.362	.392	.754	102	1	25	6.02	-4	C-30,1-10/O-4(0-4-0),2-1	6	-0.1
1898 NY-N	1	4	0	0	0	0	0	0	0	....	0	....	.000	.000	.000	.000	-103	-1	0	.00	0	/O-1	0	-0.1
1899 NY-N	98	332	49	89	8	6	0	42	43	....	16	....	.268	.359	.328	.687	92	-1	47	4.98	-8	C-31,1-29,S-19,3-15/O-6(3-0-3)	8	-0.6
Total 7	370	1280	194	339	37	15	3	171	107	45	56	....	.265	.326	.324	.650	72	-51	163	4.49	-24	C-250/1-67,S-19,3-18,O-11,2	27	-4.5

• WILSON, Preston Preston James Richard Wilson b: 7/19/1974, Bamberg, SC BR/TR, 6'2", 193 lbs. Deb: 5/7/1998 Career OF: 30-692-17

YEAR TM-L	G	AB	R	H	2B	3B	HR	RBI	BB	SO	SB	CS	AVG	OBP	SLG	OPS	OPS+	BR/A	RC	RC/G	FR	G/POS	WS	TPW
1998 NY-N	8	20	3	6	2	0	0	2	2	8	1	1	.300	.364	.400	.764	102	-0	3	5.18	-1	/O-7(4-2-1)	1	-0.1
Fla-N	14	31	4	2	0	0	1	1	4	13	0	0	.065	.194	.161	.356	-5	-5	1	1.18	0	O-11(3-7-1)	0	-0.5
Yr.	22	51	7	8	2	0	1	3	6	21	1	1	.157	.259	.255	.514	34	-5	4	2.48	-1	O-18(7-9-2)	1	-0.6
1999 Fla-N	149	482	67	135	21	4	26	71	46	156	11	4	.280	.354	.502	.856	120	14	83	6.04	1	*O-136(23-111-15)	13	1.3
2000 Fla-N	161	605	94	160	35	3	31	121	55	187	36	14	.264	.334	.486	.820	108	7	98	5.53	1	*O-158(0-158-0)	20	0.9
2001 Fla-N	123	468	70	128	30	2	23	71	36	107	20	8	.274	.333	.494	.827	114	9	73	5.41	5	*O-121(0-121-0)	10	1.4
2002 Fla-N	141	510	80	124	22	2	23	65	58	140	20	11	.243	.331	.429	.760	102	1	70	4.49	-9	*O-138(0-138-0)	11	-0.7
2003 Col-N★	155	600	94	169	43	1	36	**141**	54	139	14	7	.282	.345	.537	.882	110	7	103	5.99	-12	*O-155(0-155-0)	20	-0.4
Total 6	751	2716	412	724	153	12	140	472	255	750	102	45	.267	.338	.486	.824	109	33	431	5.43	-15	O-726	75	2.0

• WILSON, Red Robert James Wilson b: 3/7/1929, Milwaukee, WI BR/TR, 5'10", 200 lbs. Deb: 9/22/1951

YEAR TM-L	G	AB	R	H	2B	3B	HR	RBI	BB	SO	SB	CS	AVG	OBP	SLG	OPS	OPS+	BR/A	RC	RC/G	FR	G/POS	WS	TPW
1951 Chi-A	4	11	1	3	1	0	0	0	1	2	0	0	.273	.333	.364	.697	90	-0	1	1.96	0	/C-4	0	0.0
1952 Chi-A	2	3	0	0	0	0	0	0	0	1	0	0	.000	.000	.000	.000	-99	-1	0	.00	0	/C-2	0	-0.1
1953 Chi-A	71	164	21	41	6	1	0	10	26	12	2	3	.250	.353	.299	.651	75	-5	17	3.41	-2	C-63	5	-0.5
1954 Chi-A	8	20	2	4	0	0	1	1	1	2	0	0	.200	.238	.350	.588	58	-1	2	2.92	0	/C-8	1	-0.1
Det-A	54	170	22	48	11	1	2	22	27	12	3	1	.282	.381	.394	.775	115	5	26	5.01	2	C-53	8	0.9
Yr.	62	190	24	52	11	1	3	23	28	14	3	1	.274	.367	.389	.756	109	3	27	4.80	2	C-61	9	0.9
1955 Det-A	78	241	26	53	9	0	2	17	26	23	1	2	.220	.296	.282	.578	57	-15	18	2.35	-2	C-72	2	-1.4
1956 Det-A	78	228	32	66	12	2	7	38	42	18	2	1	.289	.400	.452	.852	124	10	43	6.50	-1	C-78	11	1.2
1957 Det-A	60	180	21	43	8	1	3	13	25	19	2	3	.239	.341	.344	.686	86	-3	22	4.03	2	C-60	6	0.1
1958 Det-A	103	298	31	89	13	1	3	29	35	30	10	0	.299	.376	.379	.755	101	4	45	5.39	-1	*C-101	13	0.9
1959 Det-A	67	228	28	60	17	2	4	35	10	23	2	2	.263	.300	.408	.708	88	-5	25	3.68	-3	C-64	5	-0.5
1960 Det-A	45	134	17	29	4	0	1	14	16	14	3	0	.216	.300	.269	.569	52	-8	12	3.09	-2	C-45	2	-0.8
Cle-A	32	88	5	19	3	0	1	10	6	7	0	0	.216	.274	.284	.558	53	-6	7	2.38	1	C-30	2	-0.4
Yr.	77	222	22	48	7	0	2	24	22	21	3	0	.216	.290	.275	.565	52	-14	19	2.79	-2	C-75	4	-1.2
Total 10	602	1765	206	455	84	8	24	189	215	163	25	12	.258	.341	.355	.696	87	-26	217	4.10	-7	C-580	55	-0.6

YEAR TM-L	G	AB	R	H	2B	3B	HR	RBI	BB	SO	SB	CS	AVG	OBP	SLG	OPS	OPS+	BR/A	RC	RC/G	FR	G/POS	WS	TPW
• **WILSON, Squanto**	George Francis Wilson b: 3/29/1889, Old Town, ME d: 3/26/1967, Winthrop, ME BB/TR, 5'9.5", 170 lbs. Deb: 10/2/1911																							
1911 Det-A	5	16	2	3	0	0	0	0	2	....	0	....	.188	.278	.188	.465	29	-1	1	1.60	-1	/C-5	0	-0.2
1914 Bos-A	1	0	0	0	0	0	0	0	0	0	0	....	....	....	....	....	-100	0	0	....	0	/1-1	0	0.0
Total 2	6	16	2	3	0	0	0	0	2	0	0	....	.188	.278	.188	.465	29	-1	1	1.60	-1	/C-5,1-1	0	-0.2
• **WILSON, Tack**	Michael Wilson b: 5/16/1956, Shreveport, LA BR/TR, 5'10", 185 lbs. Deb: 4/9/1983 Career OF: 4-1-0																							
1983 Min-A	5	4	4	1	1	0	0	1	0	0	0	0	.250	.250	.500	.750	97	-0	1	4.50	-0	/D-2,0-1	0	0.0
1987 Cal-A	7	2	5	1	0	0	0	0	1	0	0	0	.500	.667	.500	1.167	224	1	1	12.02	0	/0-4(4-0-0),D-2	0	0.0
Total 2	12	6	9	2	1	0	0	1	1	0	0	0	.333	.429	.500	.929	160	0	1	7.51	0	/0-5,D-4	0	0.0
• **WILSON, Tom**	Thomas Leroy Wilson b: 12/19/1970, Fullerton, CA BR/TR, 6'3", 210 lbs. Deb: 5/19/2001																							
2001 Oak-A	9	21	4	4	0	0	2	4	1	5	0	0	.190	.261	.476	.737	88	-1	2	3.27	-3	/C-9	0	-0.3
2002 Tor-A	96	265	33	68	10	0	8	37	28	79	0	0	.257	.339	.385	.724	89	-4	35	4.62	-5	C-65,D-12,1-11	7	-0.6
2003 Tor-A	96	256	37	66	19	0	5	35	28	80	0	0	.258	.333	.391	.724	89	-4	34	4.74	1	C-76,1-14/0-2(1-0-1),D-1	3	0.1
Total 3	201	542	74	138	29	0	15	76	57	164	0	0	.255	.333	.391	.724	89	-8	72	4.62	-6	C-150/1-25,D-13,0-2	10	-0.7
• **WILSON, Tom**	Thomas G. "Slats" Wilson b: 6/3/1890, Fleming, KS d: 3/7/1953, San Pedro, CA BB/TR, 6'1.5", 160 lbs. Deb: 9/8/1914																							
1914 Was-A	1	1	0	0	0	0	0	0	0	0	0	....	.000	.000	.000	.000	-96	-0	0	.00	-1	/C-1	0	-0.1
• **WILSON, Tug**	George Archer Wilson b: Brooklyn, NY d: 11/28/1914, Brooklyn, NY, 5'8", 175 lbs. Deb: 5/9/1884																							
1884 Bro-a	24	82	13	19	4	0	0	0	5	....	....	....	.232	.276	.280	.556	81	-2	7	2.84	-1	0-12(0-12-0),C-10/1-3,2-1	2	-0.2
• **WILSON, Vance**	Vance Allen Wilson b: 3/17/1973, Mesa, AZ BR/TR, 5'11", 190 lbs. Deb: 4/24/1999																							
1999 NY-N	1	0	0	0	0	0	0	0	0	0	0	0	....	....	....	....	-103	0	0	....	-1	/C-1	0	-0.1
2000 NY-N	4	4	0	0	0	0	0	0	0	2	0	0	.000	.000	.000	.000	-105	-1	0	.00	1	/C-3	0	-0.1
2001 NY-N	32	57	3	17	3	0	0	6	2	16	0	1	.298	.344	.351	.695	85	-2	7	4.15	1	C-27	1	0.1
2002 NY-N	74	163	19	40	7	0	5	26	5	32	0	1	.245	.301	.380	.682	81	-5	18	3.72	5	C-66/1-1	5	0.3
2003 NY-N	96	268	28	65	9	1	8	39	15	56	1	2	.243	.295	.373	.668	75	-11	28	3.56	6	C-89	7	0.0
Total 5	207	492	50	122	19	1	13	71	22	106	1	4	.248	.301	.370	.670	77	-20	53	3.64	12	C-186/1-1	13	0.3
• **WILSON, Willie**	Willie James Wilson b: 7/9/1955, Montgomery, AL BB/TR, 6'3", 195 lbs. Deb: 9/4/1976 Career OF: 673-1356-31																							
1976 KC-A	12	6	0	1	0	0	0	0	0	2	2	1	.167	.167	.167	.333	-2	-1	0	.00	0	/0-6(0-6-0)	0	-0.1
1977 KC-A	13	34	10	11	2	0	0	1	1	8	6	3	.324	.343	.382	.725	97	-0	4	3.51	-1	/0-9(0-9-0),D-2	1	-0.1
1978*KC-A	127	198	43	43	8	2	0	16	16	33	46	12	.217	.282	.278	.560	57	-7	18	2.82	2	*0-112(82-35-0)/D-6	4	-0.8
1979 KC-A	154	588	113	185	18	13	6	49	28	92	**83**	12	.315	.353	.420	.773	105	17	99	6.20	5	*0-152(130-23-5)/D-2	24	1.5
1980*KC-A	161	705	**133**	**230**	28	**15**	3	49	28	81	79	10	.326	.357	.421	.779	111	23	117	6.39	6	*0-159(102-62-0)	31	2.3
1981*KC-A	102	439	54	133	10	7	1	32	18	42	34	8	.303	.336	.364	.701	103	5	56	4.71	11	*0-101(83-19-0)	14	1.2
1982 KC-A★	136	585	87	194	19	**15**	3	46	26	81	37	11	**.332**	.366	.431	.797	118	17	96	6.29	5	*0-135(119-19-0)	25	1.6
1983 KC-A★	137	576	90	159	22	8	2	33	33	75	59	8	.276	.316	.352	.669	84	-4	72	4.51	-6	*0-136(63-75-0)	15	-1.4
1984*KC-A	128	541	81	163	24	9	2	44	39	56	47	5	.301	.352	.390	.742	104	12	82	5.57	3	*0-128(0-128-0)	23	1.3
1985*KC-A	141	605	87	168	25	**21**	4	43	29	94	43	11	.278	.316	.408	.724	96	-0	80	4.75	-1	*0-140(0-140-0)	19	-0.3
1986 KC-A	156	631	77	170	20	7	9	44	31	97	34	8	.269	.313	.366	.679	82	-12	76	4.27	1	*0-155(0-155-0)	15	-1.3
1987 KC-A	146	610	97	170	18	**15**	4	30	32	88	59	11	.279	.321	.377	.698	82	-8	78	4.56	2	*0-143(0-143-0)/D-2	15	-0.8
1988 KC-A	147	591	81	155	17	**11**	1	37	22	106	35	7	.262	.291	.333	.624	74	-18	61	3.55	-5	*0-142(0-143-0)	12	-2.5
1989 KC-A	112	383	58	97	17	7	3	43	27	78	24	6	.253	.304	.358	.662	86	-5	43	3.70	-3	*0-108(0-108-0)/D-1	10	-1.0
1990 KC-A	115	307	49	89	13	3	2	42	30	57	24	6	.290	.357	.371	.728	106	6	44	5.11	-4	*0-106(54-48-4)/D-1	11	0.0
1991 Oak-A	113	294	38	70	14	4	0	28	18	43	20	5	.238	.291	.313	.604	71	-9	26	2.90	-3	0-87(40-33-19)/D-9	5	-1.4
1992*Oak-A	132	396	38	107	15	5	0	37	35	65	28	8	.270	.331	.333	.664	91	-1	45	3.87	-5	*0-120(0-118-3)/D-5	10	-0.8
1993 Chi-N	105	221	29	57	11	3	1	11	11	40	7	2	.258	.302	.348	.651	75	-8	24	3.82	-2	0-82(0-82-0)	3	-0.9
1994 Chi-N	17	21	4	5	0	2	0	0	1	6	1	0	.238	.273	.429	.701	80	-1	3	4.27	0	0-10(0-10-0)	0	-0.1
Total 19	2154	7731	1169	2207	281	147	41	585	425	1144	668	134	.285	.328	.376	.704	93	5	1024	4.73	7	*0-2031/D-28	237	-3.7
• **WINCENIAK, Ed**	Edward Joseph Winceniak b: 4/16/1929, Chicago, IL BR/TR, 5'9", 165 lbs. Deb: 4/25/1956																							
1956 Chi-N	15	17	1	2	0	0	0	0	1	3	0	0	.118	.167	.118	.284	-22	-3	0	.42	-1	/3-4,2-1	0	-0.4
1957 Chi-N	17	50	5	12	3	0	1	8	2	9	0	0	.240	.269	.360	.629	68	-2	4	2.84	-1	/S-5,3-4,2-3	0	-0.3
Total 2	32	67	6	14	3	0	1	8	3	12	0	0	.209	.243	.299	.541	45	-5	5	2.16	-2	/3-8,S-5,2-4	0	-0.7
• **WINDHORN, Gordie**	Gordon Ray Windhorn b: 12/19/1933, Wateska, IL BR/TR, 6'1", 185 lbs. Deb: 9/10/1959 Career OF: 38-6-14																							
1959 NY-A	7	11	0	0	0	0	0	0	0	3	0	0	.000	.000	.000	.000	-104	-3	0	.00	0	/0-4(4-0-0)	0	-0.3
1961 LA-N	34	33	10	8	2	1	2	6	4	3	0	1	.242	.324	.545	.870	115	0	5	5.08	0	0-17(5-3-9)	1	0.0
1962 KC-A	14	19	1	3	1	0	0	1	0	3	0	0	.158	.158	.211	.368	-2	-3	1	1.08	-0	/0-7(7-0-0)	0	-0.3
LA-A	40	45	9	8	6	0	0	1	7	10	1	1	.178	.288	.311	.600	63	-3	4	2.75	-1	0-27(22-3-5)	1	-0.4
Yr.	54	64	10	11	7	0	0	2	7	13	1	1	.172	.254	.281	.535	45	-5	5	2.23	-1	0-34(29-3-5)	1	-0.7
Total 3	95	108	20	19	9	1	2	8	11	19	1	2	.176	.252	.333	.585	53	-8	10	2.78	-1	/0-55	2	-1.0
• **WINDLE, Bill**	Willis Brewer Windle b: 12/13/1904, Galena, KS d: 12/8/1981, Corpus Christi, TX BL/TL, 5'11.5", 170 lbs. Deb: 9/27/1928																							
1928 Pit-N	1	1	1	1	1	0	0	0	0	0	0	....	1.000	1.000	2.000	3.000	641	1	2	∞	0	/1-1	0	0.1
1929 Pit-N	2	1	0	0	0	0	0	0	0	1	0	....	.000	.000	.000	.000	-98	-0	0	.00	0	/1-2	0	0.0
Total 2	3	2	1	1	1	0	0	0	0	1	0	....	.500	.500	1.000	1.500	271	0	2	.00	0	/1-3	0	0.0
• **WINE, Bobby**	Robert Paul Wine, Sr. b: 9/17/1938, New York, NY BR/TR, 6'1", 187 lbs. Deb: 9/20/1960 M/C																							
1960 Phi-N	4	14	1	2	0	0	0	0	0	2	0	0	.143	.143	.143	.286	-22	-2	0	.64	0	/S-4	0	-0.2
1962 Phi-N	112	311	30	76	15	0	4	25	11	49	2	0	.244	.270	.331	.601	62	-17	23	2.38	11	S-89,3-20	5	0.0
1963 Phi-N	142	418	29	90	14	3	6	44	14	83	1	3	.215	.242	.306	.549	58	-24	28	2.15	3	*S-132/3-8	5	-1.1
1964 Phi-N	126	283	28	60	8	3	4	34	25	37	1	0	.212	.276	.304	.580	64	-13	23	2.62	6	*S-108,3-16	7	0.0
1965 Phi-N	139	394	31	90	8	1	5	33	31	69	0	0	.228	.285	.292	.577	64	-19	30	2.50	10	*S-135/1-4	7	0.2
1966 Phi-N	46	89	8	21	5	0	0	5	6	13	0	1	.236	.292	.292	.584	63	-5	7	2.66	3	S-40/0-2(2-0-0)	2	0.1
1967 Phi-N	135	363	27	69	12	5	2	28	29	77	3	2	.190	.250	.267	.517	48	-25	23	1.96	17	*S-134/1-2	7	0.2
1968 Phi-N	27	71	5	12	3	0	2	7	6	17	0	0	.169	.234	.296	.530	58	-4	4	1.70	0	S-25/3-1	1	-0.3
1969 Mon-N	121	370	23	74	8	1	3	25	28	49	0	0	.200	.256	.251	.508	42	-28	23	1.98	3	*S-118/1-1,3-1	4	-1.2
1970 Mon-N	159	501	40	116	21	3	3	51	39	94	0	1	.232	.288	.303	.592	59	-30	44	2.90	19	*S-159	11	0.6
1971 Mon-N	119	340	25	68	9	0	1	16	25	46	0	0	.200	.255	.235	.490	39	-27	20	1.82	-3	*S-119	3	-1.9
1972 Mon-N	34	18	2	4	1	0	0	0	0	2	0	0	.222	.222	.278	.500	41	-1	1	1.50	-3	3-21/S-4,2-1	0	-0.5
Total 12	1164	3172	249	682	104	16	30	268	214	538	7	7	.215	.265	.286	.552	54	-195	227	2.29	66	*S-1067/3-67,1-7,0-2,2-1	52	-3.9
• **WINE, Robbie**	Robert Paul Wine, Jr. b: 7/13/1962, Norristown, PA BR/TR, 6'2", 190 lbs. Deb: 9/2/1986																							
1986 Hou-N	9	12	2	3	1	0	0	0	1	4	0	0	.250	.308	.333	.641	79	-0	1	3.93	1	/C-8	0	0.0
1987 Hou-N	14	29	1	3	1	0	0	0	1	10	0	0	.103	.133	.138	.271	-29	-5	1	.62	1	C-12	0	-0.4
Total 2	23	41	3	6	2	0	0	0	2	14	0	0	.146	.186	.195	.381	3	-6	2	1.45	1	/C-20	0	-0.4
• **WINEGARNER, Ralph**	Ralph Lee Winegarner b: 10/29/1909, Benton, KS d: 4/14/1988, Wichita, KS BR/TR, 6', 182 lbs. Deb: 9/20/1930 C Career OF: 4-0-1 ♦																							
1930 Cle-A	5	22	5	10	1	0	0	2	1	7	0	0	.455	.478	.500	.978	143	2	5	10.56	1	/3-5	1	0.2
1932 Cle-A	7	7	1	1	0	0	0	0	0	5	0	0	.143	.143	.143	.286	-24	-0	0	.61	0	/P-5	2	0.6
1934 Cle-A	32	51	9	10	2	0	1	5	3	11	0	0	.196	.241	.294	.535	37	0	4	2.36	0	P-22/0-1	3	-0.6
1935 Cle-A	65	84	11	26	4	1	3	17	9	12	1	1	.310	.376	.488	.864	120	6	15	6.81	2	P-25/0-4(4-0-0),3-3,1-1	4	0.0
1936 Cle-A	18	16	0	2	0	0	0	2	1	6	0	0	.125	.176	.125	.301	-24	-1	0	.72	0	/P-9	1	-0.1
1949 StL-A	9	5	2	2	0	0	1	2	1	2	0	0	.400	.500	1.000	1.500	280	2	3	24.23	0	/P-9	0	-0.3
Total 6	136	185	28	51	7	1	5	28	15	43	1	1	.276	.330	.405	.735	88	9	27	5.32	2	/P-70,3-8,0-5,1-1	11	-0.2

YEAR TM-L	G	AB	R	H	2B	3B	HR	RBI	BB	SO	SB	CS	AVG	OBP	SLG	OPS	OPS+	BR/A	RC	RC/G	FR	G/POS	WS	TPW
• WINFIELD, Dave	David Mark Winfield b: 10/3/1951, St. Paul, MN BR/TR, 6'6", 220 lbs. Deb: 6/19/1973 HOF: 2001 Career OF: 466-219-1879																							
1973 SD-N	56	141	9	39	4	1	3	12	12	19	0	0	.277	.333	.383	.716	107	1	17	4.28	-1	O-36(34-2-1)/1-1	3	-0.2
1974 SD-N	145	498	57	132	18	4	20	75	40	96	9	7	.265	.321	.438	.759	116	7	66	4.53	1	*O-131(81-25-34)	17	0.1
1975 SD-N	143	509	74	136	20	2	15	76	69	82	23	4	.267	.358	.403	.761	118	17	77	5.26	3	*O-138(0-0-138)	20	1.3
1976 SD-N	137	492	81	139	26	4	13	69	65	78	26	7	.283	.370	.431	.801	138	28	80	5.69	9	*O-134(0-10-127)	25	3.2
1977 SD-N★	157	615	104	169	29	7	25	92	58	75	16	7	.275	.337	.467	.804	126	21	95	5.47	11	*O-156(0-0-156)	24	2.5
1978 SD-N★	158	587	88	181	30	5	24	97	55	81	21	9	.308	.370	.499	.869	153	40	105	6.56	-2	*O-154(1-84-112)/1-2	28	3.4
1979 SD-N★	159	597	97	184	27	10	34	**118**	85	71	15	9	.308	.396	.558	.954	**167**	**55**	132	8.24	14	*O-157(0-0-157)	**33**	**6.3**
1980 SD-N★	162	558	89	154	25	6	20	87	79	83	23	7	.276	.368	.450	.818	135	29	94	5.96	3	*O-159(0-20-154)	22	2.7
1981*NY-A★	105	388	52	114	25	1	13	68	43	41	11	1	.294	.366	.464	.830	140	22	66	5.99	-5	*O-102(80-23-0)/D-1	16	1.4
1982 NY-A★	140	539	84	151	24	8	37	106	45	64	5	3	.280	.336	.560	.896	143	29	93	5.93	5	*O-135(135-0-0)/D-4	20	2.7
1983 NY-A★	152	598	99	169	26	8	32	116	58	77	15	6	.283	.348	.513	.861	139	31	97	5.55	-7	*O-151(122-39-9)	22	1.7
1984 NY-A★	141	567	106	193	34	4	19	100	53	71	6	4	.340	.397	.515	.912	156	43	113	7.65	1	*O-140(1-16-127)	26	3.8
1985 NY-A★	155	633	105	174	34	6	26	114	52	96	19	7	.275	.330	.471	.801	119	16	94	5.22	0	*O-152(0-0-152)/D-2	21	0.8
1986 NY-A★	154	565	90	148	31	5	24	104	77	106	6	5	.262	.352	.462	.814	121	16	89	5.33	-1	*O-145(0-0-145)/D-6,3-2	17	0.8
1987 NY-A★	156	575	83	158	22	1	27	97	76	96	5	6	.275	.359	.457	.817	116	12	91	5.49	-11	*O-145(0-0-145)/D-8	18	-0.6
1988 NY-A★	149	559	96	180	37	2	25	107	69	88	9	4	.322	.398	.530	.928	159	45	115	7.68	-8	*O-141(0-0-141)/D-4	31	3.3
1990 NY-A	20	61	7	13	3	0	2	6	4	13	0	0	.213	.273	.361	.633	75	-2	6	3.01	0	O-12(12-0-0)/D-7	0	-0.3
Cal-A	112	414	63	114	18	2	19	72	48	68	0	1	.275	.352	.466	.818	130	16	65	5.45	-3	*O-108(0-0-108)/D-3	13	1.0
Yr.	132	475	70	127	21	2	21	78	52	81	0	1	.267	.342	.453	.795	123	13	71	5.12	-3	*O-120(12-0-108),D-10	13	0.7
1991 Cal-A	150	568	75	149	27	4	28	86	56	109	7	2	.262	.330	.472	.801	119	14	84	5.02	1	*O-115(0-0-115),D-34	17	1.1
1992*Tor-A	156	583	92	169	33	3	26	108	82	89	2	3	.290	.378	.491	.869	136	28	110	6.88	0	*D-130,O-26(0-0-26)	27	2.2
1993 Min-A	143	547	72	148	27	2	21	76	45	106	2	3	.271	.326	.442	.768	104	1	75	4.85	-1	*D-105,O-31(0-0-31)/1-5	10	-0.9
1994 Min-A	77	294	35	74	15	3	10	43	31	51	2	1	.252	.323	.425	.748	91	-5	40	4.64	0	D-76/O-1	5	-0.9
1995 Cle-A	46	115	11	22	5	0	2	4	14	26	1	0	.191	.285	.287	.572	49	-9	9	2.50	0	D-39	0	-1.0
Total 22	2973	11003	1669	3110	540	88	465	1833	1216	1686	223	96	.283	.355	.475	.830	131	453	1813	5.81	10	*O-2469,D-419/1-8,3-2	415	34.4
• WINGO, Al	Absalom Holbrook "Red" Wingo b: 5/6/1898, Norcross, GA d: 10/9/1964, Detroit, MI BL/TR, 5'11", 180 lbs. Deb: 9/9/1919 Career OF: 270-41-47																							
1919 Phi-A	15	59	9	18	1	3	0	2	4	12	0	....	.305	.349	.424	.773	115	1	8	5.24	-2	O-15(15-0-0)	1	-0.1
1924 Det-A	78	150	21	43	12	2	1	26	21	13	2	5	.287	.374	.413	.788	105	-0	23	5.25	0	O-43(30-7-6)	4	-0.2
1925 Det-A	130	440	104	163	34	10	5	68	69	31	14	13	.370	.456	.527	.983	151	36	106	9.23	9	*O-122(120-2-0)	22	3.3
1926 Det-A	108	298	45	84	19	0	1	45	52	32	4	2	.282	.389	.356	.744	94	0	45	5.31	1	O-74(61-0-14)/3-2	8	-0.5
1927 Det-A	75	137	15	32	8	2	0	20	25	14	1	0	.234	.352	.321	.673	75	-4	18	4.23	0	O-34(9-4-21)	2	-0.6
1928 Det-A	87	242	30	69	13	2	2	30	40	17	2	2	.285	.389	.380	.769	101	2	38	5.65	-2	O-71(35-28-6)	7	-0.4
Total 6	493	1326	224	409	87	19	9	191	211	119	23	22	.308	.404	.423	.827	114	35	238	6.47	5	O-359/3-2	44	1.4
• WINGO, Ed	Edmund Armand Wingo b: 10/8/1895, Ste. Anne de Bellevue, Canada d: 12/5/1964, Lachine, Canada BR/TR, 5'6", 145 lbs. Deb: 10/2/1920																							
1920 Phi-A	1	4	0	1	0	0	0	1	0	0	0	0	.250	.250	.250	.500	32	-0	0	2.12	1	/C-1	0	0.1
• WINGO, Ivey	Ivey Brown Wingo b: 7/8/1890, Gainesville, GA d: 3/1/1941, Norcross, GA BL/TR, 5'10", 160 lbs. Deb: 4/20/1911 M/C Career OF: 7-1-5																							
1911 StL-N	25	57	4	12	2	0	0	3	3	7	0	....	.211	.250	.246	.496	40	-5	3	1.92	-2	C-18	0	-0.5
1912 StL-N	100	310	38	82	18	8	2	44	23	45	8	....	.265	.317	.394	.711	96	-3	40	4.43	7	C-92	10	1.1
1913 StL-N	112	307	25	78	5	8	2	35	17	41	18	....	.254	.295	.342	.637	83	-8	34	3.70	3	C-98/1-5,O-1	6	0.2
1914 StL-N	80	237	24	71	8	5	4	26	18	17	15	....	.300	.352	.426	.778	132	9	38	5.88	-1	C-70/O-4(0-0-4)	11	1.3
1915 Cin-N	119	339	26	75	11	6	3	29	13	33	10	11	.221	.250	.316	.566	69	-17	27	2.46	-1	C-98/O-1	4	-1.1
1916 Cin-N	119	347	30	85	8	11	2	40	25	27	4	....	.245	.298	.349	.646	100	-1	40	3.68	4	*C-107	8	1.4
1917 Cin-N	121	399	37	106	16	11	2	39	25	13	9	....	.266	.311	.376	.687	115	6	47	4.07	-4	*C-120	15	1.3
1918 Cin-N	100	323	35	82	15	6	0	31	19	18	6	....	.254	.297	.337	.635	95	-3	33	3.44	4	C-93/O-5(3-0-1)	10	0.9
1919*Cin-N	76	245	30	67	12	6	0	27	23	19	4	....	.273	.336	.371	.707	115	5	30	4.37	3	C-75	13	1.5
1920 Cin-N	108	364	32	96	11	5	2	38	19	13	6	4	.264	.300	.338	.638	84	-7	37	3.48	-5	*C-107/2-2	11	-0.4
1921 Cin-N	97	295	20	79	7	6	3	38	21	14	3	2	.268	.319	.363	.681	84	-6	35	4.06	1	C-92/O-1	7	0.1
1922 Cin-N	80	260	24	74	13	3	3	45	23	11	1	4	.285	.343	.392	.735	91	-4	34	4.72	-3	C-78	8	-0.2
1923 Cin-N	61	171	10	45	9	2	1	24	9	11	1	1	.263	.304	.357	.661	75	-6	18	3.79	-3	C-57	5	-0.6
1924 Cin-N	66	192	21	55	5	4	1	23	14	8	1	1	.286	.338	.370	.708	91	-2	24	4.49	-2	C-65/1-1	6	0.0
1925 Cin-N	55	146	6	30	7	0	0	12	11	8	1	2	.205	.261	.253	.515	33	-15	10	2.13	-3	C-55	1	-1.4
1926 Cin-N	7	10	0	2	0	0	0	1	1	0	0	....	.200	.333	.200	.533	48	-1	1	2.54	0	/C-7	0	-0.1
1929 Cin-N	1	1	0	0	0	0	0	0	0	0	0	....	.000	.000	.000	.000	-105	-0	0	.00	0	/C-1	0	-0.1
Total 17	1327	4003	362	1039	147	81	25	455	264	285	87	25	.260	.307	.355	.662	92	-58	452	3.83	-2	*C-1233/O-12,1-6,2-2	115	3.5
• WINKELMAN, George	George Edward Winkelman b: 2/18/1865, Washington, DC d: 5/19/1960, Washington, DC BL/TL, 5'9" Deb: 8/4/1883 Career OF: 3-1-1																							
1883 Lou-a	4	13	2	0	0	0	0	0	1	....	....	....	.000	.071	.000	.071	-81	-2	0	.00	0	/O-4(3-1-0)	0	-0.2
1886 Was-N	1	5	0	1	0	0	0	0	0	1	0	....	.200	.200	.200	.400	23	-0	0	1.38	0	/O-1,P-1	0	-0.5
Total 2	5	18	2	1	0	0	0	0	1	1	0	....	.056	.105	.056	.161	-54	-3	0	.33	0	/O-5,P-1	0	-0.7
• WINN, Randy	Dwight Randolph Winn b: 6/9/1974, Los Angeles, CA BB/TR, 6'2", 193 lbs. Deb: 5/11/1998 Career OF: 193-371-86																							
1998 TB-A	109	338	51	94	9	9	1	17	29	69	26	12	.278	.337	.367	.704	82	-9	44	4.40	3	O-96(16-70-12)	5	-0.6
1999 TB-A	79	303	44	81	16	4	2	24	17	63	9	9	.267	.308	.366	.675	70	-16	33	3.73	-1	O-77(0-77-0)	4	-1.6
2000 TB-A	51	159	28	40	5	0	1	16	26	25	6	7	.252	.364	.302	.666	72	-7	19	3.84	2	O-47(29-18-0)/D-1	2	-0.6
2001 TB-A	128	429	54	117	25	6	6	50	38	81	12	10	.273	.340	.401	.741	96	-4	57	4.52	0	*O-117(9-48-62)/D-3	10	-0.7
2002 TB-A★	152	607	87	181	39	9	14	75	55	109	27	8	.298	.362	.461	.824	119	19	104	6.27	1	*O-146(0-138-8)/D-4	23	1.9
2003 Sea-A	157	600	103	177	37	4	11	75	41	108	23	5	.295	.348	.425	.773	106	8	92	5.53	-3	*O-157(139-20-4)	21	-0.1
Total 6	676	2436	367	690	131	32	35	257	206	455	103	51	.283	.345	.406	.751	97	-10	348	5.02	1	O-640/D-8	65	-1.6
• WINNINGHAM, Herm	Herman Son Winningham b: 12/1/1961, Orangeburg, SC BL/TR, 5'11", 185 lbs. Deb: 9/1/1984 Career OF: 106-547-32																							
1984 NY-N	14	27	5	11	1	1	0	5	1	7	2	1	.407	.429	.519	.947	167	2	6	9.55	-1	O-10(1-9-1)	2	0.1
1985 Mon-N	125	312	30	74	6	5	3	21	28	72	20	9	.237	.300	.317	.617	77	-9	32	3.37	0	*O-116(1-115-0)	7	-1.1
1986 Mon-N	90	185	23	40	6	3	4	11	18	51	12	7	.216	.286	.346	.632	74	-7	17	2.96	-2	O-66(3-56-7)/S-1	2	-1.1
1987 Mon-N	137	347	34	83	20	3	4	41	34	68	29	10	.239	.307	.349	.656	71	-13	37	3.42	-2	*O-131(0-131-0)	7	-1.6
1988 Mon-N	47	90	10	21	2	1	0	6	12	18	4	5	.233	.324	.278	.601	71	-4	8	2.70	-2	O-30(0-29-1)	2	-0.7
Cin-N	53	113	6	26	1	3	0	15	5	27	8	3	.230	.263	.292	.555	57	-6	9	2.67	0	O-42(14-21-8)	2	-0.7
Yr.	100	203	16	47	3	4	0	21	17	45	12	8	.232	.291	.286	.577	63	-11	17	2.68	-2	O-72(14-50-9)	4	-1.4
1989 Cin-N	115	251	40	63	11	3	3	13	24	50	14	5	.251	.316	.355	.671	89	-3	29	3.86	-2	O-85(34-41-13)	4	-0.7
1990*Cin-N	84	160	20	41	8	5	3	17	14	31	6	4	.256	.316	.425	.741	98	-1	22	4.70	1	O-64(5-58-1)	5	-0.1
1991 Cin-N	98	169	17	38	6	1	1	4	11	40	4	4	.225	.272	.290	.562	56	-11	13	2.51	-2	O-66(12-55-1)	1	-1.5
1992 Bos-A	105	234	27	55	8	1	1	14	10	53	6	5	.235	.266	.291	.557	52	-16	17	2.49	-2	O-67(36-32-0)/D-6	2	-1.6
Total 9	868	1888	212	452	69	26	19	147	157	417	105	53	.239	.298	.334	.631	74	-70	189	3.32	-8	O-677/D-6,S-1	34	-9.0
• WINSETT, Tom	John Thomas "Long Tom" Winsett b: 11/24/1909, McKenzie, TN d: 7/20/1987, Memphis, TN BL/TR, 6'2", 190 lbs. Deb: 4/20/1930 Career OF: 136-1-8																							
1930 Bos-A	1	1	0	0	0	0	0	0	0	1	0	0	.000	.000	.000	.000	-104	-0	0	.00	0	....	0	0.0
1931 Bos-A	64	76	6	15	1	0	1	7	4	21	0	0	.197	.247	.250	.497	33	-7	5	2.09	0	/O-8(8-0-0)	0	-0.7
1933 Bos-A	6	12	1	1	0	0	0	0	1	6	0	0	.083	.154	.083	.237	-36	-2	0	.45	0	/O-4(2-0-2)	0	-0.3
1935 StL-N	7	12	2	6	1	0	0	2	2	3	0	....	.500	.571	.583	1.155	203	2	4	16.90	0	/O-2(0-0-2)	1	0.2
1936 Bro-N	22	85	13	20	7	0	1	18	11	14	0	....	.235	.330	.353	.683	83	-2	10	4.22	1	O-21(21-0-0)	2	-0.2
1937 Bro-N	118	350	32	83	15	5	5	42	45	64	3	....	.237	.329	.351	.681	83	-7	44	4.28	-1	*O-101(100-1-0)/P-1	7	-1.5
1938 Bro-N	12	30	6	9	1	0	1	7	6	4	0	....	.300	.417	.433	.850	131	2	6	6.84	-1	/O-9(5-0-4)	1	0.0
Total 7	230	566	60	134	25	5	8	76	69	113	3	0	.237	.325	.341	.666	80	-15	69	4.20	-2	O-145/P-1	11	-2.6
• WINTERS, Matt	Matthew Littleton Winters b: 3/18/1960, Buffalo, NY BL/TR, 6'3", 215 lbs. Deb: 5/30/1989																							
1989 KC-A	42	107	14	25	6	0	2	9	14	23	0	0	.234	.322	.346	.668	89	-1	12	3.79	-2	O-31(0-0-31)/D-3	1	-0.4

YEAR TM-L	G	AB	R	H	2B	3B	HR	RBI	BB	SO	SB	CS	AVG	OBP	SLG	OPS	OPS+	BR/A	RC	RC/G	FR	G/POS	WS	TPW
• WIRTS, Kettle	Elwood Vernon Wirts b: 10/31/1897, Cosumnes, CA d: 7/12/1968, Sacramento, CA BR/TR, 5'11", 170 lbs. Deb: 7/20/1921																							
1921 Chi-N	7	11	0	2	0	0	0	1	0	3	0	0	.182	.182	.182	.364	-4	-2	0	1.03	0	/C-5	0	-0.1
1922 Chi-N	31	58	7	10	2	0	1	6	12	15	0	0	.172	.314	.259	.573	48	-4	5	3.02	-1	C-27	1	-0.4
1923 Chi-N	5	5	2	1	0	0	0	1	2	0	0	0	.200	.429	.200	.629	71	-0	1	4.14	0	/C-3	0	0.0
1924 Chi-A	6	12	0	1	0	0	0	0	2	2	1	0	.083	.214	.083	.298	-22	-2	0	1.08	1	/C-5	0	-0.1
Total 4	49	86	9	14	2	0	1	8	16	20	1	0	.163	.294	.221	.515	34	-7	7	2.52	0	/C-40	1	-0.5
• WISE, Bill	William E. Wise b: 3/15/1861, Washington, DC d: 5/5/1940, Washington, DC Deb: 5/2/1882 Career OF: 1-0-0 ♦																							
1882 Bal-a	5	20	2	2	1	0	0	1	0	....	....	....	.100	.100	.150	.250	-18	-2	0	.48	-0	/P-3,O-2(0-0-0)	1	-0.1
1884 Was-U	85	339	51	79	17	1	2	....	12	....	....	....	.233	.259	.307	.566	94	1	28	2.98	11	P-50,O-43(0-0-0)/3-8,S-2,1	30	1.6
1886 Was-N	1	3	0	0	0	0	0	0	0	1	0	....	.000	.000	.000	.000	-106	-1	0	.00	0	/O-1,P-1	0	-0.2
Total 3	91	362	53	81	18	1	2	1	12	1	0	....	.224	.249	.296	.544	86	-1	28	2.78	11	/P-54,O-46,3-8,S-2,1-1	31	1.3
• WISE, Casey	Kendall Cole Wise b: 9/8/1932, Lafayette, IN BB/TR, 6', 170 lbs. Deb: 4/16/1957																							
1957 Chi-N	43	106	12	19	3	1	0	7	11	14	0	0	.179	.256	.226	.483	32	-10	6	1.68	-1	2-31/S-5	1	-0.9
1958*Mil-N	31	71	8	14	1	0	0	0	4	8	1	1	.197	.240	.211	.451	23	-8	3	1.37	1	2-10/S-7,3-1	1	-0.6
1959 Mil-N	22	76	11	13	2	0	1	5	10	5	0	0	.171	.267	.237	.504	39	-6	5	1.96	-3	2-20/S-5	1	-0.8
1960 Det-A	30	68	6	10	0	2	2	5	4	9	1	0	.147	.194	.294	.489	28	-7	3	1.46	3	2-17,S-10/3-1	1	-0.3
Total 4	126	321	37	56	6	3	3	17	29	36	2	1	.174	.243	.240	.483	31	-32	17	1.63	-1	/2-78,S-27,3-2	4	-2.6
• WISE, Dewayne	Larry Dewayne Wise b: 2/24/1978, Columbia, SC BL/TL, 6'1", 180 lbs. Deb: 4/6/2000 Career OF: 20-4-29																							
2000 Tor-A	28	22	3	3	0	0	0	0	1	5	1	0	.136	.208	.136	.345	-10	-4	1	1.20	1	O-18(14-1-3)/D-2	0	-0.3
2002 Tor-A	42	112	14	20	4	1	3	13	4	15	5	0	.179	.207	.313	.519	34	-10	8	2.35	7	O-33(6-3-26)/D-2	1	-0.4
Total 2	70	134	17	23	4	1	3	13	5	20	6	0	.172	.207	.284	.491	27	-13	9	2.15	8	/O-51,D-4	1	-0.7
• WISE, Hughie	Hugh Edward Wise b: 3/9/1906, Campbellsville, KY d: 7/21/1987, Plantation, FL BB/TR, 6', 178 lbs. Deb: 9/26/1930																							
1930 Det-A	2	6	0	2	0	0	0	0	0	0	0	0	.333	.333	.333	.667	68	-0	1	4.24	0	/C-2	0	0.0
• WISE, Nick	Nicholas Joseph Wise b: 6/15/1866, Boston, MA d: 1/15/1923, Boston, MA BR/TR, 5'11", 194 lbs. Deb: 6/20/1888																							
1888 Bos-N	1	3	0	0	0	0	0	0	0	0	0	....	.000	.000	.000	.000	-96	-1	0	.00	0	/C-1,O-1	0	-0.1
• WISE, Sam	Samuel Washington "Modoc" Wise b: 8/18/1857, Akron, OH d: 1/22/1910, Akron, OH BL/TR, 5'10.5", 170 lbs. Deb: 7/30/1881 U Career OF: 12-0-36																							
1881 Det-N	1	4	0	2	0	0	0	0	0	2	....	....	.500	.500	.500	1.000	206	0	1	13.84	0	/3-1	0	0.0
1882 Bos-N	78	298	44	66	11	4	4	34	5	45	....	....	.221	.234	.326	.560	77	-8	23	2.76	-7	*S-72/3-6	6	-1.2
1883 Bos-N	96	406	73	110	25	7	4	58	13	74	....	....	.271	.294	.397	.690	105	2	48	4.50	-2	*S-96	14	0.3
1884 Bos-N	114	426	60	91	15	9	4	41	25	104	....	....	.214	.257	.319	.576	80	-9	36	2.94	4	*S-107/2-7	12	-0.1
1885 Bos-N	107	424	71	120	20	10	4	46	25	61	....	....	.283	.323	.406	.729	139	18	57	5.06	-2	*S-79,2-22/O-6(4-0-2)	19	1.9
1886 Bos-N	96	387	71	112	19	12	4	72	33	61	31	....	.289	.345	.432	.777	140	19	70	6.88	-12	1-57,2-20,S-18/O-1	17	0.3
1887 Bos-N	113	503	103	192	27	17	9	92	36	44	43	....	.382	.390	.522	.913	155	35	115	9.78	-4	S-72,O-27(4-0-23),2-16	22	2.8
1888 Bos-N	105	417	66	100	19	12	4	40	34	66	33	....	.240	.306	.372	.678	111	5	59	5.03	5	S-89/3-6,1-5,O-4(4-0-0),2	14	1.3
1889 Was-N	121	472	79	118	15	8	4	62	61	62	24	....	.250	.341	.341	.682	97	1	65	4.84	-19	2-72,S-26,3-13,O-10(0-0-10)	10	-1.3
1890 Buf-P	119	505	95	148	29	11	5	102	46	45	19	....	.293	.359	.424	.783	120	15	87	6.57	-9	*2-119	14	0.8
1891 Bal-a	103	388	70	96	14	5	1	48	62	52	33	....	.247	.364	.317	.681	94	-0	58	5.28	-2	*2-99/S-4	12	0.1
1893 Was-N	122	521	102	162	27	17	5	77	49	27	20	....	.311	.375	.457	.831	124	16	99	7.31	2	*2-91,3-31	17	1.8
Total 12	1175	4751	834	1317	221	112	48	672	389	643	203	....	.277	.332	.397	.729	114	93	718	5.61	-46	S-563,2-448/1-62,3-57,O-48	157	6.7
• WISNER, Phil	Philip N. Wisner b: 7/1869, Washington, DC d: 7/5/1936, Washington, DC TR Deb: 8/30/1895																							
1895 Was-N	1	0	0	0	0	0	0	0	0	0	0	....	....	....	....	....	-101	0	0	....	-1	/S-1	0	-0.1
• WISSMAN, Dave	David Alvin Wissman b: 2/17/1941, Greenfield, MA BL/TR, 6'2", 178 lbs. Deb: 9/15/1964																							
1964 Pit-N	16	27	2	4	0	0	0	0	1	9	0	0	.148	.179	.148	.327	-7	-4	1	.89	0	O-10(7-3-0)	0	-0.5
• WISTERZIL, Tex	George John Wisterzil b: 3/7/1888, Detroit, MI d: 6/27/1964, San Antonio, TX BR/TR, 5'9.5", 150 lbs. Deb: 4/14/1914																							
1914 Bro-F	149	534	54	137	18	10	0	66	34	47	17	....	.257	.314	.328	.642	82	-13	58	3.61	19	*3-149	16	1.1
1915 Bro-F	36	106	13	33	3	3	0	21	21	7	8	....	.311	.438	.396	.835	149	9	22	7.16	4	3-31	6	1.4
Chi-F	7	20	3	4	1	0	0	0	3	2	0	....	.200	.304	.250	.554	68	-1	2	2.55	1	/3-6	0	0.0
StL-F	8	24	1	5	1	0	0	4	2	2	2	....	.208	.296	.250	.546	58	-1	2	2.93	1	/3-8	1	0.0
Chi-F	42	144	12	36	3	1	0	14	5	10	2	....	.250	.280	.285	.565	70	-6	13	2.77	8	3-42	4	0.3
Yr.	93	294	29	78	8	4	0	39	31	21	12	....	.265	.345	.320	.665	100	1	39	4.23	13	3-87	11	1.8
Total 2	242	828	83	215	26	14	0	105	65	68	29	....	.260	.326	.325	.651	89	-12	97	3.84	32	3-236	27	2.9
• WITEK, Mickey	Nicholas Joseph Witek b: 12/19/1915, Luzerne, PA d: 8/24/1990, Kingston, PA BR/TR, 5'10", 170 lbs. Deb: 4/16/1940																							
1940 NY-N	119	433	34	111	7	0	3	31	24	17	2	....	.256	.295	.293	.589	62	-22	36	2.85	-4	S-89,2-32	7	-1.8
1941 NY-N	26	94	11	34	5	0	1	16	4	2	0	....	.362	.388	.447	.835	132	4	16	6.99	1	2-23	4	0.7
1942 NY-N	148	553	72	144	19	6	5	48	36	20	2	....	.260	.306	.344	.649	89	-9	54	3.26	2	*2-147	14	0.3
1943 NY-N	153	622	68	195	17	0	6	55	41	23	1	....	.314	.356	.370	.726	109	7	78	4.64	-5	*2-153	19	1.1
1946 NY-N	82	284	32	75	13	2	4	29	28	10	1	....	.264	.330	.366	.696	97	-2	34	4.27	-7	2-42,3-35	6	-0.7
1947 NY-N	51	160	22	35	4	1	3	17	15	12	1	....	.219	.286	.313	.598	58	-10	15	3.14	4	2-40/3-3	2	-0.4
1949 NY-A	2	1	0	1	0	0	0	0	0	0	0	0	1.000	1.000	1.000	2.000	430	0	1	∞	0	....	0	0.0
Total 7	581	2147	239	595	65	9	22	196	148	84	7	0	.277	.324	.347	.670	90	-32	235	3.82	-8	2-437/S-89,3-38	52	-0.8
• WITHROW, Corky	Raymond Wallace Withrow b: 11/28/1937, High Coal, WV BR/TR, 6'3.5", 197 lbs. Deb: 9/6/1963																							
1963 StL-N	6	9	0	0	0	0	0	1	0	2	0	0	.000	.000	.000	.000	-91	-2	0	.00	-0	/O-2(1-0-1)	0	-0.3
• WITHROW, Frank	Frank Blaine "Kid" Withrow b: 6/14/1891, Greenwood, MO d: 9/5/1966, Omaha, NE BR/TR, 5'11.5", 187 lbs. Deb: 4/15/1920																							
1920 Phi-N	48	132	8	24	4	1	0	12	8	26	0	0	.182	.239	.227	.467	33	-11	8	1.84	2	C-48	2	-0.6
1922 Phi-N	10	21	3	7	2	0	0	3	3	5	0	0	.333	.417	.429	.845	108	0	4	7.40	-1	/C-8	1	0.0
Total 2	58	153	11	31	6	1	0	15	11	31	0	0	.203	.265	.255	.520	44	-10	12	2.46	1	/C-56	3	-0.6
• WITMEYER, Ron	Ronald Herman Witmeyer b: 6/28/1967, West Islip, NY BL/TL, 6'3", 215 lbs. Deb: 8/25/1991																							
1991 Oak-A	11	19	0	1	0	0	0	0	0	5	0	0	.053	.053	.053	.105	-75	-4	0	.00	0	/1-8	0	-0.4
• WITT, Kevin	Kevin Joseph Witt b: 1/5/1976, High Point, NC BL/TR, 6'4", 200 lbs. Deb: 9/15/1998																							
1998 Tor-A	5	7	0	1	0	0	0	0	0	3	0	0	.143	.143	.143	.286	-25	-1	0	.64	0	/1-1	0	-0.1
1999 Tor-A	15	34	3	7	1	0	1	5	2	9	0	0	.206	.250	.324	.574	44	-3	3	2.82	0	D-10	0	-0.3
2001 SD-N	14	27	5	5	0	0	2	5	2	7	0	0	.185	.241	.407	.649	69	-1	3	3.30	0	/1-9	1	-0.2
2003 Det-A	93	270	25	71	9	0	10	26	15	68	1	1	.263	.304	.407	.712	92	-4	33	4.23	-0	D-36,1-27,O-13(13-0-0)/3-5	2	-0.8
Total 4	127	338	33	84	10	0	13	36	19	87	1	1	.249	.291	.393	.684	83	-10	38	3.92	0	/D-46,1-37,O-13,3-5	3	-1.5
• WITT, Whitey	Lawton Walter Witt b: 9/28/1895, Orange, MA d: 7/14/1988, Salem County, NJ BL/TR, 5'7", 150 lbs. Deb: 4/12/1916 Career OF: 50-447-232																							
1916 Phi-A	143	563	64	138	16	15	2	36	55	71	19	....	.245	.315	.337	.652	101	-1	66	3.97	-23	*S-142	10	-1.6
1917 Phi-A	128	452	62	114	13	4	0	28	65	45	12	....	.252	.346	.299	.645	98	2	50	3.71	-6	*S-111/O-7(7-0-0),3-6	13	0.4
1919 Phi-A	122	460	56	123	15	6	0	33	46	26	11	....	.267	.334	.326	.660	85	-9	52	3.90	-12	O-59(40-19-0),2-56/3-2	7	-2.4
1920 Phi-A	65	218	29	70	11	3	1	25	27	16	2	3	.321	.396	.413	.809	113	5	36	6.07	-6	O-50(0-5-45),2-10/S-2	6	-0.3
1921 Phi-A	154	629	100	198	31	11	4	45	77	52	16	15	.315	.390	.418	.809	106	6	104	5.92	-2	*O-154(0-0-154)	13	-0.8
1922*NY-A	140	528	98	157	11	6	4	40	**89**	29	5	8	.297	.400	.364	.763	98	2	81	5.55	-5	*O-139(0-109-30)	19	-0.9
1923*NY-A	146	596	113	187	18	10	6	56	67	42	2	7	.314	.386	.408	.794	107	7	95	5.80	-2	*O-144(0-144-0)	22	-0.1
1924 NY-A	147	600	88	178	26	5	1	36	45	20	9	7	.297	.346	.362	.707	83	-16	76	4.52	-7	*O-144(0-144-0)	13	-2.7
1925 NY-A	31	40	9	8	2	1	0	0	6	2	1	1	.200	.304	.300	.604	55	-3	4	3.07	0	O-10(0-9-1)	0	-0.3
1926 Bro-N	63	85	13	22	1	1	0	3	12	6	1	....	.259	.351	.294	.645	76	-2	9	3.71	-1	O-22(3-17-2)	2	-0.4
Total 10	1139	4171	632	1195	144	62	18	302	489	309	78	41	.287	.362	.364	.726	97	-9	574	4.85	-64	O-729,S-255/2-66,3-8	105	-9.0

YEAR TM-L	G	AB	R	H	2B	3B	HR	RBI	BB	SO	SB	CS	AVG	OBP	SLG	OPS	OPS+	BR/A	RC	RC/G	FR	G/POS	WS	TPW
• WITTE, Jerry	Jerome Charles Witte b: 7/30/1915, St. Louis, MO d: 4/27/2002, Houston, TX BR/TR, 6'1", 190 lbs. Deb: 9/10/1946																							
1946 StL-A	18	73	7	14	2	0	2	4	0	18	0	0	.192	.192	.301	.493	35	-7	4	1.98	-2	1-18	0	-1.0
1947 StL-A	34	99	4	14	2	1	2	12	11	22	0	0	.141	.227	.242	.470	30	-10	6	1.68	-2	1-27	0	-1.3
Total 2	**52**	**172**	**11**	**28**	**4**	**1**	**4**	**16**	**11**	**40**	**0**	**0**	**.163**	**.213**	**.267**	**.481**	**32**	**-16**	**10**	**1.80**	**-5**	**/1-45**	**0**	**-2.3**
• WOCKENFUSS, John	Johnny Bilton Wockenfuss b: 2/27/1949, Welch, WV BR/TR, 6', 190 lbs. Deb: 8/11/1974 Career OF: 42-0-69																							
1974 Det-A	13	29	1	4	1	0	0	2	3	2	0	0	.138	.219	.172	.391	13	-3	1	1.39	0	C-13	0	-0.3
1975 Det-A	35	118	15	27	6	3	4	13	10	15	0	0	.229	.289	.432	.721	97	-1	13	3.71	2	C-34	4	0.3
1976 Det-A	60	144	18	32	7	2	3	10	17	14	0	3	.222	.309	.361	.670	92	-3	15	3.50	-4	C-59	3	-0.5
1977 Det-A	53	164	26	45	8	1	9	25	14	18	0	0	.274	.331	.500	.831	117	4	28	6.28	-1	C-37/0-9(6-0-3),D-3	6	0.4
1978 Det-A	71	187	23	53	5	0	7	22	21	14	0	1	.283	.359	.422	.781	116	4	27	5.04	-4	0-60(6-0-55)/D-2	5	-0.2
1979 Det-A	87	231	27	61	9	1	15	46	18	40	2	2	.264	.323	.506	.829	116	4	34	5.05	1	1-31,C-20,D-18/0-6(5-0-1)	7	0.4
1980 Det-A	126	372	56	102	13	2	16	65	68	64	1	4	.274	.391	.449	.839	126	15	68	6.48	2	1-52,D-28,C-25,0-23(21-0-2)	15	1.4
1981 Det-A	70	172	20	37	4	0	9	25	28	22	0	0	.215	.325	.395	.720	103	1	23	4.30	-3	D-39,1-25/C-5,0-1	5	-0.4
1982 Det-A	70	193	28	58	9	0	8	32	29	21	0	0	.301	.392	.472	.863	135	10	37	7.16	-1	C-24,1-17,D-17,0-10(2-0-8)/3	9	0.8
1983 Det-A	92	245	32	66	8	1	9	44	31	37	1	1	.269	.351	.420	.772	114	5	37	5.31	2	D-39,C-29,1-13/3-1,0-1	9	0.7
1984 Phi-N	86	180	20	52	3	1	6	24	30	24	1	0	.289	.390	.417	.807	125	7	31	6.27	-5	1-39,C-21/3-2	6	0.2
1985 Phi-N	32	37	1	6	0	0	0	2	8	7	0	0	.162	.311	.162	.473	35	-3	2	1.52	-1	/1-7,C-2	0	-0.4
Total 12	**795**	**2072**	**267**	**543**	**73**	**11**	**86**	**310**	**277**	**278**	**5**	**11**	**.262**	**.351**	**.432**	**.783**	**114**	**41**	**316**	**5.31**	**-11**	**C-269,1-184,D-146,0-110/3-4**	**69**	**2.4**
• WOEHR, Andy	Andrew Emil Woehr b: 2/4/1896, Fort Wayne, IN d: 7/24/1990, Fort Wayne, IN BR/TR, 5'11", 165 lbs. Deb: 9/15/1923																							
1923 Phi-N	13	41	3	14	2	0	0	3	1	1	0	0	.341	.357	.390	.747	87	-1	6	5.32	0	3-13	1	0.0
1924 Phi-N	50	152	11	33	4	5	0	17	5	8	2	2	.217	.252	.309	.561	44	-12	12	2.47	-7	3-44/2-1	1	-1.7
Total 2	**63**	**193**	**14**	**47**	**6**	**5**	**0**	**20**	**6**	**9**	**2**	**2**	**.244**	**.274**	**.326**	**.600**	**53**	**-13**	**17**	**3.00**	**-6**	**/3-57,2-1**	**2**	**-1.6**
• WOERLIN, Joe	Joseph Woerlin b: 10/9/1864, France d: 6/22/1919, St. Louis, MO Deb: 7/21/1895																							
1895 Was-N	1	3	1	1	0	0	0	0	0	0	0	....	.333	.333	.333	.667	73	-0	0	3.99	0	/S-1	0	0.0
• WOHLFORD, Jim	James Eugene Wohlford b: 2/28/1951, Visalia, CA BR/TR, 5'11", 175 lbs. Deb: 9/1/1972 Career OF: 616-35-268																							
1972 KC-A	15	25	3	6	1	0	0	0	2	6	0	0	.240	.321	.280	.601	80	-0	3	3.55	-1	/2-8	0	-0.1
1973 KC-A	45	109	21	29	1	3	2	10	11	12	1	1	.266	.333	.385	.719	95	-1	14	4.43	3	D-19,0-13(12-0-1)	3	0.0
1974 KC-A	143	501	55	136	16	7	2	44	39	74	16	13	.271	.328	.343	.671	88	-9	55	3.75	2	*0-138(126-0-16)/D-1	10	-1.5
1975 KC-A	116	353	45	90	10	5	0	30	34	37	12	7	.255	.322	.312	.634	78	-10	38	3.56	-2	*0-102(43-0-66)/D-4	6	-1.7
1976*KC-A	107	293	47	73	10	2	1	24	29	24	22	16	.249	.319	.307	.626	83	-8	27	2.88	2	0-93(84-2-8)/D-3,2-1	5	-1.1
1977 Mil-A	129	391	41	97	16	3	2	36	21	49	17	16	.248	.288	.320	.608	65	-22	32	2.64	4	*0-125(97-4-33)/2-1,D-1	3	-2.3
1978 Mil-A	46	118	16	35	7	2	1	19	6	10	3	2	.297	.331	.415	.746	108	1	16	4.69	0	0-35(21-4-12)/D-4	3	-0.1
1979 Mil-A	63	175	19	46	13	1	1	17	8	28	6	2	.263	.295	.366	.661	77	-6	19	3.58	-4	0-55(35-14-8)/D-5	3	-1.1
1980 SF-N	91	193	17	54	6	4	1	24	13	23	1	4	.280	.329	.368	.696	96	-3	22	4.04	-1	0-49(40-4-8)/3-1	5	-0.7
1981 SF-N	50	68	4	11	3	0	1	7	4	9	0	0	.162	.208	.250	.458	30	-6	3	1.09	0	0-10(10-0-0)	0	-0.7
1982 SF-N	97	250	37	64	12	1	2	25	30	36	8	3	.256	.336	.336	.672	89	-3	28	3.72	-1	0-72(68-0-6)	6	-0.8
1983 Mon-N	83	141	7	39	8	0	1	14	5	14	0	0	.277	.301	.355	.656	82	-4	14	3.49	0	0-61(18-6-48)	2	-0.6
1984 Mon-N	95	213	20	64	13	2	5	29	14	19	3	0	.300	.344	.451	.794	127	7	34	6.14	0	0-59(44-1-14)/3-2	8	0.5
1985 Mon-N	70	125	7	24	5	1	1	15	16	18	0	2	.192	.284	.272	.556	60	-8	10	2.50	1	0-43(8-0-36)	1	-0.9
1986 Mon-N	70	94	10	25	4	2	1	11	9	17	0	2	.266	.330	.383	.713	97	-1	11	3.93	1	0-22(10-0-12)/3-6	2	-0.1
Total 15	**1220**	**3049**	**349**	**793**	**125**	**33**	**21**	**305**	**241**	**376**	**89**	**68**	**.260**	**.316**	**.343**	**.659**	**85**	**-73**	**325**	**3.57**	**3**	**0-877/D-37,2-10,3-9**	**57**	**-11.2**
• WOJCIK, John	John Joseph Wojcik b: 4/6/1942, Olean, NY BL/TR, 6', 175 lbs. Deb: 9/9/1962 Career OF: 26-2-11																							
1962 KC-A	16	43	8	13	4	0	0	9	13	4	3	0	.302	.474	.395	.869	133	4	11	9.46	0	0-12(10-0-5)	3	0.3
1963 KC-A	19	59	7	11	0	0	0	2	8	8	2	0	.186	.284	.186	.470	34	-5	4	2.17	0	0-17(10-2-6)	1	-0.6
1964 KC-A	6	22	1	3	0	0	0	0	2	8	0	0	.136	.208	.136	.345	-2	-3	1	1.04	0	/0-6(6-0-0)	0	-0.4
Total 3	**41**	**124**	**16**	**27**	**4**	**0**	**0**	**11**	**23**	**20**	**5**	**0**	**.218**	**.345**	**.250**	**.595**	**66**	**-4**	**15**	**4.20**	**0**	**/0-35**	**4**	**-0.6**
• WOLF, Jimmy	William Van Winkle "Chicken" Wolf b: 5/12/1862, Louisville, KY d: 5/16/1903, Louisville, KY BR/TR, 5'9", 190 lbs. Deb: 5/2/1882 M Career OF: 17-3-1026																							
1882 Lou-a	78	318	46	95	11	8	0	....	9	....	....	....	.299	.318	.384	.702	143	14	40	4.99	0	*0-70(3-0-67)/S-9,1-1,P-1	12	0.9
1883 Lou-a	98	389	59	102	17	9	1	0	5	....	....	....	.262	.272	.360	.631	109	5	39	3.80	11	*0-78(0-1-77),C-20/S-5,2-1	13	1.4
1884 Lou-a	110	486	79	146	24	11	3	73	4	....	....	....	.300	.310	.414	.724	140	20	64	5.17	5	*0-101(0-1-101),C-11/1-1,3,S	20	2.2
1885 Lou-a	112	483	79	141	23	17	1	52	11	....	....	....	.292	.309	.416	.725	128	13	64	5.03	0	*0-111(0-0-111)/C-2,3-1,P	16	1.0
1886 Lou-a	130	545	93	148	17	12	3	61	27	....	23	....	.272	.310	.363	.673	105	-0	70	4.77	12	*0-122(5-0-119)/1-8,C-3,2,P	14	0.5
1887 Lou-a	137	603	103	194	27	13	2	102	34	....	45	....	.322	.331	.385	.715	97	-4	89	5.91	12	*0-128(8-1-120),1-11	15	0.4
1888 Lou-a	128	538	80	154	28	11	0	67	25	....	41	....	.286	.320	.379	.700	126	14	80	5.66	4	0-85(1-0-84),S-39/3-4,C-3,1	17	1.7
1889 Lou-a	130	546	72	159	20	9	3	57	29	34	18	....	.291	.333	.377	.710	104	1	76	5.23	2	0-88(0-0-88),1-16,2-13,S-10/3	8	0.1
1890*Lou-a	134	543	100	**197**	29	11	4	98	43	....	46	....	**.363**	.421	.479	.900	169	46	132	10.12	-1	*0-123(0-0-123),3-12	27	3.8
1891 Lou-a	136	528	67	135	16	8	1	81	42	36	13	....	.256	.320	.322	.642	85	-11	60	4.05	2	*0-133(0-0-133)/1-5,3-1	9	-1.1
1892 StL-N	3	14	1	2	0	0	0	1	0	1	0	....	.143	.143	.143	.286	-14	-2	0	.66	0	/0-3(0-0-3)	0	-0.2
Total 11	**1196**	**4993**	**779**	**1473**	**212**	**109**	**18**	**592**	**229**	**71**	**186**	**....**	**.295**	**.327**	**.388**	**.715**	**119**	**96**	**715**	**5.48**	**46**	***0-1042/S-64,1-43,C-39,3,2,P**	**151**	**10.5**
• WOLF, Ray	Raymond Bernard "Grandpa" Wolf b: 7/15/1904, Chicago, IL d: 10/6/1979, Fort Worth, TX BR/TR, 5'11", 175 lbs. Deb: 7/27/1927																							
1927 Cin-N	1	1	0	0	0	0	0	0	0	0	0	....	.000	.000	.000	.000	-103	-0	0	.00	0	/1-1	0	0.0
• WOLFE, Harry	Harold "Whitey" Wolfe b: 11/24/1890, Worcester, MA d: 7/28/1971, Fort Wayne, IN BR/TR, 5'8", 160 lbs. Deb: 4/15/1917																							
1917 Chi-N	9	5	1	2	0	0	0	1	1	1	0	....	.400	.500	.400	.900	165	0	1	8.38	0	/0-2(1-0-0),S-1	0	0.0
Pit-N	3	5	0	0	0	0	0	0	1	4	0	....	.000	.167	.000	.167	-45	-1	0	.00	1	/2-1,S-1	0	0.0
Yr.	12	10	1	2	0	0	0	1	2	5	0	....	.200	.333	.200	.533	60	-0	1	3.14	0	/0-2(1-0-0),S-2,2-1	0	0.0
• WOLFE, Larry	Laurence Marcy Wolfe b: 3/2/1953, Melbourne, FL BR/TR, 5'11", 170 lbs. Deb: 9/16/1977																							
1977 Min-A	8	25	3	6	1	0	0	6	1	0	0	0	.240	.269	.280	.549	51	-2	2	2.63	0	/3-8	0	-0.2
1978 Min-A	88	235	25	55	10	1	3	25	36	27	0	1	.234	.336	.323	.659	85	-4	26	3.63	-4	3-81/S-7	5	-0.9
1979 Bos-A	47	78	12	19	4	0	3	15	17	21	0	0	.244	.385	.410	.796	109	2	14	5.89	-1	2-27/3-9,S-2,1-1,C-1,D-1	3	0.1
1980 Bos-A	18	23	3	3	1	0	1	4	0	5	0	0	.130	.130	.304	.435	15	-3	1	.77	-1	3-14/D-4	0	-0.4
Total 4	**161**	**361**	**43**	**83**	**16**	**1**	**7**	**50**	**54**	**53**	**0**	**1**	**.230**	**.332**	**.338**	**.670**	**84**	**-7**	**43**	**3.83**	**-7**	**3-112/2-27,S-9,D-5,1-1,C-1**	**8**	**-1.3**
• WOLFE, Polly	Roy Chamberlain Wolfe b: 9/1/1888, Knoxville, IL d: 11/21/1938, Morris, IL BL/TR, 5'10", 170 lbs. Deb: 9/22/1912																							
1912 Chi-A	1	1	0	0	0	0	0	0	0	....	0	....	.000	.000	.000	.000	-103	-0	0	.00	0	....	0	0.0
1914 Chi-A	8	28	0	6	0	0	0	0	3	6	1	1	.214	.290	.214	.505	53	-2	2	2.04	-1	/0-7(0-0-7)	0	-0.3
Total 2	**9**	**29**	**0**	**6**	**0**	**0**	**0**	**0**	**3**	**6**	**1**	**1**	**.207**	**.281**	**.207**	**.488**	**48**	**-2**	**2**	**1.95**	**-1**	**/0-7**	**0**	**-0.3**
• WOLSTENHOLME, Abe	Abraham Lincoln Wolstenholme b: 3/4/1861, Philadelphia, PA d: 3/4/1916, Philadelphia, PA Deb: 6/4/1883																							
1883 Phi-N	3	11	0	1	1	0	0	0	0	0	....	....	.091	.091	.182	.273	-22	-1	0	.51	0	/C-2,0-1	0	-0.2
• WOLTER, Harry	Harry Meigs Wolter b: 7/11/1884, Monterey, CA d: 7/6/1970, Palo Alto, CA BL/TL, 5'10", 175 lbs. Deb: 5/14/1907 Career OF: 5-126-361 ♦																							
1907 Cin-N	4	15	1	2	0	0	0	1	0	....	0	....	.133	.133	.133	.267	-16	-2	0	.55	-0	/0-4(0-0-4)	0	-0.2
Pit-N	1	1	0	0	0	0	0	0	0	....	0	....	.000	.000	.000	.000	-99	-0	0	.00	0	/P-1	0	-0.1
StL-N	16	47	4	16	0	0	0	6	3	....	1	....	.340	.380	.340	.720	130	2	7	5.55	2	0-12(1-6-2)/P-3	2	0.0
Yr.	21	63	5	18	0	0	0	7	3	....	1	....	.286	.318	.286	.604	94	0	7	3.98	2	0-16(1-6-6)/P-4	2	-0.3
1909 Bos-A	54	121	14	29	2	4	2	10	9	....	2	....	.240	.292	.372	.664	107	2	14	3.67	-1	1-17,P-11/0-9(0-0-9)	4	-0.7
1910 NY-A	135	479	84	128	15	9	4	42	66	....	39	....	.267	.364	.361	.725	120	14	78	5.45	-4	*0-129(1-0-128)/1-2	21	0.5
1911 NY-A	122	434	78	132	17	15	4	36	62	....	28	....	.304	.396	.440	.836	125	16	86	7.18	5	*0-113(0-7-106)/1-2	17	1.5
1912 NY-A	12	32	8	11	2	1	0	1	10	....	5	....	.344	.512	.469	.980	170	4	10	12.61	-1	/0-9(0-5-4)	2	0.3
1913 NY-A	127	425	53	108	18	6	2	43	80	50	13	....	.254	.377	.339	.716	109	9	58	4.51	-9	*0-121(0-106-14)	14	-0.6

YEAR TM-L	G	AB	R	H	2B	3B	HR	RBI	BB	SO	SB	CS	AVG	OBP	SLG	OPS	OPS+	BR/A	RC	RC/G	FR	G/POS	WS	TPW
1917 Chi-N	117	353	44	88	15	7	0	28	38	40	7	....	.249	.324	.331	.655	94	-2	39	3.71	2	0-97(3-2-94)/1-1	10	-0.5
Total 7	588	1907	286	514	69	42	12	167	268	90	95	....	.270	.365	.369	.733	113	44	292	5.22	-6	0-494/1-22,P-15	70	0.2
• WOLVERTON, Harry	Harry Sterling "Fighting Harry" Wolverton b: 12/6/1873, Mount Vernon, OH d: 2/4/1937, Oakland, CA BL/TR, 5'11", 205 lbs. Deb: 9/25/1898 M																							
1898 Chi-N	13	49	4	16	1	0	0	2	1	....	1	....	.327	.353	.347	.700	101	-0	7	5.08	2	3-13	1	0.2
1899 Chi-N	99	389	50	111	14	11	1	49	30	....	14	....	.285	.350	.386	.736	105	3	61	5.50	-10	3-98/S-1	11	-0.5
1900 Chi-N	3	11	2	2	0	0	0	0	2	....	1	....	.182	.308	.182	.490	38	-1	1	2.79	0	/3-3	0	-0.1
Phi-N	101	383	42	108	10	8	3	58	20	....	4	....	.282	.323	.373	.696	92	-5	50	4.64	-12	*3-101	9	-1.4
Yr.	104	394	44	110	10	8	3	58	22	....	5	....	.279	.322	.368	.690	91	-6	51	4.59	-12	*3-104	9	-1.5
1901 Phi-N	93	379	42	117	15	4	0	43	22	....	13	....	.309	.356	.369	.726	108	4	57	5.60	6	3-93	15	1.3
1902 Was-A	59	249	35	62	8	3	1	23	13	....	8	....	.249	.292	.317	.609	68	-11	26	3.68	3	3-59	4	-0.6
Phi-N	34	136	12	40	3	2	0	16	9	....	3	....	.294	.347	.346	.693	114	2	18	4.84	7	3-34	6	1.1
1903 Phi-N	123	494	72	152	13	12	0	53	18	....	10	....	.308	.342	.383	.725	110	5	73	5.27	4	*3-123	15	1.2
1904 Phi-N	102	398	43	106	15	5	0	49	26	....	18	....	.266	.321	.329	.650	105	2	50	4.33	-5	*3-102	12	0.1
1905 Bos-N	122	463	38	104	15	7	2	55	23	....	10	....	.225	.276	.300	.576	73	-16	43	3.06	1	*3-122	8	-1.2
1912 NY-A	34	50	6	15	1	1	0	4	2	....	1	....	.300	.340	.360	.700	94	-0	6	4.60	-2	/3-8	1	-0.2
Total 9	783	3001	346	833	95	53	7	352	166	....	83	....	.278	.326	.352	.677	97	-17	392	4.59	-5	3-756/S-1	82	-0.1
• WOMACK, Sid	Sidney Kirk "Tex" Womack b: 10/2/1896, Greensburg, LA d: 8/28/1958, Jackson, MS BR/TR, 5'11", 185 lbs. Deb: 8/15/1926																							
1926 Bos-N	1	3	0	0	0	0	0	1	0	0	0	0	.000	.000	.000	.000	-110	-1	0	.00	-0	/C-1	0	-0.1
• WOMACK, Tony	Anthony Darrell Womack b: 9/25/1969, Danville, VA BL/TR, 5'9", 160 lbs. Deb: 9/10/1993 Career OF: 0-18-126																							
1993 Pit-N	15	24	5	2	0	0	0	0	3	3	2	0	.083	.185	.083	.269	-25	-4	1	.91	2	/S-6	0	-0.2
1994 Pit-N	5	12	4	4	0	0	0	1	2	3	0	0	.333	.429	.333	.762	101	0	2	6.54	-1	/2-3,S-2	1	-0.1
1996 Pit-N	17	30	11	10	3	1	0	7	6	1	2	0	.333	.459	.500	.959	149	3	8	9.69	-2	/0-6(0-5-1),2-4	2	0.1
1997 Pit-N★	155	641	85	178	26	9	6	50	43	109	**60**	7	.278	.326	.374	.700	81	-8	87	4.91	-10	*2-152/S-4	18	-1.1
1998 Pit-N	159	655	85	185	26	7	3	45	38	94	**58**	8	.282	.322	.357	.679	77	-13	84	4.59	12	*2-152/0-5(0-5-0),S-2	17	0.6
1999★Ari-N	144	614	111	170	25	10	4	41	52	68	**72**	13	.277	.335	.370	.705	78	-11	87	4.91	4	*0-123(0-6-122),2-19,S-19	14	-1.1
2000 Ari-N	146	617	95	167	21	**14**	7	57	30	74	45	11	.271	.310	.384	.694	72	-24	77	4.37	-5	*S-143/0-2(0-0-2)	16	-1.6
2001★Ari-N	125	481	66	128	19	5	3	30	23	54	28	7	.266	.308	.345	.653	65	-23	54	3.92	1	*S-118/0-1	10	-1.2
2002★Ari-N	153	590	90	160	23	5	5	57	46	80	29	12	.271	.328	.353	.681	73	-22	70	4.09	-13	*S-149/0-1	15	-2.3
2003 Ari-N	61	219	30	52	10	3	2	15	8	27	8	3	.237	.271	.338	.609	52	-16	19	2.85	-9	S-58	2	-2.0
Col-N	21	79	9	15	2	0	0	5	0	9	3	1	.190	.200	.215	.415	7	-11	3	1.35	-5	S-14/2-7,0-1	1	-1.4
Chi-N	21	51	4	12	2	1	0	2	1	11	2	1	.235	.250	.314	.564	47	-4	4	2.69	-2	2-14/S-1	1	-0.6
Yr.	103	349	43	79	14	4	2	22	9	47	13	5	.226	.252	.307	.559	41	-30	26	2.47	-16	S-73,2-21/0-1	4	-4.0
Total 10	1022	4013	595	1083	157	55	30	310	252	533	309	63	.270	.317	.359	.676	72	-132	495	4.32	-28	S-516,2-351,0-139	97	-10.6
• WOOD,	Wood Deb: 9/30/1874																							
1874 Bal-n	1	5	0	0	0	0	0	0	0	1	0	0	.000	.000	.000	.000	-101	-1	0	.00	-1	/2-1	....	-0.1
• WOOD, Bob	Robert Lynn Wood b: 7/28/1865, Thorn Hill, OH d: 5/22/1943, Churchill, OH BR/TR, 5'8.5", 153 lbs. Deb: 5/2/1898 Career OF: 3-2-4																							
1898 Cin-N	39	109	14	30	6	0	0	16	9	....	1	....	.275	.331	.330	.661	84	-2	13	4.19	-2	C-29/1-1,0-1	3	-0.2
1899 Cin-N	62	194	34	61	11	7	0	24	25	....	3	....	.314	.406	.443	.850	130	9	37	7.33	-4	C-53/3-2,0-2(1-1-0),1-1	9	0.8
1900 Cin-N	45	139	17	37	8	1	0	22	10	....	3	....	.266	.320	.338	.658	84	-3	17	4.25	-2	C-18,3-15/0-1	3	-0.3
1901 Cle-A	98	346	45	101	23	3	1	49	12	....	6	....	.292	.327	.384	.711	101	-0	47	5.01	5	C-84/3-4,0-3(1-0-2),1-1,2,S	11	1.2
1902 Cle-A	81	258	23	76	18	2	0	40	27	....	1	....	.295	.375	.380	.754	114	6	39	5.50	-3	C-52,1-16/0-2(0-0-2),2-1,3	8	0.7
1904 Det-A	49	175	15	43	6	2	1	17	5	....	1	....	.246	.271	.320	.591	89	-3	16	3.17	10	C-47	5	1.4
1905 Det-A	8	24	1	2	1	0	0	0	1	....	0	....	.083	.120	.125	.245	-22	-3	0	.44	-1	/C-7	0	-0.4
Total 7	382	1245	149	350	73	15	2	168	89	....	15	....	.281	.339	.369	.707	101	4	169	4.92	3	C-290/3-22,1-19,0-9,2-2,S-1	39	3.3
• WOOD, Doc	Charles Spencer Wood b: 2/28/1900, Batesville, MS d: 11/3/1974, New Orleans, LA BR/TR, 5'10", 150 lbs. Deb: 7/21/1923																							
1923 Phi-A	3	3	0	1	0	0	0	0	0	0	0	0	.333	.333	.333	.667	75	-0	0	4.24	0	/S-3	0	0.0
• WOOD, Fred	Frederick Llewellyn Wood b: 7/21/1863, Hamilton, Canada d: 8/23/1933, New York, NY, 5'5", 150 lbs. Deb: 5/14/1884																							
1884 Det-N	12	42	4	2	0	0	0	1	3	18	....	....	.048	.111	.048	.159	-51	-7	0	.16	-3	/C-7,0-6(0-0-6),S-1	0	-0.8
1885 Buf-N	1	4	0	1	0	0	0	0	0	0	....	....	.250	.250	.250	.500	60	-0	0	2.31	0	/C-1	0	0.0
Total 2	13	46	4	3	0	0	0	1	3	18	....	....	.065	.122	.065	.188	-42	-7	0	.31	-3	/C-8,0-6,S-1	0	-0.8
• WOOD, George	George A. "Dandy" Wood b: 11/9/1858, Boston, MA d: 4/4/1924, Harrisburg, PA BL/TR, 5'10.5", 175 lbs. Deb: 5/1/1880 M/U Career OF: 1192-5-36																							
1880 Wor-N	81	327	37	80	16	5	0	28	10	37	....	....	.245	.267	.324	.591	91	-4	29	3.23	-5	*0-80(80-0-0)/3-2,1-1	8	-1.3
1881 Det-N	80	337	54	100	18	9	2	32	19	32	....	....	.297	.334	.421	.756	130	11	49	5.54	-3	*0-80(80-0-0)	11	0.3
1882 Det-N	84	375	69	101	12	12	**7**	29	14	30	....	....	.269	.296	.421	.717	127	11	48	4.81	-1	*0-84(84-0-0)	13	0.7
1883 Det-N	99	441	81	133	26	11	5	47	25	37	....	....	.302	.339	.444	.784	142	23	68	6.08	4	*0-99(96-3-0)/P-1	17	1.8
1884 Det-N	114	473	79	119	16	10	8	29	39	75	....	....	.252	.309	.378	.687	122	14	57	4.40	0	*0-114(114-0-1)/3-1	10	0.9
1885 Det-N	82	362	62	105	19	8	5	28	13	19	....	....	.290	.315	.428	.743	138	14	50	5.25	1	0-70(70-0-0),3-12/P-1,S-1	11	1.4
1886 Phi-N	106	450	81	123	18	15	4	50	23	75	9	....	.273	.309	.407	.715	115	7	61	5.02	-5	*0-97(96-1-0)/S-6,3-3	18	-0.1
1887 Phi-N	113	531	118	182	22	19	14	66	40	51	19	....	.343	.350	.497	.847	125	15	94	7.17	-11	*0-104(104-0-0)/2-3,3-3,S	18	0.0
1888 Phi-N	106	433	67	99	19	6	6	51	39	44	20	....	.229	.303	.342	.645	100	0	52	4.21	1	*0-104(104-0-0)/3-2,P-2	13	-0.3
1889 Phi-N	97	422	77	106	21	4	5	53	53	33	17	....	.251	.336	.355	.692	86	-9	58	4.83	-5	0-92(92-0-0)/S-6,P-1	9	-1.6
Bal-a	3	10	1	2	0	0	0	1	0	2	1	....	.200	.200	.200	.400	14	-1	1	2.04	0	/0-3(0-0-3)	0	-0.1
1890 Phi-P	132	539	115	156	20	14	9	102	51	35	20	....	.289	.360	.429	.788	107	4	92	6.52	11	*0-132(128-0-4)/3-1	16	0.8
1891 Phi-a	132	528	105	163	18	14	3	61	72	52	22	....	.309	.399	.413	.812	128	21	98	7.12	1	*0-122(122-0-0)/3-6,S-5	20	1.5
1892 Bal-N	21	76	9	17	1	1	0	10	10	8	1	....	.224	.330	.263	.593	78	-2	7	3.25	2	0-21(21-0-0)	1	-0.2
Cin-N	30	107	10	21	2	4	0	14	10	17	4	....	.196	.271	.290	.561	71	-4	10	3.05	0	0-30(1-1-28)	1	-0.5
Yr.	51	183	19	38	3	5	0	24	20	25	5	....	.208	.296	.279	.575	74	-6	17	3.13	1	0-51(22-1-28)	2	-0.7
Total 13	1280	5411	965	1507	228	132	68	601	418	547	113	....	.279	.329	.403	.732	116	100	773	5.34	-10	*0-1232/3-30,S-21,P-5,2-3,1	166	3.4
• WOOD, Harry	Harold Austin Wood b: 2/10/1885, Waterville, ME d: 5/18/1955, Bethesda, MD BL/TR, 5'10", 155 lbs. Deb: 4/19/1903																							
1903 Cin-N	2	3	0	0	0	0	0	0	1	....	0	....	.000	.250	.000	.250	-24	-0	0	.00	0	/0-2(1-0-1)	0	-0.1
• WOOD, Jake	Jacob Wood b: 6/22/1937, Elizabeth, NJ BR/TR, 6'1", 170 lbs. Deb: 4/11/1961 Career OF: 1-0-2																							
1961 Det-A	162	663	96	171	17	**14**	11	69	58	141	30	9	.258	.321	.376	.697	83	-14	84	4.39	1	*2-162	18	0.1
1962 Det-A	111	367	68	83	10	5	8	30	33	59	24	3	.226	.292	.346	.638	68	-13	40	3.70	-8	2-90	6	-1.4
1963 Det-A	85	351	50	95	11	2	11	27	24	61	18	5	.271	.330	.407	.737	102	2	50	5.08	-3	2-81/3-1	11	0.7
1964 Det-A	64	125	11	29	2	2	1	7	4	24	0	0	.232	.256	.304	.560	54	-8	10	2.80	-1	1-11,2-10/3-6,0-1	1	-1.0
1965 Det-A	58	104	12	30	3	0	2	7	10	19	3	3	.288	.357	.375	.732	107	1	12	3.76	-3	2-20/1-1,3-1,S-1	2	-0.1
1966 Det-A	98	230	39	58	9	3	2	27	28	48	4	3	.252	.336	.343	.679	94	-1	27	3.84	-5	2-52/3-4,1-2	6	-0.3
1967 Det-A	14	20	2	1	1	0	0	0	1	7	0	0	.050	.095	.100	.195	-41	-4	0	.15	0	/1-2,2-2	0	-0.4
Cin-N	16	17	1	2	0	0	0	1	1	3	0	0	.118	.167	.118	.284	-16	-3	0	.68	0	/0-2(0-0-2)	0	-0.3
Total 7	608	1877	279	469	53	26	35	168	159	362	79	23	.250	.313	.362	.675	82	-40	223	4.07	-19	2-417/1-16,3-12,0-3,S-1	44	-2.7
• WOOD, Jason	Jason William Wood b: 12/16/1969, San Bernardino, CA BR/TR, 6'1", 200 lbs. Deb: 4/1/1998																							
1998 Oak-A	3	1	1	0	0	0	0	0	0	1	0	0	.000	.000	.000	.000	-102	-0	0	.00	0	/S-2,3-1	0	0.0
Det-A	10	23	5	8	2	0	1	1	3	4	0	1	.348	.423	.565	.988	153	1	5	8.94	-1	/1-6,D-3,S-1	0	0.0
Yr.	13	24	6	8	2	0	1	1	3	5	0	1	.333	.407	.542	.949	144	1	5	8.42	0	/1-6,D-3,S-3,3-1	0	0.0
1999 Det-A	27	44	5	7	1	0	1	8	2	13	0	0	.159	.196	.250	.446	13	-6	2	1.64	-4	/3-9,S-9,1-5,2-1,D-1	0	-0.9
Total 2	40	68	11	15	3	0	2	9	5	18	0	1	.221	.274	.353	.627	60	-5	8	3.73	-5	/S-12,1-11,3-10,D-4,2-1	0	-0.9
• WOOD, Jimmy	James Leon Wood b: 12/1/1844, Brooklyn, NY d: 11/30/1886, TR, 5'8.5", 150 lbs. Deb: 5/8/1871 M																							
1871 Chi-n	28	135	45	51	10	6	1	29	11	3	18	2	.378	.425	.563	.988	163	12	41	14.99	7	*2-28	....	1.2
1872 Tro-n	25	113	40	38	11	4	2	27	2	1	3	0	.336	.348	.558	.905	172	9	24	9.73	3	2-25	....	0.8

YEAR TM-L	G	AB	R	H	2B	3B	HR	RBI	BB	SO	SB	CS	AVG	OBP	SLG	OPS	OPS+	BR/A	RC	RC/G	FR	G/POS	WS	TPW
Eck-n	7	30	10	6	1	1	0	0	4	1	1	0	.200	.294	.300	.594	98	1	3	3.89	-1	/2-7	....	0.0
Yr.	32	143	50	44	12	5	2	27	6	2	4	0	.308	.336	.503	.839	155	11	27	8.31	3	*2-32	....	0.8
1873 Phi-n	42	209	67	67	11	1	0	27	8	1	8	3	.321	.346	.383	.728	112	3	31	6.56	1	*2-42	....	0.1
Total 3 n	102	487	162	162	33	12	3	83	25	6	30	5	.333	.365	.468	.833	139	26	99	9.28	11	2-102	....	2.1

• WOOD, Joe Joseph Perry "J.P.,Little Joe" Wood b: 10/3/1919, Houston, TX d: 3/25/1985, Houston, TX BR/TR, 5'9.5", 160 lbs. Deb: 5/2/1943

YEAR TM-L	G	AB	R	H	2B	3B	HR	RBI	BB	SO	SB	CS	AVG	OBP	SLG	OPS	OPS+	BR/A	RC	RC/G	FR	G/POS	WS	TPW
1943 Det-A	60	164	22	53	4	4	1	17	6	13	2	2	.323	.347	.415	.762	114	2	21	4.65	-16	2-22,3-18	5	-1.3

• WOOD, Joe Joe "Smokey Joe" Wood
b: 10/25/1889, Kansas City, MO d: 7/27/1985, West Haven, CT BR/TR, 5'11", 180 lbs. Deb: 8/24/1908 Career OF: 106-31-295 ♦

YEAR TM-L	G	AB	R	H	2B	3B	HR	RBI	BB	SO	SB	CS	AVG	OBP	SLG	OPS	OPS+	BR/A	RC	RC/G	FR	G/POS	WS	TPW
1908 Bos-A	6	7	1	0	0	0	0	0	0	....	0	....	.000	.000	.000	.000	-97	-1	0	.00	-0	/P-6	1	-0.1
1909 Bos-A	24	55	4	9	0	1	0	3	2	....	0	....	.164	.207	.200	.407	28	-0	2	1.23	-4	P-24	13	0.3
1910 Bos-A	35	69	9	18	2	1	1	5	5	....	0	....	.261	.311	.362	.673	108	5	8	3.77	2	P-35	14	2.8
1911 Bos-A	44	88	15	23	4	2	2	11	10	....	1	....	.261	.343	.420	.764	114	8	13	4.89	2	P-44	26	4.6
1912*Bos-A	43	124	16	36	13	1	1	13	11	....	0	....	.290	.348	.435	.784	118	10	19	5.23	8	P-43	44	6.9
1913 Bos-A	25	56	10	15	5	0	0	10	4	7	1	....	.268	.317	.357	.674	95	4	6	3.86	4	P-23	13	1.8
1914 Bos-A	21	43	2	6	1	0	0	1	3	14	1	....	.140	.213	.163	.376	13	-0	2	1.26	0	P-18	8	-0.2
1915 Bos-A	29	54	6	14	1	1	1	7	5	10	1	1	.259	.322	.370	.692	111	4	7	4.07	1	P-25	20	2.7
1917 Cle-A	10	6	1	0	0	0	0	0	0	3	0	....	.000	.000	.000	.000	-93	-1	0	.00	0	/P-5	1	-0.3
1918 Cle-A	119	422	41	125	22	4	5	66	36	38	8	....	.296	.356	.403	.759	117	8	63	5.04	-1	0-95(84-1-10),2-19/1-4	16	0.4
1919 Cle-A	72	192	30	49	10	6	0	27	32	21	3	....	.255	.367	.370	.737	101	2	27	4.68	-5	0-64(15-6-43)/P-1	6	-0.6
1920*Cle-A	61	137	25	37	11	2	1	30	25	16	1	1	.270	.390	.401	.792	107	3	24	5.53	0	0-55(5-2-48)/P-1	5	-0.4
1921 Cle-A	66	194	32	71	16	5	4	60	25	17	2	0	.366	.438	.562	1.000	151	16	49	9.75	-4	0-64(0-21-56)	10	0.8
1922 Cle-A	142	505	74	150	33	8	8	92	50	63	5	1	.297	.367	.442	.809	109	8	85	5.95	1	*0-141(2-1-138)	16	-0.1
Total 14	697	1952	266	553	118	31	23	325	208	189	23	3	.283	.357	.411	.768	109	67	305	5.32	6	0-419,P-225/2-19,1-4	193	18.7

• WOOD, Ken Kenneth Lanier Wood b: 7/1/1924, Lincolnton, NC BR/TR, 6', 200 lbs. Deb: 4/28/1948 Career OF: 100-7-176

YEAR TM-L	G	AB	R	H	2B	3B	HR	RBI	BB	SO	SB	CS	AVG	OBP	SLG	OPS	OPS+	BR/A	RC	RC/G	FR	G/POS	WS	TPW
1948 StL-A	10	24	2	2	0	1	0	2	1	4	0	0	.083	.120	.167	.287	-24	-4	0	.20	0	/0-5(0-0-5)	0	-0.4
1949 StL-A	7	6	0	0	0	0	0	0	1	2	0	0	.000	.143	.000	.143	-58	-1	0	.17	-1	/0-3(2-0-1)	0	-0.2
1950 StL-A	128	369	42	83	24	0	13	62	38	58	0	4	.225	.299	.396	.695	74	-18	40	3.50	0	0-94(7-0-88)	4	-1.9
1951 StL-A	109	333	40	79	19	0	15	44	27	49	1	2	.237	.296	.429	.726	92	-7	40	3.99	-3	*0-100(29-4-69)	6	-1.3
1952 Bos-A	15	20	0	2	0	0	0	0	3	4	0	0	.100	.217	.100	.317	-9	-3	1	.92	0	0-13(1-0-12)	0	-0.4
Was-A	61	210	26	50	8	6	6	32	30	21	0	1	.238	.333	.419	.752	112	3	30	4.82	3	0-56(54-3-1)	8	0.2
Yr.	76	230	26	52	8	6	6	32	33	25	0	1	.226	.323	.391	.714	102	0	30	4.44	3	0-69(55-3-13)	8	-0.2
1953 Was-A	12	33	0	7	1	0	0	3	2	3	0	0	.212	.257	.242	.500	36	-3	2	1.99	1	/0-7(7-0-0)	0	-0.2
Total 6	342	995	110	223	52	7	34	143	102	141	1	7	.224	.298	.393	.691	82	-34	113	3.70	1	0-278	18	-4.3

• WOOD, Roy Roy Winton "Woody" Wood b: 8/29/1892, Monticello, AR d: 4/6/1974, Fayetteville, AR BR/TR, 6', 175 lbs. Deb: 6/16/1913 Career OF: 14-13-24

YEAR TM-L	G	AB	R	H	2B	3B	HR	RBI	BB	SO	SB	CS	AVG	OBP	SLG	OPS	OPS+	BR/A	RC	RC/G	FR	G/POS	WS	TPW
1913 Pit-N	14	35	4	10	4	0	0	2	1	8	0	....	.286	.306	.400	.706	105	-0	4	4.05	1	/0-8(8-0-0),1-1	1	0.0
1914 Cle-A	72	220	24	52	6	3	1	15	13	26	6	9	.236	.300	.305	.605	79	-9	19	2.84	-2	0-40(5-13-23),1-20	2	-1.4
1915 Cle-A	33	78	5	15	2	1	0	3	2	13	1	2	.192	.232	.244	.475	41	-7	4	1.70	-2	1-21/0-2(1-0-1)	0	-0.9
Total 3	119	333	33	77	12	4	1	20	16	47	7	11	.231	.285	.300	.585	73	-15	27	2.68	-2	/0-50,1-42	3	-2.3

• WOOD, Ted Edward Robert Wood b: 1/4/1967, Mansfield, OH BL/TL, 6'2", 178 lbs. Deb: 9/4/1991 Career OF: 14-0-19

YEAR TM-L	G	AB	R	H	2B	3B	HR	RBI	BB	SO	SB	CS	AVG	OBP	SLG	OPS	OPS+	BR/A	RC	RC/G	FR	G/POS	WS	TPW
1991 SF-N	10	25	0	3	0	0	0	1	2	11	0	0	.120	.185	.120	.305	-13	-4	1	.85	-1	/0-8(0-0-8)	0	-0.5
1992 SF-N	24	58	5	12	2	0	1	3	6	15	0	0	.207	.292	.293	.585	70	-2	4	2.31	0	0-16(6-0-10)	0	-0.3
1993 Mon-N	13	26	4	5	1	0	0	3	3	3	0	0	.192	.276	.231	.507	36	-2	2	2.27	0	/0-8(8-0-1)	1	-0.3
Total 3	47	109	9	20	3	0	1	7	11	29	0	0	.183	.264	.239	.503	43	-8	7	1.96	-2	/0-32	1	-1.1

• WOODALL, Larry Charles Lawrence Woodall b: 7/26/1894, Staunton, VA d: 5/6/1963, Cambridge, MA BR/TR, 5'9", 165 lbs. Deb: 5/20/1920 C

YEAR TM-L	G	AB	R	H	2B	3B	HR	RBI	BB	SO	SB	CS	AVG	OBP	SLG	OPS	OPS+	BR/A	RC	RC/G	FR	G/POS	WS	TPW
1920 Det-A	18	49	4	12	1	0	0	5	2	6	0	0	.245	.275	.265	.540	45	-4	4	2.48	0	C-15	0	-0.2
1921 Det-A	46	80	10	29	4	1	0	14	6	7	1	0	.363	.407	.438	.844	117	3	15	6.81	-1	C-25	2	0.2
1922 Det-A	50	125	19	43	2	2	0	18	8	11	0	1	.344	.388	.392	.780	107	1	19	5.88	-4	C-40	4	-0.1
1923 Det-A	71	148	20	41	12	2	1	19	22	9	2	1	.277	.371	.405	.776	106	2	24	5.53	1	C-60	6	0.6
1924 Det-A	67	165	23	51	9	2	0	25	21	5	0	0	.309	.387	.388	.775	102	2	26	5.84	-1	C-62	7	0.4
1925 Det-A	75	171	20	35	4	1	0	13	24	8	1	0	.205	.303	.240	.542	39	-15	14	2.69	-5	C-75	2	-1.5
1926 Det-A	67	146	18	34	5	0	0	15	15	2	0	0	.233	.304	.267	.571	49	-10	13	2.93	0	C-59	3	-0.7
1927 Det-A	88	246	28	69	8	6	0	39	37	9	9	1	.280	.375	.362	.736	90	-0	37	5.27	3	C-86	10	0.8
1928 Det-A	65	186	19	39	7	1	0	13	24	10	3	1	.210	.300	.258	.558	47	-13	16	2.79	2	C-62	3	-0.7
1929 Det-A	1	1	0	0	0	0	0	0	0	0	0	0	.000	.000	.000	.000	-100	-0	0	.00	0	....	0	0.0
Total 10	548	1317	161	353	52	15	1	161	159	67	16	4	.268	.347	.333	.680	78	-35	167	4.39	-4	C-484	37	-1.4

• WOODARD, Darrell Darrell Lee Woodard b: 12/10/1956, Wilma, AR BR/TR, 5'11", 160 lbs. Deb: 8/6/1978

YEAR TM-L	G	AB	R	H	2B	3B	HR	RBI	BB	SO	SB	CS	AVG	OBP	SLG	OPS	OPS+	BR/A	RC	RC/G	FR	G/POS	WS	TPW
1978 Oak-A	33	9	10	0	0	0	0	0	1	1	3	4	.000	.100	.000	.100	-73	-3	0	.00	-1	2-14/3-1,D-1	0	-0.4

• WOODARD, Mike Michael Cary Woodard b: 3/2/1960, Melrose Park, IL BL/TR, 5'9", 155 lbs. Deb: 9/11/1985

YEAR TM-L	G	AB	R	H	2B	3B	HR	RBI	BB	SO	SB	CS	AVG	OBP	SLG	OPS	OPS+	BR/A	RC	RC/G	FR	G/POS	WS	TPW
1985 SF-N	24	82	12	20	1	0	0	9	5	3	6	1	.244	.287	.256	.543	56	-4	7	2.98	-1	2-23	2	-0.4
1986 SF-N	48	79	14	20	2	1	1	5	10	9	7	2	.253	.337	.342	.679	92	0	11	4.57	0	2-23/3-2,S-2	3	0.1
1987 SF-N	10	19	0	4	1	0	0	1	0	1	0	0	.211	.211	.263	.474	26	-2	1	1.89	-0	/2-8	0	-0.2
1988 Chi-A	18	45	3	6	0	1	0	4	1	5	1	1	.133	.170	.178	.348	-2	-6	1	.77	-2	2-14/D-2	1	-0.8
Total 4	100	225	29	50	4	2	1	19	16	18	14	4	.222	.277	.271	.548	55	-12	20	2.93	-4	/2-68,3-2,D-2,S-2	6	-1.4

• WOODHEAD, Red James Woodhead b: 7/9/1851, Chelsea, MA d: 9/7/1881, Boston, MA, 5'6", 160 lbs. Deb: 4/15/1873

YEAR TM-L	G	AB	R	H	2B	3B	HR	RBI	BB	SO	SB	CS	AVG	OBP	SLG	OPS	OPS+	BR/A	RC	RC/G	FR	G/POS	WS	TPW
1873 Mar-n	1	5	1	0	0	0	0	0	0	0	0	0	.000	.000	.000	.000	-130	-1	0	.00	1	/S-1	....	0.0
1879 Syr-N	34	131	4	21	1	0	0	2	0	23	....	....	.160	.160	.168	.328	9	-11	4	.92	-4	3-34	1	-1.3

• WOODLING, Gene Eugene Richard Woodling b: 8/16/1922, Akron, OH d: 6/2/2001, Barberton, OH BL/TR, 5'9.5", 195 lbs. Deb: 9/23/1943 C Career OF: 1230-93-304

YEAR TM-L	G	AB	R	H	2B	3B	HR	RBI	BB	SO	SB	CS	AVG	OBP	SLG	OPS	OPS+	BR/A	RC	RC/G	FR	G/POS	WS	TPW
1943 Cle-A	8	25	5	8	2	1	1	5	1	5	0	0	.320	.346	.600	.946	186	2	5	8.08	0	/0-6(0-1-5)	2	0.2
1946 Cle-A	61	133	8	25	1	4	0	9	16	13	1	2	.188	.280	.256	.536	54	-9	11	2.48	-2	0-37(6-31-0)	1	-1.2
1947 Pit-N	22	79	7	21	2	2	0	10	7	5	0	....	.266	.326	.342	.667	75	-3	9	4.10	-1	0-21(1-20-0)	1	-0.4
1949*NY-A	112	296	60	80	13	7	5	44	52	21	2	2	.270	.381	.412	.793	110	5	50	5.89	-3	0-98(82-12-5)	12	-0.3
1950*NY-A	122	449	81	127	20	10	6	60	70	31	5	3	.283	.381	.412	.793	106	6	75	6.00	11	*0-118(117-2-0)	16	0.8
1951*NY-A	120	420	65	118	15	8	15	71	62	37	0	4	.281	.373	.462	.835	130	16	75	6.39	-2	*0-116(101-17-0)	19	0.6
1952*NY-A	122	408	58	126	19	6	12	63	59	31	1	4	.309	.397	.473	.870	150	27	81	7.44	4	*0-118(112-6-0)	21	2.4
1953*NY-A	125	395	64	121	26	4	10	58	82	29	2	7	.306	**.429**	.468	.898	147	29	82	7.46	2	*0-119(119-0-0)	20	2.4
1954 NY-A	97	304	33	76	12	5	3	40	53	35	3	4	.250	.361	.352	.713	99	1	42	4.76	0	0-89(89-0-0)	10	-0.5
1955 Bal-A	47	145	22	32	6	2	3	18	24	18	1	1	.221	.335	.352	.687	91	-1	18	4.15	-1	0-44(26-4-25)	3	-0.4
Cle-A	79	259	33	72	15	1	5	35	36	15	2	4	.278	.372	.402	.774	104	1	38	5.07	-3	0-70(64-0-16)	7	-0.6
Yr.	126	404	55	104	21	3	8	53	60	33	3	5	.257	.359	.384	.743	99	-0	57	4.73	-4	*0-114(90-4-41)	10	-1.0
1956 Cle-A	100	317	56	83	17	0	8	38	69	29	2	6	.262	.398	.391	.790	107	5	53	5.61	-3	0-85(85-0-2)	12	-0.3
1957 Cle-A	133	430	74	138	25	2	19	78	64	35	0	5	.321	.412	.521	.933	155	33	94	8.15	6	*0-113(113-0-0)	25	3.3
1958 Bal-A	133	413	57	114	16	1	15	65	66	49	4	2	.276	.378	.429	.807	128	19	68	5.74	-2	*0-116(61-0-68)	16	1.3
1959 Bal-A★	140	440	63	132	22	2	14	77	78	35	1	1	.300	.405	.455	.860	139	27	87	7.32	-2	*0-124(85-0-57)	20	2.0
1960 Bal-A	140	435	68	123	18	3	11	62	84	40	3	0	.283	.403	.414	.817	123	19	80	6.70	5	*0-124(124-0-1)	22	1.8
1961 Was-A	110	342	39	107	16	4	10	57	50	24	1	0	.313	.404	.471	.874	139	21	66	7.21	3	0-90(15-0-77)	14	1.9
1962 Was-A	44	107	19	30	4	0	5	16	24	5	1	0	.280	.421	.458	.879	138	7	23	7.82	-1	0-30(3-0-27)	4	0.5
NY-N	81	190	18	52	8	1	5	24	24	22	0	0	.274	.358	.405	.763	103	1	28	5.15	-1	0-48(27-0-21)	3	-0.2
Total 17	1796	5587	830	1585	257	63	147	830	921	479	29	45	.284	.388	.431	.819	124	206	986	6.29	9	*0-1566	228	13.2

• WOODRUFF, Pete Franklin Woodruff b: 6/1873, NY BR/TR Deb: 9/19/1899

YEAR TM-L	G	AB	R	H	2B	3B	HR	RBI	BB	SO	SB	CS	AVG	OBP	SLG	OPS	OPS+	BR/A	RC	RC/G	FR	G/POS	WS	TPW
1899 NY-N	20	61	11	15	1	1	2	7	9	....	3	....	.246	.343	.393	.736	105	1	9	5.47	0	0-19(0-0-19)/1-1	2	0.0

YEAR	TM-L	G	AB	R	H	2B	3B	HR	RBI	BB	SO	SB	CS	AVG	OBP	SLG	OPS	OPS+	BR/A	RC	RC/G	FR	G/POS	WS	TPW
• WOODRUFF, Sam		Orville Francis Woodruff b: 12/27/1876, Chilo, OH d: 7/22/1937, Cincinnati, OH BR/TR, 5'9", 160 lbs. Deb: 4/14/1904																							
1904	Cin-N	87	306	20	58	14	3	0	20	19	....	9	....	.190	.244	.255	.499	50	-19	23	2.31	4	3-61,2-17/S-8,O-1	3	-1.4
1910	Cin-N	21	61	6	9	1	0	0	2	7	8	2	....	.148	.235	.164	.399	18	-6	3	1.40	-2	3-17/2-4	1	-0.9
Total	**2**	**108**	**367**	**26**	**67**	**15**	**3**	**0**	**22**	**26**	**8**	**11**	**....**	**.183**	**.242**	**.240**	**.482**	**44**	**-25**	**26**	**2.15**	**1**	**/3-78,2-21,S-8,O-1**	**4**	**-2.2**
• WOODS, Al		Alvis Woods b: 8/8/1953, Oakland, CA BL/TL, 6'3", 195 lbs. Deb: 4/7/1977 Career OF: 522-0-15																							
1977	Tor-A	122	440	58	125	17	4	6	35	36	38	8	7	.284	.338	.382	.720	95	-4	55	4.32	-1	*O-115(106-0-15)/D-4	8	-1.1
1978	Tor-A	62	220	19	53	12	3	3	25	11	23	1	2	.241	.280	.364	.644	78	-8	21	3.15	-2	O-60(60-0-0)	3	-1.3
1979	Tor-A	132	436	57	121	24	4	5	36	40	28	6	4	.278	.340	.385	.725	94	-4	58	4.65	3	*O-127(127-0-0)/D-2	9	-0.6
1980	Tor-A	109	373	54	112	18	2	15	47	37	35	4	4	.300	.365	.480	.845	124	11	66	6.46	2	O-88(88-0-0),D-13	15	0.8
1981	Tor-A	85	288	20	71	15	0	1	21	19	31	3	4	.247	.293	.309	.602	69	-12	25	2.81	-1	O-77(77-0-0)/D-2	3	-1.8
1982	Tor-A	85	201	20	47	11	1	3	24	21	20	1	3	.234	.306	.343	.650	71	-9	21	3.45	-2	O-64(64-0-0),D-10	3	-1.3
1986	Min-A	23	28	5	9	1	0	2	8	3	5	0	0	.321	.387	.571	.959	153	2	6	8.76	0	/D-7	1	0.2
Total	**7**	**618**	**1986**	**233**	**538**	**98**	**14**	**35**	**196**	**167**	**180**	**23**	**24**	**.271**	**.328**	**.387**	**.716**	**93**	**-23**	**252**	**4.37**	**-2**	**O-531/D-38**	**42**	**-5.1**
• WOODS, Gary		Gary Lee Woods b: 7/20/1954, Santa Barbara, CA BR/TR, 6'2", 190 lbs. Deb: 9/14/1976 Career OF: 164-175-107																							
1976	Oak-A	6	8	0	1	0	0	0	0	0	3	0	0	.125	.125	.125	.250	-28	-1	0	.48	0	/O-4(1-2-1),D-1	0	-0.2
1977	Tor-A	60	227	21	49	9	1	0	17	7	38	5	4	.216	.246	.264	.510	39	-20	14	1.94	-3	O-60(0-60-0)	2	-2.3
1978	Tor-A	8	19	1	3	1	0	0	0	1	1	1	0	.158	.200	.211	.411	15	-2	1	1.61	-0	/O-6(0-1-5)	0	-0.2
1980*	Hou-N	19	53	8	20	5	0	2	15	2	9	1	0	.377	.400	.585	.985	186	6	12	9.71	-0	O-14(4-0-12)	3	0.6
1981*	Hou-N	54	110	10	23	4	1	0	12	11	22	2	1	.209	.281	.264	.545	58	-6	8	2.21	-1	O-40(2-3-35)	1	-0.9
1982	Chi-N	117	245	28	66	15	1	4	30	21	48	3	3	.269	.327	.388	.715	97	-2	31	4.36	1	*O-103(37-67-12)	7	-0.4
1983	Chi-N	93	190	25	46	9	0	4	22	15	27	5	3	.242	.298	.353	.650	76	-7	18	3.16	-1	O-73(40-27-13)/2-1	2	-1.0
1984*	Chi-N	87	98	13	23	4	1	3	10	15	21	2	1	.235	.336	.388	.724	94	-1	13	4.29	0	O-62(36-11-18)/2-3	3	-0.2
1985	Chi-N	81	82	11	20	3	0	0	4	14	18	0	1	.244	.354	.280	.635	72	-3	9	3.55	0	O-56(44-4-11)	1	-0.5
Total	**9**	**525**	**1032**	**117**	**251**	**50**	**4**	**13**	**110**	**86**	**187**	**19**	**13**	**.243**	**.303**	**.337**	**.640**	**76**	**-36**	**106**	**3.40**	**-5**	**O-418/2-4,D-1**	**19**	**-5.1**
• WOODS, Jim		James Jerome "Woody" Woods b: 9/17/1939, Chicago, IL BR/TR, 6', 175 lbs. Deb: 9/27/1957																							
1957	Chi-N	2	0	1	0	0	0	0	0	0	0	0	0	....	....	....	....	-102	0	0	....	0	....	0	0.0
1960	Phi-N	11	34	4	6	0	0	1	3	3	13	0	0	.176	.243	.265	.508	39	-3	2	2.23	0	3-11	0	-0.3
1961	Phi-N	23	48	6	11	3	0	2	9	4	15	0	0	.229	.302	.417	.719	89	-1	5	3.32	0	3-15	1	-0.1
Total	**3**	**36**	**82**	**11**	**17**	**3**	**0**	**3**	**12**	**7**	**28**	**0**	**0**	**.207**	**.278**	**.354**	**.631**	**69**	**-4**	**7**	**2.88**	**-1**	**/3-26**	**1**	**-0.4**
• WOODS, Ron		Ronald Lawrence Woods b: 2/1/1943, Hamilton, OH BR/TR, 5'10", 173 lbs. Deb: 4/22/1969 Career OF: 122-268-95																							
1969	Det-A	17	15	3	4	0	0	1	3	2	3	0	0	.267	.353	.467	.820	122	0	3	6.51	0	/O-7(7-1-0)	1	0.0
	NY-A	72	171	18	30	5	2	1	7	22	29	2	0	.175	.273	.246	.519	48	-11	13	2.27	1	O-67(1-66-0)	2	-1.3
	Yr.	89	186	21	34	5	2	2	10	24	32	2	0	.183	.280	.263	.543	54	-11	15	2.56	0	O-74(8-67-0)	3	-1.3
1970	NY-A	95	225	30	51	5	3	8	27	33	35	4	2	.227	.326	.382	.708	100	0	27	3.83	0	O-78(2-9-70)	6	-0.3
1971	NY-A	25	32	4	8	1	0	1	2	4	2	0	0	.250	.333	.375	.708	107	0	4	4.89	-1	/O-9(3-0-6)	1	-0.1
	Mon-N	51	138	26	41	7	3	1	17	19	18	0	2	.297	.382	.413	.795	125	4	21	5.35	3	O-45(32-23-0)	6	0.6
1972	Mon-N	97	221	21	57	5	1	10	31	22	33	3	3	.258	.325	.425	.750	110	2	30	4.67	-2	O-73(8-58-10)	7	-0.2
1973	Mon-N	135	318	45	73	11	3	3	31	56	34	12	6	.230	.345	.311	.656	80	-6	39	3.96	-7	*O-114(29-91-4)	9	-1.8
1974	Mon-N	90	127	15	26	0	0	1	12	17	17	6	5	.205	.303	.228	.532	48	-9	9	2.22	-1	O-61(40-20-5)	1	-1.3
Total	**6**	**582**	**1247**	**162**	**290**	**34**	**12**	**26**	**130**	**175**	**171**	**27**	**18**	**.233**	**.328**	**.342**	**.670**	**87**	**-19**	**146**	**3.81**	**-7**	**O-454**	**33**	**-4.2**
• WOODSON, Tracy		Tracy Michael Woodson b: 10/5/1962, Richmond, VA BR/TR, 6'3", 215 lbs. Deb: 4/7/1987																							
1987	LA-N	53	136	14	31	8	1	1	11	9	21	1	1	.228	.286	.324	.609	63	-8	12	3.09	1	3-45/1-7	2	-0.8
1988*	LA-N	65	173	15	43	4	1	3	15	7	32	1	2	.249	.282	.335	.617	79	-6	15	2.95	-5	3-41,1-25	2	-1.3
1989	LA-N	4	6	0	0	0	0	0	0	0	1	0	0	.000	.000	.000	.000	-102	-2	0	.00	0	/3-1	0	-0.2
1992	StL-N	31	114	9	35	8	0	1	22	3	10	0	0	.307	.331	.404	.734	110	1	15	5.06	-3	3-26/1-3	5	-0.2
1993	StL-N	62	77	4	16	2	0	0	2	1	14	0	0	.208	.218	.234	.452	21	-9	4	1.63	-1	3-28,1-11	0	-1.0
Total	**5**	**215**	**506**	**42**	**125**	**22**	**2**	**5**	**50**	**20**	**78**	**2**	**3**	**.247**	**.281**	**.328**	**.609**	**71**	**-23**	**47**	**3.15**	**-8**	**3-141/1-46**	**9**	**-3.4**
• WOODWARD, Chris		Christopher Michael Woodward b: 6/27/1976, Covina, CA BR/TR, 6', 173 lbs. Deb: 6/7/1999																							
1999	Tor-A	14	26	1	6	1	0	0	2	2	6	0	0	.231	.286	.269	.555	42	-2	2	2.38	0	S-10/3-2	0	-0.1
2000	Tor-A	37	104	16	19	7	0	3	14	10	28	1	0	.183	.254	.337	.591	46	-9	9	2.86	0	S-22/3-9,1-3,2-3	2	-0.6
2001	Tor-A	37	63	9	12	3	2	2	5	1	14	0	1	.190	.203	.397	.600	52	-5	4	2.15	8	2-17,3-10/S-4,1-2	1	0.3
2002	Tor-A	90	312	48	86	13	4	13	45	26	72	3	0	.276	.337	.468	.805	107	3	49	5.43	10	S-79/2-6,1-3,3-2,D-1	10	1.9
2003	Tor-A	104	349	49	91	22	2	7	45	28	72	1	2	.261	.321	.395	.716	86	-8	44	4.39	-2	*S-103	9	-0.1
Total	**5**	**282**	**854**	**123**	**214**	**46**	**8**	**25**	**111**	**67**	**192**	**5**	**3**	**.251**	**.310**	**.411**	**.721**	**85**	**-21**	**109**	**4.32**	**17**	**S-218/2-26,3-23,1-8,D-1**	**22**	**1.3**
• WOODWARD, Woody		William Frederick Woodward b: 9/23/1942, Miami, FL BR/TR, 6'2", 185 lbs. Deb: 9/9/1963																							
1963	Mil-N	10	2	1	0	0	0	0	0	0	0	0	0	.000	.000	.000	.000	-101	-1	0	.00	0	/S-5	0	-0.1
1964	Mil-N	77	115	18	24	2	1	0	11	6	28	0	1	.209	.260	.243	.504	43	-9	7	2.11	0	2-40,S-18/3-7,1-1	1	-0.6
1965	Mil-N	112	265	17	55	7	4	0	11	10	50	2	2	.208	.236	.264	.501	40	-22	16	1.98	4	*S-107/2-8	4	-1.1
1966	Atl-N	144	455	46	120	23	3	0	43	37	54	2	2	.264	.325	.327	.652	81	-11	49	3.62	-2	2-79,S-73	10	-0.1
1967	Atl-N	136	429	30	97	15	2	0	25	37	51	0	6	.226	.289	.270	.559	62	-23	32	2.42	12	*2-120,S-16	7	0.0
1968	Atl-N	12	24	2	4	1	0	0	1	1	6	1	0	.167	.200	.208	.408	23	-2	1	1.19	1	/S-6,3-2,2-1	0	0.0
	Cin-N	56	119	13	29	2	0	0	10	7	23	1	0	.244	.297	.261	.557	64	-5	10	2.83	-8	S-41/2-9,1-1	1	-1.1
	Yr.	68	143	15	33	3	0	0	11	8	29	2	0	.231	.281	.252	.533	57	-7	11	2.52	-7	S-47,2-10/3-2,1-1	1	-1.1
1969	Cin-N	97	241	36	63	12	0	0	15	24	40	3	2	.261	.333	.311	.645	77	-6	25	3.50	-5	S-93/2-2	6	-0.2
1970*	Cin-N	100	264	23	59	8	3	1	14	20	21	1	2	.223	.283	.288	.571	51	-19	21	2.64	4	S-77,3-20,2-10/1-2	3	-0.7
1971	Cin-N	136	273	22	66	9	1	0	18	27	28	4	0	.242	.310	.282	.592	72	-8	25	2.98	-1	S-85,3-63/2-9	6	-0.2
Total	**9**	**880**	**2187**	**208**	**517**	**79**	**14**	**1**	**148**	**169**	**301**	**14**	**15**	**.236**	**.295**	**.287**	**.582**	**64**	**-105**	**186**	**2.81**	**6**	**S-521,2-278/3-92,1-4**	**38**	**-3.9**
• WOOTEN, Junior		Earl Hazwell Wooten b: 1/16/1924, Pelzer, SC BR/TL, 5'11", 160 lbs. Deb: 9/16/1947 Career OF: 1-61-22																							
1947	Was-A	6	24	0	2	0	0	0	1	0	4	1	0	.083	.083	.083	.167	-55	-5	0	.13	-1	/O-6(1-6-0)	0	-0.6
1948	Was-A	88	258	34	66	8	3	1	23	24	21	2	1	.256	.324	.322	.646	74	-9	29	3.82	2	O-73(0-55-22)/1-6,P-1	6	-1.1
Total	**2**	**94**	**282**	**34**	**68**	**8**	**3**	**1**	**24**	**24**	**25**	**3**	**1**	**.241**	**.305**	**.301**	**.607**	**64**	**-14**	**29**	**3.44**	**1**	**/O-79,1-6,P-1**	**6**	**-1.7**
• WOOTEN, Shawn		William Shawn Wooten b: 7/24/1972, Glendora, CA BR/TR, 5'10", 225 lbs. Deb: 8/19/2000																							
2000	Ana-A	7	9	2	5	1	0	0	1	0	0	0	0	.556	.556	.667	1.222	202	1	3	22.50	-1	/C-4,1-3	0	0.1
2001	Ana-A	79	221	24	69	8	1	8	32	5	42	2	0	.312	.336	.466	.802	106	2	33	5.64	-3	D-27,C-25,1-21/3-1	6	-0.3
2002*	Ana-A	49	113	13	33	8	0	3	19	6	24	2	0	.292	.333	.442	.776	104	1	16	5.22	-1	D-24,1-16/C-2,3-1	3	-0.2
2003	Ana-A	98	272	25	66	8	0	7	32	24	45	0	4	.243	.306	.349	.656	75	-12	27	3.33	-1	1-32,D-25,C-19,3-17	2	-1.4
Total	**4**	**233**	**615**	**64**	**173**	**25**	**1**	**18**	**84**	**35**	**111**	**4**	**4**	**.281**	**.325**	**.413**	**.738**	**93**	**-8**	**80**	**4.62**	**-6**	**/D-76,1-72,C-50,3-19**	**11**	**-1.8**
• WORDSWORTH, Favel		Favel Perry Wordsworth b: 11/22/1850, New York, NY d: 8/12/1888, New York, NY Deb: 4/28/1873																							
1873	Res-n	12	42	5	10	0	0	0	3	2	1	0	0	.238	.273	.238	.511	57	-2	3	2.66	-6	S-11/O-1	....	-0.5
• WORKMAN, Chuck		Charles Thomas Workman b: 1/6/1915, Leeton, MO d: 1/3/1953, Kansas City, MO BL/TR, 6', 175 lbs. Deb: 9/18/1938 Career OF: 22-8-300																							
1938	Cle-A	2	5	1	2	0	0	0	0	0	0	0	0	.400	.400	.400	.800	103	0	1	6.78	0	/O-1	0	0.0
1941	Cle-A	9	4	2	0	0	0	0	0	1	1	0	0	.000	.200	.000	.200	-45	-1	0	.35	0	....	0	-0.1
1943	Bos-N	153	615	71	153	17	1	10	67	53	72	12	....	.249	.311	.328	.640	86	-11	66	3.72	12	*O-149(16-0-133)/1-3,3-1	15	-1.1
1944	Bos-N	140	418	46	87	18	3	11	53	42	41	1	....	.208	.287	.344	.631	74	-15	43	3.33	6	*O-103(0-0-103),3-19	7	-1.5
1945	Bos-N	139	514	77	141	16	2	25	87	51	58	9	....	.274	.347	.459	.806	122	14	84	5.79	-15	*3-107,O-24(0-0-24)	13	-0.1
1946	Bos-N	25	48	5	8	2	0	2	7	3	11	0	....	.167	.231	.333	.564	58	-3	4	2.34	-1	O-12(3-8-1)	0	-0.4
	Pit-N	58	145	11	32	4	1	2	16	11	19	2	....	.221	.280	.303	.584	64	-7	13	2.82	4	O-40(3-0-38)/3-1	2	-0.4
	Yr.	83	193	16	40	6	1	4	23	14	30	2	....	.207	.268	.311	.579	62	-10	16	2.70	4	O-52(6-8-39)/3-1	2	-0.9
Total	**6**	**526**	**1749**	**213**	**423**	**57**	**7**	**50**	**230**	**161**	**202**	**24**	**0**	**.242**	**.311**	**.368**	**.679**	**91**	**-24**	**209**	**4.08**	**6**	**O-329,3-128/1-3**	**37**	**-3.7**

YEAR TM-L	G	AB	R	H	2B	3B	HR	RBI	BB	SO	SB	CS	AVG	OBP	SLG	OPS	OPS+	BR/A	RC	RC/G	FR	G/POS	WS	TPW
• WORKMAN, Hank	Henry Kilgariff Workman b: 2/5/1926, Los Angeles, CA BL/TR, 6'1", 185 lbs. Deb: 9/4/1950																							
1950 NY-A	2	5	1	1	0	0	0	0	0	1	0	0	.200	.200	.200	.400	3	-1	0	1.38	0	/1-1	0	-0.1
• WORTH, Herb	Herbert Worth b: 5/2/1847, d: 4/27/1914, Brooklyn, NY Deb: 7/29/1872 U																							
1872 Atl-n	1	5	1	1	1	0	0	1	0	0	0	0	.200	.200	.400	.600	68	-0	0	3.18	-0	/0-1	....	0.0
• WORTHINGTON, Craig	Craig Richard Worthington b: 4/17/1965, Los Angeles, CA BR/TR, 6', 200 lbs. Deb: 4/26/1988																							
1988 Bal-A	26	81	5	15	2	0	2	4	9	24	1	0	.185	.267	.284	.551	56	-5	6	2.51	1	3-26	1	-0.4
1989 Bal-A	145	497	57	123	23	0	15	70	61	114	1	2	.247	.335	.384	.719	105	4	65	4.52	-6	*3-145	20	-0.1
1990 Bal-A	133	425	46	96	17	0	8	44	63	96	1	2	.226	.330	.322	.652	86	-7	47	3.57	-1	*3-131/D-2	8	-0.7
1991 Bal-A	31	102	11	23	3	0	4	12	12	14	0	1	.225	.313	.373	.686	93	-1	12	3.72	-5	3-30	2	-0.6
1992 Cle-A	9	24	0	4	0	0	0	2	2	4	0	1	.167	.231	.167	.397	13	-3	1	1.12	-1	/3-9	0	-0.4
1995 Cin-N	10	18	1	5	1	0	1	2	2	1	0	0	.278	.350	.500	.850	122	1	3	6.92	0	/1-4,3-2	0	0.0
Tex-A	26	68	4	15	4	0	2	6	7	8	0	0	.221	.293	.368	.661	69	-3	6	2.56	0	3-26	1	-0.3
1996 Tex-A	13	19	2	3	0	0	1	4	6	3	0	0	.158	.360	.316	.676	69	-1	3	3.62	1	/3-7,1-6	0	0.0
Total 7	**393**	**1234**	**126**	**284**	**50**	**0**	**33**	**144**	**162**	**264**	**3**	**6**	**.230**	**.323**	**.351**	**.674**	**90**	**-16**	**142**	**3.81**	**-12**	**3-376/1-10,D-2**	**32**	**-2.6**
• WORTHINGTON, Red	Robert Lee Worthington b: 4/24/1906, Alhambra, CA d: 12/8/1963, Sepulveda, CA BR/TR, 5'11", 170 lbs. Deb: 4/14/1931 Career OF: 221-0-28																							
1931 Bos-N	128	491	47	143	25	10	4	44	26	38	1	....	.291	.328	.407	.736	100	-1	66	4.87	0	*0-124(114-0-10)	13	-0.8
1932 Bos-N	105	435	62	132	35	8	8	61	15	24	1	....	.303	.330	.476	.806	118	9	68	5.68	-1	*0-104(104-0-0)	16	0.2
1933 Bos-N	17	45	3	7	4	0	0	0	1	3	0	....	.156	.174	.244	.418	20	-5	1	.83	0	0-10(3-0-7)	0	-0.6
1934 Bos-N	41	65	6	16	5	0	0	6	6	5	0	....	.246	.319	.323	.643	78	-2	6	3.37	-1	0-11(0-0-11)	1	-0.3
StL-N	1	1	0	0	0	0	0	0	0	1	0	....	.000	.000	.000	.000	-94	-0	0	.00	0	....	0	0.0
Yr.	42	66	6	16	5	0	0	6	6	6	0	....	.242	.315	.318	.633	76	-2	6	3.30	-1	0-11(0-0-11)	1	-0.3
Total 4	**292**	**1037**	**118**	**298**	**69**	**18**	**12**	**111**	**48**	**71**	**2**	**....**	**.287**	**.321**	**.423**	**.745**	**103**	**1**	**142**	**4.87**	**-2**	**0-249**	**30**	**-1.6**
• WORTMAN, Chuck	William Lewis Wortman b: 1/5/1892, Baltimore, MD d: 8/19/1977, Las Vegas, NV BR/TR, 5'7", 150 lbs. Deb: 7/20/1916																							
1916 Chi-N	69	234	17	47	4	2	2	16	18	22	4	....	.201	.258	.261	.519	54	-13	17	2.34	-16	S-69	1	-2.8
1917 Chi-N	75	190	24	33	4	1	0	9	18	23	6	....	.174	.245	.205	.450	36	-14	12	1.79	-16	S-65/2-1,3-1	0	-3.0
1918*Chi-N	17	17	4	2	0	0	1	3	1	2	3	....	.118	.167	.294	.461	39	-1	1	1.93	-3	/2-8,S-4	0	-0.5
Total 3	**161**	**441**	**45**	**82**	**8**	**3**	**3**	**28**	**37**	**47**	**13**	**....**	**.186**	**.249**	**.238**	**.487**	**45**	**-28**	**30**	**2.08**	**-35**	**S-138/2-9,3-1**	**1**	**-6.2**
• WOTUS, Ron	Ronald Allan Wotus b: 3/3/1961, Hartford, CT BR/TR, 6'1", 164 lbs. Deb: 9/3/1983 C																							
1983 Pit-N	5	3	0	0	0	0	0	0	0	1	0	0	.000	.000	.000	.000	-98	-1	0	.00	0	/S-2,2-1	0	-0.1
1984 Pit-N	27	55	4	12	6	0	0	2	6	8	0	0	.218	.295	.327	.622	75	-2	5	2.43	3	S-17/2-7	1	0.3
Total 2	**32**	**58**	**4**	**12**	**6**	**0**	**0**	**2**	**6**	**9**	**0**	**0**	**.207**	**.281**	**.310**	**.592**	**67**	**-3**	**5**	**2.30**	**3**	**/S-19,2-8**	**1**	**0.2**
• WOULFE, Jimmy	James Joseph Woulfe b: 11/25/1859, New Orleans, LA d: 12/20/1924, New Orleans, LA TR, 5'11" Deb: 5/16/1884																							
1884 Cin-a	8	34	3	5	0	1	0	2	1	....	....	....	.147	.171	.206	.377	21	-3	1	1.17	-3	/0-7(1-0-6),3-1	0	-0.6
Pit-a	15	53	7	6	1	0	0	1	0	....	....	....	.113	.113	.132	.245	-20	-7	1	.48	0	0-15(0-14-1)	0	-0.7
Yr.	23	87	10	11	1	1	0	3	1	....	....	....	.126	.136	.161	.297	-4	-10	2	.74	-3	0-22(1-14-7)/3-1	0	-1.2
• WRIGHT, Ab	Albert Owen Wright b: 11/16/1906, Terlton, OK d: 5/23/1995, Muskogee, OK BR/TR, 6'1.5", 200 lbs. Deb: 4/20/1935 Career OF: 40-5-50																							
1935 Cle-A	67	160	17	38	11	1	2	18	10	17	2	1	.238	.291	.356	.647	65	-9	17	3.51	0	0-47(5-5-38)	2	-1.0
1944 Bos-N	71	195	20	50	9	0	7	35	18	31	0	....	.256	.326	.410	.736	102	0	26	4.61	-1	0-47(35-0-12)	5	-0.4
Total 2	**138**	**355**	**37**	**88**	**20**	**1**	**9**	**53**	**28**	**48**	**2**	**1**	**.248**	**.310**	**.386**	**.696**	**85**	**-9**	**43**	**4.11**	**-1**	**/0-94**	**7**	**-1.4**
• WRIGHT, Al	Albert Edgar "A-1" Wright b: 11/11/1912, San Francisco, CA d: 11/13/1998, Oakland, CA BR/TR, 6'1.5", 170 lbs. Deb: 4/25/1933																							
1933 Bos-N	4	1	0	1	0	0	0	0	0	0	0	....	1.000	1.000	1.000	2.000	515	1	1	∞	-2	/2-3	0	-0.1
• WRIGHT, Bill	William Hiram Wright Deb: 9/16/1887																							
1887 Was-N	1	3	0	2	0	0	0	0	0	0	0	....	.667	.667	.667	1.333	286	1	1	36.22	-1	/C-1	0	0.0
• WRIGHT, Cy	Ceylon Wright b: 8/16/1893, Minneapolis, MN d: 11/7/1947, Hines, IL BL/TR, 5'9", 150 lbs. Deb: 6/30/1916																							
1916 Chi-A	8	18	0	0	0	0	0	0	1	7	0	....	.000	.053	.000	.053	-83	-4	0	.11	-1	/S-8	0	-0.6
• WRIGHT, Dick	Willard James Wright b: 5/5/1890, Worcester, NY d: 1/24/1952, Bethlehem, PA BR/TR, 5'10", 170 lbs. Deb: 6/30/1915																							
1915 Bro-F	4	5	0	0	0	0	0	0	0	0	0	....	.000	.000	.000	.000	-102	-1	0	.00	-1	/C-3	0	-0.2
• WRIGHT, George	George DeWitt Wright b: 12/22/1958, Oklahoma City, OK BB/TR, 5'11", 180 lbs. Deb: 4/10/1982 Career OF: 20-444-114																							
1982 Tex-A	150	557	69	147	20	5	11	50	30	78	3	7	.264	.305	.377	.682	91	-11	61	3.74	9	*0-149(0-147-3)	11	-0.4
1983 Tex-A	162	634	79	175	28	6	18	80	41	82	8	7	.276	.322	.424	.746	105	2	84	4.75	4	*0-161(0-161-0)	20	0.3
1984 Tex-A	101	383	40	93	19	4	9	48	15	54	0	2	.243	.275	.384	.659	78	-14	39	3.45	-5	0-80(0-54-26),D-18	6	-2.2
1985 Tex-A	109	363	21	69	13	0	2	18	25	49	4	7	.190	.242	.242	.485	33	-36	19	1.67	1	*0-102(0-53-55)/D-4	2	-3.8
1986 Tex-A	49	106	10	23	3	1	2	7	4	23	3	5	.217	.252	.321	.573	53	-9	7	2.07	-1	0-42(10-8-27)	1	-1.0
Mon-N	56	117	12	22	5	2	0	5	11	28	1	1	.188	.264	.265	.529	47	-9	8	2.17	0	0-32(10-21-3)	1	-1.0
Total 5	**627**	**2160**	**231**	**529**	**88**	**18**	**42**	**208**	**126**	**314**	**19**	**29**	**.245**	**.289**	**.361**	**.650**	**79**	**-76**	**218**	**3.41**	**8**	**0-566/D-22**	**41**	**-8.1**
• WRIGHT, George	George Wright b: 1/28/1847, Yonkers, NY d: 8/21/1937, Boston, MA BR/TR, 5'9.5", 150 lbs. Deb: 5/5/1871 M HOF: 1937																							
1871 Bos-n	16	80	33	33	7	5	0	11	6	1	9	1	.413	.453	.625	1.078	199	11	27	18.00	3	S-15/1-1	....	0.9
1872 Bos-n	48	255	87	86	16	6	2	32	3	1	14	4	.337	.345	.471	.816	141	12	47	8.49	14	*S-48	....	1.7
1873 Bos-n	59	325	99	126	19	8	3	50	8	2	3	5	.388	.402	.523	.925	160	20	71	10.67	9	*S-59	....	1.9
1874 Bos-n	60	313	76	103	10	**15**	2	44	5	6	2	0	.329	.340	.476	.816	150	16	53	7.51	0	*S-60/3-1	....	1.2
1875 Bos-n	79	408	106	136	20	7	2	61	2	6	13	6	.333	.337	.431	.768	159	22	65	6.92	0	*S-79/P-2	....	1.8
1876 Bos-N	70	343	72	100	18	6	1	34	8	9	....	....	.292	.315	.397	.712	133	11	43	5.11	10	*S-68/2-2,P-1	17	2.2
1877 Bos-N	61	290	58	80	15	1	0	35	9	15	....	....	.276	.298	.334	.632	95	-2	30	3.88	17	*2-58/S-3	8	1.6
1878 Bos-N	59	267	35	60	5	1	0	12	6	22	....	....	.225	.242	.251	.493	58	-13	17	2.21	10	*S-59	8	0.0
1879 Pro-N	85	388	79	107	15	10	1	42	13	20	....	....	.276	.299	.374	.673	122	9	44	4.43	13	*S-85	16	2.5
1880 Bos-N	1	4	2	1	0	0	0	0	0	0	....	....	.250	.250	.250	.500	72	-0	0	2.35	0	/S-1	0	0.0
1881 Bos-N	7	25	4	5	0	0	0	0	3	1	....	....	.200	.286	.200	.486	58	-1	1	1.98	0	/S-7	0	-0.1
1882 Pro-N	46	185	14	30	1	2	0	9	4	36	....	....	.162	.180	.189	.369	19	-16	6	1.15	-5	S-46	2	-1.8
Total 5 n	**262**	**1381**	**401**	**484**	**72**	**41**	**9**	**198**	**24**	**16**	**41**	**16**	**.350**	**.362**	**.482**	**.843**	**156**	**81**	**264**	**8.77**	**26**	**S-261/P-2,1-1,3-1**	**....**	**7.5**
Total 7	**329**	**1502**	**264**	**383**	**54**	**20**	**2**	**132**	**43**	**103**	**....**	**....**	**.255**	**.277**	**.323**	**.600**	**94**	**-11**	**142**	**3.55**	**46**	**S-269/2-60,P-1**	**51**	**4.5**
• WRIGHT, Glenn	Forest Glenn "Buckshot" Wright b: 2/6/1901, Archie, MO d: 4/6/1984, Olathe, KS BR/TR, 5'11", 170 lbs. Deb: 4/15/1924																							
1924 Pit-N	153	616	80	177	28	18	7	111	27	52	14	6	.287	.318	.425	.744	96	-3	82	4.72	19	*S-153	22	3.3
1925*Pit-N	153	614	97	189	32	10	18	121	31	32	3	7	.308	.341	.480	.822	100	-3	97	5.74	10	*S-153/3-1	24	2.2
1926 Pit-N	119	458	73	141	15	15	8	77	19	26	6	....	.308	.335	.459	.794	106	2	67	5.24	3	*S-116	17	1.7
1927*Pit-N	143	570	78	160	26	4	9	105	39	46	4	....	.281	.328	.388	.716	85	-13	71	4.33	4	*S-143	17	0.6
1928 Pit-N	108	407	63	126	20	8	8	66	21	53	3	....	.310	.343	.457	.800	103	0	61	5.38	-12	*S-101/1-1,0-1	12	-0.1
1929 Bro-N	24	25	4	5	0	0	1	6	3	6	0	....	.200	.286	.320	.606	51	-2	2	2.84	-1	/S-3	0	-0.3
1930 Bro-N	135	532	83	171	28	12	22	126	32	70	2	....	.321	.360	.543	.903	116	11	99	6.82	18	*S-134	21	3.8
1931 Bro-N	77	268	36	76	9	4	9	32	14	35	1	....	.284	.324	.448	.772	106	1	39	5.25	5	S-75	11	1.1
1932 Bro-N	127	446	50	122	31	5	11	60	12	57	4	....	.274	.293	.439	.732	96	-5	57	4.47	-6	*S-122/1-2	12	-0.2
1933 Bro-N	71	192	19	49	13	0	1	18	11	24	1	....	.255	.299	.339	.638	85	-4	18	3.11	-3	S-51/1-9,3-2	3	-0.4
1935 Chi-A	9	25	1	3	1	0	0	1	0	6	0	0	.120	.120	.160	.280	-27	-5	1	.58	-1	/2-7	0	-0.5
Total 11	**1119**	**4153**	**584**	**1219**	**203**	**76**	**94**	**723**	**209**	**407**	**38**	**13**	**.294**	**.328**	**.447**	**.775**	**99**	**-21**	**594**	**5.07**	**36**	***S-1051/1-12,2-7,3-3,0-1**	**139**	**11.2**

YEAR TM-L	G	AB	R	H	2B	3B	HR	RBI	BB	SO	SB	CS	AVG	OBP	SLG	OPS	OPS+	BR/A	RC	RC/G	FR	G/POS	WS	TPW
• WRIGHT, Harry	William Henry Wright b: 1/10/1835, Sheffield, England d: 10/3/1895, Atlantic City, NJ BR/TR, 5'9.5", 157 lbs. Deb: 5/5/1871 M/U HOF: 1953 NA OF: 0-176-1 Career OF: 0-1-1 ♦																							
1871 Bos-n	31	147	42	44	5	2	0	26	13	2	7	1	.299	.356	.361	.717	103	1	22	6.64	1	*O-30(0-30-0)/P-9,S-1	....	-0.2
1872 Bos-n	48	208	39	52	5	1	0	23	9	2	0	0	.250	.281	.284	.565	70	-7	17	3.38	0	*O-48(0-48-0)/P-7	....	-0.4
1873 Bos-n	58	266	57	67	10	4	2	35	10	3	1	1	.252	.279	.342	.621	77	-8	26	4.01	-3	*O-58(0-58-0),P-13	....	-1.0
1874 Bos-n	40	184	44	58	4	2	2	27	4	3	1	0	.315	.330	.391	.721	123	4	25	5.88	-2	*O-40(0-40-0)/P-6	....	0.2
1875 Bos-n	1	4	1	1	0	0	0	0	0	1	0	0	.250	.250	.250	.500	72	-0	0	2.52	-0	/O-1	....	0.0
1876 Bos-N	1	3	0	0	0	0	0	0	0	1	....	....	.000	.000	.000	.000	-98	-1	0	.00	0	/O-1	0	-0.1
1877 Bos-N	1	4	0	0	0	0	0	0	0	1	....	....	.000	.000	.000	.000	-97	-1	0	.00	1	/O-1	0	0.0
Total 5 n	178	809	183	222	24	9	4	111	36	11	9	2	.274	.305	.341	.646	91	-10	90	4.70	-4	O-177/P-35,S-1	....	-1.4
Total 2	2	7	0	0	0	0	0	0	0	2	....	....	.000	.000	.000	.000	-97	-1	0	.00	1	/O-2	0	-0.1
• WRIGHT, Joe	Joseph S. Wright b: 1873, Pittsburgh, PA BL/TL, 5'8", 175 lbs. Deb: 7/14/1895 Career OF: 0-55-19																							
1895 Lou-N	60	228	30	63	10	4	1	30	12	28	7	....	.276	.315	.368	.684	81	-7	30	4.79	-4	O-60(0-43-17)	3	-1.1
1896 Lou-N	2	7	0	2	0	0	0	0	0	1	0	....	.286	.286	.286	.571	53	-0	1	3.10	-0	/O-2(0-0-2)	0	0.0
Pit-N	15	52	5	16	2	1	0	6	1	2	1	....	.308	.321	.385	.705	89	-1	7	5.08	-1	O-12(0-12-0)/3-1	1	-0.3
Yr.	17	59	5	18	2	1	0	6	1	3	1	....	.305	.317	.373	.690	85	-2	7	4.84	-1	O-14(0-12-2)/3-1	1	-0.3
Total 2	77	287	35	81	12	5	1	36	13	31	8	....	.282	.316	.369	.685	82	-8	37	4.80	-5	/O-74,3-1	4	-1.5
• WRIGHT, Pat	Patrick W. Wright b: 7/5/1868, Pottsville, PA d: 5/29/1943, Springfield, IL BB/TR, 6'2", 190 lbs. Deb: 7/11/1890																							
1890 Chi-N	1	2	0	0	0	0	0	0	1	0	0	....	.000	.333	.000	.333	-1	-0	0	.00	0	/2-1	0	0.0
• WRIGHT, Rasty	William Smith Wright b: 1/31/1863, Birmingham, MI d: 10/14/1922, Duluth, MN BL, 6'1", 185 lbs. Deb: 4/17/1890																							
1890 Syr-a	88	348	82	106	10	6	0	27	69	....	30	....	.305	.428	.368	.796	150	29	69	7.59	-2	O-88(0-70-18)	17	2.1
Cle-N	13	45	7	5	1	0	0	2	12	4	3	....	.111	.298	.133	.432	27	-3	3	1.82	-1	O-13(0-0-13)	0	-0.4
• WRIGHT, Ron	Ronald Wade Wright b: 1/21/1976, Delta, UT BR/TR, 6'1", 230 lbs. Deb: 4/14/2002																							
2002 Sea-A	1	3	0	0	0	0	0	0	0	1	0	0	.000	.000	.000	.000	-104	-1	0	.00	0	/D-1	0	-0.1
• WRIGHT, Sam	Samuel Wright b: 11/25/1848, New York, NY d: 5/6/1928, Boston, MA BR/TR, 5'7.5", 146 lbs. Deb: 4/21/1875																							
1875 NH-n	33	127	10	24	4	0	0	5	1	1	1	0	.189	.195	.220	.416	51	-4	6	1.66	1	S-33	....	-0.3
1876 Bos-N	2	8	0	1	0	0	0	0	0	0	....	....	.125	.125	.125	.250	-16	-1	0	.51	-1	/S-2	0	-0.1
1880 Cin-N	9	34	0	3	0	0	0	0	0	5	....	....	.088	.088	.088	.176	-41	-5	0	.24	-1	/S-9	0	-0.6
1881 Bos-N	1	4	0	1	0	0	0	0	0	0	....	....	.250	.250	.250	.500	60	-0	0	2.31	-1	/S-1	0	-0.1
Total 3	12	46	0	5	0	0	0	0	0	5	....	....	.109	.109	.109	.217	-28	-6	1	.44	-2	/S-12	0	-0.7
• WRIGHT, Taffy	Taft Shedron Wright b: 8/10/1911, Tabor City, NC d: 10/22/1981, Orlando, FL BL/TR, 5'10", 180 lbs. Deb: 4/18/1938 Career OF: 183-1-716																							
1938 Was-A	100	263	37	92	18	10	2	36	13	17	1	2	.350	.389	.517	.906	134	12	52	7.88	0	O-60(14-1-45)	10	0.8
1939 Was-A	129	499	77	154	29	11	4	93	38	19	1	2	.309	.359	.435	.794	110	6	78	5.81	3	*O-123(39-0-84)	13	0.2
1940 Chi-A	147	581	79	196	31	9	5	88	43	25	4	7	.337	.385	.448	.832	114	10	101	6.77	-7	*O-144(0-0-144)	21	-0.6
1941 Chi-A	136	513	71	165	35	5	10	97	60	27	5	4	.322	.399	.468	.867	130	23	101	7.52	-3	*O-134(0-0-134)	25	1.2
1942 Chi-A	85	300	43	100	13	5	0	47	48	9	1	8	.333	.432	.410	.842	140	16	55	6.99	-1	O-81(81-0-1)	15	1.1
1946 Chi-A	115	422	46	116	19	4	7	52	42	17	10	3	.275	.342	.389	.731	108	6	55	4.55	-1	*O-107(8-0-99)	13	0.1
1947 Chi-A	124	401	48	130	13	0	4	54	48	17	8	6	.324	.398	.387	.784	123	14	64	5.97	-3	*O-100(35-0-66)	15	0.6
1948 Chi-A	134	455	50	127	15	6	4	61	38	18	2	1	.279	.341	.365	.706	91	-6	57	4.50	1	*O-114(6-0-108)	9	-0.8
1949 Phi-A	59	149	14	35	2	5	2	25	16	6	0	0	.235	.321	.356	.677	82	-4	16	3.52	0	O-35(0-0-35)	2	-0.5
Total 9	1029	3583	465	1115	175	55	38	553	346	155	32	33	.311	.376	.423	.799	116	77	580	6.00	-12	O-898	123	2.0
• WRIGHT, Tom	Thomas Everette Wright b: 9/22/1923, Shelby, NC BL/TR, 5'11.5", 180 lbs. Deb: 9/15/1948 Career OF: 71-0-101																							
1948 Bos-A	3	2	1	1	0	1	0	0	0	0	0	0	.500	.500	1.500	2.000	400	1	2	41.51	0	....	0	0.1
1949 Bos-A	5	4	1	1	1	0	0	1	1	1	0	0	.250	.400	.500	.900	128	0	1	8.32	0	....	0	0.0
1950 Bos-A	54	107	17	34	7	0	0	20	6	18	0	0	.318	.360	.383	.743	82	-3	15	5.35	-1	O-24(5-0-19)	2	-0.4
1951 Bos-A	28	63	8	14	1	1	1	9	11	8	0	0	.222	.347	.317	.664	73	-2	7	3.49	-1	O-18(1-0-17)	1	-0.3
1952 StL-A	29	66	6	16	0	0	1	6	12	20	1	1	.242	.359	.288	.647	79	-1	7	3.77	0	O-18(18-0-0)	1	-0.2
Chi-A	60	132	15	34	10	2	1	21	16	16	1	0	.258	.342	.386	.729	102	1	19	4.85	0	O-34(22-0-13)	4	-0.1
Yr.	89	198	21	50	10	2	2	27	28	36	2	1	.253	.348	.354	.702	94	-1	26	4.49	0	O-52(40-0-13)	5	-0.4
1953 Chi-A	77	132	14	33	5	3	2	25	12	21	0	0	.250	.322	.379	.701	86	-3	17	4.64	-2	O-33(10-0-24)	3	-0.5
1954 Was-A	76	171	13	42	4	4	1	17	18	38	0	0	.246	.325	.333	.658	85	-3	20	4.01	-2	O-43(15-0-28)	3	-0.7
1955 Was-A	7	7	0	0	0	0	0	0	0	1	0	0	.000	.000	.000	.000	-106	-2	0	.00	0	....	0	-0.2
1956 Was-A	2	1	0	0	0	0	0	0	0	0	0	0	.000	.000	.000	.000	-100	-0	0	.00	0	....	0	0.0
Total 9	341	685	75	175	28	11	6	99	76	123	2	1	.255	.336	.355	.691	85	-12	87	4.44	-5	O-170	14	-2.4
• WRIGHTSTONE, Russ	Russell Guy Wrightstone b: 3/18/1893, Bowmansdale, PA d: 2/25/1969, Harrisburg, PA BL/TR, 5'10.5", 176 lbs. Deb: 4/19/1920 Career OF: 85-0-33																							
1920 Phi-N	76	206	23	54	6	1	3	17	10	25	3	2	.262	.303	.345	.647	82	-4	21	3.64	-3	3-56/S-2,2-1	4	-0.6
1921 Phi-N	109	372	59	110	13	4	9	51	18	20	4	4	.296	.332	.425	.756	91	-5	51	4.98	-2	3-54,O-37(34-0-3)/2-4	8	-0.6
1922 Phi-N	99	331	56	101	18	6	5	33	28	17	4	5	.305	.365	.441	.806	98	-2	53	5.78	5	3-40,S-35/1-2	8	0.9
1923 Phi-N	119	392	59	107	21	7	7	57	21	19	5	2	.273	.315	.416	.731	82	-11	51	4.63	-1	3-72,S-21/2-9	7	-0.5
1924 Phi-N	118	388	55	119	24	4	7	58	27	15	5	4	.307	.363	.443	.806	102	2	62	5.94	-15	3-97/2-9,S-5,O-1	11	-0.6
1925 Phi-N	92	286	48	99	18	5	14	61	19	18	0	3	.346	.389	.591	.980	135	13	63	8.46	-7	O-45(37-0-10),S-12,3-11,2-10/1	10	0.5
1926 Phi-N	112	368	55	113	23	1	7	57	27	11	5	....	.307	.356	.432	.788	106	3	55	5.47	-4	1-53,3-37,2-13/O-5(5-0-0)	11	-0.3
1927 Phi-N	141	533	62	163	24	5	6	75	48	20	9	....	.306	.365	.403	.769	104	4	78	5.34	-6	*1-136/2-1,3-1	13	-1.1
1928 Phi-N	33	91	7	19	5	1	1	11	14	5	0	....	.209	.321	.319	.639	65	-4	10	3.42	-2	O-26(9-0-19)/1-4	1	-0.8
NY-N	30	25	3	4	0	0	1	5	3	2	0	....	.160	.250	.280	.530	38	-2	2	2.24	0	/1-2	0	-0.2
Yr.	63	116	10	23	5	1	2	16	17	7	0	....	.198	.306	.310	.616	60	-7	12	3.16	-2	O-26(9-0-19)/1-6	1	-1.0
Total 9	929	2992	427	889	152	34	60	425	215	152	35	20	.297	.349	.431	.780	99	-6	447	5.41	-35	3-368,1-203,O-114/S-75,2-47	73	-3.4
• WRIGLEY, Zeke	George Watson Wrigley b: 1/18/1874, Philadelphia, PA d: 9/28/1952, Philadelphia, PA, 5'8.5", 150 lbs. Deb: 8/31/1896 Career OF: 4-15-20																							
1896 Was-N	5	9	1	1	0	0	0	2	1	1	0	....	.111	.200	.111	.311	-17	-2	0	.68	2	/2-3,S-1	0	0.0
1897 Was-N	104	388	65	110	14	8	3	64	21	....	5	....	.284	.320	.384	.704	86	-10	52	4.74	2	O-36(4-13-19),S-33,3-30/2-9	7	-0.6
1898 Was-N	111	400	50	98	9	10	2	39	20	....	10	....	.245	.283	.333	.615	76	-14	42	3.62	-4	S-97,2-11/O-3(0-2-1),3-1	7	-1.2
1899 NY-N	4	15	1	3	0	0	0	1	1	....	1	....	.200	.250	.200	.450	25	-2	1	2.26	-1	/3-4	0	-0.2
Bro-N	15	49	4	10	2	2	0	11	3	....	2	....	.204	.250	.327	.577	56	-3	5	3.12	-3	S-14/3-1	1	-0.5
Yr.	19	64	5	13	2	2	0	12	4	....	3	....	.203	.250	.297	.547	49	-5	6	2.92	-4	S-14/3-5	1	-0.7
Total 4	239	861	121	222	25	20	5	117	46	1	18	....	.258	.296	.351	.647	78	-30	100	4.02	-4	S-145/O-39,3-36,2-23	15	-2.5
• WRONA, Rick	Richard James Wrona b: 12/10/1963, Tulsa, OK BR/TR, 6'1", 185 lbs. Deb: 9/3/1988																							
1988 Chi-N	4	6	0	0	0	0	0	0	0	1	0	0	.000	.000	.000	.000	-96	-2	0	.00	-0	/C-2	0	-0.2
1989*Chi-N	38	92	11	26	2	1	2	14	2	21	0	0	.283	.305	.391	.697	91	-1	11	4.24	0	C-37	4	0.0
1990 Chi-N	16	29	3	5	0	0	0	0	2	11	1	0	.172	.226	.172	.398	10	-3	1	1.49	0	C-16	0	-0.2
1992 Cin-N	11	23	0	4	0	0	0	0	0	3	0	0	.174	.174	.174	.348	-1	-3	0	.45	-1	C-10/1-1	0	-0.4
1993 Chi-A	4	8	0	1	0	0	0	1	0	4	0	0	.125	.125	.125	.250	-33	-1	0	.48	0	/C-4	0	-0.1
1994 Mil-A	6	10	2	5	4	0	1	3	1	1	0	0	.500	.545	1.200	1.745	319	3	6	28.76	0	/C-5,1-1	1	0.3
Total 6	79	168	16	41	6	1	3	18	5	41	1	0	.244	.270	.345	.615	68	-8	19	3.85	-1	/C-74,1-2	5	-0.6
• WUESTLING, Yats	George Wuestling b: 10/18/1903, St. Louis, MO d: 4/26/1970, St. Louis, MO BR/TR, 5'11", 167 lbs. Deb: 6/15/1929																							
1929 Det-A	54	150	13	30	4	1	0	16	9	24	1	3	.200	.250	.240	.490	27	-17	9	1.85	-4	S-52/2-1,3-1	1	-1.6
1930 Det-A	4	9	0	0	0	0	0	0	2	3	0	0	.000	.182	.000	.182	-48	-2	0	.27	-1	/S-4	0	-0.2
NY-A	25	58	5	11	0	1	0	3	4	14	0	1	.190	.242	.224	.466	20	-7	3	1.68	-1	S-21/3-3	1	-0.6

YEAR TM-L	G	AB	R	H	2B	3B	HR	RBI	BB	SO	SB	CS	AVG	OBP	SLG	OPS	OPS+	BR/A	RC	RC/G	FR	G/POS	WS	TPW
Yr.	29	67	5	11	0	1	0	3	6	17	0	1	.164	.233	.194	.427	10	-9	3	1.46	-1	S-25/3-3	1	-0.8
Total 2	83	217	18	41	4	2	0	19	15	41	1	4	.189	.245	.226	.470	21	-27	12	1.73	-6	/S-77,3-4,2-1	2	-2.4

• WYATT, Joe Loral John Wyatt b: 4/6/1900, Petersburg, IN d: 12/5/1970, Oblong, IL BR/TR, 6'1", 175 lbs. Deb: 9/11/1924

YEAR TM-L	G	AB	R	H	2B	3B	HR	RBI	BB	SO	SB	CS	AVG	OBP	SLG	OPS	OPS+	BR/A	RC	RC/G	FR	G/POS	WS	TPW
1924 Cle-A	4	12	1	2	0	0	0	1	2	1	0	0	.167	.286	.167	.452	18	-1	1	1.88	-1	/O-4(0-0-4)	0	-0.2

• WYLIE, Ren James Renwick Wylie b: 12/14/1861, Elizabeth, PA d: 8/17/1951, Wilkinsburg, PA BR/TR, 5'11", 155 lbs. Deb: 8/11/1882

YEAR TM-L	G	AB	R	H	2B	3B	HR	RBI	BB	SO	SB	CS	AVG	OBP	SLG	OPS	OPS+	BR/A	RC	RC/G	FR	G/POS	WS	TPW
1882 Pit-a	1	3	0	0	0	0	0	....	0	....	....	....	.000	.000	.000	.000	-105	-1	0	.00	1	/O-1	0	0.0

• WYMAN, Frank Frank C. Wyman b: 5/10/1862, Haverhill, MA d: 2/4/1916, Everett, MA Deb: 6/10/1884

YEAR TM-L	G	AB	R	H	2B	3B	HR	RBI	BB	SO	SB	CS	AVG	OBP	SLG	OPS	OPS+	BR/A	RC	RC/G	FR	G/POS	WS	TPW
1884 KC-U	30	124	16	27	4	0	0	....	3	....	....	....	.218	.236	.250	.486	74	-2	8	2.17	2	O-25(13-11-0)/1-3,3-3,P-3	2	-0.8
CP-U	2	8	1	3	0	0	0	....	0	....	....	....	.375	.375	.375	.750	164	1	1	6.46	0	/1-2	0	0.0
Yr.	32	132	17	30	4	0	0	....	3	....	....	....	.227	.244	.258	.502	79	-1	9	2.38	2	O-25(13-11-0)/1-5,3-3,P-3	2	-0.8

• WYNEGAR, Butch Harold Delano Wynegar b: 3/14/1956, York, PA BB/TR, 6'1", 194 lbs. Deb: 4/9/1976 C

YEAR TM-L	G	AB	R	H	2B	3B	HR	RBI	BB	SO	SB	CS	AVG	OBP	SLG	OPS	OPS+	BR/A	RC	RC/G	FR	G/POS	WS	TPW
1976 Min-A★	149	534	58	139	21	2	10	69	79	63	0	0	.260	.358	.363	.721	108	9	72	4.66	-3	*C-137,D-15	20	1.3
1977 Min-A★	144	532	76	139	22	3	10	79	68	61	2	3	.261	.347	.370	.717	97	-1	70	4.50	-2	*C-142/3-1	18	0.4
1978 Min-A	135	454	36	104	22	1	4	45	47	42	1	0	.229	.310	.308	.618	73	-15	46	3.37	0	*C-131/3-1	10	-0.9
1979 Min-A	149	504	74	136	20	0	7	57	74	36	2	2	.270	.366	.351	.717	91	-3	68	4.59	-1	*C-146/D-2	17	0.2
1980 Min-A	146	486	61	124	18	3	5	57	63	36	3	1	.255	.343	.335	.678	81	-10	59	4.15	-1	*C-142/D-1	13	-0.5
1981 Min-A	47	150	11	37	5	0	0	10	17	9	0	1	.247	.327	.280	.607	72	-5	13	2.85	3	C-37/D-9	3	-0.1
1982 Min-A	24	86	9	18	4	0	1	8	10	12	0	0	.209	.292	.291	.582	59	-5	7	2.86	0	C-24	1	-0.4
NY-A	63	191	27	56	8	1	3	20	40	21	0	1	.293	.418	.393	.811	126	9	33	5.88	-2	C-62	8	1.1
Yr.	87	277	36	74	12	1	4	28	50	33	0	1	.267	.381	.361	.742	107	5	41	4.93	-2	C-86	9	0.7
1983 NY-A	94	301	40	89	18	2	6	42	52	29	1	1	.296	.401	.429	.830	133	16	54	6.57	-8	C-93	14	1.3
1984 NY-A	129	442	48	118	13	1	6	45	65	35	1	4	.267	.361	.342	.703	99	1	53	4.10	0	*C-126	15	0.7
1985 NY-A	102	309	27	69	15	0	5	32	64	43	0	0	.223	.357	.320	.677	89	-2	38	4.03	0	C-96	10	0.3
1986 NY-A	61	194	19	40	4	1	7	29	30	21	0	0	.206	.313	.345	.658	80	-5	20	3.33	-1	C-57	3	-0.3
1987 Cal-A	31	92	4	19	2	0	0	5	9	13	0	0	.207	.277	.228	.505	37	-8	6	2.16	1	C-28/D-1	2	-0.5
1988 Cal-A	27	55	8	14	4	1	1	8	8	7	0	0	.255	.349	.418	.767	117	1	8	4.77	0	C-26	2	0.2
Total 13	1301	4330	498	1102	176	15	65	506	626	428	10	13	.255	.351	.347	.698	94	-17	549	4.29	-14	*C-1247/D-28,3-2	136	3.0

• WYNN, Jimmy James Sherman "The Toy Cannon" Wynn b: 3/12/1942, Hamilton, OH BR/TR, 5'10", 170 lbs. Deb: 7/10/1963 Career OF: 298-1181-355

YEAR TM-L	G	AB	R	H	2B	3B	HR	RBI	BB	SO	SB	CS	AVG	OBP	SLG	OPS	OPS+	BR/A	RC	RC/G	FR	G/POS	WS	TPW
1963 Hou-N	70	250	31	61	10	5	4	27	30	53	4	2	.244	.325	.372	.697	107	3	32	4.26	-2	O-53(43-10-0),S-21/3-2	9	-0.1
1964 Hou-N	67	219	19	49	7	0	5	18	24	58	5	5	.224	.303	.324	.627	81	-6	21	3.16	1	O-64(13-51-0)	4	-0.8
1965 Hou-N	157	564	90	155	30	7	22	73	84	126	43	4	.275	.374	.470	.844	146	45	108	6.72	7	*O-155(0-155-0)	31	5.0
1966 Hou-N	105	418	62	107	21	1	18	62	41	81	13	10	.256	.324	.440	.764	118	8	58	4.65	0	*O-104(0-104-0)	14	0.5
1967 Hou-N★	158	594	102	148	29	3	37	107	74	137	16	4	.249	.334	.495	.829	139	31	102	5.82	-3	*O-157(0-157-0)	28	2.5
1968 Hou-N	156	542	85	146	23	5	26	67	90	131	11	17	.269	.378	.474	.853	158	37	98	6.17	9	*O-153(56-93-7)	32	4.5
1969 Hou-N	149	495	113	133	17	1	33	87	**148**	142	23	7	.269	.440	.507	.947	168	58	126	8.92	4	*O-149(0-149-0)	36	6.0
1970 Hou-N	157	554	82	156	32	2	27	88	106	96	24	5	.282	.398	.493	.891	143	40	114	7.21	6	*O-151(66-87-0)	27	4.1
1971 Hou-N	123	404	38	82	16	0	7	45	56	63	10	5	.203	.303	.295	.598	72	-14	36	2.84	2	*O-116(1-48-72)	7	-1.8
1972 Hou-N	145	542	117	148	29	3	24	90	103	99	17	7	.273	.391	.470	.862	147	38	107	6.96	1	*O-144(0-12-132)	28	3.5
1973 Hou-N	139	481	90	106	14	5	20	55	91	102	14	11	.220	.349	.395	.744	106	5	68	4.60	-5	*O-133(2-10-125)	16	-0.7
1974*LA-N★	150	535	104	145	17	4	32	108	108	104	18	15	.271	.393	.497	.891	154	39	109	6.92	4	*O-148(0-148-0)	32	4.1
1975 LA-N★	130	412	80	102	16	0	18	58	110	77	7	3	.248	.407	.417	.825	135	26	79	6.53	-6	*O-120(21-107-0)	21	1.7
1976 Atl-N	148	449	75	93	19	1	17	66	**127**	111	16	6	.207	.382	.367	.749	107	12	75	5.34	2	*O-138(90-50-0)	18	0.7
1977 NY-A	30	77	7	11	2	1	1	3	15	16	1	0	.143	.283	.234	.516	43	-5	6	2.56	1	D-15/O-8(5-0-3)	1	-0.5
Mil-A	36	117	10	23	3	1	0	10	17	31	3	0	.197	.299	.239	.538	49	-7	10	2.80	0	O-17(1-0-16),D-15	1	-0.8
Yr.	66	194	17	34	5	2	1	13	32	47	4	0	.175	.292	.237	.529	46	-12	16	2.70	1	D-30,O-25(6-0-19)	2	-1.3
Total 15	1920	6653	1105	1665	285	39	291	964	1224	1427	225	101	.250	.369	.436	.805	130	310	1148	5.84	20	*O-1810/D-30,S-21,3-2	305	27.8

• WYNNE, Marvell Marvell Wynne b: 12/17/1959, Chicago, IL BL/TL, 5'11", 185 lbs. Deb: 6/15/1983 Career OF: 126-706-47

YEAR TM-L	G	AB	R	H	2B	3B	HR	RBI	BB	SO	SB	CS	AVG	OBP	SLG	OPS	OPS+	BR/A	RC	RC/G	FR	G/POS	WS	TPW
1983 Pit-N	103	366	66	89	16	2	7	26	38	52	12	10	.243	.319	.355	.675	84	-9	43	3.86	-4	*O-102(0-102-0)	8	-1.5
1984 Pit-N	154	653	77	174	24	11	0	39	42	81	24	19	.266	.311	.337	.648	82	-20	67	3.50	-4	*O-154(0-154-0)	12	-2.7
1985 Pit-N	103	337	21	69	6	3	2	18	18	48	10	5	.205	.247	.258	.505	42	-27	21	1.94	3	O-99(0-100-0)	3	-2.7
1986 SD-N	137	288	34	76	19	2	7	37	15	45	11	11	.264	.303	.417	.719	98	-5	32	3.77	-6	*O-125(0-125-0)	7	-1.3
1987 SD-N	98	188	17	47	8	2	2	24	20	37	11	6	.250	.322	.346	.668	80	-6	21	3.54	-1	O-71(33-40-5)	3	-0.8
1988 SD-N	128	333	37	88	13	4	11	42	31	62	3	4	.264	.327	.426	.753	117	5	47	4.90	-1	*O-113(37-84-10)	15	0.2
1989 SD-N	105	294	19	74	11	1	6	35	12	41	4	1	.252	.283	.357	.641	82	-8	30	3.52	0	O-96(39-41-25)	8	-1.0
*Chi-N	20	48	8	9	2	1	1	4	1	7	2	0	.188	.220	.333	.553	52	-3	4	2.59	-1	O-13(4-6-3)	0	-0.4
Yr.	125	342	27	83	13	2	7	39	13	48	6	1	.243	.275	.354	.628	78	-10	34	3.38	0	*O-109(43-47-28)	8	-1.4
1990 Chi-N	92	186	21	38	8	2	4	19	14	25	3	2	.204	.264	.333	.597	59	-11	16	2.72	0	O-66(13-54-4)	2	-1.3
Total 8	940	2693	300	664	107	28	40	244	191	398	80	58	.247	.298	.352	.650	81	-83	279	3.47	-13	O-839	58	-11.4

• WYROSTEK, Johnny John Barney Wyrostek b: 7/12/1919, Fairmont City, IL d: 12/12/1986, St. Louis, MO BL/TR, 6'2", 180 lbs. Deb: 9/10/1942 Career OF: 49-396-674

YEAR TM-L	G	AB	R	H	2B	3B	HR	RBI	BB	SO	SB	CS	AVG	OBP	SLG	OPS	OPS+	BR/A	RC	RC/G	FR	G/POS	WS	TPW
1942 Pit-N	9	35	0	4	0	1	0	3	3	2	0	....	.114	.184	.171	.356	4	-4	1	1.09	1	/O-8(8-0-0)	0	-0.4
1943 Pit-N	51	79	7	12	3	0	0	1	3	15	0	....	.152	.183	.190	.373	7	-10	3	1.08	-3	O-20(5-6-9)/3-2,1-1,2-1	0	-1.5
1946 Phi-N	145	545	73	153	30	4	6	45	70	42	7	....	.281	.366	.383	.749	116	13	82	5.41	0	*O-142(6-138-0)	22	0.9
1947 Phi-N	128	454	68	124	24	7	5	51	61	45	7	....	.273	.364	.390	.754	104	4	67	5.31	-2	*O-126(0-27-100)	12	-0.1
1948 Cin-N	136	512	74	140	24	9	17	76	52	63	7	....	.273	.344	.455	.799	119	12	83	5.93	-7	*O-130(0-130-0)	18	0.1
1949 Cin-N	134	474	54	118	20	4	9	46	58	63	7	....	.249	.333	.365	.698	86	-9	60	4.49	-3	*O-129(2-60-67)	11	-1.6
1950 Cin-N★	131	509	70	145	34	5	8	76	52	38	1	....	.285	.357	.418	.775	103	2	76	5.37	-3	*O-129(11-9-115)/1-4	14	-0.5
1951 Cin-N★	142	537	52	167	31	3	2	61	54	54	2	1	.311	.376	.391	.767	105	6	83	5.79	-11	*O-139(1-0-139)	18	-1.0
1952 Cin-N	30	106	12	25	1	3	1	10	18	7	1	2	.236	.347	.330	.677	89	-1	12	3.49	-1	O-29(0-25-6)/1-1	2	-0.3
Phi-N	98	321	45	88	16	3	1	37	44	26	1	7	.274	.363	.352	.715	100	-1	42	4.55	4	O-88(2-1-87)	9	0.0
Yr.	128	427	57	113	17	6	2	47	62	33	2	9	.265	.359	.347	.706	97	-2	54	4.27	4	*O-117(2-26-93)/1-1	11	-0.3
1953 Phi-N	125	409	42	111	14	2	6	47	38	43	0	3	.271	.339	.359	.699	83	-11	51	4.39	-3	*O-110(8-0-102)	8	-1.7
1954 Phi-N	92	259	28	62	12	4	3	28	29	39	0	0	.239	.318	.351	.670	74	-9	29	3.76	-1	O-55(6-0-49),1-22	4	-1.3
Total 11	1221	4240	525	1149	209	45	58	481	482	437	33	13	.271	.349	.383	.731	98	-8	589	4.94	-30	*O-1105/1-28,3-2,2-1	118	-7.3

• YAIK, Henry Henry Yaik b: 3/1/1864, Detroit, MI d: 9/21/1935, Detroit, MI BL, 5'11", 185 lbs. Deb: 10/3/1888

YEAR TM-L	G	AB	R	H	2B	3B	HR	RBI	BB	SO	SB	CS	AVG	OBP	SLG	OPS	OPS+	BR/A	RC	RC/G	FR	G/POS	WS	TPW
1888 Pit-N	2	6	0	2	0	0	0	1	1	0	0	....	.333	.429	.333	.762	158	0	1	5.93	1	/C-1,O-1	0	0.1

• YALE, Ad William M. Yale b: 4/17/1870, Bristol, CT d: 4/27/1948, Bridgeport, CT BR Deb: 9/18/1905

YEAR TM-L	G	AB	R	H	2B	3B	HR	RBI	BB	SO	SB	CS	AVG	OBP	SLG	OPS	OPS+	BR/A	RC	RC/G	FR	G/POS	WS	TPW
1905 Bro-N	4	13	1	1	0	0	0	1	1	....	0	....	.077	.143	.077	.220	-37	-2	0	.32	0	/1-4	0	-0.3

• YANCY, Hugh Hugh Yancy b: 10/16/1950, Sarasota, FL BR/TR, 5'11", 170 lbs. Deb: 7/5/1972

YEAR TM-L	G	AB	R	H	2B	3B	HR	RBI	BB	SO	SB	CS	AVG	OBP	SLG	OPS	OPS+	BR/A	RC	RC/G	FR	G/POS	WS	TPW
1972 Chi-A	3	9	0	1	0	0	0	0	0	0	0	1	.111	.111	.111	.222	-33	-2	0	.00	0	/3-3	0	-0.2
1974 Chi-A	1	0	0	0	0	0	0	0	0	0	0	0	....	....	....	....	-98	0	0	.00	0	/D-1	0	0.0
1976 Chi-A	3	10	0	1	1	0	0	0	0	3	0	0	.100	.100	.200	.300	-14	-1	0	.60	-0	/2-3	0	-0.1
Total 3	7	19	0	2	1	0	0	0	0	3	0	1	.105	.105	.158	.263	-27	-3	0	.27	0	/2-3,3-3,D-1	0	-0.3

• YANKOWSKI, George George Edward Yankowski b: 11/19/1922, Cambridge, MA BR/TR, 6', 180 lbs. Deb: 8/17/1942

YEAR TM-L	G	AB	R	H	2B	3B	HR	RBI	BB	SO	SB	CS	AVG	OBP	SLG	OPS	OPS+	BR/A	RC	RC/G	FR	G/POS	WS	TPW
1942 Phi-A	6	13	0	2	1	0	0	2	0	2	0	0	.154	.154	.231	.385	7	-2	0	.53	0	/C-6	0	-0.1
1949 Chi-A	12	18	0	3	1	0	0	2	0	2	0	0	.167	.167	.222	.389	3	-3	0	.36	0	/C-6	0	-0.2
Total 2	18	31	0	5	2	0	0	4	0	4	0	0	.161	.161	.226	.387	5	-4	0	.43	1	/C-12	0	-0.3

• YANTZ, George George Webb Yantz b: 7/27/1886, Louisville, KY d: 2/26/1967, Louisville, KY BR/TR, 5'6.5", 168 lbs. Deb: 9/30/1912

YEAR TM-L	G	AB	R	H	2B	3B	HR	RBI	BB	SO	SB	CS	AVG	OBP	SLG	OPS	OPS+	BR/A	RC	RC/G	FR	G/POS	WS	TPW
1912 Chi-N	1	1	0	1	0	0	0	0	0	0	0	....	1.000	1.000	1.000	2.000	449	0	1	∞	0	/C-1	0	0.0

YEAR TM-L	G	AB	R	H	2B	3B	HR	RBI	BB	SO	SB	CS	AVG	OBP	SLG	OPS	OPS+	BR/A	RC	RC/G	FR	G/POS	WS	TPW
• YARYAN, Yam	Clarence Everett Yaryan b: 11/5/1892, Knowlton, IA d: 11/16/1964, Birmingham, AL BR/TR, 5'10.5", 180 lbs. Deb: 4/23/1921																							
1921 Chi-A	45	102	11	31	8	2	0	15	9	16	0	0	.304	.366	.422	.788	102	0	16	5.78	0	C-34	3	0.2
1922 Chi-A	36	71	9	14	2	0	2	9	6	10	1	0	.197	.269	.310	.579	51	-5	6	2.90	0	C-26	1	-0.4
Total 2	81	173	20	45	10	2	2	24	15	26	1	0	.260	.326	.376	.702	81	-4	22	4.51	0	/C-60	4	-0.2
• YASTRZEMSKI, Carl	Carl Michael "Yaz" Yastrzemski b: 8/22/1939, Southampton, NY BL/TR, 5'11", 182 lbs. Deb: 4/11/1961 HOF: 1989 Career OF: 1917-159-7																							
1961 Bos-A	148	583	71	155	31	6	11	80	50	96	6	5	.266	.327	.396	.723	90	-10	72	4.22	-5	*O-147(147-0-0)	12	-2.3
1962 Bos-A	160	646	99	191	43	6	19	94	66	82	7	4	.296	.364	.469	.833	118	16	103	5.70	8	*O-160(160-0-0)	21	1.5
1963 Bos-A★	151	570	91	**183**	**40**	3	14	68	**95**	72	8	5	**.321**	**.419**	.475	.894	145	**39**	118	**7.81**	3	*O-151(151-1-0)	**29**	3.5
1964 Bos-A	151	567	77	164	29	9	15	67	75	90	6	5	.289	.374	.451	.826	122	18	89	5.45	12	*O-148(18-131-0)/3-2	20	2.7
1965 Bos-A★	133	494	78	154	**45**	3	20	72	70	58	7	6	.312	**.398**	**.536**	**.935**	**154**	**35**	102	**7.52**	-1	*O-130(125-7-1)	21	2.9
1966 Bos-A★	160	594	81	165	**39**	2	16	80	84	60	8	9	.278	.368	.431	.799	117	14	92	5.46	8	*O-158(157-1-0)	21	1.4
1967*Bos-A★	161	579	**112**	**189**	31	4	**44**	**121**	91	69	10	8	**.326**	**.421**	**.622**	**1.043**	**189**	**66**	155	**10.26**	2	*O-161(161-1-0)	**42**	**6.5**
1968 Bos-A★	157	539	90	162	32	2	23	74	**119**	90	13	6	**.301**	**.429**	.495	**.924**	168	**52**	121	**8.21**	7	*O-155(154-1-0)/1-3	**39**	**5.8**
1969 Bos-A★	162	603	96	154	28	2	40	111	101	91	15	7	.255	.363	.507	.871	134	28	113	6.45	4	*O-143(140-3-0),1-22	26	2.4
1970 Bos-A★	161	566	**125**	186	29	0	40	102	128	66	23	13	.329	**.453**	**.592**	**1.045**	**174**	**64**	157	**10.45**	-1	1-94,O-69(67-3-0)	**36**	**5.4**
1971 Bos-A★	148	508	75	129	21	2	15	70	106	60	8	7	.254	.384	.392	.775	112	12	80	5.33	7	*O-146(146-0-0)	21	1.1
1972 Bos-A★	125	455	70	120	18	2	12	68	67	44	5	4	.264	.363	.391	.754	118	12	66	4.94	2	O-83(83-0-0),1-42	19	0.7
1973 Bos-A★	152	540	82	160	25	4	19	95	105	58	9	7	.296	.411	.463	.874	138	31	103	6.76	-3	*1-107,3-31,O-14(14-0-0)	24	2.0
1974 Bos-A★	148	515	**93**	155	25	2	15	79	104	48	12	7	.301	.421	.445	.866	139	33	102	7.03	0	1-84,O-63(63-0-0)/D-4	24	2.4
1975*Bos-A★	149	543	91	146	30	1	14	60	87	67	8	4	.269	.372	.405	.777	110	11	84	5.43	4	*1-140/O-8(8-0-0),D-2	20	0.3
1976 Bos-A★	155	546	71	146	23	2	21	102	80	67	5	6	.267	.362	.432	.794	118	13	86	5.46	-2	1-94,O-51(51-0-0),D-10	18	0.1
1977 Bos-A★	150	558	99	165	27	3	28	102	73	40	11	1	.296	.378	.505	.884	124	22	110	7.18	7	*O-140(138-0-2)/1-7,D-6	24	2.2
1978 Bos-A★	144	523	70	145	21	2	17	81	76	44	4	5	.277	.372	.423	.795	111	10	85	5.70	6	O-71(63-8-0),1-50,D-27	19	0.9
1979 Bos-A★	147	518	69	140	28	1	21	87	62	46	3	3	.270	.351	.450	.800	108	6	81	5.46	6	D-56,1-51,O-36(36-0-0)	13	0.5
1980 Bos-A	105	364	49	100	21	1	15	50	44	38	0	2	.275	.353	.462	.814	115	7	58	5.63	-2	D-49,O-39(34-1-4),1-16	10	0.0
1981 Bos-A	91	338	36	83	14	1	7	53	49	28	0	1	.246	.341	.355	.696	95	-1	41	4.15	4	D-48,1-39	7	-0.1
1982 Bos-A★	131	459	53	126	22	1	16	72	59	50	0	1	.275	.360	.431	.791	110	7	72	5.54	1	*D-102,1-14/O-2(0-2-0)	13	0.4
1983 Bos-A★	119	380	38	101	24	0	10	56	54	29	0	0	.266	.360	.408	.768	103	3	55	5.08	0	*D-107/1-2,O-1	9	0.0
Total 23	3308	11988	1816	3419	646	59	452	1844	1845	1393	168	116	.285	.382	.462	.844	128	492	2147	6.35	67	*O-2076,1-765,D-411/3-33	488	40.3
• YATES, Al	Albert Arthur Yates b: 5/26/1945, Jersey City, NJ BR/TR, 6'2", 210 lbs. Deb: 5/13/1971																							
1971 Mil-A	24	47	5	13	2	0	1	4	3	7	1	0	.277	.320	.383	.703	99	0	5	3.89	1	O-12(3-0-9)	1	0.1
• YEABSLEY, Bert	Robert Watkins Yeabsley b: 12/17/1893, Philadelphia, PA d: 2/8/1961, Philadelphia, PA BR/TR, 5'9.5", 175 lbs. Deb: 5/28/1919																							
1919 Phi-N	3	0	0	0	0	0	0	0	1	0	0	....	....	1.000	....	1.000	200	0	0	....	0	....	0	0.0
• YEAGER, George	George J. "Doc" Yeager b: 6/4/1873, Cincinnati, OH d: 6/5/1940, Cincinnati, OH BR/TR, 5'10", 190 lbs. Deb: 9/25/1896 U Career OF: 8-5-13																							
1896 Bos-N	2	5	1	1	0	0	0	0	0	1	0	....	.200	.200	.200	.400	5	-1	0	1.36	0	/1-2	0	-0.1
1897*Bos-N	30	95	20	23	2	3	2	15	7	....	2	....	.242	.294	.389	.684	75	-4	12	4.26	-1	C-13,O-10(2-1-7)/2-4,3-1	2	-0.4
1898 Bos-N	68	221	37	59	13	1	3	24	16	....	1	....	.267	.328	.376	.703	96	-2	29	4.59	-7	C-37,1-17/O-9(6-3-1),S-2	7	-0.6
1899 Bos-N	3	8	1	1	0	0	0	0	1	....	0	....	.125	.222	.125	.347	-3	-1	0	.86	-1	/O-2(0-1-1),C-1	0	-0.1
1901 Cle-A	39	139	13	31	5	0	0	14	4	....	2	....	.223	.250	.259	.509	43	-11	10	2.40	3	C-25/1-5,O-3(0-0-3),2-2	1	-0.5
Pit-N	26	91	9	24	2	1	0	10	4	....	1	....	.264	.302	.308	.610	75	-3	9	3.54	-2	C-20/3-4,1-1	2	-0.2
1902 NY-N	39	108	6	22	2	1	0	9	11	....	1	....	.204	.277	.241	.518	60	-5	8	2.41	-1	C-27/1-3,O-1	1	-0.3
Bal-A	11	38	3	7	1	0	0	1	2	....	0	....	.184	.225	.211	.436	17	-4	2	1.58	1	C-11	0	-0.3
Total 6	218	705	90	168	25	6	5	73	45	1	7	....	.238	.290	.312	.602	69	-31	71	3.38	-8	C-134/1-28,O-25,2-6,3-5,S-2	13	-2.5
• YEAGER, Joe	Joseph F. "Little Joe" Yeager b: 8/28/1875, Philadelphia, PA d: 7/2/1937, Detroit, MI BR/TR, 5'10", 160 lbs. Deb: 4/22/1898 Career OF: 10-1-7 ♦																							
1898 Bro-N	43	134	12	23	5	1	0	15	7	....	1	....	.172	.218	.224	.442	27	-5	7	1.69	5	P-36/O-4(2-1-1),S-2,2-1	13	-0.3
1899 Bro-N	23	47	12	9	0	1	0	4	6	....	0	....	.191	.333	.234	.567	55	-1	4	2.73	1	S-11,P-10/3-1,O-1	3	-0.5
1900 Bro-N	3	9	0	3	0	0	0	0	0	....	0	....	.333	.333	.333	.667	79	0	1	4.53	-1	/P-2,3-1	0	-0.6
1901 Det-A	41	125	18	37	7	1	2	17	4	....	3	....	.296	.343	.416	.759	105	6	20	5.76	5	P-26,S-12/2-1	21	3.1
1902 Det-A	50	161	17	39	6	5	1	23	5	....	0	....	.242	.282	.360	.643	76	-1	17	3.64	3	P-19,O-13(7-0-6),2-12/S-3,3	6	-2.0
1903 Det-A	109	402	36	103	15	6	0	43	18	....	9	....	.256	.303	.323	.626	91	-4	44	3.81	-11	*3-107/P-1,S-1	9	-1.4
1905 NY-A	115	401	54	107	16	7	0	42	25	....	8	....	.267	.330	.342	.672	102	1	50	4.40	6	3-91,S-21	15	1.1
1906 NY-A	57	123	20	37	6	1	0	12	13	....	3	....	.301	.407	.366	.773	129	6	21	6.02	0	S-22,2-13/3-3	6	0.7
1907 StL-A	123	436	32	104	21	7	1	44	31	....	11	....	.239	.294	.326	.619	98	-2	47	3.66	8	3-91,2-17,S-10	13	1.0
1908 StL-A	10	15	3	5	1	0	0	1	1	....	2	....	.333	.474	.400	.874	183	2	4	9.20	0	/2-4,S-1	1	0.2
Total 10	574	1853	204	467	77	29	4	201	110	....	37	....	.252	.312	.331	.643	93	2	216	4.00	14	3-295/P-94,S-83,2-48,O-18	87	1.5
• YEAGER, Steve	Stephen Wayne Yeager b: 11/24/1948, Huntington, WV BR/TR, 6', 190 lbs. Deb: 8/2/1972																							
1972 LA-N	35	106	18	29	0	1	4	15	16	26	0	0	.274	.374	.406	.780	124	4	16	5.48	3	C-35	5	0.9
1973 LA-N	54	134	18	34	5	0	2	10	15	33	1	0	.254	.342	.336	.678	93	-1	16	4.05	-1	C-50	5	0.1
1974*LA-N	94	316	41	84	16	1	12	41	32	77	2	2	.266	.337	.437	.774	120	7	46	5.04	0	C-93	15	1.3
1975 LA-N	135	452	34	103	16	1	12	54	40	75	2	5	.228	.302	.347	.649	83	-13	45	3.16	1	*C-135	12	-0.5
1976 LA-N	117	359	42	77	11	3	11	35	30	84	3	1	.214	.288	.354	.642	83	-9	38	3.49	10	*C-115	13	0.7
1977*LA-N	125	387	53	99	21	2	16	55	43	84	1	3	.256	.336	.444	.781	108	3	57	5.11	5	*C-123	16	1.4
1978*LA-N	94	228	19	44	7	0	4	23	36	41	0	0	.193	.303	.276	.579	63	-10	20	2.92	4	C-91	6	-0.3
1979 LA-N	105	310	33	67	9	2	13	41	29	68	1	0	.216	.283	.384	.667	81	-9	31	3.22	4	*C-103	7	0.0
1980 LA-N	96	227	20	48	8	0	2	20	20	54	2	3	.211	.275	.273	.548	55	-15	16	2.23	0	C-95	4	-1.2
1981*LA-N	42	86	5	18	2	0	3	7	6	14	0	0	.209	.261	.337	.598	71	-4	7	2.82	-1	C-40	2	-0.4
1982 LA-N	82	196	13	48	5	2	2	18	13	28	0	0	.245	.295	.321	.617	74	-7	19	3.25	1	C-76	5	-0.3
1983*LA-N	113	335	31	68	8	3	15	41	23	57	1	1	.203	.256	.379	.635	74	-14	28	2.64	0	*C-112	7	-1.0
1984 LA-N	74	197	16	45	4	0	4	29	20	38	1	2	.228	.300	.310	.609	72	-8	19	3.19	1	C-65	5	-0.5
1985*LA-N	53	121	4	25	4	1	0	9	7	24	0	1	.207	.250	.256	.506	43	-10	7	1.90	3	C-48	2	-0.6
1986 Sea-A	50	130	10	27	2	0	2	12	12	23	0	0	.208	.275	.269	.544	48	-9	9	2.26	2	C-49	2	-0.5
Total 15	1269	3584	357	816	118	16	102	410	342	726	14	18	.228	.300	.355	.655	83	-93	375	3.44	32	*C-1230	106	-0.9
• YEATMAN, Bill	William Suter Yeatman b: 3/1839, Alexandria, VA d: 4/20/1901, York, PA Deb: 4/20/1872																							
1872 Nat-n	1	4	0	0	0	0	0	0	0	1	0	0	.000	.000	.000	.000	-86	-1	0	.00	-1	/O-1	....	-0.1
• YELDING, Eric	Eric Girard Yelding b: 2/22/1965, Montrose, AL BR/TR, 5'11", 165 lbs. Deb: 4/9/1989 Career OF: 14-92-10																							
1989 Hou-N	70	90	19	21	2	0	0	9	7	19	11	5	.233	.296	.256	.551	61	-4	7	2.39	-1	S-15,2-13/O-8(1-4-3)	3	-0.4
1990 Hou-N	142	511	69	130	9	5	1	28	39	87	64	25	.254	.307	.297	.605	69	-19	48	3.01	-9	O-94(11-83-6),S-40,2-10/3-3	8	-2.7
1991 Hou-N	78	276	19	67	11	1	1	20	13	46	11	9	.243	.277	.301	.578	66	-15	21	2.55	-14	S-72/O-4(0-3-1)	1	-2.4
1992 Hou-N	9	8	1	2	0	0	0	0	0	3	0	0	.250	.250	.250	.500	44	-1	1	2.25	-1	/O-2(2-1-0),S-2	0	-0.2
1993 Chi-N	69	108	14	22	5	1	1	10	11	22	3	2	.204	.277	.296	.574	54	-7	9	2.46	-3	2-32/3-7,O-1,S-1	1	-0.9
Total 5	368	993	122	242	27	7	3	67	70	177	89	41	.244	.294	.294	.588	66	-46	85	2.76	-28	S-130,O-109/2-55,3-10	13	-6.6
• YELLE, Archie	Archie Joseph Yelle b: 6/11/1892, Saginaw, MI d: 5/2/1983, Woodland, CA BR/TR, 5'10.5", 170 lbs. Deb: 5/12/1917																							
1917 Det-A	25	51	4	7	1	0	0	0	5	4	2	....	.137	.214	.157	.371	13	-5	2	1.12	-1	C-24	1	-0.6
1918 Det-A	56	144	7	25	3	0	0	7	9	15	0	....	.174	.227	.194	.422	28	-13	6	1.31	-1	C-52	2	-1.0
1919 Det-A	6	4	1	0	0	0	0	0	1	0	0	....	.000	.200	.000	.200	-42	-1	0	.00	-2	/C-6	0	-0.2
Total 3	87	199	12	32	4	0	0	7	15	19	2	....	.161	.223	.181	.404	23	-19	8	1.23	-3	/C-82	3	-1.8
• YERKES, Steve	Stephen Douglas Yerkes b: 5/15/1888, Hatboro, PA d: 1/31/1971, Lansdale, PA BR/TR, 5'9", 165 lbs. Deb: 9/29/1909																							
1909 Bos-A	5	7	0	2	0	0	0	0	0	....	0	....	.286	.286	.286	.571	79	-0	1	2.83	0	/S-2	0	0.0
1911 Bos-A	142	502	70	140	24	3	1	57	52	....	14	....	.279	.354	.345	.698	96	-1	68	4.52	-16	*S-116,2-14,3-11	13	-0.8
1912*Bos-A	131	523	73	132	22	6	0	42	41	....	4	....	.252	.312	.317	.629	76	-17	54	3.39	-6	*2-131	10	-2.1
1913 Bos-A	137	483	67	129	29	6	1	48	50	32	11	....	.267	.338	.358	.696	101	1	62	4.19	-16	*2-129	13	-1.4

YEAR	TM-L	G	AB	R	H	2B	3B	HR	RBI	BB	SO	SB	CS	AVG	OBP	SLG	OPS	OPS+	BR/A	RC	RC/G	FR	G/POS	WS	TPW
1914	Bos-A	92	293	23	64	17	2	1	23	14	23	5	6	.218	.259	.300	.559	68	-15	24	2.53	5	2-91	5	-0.8
	Pit-F	39	142	18	48	9	5	1	25	11	13	2	....	.338	.386	.493	.879	158	10	27	6.95	8	S-39	8	2.3
1915	Pit-F	121	434	44	125	17	8	1	49	30	27	17	....	.288	.337	.371	.708	104	1	58	4.66	8	*2-114/S-8	16	1.3
1916	Chi-N	44	137	12	36	6	2	1	10	9	7	1	....	.263	.308	.358	.666	94	-1	16	3.96	-5	2-41	3	-0.7
Total 7		711	2521	307	676	124	32	6	254	207	102	54	6	.268	.328	.350	.677	94	-22	310	4.08	-21	2-520,S-165/3-11	68	-2.2

• YEWCIC, Tom
Thomas "Kibby" Yewcic b: 5/9/1932, Conenaugh, PA   BR/TR, 5'11", 180 lbs.   Deb: 6/27/1957

YEAR	TM-L	G	AB	R	H	2B	3B	HR	RBI	BB	SO	SB	CS	AVG	OBP	SLG	OPS	OPS+	BR/A	RC	RC/G	FR	G/POS	WS	TPW
1957	Det-A	1	1	0	0	0	0	0	0	0	0	0	....	.000	.000	.000	.000	-98	-0	0	.00	0	/C-1	0	0.0

• YEWELL, Ed
Edwin Leonard Yewell   b: 8/22/1862, Washington, DC   d: 9/15/1940, Washington, DC   Deb: 5/12/1884

| 1884 | Was-a | 27 | 93 | 14 | 23 | 3 | 1 | 0 | 1 | .... | .... | .... | .... | .247 | .263 | .301 | .564 | 94 | -0 | 8 | 2.97 | -2 | 2-11/0-8(1-2-5),3-7,S-2 | 1 | -0.2 |
| | Was-U | 1 | 4 | 0 | 0 | 0 | 0 | 0 | 0 | .... | .... | .... | .... | .000 | .000 | .000 | .000 | -103 | -1 | 0 | .00 | 0 | /3-1 | 0 | -0.1 |

• YINGLING, Joe
Joseph Granville Yingling   b: 7/23/1866, Westminster, MD   d: 10/24/1946, Manchester, MD   BR/TL, 5'7.5", 145 lbs.   Deb: 5/28/1886 ♦

1886	Was-N	1	2	0	0	0	0	0	0	0	1	0	....	.000	.000	.000	.000	-106	-0	0	.00	0	/P-1	0	-0.3
1894	Phi-N	1	4	0	1	0	0	0	0	0	1	0	....	.250	.250	.250	.500	22	-1	0	2.22	0	/S-1	0	-0.1
Total 2		2	6	0	1	0	0	0	0	0	2	0	....	.167	.167	.167	.333	-21	-1	0	1.33	0	/P-1,S-1	0	-0.3

• YOHE, Bill
William Clyde Yohe   b: 9/2/1878, Mount Erie, IL   d: 12/24/1938, Bremerton, WA   BR/TR, 5'8", 180 lbs.   Deb: 8/30/1909

| 1909 | Was-A | 21 | 72 | 6 | 15 | 2 | 0 | 0 | 4 | 3 | .... | 2 | .... | .208 | .240 | .236 | .476 | 53 | -4 | 5 | 2.00 | 1 | 3-19 | 1 | -0.2 |

• YORK, Rudy
Rudolph Preston York   b: 8/17/1913, Ragland, AL   d: 2/5/1970, Rome, GA   BR/TR, 6'1", 209 lbs.   Deb: 8/22/1934   M/C

1934	Det-A	3	6	0	1	0	0	0	0	1	3	0	0	.167	.286	.167	.452	19	-1	0	1.83	0	/C-2	0	-0.1
1937	Det-A	104	375	72	115	18	3	35	103	41	52	3	2	.307	.375	.651	1.026	150	25	91	9.17	-9	C-54,3-41/1-2	18	2.0
1938	Det-A★	135	463	85	138	27	2	33	127	92	74	1	2	.298	.417	.579	.995	139	29	116	9.41	-3	*C-116,0-14(14-0-0)/1-1	27	2.9
1939	Det-A	102	329	66	101	16	1	20	68	41	50	5	0	.307	.387	.544	.931	126	13	70	7.93	-1	C-67,1-19	13	1.3
1940*	Det-A	155	588	105	186	46	6	33	134	89	88	3	2	.316	.410	.583	.993	104	37	147	9.44	4	*1-155	26	2.5
1941	Det-A★	155	590	91	153	29	3	27	111	92	88	3	1	.259	.360	.456	.816	104	4	101	5.96	-1	*1-155	16	-1.1
1942	Det-A★	153	577	81	150	26	4	21	90	73	71	3	3	.260	.343	.428	.771	107	5	86	5.17	14	*1-152	15	0.5
1943	Det-A★	155	571	90	155	22	11	34	118	84	88	5	5	.271	.366	.527	.893	148	34	108	6.52	11	*1-155	26	3.9
1944	Det-A★	151	583	77	161	27	7	18	98	68	73	5	5	.276	.353	.439	.792	119	14	91	5.53	-4	*1-151	22	0.8
1945*	Det-A	155	595	71	157	25	5	18	87	60	85	6	6	.264	.331	.413	.745	109	5	78	4.49	-4	*1-155	17	-0.8
1946*	Bos-A★	154	579	78	160	30	6	17	119	86	93	3	2	.276	.371	.437	.808	118	17	98	5.99	4	*1-154	22	0.8
1947	Bos-A	48	184	16	39	7	0	6	27	22	32	0	0	.212	.296	.348	.644	73	-7	18	3.08	2	1-48	2	-0.7
	Chi-A★	102	400	40	97	18	4	15	64	36	55	1	0	.243	.305	.420	.725	104	0	51	4.32	-4	*1-102	10	-0.7
	Yr.	150	584	56	136	25	4	21	91	58	87	1	0	.233	.302	.397	.699	94	-6	68	3.91	-2	*1-150	12	-1.4
1948	Phi-A	31	51	4	8	0	0	0	6	7	15	0	0	.157	.259	.157	.415	12	-6	2	1.35	-1	1-14	0	-0.7
Total 13		1603	5891	876	1621	291	52	277	1152	792	867	38	26	.275	.362	.483	.845	121	169	1057	6.35	8	*1-1263,C-239/3-41,0-14	214	10.8

• YORK, Tom
Thomas Jefferson York   b: 7/13/1851, Brooklyn, NY   d: 2/17/1936, New York, NY   BL, 5'9", 165 lbs.   Deb: 5/9/1871   M/U   NA OF: 242-31-1   Career OF: 651-3-36

1871	Tro-n	29	145	36	37	5	7	2	23	9	1	2	2	.255	.299	.428	.726	104	-1	20	5.61	1	*0-29(0-29-0)	....	0.1
1872	Bal-n	51	248	66	66	10	4	1	41	4	1	2	1	.266	.278	.351	.629	88	-5	25	4.29	8	*0-51(51-0-1)	....	0.3
1873	Bal-n	57	277	70	84	10	7	2	49	3	3	3	1	.303	.311	.412	.722	113	5	37	5.86	9	*0-57(56-1-0)	....	1.0
1874	Phi-n	50	224	36	56	4	7	0	37	5	4	1	0	.250	.266	.330	.597	87	-4	20	3.66	6	*0-50(49-1-0)	....	1.0
1875	Har-n	86	375	68	111	14	7	0	37	3	6	7	3	.296	.302	.371	.672	126	8	45	4.99	1	*0-86(86-0-0)	....	1.0
1876	Har-N	67	273	47	68	12	7	1	39	10	4	....	....	.249	.286	.369	.655	108	1	28	4.08	4	*0-67(66-1-0)	10	0.1
1877	Har-N	56	237	43	67	16	7	1	37	3	11	....	....	.283	.292	.422	.714	136	10	30	4.84	2	*0-56(56-0-0)	10	0.8
1878	Pro-N	62	269	56	83	19	10	1	26	8	19	....	....	.309	.329	.465	.793	159	16	42	6.22	6	*0-62(62-0-0)	13	1.8
1879	Pro-N	81	342	69	106	25	5	1	50	19	28	....	....	.310	.346	.421	.767	154	20	51	6.06	0	*0-81(81-0-0)	14	1.4
1880	Pro-N	53	203	21	43	9	2	0	18	8	29	....	....	.212	.242	.276	.518	77	-4	14	2.38	0	0-53(50-1-2)	4	-0.7
1881	Pro-N	85	316	57	96	23	5	2	47	29	26	....	....	.304	.362	.427	.790	149	19	50	6.15	-2	*0-85(85-0-0)	17	1.1
1882	Pro-N	81	321	48	86	23	7	1	40	19	14	....	....	.268	.309	.393	.701	123	9	40	4.67	1	*0-81(81-0-0)	13	0.6
1883	Cle-N	100	381	56	99	29	5	2	46	37	55	....	....	.260	.325	.378	.703	114	8	48	4.68	1	*0-100(100-0-0)	12	0.5
1884	Bal-a	83	314	64	70	14	7	1	0	34	....	....	....	.223	.318	.322	.640	105	3	33	3.72	-5	*0-83(68-0-15)	12	-0.4
1885	Bal-a	22	87	6	23	4	2	0	12	8	....	....	....	.264	.326	.356	.683	117	2	10	4.37	0	0-22(2-1-19)	2	0.2
Total 5 n		273	1269	276	354	43	32	5	187	24	15	15	7	.279	.292	.375	.667	106	4	148	4.86	26	0-273	....	2.7
Total 10		690	2743	467	741	174	57	10	315	175	186	....	....	.270	.317	.387	.705	126	85	347	4.79	8	0-690	107	5.5

• YORK, Tony
Tony Batton York   b: 11/27/1912, Irene, TX   d: 4/18/1970, Hillsboro, TX   BR/TR, 5'10", 165 lbs.   Deb: 4/18/1944

| 1944 | Chi-N | 28 | 85 | 4 | 20 | 1 | 0 | 0 | 7 | 4 | 11 | 0 | .... | .235 | .270 | .247 | .517 | 46 | -6 | 6 | 2.19 | 1 | S-15,3-12 | 1 | -0.3 |

• YOST, Eddie
Edward Frederick "The Walking Man" Yost   b: 10/13/1926, Brooklyn, NY   BR/TR, 5'10", 170 lbs.   Deb: 8/16/1944   M/C   Career OF: 3-0-8

1944	Was-A	7	14	3	2	0	0	0	1	2	0	0	0	.143	.200	.143	.343	-1	-2	1	1.10	-1	/3-3,S-2	0	-0.3
1946	Was-A	8	25	2	2	1	0	0	1	5	5	2	1	.080	.233	.120	.353	1	-3	1	.99	1	/3-7	0	-0.2
1947	Was-A	115	428	52	102	17	3	0	14	45	57	3	5	.238	.314	.292	.606	71	-17	41	3.19	-8	*3-114	7	-2.6
1948	Was-A	145	555	74	138	32	11	2	50	82	51	4	3	.249	.349	.357	.706	91	-6	73	4.49	-9	*3-145	14	-1.5
1949	Was-A	124	435	57	110	19	7	9	45	91	41	3	3	.253	.383	.391	.774	107	7	71	5.62	-4	*3-122	15	0.3
1950	Was-A	155	573	114	169	26	2	11	58	141	63	6	6	.295	.440	.405	.845	123	30	116	7.27	-5	*3-155	24	2.4
1951	Was-A	154	568	109	161	36	4	12	65	126	55	6	4	.283	.423	.424	.847	132	34	117	7.35	-15	*3-152/0-3(3-0-0)	27	1.8
1952	Was-A★	157	587	92	137	32	3	12	49	129	73	4	3	.233	.378	.359	.738	110	15	93	5.29	-21	*3-157	23	-0.6
1953	Was-A	152	577	107	157	30	7	9	45	123	59	7	4	.272	.403	.395	.799	119	23	103	6.27	-4	*3-152	24	1.9
1954	Was-A	155	539	101	138	26	4	11	47	131	71	7	3	.256	.406	.380	.786	123	26	97	6.21	4	*3-155	23	3.1
1955	Was-A	122	375	64	91	17	5	7	48	95	54	4	3	.243	.410	.371	.780	117	16	66	5.89	-3	*3-107	16	1.3
1956	Was-A	152	515	94	119	17	2	11	53	151	82	8	5	.231	.412	.336	.748	100	11	86	5.53	0	*3-135/0-8(0-8-0)	19	1.0
1957	Was-A	110	414	47	104	13	5	9	38	73	49	1	11	.251	.370	.372	.742	104	2	58	4.83	-16	*3-107	13	-1.5
1958	Was-A	134	406	55	91	16	0	8	37	81	43	3	6	.224	.365	.323	.688	93	-1	52	4.21	-17	*3-114/0-4(0-0-0),1-2	11	-1.9
1959	Det-A	148	521	115	145	19	0	21	61	135	77	9	2	.278	.437	.436	.873	133	35	115	7.94	-1	*3-146/2-1	27	3.4
1960	Det-A	143	497	78	129	23	2	14	49	125	69	5	4	.260	.416	.398	.814	114	18	92	6.42	-15	*3-142	17	0.2
1961	LA-A	76	213	29	43	4	0	3	15	50	48	0	1	.202	.358	.263	.621	62	-10	24	3.75	-6	3-67	3	-1.6
1962	LA-A	104	100	14	22	5	0	0	7	28	17	0	3	.240	.415	.340	.761	11	3	4	5.31	-2	3-28/1-7	4	0.0
Total 18		2109	7346	1215	1863	337	56	139	683	1614	920	72	66	.254	.395	.371	.766	109	180	1225	5.70	-120	*3-2008/0-15,1-9,S-2,2-1	267	5.1

• YOST, Ned
Edgar Frederick Yost   b: 8/19/1954, Eureka, CA   BR/TR, 6'1", 190 lbs.   Deb: 4/12/1980   M/C

1980	Mil-A	15	31	0	5	0	0	0	1	0	9	0	0	.161	.161	.161	.323	-12	-5	1	.65	0	C-15	1	-0.4
1981	Mil-A	18	27	4	6	0	0	3	3	3	6	0	0	.222	.300	.556	.856	150	2	5	6.09	0	C-16	2	0.1
1982*	Mil-A	40	98	13	27	6	3	1	8	7	20	3	1	.276	.324	.429	.752	111	2	14	5.00	-2	C-39/D-1	4	0.1
1983	Mil-A	61	196	21	44	5	1	6	28	9	36	1	0	.224	.244	.352	.596	67	-9	15	2.50	-4	C-61	2	-1.1
1984	Tex-A	80	242	15	44	4	0	6	25	6	47	1	2	.182	.202	.273	.474	29	-25	12	1.55	-2	C-78	2	-2.4
1985	Mon-N	5	11	1	2	0	0	0	0	0	0	0	0	.182	.182	.182	.364	2	-1	0	1.09	-1	/C-5	0	-0.2
Total 6		219	605	54	128	15	4	16	64	21	117	5	3	.212	.238	.329	.567	58	-37	47	2.50	-9	C-214/D-1	11	-3.8

• YOTER, Elmer
Elmer Ellsworth Yoter   b: 6/26/1900, Plainfield, PA   d: 7/26/1966, Camp Hill, PA   BR/TR, 5'7", 155 lbs.   Deb: 9/9/1921

1921	Phi-A	3	3	0	0	0	0	0	0	0	0	0	....	.000	.000	.000	.000	-99	-1	0	.00	0	....	0	-0.1
1924	Cle-A	19	66	3	18	1	1	0	7	5	8	0	0	.273	.324	.318	.642	65	-3	7	3.69	1	3-19	1	-0.1
1927	Chi-N	13	27	2	6	1	0	0	5	4	4	0	0	.222	.323	.333	.656	76	-1	3	3.73	0	3-11	1	0.0
1928	Chi-N	1	0	0	0	....	....	....	....	....	....	....	....	....	....	....	....	-101	-0	0	....	0	....	0	0.0
Total 4		36	96	5	24	2	2	0	12	9	12	0	0	.250	.314	.313	.627	64	-5	10	3.56	1	/3-31	2	-0.3

• YOUNG, Babe
Norman Robert Young   b: 7/1/1915, Astoria, NY   d: 12/25/1983, Everett, WA   BL/TL, 6'2.5", 185 lbs.   Deb: 9/26/1936   Career OF: 0-71-8

| 1936 | NY-N | 1 | 1 | 0 | 0 | 0 | 0 | 0 | 0 | 0 | 0 | 0 | .... | .000 | .000 | .000 | .000 | -101 | -0 | 0 | .00 | 0 | .... | 0 | 0.0 |

YEAR TM-L	G	AB	R	H	2B	3B	HR	RBI	BB	SO	SB	CS	AVG	OBP	SLG	OPS	OPS+	BR/A	RC	RC/G	FR	G/POS	WS	TPW
1939 NY-N	22	75	8	23	4	0	3	14	5	6	0	....	.307	.373	.480	.853	127	3	14	7.26	-2	1-22	3	-0.1
1940 NY-N	149	556	75	159	27	4	17	101	69	28	4	....	.286	.367	.441	.807	121	17	92	6.03	-3	*1-147	20	0.0
1941 NY-N	152	574	90	152	28	5	25	104	66	39	1	....	.265	.346	.462	.807	124	17	93	5.72	-7	*1-150	20	-0.4
1942 NY-N	101	287	37	80	17	1	11	59	34	22	1	....	.279	.365	.460	.825	140	14	50	6.36	1	0-54(0-54-0),1-18	14	1.4
1946 NY-N	104	291	30	81	11	0	7	33	30	21	3	....	.278	.346	.388	.734	107	3	40	5.01	-5	1-49,0-24(0-17-7)	7	-0.5
1947 NY-N	14	14	0	1	1	0	0	0	0	1	0	....	.071	.071	.143	.214	-44	-3	0	.30	0	....	0	-0.3
Cin-N	95	364	55	103	21	3	14	79	35	26	0	....	.283	.349	.473	.822	117	8	60	5.96	-2	1-93	13	0.2
Yr.	109	378	55	104	22	3	14	79	35	27	0	....	.275	.340	.460	.800	112	5	60	5.70	-2	1-93	13	0.0
1948 Cin-N	49	130	11	30	7	2	1	12	19	12	0	....	.231	.329	.338	.667	84	-3	16	4.19	1	1-31/0-1	3	-0.3
StL-N	41	111	14	27	5	2	1	13	16	6	0	....	.243	.339	.351	.690	82	-2	14	4.22	-3	1-35	2	-0.7
Yr.	90	241	25	57	12	4	2	25	35	18	0	....	.237	.333	.344	.678	83	-5	29	4.20	-3	1-66/0-1	5	-1.0
Total 8	**728**	**2403**	**320**	**656**	**121**	**17**	**79**	**415**	**274**	**161**	**9**	**....**	**.273**	**.352**	**.436**	**.788**	**117**	**53**	**379**	**5.66**	**-20**	**1-545/0-79**	**82**	**-0.6**

• YOUNG, Bobby Robert George Young b: 1/22/1925, Granite, MD d: 1/28/1985, Baltimore, MD BL/TR, 6'1", 175 lbs. Deb: 7/28/1948

YEAR TM-L	G	AB	R	H	2B	3B	HR	RBI	BB	SO	SB	CS	AVG	OBP	SLG	OPS	OPS+	BR/A	RC	RC/G	FR	G/POS	WS	TPW
1948 StL-N	3	1	0	0	0	0	0	0	0	1	0	....	.000	.000	.000	.000	-95	-0	0	.00	0	/3-1	0	-0.1
1951 StL-A	147	611	75	159	13	9	1	31	44	51	8	7	.260	.310	.316	.626	67	-29	60	3.31	-3	*2-147	9	-2.3
1952 StL-A	149	575	59	142	15	9	4	39	56	48	3	3	.247	.314	.325	.639	76	-19	62	3.75	2	*2-149	12	-0.9
1953 StL-A	148	537	48	137	22	2	4	25	41	40	2	1	.255	.309	.326	.635	70	-22	56	3.52	-15	*2-148	6	-2.5
1954 Bal-A	130	432	43	106	13	6	4	24	54	42	4	4	.245	.331	.331	.662	88	-7	49	3.82	-2	*2-127	9	0.0
1955 Bal-A	59	186	5	37	3	0	1	8	11	23	1	4	.199	.244	.231	.475	30	-20	10	1.66	-3	2-58	2	-1.9
Cle-A	18	45	7	14	1	1	0	6	1	2	0	0	.311	.326	.378	.704	86	-1	6	4.79	3	2-11/3-1	1	0.3
Yr.	77	231	12	51	4	1	1	14	12	25	1	4	.221	.259	.260	.519	41	-21	16	2.18	0	2-69/3-1	3	-1.6
1956 Cle-A	1	0	0	0	0	0	0	0	0	0	0	0	....	....	....	....	-98	0	0	....	0	....	0	0.0
1958 Phi-N	32	60	7	14	1	1	1	4	1	5	0	0	.233	.246	.333	.579	52	-4	4	1.64	-1	2-21	0	-0.4
Total 8	**687**	**2447**	**244**	**609**	**68**	**28**	**15**	**137**	**208**	**212**	**18**	**19**	**.249**	**.308**	**.318**	**.626**	**71**	**-103**	**247**	**3.38**	**-19**	**2-661/3-2**	**39**	**-7.9**

• YOUNG, Del Delmer John Young b: 10/24/1885, Macon, MO d: 12/17/1959, Cleveland, OH BL/TR, 5'11", 195 lbs. Deb: 9/24/1909 Career OF: 8-3-35

YEAR TM-L	G	AB	R	H	2B	3B	HR	RBI	BB	SO	SB	CS	AVG	OBP	SLG	OPS	OPS+	BR/A	RC	RC/G	FR	G/POS	WS	TPW
1909 Cin-N	2	7	0	2	0	0	0	1	1	....	0	....	.286	.375	.286	.661	106	0	1	3.81	1	/0-2(1-0-1)	0	0.1
1914 Buf-F	80	174	17	48	5	5	4	22	3	13	0	....	.276	.288	.431	.719	99	-2	20	4.07	-2	0-41(7-2-32)	4	-0.5
1915 Buf-F	12	15	0	2	0	0	0	0	1	0	1	....	.133	.188	.133	.321	-5	-2	0	.96	0	/0-3(0-1-2)	0	-0.3
Total 3	**94**	**196**	**17**	**52**	**5**	**5**	**4**	**23**	**5**	**13**	**1**	**....**	**.265**	**.284**	**.403**	**.687**	**91**	**-4**	**21**	**3.78**	**-2**	**/0-46**	**4**	**-0.7**

• YOUNG, Del Delmer Edward Young b: 3/11/1912, Cleveland, OH d: 12/8/1979, San Francisco, CA BB/TR, 5'11", 168 lbs. Deb: 4/19/1937

YEAR TM-L	G	AB	R	H	2B	3B	HR	RBI	BB	SO	SB	CS	AVG	OBP	SLG	OPS	OPS+	BR/A	RC	RC/G	FR	G/POS	WS	TPW
1937 Phi-N	109	360	36	70	9	2	0	24	18	55	6	....	.194	.235	.231	.465	25	-38	20	1.74	-1	*2-108	3	-3.3
1938 Phi-N	108	340	27	78	13	2	0	31	20	35	0	....	.229	.276	.279	.556	53	-22	27	2.60	-2	S-87,2-17	4	-1.7
1939 Phi-N	77	217	22	57	9	2	3	20	8	24	1	....	.263	.289	.364	.653	78	-8	22	3.48	-4	S-55,2-17	3	-0.8
1940 Phi-N	15	33	2	8	0	1	0	1	2	1	0	....	.242	.286	.303	.589	65	-2	3	2.76	-1	/S-6,2-5	0	-0.2
Total 4	**309**	**950**	**87**	**213**	**31**	**7**	**3**	**76**	**48**	**115**	**7**	**....**	**.224**	**.264**	**.281**	**.545**	**48**	**-70**	**72**	**2.46**	**-9**	**S-148,2-147**	**10**	**-6.1**

• YOUNG, Dick Richard Ennis Young b: 6/3/1928, Seattle, WA BL/TR, 5'11", 175 lbs. Deb: 9/11/1951

YEAR TM-L	G	AB	R	H	2B	3B	HR	RBI	BB	SO	SB	CS	AVG	OBP	SLG	OPS	OPS+	BR/A	RC	RC/G	FR	G/POS	WS	TPW
1951 Phi-N	15	68	7	16	5	0	0	2	3	6	0	1	.235	.268	.309	.576	55	-5	5	2.47	-2	2-15	0	-0.6
1952 Phi-N	5	9	3	2	1	0	0	0	1	3	1	0	.222	.300	.333	.633	76	-0	1	4.46	-1	/2-2	0	-0.1
Total 2	**20**	**77**	**10**	**18**	**6**	**0**	**0**	**2**	**4**	**9**	**1**	**1**	**.234**	**.272**	**.312**	**.583**	**58**	**-5**	**6**	**2.69**	**-3**	**/2-17**	**0**	**-0.7**

• YOUNG, Dmitri Dmitri Dell Young b: 10/11/1973, Vicksburg, MS BB/TR, 6'2", 215 lbs. Deb: 8/29/1996 Career OF: 382-0-101

YEAR TM-L	G	AB	R	H	2B	3B	HR	RBI	BB	SO	SB	CS	AVG	OBP	SLG	OPS	OPS+	BR/A	RC	RC/G	FR	G/POS	WS	TPW
1996*StL-N	16	29	3	7	0	0	0	2	4	5	0	1	.241	.353	.241	.594	61	-2	2	2.75	-1	1-10	0	-0.3
1997 StL-N	110	333	38	86	14	3	5	34	38	63	6	5	.258	.338	.363	.701	84	-8	41	4.16	-1	1-74,0-17(9-0-10)/D-1	5	-1.6
1998 Cin-N	144	536	81	166	48	1	14	83	47	94	2	4	.310	.368	.481	.849	120	13	90	6.18	-4	*0-105(91-0-14),1-44	16	0.2
1999 Cin-N	127	373	63	112	30	2	14	56	30	71	3	1	.300	.356	.504	.860	111	5	65	6.35	0	0-91(23-0-75)/1-9,D-1	10	0.1
2000 Cin-N	152	548	68	166	37	6	18	88	36	80	0	3	.303	.349	.491	.840	107	3	88	5.84	-4	*0-111(111-0-1),1-36/D-4	14	-0.8
2001 Cin-N	142	540	68	163	28	3	21	69	37	77	8	5	.302	.352	.481	.834	108	5	83	5.52	0	0-87(86-0-1),1-38,3-36	13	0.0
2002 Det-A	54	201	25	57	14	0	7	27	12	39	2	0	.284	.330	.458	.788	113	4	26	4.50	2	D-35,1-15/3-1,0-1	5	0.2
2003 Det-A★	155	562	78	167	34	7	29	85	58	130	2	1	.297	.374	.537	.911	148	38	110	7.14	3	D-75,0-61(61-0-0),3-16/1-1	19	3.2
Total 8	**900**	**3122**	**424**	**924**	**205**	**22**	**108**	**444**	**262**	**559**	**23**	**20**	**.296**	**.356**	**.480**	**.835**	**115**	**58**	**506**	**5.82**	**-5**	**0-473,1-227,D-116/3-53**	**82**	**1.0**

• YOUNG, Don Donald Wayne Young b: 10/18/1945, Houston, TX BR/TR, 6'2", 185 lbs. Deb: 9/9/1965 Career OF: 3-105-8

YEAR TM-L	G	AB	R	H	2B	3B	HR	RBI	BB	SO	SB	CS	AVG	OBP	SLG	OPS	OPS+	BR/A	RC	RC/G	FR	G/POS	WS	TPW
1965 Chi-N	11	35	1	2	0	0	1	2	0	11	0	0	.057	.057	.143	.200	-45	-7	0	.24	0	0-11(0-11-0)	0	-0.8
1969 Chi-N	101	272	36	65	12	3	6	27	38	74	1	5	.239	.343	.371	.714	88	-5	35	4.27	-1	*0-100(3-94-8)	8	-0.9
Total 2	**112**	**307**	**37**	**67**	**12**	**3**	**7**	**29**	**38**	**85**	**1**	**5**	**.218**	**.314**	**.345**	**.660**	**75**	**-11**	**36**	**3.74**	**-2**	**0-111**	**8**	**-1.7**

• YOUNG, Eric Eric Orlando Young b: 5/18/1967, New Brunswick, NJ BR/TR, 5'9", 180 lbs. Deb: 7/30/1992 Career OF: 126-12-1

YEAR TM-L	G	AB	R	H	2B	3B	HR	RBI	BB	SO	SB	CS	AVG	OBP	SLG	OPS	OPS+	BR/A	RC	RC/G	FR	G/POS	WS	TPW
1992 LA-N	49	132	9	34	1	0	1	11	8	9	6	1	.258	.300	.288	.588	68	-5	12	3.04	2	2-43	4	-0.1
1993 Col-N	144	490	82	132	16	8	3	42	63	41	42	19	.269	.357	.353	.710	78	-13	65	4.47	-10	2-79,0-52(46-10-0)	10	-2.1
1994 Col-N	90	228	37	62	13	1	7	30	38	17	18	7	.272	.381	.430	.810	95	0	41	5.98	-1	0-60(60-0-0)/2-1	6	-0.2
1995*Col-N	120	366	68	116	21	**9**	6	36	49	29	35	12	.317	.405	.473	.877	101	5	75	7.50	-5	2-77,0-19(19-0-0)	12	0.3
1996 Col-N★	141	568	113	184	23	4	8	74	47	31	**53**	19	.324	.396	.421	.817	94	-0	100	6.46	9	*2-139	17	1.5
1997 Col-N	118	468	78	132	29	6	6	45	57	37	32	12	.282	.366	.408	.774	83	-9	70	5.05	10	*2-117	13	0.7
LA-N	37	154	28	42	4	2	2	16	14	17	13	2	.273	.349	.364	.712	94	1	22	4.99	-5	2-37	4	-0.2
Yr.	155	622	106	174	33	8	8	61	71	54	45	14	.280	.362	.397	.759	86	-7	92	5.03	5	*2-154	17	0.5
1998 LA-N	117	452	78	129	24	1	8	43	45	32	42	13	.285	.357	.396	.753	104	7	69	5.33	-7	*2-113/D-1	17	0.5
1999 LA-N	119	456	73	128	24	2	2	41	63	26	51	22	.281	.374	.355	.729	91	-2	64	4.65	2	*2-116	14	0.5
2000 Chi-N	153	607	98	180	40	2	6	47	63	39	54	7	.297	.370	.399	.769	96	7	99	5.84	9	*2-150	18	2.2
2001 Chi-N	149	603	98	168	43	4	6	42	42	45	31	14	.279	.335	.393	.728	92	-7	78	4.36	1	*2-147	16	0.1
2002 Mil-N	138	496	57	139	29	3	3	28	39	38	31	11	.280	.340	.369	.709	88	-7	62	4.28	0	*2-123/D-2,0-2(1-0-1)	8	-0.1
2003 Mil-N	109	404	71	105	18	1	15	31	48	34	25	7	.260	.344	.421	.765	100	3	61	5.15	-9	2-99/D-1	8	-0.2
SF-N	26	71	9	14	2	0	0	3	9	10	3	5	.197	.296	.225	.522	40	-8	4	1.65	3	2-18/0-2(0-2-0)	1	-0.4
Yr.	135	475	80	119	20	1	15	34	57	44	28	12	.251	.337	.392	.729	91	-5	65	4.55	-6	*2-117/0-2(0-2-0),D-1	9	-0.6
Total 12	**1510**	**5495**	**899**	**1565**	**287**	**43**	**73**	**489**	**585**	**405**	**436**	**151**	**.285**	**.362**	**.393**	**.754**	**91**	**-26**	**823**	**5.16**	**0**	***2-1259,0-135/D-4**	**148**	**2.5**

• YOUNG, Ernie Ernest Wesley Young b: 7/8/1969, Chicago, IL BR/TR, 6'1", 190 lbs. Deb: 5/17/1994 Career OF: 25-208-62

YEAR TM-L	G	AB	R	H	2B	3B	HR	RBI	BB	SO	SB	CS	AVG	OBP	SLG	OPS	OPS+	BR/A	RC	RC/G	FR	G/POS	WS	TPW
1994 Oak-A	11	30	2	2	1	0	0	3	1	8	0	0	.067	.097	.100	.197	-54	-7	0	.20	0	0-10(7-3-1)/D-1	0	-0.6
1995 Oak-A	26	50	9	10	3	0	2	5	8	12	0	0	.200	.310	.380	.690	84	-1	6	4.07	-1	0-24(7-7-10)	1	-0.3
1996 Oak-A	141	462	72	112	19	4	19	64	52	118	7	5	.242	.328	.424	.752	91	-8	63	4.56	-0	*0-140(8-133-17)	10	-0.7
1997 Oak-A	71	175	22	39	7	0	5	15	19	57	1	3	.223	.306	.349	.655	72	-8	18	3.19	1	0-66(1-60-12)/D-1	1	-0.7
1998 KC-A	25	53	2	10	3	0	1	3	2	9	2	1	.189	.232	.302	.534	36	-5	3	1.65	1	0-24(1-5-19)	1	-0.5
1999 Ari-N	6	11	1	2	0	0	0	0	3	2	0	0	.182	.400	.182	.582	54	-1	1	3.65	2	/0-4(1-0-3)	0	0.1
2003 Det-A	5	11	0	2	0	0	0	0	4	5	0	2	.182	.400	.182	.582	66	-1	1	1.37	0	/D-4	0	-0.1
Total 7	**285**	**792**	**108**	**177**	**33**	**4**	**27**	**90**	**89**	**211**	**10**	**11**	**.223**	**.311**	**.378**	**.688**	**77**	**-31**	**92**	**3.75**	**2**	**0-268/D-6**	**13**	**-2.9**

• YOUNG, George George Joseph Young b: 4/1/1890, Brooklyn, NY d: 3/13/1950, Brightwaters, NY BL/TR, 6', 185 lbs. Deb: 8/10/1913

YEAR TM-L	G	AB	R	H	2B	3B	HR	RBI	BB	SO	SB	CS	AVG	OBP	SLG	OPS	OPS+	BR/A	RC	RC/G	FR	G/POS	WS	TPW
1913 Cle-A	2	2	0	0	0	0	0	0	0	0	0	....	.000	.000	.000	.000	-97	-0	0	.00	0	....	0	-0.1

• YOUNG, Gerald Gerald Anthony Young b: 10/22/1964, Tela, Honduras BB/TR, 6'2", 185 lbs. Deb: 7/8/1987 Career OF: 19-504-55

YEAR TM-L	G	AB	R	H	2B	3B	HR	RBI	BB	SO	SB	CS	AVG	OBP	SLG	OPS	OPS+	BR/A	RC	RC/G	FR	G/POS	WS	TPW
1987 Hou-N	71	274	44	88	9	2	1	15	26	27	26	9	.321	.382	.380	.762	107	5	44	5.93	-2	0-67(0-67-0)	10	0.2
1988 Hou-N	149	576	79	148	21	9	0	37	66	66	65	27	.257	.336	.325	.661	94	-1	67	3.81	4	*0-145(0-145-0)	21	0.1
1989 Hou-N	146	533	71	124	17	3	0	38	74	60	34	25	.233	.328	.276	.604	77	-17	51	3.06	13	*0-143(0-143-0)	18	-0.6
1990 Hou-N	57	154	15	27	4	1	1	4	20	23	6	3	.175	.270	.234	.504	41	-12	11	2.10	0	0-50(0-50-0)	1	-1.4
1991 Hou-N	108	142	26	31	3	1	1	11	24	17	16	5	.218	.331	.275	.606	77	-2	15	3.39	0	0-84(6-76-5)	3	-0.3
1992 Hou-N	74	76	14	14	1	1	0	4	10	11	6	2	.184	.279	.224	.503	46	-5	6	2.13	-2	0-57(6-14-43)	1	-0.8
1993 Col-N	19	19	5	1	0	0	0	1	4	1	0	1	.053	.217	.053	.270	-20	-4	0	.23	-1	0-11(4-3-5)	0	-0.5

YEAR TM-L	G	AB	R	H	2B	3B	HR	RBI	BB	SO	SB	CS	AVG	OBP	SLG	OPS	OPS+	BR/A	RC	RC/G	FR	G/POS	WS	TPW
1994 StL-N	16	41	5	13	3	2	0	3	3	8	2	1	.317	.364	.488	.851	122	1	7	6.25	0	0-11(3-6-2)	2	0.1
Total 8	640	1815	259	446	58	19	3	113	227	213	155	73	.246	.332	.304	.635	82	-34	200	3.59	12	0-568	56	-3.2
• YOUNG, Herman	Herman John Young b: 4/14/1886, Boston, MA d: 12/12/1966, Ipswich, MA BR/TR, 5'8", 155 lbs. Deb: 6/11/1911																							
1911 Bos-N	9	25	2	6	0	0	0	0	0	3	0	....	.240	.269	.240	.509	40	-2	2	2.20	1	/3-5,S-3	0	-0.1
• YOUNG, John	John Thomas Young b: 2/9/1949, Los Angeles, CA BL/TL, 6'3", 210 lbs. Deb: 9/9/1971																							
1971 Det-A	2	4	1	2	1	0	0	1	0	0	0	0	.500	.500	.750	1.250	240	1	2	20.25	0	/1-1	0	0.0
• YOUNG, Kevin	Kevin Stacey Young b: 6/16/1969, Alpena, MI BR/TR, 6'3", 219 lbs. Deb: 7/12/1992 Career OF: 13-0-18																							
1992 Pit-N	10	7	2	4	0	0	0	4	2	0	1	0	.571	.667	.571	1.238	256	2	3	30.24	-2	/3-7,1-1	1	0.0
1993 Pit-N	141	449	38	106	24	3	6	47	36	82	2	2	.236	.306	.343	.649	73	-18	47	3.47	3	*1-135/3-6	5	-2.5
1994 Pit-N	59	122	15	25	7	2	1	11	8	34	0	2	.205	.260	.320	.579	49	-10	9	2.36	-2	1-37,3-17/O-1	1	-1.4
1995 Pit-N	56	181	13	42	9	0	6	22	8	53	1	3	.232	.272	.381	.653	69	-10	17	2.99	-1	3-48/1-6	2	-1.1
1996 KC-A	55	132	20	32	6	0	8	23	11	32	3	3	.242	.301	.470	.770	91	-3	18	4.54	1	1-27,O-17(2-0-15)/3-7,D-3	3	-0.4
1997 Pit-N	97	333	59	100	18	3	18	74	16	89	11	2	.300	.340	.535	.874	123	11	60	6.46	0	1-77,3-12,O-11(10-0-1)	12	0.4
1998 Pit-N	159	592	88	160	40	2	27	108	44	127	15	7	.270	.332	.481	.814	109	6	89	5.15	-11	*1-157	13	-1.9
1999 Pit-N	156	584	103	174	41	6	26	106	75	124	22	10	.298	.389	.522	.911	128	26	120	7.40	-4	*1-155	21	0.8
2000 Pit-N	132	496	77	128	27	0	20	88	32	96	8	3	.258	.313	.433	.747	87	-12	64	4.44	-13	*1-129/D-1	7	-3.4
2001 Pit-N	142	449	53	104	33	0	14	65	42	119	15	11	.232	.313	.399	.711	81	-15	51	3.68	-3	*1-137	7	-2.8
2002 Pit-N	146	468	60	115	26	1	16	51	50	101	4	6	.246	.324	.408	.732	90	-9	59	4.28	-1	*1-144	7	-2.2
2003 Pit-N	52	84	8	17	4	0	2	7	12	25	1	0	.202	.302	.321	.624	62	-4	9	3.55	0	1-44/O-1	1	-0.7
Total 12	1205	3897	536	1007	235	17	144	606	336	882	83	49	.258	.327	.438	.765	96	-36	547	4.77	-33	*1-1049/3-97,O-30,D-4	80	-15.0
• YOUNG, Mike	Michael B. Young b: 10/19/1976, Covina, CA BR/TR, 6', 190 lbs. Deb: 9/29/2000																							
2000 Tex-A	2	2	0	0	0	0	0	0	0	1	0	0	.000	.000	.000	.000	-99	-1	0	.00	-1	/2-1	0	-0.1
2001 Tex-A	106	386	57	96	18	4	11	49	26	91	3	1	.249	.301	.402	.703	80	-12	46	3.95	-5	*2-104	7	-1.1
2002 Tex-A	156	573	77	150	26	8	9	62	41	112	6	7	.262	.311	.382	.693	79	-20	65	3.80	-0	*2-152,S-11/3-4	10	-1.2
2003 Tex-A	160	666	106	204	33	9	14	72	36	103	13	2	.306	.343	.446	.789	97	-2	100	5.56	-9	*2-159/S-7	21	-0.2
Total 4	424	1627	240	450	77	21	34	183	103	307	22	10	.277	.321	.412	.734	86	-34	211	4.51	-15	2-416/S-18,3-4	38	-2.7
• YOUNG, Mike	Michael Darren Young b: 3/20/1960, Oakland, CA BB/TR, 6'2", 195 lbs. Deb: 9/14/1982 Career OF: 266-8-153																							
1982 Bal-A	6	2	2	0	0	0	0	0	0	1	0	0	.000	.000	.000	.000	-100	-1	0	.00	-0	/D-2,O-1	0	-0.1
1983 Bal-A	25	36	5	6	2	1	0	2	2	8	1	0	.167	.231	.278	.509	40	-3	2	1.92	-1	O-22(14-0-8)/D-3	0	-0.4
1984 Bal-A	123	401	59	101	17	2	17	52	58	110	6	2	.252	.356	.431	.788	119	13	66	5.71	0	*O-115(40-1-85)/D-1	16	0.8
1985 Bal-A	139	450	72	123	22	1	28	81	48	104	1	5	.273	.349	.513	.862	136	19	78	6.16	0	O-90(83-0-20),D-37	17	1.4
1986 Bal-A	117	369	43	93	15	1	9	42	49	90	3	1	.252	.344	.371	.716	96	-0	47	4.34	-1	O-69(69-0-0),D-38	8	-0.6
1987 Bal-A	110	363	46	87	10	1	16	39	46	91	10	7	.240	.328	.405	.733	96	-3	48	4.49	-3	O-60(54-7-0),D-47	7	-0.9
1988 Phi-N	75	146	13	33	14	0	1	14	26	43	0	0	.226	.347	.342	.689	97	0	19	4.54	-3	O-42(3-0-39)	4	-0.4
Mil-A	8	14	2	0	0	0	0	0	2	5	0	0	.000	.176	.000	.176	-46	-3	0	.31	0	/D-5,O-2(1-0-1)	0	-0.3
1989 Cle-A	32	59	2	11	0	0	1	5	6	13	1	2	.186	.273	.237	.510	44	-5	4	2.11	-0	D-15/O-1	0	-0.5
Total 8	635	1840	244	454	80	6	72	235	237	465	22	17	.247	.339	.414	.753	107	18	266	4.92	-7	O-402,D-148	52	-1.0
• YOUNG, Pep	Lemuel Floyd Young b: 8/29/1907, Jamestown, NC d: 1/14/1962, Jamestown, NC BR/TR, 5'9", 162 lbs. Deb: 4/25/1933																							
1933 Pit-N	25	20	3	6	1	1	0	0	0	5	0	....	.300	.300	.450	.750	112	0	3	5.34	-1	/2-1,S-1	1	-0.1
1934 Pit-N	19	17	3	4	0	0	0	2	0	6	0	....	.235	.235	.235	.471	26	-2	1	2.00	1	/2-2,S-2	0	-0.1
1935 Pit-N	128	494	60	131	25	10	7	82	21	59	2	....	.265	.298	.399	.697	83	-14	58	4.10	-7	*2-107/3-6,O-6(1-0-5),S-4	9	-1.4
1936 Pit-N	125	475	47	118	23	10	6	77	29	52	3	....	.248	.293	.377	.670	77	-17	53	3.82	-5	*2-123	9	-1.3
1937 Pit-N	113	408	43	106	20	3	9	54	26	63	4	....	.260	.306	.390	.695	88	-8	49	4.18	9	S-45,3-39,2-30	12	0.7
1938 Pit-N	149	562	58	156	36	5	4	79	40	64	7	....	.278	.329	.381	.710	94	-5	70	4.46	22	*2-149	18	2.6
1939 Pit-N	84	293	34	81	14	3	3	29	23	29	1	....	.276	.333	.375	.709	92	-4	37	4.34	-2	2-84	7	0.0
1940 Pit-N	54	136	19	34	8	2	2	20	12	23	1	....	.250	.320	.382	.702	94	-1	18	4.71	-8	2-33/S-7,3-5	4	-0.7
1941 Cin-N	4	12	2	2	0	0	0	0	0	1	0	....	.167	.231	.167	.397	13	-1	1	1.41	1	/3-3	0	-0.1
StL-N	2	2	0	0	0	0	0	0	0	2	0	....	.000	.000	.000	.000	-94	-0	0	.00	0	....	0	-0.1
Yr.	6	14	2	2	0	0	0	0	0	3	0	....	.143	.200	.143	.343	-1	-2	1	1.17	1	/3-3	0	-0.1
1945 StL-N	27	47	5	7	1	0	1	4	1	8	0	....	.149	.167	.234	.401	10	-6	2	1.08	-1	S-11/3-9,2-3	1	-0.6
Total 10	730	2466	274	645	128	34	32	347	152	312	18	....	.262	.308	.380	.688	85	-58	291	4.11	8	2-532/S-70,3-62,O-6	61	-0.9
• YOUNG, Ralph	Ralph Stuart Young b: 9/19/1889, Philadelphia, PA d: 1/24/1965, Philadelphia, PA BB/TR, 5'5", 165 lbs. Deb: 4/10/1913																							
1913 NY-A	7	15	2	1	0	0	0	0	3	3	2	....	.067	.222	.067	.289	-15	-2	1	1.01	-1	/S-7	0	-0.3
1915 Det-A	123	378	44	92	6	5	0	31	53	31	12	11	.243	.339	.286	.625	83	-8	41	3.40	-8	*2-119	10	-1.5
1916 Det-A	153	528	60	139	16	6	1	45	62	43	20	20	.263	.342	.322	.664	96	-6	61	3.68	4	*2-146/S-6,3-1	17	0.2
1917 Det-A	141	503	64	116	18	2	1	35	61	35	8	....	.231	.317	.280	.598	83	-9	49	3.08	13	*2-141	12	0.7
1918 Det-A	91	298	31	56	7	1	0	21	54	17	15	....	.188	.313	.218	.531	63	-11	26	2.55	-9	2-91	4	-2.0
1919 Det-A	125	456	63	96	13	5	1	25	53	32	8	....	.211	.294	.268	.562	60	-24	43	2.72	17	*2-120/S-5	8	-0.4
1920 Det-A	150	594	84	173	21	6	0	33	85	30	8	13	.291	.382	.347	.729	96	-0	82	4.78	-22	*2-150	16	-1.9
1921 Det-A	107	401	70	120	8	3	0	29	69	23	11	9	.299	.406	.334	.740	91	-1	60	5.22	-19	*2-106	9	-1.6
1922 Phi-A	125	470	62	105	19	2	1	35	55	21	8	6	.223	.309	.279	.587	53	-32	43	3.03	-7	*2-120	4	-3.4
Total 9	1022	3643	480	898	108	30	4	254	495	235	92	59	.247	.339	.296	.635	79	-92	406	3.57	-31	2-993/S-18,3-1	80	-10.2
• YOUNG, Russ	Russell Charles Young b: 9/15/1902, Bryan, OH d: 5/13/1984, Roseville, CA BB/TR, 6', 175 lbs. Deb: 4/16/1931																							
1931 StL-A	16	34	2	4	0	0	1	2	2	4	0	0	.118	.167	.206	.373	-3	-5	1	1.06	1	C-16	1	-0.4
• YOUNGBLOOD, Joel	Joel Randolph Youngblood b: 8/28/1951, Houston, TX BR/TR, 6', 180 lbs. Deb: 4/13/1976 C Career OF: 233-107-454																							
1976 Cin-N	55	57	8	11	1	1	0	1	2	8	1	0	.193	.233	.246	.479	35	-5	3	1.90	-2	/O-9(3-3-3),3-6,2-1,C-1	0	-0.7
1977 StL-N	25	27	1	5	2	0	0	1	3	5	0	2	.185	.267	.259	.526	42	-3	1	1.40	-1	O-11(10-0-1)/3-6	0	-0.4
NY-N	70	182	16	46	11	1	0	11	13	40	1	3	.253	.303	.324	.627	72	-9	16	2.97	2	2-33,O-22(4-7-13),3-10	3	-0.6
Yr.	95	209	17	51	13	1	0	12	16	45	1	5	.244	.298	.316	.614	68	-12	17	2.74	1	2-33,O-33(14-7-14),3-16	3	-1.0
1978 NY-N	113	266	40	67	12	8	7	30	16	39	4	0	.252	.297	.436	.733	106	1	35	4.52	4	O-50(7-14-33),2-39/3-9,S-1	9	0.5
1979 NY-N	158	590	90	162	37	5	16	60	60	84	18	13	.275	.349	.436	.784	117	12	90	5.32	5	*O-147(70-5-87),2-13,3-12	18	1.0
1980 NY-N	146	514	58	142	26	2	8	69	52	69	14	11	.276	.345	.381	.726	105	2	67	4.47	5	*O-121(0-39-96),3-21/2-6	16	0.2
1981 NY-N★	43	143	16	50	10	2	4	25	12	19	2	5	.350	.408	.531	.939	167	11	28	7.18	1	O-41(4-2-36)	7	1.1
1982 NY-N	80	202	21	52	12	0	3	21	8	37	0	4	.257	.302	.361	.664	86	-6	20	3.43	-3	O-63(15-8-43)/2-8,3-1,S-1	3	-1.1
Mon-N	40	90	16	18	2	0	0	8	9	21	2	1	.200	.294	.222	.516	45	-6	6	2.27	-1	O-35(0-2-33)	1	-0.8
Yr.	120	292	37	70	14	0	3	29	17	58	2	5	.240	.300	.318	.618	73	-12	27	3.05	-3	O-98(15-10-76)/2-8,3-1,S-1	4	-2.0
1983 SF-N	124	373	59	109	20	3	17	53	33	59	7	4	.292	.358	.499	.856	139	18	64	6.09	-13	2-64,3-28,O-22(14-0-8)	16	0.8
1984 SF-N	134	469	50	119	17	1	10	51	48	86	5	6	.254	.328	.358	.686	96	-4	56	4.09	-24	*3-117,O-11(4-0-8)/2-5	9	-3.1
1985 SF-N	95	230	24	62	6	0	4	24	30	37	3	2	.270	.356	.348	.704	103	1	29	4.43	-2	O-56(7-17-34)/3-1	6	-0.2
1986 SF-N	97	184	20	47	12	0	5	28	18	34	1	1	.255	.325	.402	.727	105	1	25	4.63	-1	O-45(29-0-17)/1-7,3-5,2-4,S	5	-0.2
1987 SF-N	69	91	9	23	3	0	3	11	5	13	1	1	.253	.299	.385	.684	83	-3	10	3.55	0	O-22(9-1-14)/3-2	2	-0.3
1988 SF-N	83	123	12	31	4	0	0	16	10	17	1	1	.252	.313	.285	.598	76	-4	11	2.78	-1	O-45(22-9-18)	2	-0.6
1989 Cin-N	76	118	13	25	5	0	3	13	13	21	0	1	.212	.301	.331	.631	78	-4	11	2.82	0	O-45(35-0-10)	1	-0.5
Total 14	1408	3659	453	969	180	23	80	422	332	589	60	55	.265	.332	.392	.724	104	3	471	4.42	-28	O-745,3-218,2-173/1-7,S-3,C	98	-4.9
• YOUNGMAN, Henry	Henry Youngman b: 1865, Indiana, PA d: 1/24/1936, Pittsburgh, PA TR, 5'9" Deb: 4/19/1890																							
1890 Pit-N	13	47	6	6	1	1	0	4	6	9	1	....	.128	.226	.191	.418	25	-4	2	1.50	-4	/3-7,2-6	0	-0.7
• YOUNGS, Ross	Royce Middlebrook "Pep" Youngs b: 4/10/1897, Shiner, TX d: 10/22/1927, San Antonio, TX BL/TR, 5'8", 162 lbs. Deb: 9/25/1917 HOF: 1972 Career OF: 1-6-1192																							
1917 NY-N	7	26	5	9	2	3	0	1	1	5	1	....	.346	.370	.654	1.024	218	3	6	8.75	1	/O-7(1-6-0)	2	0.5
1918 NY-N	121	474	70	143	16	8	1	25	44	49	10	....	.302	.368	.376	.744	129	18	67	5.11	-1	*O-120(0-0-120)/2-7	22	1.3

YEAR TM-L	G	AB	R	H	2B	3B	HR	RBI	BB	SO	SB	CS	AVG	OBP	SLG	OPS	OPS+	BR/A	RC	RC/G	FR	G/POS	WS	TPW
1919 NY-N	130	489	73	152	**31**	7	2	43	51	47	24	....	.311	.384	.415	.799	142	27	84	6.23	4	*O-130(0-0-130)	27	2.6
1920 NY-N	153	581	92	204	27	14	6	78	75	55	18	18	.351	.427	.477	.904	161	47	118	7.65	7	*O-153(0-0-153)	33	5.0
1921*NY-N	141	504	90	165	24	16	3	102	71	47	21	17	.327	.411	.456	.868	129	24	96	6.77	1	*O-137(0-0-137)	23	1.4
1922*NY-N	149	559	105	185	34	10	7	86	55	50	17	9	.331	.398	.465	.863	121	20	105	6.90	8	*O-147(0-0-147)	22	1.5
1923*NY-N	152	596	**121**	200	33	12	3	87	73	36	13	19	.336	.412	.446	.859	128	23	108	6.70	2	*O-152(0-0-152)	25	1.3
1924*NY-N	133	526	112	187	33	12	10	74	77	31	11	9	.356	.441	.521	.962	161	49	123	9.19	-1	*O-132(0-0-132)/2-2	29	3.8
1925 NY-N	130	500	82	132	24	6	6	53	66	51	17	11	.264	.354	.372	.726	89	-6	69	4.66	-6	*O-127(0-0-127)/2-3	11	-2.0
1926 NY-N	95	372	62	114	12	5	4	43	37	19	21	....	.306	.372	.398	.770	109	5	55	5.34	1	O-94(0-0-94)	12	-0.1
Total 10	1211	4627	812	1491	236	93	42	592	550	390	153	83	.322	.399	.441	.839	132	210	831	6.56	17	*O-1199/2-12	206	15.2

• YOUNT, Eddie
Floyd Edwin Yount b: 12/19/1915, Newton, NC d: 10/26/1973, Newton, NC BR/TR, 6'1", 185 lbs. Deb: 9/9/1937

YEAR TM-L	G	AB	R	H	2B	3B	HR	RBI	BB	SO	SB	CS	AVG	OBP	SLG	OPS	OPS+	BR/A	RC	RC/G	FR	G/POS	WS	TPW
1937 Phi-A	4	7	1	2	0	0	0	1	0	1	0	0	.286	.286	.286	.571	45	-1	1	2.91	0	/O-2(1-1-0)	0	-0.1
1939 Pit-N	2	2	0	0	0	0	0	0	0	2	0	....	.000	.000	.000	.000	-102	-1	0	.00	0	....	0	-0.1
Total 2	6	9	1	2	0	0	0	1	0	3	0	0	.222	.222	.222	.444	12	-1	1	2.08	0	/O-2	0	-0.1

• YOUNT, Robin
Robin R. Yount b: 9/16/1955, Danville, IL BR/TR, 6', 170 lbs. Deb: 4/5/1974 C HOF: 1999 Career OF: 69-1150-0

YEAR TM-L	G	AB	R	H	2B	3B	HR	RBI	BB	SO	SB	CS	AVG	OBP	SLG	OPS	OPS+	BR/A	RC	RC/G	FR	G/POS	WS	TPW
1974 Mil-A	107	344	48	86	14	5	3	26	12	46	7	7	.250	.277	.346	.623	79	-12	31	3.07	-3	*S-107	8	-0.3
1975 Mil-A	147	558	67	149	28	2	8	52	33	69	12	4	.267	.309	.367	.677	90	-7	64	3.96	-10	*S-145	14	-0.1
1976 Mil-A	161	638	59	161	19	3	2	54	38	69	16	11	.252	.294	.301	.595	76	-21	55	2.88	9	*S-161/O-1	14	0.7
1977 Mil-A	154	605	66	174	34	4	4	49	41	80	16	7	.288	.335	.377	.712	94	-4	77	4.45	-14	*S-153	16	-0.2
1978 Mil-A	127	502	66	147	23	9	9	71	24	43	16	5	.293	.326	.428	.755	110	7	71	5.01	15	*S-125	19	3.6
1979 Mil-A	149	577	72	154	26	5	8	51	35	52	11	8	.267	.310	.371	.681	83	-16	63	3.69	5	*S-149	14	0.5
1980 Mil-A★	143	611	121	179	**49**	10	23	87	26	67	20	5	.293	.323	.519	.842	131	24	101	6.01	9	*S-133/D-9	25	4.7
1981*Mil-A	96	377	50	103	15	5	10	49	22	37	4	1	.273	.317	.419	.736	117	7	51	4.75	20	S-93/D-3	20	3.9
1982*Mil-A★	156	635	129	**210**	**46**	12	29	114	54	63	14	3	.331	.384	**.578**	**.962**	**170**	**61**	136	**7.99**	-1	*S-154/D-1	**39**	**7.6**
1983 Mil-A★	149	578	102	178	42	**10**	17	80	72	58	12	5	.308	.387	.503	.891	155	44	115	7.27	2	*S-139/D-8	33	6.1
1984 Mil-A	160	624	105	186	27	7	16	80	67	67	14	4	.298	.367	.441	.808	128	26	99	5.61	2	*S-120,D-39	27	3.9
1985 Mil-A	122	466	76	129	26	3	15	68	49	56	10	4	.277	.348	.442	.790	115	10	73	5.49	-5	*O-108(69-40-0),D-12/1-2	16	0.1
1986 Mil-A	140	522	82	163	31	7	9	46	62	73	14	5	.312	.389	.450	.840	124	20	94	6.71	-2	*O-131(0-131-0)/D-6,1-3	23	1.6
1987 Mil-A	158	635	99	198	25	9	21	103	76	94	19	9	.312	.386	.479	.865	124	24	120	6.94	-4	*O-150(0-150-0)/D-8	26	1.6
1988 Mil-A	162	621	92	190	38	**11**	13	91	63	63	22	4	.306	.373	.465	.838	132	30	106	6.16	9	*O-158(0-158-0)/D-4	31	3.6
1989 Mil-A	160	614	101	195	38	9	21	103	63	71	19	3	.318	.387	.511	.898	152	45	125	7.72	1	*O-143(0-143-0),D-17	**34**	**4.5**
1990 Mil-A	158	587	98	145	17	5	17	77	78	89	15	8	.247	.341	.380	.721	102	3	81	4.64	-6	*O-157(0-157-0)/D-1	18	-0.6
1991 Mil-A	130	503	66	131	20	4	10	77	54	79	6	4	.260	.337	.376	.713	99	-0	63	4.29	-4	*O-117(0-117-0),D-13	16	-0.6
1992 Mil-A	150	557	71	147	40	3	8	77	53	81	15	6	.264	.331	.390	.721	103	3	73	4.49	-3	*O-139(0-139-0),D-11	20	-0.3
1993 Mil-A	127	454	62	117	25	3	8	51	44	93	9	2	.258	.330	.379	.709	91	-4	57	4.28	-2	*O-114(0-114-0)/1-7,D-6	10	-0.6
Total 20	2856	11008	1632	3142	583	126	251	1406	966	1350	271	105	.285	.346	.430	.775	115	239	1655	5.31	19	*S-1479,O-1218,D-138/1-12	423	40.0

• YURAK, Jeff
Jeffrey Lynn Yurak b: 2/26/1954, Pasadena, CA BB/TR, 6'3", 195 lbs. Deb: 9/15/1978

YEAR TM-L	G	AB	R	H	2B	3B	HR	RBI	BB	SO	SB	CS	AVG	OBP	SLG	OPS	OPS+	BR/A	RC	RC/G	FR	G/POS	WS	TPW
1978 Mil-A	5	5	0	0	0	0	0	0	1	0	0	0	.000	.167	.000	.167	-49	-1	0	.23	0	/O-1	0	-0.1

• YVARS, Sal
Salvador Anthony Yvars b: 2/20/1924, New York, NY BR/TR, 5'10", 187 lbs. Deb: 9/27/1947

YEAR TM-L	G	AB	R	H	2B	3B	HR	RBI	BB	SO	SB	CS	AVG	OBP	SLG	OPS	OPS+	BR/A	RC	RC/G	FR	G/POS	WS	TPW
1947 NY-N	1	5	0	1	0	0	0	0	0	2	0	....	.200	.200	.200	.400	6	-1	0	1.35	0	/C-1	0	-0.1
1948 NY-N	15	38	4	8	1	0	1	6	3	1	0	....	.211	.286	.316	.602	62	-2	3	2.97	1	C-15	1	0.0
1949 NY-N	3	8	0	0	0	0	0	0	1	1	0	....	.000	.111	.000	.111	-68	-2	0	.10	1	/C-2	0	-0.1
1950 NY-N	9	14	0	2	0	0	0	0	1	2	0	....	.143	.200	.143	.343	-8	-2	0	1.02	-0	/C-9	0	-0.2
1951*NY-N	25	41	9	13	2	0	2	3	5	7	0	0	.317	.417	.512	.929	147	3	10	8.78	-2	C-23	2	0.2
1952 NY-N	66	151	15	37	3	0	4	18	10	16	0	0	.245	.296	.344	.641	77	-5	14	3.14	3	C-59	4	0.0
1953 NY-N	23	47	1	13	0	0	0	1	7	1	0	0	.277	.370	.277	.647	71	-2	5	3.44	1	C-20	1	0.0
StL-N	30	57	4	14	2	0	1	6	4	6	0	1	.246	.306	.333	.640	67	-3	5	2.64	1	C-26	1	-0.1
Yr.	53	104	5	27	2	0	1	7	11	7	0	1	.260	.336	.308	.644	69	-5	10	2.99	2	C-46	2	-0.2
1954 StL-N	38	57	8	14	4	0	2	8	6	5	1	0	.246	.328	.421	.749	93	-0	8	4.96	1	C-21	2	0.1
Total 8	210	418	41	102	12	0	10	42	37	41	1	1	.244	.315	.344	.659	77	-14	46	3.66	5	C-176	11	-0.2

• ZACHER, Elmer
Elmer Henry "Silver" Zacher b: 9/17/1883, Buffalo, NY d: 12/20/1944, Buffalo, NY BR/TR, 5'9", 190 lbs. Deb: 4/30/1910

YEAR TM-L	G	AB	R	H	2B	3B	HR	RBI	BB	SO	SB	CS	AVG	OBP	SLG	OPS	OPS+	BR/A	RC	RC/G	FR	G/POS	WS	TPW
1910 NY-N	1	0	0	0	0	0	0	0	0	0	0	....	....	....	....	....	-100	0	0	....	-0	/O-1	0	0.0
StL-N	47	132	7	28	5	1	0	10	10	19	3	....	.212	.278	.265	.543	61	-7	11	2.56	2	O-36(11-12-13)/2-1	1	-0.7
Yr.	48	132	7	28	5	1	0	10	10	19	3	....	.212	.278	.265	.543	61	-7	11	2.56	1	O-37(11-13-13)/2-1	1	-0.7

• ZAHNER, Fred
Frederick Joseph Zahner b: 6/5/1870, Louisville, KY d: 7/24/1900, Louisville, KY Deb: 7/23/1894

YEAR TM-L	G	AB	R	H	2B	3B	HR	RBI	BB	SO	SB	CS	AVG	OBP	SLG	OPS	OPS+	BR/A	RC	RC/G	FR	G/POS	WS	TPW
1894 Lou-N	14	49	7	9	0	1	0	4	3	6	2	....	.184	.231	.224	.455	11	-7	3	2.00	-2	C-10/O-2(0-0-2),1-1	0	-0.6
1895 Lou-N	21	49	7	10	1	1	0	6	6	4	0	....	.204	.304	.265	.569	61	-3	5	3.28	0	C-21	0	-0.1
Total 2	35	98	14	19	1	2	0	10	9	10	2	....	.194	.269	.245	.513	37	-10	8	2.62	-2	/C-31,O-2,1-1	0	-0.8

• ZAK, Frankie
Frank Thomas Zak b: 2/22/1922, Passaic, NJ d: 2/6/1972, Passaic, NJ BR/TR, 5'10", 150 lbs. Deb: 4/21/1944

YEAR TM-L	G	AB	R	H	2B	3B	HR	RBI	BB	SO	SB	CS	AVG	OBP	SLG	OPS	OPS+	BR/A	RC	RC/G	FR	G/POS	WS	TPW
1944 Pit-N★	87	160	33	48	3	1	0	11	22	18	6	....	.300	.385	.331	.716	99	1	22	5.09	-7	S-67	6	-0.2
1945 Pit-N	15	28	2	4	2	0	0	3	3	5	0	....	.143	.226	.214	.440	22	-3	2	1.72	0	S-10/2-1	0	-0.2
1946 Pit-N	21	20	8	4	0	0	0	0	1	0	0	....	.200	.238	.200	.438	24	-2	1	1.73	0	S-10	0	-0.2
Total 3	123	208	43	56	5	1	0	14	26	23	6	....	.269	.350	.303	.653	82	-4	25	4.20	-7	/S-87,2-1	6	-0.6

• ZALUSKY, Jack
John Francis Zalusky b: 6/22/1879, Minneapolis, MN d: 8/11/1935, Minneapolis, MN BR/TR, 5'11.5", 172 lbs. Deb: 9/4/1903

YEAR TM-L	G	AB	R	H	2B	3B	HR	RBI	BB	SO	SB	CS	AVG	OBP	SLG	OPS	OPS+	BR/A	RC	RC/G	FR	G/POS	WS	TPW
1903 NY-A	7	16	2	5	0	0	0	1	1	....	0	....	.313	.353	.313	.665	95	-0	2	4.36	0	/C-6,1-1	1	0.0

• ZAMBRANO, Eduardo
Eduardo Jose (Guerra) Zambrano b: 2/1/1966, Maracaibo, Venezuela BR/TR, 6'2", 175 lbs. Deb: 9/19/1993 Career OF: 10-0-21

YEAR TM-L	G	AB	R	H	2B	3B	HR	RBI	BB	SO	SB	CS	AVG	OBP	SLG	OPS	OPS+	BR/A	RC	RC/G	FR	G/POS	WS	TPW
1993 Chi-N	8	17	1	5	0	0	0	2	1	3	0	0	.294	.333	.294	.627	71	-1	1	3.03	-1	/O-4(1-0-3),1-2	0	-0.2
1994 Chi-N	67	116	17	30	7	0	6	18	16	29	2	1	.259	.353	.474	.828	115	3	20	5.86	-1	O-27(9-0-18)/1-9,3-4	4	0.0
Total 2	75	133	18	35	7	0	6	20	17	32	2	1	.263	.351	.451	.802	110	2	21	5.51	-2	/O-31,1-11,3-4	4	-0.2

• ZAPUSTAS, Joe
Joseph John Zapustas b: 7/25/1907, Boston, MA d: 1/14/2001, Brockton, MA BR/TR, 6'1", 185 lbs. Deb: 9/28/1933

YEAR TM-L	G	AB	R	H	2B	3B	HR	RBI	BB	SO	SB	CS	AVG	OBP	SLG	OPS	OPS+	BR/A	RC	RC/G	FR	G/POS	WS	TPW
1933 Phi-A	2	5	0	1	0	0	0	0	0	0	0	0	.200	.200	.200	.400	6	-1	0	1.27	0	/O-2(1-1-0)	0	-0.1

• ZARDON, Jose
Jose Antonio (Sanchez) "Guineo" Zardon b: 5/20/1923, Havana, Cuba BR/TR, 6', 150 lbs. Deb: 4/18/1945

YEAR TM-L	G	AB	R	H	2B	3B	HR	RBI	BB	SO	SB	CS	AVG	OBP	SLG	OPS	OPS+	BR/A	RC	RC/G	FR	G/POS	WS	TPW
1945 Was-A	54	131	13	38	5	3	0	13	7	11	3	1	.290	.326	.374	.700	112	2	15	4.01	-1	O-43(16-25-3)	4	-0.1

• ZARILLA, Al
Allen Lee "Zeke" Zarilla b: 5/1/1919, Los Angeles, CA d: 8/28/1996, Honolulu, HI BL/TR, 5'11", 180 lbs. Deb: 6/30/1943 C Career OF: 229-131-660

YEAR TM-L	G	AB	R	H	2B	3B	HR	RBI	BB	SO	SB	CS	AVG	OBP	SLG	OPS	OPS+	BR/A	RC	RC/G	FR	G/POS	WS	TPW
1943 StL-A	70	228	27	58	7	1	2	17	17	20	1	1	.254	.309	.320	.629	82	-5	23	3.51	-0	O-60(0-6-56)	4	-1.0
1944*StL-A	100	288	43	86	13	6	6	45	29	33	1	1	.299	.375	.448	.823	127	10	52	6.63	-1	O-79(74-2-4)	15	0.5
1946 StL-A	125	371	46	96	14	9	4	43	27	37	3	5	.259	.311	.377	.688	87	-8	43	3.98	4	*O-107(46-17-51)	9	-1.0
1947 StL-A	127	380	34	85	15	6	3	38	40	45	3	6	.224	.303	.318	.621	71	-17	39	3.31	-3	*O-110(23-22-72)	4	-2.4
1948 StL-A★	144	529	77	174	39	3	12	74	48	48	11	6	.329	.389	.482	.871	127	20	103	7.21	-10	*O-136(26-58-61)	17	0.4
1949 StL-A	15	56	10	14	1	0	1	6	8	2	1	1	.250	.354	.321	.675	76	-2	7	4.17	-1	O-15(10-1-8)	1	-0.3
Bos-A	124	474	68	133	32	4	9	71	48	51	4	4	.281	.352	.422	.774	97	-4	70	5.26	-5	*O-122(2-2-119)	12	-1.3
Yr.	139	530	78	147	33	4	10	77	56	53	5	5	.277	.352	.411	.763	95	-6	77	5.13	-6	*O-137(12-3-127)	13	-1.6
1950 Bos-A	130	471	92	153	32	10	9	74	76	47	2	3	.325	.423	.493	.915	122	18	106	8.66	-2	*O-128(0-0-128)	20	1.1
1951 Chi-A	120	382	56	98	21	2	10	60	60	57	2	4	.257	.363	.401	.764	109	5	58	5.26	-3	*O-117(7-0-112)	10	-0.1
1952 Chi-A	39	99	14	23	4	1	2	7	14	6	1	0	.232	.333	.354	.687	90	-1	13	4.33	-1	O-32(17-0-18)	2	-0.2
StL-A	48	130	20	31	6	0	1	9	27	15	2	1	.238	.373	.308	.681	88	-0	17	4.63	1	O-35(21-10-8)	4	-0.1
Bos-A	21	60	9	11	0	1	2	8	7	8	2	0	.183	.269	.317	.585	58	-3	6	3.31	1	O-19(0-6-14)	1	-0.3
Yr.	108	289	43	65	10	2	5	24	48	29	5	1	.225	.339	.325	.664	83	-4	36	4.24	2	O-86(38-16-40)	7	-0.6
1953 Bos-A	57	67	11	13	2	0	0	4	14	13	0	1	.194	.333	.224	.557	50	-4	5	2.51	0	O-18(3-7-9)	0	-0.5
Total 10	1120	3535	507	975	186	43	61	456	415	382	33	33	.276	.357	.405	.761	102	8	543	5.41	-19	O-978	99	-5.0

YEAR TM-L	G	AB	R	H	2B	3B	HR	RBI	BB	SO	SB	CS	AVG	OBP	SLG	OPS	OPS+	BR/A	RC	RC/G	FR	G/POS	WS	TPW
• ZAUCHIN, Norm	Norbert Henry Zauchin b: 11/17/1929, Royal Oak, MI d: 1/31/1999, Birmingham, AL BR/TR, 6'4.5", 220 lbs. Deb: 9/23/1951																							
1951 Bos-A	5	12	0	2	1	0	0	0	0	4	0	1	.167	.167	.250	.417	10	-2	0	.00	-0	/1-4	0	-0.2
1955 Bos-A	130	477	65	114	10	0	27	93	69	105	3	0	.239	.339	.430	.769	97	-2	73	5.23	4	*1-126	11	-0.6
1956 Bos-A	44	84	12	18	2	0	2	11	14	22	0	0	.214	.333	.310	.643	63	-4	9	3.38	-1	1-31	1	-0.7
1957 Bos-A	52	91	11	24	3	0	3	14	9	13	0	0	.264	.343	.396	.739	96	-0	11	4.09	0	1-36	2	-0.2
1958 Was-A	96	303	35	69	8	2	15	37	38	68	0	0	.228	.316	.416	.732	101	1	39	4.21	2	1-91	8	-0.2
1959 Was-A	19	71	11	15	4	0	3	4	7	14	2	0	.211	.291	.394	.686	87	-1	7	2.92	-2	1-19	1	-0.4
Total 6	346	1038	134	242	28	2	50	159	137	226	5	1	.233	.327	.408	.736	94	-9	139	4.43	2	1-307	23	-2.2
• ZAUN, Gregg	Gregory Owen Zaun b: 4/14/1971, Glendale, CA BB/TR, 5'10", 170 lbs. Deb: 6/24/1995																							
1995 Bal-A	40	104	18	27	5	0	3	14	16	14	1	1	.260	.358	.394	.753	94	-1	15	5.04	0	C-39/D-1	3	0.1
1996 Bal-A	50	108	16	25	8	1	1	13	11	15	0	0	.231	.314	.352	.666	68	-5	12	3.66	-1	C-49	2	-0.4
Fla-N	10	31	4	9	1	0	1	2	3	5	1	0	.290	.353	.419	.772	106	0	4	4.49	1	C-10	1	0.2
1997*Fla-N	58	143	21	43	10	2	2	20	26	18	1	0	.301	.415	.441	.856	130	8	28	7.21	-1	C-50/1-1	9	1.0
1998 Fla-N	106	298	19	56	12	2	5	29	35	52	5	2	.188	.275	.292	.567	51	-21	25	2.61	2	C-88/2-1	3	-1.3
1999 Tex-A	43	93	12	23	2	1	1	12	10	7	1	0	.247	.320	.323	.643	62	-5	10	3.65	-0	C-37/D-2	3	-0.3
2000 KC-A	83	234	36	64	11	0	7	33	43	34	7	3	.274	.393	.410	.803	100	2	41	6.16	-2	C-76/1-1,2-1	9	0.4
2001 KC-A	39	125	15	40	9	0	6	18	12	16	1	2	.320	.380	.536	.916	127	4	25	7.43	-2	C-35/D-2	4	0.4
2002 Hou-N	76	185	18	41	7	1	3	24	12	36	1	0	.222	.276	.319	.595	54	-13	16	2.91	-1	C-44	2	-1.1
2003 Hou-N	59	120	9	26	7	0	1	13	14	14	1	0	.217	.304	.300	.604	56	-7	11	2.90	-6	C-31	1	-1.2
Col-N	15	46	6	12	1	0	3	8	5	7	0	1	.261	.333	.478	.812	95	-1	7	5.64	-1	C-14	1	-0.1
Yr.	74	166	15	38	8	0	4	21	19	21	1	1	.229	.312	.349	.661	66	-8	18	3.60	-7	C-45	2	-1.3
Total 9	579	1487	174	366	73	7	33	186	187	218	19	9	.246	.335	.371	.706	82	-38	194	4.42	-13	C-473/D-5,1-2,2-2	38	-2.2
• ZAY,	Zay b: Pittsburgh, PA Deb: 10/7/1886																							
1886 Bal-a	1	1	0	0	0	0	0	0	0	....	0	....	.000	.000	.000	.000	-103	-0	0	.00	0	/0-1,P-1	0	-0.1
• ZDEB, Joe	Joseph Edmund Zdeb b: 6/27/1953, Compton, IL BR/TR, 5'11", 185 lbs. Deb: 4/7/1977 Career OF: 137-1-23																							
1977*KC-A	105	195	26	58	5	2	2	23	16	23	6	5	.297	.351	.374	.725	97	-1	24	4.30	0	0-93(88-1-8)/D-4,3-1	5	-0.4
1978 KC-A	60	127	18	32	2	3	0	11	7	18	3	0	.252	.291	.315	.606	69	-5	12	3.20	-1	0-52(43-0-12)/2-1,3-1,D-1	2	-0.7
1979 KC-A	15	23	3	4	1	1	0	0	2	4	1	0	.174	.240	.304	.544	45	-2	2	2.17	0	/0-9(6-0-3)	0	-0.2
Total 3	180	345	47	94	8	6	2	34	25	45	10	5	.272	.322	.348	.669	83	-8	38	3.73	-2	0-154/D-5,3-2,2-1	7	-1.3
• ZEARFOSS, Dave	David William Tilden Zearfoss b: 1/1/1868, Schenectady, NY d: 9/12/1945, Wilmington, DE TR, 5'9" Deb: 4/17/1896																							
1896 NY-N	19	60	5	13	1	1	0	6	5	5	2	....	.217	.288	.267	.555	48	-4	5	2.99	-1	C-19	0	-0.4
1897 NY-N	5	10	1	3	0	1	0	0	0	....	0	....	.300	.300	.500	.800	112	0	2	5.82	1	/C-5	1	0.1
1898 NY-N	1	1	0	1	0	0	0	0	0	....	0	....	1.000	1.000	1.000	2.000	488	0	1	∞	0	/C-1	0	0.1
1904 StL-N	27	80	7	17	2	0	0	9	10	....	0	....	.213	.300	.238	.538	70	-2	6	2.41	-4	C-25	1	-0.4
1905 StL-N	20	51	2	8	0	1	0	2	4	....	0	....	.157	.218	.196	.414	24	-5	2	1.43	0	C-19	1	-0.3
Total 5	72	202	15	42	3	3	0	17	19	5	2	....	.208	.279	.252	.532	56	-11	16	2.46	-4	/C-69	3	-0.9
• ZEBER, George	George William Zeber b: 8/29/1950, Ellwood City, PA BB/TR, 5'11", 170 lbs. Deb: 5/7/1977																							
1977*NY-A	25	65	8	21	3	0	3	10	9	11	0	0	.323	.405	.508	.913	149	5	14	8.08	0	2-21/3-2,S-2,D-1	4	0.6
1978 NY-A	3	6	0	0	0	0	0	0	0	0	0	0	.000	.000	.000	.000	-102	-2	0	.00	0	/2-1	0	-0.2
Total 2	28	71	8	21	3	0	3	10	9	11	0	0	.296	.375	.465	.840	130	3	14	7.15	-1	/2-22,3-2,S-2,D-1	4	0.4
• ZEIDER, Rollie	Rollie Hubert "Bunions" Zeider b: 11/16/1883, Auburn, IN d: 9/12/1967, Garrett, IN BR/TR, 5'10", 162 lbs. Deb: 4/14/1910 Career OF: 6-1-1																							
1910 Chi-A	136	498	57	108	9	2	0	31	62	....	49	....	.217	.305	.243	.548	76	-11	52	3.33	-7	2-87,S-45/3-4	15	-1.7
1911 Chi-A	73	217	39	55	3	0	2	21	29	....	28	....	.253	.347	.295	.642	81	-4	32	4.85	-5	1-29,S-17,3-10/2-9	7	-0.8
1912 Chi-A	130	420	57	103	12	10	1	42	50	....	47	....	.245	.330	.329	.658	91	-4	62	4.70	4	1-66,3-56/S-1	13	0.1
1913 Chi-A	16	20	4	7	0	0	0	2	4	1	3	....	.350	.458	.350	.808	139	1	4	8.03	0	/3-6,1-3,2-1	1	0.1
NY-A	50	159	15	37	2	0	0	12	25	9	3	....	.233	.341	.245	.586	72	-4	14	2.88	-5	S-24,2-19/1-4,3-2	3	-0.8
Yr.	66	179	19	44	2	0	0	14	29	10	6	....	.246	.354	.257	.611	79	-3	19	3.39	-6	S-24,2-20/3-8,1-7	4	-0.7
1914 Chi-F	119	452	60	124	13	2	1	36	44	28	35	....	.274	.344	.319	.663	95	-2	59	4.38	7	*3-117/S-1	15	0.9
1915 Chi-F	129	494	65	112	22	2	0	34	43	24	16	....	.227	.297	.279	.576	74	-16	45	2.92	13	2-83,3-30,S-21	11	0.1
1916 Chi-N	98	345	29	81	11	2	1	22	26	26	9	....	.235	.294	.287	.581	71	-11	32	3.11	0	3-55,2-33/0-7(6-0-1),S-5,1	6	-1.0
1917 Chi-N	108	354	36	86	14	2	0	27	28	30	17	....	.243	.302	.294	.596	77	-9	35	3.28	-12	S-48,3-26,2-24/1-1,0-1	8	-1.9
1918*Chi-N	82	251	31	56	3	2	0	26	23	20	16	....	.223	.288	.251	.539	63	-10	23	2.83	-1	2-79/1-1,3-1	5	-1.1
Total 9	941	3210	393	769	89	22	5	253	334	138	223	....	.240	.315	.286	.601	80	-70	359	3.63	-6	2-335,3-307,S-162,1-106/0-8	84	-6.2
• ZEILE, Todd	Todd Edward Zeile b: 9/9/1965, Van Nuys, CA BR/TR, 6'1", 190 lbs. Deb: 8/18/1989 Career OF: 3-0-0																							
1989 StL-N	28	82	7	21	3	1	1	8	9	14	0	0	.256	.330	.354	.683	92	-1	10	4.23	-2	C-23	2	-0.1
1990 StL-N	144	495	62	121	25	3	15	57	67	77	2	4	.244	.337	.398	.735	101	-0	67	4.58	2	*C-105,3-24,1-11/0-1	12	0.7
1991 StL-N	155	565	76	158	36	3	11	81	62	94	17	11	.280	.356	.412	.768	115	11	82	5.02	0	*3-154	22	1.3
1992 StL-N	126	439	51	113	18	4	7	48	68	70	7	10	.257	.357	.364	.721	108	4	57	4.37	-3	*3-124	11	0.1
1993 StL-N	157	571	82	158	36	1	17	103	70	76	5	4	.277	.356	.433	.788	112	10	87	5.37	-4	*3-153	19	0.7
1994 StL-N	113	415	62	111	25	1	19	75	52	56	1	3	.267	.353	.470	.823	114	8	67	5.52	3	*3-112	15	1.2
1995 StL-N	34	127	16	37	6	0	5	22	18	23	1	0	.291	.384	.457	.840	121	4	23	6.73	0	1-34	4	0.2
Chi-N	79	299	34	68	16	0	9	30	16	53	0	0	.227	.274	.371	.645	69	-15	28	3.03	-4	3-75/0-2(2-0-0),1-1	4	-1.7
Yr.	113	426	50	105	22	0	14	52	34	76	1	0	.246	.308	.397	.705	85	-10	51	4.05	-3	3-75,1-35/0-2(2-0-0)	8	-1.6
1996 Phi-N	134	500	61	134	24	0	20	80	67	88	1	1	.268	.356	.436	.792	106	5	77	5.35	-8	*3-106,1-28	13	-0.4
*Bal-A	29	117	17	28	8	0	5	19	15	16	0	0	.239	.326	.436	.762	91	-2	17	5.06	2	3-29	3	0.0
1997 LA-N	160	575	89	154	17	0	31	90	85	112	8	7	.268	.368	.459	.827	125	20	96	5.73	-10	*3-160	18	1.3
1998 LA-N	40	158	22	40	6	1	7	27	10	24	1	1	.253	.302	.437	.738	97	-2	19	4.17	-5	3-40/1-1	5	-0.6
Fla-N	66	234	37	68	12	1	6	39	31	34	2	3	.291	.378	.427	.806	116	5	39	5.91	1	3-65	10	0.7
Yr.	106	392	59	108	18	2	13	66	41	58	3	4	.276	.349	.431	.780	109	4	58	5.19	-4	*3-105/1-1	15	0.1
*Tex-A	52	180	26	47	14	1	6	28	28	32	1	0	.261	.364	.450	.814	106	2	31	6.02	1	3-52	6	0.4
1999*Tex-A	156	588	80	172	41	1	24	98	56	94	1	2	.293	.358	.488	.846	108	6	98	5.94	0	*3-155/1-1,D-1	19	0.7
2000*NY-N	153	544	67	146	36	3	22	79	74	85	3	4	.268	.358	.467	.825	111	8	90	5.78	2	*1-151	18	-0.3
2001 NY-N	151	531	66	141	25	1	10	62	73	102	1	0	.266	.361	.373	.734	95	-1	73	4.87	6	*1-149	18	-0.8
2002 Col-N	144	506	61	138	23	0	18	87	66	92	1	1	.273	.358	.425	.783	91	-5	72	4.82	-8	*3-139/P-1	12	-1.1
2003 NY-A	66	186	29	39	8	0	6	23	24	36	0	0	.210	.300	.349	.649	72	-8	21	3.60	4	3-30,1-23/D-8	3	-0.5
Mon-N	34	113	11	29	2	2	5	19	10	18	1	0	.257	.333	.442	.776	85	-2	17	5.13	1	3-34	3	-0.1
Total 15	2021	7225	956	1923	381	23	244	1075	901	1196	53	51	.266	.351	.427	.777	105	46	1071	5.12	-22	*3-1452,1-399,C-128/D-9,0-3,P	217	1.7
• ZELLER, Bart	Barton Wallace Zeller b: 7/22/1941, Chicago Heights, IL BR/TR, 6'1", 185 lbs. Deb: 5/21/1970 C																							
1970 StL-N	1	0	0	0	0	0	0	0	0	0	0	0	....	....	....	....	-98	0	0	....	0	/C-1	0	0.0
• ZERNIAL, Gus	Gus Edward "Ozark Ike" Zernial b: 6/27/1923, Beaumont, TX BR/TR, 6'2.5", 210 lbs. Deb: 4/19/1949 Career OF: 1006-0-1																							
1949 Chi-A	73	198	29	63	17	2	5	38	15	26	0	1	.318	.366	.500	.866	132	7	37	7.26	2	0-46(46-0-0)	7	0.7
1950 Chi-A	143	543	75	152	16	4	29	93	38	110	0	2	.280	.330	.484	.815	110	3	84	5.54	0	*0-137(137-0-0)	13	-0.7
1951 Chi-A	4	19	2	2	0	0	0	4	2	2	0	0	.105	.190	.105	.296	-19	-3	0	.78	1	/0-4(4-0-0)	0	-0.2
Phi-A	139	552	90	151	30	5	33	125	61	99	2	2	.274	.350	.525	.875	132	21	102	6.57	7	*0-138(138-0-0)	19	1.8
Yr.	143	571	92	153	30	5	**33**	**129**	63	101	2	2	.268	.345	.511	.856	127	18	102	6.34	9	*0-142(142-0-0)	19	1.5
1952 Phi-A	145	549	76	144	15	1	29	100	70	87	5	1	.262	.347	.452	.799	114	11	89	5.74	-7	*0-141(141-0-0)	21	-0.7
1953 Phi-A★	147	556	85	158	21	3	42	108	57	79	4	0	.284	.355	.559	.914	138	28	113	7.44	1	*0-141(141-0-0)	21	2.0
1954 Phi-A	97	336	42	84	8	2	14	62	30	60	0	0	.250	.319	.411	.730	98	-2	44	4.49	-3	0-90(90-0-0)/1-2	9	-1.0
1955 KC-A	120	413	62	105	9	3	30	84	30	90	1	0	.254	.309	.508	.818	116	6	59	4.82	5	*0-103(103-0-0)	13	0.5
1956 KC-A	109	272	36	61	12	0	16	44	33	66	2	0	.224	.317	.445	.762	99	-1	40	4.90	5	0-69(69-0-0)	6	0.1
1957 KC-A	131	437	56	103	20	1	27	69	34	84	1	1	.236	.292	.471	.764	103	-0	57	4.38	-3	*0-113(113-0-0)/1-1	10	-1.0

YEAR TM-L	G	AB	R	H	2B	3B	HR	RBI	BB	SO	SB	CS	AVG	OBP	SLG	OPS	OPS+	BR/A	RC	RC/G	FR	G/POS	WS	TPW
1958 Det-A	66	124	8	40	7	1	5	23	6	25	0	0	.323	.354	.516	.870	127	4	22	6.66	-1	0-24(24-0-0)	4	0.2
1959 Det-A	60	132	11	30	4	0	7	26	7	27	0	0	.227	.266	.417	.683	80	-4	14	3.52	-2	1-32/0-1	2	-0.8
Total 11	1234	4131	572	1093	159	22	237	776	383	755	15	7	.265	.331	.486	.816	115	69	661	5.62	6	*0-1007/1-35	125	0.7

• ZIEGLER, Charlie Charles Wallace Ziegler b: 1/13/1875, Canton, OH d: 4/18/1904, Canton, OH TR Deb: 9/23/1899

YEAR TM-L	G	AB	R	H	2B	3B	HR	RBI	BB	SO	SB	CS	AVG	OBP	SLG	OPS	OPS+	BR/A	RC	RC/G	FR	G/POS	WS	TPW
1899 Cle-N	2	8	2	2	0	0	0	0	0	....	0	....	.250	.250	.250	.500	40	-1	1	2.26	0	/2-1,S-1	0	-0.1
1900 Phi-N	3	11	0	3	0	0	0	1	0	....	0	....	.273	.273	.273	.545	51	-1	1	2.78	-1	/3-3	0	-0.1
Total 2	5	19	2	5	0	0	0	1	0	....	0	....	.263	.263	.263	.526	46	-1	1	2.56	-1	/3-3,2-1,S-1	0	-0.2

• ZIENTARA, Benny Benedict Joseph Zientara b: 2/14/1918, Chicago, IL d: 4/16/1985, Lake Elsinore, CA BR/TR, 5'9", 165 lbs. Deb: 9/11/1941

YEAR TM-L	G	AB	R	H	2B	3B	HR	RBI	BB	SO	SB	CS	AVG	OBP	SLG	OPS	OPS+	BR/A	RC	RC/G	FR	G/POS	WS	TPW
1941 Cin-N	9	21	3	6	0	0	0	2	1	3	0	....	.286	.318	.286	.604	71	-1	2	3.59	-1	/2-6	1	-0.1
1946 Cin-N	78	280	26	81	10	2	0	16	14	11	3	....	.289	.323	.339	.662	91	-4	30	3.75	13	2-39,3-36	7	1.2
1947 Cin-N	117	418	60	108	18	1	2	24	23	23	2	....	.258	.297	.321	.618	64	-22	39	3.14	-1	*2-100,3-13	6	-1.8
1948 Cin-N	74	187	17	35	1	2	0	7	12	11	0	....	.187	.236	.214	.450	23	-20	9	1.43	-2	2-60/3-3,S-2	2	-1.9
Total 4	278	906	106	230	29	5	2	49	50	48	5	....	.254	.293	.304	.596	64	-47	80	2.94	10	2-205/3-52,S-2	16	-2.6

• ZIES, Bill William Zies b: 6/16/1867, Rock Island, IL d: 4/16/1907, Beardstown, IL BL Deb: 8/9/1891

YEAR TM-L	G	AB	R	H	2B	3B	HR	RBI	BB	SO	SB	CS	AVG	OBP	SLG	OPS	OPS+	BR/A	RC	RC/G	FR	G/POS	WS	TPW
1891 StL-a	2	3	0	1	0	0	0	0	0	0	0	....	.333	.333	.333	.667	79	-0	0	4.53	-0	/C-2	0	0.0

• ZIMMER, Chief Charles Louis Zimmer b: 11/23/1860, Marietta, OH d: 8/22/1949, Cleveland, OH BR/TR, 6', 190 lbs. Deb: 7/18/1884 M/U Career OF: 0-1-4

YEAR TM-L	G	AB	R	H	2B	3B	HR	RBI	BB	SO	SB	CS	AVG	OBP	SLG	OPS	OPS+	BR/A	RC	RC/G	FR	G/POS	WS	TPW
1884 Det-N	8	29	0	2	1	0	0	0	1	14	....	....	.069	.100	.103	.203	-38	-4	0	.31	-1	/C-6,0-2(0-0-2)	0	-0.4
1886 NY-a	6	19	1	3	0	0	0	1	1	....	0	....	.158	.238	.158	.396	26	-1	1	1.24	2	/C-6	0	0.1
1887 Cle-a	14	56	9	16	5	0	0	4	4	....	1	....	.286	.298	.327	.625	76	-2	6	3.71	-2	C-12/1-2	1	-0.2
1888 Cle-a	65	212	27	51	11	4	0	22	18	....	15	....	.241	.312	.330	.642	109	3	27	4.56	7	C-59/1-3,0-3(0-1-2),S-1	8	1.3
1889 Cle-N	84	259	47	67	9	9	1	21	44	35	14	....	.259	.368	.375	.743	110	5	42	5.79	10	C-81/1-3	11	1.9
1890 Cle-N	125	444	54	95	16	6	2	57	46	54	15	....	.214	.303	.291	.594	75	-13	45	3.40	17	*C-125	11	1.3
1891 Cle-N	116	440	55	112	21	4	3	69	33	49	15	....	.255	.312	.341	.653	87	-9	53	4.35	22	*C-116/3-1	14	2.0
1892*Cle-N	111	413	63	109	29	13	1	64	32	47	18	....	.264	.327	.404	.732	116	6	62	5.51	-4	*C-111	18	1.2
1893 Cle-N	57	227	27	70	13	7	2	41	16	15	4	....	.308	.357	.454	.810	108	1	39	6.60	7	C-56/3-1	9	1.0
1894 Cle-N	90	341	55	97	20	5	4	65	17	31	14	....	.284	.328	.408	.735	74	-17	51	5.48	9	*C-89	10	0.0
1895*Cle-N	88	315	60	107	21	2	5	56	33	30	14	....	.340	.417	.467	.884	121	10	69	8.94	-1	C-84/1-3	17	1.4
1896*Cle-N	91	336	46	93	18	3	3	46	31	48	4	....	.277	.354	.375	.729	87	-7	48	5.11	-4	*C-91/3-1	10	-0.1
1897 Cle-N	80	294	50	93	22	3	0	40	25	....	8	....	.316	.378	.412	.789	103	1	51	6.51	2	C-80	10	0.9
1898 Cle-N	20	63	5	15	2	0	0	4	5	....	2	....	.238	.304	.270	.574	66	-3	6	3.29	0	C-19	2	-0.1
1899 Cle-N	20	73	9	25	2	1	2	14	5	....	1	....	.342	.407	.479	.887	154	5	15	8.30	3	C-20	1	0.9
Lou-N	75	262	43	78	11	3	2	29	22	....	9	....	.298	.370	.385	.755	107	3	43	5.87	1	C-62,1-11	9	0.9
Yr.	95	335	52	103	13	4	4	43	27	....	10	....	.307	.378	.406	.784	117	9	58	6.36	4	C-82,1-11	10	1.9
1900*Pit-N	82	271	27	80	7	10	0	35	17	....	4	....	.295	.361	.395	.756	108	3	42	5.60	-7	C-78/1-2	10	0.4
1901 Pit-N	69	236	17	52	7	3	0	21	20	....	6	....	.220	.292	.275	.568	63	-11	22	3.08	-8	C-68	5	-1.2
1902 Pit-N	42	142	13	38	4	2	0	17	11	....	4	....	.268	.338	.324	.662	101	0	18	4.37	-4	C-41/1-1	5	0.0
1903 Phi-N	37	118	9	26	3	1	1	19	9	....	3	....	.220	.292	.288	.580	68	-5	11	3.20	3	C-35	2	0.2
Total 19	1280	4550	617	1229	222	76	26	625	390	323	151	....	.270	.339	.369	.708	95	-34	652	5.15	53	*C-1239/1-25,0-5,3-3,S-1	153	11.6

• ZIMMER, Don Donald William Zimmer b: 1/17/1931, Cincinnati, OH BR/TR, 5'9", 177 lbs. Deb: 7/2/1954 M/C Career OF: 4-0-4

YEAR TM-L	G	AB	R	H	2B	3B	HR	RBI	BB	SO	SB	CS	AVG	OBP	SLG	OPS	OPS+	BR/A	RC	RC/G	FR	G/POS	WS	TPW
1954 Bro-N	24	33	3	6	0	1	0	0	3	8	2	0	.182	.270	.242	.513	34	-3	2	2.36	0	S-13	0	-0.2
1955*Bro-N	88	280	38	67	10	1	15	50	19	66	5	3	.239	.292	.443	.735	89	-6	34	3.98	-1	2-62,S-21/3-8	7	-0.1
1956 Bro-N	17	20	4	6	1	0	0	2	0	7	0	1	.300	.333	.350	.683	78	-1	2	2.92	-1	/S-8,3-3,2-1	0	-0.1
1957 Bro-N	84	269	23	59	9	1	6	19	16	63	1	3	.219	.263	.327	.590	52	-19	21	2.48	0	3-39,S-37/2-5	3	-1.7
1958 LA-N	127	455	52	119	15	2	17	60	28	92	14	2	.262	.306	.415	.721	86	-8	55	4.02	14	*S-114,3-12/2-1,0-1	14	1.6
1959*LA-N	97	249	21	41	7	1	4	28	37	56	3	1	.165	.275	.249	.524	38	-22	18	2.16	3	S-88/3-5,2-1	4	-1.2
1960 Chi-N	132	368	37	95	16	7	6	35	27	56	8	6	.258	.309	.389	.697	90	-6	42	3.82	-7	2-75,3-45/S-5,0-2(2-0-0)	8	-0.7
1961 Chi-N★	128	477	57	120	25	4	13	40	25	70	5	1	.252	.292	.403	.694	81	-14	52	3.69	-2	*2-116/3-5,0-1	8	-0.7
1962 NY-N	14	52	3	4	1	0	0	1	3	10	0	1	.077	.127	.096	.223	-38	-11	1	.28	2	3-14	1	-0.8
Cin-N	63	192	16	48	11	2	2	16	14	30	1	2	.250	.304	.359	.664	75	-8	20	3.54	-2	3-43,2-17/S-1	4	-0.9
Yr.	77	244	19	52	12	2	2	17	17	40	1	3	.213	.267	.303	.570	51	-18	20	2.73	0	3-57,2-17/S-1	5	-1.7
1963 LA-N	22	23	4	5	1	0	1	2	3	10	0	0	.217	.308	.391	.699	107	0	3	3.74	0	3-10/2-1,S-1	1	0.0
Was-A	83	298	37	74	12	1	13	44	18	57	3	2	.248	.296	.426	.722	100	-1	34	3.90	1	3-78/2-2	7	0.0
1964 Was-A	121	341	38	84	16	2	12	38	27	94	1	3	.246	.302	.411	.712	96	-4	40	4.02	0	3-87/0-4(2-0-3),C-2,2-1	8	-0.4
1965 Was-A	95	226	20	45	6	0	2	17	26	59	2	0	.199	.287	.252	.540	55	-12	17	2.42	1	C-33,3-26,2-12	2	-1.0
Total 12	1095	3283	353	773	130	22	91	352	246	678	45	25	.235	.291	.372	.663	76	-114	340	3.42	9	3-375,2-294,S-288/C-35,0-8	67	-6.3

• ZIMMERMAN, Bill William H. Zimmerman b: 1/20/1889, Kengen, Germany d: 10/4/1952, Newark, NJ BR/TR, 5'8.5", 172 lbs. Deb: 4/14/1915

YEAR TM-L	G	AB	R	H	2B	3B	HR	RBI	BB	SO	SB	CS	AVG	OBP	SLG	OPS	OPS+	BR/A	RC	RC/G	FR	G/POS	WS	TPW
1915 Bro-N	22	57	3	16	2	0	0	7	4	8	1	....	.281	.328	.316	.644	93	-0	6	4.01	-2	0-18(0-0-18)	2	-0.3

• ZIMMERMAN, Eddie Edward Desmond Zimmerman b: 1/4/1883, Oceanic, NJ d: 5/6/1945, Emmaus, PA BR/TR, 5'9", 160 lbs. Deb: 9/29/1906

YEAR TM-L	G	AB	R	H	2B	3B	HR	RBI	BB	SO	SB	CS	AVG	OBP	SLG	OPS	OPS+	BR/A	RC	RC/G	FR	G/POS	WS	TPW
1906 StL-N	5	14	0	3	0	0	0	1	0	....	0	....	.214	.214	.214	.429	35	-1	1	1.66	0	/3-5	0	-0.2
1911 Bro-N	122	417	31	77	10	7	3	36	34	37	9	....	.185	.249	.264	.513	46	-32	30	2.18	4	*3-122	6	-2.4
Total 2	127	431	31	80	10	7	3	37	34	37	9	....	.186	.248	.262	.511	45	-33	31	2.17	4	3-127	6	-2.6

• ZIMMERMAN, Heinie Henry Zimmerman b: 2/9/1887, New York, NY d: 3/14/1969, New York, NY BR/TR, 5'11.5", 176 lbs. Deb: 9/8/1907 Career OF: 3-8-2

YEAR TM-L	G	AB	R	H	2B	3B	HR	RBI	BB	SO	SB	CS	AVG	OBP	SLG	OPS	OPS+	BR/A	RC	RC/G	FR	G/POS	WS	TPW
1907*Chi-N	5	9	0	2	1	0	0	1	0	....	0	....	.222	.222	.333	.556	70	-0	1	2.54	-1	/2-4,0-1,S-1	0	-0.2
1908 Chi-N	46	113	17	33	4	1	0	9	1	....	2	....	.292	.298	.345	.643	101	-1	12	3.75	-5	2-20/0-8(2-4-2),3-1,S-1	3	-0.6
1909 Chi-N	65	183	23	50	9	2	0	21	3	....	7	....	.273	.285	.344	.629	93	-3	19	3.68	-7	2-31,S-12/3-4	7	-1.0
1910*Chi-N	99	335	35	95	16	6	3	38	20	36	7	....	.284	.326	.394	.720	111	2	44	4.68	-5	2-32,S-26,3-23/0-4(0-4-0),1	13	-0.1
1911 Chi-N	143	535	80	164	22	17	9	85	25	50	23	....	.307	.343	.462	.805	124	13	91	6.10	-6	*2-108,3-20,1-11	22	1.0
1912 Chi-N	145	557	95	**207**	**41**	14	**14**	99	38	60	23	....	**.372**	.418	**.571**	**.989**	**169**	**50**	141	**9.75**	-2	*3-121,1-22	34	5.0
1913 Chi-N	127	447	69	140	28	12	9	95	41	40	18	....	.313	.379	.490	.868	146	26	87	6.83	1	*3-125	25	3.2
1914 Chi-N	146	564	75	167	36	12	4	87	20	46	17	....	.296	.326	.424	.750	123	12	79	5.04	-14	*3-118,S-15,2-12	22	0.3
1915 Chi-N	139	520	65	138	28	11	3	62	21	33	19	13	.265	.300	.379	.679	105	-1	61	3.93	-5	*2-100,3-36/S-4	16	-0.4
1916 Chi-N	107	398	54	116	25	5	6	64	16	33	15	12	.291	.324	.425	.748	116	4	55	4.69	6	3-85,2-14/S-4	13	1.5
NY-N	40	151	22	41	4	0	0	19	7	10	9	8	.272	.304	.298	.602	90	-4	14	2.95	-2	3-40/2-1	4	-0.5
Yr.	147	549	76	157	29	5	6	**83**	23	43	24	20	.286	.318	.390	.708	109	1	69	4.19	4	*3-125,2-15/S-4	17	1.0
1917*NY-N	150	585	61	174	22	9	5	**102**	16	43	13	....	.297	.317	.391	.709	121	11	74	4.48	20	*3-149/2-5	26	4.0
1918 NY-N	121	463	43	126	19	10	1	56	13	23	14	....	.272	.294	.363	.656	102	-2	51	3.79	-1	*3-100,1-19	15	0.1
1919 NY-N	123	444	56	113	20	6	4	58	21	30	8	....	.255	.296	.354	.649	96	-3	48	3.56	-1	*3-123	14	0.0
Total 13	1456	5304	695	1566	275	105	58	796	242	404	175	33	.295	.331	.419	.750	120	105	776	5.12	-22	3-945,2-327/S-63,1-53,0-13	214	12.1

• ZIMMERMAN, Jerry Gerald Robert Zimmerman b: 9/21/1934, Omaha, NE d: 9/9/1998, Neskowin, OR BR/TR, 6'2", 185 lbs. Deb: 4/14/1961 C/U

YEAR TM-L	G	AB	R	H	2B	3B	HR	RBI	BB	SO	SB	CS	AVG	OBP	SLG	OPS	OPS+	BR/A	RC	RC/G	FR	G/POS	WS	TPW
1961*Cin-N	76	204	8	42	5	0	0	10	11	21	1	1	.206	.253	.230	.484	29	-21	11	1.61	-2	C-76	3	-2.0
1962 Min-A	34	62	8	17	4	0	0	7	3	5	0	0	.274	.318	.339	.657	74	-2	7	3.77	0	C-34	2	-0.1
1963 Min-A	39	56	3	13	1	0	0	3	2	8	0	0	.232	.259	.250	.509	42	-4	3	1.74	0	C-39	1	-0.3
1964 Min-A	63	120	6	24	3	0	0	12	10	15	0	0	.200	.278	.225	.503	42	-9	7	1.87	1	C-63	2	-0.7
1965*Min-A	83	154	8	33	1	1	1	11	12	23	0	0	.214	.275	.253	.529	49	-10	10	2.09	1	C-82	4	-0.7
1966 Min-A	60	119	11	30	4	1	1	15	15	23	0	0	.252	.341	.328	.668	88	-1	13	3.78	1	C-59	5	0.2
1967 Min-A	104	234	13	39	3	0	1	12	22	49	0	1	.167	.244	.192	.436	28	-21	11	1.40	-1	*C-104	5	-1.9
1968 Min-A	24	45	3	5	1	0	0	2	3	10	0	0	.111	.184	.133	.317	-3	-6	1	.90	-1	C-24	1	-0.6
Total 8	483	994	60	203	22	2	3	72	78	154	1	2	.204	.270	.239	.509	43	-74	64	2.00	0	C-481	23	-6.0

• ZIMMERMAN, Roy Roy Franklin Zimmerman b: 9/13/1916, Pine Grove, PA d: 11/22/1991, Pine Grove, PA BL/TL, 6'2", 187 lbs. Deb: 8/27/1945

YEAR TM-L	G	AB	R	H	2B	3B	HR	RBI	BB	SO	SB	CS	AVG	OBP	SLG	OPS	OPS+	BR/A	RC	RC/G	FR	G/POS	WS	TPW
1945 NY-N	27	98	14	27	1	0	5	15	5	16	1	....	.276	.330	.439	.769	111	1	14	5.19	-2	1-25/0-1	2	-0.2

YEAR TM-L	G	AB	R	H	2B	3B	HR	RBI	BB	SO	SB	CS	AVG	OBP	SLG	OPS	OPS+	BR/A	RC	RC/G	FR	G/POS	WS	TPW
• ZINN, Frank	Frank Patrick Zinn b: 12/21/1865, Phoenixville, PA d: 5/12/1936, Philadelphia, PA, 5'8", 150 lbs. Deb: 4/18/1888																							
1888 Phi-a	2	7	0	0	0	0	0	0	1	....	0	....	.000	.125	.000	.125	-59	-1	0	.00	-1	/C-2	0	-0.2
• ZINN, Guy	Guy Zinn b: 2/13/1887, Holbrook, WV d: 10/6/1949, Clarksburg, WV BL/TR, 5'10.5", 170 lbs. Deb: 9/11/1911 Career OF: 110-98-85																							
1911 NY-A	9	27	5	4	0	2	0	1	4	....	0	....	.148	.281	.296	.578	57	-2	2	2.45	0	/0-8(2-4-2)	0	-0.2
1912 NY-A	106	401	56	105	15	10	6	55	50	....	17	....	.262	.345	.394	.739	105	2	60	5.09	-14	*0-106(13-31-61)	9	-1.7
1913 Bos-N	36	138	15	41	8	2	1	15	4	23	3	....	.297	.322	.406	.727	105	0	18	4.60	3	0-35(1-34-0)	5	0.0
1914 Bal-F	61	225	30	63	10	6	3	25	16	26	6	....	.280	.336	.418	.754	115	4	32	4.93	-3	0-57(31-12-14)	7	-0.2
1915 Bal-F	102	312	30	84	18	3	5	43	35	28	2	....	.269	.343	.394	.737	109	3	42	4.59	-1	0-88(63-17-8)	8	-0.1
Total 5	314	1103	136	297	51	23	15	139	109	77	28	....	.269	.338	.398	.736	107	8	155	4.78	-15	0-294	29	-2.2
• ZINTER, Alan	Alan Michael Zinter b: 5/19/1968, El Paso, TX BB/TR, 6'2", 200 lbs. Deb: 6/18/2002																							
2002 Hou-N	39	44	5	6	2	0	2	3	0	19	0	0	.136	.136	.318	.455	14	-6	2	1.36	0	/1-8,C-1	0	-0.6
• ZIPFEL, Bud	Marion Sylvester Zipfel b: 11/18/1938, Belleville, IL BL/TR, 6'3", 200 lbs. Deb: 7/26/1961																							
1961 Was-A	50	170	17	34	7	5	4	18	15	49	1	1	.200	.265	.371	.635	71	-8	17	3.09	-4	1-44	2	-1.5
1962 Was-A	68	184	21	44	4	1	6	21	17	43	1	2	.239	.307	.370	.676	82	-6	21	4.00	-2	1-26,0-23(23-0-0)	3	-1.0
Total 2	118	354	38	78	11	6	10	39	32	92	2	3	.220	.287	.370	.657	77	-14	38	3.54	-7	/1-70,0-23	5	-2.5
• ZISK, Richie	Richard Walter Zisk b: 2/6/1949, Brooklyn, NY BR/TR, 6'1", 208 lbs. Deb: 9/8/1971 Career OF: 413-0-507																							
1971 Pit-N	7	15	2	3	1	0	1	2	4	7	0	0	.200	.368	.467	.835	134	1	3	6.66	0	/0-6(3-0-3)	1	0.1
1972 Pit-N	17	37	4	7	3	0	0	4	7	10	0	0	.189	.318	.270	.588	70	-1	3	3.04	0	0-12(12-0-1)	0	-0.2
1973 Pit-N	103	333	44	108	23	7	10	54	21	63	0	0	.324	.364	.526	.890	148	20	62	7.15	4	0-84(22-0-65)	16	2.0
1974*Pit-N	149	536	75	168	30	3	17	100	65	91	1	1	.313	.388	.476	.863	146	33	99	6.97	9	*0-141(9-0-135)	25	3.6
1975*Pit-N	147	504	69	146	27	3	20	75	68	109	0	1	.290	.376	.474	.851	136	24	90	6.50	-2	*0-140(140-0-0)	22	1.5
1976 Pit-N	155	581	91	168	35	2	21	89	52	96	1	0	.289	.348	.465	.812	128	20	90	5.49	4	*0-152(152-0-0)	24	1.6
1977 Chi-A★	141	531	78	154	17	6	30	101	55	98	0	4	.290	.360	.514	.874	135	24	94	6.25	-6	*0-109(10-0-100),D-28	20	1.1
1978 Tex-A★	140	511	68	134	19	1	22	85	58	76	3	3	.262	.341	.432	.773	116	11	74	4.95	1	0-90(48-0-42),D-49	15	0.6
1979 Tex-A	144	503	69	132	21	1	18	64	57	75	1	1	.262	.338	.416	.753	103	2	69	4.78	0	*0-134(15-0-126)/D-3	13	-0.4
1980 Tex-A	135	448	48	130	17	1	19	77	39	72	0	2	.290	.347	.460	.807	123	12	66	5.18	0	D-86,0-37(2-0-35)	11	0.8
1981 Sea-A	94	357	42	111	12	1	16	43	28	63	0	2	.311	.366	.485	.851	138	16	61	6.47	0	D-93	12	1.4
1982 Sea-A	131	503	61	147	28	1	21	62	49	89	2	1	.292	.356	.477	.833	123	16	86	6.26	0	*D-130	14	1.1
1983 Sea-A	90	285	30	69	12	0	12	36	30	61	0	0	.242	.314	.411	.725	94	-2	37	4.41	0	D-84	5	-0.5
Total 13	1453	5144	681	1477	245	26	207	792	533	910	8	15	.287	.355	.466	.821	126	175	834	5.82	10	0-905,D-473	178	12.7
• ZITZMANN, Billy	William Arthur Zitzmann b: 11/19/1895, Long Island City, NY d: 5/29/1985, Passaic, NJ BR/TR, 5'10.5", 175 lbs. Deb: 4/27/1919 Career OF: 189-57-46																							
1919 Pit-N	11	26	5	5	1	0	0	2	0	6	2	....	.192	.192	.231	.423	26	-2	1	1.68	-1	/0-8(8-0-0)	0	-0.4
Cin-N	2	1	0	0	0	0	0	0	0	0	0	....	.000	.000	.000	.000	-103	-0	0	.00	0	/0-1	0	0.0
Yr.	13	27	5	5	1	0	0	2	0	6	2	....	.185	.185	.222	.407	21	-3	1	1.60	-1	/0-9(9-0-0)	0	-0.4
1925 Cin-N	104	301	53	76	13	3	0	21	35	22	11	11	.252	.342	.316	.658	71	-14	33	3.70	-3	0-89(80-4-7)/S-1	5	-2.0
1926 Cin-N	53	94	21	23	2	1	0	3	6	7	3	....	.245	.304	.287	.591	61	-5	8	2.94	-2	0-31(22-5-2)	1	-0.8
1927 Cin-N	88	232	47	66	10	4	0	24	20	18	9	....	.284	.352	.362	.714	94	-1	30	4.27	-8	0-60(17-36-7)/S-8,3-3	6	-1.1
1928 Cin-N	101	266	53	79	9	3	3	33	13	22	13	....	.297	.337	.387	.724	90	-4	34	4.39	-2	0-78(46-12-23)/3-1	7	-1.1
1929 Cin-N	47	84	18	19	3	0	0	6	9	10	4	....	.226	.309	.262	.570	45	-7	7	2.78	-2	0-22(15-0-7)/1-5	1	-1.0
Total 6	406	1004	197	268	38	11	3	89	83	85	42	11	.267	.333	.336	.668	77	-34	114	3.80	-18	0-289/S-9,1-5,3-4	20	-6.5
• ZOCCOLILLO, Pete	Peter J. Zoccolillo b: 2/6/1977, Bronx, NY BL/TR, 6'2", 200 lbs. Deb: 9/5/2003																							
2003 Mil-N	20	37	0	4	1	0	0	3	2	13	0	0	.108	.154	.135	.289	-24	-7	1	.56	0	/0-7(3-0-4)	0	-0.7
• ZOSKY, Eddie	Edward James Zosky b: 2/10/1968, Whittier, CA BR/TR, 6', 175 lbs. Deb: 9/2/1991																							
1991 Tor-A	18	27	2	4	1	1	0	2	0	8	0	0	.148	.148	.259	.407	10	-3	1	.87	1	S-18	0	-0.2
1992 Tor-A	8	7	1	2	0	1	0	1	0	2	0	0	.286	.286	.571	.857	129	0	1	5.09	-0	/S-8	0	0.0
1995 Fla-N	6	5	0	1	0	0	0	0	0	0	0	0	.200	.200	.200	.400	6	-1	0	1.35	-2	/S-4,2-1	0	-0.2
1999 Mil-N	8	7	1	1	0	0	0	0	1	2	0	0	.143	.250	.143	.393	3	-1	0	1.42	-1	/3-4,2-2	0	-0.2
2000 Hou-N	4	4	0	0	0	0	0	0	0	1	0	0	.000	.000	.000	.000	-95	-1	0	.00	0	....	0	-0.1
Total 5	44	50	4	8	1	2	0	3	1	13	0	0	.160	.176	.260	.436	19	-6	2	1.47	-2	/S-30,3-4,2-3	0	-0.7
• ZUBER, Jon	Jon Edward Zuber b: 12/10/1969, Encino, CA BL/TL, 6'1", 190 lbs. Deb: 4/19/1996																							
1996 Phi-N	30	91	7	23	4	0	1	10	6	11	1	0	.253	.299	.330	.629	65	-5	9	3.19	-1	1-22	1	-0.7
1998 Phi-N	38	45	6	11	3	1	2	6	6	9	0	0	.244	.346	.489	.835	115	1	8	6.01	0	/0-5(5-0-0),1-4	1	0.0
Total 2	68	136	13	34	7	1	3	16	12	20	1	0	.250	.315	.382	.698	82	-4	16	4.10	-1	/1-26,0-5	2	-0.6
• ZULETA, Julio	Julio Ernesto (Tapia) Zuleta b: 3/28/1975, Panama City, Panama BR/TR, 6'6", 235 lbs. Deb: 4/6/2000																							
2000 Chi-N	30	68	13	20	8	0	3	12	2	19	0	1	.294	.342	.544	.887	122	1	12	6.11	0	1-14/0-6(6-0-0)	2	0.0
2001 Chi-N	49	106	11	23	3	0	6	24	8	32	0	1	.217	.291	.415	.706	83	-3	12	3.68	-4	1-35	1	-0.9
Total 2	79	174	24	43	11	0	9	36	10	51	0	2	.247	.311	.466	.776	98	-2	24	4.57	-4	/1-49,0-6	3	-0.9
• ZUPCIC, Bob	Robert Zupcic b: 8/18/1966, Pittsburgh, PA BR/TR, 6'4", 220 lbs. Deb: 9/7/1991 Career OF: 100-112-96																							
1991 Bos-A	18	25	3	4	0	0	1	3	1	6	0	0	.160	.192	.280	.472	28	-3	1	1.77	-1	0-16(3-7-6)	0	-0.4
1992 Bos-A	124	392	46	108	19	1	3	43	25	60	2	2	.276	.325	.352	.677	84	-9	45	4.05	1	*0-114(32-68-22)/D-5	10	-1.0
1993 Bos-A	141	286	40	69	24	2	2	26	27	54	5	2	.241	.311	.360	.671	75	-10	32	3.68	0	*0-122(48-37-54)/D-5	5	-1.2
1994 Bos-A	4	4	0	0	0	0	0	0	0	1	0	1	.000	.000	.000	.000	-95	-2	0	.00	0	/0-2(2-0-0),D-1	0	-0.2
Chi-A	32	88	10	18	4	1	1	8	4	16	0	0	.205	.239	.307	.546	40	-8	6	2.22	0	0-28(15-0-14)/3-2,1-1	1	-0.8
Yr.	36	92	10	18	4	1	1	8	4	17	0	1	.196	.229	.293	.523	35	-10	6	2.08	0	0-30(17-0-14)/3-2,1-1,D-1	1	-1.0
Total 4	319	795	99	199	47	4	7	80	57	137	7	5	.250	.305	.346	.651	73	-31	85	3.58	1	0-282/D-11,3-2,1-1	16	-3.6
• ZUPO, Frank	Frank Joseph "Noodles" Zupo b: 8/29/1939, San Francisco, CA BL/TR, 5'11", 182 lbs. Deb: 7/1/1957																							
1957 Bal-A	10	12	2	1	0	0	0	0	1	4	0	0	.083	.154	.083	.237	-36	-2	0	.48	-1	/C-8	0	-0.3
1958 Bal-A	1	2	0	0	0	0	0	0	0	1	0	0	.000	.000	.000	.000	-106	-1	0	.00	0	/C-1	0	-0.1
1961 Bal-A	5	4	1	2	1	0	0	0	1	1	0	0	.500	.600	.750	1.350	264	1	2	26.41	0	/C-4	1	0.1
Total 3	16	18	3	3	1	0	0	0	2	6	0	0	.167	.250	.222	.472	32	-2	2	3.87	-2	/C-13	1	-0.3
• ZUVELLA, Paul	Paul Zuvella b: 10/31/1958, San Mateo, CA BR/TR, 6', 178 lbs. Deb: 9/4/1982 C																							
1982 Atl-N	2	1	0	0	0	0	0	0	0	0	0	0	.000	.000	.000	.000	-96	-0	0	.00	0	/S-1	0	0.0
1983 Atl-N	3	5	0	0	0	0	0	0	2	1	0	0	.000	.375	.000	.375	11	-0	0	1.58	-1	/S-2	0	-0.1
1984 Atl-N	11	25	2	5	1	0	0	1	2	3	0	0	.200	.259	.240	.499	38	-2	2	2.28	1	/2-6,S-6	0	-0.1
1985 Atl-N	81	190	16	48	8	1	0	4	16	14	2	0	.253	.311	.305	.616	69	-7	19	3.42	1	2-42,S-33/3-5	5	-0.2
1986 NY-A	21	48	2	4	1	0	0	2	5	4	0	0	.083	.170	.104	.274	-24	-8	1	.65	1	S-21	1	-0.5
1987 NY-A	14	34	2	6	0	0	0	0	0	4	0	0	.176	.176	.176	.353	-6	-5	1	.85	0	/2-7,S-6,3-1	0	-0.4
1988 Cle-A	51	130	9	30	5	1	0	7	8	13	0	0	.231	.275	.285	.560	56	-8	10	2.52	-9	S-49	1	-1.4
1989 Cle-A	24	58	10	16	2	0	2	6	1	11	0	0	.276	.300	.414	.714	98	-0	7	4.73	-1	S-15/3-5,D-3	1	-0.1
1991 KC-A	2	0	0	0	0	0	0	0	0	0	0	0	....	....	....	....	-100	0	0	....	-1	/3-2	0	-0.1
Total 9	209	491	41	109	17	2	2	20	34	50	2	0	.222	.275	.277	.552	51	-32	41	2.70	-8	S-133/2-55,3-13,D-3	8	-2.9
• ZWILLING, Dutch	Edward Harrison Zwilling b: 11/2/1888, St. Louis, MO d: 3/27/1978, La Crescenta, CA BL/TL, 5'6.5", 160 lbs. Deb: 8/14/1910 C Career OF: 0-333-5																							
1910 Chi-A	27	87	7	16	5	0	0	5	11	....	1	....	.184	.283	.241	.524	68	-3	6	2.21	-2	0-27(0-27-0)	2	-0.7
1914 Chi-F	154	592	91	185	38	8	**16**	95	46	68	21	....	.313	.363	.485	.848	149	34	106	6.50	-3	*0-154(0-153-1)	29	2.3
1915 Chi-F	150	548	65	157	32	7	13	**94**	67	65	24	....	.286	.366	.442	.808	146	31	94	5.98	-0	*0-148(0-148-0)/1-3	30	2.3
1916 Chi-N	35	53	4	6	1	0	1	8	4	6	0	....	.113	.175	.189	.364	11	-6	2	1.05	0	0-10(0-5-4)	0	-0.7
Total 4	366	1280	167	364	76	15	30	202	128	139	46	....	.284	.351	.438	.789	136	57	208	5.67	-5	0-339/1-3	61	3.2

Chapter 61

The Pitcher Register

The Pitcher Register consists of the central pitching statistics of every major league pitcher since 1871 who either had at least one season where he was primarily a pitcher, or who pitched in at least five games in his career.

The pitchers are listed alphabetically by surname and, when more than one pitcher bears the name, alphabetically by common name—the name applied to him during his playing career, whether nickname or first name. On the whole, we have been conservative in ascribing nicknames, doing so only when the player was in fact known by that name during his playing days.

The record of a man who pitched in more than one season is given in one line for each season, plus a career total line. If he pitched for more than one team in a given year, his totals for each team are given on separate lines; and if the teams for which he pitched in his "traded year" are in the same league, then his full record is stated in both separate and combined fashion. (In the odd case of a man playing for three or more clubs in one year, with some of these clubs being in the same league, the combined total line will reflect only his play in that one league.) A man who pitched in only one year has no additional career total line since it would be identical to his seasonal listing.

A star denoting All-Star Game selection appears to the right of the team/league column. An asterisk appears to the left of the team for which a player appeared in postseason competition, thus making for easy cross-reference to the other postseason sections.

Pitching records for the National Association are included in the Pitcher Register because the editors, like most baseball historians, regard it as a major league, inasmuch as it was the only professional league of its day and supplied the National League of 1876 with most of its personnel.

Gaps remain elsewhere in the official record of baseball and in the ongoing process of statistical reconstruction. The reader will note occasional elements in biographical lines which are blank except for an ellipsis ("...."). These are neither zeroes nor typographical lapses, but rather signs that the information does not exist or has not yet been found.

For a key to the team and league abbreviations used in the Pitcher Register, please visit the last page of the book.

Looking at the biographical line for any pitcher, we see first his last and common name in bold, followed by his full given name and nickname (and any other name he may have used or been born with, such as the matronymic of a Latin American player). His date and place of birth follow "b" and his date and place of death follow "d". Then comes his manner of batting and throwing, abbreviated for a lefthanded batter who throws right as BL/TR (a switch hitter would be shown as BB for "bats both" and a switch thrower as TB for "throws both"). Next is height and weight information; then, and for most pitchers last, is the pitcher's debut date.

Some pitchers continue in major league baseball after their pitching days are through, as managers, coaches, or even umpires. A pitcher whose biographical line concludes with an M can also be located in the Manager Roster and one with a U occupies a place in the Umpire Roster. The select few who have been enshrined in the Baseball Hall of Fame are noted with a "HOF 19xx" identifier. (See also the Hall of Fame Roster in Chapter 41.)

A black diamond (◆) appears at the end of the biographical line for pitchers who also appear in the Player Register by virtue of their having played in 100 or more games at another position, or having played more than half of their total major league games at another position, or having played more games at a position other than pitcher in at least one year.

For this edition of *Total Baseball*, there are several changes to the statistical categories found in the Pitching Register.

First, the column for "Total Pitcher Index" has been changed to "Total Player Wins". TPW is basically the same as the old TPI, but includes the contributions of a player's batting and fielding at positions other than pitcher. Babe Ruth is the player most prominently affected by the change. (Old readers will recognize that TPW is the new name for what was previously called "Total Baseball Ranking.") Also, TPW does not include the pitcher's own fielding runs—those runs saved would have lowered his ERA and thus improved his own Pitching Runs, so adjusting for them separately would count them twice.

Second, TPW no longer employs the Relief Ranking Formula. All pitchers are now rated on the basis of their Pitching Runs, without regard to the relative importance of their innings.

Third, we now adjust Pitching Runs to account for the defense behind the pitcher. For instance, if a pitcher threw 10% of his team's innings, and the team had a combined FR of +20 runs, we would hold that the pitcher claimed a benefit of +2 from this defense, and his Pitching Runs would be reduced by that amount.

Fourth, in a technical change, we now calculate wins from runs without regard to the pitcher's proficiency. Previously, pitchers were credited with more wins per run saved if their ERA was lower (and vice-versa); now, we credit pitchers with the same wins per run regardless of their ERA. The effect is that pitchers will now have less extreme TPW figures; the best will be lower, and the worst will be higher.

Fifth, we have changed the definition of "ratio" to conform to common usage—hits plus walks per inning. The previous statistic included HBP and was per game rather than per inning.

Sixth, we no longer downgrade TPW for the Federal League and Union Association. We present the results as is, and leave era comparisons to the reader.

Finally, we have added two new statistics—Component ERA, and Win Shares.

The explanations for the statistical column heads follow; for more technical information, see the Glossary at the back of the book.

YEAR   Year in which a man pitched (When a space in the column is blank, this indicates that the man pitched for two or more clubs in the last year stated in the column; if those clubs were in the same league, then the man will also have a combined total line, beginning with the abbreviation "Yr" placed in the TM-L column.)

*   Denotes postseason play, World Series, League Championship Series, or Division Series

Yr   Year's totals for pitching with two or more clubs in same league (See comments for YEAR.)

TM/L   Team and League (See comments for YEAR.)

★   Named to All-Star Game

W   Wins

L   Losses

PCT   Win Percentage (Wins divided by decisions.)

G   Games pitched

GS   Games Started

CG   Complete Games

SH   Shutouts (Complete-game shutouts only.)

SV   Saves (Employing definition in force at the time, and 1969 definition for years prior to 1969.)

IP   Innings Pitched (Fractional innings included.)

H   Hits allowed (Bases on balls were counted as hits by scorers in 1887.)

R   Runs allowed

ER   Earned Runs Allowed

HR   Home Runs allowed

HB   Hit Batsmen (Data is available from 1884–1891 in the American Association, from 1887 on for the National League, for the 1890 Players League, and the Federal League in 1914–1915.)

BB   Bases on Balls allowed (Bases on balls were counted as outs by scorers in 1876.)

SO   Strikeouts

RAT   Ratio (Hits allowed plus walks allowed per inning—a rotisserie baseball staple.)

ERA   Earned Run Average (In a handful of cases, a pitcher will have allowed one or more earned runs without having retired a batter; this situation would produce an infinite ERA, expressed in the pitcher's record as ∞.)

ERA+   Adjusted Earned Run Average (Normalized to league average and adjusted for home-park factor; Higher numbers are better; league average is represented by 100.)

CERA   Component ERA (This Bill James statistic is an estimate of what the pitcher's ERA "should have been," based on the composite batting line of the batters who faced him.)

OAV   Opponents' Batting Average

BH   Base Hits (as a batter)

AVG   Batting Average (as a batter)

PR+   Adjusted Pitching Runs (Linear Weights measure of runs saved beyond what a league-average pitcher might have saved, defined as zero. Adjusted for home park and for the quality of the defense behind the pitcher. Occasionally the curious figure of -0 will appear in this column, or in the columns of other Linear Weights measures of batting, fielding, and pitching. This "negative zero" figure signifies a run contribution that falls below the league average, but to so small a degree that it cannot be said to be significant enough to score as minus 1.)

Total   For players whose careers include play in the National Association as well as other major leagues, two totals are given, as described above. A player's record of his years in the National Association is shown alongside the notation "Total x n," where x would be the number of years totaled and n stands for National Association. For players whose careers began in 1876 or later, the lifetime record is shown alongside the notation "Total y," where y stands for the number of post-1875 years totaled.

WS   Win Shares (The Bill James estimate of how many of his team's wins this player was individually responsible for, multiplied by 3.)

TPW   Total Player Wins (This is the sum of a pitcher's Adjusted Pitching Runs, Fielding Runs (at positions other than pitcher), and Adjusted Batting Runs, all divided by the Runs Per Win factor for that year—generally around 10, historically in the 9 to 11 range. For more information on the formula and the Runs Per Win concept, see the Glossary. In the lifetime line, the TPW is the sum of the seasonal TPWs. TPW includes the contributions made by pitchers who also played other positions—Babe Ruth is the player most prominently affected. TPW is the new name for what was previously called "Total Baseball Ranking." It is also similar to the former "Total Pitcher Index," with the exception that TPW also includes the player's contribution at other positions, if any.)

• AASE, Don Donald William Aase b: 9/8/1954, Orange, CA BR/TR, 6'3", 210 lbs. Deb: 7/26/1977

YEAR	TM-L	W	L	PCT	G	GS	CG	SH	SV	IP	H	R	ER	HR	HB	BB	SO	RAT	ERA	ERA+	CERA	OAV	BH	AVG	PR+	WS	TPW
1977	Bos-A	6	2	.750	13	13	4	2	0	92^1	85	36	32	6	1	19	49	1.126	3.12	144	2.74	.244	0	....	15	9	1.5
1978	Cal-A	11	8	.579	29	29	6	1	0	178^2	185	88	80	14	2	80	93	1.483	4.03	90	4.39	.270	0	....	-7	8	-0.7
1979*	Cal-A	9	10	.474	37	28	7	1	2	185^1	200	104	99	19	1	77	96	1.495	4.81	85	4.56	.277	0	....	-14	6	-1.4
1980	Cal-A	8	13	.381	40	21	5	1	2	175	193	83	79	13	1	66	74	1.480	4.06	97	4.42	.287	0	....	-2	9	-0.2
1981	Cal-A	4	4	.500	39	0	0	0	11	65^1	56	17	17	4	0	24	38	1.224	2.34	156	2.96	.234	0	....	9	8	1.0
1982	Cal-A	3	3	.500	24	0	0	0	4	52	45	20	20	5	0	23	40	1.308	3.46	117	3.56	.243	0	....	3	5	0.3
1984	Cal-A	4	1	.800	23	0	0	0	8	39	30	7	7	1	0	19	28	1.256	1.62	246	2.53	.221	0	....	10	7	1.0
1985	Bal-A	10	6	.625	54	0	0	0	14	88	83	44	37	6	1	35	67	1.341	3.78	107	3.55	.258	0	....	3	9	0.3
1986	Bal-A★	6	7	.462	66	0	0	0	34	81^2	71	29	27	6	0	28	67	1.212	2.98	139	2.95	.234	0	....	11	14	1.1
1987	Bal-A	1	0	1.000	7	0	0	0	2	8	8	2	2	1	0	4	3	1.500	2.25	195	5.01	.276	0	....	2	1	0.2
1988	Bal-A	0	0	....	35	0	0	0	0	46^2	40	22	21	4	0	37	28	1.650	4.05	96	4.58	.240	0	....	-1	2	-0.1
1989	NY-N	1	5	.167	49	0	0	0	2	59^1	56	27	26	5	1	26	34	1.382	3.94	83	3.69	.245	0	.000	-4	2	-0.5
1990	LA-N	3	1	.750	32	0	0	0	3	38	33	24	21	5	0	19	24	1.368	4.97	74	3.78	.232	0	....	-6	1	-0.6
Total	13	66	60	.524	448	91	22	5	82	1109^1	1085	503	468	89	7	457	641	1.390	3.80	102	3.88	.259	0	.000	19	81	1.8

• ABBEY, Bert Bert Wood Abbey b: 11/11/1869, Essex, VT d: 6/11/1962, Essex Junction, VT BR/TR, 5'11", 175 lbs. Deb: 6/14/1892

YEAR	TM-L	W	L	PCT	G	GS	CG	SH	SV	IP	H	R	ER	HR	HB	BB	SO	RAT	ERA	ERA+	CERA	OAV	BH	AVG	PR+	WS	TPW
1892	Was-N	5	18	.217	27	22	19	0	1	195^2	207	139	75	7	0	76	77	1.446	3.45	94	3.80	.261	9	.120	-4	8	-0.6
1893	Chi-N	2	4	.333	7	7	5	0	0	56	74	52	34	1	0	20	6	1.679	5.46	85	5.03	.309	6	.231	-5	2	-0.4
1894	Chi-N	2	7	.222	11	11	10	0	0	92	119	74	53	3	0	37	24	1.696	5.18	108	5.16	.310	5	.128	6	5	0.1
1895	Chi-N	0	1	.000	1	1	1	0	0	8	10	8	4	0	0	2	3	1.500	4.50	113	4.10	.302	1	.333	1	0	0.0
	Bro-N	5	2	.714	8	6	5	0	0	52	66	34	25	0	0	9	14	1.442	4.33	101	3.94	.305	5	.263	-0	4	0.1
	Yr.	5	3	.625	9	7	6	0	0	60	76	42	29	0	0	11	17	1.450	4.35	103	3.96	.304	6	.273	0	4	0.1
1896	Bro-N	8	8	.500	25	18	12	0	0	164^1	210	135	94	7	0	48	37	1.570	5.15	80	4.74	.308	12	.190	-18	4	-1.5
Total	5	22	40	.355	79	65	52	0	1	568	686	442	285	18	0	192	161	1.546	4.52	91	4.43	.292	38	.169	-20	23	-2.4

• ABBOTT, Dan Leander Franklin "Big Dan" Abbott b: 3/16/1862, Portage, OH d: 2/13/1930, Ottawa Lake, MI BR/TR, 5'11", 190 lbs. Deb: 4/19/1890

YEAR	TM-L	W	L	PCT	G	GS	CG	SH	SV	IP	H	R	ER	HR	HB	BB	SO	RAT	ERA	ERA+	CERA	OAV	BH	AVG	PR+	WS	TPW
1890	Tol-a	0	2	.000	3	1	1	0	1	13	19	14	9	0	0	8	1	2.077	6.23	63	....	.331	1	.143	-4	0	-0.3

• ABBOTT, Glenn William Glenn Abbott b: 2/16/1951, Little Rock, AR BR/TR, 6'6", 200 lbs. Deb: 7/29/1973

YEAR	TM-L	W	L	PCT	G	GS	CG	SH	SV	IP	H	R	ER	HR	HB	BB	SO	RAT	ERA	ERA+	CERA	OAV	BH	AVG	PR+	WS	TPW
1973	Oak-A	1	0	1.000	5	3	1	0	0	18^2	16	8	8	3	0	7	6	1.232	3.86	92	3.53	.225	0	....	-1	1	-0.1
1974	Oak-A	5	7	.417	19	17	3	0	0	96	89	38	32	4	3	34	38	1.281	3.00	111	3.22	.247	0	....	2	6	0.2
1975*	Oak-A	5	5	.500	30	15	3	1	0	114^1	109	61	54	12	2	50	51	1.391	4.25	85	3.95	.253	0	....	-8	3	-0.9
1976	Oak-A	2	4	.333	19	10	0	0	0	62^1	87	41	38	6	1	16	27	1.652	5.49	61	5.88	.333	0	....	-14	0	-1.5
1977	Sea-A	12	13	.480	36	34	7	0	0	204^1	212	111	101	32	12	56	100	1.312	4.45	92	4.46	.270	0	....	-11	10	-1.1
1978	Sea-A	7	15	.318	29	28	8	1	0	155^1	191	99	91	22	2	44	67	1.513	5.27	72	5.22	.303	0	....	-24	3	-2.5
1979	Sea-A	4	10	.286	23	19	3	0	0	116^2	138	78	67	19	3	38	25	1.509	5.17	84	5.37	.301	0	....	-10	3	-1.0
1980	Sea-A	12	12	.500	31	31	7	2	0	215	228	110	98	27	3	49	78	1.288	4.10	101	3.95	.272	0	....	2	12	0.2
1981	Sea-A	4	9	.308	22	20	1	0	0	130^1	127	64	57	14	0	28	35	1.189	3.94	98	3.30	.258	0	....	1	6	0.1
1983	Sea-A	5	3	.625	14	14	2	0	0	82^1	103	46	42	9	4	15	38	1.433	4.59	93	4.95	.311	0	....	-3	4	-0.3
	Det-A	2	1	.667	7	7	1	1	0	46^2	43	12	10	5	0	7	11	1.071	1.93	203	2.74	.244	0	....	10	4	1.0
	Yr.	7	4	.636	21	21	3	1	0	129	146	58	52	14	4	22	49	1.302	3.63	115	4.15	.288	0	....	7	8	0.7
1984	Det-A	3	4	.429	13	8	1	0	0	44	62	39	29	9	2	8	8	1.591	5.93	66	6.32	.325	0	....	-10	0	-1.0
Total	11	62	83	.428	248	206	37	5	0	1286	1405	707	627	162	32	352	484	1.366	4.39	89	4.38	.280	0	....	-67	52	-6.9

• ABBOTT, Jim James Anthony Abbott b: 9/19/1967, Flint, MI BL/TL, 6'3", 210 lbs. Deb: 4/8/1989

YEAR	TM-L	W	L	PCT	G	GS	CG	SH	SV	IP	H	R	ER	HR	HB	BB	SO	RAT	ERA	ERA+	CERA	OAV	BH	AVG	PR+	WS	TPW
1989	Cal-A	12	12	.500	29	29	4	2	0	181^1	190	95	79	13	4	74	115	1.456	3.92	97	4.27	.274	0	....	-5	8	-0.5
1990	Cal-A	10	14	.417	33	33	4	1	0	211^2	246	116	106	16	5	72	105	**1.502**	4.51	85	4.69	.295	0	....	-16	8	-1.6
1991	Cal-A	18	11	.621	34	34	5	1	0	243	222	85	78	14	5	73	158	1.214	2.89	142	3.02	.244	0	....	29	20	2.9
1992	Cal-A	7	15	.318	29	29	7	0	0	211	208	73	65	12	4	68	130	1.308	2.77	144	3.54	.263	0	....	27	18	2.8
1993	NY-A	11	14	.440	32	32	4	1	0	214	221	115	104	22	3	73	95	1.374	4.37	95	4.14	.271	0	....	-5	10	-0.5
1994	NY-A	9	8	.529	24	24	2	0	0	160^1	167	88	81	24	2	64	90	1.441	4.55	101	4.76	.273	0	....	-2	8	-0.2
1995	Chi-A	6	4	.600	17	17	3	0	0	112^1	116	50	42	10	1	35	45	1.344	3.36	132	3.90	.269	0	....	15	7	1.4
	Cal-A	5	4	.556	13	13	1	1	0	84^2	93	43	39	4	1	29	41	1.441	4.15	113	4.07	.280	0	....	4	5	0.4
	Yr.	11	8	.579	30	30	4	1	0	197	209	93	81	14	2	64	86	1.386	3.70	123	3.98	.274	0	....	20	12	1.8
1996	Cal-A	2	18	.100	27	23	1	0	0	142	171	128	118	23	4	78	58	1.754	7.48	65	6.59	.306	0	....	-41	0	-3.7
1998	Chi-A	5	0	1.000	5	5	0	0	0	31^2	35	16	16	2	1	12	14	1.484	4.55	100	4.66	.292	0	....	-0	2	0.0
1999	Mil-N	2	8	.200	20	15	0	0	0	82	110	71	63	14	2	42	37	1.854	6.91	66	7.16	.317	2	.095	-21	0	-2.1
Total	10	87	108	.446	263	254	31	6	0	1674	1779	880	791	154	32	620	888	1.433	4.25	100	4.39	.276	2	.095	-14	86	-1.1

• ABBOTT, Kyle Lawrence Kyle Abbott b: 2/18/1968, Newburyport, MA BL/TL, 6'4", 200 lbs. Deb: 9/10/1991

YEAR	TM-L	W	L	PCT	G	GS	CG	SH	SV	IP	H	R	ER	HR	HB	BB	SO	RAT	ERA	ERA+	CERA	OAV	BH	AVG	PR+	WS	TPW
1991	Cal-A	1	2	.333	5	3	0	0	0	19^2	22	11	10	2	1	13	12	1.780	4.58	90	6.27	.301	0	....	-1	1	-0.1
1992	Phi-N	1	14	.067	31	19	0	0	0	133^1	147	80	76	20	1	45	88	1.440	5.13	68	4.83	.283	2	.069	-23	0	-2.6
1995	Phi-N	2	0	1.000	18	0	0	0	0	28^1	28	12	12	3	0	16	21	1.553	3.81	111	4.89	.267	1	.500	1	2	0.1
1996	Cal-A	0	1	.000	3	0	0	0	0	4	10	9	9	1	0	5	3	3.750	20.25	24	20.74	.500	0	....	-7	0	-0.6
Total	4	4	17	.190	57	22	0	0	0	185^1	207	112	107	26	2	79	124	1.543	5.20	71	5.34	.288	3	.097	-31	3	-3.3

• ABBOTT, Paul Paul David Abbott b: 9/15/1967, Van Nuys, CA BR/TR, 6'3", 185 lbs. Deb: 8/21/1990

YEAR	TM-L	W	L	PCT	G	GS	CG	SH	SV	IP	H	R	ER	HR	HB	BB	SO	RAT	ERA	ERA+	CERA	OAV	BH	AVG	PR+	WS	TPW
1990	Min-A	0	5	.000	7	7	0	0	0	34^2	37	24	23	0	1	28	25	1.875	5.97	70	5.53	.282	0	....	-7	0	-0.7
1991	Min-A	3	1	.750	15	3	0	0	0	47^1	38	27	25	5	0	36	43	1.563	4.75	90	4.42	.232	0	....	-3	2	-0.3
1992	Min-A	0	0	....	6	0	0	0	0	11	12	4	4	1	1	5	13	1.545	3.27	124	5.10	.279	0	....	1	1	0.1
1993	Cle-A	0	1	.000	5	5	0	0	0	18^1	19	15	13	5	0	11	7	1.636	6.38	68	6.28	.260	0	....	-4	0	-0.4
1998	Sea-A	3	1	.750	4	4	0	0	0	24^2	24	11	11	2	0	10	22	1.378	4.01	115	3.85	.255	0	....	2	2	0.2
1999	Sea-A	6	2	.750	25	7	0	0	0	72^2	50	31	25	9	0	32	68	1.128	3.10	161	2.65	.193	0	....	15	7	1.4
2000*	Sea-A	9	7	.563	35	27	0	0	0	179	164	89	84	23	5	80	100	1.363	4.22	108	4.09	.243	2	.400	5	11	0.5
2001*	Sea-A	17	4	.810	28	27	1	0	0	163	145	79	77	21	7	87	118	1.423	4.25	98	4.33	.238	1	.250	-6	9	-0.6
2002	Sea-A	1	3	.250	7	5	0	0	0	26^1	40	36	35	5	1	20	22	2.278	11.96	35	9.89	.351	0	....	-22	0	-2.2
2003	KC-A	1	2	.333	10	8	0	0	0	47^2	47	29	28	8	2	26	32	1.531	5.29	98	5.17	.257	0	....	-1	2	-0.1
Total	10	40	26	.606	142	93	1	0	0	624^2	576	345	325	79	17	335	450	1.458	4.68	94	4.49	.246	3	.333	-21	34	-2.0

• ABER, Al Albert Julius "Lefty" Aber b: 7/31/1927, Cleveland, OH d: 5/20/1993, Garfield Heights, OH BL/TL, 6'2", 195 lbs. Deb: 9/15/1950

YEAR	TM-L	W	L	PCT	G	GS	CG	SH	SV	IP	H	R	ER	HR	HB	BB	SO	RAT	ERA	ERA+	CERA	OAV	BH	AVG	PR+	WS	TPW
1950	Cle-A	1	0	1.000	1	1	1	0	0	9	5	2	2	0	0	4	4	1.000	2.00	217	1.49	.167	0	.000	2	1	0.2
1953	Cle-A	1	1	.500	6	0	0	0	0	6	6	6	5	0	0	9	4	2.500	7.50	50	6.50	.240	0	....	-3	0	-0.2
	Det-A	4	3	.571	17	10	2	0	0	66^2	63	35	33	3	0	41	34	1.560	4.46	91	4.14	.260	3	.130	-1	3	-0.2
	Yr.	5	4	.556	23	10	2	0	0	72^2	69	41	38	3	0	50	38	1.638	4.71	85	4.34	.258	3	.130	-3	3	-0.4
1954	Det-A	5	11	.313	32	18	4	0	3	124^2	121	63	55	8	3	40	54	1.291	3.97	93	3.37	.257	5	.128	-4	6	-0.6
1955	Det-A	6	3	.667	39	1	0	0	3	80	86	32	30	9	0	28	37	1.425	3.38	114	4.38	.275	1	.059	4	6	0.3
1956	Det-A	4	4	.500	42	0	0	0	7	63	65	30	24	1	2	25	21	1.429	3.43	120	3.50	.270	3	.300	5	6	0.5
1957	Det-A	3	3	.500	28	0	0	0	1	37	46	33	28	6	1	11	15	1.541	6.81	57	5.44	.315	1	.125	-12	0	-1.3
	KC-A	0	0	....	3	0	0	0	0	3	6	4	4	2	0	2	0	2.667	12.00	33	17.38	.400	1	1.000	-3	0	-0.2
	Yr.	3	3	.500	31	0	0	0	1	40	52	37	32	8	1	13	15	1.625	7.20	54	6.34	.323	2	.222	-15	0	-1.5
Total	6	24	25	.490	168	30	7	0	14	389^1	398	205	181	29	6	160	169	1.433	4.18	93	4.04	.269	14	.140	-11	22	-1.5

• ABERNATHIE, Bill William Edward Abernathie b: 1/30/1929, Torrance, CA BR/TR, 5'10", 190 lbs. Deb: 9/27/1952

YEAR	TM-L	W	L	PCT	G	GS	CG	SH	SV	IP	H	R	ER	HR	HB	BB	SO	RAT	ERA	ERA+	CERA	OAV	BH	AVG	PR+	WS	TPW
1952	Cle-A	0	0	....	1	0	0	0	1	2	4	3	3	1	0	1	0	2.500	13.50	25	16.06	.444	0	.000	-2	0	-0.2

• ABERNATHY, Ted Theodore Wade Abernathy b: 3/6/1933, Stanley, NC BR/TR, 6'4", 215 lbs. Deb: 4/13/1955

YEAR	TM-L	W	L	PCT	G	GS	CG	SH	SV	IP	H	R	ER	HR	HB	BB	SO	RAT	ERA	ERA+	CERA	OAV	BH	AVG	PR+	WS	TPW
1955	Was-A	5	9	.357	40	14	3	2	0	119^1	136	87	79	9	7	67	79	1.701	5.96	64	5.59	.294	4	.154	-25	0	-2.6
1956	Was-A	1	3	.250	5	4	2	0	0	30^1	35	16	14	2	1	10	18	1.484	4.15	104	4.62	.292	2	.182	1	2	0.1
1957	Was-A	2	10	.167	26	16	2	0	0	85	100	65	64	9	4	65	50	1.941	6.78	58	7.16	.314	4	.167	-25	0	-2.6

YEAR	TM-L	W	L	PCT	G	GS	CG	SH	SV	IP	H	R	ER	HR	HB	BB	SO	RAT	ERA	ERA+	CERA	OAV	BH	AVG	PR+	WS	TPW
1960	Was-A	0	0	....	2	0	0	0	0	3	4	4	4	0	0	4	1	2.667	12.00	33	8.91	.308	1	1.000	-3	0	-0.2
1963	Cle-A	7	2	.778	43	0	0	0	12	59^1	54	25	19	3	0	29	47	1.399	2.88	126	3.51	.251	2	.400	5	8	0.7
1964	Cle-A	2	6	.250	53	0	0	0	11	72^2	66	40	35	5	2	46	57	1.541	4.33	83	4.28	.247	0	.000	-4	3	-0.5
1965	Chi-N	4	6	.400	**84**	0	0	0	**31**	136^1	113	49	39	7	5	56	104	1.240	2.57	143	2.86	.227	3	.167	18	18	1.9
1966	Chi-N	1	3	.250	20	0	0	0	4	27^2	26	19	19	4	2	17	18	1.554	6.18	60	5.21	.255	0	.000	-7	0	-0.8
	Atl-N	4	4	.500	38	0	0	0	4	65^1	58	34	28	5	0	36	42	1.439	3.86	94	3.66	.247	2	.250	-2	3	-0.1
	Yr.	5	7	.417	58	0	0	0	8	93	84	53	47	9	2	53	60	1.473	4.55	80	4.12	.249	2	.167	-9	3	-0.9
1967	Cin-N	6	3	.667	**70**	0	0	0	**28**	106^1	63	19	15	1	5	41	88	.978	1.27	295	1.55	.170	1	.059	30	24	3.1
1968	Cin-N	10	7	.588	**78**	0	0	0	13	134^2	111	43	37	9	4	55	64	1.233	2.47	128	2.89	.228	0	.000	11	13	1.2
1969	Chi-N	4	3	.571	56	0	0	0	3	85^1	75	38	30	8	1	42	55	1.371	3.16	127	3.47	.234	2	.250	8	7	0.9
1970	Chi-N	0	0	....	11	0	0	0	1	9	9	2	2	0	1	5	2	1.556	2.00	225	4.26	.281	0	....	2	1	0.2
	StL-N	1	0	1.000	11	0	0	0	1	18^1	15	6	6	0	3	12	8	1.473	2.95	140	3.56	.246	0	.000	3	2	0.2
	Yr.	1	0	1.000	22	0	0	0	2	27^1	24	8	8	0	4	17	10	1.500	2.63	160	3.79	.258	0	.000	5	3	0.5
	KC-A	9	3	.750	36	0	0	0	12	55^2	41	23	16	3	1	38	49	1.419	2.59	144	3.41	.209	3	.214	7	8	0.7
1971	KC-A	4	6	.400	63	0	0	0	23	81	60	28	23	3	6	50	55	1.358	2.56	134	3.27	.210	1	.077	8	11	0.8
1972	KC-A	3	4	.429	45	0	0	0	5	58^1	44	15	11	2	3	19	28	1.080	1.70	178	2.20	.210	0	.000	9	7	1.0
Total	14	63	69	.477	681	34	7	2	148	1147^2	1010	513	441	70	45	592	765	1.396	3.46	107	3.72	.241	25	.138	38	107	4.1

• ABERNATHY, Ted — Talmadge Lafayette Abernathy b: 10/30/1921, Bynum, NC d: 11/16/2001, Charlotte, NC BR/TL, 6'2", 210 lbs. Deb: 9/19/1942

YEAR	TM-L	W	L	PCT	G	GS	CG	SH	SV	IP	H	R	ER	HR	HB	BB	SO	RAT	ERA	ERA+	CERA	OAV	BH	AVG	PR+	WS	TPW
1942	Phi-A	0	0	....	1	0	0	0	0	2^2	2	3	3	0	0	3	1	1.875	10.13	37	4.59	.222	0	....	-2	0	-0.2
1943	Phi-A	0	3	.000	5	2	1	0	0	14^2	24	22	21	0	0	13	10	2.523	12.89	26	8.57	.353	1	.250	-15	0	-1.6
1944	Phi-A	0	0	....	1	0	0	0	0	3	5	1	1	0	0	1	2	2.000	3.00	116	7.83	.417	0	.000	0	0	0.0
Total	3	0	3	.000	7	2	1	0	0	20^1	31	26	25	0	0	17	13	2.361	11.07	31	7.94	.348	1	.200	-17	0	-1.8

• ABERNATHY, Woody — Virgil Woodrow Abernathy b: 2/1/1915, Forest City, NC d: 12/5/1994, Louisville, KY BL/TL, 6', 170 lbs. Deb: 7/28/1946

YEAR	TM-L	W	L	PCT	G	GS	CG	SH	SV	IP	H	R	ER	HR	HB	BB	SO	RAT	ERA	ERA+	CERA	OAV	BH	AVG	PR+	WS	TPW
1946	NY-N	1	1	.500	15	1	0	0	1	40	32	16	15	5	0	10	6	1.050	3.38	102	2.70	.232	0	.000	1	2	0.0
1947	NY-N	0	0	....	1	0	0	0	0	2	4	3	2	0	0	1	0	2.500	9.00	45	9.55	.400	0	....	-1	0	-0.1
Total	2	1	1	.500	16	1	0	0	1	42	36	19	17	5	0	11	6	1.119	3.64	96	3.02	.243	0	.000	-0	2	-0.1

• ABLES, Harry — Harry Terrell "Hans" Ables b: 10/4/1884, Terrell, TX d: 2/8/1951, San Antonio, TX BR/TL, 6'2.5", 200 lbs. Deb: 9/4/1905

YEAR	TM-L	W	L	PCT	G	GS	CG	SH	SV	IP	H	R	ER	HR	HB	BB	SO	RAT	ERA	ERA+	CERA	OAV	BH	AVG	PR+	WS	TPW
1905	StL-A	0	3	.000	6	3	1	0	0	30^2	37	22	13	0	0	13	11	1.630	3.82	67	4.47	.300	0	.000	-4	0	-0.6
1909	Cle-A	1	1	.500	5	3	3	0	0	29^2	26	14	7	1	1	10	24	1.213	2.12	120	2.71	.226	0	.000	1	1	0.0
1911	NY-A	0	1	.000	3	2	0	0	0	11	16	15	12	0	0	7	6	2.091	9.82	37	6.69	.333	0	.000	-7	0	-0.8
Total	3	1	5	.167	14	8	4	0	0	71^1	79	51	32	1	1	30	41	1.528	4.04	71	4.08	.276	0	.000	-10	1	-1.4

• ABRAMS, George — George Allen Abrams b: 11/9/1899, Seattle, WA d: 12/5/1986, Clearwater, FL BR/TR, 5'9", 170 lbs. Deb: 4/19/1923

YEAR	TM-L	W	L	PCT	G	GS	CG	SH	SV	IP	H	R	ER	HR	HB	BB	SO	RAT	ERA	ERA+	CERA	OAV	BH	AVG	PR+	WS	TPW
1923	Cin-N	0	0	....	3	0	0	0	0	4^2	10	5	5	0	0	3	1	2.786	9.64	40	12.60	.500	1	1.000	-3	0	-0.2

• ABREGO, Johnny — Johnny Ray Abrego b: 7/4/1962, Corpus Christi, TX BR/TR, 6', 185 lbs. Deb: 9/4/1985

YEAR	TM-L	W	L	PCT	G	GS	CG	SH	SV	IP	H	R	ER	HR	HB	BB	SO	RAT	ERA	ERA+	CERA	OAV	BH	AVG	PR+	WS	TPW
1985	Chi-N	1	1	.500	6	5	0	0	0	24	32	18	17	3	0	12	13	1.833	6.38	63	6.89	.352	0	.000	-6	0	-0.7

• ACEVEDO, Jose — Jose Omar Acevedo b: 12/18/1977, Santo Domingo, Dominican Republic BR/TR, 6', 185 lbs. Deb: 6/19/2001

YEAR	TM-L	W	L	PCT	G	GS	CG	SH	SV	IP	H	R	ER	HR	HB	BB	SO	RAT	ERA	ERA+	CERA	OAV	BH	AVG	PR+	WS	TPW
2001	Cin-N	5	7	.417	18	18	0	0	0	96	101	61	58	17	3	34	68	1.406	5.44	84	4.84	.272	4	.118	-8	2	-0.9
2002	Cin-N	4	2	.667	6	5	0	0	0	23^2	28	21	19	8	2	12	14	1.690	7.23	59	7.81	.292	1	.143	-8	0	-0.7
2003	Cin-N	2	0	1.000	5	4	1	0	0	27	17	8	8	3	1	6	23	.852	2.67	160	1.75	.183	0	.000	5	3	0.4
Total	3	11	9	.550	29	27	1	0	0	146^2	146	90	85	28	6	52	105	1.350	5.22	85	4.75	.261	5	.100	-11	5	-1.2

• ACEVEDO, Juan — Juan Carlos Acevedo b: 5/5/1970, Juarez, Mexico BR/TR, 6'2", 195 lbs. Deb: 4/30/1995

YEAR	TM-L	W	L	PCT	G	GS	CG	SH	SV	IP	H	R	ER	HR	HB	BB	SO	RAT	ERA	ERA+	CERA	OAV	BH	AVG	PR+	WS	TPW
1995	Col-N	4	6	.400	17	11	0	0	0	65^2	82	53	47	15	6	20	40	1.553	6.44	84	6.65	.317	1	.056	-6	1	-0.7
1997	NY-N	3	1	.750	25	2	0	0	0	47^2	52	24	19	6	4	22	33	1.552	3.59	113	5.34	.286	0	.000	1	3	0.1
1998	StL-N	8	3	.727	50	9	0	0	15	98^1	83	30	28	7	4	29	56	1.139	2.56	164	2.87	.236	3	.176	18	13	1.8
1999	StL-N	6	8	.429	50	12	0	0	4	102^1	115	71	67	17	4	48	52	1.593	5.89	78	5.78	.291	1	.050	-15	3	-1.6
2000	Mil-N	3	7	.300	62	0	0	0	0	82^2	77	38	35	11	1	31	51	1.306	3.81	119	3.74	.246	0	.000	6	6	0.5
2001	Col-N	0	2	.000	39	0	0	0	0	32	37	24	20	4	1	19	26	1.750	5.63	95	5.62	.285	0	....	-1	1	-0.1
	Fla-N	2	3	.400	20	0	0	0	0	28^1	31	11	8	2	1	16	21	1.659	2.54	166	5.04	.284	1	.333	5	3	0.6
	Yr.	2	5	.286	59	0	0	0	0	60^1	68	35	28	6	2	35	47	1.707	4.18	119	5.34	.285	1	.333	4	4	0.4
2002	Det-A	1	5	.167	65	0	0	0	28	74^2	68	33	22	4	5	23	43	1.219	2.65	162	3.12	.246	0	....	14	12	1.4
2003	NY-A	0	3	.000	25	0	0	0	6	25^2	34	24	22	5	2	10	19	1.714	7.71	57	6.57	.315	0	....	-9	0	-0.9
	Tor-A	1	2	.333	14	0	0	0	0	12^2	18	8	6	1	0	8	9	2.053	4.26	108	7.20	.327	0	....	1	1	0.1
	Yr.	1	5	.167	39	0	0	0	6	38^1	52	32	28	6	2	18	28	1.826	6.57	67	6.78	.319	0	....	-8	1	-0.8
Total	8	28	40	.412	367	34	0	0	53	570	597	316	274	72	28	226	350	1.444	4.33	106	4.72	.274	6	.092	15	43	1.2

• ACKER, Jim — James Justin Acker b: 9/24/1958, Freer, TX BR/TR, 6'2", 212 lbs. Deb: 4/7/1983

YEAR	TM-L	W	L	PCT	G	GS	CG	SH	SV	IP	H	R	ER	HR	HB	BB	SO	RAT	ERA	ERA+	CERA	OAV	BH	AVG	PR+	WS	TPW
1983	Tor-A	5	1	.833	38	5	0	0	1	97^2	103	52	47	7	8	38	44	1.444	4.33	99	4.51	.273	0	....	-0	6	0.0
1984	Tor-A	3	5	.375	32	3	0	0	1	72	79	39	35	3	6	25	33	1.444	4.38	94	4.34	.286	0	....	-3	3	-0.3
1985*	Tor-A	7	2	.778	61	0	0	0	10	86^1	86	35	31	7	3	43	42	1.494	3.23	130	4.59	.268	0	....	8	9	0.8
1986	Tor-A	2	4	.333	23	5	0	0	0	60	63	34	29	6	2	22	32	1.417	4.35	97	4.32	.281	0	....	-1	2	-0.1
	Atl-N	3	8	.273	21	14	0	0	0	95	100	47	40	7	1	26	37	1.326	3.79	105	3.70	.274	3	.107	3	5	0.2
1987	Atl-N	4	9	.308	68	0	0	0	14	114^2	109	57	53	11	4	51	68	1.395	4.16	104	4.08	.253	3	.214	3	10	0.3
1988	Atl-N	0	4	.000	21	1	0	0	0	42	45	26	22	6	1	14	25	1.405	4.71	78	4.45	.280	2	.400	-4	1	-0.4
1989	Atl-N	0	6	.000	59	0	0	0	2	97^2	84	29	29	5	1	20	68	1.065	2.67	137	2.30	.237	1	.143	12	8	1.2
	*Tor-A	2	1	.667	14	0	0	0	0	28^1	24	7	5	1	1	12	24	1.271	1.59	228	2.97	.235	0	....	6	3	0.6
1990	Tor-A	4	4	.500	59	0	0	0	1	91^2	103	49	39	9	3	30	54	1.451	3.83	107	4.50	.281	0	....	3	4	0.3
1991*	Tor-A	3	5	.375	54	4	0	0	1	88^1	77	53	51	16	2	36	44	1.279	5.20	81	3.94	.238	0	....	-9	3	-0.9
1992	Sea-A	0	0	....	17	0	0	0	0	30^2	45	19	18	4	0	12	11	1.859	5.28	75	6.92	.338	0	....	-4	0	-0.4
Total	10	33	49	.402	467	32	0	0	30	904^1	918	447	399	82	32	329	482	1.379	3.97	103	4.09	.267	9	.167	13	54	1.4

• ACKER, Tom — Thomas James Acker b: 3/7/1930, Paterson, NJ BR/TR, 6'4", 215 lbs. Deb: 4/20/1956

YEAR	TM-L	W	L	PCT	G	GS	CG	SH	SV	IP	H	R	ER	HR	HB	BB	SO	RAT	ERA	ERA+	CERA	OAV	BH	AVG	PR+	WS	TPW
1956	Cin-N	4	3	.571	29	7	1	1	1	83^2	60	23	22	7	2	29	54	1.064	2.37	168	2.36	.201	1	.053	16	9	1.5
1957	Cin-N	10	5	.667	49	6	1	0	4	108^2	122	63	60	16	8	41	67	1.500	4.97	83	5.22	.293	1	.053	-11	6	-1.1
1958	Cin-N	4	3	.571	38	10	3	0	1	124^2	126	64	63	10	3	43	90	1.356	4.55	91	3.85	.266	2	.067	-6	5	-0.7
1959	Cin-N	1	2	.333	37	0	0	0	2	63^1	57	31	29	10	4	37	45	1.484	4.12	98	4.88	.246	1	.111	-1	3	-0.1
Total	4	19	13	.594	153	23	5	1	8	380^1	365	181	174	43	17	150	256	1.354	4.12	99	4.09	.257	5	.065	-1	23	-0.4

• ACKLEY, Fritz — Florian Frederick Ackley b: 4/10/1937, Hayward, WI d: 5/22/2002, Duluth, MN BL/TR, 6'1.5", 202 lbs. Deb: 9/21/1963

YEAR	TM-L	W	L	PCT	G	GS	CG	SH	SV	IP	H	R	ER	HR	HB	BB	SO	RAT	ERA	ERA+	CERA	OAV	BH	AVG	PR+	WS	TPW
1963	Chi-A	1	0	1.000	2	2	0	0	0	13	7	4	3	2	0	7	11	1.077	2.08	169	2.60	.167	1	.200	2	1	0.2
1964	Chi-A	0	0	....	3	2	0	0	0	6^1	10	6	6	2	0	4	6	2.211	8.53	41	10.47	.345	1	1.000	-4	0	-0.3
Total	2	1	0	1.000	5	4	0	0	0	19^1	17	10	9	4	0	11	17	1.448	4.19	83	5.18	.239	2	.333	-2	1	-0.1

• ACOSTA, Cy — Cecilio (Miranda) Acosta b: 11/22/1946, Sabino, Mexico BR/TR, 5'10", 165 lbs. Deb: 6/4/1972

YEAR	TM-L	W	L	PCT	G	GS	CG	SH	SV	IP	H	R	ER	HR	HB	BB	SO	RAT	ERA	ERA+	CERA	OAV	BH	AVG	PR+	WS	TPW
1972	Chi-A	3	0	1.000	26	0	0	0	5	34^2	25	6	6	2	0	17	28	1.212	1.56	200	2.65	.210	0	.000	7	6	0.7
1973	Chi-A	10	6	.625	48	0	0	0	18	97	66	30	24	8	7	39	60	1.082	2.23	178	2.52	.193	0	.000	20	15	2.0
1974	Chi-A	0	3	.000	27	0	0	0	3	45^2	43	22	19	3	5	18	19	1.336	3.74	100	3.85	.256	0	.000	0	2	0.0
1975	Phi-N	0	0	....	6	0	0	0	1	8^2	9	7	6	2	0	3	2	1.385	6.23	60	5.19	.273	0	....	-3	0	-0.3
Total	4	13	9	.591	107	0	0	0	27	186	143	65	55	15	12	77	109	1.183	2.66	141	3.00	.216	0	.000	25	23	2.5

• ACOSTA, Ed — Eduardo Elixbet (Lopez) Acosta b: 3/9/1944, Boquete, Panama BB/TR, 6'5", 215 lbs. Deb: 9/7/1970

YEAR	TM-L	W	L	PCT	G	GS	CG	SH	SV	IP	H	R	ER	HR	HB	BB	SO	RAT	ERA	ERA+	CERA	OAV	BH	AVG	PR+	WS	TPW
1970	Pit-N	0	0	....	3	0	0	0	1	2^2	5	4	4	1	1	2	1	2.625	13.50	29	15.82	.417	0	....	-3	0	-0.3
1971	SD-N	3	3	.500	8	6	3	1	0	46	43	18	14	4	0	7	16	1.087	2.74	120	2.69	.246	0	.000	3	3	0.1

YEAR TM-L	W	L	PCT	G	GS	CG	SH	SV	IP	H	R	ER	HR	HB	BB	SO	RAT	ERA	ERA+	CERA	OAV	BH	AVG	PR+	WS	TPW
1972 SD-N	3	6	.333	46	2	0	0	0	89	105	49	44	7	3	30	53	1.517	4.45	74	4.72	.302	1	.083	-10	1	-1.1
Total 3	6	9	.400	57	8	3	1	1	137^2	153	71	62	12	4	39	70	1.395	4.05	82	4.25	.286	1	.034	-10	4	-1.3
• ACOSTA, Jose	Jose "Acostica" Acosta b: 3/4/1891, Havana, Cuba d: 11/16/1977, Havana, Cuba BR/TR, 5'6", 134 lbs. Deb: 7/28/1920																									
1920 Was-A	5	4	.556	17	5	4	1	1	82^2	92	40	37	1	0	26	9	1.427	4.03	92	3.77	.290	6	.240	-2	5	-0.1
1921 Was-A	5	4	.556	33	7	2	0	3	115^2	148	65	56	4	0	36	30	1.591	4.36	94	4.73	.317	2	.067	-5	7	-0.6
1922 Chi-A	0	2	.000	5	1	0	0	0	15	25	14	14	4	0	6	6	2.067	8.40	48	10.21	.417	1	.200	-7	0	-0.7
Total 3	10	10	.500	55	13	6	1	4	213^1	265	119	107	9	0	68	45	1.561	4.51	88	4.74	.314	9	.150	-15	12	-1.4
• ACRE, Mark	Mark Robert Acre b: 9/16/1968, Concord, CA BR/TR, 6'8", 235 lbs. Deb: 5/13/1994																									
1994 Oak-A	5	1	.833	34	0	0	0	0	34^1	24	13	13	4	1	23	21	1.369	3.41	130	3.58	.202	0	....	4	3	0.3
1995 Oak-A	1	2	.333	43	0	0	0	0	52	52	35	33	7	2	28	47	1.538	5.71	78	4.90	.256	0	....	-7	1	-0.7
1996 Oak-A	1	3	.250	22	0	0	0	2	25	38	17	17	4	2	9	18	1.880	6.12	80	7.43	.339	0	....	-4	1	-0.3
1997 Oak-A	2	0	1.000	15	0	0	0	0	15^2	21	10	10	1	0	8	12	1.851	5.74	78	6.19	.318	0	....	-2	1	-0.2
Total 4	9	6	.600	114	0	0	0	2	127	135	75	73	16	5	68	98	1.598	5.17	88	5.20	.270	0	....	-9	6	-0.9
• ADAMS, Ace	Ace Townsend Adams b: 3/2/1912, Willows, CA BR/TR, 5'10.5", 182 lbs. Deb: 4/15/1941																									
1941 NY-N	4	1	.800	38	0	0	0	1	71	84	43	38	3	1	35	18	1.676	4.82	77	5.08	.304	1	.083	-9	3	-1.1
1942 NY-N	7	4	.636	**61**	0	0	0	11	88	69	23	18	1	0	31	33	1.136	1.84	182	2.19	.223	1	.100	14	12	1.4
1943 NY-N★	11	7	.611	**70**	3	1	0	9	140^1	121	50	44	5	1	55	46	1.254	2.82	122	2.85	.236	4	.125	12	13	1.1
1944 NY-N	8	11	.421	**65**	4	1	0	**13**	137^2	149	71	65	8	4	58	32	1.504	4.25	86	4.27	.279	3	.103	-10	8	-1.2
1945 NY-N	11	9	.550	65	0	0	0	**15**	113	109	55	43	7	2	44	39	1.354	3.42	114	3.44	.252	3	.188	6	13	0.6
1946 NY-N	0	1	.000	3	0	0	0	0	2^2	9	5	5	2	0	1	3	3.750	16.88	20	26.82	.500	0	....	-4	0	-0.4
Total 6	41	33	.554	302	7	2	0	49	552^2	541	247	213	26	8	224	171	1.384	3.47	105	3.62	.260	12	.121	8	49	0.5
• ADAMS, Babe	Charles Benjamin Adams b: 5/18/1882, Tipton, IN d: 7/27/1968, Silver Spring, MD BL/TR, 5'11.5", 185 lbs. Deb: 4/18/1906																									
1906 StL-N	0	1	.000	1	1	0	0	0	4	9	8	6	0	0	2	0	2.750	13.50	19	12.41	.474	0	.000	-5	0	-0.5
1907 Pit-N	0	2	.000	4	3	1	0	0	22	40	25	17	1	3	3	11	1.955	6.95	35	8.48	.408	2	.286	-11	0	-1.2
1909* Pit-N	12	3	.800	25	12	7	3	2	130	88	25	16	0	3	23	65	.854	1.11	232	1.38	.196	2	.051	19	16	1.9
1910 Pit-N	18	9	.667	34	30	16	3	0	245	217	95	61	4	6	60	101	1.131	2.24	140	2.48	.240	16	.193	23	21	2.5
1911 Pit-N	22	12	.647	40	37	24	6	0	293^1	253	97	76	5	8	42	133	1.006	2.33	147	2.09	.237	26	.252	30	25	3.5
1912 Pit-N	11	8	.579	28	20	11	2	0	170^1	169	73	55	4	3	35	63	1.198	2.91	112	2.80	.262	12	.226	5	13	0.8
1913 Pit-N	21	10	.677	43	37	24	4	0	313^2	271	94	75	8	0	49	144	1.020	2.15	140	**2.03**	.235	33	.289	33	29	**4.2**
1914 Pit-N	13	16	.448	40	35	19	3	1	283	253	97	79	5	7	39	91	1.032	2.51	105	2.14	.244	16	.165	3	19	0.4
1915 Pit-N	14	14	.500	40	30	17	2	2	245	229	90	78	6	2	34	62	1.073	2.87	95	2.33	.252	12	.141	-3	13	-0.5
1916 Pit-N	2	9	.182	16	10	4	1	0	72^1	91	51	46	2	3	12	22	1.424	5.72	47	4.21	.320	6	.273	-23	1	-2.4
1918 Pit-N	1	1	.500	3	3	2	0	0	22^2	15	4	3	0	0	4	6	.838	1.19	241	1.29	.197	3	.333	3	3	0.5
1919 Pit-N	17	10	.630	34	29	23	6	1	263^1	213	66	58	1	3	23	92	.896	1.98	152	**1.52**	.220	17	.185	32	27	3.5
1920 Pit-N	17	13	.567	35	33	19	**8**	2	263	240	83	63	6	1	18	84	.981	2.16	149	**1.94**	.244	13	.146	32	25	2.9
1921 Pit-N	14	5	.737	25	20	11	2	0	160	155	57	47	4	0	18	55	1.081	2.64	**145**	**2.32**	.251	16	.254	21	18	2.4
1922 Pit-N	8	11	.421	27	19	12	4	0	171^1	191	77	68	1	4	15	39	1.202	3.57	114	2.95	.287	16	.286	12	13	1.5
1923 Pit-N	13	7	.650	26	22	11	0	1	158^2	196	83	78	8	1	25	38	1.393	4.42	90	4.11	.309	15	.273	-10	11	-0.6
1924 Pit-N	3	1	.750	9	3	2	0	0	39^2	31	9	5	1	0	3	5	.857	1.13	338	1.45	.209	2	.182	10	5	1.0
1925* Pit-N	6	5	.545	33	10	3	0	3	101^1	129	67	61	7	3	17	18	1.441	5.42	82	4.48	.306	7	.226	-13	4	-1.2
1926 Pit-N	2	3	.400	19	0	0	0	3	36^2	51	32	25	5	0	8	7	1.609	6.14	64	5.88	.347	2	.222	-10	0	-1.0
Total 19	194	140	.581	482	354	206	44	15	2995^1	2841	1133	917	68	47	430	1036	1.092	2.76	117	2.48	.253	216	.212	149	243	17.8
• ADAMS, Bob	Robert Burdette Adams b: 7/24/1901, Holyoke, MA d: 10/17/1996, Lemoyne, PA BR/TR, 5'11", 168 lbs. Deb: 9/22/1925																									
1925 Bos-A	0	0	....	2	0	0	0	0	5^2	10	5	5	1	0	3	1	2.294	7.94	57	10.53	.417	1	.333	-2	0	-0.2
• ADAMS, Bob	Robert Andrew Adams b: 1/20/1907, Birmingham, AL d: 3/6/1970, Jacksonville, FL BR/TR, 6'.5", 165 lbs. Deb: 9/27/1931																									
1931 Phi-N	0	1	.000	1	1	0	0	0	6	14	10	6	0	0	1	3	2.500	9.00	47	9.80	.424	0	.000	-3	0	-0.3
1932 Phi-N	0	0	....	4	0	0	0	0	6	7	1	1	0	0	2	2	1.500	1.50	294	4.18	.318	0	....	2	1	0.2
Total 2	0	1	.000	5	1	0	0	0	12	21	11	7	0	0	3	5	2.000	5.25	81	6.99	.382	0	.000	-1	1	-0.2
• ADAMS, Dan	Daniel Leslie "Rube" Adams b: 6/19/1887, St. Louis, MO d: 10/6/1964, St. Louis, MO BR/TR, 5'11.5", 165 lbs. Deb: 5/22/1914																									
1914 KC-F	4	9	.308	36	14	6	0	3	136	141	67	53	3	7	52	38	1.419	3.51	88	3.87	.273	7	.152	-7	5	-0.8
1915 KC-F	0	2	.000	11	2	0	0	0	35	41	20	18	2	1	13	16	1.543	4.63	63	4.64	.301	1	.111	-6	0	-0.7
Total 2	4	11	.267	47	16	6	0	3	171	182	87	71	5	8	65	54	1.444	3.74	81	4.03	.279	8	.145	-14	5	-1.6
• ADAMS, Joe	Joseph Edward Adams b: 10/28/1877, Cowden, IL d: 10/8/1952, Montgomery City, MO BR/TL, 6', 190 lbs. Deb: 4/26/1902																									
1902 StL-N	0	0	....	1	0	0	0	0	4	9	6	4	0	1	2	0	2.750	9.00	30	12.68	.442	0	.000	-3	0	-0.3
• ADAMS, Karl	Karl Tutwiler "Rebel" Adams b: 8/11/1891, Columbus, GA d: 9/17/1967, Everett, WA BR/TR, 6'2", 170 lbs. Deb: 4/19/1914																									
1914 Cin-N	0	0	....	4	0	0	0	0	8	14	10	8	0	0	5	5	2.375	9.00	33	8.83	.424	1	.500	-5	0	-0.5
1915 Chi-N	1	9	.100	26	12	3	0	0	107	105	62	56	5	2	43	57	1.383	4.71	59	3.56	.267	0	.000	-21	0	-2.8
Total 2	1	9	.100	30	12	3	0	0	115	119	72	64	5	2	48	62	1.452	5.01	56	3.93	.279	1	.031	-27	0	-3.4
• ADAMS, Red	Charles Dwight Adams b: 10/7/1921, Parlier, CA BR/TR, 6', 185 lbs. Deb: 5/5/1946 C																									
1946 Chi-N	0	1	.000	8	0	0	0	0	12	18	12	11	1	0	7	8	2.083	8.25	40	7.66	.353	0	.000	-6	0	-0.7
• ADAMS, Rick	Reuben Alexander Adams b: 12/24/1878, Paris, TX d: 3/10/1955, Paris, TX BL/TL, 6', 165 lbs. Deb: 7/13/1905																									
1905 Was-A	2	5	.286	11	6	3	1	0	62^2	63	30	25	1	8	24	25	1.388	3.59	74	3.79	.264	4	.174	-8	2	-0.8
• ADAMS, Terry	Terry Wayne Adams b: 3/6/1973, Mobile, AL BR/TR, 6'3", 205 lbs. Deb: 8/10/1995																									
1995 Chi-N	1	1	.500	18	0	0	0	1	18	22	15	13	0	0	10	15	1.778	6.50	63	4.95	.289	0	....	-5	0	-0.5
1996 Chi-N	3	6	.333	69	0	0	0	4	101	84	36	33	6	1	49	78	1.317	2.94	148	3.20	.231	0	.000	14	9	1.4
1997 Chi-N	2	9	.182	74	0	0	0	18	74	91	43	38	3	1	40	64	1.770	4.62	93	5.49	.306	0	.000	-3	5	-0.3
1998 Chi-N	7	7	.500	63	0	0	0	1	72^2	72	39	35	7	1	41	73	1.555	4.33	102	4.55	.255	0	.000	2	5	0.2
1999 Chi-N	6	3	.667	52	0	0	0	13	65	60	33	29	9	0	28	57	1.354	4.02	113	4.00	.245	0	.000	4	9	0.4
2000 LA-N	6	9	.400	66	0	0	0	2	84^1	80	42	33	6	0	39	56	1.411	3.52	123	3.77	.245	0	.000	8	6	0.7
2001 LA-N	12	8	.600	43	22	0	0	0	166^1	172	84	80	9	3	54	141	1.359	4.33	93	3.74	.267	2	.051	-5	8	-0.7
2002 Phi-N	7	9	.438	46	19	0	0	0	136^2	132	76	66	9	3	58	96	1.390	4.35	90	3.77	.255	2	.080	-8	5	-0.8
2003 Phi-N	1	4	.200	66	0	0	0	0	68	68	22	20	1	2	23	51	1.338	2.65	151	3.35	.268	0	.000	10	7	1.0
Total 9	45	56	.446	497	41	0	0	39	786	781	390	347	50	11	342	631	1.429	3.97	105	3.93	.260	4	.051	19	54	1.4
• ADAMS, Willie	William Edward Adams b: 10/8/1972, Gallup, NM BR/TR, 6'7", 215 lbs. Deb: 6/11/1996																									
1996 Oak-A	3	4	.429	12	12	1	1	0	76^1	76	39	34	11	5	23	68	1.297	4.01	122	4.13	.257	0	....	7	5	0.6
1997 Oak-A	3	5	.375	13	12	0	0	0	58^1	73	53	53	9	4	32	37	1.800	8.18	55	6.75	.307	0	....	-22	0	-2.1
Total 2	6	9	.400	25	24	1	1	0	134^2	149	92	87	20	9	55	105	1.515	5.81	80	5.26	.279	0	....	-16	5	-1.5
• ADAMS, Willie	James Irvin Adams b: 9/27/1890, Clearfield, PA d: 6/18/1937, Albany, NY BR/TR, 6'4", 180 lbs. Deb: 6/30/1912																									
1912 StL-A	2	3	.400	13	5	0	0	0	46^1	50	32	20	0	2	19	16	1.489	3.88	86	4.05	.284	0	.000	-3	1	-0.6
1913 StL-A	0	0	....	4	0	0	0	0	9	12	14	10	1	3	4	5	1.778	10.00	29	6.87	.286	0	.000	-7	0	-0.7
1914 Pit-F	1	1	.500	15	2	1	0	2	55^1	70	29	23	4	1	22	14	1.663	3.74	82	5.72	.326	1	.067	-4	2	-0.5
1918 Phi-A	5	12	.294	32	14	7	0	0	169	164	95	83	2	12	97	39	**1.544**	4.42	66	4.20	.272	8	.140	-33	2	-4.0
1919 Phi-A	0	0	....	1	0	0	0	0	4^2	7	2	2	1	1	2	0	1.929	3.86	89	10.17	.389	0	.000	-0	0	0.0
Total 5	8	16	.333	65	21	8	0	2	284^1	303	172	138	8	19	144	74	1.572	4.37	69	4.65	.288	9	.102	-48	5	-5.9
• ADAMSON, Joel	Joel Lee Adamson b: 7/2/1971, Lakewood, CA BL/TL, 6'4", 185 lbs. Deb: 4/10/1996																									
1996 Fla-N	0	0	....	9	0	0	0	0	11	18	9	9	1	1	7	7	2.273	7.36	55	9.71	.400	0	....	-4	0	-0.4

YEAR TM-L	W	L	PCT	G	GS	CG	SH	SV	IP	H	R	ER	HR	HB	BB	SO	RAT	ERA	ERA+	CERA	OAV	BH	AVG	PR+	WS	TPW
1997 Mil-A	5	3	.625	30	6	0	0	0	76^1	78	36	30	13	5	19	56	1.271	3.54	131	4.35	.265	0	.000	7	6	0.6
1998 Ari-N	0	3	.000	5	5	0	0	0	23	25	21	21	5	3	11	14	1.565	8.22	51	6.48	.284	3	.429	-10	0	-0.9
Total 3	5	6	.455	44	11	0	0	0	110^1	121	66	60	19	9	37	77	1.432	4.89	90	5.33	.283	3	.300	-8	6	-0.7
• ADAMSON, Mike	John Michael Adamson b: 9/13/1947, San Diego, CA BR/TR, 6'2", 185 lbs. Deb: 7/1/1967																									
1967 Bal-A	0	1	.000	3	2	0	0	0	9^2	9	9	9	1	0	12	8	2.172	8.38	38	7.27	.257	1	.500	-6	0	-0.5
1968 Bal-A	0	2	.000	2	2	0	0	0	7^2	9	9	8	2	0	4	4	1.696	9.39	31	6.72	.281	1	.333	-6	0	-0.6
1969 Bal-A	0	1	.000	6	0	0	0	0	8	10	4	4	0	0	6	2	2.000	4.50	79	5.79	.357	0	.000	-1	0	-0.1
Total 3	0	4	.000	11	4	0	0	0	25^1	28	22	21	3	0	22	14	1.974	7.46	42	6.64	.295	2	.333	-13	0	-1.3
• ADKINS, Dewey	John Dewey Adkins b: 5/11/1918, Norcatur, KS d: 12/26/1998, Santa Monica, CA BR/TR, 6'2", 195 lbs. Deb: 9/19/1942																									
1942 Was-A	0	0	....	1	1	0	0	0	6^1	7	8	7	0	0	6	3	2.053	9.95	37	5.41	.259	1	.500	-4	0	-0.4
1943 Was-A	0	0	....	7	0	0	0	0	10^1	9	3	3	0	0	5	1	1.355	2.61	123	3.14	.250	0	....	1	1	0.1
1949 Chi-N	2	4	.333	30	5	1	0	0	82^1	98	58	52	10	0	39	43	1.664	5.68	71	5.49	.298	4	.200	-13	1	-1.2
Total 3	2	4	.333	38	6	1	0	0	99	114	69	62	10	0	50	47	1.657	5.64	70	5.24	.291	5	.227	-17	2	-1.5
• ADKINS, Doc	Merle Theron Adkins b: 8/5/1872, Troy, WI d: 2/21/1934, Durham, NC BR/TR, 5'10.5", 220 lbs. Deb: 6/24/1902																									
1902 Bos-A	1	1	.500	4	2	1	0	0	20	30	20	9	2	0	7	3	1.850	4.05	88	6.78	.346	2	.222	-2	0	-0.2
1903 NY-A	0	0	....	2	1	0	0	1	7	10	8	6	0	1	5	0	2.143	7.71	40	7.23	.334	0	.000	-4	0	-0.4
Total 2	1	1	.500	6	3	1	0	1	27	40	28	15	2	1	12	3	1.926	5.00	68	6.90	.343	2	.167	-5	0	-0.6
• ADKINS, Grady	Grady Emmett "Butcher Boy" Adkins b: 6/29/1897, Jacksonville, AR d: 3/31/1966, Little Rock, AR BR/TR, 5'11", 175 lbs. Deb: 4/13/1928																									
1928 Chi-A	10	16	.385	36	27	14	0	1	224^2	235	113	93	12	6	89	54	1.442	3.73	109	3.96	.278	10	.143	7	13	0.4
1929 Chi-A	2	11	.154	31	15	5	0	0	138^1	168	98	82	12	1	67	24	1.699	5.33	80	5.42	.303	11	.239	-18	3	-1.4
Total 2	12	27	.308	67	42	19	0	1	363	403	211	175	24	7	156	78	1.540	4.34	96	4.51	.288	21	.181	-11	16	-1.1
• ADKINS, Jon	Jonathan Scott Adkins b: 8/30/1977, Huntington, WV BL/TR, 6', 200 lbs. Deb: 8/14/2003																									
2003 Chi-A	0	0	....	4	0	0	0	0	9^1	8	5	5	1	1	7	3	1.607	4.82	93	5.27	.250	0	....	-0	0	0.0
• ADKINS, Steve	Steven Thomas Adkins b: 10/26/1964, Chicago, IL BR/TL, 6'6", 210 lbs. Deb: 9/12/1990																									
1990 NY-A	1	2	.333	5	5	0	0	0	24	19	18	17	4	0	29	14	2.000	6.38	62	6.83	.226	0	....	-6	0	-0.7
• AFFELDT, Jeremy	Jeremy David Affeldt b: 6/6/1979, Phoenix, AZ BL/TL, 6'4", 215 lbs. Deb: 4/6/2002																									
2002 KC-A	3	4	.429	34	7	0	0	0	77^2	85	41	40	8	3	37	67	1.571	4.64	108	4.97	.274	0	....	4	5	0.4
2003 KC-A	7	6	.538	36	18	0	0	4	126	126	58	55	12	5	38	98	1.302	3.93	132	3.82	.261	2	.333	17	12	1.7
Total 2	10	10	.500	70	25	0	0	4	203^2	211	99	95	20	8	75	165	1.404	4.20	122	4.26	.266	2	.333	21	17	2.1
• AGOSTO, Juan	Juan Roberto (Gonzalez) Agosto b: 2/23/1958, Rio Piedras, Puerto Rico BL/TL, 6'2", 190 lbs. Deb: 9/7/1981																									
1981 Chi-A	0	0	....	2	0	0	0	0	5^2	5	3	3	1	1	0	3	.882	4.76	75	3.16	.238	0	....	-1	0	-0.1
1982 Chi-A	0	0	....	1	0	0	0	0	2	7	4	4	0	0	0	1	3.500	18.00	22	18.39	.538	0	....	-3	0	-0.3
1983* Chi-A	2	2	.500	39	0	0	0	7	41^2	41	20	19	2	1	11	29	1.248	4.10	102	3.36	.283	0	....	0	4	0.0
1984 Chi-A	2	1	.667	49	0	0	0	7	55^1	54	20	19	2	3	34	26	1.590	3.09	135	4.43	.270	0	....	6	6	0.6
1985 Chi-A	4	3	.571	54	0	0	0	1	60^1	45	27	24	3	3	23	39	1.127	3.58	121	2.52	.210	0	....	5	4	0.5
1986 Chi-A	0	2	.000	9	0	0	0	0	4^2	6	5	4	0	0	4	3	2.143	7.71	56	6.63	.300	0	....	-2	0	-0.2
Min-A	1	2	.333	17	1	0	0	1	20^1	43	25	20	1	2	14	9	2.803	8.85	49	12.94	.443	0	....	-10	0	-1.0
Yr.	1	4	.200	26	1	0	0	1	25	49	30	24	1	2	18	12	2.680	8.64	50	11.76	.419	0	....	-12	0	-1.2
1987 Hou-N	1	1	.500	27	0	0	0	2	27^1	26	12	8	1	0	10	6	1.317	2.63	149	3.11	.248	0	.000	4	3	0.4
1988 Hou-N	10	2	.833	75	0	0	0	4	91^2	74	27	23	6	0	30	33	1.135	2.26	147	2.38	.226	0	.000	11	11	1.2
1989 Hou-N	4	5	.444	71	0	0	0	1	83	81	32	27	3	2	32	46	1.361	2.93	116	3.28	.256	1	.200	5	6	0.5
1990 Hou-N	9	8	.529	**82**	0	0	0	4	92^1	91	46	44	4	7	39	50	1.408	4.29	87	3.83	.261	0	.000	-6	5	-0.7
1991 StL-N	5	3	.625	72	0	0	0	2	86	92	52	46	4	8	39	34	1.523	4.81	77	4.71	.291	1	.333	-11	2	-1.1
1992 StL-N	2	4	.333	22	0	0	0	0	31^2	39	24	22	2	3	9	13	1.516	6.25	54	4.92	.312	0	.000	-11	0	-1.2
Sea-A	0	0	....	17	1	0	0	0	18^1	27	12	12	0	0	3	12	1.636	5.89	67	5.02	.346	0	....	-4	0	-0.4
1993 Hou-N	0	0	....	6	0	0	0	0	6	8	4	4	1	0	0	3	1.333	6.00	65	4.69	.308	0	....	-1	0	-0.1
Total 13	40	33	.548	543	2	0	0	29	626^1	639	313	279	30	30	248	307	1.416	4.01	94	3.99	.272	2	.100	-18	41	-1.9
• AGUILERA, Rick	Richard Warren Aguilera b: 12/31/1961, San Gabriel, CA BR/TR, 6'4", 205 lbs. Deb: 6/12/1985																									
1985 NY-N	10	7	.588	21	19	2	0	0	122^1	118	49	44	8	2	37	74	1.267	3.24	107	3.36	.258	10	.278	4	8	0.7
1986* NY-N	10	7	.588	28	20	2	0	0	141^2	145	70	61	15	7	36	104	1.278	3.88	91	3.83	.263	8	.157	-6	6	-0.4
1987 NY-N	11	3	.786	18	17	1	0	0	115	124	53	46	12	3	33	77	1.365	3.60	105	4.18	.276	9	.225	4	8	0.6
1988* NY-N	0	4	.000	11	3	0	0	0	24^2	29	20	19	2	1	10	16	1.581	6.93	46	5.00	.296	1	.250	-10	0	-1.1
1989 NY-N	6	6	.500	36	0	0	0	7	69^1	59	19	18	3	2	21	80	1.154	2.34	140	2.60	.231	0	.000	8	7	0.8
Min-A	3	5	.375	11	11	3	0	0	75^2	71	32	27	5	1	17	57	1.163	3.21	129	2.89	.245	0	....	8	5	0.8
1990 Min-A	5	3	.625	56	0	0	0	32	65^1	55	27	20	5	4	19	61	1.133	2.76	151	2.77	.224	0	....	10	12	1.0
1991* Min-A★	4	5	.444	63	0	0	0	42	69	44	20	18	3	1	30	61	1.072	2.35	182	1.95	.183	0	....	14	15	1.4
1992 Min-A★	2	6	.250	64	0	0	0	41	66^2	60	28	21	7	1	17	52	1.155	2.84	143	2.99	.238	0	....	9	11	0.9
1993 Min-A★	4	3	.571	65	0	0	0	34	72^1	60	25	25	9	1	14	59	1.023	3.11	140	2.55	.223	0	....	11	14	1.0
1994 Min-A	1	4	.200	44	0	0	0	23	44^2	57	23	18	7	0	10	46	1.500	3.63	134	5.13	.306	0	....	7	6	0.6
1995 Min-A	1	1	.500	22	0	0	0	12	25	20	7	7	2	1	6	29	1.040	2.52	189	2.44	.222	0	....	6	5	0.6
*Bos-A	2	2	.500	30	0	0	0	20	30^1	26	9	9	4	0	7	23	1.088	2.67	182	2.81	.228	0	....	7	6	0.7
Yr.	3	3	.500	52	0	0	0	32	55^1	46	16	16	6	1	13	52	1.066	2.60	185	2.65	.225	0	....	14	11	1.3
1996 Min-A	8	6	.571	19	19	2	0	0	111^1	124	69	67	20	3	27	83	1.356	5.42	95	4.68	.276	0	....	-5	6	-0.4
1997 Min-A	5	4	.556	61	0	0	0	26	68^1	65	29	29	9	2	22	68	1.273	3.82	122	3.81	.257	0	....	6	9	0.6
1998 Min-A	4	9	.308	68	0	0	0	38	74^1	75	35	35	8	1	15	57	1.211	4.24	113	3.45	.262	0	....	6	12	0.5
1999 Min-A	3	1	.750	17	0	0	0	6	21^1	10	3	3	2	0	2	13	.563	1.27	401	0.86	.135	0	....	9	6	0.8
Chi-N	6	3	.667	44	0	0	0	8	46^1	44	22	19	6	2	10	32	1.165	3.69	122	3.42	.254	0	.000	5	7	0.4
2000 Chi-N	1	2	.333	54	0	0	0	29	47^2	47	28	26	11	4	18	38	1.364	4.91	92	5.06	.251	0	....	-2	4	-0.2
Total 16	86	81	.515	732	89	10	0	318	1291^1	1233	568	512	138	36	351	1030	1.227	3.57	115	3.47	.251	28	.201	90	147	9.6
• AGUIRRE, Hank	Henry John Aguirre b: 1/31/1931, Azusa, CA d: 9/5/1994, Bloomfield Hills, MI BR/TL, 6'4", 205 lbs. Deb: 9/10/1955 C																									
1955 Cle-A	2	0	1.000	4	1	1	1	0	12^2	6	3	2	0	0	12	6	1.421	1.42	281	2.62	.143	0	.000	4	2	0.3
1956 Cle-A	3	5	.375	16	9	2	1	1	65^1	63	35	27	7	1	27	31	1.378	3.72	113	4.00	.253	2	.111	4	3	0.2
1957 Cle-A	1	1	.500	10	1	0	0	0	20^1	26	15	13	0	0	13	9	1.918	5.75	65	5.42	.317	0	.000	-4	0	-0.5
1958 Det-A	3	4	.429	44	3	0	0	5	69^2	67	31	29	5	1	27	38	1.349	3.75	108	3.61	.255	3	.214	2	5	0.2
1959 Det-A	0	0	....	3	0	0	0	0	2^2	4	1	1	0	0	3	3	2.625	3.38	120	9.81	.364	0	....	0	0	0.0
1960 Det-A	5	3	.625	37	6	1	0	10	94^2	75	31	30	7	3	30	80	1.109	2.85	145	2.60	.217	1	.036	14	11	1.1
1961 Det-A	4	4	.500	45	0	0	0	8	55^1	44	22	20	5	2	38	32	1.482	3.25	126	4.04	.224	0	.000	5	6	0.4
1962 Det-A★	16	8	.667	42	22	11	2	3	216	162	67	53	14	5	65	156	1.051	**2.21**	**184**	**2.20**	**.205**	2	.027	**47**	22	**3.9**
1963 Det-A	14	15	.483	38	33	14	3	0	225^2	222	96	92	25	8	68	134	1.285	3.67	102	3.80	.256	10	.132	2	12	0.0
1964 Det-A	5	10	.333	32	27	3	0	1	161^2	134	76	68	15	8	59	88	1.194	3.79	97	3.10	.223	3	.057	-3	7	-0.7
1965 Det-A	14	10	.583	32	32	10	2	0	208^1	185	89	83	24	10	60	141	1.176	3.59	97	3.26	.236	6	.086	-1	12	-0.4
1966 Det-A	3	9	.250	30	14	2	0	0	103^2	104	50	44	14	3	26	50	1.254	3.82	91	3.82	.260	3	.120	-4	4	-0.4
1967 Det-A	0	1	.000	31	1	0	0	0	41^1	34	15	11	2	0	17	33	1.234	2.40	136	2.71	.219	1	.500	4	3	0.5
1968 LA-N	1	2	.333	25	0	0	0	3	39^1	32	8	3	0	3	13	25	1.144	0.69	403	2.27	.227	0	.000	9	5	1.0
1969 Chi-N	1	0	1.000	41	0	0	0	1	45	45	13	13	2	2	12	19	1.267	2.60	155	3.40	.269	2	.400	7	5	0.8
1970 Chi-N	3	0	1.000	17	0	0	0	1	14	13	10	7	3	1	9	11	1.571	4.50	100	5.65	.250	0	.000	-0	1	0.0
Total 16	75	72	.510	447	149	44	9	33	1375^2	1216	562	496	123	47	479	856	1.232	3.24	116	3.27	.236	33	.085	83	98	6.5
• AHEARNE, Pat	Patrick Howard Ahearne b: 12/10/1969, San Francisco, CA BR/TR, 6'3", 195 lbs. Deb: 6/14/1995																									
1995 Det-A	0	2	.000	4	3	0	0	0	10	20	13	13	2	0	5	4	2.500	11.70	41	11.49	.400	0	....	-8	0	-0.7

YEAR	TM-L	W	L	PCT	G	GS	CG	SH	SV	IP	H	R	ER	HR	HB	BB	SO	RAT	ERA	ERA+	CERA	OAV	BH	AVG	PR+	WS	TPW
• AINSWORTH, Kurt	Kurt Harold Ainsworth b: 9/9/1978, Baton Rouge, LA BR/TR, 6'3", 192 lbs. Deb: 9/5/2001																										
2001	SF-N	0	0	....	2	0	0	0	0	2	3	3	3	1	1	2	3	2.500	13.50	29	16.26	.333	0	....	-2	0	-0.2
2002	SF-N	1	2	.333	6	4	0	0	0	25^2	22	7	6	1	1	12	15	1.325	2.10	184	3.34	.237	1	.167	5	2	0.5
2003	SF-N	5	4	.556	11	11	0	0	0	66	66	31	28	7	1	26	48	1.394	3.82	107	4.19	.262	1	.045	1	4	-0.1
	Bal-A	0	1	.000	3	0	0	0	0	2^1	6	3	3	1	0	1	4	3.000	11.57	38	16.91	.429	0	....	-2	0	-0.2
Total	3	6	7	.462	22	15	0	0	0	96	97	44	40	10	3	41	70	1.438	3.75	109	4.52	.264	2	.071	1	6	0.0
• AITCHISON, Raleigh	Raleigh Leonidas Aitchison b: 12/5/1887, Tyndall, SD d: 9/26/1958, Columbus, KS BR/TL, 5'11.5", 175 lbs. Deb: 4/19/1911																										
1911	Bro-N	0	1	.000	1	0	0	0	0	1^1	1	2	0	0	0	1	0	1.500	0.00	....	3.02	.200	0	....	0	0	0.1
1914	Bro-N	12	7	.632	26	17	8	3	0	172^1	156	71	51	4	3	60	87	1.253	2.66	107	2.84	.244	10	.196	3	11	0.5
1915	Bro-N	0	4	.000	7	5	2	0	0	32^2	36	25	18	3	2	6	14	1.286	4.96	56	3.67	.267	0	.000	-8	0	-0.9
Total	3	12	12	.500	34	22	10	3	0	206^1	193	98	69	7	5	67	101	1.260	3.01	94	2.97	.248	10	.169	-5	11	-0.4
• AKER, Jack	Jackie Delane Aker b: 7/13/1940, Tulare, CA BR/TR, 6'2", 190 lbs. Deb: 5/3/1964 C																										
1964	KC-A	0	1	.000	9	0	0	0	0	16^1	17	18	16	6	6	10	7	1.653	8.82	43	9.00	.266	0	.000	-9	0	-1.0
1965	KC-A	4	3	.571	34	0	0	0	3	51^1	45	18	18	3	3	18	26	1.227	3.16	111	3.08	.242	0	.000	2	4	0.1
1966	KC-A	8	4	.667	66	0	0	0	**32**	113	81	27	25	6	3	28	68	.965	1.99	171	1.80	.201	2	.095	17	20	1.7
1967	KC-A	3	8	.273	57	0	0	0	12	88	87	44	42	9	3	32	65	1.352	4.30	74	3.93	.264	1	.125	-11	3	-1.2
1968	Oak-A	4	4	.500	54	0	0	0	11	74^2	72	39	34	6	6	33	44	1.406	4.10	69	4.04	.258	1	.143	-11	2	-1.2
1969	Sea-A	0	2	.000	15	0	0	0	3	16^2	25	15	14	4	1	13	7	2.280	7.56	48	10.17	.357	0	.000	-7	0	-0.7
	NY-A	8	4	.667	38	0	0	0	11	65^2	51	17	15	4	4	22	40	1.112	2.06	169	2.59	.217	1	.111	10	12	1.0
	Yr.	8	6	.571	53	0	0	0	14	82^1	76	32	29	8	5	35	47	1.348	3.17	112	4.12	.249	1	.100	3	12	0.3
1970	NY-A	4	2	.667	41	0	0	0	16	70	57	19	16	3	4	20	36	1.100	2.06	171	2.43	.226	1	.063	11	10	1.0
1971	NY-A	4	4	.500	41	0	0	0	4	55^2	48	20	16	3	0	26	24	1.329	2.59	125	3.00	.238	0	.000	4	5	0.4
1972	NY-A	0	0	....	4	0	0	0	0	6	5	2	2	0	1	3	1	1.333	3.00	98	3.50	.238	0	....	-0	0	0.0
	Chi-N	6	6	.500	48	0	0	0	17	67	65	31	22	4	5	23	36	1.313	2.96	129	3.56	.259	0	.000	6	8	0.6
1973	Chi-N	4	5	.444	47	0	0	0	12	63^2	76	33	29	8	2	23	25	1.555	4.10	96	5.29	.308	0	.000	0	5	0.0
1974	Atl-N	0	1	.000	17	0	0	0	0	16^2	17	11	7	3	0	9	7	1.560	3.78	100	5.42	.298	0	.000	-0	0	0.0
	NY-N	2	1	.667	24	0	0	0	2	41^1	33	18	16	4	2	14	18	1.137	3.48	102	2.83	.213	1	.500	0	4	0.1
	Yr.	2	2	.500	41	0	0	0	2	58	50	29	23	7	2	23	25	1.259	3.57	102	3.58	.236	1	.333	-0	4	0.1
Total	11	47	45	.511	495	0	0	0	123	746	679	312	272	63	40	274	404	1.277	3.28	104	3.53	.247	7	.076	14	73	0.9
• AKERFELDS, Darrel	Darrel Wayne Akerfelds b: 6/12/1962, Denver, CO BR/TR, 6'2", 210 lbs. Deb: 8/1/1986 C																										
1986	Oak-A	0	0	....	2	0	0	0	0	5^1	7	5	4	2	0	3	5	1.875	6.75	57	8.41	.304	0	....	-2	0	-0.2
1987	Cle-A	2	6	.250	16	13	1	0	0	74^2	84	60	56	18	7	38	42	1.634	6.75	67	6.72	.284	0	....	-17	0	-1.7
1989	Tex-A	0	1	.000	6	0	0	0	0	11	11	6	4	1	0	5	9	1.455	3.27	121	3.74	.250	0	....	1	0	0.1
1990	Phi-N	5	2	.714	71	0	0	0	3	93	65	45	39	10	3	54	42	1.280	3.77	101	3.16	.201	1	.167	-1	7	-0.1
1991	Phi-N	2	1	.667	30	0	0	0	0	49^2	49	30	29	5	3	27	31	1.530	5.26	70	4.54	.257	0	.000	-9	1	-0.9
Total	5	9	10	.474	125	13	1	0	3	233^2	216	146	132	36	13	127	129	1.468	5.08	80	4.74	.246	1	.111	-27	8	-2.7
• AKERS, Jerry	Albert Earl Akers b: 11/1/1887, Shelbyville, IN d: 5/15/1979, Bay Pines, FL BR/TR, 5'11", 175 lbs. Deb: 5/4/1912																										
1912	Was-A	1	1	.500	5	1	0	0	0	20^1	24	17	11	1	2	15	11	1.918	4.87	69	6.42	.300	2	.333	-4	0	-0.4
• ALBA, Gibson	Gibson Alberto (Rosado) Alba b: 1/18/1960, Santiago, Dominican Republic BL/TL, 6'2", 160 lbs. Deb: 5/3/1988																										
1988	StL-N	0	0	....	3	0	0	0	0	3^1	1	2	1	0	0	2	3	.900	2.70	129	0.97	.091	0	....	0	0	0.0
• ALBANESE, Joe	Joseph Peter Albanese b: 6/26/1933, New York, NY d: 6/17/2000, New York, NY BR/TR, 6'3", 215 lbs. Deb: 7/18/1958																										
1958	Was-A	0	0	....	6	0	0	0	0	6	8	3	3	1	0	2	3	1.667	4.50	85	6.38	.348	0	....	-0	0	0.0
• ALBERRO, Jose	Jose Edgardo Alberro b: 6/29/1969, San Juan, Puerto Rico BR/TR, 6'2", 190 lbs. Deb: 4/27/1995																										
1995	Tex-A	0	0	....	12	0	0	0	0	20^2	26	18	17	2	1	12	10	1.839	7.40	65	6.28	.299	0	....	-6	0	-0.5
1996	Tex-A	0	1	.000	5	1	0	0	0	9^1	14	6	6	1	0	7	2	2.250	5.79	91	8.88	.368	0	....	-1	0	-0.1
1997	Tex-A	0	3	.000	10	4	0	0	0	28^1	37	33	25	4	1	17	11	1.906	7.94	60	6.85	.303	0	....	-10	0	-0.9
Total	3	0	4	.000	27	5	0	0	0	58^1	77	57	48	7	2	36	23	1.937	7.41	66	6.97	.312	0	....	-16	0	-1.5
• ALBERTS, Cy	Frederick Joseph Alberts b: 1/14/1882, Grand Rapids, MI d: 8/27/1917, Fort Wayne, IN BR/TR, 6', 230 lbs. Deb: 9/17/1910																										
1910	StL-N	1	2	.333	4	3	2	0	0	27^2	35	22	19	1	0	20	10	1.988	6.18	48	6.69	.330	0	.000	-9	0	-1.0
• ALBOSTA, Ed	Edward John "Rube" Albosta b: 10/27/1918, Saginaw, MI d: 1/7/2003, Saginaw, MI BR/TR, 6'1", 175 lbs. Deb: 9/3/1941																										
1941	Bro-N	0	2	.000	2	2	0	0	0	13	11	9	9	1	0	8	5	1.462	6.23	59	3.87	.239	0	.000	-4	0	-0.5
1946	Pit-N	0	6	.000	17	6	0	0	0	39^2	41	34	27	3	1	35	19	1.916	6.13	58	5.73	.266	1	.125	-11	0	-1.2
Total	2	0	8	.000	19	8	0	0	0	52^2	52	43	36	4	1	43	24	1.804	6.15	58	5.27	.260	1	.083	-15	0	-1.7
• ALBRECHT, Ed	Edward Arthur Albrecht b: 2/28/1929, St. Louis, MO d: 12/29/1979, Centerville, IA BR/TR, 5'10.5", 165 lbs. Deb: 10/2/1949																										
1949	StL-A	1	0	1.000	1	1	1	0	0	5	1	3	3	0	0	4	1	1.000	5.40	84	1.02	.063	0	.000	-0	0	0.0
1950	StL-A	0	1	.000	2	1	0	0	0	6^2	6	7	4	0	0	7	1	1.950	5.40	92	4.94	.250	0	.000	-0	0	0.0
Total	2	1	1	.500	3	2	1	0	0	11^2	7	10	7	0	0	11	2	1.543	5.40	88	3.26	.175	0	.000	-0	0	-0.1
• ALBURY, Vic	Victor Albury b: 5/12/1947, Key West, FL BL/TL, 6', 190 lbs. Deb: 8/7/1973																										
1973	Min-A	1	0	1.000	14	0	0	0	0	23^1	13	7	7	1	0	19	13	1.371	2.70	147	2.85	.169	0	....	3	2	0.3
1974	Min-A	8	9	.471	32	22	4	1	0	164	159	83	75	19	6	80	85	1.457	4.12	91	4.61	.259	0	....	-5	7	-0.6
1975	Min-A	6	7	.462	32	15	2	0	1	135	115	82	68	16	4	97	72	1.570	4.53	85	4.75	.237	0	.000	-9	4	-0.9
1976	Min-A	3	1	.750	23	0	0	0	0	50^1	51	22	20	0	2	24	23	1.490	3.58	101	3.79	.271	0	....	0	3	0.0
Total	4	18	17	.514	101	37	6	1	1	372^2	338	194	170	36	12	220	193	1.497	4.11	92	4.44	.248	0	.000	-11	16	-1.1
• ALCALA, Santo	Santo Alcala b: 12/23/1952, San Pedro de Macoris, Dominican Republic BR/TR, 6'5", 195 lbs. Deb: 4/10/1976																										
1976	Cin-N	11	4	.733	30	21	3	1	0	132	131	72	69	12	3	67	67	1.500	4.70	74	4.45	.261	6	.140	-19	3	-2.0
1977	Cin-N	1	1	.500	7	2	0	0	0	15^2	22	11	10	1	1	7	9	1.851	5.74	68	6.74	.349	0	.000	-3	0	-0.4
	Mon-N	2	6	.250	31	10	0	0	2	101^2	104	55	53	12	2	47	64	1.485	4.69	81	4.59	.263	2	.080	-10	3	-1.1
	Yr.	3	7	.300	38	12	0	0	2	117^1	126	66	63	13	3	54	73	1.534	4.83	79	4.88	.275	2	.071	-14	3	-1.5
Total	2	14	11	.560	68	33	3	1	2	249^1	257	138	132	25	6	121	140	1.516	4.76	77	4.65	.268	8	.113	-32	6	-3.6
• ALDERSON, Dale	Dale Leonard Alderson b: 3/9/1918, Belden, NE d: 2/12/1982, Garden Grove, CA BR/TR, 5'10", 190 lbs. Deb: 9/18/1943																										
1943	Chi-N	0	1	.000	4	2	0	0	0	14	21	12	10	2	0	3	4	1.714	6.43	52	6.73	.356	0	.000	-5	0	-0.5
1944	Chi-N	0	0	....	12	1	0	0	0	21^2	31	18	16	2	0	9	7	1.846	6.65	53	6.37	.344	0	.000	-7	0	-0.8
Total	2	0	1	.000	16	3	0	0	0	35^2	52	30	26	4	0	12	11	1.794	6.56	53	6.51	.349	0	.000	-12	0	-1.3
• ALDRED, Scott	Scott Phillip Aldred b: 6/12/1968, Flint, MI BL/TL, 6'4", 195 lbs. Deb: 9/9/1990																										
1990	Det-A	1	2	.333	4	3	0	0	0	14^1	13	6	6	0	1	10	7	1.605	3.77	105	4.25	.265	0	....	-0	1	0.0
1991	Det-A	2	4	.333	11	11	1	0	0	57^1	58	37	33	9	0	30	35	1.535	5.18	80	5.03	.266	0	....	-6	1	-0.6
1992	Det-A	3	8	.273	16	13	0	0	0	65	80	51	49	12	3	33	34	1.738	6.78	58	6.66	.307	0	....	-20	0	-2.0
1993	Col-N	0	0	....	5	0	0	0	0	6^2	10	10	8	1	1	9	5	2.850	10.80	44	12.03	.357	0	....	-4	0	-0.4
	Mon-N	1	0	1.000	3	0	0	0	0	5^1	9	4	4	1	0	1	4	1.875	6.75	62	8.25	.375	0	....	-2	0	-0.2
	Yr.	1	0	1.000	8	0	0	0	0	12	19	14	12	2	1	10	9	2.417	9.00	51	10.35	.365	0	....	-6	0	-0.6
1996	Det-A	0	4	.000	11	8	0	0	0	43^1	60	52	45	9	3	26	36	1.985	9.35	54	8.26	.328	0	....	-20	0	-1.8
	Min-A	6	5	.545	25	17	0	0	0	122	134	73	69	20	3	42	75	1.443	5.09	101	4.99	.281	0	....	-1	6	-0.1
	Yr.	6	9	.400	36	25	0	0	0	165^1	194	125	114	29	6	68	111	1.585	6.21	82	5.85	.294	0	....	-20	6	-1.9
1997	Min-A	2	10	.167	17	15	0	0	0	77^1	102	66	66	20	3	28	33	1.681	7.68	61	7.36	.323	0	....	-26	0	-2.5
1998	TB-A	0	0	....	48	0	0	0	0	31^1	33	13	13	1	2	12	21	1.436	3.73	128	3.99	.280	0	....	2	3	0.2
1999	TB-A	3	2	.600	37	0	0	0	0	24^1	26	15	14	1	2	14	22	1.644	5.18	96	4.95	.274	0	....	-0	1	0.0
	Phi-N	1	1	.500	29	0	0	0	1	32^1	33	15	14	1	0	15	19	1.485	3.90	121	3.83	.277	0	.000	2	3	0.2

YEAR	TM-L	W	L	PCT	G	GS	CG	SH	SV	IP	H	R	ER	HR	HB	BB	SO	RAT	ERA	ERA+	CERA	OAV	BH	AVG	PR+	WS	TPW
2000	Phi-N	1	3	.250	23	0	0	0	0	20^1	23	14	13	3	1	10	21	1.623	5.75	81	5.65	.284	0	....	-3	0	-0.2
Total	9	20	39	.339	229	67	1	0	1	499^2	581	356	334	78	19	230	312	1.623	6.02	77	5.86	.295	0	.000	-77	15	-7.4

• ALDRICH, Jay Jay Robert Aldrich b: 4/14/1961, Alexandria, LA BR/TR, 6'3", 210 lbs. Deb: 6/5/1987

YEAR	TM-L	W	L	PCT	G	GS	CG	SH	SV	IP	H	R	ER	HR	HB	BB	SO	RAT	ERA	ERA+	CERA	OAV	BH	AVG	PR+	WS	TPW
1987	Mil-A	3	1	.750	31	0	0	0	0	58^1	71	33	32	8	2	13	22	1.440	4.94	93	4.98	.306	0	....	-2	3	-0.2
1989	Mil-A	1	0	1.000	16	0	0	0	1	26	24	11	11	3	1	13	12	1.423	3.81	101	4.33	.253	0	....	-0	2	0.0
	Atl-N	1	2	.333	8	0	0	0	0	12^1	7	5	3	0	0	6	7	1.054	2.19	167	1.51	.167	0	.000	2	1	0.2
1990	Bal-A	1	2	.333	7	0	0	0	1	12	17	13	11	1	0	7	5	2.000	8.25	46	6.42	.327	0	....	-6	0	-0.6
Total	3	6	5	.545	62	0	0	0	2	108^2	119	62	57	12	3	39	46	1.454	4.72	89	4.59	.283	0	.000	-6	6	-0.6

• ALDRIDGE, Vic Victor Eddington Aldridge b: 10/25/1893, Indian Springs, IN d: 4/17/1973, Terre Haute, IN BR/TR, 5'9.5", 175 lbs. Deb: 4/15/1917

YEAR	TM-L	W	L	PCT	G	GS	CG	SH	SV	IP	H	R	ER	HR	HB	BB	SO	RAT	ERA	ERA+	CERA	OAV	BH	AVG	PR+	WS	TPW
1917	Chi-N	6	6	.500	30	6	1	1	2	106^2	100	52	37	1	2	37	44	1.284	3.12	93	2.94	.252	4	.138	-1	4	-0.3
1918	Chi-N	0	1	.000	3	0	0	0	0	12^1	11	3	2	0	0	6	10	1.378	1.46	191	3.35	.275	1	.333	2	1	0.3
1922	Chi-N	16	15	.516	36	34	20	2	0	258^1	287	129	101	14	12	56	66	1.328	3.52	119	3.80	.286	26	.260	17	19	2.0
1923	Chi-N	16	9	.640	30	30	15	2	0	217	209	101	84	17	1	67	64	1.272	3.48	115	3.30	.251	19	.268	7	18	1.0
1924	Chi-N	15	12	.556	32	32	20	0	0	244^1	261	110	95	10	7	80	74	1.396	3.50	112	3.80	.279	15	.176	7	17	0.4
1925*	Pit-N	15	7	.682	30	26	14	1	0	213^1	218	99	86	15	5	74	88	1.369	3.63	123	3.83	.269	20	.233	15	16	1.3
1926	Pit-N	10	13	.435	30	26	12	1	1	190	204	100	86	7	4	73	61	1.458	4.07	97	3.92	.279	16	.225	-6	10	-0.7
1927*	Pit-N	15	10	.600	35	34	17	1	1	239^1	248	123	113	16	5	74	86	1.345	4.25	97	3.67	.270	21	.219	-5	12	-0.5
1928	NY-N	4	7	.364	22	16	3	0	2	119^1	133	68	64	7	3	45	33	1.492	4.83	81	4.37	.285	11	.275	-13	5	-1.1
Total	9	97	80	.548	248	204	102	8	6	1600^2	1671	785	668	87	39	512	526	1.364	3.76	106	3.71	.272	133	.229	23	102	2.4

• ALEXANDER, Bob Robert Somerville Alexander b: 8/7/1922, Vancouver, Canada d: 4/7/1993, Oceanside, CA BR/TR, 6'2.5", 205 lbs. Deb: 4/11/1955

YEAR	TM-L	W	L	PCT	G	GS	CG	SH	SV	IP	H	R	ER	HR	HB	BB	SO	RAT	ERA	ERA+	CERA	OAV	BH	AVG	PR+	WS	TPW
1955	Bal-A	1	0	1.000	4	0	0	0	0	4	8	6	6	0	1	2	1	2.500	13.50	28	11.38	.444	0	....	-4	0	-0.4
1957	Cle-A	0	1	.000	5	0	0	0	0	7	10	7	7	0	1	5	1	2.143	9.00	41	7.32	.357	0	.000	-4	0	-0.4
Total	2	1	1	.500	9	0	0	0	0	11	18	13	13	0	2	7	2	2.273	10.64	35	8.80	.391	0	.000	-8	0	-0.9

• ALEXANDER, Doyle Doyle Lafayette Alexander b: 9/4/1950, Cordova, AL BR/TR, 6'3", 205 lbs. Deb: 6/26/1971

YEAR	TM-L	W	L	PCT	G	GS	CG	SH	SV	IP	H	R	ER	HR	HB	BB	SO	RAT	ERA	ERA+	CERA	OAV	BH	AVG	PR+	WS	TPW
1971	LA-N	6	6	.500	17	12	4	0	0	92^1	105	45	39	6	1	18	30	1.332	3.80	85	3.80	.282	9	.273	-6	4	-0.4
1972	Bal-A	6	8	.429	35	9	2	2	2	106^1	78	36	29	5	1	30	49	1.016	2.45	125	1.89	.203	2	.080	5	7	0.4
1973*	Bal-A	12	8	.600	29	26	10	0	0	174^2	169	85	75	19	7	52	63	1.265	3.86	97	3.74	.258	0	....	-10	8	-1.0
1974	Bal-A	6	9	.400	30	12	2	0	0	114^1	127	65	51	7	4	43	40	1.487	4.01	86	4.48	.290	0	....	-9	3	-0.9
1975	Bal-A	8	8	.500	32	11	3	1	1	133^1	127	47	45	7	1	47	46	1.305	3.04	116	3.27	.251	0	....	3	9	0.3
1976	Bal-A	3	4	.429	11	6	2	1	0	64^1	58	27	25	3	0	24	17	1.275	3.50	93	3.09	.247	0	....	-2	3	-0.2
	*NY-A	10	5	.667	19	19	5	2	0	136^2	114	54	50	9	3	39	41	1.120	3.29	104	2.69	.229	0	....	-3	8	-0.3
	Yr.	13	9	.591	30	25	7	3	0	201	172	81	75	12	3	63	58	1.169	3.36	100	2.82	.235	0	....	-5	11	-0.5
1977	Tex-A	17	11	.607	34	34	12	1	0	237	221	103	96	24	2	82	82	1.278	3.65	112	3.53	.246	0	....	9	17	0.9
1978	Tex-A	9	10	.474	31	28	7	1	0	191	198	84	82	18	1	71	81	1.408	3.86	97	4.16	.270	0	....	-2	10	-0.2
1979	Tex-A	5	7	.417	23	18	0	0	0	113^1	114	65	56	3	1	69	50	1.615	4.45	93	4.39	.268	0	....	-5	4	-0.5
1980	Atl-N	14	11	.560	35	35	7	1	0	231^2	227	120	108	20	4	74	114	1.299	4.20	89	3.59	.256	15	.181	-11	10	-1.1
1981	SF-N	11	7	.611	24	24	1	1	0	152^1	156	51	49	11	2	44	77	1.313	2.89	119	3.61	.263	9	.176	10	11	1.3
1982	NY-A	1	7	.125	16	11	0	0	0	66^2	81	52	45	14	0	14	26	1.425	6.08	66	5.19	.298	0	....	-15	0	-1.5
1983	NY-A	0	2	.000	8	5	0	0	0	28^1	31	21	20	6	0	7	17	1.341	6.35	61	4.75	.277	0	....	-8	0	-0.8
	Tor-A	7	6	.538	17	15	5	0	0	116^2	126	55	51	14	1	26	46	1.303	3.93	109	4.08	.279	0	....	5	8	0.5
	Yr.	7	8	.467	25	20	5	0	0	145	157	76	71	20	1	33	63	1.310	4.41	95	4.21	.278	0	....	-3	8	-0.3
1984	Tor-A	17	6	.739	36	35	11	2	0	261^2	238	99	91	21	3	59	139	1.135	3.13	131	2.86	.242	0	....	27	23	2.7
1985*	Tor-A	17	10	.630	36	36	6	1	0	260^2	268	105	100	28	6	67	142	1.285	3.45	122	3.85	.266	0	....	18	20	1.7
1986	Tor-A	5	4	.556	17	17	3	0	0	111	120	56	55	18	4	20	65	1.261	4.46	95	4.18	.273	0	....	-3	5	-0.3
	Atl-N	6	6	.500	17	17	2	0	0	117^1	135	58	50	9	0	17	74	1.295	3.84	104	3.71	.287	8	.211	3	7	0.4
1987	Atl-N	5	10	.333	16	16	3	0	0	117^2	115	57	54	21	2	27	64	1.207	4.13	105	3.86	.257	1	.029	3	6	0.1
	*Det-A	9	0	1.000	11	11	3	3	0	88^1	63	16	15	3	0	26	44	1.008	1.53	276	1.90	.201	0	....	26	12	2.5
1988	Det-A★	14	11	.560	34	34	5	1	0	229	260	122	110	30	5	46	126	1.336	4.32	88	4.26	.282	0	....	-14	9	-1.5
1989	Det-A	6	18	.250	33	33	5	1	0	223	245	118	110	28	5	76	95	1.439	4.44	86	4.63	.280	0	....	-13	8	-1.3
Total	19	194	174	.527	561	464	98	18	3	3367^2	3376	1541	1406	324	53	978	1528	1.293	3.76	102	3.70	.261	44	.166	7	192	0.7

• ALEXANDER, Gerald Gerald Paul Alexander b: 3/26/1968, Baton Rouge, LA BR/TR, 5'11", 190 lbs. Deb: 9/9/1990

YEAR	TM-L	W	L	PCT	G	GS	CG	SH	SV	IP	H	R	ER	HR	HB	BB	SO	RAT	ERA	ERA+	CERA	OAV	BH	AVG	PR+	WS	TPW
1990	Tex-A	0	0	....	3	2	0	0	0	7	14	6	6	0	1	5	8	2.714	7.71	51	11.97	.438	0	....	-3	0	-0.3
1991	Tex-A	5	3	.625	30	9	0	0	0	89^1	93	56	52	11	3	48	50	1.578	5.24	77	5.05	.272	0	....	-11	2	-1.1
1992	Tex-A	1	0	1.000	3	0	0	0	0	1^2	5	5	5	1	0	1	1	3.600	27.00	14	22.63	.500	0	....	-4	0	-0.4
Total	3	6	3	.667	36	11	0	0	0	98	112	67	63	12	4	54	59	1.694	5.79	69	5.84	.292	0	....	-18	2	-1.8

• ALEXANDER, Grover Grover Cleveland "Pete" Alexander b: 1/26/1887, Elba, NE d: 11/4/1950, St. Paul, NE BR/TR, 6'1", 185 lbs. Deb: 4/15/1911 HOF: 1938

YEAR	TM-L	W	L	PCT	G	GS	CG	SH	SV	IP	H	R	ER	HR	HB	BB	SO	RAT	ERA	ERA+	CERA	OAV	BH	AVG	PR+	WS	TPW
1911	Phi-N	**28**	13	.683	48	37	**31**	**7**	3	**367**	285	133	105	5	8	129	227	1.128	2.57	133	2.22	**.219**	24	.174	34	**34**	3.2
1912	Phi-N	19	17	.528	46	34	25	3	3	**310^1**	289	133	97	11	6	105	**195**	1.270	2.81	128	3.06	.251	19	.186	27	24	2.7
1913	Phi-N	22	8	.733	47	36	23	**9**	2	306^1	288	106	95	9	3	75	159	1.185	2.79	119	2.76	.254	13	.126	19	27	1.5
1914	Phi-N	**27**	15	.643	46	39	**32**	6	1	**355**	327	133	94	8	11	76	**214**	1.135	2.38	123	2.51	.244	32	.234	**33**	26	**3.8**
1915*	Phi-N	**31**	10	.756	49	42	**36**	**12**	3	**376^1**	253	86	51	3	10	64	**241**	.842	**1.22**	**224**	**1.33**	**.191**	22	.169	**63**	**43**	**7.0**
1916	Phi-N	**33**	12	.733	48	**45**	**38**	**16**	3	**389**	323	90	67	6	10	50	**167**	.959	**1.55**	**171**	**1.83**	.230	33	.239	**48**	**44**	**6.3**
1917	Phi-N	**30**	13	.698	45	**44**	**34**	**8**	0	**388**	336	107	79	4	6	56	**200**	1.010	1.83	153	1.94	.234	30	.216	**40**	**40**	**5.0**
1918	Chi-N	2	1	.667	3	3	3	0	0	26	19	7	5	0	1	3	15	.846	1.73	161	1.41	.207	1	.100	4	2	0.3
1919	Chi-N	16	11	.593	30	27	20	**9**	1	235	180	51	45	3	0	38	121	.928	**1.72**	**167**	1.56	**.211**	12	.171	32	26	3.6
1920	Chi-N	**27**	14	.659	46	**40**	**33**	7	5	**363^1**	335	96	77	8	1	69	**173**	1.112	**1.91**	**168**	2.40	.248	27	.229	**57**	**36**	**6.6**
1921	Chi-N	15	13	.536	31	30	21	**3**	1	252	286	110	95	10	1	33	77	1.266	3.39	113	3.42	.296	29	.305	11	22	1.7
1922	Chi-N	16	13	.552	33	31	20	1	1	245^2	283	111	99	8	3	34	48	1.290	3.63	116	3.52	.295	15	.176	14	18	1.2
1923	Chi-N	22	12	.647	39	36	26	3	2	305	308	128	108	17	0	30	72	1.108	3.19	125	2.64	.259	24	.216	20	27	2.0
1924	Chi-N	12	5	.706	21	20	12	0	0	169^1	183	82	57	9	1	25	33	1.228	3.03	129	3.19	.272	15	.231	14	14	1.4
1925	Chi-N	15	11	.577	32	30	20	1	0	236	270	106	89	14	3	29	63	1.267	3.39	127	3.58	.288	19	.241	20	20	2.1
1926	Chi-N	3	3	.500	7	7	4	0	0	52	55	26	20	0	0	7	12	1.192	3.46	111	2.63	.270	7	.467	1	4	0.4
	*StL-N	9	7	.563	23	16	11	2	2	148^1	136	57	48	8	2	24	35	1.079	2.91	134	2.47	.242	6	.120	15	12	1.2
	Yr.	12	10	.545	30	23	15	2	2	200^1	191	83	68	8	2	31	47	1.108	3.05	127	**2.51**	.249	13	.200	16	16	1.5
1927	StL-N	21	10	.677	37	30	22	2	3	268	261	94	75	11	1	38	48	1.116	2.52	157	2.58	.258	23	.245	38	**28**	**4.0**
1928*	StL-N	16	9	.640	34	31	18	1	2	243^2	262	107	91	15	2	37	59	1.227	3.36	119	3.27	.277	25	.291	16	19	2.1
1929	StL-N	9	8	.529	22	19	8	0	0	132	149	65	57	10	1	23	33	1.303	3.89	120	3.69	.285	2	.049	12	10	0.7
1930	Phi-N	0	3	.000	9	3	0	0	0	21^2	40	24	22	5	0	6	6	2.123	9.14	60	9.91	.396	0	.000	-8	0	-0.7
Total	20	373	208	.642	696	600	437	90	32	5190	4868	1852	1476	164	70	951	2198	1.121	2.56	138	2.57	.250	378	.209	508	476	56.1

• ALFONSECA, Antonio Antonio Alfonseca b: 4/16/1972, La Romana, Dominican Republic BR/TR, 6'5", 235 lbs. Deb: 6/17/1997

YEAR	TM-L	W	L	PCT	G	GS	CG	SH	SV	IP	H	R	ER	HR	HB	BB	SO	RAT	ERA	ERA+	CERA	OAV	BH	AVG	PR+	WS	TPW
1997*	Fla-N	1	3	.250	17	0	0	0	0	25^2	36	16	14	3	1	10	19	1.792	4.91	82	6.41	.324	0	.000	-3	0	-0.3
1998	Fla-N	4	6	.400	58	0	0	0	8	70^2	75	32	32	10	3	33	46	1.528	4.08	100	4.96	.281	0	.000	1	3	0.0
1999	Fla-N	4	5	.444	73	0	0	0	21	77^2	79	28	28	4	4	29	46	1.391	3.24	134	3.96	.274	0	.000	10	11	0.9
2000	Fla-N	5	6	.455	68	0	0	0	**45**	70	82	35	33	7	1	24	47	1.514	4.24	104	4.79	.291	0	....	2	10	0.2
2001	Fla-N	4	4	.500	58	0	0	0	28	61^2	68	24	21	6	5	15	40	1.346	3.06	137	4.24	.281	0	....	8	9	0.7
2002	Chi-N	2	5	.286	66	0	0	0	19	74^1	73	34	33	5	3	36	61	1.466	4.00	100	4.12	.257	2	.667	1	7	0.2
2003*	Chi-N	3	1	.750	60	0	0	0	0	66^1	76	43	43	7	2	27	51	1.553	5.83	72	5.05	.290	0	....	-12	1	-1.2
Total	7	23	30	.434	400	0	0	0	121	446^1	489	212	204	42	19	174	310	1.485	4.11	102	4.62	.282	2	.167	6	41	0.5

• ALLARD, Brian Brian Marshall Allard b: 1/3/1958, Spring Valley, IL BR/TR, 6'1", 175 lbs. Deb: 8/8/1979

YEAR	TM-L	W	L	PCT	G	GS	CG	SH	SV	IP	H	R	ER	HR	HB	BB	SO	RAT	ERA	ERA+	CERA	OAV	BH	AVG	PR+	WS	TPW
1979	Tex-A	1	3	.250	7	4	2	0	0	33^1	36	17	16	4	0	13	14	1.470	4.32	96	4.71	.283	0	....	-1	1	-0.1
1980	Tex-A	0	1	.000	5	2	0	0	0	14^1	13	13	9	0	1	10	10	1.605	5.65	69	3.97	.236	0	....	-3	0	-0.3

YEAR TM-L	W	L	PCT	G	GS	CG	SH	SV	IP	H	R	ER	HR	HB	BB	SO	RAT	ERA	ERA+	CERA	OAV	BH	AVG	PR+	WS	TPW
1981 Sea-A	3	2	.600	7	7	1	0	0	48	48	22	20	5	0	8	20	1.167	3.75	103	3.31	.265	0	....	1	3	0.1
Total 3	4	6	.400	19	13	3	0	0	95^{2}	97	52	45	9	1	31	44	1.338	4.23	94	3.89	.267	0	....	-2	4	-0.2

• ALLEN, Bob Robert Earl "Thin Man" Allen b: 7/2/1914, Smithville, TN BR/TR, 6'1", 165 lbs. Deb: 9/19/1937

YEAR TM-L	W	L	PCT	G	GS	CG	SH	SV	IP	H	R	ER	HR	HB	BB	SO	RAT	ERA	ERA+	CERA	OAV	BH	AVG	PR+	WS	TPW
1937 Phi-N	0	1	.000	3	1	0	0	0	12	18	12	9	2	0	8	8	2.167	6.75	64	8.21	.321	1	.333	-3	0	-0.3

• ALLEN, Bob Robert Gray Allen b: 10/23/1937, Tatum, TX BL/TL, 6'2", 185 lbs. Deb: 4/14/1961

YEAR TM-L	W	L	PCT	G	GS	CG	SH	SV	IP	H	R	ER	HR	HB	BB	SO	RAT	ERA	ERA+	CERA	OAV	BH	AVG	PR+	WS	TPW
1961 Cle-A	3	2	.600	48	0	0	0	3	81^{2}	96	42	34	7	1	40	42	1.665	3.75	105	5.29	.294	2	.167	2	5	0.2
1962 Cle-A	1	1	.500	30	0	0	0	4	30^{2}	29	24	20	5	0	25	23	1.761	5.87	66	5.66	.250	0	.000	-7	0	-0.8
1963 Cle-A	1	2	.333	43	0	0	0	2	56	58	37	29	5	1	29	51	1.554	4.66	78	4.46	.266	1	.200	-6	1	-0.6
1966 Cle-A	2	2	.500	36	0	0	0	5	51^{1}	56	27	24	2	2	13	33	1.344	4.21	82	3.41	.273	1	.111	-4	3	-0.4
1967 Cle-A	0	5	.000	47	0	0	0	5	54^{1}	49	22	18	4	1	25	50	1.362	2.98	110	3.46	.243	0	....	2	3	0.2
Total 5	7	12	.368	204	0	0	0	19	274	288	152	125	23	5	132	199	1.533	4.11	89	4.45	.270	4	.129	-13	12	-1.4

• ALLEN, Frank Frank Leon Allen b: 8/26/1889, Newbern, AL d: 7/30/1933, Gainsville, AL BR/TL, 5'9", 175 lbs. Deb: 4/24/1912

YEAR TM-L	W	L	PCT	G	GS	CG	SH	SV	IP	H	R	ER	HR	HB	BB	SO	RAT	ERA	ERA+	CERA	OAV	BH	AVG	PR+	WS	TPW
1912 Bro-N	3	9	.250	20	15	5	1	0	109	119	70	44	1	1	57	58	1.615	3.63	92	4.25	.285	6	.167	-2	3	0.0
1913 Bro-N	4	18	.182	34	25	11	0	2	174^{2}	144	75	55	6	10	81	82	1.288	2.83	116	3.04	.231	7	.137	7	9	0.6
1914 Bro-N	8	14	.364	36	21	10	1	0	171^{1}	165	79	59	6	3	57	68	1.296	3.10	92	3.24	.265	6	.128	-5	7	-0.5
Pit-F	1	0	1.000	1	1	1	0	0	7	9	4	4	0	0	0	3	1.286	5.14	60	3.42	.321	1	.500	-2	1	-0.1
1915 Pit-F	23	13	.639	41	37	24	6	0	283^{1}	230	90	79	9	11	100	127	1.165	2.51	124	2.64	.227	7	.079	19	24	1.6
1916 Bos-N	8	2	.800	19	14	7	2	1	113	102	32	26	1	4	31	63	1.177	2.07	118	2.57	.244	7	.206	5	10	0.9
1917 Bos-N	3	10	.231	29	14	2	0	0	112	124	61	49	3	6	47	56	1.527	3.94	65	4.40	.297	5	.172	-16	1	-1.6
Total 6	50	66	.431	180	127	60	10	3	970^{1}	893	411	316	26	35	373	457	1.305	2.93	101	3.20	.252	39	.135	5	55	0.9

• ALLEN, John John Marshall Allen b: 10/27/1890, Berkeley Springs, WV d: 9/24/1967, Hagerstown, MD BR/TR, 6'1", 170 lbs. Deb: 6/2/1914

YEAR TM-L	W	L	PCT	G	GS	CG	SH	SV	IP	H	R	ER	HR	HB	BB	SO	RAT	ERA	ERA+	CERA	OAV	BH	AVG	PR+	WS	TPW
1914 Bal-F	0	0	....	1	0	0	0	0	2	2	4	4	0	1	2	2	2.000	18.00	18	7.12	.286	0	....	-3	0	-0.3

• ALLEN, Johnny John Thomas Allen b: 9/30/1905, Lenoir, NC d: 5/29/1959, St. Petersburg, FL BR/TR, 6', 180 lbs. Deb: 4/19/1932

YEAR TM-L	W	L	PCT	G	GS	CG	SH	SV	IP	H	R	ER	HR	HB	BB	SO	RAT	ERA	ERA+	CERA	OAV	BH	AVG	PR+	WS	TPW
1932* NY-A	17	4	.810	33	21	13	3	4	192	162	86	79	10	5	76	109	1.240	3.70	110	2.89	.228	9	.123	8	15	0.6
1933 NY-A	15	7	.682	25	24	10	1	1	184^{2}	171	96	90	9	4	87	119	1.397	4.39	89	3.51	.242	13	.181	-8	10	-0.8
1934 NY-A	5	2	.714	13	10	4	0	0	71^{2}	62	30	23	3	2	32	54	1.312	2.89	141	3.06	.227	5	.192	8	6	0.8
1935 NY-A	13	6	.684	23	23	12	2	0	167	149	76	67	11	4	58	113	1.240	3.61	112	3.10	**.238**	15	.224	5	12	0.6
1936 Cle-A	20	10	.667	36	31	19	4	1	243	234	108	93	5	1	97	165	1.362	3.44	146	3.26	.256	14	.161	45	25	3.7
1937 Cle-A	15	1	.938	24	20	14	0	0	173	157	55	49	4	5	60	87	1.254	2.55	181	2.94	.244	6	.090	41	20	3.2
1938 Cle-A★	14	8	.636	30	27	13	0	0	200	189	107	93	15	3	81	112	1.350	4.19	111	3.57	.246	20	.253	10	16	1.2
1939 Cle-A	9	7	.563	28	26	9	2	0	175	199	96	89	9	3	56	79	1.457	4.58	96	4.18	.291	16	.225	-3	10	-0.2
1940 Cle-A	9	8	.529	32	17	5	3	5	138^{2}	126	61	53	3	3	48	62	1.255	3.44	123	2.88	.243	10	.208	9	11	0.8
1941 StL-A	2	5	.286	20	9	2	0	1	67	89	53	49	4	2	29	27	1.761	6.58	65	5.74	.319	3	.136	-16	0	-1.6
*Bro-N	3	0	1.000	11	4	1	0	0	57^{1}	38	18	16	6	0	12	21	.872	2.51	146	1.70	.188	1	.050	6	5	0.4
1942 Bro-N	10	6	.625	27	15	5	1	3	118	106	53	42	11	2	39	50	1.229	3.20	102	3.18	.238	7	.179	-1	7	-0.1
1943 Bro-N	5	1	.833	17	1	0	0	1	38	42	21	18	3	2	25	15	1.763	4.26	79	5.53	.280	3	.429	-3	2	-0.2
NY-N	1	3	.250	15	0	0	0	2	41	37	16	14	4	0	14	24	1.244	3.07	112	3.27	.245	0	.000	2	3	0.0
Yr.	6	4	.600	32	1	0	0	3	79	79	37	32	7	2	39	39	1.494	3.65	93	4.35	.262	3	.143	-1	5	-0.1
1944 NY-N	4	7	.364	18	13	2	1	0	84	88	48	38	7	2	24	33	1.333	4.07	90	3.68	.260	2	.083	-4	3	-0.7
Total 13	142	75	.654	352	241	109	17	18	1950^{1}	1849	924	813	104	38	738	1070	1.326	3.75	111	3.38	.250	124	.173	99	145	8.0

• ALLEN, Lloyd Lloyd Cecil Allen b: 5/8/1950, Merced, CA BR/TR, 6'1", 185 lbs. Deb: 9/1/1969

YEAR TM-L	W	L	PCT	G	GS	CG	SH	SV	IP	H	R	ER	HR	HB	BB	SO	RAT	ERA	ERA+	CERA	OAV	BH	AVG	PR+	WS	TPW
1969 Cal-A	0	1	.000	4	1	0	0	0	10	5	7	6	1	0	10	5	1.500	5.40	65	3.62	.147	1	.500	-2	0	-0.2
1970 Cal-A	1	1	.500	8	2	0	0	0	24	23	7	7	0	1	11	12	1.417	2.63	138	3.47	.261	0	.000	2	2	0.2
1971 Cal-A	4	6	.400	54	1	0	0	15	94	75	29	26	4	0	40	72	1.223	2.49	130	2.61	.221	5	.294	7	12	0.9
1972 Cal-A	3	7	.300	42	6	0	0	5	85^{1}	76	38	33	7	3	55	53	1.535	3.48	84	4.31	.240	2	.118	-6	2	-0.8
1973 Cal-A	0	0	....	5	0	0	0	1	8^{2}	15	10	10	0	0	5	4	2.308	10.38	34	8.88	.417	0	....	-6	0	-0.7
Tex-A	0	6	.000	23	5	0	0	1	41	58	59	42	3	5	39	25	2.366	9.22	40	8.83	.326	0	....	-24	0	-2.5
Yr.	0	6	.000	28	5	0	0	2	49^{2}	73	69	52	3	5	44	29	2.356	9.42	39	8.84	.341	0	....	-30	0	-3.1
1974 Tex-A	0	1	.000	14	0	0	0	0	22	24	17	16	2	1	18	18	1.909	6.55	54	6.27	.276	0	....	-7	0	-0.8
Chi-A	0	1	.000	6	2	0	0	0	7	7	9	8	0	1	12	3	2.714	10.29	36	8.79	.259	0	....	-5	0	-0.5
Yr.	0	2	.000	20	2	0	0	0	29	31	26	24	2	2	30	21	2.103	7.45	49	6.88	.272	0	....	-12	0	-1.3
1975 Chi-A	0	2	.000	3	2	0	0	0	5^{1}	8	7	7	2	0	6	2	2.625	11.81	33	12.53	.348	0	....	-5	0	-0.5
Total 7	8	25	.242	159	19	0	0	22	297^{1}	291	183	155	19	11	196	194	1.638	4.69	72	4.84	.258	8	.200	-47	16	-4.7

• ALLEN, Neil Neil Patrick Allen b: 1/24/1958, Kansas City, KS BR/TR, 6'3", 190 lbs. Deb: 4/15/1979

YEAR TM-L	W	L	PCT	G	GS	CG	SH	SV	IP	H	R	ER	HR	HB	BB	SO	RAT	ERA	ERA+	CERA	OAV	BH	AVG	PR+	WS	TPW
1979 NY-N	6	10	.375	50	5	0	0	8	99	100	46	39	4	0	47	65	1.485	3.55	103	3.80	.268	0	.000	-0	6	-0.2
1980 NY-N	7	10	.412	59	0	0	0	22	97^{1}	87	43	40	7	0	40	79	1.305	3.70	96	3.24	.244	2	.143	-2	10	-0.2
1981 NY-N	7	6	.538	43	0	0	0	18	66^{2}	64	26	22	4	0	26	50	1.350	2.97	117	3.32	.259	1	.200	5	8	0.6
1982 NY-N	3	7	.300	50	0	0	0	19	64^{2}	65	22	22	5	1	30	59	1.469	3.06	119	4.20	.266	1	.167	5	8	0.6
1983 NY-N	2	7	.222	21	4	1	1	2	54	57	29	27	6	0	36	32	1.722	4.50	81	5.47	.278	0	.000	-6	1	-0.7
StL-N	10	6	.625	25	18	4	2	0	121^{2}	122	55	50	6	1	48	74	1.397	3.70	98	3.76	.265	5	.128	-1	7	-0.1
Yr.	12	13	.480	46	22	5	3	2	175^{2}	179	84	77	12	1	84	106	1.497	3.94	92	4.28	.269	5	.102	-6	8	-0.9
1984 StL-N	9	6	.600	57	1	0	0	3	119	105	54	47	6	0	49	66	1.294	3.55	98	3.07	.239	6	.240	-3	8	-0.2
1985 StL-N	1	4	.200	23	1	0	0	2	29	32	22	18	3	1	17	10	1.690	5.59	63	5.16	.283	0	.000	-7	0	-0.8
NY-A	1	0	1.000	17	0	0	0	1	29^{1}	26	9	9	1	0	13	16	1.330	2.76	145	3.18	.234	0	....	4	2	0.4
1986 Chi-A	7	2	.778	22	17	2	2	0	113	101	50	48	8	2	38	57	1.230	3.82	113	3.16	.244	0	....	4	8	0.4
1987 Chi-A	0	7	.000	15	10	0	0	0	49^{2}	74	40	39	6	2	26	26	2.013	7.07	65	8.29	.365	0	....	-15	0	-1.4
NY-A	0	1	.000	8	1	0	0	0	24^{2}	23	12	10	2	0	10	16	1.338	3.65	120	3.49	.242	0	....	2	1	0.2
Yr.	0	8	.000	23	11	0	0	0	74^{1}	97	52	49	8	2	36	42	1.789	5.93	77	6.70	.326	0	....	-13	1	-1.3
1988 NY-A	5	3	.625	41	2	0	1	0	117^{1}	121	51	50	14	2	37	61	1.347	3.84	103	4.00	.268	0	....	2	7	0.2
1989 Cle-A	0	1	.000	3	0	0	0	0	3	8	5	5	1	0	0	0	2.667	15.00	26	15.50	.500	0	....	-4	0	-0.4
Total 11	58	70	.453	434	59	7	6	75	988^{1}	985	464	426	73	9	417	611	1.419	3.88	98	3.96	.264	15	.130	-16	66	-1.7

• ALLISON, Dana Dana Eric Allison b: 8/14/1966, Front Royal, VA BR/TL, 6'3", 215 lbs. Deb: 4/12/1991

YEAR TM-L	W	L	PCT	G	GS	CG	SH	SV	IP	H	R	ER	HR	HB	BB	SO	RAT	ERA	ERA+	CERA	OAV	BH	AVG	PR+	WS	TPW
1991 Oak-A	1	1	.500	11	0	0	0	0	11	16	9	9	0	0	5	4	1.909	7.36	52	6.49	.381	0	....	-4	0	-0.4

• ALLISON, Mack Mack Pendleton Allison b: 1/23/1887, Owensboro, KY d: 3/13/1964, Mount Vernon, MO BR/TR, 6'1", 185 lbs. Deb: 9/13/1911

YEAR TM-L	W	L	PCT	G	GS	CG	SH	SV	IP	H	R	ER	HR	HB	BB	SO	RAT	ERA	ERA+	CERA	OAV	BH	AVG	PR+	WS	TPW
1911 StL-A	2	1	.667	3	3	3	0	0	26^{1}	24	9	6	0	2	5	2	1.101	2.05	164	2.57	.253	2	.200	4	2	0.3
1912 StL-A	6	17	.261	31	20	11	1	1	169	171	102	68	4	6	49	43	1.302	3.62	92	3.39	.269	7	.135	-7	6	-1.1
1913 StL-A	1	3	.250	11	4	3	0	0	51^{1}	52	24	13	0	3	13	12	1.266	2.28	128	3.41	.287	0	.000	3	2	0.1
Total 3	9	21	.300	45	27	17	1	1	246^{2}	247	135	87	4	11	67	57	1.273	3.17	103	3.31	.271	9	.118	-1	10	-0.6

• ALMANZA, Armando Armando N. Almanza b: 10/26/1972, El Paso, TX BL/TL, 6'3", 220 lbs. Deb: 7/29/1999

YEAR TM-L	W	L	PCT	G	GS	CG	SH	SV	IP	H	R	ER	HR	HB	BB	SO	RAT	ERA	ERA+	CERA	OAV	BH	AVG	PR+	WS	TPW
1999 Fla-N	0	1	.000	14	0	0	0	0	15^{2}	8	4	3	1	1	9	20	1.085	1.72	253	2.09	.154	0	.000	5	2	0.4
2000 Fla-N	4	2	.667	67	0	0	0	0	46^{1}	38	27	25	3	2	43	46	1.748	4.86	91	4.79	.228	0	.000	-2	3	-0.2
2001 Fla-N	2	2	.500	52	0	0	0	0	41	34	24	22	8	0	26	45	1.463	4.83	87	4.73	.230	0	....	-3	2	-0.3
2002 Fla-N	3	2	.600	51	0	0	0	0	45^{2}	36	22	22	8	0	23	57	1.292	4.34	91	3.85	.224	0	....	-2	3	-0.2
2003 Fla-N	4	5	.444	51	0	0	0	0	50^{1}	59	37	34	10	2	25	49	1.669	6.08	67	6.42	.296	0	....	-11	0	-1.1
Total 5	13	12	.520	235	0	0	0	2	199	175	114	106	30	5	126	217	1.513	4.79	87	4.76	.241	0	.000	-14	10	-1.4

• ALMANZAR, Carlos Carlos Manuel (Giron) Almanzar b: 11/6/1973, Santiago, Dominican Republic BR/TR, 6'2", 166 lbs. Deb: 9/4/1997

YEAR TM-L	W	L	PCT	G	GS	CG	SH	SV	IP	H	R	ER	HR	HB	BB	SO	RAT	ERA	ERA+	CERA	OAV	BH	AVG	PR+	WS	TPW
1997 Tor-A	0	1	.000	4	0	0	0	0	3^{1}	1	1	1	1	0	1	4	.600	2.70	170	1.39	.091	0	....	1	0	0.1
1998 Tor-A	2	2	.500	25	0	0	0	0	28^{2}	34	18	17	4	1	8	20	1.465	5.34	87	4.85	.286	0	....	-2	1	-0.2
1999 SD-N	0	0	....	28	0	0	0	0	37^{1}	48	32	31	6	3	15	30	1.688	7.47	56	6.54	.316	0	.000	-14	0	-1.3
2000 SD-N	4	5	.444	62	0	0	0	0	69^{2}	73	35	34	12	4	25	56	1.407	4.39	98	4.83	.266	0	.000	-2	3	-0.2

YEAR	TM-L	W	L	PCT	G	GS	CG	SH	SV	IP	H	R	ER	HR	HB	BB	SO	RAT	ERA	ERA+	CERA	OAV	BH	AVG	PR+	WS	TPW
2001	NY-A	0	1	.000	10	0	0	0	0	10^{2}	14	4	4	2	0	2	6	1.500	3.38	133	5.63	.333	0	....	2	1	0.1
2002	Cin-N	0	1	.000	8	1	0	0	0	11^{2}	6	4	3	0	0	5	7	.943	2.31	183	1.26	.158	0	....	2	1	0.2
Total	6	6	10	.375	137	1	0	0	0	161^{1}	176	94	90	25	8	56	123	1.438	5.02	86	4.95	.277	0	.000	-13	6	-1.2

• ALMONTE, Edwin Edwin Almonte b: 12/17/1976, Santiago, Dominican Republic BR/TR, 6'3", 220 lbs. Deb: 7/7/2003

YEAR	TM-L	W	L	PCT	G	GS	CG	SH	SV	IP	H	R	ER	HR	HB	BB	SO	RAT	ERA	ERA+	CERA	OAV	BH	AVG	PR+	WS	TPW
2003	NY-N	0	0	....	12	0	0	0	0	11^{1}	21	15	14	3	0	5	7	2.294	11.12	37	11.40	.412	0	.000	-9	0	-0.9

• ALMONTE, Hector Hector Radhames (Moreta) Almonte b: 10/17/1975, Santo Domingo, Dominican Republic BR/TR, 6'2", 190 lbs. Deb: 7/26/1999

YEAR	TM-L	W	L	PCT	G	GS	CG	SH	SV	IP	H	R	ER	HR	HB	BB	SO	RAT	ERA	ERA+	CERA	OAV	BH	AVG	PR+	WS	TPW
1999	Fla-N	0	2	.000	15	0	0	0	0	15	20	7	7	1	0	6	8	1.733	4.20	104	5.73	.339	0	....	0	1	0.0
2003	Bos-A	0	1	.000	7	0	0	0	0	7^{2}	9	7	7	1	0	7	6	2.087	8.22	55	7.08	.310	0	....	-3	0	-0.3
	Mon-N	1	1	.500	28	0	0	0	0	29	34	22	22	4	2	17	26	1.759	6.83	74	6.32	.291	0	.000	-6	0	-0.6
Total	2	1	4	.200	50	0	0	0	0	51^{2}	63	36	36	6	2	30	40	1.800	6.27	77	6.26	.307	0	.000	-8	1	-0.8

• ALOMA, Luis Luis (Barba) "Witto" Aloma b: 6/19/1923, Havana, Cuba d: 4/7/1997, Park Ridge, IL BR/TR, 6'2", 195 lbs. Deb: 4/19/1950

YEAR	TM-L	W	L	PCT	G	GS	CG	SH	SV	IP	H	R	ER	HR	HB	BB	SO	RAT	ERA	ERA+	CERA	OAV	BH	AVG	PR+	WS	TPW
1950	Chi-A	7	2	.778	42	0	0	0	4	87^{2}	77	44	37	6	1	53	49	1.483	3.80	118	3.82	.234	1	.067	5	8	0.3
1951	Chi-A	6	0	1.000	25	1	1	1	3	69^{1}	52	14	14	3	2	24	25	1.096	1.82	222	2.32	.215	7	.350	16	10	1.7
1952	Chi-A	3	1	.750	25	0	0	0	6	40	42	20	19	5	1	11	18	1.325	4.28	85	4.16	.278	0	.000	-3	3	-0.4
1953	Chi-A	2	0	1.000	24	0	0	0	2	38^{1}	41	20	20	7	0	23	23	1.670	4.70	86	5.85	.283	0	.000	-3	2	-0.4
Total	4	18	3	.857	116	1	1	1	15	235^{1}	212	98	90	21	4	111	115	1.373	3.44	119	3.77	.245	8	.167	15	23	1.2

• ALSTON, Garvin Garvin James Alston b: 12/8/1971, Mount Vernon, NY BR/TR, 6'2", 185 lbs. Deb: 6/6/1996

YEAR	TM-L	W	L	PCT	G	GS	CG	SH	SV	IP	H	R	ER	HR	HB	BB	SO	RAT	ERA	ERA+	CERA	OAV	BH	AVG	PR+	WS	TPW
1996	Col-N	1	0	1.000	6	0	0	0	0	6	9	6	6	1	1	3	5	2.000	9.00	58	9.02	.375	0	.000	-2	0	-0.2

• ALTAMIRANO, Porfi Porfirio (Ramirez) Altamirano b: 5/17/1952, Darillo, Nicaragua BR/TR, 6', 175 lbs. Deb: 5/9/1982

YEAR	TM-L	W	L	PCT	G	GS	CG	SH	SV	IP	H	R	ER	HR	HB	BB	SO	RAT	ERA	ERA+	CERA	OAV	BH	AVG	PR+	WS	TPW
1982	Phi-N	5	1	.833	29	0	0	0	2	39	41	19	18	2	1	14	26	1.410	4.15	88	3.83	.281	1	.250	-2	3	-0.2
1983	Phi-N	2	3	.400	31	0	0	0	0	41^{1}	38	18	17	9	2	15	24	1.282	3.70	96	4.44	.255	0	.000	-0	2	0.0
1984	Chi-N	0	0	....	5	0	0	0	0	11^{1}	8	6	6	2	0	1	7	.794	4.76	82	1.83	.195	0	.000	-1	0	-0.1
Total	3	7	4	.636	65	0	0	0	2	91^{2}	87	43	41	13	3	30	57	1.276	4.03	91	3.86	.259	1	.125	-3	5	-0.4

• ALTEN, Ernie Ernest Matthias "Lefty" Alten b: 12/1/1894, Avon, OH d: 9/9/1981, Napa, CA BR/TL, 6', 175 lbs. Deb: 4/17/1920

YEAR	TM-L	W	L	PCT	G	GS	CG	SH	SV	IP	H	R	ER	HR	HB	BB	SO	RAT	ERA	ERA+	CERA	OAV	BH	AVG	PR+	WS	TPW
1920	Det-A	0	1	.000	14	1	0	0	0	23	40	27	23	2	1	9	4	2.130	9.00	41	8.93	.392	0	.000	-13	0	-1.3

• ALTROCK, Nick Nicholas Altrock b: 9/15/1876, Cincinnati, OH d: 1/20/1965, Washington, DC BB/TL, 5'10", 197 lbs. Deb: 7/14/1898 C/U

YEAR	TM-L	W	L	PCT	G	GS	CG	SH	SV	IP	H	R	ER	HR	HB	BB	SO	RAT	ERA	ERA+	CERA	OAV	BH	AVG	PR+	WS	TPW
1898	Lou-N	3	3	.500	11	7	6	0	0	70	89	54	35	2	3	21	13	1.571	4.50	79	4.78	.307	7	.241	-7	2	-0.6
1902	Bos-A	0	2	.000	3	2	1	0	1	18	19	13	4	0	0	7	5	1.444	2.00	179	3.48	.272	0	.000	3	1	0.1
1903	Bos-A	0	1	.000	1	1	1	0	0	8	13	10	8	0	0	4	3	2.125	9.00	34	7.10	.363	2	.667	-6	0	-0.5
	Chi-A	4	3	.571	12	8	6	1	0	71	59	35	17	3	3	19	19	1.099	2.15	130	2.34	.226	9	.300	6	5	0.9
	Yr.	4	4	.500	13	9	7	1	0	79	72	45	25	3	3	23	22	1.203	2.85	101	2.82	.242	11	.333	1	5	0.5
1904	Chi-A	19	14	.576	38	36	31	6	1	307	274	117	101	2	4	48	87	1.049	2.96	83	2.06	.240	22	.198	-24	16	-2.6
1905	Chi-A	23	12	.657	38	34	31	3	0	315^{2}	274	89	66	3	2	63	97	1.068	1.88	131	2.09	.236	14	.125	11	24	0.8
1906*	Chi-A	20	13	.606	38	30	25	4	0	287^{2}	269	95	66	0	3	42	99	1.081	2.06	123	2.20	.251	16	.160	12	21	1.2
1907	Chi-A	7	13	.350	30	21	15	1	2	213^{2}	210	76	61	3	2	31	61	1.128	2.57	93	2.47	.260	13	.181	-2	13	-0.2
1908	Chi-A	5	7	.417	23	13	8	1	2	136	127	59	41	2	2	18	21	1.066	2.71	85	2.30	.240	10	.204	-5	6	-0.4
1909	Chi-A	0	1	.000	1	1	1	0	0	9	16	6	5	0	0	1	2	1.889	5.00	47	8.61	.480	0	.000	-3	0	-0.3
	Was-A	1	3	.250	9	5	2	0	0	38	55	23	23	0	1	5	9	1.579	5.45	45	4.87	.330	1	.053	-12	0	-1.7
	Yr.	1	4	.200	10	6	3	0	0	47	71	29	28	0	1	6	11	1.638	5.36	45	5.59	.355	1	.045	-15	0	-2.0
1912	Was-A	0	1	.000	1	0	0	0	0	1	1	2	2	0	0	2	0	3.000	18.00	19	8.74	.200	0	.000	-2	0	-0.2
1913	Was-A	0	0	....	4	0	0	0	0	9	7	5	5	0	1	4	2	1.222	5.00	59	2.28	.180	0	.000	-2	0	-0.2
1914	Was-A	0	0	....	1	0	0	0	0	1	3	0	0	0	0	0	0	3.000	0.00	....	17.53	.750	0	....	0	0	0.0
1915	Was-A	0	0	....	1	0	0	0	1	3	7	0	3	0	0	1	2	2.667	9.00	33	11.15	.430	0	.000	-2	0	-0.2
1918	Was-A	1	2	.333	5	3	1	0	0	24	24	11	8	1	1	6	5	1.250	3.00	91	3.05	.270	1	.125	-1	1	-0.2
1919	Was-A	0	0	....	1	0	0	0	0	0	4	4	0	0	0	0	0	....	....	....	∞	1.000	0	....	0	0	0.0
1924	Was-A	0	0	....	1	0	0	0	0	2	4	1	0	0	0	0	0	2.000	0.00	....	9.49	.500	1	1.000	1	1	0.2
Total	16	83	75	.525	218	161	128	16	7	1514	1455	600	445	16	22	272	425	1.141	2.65	96	2.52	.254	97	.176	-33	90	-3.9

• ALVAREZ, Jose Jose Lino Alvarez b: 4/12/1956, Tampa, FL BR/TR, 5'10", 170 lbs. Deb: 10/1/1981

YEAR	TM-L	W	L	PCT	G	GS	CG	SH	SV	IP	H	R	ER	HR	HB	BB	SO	RAT	ERA	ERA+	CERA	OAV	BH	AVG	PR+	WS	TPW
1981	Atl-N	0	0	....	1	0	0	0	0	2	0	0	0	0	0	0	2	.000	0.00	....	0.00	.000	0	....	1	0	0.1
1982	Atl-N	0	0	....	7	0	0	0	0	7^{2}	8	4	4	1	0	2	6	1.304	4.70	79	4.27	.308	0	....	-1	0	-0.1
1988	Atl-N	5	6	.455	60	0	0	0	3	102^{1}	88	34	34	7	6	53	81	1.378	2.99	123	3.64	.240	3	.375	9	9	1.1
1989	Atl-N	3	3	.500	30	0	0	0	2	50^{1}	44	18	16	4	1	24	45	1.351	2.86	128	3.52	.237	0	.000	5	4	0.5
Total	4	8	9	.471	98	0	0	0	5	162^{1}	140	56	54	12	7	79	134	1.349	2.99	123	3.59	.242	3	.273	14	13	1.6

• ALVAREZ, Juan Juan M. Alvarez b: 8/9/1973, Coral Gables, FL BL/TL, 6'1", 184 lbs. Deb: 9/1/1999

YEAR	TM-L	W	L	PCT	G	GS	CG	SH	SV	IP	H	R	ER	HR	HB	BB	SO	RAT	ERA	ERA+	CERA	OAV	BH	AVG	PR+	WS	TPW
1999	Ana-A	0	1	.000	8	0	0	0	0	3	1	1	1	0	0	4	4	1.667	3.00	161	3.04	.111	0	....	1	0	0.1
2000	Ana-A	0	0	....	11	0	0	0	0	6	14	9	9	3	0	7	2	3.500	13.50	38	21.26	.467	0	....	-6	0	-0.5
2002	Tex-A	0	4	.000	52	0	0	0	0	39^{2}	35	22	21	7	3	21	30	1.412	4.76	99	4.83	.241	0	....	0	2	0.0
2003	Fla-N	0	0	....	9	0	0	0	0	11^{2}	8	4	4	2	1	8	6	1.371	3.09	133	4.66	.216	0	....	1	1	0.1
Total	4	0	5	.000	80	0	0	0	0	60^{1}	58	36	35	12	4	40	42	1.624	5.22	91	6.34	.262	0	....	-4	3	-0.3

• ALVAREZ, Tavo Cesar Octavio Alvarez b: 11/25/1971, Ciudad Obregon, Mexico BR/TR, 6'3", 245 lbs. Deb: 8/21/1995

YEAR	TM-L	W	L	PCT	G	GS	CG	SH	SV	IP	H	R	ER	HR	HB	BB	SO	RAT	ERA	ERA+	CERA	OAV	BH	AVG	PR+	WS	TPW
1995	Mon-N	1	5	.167	8	8	0	0	0	37^{1}	46	30	28	2	3	14	17	1.607	6.75	64	5.22	.297	0	.000	-10	0	-1.1
1996	Mon-N	2	1	.667	11	5	0	0	0	21	19	10	7	0	1	12	9	1.476	3.00	144	3.43	.235	2	.500	3	2	0.4
Total	2	3	6	.333	19	13	0	0	0	58^{1}	65	40	35	2	4	26	26	1.560	5.40	80	4.57	.275	2	.125	-7	2	-0.7

• ALVAREZ, Victor Victor Aurelio Alvarez b: 11/8/1976, Culiacan, Mexico BL/TL, 5'10", 150 lbs. Deb: 7/30/2002

YEAR	TM-L	W	L	PCT	G	GS	CG	SH	SV	IP	H	R	ER	HR	HB	BB	SO	RAT	ERA	ERA+	CERA	OAV	BH	AVG	PR+	WS	TPW
2002	LA-N	0	1	.000	4	1	0	0	0	10^{1}	9	5	5	1	0	2	7	1.065	4.35	88	2.70	.237	0	.000	-1	0	-0.1
2003	LA-N	0	1	.000	5	0	0	0	0	5^{2}	9	8	8	1	1	6	3	2.647	12.71	32	12.90	.391	0	....	-6	0	-0.5
Total	2	0	2	.000	9	1	0	0	0	16	18	13	13	2	1	8	10	1.625	7.31	54	6.31	.295	0	.000	-6	0	-0.6

• ALVAREZ, Wilson Wilson Eduardo (Fuenmayor) Alvarez b: 3/24/1970, Maracaibo, Venezuela BL/TL, 6'1", 235 lbs. Deb: 7/24/1989

YEAR	TM-L	W	L	PCT	G	GS	CG	SH	SV	IP	H	R	ER	HR	HB	BB	SO	RAT	ERA	ERA+	CERA	OAV	BH	AVG	PR+	WS	TPW
1989	Tex-A	0	1	.000	1	1	0	0	0	0	3	3	3	2	0	2	0	....	∞	....	∞	1.000	0	....	-3	0	-0.3
1991	Chi-A	3	2	.600	10	9	2	1	0	56^{1}	47	26	22	9	0	29	32	1.349	3.51	113	4.09	.230	0	....	1	3	0.1
1992	Chi-A	5	3	.625	34	9	0	0	1	100^{1}	103	64	58	12	4	65	66	1.674	5.20	74	5.61	.272	0	....	-15	1	-1.5
1993*	Chi-A	15	8	.652	31	31	1	1	0	207^{2}	168	78	68	14	7	122	155	1.396	2.95	142	3.69	.230	0	....	28	18	2.7
1994	Chi-A★	12	8	.600	24	24	2	1	0	161^{2}	147	72	62	16	0	62	108	1.293	3.45	135	3.49	.241	0	....	22	12	2.1
1995	Chi-A	8	11	.421	29	29	3	0	0	175	171	96	84	21	2	93	118	1.509	4.32	103	4.66	.258	0	....	5	8	0.5
1996	Chi-A	15	10	.600	35	35	0	0	0	217^{1}	216	106	102	21	4	97	181	1.440	4.22	112	4.26	.258	0	....	14	13	1.3
1997	Chi-A	9	8	.529	22	22	2	1	0	145^{2}	126	61	49	9	3	55	110	1.243	3.03	145	3.05	.232	0	.000	24	12	2.3
	*SF-N	4	3	.571	11	11	0	0	0	66^{1}	54	36	33	9	1	36	69	1.357	4.48	90	3.86	.224	3	.130	-3	3	-0.3
1998	TB-A	6	14	.300	25	25	0	0	0	142^{2}	130	78	75	18	9	68	107	1.388	4.73	101	4.30	.239	0	....	-5	7	-0.4
1999	TB-A	9	9	.500	28	28	1	0	0	160	159	92	75	22	6	79	128	1.488	4.22	118	4.87	.260	0	.000	14	10	1.3
2002	TB-A	2	3	.400	23	10	0	0	1	75	80	47	44	13	4	36	56	1.547	5.28	85	5.46	.272	0	.000	-8	2	-0.8
2003	LA-N	6	2	.750	21	12	1	1	1	95	80	27	25	5	5	23	82	1.084	2.37	169	2.61	.231	5	.172	16	10	1.6
Total	12	94	82	.534	294	246	12	5	3	1603	1484	786	700	171	45	767	1212	1.404	3.93	114	4.13	.247	8	.129	91	99	8.4

• AMES, Red Leon Kessling Ames b: 8/2/1882, Warren, OH d: 10/8/1936, Warren, OH BB/TR, 5'10.5", 185 lbs. Deb: 9/14/1903

YEAR	TM-L	W	L	PCT	G	GS	CG	SH	SV	IP	H	R	ER	HR	HB	BB	SO	RAT	ERA	ERA+	CERA	OAV	BH	AVG	PR+	WS	TPW
1903	NY-N	2	0	1.000	2	2	2	1	0	14	5	2	2	0	0	8	14	.929	1.29	260	1.13	.114	0	.000	3	2	0.2
1904	NY-N	4	6	.400	16	13	11	1	3	115	94	44	29	2	3	38	93	1.148	2.27	120	2.39	.222	5	.125	3	8	0.2
1905*	NY-N	22	8	.733	34	31	21	2	0	262^{2}	220	113	80	2	3	105	198	1.237	2.74	107	2.63	.230	14	.144	7	17	0.6
1906	NY-N	12	10	.545	31	25	15	1	1	203^{1}	166	79	60	1	3	93	156	1.274	2.66	98	2.66	.223	4	.066	-2	12	-0.5
1907	NY-N	10	12	.455	39	26	17	2	1	233^{1}	184	93	56	4	10	108	146	1.251	2.16	114	2.74	.219	12	.174	16	15	2.0

YEAR TM-L	W	L	PCT	G	GS	CG	SH	SV	IP	H	R	ER	HR	HB	BB	SO	RAT	ERA	ERA+	CERA	OAV	BH	AVG	PR+	WS	TPW
1908 NY-N	7	4	.636	18	15	5	0	1	114^1	96	35	23	0	1	27	81	1.076	1.81	132	2.11	.232	7	.194	9	8	1.0
1909 NY-N	15	10	.600	34	26	20	2	1	244	217	109	73	2	4	81	156	1.221	2.69	95	2.69	.241	6	.074	-1	12	-0.7
1910 NY-N	12	11	.522	33	23	13	3	0	190^1	161	78	47	3	6	63	94	1.177	2.22	133	2.64	.237	11	.177	18	13	1.8
1911* NY-N	11	10	.524	34	23	13	1	2	205	170	80	61	0	4	54	118	1.093	2.68	125	**2.09**	.223	6	.094	18	16	1.5
1912* NY-N	11	5	.688	33	22	9	2	2	179	194	82	49	3	4	35	83	1.279	2.46	137	3.26	.281	13	.224	18	14	1.9
1913 NY-N	2	1	.667	8	5	2	0	1	41^2	35	11	10	0	1	8	30	1.032	2.16	144	2.07	.241	2	.154	4	4	0.4
Cin-N	11	13	.458	31	24	12	1	2	187^1	185	82	60	7	5	70	80	1.361	2.88	112	3.55	.265	6	.102	7	11	0.3
Yr.	13	14	.481	39	29	14	1	3	229	220	93	70	7	6	78	110	1.301	2.75	117	3.28	.261	8	.111	11	15	0.6
1914 Cin-N	15	23	.395	47	36	18	3	**6**	297	274	125	87	8	6	94	128	1.239	2.64	111	2.85	.248	12	.128	11	17	0.8
1915 Cin-N	2	4	.333	17	7	4	1	1	68	82	39	34	2	0	24	26	1.559	4.50	63	4.61	.311	1	.050	-14	0	-1.7
StL-N	9	3	.750	15	14	8	2	1	113^1	93	35	31	1	0	32	48	1.103	2.46	113	2.08	.226	4	.114	5	9	0.4
Yr.	11	7	.611	32	21	12	3	2	181^1	175	74	65	3	0	56	74	1.274	3.23	87	3.03	.259	5	.091	-9	9	-1.3
1916 StL-N	11	16	.407	45	22	10	2	**8**	228	225	100	67	3	5	57	98	1.237	2.64	100	2.88	.263	12	.176	0	12	0.1
1917 StL-N	15	10	.600	43	19	10	2	3	209	189	75	63	2	3	57	62	1.177	2.71	99	2.54	.249	12	.188	-3	17	-0.1
1918 StL-N	9	14	.391	27	25	17	0	1	206^2	192	75	53	1	5	52	68	1.181	2.31	117	2.57	.252	10	.156	8	11	0.9
1919 StL-N	3	5	.375	23	7	1	0	1	70	88	44	38	1	1	25	19	1.614	4.89	57	4.72	.314	4	.222	-17	0	-1.9
Phi-N	0	2	.000	3	2	1	0	1	16	26	12	11	0	0	3	4	1.813	6.19	52	6.44	.400	2	.400	-5	0	-0.5
Yr.	3	7	.300	26	9	2	0	2	86	114	56	49	1	1	28	23	1.651	5.13	56	5.04	.330	6	.261	-22	0	-2.4
Total 17	183	167	.523	533	367	209	26	36	3198	2896	1313	934	42	64	1034	1702	1.229	2.63	107	2.77	.245	143	.141	85	198	6.7

• AMOLE, Doc

Morris George Amole b: 7/5/1878, Coatesville, PA d: 3/7/1912, Wilmington, DE BR/TL, 5'9", 165 lbs. Deb: 8/19/1897

YEAR TM-L	W	L	PCT	G	GS	CG	SH	SV	IP	H	R	ER	HR	HB	BB	SO	RAT	ERA	ERA+	CERA	OAV	BH	AVG	PR+	WS	TPW
1897 Bal-N	4	4	.500	11	7	6	0	0	70	67	34	20	0	6	17	19	1.200	2.57	162	2.83	.250	3	.107	11	5	0.8
1898 Was-N	0	6	.000	7	5	4	0	0	49^1	83	57	43	0	6	22	11	2.128	7.84	47	7.94	.370	2	.100	-22	0	-2.2
Total 2	4	10	.286	18	12	10	0	0	119^1	150	91	63	0	12	39	30	1.584	4.75	80	4.94	.305	5	.104	-11	5	-1.5

• AMOR, Vicente

Vicente (Alvarez) Amor b: 8/8/1932, Havana, Cuba BR/TR, 6'3", 182 lbs. Deb: 4/16/1955

YEAR TM-L	W	L	PCT	G	GS	CG	SH	SV	IP	H	R	ER	HR	HB	BB	SO	RAT	ERA	ERA+	CERA	OAV	BH	AVG	PR+	WS	TPW
1955 Chi-N	0	1	.000	4	0	0	0	0	6	11	3	3	0	0	3	3	2.333	4.50	91	8.52	.407	0	....	-0	0	0.0
1957 Cin-N	1	2	.333	9	4	1	0	0	27^1	39	19	18	2	2	10	9	1.793	5.93	69	6.49	.345	1	.167	-6	0	-0.6
Total 2	1	3	.250	13	4	1	0	0	33^1	50	22	21	2	2	13	12	1.890	5.67	72	6.86	.357	1	.167	-6	0	-0.6

• ANCKER, Walter

Walter Ancker b: 4/10/1894, New York, NY d: 2/13/1954, Englewood, NJ BR/TR, 6'1", 190 lbs. Deb: 9/3/1915

YEAR TM-L	W	L	PCT	G	GS	CG	SH	SV	IP	H	R	ER	HR	HB	BB	SO	RAT	ERA	ERA+	CERA	OAV	BH	AVG	PR+	WS	TPW
1915 Phi-A	0	0	....	4	1	0	0	0	17^2	19	10	7	1	3	17	4	2.038	3.57	82	6.93	.279	0	.000	-1	0	-0.2

• ANDERSEN, Larry

Larry Eugene Andersen b: 5/6/1953, Portland, OR BR/TR, 6'3", 205 lbs. Deb: 9/5/1975

YEAR TM-L	W	L	PCT	G	GS	CG	SH	SV	IP	H	R	ER	HR	HB	BB	SO	RAT	ERA	ERA+	CERA	OAV	BH	AVG	PR+	WS	TPW
1975 Cle-A	0	0	....	3	0	0	0	0	5^2	4	3	3	0	0	2	4	1.059	4.76	79	1.76	.200	0	....	-1	0	-0.1
1977 Cle-A	0	1	.000	11	0	0	0	0	14^1	10	7	5	1	0	9	8	1.326	3.14	126	2.71	.200	0	....	1	1	0.1
1979 Cle-A	0	0	....	8	0	0	0	0	16^2	25	14	14	3	0	4	7	1.740	7.56	56	7.07	.357	0	....	-6	0	-0.6
1981 Sea-A	3	3	.500	41	0	0	0	5	67^2	57	27	20	4	2	18	40	1.108	2.66	145	2.57	.228	0	....	10	7	1.0
1982 Sea-A	0	0	....	40	1	0	0	1	79^2	100	56	53	16	4	23	32	1.544	5.99	71	6.14	.311	0	....	-15	0	-1.5
1983* Phi-N	1	0	1.000	17	0	0	0	0	26^1	19	7	7	0	0	9	14	1.063	2.39	149	1.76	.200	0	.000	4	3	0.4
1984 Phi-N	3	7	.300	64	0	0	0	4	90^2	85	32	24	5	0	25	54	1.213	2.38	153	2.86	.248	0	.000	14	8	1.4
1985 Phi-N	3	3	.500	57	0	0	0	3	73	78	41	35	5	3	26	50	1.425	4.32	85	4.14	.274	0	.000	-4	3	-0.5
1986 Phi-N	0	0	....	10	0	0	0	0	12^2	19	8	6	0	0	3	9	1.737	4.26	90	5.95	.388	0	....	-1	0	-0.1
*Hou-N	2	1	.667	38	0	0	0	1	64^2	64	22	20	2	1	23	33	1.345	2.78	129	3.29	.276	0	.000	6	5	0.5
Yr.	2	1	.667	48	0	0	0	1	77^1	83	30	26	2	1	26	42	1.409	3.03	121	3.72	.295	0	.000	5	5	0.5
1987 Hou-N	9	5	.643	67	0	0	0	5	101^2	95	46	39	7	2	41	94	1.338	3.45	113	3.37	.246	1	.167	6	9	0.6
1988 Hou-N	2	4	.333	53	0	0	0	5	82^2	82	29	27	3	1	20	66	1.234	2.94	113	2.84	.254	2	.333	4	6	0.5
1989 Hou-N	4	4	.500	60	0	0	0	3	87^2	63	19	15	2	0	24	85	.992	1.54	220	1.65	.198	1	.333	19	11	2.0
1990 Hou-N	5	2	.714	50	0	0	0	6	73^2	61	19	16	2	1	24	68	1.154	1.95	190	2.38	.229	0	.000	14	10	1.4
*Bos-A	0	0	....	15	0	0	0	1	22	18	3	3	0	1	3	25	.955	1.23	332	1.78	.220	0	....	7	3	0.8
1991 SD-N	3	4	.429	38	0	0	0	13	47	39	13	12	0	0	13	40	1.106	2.30	165	2.04	.231	0	.000	8	9	0.8
1992 SD-N	1	1	.500	34	0	0	0	2	35	26	14	13	2	1	8	35	.971	3.34	107	1.87	.202	0	.000	1	4	0.1
1993* Phi-N	3	2	.600	64	0	0	0	0	61^2	54	22	20	4	1	21	67	1.216	2.92	136	2.96	.233	1	1.000	8	7	0.8
1994 Phi-N	1	2	.333	29	0	0	0	0	32^2	33	20	16	2	0	15	27	1.469	4.41	97	3.80	.256	0	....	-0	1	0.0
Total 17	40	39	.506	699	1	0	0	49	995^1	932	402	348	58	17	311	758	1.249	3.15	121	3.15	.249	5	.132	74	87	7.8

• ANDERSON, Allan

Allan Lee Anderson b: 1/7/1964, Lancaster, OH BL/TL, 5'11.5", 186 lbs. Deb: 6/11/1986

YEAR TM-L	W	L	PCT	G	GS	CG	SH	SV	IP	H	R	ER	HR	HB	BB	SO	RAT	ERA	ERA+	CERA	OAV	BH	AVG	PR+	WS	TPW
1986 Min-A	3	6	.333	21	10	1	0	0	84^1	106	54	52	11	1	30	51	1.613	5.55	78	5.78	.316	0	....	-11	2	-1.1
1987 Min-A	1	0	1.000	4	2	0	0	0	12^1	20	15	15	3	0	10	3	2.432	10.95	42	11.70	.392	0	....	-9	0	-0.8
1988 Min-A	16	9	.640	30	30	3	1	0	202^1	199	70	55	14	7	37	83	1.166	**2.45**	**166**	3.16	.261	0	....	36	19	3.7
1989 Min-A	17	10	.630	33	33	4	1	0	196^2	214	97	83	15	7	53	69	1.358	3.80	109	4.02	.275	0	.000	8	12	0.8
1990 Min-A	7	18	.280	31	31	5	1	0	188^2	214	106	95	20	5	39	82	1.341	4.53	92	4.26	.289	0	....	-8	7	-0.8
1991 Min-A	5	11	.313	29	22	2	0	0	134^1	148	82	74	24	5	42	51	1.414	4.96	86	4.99	.281	0	....	-12	3	-1.2
Total 6	49	54	.476	148	128	15	3	0	818^2	901	424	374	87	25	211	339	1.358	4.11	102	4.32	.282	0	.000	5	43	0.6

• ANDERSON, Bill

William Edward "Lefty" Anderson b: 11/28/1895, Boston, MA d: 3/13/1983, Medford, MA BR/TL, 6'1", 165 lbs. Deb: 9/10/1925

YEAR TM-L	W	L	PCT	G	GS	CG	SH	SV	IP	H	R	ER	HR	HB	BB	SO	RAT	ERA	ERA+	CERA	OAV	BH	AVG	PR+	WS	TPW
1925 Bos-N	0	0	....	2	0	0	0	0	2^2	5	3	3	0	0	2	1	2.625	10.13	40	10.47	.500	0	.000	-2	0	-0.2

• ANDERSON, Bob

Robert Carl Anderson b: 9/29/1935, East Chicago, IN BR/TR, 6'4.5", 210 lbs. Deb: 7/31/1957

YEAR TM-L	W	L	PCT	G	GS	CG	SH	SV	IP	H	R	ER	HR	HB	BB	SO	RAT	ERA	ERA+	CERA	OAV	BH	AVG	PR+	WS	TPW
1957 Chi-N	0	1	.000	8	0	0	0	0	16^1	20	16	14	2	1	8	7	1.714	7.71	50	6.11	.317	0	.000	-7	0	-0.7
1958 Chi-N	3	3	.500	17	8	2	0	0	65^2	61	29	29	3	1	29	51	1.371	3.97	99	3.60	.255	2	.118	0	4	-0.1
1959 Chi-N	12	13	.480	37	36	7	1	0	235^1	245	117	108	21	5	77	113	1.368	4.13	96	4.04	.272	6	.075	-7	11	-1.1
1960 Chi-N	9	11	.450	38	30	5	0	1	203^2	201	105	93	26	7	68	115	1.321	4.11	92	4.01	.255	12	.169	-7	8	-0.7
1961 Chi-N	7	10	.412	57	12	1	0	8	152	162	85	72	14	2	56	96	1.434	4.26	98	4.21	.275	6	.143	1	8	0.1
1962 Chi-N	2	7	.222	57	4	0	0	4	107^2	111	70	60	9	5	60	82	1.588	5.02	83	4.81	.266	3	.130	-11	3	-1.0
1963 Det-A	3	1	.750	32	3	0	0	0	60	58	28	22	5	6	21	38	1.317	3.30	113	3.90	.258	4	.444	3	4	0.5
Total 7	36	46	.439	246	93	15	1	13	840^2	858	450	398	80	27	319	502	1.400	4.26	93	4.16	.266	33	.134	-27	38	-3.0

• ANDERSON, Brian

Brian James Anderson b: 4/26/1972, Portsmouth, VA BL/TL, 6'1", 190 lbs. Deb: 9/10/1993

YEAR TM-L	W	L	PCT	G	GS	CG	SH	SV	IP	H	R	ER	HR	HB	BB	SO	RAT	ERA	ERA+	CERA	OAV	BH	AVG	PR+	WS	TPW
1993 Cal-A	0	0	....	4	1	0	0	0	11^1	11	5	5	1	0	2	4	1.147	3.97	113	3.08	.256	0	....	1	1	0.1
1994 Cal-A	7	5	.583	18	18	0	0	0	101^2	120	63	59	13	5	27	47	1.446	5.22	93	5.05	.300	0	....	-4	6	-0.4
1995 Cal-A	6	8	.429	18	17	1	0	0	99^2	110	66	65	24	3	30	45	1.405	5.87	80	5.37	.282	0	....	-14	3	-1.3
1996 Cle-A	3	1	.750	10	9	0	0	0	51^1	58	29	28	9	0	14	21	1.403	4.91	100	4.96	.296	0	....	0	3	0.0
1997* Cle-A	4	2	.667	8	8	0	0	0	48	55	28	25	7	0	11	22	1.375	4.69	100	4.71	.301	0	....	0	2	0.0
1998 Ari-N	12	13	.480	32	32	2	1	0	208	221	100	100	39	4	24	95	1.178	4.33	97	3.99	.274	7	.106	-3	9	-0.5
1999* Ari-N	8	2	.800	31	19	2	1	1	130	144	69	66	18	1	28	75	1.323	4.57	100	4.23	.279	5	.132	-1	7	0.0
2000 Ari-N	11	7	.611	33	32	2	0	0	213^1	226	101	96	38	3	39	104	1.242	4.05	116	4.15	.275	13	.188	16	14	1.6
2001* Ari-N	4	9	.308	29	22	1	0	0	133^1	156	93	77	25	1	30	55	1.395	5.20	88	5.00	.295	5	.135	-11	2	-1.1
2002 Ari-N	6	11	.353	35	24	0	0	0	156	174	86	83	23	1	32	81	1.321	4.79	93	4.28	.284	5	.116	-4	5	-0.5
2003 Cle-A	9	10	.474	25	24	0	0	0	148	162	88	61	21	4	32	72	1.311	3.71	119	4.29	.282	0	.000	9	7	0.8
KC-A	5	1	.833	7	7	2	1	0	49^2	50	22	22	6	0	11	15	1.228	3.99	130	3.72	.272	0	....	7	5	0.6
Yr.	14	11	.560	32	31	2	1	0	197^2	212	110	83	27	4	43	87	1.290	3.78	122	4.14	.279	0	.000	15	12	1.5
Total 11	75	69	.521	250	213	10	3	1	1350^1	1487	750	687	224	22	280	636	1.309	4.58	100	4.43	.283	35	.138	-5	64	-0.6

• ANDERSON, Bud

Karl Adam Anderson b: 5/27/1956, Westbury, NY BR/TR, 6'3", 210 lbs. Deb: 6/11/1982

YEAR TM-L	W	L	PCT	G	GS	CG	SH	SV	IP	H	R	ER	HR	HB	BB	SO	RAT	ERA	ERA+	CERA	OAV	BH	AVG	PR+	WS	TPW
1982 Cle-A	3	4	.429	25	5	1	0	0	80^2	84	37	30	4	1	30	44	1.413	3.35	122	3.80	.268	0	....	7	6	0.7
1983 Cle-A	1	6	.143	39	1	0	0	7	68^1	64	34	31	8	0	32	32	1.405	4.08	104	4.04	.255	0	....	2	5	0.2
Total 2	4	10	.286	64	6	1	0	7	149	148	71	61	12	1	62	76	1.409	3.68	113	3.91	.262	0	....	9	11	0.9

YEAR TM-L	W	L	PCT	G	GS	CG	SH	SV	IP	H	R	ER	HR	HB	BB	SO	RAT	ERA	ERA+	CERA	OAV	BH	AVG	PR+	WS	TPW
• ANDERSON, Craig	Norman Craig Anderson b: 7/1/1938, Washington, DC BR/TR, 6'2", 205 lbs. Deb: 6/23/1961																									
1961 StL-N	4	3	.571	25	0	0	0	1	38^2	38	15	14	3	1	12	21	1.293	3.26	135	3.57	.255	3	.333	5	4	0.5
1962 NY-N	3	17	.150	50	14	2	0	4	131^1	150	108	78	18	5	63	62	1.622	5.35	78	5.46	.278	3	.094	-14	1	-1.6
1963 NY-N	0	2	.000	3	2	0	0	0	9^1	17	15	9	0	0	3	6	2.143	8.68	40	7.26	.362	1	.333	-5	0	-0.5
1964 NY-N	0	1	.000	4	1	0	0	0	13	21	9	8	0	0	3	5	1.846	5.54	65	6.29	.382	0	.000	-3	0	-0.3
Total 4	7	23	.233	82	17	2	0	5	192^1	226	147	109	21	6	81	94	1.596	5.10	80	5.22	.286	7	.149	-18	5	-2.0
• ANDERSON, Dave	David S. Anderson b: 10/10/1868, Chester, PA d: 3/22/1897, Chester, PA TL Deb: 8/24/1889																									
1889 Phi-N	0	1	.000	5	2	1	0	0	23	30	21	19	2	0	14	8	1.913	7.43	59	....	.305	2	.182	-7	0	-0.6
1890 Phi-N	1	1	.500	3	2	1	0	0	19^1	31	25	16	0	1	11	7	2.172	7.45	49	....	.352	1	.111	-8	0	-0.8
Pit-N	2	11	.154	13	13	13	0	0	108	116	84	56	2	7	49	41	1.528	4.67	70	....	.267	3	.071	-11	1	-1.3
Yr.	3	12	.200	16	15	14	0	0	127^1	147	109	72	2	8	60	48	1.626	5.09	66	....	.281	4	.078	-19	1	-2.1
Total 2	3	13	.188	21	17	15	0	0	150^1	177	130	91	4	8	74	56	1.670	5.45	65	....	.285	6	.097	-26	1	-2.8
• ANDERSON, Fred	John Frederick Anderson b: 12/11/1885, Calahan, NC d: 11/8/1957, Winston-Salem, NC BR/TR, 6'2", 180 lbs. Deb: 9/25/1909																									
1909 Bos-A	0	0	....	1	1	0	0	0	8	3	3	1	0	0	1	5	.500	1.13	222	0.48	.115	0	.000	1	1	0.1
1913 Bos-A	0	6	.000	10	8	4	0	0	57^1	84	51	38	0	1	21	32	1.831	5.97	49	6.41	.350	1	.050	-18	0	-2.2
1914 Buf-F	13	15	.464	37	28	21	2	0	260^1	243	115	89	8	2	64	144	1.179	3.08	108	2.75	.249	17	.189	4	15	0.2
1915 Buf-F	19	13	.594	36	28	14	5	0	240	192	80	67	5	3	72	142	1.100	2.51	122	2.24	.222	12	.150	15	20	1.3
1916 NY-N	9	13	.409	38	27	13	2	2	188	206	99	71	7	5	38	98	1.298	3.40	71	3.40	.277	8	.138	-23	3	-2.7
1917* NY-N	8	8	.500	38	18	8	1	3	162	122	40	26	1	2	34	69	.963	**1.44**	**176**	**1.62**	**.209**	3	.071	18	14	1.7
1918 NY-N	4	2	.667	18	4	2	1	**3**	70^2	62	27	21	1	2	17	24	1.118	2.67	98	2.35	.246	0	.000	-1	4	-0.4
Total 7	53	57	.482	178	114	62	11	8	986^1	912	415	313	22	15	247	514	1.175	2.86	100	2.73	.247	41	.131	-4	57	-1.9
• ANDERSON, Jason	Jason R. Anderson b: 6/9/1979, Danville, IL BL/TR, 6', 170 lbs. Deb: 3/31/2003																									
2003 NY-A	1	0	1.000	22	0	0	0	0	20^2	23	13	11	3	2	14	9	1.790	4.79	91	6.19	.280	0	....	-0	1	0.0
NY-N	0	0	....	6	0	0	0	0	10^2	10	6	6	2	1	5	7	1.406	5.06	82	4.86	.256	0	....	-1	0	-0.1
• ANDERSON, Jimmy	James Drew Anderson b: 1/22/1976, Portsmouth, VA BL/TL, 6'1", 207 lbs. Deb: 7/4/1999																									
1999 Pit-N	2	1	.667	13	4	0	0	0	29^1	25	15	13	2	1	16	13	1.398	3.99	114	3.62	.234	3	.333	2	3	0.3
2000 Pit-N	5	11	.313	27	26	1	0	0	144	169	94	84	13	7	58	73	1.576	5.25	87	5.21	.294	7	.140	-9	4	-1.0
2001 Pit-N	9	17	.346	34	34	1	0	0	206^1	232	123	117	15	11	83	89	1.527	5.10	88	4.69	.287	7	.119	-14	7	-1.4
2002 Pit-N	8	13	.381	28	25	1	0	0	140^2	167	91	85	20	5	63	47	1.635	5.44	77	5.84	.299	5	.119	-21	3	-2.2
2003 Cin-N	1	5	.167	8	7	0	0	0	38^2	60	39	38	8	0	14	13	1.914	8.84	48	8.22	.359	1	.111	-20	0	-1.9
Total 5	25	47	.347	110	96	3	0	0	559	653	362	337	58	24	234	235	1.587	5.43	81	5.30	.295	23	.136	-61	17	-6.2
• ANDERSON, John	John Charles Anderson b: 11/23/1929, St. Paul, MN d: 12/20/1998, Houston, TX BR/TR, 6'1", 190 lbs. Deb: 8/17/1958																									
1958 Phi-N	0	0	....	5	1	0	0	0	16	26	17	14	5	1	4	9	1.875	7.88	50	9.29	.361	0	.000	-7	0	-0.7
1960 Bal-A	0	0	....	4	0	0	0	0	4^2	8	7	7	0	0	4	1	2.571	13.50	28	9.39	.444	0	....	-5	0	-0.5
1962 StL-N	0	0	....	5	0	0	0	1	6^1	4	1	1	0	0	3	3	1.105	1.42	300	1.44	.182	0	....	2	1	0.2
Hou-N	0	0	....	10	0	0	0	0	17^2	26	12	10	1	0	3	6	1.642	5.09	73	5.39	.338	0	.000	-2	0	-0.3
Yr.	0	0	....	15	0	0	0	1	24	30	13	11	1	0	6	9	1.500	4.13	92	4.35	.303	0	.000	-0	1	-0.1
Total 3	0	0	....	24	1	0	0	1	44^2	64	37	32	6	1	14	19	1.746	6.45	60	6.64	.339	0	.000	-12	1	-1.3
• ANDERSON, Larry	Lawrence Dennis Anderson b: 12/3/1952, Maywood, CA BR/TR, 6'3", 190 lbs. Deb: 9/25/1974																									
1974 Mil-A	0	0	....	2	0	0	0	0	2^1	2	0	0	0	0	1	3	1.286	0.00	....	3.03	.250	0	....	1	0	0.1
1975 Mil-A	1	0	1.000	8	1	1	1	0	30^1	36	18	17	3	0	6	13	1.385	5.04	76	4.40	.298	0	....	-4	1	-0.4
1977 Chi-A	1	3	.250	6	0	0	0	0	8^2	10	10	9	1	0	15	7	2.885	9.35	44	8.95	.286	0	....	-5	0	-0.5
Total 3	2	3	.400	16	1	1	1	0	41^1	48	28	26	4	0	22	23	1.694	5.66	69	5.27	.293	0	....	-8	1	-0.8
• ANDERSON, Matt	Matthew Jason Anderson b: 8/17/1976, Louisville, KY BR/TR, 6'4", 200 lbs. Deb: 6/25/1998																									
1998 Det-A	5	1	.833	42	0	0	0	0	44	38	16	16	3	2	31	44	1.568	3.27	144	4.38	.250	0	....	6	5	0.6
1999 Det-A	2	1	.667	37	0	0	0	0	38	33	27	24	8	1	35	32	1.789	5.68	87	6.34	.232	0	....	-3	1	-0.3
2000 Det-A	3	2	.600	69	0	0	0	1	74^1	61	44	39	8	3	45	71	1.426	4.72	102	4.02	.228	0	....	1	4	0.1
2001 Det-A	3	1	.750	62	0	0	0	22	56	56	33	30	2	0	18	52	1.321	4.82	90	3.19	.257	0	....	-2	8	-0.2
2002 Det-A	2	1	.667	12	0	0	0	0	11	17	13	11	1	2	8	8	2.273	9.00	48	9.52	.378	0	....	-6	0	-0.5
2003 Det-A	0	1	.000	23	0	0	0	3	23^1	25	17	14	5	1	9	13	1.457	5.40	80	5.25	.272	0	....	-3	1	-0.3
Total 6	15	7	.682	245	0	0	0	26	246^2	230	150	134	27	9	146	220	1.524	4.89	94	4.61	.251	0	....	-6	19	-0.6
• ANDERSON, Mike	Michael James Anderson b: 7/30/1966, Austin, TX BR/TR, 6'3", 200 lbs. Deb: 9/7/1993																									
1993 Cin-N	0	0	....	3	0	0	0	0	5^1	12	11	11	3	0	3	4	2.813	18.56	22	18.35	.444	0	.000	-9	0	-0.9
• ANDERSON, Red	Arnold Revola Anderson b: 6/19/1912, Lawton, IA d: 8/7/1972, Sioux City, IA BR/TR, 6'3", 210 lbs. Deb: 9/19/1937																									
1937 Was-A	0	1	.000	2	1	0	0	0	10^2	11	9	8	0	1	11	3	2.063	6.75	66	6.15	.282	0	.000	-3	0	-0.3
1940 Was-A	1	1	.500	2	2	2	0	0	14	12	6	6	0	0	5	3	1.214	3.86	108	2.58	.245	3	.600	1	1	0.2
1941 Was-A	4	6	.400	32	6	1	0	0	112	127	69	52	7	3	53	34	1.607	4.18	97	4.91	.296	8	.258	-0	5	0.2
Total 3	5	8	.385	36	9	3	0	0	136^2	150	84	66	7	4	69	40	1.602	4.35	94	4.77	.290	11	.282	-3	6	0.0
• ANDERSON, Rick	Richard Arlen Anderson b: 11/29/1956, Everett, WA BR/TR, 6', 175 lbs. Deb: 6/9/1986																									
1986 NY-N	2	1	.667	15	5	0	0	1	49^2	45	17	15	3	0	11	21	1.128	2.72	130	2.57	.245	1	.091	4	4	0.4
1987 KC-A	0	2	.000	6	2	0	0	0	13	26	22	20	3	2	9	12	2.692	13.85	33	13.40	.394	0	....	-13	0	-1.3
1988 KC-A	2	1	.667	7	3	0	0	0	34	41	17	16	3	1	9	9	1.471	4.24	94	4.73	.308	0	....	-0	2	0.0
Total 3	4	4	.500	28	10	0	0	1	96^2	112	56	51	9	3	29	42	1.459	4.75	85	4.79	.292	1	.091	-9	6	-0.9
• ANDERSON, Rick	Richard Lee Anderson b: 12/25/1953, Inglewood, CA d: 6/23/1989, Wilmington, CA BR/TR, 6'2", 210 lbs. Deb: 9/18/1979																									
1979 NY-A	0	0	....	1	0	0	0	0	2^1	1	1	1	0	0	4	0	2.143	3.86	106	5.91	.167	0	....	0	0	0.0
1980 Sea-A	0	0	....	5	2	0	0	0	9^2	8	5	4	1	0	10	7	1.862	3.72	111	5.22	.229	0	....	1	1	0.1
Total 2	0	0	....	6	2	0	0	0	12	9	6	5	1	0	14	7	1.917	3.75	110	5.35	.220	0	....	1	1	0.1
• ANDERSON, Scott	Scott Richard Anderson b: 8/1/1962, Corvallis, OR BR/TR, 6'6", 190 lbs. Deb: 4/8/1987																									
1987 Tex-A	0	1	.000	8	0	0	0	0	11^1	17	12	12	0	1	8	6	2.206	9.53	47	7.46	.347	0	....	-6	0	-0.6
1990 Mon-N	0	1	.000	4	3	0	0	0	18	12	6	6	1	0	5	16	.944	3.00	122	1.67	.188	0	.000	1	1	0.1
1995 KC-A	1	0	1.000	6	4	0	0	0	25^1	29	15	15	3	1	8	6	1.461	5.33	90	4.98	.290	0	....	-2	1	-0.2
Total 3	1	2	.333	18	7	0	0	0	54^2	58	33	33	4	2	21	28	1.445	5.43	81	4.41	.272	0	.000	-7	2	-0.7
• ANDERSON, Varney	Varney Samuel "Varn" Anderson b: 6/18/1866, Geneva, IL d: 11/5/1941, Rockford, IL BR/TR, 5'10", 165 lbs. Deb: 8/1/1889																									
1889 Ind-N	0	1	.000	2	1	1	0	0	12	13	10	6	0	3	9	3	1.833	4.50	93	....	.267	0	.000	-1	0	-0.1
1894 Was-N	0	2	.000	2	2	2	0	0	14	15	12	11	0	1	6	3	1.500	7.07	74	3.99	.271	3	.429	-2	0	-0.1
1895 Was-N	9	16	.360	29	25	18	0	0	204^2	288	199	134	13	10	97	35	1.881	5.89	81	6.58	.327	28	.289	-21	7	-1.4
1896 Was-N	0	1	.000	2	2	1	0	0	9	23	16	13	0	0	3	0	2.889	13.00	34	13.08	.471	3	.600	-8	0	-0.6
Total 4	9	20	.310	35	30	22	0	0	239^2	339	237	164	13	14	115	41	1.894	6.16	77	6.34	.328	34	.298	-33	7	-2.3
• ANDERSON, Walter	Walter Carl "Lefty" Anderson b: 9/25/1897, Grand Rapids, MI d: 1/6/1990, Battle Creek, MI BL/TL, 6'2", 160 lbs. Deb: 5/14/1917																									
1917 Phi-A	0	0	....	14	2	0	0	0	38^2	32	16	13	0	1	21	10	1.371	3.03	91	3.00	.246	3	.429	-1	2	0.1
1919 Phi-A	1	0	1.000	3	0	0	0	0	14	13	8	6	0	1	8	10	1.500	3.86	89	2.39	.245	0	.000	-0	1	-0.1
Total 2	1	0	1.000	17	2	0	0	0	52^2	45	24	19	0	2	29	20	1.405	3.25	90	2.84	.246	3	.273	-1	3	0.0
• ANDERSON, Wingo	Wingo Charlie Anderson b: 8/13/1886, Alvarado, TX d: 12/19/1950, Fort Worth, TX BL/TL, 5'10.5", 150 lbs. Deb: 4/16/1910																									
1910 Cin-N	0	0	....	7	2	0	0	0	17^1	16	15	9	0	1	17	11	1.904	4.67	62	5.27	.258	1	.200	-3	0	-0.4

YEAR	TM-L	W	L	PCT	G	GS	CG	SH	SV	IP	H	R	ER	HR	HB	BB	SO	RAT	ERA	ERA+	CERA	OAV	BH	AVG	PR+	WS	TPW
• ANDRE, John	John Edward Andre b: 1/3/1923, Brockton, MA d: 11/25/1976, Barnstable, MA BL/TR, 6'4", 200 lbs. Deb: 4/16/1955																										
1955	Chi-N	0	1	.000	22	3	0	0	1	45	45	34	29	7	1	28	19	1.622	5.80	70	5.26	.259	1	.111	-9	0	-0.9
• ANDREWS, Clayton	Clayton John Andrews b: 5/15/1978, Dunedin, FL BR/TL, 6', 180 lbs. Deb: 4/16/2000																										
2000	Tor-A	1	2	.333	8	2	0	0	0	20^{2}	34	23	23	6	0	9	12	2.081	10.02	51	10.03	.374	0	.000	-11	0	-1.1
• ANDREWS, Elbert	Elbert DeVore Andrews b: 12/11/1901, Greenwood, SC d: 11/25/1979, Greenwood, SC BL/TR, 6', 175 lbs. Deb: 5/1/1925																										
1925	Phi-A	0	0	....	6	0	0	0	0	8	12	12	9	0	0	11	0	2.875	10.13	46	10.39	.375	0	....	-5	0	-0.4
• ANDREWS, Hub	Herbert Carl Andrews b: 8/31/1922, Burbank, CA BR/TR, 6', 170 lbs. Deb: 4/20/1947																										
1947	NY-N	0	0	....	7	0	0	0	0	8^{2}	14	7	6	1	0	4	2	2.077	6.23	65	8.13	.368	0	....	-2	0	-0.2
1948	NY-N	0	0	....	1	0	0	0	0	3	3	1	0	0	0	0	0	1.000	0.00	....	2.46	.300	0	....	1	0	0.1
Total	2	0	0	....	8	0	0	0	0	11^{2}	17	8	6	1	0	4	2	1.800	4.63	88	6.67	.354	0	....	-1	0	-0.1
• ANDREWS, Ivy	Ivy Paul "Poison" Andrews b: 5/6/1907, Dora, AL d: 11/24/1970, Birmingham, AL BR/TR, 6'1", 200 lbs. Deb: 8/15/1931																										
1931	NY-A	2	0	1.000	7	3	1	0	0	34^{1}	36	17	16	3	0	8	10	1.282	4.19	95	3.58	.273	2	.182	-1	2	-0.1
1932	NY-A	2	1	.667	4	1	1	0	0	24^{2}	20	8	5	0	0	9	7	1.176	1.82	223	2.17	.215	2	.222	6	3	0.7
	Bos-A	8	6	.571	25	19	8	0	0	141^{2}	144	76	60	4	2	53	30	1.391	3.81	118	3.50	.262	7	.137	13	10	0.9
	Yr.	10	7	.588	29	20	9	0	0	166^{1}	164	84	65	4	2	62	37	1.359	3.52	127	3.30	.255	9	.150	19	13	1.6
1933	Bos-A	7	13	.350	34	17	5	0	1	140	157	96	77	8	1	61	37	1.557	4.95	88	4.38	.279	9	.214	-9	4	-0.8
1934	StL-A	4	11	.267	43	13	2	0	3	139	166	84	72	7	0	65	51	1.662	4.66	107	5.03	.301	14	.350	3	9	0.7
1935	StL-A	13	7	.650	50	20	10	0	1	213^{1}	231	95	84	10	1	53	43	1.331	3.54	135	3.50	.273	9	.132	31	21	2.4
1936	StL-A	7	12	.368	36	25	11	0	1	191^{1}	221	109	103	19	0	50	33	1.416	4.84	111	4.28	.286	10	.169	15	15	1.3
1937	Cle-A	3	4	.429	20	4	1	1	0	59^{2}	76	33	29	3	0	9	16	1.425	4.37	105	4.20	.311	3	.250	2	4	0.3
	* NY-A	3	2	.600	11	5	3	1	1	49	49	19	17	2	0	17	17	1.347	3.12	142	3.40	.259	1	.067	6	4	0.5
	Yr.	6	6	.500	31	9	4	2	1	108^{2}	125	52	46	5	0	26	33	1.390	3.81	119	3.84	.289	4	.148	9	8	0.7
1938	NY-A	1	3	.250	19	1	1	0	1	48	51	25	16	3	0	17	13	1.417	3.00	151	3.83	.268	2	.167	8	4	0.7
Total	8	50	59	.459	249	108	43	2	8	1041	1151	562	479	59	4	342	257	1.434	4.14	115	3.99	.279	59	.185	75	76	6.4
• ANDREWS, John	John Richard Andrews b: 2/9/1949, Monterey Park, CA BL/TL, 5'10", 175 lbs. Deb: 4/8/1973																										
1973	StL-N	1	1	.500	16	0	0	0	0	18^{1}	16	10	9	3	0	11	5	1.473	4.42	82	4.54	.235	1	.500	-2	0	-0.1
• ANDREWS, Nate	Nathan Hardy Andrews b: 9/30/1913, Pembroke, NC d: 4/26/1991, Winston-Salem, NC BR/TR, 6', 195 lbs. Deb: 5/1/1937																										
1937	StL-N	0	0	....	4	0	0	0	0	9	12	4	4	1	0	3	6	1.667	4.00	99	5.92	.324	0	....	0	1	0.0
1939	StL-N	1	2	.333	11	1	0	0	0	16	24	14	12	0	0	12	6	2.250	6.75	61	7.18	.343	0	.000	-5	0	-0.5
1940	Cle-A	0	1	.000	6	0	0	0	0	12	16	9	8	1	0	6	3	1.833	6.00	70	6.39	.327	0	....	-3	0	-0.2
1941	Cle-A	0	0	....	2	0	0	0	0	2^{1}	3	4	3	0	0	2	1	2.143	11.57	34	6.35	.300	0	.000	-2	0	-0.2
1943	Bos-N	14	20	.412	36	34	23	3	0	283^{2}	253	100	81	11	6	75	80	1.156	2.57	133	2.60	.238	14	.156	23	25	2.5
1944	Bos-N★	16	15	.516	37	34	16	2	2	257^{1}	263	106	92	14	2	74	76	1.310	3.22	119	3.38	.261	10	.114	16	17	1.3
1945	Bos-N	7	12	.368	21	19	8	0	0	137^{2}	160	75	70	9	0	52	26	1.540	4.58	84	4.56	.295	9	.209	-12	6	-1.1
1946	Cin-N	2	4	.333	7	7	3	0	0	43^{1}	50	29	19	2	1	8	13	1.338	3.95	85	3.63	.281	1	.071	-4	0	-0.5
	NY-N	1	0	1.000	3	2	0	0	0	12	17	9	8	2	0	4	5	1.750	6.00	57	7.10	.362	1	.500	-3	0	-0.3
	Yr.	3	4	.429	10	9	3	0	0	55^{1}	67	38	27	4	1	12	18	1.428	4.39	77	4.38	.298	2	.125	-7	0	-0.8
Total	8	41	54	.432	127	97	50	5	2	773^{1}	798	350	297	40	9	236	216	1.337	3.46	106	3.54	.265	35	.146	11	49	1.0
• ANDRUS, Fred	Frederick Hotham Andrus b: 8/23/1850, Washington, MI d: 11/10/1937, Detroit, MI BR/TR, 6'2", 185 lbs. Deb: 7/25/1876 ♦																										
1884	Chi-N	1	0	1.000	1	1	1	0	0	9	11	3	2	1	....	2	2	1.444	2.00	157	....	.285	1	.200	1	1	0.1
• ANDUJAR, Joaquin	Joaquin Andujar b: 12/21/1952, San Pedro de Macoris, Dominican Republic BB/TR, 6', 180 lbs. Deb: 4/8/1976																										
1976	Hou-N	9	10	.474	28	25	9	4	0	172^{1}	163	74	69	8	1	75	59	1.381	3.60	89	3.60	.255	8	.140	-8	6	-0.9
1977	Hou-N★	11	8	.579	26	25	4	1	0	158^{2}	149	80	65	11	4	64	69	1.342	3.69	97	3.61	.251	10	.189	-2	7	0.0
1978	Hou-N	5	7	.417	35	13	2	0	1	110^{2}	88	45	42	3	4	58	55	1.319	3.42	97	3.00	.224	3	.130	1	6	0.1
1979	Hou-N★	12	12	.500	46	23	8	0	4	194	168	86	74	7	2	88	77	1.320	3.43	102	3.09	.233	5	.088	2	11	0.2
1980*	Hou-N	3	8	.273	35	14	0	0	2	122	132	59	53	8	0	43	75	1.434	3.91	84	4.08	.277	5	.172	-8	4	-0.6
1981	Hou-N	2	3	.400	9	3	0	0	0	23^{2}	29	17	13	2	0	12	18	1.732	4.94	67	5.51	.296	0	.000	-4	0	-0.5
	StL-N	6	1	.857	11	8	1	0	0	55^{1}	56	24	23	4	0	11	19	1.211	3.74	95	3.25	.265	0	.000	-2	3	-0.5
	Yr.	8	4	.667	20	11	1	0	0	79	85	41	36	6	0	23	37	1.367	4.10	84	3.93	.275	0	.000	-6	3	-0.9
1982*	StL-N	15	10	.600	38	37	9	5	0	265^{2}	237	85	73	11	7	50	137	1.080	2.47	146	2.45	.240	15	.158	28	22	2.8
1983	StL-N	6	16	.273	39	34	5	2	1	225	215	112	104	23	3	75	125	1.289	4.16	87	3.62	.253	6	.082	-13	7	-1.7
1984	StL-N★	**20**	14	.588	36	36	12	**4**	0	**261^{1}**	218	104	97	20	7	70	147	1.102	3.34	104	2.61	.229	11	.131	-0	17	0.2
1985*	StL-N★	21	12	.636	38	38	10	2	0	269^{2}	265	113	102	15	11	82	112	1.287	3.40	104	3.45	.260	10	.106	-2	14	-0.4
1986	Oak-A	12	7	.632	28	26	7	1	1	155^{1}	139	70	66	23	4	56	72	1.255	3.82	101	3.80	.239	0	....	1	9	0.1
1987	Oak-A	3	5	.375	13	13	1	0	0	60^{2}	63	43	41	11	3	26	32	1.467	6.08	68	5.28	.269	0	....	-13	0	-1.2
1988	Hou-N	2	5	.286	23	10	0	0	0	78^{2}	94	43	35	9	5	21	35	1.462	4.00	83	4.87	.297	4	.211	-6	2	-0.4
Total	13	127	118	.518	405	305	68	19	9	2153	2016	955	857	155	51	731	1032	1.276	3.58	98	3.39	.250	77	.127	-26	108	-2.8
• ANDUJAR, Luis	Luis (Sanchez) Andujar b: 11/22/1972, Bani, Dominican Republic BR/TR, 6'2", 175 lbs. Deb: 9/8/1995																										
1995	Chi-A	2	1	.667	5	5	0	0	0	30^{1}	26	12	11	4	1	14	9	1.319	3.26	136	3.82	.230	0	....	4	2	0.4
1996	Chi-A	0	2	.000	5	5	0	0	0	23	32	22	21	4	0	15	6	2.043	8.22	58	8.21	.337	0	....	-9	0	-0.8
	Tor-A	1	1	.500	3	2	0	0	0	14^{1}	14	8	8	4	1	1	5	1.047	5.02	100	4.12	.264	0	....	-0	1	0.0
	Yr.	1	3	.250	8	7	0	0	0	37^{1}	46	30	29	8	1	16	11	1.661	6.99	69	6.64	.311	0	....	-9	1	-0.8
1997	Tor-A	0	6	.000	17	8	0	0	0	50	76	45	36	9	0	21	28	1.940	6.48	71	7.89	.352	0	....	-11	0	-1.1
1998	Tor-A	0	0	....	5	0	0	0	0	5^{2}	12	6	6	0	0	2	1	2.471	9.53	49	10.20	.429	0	....	-3	0	-0.3
Total	4	3	10	.231	35	20	0	0	0	123^{1}	160	93	82	21	2	53	49	1.727	5.98	78	6.62	.317	0	....	-19	3	-1.8
• ANGELINI, Norm	Norman Stanley Angelini b: 9/24/1947, San Francisco, CA BL/TL, 5'11", 175 lbs. Deb: 7/22/1972																										
1972	KC-A	2	1	.667	21	0	0	0	2	16	13	4	4	1	1	12	16	1.563	2.25	135	4.39	.228	0	.000	2	2	0.2
1973	KC-A	0	0	....	7	0	0	0	1	3^{2}	2	2	2	0	0	7	3	2.455	4.91	84	6.60	.200	0	....	-0	0	0.0
Total	2	2	1	.667	28	0	0	0	3	19^{2}	15	6	6	1	1	19	19	1.729	2.75	121	4.80	.224	0	.000	1	2	0.1
• ANKIEL, Rick	Richard Alexander Ankiel b: 7/19/1979, Fort Pierce, FL BL/TL, 6'1", 210 lbs. Deb: 8/23/1999																										
1999	StL-N	0	1	.000	9	5	0	0	1	33	26	12	12	2	1	14	39	1.212	3.27	140	2.89	.215	1	.100	5	3	0.4
2000*	StL-N	11	7	.611	31	30	0	0	0	175	137	80	68	21	6	90	194	1.297	3.50	132	3.63	.219	17	.250	20	14	2.4
2001	StL-N	1	2	.333	6	6	0	0	0	24	25	21	19	7	3	25	27	2.083	7.13	60	9.17	.275	0	.000	-8	0	-0.8
Total	3	12	10	.545	46	41	0	0	1	232	188	113	99	30	10	129	260	1.366	3.84	118	4.10	.225	18	.209	16	17	2.0
• ANTONELLI, Johnny	John August Antonelli b: 4/12/1930, Rochester, NY BL/TL, 6'1.5", 190 lbs. Deb: 7/4/1948																										
1948	Bos-N	0	0	....	4	0	0	0	1	4	2	1	1	0	0	3	0	1.250	2.25	170	1.86	.143	0	....	1	1	0.1
1949	Bos-N	3	7	.300	22	10	3	1	0	96	99	49	38	6	2	42	48	1.469	3.56	106	4.15	.273	3	.120	3	5	0.2
1950	Bos-N	2	3	.400	20	6	2	1	0	57^{2}	81	46	38	3	4	22	33	1.786	5.93	65	6.13	.335	2	.125	-13	0	-1.4
1953	Mil-N	12	12	.500	31	26	11	2	1	175^{1}	167	83	62	15	1	71	131	1.357	3.18	123	3.58	.242	11	.177	13	11	1.2
1954*	NY-N★	21	7	.750	39	37	18	**6**	2	258^{2}	209	78	66	22	5	94	152	1.171	**2.30**	**176**	2.78	**.219**	16	.163	**47**	28	**4.6**
1955	NY-N	14	16	.467	38	34	14	2	1	235^{1}	206	105	87	24	11	82	143	1.224	3.33	121	3.36	.234	17	.207	18	18	2.1
1956	NY-N★	20	13	.606	41	36	15	5	1	258^{1}	225	93	82	20	3	75	145	1.161	2.86	132	2.81	.234	14	.157	**28**	25	3.0
1957	NY-N★	12	18	.400	40	30	8	3	0	212^{1}	228	98	89	19	3	67	114	1.389	3.77	104	4.08	.276	11	.153	4	13	0.8
1958	SF-N★	16	13	.552	41	34	13	0	3	241^{2}	216	101	88	31	3	87	143	1.254	3.28	116	3.52	.239	19	.226	17	18	2.0
1959	SF-N★	19	10	.655	40	38	17	**4**	1	282	247	107	97	29	3	76	165	1.145	3.10	123	2.95	.233	16	.158	23	20	2.5
1960	SF-N	6	7	.462	41	10	1	1	11	112^{1}	106	51	47	7	2	47	57	1.362	3.77	92	3.51	.253	8	.235	-2	7	0.0

YEAR	TM-L	W	L	PCT	G	GS	CG	SH	SV	IP	H	R	ER	HR	HB	BB	SO	RAT	ERA	ERA+	CERA	OAV	BH	AVG	PR+	WS	TPW
1961	Cle-A	0	4	.000	11	7	0	0	0	48	68	39	35	8	1	18	23	1.792	6.56	60	7.13	.338	4	.267	-14	0	-1.3
	Mil-N	1	0	1.000	9	0	0	0	0	10^{2}	16	9	9	2	0	3	8	1.781	7.59	49	7.12	.340	0	.000	-5	0	-0.5
Total	12	126	110	.534	377	268	102	25	21	1992^{1}	1870	860	739	186	38	687	1162	1.283	3.34	116	3.51	.247	121	.178	119	146	13.4

• APODACA, Bob

Robert John Apodaca b: 1/31/1950, Los Angeles, CA BR/TR, 5'11", 170 lbs. Deb: 9/18/1973 C

YEAR	TM-L	W	L	PCT	G	GS	CG	SH	SV	IP	H	R	ER	HR	HB	BB	SO	RAT	ERA	ERA+	CERA	OAV	BH	AVG	PR+	WS	TPW
1973	NY-N	0	0	....	1	0	0	0	0	0	0	1	0	0	0	2	0	....	....	....	∞	1.000	0	....	0	0	0.0
1974	NY-N	6	6	.500	35	8	1	0	3	103	92	47	40	7	2	42	54	1.301	3.50	102	3.26	.241	3	.120	0	7	0.1
1975	NY-N	3	4	.429	46	0	0	0	13	84^{2}	66	18	14	4	0	28	45	1.110	1.49	232	2.22	.222	4	.364	17	13	2.0
1976	NY-N	3	7	.300	43	3	0	0	5	89^{2}	71	34	28	4	3	29	45	1.115	2.81	117	2.29	.223	2	.125	4	6	0.5
1977	NY-N	4	8	.333	59	0	0	0	5	84	83	38	32	7	1	30	53	1.345	3.43	109	3.47	.255	1	.167	3	6	0.3
Total	5	16	25	.390	184	11	1	0	26	361^{1}	312	138	114	22	6	131	197	1.226	2.84	124	2.82	.236	10	.172	25	32	2.8

• APONTE, Luis

Luis Eduardo (Yuripe) Aponte b: 6/14/1953, El Tigre, Venezuela BR/TR, 6', 185 lbs. Deb: 9/4/1980

YEAR	TM-L	W	L	PCT	G	GS	CG	SH	SV	IP	H	R	ER	HR	HB	BB	SO	RAT	ERA	ERA+	CERA	OAV	BH	AVG	PR+	WS	TPW
1980	Bos-A	0	0	....	4	0	0	0	0	7	6	1	1	0	0	2	1	1.143	1.29	328	2.11	.250	0	....	2	1	0.2
1981	Bos-A	1	0	1.000	7	0	0	0	1	15^{2}	11	1	1	0	0	3	11	.894	0.57	674	1.48	.208	0	....	6	3	0.6
1982	Bos-A	2	2	.500	40	0	0	0	3	85	78	31	30	5	0	25	44	1.212	3.18	136	2.93	.246	0	....	12	8	1.2
1983	Bos-A	5	4	.556	34	0	0	0	3	62	74	28	25	7	2	23	32	1.565	3.63	120	5.28	.301	0	....	5	5	0.5
1984	Cle-A	1	0	1.000	25	0	0	0	0	50^{1}	53	25	23	5	1	15	25	1.351	4.11	99	3.99	.269	0	....	-0	2	0.0
Total	5	9	6	.600	110	0	0	0	7	220	222	86	80	17	3	68	113	1.318	3.27	130	3.70	.265	0	....	25	19	2.6

• APPIER, Kevin

Robert Kevin Appier b: 12/6/1967, Lancaster, CA BR/TR, 6'2", 195 lbs. Deb: 6/14/1989

YEAR	TM-L	W	L	PCT	G	GS	CG	SH	SV	IP	H	R	ER	HR	HB	BB	SO	RAT	ERA	ERA+	CERA	OAV	BH	AVG	PR+	WS	TPW
1989	KC-A	1	4	.200	6	5	0	0	0	21^{2}	34	22	22	3	0	12	10	2.123	9.14	42	8.72	.374	0	....	-12	0	-1.3
1990	KC-A	12	8	.600	32	24	3	3	0	185^{2}	179	67	57	13	6	54	127	1.255	2.76	139	3.34	.252	0	....	27	13	2.7
1991	KC-A	13	10	.565	34	31	6	3	0	207^{2}	205	97	79	13	2	61	158	1.281	3.42	120	3.32	.255	0	....	22	14	2.2
1992	KC-A	15	8	.652	30	30	3	0	0	208^{1}	167	59	57	10	2	68	150	1.128	2.46	165	2.41	.217	0	....	40	20	4.1
1993	KC-A	18	8	.692	34	34	5	1	0	238^{2}	183	74	68	8	1	81	186	1.106	**2.56**	**179**	**2.25**	.212	0	....	**52**	**27**	**5.1**
1994	KC-A	7	6	.538	23	23	1	0	0	155	137	68	66	11	4	63	145	1.290	3.83	131	3.31	.240	0	....	20	13	1.8
1995	KC-A★	15	10	.600	31	31	4	1	0	201^{1}	163	90	87	14	8	80	185	1.207	3.89	123	3.01	.221	0	....	17	16	1.6
1996	KC-A	14	11	.560	32	32	5	1	0	211^{1}	192	87	85	17	5	75	207	1.263	3.62	139	3.41	.245	0	....	33	19	3.0
1997	KC-A	9	13	.409	34	34	4	1	0	235^{2}	215	96	89	24	4	74	196	1.226	3.40	139	3.37	.243	0	.000	32	18	3.0
1998	KC-A	1	2	.333	3	3	0	0	0	15	21	13	13	3	1	5	9	1.733	7.80	62	7.33	.339	0	....	-5	0	-0.5
1999	KC-A	9	9	.500	22	22	1	0	0	140^{1}	153	81	76	18	6	51	78	1.454	4.87	103	4.83	.279	0	.000	-1	7	-0.1
	Oak-A	7	5	.583	12	12	0	0	0	68^{2}	77	50	44	9	1	33	53	1.602	5.77	80	5.32	.280	0	....	-8	2	-0.8
	Yr.	16	14	.533	34	34	1	0	0	209	230	131	120	27	7	84	131	1.502	5.17	94	4.99	.279	0	.000	-9	9	-0.9
2000*	Oak-A	15	11	.577	31	31	1	1	0	195^{1}	200	109	98	23	9	102	129	1.546	4.52	105	4.89	.262	1	.167	8	11	0.7
2001	NY-N	11	10	.524	33	33	1	1	0	206^{2}	181	89	82	22	15	64	172	1.185	3.57	116	3.38	.237	7	.113	12	15	1.0
2002*	Ana-A	14	12	.538	32	32	0	0	0	188^{1}	191	89	82	23	7	64	132	1.354	3.92	113	4.29	.267	0	.000	5	11	0.4
2003	Ana-A	7	7	.500	19	19	0	0	0	92^{2}	105	60	58	17	8	36	50	1.522	5.63	76	5.65	.279	0	.000	-15	2	-1.5
	KC-A	1	2	.333	4	4	0	0	0	19	15	9	9	4	0	7	5	1.158	4.26	121	3.56	.217	0	....	2	1	0.2
	Yr.	8	9	.471	23	23	0	0	0	111^{2}	120	69	67	21	8	43	55	1.460	5.40	82	5.30	.269	0	.000	-13	3	-1.3
Total	15	169	136	.554	412	400	34	12	0	2591^{1}	2418	1160	1072	232	79	930	1992	1.292	3.72	121	3.62	.247	8	.096	228	189	21.7

• APPLEGATE, Fred

Frederick Romaine Applegate b: 5/9/1879, Williamsport, PA d: 4/21/1968, Williamsport, PA BR/TR, 6'2", 180 lbs. Deb: 9/30/1904

YEAR	TM-L	W	L	PCT	G	GS	CG	SH	SV	IP	H	R	ER	HR	HB	BB	SO	RAT	ERA	ERA+	CERA	OAV	BH	AVG	PR+	WS	TPW
1904	Phi-A	1	2	.333	3	3	3	0	0	21	29	18	15	0	1	8	12	1.762	6.43	42	5.29	.328	2	.286	-8	0	-0.9

• APPLETON, Ed

Edward Samuel "Whitey" Appleton b: 2/29/1892, Arlington, TX d: 1/27/1932, Arlington, TX BR/TR, 6'.5", 173 lbs. Deb: 4/16/1915

YEAR	TM-L	W	L	PCT	G	GS	CG	SH	SV	IP	H	R	ER	HR	HB	BB	SO	RAT	ERA	ERA+	CERA	OAV	BH	AVG	PR+	WS	TPW
1915	Bro-N	4	10	.286	34	10	5	0	0	138^{1}	133	71	51	3	8	66	50	1.439	3.32	84	3.69	.263	7	.159	-9	4	-1.0
1916	Bro-N	1	2	.333	14	3	1	0	1	47	49	25	16	1	1	18	14	1.426	3.06	87	3.64	.278	2	.167	-3	1	-0.4
Total	2	5	12	.294	48	13	6	0	1	185^{1}	182	96	67	4	9	84	64	1.435	3.25	85	3.67	.267	9	.161	-12	5	-1.4

• APPLETON, Pete

Peter William "Jake" Appleton b: 5/20/1904, Terryville, CT d: 1/18/1974, Trenton, NJ BR/TR, 5'11", 180 lbs. Deb: 9/14/1927

YEAR	TM-L	W	L	PCT	G	GS	CG	SH	SV	IP	H	R	ER	HR	HB	BB	SO	RAT	ERA	ERA+	CERA	OAV	BH	AVG	PR+	WS	TPW
1927	Cin-N	2	1	.667	6	2	2	1	0	29^{2}	29	7	6	0	0	17	3	1.551	1.82	208	3.85	.261	6	.545	7	4	0.9
1928	Cin-N	3	4	.429	31	3	0	0	0	82^{2}	101	50	43	7	2	22	20	1.488	4.68	84	4.77	.311	10	.323	-7	3	-0.4
1930	Cle-A	8	7	.533	39	7	2	0	1	118^{2}	122	71	53	8	5	53	45	1.475	4.02	120	4.19	.274	8	.200	13	9	1.1
1931	Cle-A	4	4	.500	29	4	3	0	0	79^{2}	100	51	41	2	1	29	25	1.619	4.63	100	4.62	.293	5	.208	2	4	0.2
1932	Cle-A	0	0	....	4	0	0	0	0	5	11	11	9	1	0	3	1	2.800	16.20	29	13.01	.407	0	....	-6	0	-0.6
	Bos-A	0	3	.000	11	3	0	0	0	46	49	35	21	2	2	26	15	1.630	4.11	109	4.50	.265	3	.176	3	1	0.2
	Yr.	0	3	.000	15	3	0	0	0	51	60	46	30	3	2	29	16	1.745	5.29	86	5.34	.283	3	.176	-4	1	-0.4
1933	NY-A	0	0	....	1	0	0	0	0	2	3	0	0	0	0	1	0	2.000	0.00	....	7.09	.375	0	....	1	0	0.1
1936	Was-A	14	9	.609	38	20	12	1	3	201^{2}	199	94	79	7	3	77	77	1.369	3.53	135	3.42	.254	19	.250	25	18	2.4
1937	Was-A	8	15	.348	35	18	7	4	2	168	167	103	82	16	5	72	62	1.423	4.39	101	4.12	.260	11	.186	-2	7	-0.3
1938	Was-A	7	9	.438	43	10	5	0	5	164^{1}	175	99	84	12	1	61	62	1.436	4.60	98	4.01	.270	15	.254	-2	10	0.1
1939	Was-A	5	10	.333	40	4	2	0	6	102^{2}	104	62	52	7	4	48	50	1.481	4.56	95	4.15	.265	4	.160	-3	5	-0.4
1940	Chi-A	4	0	1.000	25	0	0	0	5	57^{2}	54	39	36	8	1	28	21	1.422	5.62	79	4.22	.248	3	.176	-9	3	-0.9
1941	Chi-A	0	3	.000	13	0	0	0	1	27^{1}	27	21	16	4	2	17	12	1.610	5.27	78	5.28	.257	1	.250	-4	0	-0.4
1942	Chi-A	0	0	....	4	0	0	0	0	4^{2}	2	2	2	0	0	3	2	1.071	3.86	93	1.39	.133	0	....	-0	0	0.0
	StL-A	1	1	.500	14	0	0	0	2	27^{1}	25	9	9	1	0	11	12	1.317	2.96	125	3.14	.243	1	.167	3	3	0.3
	Yr.	1	1	.500	18	0	0	0	2	32	27	11	11	1	0	14	14	1.281	3.09	119	2.89	.229	1	.167	2	3	0.3
1945	StL-A	0	0	....	2	0	0	0	0	2^{1}	3	5	4	0	0	7	1	4.286	15.43	23	13.75	.273	0	....	-3	0	-0.3
	Was-A	1	0	1.000	6	2	1	0	1	21^{1}	16	8	8	1	0	11	12	1.266	3.38	92	2.75	.211	1	.200	-1	1	-0.1
	Yr.	1	0	1.000	8	2	1	0	1	23^{2}	19	13	12	1	0	18	13	1.563	4.56	71	3.83	.218	1	.200	-4	1	-0.4
Total	14	57	66	.463	341	73	34	6	26	1141	1187	667	545	76	26	486	420	1.466	4.30	103	4.12	.268	87	.233	16	68	1.9

• AQUINO, Luis

Luis Antonio (Colon) Aquino b: 5/19/1964, Santurce, Puerto Rico BR/TR, 6', 195 lbs. Deb: 8/8/1986

YEAR	TM-L	W	L	PCT	G	GS	CG	SH	SV	IP	H	R	ER	HR	HB	BB	SO	RAT	ERA	ERA+	CERA	OAV	BH	AVG	PR+	WS	TPW
1986	Tor-A	1	1	.500	7	0	0	0	0	11^{1}	14	8	8	2	0	3	5	1.500	6.35	66	5.28	.304	0	....	-3	0	-0.3
1988	KC-A	1	0	1.000	7	5	1	1	0	29	33	15	9	1	1	17	11	1.724	2.79	143	5.19	.282	0	....	4	2	0.4
1989	KC-A	6	8	.429	34	16	2	1	0	141^{1}	148	62	55	6	4	35	68	1.295	3.50	110	3.46	.271	0	....	8	8	0.8
1990	KC-A	4	1	.800	20	3	1	0	0	68^{1}	59	25	24	6	4	27	28	1.259	3.16	121	3.35	.237	0	....	7	4	0.7
1991	KC-A	8	4	.667	38	18	1	1	3	157	152	67	60	10	4	47	80	1.268	3.44	120	3.31	.253	0	....	16	12	1.6
1992	KC-A	3	6	.333	15	13	0	0	0	67^{2}	81	35	34	5	1	20	11	1.493	4.52	90	4.71	.303	0	....	-3	2	-0.3
1993	Fla-N	6	8	.429	38	13	0	0	0	110^{2}	115	43	42	6	5	40	67	1.401	3.42	126	4.07	.276	2	.080	13	8	1.1
1994	Fla-N	2	1	.667	29	1	0	0	0	50^{2}	39	22	21	3	3	22	22	1.204	3.73	117	2.77	.210	1	.167	3	4	0.3
1995	Mon-N	0	2	.000	29	0	0	0	2	37^{1}	47	24	16	4	3	11	22	1.554	3.86	111	5.42	.301	1	.333	2	2	0.3
	SF-N	0	1	.000	5	0	0	0	0	5	10	10	8	2	0	2	4	2.400	14.40	28	12.26	.400	0	.000	-6	0	-0.6
	Yr.	0	3	.000	34	0	0	0	2	42^{1}	57	34	24	6	3	13	26	1.654	5.10	83	6.23	.315	1	.250	-4	2	-0.3
Total	9	31	32	.492	222	69	5	3	5	678^{1}	698	311	277	45	25	224	318	1.359	3.68	111	3.87	.267	4	.114	43	42	4.2

• ARCHER, Fred

Frederick Marvin "Lefty" Archer b: 3/7/1910, Johnson City, TN d: 10/31/1981, Charlotte, NC BL/TL, 6', 193 lbs. Deb: 9/5/1936

YEAR	TM-L	W	L	PCT	G	GS	CG	SH	SV	IP	H	R	ER	HR	HB	BB	SO	RAT	ERA	ERA+	CERA	OAV	BH	AVG	PR+	WS	TPW
1936	Phi-A	2	3	.400	6	5	2	0	0	36^{2}	41	28	26	3	3	15	9	1.527	6.38	80	4.89	.289	4	.267	-5	1	-0.4
1937	Phi-A	0	0	....	1	0	0	0	0	3	4	2	2	0	0	0	2	1.333	6.00	79	3.56	.333	0	....	-0	0	0.0
Total	2	2	3	.400	7	5	2	0	0	39^{2}	45	30	28	3	3	15	11	1.513	6.35	80	4.79	.292	4	.267	-6	1	-0.4

• ARCHER, Jim

James William Archer b: 5/25/1932, Max Meadows, VA BR/TL, 6', 190 lbs. Deb: 4/30/1961

YEAR	TM-L	W	L	PCT	G	GS	CG	SH	SV	IP	H	R	ER	HR	HB	BB	SO	RAT	ERA	ERA+	CERA	OAV	BH	AVG	PR+	WS	TPW
1961	KC-A	9	15	.375	39	27	9	2	5	205^{1}	204	99	73	11	5	60	110	1.286	3.20	129	3.30	.257	4	.063	23	15	1.8
1962	KC-A	0	1	.000	18	1	0	0	0	27^{2}	40	30	29	8	0	10	12	1.807	9.43	44	8.24	.342	1	1.000	-16	0	-1.6
Total	2	9	16	.360	57	28	9	2	5	233	244	129	102	19	5	70	122	1.348	3.94	105	3.89	.268	5	.078	7	15	0.2

• ARDIZOIA, Rugger

Rinaldo Joseph Ardizoia b: 11/20/1919, Oleggio, Italy BR/TR, 5'11", 180 lbs. Deb: 4/30/1947

YEAR	TM-L	W	L	PCT	G	GS	CG	SH	SV	IP	H	R	ER	HR	HB	BB	SO	RAT	ERA	ERA+	CERA	OAV	BH	AVG	PR+	WS	TPW
1947	NY-A	0	0	....	1	0	0	0	0	2	4	2	2	1	0	1	0	2.500	9.00	39	16.06	.500	0	....	-1	0	-0.1

YEAR	TM-L	W	L	PCT	G	GS	CG	SH	SV	IP	H	R	ER	HR	HB	BB	SO	RAT	ERA	ERA+	CERA	OAV	BH	AVG	PR+	WS	TPW
• ARELLANES, Frank	Frank Julian Arellanes b: 1/28/1882, Santa Cruz, CA d: 12/13/1918, San Jose, CA BR/TR, 6', 180 lbs. Deb: 7/28/1908																										
1908	Bos-A	4	3	.571	11	8	6	1	0	79	60	26	16	1	3	18	33	.987	1.82	135	1.94	.213	5	.167	4	5	0.5
1909	Bos-A	16	12	.571	45	28	17	1	**8**	230^2	192	80	56	3	5	43	82	1.019	2.18	114	2.02	.229	13	.167	4	19	0.3
1910	Bos-A	4	7	.364	18	13	2	0	0	100	106	41	32	1	3	24	33	1.300	2.88	88	3.43	.283	6	.176	-3	4	-0.3
Total	**3**	**24**	**22**	**.522**	**74**	**49**	**25**	**2**	**8**	**409^2**	**358**	**147**	**104**	**5**	**11**	**85**	**148**	**1.081**	**2.28**	**110**	**2.35**	**.240**	**24**	**.169**	**5**	**28**	**0.5**
• ARIAS, Rudy	Rodolfo (Martinez) Arias b: 6/6/1931, Las Villas, Cuba BL/TL, 5'10", 165 lbs. Deb: 4/10/1959																										
1959	Chi-A	2	0	1.000	34	0	0	0	2	44	49	23	20	7	1	20	28	1.568	4.09	92	5.14	.277	0	.000	-2	2	-0.3
• ARLICH, Don	Donald Louis Arlich b: 2/15/1943, Wayne, MI BL/TL, 6'2", 185 lbs. Deb: 10/2/1965																										
1965	Hou-N	0	0	....	1	1	0	0	0	6	5	2	2	0	0	1	0	1.000	3.00	112	1.84	.227	0	.000	0	0	0.0
1966	Hou-N	0	1	.000	7	0	0	0	0	4	11	9	7	0	1	4	1	3.750	15.75	22	18.84	.478	0	.000	-5	0	-0.6
Total	**2**	**0**	**1**	**.000**	**8**	**1**	**0**	**0**	**0**	**10**	**16**	**11**	**9**	**0**	**1**	**5**	**1**	**2.100**	**8.10**	**42**	**8.64**	**.356**	**0**	**.000**	**-5**	**0**	**-0.6**
• ARLIN, Steve	Stephen Ralph Arlin b: 9/25/1945, Seattle, WA BR/TR, 6'3.5", 195 lbs. Deb: 6/17/1969																										
1969	SD-N	0	1	.000	4	1	0	0	0	10^2	13	11	11	2	0	9	9	2.063	9.28	38	7.65	.289	0	.000	-7	0	-0.7
1970	SD-N	1	0	1.000	2	2	1	1	0	12^2	11	4	4	0	0	8	3	1.500	2.84	140	3.48	.244	0	.000	2	1	0.1
1971	SD-N	9	19	.321	36	34	10	4	0	227^2	211	114	88	8	6	103	156	1.379	3.48	95	3.42	.244	9	.123	-3	7	-0.5
1972	SD-N	10	21	.323	38	37	12	3	0	250	217	115	100	19	9	122	159	1.356	3.60	91	3.57	.237	11	.153	-5	10	-0.2
1973	SD-N	11	14	.440	34	27	7	3	0	180	196	107	102	26	1	72	98	1.489	5.10	68	4.85	.278	10	.167	-31	4	-3.1
1974	SD-N	1	7	.125	16	12	1	0	1	64	85	46	42	5	2	37	18	1.906	5.91	60	6.57	.326	2	.111	-15	0	-1.6
	Cle-A	2	5	.286	11	10	1	0	0	43^2	59	34	32	1	0	22	20	1.855	6.60	55	5.99	.333	0	....	-15	0	-1.5
Total	**6**	**34**	**67**	**.337**	**141**	**123**	**32**	**11**	**1**	**788^2**	**792**	**431**	**379**	**61**	**18**	**373**	**463**	**1.477**	**4.33**	**79**	**4.25**	**.263**	**32**	**.139**	**-73**	**22**	**-7.6**
• ARMAS, Tony	Antonio Jose Armas b: 4/29/1978, Puerto Piritu, Venezuela BR/TR, 6'4", 205 lbs. Deb: 8/16/1999																										
1999	Mon-N	0	1	.000	1	1	0	0	0	6	8	4	1	0	0	2	2	1.667	1.50	299	4.53	.320	0	.000	2	0	0.2
2000	Mon-N	7	9	.438	17	17	0	0	0	95	74	49	46	10	3	50	59	1.305	4.36	110	3.49	.218	1	.038	5	5	0.3
2001	Mon-N	9	14	.391	34	34	0	0	0	196^2	180	101	88	18	10	91	176	1.378	4.03	111	3.95	.247	8	.151	13	12	1.2
2002	Mon-N	12	12	.500	29	29	0	0	0	164^1	149	87	81	22	7	78	131	1.381	4.44	96	4.19	.243	5	.100	-3	8	-0.5
2003	Mon-N	2	1	.667	5	5	0	0	0	31	25	9	9	4	1	8	23	1.065	2.61	193	2.84	.225	2	.200	8	4	0.8
Total	**5**	**30**	**37**	**.448**	**86**	**86**	**0**	**0**	**0**	**493**	**436**	**250**	**225**	**54**	**21**	**229**	**391**	**1.349**	**4.11**	**109**	**3.88**	**.240**	**16**	**.113**	**26**	**29**	**2.0**
• ARMBRUST, Orville	Orville Martin Armbrust b: 3/2/1910, Beirne, AR d: 10/2/1967, Mobile, AL BR/TR, 5'10", 195 lbs. Deb: 9/18/1934																										
1934	Was-A	1	0	1.000	3	2	0	0	0	12^2	10	3	3	1	0	3	3	1.026	2.13	203	2.16	.208	0	.000	3	2	0.2
• ARMSTRONG, Howard	Howard Elmer Armstrong b: 12/2/1889, East Claridon, OH d: 3/8/1926, Canisteo, NY BR/TR, 5'9", 165 lbs. Deb: 9/30/1911																										
1911	Phi-A	0	1	.000	1	0	0	0	0	3	3	2	0	0	0	1	0	1.333	0.00	....	3.27	.273	0	.000	1	0	0.1
• ARMSTRONG, Jack	Jack William Armstrong b: 3/7/1965, Englewood, NJ BR/TR, 6'5", 215 lbs. Deb: 6/21/1988																										
1988	Cin-N	4	7	.364	14	13	0	0	0	65^1	63	44	42	8	0	38	45	1.546	5.79	62	4.67	.256	2	.095	-17	0	-2.0
1989	Cin-N	2	3	.400	9	8	0	0	0	42^2	40	24	22	5	0	21	23	1.430	4.64	78	4.01	.245	0	.000	-4	1	-0.5
1990*	Cin-N★	12	9	.571	29	27	2	1	0	166	151	72	63	9	6	59	110	1.265	3.42	115	3.15	.241	5	.106	7	10	0.5
1991	Cin-N	7	13	.350	27	24	1	0	0	139^2	158	90	85	25	2	54	93	1.518	5.48	69	5.48	.293	4	.093	-26	0	-2.9
1992	Cle-A	6	15	.286	35	23	1	0	0	166^2	176	100	86	23	3	67	114	1.458	4.64	84	4.72	.269	0	....	-12	4	-1.3
1993	Fla-N	9	17	.346	36	33	0	0	0	196^1	210	105	98	29	7	78	118	1.467	4.49	96	4.82	.271	10	.152	-0	7	-0.2
1994	Tex-A	0	1	.000	2	2	0	0	0	10	9	4	4	3	0	2	7	1.100	3.60	134	3.91	.231	0	....	2	1	0.1
Total	**7**	**40**	**65**	**.381**	**152**	**130**	**4**	**1**	**0**	**786^2**	**807**	**439**	**400**	**102**	**18**	**319**	**510**	**1.431**	**4.58**	**86**	**4.50**	**.265**	**21**	**.114**	**-52**	**23**	**-6.1**
• ARMSTRONG, Mike	Michael Dennis Armstrong b: 3/7/1954, Glen Cove, NY BR/TR, 6'3", 206 lbs. Deb: 8/12/1980																										
1980	SD-N	0	0	....	11	0	0	0	0	14^1	16	10	9	3	0	13	14	2.023	5.65	61	7.51	.296	0	.000	-4	0	-0.4
1981	SD-N	0	2	.000	10	0	0	0	0	12	14	9	8	1	0	11	9	2.083	6.00	54	6.73	.311	0	....	-4	0	-0.4
1982	KC-A	5	5	.500	52	0	0	0	6	112^2	88	45	40	9	3	43	75	1.163	3.20	128	2.74	.215	0	....	11	9	1.1
1983	KC-A	10	7	.588	58	0	0	0	3	102^2	86	53	44	11	3	45	52	1.276	3.86	106	3.47	.228	0	....	3	7	0.3
1984	NY-A	3	2	.600	36	0	0	0	1	54^1	47	21	21	6	0	26	43	1.344	3.48	109	3.64	.239	0	....	2	4	0.2
1985	NY-A	0	0	....	9	0	0	0	0	14^2	9	5	5	4	0	2	11	.750	3.07	131	2.06	.173	0	....	1	1	0.1
1986	NY-A	0	1	.000	7	1	0	0	0	8^2	13	9	9	4	0	5	8	2.077	9.35	44	11.25	.351	0	....	-5	0	-0.5
1987	Cle-A	1	0	1.000	14	0	0	0	1	18^2	27	18	18	4	0	10	9	1.982	8.68	52	8.37	.333	0	....	-8	0	-0.8
Total	**8**	**19**	**17**	**.528**	**197**	**1**	**0**	**0**	**11**	**338**	**300**	**170**	**154**	**42**	**6**	**155**	**221**	**1.346**	**4.10**	**97**	**3.95**	**.240**	**0**	**.000**	**-3**	**21**	**-0.3**
• ARNOLD, Jamie	James Lee Arnold b: 3/24/1974, Dearborn, MI BR/TR, 6'2", 188 lbs. Deb: 4/20/1999																										
1999	LA-N	2	4	.333	36	3	0	0	1	69	81	50	42	6	6	34	26	1.667	5.48	78	5.81	.300	2	.200	-9	1	-0.8
2000	LA-N	0	0	....	2	0	0	0	0	6^2	4	3	3	0	1	5	3	1.350	4.05	107	2.96	.174	0	....	0	0	0.0
	Chi-N	0	3	.000	12	4	0	0	1	32^2	34	28	24	1	3	19	13	1.622	6.61	69	4.83	.274	1	.111	-7	0	-0.7
	Yr.	0	3	.000	14	4	0	0	1	39^1	38	31	27	1	4	24	16	1.576	6.18	73	4.51	.259	1	.111	-7	0	-0.7
Total	**2**	**2**	**7**	**.222**	**50**	**7**	**0**	**0**	**2**	**108^1**	**119**	**81**	**69**	**7**	**10**	**58**	**42**	**1.634**	**5.73**	**76**	**5.34**	**.285**	**3**	**.158**	**-16**	**1**	**-1.5**
• ARNOLD, Scott	Scott Gentry Arnold b: 8/18/1962, Lexington, KY BR/TR, 6'2", 210 lbs. Deb: 4/7/1988																										
1988	StL-N	0	0	....	6	0	0	0	0	6^2	9	4	4	0	0	4	8	1.950	5.40	64	5.87	.321	0	....	-1	0	-0.2
• ARNOLD, Tony	Tony Dale Arnold b: 5/3/1959, El Paso, TX BR/TR, 5'11", 170 lbs. Deb: 8/9/1986																										
1986	Bal-A	0	2	.000	11	0	0	0	0	25^1	25	15	10	0	0	11	7	1.421	3.55	116	3.42	.278	0	....	2	1	0.2
1987	Bal-A	0	0	....	27	0	0	0	0	53	71	35	34	8	2	17	18	1.660	5.77	76	6.26	.330	0	....	-8	1	-0.8
Total	**2**	**0**	**2**	**.000**	**38**	**0**	**0**	**0**	**0**	**78^1**	**96**	**50**	**44**	**8**	**2**	**28**	**25**	**1.583**	**5.06**	**86**	**5.34**	**.315**	**0**	**....**	**-6**	**2**	**-0.6**
• ARNSBERG, Brad	Bradley James Arnsberg b: 8/20/1963, Seattle, WA BR/TR, 6'4", 215 lbs. Deb: 9/6/1986 C																										
1986	NY-A	0	0	....	2	1	0	0	0	8	13	3	3	1	0	1	3	1.750	3.38	121	6.52	.342	0	....	1	1	0.1
1987	NY-A	1	3	.250	6	2	0	0	0	19^1	22	12	12	5	0	13	14	1.810	5.59	79	7.03	.289	0	....	-3	0	-0.3
1989	Tex-A	2	1	.667	16	1	0	0	1	48	45	27	22	6	3	22	26	1.396	4.13	96	4.40	.247	0	....	-1	2	-0.1
1990	Tex-A	6	1	.857	53	0	0	0	5	62^2	56	20	15	4	2	33	44	1.420	2.15	182	3.75	.235	0	....	12	9	1.2
1991	Tex-A	0	1	.000	9	0	0	0	0	9^2	10	9	9	5	0	5	8	1.552	8.38	48	7.75	.256	0	....	-5	0	-0.5
1992	Cle-A	0	0	....	8	0	0	0	0	10^2	13	14	14	6	2	11	5	2.250	11.81	33	14.25	.317	0	....	-9	0	-0.9
Total	**6**	**9**	**6**	**.600**	**94**	**4**	**0**	**0**	**6**	**158^1**	**159**	**85**	**75**	**27**	**7**	**85**	**100**	**1.541**	**4.26**	**94**	**5.44**	**.259**	**0**	**....**	**-4**	**12**	**-0.4**
• ARNTZEN, Orie	Orie Edgar "Old Folks" Arntzen b: 10/18/1909, Beverly, IL d: 1/28/1970, Cedar Rapids, IA BR/TR, 6'1", 200 lbs. Deb: 4/20/1943																										
1943	Phi-A	4	13	.235	32	20	9	0	0	164^1	172	85	77	5	5	69	66	1.467	4.22	81	4.00	.277	8	.160	-11	4	-1.3
• AROCHA, Rene	Rene (Magaly) Arocha b: 2/24/1966, Havana, Cuba BR/TR, 6', 180 lbs. Deb: 4/9/1993																										
1993	StL-N	11	8	.579	32	29	1	0	0	188	197	89	79	20	3	31	96	1.213	3.78	105	3.54	.271	6	.103	4	10	0.2
1994	StL-N	4	4	.500	45	7	1	1	11	83	94	42	37	9	4	21	62	1.386	4.01	104	4.41	.286	1	.111	1	7	0.1
1995	StL-N	3	5	.375	41	0	0	0	0	49^2	55	24	22	6	3	18	25	1.470	3.99	105	4.90	.297	0	.000	0	3	0.0
1997	SF-N	0	0	....	6	0	0	0	0	10^1	17	14	13	2	1	5	7	2.129	11.32	36	9.13	.370	0	.000	-8	0	-0.8
Total	**4**	**18**	**17**	**.514**	**124**	**36**	**2**	**1**	**11**	**331**	**363**	**169**	**151**	**37**	**11**	**75**	**190**	**1.323**	**4.11**	**99**	**4.14**	**.282**	**7**	**.101**	**-3**	**20**	**-0.5**
• ARRIGO, Gerry	Gerald William Arrigo b: 6/12/1941, Chicago, IL BL/TL, 6'1", 195 lbs. Deb: 6/12/1961																										
1961	Min-A	0	1	.000	7	2	0	0	0	9^2	9	12	11	0	2	10	6	1.966	10.24	41	5.87	.265	1	.500	-6	0	-0.6
1962	Min-A	0	0	....	1	0	0	0	0	1	3	3	2	0	0	1	1	4.000	18.00	23	22.91	.600	0	....	-2	0	-0.2
1963	Min-A	1	2	.333	5	1	0	0	0	15^2	12	5	5	2	0	4	13	1.021	2.87	127	2.44	.211	0	.000	1	1	0.1
1964	Min-A	7	4	.636	41	12	2	1	1	105^1	97	48	45	11	2	45	96	1.348	3.84	93	3.77	.244	5	.172	-2	5	-0.1
1965	Cin-N	2	4	.333	27	5	0	0	2	54	75	38	37	4	2	30	43	1.944	6.17	61	6.92	.342	2	.167	-15	0	-1.5

YEAR	TM-L	W	L	PCT	G	GS	CG	SH	SV	IP	H	R	ER	HR	HB	BB	SO	RAT	ERA	ERA+	CERA	OAV	BH	AVG	PR+	WS	TPW
1966	Cin-N	0	0	....	3	0	0	0	0	7^1	7	4	4	2	0	3	3	1.364	4.91	79	4.96	.250	0	.000	-1	0	-0.1
	NY-N	3	3	.500	17	5	0	0	0	43^1	47	20	18	5	0	16	28	1.454	3.74	97	4.33	.276	5	.500	-1	4	0.3
	Yr.	3	3	.500	20	5	0	0	0	50^2	54	24	22	7	0	19	31	1.441	3.91	94	4.42	.273	5	.455	-1	4	0.2
1967	Cin-N	6	6	.500	32	5	1	1	1	74	61	31	26	6	4	35	56	1.297	3.16	119	3.41	.232	4	.211	5	5	0.7
1968	Cin-N	12	10	.545	36	31	5	1	0	205^1	181	84	76	13	4	77	140	1.256	3.33	95	3.15	.237	5	.075	-2	9	-0.5
1969	Cin-N	4	7	.364	20	16	1	0	0	91	89	50	42	9	8	61	35	1.648	4.15	91	5.30	.256	5	.161	-4	3	-0.4
1970	Chi-A	0	3	.000	5	3	0	0	0	13^1	24	20	19	4	0	9	12	2.475	12.83	30	12.14	.393	0	.000	-13	0	-1.4
Total	10	35	40	.467	194	80	9	3	4	620	605	315	285	56	22	291	433	1.445	4.14	86	4.28	.258	27	.151	-38	27	-3.7

• ARROJO, Rolando Luis Rolando (Avila) Arrojo b: 7/18/1968, Santa Clara, Cuba BR/TR, 6'4", 220 lbs. Deb: 4/1/1998

YEAR	TM-L	W	L	PCT	G	GS	CG	SH	SV	IP	H	R	ER	HR	HB	BB	SO	RAT	ERA	ERA+	CERA	OAV	BH	AVG	PR+	WS	TPW
1998	TB-A★	14	12	.538	32	32	2	2	0	202	195	84	80	21	19	65	152	1.287	3.56	135	4.03	.256	0	.000	20	17	1.8
1999	TB-A	7	12	.368	24	24	2	0	0	140^2	162	84	81	23	14	60	107	1.578	5.18	96	6.09	.296	0	....	-3	6	-0.3
2000	Col-N	5	9	.357	19	19	0	0	0	101^1	120	77	68	14	12	46	80	1.638	6.04	96	6.08	.299	3	.107	-3	4	-0.4
	Bos-A	5	2	.714	13	13	0	0	0	71^1	67	41	40	10	4	22	44	1.248	5.05	100	3.88	.245	0	....	-0	4	0.0
2001	Bos-A	5	4	.556	41	9	0	0	5	103^1	88	44	40	8	12	35	78	1.190	3.48	129	3.25	.230	0	.000	13	9	1.2
2002	Bos-A	4	3	.571	29	8	0	0	1	81^1	83	47	45	7	6	27	51	1.352	4.98	90	4.15	.269	0	.000	-6	3	-0.6
Total	5	40	42	.488	158	105	4	2	6	700	715	377	354	83	67	255	512	1.386	4.55	109	4.62	.267	3	.081	21	43	1.8

• ARROYO, Bronson Bronson Anthony Arroyo b: 2/24/1977, Key West, FL BR/TR, 6'5", 180 lbs. Deb: 6/12/2000

YEAR	TM-L	W	L	PCT	G	GS	CG	SH	SV	IP	H	R	ER	HR	HB	BB	SO	RAT	ERA	ERA+	CERA	OAV	BH	AVG	PR+	WS	TPW
2000	Pit-N	2	6	.250	20	12	0	0	0	71^2	88	61	51	10	4	36	50	1.730	6.40	72	6.18	.302	3	.143	-14	0	-1.3
2001	Pit-N	5	7	.417	24	13	1	0	0	88^1	99	54	50	12	4	34	39	1.506	5.09	88	5.09	.289	1	.048	-6	3	-0.7
2002	Pit-N	2	1	.667	9	4	0	0	0	27	30	14	12	1	0	15	22	1.667	4.00	104	4.64	.283	0	.000	0	2	0.0
2003*	Bos-A	0	0	....	6	0	0	0	1	17^1	10	5	4	0	1	4	14	.808	2.08	220	1.14	.164	0	....	5	2	0.5
Total	4	9	14	.391	59	29	1	0	1	204^1	227	134	117	23	9	89	125	1.546	5.15	87	5.08	.284	4	.083	-14	7	-1.5

• ARROYO, Fernando Fernando Arroyo b: 3/21/1952, Sacramento, CA BR/TR, 6'2", 195 lbs. Deb: 6/28/1975

YEAR	TM-L	W	L	PCT	G	GS	CG	SH	SV	IP	H	R	ER	HR	HB	BB	SO	RAT	ERA	ERA+	CERA	OAV	BH	AVG	PR+	WS	TPW
1975	Det-A	2	1	.667	14	2	1	0	0	53^1	56	28	27	5	1	22	25	1.463	4.56	88	4.41	.272	0	....	-2	3	-0.2
1977	Det-A	8	18	.308	38	28	8	1	0	209^1	227	102	97	23	1	52	60	1.333	4.17	103	4.03	.278	0	....	3	11	0.3
1978	Det-A	0	0	....	2	0	0	0	0	4^1	8	4	4	1	1	0	1	1.846	8.31	46	10.07	.400	0	....	-2	0	-0.2
1979	Det-A	1	1	.500	6	0	0	0	0	12	17	11	11	3	0	4	7	1.750	8.25	52	7.02	.340	0	....	-5	0	-0.5
1980	Min-A	6	6	.500	21	11	1	1	0	92^1	97	55	48	7	2	32	27	1.397	4.68	93	4.06	.273	0	....	-4	4	-0.4
1981	Min-A	7	10	.412	23	19	2	0	0	128^1	144	66	56	11	5	34	39	1.387	3.93	100	4.39	.290	0	....	1	6	0.1
1982	Min-A	0	1	.000	6	0	0	0	0	13^2	17	8	8	2	0	6	4	1.683	5.27	80	6.06	.321	0	....	-2	0	-0.2
	Oak-A	0	0	....	10	0	0	0	0	22^1	23	14	13	4	1	7	9	1.343	5.24	75	4.75	.271	0	....	-3	0	-0.3
	Yr.	0	1	.000	16	0	0	0	0	36	40	22	21	6	1	13	13	1.472	5.25	77	5.25	.290	0	....	-5	0	-0.5
1986	Oak-A	0	0	....	1	0	0	0	0	0	0	0	0	0	0	3	0		....	....	∞	1.000	0	....	0	0	0.0
Total	8	24	37	.393	121	60	12	2	0	535^2	589	288	264	56	11	160	172	1.398	4.44	94	4.36	.283	0	....	-14	24	-1.4

• ARROYO, Luis Luis Enrique Arroyo b: 2/18/1927, Penuelas, Puerto Rico BL/TL, 5'8.5", 190 lbs. Deb: 4/20/1955

YEAR	TM-L	W	L	PCT	G	GS	CG	SH	SV	IP	H	R	ER	HR	HB	BB	SO	RAT	ERA	ERA+	CERA	OAV	BH	AVG	PR+	WS	TPW
1955	StL-N★	11	8	.579	35	24	9	1	0	159	162	80	74	22	2	63	68	1.415	4.19	97	4.42	.261	13	.232	-0	10	0.0
1956	Pit-N	3	3	.500	18	2	1	0	0	28^2	36	17	15	5	0	12	17	1.674	4.71	80	6.03	.298	2	.500	-3	1	-0.2
1957	Pit-N	3	11	.214	54	10	0	0	1	130^2	151	76	68	19	7	31	101	1.393	4.68	81	4.59	.282	5	.156	-15	2	-1.5
1959	Cin-N	1	0	1.000	10	0	0	0	0	13^2	17	11	6	0	0	11	8	2.049	3.95	103	5.45	.321	0	.000	0	0	0.0
1960*	NY-A	5	1	.833	29	0	0	0	7	40^2	30	14	13	2	0	22	29	1.279	2.88	124	2.76	.207	0	.000	2	6	0.2
1961*	NY-A★	15	5	.750	**65**	0	0	0	**29**	119	83	34	29	5	3	49	87	1.109	2.19	169	2.17	.199	7	.280	16	23	1.8
1962	NY-A	1	3	.250	27	0	0	0	7	33^2	33	20	18	5	1	17	21	1.485	4.81	78	4.82	.262	2	.500	-4	2	-0.4
1963	NY-A	1	1	.500	6	0	0	0	0	6	12	9	9	0	0	3	5	2.500	13.50	26	9.65	.444	0	....	-7	0	-0.7
Total	8	40	32	.556	244	36	10	1	44	531^1	524	261	232	58	13	208	336	1.378	3.93	98	4.03	.256	29	.227	-10	44	-0.8

• ARROYO, Rudy Rudolph Arroyo b: 6/19/1950, New York, NY BL/TL, 6'2", 195 lbs. Deb: 6/1/1971

YEAR	TM-L	W	L	PCT	G	GS	CG	SH	SV	IP	H	R	ER	HR	HB	BB	SO	RAT	ERA	ERA+	CERA	OAV	BH	AVG	PR+	WS	TPW
1971	StL-N	0	1	.000	9	0	0	0	0	11^2	18	8	7	2	0	5	5	1.971	5.40	67	8.22	.375	0	.000	-2	0	-0.2

• ARUNDEL, Harry Harry Arundel b: 2/1855, Philadelphia, PA d: 3/25/1904, Cleveland, OH TR, 5'6", 145 lbs. Deb: 7/19/1875

YEAR	TM-L	W	L	PCT	G	GS	CG	SH	SV	IP	H	R	ER	HR	HB	BB	SO	RAT	ERA	ERA+	CERA	OAV	BH	AVG	PR+	WS	TPW
1875	Atl-n	0	1	.000	1	1	0	0	0	2^1	6	....	2	0	....	0	0	2.571	7.71	20	....	.444	0	.000	-2	....	-0.3
1882	Pit-a	4	10	.286	14	14	13	0	0	120	155	112	62	3	....	23	47	**1.483**	4.65	56	....	.294	10	.189	-27	1	-2.4
1884	Pro-N	1	0	1.000	1	1	1	0	0	9	8	2	1	0	....	4	4	1.333	1.00	282	....	.225	1	.333	2	2	0.2
Total	2	5	10	.333	15	15	14	0	0	129	163	114	63	3	....	27	51	1.473	4.40	59	....	.289	11	.196	-25	3	-2.2

• ASENCIO, Miguel Miguel (DePaula) Asencio b: 9/29/1980, Villa Mella, Dominican Republic BR/TR, 6'2", 160 lbs. Deb: 4/6/2002

YEAR	TM-L	W	L	PCT	G	GS	CG	SH	SV	IP	H	R	ER	HR	HB	BB	SO	RAT	ERA	ERA+	CERA	OAV	BH	AVG	PR+	WS	TPW
2002	KC-A	4	7	.364	31	21	0	0	0	123^1	136	73	70	17	3	64	58	1.622	5.11	98	5.55	.282	0	.000	-1	6	-0.1
2003	KC-A	2	1	.667	8	8	1	0	0	48^1	54	29	28	4	3	21	27	1.552	5.21	99	5.08	.295	0	....	-0	3	0.0
Total	2	6	8	.429	39	29	1	0	0	171^2	190	102	98	21	6	85	85	1.602	5.14	98	5.42	.286	0	.000	-1	9	-0.1

• ASH, Ken Kenneth Lowther Ash b: 9/16/1901, Anmoore, WV d: 11/15/1979, Clarksburg, WV BR/TR, 5'11", 165 lbs. Deb: 4/17/1925

YEAR	TM-L	W	L	PCT	G	GS	CG	SH	SV	IP	H	R	ER	HR	HB	BB	SO	RAT	ERA	ERA+	CERA	OAV	BH	AVG	PR+	WS	TPW
1925	Chi-A	0	0	....	2	0	0	0	0	4	7	4	4	2	0	0	0	1.750	9.00	46	10.56	.389	0	....	-2	0	-0.2
1928	Cin-N	3	3	.500	8	5	2	0	0	36	43	26	26	1	1	13	6	1.556	6.50	61	4.69	.314	1	.071	-10	0	-1.1
1929	Cin-N	1	5	.167	29	7	2	0	2	82	91	57	44	2	5	30	26	1.476	4.83	94	4.22	.292	3	.143	-3	3	-0.4
1930	Cin-N	2	0	1.000	16	1	1	0	0	39^1	37	22	15	1	0	16	15	1.347	3.43	141	3.33	.268	2	.182	6	3	0.5
Total	4	6	8	.429	55	13	5	0	2	161^1	178	109	89	6	6	59	47	1.469	4.96	88	4.27	.294	6	.130	-9	6	-1.2

• ASHBY, Andy Andrew Jason Ashby b: 7/11/1967, Kansas City, MO BR/TR, 6'1", 190 lbs. Deb: 6/10/1991

YEAR	TM-L	W	L	PCT	G	GS	CG	SH	SV	IP	H	R	ER	HR	HB	BB	SO	RAT	ERA	ERA+	CERA	OAV	BH	AVG	PR+	WS	TPW
1991	Phi-N	1	5	.167	8	8	0	0	0	42	41	28	28	5	3	19	26	1.429	6.00	61	4.54	.256	1	.083	-11	0	-1.2
1992	Phi-N	1	3	.250	10	8	0	0	0	37	42	31	31	6	1	21	24	1.703	7.54	46	6.17	.290	1	.091	-16	0	-1.8
1993	Col-N	0	4	.000	20	9	0	0	1	54	89	54	51	5	3	32	33	2.241	8.50	56	9.06	.377	4	.267	-21	0	-2.0
	SD-N	3	6	.333	12	12	0	0	0	69	79	46	42	14	1	24	44	1.493	5.48	75	5.58	.295	1	.048	-10	1	-1.1
	Yr.	3	10	.231	32	21	0	0	1	123	168	100	93	19	4	56	77	1.821	6.80	66	7.11	.333	5	.139	-31	1	-3.1
1994	SD-N	6	11	.353	24	24	4	0	0	164^1	145	75	62	16	3	43	121	1.144	3.40	121	2.82	.233	8	.163	17	9	1.6
1995	SD-N	12	10	.545	31	**31**	2	2	0	192^2	180	79	63	17	11	62	150	1.256	2.94	136	3.60	.252	8	.163	20	14	1.9
1996*	SD-N	9	5	.643	24	24	1	0	0	150^2	147	60	54	17	3	34	85	1.201	3.23	123	3.50	.259	11	.244	13	11	1.6
1997	SD-N	9	11	.450	30	30	2	0	0	200^2	207	108	92	17	5	49	144	1.276	4.13	93	3.59	.266	4	.067	-4	6	-0.7
1998*	SD-N★	17	9	.654	33	33	5	1	0	226^2	223	90	84	23	7	58	151	1.240	3.34	118	3.55	.259	8	.111	14	15	1.2
1999	SD-N★	14	10	.583	31	31	4	**3**	0	206	204	95	87	26	7	54	132	1.252	3.80	110	3.78	.258	8	.129	8	13	0.7
2000	Phi-N	4	7	.364	16	16	1	0	0	101^1	113	75	64	17	5	38	51	1.490	5.68	82	5.20	.288	5	.179	-12	2	-1.1
	*Atl-N	8	6	.571	15	15	2	1	0	98	103	49	45	12	1	23	55	1.286	4.13	111	3.84	.271	4	.121	5	6	0.4
	Yr.	12	13	.480	31	31	3	1	0	199^1	216	124	109	29	6	61	106	1.390	4.92	94	4.53	.280	9	.148	-6	8	-0.7
2001	LA-N	2	0	1.000	2	2	0	0	0	11^2	14	5	5	2	0	1	7	1.286	3.86	104	4.42	.292	1	.500	0	1	0.1
2002	LA-N	9	13	.409	30	30	0	0	0	181^2	179	85	79	20	8	65	107	1.343	3.91	97	4.10	.261	6	.125	-3	7	-0.3
2003	LA-N	3	10	.231	21	12	0	0	0	73	90	42	42	8	3	17	41	1.466	5.18	78	4.99	.311	0	.000	-11	1	-1.2
Total	13	98	110	.471	307	285	21	7	1	1808^2	1856	922	829	205	61	540	1171	1.325	4.13	99	4.06	.268	70	.134	-9	86	-1.8

• ASSENMACHER, Paul Paul Andre Assenmacher b: 12/10/1960, Detroit, MI BL/TL, 6'3", 200 lbs. Deb: 4/12/1986

YEAR	TM-L	W	L	PCT	G	GS	CG	SH	SV	IP	H	R	ER	HR	HB	BB	SO	RAT	ERA	ERA+	CERA	OAV	BH	AVG	PR+	WS	TPW
1986	Atl-N	7	3	.700	61	0	0	0	7	68^1	61	23	19	5	0	26	56	1.273	2.50	159	3.14	.241	0	.000	12	9	1.2
1987	Atl-N	1	1	.500	52	0	0	0	2	54^2	58	41	31	8	1	24	39	1.500	5.10	85	4.67	.260	0	.000	-4	2	-0.4
1988	Atl-N	8	7	.533	64	0	0	0	5	79^1	72	28	27	4	1	32	71	1.311	3.06	120	3.15	.251	1	.333	6	9	0.8
1989	Atl-N	1	3	.250	49	0	0	0	0	57^2	55	26	23	2	1	16	64	1.231	3.59	102	2.71	.249	0	.000	1	3	0.1
	*Chi-N	2	1	.667	14	0	0	0	0	19	19	11	11	1	0	12	15	1.632	5.21	72	4.65	.275	0	.000	-3	1	-0.4
	Yr.	3	4	.429	63	0	0	0	0	76^2	74	37	34	3	1	28	79	1.330	3.99	92	3.19	.255	0	.000	-2	4	-0.3
1990	Chi-N	7	2	.778	74	1	0	0	10	103	90	33	32	10	1	36	95	1.223	2.80	146	3.12	.239	0	.000	18	13	1.7
1991	Chi-N	7	8	.467	75	0	0	0	15	102^2	85	41	37	10	3	31	117	1.130	3.24	120	2.74	.223	1	.250	9	13	1.0
1992	Chi-N	4	4	.500	70	0	0	0	8	68	72	32	31	6	3	26	67	1.441	4.10	88	4.31	.271	0	.000	-4	4	-0.4

YEAR	TM-L	W	L	PCT	G	GS	CG	SH	SV	IP	H	R	ER	HR	HB	BB	SO	RAT	ERA	ERA+	CERA	OAV	BH	AVG	PR+	WS	TPW
1993	Chi-N	2	1	.667	46	0	0	0	0	38^{2}	44	15	15	5	0	13	34	1.474	3.49	114	4.79	.288	1	.500	2	3	0.2
	NY-A	2	2	.500	26	0	0	0	0	17^{1}	10	6	6	0	1	9	11	1.096	3.12	133	1.66	.175	0	....	2	2	0.2
1994	Chi-A	1	2	.333	44	0	0	0	1	33	26	13	13	2	1	13	29	1.182	3.55	132	2.75	.224	0	....	4	4	0.4
1995*	Cle-A	6	2	.750	47	0	0	0	0	38^{1}	32	13	12	3	3	12	40	1.148	2.82	167	2.87	.225	0	....	8	5	0.8
1996*	Cle-A	4	2	.667	63	0	0	0	1	46^{2}	46	18	16	1	4	14	44	1.286	3.09	159	3.19	.260	0	....	10	6	0.9
1997*	Cle-A	5	0	1.000	75	0	0	0	4	49	43	17	16	5	1	15	53	1.184	2.94	160	2.95	.231	0	....	10	7	0.9
1998*	Cle-A	2	5	.286	69	0	0	0	3	47	54	22	17	5	1	19	43	1.553	3.26	147	4.79	.286	0	....	8	5	0.8
1999*	Cle-A	2	1	.667	55	0	0	0	0	33	50	32	30	6	1	17	29	2.030	8.18	62	8.18	.347	0	....	-11	0	-1.0
Total	14	61	44	.581	884	1	0	0	56	855^{2}	817	371	336	73	22	315	807	1.323	3.53	117	3.58	.252	3	.083	67	86	6.6

• ASTACIO, Pedro Pedro Julio (Pura) Astacio b: 11/28/1968, Hato Mayor, Dominican Republic BR/TR, 6'2", 190 lbs. Deb: 7/3/1992

YEAR	TM-L	W	L	PCT	G	GS	CG	SH	SV	IP	H	R	ER	HR	HB	BB	SO	RAT	ERA	ERA+	CERA	OAV	BH	AVG	PR+	WS	TPW
1992	LA-N	5	5	.500	11	11	4	4	0	82	80	23	18	1	2	20	43	1.220	1.98	174	2.78	.255	3	.125	15	7	1.6
1993	LA-N	14	9	.609	31	31	3	2	0	186^{1}	165	80	74	14	5	68	122	1.250	3.57	107	3.24	.239	10	.161	5	12	0.4
1994	LA-N	6	8	.429	23	23	3	1	0	149	142	77	71	18	4	47	108	1.268	4.29	92	3.71	.252	3	.064	-5	6	-0.9
1995*	LA-N	7	8	.467	48	11	1	1	0	104	103	53	49	12	4	29	80	1.269	4.24	89	3.76	.261	3	.125	-5	5	-0.5
1996*	LA-N	9	8	.529	35	32	0	0	0	211^{2}	207	86	81	18	9	67	130	1.294	3.44	112	3.69	.261	6	.088	12	13	0.8
1997	LA-N	7	9	.438	26	24	2	1	0	153^{2}	151	75	70	15	4	47	115	1.289	4.10	94	3.67	.256	6	.146	-2	6	-0.3
	Col-N	5	1	.833	7	7	0	0	0	48^{2}	49	23	23	9	5	14	51	1.295	4.25	122	4.72	.262	1	.077	6	4	0.5
	Yr.	12	10	.545	33	31	2	1	0	202^{1}	200	98	93	24	9	61	166	1.290	4.14	100	3.92	.258	7	.130	3	10	0.2
1998	Col-N	13	14	.481	35	34	0	0	0	209^{1}	245	160	145	39	17	74	170	1.524	6.23	83	5.91	.294	8	.129	-25	6	-2.7
1999	Col-N	17	11	.607	34	34	7	0	0	232	258	140	130	38	11	75	210	1.435	5.04	115	5.08	.285	20	.235	21	19	2.1
2000	Col-N	12	9	.571	32	32	3	0	0	196^{1}	217	119	115	32	15	77	193	1.497	5.27	110	5.42	.281	8	.098	10	11	0.5
2001	Col-N	6	13	.316	22	22	4	1	0	141	151	91	86	21	10	50	125	1.426	5.49	97	4.94	.276	4	.095	-3	5	-0.5
	Hou-N	2	1	.667	4	4	0	0	0	28^{2}	30	10	10	1	3	4	19	1.186	3.14	145	3.43	.280	1	.091	4	2	0.4
	Yr.	8	14	.364	26	26	4	1	0	169^{2}	181	101	96	22	13	54	144	1.385	5.09	103	4.68	.276	5	.094	1	7	-0.2
2002	NY-N	12	11	.522	31	31	3	1	0	191^{2}	192	106	102	32	16	63	152	1.330	4.79	83	4.57	.262	10	.161	-16	5	-1.6
2003	NY-N	3	2	.600	7	7	0	0	0	36^{2}	47	30	30	8	3	18	20	1.773	7.36	56	7.42	.311	1	.091	-13	0	-1.3
Total	12	118	109	.520	346	303	30	11	0	1971	2037	1073	1004	258	108	653	1538	1.365	4.58	99	4.45	.269	84	.132	4	101	-1.6

• ATCHLEY, Justin Justin Scott Atchley b: 9/5/1973, Sedro Woolley, WA BL/TL, 6'3", 215 lbs. Deb: 4/7/2001

YEAR	TM-L	W	L	PCT	G	GS	CG	SH	SV	IP	H	R	ER	HR	HB	BB	SO	RAT	ERA	ERA+	CERA	OAV	BH	AVG	PR+	WS	TPW
2001	Cin-N	0	0	....	15	0	0	0	0	10^{1}	12	7	7	4	1	5	8	1.645	6.10	75	7.74	.286	0	.000	-2	0	-0.2

• ATHERTON, Keith Keith Rowe Atherton b: 2/19/1959, Newport News, VA BR/TR, 6'4", 200 lbs. Deb: 7/14/1983

YEAR	TM-L	W	L	PCT	G	GS	CG	SH	SV	IP	H	R	ER	HR	HB	BB	SO	RAT	ERA	ERA+	CERA	OAV	BH	AVG	PR+	WS	TPW
1983	Oak-A	2	5	.286	29	0	0	0	4	68^{1}	53	22	21	7	1	23	40	1.112	2.77	139	2.64	.215	0	.000	8	6	0.8
1984	Oak-A	7	6	.538	57	0	0	0	2	104	110	51	50	13	2	39	58	1.433	4.33	87	4.43	.274	0	....	-7	4	-0.7
1985	Oak-A	4	7	.364	56	0	0	0	3	104^{2}	89	51	50	17	0	42	77	1.252	4.30	90	3.58	.231	0	....	-4	4	-0.4
1986	Oak-A	1	2	.333	13	0	0	0	0	15^{1}	18	10	10	2	0	11	8	1.891	5.87	66	6.38	.295	0	....	-3	0	-0.3
	Min-A	5	8	.385	47	0	0	0	10	81^{2}	82	37	34	9	1	35	59	1.433	3.75	115	4.26	.264	0	....	6	8	0.6
	Yr.	6	10	.375	60	0	0	0	10	97	100	47	44	11	1	46	67	1.505	4.08	103	4.60	.269	0	....	3	8	0.3
1987*	Min-A	7	5	.583	59	0	0	0	2	79^{1}	81	46	40	10	4	30	51	1.399	4.54	102	4.38	.262	0	....	0	5	0.0
1988	Min-A	7	5	.583	49	0	0	0	3	74	65	29	28	10	2	22	43	1.176	3.41	119	3.23	.235	0	....	5	7	0.5
1989	Cle-A	0	3	.000	32	0	0	0	2	39	48	22	18	7	0	13	13	1.564	4.15	95	5.43	.293	0	....	-1	1	-0.1
Total	7	33	41	.446	342	0	0	0	26	566^{1}	546	268	251	75	10	215	349	1.344	3.99	101	3.99	.253	0	.000	4	35	0.4

• ATKINS, James James Curtis Atkins b: 3/10/1921, Birmingham, AL BL/TR, 6'3", 205 lbs. Deb: 9/29/1950

YEAR	TM-L	W	L	PCT	G	GS	CG	SH	SV	IP	H	R	ER	HR	HB	BB	SO	RAT	ERA	ERA+	CERA	OAV	BH	AVG	PR+	WS	TPW
1950	Bos-A	0	0	....	1	0	0	0	0	4^{2}	4	2	2	1	1	4	0	1.714	3.86	127	6.77	.235	0	.000	1	0	0.0
1952	Bos-A	0	1	.000	3	1	0	0	0	10^{1}	11	6	4	0	0	7	2	1.742	3.48	113	4.54	.275	2	.667	0	1	0.1
Total	2	0	1	.000	4	1	0	0	0	15	15	8	6	1	1	11	2	1.733	3.60	117	5.23	.263	2	.400	1	1	0.1

• ATKINS, Tommy Francis Montgomery Atkins b: 12/9/1887, Ponca, NE d: 5/7/1956, Cleveland, OH BL/TL, 5'10.5", 165 lbs. Deb: 10/2/1909

YEAR	TM-L	W	L	PCT	G	GS	CG	SH	SV	IP	H	R	ER	HR	HB	BB	SO	RAT	ERA	ERA+	CERA	OAV	BH	AVG	PR+	WS	TPW
1909	Phi-A	0	0	....	1	1	0	0	0	6	6	4	3	0	0	5	4	1.833	4.50	53	4.79	.261	0	.000	-1	0	-0.2
1910	Phi-A	3	2	.600	15	3	2	0	2	57	53	33	17	0	1	23	29	1.333	2.68	88	3.12	.254	2	.118	-3	1	-0.5
Total	2	3	2	.600	16	4	2	0	2	63	59	37	20	0	1	28	33	1.381	2.86	83	3.28	.255	2	.105	-5	1	-0.7

• ATKINSON, Al Albert Wright Atkinson b: 3/9/1861, Clinton, IL d: 6/17/1952, McNatt, MO BR/TR, 5'11.5", 165 lbs. Deb: 5/1/1884

YEAR	TM-L	W	L	PCT	G	GS	CG	SH	SV	IP	H	R	ER	HR	HB	BB	SO	RAT	ERA	ERA+	CERA	OAV	BH	AVG	PR+	WS	TPW
1884	Phi-a	11	11	.500	22	22	20	1	0	184	186	130	86	3	10	21	93	1.125	4.21	80	....	.249	16	.193	-17	10	-1.6
	CP-U	6	10	.375	16	16	16	1	0	140	127	83	43	1	....	21	104	1.057	2.76	104	....	.226	14	.206	3	9	0.0
	Bal-U	3	5	.375	8	8	8	0	0	69^{2}	60	34	18	4	....	12	50	1.033	2.33	144	....	.217	4	.138	7	6	0.4
	Yr.	9	15	.375	24	24	24	1	0	209^{2}	187	117	61	5	....	33	154	1.049	2.62	115	....	.223	18	.186	10	15	0.5
1886	Phi-a	25	17	.595	45	45	44	1	0	396^{2}	414	288	174	11	22	101	154	1.298	3.95	89	....	.257	18	.122	-11	21	-1.3
1887	Phi-a	6	8	.429	15	15	11	0	0	124^{2}	210	121	82	2	6	54	34	1.684	5.92	72	....	.361	17	.266	-24	4	-2.0
Total	3	51	51	.500	106	106	99	3	0	915	997	656	403	21	38	209	435	1.259	3.96	89	....	.264	69	.176	-41	50	-4.4

• ATKINSON, Bill William Cecil Glenn Atkinson b: 10/4/1954, Chatham, Canada BL/TR, 5'7", 165 lbs. Deb: 9/18/1976

YEAR	TM-L	W	L	PCT	G	GS	CG	SH	SV	IP	H	R	ER	HR	HB	BB	SO	RAT	ERA	ERA+	CERA	OAV	BH	AVG	PR+	WS	TPW
1976	Mon-N	0	0	....	4	0	0	0	0	5	3	0	0	0	0	1	4	.800	0.00	....	1.01	.176	0	....	2	1	0.2
1977	Mon-N	7	2	.778	55	0	0	0	7	83^{1}	72	33	31	12	0	29	56	1.212	3.35	114	3.22	.234	1	.200	4	9	0.4
1978	Mon-N	2	2	.500	29	0	0	0	3	45^{1}	45	23	22	5	1	28	32	1.610	4.37	81	4.95	.268	2	.500	-6	2	-0.5
1979	Mon-N	2	0	1.000	10	0	0	0	1	13^{2}	9	4	3	0	0	4	7	.951	1.98	185	1.32	.170	0	.000	3	2	0.2
Total	4	11	4	.733	98	0	0	0	11	147^{1}	129	60	56	17	1	62	99	1.296	3.42	108	3.50	.236	3	.300	3	14	0.3

• AUCOIN, Derek Derek Alfred Aucoin b: 3/27/1970, Lachine, Canada BR/TR, 6'7", 235 lbs. Deb: 5/21/1996

YEAR	TM-L	W	L	PCT	G	GS	CG	SH	SV	IP	H	R	ER	HR	HB	BB	SO	RAT	ERA	ERA+	CERA	OAV	BH	AVG	PR+	WS	TPW
1996	Mon-N	0	1	.000	2	0	0	0	0	2^{2}	3	1	1	0	0	1	1	1.500	3.38	128	3.84	.300	0	....	0	0	0.0

• AUGUST, Don Donald Glenn August b: 7/3/1963, Inglewood, CA BR/TR, 6'3", 190 lbs. Deb: 6/2/1988

YEAR	TM-L	W	L	PCT	G	GS	CG	SH	SV	IP	H	R	ER	HR	HB	BB	SO	RAT	ERA	ERA+	CERA	OAV	BH	AVG	PR+	WS	TPW
1988	Mil-A	13	7	.650	24	22	6	1	0	148^{1}	137	55	51	12	0	48	66	1.247	3.09	129	3.20	.245	0	....	13	12	1.3
1989	Mil-A	12	12	.500	31	25	2	1	0	142^{1}	175	93	84	17	2	58	51	1.637	5.31	72	5.62	.302	0	....	-24	2	-2.4
1990	Mil-A	0	3	.000	5	0	0	0	0	11	13	10	8	0	0	5	2	1.636	6.55	59	4.44	.295	0	....	-3	0	-0.3
1991	Mil-A	9	8	.529	28	23	1	1	0	138^{1}	166	87	84	18	3	47	62	1.540	5.47	73	5.31	.301	0	....	-23	3	-2.3
Total	4	34	30	.531	88	70	9	3	0	440	491	245	227	47	5	158	181	1.475	4.64	84	4.68	.283	0	....	-37	17	-3.7

• AUGUSTINE, Jerry Gerald Lee Augustine b: 7/24/1952, Kewaunee, WI BL/TL, 6', 185 lbs. Deb: 9/9/1975

YEAR	TM-L	W	L	PCT	G	GS	CG	SH	SV	IP	H	R	ER	HR	HB	BB	SO	RAT	ERA	ERA+	CERA	OAV	BH	AVG	PR+	WS	TPW
1975	Mil-A	2	0	1.000	5	3	1	0	0	26^{2}	26	9	9	2	1	12	8	1.425	3.04	126	4.26	.274	0	....	3	2	0.3
1976	Mil-A	9	12	.429	39	24	5	3	0	171^{2}	167	69	63	9	4	56	59	1.299	3.30	106	3.43	.261	0	....	3	10	0.4
1977	Mil-A	12	18	.400	33	33	10	1	0	209	222	119	104	23	3	72	68	1.407	4.48	91	4.35	.277	0	....	-11	9	-1.1
1978	Mil-A	13	12	.520	35	30	9	2	0	188^{1}	204	100	95	14	4	61	59	1.407	4.54	83	4.16	.280	0	....	-17	7	-1.8
1979	Mil-A	9	6	.600	43	2	0	0	5	85^{2}	95	38	33	6	1	30	41	1.459	3.47	120	4.24	.284	0	....	7	8	0.7
1980	Mil-A	4	3	.571	39	1	0	0	2	69^{2}	83	37	35	5	2	36	22	1.708	4.52	86	5.45	.301	0	....	-6	3	-0.6
1981	Mil-A	2	2	.500	27	2	0	0	2	61^{1}	75	30	29	4	1	18	26	1.516	4.26	80	4.64	.300	0	....	-6	2	-0.7
1982	Mil-A	1	3	.250	20	2	1	0	0	62	63	43	35	13	2	26	22	1.435	5.08	74	5.15	.267	0	....	-10	0	-1.0
1983	Mil-A	3	3	.500	34	7	1	0	2	64^{1}	89	45	41	11	1	25	40	1.772	5.74	65	6.78	.328	0	....	-14	0	-1.4
1984	Mil-A	0	0	....	4	0	0	0	0	5^{1}	4	1	0	0	1	4	3	1.500	0.00	....	4.04	.211	0	....	2	1	0.2
Total	10	55	59	.482	279	104	27	6	11	944	1028	491	444	87	20	340	348	1.449	4.23	90	4.45	.281	0	....	-49	42	-5.0

• AUKER, Elden Elden Le Roy "Submarine,Big Six" Auker b: 9/21/1910, Norcatur, KS BR/TR, 6'2", 194 lbs. Deb: 8/10/1933

YEAR	TM-L	W	L	PCT	G	GS	CG	SH	SV	IP	H	R	ER	HR	HB	BB	SO	RAT	ERA	ERA+	CERA	OAV	BH	AVG	PR+	WS	TPW
1933	Det-A	3	3	.500	15	6	2	1	0	55	63	34	32	3	2	25	17	1.600	5.24	82	4.75	.285	2	.118	-6	2	-0.7
1934*	Det-A	15	7	.682	43	18	10	2	1	205	234	103	78	9	3	56	86	1.415	3.42	128	3.99	.288	11	.149	21	15	1.7
1935*	Det-A	18	7	.720	36	25	13	2	0	195	213	86	83	13	9	61	63	1.405	3.83	109	4.14	.279	16	.216	6	14	0.6
1936	Det-A	13	16	.448	35	31	14	2	0	215^{1}	263	140	117	11	3	83	66	1.607	4.89	101	4.88	.302	24	.308	3	13	0.9
1937	Det-A	17	9	.654	39	32	19	1	1	252^{2}	250	127	109	13	6	97	73	1.373	3.88	120	3.63	.260	18	.198	25	22	2.7
1938	Det-A	11	10	.524	27	24	12	1	0	160^{2}	184	97	94	14	5	56	46	1.494	5.27	95	4.58	.284	5	.088	-6	9	-0.9

YEAR	TM-L	W	L	PCT	G	GS	CG	SH	SV	IP	H	R	ER	HR	HB	BB	SO	RAT	ERA	ERA+	CERA	OAV	BH	AVG	PR+	WS	TPW
1939	Bos-A	9	10	.474	31	25	6	1	0	151	183	108	90	13	1	61	43	1.616	5.36	88	5.00	.294	12	.226	-10	7	-0.8
1940	StL-A	16	11	.593	38	35	20	2	0	263^{2}	299	129	116	17	3	96	78	1.498	3.96	116	4.32	.281	19	.213	20	22	2.2
1941	StL-A	14	15	.483	34	31	13	0	0	216	268	150	132	20	1	85	60	1.634	5.50	78	5.29	.302	10	.125	-26	5	-2.8
1942	StL-A	14	13	.519	35	34	17	2	0	249	273	132	113	16	3	86	62	1.442	4.08	91	4.06	.277	14	.161	-8	11	-0.9
Total	**10**	**130**	**101**	**.563**	**333**	**261**	**126**	**14**	**2**	**1963^{1}**	**2230**	**1106**	**964**	**129**	**36**	**706**	**594**	**1.495**	**4.42**	**101**	**4.40**	**.285**	**131**	**.187**	**19**	**120**	**2.1**

• AUSANIO, Joe Joseph John Ausanio b: 12/9/1965, Kingston, NY BR/TR, 6'1", 205 lbs. Deb: 7/14/1994

YEAR	TM-L	W	L	PCT	G	GS	CG	SH	SV	IP	H	R	ER	HR	HB	BB	SO	RAT	ERA	ERA+	CERA	OAV	BH	AVG	PR+	WS	TPW
1994	NY-A	2	1	.667	13	0	0	0	0	15^{2}	16	9	9	3	0	6	15	1.404	5.17	88	4.67	.254	0	....	-1	1	-0.1
1995	NY-A	2	0	1.000	28	0	0	0	1	37^{2}	42	24	24	9	0	23	36	1.726	5.73	80	6.78	.286	0	....	-5	1	-0.5
Total	**2**	**4**	**1**	**.800**	**41**	**0**	**0**	**0**	**1**	**53^{1}**	**58**	**33**	**33**	**12**	**0**	**29**	**51**	**1.631**	**5.57**	**83**	**6.16**	**.276**	**0**	**....**	**-6**	**2**	**-0.6**

• AUST, Dennis Dennis Kay Aust b: 11/25/1940, Tecumseh, NE BR/TR, 5'11", 180 lbs. Deb: 9/6/1965

YEAR	TM-L	W	L	PCT	G	GS	CG	SH	SV	IP	H	R	ER	HR	HB	BB	SO	RAT	ERA	ERA+	CERA	OAV	BH	AVG	PR+	WS	TPW
1965	StL-N	0	0	....	6	0	0	0	1	7^{1}	6	4	4	0	0	2	7	1.091	4.91	78	1.74	.214	0	.000	-1	1	-0.1
1966	StL-N	0	1	.000	9	0	0	0	1	9^{2}	12	7	7	1	0	6	7	1.862	6.52	55	6.03	.308	0	.000	-3	0	-0.3
Total	**2**	**0**	**1**	**.000**	**15**	**0**	**0**	**0**	**2**	**17**	**18**	**11**	**11**	**1**	**0**	**8**	**14**	**1.529**	**5.82**	**63**	**4.18**	**.269**	**0**	**.000**	**-4**	**1**	**-0.5**

• AUSTIN, Jeff Jeffrey Wellington Austin b: 10/19/1976, San Bernardino, CA BR/TR, 6', 185 lbs. Deb: 6/26/2001

YEAR	TM-L	W	L	PCT	G	GS	CG	SH	SV	IP	H	R	ER	HR	HB	BB	SO	RAT	ERA	ERA+	CERA	OAV	BH	AVG	PR+	WS	TPW
2001	KC-A	0	0	....	21	0	0	0	0	26	27	17	16	4	1	14	27	1.577	5.54	89	5.31	.273	0	....	-3	1	-0.2
2002	KC-A	0	0	....	10	0	0	0	0	11	14	6	6	0	0	6	6	1.818	4.91	102	5.24	.318	0	....	0	1	0.0
2003	Cin-N	2	3	.400	7	7	0	0	0	28^{1}	28	27	27	9	0	21	22	1.729	8.58	50	7.11	.255	1	.125	-13	0	-1.4
Total	**3**	**2**	**3**	**.400**	**38**	**7**	**0**	**0**	**0**	**65^{1}**	**69**	**50**	**49**	**13**	**1**	**41**	**55**	**1.684**	**6.75**	**67**	**6.08**	**.273**	**1**	**.125**	**-16**	**2**	**-1.6**

• AUSTIN, Jim James Parker Austin b: 12/7/1963, Farmville, VA BR/TR, 6'2", 200 lbs. Deb: 7/4/1991

YEAR	TM-L	W	L	PCT	G	GS	CG	SH	SV	IP	H	R	ER	HR	HB	BB	SO	RAT	ERA	ERA+	CERA	OAV	BH	AVG	PR+	WS	TPW
1991	Mil-A	0	0	....	5	0	0	0	0	8^{2}	8	8	8	1	3	11	3	2.192	8.31	48	8.71	.276	0	....	-4	0	-0.4
1992	Mil-A	5	2	.714	47	0	0	0	0	58^{1}	38	13	12	2	2	32	30	1.200	1.85	207	2.42	.191	0	....	12	7	1.2
1993	Mil-A	1	2	.333	31	0	0	0	0	33	28	15	14	3	1	13	15	1.242	3.82	111	3.28	.230	0	....	2	2	0.2
Total	**3**	**6**	**4**	**.600**	**83**	**0**	**0**	**0**	**0**	**100**	**74**	**36**	**34**	**6**	**6**	**56**	**48**	**1.300**	**3.06**	**132**	**3.25**	**.211**	**0**	**....**	**9**	**9**	**0.9**

• AUSTIN, Rick Rick Gerald Austin b: 10/27/1946, Seattle, WA BR/TL, 6'4", 190 lbs. Deb: 6/21/1970

YEAR	TM-L	W	L	PCT	G	GS	CG	SH	SV	IP	H	R	ER	HR	HB	BB	SO	RAT	ERA	ERA+	CERA	OAV	BH	AVG	PR+	WS	TPW
1970	Cle-A	2	5	.286	31	8	1	1	3	67^{2}	74	36	36	10	3	26	53	1.478	4.79	83	4.95	.281	2	.111	-6	3	-0.6
1971	Cle-A	0	0	....	23	0	0	0	1	23	25	15	13	3	3	20	20	1.957	5.09	75	6.94	.291	0	.000	-3	0	-0.4
1975	Mil-A	2	3	.400	32	0	0	0	2	40	32	19	18	3	1	32	30	1.600	4.05	95	4.24	.222	0	....	-1	2	-0.1
1976	Mil-A	0	0	....	3	0	0	0	0	5^{1}	10	3	3	1	1	0	3	1.875	5.06	69	9.56	.435	0	....	-1	0	-0.1
Total	**4**	**4**	**8**	**.333**	**89**	**8**	**1**	**1**	**6**	**136**	**141**	**73**	**70**	**17**	**8**	**78**	**106**	**1.610**	**4.63**	**84**	**5.26**	**.273**	**2**	**.105**	**-11**	**5**	**-1.2**

• AUTRY, Al Albert Autry b: 2/29/1952, Modesto, CA BR/TR, 6'5", 225 lbs. Deb: 9/14/1976

YEAR	TM-L	W	L	PCT	G	GS	CG	SH	SV	IP	H	R	ER	HR	HB	BB	SO	RAT	ERA	ERA+	CERA	OAV	BH	AVG	PR+	WS	TPW
1976	Atl-N	1	0	1.000	1	1	0	0	0	5	4	3	3	2	0	3	3	1.400	5.40	70	6.06	.222	0	.000	-1	0	-0.1

• AVERY, Steve Steven Thomas Avery b: 4/14/1970, Trenton, MI BL/TL, 6'4", 190 lbs. Deb: 6/13/1990

YEAR	TM-L	W	L	PCT	G	GS	CG	SH	SV	IP	H	R	ER	HR	HB	BB	SO	RAT	ERA	ERA+	CERA	OAV	BH	AVG	PR+	WS	TPW
1990	Atl-N	3	11	.214	21	20	1	1	0	99	121	79	62	7	2	45	75	1.677	5.64	72	5.26	.302	4	.133	-15	0	-1.7
1991*	Atl-N	18	8	.692	35	35	3	1	0	210^{1}	189	89	79	21	3	65	137	1.208	3.38	115	3.25	.240	17	.215	12	16	1.6
1992*	Atl-N	11	11	.500	35	**35**	2	2	0	233^{2}	216	95	83	14	0	71	129	1.228	3.20	114	3.02	.246	13	.171	11	13	1.4
1993*	Atl-N★	18	6	.750	35	35	3	1	0	223^{1}	216	81	73	14	0	43	125	1.160	2.94	136	2.92	.261	12	.160	25	19	2.5
1994	Atl-N	8	3	.727	24	24	1	0	0	151^{2}	127	71	68	15	4	55	122	1.200	4.04	105	3.12	.227	5	.102	5	9	0.3
1995*	Atl-N	7	13	.350	29	29	3	1	0	173^{1}	165	92	90	22	6	52	141	1.252	4.67	91	3.73	.252	11	.208	-6	8	-0.3
1996*	Atl-N	7	10	.412	24	23	1	0	0	131	146	70	65	10	4	40	86	1.420	4.47	99	4.22	.285	11	.239	1	7	0.6
1997	Bos-A	6	7	.462	22	18	0	0	0	96^{2}	127	76	69	15	2	49	51	1.821	6.42	72	7.01	.320	0	.000	-19	1	-1.8
1998	Bos-A	10	7	.588	34	23	0	0	0	123^{2}	128	74	69	14	4	64	57	1.553	5.02	94	5.06	.269	0	.000	-5	5	-0.5
1999	Cin-N	6	7	.462	19	19	0	0	0	96	75	62	55	11	1	78	51	1.594	5.16	90	4.69	.222	2	.077	-8	3	-0.9
2003	Det-A	2	0	1.000	19	0	0	0	0	16	19	11	10	5	0	7	6	1.625	5.63	77	7.02	.302	1	1.000	-2	1	-0.2
Total	**11**	**96**	**83**	**.536**	**297**	**261**	**14**	**6**	**0**	**1554^{2}**	**1529**	**800**	**723**	**148**	**26**	**569**	**980**	**1.349**	**4.19**	**100**	**3.92**	**.259**	**76**	**.174**	**-2**	**82**	**1.0**

• AVREA, Jay James Epherium Avrea b: 7/6/1920, Cleburne, TX d: 6/26/1987, Dallas, TX BR/TR, 6'1.5", 175 lbs. Deb: 4/22/1950

YEAR	TM-L	W	L	PCT	G	GS	CG	SH	SV	IP	H	R	ER	HR	HB	BB	SO	RAT	ERA	ERA+	CERA	OAV	BH	AVG	PR+	WS	TPW
1950	Cin-N	0	0	....	2	0	0	0	0	5^{1}	6	2	2	0	0	3	2	1.688	3.38	126	4.38	.273	0	.000	1	0	0.0

• AYALA, Bobby Robert Joseph Ayala b: 7/8/1969, Ventura, CA BR/TR, 6'2", 200 lbs. Deb: 9/5/1992

YEAR	TM-L	W	L	PCT	G	GS	CG	SH	SV	IP	H	R	ER	HR	HB	BB	SO	RAT	ERA	ERA+	CERA	OAV	BH	AVG	PR+	WS	TPW
1992	Cin-N	2	1	.667	5	5	0	0	0	29	33	15	14	1	1	13	23	1.586	4.34	83	4.73	.297	0	.000	-2	1	-0.4
1993	Cin-N	7	10	.412	43	9	0	0	3	98	106	72	61	16	7	45	65	1.541	5.60	72	5.38	.274	2	.095	-16	1	-1.8
1994	Sea-A	4	3	.571	46	0	0	0	18	56^{2}	42	25	18	2	0	26	76	1.200	2.86	171	2.48	.203	0	....	13	10	1.2
1995*	Sea-A	6	5	.545	63	0	0	0	19	71	73	42	35	9	6	30	77	1.451	4.44	107	4.68	.262	0	....	4	7	0.4
1996	Sea-A	6	3	.667	50	0	0	0	3	67^{1}	65	45	44	10	2	25	61	1.337	5.88	84	4.21	.256	0	....	-7	4	-0.7
1997*	Sea-A	10	5	.667	71	0	0	0	8	96^{2}	91	45	41	14	3	41	92	1.366	3.82	118	4.39	.260	0	....	8	9	0.8
1998	Sea-A	1	10	.091	62	0	0	0	8	75^{1}	100	66	61	9	1	26	68	1.673	7.29	64	5.78	.323	0	....	-21	0	-2.0
1999	Mon-N	1	6	.143	53	0	0	0	0	66	60	36	27	6	4	34	64	1.424	3.68	122	4.00	.235	0	.000	7	4	0.7
	Chi-N	0	1	.000	13	0	0	0	0	16	11	7	5	4	2	5	15	1.000	2.81	161	3.40	.193	0	....	3	2	0.3
	Yr.	1	7	.125	66	0	0	0	0	82	71	43	32	10	6	39	79	1.341	3.51	128	3.88	.228	0	.000	10	6	1.0
Total	**8**	**37**	**44**	**.457**	**406**	**14**	**0**	**0**	**59**	**576**	**581**	**353**	**306**	**71**	**26**	**245**	**541**	**1.434**	**4.78**	**94**	**4.51**	**.263**	**2**	**.065**	**-11**	**38**	**-1.4**

• AYALA, Luis Luis Ignacio Ayala b: 1/12/1978, Los Mochis, Mexico BR/TR, 6'2", 170 lbs. Deb: 3/31/2003

YEAR	TM-L	W	L	PCT	G	GS	CG	SH	SV	IP	H	R	ER	HR	HB	BB	SO	RAT	ERA	ERA+	CERA	OAV	BH	AVG	PR+	WS	TPW
2003	Mon-N	10	3	.769	65	0	0	0	5	71	65	27	23	8	5	13	46	1.099	2.92	173	3.11	.244	0	.000	17	12	1.7

• AYBAR, Manny Manuel Antonio Aybar b: 5/4/1972, Bani, Dominican Republic BR/TR, 6'1", 165 lbs. Deb: 8/4/1997

YEAR	TM-L	W	L	PCT	G	GS	CG	SH	SV	IP	H	R	ER	HR	HB	BB	SO	RAT	ERA	ERA+	CERA	OAV	BH	AVG	PR+	WS	TPW
1997	StL-N	2	4	.333	12	12	0	0	0	68	66	33	32	8	4	29	41	1.397	4.24	98	4.40	.263	3	.143	-1	3	-0.1
1998	StL-N	6	6	.500	20	14	0	0	0	81^{1}	90	58	54	6	2	42	57	1.623	5.98	70	5.04	.281	6	.222	-16	1	-1.4
1999	StL-N	4	5	.444	65	1	0	0	3	97	104	67	59	13	4	36	74	1.443	5.47	83	4.68	.272	1	.083	-10	4	-1.0
2000	Col-N	0	1	.000	1	0	0	0	0	1^{2}	5	3	3	1	0	0	0	3.000	16.20	36	21.12	.500	0	....	-2	0	-0.2
	Cin-N	1	1	.500	32	0	0	0	0	50^{1}	51	31	27	7	2	22	31	1.450	4.83	97	4.57	.262	0	.000	-1	2	-0.1
	Fla-N	1	0	1.000	21	0	0	0	0	27^{1}	18	8	8	3	0	13	14	1.134	2.63	168	2.53	.184	0	....	6	3	0.5
	Yr.	2	2	.500	54	0	0	0	0	79^{1}	74	42	38	11	2	35	45	1.374	4.31	109	4.21	.244	0	.000	2	5	0.2
2001	Chi-N	2	1	.667	17	1	0	0	0	22^{2}	28	19	16	5	2	17	16	1.985	6.35	65	8.38	.304	3	1.000	-5	1	-0.4
2002*	SF-N	1	0	1.000	15	0	0	0	0	14^{1}	16	6	4	1	1	3	11	1.326	2.51	154	3.71	.271	0	.000	2	1	0.2
2003	SF-N	0	0	....	3	0	0	0	0	3	4	2	2	1	0	3	2	2.333	6.00	68	10.72	.333	0	....	-1	0	-0.1
Total	**7**	**17**	**18**	**.486**	**186**	**28**	**0**	**0**	**3**	**365^{2}**	**382**	**227**	**205**	**45**	**15**	**165**	**246**	**1.496**	**5.05**	**87**	**4.85**	**.269**	**13**	**.186**	**-28**	**15**	**-2.5**

• AYDELOTT, Jake Jacob Stuart Aydelott b: 7/6/1861, Marion, IN d: 10/22/1926, Detroit, MI BL/TR, 6', 180 lbs. Deb: 5/15/1884

YEAR	TM-L	W	L	PCT	G	GS	CG	SH	SV	IP	H	R	ER	HR	HB	BB	SO	RAT	ERA	ERA+	CERA	OAV	BH	AVG	PR+	WS	TPW
1884	Ind-a	5	7	.417	12	12	11	0	0	106	129	100	58	0	0	29	30	1.491	4.92	67	....	.285	5	.114	-14	2	-1.5
1886	Phi-a	0	2	.000	2	2	2	0	0	18	21	11	8	0	0	12	5	1.833	4.00	87	....	.279	0	.000	-1	1	-0.1
Total	**2**	**5**	**9**	**.357**	**14**	**14**	**13**	**0**	**0**	**124**	**150**	**111**	**66**	**0**	**0**	**41**	**35**	**1.540**	**4.79**	**69**	**....**	**.284**	**5**	**.100**	**-15**	**3**	**-1.7**

• AYERS, Bill William Oscar Ayers b: 9/27/1919, Newman, GA d: 9/24/1980, Newman, GA BR/TR, 6'3", 185 lbs. Deb: 4/17/1947

YEAR	TM-L	W	L	PCT	G	GS	CG	SH	SV	IP	H	R	ER	HR	HB	BB	SO	RAT	ERA	ERA+	CERA	OAV	BH	AVG	PR+	WS	TPW
1947	NY-N	0	3	.000	13	4	0	0	1	35^{1}	46	35	32	7	1	14	22	1.698	8.15	50	6.74	.322	2	.250	-16	0	-1.5

• AYERS, Doc Yancy Wyatt Ayers b: 5/20/1890, Fancy Gap, VA d: 5/26/1968, Pulaski, VA BR/TR, 6'1", 185 lbs. Deb: 9/9/1913

YEAR	TM-L	W	L	PCT	G	GS	CG	SH	SV	IP	H	R	ER	HR	HB	BB	SO	RAT	ERA	ERA+	CERA	OAV	BH	AVG	PR+	WS	TPW
1913	Was-A	1	1	.500	4	2	1	1	1	17^{2}	12	7	3	0	1	4	17	.906	1.53	193	1.44	.182	0	.000	3	2	0.2
1914	Was-A	11	15	.423	49	32	8	3	3	265^{1}	221	106	75	5	8	54	148	1.036	2.54	110	2.23	.238	14	.169	6	14	0.7
1915	Was-A	14	9	.609	40	16	8	2	3	211^{1}	178	66	52	1	7	38	96	1.022	2.21	134	2.06	.234	12	.190	16	19	1.4
1916	Was-A	5	8	.385	43	17	7	0	2	157	173	89	66	4	4	52	69	1.433	3.78	74	3.99	.285	6	.140	-18	2	-2.2
1917	Was-A	11	10	.524	40	15	12	3	1	207^{2}	192	67	50	3	8	59	78	1.209	2.17	121	2.93	.256	13	.206	8	15	0.9
1918	Was-A	10	12	.455	40	24	11	4	3	219^{2}	215	91	69	2	7	63	67	1.266	2.83	96	3.02	.261	10	.152	-9	10	-1.3

YEAR	TM-L	W	L	PCT	G	GS	CG	SH	SV	IP	H	R	ER	HR	HB	BB	SO	RAT	ERA	ERA+	CERA	OAV	BH	AVG	PR+	WS	TPW
1919	Was-A	0	6	.000	11	5	0	0	1	43^{2}	52	27	14	0	4	17	12	1.580	2.89	111	4.97	.317	5	.417	2	1	0.4
	Det-A	5	3	.625	24	5	3	1	0	93^{2}	88	34	28	2	3	31	32	1.270	2.69	119	3.14	.254	3	.125	7	7	0.6
	Yr.	5	9	.357	35	10	3	1	1	137^{1}	140	61	42	2	7	48	44	1.369	2.75	116	3.72	.274	8	.222	9	8	1.0
1920	Det-A	7	14	.333	46	23	8	3	1	208^{2}	217	115	90	6	8	62	103	1.337	3.88	96	3.61	.280	9	.153	0	10	-0.2
1921	Det-A	0	0	....	2	1	0	0	0	4	9	6	4	0	0	2	0	2.750	9.00	47	11.28	.450	0	....	-2	0	-0.2
Total	**9**	**64**	**78**	**.451**	**299**	**140**	**58**	**17**	**15**	**1428^{2}**	**1357**	**608**	**451**	**23**	**50**	**382**	**622**	**1.217**	**2.84**	**105**	**2.98**	**.259**	**72**	**.171**	**12**	**80**	**0.2**
• AYRAULT, Bob	Robert Cunningham Ayrault b: 4/27/1966, South Lake Tahoe, CA BR/TR, 6'4", 230 lbs. Deb: 6/7/1992																										
1992	Phi-N	2	2	.500	30	0	0	0	0	43^{1}	32	16	15	0	1	17	27	1.131	3.12	112	2.08	.209	0	....	2	3	0.2
1993	Phi-N	2	0	1.000	10	0	0	0	0	10^{1}	18	11	11	1	1	10	8	2.710	9.58	41	11.49	.375	0	.000	-6	0	-0.7
	Sea-A	1	1	.500	14	0	0	0	0	19^{2}	18	8	7	1	0	6	7	1.220	3.20	137	2.92	.254	0	....	3	2	0.2
Total	**2**	**5**	**3**	**.625**	**54**	**0**	**0**	**0**	**0**	**73^{1}**	**68**	**35**	**33**	**2**	**2**	**33**	**42**	**1.377**	**4.05**	**94**	**3.63**	**.250**	**0**	**.000**	**-2**	**5**	**-0.2**
• BABCOCK, Bob	Robert Ernest Babcock b: 8/25/1949, New Castle, PA BR/TR, 6'5", 210 lbs. Deb: 7/22/1979																										
1979	Tex-A	0	0	....	4	0	0	0	0	5^{1}	7	7	6	1	0	7	6	2.625	10.13	41	10.25	.318	0	....	-4	0	-0.4
1980	Tex-A	1	2	.333	19	0	0	0	0	23^{1}	20	13	12	3	2	8	15	1.200	4.63	84	3.54	.238	0	....	-2	1	-0.2
1981	Tex-A	1	1	.500	16	0	0	0	0	28^{2}	21	7	7	2	1	16	18	1.291	2.20	158	3.24	.219	0	....	4	2	0.4
Total	**3**	**2**	**3**	**.400**	**39**	**0**	**0**	**0**	**0**	**57^{1}**	**48**	**27**	**25**	**6**	**3**	**31**	**39**	**1.378**	**3.92**	**97**	**4.02**	**.238**	**0**	**....**	**-2**	**3**	**-0.1**
• BABICH, Johnny	John Charles Babich b: 5/14/1913, Albion, CA d: 1/19/2001, Richmond, CA BR/TR, 6'1.5", 185 lbs. Deb: 6/19/1934																										
1934	Bro-N	7	11	.389	25	18	7	0	1	135	148	76	63	5	2	51	62	1.474	4.20	93	4.05	.281	7	.140	-4	5	-0.6
1935	Bro-N	7	14	.333	37	24	7	2	0	143^{1}	191	124	106	7	2	52	55	1.695	6.66	60	5.33	.317	9	.184	-44	0	-4.3
1936	Bos-N	0	0	....	3	0	0	0	0	6	11	8	7	1	1	6	1	2.833	10.50	37	14.21	.440	0	.000	-4	0	-0.5
1940	Phi-A	14	13	.519	31	30	16	1	0	229^{1}	222	111	95	16	1	80	94	1.317	3.73	119	3.36	.248	10	.116	22	14	1.5
1941	Phi-A	2	7	.222	16	14	4	0	0	78^{1}	85	57	53	9	3	31	19	1.481	6.09	69	4.74	.281	10	.400	-17	2	-1.3
Total	**5**	**30**	**45**	**.400**	**112**	**86**	**34**	**3**	**1**	**592**	**657**	**376**	**324**	**38**	**9**	**220**	**231**	**1.481**	**4.93**	**84**	**4.29**	**.279**	**36**	**.171**	**-48**	**21**	**-5.2**
• BACKE, Brandon	Brandon Allen Backe b: 4/5/1978, Galveston, TX BR/TR, 6', 182 lbs. Deb: 7/19/2002																										
2002	TB-A	0	0	....	9	0	0	0	0	13	15	10	10	3	2	7	6	1.692	6.92	64	7.37	.288	0	....	-4	0	-0.4
2003	TB-A	1	1	.500	28	0	0	0	0	44^{2}	40	28	27	6	2	25	36	1.455	5.44	83	4.64	.247	0	....	-6	1	-0.5
Total	**2**	**1**	**1**	**.500**	**37**	**0**	**0**	**0**	**0**	**57^{2}**	**55**	**38**	**37**	**9**	**4**	**32**	**42**	**1.509**	**5.77**	**78**	**5.25**	**.257**	**0**	**....**	**-9**	**1**	**-0.9**
• BACKMAN, Les	Lester John Backman b: 3/20/1888, Cleves, OH d: 11/8/1975, Cincinnati, OH BR/TR, 6'.5", 195 lbs. Deb: 7/3/1909																										
1909	StL-N	3	11	.214	21	15	8	0	0	128^{1}	146	69	59	1	3	39	35	1.442	4.14	61	4.09	.302	4	.103	-20	2	-2.3
1910	StL-N	6	7	.462	26	11	4	0	2	116	117	55	39	4	2	53	41	1.466	3.03	98	3.91	.265	4	.114	3	5	0.3
Total	**2**	**9**	**18**	**.333**	**47**	**26**	**12**	**0**	**2**	**244^{1}**	**263**	**124**	**98**	**5**	**5**	**92**	**76**	**1.453**	**3.61**	**74**	**4.01**	**.284**	**8**	**.108**	**-17**	**7**	**-2.0**
• BACON, Eddie	Edgar Suter Bacon b: 4/8/1895, Franklin County, KY d: 10/2/1963, Louisville, KY Deb: 8/13/1917																										
1917	Phi-A	0	0	....	1	0	0	0	0	6	5	7	4	0	0	7	0	2.000	6.00	46	5.17	.238	3	.500	-2	1	-0.1
• BACSIK, Mike	Michael Joseph Bacsik b: 11/11/1977, Dallas, TX BL/TL, 6'3", 190 lbs. Deb: 8/5/2001																										
2001	Cle-A	0	0	....	3	0	0	0	0	9	13	10	9	0	1	3	4	1.778	9.00	50	5.56	.325	0	....	-4	0	-0.4
2002	NY-N	3	2	.600	11	9	1	0	0	55^{2}	63	29	27	8	4	19	30	1.473	4.37	91	5.13	.289	2	.111	-2	2	-0.3
2003	NY-N	1	2	.333	5	3	0	0	0	17^{2}	28	21	20	5	0	8	12	2.038	10.19	41	9.79	.368	0	.000	-12	0	-1.2
Total	**3**	**4**	**4**	**.500**	**19**	**12**	**1**	**0**	**0**	**82^{1}**	**104**	**60**	**56**	**13**	**5**	**30**	**46**	**1.628**	**6.12**	**67**	**6.18**	**.311**	**2**	**.095**	**-18**	**2**	**-1.9**
• BACSIK, Mike	Michael James Bacsik b: 4/1/1952, Dallas, TX BR/TR, 6'2", 185 lbs. Deb: 6/15/1975																										
1975	Tex-A	1	2	.333	7	3	0	0	0	26^{2}	28	17	11	1	1	9	13	1.388	3.71	101	3.73	.275	0	....	0	1	0.0
1976	Tex-A	3	2	.600	23	0	0	0	0	55	66	31	26	3	2	26	21	1.673	4.25	84	5.23	.308	0	....	-4	2	-0.5
1977	Tex-A	0	0	....	2	0	0	0	0	2^{1}	9	5	5	1	0	0	1	3.857	19.29	21	26.55	.563	0	....	-4	0	-0.4
1979	Min-A	4	2	.667	31	0	0	0	0	65^{2}	61	39	32	6	0	29	33	1.371	4.39	100	3.66	.249	0	....	0	3	0.0
1980	Min-A	0	0	....	10	0	0	0	0	23	26	12	11	1	0	11	9	1.609	4.30	101	4.68	.286	0	....	0	1	0.0
Total	**5**	**8**	**6**	**.571**	**73**	**3**	**0**	**0**	**0**	**172^{2}**	**190**	**104**	**85**	**12**	**3**	**75**	**77**	**1.535**	**4.43**	**90**	**4.62**	**.284**	**0**	**....**	**-8**	**7**	**-0.8**
• BACZEWSKI, Fred	Frederic John "Lefty" Baczewski b: 5/15/1926, St. Paul, MN d: 11/14/1976, Culver City, CA BL/TL, 6'2.5", 185 lbs. Deb: 4/26/1953																										
1953	Chi-N	0	0	....	9	0	0	0	0	10	20	9	7	1	1	6	3	2.600	6.30	71	12.33	.435	1	.500	-2	0	-0.1
	Cin-N	11	4	.733	24	18	10	1	1	138^{1}	125	56	53	13	1	52	58	1.280	3.45	126	3.40	.244	8	.178	11	13	1.1
	Yr.	11	4	.733	33	18	10	1	1	148^{1}	145	65	60	14	2	58	61	1.369	3.64	120	4.00	.260	9	.191	9	13	0.9
1954	Cin-N	6	6	.500	29	22	4	1	0	130	159	82	76	22	1	53	43	1.631	5.26	80	5.90	.305	3	.071	-17	3	-2.0
1955	Cin-N	0	0	....	1	0	0	0	0	1	2	2	2	2	0	0	0	2.000	18.00	24	25.07	.400	0	....	-2	0	-0.2
Total	**3**	**17**	**10**	**.630**	**63**	**40**	**14**	**2**	**1**	**279^{1}**	**306**	**149**	**138**	**38**	**3**	**111**	**104**	**1.493**	**4.45**	**96**	**4.96**	**.282**	**12**	**.135**	**-9**	**16**	**-1.2**
• BADER, Lore	Lore Verne "King" Bader b: 4/27/1888, Bader, IL d: 6/2/1973, Le Roy, KS BL/TR, 6', 175 lbs. Deb: 9/30/1912 C																										
1912	NY-N	2	0	1.000	2	1	1	0	0	10	9	2	1	0	1	6	3	1.500	0.90	375	3.63	.250	0	.000	3	2	0.2
1917	Bos-A	2	0	1.000	15	1	0	0	1	38^{1}	48	15	10	1	1	18	14	1.722	2.35	110	5.26	.306	3	.300	1	3	0.2
1918	Bos-A	1	3	.250	5	4	2	1	0	27	26	13	10	1	3	12	10	1.407	3.33	80	3.99	.271	1	.111	-2	0	-0.3
Total	**3**	**5**	**3**	**.625**	**22**	**6**	**3**	**1**	**1**	**75^{1}**	**83**	**30**	**21**	**2**	**5**	**36**	**27**	**1.580**	**2.51**	**106**	**4.59**	**.287**	**4**	**.182**	**1**	**5**	**0.1**
• BAECHT, Ed	Edward Joseph Baecht b: 5/15/1907, Paden, OK d: 8/15/1957, Grafton, IL BR/TR, 6'3", 195 lbs. Deb: 4/24/1926																										
1926	Phi-N	2	0	1.000	28	1	1	0	0	56	73	43	38	4	1	28	14	1.804	6.11	68	5.82	.324	2	.143	-10	1	-1.1
1927	Phi-N	0	1	.000	1	1	0	0	0	6	12	8	8	0	0	2	0	2.333	12.00	34	9.16	.429	0	.000	-5	0	-0.5
1928	Phi-N	1	1	.500	9	1	0	0	0	24	37	16	16	1	0	9	10	1.917	6.00	71	6.97	.385	1	.143	-4	1	-0.5
1931	Chi-N	2	4	.333	22	6	2	0	0	67	64	34	28	1	8	32	34	1.433	3.76	103	3.75	.250	5	.278	1	3	0.2
1932	Chi-N	0	0	....	1	0	0	0	0	1	1	0	0	0	0	1	0	2.000	0.00	....	6.60	.333	0	....	0	0	0.0
1937	StL-A	0	0	....	3	0	0	0	0	6^{1}	13	15	9	3	2	6	3	3.000	12.79	38	19.07	.419	0	.000	-6	0	-0.5
Total	**6**	**5**	**6**	**.455**	**64**	**9**	**3**	**0**	**0**	**160^{1}**	**200**	**116**	**99**	**9**	**11**	**78**	**61**	**1.734**	**5.56**	**74**	**5.78**	**.313**	**8**	**.190**	**-24**	**5**	**-2.4**
• BAEZ, Benito	Benito (Ceri) Baez b: 5/6/1977, Bonao, Dominican Republic BL/TL, 6', 160 lbs. Deb: 8/25/2001																										
2001	Fla-N	0	0	....	8	0	0	0	0	9^{1}	22	14	14	3	0	6	14	3.000	13.50	31	16.75	.449	0	.000	-10	0	-1.0
• BAEZ, Danys	Denis (Gonzalez) Baez b: 9/10/1977, Pinar del Rio, Cuba BR/TR, 6'3", 225 lbs. Deb: 5/13/2001																										
2001*	Cle-A	5	3	.625	43	0	0	0	0	50^{1}	34	22	14	5	3	20	52	1.073	2.50	180	2.51	.191	0	....	12	6	1.2
2002	Cle-A	10	11	.476	39	26	1	0	6	165^{1}	160	84	81	14	9	82	130	1.464	4.41	100	4.35	.256	0	.000	2	11	0.1
2003	Cle-A	2	9	.182	73	0	0	0	25	75^{2}	65	36	32	9	4	23	66	1.163	3.81	116	3.22	.229	0	.000	4	9	0.3
Total	**3**	**17**	**23**	**.425**	**155**	**26**	**1**	**0**	**31**	**291^{1}**	**259**	**142**	**127**	**28**	**16**	**125**	**248**	**1.318**	**3.92**	**112**	**3.74**	**.238**	**0**	**.000**	**17**	**26**	**1.6**
• BAGBY, Jim	James Charles Jacob "Sarge" Bagby, Sr. b: 10/5/1889, Barnett, GA d: 7/28/1954, Marietta, GA BB/TR, 6', 170 lbs. Deb: 4/22/1912																										
1912	Cin-N	2	1	.667	5	1	0	0	0	17^{1}	17	6	6	2	0	9	10	1.500	3.12	107	4.65	.270	0	.000	1	2	0.0
1916	Cle-A	17	16	.515	48	27	14	3	5	272^{2}	253	109	79	2	8	67	88	1.174	2.61	115	2.67	.251	15	.167	11	17	1.2
1917	Cle-A	23	13	.639	49	37	26	8	7	320^{2}	277	90	70	6	6	73	83	1.091	1.96	144	2.29	.235	25	.231	22	34	2.8
1918	Cle-A	17	16	.515	**45**	31	23	2	6	271^{1}	274	108	81	0	2	78	57	1.297	2.69	111	2.96	.276	21	.212	15	19	1.7
1919	Cle-A	17	11	.607	35	32	21	0	3	241^{1}	258	96	75	3	4	44	61	1.251	2.80	119	3.12	.275	23	.258	16	21	2.1
1920*	Cle-A	**31**	12	.721	**48**	38	**30**	3	0	**339^{2}**	338	122	109	9	5	79	73	1.228	2.89	131	3.04	.266	33	.252	28	**34**	3.2
1921	Cle-A	14	12	.538	40	26	13	0	4	191^{2}	238	112	100	14	4	44	37	1.471	4.70	91	4.60	.308	15	.197	-9	10	-1.0
1922	Cle-A	4	5	.444	25	10	4	0	1	98^{1}	134	77	69	5	3	39	25	1.759	6.32	63	5.93	.340	11	.262	-23	1	-2.0
1923	Pit-N	3	2	.600	21	6	2	0	3	68^{2}	95	49	40	6	1	25	16	1.748	5.24	76	6.02	.336	1	.050	-11	1	-1.2
Total	**9**	**128**	**88**	**.593**	**316**	**208**	**133**	**16**	**29**	**1821^{2}**	**1884**	**769**	**629**	**47**	**33**	**458**	**450**	**1.286**	**3.11**	**111**	**3.30**	**.273**	**144**	**.218**	**50**	**139**	**6.9**
• BAGBY, Jim	James Charles Jacob Bagby, Jr. b: 9/8/1916, Cleveland, OH d: 9/2/1988, Marietta, GA BR/TR, 6'2", 170 lbs. Deb: 4/18/1938																										
1938	Bos-A	15	11	.577	43	25	10	1	2	198^{2}	218	110	93	9	3	90	73	1.550	4.21	117	4.44	.283	13	.191	14	15	1.2
1939	Bos-A	5	5	.500	21	11	3	0	0	80	119	66	63	7	2	36	35	1.938	7.09	67	7.09	.347	10	.294	-21	2	-1.7

YEAR TM-L	W	L	PCT	G	GS	CG	SH	SV	IP	H	R	ER	HR	HB	BB	SO	RAT	ERA	ERA+	CERA	OAV	BH	AVG	PR+	WS	TPW
1940 Bos-A	10	16	.385	36	21	6	1	2	182^{2}	217	104	96	15	1	83	57	1.642	4.73	95	5.15	.296	15	.203	-3	10	-0.4
1941 Cle-A	9	15	.375	33	27	12	0	2	200^{2}	214	104	90	10	6	76	53	1.445	4.04	98	4.02	.273	18	.243	-3	11	-0.1
1942 Cle-A★	17	9	.654	38	**35**	16	4	1	270^{2}	267	105	89	19	1	64	54	1.223	2.96	116	3.17	.258	18	.189	10	20	1.1
1943 Cle-A★	17	14	.548	36	**33**	16	3	1	**273**	248	112	94	15	3	80	70	1.201	3.10	100	2.83	.240	30	.268	-6	14	-0.1
1944 Cle-A	4	5	.444	13	10	2	0	0	79	101	48	38	2	4	34	12	1.709	4.33	76	5.28	.312	7	.226	-10	2	-1.0
1945 Cle-A	8	11	.421	25	19	11	3	1	159^{1}	171	70	66	3	2	59	38	1.444	3.73	87	3.77	.279	17	.293	-7	9	-0.4
1946* Bos-A	7	6	.538	21	11	6	1	0	106^{2}	117	55	44	4	1	49	16	1.556	3.71	99	4.30	.279	5	.119	-1	5	-0.3
1947 Pit-N	5	4	.556	37	6	2	0	0	115^{2}	143	75	60	14	5	37	23	1.556	4.67	90	5.35	.304	7	.219	-5	4	-0.4
Total 10	97	96	.503	303	198	84	13	9	1666^{1}	1815	849	733	98	28	608	431	1.454	3.96	97	4.15	.278	140	.226	-32	92	-2.1
• BAHNSEN, Stan	Stanley Raymond Bahnsen b: 12/15/1944, Council Bluffs, IA BR/TR, 6'2", 203 lbs. Deb: 9/9/1966																									
1966 NY-A	1	1	.500	4	3	1	0	1	23	15	9	9	3	0	7	16	.957	3.52	94	2.12	.181	1	.143	-0	1	-0.1
1968 NY-A	17	12	.586	37	34	10	1	0	267^{1}	216	72	61	14	2	68	162	1.062	2.05	141	2.24	.221	4	.049	28	23	2.8
1969 NY-A	9	16	.360	40	33	5	2	1	220^{2}	222	102	94	28	0	90	130	1.414	3.83	91	4.25	.260	5	.083	-10	9	-1.3
1970 NY-A	14	11	.560	36	35	6	2	0	232^{2}	227	100	86	23	2	75	116	1.298	3.33	106	3.66	.256	11	.149	5	12	0.4
1971 NY-A	14	12	.538	36	34	14	3	0	242	221	99	90	20	5	72	110	1.211	3.35	97	3.17	.248	12	.152	-2	13	-0.2
1972 Chi-A	21	16	.568	43	41	5	1	0	252^{1}	263	107	101	22	6	73	157	1.332	3.60	87	3.88	.268	14	.152	-8	12	-1.0
1973 Chi-A	18	21	.462	42	42	14	4	0	282^{1}	290	128	112	20	5	117	120	1.442	3.57	111	4.18	.269	0	....	16	18	1.6
1974 Chi-A	12	15	.444	38	35	10	1	0	216^{1}	230	128	113	17	4	110	102	**1.572**	4.70	79	4.80	.277	0	....	-21	6	-2.2
1975 Chi-A	4	6	.400	12	12	2	0	0	67^{1}	78	49	45	9	3	40	31	1.752	6.01	64	6.32	.291	0	....	-15	0	-1.5
Oak-A	6	7	.462	21	16	2	0	0	100	88	42	36	2	3	37	49	1.250	3.24	112	2.86	.238	0	.000	4	5	0.4
Yr.	10	13	.435	33	28	4	0	0	167^{1}	166	91	81	11	6	77	80	1.452	4.36	86	4.25	.261	0	.000	-11	5	-1.1
1976 Oak-A	8	7	.533	35	14	1	1	0	143	124	55	53	13	2	43	82	1.168	3.34	101	2.94	.232	0	....	3	8	0.3
1977 Oak-A	1	2	.333	11	2	0	0	1	22	24	16	15	5	1	13	21	1.682	6.14	66	6.29	.286	0	....	-5	0	-0.5
Mon-N	8	9	.471	23	22	3	1	0	127^{1}	142	76	68	14	0	38	58	1.414	4.81	79	4.39	.283	5	.119	-15	3	-1.5
1978 Mon-N	1	5	.167	44	1	0	0	7	75	74	35	32	9	0	31	44	1.400	3.84	92	4.24	.261	1	.091	-5	3	-0.6
1979 Mon-N	3	1	.750	55	0	0	0	5	94^{1}	80	34	33	10	0	42	71	1.293	3.15	116	3.49	.236	1	.071	5	7	0.5
1980 Mon-N	7	6	.538	57	0	0	0	4	91^{1}	80	40	31	7	0	33	48	1.237	3.05	117	3.01	.235	1	.111	6	7	0.7
1981* Mon-N	2	1	.667	25	3	0	0	1	49	45	27	27	7	1	24	28	1.408	4.96	70	4.47	.247	1	.111	-8	1	-0.9
1982 Cal-A	0	1	.000	7	0	0	0	0	9^{2}	13	6	5	0	0	8	5	2.172	4.66	87	6.65	.310	0	....	-1	0	-0.1
Phi-N	0	0	....	8	0	0	0	0	13^{1}	8	2	2	0	0	3	9	.825	1.35	272	1.17	.182	0	....	3	2	0.4
Total 16	146	149	.495	574	327	73	16	20	2529	2440	1127	1013	223	34	924	1359	1.330	3.60	97	3.74	.255	56	.117	-20	130	-2.9
• BAHR, Ed	Edson Garfield Bahr b: 10/16/1919, Rouleau, Canada BR/TR, 6'1.5", 172 lbs. Deb: 5/1/1946																									
1946 Pit-N	8	6	.571	27	14	7	0	0	136^{2}	128	57	40	8	5	52	44	1.317	2.63	134	3.44	.254	8	.178	15	11	1.6
1947 Pit-N	3	5	.375	19	11	1	0	0	82^{1}	82	45	42	5	3	43	25	1.518	4.59	92	4.32	.263	2	.087	-3	3	-0.5
Total 2	11	11	.500	46	25	8	0	0	219	210	102	82	13	8	95	69	1.393	3.37	114	3.77	.257	10	.147	13	14	1.1
• BAICHLEY, Grover	Grover Cleveland Baichley b: 12/10/1889, Toledo, IL d: 6/28/1956, San Jose, CA BR/TR, 5'8", 165 lbs. Deb: 8/24/1914																									
1914 StL-A	0	0	....	4	0	0	0	0	7	9	5	4	0	0	3	3	1.714	5.14	52	5.55	.346	0	.000	-2	0	-0.2
• BAILES, Scott	Scott Alan Bailes b: 12/18/1961, Chillicothe, OH BL/TL, 6'2", 184 lbs. Deb: 4/9/1986																									
1986 Cle-A	10	10	.500	62	10	0	0	7	112^{2}	123	70	62	12	1	43	60	1.473	4.95	84	4.47	.276	0	....	-9	6	-0.9
1987 Cle-A	7	8	.467	39	17	0	0	6	120^{1}	145	75	62	21	4	47	65	1.596	4.64	98	5.86	.296	0	....	0	6	0.0
1988 Cle-A	9	14	.391	37	21	5	2	0	145	149	89	79	22	2	46	53	1.345	4.90	84	4.34	.266	0	....	-10	4	-1.0
1989 Cle-A	5	9	.357	34	11	0	0	0	113^{2}	116	57	54	7	3	29	47	1.276	4.28	93	3.46	.269	0	....	-3	5	-0.4
1990 Cal-A	2	0	1.000	27	0	0	0	0	35^{1}	46	30	25	8	1	20	16	1.868	6.37	60	7.60	.315	0	....	-10	0	-1.0
1991 Cal-A	1	2	.333	42	0	0	0	0	51^{2}	41	26	24	5	4	22	41	1.219	4.18	98	3.16	.218	0	....	-1	2	-0.1
1992 Cal-A	3	1	.750	32	0	0	0	0	38^{2}	59	34	32	7	1	28	25	2.250	7.45	53	9.37	.351	0	....	-15	0	-1.5
1997 Tex-A	1	0	1.000	24	0	0	0	0	22	18	9	7	2	0	10	14	1.273	2.86	167	3.15	.231	0	....	5	2	0.5
1998 Tex-A	1	0	1.000	46	0	0	0	0	40^{1}	61	33	29	5	0	11	30	1.785	6.47	75	6.87	.351	0	....	-7	1	-0.6
Total 9	39	44	.470	343	59	5	2	13	679^{2}	758	423	374	89	16	256	351	1.492	4.95	84	4.96	.283	0	....	-51	26	-5.1
• BAILEY, Bill	William F. Bailey b: 4/12/1889, Fort Smith, AR d: 11/2/1926, Houston, TX BL/TL, 5'11", 165 lbs. Deb: 9/17/1907																									
1907 StL-A	4	1	.800	6	5	3	0	0	48^{1}	39	16	13	0	4	15	17	1.117	2.42	104	2.32	.224	3	.150	0	3	-0.1
1908 StL-A	3	5	.375	22	12	7	0	0	106^{2}	85	53	36	2	3	50	42	1.266	3.04	79	2.76	.220	3	.088	-13	2	-1.7
1909 StL-A	9	10	.474	32	20	17	1	0	199	174	71	54	2	6	75	114	1.251	2.44	99	2.94	.248	22	.286	-1	13	0.5
1910 StL-A	3	18	.143	34	20	13	0	0	192^{1}	186	133	71	2	10	97	90	**1.471**	3.32	74	3.87	.262	13	.206	-17	2	-1.8
1911 StL-A	0	3	.000	7	2	2	0	0	31^{2}	42	26	16	1	2	16	8	1.832	4.55	74	6.39	.339	0	.000	-4	0	-0.6
1912 StL-A	0	1	.000	3	2	0	0	0	10^{2}	15	12	11	0	0	10	2	2.344	9.28	36	7.84	.341	1	.500	-7	0	-0.6
1914 Bal-F	7	9	.438	19	18	10	1	0	128^{2}	106	58	44	2	7	68	131	1.352	3.08	103	3.19	.230	7	.163	4	8	0.4
1915 Bal-F	6	19	.240	36	23	11	2	0	190^{1}	179	118	98	8	9	115	98	1.545	4.63	73	4.12	.255	15	.231	-23	3	-2.4
Chi-F	3	1	.750	5	5	3	3	0	33^{1}	23	9	8	1	0	10	24	.990	2.16	129	1.70	.202	2	.222	2	3	0.3
Yr.	9	20	.310	41	28	14	5	0	223^{2}	202	127	106	9	9	125	122	1.462	4.27	78	3.76	.248	17	.230	-21	6	-2.2
1918 Det-A	1	2	.333	8	4	1	0	0	37^{2}	53	34	25	0	1	26	13	2.097	5.97	44	7.17	.368	1	.077	-12	0	-1.5
1921 StL-N	2	5	.286	19	6	3	1	0	74	95	41	35	1	2	22	20	1.581	4.26	86	4.70	.330	2	.091	-5	2	-0.7
1922 StL-N	0	2	.000	12	0	0	0	0	31^{2}	38	22	19	1	0	23	11	1.926	5.40	72	5.93	.325	2	.286	-5	1	-0.4
Total 11	38	76	.333	203	117	70	8	0	1084^{1}	1035	593	430	20	44	527	570	1.441	3.57	81	3.76	.261	71	.194	-80	37	-8.5
• BAILEY, Cory	Phillip Cory Bailey b: 1/24/1971, Herrin, IL BR/TR, 6', 202 lbs. Deb: 9/1/1993																									
1993 Bos-A	0	1	.000	11	0	0	0	0	15^{2}	12	7	6	0	0	12	11	1.532	3.45	134	3.29	.231	0	....	2	1	0.2
1994 Bos-A	0	1	.000	5	0	0	0	0	4^{1}	10	6	6	2	0	3	4	3.000	12.46	40	18.76	.476	0	....	-4	0	-0.3
1995 StL-N	0	0	....	3	0	0	0	0	3^{2}	2	3	3	0	0	2	5	1.091	7.36	57	1.37	.154	0	....	-1	0	-0.1
1996 StL-N	5	2	.714	51	0	0	0	0	57	57	21	19	1	1	30	38	1.526	3.00	140	3.97	.263	0	.000	6	6	0.7
1997 SF-N	0	1	.000	7	0	0	0	0	9^{2}	15	9	9	1	0	4	5	1.966	8.38	48	7.87	.375	1	1.000	-5	0	-0.4
1998 SF-N	0	0	....	5	0	0	0	0	3^{1}	2	1	1	1	0	1	2	.900	2.70	147	2.70	.167	0	....	0	0	0.0
2001 KC-A	1	1	.500	53	0	0	0	0	67^{1}	57	28	26	3	0	33	61	1.337	3.48	141	3.20	.234	0	....	9	6	0.9
2002 KC-A	3	4	.429	37	0	0	0	1	46	53	24	21	5	2	31	24	1.826	4.11	122	6.30	.306	0	....	5	3	0.5
Total 8	9	10	.474	172	0	0	0	1	207	208	99	91	13	3	116	150	1.565	3.96	117	4.61	.269	1	.500	13	16	1.4
• BAILEY, Harvey	Harvey Francis Bailey b: 11/24/1876, Adrian, MI d: 7/10/1922, Toledo, OH TL, 6', 160 lbs. Deb: 6/30/1899																									
1899 Bos-N	6	4	.600	12	11	8	0	0	86^{2}	83	42	38	7	6	35	26	1.362	3.95	105	3.89	.252	8	.235	-1	7	-0.1
1900 Bos-N	0	0	....	4	1	0	0	0	20	24	16	11	0	2	11	9	1.750	4.95	83	5.25	.297	2	.222	-2	1	-0.2
Total 2	6	4	.600	16	12	8	0	0	106^{2}	107	58	49	7	8	46	35	1.434	4.13	100	4.14	.261	10	.233	-4	8	-0.2
• BAILEY, Howard	Howard L Bailey b: 7/31/1957, Grand Haven, MI BR/TL, 6', 195 lbs. Deb: 4/12/1981																									
1981 Det-A	1	4	.200	9	5	0	0	0	36^{2}	45	31	30	4	3	13	17	1.582	7.36	51	5.60	.308	0	....	-15	0	-1.6
1982 Det-A	0	0	....	8	0	0	0	1	10	6	0	0	0	0	2	3	.800	0.00	....	1.06	.182	0	....	4	2	0.4
1983 Det-A	5	5	.500	33	3	0	0	0	72	69	45	39	11	2	25	21	1.306	4.88	80	4.10	.255	0	....	-9	2	-0.9
Total 3	6	9	.400	50	8	0	0	1	118^{2}	120	76	69	15	5	40	41	1.348	5.23	74	4.31	.267	0	....	-20	4	-2.1
• BAILEY, Jim	James Hopkins Bailey b: 12/16/1934, Strawberry Plains, TN BB/TL, 6'2.5", 210 lbs. Deb: 9/10/1959																									
1959 Cin-N	0	1	.000	3	1	0	0	0	11^{2}	17	8	8	1	1	6	7	1.971	6.17	66	7.35	.333	0	.000	-3	0	-0.3
• BAILEY, King	Linwood C. Bailey b: 11/1870, VA d: 11/19/1917, Macon, GA BL/TL, 6', 185 lbs. Deb: 9/21/1895																									
1895 Cin-N	1	0	1.000	1	1	1	0	0	8	13	8	5	0	0	0	0	1.625	5.63	88	5.33	.359	2	.500	-1	1	0.0
• BAILEY, Roger	Charles Roger Bailey b: 10/3/1970, Chattahoochee, FL BR/TR, 6'1", 180 lbs. Deb: 4/27/1995																									
1995 Col-N	7	6	.538	39	6	0	0	0	81^{1}	88	49	45	9	1	39	33	1.561	4.98	108	4.99	.283	2	.125	6	5	0.5
1996 Col-N	2	3	.400	24	11	0	0	1	83^{2}	94	64	58	7	1	52	45	1.745	6.24	84	5.67	.288	5	.263	-8	4	-0.5

YEAR	TM-L	W	L	PCT	G	GS	CG	SH	SV	IP	H	R	ER	HR	HB	BB	SO	RAT	ERA	ERA+	CERA	OAV	BH	AVG	PR+	WS	TPW
1997	Col-N	9	10	.474	29	29	5	2	0	191	210	103	91	27	13	70	84	1.466	4.29	121	5.16	.283	13	.210	21	13	2.2
Total	**3**	**18**	**19**	**.486**	**92**	**46**	**5**	**2**	**1**	**356**	**392**	**216**	**194**	**43**	**15**	**161**	**162**	**1.553**	**4.90**	**107**	**5.24**	**.284**	**20**	**.206**	**20**	**22**	**2.2**
• BAILEY, Steve	Steven John Bailey b: 2/12/1942, Bronx, NY BR/TR, 6'1", 194 lbs. Deb: 4/14/1967																										
1967	Cle-A	2	5	.286	32	1	0	0	2	64^{2}	62	31	28	5	3	42	46	1.608	3.90	84	4.78	.259	0	.000	-4	2	-0.5
1968	Cle-A	0	1	.000	2	1	0	0	0	5	4	3	2	1	0	2	1	1.200	3.60	82	3.57	.235	0	....	-0	0	0.0
Total	**2**	**2**	**6**	**.250**	**34**	**2**	**0**	**0**	**2**	**69^{2}**	**66**	**34**	**30**	**6**	**3**	**44**	**47**	**1.579**	**3.88**	**84**	**4.70**	**.258**	**0**	**.000**	**-4**	**2**	**-0.6**
• BAILEY, Sweetbreads	Abraham Lincoln Bailey b: 2/12/1895, Joliet, IL d: 9/27/1939, Joliet, IL BR/TR, 6', 184 lbs. Deb: 5/23/1919																										
1919	Chi-N	3	5	.375	21	5	0	0	0	71^{1}	75	30	25	2	3	20	19	1.332	3.15	91	3.66	.288	7	.389	-2	4	0.2
1920	Chi-N	1	2	.333	21	1	0	0	0	36^{2}	55	38	29	1	2	11	8	1.800	7.12	45	6.12	.359	1	.143	-16	0	-1.7
1921	Chi-N	0	0	....	3	0	0	0	0	5	6	2	2	0	1	2	2	1.600	3.60	106	4.93	.300	0	....	0	0	0.0
	Bro-N	0	0	....	7	0	0	0	0	24^{1}	35	15	14	1	1	7	6	1.726	5.18	75	6.18	.368	0	.000	-3	1	-0.4
	Yr.	0	0	....	10	0	0	0	0	29^{1}	41	17	16	1	2	9	8	1.705	4.91	79	5.97	.356	0	.000	-3	1	-0.4
Total	**3**	**4**	**7**	**.364**	**52**	**6**	**0**	**0**	**0**	**137^{1}**	**171**	**85**	**70**	**4**	**7**	**40**	**35**	**1.536**	**4.59**	**70**	**4.81**	**.323**	**8**	**.267**	**-20**	**5**	**-1.9**
• BAIN, Loren	Herbert Loren Bain b: 7/4/1922, Staples, MN d: 11/24/1996, Chetek, WI BR/TR, 6', 190 lbs. Deb: 6/23/1945																										
1945	NY-N	0	0	....	3	0	0	0	0	8	10	7	7	1	1	4	1	1.750	7.88	50	6.54	.323	1	.333	-4	0	-0.3
• BAIR, Doug	Charles Douglas Bair b: 8/22/1949, Defiance, OH BR/TR, 6', 180 lbs. Deb: 9/13/1976																										
1976	Pit-N	0	0	....	4	0	0	0	0	6^{1}	4	4	4	0	0	5	4	1.421	5.68	61	2.50	.174	0	....	-2	0	-0.2
1977	Oak-A	4	6	.400	45	0	0	0	8	83^{1}	78	39	32	11	0	57	68	1.620	3.46	116	4.89	.253	0	....	6	6	0.6
1978	Cin-N	7	6	.538	70	0	0	0	28	100^{1}	87	23	22	6	0	38	91	1.246	1.97	180	2.98	.236	2	.143	19	18	2.0
1979*	Cin-N	11	7	.611	65	0	0	0	16	94^{1}	93	47	45	7	3	51	86	1.527	4.29	87	4.15	.256	0	.000	-6	8	-0.7
1980	Cin-N	3	6	.333	61	0	0	0	6	85	91	42	40	7	1	39	62	1.529	4.24	84	4.43	.277	0	.000	-5	4	-0.6
1981	Cin-N	2	2	.500	24	0	0	0	0	39	42	28	25	5	0	17	16	1.513	5.77	62	4.64	.271	1	.333	-10	0	-1.0
	StL-N	2	0	1.000	11	0	0	0	1	15^{2}	13	6	6	0	0	2	14	.957	3.45	103	1.69	.224	0	.000	-0	2	0.0
	Yr.	4	2	.667	35	0	0	0	1	54^{2}	55	34	31	5	0	19	30	1.354	5.10	70	3.79	.258	1	.167	-10	2	-1.0
1982*	StL-N	5	3	.625	63	0	0	0	8	91^{2}	69	27	26	7	1	36	68	1.145	2.55	142	2.45	.211	1	.077	9	11	0.8
1983	StL-N	1	1	.500	26	0	0	0	1	29^{2}	24	11	10	4	0	13	21	1.247	3.03	119	3.32	.224	0	.000	2	2	0.2
	Det-A	7	3	.700	27	1	0	0	4	55^{2}	51	27	24	8	1	19	39	1.257	3.88	101	3.65	.242	0	....	-1	4	-0.1
1984*	Det-A	5	3	.625	47	1	0	0	4	93^{2}	82	42	39	10	0	36	57	1.260	3.75	105	3.40	.238	0	....	1	6	0.1
1985	Det-A	2	0	1.000	21	3	0	0	0	49	54	38	34	3	1	25	30	1.612	6.24	65	4.65	.281	0	....	-12	0	-1.2
	StL-N	0	0	....	2	0	0	0	0	2	1	0	0	0	0	2	0	1.500	0.00	....	3.21	.167	0	....	1	0	0.1
1986	Oak-A	2	3	.400	31	0	0	0	4	45	37	15	15	5	0	18	40	1.222	3.00	129	3.14	.224	0	....	4	4	0.4
1987	Phi-N	2	0	1.000	11	0	0	0	0	13^{2}	17	9	9	4	0	5	10	1.610	5.93	72	6.94	.309	0	.000	-3	0	-0.3
1988	Tor-A	0	0	....	10	0	0	0	0	13^{1}	14	6	6	2	0	3	8	1.275	4.05	97	4.07	.280	0	....	-0	1	0.0
1989	Pit-N	2	3	.400	44	0	0	0	1	67^{1}	52	19	17	4	0	28	56	1.188	2.27	148	2.46	.211	1	.200	8	6	0.9
1990	Pit-N	0	0	....	22	0	0	0	0	24^{1}	30	15	13	3	0	11	19	1.685	4.81	75	5.73	.306	0	.000	-4	0	-0.4
Total	**15**	**55**	**43**	**.561**	**584**	**5**	**0**	**0**	**81**	**909^{1}**	**839**	**398**	**367**	**86**	**7**	**405**	**689**	**1.368**	**3.63**	**103**	**3.71**	**.246**	**5**	**.096**	**9**	**72**	**0.8**
• BAIRD, Bob	Robert Allen Baird b: 1/16/1940, Knoxville, TN d: 4/11/1974, Chattanooga, TN BL/TL, 6'4", 195 lbs. Deb: 9/3/1962																										
1962	Was-A	0	1	.000	3	3	0	0	0	10^{2}	13	8	8	0	0	8	3	1.969	6.75	60	5.91	.310	0	.000	-3	0	-0.4
1963	Was-A	0	3	.000	5	3	0	0	0	11^{2}	12	15	10	1	1	7	7	1.629	7.71	48	4.94	.261	1	.333	-5	0	-0.5
Total	**2**	**0**	**4**	**.000**	**8**	**6**	**0**	**0**	**0**	**22^{1}**	**25**	**23**	**18**	**1**	**1**	**15**	**10**	**1.791**	**7.25**	**53**	**5.41**	**.284**	**1**	**.167**	**-8**	**0**	**-0.9**
• BAKELY, Jersey	Edward Enoch Bakely b: 4/17/1864, Blackwood, NJ d: 12/17/1915, Philadelphia, PA BR/TR, 5'8" Deb: 5/11/1883 U																										
1883	Phi-a	5	3	.625	8	8	7	0	0	61^{1}	65	47	22	0	....	12	14	1.255	3.23	107	....	.255	5	.192	3	4	0.4
1884	Phi-U	14	25	.359	39	38	38	1	0	344^{2}	390	305	171	0	....	76	204	1.352	4.47	65	....	.267	22	.132	-43	5	-4.5
	Wil-U	0	2	.000	2	2	2	0	0	17	24	17	8	0	....	1	9	1.471	4.24	79	....	.312	0	.000	-1	0	-0.2
	KC-U	2	3	.400	5	5	3	0	0	33	29	16	9	0	....	4	13	1.000	2.45	114	....	.220	3	.150	1	1	0.0
	Yr.	16	30	.348	46	45	43	1	0	394^{2}	443	338	188	0	....	81	226	1.328	4.29	68	....	.265	25	.130	-43	6	-4.7
1888	Cle-a	25	33	.431	61	61	60	4	0	532^{2}	518	321	176	14	15	128	212	1.213	2.97	104	....	.246	26	.134	10	21	0.7
1889	Cle-N	12	22	.353	36	34	33	2	0	304^{1}	296	169	100	9	8	106	105	1.321	2.96	136	....	.247	15	.135	27	22	2.3
1890	Cle-P	12	25	.324	43	38	32	0	0	326^{1}	412	307	162	13	6	147	67	1.713	4.47	89	....	.295	28	.203	-19	11	-1.5
1891	Was-a	2	10	.167	13	12	11	0	0	104^{1}	127	107	62	6	1	60	32	1.792	5.35	70	....	.291	10	.222	-13	1	-1.1
	Bal-a	4	2	.667	8	6	5	0	0	59	48	32	15	1	7	30	13	1.322	2.29	163	....	.215	2	.095	10	5	0.9
	Yr.	6	12	.333	21	18	16	0	0	163^{1}	175	139	77	7	8	90	45	1.622	4.24	88	....	.265	12	.182	-2	6	-0.1
Total	**6**	**76**	**125**	**.378**	**215**	**204**	**191**	**7**	**0**	**1782^{2}**	**1909**	**1321**	**725**	**43**	**37**	**564**	**669**	**1.387**	**3.66**	**92**	**....**	**.262**	**111**	**.153**	**-25**	**70**	**-3.0**
• BAKENHASTER, Dave	David Lee Bakenhaster b: 3/5/1945, Columbus, OH BR/TR, 5'10", 168 lbs. Deb: 6/20/1964																										
1964	StL-N	0	0	....	2	0	0	0	0	3	9	6	2	1	0	1	0	3.333	6.00	63	19.02	.474	0	....	-1	0	-0.1
• BAKER, Al	Albert Jones Baker b: 2/28/1906, Batesville, MS d: 11/6/1982, Kenedy, TX BR/TR, 5'11", 170 lbs. Deb: 8/20/1938																										
1938	Bos-A	0	0	....	3	0	0	0	0	7^{2}	13	8	8	2	1	2	2	1.957	9.39	53	9.74	.371	0	.000	-4	0	-0.4
• BAKER, Bock	Charles "Smiling Bock" Baker b: 7/17/1878, Troy, NY d: 8/17/1940, New York, NY TL, 5'9", 181 lbs. Deb: 4/28/1901																										
1901	Cle-A	0	1	.000	1	1	1	0	0	8	23	13	5	0	1	6	0	3.625	5.63	63	18.64	.499	0	.000	-2	0	-0.2
	Phi-A	0	1	.000	1	1	0	0	0	6	6	11	7	0	0	6	1	2.000	10.50	36	4.65	.257	1	.333	-4	0	-0.4
	Yr.	0	2	.000	2	2	1	0	0	14	29	24	12	0	1	12	1	2.929	7.71	48	12.64	.418	1	.143	-6	0	-0.6
• BAKER, Ernie	Earnest Gould Baker b: 8/8/1875, Concord, MI d: 10/25/1945, Homer, MI BR/TR, 5'10", 160 lbs. Deb: 8/18/1905																										
1905	Cin-N	0	0	....	1	0	0	0	0	4	7	4	2	1	1	0	1	1.750	4.50	73	10.18	.412	0	.000	-1	0	-0.1
• BAKER, Jesse	Jesse Ormond Baker b: 6/3/1888, Anderson Island, WA d: 9/26/1972, Tacoma, WA BL/TL, 5'11", 188 lbs. Deb: 4/23/1911																										
1911	Chi-A	2	7	.222	22	8	3	0	1	94	101	52	41	3	4	30	51	1.394	3.93	83	4.02	.288	3	.103	-7	3	-0.9
• BAKER, Kirtley	Kirtley "Whitey" Baker b: 6/24/1869, Aurora, IN d: 4/15/1927, Covington, KY BR/TR, 5'9", 160 lbs. Deb: 5/7/1890																										
1890	Pit-N	3	19	.136	25	21	19	2	0	178^{1}	209	176	111	11	20	86	76	1.654	5.60	59	....	.284	10	.147	-36	1	-3.2
1893	Bal-N	3	8	.273	15	12	8	0	0	91^{2}	138	111	86	5	5	58	26	2.138	8.44	56	7.79	.337	17	.298	-36	1	-2.6
1894	Bal-N	0	1	.000	1	0	0	0	0	0	1	5	0	0	2	2	0	....	....	....	∞	1.000	0	.000	0	0	0.0
1898	Was-N	2	3	.400	6	5	4	0	0	47	56	31	16	1	0	18	7	1.574	3.06	119	4.41	.294	5	.278	4	3	0.5
1899	Was-N	1	7	.125	11	6	3	0	0	54	79	65	41	3	6	22	6	1.870	6.83	57	6.84	.340	3	.158	-15	0	-1.5
Total	**5**	**9**	**38**	**.191**	**58**	**44**	**34**	**2**	**0**	**371**	**483**	**388**	**254**	**20**	**33**	**186**	**115**	**1.803**	**6.16**	**62**	**3.48**	**.308**	**35**	**.211**	**-83**	**5**	**-6.8**
• BAKER, Neal	Neal Vernon Baker b: 4/30/1904, LaPorte, TX d: 1/5/1982, Houston, TX BR/TR, 6'1", 175 lbs. Deb: 6/26/1927																										
1927	Phi-A	0	0	....	5	2	0	0	0	17^{1}	27	17	11	2	0	7	3	1.962	5.71	75	7.50	.365	1	.167	-3	0	-0.3
• BAKER, Norm	Norman Leslie Baker b: 10/14/1862, Philadelphia, PA d: 2/20/1949, Hurffville, NJ Deb: 5/21/1883																										
1883	Pit-a	0	2	.000	3	3	2	0	0	19	24	16	7	0	....	11	5	1.842	3.32	97	....	.289	0	.000	0	0	-0.2
1885	Lou-a	13	12	.520	25	24	24	1	0	217	210	142	82	3	10	69	79	1.286	3.40	95	....	.243	18	.207	-4	12	-0.4
1890	Bal-a	1	1	.500	2	2	2	0	0	17	16	9	7	0	0	6	10	1.294	3.71	115	....	.241	0	.000	1	1	0.0
Total	**3**	**14**	**15**	**.483**	**30**	**29**	**28**	**1**	**0**	**253**	**250**	**167**	**96**	**3**	**10**	**86**	**94**	**1.328**	**3.42**	**96**	**....**	**.247**	**18**	**.170**	**-3**	**13**	**-0.5**
• BAKER, Scott	Scott Baker b: 5/18/1970, San Jose, CA BL/TL, 6'2", 175 lbs. Deb: 7/17/1995																										
1995	Oak-A	0	0	....	1	0	0	0	0	3^{2}	5	4	4	0	1	5	3	2.727	9.82	45	10.42	.333	0	....	-2	0	-0.2
• BAKER, Steve	Steven Byrne Baker b: 8/30/1956, Eugene, OR BR/TR, 6', 185 lbs. Deb: 5/25/1978																										
1978	Det-A	2	4	.333	15	10	0	0	0	63^{1}	66	37	32	6	0	42	39	1.705	4.55	85	5.38	.276	0	....	-6	2	-0.6
1979	Det-A	1	7	.125	21	12	0	0	1	84	97	63	62	13	6	51	54	1.762	6.64	65	6.63	.296	0	....	-23	0	-2.2
1982	Oak-A	1	1	.500	5	3	0	0	0	25^{2}	30	14	13	3	0	4	14	1.325	4.56	86	4.11	.288	0	....	-2	1	-0.2

YEAR	TM-L	W	L	PCT	G	GS	CG	SH	SV	IP	H	R	ER	HR	HB	BB	SO	RAT	ERA	ERA+	CERA	OAV	BH	AVG	PR+	WS	TPW
1983	Oak-A	3	3	.500	35	1	0	0	5	54	59	32	26	4	2	26	23	1.574	4.33	89	4.74	.282	0	....	-3	2	-0.3
	StL-N	0	1	.000	8	0	0	0	0	10	10	4	2	0	1	4	1	1.400	1.80	201	3.65	.286	0	....	2	1	0.2
Total	4	7	16	.304	84	26	0	0	6	237	262	150	135	26	9	127	131	1.641	5.13	79	5.47	.286	0	....	-31	6	-3.1

• BAKER, Tom

Thomas Calvin "Rattlesnake" Baker b: 6/11/1913, Nursery, TX d: 1/3/1991, Fort Worth, TX BR/TR, 6'1.5", 180 lbs. Deb: 8/15/1935

YEAR	TM-L	W	L	PCT	G	GS	CG	SH	SV	IP	H	R	ER	HR	HB	BB	SO	RAT	ERA	ERA+	CERA	OAV	BH	AVG	PR+	WS	TPW
1935	Bro-N	1	0	1.000	11	1	1	0	0	42	48	25	20	2	0	20	10	1.619	4.29	93	4.55	.277	9	.474	-2	3	0.2
1936	Bro-N	1	8	.111	35	8	2	0	2	87^{2}	98	56	46	3	2	48	35	1.665	4.72	87	4.77	.288	7	.233	-5	3	-0.4
1937	Bro-N	0	1	.000	7	0	0	0	0	8^{1}	14	10	8	1	1	5	2	2.280	8.64	47	9.95	.378	0	....	-4	0	-0.4
	NY-N	1	0	1.000	13	0	0	0	0	31	30	15	14	0	0	16	11	1.484	4.06	96	3.57	.268	2	.222	-1	2	-0.1
	Yr.	1	1	.500	20	0	0	0	0	39^{1}	44	25	22	1	1	21	13	1.653	5.03	78	4.92	.295	2	.222	-5	2	-0.5
1938	NY-N	0	0	....	2	0	0	0	0	4	5	3	3	0	0	3	0	2.000	6.75	56	5.75	.313	0	....	-1	0	-0.1
Total	4	3	9	.250	68	9	3	0	2	173	195	109	91	6	3	92	58	1.659	4.73	85	4.77	.288	18	.310	-13	8	-0.9

• BAKER, Tom

Thomas Henry Baker b: 5/6/1934, Port Townsend, WA d: 3/9/1980, Port Townsend, WA BL/TL, 6', 195 lbs. Deb: 8/2/1963

YEAR	TM-L	W	L	PCT	G	GS	CG	SH	SV	IP	H	R	ER	HR	HB	BB	SO	RAT	ERA	ERA+	CERA	OAV	BH	AVG	PR+	WS	TPW
1963	Chi-N	0	1	.000	10	1	0	0	0	18	20	12	6	2	1	7	14	1.500	3.00	117	4.92	.282	0	.000	1	0	0.0

• BALAS, Mike

Mitchell Francis Balas b: 5/17/1910, Lowell, MA BR/TR, 6', 195 lbs. Deb: 4/27/1938

YEAR	TM-L	W	L	PCT	G	GS	CG	SH	SV	IP	H	R	ER	HR	HB	BB	SO	RAT	ERA	ERA+	CERA	OAV	BH	AVG	PR+	WS	TPW
1938	Bos-N	0	0	....	1	0	0	0	0	1^{1}	3	3	1	0	0	0	0	2.250	6.75	51	7.92	.375	0	....	-0	0	-0.1

• BALDSCHUN, Jack

Jack Edward Baldschun b: 10/16/1936, Greenville, OH BR/TR, 6'1", 190 lbs. Deb: 4/28/1961

YEAR	TM-L	W	L	PCT	G	GS	CG	SH	SV	IP	H	R	ER	HR	HB	BB	SO	RAT	ERA	ERA+	CERA	OAV	BH	AVG	PR+	WS	TPW
1961	Phi-N	5	3	.625	**65**	0	0	0	3	99^{2}	90	53	43	7	5	49	59	1.395	3.88	105	3.68	.243	0	.000	1	6	-0.1
1962	Phi-N	12	7	.632	67	0	0	0	13	112^{2}	95	41	37	6	2	58	95	1.358	2.96	131	3.30	.231	1	.063	11	14	1.0
1963	Phi-N	11	7	.611	65	0	0	0	16	113^{2}	99	37	29	7	3	42	89	1.240	2.30	141	2.96	.232	0	.000	10	13	0.9
1964	Phi-N	6	9	.400	71	0	0	0	21	118^{1}	111	50	41	8	3	40	96	1.276	3.12	111	3.22	.246	4	.250	4	12	0.6
1965	Phi-N	5	8	.385	65	0	0	0	6	99	102	53	42	4	4	42	81	1.455	3.82	91	3.84	.273	0	.000	-4	5	-0.5
1966	Cin-N	1	5	.167	42	0	0	0	0	57^{1}	71	35	35	4	4	25	44	1.674	5.49	71	5.53	.318	1	.333	-9	1	-1.0
1967	Cin-N	0	0	....	9	0	0	0	0	13	15	6	6	0	0	9	12	1.846	4.15	90	4.83	.283	0	.000	-1	0	-0.1
1969	SD-N	7	2	.778	61	0	0	0	1	77	80	45	41	7	2	29	67	1.416	4.79	74	4.04	.264	1	.250	-10	4	-1.0
1970	SD-N	1	0	1.000	12	0	0	0	0	13^{1}	24	15	15	2	0	4	12	2.100	10.13	39	8.45	.375	0	....	-9	0	-0.9
Total	9	48	41	.539	457	0	0	0	60	704	687	335	289	45	23	298	555	1.399	3.69	99	3.75	.257	7	.090	-8	55	-1.0

• BALDWIN, Dave

David George Baldwin b: 3/30/1938, Tucson, AZ BR/TR, 6'2", 200 lbs. Deb: 9/6/1966

YEAR	TM-L	W	L	PCT	G	GS	CG	SH	SV	IP	H	R	ER	HR	HB	BB	SO	RAT	ERA	ERA+	CERA	OAV	BH	AVG	PR+	WS	TPW
1966	Was-A	0	0	....	4	0	0	0	0	7	8	3	3	0	0	1	4	1.286	3.86	90	2.98	.267	0	....	-0	0	0.0
1967	Was-A	2	4	.333	58	0	0	0	12	68^{2}	53	19	13	2	4	20	52	1.063	1.70	186	2.16	.215	0	.000	11	10	1.2
1968	Was-A	0	2	.000	40	0	0	0	5	42	40	19	19	7	0	12	30	1.238	4.07	72	3.85	.260	0	.000	-5	1	-0.5
1969	Was-A	2	4	.333	43	0	0	0	4	66^{2}	57	31	30	4	5	34	51	1.365	4.05	86	3.69	.236	0	.000	-5	3	-0.6
1970	Mil-A	2	1	.667	28	0	0	0	1	35^{1}	25	11	10	4	0	18	26	1.217	2.55	149	2.82	.205	1	.500	6	3	0.6
1973	Chi-A	0	0	....	3	0	0	0	0	5	7	2	2	0	0	4	1	2.200	3.60	110	7.62	.368	0	....	0	0	0.0
Total	6	6	11	.353	176	0	0	0	22	224^{2}	190	85	77	17	9	89	164	1.242	3.08	107	3.18	.234	1	.067	7	17	0.6

• BALDWIN, Harry

Howard Edward Baldwin b: 6/3/1900, Baltimore, MD d: 1/23/1958, Baltimore, MD BR/TR, 5'11", 160 lbs. Deb: 5/4/1924

YEAR	TM-L	W	L	PCT	G	GS	CG	SH	SV	IP	H	R	ER	HR	HB	BB	SO	RAT	ERA	ERA+	CERA	OAV	BH	AVG	PR+	WS	TPW
1924*	NY-N	3	1	.750	10	2	1	0	0	33^{2}	42	18	16	5	0	11	5	1.574	4.28	86	5.52	.309	4	.364	-2	2	-0.2
1925	NY-N	0	0	....	1	0	0	0	0	1	3	2	1	0	0	1	0	4.000	9.00	45	19.12	.500	0	....	-1	0	-0.1
Total	2	3	1	.750	11	2	1	0	0	34^{2}	45	20	17	5	0	12	5	1.644	4.41	83	5.91	.317	4	.364	-3	2	-0.2

• BALDWIN, James

James J. Baldwin b: 7/15/1971, Southern Pines, NC BR/TR, 6'3", 210 lbs. Deb: 4/30/1995

YEAR	TM-L	W	L	PCT	G	GS	CG	SH	SV	IP	H	R	ER	HR	HB	BB	SO	RAT	ERA	ERA+	CERA	OAV	BH	AVG	PR+	WS	TPW
1995	Chi-A	0	1	.000	6	4	0	0	0	14^{2}	32	22	21	6	0	9	10	2.795	12.89	35	16.49	.444	0	....	-14	0	-1.3
1996	Chi-A	11	6	.647	28	28	0	0	0	169	168	88	83	24	4	57	127	1.331	4.42	107	4.17	.257	0	....	7	10	0.7
1997	Chi-A	12	15	.444	32	32	1	0	0	200	205	128	117	19	5	83	140	1.440	5.27	83	4.28	.262	0	.000	-17	6	-1.6
1998	Chi-A	13	6	.684	37	24	1	0	0	159	176	103	94	18	10	60	108	1.484	5.32	86	4.89	.278	0	.000	-14	6	-1.3
1999	Chi-A	12	13	.480	35	33	1	0	0	199^{1}	219	119	113	34	7	81	123	1.505	5.10	96	5.33	.278	1	.500	-4	9	-0.2
2000*	Chi-A★	14	7	.667	29	28	2	1	0	178	185	96	92	34	8	59	116	1.371	4.65	107	4.91	.272	0	.000	4	11	0.3
2001	Chi-A	7	5	.583	17	16	2	1	0	95^{2}	109	56	49	15	4	38	42	1.537	4.61	100	5.44	.286	0	.000	-1	5	-0.1
	LA-N	3	6	.333	12	12	0	0	0	79^{1}	82	39	37	10	3	25	53	1.349	4.20	95	4.35	.274	2	.077	-1	3	-0.3
2002	Sea-A	7	10	.412	30	23	0	0	0	150	179	95	88	26	7	49	88	1.520	5.28	80	5.70	.298	1	.500	-16	3	-1.5
2003	Min-A	0	1	.000	10	0	0	0	1	15	21	10	9	6	0	4	7	1.667	5.40	84	8.09	.333	0	....	-1	0	-0.1
Total	9	79	70	.530	236	200	7	2	1	1260	1376	756	703	192	48	465	814	1.461	5.02	91	5.05	.278	4	.098	-56	53	-5.5

• BALDWIN, Lady

Charles Busted Baldwin b: 4/8/1859, Oramel, NY d: 3/7/1937, Hastings, MI BL/TL, 5'11", 160 lbs. Deb: 9/30/1884 ♦

YEAR	TM-L	W	L	PCT	G	GS	CG	SH	SV	IP	H	R	ER	HR	HB	BB	SO	RAT	ERA	ERA+	CERA	OAV	BH	AVG	PR+	WS	TPW
1884	Mil-U	1	1	.500	2	2	2	0	0	17	7	5	5	0	....	1	21	.471	2.65	115	....	.117	6	.222	-1	3	-0.1
1885	Det-N	11	9	.550	21	20	19	1	1	179^{1}	137	84	37	2	....	28	135	.920	1.86	153	....	.202	30	.242	22	14	2.3
1886	Det-N	**42**	13	.764	56	56	55	**7**	0	487	371	194	121	11	....	100	**323**	.967	2.24	147	....	**.203**	41	.201	51	**53**	4.9
1887*	Det-N	13	10	.565	24	24	24	1	0	211	225	136	90	8	5	61	60	1.066	3.84	105	....	.315	33	.347	3	14	0.5
1888	Det-N	3	3	.500	6	6	5	0	0	53	76	50	32	5	1	15	26	1.717	5.43	51	....	.325	6	.261	-15	0	-1.2
1890	Bro-N	1	0	1.000	2	1	0	0	0	7^{2}	15	6	6	0	0	4	4	2.478	7.04	49	....	.398	0	.000	-3	0	-0.3
	Buf-P	2	5	.286	7	7	7	0	0	62	90	72	31	5	3	24	13	1.839	4.50	91	....	.325	8	.286	-2	1	0.0
Total	6	73	41	.640	118	116	112	9	1	1017	921	547	322	31	9	233	582	1.075	2.85	119	....	.240	124	.246	55	85	6.2

• BALDWIN, Mark

Marcus Elmore "Fido" Baldwin b: 10/29/1863, Pittsburgh, PA d: 11/10/1929, Pittsburgh, PA BR/TR, 6', 190 lbs. Deb: 5/2/1887 U

YEAR	TM-L	W	L	PCT	G	GS	CG	SH	SV	IP	H	R	ER	HR	HB	BB	SO	RAT	ERA	ERA+	CERA	OAV	BH	AVG	PR+	WS	TPW
1887	Chi-N	18	17	.514	40	39	35	1	**1**	334	451	218	126	23	17	122	164	1.350	3.40	131	....	.314	36	.242	40	27	3.0
1888	Chi-N	13	15	.464	30	30	27	2	0	251	241	137	77	13	13	99	157	1.355	2.76	109	....	.243	16	.151	1	15	0.1
1889	Col-a	27	33	.450	**63**	**59**	54	6	1	**513**^{2}	458	358	206	9	0	274	**368**	1.425	3.61	100	....	.231	39	.188	1	27	0.2
1890	Chi-P	**33**	21	.611	**58**	**56**	**53**	1	0	**492**	494	321	184	10	12	249	**206**	1.510	3.37	129	....	.250	45	.212	52	42	4.2
1891	Pit-N	21	28	.429	53	51	48	2	1	437^{2}	385	278	134	10	0	227	197	1.398	2.76	119	....	.227	27	.153	29	25	2.4
1892	Pit-N	26	27	.491	56	53	45	0	0	440^{1}	447	272	170	11	0	194	157	1.456	3.47	95	3.67	.253	18	.101	-23	20	-3.1
1893	Pit-N	0	0	....	1	1	0	0	0	2^{1}	6	4	3	0	0	1	0	3.000	11.57	39	13.64	.465	0	.000	-2	0	-0.2
	NY-N	16	20	.444	45	39	33	2	2	331^{1}	335	228	151	6	0	141	100	1.437	4.10	113	3.55	.255	17	.127	17	20	0.5
	Yr.	16	20	.444	46	40	33	2	**2**	333^{2}	341	232	154	6	0	142	100	1.448	4.15	112	3.62	.257	17	.126	15	20	0.4
Total	7	154	161	.489	346	328	295	14	5	2802^{1}	2817	1816	1051	82	42	1307	1349	1.428	3.38	112	1.01	.252	198	.170	114	176	7.1

• BALDWIN, O.F.

Orson F. Baldwin b: 11/3/1881, Carson City, MI d: 2/16/1942, Los Angeles, CA TR, 185 lbs. Deb: 9/6/1908

YEAR	TM-L	W	L	PCT	G	GS	CG	SH	SV	IP	H	R	ER	HR	HB	BB	SO	RAT	ERA	ERA+	CERA	OAV	BH	AVG	PR+	WS	TPW
1908	StL-N	1	3	.250	4	4	0	0	0	14^{2}	16	10	10	0	3	11	5	1.841	6.14	38	6.18	.302	0	.000	-6	0	-0.8

• BALDWIN, Rick

Rickey Alan Baldwin b: 6/1/1953, Fresno, CA BL/TR, 6'3", 180 lbs. Deb: 4/10/1975

YEAR	TM-L	W	L	PCT	G	GS	CG	SH	SV	IP	H	R	ER	HR	HB	BB	SO	RAT	ERA	ERA+	CERA	OAV	BH	AVG	PR+	WS	TPW
1975	NY-N	3	5	.375	54	0	0	0	6	97^{1}	97	39	36	4	4	34	54	1.346	3.33	104	3.54	.263	3	.200	0	6	0.0
1976	NY-N	0	0	....	11	0	0	0	0	22^{2}	14	6	6	0	2	10	9	1.059	2.38	138	1.97	.189	1	.333	2	2	0.3
1977	NY-N	1	2	.333	40	0	0	0	1	62^{2}	62	32	31	6	5	31	23	1.484	4.45	84	4.53	.265	2	.500	-5	3	-0.4
Total	3	4	7	.364	105	0	0	0	7	182^{2}	173	77	73	10	11	75	86	1.358	3.60	99	3.68	.256	6	.273	-3	11	-0.2

• BALE, John

John Robert Bale b: 5/22/1974, Cheverly, MD BL/TL, 6'4", 205 lbs. Deb: 9/30/1999

YEAR	TM-L	W	L	PCT	G	GS	CG	SH	SV	IP	H	R	ER	HR	HB	BB	SO	RAT	ERA	ERA+	CERA	OAV	BH	AVG	PR+	WS	TPW
1999	Tor-A	0	0	....	1	0	0	0	0	2	2	3	3	1	0	2	4	2.000	13.50	36	9.87	.250	0	....	-2	0	-0.2
2000	Tor-A	0	0	....	2	0	0	0	0	3^{2}	5	7	6	1	2	3	6	2.182	14.73	34	11.52	.313	0	....	-4	0	-0.4
2001	Bal-A	1	0	1.000	14	0	0	0	0	26^{2}	18	14	9	2	1	17	21	1.313	3.04	141	3.21	.194	0	....	3	2	0.3
2003	Cin-N	1	2	.333	10	9	0	0	0	46^{1}	50	24	23	7	2	12	37	1.338	4.47	95	4.52	.281	2	.118	-1	2	-0.2
Total	4	2	2	.500	27	9	0	0	0	78^{2}	75	48	41	11	5	34	68	1.386	4.69	94	4.54	.254	2	.118	-3	4	-0.4

• BALFOUR, Grant

Grant Robert Balfour b: 12/30/1977, Sydney, Australia BR/TR, 6'2", 175 lbs. Deb: 7/22/2001

YEAR	TM-L	W	L	PCT	G	GS	CG	SH	SV	IP	H	R	ER	HR	HB	BB	SO	RAT	ERA	ERA+	CERA	OAV	BH	AVG	PR+	WS	TPW
2001	Min-A	0	0	....	2	0	0	0	0	2^{2}	3	4	4	2	0	3	2	2.250	13.50	34	13.78	.333	0	....	-3	0	-0.3
2003	Min-A	1	0	1.000	17	1	0	0	0	26	23	12	12	4	0	14	30	1.423	4.15	109	4.14	.235	0	....	2	2	0.2
Total	2	1	0	1.000	19	1	0	0	0	28^{2}	26	16	16	6	0	17	32	1.500	5.02	91	5.04	.243	0	....	-1	2	-0.1

YEAR TM-L	W	L	PCT	G	GS	CG	SH	SV	IP	H	R	ER	HR	HB	BB	SO	RAT	ERA	ERA+	CERA	OAV	BH	AVG	PR+	WS	TPW
• BALLARD, Jeff Jeffrey Scott Ballard b: 8/13/1963, Billings, MT BL/TL, 6'3", 198 lbs. Deb: 5/9/1987																										
1987 Bal-A	2	8	.200	14	14	0	0	0	69^2	100	60	51	15	0	35	27	1.938	6.59	67	8.37	.344	0	....	-17	0	-1.6
1988 Bal-A	8	12	.400	25	25	6	1	0	153^1	167	83	75	15	6	42	41	1.363	4.40	89	4.24	.278	0	....	-10	6	-1.0
1989 Bal-A	18	8	.692	35	35	4	1	0	215^1	240	95	82	16	4	57	62	1.379	3.43	111	4.11	.287	0	....	7	15	0.7
1990 Bal-A	2	11	.154	44	17	0	0	0	133^1	152	79	73	22	3	42	50	1.455	4.93	77	5.08	.289	0	....	-18	2	-1.8
1991 Bal-A	6	12	.333	26	22	0	0	0	123^2	153	91	77	16	2	28	37	1.464	5.60	70	5.01	.302	0	....	-23	0	-2.3
1993 Pit-N	4	1	.800	25	5	0	0	0	53^2	70	31	29	3	2	15	16	1.584	4.86	83	5.26	.332	4	.364	-5	3	-0.4
1994 Pit-N	1	1	.500	28	0	0	0	2	24^1	32	19	18	5	1	10	11	1.726	6.66	65	6.89	.323	1	.500	-7	0	-0.6
Total 7	41	53	.436	197	118	10	2	2	773^1	914	458	405	92	18	229	244	1.478	4.71	84	5.00	.298	5	.385	-72	26	-7.0
• BALLER, Jay Jay Scot Baller b: 10/6/1960, Stayton, OR BR/TR, 6'6", 225 lbs. Deb: 9/19/1982																										
1982 Phi-N	0	0	....	4	1	0	0	0	8	7	4	3	1	1	2	7	1.125	3.38	109	3.28	.226	0	....	0	0	0.1
1985 Chi-N	2	3	.400	20	4	0	0	1	52	52	21	20	8	1	17	31	1.327	3.46	115	3.99	.260	0	.000	4	4	0.3
1986 Chi-N	2	4	.333	36	0	0	0	5	53^2	58	37	32	7	2	28	42	1.602	5.37	75	5.18	.275	0	.000	-7	1	-0.8
1987 Chi-N	0	1	.000	23	0	0	0	0	29^1	38	22	22	4	0	20	27	1.977	6.75	63	7.42	.325	1	1.000	-7	0	-0.7
1990 KC-A	0	1	.000	3	0	0	0	0	2^1	4	4	4	1	1	2	1	2.571	15.43	25	14.93	.364	0	....	-3	0	-0.3
1992 Phi-N	0	0	....	8	0	0	0	0	11	10	10	10	5	0	10	9	1.818	8.18	43	8.74	.250	0	....	-6	0	-0.6
Total 6	4	9	.308	94	5	0	0	6	156^1	169	98	91	26	5	79	117	1.586	5.24	76	5.50	.277	1	.071	-19	5	-2.0
• BALLINGER, Mark Mark Alan Ballinger b: 1/31/1949, Glendale, CA BR/TR, 6'6", 205 lbs. Deb: 8/6/1971																										
1971 Cle-A	1	2	.333	18	0	0	0	0	34^2	30	21	18	3	1	13	25	1.240	4.67	82	3.13	.233	1	.200	-3	1	-0.4
• BALLOU, Win Noble Winfield Ballou b: 11/30/1897, Mount Morgan, KY d: 1/29/1963, San Francisco, CA BR/TL, 5'10.5", 170 lbs. Deb: 8/24/1925																										
1925* Was-A	1	1	.500	10	1	1	0	0	27^2	38	17	14	1	0	13	13	1.843	4.55	93	6.22	.342	1	.143	-2	1	-0.2
1926 StL-A	11	10	.524	43	14	5	0	2	154	186	99	82	12	4	71	59	**1.669**	4.79	89	5.35	.311	2	.048	-10	7	-1.2
1927 StL-A	5	6	.455	21	11	4	0	0	90^1	105	56	48	4	1	46	17	1.672	4.78	91	5.15	.309	1	.036	-5	4	-0.8
1929 Bro-N	2	3	.400	25	2	0	0	0	57^2	69	52	43	5	0	38	20	1.855	6.71	69	5.96	.304	1	.063	-12	0	-1.3
Total 4	19	20	.487	99	28	10	0	2	329^2	398	224	187	22	5	168	109	1.717	5.11	86	5.47	.312	5	.054	-29	12	-3.5
• BALSAMO, Tony Anthony Fred Balsamo b: 11/21/1937, Brooklyn, NY BR/TR, 6'2", 185 lbs. Deb: 4/14/1962																										
1962 Chi-N	0	1	.000	18	0	0	0	0	29^1	34	22	21	1	1	20	27	1.841	6.44	64	5.59	.293	1	.200	-8	0	-0.7
• BAMBERGER, George George Irvin Bamberger b: 8/1/1925, Staten Island, NY d: 4/4/2004, North Redington Beach, FL BR/TR, 6', 175 lbs. Deb: 4/19/1951 M/C																										
1951 NY-N	0	0	....	2	0	0	0	0	2	4	4	4	2	0	2	1	3.000	18.00	22	24.73	.444	0	....	-3	0	-0.3
1952 NY-N	0	0	....	5	0	0	0	0	4	6	4	4	1	0	6	0	3.000	9.00	41	13.52	.353	0	....	-2	0	-0.2
1959 Bal-A	0	0	....	3	1	0	0	1	8^1	15	7	7	1	0	2	2	2.040	7.56	50	9.00	.405	0	.000	-4	0	-0.4
Total 3	0	0	....	10	1	0	0	1	14^1	25	15	15	4	0	10	3	2.442	9.42	40	12.46	.397	0	.000	-9	0	-0.9
• BANE, Eddie Edward Norman Bane b: 3/22/1952, Chicago, IL BR/TL, 5'9", 160 lbs. Deb: 7/4/1973																										
1973 Min-A	0	5	.000	23	6	0	0	2	60^1	62	40	33	5	2	30	42	1.525	4.92	80	4.64	.270	0	....	-6	1	-0.6
1975 Min-A	3	1	.750	4	4	0	0	0	28^1	28	11	9	2	1	15	14	1.518	2.86	135	4.44	.262	0	....	3	3	0.3
1976 Min-A	4	7	.364	17	15	1	0	0	79^1	92	52	45	6	0	39	24	1.651	5.11	70	5.16	.290	0	....	-13	0	-1.4
Total 3	7	13	.350	44	25	1	0	2	168	182	103	87	13	3	84	80	1.583	4.66	81	4.85	.278	0	....	-16	4	-1.7
• BANEY, Dick Richard Lee Baney b: 11/1/1946, Fullerton, CA BR/TR, 6', 185 lbs. Deb: 7/11/1969																										
1969 Sea-A	1	0	1.000	9	1	0	0	0	18^2	21	8	8	2	0	7	9	1.500	3.86	94	4.72	.292	0	.000	0	1	0.0
1973 Cin-N	2	1	.667	11	1	0	0	2	30^2	26	10	10	1	4	6	17	1.043	2.93	116	2.60	.234	2	.222	1	3	0.2
1974 Cin-N	1	0	1.000	22	1	0	0	1	41	51	27	25	4	0	17	12	1.659	5.49	64	5.41	.305	0	.000	-10	0	-1.1
Total 3	4	1	.800	42	3	0	0	3	90^1	98	45	43	7	4	30	38	1.417	4.28	82	4.31	.280	2	.125	-9	4	-1.0
• BANKHEAD, Dan Daniel Robert Bankhead b: 5/3/1920, Empire, AL d: 5/2/1976, Houston, TX BR/TR, 6'1", 184 lbs. Deb: 8/26/1947																										
1947* Bro-N	0	0	....	4	0	0	0	1	10	15	8	8	1	1	8	6	2.300	7.20	57	8.83	.341	1	.250	-4	0	-0.2
1950 Bro-N	9	4	.692	41	12	2	1	3	129^1	119	84	79	16	2	88	96	1.601	5.50	75	4.90	.252	9	.231	-23	4	-2.1
1951 Bro-N	0	1	.000	7	1	0	0	0	14	27	24	24	5	0	14	9	2.929	15.43	25	15.59	.422	0	.000	-18	0	-1.9
Total 3	9	5	.643	52	13	2	1	4	153^1	161	116	111	22	3	110	111	1.767	6.52	62	6.13	.277	10	.222	-45	4	-4.2
• BANKHEAD, Scott Michael Scott Bankhead b: 7/31/1963, Raleigh, NC BR/TR, 5'10", 185 lbs. Deb: 5/25/1986																										
1986 KC-A	8	9	.471	24	17	0	0	0	121	121	66	62	14	3	37	94	1.306	4.61	92	3.79	.259	0	....	-3	6	-0.3
1987 Sea-A	9	8	.529	27	25	2	0	0	149^1	168	96	90	35	3	37	95	1.373	5.42	87	5.21	.283	0	....	-13	6	-1.2
1988 Sea-A	7	9	.438	21	21	2	1	0	135	115	53	46	8	1	38	102	1.133	3.07	136	2.52	.224	0	....	17	10	1.7
1989 Sea-A	14	6	.700	33	33	3	2	0	210^1	187	84	78	19	3	63	140	1.189	3.34	121	3.10	.239	0	....	16	15	1.6
1990 Sea-A	0	2	.000	4	4	0	0	0	13	18	16	16	2	0	7	10	1.923	11.08	36	7.38	.333	0	....	-10	0	-1.0
1991 Sea-A	3	6	.333	17	9	0	0	0	60^2	73	35	33	8	2	21	28	1.549	4.90	84	5.37	.297	0	....	-6	2	-0.6
1992 Cin-N	10	4	.714	54	0	0	0	1	70^2	57	26	23	4	3	29	53	1.217	2.93	123	2.80	.218	2	.222	5	8	0.6
1993 Bos-A	2	1	.667	40	0	0	0	0	64^1	59	28	25	7	0	29	47	1.368	3.50	132	3.86	.250	0	....	8	5	0.7
1994 Bos-A	3	2	.600	27	0	0	0	0	37^2	34	21	19	5	0	12	25	1.221	4.54	111	3.33	.239	0	....	2	3	0.2
1995 NY-A	1	1	.500	20	1	0	0	0	39	44	26	26	9	0	16	20	1.538	6.00	77	5.78	.278	0	....	-6	1	-0.6
Total 10	57	48	.543	267	110	7	3	1	901	876	451	418	111	15	289	614	1.293	4.18	103	3.83	.254	2	.222	8	56	1.0
• BANKS, Bill William John Banks b: 2/26/1874, Danville, PA d: 9/8/1936, Danville, PA BR/TR, 5'11", 150 lbs. Deb: 9/27/1895																										
1895 Bos-N	1	0	1.000	1	1	1	0	0	7	7	2	0	0	0	4	4	1.571	0.00	....	3.85	.257	0	.000	4	1	0.3
1896 Bos-N	0	3	.000	4	3	2	0	0	23	42	31	27	2	0	13	6	2.391	10.57	43	9.76	.389	3	.273	-16	0	-1.3
Total 2	1	3	.250	5	4	3	0	0	30	49	33	27	2	0	17	10	2.200	8.10	56	8.38	.362	3	.214	-12	1	-1.1
• BANKS, Willie Willie Anthony Banks b: 2/27/1969, Jersey City, NJ BR/TR, 6'1", 202 lbs. Deb: 7/31/1991																										
1991 Min-A	1	1	.500	5	3	0	0	0	17^1	21	15	11	1	0	12	16	1.904	5.71	75	6.02	.288	0	....	-3	0	-0.3
1992 Min-A	4	4	.500	16	12	0	0	0	71	80	46	45	6	2	37	37	1.648	5.70	71	5.30	.288	0	....	-14	1	-1.4
1993 Min-A	11	12	.478	31	30	0	0	0	171^1	186	91	77	17	3	78	138	1.541	4.04	108	4.90	.280	0	....	7	11	0.7
1994 Chi-N	8	12	.400	23	23	1	1	0	138^1	139	88	83	16	2	56	91	1.410	5.40	77	4.27	.261	5	.122	-20	2	-2.1
1995 Chi-N	0	1	.000	10	0	0	0	0	11^2	27	23	20	5	0	12	9	3.343	15.43	27	18.75	.458	0	.000	-15	0	-1.5
LA-N	0	2	.000	6	6	0	0	0	29	36	21	13	2	1	16	23	1.793	4.03	94	5.82	.303	1	.125	-1	0	0.0
Fla-N	2	3	.400	9	9	0	0	0	50	43	27	24	7	1	30	30	1.460	4.32	98	4.42	.235	6	.353	-1	2	0.1
Yr.	2	6	.250	25	15	0	0	0	90^2	106	71	57	14	2	58	62	1.809	5.66	72	6.71	.294	7	.269	-16	2	-1.4
1997 NY-A	3	0	1.000	5	1	0	0	0	14	9	3	3	0	1	6	8	1.071	1.93	231	1.96	.188	0	....	4	2	0.4
1998 NY-A	1	1	.500	9	0	0	0	0	14^1	20	16	16	4	1	12	8	2.233	10.05	44	9.74	.323	0	....	-9	0	-0.9
Ari-N	1	2	.333	33	0	0	0	1	43^2	34	21	15	2	1	25	32	1.351	3.09	136	3.14	.217	0	.000	5	3	0.5
2001 Bos-A	0	0	....	5	0	0	0	0	10^2	5	4	1	0	0	4	10	.844	0.84	531	1.06	.132	0	....	5	1	0.4
2002 Bos-A	2	1	.667	29	0	0	0	1	39	32	15	14	5	3	14	26	1.179	3.23	139	3.45	.222	0	....	5	3	0.5
Total 9	33	39	.458	181	84	1	1	2	610^1	632	370	322	65	15	302	428	1.530	4.75	89	4.86	.268	12	.176	-36	25	-3.5
• BANNISTER, Floyd Floyd Franklin Bannister b: 6/10/1955, Pierre, SD BL/TL, 6'1", 195 lbs. Deb: 4/19/1977																										
1977 Hou-N	8	9	.471	24	23	4	1	0	142^2	138	70	64	11	4	68	112	1.444	4.04	88	4.14	.254	9	.188	-7	5	-0.7
1978 Hou-N	3	9	.250	28	16	2	2	0	110^1	120	59	59	13	1	63	94	1.659	4.81	69	5.40	.280	5	.161	-16	1	-1.7
1979 Sea-A	10	15	.400	30	30	6	2	0	182^1	185	92	82	25	4	68	115	1.388	4.05	108	4.34	.260	0	....	7	11	0.7
1980 Sea-A	9	13	.409	32	32	8	0	0	217^2	200	96	84	24	2	66	155	1.222	3.47	119	3.26	.239	0	....	18	15	1.8
1981 Sea-A	9	9	.500	21	20	5	2	0	121^1	128	62	60	14	3	39	85	1.376	4.45	87	4.29	.268	0	....	-6	6	-0.7
1982 Sea-A★	12	13	.480	35	35	5	3	0	247	225	112	94	32	3	77	**209**	1.223	3.43	124	3.51	.243	0	....	23	17	2.3
1983* Chi-A	16	10	.615	34	34	5	2	0	217^1	191	88	81	19	2	71	193	1.206	3.35	125	3.06	.233	0	....	19	17	1.9
1984 Chi-A	14	11	.560	34	33	4	0	0	218	211	127	117	30	6	80	152	1.335	4.83	86	4.10	.252	0	.000	-18	9	-1.8
1985 Chi-A	10	14	.417	34	34	4	1	0	210^2	211	121	114	30	4	100	198	1.476	4.87	89	4.72	.261	0	....	-14	7	-1.4

YEAR TM-L	W	L	PCT	G	GS	CG	SH	SV	IP	H	R	ER	HR	HB	BB	SO	RAT	ERA	ERA+	CERA	OAV	BH	AVG	PR+	WS	TPW
1986 Chi-A	10	14	.417	28	27	6	1	0	165^1	162	81	65	17	2	48	92	1.270	3.54	122	3.64	.259	0	....	11	11	1.0
1987 Chi-A	16	11	.593	34	34	11	2	0	228^2	216	100	91	38	0	49	124	1.159	3.58	128	3.46	.246	0	....	19	17	1.8
1988 KC-A	12	13	.480	31	31	2	0	0	189^1	182	102	91	22	5	68	113	1.320	4.33	92	3.82	.248	0	....	-4	8	-0.4
1989 KC-A	4	1	.800	14	14	0	0	0	75^1	87	40	39	8	1	18	35	1.394	4.66	83	4.41	.290	0	....	-6	3	-0.6
1991 Cal-A	0	0	....	16	0	0	0	0	25	25	12	11	5	0	10	16	1.400	3.96	104	4.91	.266	0	....	0	1	0.0
1992 Tex-A	1	1	.500	36	0	0	0	0	37	39	27	26	3	3	21	30	1.622	6.32	60	4.84	.281	0	....	-10	0	-1.0
Total 15	134	143	.484	431	363	62	16	0	2388	2320	1189	1078	291	40	846	1723	1.326	4.06	101	3.93	.253	14	.175	16	128	1.3

• BANTA, Jack Jackie Kay Banta b: 6/24/1925, Hutchinson, KS BL/TR, 6'2.5", 175 lbs. Deb: 9/18/1947

YEAR TM-L	W	L	PCT	G	GS	CG	SH	SV	IP	H	R	ER	HR	HB	BB	SO	RAT	ERA	ERA+	CERA	OAV	BH	AVG	PR+	WS	TPW
1947 Bro-N	0	1	.000	3	1	0	0	0	7^2	7	6	6	1	1	4	3	1.435	7.04	59	4.12	.226	0	.000	-3	0	-0.3
1948 Bro-N	0	1	.000	2	1	0	0	0	3^1	5	6	3	0	0	5	1	3.000	8.10	49	10.75	.385	0	.000	-2	0	-0.2
1949* Bro-N	10	6	.625	48	12	2	1	3	152^1	125	63	57	12	6	68	97	1.267	3.37	122	3.17	.223	5	.109	10	11	0.8
1950 Bro-N	4	4	.500	16	5	1	0	2	41^1	39	22	20	2	3	36	15	1.815	4.35	94	5.27	.252	2	.167	-2	3	-0.2
Total 4	14	12	.538	69	19	3	1	5	204^2	176	97	86	15	10	113	116	1.412	3.78	108	3.76	.232	7	.115	3	14	0.1

• BAPTIST, Travis Travis Steven Baptist b: 12/30/1971, Forest Grove, OR BL/TR, 6' Deb: 8/1/1998

YEAR TM-L	W	L	PCT	G	GS	CG	SH	SV	IP	H	R	ER	HR	HB	BB	SO	RAT	ERA	ERA+	CERA	OAV	BH	AVG	PR+	WS	TPW
1998 Min-A	0	1	.000	13	0	0	0	0	27	34	18	17	5	0	11	11	1.667	5.67	84	6.24	.321	0	....	-2	1	-0.2

• BARBER, Brian Brian Scott Barber b: 3/4/1973, Hamilton, OH BR/TR, 6'1", 170 lbs. Deb: 8/12/1995

YEAR TM-L	W	L	PCT	G	GS	CG	SH	SV	IP	H	R	ER	HR	HB	BB	SO	RAT	ERA	ERA+	CERA	OAV	BH	AVG	PR+	WS	TPW
1995 StL-N	2	1	.667	9	4	0	0	0	29^1	31	17	17	4	0	16	27	1.602	5.22	80	5.36	.279	1	.125	-4	1	-0.4
1996 StL-N	0	0	....	1	1	0	0	0	3	4	5	5	0	1	6	1	3.333	15.00	28	13.28	.364	0	....	-4	0	-0.4
1998 KC-A	2	4	.333	8	8	0	0	0	42	45	28	28	5	1	13	24	1.381	6.00	80	4.34	.276	0	....	-5	1	-0.5
1999 KC-A	1	3	.250	8	3	0	0	1	18^2	31	20	20	6	2	10	7	2.196	9.64	52	11.42	.383	0	....	-10	0	-0.9
Total 4	5	8	.385	26	16	0	0	1	93	111	70	70	15	4	45	59	1.677	6.77	69	6.37	.303	1	.125	-22	2	-2.1

• BARBER, Steve Stephen David Barber b: 2/22/1938, Takoma Park, MD BL/TL, 6', 200 lbs. Deb: 4/21/1960

YEAR TM-L	W	L	PCT	G	GS	CG	SH	SV	IP	H	R	ER	HR	HB	BB	SO	RAT	ERA	ERA+	CERA	OAV	BH	AVG	PR+	WS	TPW
1960 Bal-A	10	7	.588	36	27	6	1	2	181^2	148	78	65	10	3	113	112	1.437	3.22	118	3.68	.226	3	.056	8	12	0.5
1961 Bal-A	18	12	.600	37	34	14	**8**	1	248^1	194	102	92	13	2	130	150	1.305	3.33	117	3.08	.218	13	.163	12	19	1.4
1962 Bal-A	9	6	.600	28	19	5	2	0	140^1	145	66	54	9	1	61	89	1.468	3.46	108	4.06	.262	3	.071	3	8	0.1
1963 Bal-A★	20	13	.606	39	36	11	2	0	258^2	253	99	79	12	4	92	180	1.334	2.75	128	3.43	.258	12	.138	23	18	2.3
1964 Bal-A	9	13	.409	36	26	4	0	1	157	144	72	67	15	7	81	118	1.433	3.84	93	4.22	.248	7	.149	-9	7	-0.9
1965 Bal-A	15	10	.600	37	32	7	2	0	220^2	177	79	66	16	2	81	130	1.169	2.69	129	2.76	.224	5	.077	16	16	1.5
1966 Bal-A★	10	5	.667	25	22	5	3	0	133^1	104	38	34	6	3	49	91	1.148	2.30	145	2.57	.218	3	.068	15	11	1.2
1967 Bal-A	4	9	.308	15	15	1	1	0	74^2	47	39	34	5	5	61	48	1.446	4.10	77	3.58	.185	2	.091	-9	1	-1.1
NY-A	6	9	.400	17	17	3	1	0	97^2	103	47	44	4	3	54	70	1.608	4.05	77	4.62	.278	5	.172	-9	3	-0.9
Yr.	10	18	.357	32	32	4	2	0	172^1	150	86	78	9	8	115	118	**1.538**	4.07	77	4.17	.240	7	.137	-18	4	-1.9
1968 NY-A	6	5	.545	20	19	3	1	0	128^1	127	63	46	7	3	64	87	1.488	3.23	90	4.04	.256	2	.051	-3	4	-0.5
1969 Sea-A	4	7	.364	25	16	0	0	0	86^1	99	51	46	9	1	48	69	1.703	4.80	76	5.68	.292	5	.200	-9	2	-0.8
1970 Chi-N	0	1	.000	5	0	0	0	0	5^2	10	6	6	0	0	6	3	2.824	9.53	47	9.97	.417	0	....	-3	0	-0.3
Atl-N	0	1	.000	5	2	0	0	0	14^2	17	10	8	3	1	5	11	1.500	4.91	87	5.79	.288	1	.250	-1	0	-0.1
Yr.	0	2	.000	10	2	0	0	0	20^1	27	16	14	3	1	11	14	1.869	6.20	71	6.95	.325	1	.250	-4	0	-0.4
1971 Atl-N	3	1	.750	39	3	0	0	2	75	92	42	40	6	2	25	40	1.560	4.80	77	5.01	.301	2	.154	-9	3	-0.9
1972 Atl-N	0	0	....	5	0	0	0	0	15^2	18	10	10	1	1	6	6	1.532	5.74	66	4.79	.290	1	.200	-3	0	-0.3
Cal-A	4	4	.500	34	3	0	0	2	58	37	16	13	4	1	30	34	1.155	2.02	144	2.23	.188	1	.143	5	6	0.7
1973 Cal-A	3	2	.600	50	1	0	0	4	89^1	90	40	35	5	3	32	58	1.366	3.53	101	3.70	.265	0	....	1	6	0.1
1974 SF-N	0	1	.000	13	0	0	0	1	13^2	13	12	8	0	0	12	13	1.829	5.27	72	4.60	.255	0	....	-2	0	-0.2
Total 15	121	106	.533	466	272	59	21	13	1999	1818	870	747	125	42	950	1309	1.385	3.36	105	3.67	.245	65	.115	27	116	2.0

• BARBER, Steve Steven Lee Barber b: 3/13/1948, Grand Rapids, MI BR/TR, 6'1", 190 lbs. Deb: 4/9/1970

YEAR TM-L	W	L	PCT	G	GS	CG	SH	SV	IP	H	R	ER	HR	HB	BB	SO	RAT	ERA	ERA+	CERA	OAV	BH	AVG	PR+	WS	TPW
1970 Min-A	0	0	....	18	0	0	0	2	27^1	26	14	14	1	2	18	14	1.610	4.61	81	4.48	.263	0	.000	-3	1	-0.3
1971 Min-A	1	0	1.000	4	2	0	0	0	11^2	8	9	8	2	0	13	4	1.800	6.17	58	5.38	.190	0	.000	-3	0	-0.4
Total 2	1	0	1.000	22	2	0	0	2	39	34	23	22	3	2	31	18	1.667	5.08	72	4.75	.241	0	.000	-6	1	-0.7

• BARBERICH, Frank Frank Frederick Barberich b: 2/3/1882, New Town, NY d: 5/1/1965, Ocala, FL BB/TR, 5'10.5", 175 lbs. Deb: 9/17/1907

YEAR TM-L	W	L	PCT	G	GS	CG	SH	SV	IP	H	R	ER	HR	HB	BB	SO	RAT	ERA	ERA+	CERA	OAV	BH	AVG	PR+	WS	TPW
1907 Bos-N	1	1	.500	2	2	1	0	0	12^1	19	10	8	0	0	5	1	1.946	5.84	44	6.57	.358	0	.000	-5	0	-0.6
1910 Bos-A	0	0	....	2	0	0	0	0	5	7	6	4	0	0	2	0	1.800	7.20	35	5.90	.350	0	.000	-3	0	-0.3
Total 2	1	1	.500	4	2	1	0	0	17^1	26	16	12	0	0	7	1	1.904	6.23	41	6.37	.356	0	.000	-7	0	-0.9

• BARCELO, Lorenzo Lorenzo Antonio Barcelo b: 8/10/1977, San Pedro de Macoris, Dominican Republic BR/TR, 6'4", 230 lbs. Deb: 7/22/2000

YEAR TM-L	W	L	PCT	G	GS	CG	SH	SV	IP	H	R	ER	HR	HB	BB	SO	RAT	ERA	ERA+	CERA	OAV	BH	AVG	PR+	WS	TPW
2000* Chi-A	4	2	.667	22	1	0	0	0	39	34	17	16	5	0	9	26	1.103	3.69	135	2.90	.231	0	....	5	3	0.5
2001 Chi-A	1	0	1.000	17	0	0	0	0	21	24	13	11	1	1	8	15	1.524	4.71	98	4.33	.282	0	....	-0	1	0.0
2002 Chi-A	0	1	.000	4	0	0	0	0	6	9	6	6	1	0	1	1	1.667	9.00	51	6.43	.333	0	....	-3	0	-0.3
Total 3	5	3	.625	43	1	0	0	0	66	67	36	33	7	1	18	42	1.288	4.50	106	3.67	.259	0	....	2	4	0.1

• BARCLAY, Curt Curtis Cordell Barclay b: 8/22/1931, Chicago, IL d: 3/25/1985, Missoula, MT BR/TR, 6'3", 210 lbs. Deb: 4/21/1957

YEAR TM-L	W	L	PCT	G	GS	CG	SH	SV	IP	H	R	ER	HR	HB	BB	SO	RAT	ERA	ERA+	CERA	OAV	BH	AVG	PR+	WS	TPW
1957 NY-N	9	9	.500	37	28	5	2	0	183	196	85	70	21	2	48	67	1.333	3.44	114	4.04	.274	11	.190	11	11	1.1
1958 SF-N	1	0	1.000	6	1	0	0	0	16	16	5	5	3	3	5	6	1.313	2.81	136	4.84	.258	4	.667	2	2	0.4
1959 SF-N	0	0	....	1	0	0	0	0	0^1	2	5	2	0	0	2	0	12.00	54.00	7	59.81	.500	0	....	-2	0	-0.2
Total 3	10	9	.526	44	29	5	2	0	199^1	214	95	77	24	5	55	73	1.349	3.48	113	4.19	.274	15	.234	11	13	1.3

• BARE, Ray Raymond Douglas Bare b: 4/15/1949, Miami, FL d: 3/29/1994, Miami, FL BR/TR, 6'2", 195 lbs. Deb: 7/30/1972

YEAR TM-L	W	L	PCT	G	GS	CG	SH	SV	IP	H	R	ER	HR	HB	BB	SO	RAT	ERA	ERA+	CERA	OAV	BH	AVG	PR+	WS	TPW
1972 StL-N	0	1	.000	14	0	0	0	1	16^2	18	2	1	0	0	6	5	1.440	0.54	630	3.52	.281	0	....	5	3	0.6
1974 StL-N	1	2	.333	10	3	0	0	0	24^1	25	17	16	2	0	9	6	1.397	5.92	60	4.11	.281	1	.200	-7	0	-0.7
1975 Det-A	8	13	.381	29	21	6	1	0	150^2	174	81	75	10	1	47	71	1.467	4.48	90	4.36	.293	0	....	-5	7	-0.5
1976 Det-A	7	8	.467	30	21	3	2	0	134	157	85	69	13	0	51	59	1.552	4.63	80	4.90	.293	0	....	-12	3	-1.3
1977 Det-A	0	2	.000	5	4	0	0	0	14^1	24	21	20	3	0	7	4	2.163	12.56	34	9.72	.381	0	....	-13	0	-1.3
Total 5	16	26	.381	88	49	9	3	1	340	398	206	181	28	1	120	145	1.524	4.79	81	4.74	.296	1	.200	-32	13	-3.2

• BARFIELD, John John David Barfield b: 10/15/1964, Pine Bluff, AR BL/TL, 6'1", 185 lbs. Deb: 9/7/1989

YEAR TM-L	W	L	PCT	G	GS	CG	SH	SV	IP	H	R	ER	HR	HB	BB	SO	RAT	ERA	ERA+	CERA	OAV	BH	AVG	PR+	WS	TPW
1989 Tex-A	0	1	.000	4	2	0	0	0	11^2	15	10	8	0	0	4	9	1.629	6.17	64	4.79	.319	0	....	-3	0	-0.3
1990 Tex-A	4	3	.571	33	0	0	0	1	44^1	42	25	23	2	1	13	17	1.241	4.67	84	3.14	.268	0	....	-4	2	-0.4
1991 Tex-A	4	4	.500	28	9	0	0	1	83^1	96	51	42	11	0	22	27	1.416	4.54	89	4.55	.289	0	....	-3	3	-0.3
Total 3	8	8	.500	65	11	0	0	2	139^1	153	86	73	13	1	39	53	1.378	4.72	85	4.12	.285	0	....	-10	5	-1.0

• BARFOOT, Clyde Clyde Raymond "Foots" Barfoot b: 7/8/1891, Richmond, VA d: 3/11/1971, Highland Park, CA BR/TR, 6', 170 lbs. Deb: 4/13/1922

YEAR TM-L	W	L	PCT	G	GS	CG	SH	SV	IP	H	R	ER	HR	HB	BB	SO	RAT	ERA	ERA+	CERA	OAV	BH	AVG	PR+	WS	TPW
1922 StL-N	4	5	.444	42	2	1	0	2	117^2	139	75	55	2	10	30	19	1.436	4.21	92	4.16	.307	12	.353	-2	7	0.3
1923 StL-N	3	3	.500	33	2	1	1	1	101^1	112	49	42	7	1	27	23	1.372	3.73	105	3.96	.289	7	.189	3	6	0.2
1926 Det-A	1	2	.333	11	1	0	0	2	31^1	42	27	17	4	0	9	7	1.628	4.88	83	5.64	.318	1	.200	-3	0	-0.2
Total 3	8	10	.444	86	5	2	1	5	250^1	293	151	114	13	11	66	49	1.434	4.10	95	4.26	.301	20	.263	-2	13	0.2

• BARGAR, Greg Greg Robert Bargar b: 1/27/1959, Inglewood, CA BR/TR, 6'2", 185 lbs. Deb: 7/17/1983

YEAR TM-L	W	L	PCT	G	GS	CG	SH	SV	IP	H	R	ER	HR	HB	BB	SO	RAT	ERA	ERA+	CERA	OAV	BH	AVG	PR+	WS	TPW
1983 Mon-N	2	0	1.000	8	3	0	0	0	20	23	15	15	6	1	8	9	1.550	6.75	53	6.39	.271	1	.167	-7	0	-0.8
1984 Mon-N	0	1	.000	3	1	0	0	0	8	8	7	7	1	0	7	2	1.875	7.88	43	6.35	.286	0	.000	-4	0	-0.4
1986 StL-N	0	2	.000	22	0	0	0	0	27^1	36	19	17	3	3	10	12	1.683	5.60	65	6.39	.330	0	.000	-7	0	-0.7
Total 3	2	3	.400	33	4	0	0	0	55^1	67	41	39	10	4	25	23	1.663	6.34	56	6.38	.302	1	.111	-18	0	-1.9

• BARGER, Cy Eros Bolivar Barger b: 5/18/1885, Jamestown, KY d: 9/23/1964, Columbia, KY BL/TR, 6', 160 lbs. Deb: 8/30/1906

YEAR TM-L	W	L	PCT	G	GS	CG	SH	SV	IP	H	R	ER	HR	HB	BB	SO	RAT	ERA	ERA+	CERA	OAV	BH	AVG	PR+	WS	TPW
1906 NY-A	0	0	....	2	1	0	0	1	5^1	7	8	6	0	0	3	3	1.875	10.13	29	5.59	.319	1	.333	-4	0	-0.4
1907 NY-A	0	0	....	1	0	0	0	0	6	10	2	2	0	1	1	0	1.833	3.00	93	8.17	.373	0	.000	-0	0	0.0
1910 Bro-N	15	15	.500	35	30	25	2	1	271^2	267	105	87	2	6	107	87	1.377	2.88	105	3.59	.275	24	.231	2	19	0.6

YEAR TM-L	W	L	PCT	G	GS	CG	SH	SV	IP	H	R	ER	HR	HB	BB	SO	RAT	ERA	ERA+	CERA	OAV	BH	AVG	PR+	WS	TPW
1911 Bro-N	11	15	.423	30	30	21	1	0	217^1	224	112	85	4	7	71	60	1.357	3.52	94	3.65	.279	33	.228	-4	12	-0.6
1912 Bro-N	1	9	.100	16	11	6	0	0	94	120	78	57	4	4	42	30	1.723	5.46	61	5.62	.326	7	.189	-21	0	-2.0
1914 Pit-F	10	16	.385	33	26	18	1	1	228^1	252	125	110	7	6	63	70	1.380	4.34	71	3.90	.290	17	.205	-31	7	-3.2
1915 Pit-F	9	8	.529	34	13	8	1	6	153	130	49	39	1	4	47	47	1.157	2.29	135	2.51	.238	15	.278	14	16	1.7
Total 7	46	63	.422	151	111	78	5	9	975^2	1010	479	386	18	28	334	297	1.378	3.56	88	3.74	.280	97	.227	-44	54	-4.0

• BARK, Brian Brian Stuart Bark b: 8/26/1968, Baltimore, MD BL/TL, 5'9", 170 lbs. Deb: 7/6/1995

YEAR TM-L	W	L	PCT	G	GS	CG	SH	SV	IP	H	R	ER	HR	HB	BB	SO	RAT	ERA	ERA+	CERA	OAV	BH	AVG	PR+	WS	TPW
1995 Bos-A	0	0	....	3	0	0	0	0	2^1	2	0	0	0	0	1	0	1.286	0.00	....	3.48	.286	0	....	1	0	0.1

• BARKER, Len Leonard Harold Barker b: 7/27/1955, Fort Knox, KY BR/TR, 6'5", 225 lbs. Deb: 9/14/1976

YEAR TM-L	W	L	PCT	G	GS	CG	SH	SV	IP	H	R	ER	HR	HB	BB	SO	RAT	ERA	ERA+	CERA	OAV	BH	AVG	PR+	WS	TPW
1976 Tex-A	1	0	1.000	2	2	1	1	0	15	7	4	4	0	2	6	7	.867	2.40	149	1.48	.149	0	....	2	1	0.2
1977 Tex-A	4	1	.800	15	3	0	0	1	47^1	36	15	14	1	1	24	51	1.268	2.66	153	2.69	.217	0	....	7	5	0.7
1978 Tex-A	1	5	.167	29	0	0	0	4	52^1	63	31	28	6	2	29	33	1.758	4.82	78	6.18	.304	0	....	-6	1	-0.6
1979 Cle-A	6	6	.500	29	19	2	0	0	137^1	146	79	75	6	2	70	93	1.573	4.92	87	4.54	.277	0	....	-7	6	-0.7
1980 Cle-A	19	12	.613	36	36	8	1	0	246^1	237	127	114	17	3	92	**187**	1.336	4.17	98	3.57	.252	0	....	-1	15	-0.1
1981 Cle-A★	8	7	.533	22	22	9	3	0	154^1	150	72	67	7	1	46	**127**	1.270	3.91	93	3.11	.249	0	....	0	8	0.0
1982 Cle-A	15	11	.577	33	33	10	1	0	244^2	211	117	106	17	3	88	187	1.222	3.90	105	3.00	.232	0	....	7	16	0.7
1983 Cle-A	8	13	.381	24	24	4	1	0	149^2	150	92	85	16	2	52	105	1.350	5.11	83	4.00	.266	0	....	-13	5	-1.3
Atl-N	1	3	.250	6	6	0	0	0	33	31	17	14	0	0	14	21	1.364	3.82	102	2.99	.248	1	.125	-0	1	0.0
1984 Atl-N	7	8	.467	21	20	1	0	0	126^1	120	59	54	10	2	38	95	1.251	3.85	100	3.32	.254	2	.053	1	6	0.0
1985 Atl-N	2	9	.182	20	18	0	0	0	73^2	84	55	52	10	1	37	47	1.643	6.35	61	5.62	.288	0	.000	-20	0	-2.3
1987 Mil-A	2	1	.667	11	11	0	0	0	43^2	54	27	26	6	2	17	22	1.626	5.36	85	5.90	.303	0	....	-3	2	-0.3
Total 11	74	76	.493	248	194	35	7	5	1323^2	1289	695	639	96	21	513	975	1.361	4.34	92	3.76	.256	3	.048	-34	66	-3.8

• BARKER, Richie Richard Frank Barker b: 10/29/1972, Revere, MA BR/TR, 6'2", 220 lbs. Deb: 4/25/1999

YEAR TM-L	W	L	PCT	G	GS	CG	SH	SV	IP	H	R	ER	HR	HB	BB	SO	RAT	ERA	ERA+	CERA	OAV	BH	AVG	PR+	WS	TPW
1999 Chi-N	0	0	....	5	0	0	0	0	5	6	4	4	0	0	4	3	2.000	7.20	63	5.47	.300	0	....	-1	0	-0.1

• BARKLEY, Brian Brian Edward Barkley b: 12/8/1975, Conroe, TX BL/TL, 6'2" Deb: 5/28/1998

YEAR TM-L	W	L	PCT	G	GS	CG	SH	SV	IP	H	R	ER	HR	HB	BB	SO	RAT	ERA	ERA+	CERA	OAV	BH	AVG	PR+	WS	TPW
1998 Bos-A	0	0	....	6	0	0	0	0	11	16	13	12	2	1	9	2	2.273	9.82	48	9.46	.340	0	....	-6	0	-0.6

• BARKLEY, Jeff Jeffrey Carver Barkley b: 11/21/1959, Hickory, NC BB/TR, 6'3", 185 lbs. Deb: 9/16/1984

YEAR TM-L	W	L	PCT	G	GS	CG	SH	SV	IP	H	R	ER	HR	HB	BB	SO	RAT	ERA	ERA+	CERA	OAV	BH	AVG	PR+	WS	TPW
1984 Cle-A	0	0	....	3	0	0	0	0	4	6	3	3	0	0	1	4	1.750	6.75	61	5.46	.353	0	....	-1	0	-0.1
1985 Cle-A	0	3	.000	21	0	0	0	1	41	37	26	24	5	0	15	30	1.268	5.27	78	3.39	.243	0	....	-5	1	-0.5
Total 2	0	3	.000	24	0	0	0	1	45	43	29	27	5	0	16	34	1.311	5.40	76	3.58	.254	0	....	-6	1	-0.6

• BARLOW, Mike Michael Roswell Barlow b: 4/30/1948, Stamford, NY BL/TR, 6'6", 215 lbs. Deb: 6/18/1975

YEAR TM-L	W	L	PCT	G	GS	CG	SH	SV	IP	H	R	ER	HR	HB	BB	SO	RAT	ERA	ERA+	CERA	OAV	BH	AVG	PR+	WS	TPW
1975 StL-N	0	0	....	9	0	0	0	0	7^2	11	6	4	0	1	3	2	1.826	4.70	80	6.09	.355	0	....	-1	0	-0.1
1976 Hou-N	2	2	.500	16	0	0	0	0	22	27	13	11	0	0	17	11	2.000	4.50	71	6.02	.318	0	.000	-3	0	-0.4
1977 Cal-A	4	2	.667	20	1	0	0	1	59	53	33	30	3	4	27	25	1.356	4.58	85	3.57	.249	0	....	-4	2	-0.4
1978 Cal-A	0	0	....	1	0	0	0	0	2	3	1	1	0	0	0	1	1.500	4.50	80	5.09	.375	0	....	-0	0	0.0
1979★ Cal-A	1	1	.500	35	0	0	0	0	86	106	54	49	8	4	30	33	1.581	5.13	79	5.48	.314	0	....	-10	2	-1.0
1980 Tor-A	3	1	.750	40	1	0	0	5	55	57	29	25	4	2	21	19	1.418	4.09	105	4.08	.273	0	....	1	4	0.1
1981 Tor-A	0	0	....	12	0	0	0	0	15	22	11	7	1	4	6	5	2.800	4.20	94	7.33	.338	0	....	-0	0	0.0
Total 7	10	6	.625	133	2	0	0	6	246^2	279	147	127	16	15	104	96	1.553	4.63	85	4.89	.294	0	.000	-17	8	-1.8

• BARNABE, Charlie Charles Edward Barnabe b: 6/12/1900, Russell Gulch, CO d: 8/16/1977, Waco, TX BL/TL, 5'11.5", 164 lbs. Deb: 4/14/1927

YEAR TM-L	W	L	PCT	G	GS	CG	SH	SV	IP	H	R	ER	HR	HB	BB	SO	RAT	ERA	ERA+	CERA	OAV	BH	AVG	PR+	WS	TPW
1927 Chi-A	0	5	.000	17	4	1	0	0	61	86	46	36	2	5	20	5	1.738	5.31	76	5.95	.351	3	.158	-10	0	-0.8
1928 Chi-A	0	2	.000	7	2	0	0	0	9^2	17	9	7	0	1	0	3	1.759	6.52	62	6.69	.395	4	.500	-3	1	0.0
Total 2	0	7	.000	24	6	1	0	0	70^2	103	55	43	2	6	20	8	1.741	5.48	74	6.05	.358	7	.259	-12	1	-0.8

• BARNES, Bob Robert Avery "Lefty" Barnes b: 1/6/1902, Washburn, IL d: 12/8/1993, Peoria, IL BL/TL, 5'11.5", 150 lbs. Deb: 7/8/1924

YEAR TM-L	W	L	PCT	G	GS	CG	SH	SV	IP	H	R	ER	HR	HB	BB	SO	RAT	ERA	ERA+	CERA	OAV	BH	AVG	PR+	WS	TPW
1924 Chi-A	0	0	....	2	0	0	0	0	4^2	14	11	10	1	0	0	1	3.000	19.29	21	16.27	.519	0	.000	-8	0	-0.8

• BARNES, Brian Brian Keith Barnes b: 3/25/1967, Roanoke Rapids, NC BL/TL, 5'9", 170 lbs. Deb: 9/14/1990

YEAR TM-L	W	L	PCT	G	GS	CG	SH	SV	IP	H	R	ER	HR	HB	BB	SO	RAT	ERA	ERA+	CERA	OAV	BH	AVG	PR+	WS	TPW
1990 Mon-N	1	1	.500	4	4	1	0	0	28	25	10	9	2	0	7	23	1.143	2.89	126	2.73	.236	0	.000	2	2	0.2
1991 Mon-N	5	8	.385	28	27	1	0	0	160	135	82	75	16	6	84	117	1.369	4.22	86	3.87	.233	4	.082	-12	4	-1.4
1992 Mon-N	6	6	.500	21	17	0	0	0	100	77	34	33	9	3	46	65	1.230	2.97	117	3.11	.213	8	.276	6	7	0.8
1993 Mon-N	2	6	.250	52	8	0	0	3	100	105	53	49	9	0	48	60	1.530	4.41	95	4.58	.274	3	.150	-3	4	-0.3
1994 Cle-A	0	1	.000	6	0	0	0	0	13^1	12	10	8	2	0	15	5	2.025	5.40	87	6.40	.235	0	....	-1	0	-0.1
LA-N	0	0	....	5	0	0	0	0	5	10	4	4	1	0	4	5	2.800	7.20	55	12.73	.400	0	....	-2	0	-0.2
Total 5	14	22	.389	116	56	2	0	3	406^1	364	193	178	39	9	204	275	1.398	3.94	96	3.97	.242	15	.140	-10	17	-0.9

• BARNES, Frank Frank Samuel "Lefty" Barnes b: 1/9/1900, Dallas, TX d: 9/27/1967, Houston, TX BL/TL, 6'2.5", 195 lbs. Deb: 4/18/1929

YEAR TM-L	W	L	PCT	G	GS	CG	SH	SV	IP	H	R	ER	HR	HB	BB	SO	RAT	ERA	ERA+	CERA	OAV	BH	AVG	PR+	WS	TPW
1929 Det-A	0	1	.000	4	1	0	0	0	5	10	8	4	0	1	3	0	2.600	7.20	60	10.80	.400	0	.000	-1	0	-0.2
1930 NY-A	0	1	.000	2	2	0	0	0	12^1	13	11	11	0	1	13	2	2.108	8.03	54	6.17	.283	2	.333	-5	0	-0.4
Total 2	0	2	.000	6	3	0	0	0	17^1	23	19	15	0	2	16	2	2.250	7.79	55	7.50	.324	2	.286	-6	0	-0.5

• BARNES, Frank Frank Barnes b: 8/26/1926, Longwood, MS BR/TR, 6', 170 lbs. Deb: 9/22/1957

YEAR TM-L	W	L	PCT	G	GS	CG	SH	SV	IP	H	R	ER	HR	HB	BB	SO	RAT	ERA	ERA+	CERA	OAV	BH	AVG	PR+	WS	TPW
1957 StL-N	0	1	.000	3	1	0	0	0	10	13	5	5	0	0	9	5	2.200	4.50	88	6.96	.317	0	.000	-1	0	-0.1
1958 StL-N	1	1	.500	8	1	0	0	0	19	19	16	16	3	2	16	17	1.842	7.58	55	6.72	.260	1	.167	-7	0	-0.8
1960 StL-N	0	1	.000	4	1	0	0	1	7^2	8	5	3	1	1	9	8	2.217	3.52	116	8.19	.267	0	.000	1	0	0.0
Total 3	1	3	.250	15	3	0	0	1	36^2	40	26	24	4	3	34	30	2.018	5.89	69	7.09	.278	1	.100	-7	0	-0.9

• BARNES, Jesse Jesse Lawrence "Nubby" Barnes b: 8/26/1892, Perkins, OK d: 9/9/1961, Santa Rosa, NM BL/TR, 6', 170 lbs. Deb: 7/30/1915

YEAR TM-L	W	L	PCT	G	GS	CG	SH	SV	IP	H	R	ER	HR	HB	BB	SO	RAT	ERA	ERA+	CERA	OAV	BH	AVG	PR+	WS	TPW
1915 Bos-N	3	0	1.000	9	3	2	0	0	45^1	41	14	7	1	4	10	16	1.125	1.39	192	2.70	.244	3	.176	6	4	0.7
1916 Bos-N	6	15	.286	33	18	9	3	1	163	154	63	43	3	5	37	55	1.172	2.37	103	2.68	.254	9	.188	2	7	0.2
1917 Bos-N	13	21	.382	50	33	26	2	1	295	261	115	88	3	3	50	107	1.054	2.68	95	2.10	.241	24	.238	-1	16	0.4
1918 NY-N	6	1	.857	9	9	4	2	0	54^2	53	15	11	0	0	13	12	1.207	1.81	145	2.61	.255	4	.222	5	5	0.5
1919 NY-N	**25**	9	.735	38	34	23	4	1	295^2	263	98	79	8	2	35	92	1.008	2.40	116	2.00	.236	32	.267	9	24	1.5
1920 NY-N	20	15	.571	43	34	23	2	0	292^2	271	108	86	9	2	56	63	1.117	2.64	113	2.44	.250	22	.204	7	19	0.5
1921★ NY-N	15	9	.625	42	31	15	1	6	258^2	298	108	89	13	3	44	56	1.322	3.10	118	3.76	.299	19	.207	9	18	0.7
1922★ NY-N	13	8	.619	37	29	14	2	0	212^2	236	108	83	10	3	38	52	1.288	3.51	114	3.42	.278	14	.182	5	13	0.4
1923 NY-N	3	1	.750	12	4	1	0	1	36	48	25	25	1	0	13	12	1.694	6.25	61	5.33	.329	3	.273	-10	1	-1.0
Bos-N	10	14	.417	31	23	12	5	2	195^1	204	86	60	8	0	43	41	1.265	2.76	144	3.19	.270	10	.147	28	15	2.4
Yr.	13	15	.464	43	27	13	5	3	231^1	252	111	85	9	0	56	53	1.331	3.31	119	3.52	.280	13	.165	18	16	1.4
1924 Bos-N	15	20	.429	37	32	21	**4**	0	267^2	292	115	96	7	0	53	49	1.289	3.23	118	3.29	.284	20	.222	20	21	1.9
1925 Bos-N	11	16	.407	32	28	17	0	0	216^1	255	127	109	14	1	63	55	1.470	4.53	88	4.29	.297	16	.198	-16	9	-1.5
1926 Bro-N	10	11	.476	31	24	10	1	1	158	204	104	92	6	2	35	29	1.513	5.24	73	4.60	.321	14	.237	-22	4	-2.2
1927 Bro-N	2	10	.167	18	10	2	0	0	78^2	106	64	50	5	0	25	14	1.665	5.72	69	5.37	.331	5	.217	-16	0	-1.6
Total 13	152	150	.503	422	312	179	26	13	2569^2	2686	1150	918	88	25	515	653	1.246	3.22	105	3.15	.273	195	.214	26	156	2.9

• BARNES, Junie Junie Shoaf "Lefty" Barnes b: 12/1/1911, Linwood, NC d: 12/31/1963, Jacksonville, NC BL/TL, 5'11.5", 170 lbs. Deb: 9/12/1934

YEAR TM-L	W	L	PCT	G	GS	CG	SH	SV	IP	H	R	ER	HR	HB	BB	SO	RAT	ERA	ERA+	CERA	OAV	BH	AVG	PR+	WS	TPW
1934 Cin-N	0	0	....	2	0	0	0	0	0^1	0	0	0	0	0	1	0	3.000	0.00	....	5.85	.000	0	....	0	0	0.0

• BARNES, Rich Richard Monroe Barnes b: 7/21/1959, Palm Beach, FL BR/TL, 6'4", 186 lbs. Deb: 7/18/1982

YEAR TM-L	W	L	PCT	G	GS	CG	SH	SV	IP	H	R	ER	HR	HB	BB	SO	RAT	ERA	ERA+	CERA	OAV	BH	AVG	PR+	WS	TPW
1982 Chi-A	0	2	.000	6	2	0	0	1	17	21	15	9	1	2	4	6	1.471	4.76	85	4.73	.292	0	....	-1	0	-0.1
1983 Cle-A	1	1	.500	4	2	0	0	0	11^2	18	10	9	0	0	10	2	2.400	6.94	61	8.44	.375	0	....	-3	0	-0.3
Total 2	1	3	.250	10	4	0	0	1	28^2	39	25	18	1	2	14	8	1.849	5.65	73	6.24	.325	0	....	-5	0	-0.5

• BARNES, Virgil Virgil Jennings "Zeke" Barnes b: 3/5/1897, Ontario, KS d: 7/24/1958, Wichita, KS BR/TR, 6', 165 lbs. Deb: 9/25/1919

YEAR TM-L	W	L	PCT	G	GS	CG	SH	SV	IP	H	R	ER	HR	HB	BB	SO	RAT	ERA	ERA+	CERA	OAV	BH	AVG	PR+	WS	TPW
1919 NY-N	0	0	....	1	0	0	0	0	2	6	4	4	0	0	1	1	3.500	18.00	16	18.28	.545	0	....	-3	0	-0.4

YEAR	TM-L	W	L	PCT	G	GS	CG	SH	SV	IP	H	R	ER	HR	HB	BB	SO	RAT	ERA	ERA+	CERA	OAV	BH	AVG	PR+	WS	TPW
1920	NY-N	0	1	.000	1	1	0	0	0	7	9	3	3	0	0	1	2	1.429	3.86	78	3.95	.310	0	.000	-1	0	-0.1
1922	NY-N	1	0	1.000	22	2	1	0	2	51^2	46	27	20	1	0	11	16	1.103	3.48	115	2.29	.243	2	.167	1	4	0.1
1923*	NY-N	2	3	.400	22	2	0	0	1	53	59	31	23	2	0	19	6	1.472	3.91	98	4.00	.285	0	.000	-1	2	-0.3
1924*	NY-N	16	10	.615	35	29	15	1	3	229^1	239	87	78	10	0	57	59	1.291	3.06	120	3.30	.270	14	.182	15	16	1.2
1925	NY-N	15	11	.577	32	27	17	1	2	221^2	242	110	87	9	1	53	53	1.331	3.53	114	3.53	.281	9	.101	13	17	0.4
1926	NY-N	8	13	.381	31	25	9	2	1	185	183	73	59	4	3	56	54	1.292	2.87	131	3.11	.261	3	.054	16	14	0.8
1927	NY-N	14	11	.560	35	29	12	2	2	228^2	251	116	101	14	4	51	66	1.321	3.98	97	3.70	.283	9	.108	-2	12	-0.9
1928	NY-N	3	3	.500	10	9	3	1	0	55^1	71	32	31	3	0	18	11	1.608	5.04	78	5.06	.330	2	.091	-8	2	-0.9
	Bos-N	2	7	.222	16	10	1	0	0	60^1	86	42	39	3	0	26	7	1.856	5.82	67	6.20	.344	1	.059	-11	0	-1.2
	Yr.	5	10	.333	26	19	4	1	0	115^2	157	74	70	6	0	44	18	1.738	5.45	72	5.66	.338	3	.077	-18	2	-2.1
Total	9	61	59	.508	205	134	58	7	11	1094	1192	525	445	46	8	293	275	1.357	3.66	105	3.67	.281	40	.108	18	67	-1.4

• BARNEY, Rex Rex Edward Barney b: 12/19/1924, Omaha, NE d: 8/12/1997, Baltimore, MD BR/TR, 6'3", 185 lbs. Deb: 8/18/1943

YEAR	TM-L	W	L	PCT	G	GS	CG	SH	SV	IP	H	R	ER	HR	HB	BB	SO	RAT	ERA	ERA+	CERA	OAV	BH	AVG	PR+	WS	TPW
1943	Bro-N	2	2	.500	9	8	1	0	0	45^1	36	32	32	4	2	41	23	1.699	6.35	53	4.60	.217	1	.056	-14	0	-1.7
1946	Bro-N	2	5	.286	16	9	1	0	0	53^2	46	42	35	2	0	51	36	1.807	5.87	58	4.70	.240	4	.235	-15	0	-1.6
1947*	Bro-N	5	2	.714	28	9	0	0	0	77^2	66	52	41	4	2	59	36	1.609	4.75	87	4.29	.240	3	.111	-7	2	-0.8
1948	Bro-N	15	13	.536	44	34	12	4	0	246^2	193	101	85	17	6	122	138	1.277	3.10	129	3.06	.217	14	.167	19	18	1.7
1949*	Bro-N	9	8	.529	38	20	6	2	1	140^2	108	75	69	15	3	89	80	1.400	4.41	93	3.77	.216	10	.213	-7	7	-0.7
1950	Bro-N	2	1	.667	20	1	0	0	0	33^2	25	26	24	6	2	48	23	2.168	6.42	64	7.40	.214	1	.125	-9	0	-0.9
Total	6	35	31	.530	155	81	20	6	1	597^2	474	328	286	48	15	410	336	1.479	4.31	90	3.90	.221	33	.164	-35	27	-4.0

• BARNHART, Edgar Edgar Vernon Barnhart b: 9/16/1904, Providence, MO d: 9/14/1984, Columbia, MO BL/TR, 5'10", 160 lbs. Deb: 9/23/1924

YEAR	TM-L	W	L	PCT	G	GS	CG	SH	SV	IP	H	R	ER	HR	HB	BB	SO	RAT	ERA	ERA+	CERA	OAV	BH	AVG	PR+	WS	TPW
1924	StL-A	0	0	....	1	0	0	0	0	1	0	0	0	0	0	2	0	2.000	0.00	....	2.86	.000	0	....	0	0	0.0

• BARNHART, Les Leslie Earl "Barney" Barnhart b: 2/23/1905, Hoxie, KS d: 10/7/1971, Scottsdale, AZ BR/TR, 6', 180 lbs. Deb: 9/22/1928

YEAR	TM-L	W	L	PCT	G	GS	CG	SH	SV	IP	H	R	ER	HR	HB	BB	SO	RAT	ERA	ERA+	CERA	OAV	BH	AVG	PR+	WS	TPW
1928	Cle-A	0	1	.000	2	1	0	0	0	9	13	7	7	1	0	4	1	1.889	7.00	59	6.73	.325	1	.500	-3	0	-0.2
1930	Cle-A	1	0	1.000	1	1	0	0	0	8^1	12	7	6	0	0	4	1	1.920	6.48	74	6.05	.364	0	.000	-1	0	-0.2
Total	2	1	1	.500	3	2	0	0	0	17^1	25	14	13	1	0	8	2	1.904	6.75	66	6.40	.343	1	.200	-4	0	-0.4

• BARNICLE, George George Bernard "Barney" Barnicle b: 8/26/1917, Fitchburg, MA d: 10/10/1990, Largo, FL BR/TR, 6'2", 175 lbs. Deb: 9/6/1939

YEAR	TM-L	W	L	PCT	G	GS	CG	SH	SV	IP	H	R	ER	HR	HB	BB	SO	RAT	ERA	ERA+	CERA	OAV	BH	AVG	PR+	WS	TPW
1939	Bos-N	2	2	.500	6	1	0	0	0	18^1	16	11	10	1	0	8	15	1.309	4.91	75	3.04	.235	0	.000	-3	0	-0.3
1940	Bos-N	1	0	1.000	13	2	1	0	0	32^2	28	28	27	1	6	31	11	1.806	7.44	50	5.25	.233	0	.000	-14	0	-1.6
1941	Bos-N	0	1	.000	1	1	0	0	0	6^2	5	5	5	0	1	4	2	1.350	6.75	53	3.15	.238	0	.000	-2	0	-0.3
Total	3	3	3	.500	20	4	1	0	0	57^2	49	44	42	2	7	43	28	1.595	6.55	56	4.30	.234	0	.000	-19	0	-2.2

• BARNOWSKI, Ed Edward Anthony Barnowski b: 8/23/1943, Scranton, PA BR/TR, 6'2", 195 lbs. Deb: 9/8/1965

YEAR	TM-L	W	L	PCT	G	GS	CG	SH	SV	IP	H	R	ER	HR	HB	BB	SO	RAT	ERA	ERA+	CERA	OAV	BH	AVG	PR+	WS	TPW
1965	Bal-A	0	0	....	4	0	0	0	0	4^1	3	1	1	0	0	7	6	2.308	2.08	167	6.30	.200	0	....	1	0	0.1
1966	Bal-A	0	0	....	2	0	0	0	0	3	4	1	1	0	0	1	2	1.667	3.00	111	5.24	.364	0	....	0	0	0.0
Total	2	0	0	....	6	0	0	0	0	7^1	7	2	2	0	0	8	8	2.045	2.45	138	5.87	.269	0	....	1	0	0.1

• BAROJAS, Salome Salome (Romero) Barojas b: 6/16/1957, Cordoba, Mexico BR/TR, 5'9", 188 lbs. Deb: 4/11/1982

YEAR	TM-L	W	L	PCT	G	GS	CG	SH	SV	IP	H	R	ER	HR	HB	BB	SO	RAT	ERA	ERA+	CERA	OAV	BH	AVG	PR+	WS	TPW
1982	Chi-A	6	6	.500	61	0	0	0	21	106^2	96	43	42	9	1	46	56	1.331	3.54	114	3.56	.244	0	....	7	11	0.7
1983*	Chi-A	3	3	.500	52	0	0	0	12	87^1	70	24	24	2	5	32	38	1.168	2.47	169	2.63	.224	0	....	16	12	1.6
1984	Chi-A	3	2	.600	24	0	0	0	1	39^1	48	24	20	3	0	19	18	1.703	4.58	91	5.59	.310	0	....	-2	2	-0.2
	Sea-A	6	5	.545	19	14	0	0	1	95^1	88	46	42	12	3	41	37	1.353	3.97	101	4.17	.249	0	....	2	7	0.2
	Yr.	9	7	.563	43	14	0	0	2	134^2	136	70	62	15	3	60	55	1.455	4.14	98	4.58	.268	0	....	0	9	0.0
1985	Sea-A	0	5	.000	17	4	0	0	0	52^2	65	40	35	6	0	33	27	1.861	5.98	70	6.34	.305	0	....	-10	0	-1.0
1988	Phi-N	0	0	....	6	0	0	0	0	8^2	7	9	8	1	0	8	1	1.731	8.31	43	5.33	.250	0	....	-4	0	-0.5
Total	5	18	21	.462	179	18	0	0	35	390	374	186	171	33	9	179	177	1.418	3.95	103	4.12	.257	0	....	9	32	0.9

• BARR, Bob Robert McClelland Barr b: 12/1856, Washington, DC d: 3/11/1930, Washington, DC BR/TR, 6'1", 192 lbs. Deb: 6/23/1883

YEAR	TM-L	W	L	PCT	G	GS	CG	SH	SV	IP	H	R	ER	HR	HB	BB	SO	RAT	ERA	ERA+	CERA	OAV	BH	AVG	PR+	WS	TPW
1883	Pit-a	6	18	.250	26	23	19	0	**1**	203^1	263	166	99	5	....	28	81	1.431	4.38	73	....	.294	35	.246	-23	7	-1.8
1884	Was-a	9	23	.281	32	32	32	2	0	281	311	210	108	9	13	31	138	1.217	3.46	87	....	.266	20	.148	4	4	0.1
	Ind-a	3	11	.214	16	16	15	0	0	132	160	117	73	2	5	19	69	1.356	4.98	66	....	.284	12	.185	-19	2	-1.7
	Yr.	12	34	.261	48	48	47	2	0	413	471	327	181	11	18	50	207	1.262	3.94	79	....	.272	32	.160	-15	6	-1.6
1886	Was-N	3	18	.143	22	23	21	1	0	191^2	221	153	91	7	....	54	80	1.435	4.27	76	....	.278	13	.165	-21	4	-2.0
1890	Roc-a	28	24	.538	57	54	52	3	0	493^1	458	267	178	7	16	219	209	1.372	3.25	109	....	.239	36	.179	14	31	1.2
1891	NY-N	0	4	.000	5	4	2	0	0	27	47	25	16	1	0	12	11	2.185	5.33	60	....	.368	1	.091	-7	0	-0.6
Total	5	49	98	.333	158	152	141	6	1	1328^1	1460	938	565	31	34	363	588	1.372	3.83	86	....	.267	117	.185	-52	48	-4.8

• BARR, Bob Robert Alexander Barr b: 3/12/1908, Newton, MA d: 7/25/2002, Dover, NH BR/TR, 6', 175 lbs. Deb: 9/11/1935

YEAR	TM-L	W	L	PCT	G	GS	CG	SH	SV	IP	H	R	ER	HR	HB	BB	SO	RAT	ERA	ERA+	CERA	OAV	BH	AVG	PR+	WS	TPW
1935	Bro-N	0	0	....	2	0	0	0	0	2^1	5	3	1	0	0	2	0	3.000	3.86	103	11.20	.385	0	....	0	0	0.0

• BARR, Jim James Leland Barr b: 2/10/1948, Lynwood, CA BR/TR, 6'3", 205 lbs. Deb: 7/31/1971

YEAR	TM-L	W	L	PCT	G	GS	CG	SH	SV	IP	H	R	ER	HR	HB	BB	SO	RAT	ERA	ERA+	CERA	OAV	BH	AVG	PR+	WS	TPW
1971*	SF-N	1	1	.500	17	0	0	0	0	35^1	33	15	14	3	1	5	16	1.075	3.57	95	2.73	.254	0	.000	-0	2	-0.1
1972	SF-N	8	10	.444	44	18	8	2	2	179	166	66	57	16	3	41	86	1.156	2.87	122	2.97	.246	9	.184	12	11	1.4
1973	SF-N	11	17	.393	41	33	8	3	2	231^1	240	105	98	24	5	49	88	1.249	3.81	100	3.62	.268	10	.152	2	12	0.2
1974	SF-N	13	9	.591	44	27	11	5	2	239^2	223	81	73	17	2	47	84	1.127	2.74	139	2.77	.251	18	.254	29	23	3.5
1975	SF-N	13	14	.481	35	33	12	2	0	244	244	94	83	17	3	58	77	1.238	3.06	124	3.28	.265	9	.118	20	17	1.8
1976	SF-N	15	12	.556	37	37	8	3	0	252^1	260	104	81	9	2	60	75	1.268	2.89	126	3.17	.266	12	.162	24	20	**2.8**
1977	SF-N	12	16	.429	38	38	6	2	0	234^1	286	130	124	18	3	56	97	1.459	4.76	82	4.61	.306	10	.132	-19	8	-2.1
1978	SF-N	8	11	.421	32	25	5	2	1	163	180	69	64	7	0	35	44	1.319	3.53	98	3.47	.281	5	.100	-1	8	-0.4
1979	Cal-A	10	12	.455	36	25	5	0	0	197	217	100	92	22	3	55	69	1.381	4.20	97	4.40	.287	0	....	-2	9	-0.2
1980	Cal-A	1	4	.200	24	7	0	0	1	68	90	43	42	12	3	23	22	1.662	5.56	71	6.51	.323	0	....	-12	1	-1.2
1982	SF-N	4	3	.571	53	9	1	1	2	128^2	125	54	47	9	4	20	36	1.127	3.29	109	2.89	.262	8	.250	7	8	0.9
1983	SF-N	5	3	.625	53	0	0	0	2	92^2	106	47	41	7	1	20	47	1.360	3.98	89	3.88	.294	2	.133	-4	4	-0.4
Total	12	101	112	.474	454	252	64	20	12	2065^1	2170	908	816	161	30	469	741	1.278	3.56	105	3.59	.273	83	.162	57	123	6.2

• BARR, Steve Steven Charles Barr b: 9/8/1951, St. Louis, MO BL/TL, 6'4", 200 lbs. Deb: 10/1/1974

YEAR	TM-L	W	L	PCT	G	GS	CG	SH	SV	IP	H	R	ER	HR	HB	BB	SO	RAT	ERA	ERA+	CERA	OAV	BH	AVG	PR+	WS	TPW
1974	Bos-A	1	0	1.000	1	1	1	0	0	9	7	4	4	0	0	6	3	1.444	4.00	96	3.17	.212	0	....	-0	1	0.0
1975	Bos-A	0	1	.000	3	2	0	0	0	7	11	9	2	1	0	7	2	2.571	2.57	158	10.80	.367	0	....	1	0	0.1
1976	Tex-A	2	6	.250	20	10	3	0	0	67^2	70	51	42	10	0	44	27	1.685	5.59	64	5.66	.269	0	....	-15	0	-1.6
Total	3	3	7	.300	24	13	4	0	0	83^2	88	64	48	11	0	57	32	1.733	5.16	70	5.82	.272	0	....	-14	1	-1.5

• BARRETT, Dick Tracy Souter "Kewpie Dick" Barrett b: 9/28/1906, Montoursville, PA d: 10/30/1966, Seattle, WA BR/TR, 5'9", 175 lbs. Deb: 6/27/1933

YEAR	TM-L	W	L	PCT	G	GS	CG	SH	SV	IP	H	R	ER	HR	HB	BB	SO	RAT	ERA	ERA+	CERA	OAV	BH	AVG	PR+	WS	TPW
1933	Phi-A	4	4	.500	15	7	3	0	0	70^1	74	51	45	2	1	49	26	1.749	5.76	74	4.81	.272	6	.286	-9	2	-0.8
1934	Bos-N	1	3	.250	15	3	0	0	0	32^1	50	27	24	2	0	12	14	1.918	6.68	57	7.03	.365	1	.143	-10	0	-1.0
1943	Chi-N	0	4	.000	15	4	0	0	0	45	52	28	24	2	1	28	20	1.778	4.80	69	5.33	.291	1	.111	-6	0	-0.8
	Phi-N	10	9	.526	23	20	10	2	1	169^1	137	53	45	5	2	51	65	1.110	2.39	141	2.26	.221	7	.143	20	14	2.2
	Yr.	10	13	.435	38	24	10	2	1	214^1	189	81	69	7	3	79	85	1.250	2.90	116	2.90	.237	8	.138	14	14	1.4
1944	Phi-N	12	18	.400	37	28	11	1	0	221^1	223	110	95	7	3	88	74	1.405	3.86	94	3.54	.262	16	.216	-6	11	-0.4
1945	Phi-N	8	20	.286	36	30	8	0	1	190^2	217	129	114	11	7	92	72	**1.621**	5.38	71	4.79	.281	9	.145	-28	3	-2.9
Total	5	35	58	.376	141	92	32	3	2	729	753	398	347	29	14	320	271	1.472	4.28	87	3.96	.266	40	.180	-39	30	-3.6

• BARRETT, Frank Francis Joseph "Red" Barrett b: 7/1/1913, Fort Lauderdale, FL d: 3/6/1998, Leesburg, FL BR/TR, 6'2", 173 lbs. Deb: 10/1/1939

YEAR	TM-L	W	L	PCT	G	GS	CG	SH	SV	IP	H	R	ER	HR	HB	BB	SO	RAT	ERA	ERA+	CERA	OAV	BH	AVG	PR+	WS	TPW
1939	StL-N	0	1	.000	1	0	0	0	0	1^2	1	1	1	0	0	1	3	1.200	5.40	76	1.90	.167	0	....	-0	0	0.0
1944	Bos-A	8	7	.533	38	2	0	0	8	90^1	93	45	37	5	1	42	40	1.494	3.69	92	4.11	.271	4	.143	-3	5	-0.5
1945	Bos-A	4	3	.571	37	0	0	0	3	86	77	30	25	0	0	29	35	1.233	2.62	130	2.65	.249	5	.250	7	8	0.8
1946	Bos-N	2	4	.333	23	0	0	0	1	35^1	35	21	20	2	1	17	12	1.472	5.09	67	3.87	.252	0	.000	-6	0	-0.8

YEAR	TM-L	W	L	PCT	G	GS	CG	SH	SV	IP	H	R	ER	HR	HB	BB	SO	RAT	ERA	ERA+	CERA	OAV	BH	AVG	PR+	WS	TPW
1950	Pit-N	1	2	.333	5	0	0	0	0	4^1	5	3	2	1	0	1	0	1.385	4.15	105	6.06	.357	0	....	0	0	0.0
Total	5	15	17	.469	104	2	0	0	12	217^2	211	100	85	8	2	90	90	1.383	3.51	98	3.52	.260	9	.167	-3	13	-0.4
• BARRETT, Red		Charles Henry Barrett b: 2/14/1915, Santa Barbara, CA d: 7/28/1990, Wilson, NC BR/TR, 5'11", 183 lbs. Deb: 9/15/1937																									
1937	Cin-N	0	0	....	1	0	0	0	0	6^1	5	1	1	0	0	2	1	1.105	1.42	262	2.15	.227	0	.000	2	1	0.1
1938	Cin-N	2	0	1.000	6	2	2	0	0	28^2	28	13	10	2	0	15	5	1.500	3.14	116	4.08	.257	1	.143	1	2	0.1
1939	Cin-N	0	0	....	2	0	0	0	0	5^1	5	1	1	0	0	1	1	1.125	1.69	227	2.23	.263	0	.000	1	1	0.1
1940	Cin-N	1	0	1.000	3	0	0	0	0	2^2	5	2	2	0	0	1	0	2.250	6.75	56	9.67	.455	0	....	-1	0	-0.1
1943	Bos-N	12	18	.400	38	31	14	3	0	255	240	107	90	11	2	63	64	1.188	3.18	107	2.77	.250	11	.136	4	16	0.0
1944	Bos-N	9	16	.360	42	30	11	1	2	230^1	257	124	104	13	2	63	54	1.389	4.06	94	3.83	.279	13	.173	-7	8	-0.8
1945	Bos-N	2	3	.400	9	5	2	0	2	38	43	22	20	6	1	16	13	1.553	4.74	81	5.22	.281	2	.222	-4	2	-0.4
	StL-N★	21	9	.700	36	29	22	3	0	246^2	244	84	75	12	1	38	63	1.143	2.74	137	2.74	.256	10	.112	22	22	1.7
	Yr.	**23**	12	.657	45	34	**24**	3	2	**284^2**	287	106	95	18	2	54	76	1.198	3.00	125	3.08	.259	12	.122	18	**24**	1.3
1946	StL-N	3	2	.600	23	9	1	1	2	67	75	35	30	5	2	24	22	1.478	4.03	86	4.37	.282	1	.059	-5	2	-0.7
1947	Bos-N	11	12	.478	36	30	12	3	1	210^2	200	102	83	16	2	53	53	1.201	3.55	110	3.01	.244	8	.111	10	12	0.8
1948★	Bos-N	7	8	.467	34	13	3	0	0	128^1	132	56	52	9	0	26	40	1.231	3.65	105	3.26	.268	7	.179	2	7	0.1
1949	Bos-N	1	1	.500	23	0	0	0	0	44^1	58	32	28	4	2	10	17	1.534	5.68	66	5.23	.326	1	.200	-9	0	-0.9
Total	11	69	69	.500	253	149	67	11	7	1263^1	1292	579	496	78	12	312	333	1.270	3.53	105	3.33	.264	54	.136	15	73	-0.1
• BARRETT, Tim		Timothy Wayne Barrett b: 1/24/1961, Huntingburg, IN BL/TR, 6'1", 185 lbs. Deb: 7/18/1988																									
1988	Mon-N	0	0	....	4	0	0	0	1	9^1	10	6	6	2	0	2	5	1.286	5.79	62	4.54	.270	0	.000	-2	0	-0.3
• BARRIOS, Francisco		Francisco Javier (Jimenez) Barrios b: 6/10/1953, Hermosillo, Mexico d: 4/9/1982, Hermosillo, Mexico BR/TR, 5'11", 195 lbs. Deb: 8/18/1974																									
1974	Chi-A	0	0	....	2	0	0	0	0	2	7	6	6	0	0	2	2	4.500	27.00	14	23.57	.538	0	....	-5	0	-0.5
1976	Chi-A	5	9	.357	35	14	6	0	3	141^2	136	72	68	13	4	46	81	1.285	4.32	82	3.60	.255	0	....	-10	6	-1.1
1977	Chi-A	14	7	.667	33	31	9	0	0	231^1	241	117	106	22	5	58	119	1.293	4.12	99	3.75	.267	0	....	6	13	0.6
1978	Chi-A	9	15	.375	33	32	9	2	0	195^2	180	93	88	13	7	85	79	1.354	4.05	94	3.64	.246	0	....	-4	10	-0.4
1979	Chi-A	8	3	.727	15	15	2	0	0	94^2	88	49	38	9	5	33	28	1.278	3.61	118	3.60	.242	0	....	6	6	0.6
1980	Chi-A	1	1	.500	3	3	0	0	0	16^1	21	9	9	4	1	8	2	1.776	4.96	81	7.87	.323	0	....	-2	1	-0.2
1981	Chi-A	1	3	.250	8	7	1	0	0	36^1	45	23	16	3	1	14	12	1.624	3.96	90	5.16	.292	0	....	-2	1	-0.2
Total	7	38	38	.500	129	102	27	2	3	718	718	369	331	64	23	246	323	1.343	4.15	93	3.89	.260	0	....	-10	37	-1.1
• BARRIOS, Manuel		Manuel Antonio Barrios b: 9/21/1974, Cabecera, Panama BR/TR, 6', 170 lbs. Deb: 9/16/1997																									
1997	Hou-N	0	0	....	2	0	0	0	0	3	6	4	4	0	0	3	3	3.000	12.00	33	12.01	.400	0	....	-3	0	-0.3
1998	Fla-N	0	0	....	2	0	0	0	0	2^2	4	1	1	1	0	2	1	2.250	3.38	121	11.95	.364	0	....	0	0	0.0
	LA-N	0	0	....	1	0	0	0	0	1	0	0	0	0	0	2	0	2.000	0.00	....	4.48	.000	0	....	0	0	0.0
	Yr.	0	0	....	3	0	0	0	0	3^2	4	1	1	1	0	4	1	2.182	2.45	167	9.91	.364	0	....	1	0	0.1
Total	2	0	0	....	5	0	0	0	0	6^2	10	5	5	1	0	7	4	2.550	6.75	60	10.86	.385	0	....	-2	0	-0.2
• BARRON, Frank		Frank John Barron b: 8/6/1890, St. Marys, WV d: 9/18/1964, St. Marys, WV BL/TL, 6'1", 175 lbs. Deb: 8/19/1914																									
1914	Was-A	0	0	....	1	0	0	0	0	1	1	0	0	0	0	0	1	1.000	0.00	....	2.02	.333	0	....	0	0	0.0
• BARRY, Ed		Edward "Jumbo" Barry b: 10/2/1882, Madison, WI d: 6/19/1920, Montague, MA BR/TL, 6'3", 185 lbs. Deb: 8/21/1905																									
1905	Bos-A	1	2	.333	7	5	2	0	0	40^2	38	19	13	2	4	15	18	1.303	2.88	94	3.51	.250	1	.091	-1	2	-0.1
1906	Bos-A	0	3	.000	3	3	3	0	0	21	23	22	14	2	3	5	10	1.333	6.00	46	4.10	.281	1	.111	-7	0	-0.8
1907	Bos-A	0	1	.000	2	2	1	0	0	17^1	13	6	4	1	1	5	6	1.038	2.08	124	2.27	.211	0	.000	0	1	0.0
Total	3	1	6	.143	12	10	6	0	0	79	74	47	31	5	8	25	34	1.253	3.53	76	3.40	.250	2	.087	-8	3	-1.0
• BARRY, Hardin		Hardin "Finn" Barry b: 3/26/1891, Susanville, CA d: 11/5/1969, Carson City, NV BR/TR, 6', 185 lbs. Deb: 6/21/1912																									
1912	Phi-A	0	0	....	3	0	0	0	0	13	18	11	11	0	1	4	3	1.692	7.62	41	5.95	.360	0	.000	-7	0	-0.7
• BARRY, Tom		Thomas Arthur Barry b: 4/10/1879, St. Louis, MO d: 6/4/1946, St. Louis, MO TR, 5'9", 155 lbs. Deb: 4/15/1904																									
1904	Phi-N	0	1	.000	1	1	0	0	0	0^2	6	5	3	0	0	1	1	10.50	40.50	7	67.26	.667	0	....	-3	0	-0.3
• BARTHELSON, Bob		Robert Edward Barthelson b: 7/15/1924, New Haven, CT d: 4/14/2000, Branford, CT BR/TR, 6', 185 lbs. Deb: 7/4/1944																									
1944	NY-N	1	1	.500	7	1	0	0	0	9^2	13	9	5	2	0	5	4	1.862	4.66	79	7.21	.310	0	....	-1	0	-0.1
• BARTHOLD, John		John Francis "Hans" Barthold b: 4/14/1882, Philadelphia, PA d: 11/4/1946, Fairview Village, PA BB/TR, 5'11", 180 lbs. Deb: 5/17/1904																									
1904	Phi-A	0	0	....	4	0	0	0	0	10^2	12	9	6	0	1	8	5	1.875	5.06	53	5.46	.285	1	.333	-3	0	-0.2
• BARTHOLOMEW, Les		Lester Justin Bartholomew b: 4/4/1903, Madison, WI d: 9/19/1972, Barrington, IL BR/TL, 5'11.5", 195 lbs. Deb: 4/11/1928																									
1928	Pit-N	0	0	....	6	0	0	0	0	22^2	31	18	18	2	0	9	6	1.765	7.15	57	6.19	.356	1	.143	-8	0	-0.8
1932	Chi-A	0	0	....	3	0	0	0	0	5^1	5	3	3	0	0	6	1	2.063	5.06	85	5.24	.250	0	.000	-0	0	0.0
Total	2	0	0	....	9	0	0	0	0	28	36	21	21	2	0	15	7	1.821	6.75	61	6.01	.336	1	.125	-8	0	-0.8
• BARTLEY, Bill		William Jackson Bartley b: 1/8/1885, Cincinnati, OH d: 5/17/1965, Cincinnati, OH BR/TR, 5'11.5", 190 lbs. Deb: 9/15/1903																									
1903	NY-N	0	0	....	1	0	0	0	0	3	3	4	0	0	0	4	2	2.333	0.00	....	6.79	.273	0	.000	1	0	0.1
1906	Phi-A	0	0	....	3	0	0	0	1	8^2	10	9	9	0	0	6	6	1.846	9.35	29	5.13	.292	1	.333	-6	0	-0.6
1907	Phi-A	0	1	.000	15	3	2	0	0	56^1	44	22	14	0	0	19	16	1.118	2.24	116	2.02	.218	2	.095	2	3	0.1
Total	3	0	1	.000	19	3	2	0	1	68	57	35	23	0	0	29	24	1.265	3.04	87	2.63	.231	3	.120	-3	3	-0.5
• BARTON, Shawn		Shawn Edward Barton b: 5/14/1963, Los Angeles, CA BR/TL, 6'3", 195 lbs. Deb: 8/6/1992																									
1992	Sea-A	0	1	.000	14	0	0	0	0	12^1	10	5	4	1	0	7	4	1.378	2.92	136	3.51	.238	0	....	1	1	0.1
1995	SF-N	4	1	.800	52	0	0	0	1	44^1	37	22	21	3	2	19	22	1.263	4.26	96	3.33	.237	0	....	-1	3	-0.1
1996	SF-N	0	0	....	7	0	0	0	0	8^1	19	12	9	2	0	1	3	2.400	9.72	42	12.24	.442	0	....	-5	0	-0.5
Total	3	4	2	.667	73	0	0	0	1	65	66	39	34	6	2	27	29	1.431	4.71	87	4.51	.274	0	....	-5	4	-0.5
• BARTSON, Charlie		Charles Franklin Bartson b: 3/13/1865, Peoria, IL d: 6/9/1936, Peoria, IL, 6', 170 lbs. Deb: 5/14/1890																									
1890	Chi-P	9	10	.474	25	20	16	0	1	197	226	145	89	8	13	66	52	1.482	4.07	107	....	.276	13	.167	5	12	0.3
• BASKETTE, Jim		James Blaine "Big Jim" Baskette b: 12/10/1887, Athens, TN d: 7/30/1942, Athens, TN BR/TR, 6'2", 185 lbs. Deb: 9/22/1911																									
1911	Cle-A	1	2	.333	4	2	2	0	0	21^1	21	8	8	0	1	9	8	1.406	3.38	101	3.68	.273	2	.333	-0	2	0.0
1912	Cle-A	8	4	.667	29	11	7	1	1	116	109	50	41	2	7	46	51	1.336	3.18	108	3.37	.252	5	.125	1	8	0.1
1913	Cle-A	0	0	....	2	1	0	0	0	4^2	8	3	3	1	0	2	0	2.143	5.79	52	10.25	.400	1	1.000	-1	0	-0.1
Total	3	9	6	.600	35	14	9	1	1	142	138	61	52	3	8	57	59	1.373	3.30	103	3.65	.261	8	.170	-1	10	0.0
• BASS, Dick		Richard William Bass b: 7/7/1906, Rogersville, TN d: 2/3/1989, Graceville, FL BR/TR, 6'2", 175 lbs. Deb: 9/21/1939																									
1939	Was-A	0	1	.000	1	1	0	0	0	8	7	6	6	0	1	6	1	1.625	6.75	64	4.18	.241	0	.000	-2	0	-0.2
• BASS, Norm		Norman Delaney Bass b: 1/21/1939, Laurel, MS BR/TR, 6'3", 205 lbs. Deb: 4/23/1961																									
1961	KC-A	11	11	.500	40	23	6	2	0	170^2	164	98	89	17	4	82	74	1.441	4.69	88	4.28	.255	7	.119	-9	7	-1.1
1962	KC-A	2	6	.250	22	10	0	0	0	75^1	96	55	51	7	0	46	33	1.885	6.09	68	6.50	.317	1	.045	-16	0	-1.7
1963	KC-A	0	0	....	3	1	0	0	0	7^2	11	11	10	2	0	9	4	2.609	11.74	33	11.29	.333	0	.000	-7	0	-0.7
Total	3	13	17	.433	65	34	6	2	0	253^2	271	164	150	26	4	137	111	1.608	5.32	77	5.15	.277	8	.098	-32	7	-3.6
• BATCHELDER, Joe		Joseph Edward "Win" Batchelder b: 7/11/1898, Wenham, MA d: 5/5/1989, Beverly, MA BR/TL, 5'7", 165 lbs. Deb: 9/29/1923																									
1923	Bos-N	1	0	1.000	4	1	1	0	0	9	12	7	7	2	1	1	2	1.444	7.00	57	6.53	.353	0	.000	-3	0	-0.3
1924	Bos-N	0	0	....	3	0	0	0	0	4^2	4	2	2	0	0	2	2	1.286	3.86	99	2.74	.235	0	.000	0	0	0.0
1925	Bos-N	0	0	....	4	0	0	0	0	7	10	5	4	0	0	1	2	1.571	5.14	78	4.28	.357	0	.000	-1	0	-0.1
Total	3	1	0	1.000	11	1	1	0	0	20^2	26	14	13	2	1	4	6	1.452	5.66	70	4.91	.329	0	.000	-4	0	-0.4

YEAR TM-L	W	L	PCT	G	GS	CG	SH	SV	IP	H	R	ER	HR	HB	BB	SO	RAT	ERA	ERA+	CERA	OAV	BH	AVG	PR+	WS	TPW
• BATCHELOR, Rich	Richard Anthony Batchelor b: 4/8/1967, Florence, SC BR/TR, 6'1", 195 lbs. Deb: 9/3/1993																									
1993 StL-N	0	0	....	9	0	0	0	0	10	14	12	9	1	0	3	4	1.700	8.10	49	5.97	.359	0	.000	-5	0	-0.5
1996 StL-N	2	0	1.000	11	0	0	0	0	15	9	2	2	0	0	1	11	.667	1.20	349	0.88	.173	0	.000	5	2	0.4
1997 StL-N	1	1	.500	10	0	0	0	0	16	21	12	8	0	2	7	8	1.750	4.50	92	5.64	.323	0	....	-1	0	-0.1
SD-N	2	0	1.000	13	0	0	0	0	12^2	19	11	11	2	1	7	10	2.053	7.82	49	8.73	.358	0	....	-5	0	-0.5
Yr.	3	1	.750	23	0	0	0	0	28^2	40	23	19	2	3	14	18	1.884	5.97	66	7.01	.339	0	....	-6	0	-0.6
Total 3	5	1	.833	43	0	0	0	0	53^2	63	37	30	3	3	18	33	1.509	5.03	79	5.10	.301	0	.000	-6	2	-0.6
• BATES, Dick	Charles Richard Bates b: 10/7/1945, McArthur, OH BL/TR, 6', 190 lbs. Deb: 4/27/1969																									
1969 Sea-A	0	0	....	1	0	0	0	0	1^2	3	5	5	1	0	3	3	3.600	27.00	13	21.45	.375	0	....	-4	0	-0.4
• BATES, Frank	Creed Frank Bates b: Chattanooga, TN TR Deb: 10/7/1898																									
1898 Cle-N	2	1	.667	4	4	4	0	0	29	30	15	10	0	1	11	5	1.414	3.10	116	3.50	.265	1	.111	1	2	0.1
1899 Cle-N	1	18	.053	20	19	17	0	0	153	239	181	123	6	23	105	13	2.248	7.24	51	8.62	.355	14	.215	-53	1	-4.8
StL-N	0	0	....	2	0	0	0	0	8^2	7	2	1	0	0	5	0	1.385	1.04	383	2.87	.221	1	.333	3	1	0.3
Yr.	1	18	.053	22	19	17	0	0	161^2	246	183	124	6	23	110	13	**2.202**	6.90	53	8.31	.349	15	.221	-50	2	-4.5
Total 2	3	19	.136	26	23	21	0	0	190^2	276	198	134	6	24	121	18	2.082	6.33	58	7.58	.337	16	.208	-49	4	-4.3
• BATES, John	John William Bates b: 5/28/1868, OH d: 3/24/1919, Oakland, CA Deb: 8/25/1889																									
1889 KC-a	0	1	.000	1	1	1	0	0	8	15	14	12	0	0	5	3	2.500	13.50	31	....	.388	0	.000	-8	0	-0.7
• BATISTA, Miguel	Miguel Jerez (Decartes) Batista b: 2/19/1971, Santo Domingo, Dominican Republic BR/TR, 6', 160 lbs. Deb: 4/11/1992																									
1992 Pit-N	0	0	....	1	0	0	0	0	2	4	2	2	1	0	3	1	3.500	9.00	38	20.26	.400	0	....	-1	0	-0.1
1996 Fla-N	0	0	....	9	0	0	0	0	11^1	9	8	7	0	0	7	6	1.412	5.56	73	2.77	.231	0	....	-2	0	-0.2
1997 Chi-N	0	5	.000	11	6	0	0	0	36^1	36	24	23	4	1	24	27	1.651	5.70	76	5.09	.267	0	.000	-6	0	-0.6
1998 Mon-N	3	5	.375	56	13	0	0	0	135	141	66	57	12	6	65	92	1.526	3.80	111	4.70	.274	0	.000	8	6	0.4
1999 Mon-N	8	7	.533	39	17	2	1	1	134^2	146	88	73	10	7	58	95	1.515	4.88	92	4.62	.280	7	.200	-3	6	-0.1
2000 Mon-N	0	1	.000	4	0	0	0	0	8^1	19	14	13	2	2	3	7	2.640	14.04	34	14.73	.452	0	.000	-8	0	-0.8
KC-A	2	6	.250	14	9	0	0	0	57	66	54	49	17	0	34	30	1.754	7.74	66	7.50	.292	0	.000	-18	0	-1.7
2001* Ari-N	11	8	.579	48	18	0	0	0	139^1	113	57	52	13	10	60	90	1.242	3.36	136	3.43	.226	2	.063	17	11	1.5
2002* Ari-N	8	9	.471	36	29	1	0	0	184^2	172	99	88	12	6	70	112	1.310	4.29	103	3.45	.245	8	.157	5	9	0.6
2003 Ari-N	10	9	.526	36	29	2	1	0	193^1	197	85	76	13	8	60	142	1.329	3.54	132	3.77	.267	4	.070	26	14	2.2
Total 9	42	50	.457	254	121	5	2	1	902	903	497	440	84	40	384	602	1.427	4.39	103	4.33	.263	21	.096	18	46	1.2
• BATTON, Chris	Christopher Sean Batton b: 8/24/1954, Los Angeles, CA BR/TR, 6'4", 195 lbs. Deb: 9/19/1976																									
1976 Oak-A	0	0	....	2	1	0	0	0	4	5	4	4	1	0	3	4	2.000	9.00	37	8.64	.313	0	....	-2	0	-0.3
• BAUER, Al	Albert Bauer b: 8/7/1859, Columbus, OH d: 2/23/1944, Columbus, OH TL Deb: 9/22/1884 U																									
1884 Col-a	1	2	.333	3	3	3	0	0	25	22	21	13	1	0	14	13	1.440	4.68	65	....	.224	3	.273	-5	1	-0.4
1886 StL-N	0	4	.000	4	4	3	0	0	28^2	31	27	19	1	....	27	13	2.023	5.97	54	....	.266	2	.167	-10	0	-0.9
Total 2	1	6	.143	7	7	6	0	0	53^2	53	48	32	2	0	41	26	1.752	5.37	58	....	.246	5	.217	-15	1	-1.4
• BAUER, Lou	Louis Walter Bauer b: 11/30/1898, Egg Harbor City, NJ d: 2/4/1979, Pomona, NJ BR/TR, 6', 175 lbs. Deb: 8/13/1918																									
1918 Phi-A	0	0	....	1	0	0	0	0	0	0	2	1	0	0	2	0	....	∞	....	∞	.000	0	....	-1	0	-0.1
• BAUER, Rick	Richard Edward Bauer b: 1/10/1977, Garden Grove, CA BR/TR, 6'6", 212 lbs. Deb: 9/2/2001																									
2001 Bal-A	0	5	.000	6	6	0	0	0	33	35	22	17	7	1	9	16	1.333	4.64	92	4.74	.265	0	....	-2	0	-0.2
2002 Bal-A	6	7	.462	56	1	0	0	1	83^2	84	41	37	12	4	36	45	1.434	3.98	108	4.78	.268	0	....	2	5	0.2
2003 Bal-A	0	0	....	35	0	0	0	0	61^1	58	36	31	5	4	24	43	1.337	4.55	97	3.87	.256	0	....	-1	2	-0.1
Total 3	6	12	.333	97	7	0	0	1	178	177	99	85	24	9	69	104	1.382	4.30	101	4.46	.263	0	....	-1	7	-0.1
• BAUERS, Russ	Russell Lee Bauers b: 5/10/1914, Townsend, WI d: 1/21/1995, Hines, IL BL/TR, 6'3", 195 lbs. Deb: 8/20/1936																									
1936 Pit-N	0	0	....	1	1	0	0	0	1^1	2	5	5	0	0	4	0	4.500	33.75	12	14.66	.400	0	....	-4	0	-0.4
1937 Pit-N	13	6	.684	34	19	11	2	1	187^2	174	70	60	2	4	80	118	1.353	2.88	134	3.11	.245	15	.217	19	17	2.0
1938 Pit-N	13	14	.481	40	34	12	2	3	243	207	102	83	7	6	99	117	1.259	3.07	123	2.86	.233	21	.239	15	19	1.9
1939 Pit-N	2	4	.333	15	8	1	0	1	53^2	46	27	20	4	1	25	12	1.323	3.35	114	3.37	.240	4	.211	4	3	0.4
1940 Pit-N	0	2	.000	15	2	0	0	0	30^2	42	29	26	2	2	18	11	1.957	7.63	50	6.73	.323	2	.286	-12	0	-1.2
1941 Pit-N	1	3	.250	8	5	1	0	0	37^1	40	28	23	1	0	25	20	1.741	5.54	65	4.69	.267	5	.357	-8	1	-0.7
1946 Chi-N	2	1	.667	15	2	2	0	1	43^1	45	17	17	1	1	19	22	1.477	3.53	94	3.88	.273	3	.300	-0	3	0.1
1950 StL-A	0	0	....	1	0	0	0	0	2	6	4	1	0	0	1	0	3.500	4.50	110	19.99	.600	0	....	0	0	0.0
Total 8	31	30	.508	129	71	27	4	6	599	562	282	235	17	14	271	300	1.391	3.53	107	3.45	.250	50	.242	15	43	2.1
• BAUMANN, Frank	Frank Matt "Beau" Baumann b: 7/1/1933, St. Louis, MO BL/TL, 6', 210 lbs. Deb: 7/31/1955																									
1955 Bos-A	2	1	.667	7	5	0	0	0	34	38	28	22	2	1	17	27	1.618	5.82	74	4.90	.281	3	.231	-5	0	-0.5
1956 Bos-A	2	1	.667	7	1	0	0	0	24^2	22	11	9	3	0	14	18	1.459	3.28	141	4.27	.234	3	.333	4	3	0.5
1957 Bos-A	1	0	1.000	4	1	0	0	0	12	13	5	5	1	1	3	7	1.333	3.75	106	4.15	.277	1	.500	1	1	0.1
1958 Bos-A	2	2	.500	10	7	2	0	0	52^1	56	27	26	4	4	27	31	1.586	4.47	90	5.05	.276	3	.214	-2	3	-0.1
1959 Bos-A	6	4	.600	26	10	2	0	1	95^2	96	47	43	11	1	55	48	1.578	4.05	100	4.86	.259	6	.207	-0	6	0.1
1960 Chi-A	13	6	.684	47	20	7	2	3	185^1	169	67	55	11	1	53	71	1.198	**2.67**	141	2.93	.247	8	.154	20	16	2.1
1961 Chi-A	10	13	.435	53	23	5	1	3	187^2	249	128	117	22	2	59	75	**1.641**	5.61	70	5.73	.318	16	.262	-34	4	-2.8
1962 Chi-A	7	6	.538	40	10	3	1	4	119^2	117	46	45	10	2	36	55	1.279	3.38	115	3.50	.258	8	.267	8	11	1.2
1963 Chi-A	2	1	.667	24	1	0	0	1	50^1	52	22	17	2	0	17	31	1.371	3.04	115	3.54	.265	1	.091	2	3	0.2
1964 Chi-A	0	3	.000	22	0	0	0	1	32	40	22	22	4	0	16	19	1.750	6.19	56	5.75	.320	0	.000	-11	0	-1.2
1965 Chi-N	0	1	.000	4	0	0	0	0	3^2	4	3	3	0	0	3	2	1.909	7.36	50	5.65	.286	0	....	-1	0	-0.2
Total 11	45	38	.542	244	78	19	4	13	797^1	856	406	364	70	12	300	384	1.450	4.11	95	4.35	.276	49	.218	-19	47	-0.6
• BAUMGARDNER, George	George Washington Baumgardner b: 7/22/1891, Barboursville, WV d: 12/13/1970, Barboursville, WV BL/TR, 5'11", 178 lbs. Deb: 4/14/1912																									
1912 StL-A	11	13	.458	30	27	18	2	0	218^1	222	101	82	1	11	79	102	1.379	3.38	99	3.62	.274	11	.145	-4	13	-0.3
1913 StL-A	10	20	.333	38	31	23	2	1	253^1	267	119	88	6	10	84	78	1.386	3.13	94	3.97	.283	13	.167	-9	12	-0.7
1914 StL-A	16	14	.533	45	18	9	3	3	183^2	152	72	57	3	8	84	93	1.285	2.79	97	2.94	.229	7	.132	0	12	-0.1
1915 StL-A	0	2	.000	7	1	1	0	0	22^1	29	15	11	0	0	11	6	1.791	4.43	65	6.03	.358	0	.000	-4	0	-0.5
1916 StL-A	1	0	1.000	4	2	0	0	0	8	12	8	7	0	0	5	4	2.125	7.88	35	7.38	.364	0	.000	-5	0	-0.5
Total 5	38	49	.437	124	79	51	7	4	685^2	682	315	245	10	29	263	283	1.378	3.22	93	3.69	.269	31	.144	-22	37	-2.2
• BAUMGARTEN, Ross	Ross Baumgarten b: 5/27/1955, Highland Park, IL BL/TL, 6'1", 180 lbs. Deb: 8/16/1978																									
1978 Chi-A	2	2	.500	7	4	1	1	0	23	29	15	15	3	1	9	15	1.652	5.87	65	5.96	.315	0	....	-5	0	-0.5
1979 Chi-A	13	8	.619	28	28	4	3	0	190^2	175	82	75	18	1	83	72	1.353	3.54	120	3.71	.243	0	....	14	13	1.4
1980 Chi-A	2	12	.143	24	23	3	1	0	136	127	60	52	10	1	52	66	1.316	3.44	117	3.56	.256	0	....	10	8	1.0
1981 Chi-A	5	9	.357	19	19	2	1	0	101^2	101	56	46	9	1	40	52	1.387	4.07	88	3.95	.260	0	....	-7	3	-0.7
1982 Pit-N	0	5	.000	12	10	0	0	0	44	60	33	33	3	0	27	17	1.977	6.75	55	7.05	.349	1	.083	-15	0	-1.6
Total 5	22	36	.379	90	84	10	6	0	495^1	492	246	221	43	4	211	222	1.419	4.02	98	4.12	.263	1	.083	-2	24	-0.4
• BAUMGARTNER, Harry	Harry E. Baumgartner b: 10/6/1892, South Pittsburg, TN d: 12/3/1930, Augusta, GA BR/TR, 5'11", 175 lbs. Deb: 9/6/1920																									
1920 Det-A	0	1	.000	9	0	0	0	0	18	18	10	8	1	0	6	7	1.333	4.00	93	3.67	.273	1	.250	-0	1	0.0
• BAUMGARTNER, Stan	Stanwood Fulton Baumgartner b: 12/14/1894, Houston, TX d: 10/4/1955, Philadelphia, PA BL/TL, 6', 175 lbs. Deb: 6/26/1914																									
1914 Phi-N	2	2	.500	15	3	2	1	0	60^1	60	29	22	0	2	16	24	1.260	3.28	89	2.99	.270	1	.053	-0	2	-0.2
1915 Phi-N	0	2	.000	16	1	0	0	0	48^1	38	22	13	2	1	23	27	1.262	2.42	113	2.88	.226	1	.083	2	2	0.1
1916 Phi-N	0	0	....	1	0	0	0	0	4	5	2	1	0	0	1	0	1.500	2.25	118	4.25	.333	0	.000	0	0	0.0
1921 Phi-N	3	6	.333	22	7	2	0	0	66^2	103	72	52	8	2	22	13	1.875	7.02	60	7.05	.355	6	.200	-19	0	-1.9
1922 Phi-N	1	1	.500	6	1	0	0	0	9^2	18	9	7	1	0	5	2	2.379	6.52	72	9.90	.409	1	.333	-2	0	-0.1

YEAR	TM-L	W	L	PCT	G	GS	CG	SH	SV	IP	H	R	ER	HR	HB	BB	SO	RAT	ERA	ERA+	CERA	OAV	BH	AVG	PR+	WS	TPW
1924	Phi-A	13	6	.684	36	16	12	1	4	181	181	72	58	6	4	73	45	1.403	2.88	**149**	3.63	.271	13	.217	30	20	2.8
1925	Phi-A	6	3	.667	37	11	2	1	3	113^{1}	120	55	45	2	7	35	18	1.368	3.57	130	3.57	.275	7	.233	15	10	1.4
1926	Phi-A	1	1	.500	10	1	0	0	0	22^{1}	28	10	10	0	2	10	0	1.701	4.03	103	5.23	.326	1	.333	0	2	0.1
Total	8	26	21	.553	143	40	18	3	7	505^{2}	553	271	208	19	18	185	129	1.459	3.70	108	4.11	.287	30	.190	25	36	2.2

• BAUSEWINE, George George W. Bausewine b: 3/22/1869, Philadelphia, PA d: 7/29/1947, Norristown, PA, 6'2", 207 lbs. Deb: 9/14/1889 U

YEAR	TM-L	W	L	PCT	G	GS	CG	SH	SV	IP	H	R	ER	HR	HB	BB	SO	RAT	ERA	ERA+	CERA	OAV	BH	AVG	PR+	WS	TPW
1889	Phi-a	1	4	.200	7	6	6	0	0	55^{1}	64	46	24	1	0	33	18	1.753	3.90	97	....	.281	1	.048	-3	2	-0.4

• BAUTA, Ed Eduardo (Galvez) Bauta b: 1/6/1935, Florida, Cuba BR/TR, 6'3", 200 lbs. Deb: 7/6/1960

YEAR	TM-L	W	L	PCT	G	GS	CG	SH	SV	IP	H	R	ER	HR	HB	BB	SO	RAT	ERA	ERA+	CERA	OAV	BH	AVG	PR+	WS	TPW
1960	StL-N	0	0	....	9	0	0	0	1	15^{2}	14	11	11	4	1	11	6	1.596	6.32	65	5.99	.237	0	.000	-4	0	-0.4
1961	StL-N	2	0	1.000	13	0	0	0	5	19^{1}	12	5	3	2	0	5	12	.879	1.40	315	1.60	.171	2	.500	6	5	0.7
1962	StL-N	1	0	1.000	20	0	0	0	1	32^{1}	28	18	18	5	1	21	25	1.515	5.01	85	4.86	.239	1	.250	-3	1	-0.3
1963	StL-N	3	4	.429	38	0	0	0	3	52^{2}	55	26	23	2	2	21	30	1.443	3.93	90	3.98	.279	0	.000	-2	3	-0.3
	NY-N	0	0	....	9	0	0	0	0	19	22	11	11	0	0	9	13	1.632	5.21	67	4.50	.289	0	.000	-3	0	-0.4
	Yr.	3	4	.429	47	0	0	0	3	71^{2}	77	37	34	2	2	30	43	1.493	4.27	83	4.12	.282	0	.000	-6	3	-0.7
1964	NY-N	0	2	.000	8	0	0	0	1	10	17	6	6	1	0	3	3	2.000	5.40	66	8.08	.395	0	....	-2	0	-0.2
Total	5	6	6	.500	97	0	0	0	11	149	148	77	72	14	4	70	89	1.463	4.35	88	4.41	.263	3	.176	-8	9	-0.9

• BAUTISTA, Jose Jose Joaquin (Arias) Bautista b: 7/25/1964, Bani, Dominican Republic BR/TR, 6'1", 205 lbs. Deb: 4/9/1988

YEAR	TM-L	W	L	PCT	G	GS	CG	SH	SV	IP	H	R	ER	HR	HB	BB	SO	RAT	ERA	ERA+	CERA	OAV	BH	AVG	PR+	WS	TPW
1988	Bal-A	6	15	.286	33	25	3	0	0	171^{2}	171	86	82	21	7	45	76	1.258	4.30	91	3.81	.258	0	....	-9	7	-0.9
1989	Bal-A	3	4	.429	15	10	0	0	0	78	84	46	46	17	1	15	30	1.269	5.31	71	4.56	.274	0	....	-14	1	-1.4
1990	Bal-A	1	0	1.000	22	0	0	0	0	26^{2}	28	15	12	4	0	7	15	1.313	4.05	94	4.01	.272	0	....	-1	1	-0.1
1991	Bal-A	0	1	.000	5	0	0	0	0	5^{1}	13	10	10	1	1	5	3	3.375	16.88	23	18.61	.464	0	....	-8	0	-0.8
1993	Chi-N	10	3	.769	58	7	1	0	2	111^{2}	105	38	35	11	5	27	63	1.182	2.82	141	3.30	.250	4	.190	13	13	1.3
1994	Chi-N	4	5	.444	58	0	0	0	1	69^{1}	75	30	30	10	3	17	45	1.327	3.89	107	4.30	.284	0	.000	2	5	0.1
1995	SF-N	3	8	.273	52	6	0	0	0	100^{2}	120	77	72	24	5	26	45	1.450	6.44	63	5.68	.295	0	.000	-27	0	-2.8
1996	SF-N	3	4	.429	37	1	0	0	0	69^{2}	66	32	26	10	2	15	28	1.163	3.36	122	3.33	.249	1	.111	5	4	0.5
1997	Det-A	2	2	.500	21	0	0	0	0	40^{1}	55	32	30	6	2	12	19	1.661	6.69	69	6.29	.324	0	....	-10	0	-0.9
	StL-N	0	0	....	11	0	0	0	0	12^{1}	15	10	9	2	1	2	4	1.378	6.57	63	4.78	.300	0	....	-3	0	-0.3
Total	9	32	42	.432	312	49	4	0	3	685^{2}	732	376	352	106	27	171	328	1.317	4.62	87	4.37	.273	5	.100	-52	31	-5.4

• BAYNE, Bill William Lear "Beverly" Bayne b: 4/18/1899, Pittsburgh, PA d: 5/22/1981, St. Louis, MO BL/TL, 5'9", 160 lbs. Deb: 9/20/1919

YEAR	TM-L	W	L	PCT	G	GS	CG	SH	SV	IP	H	R	ER	HR	HB	BB	SO	RAT	ERA	ERA+	CERA	OAV	BH	AVG	PR+	WS	TPW
1919	StL-A	1	1	.500	2	2	1	0	0	12	16	8	7	0	0	6	0	1.833	5.25	63	5.55	.320	2	.400	-3	0	-0.2
1920	StL-A	5	6	.455	18	13	6	1	0	99^{2}	102	51	41	3	7	41	38	1.435	3.70	106	4.03	.279	6	.171	2	6	0.0
1921	StL-A	11	5	.688	47	14	6	1	3	164	167	103	86	8	5	80	82	1.506	4.72	95	4.13	.270	18	.300	-4	11	0.1
1922	StL-A	4	5	.444	26	9	3	0	2	92^{2}	86	49	47	5	9	37	38	1.327	4.56	91	3.56	.249	7	.233	-7	4	-0.7
1923	StL-A	2	2	.500	19	2	0	0	0	46	49	25	23	4	3	31	15	1.739	4.50	93	5.71	.287	3	.231	-2	2	-0.2
1924	StL-A	1	3	.250	22	3	0	0	0	50^{2}	47	29	25	4	7	29	20	1.500	4.44	102	4.48	.250	6	.429	-0	4	0.2
1928	Cle-A	2	5	.286	37	6	3	0	3	108^{2}	128	68	62	3	10	43	39	1.574	5.13	81	4.78	.309	11	.367	-11	5	-0.9
1929	Bos-A	5	5	.500	27	6	2	0	0	84^{1}	111	72	63	9	8	29	26	1.660	6.72	64	6.00	.326	8	.320	-23	1	-1.9
1930	Bos-A	0	0	....	1	0	0	0	0	4	5	2	2	1	0	1	1	1.500	4.50	102	5.82	.294	1	.500	0	0	0.0
Total	9	31	32	.492	199	55	21	2	8	662	711	407	356	37	49	297	259	1.523	4.84	87	4.55	.283	62	.290	-47	33	-3.5

• BEALL, Walter Walter Esau Beall b: 7/29/1899, Washington, DC d: 1/28/1959, Suitland, MD BR/TR, 5'10", 178 lbs. Deb: 9/3/1924

YEAR	TM-L	W	L	PCT	G	GS	CG	SH	SV	IP	H	R	ER	HR	HB	BB	SO	RAT	ERA	ERA+	CERA	OAV	BH	AVG	PR+	WS	TPW
1924	NY-A	2	0	1.000	4	2	0	0	0	23	19	11	9	2	0	17	18	1.565	3.52	118	4.35	.237	1	.143	1	2	0.1
1925	NY-A	0	1	.000	8	1	0	0	0	11^{1}	11	17	16	0	3	19	8	2.647	12.71	34	8.90	.282	0	.000	-11	0	-1.0
1926	NY-A	2	4	.333	20	9	1	0	1	81^{2}	71	46	32	2	6	68	56	1.702	3.53	109	4.41	.240	3	.136	4	4	0.4
1927	NY-A	0	0	....	1	0	0	0	0	1	1	1	1	0	0	0	0	1.000	9.00	43	1.95	.333	0	....	-1	0	-0.1
1929	Was-A	1	0	1.000	3	0	0	0	0	7	8	4	3	0	0	7	3	2.143	3.86	110	6.39	.348	0	.000	0	0	0.0
Total	5	5	5	.500	36	12	1	0	1	124	110	79	61	4	9	111	85	1.782	4.43	91	4.90	.249	4	.114	-5	6	-0.6

• BEAM, Alex Alexander Rodger Beam b: 11/21/1870, Johnstown, PA d: 4/17/1938, Nogales, AZ Deb: 5/25/1889

YEAR	TM-L	W	L	PCT	G	GS	CG	SH	SV	IP	H	R	ER	HR	HB	BB	SO	RAT	ERA	ERA+	CERA	OAV	BH	AVG	PR+	WS	TPW
1889	Pit-N	1	1	.500	2	2	2	0	0	18	11	16	13	0	0	15	1	1.444	6.50	58	....	.171	1	.167	-6	0	-0.5

• BEAM, Ernie Ernest Joseph Beam b: 3/17/1867, Mansfield, OH d: 9/13/1918, Mansfield, OH TR, 6'.5", 185 lbs. Deb: 5/2/1895

YEAR	TM-L	W	L	PCT	G	GS	CG	SH	SV	IP	H	R	ER	HR	HB	BB	SO	RAT	ERA	ERA+	CERA	OAV	BH	AVG	PR+	WS	TPW
1895	Phi-N	0	2	.000	9	1	1	0	**3**	24^{2}	33	33	31	1	0	25	3	2.351	11.31	42	7.86	.316	2	.182	-18	0	-1.5

• BEAMON, Charlie Charles Alfonzo Beamon, Sr. b: 12/25/1934, Oakland, CA BR/TR, 5'11", 195 lbs. Deb: 9/26/1956

YEAR	TM-L	W	L	PCT	G	GS	CG	SH	SV	IP	H	R	ER	HR	HB	BB	SO	RAT	ERA	ERA+	CERA	OAV	BH	AVG	PR+	WS	TPW
1956	Bal-A	2	0	1.000	2	1	1	1	0	13	9	2	2	0	0	8	14	1.308	1.38	283	2.55	.191	0	.000	4	2	0.3
1957	Bal-A	0	0	....	4	1	0	0	0	8^{2}	8	6	5	1	1	7	5	1.731	5.19	69	5.57	.229	0	.000	-2	0	-0.2
1958	Bal-A	1	3	.250	21	3	0	0	0	49^{2}	47	27	24	3	6	21	26	1.369	4.35	83	4.21	.266	0	.000	-4	1	-0.5
Total	3	3	3	.500	27	5	1	1	0	71^{1}	64	35	31	4	7	36	45	1.402	3.91	92	4.07	.247	0	.000	-2	3	-0.4

• BEAN, Belve Beveric Benton "Bill" Bean b: 4/25/1905, Mullin, TX d: 6/1/1988, Comanche, TX BR/TR, 6'1.5", 197 lbs. Deb: 5/30/1930

YEAR	TM-L	W	L	PCT	G	GS	CG	SH	SV	IP	H	R	ER	HR	HB	BB	SO	RAT	ERA	ERA+	CERA	OAV	BH	AVG	PR+	WS	TPW
1930	Cle-A	3	3	.500	23	3	1	0	2	74^{1}	99	58	45	7	0	32	19	1.762	5.45	88	6.11	.331	9	.346	-4	4	-0.2
1931	Cle-A	0	1	.000	4	0	0	0	0	7	11	5	5	0	1	4	3	2.143	6.43	72	7.59	.379	0	.000	-1	0	-0.1
1933	Cle-A	1	2	.333	27	2	0	0	0	70^{1}	80	43	41	6	1	20	41	1.422	5.25	85	4.47	.300	4	.182	-6	2	-0.7
1934	Cle-A	5	1	.833	21	1	0	0	0	51^{1}	53	25	22	2	3	21	20	1.442	3.86	118	3.95	.265	3	.200	4	4	0.4
1935	Cle-A	0	0	....	1	0	0	0	0	1	2	1	1	1	0	0	0	2.000	9.00	50	16.28	.400	0	....	-0	0	0.0
	Was-A	2	0	1.000	10	2	0	0	0	31	43	28	25	5	0	19	6	2.000	7.26	60	7.81	.339	3	.375	-10	1	-0.7
	Yr.	2	0	1.000	11	2	0	0	0	32	45	29	26	6	0	19	6	2.000	7.31	59	8.07	.341	3	.375	-10	1	-0.7
Total	5	11	7	.611	86	8	1	0	2	235	288	160	139	21	5	96	89	1.634	5.32	86	5.46	.311	19	.264	-18	11	-1.3

• BEARD, Dave Charles David Beard b: 10/2/1959, Atlanta, GA BL/TR, 6'5", 215 lbs. Deb: 7/16/1980

YEAR	TM-L	W	L	PCT	G	GS	CG	SH	SV	IP	H	R	ER	HR	HB	BB	SO	RAT	ERA	ERA+	CERA	OAV	BH	AVG	PR+	WS	TPW
1980	Oak-A	0	1	.000	13	0	0	0	1	16	12	6	6	0	1	7	12	1.188	3.38	112	2.49	.218	0	....	1	1	0.1
1981*	Oak-A	1	1	.500	8	0	0	0	3	13	9	5	4	1	1	4	15	1.000	2.77	126	2.13	.191	0	....	1	2	0.1
1982	Oak-A	10	9	.526	54	2	0	0	11	91^{2}	85	41	35	9	1	35	73	1.309	3.44	114	3.44	.244	0	....	5	9	0.5
1983	Oak-A	5	5	.500	43	0	0	0	10	61	55	39	38	8	2	36	40	1.492	5.61	69	4.56	.246	0	....	-12	2	-1.2
1984	Sea-A	3	2	.600	43	0	0	0	5	76	88	56	49	15	4	33	40	1.592	5.80	69	5.90	.291	0	....	-14	1	-1.4
1985	Chi-N	0	0	....	9	0	0	0	0	12^{2}	16	9	9	2	0	7	4	1.816	6.39	62	6.52	.314	0	....	-3	0	-0.3
1989	Det-A	0	2	.000	2	1	0	0	0	5^{1}	9	7	3	2	1	2	1	2.063	5.06	75	11.90	.375	0	....	-1	0	-0.1
Total	7	19	20	.487	172	3	0	0	30	275^{2}	274	163	144	37	10	124	185	1.444	4.70	83	4.56	.261	0	....	-24	15	-2.4

• BEARD, Mike Michael Richard Beard b: 6/21/1950, Little Rock, AR BL/TL, 6'1", 185 lbs. Deb: 9/7/1974

YEAR	TM-L	W	L	PCT	G	GS	CG	SH	SV	IP	H	R	ER	HR	HB	BB	SO	RAT	ERA	ERA+	CERA	OAV	BH	AVG	PR+	WS	TPW
1974	Atl-N	0	0	....	6	0	0	0	0	9^{1}	5	3	3	1	1	1	7	.643	2.89	131	1.36	.156	0	....	1	1	0.1
1975	Atl-N	4	0	1.000	34	2	0	0	0	70^{1}	71	31	25	4	2	28	27	1.408	3.20	118	3.75	.265	1	.111	6	5	0.6
1976	Atl-N	0	2	.000	30	0	0	0	1	33^{2}	38	18	16	1	0	14	8	1.545	4.28	89	4.17	.299	0	.000	-1	1	-0.1
1977	Atl-N	0	0	....	4	0	0	0	0	4^{2}	14	11	5	3	0	2	1	3.429	9.64	46	21.96	.452	0	....	-3	0	-0.3
Total	4	4	2	.667	74	2	0	0	1	118	128	63	49	9	3	45	43	1.466	3.74	103	4.40	.279	1	.100	3	7	0.3

• BEARD, Ralph Ralph William Beard b: 2/11/1929, Cincinnati, OH d: 2/10/2003, West Palm Beach, FL BR/TR, 6'5", 200 lbs. Deb: 6/29/1954

YEAR	TM-L	W	L	PCT	G	GS	CG	SH	SV	IP	H	R	ER	HR	HB	BB	SO	RAT	ERA	ERA+	CERA	OAV	BH	AVG	PR+	WS	TPW
1954	StL-N	0	4	.000	13	10	0	0	0	58	62	32	24	2	2	28	17	1.552	3.72	110	4.29	.278	1	.059	3	2	0.2

• BEARDEN, Gene Henry Eugene Bearden b: 9/5/1920, Lexa, AR BL/TL, 6'3", 204 lbs. Deb: 5/10/1947

YEAR	TM-L	W	L	PCT	G	GS	CG	SH	SV	IP	H	R	ER	HR	HB	BB	SO	RAT	ERA	ERA+	CERA	OAV	BH	AVG	PR+	WS	TPW
1947	Cle-A	0	0	....	1	0	0	0	0	0^{1}	2	3	3	0	0	1	0	9.000	81.00	4	54.30	.667	0	....	-3	0	-0.3
1948*	Cle-A	20	7	.741	37	29	15	6	1	229^{2}	187	72	62	9	3	106	80	1.276	**2.43**	**167**	2.95	.229	23	.256	37	22	4.0
1949	Cle-A	8	8	.500	32	19	5	0	0	127	140	77	72	6	2	92	41	1.827	5.10	78	5.47	.286	5	.111	-17	2	-2.0
1950	Cle-A	1	3	.250	14	3	0	0	0	45^{1}	57	32	31	5	0	32	10	1.963	6.15	70	7.07	.328	2	.154	-9	0	-0.8
	Was-A	3	5	.375	12	9	4	0	0	68^{1}	81	35	32	1	2	33	20	1.668	4.21	107	4.84	.297	5	.227	2	5	0.3
	Yr.	4	8	.333	26	12	4	0	0	113^{2}	138	67	63	6	2	65	30	1.786	4.99	88	5.73	.309	7	.200	-7	5	-0.5

YEAR	TM-L	W	L	PCT	G	GS	CG	SH	SV	IP	H	R	ER	HR	HB	BB	SO	RAT	ERA	ERA+	CERA	OAV	BH	AVG	PR+	WS	TPW
1951	Was-A	0	0	....	1	1	0	0	0	2^2	6	5	5	0	0	2	1	3.000	16.88	24	12.35	.429	0	....	-4	0	-0.4
	Det-A	3	4	.429	37	4	2	1	0	106	112	58	51	6	1	58	38	1.604	4.33	96	4.56	.275	6	.188	-1	6	0.0
	Yr.	3	4	.429	38	5	2	1	0	108^2	118	63	56	6	1	60	39	1.638	4.64	90	4.75	.280	6	.188	-5	6	-0.4
1952	StL-A	7	8	.467	34	16	3	0	0	150^2	158	89	72	13	1	78	45	1.566	4.30	91	4.59	.270	23	.354	-7	7	-0.1
1953	Chi-A	3	3	.500	25	3	0	0	0	58^1	48	27	19	8	0	33	24	1.389	2.93	137	3.88	.223	4	.190	7	4	0.6
Total	**7**	**45**	**38**	**.542**	**193**	**84**	**29**	**7**	**1**	**788^1**	**791**	**398**	**347**	**48**	**9**	**435**	**259**	**1.555**	**3.96**	**103**	**4.41**	**.266**	**68**	**.236**	**4**	**46**	**1.4**

• BEARE, Gary

Gary Ray Beare b: 8/22/1952, San Diego, CA BR/TR, 6'4", 205 lbs. Deb: 9/7/1976

YEAR	TM-L	W	L	PCT	G	GS	CG	SH	SV	IP	H	R	ER	HR	HB	BB	SO	RAT	ERA	ERA+	CERA	OAV	BH	AVG	PR+	WS	TPW
1976	Mil-A	2	3	.400	6	5	2	0	0	41	43	16	15	4	0	15	32	1.415	3.29	106	4.31	.274	0	....	1	2	0.1
1977	Mil-A	3	3	.500	17	6	0	0	0	58^2	63	46	42	6	1	38	32	1.722	6.44	63	5.47	.276	0	....	-16	0	-1.6
Total	**2**	**5**	**6**	**.455**	**23**	**11**	**2**	**0**	**0**	**99^2**	**106**	**62**	**57**	**10**	**1**	**53**	**64**	**1.595**	**5.15**	**76**	**4.99**	**.275**	**0**	**....**	**-15**	**2**	**-1.5**

• BEARNARTH, Larry

Lawrence Donald Bearnarth b: 9/11/1941, New York, NY d: 12/31/1999, Seminole, FL BR/TR, 6'2", 203 lbs. Deb: 4/16/1963 C

YEAR	TM-L	W	L	PCT	G	GS	CG	SH	SV	IP	H	R	ER	HR	HB	BB	SO	RAT	ERA	ERA+	CERA	OAV	BH	AVG	PR+	WS	TPW
1963	NY-N	3	8	.273	58	2	0	0	4	126^1	127	61	48	7	5	47	48	1.377	3.42	102	3.73	.268	6	.200	2	8	0.4
1964	NY-N	5	5	.500	44	1	0	0	3	78	79	38	36	6	2	38	31	1.500	4.15	86	4.43	.271	2	.143	-6	3	-0.6
1965	NY-N	3	5	.375	40	3	0	0	1	60^2	75	43	31	6	4	28	16	1.698	4.60	77	5.84	.304	1	.111	-7	1	-0.7
1966	NY-N	2	3	.400	29	1	0	0	0	54^2	59	31	27	11	1	20	27	1.445	4.45	82	5.04	.281	1	.111	-5	2	-0.5
1971	Mil-A	0	0	....	2	0	0	0	0	3	10	6	6	1	0	2	2	4.000	18.00	19	25.96	.556	0	....	-5	0	-0.5
Total	**5**	**13**	**21**	**.382**	**173**	**7**	**0**	**0**	**8**	**322^2**	**350**	**179**	**148**	**31**	**12**	**135**	**124**	**1.503**	**4.13**	**86**	**4.72**	**.282**	**10**	**.161**	**-20**	**14**	**-2.0**

• BEARSE, Kevin

Kevin Gerard Bearse b: 11/7/1965, Jersey City, NJ BL/TL, 6'2", 195 lbs. Deb: 4/15/1990

YEAR	TM-L	W	L	PCT	G	GS	CG	SH	SV	IP	H	R	ER	HR	HB	BB	SO	RAT	ERA	ERA+	CERA	OAV	BH	AVG	PR+	WS	TPW
1990	Cle-A	0	2	.000	3	3	0	0	0	7^2	16	11	11	2	2	5	2	2.739	12.91	30	15.45	.421	0	....	-8	0	-0.8

• BEASLEY, Chris

Christopher Charles Beasley b: 6/23/1962, Jackson, TN BR/TR, 6'2", 190 lbs. Deb: 7/20/1991

YEAR	TM-L	W	L	PCT	G	GS	CG	SH	SV	IP	H	R	ER	HR	HB	BB	SO	RAT	ERA	ERA+	CERA	OAV	BH	AVG	PR+	WS	TPW
1991	Cal-A	0	1	.000	22	0	0	0	0	26^2	26	14	10	2	1	10	14	1.350	3.38	122	3.81	.257	0	....	2	1	0.2

• BEATIN, Ed

Ebenezer Ambrose Beatin b: 8/10/1866, Baltimore, MD d: 5/9/1925, Baltimore, MD BR/TL, 5'9", 162 lbs. Deb: 8/2/1887 U

YEAR	TM-L	W	L	PCT	G	GS	CG	SH	SV	IP	H	R	ER	HR	HB	BB	SO	RAT	ERA	ERA+	CERA	OAV	BH	AVG	PR+	WS	TPW
1887	Det-N	1	1	.500	2	2	2	0	0	18	21	11	8	2	1	8	6	1.167	4.00	100	....	.283	0	.000	-0	1	-0.1
1888	Det-N	5	7	.417	12	12	12	1	0	107	111	60	34	6	2	16	44	1.187	2.86	96	....	.258	14	.250	1	6	0.6
1889	Cle-N	20	15	.571	36	36	35	3	0	317^2	316	179	126	12	6	141	126	1.439	3.57	113	....	.251	14	.116	6	22	0.2
1890	Cle-N	22	30	.423	54	54	53	1	0	474^1	518	300	202	11	0	186	155	1.484	3.83	93	....	.270	27	.141	-15	22	-2.0
1891	Cle-N	0	3	.000	5	4	2	0	0	29	39	44	17	1	0	21	4	2.069	5.28	65	....	.310	1	.077	-6	0	-0.6
Total	**5**	**48**	**56**	**.462**	**109**	**108**	**104**	**5**	**0**	**946**	**1005**	**594**	**387**	**32**	**9**	**372**	**335**	**1.447**	**3.68**	**98**	**....**	**.264**	**56**	**.144**	**-13**	**51**	**-2.0**

• BEATTIE, Jim

James Louis Beattie b: 7/4/1954, Hampton, VA BR/TR, 6'5", 220 lbs. Deb: 4/25/1978

YEAR	TM-L	W	L	PCT	G	GS	CG	SH	SV	IP	H	R	ER	HR	HB	BB	SO	RAT	ERA	ERA+	CERA	OAV	BH	AVG	PR+	WS	TPW
1978*	NY-A	6	9	.400	25	22	0	0	0	128	123	60	53	8	8	51	65	1.359	3.73	97	3.81	.255	0	....	-3	6	-0.3
1979	NY-A	3	6	.333	15	13	1	1	0	76	85	45	44	5	0	41	32	1.658	5.21	78	5.10	.294	0	....	-11	2	-1.1
1980	Sea-A	5	15	.250	33	29	3	0	0	187^1	205	115	101	19	4	98	67	**1.617**	4.85	85	5.25	.286	0	....	-13	6	-1.3
1981	Sea-A	3	2	.600	13	9	0	0	1	66^2	59	24	22	2	2	18	36	1.155	2.97	130	2.62	.232	0	....	8	6	0.8
1982	Sea-A	8	12	.400	28	26	6	1	0	172^1	149	73	64	13	1	65	140	1.242	3.34	127	3.13	.233	0	....	18	13	1.8
1983	Sea-A	10	15	.400	30	29	8	2	0	196^2	197	89	84	12	3	66	132	1.337	3.84	111	3.59	.259	0	....	9	13	0.9
1984	Sea-A	12	16	.429	32	32	12	2	0	211	206	86	80	13	5	75	119	1.332	3.41	117	3.63	.260	0	....	18	17	1.8
1985	Sea-A	5	6	.455	18	15	1	1	0	70^1	93	61	57	9	3	33	45	1.791	7.29	58	6.64	.316	0	....	-24	0	-2.4
1986	Sea-A	0	6	.000	9	7	0	0	0	40^1	57	28	27	7	3	14	24	1.760	6.02	70	7.27	.341	0	....	-8	0	-0.8
Total	**9**	**52**	**87**	**.374**	**203**	**182**	**31**	**7**	**1**	**1148^2**	**1174**	**581**	**532**	**88**	**29**	**461**	**660**	**1.423**	**4.17**	**98**	**4.19**	**.267**	**0**	**....**	**-6**	**63**	**-0.5**

• BEATTY, Blaine

Gordon Blaine Beatty b: 4/25/1964, Victoria, TX BL/TL, 6'2", 185 lbs. Deb: 9/16/1989

YEAR	TM-L	W	L	PCT	G	GS	CG	SH	SV	IP	H	R	ER	HR	HB	BB	SO	RAT	ERA	ERA+	CERA	OAV	BH	AVG	PR+	WS	TPW
1989	NY-N	0	0	....	2	1	0	0	0	6	5	1	1	1	0	2	3	1.167	1.50	217	3.28	.217	1	.500	1	1	0.2
1991	NY-N	0	0	....	5	0	0	0	0	9^2	9	3	3	0	0	4	7	1.345	2.79	130	2.82	.250	0	....	1	1	0.1
Total	**2**	**0**	**0**	**....**	**7**	**1**	**0**	**0**	**0**	**15^2**	**14**	**4**	**4**	**1**	**0**	**6**	**10**	**1.277**	**2.30**	**154**	**3.00**	**.237**	**1**	**.500**	**2**	**2**	**0.3**

• BEAZLEY, Johnny

John Andrew "Nig" Beazley b: 5/25/1918, Nashville, TN d: 4/21/1990, Nashville, TN BR/TR, 6'1.5", 190 lbs. Deb: 9/28/1941

YEAR	TM-L	W	L	PCT	G	GS	CG	SH	SV	IP	H	R	ER	HR	HB	BB	SO	RAT	ERA	ERA+	CERA	OAV	BH	AVG	PR+	WS	TPW
1941	StL-N	1	0	1.000	1	1	1	0	0	9	10	1	1	0	0	3	4	1.444	1.00	377	3.87	.294	0	.000	3	1	0.2
1942*	StL-N	21	6	.778	43	23	13	3	3	215^1	181	67	51	4	3	73	91	1.180	2.13	161	2.43	.226	10	.137	28	22	2.9
1946*	StL-N	7	5	.583	19	18	5	0	0	103	109	55	51	6	4	55	36	1.592	4.46	78	4.69	.275	8	.242	-13	3	-1.3
1947	Bos-N	2	0	1.000	9	2	2	0	0	28^2	30	15	14	1	0	19	12	1.709	4.40	89	4.64	.273	0	.000	-1	1	-0.2
1948	Bos-N	0	1	.000	3	2	0	0	0	16	19	13	8	2	0	7	4	1.625	4.50	85	5.18	.284	0	.000	-1	0	-0.2
1949	Bos-N	0	0	....	1	0	0	0	0	2	0	0	0	0	0	0	0	.000	0.00	....	0.00	.000	0	....	1	0	0.1
Total	**6**	**31**	**12**	**.721**	**76**	**46**	**21**	**3**	**3**	**374**	**349**	**151**	**125**	**13**	**7**	**157**	**147**	**1.353**	**3.01**	**117**	**3.36**	**.248**	**18**	**.150**	**16**	**27**	**1.6**

• BECANNON, Buck

James Melvin Becannon b: 8/22/1859, New York, NY d: 11/5/1923, New York, NY, 5'10", 165 lbs. Deb: 10/15/1884 U ♦

YEAR	TM-L	W	L	PCT	G	GS	CG	SH	SV	IP	H	R	ER	HR	HB	BB	SO	RAT	ERA	ERA+	CERA	OAV	BH	AVG	PR+	WS	TPW
1884*	NY-a	1	0	1.000	1	1	1	0	0	6	2	2	1	0	0	2	2	.667	1.50	208	....	.098	0	.000	1	1	0.0
1885	NY-a	2	8	.200	10	10	10	0	0	85	108	84	59	5	5	24	13	1.553	6.25	47	....	.297	10	.303	-31	1	-2.5
Total	**2**	**3**	**8**	**.273**	**11**	**11**	**11**	**0**	**0**	**91**	**110**	**86**	**60**	**5**	**5**	**26**	**15**	**1.495**	**5.93**	**50**	**....**	**.286**	**10**	**.244**	**-30**	**2**	**-2.5**

• BECHLER, Steve

Steven Scott Bechler b: 11/18/1979, Medford, OR d: 2/17/2003, Fort Lauderdale, FL BR/TR, 6'2", 225 lbs. Deb: 9/6/2002

YEAR	TM-L	W	L	PCT	G	GS	CG	SH	SV	IP	H	R	ER	HR	HB	BB	SO	RAT	ERA	ERA+	CERA	OAV	BH	AVG	PR+	WS	TPW
2002	Bal-A	0	0	....	3	0	0	0	0	4^2	6	7	7	3	1	4	3	2.143	13.50	32	13.72	.300	0	....	-5	0	-0.5

• BECHTEL, George

George A. Bechtel b: 9/2/1848, Philadelphia, PA, 5'11", 165 lbs. Deb: 5/20/1871 U ♦

YEAR	TM-L	W	L	PCT	G	GS	CG	SH	SV	IP	H	R	ER	HR	HB	BB	SO	RAT	ERA	ERA+	CERA	OAV	BH	AVG	PR+	WS	TPW
1871	Ath-n	1	2	.333	3	3	2	0	0	26	43	42	23	0	....	11	1	2.077	7.96	51	....	.325	33	.351	-12	....	-0.3
1873	Phi-n	0	2	.000	3	2	1	0	0	16	27	24	8	0	....	2	0	1.813	4.50	73	....	.334	63	.244	-3	....	-0.1
1874	Phi-n	1	3	.250	6	4	4	0	0	39	57	42	7	0	....	1	0	1.487	1.62	73	....	.306	42	.278	-4	....	-0.3
1875	Cen-n	2	12	.143	14	14	14	0	0	126	169	138	38	0	....	5	6	1.381	2.71	61	....	.294	17	.279	-6	....	-0.2
	Ath-n	3	1	.750	4	4	4	0	0	36	41	19	10	0	....	3	3	1.222	2.50	118	....	.261	46	.280	0	....	0.3
	Yr.	5	13	.278	18	18	18	0	0	162	210	157	48	0	....	8	9	1.346	2.67	69	....	.287	63	.280	-6	....	0.1
Total	**4 n**	**7**	**20**	**.259**	**30**	**27**	**25**	**0**	**0**	**243**	**337**	**265**	**86**	**0**	**....**	**22**	**10**	**1.477**	**3.19**	**67**	**....**	**.298**	**275**	**.282**	**-25**	**....**	**-0.7**

• BECK, Boom-Boom

Walter William Beck b: 10/16/1904, Decatur, IL d: 5/7/1987, Champaign, IL BR/TR, 6'2", 200 lbs. Deb: 9/22/1924 C

YEAR	TM-L	W	L	PCT	G	GS	CG	SH	SV	IP	H	R	ER	HR	HB	BB	SO	RAT	ERA	ERA+	CERA	OAV	BH	AVG	PR+	WS	TPW
1924	StL-A	0	0	....	1	0	0	0	0	1	2	0	0	0	0	1	0	3.000	0.00	....	14.07	.667	0	....	0	0	0.0
1927	StL-A	1	0	1.000	3	1	1	0	0	11^1	15	8	7	0	1	5	6	1.765	5.56	78	5.61	.333	1	.250	-2	1	-0.2
1928	StL-A	2	3	.400	16	4	2	0	0	49	52	29	24	4	4	20	17	1.469	4.41	95	4.42	.289	6	.429	-1	3	0.0
1933	Bro-N	12	20	.375	43	**35**	15	3	1	257	270	128	101	9	11	69	89	1.319	3.54	91	3.42	.267	18	.189	-3	10	-0.2
1934	Bro-N	2	6	.250	22	9	2	0	0	57	72	50	47	6	5	32	24	1.825	7.42	53	6.41	.301	4	.235	-22	0	-2.1
1939	Phi-N	7	14	.333	34	16	12	0	3	182^2	203	104	96	11	3	64	77	1.462	4.73	83	4.12	.284	9	.132	-16	6	-1.9
1940	Phi-N	4	9	.308	29	15	4	0	0	129^1	147	69	62	13	9	41	38	1.454	4.31	90	4.69	.286	2	.056	-6	6	-0.9
1941	Phi-N	1	9	.100	34	7	2	0	0	95^1	104	52	49	8	2	35	34	1.458	4.63	80	4.29	.276	3	.120	-9	2	-1.1
1942	Phi-N	0	1	.000	26	1	0	0	0	53	69	30	28	4	1	17	10	1.623	4.75	70	5.41	.325	4	.333	-9	1	-0.8
1943	Phi-N	0	0	....	4	0	0	0	0	13^2	24	15	15	1	2	5	3	2.122	9.88	34	9.22	.393	2	.500	-10	0	-1.0
1944	Det-A	1	2	.333	28	2	0	0	1	74	67	36	32	5	3	27	25	1.270	3.89	92	3.20	.243	7	.318	-2	4	-0.1
1945	Cin-N	2	4	.333	11	6	2	0	1	47^2	42	21	18	0	1	12	9	1.133	3.40	110	2.25	.236	3	.214	2	3	0.2
	Pit-N	6	1	.857	14	5	4	0	0	63	54	19	15	2	0	14	20	1.079	2.14	184	2.25	.234	2	.125	13	7	1.3
	Yr.	8	5	.615	25	11	6	0	1	110^2	96	40	33	2	1	26	29	1.102	2.68	143	2.25	.235	5	.167	15	10	1.4
Total	**12**	**38**	**69**	**.355**	**265**	**101**	**44**	**3**	**6**	**1034**	**1121**	**561**	**494**	**63**	**42**	**342**	**352**	**1.415**	**4.30**	**85**	**4.07**	**.277**	**61**	**.187**	**-63**	**43**	**-6.6**

• BECK, Frank

Frank J. Beck b: 11/1858, Poughkeepsie, NY d: 2/8/1941, Detroit, MI TR, 5'9", 141 lbs. Deb: 5/2/1884 ♦

YEAR	TM-L	W	L	PCT	G	GS	CG	SH	SV	IP	H	R	ER	HR	HB	BB	SO	RAT	ERA	ERA+	CERA	OAV	BH	AVG	PR+	WS	TPW
1884	Pit-a	0	3	.000	3	3	3	0	0	25	33	29	17	0	5	6	11	1.560	6.12	55	....	.302	4	.333	-7	0	-0.5
	Bal-U	0	2	.000	2	2	1	0	0	9	17	13	8	0	....	4	7	2.333	8.00	42	....	.378	2	.100	-5	0	-0.7

• BECK, George

Ernest George B. Beck b: 2/21/1890, South Bend, IN d: 10/29/1973, South Bend, IN BR/TR, 5'11", 165 lbs. Deb: 5/15/1914

YEAR	TM-L	W	L	PCT	G	GS	CG	SH	SV	IP	H	R	ER	HR	HB	BB	SO	RAT	ERA	ERA+	CERA	OAV	BH	AVG	PR+	WS	TPW
1914	Cle-A	0	0	....	1	0	0	0	0	1	1	0	0	0	1	0	0	1.000	0.00	....	5.17	.250	0	....	0	0	0.0

YEAR	TM-L	W	L	PCT	G	GS	CG	SH	SV	IP	H	R	ER	HR	HB	BB	SO	RAT	ERA	ERA+	CERA	OAV	BH	AVG	PR+	WS	TPW
• BECK, Rich					Richard Henry Beck b: 1/21/1941, Pasco, WA BB/TR, 6'3", 190 lbs. Deb: 9/14/1965																						
1965	NY-A	2	1	.667	3	3	1	1	0	21	22	6	5	1	0	7	10	1.381	2.14	159	3.73	.275	0	.000	3	2	0.3
• BECK, Rod					Rodney Roy Beck b: 8/3/1968, Burbank, CA BR/TR, 6'1", 236 lbs. Deb: 5/6/1991																						
1991	SF-N	1	1	.500	31	0	0	0	1	52^{1}	53	22	22	4	1	13	38	1.261	3.78	95	3.52	.273	1	.500	-2	3	-0.1
1992	SF-N	3	3	.500	65	0	0	0	17	92	62	20	18	4	2	15	87	.837	1.76	188	1.44	.190	1	.500	14	16	1.5
1993	SF-N★	3	1	.750	76	0	0	0	48	79^{1}	57	20	19	11	3	13	86	.882	2.16	181	2.05	.201	0	.000	13	16	1.3
1994	SF-N★	2	4	.333	48	0	0	0	28	48^{2}	49	17	15	10	0	13	39	1.274	2.77	145	4.17	.261	0	.000	5	7	0.4
1995	SF-N	5	6	.455	60	0	0	0	33	58^{2}	60	31	29	7	2	21	42	1.381	4.45	92	4.20	.267	1	.333	-3	7	-0.3
1996	SF-N	0	9	.000	63	0	0	0	35	62	56	23	23	9	1	10	48	1.065	3.34	123	2.95	.238	1	.333	5	10	0.5
1997*	SF-N★	7	4	.636	73	0	0	0	37	70	67	31	27	7	2	8	53	1.071	3.47	116	2.84	.248	0	....	5	12	0.5
1998*	Chi-N	3	4	.429	**81**	0	0	0	51	80^{1}	86	33	27	11	2	20	81	1.320	3.02	146	4.05	.269	0	.000	14	13	1.3
1999	Chi-N	2	4	.333	31	0	0	0	7	30	41	26	26	5	0	13	13	1.800	7.80	58	6.75	.331	0	....	-11	0	-1.0
	*Bos-A	0	1	.000	12	0	0	0	3	14	9	3	3	0	1	5	12	1.000	1.93	257	1.79	.184	0	....	5	3	0.4
2000	Bos-A	3	0	1.000	34	0	0	0	0	40^{2}	34	15	14	2	2	12	35	1.131	3.10	163	2.59	.222	0	....	9	5	0.8
2001	Bos-A	6	4	.600	68	0	0	0	6	80^{2}	77	42	35	15	3	28	63	1.302	3.90	115	4.25	.252	0	.000	7	7	0.6
2003	SD-N	3	2	.600	36	0	0	0	20	35^{1}	25	7	7	4	1	11	32	1.019	1.78	221	2.35	.197	0	....	9	6	0.9
Total	**12**	**38**	**43**	**.469**	**678**	**0**	**0**	**0**	**286**	**744**	**676**	**290**	**265**	**89**	**20**	**182**	**629**	**1.153**	**3.21**	**128**	**3.22**	**.241**	**4**	**.211**	**69**	**105**	**6.9**
• BECKER, Bob					Robert Charles Becker b: 8/15/1875, Syracuse, NY d: 10/11/1951, Syracuse, NY TL Deb: 9/6/1897																						
1897	Phi-N	0	2	.000	5	2	2	0	0	24	32	18	15	0	1	7	10	1.625	5.63	75	4.87	.317	1	.111	-3	1	-0.3
1898	Phi-N	0	0	....	1	0	0	0	0	5	6	6	6	0	0	5	0	2.200	10.80	32	6.53	.295	0	.000	-4	0	-0.4
Total	**2**	**0**	**2**	**.000**	**6**	**2**	**2**	**0**	**0**	**29**	**38**	**24**	**21**	**0**	**1**	**12**	**10**	**1.724**	**6.52**	**60**	**5.16**	**.314**	**1**	**.100**	**-7**	**1**	**-0.7**
• BECKER, Charlie					Charles S. "Buck" Becker b: 10/14/1888, Washington, DC d: 7/30/1928, Washington, DC BL/TL, 6'2", 180 lbs. Deb: 8/2/1911																						
1911	Was-A	3	5	.375	11	5	5	1	0	71^{1}	80	44	32	2	7	23	31	1.444	4.04	81	4.03	.268	5	.227	-6	3	-0.6
1912	Was-A	0	0	....	4	0	0	0	0	9	8	6	3	0	0	6	5	1.556	3.00	112	3.90	.258	1	.500	0	0	0.0
Total	**2**	**3**	**5**	**.375**	**15**	**5**	**5**	**1**	**0**	**80^{1}**	**88**	**50**	**35**	**2**	**7**	**29**	**36**	**1.456**	**3.92**	**84**	**4.02**	**.267**	**6**	**.250**	**-6**	**3**	**-0.6**
• BECKETT, Josh					Joshua Patrick Beckett b: 5/15/1980, Spring, TX BR/TR, 6'4", 190 lbs. Deb: 9/4/2001																						
2001	Fla-N	2	2	.500	4	4	0	0	0	24	14	9	4	3	1	11	24	1.042	1.50	281	2.36	.161	2	.286	7	3	0.8
2002	Fla-N	6	7	.462	23	21	0	0	0	107^{2}	93	56	49	13	1	44	113	1.272	4.10	96	3.50	.232	1	.032	-2	5	-0.5
2003*	Fla-N	9	8	.529	24	23	0	0	0	142	132	54	48	9	2	56	152	1.324	3.04	135	3.44	.246	7	.152	16	11	1.6
Total	**3**	**17**	**17**	**.500**	**51**	**48**	**0**	**0**	**0**	**273^{2}**	**239**	**119**	**101**	**25**	**4**	**111**	**289**	**1.279**	**3.32**	**121**	**3.37**	**.233**	**10**	**.119**	**21**	**19**	**1.8**
• BECKETT, Robbie					Robert Joseph Beckett b: 7/16/1972, Austin, TX BR/TL, 6'5", 235 lbs. Deb: 9/12/1996																						
1996	Col-N	0	0	....	5	0	0	0	0	5^{1}	6	8	8	3	0	9	6	2.813	13.50	39	15.01	.286	0	....	-5	0	-0.5
1997	Col-N	0	0	....	2	0	0	0	0	1^{2}	1	1	1	0	0	1	2	1.200	5.40	96	1.29	.167	0	....	-0	0	0.0
Total	**2**	**0**	**0**	**....**	**7**	**0**	**0**	**0**	**0**	**7**	**7**	**9**	**9**	**3**	**0**	**10**	**8**	**2.429**	**11.57**	**45**	**11.75**	**.259**	**0**	**....**	**-5**	**0**	**-0.5**
• BECKMAN, Jim					James Joseph Beckman b: 3/1/1905, Cincinnati, OH d: 12/5/1974, Montgomery, OH BR/TR, 5'10", 172 lbs. Deb: 7/27/1927																						
1927	Cin-N	0	1	.000	4	1	0	0	0	12^{1}	18	10	8	2	1	6	0	1.946	5.84	65	7.77	.340	0	.000	-3	0	-0.3
1928	Cin-N	0	1	.000	6	0	0	0	0	15^{1}	19	12	10	1	0	9	4	1.826	5.87	67	5.40	.306	0	.000	-3	0	-0.4
Total	**2**	**0**	**2**	**.000**	**10**	**1**	**0**	**0**	**0**	**27^{2}**	**37**	**22**	**18**	**3**	**1**	**15**	**4**	**1.880**	**5.86**	**66**	**6.46**	**.322**	**0**	**.000**	**-6**	**0**	**-0.6**
• BECKMANN, Bill					William Aloysius Beckmann b: 12/8/1907, Clayton, MO d: 1/2/1990, Florissant, MO BR/TR, 6', 175 lbs. Deb: 5/2/1939																						
1939	Phi-A	7	11	.389	27	19	7	2	0	155^{1}	198	104	93	15	1	41	20	1.539	5.39	87	5.02	.312	13	.250	-7	6	-0.5
1940	Phi-A	8	4	.667	34	9	6	2	1	127^{1}	132	68	59	11	1	35	47	1.312	4.17	107	3.63	.265	8	.205	6	7	0.5
1941	Phi-A	5	9	.357	22	15	4	0	1	130	141	76	66	11	2	33	28	1.338	4.57	92	3.81	.270	9	.191	-6	6	-0.6
1942	Phi-A	0	1	.000	5	1	0	0	0	20^{1}	24	17	16	1	0	9	10	1.623	7.08	53	4.76	.289	2	.500	-7	1	-0.6
	StL-N	1	0	1.000	2	0	0	0	0	7	4	0	0	0	0	1	3	.714	0.00	....	1.08	.200	0	.000	3	1	0.3
Total	**4**	**21**	**25**	**.457**	**90**	**44**	**17**	**4**	**2**	**440**	**499**	**265**	**234**	**38**	**4**	**119**	**108**	**1.405**	**4.79**	**92**	**4.18**	**.284**	**32**	**.224**	**-12**	**21**	**-1.0**
• BECKWITH, Joe					Thomas Joseph Beckwith b: 1/28/1955, Auburn, AL BL/TR, 6'3", 200 lbs. Deb: 7/21/1979																						
1979	LA-N	1	2	.333	17	0	0	0	2	37^{1}	42	18	18	4	0	15	28	1.527	4.34	84	4.72	.284	0	.000	-2	2	-0.3
1980	LA-N	3	3	.500	38	0	0	0	0	59^{2}	60	17	13	1	1	23	40	1.391	1.96	178	3.40	.263	0	.000	9	6	1.0
1982	LA-N	2	1	.667	19	1	0	0	1	40	38	14	12	2	0	14	33	1.300	2.70	128	3.04	.252	0	.000	4	3	0.3
1983*	LA-N	3	4	.429	42	3	0	0	1	71	73	40	28	5	1	35	50	1.521	3.55	101	4.08	.264	1	.200	2	3	0.2
1984	KC-A	8	4	.667	49	1	0	0	2	100^{2}	92	39	38	13	2	25	75	1.162	3.40	119	3.31	.247	0	....	6	8	0.6
1985*	KC-A	1	5	.167	49	0	0	0	1	95	99	45	43	9	3	32	80	1.379	4.07	102	4.01	.269	0	....	2	5	0.2
1986	LA-N	0	0	....	15	0	0	0	0	18^{1}	28	16	14	5	0	6	13	1.855	6.87	50	8.53	.350	0	....	-7	0	-0.7
Total	**7**	**18**	**19**	**.486**	**229**	**5**	**0**	**0**	**7**	**422**	**432**	**189**	**166**	**39**	**7**	**150**	**319**	**1.379**	**3.54**	**107**	**3.94**	**.266**	**1**	**.053**	**14**	**27**	**1.4**
• BEDARD, Erik					Erik Joseph Bedard b: 3/5/1979, Navan, Canada BL/TL, 6'1", 186 lbs. Deb: 4/17/2002																						
2002	Bal-A	0	0	....	2	0	0	0	0	0^{2}	2	1	1	0	0	0	1	3.000	13.50	32	14.52	.500	0	....	-1	0	-0.1
• BEDGOOD, Phil					Phillip Burlette Bedgood b: 3/8/1898, Harrison, GA d: 11/8/1927, Fort Pierce, FL BR/TR, 6'3", 218 lbs. Deb: 9/20/1922																						
1922	Cle-A	1	0	1.000	1	1	1	0	0	9	7	4	4	0	3	4	5	1.222	4.00	100	3.55	.233	0	.000	0	1	0.0
1923	Cle-A	0	2	.000	9	2	0	0	0	18^{2}	16	13	11	0	2	14	7	1.607	5.30	75	3.62	.246	1	.250	-3	0	-0.2
Total	**2**	**1**	**2**	**.333**	**10**	**3**	**1**	**0**	**0**	**27^{2}**	**23**	**17**	**15**	**0**	**5**	**18**	**12**	**1.482**	**4.88**	**81**	**3.60**	**.242**	**1**	**.167**	**-2**	**1**	**-0.2**
• BEDIENT, Hugh					Hugh Carpenter Bedient b: 10/23/1889, Gerry, NY d: 7/21/1965, Jamestown, NY BR/TR, 6', 185 lbs. Deb: 4/26/1912																						
1912*	Bos-A	20	9	.690	41	28	19	0	2	231	206	93	75	6	3	55	122	1.130	2.92	117	2.49	.240	14	.192	13	21	1.4
1913	Bos-A	15	14	.517	43	28	15	1	5	259	255	104	80	0	6	67	122	1.243	2.78	106	2.90	.261	10	.125	9	17	0.7
1914	Bos-A	8	12	.400	42	16	7	1	2	177^{1}	187	97	71	4	5	45	70	1.308	3.60	74	3.52	.281	5	.100	-21	3	-2.6
1915	Buf-F	16	18	.471	53	30	16	2	**10**	269^{1}	284	131	95	5	3	69	106	1.311	3.17	96	3.34	.274	9	.108	-3	15	-0.7
Total	**4**	**59**	**53**	**.527**	**179**	**102**	**57**	**4**	**19**	**936^{2}**	**932**	**425**	**321**	**15**	**17**	**236**	**420**	**1.247**	**3.08**	**98**	**3.04**	**.263**	**38**	**.133**	**-1**	**56**	**-1.1**
• BEDNAR, Andy					Andrew Jackson Bednar b: 8/16/1908, Streator, IL d: 11/26/1937, Graham, TX BR/TR, 5'10.5", 180 lbs. Deb: 9/6/1930																						
1930	Pit-N	0	0	....	2	0	0	0	0	1^{1}	4	4	4	0	0	1	1	3.750	27.00	18	16.12	.500	0	....	-3	0	-0.3
1931	Pit-N	0	0	....	3	0	0	0	0	4	10	5	5	1	0	0	2	2.500	11.25	34	13.36	.476	0	....	-3	0	-0.3
Total	**2**	**0**	**0**	**....**	**5**	**0**	**0**	**0**	**0**	**5^{1}**	**14**	**9**	**9**	**1**	**0**	**1**	**3**	**2.813**	**15.19**	**28**	**14.05**	**.483**	**0**	**....**	**-7**	**0**	**-0.6**
• BEDROSIAN, Steve					Stephen Wayne Bedrosian b: 12/6/1957, Methuen, MA BR/TR, 6'3", 200 lbs. Deb: 8/14/1981																						
1981	Atl-N	1	2	.333	15	1	0	0	0	24^{1}	15	14	12	2	1	15	9	1.233	4.44	81	2.63	.169	0	.000	-2	1	-0.3
1982*	Atl-N	8	6	.571	64	3	0	0	11	137^{2}	102	39	37	7	4	57	123	1.155	2.42	154	2.49	.206	1	.038	20	15	1.9
1983	Atl-N	9	10	.474	70	1	0	0	19	120	100	50	48	11	4	51	114	1.258	3.60	108	3.24	.229	2	.105	2	12	0.2
1984	Atl-N	9	6	.600	40	4	0	0	11	83^{2}	65	23	22	5	1	33	81	1.171	2.37	163	2.56	.210	2	.118	14	12	1.4
1985	Atl-N	7	15	.318	37	37	0	0	0	206^{2}	198	101	88	17	5	111	134	1.495	3.83	100	4.33	.254	5	.078	2	10	-0.2
1986	Phi-N	8	6	.571	68	0	0	0	29	90^{1}	79	39	34	12	0	34	82	1.251	3.39	114	3.31	.232	1	.200	5	13	0.5
1987	Phi-N★	5	3	.625	65	0	0	0	**40**	89	79	31	28	11	1	28	74	1.202	2.83	150	3.28	.237	0	.000	13	16	1.2
1988	Phi-N	6	6	.500	57	0	0	0	28	74^{1}	75	34	31	6	0	27	61	1.372	3.75	95	3.69	.257	0	.000	-1	8	-0.1
1989	Phi-N	2	3	.400	28	0	0	0	6	33^{2}	21	13	12	7	1	17	24	1.129	3.21	111	3.31	.183	0	....	1	3	0.2
	*SF-N	1	4	.200	40	0	0	0	17	51	35	18	15	5	0	22	34	1.118	2.65	127	2.42	.192	1	.167	3	7	0.3
	Yr.	3	7	.300	68	0	0	0	23	84^{2}	56	31	27	12	1	39	58	1.122	2.87	120	2.77	.189	1	.167	4	10	0.5
1990	SF-N	9	9	.500	68	0	0	0	17	79^{1}	72	40	37	6	2	44	43	1.462	4.20	87	3.88	.241	2	.500	-5	7	-0.5
1991*	Min-A	5	3	.625	56	0	0	0	6	77^{1}	70	42	38	11	3	35	44	1.358	4.42	96	4.10	.243	0	....	-2	5	-0.2
1993	Atl-N	5	2	.714	49	0	0	0	0	49^{2}	34	11	9	4	2	14	33	.966	1.63	246	1.98	.194	0	.000	13	7	1.2
1994	Atl-N	0	2	.000	46	0	0	0	0	46	41	20	17	4	2	18	43	1.283	3.33	128	3.34	.243	1	.500	5	3	0.5

YEAR	TM-L	W	L	PCT	G	GS	CG	SH	SV	IP	H	R	ER	HR	HB	BB	SO	RAT	ERA	ERA+	CERA	OAV	BH	AVG	PR+	WS	TPW
1995	Atl-N	1	2	.333	29	0	0	0	0	28	40	21	19	6	1	12	22	1.857	6.11	70	8.09	.354	0	....	-5	0	-0.5
Total	**14**	**76**	**79**	**.490**	**732**	**46**	**0**	**0**	**184**	**1191**	**1026**	**496**	**447**	**114**	**27**	**518**	**921**	**1.296**	**3.38**	**114**	**3.45**	**.232**	**15**	**.098**	**63**	**119**	**5.7**
• BEEBE, Fred	Frederick Leonard Beebe b: 12/31/1880, Lincoln, NE d: 10/30/1957, Elgin, IL BR/TR, 6'1", 190 lbs. Deb: 4/17/1906 U																										
1906	Chi-N	6	1	.857	14	6	4	0	1	70	56	27	21	1	5	32	55	1.257	2.70	97	2.69	.210	3	.103	-2	5	-0.4
	StL-N	9	9	.500	20	19	16	1	0	160^2	115	65	54	1	9	68	116	1.139	3.02	87	2.30	.208	10	.172	-6	9	-0.6
	Yr.	15	10	.600	34	25	20	1	1	230^2	171	92	75	2	14	100	**171**	1.175	2.93	90	2.42	.209	13	.149	-8	14	-1.0
1907	StL-N	7	19	.269	31	29	24	4	0	238^1	192	95	72	1	10	109	141	1.263	2.72	92	2.81	.230	11	.128	-5	10	-0.8
1908	StL-N	5	13	.278	29	19	12	0	0	174^1	134	88	51	3	4	66	72	1.147	2.63	89	2.06	**.193**	7	.125	-1	5	-0.4
1909	StL-N	15	21	.417	44	34	18	1	1	287^2	256	142	90	5	7	104	105	1.251	2.82	90	2.72	.229	18	.167	-2	8	-0.4
1910	Cin-N	12	14	.462	35	26	11	2	0	214^1	193	101	73	3	7	94	93	1.339	3.07	95	3.22	.246	12	.164	-2	10	-0.4
1911	Phi-N	3	3	.500	9	8	3	0	0	48^1	52	26	24	2	3	24	20	1.572	4.47	77	4.96	.297	5	.263	-6	3	-0.4
1916	Cle-A	5	3	.625	20	12	5	1	2	100^2	92	43	27	1	1	37	32	1.281	2.41	124	2.98	.251	6	.214	6	6	0.8
Total	**7**	**62**	**83**	**.428**	**202**	**153**	**93**	**9**	**4**	**1294^1**	**1090**	**587**	**412**	**17**	**46**	**534**	**634**	**1.255**	**2.86**	**92**	**2.78**	**.227**	**72**	**.158**	**-17**	**56**	**-2.7**
• BEECH, Matt	Lucas Matthew Beech b: 1/20/1972, Oakland, CA BL/TL, 6'2", 190 lbs. Deb: 8/8/1996																										
1996	Phi-N	1	4	.200	8	8	0	0	0	41^1	49	32	32	8	3	11	33	1.452	6.97	62	5.63	.306	1	.071	-12	0	-1.3
1997	Phi-N	4	9	.308	24	24	0	0	0	136^2	147	81	77	25	5	57	120	1.493	5.07	84	5.27	.279	5	.167	-12	4	-1.2
1998	Phi-N	3	9	.250	21	21	0	0	0	117	126	78	67	19	4	63	113	1.615	5.15	84	5.69	.275	5	.152	-11	2	-1.2
Total	**3**	**8**	**22**	**.267**	**53**	**53**	**0**	**0**	**0**	**295**	**322**	**191**	**176**	**52**	**12**	**131**	**266**	**1.536**	**5.37**	**80**	**5.49**	**.281**	**11**	**.143**	**-35**	**6**	**-3.7**
• BEECHER, Roy	Leroy "Colonel" Beecher b: 5/10/1884, Swanton, OH d: 10/11/1952, Toledo, OH BL/TR, 6'2", 180 lbs. Deb: 9/29/1907																										
1907	NY-N	0	2	.000	2	2	2	0	0	14	17	8	4	0	0	6	5	1.643	2.57	96	4.49	.293	0	.000	0	0	0.0
1908	NY-N	0	0	....	2	0	0	0	1	5^2	11	5	5	0	0	3	0	2.471	7.94	30	10.33	.440	1	.333	-3	0	-0.3
Total	**2**	**0**	**2**	**.000**	**4**	**2**	**2**	**0**	**1**	**19^2**	**28**	**13**	**9**	**0**	**0**	**9**	**5**	**1.881**	**4.12**	**59**	**6.17**	**.337**	**1**	**.125**	**-3**	**0**	**-0.4**
• BEENE, Andy	Ramon Andrew Beene b: 10/13/1956, Freeport, TX BR/TR, 6'3", 205 lbs. Deb: 9/22/1983																										
1983	Mil-A	0	0	....	1	0	0	0	0	2	3	3	1	0	0	1	0	2.000	4.50	83	5.47	.333	0	....	-0	0	0.0
1984	Mil-A	0	2	.000	5	3	0	0	0	18^2	28	23	23	1	2	9	11	1.982	11.09	35	7.59	.350	0	....	-15	0	-1.5
Total	**2**	**0**	**2**	**.000**	**6**	**3**	**0**	**0**	**0**	**20^2**	**31**	**26**	**24**	**1**	**2**	**10**	**11**	**1.984**	**10.45**	**37**	**7.39**	**.348**	**0**	**....**	**-15**	**0**	**-1.5**
• BEENE, Fred	Freddy Ray Beene b: 11/24/1942, Angleton, TX BB/TR, 5'9", 160 lbs. Deb: 9/18/1968																										
1968	Bal-A	0	0	....	1	0	0	0	0	1	2	1	1	0	0	1	1	3.000	9.00	32	12.01	.500	0	....	-1	0	-0.1
1969	Bal-A	0	0	....	2	0	0	0	0	2^2	2	0	0	0	0	1	0	1.125	0.00	....	2.01	.200	0	....	1	0	0.1
1970	Bal-A	0	0	....	4	0	0	0	0	6	8	5	4	1	0	5	4	2.167	6.00	61	6.95	.320	0	....	-2	0	-0.2
1972	NY-A	1	3	.250	29	1	0	0	3	57^2	55	21	15	3	1	24	37	1.370	2.34	126	3.57	.256	0	.000	4	3	0.3
1973	NY-A	6	0	1.000	19	4	0	0	1	91	67	21	17	5	1	27	49	1.033	1.68	218	2.10	.209	0	....	19	10	2.0
1974	NY-A	0	0	....	6	0	0	0	1	10	9	4	3	1	1	2	10	1.100	2.70	129	3.09	.231	0	....	1	1	0.1
	Cle-A	4	4	.500	32	0	0	0	2	73	68	44	40	7	1	26	35	1.288	4.93	73	3.54	.247	0	....	-11	2	-1.1
	Yr.	4	4	.500	38	0	0	0	3	83	77	48	43	8	2	28	45	1.265	4.66	77	3.48	.245	0	....	-10	3	-1.1
1975	Cle-A	1	0	1.000	19	1	0	0	1	46^2	63	42	36	4	3	25	20	1.886	6.94	54	6.72	.323	0	....	-17	0	-1.7
Total	**7**	**12**	**7**	**.632**	**112**	**6**	**0**	**0**	**8**	**288**	**274**	**138**	**116**	**21**	**7**	**111**	**156**	**1.337**	**3.63**	**98**	**3.67**	**.253**	**0**	**.000**	**-5**	**16**	**-0.7**
• BEERS, Clarence	Clarence Scott Beers b: 12/9/1918, El Dorado, KS BR/TR, 6', 175 lbs. Deb: 5/2/1948																										
1948	StL-N	0	0	....	1	0	0	0	0	0^2	3	4	1	0	0	1	0	6.000	13.50	30	28.95	.500	0	....	-1	0	-0.1
• BEGGS, Joe	Joseph Stanley "Fireman" Beggs b: 11/4/1910, Rankin, PA d: 7/19/1983, Indianapolis, IN BR/TR, 6'1", 182 lbs. Deb: 4/19/1938																										
1938	NY-A	3	2	.600	14	9	4	0	0	58^1	69	41	35	7	0	20	8	1.526	5.40	84	4.98	.299	5	.250	-6	2	-0.5
1940*	Cin-N	12	3	.800	37	1	0	0	**7**	76^2	68	19	17	1	1	21	25	1.161	2.00	190	2.52	.243	4	.190	13	13	1.2
1941	Cin-N	4	3	.571	37	0	0	0	5	57	57	29	24	2	0	27	19	1.474	3.79	95	3.62	.257	3	.300	-1	4	0.0
1942	Cin-N	6	5	.545	38	0	0	0	8	88^2	65	28	21	4	1	33	24	1.105	2.13	154	2.18	.206	0	.000	11	10	0.9
1943	Cin-N	7	6	.538	39	4	4	2	6	115^1	121	38	30	0	0	25	28	1.266	2.34	142	2.94	.276	5	.143	9	11	0.9
1944	Cin-N	1	0	1.000	1	1	1	0	0	9	8	2	2	0	0	0	2	.889	2.00	174	1.49	.222	0	.000	1	1	0.1
1946	Cin-N	12	10	.545	28	22	14	2	1	190	175	63	49	15	1	39	38	1.126	2.32	144	2.80	.247	14	.222	16	17	2.0
1947	Cin-N	0	3	.000	11	4	0	0	0	32^1	42	26	19	4	0	6	11	1.485	5.29	78	5.12	.316	1	.091	-4	0	-0.5
	NY-N	3	3	.500	32	0	0	0	2	66	81	38	31	6	1	18	23	1.500	4.23	96	4.70	.300	1	.077	-1	3	-0.2
	Yr.	3	6	.333	43	4	0	0	2	98^1	123	64	50	10	1	24	34	1.495	4.58	89	4.84	.305	2	.083	-5	3	-0.7
1948	NY-N	0	0	....	1	0	0	0	0	0^1	2	0	0	0	0	0	0	6.000	0.00	....	39.65	.667	0	....	0	0	0.0
Total	**9**	**48**	**35**	**.578**	**238**	**41**	**23**	**4**	**29**	**693^2**	**688**	**284**	**228**	**39**	**4**	**189**	**178**	**1.264**	**2.96**	**125**	**3.25**	**.261**	**33**	**.167**	**38**	**61**	**3.8**
• BEGLEY, Ed	Edward N. Begley b: 1863, New York, NY d: 7/24/1919, Waterbury, CT Deb: 5/3/1884																										
1884	NY-N	12	18	.400	31	30	30	0	0	266	296	209	123	9	....	99	104	1.485	4.16	71	....	.267	22	.182	-36	9	-3.4
1885	NY-a	4	9	.308	15	14	10	0	0	115	131	102	63	5	8	48	44	1.557	4.93	60	....	.275	9	.173	-25	1	-2.3
Total	**2**	**16**	**27**	**.372**	**46**	**44**	**40**	**0**	**0**	**381**	**427**	**311**	**186**	**14**	**8**	**147**	**148**	**1.507**	**4.39**	**68**	**....**	**.269**	**31**	**.179**	**-60**	**10**	**-5.8**
• BEHAN, Petie	Charles Frederick Behan b: 12/11/1887, Dallas City, PA d: 1/22/1957, Bradford, PA BR/TR, 5'10", 160 lbs. Deb: 9/16/1921																										
1921	Phi-N	0	1	.000	2	2	1	0	0	10^2	17	8	7	0	0	1	3	1.688	5.91	72	5.35	.354	0	.000	-2	0	-0.2
1922	Phi-N	4	2	.667	7	5	3	1	0	47^1	49	27	13	3	1	14	13	1.331	2.47	189	3.51	.259	5	.250	12	4	1.1
1923	Phi-N	3	12	.200	31	17	5	0	2	131	182	102	80	11	1	57	27	1.824	5.50	84	6.39	.336	8	.186	-9	3	-1.0
Total	**3**	**7**	**15**	**.318**	**40**	**24**	**9**	**1**	**2**	**189**	**248**	**137**	**100**	**14**	**2**	**72**	**43**	**1.693**	**4.76**	**96**	**5.61**	**.318**	**13**	**.194**	**1**	**7**	**-0.2**
• BEHENNA, Rick	Richard Kipp Behenna b: 3/6/1960, Miami, FL BR/TR, 6'2", 170 lbs. Deb: 4/12/1983																										
1983	Atl-N	3	3	.500	14	6	0	0	0	37^1	37	20	19	7	1	12	17	1.313	4.58	85	4.31	.255	4	.333	-3	2	-0.2
	Cle-A	0	2	.000	5	4	0	0	0	26	22	13	12	0	1	14	9	1.385	4.15	102	3.18	.232	0	....	0	1	0.0
1984	Cle-A	0	3	.000	3	3	0	0	0	9^2	17	15	15	5	1	8	6	2.586	13.97	29	15.69	.386	0	....	-11	0	-1.1
1985	Cle-A	0	2	.000	4	4	0	0	0	19^2	29	17	17	3	0	8	4	1.881	7.78	53	7.66	.354	0	....	-8	0	-0.8
Total	**3**	**3**	**10**	**.231**	**26**	**17**	**0**	**0**	**0**	**92^2**	**105**	**65**	**63**	**15**	**3**	**42**	**36**	**1.586**	**6.12**	**66**	**5.89**	**.287**	**4**	**.333**	**-21**	**3**	**-2.0**
• BEHNEY, Mel	Melvin Brian Behney b: 9/2/1947, Newark, NJ BL/TL, 6'2", 180 lbs. Deb: 8/14/1970																										
1970	Cin-N	0	2	.000	5	1	0	0	0	10	15	11	5	1	0	8	2	2.300	4.50	93	8.42	.341	0	.000	-0	0	-0.1
• BEHRMAN, Hank	Henry Bernard Behrman b: 6/27/1921, Brooklyn, NY d: 1/20/1987, New York, NY BR/TR, 5'11", 174 lbs. Deb: 4/17/1946																										
1946	Bro-N	11	5	.688	47	11	2	0	4	150^2	138	63	49	3	2	69	78	1.374	2.93	116	3.16	.241	4	.095	6	11	0.4
1947*	Bro-N	0	0	....	2	0	0	0	0	3^2	3	4	4	1	0	4	2	1.909	9.82	42	10.46	.375	0	....	-2	0	-0.2
	Pit-N	0	2	.000	10	2	0	0	0	24^2	33	26	25	6	2	17	11	2.027	9.12	46	9.34	.347	0	.000	-13	0	-1.4
	*Bro-N	5	3	.625	38	6	0	0	8	88^1	94	64	52	9	0	44	31	1.562	5.30	78	4.74	.275	6	.231	-13	3	-1.2
	Yr.	5	5	.500	50	8	0	0	8	116^2	130	94	81	16	2	65	44	1.671	6.25	67	5.90	.292	6	.188	-29	3	-2.8
1948	Bro-N	5	4	.556	34	4	2	1	7	91	95	51	41	7	3	42	42	1.505	4.05	98	4.41	.268	3	.107	-3	5	-0.4
1949	NY-N	3	3	.500	43	4	1	1	0	71^1	64	46	39	5	0	52	25	1.626	4.92	81	4.32	.239	1	.077	-7	2	-0.8
Total	**4**	**24**	**17**	**.585**	**174**	**27**	**5**	**2**	**19**	**429^2**	**427**	**254**	**210**	**31**	**7**	**228**	**189**	**1.524**	**4.40**	**88**	**4.36**	**.260**	**14**	**.122**	**-33**	**21**	**-3.7**
• BEIMEL, Joe	Joseph Ronald Beimel b: 4/19/1977, St. Mary's, PA BL/TL, 6'3", 201 lbs. Deb: 4/8/2001																										
2001	Pit-N	7	11	.389	42	15	0	0	0	115^1	131	72	67	12	6	49	58	1.561	5.23	86	5.24	.290	7	.269	-9	4	-0.7
2002	Pit-N	2	5	.286	53	8	0	0	0	85^1	88	49	44	9	4	45	53	1.559	4.64	90	4.68	.267	3	.300	-5	3	-0.4
2003	Pit-N	1	3	.250	69	0	0	0	0	62^1	69	35	35	7	4	33	42	1.636	5.05	87	5.62	.299	0	.000	-5	2	-0.5
Total	**3**	**10**	**19**	**.345**	**164**	**23**	**0**	**0**	**0**	**263**	**288**	**156**	**146**	**28**	**14**	**127**	**153**	**1.578**	**5.00**	**87**	**5.15**	**.284**	**10**	**.244**	**-19**	**9**	**-1.6**
• BEIRNE, Kevin	Kevin Patrick Beirne b: 1/1/1974, Houston, TX BL/TR, 6'4", 210 lbs. Deb: 5/17/2000																										
2000	Chi-A	1	3	.250	29	1	0	0	0	49^2	50	41	37	9	4	20	41	1.409	6.70	74	4.97	.263	0	....	-10	0	-0.9
2001	Tor-A	0	0	....	5	0	0	0	0	7	13	10	10	1	0	6	5	2.714	12.86	36	11.51	.394	0	....	-6	0	-0.6

YEAR	TM-L	W	L	PCT	G	GS	CG	SH	SV	IP	H	R	ER	HR	HB	BB	SO	RAT	ERA	ERA+	CERA	OAV	BH	AVG	PR+	WS	TPW
2002	LA-N	2	0	1.000	12	3	0	0	0	29	26	11	11	4	2	17	17	1.483	3.41	112	4.75	.245	2	.400	1	2	0.2
Total	3	3	3	.500	46	4	0	0	0	85^2	89	62	58	14	6	43	63	1.541	6.09	76	5.43	.271	2	.400	-16	2	-1.4

• BELCHER, Tim Timothy Wayne Belcher b: 10/19/1961, Mount Gilead, OH BR/TR, 6'3", 220 lbs. Deb: 9/6/1987

YEAR	TM-L	W	L	PCT	G	GS	CG	SH	SV	IP	H	R	ER	HR	HB	BB	SO	RAT	ERA	ERA+	CERA	OAV	BH	AVG	PR+	WS	TPW
1987	LA-N	4	2	.667	6	5	0	0	0	34	30	11	9	2	0	7	23	1.088	2.38	167	2.51	.240	2	.200	6	4	0.6
1988*	LA-N	12	6	.667	36	27	4	1	4	179^2	143	65	58	8	2	51	152	1.080	2.91	115	2.24	.217	4	.071	10	13	0.9
1989	LA-N	15	12	.556	39	30	**10**	**8**	1	230	182	81	72	20	7	80	200	1.139	2.82	121	2.79	.217	7	.100	14	15	1.2
1990	LA-N	9	9	.500	24	24	5	2	0	153	136	76	68	17	2	48	102	1.203	4.00	92	3.30	.240	7	.163	-7	6	-0.6
1991	LA-N	10	9	.526	33	33	2	1	0	209^1	189	76	61	10	2	75	156	1.261	2.62	137	3.04	.240	8	.119	22	15	2.1
1992	Cin-N	15	14	.517	35	34	2	1	0	227^2	201	104	99	17	3	80	149	1.234	3.91	92	3.12	.238	8	.105	-8	10	-1.1
1993	Cin-N	9	6	.600	22	22	4	2	0	137	134	72	68	11	7	47	101	1.321	4.47	90	3.72	.254	10	.200	-6	7	-0.5
	*Chi-A	3	5	.375	12	11	1	1	0	71^2	64	36	35	8	1	27	34	1.270	4.40	95	3.61	.242	0	....	-2	3	-0.2
1994	Det-A	7	15	.318	25	**25**	3	0	0	162	192	124	106	21	4	78	76	1.667	5.89	82	5.65	.290	0	....	-16	3	-1.5
1995*	Sea-A	10	12	.455	28	28	1	0	0	179^1	188	101	90	19	5	88	96	1.539	4.52	105	4.82	.269	0	....	9	9	0.8
1996	KC-A	15	11	.577	35	35	4	1	0	238^2	262	117	104	28	6	68	113	1.383	3.92	128	4.41	.281	0	....	29	19	2.6
1997	KC-A	13	12	.520	32	32	3	1	0	213^1	242	128	119	31	5	70	113	1.463	5.02	94	5.02	.288	0	.000	-9	9	-0.9
1998	KC-A	14	14	.500	34	34	2	0	0	234	247	127	111	37	7	73	130	1.368	4.27	113	4.59	.272	1	.200	17	17	1.6
1999	Ana-A	6	8	.429	24	24	0	0	0	132^1	168	104	99	27	5	46	52	1.617	6.73	72	6.44	.315	1	.200	-29	1	-2.6
2000	Ana-A	4	5	.444	9	9	1	0	0	40^2	45	31	31	8	2	22	22	1.648	6.86	74	6.23	.281	0	....	-9	1	-0.8
Total	14	146	140	.510	394	373	42	18	5	2442^2	2423	1253	1130	264	58	860	1519	1.344	4.16	102	4.03	.259	48	.124	21	132	1.6

• BELINDA, Stan Stanley Peter Belinda b: 8/6/1966, Huntingdon, PA BR/TR, 6'3", 187 lbs. Deb: 9/8/1989

YEAR	TM-L	W	L	PCT	G	GS	CG	SH	SV	IP	H	R	ER	HR	HB	BB	SO	RAT	ERA	ERA+	CERA	OAV	BH	AVG	PR+	WS	TPW
1989	Pit-N	0	1	.000	8	0	0	0	0	10^1	13	8	7	0	0	2	10	1.452	6.10	55	3.88	.295	0	....	-3	0	-0.3
1990*	Pit-N	3	4	.429	55	0	0	0	8	58^1	48	23	23	4	1	29	55	1.320	3.55	102	3.30	.227	0	.000	-0	5	-0.1
1991*	Pit-N	7	5	.583	60	0	0	0	16	78^1	50	30	30	10	4	35	71	1.085	3.45	104	2.65	.184	0	.000	1	9	0.0
1992*	Pit-N	6	4	.600	59	0	0	0	18	71^1	58	26	25	8	0	29	57	1.220	3.15	109	3.03	.223	2	.667	2	10	0.3
1993	Pit-N	3	1	.750	40	0	0	0	19	42^1	35	18	17	4	1	11	30	1.087	3.61	112	2.56	.224	0	.000	2	8	0.2
	KC-A	1	1	.500	23	0	0	0	0	27^1	30	13	13	2	1	6	25	1.317	4.28	107	3.88	.280	0	....	1	2	0.1
1994	KC-A	2	2	.500	37	0	0	0	1	49	47	36	28	6	5	24	37	1.449	5.14	97	4.62	.250	0	....	-1	2	-0.1
1995*	Bos-A	8	1	.889	63	0	0	0	10	69^2	51	25	24	5	4	28	57	1.134	3.10	157	2.65	.205	0	....	13	12	1.3
1996	Bos-A	2	1	.667	31	0	0	0	2	28^2	31	22	21	3	4	20	18	1.779	6.59	77	6.25	.272	0	....	-4	1	-0.4
1997	Cin-N	1	5	.167	84	0	0	0	1	99^1	84	42	41	11	9	33	114	1.178	3.71	116	3.27	.229	1	.333	6	8	0.6
1998	Cin-N	4	8	.333	40	0	0	0	1	61^1	46	23	22	7	1	28	57	1.207	3.23	133	2.97	.212	0	.000	7	5	0.7
1999	Cin-N	3	1	.750	29	0	0	0	2	42^2	42	26	25	11	1	18	40	1.406	5.27	88	5.20	.258	1	.250	-4	2	-0.4
2000	Col-N	1	3	.250	46	0	0	0	1	35^2	39	32	28	10	2	17	40	1.570	7.07	82	6.18	.277	0	.000	-5	1	-0.5
	Atl-N	0	0	....	10	0	0	0	0	11	16	12	12	4	1	5	11	1.909	9.82	47	9.59	.348	0	....	-6	0	-0.6
	Yr.	1	3	.250	56	0	0	0	1	46^2	55	44	40	14	3	22	51	1.650	7.71	70	6.98	.294	0	.000	-12	1	-1.1
Total	12	41	37	.526	585	0	0	0	79	685^1	590	336	316	85	34	285	622	1.277	4.15	104	3.67	.233	4	.160	7	65	0.8

• BELINSKY, Bo Robert Belinsky b: 12/7/1936, New York, NY d: 11/23/2001, Las Vegas, NV BL/TL, 6'2", 191 lbs. Deb: 4/18/1962

YEAR	TM-L	W	L	PCT	G	GS	CG	SH	SV	IP	H	R	ER	HR	HB	BB	SO	RAT	ERA	ERA+	CERA	OAV	BH	AVG	PR+	WS	TPW
1962	LA-A	10	11	.476	33	31	5	3	1	187^1	149	86	74	12	13	122	145	1.447	3.56	108	3.82	.216	10	.167	8	11	0.9
1963	LA-A	2	9	.182	13	13	2	0	0	76^2	78	54	49	12	4	35	60	1.474	5.75	60	4.96	.262	2	.074	-20	0	-2.3
1964	LA-A	9	8	.529	23	22	4	1	0	135^1	120	45	43	8	6	49	91	1.249	2.86	115	3.22	.240	4	.095	5	9	0.4
1965	Phi-N	4	9	.308	30	14	3	0	1	109^2	103	72	59	13	6	48	71	1.377	4.84	71	4.10	.248	6	.188	-17	0	-1.8
1966	Phi-N	0	2	.000	9	1	0	0	0	15^1	14	5	5	3	3	5	8	1.239	2.93	122	4.86	.250	1	.333	1	1	0.1
1967	Hou-N	3	9	.250	27	18	0	0	0	115^1	112	74	60	12	8	54	80	1.439	4.68	71	4.48	.255	3	.077	-15	0	-1.8
1969	Pit-N	0	3	.000	8	3	0	0	0	17^2	17	10	9	1	2	14	15	1.755	4.58	76	5.37	.266	0	.000	-2	0	-0.2
1970	Cin-N	0	0	....	3	0	0	0	0	8	10	6	4	0	0	6	6	2.000	4.50	93	5.98	.294	1	1.000	-0	0	0.0
Total	8	28	51	.354	146	102	14	4	2	665^1	603	352	303	61	42	333	476	1.407	4.10	85	4.08	.241	27	.131	-40	21	-4.6

• BELISLE, Matt Matthew Thomas Belisle b: 6/6/1980, Austin, TX BB/TR, 6'3", 195 lbs. Deb: 9/7/2003

YEAR	TM-L	W	L	PCT	G	GS	CG	SH	SV	IP	H	R	ER	HR	HB	BB	SO	RAT	ERA	ERA+	CERA	OAV	BH	AVG	PR+	WS	TPW
2003	Cin-N	1	1	.500	6	0	0	0	0	8^2	10	5	5	1	1	2	6	1.385	5.19	82	4.73	.303	0	.000	-1	0	-0.1

• BELITZ, Todd Todd Stephen Belitz b: 10/23/1975, Des Moines, IA BL/TL, 6'1", 200 lbs. Deb: 9/4/2000

YEAR	TM-L	W	L	PCT	G	GS	CG	SH	SV	IP	H	R	ER	HR	HB	BB	SO	RAT	ERA	ERA+	CERA	OAV	BH	AVG	PR+	WS	TPW
2000	Oak-A	0	0	....	5	0	0	0	0	3^1	4	2	1	0	0	4	3	2.400	2.70	176	7.07	.267	0	....	1	0	0.1
2001	Col-N	1	1	.500	8	0	0	0	0	9^1	9	8	8	2	0	3	5	1.286	7.71	69	4.25	.250	0	.000	-3	0	-0.3
Total	2	1	1	.500	13	0	0	0	0	12^2	13	10	9	2	0	7	8	1.579	6.39	82	4.99	.255	0	.000	-2	0	-0.2

• BELL, Bill William Samuel "Ding Dong" Bell b: 10/24/1933, Goldsboro, NC d: 10/11/1962, Durham, NC BR/TR, 6'3", 200 lbs. Deb: 9/5/1952

YEAR	TM-L	W	L	PCT	G	GS	CG	SH	SV	IP	H	R	ER	HR	HB	BB	SO	RAT	ERA	ERA+	CERA	OAV	BH	AVG	PR+	WS	TPW
1952	Pit-N	0	1	.000	4	1	0	0	0	15^2	16	11	8	3	0	13	4	1.851	4.60	87	6.23	.254	0	.000	-1	0	-0.1
1955	Pit-N	0	0	....	1	0	0	0	0	1	0	0	0	0	0	1	0	1.000	0.00	....	0.95	.000	0	....	0	0	0.0
Total	2	0	1	.000	5	1	0	0	0	16^2	16	11	8	3	0	14	4	1.800	4.32	92	5.91	.254	0	.000	-0	0	-0.1

• BELL, Charlie Charles C. Bell b: 8/12/1868, Cincinnati, OH d: 2/7/1937, Cincinnati, OH TR Deb: 10/13/1889

YEAR	TM-L	W	L	PCT	G	GS	CG	SH	SV	IP	H	R	ER	HR	HB	BB	SO	RAT	ERA	ERA+	CERA	OAV	BH	AVG	PR+	WS	TPW
1889	KC-a	1	0	1.000	1	1	1	0	0	9	4	5	1	0	0	3	3	.778	1.00	417	....	.131	1	.167	3	1	0.3
1891	Lou-a	2	6	.250	10	9	8	0	0	77	93	65	40	4	0	20	16	1.468	4.68	78	....	.289	1	.036	-9	2	-1.0
	Cin-a	1	0	1.000	1	1	1	0	0	9	2	2	0	0	0	3	1	.556	0.00	....	....	.070	2	.500	4	1	0.4
	Yr.	3	6	.333	11	10	9	0	0	86	95	67	40	4	0	23	17	1.372	4.19	87	....	.271	3	.094	-5	3	-0.6
Total	2	4	6	.400	12	11	10	0	0	95	99	72	41	4	0	26	20	1.316	3.88	94	....	.260	4	.105	-2	4	-0.3

• BELL, Eric Eric Alvin Bell b: 10/27/1963, Modesto, CA BL/TL, 6', 195 lbs. Deb: 9/24/1985

YEAR	TM-L	W	L	PCT	G	GS	CG	SH	SV	IP	H	R	ER	HR	HB	BB	SO	RAT	ERA	ERA+	CERA	OAV	BH	AVG	PR+	WS	TPW
1985	Bal-A	0	0	....	4	0	0	0	0	5^2	4	3	3	1	0	4	4	1.412	4.76	85	4.28	.200	0	....	-0	0	0.0
1986	Bal-A	1	2	.333	4	4	0	0	0	23^1	23	14	13	4	0	14	18	1.586	5.01	82	5.33	.258	0	....	-2	1	-0.2
1987	Bal-A	10	13	.435	33	29	2	0	0	165	174	113	100	32	2	78	111	1.527	5.45	81	5.47	.271	0	....	-19	5	-1.8
1991	Cle-A	4	0	1.000	10	0	0	0	0	18	5	2	1	0	1	5	7	.556	0.50	831	0.60	.091	0	....	8	3	0.8
1992	Cle-A	0	2	.000	7	1	0	0	0	15^1	22	13	13	1	1	9	10	2.022	7.63	51	7.61	.349	0	....	-6	0	-0.6
1993	Hou-N	0	1	.000	10	0	0	0	0	7^1	10	5	5	0	0	2	2	1.636	6.14	63	4.76	.313	0	....	-2	0	-0.2
Total	6	15	18	.455	68	34	2	0	0	234^2	238	150	135	38	4	112	152	1.491	5.18	83	5.17	.264	0	....	-22	9	-2.1

• BELL, Gary Gary Bell b: 11/17/1936, San Antonio, TX BR/TR, 6'1", 198 lbs. Deb: 6/1/1958

YEAR	TM-L	W	L	PCT	G	GS	CG	SH	SV	IP	H	R	ER	HR	HB	BB	SO	RAT	ERA	ERA+	CERA	OAV	BH	AVG	PR+	WS	TPW
1958	Cle-A	12	10	.545	33	23	10	0	1	182	141	70	67	17	5	73	110	1.176	3.31	110	2.94	.213	11	.196	6	12	0.8
1959	Cle-A	16	11	.593	44	28	12	1	5	234	208	107	105	28	5	105	136	1.338	4.04	91	3.82	.238	18	.240	-11	14	-0.9
1960	Cle-A★	9	10	.474	28	23	6	2	1	154^2	139	78	71	15	7	82	109	1.429	4.13	91	4.18	.242	7	.149	-7	7	-0.7
1961	Cle-A	12	16	.429	34	34	11	2	0	228^1	214	125	104	32	6	100	163	1.375	4.10	96	4.20	.245	16	.198	-4	10	-0.3
1962	Cle-A	10	9	.526	57	6	1	0	12	107^2	104	56	51	14	3	52	80	1.449	4.26	91	4.51	.264	5	.208	-6	8	-0.4
1963	Cle-A	8	5	.615	58	7	0	0	5	119	91	48	39	13	4	52	98	1.202	2.95	123	2.96	.208	3	.115	10	10	0.9
1964	Cle-A	8	6	.571	56	2	0	0	4	106	106	56	51	15	4	53	89	1.500	4.33	83	4.85	.260	6	.375	-6	5	-0.4
1965	Cle-A	6	5	.545	60	0	0	0	17	103^2	86	43	35	7	2	50	86	1.312	3.04	115	3.15	.226	1	.063	5	10	0.5
1966	Cle-A★	14	15	.483	40	37	12	0	0	254^1	211	102	91	19	4	79	194	1.140	3.22	107	2.75	.228	10	.132	10	16	1.0
1967	Cle-A	1	5	.167	9	9	1	0	0	60^2	50	28	25	7	1	24	39	1.220	3.71	88	3.30	.234	0	.000	-2	1	-0.4
	*Bos-A	12	8	.600	29	24	8	0	3	165^1	143	70	58	16	4	47	115	1.149	3.16	110	2.93	.231	12	.203	7	11	0.9
	Yr.	13	13	.500	38	33	9	0	3	226	193	98	83	23	5	71	154	1.168	3.31	103	3.03	.232	12	.162	4	12	0.4
1968	Bos-A★	11	11	.500	35	27	9	3	1	199^1	177	82	69	7	5	68	103	1.229	3.12	101	2.88	.239	13	.220	2	11	0.5
1969	Sea-A	2	6	.250	13	11	1	1	2	61^1	76	40	32	8	2	34	30	1.793	4.70	77	6.25	.305	3	.214	-6	1	-0.4
	Chi-A	0	0	....	23	2	0	0	0	38^2	48	27	27	8	2	23	26	1.836	6.28	61	7.39	.308	0	.000	-10	0	-1.1
	Yr.	2	6	.250	36	13	1	1	2	100	124	67	59	16	4	57	56	1.810	5.31	70	6.69	.306	3	.158	-15	1	-1.5
Total	12	121	117	.508	519	233	71	9	51	2015	1794	932	825	206	54	842	1378	1.308	3.68	98	3.64	.239	105	.185	-12	116	-0.1

• BELL, George George Glenn "Farmer" Bell b: 11/2/1874, Greenwood, NY d: 12/25/1941, New York, NY BR/TR, 6', 195 lbs. Deb: 4/17/1907

YEAR	TM-L	W	L	PCT	G	GS	CG	SH	SV	IP	H	R	ER	HR	HB	BB	SO	RAT	ERA	ERA+	CERA	OAV	BH	AVG	PR+	WS	TPW
1907	Bro-N	8	16	.333	35	27	20	3	1	263^2	222	102	66	1	6	77	88	1.134	2.25	104	2.41	.238	8	.095	5	13	0.3

YEAR	TM-L	W	L	PCT	G	GS	CG	SH	SV	IP	H	R	ER	HR	HB	BB	SO	RAT	ERA	ERA+	CERA	OAV	BH	AVG	PR+	WS	TPW
1908	Bro-N	4	15	.211	29	19	12	2	1	155^1	162	80	62	3	2	45	63	**1.333**	3.59	65	3.39	.270	8	.170	-23	1	-2.5
1909	Bro-N	16	15	.516	33	30	29	6	1	256	236	103	77	6	4	73	95	1.207	2.71	95	2.84	.251	15	.167	-1	15	0.1
1910	Bro-N	10	27	.270	44	36	25	4	1	310	267	127	91	4	4	82	102	1.126	2.64	114	2.32	.241	13	.134	11	17	0.7
1911	Bro-N	5	6	.455	19	12	6	2	0	101	123	59	48	2	2	28	28	1.495	4.28	78	4.52	.315	4	.121	-10	3	-1.2
Total	5	43	79	.352	160	124	92	17	4	1086	1010	471	344	16	18	305	376	1.211	2.85	93	2.82	.254	48	.137	-19	49	-2.5

• BELL, Hi Herman S. Bell b: 7/16/1897, Mount Sherman, KY d: 6/7/1949, Glendale, CA BR/TR, 6', 185 lbs. Deb: 4/16/1924

YEAR	TM-L	W	L	PCT	G	GS	CG	SH	SV	IP	H	R	ER	HR	HB	BB	SO	RAT	ERA	ERA+	CERA	OAV	BH	AVG	PR+	WS	TPW
1924	StL-N	3	8	.273	28	11	5	0	1	113^1	124	68	62	5	5	29	29	1.350	4.92	77	3.86	.292	2	.065	-14	3	-1.6
1926*	StL-N	6	6	.500	27	7	3	0	2	85	82	41	30	1	2	17	27	1.165	3.18	123	2.55	.255	3	.120	6	6	0.5
1927	StL-N	1	3	.250	25	1	0	0	0	57^1	71	37	25	5	1	22	31	1.622	3.92	101	5.37	.317	1	.091	-1	2	-0.2
1929	StL-N	0	2	.000	7	0	0	0	0	13	19	15	10	1	0	4	4	1.769	6.92	67	5.80	.339	0	.000	-3	0	-0.3
1930*	StL-N	4	3	.571	39	9	2	0	**8**	115^1	143	65	50	4	2	23	42	1.439	3.90	129	4.08	.299	2	.077	14	10	1.0
1932	NY-N	8	4	.667	35	10	3	0	2	120	132	58	49	12	2	16	25	1.233	3.68	101	3.63	.280	3	.088	3	7	0.0
1933*	NY-N	6	5	.545	38	7	1	1	5	105^1	100	31	24	4	2	20	24	1.139	2.05	156	2.62	.246	4	.138	12	10	1.2
1934	NY-N	4	3	.571	22	2	0	0	6	54	72	25	22	2	2	12	9	1.556	3.67	106	4.89	.319	2	.105	1	4	-0.1
Total	8	32	34	.485	221	47	14	1	24	663^1	743	340	272	34	16	143	191	1.336	3.69	107	3.74	.285	17	.096	17	42	0.5

• BELL, Jerry Jerry Houston Bell b: 10/6/1947, Madison, TN BB/TR, 6'4", 190 lbs. Deb: 9/6/1971

YEAR	TM-L	W	L	PCT	G	GS	CG	SH	SV	IP	H	R	ER	HR	HB	BB	SO	RAT	ERA	ERA+	CERA	OAV	BH	AVG	PR+	WS	TPW
1971	Mil-A	2	1	.667	8	0	0	0	0	14^2	10	5	5	0	0	6	8	1.091	3.07	113	1.80	.200	0	....	1	1	0.1
1972	Mil-A	5	1	.833	25	3	0	0	0	70^2	50	15	13	1	3	33	20	1.175	1.66	183	2.41	.209	1	.071	11	7	1.1
1973	Mil-A	9	9	.500	31	25	8	0	1	183^2	185	95	81	14	5	70	57	1.388	3.97	95	3.97	.263	0	....	-3	8	-0.3
1974	Mil-A	1	0	1.000	5	0	0	0	0	14	17	6	4	2	0	5	4	1.571	2.57	141	5.83	.315	0	....	2	1	0.2
Total	4	17	11	.607	69	28	8	0	1	283	262	121	103	17	8	114	89	1.329	3.28	111	3.56	.250	1	.071	10	17	1.0

• BELL, Ralph Ralph Albert "Lefty" Bell b: 11/6/1890, Kahoka, MO d: 10/18/1959, Burlington, IA BL/TL, 5'11.5", 170 lbs. Deb: 7/16/1912

YEAR	TM-L	W	L	PCT	G	GS	CG	SH	SV	IP	H	R	ER	HR	HB	BB	SO	RAT	ERA	ERA+	CERA	OAV	BH	AVG	PR+	WS	TPW
1912	Chi-A	0	0	....	3	0	0	0	0	6	8	7	6	1	0	8	5	2.667	9.00	36	10.82	.333	0	.000	-4	0	-0.4

• BELL, Rob Robert Allen Bell b: 1/17/1977, Newburgh, NY BR/TR, 6'5", 225 lbs. Deb: 4/8/2000

YEAR	TM-L	W	L	PCT	G	GS	CG	SH	SV	IP	H	R	ER	HR	HB	BB	SO	RAT	ERA	ERA+	CERA	OAV	BH	AVG	PR+	WS	TPW
2000	Cin-N	7	8	.467	26	26	1	0	0	140^1	130	84	78	32	1	73	112	1.447	5.00	94	4.98	.243	3	.067	-6	5	-0.9
2001	Cin-N	0	5	.000	9	9	0	0	0	44^1	46	28	27	9	3	17	33	1.421	5.48	83	5.43	.275	1	.143	-4	1	-0.4
	Tex-A	5	5	.500	18	18	0	0	0	105^1	130	87	84	23	4	47	64	1.680	7.18	65	6.82	.310	0	....	-29	0	-2.7
2002	Tex-A	4	3	.571	17	15	0	0	0	94	113	69	65	16	1	35	70	1.574	6.22	76	5.67	.296	0	.000	-15	2	-1.4
2003	TB-A	5	4	.556	19	18	0	0	0	101	103	64	62	15	5	39	44	1.406	5.52	82	4.67	.263	0	.000	-14	3	-1.3
Total	4	21	25	.457	89	86	1	0	0	485	522	332	316	95	14	211	323	1.511	5.86	79	5.49	.275	4	.073	-67	11	-6.7

• BELTRAN, Francis Francis LeBron Beltran b: 11/29/1979, Santo Domingo, Dominican Republic BR/TR, 6'5", 220 lbs. Deb: 6/28/2002

YEAR	TM-L	W	L	PCT	G	GS	CG	SH	SV	IP	H	R	ER	HR	HB	BB	SO	RAT	ERA	ERA+	CERA	OAV	BH	AVG	PR+	WS	TPW
2002	Chi-N	0	0	....	11	0	0	0	0	12	14	11	10	2	0	16	11	2.500	7.50	54	9.45	.311	0	.000	-5	0	-0.5

• BELTRAN, Rigo Rigoberto Beltran b: 11/13/1969, Tijuana, Mexico BL/TL, 5'11", 185 lbs. Deb: 6/2/1997

YEAR	TM-L	W	L	PCT	G	GS	CG	SH	SV	IP	H	R	ER	HR	HB	BB	SO	RAT	ERA	ERA+	CERA	OAV	BH	AVG	PR+	WS	TPW
1997	StL-N	1	2	.333	35	4	0	0	1	54^1	47	25	21	3	0	17	50	1.178	3.48	119	2.72	.237	1	.143	4	3	0.4
1998	NY-N	0	0	....	7	0	0	0	0	8	6	3	3	1	0	4	5	1.250	3.38	123	3.32	.214	0	.000	1	1	0.1
1999	NY-N	1	1	.500	21	0	0	0	0	31	30	15	12	5	0	12	35	1.355	3.48	126	4.11	.250	0	.000	3	2	0.3
	Col-N	0	0	....	12	0	0	0	0	11	20	9	9	2	1	7	15	2.455	7.36	79	11.14	.385	1	.500	-2	0	-0.2
	Yr.	1	1	.500	33	0	0	0	0	42	50	24	21	7	1	19	50	1.643	4.50	109	5.95	.291	1	.333	1	2	0.1
2000	Col-N	0	0	....	1	1	0	0	0	1^1	6	6	6	2	0	3	1	6.750	40.50	14	61.44	.600	0	....	-5	0	-0.5
Total	4	2	3	.400	76	5	0	0	1	105^2	109	58	51	13	1	43	106	1.438	4.34	106	4.79	.267	2	.182	0	6	0.1

• BENDER, Chief Charles Albert Bender b: 5/5/1884, Crow Wing County, MN d: 5/22/1954, Philadelphia, PA BR/TR, 6'2", 185 lbs. Deb: 4/20/1903 C/U HOF: 1953

YEAR	TM-L	W	L	PCT	G	GS	CG	SH	SV	IP	H	R	ER	HR	HB	BB	SO	RAT	ERA	ERA+	CERA	OAV	BH	AVG	PR+	WS	TPW
1903	Phi-A	17	14	.548	36	33	29	2	0	270	239	115	92	6	25	65	127	1.126	3.07	99	2.72	.237	22	.183	2	18	0.0
1904	Phi-A	10	11	.476	29	20	18	4	0	203^2	167	90	65	1	4	59	149	1.110	2.87	93	2.11	.225	18	.228	0	11	0.4
1905*	Phi-A	18	11	.621	35	23	18	4	0	229	193	103	72	5	11	90	142	1.236	2.83	94	2.77	.231	20	.217	2	15	0.5
1906	Phi-A	15	10	.600	36	27	24	0	**3**	238^1	208	98	67	5	8	48	159	1.074	2.53	108	2.27	.238	25	.253	5	17	1.5
1907	Phi-A	16	8	.667	33	24	20	4	3	219^1	185	67	50	1	3	34	112	.998	2.05	127	1.76	.231	23	.230	12	22	1.5
1908	Phi-A	8	9	.471	18	17	14	2	1	138^2	121	48	27	1	3	21	85	1.024	1.75	146	2.05	.236	11	.220	16	12	2.2
1909	Phi-A	18	8	.692	34	29	24	5	1	250	196	68	46	1	5	45	161	.964	1.66	145	1.68	.214	20	.215	18	22	2.5
1910*	Phi-A	23	5	.821	30	28	25	3	0	250	182	63	44	1	10	47	155	.916	1.58	150	1.61	.207	25	.269	17	26	2.7
1911*	Phi-A	17	5	.773	31	24	16	2	3	216^1	198	66	52	2	4	58	114	1.183	2.16	145	2.70	.252	13	.165	22	18	1.9
1912	Phi-A	13	8	.619	27	19	12	1	2	171	169	63	52	1	1	33	90	1.181	2.74	113	2.87	.277	9	.150	4	13	0.3
1913*	Phi-A	21	10	.677	48	21	14	2	**13**	236^2	208	78	58	2	3	59	135	1.128	2.21	125	2.25	.228	12	.154	14	20	1.5
1914*	Phi-A	17	3	.850	28	23	14	7	2	179	159	49	45	4	1	55	107	1.196	2.26	115	2.66	.240	9	.145	6	15	0.7
1915	Bal-F	4	16	.200	26	23	15	0	1	178^1	198	103	79	5	7	37	89	1.318	3.99	85	3.83	.298	16	.267	-9	6	-0.5
1916	Phi-N	7	7	.500	27	13	4	0	3	122^2	137	71	51	3	10	34	43	1.394	3.74	71	3.91	.287	12	.279	-15	3	-1.3
1917	Phi-N	8	2	.800	20	10	8	4	2	113	84	24	21	1	7	26	43	.973	1.67	168	1.83	.215	8	.205	14	13	1.7
1925	Chi-A	0	0	....	1	0	0	0	0	1	1	2	2	1	0	1	0	2.000	18.00	23	13.97	.333	0	....	-2	0	-0.1
Total	16	212	127	.625	459	334	255	40	34	3017	2645	1108	823	40	102	712	1711	1.113	2.46	113	2.42	.239	243	.212	108	231	15.4

• BENES, Alan Alan Paul Benes b: 1/21/1972, Evansville, IN BR/TR, 6'5", 215 lbs. Deb: 9/19/1995

YEAR	TM-L	W	L	PCT	G	GS	CG	SH	SV	IP	H	R	ER	HR	HB	BB	SO	RAT	ERA	ERA+	CERA	OAV	BH	AVG	PR+	WS	TPW
1995	StL-N	1	2	.333	3	3	0	0	0	16	24	15	15	2	1	4	20	1.750	8.44	50	6.84	.343	0	.000	-8	0	-0.8
1996*	StL-N	13	10	.565	34	32	3	1	0	191	192	120	104	27	7	87	131	1.461	4.90	86	4.76	.266	9	.148	-19	5	-1.9
1997	StL-N	9	9	.500	23	23	2	0	0	161^2	128	60	52	13	4	68	160	1.212	2.89	143	3.01	.219	9	.173	22	12	2.2
1999	StL-N	0	0	....	2	0	0	0	0	2	2	0	0	0	0	0	2	1.000	0.00	....	2.31	.286	0	....	1	0	0.1
2000	StL-N	2	2	.500	30	0	0	0	0	46	54	33	29	7	2	23	26	1.674	5.67	81	5.96	.290	2	.500	-6	1	-0.5
2001	StL-N	2	0	1.000	9	1	0	0	0	14^2	14	12	12	5	0	12	10	1.773	7.36	58	7.55	.250	1	.500	-5	0	-0.5
2002	Chi-N	2	2	.500	7	7	0	0	0	39^1	42	22	19	3	0	12	32	1.373	4.35	92	3.91	.276	1	.077	-1	1	-0.2
2003	Chi-N	0	0	....	3	0	0	0	1	8^1	8	2	2	0	0	6	9	1.680	2.16	195	4.60	.267	0	.000	2	1	0.2
	Tex-A	0	3	.000	4	4	0	0	0	15	29	20	19	2	0	8	11	2.467	11.40	44	11.17	.414	0	....	-11	0	-1.0
Total	8	29	28	.509	115	70	5	1	1	494	493	284	252	59	14	220	401	1.443	4.59	93	4.56	.263	22	.158	-25	20	-2.4

• BENES, Andy Andrew Charles Benes b: 8/20/1967, Evansville, IN BR/TR, 6'6", 240 lbs. Deb: 8/11/1989

YEAR	TM-L	W	L	PCT	G	GS	CG	SH	SV	IP	H	R	ER	HR	HB	BB	SO	RAT	ERA	ERA+	CERA	OAV	BH	AVG	PR+	WS	TPW
1989	SD-N	6	3	.667	10	10	0	0	0	66^2	51	28	26	7	1	31	66	1.230	3.51	100	3.12	.213	6	.250	-1	5	0.1
1990	SD-N	10	11	.476	32	31	2	0	0	192^1	177	87	77	18	1	69	140	1.279	3.60	106	3.40	.242	6	.100	4	10	0.2
1991	SD-N	15	11	.577	33	33	4	1	0	223	194	76	75	23	4	59	167	1.135	3.03	126	2.92	.232	2	.032	18	16	1.7
1992	SD-N	13	14	.481	34	34	2	2	0	231^1	230	90	86	14	5	61	169	1.258	3.35	107	3.33	.264	10	.149	7	16	0.9
1993	SD-N★	15	15	.500	34	34	4	2	0	230^2	200	111	97	23	4	86	179	1.240	3.78	109	3.25	.232	9	.125	10	12	1.0
1994	SD-N	6	14	.300	25	25	2	2	0	172^1	155	82	74	20	1	51	**189**	1.195	3.86	106	3.21	.237	8	.163	9	8	0.9
1995	SD-N	4	7	.364	19	19	1	1	0	118^2	121	65	55	10	4	45	126	1.399	4.17	96	4.05	.262	6	.150	-4	4	-0.4
	*Sea-A	7	2	.778	12	12	0	0	0	63	72	42	41	8	2	33	45	1.667	5.86	81	5.66	.287	0	....	-6	3	-0.6
1996*	StL-N	18	10	.643	36	34	3	1	1	230^1	215	107	98	28	6	77	160	1.268	3.83	109	3.69	.247	11	.151	4	14	0.4
1997	StL-N	10	7	.588	26	26	0	0	0	177	149	64	61	9	5	61	175	1.186	3.10	134	2.80	.230	12	.218	20	14	2.2
1998	Ari-N	14	13	.519	34	34	1	0	0	231^1	221	111	102	25	6	74	164	1.275	3.97	106	3.64	.251	11	.169	6	14	0.9
1999	Ari-N	13	12	.520	33	32	0	0	0	198^1	216	117	106	34	4	82	141	1.503	4.81	95	5.18	.273	9	.155	-6	8	-0.5
2000*	StL-N	12	9	.571	30	27	1	0	0	166	174	95	90	30	1	68	137	1.458	4.88	94	5.05	.275	4	.080	-7	8	-0.8
2001	StL-N	7	7	.500	27	19	0	0	0	107^1	122	92	88	30	6	61	78	1.705	7.38	58	7.27	.286	5	.156	-39	0	-3.8
2002*	StL-N	5	4	.556	18	17	1	0	0	97	80	39	30	10	5	51	64	1.351	2.78	142	3.78	.228	7	.206	11	7	1.3
Total	14	155	139	.527	403	387	21	9	1	2505^1	2377	1206	1106	289	55	909	2000	1.312	3.97	104	3.84	.250	106	.143	25	139	3.5

• BENGE, Ray Raymond Adelphia Benge b: 4/22/1902, Jacksonville, TX d: 6/27/1997, Centerville, TX BR/TR, 5'9.5", 160 lbs. Deb: 9/26/1925

YEAR	TM-L	W	L	PCT	G	GS	CG	SH	SV	IP	H	R	ER	HR	HB	BB	SO	RAT	ERA	ERA+	CERA	OAV	BH	AVG	PR+	WS	TPW
1925	Cle-A	1	0	1.000	2	2	1	1	0	11^2	9	2	2	0	0	3	3	1.029	1.54	286	1.66	.205	2	.400	4	2	0.4
1926	Cle-A	1	0	1.000	8	0	0	0	0	11^2	15	11	5	0	0	4	3	1.629	3.86	105	4.41	.313	1	.333	-0	1	0.0
1928	Phi-N	8	18	.308	40	28	12	1	1	201^2	219	117	102	15	5	88	68	1.522	4.55	94	4.50	.286	12	.207	-3	10	-0.2

YEAR	TM-L	W	L	PCT	G	GS	CG	SH	SV	IP	H	R	ER	HR	HB	BB	SO	RAT	ERA	ERA+	CERA	OAV	BH	AVG	PR+	WS	TPW
1929	Phi-N	11	15	.423	38	26	9	2	4	199	255	147	139	24	4	77	78	1.668	6.29	82	5.83	.322	15	.203	-20	8	-2.1
1930	Phi-N	11	15	.423	38	29	14	0	1	225^2	305	178	143	22	1	81	70	1.710	5.70	96	5.78	.328	18	.205	-0	9	-0.3
1931	Phi-N	14	18	.438	38	31	16	2	2	247	251	107	87	12	5	61	117	1.263	3.17	134	3.21	.262	18	.205	32	21	**3.1**
1932	Phi-N	13	12	.520	41	28	13	2	6	222^1	247	119	100	15	4	58	89	1.372	4.05	109	3.93	.281	13	.173	9	15	0.7
1933	Bro-N	10	17	.370	37	30	16	2	1	228^2	238	104	87	11	6	55	74	1.281	3.42	94	3.35	.268	14	.184	1	10	0.1
1934	Bro-N	14	12	.538	36	32	14	1	0	227	252	124	109	11	3	61	64	1.379	4.32	90	3.70	.272	15	.169	-9	10	-1.1
1935	Bro-N	9	9	.500	23	17	5	1	1	124^2	142	77	62	12	1	47	39	1.516	4.48	89	4.75	.289	9	.191	-8	4	-0.9
1936	Bos-N	7	9	.438	21	19	2	0	0	115	161	79	74	6	1	38	32	1.730	5.79	66	5.77	.333	6	.140	-26	0	-2.8
	Phi-N	1	4	.200	15	6	0	0	1	45^2	70	35	24	3	0	19	13	1.949	4.73	96	6.94	.350	0	.000	0	1	-0.1
	Yr.	8	13	.381	36	25	2	0	1	160^2	231	114	98	9	1	57	45	**1.793**	5.49	73	6.10	.338	6	.113	-26	1	-2.9
1938	Cin-N	1	1	.500	9	0	0	0	2	15^1	13	8	7	1	0	6	5	1.239	4.11	89	2.95	.228	1	.333	-1	1	-0.1
Total	**12**	**101**	**130**	**.437**	**346**	**248**	**102**	**12**	**19**	**1875^1**	**2177**	**1108**	**941**	**132**	**30**	**598**	**655**	**1.480**	**4.52**	**95**	**4.44**	**.292**	**124**	**.188**	**-22**	**92**	**-3.3**
• BENITEZ, Armando	Armando German Benitez b: 11/3/1972, Ramon Santana, Dominican Republic BR/TR, 6'4", 180 lbs. Deb: 7/28/1994																										
1994	Bal-A	0	0	....	3	0	0	0	0	10	8	1	1	0	1	4	14	1.200	0.90	556	2.71	.216	0	....	4	1	0.4
1995	Bal-A	1	5	.167	44	0	0	0	2	47^2	37	33	30	8	5	37	56	1.552	5.66	84	5.06	.213	0	....	-5	1	-0.5
1996*	Bal-A	1	0	1.000	18	0	0	0	4	14^1	7	6	6	2	0	6	20	.907	3.77	131	1.78	.143	0	....	2	3	0.2
1997*	Bal-A	4	5	.444	71	0	0	0	9	73^1	49	22	20	7	1	43	106	1.255	2.45	179	2.92	.191	0	....	16	11	1.5
1998	Bal-A	5	6	.455	71	0	0	0	22	68^1	48	29	29	10	4	39	87	1.273	3.82	119	3.63	.199	0	....	6	10	0.6
1999*	NY-N	4	3	.571	77	0	0	0	22	78	40	17	16	4	0	41	128	1.038	1.85	237	1.69	.148	0	.000	21	19	2.0
2000*	NY-N	4	4	.500	76	0	0	0	41	76	39	24	22	10	0	38	106	1.013	2.61	169	2.08	.148	0	....	16	17	1.5
2001	NY-N	6	4	.600	73	0	0	0	43	76^1	59	32	32	12	1	40	93	1.297	3.77	109	3.67	.214	0	.000	3	14	0.2
2002	NY-N	1	0	1.000	62	0	0	0	33	67^1	46	20	17	8	3	25	79	1.054	2.27	174	2.55	.190	0	....	13	12	1.3
2003	NY-N★	3	3	.500	45	0	0	0	21	49^1	41	18	17	5	0	24	50	1.318	3.10	134	3.46	.223	0	.000	6	8	0.6
	NY-A	1	1	.500	9	0	0	0	0	9^1	8	4	2	0	0	6	10	1.500	1.93	226	3.40	.235	0	....	3	1	0.3
	Sea-A	0	0	....	15	0	0	0	0	14^1	10	5	5	1	0	11	15	1.465	3.14	138	3.40	.189	0	....	1	1	0.1
	Yr.	1	1	.500	24	0	0	0	0	23^2	18	9	7	1	0	17	25	1.479	2.66	163	3.40	.207	0	....	4	2	0.4
Total	**10**	**30**	**31**	**.492**	**564**	**0**	**0**	**0**	**197**	**584^1**	**392**	**211**	**197**	**67**	**15**	**314**	**764**	**1.208**	**3.03**	**144**	**2.99**	**.188**	**0**	**.000**	**86**	**98**	**8.1**
• BENN, Henry	Henry Omer Benn b: 1/25/1890, Viola, WI d: 6/4/1967, Madison, WI BR/TR, 6', 190 lbs. Deb: 9/24/1914																										
1914	Cle-A	0	0	....	1	0	0	0	0	1	0	0	0	0	0	0	1	.000	0.00	....	0.00	.000	0	....	0	0	0.0
• BENNETT, Bugs	Joseph Harley Bennett b: 4/19/1892, Kansas City, MO d: 11/21/1957, Noel, MO BR/TR, 5'9.5", 163 lbs. Deb: 7/20/1918																										
1918	StL-A	0	2	.000	4	2	0	0	0	10^1	12	7	4	1	0	7	0	1.839	3.48	78	6.05	.308	1	.250	-1	0	-0.1
1921	Chi-A	0	3	.000	3	2	1	0	0	17^2	19	14	12	1	0	16	2	1.981	6.11	69	6.00	.297	2	.333	-4	0	-0.3
	StL-A	0	0	....	3	1	0	0	0	5^2	11	10	9	1	2	6	3	3.000	14.29	31	15.42	.407	1	1.000	-6	0	-0.5
	Yr.	0	3	.000	6	3	1	0	0	23^1	30	24	21	2	2	22	5	2.229	8.10	53	8.29	.330	3	.429	-10	0	-0.9
Total	**2**	**0**	**5**	**.000**	**10**	**5**	**1**	**0**	**0**	**33^2**	**42**	**31**	**25**	**3**	**2**	**29**	**5**	**2.109**	**6.68**	**59**	**7.60**	**.323**	**4**	**.364**	**-11**	**0**	**-1.0**
• BENNETT, Dave	David Hans Bennett b: 11/7/1945, Berkeley, CA BR/TR, 6'5", 195 lbs. Deb: 6/12/1964																										
1964	Phi-N	0	0	....	1	0	0	0	0	1	2	1	1	0	0	0	1	2.000	9.00	39	7.48	.400	0	....	-1	0	-0.1
• BENNETT, Dennis	Dennis John Bennett b: 10/5/1939, Oakland, CA BL/TL, 6'3", 205 lbs. Deb: 5/12/1962																										
1962	Phi-N	9	9	.500	31	24	7	2	3	174^2	144	78	74	17	6	68	149	1.214	3.81	101	3.20	.224	8	.127	-0	11	-0.1
1963	Phi-N	9	5	.643	23	16	6	1	1	119^1	102	44	35	12	4	33	82	1.131	2.64	123	2.90	.231	9	.225	6	9	0.9
1964	Phi-N	12	14	.462	41	32	7	2	1	208	222	92	85	23	5	58	125	1.346	3.68	94	4.13	.280	13	.197	-6	10	-0.3
1965	Bos-A	5	7	.417	34	18	3	0	0	141^2	152	76	69	15	6	53	85	1.447	4.38	85	4.54	.279	7	.179	-8	5	-0.6
1966	Bos-A	3	3	.500	16	13	0	0	0	75	75	30	27	9	1	23	47	1.307	3.24	117	3.88	.261	3	.130	5	5	0.6
1967	Bos-A	4	3	.571	13	11	4	1	0	69^2	72	32	30	12	2	22	34	1.349	3.88	90	4.49	.268	3	.120	-3	3	-0.3
	NY-N	1	1	.500	8	6	0	0	0	26^1	37	15	15	4	1	7	14	1.671	5.13	66	6.43	.336	2	.250	-5	0	-0.5
1968	Cal-A	0	5	.000	16	7	1	0	1	48^1	46	22	19	6	4	17	36	1.303	3.54	82	4.02	.250	1	.077	-4	1	-0.5
Total	**7**	**43**	**47**	**.478**	**182**	**127**	**28**	**6**	**6**	**863**	**850**	**389**	**354**	**98**	**29**	**281**	**572**	**1.311**	**3.69**	**96**	**3.91**	**.260**	**46**	**.166**	**-15**	**44**	**-0.9**
• BENNETT, Erik	Erik Hans Bennett b: 9/13/1968, Yreka, CA BR/TR, 6'2", 205 lbs. Deb: 5/15/1995																										
1995	Cal-A	0	0	....	1	0	0	0	0	0^1	0	0	0	0	0	0	0	.000	0.00	....	0.00	.000	0	....	0	0	0.0
1996	Min-A	2	0	1.000	24	0	0	0	1	27^1	33	24	24	7	2	16	13	1.793	7.90	65	7.64	.306	0	....	-9	0	-0.8
Total	**2**	**2**	**0**	**1.000**	**25**	**0**	**0**	**0**	**1**	**27^2**	**33**	**24**	**24**	**7**	**2**	**16**	**13**	**1.771**	**7.81**	**66**	**7.55**	**.306**	**0**	**....**	**-9**	**0**	**-0.8**
• BENNETT, Frank	Francis Allen "Chip" Bennett b: 10/27/1904, Mardela Springs, MD d: 3/18/1966, Wilmington, DE BR/TR, 5'10.5", 163 lbs. Deb: 9/17/1927																										
1927	Bos-A	0	1	.000	4	1	0	0	0	12^1	15	4	4	0	0	6	1	1.703	2.92	144	5.22	.333	0	.000	2	1	0.1
1928	Bos-A	0	0	....	1	0	0	0	0	1	1	0	0	0	0	0	0	1.000	0.00	....	1.95	.250	0	....	0	0	0.0
Total	**2**	**0**	**1**	**.000**	**5**	**1**	**0**	**0**	**0**	**13^1**	**16**	**4**	**4**	**0**	**0**	**6**	**1**	**1.650**	**2.70**	**156**	**4.97**	**.326**	**0**	**.000**	**2**	**1**	**0.2**
• BENNETT, Joel	Joel Todd Bennett b: 1/31/1970, Binghamton, NY BR/TR, 6'1", 171 lbs. Deb: 7/15/1998																										
1998	Bal-A	0	0	....	2	0	0	0	0	2	2	1	1	0	0	3	0	2.500	4.50	101	7.45	.250	0	....	0	0	0.0
1999	Phi-N	2	1	.667	5	3	0	0	0	17	26	17	17	10	0	7	13	1.941	9.00	52	11.52	.351	0	.000	-8	0	-0.8
Total	**2**	**2**	**1**	**.667**	**7**	**3**	**0**	**0**	**0**	**19**	**28**	**18**	**18**	**10**	**0**	**10**	**13**	**2.000**	**8.53**	**55**	**11.09**	**.341**	**0**	**.000**	**-8**	**0**	**-0.8**
• BENNETT, Shayne	Shayne Anthony Bennett b: 4/10/1972, Adelaide, Australia BR/TR, 6'5", 200 lbs. Deb: 8/22/1997																										
1997	Mon-N	0	1	.000	16	0	0	0	0	22^2	21	9	8	2	0	9	8	1.324	3.18	132	3.29	.247	0	.000	3	2	0.3
1998	Mon-N	5	5	.500	62	0	0	0	1	91^2	97	61	56	8	6	45	59	1.549	5.50	77	4.83	.276	0	.000	-12	2	-1.2
1999	Mon-N	0	1	.000	5	1	0	0	0	11^1	24	18	18	4	1	3	4	2.382	14.29	31	14.07	.444	0	.000	-12	0	-1.2
Total	**3**	**5**	**7**	**.417**	**83**	**1**	**0**	**0**	**1**	**125^2**	**142**	**88**	**82**	**14**	**7**	**57**	**71**	**1.584**	**5.87**	**73**	**5.39**	**.290**	**0**	**.000**	**-21**	**4**	**-2.1**
• BENOIT, Joaquin	Joaquin Antonio (Pena) Benoit b: 7/26/1977, Santiago, Dominican Republic BR/TR, 6'3", 205 lbs. Deb: 8/8/2001																										
2001	Tex-A	0	0	....	1	1	0	0	0	5	8	6	6	3	0	3	4	2.200	10.80	43	13.11	.364	0	....	-3	0	-0.3
2002	Tex-A	4	5	.444	17	13	0	0	1	84^2	91	51	50	6	5	58	59	1.760	5.31	89	5.52	.272	0	....	-5	4	-0.4
2003	Tex-A	8	5	.615	25	17	0	0	0	105	99	67	64	23	3	51	87	1.429	5.49	90	5.03	.246	0	.000	-5	5	-0.5
Total	**3**	**12**	**10**	**.545**	**43**	**31**	**0**	**0**	**1**	**194^2**	**198**	**124**	**120**	**32**	**8**	**112**	**150**	**1.592**	**5.55**	**87**	**5.45**	**.261**	**0**	**.000**	**-13**	**9**	**-1.2**
• BENSON, Allen	Allen Wilbert "Bullet Ben" Benson b: 7/12/1908, Hurley, SD d: 11/16/1999, Viborg, SD BR/TR, 6'1", 185 lbs. Deb: 8/19/1934																										
1934	Was-A	0	1	.000	2	2	0	0	0	9^2	19	14	13	0	2	5	4	2.483	12.10	36	10.65	.413	0	.000	-8	0	-0.8
• BENSON, Kris	Kristen James Benson b: 11/7/1974, Kennesaw, GA BR/TR, 6'4", 200 lbs. Deb: 4/9/1999																										
1999	Pit-N	11	14	.440	31	31	2	0	0	196^2	184	105	89	16	6	83	139	1.358	4.07	112	3.78	.249	10	.154	11	12	1.1
2000	Pit-N	10	12	.455	32	32	2	1	0	217^2	206	104	93	24	10	86	184	1.342	3.85	119	3.97	.249	6	.092	21	14	1.8
2002	Pit-N	9	6	.600	25	25	0	0	0	130^1	152	76	68	18	3	50	79	1.550	4.70	89	5.31	.295	7	.175	-8	5	-0.9
2003	Pit-N	5	9	.357	18	18	0	0	0	105	127	67	58	14	1	36	68	1.552	4.97	88	5.20	.295	0	.000	-7	2	-1.0
Total	**4**	**35**	**41**	**.461**	**106**	**106**	**4**	**1**	**0**	**649^2**	**669**	**352**	**308**	**72**	**20**	**255**	**470**	**1.422**	**4.27**	**104**	**4.38**	**.266**	**23**	**.115**	**17**	**33**	**1.1**
• BENTLEY, Cy	Clytus G. Bentley b: 11/23/1850, East Haven, CT d: 2/26/1873, Middletown, CT Deb: 4/26/1872																										
1872	Man-n	2	15	.118	18	17	14	0	0	144	268	252	101	4	....	12	5	1.944	6.31	56	....	.352	27	.235	-32	....	-2.3
• BENTLEY, Jack	Jack Needles Bentley b: 3/8/1895, Sandy Spring, MD d: 10/24/1969, Olney, MD BL/TL, 5'11.5", 200 lbs. Deb: 9/6/1913 ♦																										
1913	Was-A	1	0	1.000	3	1	0	0	1	11	5	0	0	0	1	2	5	.636	0.00	....	0.86	.147	0	.000	3	2	0.3
1914	Was-A	5	7	.417	30	11	3	2	**4**	125^1	110	49	33	3	3	53	55	1.301	2.37	119	3.20	.249	11	.275	5	9	0.8
1915	Was-A	0	2	.000	4	2	0	0	0	11^1	8	4	1	0	0	3	0	.971	0.79	373	1.58	.200	0	.000	3	1	0.2
1916	Was-A	0	0	....	2	0	0	0	0	1^1	0	0	0	0	0	1	1	.750	0.00	....	0.49	.000	0	....	0	0	0.0
1923*	NY-N	13	8	.619	31	26	12	1	3	183	198	102	91	10	5	67	80	1.448	4.48	85	4.10	.277	38	.427	-16	15	-0.1
1924*	NY-N	16	5	.762	28	24	13	1	1	188	196	85	79	11	4	56	60	1.340	3.78	97	3.71	.273	26	.265	-3	12	0.0
1925	NY-N	11	9	.550	28	22	11	0	0	157	200	90	88	10	1	59	47	1.650	5.04	80	5.30	.323	30	.303	-17	12	-0.6

YEAR	TM-L	W	L	PCT	G	GS	CG	SH	SV	IP	H	R	ER	HR	HB	BB	SO	RAT	ERA	ERA+	CERA	OAV	BH	AVG	PR+	WS	TPW
1926	Phi-N	0	2	.000	7	3	0	0	0	25^1	37	28	23	2	0	10	7	1.855	8.17	51	6.25	.327	62	.258	-11	1	-3.0
	NY-N	0	0	....	1	0	0	0	0	2	0	0	0	0	0	2	1	1.000	0.00	....	0.80	.311	1	.250	1	0	0.1
	Yr.	0	2	.000	8	3	0	0	0	27^1	37	28	23	2	0	12	8	1.793	7.57	55	5.85	.327	63	.258	-10	1	-2.9
1927	NY-N	0	0	....	4	0	0	0	0	9^2	7	7	3	1	1	10	3	1.759	2.79	138	4.96	.333	2	.222	1	1	0.2
Total	9	46	33	.582	138	89	39	4	9	714	761	365	318	37	15	263	259	1.434	4.01	93	4.08	.282	170	.291	-33	53	-1.9

• BENTON, Al John Alton Benton b: 3/18/1911, Noble, OK d: 4/14/1968, Lynwood, CA BR/TR, 6'4", 215 lbs. Deb: 4/18/1934

YEAR	TM-L	W	L	PCT	G	GS	CG	SH	SV	IP	H	R	ER	HR	HB	BB	SO	RAT	ERA	ERA+	CERA	OAV	BH	AVG	PR+	WS	TPW
1934	Phi-A	7	9	.438	32	21	7	0	1	155	145	98	84	7	2	88	58	1.503	4.88	90	3.88	.249	6	.109	-10	7	-1.3
1935	Phi-A	3	4	.429	27	9	0	0	0	78^1	110	81	67	7	1	47	42	2.004	7.70	59	7.06	.328	1	.040	-26	0	-2.7
1938	Det-A	5	3	.625	19	10	6	0	0	95^1	93	40	35	10	1	39	33	1.385	3.30	151	3.96	.259	4	.121	17	10	1.3
1939	Det-A	6	8	.429	37	16	3	0	5	150	182	94	76	11	1	58	67	1.600	4.56	107	4.83	.294	4	.091	5	8	0.1
1940	Det-A	6	10	.375	42	0	0	0	**17**	79^1	93	44	39	5	0	36	50	1.626	4.42	107	4.84	.294	0	.000	4	8	0.2
1941	Det-A★	15	6	.714	38	14	7	1	7	157^2	130	63	52	11	3	65	63	1.237	2.97	153	2.92	**.221**	3	.060	32	20	2.7
1942	Det-A★	7	13	.350	35	30	9	1	2	226^2	210	87	73	9	0	84	110	1.297	2.90	136	3.07	.246	5	.075	29	17	2.5
1945*	Det-A	13	8	.619	31	27	12	5	3	191^2	175	68	43	7	2	63	76	1.242	2.02	174	2.82	.241	4	.063	31	17	2.7
1946	Det-A	11	7	.611	28	15	6	1	1	140^2	132	69	57	9	1	58	60	1.351	3.65	100	3.42	.245	9	.184	2	8	0.1
1947	Det-A	6	7	.462	36	14	4	0	7	133	147	77	65	11	1	61	33	1.564	4.40	86	4.73	.288	6	.154	-6	5	-0.8
1948	Det-A	2	2	.500	30	0	0	0	3	44^1	45	34	28	4	1	36	18	1.827	5.68	77	5.59	.273	2	.182	-5	1	-0.6
1949	Cle-A	9	6	.600	40	11	4	2	10	135^2	116	33	32	7	1	51	41	1.231	2.12	188	2.93	.238	5	.132	27	18	2.4
1950	Cle-A	4	2	.667	36	0	0	0	4	63	57	32	25	7	1	30	26	1.381	3.57	121	3.90	.243	1	.083	5	5	0.4
1952	Bos-A	4	3	.571	24	0	0	0	6	37^2	37	11	10	1	0	17	20	1.434	2.39	165	3.67	.268	0	.000	6	5	0.5
Total	14	98	88	.527	455	167	58	10	66	1688^1	1672	831	686	106	15	733	697	1.424	3.66	116	3.84	.259	50	.098	111	129	7.4

• BENTON, Larry Lawrence James Benton b: 11/20/1897, St. Louis, MO d: 4/3/1953, Amberley, OH BR/TR, 5'11", 165 lbs. Deb: 4/25/1923

YEAR	TM-L	W	L	PCT	G	GS	CG	SH	SV	IP	H	R	ER	HR	HB	BB	SO	RAT	ERA	ERA+	CERA	OAV	BH	AVG	PR+	WS	TPW
1923	Bos-N	5	9	.357	35	9	1	0	0	128	141	78	71	4	4	57	42	1.547	4.99	80	4.41	.293	5	.161	-13	4	-1.3
1924	Bos-N	5	7	.417	30	13	4	0	1	128	129	63	59	4	3	64	41	1.508	4.15	92	4.05	.274	3	.091	-4	7	-0.6
1925	Bos-N	14	7	.667	31	21	16	2	1	183^1	170	72	63	6	2	70	49	1.309	3.09	129	3.11	.249	14	.241	16	17	1.7
1926	Bos-N	14	14	.500	43	27	12	1	1	231^2	244	113	99	10	7	81	103	1.403	3.85	92	3.83	.280	12	.154	-5	11	-0.8
1927	Bos-N	4	2	.667	11	10	3	0	0	60^1	72	33	30	3	2	27	25	1.641	4.48	83	5.13	.310	4	.222	-4	3	-0.3
	NY-N	13	5	.722	29	23	8	1	2	173	183	83	76	9	2	54	65	1.370	3.95	97	3.71	.275	8	.160	-1	11	-0.3
	Yr.	17	7	.708	40	33	11	1	2	233^1	255	116	106	12	4	81	90	1.440	4.09	93	4.08	.284	12	.176	-5	14	-0.7
1928	NY-N	**25**	9	.735	42	36	**28**	2	4	310^1	299	106	94	14	0	71	90	1.192	2.73	143	2.85	.258	16	.143	38	30	3.3
1929	NY-N	11	17	.393	39	31	14	3	3	237	276	129	109	16	0	61	63	1.422	4.14	111	4.17	.297	9	.105	8	13	0.2
1930	NY-N	1	3	.250	8	4	1	0	1	30	42	31	26	8	0	14	16	1.867	7.80	61	7.80	.323	3	.300	-10	0	-0.8
	Cin-N	7	12	.368	35	22	9	0	1	177^2	246	124	101	7	0	45	47	1.638	5.12	94	5.20	.337	11	.177	-4	7	-0.6
	Yr.	8	15	.348	43	26	10	0	2	207^2	288	155	127	15	0	59	63	1.671	5.50	87	5.58	.335	14	.194	-15	7	-1.4
1931	Cin-N	10	15	.400	38	23	12	2	2	204^1	240	98	76	6	1	53	35	1.434	3.35	111	3.99	.299	11	.167	7	12	0.6
1932	Cin-N	6	13	.316	35	22	7	0	2	179^2	201	104	86	10	0	27	35	1.269	4.31	89	3.45	.285	11	.204	-9	6	-0.8
1933	Cin-N	10	11	.476	34	19	7	2	2	152^2	160	70	63	5	3	36	33	1.284	3.71	91	3.25	.271	9	.170	-4	8	-0.5
1934	Cin-N	0	1	.000	16	1	0	0	2	29	53	25	21	1	0	7	5	2.069	6.52	63	7.90	.393	2	.286	-7	0	-0.7
1935	Bos-N	2	3	.400	29	0	0	0	0	72	103	61	55	6	1	24	21	1.764	6.88	55	6.24	.338	4	.200	-22	0	-2.1
Total	13	127	128	.498	455	261	122	13	22	2297	2559	1190	1029	109	25	691	670	1.415	4.03	98	3.98	.288	122	.165	-14	129	-3.0

• BENTON, Rube John Clebon Benton b: 6/27/1887, Clinton, NC d: 12/12/1937, Dothan, AL BL/TL, 6'1", 190 lbs. Deb: 6/28/1910

YEAR	TM-L	W	L	PCT	G	GS	CG	SH	SV	IP	H	R	ER	HR	HB	BB	SO	RAT	ERA	ERA+	CERA	OAV	BH	AVG	PR+	WS	TPW
1910	Cin-N	0	1	.000	12	2	0	0	0	38	44	34	20	1	1	23	15	1.763	4.74	61	5.08	.282	1	.091	-7	0	-0.9
1911	Cin-N	3	3	.500	6	6	5	0	0	44^2	44	18	10	0	3	23	28	1.500	2.01	164	4.03	.270	2	.143	6	3	0.6
1912	Cin-N	18	20	.474	**50**	**39**	22	2	2	302	316	143	104	2	18	118	162	1.437	3.10	108	3.81	.278	14	.135	12	18	0.6
1913	Cin-N	11	7	.611	23	22	9	1	0	144^1	140	76	56	4	9	60	68	1.386	3.49	93	3.63	.265	10	.208	-4	7	-0.3
1914	Cin-N	16	18	.471	41	35	16	5	2	271	223	124	89	3	11	95	121	1.173	2.96	99	2.45	.228	13	.143	0	14	-0.3
1915	Cin-N	6	13	.316	35	21	6	2	4	176^1	165	79	65	2	14	67	83	1.316	3.32	86	3.26	.257	11	.208	-13	7	-1.5
	NY-N	3	5	.375	10	6	3	0	1	60^2	57	26	19	0	5	9	26	1.088	2.82	91	2.43	.253	5	.217	-1	3	0.0
	Yr.	9	18	.333	45	27	9	2	5	237	222	105	84	2	19	76	109	1.257	3.19	87	3.04	.256	16	.211	-14	10	-1.5
1916	NY-N	16	8	.667	38	29	15	3	2	238^2	210	84	76	5	10	58	115	1.123	2.87	85	2.49	.241	7	.090	-15	12	-2.3
1917*	NY-N	15	9	.625	35	25	14	3	3	215	190	78	65	5	7	41	70	1.074	2.72	94	2.29	.238	12	.167	-7	12	-0.8
1918	NY-N	1	2	.333	3	3	2	0	0	24	17	8	5	0	0	3	9	.833	1.88	140	1.28	.202	1	.143	2	2	0.3
1919	NY-N	17	11	.607	35	28	11	1	2	209	181	71	61	5	4	52	53	1.115	2.63	107	2.34	.237	13	.194	1	14	0.0
1920	NY-N	9	16	.360	33	25	12	4	2	193^1	222	82	65	8	3	31	52	1.309	3.03	99	3.56	.291	6	.092	-4	9	-1.1
1921	NY-N	5	2	.714	18	9	3	1	0	72	72	28	23	2	0	17	11	1.236	2.88	127	2.94	.266	3	.143	4	5	0.3
1923	Cin-N	14	10	.583	33	26	15	0	1	219	243	106	89	10	5	57	59	1.370	3.66	105	3.79	.284	23	.288	5	16	0.8
1924	Cin-N	7	9	.438	32	19	6	1	1	162^2	166	70	50	2	4	24	42	1.168	2.77	136	2.70	.266	12	.261	18	13	2.0
1925	Cin-N	9	10	.474	33	16	6	1	1	146^2	182	88	66	3	1	34	36	1.473	4.05	101	4.11	.301	9	.200	-1	7	-0.1
Total	15	150	144	.510	437	311	145	24	21	2517^1	2472	1115	863	52	95	712	950	1.265	3.09	100	3.10	.261	142	.172	-4	142	-2.6

• BENTON, Sid Sidney Wright Benton b: 8/4/1895, Buckner, AR d: 3/8/1977, Fayetteville, AR BR/TR, 6'1", 170 lbs. Deb: 4/18/1922

YEAR	TM-L	W	L	PCT	G	GS	CG	SH	SV	IP	H	R	ER	HR	HB	BB	SO	RAT	ERA	ERA+	CERA	OAV	BH	AVG	PR+	WS	TPW
1922	StL-N	0	0	....	1	0	0	0	0	0	0	0	0	0	0	2	0	....	....	....	∞	.000	0	....	0	0	0.0

• BENZ, Joe Joseph Louis "Blitzen,Butcher Boy" Benz b: 1/21/1886, New Alsace, IN d: 4/22/1957, Chicago, IL BR/TR, 6'1.5", 196 lbs. Deb: 8/16/1911

YEAR	TM-L	W	L	PCT	G	GS	CG	SH	SV	IP	H	R	ER	HR	HB	BB	SO	RAT	ERA	ERA+	CERA	OAV	BH	AVG	PR+	WS	TPW
1911	Chi-A	3	2	.600	12	6	1	0	0	55^2	52	23	14	0	2	13	28	1.168	2.26	143	2.62	.251	1	.059	6	4	0.4
1912	Chi-A	13	17	.433	42	31	12	3	0	238^2	231	107	77	5	8	70	97	1.261	2.90	111	3.15	.259	10	.132	13	14	0.8
1913	Chi-A	7	10	.412	33	17	6	1	1	151	146	64	46	1	2	59	79	1.358	2.74	106	3.21	.254	9	.180	3	8	0.2
1914	Chi-A	15	19	.441	48	35	16	4	2	283^1	245	103	71	4	2	66	142	1.098	2.26	119	2.27	.236	12	.130	14	20	1.2
1915	Chi-A	15	11	.577	39	28	17	2	0	238^1	209	78	56	4	3	43	81	1.057	2.11	141	2.24	.238	10	.127	25	17	2.1
1916	Chi-A	9	5	.643	28	16	6	4	0	142	108	40	32	0	3	32	57	.986	2.03	136	1.74	.214	3	.065	10	12	0.7
1917	Chi-A	7	3	.700	19	13	7	2	0	94^2	76	36	26	1	2	23	25	1.046	2.47	107	2.01	.220	5	.167	3	5	0.2
1918	Chi-A	8	8	.500	29	17	10	1	0	154	156	57	45	1	2	28	30	1.195	2.63	104	2.89	.269	11	.216	4	9	0.4
1919	Chi-A	0	0	....	1	0	0	0	0	2	2	1	0	0	0	0	0	1.000	0.00	....	1.95	.250	0	....	1	0	0.1
Total	9	77	75	.507	251	163	75	17	3	1359^2	1225	509	367	16	24	334	539	1.147	2.43	119	2.53	.244	61	.138	78	89	6.1

• BERE, Jason Jason Phillip Bere b: 5/26/1971, Cambridge, MA BR/TR, 6'3", 185 lbs. Deb: 5/27/1993

YEAR	TM-L	W	L	PCT	G	GS	CG	SH	SV	IP	H	R	ER	HR	HB	BB	SO	RAT	ERA	ERA+	CERA	OAV	BH	AVG	PR+	WS	TPW
1993*	Chi-A	12	5	.706	24	24	1	0	0	142^2	109	60	55	12	5	81	129	1.332	3.47	120	3.46	.210	0	....	11	11	1.1
1994	Chi-A★	12	2	.857	24	24	0	0	0	141^2	119	65	60	17	1	80	127	1.405	3.81	122	4.03	.229	0	....	14	10	1.3
1995	Chi-A	8	15	.348	27	27	1	0	0	137^2	151	120	110	21	6	106	110	1.867	7.19	62	6.63	.277	0	....	-40	0	-3.8
1996	Chi-A	0	1	.000	5	5	0	0	0	16^2	26	19	19	3	0	18	19	2.640	10.26	46	11.16	.356	0	....	-10	0	-0.9
1997	Chi-A	4	2	.667	6	6	0	0	0	28^2	20	15	15	4	3	17	21	1.291	4.71	93	3.86	.198	0	....	-1	2	-0.1
1998	Chi-A	3	7	.300	18	15	0	0	0	83^2	98	71	60	14	2	58	53	1.865	6.45	71	6.90	.293	0	....	-18	0	-1.7
	Cin-N	3	2	.600	9	7	0	0	0	43^2	39	20	20	3	1	20	31	1.351	4.12	104	3.65	.242	0	.000	1	2	0.0
1999	Cin-N	3	0	1.000	12	10	0	0	0	43^1	56	37	33	6	2	40	28	2.215	6.85	68	8.60	.326	4	.286	-12	0	-1.0
	Mil-N	2	0	1.000	5	4	0	0	0	23^1	23	15	12	3	0	10	19	1.414	4.63	98	4.26	.256	3	.375	0	1	0.1
	Yr.	5	0	1.000	17	14	0	0	0	66^2	79	52	45	9	2	50	47	1.935	6.08	76	7.08	.302	7	.318	-12	1	-0.9
2000	Mil-N	6	7	.462	20	20	0	0	0	115	115	66	63	19	1	63	98	1.548	4.93	92	5.06	.264	8	.205	-7	5	-0.5
	Cle-A	6	3	.667	11	11	0	0	0	54^1	65	41	40	6	4	26	44	1.675	6.63	75	5.94	.297	0	....	-9	2	-0.9
2001	Chi-N	11	11	.500	32	32	2	0	0	188	171	99	90	24	1	77	175	1.319	4.31	96	3.75	.241	12	.194	-0	9	0.2
2002	Chi-N	1	10	.091	16	16	0	0	0	85^2	98	63	54	13	3	28	65	1.471	5.67	71	5.09	.290	3	.125	-15	0	-1.5
2003	Cle-A	0	0	....	2	2	0	0	0	6^2	5	3	3	0	0	2	1	1.050	4.05	109	1.70	.208	0	....	0	0	0.0
Total	11	71	65	.522	211	203	4	0	0	1111	1095	694	634	145	29	626	920	1.549	5.14	86	4.99	.258	30	.186	-86	42	-7.8

• BERENGUER, Juan Juan Bautista Berenguer b: 11/30/1954, Aguadulce, Panama BR/TR, 5'11", 215 lbs. Deb: 8/17/1978

YEAR	TM-L	W	L	PCT	G	GS	CG	SH	SV	IP	H	R	ER	HR	HB	BB	SO	RAT	ERA	ERA+	CERA	OAV	BH	AVG	PR+	WS	TPW
1978	NY-N	0	2	.000	5	3	0	0	0	13	17	12	12	1	1	11	8	2.154	8.31	42	8.14	.327	0	.000	-7	0	-0.8
1979	NY-N	1	1	.500	5	5	0	0	0	30^2	28	13	10	2	1	12	25	1.304	2.93	124	3.59	.252	1	.143	2	2	0.3
1980	NY-N	0	1	.000	6	0	0	0	0	9^1	9	9	6	1	0	10	7	2.036	5.79	61	6.20	.250	0	....	-2	0	-0.2

YEAR	TM-L	W	L	PCT	G	GS	CG	SH	SV	IP	H	R	ER	HR	HB	BB	SO	RAT	ERA	ERA+	CERA	OAV	BH	AVG	PR+	WS	TPW
1981	KC-A	0	4	.000	8	3	0	0	0	19^{2}	22	21	19	4	2	16	20	1.932	8.69	41	7.82	.289	0	....	-11	0	-1.2
	Tor-A	2	9	.182	12	11	1	0	0	71	62	41	34	7	3	35	29	1.366	4.31	91	3.85	.235	0	....	-2	2	-0.3
	Yr.	2	13	.133	20	14	1	0	0	90^{2}	84	62	53	11	5	51	49	1.489	5.26	73	4.71	.247	0	....	-14	2	-1.4
1982	Det-A	0	0	....	2	1	0	0	0	6^{2}	5	5	5	0	0	9	8	2.100	6.75	60	5.03	.200	0	....	-2	0	-0.2
1983	Det-A	9	5	.643	37	19	2	1	1	157^{2}	110	58	55	19	6	71	129	1.148	3.14	124	2.90	.193	0	....	11	11	1.1
1984	Det-A	11	10	.524	31	27	2	1	0	168^{1}	146	75	65	14	5	79	118	1.337	3.48	113	3.59	.232	0	....	7	9	0.7
1985	Det-A	5	6	.455	31	13	0	0	0	95	96	67	59	12	1	48	82	1.516	5.59	73	4.70	.259	0	....	-16	1	-1.6
1986	SF-N	2	3	.400	46	4	0	0	4	73^{1}	64	23	22	4	2	44	72	1.473	2.70	130	3.97	.242	1	.143	6	6	0.6
1987*	Min-A	8	1	.889	47	6	0	0	4	112	100	51	49	10	0	47	110	1.313	3.94	117	3.40	.238	0	....	8	10	0.8
1988	Min-A	8	4	.667	57	1	0	0	2	100	74	44	44	7	1	61	99	1.350	3.96	103	3.17	.207	0	....	1	8	0.1
1989	Min-A	9	3	.750	56	0	0	0	3	106	96	44	41	11	2	47	93	1.349	3.48	119	3.84	.246	0	....	8	9	0.8
1990	Min-A	8	5	.615	51	0	0	0	0	100^{1}	85	43	38	9	2	58	77	1.425	3.41	122	3.88	.232	0	....	8	8	0.8
1991	Atl-N	0	3	.000	49	0	0	0	17	64^{1}	43	18	16	5	3	20	53	.979	2.24	174	2.05	.189	0	.000	12	11	1.2
1992	Atl-N	3	1	.750	28	0	0	0	1	33^{1}	35	22	19	7	1	16	19	1.530	5.13	71	5.46	.269	0	.000	-6	0	-0.6
	KC-A	1	4	.200	19	2	0	0	0	44^{2}	42	30	28	3	1	20	26	1.388	5.64	72	3.63	.247	0	....	-7	0	-0.7
Total	15	67	62	.519	490	95	5	2	32	1205^{1}	1034	576	522	116	31	604	975	1.359	3.90	102	3.74	.232	2	.083	10	77	0.8

• BERENYI, Bruce Bruce Michael Berenyi b: 8/21/1954, Bryan, OH BR/TR, 6'3", 215 lbs. Deb: 7/5/1980

YEAR	TM-L	W	L	PCT	G	GS	CG	SH	SV	IP	H	R	ER	HR	HB	BB	SO	RAT	ERA	ERA+	CERA	OAV	BH	AVG	PR+	WS	TPW
1980	Cin-N	2	2	.500	6	6	0	0	0	27^{2}	34	26	24	1	0	23	19	2.060	7.81	46	6.93	.318	0	.000	-13	0	-1.4
1981	Cin-N	9	6	.600	21	20	5	3	0	126	97	55	49	3	0	77	106	1.381	3.50	102	3.07	.211	8	.190	-1	8	0.1
1982	Cin-N	9	18	.333	34	34	4	1	0	222^{1}	208	90	83	8	2	96	157	1.367	3.36	110	3.45	.255	15	.242	7	13	1.0
1983	Cin-N	9	14	.391	32	31	4	1	0	186^{1}	173	92	80	9	2	102	151	1.476	3.86	98	3.90	.247	12	.218	-1	10	0.1
1984	Cin-N	3	7	.300	13	11	0	0	0	51	63	35	34	0	0	42	53	2.059	6.00	63	6.29	.306	1	.063	-12	0	-1.4
	NY-N	9	6	.600	19	19	0	0	0	115	100	58	48	6	1	53	81	1.330	3.76	94	3.30	.238	9	.243	-3	6	-0.1
	Yr.	12	13	.480	32	30	0	0	0	166	163	93	82	6	1	95	134	1.554	4.45	82	4.22	.260	10	.189	-15	6	-1.5
1985	NY-N	1	0	1.000	3	3	0	0	0	13^{2}	8	6	4	0	1	10	10	1.317	2.63	131	2.70	.170	1	.250	1	1	0.2
1986	NY-N	2	2	.500	14	7	0	0	0	39^{2}	47	30	28	5	1	22	30	1.739	6.35	56	6.14	.299	0	.000	-13	0	-1.4
Total	7	44	55	.444	142	131	13	5	0	781^{2}	730	392	350	32	7	425	607	1.478	4.03	91	3.90	.251	46	.197	-33	38	-3.0

• BERGER, Heinie Charles Berger b: 1/7/1882, LaSalle, IL d: 2/10/1954, Lakewood, OH TR, 5'9.5" Deb: 5/6/1907

YEAR	TM-L	W	L	PCT	G	GS	CG	SH	SV	IP	H	R	ER	HR	HB	BB	SO	RAT	ERA	ERA+	CERA	OAV	BH	AVG	PR+	WS	TPW
1907	Cle-A	3	3	.500	14	7	5	1	0	87^{1}	74	35	29	0	1	20	50	1.076	2.99	84	2.06	.232	5	.179	-6	4	-0.7
1908	Cle-A	13	8	.619	29	24	16	0	0	199^{1}	152	60	47	1	4	66	101	1.094	2.12	112	2.13	.219	8	.108	4	14	0.0
1909	Cle-A	13	14	.481	34	29	19	4	1	247	221	95	75	2	12	58	162	1.130	2.73	93	2.68	.256	11	.133	-7	14	-0.9
1910	Cle-A	3	4	.429	13	8	2	0	0	65^{1}	57	25	22	0	3	32	24	1.362	3.03	85	3.21	.243	3	.143	-4	3	-0.5
Total	4	32	29	.525	90	68	42	5	1	599	504	215	173	3	20	176	337	1.135	2.60	96	2.46	.239	27	.131	-13	35	-2.1

• BERGMAN, Sean Sean Frederick Bergman b: 4/11/1970, Joliet, IL BR/TR, 6'4", 205 lbs. Deb: 7/7/1993

YEAR	TM-L	W	L	PCT	G	GS	CG	SH	SV	IP	H	R	ER	HR	HB	BB	SO	RAT	ERA	ERA+	CERA	OAV	BH	AVG	PR+	WS	TPW
1993	Det-A	1	4	.200	9	6	1	0	0	39^{2}	47	29	25	6	1	23	19	1.765	5.67	76	6.17	.294	0	....	-6	0	-0.6
1994	Det-A	2	1	.667	3	3	0	0	0	17^{2}	22	11	11	2	1	7	12	1.642	5.60	86	5.77	.301	0	....	-1	1	-0.1
1995	Det-A	7	10	.412	28	28	1	1	0	135^{1}	169	95	77	19	4	67	86	1.744	5.12	93	6.29	.307	0	....	-4	5	-0.3
1996	SD-N	6	8	.429	41	14	0	0	0	113^{1}	119	63	55	14	2	33	85	1.341	4.37	91	4.13	.274	3	.100	-5	4	-0.5
1997	SD-N	2	4	.333	44	9	0	0	0	99	126	72	67	11	3	38	74	1.657	6.09	63	5.78	.316	3	.231	-23	0	-2.2
1998	Hou-N	12	9	.571	31	27	1	0	0	172	183	81	71	20	5	42	100	1.308	3.72	109	4.00	.268	5	.083	6	9	0.3
1999	Hou-N	4	6	.400	19	16	2	1	0	99	130	60	59	9	3	26	38	1.576	5.36	82	5.62	.332	3	.107	-11	2	-1.0
	Atl-N	1	0	1.000	6	0	0	0	0	6^{1}	5	2	2	0	0	3	6	1.263	2.84	158	2.50	.217	0	....	1	1	0.1
	Yr.	5	6	.455	25	16	2	1	0	105^{1}	135	62	61	9	3	29	44	1.557	5.21	85	5.43	.325	3	.107	-10	3	-0.9
2000	Min-A	4	5	.444	15	14	0	0	0	68	111	76	73	18	2	33	35	2.118	9.66	53	10.16	.374	1	.500	-33	0	-3.0
Total	8	39	47	.453	196	117	5	2	0	750^{1}	912	489	440	99	21	272	455	1.578	5.28	82	5.58	.303	15	.113	-76	22	-7.4

• BERLY, Jack John Chambers Berly b: 5/24/1903, Natchitoches, LA d: 6/26/1977, Houston, TX BR/TR, 5'11.5", 190 lbs. Deb: 4/22/1924

YEAR	TM-L	W	L	PCT	G	GS	CG	SH	SV	IP	H	R	ER	HR	HB	BB	SO	RAT	ERA	ERA+	CERA	OAV	BH	AVG	PR+	WS	TPW
1924	StL-N	0	0	....	4	0	0	0	0	8	8	5	5	2	0	4	2	1.500	5.63	67	5.68	.267	0	.000	-2	0	-0.2
1931	NY-N	7	8	.467	27	11	4	1	0	111^{1}	114	55	48	6	4	51	45	1.482	3.88	95	4.14	.270	6	.171	-3	5	-0.4
1932	Phi-N	1	2	.333	21	1	1	0	2	46	61	42	39	4	1	21	15	1.783	7.63	58	6.11	.333	0	.000	-16	0	-1.8
1933	Phi-N	2	3	.400	13	6	1	1	0	50	62	30	28	5	2	22	4	1.680	5.04	76	5.66	.307	4	.308	-7	2	-0.7
Total	4	10	13	.435	65	18	6	2	2	215^{1}	245	132	120	17	7	98	66	1.593	5.02	78	4.97	.293	10	.167	-28	7	-3.0

• BERNAL, Victor Victor Hugo Bernal b: 10/6/1953, Los Angeles, CA BR/TR, 6'1", 175 lbs. Deb: 4/6/1977

YEAR	TM-L	W	L	PCT	G	GS	CG	SH	SV	IP	H	R	ER	HR	HB	BB	SO	RAT	ERA	ERA+	CERA	OAV	BH	AVG	PR+	WS	TPW
1977	SD-N	1	1	.500	15	0	0	0	0	20^{1}	23	13	12	4	0	9	6	1.574	5.31	67	5.71	.288	0	.000	-4	0	-0.4

• BERNARD, Dwight Dwight Vern Bernard b: 5/31/1952, Mount Vernon, IL BR/TR, 6'2", 170 lbs. Deb: 6/29/1978

YEAR	TM-L	W	L	PCT	G	GS	CG	SH	SV	IP	H	R	ER	HR	HB	BB	SO	RAT	ERA	ERA+	CERA	OAV	BH	AVG	PR+	WS	TPW
1978	NY-N	1	4	.200	30	1	0	0	0	48	54	25	23	4	0	27	26	1.688	4.31	81	5.40	.297	1	.200	-5	1	-0.5
1979	NY-N	0	3	.000	32	1	0	0	0	44	59	26	23	2	0	26	20	1.932	4.70	77	6.39	.331	0	....	-6	0	-0.6
1981*	Mil-A	0	0	....	6	0	0	0	0	5	5	3	2	0	0	6	1	2.200	3.60	95	5.59	.263	0	....	-0	0	0.0
1982*	Mil-A	3	1	.750	47	0	0	0	6	79	78	39	33	4	1	27	45	1.329	3.76	101	3.50	.263	0	....	-1	4	-0.1
Total	4	4	8	.333	115	2	0	0	6	176	196	93	81	10	1	86	92	1.602	4.14	88	4.80	.290	1	.200	-12	5	-1.1

• BERNARD, Joe Joseph Carl "J.C." Bernard b: 3/24/1882, Brighton, IL d: 9/22/1960, Springfield, IL BR/TR, 6'1", 175 lbs. Deb: 9/23/1909

YEAR	TM-L	W	L	PCT	G	GS	CG	SH	SV	IP	H	R	ER	HR	HB	BB	SO	RAT	ERA	ERA+	CERA	OAV	BH	AVG	PR+	WS	TPW
1909	StL-N	0	0	....	1	0	0	0	0	1	1	0	0	0	0	2	2	3.000	0.00	....	8.74	.250	0	....	0	0	0.0

• BERNERO, Adam Adam Gino Bernero b: 11/28/1976, San Jose, CA BR/TR, 6'4", 205 lbs. Deb: 8/1/2000

YEAR	TM-L	W	L	PCT	G	GS	CG	SH	SV	IP	H	R	ER	HR	HB	BB	SO	RAT	ERA	ERA+	CERA	OAV	BH	AVG	PR+	WS	TPW
2000	Det-A	0	1	.000	12	4	0	0	0	34^{1}	33	18	16	3	1	13	20	1.340	4.19	115	3.94	.270	0	....	3	2	0.2
2001	Det-A	0	0	....	5	0	0	0	0	12^{1}	13	13	10	4	1	4	8	1.378	7.30	59	5.79	.260	0	....	-4	0	-0.4
2002	Det-A	4	7	.364	28	11	0	0	0	101^{2}	128	74	70	17	6	31	69	1.564	6.20	69	5.95	.309	0	.000	-21	1	-2.0
2003	Det-A	1	12	.077	18	17	0	0	0	100^{2}	104	68	68	14	7	41	54	1.440	6.08	71	4.83	.267	0	.000	-20	1	-1.9
	Col-N	0	2	.000	31	0	0	0	0	32^{2}	33	22	19	5	1	13	26	1.408	5.23	94	4.58	.266	0	.000	-1	1	-0.1
Total	4	5	22	.185	94	32	0	0	0	281^{2}	311	195	183	43	16	102	177	1.466	5.85	75	5.14	.283	0	.000	-43	5	-4.2

• BERNHARD, Bill William Henry "Strawberry Bill" Bernhard b: 3/16/1871, Clarence, NY d: 3/30/1949, San Diego, CA BB/TR, 6'1", 205 lbs. Deb: 4/24/1899 U

YEAR	TM-L	W	L	PCT	G	GS	CG	SH	SV	IP	H	R	ER	HR	HB	BB	SO	RAT	ERA	ERA+	CERA	OAV	BH	AVG	PR+	WS	TPW
1899	Phi-N	6	6	.500	21	12	10	1	0	132^{1}	120	66	39	3	6	36	23	1.179	2.65	139	2.70	.242	13	.241	13	10	1.2
1900	Phi-N	15	10	.600	32	27	20	0	2	218^{2}	284	151	116	3	5	74	49	1.637	4.77	76	4.88	.313	14	.154	-27	9	-2.9
1901	Phi-A	17	10	.630	31	27	26	1	0	257	328	169	129	6	2	50	58	1.471	4.52	83	4.25	.307	20	.187	-22	13	-2.0
1902	Phi-A	1	0	1.000	1	1	1	0	0	9	7	1	1	0	0	3	1	1.111	1.00	367	2.00	.215	0	.000	3	1	0.2
	Cle-A	17	5	.773	27	24	22	3	1	217	169	78	53	4	5	34	57	.935	2.20	157	1.68	.216	18	.200	29	19	2.7
	Yr.	18	5	.783	28	25	23	3	1	226	176	79	54	4	5	37	58	.942	2.15	160	**1.69**	**.216**	18	.191	32	20	2.9
1903	Cle-A	14	5	.737	20	19	18	3	0	165^{2}	151	62	39	1	0	21	60	1.038	2.12	135	2.02	.242	12	.185	12	12	1.2
1904	Cle-A	23	13	.639	38	37	35	4	0	320^{2}	323	107	76	3	4	55	137	1.179	2.13	119	2.60	.263	22	.177	13	22	1.4
1905	Cle-A	7	13	.350	22	19	17	0	0	174^{1}	185	93	65	5	1	34	56	1.256	3.36	78	3.13	.274	6	.087	-14	4	-2.2
1906	Cle-A	16	15	.516	31	30	23	2	0	255^{1}	235	99	72	1	5	47	85	1.104	2.54	103	2.29	.248	21	.212	-3	14	-0.1
1907	Cle-A	0	4	.000	8	4	3	0	0	42	58	32	15	0	0	11	19	1.643	3.21	78	4.86	.330	3	.200	-4	0	-0.5
Total	9	116	81	.589	231	200	175	14	3	1792	1860	858	605	26	28	365	545	1.242	3.04	102	3.02	.268	129	.180	0	104	-1.0

• BERNHARDT, Walter Walter Jacob Bernhardt b: 5/20/1893, Pleasant Village, PA d: 7/26/1958, Watertown, NY BR/TR, 6'2", 175 lbs. Deb: 7/16/1918

YEAR	TM-L	W	L	PCT	G	GS	CG	SH	SV	IP	H	R	ER	HR	HB	BB	SO	RAT	ERA	ERA+	CERA	OAV	BH	AVG	PR+	WS	TPW
1918	NY-A	0	0	....	1	0	0	0	0	0^{2}	0	0	0	0	0	0	1	.000	0.00	....	0.00	.000	0	....	0	0	0.0

• BERRY, Joe Jonas Arthur "Jittery Joe" Berry b: 12/16/1904, Huntsville, AR d: 9/27/1958, Anaheim, CA BL/TR, 5'10.5", 145 lbs. Deb: 9/6/1942

YEAR	TM-L	W	L	PCT	G	GS	CG	SH	SV	IP	H	R	ER	HR	HB	BB	SO	RAT	ERA	ERA+	CERA	OAV	BH	AVG	PR+	WS	TPW
1942	Chi-N	0	0	....	2	0	0	0	0	2	7	4	4	0	0	2	1	4.500	18.00	18	21.64	.538	0	....	-3	0	-0.3
1944	Phi-A	10	8	.556	53	0	0	0	**12**	111^{1}	78	32	24	4	2	23	44	.907	1.94	180	1.53	.192	3	.120	19	18	1.9
1945	Phi-A	8	7	.533	**52**	0	0	0	5	130^{1}	114	40	34	5	0	38	51	1.166	2.35	146	2.52	.232	5	.143	16	14	1.6

YEAR	TM-L	W	L	PCT	G	GS	CG	SH	SV	IP	H	R	ER	HR	HB	BB	SO	RAT	ERA	ERA+	CERA	OAV	BH	AVG	PR+	WS	TPW
1946	Phi-A	0	1	.000	5	0	0	0	0	13	15	5	4	1	1	3	5	1.385	2.77	128	4.31	.288	1	.333	1	1	0.1
	Cle-A	3	6	.333	21	0	0	0	1	37^1	32	18	14	4	0	21	16	1.420	3.38	98	3.87	.235	2	.286	-0	2	0.0
	Yr.	3	7	.300	26	0	0	0	1	50^1	47	23	18	5	1	24	21	1.411	3.22	104	3.98	.250	3	.300	1	3	0.2
Total	**4**	**21**	**22**	**.488**	**133**	**0**	**0**	**0**	**18**	**294**	**246**	**99**	**80**	**14**	**3**	**87**	**117**	**1.133**	**2.45**	**139**	**2.52**	**.224**	**11**	**.157**	**33**	**35**	**3.4**

• BERTAINA, Frank Frank Louis Bertaina b: 4/14/1944, San Francisco, CA BL/TL, 5'11", 180 lbs. Deb: 8/1/1964

YEAR	TM-L	W	L	PCT	G	GS	CG	SH	SV	IP	H	R	ER	HR	HB	BB	SO	RAT	ERA	ERA+	CERA	OAV	BH	AVG	PR+	WS	TPW
1964	Bal-A	1	0	1.000	6	4	1	1	0	26	18	8	8	3	0	13	18	1.192	2.77	129	2.83	.198	0	.000	2	2	0.1
1965	Bal-A	0	0	....	2	1	0	0	0	6	9	4	4	0	0	4	5	2.167	6.00	58	7.17	.360	0	.000	-2	0	-0.2
1966	Bal-A	2	5	.286	16	9	0	0	0	63^1	52	29	22	3	4	36	46	1.389	3.13	107	3.56	.226	2	.105	1	2	0.1
1967	Bal-A	1	1	.500	5	2	0	0	0	21^2	17	9	8	4	0	14	19	1.431	3.32	95	4.51	.224	1	.111	-1	1	-0.1
	Was-A	6	5	.545	18	17	4	4	0	95^2	90	36	31	8	0	37	67	1.328	2.92	108	3.62	.251	2	.057	2	6	0.0
	Yr.	7	6	.538	23	19	4	4	0	117^1	107	45	39	12	0	51	86	1.347	2.99	106	3.78	.247	3	.068	2	7	-0.2
1968	Was-A	7	13	.350	27	23	1	0	0	127^1	133	76	66	15	6	69	81	1.586	4.66	62	5.23	.273	5	.132	-23	0	-2.7
1969	Was-A	1	3	.250	14	5	0	0	0	35^2	43	30	26	8	0	23	25	1.850	6.56	53	7.19	.291	4	.364	-12	0	-1.0
	Bal-A	0	0	....	3	0	0	0	0	6	1	0	0	0	0	3	5	.667	0.00	....	0.63	.063	1	1.000	2	1	0.3
	Yr.	1	3	.250	17	5	0	0	0	41^2	44	30	26	8	0	26	30	1.680	5.62	62	6.24	.268	5	.417	-10	1	-0.7
1970	StL-N	1	2	.333	8	5	0	0	0	31^1	36	16	11	1	0	15	14	1.628	3.16	130	4.53	.293	1	.143	4	2	0.4
Total	**7**	**19**	**29**	**.396**	**99**	**66**	**6**	**5**	**0**	**413**	**399**	**208**	**176**	**42**	**10**	**214**	**280**	**1.484**	**3.84**	**83**	**4.49**	**.257**	**16**	**.127**	**-27**	**14**	**-3.2**

• BERTOTTI, Mike Michael David Bertotti b: 1/18/1970, Jersey City, NJ BL/TL, 6'1", 185 lbs. Deb: 7/29/1995

YEAR	TM-L	W	L	PCT	G	GS	CG	SH	SV	IP	H	R	ER	HR	HB	BB	SO	RAT	ERA	ERA+	CERA	OAV	BH	AVG	PR+	WS	TPW
1995	Chi-A	1	1	.500	4	4	0	0	0	14^1	23	20	20	6	3	11	15	2.372	12.56	35	13.43	.365	0	....	-13	0	-1.2
1996	Chi-A	2	0	1.000	15	2	0	0	0	28	28	18	16	5	0	20	19	1.714	5.14	92	5.73	.257	0	....	-1	1	-0.1
1997	Chi-A	0	0	....	9	0	0	0	0	3^2	9	3	3	0	0	2	4	3.000	7.36	60	12.56	.450	0	....	-1	0	-0.1
Total	**3**	**3**	**1**	**.750**	**28**	**6**	**0**	**0**	**0**	**46**	**60**	**41**	**39**	**11**	**3**	**33**	**38**	**2.022**	**7.63**	**60**	**8.68**	**.313**	**0**	**....**	**-15**	**1**	**-1.4**

• BERTRAND, Lefty Roman Mathias Bertrand b: 2/28/1909, Cobden, MN d: 3/17/2002, The Dalles, OR BR/TL, 6', 180 lbs. Deb: 4/15/1936

YEAR	TM-L	W	L	PCT	G	GS	CG	SH	SV	IP	H	R	ER	HR	HB	BB	SO	RAT	ERA	ERA+	CERA	OAV	BH	AVG	PR+	WS	TPW
1936	Phi-N	0	0	....	1	0	0	0	0	2	3	2	2	1	0	2	1	2.500	9.00	50	13.23	.333	0	....	-1	0	-0.1

• BERUMEN, Andres Andres Berumen b: 4/5/1971, Tijuana, Mexico BR/TR, 6'2", 210 lbs. Deb: 4/27/1995

YEAR	TM-L	W	L	PCT	G	GS	CG	SH	SV	IP	H	R	ER	HR	HB	BB	SO	RAT	ERA	ERA+	CERA	OAV	BH	AVG	PR+	WS	TPW
1995	SD-N	2	3	.400	37	0	0	0	1	44^1	37	29	28	3	3	36	42	1.647	5.68	70	4.57	.226	0	.000	-9	1	-0.9
1996	SD-N	0	0	....	3	0	0	0	0	3^1	3	2	2	1	1	2	4	1.500	5.40	73	6.44	.231	0	....	-1	0	-0.1
Total	**2**	**2**	**3**	**.400**	**40**	**0**	**0**	**0**	**1**	**47^2**	**40**	**31**	**30**	**4**	**4**	**38**	**46**	**1.636**	**5.66**	**71**	**4.70**	**.226**	**0**	**.000**	**-9**	**1**	**-0.9**

• BESANA, Fred Frederick Cyril Besana b: 4/5/1931, Lincoln, CA BR/TL, 6'3.5", 200 lbs. Deb: 4/18/1956

YEAR	TM-L	W	L	PCT	G	GS	CG	SH	SV	IP	H	R	ER	HR	HB	BB	SO	RAT	ERA	ERA+	CERA	OAV	BH	AVG	PR+	WS	TPW
1956	Bal-A	1	0	1.000	7	2	0	0	0	17^2	22	12	11	0	2	14	7	2.038	5.60	70	6.42	.310	0	.000	-3	0	-0.3

• BESSE, Herman Herman A. Besse b: 8/16/1911, St. Louis, MO d: 8/13/1972, Los Angeles, CA BL/TL, 6'2", 190 lbs. Deb: 4/19/1940

YEAR	TM-L	W	L	PCT	G	GS	CG	SH	SV	IP	H	R	ER	HR	HB	BB	SO	RAT	ERA	ERA+	CERA	OAV	BH	AVG	PR+	WS	TPW
1940	Phi-A	0	3	.000	17	5	0	0	0	53	70	56	52	10	3	34	19	1.962	8.83	50	7.78	.315	5	.263	-25	0	-2.2
1941	Phi-A	2	0	1.000	6	2	1	0	0	19^2	28	22	22	4	0	12	8	2.034	10.07	42	8.26	.329	1	.200	-13	0	-1.3
1942	Phi-A	2	9	.182	30	14	4	0	1	133	163	99	91	7	4	69	78	1.744	6.16	61	5.38	.300	12	.226	-32	0	-3.1
1943	Phi-A	1	1	.500	5	1	0	0	0	16^1	18	6	6	2	1	4	3	1.347	3.31	103	4.54	.295	0	.000	1	1	-0.1
1946	Phi-A	0	2	.000	7	3	0	0	1	20^2	19	12	12	1	0	9	10	1.355	5.23	68	3.27	.247	0	.000	-4	0	-0.4
Total	**5**	**5**	**15**	**.250**	**65**	**25**	**5**	**0**	**2**	**242^2**	**298**	**195**	**183**	**24**	**8**	**128**	**118**	**1.755**	**6.79**	**58**	**5.90**	**.302**	**18**	**.200**	**-73**	**1**	**-7.0**

• BESSENT, Don Fred Donald Bessent b: 3/13/1931, Jacksonville, FL d: 7/7/1990, Jacksonville, FL BR/TR, 6', 175 lbs. Deb: 7/17/1955

YEAR	TM-L	W	L	PCT	G	GS	CG	SH	SV	IP	H	R	ER	HR	HB	BB	SO	RAT	ERA	ERA+	CERA	OAV	BH	AVG	PR+	WS	TPW
1955*	Bro-N	8	1	.889	24	2	1	0	3	63^1	51	19	19	7	0	21	29	1.137	2.70	150	2.84	.220	2	.100	9	7	0.7
1956*	Bro-N	4	3	.571	38	0	0	0	9	79^1	63	23	22	5	0	31	52	1.185	2.50	159	2.62	.221	2	.111	11	10	1.1
1957	Bro-N	1	3	.250	27	0	0	0	0	44	58	28	28	5	0	19	24	1.750	5.73	73	6.08	.328	1	.250	-8	1	-0.8
1958	LA-N	1	0	1.000	19	0	0	0	0	24^1	24	14	9	3	1	17	13	1.685	3.33	123	5.86	.270	0	.000	2	1	0.2
Total	**4**	**14**	**7**	**.667**	**108**	**2**	**1**	**0**	**12**	**211**	**196**	**84**	**78**	**20**	**1**	**88**	**118**	**1.346**	**3.33**	**122**	**3.78**	**.250**	**5**	**.114**	**15**	**19**	**1.2**

• BEST, Karl Karl Jon Best b: 3/6/1959, Aberdeen, WA BR/TR, 6'4", 210 lbs. Deb: 8/19/1983

YEAR	TM-L	W	L	PCT	G	GS	CG	SH	SV	IP	H	R	ER	HR	HB	BB	SO	RAT	ERA	ERA+	CERA	OAV	BH	AVG	PR+	WS	TPW
1983	Sea-A	0	1	.000	4	0	0	0	0	5^1	14	9	8	2	2	5	3	3.563	13.50	32	23.50	.483	0	....	-5	0	-0.5
1984	Sea-A	1	1	.500	5	0	0	0	0	6	7	2	2	0	0	0	6	1.167	3.00	133	2.72	.292	0	....	1	1	0.1
1985	Sea-A	2	1	.667	15	0	0	0	4	32^1	25	9	7	1	1	6	32	.959	1.95	216	1.83	.207	0	....	8	5	0.8
1986	Sea-A	2	3	.400	26	0	0	0	1	35^2	35	19	16	3	1	21	23	1.570	4.04	105	4.52	.255	0	....	1	2	0.1
1988	Min-A	0	0	....	11	0	0	0	0	12	15	9	8	1	0	7	9	1.833	6.00	68	5.75	.306	0	....	-3	0	-0.3
Total	**5**	**5**	**6**	**.455**	**61**	**0**	**0**	**0**	**5**	**91^1**	**96**	**48**	**41**	**7**	**4**	**39**	**73**	**1.478**	**4.04**	**104**	**4.72**	**.267**	**0**	**....**	**2**	**8**	**0.2**

• BETANCOURT, Rafael Rafael Jose Betancourt b: 4/29/1975, Cumana, Venezuela BR/TR, 6'2", 176 lbs. Deb: 7/13/2003

YEAR	TM-L	W	L	PCT	G	GS	CG	SH	SV	IP	H	R	ER	HR	HB	BB	SO	RAT	ERA	ERA+	CERA	OAV	BH	AVG	PR+	WS	TPW
2003	Cle-A	2	2	.500	33	0	0	0	1	38	27	11	9	5	1	13	36	1.053	2.13	207	2.54	.196	0	....	9	4	0.8

• BETHKE, Jim James Charles Bethke b: 11/5/1946, Falls City, NE BR/TR, 6'3", 185 lbs. Deb: 4/12/1965

YEAR	TM-L	W	L	PCT	G	GS	CG	SH	SV	IP	H	R	ER	HR	HB	BB	SO	RAT	ERA	ERA+	CERA	OAV	BH	AVG	PR+	WS	TPW
1965	NY-N	2	0	1.000	25	0	0	0	0	40	41	24	19	3	6	22	19	1.575	4.28	82	5.15	.266	0	.000	-3	2	-0.4

• BETTENDORF, Jeff Jeffrey Allen Bettendorf b: 12/10/1960, Lompoc, CA BR/TR, 6'3", 180 lbs. Deb: 4/8/1984

YEAR	TM-L	W	L	PCT	G	GS	CG	SH	SV	IP	H	R	ER	HR	HB	BB	SO	RAT	ERA	ERA+	CERA	OAV	BH	AVG	PR+	WS	TPW
1984	Oak-A	0	0	....	3	0	0	0	1	9^2	9	5	5	3	0	5	5	1.448	4.66	80	5.70	.243	0	....	-1	0	-0.1

• BETTS, Harry Harold Matthew "Chubby,Ginger" Betts b: 6/19/1881, Alliance, OH d: 5/22/1946, San Antonio, TX BR/TR, 5'10", 200 lbs. Deb: 9/22/1903

YEAR	TM-L	W	L	PCT	G	GS	CG	SH	SV	IP	H	R	ER	HR	HB	BB	SO	RAT	ERA	ERA+	CERA	OAV	BH	AVG	PR+	WS	TPW
1903	StL-N	0	1	.000	1	1	1	0	0	9	11	10	10	0	2	5	2	1.778	10.00	33	5.83	.297	0	.000	-7	0	-0.7
1913	Cin-N	0	0	....	1	0	0	0	0	3^1	1	1	1	0	1	3	0	1.200	2.70	120	2.83	.143	0	.000	0	0	0.0
Total	**2**	**0**	**1**	**.000**	**2**	**1**	**1**	**0**	**0**	**12^1**	**12**	**11**	**11**	**0**	**3**	**8**	**2**	**1.622**	**8.03**	**41**	**5.02**	**.273**	**0**	**.000**	**-7**	**0**	**-0.7**

• BETTS, Huck Walter Martin Betts b: 2/18/1897, Millsboro, DE d: 6/13/1987, Millsboro, DE BR/TR, 5'11", 170 lbs. Deb: 4/26/1920

YEAR	TM-L	W	L	PCT	G	GS	CG	SH	SV	IP	H	R	ER	HR	HB	BB	SO	RAT	ERA	ERA+	CERA	OAV	BH	AVG	PR+	WS	TPW
1920	Phi-N	1	1	.500	27	4	1	0	0	88^1	86	48	35	3	2	33	18	1.347	3.57	96	3.37	.261	2	.080	-1	4	-0.4
1921	Phi-N	3	7	.300	32	2	1	0	4	100^2	141	65	50	8	4	14	28	1.540	4.47	94	5.24	.337	8	.267	-1	5	0.0
1922	Phi-N	1	0	1.000	7	0	0	0	0	15	23	17	16	3	0	8	4	2.067	9.60	49	8.45	.348	0	.000	-8	0	-0.8
1923	Phi-N	2	4	.333	19	4	3	0	1	84^1	100	38	29	7	4	14	18	1.352	3.09	148	4.28	.314	3	.097	17	6	1.3
1924	Phi-N	7	10	.412	37	9	2	0	2	144^1	160	76	69	8	5	42	46	1.400	4.30	104	4.00	.286	7	.156	6	9	0.4
1925	Phi-N	4	5	.444	35	7	1	0	1	97^1	146	86	60	10	3	38	28	1.890	5.55	86	6.97	.342	10	.294	-5	3	-0.2
1932	Bos-N	13	11	.542	31	27	16	3	1	221^2	229	84	69	9	0	35	32	1.191	2.80	134	2.90	.267	19	.241	23	18	2.5
1933	Bos-N	11	11	.500	35	26	17	2	4	242	225	79	75	9	0	55	40	1.157	2.79	110	2.60	.248	17	.224	9	19	1.1
1934	Bos-N	17	10	.630	40	27	10	2	3	213	258	105	96	17	3	42	69	1.408	4.06	94	4.27	.296	13	.188	-5	13	-0.5
1935	Bos-N	2	9	.182	44	19	2	1	0	159^2	213	118	97	9	2	40	40	1.585	5.47	69	5.00	.321	7	.159	-24	1	-2.4
Total	**10**	**61**	**68**	**.473**	**307**	**125**	**53**	**8**	**16**	**1366^1**	**1581**	**716**	**596**	**83**	**23**	**321**	**323**	**1.392**	**3.93**	**99**	**4.06**	**.292**	**86**	**.197**	**10**	**78**	**1.0**

• BEVENS, Bill Floyd Clifford Bevens b: 10/21/1916, Hubbard, OR d: 10/26/1991, Salem, OR BR/TR, 6'3.5", 210 lbs. Deb: 5/12/1944

YEAR	TM-L	W	L	PCT	G	GS	CG	SH	SV	IP	H	R	ER	HR	HB	BB	SO	RAT	ERA	ERA+	CERA	OAV	BH	AVG	PR+	WS	TPW
1944	NY-A	4	1	.800	8	5	3	0	0	43^2	44	18	13	4	1	13	16	1.305	2.68	130	3.79	.273	1	.063	3	4	0.2
1945	NY-A	13	9	.591	29	25	14	2	0	184	174	83	75	12	1	68	76	1.315	3.67	94	3.38	.254	7	.111	-8	9	-1.4
1946	NY-A	16	13	.552	31	31	18	3	0	249^2	213	73	62	11	1	78	120	1.166	2.23	154	2.58	.232	7	.083	26	21	2.3
1947*	NY-A	7	13	.350	28	23	11	1	0	165	167	79	70	13	1	77	77	1.479	3.82	93	4.15	.264	7	.121	-6	5	-1.0
Total	**4**	**40**	**36**	**.526**	**96**	**84**	**46**	**6**	**0**	**642^1**	**598**	**253**	**220**	**40**	**4**	**236**	**289**	**1.298**	**3.08**	**113**	**3.29**	**.250**	**22**	**.100**	**15**	**39**	**0.2**

• BEVERLIN, Jason Jason Robert Beverlin b: 11/27/1973, Ashtabula, OH BL/TR, 6'5", 220 lbs. Deb: 7/29/2002

YEAR	TM-L	W	L	PCT	G	GS	CG	SH	SV	IP	H	R	ER	HR	HB	BB	SO	RAT	ERA	ERA+	CERA	OAV	BH	AVG	PR+	WS	TPW
2002	Cle-A	0	0	....	4	0	0	0	0	7^1	9	7	6	1	0	4	9	1.773	7.36	60	6.16	.290	0	....	-2	0	-0.2
	Det-A	0	3	.000	3	3	0	0	0	12^1	18	15	13	2	0	5	7	1.865	9.49	45	7.21	.327	0	....	-7	0	-0.7
	Yr.	0	3	.000	7	3	0	0	0	19^2	27	22	19	3	0	9	16	1.831	8.69	50	6.82	.314	0	....	-9	0	-0.9

• BEVIL, Brian Brian Scott Bevil b: 9/5/1971, Houston, TX BR/TR, 6'3", 190 lbs. Deb: 6/17/1996

YEAR	TM-L	W	L	PCT	G	GS	CG	SH	SV	IP	H	R	ER	HR	HB	BB	SO	RAT	ERA	ERA+	CERA	OAV	BH	AVG	PR+	WS	TPW
1996	KC-A	1	0	1.000	3	1	0	0	0	11	9	7	7	2	0	5	7	1.273	5.73	88	4.06	.237	0	....	-1	1	-0.1
1997	KC-A	1	2	.333	18	0	0	0	1	16^1	16	13	12	1	1	9	13	1.531	6.61	71	4.37	.267	0	....	-4	0	-0.3

YEAR	TM-L	W	L	PCT	G	GS	CG	SH	SV	IP	H	R	ER	HR	HB	BB	SO	RAT	ERA	ERA+	CERA	OAV	BH	AVG	PR+	WS	TPW
1998	KC-A	3	1	.750	39	0	0	0	0	40	47	29	28	4	3	22	47	1.725	6.30	77	5.76	.283	0	....	-6	1	-0.6
Total	3	5	3	.625	60	1	0	0	1	67^1	72	49	47	7	4	36	67	1.604	6.28	77	5.15	.273	0	....	-11	2	-1.0

• BEVIL, Lou Louis Eugene Bevil b: 11/27/1922, Nelson, IL d: 2/1/1973, Dixon, IL BB/TR, 5'11.5", 190 lbs. Deb: 9/2/1942

YEAR	TM-L	W	L	PCT	G	GS	CG	SH	SV	IP	H	R	ER	HR	HB	BB	SO	RAT	ERA	ERA+	CERA	OAV	BH	AVG	PR+	WS	TPW
1942	Was-A	0	1	.000	4	1	0	0	0	9^2	9	7	7	0	1	11	2	2.069	6.52	56	5.99	.265	0	.000	-3	0	-0.3

• BEVILLE, Ben Clarence Benjamin Beville b: 8/28/1877, Colusa, CA d: 1/5/1937, Yountville, CA BR/TR, 5'9", 190 lbs. Deb: 5/24/1901

YEAR	TM-L	W	L	PCT	G	GS	CG	SH	SV	IP	H	R	ER	HR	HB	BB	SO	RAT	ERA	ERA+	CERA	OAV	BH	AVG	PR+	WS	TPW
1901	Bos-A	0	2	.000	2	2	1	0	0	9	8	7	4	0	1	9	1	1.889	4.00	88	5.05	.236	2	.286	-1	0	-0.1

• BIBBY, Jim James Blair Bibby b: 10/29/1944, Franklinton, NC BR/TR, 6'5", 235 lbs. Deb: 9/4/1972

YEAR	TM-L	W	L	PCT	G	GS	CG	SH	SV	IP	H	R	ER	HR	HB	BB	SO	RAT	ERA	ERA+	CERA	OAV	BH	AVG	PR+	WS	TPW
1972	StL-N	1	3	.250	6	6	0	0	0	40^1	29	18	15	4	1	19	28	1.190	3.35	102	2.81	.206	1	.125	0	2	0.1
1973	StL-N	0	2	.000	6	3	0	0	0	16	19	17	17	2	2	17	12	2.250	9.56	38	8.62	.306	0	.000	-11	0	-1.1
	Tex-A	9	10	.474	26	23	11	2	1	180^1	121	73	65	14	6	106	155	1.259	3.24	115	2.99	**.192**	0	....	14	10	1.5
1974	Tex-A	19	19	.500	41	41	11	5	0	264	255	146	139	25	9	113	149	1.394	4.74	75	4.11	.255	0	....	-36	8	-3.7
1975	Tex-A	2	6	.250	12	12	4	1	0	68^1	73	41	38	2	2	28	31	1.478	5.00	75	4.08	.274	0	....	-9	1	-0.9
	Cle-A	5	9	.357	24	12	2	0	1	112^2	99	48	40	7	0	50	62	1.322	3.20	118	3.27	.235	0	....	7	7	0.7
	Yr.	7	15	.318	36	24	6	1	1	181	172	89	78	9	2	78	93	1.381	3.88	97	3.57	.250	0	....	-3	8	-0.3
1976	Cle-A	13	7	.650	34	21	4	3	1	163^1	162	61	58	6	1	56	84	1.335	3.20	109	3.45	.266	0	....	5	11	0.5
1977	Cle-A	12	13	.480	37	30	9	2	2	206^2	197	100	82	17	4	73	141	1.306	3.57	110	3.58	.250	0	....	8	13	0.8
1978	Pit-N	8	7	.533	34	14	3	2	1	107	100	52	42	10	2	39	72	1.299	3.53	105	3.44	.246	4	.129	3	6	0.4
1979*	Pit-N	12	4	.750	34	17	4	1	0	137^2	110	51	43	9	4	47	103	1.140	2.81	138	2.62	.218	8	.178	15	12	1.7
1980	Pit-N★	19	6	.760	35	34	6	1	0	238^1	210	95	88	20	6	88	144	1.250	3.32	110	3.34	.238	12	.156	6	17	0.9
1981	Pit-N	6	3	.667	14	14	2	2	0	93^2	79	30	26	4	2	26	48	1.121	2.50	144	2.46	.225	4	.143	12	8	1.4
1983	Pit-N	5	12	.294	29	12	0	0	2	78	92	60	58	10	1	51	44	1.833	6.69	55	6.52	.297	2	.111	-25	0	-2.7
1984	Tex-A	0	0	....	8	0	0	0	0	16^1	19	8	8	1	0	10	6	1.776	4.41	94	5.56	.297	0	....	-0	1	0.0
Total	12	111	101	.524	340	239	56	19	8	1722^2	1565	800	719	131	40	723	1079	1.328	3.76	98	3.59	.243	31	.148	-11	96	-0.6

• BICKFORD, Vern Vernon Edgell Bickford b: 8/17/1920, Hellier, KY d: 5/6/1960, Concord, VA BR/TR, 6', 185 lbs. Deb: 4/24/1948

YEAR	TM-L	W	L	PCT	G	GS	CG	SH	SV	IP	H	R	ER	HR	HB	BB	SO	RAT	ERA	ERA+	CERA	OAV	BH	AVG	PR+	WS	TPW
1948*	Bos-N	11	5	.688	33	22	10	1	1	146	125	59	53	9	3	63	60	1.288	3.27	117	3.07	.226	10	.204	8	11	0.9
1949	Bos-N★	16	11	.593	37	36	15	2	0	230^2	246	125	109	20	6	106	101	1.526	4.25	89	4.57	.273	15	.185	-11	10	-1.2
1950	Bos-N	19	14	.576	40	**39**	**27**	2	0	**311**^{2}	293	135	120	25	6	122	126	1.332	3.47	111	3.56	.248	16	.138	15	18	1.1
1951	Bos-N	11	9	.550	25	20	12	3	0	164^2	146	68	57	7	6	76	76	1.348	3.12	118	3.36	.240	6	.115	12	11	1.0
1952	Bos-N	7	12	.368	26	22	7	1	0	161^1	165	73	67	7	2	64	62	1.419	3.74	97	3.79	.269	9	.176	1	7	0.0
1953	Mil-N	2	5	.286	20	9	2	0	1	58	60	35	34	8	2	35	25	1.638	5.28	74	5.52	.279	1	.067	-9	0	-1.0
1954	Bal-A	0	1	.000	1	1	0	0	0	4	5	5	4	0	0	1	0	1.500	9.00	40	3.53	.333	0	.000	-2	0	-0.3
Total	7	66	57	.537	182	149	73	9	2	1076^1	1040	500	444	76	25	467	450	1.400	3.71	102	3.82	.254	57	.156	13	57	0.5

• BICKHAM, Dan Daniel Denison Bickham b: 10/31/1864, Dayton, OH d: 3/3/1951, Dayton, OH BR/TR, 5'10", 160 lbs. Deb: 8/13/1886

YEAR	TM-L	W	L	PCT	G	GS	CG	SH	SV	IP	H	R	ER	HR	HB	BB	SO	RAT	ERA	ERA+	CERA	OAV	BH	AVG	PR+	WS	TPW
1886	Cin-a	1	0	1.000	1	1	1	0	0	9	13	11	3	0	0	3	6	1.778	3.00	117	....	.323	1	.333	0	0	0.1

• BICKNELL, Charlie Charles Stephen "Bud" Bicknell b: 7/27/1928, Plainfield, NJ BR/TR, 5'11", 170 lbs. Deb: 4/22/1948

YEAR	TM-L	W	L	PCT	G	GS	CG	SH	SV	IP	H	R	ER	HR	HB	BB	SO	RAT	ERA	ERA+	CERA	OAV	BH	AVG	PR+	WS	TPW
1948	Phi-N	0	1	.000	17	1	0	0	0	25^2	29	20	17	5	0	17	5	1.792	5.96	66	6.52	.287	0	.000	-6	0	-0.6
1949	Phi-N	0	0	....	13	0	0	0	0	28^1	32	24	24	3	2	17	4	1.729	7.62	52	5.83	.291	0	.000	-12	0	-1.1
Total	2	0	1	.000	30	1	0	0	0	54	61	44	41	8	2	34	9	1.759	6.83	58	6.16	.289	0	.000	-18	0	-1.8

• BIDDLE, Rocky Lee Francis Biddle b: 5/21/1976, Las Vegas, NV BR/TR, 6'3", 230 lbs. Deb: 8/10/2000

YEAR	TM-L	W	L	PCT	G	GS	CG	SH	SV	IP	H	R	ER	HR	HB	BB	SO	RAT	ERA	ERA+	CERA	OAV	BH	AVG	PR+	WS	TPW
2000	Chi-A	1	2	.333	4	4	0	0	0	22^2	31	25	21	5	0	8	7	1.721	8.34	60	7.01	.326	0	....	-9	0	-0.8
2001	Chi-A	7	8	.467	30	21	0	0	0	128^2	137	87	77	16	8	52	85	1.469	5.39	86	4.85	.272	0	.000	-12	4	-1.1
2002	Chi-A	3	4	.429	44	7	0	0	1	77^2	72	42	35	13	5	39	64	1.429	4.06	112	4.78	.245	0	....	4	4	0.4
2003	Mon-N	5	8	.385	73	0	0	0	34	71^2	71	43	37	10	6	40	54	1.549	4.65	109	5.08	.254	0	.000	3	9	0.3
Total	4	16	22	.421	151	32	0	0	35	300^2	311	197	170	44	19	139	210	1.497	5.09	93	5.05	.265	0	.000	-14	17	-1.3

• BIELECKI, Mike Michael Joseph Bielecki b: 7/31/1959, Baltimore, MD BR/TR, 6'3", 195 lbs. Deb: 9/14/1984

YEAR	TM-L	W	L	PCT	G	GS	CG	SH	SV	IP	H	R	ER	HR	HB	BB	SO	RAT	ERA	ERA+	CERA	OAV	BH	AVG	PR+	WS	TPW
1984	Pit-N	0	0	....	4	0	0	0	0	4^1	4	0	0	0	0	0	1	.923	0.00	....	1.64	.250	0	....	2	1	0.2
1985	Pit-N	2	3	.400	12	7	0	0	0	45^2	45	26	23	5	1	31	22	1.664	4.53	79	5.18	.257	0	.000	-4	1	-0.5
1986	Pit-N	6	11	.353	31	27	0	0	0	148^2	149	87	77	10	2	83	83	1.561	4.66	82	4.47	.262	3	.063	-14	2	-1.7
1987	Pit-N	2	3	.400	8	8	2	0	0	45^2	43	25	24	6	1	12	25	1.204	4.73	87	3.46	.250	1	.063	-4	2	-0.5
1988	Chi-N	2	2	.500	19	5	0	0	0	48^1	55	22	18	4	0	16	33	1.469	3.35	108	4.34	.284	1	.100	2	3	0.2
1989*	Chi-N	18	7	.720	33	33	4	3	0	212^1	187	82	74	16	0	81	147	1.262	3.14	120	3.16	.237	3	.043	15	16	1.2
1990	Chi-N	8	11	.421	36	29	0	0	1	168	188	101	92	13	5	70	103	**1.536**	4.93	83	4.66	.287	7	.163	-11	5	-1.1
1991	Chi-N	13	11	.542	39	25	0	0	0	172	169	91	86	18	2	54	72	1.297	4.50	86	3.72	.262	3	.065	-9	7	-1.2
	Atl-N	0	0	....	2	0	0	0	0	1^2	2	0	0	0	0	2	3	2.400	0.00	....	7.49	.286	0	....	1	0	0.1
	Yr.	13	11	.542	41	25	0	0	0	173^2	171	91	86	18	2	56	75	1.307	4.46	87	3.75	.262	3	.065	-8	7	-1.1
1992	Atl-N	2	4	.333	19	14	1	1	0	80^2	77	27	23	2	1	27	62	1.289	2.57	142	3.14	.254	3	.125	10	5	0.9
1993	Cle-A	4	5	.444	13	13	0	0	0	68^2	90	47	45	8	2	23	38	1.646	5.90	73	5.73	.310	0	....	-12	1	-1.2
1994	Atl-N	2	0	1.000	19	1	0	0	0	27	28	12	12	2	1	12	18	1.481	4.00	106	4.54	.277	0	.000	1	2	0.1
1995	Cal-A	4	6	.400	22	11	0	0	0	75^1	80	56	50	15	3	31	45	1.473	5.97	79	5.33	.273	0	....	-11	1	-1.1
1996*	Atl-N	4	3	.571	40	5	0	0	2	75^1	63	24	22	8	0	33	71	1.274	2.63	168	3.24	.224	1	.100	16	8	1.6
1997	Atl-N	3	7	.300	50	0	0	0	2	57^1	56	33	26	9	1	21	60	1.343	4.08	103	4.10	.250	0	.000	0	3	0.1
Total	14	70	73	.490	347	178	7	4	5	1231	1236	633	572	116	19	496	783	1.407	4.18	96	4.09	.262	22	.078	-18	57	-3.0

• BIEMILLER, Harry Harry Lee Biemiller b: 10/9/1897, Baltimore, MD d: 5/25/1965, Orlando, FL BR/TR, 6'1", 171 lbs. Deb: 8/26/1920

YEAR	TM-L	W	L	PCT	G	GS	CG	SH	SV	IP	H	R	ER	HR	HB	BB	SO	RAT	ERA	ERA+	CERA	OAV	BH	AVG	PR+	WS	TPW
1920	Was-A	1	0	1.000	5	2	1	0	0	17	21	13	9	1	0	13	10	2.000	4.76	78	6.75	.318	0	.000	-2	0	-0.2
1925	Cin-N	0	1	.000	23	1	0	0	2	47	45	28	21	2	7	21	9	1.404	4.02	102	4.30	.280	0	.000	-0	2	-0.1
Total	2	1	1	.500	28	3	1	0	2	64	66	41	30	3	7	34	19	1.563	4.22	94	4.95	.291	0	.000	-2	2	-0.3

• BIERBRODT, Nick Nicholas Raymond Bierbrodt b: 5/16/1978, Tarzana, CA BL/TL, 6'5", 185 lbs. Deb: 6/7/2001

YEAR	TM-L	W	L	PCT	G	GS	CG	SH	SV	IP	H	R	ER	HR	HB	BB	SO	RAT	ERA	ERA+	CERA	OAV	BH	AVG	PR+	WS	TPW
2001	Ari-N	2	2	.500	5	5	0	0	0	23	29	21	21	6	0	12	17	1.783	8.22	56	7.43	.305	4	.667	-10	0	-0.7
	TB-A	3	4	.429	11	11	0	0	0	61^1	71	38	31	11	4	27	56	1.598	4.55	99	5.99	.285	0	....	-1	3	-0.1
2003	TB-A	0	2	.000	13	5	0	0	0	35^1	59	41	38	9	5	23	20	2.321	9.68	47	11.32	.376	0	....	-21	0	-2.0
	Cle-A	0	0	....	5	0	0	0	0	8	5	6	6	0	0	4	9	1.125	6.75	65	1.84	.185	0	....	-2	0	-0.2
	Yr.	0	2	.000	18	5	0	0	0	43^1	64	47	44	9	5	27	29	2.100	9.14	49	9.57	.348	0	....	-23	0	-2.2
Total	2	5	8	.385	34	21	0	0	0	127^2	164	106	96	26	9	66	102	1.802	6.77	67	7.47	.311	4	.667	-34	3	-3.0

• BIGBEE, Lyle Lyle Randolph "Al" Bigbee b: 8/22/1893, Sweet Home, OR d: 8/5/1942, Portland, OR BL/TR, 6', 180 lbs. Deb: 4/15/1920 ♦

YEAR	TM-L	W	L	PCT	G	GS	CG	SH	SV	IP	H	R	ER	HR	HB	BB	SO	RAT	ERA	ERA+	CERA	OAV	BH	AVG	PR+	WS	TPW
1920	Phi-A	0	3	.000	12	2	0	0	0	45	66	42	40	5	0	25	12	2.022	8.00	50	7.96	.369	14	.187	-19	0	-2.5
1921	Pit-N	0	0	....	5	0	0	0	0	8	4	1	1	0	0	4	1	1.000	1.13	341	1.43	.154	0	.000	2	1	0.2
Total	2	0	3	.000	17	2	0	0	0	53	70	43	41	5	0	29	13	1.868	6.96	58	6.97	.342	14	.182	-17	1	-2.3

• BIGGS, Charlie Charles Orval Biggs b: 9/15/1906, French Lick, IN d: 5/24/1954, French Lick, IN BR/TR, 6'1", 185 lbs. Deb: 9/3/1932

YEAR	TM-L	W	L	PCT	G	GS	CG	SH	SV	IP	H	R	ER	HR	HB	BB	SO	RAT	ERA	ERA+	CERA	OAV	BH	AVG	PR+	WS	TPW
1932	Chi-A	1	1	.500	6	4	0	0	0	24^2	32	22	19	2	3	12	1	1.784	6.93	62	6.44	.314	1	.111	-7	0	-0.7

• BILBREY, Jim James Melvin Bilbrey b: 4/20/1924, Rickman, TN d: 12/26/1985, Toledo, OH BR/TR, 6'2.5", 205 lbs. Deb: 5/17/1949

YEAR	TM-L	W	L	PCT	G	GS	CG	SH	SV	IP	H	R	ER	HR	HB	BB	SO	RAT	ERA	ERA+	CERA	OAV	BH	AVG	PR+	WS	TPW
1949	StL-A	0	0	....	1	0	0	0	0	1	1	2	2	0	0	3	0	4.000	18.00	25	12.51	.250	0	....	-1	0	-0.1

• BILDILLI, Emil Emil "Hill Billy" Bildilli b: 9/16/1912, Diamond, IN d: 9/16/1946, Hartford City, IN BR/TL, 5'10", 170 lbs. Deb: 8/24/1937

YEAR	TM-L	W	L	PCT	G	GS	CG	SH	SV	IP	H	R	ER	HR	HB	BB	SO	RAT	ERA	ERA+	CERA	OAV	BH	AVG	PR+	WS	TPW
1937	StL-A	0	1	.000	4	1	0	0	0	8	12	9	9	1	0	3	2	1.875	10.13	48	7.32	.353	0	.000	-5	0	-0.5
1938	StL-A	1	2	.333	5	3	2	0	0	21^2	33	18	17	3	0	11	11	2.031	7.06	70	8.04	.359	2	.250	-5	0	-0.4
1939	StL-A	1	1	.500	2	2	2	0	0	19	21	8	7	0	0	6	8	1.421	3.32	147	3.40	.266	0	.000	4	1	0.3
1940	StL-A	2	4	.333	28	11	3	0	1	97	113	68	60	12	2	52	32	1.701	5.57	82	5.86	.298	6	.200	-10	3	-1.0

YEAR TM-L	W	L	PCT	G	GS	CG	SH	SV	IP	H	R	ER	HR	HB	BB	SO	RAT	ERA	ERA+	CERA	OAV	BH	AVG	PR+	WS	TPW
1941 StL-A	0	0	....	2	0	0	0	0	2^1	5	3	3	0	0	3	2	3.429	11.57	37	13.86	.417	0	....	-2	0	-0.2
Total 5	4	8	.333	41	17	7	0	1	148	184	106	96	16	2	75	55	1.750	5.84	80	6.07	.309	8	.178	-18	4	-1.8
• BILLIARD, Harry	Harry Pree "Pree" Billiard b: 11/11/1883, Monroe, IN d: 6/3/1923, Wooster, OH BR/TR, 6', 190 lbs. Deb: 7/31/1908																									
1908 NY-A	0	0	....	6	0	0	0	0	17	15	15	5	1	5	14	10	1.706	2.65	93	5.56	.234	1	.167	0	0	0.0
1914 Ind-F	8	7	.533	32	16	5	0	2	125^2	117	71	52	4	7	63	45	1.432	3.72	93	3.86	.257	7	.184	-5	6	-0.6
1915 New-F	0	1	.000	14	2	0	0	1	28^1	32	23	18	0	2	28	7	2.118	5.72	50	6.31	.291	2	.333	-9	0	-0.9
Total 3	8	8	.500	52	18	5	0	3	171	164	109	75	5	14	105	62	1.573	3.95	81	4.44	.261	10	.200	-14	6	-1.5
• BILLINGHAM, Jack	John Eugene Billingham b: 2/21/1943, Orlando, FL BR/TR, 6'4", 215 lbs. Deb: 4/11/1968																									
1968 LA-N	3	0	1.000	50	1	0	0	8	70^2	54	18	17	0	2	30	46	1.189	2.17	128	2.18	.215	0	.000	4	8	0.5
1969 Hou-N	6	7	.462	52	4	1	0	2	82^2	92	45	39	12	5	29	71	1.464	4.25	83	4.99	.290	1	.071	-6	3	-0.6
1970 Hou-N	13	9	.591	46	24	8	2	0	187^2	190	102	83	10	10	63	134	1.348	3.98	97	3.70	.259	6	.103	-2	9	-0.4
1971 Hou-N	10	16	.385	33	33	8	3	0	228^1	205	98	86	9	16	68	139	1.196	3.39	99	2.99	.243	9	.123	-2	9	-0.5
1972* Cin-N	12	12	.500	36	31	8	4	1	217^2	197	83	77	18	7	64	137	1.199	3.18	101	3.12	.241	5	.070	-4	10	-0.8
1973* Cin-N★	19	10	.655	40	**40**	16	**7**	0	**293^1**	257	112	99	20	10	95	155	1.200	3.04	112	3.03	.236	6	.065	6	19	0.0
1974 Cin-N	19	11	.633	36	35	8	3	0	212^1	233	105	93	16	6	64	103	1.399	3.94	88	4.20	.288	5	.075	-15	9	-2.1
1975* Cin-N	15	10	.600	33	32	5	0	0	208	222	100	95	22	9	76	79	1.433	4.11	87	4.54	.279	7	.108	-18	8	-2.0
1976* Cin-N	12	10	.545	34	29	5	2	1	177	190	96	85	17	4	62	76	1.424	4.32	81	4.36	.279	14	.237	-18	5	-1.5
1977 Cin-N	10	10	.500	36	23	3	2	0	161^2	195	105	94	16	10	56	76	1.553	5.23	75	5.24	.306	9	.161	-25	2	-2.6
1978 Det-A	15	8	.652	30	30	10	4	0	201^2	218	95	87	16	8	65	59	1.403	3.88	99	4.32	.284	0	....	-3	12	-0.3
1979 Det-A	10	7	.588	35	19	2	0	3	158	163	74	58	13	7	60	59	1.411	3.30	131	4.25	.275	0	....	16	12	1.6
1980 Det-A	0	0	....	8	0	0	0	0	7^1	11	6	6	1	0	6	3	2.318	7.36	56	9.06	.355	0	....	-3	0	-0.3
Bos-A	1	3	.250	7	4	0	0	0	24^1	45	30	30	6	4	12	4	2.342	11.10	38	12.46	.413	0	....	-19	0	-1.9
Yr.	1	3	.250	15	4	0	0	0	31^2	56	36	36	7	4	18	7	2.337	10.23	41	11.68	.400	0	....	-21	0	-2.1
Total 13	145	113	.562	476	305	74	27	15	2230^2	2272	1069	949	176	98	750	1141	1.355	3.83	94	3.98	.268	62	.111	-87	106	-10.9
• BILLINGS, Josh	Haskell Clark Billings b: 9/27/1907, New York, NY d: 12/26/1983, Greenbrae, CA BR/TR, 5'11", 180 lbs. Deb: 8/17/1927																									
1927 Det-A	5	4	.556	10	9	5	0	0	67	64	36	36	3	6	39	18	1.537	4.84	87	4.30	.259	7	.259	-4	4	-0.3
1928 Det-A	5	10	.333	21	16	3	1	0	110^2	118	83	63	4	5	59	48	1.599	5.12	80	4.40	.276	10	.286	-12	3	-0.9
1929 Det-A	0	1	.000	8	0	0	0	0	19^1	27	14	11	0	1	9	1	1.862	5.12	84	5.91	.365	0	.000	-1	0	-0.2
Total 3	10	15	.400	39	25	8	1	0	197	209	133	110	7	12	107	67	1.604	5.03	83	4.51	.279	17	.250	-18	7	-1.4
• BILLINGSLEY, Brent	Brett Aaron Billingsley b: 4/19/1975, Downey, CA BL/TL, 6'2", 200 lbs. Deb: 5/20/1999																									
1999 Fla-N	0	0	....	8	0	0	0	0	7^2	11	14	14	3	2	10	3	2.739	16.43	26	16.37	.379	0	....	-10	0	-1.0
• BIRD, Doug	James Douglas Bird b: 3/5/1950, Corona, CA BR/TR, 6'4", 180 lbs. Deb: 4/29/1973																									
1973 KC-A	4	4	.500	54	0	0	0	20	102^1	81	37	34	10	2	30	83	1.085	2.99	137	2.53	.217	0	....	14	15	1.4
1974 KC-A	7	6	.538	55	1	1	0	10	92^1	100	31	28	6	1	27	62	1.375	2.73	140	3.82	.286	0	....	12	10	1.3
1975 KC-A	9	6	.600	51	4	0	0	11	105^1	100	42	38	7	2	40	81	1.329	3.25	119	3.45	.258	0	....	9	11	0.9
1976* KC-A	12	10	.545	39	27	2	1	2	197^2	191	90	74	17	3	31	107	1.123	3.37	104	2.89	.251	0	....	3	10	0.3
1977* KC-A	11	4	.733	53	5	0	0	14	118^1	120	52	51	14	3	29	83	1.259	3.88	104	3.78	.270	0	....	1	11	0.1
1978* KC-A	6	6	.500	40	6	0	0	1	98^2	110	63	58	8	2	31	48	1.429	5.29	72	4.19	.284	0	....	-17	1	-1.7
1979 Phi-N	2	0	1.000	32	1	1	0	0	61	73	35	35	7	2	16	33	1.459	5.16	74	4.88	.305	1	.167	-10	2	-1.0
1980 NY-A	3	0	1.000	22	1	0	0	1	50^2	47	16	15	3	1	14	17	1.204	2.66	147	3.08	.257	0	....	7	5	0.7
1981 NY-A	5	1	.833	17	4	0	0	0	53^1	58	19	16	5	0	16	28	1.388	2.70	132	4.04	.280	0	....	5	4	0.5
Chi-N	4	5	.444	12	12	2	1	0	75^1	72	34	30	5	1	16	34	1.168	3.58	103	2.94	.254	2	.100	3	4	0.2
1982 Chi-N	9	14	.391	35	33	2	1	0	191	230	119	109	26	3	30	71	1.361	5.14	73	4.54	.297	8	.143	-28	2	-3.1
1983 Bos-A	1	4	.200	22	6	0	0	1	67^2	91	52	50	14	2	16	33	1.581	6.65	65	6.31	.324	0	....	-17	0	-1.7
Total 11	73	60	.549	432	100	8	3	60	1213^2	1273	590	538	122	22	296	680	1.293	3.99	96	3.78	.272	11	.134	-18	75	-2.1
• BIRD, Red	James Edward Bird b: 4/25/1890, Stephenville, TX d: 3/23/1972, Murfreesboro, AR BL/TL, 5'11", 170 lbs. Deb: 9/17/1921																									
1921 Was-A	0	0	....	1	0	0	0	0	5	5	3	3	0	1	1	2	1.200	5.40	76	3.36	.294	0	.000	-1	0	-0.1
• BIRKBECK, Mike	Michael Lawrence Birkbeck b: 3/10/1961, Orrville, OH BR/TR, 6'1", 190 lbs. Deb: 8/17/1986																									
1986 Mil-A	1	1	.500	7	4	0	0	0	22	24	12	11	0	0	12	13	1.636	4.50	96	4.53	.282	0	....	-0	1	0.0
1987 Mil-A	1	4	.200	10	10	1	0	0	45	63	33	31	8	0	19	25	1.822	6.20	74	7.29	.335	0	....	-8	0	-0.7
1988 Mil-A	10	8	.556	23	23	0	0	0	124	141	69	65	10	1	37	64	1.435	4.72	84	4.33	.285	0	....	-11	5	-1.1
1989 Mil-A	0	4	.000	9	9	1	0	0	44^2	57	32	27	4	3	22	31	1.769	5.44	71	6.10	.310	0	....	-8	0	-0.8
1992 NY-N	0	1	.000	1	1	0	0	0	7	12	7	7	3	0	1	2	1.857	9.00	39	9.94	.387	0	.000	-4	0	-0.5
1995 NY-N	0	1	.000	4	4	0	0	0	27^2	22	5	5	2	0	2	14	.867	1.63	249	1.74	.220	2	.333	7	3	0.8
Total 6	12	19	.387	54	51	2	0	0	270^1	319	158	146	27	4	93	149	1.524	4.86	84	5.01	.295	2	.250	-24	9	-2.4
• BIRKOFER, Ralph	Ralph Joseph "Lefty" Birkofer b: 11/5/1908, Cincinnati, OH d: 3/16/1971, Cincinnati, OH BL/TL, 5'11", 213 lbs. Deb: 4/25/1933																									
1933 Pit-N	4	2	.667	9	8	3	1	0	50^2	43	22	13	1	1	17	20	1.184	2.31	144	2.53	.229	7	.318	5	4	0.7
1934 Pit-N	11	12	.478	41	24	11	0	1	204	227	106	93	11	5	66	71	1.436	4.10	100	4.04	.277	17	.227	2	11	0.3
1935 Pit-N	9	7	.563	37	18	8	1	1	150^1	173	87	68	5	6	42	80	1.430	4.07	101	3.91	.283	14	.241	2	8	0.4
1936 Pit-N	7	5	.583	34	13	2	0	0	109^1	130	73	57	4	5	41	44	1.564	4.69	86	4.62	.295	9	.220	-7	4	-0.7
1937 Bro-N	0	2	.000	11	1	0	0	0	29^2	45	28	22	3	0	9	9	1.820	6.67	60	6.43	.341	3	.273	-8	0	-0.7
Total 5	31	28	.525	132	64	24	2	2	544	618	316	253	24	17	175	224	1.458	4.19	97	4.11	.282	50	.242	-5	27	-0.1
• BIRRER, Babe	Werner Joseph Birrer b: 7/4/1928, Buffalo, NY BR/TR, 6', 195 lbs. Deb: 6/5/1955																									
1955 Det-A	4	3	.571	36	3	1	0	3	80^1	77	39	37	9	0	29	28	1.320	4.15	93	3.66	.248	3	.158	-3	5	0.0
1956 Bal-A	0	0	....	4	0	0	0	0	5^1	9	5	4	0	0	1	1	1.875	6.75	58	6.33	.360	0	.000	-2	0	-0.2
1958 LA-N	0	0	....	16	0	0	0	1	34	43	20	17	4	1	7	16	1.471	4.50	91	4.93	.309	4	.571	-2	2	0.0
Total 3	4	3	.571	56	3	1	0	4	119^2	129	64	58	13	1	37	45	1.387	4.36	90	4.14	.272	7	.259	-6	7	-0.2
• BIRTSAS, Tim	Timothy Dean Birtsas b: 9/5/1960, Pontiac, MI BL/TL, 6'7", 240 lbs. Deb: 5/3/1985																									
1985 Oak-A	10	6	.625	29	25	2	0	0	141^1	124	72	63	18	3	91	94	1.521	4.01	96	4.67	.238	0	....	-1	6	-0.1
1986 Oak-A	0	0	....	2	0	0	0	0	2	2	5	5	1	0	4	1	3.000	22.50	17	13.74	.286	0	....	-4	0	-0.4
1988 Cin-N	1	3	.250	36	4	0	0	0	64^1	61	34	30	6	3	24	38	1.321	4.20	85	3.67	.250	0	.000	-6	1	-0.7
1989 Cin-N	2	2	.500	42	1	0	0	1	69^2	68	33	29	5	3	27	57	1.364	3.75	96	3.68	.261	1	.250	-0	4	0.1
1990 Cin-N	1	3	.250	29	0	0	0	0	51^1	69	24	22	7	1	24	41	1.812	3.86	102	6.67	.325	0	.000	-0	2	-0.1
Total 5	14	14	.500	138	30	2	0	1	328^2	324	168	149	37	10	170	231	1.503	4.08	92	4.63	.260	1	.056	-12	13	-1.3
• BISCAN, Frank	Frank Stephen "Porky" Biscan b: 3/13/1920, Mount Olive, IL d: 5/22/1959, St. Louis, MO BL/TL, 5'11", 190 lbs. Deb: 5/3/1942																									
1942 StL-A	0	1	.000	11	0	0	0	1	27	13	8	7	1	0	11	10	.889	2.33	159	1.28	.143	0	.000	4	3	0.4
1946 StL-A	1	1	.500	16	0	0	0	1	22^2	28	13	13	0	0	22	9	2.206	5.16	72	6.84	.318	0	.000	-4	1	-0.4
1948 StL-A	6	7	.462	47	4	1	0	2	98^2	129	78	67	3	9	71	45	2.027	6.11	75	6.75	.323	5	.192	-15	2	-1.4
Total 3	7	9	.438	74	4	1	0	4	148^1	170	99	87	4	9	104	64	1.847	5.28	82	5.77	.294	5	.143	-14	6	-1.4
• BISHOP, Bill	William Robinson Bishop b: 12/27/1869, Adamsburg, PA d: 12/15/1932, Pittsburgh, PA BR/TR, 5'8" Deb: 9/13/1886																									
1886 Pit-a	0	1	.000	2	2	2	0	0	17	17	14	6	0	1	11	4	1.647	3.18	106	....	.249	1	.143	0	0	0.0
1887 Pit-N	0	3	.000	3	3	3	0	0	27	67	46	40	2	2	22	4	2.481	13.33	29	....	.457	1	.100	-28	0	-2.5
1889 Chi-N	0	0	....	2	0	0	0	**2**	3	6	13	6	0	0	6	1	4.000	18.00	23	....	.403	0	.000	-5	0	-0.4
Total 3	0	4	.000	7	5	5	0	2	47	90	73	52	2	3	39	9	2.277	9.96	38	....	.391	2	.111	-33	0	-2.9
• BISHOP, Bill	William Henry "Lefty" Bishop b: 10/22/1900, Houtzdale, PA d: 2/14/1956, St. Joseph, MO BL/TL, 5'8", 170 lbs. Deb: 9/15/1921																									
1921 Phi-A	0	0	....	2	0	0	0	0	7	8	9	7	0	0	10	4	2.571	9.00	49	7.16	.267	0	.000	-3	0	-0.4

YEAR TM-L	W	L	PCT	G	GS	CG	SH	SV	IP	H	R	ER	HR	HB	BB	SO	RAT	ERA	ERA+	CERA	OAV	BH	AVG	PR+	WS	TPW
• BISHOP, Charlie	Charles Tuller Bishop b: 1/1/1924, Atlanta, GA d: 7/5/1993, Lawrenceville, GA BR/TR, 6'2", 195 lbs. Deb: 8/22/1952																									
1952 Phi-A	2	2	.500	6	5	1	0	0	30^2	29	24	22	2	0	24	17	1.728	6.46	61	4.56	.238	1	.111	-8	0	-0.9
1953 Phi-A	3	14	.176	39	20	1	1	2	160^2	174	106	101	15	5	86	66	1.618	5.66	76	5.09	.282	5	.089	-24	2	-2.8
1954 Phi-A	4	6	.400	20	12	4	0	1	96	98	49	47	10	5	50	34	1.542	4.41	89	4.82	.275	4	.121	-4	5	-0.6
1955 KC-A	1	0	1.000	4	0	0	0	0	6^2	6	7	4	1	3	8	4	2.100	5.40	77	8.48	.261	1	.500	-1	0	-0.1
Total 4	10	22	.313	69	37	6	1	3	294	307	186	174	28	13	168	121	1.616	5.33	78	5.02	.275	11	.110	-37	7	-4.3
• BISHOP, Jim	James Morton Bishop b: 1/28/1898, Montgomery City, MO d: 9/20/1973, Montgomery City, MO BR/TR, 6', 195 lbs. Deb: 4/26/1923																									
1923 Phi-N	0	3	.000	15	0	0	0	1	32^2	48	31	23	2	3	11	5	1.806	6.34	72	6.71	.353	0	.000	-5	0	-0.7
1924 Phi-N	0	1	.000	7	1	0	0	0	16^2	24	14	12	3	0	7	3	1.860	6.48	69	7.48	.348	1	.200	-3	0	-0.4
Total 2	0	4	.000	22	1	0	0	1	49^1	72	45	35	5	3	18	8	1.824	6.39	71	6.97	.351	1	.067	-9	0	-1.0
• BISHOP, Lloyd	Lloyd Clifton Bishop b: 4/25/1890, Conway Springs, KS d: 6/18/1968, Wichita, KS BR/TR, 6', 180 lbs. Deb: 9/5/1914																									
1914 Cle-A	0	1	.000	3	1	0	0	0	8	14	5	5	0	0	3	1	2.125	5.63	51	7.81	.389	0	.000	-2	0	-0.3
• BITHORN, Hi	Hiram Gabriel (Sosa) Bithorn b: 3/18/1916, Santurce, Puerto Rico d: 1/1/1952, El Mante, Mexico BR/TR, 6'1", 200 lbs. Deb: 4/15/1942																									
1942 Chi-N	9	14	.391	38	16	9	0	2	171^1	191	93	70	8	0	81	65	**1.588**	3.68	87	4.65	.296	7	.123	-6	5	-0.7
1943 Chi-N	18	12	.600	39	30	19	**7**	2	249^2	227	79	72	8	2	65	86	1.170	2.60	128	2.61	.244	16	.174	25	19	2.7
1946 Chi-N	6	5	.545	26	7	2	1	1	86^2	97	42	37	5	0	25	34	1.408	3.84	86	3.90	.283	5	.179	-3	3	-0.4
1947 Chi-A	1	0	1.000	2	0	0	0	0	2	2	0	0	0	0	0	0	1.000	0.00	....	2.31	.286	0	....	1	1	0.1
Total 4	34	31	.523	105	53	30	8	5	509^2	517	214	179	21	2	171	185	1.350	3.16	104	3.51	.268	28	.158	17	28	1.6
• BITKER, Joe	Joseph Anthony Bitker b: 2/12/1964, Glendale, CA BR/TR, 6'1", 175 lbs. Deb: 7/31/1990																									
1990 Oak-A	0	0	....	1	0	0	0	0	3	1	0	0	0	0	1	2	.667	0.00	....	0.75	.111	0	....	1	0	0.1
Tex-A	0	0	....	5	0	0	0	0	9	7	3	3	0	1	3	6	1.111	3.00	131	2.35	.212	0	....	1	1	0.1
Yr.	0	0	....	6	0	0	0	0	12	8	3	3	0	1	4	8	1.000	2.25	174	1.95	.190	0	....	2	1	0.2
1991 Tex-A	1	0	1.000	9	0	0	0	0	14^2	17	11	11	4	0	8	16	1.705	6.75	60	6.36	.274	0	....	-4	0	-0.4
Total 2	1	0	1.000	15	0	0	0	0	26^2	25	14	14	4	1	12	24	1.388	4.73	85	4.37	.240	0	....	-2	1	-0.2
• BITTIGER, Jeff	Jeffrey Scott Bittiger b: 4/13/1962, Jersey City, NJ BR/TR, 5'10", 175 lbs. Deb: 9/2/1986																									
1986 Phi-N	1	1	.500	3	3	0	0	0	14^2	16	10	9	2	1	7	8	1.568	5.52	70	5.22	.271	1	.333	-3	0	-0.2
1987 Min-A	1	0	1.000	3	1	0	0	0	8^1	11	5	5	2	1	0	5	1.320	5.40	85	5.82	.314	0	....	-1	0	-0.1
1988 Chi-A	2	4	.333	25	7	0	0	0	61^2	59	31	29	11	0	29	33	1.427	4.23	94	4.61	.255	0	....	-3	2	-0.3
1989 Chi-A	0	1	.000	2	1	0	0	0	9^2	9	7	7	2	0	6	7	1.552	6.52	58	5.67	.257	0	....	-3	0	-0.3
Total 4	4	6	.400	33	12	0	0	0	94^1	95	53	50	17	2	42	53	1.452	4.77	83	4.92	.264	1	.333	-9	2	-0.8
• BIVIN, Jim	James Nathaniel Bivin b: 12/11/1909, Jackson, MS d: 11/7/1982, Pueblo, CO BR/TR, 6', 155 lbs. Deb: 4/16/1935																									
1935 Phi-N	2	9	.182	47	14	0	0	1	161^2	220	129	104	20	3	65	54	**1.763**	5.79	78	6.22	.316	7	.146	-20	3	-2.0
• BLACK, Bob	Robert Benjamin Black b: 12/10/1862, Cincinnati, OH d: 3/21/1933, Sioux City, IA, 5'5.5", 155 lbs. Deb: 8/19/1884 ♦																									
1884 KC-U	4	9	.308	16	15	13	0	0	123	127	79	44	1	....	17	93	1.171	3.22	87	....	.249	36	.247	-6	7	0.1
• BLACK, Bud	William Carroll Black b: 7/9/1932, St. Louis, MO BR/TR, 6'3", 197 lbs. Deb: 9/13/1952																									
1952 Det-A	0	1	.000	2	2	0	0	0	8	14	11	9	0	0	5	0	2.375	10.13	38	8.61	.389	0	.000	-5	0	-0.6
1955 Det-A	1	1	.500	3	2	1	1	0	14	12	5	2	0	2	8	7	1.429	1.29	299	3.71	.231	1	.250	4	1	0.4
1956 Det-A	1	1	.500	5	1	0	0	0	10	10	4	4	2	0	5	7	1.500	3.60	114	5.10	.256	0	.000	1	1	0.0
Total 3	2	3	.400	10	5	1	1	0	32	36	20	15	2	2	18	14	1.688	4.22	92	5.37	.283	1	.111	-1	2	-0.2
• BLACK, Bud	Harry Ralston Black b: 6/30/1957, San Mateo, CA BL/TL, 6'2", 180 lbs. Deb: 9/5/1981 C																									
1981 Sea-A	0	0	....	2	0	0	0	0	1	2	0	0	0	0	3	0	5.000	0.00	....	21.00	.500	0	....	0	0	0.0
1982 KC-A	4	6	.400	22	14	0	0	0	88^1	92	48	45	10	3	34	40	1.426	4.58	89	4.36	.269	0	....	-5	3	-0.5
1983 KC-A	10	7	.588	24	24	3	0	0	161^1	159	75	68	19	2	43	58	1.252	3.79	107	3.65	.257	0	....	6	10	0.6
1984* KC-A	17	12	.586	35	35	8	1	0	257	226	99	89	22	4	64	140	1.128	3.12	129	2.82	.233	0	....	24	20	2.4
1985* KC-A	10	15	.400	33	33	5	2	0	205^2	216	111	99	17	8	59	122	1.337	4.33	96	3.89	.268	0	....	-2	10	-0.1
1986 KC-A	5	10	.333	56	4	0	0	9	121	100	49	43	14	7	43	68	1.182	3.20	133	3.24	.225	0	....	16	12	1.5
1987 KC-A	8	6	.571	29	18	0	0	1	122^1	126	63	49	16	5	35	61	1.316	3.60	126	4.16	.265	0	....	15	9	1.4
1988 KC-A	2	1	.667	17	0	0	0	0	22	23	12	12	2	0	11	19	1.545	4.91	81	4.49	.267	0	....	-2	1	-0.2
Cle-A	2	3	.400	16	7	0	0	1	59	59	35	33	6	4	23	44	1.390	5.03	82	4.24	.262	0	....	-5	2	-0.5
Yr.	4	4	.500	33	7	0	0	1	81	82	47	45	8	4	34	63	1.432	5.00	82	4.31	.264	0	....	-7	3	-0.7
1989 Cle-A	12	11	.522	33	32	6	3	0	222^1	213	95	83	14	1	52	88	1.192	3.36	118	3.00	.252	0	....	16	15	1.6
1990 Cle-A	11	10	.524	29	29	5	2	0	191	171	79	75	17	4	58	103	1.199	3.53	111	3.12	.236	0	....	11	11	1.2
Tor-A	2	1	.667	3	2	0	0	0	15^2	10	7	7	2	1	3	3	.830	4.02	102	1.85	.189	0	....	0	1	0.0
Yr.	13	11	.542	32	31	5	2	0	206^2	181	86	82	19	5	61	106	1.171	3.57	110	3.02	.233	0	....	11	12	1.2
1991 SF-N	12	16	.429	34	34	3	3	0	214^1	201	104	95	25	4	71	104	1.269	3.99	90	3.63	.251	13	.183	-12	8	-1.1
1992 SF-N	10	12	.455	28	28	2	1	0	177	178	88	78	23	1	59	82	1.339	3.97	83	4.00	.263	3	.056	-17	5	-2.1
1993 SF-N	8	2	.800	16	16	0	0	0	93^2	89	44	37	13	2	33	45	1.302	3.56	110	3.97	.256	9	.243	1	6	0.3
1994 SF-N	4	2	.667	10	10	0	0	0	54^1	50	31	27	9	3	16	28	1.215	4.47	90	3.87	.245	1	.059	-5	2	-0.6
1995 Cle-A	4	2	.667	11	10	0	0	0	47^1	63	42	36	8	0	16	34	1.669	6.85	69	6.14	.317	0	....	-11	0	-1.0
Total 15	121	116	.511	398	296	32	12	11	2053^1	1978	982	876	217	49	623	1039	1.267	3.84	103	3.61	.253	26	.145	32	115	2.9
• BLACK, Dave	David Black b: 4/19/1892, Chicago, IL d: 10/27/1936, Pittsburgh, PA BL/TR, 6'2", 175 lbs. Deb: 5/2/1914																									
1914 Chi-F	1	0	1.000	8	1	1	0	0	25	28	19	17	1	0	4	19	1.280	6.12	48	3.37	.311	2	.286	-9	0	-0.9
1915 Chi-F	6	7	.462	25	10	2	0	0	121^1	104	46	33	3	6	33	43	1.129	2.45	114	2.49	.241	4	.108	5	7	0.3
Bal-F	1	3	.250	8	4	1	0	0	34	32	18	14	2	2	15	10	1.382	3.71	91	3.73	.260	3	.250	-1	1	0.0
Yr.	7	10	.412	33	14	3	0	0	155^1	136	64	47	5	8	48	53	1.185	2.72	108	2.76	.245	7	.143	4	8	0.2
1923 Bos-A	0	0	....	2	0	0	0	0	1	2	0	0	0	0	0	0	2.000	0.00	....	7.48	.500	0	....	0	0	0.0
Total 3	8	10	.444	43	15	4	0	0	181^1	166	83	64	6	8	52	72	1.202	3.18	93	2.87	.256	9	.161	-5	8	-0.6
• BLACK, Don	Donald Paul Black b: 7/20/1916, Salix, IA d: 4/21/1959, Cuyahoga Falls, OH BR/TR, 6', 185 lbs. Deb: 4/24/1943																									
1943 Phi-A	6	16	.273	33	26	12	1	1	208	193	105	97	8	6	110	65	1.457	4.20	81	3.67	.247	13	.188	-13	6	-1.5
1944 Phi-A	10	12	.455	29	27	8	0	0	177^1	177	94	80	6	4	75	78	1.421	4.06	86	3.64	.259	11	.186	-11	7	-1.2
1945 Phi-A	5	11	.313	26	18	8	0	0	125^1	154	77	72	5	0	69	47	1.779	5.17	66	5.40	.307	6	.162	-24	0	-2.8
1946 Cle-A	1	2	.333	18	4	0	0	0	43^2	45	26	22	5	1	21	15	1.511	4.53	73	4.71	.273	2	.200	-6	0	-0.6
1947 Cle-A	10	12	.455	30	28	8	3	0	190^2	177	90	83	17	1	85	72	1.374	3.92	89	3.75	.249	12	.182	-12	6	-1.4
1948 Cle-A	2	2	.500	18	10	1	0	0	52	57	33	31	5	1	40	16	1.865	5.37	76	5.94	.282	3	.200	-9	0	-0.9
Total 6	34	55	.382	154	113	37	4	1	797	803	425	385	46	13	400	293	1.509	4.35	80	4.16	.264	47	.184	-75	19	-8.3
• BLACK, Joe	Joseph Black b: 2/8/1924, Plainfield, NJ d: 5/17/2002, Scottsdale, AZ BR/TR, 6'2", 220 lbs. Deb: 5/1/1952																									
1952* Bro-N	15	4	.789	56	2	1	0	15	142^1	102	40	34	9	1	41	85	1.005	2.15	169	1.97	.201	5	.139	22	20	2.2
1953* Bro-N	6	3	.667	34	3	0	0	5	72^2	74	46	43	12	1	27	42	1.390	5.33	80	4.46	.259	4	.235	-10	4	-0.9
1954 Bro-N	0	0	....	5	0	0	0	0	7	11	9	9	3	0	5	3	2.286	11.57	35	11.67	.355	0	....	-6	0	-0.6
1955 Bro-N	1	0	1.000	6	0	0	0	0	15^1	15	5	5	1	0	5	9	1.304	2.93	138	3.50	.273	1	.333	2	1	0.2
Cin-N	5	2	.714	32	11	1	0	3	102^1	106	58	48	13	0	25	54	1.280	4.22	100	3.70	.263	3	.100	0	5	-0.2
Yr.	6	2	.750	38	11	1	0	3	117^2	121	63	53	14	0	30	63	1.283	4.05	104	3.68	.264	4	.121	2	6	0.0
1956 Cin-N	3	2	.600	32	0	0	0	2	61^2	61	31	31	11	0	25	27	1.395	4.52	88	4.54	.256	0	.000	-3	3	-0.4
1957 Was-A	0	1	.000	7	0	0	0	0	12^2	22	11	10	4	0	1	2	1.816	7.11	55	8.95	.393	0	....	-4	0	-0.4
Total 6	30	12	.714	172	16	2	0	25	414	391	200	180	53	2	129	222	1.256	3.91	103	3.66	.248	13	.135	1	33	-0.2
• BLACKBURN, Charlie	Foster Edwin Blackburn b: 1/6/1895, Chicago, IL d: 3/9/1984, New Port Richey, FL BR/TR, 6'1", 165 lbs. Deb: 4/17/1915																									
1915 KC-F	0	1	.000	7	2	0	0	0	15^2	19	15	15	2	0	13	7	2.043	8.62	34	7.14	.306	0	.000	-10	0	-1.1

YEAR TM-L	W	L	PCT	G	GS	CG	SH	SV	IP	H	R	ER	HR	HB	BB	SO	RAT	ERA	ERA+	CERA	OAV	BH	AVG	PR+	WS	TPW
1921 Chi-A	0	0	....	1	0	0	0	0	1	0	0	0	0	0	1	0	1.000	0.00	....	0.82	.000	0	....	0	0	0.0
Total 2	0	1	.000	8	2	0	0	0	16^{2}	19	15	15	2	0	14	7	1.980	8.10	36	6.77	.306	0	.000	-9	0	-1.1

• BLACKBURN, George George W. "Smiling George" Blackburn b: 9/21/1871, Ozark, MO TR, 5'11", 184 lbs. Deb: 7/6/1897

YEAR TM-L	W	L	PCT	G	GS	CG	SH	SV	IP	H	R	ER	HR	HB	BB	SO	RAT	ERA	ERA+	CERA	OAV	BH	AVG	PR+	WS	TPW
1897 Bal-N	2	2	.500	5	4	3	0	0	33	34	30	25	2	1	12	1	1.394	6.82	61	3.86	.264	1	.077	-10	0	-1.0

• BLACKBURN, Jim James Ray "Bones" Blackburn b: 6/19/1924, Warsaw, KY d: 10/26/1969, Cincinnati, OH BR/TR, 6'4", 175 lbs. Deb: 7/24/1948

YEAR TM-L	W	L	PCT	G	GS	CG	SH	SV	IP	H	R	ER	HR	HB	BB	SO	RAT	ERA	ERA+	CERA	OAV	BH	AVG	PR+	WS	TPW
1948 Cin-N	0	2	.000	16	0	0	0	0	32^{1}	38	18	15	1	0	14	10	1.608	4.18	94	4.62	.302	0	.000	-0	1	-0.1
1951 Cin-N	0	0	....	2	0	0	0	0	3^{2}	8	7	7	3	2	2	1	2.727	17.18	24	23.76	.444	0	....	-5	0	-0.5
Total 2	0	2	.000	18	0	0	0	0	36	46	25	22	4	2	16	11	1.722	5.50	72	6.57	.319	0	.000	-6	1	-0.6

• BLACKBURN, Ron Ronald Hamilton Blackburn b: 4/23/1935, Mount Airy, NC d: 4/29/1998, Morganton, NC BR/TR, 6'.5", 160 lbs. Deb: 4/15/1958

YEAR TM-L	W	L	PCT	G	GS	CG	SH	SV	IP	H	R	ER	HR	HB	BB	SO	RAT	ERA	ERA+	CERA	OAV	BH	AVG	PR+	WS	TPW
1958 Pit-N	2	1	.667	38	2	0	0	3	63^{2}	61	33	24	7	3	27	31	1.382	3.39	114	4.03	.261	2	.286	2	4	0.3
1959 Pit-N	1	1	.500	26	0	0	0	1	44^{1}	50	21	18	5	2	15	19	1.466	3.65	106	4.59	.286	1	.200	1	3	0.2
Total 2	3	2	.600	64	2	0	0	4	108	111	54	42	12	5	42	50	1.417	3.50	110	4.26	.271	3	.250	3	7	0.5

• BLACKWELL, Ewell Ewell "The Whip" Blackwell b: 10/23/1922, Fresno, CA d: 10/29/1996, Hendersonville, NC BR/TR, 6'6", 195 lbs. Deb: 4/21/1942

YEAR TM-L	W	L	PCT	G	GS	CG	SH	SV	IP	H	R	ER	HR	HB	BB	SO	RAT	ERA	ERA+	CERA	OAV	BH	AVG	PR+	WS	TPW
1942 Cin-N	0	0	....	2	0	0	0	0	3	3	4	2	0	0	3	1	2.000	6.00	55	4.81	.231	0	.000	-1	0	-0.1
1946 Cin-N★	9	13	.409	33	25	10	**5**	0	194^{1}	160	62	53	1	4	79	100	1.230	2.45	136	2.53	.226	6	.107	14	14	1.1
1947 Cin-N★	**22**	8	.733	33	33	**23**	6	0	273	227	91	75	10	4	95	**193**	1.179	2.47	166	2.66	.234	13	.123	53	28	4.7
1948 Cin-N★	7	9	.438	22	20	4	1	1	138^{2}	134	73	70	12	4	52	114	1.341	4.54	86	3.67	.251	11	.229	-8	8	-0.6
1949 Cin-N★	5	5	.500	30	4	0	0	1	76^{2}	80	36	36	7	3	34	55	1.487	4.23	99	4.53	.271	4	.211	-0	5	0.0
1950 Cin-N★	17	15	.531	40	32	18	1	4	261	203	105	86	12	13	112	188	1.207	2.97	143	**2.68**	**.210**	13	.146	**40**	**26**	**3.7**
1951 Cin-N★	16	15	.516	38	32	11	2	2	232^{2}	204	110	89	16	9	97	120	1.294	3.44	118	3.26	.233	24	.293	18	19	2.5
1952 Cin-N	3	12	.200	23	17	3	0	0	102	107	66	61	6	5	60	48	1.637	5.38	70	4.87	.275	5	.156	-19	0	-1.9
*NY-A	1	0	1.000	5	2	0	0	1	16	12	2	1	0	0	12	7	1.500	0.56	590	3.02	.203	1	.200	4	2	0.4
1953 NY-A	2	0	1.000	8	4	0	0	1	19^{2}	17	10	8	2	1	13	11	1.525	3.66	101	4.36	.233	0	.000	-0	1	-0.1
1955 KC-A	0	1	.000	2	0	0	0	0	4	3	3	3	1	1	5	2	2.000	6.75	62	9.74	.250	0	....	-1	0	-0.1
Total 10	82	78	.513	236	169	69	15	10	1321	1150	562	484	67	44	562	839	1.296	3.30	120	3.19	.235	77	.174	100	103	9.6

• BLAEHOLDER, George George Franklin Blaeholder b: 1/26/1904, Orange, CA d: 12/29/1947, Garden Grove, CA BR/TR, 5'11", 175 lbs. Deb: 4/20/1925

YEAR TM-L	W	L	PCT	G	GS	CG	SH	SV	IP	H	R	ER	HR	HB	BB	SO	RAT	ERA	ERA+	CERA	OAV	BH	AVG	PR+	WS	TPW
1925 StL-A	0	0	....	2	0	0	0	0	2	6	7	7	3	1	1	1	3.500	31.50	15	40.93	.600	0	....	-6	0	-0.6
1927 StL-A	0	1	.000	1	1	1	0	0	9	8	5	5	1	1	4	2	1.333	5.00	87	4.27	.258	1	.333	-1	1	0.0
1928 StL-A	10	15	.400	38	26	9	1	3	214^{1}	235	123	104	23	2	52	87	1.339	4.37	96	3.84	.280	15	.211	-4	12	-0.2
1929 StL-A	14	15	.483	42	24	13	**4**	2	222	237	113	103	18	0	61	72	1.342	4.18	106	3.72	.275	9	.122	4	15	0.0
1930 StL-A	11	13	.458	37	23	10	1	4	191^{1}	235	119	98	20	2	46	70	1.469	4.61	106	4.72	.303	12	.185	3	13	0.2
1931 StL-A	11	15	.423	35	32	13	1	0	226^{1}	280	137	114	15	1	56	79	1.485	4.53	102	4.42	.295	11	.143	2	13	0.0
1932 StL-A	14	14	.500	42	36	16	1	0	258^{1}	304	163	135	19	3	76	80	1.471	4.70	103	4.39	.290	12	.136	3	14	0.0
1933 StL-A	15	19	.441	38	36	14	3	0	255^{2}	283	146	134	24	0	69	63	1.377	4.72	99	4.07	.280	14	.182	-7	14	-0.6
1934 StL-A	14	18	.438	39	33	14	1	3	234^{1}	276	130	110	16	0	68	66	1.468	4.22	118	4.35	.296	7	.093	17	16	1.1
1935 StL-A	1	1	.500	6	2	0	0	0	17^{2}	25	15	14	3	0	6	0	1.755	7.13	67	6.69	.342	0	.000	-4	0	-0.5
Phi-A	6	10	.375	23	22	10	1	0	149	173	78	66	10	0	49	22	1.490	3.99	114	4.33	.289	2	.043	11	8	0.5
Yr.	7	11	.389	29	24	10	1	0	166^{2}	198	93	80	13	0	55	22	1.518	4.32	106	4.58	.295	2	.040	7	8	0.0
1936 Cle-A	8	4	.667	35	16	6	1	0	134^{1}	158	83	76	21	3	47	30	1.526	5.09	99	5.33	.295	6	.130	0	8	-0.2
Total 11	104	125	.454	338	251	106	14	12	1914^{1}	2220	1119	966	173	13	535	572	1.439	4.54	103	4.36	.290	89	.142	19	114	-0.2

• BLAIR, Bill William Ellsworth Blair b: 9/17/1863, Pittsburgh, PA d: 2/22/1890, Pittsburgh, PA BL/TL, 5'8.5", 172 lbs. Deb: 7/19/1888

YEAR TM-L	W	L	PCT	G	GS	CG	SH	SV	IP	H	R	ER	HR	HB	BB	SO	RAT	ERA	ERA+	CERA	OAV	BH	AVG	PR+	WS	TPW
1888 Phi-a	1	3	.250	4	4	3	0	0	31	29	21	9	0	0	8	16	1.194	2.61	114	....	.239	4	.308	1	2	0.2

• BLAIR, Dennis Dennis Herman Blair b: 6/5/1954, Middletown, OH BR/TR, 6'5", 182 lbs. Deb: 5/26/1974

YEAR TM-L	W	L	PCT	G	GS	CG	SH	SV	IP	H	R	ER	HR	HB	BB	SO	RAT	ERA	ERA+	CERA	OAV	BH	AVG	PR+	WS	TPW
1974 Mon-N	11	7	.611	22	22	4	1	0	146	113	61	53	7	5	72	76	1.267	3.27	117	2.90	.210	6	.118	10	10	0.8
1975 Mon-N	8	15	.348	30	27	1	0	0	163^{1}	150	77	69	14	3	106	82	1.567	3.80	101	4.63	.251	7	.143	0	9	-0.1
1976 Mon-N	0	2	.000	5	4	1	0	0	15^{2}	21	11	7	1	2	11	9	2.043	4.02	92	7.15	.300	0	.000	-0	0	-0.1
1980 SD-N	0	1	.000	5	1	0	0	0	14	18	10	10	3	0	3	11	1.500	6.43	53	5.88	.310	1	.200	-5	0	-0.5
Total 4	19	25	.432	62	54	6	1	0	339	302	159	139	25	10	192	178	1.457	3.69	103	4.05	.239	14	.128	5	19	0.1

• BLAIR, Willie William Allen Blair b: 12/18/1965, Paintsville, KY BR/TR, 6'1", 185 lbs. Deb: 4/11/1990

YEAR TM-L	W	L	PCT	G	GS	CG	SH	SV	IP	H	R	ER	HR	HB	BB	SO	RAT	ERA	ERA+	CERA	OAV	BH	AVG	PR+	WS	TPW
1990 Tor-A	3	5	.375	27	6	0	0	0	68^{2}	66	33	31	4	1	28	43	1.369	4.06	101	3.53	.250	0	....	0	3	0.0
1991 Cle-A	2	3	.400	11	5	0	0	0	36	58	27	27	7	1	10	13	1.889	6.75	62	8.48	.377	0	....	-10	0	-1.0
1992 Hou-N	5	7	.417	29	8	0	0	0	78^{2}	74	47	35	5	2	25	48	1.258	4.00	84	3.24	.249	1	.059	-5	1	-0.7
1993 Col-N	6	10	.375	46	18	1	0	0	146	184	90	77	20	3	42	84	1.548	4.75	100	5.34	.306	4	.111	5	7	0.4
1994 Col-N	0	5	.000	47	1	0	0	3	77^{2}	98	57	50	9	4	39	68	1.764	5.79	86	6.33	.308	0	.000	-5	2	-0.5
1995 SD-N	7	5	.583	40	12	0	0	0	114	112	60	55	11	2	45	83	1.377	4.34	92	4.01	.262	0	.000	-6	5	-0.8
1996*SD-N	2	6	.250	60	0	0	0	1	88	80	52	45	13	7	29	67	1.239	4.60	86	3.80	.240	0	.000	-6	3	-0.6
1997 Det-A	16	8	.667	29	27	2	0	0	175	186	85	81	18	3	46	90	1.326	4.17	110	3.99	.273	0	.000	6	13	0.5
1998 Ari-N	4	15	.211	23	23	0	0	0	146^{2}	165	91	87	27	3	51	71	1.473	5.34	79	5.36	.292	4	.083	-19	2	-2.1
NY-N	1	1	.500	11	2	0	0	0	28^{2}	23	10	10	4	1	10	21	1.151	3.14	132	3.27	.228	1	.250	3	3	0.4
Yr.	5	16	.238	34	25	0	0	0	175^{1}	188	101	97	31	4	61	92	1.420	4.98	84	5.02	.282	5	.096	-15	5	-1.7
1999 Det-A	3	11	.214	39	16	0	0	0	134	169	107	102	29	4	44	82	1.590	6.85	72	6.35	.308	0	.000	-28	1	-2.6
2000 Det-A	10	6	.625	47	17	0	0	0	156^{2}	185	89	85	20	2	35	74	1.404	4.88	99	4.69	.296	1	.333	-0	8	0.0
2001 Det-A	1	4	.200	9	4	0	0	0	24	38	30	28	3	3	11	15	2.042	10.50	41	8.45	.369	0	.000	-16	0	-1.6
Total 12	60	86	.411	418	139	3	0	4	1274	1438	778	713	170	36	415	759	1.454	5.04	88	4.89	.286	11	.074	-81	48	-8.6

• BLAISDELL, Dick Howard Carleton Blaisdell b: 6/18/1862, Bradford, MA d: 8/20/1886, Malden, MA Deb: 7/9/1884

YEAR TM-L	W	L	PCT	G	GS	CG	SH	SV	IP	H	R	ER	HR	HB	BB	SO	RAT	ERA	ERA+	CERA	OAV	BH	AVG	PR+	WS	TPW
1884 KC-U	0	3	.000	3	3	3	0	0	26	49	39	25	0	....	4	8	2.038	8.65	32	....	.377	5	.313	-17	1	-1.4

• BLAKE, Ed Edward James Blake b: 12/23/1925, East St. Louis, IL BR/TR, 5'11", 175 lbs. Deb: 5/1/1951

YEAR TM-L	W	L	PCT	G	GS	CG	SH	SV	IP	H	R	ER	HR	HB	BB	SO	RAT	ERA	ERA+	CERA	OAV	BH	AVG	PR+	WS	TPW
1951 Cin-N	0	0	....	3	0	0	0	0	4	10	5	5	3	0	1	1	2.750	11.25	36	19.01	.476	0	....	-3	0	-0.3
1952 Cin-N	0	0	....	2	0	0	0	0	3	3	0	0	0	0	0	0	1.000	0.00	....	1.95	.250	0	....	1	1	0.1
1953 Cin-N	0	0	....	1	0	0	0	0	0	1	2	0	0	0	1	0	....	....	....	∞	1.000	0	....	0	0	0.0
1957 KC-A	0	0	....	2	0	0	0	0	1^{2}	1	1	1	1	0	2	0	1.800	5.40	73	7.78	.167	0	....	-0	0	0.0
Total 4	0	0	....	8	0	0	0	0	8^{2}	15	8	6	4	0	4	1	2.192	6.23	65	10.95	.375	0	....	-2	1	-0.2

• BLAKE, Sheriff John Frederick Blake b: 9/17/1899, Ansted, WV d: 10/31/1982, Beckley, WV BB/TR, 6', 180 lbs. Deb: 6/29/1920

YEAR TM-L	W	L	PCT	G	GS	CG	SH	SV	IP	H	R	ER	HR	HB	BB	SO	RAT	ERA	ERA+	CERA	OAV	BH	AVG	PR+	WS	TPW
1920 Pit-N	0	0	....	6	0	0	0	0	13^{1}	21	14	12	0	1	6	7	2.025	8.10	40	7.35	.368	1	.250	-7	0	-0.8
1924 Chi-N	6	6	.500	29	11	4	0	1	106^{1}	123	58	54	3	2	44	42	1.571	4.57	85	4.52	.299	9	.290	-9	5	-0.8
1925 Chi-N	10	18	.357	36	31	14	0	2	231^{1}	260	144	125	17	5	114	93	1.617	4.86	89	4.92	.287	12	.152	-18	9	-2.1
1926 Chi-N	11	12	.478	39	27	11	4	1	197^{2}	204	91	79	7	6	92	95	1.497	3.60	107	4.16	.280	14	.215	1	12	0.1
1927 Chi-N	13	14	.481	32	27	13	2	0	224^{1}	238	101	82	3	4	82	64	1.426	3.29	117	3.68	.282	16	.193	10	15	0.7
1928 Chi-N	17	11	.607	34	29	16	**4**	1	240^{2}	209	80	66	4	3	101	78	1.288	2.47	156	2.88	.240	19	.216	29	24	2.8
1929*Chi-N	14	13	.519	35	29	13	1	1	218^{1}	244	122	104	8	2	103	70	1.589	4.29	108	4.55	.291	14	.173	4	13	0.2
1930 Chi-N	10	14	.417	34	24	7	0	0	186^{2}	213	127	100	14	3	99	80	1.671	4.82	101	5.13	.291	15	.227	2	9	0.1
1931 Chi-N	0	4	.000	16	5	0	0	0	50	64	34	29	4	1	26	29	1.800	5.22	74	5.92	.312	8	.500	-7	1	-0.5
Phi-N	4	5	.444	14	9	1	0	1	71	90	49	44	2	3	35	31	1.761	5.58	76	5.42	.305	6	.240	-10	2	-0.9
Yr.	4	9	.308	30	14	1	0	1	121	154	83	73	6	4	61	60	1.777	5.43	75	5.62	.308	14	.341	-17	3	-1.4
1937 StL-A	2	2	.500	15	1	0	0	1	36^{2}	55	33	31	5	0	20	12	2.045	7.61	63	7.94	.350	1	.100	-11	0	-1.1
StL-N	0	3	.000	14	2	2	0	0	43^{2}	45	23	18	1	0	18	20	1.443	3.71	107	3.58	.271	3	.300	2	2	0.2
Total 10	87	102	.460	304	195	81	11	8	1620	1766	876	744	68	30	740	621	1.547	4.13	102	4.41	.284	118	.211	-15	92	-2.1

• BLANCHE, Al Prosper Albert Blanche b: 9/21/1909, Somerville, MA d: 4/2/1997, Melrose, MA BR/TR, 6', 178 lbs. Deb: 8/23/1935

YEAR TM-L	W	L	PCT	G	GS	CG	SH	SV	IP	H	R	ER	HR	HB	BB	SO	RAT	ERA	ERA+	CERA	OAV	BH	AVG	PR+	WS	TPW
1935 Bos-N	0	0	....	6	0	0	0	0	17^{1}	14	3	3	0	0	5	4	1.096	1.56	243	2.02	.230	1	.167	5	1	0.5

YEAR TM-L	W	L	PCT	G	GS	CG	SH	SV	IP	H	R	ER	HR	HB	BB	SO	RAT	ERA	ERA+	CERA	OAV	BH	AVG	PR+	WS	TPW
1936 Bos-N	0	1	.000	11	0	0	0	1	16	20	15	11	1	1	8	4	1.750	6.19	62	5.60	.303	1	.250	-4	0	-0.4
Total 2	0	1	.000	17	0	0	0	1	33^1	34	18	14	1	1	13	8	1.410	3.78	101	3.73	.268	2	.200	1	1	0.0
• BLANCO, Gil	Gilbert Henry Blanco b: 12/15/1945, Phoenix, AZ BL/TL, 6'5", 205 lbs. Deb: 4/24/1965																									
1965 NY-A	1	1	.500	17	1	0	0	0	20^1	16	10	9	1	1	12	14	1.377	3.98	85	3.51	.232	0	....	-1	1	-0.1
1966 KC-A	2	4	.333	11	8	0	0	0	38^1	31	26	20	3	4	36	21	1.748	4.70	72	5.52	.237	2	.167	-6	0	-0.6
Total 2	3	5	.375	28	9	0	0	0	58^2	47	36	29	4	5	48	35	1.619	4.45	76	4.82	.235	2	.167	-7	1	-0.8
• BLAND, Nate	Nathan Garrett Bland b: 12/27/1974, Birmingham, AL BL/TL, 6'5", 190 lbs. Deb: 5/5/2003																									
2003 Hou-N	1	2	.333	22	0	0	0	0	20^1	22	13	13	3	2	12	18	1.672	5.75	77	5.85	.286	0	....	-3	0	-0.3
• BLANDING, Fred	Frederick James "Fritz" Blanding b: 2/8/1888, Redlands, CA d: 7/16/1950, Salem, VA BR/TR, 6', 185 lbs. Deb: 9/15/1910																									
1910 Cle-A	2	2	.500	6	5	4	1	0	45^1	43	19	14	0	4	12	25	1.213	2.78	93	2.96	.254	2	.111	-1	2	-0.3
1911 Cle-A	7	11	.389	29	16	11	0	2	176	190	95	72	5	6	60	80	1.420	3.68	93	3.98	.283	17	.262	-8	11	-0.6
1912 Cle-A	18	14	.563	39	31	23	1	1	262	259	117	85	4	3	79	75	1.290	2.92	117	3.20	.267	21	.226	10	20	1.2
1913 Cle-A	15	10	.600	41	22	14	3	0	215	234	79	61	6	2	72	63	1.423	2.55	119	3.87	.282	21	.244	8	18	1.3
1914 Cle-A	4	9	.308	29	12	5	0	0	116	133	82	51	0	1	54	35	1.612	3.96	73	4.57	.301	4	.103	-12	1	-1.6
Total 5	46	46	.500	144	86	57	5	3	814^1	859	392	283	15	16	277	278	1.395	3.13	101	3.73	.279	65	.216	-3	52	0.1
• BLANK, Fred	Frederick August Blank b: 6/18/1874, DeSoto, MO d: 2/5/1936, St. Louis, MO BL/TL, 6'.5", 175 lbs. Deb: 6/20/1894																									
1894 Cin-N	0	1	.000	1	1	1	0	0	8	5	4	4	0	0	9	1	1.750	4.50	123	3.63	.179	0	.000	1	1	0.0
• BLANK, Matt	Clarence Matthew Blank b: 4/5/1976, Texarkana, TX BL/TL, 6'2", 195 lbs. Deb: 4/3/2000																									
2000 Mon-N	0	1	.000	13	0	0	0	0	14	12	8	8	1	1	5	4	1.214	5.14	93	2.86	.222	0	.000	-0	1	-0.1
2001 Mon-N	2	2	.500	5	4	0	0	0	22^2	23	14	13	5	2	13	11	1.588	5.16	86	6.08	.267	4	.500	-1	2	0.0
Total 2	2	3	.400	18	4	0	0	0	36^2	35	22	21	6	3	18	15	1.445	5.15	89	4.85	.250	4	.444	-2	3	0.0
• BLANKENSHIP, Homer	Homer "Si" Blankenship b: 8/4/1902, Bonham, TX d: 6/22/1974, Longview, TX BR/TR, 6', 185 lbs. Deb: 9/6/1922																									
1922 Chi-A	0	0	....	4	0	0	0	0	13	21	7	7	1	0	5	3	2.000	4.85	84	7.92	.389	0	.000	-1	0	-0.2
1923 Chi-A	1	1	.500	4	0	0	0	1	5	9	5	2	0	0	1	1	2.000	3.60	110	7.34	.429	0	....	0	0	0.0
1928 Pit-N	0	2	.000	5	2	1	0	0	21^2	27	15	14	1	0	9	6	1.662	5.82	70	5.07	.321	3	.375	-4	0	-0.3
Total 3	1	3	.250	13	2	1	0	1	39^2	57	27	23	2	0	15	10	1.815	5.22	78	6.29	.358	3	.250	-5	0	-0.5
• BLANKENSHIP, Kevin	Kevin De Wayne Blankenship b: 1/26/1963, Anaheim, CA BR/TR, 6', 180 lbs. Deb: 9/20/1988																									
1988 Atl-N	0	1	.000	2	2	0	0	0	10^2	7	4	4	0	1	7	5	1.313	3.38	109	2.98	.194	0	.000	0	1	0.0
Chi-N	1	0	1.000	1	1	0	0	0	5	7	4	4	2	0	1	4	1.600	7.20	50	7.74	.318	0	.000	-2	0	-0.2
Yr.	1	1	.500	3	3	0	0	0	15^2	14	8	8	2	1	8	9	1.404	4.60	79	4.50	.241	0	.000	-1	1	-0.2
1989 Chi-N	0	0	....	2	0	0	0	0	5^1	4	1	1	0	0	2	2	1.125	1.69	223	2.01	.200	0	.000	1	1	0.1
1990 Chi-N	0	2	.000	3	2	0	0	0	12^1	13	10	8	1	0	6	5	1.541	5.84	70	4.38	.265	0	.000	-2	0	-0.3
Total 3	1	3	.250	8	5	0	0	0	33^1	31	19	17	3	1	16	16	1.410	4.59	84	4.06	.244	0	.000	-2	2	-0.3
• BLANKENSHIP, Ted	Theodore Blankenship b: 5/10/1901, Bonham, TX d: 1/14/1945, Atoka, OK BR/TR, 6'1", 170 lbs. Deb: 7/2/1922																									
1922 Chi-A	8	10	.444	24	15	7	0	1	127^2	124	58	54	4	2	47	42	1.339	3.81	107	3.39	.266	7	.171	2	8	0.1
1923 Chi-A	9	14	.391	44	23	9	1	0	204^2	219	115	99	8	4	100	57	1.559	4.35	91	4.34	.287	16	.211	-8	9	-0.6
1924 Chi-A	7	6	.538	25	11	7	0	1	129^1	167	79	72	1	1	38	36	1.585	5.01	82	4.55	.317	15	.326	-12	7	-0.6
1925 Chi-A	17	8	.680	40	23	16	3	1	232	218	90	78	11	0	69	81	1.237	3.03	137	2.98	.253	18	.205	29	22	2.8
1926 Chi-A	13	10	.565	29	26	15	1	1	209^1	217	96	84	13	1	65	66	1.347	3.61	107	3.63	.273	10	.132	4	13	0.2
1927 Chi-A	12	17	.414	37	34	11	3	0	236^2	280	156	133	14	2	74	51	1.496	5.06	80	4.42	.299	15	.188	-30	7	-2.6
1928 Chi-A	9	11	.450	27	22	8	0	0	158	186	92	81	9	2	80	36	1.684	4.61	88	4.96	.306	10	.169	-11	6	-1.2
1929 Chi-A	0	2	.000	8	1	0	0	0	18^1	28	18	18	3	0	9	7	2.018	8.84	48	8.09	.359	1	.250	-10	0	-0.9
1930 Chi-A	2	1	.667	7	1	0	0	0	14^2	23	15	15	0	1	7	2	2.045	9.20	50	7.02	.371	1	.200	-7	0	-0.7
Total 9	77	79	.494	241	156	73	8	4	1330^2	1462	719	634	63	13	489	378	1.466	4.29	94	4.09	.287	93	.196	-44	72	-3.5
• BLANTON, Cy	Darrell Elijah Blanton b: 7/6/1908, Waurika, OK d: 9/13/1945, Norman, OK BL/TR, 5'11.5", 180 lbs. Deb: 9/23/1934																									
1934 Pit-N	0	1	.000	1	1	0	0	0	8	5	3	3	1	1	4	5	1.125	3.38	122	2.69	.161	0	.000	1	0	0.1
1935 Pit-N	18	13	.581	35	31	23	**4**	1	254^1	220	93	73	3	2	55	142	1.081	**2.58**	**159**	**2.08**	**.229**	13	.134	**45**	24	**4.0**
1936 Pit-N	13	15	.464	44	32	15	**4**	3	235^2	235	114	92	9	3	55	127	1.231	3.51	115	2.96	.257	13	.155	16	15	1.2
1937 Pit-N★	14	12	.538	36	**34**	14	4	0	242^2	250	115	89	13	5	76	143	1.343	3.30	117	3.59	.266	14	.165	14	16	1.3
1938 Pit-N	11	7	.611	29	25	10	1	0	172^2	190	84	71	13	2	46	80	1.367	3.70	102	3.98	.281	13	.203	-1	9	-0.2
1939 Pit-N	2	3	.400	10	6	1	0	0	42	45	23	20	4	0	10	11	1.310	4.29	90	3.64	.266	4	.286	-1	2	0.0
1940 Phi-N	4	3	.571	13	10	5	0	0	77	82	43	37	7	1	21	24	1.338	4.32	90	3.83	.272	2	.083	-4	4	-0.5
1941 Phi-N★	6	13	.316	28	25	7	1	0	163^2	186	98	82	11	3	57	64	1.485	4.51	82	4.34	.284	6	.118	-14	5	-1.6
1942 Phi-N	0	4	.000	6	3	0	0	0	22^1	30	15	14	3	1	13	15	1.925	5.64	59	7.61	.345	1	.125	-6	0	-0.7
Total 9	68	71	.489	202	167	75	14	4	1218^1	1243	588	481	64	18	337	611	1.297	3.55	109	3.39	.262	66	.154	50	75	3.6
• BLASINGAME, Wade	Wade Allen Blasingame b: 11/22/1943, Deming, NM BL/TL, 6'1", 185 lbs. Deb: 9/17/1963																									
1963 Mil-N	0	0	....	2	0	0	0	0	3	7	4	4	0	0	2	6	3.000	12.00	27	12.85	.467	0	....	-3	0	-0.3
1964 Mil-N	9	5	.643	28	13	3	1	2	116^2	113	58	55	15	0	51	70	1.406	4.24	83	4.31	.257	7	.175	-10	6	-0.6
1965 Mil-N	16	10	.615	38	36	10	1	1	224^2	200	103	94	17	5	116	117	1.407	3.77	93	3.84	.244	15	.185	-7	12	-0.4
1966 Atl-N	3	7	.300	16	12	0	0	0	67^2	71	42	40	5	2	25	34	1.419	5.32	68	4.18	.272	5	.217	-13	0	-1.2
1967 Atl-N	1	0	1.000	10	4	0	0	0	25^1	27	13	13	1	1	21	20	1.895	4.62	72	5.93	.287	1	.143	-4	1	-0.4
Hou-N	4	7	.364	15	14	0	0	0	77	91	57	51	9	2	27	46	1.532	5.96	56	5.16	.298	4	.182	-21	0	-2.1
Yr.	5	7	.417	25	18	0	0	0	102^1	118	70	64	10	3	48	66	1.622	5.63	59	5.35	.296	5	.172	-25	1	-2.5
1968 Hou-N	1	2	.333	22	2	0	0	1	36	45	21	19	3	0	10	22	1.528	4.75	62	4.82	.308	0	.000	-6	0	-0.7
1969 Hou-N	0	5	.000	26	5	0	0	1	52	66	47	31	4	2	33	33	1.904	5.37	66	6.16	.306	0	.000	-10	0	-1.2
1970 Hou-N	3	3	.500	13	13	1	0	0	77^2	76	34	30	4	2	23	55	1.275	3.48	112	3.35	.261	2	.083	4	5	0.3
1971 Hou-N	9	11	.450	30	28	2	0	0	158^1	177	90	81	11	13	45	93	1.402	4.60	73	4.34	.285	10	.204	-23	3	-2.0
1972 Hou-N	0	0	....	10	0	0	0	0	8^1	4	9	8	1	2	8	9	1.440	8.64	39	4.17	.148	0	....	-5	0	-0.5
NY-A	0	1	.000	12	1	0	0	0	17	14	8	8	5	1	11	7	1.471	4.24	70	5.94	.250	0	.000	-2	0	-0.3
Total 10	46	51	.474	222	128	16	2	5	863^2	891	486	434	75	30	372	512	1.462	4.52	76	4.41	.271	44	.166	-100	27	-9.3
• BLASS, Steve	Stephen Robert Blass b: 4/18/1942, Canaan, CT BR/TR, 6', 165 lbs. Deb: 5/10/1964																									
1964 Pit-N	5	8	.385	24	13	3	1	0	104^2	107	52	47	9	1	45	67	1.452	4.04	87	4.16	.266	2	.067	-5	3	-0.6
1966 Pit-N	11	7	.611	34	25	1	0	0	155^2	173	80	67	12	2	46	76	1.407	3.87	92	4.24	.284	12	.231	-8	7	-0.7
1967 Pit-N	6	8	.429	32	16	2	0	0	126^2	126	65	50	12	2	47	72	1.366	3.55	95	3.89	.261	5	.128	-4	4	-0.6
1968 Pit-N	18	6	.750	33	31	12	7	0	220^1	191	64	52	13	4	57	132	1.126	2.12	138	2.66	.234	11	.138	17	17	1.8
1969 Pit-N	16	10	.615	38	32	9	0	2	210	207	119	104	21	6	86	147	1.395	4.46	78	4.14	.258	21	.250	-21	7	-1.7
1970 Pit-N	10	12	.455	31	31	6	1	0	196^2	187	92	77	14	5	73	120	1.322	3.52	110	3.59	.254	8	.114	3	10	0.1
1971* Pit-N	15	8	.652	33	33	12	**5**	0	240	226	81	76	16	2	68	136	1.225	2.85	120	3.08	.249	10	.120	13	15	1.0
1972* Pit-N★	19	8	.704	33	32	11	2	0	249^2	227	80	69	18	4	84	117	1.246	2.49	133	3.24	.246	15	.183	20	19	2.2
1973 Pit-N	3	9	.250	23	18	1	0	0	88^2	109	98	97	11	12	84	27	2.177	9.85	36	8.59	.313	10	.417	-62	1	-6.1
1974 Pit-N	0	0	....	1	0	0	0	0	5	5	8	5	2	0	7	2	2.400	9.00	38	10.54	.238	0	.000	-3	0	-0.4
Total 10	103	76	.575	282	231	57	16	2	1597^1	1558	739	644	128	38	597	896	1.349	3.63	95	3.83	.258	94	.172	-52	83	-4.9
• BLATERIC, Steve	Stephen Lawrence Blateric b: 3/20/1944, Denver, CO BR/TR, 6'3", 200 lbs. Deb: 9/17/1971																									
1971 Cin-N	0	0	....	2	0	0	0	0	2^2	5	4	4	2	1	0	4	1.875	13.50	24	15.40	.385	0	....	-3	0	-0.3
1972 NY-A	0	0	....	1	0	0	0	0	4	2	0	0	0	0	0	4	.500	0.00	....	0.54	.143	0	.000	1	0	0.1
1975 Cal-A	0	0	....	2	0	0	0	0	4^1	9	5	3	0	0	1	5	2.308	6.23	57	8.62	.429	0	....	-1	0	-0.1
Total 3	0	0	....	5	0	0	0	0	11	16	9	7	2	1	1	13	1.545	5.73	59	7.33	.333	0	.000	-3	0	-0.3

YEAR	TM-L	W	L	PCT	G	GS	CG	SH	SV	IP	H	R	ER	HR	HB	BB	SO	RAT	ERA	ERA+	CERA	OAV	BH	AVG	PR+	WS	TPW
• BLAUVELT, Henry	Henry Russell Blauvelt b: 4/8/1873, Rochester, NY d: 12/28/1926, Portland, OR Deb: 6/22/1890																										
1890	Roc-a	0	0	....	2	0	0	0	0	12^1	19	23	14	0	0	8	5	2.189	10.22	35	....	.342	3	.500	-9	0	-0.7
• BLAYLOCK, Bob	Robert Edward Blaylock b: 6/28/1935, Chattanooga, TN BR/TR, 6'1", 185 lbs. Deb: 7/22/1956																										
1956	StL-N	1	6	.143	14	6	0	0	0	41	45	32	29	7	0	24	39	1.683	6.37	59	5.87	.276	1	.091	-12	0	-1.3
1959	StL-N	0	1	.000	3	1	0	0	0	9	8	5	4	1	0	3	3	1.222	4.00	106	3.22	.229	0	.000	0	0	0.0
Total	**2**	**1**	**7**	**.125**	**17**	**7**	**0**	**0**	**0**	**50**	**53**	**37**	**33**	**8**	**0**	**27**	**42**	**1.600**	**5.94**	**65**	**5.39**	**.268**	**1**	**.083**	**-11**	**0**	**-1.3**
• BLAYLOCK, Gary	Gary Nelson Blaylock b: 10/11/1931, Clarkton, MO BR/TR, 6', 196 lbs. Deb: 4/10/1959 C																										
1959	StL-N	4	5	.444	26	12	3	0	0	100	117	61	57	14	2	43	61	1.600	5.13	83	5.56	.298	4	.118	-9	3	-0.9
	NY-A	0	1	.000	15	1	0	0	0	25^2	30	13	10	0	1	15	20	1.753	3.51	104	5.25	.306	1	.500	0	1	0.1
• BLAZIER, Ron	Ronald Patrick Blazier b: 7/30/1971, Altoona, PA BR/TR, 6'6", 215 lbs. Deb: 5/31/1996																										
1996	Phi-N	3	1	.750	27	0	0	0	0	38^1	49	30	25	6	0	10	25	1.539	5.87	74	5.31	.310	1	1.000	-7	1	-0.6
1997	Phi-N	1	1	.500	36	0	0	0	0	53^2	62	31	30	8	0	21	42	1.547	5.03	84	5.17	.290	2	.400	-4	2	-0.4
Total	**2**	**4**	**2**	**.667**	**63**	**0**	**0**	**0**	**0**	**92**	**111**	**61**	**55**	**14**	**0**	**31**	**67**	**1.543**	**5.38**	**80**	**5.23**	**.298**	**3**	**.500**	**-11**	**3**	**-1.0**
• BLEMKER, Ray	Raymond Blemker b: 8/9/1937, Huntingburg, IN d: 2/15/1994, Evansville, IN BR/TL, 5'11", 190 lbs. Deb: 7/3/1960																										
1960	KC-A	0	0	....	1	0	0	0	0	1^2	3	5	5	1	1	2	0	3.000	27.00	15	21.45	.375	0	....	-4	0	-0.4
• BLETHEN, Clarence	Clarence Waldo "Climax" Blethen b: 7/11/1893, Dover-Foxcroft, ME d: 4/11/1973, Frederick, MD BL/TR, 5'11", 165 lbs. Deb: 9/17/1923																										
1923	Bos-A	0	0	....	5	0	0	0	0	17^2	29	18	14	0	0	7	2	2.038	7.13	58	6.97	.382	0	.000	-6	0	-0.7
1929	Bro-N	0	0	....	2	0	0	0	0	2	4	2	2	0	0	3	0	3.500	9.00	51	13.72	.444	0	....	-1	0	-0.1
Total	**2**	**0**	**0**	**....**	**7**	**0**	**0**	**0**	**0**	**19^2**	**33**	**20**	**16**	**0**	**0**	**10**	**2**	**2.186**	**7.32**	**57**	**7.66**	**.389**	**0**	**.000**	**-7**	**0**	**-0.7**
• BLEWETT, Bob	Robert Lawrence Blewett b: 6/28/1877, Fond du Lac, WI d: 3/17/1958, Sedro Woolley, WA BL/TL, 5'11", 170 lbs. Deb: 6/17/1902																										
1902	NY-N	0	2	.000	5	3	2	0	0	28	39	26	15	0	1	7	8	1.643	4.82	58	5.04	.329	0	.000	-6	0	-0.8
• BLISS, Elmer	Elmer Ward Bliss b: 3/9/1875, Penfield, PA d: 3/18/1962, Bradford, PA BL/TR, 6', 180 lbs. Deb: 9/28/1903 ♦																										
1903	NY-A	1	0	1.000	1	0	0	0	0	7	4	1	0	0	0	0	3	.571	0.00	....	0.66	.167	0	.000	2	1	0.2
• BLOMDAHL, Ben	Benjamin Earl Blomdahl b: 12/30/1970, Long Beach, CA BR/TR, 6'2", 185 lbs. Deb: 4/28/1995																										
1995	Det-A	0	0	....	14	0	0	0	1	24^1	36	21	21	5	0	13	15	2.014	7.77	61	8.85	.356	0	....	-8	0	-0.7
• BLONG, Joe	Joseph Myles Blong b: 9/17/1853, St. Louis, MO d: 9/17/1892, St. Louis, MO BR/TR Deb: 5/4/1875 ♦																										
1875	RS-n	3	12	.200	15	15	12	1	0	129	169	....	44	0	....	2	11	1.326	3.07	72	....	.289	10	.147	-4	....	-0.5
1876	StL-N	0	0	....	1	0	0	0	0	4	2	0	0	0	....	1	0	.750	0.00	....	....	.129	62	.233	1	7	-0.2
1877	StL-N	10	9	.526	25	21	17	0	0	187^1	203	121	57	0	....	38	51	1.286	2.74	95	....	.261	47	.216	-2	14	-1.0
Total	**2**	**10**	**9**	**.526**	**26**	**21**	**17**	**0**	**0**	**191^1**	**205**	**121**	**57**	**0**	**....**	**39**	**51**	**1.275**	**2.68**	**97**	**....**	**.258**	**109**	**.225**	**-2**	**21**	**-1.2**
• BLUE, Vida	Vida Rochelle Blue b: 7/28/1949, Mansfield, LA BB/TL, 6', 189 lbs. Deb: 7/20/1969																										
1969	Oak-A	1	1	.500	12	4	0	0	1	42	49	34	31	13	0	18	24	1.595	6.64	52	6.66	.290	0	.000	-15	0	-1.6
1970	Oak-A	2	0	1.000	6	6	2	2	0	38^2	20	12	9	0	1	12	35	.828	2.09	169	1.16	.152	3	.200	6	3	0.8
1971*	Oak-A★	24	8	.750	39	39	24	**8**	0	312	209	73	63	19	4	88	301	.952	**1.82**	183	**1.81**	**.189**	12	.118	47	30	4.8
1972*	Oak-A	6	10	.375	25	23	5	4	0	151	117	55	47	11	1	48	111	1.093	2.80	101	2.43	.215	2	.044	-1	6	-0.4
1973*	Oak-A	20	9	.690	37	37	13	4	0	263^2	214	108	96	26	4	105	158	1.210	3.28	108	3.13	.224	0	.000	1	15	0.1
1974*	Oak-A	17	15	.531	40	40	12	1	0	282^1	246	118	102	17	1	98	174	1.218	3.25	102	2.93	.236	0	....	-2	16	-0.2
1975*	Oak-A★	22	11	.667	39	38	13	2	1	278	243	103	93	21	5	99	189	1.230	3.01	120	3.13	.236	0	....	18	19	1.8
1976	Oak-A	18	13	.581	37	37	20	6	0	298^1	268	90	78	9	1	63	166	1.109	2.35	143	2.39	.239	0	....	38	25	4.0
1977	Oak-A★	14	19	.424	38	38	16	1	0	279^2	284	138	119	23	1	86	157	1.323	3.83	105	3.67	.264	0	.000	9	14	0.9
1978	SF-N★	18	10	.643	35	35	9	4	0	258	233	87	80	12	0	70	171	1.174	2.79	123	2.75	.246	6	.076	19	22	2.2
1979	SF-N	14	14	.500	34	34	10	0	0	237	246	143	132	23	1	111	138	1.506	5.01	70	4.50	.272	10	.120	-37	3	-3.8
1980	SF-N★	14	10	.583	31	31	10	3	0	224	202	79	74	14	0	61	129	1.174	2.97	119	2.79	.242	5	.074	19	16	1.6
1981	SF-N★	8	6	.571	18	18	1	0	0	124^2	97	40	34	7	1	54	63	1.211	2.45	140	2.75	.217	7	.200	15	10	1.8
1982	KC-A	13	12	.520	31	31	6	2	0	181	163	80	76	20	0	80	103	1.343	3.78	108	3.72	.238	0	....	6	11	0.6
1983	KC-A	0	5	.000	19	14	1	0	0	85^1	96	62	57	12	2	35	53	1.535	6.01	68	5.21	.286	0	....	-18	0	-1.8
1985	SF-N	8	8	.500	33	20	1	0	0	131	115	70	65	17	1	80	103	1.489	4.47	77	4.48	.240	4	.133	-13	4	-1.3
1986	SF-N	10	10	.500	28	28	0	0	0	156^2	137	65	57	19	0	77	100	1.366	3.27	108	3.91	.239	4	.093	2	8	0.3
Total	**17**	**209**	**161**	**.565**	**502**	**473**	**143**	**37**	**2**	**3343^1**	**2939**	**1357**	**1213**	**263**	**23**	**1185**	**2175**	**1.234**	**3.27**	**108**	**3.16**	**.237**	**53**	**.104**	**93**	**202**	**9.7**
• BLUEJACKET, Jim	James Bluejacket b: 7/8/1887, Adair, OK d: 3/26/1947, Pekin, IL BR/TR, 6'2.5", 200 lbs. Deb: 8/6/1914																										
1914	Bro-F	4	5	.444	17	7	3	1	1	67	77	34	28	2	0	19	29	1.433	3.76	86	4.14	.302	3	.136	-3	3	-0.4
1915	Bro-F	10	11	.476	24	21	10	2	0	162^2	155	74	57	2	0	75	48	1.414	3.15	94	3.46	.258	8	.131	-4	7	-0.8
1916	Cin-N	0	1	.000	3	2	0	0	0	7	12	6	6	0	0	3	1	2.143	7.71	34	8.11	.400	0	.000	-4	0	-0.5
Total	**3**	**14**	**17**	**.452**	**44**	**30**	**13**	**3**	**1**	**236^2**	**244**	**114**	**91**	**4**	**0**	**97**	**78**	**1.441**	**3.46**	**87**	**3.79**	**.275**	**11**	**.129**	**-11**	**10**	**-1.7**
• BLUMA, Jaime	James Andrew Bluma b: 5/18/1972, Beaufort, SC BR/TR, 5'11", 195 lbs. Deb: 8/9/1996																										
1996	KC-A	0	0	....	17	0	0	0	5	20	18	9	8	2	2	4	14	1.100	3.60	139	3.10	.247	0	....	3	3	0.3
• BLUME, Clint	Clinton Willis Blume b: 10/17/1898, Brooklyn, NY d: 6/12/1973, Islip, NY BR/TR, 5'11", 175 lbs. Deb: 9/30/1922																										
1922	NY-N	1	0	1.000	1	1	1	0	0	9	7	3	1	0	0	1	2	.889	1.00	400	1.42	.212	1	1.000	3	2	0.4
1923	NY-N	2	0	1.000	12	1	0	0	0	24	22	11	10	0	2	20	2	1.750	3.75	102	4.69	.265	0	.000	-0	2	-0.1
Total	**2**	**3**	**0**	**1.000**	**13**	**2**	**1**	**0**	**0**	**33**	**29**	**14**	**11**	**0**	**2**	**21**	**4**	**1.515**	**3.00**	**128**	**3.80**	**.250**	**1**	**.167**	**3**	**4**	**0.3**
• BLYLEVEN, Bert	Rik Aalbert Blyleven b: 4/6/1951, Zeist, Holland BR/TR, 6'3", 207 lbs. Deb: 6/5/1970																										
1970*	Min-A	10	9	.526	27	25	5	1	0	164	143	66	58	17	2	47	135	1.159	3.18	117	2.96	.232	7	.140	9	10	0.8
1971	Min-A	16	15	.516	38	38	17	5	0	278^1	267	95	87	21	5	59	224	1.171	2.81	126	3.10	.255	12	.132	28	20	2.7
1972	Min-A	17	17	.500	39	38	11	3	0	287^1	247	93	87	22	10	69	228	1.100	2.73	118	2.70	.233	15	.160	13	19	1.4
1973	Min-A★	20	17	.541	40	40	25	**9**	0	325	296	109	91	16	9	67	258	1.117	2.52	**157**	2.64	.242	0	....	**53**	**29**	**5.5**
1974	Min-A	17	17	.500	37	37	19	3	0	281	244	99	83	14	9	77	249	1.142	2.66	141	2.69	.233	0	....	36	23	3.8
1975	Min-A	15	10	.600	35	35	20	3	0	275^2	219	104	92	24	4	84	233	1.099	3.00	128	2.63	.219	0	....	28	21	2.9
1976	Min-A	4	5	.444	12	12	4	0	0	95^1	101	39	33	3	4	35	75	1.427	3.12	116	3.97	.283	0	....	5	5	0.5
	Tex-A	9	11	.450	24	24	14	6	0	202^1	182	67	62	11	8	46	144	1.127	2.76	130	2.77	.242	0	....	18	15	1.9
	Yr.	13	16	.448	36	36	18	6	0	297^2	283	106	95	14	12	81	219	1.223	2.87	125	3.15	.255	0	....	23	20	2.4
1977	Tex-A	14	12	.538	30	30	15	5	0	234^2	181	81	71	20	7	69	182	1.065	2.72	150	**2.53**	.214	0	....	33	21	3.2
1978	Pit-N	14	10	.583	34	34	11	4	0	243^2	217	94	82	17	6	66	182	1.161	3.03	122	2.83	.235	11	.129	21	16	2.0
1979*	Pit-N	12	5	.706	37	37	4	0	0	237^1	238	102	95	21	6	92	172	1.390	3.60	108	4.04	.265	9	.129	5	13	0.2
1980	Pit-N	8	13	.381	34	32	5	2	0	216^2	219	102	92	20	0	59	168	1.283	3.82	95	3.56	.262	5	.082	-6	9	-1.0
1981	Cle-A	11	7	.611	20	20	9	1	0	159^1	145	52	51	9	5	40	107	1.161	2.88	126	2.92	.245	0	....	19	14	2.0
1982	Cle-A	2	2	.500	4	4	0	0	0	20^1	16	14	11	2	0	11	19	1.328	4.87	84	3.32	.211	0	....	-2	1	-0.2
1983	Cle-A	7	10	.412	24	24	5	0	0	156^1	160	74	68	8	10	44	123	1.305	3.91	108	3.66	.267	0	....	7	10	0.7
1984	Cle-A	19	7	.731	33	32	12	4	0	245	204	86	78	19	6	74	170	1.135	2.87	143	**2.73**	.224	0	....	32	20	3.2
1985	Cle-A★	9	11	.450	23	23	15	4	0	179^2	163	76	65	14	7	49	129	1.180	3.26	127	3.09	.240	0	....	18	12	1.8
	Min-A	8	5	.615	14	14	9	1	0	114	101	45	38	9	2	26	77	1.114	3.00	147	2.77	.237	0	....	18	11	1.8
	Yr.	17	16	.515	37	**37**	**24**	**5**	0	**293^2**	264	121	103	23	9	75	**206**	1.154	3.16	134	2.97	.239	0	....	36	23	3.5
1986	Min-A	17	14	.548	36	36	16	3	0	**271^2**	262	134	121	50	10	58	215	1.178	4.01	107	3.82	.250	0	....	12	18	1.2
1987*	Min-A	15	12	.556	37	37	8	1	0	267	249	132	119	46	9	101	196	1.311	4.01	115	4.29	.249	0	....	17	18	1.6
1988	Min-A	10	17	.370	33	33	7	0	0	207^1	240	128	125	21	16	51	145	1.404	5.43	75	4.75	.294	0	....	-32	4	-3.2
1989	Cal-A	17	5	.773	33	33	8	**5**	0	241	225	76	73	14	8	44	131	1.116	2.73	140	2.77	.248	0	....	25	22	2.6
1990	Cal-A	8	7	.533	23	23	2	0	0	134	163	85	78	15	7	25	69	1.403	5.24	73	4.80	.303	0	....	-21	3	-2.1

YEAR TM-L	W	L	PCT	G	GS	CG	SH	SV	IP	H	R	ER	HR	HB	BB	SO	RAT	ERA	ERA+	CERA	OAV	BH	AVG	PR+	WS	TPW
1992 Cal-A	8	12	.400	25	24	1	0	0	133	150	76	70	17	5	29	70	1.346	4.74	84	4.42	.285	0	....	-12	5	-1.2
Total 22	287	250	.534	692	685	242	60	0	4970	4632	2029	1830	430	155	1322	3701	1.198	3.31	117	3.24	.247	59	.131	324	339	32.0

• BLYZKA, Mike Michael John Blyzka b: 12/25/1928, Hamtramck, MI BR/TR, 5'11.5", 190 lbs. Deb: 4/21/1953

YEAR TM-L	W	L	PCT	G	GS	CG	SH	SV	IP	H	R	ER	HR	HB	BB	SO	RAT	ERA	ERA+	CERA	OAV	BH	AVG	PR+	WS	TPW
1953 StL-A	2	6	.250	33	9	2	0	0	94^{1}	110	78	67	6	0	56	23	1.760	6.39	66	5.35	.292	0	.000	-22	0	-2.5
1954 Bal-A	1	5	.167	37	0	0	0	1	86^{1}	83	48	45	2	0	51	35	1.552	4.69	76	3.85	.254	2	.133	-10	2	-1.1
Total 2	3	11	.214	70	9	2	0	1	180^{2}	193	126	112	8	0	107	58	1.661	5.58	70	4.63	.274	2	.053	-32	2	-3.7

• BOARDMAN, Charlie Charles Louis Boardman b: 3/27/1893, Seneca Falls, NY d: 8/10/1968, Sacramento, CA BL/TL, 6'2.5", 194 lbs. Deb: 9/26/1913

YEAR TM-L	W	L	PCT	G	GS	CG	SH	SV	IP	H	R	ER	HR	HB	BB	SO	RAT	ERA	ERA+	CERA	OAV	BH	AVG	PR+	WS	TPW
1913 Phi-A	0	2	.000	2	2	1	0	0	9	10	5	2	0	0	6	4	1.778	2.00	138	5.05	.294	0	.000	1	0	0.0
1914 Phi-A	0	0	....	2	0	0	0	0	7^{1}	10	5	4	0	0	4	2	1.909	4.91	53	6.46	.357	0	.000	-2	0	-0.2
1915 StL-N	1	0	1.000	3	1	1	0	0	19	12	4	3	0	2	15	7	1.421	1.42	196	3.22	.188	2	.286	3	2	0.4
Total 3	1	2	.333	7	3	2	0	0	35^{1}	32	14	9	0	2	25	13	1.613	2.29	118	4.36	.254	2	.167	2	2	0.2

• BOCHTLER, Doug Douglas Eugene Bochtler b: 7/5/1970, West Palm Beach, FL BR/TR, 6'3", 205 lbs. Deb: 5/5/1995

YEAR TM-L	W	L	PCT	G	GS	CG	SH	SV	IP	H	R	ER	HR	HB	BB	SO	RAT	ERA	ERA+	CERA	OAV	BH	AVG	PR+	WS	TPW
1995 SD-N	4	4	.500	34	0	0	0	1	45^{1}	38	18	18	5	0	19	45	1.257	3.57	112	3.52	.239	0	.000	1	4	0.1
1996* SD-N	2	4	.333	63	0	0	0	3	65^{2}	45	25	22	6	1	39	68	1.279	3.02	131	2.91	.195	0	....	7	7	0.7
1997 SD-N	3	6	.333	54	0	0	0	2	60^{1}	51	35	32	3	1	50	46	1.674	4.77	80	4.35	.229	0	....	-5	2	-0.5
1998 Det-A	0	2	.000	51	0	0	0	0	67^{1}	73	46	46	17	3	42	45	1.708	6.15	77	6.77	.279	0	....	-12	1	-1.1
1999 LA-N	0	0	....	12	0	0	0	0	13	11	8	8	3	1	6	7	1.308	5.54	77	4.38	.224	0	....	-2	0	-0.2
2000 KC-A	0	2	.000	6	0	0	0	0	8^{1}	13	6	6	2	0	10	4	2.760	6.48	79	11.73	.371	0	....	-1	0	-0.1
Total 6	9	18	.333	220	0	0	0	6	260	231	138	132	36	6	166	215	1.527	4.57	93	4.71	.241	0	.000	-12	14	-1.1

• BOCKUS, Randy Randy Walter Bockus b: 10/5/1960, Canton, OH BL/TR, 6'2", 190 lbs. Deb: 9/10/1986

YEAR TM-L	W	L	PCT	G	GS	CG	SH	SV	IP	H	R	ER	HR	HB	BB	SO	RAT	ERA	ERA+	CERA	OAV	BH	AVG	PR+	WS	TPW
1986 SF-N	0	0	....	5	0	0	0	0	7	7	5	2	1	0	6	4	1.857	2.57	137	5.50	.241	0	.000	1	0	0.0
1987 SF-N	1	0	1.000	12	0	0	0	0	17^{1}	17	8	7	2	0	4	9	1.212	3.63	106	3.54	.266	0	.000	0	1	0.0
1988 SF-N	1	1	.500	20	0	0	0	0	32	35	19	17	2	1	13	18	1.500	4.78	68	4.50	.297	1	.167	-5	0	-0.6
1989 Det-A	0	0	....	2	0	0	0	0	5^{1}	7	3	3	0	0	2	2	1.688	5.06	75	4.97	.333	0	....	-1	0	-0.1
Total 4	2	1	.667	39	0	0	0	0	61^{2}	66	35	29	5	1	25	33	1.476	4.23	82	4.39	.284	1	.125	-5	1	-0.6

• BODDICKER, Mike Michael James Boddicker b: 8/23/1957, Cedar Rapids, IA BR/TR, 5'11", 172 lbs. Deb: 10/4/1980

YEAR TM-L	W	L	PCT	G	GS	CG	SH	SV	IP	H	R	ER	HR	HB	BB	SO	RAT	ERA	ERA+	CERA	OAV	BH	AVG	PR+	WS	TPW
1980 Bal-A	0	1	.000	1	1	0	0	0	7^{1}	6	6	5	1	0	5	4	1.500	6.14	64	4.18	.207	0	....	-2	0	-0.2
1981 Bal-A	0	0	....	2	0	0	0	0	5^{2}	6	4	3	1	0	2	2	1.412	4.76	76	4.66	.261	0	....	-1	0	-0.1
1982 Bal-A	1	0	1.000	7	0	0	0	0	25^{2}	25	10	10	2	0	12	20	1.442	3.51	115	3.97	.258	0	....	1	2	0.1
1983* Bal-A	16	8	.667	27	26	10	**5**	0	179	141	65	55	13	0	52	120	1.078	2.77	143	**2.41**	**.216**	0	....	24	16	2.4
1984 Bal-A★	**20**	11	.645	34	34	16	4	0	261^{1}	218	95	81	23	5	81	128	1.144	**2.79**	139	2.90	.228	0	....	26	23	2.6
1985 Bal-A	12	17	.414	32	32	9	2	0	203^{1}	227	104	92	13	5	89	135	1.554	4.07	99	4.72	.286	0	....	1	10	0.1
1986 Bal-A	14	12	.538	33	33	7	0	0	218^{1}	214	125	114	30	11	74	175	1.319	4.70	88	4.16	.255	0	....	-12	9	-1.2
1987 Bal-A	10	12	.455	33	33	7	2	0	226	212	114	105	29	7	78	152	1.283	4.18	105	3.83	.248	0	....	6	14	0.5
1988 Bal-A	6	12	.333	21	21	4	0	0	147	149	72	63	14	11	51	100	1.361	3.86	101	4.16	.265	0	....	-0	7	0.0
*Bos-A	7	3	.700	15	14	1	1	0	89	85	30	26	3	3	26	56	1.247	2.63	156	3.17	.257	0	....	16	8	1.6
Yr.	13	15	.464	36	35	5	1	0	236	234	102	89	17	14	77	156	1.318	3.39	117	3.79	.262	0	....	15	15	1.6
1989 Bos-A	15	11	.577	34	34	3	2	0	211^{2}	217	101	94	19	10	71	145	1.361	4.00	103	4.05	.267	0	....	4	11	0.4
1990* Bos-A	17	8	.680	34	34	4	0	0	228	225	92	85	16	10	69	143	1.289	3.36	121	3.60	.258	0	....	23	19	2.3
1991 KC-A	12	12	.500	30	29	1	0	0	180^{2}	188	89	82	13	13	59	79	1.367	4.08	101	4.15	.272	0	....	6	10	0.6
1992 KC-A	1	4	.200	29	8	0	0	3	86^{2}	92	50	48	5	8	37	47	1.488	4.98	81	4.47	.269	0	....	-8	2	-0.8
1993 Mil-A	3	5	.375	10	10	1	0	0	54	77	35	34	6	4	15	24	1.704	5.67	75	6.56	.338	0	....	-8	1	-0.8
Total 14	134	116	.536	342	309	63	16	3	2123^{2}	2082	992	897	188	87	721	1330	1.320	3.80	107	3.84	.257	0	....	76	132	7.7

• BOEHLER, George George Henry Boehler b: 1/2/1892, Lawrenceburg, IN d: 6/23/1958, Lawrenceburg, IN BR/TR, 6'2", 180 lbs. Deb: 9/13/1912

YEAR TM-L	W	L	PCT	G	GS	CG	SH	SV	IP	H	R	ER	HR	HB	BB	SO	RAT	ERA	ERA+	CERA	OAV	BH	AVG	PR+	WS	TPW
1912 Det-A	0	2	.000	5	4	2	0	0	32	50	31	23	0	2	14	15	2.000	6.47	51	7.34	.365	1	.100	-11	0	-1.2
1913 Det-A	0	1	.000	1	1	1	0	0	8	11	9	6	0	2	6	2	2.125	6.75	43	8.26	.355	1	.333	-3	0	-0.3
1914 Det-A	2	3	.400	18	6	2	0	0	63	54	39	25	1	8	48	37	1.619	3.57	78	4.47	.242	3	.176	-5	1	-0.4
1915 Det-A	1	1	.500	8	0	0	0	0	15	19	10	3	0	1	4	7	1.533	1.80	168	4.83	.328	3	.750	2	1	0.4
1916 Det-A	1	1	.500	5	2	1	0	0	13^{1}	12	8	7	0	2	9	8	1.575	4.73	61	4.51	.261	0	.000	-3	0	-0.3
1920 StL-A	0	1	.000	3	1	0	0	0	7	10	10	6	1	0	4	2	2.000	7.71	51	6.99	.303	0	.000	-3	0	-0.3
1921 StL-A	0	0	....	1	0	0	0	0	1	1	0	0	0	0	0	0	1.000	0.00	....	2.02	.500	0		1	0	0.0
1923 Pit-N	1	3	.250	10	3	1	0	0	28^{1}	33	26	19	1	1	26	12	2.082	6.04	66	6.69	.314	3	.300	-7	0	-0.6
1926 Bro-N	1	0	1.000	10	1	0	0	0	34^{2}	42	23	17	1	3	23	10	1.875	4.41	87	5.77	.302	3	.250	-2	1	-0.1
Total 9	6	12	.333	61	18	7	0	0	202^{1}	232	156	106	4	19	134	93	1.809	4.71	70	5.71	.300	14	.233	-30	3	-2.7

• BOEHLING, Joe John Joseph Boehling b: 3/20/1891, Richmond, VA d: 9/8/1941, Richmond, VA BL/TL, 5'11", 168 lbs. Deb: 6/20/1912

YEAR TM-L	W	L	PCT	G	GS	CG	SH	SV	IP	H	R	ER	HR	HB	BB	SO	RAT	ERA	ERA+	CERA	OAV	BH	AVG	PR+	WS	TPW
1912 Was-A	0	0	....	3	0	0	0	0	5	4	4	4	0	2	6	2	2.000	7.20	47	6.58	.235	0	....	-2	0	-0.2
1913 Was-A	17	7	.708	38	25	18	3	4	235^{1}	197	82	56	3	9	82	110	1.186	2.14	138	2.57	.229	19	.221	17	23	1.9
1914 Was-A	13	8	.619	27	24	14	2	0	196	180	76	66	3	9	76	91	1.306	3.03	93	3.31	.258	17	.239	-6	12	-0.3
1915 Was-A	14	13	.519	40	32	14	2	0	229^{1}	217	105	82	5	9	119	108	1.465	3.22	92	3.80	.255	13	.173	-9	12	-0.9
1916 Was-A	9	11	.450	27	19	7	2	0	139^{2}	134	62	48	1	3	54	52	1.346	3.09	90	3.29	.260	7	.171	-6	7	-0.5
Cle-A	2	4	.333	12	9	3	0	0	60^{2}	63	23	18	0	2	23	18	1.418	2.67	112	3.75	.281	5	.263	2	4	0.3
Yr.	11	15	.423	39	28	10	2	0	200^{1}	197	85	66	1	5	77	70	1.368	2.97	96	3.43	.266	12	.200	-3	11	-0.2
1917 Cle-A	1	6	.143	12	7	1	0	0	46^{1}	50	27	24	1	3	16	11	1.424	4.66	61	4.16	.291	3	.188	-11	0	-1.2
1920 Cle-A	0	1	.000	3	2	0	0	0	13	16	10	7	0	0	10	4	2.000	4.85	78	6.46	.333	2	.500	-2	0	-0.1
Total 7	56	50	.528	162	118	57	9	4	925^{1}	861	389	305	13	37	386	396	1.348	2.97	98	3.37	.254	66	.212	-16	58	-0.9

• BOEHRINGER, Brian Brian Edward Boehringer b: 1/8/1969, St. Louis, MO BB/TR, 6'2", 180 lbs. Deb: 4/30/1995

YEAR TM-L	W	L	PCT	G	GS	CG	SH	SV	IP	H	R	ER	HR	HB	BB	SO	RAT	ERA	ERA+	CERA	OAV	BH	AVG	PR+	WS	TPW
1995 NY-A	0	3	.000	7	3	0	0	0	17^{2}	24	27	27	5	1	22	10	2.604	13.75	34	11.86	.320	0	....	-18	0	-1.7
1996* NY-A	2	4	.333	15	3	0	0	0	46^{1}	46	28	28	6	1	21	37	1.446	5.44	91	4.42	.260	0	....	-2	2	-0.2
1997* NY-A	3	2	.600	34	0	0	0	0	48	39	16	14	4	0	32	53	1.479	2.63	170	3.74	.225	0	....	10	4	1.0
1998* SD-N	5	2	.714	56	1	0	0	0	76^{1}	75	38	37	10	4	45	67	1.572	4.36	90	5.06	.257	0	.000	-4	4	-0.4
1999 SD-N	6	5	.545	33	11	0	0	0	94^{1}	97	38	34	10	1	35	64	1.399	3.24	129	4.12	.267	1	.063	9	7	0.8
2000 SD-N	0	3	.000	7	3	0	0	0	15^{2}	18	15	10	4	0	10	9	1.787	5.74	75	7.15	.286	1	.250	-3	0	-0.2
2001 NY-A	0	1	.000	22	0	0	0	1	34^{2}	35	15	12	3	3	12	33	1.356	3.12	144	4.03	.255	0	....	6	3	0.6
SF-N	0	3	.000	29	0	0	0	1	34^{1}	32	20	16	4	2	17	27	1.427	4.19	95	4.01	.239	0	.000	-1	1	-0.1
2002 Pit-N	4	4	.500	70	0	0	0	1	79^{2}	65	30	30	5	2	33	65	1.230	3.39	123	2.92	.229	0	....	6	9	0.6
2003 Pit-N	5	4	.556	62	0	0	0	0	62^{1}	64	39	38	11	3	30	47	1.508	5.49	80	5.24	.267	0	....	-8	2	-0.7
Total 9	25	31	.446	335	21	0	0	3	509^{1}	495	266	246	62	17	257	412	1.476	4.35	99	4.55	.255	2	.067	-3	32	-0.3

• BOERNER, Larry Lawrence Hyer Boerner b: 1/21/1905, Staunton, VA d: 10/16/1969, Staunton, VA BR/TR, 6'4.5", 175 lbs. Deb: 6/30/1932

YEAR TM-L	W	L	PCT	G	GS	CG	SH	SV	IP	H	R	ER	HR	HB	BB	SO	RAT	ERA	ERA+	CERA	OAV	BH	AVG	PR+	WS	TPW
1932 Bos-A	0	4	.000	21	5	0	0	0	61	71	41	34	2	3	37	19	1.770	5.02	90	5.39	.302	0	.000	-2	2	-0.5

• BOEVER, Joe Joseph Martin Boever b: 10/4/1960, Kirkwood, MO BR/TR, 6'1", 200 lbs. Deb: 7/19/1985

YEAR TM-L	W	L	PCT	G	GS	CG	SH	SV	IP	H	R	ER	HR	HB	BB	SO	RAT	ERA	ERA+	CERA	OAV	BH	AVG	PR+	WS	TPW
1985 StL-N	0	0	....	13	0	0	0	0	16^{1}	17	8	8	3	0	4	20	1.286	4.41	80	4.14	.270	0	....	-2	0	-0.2
1986 StL-N	0	1	.000	11	0	0	0	0	21^{2}	19	5	4	2	0	11	8	1.385	1.66	219	3.76	.232	1	.500	4	2	0.5
1987 Atl-N	1	0	1.000	14	0	0	0	0	18^{1}	29	15	15	4	0	12	18	2.236	7.36	59	9.90	.367	0	....	-6	0	-0.6
1988 Atl-N	0	2	.000	16	0	0	0	1	20^{1}	12	4	4	1	1	1	7	.639	1.77	208	1.13	.182	0	....	5	2	0.5
1989 Atl-N	4	11	.267	66	0	0	0	21	82^{1}	78	37	36	6	1	34	68	1.360	3.94	93	3.64	.252	0	.000	-2	8	-0.2
1990 Atl-N	1	3	.250	33	0	0	0	8	42^{1}	40	23	22	6	0	35	35	1.772	4.68	86	5.35	.252	0	.000	-2	2	-0.2
Phi-N	2	3	.400	34	0	0	0	6	46	37	12	11	0	0	16	40	1.152	2.15	178	2.12	.215	0	.000	8	7	0.8
Yr.	3	6	.333	67	0	0	0	14	88^{1}	77	35	33	6	0	51	75	1.449	3.36	118	3.67	.233	0	.000	6	9	0.6
1991 Phi-N	3	5	.375	68	0	0	0	0	98^{1}	90	45	42	10	0	54	89	1.464	3.84	95	4.00	.245	1	.333	-2	5	-0.1
1992 Hou-N	3	6	.333	**81**	0	0	0	2	111^{1}	103	38	31	3	4	45	67	1.329	2.51	134	3.15	.248	0	.000	11	7	1.1

YEAR	TM-L	W	L	PCT	G	GS	CG	SH	SV	IP	H	R	ER	HR	HB	BB	SO	RAT	ERA	ERA+	CERA	OAV	BH	AVG	PR+	WS	TPW
1993	Oak-A	4	2	.667	42	0	0	0	0	79^1	87	40	34	8	4	33	49	1.513	3.86	106	4.83	.280	0	....	2	4	0.2
	Det-A	2	1	.667	19	0	0	0	3	23	14	10	7	1	0	11	14	1.087	2.74	157	1.74	.179	0	....	4	3	0.4
	Yr.	6	3	.667	61	0	0	0	3	102^1	101	50	41	9	4	44	63	1.417	3.61	114	4.13	.260	0	....	6	7	0.6
1994	Det-A	9	2	.818	46	0	0	0	3	81^1	80	40	36	12	2	37	49	1.439	3.98	122	4.49	.263	0	....	9	7	0.8
1995	Det-A	5	7	.417	60	0	0	0	3	98^2	128	74	70	17	3	44	71	1.743	6.39	74	6.48	.319	0	....	-16	2	-1.5
1996	Pit-N	0	2	.000	13	0	0	0	2	15	17	11	9	2	1	6	6	1.533	5.40	81	5.33	.288	0	.000	-2	0	-0.2
Total	**12**	**34**	**45**	**.430**	**516**	**0**	**0**	**0**	**49**	**754^1**	**751**	**362**	**329**	**75**	**16**	**343**	**541**	**1.450**	**3.93**	**103**	**4.28**	**.262**	**2**	**.118**	**11**	**49**	**1.2**

• BOGART, John
John Renzie "Big John" Bogart b: 9/21/1900, Bloomsburg, PA d: 12/7/1986, Clarence, NY BR/TR, 6'2", 195 lbs. Deb: 9/17/1920

YEAR	TM-L	W	L	PCT	G	GS	CG	SH	SV	IP	H	R	ER	HR	HB	BB	SO	RAT	ERA	ERA+	CERA	OAV	BH	AVG	PR+	WS	TPW
1920	Det-A	2	1	.667	4	2	0	0	0	23^2	16	12	8	0	0	18	5	1.437	3.04	122	2.86	.195	2	.250	2	2	0.2

• BOGGS, Ray
Raymond Joseph "Lefty" Boggs b: 12/12/1904, Reamsville, KS d: 11/27/1989, Grand Junction, CO BL/TL, 6'.5", 170 lbs. Deb: 9/1/1928

YEAR	TM-L	W	L	PCT	G	GS	CG	SH	SV	IP	H	R	ER	HR	HB	BB	SO	RAT	ERA	ERA+	CERA	OAV	BH	AVG	PR+	WS	TPW
1928	Bos-N	0	0	....	4	0	0	0	0	5	2	3	3	0	3	7	0	1.800	5.40	72	6.00	.167	0	....	-1	0	-0.1

• BOGGS, Tommy
Thomas Winton Boggs b: 10/25/1955, Poughkeepsie, NY BR/TR, 6'2", 200 lbs. Deb: 7/19/1976

YEAR	TM-L	W	L	PCT	G	GS	CG	SH	SV	IP	H	R	ER	HR	HB	BB	SO	RAT	ERA	ERA+	CERA	OAV	BH	AVG	PR+	WS	TPW
1976	Tex-A	1	7	.125	13	13	3	0	0	90^1	87	42	35	7	1	34	36	1.339	3.49	103	3.67	.257	0	....	1	4	0.1
1977	Tex-A	0	3	.000	6	6	0	0	0	27^1	40	18	18	1	1	12	15	1.902	5.93	69	6.74	.351	0	....	-6	0	-0.6
1978	Atl-N	2	8	.200	16	12	1	1	0	59	80	46	44	8	1	26	21	1.797	6.71	60	6.50	.323	3	.167	-17	0	-1.7
1979	Atl-N	0	2	.000	3	3	0	0	0	12^2	21	11	9	0	1	4	1	1.974	6.39	63	7.02	.362	1	.250	-3	0	-0.3
1980	Atl-N	12	9	.571	32	26	4	3	0	192^1	180	80	73	14	4	46	84	1.175	3.42	110	3.02	.249	10	.159	7	13	0.6
1981	Atl-N	3	13	.188	25	24	2	0	0	142^2	140	72	65	11	3	54	81	1.360	4.10	87	3.81	.265	7	.152	-8	3	-1.0
1982	Atl-N	2	2	.500	10	10	0	0	0	46^1	43	22	17	2	2	22	29	1.403	3.30	113	3.79	.253	4	.235	2	3	0.3
1983	Atl-N	0	0	....	5	0	0	0	0	6^1	8	4	4	1	0	1	5	1.421	5.68	68	5.10	.320	0	....	-1	0	-0.1
1985	Tex-A	0	0	....	4	0	0	0	0	7	13	9	9	3	0	2	6	2.143	11.57	37	11.75	.382	0	....	-6	0	-0.6
Total	**9**	**20**	**44**	**.313**	**114**	**94**	**10**	**4**	**0**	**584**	**612**	**304**	**274**	**47**	**13**	**201**	**278**	**1.392**	**4.22**	**89**	**4.11**	**.273**	**25**	**.169**	**-31**	**23**	**-3.3**

• BOGLE, Warren
Warren Frederick Bogle b: 10/19/1946, Passaic, NJ BL/TL, 6'4", 220 lbs. Deb: 7/31/1968

YEAR	TM-L	W	L	PCT	G	GS	CG	SH	SV	IP	H	R	ER	HR	HB	BB	SO	RAT	ERA	ERA+	CERA	OAV	BH	AVG	PR+	WS	TPW
1968	Oak-A	0	0	....	16	1	0	0	0	23	26	12	11	3	0	8	26	1.478	4.30	65	4.64	.283	0	.000	-4	0	-0.5

• BOHANON, Brian
Brian Edward Bohanon b: 8/1/1968, Denton, TX BL/TL, 6'2", 220 lbs. Deb: 4/10/1990

YEAR	TM-L	W	L	PCT	G	GS	CG	SH	SV	IP	H	R	ER	HR	HB	BB	SO	RAT	ERA	ERA+	CERA	OAV	BH	AVG	PR+	WS	TPW
1990	Tex-A	0	3	.000	11	6	0	0	0	34	40	30	25	6	2	18	15	1.706	6.62	59	6.53	.296	0	....	-10	0	-1.1
1991	Tex-A	4	3	.571	11	11	1	0	0	61^1	66	35	33	4	2	23	34	1.451	4.84	83	4.21	.274	0	....	-5	2	-0.5
1992	Tex-A	1	1	.500	18	7	0	0	0	45^2	57	38	32	7	1	25	29	1.796	6.31	60	6.53	.297	0	....	-12	0	-1.2
1993	Tex-A	4	4	.500	36	8	0	0	0	92^2	107	54	49	8	4	46	45	1.651	4.76	87	5.47	.296	0	....	-5	3	-0.4
1994	Tex-A	2	2	.500	11	5	0	0	0	37^1	51	31	30	7	1	8	26	1.580	7.23	67	6.16	.321	0	....	-9	0	-0.8
1995	Det-A	1	1	.500	52	10	0	0	1	105^2	121	68	65	10	4	41	63	1.533	5.54	86	4.87	.285	0	....	-8	5	-0.7
1996	Tor-A	0	1	.000	20	0	0	0	1	22	27	19	19	4	2	19	17	2.091	7.77	64	8.11	.303	0	....	-7	0	-0.7
1997	NY-N	6	4	.600	19	14	0	0	0	94^1	95	49	40	9	4	34	66	1.367	3.82	106	4.01	.258	6	.182	0	5	0.0
1998	NY-N	2	4	.333	25	4	0	0	0	54^1	47	21	19	4	6	21	39	1.252	3.15	132	3.50	.234	6	.429	6	5	0.8
	LA-N	5	7	.417	14	14	2	0	0	97^1	74	35	26	9	5	36	72	1.130	2.40	165	2.87	.213	6	.207	17	8	1.9
	Yr.	7	11	.389	39	18	2	0	0	151^2	121	56	45	13	11	57	111	1.174	2.67	151	3.10	.220	12	.279	23	13	2.7
1999	Col-N	12	12	.500	33	33	3	1	0	197^1	236	146	136	30	14	92	120	1.662	6.20	94	6.27	.304	14	.197	-8	9	-0.6
2000	Col-N	12	10	.545	34	26	2	1	0	177	181	101	92	24	6	79	98	1.469	4.68	124	4.80	.266	11	.208	21	13	2.2
2001	Col-N	5	8	.385	20	19	0	0	0	97	127	79	77	20	7	47	47	1.794	7.14	75	7.52	.323	10	.323	-20	2	-1.7
Total	**12**	**54**	**60**	**.474**	**304**	**157**	**8**	**2**	**2**	**1116**	**1229**	**706**	**643**	**142**	**58**	**489**	**671**	**1.539**	**5.19**	**93**	**5.26**	**.281**	**53**	**.229**	**-39**	**52**	**-2.7**

• BOHEN, Pat
Leo Ignatius Bohen b: 9/30/1890, Oakland, IA d: 4/8/1942, Napa, CA BR/TR, 5'10.5", 155 lbs. Deb: 10/1/1913

YEAR	TM-L	W	L	PCT	G	GS	CG	SH	SV	IP	H	R	ER	HR	HB	BB	SO	RAT	ERA	ERA+	CERA	OAV	BH	AVG	PR+	WS	TPW
1913	Phi-A	0	1	.000	1	1	1	0	0	8	3	1	1	0	0	2	5	.625	1.13	245	0.65	.115	0	.000	1	1	0.1
1914	Pit-N	0	0	....	1	0	0	0	0	1	2	2	2	0	1	2	0	4.000	18.00	15	22.96	.500	0	.000	-2	0	-0.2
Total	**2**	**0**	**1**	**.000**	**2**	**1**	**1**	**0**	**0**	**9**	**5**	**3**	**3**	**0**	**1**	**4**	**5**	**1.000**	**3.00**	**89**	**3.13**	**.166**	**0**	**.000**	**-0**	**1**	**-0.1**

• BOHN, Charlie
Charles Bohn b: 1857, Cleveland, OH d: 8/1/1903, Cleveland, OH BR/TR, 5'9", 165 lbs. Deb: 6/20/1882 ♦

YEAR	TM-L	W	L	PCT	G	GS	CG	SH	SV	IP	H	R	ER	HR	HB	BB	SO	RAT	ERA	ERA+	CERA	OAV	BH	AVG	PR+	WS	TPW
1882	Lou-a	1	1	.500	2	2	2	0	0	18	21	8	6	0	....	3	1	1.333	3.00	83	....	.273	2	.154	-1	1	-0.2

• BOHNET, John
John Kelly Bohnet b: 1/18/1961, Pasadena, CA BB/TL, 6', 175 lbs. Deb: 5/10/1982

YEAR	TM-L	W	L	PCT	G	GS	CG	SH	SV	IP	H	R	ER	HR	HB	BB	SO	RAT	ERA	ERA+	CERA	OAV	BH	AVG	PR+	WS	TPW
1982	Cle-A	0	0	....	3	3	0	0	0	11^2	11	9	9	4	1	7	4	1.543	6.94	59	6.78	.250	0	....	-4	0	-0.4

• BOITANO, Dan
Danny Jon Boitano b: 3/22/1953, Sacramento, CA BR/TR, 6', 185 lbs. Deb: 10/1/1978

YEAR	TM-L	W	L	PCT	G	GS	CG	SH	SV	IP	H	R	ER	HR	HB	BB	SO	RAT	ERA	ERA+	CERA	OAV	BH	AVG	PR+	WS	TPW
1978	Phi-N	0	0	....	1	0	0	0	0	1	0	0	0	0	0	1	0	1.000	0.00	....	0.95	.000	0	....	0	0	0.0
1979	Mil-A	0	0	....	5	0	0	0	0	6	6	1	1	1	0	3	5	1.500	1.50	278	5.06	.273	0	....	2	1	0.2
1980	Mil-A	0	1	.000	11	0	0	0	0	17^2	26	17	16	7	1	6	11	1.811	8.15	47	9.34	.342	0	....	-9	0	-0.9
1981	NY-N	2	1	.667	15	0	0	0	0	16^1	21	10	10	2	2	5	8	1.592	5.51	63	5.99	.309	0	....	-3	0	-0.4
1982	Tex-A	0	0	....	19	0	0	0	0	30^1	33	19	18	5	2	13	28	1.516	5.34	73	5.34	.280	0	....	-5	0	-0.5
Total	**5**	**2**	**2**	**.500**	**51**	**0**	**0**	**0**	**0**	**71^1**	**86**	**47**	**45**	**15**	**5**	**28**	**52**	**1.598**	**5.68**	**67**	**6.40**	**.303**	**0**	**....**	**-15**	**1**	**-1.5**

• BOKELMANN, Dick
Richard Werner Bokelmann b: 10/26/1926, Arlington Heights, IL BR/TR, 6'.5", 180 lbs. Deb: 8/3/1951

YEAR	TM-L	W	L	PCT	G	GS	CG	SH	SV	IP	H	R	ER	HR	HB	BB	SO	RAT	ERA	ERA+	CERA	OAV	BH	AVG	PR+	WS	TPW
1951	StL-N	3	3	.500	20	1	0	0	3	52^1	49	30	22	2	1	31	22	1.529	3.78	105	3.87	.245	0	.000	0	3	-0.2
1952	StL-N	0	1	.000	11	0	0	0	0	12^2	20	17	13	0	0	7	5	2.132	9.24	40	7.01	.357	0	....	-8	0	-0.8
1953	StL-N	0	0	....	3	0	0	0	0	3	4	2	2	0	0	0	0	1.333	6.00	71	3.56	.308	0	....	-1	0	-0.1
Total	**3**	**3**	**4**	**.429**	**34**	**1**	**0**	**0**	**3**	**68**	**73**	**49**	**37**	**2**	**1**	**38**	**27**	**1.632**	**4.90**	**79**	**4.45**	**.271**	**0**	**.000**	**-8**	**3**	**-1.0**

• BOKINA, Joe
Joseph Bokina b: 4/4/1910, Northampton, MA d: 10/25/1991, Chattanooga, TN BR/TR, 6', 184 lbs. Deb: 4/16/1936

YEAR	TM-L	W	L	PCT	G	GS	CG	SH	SV	IP	H	R	ER	HR	HB	BB	SO	RAT	ERA	ERA+	CERA	OAV	BH	AVG	PR+	WS	TPW
1936	Was-A	0	2	.000	5	1	0	0	0	8^1	15	8	8	0	0	6	5	2.520	8.64	55	9.55	.395	0	.000	-4	0	-0.3

• BOLAND, Bernie
Bernard Anthony Boland b: 1/21/1892, Rochester, NY d: 9/12/1973, Detroit, MI BR/TR, 5'8.5", 168 lbs. Deb: 4/14/1915

YEAR	TM-L	W	L	PCT	G	GS	CG	SH	SV	IP	H	R	ER	HR	HB	BB	SO	RAT	ERA	ERA+	CERA	OAV	BH	AVG	PR+	WS	TPW
1915	Det-A	13	7	.650	45	18	8	1	2	202^2	167	86	70	2	6	75	72	1.194	3.11	97	2.57	.230	11	.175	2	13	0.2
1916	Det-A	10	3	.769	46	9	5	1	3	130^1	111	69	57	1	4	73	59	1.412	3.94	73	3.37	.240	8	.250	-13	6	-1.2
1917	Det-A	16	11	.593	43	28	13	3	6	238	192	89	71	0	6	95	89	1.206	2.68	98	2.49	.226	4	.056	3	13	-0.3
1918	Det-A	14	10	.583	29	25	14	4	0	204	176	69	60	1	6	67	63	1.191	2.65	100	2.52	.236	12	.174	10	12	1.2
1919	Det-A	14	16	.467	35	30	18	1	1	242^2	222	93	82	7	3	80	71	1.245	3.04	105	3.03	.253	8	.108	8	16	0.5
1920	Det-A	0	2	.000	4	3	1	0	0	17^1	23	18	15	0	2	14	4	2.135	7.79	48	7.66	.348	1	.143	-7	0	-0.7
1921	StL-A	1	4	.200	7	6	0	0	0	27	34	36	28	2	2	28	6	2.296	9.33	48	7.62	.309	1	.100	-14	0	-1.4
Total	**7**	**68**	**53**	**.562**	**209**	**119**	**59**	**10**	**12**	**1062**	**925**	**460**	**383**	**13**	**29**	**432**	**364**	**1.278**	**3.25**	**92**	**2.96**	**.241**	**45**	**.138**	**-11**	**60**	**-1.8**

• BOLDEN, Bill
William Horace "Big Bill" Bolden b: 5/9/1893, Dandridge, TN d: 12/8/1966, Jefferson City, TN BR/TR, 6'4", 200 lbs. Deb: 6/27/1919

YEAR	TM-L	W	L	PCT	G	GS	CG	SH	SV	IP	H	R	ER	HR	HB	BB	SO	RAT	ERA	ERA+	CERA	OAV	BH	AVG	PR+	WS	TPW
1919	StL-N	0	1	.000	3	1	0	0	0	12	17	7	7	0	1	4	4	1.750	5.25	53	5.73	.340	1	.333	-3	0	-0.4

• BOLEN, Stew
Stewart O'Neal Bolen b: 10/12/1902, Jackson, AL d: 8/30/1969, Mobile, AL BL/TL, 5'11", 180 lbs. Deb: 4/15/1926

YEAR	TM-L	W	L	PCT	G	GS	CG	SH	SV	IP	H	R	ER	HR	HB	BB	SO	RAT	ERA	ERA+	CERA	OAV	BH	AVG	PR+	WS	TPW
1926	StL-A	0	0	....	5	0	0	0	0	14^2	21	10	10	2	0	6	7	1.841	6.14	70	7.27	.356	2	.500	-3	0	-0.2
1927	StL-A	0	1	.000	3	1	1	0	0	9^2	14	9	9	0	0	5	7	1.966	8.38	52	6.68	.368	1	.333	-4	0	-0.4
1931	Phi-N	3	12	.200	28	16	2	0	0	98^2	117	75	70	5	4	63	55	1.824	6.39	66	5.68	.297	5	.156	-22	0	-2.3
1932	Phi-N	0	0	....	5	0	0	0	0	16	18	8	5	0	2	10	3	1.750	2.81	157	5.17	.281	1	.143	3	1	0.2
Total	**4**	**3**	**13**	**.188**	**41**	**17**	**3**	**0**	**0**	**139**	**170**	**102**	**94**	**7**	**6**	**84**	**72**	**1.827**	**6.09**	**70**	**5.86**	**.306**	**9**	**.196**	**-27**	**1**	**-2.7**

• BOLIN, Bobby
Bobby Donald Bolin b: 1/29/1939, Hickory Grove, SC BR/TR, 6'4", 200 lbs. Deb: 4/18/1961

YEAR	TM-L	W	L	PCT	G	GS	CG	SH	SV	IP	H	R	ER	HR	HB	BB	SO	RAT	ERA	ERA+	CERA	OAV	BH	AVG	PR+	WS	TPW
1961	SF-N	2	2	.500	37	1	0	0	5	48	37	20	17	6	3	37	48	1.542	3.19	119	4.20	.210	2	.286	4	4	0.4
1962*	SF-N	7	3	.700	41	5	2	0	5	92	84	41	37	10	5	35	74	1.293	3.62	105	3.68	.243	6	.261	2	8	0.4
1963	SF-N	10	6	.625	47	12	2	0	7	137^1	128	73	50	13	7	57	134	1.347	3.28	98	3.78	.242	5	.143	1	7	0.4
1964	SF-N	6	9	.400	38	23	5	3	1	174^2	143	71	63	16	10	77	146	1.260	3.25	110	3.36	.220	5	.100	5	10	0.6
1965	SF-N	14	6	.700	45	13	2	0	2	163	125	51	50	17	4	56	135	1.110	2.76	130	2.75	.214	9	.167	17	15	2.0
1966	SF-N	11	10	.524	36	34	10	4	1	224^1	174	85	72	25	10	70	143	1.088	2.89	127	2.71	.211	13	.171	19	17	2.4
1967	SF-N	6	8	.429	37	15	0	0	0	120	120	71	65	16	3	50	69	1.417	4.88	67	4.32	.258	8	.242	-21	1	-2.1

YEAR	TM-L	W	L	PCT	G	GS	CG	SH	SV	IP	H	R	ER	HR	HB	BB	SO	RAT	ERA	ERA+	CERA	OAV	BH	AVG	PR+	WS	TPW
1968	SF-N	10	5	.667	34	19	6	3	0	176^2	128	44	39	9	4	46	126	.985	1.99	148	1.89	.200	5	.091	20	15	2.2
1969	SF-N	7	7	.500	30	22	2	0	0	146^1	149	86	72	17	7	49	102	1.353	4.43	79	4.13	.260	6	.154	-14	4	-1.1
1970	Mil-A	5	11	.313	32	20	3	0	1	132	131	84	72	20	4	67	81	1.500	4.91	77	4.79	.256	7	.194	-14	2	-1.2
	Bos-A	2	0	1.000	6	0	0	0	2	8	2	0	0	0	1	5	8	.875	0.00	....	0.94	.080	0	.000	4	3	0.4
	Yr.	7	11	.389	38	20	3	0	3	140	133	84	72	20	5	72	89	1.464	4.63	82	4.57	.248	7	.189	-10	5	-0.8
1971	Bos-A	5	3	.625	52	0	0	0	6	69^2	74	34	33	7	0	24	51	1.407	4.26	87	4.06	.273	3	.250	-4	5	-0.3
1972	Bos-A	0	1	.000	21	0	0	0	5	30^2	24	11	10	3	1	11	27	1.141	2.93	110	2.77	.209	0	.000	2	3	0.2
1973	Bos-A	3	4	.429	39	0	0	0	15	53^1	45	16	16	5	1	13	31	1.088	2.70	149	2.69	.232	0	....	8	9	0.8
Total	**13**	**88**	**75**	**.540**	**495**	**164**	**32**	**10**	**50**	**1576**	**1364**	**687**	**596**	**164**	**60**	**597**	**1175**	**1.244**	**3.40**	**103**	**3.37**	**.231**	**69**	**.163**	**29**	**103**	**4.8**

• BOLLO, Greg

Gregory Gene Bollo b: 11/16/1943, Detroit, MI BR/TR, 6'4", 183 lbs. Deb: 5/9/1965

YEAR	TM-L	W	L	PCT	G	GS	CG	SH	SV	IP	H	R	ER	HR	HB	BB	SO	RAT	ERA	ERA+	CERA	OAV	BH	AVG	PR+	WS	TPW
1965	Chi-A	0	0	....	15	0	0	0	0	22^2	12	11	9	5	2	9	16	.926	3.57	89	2.61	.152	0	....	-1	1	-0.1
1966	Chi-A	0	1	.000	3	1	0	0	0	7	7	2	2	0	1	3	4	1.429	2.57	123	4.18	.269	0	.000	0	0	0.0
Total	**2**	**0**	**1**	**.000**	**18**	**1**	**0**	**0**	**0**	**29^2**	**19**	**13**	**11**	**5**	**3**	**12**	**20**	**1.045**	**3.34**	**96**	**2.98**	**.181**	**0**	**.000**	**-1**	**1**	**-0.1**

• BOLTON, Rod

Rodney Earl Bolton b: 9/23/1968, Chattanooga, TN BR/TR, 6'2", 190 lbs. Deb: 4/10/1993

YEAR	TM-L	W	L	PCT	G	GS	CG	SH	SV	IP	H	R	ER	HR	HB	BB	SO	RAT	ERA	ERA+	CERA	OAV	BH	AVG	PR+	WS	TPW
1993	Chi-A	2	6	.250	9	8	0	0	0	42^1	55	40	35	4	1	16	17	1.677	7.44	56	5.71	.314	0	....	-15	0	-1.5
1995	Chi-A	0	2	.000	8	3	0	0	0	22	33	23	20	4	0	14	10	2.136	8.18	54	8.95	.351	0	....	-9	0	-0.8
Total	**2**	**2**	**8**	**.200**	**17**	**11**	**0**	**0**	**0**	**64^1**	**88**	**63**	**55**	**8**	**1**	**30**	**27**	**1.834**	**7.69**	**56**	**6.82**	**.327**	**0**	**....**	**-24**	**0**	**-2.3**

• BOLTON, Tom

Thomas Edward Bolton b: 5/6/1962, Nashville, TN BL/TL, 6'2", 175 lbs. Deb: 5/17/1987

YEAR	TM-L	W	L	PCT	G	GS	CG	SH	SV	IP	H	R	ER	HR	HB	BB	SO	RAT	ERA	ERA+	CERA	OAV	BH	AVG	PR+	WS	TPW
1987	Bos-A	1	0	1.000	29	0	0	0	0	61^2	83	33	30	5	2	27	49	1.784	4.38	104	6.28	.329	0	....	1	3	0.1
1988	Bos-A	1	3	.250	28	0	0	0	1	30^1	35	17	16	1	0	14	21	1.615	4.75	87	4.51	.285	0	....	-2	1	-0.2
1989	Bos-A	0	4	.000	4	4	0	0	0	17^1	21	18	16	1	0	10	9	1.788	8.31	49	5.44	.292	0	....	-8	0	-0.8
1990*	Bos-A	10	5	.667	21	16	3	0	0	119^2	111	46	45	6	3	47	65	1.320	3.38	120	3.43	.251	0	....	11	10	1.2
1991	Bos-A	8	9	.471	25	19	0	0	0	110	136	72	64	16	1	51	64	1.700	5.24	82	6.19	.308	0	....	-11	3	-1.1
1992	Bos-A	1	2	.333	21	1	0	0	0	29	34	11	11	0	2	14	23	1.655	3.41	123	4.77	.286	0	....	3	2	0.3
	Cin-N	3	3	.500	16	8	0	0	0	46^1	52	28	27	9	2	23	27	1.619	5.24	69	6.06	.284	0	.000	-9	0	-1.1
1993	Det-A	6	6	.500	43	8	0	0	0	102^2	113	57	51	5	7	45	66	1.539	4.47	96	4.51	.282	0	....	-2	5	-0.2
1994	Bal-A	1	2	.333	22	0	0	0	0	23^1	29	15	14	3	0	13	12	1.800	5.40	93	6.34	.309	0	....	-1	1	-0.1
Total	**8**	**31**	**34**	**.477**	**209**	**56**	**3**	**0**	**1**	**540^1**	**614**	**297**	**274**	**46**	**17**	**244**	**336**	**1.588**	**4.56**	**92**	**5.07**	**.289**	**0**	**.000**	**-17**	**25**	**-1.9**

• BOMBACK, Mark

Mark Vincent Bomback b: 4/14/1953, Portsmouth, VA BR/TR, 5'11", 170 lbs. Deb: 9/12/1978

YEAR	TM-L	W	L	PCT	G	GS	CG	SH	SV	IP	H	R	ER	HR	HB	BB	SO	RAT	ERA	ERA+	CERA	OAV	BH	AVG	PR+	WS	TPW
1978	Mil-A	0	0	....	2	1	0	0	0	1^2	5	3	3	1	0	1	1	3.600	16.20	23	24.74	.500	0	....	-2	0	-0.2
1980	NY-N	10	8	.556	36	25	2	1	0	162^2	191	80	74	17	4	49	68	1.475	4.09	87	4.82	.297	10	.233	-10	8	-0.7
1981	Tor-A	5	5	.500	20	11	0	0	0	90^1	84	42	39	6	1	35	33	1.317	3.89	101	3.48	.251	0	....	1	5	0.1
1982	Tor-A	1	5	.167	16	8	0	0	0	59^2	87	44	40	10	3	25	22	1.877	6.03	74	7.74	.343	0	....	-10	0	-1.0
Total	**4**	**16**	**18**	**.471**	**74**	**45**	**2**	**1**	**0**	**314^1**	**367**	**169**	**156**	**34**	**8**	**110**	**124**	**1.517**	**4.47**	**86**	**5.09**	**.295**	**10**	**.233**	**-21**	**13**	**-1.8**

• BOND, Tommy

Thomas Henry Bond b: 4/2/1856, Granard, Ireland d: 1/24/1941, Boston, MA BR/TR, 5'7.5", 160 lbs. Deb: 5/5/1874 M/U ♦

YEAR	TM-L	W	L	PCT	G	GS	CG	SH	SV	IP	H	R	ER	HR	HB	BB	SO	RAT	ERA	ERA+	CERA	OAV	BH	AVG	PR+	WS	TPW
1874	Atl-n	22	32	.407	55	55	55	1	0	497	606	....	112	16	....	8	92	1.235	2.03	88	....	.269	54	.220	-23	....	-1.5
1875	Har-n	19	16	.543	40	39	37	6	0	352	302	....	56	3	....	7	20	.878	1.43	166	....	.210	77	.266	30	....	3.2
1876	Har-N	31	13	.705	45	45	45	6	0	408	355	164	76	2	....	13	88	.902	1.68	141	....	.216	50	.275	11	47	1.0
1877	Bos-N	**40**	17	.702	58	58	58	**6**	0	521	530	248	122	5	....	36	**170**	1.086	**2.11**	133	....	**.249**	59	.228	**41**	47	3.4
1878	Bos-N	**40**	19	.678	**59**	**59**	**57**	**9**	0	**532^2**	571	222	122	5	....	33	**182**	1.134	2.06	114	....	.261	50	.212	8	**60**	0.3
1879	Bos-N	43	19	.694	64	64	59	**11**	0	555^1	543	206	121	8	....	24	155	1.021	**1.96**	**127**	....	.240	62	.241	10	50	1.0
1880	Bos-N	26	29	.473	63	57	49	3	0	493	559	298	146	1	....	45	118	1.225	2.67	85	....	.271	62	.220	-11	21	-1.0
1881	Bos-N	0	3	.000	3	3	2	0	0	25^1	40	17	12	3	....	2	2	1.658	4.26	62	....	.344	2	.200	-4	1	-0.4
1882	Wor-N	0	1	.000	2	2	0	0	0	12^1	12	13	6	0	....	7	2	1.541	4.38	71	....	.241	4	.133	-1	0	-0.6
1884	Bos-U	13	9	.591	23	21	19	0	0	189	185	120	63	3	....	14	128	1.053	3.00	99	....	.239	48	.296	-3	17	0.2
	Ind-a	0	5	.000	5	5	5	0	0	43	62	51	27	5	2	4	15	1.535	5.65	58	....	.321	3	.130	-9	0	-1.0
Total	**2 n**	**41**	**48**	**.461**	**95**	**94**	**92**	**7**	**0**	**849**	**908**	**....**	**168**	**19**	**....**	**15**	**112**	**1.087**	**1.78**	**110**	**....**	**.246**	**131**	**.245**	**7**	**....**	**1.7**
Total	**8**	**193**	**115**	**.627**	**322**	**314**	**294**	**35**	**0**	**2779^2**	**2857**	**1339**	**695**	**32**	**2**	**178**	**860**	**1.092**	**2.25**	**112**	**....**	**.250**	**340**	**.236**	**41**	**243**	**2.9**

• BONDERMAN, Jeremy

Jeremy Allen Bonderman b: 10/28/1982, Kennewick, WA BR/TR, 6'2", 210 lbs. Deb: 4/2/2003

YEAR	TM-L	W	L	PCT	G	GS	CG	SH	SV	IP	H	R	ER	HR	HB	BB	SO	RAT	ERA	ERA+	CERA	OAV	BH	AVG	PR+	WS	TPW
2003	Det-A	6	19	.240	33	28	0	0	0	162	193	118	100	23	4	58	108	1.549	5.56	78	5.39	.294	0	.000	-23	2	-2.2

• BONES, Ricky

Ricardo Ricky Bones b: 4/7/1969, Salinas, Puerto Rico BR/TR, 5'10", 190 lbs. Deb: 8/11/1991

YEAR	TM-L	W	L	PCT	G	GS	CG	SH	SV	IP	H	R	ER	HR	HB	BB	SO	RAT	ERA	ERA+	CERA	OAV	BH	AVG	PR+	WS	TPW
1991	SD-N	4	6	.400	11	11	0	0	0	54	57	33	29	3	0	18	31	1.389	4.83	79	3.77	.269	1	.077	-6	1	-0.7
1992	Mil-A	9	10	.474	31	28	0	0	0	163^1	169	90	83	27	9	48	65	1.329	4.57	84	4.50	.264	0	....	-17	4	-1.7
1993	Mil-A	11	11	.500	32	31	3	0	0	203^2	222	122	110	28	8	63	63	1.399	4.86	87	4.64	.278	0	....	-12	8	-1.2
1994	Mil-A★	10	9	.526	24	24	4	1	0	170^2	166	76	65	17	3	45	57	1.236	3.43	147	3.48	.255	0	....	25	14	2.3
1995	Mil-A	10	12	.455	32	31	3	0	0	200^1	218	108	103	26	4	83	77	1.502	4.63	108	4.98	.281	0	....	4	11	0.4
1996	Mil-A	7	14	.333	32	23	0	0	0	145	170	104	94	28	9	62	59	1.600	5.83	89	6.19	.294	0	....	-13	4	-1.2
	NY-A	0	0	....	4	1	0	0	0	7	14	11	11	2	1	6	4	2.857	14.14	35	15.54	.438	0	....	-7	0	-0.6
	Yr.	7	14	.333	36	24	0	0	0	152	184	115	105	30	10	68	63	1.658	6.22	83	6.62	.301	0	....	-20	4	-1.8
1997	Cin-N	0	1	.000	9	2	0	0	0	17^2	31	22	20	2	2	11	8	2.377	10.19	42	9.89	.378	0	.000	-12	0	-1.2
	KC-A	4	7	.364	21	11	1	0	0	78^1	102	59	52	10	5	25	36	1.621	5.97	79	6.08	.325	0	....	-12	1	-1.1
1998	KC-A	2	2	.500	32	0	0	0	1	53^1	49	18	18	4	1	24	38	1.369	3.04	159	3.53	.244	0	.000	11	6	1.0
1999	Bal-A	0	3	.000	30	2	0	0	0	43^2	59	29	29	7	2	19	26	1.786	5.98	78	6.99	.322	0	....	-7	1	-0.7
2000	Fla-N	2	3	.400	56	0	0	0	0	77^1	94	43	39	6	3	27	59	1.565	4.54	98	4.85	.303	0	.000	-1	4	0.0
2001	Fla-N	4	4	.500	61	0	0	0	0	64	71	39	36	7	3	33	41	1.625	5.06	83	5.27	.286	1	.500	-6	2	-0.6
Total	**11**	**63**	**82**	**.434**	**375**	**164**	**11**	**1**	**1**	**1278^1**	**1422**	**754**	**689**	**167**	**50**	**464**	**564**	**1.475**	**4.85**	**93**	**4.96**	**.283**	**2**	**.100**	**-53**	**56**	**-5.3**

• BONETTI, Julio

Julio Giacomo Bonetti b: 7/14/1911, Genoa, Italy d: 6/17/1952, Belmont, CA BR/TR, 6', 180 lbs. Deb: 4/22/1937

YEAR	TM-L	W	L	PCT	G	GS	CG	SH	SV	IP	H	R	ER	HR	HB	BB	SO	RAT	ERA	ERA+	CERA	OAV	BH	AVG	PR+	WS	TPW
1937	StL-A	4	11	.267	28	16	7	0	1	143^1	190	103	93	13	2	60	43	1.744	5.84	83	5.97	.321	7	.149	-15	5	-1.5
1938	StL-A	2	3	.400	17	0	0	0	0	28^1	41	21	20	1	0	13	7	1.906	6.35	78	6.56	.350	0	.000	-4	1	-0.5
1940	Chi-N	0	0	....	1	0	0	0	0	1^1	3	3	3	0	0	4	0	5.250	20.25	19	21.99	.500	0	....	-2	0	-0.2
Total	**3**	**6**	**14**	**.300**	**46**	**16**	**7**	**0**	**1**	**173**	**234**	**127**	**116**	**14**	**2**	**77**	**50**	**1.798**	**6.03**	**80**	**6.19**	**.327**	**7**	**.127**	**-22**	**6**	**-2.2**

• BONEY, Hank

Henry Tate "Haney" Boney b: 10/28/1903, Wallace, NC d: 6/12/2002, Lake Worth, FL BL/TR, 5'11", 176 lbs. Deb: 6/28/1927

YEAR	TM-L	W	L	PCT	G	GS	CG	SH	SV	IP	H	R	ER	HR	HB	BB	SO	RAT	ERA	ERA+	CERA	OAV	BH	AVG	PR+	WS	TPW
1927	NY-N	0	0	....	3	0	0	0	0	4	4	1	1	0	0	2	0	1.500	2.25	171	3.74	.267	0	....	1	0	0.1

• BONG, Jung

Jung Keun Bong b: 7/15/1980, Seoul, South Korea BL/TL, 6'3", 175 lbs. Deb: 4/23/2002

YEAR	TM-L	W	L	PCT	G	GS	CG	SH	SV	IP	H	R	ER	HR	HB	BB	SO	RAT	ERA	ERA+	CERA	OAV	BH	AVG	PR+	WS	TPW
2002	Atl-N	0	1	.000	1	1	0	0	0	6	8	5	5	0	0	2	4	1.667	7.50	55	5.03	.320	0	.000	-2	0	-0.3
2003	Atl-N	6	2	.750	44	0	0	0	1	57	56	32	32	8	2	31	47	1.526	5.05	83	4.97	.267	0	.000	-5	3	-0.5
Total	**2**	**6**	**3**	**.667**	**45**	**1**	**0**	**0**	**1**	**63**	**64**	**37**	**37**	**8**	**2**	**33**	**51**	**1.540**	**5.29**	**79**	**4.98**	**.272**	**0**	**.000**	**-7**	**3**	**-0.8**

• BONHAM, Bill

William Gordon Bonham b: 10/1/1948, Glendale, CA BR/TR, 6'3", 195 lbs. Deb: 4/7/1971

YEAR	TM-L	W	L	PCT	G	GS	CG	SH	SV	IP	H	R	ER	HR	HB	BB	SO	RAT	ERA	ERA+	CERA	OAV	BH	AVG	PR+	WS	TPW
1971	Chi-N	2	1	.667	33	2	0	0	0	60	63	38	31	6	5	36	41	1.650	4.65	85	5.47	.281	2	.167	-4	1	-0.4
1972	Chi-N	1	1	.500	19	4	0	0	4	57^2	56	22	20	4	1	25	49	1.405	3.12	122	3.92	.260	4	.286	4	5	0.6
1973	Chi-N	7	5	.583	44	15	3	0	6	152	126	55	51	10	4	64	121	1.250	3.02	131	3.09	.230	4	.093	19	15	1.7
1974	Chi-N	11	22	.333	44	36	10	2	1	242^2	246	133	104	13	6	109	191	1.463	3.86	99	3.99	.263	12	.143	11	11	0.9
1975	Chi-N	13	15	.464	38	36	7	2	0	229^1	254	133	120	15	5	109	165	1.583	4.71	82	4.75	.281	15	.183	-15	9	-1.5
1976	Chi-N	9	13	.409	32	31	3	0	0	196	215	102	93	11	2	96	110	**1.587**	4.27	90	4.69	.283	13	.200	-6	9	-0.4
1977	Chi-N	10	13	.435	34	34	1	0	0	214^2	207	111	104	15	3	82	134	1.346	4.36	101	3.54	.254	15	.231	5	12	0.6
1978	Cin-N	11	5	.688	23	23	1	0	0	140^1	151	59	55	9	1	50	83	1.432	3.53	101	4.00	.276	8	.186	3	10	0.5
1979	Cin-N	9	7	.563	29	29	2	0	0	175^2	173	80	74	14	8	60	78	1.326	3.79	98	3.84	.261	8	.140	-1	9	-0.3
1980	Cin-N	2	1	.667	4	4	0	0	0	19	21	10	10	1	0	5	13	1.368	4.74	76	3.80	.276	0	.000	-2	1	-0.3
Total	**10**	**75**	**83**	**.475**	**300**	**214**	**27**	**4**	**11**	**1487^1**	**1512**	**743**	**662**	**98**	**35**	**636**	**985**	**1.444**	**4.01**	**97**	**4.08**	**.266**	**81**	**.172**	**14**	**82**	**1.4**

YEAR	TM-L	W	L	PCT	G	GS	CG	SH	SV	IP	H	R	ER	HR	HB	BB	SO	RAT	ERA	ERA+	CERA	OAV	BH	AVG	PR+	WS	TPW
• BONHAM, Tiny	Ernest Edward Bonham b: 8/16/1913, Ione, CA d: 9/15/1949, Pittsburgh, PA BR/TR, 6'2", 215 lbs. Deb: 8/5/1940																										
1940	NY-A	9	3	.750	12	12	10	3	0	99^1	83	24	21	4	0	13	37	.966	1.90	212	1.89	.224	7	.189	22	13	2.1
1941*	NY-A	9	6	.600	23	14	7	1	2	126^2	118	44	42	12	1	31	43	1.176	2.98	132	3.07	.246	8	.160	9	11	0.7
1942*	NY-A★	21	5	.808	28	27	**22**	**6**	0	226	199	65	57	11	1	24	71	.987	2.27	152	**2.11**	.237	9	.122	20	21	1.8
1943*	NY-A★	15	8	.652	28	26	17	4	1	225^2	197	63	57	13	1	52	71	1.103	2.27	141	2.50	.236	15	.197	20	20	2.2
1944	NY-A	12	9	.571	26	25	17	1	0	213^2	228	84	71	14	0	41	54	1.259	2.99	117	3.38	.273	10	.133	8	15	0.6
1945	NY-A	8	11	.421	23	23	12	0	0	180^2	186	72	66	11	1	22	42	1.151	3.29	105	2.91	.265	15	.238	-1	11	0.2
1946	NY-A	5	8	.385	18	14	6	2	3	104^2	97	47	43	6	0	23	30	1.146	3.70	93	2.65	.243	4	.129	-6	5	-0.7
1947	Pit-N	11	8	.579	33	18	7	3	3	149^2	167	67	64	17	2	35	63	1.350	3.85	110	4.13	.277	7	.156	7	10	0.7
1948	Pit-N	6	10	.375	22	20	7	0	0	135^2	145	71	65	18	3	23	42	1.238	4.31	94	3.89	.276	8	.163	-4	6	-0.6
1949	Pit-N	7	4	.636	18	14	5	1	0	89	81	43	42	11	0	23	25	1.169	4.25	99	3.24	.246	1	.045	0	6	-0.1
Total	**10**	**103**	**72**	**.589**	**231**	**193**	**110**	**21**	**9**	**1551**	**1501**	**580**	**528**	**117**	**9**	**287**	**478**	**1.153**	**3.06**	**120**	**2.95**	**.254**	**84**	**.161**	**75**	**118**	**6.9**
• BONIKOWSKI, Joe	Joseph Peter Bonikowski b: 1/16/1941, Philadelphia, PA BR/TR, 6', 175 lbs. Deb: 4/12/1962																										
1962	Min-A	5	7	.417	30	13	3	0	2	99^2	95	47	43	6	1	38	45	1.334	3.88	105	3.54	.255	4	.148	2	6	0.1
• BONNESS, Bill	William John "Lefty" Bonness b: 12/15/1923, Cleveland, OH d: 12/3/1977, Detroit, MI BR/TL, 6'4", 200 lbs. Deb: 9/26/1944																										
1944	Cle-A	0	1	.000	2	1	0	0	0	7	11	6	6	0	2	5	1	2.286	7.71	43	8.95	.367	0	.000	-4	0	-0.4
• BONO, Gus	Adlai Wendell Bono b: 8/29/1894, Doe Run, MO d: 12/3/1948, Dearborn, MI BR/TR, 5'11", 175 lbs. Deb: 9/13/1920																										
1920	Was-A	0	2	.000	4	1	0	0	0	12^1	17	13	12	0	0	6	4	1.865	8.76	42	5.55	.315	0	.000	-7	0	-0.7
• BOOKER, Greg	Gregory Scott Booker b: 6/22/1960, Lynchburg, VA BR/TR, 6'6", 233 lbs. Deb: 9/11/1983 C																										
1983	SD-N	0	1	.000	6	1	0	0	0	11^2	18	10	10	2	0	9	5	2.314	7.71	45	10.22	.375	0	.000	-6	0	-0.6
1984*	SD-N	1	1	.500	32	1	0	0	0	57^1	67	27	21	4	0	27	28	1.640	3.30	108	4.93	.295	2	.286	1	3	0.1
1985	SD-N	0	1	.000	17	0	0	0	0	22^1	20	17	17	3	1	17	7	1.657	6.85	52	5.24	.247	0	.000	-9	0	-0.9
1986	SD-N	1	0	1.000	9	0	0	0	0	11	10	5	2	0	0	4	7	1.273	1.64	223	2.44	.233	0	....	2	1	0.3
1987	SD-N	1	1	.500	44	0	0	0	1	68^1	62	29	24	5	3	30	17	1.346	3.16	125	3.76	.246	0	.000	5	5	0.5
1988	SD-N	2	2	.500	34	2	0	0	0	63^2	68	31	24	5	1	19	43	1.366	3.39	100	3.93	.278	2	.250	-1	3	0.0
1989	SD-N	0	1	.000	11	0	0	0	0	19	15	10	9	2	0	10	8	1.316	4.26	82	3.44	.224	0	....	-2	0	-0.2
	Min-A	0	0	....	6	0	0	0	0	8^2	11	4	4	1	0	2	3	1.500	4.15	100	5.07	.306	0	....	0	0	0.0
1990	SF-N	0	0	....	2	0	0	0	0	2	7	3	3	0	0	0	1	3.500	13.50	27	18.39	.538	0	....	-2	0	-0.2
Total	**8**	**5**	**7**	**.417**	**161**	**4**	**0**	**0**	**1**	**264**	**278**	**136**	**114**	**22**	**5**	**118**	**119**	**1.500**	**3.89**	**93**	**4.54**	**.275**	**4**	**.174**	**-11**	**12**	**-1.1**
• BOOLES, Red	Seabron Jesse Booles b: 7/14/1880, Bernice, LA d: 3/16/1955, Monroe, LA BL/TL, 5'10", 150 lbs. Deb: 7/30/1909																										
1909	Cle-A	0	1	.000	4	1	0	0	0	22^2	20	12	5	0	1	8	6	1.235	1.99	128	2.70	.235	1	.167	1	1	0.2
• BOONE, Dan	James Albert Boone b: 1/19/1895, Samantha, AL d: 6/11/1968, Tuscaloosa, AL BR/TR, 6'2", 190 lbs. Deb: 9/10/1919																										
1919	Phi-A	0	1	.000	3	2	0	0	0	14^2	24	14	11	0	0	10	1	2.318	6.75	51	8.34	.375	0	.000	-5	0	-0.6
1921	Det-A	0	0	....	1	0	0	0	0	2	1	1	0	0	0	2	0	1.500	0.00	....	2.54	.200	0	.000	1	0	0.1
1922	Cle-A	4	6	.400	11	10	4	2	0	75^1	87	39	34	3	1	19	9	1.407	4.06	98	3.99	.298	5	.192	1	4	0.1
1923	Cle-A	4	6	.400	27	4	2	0	0	70^1	93	56	47	3	3	31	15	1.763	6.01	66	5.62	.322	4	.211	-15	1	-1.4
Total	**4**	**8**	**13**	**.381**	**42**	**16**	**6**	**2**	**0**	**162^1**	**205**	**110**	**92**	**6**	**4**	**62**	**25**	**1.645**	**5.10**	**77**	**5.07**	**.315**	**9**	**.180**	**-18**	**5**	**-1.9**
• BOONE, Danny	Daniel Hugh Boone b: 1/14/1954, Long Beach, CA BL/TL, 5'8", 150 lbs. Deb: 4/11/1981																										
1981	SD-N	1	0	1.000	37	0	0	0	2	63^1	63	23	20	2	1	21	43	1.326	2.84	115	3.30	.267	2	.500	3	4	0.4
1982	SD-N	1	0	1.000	10	0	0	0	1	16	21	10	10	2	0	3	8	1.500	5.63	61	5.31	.323	1	.200	-4	0	-0.4
	Hou-N	0	1	.000	10	0	0	0	1	12^2	7	6	5	1	0	4	4	.868	3.55	93	1.49	.171	0	.000	-0	1	-0.1
	Yr.	1	1	.500	20	0	0	0	2	28^2	28	16	15	3	0	7	12	1.221	4.71	72	3.62	.264	1	.167	-4	1	-0.4
1990	Bal-A	0	0	....	4	1	0	0	0	9^2	12	3	3	1	1	3	2	1.552	2.79	136	5.71	.308	0	....	1	1	0.1
Total	**3**	**2**	**1**	**.667**	**61**	**1**	**0**	**0**	**4**	**101^2**	**103**	**42**	**38**	**6**	**2**	**31**	**57**	**1.318**	**3.36**	**99**	**3.62**	**.270**	**3**	**.300**	**-1**	**6**	**0.0**
• BOONE, George	George Morris Boone b: 3/1/1871, Louisville, KY d: 9/24/1910, Louisville, KY Deb: 4/23/1891																										
1891	Lou-a	0	0	....	4	1	0	0	1	15	15	15	13	0	0	9	4	1.600	7.80	47	....	.252	2	.333	-7	0	-0.6
• BOOTCHECK, Chris	Christopher Brandon Bootcheck b: 10/24/1978, La Porte, IN BR/TR, 6'5", 200 lbs. Deb: 9/9/2003																										
2003	Ana-A	0	1	.000	4	1	0	0	0	10^1	16	13	11	5	0	6	7	2.129	9.58	45	11.53	.340	0	....	-6	0	-0.6
• BOOTH, Amos	Amos Smith "Darling" Booth b: 9/4/1852, Cincinnati, OH d: 7/1/1921, Miamisburg, OH BR/TR, 5'9", 159 lbs. Deb: 4/25/1876 U ♦																										
1876	Cin-N	0	1	.000	3	1	0	0	0	9^2	22	18	10	0	....	0	0	2.276	9.31	24	....	.422	71	.253	-7	4	-1.1
1877	Cin-N	1	7	.125	12	8	6	0	0	86	114	75	34	1	....	13	18	1.477	3.56	74	....	.301	27	.172	-4	2	-1.4
Total	**2**	**1**	**8**	**.111**	**15**	**9**	**6**	**0**	**0**	**95^2**	**136**	**93**	**44**	**1**	**....**	**13**	**18**	**1.557**	**4.14**	**61**	**....**	**.316**	**98**	**.219**	**-11**	**6**	**-2.5**
• BOOZER, John	John Morgan Boozer b: 7/6/1938, Columbia, SC d: 1/24/1986, Lexington, SC BR/TR, 6'3", 205 lbs. Deb: 7/22/1962																										
1962	Phi-N	0	0	....	9	0	0	0	0	20^1	22	13	13	3	0	10	13	1.574	5.75	67	5.39	.282	0	.000	-4	0	-0.5
1963	Phi-N	3	4	.429	26	8	2	0	1	83	67	31	27	11	1	33	69	1.205	2.93	110	3.28	.227	3	.143	1	5	0.1
1964	Phi-N	3	4	.429	22	3	0	0	2	60^1	64	37	34	6	2	18	51	1.359	5.07	68	4.11	.271	1	.077	-11	0	-1.2
1966	Phi-N	0	0	....	2	2	0	0	0	5^1	8	5	4	1	0	3	5	2.063	6.75	53	8.42	.348	0	.000	-2	0	-0.2
1967	Phi-N	5	4	.556	28	7	1	0	1	74^2	86	39	34	6	1	24	48	1.473	4.10	83	4.47	.292	4	.211	-6	3	-0.5
1968	Phi-N	2	2	.500	38	0	0	0	5	68^2	76	32	28	3	2	15	49	1.325	3.67	82	3.57	.279	1	.111	-4	3	-0.5
1969	Phi-N	1	2	.333	46	2	0	0	6	82	91	46	39	12	0	36	47	1.549	4.28	83	5.15	.283	3	.333	-7	3	-0.6
Total	**7**	**14**	**16**	**.467**	**171**	**22**	**3**	**0**	**15**	**394^1**	**414**	**203**	**179**	**42**	**6**	**139**	**282**	**1.402**	**4.09**	**83**	**4.25**	**.272**	**12**	**.162**	**-33**	**14**	**-3.5**
• BORBON, Pedro	Pedro (Rodriguez) Borbon b: 12/2/1946, Valverde de Mao, Dominican Republic BR/TR, 6'2", 185 lbs. Deb: 4/9/1969																										
1969	Cal-A	2	3	.400	22	0	0	0	0	41	55	31	28	5	4	11	20	1.610	6.15	57	6.02	.324	0	.000	-13	0	-1.4
1970	Cin-N	0	2	.000	12	1	0	0	0	17^1	21	15	13	2	3	6	6	1.558	6.75	62	5.91	.309	0	.000	-5	0	-0.5
1971	Cin-N	0	0	....	3	0	0	0	0	4^1	3	3	2	1	0	1	4	.923	4.15	78	2.74	.200	0	....	-1	0	-0.1
1972*	Cin-N	8	3	.727	62	2	0	0	11	122	115	45	43	5	3	32	48	1.205	3.17	101	2.84	.254	1	.048	-2	9	-0.3
1973*	Cin-N	11	4	.733	80	0	0	0	14	121	137	33	29	4	1	35	60	1.421	2.16	158	3.79	.298	5	.333	14	15	1.6
1974	Cin-N	10	7	.588	73	0	0	0	14	139	133	54	50	11	4	32	53	1.187	3.24	108	3.02	.255	5	.192	1	12	0.1
1975*	Cin-N	9	5	.643	67	0	0	0	5	125	145	47	41	6	3	21	29	1.328	2.95	122	3.78	.301	7	.292	5	10	0.7
1976*	Cin-N	4	3	.571	69	1	0	0	8	121	135	49	45	4	4	31	53	1.372	3.35	105	3.71	.292	4	.222	1	8	0.1
1977	Cin-N	10	5	.667	73	0	0	0	18	127	131	48	45	7	3	24	48	1.220	3.19	123	3.20	.268	4	.182	10	14	1.0
1978	Cin-N	8	2	.800	62	0	0	0	4	99^1	102	56	55	6	3	27	35	1.299	4.98	71	3.47	.274	2	.182	-14	4	-1.5
1979	Cin-N	2	2	.500	30	0	0	0	2	44^2	48	17	17	2	0	8	23	1.254	3.43	109	3.09	.277	2	.333	1	4	0.2
	SF-N	4	3	.571	30	0	0	0	3	46	56	28	25	7	0	13	26	1.500	4.89	71	5.14	.303	1	.333	-7	1	-0.7
	Yr.	6	5	.545	60	0	0	0	5	90^2	104	45	42	9	0	21	49	1.379	4.17	86	4.13	.291	3	.333	-5	5	-0.5
1980	StL-N	1	0	1.000	10	0	0	0	1	19	17	10	8	3	0	10	4	1.421	3.79	97	4.13	.250	1	.250	-0	1	0.0
Total	**12**	**69**	**39**	**.639**	**593**	**4**	**0**	**0**	**80**	**1026^2**	**1098**	**436**	**401**	**63**	**28**	**251**	**409**	**1.314**	**3.52**	**101**	**3.62**	**.280**	**32**	**.205**	**-9**	**78**	**-0.8**
• BORBON, Pedro	Pedro Felix (Marte) Borbon b: 11/15/1967, Valverde de Mao, Dominican Republic BR/TL, 6'1", 205 lbs. Deb: 10/2/1992																										
1992	Atl-N	0	1	.000	2	0	0	0	0	1^1	2	1	1	0	0	1	1	2.250	6.75	54	5.90	.333	0	....	-0	0	0.0
1993	Atl-N	0	0	....	3	0	0	0	0	1^2	3	4	4	0	0	3	2	3.600	21.60	19	14.26	.429	0	....	-3	0	-0.3
1995*	Atl-N	2	2	.500	41	0	0	0	2	32	29	12	11	2	1	17	33	1.438	3.09	138	3.61	.240	0	.000	5	4	0.4
1996	Atl-N	3	0	1.000	43	0	0	0	1	36	26	12	11	1	1	7	31	.917	2.75	160	1.64	.203	1	1.000	7	5	0.7
1999	LA-N	4	3	.571	70	0	0	0	1	50^2	39	23	23	5	1	29	33	1.342	4.09	105	3.45	.209	0	.000	1	4	0.1
2000	Tor-A	1	1	.500	59	0	0	0	1	41^2	45	37	30	5	5	38	29	1.992	6.48	78	6.91	.280	0	....	-7	0	-0.6
2001	Tor-A	2	4	.333	71	0	0	0	0	53^1	48	24	22	8	4	12	45	1.125	3.71	124	3.44	.244	0	....	5	4	0.5
2002	Tor-A	1	2	.333	16	0	0	0	0	12^2	12	8	7	3	1	6	11	1.421	4.97	93	4.61	.231	0	....	-0	0	0.0
	Hou-N	3	2	.600	56	0	0	0	1	37^2	41	24	23	7	2	19	39	1.593	5.50	77	5.63	.287	0	.000	-5	1	-0.5

YEAR TM-L	W	L	PCT	G	GS	CG	SH	SV	IP	H	R	ER	HR	HB	BB	SO	RAT	ERA	ERA+	CERA	OAV	BH	AVG	PR+	WS	TPW
2003 StL-N	0	1	.000	7	0	0	0	0	4	14	9	9	2	1	2	0	4.000	20.25	20	28.24	.560	0	....	-7	0	-0.7
Total 9	16	16	.500	368	0	0	0	6	271	259	154	141	33	16	134	224	1.450	4.68	95	4.56	.252	1	.143	-5	18	-0.5

• BORCHERS, George
George Bernard "Chief" Borchers b: 4/18/1869, Sacramento, CA d: 10/24/1938, Sacramento, CA BB/TR, 5'10", 180 lbs. Deb: 5/18/1888

YEAR TM-L	W	L	PCT	G	GS	CG	SH	SV	IP	H	R	ER	HR	HB	BB	SO	RAT	ERA	ERA+	CERA	OAV	BH	AVG	PR+	WS	TPW
1888 Chi-N	4	4	.500	10	10	7	1	0	67	67	45	26	2	6	29	26	1.433	3.49	86	....	.251	2	.061	-5	2	-0.9
1895 Lou-N	0	1	.000	1	1	0	0	0	0^2	1	2	2	0	0	3	0	6.000	27.00	17	22.90	.341	0	....	-2	0	-0.1
Total 2	4	5	.444	11	11	7	1	0	67^2	68	47	28	2	6	32	26	1.478	3.72	83	0.23	.252	2	.061	-7	2	-1.0

• BORDEN, Joe
Joseph Emley Borden b: 5/9/1854, Jacobstown, NJ d: 10/14/1929, Yeadon, PA BR/TR, 5'9", 140 lbs. Deb: 7/24/1875

YEAR TM-L	W	L	PCT	G	GS	CG	SH	SV	IP	H	R	ER	HR	HB	BB	SO	RAT	ERA	ERA+	CERA	OAV	BH	AVG	PR+	WS	TPW
1875 Phi-n	2	4	.333	7	7	7	2	0	66	47	....	11	0	....	7	7	.818	1.50	154	....	**.181**	3	.107	6	....	0.3
1876 Bos-N	11	12	.478	29	24	16	2	1	218^1	257	155	70	4	....	51	34	1.411	2.89	78	....	.260	25	.202	-15	10	-1.8

• BORDI, Rich
Richard Albert Bordi b: 4/18/1959, San Francisco, CA BR/TR, 6'7", 220 lbs. Deb: 7/16/1980

YEAR TM-L	W	L	PCT	G	GS	CG	SH	SV	IP	H	R	ER	HR	HB	BB	SO	RAT	ERA	ERA+	CERA	OAV	BH	AVG	PR+	WS	TPW
1980 Oak-A	0	0	....	1	0	0	0	0	2	4	1	1	0	0	0	0	2.000	4.50	84	7.48	.400	0	....	-0	0	0.0
1981 Oak-A	0	0	....	2	0	0	0	0	2	1	0	0	0	0	1	0	1.000	0.00	....	1.41	.143	0	....	1	0	0.1
1982 Sea-A	0	2	.000	7	2	0	0	0	13	18	12	12	4	1	1	10	1.462	8.31	51	6.59	.310	0	....	-6	0	-0.6
1983 Chi-N	0	2	.000	11	1	0	0	1	25^1	34	15	14	2	0	12	20	1.816	4.97	76	6.17	.321	0	.000	-3	0	-0.4
1984 Chi-N	5	2	.714	31	7	0	0	4	83^1	78	37	32	11	0	20	41	1.176	3.46	113	3.19	.242	1	.053	5	7	0.4
1985 NY-A	6	8	.429	51	3	0	0	2	98	95	41	35	5	1	29	64	1.265	3.21	125	3.12	.253	0	....	7	6	0.7
1986 Bal-A	6	4	.600	52	1	0	0	3	107	105	56	53	13	4	41	83	1.364	4.46	93	4.10	.254	0	....	-3	6	-0.3
1987 NY-A	3	1	.750	16	1	0	0	0	33	42	28	28	7	0	12	23	1.636	7.64	57	6.43	.309	0	....	-12	0	-1.2
1988 Oak-A	0	1	.000	2	2	0	0	0	7^2	6	6	4	0	0	5	6	1.435	4.70	81	3.05	.214	0	....	-1	0	-0.1
Total 9	20	20	.500	173	17	0	0	10	371^1	383	196	179	42	6	121	247	1.357	4.34	94	4.05	.263	1	.043	-12	19	-1.3

• BORDLEY, Bill
William Clarke Bordley b: 1/9/1958, Rolling Hills Estate, CA BR/TL, 6'3", 185 lbs. Deb: 6/30/1980

YEAR TM-L	W	L	PCT	G	GS	CG	SH	SV	IP	H	R	ER	HR	HB	BB	SO	RAT	ERA	ERA+	CERA	OAV	BH	AVG	PR+	WS	TPW
1980 SF-N	2	3	.400	8	6	0	0	0	30^2	34	19	16	3	0	21	11	1.793	4.70	75	5.91	.288	1	.167	-3	0	-0.3

• BORIS, Paul
Paul Stanley Boris b: 12/13/1955, Irvington, NJ BR/TR, 6'2", 200 lbs. Deb: 5/21/1982

YEAR TM-L	W	L	PCT	G	GS	CG	SH	SV	IP	H	R	ER	HR	HB	BB	SO	RAT	ERA	ERA+	CERA	OAV	BH	AVG	PR+	WS	TPW
1982 Min-A	1	2	.333	23	0	0	0	0	49^2	46	24	22	8	2	19	30	1.309	3.99	106	4.01	.246	0	....	1	3	0.1

• BORK, Frank
Frank Bernard Bork b: 7/13/1940, Buffalo, NY BR/TL, 6'2", 175 lbs. Deb: 4/15/1964

YEAR TM-L	W	L	PCT	G	GS	CG	SH	SV	IP	H	R	ER	HR	HB	BB	SO	RAT	ERA	ERA+	CERA	OAV	BH	AVG	PR+	WS	TPW
1964 Pit-N	2	2	.500	33	2	0	0	2	42	51	22	19	6	1	11	31	1.476	4.07	86	5.03	.295	1	.200	-2	2	-0.2

• BORKOWSKI, Dave
David Richard Borkowski b: 2/7/1977, Detroit, MI BR/TR, 6'1", 200 lbs. Deb: 7/17/1999

YEAR TM-L	W	L	PCT	G	GS	CG	SH	SV	IP	H	R	ER	HR	HB	BB	SO	RAT	ERA	ERA+	CERA	OAV	BH	AVG	PR+	WS	TPW
1999 Det-A	2	6	.250	17	12	0	0	0	76^2	86	58	52	10	4	40	50	1.643	6.10	81	5.75	.283	0	.000	-10	1	-0.9
2000 Det-A	0	1	.000	2	1	0	0	0	5^1	11	13	13	2	0	7	1	3.375	21.94	22	17.78	.423	0	....	-10	0	-0.9
2001 Det-A	0	2	.000	15	0	0	0	0	29^2	30	21	21	5	3	15	30	1.517	6.37	68	5.28	.261	0	....	-6	0	-0.6
Total 3	2	9	.182	34	13	0	0	0	111^2	127	92	86	17	7	62	81	1.693	6.93	69	6.20	.285	0	.000	-26	1	-2.5

• BORLAND, Toby
Toby Shawn Borland b: 5/29/1969, Ruston, LA BR/TR, 6'6", 186 lbs. Deb: 5/27/1994

YEAR TM-L	W	L	PCT	G	GS	CG	SH	SV	IP	H	R	ER	HR	HB	BB	SO	RAT	ERA	ERA+	CERA	OAV	BH	AVG	PR+	WS	TPW
1994 Phi-N	1	0	1.000	24	0	0	0	1	34^1	31	10	9	1	4	14	26	1.311	2.36	182	3.50	.248	0	.000	8	3	0.7
1995 Phi-N	1	3	.250	50	0	0	0	6	74	81	37	31	3	5	37	59	1.595	3.77	112	4.62	.277	1	.200	3	5	0.3
1996 Phi-N	7	3	.700	69	0	0	0	0	90^2	83	51	41	9	3	43	76	1.390	4.07	106	3.89	.239	0	.000	2	6	0.1
1997 NY-N	0	1	.000	13	0	0	0	1	13^1	11	9	9	1	1	14	7	1.875	6.08	67	5.68	.220	0	....	-3	0	-0.3
Bos-A	0	0	....	3	0	0	0	0	3^1	6	5	5	1	2	7	1	3.900	13.50	34	23.38	.400	0	....	-3	0	-0.3
1998 Phi-N	0	0	....	6	0	0	0	0	9	8	5	5	1	0	5	9	1.444	5.00	87	4.17	.242	0	....	-1	0	-0.1
2001 Ana-A	0	1	.000	2	0	0	0	0	3^1	8	5	4	1	0	1	0	2.700	10.80	42	14.71	.471	0	....	-2	0	-0.2
2002 Fla-N	1	0	1.000	15	0	0	0	0	13^2	14	8	8	3	3	5	11	1.390	5.27	75	5.85	.269	0	....	-2	1	-0.2
2003 Fla-N	0	0	....	7	0	0	0	0	9^2	3	3	2	0	0	8	4	1.138	1.86	220	1.40	.097	0	....	2	1	0.2
Total 8	10	8	.556	189	0	0	0	8	251^1	245	133	114	20	18	134	193	1.508	4.08	104	4.57	.254	1	.083	3	16	0.3

• BORLAND, Tom
Thomas Bruce "Spike" Borland b: 2/14/1933, El Dorado, KS BL/TL, 6'3", 172 lbs. Deb: 5/15/1960

YEAR TM-L	W	L	PCT	G	GS	CG	SH	SV	IP	H	R	ER	HR	HB	BB	SO	RAT	ERA	ERA+	CERA	OAV	BH	AVG	PR+	WS	TPW
1960 Bos-A	0	4	.000	26	4	0	0	3	51	67	40	37	4	0	23	32	1.765	6.53	62	5.85	.322	0	.000	-13	0	-1.5
1961 Bos-A	0	0	....	1	0	0	0	0	1	3	2	2	0	0	0	0	3.000	18.00	23	14.52	.500	0	....	-2	0	-0.2
Total 2	0	4	.000	27	4	0	0	3	52	70	42	39	4	0	23	32	1.788	6.75	60	6.02	.327	0	.000	-14	0	-1.6

• BOROWSKI, Joe
Joseph Thomas Borowski b: 5/4/1971, Bayonne, NJ BR/TR, 6'2", 225 lbs. Deb: 7/9/1995

YEAR TM-L	W	L	PCT	G	GS	CG	SH	SV	IP	H	R	ER	HR	HB	BB	SO	RAT	ERA	ERA+	CERA	OAV	BH	AVG	PR+	WS	TPW
1995 Bal-A	0	0	....	6	0	0	0	0	7^1	5	1	1	0	0	4	3	1.227	1.23	387	2.32	.192	0	....	3	1	0.3
1996 Atl-N	2	4	.333	22	0	0	0	0	26	33	15	14	4	1	13	15	1.769	4.85	91	6.46	.324	0	.000	-1	1	-0.1
1997 Atl-N	2	2	.500	20	0	0	0	0	24	27	11	10	2	0	16	6	1.792	3.75	112	5.51	.287	0	....	1	2	0.1
NY-A	0	1	.000	1	0	0	0	0	2	2	2	2	0	0	4	2	3.000	9.00	49	8.25	.250	0	....	-1	0	-0.1
1998 NY-A	1	0	1.000	8	0	0	0	0	9^2	11	7	7	0	0	4	7	1.552	6.52	67	4.27	.289	0	....	-2	0	-0.2
2001 Chi-N	0	1	.000	1	1	0	0	0	1^2	6	6	6	1	0	3	1	5.400	32.40	13	39.91	.667	0	....	-5	0	-0.5
2002 Chi-N	4	4	.500	73	0	0	0	2	95^2	84	31	29	10	1	29	97	1.181	2.73	147	3.05	.238	2	.286	14	8	1.5
2003* Chi-N	2	2	.500	68	0	0	0	33	68^1	53	23	20	5	1	19	66	1.054	2.63	160	2.26	.207	0	....	12	14	1.2
Total 7	11	14	.440	199	1	0	0	35	234^2	221	96	89	22	3	92	197	1.334	3.41	123	3.78	.249	2	.222	21	26	2.1

• BOROWY, Hank
Henry Ludwig Borowy b: 5/12/1916, Bloomfield, NJ BR/TR, 6', 175 lbs. Deb: 4/18/1942

YEAR TM-L	W	L	PCT	G	GS	CG	SH	SV	IP	H	R	ER	HR	HB	BB	SO	RAT	ERA	ERA+	CERA	OAV	BH	AVG	PR+	WS	TPW
1942* NY-A	15	4	.789	25	21	13	4	1	178^1	157	56	50	6	0	66	85	1.250	2.52	136	2.78	.233	11	.157	11	15	1.0
1943* NY-A	14	9	.609	29	27	14	3	0	217^1	195	75	68	11	2	72	113	1.229	2.82	114	2.92	.241	15	.203	6	15	0.9
1944 NY-A★	17	12	.586	35	30	19	3	2	252^2	224	93	74	15	0	88	107	1.235	2.64	132	2.94	.236	12	.133	19	20	1.7
1945 NY-A★	10	5	.667	18	18	7	1	0	132^1	107	61	46	6	1	58	35	1.247	3.13	111	2.75	.221	11	.220	2	8	0.3
*Chi-N	11	2	.846	15	14	11	1	1	122^1	105	33	29	2	0	47	47	1.243	**2.13**	171	2.63	.231	7	.171	19	14	1.9
1946 Chi-N	12	10	.545	32	28	8	1	0	201	220	96	84	9	1	61	95	1.398	3.76	88	3.70	.274	13	.181	-6	9	-0.6
1947 Chi-N	8	12	.400	40	25	7	1	2	183	190	99	89	19	1	63	75	1.383	4.38	90	4.05	.267	7	.125	-8	9	-0.9
1948 Chi-N	5	10	.333	39	17	2	1	1	127	156	80	69	9	0	49	50	1.614	4.89	80	5.09	.308	8	.222	-13	3	-1.1
1949 Phi-N	12	12	.500	28	28	12	1	0	193^1	188	99	90	19	0	63	43	1.298	4.19	94	3.64	.259	13	.213	-7	12	-0.4
1950 Phi-N	0	0	....	3	0	0	0	0	6^1	5	4	4	0	0	4	3	1.421	5.68	71	3.27	.250	0	....	-1	0	-0.1
Pit-N	1	3	.250	11	3	0	0	0	25^1	32	19	18	6	1	9	9	1.618	6.39	69	6.60	.311	1	.167	-6	0	-0.6
Yr.	1	3	.250	14	3	0	0	0	31^2	37	23	22	6	1	13	12	1.579	6.25	69	5.93	.301	1	.167	-7	0	-0.7
Det-A	1	1	.500	13	2	1	0	0	32^2	23	15	12	3	0	16	12	1.194	3.31	142	2.70	.205	1	.143	5	3	0.4
1951 Det-A	2	2	.500	26	1	0	0	0	45^1	58	39	35	3	1	27	16	1.875	6.95	60	6.10	.314	0	.000	-14	0	-1.5
Total 10	108	82	.568	314	214	94	16	7	1717	1660	769	668	108	7	623	690	1.330	3.50	105	3.46	.254	99	.173	7	108	1.1

• BOSIO, Chris
Christopher Louis Bosio b: 4/3/1963, Carmichael, CA BR/TR, 6'3", 225 lbs. Deb: 8/3/1986

YEAR TM-L	W	L	PCT	G	GS	CG	SH	SV	IP	H	R	ER	HR	HB	BB	SO	RAT	ERA	ERA+	CERA	OAV	BH	AVG	PR+	WS	TPW
1986 Mil-A	0	4	.000	10	4	0	0	0	34^2	41	27	27	9	0	13	29	1.558	7.01	62	6.27	.293	0	....	-10	0	-1.0
1987 Mil-A	11	8	.579	46	19	2	1	2	170	187	102	99	18	1	50	150	1.394	5.24	87	4.24	.276	0	....	-11	8	-1.1
1988 Mil-A	7	15	.318	38	22	9	1	6	182	190	80	68	13	2	38	84	1.253	3.36	118	3.35	.268	0	....	11	12	1.1
1989 Mil-A	15	10	.600	33	33	8	2	0	234^2	225	90	77	16	6	48	173	1.163	2.95	130	2.97	.249	0	....	22	17	2.2
1990 Mil-A	4	9	.308	20	20	4	1	0	132^2	131	67	59	15	3	38	76	1.274	4.00	97	3.74	.258	0	....	-0	5	0.0
1991 Mil-A	14	10	.583	32	32	5	1	0	204^2	187	80	74	15	8	58	117	1.197	3.25	122	3.18	.244	0	....	16	14	1.6
1992 Mil-A	16	6	.727	33	33	4	2	0	231^1	223	100	93	21	4	44	120	1.154	3.62	106	3.12	.254	0	....	1	13	0.1
1993 Sea-A	9	9	.500	29	24	3	1	1	164^1	138	75	63	14	6	59	119	1.199	3.45	128	3.10	.229	0	....	17	12	1.6
1994 Sea-A	4	10	.286	19	19	4	0	0	125	137	72	60	15	2	40	67	1.416	4.32	113	4.43	.277	0	....	9	7	0.9
1995* Sea-A	10	8	.556	31	31	0	0	0	170	211	98	93	18	5	69	85	**1.647**	4.92	96	5.73	.312	0	....	1	8	0.1
1996 Sea-A	4	4	.500	18	9	0	0	0	60^2	72	44	40	8	4	24	39	1.582	5.93	83	5.58	.299	0	....	-7	2	-0.6
Total 11	94	93	.503	309	246	39	9	9	1710	1742	835	753	162	41	481	1059	1.300	3.96	107	3.80	.264	0	....	48	98	4.9

• BOSKIE, Shawn
Shawn Kealoha Boskie b: 3/28/1967, Hawthorne, NV BR/TR, 6'3", 200 lbs. Deb: 5/20/1990

YEAR TM-L	W	L	PCT	G	GS	CG	SH	SV	IP	H	R	ER	HR	HB	BB	SO	RAT	ERA	ERA+	CERA	OAV	BH	AVG	PR+	WS	TPW
1990 Chi-N	5	6	.455	15	15	1	0	0	97^2	99	42	40	8	1	31	49	1.331	3.69	111	3.70	.265	8	.222	7	7	0.9
1991 Chi-N	4	9	.308	28	20	0	0	0	129	150	78	75	14	5	52	62	1.566	5.23	74	5.18	.294	7	.171	-17	2	-1.6

YEAR	TM-L	W	L	PCT	G	GS	CG	SH	SV	IP	H	R	ER	HR	HB	BB	SO	RAT	ERA	ERA+	CERA	OAV	BH	AVG	PR+	WS	TPW
1992	Chi-N	5	11	.313	23	18	0	0	0	91^{2}	96	55	51	14	4	36	39	1.440	5.01	72	4.95	.284	5	.185	-15	0	-1.5
1993	Chi-N	5	3	.625	39	2	0	0	0	65^{2}	63	30	25	7	7	21	39	1.279	3.43	116	4.03	.258	3	.273	3	5	0.4
1994	Chi-N	0	0	....	2	0	0	0	0	3^{2}	3	0	0	0	0	0	2	.818	0.00	....	1.32	.214	0	....	2	1	0.2
	Phi-N	4	6	.400	18	14	1	0	0	84^{1}	85	56	49	14	3	29	59	1.352	5.23	82	4.41	.258	3	.115	-8	1	-0.7
	Yr.	4	6	.400	20	14	1	0	0	88	88	56	49	14	3	29	61	1.330	5.01	86	4.28	.256	3	.115	-6	2	-0.6
	Sea-A	0	1	.000	2	1	0	0	0	2^{2}	4	2	2	1	0	1	0	1.875	6.75	72	8.41	.333	0	....	-1	0	0.0
1995	Cal-A	7	7	.500	20	20	1	0	0	111^{2}	127	73	70	16	7	25	51	1.361	5.64	83	4.60	.281	0	....	-13	4	-1.2
1996	Cal-A	12	11	.522	37	28	1	0	0	189^{1}	226	126	112	40	13	67	133	1.548	5.32	92	6.05	.294	0	....	-9	8	-0.8
1997	Bal-A	6	6	.500	28	9	0	0	1	77	95	57	55	14	2	26	50	1.571	6.43	69	5.84	.304	0	....	-18	1	-1.7
1998	Mon-N	1	3	.250	5	5	0	0	0	17^{2}	34	21	18	5	2	4	10	2.151	9.17	46	11.44	.415	0	.000	-9	0	-0.9
Total	**9**	**49**	**63**	**.438**	**217**	**132**	**4**	**0**	**1**	**870^{1}**	**982**	**540**	**497**	**133**	**44**	**292**	**494**	**1.464**	**5.14**	**83**	**5.12**	**.286**	**26**	**.179**	**-77**	**29**	**-7.0**

• BOSMAN, Dick Richard Allen Bosman b: 2/17/1944, Kenosha, WI BR/TR, 6'2", 208 lbs. Deb: 6/1/1966 C

YEAR	TM-L	W	L	PCT	G	GS	CG	SH	SV	IP	H	R	ER	HR	HB	BB	SO	RAT	ERA	ERA+	CERA	OAV	BH	AVG	PR+	WS	TPW
1966	Was-A	2	6	.250	13	7	0	0	0	39	60	36	33	4	0	12	20	1.846	7.62	45	6.78	.361	3	.250	-18	0	-1.9
1967	Was-A	3	1	.750	7	7	2	1	0	51^{1}	38	12	10	3	0	10	25	.935	1.75	180	1.75	.204	3	.200	8	6	0.9
1968	Was-A	2	9	.182	46	10	0	0	1	139	139	63	57	9	4	35	63	1.252	3.69	79	3.33	.262	6	.200	-10	4	-1.0
1969	Was-A	14	5	.737	31	26	5	2	1	193	156	59	47	11	2	39	99	1.010	**2.19**	**158**	2.14	.220	6	.094	26	17	2.6
1970	Was-A	16	12	.571	36	34	7	3	0	230^{2}	212	81	77	16	2	71	134	1.227	3.00	118	3.09	.245	11	.138	11	16	0.9
1971	Was-A	12	16	.429	35	35	7	1	0	236^{2}	245	110	98	29	5	71	113	1.335	3.73	89	4.14	.272	7	.093	-12	9	-1.4
1972	Tex-A	8	10	.444	29	29	1	1	0	173^{1}	183	87	70	11	6	48	105	1.333	3.63	83	3.75	.273	5	.094	-9	4	-1.2
1973	Tex-A	2	5	.286	7	7	1	1	0	40^{1}	42	24	19	6	1	17	14	1.463	4.24	88	4.85	.268	0	....	-1	1	-0.1
	Cle-A	1	8	.111	22	17	2	0	0	97	130	74	67	19	6	29	41	1.639	6.22	63	6.59	.320	0	....	-24	0	-2.5
	Yr.	3	13	.188	29	24	3	1	0	137^{1}	172	98	86	25	7	46	55	1.587	5.64	69	6.08	.306	0	....	-26	1	-2.6
1974	Cle-A	7	5	.583	25	18	2	1	0	127^{1}	126	69	58	13	1	29	56	1.217	4.10	88	3.35	.255	0	....	-7	5	-0.8
1975	Cle-A	0	2	.000	6	3	0	0	0	28^{2}	33	17	13	3	3	8	11	1.430	4.08	93	4.86	.292	0	....	-1	1	-0.1
	* Oak-A	11	4	.733	22	21	2	0	0	122^{2}	112	50	48	12	3	24	42	1.109	3.52	103	2.86	.240	0	....	1	7	0.1
	Yr.	11	6	.647	28	24	2	0	0	151^{1}	145	67	61	15	6	32	53	1.170	3.63	101	3.24	.250	0	....	-0	8	0.0
1976	Oak-A	4	2	.667	27	15	0	0	0	112	118	54	51	13	1	19	34	1.223	4.10	82	3.65	.274	0	....	-7	4	-0.8
Total	**11**	**82**	**85**	**.491**	**306**	**229**	**29**	**10**	**2**	**1591**	**1594**	**736**	**648**	**149**	**34**	**412**	**757**	**1.261**	**3.67**	**93**	**3.60**	**.261**	**41**	**.125**	**-45**	**74**	**-5.3**

• BOSSER, Mel Melvin Edward Bosser b: 2/8/1914, Johnstown, PA d: 3/26/1986, Crossville, TN BR/TR, 6', 173 lbs. Deb: 4/29/1945

YEAR	TM-L	W	L	PCT	G	GS	CG	SH	SV	IP	H	R	ER	HR	HB	BB	SO	RAT	ERA	ERA+	CERA	OAV	BH	AVG	PR+	WS	TPW
1945	Cin-N	2	0	1.000	7	2	0	0	0	16	9	6	6	0	0	17	3	1.625	3.38	111	3.02	.158	0	.000	1	2	0.0

• BOSWELL, Andy Andrew Cottrell Boswell b: 9/5/1874, New Gretna, NJ d: 2/3/1936, Ocean City, NJ TR, 6'1", 165 lbs. Deb: 5/10/1895

YEAR	TM-L	W	L	PCT	G	GS	CG	SH	SV	IP	H	R	ER	HR	HB	BB	SO	RAT	ERA	ERA+	CERA	OAV	BH	AVG	PR+	WS	TPW
1895	NY-N	2	2	.500	5	4	3	0	0	34	41	35	22	1	0	22	18	1.853	5.82	80	5.52	.294	3	.188	-5	1	-0.5
	Was-N	1	2	.333	6	3	3	0	0	30	44	32	20	1	0	19	12	2.100	6.00	80	7.12	.336	4	.286	-3	1	-0.3
	Yr.	3	4	.429	11	7	6	0	0	64	85	67	42	2	0	41	30	1.969	5.91	80	6.27	.314	7	.233	-8	2	-0.8

• BOSWELL, Dave David Wilson Boswell b: 1/20/1945, Baltimore, MD BR/TR, 6'3", 185 lbs. Deb: 9/18/1964

YEAR	TM-L	W	L	PCT	G	GS	CG	SH	SV	IP	H	R	ER	HR	HB	BB	SO	RAT	ERA	ERA+	CERA	OAV	BH	AVG	PR+	WS	TPW
1964	Min-A	2	0	1.000	4	4	0	0	0	23^{1}	21	11	11	4	0	12	25	1.414	4.24	84	4.40	.236	2	.222	-1	1	-0.1
1965*	Min-A	6	5	.545	27	12	1	0	0	106	77	43	40	20	5	46	85	1.160	3.40	105	3.52	.204	12	.316	1	7	0.4
1966	Min-A	12	5	.706	28	21	8	1	0	169^{1}	120	66	59	19	5	65	173	1.093	3.14	115	2.63	.197	9	.143	10	12	0.9
1967	Min-A	14	12	.538	37	32	11	3	0	222^{2}	162	84	81	14	7	107	204	1.208	3.27	106	2.78	.202	16	.219	8	15	1.3
1968	Min-A	10	13	.435	34	28	7	2	0	190	148	79	70	19	7	87	143	1.237	3.32	93	3.22	.213	14	.233	-2	10	0.3
1969*	Min-A	20	12	.625	39	38	10	0	0	256^{1}	215	105	92	18	8	99	190	1.225	3.23	113	3.06	.226	16	.170	9	16	1.2
1970	Min-A	3	7	.300	18	15	0	0	0	68^{2}	80	55	49	12	2	44	45	1.806	6.42	58	6.69	.292	4	.160	-21	0	-2.2
1971	Det-A	0	0	....	3	0	0	0	0	4^{1}	3	3	3	0	0	6	3	2.077	6.23	58	5.14	.200	0	....	-1	0	-0.1
	Bal-A	1	2	.333	15	1	0	0	0	24^{2}	32	16	12	4	0	15	14	1.905	4.38	76	7.00	.305	1	.200	-3	0	-0.3
	Yr.	1	2	.333	18	1	0	0	0	29	35	19	15	4	0	21	17	1.931	4.66	73	6.72	.292	1	.200	-4	0	-0.4
Total	**8**	**68**	**56**	**.548**	**205**	**151**	**37**	**6**	**0**	**1065^{1}**	**858**	**462**	**417**	**110**	**34**	**481**	**882**	**1.257**	**3.52**	**99**	**3.37**	**.219**	**74**	**.202**	**-2**	**61**	**1.3**

• BOTELHO, Derek Derek Wayne Botelho b: 8/2/1956, Long Beach, CA BR/TR, 6'2", 180 lbs. Deb: 7/18/1982

YEAR	TM-L	W	L	PCT	G	GS	CG	SH	SV	IP	H	R	ER	HR	HB	BB	SO	RAT	ERA	ERA+	CERA	OAV	BH	AVG	PR+	WS	TPW
1982	KC-A	2	1	.667	8	4	0	0	0	24	25	11	11	4	0	8	12	1.375	4.13	99	4.66	.275	0	....	-0	1	0.0
1985	Chi-N	1	3	.250	11	7	1	0	0	44	52	27	26	8	2	23	23	1.705	5.32	75	6.51	.299	2	.143	-6	1	-0.6
Total	**2**	**3**	**4**	**.429**	**19**	**11**	**1**	**0**	**0**	**68**	**77**	**38**	**37**	**12**	**2**	**31**	**35**	**1.588**	**4.90**	**82**	**5.85**	**.291**	**2**	**.143**	**-6**	**2**	**-0.6**

• BOTTALICO, Ricky Ricky Paul Bottalico b: 8/26/1969, New Britain, CT BL/TR, 6'1", 200 lbs. Deb: 7/29/1994

YEAR	TM-L	W	L	PCT	G	GS	CG	SH	SV	IP	H	R	ER	HR	HB	BB	SO	RAT	ERA	ERA+	CERA	OAV	BH	AVG	PR+	WS	TPW
1994	Phi-N	0	0	....	3	0	0	0	0	3	3	0	0	0	0	1	3	1.333	0.00	....	3.05	.250	0	....	1	0	0.1
1995	Phi-N	5	3	.625	62	0	0	0	1	87^{2}	50	25	24	7	4	42	87	1.049	2.46	172	2.17	.167	0	.000	16	11	1.6
1996	Phi-N★	4	5	.444	61	0	0	0	34	67^{2}	47	24	24	6	2	23	74	1.034	3.19	135	2.29	.197	1	.333	8	13	0.8
1997	Phi-N	2	5	.286	69	0	0	0	34	74	68	31	30	7	2	42	89	1.486	3.65	116	4.29	.245	0	.000	5	10	0.5
1998	Phi-N	1	5	.167	39	0	0	0	6	43^{1}	54	31	31	7	1	25	27	1.823	6.44	67	6.63	.305	0	....	-10	0	-1.0
1999	StL-N	3	7	.300	68	0	0	0	20	73^{1}	83	45	40	8	3	49	66	1.800	4.91	93	6.16	.284	0	.000	-3	4	-0.3
2000	KC-A	9	6	.600	62	0	0	0	16	72^{2}	65	40	39	12	2	41	56	1.459	4.83	106	4.65	.239	0	....	1	8	0.1
2001	Phi-N	3	4	.429	66	0	0	0	3	67	58	31	29	11	4	25	57	1.239	3.90	109	3.88	.241	1	.333	2	6	0.2
2002	Phi-N	0	3	.000	30	0	0	0	0	27^{1}	33	16	14	3	2	13	24	1.683	4.61	85	5.80	.300	0	....	-2	0	-0.2
2003	Ari-N	1	0	1.000	2	0	0	0	0	1^{2}	3	1	1	0	0	2	2	3.000	5.40	86	10.00	.375	0	....	-0	0	0.0
Total	**10**	**28**	**38**	**.424**	**462**	**0**	**0**	**0**	**114**	**517^{2}**	**464**	**244**	**232**	**61**	**20**	**263**	**485**	**1.404**	**4.03**	**110**	**4.22**	**.241**	**2**	**.133**	**18**	**52**	**1.8**

• BOTTENFIELD, Kent Kent Dennis Bottenfield b: 11/14/1968, Portland, OR BR/TR, 6'3", 237 lbs. Deb: 7/6/1992

YEAR	TM-L	W	L	PCT	G	GS	CG	SH	SV	IP	H	R	ER	HR	HB	BB	SO	RAT	ERA	ERA+	CERA	OAV	BH	AVG	PR+	WS	TPW
1992	Mon-N	1	2	.333	10	4	0	0	1	32^{1}	26	9	8	1	1	11	14	1.144	2.23	156	2.39	.217	3	.375	4	3	0.6
1993	Mon-N	2	5	.286	23	11	0	0	0	83	93	49	38	11	5	33	33	1.518	4.12	101	5.19	.288	4	.167	0	2	0.0
	Col-N	3	5	.375	14	14	1	0	0	76^{2}	86	53	52	13	1	38	30	1.617	6.10	78	5.93	.302	7	.269	-9	3	-0.8
	Yr.	5	10	.333	37	25	1	0	0	159^{2}	179	102	90	24	6	71	63	1.566	5.07	89	5.54	.294	11	.220	-9	5	-0.7
1994	Col-N	3	1	.750	15	1	0	0	1	24^{2}	28	16	16	1	2	10	15	1.541	5.84	85	4.71	.283	0	.000	-2	2	-0.2
	SF-N	0	0	....	1	0	0	0	0	1^{2}	5	2	2	1	0	0	0	3.000	10.80	37	23.52	.556	0	....	-1	0	-0.1
	Yr.	3	1	.750	16	1	0	0	1	26^{1}	33	18	18	2	2	10	15	1.633	6.15	79	5.90	.306	0	.000	-3	2	-0.3
1996	Chi-N	3	5	.375	48	0	0	0	1	61^{2}	59	25	18	3	3	19	33	1.265	2.63	165	3.26	.255	1	.500	11	6	1.1
1997	Chi-N	2	3	.400	64	0	0	0	2	84	82	39	36	13	2	35	74	1.393	3.86	112	4.39	.259	0	.000	4	6	0.4
1998	StL-N	4	6	.400	44	17	0	0	4	133^{2}	128	72	66	13	4	57	98	1.384	4.44	94	4.00	.254	3	.088	-3	6	-0.5
1999	StL-N★	18	7	.720	31	31	0	0	0	190^{1}	197	91	84	21	5	89	124	1.503	3.97	115	4.68	.270	9	.148	13	14	1.2
2000	Ana-A	7	8	.467	21	21	0	0	0	127^{2}	144	82	81	25	3	56	75	1.567	5.71	89	5.77	.285	2	.667	-12	5	-1.0
	Phi-N	1	2	.333	8	8	1	1	0	44	41	24	22	5	0	21	31	1.409	4.50	104	4.00	.240	0	.000	1	2	-0.1
2001	Hou-N	2	5	.286	13	9	0	0	1	52	61	44	37	16	2	16	39	1.481	6.40	71	6.27	.288	2	.143	-11	0	-1.1
Total	**9**	**46**	**49**	**.484**	**292**	**116**	**2**	**1**	**10**	**911^{2}**	**950**	**506**	**460**	**123**	**28**	**385**	**566**	**1.464**	**4.54**	**100**	**4.77**	**.271**	**31**	**.162**	**-4**	**49**	**-0.5**

• BOTTING, Ralph Ralph Wayne Botting b: 5/12/1955, Houlton, ME BL/TL, 6', 195 lbs. Deb: 6/28/1979

YEAR	TM-L	W	L	PCT	G	GS	CG	SH	SV	IP	H	R	ER	HR	HB	BB	SO	RAT	ERA	ERA+	CERA	OAV	BH	AVG	PR+	WS	TPW
1979	Cal-A	2	0	1.000	12	1	0	0	0	29^{2}	46	30	29	6	1	15	22	2.056	8.80	46	9.03	.362	0	....	-15	0	-1.5
1980	Cal-A	0	3	.000	6	6	0	0	0	26^{1}	40	20	17	1	0	13	12	2.013	5.81	68	7.02	.348	0	....	-5	0	-0.5
Total	**2**	**2**	**3**	**.400**	**18**	**7**	**0**	**0**	**0**	**56**	**86**	**50**	**46**	**7**	**1**	**28**	**34**	**2.036**	**7.39**	**54**	**8.08**	**.355**	**0**	**....**	**-21**	**0**	**-2.0**

• BOTZ, Bob Robert Allen Botz b: 4/28/1935, Milwaukee, WI BR/TR, 5'11", 170 lbs. Deb: 5/8/1962

YEAR	TM-L	W	L	PCT	G	GS	CG	SH	SV	IP	H	R	ER	HR	HB	BB	SO	RAT	ERA	ERA+	CERA	OAV	BH	AVG	PR+	WS	TPW
1962	LA-A	2	1	.667	35	0	0	0	2	63	71	30	24	7	2	11	24	1.302	3.43	112	4.08	.285	0	.000	4	4	0.2

• BOUCHER, Denis Denis Boucher b: 3/7/1968, Montreal, Canada BR/TL, 6'1", 195 lbs. Deb: 4/12/1991

YEAR	TM-L	W	L	PCT	G	GS	CG	SH	SV	IP	H	R	ER	HR	HB	BB	SO	RAT	ERA	ERA+	CERA	OAV	BH	AVG	PR+	WS	TPW
1991	Tor-A	0	3	.000	7	7	0	0	0	35^{1}	39	20	18	6	2	16	16	1.557	4.58	92	5.51	.279	0	....	-1	1	-0.1
	Cle-A	1	4	.200	5	5	0	0	0	22^{2}	35	21	21	6	0	8	13	1.897	8.34	50	8.65	.350	0	....	-10	0	-1.0
	Yr.	1	7	.125	12	12	0	0	0	58	74	41	39	12	2	24	29	1.690	6.05	69	6.74	.308	0	....	-12	1	-1.2
1992	Cle-A	2	2	.500	8	7	0	0	0	41	48	29	29	9	1	20	17	1.659	6.37	61	6.63	.302	0	....	-11	0	-1.1
1993	Mon-N	3	1	.750	5	5	0	0	0	28^{1}	24	7	6	1	0	3	14	.953	1.91	219	1.79	.229	1	.167	7	3	0.7

YEAR	TM-L	W	L	PCT	G	GS	CG	SH	SV	IP	H	R	ER	HR	HB	BB	SO	RAT	ERA	ERA+	CERA	OAV	BH	AVG	PR+	WS	TPW
1994	Mon-N	0	1	.000	10	2	0	0	0	18^{2}	24	16	14	6	0	7	17	1.661	6.75	63	7.52	.324	1	.333	-5	0	-0.5
Total	**4**	**6**	**11**	**.353**	**35**	**26**	**0**	**0**	**0**	**146**	**170**	**93**	**88**	**28**	**3**	**54**	**77**	**1.534**	**5.42**	**75**	**5.85**	**.294**	**2**	**.222**	**-21**	**4**	**-2.0**
• BOULDIN, Carl	Carl Edward Bouldin b: 9/17/1939, Germantown, KY BB/TR, 6'2", 180 lbs. Deb: 9/2/1961																										
1961	Was-A	0	1	.000	2	1	0	0	0	3^{1}	9	6	6	0	0	2	2	3.300	16.20	24	16.03	.500	0	.000	-5	0	-0.5
1962	Was-A	1	2	.333	6	3	1	0	0	20	26	13	13	0	1	9	12	1.750	5.85	69	5.47	.321	0	.000	-4	0	-0.5
1963	Was-A	2	2	.500	10	3	0	0	0	23^{1}	31	18	15	3	0	8	10	1.671	5.79	64	5.66	.307	0	.000	-5	0	-0.6
1964	Was-A	0	3	.000	9	3	0	0	0	25	30	20	15	2	2	11	12	1.640	5.40	69	5.28	.294	0	.000	-5	0	-0.6
Total	**4**	**3**	**8**	**.273**	**27**	**10**	**1**	**0**	**0**	**71^{2}**	**96**	**57**	**49**	**5**	**3**	**30**	**36**	**1.758**	**6.15**	**62**	**5.96**	**.318**	**0**	**.000**	**-19**	**0**	**-2.2**
• BOULTES, Jake	Jacob John Boultes b: 8/6/1884, St. Louis, MO d: 12/24/1955, St. Louis, MO BR/TR, 6'3" Deb: 4/18/1907																										
1907	Bos-N	5	9	.357	24	12	11	0	0	139^{2}	140	74	42	1	8	50	49	1.360	2.71	94	3.66	.266	9	.132	-4	4	-0.7
1908	Bos-N	3	5	.375	17	5	1	0	0	74^{2}	80	40	25	7	1	8	28	1.179	3.01	79	2.40	.274	3	.143	-7	2	-0.8
1909	Bos-N	0	0	....	1	0	0	0	0	8	9	7	6	2	1	0	1	1.125	6.75	42	4.86	.290	1	.333	-4	0	-0.3
Total	**3**	**8**	**14**	**.364**	**42**	**17**	**12**	**0**	**0**	**222^{1}**	**229**	**121**	**73**	**10**	**10**	**58**	**78**	**1.291**	**2.96**	**85**	**3.28**	**.270**	**13**	**.141**	**-14**	**6**	**-1.9**
• BOURGEOIS, Steve	Steven James Bourgeois b: 8/4/1972, Lutcher, LA BR/TR, 6'1", 220 lbs. Deb: 4/3/1996																										
1996	SF-N	1	3	.250	15	5	0	0	0	40	60	35	28	4	4	21	17	2.025	6.30	65	7.99	.355	3	.273	-10	0	-0.8
• BOUTON, Jim	James Alan "Bulldog" Bouton b: 3/8/1939, Newark, NJ BR/TR, 6', 185 lbs. Deb: 4/22/1962																										
1962	NY-A	7	7	.500	36	16	3	1	2	133	124	63	59	9	0	59	71	1.376	3.99	94	3.71	.254	2	.063	-5	6	-0.7
1963*	NY-A★	21	7	.750	40	30	12	6	1	249^{1}	191	79	70	18	3	87	148	1.115	2.53	139	2.54	.212	6	.072	23	22	1.8
1964*	NY-A	18	13	.581	38	**37**	11	4	0	271^{1}	227	100	91	32	6	60	125	1.058	3.02	120	2.72	.225	13	.130	16	18	1.4
1965	NY-A	4	15	.211	30	25	2	0	0	151^{1}	158	89	81	23	5	60	97	1.441	4.82	71	4.79	.269	4	.093	-23	0	-2.5
1966	NY-A	3	8	.273	24	19	3	0	1	120^{1}	117	49	36	13	1	38	65	1.288	2.69	123	3.61	.257	4	.105	9	6	0.8
1967	NY-A	1	0	1.000	17	1	0	0	0	44^{1}	47	31	23	5	1	18	31	1.466	4.67	67	4.43	.275	0	.000	-7	0	-0.8
1968	NY-A	1	1	.500	12	3	1	0	0	44	49	20	18	5	2	9	24	1.318	3.68	79	4.24	.287	0	.000	-3	1	-0.4
1969	Sea-A	2	1	.667	57	1	0	0	1	92	77	48	40	12	2	38	68	1.250	3.91	93	3.37	.219	0	.000	-0	4	-0.1
	Hou-N	0	2	.000	16	1	1	0	1	30^{2}	32	16	14	1	2	12	32	1.435	4.11	86	3.99	.267	0	.000	-2	1	-0.2
1970	Hou-N	4	6	.400	29	6	1	0	0	73^{1}	84	53	44	5	1	33	49	1.595	5.40	72	4.76	.285	6	.353	-12	1	-1.0
1978	Atl-N	1	3	.250	5	5	0	0	0	29	25	18	16	4	0	21	10	1.586	4.97	81	4.85	.234	0	.000	-3	1	-0.3
Total	**10**	**62**	**63**	**.496**	**304**	**144**	**34**	**11**	**6**	**1238^{2}**	**1131**	**566**	**492**	**127**	**23**	**435**	**720**	**1.264**	**3.57**	**99**	**3.49**	**.243**	**35**	**.101**	**-7**	**60**	**-2.1**
• BOVEE, Mike	Michael Craig Bovee b: 8/21/1973, San Diego, CA BR/TR, 5'10", 200 lbs. Deb: 9/13/1997																										
1997	Ana-A	0	0	....	3	0	0	0	0	3^{1}	3	2	2	1	0	1	5	1.200	5.40	85	4.34	.231	0	....	-0	0	0.0
• BOWEN, Cy	Sutherland McCoy Bowen b: 2/17/1871, Kingston, IN d: 1/25/1925, Greensburg, IN BR/TR, 6', 175 lbs. Deb: 4/28/1896																										
1896	NY-N	0	1	.000	2	1	1	0	0	12	12	13	8	0	0	9	3	1.750	6.00	70	4.45	.259	1	.333	-2	0	-0.2
• BOWEN, Ryan	Ryan Eugene Bowen b: 2/10/1968, Hanford, CA BR/TR, 6', 185 lbs. Deb: 7/22/1991																										
1991	Hou-N	6	4	.600	14	13	0	0	0	71^{2}	73	43	41	4	3	36	49	1.521	5.15	68	4.40	.268	4	.182	-13	1	-1.2
1992	Hou-N	0	7	.000	11	9	0	0	0	33^{2}	48	43	41	8	2	30	22	2.317	10.96	31	10.12	.333	1	.111	-28	0	-3.1
1993	Fla-N	8	12	.400	27	27	2	1	0	156^{2}	156	83	77	11	3	87	98	1.551	4.42	98	4.49	.263	6	.118	1	6	0.0
1994	Fla-N	1	5	.167	8	8	1	0	0	47^{1}	50	28	26	9	2	19	32	1.458	4.94	88	5.26	.273	5	.357	-4	2	-0.1
1995	Fla-N	2	0	1.000	4	3	0	0	0	16^{2}	23	11	7	3	0	12	15	2.100	3.78	111	8.03	.329	2	.333	1	1	0.1
Total	**5**	**17**	**28**	**.378**	**64**	**60**	**3**	**1**	**0**	**326**	**350**	**208**	**192**	**35**	**10**	**184**	**216**	**1.638**	**5.30**	**73**	**5.34**	**.277**	**18**	**.176**	**-43**	**10**	**-4.4**
• BOWERS, Shane	Shane Patrick Bowers b: 7/27/1971, Glendora, CA BR/TR, 6'4", 215 lbs. Deb: 7/26/1997																										
1997	Min-A	0	3	.000	5	5	0	0	0	19	27	20	17	2	1	8	7	1.842	8.05	58	6.87	.329	0	....	-7	0	-0.7
• BOWERS, Stew	Stewart Cole "Doc" Bowers b: 2/26/1915, New Freedom, PA BB/TR, 6', 170 lbs. Deb: 8/5/1935																										
1935	Bos-A	2	1	.667	10	2	1	0	0	23^{2}	26	14	9	1	0	17	5	1.817	3.42	139	5.11	.283	1	.200	3	2	0.3
1936	Bos-A	0	0	....	5	0	0	0	0	5^{2}	10	7	6	1	0	2	0	2.118	9.53	56	9.01	.370	0	....	-3	0	-0.2
Total	**2**	**2**	**1**	**.667**	**15**	**2**	**1**	**0**	**0**	**29^{1}**	**36**	**21**	**15**	**2**	**0**	**19**	**5**	**1.875**	**4.60**	**108**	**5.87**	**.303**	**1**	**.200**	**1**	**2**	**0.1**
• BOWIE, Micah	Micah Andrew Bowie b: 11/10/1974, Humble, TX BL/TL, 6'4", 210 lbs. Deb: 7/24/1999																										
1999	Atl-N	0	1	.000	3	0	0	0	0	4	8	6	6	1	0	4	2	3.000	13.50	33	15.43	.421	0	....	-4	0	-0.4
	Chi-N	2	6	.250	11	11	0	0	0	47	73	54	52	8	2	30	39	2.191	9.96	45	9.23	.358	3	.214	-28	0	-2.6
	Yr.	2	7	.222	14	11	0	0	0	51	81	60	58	9	2	34	41	2.255	10.24	44	9.72	.363	3	.214	-32	0	-3.0
2002*	Oak-A	2	0	1.000	13	0	0	0	0	12	12	2	2	1	1	8	8	1.667	1.50	293	5.26	.261	0	....	4	2	0.4
2003	Oak-A	0	1	.000	6	0	0	0	0	8^{1}	13	7	7	1	0	2	4	1.800	7.56	60	7.15	.361	0	....	-3	0	-0.3
Total	**3**	**4**	**8**	**.333**	**33**	**11**	**0**	**0**	**0**	**71^{1}**	**106**	**69**	**67**	**11**	**3**	**44**	**53**	**2.103**	**8.45**	**53**	**8.67**	**.348**	**3**	**.214**	**-31**	**2**	**-2.8**
• BOWLER, Grant	Grant Tierney "Moose" Bowler b: 10/24/1907, Denver, CO d: 6/25/1968, Denver, CO BR/TR, 6', 190 lbs. Deb: 8/21/1931																										
1931	Chi-A	0	1	.000	13	3	1	0	0	35^{1}	40	26	21	1	0	24	15	1.811	5.35	80	5.22	.288	1	.100	-4	1	-0.4
1932	Chi-A	0	0	....	4	0	0	0	0	6^{1}	15	12	11	1	0	3	2	2.842	15.63	28	14.51	.484	0	.000	-8	0	-0.8
Total	**2**	**0**	**1**	**.000**	**17**	**3**	**1**	**0**	**0**	**41^{2}**	**55**	**38**	**32**	**2**	**0**	**27**	**17**	**1.968**	**6.91**	**62**	**6.63**	**.324**	**1**	**.083**	**-12**	**1**	**-1.1**
• BOWLES, Brian	Brian Christopher Bowles b: 8/18/1976, Harbor City, CA BR/TR, 6'5", 220 lbs. Deb: 6/27/2001																										
2001	Tor-A	0	0	....	2	0	0	0	0	3^{2}	4	0	0	0	0	1	4	1.364	0.00	....	3.55	.286	0	....	2	1	0.2
2002	Tor-A	2	1	.667	17	0	0	0	0	20	13	11	9	0	3	14	19	1.350	4.05	114	3.00	.183	0	....	1	1	0.1
2003	Tor-A	0	0	....	5	0	0	0	0	7	8	4	2	1	2	2	2	1.429	2.57	179	5.62	.267	0	....	2	0	0.2
Total	**3**	**2**	**1**	**.667**	**24**	**0**	**0**	**0**	**0**	**30^{2}**	**25**	**15**	**11**	**1**	**5**	**17**	**25**	**1.370**	**3.23**	**143**	**3.67**	**.217**	**0**	**....**	**5**	**2**	**0.5**
• BOWLES, Charlie	Charles James Bowles b: 3/15/1917, Norwood, MA BR/TR, 6'3", 180 lbs. Deb: 9/25/1943																										
1943	Phi-A	1	1	.500	2	2	2	0	0	18	17	10	6	0	0	4	6	1.167	3.00	113	2.49	.258	1	.125	1	1	0.1
1945	Phi-A	0	3	.000	8	4	1	0	0	33^{1}	35	19	19	3	0	23	11	1.740	5.13	67	5.27	.273	5	.238	-6	0	-0.6
Total	**2**	**1**	**4**	**.200**	**10**	**6**	**3**	**0**	**0**	**51^{1}**	**52**	**29**	**25**	**3**	**0**	**27**	**17**	**1.539**	**4.38**	**78**	**4.29**	**.268**	**6**	**.207**	**-5**	**1**	**-0.6**
• BOWLES, Emmett	Emmett Jerome "Chief" Bowles b: 8/2/1898, Wanette, OK d: 9/3/1959, Flagstaff, AZ BR/TR, 6', 180 lbs. Deb: 9/12/1922																										
1922	Chi-A	0	0	....	1	0	0	0	0	1	2	3	3	0	0	1	0	3.000	27.00	15	11.63	.500	0	....	-3	0	-0.2
• BOWMAN, Abe	Alvah Edson Bowman b: 1/25/1893, Greenup, IL d: 10/11/1979, Longview, TX BR/TR, 6'1", 190 lbs. Deb: 5/19/1914																										
1914	Cle-A	2	7	.222	22	10	2	1	0	72^{2}	74	45	36	0	4	45	27	1.638	4.46	65	4.55	.277	1	.048	-12	1	-1.5
1915	Cle-A	0	1	.000	2	1	0	0	0	1^{1}	1	4	3	0	0	3	0	3.000	20.25	15	9.24	.250	0	....	-3	0	-0.3
Total	**2**	**2**	**8**	**.200**	**24**	**11**	**2**	**1**	**0**	**74**	**75**	**49**	**39**	**0**	**4**	**48**	**27**	**1.662**	**4.74**	**61**	**4.63**	**.277**	**1**	**.048**	**-14**	**1**	**-1.8**
• BOWMAN, Bob	Robert James Bowman b: 10/3/1910, Keystone, WV d: 9/4/1972, Bluefield, WV BR/TR, 5'10.5", 160 lbs. Deb: 4/21/1939																										
1939	StL-N	13	5	.722	51	15	4	2	**9**	169^{1}	141	54	49	8	1	60	78	1.187	2.60	158	2.64	.232	4	.085	27	19	2.4
1940	StL-N	7	5	.583	28	17	7	0	0	114^{1}	118	66	55	9	4	43	43	1.408	4.33	92	4.02	.267	2	.061	-2	5	-0.4
1941	NY-N	6	7	.462	29	6	2	0	1	80^{1}	100	55	51	10	1	36	25	1.693	5.71	65	5.78	.302	1	.048	-18	1	-2.0
1942	Chi-N	0	0	....	1	0	0	0	0	1	1	0	0	0	0	0	0	1.000	0.00	....	1.95	.250	0	....	0	0	0.0
Total	**4**	**26**	**17**	**.605**	**109**	**38**	**13**	**2**	**10**	**365**	**360**	**175**	**155**	**27**	**6**	**139**	**146**	**1.367**	**3.82**	**103**	**3.76**	**.260**	**7**	**.069**	**6**	**25**	**0.0**
• BOWMAN, Joe	Joseph Emil Bowman b: 6/17/1910, Kansas City, KS d: 11/22/1990, Kansas City, MO BL/TR, 6'2", 190 lbs. Deb: 4/18/1932																										
1932	Phi-A	0	1	.000	7	0	0	0	0	11	14	10	10	2	3	6	4	1.818	8.18	55	7.92	.318	1	1.000	-5	0	-0.4
1934	NY-N	5	4	.556	30	10	3	0	3	107^{1}	119	52	43	9	2	36	36	1.444	3.61	107	4.29	.279	5	.172	2	7	0.2
1935	Phi-N	7	10	.412	33	17	6	1	1	148^{1}	157	86	70	13	4	56	58	1.436	4.25	107	4.20	.269	13	.194	7	10	0.7
1936	Phi-N	9	20	.310	40	28	12	0	1	203^{2}	243	140	114	14	7	53	80	1.453	5.04	90	4.37	.289	15	.195	-5	7	-0.5
1937	Pit-N	8	8	.500	30	19	7	0	1	128	161	78	65	11	1	35	38	1.531	4.57	84	4.91	.306	10	.213	-11	5	-0.9
1938	Pit-N	3	4	.429	17	1	0	0	1	60	68	33	31	2	0	20	25	1.467	4.65	82	3.94	.285	7	.333	-7	3	-0.4

YEAR	TM-L	W	L	PCT	G	GS	CG	SH	SV	IP	H	R	ER	HR	HB	BB	SO	RAT	ERA	ERA+	CERA	OAV	BH	AVG	PR+	WS	TPW
1939	Pit-N	10	14	.417	37	27	10	1	1	184^2	217	105	92	15	7	43	58	1.408	4.48	86	4.29	.292	33	.344	-9	11	0.3
1940	Pit-N	9	10	.474	32	24	10	0	2	187^2	209	113	93	10	7	66	57	1.465	4.46	85	4.13	.274	22	.244	-8	8	0.2
1941	Pit-N	3	2	.600	18	7	1	1	1	69^1	77	24	23	3	1	28	22	1.514	2.99	121	4.19	.278	8	.258	6	6	0.7
1944	Bos-A	12	8	.600	26	24	10	1	0	168^1	175	95	90	14	2	64	53	1.420	4.81	71	4.09	.269	20	.200	-27	5	-2.5
1945	Bos-A	0	2	.000	3	3	0	0	0	11^2	18	12	12	1	0	9	0	2.314	9.26	37	8.60	.360	2	.222	-8	0	-0.8
	Cin-N	11	13	.458	25	24	15	1	0	185^2	198	89	74	8	7	68	71	1.433	3.59	105	3.86	.270	5	.070	4	10	-0.1
Total	**11**	**77**	**96**	**.445**	**298**	**184**	**74**	**5**	**11**	**1465^2**	**1656**	**837**	**717**	**102**	**41**	**484**	**502**	**1.460**	**4.40**	**89**	**4.29**	**.282**	**141**	**.221**	**-61**	**72**	**-3.6**

• BOWMAN, Roger Roger Clinton Bowman b: 8/18/1927, Amsterdam, NY d: 7/21/1997, Los Angeles, CA BR/TL, 6', 175 lbs. Deb: 9/22/1949

YEAR	TM-L	W	L	PCT	G	GS	CG	SH	SV	IP	H	R	ER	HR	HB	BB	SO	RAT	ERA	ERA+	CERA	OAV	BH	AVG	PR+	WS	TPW
1949	NY-N	0	0	....	2	2	0	0	0	6^1	6	3	3	1	0	7	4	2.053	4.26	93	6.87	.261	0	.000	-0	0	0.0
1951	NY-N	2	4	.333	9	5	0	0	0	26^1	35	18	18	2	1	22	24	2.165	6.15	64	7.10	.297	0	.000	-7	0	-0.7
1952	NY-N	0	0	....	2	1	0	0	0	3	6	4	4	0	1	3	3	3.000	12.00	31	13.78	.429	0	.000	-3	0	-0.3
1953	Pit-N	0	4	.000	30	2	0	0	0	65^1	65	42	35	9	1	29	36	1.439	4.82	93	4.39	.261	2	.286	-2	3	-0.1
1955	Pit-N	0	3	.000	7	2	0	0	0	16^2	25	18	16	2	1	10	8	2.100	8.64	48	8.10	.347	1	.500	-8	0	-0.8
Total	**5**	**2**	**11**	**.154**	**50**	**12**	**0**	**0**	**0**	**117^2**	**137**	**85**	**76**	**14**	**4**	**71**	**75**	**1.768**	**5.81**	**72**	**5.89**	**.288**	**3**	**.167**	**-20**	**3**	**-2.0**

• BOWMAN, Sumner Sumner Sallade Bowman b: 2/9/1867, Millersburg, PA d: 1/11/1954, Millersburg, PA BL/TL, 6', 160 lbs. Deb: 6/11/1890

YEAR	TM-L	W	L	PCT	G	GS	CG	SH	SV	IP	H	R	ER	HR	HB	BB	SO	RAT	ERA	ERA+	CERA	OAV	BH	AVG	PR+	WS	TPW
1890	Phi-N	0	0	....	1	1	0	0	0	8	11	7	7	0	0	2	2	1.625	7.88	46	....	.318	2	.500	-4	0	-0.3
	Pit-N	2	5	.286	9	7	6	0	0	70^2	100	90	52	1	11	50	22	2.123	6.62	50	....	.324	10	.278	-22	1	-1.8
	Yr.	2	5	.286	10	8	6	0	0	78^2	111	97	59	1	11	52	24	2.072	6.75	49	....	.323	12	.300	-26	1	-2.1
1891	Phi-a	2	5	.286	8	8	8	0	0	68	73	54	26	0	0	37	22	1.618	3.44	111	....	.265	13	.241	3	4	0.3
Total	**2**	**4**	**10**	**.286**	**18**	**16**	**14**	**0**	**0**	**146^2**	**184**	**151**	**85**	**1**	**11**	**89**	**46**	**1.861**	**5.22**	**66**	**....**	**.297**	**25**	**.266**	**-23**	**5**	**-1.8**

• BOWSFIELD, Ted Edward Oliver Bowsfield b: 1/10/1935, Vernon, Canada BR/TL, 6'1", 190 lbs. Deb: 7/20/1958

YEAR	TM-L	W	L	PCT	G	GS	CG	SH	SV	IP	H	R	ER	HR	HB	BB	SO	RAT	ERA	ERA+	CERA	OAV	BH	AVG	PR+	WS	TPW
1958	Bos-A	4	2	.667	16	10	2	0	0	65^2	58	32	28	3	1	36	38	1.431	3.84	104	3.58	.233	4	.154	2	4	0.1
1959	Bos-A	0	1	.000	5	2	0	0	0	9	16	15	15	2	0	9	4	2.778	15.00	27	13.34	.390	0	.000	-11	0	-1.1
1960	Bos-A	1	2	.333	17	2	0	0	2	21	20	12	12	1	1	13	18	1.571	5.14	79	4.50	.260	1	.250	-2	1	-0.2
	Cle-A	3	4	.429	11	6	1	1	0	40^2	47	30	23	1	0	20	14	1.648	5.09	73	4.78	.296	1	.100	-6	0	-0.7
	Yr.	4	6	.400	28	8	1	1	2	61^2	67	42	35	2	1	33	32	1.622	5.11	75	4.69	.284	2	.143	-8	1	-0.9
1961	LA-A	11	8	.579	41	21	4	1	0	157	154	75	65	18	1	63	88	1.382	3.73	121	4.02	.255	7	.137	15	11	1.4
1962	LA-A	9	8	.529	34	25	1	0	1	139	154	82	68	12	2	40	52	1.396	4.40	88	4.12	.277	6	.162	-7	5	-0.6
1963	KC-A	5	7	.417	41	11	2	1	3	111^1	115	60	55	14	3	47	67	1.455	4.45	86	4.57	.269	1	.043	-7	5	-0.8
1964	KC-A	4	7	.364	50	9	2	1	0	118^2	135	63	54	12	4	31	45	1.399	4.10	93	4.31	.285	2	.095	-2	5	-0.2
Total	**7**	**37**	**39**	**.487**	**215**	**86**	**12**	**4**	**6**	**662^1**	**699**	**369**	**320**	**63**	**12**	**259**	**326**	**1.446**	**4.35**	**92**	**4.33**	**.270**	**22**	**.127**	**-17**	**31**	**-2.1**

• BOYD, Gary Gary Lee Boyd b: 8/22/1946, Pasadena, CA BR/TR, 6'4", 200 lbs. Deb: 8/1/1969

YEAR	TM-L	W	L	PCT	G	GS	CG	SH	SV	IP	H	R	ER	HR	HB	BB	SO	RAT	ERA	ERA+	CERA	OAV	BH	AVG	PR+	WS	TPW
1969	Cle-A	0	2	.000	8	3	0	0	0	11	8	11	11	1	0	14	9	2.000	9.00	42	5.55	.205	0	.000	-6	0	-0.7

• BOYD, Jake Jacob Henry Boyd b: 1/19/1874, Martinsburg, WV d: 8/12/1932, Gettysburg, PA TL, 160 lbs. Deb: 9/20/1894 ♦

YEAR	TM-L	W	L	PCT	G	GS	CG	SH	SV	IP	H	R	ER	HR	HB	BB	SO	RAT	ERA	ERA+	CERA	OAV	BH	AVG	PR+	WS	TPW
1894	Was-N	0	3	.000	3	3	3	0	0	19	37	35	18	1	0	14	3	2.684	8.53	62	11.01	.404	3	.143	-6	0	-0.7
1895	Was-N	2	11	.154	14	13	8	0	0	92	132	95	67	1	0	40	18	1.870	6.55	73	5.95	.331	43	.270	-16	3	-2.0
1896	Was-N	1	2	.333	4	2	2	0	0	32	45	34	24	0	0	15	6	1.875	6.75	65	5.81	.329	1	.077	-8	0	-0.8
Total	**3**	**3**	**16**	**.158**	**21**	**18**	**13**	**0**	**0**	**143**	**214**	**164**	**109**	**2**	**0**	**69**	**27**	**1.979**	**6.86**	**70**	**6.59**	**.341**	**47**	**.244**	**-31**	**3**	**-3.4**

• BOYD, Jason Jason Pernell Boyd b: 2/23/1973, St. Clair, IL BR/TR, 6'3", 173 lbs. Deb: 9/10/1999

YEAR	TM-L	W	L	PCT	G	GS	CG	SH	SV	IP	H	R	ER	HR	HB	BB	SO	RAT	ERA	ERA+	CERA	OAV	BH	AVG	PR+	WS	TPW
1999	Pit-N	0	0	....	4	0	0	0	0	5^1	5	2	2	0	1	2	4	1.313	3.38	135	3.53	.250	0	.000	1	0	0.1
2000	Phi-N	0	1	.000	30	0	0	0	0	34^1	39	28	25	2	1	24	32	1.835	6.55	71	5.71	.293	0	....	-7	0	-0.7
2002	SD-N	1	0	1.000	23	0	0	0	0	28^1	33	29	25	6	0	15	18	1.694	7.94	47	6.35	.300	0	....	-13	0	-1.3
2003	Cle-A	3	1	.750	44	0	0	0	0	52^1	38	25	25	4	3	26	31	1.223	4.30	103	2.98	.200	0	....	-0	3	0.0
Total	**4**	**4**	**2**	**.667**	**101**	**0**	**0**	**0**	**0**	**120^1**	**115**	**84**	**77**	**12**	**5**	**67**	**85**	**1.512**	**5.76**	**74**	**4.58**	**.254**	**0**	**.000**	**-20**	**3**	**-2.0**

• BOYD, Oil Can Dennis Ray Boyd b: 10/6/1959, Meridian, MS BR/TR, 6'1", 155 lbs. Deb: 9/13/1982

YEAR	TM-L	W	L	PCT	G	GS	CG	SH	SV	IP	H	R	ER	HR	HB	BB	SO	RAT	ERA	ERA+	CERA	OAV	BH	AVG	PR+	WS	TPW
1982	Bos-A	0	1	.000	3	1	0	0	0	8^1	11	5	5	2	0	2	2	1.560	5.40	80	6.38	.314	0	....	-1	0	-0.1
1983	Bos-A	4	8	.333	15	13	5	0	0	98^2	103	46	36	9	1	23	43	1.277	3.28	132	3.66	.269	0	....	12	6	1.2
1984	Bos-A	12	12	.500	29	26	10	3	0	197^2	207	109	96	18	1	53	134	1.315	4.37	95	3.75	.269	0	....	2	10	0.2
1985	Bos-A	15	13	.536	35	35	13	3	0	272^1	273	117	112	26	4	67	154	1.248	3.70	116	3.52	.261	0	....	22	17	2.2
1986*	Bos-A	16	10	.615	30	30	10	0	0	214^1	222	99	90	32	2	45	129	1.246	3.78	110	3.89	.265	0	....	11	15	1.1
1987	Bos-A	1	3	.250	7	7	0	0	0	36^2	47	31	24	6	2	9	12	1.527	5.89	77	5.64	.315	0	....	-5	0	-0.5
1988	Bos-A	9	7	.563	23	23	1	0	0	129^2	147	82	77	25	2	41	71	1.450	5.34	77	5.28	.289	0	....	-16	3	-1.6
1989	Bos-A	3	2	.600	10	10	0	0	0	59	57	31	29	8	0	19	26	1.288	4.42	93	3.86	.253	0	....	-2	3	-0.2
1990	Mon-N	10	6	.625	31	31	3	3	0	190^2	164	64	62	19	3	52	113	1.133	2.93	125	2.84	.233	3	.051	15	13	1.1
1991	Mon-N	6	8	.429	19	19	1	1	0	120^1	115	49	47	9	0	40	82	1.288	3.52	103	3.45	.256	3	.083	0	6	-0.1
	Tex-A	2	7	.222	12	12	0	0	0	62	81	47	46	12	0	17	33	1.581	6.68	60	6.05	.314	0	....	-17	0	-1.7
Total	**10**	**78**	**77**	**.503**	**214**	**207**	**43**	**10**	**0**	**1389^2**	**1427**	**680**	**624**	**166**	**15**	**368**	**799**	**1.292**	**4.04**	**101**	**3.89**	**.266**	**6**	**.063**	**22**	**73**	**1.6**

• BOYD, Ray Raymond C. Boyd b: 2/11/1887, Hortonville, IN d: 2/11/1920, Hortonville, IN BR/TR, 5'10", 160 lbs. Deb: 9/24/1910

YEAR	TM-L	W	L	PCT	G	GS	CG	SH	SV	IP	H	R	ER	HR	HB	BB	SO	RAT	ERA	ERA+	CERA	OAV	BH	AVG	PR+	WS	TPW
1910	StL-A	0	2	.000	3	2	1	0	0	14^1	16	9	7	0	1	5	6	1.465	4.40	56	4.06	.286	1	.200	-3	0	-0.3
1911	Cin-N	2	2	.500	7	4	3	0	1	44	34	22	13	0	2	19	20	1.205	2.66	124	2.31	.206	1	.083	3	2	0.3
Total	**2**	**2**	**4**	**.333**	**10**	**6**	**4**	**0**	**1**	**58^1**	**50**	**31**	**20**	**0**	**3**	**24**	**26**	**1.269**	**3.09**	**96**	**2.74**	**.226**	**2**	**.118**	**0**	**2**	**0.0**

• BOYER, Cloyd Cloyd Victor "Junior" Boyer b: 9/1/1927, Alba, MO BR/TR, 6'1", 188 lbs. Deb: 4/23/1949 C

YEAR	TM-L	W	L	PCT	G	GS	CG	SH	SV	IP	H	R	ER	HR	HB	BB	SO	RAT	ERA	ERA+	CERA	OAV	BH	AVG	PR+	WS	TPW
1949	StL-N	0	0	....	4	1	0	0	0	3^1	5	4	4	0	0	7	0	3.600	10.80	39	13.19	.357	0	....	-2	0	-0.2
1950	StL-N	7	7	.500	36	14	6	1	1	120^1	105	52	47	15	3	49	82	1.280	3.52	122	3.57	.233	6	.182	11	10	1.1
1951	StL-N	2	5	.286	19	8	1	0	1	63^1	68	42	37	9	3	46	40	1.800	5.26	75	6.44	.286	4	.200	-10	1	-1.0
1952	StL-N	6	6	.500	23	14	4	2	0	110^1	108	56	52	11	4	47	44	1.405	4.24	87	4.12	.258	8	.211	-7	5	-0.5
1955	KC-A	5	5	.500	30	11	2	0	0	98^1	107	81	68	21	7	69	32	1.790	6.22	67	7.05	.282	2	.069	-22	0	-2.4
Total	**5**	**20**	**23**	**.465**	**112**	**48**	**13**	**3**	**2**	**395^2**	**393**	**235**	**208**	**56**	**17**	**218**	**198**	**1.544**	**4.73**	**85**	**5.13**	**.262**	**20**	**.167**	**-30**	**16**	**-3.0**

• BOYLE, Henry Henry J. "Handsome Henry" Boyle b: 9/20/1860, Philadelphia, PA d: 5/25/1932, Philadelphia, PA BR/TR, 6'1" Deb: 7/9/1884 U ♦

YEAR	TM-L	W	L	PCT	G	GS	CG	SH	SV	IP	H	R	ER	HR	HB	BB	SO	RAT	ERA	ERA+	CERA	OAV	BH	AVG	PR+	WS	TPW
1884	StL-U	15	3	.833	19	16	16	2	1	150	118	63	29	3	....	10	88	.853	1.74	171	....	.202	68	.260	14	25	1.9
1885	StL-N	16	24	.400	42	39	39	1	0	366^2	346	207	112	2	....	100	133	1.216	2.75	100	....	.238	52	.202	-12	24	-1.5
1886	StL-N	9	15	.375	25	24	23	2	0	210	183	106	41	5	....	46	101	1.090	**1.76**	**182**	....	.226	27	.250	28	15	3.0
1887	Ind-N	13	24	.351	38	38	37	0	0	328	425	204	133	11	12	69	85	1.296	3.65	113	....	.305	36	.240	14	15	1.1
1888	Ind-N	15	22	.405	37	37	36	3	0	323	315	179	117	11	10	58	98	1.155	3.26	90	....	.246	18	.144	-7	13	-0.8
1889	Ind-N	21	23	.477	46	45	38	2	0	378^2	422	224	165	14	14	95	97	1.365	3.92	107	....	.273	38	.245	6	28	1.0
Total	**6**	**89**	**111**	**.445**	**207**	**199**	**189**	**10**	**1**	**1756^1**	**1809**	**983**	**597**	**46**	**36**	**378**	**602**	**1.206**	**3.06**	**111**	**....**	**.256**	**239**	**.226**	**43**	**120**	**4.7**

• BOYLES, Harry Harry "Stretch" Boyles b: 11/29/1911, Granite City, IL BR/TR, 6'5", 185 lbs. Deb: 8/3/1938

YEAR	TM-L	W	L	PCT	G	GS	CG	SH	SV	IP	H	R	ER	HR	HB	BB	SO	RAT	ERA	ERA+	CERA	OAV	BH	AVG	PR+	WS	TPW
1938	Chi-A	0	4	.000	9	2	1	0	1	29^1	31	27	17	2	2	25	18	1.909	5.22	94	5.78	.263	1	.125	-1	0	-0.1
1939	Chi-A	0	0	....	2	0	0	0	0	3^1	4	4	4	0	0	6	1	3.000	10.80	44	9.84	.308	0	.000	-2	0	-0.2
Total	**2**	**0**	**4**	**.000**	**11**	**2**	**1**	**0**	**1**	**32^2**	**35**	**31**	**21**	**2**	**2**	**31**	**19**	**2.020**	**5.79**	**84**	**6.19**	**.267**	**1**	**.111**	**-3**	**0**	**-0.4**

• BOZE, Marshall Marshall Wayne Boze b: 5/23/1971, San Manuel, AZ BR/TR, 6'1", 214 lbs. Deb: 4/28/1996

YEAR	TM-L	W	L	PCT	G	GS	CG	SH	SV	IP	H	R	ER	HR	HB	BB	SO	RAT	ERA	ERA+	CERA	OAV	BH	AVG	PR+	WS	TPW
1996	Mil-A	0	2	.000	25	0	0	0	1	32^1	47	29	28	5	6	25	19	2.227	7.79	67	9.94	.362	0	....	-10	0	-0.9

• BRABENDER, Gene Eugene Mathew Brabender b: 8/16/1941, Madison, WI d: 12/27/1996, Madison, WI BR/TR, 6'5.5", 225 lbs. Deb: 5/11/1966

YEAR	TM-L	W	L	PCT	G	GS	CG	SH	SV	IP	H	R	ER	HR	HB	BB	SO	RAT	ERA	ERA+	CERA	OAV	BH	AVG	PR+	WS	TPW
1966	Bal-A	4	3	.571	31	1	0	0	2	71	57	30	28	4	1	29	62	1.211	3.55	94	2.91	.229	1	.077	-2	4	-0.3
1967	Bal-A	6	4	.600	14	14	3	1	0	94	77	38	35	6	1	23	71	1.064	3.35	94	2.34	.220	2	.071	-4	4	-0.5
1968	Bal-A	6	7	.462	37	15	3	2	3	125	116	52	46	9	3	48	92	1.312	3.31	88	3.48	.248	3	.086	-8	4	-0.9
1969	Sea-A	13	14	.481	40	29	7	1	0	202^1	193	111	98	26	13	103	139	1.463	4.36	83	4.69	.254	9	.129	-11	7	-1.2

YEAR TM-L	W	L	PCT	G	GS	CG	SH	SV	IP	H	R	ER	HR	HB	BB	SO	RAT	ERA	ERA+	CERA	OAV	BH	AVG	PR+	WS	TPW
1970 Mil-A	6	15	.286	29	21	2	0	1	128^{2}	127	94	86	8	2	79	76	1.601	6.02	63	4.48	.255	4	.098	-29	0	-3.2
Total 5	35	43	.449	151	80	15	4	6	621	570	325	293	53	20	282	440	1.372	4.25	81	3.84	.245	19	.102	-53	19	-6.2
• BRACKEN, Jack	John James Bracken b: 4/14/1881, Cleveland, OH d: 7/16/1954, Highland Park, MI BR/TR, 5'11", 175 lbs. Deb: 8/7/1901																									
1901 Cle-A	4	8	.333	12	12	12	0	0	100	137	94	69	4	10	31	18	1.680	6.21	57	5.65	.322	10	.227	-29	1	-2.6
• BRACKENRIDGE, John	John Givler Brackenridge b: 12/24/1880, Harrisburg, PA d: 3/20/1953, Harrisburg, PA BR/TR, 6' Deb: 4/15/1904																									
1904 Phi-N	0	1	.000	7	1	0	0	0	34	37	32	21	4	4	16	11	1.559	5.56	48	5.79	.298	2	.154	-10	0	-1.1
• BRADEY, Don	Donald Eugene Bradey b: 10/4/1934, Charlotte, NC BR/TR, 5'9", 180 lbs. Deb: 9/25/1964																									
1964 Hou-N	0	2	.000	3	1	0	0	0	2^{1}	6	7	5	0	0	3	2	3.857	19.29	18	14.52	.429	0	....	-4	0	-0.4
• BRADFORD, Bill	William D. Bradford b: 8/28/1921, Choctaw, AR d: 8/22/2000, Fairfield Bay, AR BR/TR, 6'2", 180 lbs. Deb: 4/24/1956																									
1956 KC-A	0	0	....	1	0	0	0	0	2	2	2	2	2	0	1	0	1.500	9.00	48	10.96	.250	0	....	-1	0	-0.1
• BRADFORD, Chad	Chadwick Lee Bradford b: 9/14/1974, Jackson, MS BR/TR, 6'5", 205 lbs. Deb: 8/1/1998																									
1998 Chi-A	2	1	.667	29	0	0	0	1	30^{2}	27	16	11	0	0	7	11	1.109	3.23	141	2.16	.229	0	....	4	3	0.4
1999 Chi-A	0	0	....	3	0	0	0	0	3^{2}	9	8	8	1	0	5	0	3.818	19.64	25	21.34	.474	0	....	-6	0	-0.6
2000* Chi-A	1	0	1.000	12	0	0	0	0	13^{2}	13	4	3	0	0	1	9	1.024	1.98	252	2.01	.255	0	....	4	2	0.4
2001* Oak-A	2	1	.667	35	0	0	0	1	36^{2}	41	12	11	6	1	6	34	1.282	2.70	164	4.36	.281	0	....	7	3	0.7
2002* Oak-A	4	2	.667	75	0	0	0	2	75^{1}	73	29	26	2	5	14	56	1.155	3.11	141	2.77	.253	0	....	11	9	1.1
2003* Oak-A	7	4	.636	72	0	0	0	2	77	67	28	26	7	7	30	62	1.260	3.04	149	3.50	.236	0	....	13	9	1.2
Total 6	16	8	.667	226	0	0	0	6	237	230	97	85	16	13	63	172	1.236	3.23	140	3.42	.254	0	....	34	26	3.2
• BRADFORD, Larry	Larry Bradford b: 12/21/1949, Chicago, IL d: 9/11/1998, Atlanta, GA BR/TL, 6'1", 200 lbs. Deb: 9/24/1977																									
1977 Atl-N	0	0	....	2	0	0	0	0	2^{2}	3	1	1	1	0	0	1	1.125	3.38	132	4.77	.273	0	....	0	0	0.0
1979 Atl-N	1	0	1.000	21	0	0	0	2	19	11	5	2	0	1	10	11	1.105	0.95	427	1.77	.172	0	.000	7	3	0.7
1980 Atl-N	3	4	.429	56	0	0	0	4	55^{1}	49	20	15	3	1	22	32	1.283	2.44	153	3.00	.243	0	.000	8	6	0.8
1981 Atl-N	2	0	1.000	25	0	0	0	1	26^{2}	26	13	11	1	0	12	14	1.425	3.71	97	3.78	.268	1	1.000	-0	2	0.0
Total 4	6	4	.600	104	0	0	0	7	103^{2}	89	39	29	5	2	44	58	1.283	2.52	148	3.02	.238	1	.200	15	11	1.6
• BRADLEY, Bert	Steven Bert Bradley b: 12/23/1956, Athens, GA BB/TR, 6'1", 190 lbs. Deb: 9/3/1983																									
1983 Oak-A	0	0	....	6	0	0	0	0	8^{1}	14	7	6	1	0	4	3	2.160	6.48	59	9.04	.400	0	....	-2	0	-0.2
• BRADLEY, Foghorn	George H. Bradley b: 7/1/1855, Medford, MA d: 3/31/1900, Philadelphia, PA BR/TR, 6' Deb: 8/23/1876 U																									
1876 Bos-N	9	10	.474	22	21	16	1	1	173^{1}	201	116	48	1	....	16	16	1.252	2.49	90	....	.265	19	.226	-4	9	-0.4
• BRADLEY, Fred	Fred Langdon Bradley b: 7/31/1920, Parsons, KS BR/TR, 6'1", 180 lbs. Deb: 5/1/1948																									
1948 Chi-A	0	0	....	8	0	0	0	0	15^{2}	11	12	8	2	1	4	2	.957	4.60	93	2.16	.190	0	.000	-1	0	-0.1
1949 Chi-A	0	0	....	1	1	0	0	0	2	4	3	3	0	0	3	0	3.500	13.50	31	14.91	.444	0	.000	-2	0	-0.2
Total 2	0	0	....	9	1	0	0	0	17^{2}	15	15	11	2	1	7	2	1.245	5.60	76	3.61	.224	0	.000	-3	0	-0.3
• BRADLEY, George	George Washington "Grin" Bradley b: 7/13/1852, Reading, PA d: 10/2/1931, Philadelphia, PA BR/TR, 5'10.5", 175 lbs. Deb: 5/4/1875 U ♦																									
1875 StL-n	33	26	.559	60	60	57	4	0	535^{2}	538	....	127	3	....	16	9	1.034	2.13	108	....	.238	62	.244	-1	....	0.5
1876 StL-N	45	19	.703	64	64	63	**16**	0	573	470	229	78	3	....	38	103	.887	**1.23**	**174**	....	**.205**	66	.246	21	**57**	2.3
1877 Chi-N	18	23	.439	50	44	35	2	0	394	452	266	145	4	....	39	59	1.246	3.31	90	....	.272	52	.243	-12	19	-1.4
1879 Tro-N	13	40	.245	54	54	53	3	0	487	590	361	154	12	....	26	133	1.265	2.85	88	....	.281	62	.247	-4	14	0.4
1880 Pro-N	13	8	.619	28	20	16	4	1	196	158	66	30	2	....	6	54	.837	1.38	160	....	.209	70	.227	14	24	**2.6**
1881 Cle-N	2	4	.333	6	6	5	0	0	51	70	36	22	2	....	3	6	1.431	3.88	68	....	.313	60	.249	-8	5	-1.2
1882 Cle-N	6	9	.400	18	16	15	0	0	147	164	102	61	5	....	22	32	1.265	3.73	75	....	.267	21	.183	-21	5	-2.5
1883 Phi-a	16	7	.696	26	23	22	0	0	214^{1}	215	129	75	7	....	22	56	1.106	3.15	110	....	.244	73	.234	14	22	0.8
1884 Cin-U	25	15	.625	41	38	36	3	0	342	350	203	103	7	....	23	168	1.091	2.71	118	....	.248	43	.190	19	28	0.8
Total 8	138	125	.525	287	265	245	28	1	2404^{1}	2469	1392	668	42	....	179	611	1.101	2.50	109	....	.248	456	.227	23	174	1.8
• BRADLEY, Herb	Herbert Theodore Bradley b: 1/3/1903, Agenda, KS d: 10/16/1959, Clay Center, KS BR/TR, 6', 170 lbs. Deb: 5/9/1927																									
1927 Bos-A	1	1	.500	6	2	2	0	0	23	16	9	8	0	2	7	6	1.000	3.13	135	1.79	.198	3	.429	3	2	0.4
1928 Bos-A	0	3	.000	15	5	1	1	0	47^{1}	64	41	38	2	2	16	14	1.690	7.23	57	5.60	.339	2	.154	-17	0	-1.7
1929 Bos-A	0	0	....	3	0	0	0	0	4	7	3	3	1	0	2	0	2.250	6.75	63	10.79	.438	0	.000	-1	0	-0.1
Total 3	1	4	.200	24	7	3	1	0	74^{1}	87	53	49	3	4	25	20	1.507	5.93	70	4.70	.305	5	.238	-15	2	-1.4
• BRADLEY, Ryan	Ryan J. Bradley b: 10/26/1975, Covina, CA BR/TR, 6'4" Deb: 8/22/1998																									
1998 NY-A	2	1	.667	5	1	0	0	0	12^{2}	12	9	8	2	1	9	13	1.658	5.68	77	5.77	.250	0	....	-2	1	-0.2
• BRADLEY, Tom	Thomas William Bradley b: 3/16/1947, Asheville, NC BR/TR, 6'2.5", 185 lbs. Deb: 9/9/1969																									
1969 Cal-A	0	1	.000	3	0	0	0	0	2	9	9	6	1	0	0	2	4.500	27.00	13	33.18	.600	0	....	-5	0	-0.6
1970 Cal-A	2	5	.286	17	11	1	1	0	69^{2}	71	38	32	3	1	33	53	1.493	4.13	87	4.02	.270	3	.167	-6	1	-0.6
1971 Chi-A	15	15	.500	45	39	7	6	2	285^{2}	273	111	94	16	2	74	206	1.215	2.96	121	2.96	.248	15	.156	25	20	2.6
1972 Chi-A	15	14	.517	40	40	11	2	0	260	225	94	86	19	2	65	209	1.115	2.98	105	2.63	.231	12	.132	10	16	0.9
1973 SF-N	13	12	.520	35	34	6	1	0	224	212	109	97	26	3	69	136	1.254	3.90	98	3.49	.246	15	.195	0	11	0.1
1974 SF-N	8	11	.421	30	21	2	0	0	134^{1}	152	90	77	15	1	52	72	1.519	5.16	74	4.71	.282	3	.075	-20	2	-2.3
1975 SF-N	2	3	.400	13	6	0	0	0	42	57	33	29	6	1	18	13	1.786	6.21	61	6.54	.326	0	.000	-11	0	-1.3
Total 7	55	61	.474	183	151	27	10	2	1017^{2}	999	484	421	86	10	311	691	1.287	3.72	96	3.50	.254	48	.145	-7	50	-1.1
• BRADSHAW, Joe	Joe Siah Bradshaw b: 8/17/1897, Ro Ellen, TN d: 1/30/1985, Tavares, FL BR/TR, 6'2.5", 200 lbs. Deb: 5/9/1929																									
1929 Bro-N	0	0	....	2	0	0	0	0	4	3	3	2	0	2	4	1	1.750	4.50	102	5.72	.231	0	....	0	0	0.0
• BRADY, Bill	William Aloysius "King" Brady b: 8/18/1889, New York, NY BR/TR, 6'1.5" Deb: 7/9/1912																									
1912 Bos-N	0	0	....	1	0	0	0	0	1	2	0	0	0	0	0	0	2.000	0.00	....	9.49	.500	0	....	0	0	0.0
• BRADY, Jim	James Joseph "Diamond Jim" Brady b: 3/2/1936, Jersey City, NJ BL/TL, 6'2", 185 lbs. Deb: 5/12/1956																									
1956 Det-A	0	0	....	6	0	0	0	0	6^{1}	15	21	20	3	0	11	3	4.105	28.42	14	24.95	.484	0	....	-17	0	-1.6
• BRADY, King	James Ward Brady b: 5/28/1881, Elmer, NJ d: 8/21/1947, Albany, NY BR/TR, 6', 190 lbs. Deb: 9/21/1905																									
1905 Phi-N	1	1	.500	2	2	2	0	0	13	19	7	5	0	0	2	3	1.615	3.46	84	4.90	.333	1	.200	-1	0	-0.1
1906 Pit-N	1	1	.500	3	2	1	0	0	23	30	7	6	0	0	4	14	1.478	2.35	113	4.15	.313	1	.100	1	1	0.0
1907 Pit-N	0	0	....	1	0	0	0	0	2	2	1	0	0	0	1	0	1.500	0.00	....	4.01	.286	0	....	1	0	0.1
1908 Bos-A	1	0	1.000	1	1	1	1	0	9	8	0	0	0	0	0	3	.889	0.00	....	1.62	.242	0	.000	2	1	0.2
1912 Bos-N	0	0	....	1	0	0	0	0	2^{2}	5	6	6	0	0	3	0	3.000	20.25	18	12.06	.313	0	.000	-5	0	-0.5
Total 5	3	2	.600	8	5	4	1	0	49^{2}	64	21	17	0	0	10	20	1.490	3.08	98	4.31	.306	2	.111	-2	2	-0.3
• BRADY, Neal	Cornelius Joseph Brady b: 3/4/1897, Covington, KY d: 6/19/1947, Fort Mitchell, KY BR/TR, 6'.5", 197 lbs. Deb: 9/25/1915																									
1915 NY-A	0	0	....	2	1	0	0	0	8^{2}	9	3	3	0	0	7	6	1.846	3.12	94	5.14	.281	0	.000	-0	0	-0.1
1917 NY-A	1	0	1.000	2	1	0	0	0	9	6	2	2	0	0	5	4	1.222	2.00	134	2.14	.188	1	.500	1	1	0.1
1925 Cin-N	1	3	.250	20	3	2	0	1	63^{2}	73	44	33	4	4	20	12	1.461	4.66	88	4.35	.289	6	.240	-5	2	-0.4
Total 3	2	3	.400	24	5	2	0	1	81^{1}	88	49	38	4	4	32	22	1.475	4.20	92	4.19	.278	7	.226	-5	3	-0.4
• BRAGGINS, Dick	Richard Realf Braggins b: 12/25/1879, Mercer, PA d: 8/16/1963, Lake Wales, FL BR/TR, 5'11", 170 lbs. Deb: 5/16/1901																									
1901 Cle-A	1	2	.333	4	3	2	0	0	32	44	28	17	1	1	15	1	1.844	4.78	74	6.01	.323	2	.154	-4	1	-0.5
• BRAINARD, Asa	Asa "Count" Brainard b: 1841, Albany, NY d: 12/29/1888, Denver, CO TR, 5'8.5", 150 lbs. Deb: 5/5/1871 U																									
1871 Oly-n	12	15	.444	30	30	30	0	0	264	361	....	132	4	....	37	13	1.508	4.50	93	....	.285	30	.224	-29	....	-2.1

YEAR	TM-L	W	L	PCT	G	GS	CG	SH	SV	IP	H	R	ER	HR	HB	BB	SO	RAT	ERA	ERA+	CERA	OAV	BH	AVG	PR+	WS	TPW
1872	Oly-n	2	7	.222	9	9	9	0	0	79	147	....	56	0	....	5	1	1.924	6.38	58	....	.352	16	.372	-19	....	-1.0
	Man-n	0	2	.000	2	2	1	0	0	8	14	....	7	1	....	0	0	1.750	7.88	47	....	.338	5	.200	-3	....	-0.5
	Yr.	2	9	.182	11	11	10	0	0	87	161	....	63	1	....	5	1	1.908	6.52	56	....	.351	21	.309	-22	....	-1.5
1873	Bal-n	5	7	.417	14	14	12	0	0	108^2	182	....	50	0	....	9	3	1.758	4.14	79	....	.332	18	.261	-14	....	-1.0
1874	Bal-n	5	22	.185	30	27	25	0	0	240	405	....	99	1	....	27	8	**1.800**	3.71	82	....	.337	47	.240	-15	....	-2.2
Total	4 n	24	53	.312	85	82	77	0	0	699^2	1109	....	344	6	....	78	25	1.697	4.42	80	....	.319	116	.248	-80	....	-6.8
• BRAITHWOOD, Al	Alfred Braithwood b: 2/15/1892, Braceville, IL d: 11/24/1960, Rowlesburg, WV BR/TL, 6'1.5", 145 lbs. Deb: 9/1/1915																										
1915	Pit-F	0	0	....	2	0	0	0	0	3	0	0	0	0	0	0	2	.000	0.00	....	0.00	.000	0	....	1	1	0.1
• BRAME, Erv	Ervin Beckham Brame b: 10/12/1901, Big Rock, TN d: 11/22/1949, Hopkinsville, KY BL/TR, 6'2", 190 lbs. Deb: 4/14/1928																										
1928	Pit-N	7	4	.636	24	11	6	0	0	95^2	110	62	54	5	1	44	22	1.610	5.08	80	4.67	.291	13	.265	-11	5	-0.7
1929	Pit-N	16	11	.593	37	28	19	1	0	229^2	250	123	116	17	0	71	68	1.398	4.55	105	3.93	.278	36	.310	2	18	1.2
1930	Pit-N	17	8	.680	32	29	**22**	0	1	235^2	291	153	123	21	5	56	55	1.472	4.70	106	4.65	.305	41	.353	8	18	1.6
1931	Pit-N	9	13	.409	26	21	15	2	0	179^2	211	102	84	14	0	45	33	1.425	4.21	91	4.22	.295	26	.274	-10	9	-0.4
1932	Pit-N	3	1	.750	23	3	0	0	0	51	84	52	42	6	0	16	10	1.961	7.41	51	7.70	.365	5	.250	-21	0	-2.0
Total	5	52	37	.584	142	92	62	3	1	791^2	946	492	419	63	6	232	188	1.488	4.76	92	4.54	.298	121	.306	-33	50	-0.3
• BRANCA, Ralph	Ralph Theodore Joseph "Hawk" Branca b: 1/6/1926, Mount Vernon, NY BR/TR, 6'3", 220 lbs. Deb: 6/12/1944																										
1944	Bro-N	0	2	.000	21	1	0	0	1	44^2	46	36	35	2	5	32	16	1.746	7.05	50	5.21	.274	0	.000	-16	0	-1.7
1945	Bro-N	5	6	.455	16	15	7	0	1	109^2	73	44	37	4	0	79	69	1.386	3.04	124	2.82	.189	4	.100	9	7	0.7
1946	Bro-N	3	1	.750	24	10	2	2	3	67^1	62	34	29	4	0	41	42	1.530	3.88	87	4.01	.246	2	.111	-4	3	-0.4
1947*	Bro-N★	21	12	.636	43	**36**	15	4	1	280	251	100	83	22	6	98	148	1.246	2.67	155	3.22	.240	12	.124	40	26	3.6
1948	Bro-N★	14	9	.609	36	28	11	1	1	215^2	189	93	84	24	4	80	122	1.247	3.51	114	3.34	.232	15	.203	7	15	0.8
1949*	Bro-N★	13	5	.722	34	27	9	2	1	186^2	181	100	91	21	2	91	109	1.457	4.39	93	4.28	.253	5	.081	-9	8	-1.1
1950	Bro-N	7	9	.438	43	15	5	0	7	142	152	80	74	24	0	55	100	1.458	4.69	87	4.82	.271	4	.118	-13	7	-1.1
1951	Bro-N	13	12	.520	42	27	13	3	3	204	180	81	74	19	3	85	118	1.299	3.26	120	3.44	.237	11	.175	10	14	1.0
1952	Bro-N	4	2	.667	16	7	2	0	0	61	52	29	26	8	4	21	26	1.197	3.84	95	3.49	.232	3	.158	-2	3	-0.2
1953	Bro-N	0	0	....	7	0	0	0	0	11	15	12	12	4	2	5	5	1.818	9.82	43	9.98	.341	0	....	-7	0	-0.7
	Det-A	4	7	.364	17	14	7	0	1	102	98	55	47	7	2	31	50	1.265	4.15	98	3.23	.253	4	.118	2	4	0.1
1954	Det-A	3	3	.500	17	5	0	0	0	45^1	63	33	29	10	2	30	15	2.051	5.76	64	8.58	.330	4	.308	-11	0	-0.9
	NY-A	1	0	1.000	5	3	0	0	0	12^2	9	5	4	0	1	13	7	1.737	2.84	121	3.91	.209	2	.500	1	1	0.1
	Yr.	4	3	.571	22	8	0	0	0	58	72	38	33	10	3	43	22	1.983	5.12	71	7.56	.308	6	.353	-10	1	-0.8
1956	Bro-N	0	0	....	1	0	0	0	0	2	1	0	0	0	0	2	2	1.500	0.00	....	2.80	.143	0	....	1	0	0.1
Total	12	88	68	.564	322	188	71	12	19	1484	1372	702	625	149	31	663	829	1.371	3.79	104	3.85	.245	66	.142	8	88	0.1
• BRANCH, Harvey	Harvey Alfred Branch b: 2/8/1939, Memphis, TN BR/TL, 6', 175 lbs. Deb: 9/18/1962																										
1962	StL-N	0	1	.000	1	1	0	0	0	5	5	3	3	1	0	5	2	2.000	5.40	79	7.56	.263	0	.000	-1	0	-0.1
• BRANCH, Norm	Norman Downs "Red" Branch b: 3/22/1915, Spokane, WA d: 11/21/1971, Navasota, TX BR/TR, 6'3", 200 lbs. Deb: 5/5/1941																										
1941	NY-A	5	1	.833	27	0	0	0	2	47	37	16	15	2	0	26	28	1.340	2.87	137	3.06	.224	0	.000	4	5	0.3
1942	NY-A	0	1	.000	10	0	0	0	2	15^2	18	15	11	3	0	16	13	2.170	6.32	54	7.99	.290	1	.333	-6	0	-0.6
Total	2	5	2	.714	37	0	0	0	4	62^2	55	31	26	5	0	42	41	1.548	3.73	99	4.30	.242	1	.077	-2	5	-0.3
• BRANCH, Roy	Roy Branch b: 7/12/1953, St. Louis, MO BR/TR, 6', 175 lbs. Deb: 9/11/1979																										
1979	Sea-A	0	1	.000	2	2	0	0	0	11^1	12	11	10	2	0	7	6	1.676	7.94	55	5.72	.273	0	....	-4	0	-0.4
• BRANDENBURG, Mark	Mark Clay Brandenburg b: 7/14/1970, Houston, TX BR/TR, 6', 180 lbs. Deb: 7/20/1995																										
1995	Tex-A	0	1	.000	11	0	0	0	0	27^1	36	18	18	5	1	7	21	1.573	5.93	81	6.08	.316	0	....	-3	1	-0.3
1996	Tex-A	1	3	.250	26	0	0	0	0	47^2	48	22	17	3	2	25	37	1.531	3.21	163	4.41	.262	0	....	11	4	1.0
	Bos-A	4	2	.667	29	0	0	0	0	28^1	28	13	12	5	1	8	29	1.271	3.81	133	4.02	.250	0	....	5	3	0.4
	Yr.	5	5	.500	55	0	0	0	0	76	76	35	29	8	3	33	66	1.434	3.43	151	4.27	.258	0	....	15	7	1.4
1997	Bos-A	0	2	.000	31	0	0	0	0	41	49	25	25	3	2	16	34	1.585	5.49	84	5.01	.299	0	....	-4	1	-0.4
Total	3	5	8	.385	97	0	0	0	0	144^1	161	78	72	16	6	56	121	1.503	4.49	109	4.82	.281	0	....	8	9	0.7
• BRANDOM, Chick	Chester Milton Brandom b: 3/31/1887, Coldwater, KS d: 10/7/1958, Santa Ana, CA BR/TR, 5'8", 161 lbs. Deb: 9/3/1908																										
1908	Pit-N	1	0	1.000	3	1	1	0	1	17	13	5	1	0	1	4	8	1.000	0.53	431	2.04	.228	1	.143	3	2	0.4
1909	Pit-N	1	0	1.000	13	2	0	0	2	40^2	33	12	5	0	1	10	21	1.057	1.11	232	2.19	.239	1	.100	6	4	0.6
1915	New-F	1	1	.500	16	1	1	0	0	50^1	55	36	19	0	1	15	15	1.391	3.40	84	3.74	.293	2	.200	-3	1	-0.3
Total	3	3	1	.750	32	4	2	0	3	108	101	53	25	0	3	29	44	1.204	2.08	132	2.89	.264	4	.148	6	7	0.7
• BRANDON, Bucky	Darrell G Brandon b: 7/8/1940, Nacogdoches, TX BR/TR, 6'2", 200 lbs. Deb: 4/19/1966																										
1966	Bos-A	8	8	.500	40	17	5	2	2	157^2	129	70	58	13	4	70	101	1.262	3.31	115	3.23	.222	8	.182	10	10	1.2
1967	Bos-A	5	11	.313	39	19	2	0	3	157^2	147	86	73	21	7	59	96	1.307	4.17	84	3.86	.245	8	.186	-11	4	-1.1
1968	Bos-A	0	0	....	8	0	0	0	0	12^2	19	11	9	1	1	9	10	2.211	6.39	49	8.44	.333	0	.000	-4	0	-0.5
1969	Sea-A	0	1	.000	8	1	0	0	0	15	15	15	14	4	2	16	10	2.067	8.40	43	8.59	.250	0	....	-8	0	-0.8
	Min-A	0	0	....	3	0	0	0	0	3^1	5	3	1	1	0	3	1	2.400	2.70	135	8.71	.357	0	.000	0	0	0.1
	Yr.	0	1	.000	11	1	0	0	0	18^1	20	18	15	5	2	19	11	2.127	7.36	49	8.61	.270	0	.000	-7	0	-0.7
1971	Phi-N	6	6	.500	52	0	0	0	4	83	81	42	36	5	0	47	44	1.542	3.90	90	4.17	.264	2	.154	-4	5	-0.5
1972	Phi-N	7	7	.500	42	6	0	0	2	104^1	106	49	40	9	6	46	67	1.457	3.45	104	4.39	.268	1	.067	0	6	-0.1
1973	Phi-N	2	4	.333	36	0	0	0	2	56^1	54	35	34	5	3	25	25	1.402	5.43	70	3.98	.261	1	.200	-11	1	-1.1
Total	7	28	37	.431	228	43	7	2	13	590	556	311	265	59	23	275	354	1.408	4.04	89	4.09	.250	20	.164	-28	26	-2.9
• BRANDT, Bill	William George Brandt b: 3/21/1915, Aurora, IN d: 5/16/1968, Fort Wayne, IN BR/TR, 5'8.5", 170 lbs. Deb: 9/20/1941																										
1941	Pit-N	0	1	.000	2	1	0	0	0	7	5	3	3	0	0	3	0	1.143	3.86	94	2.02	.200	0	.000	-0	0	0.0
1942	Pit-N	1	1	.500	3	3	1	0	0	16^1	23	10	9	1	0	5	4	1.714	4.96	68	5.89	.343	1	.143	-3	0	-0.3
1943	Pit-N	4	1	.800	29	3	0	0	0	57^1	57	25	20	3	1	19	17	1.326	3.14	111	3.27	.248	1	.143	2	3	0.2
Total	3	5	3	.625	34	7	1	0	0	80^2	85	38	32	4	1	27	21	1.388	3.57	97	3.69	.264	2	.133	-1	3	-0.1
• BRANDT, Ed	Edward Arthur "Big Ed" Brandt b: 2/17/1905, Spokane, WA d: 11/1/1944, Spokane, WA BL/TL, 6'1", 190 lbs. Deb: 4/26/1928																										
1928	Bos-N	9	21	.300	38	31	12	1	0	225^1	234	141	127	22	7	109	84	1.522	5.07	77	4.61	.273	17	.243	-21	6	-1.6
1929	Bos-N	8	13	.381	26	21	13	0	0	167^2	196	111	103	12	5	83	50	1.664	5.53	85	5.25	.302	15	.234	-15	7	-1.2
1930	Bos-N	4	11	.267	41	13	4	1	1	147^1	168	88	82	15	0	59	65	1.541	5.01	99	4.77	.291	12	.240	-1	8	0.0
1931	Bos-N	18	11	.621	33	29	23	3	2	250	228	94	81	11	4	77	112	1.220	2.92	130	2.88	.244	21	.256	26	**27**	3.1
1932	Bos-N	16	16	.500	35	31	19	2	1	254	271	122	112	11	5	57	79	1.291	3.97	95	3.42	.275	19	.207	-6	13	-0.7
1933	Bos-N	18	14	.563	41	32	23	4	4	287^2	256	85	83	10	3	77	104	1.158	2.60	118	2.59	.245	30	.309	17	29	2.7
1934	Bos-N	16	14	.533	40	28	20	3	5	255	249	111	100	13	4	83	106	1.302	3.53	108	3.30	.254	23	.240	9	19	1.3
1935	Bos-N	5	19	.208	29	25	12	0	0	174^2	224	110	97	12	1	66	61	1.660	5.00	76	5.33	.319	13	.210	-17	4	-1.7
1936	Bro-N	11	13	.458	38	29	12	1	2	234	246	105	91	14	4	65	104	1.329	3.50	118	3.56	.268	16	.190	19	17	1.9
1937	Pit-N	11	10	.524	33	25	7	2	2	176^1	177	73	61	11	2	67	74	1.384	3.11	124	3.75	.263	10	.169	14	14	1.5
1938	Pit-N	5	4	.556	24	14	5	1	0	96^1	93	44	37	3	0	35	38	1.329	3.46	110	3.14	.250	11	.297	2	7	0.4
Total	11	121	146	.453	378	278	150	18	17	2268^1	2342	1084	974	134	35	778	877	1.375	3.86	101	3.76	.269	187	.236	24	151	5.8
• BRANTLEY, Cliff	Clifford Brantley b: 4/12/1968, Staten Island, NY BR/TR, 6'2", 190 lbs. Deb: 9/3/1991																										
1991	Phi-N	2	2	.500	6	5	0	0	0	31^2	26	12	12	0	2	19	25	1.421	3.41	107	3.33	.228	0	.000	1	2	0.0
1992	Phi-N	2	6	.250	28	9	0	0	0	76^1	71	45	39	6	4	58	32	1.690	4.60	76	5.06	.251	3	.214	-9	1	-0.8
Total	2	4	8	.333	34	14	0	0	0	108	97	57	51	6	6	77	57	1.611	4.25	83	4.55	.244	3	.136	-8	3	-0.8
• BRANTLEY, Jeff	Jeffrey Hoke Brantley b: 9/5/1963, Florence, AL BR/TR, 5'11", 190 lbs. Deb: 8/5/1988																										
1988	SF-N	0	1	.000	9	1	0	0	1	20^2	22	13	13	2	1	6	11	1.355	5.66	58	4.15	.275	1	.500	-6	0	-0.6
1989*	SF-N	7	1	.875	59	1	0	0	0	97^1	101	50	44	10	2	37	69	1.418	4.07	83	4.18	.271	1	.083	-10	3	-1.1

YEAR	TM-L	W	L	PCT	G	GS	CG	SH	SV	IP	H	R	ER	HR	HB	BB	SO	RAT	ERA	ERA+	CERA	OAV	BH	AVG	PR+	WS	TPW
1990	SF-N★	5	3	.625	55	0	0	0	19	86^2	77	18	15	3	3	33	61	1.269	1.56	234	3.02	.240	2	.286	20	15	2.1
1991	SF-N	5	2	.714	67	0	0	0	15	95^1	78	27	26	8	5	52	81	1.364	2.45	146	3.56	.225	0	.000	11	11	1.1
1992	SF-N	7	7	.500	56	4	0	0	7	91^2	67	32	30	8	3	45	86	1.222	2.95	112	2.95	.207	1	.111	2	8	0.2
1993	SF-N	5	6	.455	53	12	0	0	0	113^2	112	60	54	19	7	46	76	1.390	4.28	91	4.71	.259	3	.107	-8	3	-0.9
1994	Cin-N	6	6	.500	50	0	0	0	15	65^1	46	20	18	6	0	28	63	1.133	2.48	167	2.51	.202	0	.000	12	10	1.2
1995*	Cin-N	3	2	.600	56	0	0	0	28	70^1	53	22	22	11	1	20	62	1.038	2.82	146	2.66	.206	0	.000	9	13	0.8
1996	Cin-N	1	2	.333	66	0	0	0	**44**	71	54	21	19	7	0	28	76	1.155	2.41	173	2.68	.215	0	.000	13	14	1.3
1997	Cin-N	1	1	.500	13	0	0	0	1	11^2	9	5	5	2	2	7	16	1.371	3.86	112	4.53	.205	0	....	1	1	0.1
1998	StL-N	0	5	.000	48	0	0	0	14	50^2	40	26	25	12	1	18	48	1.145	4.44	95	3.60	.220	0	....	-1	5	-0.1
1999	Phi-N	1	2	.333	10	0	0	0	5	8^2	5	6	5	0	0	8	11	1.500	5.19	91	2.84	.161	0	....	-1	1	-0.1
2000	Phi-N	2	7	.222	55	0	0	0	23	55^1	64	36	36	12	2	29	57	1.681	5.86	80	6.57	.288	0	....	-7	3	-0.7
2001	Tex-A	0	1	.000	18	0	0	0	0	21	26	12	12	5	0	9	11	1.667	5.14	91	6.74	.310	0	....	-1	1	-0.1
Total	**14**	**43**	**46**	**.483**	**615**	**18**	**0**	**0**	**172**	**859^1**	**754**	**348**	**324**	**105**	**27**	**366**	**728**	**1.303**	**3.39**	**114**	**3.73**	**.237**	**8**	**.118**	**33**	**88**	**3.2**

• BRASHEAR, Kitty
Norman C. Brashear b: 8/27/1877, Mansfield, OH d: 12/22/1934, Los Angeles, CA BR/TR, 5'11" Deb: 6/25/1899

YEAR	TM-L	W	L	PCT	G	GS	CG	SH	SV	IP	H	R	ER	HR	HB	BB	SO	RAT	ERA	ERA+	CERA	OAV	BH	AVG	PR+	WS	TPW
1899	Lou-N	1	0	1.000	3	0	0	0	0	8	8	7	4	0	1	2	5	1.250	4.50	86	3.20	.260	1	.500	-0	0	0.0

• BRAUN, John
John Paul Braun b: 12/26/1939, Madison, WI BR/TR, 6'5", 218 lbs. Deb: 10/2/1964

YEAR	TM-L	W	L	PCT	G	GS	CG	SH	SV	IP	H	R	ER	HR	HB	BB	SO	RAT	ERA	ERA+	CERA	OAV	BH	AVG	PR+	WS	TPW
1964	Mil-N	0	0	....	1	0	0	0	0	2	2	0	0	0	0	1	1	1.500	0.00	....	3.63	.286	0	....	1	0	0.1

• BRAXTON, Garland
Edgar Garland Braxton b: 6/10/1900, Snow Camp, NC d: 2/26/1966, Norfolk, VA BB/TL, 5'11", 152 lbs. Deb: 5/27/1921

YEAR	TM-L	W	L	PCT	G	GS	CG	SH	SV	IP	H	R	ER	HR	HB	BB	SO	RAT	ERA	ERA+	CERA	OAV	BH	AVG	PR+	WS	TPW
1921	Bos-N	1	3	.250	17	2	0	0	0	37^1	44	26	20	0	2	17	16	1.634	4.82	76	4.79	.310	0	.000	-5	0	-0.6
1922	Bos-N	1	2	.333	25	5	2	0	0	66^2	75	37	25	3	4	24	15	1.485	3.38	118	4.33	.286	1	.063	5	4	0.3
1925	NY-A	1	1	.500	3	2	0	0	0	19^1	26	14	14	1	1	5	11	1.603	6.52	65	5.46	.338	2	.333	-5	0	-0.4
1926	NY-A	5	1	.833	37	1	0	0	2	67^1	71	28	20	1	0	19	30	1.337	2.67	144	3.28	.275	6	.300	10	7	1.1
1927	Was-A	10	9	.526	**58**	2	0	0	**13**	155^1	144	62	51	5	2	33	96	1.139	2.95	137	2.52	.246	9	.231	17	17	1.7
1928	Was-A	13	11	.542	38	24	15	2	6	218^1	177	78	61	7	5	44	94	1.012	**2.51**	**159**	**1.92**	**.222**	9	.125	33	21	2.8
1929	Was-A	12	10	.545	37	20	9	0	4	182	219	116	98	6	2	51	59	1.484	4.85	87	4.16	.299	8	.148	-15	8	-1.4
1930	Was-A	3	2	.600	15	0	0	0	5	27^1	22	11	10	3	0	9	7	1.134	3.29	139	2.74	.222	0	.000	3	4	0.2
	Chi-A	4	10	.286	19	10	2	0	1	90^2	127	80	65	9	1	33	44	1.765	6.45	72	6.26	.333	2	.087	-16	1	-1.6
	Yr.	7	12	.368	34	10	2	0	6	118	149	91	75	12	1	42	51	1.619	5.72	81	5.44	.310	2	.071	-13	5	-1.4
1931	Chi-A	0	3	.000	17	3	0	0	1	47^1	71	43	36	1	2	23	28	1.986	6.85	62	6.56	.338	1	.091	-13	0	-1.3
	StL-A	0	0	....	11	1	0	0	0	18	27	24	21	2	1	10	7	2.056	10.50	44	8.34	.370	2	.667	-12	0	-1.0
	Yr.	0	3	.000	28	4	0	0	1	65^1	98	67	57	3	3	33	35	2.005	7.85	56	7.05	.346	3	.214	-25	0	-2.3
1933	StL-A	0	1	.000	5	1	0	0	0	8^1	11	10	9	0	1	8	5	2.280	9.72	48	6.89	.289	0	.000	-5	0	-0.5
Total	**10**	**50**	**53**	**.485**	**282**	**71**	**28**	**2**	**32**	**938**	**1014**	**529**	**430**	**38**	**21**	**276**	**412**	**1.375**	**4.13**	**102**	**3.75**	**.277**	**40**	**.156**	**-1**	**62**	**-0.6**

• BRAZELTON, Dewon
Dewon Cortez Brazelton b: 6/16/1980, Tullahoma, TN BR/TR, 6'4", 214 lbs. Deb: 9/13/2002

YEAR	TM-L	W	L	PCT	G	GS	CG	SH	SV	IP	H	R	ER	HR	HB	BB	SO	RAT	ERA	ERA+	CERA	OAV	BH	AVG	PR+	WS	TPW
2002	TB-A	0	1	.000	2	2	0	0	0	13	12	7	7	3	2	6	5	1.385	4.85	92	6.29	.279	0	....	-1	1	-0.1
2003	TB-A	1	6	.143	10	10	0	0	0	48^1	57	49	37	9	3	23	24	1.655	6.89	66	6.29	.292	0	.000	-14	0	-1.3
Total	**2**	**1**	**7**	**.125**	**12**	**12**	**0**	**0**	**0**	**61^1**	**69**	**56**	**44**	**12**	**5**	**29**	**29**	**1.598**	**6.46**	**70**	**6.29**	**.290**	**0**	**.000**	**-15**	**1**	**-1.4**

• BRAZLE, Al
Alpha Eugene "Cotton" Brazle b: 10/19/1913, Loyal, OK d: 10/24/1973, Grand Junction, CO BL/TL, 6'2", 185 lbs. Deb: 7/25/1943

YEAR	TM-L	W	L	PCT	G	GS	CG	SH	SV	IP	H	R	ER	HR	HB	BB	SO	RAT	ERA	ERA+	CERA	OAV	BH	AVG	PR+	WS	TPW
1943*	StL-N	8	2	.800	13	9	8	1	0	88	74	18	15	0	0	29	26	1.170	1.53	219	2.33	.231	9	.281	16	12	1.9
1946*	StL-N	11	10	.524	37	15	6	2	0	153^1	152	69	56	1	2	55	58	1.350	3.29	105	3.20	.261	11	.212	1	8	0.0
1947	StL-N	14	8	.636	44	19	7	0	4	168	186	65	53	7	2	48	85	1.393	2.84	146	3.85	.284	14	.219	24	16	2.4
1948	StL-N	10	6	.625	42	23	6	2	1	156^1	171	77	66	8	0	50	55	1.414	3.80	108	3.87	.281	8	.145	6	9	0.4
1949	StL-N	14	8	.636	39	25	9	1	0	206^1	208	85	73	18	6	61	75	1.304	3.18	131	3.69	.263	11	.134	21	16	1.7
1950	StL-N	11	9	.550	46	12	3	0	6	164^2	188	81	75	12	4	80	47	1.628	4.10	105	5.11	.296	13	.213	5	11	0.4
1951	StL-N	6	5	.545	56	8	5	0	7	154^1	139	61	53	13	5	60	66	1.289	3.09	128	3.43	.245	5	.109	13	14	1.0
1952	StL-N	12	5	.706	46	6	3	1	**16**	109^1	75	38	33	7	1	42	55	1.070	2.72	137	2.16	.198	4	.125	12	15	1.1
1953	StL-N	6	7	.462	60	0	0	0	**18**	92	101	47	43	8	2	43	57	1.565	4.21	101	4.71	.280	5	.333	2	9	0.3
1954	StL-N	5	4	.556	58	0	0	0	8	84^1	93	48	39	10	3	24	30	1.387	4.16	99	4.42	.288	0	.000	0	5	-0.2
Total	**10**	**97**	**64**	**.602**	**441**	**117**	**47**	**7**	**60**	**1376^2**	**1387**	**589**	**506**	**84**	**25**	**492**	**554**	**1.365**	**3.31**	**121**	**3.72**	**.266**	**80**	**.177**	**98**	**115**	**9.0**

• BREA, Lesli
Lesli Guillermo Brea b: 10/12/1973, San Pedro de Macoris, Dominican Republic BR/TR, 5'10", 170 lbs. Deb: 8/13/2000

YEAR	TM-L	W	L	PCT	G	GS	CG	SH	SV	IP	H	R	ER	HR	HB	BB	SO	RAT	ERA	ERA+	CERA	OAV	BH	AVG	PR+	WS	TPW
2000	Bal-A	0	1	.000	6	1	0	0	0	9	12	11	11	1	1	10	5	2.444	11.00	43	9.77	.324	0	....	-6	0	-0.6
2001	Bal-A	0	0	....	2	0	0	0	0	2	6	4	4	2	0	3	0	4.500	18.00	24	37.82	.545	0	....	-3	0	-0.3
Total	**2**	**0**	**1**	**.000**	**8**	**1**	**0**	**0**	**0**	**11**	**18**	**15**	**15**	**3**	**1**	**13**	**5**	**2.818**	**12.27**	**37**	**14.87**	**.375**	**0**	**....**	**-9**	**0**	**-0.9**

• BRECHEEN, Harry
Harry David "Harry The Cat" Brecheen b: 10/14/1914, Broken Bow, OK BL/TL, 5'10", 160 lbs. Deb: 4/22/1940 C

YEAR	TM-L	W	L	PCT	G	GS	CG	SH	SV	IP	H	R	ER	HR	HB	BB	SO	RAT	ERA	ERA+	CERA	OAV	BH	AVG	PR+	WS	TPW
1940	StL-N	0	0	....	3	0	0	0	0	3^1	2	1	0	0	0	2	4	1.200	0.00	....	1.90	.167	0	....	2	0	0.2
1943*	StL-N	9	6	.600	29	13	8	1	4	135^1	98	41	34	4	3	39	68	1.012	2.26	149	1.90	.206	8	.190	13	15	1.5
1944*	StL-N	16	5	.762	30	22	13	3	0	189^1	174	67	60	8	3	46	88	1.162	2.85	124	2.69	.242	11	.162	10	15	1.1
1945	StL-N	15	4	.789	24	18	13	3	2	157^1	136	48	44	5	5	44	63	1.144	2.52	149	2.59	.238	7	.123	18	17	1.6
1946*	StL-N	15	15	.500	36	30	14	**5**	3	231^1	212	73	64	8	4	67	117	1.206	2.49	139	2.79	.244	11	.133	21	20	1.9
1947	StL-N★	16	11	.593	29	28	18	1	1	223^1	220	92	82	20	3	66	89	1.281	3.30	125	3.55	.260	20	.241	20	19	2.5
1948	StL-N★	20	7	.741	33	30	21	**7**	1	233^1	193	62	58	6	2	49	**149**	1.037	**2.24**	**183**	**2.01**	.222	12	.146	**49**	27	**4.8**
1949	StL-N	14	11	.560	32	31	14	2	1	214^2	207	96	80	18	7	65	88	1.267	3.35	124	3.43	.252	21	.273	18	18	2.3
1950	StL-N	8	11	.421	27	23	12	2	1	163^1	151	77	69	18	3	45	80	1.200	3.80	113	3.26	.244	14	.241	10	12	1.3
1951	StL-N	8	4	.667	24	16	5	0	2	138^2	134	54	50	11	1	54	57	1.356	3.25	122	3.71	.256	12	.218	9	12	1.1
1952	StL-N	7	5	.583	25	13	4	1	2	100^1	82	39	37	12	3	28	54	1.096	3.32	112	2.81	.223	6	.207	4	8	0.6
1953	StL-A	5	13	.278	26	16	3	0	1	117^1	122	51	40	7	3	31	44	1.304	3.07	137	3.55	.269	7	.179	16	10	1.4
Total	**12**	**133**	**92**	**.591**	**318**	**240**	**125**	**25**	**18**	**1907^2**	**1731**	**701**	**618**	**117**	**37**	**536**	**901**	**1.188**	**2.92**	**133**	**2.92**	**.242**	**129**	**.192**	**190**	**173**	**20.3**

• BRECKINRIDGE, Bill
William Robertson Breckinridge b: 10/16/1907, Tulsa, OK d: 8/23/1958, Tulsa, OK BR/TR, 5'11", 175 lbs. Deb: 6/30/1929

YEAR	TM-L	W	L	PCT	G	GS	CG	SH	SV	IP	H	R	ER	HR	HB	BB	SO	RAT	ERA	ERA+	CERA	OAV	BH	AVG	PR+	WS	TPW
1929	Phi-A	0	0	....	3	1	0	0	0	10	10	10	9	0	0	16	2	2.600	8.10	52	7.43	.270	0	.000	-4	0	-0.5

• BREINING, Fred
Fred Lawrence Breining b: 11/15/1955, San Francisco, CA BR/TR, 6'4", 185 lbs. Deb: 9/4/1980

YEAR	TM-L	W	L	PCT	G	GS	CG	SH	SV	IP	H	R	ER	HR	HB	BB	SO	RAT	ERA	ERA+	CERA	OAV	BH	AVG	PR+	WS	TPW
1980	SF-N	0	0	....	5	0	0	0	0	6^2	8	4	4	0	1	4	3	1.800	5.40	66	5.98	.333	0	....	-1	0	-0.1
1981	SF-N	5	2	.714	45	1	0	0	1	77^2	66	28	22	4	2	38	37	1.339	2.55	135	3.26	.243	0	.000	8	6	0.8
1982	SF-N	11	6	.647	54	9	2	0	0	143^1	146	61	49	6	1	52	98	1.381	3.08	117	3.55	.269	6	.207	11	10	1.3
1983	SF-N	11	12	.478	32	32	6	0	0	202^2	202	97	86	15	5	60	117	1.293	3.82	92	3.44	.259	10	.149	-5	8	-0.4
1984	Mon-N	0	0	....	4	0	0	0	0	6^2	4	1	1	0	0	5	5	1.350	1.35	254	2.71	.190	0	.000	1	1	0.1
Total	**5**	**27**	**20**	**.574**	**140**	**42**	**8**	**0**	**1**	**437**	**426**	**191**	**162**	**25**	**9**	**159**	**260**	**1.339**	**3.34**	**106**	**3.47**	**.260**	**16**	**.148**	**15**	**25**	**1.7**

• BREITENSTEIN, Alonzo
Alonzo Breitenstein b: 11/9/1857, Utica, NY d: 6/19/1932, Utica, NY Deb: 7/7/1883

YEAR	TM-L	W	L	PCT	G	GS	CG	SH	SV	IP	H	R	ER	HR	HB	BB	SO	RAT	ERA	ERA+	CERA	OAV	BH	AVG	PR+	WS	TPW
1883	Phi-N	0	1	.000	1	1	0	0	0	5	8	9	5	0	....	2	0	2.000	9.00	34	....	.342	0	.000	-3	0	-0.3

• BREITENSTEIN, Ted
Theodore P. "Theo" Breitenstein b: 6/1/1869, St. Louis, MO d: 5/3/1935, St. Louis, MO BL/TL, 5'9", 167 lbs. Deb: 4/28/1891 U

YEAR	TM-L	W	L	PCT	G	GS	CG	SH	SV	IP	H	R	ER	HR	HB	BB	SO	RAT	ERA	ERA+	CERA	OAV	BH	AVG	PR+	WS	TPW
1891	StL-a	2	0	1.000	6	1	1	1	1	28^2	15	14	7	2	0	14	13	1.012	2.20	191	....	.150	0	.000	6	3	0.4
1892	StL-N	9	19	.321	39	32	28	1	0	282^1	280	192	147	8	0	148	126	1.516	4.69	68	3.86	.249	16	.122	-37	8	-4.0
1893	StL-N	19	24	.442	48	42	38	1	1	382^2	359	197	135	8	0	156	102	1.346	**3.18**	**149**	**3.13**	.241	29	.181	67	30	5.1
1894	StL-N	27	23	.540	**56**	**50**	**46**	1	0	**447^1**	497	320	238	21	0	191	140	1.538	4.79	113	4.32	.279	40	.220	31	36	2.3
1895	StL-N	19	30	.388	55	**51**	**47**	1	1	438	468	299	212	16	0	182	131	1.484	4.36	111	3.96	.270	42	.193	35	25	1.9
1896	StL-N	18	26	.409	44	43	37	1	0	339^2	376	236	169	12	0	138	114	1.513	4.48	97	4.13	.279	42	.259	4	22	0.5
1897	Cin-N	23	12	.657	40	39	32	2	0	320^1	345	172	129	3	9	91	98	1.361	3.62	125	3.45	.273	33	.266	33	34	3.1
1898	Cin-N	20	14	.588	39	37	32	3	0	315^2	313	170	120	2	11	123	68	1.381	3.42	112	3.36	.257	26	.215	11	25	1.1
1899	Cin-N	13	9	.591	26	24	21	0	0	210^2	219	111	84	2	9	71	59	1.377	3.59	109	3.49	.268	37	.352	7	19	1.5
1900	Cin-N	10	10	.500	24	20	18	1	0	192^1	205	111	78	4	14	79	39	1.477	3.65	100	4.06	.272	24	.190	-0	10	-0.5

YEAR	TM-L	W	L	PCT	G	GS	CG	SH	SV	IP	H	R	ER	HR	HB	BB	SO	RAT	ERA	ERA+	CERA	OAV	BH	AVG	PR+	WS	TPW
1901	StL-N	0	3	.000	3	3	1	0	0	15	24	26	11	1	0	14	3	2.533	6.60	48	9.55	.358	2	.333	-6	0	-0.6
Total	11	160	170	.485	380	342	301	12	3	2972^{2}	3101	1848	1330	79	43	1207	893	1.449	4.03	107	3.76	.265	291	.216	150	212	11.0

• BRENNAN, Ad Addison Foster Brennan b: 7/18/1881, La Harpe, KS d: 1/7/1962, Kansas City, MO BL/TL, 5'11", 170 lbs. Deb: 5/19/1910

YEAR	TM-L	W	L	PCT	G	GS	CG	SH	SV	IP	H	R	ER	HR	HB	BB	SO	RAT	ERA	ERA+	CERA	OAV	BH	AVG	PR+	WS	TPW
1910	Phi-N	2	0	1.000	19	5	2	0	0	73^{1}	72	36	19	2	3	28	28	1.364	2.33	134	3.60	.264	7	.280	6	5	0.8
1911	Phi-N	2	1	.667	5	3	1	0	0	22^{2}	22	12	9	0	1	12	12	1.500	3.57	96	3.80	.259	2	.222	-0	1	0.0
1912	Phi-N	11	9	.550	27	19	13	1	2	174	185	88	69	4	3	49	78	1.345	3.57	101	3.42	.274	15	.254	0	12	0.4
1913	Phi-N	14	12	.538	40	24	12	1	1	207	204	76	55	5	6	46	94	1.208	2.39	139	2.94	.268	11	.164	22	19	2.1
1914	Chi-F	5	5	.500	16	11	5	1	0	85^{2}	84	44	34	6	2	21	31	1.226	3.57	83	3.26	.256	8	.250	-8	3	-0.7
1915	Chi-F	3	9	.250	19	13	7	2	0	106	117	55	44	4	7	30	40	1.387	3.74	75	3.23	.287	5	.185	-11	2	-1.1
1918	Was-A	0	0	....	2	1	0	0	0	5^{1}	7	4	3	0	1	5	0	2.250	5.06	54	8.44	.241	0	.000	-2	0	-0.2
	Cle-A	0	0	....	1	0	0	0	0	3	3	1	1	0	0	3	0	2.000	3.00	100	6.60	.333	0	....	0	0	0.0
	Yr.	0	0	....	3	1	0	0	0	8^{1}	10	5	4	0	1	8	0	2.160	4.32	64	7.78	.263	0	.000	-1	0	-0.2
Total	7	37	36	.507	129	76	40	5	3	677	694	316	234	21	23	194	283	1.312	3.11	103	3.31	.270	48	.218	7	42	1.2

• BRENNAN, Don James Donald Brennan b: 12/2/1903, Augusta, ME d: 4/26/1953, Boston, MA BR/TR, 6', 210 lbs. Deb: 4/16/1933

YEAR	TM-L	W	L	PCT	G	GS	CG	SH	SV	IP	H	R	ER	HR	HB	BB	SO	RAT	ERA	ERA+	CERA	OAV	BH	AVG	PR+	WS	TPW
1933	NY-A	5	1	.833	18	10	3	0	3	85	92	56	47	4	0	47	46	1.635	4.98	78	4.52	.275	7	.259	-9	4	-0.7
1934	Cin-N	4	3	.571	28	7	2	0	2	78	89	51	33	3	1	35	31	1.590	3.81	107	4.56	.290	5	.227	4	4	0.5
1935	Cin-N	5	5	.500	38	5	2	1	5	114^{1}	101	43	40	4	4	44	48	1.268	3.15	126	3.01	.242	3	.100	12	11	1.0
1936	Cin-N	5	2	.714	41	4	0	0	9	94^{1}	117	60	46	2	1	35	40	1.611	4.39	87	4.70	.305	2	.080	-5	5	-0.8
1937	Cin-N	1	1	.500	10	0	0	0	0	16	25	14	12	1	0	10	6	2.188	6.75	55	7.87	.347	0	.000	-5	0	-0.6
	*NY-N	1	0	1.000	6	0	0	0	0	9^{1}	12	8	7	0	1	9	1	2.250	6.75	58	7.14	.316	0	.000	-3	0	-0.3
	Yr.	2	1	.667	16	0	0	0	0	25^{1}	37	22	19	1	1	19	7	2.211	6.75	56	7.60	.336	0	.000	-8	0	-0.9
Total	5	21	12	.636	141	26	7	1	19	397	436	232	185	14	7	180	172	1.552	4.19	93	4.33	.281	17	.155	-7	24	-0.9

• BRENNAN, Tom Thomas Martin Brennan b: 10/30/1952, Chicago, IL BR/TR, 6'1", 180 lbs. Deb: 9/5/1981

YEAR	TM-L	W	L	PCT	G	GS	CG	SH	SV	IP	H	R	ER	HR	HB	BB	SO	RAT	ERA	ERA+	CERA	OAV	BH	AVG	PR+	WS	TPW
1981	Cle-A	2	2	.500	7	6	1	0	0	48^{1}	49	20	17	5	0	14	15	1.303	3.17	114	3.69	.259	0	....	4	3	0.4
1982	Cle-A	4	2	.667	30	4	0	0	2	92^{2}	112	51	44	9	2	10	46	1.317	4.27	95	4.14	.300	0	....	-1	5	-0.1
1983	Cle-A	2	2	.500	11	5	1	1	0	39^{2}	45	22	17	3	1	8	21	1.336	3.86	110	3.99	.288	0	....	2	2	0.2
1984	Chi-A	0	1	.000	4	1	0	0	0	6^{2}	8	5	3	1	0	3	3	1.650	4.05	103	5.90	.308	0	....	0	0	0.0
1985	LA-N	1	3	.250	12	4	0	0	0	31^{2}	41	26	26	2	0	11	17	1.642	7.39	47	5.04	.333	1	.125	-14	0	-1.5
Total	5	9	10	.474	64	20	2	1	2	219	255	124	107	20	3	46	102	1.374	4.40	88	4.20	.294	1	.125	-9	10	-1.0

• BRENNAN, William William Raymond Brennan b: 1/15/1963, Tampa, FL BR/TR, 6'3", 200 lbs. Deb: 7/19/1988

YEAR	TM-L	W	L	PCT	G	GS	CG	SH	SV	IP	H	R	ER	HR	HB	BB	SO	RAT	ERA	ERA+	CERA	OAV	BH	AVG	PR+	WS	TPW
1988	LA-N	0	1	.000	4	2	0	0	0	9^{1}	13	7	7	0	0	6	7	2.036	6.75	49	6.65	.342	0	.000	-3	0	-0.4
1993	Chi-N	2	1	.667	8	1	0	0	0	15	16	8	7	2	1	8	11	1.600	4.20	95	5.73	.291	0	.000	-1	1	0.0
Total	2	2	2	.500	12	3	0	0	0	24^{1}	29	15	14	2	1	14	18	1.767	5.18	70	6.08	.312	0	.000	-4	1	-0.4

• BRENNEMAN, Jim James Leroy Brenneman b: 2/13/1941, San Diego, CA d: 3/10/1994, Pearl, MS BR/TR, 6'2", 180 lbs. Deb: 7/9/1965

YEAR	TM-L	W	L	PCT	G	GS	CG	SH	SV	IP	H	R	ER	HR	HB	BB	SO	RAT	ERA	ERA+	CERA	OAV	BH	AVG	PR+	WS	TPW
1965	NY-A	0	0	....	3	0	0	0	0	2	5	5	4	1	0	3	2	4.000	18.00	19	24.40	.455	0	....	-3	0	-0.3

• BRENNER, Bert Delbert Henry "Dutch" Brenner b: 7/18/1887, Minneapolis, MN d: 4/11/1971, St. Louis Park, MN BR/TR, 6', 175 lbs. Deb: 9/21/1912

YEAR	TM-L	W	L	PCT	G	GS	CG	SH	SV	IP	H	R	ER	HR	HB	BB	SO	RAT	ERA	ERA+	CERA	OAV	BH	AVG	PR+	WS	TPW
1912	Cle-A	1	0	1.000	2	1	1	0	0	13	14	8	4	0	0	4	3	1.385	2.77	124	3.56	.286	0	.000	1	1	0.0

• BRENTON, Lynn Lynn Davis "Buck,Herb" Brenton b: 10/7/1890, Peoria, IL d: 10/14/1968, Los Angeles, CA BR/TR, 5'10", 165 lbs. Deb: 8/10/1913

YEAR	TM-L	W	L	PCT	G	GS	CG	SH	SV	IP	H	R	ER	HR	HB	BB	SO	RAT	ERA	ERA+	CERA	OAV	BH	AVG	PR+	WS	TPW
1913	Cle-A	0	0	....	1	0	0	0	0	2	4	2	2	0	0	0	2	2.000	9.00	34	7.48	.400	0	....	-1	0	-0.1
1915	Cle-A	2	3	.400	11	5	1	1	0	51	60	31	19	1	2	20	18	1.569	3.35	91	4.77	.308	2	.118	-1	2	-0.3
1920	Cin-N	2	1	.667	5	1	1	0	1	18^{1}	17	14	10	0	0	4	13	1.145	4.91	62	2.24	.236	2	.250	-4	0	-0.4
1921	Cin-N	1	8	.111	17	8	2	0	1	60	80	35	27	0	1	17	19	1.617	4.05	88	4.87	.342	2	.133	-2	2	-0.2
Total	4	5	12	.294	34	14	4	1	2	131^{1}	161	82	58	1	3	41	52	1.538	3.97	82	4.50	.315	6	.150	-9	4	-1.1

• BRESNAHAN, Roger Roger Philip "The Duke Of Tralee" Bresnahan
b: 6/11/1879, Toledo, OH d: 12/4/1944, Toledo, OH BR/TR, 5'9", 200 lbs. Deb: 8/27/1897 M/C HOF: 1945 ♦

YEAR	TM-L	W	L	PCT	G	GS	CG	SH	SV	IP	H	R	ER	HR	HB	BB	SO	RAT	ERA	ERA+	CERA	OAV	BH	AVG	PR+	WS	TPW
1897	Was-N	4	0	1.000	6	5	3	1	0	41	52	21	18	1	3	10	12	1.512	3.95	110	4.63	.307	6	.375	1	3	0.2
1901	Bal-A	0	1	.000	2	1	0	0	0	6	10	8	4	0	0	4	3	2.333	6.00	64	8.24	.366	79	.268	-1	6	-1.0
1910	StL-N	0	0	....	1	0	0	0	0	3^{1}	6	1	0	0	0	1	0	2.100	0.00	....	7.92	.400	65	.278	1	13	2.0
Total	3	4	1	.800	9	6	3	1	0	50^{1}	68	30	22	1	3	15	15	1.649	3.93	108	5.28	.321	1252	.279	1	22	1.1

• BRESSLER, Rube Raymond Bloom Bressler b: 10/23/1894, Coder, PA d: 11/7/1966, Mount Washington, OH BR/TL, 6', 187 lbs. Deb: 4/24/1914 ♦

YEAR	TM-L	W	L	PCT	G	GS	CG	SH	SV	IP	H	R	ER	HR	HB	BB	SO	RAT	ERA	ERA+	CERA	OAV	BH	AVG	PR+	WS	TPW
1914	Phi-A	10	4	.714	29	10	8	1	2	147^{2}	112	37	29	1	4	56	96	1.138	1.77	147	2.31	.220	11	.216	13	14	1.9
1915	Phi-A	4	17	.190	32	20	7	1	0	178^{1}	183	133	103	3	7	118	69	**1.688**	5.20	56	4.91	.283	8	.145	-44	1	-4.5
1916	Phi-A	0	2	.000	4	2	0	0	0	15	16	11	11	0	2	14	8	2.000	6.60	43	6.43	.296	1	.200	-6	0	-0.6
1917	Cin-N	0	0	....	2	1	0	0	0	9	15	11	6	0	0	5	2	2.222	6.00	43	8.14	.429	1	.200	-3	0	-0.4
1918	Cin-N	8	5	.615	17	13	10	0	0	128	124	48	35	3	1	39	37	1.273	2.46	108	3.01	.261	17	.274	2	9	0.6
1919	Cin-N	2	4	.333	13	4	1	0	0	41^{2}	37	19	16	1	0	8	13	1.080	3.46	80	2.28	.248	34	.206	-4	6	-0.8
1920	Cin-N	2	0	1.000	10	2	1	1	0	20^{1}	24	8	4	0	0	2	4	1.279	1.77	171	3.15	.300	8	.267	3	2	0.2
Total	7	26	32	.448	107	52	27	3	2	540	511	267	204	8	14	242	229	1.394	3.40	82	3.58	.262	1170	.301	-39	32	-3.6

• BRETT, Herb Herbert James "Duke" Brett b: 5/23/1900, Lawrenceville, VA d: 11/25/1974, St. Petersburg, FL BR/TR, 6', 175 lbs. Deb: 8/8/1924

YEAR	TM-L	W	L	PCT	G	GS	CG	SH	SV	IP	H	R	ER	HR	HB	BB	SO	RAT	ERA	ERA+	CERA	OAV	BH	AVG	PR+	WS	TPW
1924	Chi-N	0	0	....	1	1	0	0	0	5^{1}	6	4	3	0	0	7	1	2.438	5.06	77	7.02	.300	0	.000	-1	0	-0.1
1925	Chi-N	1	1	.500	10	1	0	0	0	17^{1}	12	7	7	0	1	3	6	.865	3.63	119	1.38	.194	0	.000	1	1	0.1
Total	2	1	1	.500	11	2	0	0	0	22^{2}	18	11	10	0	1	10	7	1.235	3.97	105	2.71	.220	0	.000	0	1	0.0

• BRETT, Ken Kenneth Alven "Kemer" Brett b: 9/18/1948, Brooklyn, NY BL/TL, 6', 195 lbs. Deb: 9/27/1967

YEAR	TM-L	W	L	PCT	G	GS	CG	SH	SV	IP	H	R	ER	HR	HB	BB	SO	RAT	ERA	ERA+	CERA	OAV	BH	AVG	PR+	WS	TPW
1967*	Bos-A	0	0	....	1	0	0	0	0	2	3	1	1	0	0	0	2	1.500	4.50	77	5.09	.375	0	....	-0	0	0.0
1969	Bos-A	2	3	.400	8	8	0	0	0	39^{1}	41	24	23	6	3	22	23	1.602	5.26	72	5.71	.275	3	.300	-6	1	-0.4
1970	Bos-A	8	9	.471	41	14	1	0	2	139^{1}	118	71	63	17	3	79	155	1.414	4.07	97	3.97	.223	13	.317	1	9	0.7
1971	Bos-A	0	3	.000	29	2	0	0	1	59	57	38	35	7	1	35	57	1.559	5.34	69	4.68	.253	2	.200	-10	0	-1.1
1972	Mil-A	7	12	.368	26	22	2	1	0	133	121	76	67	13	1	49	74	1.278	4.53	67	3.37	.242	10	.227	-22	1	-2.3
1973	Phi-N	13	9	.591	31	25	10	1	0	211^{2}	206	91	81	19	0	74	111	1.323	3.44	110	3.64	.259	20	.250	6	17	1.5
1974*	Pit-N★	13	9	.591	27	27	10	3	0	191	192	81	70	9	2	52	96	1.277	3.30	104	3.20	.257	27	.310	2	14	1.3
1975*	Pit-N	9	5	.643	23	16	4	1	0	118	110	47	44	10	2	43	47	1.297	3.36	105	3.52	.250	12	.231	2	8	0.6
1976	NY-A	0	0	....	2	0	0	0	1	2^{1}	2	0	0	0	0	0	1	.857	0.00	....	1.44	.222	0	....	1	1	0.1
	Chi-A	10	12	.455	27	26	16	1	1	200^{2}	171	82	74	5	3	76	91	1.231	3.32	107	2.78	.234	1	.083	8	13	0.9
	Yr.	10	12	.455	29	26	16	1	2	203	173	82	74	5	3	76	92	1.227	3.28	109	2.76	.233	1	.083	9	14	1.0
1977	Chi-A	6	4	.600	13	13	2	0	0	82^{2}	101	47	46	10	1	15	39	1.403	5.01	82	4.73	.305	0	....	-6	3	-0.6
	Cal-A	7	10	.412	21	21	5	0	0	142	157	73	67	15	3	38	41	1.373	4.25	92	4.37	.287	0	....	-4	5	-0.4
	Yr.	13	14	.481	34	34	7	0	0	224^{2}	258	120	113	25	4	53	80	1.384	4.53	88	4.50	.294	0	....	-10	8	-1.0
1978	Cal-A	3	5	.375	31	10	1	1	1	100	100	60	55	12	1	42	43	1.420	4.95	73	4.32	.262	0	....	-14	1	-1.5
1979	Min-A	0	0	....	9	0	0	0	0	12^{2}	16	7	7	1	0	6	3	1.737	4.97	88	5.82	.320	0	....	-1	1	-0.1
	LA-N	4	3	.571	30	0	0	0	2	47	52	20	18	1	1	12	13	1.362	3.45	105	3.55	.277	3	.273	2	3	0.2
1980	KC-A	0	0	....	8	0	0	0	1	13^{1}	8	0	0	0	1	5	4	.975	0.00	....	1.61	.174	0	....	6	2	0.6
1981	KC-A	1	1	.500	22	0	0	0	2	32^{1}	35	16	15	2	1	14	7	1.515	4.18	86	4.29	.282	0	....	-2	1	-0.2
Total	14	83	85	.494	349	184	51	8	11	1526^{1}	1490	734	666	127	23	562	807	1.344	3.93	93	3.74	.257	91	.262	-37	80	-0.5

• BREUER, Marv Marvin Howard "Baby Face" Breuer b: 4/29/1914, Rolla, MO d: 1/17/1991, Rolla, MO BR/TR, 6'2", 185 lbs. Deb: 5/4/1939

YEAR	TM-L	W	L	PCT	G	GS	CG	SH	SV	IP	H	R	ER	HR	HB	BB	SO	RAT	ERA	ERA+	CERA	OAV	BH	AVG	PR+	WS	TPW
1939	NY-A	0	0	....	1	0	0	0	0	1	2	1	1	0	0	1	0	3.000	9.00	48	11.63	.667	0	....	-1	0	-0.1
1940	NY-A	8	9	.471	27	22	10	0	0	164	175	89	83	20	0	61	71	1.439	4.55	89	4.34	.267	2	.037	-12	7	-1.6
1941*	NY-A	9	7	.563	26	18	7	1	2	141	131	73	64	10	2	49	77	1.277	4.09	96	3.25	.243	4	.087	-8	7	-1.1
1942*	NY-A	8	9	.471	27	19	6	0	1	164^{1}	157	67	56	11	1	37	72	1.181	3.07	112	2.96	.252	3	.056	-0	9	-0.4

YEAR TM-L	W	L	PCT	G	GS	CG	SH	SV	IP	H	R	ER	HR	HB	BB	SO	RAT	ERA	ERA+	CERA	OAV	BH	AVG	PR+	WS	TPW
1943 NY-A	0	1	.000	5	1	0	0	0	14	22	16	13	0	0	6	6	2.000	8.36	38	6.49	.349	1	.333	-8	0	-0.8
Total 5	25	26	.490	86	60	23	1	3	484^1	487	246	217	41	3	154	226	1.323	4.03	94	3.63	.258	10	.064	-28	23	-3.8
• BREWER, Billy	William Robert Brewer b: 4/15/1968, Fort Worth, TX BL/TL, 6'1", 175 lbs. Deb: 4/8/1993																									
1993 KC-A	2	2	.500	46	0	0	0	0	39	31	16	15	6	0	20	28	1.308	3.46	132	3.81	.230	0	....	5	4	0.4
1994 KC-A	4	1	.800	50	0	0	0	3	38^2	28	11	11	4	2	16	25	1.138	2.56	195	2.89	.207	0	....	10	7	1.0
1995 KC-A	2	4	.333	48	0	0	0	0	45^1	54	28	28	9	2	20	31	1.632	5.56	86	6.23	.290	0	....	-5	1	-0.4
1996 NY-A	1	0	1.000	4	0	0	0	0	5^2	7	6	6	0	0	8	8	2.647	9.53	52	8.60	.292	0	....	-3	0	-0.3
1997 Oak-A	0	0	....	3	0	0	0	0	2	4	3	3	1	0	2	1	3.000	13.50	33	17.51	.444	0	....	-2	0	-0.2
Phi-N	1	2	.333	25	0	0	0	0	22	15	8	8	2	0	11	16	1.182	3.27	130	2.62	.188	0	.000	2	2	0.2
1998 Phi-N	0	1	.000	2	0	0	0	0	0^1	3	4	4	0	0	2	0	15.00	108.00	4	100.03	.750	0	....	-4	0	-0.4
1999 Phi-N	1	1	.500	25	0	0	0	2	25^2	30	20	20	4	0	14	28	1.714	7.01	67	6.05	.294	0	....	-7	0	-0.7
Total 7	11	11	.500	203	0	0	0	5	178^2	172	96	95	26	4	93	137	1.483	4.79	98	4.88	.255	0	.000	-2	14	-0.2
• BREWER, Jack	John Herndon "Buddy" Brewer b: 7/21/1919, Los Angeles, CA BR/TR, 6'2", 170 lbs. Deb: 7/15/1944																									
1944 NY-N	1	4	.200	14	7	2	0	0	55	66	40	34	8	3	16	21	1.491	5.56	66	5.09	.288	4	.211	-12	0	-1.2
1945 NY-N	8	6	.571	28	21	8	0	0	159^2	162	77	68	14	3	58	49	1.378	3.83	102	3.89	.260	10	.179	1	9	0.0
1946 NY-N	0	0	....	1	0	0	0	0	2	3	3	3	0	0	2	3	2.500	13.50	26	8.24	.333	0	....	-2	0	-0.2
Total 3	9	10	.474	43	28	10	0	0	216^2	231	120	105	22	6	76	73	1.417	4.36	87	4.24	.268	14	.187	-13	9	-1.4
• BREWER, Jim	James Thomas Brewer b: 11/14/1937, Merced, CA d: 11/16/1987, Tyler, TX BL/TL, 6'1", 195 lbs. Deb: 7/17/1960 C																									
1960 Chi-N	0	3	.000	5	4	0	0	0	21^2	25	14	14	2	1	6	7	1.431	5.82	65	4.22	.272	1	.167	-5	0	-0.5
1961 Chi-N	1	7	.125	36	11	0	0	0	86^2	116	65	56	17	1	21	57	1.581	5.82	72	6.17	.321	4	.182	-14	0	-1.4
1962 Chi-N	0	1	.000	6	1	0	0	0	5^2	10	6	6	2	0	3	1	2.294	9.53	44	13.00	.435	0	....	-3	0	-0.3
1963 Chi-N	3	2	.600	29	1	0	0	0	49^2	59	32	27	10	0	15	35	1.490	4.89	72	5.38	.294	0	.000	-8	1	-0.9
1964 LA-N	4	3	.571	34	5	1	1	1	93	79	33	31	5	0	25	63	1.118	3.00	108	2.44	.232	6	.273	3	6	0.5
1965* LA-N	3	2	.600	19	2	0	0	2	49^1	33	13	10	1	0	28	31	1.236	1.82	179	2.40	.196	0	.000	7	5	0.7
1966* LA-N	0	2	.000	13	0	0	0	2	22	17	9	9	0	0	11	8	1.273	3.68	90	2.54	.221	0	....	-1	1	-0.1
1967 LA-N	5	4	.556	30	11	0	0	1	100^2	78	32	30	8	1	31	74	1.083	2.68	115	2.43	.218	1	.045	6	8	0.5
1968 LA-N	8	3	.727	54	0	0	0	14	76^1	59	22	21	5	0	33	75	1.205	2.48	112	2.56	.219	2	.222	2	10	0.2
1969 LA-N	7	6	.538	59	0	0	0	20	88^1	71	30	25	5	4	41	92	1.268	2.55	131	3.04	.221	1	.091	7	12	0.7
1970 LA-N	7	6	.538	58	0	0	0	24	89	66	36	31	10	0	33	91	1.112	3.13	122	2.53	.207	1	.083	5	13	0.5
1971 LA-N	6	5	.545	55	0	0	0	22	81^1	55	17	17	4	0	24	66	.971	1.88	172	1.70	.194	3	.333	12	15	1.4
1972 LA-N	8	7	.533	51	0	0	0	17	78^1	41	16	11	6	2	25	69	.843	1.26	264	1.34	.157	0	.000	18	16	1.9
1973 LA-N★	6	8	.429	56	0	0	0	20	71^2	58	26	24	8	0	25	56	1.158	3.01	114	2.77	.229	2	.400	2	11	0.3
1974* LA-N	4	4	.500	24	0	0	0	0	39^1	29	14	11	5	0	10	26	.992	2.52	135	2.28	.207	0	.000	4	3	0.4
1975 LA-N	3	1	.750	21	0	0	0	2	33	44	20	19	2	1	12	21	1.697	5.18	66	5.60	.333	0	.000	-7	0	-0.8
Cal-A	1	0	1.000	21	0	0	0	5	34^2	38	9	7	2	0	11	22	1.413	1.82	195	3.93	.281	0	....	7	4	0.7
1976 Cal-A	3	1	.750	13	0	0	0	2	20	20	7	6	0	0	6	16	1.300	2.70	123	2.98	.256	0	....	1	3	0.2
Total 17	69	65	.515	584	35	1	1	132	1040^2	898	401	355	92	10	360	810	1.209	3.07	113	3.09	.236	21	.150	35	108	4.0
• BREWER, Tom	Thomas Austin Brewer b: 9/3/1931, Wadesboro, SC BR/TR, 6'1", 175 lbs. Deb: 4/18/1954																									
1954 Bos-A	10	9	.526	33	23	7	0	0	162^2	152	90	84	15	7	95	69	1.518	4.65	88	4.37	.249	16	.267	-8	7	-0.5
1955 Bos-A	11	10	.524	31	28	9	2	0	192^2	198	101	90	21	8	87	91	1.479	4.20	102	4.62	.263	11	.151	4	10	0.2
1956 Bos-A★	19	9	.679	32	32	15	4	0	244^1	200	103	95	14	5	112	127	1.277	3.50	132	3.03	.220	28	.298	31	24	3.5
1957 Bos-A	16	13	.552	32	32	15	2	0	238^1	225	113	102	24	7	93	128	1.334	3.85	104	3.81	.250	19	.202	7	16	0.7
1958 Bos-A	12	12	.500	33	32	10	1	0	227^1	227	122	94	21	8	93	124	1.408	3.72	108	4.16	.259	16	.195	11	12	1.1
1959 Bos-A	10	12	.455	36	32	11	3	2	215^1	219	96	90	14	2	88	121	1.426	3.76	108	3.99	.265	8	.111	6	13	0.3
1960 Bos-A	10	15	.400	34	29	8	1	1	186^2	220	115	100	13	6	72	60	**1.564**	4.82	84	4.94	.301	12	.194	-11	6	-1.1
1961 Bos-A	3	2	.600	10	9	0	0	0	42	37	21	16	4	0	29	13	1.571	3.43	122	4.48	.242	4	.286	4	4	0.5
Total 8	91	82	.526	241	217	75	13	3	1509^1	1478	761	671	126	43	669	733	1.422	4.00	104	4.08	.257	114	.207	44	92	4.7
• BREWINGTON, Jamie	Jamie Chancellor Brewington b: 9/28/1971, Greenville, NC BR/TR, 6'4", 180 lbs. Deb: 7/24/1995																									
1995 SF-N	6	4	.600	13	13	0	0	0	75^1	68	38	38	8	4	45	45	1.500	4.54	90	4.44	.245	5	.217	-4	4	-0.4
2000 Cle-A	3	0	1.000	26	0	0	0	0	45^1	56	28	27	3	2	19	34	1.654	5.36	93	5.53	.311	0	.000	-2	2	-0.1
Total 2	9	4	.692	39	13	0	0	0	120^2	124	66	65	11	6	64	79	1.558	4.85	91	4.85	.271	5	.208	-6	6	-0.5
• BRICE, Alan	Alan Healey Brice b: 10/1/1937, New York, NY BR/TR, 6'5", 215 lbs. Deb: 9/22/1961																									
1961 Chi-A	0	1	.000	3	0	0	0	0	3^1	4	2	0	0	0	3	3	2.100	0.00	....	6.70	.308	0	....	1	0	0.1
• BRICKNER, Ralph	Ralph Harold "Brick" Brickner b: 5/2/1925, Cincinnati, OH d: 5/9/1994, Bridgetown, OH BR/TR, 6'3.5", 215 lbs. Deb: 5/4/1952																									
1952 Bos-A	3	1	.750	14	1	0	0	1	33	32	8	8	1	0	11	9	1.303	2.18	180	3.21	.264	2	.250	6	4	0.7
• BRIDGES, Marshall	Marshall "Fox,Sheriff" Bridges b: 6/2/1931, Jackson, MS d: 9/3/1990, Jackson, MS BB/TL, 6'1", 180 lbs. Deb: 6/17/1959																									
1959 StL-N	6	3	.667	27	4	1	0	1	76	67	38	36	10	0	37	76	1.368	4.26	99	3.78	.240	5	.217	0	6	0.2
1960 StL-N	2	2	.500	20	1	0	0	1	31^1	33	15	12	2	1	16	27	1.564	3.45	119	4.50	.266	0	.000	2	2	0.2
Cin-N	4	0	1.000	14	0	0	0	2	25^1	14	3	3	1	0	7	26	.829	1.07	359	1.31	.161	1	.250	8	5	0.8
Yr.	6	2	.750	34	1	0	0	3	56^2	47	18	15	3	1	23	53	1.235	2.38	169	3.07	.223	1	.100	10	7	1.0
1961 Cin-N	0	1	.000	13	0	0	0	0	20^2	26	19	18	4	1	11	17	1.790	7.84	52	7.13	.317	0	.000	-9	0	-0.9
1962* NY-A	8	4	.667	52	0	0	0	18	71^2	49	30	25	4	0	48	66	1.353	3.14	119	2.93	.194	0	.000	4	10	0.2
1963 NY-A	2	0	1.000	23	0	0	0	1	33	27	18	14	2	1	30	35	1.727	3.82	92	4.78	.237	0	....	-2	1	-0.2
1964 Was-A	0	3	.000	17	0	0	0	2	30	37	22	19	3	0	17	16	1.800	5.70	65	6.00	.303	0	.000	-7	0	-0.7
1965 Was-A	1	2	.333	40	0	0	0	0	57^1	62	26	17	3	0	25	39	1.517	2.67	130	4.10	.268	1	.143	6	3	0.6
Total 7	23	15	.605	206	5	1	0	25	345^1	315	171	144	29	3	191	302	1.465	3.75	103	4.03	.244	7	.119	3	27	0.4
• BRIDGES, Tommy	Thomas Jefferson Davis Bridges b: 12/28/1906, Gordonsville, TN d: 4/19/1968, Nashville, TN BR/TR, 5'10.5", 155 lbs. Deb: 8/13/1930 C																									
1930 Det-A	3	2	.600	8	5	2	0	0	37^2	28	18	17	4	0	23	17	1.354	4.06	118	3.45	.215	3	.300	3	3	0.3
1931 Det-A	8	16	.333	35	23	8	2	0	173	182	120	96	13	0	108	105	1.676	4.99	92	4.78	.263	8	.148	-8	7	-0.9
1932 Det-A	14	12	.538	34	26	10	**4**	1	201	174	95	75	14	1	119	108	1.458	3.36	140	3.71	.233	11	.164	27	16	2.4
1933 Det-A	14	12	.538	33	28	17	2	2	233	192	102	80	8	6	110	120	1.296	3.09	139	**2.94**	**.226**	16	.205	30	20	3.0
1934* Det-A★	22	11	.667	36	**35**	23	3	1	275	249	117	112	16	3	104	151	1.284	3.67	120	3.16	.241	12	.122	20	22	1.5
1935* Det-A★	21	10	.677	36	34	23	4	1	274^1	277	129	107	22	3	113	**163**	1.422	3.51	119	3.95	.259	26	.239	18	19	1.9
1936 Det-A★	**23**	11	.676	39	**38**	26	5	0	294^2	289	141	118	21	5	115	**175**	1.371	3.60	137	3.67	.255	25	.212	47	26	4.1
1937 Det-A★	15	12	.556	34	31	18	3	0	245^1	267	129	111	15	3	91	138	1.459	4.07	115	4.11	.274	23	.240	19	19	2.0
1938 Det-A	13	9	.591	25	20	13	0	1	151	171	83	77	14	2	58	101	1.517	4.59	109	4.69	.287	7	.130	6	12	0.4
1939 Det-A★	17	7	.708	29	26	16	2	2	198	186	87	77	11	6	61	129	1.247	3.50	140	3.09	.243	14	.197	30	19	2.8
1940* Det-A★	12	9	.571	29	28	12	2	0	197^2	171	89	74	11	0	88	133	1.310	3.37	141	3.07	.229	12	.176	34	16	3.0
1941 Det-A	9	12	.429	25	22	10	1	0	147^2	128	66	56	10	1	70	90	1.341	3.41	133	3.31	.233	4	.085	23	13	2.0
1942 Det-A	9	7	.563	23	22	11	2	1	174	164	66	53	6	4	61	97	1.293	2.74	144	3.09	.246	6	.095	26	15	2.4
1943 Det-A	12	7	.632	25	22	11	3	0	191^2	159	57	51	9	0	61	124	1.148	2.39	147	2.49	.226	14	.219	25	17	2.9
1945* Det-A	1	0	1.000	4	1	0	0	0	11	14	6	4	2	0	2	6	1.455	3.27	107	5.30	.311	0	.000	0	1	0.0
1946 Det-A	1	1	.500	9	1	0	0	1	21^1	24	16	14	5	1	8	17	1.500	5.91	62	5.79	.279	0	.000	-5	0	-0.5
Total 16	194	138	.584	424	362	200	33	10	2826^1	2675	1321	1122	181	35	1192	1674	1.368	3.57	126	3.55	.248	181	.180	293	225	27.3
• BRIGGS, Buttons	Herbert Theodore Briggs b: 7/8/1875, Poughkeepsie, NY d: 2/18/1911, Cleveland, OH BR/TR, 6'1", 180 lbs. Deb: 4/23/1896																									
1896 Chi-N	12	8	.600	26	21	19	0	1	194	202	129	93	6	0	108	84	1.598	4.31	105	4.26	.266	10	.128	2	14	-0.3
1897 Chi-N	4	17	.190	22	22	21	0	0	186^2	246	166	109	6	9	85	60	1.773	5.26	85	5.68	.315	13	.160	-15	4	-1.7
1898 Chi-N	1	3	.250	4	4	3	0	0	30	38	22	19	0	1	10	14	1.600	5.70	63	4.61	.307	6	.429	-7	1	-0.5
1904 Chi-N	19	11	.633	34	30	28	3	3	277	252	101	63	3	8	77	112	1.188	2.05	130	2.69	.246	16	.170	14	24	1.4

YEAR	TM-L	W	L	PCT	G	GS	CG	SH	SV	IP	H	R	ER	HR	HB	BB	SO	RAT	ERA	ERA+	CERA	OAV	BH	AVG	PR+	WS	TPW
1905	Chi-N	8	8	.500	20	20	13	5	0	168	141	58	40	1	6	52	68	1.149	2.14	139	2.59	.237	3	.053	9	12	0.5
Total	5	44	47	.484	106	97	84	8	4	855^2	879	476	324	16	24	332	338	1.415	3.41	109	3.75	.268	48	.148	3	55	-0.6
• BRIGGS, John					Jonathan Tift Briggs b: 1/24/1934, Natoma, CA BR/TR, 5'10", 175 lbs. Deb: 4/17/1956																						
1956	Chi-N	0	0	....	3	0	0	0	0	5^1	5	1	1	1	3	4	1	1.688	1.69	223	7.68	.238	0	....	1	1	0.1
1957	Chi-N	0	1	.000	3	0	0	0	0	4^1	7	6	6	2	0	3	1	2.308	12.46	31	12.43	.368	0	....	-4	0	-0.4
1958	Chi-N	5	5	.500	20	17	3	1	0	95^2	99	52	48	12	1	45	46	1.505	4.52	87	4.83	.270	9	.257	-5	4	-0.4
1959	Cle-A	0	1	.000	4	1	0	0	0	12^2	12	5	3	1	0	3	5	1.184	2.13	173	2.96	.245	0	.000	2	1	0.2
1960	Cle-A	4	2	.667	21	2	0	0	1	36^1	32	20	18	4	1	15	19	1.294	4.46	84	3.79	.250	1	.125	-3	2	-0.3
	KC-A	0	2	.000	8	1	0	0	0	11^1	19	17	16	3	0	12	8	2.735	12.71	31	13.22	.380	0	.000	-11	0	-1.1
	Yr.	4	4	.500	29	3	0	0	1	47^2	51	37	34	7	1	27	27	1.636	6.42	60	6.03	.287	1	.091	-14	2	-1.5
Total	5	9	11	.450	59	21	3	1	1	165^2	174	101	92	23	5	82	80	1.545	5.00	78	5.32	.275	10	.208	-20	8	-2.0
• BRILES, Nelson					Nelson Kelley Briles b: 8/5/1943, Dorris, CA BR/TR, 5'11", 200 lbs. Deb: 4/19/1965																						
1965	StL-N	3	3	.500	37	2	0	0	4	82^1	79	33	32	4	6	26	52	1.275	3.50	110	3.45	.258	2	.133	3	6	0.3
1966	StL-N	4	15	.211	49	17	0	0	6	154	162	65	55	14	7	54	100	1.403	3.21	112	4.29	.279	3	.079	5	8	0.3
1967★	StL-N	14	5	.737	49	14	4	2	6	155^1	139	45	42	8	5	40	94	1.152	2.43	133	2.69	.236	6	.150	14	16	1.5
1968★	StL-N	19	11	.633	33	33	13	4	0	243^2	251	90	76	18	7	55	141	1.256	2.81	103	3.42	.266	11	.138	0	14	0.1
1969	StL-N	15	13	.536	36	33	10	3	0	227^2	218	104	89	17	2	63	126	1.234	3.52	102	3.16	.251	8	.105	-1	11	-0.2
1970	StL-N	6	7	.462	30	19	1	1	0	106^2	129	84	74	14	2	36	59	1.547	6.24	66	5.14	.297	7	.179	-24	0	-2.2
1971★	Pit-N	8	4	.667	37	14	4	2	1	136	131	51	46	12	3	35	76	1.221	3.04	112	3.20	.250	10	.256	4	9	0.9
1972★	Pit-N	14	11	.560	28	27	9	2	0	195^2	185	83	67	14	1	43	120	1.165	3.08	108	2.87	.249	11	.157	2	10	0.2
1973	Pit-N	14	13	.519	33	33	7	1	0	218^2	201	87	69	19	1	51	94	1.152	2.84	124	2.92	.244	14	.194	16	12	2.0
1974	KC-A	5	7	.417	18	17	3	0	0	103	118	48	46	9	2	21	41	1.350	4.02	95	4.18	.293	0	....	-1	5	-0.1
1975	KC-A	6	6	.500	24	16	3	0	2	112	127	60	53	19	5	25	73	1.357	4.26	90	4.84	.285	0	....	-4	5	-0.4
1976	Tex-A	11	9	.550	32	31	7	1	1	210	224	87	76	17	2	47	98	1.290	3.26	110	3.69	.273	0	....	7	13	0.7
1977	Tex-A	6	4	.600	28	15	2	1	1	108^1	114	58	51	13	6	30	57	1.329	4.24	96	4.32	.275	0	....	-3	6	-0.3
	Bal-A	0	0	....	2	0	0	0	1	4	5	3	3	2	0	0	2	1.250	6.75	56	6.37	.294	0	....	-1	0	-0.1
	Yr.	6	4	.600	30	15	2	1	2	112^1	119	61	54	15	6	30	59	1.326	4.33	94	4.40	.276	0	....	-5	6	-0.5
1978	Bal-A	4	4	.500	16	8	1	0	0	54^1	58	31	28	6	2	21	30	1.454	4.64	75	4.63	.279	0	....	-8	1	-0.8
Total	14	129	112	.535	452	279	64	17	22	2111^2	2141	929	807	186	51	547	1163	1.273	3.44	103	3.59	.264	72	.154	11	116	1.8
• BRILL, Frank					Francis Hasbrouck Brill b: 3/28/1864, Astoria, NY d: 11/19/1944, Flushing, NY BR/TR, 5'8", 155 lbs. Deb: 6/23/1884																						
1884	Det-N	2	10	.167	12	12	12	1	0	103	148	98	63	7	....	26	18	1.689	5.50	53	....	.320	6	.136	-26	1	-2.6
• BRILLHEART, Jim					James Benson Brillheart b: 9/28/1903, Dublin, VA d: 9/2/1972, Radford, VA BR/TL, 5'11", 170 lbs. Deb: 4/17/1922																						
1922	Was-A	4	6	.400	31	10	3	0	1	119^2	120	58	48	3	8	72	47	1.604	3.61	107	4.47	.275	3	.083	-0	6	-0.4
1923	Was-A	0	1	.000	12	0	0	0	0	18	27	15	14	1	1	12	8	2.167	7.00	54	8.15	.360	0	.000	-7	0	-0.7
1927	Chi-N	4	2	.667	32	12	4	0	0	128^2	140	67	59	4	4	38	36	1.383	4.13	94	3.70	.286	1	.023	-6	5	-1.2
1931	Bos-A	0	0	....	11	1	0	0	0	19^2	27	16	12	2	0	15	7	2.136	5.49	78	7.54	.325	2	.500	-3	1	-0.1
Total	4	8	9	.471	86	23	7	0	1	286	314	156	133	10	13	137	98	1.577	4.19	93	4.57	.290	6	.070	-16	12	-2.3
• BRINK, Brad					Bradford Albert Brink b: 1/20/1965, Roseville, CA BR/TR, 6'2", 195 lbs. Deb: 5/17/1992																						
1992	Phi-N	0	4	.000	8	7	0	0	0	41^1	53	27	19	2	1	13	16	1.597	4.14	84	4.96	.308	1	.083	-3	0	-0.3
1993	Phi-N	0	0	....	2	0	0	0	0	6	3	2	2	1	0	3	8	1.000	3.00	132	2.24	.143	0	.000	1	0	0.1
1994	SF-N	0	0	....	4	0	0	0	0	8^1	4	1	1	1	0	4	3	.960	1.08	371	1.76	.143	0	.000	2	1	0.2
Total	3	0	4	.000	14	7	0	0	0	55^2	60	30	22	4	1	20	27	1.437	3.56	100	4.19	.271	1	.071	0	1	0.0
• BRISCOE, John					John Eric Briscoe b: 9/22/1967, La Grange, IL BR/TR, 6'3", 185 lbs. Deb: 4/18/1991																						
1991	Oak-A	0	0	....	11	0	0	0	0	14	12	11	11	3	0	10	9	1.571	7.07	54	5.45	.235	0	....	-5	0	-0.5
1992	Oak-A	0	1	.000	2	2	0	0	0	7	12	6	5	0	0	9	4	3.000	6.43	58	11.89	.400	0	....	-2	0	-0.2
1993	Oak-A	1	0	1.000	17	0	0	0	0	24^2	26	25	22	2	0	26	24	2.108	8.03	51	6.72	.277	0	....	-11	0	-1.0
1994	Oak-A	4	2	.667	37	0	0	0	1	49^1	31	24	22	7	1	39	45	1.419	4.01	110	3.94	.185	0	....	2	4	0.2
1995	Oak-A	0	1	.000	16	0	0	0	0	18^1	25	17	17	4	2	21	19	2.509	8.35	53	11.34	.347	0	....	-8	0	-0.7
1996	Oak-A	0	1	.000	17	0	0	0	1	26^1	18	11	11	2	0	24	14	1.595	3.76	130	4.06	.205	0	....	3	2	0.3
Total	6	5	5	.500	100	2	0	0	2	139^2	124	94	88	18	3	129	115	1.811	5.67	75	5.98	.247	0	....	-21	6	-2.1
• BRISSIE, Lou					Leland Victor Brissie b: 6/5/1924, Anderson, SC BL/TL, 6'4.5", 215 lbs. Deb: 9/28/1947																						
1947	Phi-A	0	1	.000	1	1	0	0	0	7	9	5	5	1	0	5	4	2.000	6.43	59	7.31	.310	0	.000	-2	0	-0.3
1948	Phi-A	14	10	.583	39	25	11	0	5	194	202	100	89	6	2	95	127	1.531	4.13	104	4.05	.269	18	.237	2	15	0.2
1949	Phi-A★	16	11	.593	34	29	18	0	3	229^1	220	113	109	20	5	118	118	1.474	4.28	96	4.17	.251	24	.267	-10	15	-0.6
1950	Phi-A	7	19	.269	46	31	15	2	8	246	237	127	110	22	4	117	101	1.439	4.02	113	3.99	.253	15	.172	16	15	1.2
1951	Phi-A	0	2	.000	2	2	0	0	0	13^1	20	10	10	0	0	8	3	2.100	6.75	63	7.16	.357	1	.200	-4	0	-0.4
	Cle-A	4	3	.571	54	4	1	0	9	112^1	90	44	40	5	3	61	50	1.344	3.20	118	3.13	.223	6	.261	7	11	0.8
	Yr.	4	5	.444	56	6	1	0	9	125^2	110	54	50	5	3	69	53	1.424	3.58	108	3.56	.239	7	.250	3	11	0.3
1952	Cle-A	3	2	.600	42	1	0	0	2	82^2	68	41	32	5	0	34	28	1.234	3.48	96	2.72	.221	3	.250	-1	4	0.0
1953	Cle-A	0	0	....	16	0	0	0	2	13	21	11	11	2	0	13	5	2.615	7.62	49	11.22	.389	0	....	-6	0	-0.6
Total	7	44	48	.478	234	93	45	2	29	897^2	867	451	406	61	14	451	436	1.468	4.07	102	4.00	.254	67	.227	3	60	0.3
• BRITT, Jim					James Edward Britt b: 2/25/1856, Brooklyn, NY d: 2/28/1923, San Francisco, CA Deb: 5/2/1872																						
1872	Atl-n	9	28	.243	37	37	37	0	0	336	570	....	162	6	....	19	13	1.753	4.34	91	....	.332	40	.256	-11	....	-0.9
1873	Atl-n	17	36	.321	54	**54**	**51**	1	0	480^2	696	....	208	6	....	40	15	1.531	3.89	78	....	.301	47	.196	-53	....	-3.9
Total	2 n	26	64	.289	91	91	88	1	0	816^2	1266	....	370	12	....	59	28	1.622	4.08	83	....	.314	87	.220	-64	....	-4.8
• BRITTIN, Jack					John Albert Brittin b: 3/4/1924, Athens, IL d: 1/5/1994, Springfield, IL BR/TR, 5'11", 175 lbs. Deb: 9/15/1950																						
1950	Phi-N	0	0	....	3	0	0	0	0	4	2	2	2	0	0	3	3	1.250	4.50	90	1.86	.143	0	....	-0	0	0.0
1951	Phi-N	0	0	....	3	0	0	0	0	4	5	5	4	0	0	6	3	2.750	9.00	43	8.52	.294	0	....	-2	0	-0.2
Total	2	0	0	....	6	0	0	0	0	8	7	7	6	0	0	9	6	2.000	6.75	58	5.19	.226	0	....	-2	0	-0.2
• BRITTON, Jim					James Allan Britton b: 3/25/1944, North Tonawanda, NY BR/TR, 6'5", 225 lbs. Deb: 9/20/1967																						
1967	Atl-N	0	2	.000	2	2	0	0	0	13^1	15	9	9	2	0	2	4	1.275	6.08	55	4.10	.278	0	.000	-4	0	-0.5
1968	Atl-N	4	6	.400	34	9	2	2	3	90	81	35	31	1	2	34	61	1.278	3.10	97	2.86	.245	3	.143	-1	5	-0.2
1969★	Atl-N	7	5	.583	24	13	2	1	1	88	69	38	37	10	0	49	60	1.341	3.78	95	3.55	.218	4	.190	-1	6	-0.1
1971	Mon-N	2	3	.400	16	6	0	0	0	45^2	49	33	29	10	2	27	23	1.664	5.72	62	6.38	.274	0	.000	-11	0	-1.3
Total	4	13	16	.448	76	30	4	3	4	237	214	115	106	23	4	112	148	1.376	4.03	83	3.87	.243	7	.127	-18	11	-2.1
• BRIZZOLARA, Tony					Anthony John Brizzolara b: 1/14/1957, Santa Monica, CA BR/TR, 6'5", 215 lbs. Deb: 5/19/1979																						
1979	Atl-N	6	9	.400	20	19	2	0	0	107^1	133	70	63	6	3	33	64	1.547	5.28	77	4.76	.303	1	.029	-12	2	-1.5
1983	Atl-N	1	0	1.000	14	0	0	0	1	20^1	22	8	8	2	0	6	17	1.377	3.54	109	4.06	.278	0	....	1	2	0.1
1984	Atl-N	1	2	.333	10	4	0	0	0	29	33	22	17	4	0	13	17	1.586	5.28	73	5.21	.284	0	.000	-4	0	-0.5
Total	3	8	11	.421	44	23	2	0	1	156^2	188	100	88	12	3	52	98	1.532	5.06	79	4.75	.297	1	.024	-15	4	-2.0
• BROACA, Johnny					John Joseph Broaca b: 10/3/1909, Lawrence, MA d: 5/16/1985, Lawrence, MA BR/TR, 5'11", 190 lbs. Deb: 6/2/1934																						
1934	NY-A	12	9	.571	26	24	13	1	0	177^1	203	94	82	9	1	65	74	1.511	4.16	98	4.27	.284	2	.030	-5	9	-1.1
1935	NY-A	15	7	.682	29	27	14	2	0	201	199	96	80	16	0	79	78	1.383	3.58	113	3.70	.254	12	.150	7	12	0.3
1936	NY-A	12	7	.632	37	27	12	1	3	206	235	110	97	16	0	66	84	1.461	4.24	110	4.29	.284	9	.110	8	12	0.1
1937	NY-A	1	4	.200	7	6	3	0	0	44	58	27	23	5	0	17	9	1.705	4.70	94	5.93	.324	0	.000	-2	1	-0.4
1939	Cle-A	4	2	.667	22	2	0	0	0	46	53	39	24	5	0	28	13	1.761	4.70	94	5.66	.288	0	.000	-1	1	-0.3
Total	5	44	29	.603	121	86	42	4	3	674^1	748	366	306	51	1	255	258	1.487	4.08	105	4.31	.278	23	.091	7	35	-1.4

• BROBERG, Pete Peter Sven Broberg b: 3/2/1950, West Palm Beach, FL BR/TR, 6'3", 205 lbs. Deb: 6/20/1971

YEAR	TM-L	W	L	PCT	G	GS	CG	SH	SV	IP	H	R	ER	HR	HB	BB	SO	RAT	ERA	ERA+	CERA	OAV	BH	AVG	PR+	WS	TPW
1971	Was-A	5	9	.357	18	18	7	1	0	124^{2}	104	57	48	10	10	53	89	1.259	3.47	95	3.44	.228	5	.114	-3	5	-0.3
1972	Tex-A	5	12	.294	39	25	3	2	1	176^{1}	153	93	84	14	13	85	133	1.350	4.29	70	3.79	.237	4	.078	-21	2	-2.7
1973	Tex-A	5	9	.357	22	20	6	1	0	118^{2}	130	77	74	8	5	66	57	1.652	5.61	66	5.14	.283	0	....	-22	2	-2.2
1974	Tex-A	0	4	.000	12	2	0	0	0	29	29	29	26	7	1	13	15	1.448	8.07	44	5.42	.264	0	....	-15	0	-1.5
1975	Mil-A	14	16	.467	38	32	7	2	0	220^{1}	219	114	101	17	16	106	100	1.475	4.13	93	4.53	.263	0	....	-6	10	-0.6
1976	Mil-A	1	7	.125	20	11	1	0	0	92^{1}	99	59	51	5	4	72	28	1.852	4.97	70	5.76	.281	0	....	-15	0	-1.6
1977	Chi-N	1	2	.333	22	0	0	0	0	36	34	22	19	8	0	18	20	1.444	4.75	92	4.82	.256	0	.000	-1	1	-0.1
1978	Oak-A	10	12	.455	35	26	2	0	0	165^{2}	174	101	85	16	3	65	94	1.443	4.62	79	4.29	.270	0	....	-15	5	-1.6
Total	**8**	**41**	**71**	**.366**	**206**	**134**	**26**	**6**	**1**	**963**	**942**	**552**	**488**	**85**	**52**	**478**	**536**	**1.475**	**4.56**	**77**	**4.44**	**.259**	**9**	**.089**	**-98**	**25**	**-10.7**

• BROCAIL, Doug Douglas Keith Brocail b: 5/16/1967, Clearfield, PA BL/TR, 6'5", 235 lbs. Deb: 9/8/1992

YEAR	TM-L	W	L	PCT	G	GS	CG	SH	SV	IP	H	R	ER	HR	HB	BB	SO	RAT	ERA	ERA+	CERA	OAV	BH	AVG	PR+	WS	TPW
1992	SD-N	0	0	....	3	3	0	0	0	14	17	10	10	2	0	5	15	1.571	6.43	56	5.33	.298	1	.200	-4	0	-0.5
1993	SD-N	4	13	.235	24	24	0	0	0	128^{1}	143	75	65	16	4	42	70	1.442	4.56	91	4.60	.282	6	.182	-6	4	-0.5
1994	SD-N	0	0	....	12	0	0	0	0	17	21	13	11	1	2	5	11	1.529	5.82	71	4.79	.304	0	.000	-3	0	-0.3
1995	Hou-N	6	4	.600	36	7	0	0	1	77^{1}	87	40	36	10	4	22	39	1.409	4.19	92	4.68	.280	4	.250	-1	3	0.0
1996	Hou-N	1	5	.167	23	4	0	0	0	53	58	31	27	7	2	23	34	1.528	4.58	84	5.26	.289	0	.000	-3	1	-0.4
1997	Det-A	3	4	.429	61	4	0	0	2	78	74	31	28	10	3	36	60	1.410	3.23	142	4.42	.256	0	....	11	7	1.0
1998	Det-A	5	2	.714	60	0	0	0	0	62^{2}	47	23	19	2	1	18	55	1.037	2.73	173	1.99	.211	0	....	13	8	1.2
1999	Det-A	4	4	.500	70	0	0	0	2	82	60	23	23	7	4	25	78	1.037	2.52	196	2.43	.206	0	....	22	12	2.0
2000	Det-A	5	4	.556	49	0	0	0	0	50^{2}	57	25	23	5	1	14	41	1.401	4.09	118	4.25	.285	0	....	4	5	0.4
Total	**9**	**28**	**36**	**.438**	**338**	**42**	**0**	**0**	**5**	**563**	**564**	**271**	**242**	**60**	**21**	**190**	**403**	**1.339**	**3.87**	**110**	**4.03**	**.263**	**11**	**.164**	**33**	**40**	**3.0**

• BROCK, Chris Terrence Christopher Brock b: 2/5/1970, Orlando, FL BR/TR, 6', 175 lbs. Deb: 6/11/1997

YEAR	TM-L	W	L	PCT	G	GS	CG	SH	SV	IP	H	R	ER	HR	HB	BB	SO	RAT	ERA	ERA+	CERA	OAV	BH	AVG	PR+	WS	TPW
1997	Atl-N	0	0	....	7	6	0	0	0	30^{2}	34	23	19	2	0	19	16	1.728	5.58	75	5.10	.288	1	.100	-5	0	-0.5
1998	SF-N	0	0	....	13	0	0	0	0	27^{2}	31	13	12	3	0	7	19	1.373	3.90	102	4.11	.279	1	.250	0	1	0.0
1999	SF-N	6	8	.429	19	19	0	0	0	106^{2}	124	69	65	18	4	41	76	1.547	5.48	77	5.59	.291	7	.200	-15	2	-1.3
2000	Phi-N	7	8	.467	63	5	0	0	1	93^{1}	85	48	45	21	3	41	69	1.350	4.34	107	4.71	.239	2	.222	3	7	0.4
2001	Phi-N	3	0	1.000	24	0	0	0	0	32^{2}	35	16	15	6	2	15	26	1.531	4.13	103	5.50	.276	1	.333	0	3	0.0
2002	Bal-A	2	1	.667	22	0	0	0	0	44	52	24	23	6	1	14	21	1.500	4.70	91	5.19	.297	0	.000	-3	2	-0.3
Total	**6**	**18**	**17**	**.514**	**148**	**30**	**0**	**0**	**1**	**335**	**361**	**193**	**179**	**56**	**10**	**137**	**227**	**1.487**	**4.81**	**90**	**5.12**	**.275**	**12**	**.190**	**-19**	**15**	**-1.6**

• BROCKETT, Lew Lewis Albert "King" Brockett b: 7/23/1880, Brownsville, IL d: 9/19/1960, Norris City, IL BR/TR, 5'10.5", 168 lbs. Deb: 4/25/1907

YEAR	TM-L	W	L	PCT	G	GS	CG	SH	SV	IP	H	R	ER	HR	HB	BB	SO	RAT	ERA	ERA+	CERA	OAV	BH	AVG	PR+	WS	TPW
1907	NY-A	1	2	.333	8	4	1	0	0	46^{1}	58	36	32	1	2	26	13	1.813	6.22	45	5.61	.309	4	.182	-17	0	-1.9
1909	NY-A	10	8	.556	26	18	10	3	1	170	148	68	40	3	6	59	70	1.218	2.12	119	2.87	.245	17	.283	12	11	1.8
1911	NY-A	2	4	.333	16	8	2	0	0	75^{1}	73	45	39	3	5	39	25	1.487	4.66	77	4.10	.256	12	.308	-7	4	-0.5
Total	**3**	**13**	**14**	**.481**	**50**	**30**	**13**	**3**	**1**	**291^{2}**	**279**	**149**	**111**	**7**	**13**	**124**	**108**	**1.382**	**3.43**	**85**	**3.62**	**.259**	**33**	**.273**	**-12**	**15**	**-0.6**

• BRODOWSKI, Dick Richard Stanley Brodowski b: 7/26/1932, Bayonne, NJ BR/TR, 6'1", 190 lbs. Deb: 6/15/1952

YEAR	TM-L	W	L	PCT	G	GS	CG	SH	SV	IP	H	R	ER	HR	HB	BB	SO	RAT	ERA	ERA+	CERA	OAV	BH	AVG	PR+	WS	TPW
1952	Bos-A	5	5	.500	20	12	4	0	0	114^{2}	111	66	56	12	3	50	42	1.404	4.40	90	4.03	.252	8	.205	-6	4	-0.6
1955	Bos-A	1	0	1.000	16	0	0	0	0	32	36	25	20	5	1	25	10	1.906	5.63	76	6.95	.295	5	.500	-4	1	-0.2
1956	Was-A	0	3	.000	7	3	1	0	0	17^{2}	31	18	18	5	0	12	8	2.434	9.17	47	11.92	.397	0	.000	-9	0	-1.0
1957	Was-A	0	1	.000	6	0	0	0	0	11^{1}	12	15	14	2	1	10	4	1.941	11.12	35	7.27	.261	0	.000	-9	0	-0.9
1958	Cle-A	1	0	1.000	5	0	0	0	0	10	3	0	0	0	0	6	12	.900	0.00	....	1.10	.100	0	.000	4	2	0.4
1959	Cle-A	2	2	.500	18	0	0	0	5	30	19	13	6	3	3	21	9	1.333	1.80	205	3.46	.181	2	.333	6	4	0.7
Total	**6**	**9**	**11**	**.450**	**72**	**15**	**5**	**0**	**5**	**215^{2}**	**212**	**137**	**114**	**27**	**8**	**124**	**85**	**1.558**	**4.76**	**85**	**5.07**	**.258**	**15**	**.242**	**-19**	**11**	**-1.6**

• BROGLIO, Ernie Ernest Gilbert Broglio b: 8/27/1935, Berkeley, CA BR/TR, 6'2", 200 lbs. Deb: 4/11/1959

YEAR	TM-L	W	L	PCT	G	GS	CG	SH	SV	IP	H	R	ER	HR	HB	BB	SO	RAT	ERA	ERA+	CERA	OAV	BH	AVG	PR+	WS	TPW
1959	StL-N	7	12	.368	35	25	6	3	0	181^{1}	174	104	95	20	0	89	133	**1.450**	4.72	90	4.17	.250	6	.098	-8	7	-1.1
1960	StL-N	**21**	9	.700	52	24	9	3	0	226^{1}	172	76	69	18	2	100	188	1.202	2.74	**149**	2.86	.213	14	.206	**35**	24	**3.9**
1961	StL-N	9	12	.429	29	26	7	2	0	174^{2}	166	97	80	19	1	75	113	1.380	4.12	107	3.88	.248	9	.145	5	9	0.3
1962	StL-N	12	9	.571	34	30	11	4	0	222^{1}	193	80	74	22	2	93	132	1.286	3.00	143	3.48	.237	10	.139	30	17	2.8
1963	StL-N	18	8	.692	39	35	11	5	0	250	202	97	83	24	4	90	145	1.168	2.99	119	2.87	.216	10	.112	15	17	1.3
1964	StL-N	3	5	.375	11	11	3	1	0	69^{1}	65	33	27	7	1	26	36	1.313	3.50	108	3.67	.247	2	.095	2	4	0.2
	Chi-N	4	7	.364	18	16	3	0	1	100^{1}	111	51	45	12	0	30	46	1.405	4.04	92	4.39	.281	10	.286	-3	5	0.0
	Yr.	7	12	.368	29	27	6	1	1	169^{2}	176	84	72	19	1	56	82	1.367	3.82	98	4.09	.267	12	.214	-1	9	0.2
1965	Chi-N	1	6	.143	26	6	0	0	0	50^{2}	63	44	39	7	0	46	22	2.151	6.93	53	7.83	.313	0	.000	-18	0	-1.9
1966	Chi-N	2	6	.250	15	11	2	0	1	62^{1}	70	46	44	14	0	38	34	1.733	6.35	58	6.65	.290	7	.368	-18	1	-1.6
Total	**8**	**77**	**74**	**.510**	**259**	**184**	**52**	**18**	**2**	**1337^{1}**	**1216**	**628**	**556**	**143**	**10**	**587**	**849**	**1.348**	**3.74**	**106**	**3.80**	**.242**	**68**	**.158**	**40**	**84**	**4.0**

• BROHAWN, Troy Michael Troy Brohawn b: 1/14/1973, Cambridge, MD BL/TL, 6'1", 190 lbs. Deb: 4/14/2001

YEAR	TM-L	W	L	PCT	G	GS	CG	SH	SV	IP	H	R	ER	HR	HB	BB	SO	RAT	ERA	ERA+	CERA	OAV	BH	AVG	PR+	WS	TPW
2001★	Ari-N	2	3	.400	59	0	0	0	1	49^{1}	55	27	27	5	1	23	30	1.581	4.93	93	5.07	.289	0	.000	-3	2	-0.3
2002	SF-N	0	1	.000	11	0	0	0	0	5^{2}	5	4	4	1	2	1	3	1.059	6.35	61	4.37	.227	0	....	-2	0	-0.2
2003	LA-N	2	0	1.000	12	0	0	0	0	11^{2}	10	6	5	2	0	4	13	1.200	3.86	104	3.56	.227	1	1.000	0	1	0.0
Total	**3**	**4**	**4**	**.500**	**82**	**0**	**0**	**0**	**1**	**66^{2}**	**70**	**37**	**36**	**8**	**3**	**28**	**46**	**1.470**	**4.86**	**91**	**4.75**	**.273**	**1**	**.500**	**-4**	**3**	**-0.4**

• BRONDELL, Ken Kenneth Leroy Brondell b: 10/17/1921, Bradshaw, NE BR/TR, 6'1", 195 lbs. Deb: 5/3/1944

YEAR	TM-L	W	L	PCT	G	GS	CG	SH	SV	IP	H	R	ER	HR	HB	BB	SO	RAT	ERA	ERA+	CERA	OAV	BH	AVG	PR+	WS	TPW
1944	NY-N	0	1	.000	7	2	1	0	0	19^{1}	27	18	18	3	0	8	1	1.810	8.38	44	6.75	.329	0	.000	-10	0	-1.1

• BRONKEY, Jeff Jacob Jeffery Bronkey b: 9/18/1965, Kabul, Afghanistan BR/TR, 6'3", 215 lbs. Deb: 5/2/1993

YEAR	TM-L	W	L	PCT	G	GS	CG	SH	SV	IP	H	R	ER	HR	HB	BB	SO	RAT	ERA	ERA+	CERA	OAV	BH	AVG	PR+	WS	TPW
1993	Tex-A	1	1	.500	21	0	0	0	1	36	39	20	16	4	1	11	18	1.389	4.00	104	4.29	.285	0	.000	1	2	0.1
1994	Mil-A	1	1	.500	16	0	0	0	1	20^{2}	20	10	10	3	0	12	13	1.548	4.35	116	4.56	.247	0	....	1	2	0.1
1995	Mil-A	0	0	....	8	0	0	0	0	12^{1}	15	6	5	0	0	6	5	1.703	3.65	137	4.94	.313	0	....	2	1	0.1
Total	**3**	**2**	**2**	**.500**	**45**	**0**	**0**	**0**	**2**	**69**	**74**	**36**	**31**	**7**	**1**	**29**	**36**	**1.493**	**4.04**	**112**	**4.49**	**.278**	**0**	**.000**	**4**	**5**	**0.3**

• BRONSTAD, Jim James Warren Bronstad b: 6/22/1936, Fort Worth, TX BR/TR, 6'3", 196 lbs. Deb: 6/7/1959

YEAR	TM-L	W	L	PCT	G	GS	CG	SH	SV	IP	H	R	ER	HR	HB	BB	SO	RAT	ERA	ERA+	CERA	OAV	BH	AVG	PR+	WS	TPW
1959	NY-A	0	3	.000	16	3	0	0	2	29^{1}	34	19	17	2	1	13	14	1.602	5.22	70	5.05	.288	0	.000	-5	0	-0.6
1963	Was-A	1	3	.250	25	0	0	0	1	57^{1}	66	38	36	9	1	22	22	1.535	5.65	66	5.47	.297	0	.000	-12	0	-1.4
1964	Was-A	0	1	.000	4	0	0	0	0	7	10	4	4	0	0	2	9	1.714	5.14	72	5.56	.345	0	....	-1	0	-0.1
Total	**3**	**1**	**7**	**.125**	**45**	**3**	**0**	**0**	**3**	**93^{2}**	**110**	**61**	**57**	**11**	**2**	**37**	**45**	**1.569**	**5.48**	**67**	**5.35**	**.298**	**0**	**.000**	**-19**	**0**	**-2.1**

• BROOKENS, Ike Edward Dwain Brookens b: 1/3/1949, Chambersburg, PA BR/TR, 6'5", 170 lbs. Deb: 6/17/1975

YEAR	TM-L	W	L	PCT	G	GS	CG	SH	SV	IP	H	R	ER	HR	HB	BB	SO	RAT	ERA	ERA+	CERA	OAV	BH	AVG	PR+	WS	TPW
1975	Det-A	0	0	....	3	0	0	0	0	10^{1}	11	6	6	3	1	5	8	1.548	5.23	77	6.84	.282	0	....	-1	0	-0.1

• BROSNAN, Jim James Patrick Brosnan b: 10/24/1929, Cincinnati, OH BR/TR, 6'4", 210 lbs. Deb: 4/15/1954

YEAR	TM-L	W	L	PCT	G	GS	CG	SH	SV	IP	H	R	ER	HR	HB	BB	SO	RAT	ERA	ERA+	CERA	OAV	BH	AVG	PR+	WS	TPW
1954	Chi-N	1	0	1.000	18	0	0	0	0	33^{1}	44	35	35	9	1	18	17	1.860	9.45	44	8.07	.331	1	.125	-19	0	-1.9
1956	Chi-N	5	9	.357	30	10	1	1	1	95	95	44	40	9	0	45	51	1.474	3.79	100	4.24	.270	4	.182	-2	5	-0.2
1957	Chi-N	5	5	.500	41	5	1	0	0	98^{2}	79	38	37	11	1	46	73	1.267	3.38	115	3.31	.219	5	.250	7	8	0.9
1958	Chi-N	3	4	.429	8	8	2	0	0	51^{2}	41	20	18	3	0	29	24	1.355	3.14	125	3.28	.225	2	.105	5	4	0.4
	StL-N	8	4	.667	33	12	2	0	7	115	107	46	44	10	1	50	65	1.365	3.44	120	3.78	.250	3	.097	9	12	0.8
	Yr.	11	8	.579	41	20	4	0	7	166^{2}	148	66	62	13	1	79	89	1.362	3.35	121	3.62	.243	5	.100	14	16	1.2
1959	StL-N	1	3	.250	20	1	0	0	2	33	34	18	18	5	1	15	18	1.485	4.91	86	4.85	.276	2	.286	-2	2	-0.1
	Cin-N	8	3	.727	26	9	1	1	2	83^{1}	79	35	31	7	5	26	56	1.260	3.35	121	3.47	.248	1	.043	6	7	0.5
	Yr.	9	6	.600	46	10	1	1	4	116^{1}	113	53	49	12	6	41	74	1.324	3.79	109	3.87	.256	3	.100	4	9	0.3
1960	Cin-N	7	2	.778	57	2	0	0	12	99	79	31	26	4	0	22	62	1.020	2.36	162	2.02	.225	3	.200	16	14	1.8
1961★	Cin-N	10	4	.714	53	0	0	0	16	80	77	34	27	7	0	18	40	1.188	3.04	134	3.00	.249	2	.154	9	13	0.9
1962	Cin-N	4	4	.500	48	0	0	0	13	64^{2}	76	27	24	6	0	18	51	1.454	3.34	120	4.36	.292	0	.000	5	7	0.4
1963	Cin-N	0	1	.000	6	0	0	0	0	4^{2}	8	4	4	2	0	3	4	2.357	7.71	43	12.12	.421	0	....	-2	0	-0.2
	Chi-A	3	8	.273	45	0	0	0	14	73	71	24	23	7	0	22	46	1.274	2.84	124	3.50	.263	4	.308	5	8	0.6
Total	**9**	**55**	**47**	**.539**	**385**	**47**	**7**	**2**	**67**	**831^{1}**	**790**	**356**	**327**	**80**	**9**	**312**	**507**	**1.326**	**3.54**	**112**	**3.71**	**.254**	**27**	**.153**	**36**	**80**	**3.8**

YEAR	TM-L	W	L	PCT	G	GS	CG	SH	SV	IP	H	R	ER	HR	HB	BB	SO	RAT	ERA	ERA+	CERA	OAV	BH	AVG	PR+	WS	TPW
• BROSS, Terry	Terrence Paul Bross b: 3/30/1966, El Paso, TX BR/TR, 6'9", 234 lbs. Deb: 9/4/1991																										
1991	NY-N	0	0	....	8	0	0	0	0	10	7	2	2	1	0	3	5	1.000	1.80	202	2.20	.200	0	....	2	1	0.2
1993	SF-N	0	0	....	2	0	0	0	0	2	3	2	2	1	0	1	1	2.000	9.00	43	10.88	.333	0	....	-1	0	-0.1
Total	2	0	0	....	10	0	0	0	0	12	10	4	4	2	0	4	6	1.167	3.00	126	3.64	.227	0	....	1	1	0.1
• BROSSEAU, Frank	Franklin Lee Brosseau b: 7/31/1944, Drayton, ND BR/TR, 6'1", 180 lbs. Deb: 9/10/1969																										
1969	Pit-N	0	0	....	2	0	0	0	0	1^2	2	2	2	0	0	2	2	2.400	10.80	32	6.15	.286	0	....	-1	0	-0.1
1971	Pit-N	0	0	....	1	0	0	0	0	2	1	0	0	0	0	0	0	.500	0.00	....	0.55	.200	0	....	1	0	0.1
Total	2	0	0	....	3	0	0	0	0	3^2	3	2	2	0	0	2	2	1.364	4.91	71	3.09	.250	0	....	-1	0	-0.1
• BROW, Scott	Scott John Brow b: 3/17/1969, Butte, MT BR/TR, 6'3", 200 lbs. Deb: 4/28/1993																										
1993	Tor-A	1	1	.500	6	3	0	0	0	18	19	15	12	2	1	10	7	1.611	6.00	72	5.17	.275	0	....	-3	0	-0.3
1994	Tor-A	0	3	.000	18	0	0	0	2	29	34	27	19	4	1	19	15	1.828	5.90	82	6.31	.288	0	....	-3	0	-0.3
1996	Tor-A	1	0	1.000	18	1	0	0	0	38^2	45	25	24	5	0	25	23	1.810	5.59	90	6.31	.294	0	....	-3	1	-0.3
1998	Ari-N	1	0	1.000	17	0	0	0	0	21^1	22	17	17	2	0	14	13	1.688	7.17	59	5.05	.272	0	.000	-7	0	-0.7
Total	4	3	4	.429	59	4	0	0	2	107	120	84	72	13	2	68	58	1.757	6.06	76	5.87	.285	0	.000	-17	1	-1.6
• BROWER, Jim	James Robert Brower b: 12/29/1972, Edina, MN BR/TR, 6'2" Deb: 9/5/1999																										
1999	Cle-A	3	1	.750	9	2	0	0	0	25^2	27	13	13	8	1	10	18	1.442	4.56	110	5.96	.270	0	....	2	2	0.1
2000	Cle-A	2	3	.400	17	11	0	0	0	62	80	45	43	11	2	31	32	1.790	6.24	80	6.95	.309	0	.000	-8	1	-0.8
2001	Cin-N	7	10	.412	46	10	0	0	1	129^1	119	65	57	17	5	60	94	1.384	3.97	115	4.21	.247	8	.308	10	8	1.2
2002	Cin-N	2	0	1.000	22	0	0	0	0	39^1	38	18	17	2	0	10	24	1.220	3.89	109	3.08	.260	0	.000	1	3	0.1
	Mon-N	1	2	.333	30	0	0	0	0	41	39	22	22	5	4	22	33	1.488	4.83	88	4.79	.245	0	.000	-3	2	-0.3
	Yr.	3	2	.600	52	0	0	0	0	80^1	77	40	39	7	4	32	57	1.357	4.37	97	3.95	.252	0	.000	-1	5	-0.2
2003*	SF-N	8	5	.615	51	5	0	0	2	100	90	48	44	8	1	39	65	1.290	3.96	104	3.46	.249	3	.176	-1	7	0.0
Total	5	23	21	.523	175	28	0	0	3	397^1	393	211	196	51	13	172	266	1.422	4.44	101	4.51	.261	11	.200	2	23	0.3
• BROWN, Alton	Alton Leo "Deacon" Brown b: 4/16/1925, Norfolk, VA BR/TR, 6'2", 195 lbs. Deb: 4/21/1951																										
1951	Was-A	0	0	....	7	0	0	0	0	11^2	14	12	12	1	1	12	7	2.229	9.26	44	7.86	.298	0	.000	-7	0	-0.7
• BROWN, Boardwalk	Carroll William Brown b: 2/20/1887, Woodbury, NJ d: 2/8/1977, Burlington, NJ BR/TR, 6'1.5", 178 lbs. Deb: 9/27/1911																										
1911	Phi-A	0	1	.000	2	1	1	0	0	12	12	7	6	0	0	2	6	1.167	4.50	70	2.65	.267	0	.000	-2	0	-0.2
1912	Phi-A	13	11	.542	34	24	15	3	0	199	204	115	81	2	9	87	64	1.462	3.66	85	4.06	.283	11	.145	-16	7	-1.9
1913	Phi-A	17	11	.607	43	35	11	3	1	235^1	200	94	77	6	10	87	70	1.220	2.94	94	2.64	.219	13	.159	-5	12	-0.7
1914	Phi-A	1	6	.143	15	7	2	0	0	66	64	34	30	1	0	26	20	1.364	4.09	64	3.44	.268	0	.000	-11	0	-1.4
	NY-A	6	5	.545	20	14	8	0	0	122^1	123	57	44	2	1	42	57	1.349	3.24	85	3.44	.271	8	.182	-8	6	-0.7
	Yr.	7	11	.389	35	21	10	0	0	188^1	187	91	74	3	1	68	77	1.354	3.54	76	3.44	.270	8	.125	-19	6	-2.1
1915	NY-A	3	6	.333	19	11	5	0	0	96^2	95	49	44	4	5	47	34	1.469	4.10	72	4.29	.275	6	.188	-14	2	-1.5
Total	5	40	40	.500	133	92	42	6	1	731^1	698	356	282	15	25	291	251	1.352	3.47	82	3.45	.257	38	.147	-56	27	-6.6
• BROWN, Bob	Robert Murray Brown b: 4/1/1911, Dorchester, MA d: 8/3/1990, Pembroke, MA BR/TR, 6'.5", 190 lbs. Deb: 4/21/1930																										
1930	Bos-N	0	0	....	3	0	0	0	0	6	10	7	7	0	0	8	1	3.000	10.50	47	11.33	.417	0	.000	-4	0	-0.4
1931	Bos-N	0	1	.000	3	1	0	0	0	6^1	9	7	6	0	0	3	2	1.895	8.53	44	5.75	.375	1	.500	-3	0	-0.3
1932	Bos-N	14	7	.667	35	28	9	0	1	213	187	89	78	6	2	104	110	1.366	3.30	114	3.17	.238	13	.194	11	15	1.0
1933	Bos-N	0	0	....	5	0	0	0	0	6^2	6	4	2	0	0	3	3	1.350	2.70	113	2.97	.250	0	.000	0	0	0.0
1934	Bos-N	1	3	.250	16	8	2	1	0	58^1	59	40	37	2	3	36	21	1.629	5.71	67	4.44	.262	5	.238	-12	0	-1.1
1935	Bos-N	1	8	.111	15	10	2	1	0	65	79	55	46	2	0	36	17	1.769	6.37	59	5.21	.302	2	.105	-16	0	-1.7
1936	Bos-N	0	2	.000	2	2	0	0	0	8^1	10	5	5	1	0	3	5	1.560	5.40	71	4.85	.278	0	.000	-2	0	-0.2
Total	7	16	21	.432	79	49	13	2	1	363^2	360	207	181	11	5	193	159	1.521	4.48	85	3.96	.261	21	.183	-26	15	-2.7
• BROWN, Buster	Charles Edward "Yank" Brown b: 8/31/1881, Boone, IA d: 2/9/1914, Sioux City, IA BR/TR, 6', 180 lbs. Deb: 6/22/1905																										
1905	StL-N	8	11	.421	23	21	17	3	0	178^2	172	80	59	5	10	62	57	1.310	2.97	100	3.43	.260	6	.092	6	8	0.4
1906	StL-N	8	16	.333	32	27	21	0	0	238^1	208	98	70	2	11	112	109	1.343	2.64	99	3.09	.234	14	.165	2	12	0.3
1907	StL-N	1	6	.143	9	8	6	0	0	63^2	57	38	24	2	5	45	17	1.602	3.39	74	4.67	.263	7	.269	-6	1	-0.5
	Phi-N	9	6	.600	21	16	13	4	0	130	118	47	35	3	6	56	38	1.338	2.42	100	3.32	.246	10	.189	-2	9	-0.1
	Yr.	10	12	.455	30	24	19	4	0	193^2	175	85	59	5	11	101	55	**1.425**	2.74	89	3.77	.251	17	.215	-8	10	-0.5
1908	Phi-N	0	0	....	3	0	0	0	0	7	9	6	2	0	1	5	3	2.000	2.57	93	7.22	.346	1	.200	-0	0	0.0
1909	Phi-N	0	0	....	7	1	0	0	0	25	22	10	9	1	1	16	10	1.520	3.24	80	4.27	.259	0	.000	-2	1	-0.4
	Bos-N	4	8	.333	18	17	8	2	0	123^1	108	45	43	1	7	56	32	1.330	3.14	90	3.22	.244	7	.146	-5	6	-0.7
	Yr.	4	8	.333	25	18	8	2	0	148^1	130	55	52	2	8	72	42	1.362	3.16	88	3.40	.246	7	.123	-7	7	-1.0
1910	Bos-N	9	23	.281	46	29	16	1	2	263	251	113	78	4	4	94	88	1.312	2.67	124	3.32	.268	16	.198	15	19	1.6
1911	Bos-N	8	18	.308	42	25	13	0	2	241	258	161	115	11	10	116	76	1.552	4.29	89	4.63	.284	21	.250	-8	6	-0.4
1912	Bos-N	4	15	.211	31	21	12	0	0	168^1	146	107	75	7	2	66	68	1.259	4.01	89	2.87	.239	13	.213	-6	7	-0.4
1913	Bos-N	0	0	....	2	0	0	0	0	13^1	19	10	7	0	2	3	3	1.650	4.73	69	6.39	.396	0	.000	-2	0	-0.2
Total	9	51	103	.331	234	165	106	10	4	1451^2	1368	715	517	36	59	631	501	1.377	3.21	96	3.58	.258	95	.182	-9	69	-0.3
• BROWN, Charlie	Charles Edward Brown b: 8/17/1871, Bluffton, IN d: 4/3/1938, Monclova, OH TL, 6', 180 lbs. Deb: 8/4/1897																										
1897	Cle-N	1	2	.333	4	4	2	0	0	24^1	30	25	21	2	5	17	8	1.932	7.77	58	7.15	.301	3	.273	-10	0	-0.9
• BROWN, Clint	Clinton Harold Brown b: 7/8/1903, Blackash, PA d: 12/31/1955, Rocky River, OH BL/TR, 6'1", 190 lbs. Deb: 9/27/1928																										
1928	Cle-A	0	1	.000	2	1	1	0	0	11	14	6	6	0	0	2	2	1.455	4.91	84	3.87	.304	1	.200	-1	0	-0.1
1929	Cle-A	0	2	.000	3	1	1	0	0	16^1	18	8	6	0	0	6	1	1.469	3.31	134	3.72	.286	0	.000	2	1	0.1
1930	Cle-A	11	13	.458	35	31	16	**3**	1	213^2	271	138	118	14	4	51	54	1.507	4.97	97	4.70	.314	18	.247	0	13	0.2
1931	Cle-A	11	15	.423	39	33	12	2	0	233^1	284	143	122	10	1	55	50	1.453	4.71	98	4.14	.295	15	.172	5	12	0.3
1932	Cle-A	15	12	.556	37	32	21	1	1	262^2	298	143	119	14	4	50	59	1.325	4.08	116	3.61	.279	25	.250	24	21	2.8
1933	Cle-A	11	12	.478	33	23	10	2	1	185	202	83	70	10	2	34	47	1.276	3.41	131	3.39	.276	9	.145	21	15	1.7
1934	Cle-A	4	3	.571	17	2	0	0	1	50^1	83	42	33	3	0	14	15	1.927	5.90	77	6.87	.359	5	.294	-7	1	-0.5
1935	Cle-A	4	3	.571	23	5	1	0	2	49	61	34	28	3	1	14	20	1.531	5.14	88	4.56	.300	2	.200	-3	2	-0.2
1936	Chi-A	6	2	.750	38	2	0	0	5	83	106	50	46	5	3	24	19	1.566	4.99	104	5.05	.315	4	.160	1	6	0.1
1937	Chi-A	7	7	.500	**53**	0	0	0	**18**	100	92	47	38	7	1	36	51	1.280	3.42	135	3.18	.242	4	.222	11	14	1.1
1938	Chi-A	1	3	.250	8	0	0	0	2	13^2	16	8	7	0	0	9	2	1.829	4.61	106	5.32	.333	1	.500	0	1	0.1
1939	Chi-A	11	10	.524	**61**	0	0	0	18	118^1	127	58	51	8	0	27	41	1.301	3.88	122	3.54	.281	4	.211	10	16	1.0
1940	Chi-A	4	6	.400	37	0	0	0	10	66	75	30	27	5	2	16	23	1.379	3.68	120	4.00	.284	1	.071	4	7	0.3
1941	Cle-A	3	3	.500	41	0	0	0	5	74^1	77	30	27	3	1	28	22	1.413	3.27	121	3.86	.279	2	.118	5	7	0.5
1942	Cle-A	1	1	.500	7	0	0	0	0	9	16	10	6	2	1	2	4	2.000	6.00	57	9.01	.356	0	.000	-3	0	-0.3
Total	15	89	93	.489	434	130	62	8	64	1485^2	1740	830	704	84	20	368	410	1.419	4.26	109	4.09	.291	91	.199	70	116	7.2
• BROWN, Curly	Charles Roy "Lefty" Brown b: 12/9/1888, Spring Hill, KS d: 6/10/1968, Spring Hill, KS BL/TL, 5'10.5", 165 lbs. Deb: 9/8/1911																										
1911	StL-A	1	2	.333	3	2	2	0	0	23	22	9	7	0	1	5	8	1.174	2.74	123	2.60	.247	0	.000	1	1	0.0
1912	StL-A	1	3	.250	16	4	2	1	0	64^2	69	56	35	0	3	35	28	1.608	4.87	69	4.38	.277	5	.208	-12	0	-1.2
1913	StL-A	1	1	.500	2	2	2	0	0	14	12	5	4	0	0	4	3	1.143	2.57	114	2.41	.245	2	.400	0	1	0.1
1915	Cin-N	0	2	.000	7	3	0	0	0	27	26	20	14	2	2	6	13	1.185	4.67	61	3.13	.245	4	.364	-6	1	-0.5
Total	4	3	8	.273	28	11	6	1	0	128^2	129	90	60	2	6	50	52	1.391	4.20	76	3.58	.262	11	.224	-16	3	-1.6
• BROWN, Curt	Curtis Steven Brown b: 1/15/1960, Fort Lauderdale, FL BR/TR, 6'5", 200 lbs. Deb: 6/10/1983																										
1983	Cal-A	1	1	.500	10	0	0	0	0	16	25	13	13	1	0	4	7	1.813	7.31	55	6.60	.368	0	....	-6	0	-0.6
1984	NY-A	1	1	.500	13	0	0	0	0	16^2	18	5	5	1	0	4	10	1.320	2.70	140	3.59	.281	0	....	2	1	0.2
1986	Mon-N	0	1	.000	6	0	0	0	0	12	15	6	4	0	0	2	4	1.417	3.00	123	3.47	.319	0	.000	1	1	0.1
1987	Mon-N	0	1	.000	5	0	0	0	0	7	10	7	6	2	0	4	6	2.000	7.71	54	8.56	.333	0	....	-3	0	-0.3
Total	4	2	4	.333	34	0	0	0	0	51^2	68	31	28	4	0	14	27	1.587	4.88	81	5.17	.325	0	.000	-5	2	-0.5

• BROWN, Elmer Elmer Young "Shook" Brown b: 3/25/1883, Southport, IN d: 1/23/1955, Indianapolis, IN BL/TR, 5'11.5", 172 lbs. Deb: 9/16/1911

YEAR TM-L	W	L	PCT	G	GS	CG	SH	SV	IP	H	R	ER	HR	HB	BB	SO	RAT	ERA	ERA+	CERA	OAV	BH	AVG	PR+	WS	TPW
1911 StL-A	1	1	.500	5	3	1	1	0	16^{2}	16	14	12	0	0	14	5	1.800	6.48	52	4.41	.242	1	.125	-6	0	-0.6
1912 StL-A	5	8	.385	23	13	2	1	0	120^{1}	122	56	40	2	12	42	45	1.363	2.99	112	3.92	.280	6	.167	3	7	0.2
1913 Bro-N	0	0	....	3	1	0	0	0	13	6	3	3	0	1	10	6	1.231	2.08	158	2.19	.158	0	.000	2	1	0.1
1914 Bro-N	1	2	.333	11	5	1	0	0	36^{2}	33	24	16	2	7	23	22	1.527	3.93	73	4.53	.402	1	.083	-5	0	-0.6
1915 Bro-N	0	0	....	1	0	0	0	0	2	4	4	2	0	0	3	1	3.500	9.00	31	16.31	.500	0	....	-1	0	-0.2
Total 5	7	11	.389	43	22	4	2	0	188^{2}	181	101	73	4	20	92	79	1.447	3.48	92	4.10	.287	8	.133	-7	8	-1.0

• BROWN, Hal Hector Harold "Skinny" Brown b: 12/11/1924, Greensboro, NC BR/TR, 6'2", 182 lbs. Deb: 4/19/1951 C

YEAR TM-L	W	L	PCT	G	GS	CG	SH	SV	IP	H	R	ER	HR	HB	BB	SO	RAT	ERA	ERA+	CERA	OAV	BH	AVG	PR+	WS	TPW
1951 Chi-A	0	0	....	3	0	0	0	1	8^{2}	15	9	9	3	0	4	4	2.192	9.35	43	11.09	.385	2	1.000	-5	0	-0.4
1952 Chi-A	2	3	.400	24	8	1	0	0	72^{1}	82	39	34	8	0	21	31	1.424	4.23	86	4.38	.284	3	.158	-5	2	-0.5
1953 Bos-A	11	6	.647	30	25	6	1	0	166^{1}	177	94	86	16	0	57	62	1.407	4.65	90	4.07	.269	17	.293	-9	10	-0.5
1954 Bos-A	1	8	.111	40	5	1	0	0	118	126	64	54	6	3	41	66	1.415	4.12	100	3.80	.269	3	.125	1	4	0.1
1955 Bos-A	1	0	1.000	2	0	0	0	0	4	2	1	1	0	0	2	2	1.000	2.25	191	1.41	.143	1	1.000	1	1	0.1
Bal-A	0	4	.000	15	5	1	0	0	57	51	30	26	5	0	26	26	1.351	4.11	93	3.55	.241	0	.000	-1	2	-0.3
Yr.	1	4	.200	17	5	1	0	0	61	53	31	27	5	0	28	28	1.328	3.98	96	3.41	.235	1	.059	-0	3	-0.1
1956 Bal-A	9	7	.563	35	14	4	1	2	151^{2}	142	72	68	18	1	37	57	1.180	4.04	97	3.27	.247	8	.190	-1	12	0.1
1957 Bal-A	7	8	.467	25	20	7	2	1	150	132	68	65	17	2	37	62	1.127	3.90	92	2.97	.236	10	.208	-8	7	-0.6
1958 Bal-A	7	5	.583	19	17	4	2	1	96^{2}	96	35	33	9	0	20	44	1.200	3.07	117	3.27	.259	4	.148	6	8	0.5
1959 Bal-A	11	9	.550	31	21	2	0	3	164	158	73	69	16	1	32	81	1.159	3.79	100	3.04	.252	2	.048	-1	10	-0.4
1960 Bal-A	12	5	.706	30	20	6	1	0	159	155	61	54	14	1	22	66	1.113	3.06	125	2.91	.258	8	.182	10	14	1.3
1961 Bal-A	10	6	.625	27	23	6	3	1	166^{2}	153	62	59	14	1	33	61	1.116	3.19	123	2.83	.247	7	.140	11	13	1.1
1962 Bal-A	6	4	.600	22	11	0	0	1	85^{2}	88	41	39	12	3	21	25	1.272	4.10	92	4.03	.268	8	.286	-4	5	-0.2
NY-A	0	1	.000	2	1	0	0	0	6^{2}	9	10	5	3	0	2	2	1.650	6.75	55	7.77	.333	0	.000	-2	0	-0.2
Yr.	6	5	.545	24	12	0	0	1	92^{1}	97	51	44	15	3	23	27	1.300	4.29	88	4.30	.273	8	.276	-6	5	-0.5
1963 Hou-N	5	11	.313	26	20	6	3	0	141^{1}	137	54	52	14	0	8	68	1.026	3.31	95	2.58	.255	4	.093	1	7	-0.1
1964 Hou-N	3	15	.167	27	21	3	0	1	132	154	68	58	18	2	26	53	1.364	3.95	86	4.37	.292	5	.128	-6	3	-0.7
Total 14	85	92	.480	358	211	47	13	11	1680	1677	781	712	173	14	389	710	1.230	3.81	98	3.44	.260	82	.169	-13	98	-0.7

• BROWN, Jackie Jackie Gene Brown b: 5/31/1943, Holdenville, OK BR/TR, 6'1", 195 lbs. Deb: 7/2/1970 C

YEAR TM-L	W	L	PCT	G	GS	CG	SH	SV	IP	H	R	ER	HR	HB	BB	SO	RAT	ERA	ERA+	CERA	OAV	BH	AVG	PR+	WS	TPW
1970 Was-A	2	2	.500	24	5	1	0	0	57	49	28	25	8	0	37	47	1.509	3.95	90	4.57	.231	2	.154	-3	2	-0.4
1971 Was-A	3	4	.429	14	9	0	0	0	47	60	34	31	9	1	27	21	1.851	5.94	56	7.27	.316	2	.133	-14	0	-1.6
1973 Tex-A	5	5	.500	25	3	2	1	2	66^{2}	82	31	29	7	2	25	45	1.605	3.92	95	5.64	.309	0	....	0	3	0.0
1974 Tex-A	13	12	.520	35	26	9	2	0	216^{2}	219	97	86	13	4	74	134	1.352	3.57	100	3.73	.265	0	....	-1	12	-0.1
1975 Tex-A	5	5	.500	17	7	2	1	0	70^{1}	70	37	33	7	2	35	35	1.493	4.22	89	4.60	.266	0	....	-3	3	-0.4
Cle-A	1	2	.333	25	3	1	0	1	69^{1}	72	40	33	9	0	29	41	1.457	4.28	88	4.51	.276	0	....	-4	2	-0.4
Yr.	6	7	.462	42	10	3	1	1	139^{2}	142	77	66	16	2	64	76	1.475	4.25	89	4.56	.271	0	....	-8	5	-0.8
1976 Cle-A	9	11	.450	32	27	5	2	0	180	193	94	85	14	7	55	104	1.378	4.25	82	4.07	.276	0	....	-16	5	-1.7
1977 Mon-N	9	12	.429	42	25	6	2	0	185^{2}	189	99	93	15	4	71	89	1.400	4.51	84	4.01	.264	7	.125	-15	6	-1.8
Total 7	47	53	.470	214	105	26	8	3	892^{2}	934	460	415	82	20	353	516	1.442	4.18	86	4.37	.272	11	.131	-57	33	-6.3

• BROWN, Jim James W. H. Brown b: 12/12/1860, Clinton County, PA d: 4/6/1908, Williamsport, PA Deb: 4/17/1884 ♦

YEAR TM-L	W	L	PCT	G	GS	CG	SH	SV	IP	H	R	ER	HR	HB	BB	SO	RAT	ERA	ERA+	CERA	OAV	BH	AVG	PR+	WS	TPW
1884 Alt-U	1	9	.100	11	11	7	0	0	74	99	80	44	0	....	36	39	1.824	5.35	62	....	.301	22	.250	-10	2	-1.3
NY-N	0	1	.000	1	1	1	0	0	9	10	9	5	0	....	8	2	2.000	5.00	59	....	.266	0	.000	-2	0	-0.2
StP-U	1	4	.200	6	6	4	1	0	36	43	34	15	1	....	14	20	1.583	3.75	81	....	.278	5	.313	-5	2	-0.3
Yr.	2	13	.133	17	17	11	1	0	110	142	114	59	1	....	50	59	1.745	4.83	67	....	.293	27	.260	-15	4	-1.5
1886 Phi-a	0	1	.000	1	1	1	0	0	8^{1}	9	5	3	0	0	3	4	1.440	3.24	108	....	.263	0	.000	0	0	0.0
Total 2	2	15	.118	19	19	13	1	0	127^{1}	161	128	67	1	0	61	65	1.743	4.74	68	....	.290	27	.245	-17	4	-1.8

• BROWN, Joe Joseph E. Brown b: 4/4/1859, Warren, PA d: 6/28/1888, Warren, PA, 5'10", 162 lbs. Deb: 8/16/1884 ♦

YEAR TM-L	W	L	PCT	G	GS	CG	SH	SV	IP	H	R	ER	HR	HB	BB	SO	RAT	ERA	ERA+	CERA	OAV	BH	AVG	PR+	WS	TPW
1884 Chi-N	4	2	.667	7	6	5	0	0	50	56	36	26	4	....	7	27	1.260	4.68	67	....	.268	13	.213	-11	2	-1.3
1885 Bal-a	0	4	.000	4	4	4	0	0	38	52	33	24	0	0	4	9	1.474	5.68	57	....	.313	3	.158	-9	0	-0.9
Total 2	4	6	.400	11	10	9	0	0	88	108	69	50	4	0	11	36	1.352	5.11	62	....	.288	16	.200	-20	2	-2.2

• BROWN, Joe Joseph Henry Brown b: 7/3/1900, Little Rock, AR d: 3/7/1950, Los Angeles, CA BR/TR, 6', 176 lbs. Deb: 5/17/1927

YEAR TM-L	W	L	PCT	G	GS	CG	SH	SV	IP	H	R	ER	HR	HB	BB	SO	RAT	ERA	ERA+	CERA	OAV	BH	AVG	PR+	WS	TPW
1927 Chi-A	0	0	....	1	1	0	0	0	0	2	3	0	0	0	1	0	....	....	....	∞	1.000	0	....	0	0	0.0

• BROWN, John John J. "Ad" Brown b: Trenton, NJ Deb: 8/11/1897

YEAR TM-L	W	L	PCT	G	GS	CG	SH	SV	IP	H	R	ER	HR	HB	BB	SO	RAT	ERA	ERA+	CERA	OAV	BH	AVG	PR+	WS	TPW
1897 Bro-N	0	1	.000	1	1	0	0	0	5	7	8	4	0	3	4	0	2.200	7.20	57	9.37	.328	1	.500	-2	0	-0.1

• BROWN, Jophrey Jophrey Clifford Brown b: 1/22/1945, Grambling, LA BL/TR, 6'2", 190 lbs. Deb: 9/21/1968

YEAR TM-L	W	L	PCT	G	GS	CG	SH	SV	IP	H	R	ER	HR	HB	BB	SO	RAT	ERA	ERA+	CERA	OAV	BH	AVG	PR+	WS	TPW
1968 Chi-N	0	0	....	1	0	0	0	0	2	2	1	1	0	0	1	0	1.500	4.50	70	2.79	.286	0	....	-0	0	0.0

• BROWN, Jumbo Walter George Brown b: 4/30/1907, Greene, RI d: 10/2/1966, Freeport, NY BR/TR, 6'4", 295 lbs. Deb: 8/26/1925

YEAR TM-L	W	L	PCT	G	GS	CG	SH	SV	IP	H	R	ER	HR	HB	BB	SO	RAT	ERA	ERA+	CERA	OAV	BH	AVG	PR+	WS	TPW
1925 Chi-N	0	0	....	2	0	0	0	0	6	5	5	2	0	0	4	0	1.500	3.00	144	3.05	.217	0	.000	1	0	0.1
1927 Cle-A	0	2	.000	8	0	0	0	0	18^{2}	19	14	13	3	1	26	8	2.411	6.27	67	8.80	.284	2	.667	-4	1	-0.3
1928 Cle-A	0	1	.000	5	0	0	0	0	14^{2}	19	15	11	0	0	15	12	2.318	6.75	61	7.77	.365	2	.667	-4	1	-0.3
1932 NY-A	5	2	.714	19	3	3	1	1	55^{2}	58	30	28	1	2	30	31	1.581	4.53	90	4.24	.270	4	.174	-3	3	-0.3
1933 NY-A	7	5	.583	21	8	1	0	0	74	78	48	43	3	0	52	55	1.757	5.23	74	4.84	.269	5	.179	-10	2	-1.0
1935 NY-A	6	5	.545	20	8	3	1	0	87^{1}	94	41	35	2	0	37	41	1.500	3.61	112	3.96	.279	10	.313	3	6	0.5
1936 NY-A	1	4	.200	20	3	0	0	1	64	93	47	42	4	0	29	19	1.906	5.91	79	6.68	.352	0	.000	-9	1	-1.1
1937 Cin-N	1	0	1.000	4	1	0	0	0	9^{2}	16	10	9	0	0	3	4	1.966	8.38	45	7.20	.390	0	.000	-5	0	-0.5
NY-N	1	0	1.000	4	0	0	0	0	8^{2}	5	2	1	0	0	5	4	1.154	1.04	374	1.80	.172	0	....	3	1	0.3
Yr.	2	0	1.000	8	1	0	0	0	18^{1}	21	12	10	0	0	8	8	1.582	4.91	76	4.65	.300	0	.000	-2	1	-0.2
1938 NY-N	5	3	.625	43	0	0	0	5	90	65	26	18	5	1	28	42	1.033	1.80	209	2.04	.204	3	.188	20	12	2.0
1939 NY-N	4	0	1.000	31	0	0	0	7	56^{1}	69	30	26	1	1	25	24	1.669	4.15	95	4.80	.304	4	.364	-1	5	0.0
1940 NY-N	2	4	.333	41	0	0	0	**7**	55^{1}	49	25	21	5	0	25	31	1.337	3.42	114	3.39	.232	1	.100	3	5	0.2
1941 NY-N	1	5	.167	31	0	0	0	**8**	57	49	23	21	2	0	21	30	1.228	3.32	111	2.70	.238	1	.111	2	6	0.2
Total 12	33	31	.516	249	23	7	2	29	597^{1}	619	316	270	26	5	300	301	1.539	4.07	99	4.26	.272	32	.204	-6	43	-0.2

• BROWN, Keith Keith Edward Brown b: 2/14/1964, Flagstaff, AZ BB/TR, 6'4", 215 lbs. Deb: 8/25/1988

YEAR TM-L	W	L	PCT	G	GS	CG	SH	SV	IP	H	R	ER	HR	HB	BB	SO	RAT	ERA	ERA+	CERA	OAV	BH	AVG	PR+	WS	TPW
1988 Cin-N	2	1	.667	4	3	0	0	0	16^{1}	14	5	5	1	0	4	6	1.102	2.76	130	2.64	.237	0	.000	1	2	0.1
1990 Cin-N	0	0	....	8	0	0	0	0	11^{1}	12	6	6	2	0	3	8	1.324	4.76	83	4.61	.286	0	....	-1	0	-0.1
1991 Cin-N	0	0	....	11	0	0	0	0	12	15	4	3	0	0	6	4	1.750	2.25	169	4.94	.306	0	....	2	1	0.2
1992 Cin-N	0	1	.000	2	2	0	0	0	8	10	5	4	2	0	5	5	1.875	4.50	80	8.04	.313	0	.000	-1	0	-0.1
Total 4	2	2	.500	25	5	0	0	0	47^{2}	51	20	18	5	0	18	23	1.448	3.40	110	4.59	.280	0	.000	1	3	0.1

• BROWN, Kevin Kevin Dewayne Brown b: 3/5/1966, Oroville, CA BL/TL, 6'1", 185 lbs. Deb: 7/27/1990

YEAR TM-L	W	L	PCT	G	GS	CG	SH	SV	IP	H	R	ER	HR	HB	BB	SO	RAT	ERA	ERA+	CERA	OAV	BH	AVG	PR+	WS	TPW
1990 NY-N	0	0	....	2	0	0	0	0	2	2	0	0	0	0	1	0	1.500	0.00	....	3.63	.250	0	....	1	0	0.1
Mil-A	1	1	.500	5	3	0	0	0	21	14	7	6	1	1	7	12	1.000	2.57	150	1.82	.182	0	....	3	2	0.3
1991 Mil-A	2	4	.333	15	10	0	0	0	63^{2}	66	39	39	6	1	34	30	1.571	5.51	72	4.79	.270	0	....	-11	1	-1.1
1992 Sea-A	0	0	....	2	0	0	0	0	3	4	3	3	1	0	3	2	2.333	9.00	44	11.47	.333	0	....	-2	0	-0.2
Total 3	3	5	.375	24	13	0	0	0	89^{2}	86	49	48	8	2	45	44	1.461	4.82	82	4.30	.252	0	....	-8	3	-0.8

• BROWN, Kevin James Kevin Brown b: 3/14/1965, Milledgeville, GA BR/TR, 6'4", 195 lbs. Deb: 9/30/1986

YEAR TM-L	W	L	PCT	G	GS	CG	SH	SV	IP	H	R	ER	HR	HB	BB	SO	RAT	ERA	ERA+	CERA	OAV	BH	AVG	PR+	WS	TPW
1986 Tex-A	1	0	1.000	1	1	0	0	0	5	6	2	2	0	0	0	4	1.200	3.60	119	3.25	.316	0	....	0	0	0.0
1988 Tex-A	1	1	.500	4	4	1	0	0	23^{1}	33	15	11	2	1	8	12	1.757	4.24	96	6.33	.330	0	....	-1	1	-0.1
1989 Tex-A	12	9	.571	28	28	7	0	0	191	167	81	71	10	4	70	104	1.241	3.35	118	3.02	.234	0	....	14	13	1.5
1990 Tex-A	12	10	.545	26	26	6	2	0	180	175	84	72	13	3	60	88	1.306	3.60	109	3.54	.255	0	.000	5	12	0.6
1991 Tex-A	9	12	.429	33	33	0	0	0	210^{2}	233	116	103	17	13	90	96	1.533	4.40	92	4.92	.284	0	....	-5	7	-0.5

YEAR	TM-L	W	L	PCT	G	GS	CG	SH	SV	IP	H	R	ER	HR	HB	BB	SO	RAT	ERA	ERA+	CERA	OAV	BH	AVG	PR+	WS	TPW
1992	Tex-A★	**21**	11	.656	35	35	11	1	0	**265^{2}**	262	117	98	11	10	76	173	1.272	3.32	114	3.34	.260	0	....	19	18	1.9
1993	Tex-A	15	12	.556	34	34	12	3	0	233	228	105	93	14	15	74	142	1.296	3.59	116	3.55	.252	0	....	19	15	1.8
1994	Tex-A	7	9	.438	26	**25**	3	0	0	170	218	109	91	18	6	50	123	1.576	4.82	100	5.49	.314	0	....	4	7	0.4
1995	Bal-A	10	9	.526	26	26	3	1	0	172^{1}	155	73	69	10	9	48	117	1.178	3.60	132	3.03	.241	0	....	20	13	1.8
1996	Fla-N★	17	11	.607	32	32	5	**3**	0	233	187	60	49	8	16	33	159	.944	**1.89**	**215**	**2.00**	.220	9	.120	**53**	26	**5.1**
1997*	Fla-N★	16	8	.667	33	33	6	2	0	237^{1}	214	77	71	10	14	66	205	1.180	2.69	150	2.92	.240	9	.125	34	23	3.3
1998*	SD-N★	18	7	.720	36	**35**	7	3	0	257	225	77	68	8	10	49	257	1.066	2.38	165	2.35	.235	17	.207	43	**26**	4.6
1999	LA-N	18	9	.667	35	**35**	5	1	0	252^{1}	210	99	84	19	7	59	221	1.066	3.00	143	2.51	.222	5	.064	38	19	3.1
2000	LA-N★	13	6	.684	33	33	5	1	0	230	181	76	66	21	9	47	216	.991	**2.58**	168	**2.30**	**.213**	5	.076	46	20	4.0
2001	LA-N	10	4	.714	20	19	1	0	0	115^{2}	94	41	34	8	2	38	104	1.141	2.65	151	2.71	.224	3	.083	18	11	1.8
2002	LA-N	3	4	.429	17	10	0	0	0	63^{2}	68	36	34	9	5	23	58	1.429	4.81	79	4.96	.274	5	.250	-7	1	-0.5
2003	LA-N★	14	9	.609	32	32	0	0	0	211	184	67	56	11	5	56	185	1.137	2.39	168	2.68	.236	10	.159	35	20	3.4
Total	17	197	131	.601	451	441	72	17	0	3051	2840	1235	1072	189	129	847	2264	1.208	3.16	131	3.18	.246	63	.128	335	232	32.2

• BROWN, Lloyd Lloyd Andrew "Gimpy" Brown b: 12/25/1904, Beeville, TX d: 1/14/1974, Opa-locka, FL BL/TL, 5'9", 170 lbs. Deb: 7/17/1925

YEAR	TM-L	W	L	PCT	G	GS	CG	SH	SV	IP	H	R	ER	HR	HB	BB	SO	RAT	ERA	ERA+	CERA	OAV	BH	AVG	PR+	WS	TPW
1925	Bro-N	0	3	.000	17	5	1	0	0	63^{1}	79	39	29	1	2	25	23	1.642	4.12	101	5.01	.319	2	.087	2	2	0.0
1928	Was-A	4	4	.500	27	10	2	0	1	107	112	62	48	7	2	40	38	1.421	4.04	99	3.86	.273	5	.161	-2	5	-0.1
1929	Was-A	8	7	.533	40	15	7	1	0	168	186	92	78	7	1	69	48	1.518	4.18	101	4.31	.297	11	.220	-1	10	0.2
1930	Was-A	16	12	.571	38	22	10	1	0	197	220	99	93	6	5	65	59	1.447	4.25	108	4.04	.293	14	.215	1	15	0.3
1931	Was-A	15	14	.517	42	32	15	1	0	258^{2}	256	121	92	13	0	79	79	1.295	3.20	134	3.24	.257	22	.229	29	19	2.9
1932	Was-A	15	12	.556	46	24	10	2	5	202^{2}	239	115	100	11	1	55	53	1.451	4.44	97	4.25	.296	7	.100	-8	12	-1.2
1933	StL-A	1	6	.143	8	6	0	0	0	39	57	35	31	1	0	17	7	1.897	7.15	65	6.21	.350	3	.273	-12	0	-1.0
	Bos-A	8	11	.421	33	21	9	2	1	163^{1}	180	93	73	4	0	64	37	1.494	4.02	109	3.93	.281	16	.281	7	10	1.2
	Yr.	9	17	.346	41	27	9	2	1	202^{1}	237	128	104	5	0	81	44	1.572	4.63	96	4.37	.295	19	.279	-5	10	0.2
1934	Cle-A	5	10	.333	38	15	5	0	6	117	116	67	50	7	2	51	39	1.427	3.85	118	3.88	.263	7	.233	10	8	1.0
1935	Cle-A	8	7	.533	42	8	4	2	4	122	123	52	49	6	3	37	45	1.311	3.61	125	3.43	.265	4	.108	14	11	1.1
1936	Cle-A	8	10	.444	24	16	12	1	1	140^{1}	166	78	65	13	3	45	34	1.504	4.17	121	4.74	.294	10	.222	15	11	1.5
1937	Cle-A	2	6	.250	31	5	2	0	0	77	107	59	56	4	3	27	32	1.740	6.55	70	5.84	.329	4	.167	-16	0	-1.5
1940	Phi-N	1	3	.250	18	2	0	0	3	37^{2}	58	26	26	3	0	16	16	1.965	6.21	63	7.06	.354	1	.077	-10	0	-1.1
Total	12	91	105	.464	404	181	77	10	21	1693	1899	938	790	83	22	590	510	1.470	4.20	105	4.18	.288	106	.192	29	103	3.1

• BROWN, Mace Mace Stanley Brown b: 5/21/1909, North English, IA d: 3/24/2002, Greensboro, NC BR/TR, 6'1", 190 lbs. Deb: 5/21/1935 C

YEAR	TM-L	W	L	PCT	G	GS	CG	SH	SV	IP	H	R	ER	HR	HB	BB	SO	RAT	ERA	ERA+	CERA	OAV	BH	AVG	PR+	WS	TPW
1935	Pit-N	4	1	.800	18	5	2	0	0	72^{2}	84	41	29	5	0	22	28	1.459	3.59	114	4.25	.287	4	.167	5	4	0.4
1936	Pit-N	10	11	.476	47	10	3	0	3	165	178	89	71	8	1	55	56	1.412	3.87	105	3.80	.275	10	.167	5	9	0.3
1937	Pit-N	7	2	.778	50	2	0	0	**7**	107^{2}	109	59	50	2	1	45	60	1.430	4.18	92	3.53	.261	9	.300	-4	8	-0.2
1938	Pit-N★	15	9	.625	**51**	2	0	0	5	132^{2}	155	68	56	5	0	44	55	1.500	3.80	100	4.20	.294	5	.132	-2	9	-0.4
1939	Pit-N	9	13	.409	47	19	8	1	7	200^{1}	232	90	75	8	2	52	71	1.418	3.37	114	3.92	.293	7	.109	15	14	1.1
1940	Pit-N	10	9	.526	48	17	5	1	**7**	173	181	78	67	5	2	49	73	1.329	3.49	109	3.35	.267	6	.115	11	11	1.0
1941	Pit-N	0	0	....	1	0	0	0	0	1^{1}	2	0	0	0	0	0	0	1.500	0.00	....	4.47	.333	0	....	1	0	0.1
	Bro-N	3	2	.600	24	0	0	0	3	42^{2}	31	17	15	3	1	26	22	1.336	3.16	116	3.14	.208	0	.000	2	4	0.1
	Yr.	3	2	.600	25	0	0	0	3	44	33	17	15	3	1	26	22	1.341	3.07	119	3.18	.213	0	.000	2	4	0.1
1942	Bos-A	9	3	.750	34	0	0	0	6	60^{1}	56	27	23	4	0	28	20	1.392	3.43	109	3.70	.255	1	.067	1	6	0.0
1943	Bos-A	6	6	.500	**49**	0	0	0	9	93^{1}	71	26	22	2	0	51	40	1.307	2.12	156	2.78	.222	1	.059	12	11	1.1
1946*	Bos-A	3	1	.750	18	0	0	0	1	26^{1}	26	7	6	2	0	16	10	1.595	2.05	179	4.58	.268	0	.000	5	3	0.4
Total	10	76	57	.571	387	55	18	2	48	1075^{1}	1125	502	414	44	7	388	435	1.407	3.46	111	3.70	.271	43	.137	48	79	3.8

• BROWN, Mark Mark Anthony Brown b: 7/13/1959, Bellows Falls, VT BB/TR, 6'2", 190 lbs. Deb: 8/9/1984

YEAR	TM-L	W	L	PCT	G	GS	CG	SH	SV	IP	H	R	ER	HR	HB	BB	SO	RAT	ERA	ERA+	CERA	OAV	BH	AVG	PR+	WS	TPW
1984	Bal-A	1	2	.333	9	0	0	0	0	23	22	11	10	2	1	7	10	1.261	3.91	99	3.68	.256	0	....	-1	1	-0.1
1985	Min-A	0	0	....	6	0	0	0	0	15^{2}	21	13	12	1	0	7	5	1.787	6.89	64	6.01	.333	0	....	-4	0	-0.4
Total	2	1	2	.333	15	0	0	0	0	38^{2}	43	24	22	3	1	14	15	1.474	5.12	81	4.62	.289	0	....	-5	1	-0.5

• BROWN, Mike Michael Gary Brown b: 3/24/1959, Camden County, NJ BR/TR, 6'2", 195 lbs. Deb: 9/16/1982 C

YEAR	TM-L	W	L	PCT	G	GS	CG	SH	SV	IP	H	R	ER	HR	HB	BB	SO	RAT	ERA	ERA+	CERA	OAV	BH	AVG	PR+	WS	TPW
1982	Bos-A	1	0	1.000	3	0	0	0	0	6	7	0	0	0	0	1	4	1.333	0.00	....	3.63	.304	0	....	3	1	0.3
1983	Bos-A	6	6	.500	19	18	3	1	0	104	110	62	54	12	2	43	35	1.471	4.67	93	4.66	.276	0	....	-3	4	-0.3
1984	Bos-A	1	8	.111	15	11	0	0	0	67	104	63	51	9	3	19	32	1.836	6.85	61	7.22	.347	0	....	-18	0	-1.8
1985	Bos-A	0	0	....	2	1	0	0	0	3^{1}	9	8	8	0	0	3	3	3.600	21.60	20	16.72	.500	0	....	-6	0	-0.6
1986	Bos-A	4	4	.500	15	10	0	0	0	57^{1}	72	35	34	10	1	25	32	1.692	5.34	78	6.47	.316	0	....	-7	2	-0.7
	Sea-A	0	2	.000	6	2	0	0	0	15^{2}	19	14	13	4	0	11	9	1.915	7.47	57	8.09	.302	0	....	-6	0	-0.5
	Yr.	4	6	.400	21	12	0	0	0	73	91	49	47	14	1	36	41	1.740	5.79	72	6.82	.313	0	....	-13	2	-1.2
1987	Sea-A	0	0	....	1	0	0	0	0	0^{1}	3	2	2	0	0	0	0	9.000	54.00	9	67.29	.750	0	....	-2	0	-0.2
Total	6	12	20	.375	61	42	3	1	0	253^{2}	324	184	162	35	6	102	115	1.679	5.75	74	6.18	.313	0	....	-39	7	-3.8

• BROWN, Mordecai Mordecai Peter Centennial "Three Finger,Miner" Brown
b: 10/19/1876, Nyesville, IN d: 2/14/1948, Terre Haute, IN BB/TR, 5'10", 175 lbs. Deb: 4/19/1903 M HOF: 1949

YEAR	TM-L	W	L	PCT	G	GS	CG	SH	SV	IP	H	R	ER	HR	HB	BB	SO	RAT	ERA	ERA+	CERA	OAV	BH	AVG	PR+	WS	TPW
1903	StL-N	9	13	.409	26	24	19	1	0	201	231	105	58	7	6	59	83	1.443	2.60	125	4.05	.293	15	.195	11	12	1.0
1904	Chi-N	15	10	.600	26	23	21	4	1	212^{1}	155	74	44	1	6	50	81	.965	1.86	142	**1.60**	**.199**	19	.213	15	20	1.6
1905	Chi-N	18	12	.600	30	24	24	4	0	249	219	89	60	3	1	44	89	1.056	2.17	137	2.06	.235	13	.140	13	20	1.3
1906*	Chi-N	26	6	.813	36	32	27	**9**	3	277^{1}	198	56	32	1	4	61	144	.934	**1.04**	**253**	**1.53**	.202	20	.204	**43**	**35**	**4.9**
1907*	Chi-N	20	6	.769	34	27	20	6	3	233	180	51	36	2	6	40	107	.944	1.39	179	1.70	.221	13	.153	23	29	2.5
1908*	Chi-N	29	9	.763	44	31	27	9	5	312^{1}	214	64	51	1	5	49	123	.842	1.47	159	**1.31**	.195	25	.207	27	34	3.2
1909	Chi-N	**27**	9	.750	**50**	34	**32**	8	**7**	**342^{2}**	246	78	50	1	7	53	172	.873	1.31	193	1.42	.202	22	.176	44	**36**	5.0
1910*	Chi-N	25	14	.641	46	31	**27**	**6**	**7**	295^{1}	256	95	61	3	4	64	143	1.084	1.86	155	**2.15**	.232	18	.175	30	29	3.1
1911	Chi-N	21	11	.656	**53**	27	21	0	**13**	270	267	110	84	5	6	55	129	1.193	2.80	118	2.79	.262	23	.253	10	25	1.5
1912	Chi-N	5	6	.455	15	8	5	2	0	88^{2}	92	35	26	2	1	20	34	1.263	2.64	126	3.13	.274	9	.290	5	8	0.6
1913	Cin-N	11	12	.478	39	16	11	1	6	173^{1}	174	79	56	7	1	44	41	1.258	2.91	111	3.21	.277	11	.204	6	11	0.6
1914	StL-F	12	6	.667	26	18	13	2	0	175	172	73	64	7	3	43	81	1.229	3.29	105	3.02	.254	15	.254	7	14	0.9
	Bro-F	2	5	.286	9	8	5	0	0	57^{2}	63	33	27	1	0	18	32	1.405	4.21	77	3.57	.276	4	.211	-6	1	-0.6
	Yr.	14	11	.560	35	26	18	2	0	232^{2}	235	106	91	8	3	61	113	1.272	3.52	97	3.16	.260	19	.244	1	15	0.3
1915	Chi-F	17	8	.680	35	25	17	3	4	236^{1}	189	75	55	2	7	64	95	1.071	2.09	133	2.04	.220	24	.293	18	21	2.6
1916	Chi-N	2	3	.400	12	4	2	0	0	48^{1}	52	27	21	0	4	9	21	1.262	3.91	74	3.27	.289	4	.250	-5	1	-0.5
Total	14	239	130	.648	481	332	271	55	49	3172^{1}	2708	1044	725	43	61	673	1375	1.066	2.06	142	2.20	.233	235	.206	241	296	27.7

• BROWN, Myrl Myrl Lincoln Brown b: 10/10/1894, Waynesboro, PA d: 2/23/1981, Harrisburg, PA BR/TR, 5'11", 172 lbs. Deb: 8/19/1922

YEAR	TM-L	W	L	PCT	G	GS	CG	SH	SV	IP	H	R	ER	HR	HB	BB	SO	RAT	ERA	ERA+	CERA	OAV	BH	AVG	PR+	WS	TPW
1922	Pit-N	3	1	.750	7	5	2	0	0	34^{2}	42	25	23	2	0	13	9	1.587	5.97	68	4.75	.296	3	.273	-7	1	-0.6

• BROWN, Norm Norman Ladelle Brown b: 2/1/1919, Evergreen, NC d: 5/31/1995, Bennettsville, SC BB/TR, 6'3", 180 lbs. Deb: 10/3/1943

YEAR	TM-L	W	L	PCT	G	GS	CG	SH	SV	IP	H	R	ER	HR	HB	BB	SO	RAT	ERA	ERA+	CERA	OAV	BH	AVG	PR+	WS	TPW
1943	Phi-A	0	0	....	1	1	0	0	0	7	5	4	0	0	0	0	1	.714	0.00	....	1.00	.185	0	.000	3	1	0.3
1946	Phi-A	0	1	.000	4	0	0	0	0	7^{1}	8	8	5	2	0	6	3	1.909	6.14	58	7.18	.267	0	....	-2	0	-0.2
Total	2	0	1	.000	5	1	0	0	0	14^{1}	13	12	5	2	0	6	4	1.326	3.14	113	4.16	.228	0	.000	1	1	0.0

• BROWN, Paul Paul Dwayne Brown b: 6/18/1941, Fort Smith, AR BR/TR, 6'1", 190 lbs. Deb: 7/23/1961

YEAR	TM-L	W	L	PCT	G	GS	CG	SH	SV	IP	H	R	ER	HR	HB	BB	SO	RAT	ERA	ERA+	CERA	OAV	BH	AVG	PR+	WS	TPW
1961	Phi-N	0	1	.000	5	1	0	0	0	10	13	9	9	3	1	8	1	2.100	8.10	50	10.09	.325	1	.500	-5	0	-0.4
1962	Phi-N	0	6	.000	23	9	0	0	1	63^{2}	74	45	42	9	3	33	29	1.681	5.94	65	6.09	.298	2	.154	-15	0	-1.5
1963	Phi-N	0	1	.000	6	2	0	0	0	15^{1}	15	10	7	2	2	5	11	1.304	4.11	79	4.09	.238	1	.500	-2	0	-0.1
1968	Phi-N	0	0	....	2	0	0	0	0	4	6	4	4	0	0	1	4	1.750	9.00	33	5.46	.353	0	....	-3	0	-0.3
Total	4	0	8	.000	36	12	0	0	1	93	108	68	62	14	6	47	45	1.667	6.00	62	6.16	.293	4	.235	-24	0	-2.3

• BROWN, Ray Paul Percival Brown b: 1/31/1889, Chicago, IL d: 5/29/1955, Los Angeles, CA BR/TR, 6'1", 172 lbs. Deb: 9/29/1909

YEAR	TM-L	W	L	PCT	G	GS	CG	SH	SV	IP	H	R	ER	HR	HB	BB	SO	RAT	ERA	ERA+	CERA	OAV	BH	AVG	PR+	WS	TPW
1909	Chi-N	1	0	1.000	1	1	1	0	0	9	5	3	2	0	0	4	2	1.000	2.00	127	1.53	.172	0	.000	0	1	0.0

YEAR	TM-L	W	L	PCT	G	GS	CG	SH	SV	IP	H	R	ER	HR	HB	BB	SO	RAT	ERA	ERA+	CERA	OAV	BH	AVG	PR+	WS	TPW
• BROWN, Scott	Scott Edward Brown b: 8/30/1956, DeQuincy, LA BR/TR, 6'2", 220 lbs. Deb: 8/11/1981																										
1981	Cin-N	1	0	1.000	10	0	0	0	0	13	16	4	4	0	0	1	7	1.308	2.77	128	3.41	.314	0	.000	1	1	0.1
• BROWN, Steve	Steven Elbert Brown b: 2/12/1957, San Francisco, CA BR/TR, 6'5", 200 lbs. Deb: 8/1/1983																										
1983	Cal-A	2	3	.400	12	4	2	1	0	46	45	19	18	4	0	16	23	1.326	3.52	114	3.63	.256	0	....	3	3	0.3
1984	Cal-A	0	1	.000	3	3	0	0	0	11	16	13	11	0	0	9	5	2.273	9.00	44	7.46	.340	0	....	-6	0	-0.6
Total	**2**	**2**	**4**	**.333**	**15**	**7**	**2**	**1**	**0**	**57**	**61**	**32**	**29**	**4**	**0**	**25**	**28**	**1.509**	**4.58**	**87**	**4.37**	**.274**	**0**	**....**	**-4**	**3**	**-0.4**
• BROWN, Stub	Richard P. Brown b: 8/3/1870, Baltimore, MD d: 3/10/1948, Baltimore, MD TL, 6'2", 220 lbs. Deb: 8/15/1893																										
1893	Bal-N	0	0	....	2	0	0	0	0	9	13	8	6	0	0	5	0	2.000	6.00	79	6.37	.328	1	.200	-1	0	-0.1
1894	Bal-N	4	0	1.000	9	6	3	0	0	49^{2}	59	39	27	3	0	24	8	1.671	4.89	111	5.07	.292	2	.087	2	3	-0.2
1897	Cin-N	0	1	.000	2	1	1	0	0	13	17	8	6	1	0	8	2	1.923	4.15	109	6.44	.313	0	.000	1	1	0.0
Total	**3**	**4**	**1**	**.800**	**13**	**7**	**4**	**0**	**0**	71^{2}	**89**	**55**	**39**	**4**	**0**	**37**	**10**	**1.758**	**4.90**	**106**	**5.48**	**.301**	**3**	**.091**	**1**	**4**	**-0.3**
• BROWN, Tom	Thomas Dale Brown b: 8/10/1949, Lafayette, LA BR/TR, 6'1", 170 lbs. Deb: 9/14/1978																										
1978	Sea-A	0	0	....	6	0	0	0	0	13	14	6	6	2	0	4	8	1.385	4.15	92	4.79	.286	0	....	-0	1	0.0
• BROWN, Tom	Thomas Tarlton Brown b: 9/21/1860, Liverpool, England d: 10/25/1927, Washington, DC BL/TR, 5'10", 168 lbs. Deb: 7/6/1882 M/U ♦																										
1882	Bal-a	0	0	....	2	0	0	0	0	8^{1}	13	7	1	0	....	6	2	2.280	1.08	255	....	.334	55	.304	2	8	0.9
1883	Col-a	0	1	.000	3	1	1	0	0	14	14	17	9	0	....	10	6	1.714	5.79	53	....	.244	115	.274	-4	12	0.7
1884	Col-a	2	1	.667	4	0	0	0	0	19	27	24	15	0	0	7	5	1.789	7.11	43	....	.317	123	.273	-9	18	0.6
1885	Pit-a	0	0	....	2	0	0	0	0	6	0	3	2	0	3	3	2	.500	3.00	107	....	.000	134	.307	0	20	2.0
1886	Pit-a	0	0	....	1	0	0	0	0	2	2	4	2	0	0	5	1	3.500	9.00	38	....	.249	131	.285	-1	19	1.5
Total	**5**	**2**	**2**	**.500**	**12**	**1**	**1**	**0**	**0**	49^{1}	**56**	**55**	**29**	**0**	**3**	**31**	**16**	**1.764**	**5.29**	**58**	**....**	**.296**	**1973**	**.267**	**-13**	**77**	**5.7**
• BROWN, Walter	Walter Irving Brown b: 4/23/1915, Jamestown, NY d: 2/3/1991, Westfield, NY BR/TR, 5'11", 175 lbs. Deb: 5/16/1947																										
1947	StL-A	1	0	1.000	19	0	0	0	0	46	50	27	25	3	0	28	10	1.696	4.89	79	5.22	.294	0	.000	-5	1	-0.6
• BROWNING, Cal	Calvin Duane Browning b: 3/16/1938, Burns Flat, OK BL/TL, 5'11", 190 lbs. Deb: 6/12/1960																										
1960	StL-N	0	0	....	1	0	0	0	0	0^{2}	5	3	3	1	0	1	0	9.000	40.50	10	86.39	.714	0	....	-3	0	-0.3
• BROWNING, Frank	Frank "Dutch" Browning b: 10/29/1882, Falmouth, KY d: 5/19/1948, San Antonio, TX BR/TR, 5'5", 155 lbs. Deb: 4/16/1910																										
1910	Det-A	2	2	.500	11	6	2	0	3	49	51	17	14	0	0	10	16	1.245	2.57	102	2.81	.262	0	.000	0	4	-0.1
• BROWNING, Tom	Thomas Leo Browning b: 4/28/1960, Casper, WY BL/TL, 6'1", 190 lbs. Deb: 9/9/1984																										
1984	Cin-N	1	0	1.000	3	3	0	0	0	23^{1}	27	4	4	0	0	5	14	1.371	1.54	245	3.72	.303	1	.143	6	3	0.6
1985	Cin-N	20	9	.690	38	38	6	4	0	261^{1}	242	111	103	29	3	73	155	1.205	3.55	107	3.27	.245	17	.193	4	18	0.7
1986	Cin-N	14	13	.519	39	**39**	4	2	0	243^{1}	225	123	103	26	1	70	147	1.212	3.81	101	3.22	.245	14	.163	3	12	0.2
1987	Cin-N	10	13	.435	32	31	2	0	0	183	201	107	102	27	5	61	117	1.432	5.02	85	4.81	.284	8	.154	-17	6	-1.6
1988	Cin-N	18	5	.783	36	**36**	5	2	0	250^{2}	205	98	95	36	7	64	124	1.073	3.41	105	2.95	.224	12	.145	0	16	0.2
1989	Cin-N	15	12	.556	37	**37**	9	2	0	249^{2}	241	109	94	31	3	64	118	1.222	3.39	106	3.50	.255	7	.090	9	14	0.5
1990*	Cin-N	15	9	.625	35	**35**	2	1	0	227^{2}	235	98	96	24	5	52	99	1.261	3.80	104	3.61	.266	7	.093	-0	13	-0.3
1991	Cin-N★	14	14	.500	36	36	1	0	0	230^{1}	241	124	107	32	4	56	115	1.289	4.18	91	3.97	.266	12	.171	-9	9	-0.8
1992	Cin-N	6	5	.545	16	16	0	0	0	87	108	49	49	6	2	28	33	1.563	5.07	71	4.92	.311	7	.226	-14	1	-1.4
1993	Cin-N	7	7	.500	21	20	0	0	0	114	159	61	60	15	1	20	53	1.570	4.74	85	5.77	.333	8	.216	-8	5	-0.6
1994	Cin-N	3	1	.750	7	7	2	1	0	40^{2}	34	20	19	8	1	13	22	1.156	4.20	98	3.51	.222	2	.143	-0	2	0.0
1995	KC-A	0	2	.000	2	2	0	0	0	10	13	9	9	2	0	5	3	1.800	8.10	59	6.78	.302	0	....	-4	0	-0.4
Total	**12**	**123**	**90**	**.577**	**302**	**300**	**31**	**12**	**0**	**1921**	**1931**	**913**	**841**	**236**	**32**	**511**	**1000**	**1.271**	**3.94**	**97**	**3.78**	**.262**	**95**	**.153**	**-31**	**99**	**-2.7**
• BROWNSON, Mark	Mark Phillip Brownson b: 6/17/1975, Lake Worth, FL BL/TR, 6'2", 185 lbs. Deb: 7/21/1998																										
1998	Col-N	1	0	1.000	2	2	1	1	0	13^{1}	16	7	7	2	1	2	8	1.350	4.73	110	4.94	.296	0	.000	1	1	0.0
1999	Col-N	0	2	.000	7	7	0	0	0	29^{2}	42	26	26	8	1	8	21	1.685	7.89	74	7.40	.333	1	.111	-7	0	-0.7
2000	Phi-N	1	0	1.000	2	0	0	0	0	5	7	4	4	1	0	3	3	2.000	7.20	65	8.04	.333	0	....	-1	0	-0.1
Total	**3**	**2**	**2**	**.500**	**11**	**9**	**1**	**1**	**0**	**48**	**65**	**37**	**37**	**11**	**2**	**13**	**32**	**1.625**	**6.94**	**80**	**6.78**	**.323**	**1**	**.071**	**-8**	**1**	**-0.8**
• BRUBAKER, Bruce	Bruce Ellsworth Brubaker b: 12/29/1941, Harrisburg, PA BR/TR, 6'1", 198 lbs. Deb: 4/15/1967																										
1967	LA-N	0	0	....	1	0	0	0	0	1^{1}	3	3	3	1	0	0	2	2.250	20.25	15	16.20	.429	0	....	-3	0	-0.3
1970	Mil-A	0	0	....	1	0	0	0	0	2	2	2	2	1	0	1	0	1.500	9.00	42	7.30	.250	0	....	-1	0	-0.1
Total	**2**	**0**	**0**	**....**	**2**	**0**	**0**	**0**	**0**	3^{1}	**5**	**5**	**5**	**2**	**0**	**1**	**2**	**1.800**	**13.50**	**25**	**10.86**	**.333**	**0**	**....**	**-4**	**0**	**-0.4**
• BRUCE, Bob	Robert James Bruce b: 5/16/1933, Detroit, MI BR/TR, 6'3", 210 lbs. Deb: 9/14/1959																										
1959	Det-A	0	1	.000	2	1	0	0	0	2	2	5	2	1	0	3	1	2.500	9.00	45	11.36	.250	0	....	-1	0	-0.1
1960	Det-A	4	7	.364	34	15	1	0	0	130	127	68	54	16	5	56	76	1.408	3.74	110	4.32	.250	7	.179	6	6	0.6
1961	Det-A	1	2	.333	14	6	0	0	0	44^{2}	57	28	22	6	2	24	25	1.813	4.43	93	6.75	.320	1	.111	-2	1	-0.1
1962	Hou-N	10	9	.526	32	27	6	0	0	175	164	92	79	16	12	82	135	1.406	4.06	92	4.18	.248	11	.200	-3	9	0.2
1963	Hou-N	5	9	.357	30	25	1	1	0	170^{1}	162	73	68	7	8	60	123	1.303	3.59	88	3.36	.250	7	.127	-5	8	-0.3
1964	Hou-N	15	9	.625	35	29	9	4	0	202^{1}	191	70	62	8	3	33	135	1.107	2.76	124	2.49	.246	12	.190	17	18	2.1
1965	Hou-N	9	18	.333	35	34	7	1	0	229^{2}	241	107	95	22	9	38	145	1.215	3.72	90	3.54	.270	9	.122	-5	8	-0.7
1966	Hou-N	3	13	.188	25	23	1	0	0	129^{2}	160	83	77	16	8	29	71	1.458	5.34	64	5.07	.301	3	.077	-26	0	-3.0
1967	Atl-N	2	3	.400	12	7	1	0	1	38^{2}	42	25	21	3	1	15	22	1.474	4.89	68	4.20	.269	2	.167	-7	0	-0.7
Total	**9**	**49**	**71**	**.408**	**219**	**167**	**26**	**6**	**1**	1122^{1}	**1146**	**551**	**480**	**95**	**48**	**340**	**733**	**1.324**	**3.85**	**91**	**3.85**	**.263**	**52**	**.150**	**-26**	**50**	**-2.1**
• BRUCKBAUER, Fred	Frederick John Bruckbauer b: 5/27/1938, New Ulm, MN BR/TR, 6'1", 185 lbs. Deb: 4/25/1961																										
1961	Min-A	0	0	....	1	0	0	0	0	0	3	3	3	0	0	1	0	....	∞	....	∞	1.000	0	....	-3	0	-0.3
• BRUCKMILLER, Andy	Andrew Bruckmiller b: 1/1/1882, McKeesport, PA d: 1/12/1970, McKeesport, PA BR/TR, 5'11", 175 lbs. Deb: 6/26/1905																										
1905	Det-A	0	0	....	1	0	0	0	0	1	4	3	3	0	0	1	1	5.000	27.00	10	27.96	.587	0	.000	-3	0	-0.3
• BRUHERT, Mike	Michael Edwin Bruhert b: 6/24/1951, Jamaica, NY BR/TR, 6'6", 220 lbs. Deb: 4/9/1978																										
1978	NY-N	4	11	.267	27	22	1	1	0	133^{2}	171	83	71	6	1	34	56	1.534	4.78	73	4.71	.317	3	.075	-20	0	-2.4
• BRUMLEY, Duff	Duff Lechaun Brumley b: 8/25/1970, Cleveland, TN BR/TR, 6'4", 195 lbs. Deb: 6/1/1994																										
1994	Tex-A	0	0	....	2	0	0	0	0	3^{1}	6	6	6	1	0	5	4	3.300	16.20	30	15.57	.400	0	....	-4	0	-0.4
• BRUMMETT, Greg	Gregory Scott Brummett b: 4/20/1967, Wichita, KS BR/TR, 6', 180 lbs. Deb: 5/29/1993																										
1993	SF-N	2	3	.400	8	8	0	0	0	46	53	25	24	9	0	13	20	1.435	4.70	83	5.23	.294	0	.000	-5	1	-0.7
	Min-A	2	1	.667	5	5	0	0	0	26^{2}	29	17	17	3	0	15	10	1.650	5.74	76	5.58	.299	0	....	-4	1	-0.4
• BRUNER, Jack	Jack Raymond Bruner b: 7/1/1924, Waterloo, IA d: 6/24/2003, Lincoln, NE BL/TL, 6'1", 185 lbs. Deb: 9/16/1949																										
1949	Chi-A	1	2	.333	4	2	0	0	0	7^{2}	10	7	7	0	0	8	4	2.348	8.22	51	8.23	.357	0	.000	-3	0	-0.4
1950	Chi-A	0	0	....	9	0	0	0	0	12^{1}	7	6	5	0	1	14	8	1.703	3.65	123	3.80	.184	0	....	1	1	0.1
	StL-A	1	2	.333	13	1	0	0	1	35	36	21	18	4	2	23	16	1.686	4.63	107	5.43	.267	0	.000	2	2	0.1
	Yr.	1	2	.333	22	1	0	0	1	47^{1}	43	27	23	4	3	37	24	1.690	4.37	111	5.01	.249	0	.000	3	3	0.2
Total	**2**	**2**	**4**	**.333**	**26**	**3**	**0**	**0**	**1**	**55**	**53**	**34**	**30**	**4**	**3**	**45**	**28**	**1.782**	**4.91**	**95**	**5.45**	**.264**	**0**	**.000**	**-0**	**3**	**-0.1**
• BRUNER, Roy	Walter Roy Bruner b: 2/10/1917, Cecilia, KY d: 11/30/1986, St. Matthews, KY BR/TR, 6', 165 lbs. Deb: 9/14/1939																										
1939	Phi-N	0	4	.000	4	4	2	0	0	27	38	22	20	3	0	13	11	1.889	6.67	59	6.93	.339	1	.111	-8	0	-0.9
1940	Phi-N	0	0	....	2	0	0	0	0	6^{1}	5	4	4	2	0	6	4	1.737	5.68	69	6.62	.227	1	.500	-1	0	-0.1
1941	Phi-N	0	3	.000	13	1	0	0	0	29^{1}	37	17	16	1	0	25	13	2.114	4.91	75	6.95	.336	0	.000	-4	0	-0.4
Total	**3**	**0**	**7**	**.000**	**19**	**5**	**2**	**0**	**0**	62^{2}	**80**	**43**	**40**	**6**	**0**	**44**	**28**	**1.979**	**5.74**	**67**	**6.91**	**.328**	**2**	**.118**	**-13**	**0**	**-1.4**

YEAR	TM-L	W	L	PCT	G	GS	CG	SH	SV	IP	H	R	ER	HR	HB	BB	SO	RAT	ERA	ERA+	CERA	OAV	BH	AVG	PR+	WS	TPW
• BRUNET, George					George Stuart "Lefty" Brunet b: 6/8/1935, Houghton, MI d: 10/25/1991, Poza Rica, Mexico BR/TL, 6'1", 210 lbs. Deb: 9/14/1956																						
1956	KC-A	0	0	....	6	1	0	0	0	9	10	8	7	1	0	11	5	2.333	7.00	62	8.27	.286	0	.000	-3	0	-0.3
1957	KC-A	0	1	.000	4	2	0	0	0	11^1	13	7	7	2	0	4	3	1.500	5.56	71	5.17	.277	0	.000	-2	0	-0.2
1959	KC-A	0	0	....	2	0	0	0	0	4^2	10	9	6	2	1	7	7	3.643	11.57	35	21.11	.435	0	....	-4	0	-0.4
1960	KC-A	0	2	.000	3	2	0	0	0	10^1	12	6	5	0	1	10	4	2.129	4.35	91	6.55	.308	0	.000	-0	0	-0.1
	Mil-N	2	0	1.000	17	6	0	0	0	49^2	53	31	28	6	1	22	39	1.510	5.07	68	4.67	.275	1	.091	-8	0	-0.9
1961	Mil-N	0	0	....	5	0	0	0	0	5	7	3	3	1	0	2	0	1.800	5.40	69	7.46	.412	0	....	-1	0	-0.1
1962	Hou-N	2	4	.333	17	11	2	0	0	54	62	31	27	2	0	21	36	1.537	4.50	83	4.40	.291	1	.059	-4	1	-0.5
1963	Hou-N	0	3	.000	5	2	0	0	0	12^2	24	11	10	2	0	6	11	2.368	7.11	44	10.41	.393	0	.000	-5	0	-0.6
	Bal-A	0	1	.000	16	0	0	0	1	20	25	15	12	3	1	9	13	1.700	5.40	65	6.29	.301	0	.000	-4	0	-0.4
1964	LA-A	2	2	.500	10	7	0	0	0	42^1	38	17	17	2	0	25	36	1.488	3.61	91	3.77	.238	2	.182	-2	2	-0.2
1965	Cal-A	9	11	.450	41	26	8	3	2	197	149	64	56	9	3	69	141	1.107	2.56	133	2.28	.209	3	.054	18	15	1.6
1966	Cal-A	13	13	.500	41	32	8	2	0	212	183	88	78	21	5	106	148	1.363	3.31	101	3.72	.234	7	.103	-1	12	-0.3
1967	Cal-A	11	19	.367	40	37	7	2	1	250	203	99	92	19	4	90	165	1.172	3.31	95	2.78	.223	6	.077	-7	11	-1.3
1968	Cal-A	13	17	.433	39	36	8	5	0	245^1	191	83	78	23	2	68	132	1.056	2.86	102	2.46	.215	6	.081	-2	13	-0.6
1969	Cal-A	6	7	.462	23	19	2	2	0	100^2	98	51	43	15	1	39	56	1.361	3.84	91	4.17	.255	1	.037	-6	4	-0.7
	Sea-A	2	5	.286	12	11	2	0	0	63^2	70	41	38	11	0	28	37	1.539	5.37	68	5.25	.280	3	.150	-10	0	-1.0
	Yr.	8	12	.400	35	30	4	2	0	164^1	168	92	81	26	1	67	93	1.430	4.44	80	4.59	.265	4	.085	-16	4	-1.7
1970	Was-A	8	6	.571	24	20	2	1	0	118	124	64	58	10	1	48	67	1.458	4.42	80	4.32	.275	6	.158	-13	4	-1.2
	Pit-N	1	1	.500	12	1	0	0	0	16^2	19	5	5	1	1	9	17	1.680	2.70	144	5.43	.311	0	.000	2	1	0.1
1971	StL-N	0	1	.000	7	0	0	0	0	9^1	12	6	6	3	0	7	4	2.036	5.79	62	9.26	.316	1	.333	-2	0	-0.2
Total	**15**	**69**	**93**	**.426**	**324**	**213**	**39**	**15**	**4**	**1431^2**	**1303**	**639**	**576**	**133**	**21**	**581**	**921**	**1.316**	**3.62**	**93**	**3.63**	**.244**	**37**	**.089**	**-55**	**63**	**-7.3**
• BRUNETTE, Justin					Justin Thomas Brunette b: 10/7/1975, Los Alamitos, CA BL/TL, 6'1", 200 lbs. Deb: 4/13/2000																						
2000	StL-N	0	0	....	4	0	0	0	0	4^2	8	3	3	0	0	5	2	2.786	5.79	80	10.34	.364	1	1.000	-1	0	0.0
• BRUNO, Tom					Thomas Michael Bruno b: 1/26/1953, Chicago, IL BR/TR, 6'5", 210 lbs. Deb: 8/1/1976																						
1976	KC-A	1	0	1.000	12	0	0	0	0	17^1	20	13	13	3	0	9	11	1.673	6.75	52	5.87	.290	0	....	-6	0	-0.7
1977	Tor-A	0	1	.000	12	0	0	0	0	18^1	30	18	16	4	1	13	9	2.345	7.85	53	10.36	.366	0	....	-7	0	-0.7
1978	StL-N	4	3	.571	18	3	0	0	1	49^2	38	12	11	3	0	17	33	1.107	1.99	176	2.35	.209	1	.083	8	5	0.8
1979	StL-N	2	3	.400	27	1	0	0	0	38^1	37	18	18	1	2	22	27	1.539	4.23	89	3.92	.253	1	.200	-3	2	-0.3
Total	**4**	**7**	**7**	**.500**	**69**	**4**	**0**	**0**	**1**	**123^2**	**125**	**61**	**58**	**11**	**3**	**61**	**80**	**1.504**	**4.22**	**89**	**4.52**	**.261**	**2**	**.118**	**-8**	**7**	**-0.9**
• BRUNSON, Will					William Donald Brunson b: 3/20/1970, Irving, TX BL/TL, 6'4", 185 lbs. Deb: 6/21/1998																						
1998	LA-N	0	1	.000	2	0	0	0	0	2^1	3	3	3	0	0	2	1	2.143	11.57	34	7.28	.333	0	....	-2	0	-0.2
	Det-A	0	0	....	8	0	0	0	0	3	2	0	0	0	0	1	1	1.000	0.00	....	1.73	.200	0	....	2	1	0.1
1999	Det-A	1	0	1.000	17	0	0	0	0	12	18	9	8	3	0	6	9	2.000	6.00	82	8.82	.367	0	....	-1	0	-0.1
Total	**2**	**1**	**1**	**.500**	**27**	**0**	**0**	**0**	**0**	**17^1**	**23**	**12**	**11**	**3**	**0**	**9**	**11**	**1.846**	**5.71**	**81**	**7.39**	**.338**	**0**	**....**	**-2**	**1**	**-0.2**
• BRUSKE, Jim					James Scott Bruske b: 10/7/1964, East St. Louis, IL BR/TR, 6'1", 185 lbs. Deb: 8/25/1995																						
1995	LA-N	0	0	....	9	0	0	0	1	10	12	7	5	0	1	4	5	1.600	4.50	84	4.95	.300	0	....	-1	0	-0.1
1996	LA-N	0	0	....	11	0	0	0	0	12^2	17	8	8	2	1	3	12	1.579	5.68	68	6.01	.315	0	....	-2	0	-0.2
1997	SD-N	4	1	.800	28	0	0	0	0	44^2	37	22	18	4	1	25	32	1.388	3.63	106	3.72	.228	1	.167	2	2	0.2
1998	LA-N	3	0	1.000	35	0	0	0	1	44	47	18	17	2	3	19	31	1.500	3.48	114	4.44	.272	0	.000	3	4	0.2
	SD-N	0	0	....	4	0	0	0	0	7	10	4	3	1	0	4	4	2.000	3.86	102	7.24	.333	0	....	0	0	0.0
	Yr.	3	0	1.000	39	0	0	0	1	51	57	22	20	3	3	23	35	1.569	3.53	112	4.83	.281	0	.000	3	4	0.2
	NY-A	1	0	1.000	3	1	0	0	0	9	9	3	3	2	0	1	3	1.111	3.00	146	3.75	.257	0	....	1	1	0.1
2000	Mil-N	1	0	1.000	15	0	0	0	0	16^2	22	15	12	5	2	12	8	2.040	6.48	70	9.52	.314	0	.000	-4	0	-0.4
Total	**5**	**9**	**1**	**.900**	**105**	**1**	**0**	**0**	**2**	**144**	**154**	**77**	**66**	**16**	**8**	**68**	**95**	**1.542**	**4.13**	**97**	**5.07**	**.273**	**1**	**.100**	**-2**	**7**	**-0.2**
• BRUSSTAR, Warren					Warren Scott Brusstar b: 2/2/1952, Oakland, CA BR/TR, 6'3", 200 lbs. Deb: 5/6/1977																						
1977*	Phi-N	7	2	.778	46	0	0	0	3	71^1	64	26	21	7	1	24	46	1.234	2.65	151	3.42	.250	0	.000	9	7	0.9
1978*	Phi-N	6	3	.667	58	0	0	0	0	88^2	74	25	23	0	3	30	60	1.173	2.33	153	2.47	.239	1	.143	10	8	1.1
1979	Phi-N	1	0	1.000	13	0	0	0	1	14^1	23	12	11	1	0	4	3	1.884	6.91	55	6.95	.383	0	....	-5	0	-0.5
1980*	Phi-N	2	2	.500	26	0	0	0	0	38^2	42	16	16	3	0	13	21	1.422	3.72	102	4.13	.286	0	.000	0	2	0.0
1981*	Phi-N	0	1	.000	14	0	0	0	0	12^1	12	6	6	0	1	10	8	1.784	4.38	83	4.29	.250	0	....	-1	0	-0.1
1982	Phi-N	2	3	.400	22	0	0	0	2	22^2	31	12	12	2	1	5	11	1.588	4.76	77	5.37	.348	0	.000	-3	1	-0.3
	Chi-A	2	0	1.000	10	0	0	0	0	18^1	19	7	7	2	1	3	8	1.200	3.44	117	3.54	.257	0	....	1	2	0.1
1983	Chi-N	3	1	.750	59	0	0	0	1	80^1	67	21	21	1	2	37	46	1.295	2.35	161	2.76	.234	0	.000	14	7	1.4
1984*	Chi-N	1	1	.500	41	0	0	0	3	63^2	57	23	22	4	1	21	36	1.225	3.11	126	2.96	.247	1	.200	6	6	0.7
1985	Chi-N	4	3	.571	51	0	0	0	4	74^1	87	55	50	8	3	36	34	1.655	6.05	66	5.28	.292	1	.143	-16	0	-1.7
Total	**9**	**28**	**16**	**.636**	**340**	**0**	**0**	**0**	**14**	**484^2**	**476**	**203**	**189**	**28**	**13**	**183**	**273**	**1.360**	**3.51**	**110**	**3.64**	**.265**	**3**	**.094**	**17**	**33**	**1.7**
• BRYANT, Clay					Claiborne Henry Bryant b: 11/26/1911, Madison Heights, VA d: 4/9/1999, Boca Raton, FL BR/TR, 6'2.5", 195 lbs. Deb: 4/19/1935 C																						
1935	Chi-N	1	2	.333	9	1	0	0	2	22^2	34	15	13	1	0	7	13	1.809	5.16	76	6.22	.358	2	.333	-4	1	-0.2
1936	Chi-N	1	2	.333	26	0	0	0	0	57^1	57	25	21	0	2	24	35	1.413	3.30	121	3.39	.259	5	.417	3	4	0.4
1937	Chi-N	9	3	.750	38	10	4	1	3	135^1	117	69	64	1	1	78	75	1.441	4.26	93	3.23	.232	14	.311	-5	10	0.0
1938*	Chi-N	19	11	.633	44	30	17	3	2	270^1	235	105	93	6	1	125	**135**	1.332	3.10	123	2.97	.235	24	.226	20	23	2.4
1939	Chi-N	2	1	.667	4	4	2	0	0	31^1	42	23	20	3	1	14	9	1.787	5.74	68	5.96	.307	3	.214	-5	0	-0.5
1940	Chi-N	0	1	.000	8	0	0	0	0	26^1	26	17	14	2	0	14	5	1.519	4.78	78	4.22	.265	3	.333	-3	0	-0.2
Total	**6**	**32**	**20**	**.615**	**129**	**45**	**23**	**4**	**7**	**543^1**	**511**	**254**	**225**	**13**	**5**	**262**	**272**	**1.423**	**3.73**	**104**	**3.45**	**.249**	**51**	**.266**	**6**	**38**	**1.9**
• BRYANT, Ron					Ronald Raymond Bryant b: 11/12/1947, Redlands, CA BB/TL, 6', 190 lbs. Deb: 9/29/1967																						
1967	SF-N	0	0	....	1	0	0	0	0	4	3	2	2	0	1	0	2	.750	4.50	73	1.65	.200	0	.000	-1	0	-0.1
1969	SF-N	4	3	.571	16	8	0	0	1	57^2	60	29	28	8	2	25	30	1.474	4.37	80	4.89	.271	3	.188	-5	3	-0.5
1970	SF-N	5	8	.385	34	11	1	0	0	96	103	58	51	7	2	38	66	1.469	4.78	83	4.32	.274	3	.111	-7	3	-0.8
1971*	SF-N	7	10	.412	27	22	3	2	0	140	146	69	59	9	3	49	79	1.393	3.79	90	3.93	.272	10	.200	-5	5	-0.5
1972	SF-N	14	7	.667	35	28	11	4	0	214	176	81	69	20	2	77	107	1.182	2.90	120	2.94	.224	12	.171	14	13	1.6
1973	SF-N	**24**	12	.667	41	39	8	0	0	270	240	125	106	23	9	115	143	1.315	3.53	108	3.47	.234	16	.168	11	17	1.3
1974	SF-N	3	15	.167	41	23	0	0	0	126^2	142	92	79	11	4	68	75	1.658	5.61	68	5.17	.286	4	.129	-25	0	-2.7
1975	StL-N	0	1	.000	10	1	0	0	0	8^2	20	17	16	2	0	7	7	3.115	16.62	23	15.03	.444	0	.000	-12	0	-1.3
Total	**8**	**57**	**56**	**.504**	**205**	**132**	**23**	**6**	**1**	**917**	**890**	**473**	**410**	**80**	**23**	**379**	**509**	**1.384**	**4.02**	**91**	**3.93**	**.254**	**48**	**.165**	**-29**	**41**	**-2.9**
• BRYDEN, T.R.					Thomas Ray Bryden b: 1/17/1959, Moses Lake, WA BR/TR, 6'4", 190 lbs. Deb: 4/10/1986																						
1986	Cal-A	2	1	.667	16	0	0	0	0	34^1	38	25	25	4	2	21	25	1.718	6.55	63	5.99	.290	0	....	-10	0	-1.0
• BRYNAN, Tod					Charles Ruley Brynan b: 7/1863, Philadelphia, PA d: 5/10/1925, Philadelphia, PA BR/TR, 5'10" Deb: 6/22/1888																						
1888	Chi-N	2	1	.667	3	3	2	0	0	25	29	26	18	2	2	7	11	1.440	6.48	46	....	.280	2	.182	-10	0	-1.0
1891	Bos-N	0	1	.000	1	1	0	0	0	1	4	6	6	0	0	3	0	7.000	54.00	7	....	.572	0	....	-6	0	-0.5
Total	**2**	**2**	**2**	**.500**	**4**	**4**	**2**	**0**	**0**	**26**	**33**	**32**	**24**	**2**	**2**	**10**	**11**	**1.654**	**8.31**	**38**	**....**	**.298**	**2**	**.182**	**-16**	**0**	**-1.5**
• BUCHANAN, Bob					Robert Gordon Buchanan b: 5/3/1961, Ridley Park, PA BL/TL, 6'1", 185 lbs. Deb: 7/13/1985																						
1985	Cin-N	1	0	1.000	14	0	0	0	0	16	25	15	15	4	0	9	3	2.125	8.44	45	9.92	.368	0	.000	-8	0	-0.9
1989	KC-A	0	0	....	2	0	0	0	0	3^1	5	6	6	1	0	3	3	2.400	16.20	24	9.75	.333	0	....	-5	0	-0.5
Total	**2**	**1**	**0**	**1.000**	**16**	**0**	**0**	**0**	**0**	**19^1**	**30**	**21**	**21**	**5**	**0**	**12**	**6**	**2.172**	**9.78**	**39**	**9.89**	**.361**	**0**	**.000**	**-13**	**0**	**-1.4**
• BUCHANAN, Jim					James Forrest Buchanan b: 7/1/1876, Chatham Hill, VA d: 6/15/1949, Norfolk, NE BL/TR, 5'10", 165 lbs. Deb: 4/16/1905																						
1905	StL-A	5	9	.357	22	15	12	1	**2**	141^1	149	76	55	2	2	27	54	1.245	3.50	73	3.01	.273	7	.152	-13	3	-1.4

YEAR TM-L	W	L	PCT	G	GS	CG	SH	SV	IP	H	R	ER	HR	HB	BB	SO	RAT	ERA	ERA+	CERA	OAV	BH	AVG	PR+	WS	TPW
• BUCKELS, Gary	Gary Scott Buckels b: 7/22/1965, La Mirada, CA BR/TR, 6', 185 lbs. Deb: 7/23/1994																									
1994 StL-N	0	1	.000	10	0	0	0	0	12	8	5	3	2	0	7	9	1.250	2.25	185	3.23	.186	0	.000	3	1	0.2
• BUCKEYE, Garland	Garland Maiers "Gob" Buckeye b: 10/16/1897, Heron Lake, MN d: 11/14/1975, Stone Lake, WI BB/TL, 6', 260 lbs. Deb: 6/19/1918																									
1918 Was-A	0	0	....	1	0	0	0	0	2	3	4	4	0	0	6	2	4.500	18.00	15	16.18	.333	0	....	-3	0	-0.4
1925 Cle-A	13	8	.619	30	18	11	1	0	153	161	74	62	3	6	58	49	1.431	3.65	121	3.65	.267	14	.226	14	13	1.5
1926 Cle-A	6	9	.400	32	18	5	1	0	165^{2}	160	79	57	3	6	69	36	1.382	3.10	131	3.40	.264	12	.200	14	11	1.5
1927 Cle-A	10	17	.370	35	25	13	2	1	204^{2}	231	106	90	6	5	74	38	1.490	3.96	106	4.14	.296	19	.268	6	13	0.8
1928 Cle-A	1	5	.167	9	6	0	0	0	35	58	32	26	2	2	5	6	1.800	6.69	62	6.88	.389	1	.111	-10	0	-1.0
NY-N	0	0	....	1	0	0	0	0	3^{2}	9	6	6	1	0	2	3	3.000	14.73	27	14.57	.409	1	.500	-4	0	-0.4
Total 5	30	39	.435	108	67	29	4	1	564	622	301	245	15	19	214	134	1.482	3.91	107	4.07	.287	47	.230	16	37	2.1
• BUCKINGHAM, Ed	Edward Taylor Buckingham b: 5/22/1874, Metuchen, NJ d: 7/30/1942, Bridgeport, CT Deb: 8/30/1895																									
1895 Was-N	0	0	....	1	1	0	0	0	3	6	5	2	0	0	2	1	2.667	6.00	80	10.52	.409	0	.000	-0	0	0.0
• BUCKLES, Jess	Jesse Robert "Jim" Buckles b: 5/20/1890, LaVerne, CA d: 8/2/1975, Westminster, CA BL/TL, 6'2.5", 205 lbs. Deb: 9/17/1916																									
1916 NY-A	0	0	....	2	0	0	0	0	4	3	2	1	0	0	1	2	1.000	2.25	128	1.52	.188	0	.000	0	0	0.0
• BUCKLEY, John	John Edward Buckley b: 3/20/1870, Marlboro, MA d: 3/3/1942, Westborough, MA BL/TR, 6'1", 200 lbs. Deb: 7/15/1890																									
1890 Buf-P	1	3	.250	4	4	4	0	0	34	49	32	29	5	0	16	4	1.912	7.68	53	....	.324	0	.000	-13	0	-1.2
• BUDDIE, Mike	Michael Joseph Buddie b: 12/12/1970, Berea, OH BR/TR, 6'3", 215 lbs. Deb: 4/6/1998																									
1998 NY-A	4	1	.800	24	2	0	0	0	41^{2}	46	29	26	5	3	13	20	1.416	5.62	78	4.80	.284	0	....	-6	1	-0.6
1999 NY-A	0	0	....	2	0	0	0	0	2	3	1	1	1	0	0	1	1.500	4.50	105	8.13	.333	0	....	0	0	0.0
2000 Mil-N	0	0	....	5	0	0	0	0	6	8	3	3	0	0	1	5	1.500	4.50	101	3.91	.320	0	....	-0	0	0.0
2001 Mil-N	0	1	.000	31	0	0	0	2	41^{2}	34	20	18	2	4	17	22	1.224	3.89	110	3.09	.225	1	.250	2	3	0.2
2002 Mil-N	1	2	.333	25	0	0	0	0	39^{2}	46	23	20	5	1	21	28	1.689	4.54	90	5.44	.293	0	.000	-2	1	-0.2
Total 5	5	4	.556	87	2	0	0	2	131	137	76	68	13	8	52	76	1.443	4.67	92	4.46	.272	1	.167	-7	5	-0.6
• BUDNICK, Mike	Michael Joe Budnick b: 9/15/1919, Astoria, OR d: 12/2/1999, Seattle, WA BR/TR, 6'1", 200 lbs. Deb: 4/18/1946																									
1946 NY-N	2	3	.400	35	7	1	1	3	88^{1}	75	40	31	13	0	48	36	1.392	3.16	109	4.00	.231	6	.300	4	6	0.7
1947 NY-N	0	0	....	7	1	0	0	0	12	16	16	14	0	0	10	6	2.167	10.50	39	6.55	.314	1	.250	-9	0	-0.8
Total 2	2	3	.400	42	8	1	1	3	100^{1}	91	56	45	13	0	58	42	1.485	4.04	90	4.31	.242	7	.292	-5	6	-0.1
• BUEHRLE, Mark	Mark Anthony Buehrle b: 3/23/1979, St. Charles, MO BL/TL, 6'2", 200 lbs. Deb: 7/16/2000																									
2000* Chi-A	4	1	.800	28	3	0	0	0	51^{1}	55	27	24	5	3	19	37	1.442	4.21	118	4.56	.272	0	....	4	4	0.3
2001 Chi-A	16	8	.667	32	32	4	2	0	221^{1}	188	89	81	24	8	48	126	1.066	3.29	140	2.79	.230	0	.000	31	18	3.0
2002 Chi-A★	19	12	.613	34	34	5	2	0	239	236	102	95	25	3	61	134	1.243	3.58	127	3.53	.260	1	.167	24	17	2.3
2003 Chi-A	14	14	.500	35	35	2	0	0	230^{1}	250	124	106	22	5	61	119	1.350	4.14	108	4.10	.278	1	.167	6	13	0.6
Total 4	53	35	.602	129	104	11	4	0	742	729	342	306	76	19	189	416	1.237	3.71	123	3.56	.258	2	.133	64	52	6.2
• BUFFINTON, Charlie	Charles G. Buffinton b: 6/14/1861, Fall River, MA d: 9/23/1907, Fall River, MA BR/TR, 6'1" Deb: 5/17/1882 M/U ♦																									
1882 Bos-N	2	3	.400	5	5	4	1	0	42	53	34	19	2	....	14	17	1.595	4.07	70	....	.291	13	.260	-5	2	-0.7
1883 Bos-N	25	14	.641	43	41	34	4	1	333	346	187	112	4	....	51	188	1.192	3.03	102	....	.252	81	.238	6	28	-1.0
1884 Bos-N	48	16	.750	67	67	63	8	0	587	506	225	140	15	....	76	417	.991	2.15	134	....	.220	94	.267	39	62	4.2
1885 Bos-N	22	27	.449	51	50	49	6	0	434^{1}	425	238	139	10	....	112	242	1.236	2.88	93	....	.244	81	.240	8	28	0.3
1886 Bos-N	7	10	.412	18	17	16	0	0	151	203	129	77	4	....	39	47	**1.603**	4.59	69	....	.310	51	.290	-20	8	-2.0
1887 Phi-N	21	17	.553	40	38	35	1	0	332^{1}	444	224	135	16	4	92	160	1.336	3.66	115	....	.312	83	.296	28	23	1.8
1888 Phi-N	28	17	.622	46	46	43	6	0	400^{1}	324	139	85	6	4	59	199	.957	1.91	154	....	.213	29	.181	**52**	**44**	**5.2**
1889 Phi-N	28	16	.636	47	43	37	2	0	380	390	196	137	10	6	121	153	1.345	3.24	134	....	.257	32	.208	61	33	5.2
1890 Phi-P	19	15	.559	36	33	28	0	1	283^{1}	312	211	120	8	6	126	89	1.546	3.81	112	....	.268	41	.273	15	21	1.5
1891 Bos-a	29	9	.763	48	43	33	2	1	363^{2}	303	153	103	8	0	120	158	1.163	2.55	137	....	.219	34	.188	30	31	2.3
1892 Bal-N	4	8	.333	13	13	9	0	0	97	130	88	53	4	0	46	30	1.814	4.92	70	5.78	.309	15	.349	-12	3	-0.7
Total 11	233	152	.605	414	396	351	30	3	3404	3436	1824	1120	87	20	856	1700	1.234	2.96	114	0.16	.251	554	.249	200	283	16.0
• BUHL, Bob	Robert Ray Buhl b: 8/12/1928, Saginaw, MI d: 2/16/2001, Titusville, FL BR/TR, 6'2", 190 lbs. Deb: 4/17/1953																									
1953 Mil-N	13	8	.619	30	18	8	3	0	154^{1}	133	59	51	9	3	73	83	1.335	2.97	132	3.33	.235	6	.113	15	12	1.1
1954 Mil-N	2	7	.222	31	14	2	1	3	110^{1}	117	54	49	5	2	65	57	1.650	4.00	93	4.63	.277	1	.032	-5	4	-0.8
1955 Mil-N	13	11	.542	38	27	11	1	1	201^{2}	168	85	72	13	1	109	117	1.374	3.21	117	3.43	.227	6	.105	12	13	0.8
1956 Mil-N	18	8	.692	38	33	13	2	0	216^{2}	190	96	80	18	2	105	86	1.362	3.32	104	3.61	.236	7	.096	1	12	-0.3
1957* Mil-N	18	7	.720	34	31	14	2	0	216^{2}	191	77	66	15	0	121	117	1.440	2.74	128	3.86	.241	6	.082	14	16	1.1
1958 Mil-N	5	2	.714	11	10	3	0	1	73	74	33	28	5	1	30	27	1.425	3.45	102	3.99	.260	5	.200	-0	4	0.0
1959 Mil-N	15	9	.625	31	25	12	**4**	0	198	181	76	63	19	2	74	105	1.288	2.86	124	3.50	.243	4	.057	16	15	1.1
1960 Mil-N★	16	9	.640	36	33	11	2	0	238^{2}	202	89	82	23	3	103	121	1.278	3.09	111	3.33	.229	14	.157	12	16	1.0
1961 Mil-N	9	10	.474	32	28	9	1	0	188^{1}	180	99	86	23	5	98	77	1.476	4.11	91	4.60	.256	4	.067	-7	7	-1.1
1962 Mil-N	0	1	.000	1	1	0	0	0	2	6	5	5	0	0	4	1	5.000	22.50	17	23.01	.545	0	.000	-4	0	-0.4
Chi-N	12	13	.480	34	30	8	1	0	212	204	108	87	23	6	94	109	1.406	3.69	112	4.19	.255	0	.000	10	13	0.4
Yr.	12	14	.462	35	31	8	1	0	214	210	113	92	23	6	98	110	1.439	3.87	107	4.36	.259	0	.000	6	13	0.0
1963 Chi-N	11	14	.440	37	34	6	0	0	226	219	96	85	24	3	62	108	1.243	3.38	104	3.61	.259	8	.108	-0	13	-0.3
1964 Chi-N	15	14	.517	36	35	11	3	0	227^{2}	208	103	97	22	5	68	107	1.212	3.83	97	3.27	.244	7	.096	-1	14	-0.2
1965 Chi-N	13	11	.542	32	31	2	0	0	184^{1}	207	100	90	26	0	57	92	1.432	4.39	84	4.65	.284	4	.060	-13	6	-1.8
1966 Chi-N	0	0	....	1	1	0	0	0	2^{1}	4	4	4	1	0	1	1	2.143	15.43	24	11.45	.400	0	.000	-3	0	-0.3
Phi-N	6	8	.429	32	18	1	0	1	132	156	74	70	10	4	39	59	1.477	4.77	75	4.64	.298	4	.098	-18	2	-2.0
Yr.	6	8	.429	33	19	1	0	1	134^{1}	160	78	74	11	4	40	60	1.489	4.96	73	4.75	.300	4	.095	-21	2	-2.3
1967 Phi-N	0	0	....	3	0	0	0	0	3	6	4	4	2	0	2	1	2.667	12.00	28	19.77	.462	0	....	-3	0	-0.3
Total 15	166	132	.557	457	369	111	20	6	2587	2446	1162	1019	238	37	1105	1268	1.373	3.55	103	3.88	.251	76	.089	28	147	-1.9
• BUICE, De Wayne	De Wayne Allison Buice b: 8/20/1957, Lynwood, CA BR/TR, 6', 170 lbs. Deb: 4/25/1987																									
1987 Cal-A	6	7	.462	57	0	0	0	17	114	87	45	43	12	2	40	109	1.114	3.39	127	2.75	.213	0	....	11	13	1.1
1988 Cal-A	2	4	.333	32	0	0	0	3	41^{1}	45	29	27	5	0	19	38	1.548	5.88	66	4.88	.287	0	....	-9	0	-0.9
1989 Tor-A	1	0	1.000	7	0	0	0	0	17	13	12	11	2	0	13	10	1.529	5.82	62	4.30	.220	0	....	-4	0	-0.4
Total 3	9	11	.450	96	0	0	0	20	172^{1}	145	86	81	19	2	72	157	1.259	4.23	96	3.41	.232	0	....	-2	13	-0.3
• BUKER, Cy	Cyril Owen Buker b: 2/5/1919, Greenwood, WI BL/TR, 5'11", 190 lbs. Deb: 5/17/1945																									
1945 Bro-N	7	2	.778	42	4	0	0	5	87^{1}	90	41	32	2	1	45	48	1.546	3.30	114	4.01	.268	3	.188	5	7	0.5
• BUKVICH, Ryan	Ryan Adrien Bukvich b: 5/13/1978, Naperville, IL BR/TR, 6'2", 250 lbs. Deb: 7/12/2002																									
2002 KC-A	1	0	1.000	26	0	0	0	0	25	26	19	17	2	1	19	20	1.800	6.12	82	5.39	.277	0	....	-3	1	-0.3
2003 KC-A	1	0	1.000	9	0	0	0	0	10^{1}	12	11	11	2	0	9	8	2.032	9.58	54	7.65	.293	0	....	-5	0	-0.5
Total 2	2	0	1.000	35	0	0	0	0	35^{1}	38	30	28	4	1	28	28	1.868	7.13	71	6.05	.281	0	....	-8	1	-0.8
• BULLINGER, Jim	James Eric Bullinger b: 8/21/1965, New Orleans, LA BR/TR, 6'2", 185 lbs. Deb: 5/27/1992																									
1992 Chi-N	2	8	.200	39	9	1	0	7	85	72	49	44	9	4	54	36	1.482	4.66	77	4.20	.233	5	.250	-10	2	-0.9
1993 Chi-N	1	0	1.000	15	0	0	0	1	16^{2}	18	9	8	1	0	9	10	1.620	4.32	92	4.80	.277	0	.000	-1	1	-0.1
1994 Chi-N	6	2	.750	33	10	1	0	2	100	87	43	40	6	1	34	72	1.210	3.60	116	2.91	.235	3	.136	6	7	0.6
1995 Chi-N	12	8	.600	24	24	1	1	0	150	152	80	69	14	9	65	93	1.447	4.14	99	4.36	.265	6	.128	-2	8	-0.1
1996 Chi-N	6	10	.375	37	20	1	1	1	129^{1}	144	101	94	15	8	68	90	1.639	6.54	66	5.51	.283	8	.250	-33	1	-2.7
1997 Mon-N	7	12	.368	36	25	2	2	0	155^{1}	165	106	96	17	12	74	87	1.539	5.56	76	5.10	.276	9	.209	-24	2	-2.2
1998 Sea-A	0	1	.000	2	1	0	0	0	5^{2}	13	10	10	3	0	2	4	2.647	15.88	29	16.02	.433	0	....	-7	0	-0.7
Total 7	34	41	.453	186	89	6	4	11	642	651	398	361	65	34	306	392	1.491	5.06	82	4.64	.265	31	.188	-71	21	-6.0

YEAR	TM-L	W	L	PCT	G	GS	CG	SH	SV	IP	H	R	ER	HR	HB	BB	SO	RAT	ERA	ERA+	CERA	OAV	BH	AVG	PR+	WS	TPW
• BULLINGER, Kirk					Kirk Matthew Bullinger b: 10/28/1969, New Orleans, LA BR/TR, 6'2", 170 lbs. Deb: 8/30/1998																						
1998	Mon-N	1	0	1.000	8	0	0	0	0	7	14	8	7	1	0	0	2	2.000	9.00	47	8.74	.400	0	.000	-4	0	-0.4
1999	Bos-A	0	0	....	4	0	0	0	0	2	2	1	1	0	0	2	0	2.000	4.50	110	6.15	.286	0	....	0	0	0.0
2000	Phi-N	0	0	....	3	0	0	0	0	3^1	4	2	2	0	0	0	4	1.200	5.40	86	2.89	.308	0	....	-0	0	0.0
2003	Hou-N	0	0	....	7	0	0	0	0	8	7	6	6	2	0	1	5	1.000	6.75	66	3.06	.219	0	....	-2	0	-0.2
Total	**4**	**1**	**0**	**1.000**	**22**	**0**	**0**	**0**	**0**	20^1	**27**	**17**	**16**	**3**	**0**	**3**	**11**	**1.475**	**7.08**	**62**	**5.29**	**.310**	**0**	**.000**	**-6**	**0**	**-0.6**
• BULLOCK, Red					Malton Joseph Bullock b: 10/12/1911, Biloxi, MS d: 6/27/1988, Pascagoula, MS BL/TL, 6'1", 192 lbs. Deb: 5/19/1936																						
1936	Phi-A	0	2	.000	12	2	0	0	0	16^2	19	32	26	0	0	37	7	3.360	14.04	36	10.30	.271	0	.000	-17	0	-1.5
• BUMP, Nate					Nathan Louis Bump b: 7/24/1976, Towanda, PA BR/TR, 6'2", 185 lbs. Deb: 6/28/2003																						
2003*	Fla-N	4	0	1.000	32	0	0	0	0	36^1	34	21	19	3	7	20	17	1.486	4.71	87	4.91	.246	0	....	-3	2	-0.3
• BUNCH, Melvin					Melvin Lynn Bunch b: 11/4/1971, Texarkana, TX BR/TR, 6'1", 165 lbs. Deb: 5/6/1995																						
1995	KC-A	1	3	.250	13	5	0	0	0	40	42	25	25	11	0	14	19	1.400	5.63	85	5.28	.261	0	....	-4	1	-0.4
1999	Sea-A	0	0	....	5	1	0	0	0	10	20	13	13	3	0	7	4	2.700	11.70	43	14.28	.426	0	....	-7	0	-0.7
Total	**2**	**1**	**3**	**.250**	**18**	**6**	**0**	**0**	**0**	**50**	**62**	**38**	**38**	**14**	**0**	**21**	**23**	**1.660**	**6.84**	**71**	**7.08**	**.298**	**0**	**....**	**-12**	**1**	**-1.1**
• BUNKER, Wally					Wallace Edward Bunker b: 1/25/1945, Seattle, WA BR/TR, 6'2", 197 lbs. Deb: 9/29/1963																						
1963	Bal-A	0	1	.000	1	1	0	0	0	4	10	6	6	1	0	3	1	3.250	13.50	26	17.33	.476	1	.500	-4	0	-0.4
1964	Bal-A	19	5	.792	29	29	12	1	0	214	161	72	64	17	3	62	96	1.042	2.69	133	2.29	.207	5	.069	15	19	1.5
1965	Bal-A	10	8	.556	34	27	4	1	2	189	170	79	71	16	4	58	84	1.206	3.38	103	3.17	.242	4	.073	-1	10	-0.3
1966*	Bal-A	10	6	.625	29	24	3	0	0	142^2	151	74	68	16	2	48	89	1.395	4.29	78	4.28	.269	5	.104	-16	4	-1.7
1967	Bal-A	3	7	.300	29	9	1	0	1	88	83	46	40	7	2	31	51	1.295	4.09	77	3.59	.254	2	.077	-11	1	-1.4
1968	Bal-A	2	0	1.000	18	10	2	1	0	71	59	25	19	4	1	14	44	1.028	2.41	121	2.22	.225	2	.111	3	4	0.3
1969	KC-A	12	11	.522	35	31	10	1	2	222^2	198	89	80	29	4	62	130	1.168	3.23	114	3.29	.238	10	.143	14	16	1.5
1970	KC-A	2	11	.154	24	15	2	1	0	121^2	109	63	57	16	0	50	59	1.307	4.22	89	3.74	.238	2	.065	-8	3	-0.8
1971	KC-A	2	3	.400	7	6	0	0	0	32^1	35	19	18	7	0	6	15	1.268	5.01	68	4.44	.271	0	.000	-6	0	-0.7
Total	**9**	**60**	**52**	**.536**	**206**	**152**	**34**	**5**	**5**	1085^1	**976**	**473**	**423**	**113**	**16**	**334**	**569**	**1.207**	**3.51**	**99**	**3.29**	**.240**	**31**	**.094**	**-13**	**57**	**-2.0**
• BUNNING, Jim					James Paul David Bunning b: 10/23/1931, Southgate, KY BR/TR, 6'3", 195 lbs. Deb: 7/20/1955 HOF: 1996																						
1955	Det-A	3	5	.375	15	8	0	0	1	51	59	38	36	8	3	32	37	1.784	6.35	60	6.59	.291	3	.200	-14	0	-1.4
1956	Det-A	5	1	.833	15	3	0	0	1	53^1	55	24	22	6	0	28	34	1.556	3.71	111	4.56	.257	6	.333	2	4	0.4
1957	Det-A★	**20**	8	.714	45	30	14	1	1	**267^1**	214	91	80	33	11	72	182	1.070	2.69	143	2.80	.218	20	.213	33	**26**	3.7
1958	Det-A	14	12	.538	35	34	10	3	0	219^2	188	96	86	28	10	79	177	1.215	3.52	115	3.45	.228	14	.187	10	14	1.0
1959	Det-A★	17	13	.567	40	35	14	1	1	249^2	220	111	108	37	11	75	**201**	1.182	3.89	104	3.53	.234	17	.191	4	17	0.5
1960	Det-A	11	14	.440	36	34	10	3	0	252	217	92	78	20	11	64	**201**	1.115	2.79	**148**	**2.79**	.236	13	.160	**38**	**20**	**3.6**
1961	Det-A★	17	11	.607	38	37	12	4	1	268	232	113	95	25	9	71	194	1.131	3.19	129	2.87	.229	13	.130	27	19	2.2
1962	Det-A★	19	10	.655	41	35	12	2	6	258	262	112	103	28	13	74	184	1.302	3.59	113	3.94	.261	23	.242	16	21	2.1
1963	Det-A★	12	13	.480	39	35	6	2	1	248^1	245	119	107	38	5	69	196	1.264	3.88	96	3.91	.254	13	.155	-4	11	-0.5
1964	Phi-N★	19	8	.704	41	39	13	5	2	284^1	248	99	83	23	14	46	219	1.034	2.63	132	2.55	.233	12	.121	25	22	2.4
1965	Phi-N	19	9	.679	39	39	15	7	0	291	253	92	84	23	12	62	268	1.082	2.60	133	2.62	.232	22	.214	28	27	3.3
1966	Phi-N★	19	14	.576	43	**41**	16	**5**	1	314	260	91	84	26	19	55	252	1.003	2.41	149	2.42	.223	19	.179	41	30	4.3
1967	Phi-N	17	15	.531	40	**40**	16	**6**	0	**302^1**	241	94	77	18	13	73	**253**	1.039	2.29	149	2.24	.217	17	.163	**38**	**25**	**4.3**
1968	Pit-N	4	14	.222	27	26	3	1	0	160	168	75	69	14	8	48	95	1.350	3.88	75	4.04	.272	5	.098	-19	1	-2.4
1969	Pit-N	10	9	.526	25	25	4	0	0	156	147	74	66	10	6	49	124	1.256	3.81	92	3.31	.249	2	.043	-5	6	-0.8
	LA-N	3	1	.750	9	9	1	0	0	56^1	65	23	21	5	1	10	33	1.331	3.36	99	4.08	.288	2	.111	-1	3	-0.2
	Yr.	13	10	.565	34	34	5	0	0	212^1	212	97	87	15	7	59	157	1.276	3.69	93	3.51	.259	4	.062	-5	9	-1.0
1970	Phi-N	10	15	.400	34	33	4	0	0	219	233	111	100	19	8	56	147	1.320	4.11	97	3.84	.274	9	.127	-1	11	-0.3
1971	Phi-N	5	12	.294	29	16	1	0	1	110	126	72	67	11	6	37	58	1.482	5.48	64	4.80	.297	3	.120	-25	0	-2.7
Total	**17**	**224**	**184**	**.549**	**591**	**519**	**151**	**40**	**16**	3760^1	**3433**	**1527**	**1366**	**372**	**160**	**1000**	**2855**	**1.179**	**3.27**	**114**	**3.22**	**.242**	**213**	**.167**	**194**	**257**	**19.6**
• BURBA, Dave					David Allen Burba b: 7/7/1966, Dayton, OH BR/TR, 6'4", 240 lbs. Deb: 9/8/1990																						
1990	Sea-A	0	0	....	6	0	0	0	0	8	8	6	4	0	1	2	4	1.250	4.50	88	3.19	.267	0	....	-0	0	0.0
1991	Sea-A	2	2	.500	22	2	0	0	1	36^2	34	16	15	6	0	14	16	1.309	3.68	112	3.97	.245	0	....	1	2	0.1
1992	SF-N	2	7	.222	23	11	0	0	0	70^2	80	43	39	4	2	31	47	1.571	4.97	66	4.71	.287	1	.067	-15	0	-1.6
1993	SF-N	10	3	.769	54	5	0	0	0	95^1	95	49	45	14	3	37	88	1.385	4.25	92	4.44	.265	5	.294	-6	5	-0.5
1994	SF-N	3	6	.333	57	0	0	0	0	74	59	39	36	5	6	45	84	1.405	4.38	92	3.80	.221	0	.000	-6	3	-0.6
1995	SF-N	4	2	.667	37	0	0	0	0	43^1	38	26	24	5	0	25	46	1.454	4.98	82	4.07	.235	0	....	-5	2	-0.5
*	Cin-N	6	2	.750	15	9	1	1	0	63^1	52	24	23	4	0	26	50	1.232	3.27	126	2.93	.223	1	.067	4	5	0.4
	Yr.	10	4	.714	52	9	1	1	0	106^2	90	50	47	9	0	51	96	1.322	3.97	103	3.39	.228	1	.067	-0	7	0.0
1996	Cin-N	11	13	.458	34	33	0	0	0	195	179	96	83	18	2	97	148	1.415	3.83	109	3.89	.244	7	.104	5	10	0.5
1997	Cin-N	11	10	.524	30	27	2	0	0	160	157	88	84	22	9	73	131	1.438	4.73	91	4.57	.255	9	.196	-8	7	-0.7
1998*	Cle-A	15	10	.600	32	31	0	0	0	203^2	210	100	93	30	7	69	132	1.370	4.11	116	4.50	.269	1	.167	16	15	1.5
1999*	Cle-A	15	9	.625	34	34	1	0	0	220	211	113	104	30	8	96	174	1.395	4.25	118	4.45	.254	1	.333	20	15	1.9
2000	Cle-A	16	6	.727	32	32	0	0	0	191^1	199	99	95	19	2	91	180	1.516	4.47	111	4.62	.267	0	.000	12	13	1.1
2001*	Cle-A	10	10	.500	32	27	1	0	0	150^2	188	112	104	16	3	54	118	1.606	6.21	73	5.43	.306	0	.000	-25	3	-2.5
2002	Tex-A	4	5	.444	23	18	1	0	0	111^1	125	71	67	13	7	40	70	1.482	5.42	87	4.90	.279	1	.200	-7	4	-0.7
	Cle-A	1	0	1.000	12	3	0	0	0	34	30	20	17	3	2	17	25	1.382	4.50	98	3.98	.236	0	....	-0	2	0.0
	Yr.	5	5	.500	35	21	1	0	0	145^1	155	91	84	16	9	57	95	1.459	5.20	89	4.69	.270	1	.200	-7	6	-0.7
2003	Mil-N	1	1	.500	17	2	0	0	0	43^1	42	19	17	5	4	19	35	1.408	3.53	120	4.40	.250	0	.000	4	3	0.3
Total	**14**	**111**	**86**	**.563**	**460**	**234**	**6**	**1**	**1**	1700^2	**1707**	**921**	**850**	**194**	**56**	**736**	**1348**	**1.436**	**4.50**	**98**	**4.43**	**.261**	**26**	**.137**	**-9**	**89**	**-1.1**
• BURBACH, Bill					William David Burbach b: 8/22/1947, Dickeyville, WI BR/TR, 6'4", 215 lbs. Deb: 4/11/1969																						
1969	NY-A	6	8	.429	31	24	2	1	0	140^2	112	68	57	15	2	102	82	1.521	3.65	95	4.30	.219	4	.100	-3	6	-0.4
1970	NY-A	0	2	.000	4	4	0	0	0	16^2	23	19	19	2	1	9	10	1.920	10.26	34	7.21	.324	0	.000	-13	0	-1.4
1971	NY-A	0	1	.000	2	0	0	0	0	3^1	6	6	4	0	0	5	3	3.300	10.80	30	10.76	.400	0	.000	-3	0	-0.3
Total	**3**	**6**	**11**	**.353**	**37**	**28**	**2**	**1**	**0**	160^2	**141**	**93**	**80**	**17**	**3**	**116**	**95**	**1.600**	**4.48**	**78**	**4.74**	**.236**	**4**	**.085**	**-19**	**6**	**-2.1**
• BURCHART, Larry					Larry Wayne Burchart b: 2/8/1946, Tulsa, OK BR/TR, 6'3", 205 lbs. Deb: 4/10/1969																						
1969	Cle-A	0	2	.000	29	0	0	0	0	42^1	42	28	20	2	1	24	26	1.559	4.25	89	4.24	.266	0	....	-2	0	-0.2
• BURCHELL, Fred					Frederick Duff Burchell b: 7/14/1879, Perth Amboy, NJ d: 11/20/1951, Jordan, NY BR/TL, 5'11", 175 lbs. Deb: 4/17/1903																						
1903	Phi-N	0	3	.000	6	3	2	0	0	44	48	28	14	0	2	14	12	1.409	2.86	114	3.89	.293	3	.188	1	1	0.1
1907	Bos-A	0	1	.000	2	1	0	0	0	10	8	5	3	0	1	2	6	1.000	2.70	95	2.14	.222	1	.200	-1	0	-0.1
1908	Bos-A	10	8	.556	31	19	9	0	0	179^2	161	84	59	2	11	65	94	1.258	2.96	83	3.05	.247	17	.246	-14	7	-1.5
1909	Bos-A	3	3	.500	10	5	1	0	0	52	51	22	17	1	2	11	12	1.192	2.94	85	3.05	.271	3	.158	-3	3	-0.4
Total	**4**	**13**	**15**	**.464**	**49**	**28**	**12**	**0**	**0**	285^2	**268**	**139**	**93**	**3**	**16**	**92**	**124**	**1.260**	**2.93**	**87**	**3.15**	**.258**	**24**	**.220**	**-17**	**11**	**-1.9**
• BURDETTE, Freddie					Freddie Thomason Burdette b: 9/15/1936, Moultrie, GA BR/TR, 6'1", 170 lbs. Deb: 9/5/1962																						
1962	Chi-N	0	0	....	8	0	0	0	1	9^2	5	4	4	2	0	8	5	1.345	3.72	111	3.46	.161	0	.000	0	1	0.0
1963	Chi-N	0	0	....	4	0	0	0	0	4^2	5	2	2	1	0	2	1	1.500	3.86	91	5.94	.313	0	....	-0	0	0.0
1964	Chi-N	1	0	1.000	18	0	0	0	0	20	17	7	7	2	1	10	4	1.350	3.15	118	3.68	.243	1	1.000	1	2	0.2
Total	**3**	**1**	**0**	**1.000**	**30**	**0**	**0**	**0**	**1**	34^1	**27**	**13**	**13**	**5**	**1**	**20**	**10**	**1.369**	**3.41**	**111**	**3.92**	**.231**	**1**	**.500**	**2**	**3**	**0.2**
• BURDETTE, Lew					Selva Lewis Burdette b: 11/22/1926, Nitro, WV BR/TR, 6'2", 190 lbs. Deb: 9/26/1950 C																						
1950	NY-A	0	0	....	2	0	0	0	0	1^1	3	1	1	0	0	0	0	2.250	6.75	64	10.75	.500	0	....	-0	0	0.0
1951	Bos-N	0	0	....	3	0	0	0	0	4^1	6	4	3	0	1	5	1	2.538	6.23	59	9.79	.375	0	.000	-1	0	-0.1
1952	Bos-N	6	11	.353	45	9	5	0	7	137	138	58	55	8	2	47	47	1.350	3.61	100	3.62	.265	4	.114	2	8	0.2
1953	Mil-N	15	5	.750	46	13	6	1	8	175	177	73	63	7	5	56	58	1.331	3.24	121	3.47	.264	9	.170	11	15	0.9

YEAR	TM-L	W	L	PCT	G	GS	CG	SH	SV	IP	H	R	ER	HR	HB	BB	SO	RAT	ERA	ERA+	CERA	OAV	BH	AVG	PR+	WS	TPW
1954	Mil-N	15	14	.517	38	32	13	4	0	238	224	87	73	17	4	62	79	1.202	2.76	135	3.08	.251	7	.089	22	18	1.7
1955	Mil-N	13	8	.619	42	33	11	2	0	230	253	114	103	25	6	73	70	1.417	4.03	93	4.41	.280	20	.233	-7	11	-0.4
1956	Mil-N	19	10	.655	39	35	16	**6**	1	256^{1}	234	92	77	22	3	52	110	1.116	**2.70**	128	2.79	.241	16	.186	19	20	2.0
1957*	Mil-N★	17	9	.654	37	33	14	1	0	256^{2}	260	117	106	25	2	59	78	1.243	3.72	94	3.46	.264	13	.148	-11	12	-1.0
1958*	Mil-N	20	10	.667	40	36	19	3	0	275^{1}	279	102	89	18	5	50	113	1.195	2.91	121	3.16	.264	24	.242	16	23	2.4
1959	Mil-N★	**21**	15	.583	41	**39**	20	**4**	1	289^{2}	312	144	131	38	1	38	105	1.208	4.07	87	3.66	.273	21	.202	-15	14	-1.0
1960	Mil-N	19	13	.594	45	32	**18**	4	4	275^{2}	277	116	103	19	5	35	83	1.132	3.36	102	2.91	.260	16	.176	6	18	1.1
1961	Mil-N	18	11	.621	40	36	14	3	0	**272**^{1}	295	131	121	31	3	33	92	1.204	4.00	93	3.56	.273	21	.204	-7	15	-0.3
1962	Mil-N	10	9	.526	37	19	6	1	2	143^{2}	172	85	78	26	2	23	59	1.357	4.89	78	4.82	.298	9	.176	-18	4	-1.8
1963	Mil-N	6	5	.545	15	13	4	1	0	84	71	40	34	15	1	24	28	1.131	3.64	88	3.28	.228	1	.038	-5	3	-0.6
	StL-N	3	8	.273	21	14	3	0	2	98	106	50	41	6	7	16	45	1.245	3.77	94	3.56	.278	3	.097	-3	3	-0.4
	Yr.	9	13	.409	36	27	7	1	2	182	177	90	75	21	8	40	73	1.192	3.71	91	3.43	.255	4	.070	-8	6	-1.0
1964	StL-N	1	0	1.000	8	0	0	0	0	10	10	3	2	1	0	3	3	1.300	1.80	211	3.60	.256	0	.000	2	1	0.2
	Chi-N	9	9	.500	28	17	8	2	0	131	152	74	71	15	1	19	40	1.305	4.88	76	4.10	.292	12	.279	-16	6	-1.0
	Yr.	10	9	.526	36	17	8	2	0	141	162	77	73	16	1	22	43	1.305	4.66	80	4.06	.290	12	.273	-13	7	-0.8
1965	Chi-N	0	2	.000	7	3	0	0	0	20^{1}	26	17	12	3	1	4	5	1.475	5.31	69	5.14	.299	2	.333	-3	0	-0.3
	Phi-N	3	3	.500	19	9	1	1	0	70^{2}	95	50	43	5	5	17	23	1.585	5.48	63	5.49	.329	6	.300	-16	0	-1.5
	Yr.	3	5	.375	26	12	1	1	0	91	121	67	55	8	6	21	28	1.560	5.44	64	5.41	.322	8	.308	-19	0	-1.8
1966	Cal-A	7	2	.778	54	0	0	0	5	79^{2}	80	32	30	4	1	12	27	1.155	3.39	99	2.93	.268	1	.125	-1	7	-0.1
1967	Cal-A	1	0	1.000	19	0	0	0	1	18^{1}	16	10	10	4	1	0	8	.873	4.91	64	2.76	.232	0	....	-4	0	-0.4
Total	**18**	**203**	**144**	**.585**	**626**	**373**	**158**	**33**	**31**	**3067**^{1}	**3186**	**1400**	**1246**	**289**	**56**	**628**	**1074**	**1.243**	**3.66**	**98**	**3.55**	**.268**	**185**	**.183**	**-28**	**178**	**-0.4**

• BURDICK, Bill William Byron Burdick b: 10/11/1859, Austin, MN d: 10/23/1949, Spokane, WA BR/TR Deb: 7/23/1888

YEAR	TM-L	W	L	PCT	G	GS	CG	SH	SV	IP	H	R	ER	HR	HB	BB	SO	RAT	ERA	ERA+	CERA	OAV	BH	AVG	PR+	WS	TPW
1888	Ind-N	10	10	.500	20	20	20	0	0	176	168	88	55	12	6	43	55	1.199	2.81	105	....	.242	10	.147	5	9	0.3
1889	Ind-N	2	4	.333	10	4	2	0	1	45^{2}	58	42	23	7	0	13	16	1.555	4.53	92	....	.300	2	.118	-2	2	-0.2
Total	**2**	**12**	**14**	**.462**	**30**	**24**	**22**	**0**	**1**	**221**^{2}	**226**	**130**	**78**	**19**	**6**	**56**	**71**	**1.272**	**3.17**	**102**	**....**	**.255**	**12**	**.141**	**3**	**11**	**0.1**

• BURGMEIER, Tom Thomas Henry Burgmeier b: 8/2/1943, St. Paul, MN BL/TL, 5'11", 185 lbs. Deb: 4/10/1968 C

YEAR	TM-L	W	L	PCT	G	GS	CG	SH	SV	IP	H	R	ER	HR	HB	BB	SO	RAT	ERA	ERA+	CERA	OAV	BH	AVG	PR+	WS	TPW
1968	Cal-A	1	4	.200	56	2	0	0	5	72^{2}	65	41	35	5	0	24	33	1.225	4.33	67	3.05	.250	0	.000	-12	1	-1.4
1969	KC-A	3	1	.750	31	0	0	0	0	54	67	31	25	5	1	21	23	1.630	4.17	88	5.38	.316	3	.167	-2	2	-0.3
1970	KC-A	6	6	.500	41	0	0	0	1	68^{1}	59	31	24	6	0	23	43	1.200	3.16	118	2.98	.236	2	.143	4	5	0.4
1971	KC-A	9	7	.563	67	0	0	0	17	88^{1}	71	23	17	3	7	30	44	1.143	1.73	198	2.62	.223	5	.250	17	15	2.0
1972	KC-A	6	2	.750	51	0	0	0	9	55^{1}	67	32	26	0	1	33	18	1.807	4.23	72	5.16	.313	4	.333	-7	2	-0.6
1973	KC-A	0	0	....	6	0	0	0	1	10	13	6	6	2	1	4	4	1.700	5.40	76	7.09	.310	0	....	-1	0	-0.1
1974	Min-A	5	3	.625	50	0	0	0	4	91^{2}	92	46	46	7	2	26	34	1.287	4.52	83	3.60	.270	0	....	-7	5	-0.7
1975	Min-A	5	8	.385	46	0	0	0	11	75^{2}	76	32	26	7	1	23	41	1.308	3.09	125	3.72	.264	0	....	7	7	0.7
1976	Min-A	8	1	.889	57	0	0	0	1	115^{1}	95	36	32	11	2	29	45	1.075	2.50	144	2.65	.226	0	....	14	10	1.5
1977	Min-A	6	4	.600	61	0	0	0	7	97^{1}	113	56	55	15	2	33	35	1.500	5.09	78	5.34	.299	0	....	-12	4	-1.2
1978	Bos-A	2	1	.667	35	1	0	0	4	61^{1}	74	33	30	7	3	23	24	1.582	4.40	93	5.49	.302	0	....	-2	3	-0.3
1979	Bos-A	3	2	.600	44	0	0	0	4	88^{2}	89	32	27	8	4	16	60	1.184	2.74	161	3.29	.263	0	....	17	9	1.7
1980	Bos-A★	5	4	.556	62	0	0	0	24	99	87	30	22	3	2	20	54	1.081	2.00	211	2.36	.241	0	....	24	17	2.4
1981	Bos-A	4	5	.444	32	0	0	0	6	59^{2}	61	23	19	5	4	17	35	1.307	2.87	135	3.80	.268	0	....	8	6	0.8
1982	Bos-A	7	0	1.000	40	0	0	0	2	102^{1}	98	30	26	6	2	22	44	1.173	2.29	188	2.91	.259	0	....	25	13	2.5
1983	Oak-A	6	7	.462	49	0	0	0	4	96	89	33	30	2	0	32	39	1.260	2.81	137	2.71	.244	0	....	10	8	1.0
1984	Oak-A	3	0	1.000	17	0	0	0	2	23	15	6	6	2	0	8	8	1.000	2.35	159	1.85	.190	0	....	4	3	0.4
Total	**17**	**79**	**55**	**.590**	**745**	**3**	**0**	**0**	**102**	**1258**^{2}	**1231**	**521**	**452**	**94**	**32**	**384**	**584**	**1.283**	**3.23**	**116**	**3.52**	**.261**	**14**	**.212**	**86**	**110**	**8.7**

• BURGOS, Enrique Enrique (Calles) Burgos b: 10/7/1965, Chorrera, Panama BL/TL, 6'4", 195 lbs. Deb: 7/15/1993

YEAR	TM-L	W	L	PCT	G	GS	CG	SH	SV	IP	H	R	ER	HR	HB	BB	SO	RAT	ERA	ERA+	CERA	OAV	BH	AVG	PR+	WS	TPW
1993	KC-A	0	1	.000	5	0	0	0	0	5	5	5	5	0	1	6	6	2.200	9.00	51	6.34	.238	0	....	-2	0	-0.2
1995	SF-N	0	0	....	5	0	0	0	0	8^{1}	14	8	8	1	1	6	12	2.400	8.64	47	10.78	.378	0	....	-4	0	-0.4
Total	**2**	**0**	**1**	**.000**	**10**	**0**	**0**	**0**	**0**	**13**^{1}	**19**	**13**	**13**	**1**	**2**	**12**	**18**	**2.325**	**8.78**	**49**	**9.12**	**.328**	**0**	**....**	**-7**	**0**	**-0.7**

• BURK, Sandy Charles Sanford Burk b: 4/22/1887, Columbus, OH d: 10/11/1934, Brooklyn, NY BR/TR, 5'8", 155 lbs. Deb: 9/12/1910

YEAR	TM-L	W	L	PCT	G	GS	CG	SH	SV	IP	H	R	ER	HR	HB	BB	SO	RAT	ERA	ERA+	CERA	OAV	BH	AVG	PR+	WS	TPW
1910	Bro-N	0	3	.000	4	3	1	0	0	19^{1}	17	16	13	0	2	27	14	2.276	6.05	50	6.83	.258	0	.000	-7	0	-0.8
1911	Bro-N	1	3	.250	13	7	1	0	0	58	54	36	33	1	3	47	15	1.741	5.12	65	4.87	.261	2	.105	-11	0	-1.3
1912	Bro-N	0	0	....	2	0	0	0	0	8^{1}	9	3	3	0	0	3	2	1.440	3.24	103	3.57	.273	1	.250	0	0	0.1
	StL-N	1	3	.250	12	4	2	0	1	44^{2}	37	19	12	0	1	12	17	1.097	2.42	141	2.14	.236	0	.000	5	3	0.3
	Yr.	1	3	.250	14	4	2	0	1	53	46	22	15	0	1	15	19	1.151	2.55	133	2.37	.242	1	.067	5	3	0.4
1913	StL-N	0	2	.000	19	7	0	0	1	70	81	45	40	1	6	33	29	1.629	5.14	63	4.68	.290	2	.091	-15	1	-1.7
1915	Pit-F	2	0	1.000	2	2	1	0	0	18	8	3	2	0	0	11	9	1.056	1.00	310	1.42	.140	1	.167	4	3	0.4
Total	**5**	**4**	**11**	**.267**	**52**	**23**	**5**	**0**	**2**	**218**^{1}	**206**	**122**	**103**	**2**	**12**	**133**	**86**	**1.553**	**4.25**	**77**	**4.09**	**.258**	**6**	**.090**	**-24**	**7**	**-3.0**

• BURKART, Elmer Elmer Robert "Swede" Burkart b: 2/1/1917, Philadelphia, PA d: 2/6/1995, Baltimore, MD BR/TR, 6'2", 190 lbs. Deb: 9/14/1936

YEAR	TM-L	W	L	PCT	G	GS	CG	SH	SV	IP	H	R	ER	HR	HB	BB	SO	RAT	ERA	ERA+	CERA	OAV	BH	AVG	PR+	WS	TPW
1936	Phi-N	0	0	....	2	2	0	0	0	7^{2}	4	3	3	0	0	12	2	2.087	3.52	129	4.60	.160	0	.000	1	1	0.1
1937	Phi-N	0	0	....	7	0	0	0	0	16	20	11	11	0	0	9	4	1.813	6.19	70	5.39	.323	0	.000	-3	0	-0.4
1938	Phi-N	0	1	.000	2	1	1	0	0	10	12	5	5	0	1	3	1	1.500	4.50	89	4.23	.286	0	.000	-0	0	-0.1
1939	Phi-N	1	0	1.000	5	0	0	0	0	8^{1}	11	4	4	0	0	2	2	1.560	4.32	91	4.75	.344	1	1.000	-0	1	0.0
Total	**4**	**1**	**1**	**.500**	**16**	**3**	**1**	**0**	**0**	**42**	**47**	**23**	**23**	**0**	**1**	**26**	**9**	**1.738**	**4.93**	**85**	**4.84**	**.292**	**1**	**.083**	**-3**	**2**	**-0.3**

• BURKE, Billy William Ignatius Burke b: 7/11/1889, Clinton, MA d: 2/9/1967, Worcester, MA BL/TL, 5'10", 165 lbs. Deb: 4/30/1910

YEAR	TM-L	W	L	PCT	G	GS	CG	SH	SV	IP	H	R	ER	HR	HB	BB	SO	RAT	ERA	ERA+	CERA	OAV	BH	AVG	PR+	WS	TPW
1910	Bos-N	1	0	1.000	19	1	1	0	0	64	68	32	29	1	2	29	22	1.516	4.08	81	4.50	.302	4	.190	-6	3	-0.7
1911	Bos-N	0	1	.000	2	1	0	0	0	3^{1}	6	7	7	0	0	5	1	3.300	18.90	20	13.63	.429	1	1.000	-6	0	-0.5
Total	**2**	**1**	**1**	**.500**	**21**	**2**	**1**	**0**	**0**	**67**^{1}	**74**	**39**	**36**	**1**	**2**	**34**	**23**	**1.604**	**4.81**	**71**	**4.96**	**.309**	**5**	**.227**	**-12**	**3**	**-1.2**

• BURKE, Bobby Robert James "Lefty" Burke b: 1/23/1907, Joliet, IL d: 2/8/1971, Joliet, IL BL/TL, 6'.5", 150 lbs. Deb: 4/16/1927

YEAR	TM-L	W	L	PCT	G	GS	CG	SH	SV	IP	H	R	ER	HR	HB	BB	SO	RAT	ERA	ERA+	CERA	OAV	BH	AVG	PR+	WS	TPW
1927	Was-A	3	2	.600	36	6	1	0	0	100	91	48	44	6	7	32	20	1.230	3.96	103	3.25	.245	3	.125	0	5	-0.2
1928	Was-A	2	4	.333	26	7	2	1	0	85^{1}	87	44	37	1	2	18	27	1.230	3.90	103	2.92	.277	5	.250	-0	5	0.1
1929	Was-A	6	8	.429	37	17	4	0	0	141	154	91	75	6	4	55	51	1.482	4.79	88	4.10	.279	6	.140	-10	5	-1.2
1930	Was-A	3	4	.429	24	4	2	0	3	74^{1}	62	41	30	2	3	29	35	1.224	3.63	126	2.70	.229	4	.174	6	6	0.4
1931	Was-A	8	3	.727	30	13	3	1	2	128^{2}	124	67	61	6	2	50	38	1.352	4.27	101	3.44	.255	10	.213	-1	8	-0.1
1932	Was-A	3	6	.333	22	10	2	0	0	91	98	55	52	4	1	44	32	1.560	5.14	84	4.30	.272	5	.200	-11	3	-1.0
1933	Was-A	4	3	.571	25	6	4	1	0	64	64	29	23	1	2	31	28	1.484	3.23	129	3.70	.256	4	.235	5	5	0.5
1934	Was-A	8	8	.500	37	15	7	1	0	168	155	67	60	2	1	72	52	1.351	3.21	134	3.04	.245	13	.228	21	15	2.1
1935	Was-A	1	8	.111	15	10	2	0	0	66^{1}	90	63	55	7	2	27	16	1.764	7.46	58	6.28	.327	4	.182	-23	0	-2.2
1937	Phi-N	0	0	....	2	0	0	0	0	0	1	1	0	0	0	2	0	....	....	....	∞	.500	0	....	0	0	0.0
Total	**10**	**38**	**46**	**.452**	**254**	**88**	**27**	**4**	**5**	**918**^{2}	**926**	**506**	**437**	**35**	**24**	**360**	**299**	**1.400**	**4.28**	**99**	**3.65**	**.263**	**54**	**.194**	**-13**	**52**	**-1.6**

• BURKE, James James Burke b: Attleboro, MA Deb: 6/10/1882

YEAR	TM-L	W	L	PCT	G	GS	CG	SH	SV	IP	H	R	ER	HR	HB	BB	SO	RAT	ERA	ERA+	CERA	OAV	BH	AVG	PR+	WS	TPW
1882	Buf-N	0	1	.000	1	1	0	0	0	4	10	9	5	0	....	0	0	2.500	11.25	26	....	.449	0	.000	-4	0	-0.4
1883	Buf-N	0	0	....	1	1	0	0	0	8	9	8	5	0	....	3	1	1.500	5.63	56	....	.268	1	.200	-2	0	-0.2
1884	Bos-U	19	15	.559	38	36	34	0	0	322	326	201	102	10	....	31	255	1.109	2.85	104	....	.246	41	.223	-0	24	0.1
Total	**3**	**19**	**16**	**.543**	**40**	**38**	**34**	**0**	**0**	**334**	**345**	**218**	**112**	**10**	**....**	**34**	**256**	**1.135**	**3.02**	**99**	**....**	**.249**	**42**	**.218**	**-6**	**24**	**-0.6**

• BURKE, John John Patrick Burke b: 1/27/1877, Hazleton, PA d: 8/4/1950, Jersey City, NJ BR/TR Deb: 6/27/1902 ♦

YEAR	TM-L	W	L	PCT	G	GS	CG	SH	SV	IP	H	R	ER	HR	HB	BB	SO	RAT	ERA	ERA+	CERA	OAV	BH	AVG	PR+	WS	TPW
1902	NY-N	0	1	.000	2	1	1	0	0	14	21	11	9	0	0	3	3	1.714	5.79	48	5.41	.346	2	.154	-5	0	-0.6

• BURKE, John John C. Burke b: 2/9/1970, Durango, CO BB/TR, 6'4", 220 lbs. Deb: 8/13/1996

YEAR	TM-L	W	L	PCT	G	GS	CG	SH	SV	IP	H	R	ER	HR	HB	BB	SO	RAT	ERA	ERA+	CERA	OAV	BH	AVG	PR+	WS	TPW
1996	Col-N	2	1	.667	11	0	0	0	0	15^{2}	21	13	13	3	1	7	19	1.787	7.47	70	7.27	.318	1	.500	-4	1	-0.3
1997	Col-N	2	5	.286	17	9	0	0	0	59	83	46	43	13	6	26	39	1.847	6.56	79	8.11	.329	3	.158	-8	1	-0.9
Total	**2**	**4**	**6**	**.400**	**28**	**9**	**0**	**0**	**0**	**74**^{2}	**104**	**59**	**56**	**16**	**7**	**33**	**58**	**1.835**	**6.75**	**77**	**7.94**	**.327**	**4**	**.190**	**-12**	**2**	**-1.2**

YEAR	TM-L	W	L	PCT	G	GS	CG	SH	SV	IP	H	R	ER	HR	HB	BB	SO	RAT	ERA	ERA+	CERA	OAV	BH	AVG	PR+	WS	TPW
• BURKE, Steve	Steven Michael Burke b: 3/5/1955, Stockton, CA BB/TR, 6'2", 200 lbs. Deb: 9/10/1977																										
1977	Sea-A	0	1	.000	6	0	0	0	0	15^2	12	6	5	0	0	7	6	1.213	2.87	143	2.30	.226	0	....	2	1	0.2
1978	Sea-A	0	1	.000	18	0	0	0	0	49	46	22	19	2	1	24	16	1.429	3.49	109	3.87	.258	0	....	2	3	0.2
Total	2	0	2	.000	24	0	0	0	0	64^2	58	28	24	2	1	31	22	1.376	3.34	116	3.49	.251	0	....	4	4	0.4
• BURKE, Tim	Timothy Philip Burke b: 2/19/1959, Omaha, NE BR/TR, 6'3", 205 lbs. Deb: 4/8/1985																										
1985	Mon-N	9	4	.692	**78**	0	0	0	8	120^1	86	32	32	9	7	44	87	1.080	2.39	142	2.38	.204	1	.100	12	13	1.3
1986	Mon-N	9	7	.563	68	2	0	0	4	101^1	103	37	33	7	4	46	82	1.470	2.93	126	4.05	.262	0	.000	8	9	0.8
1987	Mon-N	7	0	1.000	55	0	0	0	18	91	64	18	12	3	0	17	58	.890	1.19	354	1.44	.196	0	.000	32	20	3.1
1988	Mon-N	3	5	.375	61	0	0	0	18	82	84	36	31	7	3	25	42	1.329	3.40	106	3.63	.272	0	.000	1	7	0.0
1989	Mon-N★	9	3	.750	68	0	0	0	28	84^2	68	24	24	6	0	22	54	1.063	2.55	138	2.28	.225	0	.000	10	17	1.0
1990	Mon-N	3	3	.500	58	0	0	0	20	75	71	29	21	6	2	21	47	1.227	2.52	145	3.13	.247	1	.167	9	10	1.0
1991	Mon-N	3	4	.429	37	0	0	0	5	46	41	24	21	3	4	14	25	1.196	4.11	88	3.08	.243	0	.000	-3	3	-0.3
	NY-N	3	3	.500	35	0	0	0	1	55^2	55	22	17	5	0	12	34	1.204	2.75	132	3.16	.255	0	.000	7	5	0.6
	Yr.	6	7	.462	72	0	0	0	6	101^2	96	46	38	8	4	26	59	1.200	3.36	108	3.12	.249	0	.000	4	8	0.3
1992	NY-N	1	2	.333	15	0	0	0	0	15^2	26	15	10	1	0	3	7	1.851	5.74	60	6.71	.366	0	....	-4	0	-0.4
	NY-A	2	2	.500	23	0	0	0	0	27^2	26	14	10	2	1	15	8	1.482	3.25	120	3.99	.250	0	....	2	2	0.2
Total	8	49	33	.598	498	2	0	0	102	699^1	624	251	211	49	21	219	444	1.205	2.72	133	2.98	.240	2	.045	74	86	7.3
• BURKE, Turk	William R. Burke b: 11/1865, Cincinnati, OH d: 3/17/1939, Atchison, KS, 6'3", 200 lbs. Deb: 7/20/1887																										
1887	Det-N	0	1	.000	2	2	1	0	0	15	26	14	10	0	2	5	3	1.733	6.00	67	....	.370	2	.250	-3	0	-0.3
• BURKETT, Jesse	Jesse Cail "Crab" Burkett b: 12/4/1868, Wheeling, WV d: 5/27/1953, Worcester, MA BL/TL, 5'8", 155 lbs. Deb: 4/22/1890 C HOF: 1946 ♦																										
1890	NY-N	3	10	.231	21	14	6	0	0	118	134	123	73	3	0	92	82	1.915	5.57	63	....	.278	124	.309	-28	14	-0.4
1894	Cle-N	0	0	....	1	0	0	0	0	4	6	2	2	0	0	1	0	1.750	4.50	121	5.54	.343	187	.358	0	21	0.7
1902	StL-A	0	1	.000	1	0	0	0	0	1	4	4	1	0	0	1	2	5.000	9.00	39	27.96	.585	169	.306	-1	25	1.9
Total	3	3	11	.214	23	14	6	0	0	123	144	129	76	3	0	94	84	1.935	5.56	63	0.41	.284	2850	.338	-28	60	2.2
• BURKETT, John	John David Burkett b: 11/28/1964, New Brighton, PA BR/TR, 6'2", 211 lbs. Deb: 9/15/1987																										
1987	SF-N	0	0	....	3	0	0	0	0	6	7	4	3	2	1	3	5	1.667	4.50	85	8.25	.304	0	.000	-1	0	-0.1
1990	SF-N	14	7	.667	33	32	2	0	1	204	201	92	86	18	4	61	118	1.284	3.79	96	3.56	.257	3	.048	-5	11	-0.8
1991	SF-N	12	11	.522	36	34	3	1	0	206^2	223	103	96	19	10	60	131	1.369	4.18	86	4.22	.277	5	.091	-16	6	-1.8
1992	SF-N	13	9	.591	32	32	3	1	0	189^2	194	96	81	13	4	45	107	1.260	3.84	86	3.37	.264	1	.018	-15	7	-2.0
1993	SF-N★	**22**	7	.759	34	34	2	1	0	231^2	224	100	94	18	11	40	145	1.140	3.65	107	3.07	.255	9	.118	0	14	-0.1
1994	SF-N	6	8	.429	25	25	0	0	0	159^1	176	72	64	14	7	36	85	1.331	3.62	111	4.03	.286	3	.059	1	8	-0.3
1995	Fla-N	14	14	.500	30	30	4	0	0	188^1	208	95	90	22	6	57	126	1.407	4.30	98	4.53	.282	7	.106	-2	8	-0.4
1996	Fla-N	6	10	.375	24	24	1	0	0	154	154	84	74	15	3	42	108	1.273	4.32	94	3.64	.263	9	.173	-7	6	-0.6
	* Tex-A	5	2	.714	10	10	1	1	0	68^2	75	33	31	4	2	16	47	1.325	4.06	129	3.76	.280	0	....	9	6	0.8
1997	Tex-A	9	12	.429	30	30	2	0	0	189^1	240	106	96	20	4	30	139	1.426	4.56	105	4.72	.307	1	.200	7	10	0.7
1998	Tex-A	9	13	.409	32	32	0	0	0	195	230	131	123	19	8	46	131	1.415	5.68	85	4.55	.292	0	.000	-16	7	-1.5
1999	Tex-A	9	8	.529	30	25	0	0	0	147^1	184	95	92	18	3	46	96	1.561	5.62	90	5.44	.307	0	.000	-7	6	-0.7
2000*	Atl-N	10	6	.625	31	22	0	0	0	134^1	162	79	73	13	4	51	110	1.586	4.89	94	5.28	.303	6	.143	-4	7	-0.4
2001*	Atl-N★	12	12	.500	34	34	1	1	0	219^1	187	83	74	17	6	70	187	1.172	3.04	145	2.86	.230	6	.092	32	17	2.9
2002	Bos-A	13	8	.619	29	29	1	1	0	173	199	93	87	25	8	50	124	1.439	4.53	99	4.95	.287	0	.000	-3	8	-0.3
2003*	Bos-A	12	9	.571	32	30	1	0	0	181^2	202	108	104	20	9	47	107	1.371	5.15	89	4.41	.281	0	.000	-8	8	-0.8
Total	15	166	136	.550	445	423	21	6	1	2648^1	2866	1374	1268	257	90	700	1766	1.347	4.31	98	4.11	.277	50	.093	-34	129	-5.5
• BURKHART, Ken	Kenneth William Burkhart b: 11/18/1916, Knoxville, TN BR/TR, 6'1", 190 lbs. Deb: 4/21/1945																										
1945	StL-N	18	8	.692	42	22	12	4	2	217^1	206	76	70	9	3	66	67	1.252	2.90	129	3.04	.251	13	.181	15	20	1.6
1946	StL-N	6	3	.667	25	13	5	2	2	100	111	34	32	4	2	36	32	1.470	2.88	120	4.13	.282	5	.147	5	8	0.5
1947	StL-N	3	6	.333	34	6	1	0	1	95	108	55	55	13	4	23	44	1.379	5.21	79	4.67	.292	3	.125	-11	2	-1.3
1948	StL-N	0	0	....	20	0	0	0	1	37^1	50	24	23	4	2	14	16	1.714	5.54	74	6.25	.331	1	.250	-6	1	-0.6
	Cin-N	0	3	.000	16	0	0	0	0	41^2	42	34	32	3	1	16	14	1.392	6.91	57	3.80	.255	3	.333	-13	1	-1.1
	Yr.	0	3	.000	36	0	0	0	1	79	92	58	55	7	3	30	30	1.544	6.27	64	4.96	.291	4	.308	-19	2	-1.7
1949	Cin-N	0	0	....	11	0	0	0	1	28^1	29	10	10	2	0	10	8	1.376	3.18	132	3.97	.282	2	.286	3	3	0.3
Total	5	27	20	.574	148	41	18	6	7	519^2	546	233	222	35	12	165	181	1.368	3.84	100	3.89	.273	27	.180	-7	35	-0.5
• BURNETT, A.J.	Allan James Burnett b: 1/3/1977, North Little Rock, AR BR/TR, 6'5", 205 lbs. Deb: 8/17/1999																										
1999	Fla-N	4	2	.667	7	7	0	0	0	41^1	37	23	16	3	0	25	33	1.500	3.48	125	4.00	.242	2	.118	4	3	0.3
2000	Fla-N	3	7	.300	13	13	0	0	0	82^2	80	46	44	8	2	44	57	1.500	4.79	93	4.45	.259	7	.280	-3	5	0.1
2001	Fla-N	11	12	.478	27	27	2	1	0	173^1	145	82	78	20	7	83	128	1.315	4.05	104	3.76	.231	4	.080	2	9	0.0
2002	Fla-N	12	9	.571	31	29	7	**5**	0	204^1	153	84	75	12	9	90	203	1.189	3.30	119	2.77	.209	6	.105	14	14	1.4
2003	Fla-N	0	2	.000	4	4	0	0	0	23	18	13	12	2	2	18	21	1.565	4.70	87	4.36	.217	1	.143	-2	0	-0.1
Total	5	30	32	.484	82	80	9	6	0	524^2	433	248	225	45	20	260	442	1.321	3.86	108	3.53	.227	20	.128	15	31	1.8
• BURNETTE, Wally	Wallace Harper Burnette b: 6/20/1929, Blairs, VA d: 2/12/2003, Danville, VA BR/TR, 6'.5", 178 lbs. Deb: 7/15/1956																										
1956	KC-A	6	8	.429	18	14	4	1	0	121^1	115	48	39	13	2	39	54	1.269	2.89	150	3.58	.252	2	.051	18	10	1.3
1957	KC-A	7	12	.368	38	9	1	0	1	113	115	62	54	8	1	44	57	1.407	4.30	92	3.94	.268	8	.250	-4	5	-0.3
1958	KC-A	1	1	.500	12	4	0	0	0	28^1	29	14	11	2	0	14	11	1.518	3.49	112	4.37	.264	1	.167	1	2	0.2
Total	3	14	21	.400	68	27	5	1	1	262^2	259	124	104	23	3	97	122	1.355	3.56	115	3.82	.260	11	.143	16	17	1.2
• BURNS, Bill	William Thomas "Sleepy Bill" Burns b: 1/29/1880, San Saba, TX d: 6/6/1953, Ramona, CA BB/TL, 6'2", 195 lbs. Deb: 4/18/1908																										
1908	Was-A	6	11	.353	23	19	11	2	0	164	135	58	31	3	4	18	55	.933	1.70	134	1.81	....	8	.148	10	10	1.1
1909	Was-A	1	1	.500	6	4	1	0	0	29^1	25	7	4	0	3	7	13	1.091	1.23	198	2.39	.229	3	.273	4	2	0.5
	Chi-A	7	13	.350	23	19	10	3	0	168	161	64	38	2	8	34	50	1.161	2.04	115	3.06	.264	9	.153	6	9	0.8
	Yr.	8	14	.364	29	23	11	3	0	197^1	186	71	42	2	11	41	63	1.150	1.92	122	2.96	.259	12	.171	10	11	1.3
1910	Chi-A	0	0	....	1	0	0	0	0	0^1	0	0	0	0	0	1	0	3.000	0.00	....	6.02	.000	0	....	0	0	0.0
	Cin-N	8	13	.381	31	21	13	2	0	178^2	183	103	69	3	12	49	57	1.299	3.48	84	3.48	.273	16	.262	-10	6	-0.7
1911	Cin-N	1	0	1.000	6	3	0	0	1	17^2	17	11	6	1	3	3	5	1.132	3.06	108	3.34	.254	3	.429	1	2	0.2
	Phi-N	6	10	.375	21	14	8	3	1	121	132	59	46	5	6	26	47	1.306	3.42	100	3.78	.287	6	.150	-0	7	-0.1
	Yr.	7	10	.412	27	17	8	3	2	138^2	149	70	52	6	9	29	52	1.284	3.38	101	3.72	.283	9	.191	1	9	0.1
1912	Det-A	1	4	.200	6	5	2	0	0	38^2	52	29	23	0	2	9	6	1.578	5.35	61	5.07	.338	3	.231	-9	1	-0.7
Total	5	30	52	.366	117	85	45	10	2	717^2	705	331	217	14	38	147	233	1.187	2.72	103	3.09	.341	48	.196	2	37	1.0
• BURNS, Britt	Robert Britt Burns b: 6/8/1959, Houston, TX BL/TL, 6'5", 218 lbs. Deb: 8/5/1978																										
1978	Chi-A	0	2	.000	2	2	0	0	0	7^2	14	12	11	2	0	3	3	2.217	12.91	29	10.25	.378	0	....	-8	0	-0.8
1979	Chi-A	0	0	....	6	0	0	0	0	5	10	5	3	1	0	1	2	2.200	5.40	79	10.23	.435	0	....	-1	0	-0.1
1980	Chi-A	15	13	.536	34	32	11	1	0	238	213	83	75	17	4	63	133	1.160	2.84	142	2.89	.241	0	....	33	21	3.3
1981	Chi-A★	10	6	.625	24	23	5	1	0	156^2	139	52	46	14	6	49	108	1.200	2.64	135	3.20	.238	0	....	15	12	1.5
1982	Chi-A	13	5	.722	28	28	5	1	0	169^1	168	89	76	12	3	67	116	1.388	4.04	100	3.83	.257	0	....	2	9	0.2
1983*	Chi-A	10	11	.476	29	26	8	4	0	173^2	165	79	69	14	5	55	115	1.267	3.58	117	3.44	.249	0	....	11	11	1.1
1984	Chi-A	4	12	.250	34	16	2	0	3	117	130	74	65	7	4	45	85	1.496	5.00	83	4.47	.280	0	....	-12	3	-1.2
1985	Chi-A	18	11	.621	36	34	8	4	0	227	206	105	100	26	2	79	172	1.256	3.96	109	3.52	.242	0	....	8	15	0.8
Total	8	70	60	.538	193	161	39	11	3	1094^1	1045	499	445	93	24	362	734	1.286	3.66	111	3.55	.251	0	....	49	71	4.9
• BURNS, Dennis	Dennis Burns b: 5/24/1898, Tiff City, MO d: 5/21/1969, Tulsa, OK BR/TR, 5'10", 180 lbs. Deb: 9/22/1923																										
1923	Phi-A	2	1	.667	4	3	2	0	0	27	21	9	6	1	0	7	8	1.037	2.00	205	1.90	.210	1	.111	7	3	0.6
1924	Phi-A	6	8	.429	37	17	7	0	1	154	191	101	87	3	1	68	26	**1.682**	5.08	84	4.89	.314	6	.143	-12	6	-1.3
Total	2	8	9	.471	41	20	9	0	1	181	212	110	93	4	1	75	34	1.586	4.62	92	4.44	.299	7	.137	-5	9	-0.7

YEAR	TM-L	W	L	PCT	G	GS	CG	SH	SV	IP	H	R	ER	HR	HB	BB	SO	RAT	ERA	ERA+	CERA	OAV	BH	AVG	PR+	WS	TPW
• **BURNS, Dick**	Richard Simon Burns b: 12/26/1863, Holyoke, MA d: 11/16/1937, Holyoke, MA BL/TL, 5'7", 140 lbs. Deb: 5/3/1883 ♦																										
1883	Det-N	2	12	.143	17	13	13	0	0	127^2	172	122	64	8	....	33	30	1.606	4.51	69	....	.305	26	.186	-18	2	-2.5
1884	Cin-U	23	15	.605	40	40	34	1	0	329^2	298	179	90	7	....	47	167	1.047	2.46	130	....	.225	107	.306	27	41	3.5
1885	StL-N	0	0	....	1	0	0	0	0	3	3	3	3	0	....	0	2	1.000	9.00	30	....	.248	12	.222	-2	1	-0.5
Total	**3**	**25**	**27**	**.481**	**58**	**53**	**47**	**1**	**0**	**460^1**	**473**	**304**	**157**	**15**	**....**	**80**	**199**	**1.201**	**3.07**	**102**	**....**	**.249**	**145**	**.267**	**7**	**44**	**0.5**
• **BURNS, Farmer**	James "Slab" Burns b: Ashtabula, OH TR, 5'7", 168 lbs. Deb: 7/6/1901																										
1901	StL-N	0	0	....	1	0	0	0	0	1	2	1	1	0	1	1	0	3.000	9.00	35	16.23	.411	0	....	-1	0	0.0
• **BURNS, Oyster**	Thomas P. Burns b: 9/6/1864, Philadelphia, PA d: 11/11/1928, Brooklyn, NY BR/TR, 5'8", 183 lbs. Deb: 8/18/1884 U ♦																										
1884	Bal-a	0	0	....	2	0	0	0	**1**	9	12	5	3	0	0	2	6	1.556	3.00	115	....	.304	39	.298	1	9	0.8
1885	Bal-a	7	4	.636	15	11	10	1	**3**	105^2	112	76	42	2	13	21	30	1.259	3.58	91	....	.261	74	.231	-1	13	0.1
1887	Bal-a	1	0	1.000	3	0	0	0	0	11^1	20	16	12	0	3	4	2	1.765	9.53	43	....	.372	251	.409	-7	28	2.9
1888	Bal-a	0	1	.000	5	0	0	0	0	12^2	12	8	6	0	0	3	2	1.184	4.26	70	....	.241	97	.298	-2	15	1.1
Total	**4**	**8**	**5**	**.615**	**25**	**11**	**10**	**1**	**4**	**138^2**	**156**	**105**	**63**	**2**	**16**	**30**	**40**	**1.313**	**4.09**	**82**	**....**	**.272**	**1453**	**.309**	**-9**	**65**	**4.9**
• **BURNS, Todd**	Todd Edward Burns b: 7/6/1963, Maywood, CA BR/TR, 6'2", 190 lbs. Deb: 5/31/1988																										
1988*	Oak-A	8	2	.800	17	14	2	0	1	102^2	93	38	36	8	1	34	57	1.237	3.16	120	3.20	.241	0	....	6	7	0.6
1989*	Oak-A	6	5	.545	50	2	0	0	8	96^1	66	27	24	3	1	28	49	.976	2.24	164	1.68	.196	0	....	14	11	1.4
1990*	Oak-A	3	3	.500	43	2	0	0	3	78^2	78	28	26	8	0	32	43	1.398	2.97	125	4.01	.263	0	....	5	5	0.5
1991	Oak-A	1	0	1.000	9	0	0	0	0	13^1	10	5	5	2	0	8	3	1.350	3.38	114	3.70	.217	0	....	1	1	0.1
1992	Tex-A	3	5	.375	35	10	0	0	1	103	97	54	44	8	4	32	55	1.252	3.84	99	3.40	.248	0	....	1	5	0.1
1993	Tex-A	0	4	.000	25	5	0	0	0	65	63	36	33	6	2	32	35	1.462	4.57	91	4.21	.253	0	....	-2	2	-0.2
	StL-N	0	4	.000	24	0	0	0	0	30^2	32	21	21	8	0	9	10	1.337	6.16	64	4.67	.274	0	.000	-8	0	-0.8
Total	**6**	**21**	**23**	**.477**	**203**	**33**	**2**	**0**	**13**	**489^2**	**439**	**209**	**189**	**43**	**8**	**175**	**252**	**1.254**	**3.47**	**111**	**3.31**	**.241**	**0**	**.000**	**17**	**31**	**1.7**
• **BURNSIDE, Pete**	Peter Willits Burnside b: 7/2/1930, Evanston, IL BR/TL, 6'2", 190 lbs. Deb: 9/20/1955																										
1955	NY-N	1	0	1.000	2	2	1	0	0	12^2	10	9	4	1	0	9	2	1.500	2.84	142	3.78	.204	1	.200	2	1	0.2
1957	NY-N	1	4	.200	10	9	1	1	0	30^2	47	30	30	5	1	13	18	1.957	8.80	45	8.10	.356	0	.000	-17	0	-1.8
1958	SF-N	0	0	....	6	1	0	0	0	10^2	20	10	8	3	0	5	4	2.344	6.75	57	11.89	.400	0	....	-3	0	-0.3
1959	Det-A	1	3	.250	30	0	0	0	1	62	55	31	26	7	2	25	49	1.290	3.77	108	3.64	.237	0	.000	2	3	0.1
1960	Det-A	7	7	.500	31	15	2	0	2	113^2	122	56	54	14	4	50	71	1.513	4.28	96	4.95	.277	4	.148	-1	6	-0.2
1961	Was-A	4	9	.308	33	16	4	2	2	113^1	106	66	57	11	3	51	56	1.385	4.53	87	3.94	.251	2	.059	-8	3	-1.1
1962	Was-A	5	11	.313	40	20	6	0	2	149^2	152	82	74	20	2	51	74	1.356	4.45	91	4.15	.263	2	.057	-7	5	-0.9
1963	Bal-A	0	1	.000	6	0	0	0	0	7^1	11	4	4	0	1	2	6	1.773	4.91	72	6.30	.344	0	.000	-1	0	-0.1
	Was-A	0	1	.000	38	1	0	0	0	67^1	84	49	46	12	0	24	23	1.604	6.15	60	5.86	.308	1	.091	-18	0	-1.9
	Yr.	0	2	.000	44	1	0	0	0	74^2	95	53	50	12	1	26	29	1.621	6.03	61	5.90	.311	1	.083	-19	0	-2.1
Total	**8**	**19**	**36**	**.345**	**196**	**64**	**14**	**3**	**7**	**567^1**	**607**	**337**	**303**	**73**	**13**	**230**	**303**	**1.475**	**4.81**	**82**	**4.80**	**.275**	**10**	**.076**	**-52**	**18**	**-6.1**
• **BURNSIDE, Sheldon**	Sheldon John Burnside b: 12/22/1954, South Bend, IN BR/TL, 6'5", 200 lbs. Deb: 9/4/1978																										
1978	Det-A	0	0	....	2	0	0	0	0	4	4	4	4	0	0	2	3	1.500	9.00	43	3.63	.250	0	....	-2	0	-0.2
1979	Det-A	1	1	.500	10	0	0	0	0	21^1	28	16	15	2	1	8	13	1.688	6.33	68	5.96	.333	0	....	-5	0	-0.5
1980	Cin-N	1	0	1.000	7	0	0	0	0	4^2	6	1	1	1	0	1	2	1.500	1.93	186	6.34	.333	0	.000	1	1	0.1
Total	**3**	**2**	**1**	**.667**	**19**	**0**	**0**	**0**	**0**	**30**	**38**	**21**	**20**	**3**	**1**	**11**	**18**	**1.633**	**6.00**	**70**	**5.71**	**.322**	**0**	**.000**	**-6**	**1**	**-0.6**
• **BURPO, George**	George Harvie Burpo b: 6/19/1922, Jenkins, KY BR/TL, 6', 195 lbs. Deb: 6/9/1946																										
1946	Cin-N	0	0	....	2	0	0	0	0	2^1	4	4	4	0	0	5	1	3.857	15.43	22	15.28	.400	0	....	-3	0	-0.3
• **BURRELL, Harry**	Harry J. Burrell b: 5/26/1869, Bethel, VT d: 12/11/1914, Omaha, NE BR/TL Deb: 9/13/1891																										
1891	StL-a	4	2	.667	7	4	3	0	0	43	51	36	23	4	0	21	19	1.674	4.81	87	....	.285	5	.227	-3	2	-0.2
• **BURRIS, Al**	Alva Burton Burris b: 1/28/1874, Warwick, MD d: 3/25/1938, Salisbury, MD BR/TR Deb: 6/22/1894																										
1894	Phi-N	0	0	....	1	0	0	0	0	5	14	10	10	0	0	2	0	3.200	18.00	28	15.25	.493	2	.500	-7	0	-0.5
• **BURRIS, Ray**	Bertram Ray Burris b: 8/22/1950, Idabel, OK BR/TR, 6'5", 200 lbs. Deb: 4/8/1973 C																										
1973	Chi-N	1	1	.500	31	1	0	0	0	64^2	65	22	21	2	0	27	57	1.423	2.92	135	3.47	.261	1	.143	9	6	0.9
1974	Chi-N	3	5	.375	40	5	0	0	1	75	91	61	55	8	4	26	40	1.560	6.60	58	5.12	.300	1	.077	-20	0	-2.1
1975	Chi-N	15	10	.600	36	35	8	2	0	238^1	259	121	109	25	4	73	108	1.393	4.12	93	4.29	.281	15	.183	1	14	0.2
1976	Chi-N	15	13	.536	37	36	10	4	0	249	251	102	86	22	5	70	112	1.289	3.11	124	3.62	.263	9	.111	25	19	2.2
1977	Chi-N	14	16	.467	39	39	5	1	0	221	270	132	116	29	3	67	105	1.525	4.72	93	5.24	.305	12	.174	-4	10	-0.2
1978	Chi-N	7	13	.350	40	32	4	1	1	198^2	210	112	105	15	10	79	94	1.455	4.76	85	4.34	.274	7	.115	-15	6	-1.6
1979	Chi-N	0	0	....	14	0	0	0	0	21^2	23	17	15	0	1	15	14	1.754	6.23	66	5.08	.284	0	.000	-5	0	-0.5
	NY-A	1	3	.250	15	0	0	0	0	27^2	40	22	19	5	0	10	19	1.807	6.18	66	7.07	.342	0	....	-7	0	-0.7
	NY-N	0	2	.000	4	4	0	0	0	21^2	21	10	8	2	1	6	10	1.246	3.32	109	3.26	.247	1	.167	1	1	0.0
	Yr.	0	2	.000	18	4	0	0	0	43^1	44	27	23	2	2	21	24	1.500	4.78	82	4.17	.265	1	.143	-4	1	-0.4
1980	NY-N	7	13	.350	29	29	1	0	0	170^1	181	86	76	20	4	54	83	1.380	4.02	88	4.32	.277	5	.098	-9	5	-1.3
1981*	Mon-N	9	7	.563	22	21	4	0	0	135^2	117	56	46	9	3	41	52	1.165	3.05	115	2.83	.235	7	.189	6	8	0.8
1982	Mon-N	4	14	.222	37	15	2	0	2	123^2	143	77	65	14	2	53	55	1.585	4.73	77	5.23	.297	5	.179	-16	1	-1.5
1983	Mon-N	4	7	.364	40	17	2	1	0	154	139	68	63	13	2	56	100	1.266	3.68	97	3.34	.244	9	.231	-4	8	-0.1
1984	Oak-A	13	10	.565	34	28	5	1	0	211^2	193	84	74	15	8	90	93	1.337	3.15	119	3.65	.244	0	....	13	12	1.4
1985	Mil-A	9	13	.409	29	28	6	0	0	170^1	182	95	91	25	3	53	81	1.380	4.81	87	4.48	.272	0	....	-12	7	-1.2
1986	StL-N	4	5	.444	23	10	0	0	0	82	92	52	51	13	4	32	34	1.512	5.60	65	5.37	.287	4	.148	-21	0	-2.1
1987	Mil-A	2	2	.500	10	2	0	0	0	23	33	16	15	4	0	12	8	1.957	5.87	78	7.79	.351	0	....	-3	1	-0.3
Total	**15**	**108**	**134**	**.446**	**480**	**302**	**47**	**10**	**4**	**2188^1**	**2310**	**1133**	**1015**	**221**	**54**	**764**	**1065**	**1.405**	**4.17**	**93**	**4.28**	**.274**	**76**	**.151**	**-60**	**98**	**-6.1**
• **BURROWS, John**	John Burrows b: 10/30/1913, Winnfield, LA d: 4/27/1987, Coal Run, OH BR/TL, 5'10", 200 lbs. Deb: 4/25/1943																										
1943	Phi-A	0	1	.000	4	1	0	0	0	7^2	8	7	7	0	1	9	3	2.217	8.22	41	6.67	.276	0	.000	-4	0	-0.4
	Chi-N	0	2	.000	23	1	0	0	2	32^2	25	17	14	0	2	16	18	1.255	3.86	86	2.53	.205	2	.667	-1	2	0.0
1944	Chi-N	0	0	....	3	0	0	0	0	3	7	7	6	0	0	3	1	3.333	18.00	20	14.04	.467	0	....	-5	0	-0.5
Total	**2**	**0**	**3**	**.000**	**30**	**2**	**0**	**0**	**2**	**43^1**	**40**	**31**	**27**	**0**	**3**	**28**	**22**	**1.569**	**5.61**	**60**	**4.06**	**.241**	**2**	**.500**	**-10**	**2**	**-0.9**
• **BURROWS, Terry**	Terry Dale Burrows b: 11/28/1968, Lake Charles, LA BL/TL, 6'1", 185 lbs. Deb: 6/12/1994																										
1994	Tex-A	0	0	....	1	0	0	0	0	1	1	1	1	1	0	1	0	2.000	9.00	53	14.27	.250	0	....	-0	0	0.0
1995	Tex-A	2	2	.500	28	3	0	0	1	44^2	60	37	32	11	2	19	22	1.769	6.45	75	7.77	.323	0	....	-8	0	-0.7
1996	Mil-A	2	0	1.000	8	0	0	0	0	12^2	12	4	4	2	1	10	5	1.737	2.84	183	6.33	.261	0	....	3	2	0.3
1997	SD-N	0	2	.000	13	0	0	0	0	10^1	12	13	12	1	1	8	8	1.935	10.45	37	6.59	.286	0	....	-7	0	-0.7
Total	**4**	**4**	**4**	**.500**	**50**	**3**	**0**	**0**	**1**	**68^2**	**85**	**55**	**49**	**15**	**4**	**38**	**35**	**1.791**	**6.42**	**71**	**7.42**	**.306**	**0**	**....**	**-13**	**2**	**-1.2**
• **BURTON, Jim**	Jim Scott Burton b: 10/27/1949, Royal Oak, MI BR/TL, 6'3", 195 lbs. Deb: 6/10/1975																										
1975*	Bos-A	1	2	.333	29	4	0	0	1	53	58	30	17	6	0	19	39	1.453	2.89	141	4.45	.276	0	....	7	3	0.7
1977	Bos-A	0	0	....	1	0	0	0	0	2^2	2	0	0	0	0	1	3	1.125	0.00	....	2.01	.200	0	....	1	0	0.1
Total	**2**	**1**	**2**	**.333**	**30**	**4**	**0**	**0**	**1**	**55^2**	**60**	**30**	**17**	**6**	**0**	**20**	**42**	**1.437**	**2.75**	**148**	**4.34**	**.273**	**0**	**....**	**8**	**3**	**0.8**
• **BURTSCHY, Moe**	Edward Frank Burtschy b: 4/18/1922, Cincinnati, OH BR/TR, 6'3", 208 lbs. Deb: 6/17/1950																										
1950	Phi-A	0	1	.000	9	1	0	0	0	19	22	16	15	2	1	21	12	2.263	7.11	64	7.76	.289	0	.000	-5	0	-0.5
1951	Phi-A	0	0	....	7	0	0	0	0	17	18	11	10	0	1	12	4	1.765	5.29	81	4.90	.277	1	.333	-2	0	-0.2
1954	Phi-A	5	4	.556	46	0	0	0	4	94^2	80	45	40	7	8	53	54	1.405	3.80	103	3.84	.234	2	.118	2	7	0.2
1955	KC-A	2	0	1.000	7	0	0	0	0	11^1	17	13	13	0	1	10	9	2.382	10.32	40	8.55	.354	1	.333	-8	0	-0.8
1956	KC-A	3	1	.750	21	0	0	0	0	43^1	41	22	19	6	3	30	18	1.638	3.95	110	5.48	.263	1	.125	1	3	0.1
Total	**5**	**10**	**6**	**.625**	**90**	**1**	**0**	**0**	**4**	**185^1**	**178**	**107**	**97**	**15**	**14**	**126**	**97**	**1.640**	**4.71**	**88**	**5.01**	**.259**	**5**	**.139**	**-11**	**10**	**-1.2**

YEAR TM-L	W	L	PCT	G	GS	CG	SH	SV	IP	H	R	ER	HR	HB	BB	SO	RAT	ERA	ERA+	CERA	OAV	BH	AVG	PR+	WS	TPW
• BURTT, Dennis	Dennis Allen Burtt b: 11/29/1957, San Diego, CA BB/TR, 6', 180 lbs. Deb: 9/4/1985																									
1985 Min-A	2	2	.500	5	2	0	0	0	28^1	20	13	12	2	0	7	9	.953	3.81	116	1.89	.200	0	....	2	2	0.2
1986 Min-A	0	0	....	3	0	0	0	0	2	7	7	7	1	0	3	1	5.000	31.50	14	31.45	.538	0	....	-6	0	-0.6
Total 2	2	2	.500	8	2	0	0	0	30^1	27	20	19	3	0	10	10	1.220	5.64	78	3.84	.239	0	....	-4	2	-0.4
• BURWELL, Bill	William Edwin Burwell b: 3/27/1895, Jarbalo, KS d: 6/11/1973, Ormond Beach, FL BL/TR, 5'11", 175 lbs. Deb: 5/1/1920 M/C																									
1920 StL-A	6	4	.600	33	2	0	0	4	113^1	133	55	46	5	4	42	30	1.544	3.65	107	4.73	.303	7	.167	3	8	0.1
1921 StL-A	2	4	.333	33	3	1	0	2	84^1	102	62	48	2	2	29	17	1.553	5.12	87	4.45	.309	6	.240	-6	3	-0.5
1928 Pit-N	1	0	1.000	4	1	0	0	0	20^2	18	12	12	2	0	8	2	1.258	5.23	78	3.19	.234	2	.222	-3	1	-0.3
Total 3	9	8	.529	70	6	1	0	6	218^1	253	129	106	9	6	79	49	1.521	4.37	95	4.48	.299	15	.197	-5	12	-0.7
• BURWELL, Dick	Richard Matthew Burwell b: 1/23/1940, Alton, IL BR/TR, 6'1", 190 lbs. Deb: 9/13/1960																									
1960 Chi-N	0	0	....	3	1	0	0	0	9^2	11	6	6	2	1	7	1	1.862	5.59	68	8.15	.306	1	.333	-2	0	-0.2
1961 Chi-N	0	0	....	2	0	0	0	0	4	6	4	4	0	0	4	0	2.500	9.00	46	9.02	.375	0	.000	-2	0	-0.2
Total 2	0	0	....	5	1	0	0	0	13^2	17	10	10	2	1	11	1	2.049	6.59	60	8.40	.327	1	.250	-4	0	-0.4
• BUSBY, Mike	Michael James Busby b: 12/27/1972, Lomita, CA BR/TR, 6'4", 210 lbs. Deb: 4/7/1996																									
1996 StL-N	0	1	.000	1	1	0	0	0	4	9	13	8	4	1	4	4	3.250	18.00	23	24.89	.409	1	.500	-6	0	-0.6
1997 StL-N	0	2	.000	3	3	0	0	0	14^1	24	14	14	2	0	4	6	1.953	8.79	47	8.34	.393	2	.500	-7	0	-0.7
1998 StL-N	5	2	.714	26	2	0	0	0	46	45	23	23	3	5	15	33	1.304	4.50	93	3.77	.254	0	.000	-1	3	-0.1
1999 StL-N	0	1	.000	15	0	0	0	0	17^2	21	15	14	2	2	14	7	1.981	7.13	64	7.62	.300	0	....	-5	0	-0.5
Total 4	5	6	.455	45	6	0	0	0	82	99	65	59	11	8	37	50	1.659	6.48	66	6.43	.300	3	.333	-20	3	-1.8
• BUSBY, Steve	Steven Lee Busby b: 9/29/1949, Burbank, CA BR/TR, 6'2", 205 lbs. Deb: 9/8/1972																									
1972 KC-A	3	1	.750	5	5	3	0	0	40	28	9	7	1	0	8	31	.900	1.58	192	1.52	.200	3	.200	7	5	0.8
1973 KC-A	16	15	.516	37	37	7	1	0	238^1	246	125	112	18	6	105	174	1.473	4.23	97	4.34	.271	0	....	-0	14	0.0
1974 KC-A★	22	14	.611	38	38	20	3	0	292^1	284	118	110	14	9	92	198	1.286	3.39	113	3.37	.258	0	....	18	22	1.9
1975 KC-A★	18	12	.600	34	34	18	3	0	260^1	233	96	89	18	3	81	160	1.206	3.08	125	3.03	.242	0	....	26	22	2.6
1976 KC-A	3	3	.500	13	13	1	0	0	71^2	58	42	35	7	3	49	29	1.493	4.40	80	4.16	.218	0	....	-7	1	-0.8
1978 KC-A	1	0	1.000	7	5	0	0	0	21^1	24	18	18	2	2	15	10	1.828	7.59	50	6.20	.282	0	....	-9	0	-0.9
1979 KC-A	6	6	.500	22	12	4	0	0	94^1	71	45	38	10	0	64	45	1.431	3.63	118	3.83	.220	0	....	6	6	0.6
1980 KC-A	1	3	.250	11	6	0	0	0	42^1	59	30	29	3	2	19	12	1.843	6.17	66	6.70	.335	0	....	-10	0	-1.0
Total 8	70	54	.565	167	150	53	7	0	1060^2	1003	483	438	73	25	433	659	1.354	3.72	105	3.72	.253	3	.200	31	70	3.3
• BUSCHHORN, Don	Donald Lee Buschhorn b: 4/29/1946, Independence, MO BR/TR, 6', 170 lbs. Deb: 5/15/1965																									
1965 KC-A	0	1	.000	12	3	0	0	0	31	36	17	15	7	1	8	9	1.419	4.35	80	5.56	.295	2	.500	-3	1	-0.2
• BUSH, Guy	Guy Terrell "The Mississippi Mudcat" Bush b: 8/23/1901, Aberdeen, MS d: 7/2/1985, Shannon, MS BR/TR, 6', 175 lbs. Deb: 9/17/1923																									
1923 Chi-N	0	0	....	1	0	0	0	0	1	1	0	0	0	0	0	2	1.000	0.00	....	1.95	.250	0	....	0	0	0.0
1924 Chi-N	2	5	.286	16	8	4	0	0	80^2	91	51	36	7	2	24	36	1.426	4.02	97	4.34	.285	4	.154	-2	2	-0.3
1925 Chi-N	6	13	.316	42	15	5	0	**4**	182	213	102	87	15	3	52	76	1.456	4.30	100	4.48	.300	11	.193	-3	10	-0.4
1926 Chi-N	13	9	.591	35	16	7	2	2	157^1	149	58	50	3	3	42	32	1.214	2.86	134	2.82	.258	8	.167	14	14	1.1
1927 Chi-N	10	10	.500	36	22	9	1	2	193^1	177	76	65	3	6	79	62	1.324	3.03	128	3.12	.250	8	.123	14	15	1.0
1928 Chi-N	15	6	.714	42	24	9	2	2	204^1	229	104	87	10	5	86	61	1.542	3.83	100	4.52	.293	6	.082	-7	12	-1.3
1929* Chi-N	18	7	.720	**50**	29	18	2	**8**	270^2	277	135	110	16	4	107	82	1.419	3.66	126	3.84	.265	15	.165	24	21	1.9
1930 Chi-N	15	10	.600	46	25	11	0	3	225	291	174	155	22	2	86	75	1.676	6.20	79	5.62	.316	22	.282	-32	8	-2.5
1931 Chi-N	16	8	.667	39	24	14	1	2	180^1	190	104	90	9	2	66	54	1.420	4.49	86	3.78	.268	7	.123	-11	7	-1.3
1932* Chi-N	19	11	.633	40	30	15	1	0	238^2	262	106	85	13	7	70	73	1.391	3.21	117	3.91	.278	15	.179	11	19	1.1
1933 Chi-N	20	12	.625	41	32	20	4	2	259	261	95	79	9	1	68	84	1.270	2.75	119	3.05	.257	11	.125	9	18	0.9
1934 Chi-N	18	10	.643	40	27	15	1	2	209^1	213	96	89	15	1	54	75	1.275	3.83	101	3.37	.262	16	.229	-0	16	0.0
1935 Pit-N	11	11	.500	41	25	8	1	2	204^1	237	115	98	16	5	40	42	1.356	4.32	95	3.98	.285	8	.127	-3	10	-0.4
1936 Pit-N	1	3	.250	16	0	0	0	2	34^2	49	28	23	3	0	11	10	1.731	5.97	68	5.95	.336	3	.333	-7	0	-0.6
Bos-N	4	5	.444	15	11	5	0	0	90^1	98	38	34	2	0	20	28	1.306	3.39	113	3.32	.281	3	.120	4	6	0.3
Yr.	5	8	.385	31	11	5	0	2	125	147	66	57	5	0	31	38	1.424	4.10	95	4.05	.297	6	.176	-3	6	-0.4
1937 Bos-N	8	15	.348	32	20	11	1	1	180^2	201	77	71	8	0	48	56	1.378	3.54	101	3.72	.282	6	.111	-3	9	-0.5
1938 StL-N	0	1	.000	6	0	0	0	1	6	6	3	3	1	0	3	1	1.500	4.50	88	5.39	.286	0	....	-0	0	0.0
1945 Cin-N	0	0	....	4	0	0	0	1	4^1	5	4	4	0	0	3	1	1.846	8.31	45	4.99	.278	0	....	-2	0	-0.2
Total 17	176	136	.564	542	308	151	16	34	2722	2950	1366	1166	152	41	859	850	1.399	3.86	104	3.89	.278	143	.161	5	167	-1.5
• BUSH, Joe	Leslie Ambrose "Bullet Joe" Bush b: 11/27/1892, Brainerd, MN d: 11/1/1974, Fort Lauderdale, FL BR/TR, 5'9", 173 lbs. Deb: 9/30/1912																									
1912 Phi-A	0	0	....	1	1	0	0	0	8	14	10	7	0	0	4	3	2.250	7.88	39	7.90	.368	2	.500	-4	1	-0.3
1913* Phi-A	15	6	.714	39	16	6	1	3	200^1	199	95	85	3	5	66	81	1.323	3.82	72	3.11	.248	11	.157	-24	8	-2.6
1914* Phi-A	17	13	.567	38	23	14	3	2	206	184	84	70	2	8	81	109	1.286	3.06	85	2.99	.242	14	.189	-11	11	-1.0
1915 Phi-A	5	15	.250	25	18	8	0	0	145^2	137	86	67	3	4	89	89	1.551	4.14	71	4.18	.263	7	.143	-19	2	-2.3
1916 Phi-A	15	24	.385	40	33	25	8	0	286^2	222	109	82	3	3	130	157	1.228	2.57	111	2.54	.219	14	.140	15	7	1.3
1917 Phi-A	11	17	.393	37	31	17	4	2	233^1	207	101	64	3	1	111	121	1.363	2.47	111	2.94	.241	16	.200	11	10	1.4
1918* Bos-A	15	15	.500	36	31	26	7	2	272^2	241	88	64	3	3	91	125	1.218	2.11	127	2.61	.242	27	.276	16	21	2.4
1919 Bos-A	0	0	....	3	2	0	0	0	9	11	5	5	0	0	4	3	1.667	5.00	60	5.04	.324	2	.400	-2	0	-0.2
1920 Bos-A	15	15	.500	35	32	18	0	1	243^2	287	138	115	3	10	94	88	1.564	4.25	86	4.48	.300	25	.245	-20	12	-1.8
1921 Bos-A	16	9	.640	37	32	21	3	1	254^1	244	111	99	10	6	93	96	1.325	3.50	121	3.36	.260	39	.325	15	24	2.2
1922* NY-A	26	7	.788	39	30	20	0	3	255^1	240	109	94	16	1	85	92	1.273	3.31	121	3.21	.252	31	.326	17	26	2.4
1923* NY-A	19	15	.559	37	30	22	3	0	275^2	263	115	105	7	5	117	125	1.378	3.43	115	3.39	.260	31	.274	13	24	1.9
1924 NY-A	17	16	.515	39	31	19	3	1	252	262	117	100	9	7	109	80	1.472	3.57	116	3.93	.273	42	.339	15	23	2.6
1925 StL-A	14	14	.500	33	30	15	2	0	208^2	230	129	118	18	2	91	63	1.538	5.09	92	4.58	.284	26	.255	-12	14	-0.6
1926 Was-A	1	8	.111	12	11	3	0	0	71^1	83	54	53	6	5	35	27	1.654	6.69	58	5.36	.292	7	.233	-23	0	-2.2
Pit-N	6	6	.500	19	12	9	2	3	110^2	97	45	37	7	2	35	38	1.193	3.01	131	2.84	.236	13	.265	10	10	1.2
1927 Pit-N	1	2	.333	5	3	0	0	0	6^2	14	14	10	1	0	5	1	2.850	13.50	30	11.93	.412	3	.600	-7	1	-0.6
NY-N	1	1	.500	3	2	1	0	0	12	18	10	10	1	0	5	6	1.917	7.50	51	6.85	.340	2	.500	-5	0	-0.4
Yr.	2	3	.400	8	5	1	0	0	18^2	32	24	20	2	0	10	7	2.250	9.64	41	8.67	.368	5	.556	-12	1	-1.0
1928 Phi-A	2	1	.667	11	2	1	0	1	35^1	39	21	20	1	1	18	15	1.613	5.09	79	4.37	.300	1	.067	-4	1	-0.6
Total 17	196	184	.516	489	370	225	36	19	3087^1	2992	1441	1205	96	63	1263	1319	1.378	3.51	99	3.48	.259	313	.253	-19	195	3.0
• BUSHELMAN, Jack	John Francis Bushelman b: 8/29/1885, Cincinnati, OH d: 10/26/1955, Roanoke, VA BR/TR, 6'2", 175 lbs. Deb: 10/5/1909																									
1909 Cin-N	0	1	.000	1	1	1	0	0	7	7	7	2	1	0	4	3	1.571	2.57	101	4.99	.241	0	.000	-0	0	0.0
1911 Bos-A	0	1	.000	3	1	1	0	0	12	8	9	4	0	1	10	5	1.500	3.00	109	3.04	.186	0	.000	0	0	0.0
1912 Bos-A	1	0	1.000	3	0	0	0	0	7^2	9	4	4	0	0	5	5	1.826	4.70	73	5.45	.310	0	.000	-1	0	-0.1
Total 3	1	2	.333	7	2	2	0	0	26^2	24	20	10	1	1	19	13	1.613	3.38	94	4.25	.237	0	.000	-1	0	-0.2
• BUSHEY, Frank	Francis Clyde Bushey b: 8/1/1906, Wheaton, KS d: 3/18/1972, Topeka, KS BR/TR, 6', 180 lbs. Deb: 9/17/1927																									
1927 Bos-A	0	0	....	1	0	0	0	0	1^1	2	1	1	0	0	2	0	3.000	6.75	62	13.77	.500	0	....	-0	0	0.0
1930 Bos-A	0	1	.000	11	0	0	0	0	30	34	22	21	1	2	15	4	1.633	6.30	73	4.90	.306	1	.111	-6	0	-0.6
Total 2	0	1	.000	12	0	0	0	0	31^1	36	23	22	1	2	17	4	1.691	6.32	73	5.27	.313	1	.111	-6	0	-0.7
• BUSHING, Chris	Christopher Shaun Bushing b: 11/4/1967, Rockville Centre, NY BR/TR, 6', 190 lbs. Deb: 9/3/1993																									
1993 Cin-N	0	0	....	6	0	0	0	0	4^1	9	7	6	1	0	4	3	3.000	12.46	32	15.35	.450	0	....	-4	0	-0.4
• BUSKEY, Tom	Thomas William Buskey b: 2/20/1947, Harrisburg, PA d: 6/7/1998, Harrisburg, PA BR/TR, 6'3", 220 lbs. Deb: 8/5/1973																									
1973 NY-A	0	1	.000	8	0	0	0	1	16^2	18	12	10	2	1	4	8	1.320	5.40	68	4.23	.286	0	....	-3	0	-0.3

YEAR	TM-L	W	L	PCT	G	GS	CG	SH	SV	IP	H	R	ER	HR	HB	BB	SO	RAT	ERA	ERA+	CERA	OAV	BH	AVG	PR+	WS	TPW
1974	NY-A	0	1	.000	4	0	0	0	1	5^2	10	4	4	1	1	3	3	2.294	6.35	55	10.77	.400	0	....	-2	0	-0.2
	Cle-A	2	6	.250	51	0	0	0	17	93	93	36	33	10	1	33	40	1.355	3.19	113	3.83	.263	0	....	4	9	0.4
	Yr.	2	7	.222	55	0	0	0	18	98^2	103	40	37	11	2	36	43	1.409	3.38	107	4.23	.272	0	....	2	9	0.2
1975	Cle-A	5	3	.625	50	0	0	0	7	77	69	27	22	7	1	29	29	1.273	2.57	147	3.30	.252	0	....	10	8	1.0
1976	Cle-A	5	4	.556	39	0	0	0	1	94^1	88	42	38	9	3	34	32	1.293	3.63	96	3.60	.256	0	....	-2	5	-0.2
1977	Cle-A	0	0	....	21	0	0	0	0	34	45	24	20	6	1	8	15	1.559	5.29	74	5.76	.313	0	....	-5	0	-0.5
1978	Tor-A	0	1	.000	8	0	0	0	0	13^1	14	5	5	1	0	5	7	1.425	3.38	116	3.49	.275	0	....	1	1	0.1
1979	Tor-A	6	10	.375	44	0	0	0	7	78^2	74	33	30	10	1	25	44	1.258	3.43	126	3.53	.249	0	....	8	8	0.7
1980	Tor-A	3	1	.750	33	0	0	0	0	66^2	68	35	33	11	0	26	34	1.410	4.46	97	4.63	.278	0	....	-2	3	-0.2
Total	**8**	**21**	**27**	**.438**	**258**	**0**	**0**	**0**	**34**	**479^1**	**479**	**218**	**195**	**57**	**9**	**167**	**212**	**1.348**	**3.66**	**105**	**3.99**	**.267**	**0**	**....**	**8**	**34**	**0.8**

• BUTCHER, John — John Daniel Butcher b: 3/8/1957, Glendale, CA BR/TR, 6'4", 190 lbs. Deb: 9/8/1980

YEAR	TM-L	W	L	PCT	G	GS	CG	SH	SV	IP	H	R	ER	HR	HB	BB	SO	RAT	ERA	ERA+	CERA	OAV	BH	AVG	PR+	WS	TPW
1980	Tex-A	3	3	.500	6	6	1	0	0	35^1	34	19	16	2	0	13	27	1.330	4.08	95	3.39	.248	0	....	-0	2	0.0
1981	Tex-A	1	2	.333	5	3	1	1	0	27^2	18	6	5	0	0	8	19	.940	1.63	213	1.44	.186	0	....	5	3	0.5
1982	Tex-A	1	5	.167	18	13	2	0	1	94^1	102	53	51	10	2	34	39	1.442	4.87	80	4.51	.280	0	....	-10	3	-1.0
1983	Tex-A	6	6	.500	38	6	1	1	5	123	128	50	48	8	1	41	58	1.374	3.51	114	3.82	.270	0	....	7	9	0.7
1984	Min-A	13	11	.542	34	34	8	1	0	225	242	98	86	18	4	53	83	1.311	3.44	122	3.79	.276	0	....	14	17	1.4
1985	Min-A	11	14	.440	34	33	8	2	0	207^2	239	125	115	24	6	43	92	1.358	4.98	88	4.34	.289	0	....	-13	8	-1.3
1986	Min-A	0	3	.000	16	10	1	0	0	70	82	50	49	11	1	24	29	1.514	6.30	68	5.33	.294	0	....	-15	0	-1.4
	Cle-A	1	5	.167	13	8	1	1	0	50^2	86	43	39	6	3	13	16	1.954	6.93	60	8.25	.381	0	....	-15	0	-1.5
	Yr.	1	8	.111	29	18	2	1	0	120^2	168	93	88	17	4	37	45	1.699	6.56	64	6.56	.333	0	....	-30	0	-3.0
Total	**7**	**36**	**49**	**.424**	**164**	**113**	**23**	**6**	**6**	**833^2**	**931**	**444**	**409**	**79**	**17**	**229**	**363**	**1.391**	**4.42**	**94**	**4.32**	**.284**	**0**	**....**	**-27**	**42**	**-2.6**

• BUTCHER, Max — Albert Maxwell Butcher b: 9/21/1910, Holden, WV d: 9/15/1957, Man, WV BR/TR, 6'2", 220 lbs. Deb: 4/20/1936

YEAR	TM-L	W	L	PCT	G	GS	CG	SH	SV	IP	H	R	ER	HR	HB	BB	SO	RAT	ERA	ERA+	CERA	OAV	BH	AVG	PR+	WS	TPW
1936	Bro-N	6	6	.500	38	15	5	0	2	147^2	154	85	65	11	1	59	55	1.442	3.96	104	4.05	.268	6	.125	5	8	0.2
1937	Bro-N	11	15	.423	39	24	8	1	0	191^2	203	106	91	12	5	75	57	1.450	4.27	94	4.19	.280	10	.161	-0	10	-0.1
1938	Bro-N	5	4	.556	24	8	3	0	2	72^2	104	66	53	9	1	39	21	1.968	6.56	59	7.34	.334	4	.160	-21	0	-2.1
	Phi-N	4	8	.333	12	12	11	0	0	98^1	94	40	32	6	2	31	29	1.271	2.93	137	3.24	.253	9	.257	15	7	1.6
	Yr.	9	12	.429	36	20	14	0	2	171	198	106	85	15	3	70	50	1.567	4.47	88	4.98	.290	13	.217	-6	7	-0.5
1939	Phi-N	2	13	.133	19	16	3	0	0	104^1	131	72	65	10	1	51	27	1.744	5.61	70	5.72	.308	7	.184	-19	1	-2.0
	Pit-N	4	4	.500	14	12	5	2	0	86^2	104	37	33	2	0	23	21	1.465	3.43	112	4.00	.297	3	.097	6	5	0.4
	Yr.	6	17	.261	33	28	8	2	0	191	235	109	98	12	1	74	48	1.618	4.62	85	4.94	.303	10	.145	-13	6	-1.6
1940	Pit-N	8	9	.471	35	24	6	2	2	136^1	161	99	91	13	1	46	40	1.518	6.01	63	4.72	.290	15	.300	-29	2	-2.5
1941	Pit-N	17	12	.586	33	32	19	0	0	236	249	98	80	11	1	66	61	1.335	3.05	118	3.43	.265	15	.183	17	17	1.7
1942	Pit-N	5	8	.385	24	18	9	0	1	150^2	144	59	49	7	2	44	49	1.248	2.93	116	2.97	.247	7	.143	9	10	0.8
1943	Pit-N	10	8	.556	33	21	10	2	1	193^2	191	65	56	4	2	57	45	1.281	2.60	134	3.07	.262	10	.164	19	14	1.9
1944	Pit-N	13	11	.542	35	27	13	5	1	199	216	83	69	8	1	46	43	1.317	3.12	119	3.38	.273	12	.190	15	15	1.5
1945	Pit-N	10	8	.556	28	20	12	2	0	169^1	184	76	57	7	4	46	37	1.358	3.03	130	3.65	.277	12	.222	19	13	1.9
Total	**10**	**95**	**106**	**.473**	**334**	**229**	**104**	**14**	**9**	**1786^1**	**1935**	**886**	**741**	**100**	**21**	**583**	**485**	**1.410**	**3.73**	**102**	**3.91**	**.276**	**110**	**.184**	**35**	**102**	**3.2**

• BUTCHER, Mike — Michael Dana Butcher b: 5/10/1965, Davenport, IA BR/TR, 6'1", 200 lbs. Deb: 7/6/1992

YEAR	TM-L	W	L	PCT	G	GS	CG	SH	SV	IP	H	R	ER	HR	HB	BB	SO	RAT	ERA	ERA+	CERA	OAV	BH	AVG	PR+	WS	TPW
1992	Cal-A	2	2	.500	19	0	0	0	0	27^2	29	11	10	3	2	13	24	1.518	3.25	122	4.89	.264	0	....	2	2	0.2
1993	Cal-A	1	0	1.000	23	0	0	0	8	28^1	21	12	9	2	2	15	24	1.271	2.86	158	3.07	.204	0	....	5	5	0.5
1994	Cal-A	2	1	.667	33	0	0	0	1	29^2	31	24	22	2	2	23	19	1.820	6.67	73	5.59	.274	0	....	-6	1	-0.6
1995	Cal-A	6	1	.857	40	0	0	0	0	51^1	49	28	27	7	1	31	29	1.558	4.73	99	4.98	.257	0	....	-1	3	-0.1
Total	**4**	**11**	**4**	**.733**	**115**	**0**	**0**	**0**	**9**	**137**	**130**	**75**	**68**	**14**	**7**	**82**	**96**	**1.547**	**4.47**	**103**	**4.70**	**.251**	**0**	**....**	**0**	**11**	**0.1**

• BUTLAND, Bill — Wilburn Rue Butland b: 3/22/1918, Terre Haute, IN d: 9/19/1997, Terre Haute, IN BR/TR, 6'5", 185 lbs. Deb: 5/29/1940

YEAR	TM-L	W	L	PCT	G	GS	CG	SH	SV	IP	H	R	ER	HR	HB	BB	SO	RAT	ERA	ERA+	CERA	OAV	BH	AVG	PR+	WS	TPW
1940	Bos-A	1	2	.333	3	3	1	0	0	21	27	13	13	0	0	10	5	1.762	5.57	81	5.03	.307	0	.000	-2	1	-0.3
1942	Bos-A	7	1	.875	23	10	6	2	1	111^1	85	35	31	8	3	33	46	1.060	2.51	149	2.28	.206	1	.036	13	11	1.2
1946	Bos-A	1	0	1.000	5	2	0	0	0	16^1	23	20	20	3	0	13	10	2.204	11.02	33	9.04	.343	1	.250	-13	0	-1.4
1947	Bos-A	0	0	....	1	0	0	0	0	2	3	1	1	0	0	0	1	1.500	4.50	86	4.47	.333	0	....	-0	0	0.0
Total	**4**	**9**	**3**	**.750**	**32**	**15**	**7**	**2**	**1**	**150^2**	**138**	**69**	**65**	**11**	**3**	**56**	**62**	**1.288**	**3.88**	**99**	**3.43**	**.240**	**2**	**.051**	**-3**	**12**	**-0.5**

• BUTLER, Adam — Adam Christopher Butler b: 8/17/1973, Fairfax, VA BL/TL, 6'2" Deb: 3/31/1998

YEAR	TM-L	W	L	PCT	G	GS	CG	SH	SV	IP	H	R	ER	HR	HB	BB	SO	RAT	ERA	ERA+	CERA	OAV	BH	AVG	PR+	WS	TPW
1998	Atl-N	0	1	.000	8	0	0	0	0	5	5	7	6	1	1	6	7	2.200	10.80	39	8.22	.278	0		-4	0	-0.4

• BUTLER, Bill — William Franklin Butler b: 3/12/1947, Hyattsville, MD BL/TL, 6'2", 210 lbs. Deb: 4/9/1969

YEAR	TM-L	W	L	PCT	G	GS	CG	SH	SV	IP	H	R	ER	HR	HB	BB	SO	RAT	ERA	ERA+	CERA	OAV	BH	AVG	PR+	WS	TPW
1969	KC-A	9	10	.474	34	29	5	4	0	193^2	174	91	84	15	3	91	156	1.368	3.90	94	3.63	.240	3	.050	-2	9	-0.6
1970	KC-A	4	12	.250	25	25	2	1	0	140^2	117	66	59	17	1	87	75	1.450	3.77	99	4.19	.229	2	.045	-2	5	-0.5
1971	KC-A	1	2	.333	14	6	0	0	0	44^1	45	19	17	6	0	18	32	1.421	3.45	99	4.49	.268	1	.083	0	2	-0.1
1972	Cle-A	0	0	....	6	2	0	0	0	11^2	9	3	2	1	0	10	6	1.629	1.54	208	4.54	.220	0	.000	2	1	0.2
1974	Min-A	4	6	.400	26	12	2	0	1	98^2	91	47	45	9	1	56	79	1.490	4.10	91	4.32	.251	0	....	-3	4	-0.3
1975	Min-A	5	4	.556	23	8	1	0	0	81^2	100	61	54	12	0	35	55	1.653	5.95	65	5.78	.301	0	....	-18	0	-1.9
1977	Min-A	0	1	.000	6	4	0	0	0	21	19	17	16	5	1	15	5	1.619	6.86	58	6.21	.244	0	....	-7	0	-0.7
Total	**7**	**23**	**35**	**.397**	**134**	**86**	**10**	**5**	**1**	**591^2**	**555**	**304**	**277**	**65**	**6**	**312**	**408**	**1.465**	**4.21**	**89**	**4.35**	**.250**	**6**	**.051**	**-30**	**21**	**-3.8**

• BUTLER, Cecil — Cecil Dean "Slewfoot" Butler b: 10/23/1937, Dallas, GA BR/TR, 6'4", 195 lbs. Deb: 4/23/1962

YEAR	TM-L	W	L	PCT	G	GS	CG	SH	SV	IP	H	R	ER	HR	HB	BB	SO	RAT	ERA	ERA+	CERA	OAV	BH	AVG	PR+	WS	TPW
1962	Mil-N	2	0	1.000	9	2	1	0	0	31	26	13	9	4	0	9	22	1.129	2.61	145	2.82	.217	0	.000	4	3	0.3
1964	Mil-N	0	0	....	2	0	0	0	0	4^1	7	4	4	2	0	0	2	1.615	8.31	42	9.16	.368	0	....	-2	0	-0.2
Total	**2**	**2**	**0**	**1.000**	**11**	**2**	**1**	**0**	**0**	**35^1**	**33**	**17**	**13**	**6**	**0**	**9**	**24**	**1.189**	**3.31**	**112**	**3.60**	**.237**	**0**	**.000**	**2**	**3**	**0.1**

• BUTLER, Charlie — Charles Thomas Butler b: 5/12/1906, Green Cove Springs, FL d: 5/10/1964, Brunswick, GA BR/TL, 6'1.5", 210 lbs. Deb: 5/1/1933

YEAR	TM-L	W	L	PCT	G	GS	CG	SH	SV	IP	H	R	ER	HR	HB	BB	SO	RAT	ERA	ERA+	CERA	OAV	BH	AVG	PR+	WS	TPW
1933	Phi-N	0	0	....	1	0	0	0	0	1	1	1	1	0	0	2	0	3.000	9.00	42	8.74	.250	0	....	-1	0	-0.1

• BUTLER, Ike — Isaac Burr Butler b: 8/22/1873, Langston, MI d: 3/17/1948, Oakland, CA TR, 6', 175 lbs. Deb: 8/5/1902

YEAR	TM-L	W	L	PCT	G	GS	CG	SH	SV	IP	H	R	ER	HR	HB	BB	SO	RAT	ERA	ERA+	CERA	OAV	BH	AVG	PR+	WS	TPW
1902	Bal-A	1	10	.091	16	14	12	0	0	116^1	168	103	69	1	2	45	13	1.831	5.34	71	5.87	.338	6	.113	-14	0	-1.8

• BUTTERS, Tom — Thomas Arden Butters b: 4/8/1938, Delaware, OH BR/TR, 6'2", 195 lbs. Deb: 9/8/1962

YEAR	TM-L	W	L	PCT	G	GS	CG	SH	SV	IP	H	R	ER	HR	HB	BB	SO	RAT	ERA	ERA+	CERA	OAV	BH	AVG	PR+	WS	TPW
1962	Pit-N	0	0	....	4	0	0	0	0	6	5	1	1	0	1	6	10	1.833	1.50	262	4.99	.238	0	....	2	1	0.2
1963	Pit-N	0	0	....	6	1	0	0	0	16^1	15	8	8	1	2	8	11	1.408	4.41	75	4.18	.259	1	.333	-2	0	-0.2
1964	Pit-N	2	2	.500	28	4	0	0	0	64^1	52	21	17	3	0	37	58	1.383	2.38	147	3.27	.221	2	.182	9	5	0.9
1965	Pit-N	0	1	.000	5	0	0	0	0	9	9	8	7	2	0	5	6	1.556	7.00	50	5.50	.250	0	.000	-4	0	-0.4
Total	**4**	**2**	**3**	**.400**	**43**	**5**	**0**	**0**	**0**	**95^2**	**81**	**38**	**33**	**6**	**3**	**56**	**85**	**1.432**	**3.10**	**112**	**3.75**	**.231**	**3**	**.200**	**5**	**6**	**0.5**

• BUTTERY, Frank — Frank Buttery b: 5/13/1851, Silvermine, CT d: 12/16/1902, Silvermine, CT Deb: 4/26/1872 ♦

YEAR	TM-L	W	L	PCT	G	GS	CG	SH	SV	IP	H	R	ER	HR	HB	BB	SO	RAT	ERA	ERA+	CERA	OAV	BH	AVG	PR+	WS	TPW
1872	Man-n	3	2	.600	8	5	5	0	0	59	93	78	27	0	....	2	0	1.610	4.12	86	....	.315	24	.258	2	....	-0.1

• BUXTON, Ralph — Ralph Stanley "Buck" Buxton b: 6/7/1911, Weyburn, Canada d: 1/6/1988, San Leandro, CA BR/TR, 5'11.5", 163 lbs. Deb: 9/11/1938

YEAR	TM-L	W	L	PCT	G	GS	CG	SH	SV	IP	H	R	ER	HR	HB	BB	SO	RAT	ERA	ERA+	CERA	OAV	BH	AVG	PR+	WS	TPW
1938	Phi-A	0	1	.000	5	0	0	0	0	9^1	12	7	5	1	0	5	9	1.821	4.82	100	6.39	.324	0	.000	0	0	0.0
1949	NY-A	0	1	.000	14	0	0	0	2	26^2	22	13	12	3	0	16	14	1.425	4.05	100	3.92	.229	0	.000	-1	1	-0.1
Total	**2**	**0**	**2**	**.000**	**19**	**0**	**0**	**0**	**2**	**36**	**34**	**20**	**17**	**4**	**0**	**21**	**23**	**1.528**	**4.25**	**100**	**4.56**	**.256**	**0**	**.000**	**-0**	**1**	**-0.1**

• BUZHARDT, John — John William Buzhardt b: 8/17/1936, Prosperity, SC BR/TR, 6'2.5", 198 lbs. Deb: 9/10/1958

YEAR	TM-L	W	L	PCT	G	GS	CG	SH	SV	IP	H	R	ER	HR	HB	BB	SO	RAT	ERA	ERA+	CERA	OAV	BH	AVG	PR+	WS	TPW
1958	Chi-N	3	0	1.000	6	2	1	0	0	24^1	16	5	5	2	0	7	9	.945	1.85	212	1.78	.184	1	.125	6	3	0.5
1959	Chi-N	4	5	.444	31	10	1	1	0	101^1	107	64	56	12	1	29	33	1.342	4.97	79	3.97	.271	2	.069	-12	2	-1.4
1960	Phi-N	5	16	.238	30	29	5	0	0	200^1	198	101	86	14	2	68	73	1.328	3.86	100	3.52	.259	10	.161	-0	9	-0.1
1961	Phi-N	6	18	.250	41	27	6	1	0	202^1	200	107	101	28	6	65	92	1.310	4.49	91	4.11	.263	6	.105	-13	7	-1.5
1962	Chi-A	8	12	.400	28	25	8	2	0	152^1	156	75	71	16	4	59	64	1.411	4.19	93	4.25	.264	6	.118	-4	6	-0.6
1963	Chi-A	9	4	.692	19	18	6	3	0	126^1	100	35	34	8	5	31	59	1.037	2.42	145	2.30	.216	4	.083	14	11	1.2
1964	Chi-A	10	8	.556	31	25	8	3	0	160	150	60	53	13	4	35	97	1.156	2.98	116	3.01	.250	11	.204	4	10	0.6

YEAR	TM-L	W	L	PCT	G	GS	CG	SH	SV	IP	H	R	ER	HR	HB	BB	SO	RAT	ERA	ERA+	CERA	OAV	BH	AVG	PR+	WS	TPW
1965	Chi-A	13	8	.619	32	30	4	1	1	188^2	167	69	63	12	7	56	108	1.182	3.01	106	2.99	.242	7	.125	2	11	0.2
1966	Chi-A	6	11	.353	33	22	5	4	1	150^1	144	74	64	13	4	30	66	1.157	3.83	83	3.00	.248	5	.116	-12	3	-1.4
1967	Chi-A	3	9	.250	28	7	0	0	0	88^2	100	44	39	11	6	37	33	1.545	3.96	78	5.37	.294	4	.200	-9	1	-0.9
	Bal-A	0	1	.000	7	1	0	0	0	11^2	14	6	6	1	0	5	7	1.629	4.63	68	5.06	.298	0	.000	-2	0	-0.2
	Yr.	3	10	.231	35	8	0	0	0	100^1	114	50	45	12	6	42	40	1.555	4.04	77	5.34	.295	4	.190	-11	1	-1.2
	Hou-N	0	0	....	1	0	0	0	0	0^2	0	0	0	0	0	0	0	.000	0.00	....	0.00	.000	0	....	0	0	0.0
1968	Hou-N	4	4	.500	39	4	0	0	5	83^2	73	35	29	0	4	35	37	1.291	3.12	95	2.69	.239	4	.250	0	6	0.1
Total	**11**	**71**	**96**	**.425**	**326**	**200**	**44**	**15**	**7**	**1490^2**	**1425**	**675**	**607**	**130**	**43**	**457**	**678**	**1.263**	**3.66**	**97**	**3.47**	**.253**	**60**	**.135**	**-26**	**69**	**-3.4**
• BYERLY, Bud		Eldred William Byerly b: 10/26/1920, Webster Groves, MO BR/TR, 6'2.5", 185 lbs. Deb: 9/26/1943																									
1943	StL-N	1	0	1.000	2	2	0	0	0	13	14	6	5	0	0	5	6	1.462	3.46	97	3.67	.280	0	.000	-0	1	-0.1
1944*	StL-N	2	2	.500	9	4	2	0	0	42^1	37	18	16	2	0	20	13	1.346	3.40	104	3.11	.228	2	.167	-0	2	-0.1
1945	StL-N	4	5	.444	33	8	2	0	0	95	111	61	50	3	1	41	39	1.600	4.74	79	4.53	.288	5	.217	-13	2	-1.2
1950	Cin-N	0	1	.000	4	1	0	0	0	14^2	12	4	4	1	0	4	5	1.091	2.45	173	2.39	.218	0	.000	3	1	0.3
1951	Cin-N	2	1	.667	40	0	0	0	0	66	69	33	24	6	2	25	28	1.424	3.27	125	4.18	.267	0	.000	6	4	0.6
1952	Cin-N	0	1	.000	12	2	0	0	1	24^2	29	15	14	0	0	7	14	1.459	5.11	74	3.99	.309	1	.200	-4	0	-0.4
1956	Was-A	2	4	.333	25	0	0	0	4	51^2	45	19	17	6	2	14	19	1.142	2.96	146	3.15	.243	1	.091	9	6	0.8
1957	Was-A	6	6	.500	47	0	0	0	6	95	94	38	33	6	1	22	39	1.221	3.13	125	3.05	.264	1	.067	10	8	1.0
1958	Was-A	2	0	1.000	17	0	0	0	1	24	34	20	18	4	1	11	13	1.875	6.75	57	7.51	.347	0	.000	-7	0	-0.8
	Bos-A	1	2	.333	18	0	0	0	0	30^1	31	12	6	1	1	7	16	1.253	1.78	225	3.04	.272	0	.000	8	3	0.8
	Yr.	3	2	.600	35	0	0	0	1	54^1	65	32	24	5	2	18	29	1.528	3.98	97	5.02	.307	0	.000	1	3	0.0
1959	SF-N	1	0	1.000	11	0	0	0	0	13	11	2	2	2	0	5	4	1.231	1.38	275	3.58	.234	0	....	4	2	0.4
1960	SF-N	1	0	1.000	19	0	0	0	2	22	32	14	13	3	1	6	13	1.727	5.32	65	6.51	.340	0	.000	-4	0	-0.5
Total	**11**	**22**	**22**	**.500**	**237**	**17**	**4**	**0**	**14**	**491^2**	**519**	**242**	**202**	**34**	**9**	**167**	**209**	**1.395**	**3.70**	**103**	**3.93**	**.273**	**10**	**.118**	**12**	**29**	**0.8**
• BYNUM, Mike		Michael Allen Bynum b: 3/20/1978, Tampa, FL BL/TL, 6'4", 200 lbs. Deb: 8/17/2002																									
2002	SD-N	1	0	1.000	14	3	0	0	0	27^1	33	16	16	3	3	15	17	1.756	5.27	71	6.31	.308	0	.000	-4	0	-0.5
2003	SD-N	1	4	.200	13	5	0	0	0	36	44	35	35	14	1	15	35	1.639	8.75	45	7.83	.297	3	.300	-19	0	-1.8
Total	**2**	**2**	**4**	**.333**	**27**	**8**	**0**	**0**	**0**	**63^1**	**77**	**51**	**51**	**17**	**4**	**30**	**52**	**1.689**	**7.25**	**54**	**7.17**	**.302**	**3**	**.167**	**-23**	**0**	**-2.3**
• BYRD, Harry		Harry Gladwin Byrd b: 2/3/1925, Darlington, SC d: 5/14/1985, Darlington, SC BR/TR, 6'1", 188 lbs. Deb: 4/21/1950																									
1950	Phi-A	0	0	....	6	0	0	0	0	10^2	25	20	20	3	2	9	2	3.188	16.88	27	18.36	.481	0	.000	-15	0	-1.4
1952	Phi-A	15	15	.500	37	28	15	3	2	228^1	244	100	84	12	7	98	116	1.498	3.31	119	4.24	.274	10	.133	20	18	1.8
1953	Phi-A	11	20	.355	40	**37**	11	2	0	236^2	279	155	145	23	14	115	122	**1.665**	5.51	78	5.55	.294	18	.222	-32	5	-3.2
1954	NY-A	9	7	.563	25	21	5	1	0	132^1	131	56	44	10	7	43	52	1.315	2.99	115	3.66	.258	9	.196	3	8	0.4
1955	Bal-A	3	2	.600	14	8	1	1	1	65^1	64	33	33	7	7	28	25	1.408	4.55	84	4.55	.261	3	.158	-4	2	-0.5
	Chi-A	4	6	.400	25	12	1	1	1	91	85	49	47	10	2	30	44	1.264	4.65	85	3.55	.251	2	.067	-8	3	-1.1
	Yr.	7	8	.467	39	20	2	2	2	156^1	149	82	80	17	9	58	69	1.324	4.61	84	3.97	.255	5	.102	-13	5	-1.6
1956	Chi-A	0	1	.000	3	1	0	0	0	4^1	9	6	5	0	0	4	0	3.000	10.38	40	12.21	.474	0	.000	-3	0	-0.3
1957	Det-A	4	3	.571	37	1	0	0	5	59	53	23	22	6	2	28	20	1.373	3.36	115	3.88	.249	0	.000	3	6	0.2
Total	**7**	**46**	**54**	**.460**	**187**	**108**	**33**	**8**	**9**	**827^2**	**890**	**442**	**400**	**71**	**41**	**355**	**381**	**1.504**	**4.35**	**92**	**4.67**	**.277**	**42**	**.160**	**-36**	**42**	**-4.2**
• BYRD, Jeff		Jeffrey Alan Byrd b: 11/11/1956, La Mesa, CA BR/TR, 6'3", 195 lbs. Deb: 6/20/1977																									
1977	Tor-A	2	13	.133	17	17	1	0	0	87^1	98	68	60	5	0	68	40	1.901	6.18	68	5.97	.286	0	....	-17	0	-1.7
• BYRD, Paul		Paul Gregory Byrd b: 12/3/1970, Louisville, KY BR/TR, 6'1", 185 lbs. Deb: 7/28/1995																									
1995	NY-N	2	0	1.000	17	0	0	0	0	22	18	6	5	1	1	7	26	1.136	2.05	198	2.53	.222	1	1.000	5	3	0.5
1996	NY-N	1	2	.333	38	0	0	0	0	46^2	48	22	22	7	0	21	31	1.479	4.24	95	4.67	.265	0	.000	-2	2	-0.2
1997	Atl-N	4	4	.500	31	4	0	0	0	53	47	34	31	6	4	28	37	1.415	5.26	80	4.15	.235	1	.143	-7	1	-0.7
1998	Atl-N	0	0	....	1	0	0	0	0	2	4	3	3	0	0	1	1	2.500	13.50	31	9.72	.400	0	....	-2	0	-0.2
	Phi-N	5	2	.714	8	8	2	1	0	55	41	16	14	6	0	17	38	1.055	2.29	189	2.41	.203	3	.167	12	7	1.3
	Yr.	5	2	.714	9	8	2	1	0	57	45	19	17	6	0	18	39	1.105	2.68	160	2.66	.212	3	.167	10	7	1.0
1999	Phi-N★	15	11	.577	32	32	1	0	0	199^2	205	119	102	34	17	70	106	1.377	4.60	103	4.87	.265	7	.127	-0	10	-0.1
2000	Phi-N	2	9	.182	17	15	0	0	0	83	89	67	60	17	3	35	53	1.494	6.51	72	5.42	.271	3	.150	-17	0	-1.6
2001	Phi-N	0	1	.000	3	1	0	0	0	10	10	9	9	1	1	4	3	1.400	8.10	52	4.36	.278	1	.500	-4	0	-0.4
	KC-A	6	6	.500	16	15	1	0	0	93^1	110	45	42	11	1	22	49	1.414	4.05	121	4.65	.297	0	.000	6	6	0.6
2002	KC-A	17	11	.607	33	33	**7**	2	0	228^1	224	111	99	36	7	38	129	1.147	3.90	129	3.55	.256	0	.000	29	18	2.8
Total	**8**	**52**	**46**	**.531**	**196**	**108**	**11**	**3**	**0**	**793**	**796**	**432**	**387**	**119**	**34**	**243**	**473**	**1.310**	**4.39**	**106**	**4.23**	**.260**	**16**	**.144**	**21**	**47**	**2.0**
• BYRDAK, Tim		Timothy Christopher Byrdak b: 10/31/1973, Oak Lawn, IL BL/TL, 5'11", 190 lbs. Deb: 8/7/1998																									
1998	KC-A	0	0	....	3	0	0	0	0	1^2	5	1	1	1	0	0	1	3.000	5.40	89	23.52	.556	0	....	-0	0	0.0
1999	KC-A	0	3	.000	33	0	0	0	1	24^2	32	24	21	5	1	20	17	2.108	7.66	65	8.29	.308	1	.500	-8	0	-0.7
2000	KC-A	0	1	.000	12	0	0	0	0	6^1	11	8	8	3	0	4	8	2.368	11.37	45	13.14	.367	0	....	-5	0	-0.4
Total	**3**	**0**	**4**	**.000**	**48**	**0**	**0**	**0**	**1**	**32^2**	**48**	**33**	**30**	**9**	**1**	**24**	**26**	**2.204**	**8.27**	**61**	**10.01**	**.336**	**1**	**.500**	**-12**	**0**	**-1.1**
• BYRNE, Jerry		Gerald Wilfred Byrne b: 2/2/1907, Parnell, MI d: 8/11/1955, Lansing, MI BR/TR, 6', 170 lbs. Deb: 8/31/1929																									
1929	Chi-A	0	1	.000	3	1	0	0	0	7^1	11	6	6	0	0	6	1	2.318	7.36	58	7.75	.379	0	.000	-3	0	-0.3
• BYRNE, Tommy		Thomas Joseph Byrne b: 12/31/1919, Baltimore, MD BL/TL, 6'1", 182 lbs. Deb: 4/27/1943																									
1943	NY-A	2	1	.667	11	2	0	0	0	31^2	28	26	23	1	3	35	22	1.989	6.54	49	5.63	.248	1	.091	-12	0	-1.3
1946	NY-A	0	1	.000	4	1	0	0	0	9^1	7	8	6	1	1	8	5	1.607	5.79	60	4.42	.194	2	.222	-3	0	-0.2
1947	NY-A	0	0	....	4	1	0	0	0	4^1	5	2	2	0	0	6	2	2.538	4.15	85	7.82	.294	0	....	-0	0	0.0
1948	NY-A	8	5	.615	31	11	5	1	2	133^2	79	55	49	8	9	101	93	1.347	3.30	124	2.96	.172	15	.326	10	12	1.5
1949*	NY-A	15	7	.682	32	30	12	3	0	196	125	84	81	11	13	179	129	1.551	3.72	109	3.70	**.183**	16	.193	3	13	0.3
1950	NY-A★	15	9	.625	31	31	10	2	0	203^1	188	115	107	23	17	160	118	**1.711**	4.74	91	5.39	.245	22	.272	-13	12	-0.6
1951	NY-A	2	1	.667	9	3	0	0	0	21	16	17	16	0	3	36	14	2.476	6.86	56	6.90	.213	2	.222	-7	0	-0.7
	StL-A	4	10	.286	19	17	7	2	0	122^2	104	56	52	5	12	114	57	1.777	3.82	115	4.94	.235	16	.281	11	9	1.4
	Yr.	6	11	.353	28	20	7	2	0	143^2	120	73	68	5	15	150	71	1.879	4.26	100	5.23	.232	18	.273	3	9	0.7
1952	StL-A	7	14	.333	29	24	14	0	0	196	182	117	102	16	10	112	91	1.500	4.68	83	4.23	.247	21	.250	-18	6	-1.3
1953	Chi-A	2	0	1.000	6	6	0	0	0	16	18	18	18	0	0	26	4	2.750	10.13	40	8.47	.295	3	.167	-11	0	-1.0
	Was-A	0	5	.000	6	5	2	0	0	33^2	35	17	16	3	1	22	22	1.693	4.28	91	5.18	.276	1	.059	-2	0	-0.3
	Yr.	2	5	.286	12	11	2	0	0	49^2	53	35	34	3	1	48	26	2.034	6.16	64	6.24	.282	4	.114	-13	0	-1.3
1954	NY-A	3	2	.600	5	5	4	1	0	40	36	13	12	1	0	19	24	1.375	2.70	127	3.22	.240	7	.368	2	5	0.6
1955*	NY-A	16	5	.762	27	22	9	3	2	160	137	69	56	12	7	87	76	1.400	3.15	119	3.84	.237	16	.205	4	12	0.8
1956*	NY-A	7	3	.700	37	8	1	0	6	109^2	108	50	41	9	2	72	52	1.641	3.36	115	4.93	.262	14	.269	4	9	0.9
1957*	NY-A	4	6	.400	30	4	1	0	2	84^2	70	41	41	8	7	60	57	1.535	4.36	82	4.54	.227	7	.189	-8	3	-0.5
Total	**13**	**85**	**69**	**.552**	**281**	**170**	**65**	**12**	**12**	**1362**	**1138**	**688**	**622**	**98**	**85**	**1037**	**766**	**1.597**	**4.11**	**96**	**4.43**	**.229**	**143**	**.238**	**-41**	**81**	**-0.4**
• BYSTROM, Marty		Martin Eugene Bystrom b: 7/26/1958, Coral Gables, FL BR/TR, 6'5", 200 lbs. Deb: 9/7/1980																									
1980*	Phi-N	5	0	1.000	6	5	1	1	0	36	26	6	6	1	0	9	21	.972	1.50	253	1.69	.195	1	.071	9	5	0.9
1981	Phi-N	4	3	.571	9	9	1	0	0	53^2	55	21	20	3	1	16	24	1.323	3.35	108	3.57	.264	2	.118	1	3	0.0
1982	Phi-N	5	6	.455	19	16	1	0	0	89	93	53	48	2	5	35	50	1.438	4.85	76	3.92	.277	3	.125	-12	1	-1.3
1983*	Phi-N	6	9	.400	24	23	1	1	0	119^1	136	75	61	6	7	44	87	1.508	4.60	78	4.51	.285	9	.237	-12	2	-1.0
1984	Phi-N	4	4	.500	11	11	0	0	0	56^2	66	36	32	5	0	22	36	1.553	5.08	71	4.73	.283	3	.158	-8	1	-0.9
	NY-A	2	2	.500	7	7	0	0	0	39^1	34	16	13	3	1	13	24	1.195	2.97	128	2.94	.228	0	....	4	3	0.4
1985	NY-A	3	2	.600	8	8	0	0	0	41	44	29	26	8	1	19	16	1.537	5.71	70	5.68	.280	0	....	-8	0	-0.8
Total	**6**	**29**	**26**	**.527**	**84**	**79**	**4**	**2**	**0**	**435**	**454**	**236**	**206**	**28**	**15**	**158**	**258**	**1.407**	**4.26**	**86**	**4.04**	**.268**	**18**	**.161**	**-26**	**15**	**-2.7**
• CABRERA, Jose		Jose Alberto Cabrera b: 3/24/1972, La Delgada, Dominican Republic BR/TR, 6', 200 lbs. Deb: 7/15/1997																									
1997	Hou-N	0	0	....	12	0	0	0	0	15^1	6	2	2	1	0	6	18	.783	1.17	341	1.16	.125	0	.000	5	2	0.4

YEAR	TM-L	W	L	PCT	G	GS	CG	SH	SV	IP	H	R	ER	HR	HB	BB	SO	RAT	ERA	ERA+	CERA	OAV	BH	AVG	PR+	WS	TPW
1998	Hou-N	0	0	....	3	0	0	0	0	4^1	7	4	4	0	0	1	1	1.846	8.31	49	6.28	.389	0	....	-2	0	-0.2
1999*	Hou-N	4	0	1.000	26	0	0	0	0	29^1	21	7	7	3	0	9	28	1.023	2.15	205	2.12	.196	0	....	7	5	0.7
2000	Hou-N	2	3	.400	52	0	0	0	2	59^1	74	40	39	10	3	17	41	1.534	5.92	82	5.72	.308	0	.000	-6	2	-0.6
2001	Atl-N	7	4	.636	55	0	0	0	2	59^1	52	24	19	5	2	25	43	1.298	2.88	153	3.38	.239	0	.000	10	7	0.9
2002	Mil-N	6	10	.375	50	11	0	0	0	103^1	131	84	78	23	9	36	61	1.616	6.79	60	6.64	.314	2	.105	-31	0	-3.2
Total	6	19	17	.528	198	11	0	0	4	271	291	161	149	42	14	94	192	1.421	4.95	87	4.92	.278	2	.087	-17	16	-1.9

• CADARET, Greg Gregory James Cadaret b: 2/27/1962, Detroit, MI BL/TL, 6'3", 214 lbs. Deb: 7/5/1987

YEAR	TM-L	W	L	PCT	G	GS	CG	SH	SV	IP	H	R	ER	HR	HB	BB	SO	RAT	ERA	ERA+	CERA	OAV	BH	AVG	PR+	WS	TPW
1987	Oak-A	6	2	.750	29	0	0	0	0	39^2	37	22	20	6	1	24	30	1.538	4.54	91	4.99	.252	0	....	-1	2	-0.1
1988*	Oak-A	5	2	.714	58	0	0	0	3	71^2	60	26	23	2	1	36	64	1.340	2.89	131	3.05	.226	0	....	6	7	0.6
1989	Oak-A	0	0	....	26	0	0	0	0	27^2	21	9	7	0	0	19	14	1.446	2.28	162	2.98	.214	0	....	4	2	0.4
	NY-A	5	5	.500	20	13	3	1	0	92^1	109	53	47	7	2	38	66	1.592	4.58	84	5.10	.298	0	....	-8	3	-0.8
	Yr.	5	5	.500	46	13	3	1	0	120	130	62	54	7	2	57	80	1.558	4.05	95	4.62	.280	0	....	-4	5	-0.4
1990	NY-A	5	4	.556	54	6	0	0	3	121^1	120	62	56	8	1	64	80	1.516	4.15	96	4.33	.268	0	....	-3	7	-0.3
1991	NY-A	8	6	.571	68	5	0	0	3	121^2	110	52	49	8	2	59	105	1.389	3.62	114	3.68	.246	0	....	7	9	0.7
1992	NY-A	4	8	.333	46	11	1	1	1	103^2	104	53	49	12	2	74	73	1.717	4.25	92	5.55	.267	0	....	-4	4	-0.4
1993	Cin-N	2	1	.667	34	0	0	0	1	32^2	40	19	18	3	1	23	23	1.929	4.96	81	6.43	.305	0	.000	-3	1	-0.3
	KC-A	1	1	.500	13	0	0	0	0	15^1	14	5	5	0	1	7	2	1.370	2.93	156	3.63	.264	0	....	3	2	0.3
1994	Tor-A	0	1	.000	21	0	0	0	0	20	24	15	13	4	0	17	15	2.050	5.85	82	7.74	.289	0	....	-2	0	-0.2
	Det-A	1	0	1.000	17	0	0	0	2	20	17	9	8	0	0	16	14	1.650	3.60	134	3.73	.227	0	....	3	2	0.3
	Yr.	1	1	.500	38	0	0	0	2	40	41	24	21	4	0	33	29	1.850	4.73	102	5.73	.259	0	....	1	2	0.1
1997	Ana-A	0	0	....	15	0	0	0	0	13^2	11	5	5	1	2	8	11	1.390	3.29	140	3.79	.220	0	....	2	1	0.2
1998	Ana-A	1	2	.333	39	0	0	0	1	37	38	17	17	6	3	15	37	1.432	4.14	113	4.92	.257	0	....	3	3	0.2
	Tex-A	0	0	....	11	0	0	0	0	7^2	11	4	4	1	0	3	5	1.826	4.70	103	6.93	.355	0	....	0	0	0.0
	Yr.	1	2	.333	50	0	0	0	1	44^2	49	21	21	7	3	18	42	1.500	4.23	111	5.27	.274	0	....	3	3	0.3
Total	10	38	32	.543	451	35	4	2	14	724^1	716	351	321	58	16	403	539	1.545	3.99	102	4.56	.262	0	.000	7	43	0.6

• CADORE, Leon Leon Joseph "Caddy" Cadore b: 11/20/1890, Chicago, IL d: 3/16/1958, Spokane, WA BR/TR, 6'1", 190 lbs. Deb: 4/28/1915

YEAR	TM-L	W	L	PCT	G	GS	CG	SH	SV	IP	H	R	ER	HR	HB	BB	SO	RAT	ERA	ERA+	CERA	OAV	BH	AVG	PR+	WS	TPW
1915	Bro-N	0	2	.000	7	2	1	0	0	21	28	15	13	0	2	8	12	1.714	5.57	50	5.68	.337	0	.000	-7	0	-0.8
1916	Bro-N	0	0	....	1	0	0	0	0	6	10	4	3	0	0	0	2	1.667	4.50	59	5.65	.370	0	.000	-1	0	-0.2
1917	Bro-N	13	13	.500	37	30	21	1	3	264	231	86	72	3	7	63	115	1.114	2.45	114	2.31	.241	24	.261	7	21	1.4
1918	Bro-N	1	0	1.000	2	2	1	1	0	17	6	1	1	0	1	2	5	.471	0.53	526	0.51	.115	0	.000	4	3	0.4
1919	Bro-N	14	12	.538	35	27	16	3	0	250^2	228	80	66	5	6	39	94	1.065	2.37	125	2.28	.245	14	.161	22	18	2.1
1920*	Bro-N	15	14	.517	35	30	16	4	0	254^1	256	91	74	4	3	56	79	1.227	2.62	122	2.92	.270	20	.220	20	21	2.4
1921	Bro-N	13	14	.481	35	30	12	1	0	211^2	243	112	98	17	6	46	79	1.365	4.17	93	4.11	.292	14	.187	-6	12	-0.7
1922	Bro-N	8	15	.348	29	21	13	0	0	190^1	224	115	92	13	1	57	49	1.476	4.35	93	4.36	.299	19	.268	-5	8	-0.1
1923	Bro-N	4	1	.800	8	4	3	0	0	36	39	14	13	2	0	13	5	1.444	3.25	119	4.11	.291	1	.077	3	3	0.1
	Chi-A	0	1	.000	1	1	0	0	0	2^1	6	7	6	0	0	2	3	3.429	23.14	17	15.18	.500	0	....	-5	0	-0.5
1924	NY-N	0	0	....	2	0	0	0	0	4	2	0	0	0	0	3	2	1.250	0.00	....	2.01	.154	0	....	2	1	0.2
Total	10	68	72	.486	192	147	83	10	3	1257^1	1273	525	438	44	26	289	445	1.242	3.14	107	3.16	.269	92	.208	34	87	4.4

• CADY, Charlie Charles B. Cady b: 12/1865, Chicago, IL d: 6/7/1909, Kankakee, IL, 5'11", 180 lbs. Deb: 9/5/1883 ♦

YEAR	TM-L	W	L	PCT	G	GS	CG	SH	SV	IP	H	R	ER	HR	HB	BB	SO	RAT	ERA	ERA+	CERA	OAV	BH	AVG	PR+	WS	TPW
1883	Cle-N	0	1	.000	1	1	1	0	0	8	13	13	7	0	....	4	5	2.125	7.88	40	....	.346	0	.000	-5	0	-0.6
1884	CP-U	3	1	.750	4	4	4	0	0	35	37	25	11	0	....	13	15	1.429	2.83	102	....	.254	2	.100	1	2	-0.1
Total	2	3	2	.600	5	5	5	0	0	43	50	38	18	0	....	17	20	1.558	3.77	79	....	.273	2	.059	-4	2	-0.6

• CAHILL, John John Patrick Parnell "Patsy" Cahill b: 4/30/1865, San Francisco, CA d: 10/31/1901, Pleasanton, CA BR/TR, 5'7.5", 168 lbs. Deb: 5/31/1884 ♦

YEAR	TM-L	W	L	PCT	G	GS	CG	SH	SV	IP	H	R	ER	HR	HB	BB	SO	RAT	ERA	ERA+	CERA	OAV	BH	AVG	PR+	WS	TPW
1884	Col-a	1	0	1.000	2	1	1	0	0	16	15	15	9	0	3	4	1	1.188	5.06	60	....	.235	46	.219	-4	3	-0.9
1886	StL-N	1	0	1.000	2	0	0	0	0	12	11	5	4	0	....	3	2	1.167	3.00	107	....	.235	92	.199	-0	3	-2.5
1887	Ind-N	0	2	.000	6	1	1	0	0	22	59	38	35	2	2	19	5	2.682	14.32	29	....	.476	63	.232	-25	1	-4.4
Total	3	2	2	.500	10	2	2	0	0	50	85	58	48	2	5	26	8	1.840	8.64	44	....	.362	201	.213	-29	7	-7.8

• CAIN, Bob Robert Max "Sugar" Cain b: 10/16/1924, Longford, KS d: 4/8/1997, Cleveland, OH BL/TL, 6', 165 lbs. Deb: 9/18/1949

YEAR	TM-L	W	L	PCT	G	GS	CG	SH	SV	IP	H	R	ER	HR	HB	BB	SO	RAT	ERA	ERA+	CERA	OAV	BH	AVG	PR+	WS	TPW
1949	Chi-A	0	0	....	6	0	0	0	1	11	7	3	3	0	0	5	5	1.091	2.45	170	1.71	.179	0	.000	2	1	0.2
1950	Chi-A	9	12	.429	34	23	11	1	2	171^2	153	80	75	12	5	109	77	1.526	3.93	114	4.17	.244	12	.197	7	13	0.6
1951	Chi-A	1	2	.333	4	4	1	0	0	26^1	25	14	11	3	3	13	3	1.443	3.76	107	4.49	.248	3	.333	0	1	0.1
	Det-A	11	10	.524	35	22	6	1	2	149^1	135	88	78	12	11	82	58	1.453	4.70	89	4.09	.239	13	.245	-7	8	-0.5
	Yr.	12	12	.500	39	26	7	1	2	175^2	160	102	89	15	14	95	61	1.452	4.56	91	4.15	.241	16	.258	-7	9	-0.4
1952	StL-A	12	10	.545	29	27	8	1	2	170	169	79	78	15	2	62	70	1.359	4.13	95	3.83	.264	8	.138	-5	9	-0.7
1953	StL-A	4	10	.286	32	13	1	0	1	99^2	129	74	69	8	1	45	36	1.746	6.23	67	5.74	.310	6	.200	-22	0	-2.2
Total	5	37	44	.457	140	89	27	3	8	628	618	338	314	50	22	316	249	1.487	4.50	93	4.28	.259	42	.196	-25	32	-2.5

• CAIN, Les Leslie Cain b: 1/13/1948, San Luis Obispo, CA BL/TL, 6'1", 200 lbs. Deb: 4/28/1968

YEAR	TM-L	W	L	PCT	G	GS	CG	SH	SV	IP	H	R	ER	HR	HB	BB	SO	RAT	ERA	ERA+	CERA	OAV	BH	AVG	PR+	WS	TPW
1968	Det-A	1	0	1.000	8	4	0	0	0	24	25	9	8	1	0	20	13	1.875	3.00	100	5.51	.269	1	.143	-0	1	0.0
1970	Det-A	12	7	.632	29	29	5	0	0	180^2	167	92	77	15	7	98	156	1.467	3.84	97	4.25	.247	11	.162	3	11	0.3
1971	Det-A	10	9	.526	26	26	3	1	0	144^2	121	77	70	14	6	91	118	1.465	4.35	82	4.21	.228	8	.145	-12	4	-1.3
1972	Det-A	0	3	.000	5	5	0	0	0	23^2	18	12	10	2	0	16	16	1.437	3.80	83	3.70	.209	1	.143	-2	0	-0.2
Total	4	23	19	.548	68	64	8	1	0	373	331	190	165	32	13	225	303	1.491	3.98	90	4.28	.239	21	.153	-11	16	-1.2

• CAIN, Sugar Merritt Patrick Cain b: 4/5/1907, Macon, GA d: 4/3/1975, Atlanta, GA BL/TR, 5'11", 190 lbs. Deb: 4/15/1932

YEAR	TM-L	W	L	PCT	G	GS	CG	SH	SV	IP	H	R	ER	HR	HB	BB	SO	RAT	ERA	ERA+	CERA	OAV	BH	AVG	PR+	WS	TPW
1932	Phi-A	3	4	.429	10	6	3	0	0	45	42	27	25	1	0	28	24	1.556	5.00	91	3.89	.256	3	.250	-3	2	-0.2
1933	Phi-A	13	12	.520	38	32	16	1	1	218	244	132	103	18	3	137	43	**1.748**	4.25	101	5.34	.280	16	.200	7	11	0.6
1934	Phi-A	9	17	.346	36	32	15	0	0	230^2	235	128	113	15	3	128	66	1.574	4.41	99	4.43	.266	13	.159	-3	12	-0.6
1935	Phi-A	0	5	.000	6	5	0	0	0	26	39	22	19	1	0	19	5	2.231	6.58	69	8.14	.382	0	.000	-5	0	-0.6
	StL-A	9	8	.529	31	24	8	0	0	167^2	197	112	98	7	4	104	68	1.795	5.26	91	5.38	.290	11	.193	-8	9	-0.9
	Yr.	9	13	.409	37	29	8	0	0	193^2	236	134	117	8	4	123	73	**1.854**	5.44	87	5.75	.302	11	.169	-13	9	-1.6
1936	StL-A	1	1	.500	4	3	1	0	0	16^1	20	13	12	0	0	9	8	1.776	6.61	81	4.82	.286	2	.286	-2	1	-0.2
	Chi-A	14	10	.583	30	26	14	1	0	195^1	228	112	103	18	5	75	42	1.551	4.75	110	4.97	.293	7	.103	8	13	0.3
	Yr.	15	11	.577	34	29	15	1	0	211^2	248	125	115	18	5	84	50	1.569	4.89	107	4.96	.292	9	.120	6	14	0.2
1937	Chi-A	4	2	.667	18	6	1	0	0	68^2	88	48	47	7	0	51	17	2.024	6.16	75	7.19	.325	4	.182	-13	2	-1.3
1938	Chi-A	0	1	.000	5	3	0	0	0	19^2	26	17	10	0	0	18	6	2.237	4.58	107	6.93	.321	0	.000	1	0	0.0
Total	7	53	60	.469	178	137	58	2	1	987^1	1119	611	530	67	15	569	279	1.710	4.83	96	5.22	.287	56	.163	-18	50	-2.9

• CAIRNCROSS, Cameron Cameron Cairncross b: 5/11/1972, Queensland, Australia BL/TL, 6', 210 lbs. Deb: 7/20/2000

YEAR	TM-L	W	L	PCT	G	GS	CG	SH	SV	IP	H	R	ER	HR	HB	BB	SO	RAT	ERA	ERA+	CERA	OAV	BH	AVG	PR+	WS	TPW
2000	Cle-A	1	0	1.000	15	0	0	0	0	9^1	11	4	4	1	0	3	8	1.500	3.86	129	4.79	.306	0	....	1	1	0.1

• CALDWELL, Charlie Charles William "Chuck" Caldwell b: 8/2/1901, Bristol, VA d: 11/1/1957, Princeton, NJ BR/TR, 5'10", 180 lbs. Deb: 7/7/1925

YEAR	TM-L	W	L	PCT	G	GS	CG	SH	SV	IP	H	R	ER	HR	HB	BB	SO	RAT	ERA	ERA+	CERA	OAV	BH	AVG	PR+	WS	TPW
1925	NY-A	0	0	....	3	0	0	0	0	2^2	7	6	5	0	0	3	1	3.750	16.88	25	16.77	.467	0	.000	-4	0	-0.4

• CALDWELL, Earl Earl Welton "Teach" Caldwell b: 4/9/1905, Sparks, TX d: 9/15/1981, Mission, TX BR/TR, 6'1", 178 lbs. Deb: 9/8/1928

YEAR	TM-L	W	L	PCT	G	GS	CG	SH	SV	IP	H	R	ER	HR	HB	BB	SO	RAT	ERA	ERA+	CERA	OAV	BH	AVG	PR+	WS	TPW
1928	Phi-N	1	4	.200	5	5	1	1	0	34^2	46	23	22	5	0	17	6	1.817	5.71	75	7.05	.348	1	.111	-5	1	-0.5
1935	StL-A	3	2	.600	6	5	2	1	0	36^2	34	16	15	2	0	17	5	1.391	3.68	130	3.50	.245	2	.182	5	4	0.4
1936	StL-A	7	16	.304	41	25	10	2	2	189	252	146	126	15	15	83	59	1.772	6.00	90	6.19	.319	11	.190	-9	8	-0.9
1937	StL-A	0	0	....	9	2	0	0	0	29	39	22	22	3	2	13	8	1.793	6.83	71	6.49	.317	2	.222	-6	1	-0.6
1945	Chi-A	6	7	.462	27	11	5	1	4	105^1	108	50	42	8	3	37	45	1.377	3.59	92	3.86	.265	8	.216	-2	6	-0.2
1946	Chi-A	13	4	.765	39	0	0	0	8	90^2	60	28	21	2	1	29	42	.982	2.08	164	1.61	.186	3	.167	13	14	1.4
1947	Chi-A	1	4	.200	40	0	0	0	8	54^1	53	23	22	4	1	30	22	1.528	3.64	100	4.31	.261	0	.000	0	4	-0.1

YEAR TM-L	W	L	PCT	G	GS	CG	SH	SV	IP	H	R	ER	HR	HB	BB	SO	RAT	ERA	ERA+	CERA	OAV	BH	AVG	PR+	WS	TPW
1948 Bos-A	1	1	.500	8	0	0	0	0	9	11	14	13	2	1	11	5	2.444	13.00	34	10.88	.333	1	.333	-9	0	-0.8
Chi-A	1	5	.167	25	1	0	0	3	39	53	25	23	3	2	22	10	1.923	5.31	80	6.92	.335	0	.000	-5	1	-0.5
Yr.	2	6	.250	33	1	0	0	3	48	64	39	36	5	3	33	15	2.021	6.75	64	7.67	.335	1	.125	-14	1	-1.3
Total 8	33	43	.434	200	49	18	5	25	587^2	656	347	306	44	25	259	202	1.557	4.69	94	4.91	.284	28	.178	-19	39	-1.8
• CALDWELL, Mike	Ralph Michael Caldwell b: 1/22/1949, Tarboro, NC BR/TL, 6', 185 lbs. Deb: 9/4/1971																									
1971 SD-N	1	0	1.000	6	0	0	0	0	6^2	4	0	0	0	0	3	5	1.050	0.00	....	1.22	.174	1	1.000	2	2	0.4
1972 SD-N	7	11	.389	42	20	4	2	2	163^2	183	92	73	10	4	49	102	1.418	4.01	82	4.00	.282	7	.140	-10	3	-1.3
1973 SD-N	5	14	.263	55	13	3	1	10	149	146	77	62	8	2	53	86	1.336	3.74	93	3.43	.260	5	.143	-3	8	-0.4
1974 SF-N	14	5	.737	31	27	6	2	0	189^1	176	80	62	17	4	63	83	1.262	2.95	129	3.47	.249	9	.143	19	15	1.7
1975 SF-N	7	13	.350	38	21	4	0	1	163^1	194	102	87	16	5	48	57	1.482	4.79	79	4.74	.296	7	.159	-18	2	-1.9
1976 SF-N	1	7	.125	50	9	0	0	2	107^1	145	74	58	5	2	20	55	1.537	4.86	75	4.85	.324	3	.158	-13	0	-1.4
1977 Cin-N	0	0	....	14	0	0	0	1	24^2	25	11	11	1	0	8	11	1.338	4.01	98	3.37	.260	2	.500	-0	2	0.1
Mil-A	5	8	.385	21	12	2	0	0	94^1	101	58	48	6	2	36	38	1.452	4.58	89	4.05	.271	0	....	-6	3	-0.6
1978 Mil-A	22	9	.710	37	34	**23**	6	1	293^1	258	90	77	14	7	54	131	1.064	2.36	159	2.39	.234	0	....	44	28	4.6
1979 Mil-A	16	6	.727	30	30	16	4	0	235	252	96	86	18	4	39	89	1.238	3.29	126	3.51	.278	0	....	24	20	2.3
1980 Mil-A	13	11	.542	34	33	11	2	1	225^1	248	112	101	29	2	56	74	1.349	4.03	96	4.37	.285	0	....	-7	10	-0.7
1981* Mil-A	11	9	.550	24	23	3	0	0	144^1	151	70	63	18	1	38	41	1.309	3.93	87	3.96	.272	0	....	-10	6	-1.0
1982* Mil-A	17	13	.567	35	34	12	3	0	258	269	119	112	30	0	58	75	1.267	3.91	97	3.78	.271	0	....	-7	12	-0.7
1983 Mil-A	12	11	.522	32	32	10	2	0	228^1	269	125	115	35	1	51	58	1.401	4.53	82	4.85	.296	0	....	-20	8	-2.0
1984 Mil-A	6	13	.316	26	19	4	1	0	126	160	76	65	11	1	21	34	1.437	4.64	83	4.61	.314	0	....	-10	3	-1.0
Total 14	137	130	.513	475	307	98	23	18	2408^2	2581	1182	1020	218	35	597	939	1.319	3.81	98	3.88	.276	34	.157	-15	122	-1.9
• CALDWELL, Ralph	Ralph Grant "Lefty" Caldwell b: 1/18/1884, Philadelphia, PA d: 8/5/1969, West Trenton, NJ BL/TL, 5'9", 155 lbs. Deb: 9/10/1904																									
1904 Phi-N	2	2	.500	6	5	5	0	0	41	40	29	19	1	2	15	30	1.341	4.17	64	3.23	.242	8	.444	-6	2	-0.3
1905 Phi-N	1	3	.250	7	2	1	0	1	34	44	25	16	1	3	7	29	1.500	4.24	69	4.92	.321	0	.000	-6	0	-0.8
Total 2	3	5	.375	13	7	6	0	1	75	84	54	35	2	5	22	59	1.413	4.20	66	4.00	.278	8	.242	-12	2	-1.1
• CALDWELL, Ray	Raymond Benjamin "Rube,Sum,Slim" Caldwell b: 4/26/1888, Croydon, PA d: 8/17/1967, Salamanca, NY BL/TR, 6'2", 190 lbs. Deb: 9/9/1910																									
1910 NY-A	1	0	1.000	6	2	1	0	1	19^1	19	8	8	1	1	9	17	1.448	3.72	71	4.06	.260	0	.000	-2	1	-0.3
1911 NY-A	14	14	.500	41	26	19	1	1	255	240	115	95	7	13	79	145	1.251	3.35	107	3.24	.260	40	.272	12	23	1.4
1912 NY-A	8	16	.333	30	26	13	3	0	183^1	196	111	91	1	6	67	95	1.435	4.47	81	3.77	.277	18	.237	-7	7	-0.6
1913 NY-A	9	8	.529	27	16	15	2	1	164^1	131	59	44	5	9	60	87	1.162	2.41	124	2.62	.219	28	.289	11	14	1.7
1914 NY-A	18	9	.667	31	23	22	5	1	213	153	53	46	5	4	51	92	.958	1.94	142	1.74	.205	22	.195	17	22	1.8
1915 NY-A	19	16	.543	36	35	31	3	0	305	266	115	98	6	5	107	130	1.223	2.89	101	2.83	.244	35	.243	-3	24	0.5
1916 NY-A	5	12	.294	21	18	14	1	0	165^2	142	62	55	6	8	65	76	1.249	2.99	97	3.13	.243	19	.204	-4	8	-0.5
1917 NY-A	13	16	.448	32	29	21	1	0	236	199	92	75	8	6	76	102	1.165	2.86	94	2.66	.234	32	.258	-5	18	0.4
1918 NY-A	9	8	.529	24	21	14	1	1	176^2	173	69	60	2	1	62	59	1.330	3.06	92	3.14	.261	44	.291	-10	13	-0.3
1919 Bos-A	7	4	.636	18	12	6	1	0	86^1	92	49	38	1	3	31	23	1.425	3.96	76	3.83	.279	13	.271	-10	3	-0.9
Cle-A	5	1	.833	6	6	4	1	0	52^2	33	13	10	1	2	19	24	.987	1.71	195	1.68	.181	8	.348	10	7	1.3
Yr.	12	5	.706	24	18	10	2	0	139	125	62	48	2	5	50	47	1.259	3.11	99	3.02	.244	21	.296	-0	10	0.3
1920* Cle-A	20	10	.667	34	33	20	1	0	237^2	286	135	102	9	4	63	80	1.468	3.86	98	4.37	.303	19	.213	-6	14	-0.6
1921 Cle-A	6	6	.500	37	12	4	1	4	147	159	91	80	7	2	49	76	1.415	4.90	87	3.81	.275	11	.208	-10	7	-0.9
Total 12	134	120	.528	343	259	184	21	9	2242	2089	972	802	59	64	738	1006	1.261	3.22	100	3.11	.253	289	.248	-9	161	3.1
• CALERO, Kiko	Enrique Nomar Calero b: 1/9/1975, Santurce, Puerto Rico BR/TR, 6'1", 180 lbs. Deb: 4/2/2003																									
2003 StL-N	1	1	.500	26	1	0	0	1	38^1	29	12	12	5	1	20	51	1.278	2.82	144	3.44	.212	1	.250	5	3	0.5
• CALHOUN, Jeff	Jeffrey Wilton Calhoun b: 4/11/1958, LaGrange, GA BL/TL, 6'2", 190 lbs. Deb: 9/2/1984																									
1984 Hou-N	0	1	.000	9	0	0	0	0	15^1	5	3	2	0	0	2	11	.457	1.17	283	0.32	.100	0	....	3	1	0.4
1985 Hou-N	2	5	.286	44	0	0	0	4	63^2	56	21	18	2	0	24	47	1.257	2.54	136	2.87	.243	0	.000	6	5	0.6
1986* Hou-N	1	0	1.000	20	0	0	0	0	26^2	28	16	11	3	0	12	14	1.500	3.71	97	4.52	.264	0	....	-0	1	0.0
1987 Phi-N	3	1	.750	42	0	0	0	1	42^2	25	13	7	1	1	26	31	1.195	1.48	287	1.90	.168	0	.000	13	6	1.2
1988 Phi-N	0	0	....	3	0	0	0	0	2^1	6	4	4	2	0	1	1	3.000	15.43	23	22.87	.462	0	....	-3	0	-0.3
Total 5	6	7	.462	118	0	0	0	5	150^2	120	57	42	8	1	65	104	1.228	2.51	144	2.94	.219	0	.000	18	13	1.8
• CALIGIURI, Fred	Frederick John Caligiuri b: 10/22/1918, West Hickory, PA BR/TR, 6', 190 lbs. Deb: 9/3/1941																									
1941 Phi-A	2	2	.500	5	5	4	0	0	43	45	22	14	2	0	14	7	1.372	2.93	143	3.41	.257	4	.200	6	3	0.7
1942 Phi-A	0	3	.000	13	2	0	0	1	36^2	45	27	26	2	2	18	20	1.718	6.38	59	5.44	.300	1	.083	-10	0	-1.0
Total 2	2	5	.286	18	7	4	0	1	79^2	90	49	40	4	2	32	27	1.531	4.52	87	4.35	.277	5	.156	-4	3	-0.4
• CALIHAN, Will	William T. Calihan b: 1869, Oswego, NY d: 12/20/1917, Rochester, NY, 5'8", 150 lbs. Deb: 4/17/1890																									
1890 Roc-a	18	15	.545	37	36	31	0	0	296^1	276	170	108	4	16	125	127	1.353	3.28	108	....	.239	23	.145	7	17	0.0
1891 Phi-a	6	6	.500	13	11	11	0	0	112	151	103	80	7	12	47	28	1.768	6.43	59	....	.312	11	.196	-32	2	-2.9
Total 2	24	21	.533	50	47	42	0	0	408^1	427	273	188	11	28	172	155	1.467	4.14	88	....	.261	34	.158	-25	19	-2.8
• CALLAHAN, Ben	Benjamin Franklin Callahan b: 5/19/1957, Mount Airy, NC BR/TR, 6'7", 230 lbs. Deb: 6/22/1983																									
1983 Oak-A	1	2	.333	4	2	0	0	0	9^1	18	16	13	0	0	5	2	2.464	12.54	31	8.97	.400	0	....	-9	0	-0.9
• CALLAHAN, Joe	Joseph Thomas Callahan b: 10/8/1916, East Boston, MA d: 5/24/1949, South Boston, MA BR/TR, 6'2", 170 lbs. Deb: 9/13/1939																									
1939 Bos-N	1	0	1.000	4	1	1	0	0	17^1	17	6	6	0	1	3	8	1.154	3.12	119	2.56	.250	0	.000	1	1	0.1
1940 Bos-N	0	2	.000	6	2	0	0	0	15	20	17	17	1	0	13	3	2.200	10.20	36	7.95	.351	0	.000	-11	0	-1.2
Total 2	1	2	.333	10	3	1	0	0	32^1	37	23	23	1	1	16	11	1.639	6.40	58	5.06	.296	0	.000	-10	1	-1.1
• CALLAHAN, John	John W. Callahan b: Moberly, MO Deb: 9/3/1898																									
1898 StL-N	0	2	.000	2	2	1	0	0	8^1	18	20	15	2	2	7	2	3.000	16.20	23	16.27	.430	0	.000	-11	0	-1.1
• CALLAHAN, Nixey	James Joseph Callahan b: 3/18/1874, Fitchburg, MA d: 10/4/1934, Boston, MA BR/TR, 5'10.5", 180 lbs. Deb: 5/12/1894 M/U ♦																									
1894 Phi-N	1	2	.333	9	2	1	0	2	33^2	64	52	37	3	5	17	9	2.406	9.89	52	10.70	.398	5	.238	-18	0	-1.4
1897 Chi-N	12	9	.571	23	22	21	1	0	189^2	221	111	85	6	8	55	52	1.455	4.03	110	4.16	.289	105	.292	11	19	0.5
1898 Chi-N	20	10	.667	31	31	30	2	0	274^1	267	137	75	2	10	71	73	1.232	2.46	145	2.86	.254	43	.262	33	23	3.2
1899 Chi-N	21	12	.636	35	34	33	3	0	294^1	327	155	100	5	24	76	77	1.369	3.06	122	3.78	.281	39	.260	22	23	2.3
1900 Chi-N	13	16	.448	32	32	32	2	0	285^1	347	195	121	5	22	74	77	1.475	3.82	94	4.35	.299	27	.235	-2	14	0.1
1901 Chi-A	15	8	.652	27	22	20	1	0	215^1	195	94	58	4	9	50	70	1.138	2.42	144	2.53	.239	39	.331	25	23	3.2
1902 Chi-A	16	14	.533	35	31	29	2	0	282^1	287	150	113	8	11	89	75	1.332	3.60	94	3.41	.264	51	.234	-12	16	-1.4
1903 Chi-A	1	2	.333	3	3	3	0	0	28	40	24	14	0	1	5	12	1.607	4.50	62	4.85	.334	128	.292	-5	16	0.2
Total 8	99	73	.576	195	177	169	11	2	1603	1748	918	603	33	90	437	445	1.363	3.39	109	3.70	.276	901	.273	55	134	6.6
• CALLAHAN, Ray	Raymond James "Pat" Callahan b: 8/29/1891, Ashland, WI d: 1/23/1973, Olympia, WA BL/TL, 5'10.5", 170 lbs. Deb: 9/12/1915																									
1915 Cin-N	0	0	....	3	0	0	0	0	6^1	12	7	6	1	0	1	4	2.053	8.53	33	8.31	.364	1	.333	-4	0	-0.4
• CALLAWAY, Mickey	Michael Christopher Callaway b: 5/13/1975, Memphis, TN BR/TR, 6'2", 190 lbs. Deb: 6/12/1999																									
1999 TB-A	1	2	.333	5	4	0	0	0	19^1	30	20	16	2	0	14	11	2.276	7.45	67	8.89	.357	2	.667	-5	0	-0.4
2001 TB-A	0	0	....	2	0	0	0	0	5	3	4	4	2	0	2	2	1.000	7.20	62	3.65	.167	0	....	-2	0	-0.1
2002 Ana-A	2	1	.667	6	6	0	0	0	34^1	31	20	16	4	3	11	23	1.223	4.19	106	3.63	.235	0	....	-0	2	0.0
2003 Ana-A	1	4	.200	17	4	0	0	0	38^1	57	32	29	7	1	16	22	1.904	6.81	63	7.91	.345	0	....	-11	0	-1.1
Tex-A	0	3	.000	6	3	0	0	0	22^1	27	18	16	0	1	8	19	1.567	6.45	77	4.55	.314	0	....	-3	0	-0.3
Yr.	1	7	.125	23	7	0	0	0	60^2	84	50	45	7	2	24	41	1.780	6.68	68	6.67	.335	0	....	-15	0	-1.4
Total 4	4	10	.286	36	17	0	0	0	119^1	148	94	81	15	5	51	77	1.668	6.11	75	6.03	.305	2	.667	-22	2	-2.0

• CALMUS, Dick

Richard Lee Calmus b: 1/7/1944, Los Angeles, CA BR/TR, 6'4", 187 lbs. Deb: 4/22/1963

YEAR TM-L	W	L	PCT	G	GS	CG	SH	SV	IP	H	R	ER	HR	HB	BB	SO	RAT	ERA	ERA+	CERA	OAV	BH	AVG	PR+	WS	TPW
1963 LA-N	3	1	.750	21	1	0	0	0	44	32	14	13	3	0	16	25	1.091	2.66	114	2.36	.204	0	.000	2	3	0.2
1967 Chi-N	0	0	....	1	1	0	0	0	4^{1}	5	4	4	2	0	0	1	1.154	8.31	43	5.48	.278	1	.500	-2	0	-0.2
Total 2	3	1	.750	22	2	0	0	0	48^{1}	37	18	17	5	0	16	26	1.097	3.17	99	2.64	.211	1	.125	-0	3	-0.1

• CALVERT, Mark

Mark Calvert b: 9/29/1956, Tulsa, OK BR/TR, 6'1", 195 lbs. Deb: 4/17/1983

YEAR TM-L	W	L	PCT	G	GS	CG	SH	SV	IP	H	R	ER	HR	HB	BB	SO	RAT	ERA	ERA+	CERA	OAV	BH	AVG	PR+	WS	TPW
1983 SF-N	1	4	.200	18	4	0	0	0	37^{1}	46	33	26	2	3	34	14	2.143	6.27	56	7.31	.307	0	.000	-11	0	-1.2
1984 SF-N	2	4	.333	10	5	1	0	0	32	40	21	18	4	1	9	5	1.531	5.06	69	5.17	.303	0	.000	-5	0	-0.6
Total 2	3	8	.273	28	9	1	0	0	69^{1}	86	54	44	6	4	43	19	1.861	5.71	62	6.32	.305	0	.000	-16	0	-1.8

• CALVERT, Paul

Paul Leo Emile Calvert b: 10/6/1917, Montreal, Canada d: 2/1/1999, Sherbrooke, Canada BR/TR, 6', 185 lbs. Deb: 9/24/1942

YEAR TM-L	W	L	PCT	G	GS	CG	SH	SV	IP	H	R	ER	HR	HB	BB	SO	RAT	ERA	ERA+	CERA	OAV	BH	AVG	PR+	WS	TPW
1942 Cle-A	0	0	....	1	0	0	0	0	2	0	0	0	0	0	2	2	1.000	0.00	....	0.92	.000	0	....	1	0	0.1
1943 Cle-A	0	0	....	5	0	0	0	0	8^{1}	6	4	4	0	1	6	2	1.440	4.32	72	3.24	.200	0	.000	-1	0	-0.2
1944 Cle-A	1	3	.250	35	4	0	0	0	77	89	48	39	4	0	38	31	1.649	4.56	72	4.79	.289	4	.267	-12	1	-1.1
1945 Cle-A	0	0	....	1	0	0	0	0	1^{1}	3	2	2	0	0	1	1	3.000	13.50	24	12.35	.429	0	....	-2	0	-0.2
1949 Was-A	6	17	.261	34	23	5	0	1	160^{2}	175	111	97	11	2	86	52	1.624	5.43	78	4.73	.279	7	.137	-15	3	-1.7
1950 Det-A	2	2	.500	32	0	0	0	4	51^{1}	71	42	36	7	2	25	14	1.870	6.31	74	6.95	.324	0	.000	-10	0	-0.9
1951 Det-A	0	0	....	1	0	0	0	0	1	1	0	0	0	0	0	0	1.000	0.00	....	1.95	.250	0	....	0	0	0.0
Total 7	9	22	.290	109	27	5	0	5	301^{2}	345	207	178	22	5	158	102	1.667	5.31	76	5.08	.289	11	.149	-38	4	-4.0

• CAMACHO, Ernie

Ernest Carlos Camacho b: 2/1/1955, Salinas, CA BR/TR, 6'1", 180 lbs. Deb: 5/22/1980

YEAR TM-L	W	L	PCT	G	GS	CG	SH	SV	IP	H	R	ER	HR	HB	BB	SO	RAT	ERA	ERA+	CERA	OAV	BH	AVG	PR+	WS	TPW
1980 Oak-A	0	0	....	5	0	0	0	0	11^{2}	20	9	9	2	1	5	9	2.143	6.94	54	9.50	.364	0	....	-4	0	-0.4
1981 Pit-N	0	1	.000	7	3	0	0	0	21^{2}	23	13	12	0	0	15	11	1.754	4.98	72	4.95	.295	0	.000	-3	0	-0.4
1983 Cle-A	0	1	.000	4	0	0	0	0	5^{1}	5	3	3	1	1	2	2	1.313	5.06	84	5.14	.250	0	....	-0	0	0.0
1984 Cle-A	5	9	.357	69	0	0	0	23	100	83	31	27	6	1	37	48	1.200	2.43	168	2.77	.229	0	....	18	14	1.8
1985 Cle-A	0	1	.000	2	0	0	0	0	3^{1}	4	3	3	0	0	1	2	1.500	8.10	51	3.97	.333	0	....	-1	0	-0.1
1986 Cle-A	2	4	.333	51	0	0	0	20	57^{1}	60	26	26	1	2	31	36	1.587	4.08	101	4.06	.269	0	....	1	7	0.1
1987 Cle-A	0	1	.000	15	0	0	0	1	13^{2}	21	14	14	1	3	5	9	1.902	9.22	49	7.69	.350	0	....	-7	0	-0.7
1988 Hou-N	0	3	.000	13	0	0	0	1	17^{2}	25	15	15	1	0	12	13	2.094	7.64	43	7.42	.352	0	.000	-8	0	-0.9
1989 SF-N	3	0	1.000	13	0	0	0	0	16^{1}	10	5	5	1	0	11	14	1.286	2.76	122	2.52	.175	0	.000	1	2	0.1
1990 SF-N	0	0	....	8	0	0	0	0	10	10	4	4	1	0	3	8	1.300	3.60	101	3.70	.256	0	....	-0	1	0.0
StL-N	0	0	....	6	0	0	0	0	5^{2}	7	6	5	2	0	6	7	2.294	7.94	48	10.11	.318	0	....	-3	0	-0.3
Yr.	0	0	....	14	0	0	0	0	15^{2}	17	10	9	3	0	9	15	1.660	5.17	72	6.02	.279	0	....	-3	1	-0.3
Total 10	10	20	.333	193	3	0	0	45	262^{2}	268	129	123	16	8	128	159	1.508	4.21	93	4.34	.268	0	.000	-8	24	-0.9

• CAMBRIA, Fred

Frederick Dennis Cambria b: 1/22/1948, Cambria Heights, NY BR/TR, 6'2", 195 lbs. Deb: 8/26/1970

YEAR TM-L	W	L	PCT	G	GS	CG	SH	SV	IP	H	R	ER	HR	HB	BB	SO	RAT	ERA	ERA+	CERA	OAV	BH	AVG	PR+	WS	TPW
1970 Pit-N	1	2	.333	6	5	0	0	0	33^{1}	37	15	13	2	1	12	14	1.470	3.51	111	4.25	.272	2	.200	1	2	0.1

• CAMMACK, Eric

Eric Wade Cammack b: 8/14/1975, Nederland, TX BR/TR, 6'1", 180 lbs. Deb: 4/28/2000

YEAR TM-L	W	L	PCT	G	GS	CG	SH	SV	IP	H	R	ER	HR	HB	BB	SO	RAT	ERA	ERA+	CERA	OAV	BH	AVG	PR+	WS	TPW
2000 NY-N	0	0	....	8	0	0	0	0	10	7	7	7	1	1	10	9	1.700	6.30	70	4.79	.194	1	1.000	-2	0	-0.1

• CAMNITZ, Harry

Henry Richardson Camnitz b: 10/26/1884, McKinney, KY d: 1/6/1951, Louisville, KY BR/TR, 6'1", 168 lbs. Deb: 9/29/1909

YEAR TM-L	W	L	PCT	G	GS	CG	SH	SV	IP	H	R	ER	HR	HB	BB	SO	RAT	ERA	ERA+	CERA	OAV	BH	AVG	PR+	WS	TPW
1909 Pit-N	0	0	....	1	0	0	0	0	4	6	2	2	0	0	1	1	1.750	4.50	57	5.72	.353	0	.000	-1	0	-0.1
1911 StL-N	1	0	1.000	2	0	0	0	0	2	0	0	0	0	0	1	2	.500	0.00	....	0.23	.000	0	....	1	1	0.1
Total 2	1	0	1.000	3	0	0	0	0	6	6	2	2	0	0	2	3	1.333	3.00	86	3.89	.353	0	.000	-0	1	-0.1

• CAMNITZ, Howie

Samuel Howard "Red" Camnitz b: 8/22/1881, Covington, KY d: 3/2/1960, Louisville, KY BR/TR, 5'9", 169 lbs. Deb: 4/22/1904

YEAR TM-L	W	L	PCT	G	GS	CG	SH	SV	IP	H	R	ER	HR	HB	BB	SO	RAT	ERA	ERA+	CERA	OAV	BH	AVG	PR+	WS	TPW
1904 Pit-N	1	4	.200	10	2	2	0	0	49	48	37	23	0	3	20	21	1.388	4.22	65	3.49	.259	1	.063	-8	0	-1.0
1906 Pit-N	1	0	1.000	2	1	1	1	0	9	6	2	2	0	0	5	5	1.222	2.00	133	2.14	.188	0	.000	1	1	0.0
1907 Pit-N	13	8	.619	31	19	15	4	1	180	135	65	43	0	3	59	85	1.078	2.15	113	1.97	.211	3	.050	8	12	0.4
1908 Pit-N	16	9	.640	38	26	17	3	2	236^{2}	182	76	41	6	5	69	118	1.061	1.56	146	2.06	.210	6	.083	19	16	1.9
1909* Pit-N	25	6	.806	41	30	20	6	3	283	207	75	51	1	7	68	133	.972	1.62	158	1.72	.211	12	.138	26	30	2.9
1910 Pit-N	12	13	.480	38	31	16	1	2	260	246	110	93	1	12	61	120	1.181	3.22	97	2.77	.256	11	.125	-4	15	-0.8
1911 Pit-N	20	15	.571	40	33	18	1	1	267^{2}	245	112	93	8	4	84	139	1.229	3.13	109	2.92	.248	12	.143	4	16	0.1
1912 Pit-N	22	12	.647	41	32	22	2	2	276^{2}	256	104	87	8	13	82	121	1.222	2.83	115	2.95	.251	23	.235	10	23	1.1
1913 Pit-N	6	17	.261	36	22	5	1	2	192^{1}	203	106	80	7	8	84	64	1.492	3.74	80	4.18	.282	9	.153	-14	4	-1.6
Phi-N	3	3	.500	9	5	1	0	1	49	49	25	20	1	2	23	21	1.469	3.67	91	3.85	.268	1	.063	-2	3	-0.3
Yr.	9	20	.310	45	27	6	1	3	241^{1}	252	131	100	8	10	107	85	1.488	3.73	82	4.11	.279	10	.133	-16	7	-1.9
1914 Pit-F	14	19	.424	36	34	20	1	1	262	256	132	94	8	8	90	82	1.321	3.23	95	3.36	.258	14	.161	-4	13	-0.7
1915 Pit-F	0	0	....	4	2	0	0	0	20	19	11	10	1	0	11	6	1.500	4.50	69	3.88	.257	0	.000	-3	0	-0.4
Total 11	133	106	.556	326	237	137	20	15	2085^{1}	1852	855	637	41	65	656	915	1.203	2.75	108	2.78	.242	92	.136	33	133	1.5

• CAMP, Kid

Winfield Scott Camp b: 12/8/1869, New Albany, OH d: 3/2/1895, Omaha, NE BB/TR, 6', 160 lbs. Deb: 5/3/1892

YEAR TM-L	W	L	PCT	G	GS	CG	SH	SV	IP	H	R	ER	HR	HB	BB	SO	RAT	ERA	ERA+	CERA	OAV	BH	AVG	PR+	WS	TPW
1892 Pit-N	0	1	.000	4	1	1	0	0	23	31	23	16	4	1	9	6	1.739	6.26	53	6.79	.310	1	.091	-8	0	-0.9
1894 Chi-N	0	1	.000	3	2	2	0	0	22	34	24	16	0	1	12	6	2.091	6.55	86	7.15	.350	0	.000	-2	1	-0.3
Total 2	0	2	.000	7	3	3	0	0	45	65	47	32	4	2	21	12	1.911	6.40	65	6.96	.330	1	.045	-10	1	-1.2

• CAMP, Rick

Rick Lamar Camp b: 6/10/1953, Trion, GA BR/TR, 6'1", 198 lbs. Deb: 9/15/1976

YEAR TM-L	W	L	PCT	G	GS	CG	SH	SV	IP	H	R	ER	HR	HB	BB	SO	RAT	ERA	ERA+	CERA	OAV	BH	AVG	PR+	WS	TPW
1976 Atl-N	0	1	.000	5	1	0	0	0	11^{1}	13	9	8	0	0	2	6	1.324	6.35	60	3.49	.302	0	.000	-3	0	-0.3
1977 Atl-N	6	3	.667	54	0	0	0	10	78^{2}	89	47	35	6	1	47	51	1.729	4.00	111	5.04	.283	0	.000	6	6	0.6
1978 Atl-N	2	4	.333	42	4	0	0	0	74^{1}	99	42	31	5	3	32	23	1.762	3.75	108	5.89	.329	0	.000	4	4	0.3
1980 Atl-N	6	4	.600	77	0	0	0	22	108^{1}	92	26	23	3	4	29	33	1.117	1.91	196	2.37	.235	1	.111	22	20	2.3
1981 Atl-N	9	3	.750	48	0	0	0	17	76	68	17	15	5	1	12	47	1.053	1.78	202	2.40	.239	0	.000	15	14	1.5
1982* Atl-N	11	13	.458	51	21	3	0	5	177^{1}	199	84	72	18	1	52	68	1.415	3.65	102	4.34	.291	1	.024	1	10	-0.2
1983 Atl-N	10	9	.526	40	16	1	0	0	140	146	64	59	16	4	38	61	1.314	3.79	102	4.04	.270	3	.077	-0	7	-0.2
1984 Atl-N	8	6	.571	31	21	1	0	0	148^{2}	134	59	54	11	2	63	69	1.325	3.27	118	3.54	.245	5	.111	11	10	1.0
1985 Atl-N	4	6	.400	66	2	0	0	3	127^{2}	130	72	56	8	5	61	49	1.496	3.95	97	4.19	.263	3	.231	-0	6	0.1
Total 9	56	49	.533	414	65	5	0	57	942^{1}	970	420	353	72	21	336	407	1.386	3.37	115	3.94	.269	13	.074	55	77	5.0

• CAMPBELL, Archie

Archibald Stewart "Iron Man" Campbell b: 10/20/1903, Maplewood, NJ d: 12/22/1989, Sparks, NV BR/TR, 6', 180 lbs. Deb: 4/21/1928

YEAR TM-L	W	L	PCT	G	GS	CG	SH	SV	IP	H	R	ER	HR	HB	BB	SO	RAT	ERA	ERA+	CERA	OAV	BH	AVG	PR+	WS	TPW
1928 NY-A	0	1	.000	13	1	0	0	2	24	30	22	14	0	0	11	9	1.708	5.25	72	4.40	.288	1	.250	-4	0	-0.4
1929 Was-A	0	1	.000	4	0	0	0	0	4	10	7	7	1	0	5	1	3.750	15.75	27	21.02	.500	0	....	-5	0	-0.5
1930 Cin-N	2	4	.333	23	3	1	0	4	58	71	38	35	2	1	31	19	1.759	5.43	89	5.30	.311	4	.267	-3	3	-0.3
Total 3	2	6	.250	40	4	1	0	6	86	111	67	56	3	1	47	29	1.837	5.86	76	5.78	.315	5	.263	-12	3	-1.1

• CAMPBELL, Bill

William Richard Campbell b: 8/9/1948, Highland Park, MI BR/TR, 6'3", 190 lbs. Deb: 7/14/1973 C

YEAR TM-L	W	L	PCT	G	GS	CG	SH	SV	IP	H	R	ER	HR	HB	BB	SO	RAT	ERA	ERA+	CERA	OAV	BH	AVG	PR+	WS	TPW
1973 Min-A	3	3	.500	28	2	0	0	7	51^{2}	44	20	18	5	1	20	42	1.239	3.14	126	3.21	.226	0	....	5	6	0.5
1974 Min-A	8	7	.533	63	0	0	0	19	120^{1}	109	37	35	4	2	55	89	1.363	2.62	143	3.33	.242	0	....	16	15	1.7
1975 Min-A	4	6	.400	47	7	2	1	5	121	119	58	51	13	2	46	76	1.364	3.79	102	4.06	.262	0	.000	2	7	0.2
1976 Min-A	17	5	.773	**78**	0	0	0	20	167^{2}	145	63	56	9	5	62	115	1.235	3.01	120	2.93	.234	0	....	11	17	1.1
1977 Bos-A★	13	9	.591	69	0	0	0	**31**	140	112	48	46	13	5	60	114	1.229	2.96	152	3.10	.224	0	....	26	23	2.6
1978 Bos-A	7	5	.583	29	0	0	0	4	50^{2}	62	25	22	3	0	17	47	1.559	3.91	105	4.68	.308	0	....	1	4	0.1
1979 Bos-A	3	4	.429	41	0	0	0	9	54^{2}	55	28	26	5	1	23	25	1.427	4.28	103	4.00	.262	0	....	1	5	0.1
1980 Bos-A	4	0	1.000	23	0	0	0	0	41^{1}	44	26	22	1	0	22	17	1.597	4.79	88	4.54	.284	0	....	-3	2	-0.3
1981 Bos-A	1	1	.500	30	0	0	0	7	48^{1}	45	23	17	5	0	20	37	1.345	3.17	122	3.60	.245	0	....	5	4	0.5
1982 Chi-N	3	6	.333	62	0	0	0	8	100	89	44	41	6	0	40	71	1.290	3.69	101	3.00	.245	1	.143	1	7	0.1
1983 Chi-N	6	8	.429	**82**	0	0	0	8	122^{1}	128	65	61	4	1	49	97	1.447	4.49	84	3.66	.275	1	.100	-8	6	-0.9
1984 Phi-N	6	5	.545	57	0	0	0	1	81^{1}	68	43	31	2	0	35	52	1.266	3.43	106	2.47	.222	0	.000	3	4	0.3
1985* StL-N	5	3	.625	50	0	0	0	4	64^{1}	55	32	25	5	2	21	41	1.181	3.50	101	2.73	.230	2	.333	-1	4	0.0
1986 Det-A	3	6	.333	34	0	0	0	3	55^{2}	46	26	24	5	1	21	37	1.204	3.88	106	2.95	.230	0	....	1	3	0.1

YEAR	TM-L	W	L	PCT	G	GS	CG	SH	SV	IP	H	R	ER	HR	HB	BB	SO	RAT	ERA	ERA+	CERA	OAV	BH	AVG	PR+	WS	TPW
1987	Mon-N	0	0	....	7	0	0	0	0	10	18	12	9	2	0	4	4	2.200	8.10	52	9.04	.360	0	.000	-4	0	-0.4
Total	**15**	**83**	**68**	**.550**	**700**	**9**	**2**	**1**	**126**	**1229^1**	**1139**	**550**	**484**	**82**	**20**	**495**	**864**	**1.329**	**3.54**	**110**	**3.40**	**.248**	**4**	**.154**	**56**	**107**	**5.8**
• CAMPBELL, Billy	William James Campbell b: 11/5/1873, Pittsburgh, PA d: 10/6/1957, Cincinnati, OH BL/TL, 5'10", 165 lbs. Deb: 4/17/1905																										
1905	StL-N	1	1	.500	2	2	2	0	0	17	27	17	14	0	0	7	2	2.000	7.41	40	6.88	.365	1	.143	-8	0	-0.8
1907	Cin-N	3	0	1.000	3	3	3	0	0	21	19	5	5	0	0	3	4	1.048	2.14	121	2.08	.244	2	.250	1	2	0.1
1908	Cin-N	12	13	.480	35	24	19	2	2	221^1	203	99	64	3	10	44	73	1.116	2.60	88	2.60	.252	6	.083	-4	10	-0.9
1909	Cin-N	7	11	.389	30	15	7	0	2	148^1	162	65	44	0	9	39	37	1.355	2.67	97	3.69	.288	6	.140	-2	6	-0.3
Total	**4**	**23**	**25**	**.479**	**70**	**44**	**31**	**2**	**4**	**407^2**	**411**	**186**	**127**	**3**	**19**	**93**	**116**	**1.236**	**2.80**	**88**	**3.15**	**.270**	**15**	**.115**	**-14**	**18**	**-1.9**
• CAMPBELL, Dave	David Alan Campbell b: 9/3/1951, Princeton, IN BR/TR, 6'3", 210 lbs. Deb: 5/6/1977																										
1977	Atl-N	0	6	.000	65	0	0	0	13	88^2	78	32	30	7	3	33	42	1.252	3.05	146	3.17	.239	1	.083	16	11	1.6
1978	Atl-N	4	4	.500	53	0	0	0	1	69^1	67	39	37	10	5	49	45	1.673	4.80	84	5.43	.258	0	....	-5	3	-0.5
Total	**2**	**4**	**10**	**.286**	**118**	**0**	**0**	**0**	**14**	**158**	**145**	**71**	**67**	**17**	**8**	**82**	**87**	**1.437**	**3.82**	**110**	**4.16**	**.247**	**1**	**.083**	**12**	**14**	**1.1**
• CAMPBELL, Hugh	Hugh F. Campbell b: 1846, Ireland d: 3/1/1881, Newark, NJ Deb: 4/28/1873																										
1873	Res-n	2	16	.111	19	18	18	0	0	165	250	213	52	6	....	7	5	1.558	2.84	118	....	.311	13	.149	29	....	1.8
• CAMPBELL, Jim	James Marcus Campbell b: 5/19/1966, Santa Maria, CA BL/TL, 5'11", 175 lbs. Deb: 8/21/1990																										
1990	KC-A	1	0	1.000	2	2	0	0	0	9^2	15	9	9	1	0	1	2	1.655	8.38	46	6.13	.349	0	....	-5	0	-0.5
• CAMPBELL, John	John Millard Campbell b: 9/13/1907, Washington, DC d: 4/24/1995, Daytona Beach, FL BR/TR, 6'1.5", 184 lbs. Deb: 7/23/1933																										
1933	Was-A	0	0	....	1	0	0	0	0	1	1	1	0	0	0	1	0	2.000	0.00	....	4.22	.200	0	....	0	0	0.0
• CAMPBELL, Kevin	Kevin Wade Campbell b: 12/6/1964, Marianna, AR BR/TR, 6'2", 225 lbs. Deb: 7/19/1991																										
1991	Oak-A	1	0	1.000	14	0	0	0	0	23	13	7	7	4	1	14	16	1.174	2.74	140	3.25	.167	0	....	3	2	0.3
1992	Oak-A	2	3	.400	32	5	0	0	1	65	66	39	37	4	0	45	38	1.708	5.12	73	4.98	.267	0	....	-11	1	-1.1
1993	Oak-A	0	0	....	11	0	0	0	0	16	20	13	13	1	1	11	9	1.938	7.31	56	6.67	.313	0	....	-6	0	-0.6
1994	Min-A	1	0	1.000	14	0	0	0	0	24^2	20	8	8	2	1	5	15	1.014	2.92	167	2.43	.233	0	....	6	3	0.5
1995	Min-A	0	0	....	6	0	0	0	0	9^2	8	5	5	0	0	5	5	1.345	4.66	102	3.08	.235	0	....	0	1	0.0
Total	**5**	**4**	**3**	**.571**	**77**	**5**	**0**	**0**	**1**	**138^1**	**127**	**72**	**70**	**11**	**3**	**80**	**83**	**1.496**	**4.55**	**87**	**4.30**	**.250**	**0**	**....**	**-7**	**7**	**-0.8**
• CAMPBELL, Mike	Michael Thomas Campbell b: 2/17/1964, Seattle, WA BR/TR, 6'3", 210 lbs. Deb: 7/4/1987																										
1987	Sea-A	1	4	.200	9	9	1	0	0	49^1	41	29	26	9	2	25	35	1.338	4.74	99	4.16	.224	0	....	-0	2	0.0
1988	Sea-A	6	10	.375	20	20	2	0	0	114^2	128	81	75	18	0	43	63	1.491	5.89	71	5.01	.280	0	....	-22	1	-2.2
1989	Sea-A	1	2	.333	5	5	0	0	0	21	28	22	17	4	0	10	6	1.810	7.29	55	6.82	.301	0	....	-8	0	-0.8
1992	Tex-A	0	1	.000	1	0	0	0	0	3^2	3	4	4	1	0	2	2	1.364	9.82	39	5.10	.231	0	....	-2	0	-0.2
1994	SD-N	1	1	.500	3	2	0	0	0	8^1	13	12	12	5	0	5	10	2.160	12.96	32	12.79	.351	1	.333	-8	0	-0.8
1996	Chi-N	3	1	.750	13	5	0	0	0	36^1	29	19	18	7	0	10	19	1.073	4.46	97	3.06	.216	4	.364	-1	2	0.1
Total	**6**	**12**	**19**	**.387**	**51**	**41**	**3**	**0**	**0**	**233^1**	**242**	**167**	**152**	**44**	**2**	**95**	**135**	**1.444**	**5.86**	**72**	**4.97**	**.264**	**5**	**.357**	**-41**	**5**	**-3.9**
• CAMPER, Cardell	Cardell Camper b: 7/6/1952, Boley, OK BR/TR, 6'3", 208 lbs. Deb: 9/11/1977																										
1977	Cle-A	1	0	1.000	3	1	0	0	0	9^1	7	4	4	0	0	4	9	1.179	3.86	102	1.96	.200	0	....	0	1	0.0
• CAMPFIELD, Sal	William Holton Campfield b: 2/19/1868, Meadville, PA d: 5/16/1952, Meadville, PA BR/TR, 6'.5" Deb: 5/15/1896																										
1896	NY-N	1	1	.500	6	2	2	0	0	27	31	15	12	1	2	6	6	1.370	4.00	105	3.98	.286	2	.167	0	2	0.0
• CAMPISI, Sal	Salvatore John Campisi b: 8/11/1942, Brooklyn, NY BR/TR, 6'2", 210 lbs. Deb: 8/15/1969																										
1969	StL-N	1	0	1.000	7	0	0	0	0	9^2	4	1	1	0	0	6	7	1.034	0.93	384	1.17	.121	0	....	3	2	0.3
1970	StL-N	2	2	.500	37	0	0	0	4	49^1	53	19	16	2	3	37	26	1.824	2.92	141	5.31	.282	0	.000	7	4	0.7
1971	Min-A	0	0	....	6	0	0	0	0	4^1	5	2	2	1	0	4	2	2.077	4.15	85	8.58	.294	0	....	-0	0	0.0
Total	**3**	**3**	**2**	**.600**	**50**	**0**	**0**	**0**	**4**	**63^1**	**62**	**22**	**19**	**3**	**3**	**47**	**35**	**1.721**	**2.70**	**149**	**4.91**	**.261**	**0**	**.000**	**10**	**6**	**1.0**
• CANAVAN, Hugh	Hugh Edward "Hugo" Canavan b: 5/13/1897, Worcester, MA d: 9/4/1967, Boston, MA BL/TL, 5'8", 160 lbs. Deb: 4/23/1918																										
1918	Bos-N	0	4	.000	11	3	3	0	0	46^2	70	42	33	0	5	15	18	1.821	6.36	42	6.36	.366	2	.095	-18	0	-2.2
• CANDELARIA, John	John Robert "Candy Man" Candelaria b: 11/6/1953, New York, NY BL/TL, 6'7", 232 lbs. Deb: 6/8/1975																										
1975*	Pit-N	8	6	.571	18	18	4	1	0	120^2	95	47	37	8	2	36	95	1.086	2.76	128	2.27	.212	6	.140	10	8	1.0
1976	Pit-N	16	7	.696	32	31	11	4	1	220	173	87	77	22	2	60	138	1.059	3.15	111	2.48	.216	14	.184	7	15	1.1
1977	Pit-N★	20	5	.800	33	33	6	1	0	230^2	197	64	60	29	2	50	133	1.071	**2.34**	**170**	2.82	.232	18	.225	39	**26**	4.3
1978	Pit-N	12	11	.522	30	29	3	1	1	189	191	73	68	15	5	49	94	1.270	3.24	114	3.50	.261	9	.173	12	14	1.7
1979*	Pit-N	14	9	.609	33	30	8	0	0	207	201	83	74	25	3	41	101	1.169	3.22	120	3.29	.253	9	.132	13	14	1.2
1980	Pit-N	11	14	.440	35	34	7	0	1	233^1	246	114	104	14	3	50	97	1.269	4.01	91	3.44	.276	15	.195	-12	10	-1.0
1981	Pit-N	2	2	.500	6	6	0	0	0	40^2	42	17	16	3	0	11	14	1.303	3.54	102	3.62	.271	3	.231	0	2	0.1
1982	Pit-N	12	7	.632	31	30	1	1	1	174^2	166	62	57	13	4	37	133	1.162	2.94	126	3.05	.255	12	.222	16	14	2.0
1983	Pit-N	15	8	.652	33	32	2	0	0	197^2	191	73	71	15	2	45	157	1.194	3.23	115	3.17	.257	9	.138	11	15	1.2
1984	Pit-N	12	11	.522	33	28	3	1	2	185^1	179	69	56	19	1	34	133	1.149	2.72	132	3.10	.256	8	.129	16	12	1.7
1985	Pit-N	2	4	.333	37	0	0	0	9	54^1	57	23	22	7	1	14	47	1.307	3.64	98	4.03	.275	0	.000	0	5	0.0
	Cal-A	7	3	.700	13	13	1	1	0	71	70	33	30	7	3	24	53	1.324	3.80	108	3.93	.262	0	....	0	5	0.0
1986*	Cal-A	10	2	.833	16	16	1	1	0	91^2	68	30	26	4	3	26	81	1.025	2.55	161	2.07	.206	0	....	14	9	1.4
1987	Cal-A	8	6	.571	20	20	0	0	0	116^2	127	70	61	17	1	20	74	1.260	4.71	91	4.01	.279	0	....	-6	5	-0.5
	NY-N	2	0	1.000	3	3	0	0	0	12^1	17	8	8	1	0	3	10	1.622	5.84	65	5.36	.333	1	.200	-3	0	-0.3
1988	NY-A	13	7	.650	25	24	6	2	1	157	150	69	59	18	2	23	121	1.102	3.38	116	2.96	.248	0	....	11	11	1.1
1989	NY-A	3	3	.500	10	6	1	0	0	49	49	28	28	8	0	12	37	1.245	5.14	75	3.81	.258	0	....	-7	2	-0.7
	Mon-N	0	2	.000	12	0	0	0	0	16^1	17	8	6	3	0	4	14	1.286	3.31	107	4.11	.283	0	....	0	1	0.1
1990	Min-A	7	3	.700	34	1	0	0	4	58^1	55	23	22	9	0	9	44	1.097	3.39	122	3.05	.244	0	....	5	7	0.5
	Tor-A	0	3	.000	13	2	0	0	1	21^1	32	13	13	2	2	11	19	2.016	5.48	75	7.72	.356	0	....	-3	0	-0.3
	Yr.	7	6	.538	47	3	0	0	5	79^2	87	36	35	11	2	20	63	1.343	3.95	104	4.30	.276	0	....	2	7	0.2
1991	LA-N	1	1	.500	59	0	0	0	2	33^2	31	16	14	3	0	11	38	1.248	3.74	96	3.26	.252	0	....	-1	3	-0.1
1992	LA-N	2	5	.286	50	0	0	0	5	25^1	20	9	8	1	0	13	23	1.303	2.84	121	2.74	.220	0	....	2	4	0.3
1993	Pit-N	0	3	.000	24	0	0	0	1	19^2	25	19	18	2	1	9	17	1.729	8.24	49	6.03	.313	0	....	-9	0	-0.9
Total	**19**	**177**	**122**	**.592**	**600**	**356**	**54**	**13**	**29**	**2525^2**	**2399**	**1038**	**935**	**245**	**37**	**592**	**1673**	**1.184**	**3.33**	**113**	**3.20**	**.251**	**104**	**.174**	**118**	**182**	**13.8**
• CANDINI, Milo	Milo Cain Candini b: 8/3/1917, Manteca, CA d: 3/17/1998, Manteca, CA BR/TR, 6', 187 lbs. Deb: 5/1/1943																										
1943	Was-A	11	7	.611	28	21	8	3	1	166	144	55	46	3	1	65	67	1.259	2.49	128	2.78	.238	9	.161	13	12	1.3
1944	Was-A	6	7	.462	28	10	4	2	1	103	110	53	47	3	1	49	31	1.544	4.11	79	4.15	.276	10	.313	-9	4	-0.6
1946	Was-A	2	0	1.000	9	0	0	0	1	21^2	15	5	5	1	0	4	6	.877	2.08	161	1.52	.192	2	.333	3	3	0.4
1947	Was-A	3	4	.429	38	2	0	0	1	87	96	53	50	5	0	35	31	1.506	5.17	72	4.12	.273	3	.167	-13	1	-1.3
1948	Was-A	2	3	.400	35	4	1	0	3	94^1	96	56	54	1	1	63	23	1.686	5.15	84	4.41	.267	8	.364	-7	5	-0.4
1949	Was-A	0	0	....	3	0	0	0	1	5^2	4	3	3	0	0	1	1	.882	4.76	89	1.40	.200	1	1.000	-0	1	0.0
1950	Phi-N	1	0	1.000	18	0	0	0	0	30	32	11	9	2	0	15	10	1.567	2.70	150	4.62	.281	1	.167	4	3	0.4
1951	Phi-N	1	0	1.000	15	0	0	0	1	30	33	22	20	3	0	18	14	1.700	6.00	64	5.25	.275	1	.333	-7	0	-0.7
Total	**8**	**26**	**21**	**.553**	**174**	**37**	**13**	**5**	**8**	**537^2**	**530**	**258**	**234**	**18**	**3**	**250**	**183**	**1.451**	**3.92**	**93**	**3.72**	**.259**	**35**	**.243**	**-14**	**29**	**-0.7**
• CANDIOTTI, Tom	Thomas Caesar Candiotti b: 8/31/1957, Walnut Creek, CA BR/TR, 6'3", 200 lbs. Deb: 8/8/1983																										
1983	Mil-A	4	4	.500	10	8	2	1	0	55^2	62	21	20	4	2	16	21	1.401	3.23	115	4.39	.291	0	....	3	4	0.3
1984	Mil-A	2	2	.500	8	6	0	0	0	32^1	38	21	19	5	0	10	23	1.485	5.29	73	4.92	.277	0	....	-5	0	-0.5
1986	Cle-A	16	12	.571	36	34	**17**	3	0	252^1	234	112	100	18	8	106	167	1.347	3.57	116	3.69	.246	0	....	18	17	1.8
1987	Cle-A	7	18	.280	32	32	7	2	0	201^2	193	132	107	28	4	93	111	1.418	4.78	95	4.35	.250	0	....	-3	8	-0.3
1988	Cle-A	14	8	.636	31	31	11	1	0	216^2	225	86	79	15	6	53	137	1.283	3.28	125	3.61	.272	0	....	24	17	2.4
1989	Cle-A	13	10	.565	31	31	4	0	0	206	188	80	71	10	4	55	124	1.180	3.10	128	2.81	.242	0	....	21	16	2.1

YEAR	TM-L	W	L	PCT	G	GS	CG	SH	SV	IP	H	R	ER	HR	HB	BB	SO	RAT	ERA	ERA+	CERA	OAV	BH	AVG	PR+	WS	TPW
1990	Cle-A	15	11	.577	31	29	3	1	0	202	207	92	82	23	6	55	128	1.297	3.65	107	3.92	.263	0	....	9	12	0.9
1991	Cle-A	7	6	.538	15	15	3	0	0	108^1	88	35	27	6	2	28	86	1.071	2.24	185	2.32	.218	0	....	25	10	2.5
	*Tor-A	6	7	.462	19	19	3	0	0	129^2	114	47	43	6	4	45	81	1.226	2.98	141	2.98	.236	0	....	18	11	1.8
	Yr.	13	13	.500	34	34	6	0	0	238	202	82	70	12	6	73	167	1.155	2.65	158	2.68	.228	0	....	43	21	4.3
1992	LA-N	11	15	.423	32	30	6	2	0	203^2	177	78	68	13	3	63	152	1.178	3.00	115	2.81	.237	6	.107	15	12	1.4
1993	LA-N	8	10	.444	33	32	2	0	0	213^2	192	86	74	12	6	71	155	1.231	3.12	122	3.05	.241	8	.133	17	14	1.6
1994	LA-N	7	7	.500	23	22	5	0	0	153	149	77	70	9	5	54	102	1.327	4.12	95	3.57	.259	7	.140	-3	7	-0.3
1995	LA-N	7	14	.333	30	30	1	1	0	190^1	187	93	74	18	9	58	141	1.287	3.50	108	3.72	.255	6	.109	6	9	0.4
1996*	LA-N	9	11	.450	28	27	1	0	0	152^1	172	91	76	18	3	43	79	1.411	4.49	86	4.54	.288	4	.089	-9	4	-1.1
1997	LA-N	10	7	.588	41	18	0	0	0	135	128	60	54	21	11	40	89	1.244	3.60	107	4.03	.248	3	.094	6	8	0.4
1998	Oak-A	11	16	.407	33	33	3	0	0	201	222	124	108	30	9	63	98	1.418	4.84	94	4.84	.281	1	1.000	-4	8	-0.3
1999	Oak-A	3	5	.375	11	11	0	0	0	56^2	67	46	40	11	2	23	30	1.588	6.35	73	6.10	.298	0	....	-10	1	-1.0
	Cle-A	1	1	.500	7	2	0	0	0	14^2	19	18	18	3	1	7	11	1.773	11.05	46	7.04	.306	0	....	-10	0	-0.9
	Yr.	4	6	.400	18	13	0	0	0	71^1	86	64	58	14	3	30	41	1.626	7.32	65	6.29	.300	0	....	-20	1	-1.9
Total	**16**	**151**	**164**	**.479**	**451**	**410**	**68**	**11**	**0**	**2725**	**2662**	**1299**	**1130**	**250**	**85**	**883**	**1735**	**1.301**	**3.73**	**109**	**3.72**	**.256**	**35**	**.117**	**118**	**158**	**11.4**

• CANEIRA, John John Cascaes Caneira b: 10/7/1952, Waterbury, CT BR/TR, 6'3", 180 lbs. Deb: 9/10/1977

YEAR	TM-L	W	L	PCT	G	GS	CG	SH	SV	IP	H	R	ER	HR	HB	BB	SO	RAT	ERA	ERA+	CERA	OAV	BH	AVG	PR+	WS	TPW
1977	Cal-A	2	2	.500	6	4	0	0	0	28^2	27	15	13	5	0	16	17	1.500	4.08	96	4.86	.252	0	....	-0	1	0.0
1978	Cal-A	0	0	....	2	2	0	0	0	7^2	8	6	6	2	0	3	0	1.435	7.04	51	5.70	.286	0	....	-3	0	-0.3
Total	**2**	**2**	**2**	**.500**	**8**	**6**	**0**	**0**	**0**	**36^1**	**35**	**21**	**19**	**7**	**0**	**19**	**17**	**1.486**	**4.71**	**81**	**5.04**	**.259**	**0**	**....**	**-3**	**1**	**-0.3**

• CANO, Jose Joselito (Soriano) Cano b: 3/7/1962, Boca de Soco, Dominican Republic BR/TR, 6'3", 175 lbs. Deb: 8/28/1989

YEAR	TM-L	W	L	PCT	G	GS	CG	SH	SV	IP	H	R	ER	HR	HB	BB	SO	RAT	ERA	ERA+	CERA	OAV	BH	AVG	PR+	WS	TPW
1989	Hou-N	1	1	.500	6	3	1	0	0	23	24	13	13	2	0	7	8	1.348	5.09	67	3.67	.267	0	.000	-4	0	-0.5

• CANTRELL, Guy Guy Dewey "Gunner" Cantrell b: 4/9/1904, Clarita, OK d: 1/31/1961, McAlester, OK BR/TR, 6', 190 lbs. Deb: 8/18/1925

YEAR	TM-L	W	L	PCT	G	GS	CG	SH	SV	IP	H	R	ER	HR	HB	BB	SO	RAT	ERA	ERA+	CERA	OAV	BH	AVG	PR+	WS	TPW
1925	Bro-N	1	0	1.000	14	3	1	0	0	36	42	27	12	0	1	14	13	1.556	3.00	139	4.22	.294	0	.000	6	2	0.4
1927	Bro-N	0	0	....	6	0	0	0	0	10	10	3	3	0	0	6	5	1.600	2.70	147	3.74	.250	1	.333	1	1	0.2
	Phi-A	0	2	.000	2	2	2	0	0	18	25	10	10	0	0	7	7	1.778	5.00	85	5.54	.338	1	.167	-1	1	-0.2
1930	Det-A	1	5	.167	16	2	1	0	0	35	38	30	22	5	1	20	20	1.657	5.66	85	5.28	.271	0	.000	-3	0	-0.5
Total	**3**	**2**	**7**	**.222**	**38**	**7**	**4**	**0**	**0**	**99**	**115**	**70**	**47**	**5**	**2**	**47**	**45**	**1.636**	**4.27**	**104**	**4.79**	**.290**	**2**	**.074**	**3**	**4**	**0.0**

• CANTWELL, Ben Benjamin Caldwell Cantwell b: 4/13/1902, Milan, TN d: 12/4/1962, Salem, MO BR/TR, 6'1", 168 lbs. Deb: 8/19/1927

YEAR	TM-L	W	L	PCT	G	GS	CG	SH	SV	IP	H	R	ER	HR	HB	BB	SO	RAT	ERA	ERA+	CERA	OAV	BH	AVG	PR+	WS	TPW
1927	NY-N	1	1	.500	5	2	1	0	0	19^2	26	9	9	1	1	2	6	1.424	4.12	93	4.46	.313	2	.250	-1	1	0.0
1928	NY-N	1	0	1.000	7	1	0	0	1	18^1	20	10	9	1	1	4	0	1.309	4.42	88	3.66	.282	2	.500	-1	1	-0.1
	Bos-N	3	3	.500	22	10	3	0	0	90	112	63	51	7	2	36	18	1.644	5.10	77	5.26	.304	5	.172	-9	2	-1.0
	Yr.	4	3	.571	29	11	3	0	1	108^1	132	73	60	8	3	40	18	1.588	4.98	78	4.99	.300	7	.212	-10	3	-1.0
1929	Bos-N	4	13	.235	27	20	8	0	2	157	171	98	78	11	2	52	25	1.420	4.47	105	4.04	.280	9	.180	4	8	0.4
1930	Bos-N	9	15	.375	31	21	10	0	2	173^1	213	99	94	15	1	45	43	1.488	4.88	101	4.73	.312	19	.302	1	12	0.3
1931	Bos-N	7	9	.438	33	16	9	2	2	156^1	160	73	63	4	0	34	32	1.241	3.63	104	2.91	.262	13	.228	4	11	0.4
1932	Bos-N	13	11	.542	37	9	3	1	5	146	133	56	48	6	5	33	33	1.137	2.96	127	2.68	.247	14	.280	13	14	1.5
1933	Bos-N	20	10	.667	40	29	18	2	2	254^2	242	89	74	12	3	54	57	1.162	2.62	117	2.74	.249	12	.141	14	21	1.4
1934	Bos-N	5	11	.313	27	19	6	1	5	143^1	163	88	69	8	2	34	45	1.374	4.33	88	3.85	.285	12	.279	-8	6	-0.6
1935	Bos-N	4	25	.138	39	24	13	0	0	210^2	235	117	108	15	2	44	34	1.324	4.61	82	3.73	.282	19	.284	-12	6	-0.8
1936	Bos-N	9	9	.500	34	12	4	0	2	133^1	127	55	45	8	4	35	42	1.215	3.04	126	3.07	.252	8	.195	11	11	0.9
1937	NY-N	0	1	.000	1	1	0	0	0	4	6	4	4	1	0	1	1	1.750	9.00	43	7.86	.375	0	....	-2	0	-0.2
	Bro-N	0	0	....	13	0	0	0	0	27^1	32	17	14	1	0	8	12	1.463	4.61	88	3.83	.288	1	.167	-1	1	-0.1
	Yr.	0	1	.000	14	1	0	0	0	31^1	38	21	18	2	0	9	13	1.500	5.17	77	4.34	.299	1	.167	-3	1	-0.3
Total	**11**	**76**	**108**	**.413**	**316**	**164**	**75**	**6**	**21**	**1534**	**1640**	**778**	**666**	**90**	**23**	**382**	**348**	**1.318**	**3.91**	**100**	**3.59**	**.275**	**116**	**.231**	**12**	**94**	**2.1**

• CANTWELL, Mike Michael Joseph Cantwell b: 1/15/1896, Washington, DC d: 1/5/1953, Oteen, NC BL/TL, 6', 155 lbs. Deb: 9/17/1916

YEAR	TM-L	W	L	PCT	G	GS	CG	SH	SV	IP	H	R	ER	HR	HB	BB	SO	RAT	ERA	ERA+	CERA	OAV	BH	AVG	PR+	WS	TPW
1916	NY-A	0	0	....	1	0	0	0	0	2	0	2	0	0	0	2	0	1.000	0.00	....	0.82	.000	0	....	1	0	0.1
1919	Phi-N	1	3	.250	5	3	2	0	0	27^1	36	19	17	1	2	9	6	1.646	5.60	57	5.67	.343	2	.222	-7	0	-0.8
1920	Phi-N	0	3	.000	5	1	0	0	0	23^1	25	18	10	1	3	15	8	1.714	3.86	89	5.25	.284	1	.143	-1	0	-0.2
Total	**3**	**1**	**6**	**.143**	**11**	**4**	**2**	**0**	**0**	**52^2**	**61**	**39**	**27**	**2**	**5**	**26**	**14**	**1.652**	**4.61**	**71**	**5.30**	**.316**	**3**	**.188**	**-8**	**0**	**-0.9**

• CANTWELL, Tom Thomas Aloysius Cantwell b: 12/23/1888, Washington, DC d: 4/1/1968, Washington, DC BL/TR, 6'1", 170 lbs. Deb: 5/19/1909

YEAR	TM-L	W	L	PCT	G	GS	CG	SH	SV	IP	H	R	ER	HR	HB	BB	SO	RAT	ERA	ERA+	CERA	OAV	BH	AVG	PR+	WS	TPW
1909	Cin-N	1	0	1.000	6	1	1	0	0	21^2	16	10	4	0	1	7	7	1.062	1.66	156	1.95	.205	3	.600	2	2	0.4
1910	Cin-N	0	0	....	2	0	0	0	0	1^1	2	2	2	0	0	3	0	3.750	13.50	22	14.88	.400	0	....	-2	0	-0.2
Total	**2**	**1**	**0**	**1.000**	**8**	**1**	**1**	**0**	**0**	**23**	**18**	**12**	**6**	**0**	**1**	**10**	**7**	**1.217**	**2.35**	**114**	**2.70**	**.217**	**3**	**.600**	**1**	**2**	**0.2**

• CAPEL, Mike Michael Lee Capel b: 10/13/1961, Marshall, TX BR/TR, 6'1", 175 lbs. Deb: 5/7/1988

YEAR	TM-L	W	L	PCT	G	GS	CG	SH	SV	IP	H	R	ER	HR	HB	BB	SO	RAT	ERA	ERA+	CERA	OAV	BH	AVG	PR+	WS	TPW
1988	Chi-N	2	1	.667	22	0	0	0	0	29^1	34	19	16	5	3	13	19	1.602	4.91	73	6.08	.293	0	.000	-4	1	-0.4
1990	Mil-A	0	0	....	2	0	0	0	0	0^1	6	6	5	0	1	1	1	21.00	135.00	3	187.16	.857	0	....	-5	0	-0.5
1991	Hou-N	1	3	.250	25	0	0	0	3	32^2	33	14	11	3	0	15	23	1.469	3.03	116	4.25	.266	0	....	2	2	0.2
Total	**3**	**3**	**4**	**.429**	**49**	**0**	**0**	**0**	**3**	**62^1**	**73**	**39**	**32**	**8**	**4**	**29**	**43**	**1.636**	**4.62**	**78**	**6.09**	**.296**	**0**	**.000**	**-7**	**3**	**-0.7**

• CAPILLA, Doug Douglas Edmund Capilla b: 1/7/1952, Honolulu, HI BL/TL, 5'11", 175 lbs. Deb: 9/12/1976

YEAR	TM-L	W	L	PCT	G	GS	CG	SH	SV	IP	H	R	ER	HR	HB	BB	SO	RAT	ERA	ERA+	CERA	OAV	BH	AVG	PR+	WS	TPW
1976	StL-N	1	0	1.000	7	0	0	0	0	8^1	8	5	5	0	0	4	5	1.440	5.40	65	3.35	.242	0	....	-2	0	-0.2
1977	StL-N	0	0	....	2	0	0	0	0	2^1	2	4	4	0	0	2	1	1.714	15.43	25	4.14	.222	0	....	-3	0	-0.3
	Cin-N	7	8	.467	22	16	1	0	0	106^1	94	53	50	10	2	59	74	1.439	4.23	93	4.08	.237	2	.059	-4	4	-0.7
	Yr.	7	8	.467	24	16	1	0	0	108^2	96	57	54	10	2	61	75	1.445	4.47	88	4.08	.236	2	.059	-7	4	-1.0
1978	Cin-N	0	1	.000	6	3	0	0	0	11	14	12	12	1	0	11	9	2.273	9.82	36	8.14	.318	0	.000	-7	0	-0.8
1979	Cin-N	1	0	1.000	5	0	0	0	0	6^1	7	6	6	1	1	5	0	1.895	8.53	44	7.30	.269	1	1.000	-3	0	-0.3
	Chi-N	0	1	.000	13	1	0	0	0	17^1	14	6	5	1	0	7	10	1.212	2.60	159	2.56	.206	0	....	3	1	0.3
	Yr.	1	1	.500	18	1	0	0	0	23^2	21	12	11	2	1	12	10	1.394	4.18	93	3.83	.223	1	1.000	-0	1	0.0
1980	Chi-N	2	8	.200	39	11	0	0	0	89^2	82	46	41	7	3	51	51	1.483	4.12	95	4.24	.253	4	.190	-1	3	0.0
1981	Chi-N	1	0	1.000	42	0	0	0	0	51	52	20	18	1	2	34	28	1.686	3.18	116	4.89	.284	0	.000	4	4	0.4
Total	**6**	**12**	**18**	**.400**	**136**	**31**	**1**	**0**	**0**	**292^1**	**273**	**152**	**141**	**21**	**8**	**173**	**178**	**1.526**	**4.34**	**88**	**4.38**	**.252**	**7**	**.115**	**-13**	**12**	**-1.6**

• CAPPUZZELLO, George George Angelo Cappuzzello b: 1/15/1954, Youngstown, OH BR/TL, 6', 175 lbs. Deb: 5/31/1981

YEAR	TM-L	W	L	PCT	G	GS	CG	SH	SV	IP	H	R	ER	HR	HB	BB	SO	RAT	ERA	ERA+	CERA	OAV	BH	AVG	PR+	WS	TPW
1981	Det-A	1	1	.500	18	3	0	0	1	33^2	28	14	13	2	2	18	19	1.366	3.48	109	3.50	.222	0	....	0	2	0.0
1982	Hou-N	0	1	.000	17	0	0	0	0	19^1	16	6	6	2	3	7	13	1.190	2.79	119	3.59	.232	0	.000	1	1	0.1
Total	**2**	**1**	**2**	**.333**	**35**	**3**	**0**	**0**	**1**	**53**	**44**	**20**	**19**	**4**	**5**	**25**	**32**	**1.302**	**3.23**	**112**	**3.54**	**.226**	**0**	**.000**	**1**	**3**	**0.1**

• CAPRA, Buzz Lee William Capra b: 10/1/1947, Chicago, IL BR/TR, 5'10", 168 lbs. Deb: 9/15/1971

YEAR	TM-L	W	L	PCT	G	GS	CG	SH	SV	IP	H	R	ER	HR	HB	BB	SO	RAT	ERA	ERA+	CERA	OAV	BH	AVG	PR+	WS	TPW
1971	NY-N	0	1	.000	3	0	0	0	0	5^1	3	6	5	0	0	5	6	1.500	8.44	40	2.58	.167	0	.000	-3	0	-0.3
1972	NY-N	3	2	.600	14	6	0	0	0	53	50	27	27	7	0	27	45	1.453	4.58	73	4.48	.253	3	.250	-7	2	-0.6
1973	NY-N	2	7	.222	24	0	0	0	4	42	35	18	18	4	2	28	35	1.500	3.86	94	3.93	.233	0	.000	-1	2	-0.1
1974	Atl-N★	16	8	.667	39	27	11	5	1	217	163	67	55	13	3	84	137	1.138	**2.28**	**166**	2.47	**.208**	11	.164	33	21	3.4
1975	Atl-N	4	7	.364	12	12	5	0	0	78^1	77	41	37	8	1	28	35	1.340	4.25	89	3.83	.257	1	.043	-2	3	-0.4
1976	Atl-N	0	1	.000	5	0	0	0	0	9^1	9	9	9	0	0	6	4	1.607	8.68	44	3.48	.265	0	....	-5	0	-0.5
1977	Atl-N	6	11	.353	45	16	0	0	0	139^1	142	88	83	28	4	80	100	1.593	5.36	83	5.61	.263	4	.111	-10	4	-1.1
Total	**7**	**31**	**37**	**.456**	**142**	**61**	**16**	**5**	**5**	**544^1**	**479**	**256**	**234**	**60**	**10**	**258**	**362**	**1.354**	**3.87**	**101**	**3.80**	**.237**	**19**	**.135**	**4**	**32**	**0.3**

• CAPUANO, Chris Christopher Frank Capuano b: 8/19/1978, Springfield, MA BL/TL, 6'3", 210 lbs. Deb: 5/4/2003

YEAR	TM-L	W	L	PCT	G	GS	CG	SH	SV	IP	H	R	ER	HR	HB	BB	SO	RAT	ERA	ERA+	CERA	OAV	BH	AVG	PR+	WS	TPW
2003	Ari-N	2	4	.333	9	5	0	0	0	33	27	19	17	3	6	11	23	1.152	4.64	101	3.45	.231	0	.000	0	2	0.0

• CARAWAY, Pat Cecil Bradford Patrick Caraway b: 9/26/1905, Erath County, TX d: 6/9/1974, El Paso, TX BL/TL, 6'4", 175 lbs. Deb: 4/19/1930

YEAR	TM-L	W	L	PCT	G	GS	CG	SH	SV	IP	H	R	ER	HR	HB	BB	SO	RAT	ERA	ERA+	CERA	OAV	BH	AVG	PR+	WS	TPW
1930	Chi-A	10	10	.500	38	21	9	1	1	193^1	194	96	83	11	3	57	83	1.298	3.86	119	3.40	.267	11	.172	21	15	1.8
1931	Chi-A	10	24	.294	51	32	11	1	2	220	268	177	152	17	7	101	55	**1.677**	6.22	68	5.27	.295	14	.194	-44	2	-4.1

YEAR	TM-L	W	L	PCT	G	GS	CG	SH	SV	IP	H	R	ER	HR	HB	BB	SO	RAT	ERA	ERA+	CERA	OAV	BH	AVG	PR+	WS	TPW
1932	Chi-A	2	6	.250	19	9	1	0	0	64^2	80	55	49	6	3	37	13	1.809	6.82	63	6.13	.304	3	.143	-17	0	-1.7
Total	3	22	40	.355	108	62	21	2	3	478	542	328	284	34	13	195	151	1.542	5.35	82	4.63	.286	28	.178	-40	17	-4.0
• CARDEN, John					John Bruton Carden b: 5/19/1921, Killeen, TX d: 2/8/1949, Mexia, TX BR/TR, 6'5", 210 lbs. Deb: 5/18/1946																						
1946	NY-N	0	0	....	1	0	0	0	0	2	4	7	5	0	1	4	1	4.000	22.50	15	17.92	.400	0	....	-4	0	-0.4
• CARDINAL, Conrad					Conrad Seth Cardinal b: 3/30/1942, Brooklyn, NY BR/TR, 6'1", 190 lbs. Deb: 4/11/1963																						
1963	Hou-N	0	1	.000	6	1	0	0	0	13^1	15	14	9	0	0	7	7	1.650	6.08	52	4.31	.283	0	.000	-4	0	-0.5
• CARDONI, Ben					Armand Joseph "Big Ben" Cardoni b: 8/21/1920, Jessup, PA d: 4/2/1969, Jessup, PA BR/TR, 6'3", 195 lbs. Deb: 8/22/1943																						
1943	Bos-N	0	0	....	11	0	0	0	1	28	38	20	20	1	1	14	5	1.857	6.43	53	6.20	.336	0	.000	-10	0	-1.1
1944	Bos-N	0	6	.000	22	5	1	0	0	75^2	83	40	33	5	1	37	24	1.586	3.93	97	4.63	.284	4	.235	-1	2	-0.1
1945	Bos-N	0	0	....	3	0	0	0	0	4	6	5	4	0	1	3	5	2.250	9.00	43	7.50	.300	0	....	-2	0	-0.2
Total	3	0	6	.000	36	5	1	0	1	107^2	127	65	57	6	3	54	34	1.681	4.76	77	5.15	.299	4	.167	-13	2	-1.5
• CARDWELL, Don					Donald Eugene Cardwell b: 12/7/1935, Winston-Salem, NC BR/TR, 6'4", 210 lbs. Deb: 4/21/1957																						
1957	Phi-N	4	8	.333	30	19	5	1	1	128^1	122	71	70	17	4	42	92	1.278	4.91	77	3.87	.251	7	.200	-15	4	-1.4
1958	Phi-N	3	6	.333	16	14	3	0	0	107^2	99	55	54	16	2	37	77	1.263	4.51	88	3.76	.241	8	.211	-5	4	-0.4
1959	Phi-N	9	10	.474	25	22	5	1	0	153	135	77	69	22	4	65	106	1.307	4.06	101	3.88	.238	3	.055	1	8	-0.2
1960	Phi-N	1	2	.333	5	4	0	0	0	28^1	28	14	14	4	1	11	21	1.376	4.45	87	4.44	.262	2	.250	-2	2	0.0
	Chi-N	8	14	.364	31	26	6	1	0	177	166	101	86	19	5	68	129	1.322	4.37	86	3.75	.249	14	.203	-11	6	-0.8
	Yr.	9	16	.360	36	30	6	1	0	205^1	194	115	100	23	6	79	150	1.330	4.38	86	3.85	.251	16	.208	-13	8	-0.8
1961	Chi-N	15	14	.517	39	**38**	13	3	0	259^1	243	121	110	22	10	88	156	1.276	3.82	109	3.51	.246	10	.105	14	16	1.4
1962	Chi-N	7	16	.304	41	29	6	1	4	195^2	205	116	107	27	9	60	104	1.354	4.92	84	4.34	.267	9	.148	-17	7	-1.7
1963	Pit-N	13	15	.464	33	32	7	2	0	213^2	195	92	73	21	16	52	112	1.156	3.07	107	3.23	.245	6	.085	4	11	0.2
1964	Pit-N	1	2	.333	4	4	1	1	0	19^1	15	9	6	1	3	7	10	1.138	2.79	126	2.88	.217	1	.143	2	1	0.2
1965	Pit-N	13	10	.565	37	34	12	2	0	240^1	214	101	85	21	12	59	107	1.136	3.18	110	3.04	.239	12	.162	4	14	0.7
1966	Pit-N	6	6	.500	32	14	1	0	1	101^2	112	58	52	15	6	27	60	1.367	4.60	78	4.61	.282	3	.103	-14	2	-1.5
1967	NY-N	5	9	.357	26	16	3	3	0	118^1	112	55	47	8	7	39	71	1.276	3.57	95	3.44	.249	6	.158	-3	6	-0.1
1968	NY-N	7	13	.350	29	25	5	1	1	179^2	156	69	59	9	10	50	82	1.147	2.96	102	2.68	.233	3	.049	-1	8	-0.5
1969*	NY-N	8	10	.444	30	21	4	0	0	152^1	145	63	51	15	5	47	60	1.260	3.01	121	3.51	.252	8	.170	7	10	0.8
1970	NY-N	0	2	.000	16	1	0	0	0	25	31	19	18	3	3	6	8	1.480	6.48	62	5.41	.316	0	.000	-7	0	-0.8
	Atl-N	2	1	.667	16	2	1	1	0	23	31	23	23	5	1	13	16	1.913	9.00	48	7.94	.326	2	.400	-11	0	-1.1
	Yr.	2	3	.400	32	3	1	1	0	48	62	42	41	8	4	19	24	1.688	7.69	54	6.62	.321	2	.200	-19	0	-1.9
Total	14	102	138	.425	410	301	72	17	7	2122^2	2009	1044	924	225	98	671	1211	1.263	3.92	95	3.64	.250	94	.135	-54	99	-5.2
• CARLETON, Tex					James Otto Carleton b: 8/19/1906, Comanche, TX d: 1/11/1977, Fort Worth, TX BB/TR, 6'1.5", 180 lbs. Deb: 4/17/1932																						
1932	StL-N	10	13	.435	44	22	9	3	0	196^1	198	94	89	12	3	70	113	1.365	4.08	96	3.64	.261	9	.150	-2	11	-0.4
1933	StL-N	17	11	.607	44	33	15	4	3	277	263	117	104	15	4	97	147	1.300	3.38	103	3.27	.249	17	.187	3	18	0.4
1934*	StL-N	16	11	.593	40	31	16	0	2	240^2	260	126	114	14	7	52	103	1.296	4.26	99	3.54	.271	17	.193	-4	15	-0.3
1935*	Chi-N	11	8	.579	31	22	8	0	1	171	169	82	74	17	3	60	84	1.339	3.89	101	3.76	.257	8	.129	-6	9	-0.9
1936	Chi-N	14	10	.583	35	26	12	**4**	1	197^1	204	85	80	14	6	67	88	1.373	3.65	109	3.86	.268	14	.233	3	16	0.9
1937	Chi-N	16	8	.667	32	27	18	4	0	208^1	183	80	73	10	4	94	105	1.330	3.15	126	3.20	.236	12	.169	18	18	1.9
1938*	Chi-N	10	9	.526	33	24	9	0	0	167^2	213	118	101	11	8	74	80	**1.712**	5.42	70	5.57	.307	15	.231	-31	2	-2.8
1940	Bro-N	6	6	.500	34	17	4	1	2	149	140	68	63	12	3	47	88	1.255	3.81	105	3.28	.245	8	.186	4	9	0.4
Total	8	100	76	.568	293	202	91	16	9	1607^1	1630	770	698	105	38	561	808	1.363	3.91	100	3.71	.261	100	.185	-14	98	-0.8
• CARLOS, Cisco					Francisco Manuel Carlos b: 9/17/1940, Monrovia, CA BR/TR, 6'3", 205 lbs. Deb: 8/25/1967																						
1967	Chi-A	2	0	1.000	8	7	1	1	0	41^2	23	5	4	0	1	9	27	.768	0.86	359	1.06	.161	1	.063	10	5	1.0
1968	Chi-A	4	14	.222	29	21	0	0	0	122^1	121	64	53	13	10	37	57	1.292	3.90	78	3.93	.258	2	.065	-11	0	-1.5
1969	Chi-A	4	3	.571	25	4	0	0	0	49^1	52	33	31	4	5	23	28	1.520	5.66	68	4.85	.274	0	.000	-9	1	-1.0
	Was-A	1	1	.500	6	4	0	0	0	17^2	23	9	9	2	0	6	5	1.642	4.58	76	5.95	.348	1	.200	-2	1	-0.2
	Yr.	5	4	.556	31	8	0	0	0	67	75	42	40	6	5	29	33	1.552	5.37	70	5.14	.293	1	.067	-11	2	-1.2
1970	Was-A	0	0	....	5	0	0	0	0	6	3	1	1	0	0	4	2	1.167	1.50	237	1.79	.150	0	....	1	1	0.1
Total	4	11	18	.379	73	36	1	1	0	237	222	112	98	19	16	79	119	1.270	3.72	89	3.71	.250	4	.065	-11	8	-1.5
• CARLSEN, Don					Donald Herbert Carlsen b: 10/15/1926, Chicago, IL d: 9/22/2002, Denver, CO BR/TR, 6'1", 175 lbs. Deb: 4/28/1948																						
1948	Chi-N	0	0	....	1	0	0	0	0	1	5	4	4	0	0	2	1	7.000	36.00	11	40.61	.625	0	....	-4	0	-0.4
1951	Pit-N	2	3	.400	7	6	2	0	0	43	50	22	20	4	1	14	20	1.488	4.19	101	4.68	.292	4	.250	1	2	0.1
1952	Pit-N	0	1	.000	5	1	0	0	0	10	20	13	12	1	0	5	2	2.500	10.80	37	10.97	.417	1	.333	-7	0	-0.8
Total	3	2	4	.333	13	7	2	0	0	54	75	39	36	5	1	21	23	1.778	6.00	68	6.51	.330	5	.263	-10	2	-1.0
• CARLSON, Dan					Daniel Steven Carlson b: 1/26/1970, Portland, OR BR/TR, 6'1", 185 lbs. Deb: 9/13/1996																						
1996	SF-N	1	0	1.000	5	0	0	0	0	10	13	6	3	2	0	2	4	1.500	2.70	152	5.46	.310	0	.000	1	1	0.1
1997	SF-N	0	0	....	6	0	0	0	0	15^1	20	14	13	5	0	8	14	1.826	7.63	53	8.22	.317	0	.000	-6	0	-0.6
1998	TB-A	0	0	....	10	0	0	0	0	17^2	25	15	15	3	3	8	16	1.868	7.64	63	8.27	.347	0	....	-6	0	-0.6
1999	Ari-N	0	0	....	2	0	0	0	0	4	5	4	4	0	0	0	3	1.250	9.00	51	2.93	.278	0	....	-2	0	-0.2
Total	4	1	0	1.000	23	0	0	0	0	47	63	39	35	10	3	18	37	1.723	6.70	66	7.20	.323	0	.000	-13	1	-1.3
• CARLSON, Hal					Harold Gust Carlson b: 5/17/1892, Rockford, IL d: 5/28/1930, Chicago, IL BR/TR, 6', 180 lbs. Deb: 4/13/1917																						
1917	Pit-N	7	11	.389	34	17	9	1	1	161^1	140	64	52	0	4	49	68	1.171	2.90	98	2.42	.241	6	.122	0	7	-0.2
1918	Pit-N	0	1	.000	3	2	0	0	0	12	12	5	5	1	0	5	5	1.417	3.75	77	4.18	.286	1	.200	-2	0	-0.2
1919	Pit-N	8	10	.444	22	14	7	1	0	141	114	41	35	0	2	39	49	1.085	2.23	135	2.18	.243	7	.163	13	12	1.4
1920	Pit-N	14	13	.519	39	31	16	3	3	246^2	262	102	92	4	8	63	62	1.318	3.36	96	3.39	.281	23	.271	-3	17	0.0
1921	Pit-N	4	8	.333	31	10	3	0	4	109^2	121	59	52	6	2	23	37	1.313	4.27	90	3.64	.290	10	.294	-6	6	-0.4
1922	Pit-N	9	12	.429	39	18	6	0	2	145^1	193	106	92	10	4	58	64	1.727	5.70	71	5.66	.323	15	.268	-24	4	-2.0
1923	Pit-N	0	0	....	4	0	0	0	0	13^1	19	9	7	2	1	2	4	1.575	4.73	85	6.37	.358	0	.000	-1	0	-0.2
1924	Phi-N	8	17	.320	38	23	12	1	2	203^2	267	122	110	9	3	55	66	1.581	4.86	92	5.02	.329	21	.276	-5	10	-0.2
1925	Phi-N	13	14	.481	35	32	18	**4**	0	234	281	131	110	19	6	52	80	1.423	4.23	113	4.38	.298	17	.183	23	17	2.0
1926	Phi-N	17	12	.586	35	34	20	3	0	267^1	293	116	96	9	2	47	55	1.272	3.23	128	3.30	.281	23	.240	**36**	23	**3.8**
1927	Phi-N	4	5	.444	11	9	4	0	1	63^2	80	41	37	7	0	18	13	1.539	5.23	79	5.13	.316	6	.240	-7	2	-0.6
	Chi-N	12	8	.600	27	22	15	2	0	184^1	201	73	65	9	2	27	27	1.237	3.17	122	3.27	.280	11	.164	10	14	0.7
	Yr.	16	13	.552	38	31	19	2	1	248	281	114	102	16	2	45	40	1.315	3.70	107	3.75	.289	17	.185	4	16	0.1
1928	Chi-N	3	2	.600	20	4	2	0	4	56^1	74	42	37	4	0	15	11	1.580	5.91	65	5.12	.329	5	.263	-15	0	-1.4
1929*	Chi-N	11	5	.688	31	13	6	2	2	111^2	131	71	64	8	1	31	35	1.451	5.16	89	4.27	.292	9	.231	-9	6	-0.7
1930	Chi-N	4	2	.667	8	6	3	0	0	51^2	68	31	29	5	1	14	14	1.587	5.05	97	5.30	.313	5	.250	-1	3	-0.1
Total	14	114	120	.487	377	235	121	17	19	2002	2256	1013	883	93	36	498	590	1.376	3.97	99	3.89	.291	159	.223	11	121	1.9
• CARLSON, Leon					Leon Alton "Swede" Carlson b: 2/17/1895, Jamestown, NY d: 9/15/1961, Jamestown, NY BR/TR, 6'3", 195 lbs. Deb: 5/31/1920																						
1920	Was-A	0	0	....	3	0	0	0	0	12^1	14	7	5	1	0	2	3	1.297	3.65	102	3.88	.292	1	.167	0	1	0.0
• CARLTON, Steve					Steven Norman "Lefty" Carlton b: 12/22/1944, Miami, FL BL/TL, 6'4", 210 lbs. Deb: 4/12/1965 HOF: 1994																						
1965	StL-N	0	0	....	15	2	0	0	0	25	27	7	7	3	1	8	21	1.400	2.52	152	4.67	.287	0	.000	4	2	0.4
1966	StL-N	3	3	.500	9	9	2	1	0	52	56	22	18	2	0	18	25	1.423	3.12	116	3.86	.280	4	.267	2	3	0.3
1967*	StL-N	14	9	.609	30	28	11	2	1	193	173	71	64	10	2	62	168	1.218	2.98	109	2.93	.238	11	.153	5	13	0.6
1968*	StL-N★	13	11	.542	34	33	10	5	0	231^2	214	87	77	11	3	61	162	1.187	2.99	97	2.83	.246	12	.164	-4	11	-0.3
1969	StL-N★	17	11	.607	31	31	12	2	0	236^1	185	66	57	15	4	93	210	1.176	2.17	165	2.70	.216	17	.213	35	24	4.2
1970	StL-N	10	19	.345	34	33	13	2	0	253^2	239	123	105	25	2	109	193	1.372	3.73	110	3.80	.251	16	.200	15	14	1.6
1971	StL-N★	20	9	.690	37	36	18	4	0	273^1	275	120	108	23	5	98	172	1.365	3.56	101	3.85	.262	17	.177	7	16	0.9
1972	Phi-N★	**27**	10	.730	41	**41**	**30**	8	0	**346^1**	257	84	76	17	1	87	**310**	.993	**1.97**	**182**	1.92	.206	23	.197	**58**	**40**	**6.8**
1973	Phi-N	13	20	.394	40	**40**	**18**	3	0	**293^1**	293	146	127	29	3	113	223	1.384	3.90	97	3.98	.260	16	.160	-7	14	-0.6

YEAR	TM-L	W	L	PCT	G	GS	CG	SH	SV	IP	H	R	ER	HR	HB	BB	SO	RAT	ERA	ERA+	CERA	OAV	BH	AVG	PR+	WS	TPW
1974	Phi-N★	16	13	.552	39	39	17	1	0	291	249	118	104	21	5	136	**240**	1.323	3.22	117	3.41	.234	25	.245	12	22	1.5
1975	Phi-N	15	14	.517	37	37	14	3	0	255^1	217	116	101	24	2	104	192	1.257	3.56	105	3.27	.233	14	.156	-2	14	-0.3
1976*	Phi-N	20	7	.741	35	35	13	2	0	252^2	224	94	88	19	1	72	195	1.172	3.13	113	2.88	.237	20	.217	8	18	1.1
1977*	Phi-N★	**23**	10	.697	36	36	17	2	0	283	229	99	83	25	4	89	198	1.124	2.64	151	2.74	.223	26	.268	38	**26**	4.6
1978*	Phi-N	16	13	.552	34	34	12	3	0	247^1	228	91	78	30	3	63	161	1.177	2.84	126	3.28	.246	25	.291	15	20	2.4
1979	Phi-N★	18	11	.621	35	35	13	4	0	251	202	112	101	25	5	89	213	1.159	3.62	106	2.88	.219	21	.223	3	18	0.7
1980*	Phi-N★	**24**	9	.727	38	**38**	13	3	0	**304**	243	87	79	15	2	90	**286**	1.095	2.34	**162**	2.29	.218	19	.188	**49**	**29**	**5.2**
1981*	Phi-N★	13	4	.765	24	24	10	1	0	190	152	59	51	9	1	62	179	1.126	2.42	150	2.45	.222	9	.134	24	16	2.5
1982	Phi-N★	**23**	11	.676	38	**38**	**19**	**6**	0	**295^2**	253	114	102	17	1	86	**286**	1.147	3.10	118	2.65	.232	22	.218	18	**25**	2.4
1983*	Phi-N	15	16	.484	37	37	8	3	0	**283^2**	277	117	98	20	3	84	**275**	1.273	3.11	115	3.36	.258	19	.196	18	18	2.2
1984	Phi-N	13	7	.650	33	33	1	0	0	229	214	104	91	14	0	79	163	1.279	3.58	102	3.19	.246	16	.190	5	12	0.7
1985	Phi-N	1	8	.111	16	16	0	0	0	92	84	43	34	6	0	53	48	1.489	3.33	111	3.98	.249	5	.179	5	4	0.6
1986	Phi-N	4	8	.333	16	16	0	0	0	83	102	70	57	15	0	45	62	1.771	6.18	62	6.48	.297	7	.206	-21	0	-2.1
	SF-N	1	3	.250	6	6	0	0	0	30	36	20	17	4	1	16	18	1.733	5.10	69	6.20	.303	2	.182	-6	0	-0.5
	Yr.	5	11	.313	22	22	0	0	0	113	138	90	74	19	1	61	80	1.761	5.89	64	6.40	.299	9	.200	-27	0	-2.6
	Chi-A	4	3	.571	10	10	0	0	0	63^1	58	30	26	6	0	25	40	1.311	3.69	117	3.70	.252	0	....	3	4	0.3
1987	Cle-A	5	9	.357	23	14	3	0	1	109	111	76	65	17	2	63	71	1.596	5.37	84	5.34	.266	0	....	-9	3	-0.8
	Min-A	1	5	.167	9	7	0	0	0	43	54	35	32	7	2	23	20	1.791	6.70	69	6.95	.310	0	....	-10	0	-1.0
	Yr.	6	14	.300	32	21	3	0	1	152	165	111	97	24	4	86	91	1.651	5.74	79	5.80	.279	0	....	-19	3	-1.8
1988	Min-A	0	1	.000	4	1	0	0	0	9^2	20	19	18	5	0	5	5	2.586	16.76	24	15.30	.408	0	....	-14	0	-1.4
Total	24	329	244	.574	741	709	254	55	2	5217^1	4672	2130	1864	414	53	1833	4136	1.247	3.22	115	3.23	.240	346	.201	252	366	32.0

• CARLYLE, Buddy
Earl L. Carlyle b: 12/21/1977, Omaha, NE BL/TR, 6'3", 175 lbs. Deb: 8/29/1999

YEAR	TM-L	W	L	PCT	G	GS	CG	SH	SV	IP	H	R	ER	HR	HB	BB	SO	RAT	ERA	ERA+	CERA	OAV	BH	AVG	PR+	WS	TPW
1999	SD-N	1	3	.250	7	7	0	0	0	37^2	36	28	25	7	2	17	29	1.407	5.97	70	4.95	.257	2	.222	-8	0	-0.6
2000	SD-N	0	0	....	4	0	0	0	0	3	6	7	7	0	0	3	2	3.000	21.00	21	12.01	.400	0	....	-6	0	-0.5
Total	2	1	3	.250	11	7	0	0	0	40^2	42	35	32	7	2	20	31	1.525	7.08	60	5.47	.271	2	.222	-13	0	-1.2

• CARMAN, Don
Donald Wayne Carman b: 8/14/1959, Oklahoma City, OK BL/TL, 6'3", 195 lbs. Deb: 10/1/1983

YEAR	TM-L	W	L	PCT	G	GS	CG	SH	SV	IP	H	R	ER	HR	HB	BB	SO	RAT	ERA	ERA+	CERA	OAV	BH	AVG	PR+	WS	TPW
1983	Phi-N	0	0	....	1	0	0	0	1	1	0	0	0	0	0	0	0	.000	0.00	....	0.00	.000	0	....	0	0	0.0
1984	Phi-N	0	1	.000	11	0	0	0	0	13^1	14	9	8	2	0	6	16	1.500	5.40	67	4.23	.255	0	.000	-2	0	-0.3
1985	Phi-N	9	4	.692	71	0	0	0	7	86^1	52	25	20	6	2	38	87	1.042	2.08	177	2.06	.178	0	.000	16	12	1.7
1986	Phi-N	10	5	.667	50	14	2	1	1	134^1	113	50	48	11	3	52	98	1.228	3.22	120	3.11	.234	0	.000	10	10	0.7
1987	Phi-N	13	11	.542	35	35	3	2	0	211	194	110	99	34	5	69	125	1.246	4.22	100	3.79	.244	5	.082	-2	10	-0.5
1988	Phi-N	10	14	.417	36	32	2	0	0	201^1	211	101	96	20	4	70	116	1.396	4.29	83	4.15	.270	3	.048	-14	6	-2.0
1989	Phi-N	5	15	.250	49	20	0	0	0	149^1	152	98	87	21	3	86	81	1.594	5.24	68	5.13	.260	1	.029	-27	0	-3.3
1990	Phi-N	6	2	.750	59	1	0	0	1	86^2	69	43	40	13	4	38	58	1.235	4.15	92	3.46	.218	3	.273	-4	6	-0.4
1991	Cin-N	0	2	.000	28	0	0	0	1	36	40	23	21	8	1	19	15	1.639	5.25	72	6.29	.286	0	.000	-6	0	-0.7
1992	Tex-A	0	0	....	2	0	0	0	0	2^1	4	3	2	0	0	0	2	1.714	7.71	49	5.71	.364	0	....	-1	0	-0.1
Total	10	53	54	.495	342	102	7	3	11	921^2	849	462	421	115	22	378	598	1.331	4.11	92	3.90	.246	12	.057	-30	44	-4.7

• CARMICHAEL, Chet
Chester Keller Carmichael b: 1/9/1888, Muncie, IN d: 8/22/1960, Rochester, NY BR/TR, 5'11.5", 200 lbs. Deb: 9/5/1909

YEAR	TM-L	W	L	PCT	G	GS	CG	SH	SV	IP	H	R	ER	HR	HB	BB	SO	RAT	ERA	ERA+	CERA	OAV	BH	AVG	PR+	WS	TPW
1909	Cin-N	0	0	....	2	0	0	0	0	7	9	6	0	0	2	3	2	1.714	0.00	....	6.22	.321	0	.000	2	0	0.2

• CARMONA, Rafael
Rafael Carmona b: 10/2/1972, Rio Piedras, Puerto Rico BL/TR, 6'2", 185 lbs. Deb: 5/18/1995

YEAR	TM-L	W	L	PCT	G	GS	CG	SH	SV	IP	H	R	ER	HR	HB	BB	SO	RAT	ERA	ERA+	CERA	OAV	BH	AVG	PR+	WS	TPW
1995	Sea-A	2	4	.333	15	3	0	0	1	47^2	55	31	30	9	2	34	28	1.867	5.66	84	7.14	.293	0	....	-4	1	-0.3
1996	Sea-A	8	3	.727	53	1	0	0	1	90^1	95	47	43	11	3	55	62	1.661	4.28	116	5.33	.273	0	....	6	6	0.6
1997	Sea-A	0	0	....	4	0	0	0	0	5^2	3	3	2	1	0	2	6	.882	3.18	142	1.94	.150	0	....	1	0	0.1
1999	Sea-A	1	0	1.000	9	0	0	0	0	11^1	18	11	10	3	0	9	0	2.382	7.94	63	11.44	.409	0	....	-4	0	-0.3
Total	4	11	7	.611	81	4	0	0	2	155	171	92	85	24	5	100	96	1.748	4.94	99	6.21	.285	0	....	-0	7	0.0

• CARNETT, Eddie
Edwin Elliott "Lefty" Carnett b: 10/21/1916, Springfield, MO BL/TL, 6', 185 lbs. Deb: 4/19/1941 ♦

YEAR	TM-L	W	L	PCT	G	GS	CG	SH	SV	IP	H	R	ER	HR	HB	BB	SO	RAT	ERA	ERA+	CERA	OAV	BH	AVG	PR+	WS	TPW
1941	Bos-N	0	0	....	2	0	0	0	0	1^1	4	3	3	0	0	3	2	5.250	20.25	18	24.75	.500	0	....	-2	0	-0.3
1944	Chi-A	0	0	....	2	0	0	0	0	2	3	2	2	1	0	0	1	1.500	9.00	38	8.13	.333	126	.276	-1	13	-1.8
1945	Cle-A	0	0	....	2	0	0	0	0	2	0	0	0	0	0	0	1	.000	0.00	....	0.00	.000	16	.219	1	1	-0.5
Total	3	0	0	....	6	0	0	0	0	5^1	7	5	5	1	0	3	4	1.875	8.44	42	9.24	.412	142	.268	-3	14	-2.6

• CARNEY, Pat
Patrick Joseph "Doc" Carney b: 8/7/1876, Holyoke, MA d: 1/9/1953, Worcester, MA BL/TL, 6', 200 lbs. Deb: 9/20/1901 ♦

YEAR	TM-L	W	L	PCT	G	GS	CG	SH	SV	IP	H	R	ER	HR	HB	BB	SO	RAT	ERA	ERA+	CERA	OAV	BH	AVG	PR+	WS	TPW
1902	Bos-N	0	1	.000	2	1	0	0	0	5	6	5	5	1	1	3	3	1.800	9.00	31	7.60	.297	141	.270	-3	17	-1.3
1903	Bos-N	4	5	.444	10	9	9	0	0	78	93	52	35	2	2	31	29	1.590	4.04	79	4.45	.284	94	.240	-9	8	-2.4
1904	Bos-N	0	4	.000	4	3	1	0	0	26^1	40	27	17	1	1	12	5	1.975	5.81	47	7.29	.364	57	.204	-8	1	-2.8
Total	3	4	10	.286	16	13	10	0	0	109^1	139	84	57	4	4	46	37	1.692	4.69	64	5.28	.304	308	.247	-21	26	-6.6

• CARPENTER, Bob
Robert Louis Carpenter b: 12/12/1917, Chicago, IL BR/TR, 6'3", 195 lbs. Deb: 9/12/1940

YEAR	TM-L	W	L	PCT	G	GS	CG	SH	SV	IP	H	R	ER	HR	HB	BB	SO	RAT	ERA	ERA+	CERA	OAV	BH	AVG	PR+	WS	TPW
1940	NY-N	2	0	1.000	5	3	2	0	0	33	29	11	10	2	0	14	25	1.303	2.73	142	3.20	.238	1	.100	4	3	0.4
1941	NY-N	11	6	.647	29	19	8	1	2	131^2	138	71	56	15	2	42	42	1.367	3.83	97	4.08	.265	7	.156	-3	8	-0.3
1942	NY-N	11	10	.524	28	25	12	2	0	185^2	192	73	65	13	1	51	53	1.309	3.15	107	3.50	.263	12	.185	3	11	0.2
1946	NY-N	1	3	.250	12	6	1	1	0	39	37	22	21	7	0	18	13	1.410	4.85	71	4.41	.245	1	.100	-6	1	-0.6
1947	NY-N	0	0	....	2	0	0	0	0	3	5	5	4	0	0	3	0	2.667	12.00	34	9.34	.385	0	....	-3	0	-0.3
	Chi-N	0	1	.000	4	1	0	0	0	7^1	10	5	4	1	0	4	1	1.909	4.91	80	7.06	.323	1	1.000	-1	0	0.0
	Yr.	0	1	.000	6	1	0	0	0	10^1	15	10	8	1	0	7	1	2.129	6.97	58	7.72	.341	1	1.000	-3	0	-0.3
Total	5	25	20	.556	80	54	23	4	2	399^2	411	187	160	38	3	132	134	1.359	3.60	98	3.86	.262	22	.168	-5	23	-0.6

• CARPENTER, Chris
Chistopher John Carpenter b: 4/27/1975, Exeter, NH BR/TR, 6'6", 215 lbs. Deb: 5/12/1997

YEAR	TM-L	W	L	PCT	G	GS	CG	SH	SV	IP	H	R	ER	HR	HB	BB	SO	RAT	ERA	ERA+	CERA	OAV	BH	AVG	PR+	WS	TPW
1997	Tor-A	3	7	.300	14	13	1	1	0	81^1	108	55	46	7	2	37	55	1.783	5.09	90	6.38	.325	0	....	-6	2	-0.6
1998	Tor-A	12	7	.632	33	24	1	1	0	175	177	97	85	18	5	61	136	1.360	4.37	107	4.12	.265	0	.000	6	11	0.5
1999	Tor-A	9	8	.529	24	24	4	1	0	150	177	81	73	16	3	48	106	1.500	4.38	112	4.90	.294	0	.000	9	9	0.8
2000	Tor-A	10	12	.455	34	27	2	0	0	175^1	204	130	122	30	5	83	113	1.637	6.26	81	6.04	.290	0	.000	-23	5	-2.1
2001	Tor-A	11	11	.500	34	34	3	2	0	215^2	229	112	98	29	16	75	157	1.410	4.09	112	4.82	.274	1	.167	11	13	1.0
2002	Tor-A	4	5	.444	13	13	1	0	0	73^1	89	45	43	11	4	27	45	1.582	5.28	87	5.91	.306	1	1.000	-5	3	-0.4
Total	6	49	50	.495	152	135	12	5	0	870^2	984	520	467	111	35	331	612	1.510	4.83	99	5.18	.287	2	.182	-9	43	-0.8

• CARPENTER, Cris
Cris Howell Carpenter b: 4/5/1965, St. Augustine, FL BR/TR, 6'1", 185 lbs. Deb: 5/14/1988

YEAR	TM-L	W	L	PCT	G	GS	CG	SH	SV	IP	H	R	ER	HR	HB	BB	SO	RAT	ERA	ERA+	CERA	OAV	BH	AVG	PR+	WS	TPW
1988	StL-N	2	3	.400	8	8	1	0	0	47^2	56	27	25	3	1	9	24	1.364	4.72	74	4.00	.298	2	.143	-7	1	-0.8
1989	StL-N	4	4	.500	36	5	0	0	0	68	70	30	24	4	2	26	35	1.412	3.18	114	3.66	.262	4	.444	3	4	0.4
1990	StL-N	0	0	....	4	0	0	0	0	8	5	4	4	2	0	2	6	.875	4.50	85	2.15	.167	0	.000	-1	0	-0.1
1991	StL-N	10	4	.714	59	0	0	0	0	66	53	31	31	6	0	20	47	1.106	4.23	88	2.43	.220	1	.333	-4	5	-0.4
1992	StL-N	5	4	.556	73	0	0	0	1	88	69	29	29	10	4	27	46	1.091	2.97	114	2.74	.220	1	.333	3	7	0.3
1993	Fla-N	0	1	.000	29	0	0	0	0	37^1	29	15	12	1	2	13	26	1.125	2.89	149	2.34	.212	0	....	7	3	0.7
	Tex-A	4	1	.800	27	0	0	0	1	32	35	15	15	4	2	12	27	1.469	4.22	98	5.01	.289	0	....	0	3	0.0
1994	Tex-A	2	5	.286	47	0	0	0	5	59	69	35	33	7	0	20	39	1.508	5.03	96	4.68	.291	0	....	0	3	0.0
1996	Mil-A	0	0	....	8	0	0	0	0	8^1	12	8	7	1	0	2	2	1.680	7.56	69	6.02	.333	0	....	-2	0	-0.2
Total	8	27	22	.551	291	13	1	0	7	414^1	398	194	180	38	11	131	252	1.277	3.91	99	3.46	.254	8	.267	-2	26	0.0

• CARPENTER, Lew
Lewis Emmett Carpenter b: 8/16/1913, Woodstock, GA d: 4/25/1979, Marietta, GA BR/TR, 6'2", 195 lbs. Deb: 5/1/1943

YEAR	TM-L	W	L	PCT	G	GS	CG	SH	SV	IP	H	R	ER	HR	HB	BB	SO	RAT	ERA	ERA+	CERA	OAV	BH	AVG	PR+	WS	TPW
1943	Was-A	0	0	....	4	0	0	0	0	3^1	1	0	0	0	1	4	1	1.500	0.00	....	3.79	.125	0	....	1	0	0.1

• CARPENTER, Paul
Paul Calvin Carpenter b: 8/12/1894, Granville, OH d: 3/14/1968, Newark, OH BR/TR, 5'11", 165 lbs. Deb: 7/26/1916

YEAR	TM-L	W	L	PCT	G	GS	CG	SH	SV	IP	H	R	ER	HR	HB	BB	SO	RAT	ERA	ERA+	CERA	OAV	BH	AVG	PR+	WS	TPW
1916	Pit-N	0	0	....	5	0	0	0	0	7^2	8	3	1	0	0	4	5	1.565	1.17	228	3.68	.258	0	.000	1	0	0.1

• CARPIN, Frank
Frank Dominic Carpin b: 9/14/1938, Brooklyn, NY BL/TL, 5'10", 172 lbs. Deb: 5/25/1965

YEAR	TM-L	W	L	PCT	G	GS	CG	SH	SV	IP	H	R	ER	HR	HB	BB	SO	RAT	ERA	ERA+	CERA	OAV	BH	AVG	PR+	WS	TPW
1965	Pit-N	3	1	.750	39	0	0	0	4	39^2	35	16	14	0	3	24	27	1.487	3.18	111	3.64	.243	0	.000	1	3	0.1

YEAR TM-L	W	L	PCT	G	GS	CG	SH	SV	IP	H	R	ER	HR	HB	BB	SO	RAT	ERA	ERA+	CERA	OAV	BH	AVG	PR+	WS	TPW
1966 Hou-N	1	0	1.000	10	0	0	0	0	6	9	7	5	0	0	6	2	2.500	7.50	46	8.58	.346	0	....	-3	0	-0.3
Total 2	4	1	.800	49	0	0	0	4	45^{2}	44	23	19	0	3	30	29	1.620	3.74	93	4.29	.259	0	.000	-2	3	-0.2

• CARRARA, Giovanni Giovanni (Jimenez) Carrara b: 3/4/1968, Edo Anzoategui, Venezuela BR/TR, 6'2", 210 lbs. Deb: 7/29/1995

YEAR TM-L	W	L	PCT	G	GS	CG	SH	SV	IP	H	R	ER	HR	HB	BB	SO	RAT	ERA	ERA+	CERA	OAV	BH	AVG	PR+	WS	TPW
1995 Tor-A	2	4	.333	12	7	1	0	0	48^{2}	64	46	39	10	1	25	27	1.829	7.21	65	7.43	.320	0	....	-14	0	-1.3
1996 Tor-A	0	1	.000	11	0	0	0	0	15	23	19	19	5	0	12	10	2.333	11.40	44	11.46	.359	0	....	-11	0	-1.0
Cin-N	1	0	1.000	8	5	0	0	0	23	31	17	15	6	2	13	13	1.913	5.87	71	8.62	.323	0	.000	-5	0	-0.5
1997 Cin-N	0	1	.000	2	2	0	0	0	10^{1}	14	9	9	4	0	6	5	1.935	7.84	55	9.47	.333	0	.000	-4	0	-0.4
2000 Col-N	0	1	.000	8	0	0	0	0	13^{1}	21	19	19	5	1	11	15	2.400	12.83	45	12.21	.356	0	.000	-10	0	-1.0
2001 LA-N	6	1	.857	47	3	0	0	0	85^{1}	73	30	30	12	1	24	70	1.137	3.16	127	3.10	.231	3	.250	8	8	0.9
2002 LA-N	6	3	.667	63	1	0	0	1	90^{2}	83	34	33	14	6	32	56	1.268	3.28	116	3.97	.243	0	.000	5	7	0.5
2003 Sea-A	2	0	1.000	23	0	0	0	0	29	40	22	22	6	2	14	13	1.862	6.83	63	8.10	.333	0	....	-9	0	-0.8
Total 7	17	11	.607	174	18	1	0	1	315^{1}	349	196	186	62	13	137	209	1.541	5.31	83	5.87	.282	3	.107	-39	15	-3.7

• CARRASCO, D.J. Daniel Carrasco b: 4/12/1977, Safford, AZ BR/TR, 6'1", 215 lbs. Deb: 4/2/2003

YEAR TM-L	W	L	PCT	G	GS	CG	SH	SV	IP	H	R	ER	HR	HB	BB	SO	RAT	ERA	ERA+	CERA	OAV	BH	AVG	PR+	WS	TPW
2003 KC-A	6	5	.545	50	2	0	0	2	80^{1}	82	44	43	8	7	40	57	1.519	4.82	107	4.94	.271	0	.000	3	6	0.3

• CARRASCO, Hector Hector (Pacheco) Carrasco b: 10/22/1969, San Pedro de Macoris, Dominican Republic BR/TR, 6'2", 175 lbs. Deb: 4/4/1994

YEAR TM-L	W	L	PCT	G	GS	CG	SH	SV	IP	H	R	ER	HR	HB	BB	SO	RAT	ERA	ERA+	CERA	OAV	BH	AVG	PR+	WS	TPW
1994 Cin-N	5	6	.455	45	0	0	0	6	56^{1}	42	17	14	3	2	30	41	1.278	2.24	185	3.01	.210	0	.000	12	7	1.1
1995* Cin-N	2	7	.222	64	0	0	0	5	87^{1}	86	45	40	1	2	46	64	1.511	4.12	100	3.77	.257	0	.000	-2	5	-0.3
1996 Cin-N	4	3	.571	56	0	0	0	0	74^{1}	58	37	31	6	1	45	59	1.386	3.75	111	3.41	.214	1	.200	3	5	0.3
1997 Cin-N	1	2	.333	38	0	0	0	0	51^{1}	51	25	21	3	4	25	46	1.481	3.68	117	4.14	.250	0	....	3	3	0.3
KC-A	1	6	.143	28	0	0	0	0	34^{2}	29	21	21	4	4	16	30	1.298	5.45	87	3.79	.227	0	....	-3	1	-0.3
1998 Min-A	4	2	.667	63	0	0	0	1	61^{2}	75	30	30	4	1	31	46	1.719	4.38	109	5.47	.304	0	....	4	5	0.3
1999 Min-A	2	3	.400	39	0	0	0	1	49	48	29	26	3	1	18	35	1.347	4.78	106	3.76	.261	0	....	2	3	0.2
2000 Min-A	4	3	.571	61	0	0	0	1	72	75	38	34	6	3	33	57	1.500	4.25	121	4.52	.270	0	....	8	6	0.8
Bos-A	1	1	.500	8	1	0	0	0	6^{2}	15	8	7	2	1	5	7	3.000	9.45	53	16.76	.469	0	....	-3	0	-0.3
Yr.	5	4	.556	69	1	0	0	1	78^{2}	90	46	41	8	4	38	64	1.627	4.69	109	5.56	.290	0	....	5	6	0.5
2001 Min-A	4	3	.571	56	0	0	0	1	73^{2}	77	40	38	8	0	30	70	1.452	4.64	99	4.42	.277	0	....	0	4	0.0
2003 Bal-A	2	6	.250	40	0	0	0	1	38^{1}	40	22	21	5	2	20	27	1.565	4.93	89	5.09	.270	0	....	-2	2	-0.2
Total 9	30	42	.417	498	1	0	0	16	605^{1}	596	312	283	45	21	299	482	1.479	4.21	108	4.25	.259	1	.056	21	41	1.9

• CARRASQUEL, Alex Alejandro Eloy (Aparicio) Carrasquel b: 7/24/1912, Caracas, Venezuela d: 8/19/1969, Caracas, Venezuela BR/TR, 6'1", 182 lbs. Deb: 4/23/1939

YEAR TM-L	W	L	PCT	G	GS	CG	SH	SV	IP	H	R	ER	HR	HB	BB	SO	RAT	ERA	ERA+	CERA	OAV	BH	AVG	PR+	WS	TPW
1939 Was-A	5	9	.357	40	17	7	0	2	159^{1}	165	89	83	7	1	68	41	1.462	4.69	93	3.85	.266	7	.167	-7	8	-0.6
1940 Was-A	6	2	.750	28	0	0	0	0	48	42	26	26	4	0	29	19	1.479	4.88	86	3.95	.240	0	.000	-3	3	-0.4
1941 Was-A	6	2	.750	35	5	4	0	2	96^{2}	103	44	37	7	1	49	30	1.572	3.44	117	4.69	.278	2	.095	8	8	0.8
1942 Was-A	7	7	.500	35	15	7	1	4	152^{1}	161	74	58	7	1	53	40	1.405	3.43	107	3.67	.267	6	.136	10	7	1.0
1943 Was-A	11	7	.611	39	13	4	1	5	144^{1}	160	76	59	3	1	54	48	1.483	3.68	87	3.87	.279	8	.186	-7	6	-0.7
1944 Was-A	8	7	.533	43	7	3	0	2	134	143	68	51	8	2	50	35	1.440	3.43	95	3.98	.273	7	.194	-1	6	0.0
1945 Was-A	7	5	.583	35	7	5	2	1	122^{2}	105	43	37	5	0	40	38	1.182	2.71	114	2.56	.228	3	.083	6	8	0.5
1949 Chi-A	0	0	....	3	0	0	0	0	3^{2}	8	6	6	1	0	4	1	3.273	14.73	28	16.45	.421	0	....	-4	0	-0.4
Total 8	50	39	.562	258	64	30	4	16	861	887	426	357	42	6	347	252	1.433	3.73	98	3.81	.265	33	.144	0	46	0.1

• CARRENO, Amalio Amalio Rafael (Adrian) Carreno b: 4/11/1964, Chacachacare, Venezuela BR/TR, 6', 170 lbs. Deb: 7/7/1991

YEAR TM-L	W	L	PCT	G	GS	CG	SH	SV	IP	H	R	ER	HR	HB	BB	SO	RAT	ERA	ERA+	CERA	OAV	BH	AVG	PR+	WS	TPW
1991 Phi-N	0	0	....	3	0	0	0	0	3^{1}	5	6	6	1	2	3	2	2.400	16.20	23	14.06	.333	0	.000	-5	0	-0.5

• CARRICK, Bill William Martin "Doughnut Bill" Carrick b: 9/5/1873, Erie, PA d: 3/7/1932, Philadelphia, PA TR, 5'10" Deb: 7/30/1898 U

YEAR TM-L	W	L	PCT	G	GS	CG	SH	SV	IP	H	R	ER	HR	HB	BB	SO	RAT	ERA	ERA+	CERA	OAV	BH	AVG	PR+	WS	TPW
1898 NY-N	3	1	.750	5	4	4	0	0	39^{2}	39	23	15	0	5	21	10	1.513	3.40	102	4.04	.255	3	.167	0	2	0.0
1899 NY-N	16	27	.372	44	**43**	**40**	3	0	361^{2}	485	250	187	4	23	122	60	1.678	4.65	81	5.26	.321	18	.138	-40	13	-4.1
1900 NY-N	19	22	.463	**45**	**41**	32	1	0	341^{2}	415	224	134	7	13	92	63	1.484	3.53	102	4.26	.299	20	.174	2	17	0.0
1901 Was-A	14	22	.389	42	37	34	0	0	324	367	198	135	12	20	93	70	1.420	3.75	98	3.98	.282	20	.159	-2	18	-0.6
1902 Was-A	11	17	.393	31	30	28	0	0	257^{2}	344	194	139	10	10	72	36	1.614	4.86	76	5.14	.320	20	.185	-28	7	-2.9
Total 5	63	89	.414	167	155	138	4	0	1324^{2}	1650	889	610	33	71	400	239	1.548	4.14	89	4.63	.304	81	.163	-67	57	-7.5

• CARRITHERS, Don Donald George Carrithers b: 9/15/1949, Lynwood, CA BR/TR, 6'2", 180 lbs. Deb: 8/1/1970

YEAR TM-L	W	L	PCT	G	GS	CG	SH	SV	IP	H	R	ER	HR	HB	BB	SO	RAT	ERA	ERA+	CERA	OAV	BH	AVG	PR+	WS	TPW
1970 SF-N	2	1	.667	11	2	0	0	0	22	31	19	18	5	0	14	14	2.045	7.36	54	8.67	.333	0	.000	-8	0	-0.8
1971* SF-N	5	3	.625	22	12	2	1	1	80^{1}	77	48	36	6	2	37	41	1.419	4.03	84	3.93	.254	3	.176	-5	3	-0.5
1972 SF-N	4	8	.333	25	14	2	0	1	90	108	66	58	10	5	42	42	1.667	5.80	60	5.73	.296	6	.207	-23	0	-2.4
1973 SF-N	1	2	.333	25	3	0	0	0	58	64	40	31	2	4	35	36	1.707	4.81	79	5.12	.278	4	.250	-6	1	-0.6
1974 Mon-N	5	2	.714	22	3	0	0	1	60	56	22	20	6	3	17	31	1.217	3.00	128	3.34	.249	4	.286	6	6	0.7
1975 Mon-N	5	3	.625	19	14	5	2	0	101	90	39	37	7	4	38	37	1.267	3.30	116	3.34	.240	6	.176	6	8	0.6
1976 Mon-N	6	12	.333	34	19	2	0	0	140^{1}	153	84	69	9	7	78	71	1.646	4.43	84	4.98	.286	4	.108	-11	3	-1.3
1977 Min-A	0	1	.000	7	0	0	0	0	14^{1}	16	13	11	2	1	6	3	1.535	6.91	58	4.99	.271	0	....	-5	0	-0.5
Total 8	28	32	.467	165	67	11	3	3	566	595	331	280	47	26	267	275	1.523	4.45	83	4.64	.272	27	.176	-46	21	-4.7

• CARROLL, Clay Clay Palmer "Hawk" Carroll b: 5/2/1941, Clanton, AL BR/TR, 6'1", 200 lbs. Deb: 9/2/1964

YEAR TM-L	W	L	PCT	G	GS	CG	SH	SV	IP	H	R	ER	HR	HB	BB	SO	RAT	ERA	ERA+	CERA	OAV	BH	AVG	PR+	WS	TPW
1964 Mil-N	2	0	1.000	11	1	0	0	1	20^{1}	15	4	4	1	0	3	17	.885	1.77	199	1.54	.200	0	.000	4	2	0.4
1965 Mil-N	0	1	.000	19	1	0	0	1	34^{2}	35	18	17	3	1	13	16	1.385	4.41	80	4.01	.269	0	.000	-4	1	-0.4
1966 Atl-N	8	7	.533	**73**	3	0	0	11	144^{1}	127	45	38	8	4	29	67	1.081	2.37	153	2.47	.236	3	.100	20	14	1.9
1967 Atl-N	6	12	.333	42	7	1	0	0	93	111	62	57	6	3	29	35	1.505	5.52	60	4.52	.304	1	.063	-23	0	-2.6
1968 Atl-N	0	1	.000	10	0	0	0	0	22^{1}	26	15	12	1	0	6	10	1.433	4.84	62	3.97	.310	0	.000	-5	0	-0.6
Cin-N	7	7	.500	58	1	0	0	17	121^{2}	102	35	31	3	6	32	61	1.101	2.29	138	2.34	.230	6	.250	13	14	1.6
Yr.	7	8	.467	68	1	0	0	17	144	128	50	43	4	6	38	71	1.153	2.69	116	2.59	.242	6	.207	8	14	1.0
1969 Cin-N	12	6	.667	71	4	0	0	7	150^{2}	149	70	59	9	7	78	90	1.507	3.52	107	4.13	.262	6	.207	4	10	0.7
1970* Cin-N	9	4	.692	65	0	0	0	16	104^{1}	104	38	30	4	2	27	63	1.256	2.59	161	3.04	.259	1	.071	18	14	1.7
1971 Cin-N★	10	4	.714	61	0	0	0	15	93^{2}	78	26	26	5	2	42	64	1.281	2.50	130	3.04	.234	1	.100	6	13	0.5
1972* Cin-N★	6	4	.600	**65**	0	0	0	**37**	96	89	27	24	5	1	32	51	1.260	2.25	143	3.09	.256	2	.182	8	13	0.9
1973* Cin-N	8	8	.500	53	5	0	0	14	92^{2}	111	47	38	5	5	34	41	1.565	3.69	92	4.77	.307	3	.214	-5	5	-0.5
1974 Cin-N	12	5	.706	57	3	0	0	6	100^{2}	96	27	24	3	0	30	46	1.252	2.15	162	2.84	.256	3	.167	13	12	1.3
1975* Cin-N	7	5	.583	56	2	0	0	7	96^{1}	93	30	28	2	3	32	44	1.298	2.62	137	3.08	.255	0	.000	7	9	0.5
1976 Chi-A	4	4	.500	29	0	0	0	6	77^{1}	67	26	22	1	2	24	38	1.177	2.56	139	2.60	.242	0	....	10	8	1.0
1977 StL-N	4	2	.667	51	1	0	0	4	90	77	28	25	8	1	24	34	1.122	2.50	154	2.73	.238	1	.091	12	8	1.1
Chi-A	1	3	.250	8	0	0	0	1	11^{1}	14	7	6	3	0	4	4	1.588	4.76	86	6.79	.311	0	....	-1	0	-0.1
1978 Pit-N	0	0	....	2	0	0	0	0	4	2	1	1	0	0	3	0	1.250	2.25	164	2.03	.143	0	....	1	0	0.1
Total 15	96	73	.568	731	28	1	0	143	1353^{1}	1296	506	442	67	37	442	681	1.284	2.94	119	3.25	.257	27	.130	78	123	7.6

• CARROLL, Dick Richard Thomas "Shadow" Carroll b: 7/21/1884, Cleveland, OH d: 11/22/1945, Cleveland, OH BR/TR, 6'2" Deb: 9/25/1909

YEAR TM-L	W	L	PCT	G	GS	CG	SH	SV	IP	H	R	ER	HR	HB	BB	SO	RAT	ERA	ERA+	CERA	OAV	BH	AVG	PR+	WS	TPW
1909 NY-A	0	0	....	2	1	0	0	0	5	7	6	2	1	0	1	1	1.600	3.60	70	5.62	.292	1	.500	-0	0	0.0

• CARROLL, Ed Edgar Fleischer Carroll b: 7/27/1907, Baltimore, MD d: 10/13/1984, Rossville, MD BR/TR, 6'3", 185 lbs. Deb: 5/1/1929

YEAR TM-L	W	L	PCT	G	GS	CG	SH	SV	IP	H	R	ER	HR	HB	BB	SO	RAT	ERA	ERA+	CERA	OAV	BH	AVG	PR+	WS	TPW
1929 Bos-A	1	0	1.000	24	2	0	0	0	67^{1}	77	46	42	6	4	20	13	1.441	5.61	76	4.59	.291	1	.063	-10	1	-1.1

• CARROLL, Ownie Owen Thomas Carroll b: 11/11/1902, Kearny, NJ d: 6/8/1975, Orange, NJ BR/TR, 5'10.5", 165 lbs. Deb: 6/20/1925

YEAR TM-L	W	L	PCT	G	GS	CG	SH	SV	IP	H	R	ER	HR	HB	BB	SO	RAT	ERA	ERA+	CERA	OAV	BH	AVG	PR+	WS	TPW
1925 Det-A	2	2	.500	10	4	1	0	0	40^{2}	46	30	17	1	2	28	12	1.820	3.76	114	5.43	.293	6	.375	2	2	0.4
1927 Det-A	10	6	.625	31	15	8	0	0	172	186	99	76	5	6	73	41	1.506	3.98	106	4.13	.281	12	.174	6	10	0.4
1928 Det-A	16	12	.571	34	28	19	2	2	231	219	100	84	6	7	87	51	1.325	3.27	125	3.27	.262	19	.194	22	18	1.9
1929 Det-A	9	17	.346	34	26	12	0	1	202	249	133	104	10	8	86	54	1.658	4.63	92	5.17	.310	17	.230	-1	8	0.1
1930 Det-A	0	5	.000	6	3	0	0	0	20^{1}	30	24	24	3	0	9	4	1.918	10.62	45	7.31	.333	1	.143	-13	0	-1.2
NY-A	0	1	.000	10	1	0	0	0	32^{2}	49	32	24	2	4	18	8	2.051	6.61	65	7.90	.374	2	.200	-8	0	-0.7
Yr.	0	6	.000	16	4	0	0	0	53	79	56	48	5	4	27	12	2.000	8.15	56	7.67	.357	3	.176	-21	0	-2.0
Cin-N	0	1	.000	3	2	1	0	0	14	17	9	7	3	0	3	0	1.429	4.50	107	5.49	.309	1	.200	1	1	0.0

YEAR	TM-L	W	L	PCT	G	GS	CG	SH	SV	IP	H	R	ER	HR	HB	BB	SO	RAT	ERA	ERA+	CERA	OAV	BH	AVG	PR+	WS	TPW
1931	Cin-N	3	9	.250	29	12	4	0	0	107^1	135	76	66	6	4	51	24	1.733	5.53	67	5.56	.314	7	.206	-22	0	-2.2
1932	Cin-N	10	19	.345	32	26	15	0	1	210	245	124	105	7	9	44	55	1.376	4.50	86	3.84	.286	16	.208	-15	7	-1.2
1933	Bro-N	13	15	.464	33	31	11	0	0	226^1	248	117	95	9	7	54	45	1.334	3.78	85	3.61	.281	11	.149	-8	8	-1.0
1934	Bro-N	1	3	.250	26	5	0	0	1	74^1	108	64	53	9	1	33	17	1.897	6.42	61	7.17	.342	6	.240	-20	0	-1.8
Total	9	64	90	.416	248	153	71	2	5	1330^2	1532	808	655	61	48	486	311	1.517	4.43	89	4.48	.294	98	.200	-57	54	-5.4

• CARROLL, Tom Thomas Michael Carroll b: 11/5/1952, Oriskany, NY BL/TR, 6'3", 190 lbs. Deb: 7/7/1974

YEAR	TM-L	W	L	PCT	G	GS	CG	SH	SV	IP	H	R	ER	HR	HB	BB	SO	RAT	ERA	ERA+	CERA	OAV	BH	AVG	PR+	WS	TPW
1974	Cin-N	4	3	.571	16	13	0	0	0	78^1	68	44	32	11	0	44	37	1.430	3.68	95	4.15	.231	4	.154	-3	3	-0.4
1975	Cin-N	4	1	.800	12	7	0	0	0	47	52	28	26	1	2	26	14	1.660	4.98	72	4.95	.284	0	.000	-9	1	-1.1
Total	2	8	4	.667	28	20	0	0	0	125^1	120	72	58	12	2	70	51	1.516	4.16	85	4.45	.252	4	.100	-12	4	-1.5

• CARSEY, Kid Wilfred Carsey b: 10/22/1870, New York, NY d: 3/29/1960, Miami, FL BL/TR, 5'7", 168 lbs. Deb: 4/8/1891 U

YEAR	TM-L	W	L	PCT	G	GS	CG	SH	SV	IP	H	R	ER	HR	HB	BB	SO	RAT	ERA	ERA+	CERA	OAV	BH	AVG	PR+	WS	TPW
1891	Was-a	14	37	.275	54	53	46	1	0	415	513	358	230	17	0	161	174	**1.624**	4.99	75	....	.294	28	.150	-34	9	-3.3
1892	Phi-N	19	16	.543	43	36	30	1	1	317^2	320	166	110	6	0	104	76	1.335	3.12	104	3.21	.252	20	.153	-0	21	-0.3
1893	Phi-N	20	15	.571	39	35	30	1	0	318^1	375	229	170	7	0	124	50	1.568	4.81	95	4.36	.285	27	.186	-13	17	-1.7
1894	Phi-N	18	12	.600	37	32	26	0	0	277	349	229	171	22	0	102	41	1.628	5.56	95	5.18	.306	34	.272	-4	15	-0.1
1895	Phi-N	24	16	.600	44	40	35	0	1	342^1	460	274	187	14	0	118	64	1.688	4.92	97	5.31	.317	41	.291	-4	21	0.0
1896	Phi-N	11	11	.500	27	21	18	1	1	187^1	273	164	117	4	0	72	36	1.842	5.62	77	5.98	.337	18	.222	-25	8	-2.0
1897	Phi-N	2	1	.667	4	4	2	0	0	28	35	20	16	0	1	16	1	1.821	5.14	82	5.39	.304	3	.231	-2	1	-0.2
	StL-N	3	8	.273	12	11	11	0	0	99	133	81	66	5	4	31	14	1.657	6.00	73	5.42	.319	13	.302	-14	2	-1.0
	Yr.	5	9	.357	16	15	13	0	0	127	168	101	82	5	5	47	15	1.693	5.81	75	5.41	.316	16	.286	-16	3	-1.2
1898	StL-N	2	12	.143	20	13	10	0	0	123^2	177	112	87	2	10	37	10	1.730	6.33	60	5.76	.333	21	.200	-31	0	-3.6
1899	Cle-N	1	8	.111	10	9	8	0	0	77^2	109	66	49	2	2	24	11	1.712	5.68	65	5.50	.331	10	.278	-13	3	-1.0
	Was-N	1	2	.333	4	3	2	0	0	29	27	14	12	0	1	4	3	1.069	3.72	105	2.22	.247	0	.000	2	1	0.0
	Yr.	2	10	.167	14	12	10	0	0	106^2	136	80	61	2	3	28	14	1.538	5.15	72	4.61	.310	10	.213	-12	4	-1.0
1901	Bro-N	1	0	1.000	2	0	0	0	0	7	9	9	8	1	1	3	4	1.714	10.29	33	6.70	.310	0	.000	-5	0	-0.6
Total	10	116	138	.457	296	257	218	4	3	2222	2780	1722	1223	80	19	796	484	1.609	4.95	85	3.92	.300	221	.213	-146	98	-13.8

• CARSON, Al Albert James "Soldier" Carson b: 8/22/1882, Chicago, IL d: 11/26/1962, San Diego, CA BR/TR, 5'10.5" Deb: 5/6/1910

YEAR	TM-L	W	L	PCT	G	GS	CG	SH	SV	IP	H	R	ER	HR	HB	BB	SO	RAT	ERA	ERA+	CERA	OAV	BH	AVG	PR+	WS	TPW
1910	Chi-N	0	0	....	2	0	0	0	0	6^2	6	5	3	0	0	1	2	1.050	4.05	71	2.05	.240	0	.000	-1	0	-0.1

• CARTER, Andy Andrew Godfrey Carter b: 11/9/1968, Philadelphia, PA BL/TL, 6'5", 200 lbs. Deb: 5/3/1994

YEAR	TM-L	W	L	PCT	G	GS	CG	SH	SV	IP	H	R	ER	HR	HB	BB	SO	RAT	ERA	ERA+	CERA	OAV	BH	AVG	PR+	WS	TPW
1994	Phi-N	0	2	.000	20	0	0	0	0	34^1	34	18	17	5	6	12	18	1.340	4.46	96	4.85	.268	0	.000	-0	1	-0.1
1995	Phi-N	0	0	....	4	0	0	0	0	7^1	4	5	5	3	1	2	6	.818	6.14	69	3.40	.167	1	1.000	-2	0	-0.1
Total	2	0	2	.000	24	0	0	0	0	41^2	38	23	22	8	7	14	24	1.248	4.75	90	4.60	.252	1	.143	-2	1	-0.2

• CARTER, Arnold Arnold Lee "Hook,Lefty" Carter b: 3/14/1918, Rainelle, WV d: 4/12/1989, Louisville, KY BL/TL, 5'10", 170 lbs. Deb: 4/29/1944

YEAR	TM-L	W	L	PCT	G	GS	CG	SH	SV	IP	H	R	ER	HR	HB	BB	SO	RAT	ERA	ERA+	CERA	OAV	BH	AVG	PR+	WS	TPW
1944	Cin-N	11	7	.611	33	18	9	3	3	148^2	143	54	43	1	3	40	33	1.231	2.60	134	2.77	.256	12	.250	11	16	1.7
1945	Cin-N	2	4	.333	13	6	2	1	0	46^2	54	21	16	2	2	13	4	1.436	3.09	122	4.05	.286	3	.176	4	3	0.4
Total	2	13	11	.542	46	24	11	4	3	195^1	197	75	59	3	5	53	37	1.280	2.72	131	3.08	.264	15	.231	15	19	2.0

• CARTER, Jeff Jeffrey Allen Carter b: 12/3/1964, Tampa, FL BR/TR, 6'3", 195 lbs. Deb: 7/31/1991

YEAR	TM-L	W	L	PCT	G	GS	CG	SH	SV	IP	H	R	ER	HR	HB	BB	SO	RAT	ERA	ERA+	CERA	OAV	BH	AVG	PR+	WS	TPW
1991	Chi-A	0	1	.000	5	2	0	0	0	12	8	8	7	1	0	5	2	1.083	5.25	76	2.26	.182	0	....	-2	0	-0.2

• CARTER, Lance Lance David Carter b: 12/18/1974, Bradenton, FL BR/TR, 6'1", 190 lbs. Deb: 9/15/1999

YEAR	TM-L	W	L	PCT	G	GS	CG	SH	SV	IP	H	R	ER	HR	HB	BB	SO	RAT	ERA	ERA+	CERA	OAV	BH	AVG	PR+	WS	TPW
1999	KC-A	0	1	.000	6	0	0	0	0	5^1	3	3	3	2	0	3	3	1.125	5.06	99	4.22	.167	0	....	-0	0	0.0
2002	TB-A	2	0	1.000	8	0	0	0	2	20^1	15	3	3	2	0	5	14	.984	1.33	336	2.12	.203	0	....	7	4	0.6
2003	TB-A★	7	5	.583	62	0	0	0	26	79	72	39	38	12	4	19	47	1.152	4.33	105	3.38	.242	0	....	-0	10	0.0
Total	3	9	6	.600	76	0	0	0	28	104^2	90	45	44	16	4	27	64	1.118	3.78	120	3.17	.231	0	....	7	14	0.6

• CARTER, Larry Larry Gene Carter b: 5/22/1965, Charleston, WV BR/TR, 6'5", 195 lbs. Deb: 9/6/1992

YEAR	TM-L	W	L	PCT	G	GS	CG	SH	SV	IP	H	R	ER	HR	HB	BB	SO	RAT	ERA	ERA+	CERA	OAV	BH	AVG	PR+	WS	TPW
1992	SF-N	1	5	.167	6	6	0	0	0	33	34	17	17	6	0	18	21	1.576	4.64	71	5.49	.270	2	.200	-6	0	-0.5

• CARTER, Nick Conrad Powell Carter b: 5/19/1879, Oatlands, VA d: 11/23/1961, Grasonville, MD BL/TR, 5'8", 140 lbs. Deb: 4/14/1908

YEAR	TM-L	W	L	PCT	G	GS	CG	SH	SV	IP	H	R	ER	HR	HB	BB	SO	RAT	ERA	ERA+	CERA	OAV	BH	AVG	PR+	WS	TPW
1908	Phi-A	2	5	.286	14	4	2	0	0	60^2	58	26	20	1	2	17	17	1.236	2.97	86	3.16	.270	2	.100	-1	2	-0.3

• CARTER, Paul Paul Warren "Nick" Carter b: 5/1/1894, Lake Park, GA d: 9/11/1984, Lake Park, GA BL/TR, 6'3", 175 lbs. Deb: 9/15/1914

YEAR	TM-L	W	L	PCT	G	GS	CG	SH	SV	IP	H	R	ER	HR	HB	BB	SO	RAT	ERA	ERA+	CERA	OAV	BH	AVG	PR+	WS	TPW
1914	Cle-A	1	3	.250	5	4	1	0	0	24^2	35	15	8	0	0	5	9	1.622	2.92	99	5.04	.340	0	.000	0	1	-0.1
1915	Cle-A	1	1	.500	11	2	2	0	0	42	44	22	15	1	0	18	14	1.476	3.21	95	3.88	.272	3	.214	-1	2	0.0
1916	Chi-N	2	2	.500	8	5	2	0	0	36	26	16	11	1	3	17	14	1.194	2.75	105	2.60	.203	2	.167	1	2	0.1
1917	Chi-N	5	8	.385	23	13	6	0	2	113^1	115	47	41	2	3	19	34	1.182	3.26	89	2.89	.276	6	.171	-3	5	-0.3
1918	Chi-N	3	2	.600	21	4	1	0	2	73	78	29	22	2	1	19	13	1.329	2.71	103	3.45	.290	6	.240	2	4	0.3
1919	Chi-N	5	4	.556	28	7	2	0	1	85	81	36	25	1	2	28	17	1.282	2.65	109	2.95	.252	7	.269	3	6	0.4
1920	Chi-N	3	6	.333	31	8	2	0	2	106	131	68	55	3	5	36	14	1.575	4.67	69	4.87	.324	6	.171	-16	0	-1.8
Total	7	20	26	.435	127	43	16	0	7	480	510	233	177	10	14	142	115	1.358	3.32	90	3.60	.283	30	.195	-13	20	-1.4

• CARTER, Sol Solomon Mobley "Buck" Carter b: 12/23/1908, Picayune, MS BR/TR, 6', 178 lbs. Deb: 4/15/1931

YEAR	TM-L	W	L	PCT	G	GS	CG	SH	SV	IP	H	R	ER	HR	HB	BB	SO	RAT	ERA	ERA+	CERA	OAV	BH	AVG	PR+	WS	TPW
1931	Phi-A	0	0	....	2	0	0	0	0	2^1	1	5	5	0	0	4	1	2.143	19.29	23	4.73	.143	0	....	-4	0	-0.4

• CARUTHERS, Bob Robert Lee "Parisian Bob" Caruthers b: 1/5/1864, Memphis, TN d: 8/5/1911, Peoria, IL BL/TR, 5'7", 138 lbs. Deb: 9/7/1884 M/U ♦

YEAR	TM-L	W	L	PCT	G	GS	CG	SH	SV	IP	H	R	ER	HR	HB	BB	SO	RAT	ERA	ERA+	CERA	OAV	BH	AVG	PR+	WS	TPW
1884	StL-a	7	2	.778	13	7	7	0	0	82^2	61	34	24	1	3	15	58	.919	2.61	124	....	.195	22	.268	4	10	0.3
1885★	StL-a	**40**	13	.755	53	53	53	6	0	482^1	430	196	111	3	19	57	190	1.010	**2.07**	**158**	....	.229	50	.225	50	51	5.1
1886★	StL-a	30	14	.682	44	43	42	2	0	387^1	323	164	100	3	7	86	166	1.056	2.32	148	....	.216	106	.334	45	57	**7.7**
1887★	StL-a	29	9	.763	39	39	39	2	0	341	398	185	125	6	16	61	74	1.167	3.30	137	....	**.281**	196	.456	39	**54**	6.5
1888	Bro-a	29	15	.659	44	43	42	4	0	391^2	337	176	104	4	10	53	140	.996	2.39	125	....	.224	77	.230	25	46	3.3
1889★	Bro-a	**40**	11	.784	56	50	46	**7**	1	445	444	215	155	16	13	104	118	1.231	3.13	119	....	.252	43	.250	29	**46**	3.9
1890★	Bro-N	23	11	.676	37	33	30	1	0	300	292	163	103	9	12	87	64	1.263	3.09	111	....	.248	63	.265	11	30	1.6
1891	Bro-N	18	14	.563	38	32	29	2	1	297	323	185	103	7	13	107	69	1.448	3.12	106	....	.267	48	.281	13	22	2.2
1892	StL-N	2	10	.167	16	10	10	0	1	101^2	131	75	66	10	6	27	21	1.554	5.84	55	5.36	.301	142	.277	-26	19	-1.7
Total	9	218	99	.688	340	310	298	24	3	2828^2	2739	1393	891	59	99	597	900	1.158	2.83	122	0.19	.245	761	.301	189	335	28.7

• CARY, Chuck Charles Douglas Cary b: 3/3/1960, Whittier, CA BL/TL, 6'4", 210 lbs. Deb: 8/22/1985

YEAR	TM-L	W	L	PCT	G	GS	CG	SH	SV	IP	H	R	ER	HR	HB	BB	SO	RAT	ERA	ERA+	CERA	OAV	BH	AVG	PR+	WS	TPW
1985	Det-A	0	1	.000	16	0	0	0	2	23^2	16	9	9	2	2	8	22	1.014	3.42	119	2.33	.190	0	....	2	2	0.2
1986	Det-A	1	2	.333	22	0	0	0	0	31^2	33	18	12	3	0	15	21	1.516	3.41	121	4.35	.273	0	....	2	1	0.2
1987	Atl-N	1	1	.500	13	0	0	0	1	16^2	17	7	7	3	1	4	15	1.260	3.78	115	4.10	.266	0	.000	1	1	0.1
1988	Atl-N	0	0	....	7	0	0	0	0	8^1	8	6	6	1	1	4	7	1.440	6.48	57	4.54	.250	0	....	-2	0	-0.3
1989	NY-A	4	4	.500	22	11	2	0	0	99^1	78	42	36	13	0	29	79	1.077	3.26	119	2.60	.209	0	....	6	6	0.7
1990	NY-A	6	12	.333	28	27	2	0	0	156^2	155	77	73	21	1	55	134	1.340	4.19	95	4.12	.260	0	....	-4	7	-0.4
1991	NY-A	1	6	.143	10	9	0	0	0	53^1	61	35	35	6	0	32	34	1.744	5.91	70	5.77	.285	0	....	-10	0	-1.0
1993	Chi-A	1	0	1.000	16	0	0	0	0	20^2	22	12	12	1	3	11	10	1.597	5.23	80	5.13	.286	0	....	-2	1	-0.2
Total	8	14	26	.350	134	47	4	0	3	410^1	390	206	190	50	8	158	322	1.336	4.17	96	3.94	.250	0	.000	-8	18	-0.8

• CARY, Scott Scott Russell "Red" Cary b: 4/11/1923, Kendallville, IN BL/TL, 5'11.5", 168 lbs. Deb: 5/1/1947

YEAR	TM-L	W	L	PCT	G	GS	CG	SH	SV	IP	H	R	ER	HR	HB	BB	SO	RAT	ERA	ERA+	CERA	OAV	BH	AVG	PR+	WS	TPW
1947	Was-A	3	1	.750	23	3	1	0	0	54^2	73	38	36	5	1	20	25	1.701	5.93	63	5.64	.312	1	.077	-12	0	-1.4

• CASALE, Jerry Jerry Joseph Casale b: 9/27/1933, Brooklyn, NY BR/TR, 6'2", 200 lbs. Deb: 9/14/1958

YEAR	TM-L	W	L	PCT	G	GS	CG	SH	SV	IP	H	R	ER	HR	HB	BB	SO	RAT	ERA	ERA+	CERA	OAV	BH	AVG	PR+	WS	TPW
1958	Bos-A	0	0	....	2	0	0	0	0	3	1	0	0	0	0	2	3	1.000	0.00	....	1.37	.111	0	....	1	0	0.1
1959	Bos-A	13	8	.619	31	26	9	3	0	179^2	162	89	86	20	5	89	93	1.397	4.31	94	4.06	.238	10	.169	-6	11	-0.3
1960	Bos-A	2	9	.182	29	14	1	0	0	96^1	113	78	66	14	1	67	54	1.869	6.17	66	6.50	.294	9	.273	-20	1	-1.7

YEAR	TM-L	W	L	PCT	G	GS	CG	SH	SV	IP	H	R	ER	HR	HB	BB	SO	RAT	ERA	ERA+	CERA	OAV	BH	AVG	PR+	WS	TPW
1961	LA-A	1	5	.167	13	7	0	0	1	42^2	52	34	31	9	1	25	35	1.805	6.54	69	7.15	.297	6	.462	-9	1	-0.6
	Det-A	0	0	....	3	1	0	0	0	12	15	8	7	3	0	3	6	1.500	5.25	78	6.26	.313	0	.000	-2	0	-0.2
	Yr.	1	5	.167	16	8	0	0	1	54^2	67	42	38	12	1	28	41	1.738	6.26	71	6.95	.300	6	.375	-11	1	-0.8
1962	Det-A	1	2	.333	18	1	0	0	0	36^2	33	19	19	5	0	18	16	1.391	4.66	87	3.97	.236	0	.000	-2	1	-0.3
Total	5	17	24	.415	96	49	10	3	1	370^1	376	228	209	51	7	204	207	1.566	5.08	81	5.09	.262	25	.216	-37	14	-2.9

• CASCARELLA, Joe Joseph Thomas "Crooning Joe" Cascarella b: 6/28/1907, Philadelphia, PA d: 5/22/2002, Baltimore, MD BR/TR, 5'10.5", 175 lbs. Deb: 4/17/1934

YEAR	TM-L	W	L	PCT	G	GS	CG	SH	SV	IP	H	R	ER	HR	HB	BB	SO	RAT	ERA	ERA+	CERA	OAV	BH	AVG	PR+	WS	TPW
1934	Phi-A	12	15	.444	42	22	9	2	1	194^1	214	111	101	8	3	104	71	1.636	4.68	94	4.73	.288	6	.094	-8	10	-1.1
1935	Phi-A	1	6	.143	9	3	1	0	0	32^1	29	21	19	1	0	22	15	1.577	5.29	86	3.87	.252	1	.125	-2	1	-0.3
	Bos-A	0	3	.000	6	4	0	0	0	17	25	17	13	3	0	11	9	2.118	6.88	69	8.21	.329	0	.000	-4	0	-0.4
	Yr.	1	9	.100	15	7	1	0	0	49^1	54	38	32	4	0	33	24	1.764	5.84	79	5.37	.283	1	.100	-6	1	-0.7
1936	Bos-A	0	2	.000	10	1	0	0	0	20^2	27	16	16	0	0	9	7	1.742	6.97	76	5.37	.329	0	.000	-4	0	-0.4
	Was-A	9	8	.529	22	16	7	1	1	139^1	147	66	63	7	6	54	34	1.443	4.07	117	4.08	.276	7	.143	9	10	0.6
	Yr.	9	10	.474	32	17	7	1	1	160	174	82	79	7	6	63	41	1.481	4.44	110	4.25	.283	7	.132	5	10	0.2
1937	Was-A	0	5	.000	10	4	1	0	1	32^1	50	41	29	3	1	23	10	2.258	8.07	55	8.48	.347	2	.222	-14	0	-1.3
	Cin-N	1	2	.333	11	3	2	0	1	43^2	44	24	19	1	0	22	16	1.511	3.92	95	3.81	.263	1	.091	-1	1	-0.1
1938	Cin-N	4	7	.364	33	1	0	0	4	61	66	33	31	2	0	22	30	1.443	4.57	80	3.74	.275	3	.167	-7	3	-0.8
Total	5	27	48	.360	143	54	20	3	8	540^2	602	329	291	25	10	267	192	1.607	4.84	91	4.68	.287	20	.121	-31	25	-3.8

• CASE, Charlie Charles Emmett Case b: 9/7/1879, Smith's Landing, OH d: 4/16/1964, Batavia, OH BR/TR, 6', 170 lbs. Deb: 7/5/1901

YEAR	TM-L	W	L	PCT	G	GS	CG	SH	SV	IP	H	R	ER	HR	HB	BB	SO	RAT	ERA	ERA+	CERA	OAV	BH	AVG	PR+	WS	TPW
1901	Cin-N	1	2	.333	3	3	3	0	0	27	34	21	14	0	0	6	5	1.481	4.67	68	3.98	.305	1	.100	-4	0	-0.5
1904	Pit-N	10	5	.667	18	17	14	3	0	141	129	56	46	0	4	31	49	1.135	2.94	93	2.41	.243	9	.170	-4	9	-0.3
1905	Pit-N	11	11	.500	31	24	18	3	1	217	202	81	62	2	15	66	57	1.235	2.57	116	3.00	.251	7	.103	6	17	0.5
1906	Pit-N	1	1	.500	2	2	1	0	0	11	8	9	7	0	1	5	3	1.182	5.73	47	2.25	.190	1	.500	-4	0	-0.4
Total	4	23	19	.548	54	46	36	6	1	396	373	167	129	2	20	108	114	1.215	2.93	99	2.84	.250	18	.135	-6	26	-0.6

• CASEY, Bill William B. Casey b: St. Louis, MO Deb: 8/17/1887

YEAR	TM-L	W	L	PCT	G	GS	CG	SH	SV	IP	H	R	ER	HR	HB	BB	SO	RAT	ERA	ERA+	CERA	OAV	BH	AVG	PR+	WS	TPW
1887	Phi-a	0	0	....	1	0	0	0	0	1	5	3	2	0	0	1	0	5.000	18.00	24	....	.626	0	....	-2	0	-0.1

• CASEY, Dan Daniel Maurice Casey b: 11/20/1862, Binghamton, NY d: 2/8/1943, Washington, DC BR/TL, 6', 180 lbs. Deb: 8/18/1884 U

YEAR	TM-L	W	L	PCT	G	GS	CG	SH	SV	IP	H	R	ER	HR	HB	BB	SO	RAT	ERA	ERA+	CERA	OAV	BH	AVG	PR+	WS	TPW
1884	Wil-U	1	1	.500	2	2	2	0	0	18	23	17	2	0	....	4	10	1.500	1.00	334	....	.291	1	.167	5	1	0.4
1885	Det-N	4	8	.333	12	12	12	1	0	104	105	61	38	1	....	35	79	1.346	3.29	86	....	.250	5	.116	-4	4	-0.6
1886	Phi-N	24	18	.571	44	44	39	4	0	369	326	169	99	8	....	104	193	1.165	2.41	136	....	.228	23	.152	45	29	3.7
1887	Phi-N	28	13	.683	45	45	43	**4**	0	390^1	492	199	124	15	14	115	119	1.260	**2.86**	**147**	....	.299	33	.194	67	30	4.9
1888	Phi-N	14	18	.438	33	33	31	2	0	285^2	298	156	100	6	5	48	108	1.211	3.15	94	....	.259	18	.153	-2	18	-0.5
1889	Phi-N	6	10	.375	20	20	15	1	0	152^2	170	92	64	4	8	72	65	1.585	3.77	116	....	.273	15	.221	16	10	1.3
1890	Syr-a	19	22	.463	45	42	40	2	0	360^2	365	249	166	8	14	165	169	1.470	4.14	85	....	.255	26	.163	-18	13	-1.8
Total	7	96	90	.516	201	198	182	14	0	1680^1	1779	943	593	42	41	543	743	1.313	3.18	110	....	.262	121	.169	110	105	7.3

• CASEY, Hugh Hugh Thomas Casey b: 10/14/1913, Atlanta, GA d: 7/3/1951, Atlanta, GA BR/TR, 6'1", 207 lbs. Deb: 4/29/1935

YEAR	TM-L	W	L	PCT	G	GS	CG	SH	SV	IP	H	R	ER	HR	HB	BB	SO	RAT	ERA	ERA+	CERA	OAV	BH	AVG	PR+	WS	TPW
1935	Chi-N	0	0	....	13	0	0	0	0	25^2	29	13	11	2	0	14	10	1.675	3.86	102	5.01	.279	1	.167	-1	1	-0.1
1939	Bro-N	15	10	.600	40	25	15	0	1	227^1	228	88	74	13	11	54	79	1.240	2.93	137	3.27	.260	15	.203	29	21	2.9
1940	Bro-N	11	8	.579	44	10	5	2	2	154	136	63	62	13	6	51	53	1.214	3.62	110	3.11	.237	9	.250	7	13	0.9
1941*	Bro-N	14	11	.560	45	18	4	1	7	162	155	81	70	8	1	57	61	1.309	3.89	94	3.26	.251	6	.120	-7	9	-0.8
1942	Bro-N	6	3	.667	50	2	0	0	**13**	112	91	32	28	3	2	44	54	1.205	2.25	145	2.57	.221	4	.148	11	13	1.2
1946	Bro-N	11	5	.688	46	1	0	0	5	99^2	101	31	22	2	2	33	31	1.344	1.99	170	3.29	.267	3	.136	14	11	1.5
1947*	Bro-N	10	4	.714	46	0	0	0	**18**	76^2	75	36	34	7	2	29	40	1.357	3.99	104	3.87	.260	1	.056	-0	10	-0.2
1948	Bro-N	3	0	1.000	22	0	0	0	4	36	59	36	32	6	2	17	7	2.111	8.00	50	9.60	.391	0	.000	-17	0	-1.8
1949	Pit-N	4	1	.800	33	0	0	0	5	38^2	50	24	20	4	1	14	9	1.655	4.66	90	5.69	.314	1	.333	-2	3	-0.1
	NY-A	1	0	1.000	4	0	0	0	0	7^2	11	10	7	0	0	8	5	2.478	8.22	49	7.98	.324	0	.000	-4	0	-0.4
Total	9	75	42	.641	343	56	24	3	55	939^2	935	414	360	58	27	321	349	1.337	3.45	112	3.64	.260	40	.164	31	81	3.1

• CASHION, Carl Jay Carl Cashion b: 6/6/1891, Mecklenberg, NC d: 11/17/1935, Lake Millicent, WI BL/TR, 6'2", 200 lbs. Deb: 8/4/1911

YEAR	TM-L	W	L	PCT	G	GS	CG	SH	SV	IP	H	R	ER	HR	HB	BB	SO	RAT	ERA	ERA+	CERA	OAV	BH	AVG	PR+	WS	TPW
1911	Was-A	1	5	.167	11	9	5	0	0	71^1	67	45	33	4	7	47	26	1.598	4.16	79	4.14	.220	12	.324	-7	3	-0.5
1912	Was-A	10	6	.625	26	17	13	1	1	170^1	150	84	60	4	5	103	84	1.485	3.17	106	3.85	.250	22	.214	-3	12	-0.2
1913	Was-A	1	1	.500	4	3	0	0	0	9	7	11	6	0	3	14	3	2.333	6.00	49	8.31	.269	3	.250	-3	0	-0.4
1914	Was-A	0	1	.000	2	1	0	0	0	5	4	7	6	0	1	6	1	2.000	10.80	26	6.15	.250	0	.000	-4	0	-0.5
Total	4	12	13	.480	43	30	18	1	1	255^2	228	147	105	8	16	170	114	1.557	3.70	88	4.13	.241	37	.242	-17	15	-1.6

• CASIAN, Larry Lawrence Paul Casian b: 10/28/1965, Lynwood, CA BR/TL, 6', 170 lbs. Deb: 9/9/1990

YEAR	TM-L	W	L	PCT	G	GS	CG	SH	SV	IP	H	R	ER	HR	HB	BB	SO	RAT	ERA	ERA+	CERA	OAV	BH	AVG	PR+	WS	TPW
1990	Min-A	2	1	.667	5	3	0	0	0	22^1	26	9	8	2	0	4	11	1.343	3.22	129	4.30	.306	0	....	2	2	0.2
1991	Min-A	0	0	....	15	0	0	0	0	18^1	28	16	15	4	1	7	6	1.909	7.36	58	8.46	.354	0	....	-7	0	-0.7
1992	Min-A	1	0	1.000	6	0	0	0	0	6^2	7	2	2	0	0	1	2	1.200	2.70	150	2.67	.259	0	....	1	1	0.1
1993	Min-A	5	3	.625	54	0	0	0	1	56^2	59	23	19	1	1	14	31	1.288	3.02	144	3.13	.268	0	....	9	7	0.9
1994	Min-A	1	3	.250	33	0	0	0	1	40^2	57	34	32	11	2	12	18	1.697	7.08	69	7.57	.343	0	....	-9	0	-0.9
	Cle-A	0	2	.000	7	0	0	0	0	8^1	16	9	8	1	0	4	2	2.400	8.64	55	10.49	.421	0	....	-4	0	-0.3
	Yr.	1	5	.167	40	0	0	0	1	49	73	43	40	12	2	16	20	1.816	7.35	66	8.07	.358	0	....	-13	0	-1.2
1995	Chi-N	1	0	1.000	42	0	0	0	0	23^1	23	6	5	1	0	15	11	1.629	1.93	213	3.98	.258	0	.000	5	3	0.5
1996	Chi-N	1	1	.500	35	0	0	0	0	24	14	5	5	2	1	11	15	1.042	1.88	231	2.21	.187	0	....	6	3	0.6
1997	Chi-N	0	1	.000	12	0	0	0	0	9^2	16	9	8	3	1	2	7	1.862	7.45	58	8.94	.364	0	.000	-3	0	-0.3
	KC-A	0	2	.000	32	0	0	0	0	26^2	32	15	15	5	0	6	16	1.425	5.06	93	5.10	.299	0	....	-1	1	-0.1
1998	Chi-A	0	0	....	4	0	0	0	0	4	8	5	5	0	2	1	6	2.250	11.25	40	10.86	.400	0	....	-3	0	-0.3
Total	9	11	13	.458	245	3	0	0	2	240^2	286	133	122	30	8	77	125	1.508	4.56	99	5.21	.301	0	.000	-3	17	-0.3

• CASKEY, Craig Craig Douglas Caskey b: 12/11/1949, Visalia, CA BB/TL, 5'11", 185 lbs. Deb: 7/19/1973

YEAR	TM-L	W	L	PCT	G	GS	CG	SH	SV	IP	H	R	ER	HR	HB	BB	SO	RAT	ERA	ERA+	CERA	OAV	BH	AVG	PR+	WS	TPW
1973	Mon-N	0	0	....	9	1	0	0	0	14^1	15	11	9	3	1	4	6	1.326	5.65	67	4.97	.278	0	.000	-3	0	-0.3

• CASSIAN, Ed Edwin T. Cassian b: 11/28/1867, Wilbraham, MA d: 9/10/1918, Meriden, CT TR, 5'8", 160 lbs. Deb: 6/26/1891

YEAR	TM-L	W	L	PCT	G	GS	CG	SH	SV	IP	H	R	ER	HR	HB	BB	SO	RAT	ERA	ERA+	CERA	OAV	BH	AVG	PR+	WS	TPW
1891	Phi-N	1	3	.250	6	4	3	0	0	38	40	20	12	0	3	16	10	1.474	2.84	120	....	.261	2	.118	2	2	0.1
	Was-a	2	4	.333	7	5	5	0	0	53	73	63	33	4	5	35	14	2.038	5.60	67	....	.317	9	.346	-8	1	-0.5

• CASSIDY, John John P. Cassidy b: 1855, Brooklyn, NY d: 7/3/1891, Brooklyn, NY BR/TL, 5'8", 168 lbs. Deb: 4/24/1875 U ♦

YEAR	TM-L	W	L	PCT	G	GS	CG	SH	SV	IP	H	R	ER	HR	HB	BB	SO	RAT	ERA	ERA+	CERA	OAV	BH	AVG	PR+	WS	TPW
1875	Atl-n	1	21	.045	30	22	18	0	0	213^2	284	242	72	6	....	11	9	1.381	3.03	58	....	.292	29	.175	-25	....	-2.5
1877	Har-N	1	1	.500	2	2	2	0	0	18	24	11	10	0	....	1	2	1.389	5.00	49	....	.303	95	.378	-6	13	1.3

• CASSIDY, Scott Scott Robert Cassidy b: 10/3/1975, Syracuse, NY BR/TR, 6'2", 175 lbs. Deb: 4/1/2002

YEAR	TM-L	W	L	PCT	G	GS	CG	SH	SV	IP	H	R	ER	HR	HB	BB	SO	RAT	ERA	ERA+	CERA	OAV	BH	AVG	PR+	WS	TPW
2002	Tor-A	1	4	.200	58	0	0	0	0	66	52	42	42	12	7	32	48	1.273	5.73	81	4.17	.222	0	....	-8	2	-0.7

• CASTER, George George Jasper "Ug" Caster b: 8/4/1907, Colton, CA d: 12/18/1955, Lakewood, CA BR/TR, 6'1.5", 180 lbs. Deb: 9/10/1934

YEAR	TM-L	W	L	PCT	G	GS	CG	SH	SV	IP	H	R	ER	HR	HB	BB	SO	RAT	ERA	ERA+	CERA	OAV	BH	AVG	PR+	WS	TPW
1934	Phi-A	3	2	.600	5	3	2	0	0	37	32	16	14	3	3	14	15	1.243	3.41	129	3.37	.235	4	.267	4	3	0.4
1935	Phi-A	1	4	.200	25	1	0	0	1	63^1	86	59	44	8	2	37	24	1.942	6.25	73	7.08	.322	5	.227	-11	0	-1.0
1937	Phi-A	12	19	.387	34	33	19	3	0	231^2	227	141	114	23	2	107	100	1.442	4.43	106	4.14	.258	19	.211	7	11	0.6
1938	Phi-A	16	20	.444	42	**40**	20	2	1	281^1	310	156	136	25	3	117	112	1.518	4.35	111	4.55	.277	20	.198	23	19	2.2
1939	Phi-A	9	9	.500	28	17	7	1	0	136	144	82	74	16	3	45	59	1.390	4.90	96	4.29	.276	9	.209	2	7	0.0
1940	Phi-A	4	19	.174	36	24	11	0	2	178^1	234	160	130	18	3	69	75	1.699	6.56	68	5.72	.312	8	.129	-39	0	-4.0
1941	StL-A	3	7	.300	32	9	3	0	3	104^1	105	66	58	12	2	37	36	1.361	5.00	86	3.99	.259	3	.103	-7	4	-0.9
1942	StL-A	8	2	.800	39	0	0	0	5	80	62	30	25	3	3	39	34	1.263	2.81	132	2.80	.217	1	.067	9	9	0.8
1943	StL-A	6	8	.429	35	0	0	0	8	76^1	69	22	18	4	1	41	43	1.441	2.12	157	3.66	.246	3	.136	11	8	1.2
1944	StL-A	6	6	.500	42	0	0	0	**12**	81	91	37	22	5	0	33	46	1.531	2.44	147	4.43	.284	5	.250	12	8	1.3

YEAR TM-L	W	L	PCT	G	GS	CG	SH	SV	IP	H	R	ER	HR	HB	BB	SO	RAT	ERA	ERA+	CERA	OAV	BH	AVG	PR+	WS	TPW
1945 StL-A	1	2	.333	10	0	0	0	1	15^{2}	20	13	12	0	0	7	9	1.723	6.89	51	4.89	.308	1	.333	-6	0	-0.6
*Det-A	5	1	.833	22	0	0	0	2	51^{1}	47	25	22	3	2	27	23	1.442	3.86	91	3.86	.250	2	.182	-2	3	-0.2
Yr.	6	3	.667	32	0	0	0	3	67	67	38	34	3	2	34	32	1.507	4.57	77	4.10	.265	3	.214	-8	3	-0.8
1946 Det-A	2	1	.667	26	0	0	0	4	41^{1}	42	26	26	1	1	24	19	1.597	5.66	65	4.27	.264	1	.143	-9	1	-0.9
Total 12	76	100	.432	376	127	62	6	39	1377^{2}	1469	833	695	121	25	597	595	1.500	4.54	96	4.46	.273	81	.184	-7	73	-1.1
• CASTILLO, Bobby	Robert Ernie Castillo b: 4/18/1955, Los Angeles, CA BR/TR, 5'10", 170 lbs. Deb: 9/10/1977																									
1977 LA-N	1	0	1.000	6	1	0	0	0	11^{1}	12	5	5	2	0	2	7	1.235	3.97	96	4.13	.279	0	.000	-0	1	0.0
1978 LA-N	0	4	.000	18	0	0	0	1	34	28	19	15	2	0	33	30	1.794	3.97	88	4.56	.239	0	.000	-2	0	-0.3
1979 LA-N	2	0	1.000	19	0	0	0	7	24^{1}	26	5	3	0	1	13	25	1.603	1.11	327	4.32	.277	0	.000	7	4	0.7
1980 LA-N	8	6	.571	61	0	0	0	5	98^{1}	70	31	30	4	1	45	60	1.169	2.75	127	2.42	.206	1	.111	7	10	0.6
1981* LA-N	2	4	.333	34	1	0	0	5	50^{2}	50	31	30	5	0	24	35	1.461	5.33	62	4.18	.262	4	.444	-11	1	-1.0
1982 Min-A	13	11	.542	40	25	6	1	0	218^{2}	194	96	89	26	0	85	123	1.276	3.66	116	3.56	.241	0	....	12	14	1.2
1983 Min-A	8	12	.400	27	25	3	0	0	158^{1}	170	91	84	17	1	65	90	1.484	4.77	89	4.64	.278	0	....	-11	6	-1.1
1984 Min-A	2	1	.667	10	2	0	0	0	25^{1}	14	7	5	2	0	19	7	1.303	1.78	237	2.93	.177	0	....	6	3	0.6
1985* LA-N	2	2	.500	35	5	0	0	0	68	59	42	41	9	1	41	57	1.471	5.43	64	4.24	.230	1	.100	-15	0	-1.6
Total 9	38	40	.487	250	59	9	1	18	689	623	327	302	67	4	327	434	1.379	3.94	98	3.82	.246	6	.154	-8	39	-0.9
• CASTILLO, Carlos	Carlos Castillo b: 4/21/1975, Boston, MA BR/TR, 6'2", 240 lbs. Deb: 4/2/1997																									
1997 Chi-A	2	1	.667	37	2	0	0	1	66^{1}	68	35	33	9	1	33	43	1.523	4.48	98	4.85	.265	1	1.000	0	4	0.1
1998 Chi-A	6	4	.600	54	2	0	0	0	100^{1}	94	61	57	17	5	35	64	1.286	5.11	89	4.14	.246	0	.000	-7	4	-0.6
1999 Chi-A	2	2	.500	18	2	0	0	0	41	45	26	26	10	0	14	23	1.439	5.71	85	5.40	.274	0	....	-4	2	-0.3
2001 Bos-A	0	0	....	2	0	0	0	0	3	3	2	2	1	0	0	0	1.000	6.00	75	3.79	.273	0	....	-0	0	0.0
Total 4	10	7	.588	111	6	0	0	1	210^{2}	210	124	118	37	6	82	130	1.386	5.04	91	4.60	.258	1	.500	-10	10	-0.9
• CASTILLO, Frank	Frank Anthony Castillo b: 4/1/1969, El Paso, TX BR/TR, 6'1", 190 lbs. Deb: 6/27/1991																									
1991 Chi-N	6	7	.462	18	18	4	0	0	111^{2}	107	56	54	5	0	33	73	1.254	4.35	89	3.04	.252	5	.143	-4	4	-0.5
1992 Chi-N	10	11	.476	33	33	0	0	0	205^{1}	179	91	79	19	6	63	135	1.179	3.46	104	3.02	.232	6	.092	3	10	0.1
1993 Chi-N	5	8	.385	29	25	2	0	0	141^{1}	162	83	76	20	9	39	84	1.422	4.84	82	4.98	.293	7	.163	-15	4	-1.5
1994 Chi-N	2	1	.667	4	4	1	0	0	23	25	13	11	3	0	5	19	1.304	4.30	97	4.09	.278	0	.000	-1	1	-0.1
1995 Chi-N	11	10	.524	29	29	2	2	0	188	179	75	67	22	6	52	135	1.229	3.21	128	3.49	.248	6	.102	18	13	1.5
1996 Chi-N	7	16	.304	33	33	1	1	0	182^{1}	209	112	107	28	8	46	139	1.399	5.28	82	4.87	.288	5	.088	-21	3	-2.4
1997 Chi-N	6	9	.400	20	19	0	0	0	98	113	64	59	9	4	44	67	1.602	5.42	80	5.23	.292	5	.152	-12	2	-1.3
Col-N	6	3	.667	14	14	0	0	0	86^{1}	107	57	52	16	4	25	59	1.529	5.42	96	5.83	.308	2	.080	-1	4	-0.3
Yr.	12	12	.500	34	33	0	0	0	184^{1}	220	121	111	25	8	69	126	**1.568**	5.42	86	5.51	.300	7	.121	-13	6	-1.5
1998 Det-A	3	9	.250	27	19	0	0	1	116	150	91	88	17	5	44	81	1.672	6.83	69	6.32	.316	0	.000	-29	0	-2.7
2000 Tor-A	10	5	.667	25	24	0	0	0	138	112	58	55	18	5	56	104	1.217	3.59	141	3.42	.220	1	.143	23	12	2.1
2001 Bos-A	10	9	.526	26	26	0	0	0	136^{2}	138	72	64	14	5	35	89	1.266	4.21	106	3.68	.260	0	.000	7	8	0.6
2002 Bos-A	6	15	.286	36	23	0	0	1	163^{1}	174	101	92	19	7	58	112	1.420	5.07	89	4.51	.274	0	.000	-13	4	-1.3
Total 11	82	103	.443	294	267	10	3	2	1590	1655	873	804	190	59	500	1097	1.355	4.55	95	4.25	.268	37	.110	-47	65	-5.8
• CASTILLO, Juan	Juan Francisco (Azdura) Castillo b: 6/23/1970, Caracas, Venezuela BR/TR, 6'5" Deb: 7/26/1994																									
1994 NY-N	0	0	....	2	2	0	0	0	11^{2}	17	9	9	2	0	5	1	1.886	6.94	60	7.82	.362	1	.200	-4	0	-0.4
• CASTILLO, Tony	Antonio Jose (Jimenez) Castillo b: 3/1/1963, Quibor, Venezuela BL/TL, 5'10", 188 lbs. Deb: 8/14/1988																									
1988 Tor-A	1	0	1.000	14	0	0	0	0	15	10	5	5	2	0	2	14	.800	3.00	131	1.73	.200	0	....	1	1	0.1
1989 Tor-A	1	1	.500	17	0	0	0	1	17^{2}	23	14	12	0	1	10	10	1.868	6.11	59	5.29	.333	0	....	-5	0	-0.5
Atl-N	0	1	.000	12	0	0	0	0	9^{1}	8	5	5	0	0	4	5	1.286	4.82	76	2.44	.222	0	.000	-1	0	-0.1
1990 Atl-N	5	1	.833	52	3	0	0	1	76^{2}	93	41	36	5	1	20	64	1.474	4.23	95	4.45	.302	1	.143	0	4	0.0
1991 Atl-N	1	1	.500	7	0	0	0	0	8^{2}	13	9	7	3	0	5	8	2.077	7.27	53	9.91	.342	0	....	-3	0	-0.3
NY-N	1	0	1.000	10	3	0	0	0	23^{2}	27	7	5	1	0	6	10	1.394	1.90	191	3.71	.281	0	.000	5	2	0.5
Yr.	2	1	.667	17	3	0	0	0	32^{1}	40	16	12	4	0	11	18	1.577	3.34	113	5.37	.299	0	.000	2	2	0.1
1993* Tor-A	3	2	.600	51	0	0	0	0	50^{2}	44	19	19	4	0	22	28	1.303	3.38	128	3.24	.242	0	....	6	5	0.6
1994 Tor-A	5	2	.714	41	0	0	0	1	68	66	22	19	7	3	28	43	1.382	2.51	192	4.19	.260	0	....	18	8	1.7
1995 Tor-A	1	5	.167	55	0	0	0	13	72^{2}	64	27	26	7	3	24	38	1.211	3.22	146	3.34	.243	0	....	12	9	1.1
1996 Tor-A	2	3	.400	40	0	0	0	1	72^{1}	72	38	34	9	2	20	48	1.272	4.23	118	3.83	.260	0	....	5	5	0.4
Chi-A	3	1	.750	15	0	0	0	1	22^{2}	23	7	4	1	1	4	9	1.191	1.59	299	3.03	.267	0	....	8	3	0.7
Yr.	5	4	.556	55	0	0	0	2	95	95	45	38	10	3	24	57	1.253	3.60	138	3.64	.262	0	....	13	8	1.2
1997 Chi-A	4	4	.500	64	0	0	0	4	62^{1}	74	48	34	6	1	23	42	1.556	4.91	89	4.78	.296	0	.000	-3	3	-0.3
1998 Chi-A	1	2	.333	25	0	0	0	0	27	38	25	24	7	2	11	14	1.815	8.00	57	8.25	.328	0	....	-10	0	-1.0
Total 10	28	23	.549	403	6	0	0	22	526^{2}	555	267	230	52	14	179	333	1.394	3.93	111	4.21	.274	1	.077	33	40	3.0
• CASTLEMAN, Slick	Clydell Castleman b: 9/8/1913, Donelson, TN d: 3/2/1998, Nashville, TN BR/TR, 6', 185 lbs. Deb: 5/9/1934																									
1934 NY-N	1	0	1.000	7	0	0	0	0	16^{2}	18	11	10	1	0	10	5	1.680	5.40	72	4.80	.277	1	.250	-3	1	-0.2
1935 NY-N	15	6	.714	29	25	9	1	0	173^{2}	186	93	79	14	1	64	64	1.440	4.09	94	4.04	.268	12	.179	-5	10	-0.6
1936* NY-N	4	7	.364	29	12	2	1	1	111^{2}	148	80	70	6	5	56	54	1.827	5.64	69	6.09	.323	5	.128	-25	0	-2.6
1937 NY-N	11	6	.647	23	23	10	2	0	160^{1}	148	66	59	19	0	33	78	1.129	3.31	117	3.06	.247	4	.070	7	12	0.2
1938 NY-N	4	5	.444	21	14	4	0	0	90^{2}	108	55	42	4	3	37	18	1.599	4.17	90	4.78	.296	3	.097	-4	3	-0.6
1939 NY-N	1	2	.333	12	4	0	0	0	33^{2}	36	18	17	1	0	23	6	1.752	4.54	86	5.00	.286	3	.333	-2	2	-0.2
Total 6	36	26	.581	121	78	25	4	1	586^{2}	644	323	277	45	9	223	225	1.478	4.25	91	4.35	.279	28	.135	-33	28	-3.9
• CASTLETON, Roy	Royal Eugene Castleton b: 7/26/1885, Salt Lake City, UT d: 6/24/1967, Los Angeles, CA BR/TL, 5'11", 167 lbs. Deb: 4/16/1907																									
1907 NY-A	1	1	.500	3	2	1	0	0	16	11	6	5	1	0	3	3	.875	2.81	99	1.56	.197	0	.000	0	1	-0.1
1909 Cin-N	1	1	.500	4	1	1	0	0	14	14	6	3	0	2	6	5	1.429	1.93	134	4.10	.275	2	.667	1	1	0.2
1910 Cin-N	1	2	.333	4	2	1	0	0	13^{2}	15	5	5	0	1	6	5	1.537	3.29	88	4.37	.288	0	.000	-0	1	-0.1
Total 3	3	4	.429	11	5	3	0	0	43^{2}	40	17	13	1	3	15	13	1.260	2.68	104	3.26	.252	2	.154	1	3	0.0
• CASTNER, Paul	Paul Henry "Lefty" Castner b: 2/16/1897, St. Paul, MN d: 3/3/1986, St. Paul, MN BL/TL, 5'11", 187 lbs. Deb: 8/6/1923																									
1923 Chi-A	0	0	....	6	0	0	0	0	10	14	9	7	0	0	5	0	1.900	6.30	63	5.48	.326	0	.000	-3	0	-0.3
• CASTRO, Bill	William Radhames (Checo) Castro b: 12/13/1953, Santiago, Dominican Republic BR/TR, 5'11", 170 lbs. Deb: 8/20/1974 C																									
1974 Mil-A	0	0	....	8	0	0	0	0	18	19	10	9	2	0	5	10	1.333	4.50	80	3.89	.264	0	....	-2	0	-0.2
1975 Mil-A	3	2	.600	18	5	0	0	1	75	78	28	21	3	2	17	25	1.267	2.52	152	3.23	.272	0	....	11	6	1.2
1976 Mil-A	4	6	.400	39	0	0	0	8	70^{1}	70	29	27	4	3	19	23	1.265	3.45	101	3.38	.265	0	....	0	5	0.0
1977 Mil-A	8	6	.571	51	0	0	0	13	69^{1}	76	34	32	7	2	23	28	1.428	4.15	98	4.31	.293	0	....	-1	7	-0.1
1978 Mil-A	5	4	.556	42	0	0	0	8	49^{2}	43	14	10	2	6	14	17	1.148	1.81	207	2.76	.234	0	....	11	7	1.1
1979 Mil-A	3	1	.750	39	0	0	0	6	44^{1}	40	14	10	2	0	13	10	1.195	2.03	205	2.65	.244	0	....	11	7	1.0
1980 Mil-A	2	4	.333	56	0	0	0	8	84^{1}	89	35	26	2	2	17	32	1.257	2.77	139	3.11	.274	0	....	9	7	0.9
1981 NY-A	1	1	.500	11	0	0	0	0	19	26	13	8	2	0	5	4	1.632	3.79	94	5.62	.329	0	....	-1	0	-0.1
1982 KC-A	3	2	.600	21	4	0	0	1	75^{2}	72	34	29	8	2	20	37	1.216	3.45	118	3.26	.243	0	....	5	5	0.5
1983 KC-A	2	0	1.000	18	0	0	0	0	40^{2}	51	34	30	4	5	12	17	1.549	6.64	61	5.44	.300	0	....	-11	0	-1.1
Total 10	31	26	.544	303	9	0	0	45	546^{1}	564	245	202	36	22	145	203	1.298	3.33	117	3.55	.269	0	....	33	44	3.3
• CATES, Eli	Eli Eldo Cates b: 1/26/1877, Greens Fork, IN d: 5/29/1964, Anderson, IN BR/TR, 5'9.5", 175 lbs. Deb: 4/20/1908																									
1908 Was-A	4	8	.333	19	10	7	0	0	113	112	46	32	3	1	32	33	1.274	2.55	90	3.16	....	11	.186	-4	5	-0.3
• CATHER, Mike	Michael Peter Cather b: 12/17/1970, San Diego, CA BR/TR, 6'2", 195 lbs. Deb: 7/13/1997																									
1997* Atl-N	2	4	.333	35	0	0	0	0	37^{2}	23	12	10	1	2	19	29	1.115	2.39	176	1.99	.174	0	.000	7	4	0.7
1998 Atl-N	2	2	.500	36	0	0	0	0	41^{1}	39	21	18	7	2	12	33	1.234	3.92	106	3.97	.255	0	....	1	2	0.1

YEAR TM-L	W	L	PCT	G	GS	CG	SH	SV	IP	H	R	ER	HR	HB	BB	SO	RAT	ERA	ERA+	CERA	OAV	BH	AVG	PR+	WS	TPW
1999 Atl-N	1	0	1.000	4	0	0	0	0	2^{2}	5	3	3	2	0	1	0	2.250	10.13	44	16.62	.417	0	....	-2	0	-0.2
Total 3	**5**	**6**	**.455**	**75**	**0**	**0**	**0**	**0**	**81^{2}**	**67**	**36**	**31**	**10**	**4**	**32**	**62**	**1.212**	**3.42**	**123**	**3.47**	**.226**	**0**	**.000**	**6**	**6**	**0.6**

• CATHEY, Hardin — Hardin Abner "Lil Abner" Cathey b: 7/6/1919, Burns, TN d: 7/27/1997, Nashville, TN BR/TR, 6'4", 190 lbs. Deb: 4/16/1942

YEAR TM-L	W	L	PCT	G	GS	CG	SH	SV	IP	H	R	ER	HR	HB	BB	SO	RAT	ERA	ERA+	CERA	OAV	BH	AVG	PR+	WS	TPW
1942 Was-A	1	1	.500	12	2	0	0	0	30^{1}	44	26	25	1	0	16	8	1.978	7.42	49	6.61	.341	3	.375	-11	0	-1.1

• CATO, Keefe — John Keefe Cato b: 5/6/1958, Yonkers, NY BR/TR, 6'1", 185 lbs. Deb: 6/13/1983

YEAR TM-L	W	L	PCT	G	GS	CG	SH	SV	IP	H	R	ER	HR	HB	BB	SO	RAT	ERA	ERA+	CERA	OAV	BH	AVG	PR+	WS	TPW
1983 Cin-N	1	0	1.000	4	0	0	0	0	3^{2}	2	1	1	0	0	1	3	.818	2.45	155	1.10	.154	0	....	1	1	0.1
1984 Cin-N	0	1	.000	8	0	0	0	1	15^{2}	22	14	14	5	0	4	12	1.660	8.04	47	7.54	.344	2	.500	-7	0	-0.7
Total 2	**1**	**1**	**.500**	**12**	**0**	**0**	**0**	**1**	**19^{1}**	**24**	**15**	**15**	**5**	**0**	**5**	**15**	**1.500**	**6.98**	**54**	**6.32**	**.312**	**2**	**.500**	**-7**	**1**	**-0.6**

• CATTANACH, John — John Leckie Cattanach b: 5/10/1863, Providence, RI d: 11/10/1926, Providence, RI, 5'10", 190 lbs. Deb: 6/5/1884

YEAR TM-L	W	L	PCT	G	GS	CG	SH	SV	IP	H	R	ER	HR	HB	BB	SO	RAT	ERA	ERA+	CERA	OAV	BH	AVG	PR+	WS	TPW
1884 Pro-N	0	0	....	1	1	0	0	0	5	2	7	5	0	....	4	2	1.200	9.00	31	....	.116	0	.000	-4	0	-0.4
StL-U	1	1	.500	2	2	2	0	0	17	12	10	4	0	....	4	13	.941	2.12	141	....	.185	0	.000	1	1	0.0

• CAUDILL, Bill — William Holland Caudill b: 7/13/1956, Santa Monica, CA BR/TR, 6'1", 210 lbs. Deb: 5/12/1979

YEAR TM-L	W	L	PCT	G	GS	CG	SH	SV	IP	H	R	ER	HR	HB	BB	SO	RAT	ERA	ERA+	CERA	OAV	BH	AVG	PR+	WS	TPW
1979 Chi-N	1	7	.125	29	12	0	0	0	90	89	57	48	16	4	41	104	1.444	4.80	86	4.80	.255	1	.059	-5	2	-0.7
1980 Chi-N	4	6	.400	72	2	0	0	1	127^{2}	100	37	31	10	1	59	112	1.245	2.19	179	2.92	.223	2	.222	26	12	2.8
1981 Chi-N	1	5	.167	30	10	0	0	0	71	87	50	46	9	2	31	45	1.662	5.83	63	5.71	.301	2	.143	-15	0	-1.6
1982 Sea-A	12	9	.571	70	0	0	0	26	95^{2}	65	25	25	9	1	35	111	1.045	2.35	180	2.25	.192	0	....	20	20	2.0
1983 Sea-A	2	8	.200	63	0	0	0	26	72^{2}	70	39	38	10	2	38	73	1.486	4.71	90	4.67	.257	0	....	-4	6	-0.4
1984 Oak-A★	9	7	.563	68	0	0	0	36	96^{1}	77	30	29	9	0	31	89	1.121	2.71	138	2.59	.218	0	.000	11	14	1.1
1985 Tor-A	4	6	.400	67	0	0	0	14	69^{1}	53	26	23	9	2	35	46	1.269	2.99	141	3.32	.209	0	....	8	9	0.8
1986 Tor-A	2	4	.333	40	0	0	0	2	36^{1}	36	25	25	6	2	17	32	1.459	6.19	68	4.87	.254	0	....	-8	1	-0.8
1987 Oak-A	0	0	....	6	0	0	0	1	8	10	8	8	3	0	1	8	1.375	9.00	46	6.18	.294	0	....	-4	0	-0.4
Total 9	**35**	**52**	**.402**	**445**	**24**	**0**	**0**	**106**	**667**	**587**	**297**	**273**	**81**	**14**	**288**	**620**	**1.312**	**3.68**	**109**	**3.71**	**.237**	**5**	**.122**	**29**	**64**	**2.9**

• CAUSEY, Red — Cecil Algernon Causey b: 8/11/1893, Georgetown, FL d: 11/11/1960, Avon Park, FL BR/TR, 6'1", 160 lbs. Deb: 4/26/1918

YEAR TM-L	W	L	PCT	G	GS	CG	SH	SV	IP	H	R	ER	HR	HB	BB	SO	RAT	ERA	ERA+	CERA	OAV	BH	AVG	PR+	WS	TPW
1918 NY-N	11	6	.647	29	18	10	2	2	158^{1}	143	58	49	2	7	42	48	1.168	2.79	94	2.60	.245	6	.125	-3	9	-0.7
1919 NY-N	9	3	.750	19	16	6	0	0	105	99	52	43	5	2	38	25	1.305	3.69	76	3.24	.251	5	.132	-12	3	-1.5
Bos-N	4	5	.444	10	10	3	0	0	69	81	38	35	1	1	20	14	1.464	4.57	63	4.14	.308	2	.095	-13	1	-1.7
Yr.	13	8	.619	29	26	9	0	0	174	180	90	78	6	3	58	39	1.368	4.03	70	3.60	.274	7	.119	-25	4	-3.1
1920 Phi-N	7	14	.333	35	26	11	1	3	181^{1}	203	109	87	4	5	79	30	**1.555**	4.32	79	4.38	.299	11	.186	-18	6	-2.1
1921 Phi-N	3	3	.500	7	7	4	0	0	50^{2}	58	22	16	4	1	11	8	1.362	2.84	149	4.10	.294	3	.150	9	4	0.8
NY-N	1	1	.500	7	1	0	0	0	14^{2}	13	8	4	0	0	6	1	1.295	2.45	149	2.56	.228	1	.333	2	1	0.2
Yr.	4	4	.500	14	8	4	0	0	65^{1}	71	30	20	4	1	17	9	1.347	2.76	149	3.76	.279	4	.174	10	5	1.0
1922 NY-N	4	3	.571	24	2	1	0	1	70^{2}	69	34	25	2	0	34	13	1.458	3.18	126	3.56	.262	5	.238	4	5	0.4
Total 5	**39**	**35**	**.527**	**131**	**80**	**35**	**3**	**6**	**649^{2}**	**666**	**321**	**259**	**18**	**16**	**230**	**139**	**1.379**	**3.59**	**87**	**3.59**	**.273**	**33**	**.157**	**-32**	**29**	**-4.6**

• CAVET, Pug — Tillar H. Cavet b: 12/26/1889, McGregor, TX d: 8/4/1966, San Luis Obispo, CA BL/TL, 6'3", 176 lbs. Deb: 4/25/1911

YEAR TM-L	W	L	PCT	G	GS	CG	SH	SV	IP	H	R	ER	HR	HB	BB	SO	RAT	ERA	ERA+	CERA	OAV	BH	AVG	PR+	WS	TPW
1911 Det-A	0	0	....	1	1	0	0	0	4	6	5	2	0	0	1	1	1.750	4.50	77	5.09	.316	0	.000	-0	0	-0.1
1914 Det-A	7	7	.500	31	14	6	1	2	151^{1}	129	61	41	2	9	44	51	1.143	2.44	115	2.61	.238	5	.106	8	9	0.7
1915 Det-A	4	2	.667	17	7	2	0	1	71	83	39	32	1	2	22	26	1.479	4.06	75	4.24	.300	6	.250	-7	3	-0.6
Total 3	**11**	**9**	**.550**	**49**	**22**	**8**	**1**	**3**	**226^{1}**	**218**	**105**	**75**	**3**	**11**	**67**	**78**	**1.259**	**2.98**	**98**	**3.17**	**.260**	**11**	**.153**	**1**	**12**	**0.1**

• CECCARELLI, Art — Arthur Edward "Chic" Ceccarelli b: 4/2/1930, New Haven, CT BR/TL, 6', 190 lbs. Deb: 5/3/1955

YEAR TM-L	W	L	PCT	G	GS	CG	SH	SV	IP	H	R	ER	HR	HB	BB	SO	RAT	ERA	ERA+	CERA	OAV	BH	AVG	PR+	WS	TPW
1955 KC-A	4	7	.364	31	16	3	1	0	123^{2}	123	81	73	20	0	71	68	1.569	5.31	78	5.14	.258	3	.079	-15	3	-1.8
1956 KC-A	0	1	.000	3	2	0	0	0	10	13	13	8	3	1	4	2	1.700	7.20	60	7.40	.317	0	.000	-3	0	-0.3
1957 Bal-A	0	5	.000	20	8	1	0	0	58	62	34	29	3	2	31	30	1.603	4.50	80	4.67	.278	0	.000	-7	0	-0.9
1959 Chi-N	5	5	.500	18	15	4	2	0	102	95	58	54	19	1	37	56	1.294	4.76	83	4.07	.245	3	.091	-10	3	-1.1
1960 Chi-N	0	0	....	7	1	0	0	0	13	16	12	8	1	0	4	10	1.538	5.54	68	4.73	.296	0	....	-3	0	-0.3
Total 5	**9**	**18**	**.333**	**79**	**42**	**8**	**3**	**0**	**306^{2}**	**309**	**198**	**172**	**46**	**4**	**147**	**166**	**1.487**	**5.05**	**79**	**4.75**	**.261**	**6**	**.068**	**-38**	**6**	**-4.4**

• CECENA, Jose — Jose Isabel (Lugo) Cecena b: 8/20/1963, Ciudad Obregon, Mexico BR/TR, 5'11", 180 lbs. Deb: 4/6/1988

YEAR TM-L	W	L	PCT	G	GS	CG	SH	SV	IP	H	R	ER	HR	HB	BB	SO	RAT	ERA	ERA+	CERA	OAV	BH	AVG	PR+	WS	TPW
1988 Tex-A	0	0	....	22	0	0	0	1	26^{1}	20	16	14	2	2	23	27	1.633	4.78	85	4.61	.213	0	....	-2	1	-0.2

• CECIL, Rex — Rex Rolston Cecil b: 10/8/1916, Lindsay, OK d: 10/30/1966, Long Beach, CA BL/TR, 6'3", 195 lbs. Deb: 8/13/1944

YEAR TM-L	W	L	PCT	G	GS	CG	SH	SV	IP	H	R	ER	HR	HB	BB	SO	RAT	ERA	ERA+	CERA	OAV	BH	AVG	PR+	WS	TPW
1944 Bos-A	4	5	.444	11	9	4	0	0	61	72	44	35	5	1	33	33	1.721	5.16	66	5.29	.286	5	.278	-12	0	-1.1
1945 Bos-A	2	5	.286	7	7	1	0	0	45	46	37	26	4	0	27	30	1.622	5.20	65	4.66	.261	6	.300	-9	0	-0.9
Total 2	**6**	**10**	**.375**	**18**	**16**	**5**	**0**	**0**	**106**	**118**	**81**	**61**	**9**	**1**	**60**	**63**	**1.679**	**5.18**	**66**	**5.02**	**.276**	**11**	**.289**	**-21**	**0**	**-2.0**

• CENTER, Pete — Marvin Earl Center b: 4/22/1912, Hazel Green, KY BR/TR, 6'4", 190 lbs. Deb: 9/11/1942

YEAR TM-L	W	L	PCT	G	GS	CG	SH	SV	IP	H	R	ER	HR	HB	BB	SO	RAT	ERA	ERA+	CERA	OAV	BH	AVG	PR+	WS	TPW
1942 Cle-A	0	0	....	1	0	0	0	0	3^{1}	7	6	6	0	1	4	0	3.300	16.20	21	14.45	.438	0	.000	-5	0	-0.5
1943 Cle-A	1	2	.333	24	1	0	0	1	42^{1}	29	18	13	3	0	18	10	1.110	2.76	112	2.33	.201	0	.000	1	2	0.0
1945 Cle-A	6	3	.667	31	8	2	0	1	85^{2}	89	42	38	2	1	28	34	1.366	3.99	81	3.41	.270	2	.091	-6	4	-0.9
1946 Cle-A	0	2	.000	21	0	0	0	1	29	29	16	16	2	1	20	6	1.690	4.97	67	5.04	.269	0	.000	-5	0	-0.6
Total 4	**7**	**7**	**.500**	**77**	**9**	**2**	**0**	**3**	**160^{1}**	**154**	**82**	**73**	**7**	**3**	**70**	**50**	**1.397**	**4.10**	**79**	**3.65**	**.258**	**2**	**.065**	**-16**	**6**	**-2.0**

• CERDA, Jaime — Jaime M. Cerda b: 10/26/1978, Fresno, CA BL/TL, 6', 175 lbs. Deb: 6/28/2002

YEAR TM-L	W	L	PCT	G	GS	CG	SH	SV	IP	H	R	ER	HR	HB	BB	SO	RAT	ERA	ERA+	CERA	OAV	BH	AVG	PR+	WS	TPW
2002 NY-N	0	0	....	32	0	0	0	0	25^{2}	22	7	7	0	1	14	21	1.403	2.45	161	3.23	.232	0	.000	5	2	0.4
2003 NY-N	1	1	.500	27	0	0	0	0	32^{1}	32	21	21	4	0	20	19	1.608	5.85	71	5.08	.267	0	.000	-6	0	-0.6
Total 2	**1**	**1**	**.500**	**59**	**0**	**0**	**0**	**0**	**58**	**54**	**28**	**28**	**4**	**1**	**34**	**40**	**1.517**	**4.34**	**94**	**4.26**	**.251**	**0**	**.000**	**-1**	**2**	**-0.2**

• CERROS, Juan — R. Juan Cerros b: 9/25/1976, Monterrey, Mexico BR/TR, 6'1", 200 lbs. Deb: 9/8/2003

YEAR TM-L	W	L	PCT	G	GS	CG	SH	SV	IP	H	R	ER	HR	HB	BB	SO	RAT	ERA	ERA+	CERA	OAV	BH	AVG	PR+	WS	TPW
2003 Cin-N	0	0	....	11	0	0	0	0	13	11	7	7	1	2	5	9	1.231	4.85	88	3.27	.224	0	....	-1	0	-0.1

• CERUTTI, John — John Joseph Cerutti b: 4/28/1960, Albany, NY BL/TL, 6'2", 200 lbs. Deb: 9/1/1985

YEAR TM-L	W	L	PCT	G	GS	CG	SH	SV	IP	H	R	ER	HR	HB	BB	SO	RAT	ERA	ERA+	CERA	OAV	BH	AVG	PR+	WS	TPW
1985 Tor-A	0	2	.000	4	1	0	0	0	6^{2}	10	7	4	1	1	4	5	2.100	5.40	78	8.67	.323	0	....	-1	0	-0.1
1986 Tor-A	9	4	.692	34	20	2	1	1	145^{1}	150	73	67	25	1	47	89	1.356	4.15	102	4.50	.268	0	....	1	8	0.1
1987 Tor-A	11	4	.733	44	21	2	0	0	151^{1}	144	75	74	30	1	59	92	1.341	4.40	102	4.48	.251	0	....	-1	9	-0.1
1988 Tor-A	6	7	.462	46	12	0	0	1	123^{2}	120	56	43	12	3	42	65	1.310	3.13	126	3.68	.256	0	....	10	8	1.1
1989* Tor-A	11	11	.500	33	31	3	1	0	205^{1}	214	90	70	19	6	53	69	1.300	3.07	118	3.88	.273	0	....	12	12	1.2
1990 Tor-A	9	9	.500	30	23	0	0	0	140	162	77	74	23	4	49	49	1.507	4.76	86	5.46	.297	0	....	-10	5	-1.0
1991 Det-A	3	6	.333	38	8	1	0	2	88^{2}	94	49	45	9	2	37	29	1.477	4.57	91	4.43	.276	0	....	-4	3	-0.4
Total 7	**49**	**43**	**.533**	**229**	**116**	**8**	**2**	**4**	**861**	**894**	**427**	**377**	**119**	**18**	**291**	**398**	**1.376**	**3.94**	**103**	**4.41**	**.271**	**0**	**....**	**8**	**45**	**0.9**

• CHACON, Shawn — Shawn Anthony Chacon b: 12/23/1977, Anchorage, AK BR/TR, 6'3", 195 lbs. Deb: 4/29/2001

YEAR TM-L	W	L	PCT	G	GS	CG	SH	SV	IP	H	R	ER	HR	HB	BB	SO	RAT	ERA	ERA+	CERA	OAV	BH	AVG	PR+	WS	TPW
2001 Col-N	6	10	.375	27	27	0	0	0	160	157	96	90	26	10	87	134	1.525	5.06	105	5.22	.260	2	.043	4	7	0.0
2002 Col-N	5	11	.313	21	21	0	0	0	119^{1}	122	84	76	25	7	60	67	1.525	5.73	83	5.63	.263	9	.257	-11	4	-1.0
2003 Col-N★	11	8	.579	23	23	0	0	0	137	124	73	70	12	12	58	93	1.328	4.60	107	3.82	.243	9	.196	7	8	0.8
Total 3	**22**	**29**	**.431**	**71**	**71**	**0**	**0**	**0**	**416^{1}**	**403**	**253**	**236**	**63**	**29**	**205**	**294**	**1.460**	**5.10**	**98**	**4.88**	**.255**	**20**	**.156**	**-0**	**19**	**-0.2**

• CHADWICK, Ray — Ray Charles Chadwick b: 11/17/1962, Durham, NC BB/TR, 6'2" Deb: 7/29/1986

YEAR TM-L	W	L	PCT	G	GS	CG	SH	SV	IP	H	R	ER	HR	HB	BB	SO	RAT	ERA	ERA+	CERA	OAV	BH	AVG	PR+	WS	TPW
1986 Cal-A	0	5	.000	7	7	0	0	0	27^{1}	39	26	22	5	1	15	9	1.976	7.24	57	8.25	.336	0	....	-10	0	-1.0

• CHAGNON, Leon — Leon Wilbur Chagnon b: 9/28/1902, Pittsfield, NH d: 7/30/1953, Amesbury, MA BR/TR, 6', 182 lbs. Deb: 10/5/1929

YEAR TM-L	W	L	PCT	G	GS	CG	SH	SV	IP	H	R	ER	HR	HB	BB	SO	RAT	ERA	ERA+	CERA	OAV	BH	AVG	PR+	WS	TPW
1929 Pit-N	0	0	....	1	1	0	0	0	7	11	7	7	1	0	1	4	1.714	9.00	53	6.34	.333	0	.000	-3	0	-0.3
1930 Pit-N	0	3	.000	18	4	3	0	0	62	92	52	47	9	5	23	27	1.855	6.82	73	7.46	.355	4	.200	-13	1	-1.2
1932 Pit-N	9	6	.600	30	10	4	1	0	128	140	62	56	10	2	34	52	1.359	3.94	97	3.84	.276	9	.225	-3	8	-0.1
1933 Pit-N	6	4	.600	39	5	1	0	1	100	100	48	41	2	3	17	35	1.170	3.69	90	2.71	.259	1	.048	-5	5	-0.7
1934 Pit-N	4	1	.800	33	0	0	0	1	58	68	32	31	5	1	24	19	1.586	4.81	86	4.77	.288	3	.231	-4	3	-0.4

YEAR	TM-L	W	L	PCT	G	GS	CG	SH	SV	IP	H	R	ER	HR	HB	BB	SO	RAT	ERA	ERA+	CERA	OAV	BH	AVG	PR+	WS	TPW
1935	NY-N	0	2	.000	14	1	0	0	1	38^1	32	17	15	7	0	5	16	.965	3.52	109	2.68	.232	0	.000	1	2	0.0
Total	6	19	16	.543	135	21	8	1	3	393^1	443	218	197	34	11	104	153	1.391	4.51	88	4.19	.284	17	.162	-26	19	-2.7

• CHAKALES, Bob Robert Edward Chakales b: 8/10/1927, Asheville, NC BR/TR, 6'1" Deb: 4/21/1951

YEAR	TM-L	W	L	PCT	G	GS	CG	SH	SV	IP	H	R	ER	HR	HB	BB	SO	RAT	ERA	ERA+	CERA	OAV	BH	AVG	PR+	WS	TPW
1951	Cle-A	3	4	.429	17	10	2	1	0	68^1	80	40	36	3	0	43	32	1.800	4.74	80	5.35	.292	7	.350	-7	2	-0.5
1952	Cle-A	1	2	.333	5	1	0	0	0	12	19	13	13	2	0	8	7	2.250	9.75	34	9.88	.388	2	.500	-8	0	-0.8
1953	Cle-A	0	2	.000	7	3	1	0	0	27	28	13	8	2	1	10	6	1.407	2.67	141	4.08	.283	2	.286	3	2	0.3
1954	Cle-A	2	0	1.000	3	0	0	0	0	10^1	4	1	1	0	0	12	3	1.548	0.87	422	2.45	.114	1	.333	3	2	0.4
	Bal-A	3	7	.300	38	6	0	0	3	89^1	81	43	37	8	1	43	44	1.388	3.73	96	3.71	.245	8	.364	-1	6	0.2
	Yr.	5	7	.417	41	6	0	0	3	99^2	85	44	38	8	1	55	47	1.405	3.43	104	3.58	.232	9	.360	2	8	0.6
1955	Chi-A	0	0	....	7	0	0	0	0	12^1	11	2	2	2	0	6	6	1.378	1.46	270	4.40	.256	0	.000	3	1	0.3
	Was-A	2	3	.400	29	0	0	0	0	54^2	55	38	32	4	1	25	28	1.463	5.27	73	4.07	.263	0	.000	-7	1	-0.8
	Yr.	2	3	.400	36	0	0	0	0	67	66	40	34	6	1	31	34	1.448	4.57	84	4.13	.262	0	.000	-4	2	-0.5
1956	Was-A	4	4	.500	43	1	0	0	4	96	94	53	43	3	3	57	33	1.573	4.03	107	4.29	.268	3	.150	6	7	0.5
1957	Was-A	0	1	.000	4	2	0	0	0	18^1	20	13	11	2	0	10	12	1.636	5.40	72	5.03	.274	1	.143	-3	0	-0.2
	Bos-A	0	2	.000	18	0	0	0	3	32	53	30	29	5	1	11	16	2.000	8.16	49	8.66	.379	2	.667	-14	0	-1.4
	Yr.	0	3	.000	22	2	0	0	3	50^1	73	43	40	7	1	21	28	1.868	7.15	55	7.33	.343	3	.300	-17	0	-1.6
Total	7	15	25	.375	171	23	3	1	10	420^1	445	246	212	31	7	225	187	1.594	4.54	85	4.78	.277	26	.271	-25	21	-2.1

• CHALMERS, George George W. "Dut" Chalmers b: 6/7/1888, Edinburgh, Scotland d: 8/5/1960, Bronx, NY BR/TR, 6'1" Deb: 9/21/1910

YEAR	TM-L	W	L	PCT	G	GS	CG	SH	SV	IP	H	R	ER	HR	HB	BB	SO	RAT	ERA	ERA+	CERA	OAV	BH	AVG	PR+	WS	TPW
1910	Phi-N	1	1	.500	4	3	2	0	0	22	21	17	13	0	1	11	12	1.455	5.32	59	3.96	.280	1	.143	-6	0	-0.6
1911	Phi-N	13	10	.565	38	22	11	3	4	208^2	196	107	72	5	4	101	101	1.423	3.11	110	3.63	.256	13	.178	7	14	0.6
1912	Phi-N	3	4	.429	12	8	3	0	0	57^2	64	34	21	4	2	37	22	1.751	3.28	110	5.59	.296	3	.188	2	3	0.2
1913	Phi-N	3	10	.231	26	15	4	0	1	116	133	75	62	3	5	51	46	1.586	4.81	69	4.65	.296	7	.212	-19	1	-2.0
1914	Phi-N	0	3	.000	3	2	1	0	0	18	23	17	11	0	1	15	6	2.111	5.50	53	6.82	.324	0	.000	-5	0	-0.6
1915*	Phi-N	8	9	.471	26	20	13	1	1	170^1	159	58	47	3	0	45	82	1.198	2.48	110	2.68	.255	10	.169	5	12	0.4
1916	Phi-N	1	4	.200	12	8	2	0	0	53^2	49	31	19	2	2	19	21	1.267	3.19	83	2.96	.244	0	.000	-3	0	-0.6
Total	7	29	41	.414	121	78	36	4	6	646^1	645	339	245	17	15	279	290	1.430	3.41	92	3.78	.269	34	.163	-18	30	-2.6

• CHAMBERLAIN, Bill William Vincent Chamberlain b: 4/21/1909, Stoughton, MA d: 2/6/1994, Brockton, MA BR/TL, 5'10.5" Deb: 8/2/1932

YEAR	TM-L	W	L	PCT	G	GS	CG	SH	SV	IP	H	R	ER	HR	HB	BB	SO	RAT	ERA	ERA+	CERA	OAV	BH	AVG	PR+	WS	TPW
1932	Chi-A	0	5	.000	12	5	0	0	0	41^1	39	30	21	3	0	25	11	1.548	4.57	95	4.14	.250	1	.100	-1	1	-0.1

• CHAMBERLAIN, Craig Craig Phillip Chamberlain b: 2/2/1957, Hollywood, CA BR/TR, 6'1" Deb: 8/12/1979

YEAR	TM-L	W	L	PCT	G	GS	CG	SH	SV	IP	H	R	ER	HR	HB	BB	SO	RAT	ERA	ERA+	CERA	OAV	BH	AVG	PR+	WS	TPW
1979	KC-A	4	4	.500	10	10	4	0	0	69^2	68	31	29	7	1	18	30	1.234	3.75	114	3.50	.261	0	....	3	5	0.3
1980	KC-A	0	1	.000	5	0	0	0	0	9^1	10	8	7	3	0	5	3	1.607	6.75	60	6.23	.270	0	....	-3	0	-0.3
Total	2	4	5	.444	15	10	4	0	0	79	78	39	36	10	1	23	33	1.278	4.10	103	3.82	.262	0	....	1	5	0.0

• CHAMBERLAIN, Elton Elton P. "Icebox" Chamberlain b: 11/5/1867, Buffalo, NY d: 9/22/1929, Baltimore, MD BR/TR, 5'9", 168 lbs. Deb: 9/13/1886 U

YEAR	TM-L	W	L	PCT	G	GS	CG	SH	SV	IP	H	R	ER	HR	HB	BB	SO	RAT	ERA	ERA+	CERA	OAV	BH	AVG	PR+	WS	TPW
1886	Lou-a	0	3	.000	4	4	4	0	0	31^1	39	43	23	0	0	17	18	1.787	6.61	55	....	.292	3	.158	-11	0	-1.1
1887	Lou-a	18	16	.529	36	36	35	1	0	309	457	226	130	8	14	117	118	1.479	3.79	116	....	.332	38	.266	15	22	1.0
1888	Lou-a	14	9	.609	24	24	21	1	0	196	177	123	55	2	0	59	119	1.204	2.53	122	....	.232	18	.191	17	7	1.6
	*StL-a	11	2	.846	14	14	13	1	0	112	61	34	20	1	0	27	57	.786	1.61	203	....	.154	5	.100	18	13	1.4
	Yr.	25	11	.694	38	38	34	2	0	308	238	157	75	3	0	86	176	1.052	2.19	142	....	.206	23	.160	35	20	3.0
1889	StL-a	32	15	.681	53	51	44	3	1	421^2	376	220	139	18	0	165	202	1.283	2.97	142	....	.231	34	.199	49	42	4.1
1890	StL-a	3	1	.750	5	5	3	0	0	35	47	37	23	1	7	26	14	2.086	5.91	73	....	.312	2	.133	-6	1	-0.7
	Col-a	12	6	.667	25	21	19	6	0	175	128	69	43	2	0	70	114	1.131	2.21	162	....	.198	15	.231	20	16	2.0
	Yr.	15	7	.682	30	26	22	**6**	0	210	175	106	66	3	7	96	128	1.290	2.83	135	....	.220	17	.213	13	17	1.3
1891	Phi-a	22	23	.489	49	46	44	0	0	405^2	397	263	190	10	0	206	204	1.486	4.22	91	....	.248	33	.188	-18	27	-1.2
1892	Cin-N	19	23	.452	52	49	43	2	0	406^1	391	230	153	8	0	170	169	1.381	3.39	96	3.28	.243	36	.225	-13	26	-0.9
1893	Cin-N	16	12	.571	34	27	19	1	0	241	248	148	100	3	0	112	59	1.494	3.73	128	3.74	.258	19	.196	24	20	1.8
1894	Cin-N	10	9	.526	23	22	18	1	0	177^2	220	155	114	10	0	91	57	1.750	5.77	96	5.44	.301	22	.314	-5	11	0.0
1896	Cle-N	0	1	.000	2	2	1	0	0	11	21	12	9	0	0	5	2	2.364	7.36	61	8.99	.400	0	.000	-3	0	-0.3
Total	10	157	120	.567	321	301	264	16	1	2521^2	2562	1560	999	63	21	1065	1133	1.392	3.57	112	1.31	.255	225	.212	86	185	7.7

• CHAMBERS, Bill William Christopher Chambers b: 9/13/1889, Cameron, WV d: 3/27/1962, Fort Wayne, IN BR/TR, 5'9" Deb: 7/11/1910

YEAR	TM-L	W	L	PCT	G	GS	CG	SH	SV	IP	H	R	ER	HR	HB	BB	SO	RAT	ERA	ERA+	CERA	OAV	BH	AVG	PR+	WS	TPW
1910	StL-N	0	0	....	1	0	0	0	0	1	1	1	0	0	0	0	0	1.000	0.00	....	1.95	.250	0	....	0	0	0.0

• CHAMBERS, Cliff Clifford Day "Lefty" Chambers b: 1/10/1922, Portland, OR BL/TL, 6'3" Deb: 4/24/1948

YEAR	TM-L	W	L	PCT	G	GS	CG	SH	SV	IP	H	R	ER	HR	HB	BB	SO	RAT	ERA	ERA+	CERA	OAV	BH	AVG	PR+	WS	TPW
1948	Chi-N	2	9	.182	29	12	3	1	0	103^2	100	57	51	4	3	48	51	1.428	4.43	88	3.67	.254	4	.133	-5	3	-0.6
1949	Pit-N	13	7	.650	34	21	10	1	0	177^1	186	89	78	15	5	58	93	1.376	3.96	106	3.97	.268	13	.236	6	14	0.9
1950	Pit-N	12	15	.444	37	33	11	2	0	249^1	262	138	119	18	6	92	93	1.420	4.30	102	3.98	.265	26	.289	4	14	1.1
1951	Pit-N	3	6	.333	10	10	2	1	0	59^2	64	38	37	5	4	31	19	1.592	5.58	76	4.95	.276	7	.333	-8	2	-0.6
	StL-N	11	6	.647	21	16	9	1	0	129^1	120	59	55	13	0	56	45	1.361	3.83	104	3.78	.251	8	.163	0	9	0.0
	Yr.	14	12	.538	31	26	11	2	0	189	184	97	92	18	4	87	64	1.434	4.38	93	4.15	.259	15	.214	-8	11	-0.6
1952	StL-N	4	4	.500	26	13	2	1	1	98^1	110	51	45	8	2	33	47	1.454	4.12	90	4.37	.285	9	.281	-5	5	-0.1
1953	StL-N	3	6	.333	32	8	0	0	0	79^2	82	50	43	7	1	43	26	1.569	4.86	88	4.54	.266	2	.118	-4	2	-0.5
Total	6	48	53	.475	189	113	37	7	1	897^1	924	482	428	70	21	361	374	1.432	4.29	96	4.07	.266	69	.235	-13	49	0.2

• CHAMBERS, Johnnie Johnnie Monroe Chambers b: 9/10/1911, Copperhill, TN d: 5/11/1977, Palatka, FL BL/TR, 6', 185 lbs. Deb: 5/4/1937

YEAR	TM-L	W	L	PCT	G	GS	CG	SH	SV	IP	H	R	ER	HR	HB	BB	SO	RAT	ERA	ERA+	CERA	OAV	BH	AVG	PR+	WS	TPW
1937	StL-N	0	0	....	2	0	0	0	0	2	5	4	4	0	0	2	1	3.500	18.00	22	15.27	.455	0	....	-3	0	-0.3

• CHAMBERS, Rome Richard Jerome Chambers b: 8/31/1875, Weaverville, NC d: 8/30/1902, Weaverville, NC BL/TL, 6'2", 173 lbs. Deb: 5/7/1900

YEAR	TM-L	W	L	PCT	G	GS	CG	SH	SV	IP	H	R	ER	HR	HB	BB	SO	RAT	ERA	ERA+	CERA	OAV	BH	AVG	PR+	WS	TPW
1900	Bos-N	0	0	....	1	0	0	0	1	4	5	6	5	0	0	5	2	2.500	11.25	37	7.79	.305	0	.000	-3	0	-0.3

• CHAMPION, Bill Buford Billy Champion b: 9/18/1947, Shelby, NC BR/TR, 6'4" Deb: 6/4/1969

YEAR	TM-L	W	L	PCT	G	GS	CG	SH	SV	IP	H	R	ER	HR	HB	BB	SO	RAT	ERA	ERA+	CERA	OAV	BH	AVG	PR+	WS	TPW
1969	Phi-N	5	10	.333	23	20	4	2	1	116^2	130	68	65	7	3	63	70	1.654	5.01	71	5.01	.286	6	.171	-19	2	-2.0
1970	Phi-N	0	2	.000	7	1	0	0	0	14	21	14	14	3	1	10	12	2.214	9.00	44	9.97	.375	0	.000	-8	0	-0.8
1971	Phi-N	3	5	.375	37	9	0	0	0	108^2	100	61	53	10	3	48	49	1.362	4.39	80	3.80	.249	3	.111	-12	2	-1.4
1972	Phi-N	4	14	.222	30	22	2	0	0	132^2	155	80	75	11	1	54	54	1.575	5.09	71	4.96	.301	5	.147	-24	0	-2.5
1973	Mil-A	5	8	.385	37	11	2	0	1	136^1	139	58	56	10	4	62	67	1.474	3.70	102	4.34	.267	0	....	2	7	0.2
1974	Mil-A	11	4	.733	31	23	2	0	0	161^2	168	72	65	12	0	49	60	1.342	3.62	100	3.75	.270	0	....	-1	10	-0.1
1975	Mil-A	6	6	.500	27	13	3	1	0	110	125	77	72	11	0	55	40	1.636	5.89	65	5.17	.290	0	....	-25	1	-2.5
1976	Mil-A	0	1	.000	10	3	0	0	0	24^1	35	20	19	0	1	13	8	1.973	7.03	50	6.66	.361	0	....	-10	0	-1.0
Total	8	34	50	.405	202	102	13	3	2	804^1	873	450	419	64	13	354	360	1.525	4.69	78	4.63	.282	14	.141	-95	22	-10.1

• CHANCE, Dean Wilmer Dean Chance b: 6/1/1941, Wooster, OH BR/TR, 6'3", 200 lbs. Deb: 9/11/1961

YEAR	TM-L	W	L	PCT	G	GS	CG	SH	SV	IP	H	R	ER	HR	HB	BB	SO	RAT	ERA	ERA+	CERA	OAV	BH	AVG	PR+	WS	TPW
1961	LA-A	0	2	.000	5	4	0	0	0	18^1	33	15	14	0	1	5	11	2.073	6.87	66	8.07	.413	0	.000	-5	0	-0.5
1962	LA-A	14	10	.583	50	24	6	2	8	206^2	195	83	68	14	5	66	127	1.263	2.96	130	3.31	.250	4	.062	22	17	1.8
1963	LA-A	13	18	.419	45	35	6	2	3	248	229	109	88	10	10	90	168	1.286	3.19	107	3.19	.243	12	.150	7	12	0.6
1964	LA-A★	**20**	9	.690	46	35	**15**	**11**	4	**278^1**	194	56	51	7	2	86	207	1.006	**1.65**	**199**	1.76	.195	7	.079	**49**	**32**	**4.6**
1965	Cal-A	15	10	.600	36	33	10	4	0	225^2	197	86	79	12	9	101	164	1.321	3.15	108	3.38	.238	7	.093	5	14	0.4
1966	Cal-A	12	17	.414	41	37	11	2	1	259^2	206	113	89	18	7	114	180	1.232	3.08	109	3.02	.222	2	.026	6	14	-0.1
1967	Min-A★	20	14	.588	41	**39**	**18**	5	1	**283^2**	244	109	86	17	7	68	220	1.100	2.73	127	2.51	.229	3	.033	27	20	2.4
1968	Min-A	16	16	.500	43	39	15	6	1	292	224	96	82	15	10	63	234	.983	2.53	122	1.99	.211	5	.054	23	21	2.0
1969*	Min-A	5	4	.556	20	15	1	0	0	88^1	76	39	29	6	4	35	50	1.257	2.95	124	3.22	.233	1	.042	6	5	0.5
1970	Cle-A	9	8	.529	45	19	1	1	4	155	172	80	73	18	6	59	109	1.490	4.24	93	4.85	.287	3	.071	-5	9	-0.8
	NY-N	0	1	.000	3	0	0	0	1	2	3	3	3	0	0	2	0	2.500	13.50	30	8.24	.500	0	....	-2	0	-0.2
1971	Det-A	4	6	.400	31	14	0	0	0	89^2	91	43	35	5	4	50	64	1.572	3.51	102	4.54	.265	0	.000	1	4	-0.2
Total	11	128	115	.527	406	294	83	33	23	2147^1	1864	832	697	122	65	739	1534	1.212	2.92	119	2.99	.234	44	.066	133	148	10.4

YEAR	TM-L	W	L	PCT	G	GS	CG	SH	SV	IP	H	R	ER	HR	HB	BB	SO	RAT	ERA	ERA+	CERA	OAV	BH	AVG	PR+	WS	TPW
• CHANDLER, Ed	Edward Oliver Chandler b: 2/17/1922, Pinson, AL d: 7/6/2003, Las Vegas, NV BR/TR, 6'2", 190 lbs. Deb: 4/18/1947																										
1947	Bro-N	0	1	.000	15	1	0	0	1	29^2	31	23	21	7	0	12	8	1.449	6.37	65	5.16	.263	0	.000	-8	0	-0.8
• CHANDLER, Spud	Spurgeon Ferdinand Chandler b: 9/12/1907, Commerce, GA d: 1/9/1990, South Pasadena, FL BR/TR, 6', 181 lbs. Deb: 5/6/1937 C																										
1937	NY-A	7	4	.636	12	10	6	2	0	82^1	79	31	26	8	1	20	31	1.202	2.84	156	3.27	.253	4	.133	13	7	1.0
1938	NY-A	14	5	.737	23	23	14	2	0	172	183	86	77	7	2	47	36	1.337	4.03	113	3.47	.271	14	.203	8	13	0.9
1939	NY-A	3	0	1.000	11	0	0	0	0	19	26	7	6	0	0	9	4	1.842	2.84	153	5.58	.329	2	.400	2	2	0.3
1940	NY-A	8	7	.533	27	24	6	1	0	172	184	100	88	12	6	60	56	1.419	4.60	88	4.14	.275	9	.150	-13	7	-1.2
1941*	NY-A	10	4	.714	28	20	11	4	4	163^2	146	68	58	5	0	60	60	1.259	3.19	123	2.82	.239	11	.183	7	13	0.6
1942*	NY-A★	16	5	.762	24	24	17	3	0	200^2	176	64	53	13	4	74	74	1.246	2.38	145	3.09	.237	15	.211	15	19	1.9
1943*	NY-A★	**20**	4	.833	30	30	**20**	**5**	0	253	197	62	46	5	4	54	134	.992	**1.64**	**197**	**1.82**	.215	25	.258	**40**	**29**	**5.0**
1944	NY-A	0	0	....	1	1	0	0	0	6	6	3	3	1	1	1	1	1.167	4.50	77	4.49	.300	0	.000	-1	0	-0.1
1945	NY-A	2	1	.667	4	4	2	1	0	31	30	16	16	2	0	7	12	1.194	4.65	74	2.97	.250	4	.333	-5	1	-0.4
1946	NY-A★	20	8	.714	34	32	20	6	2	257^1	200	71	60	7	1	90	138	1.127	2.10	164	2.25	.218	14	.149	31	25	3.2
1947*	NY-A★	9	5	.643	17	16	13	2	0	128	100	41	35	4	0	41	68	1.102	2.46	144	2.13	.214	12	.245	15	11	1.9
Total	11	109	43	.717	211	184	109	26	6	1485	1327	549	468	64	19	463	614	1.205	2.84	134	2.83	.240	110	.201	114	127	13.2
• CHANEY, Esty	Esty Clyon Chaney b: 1/29/1891, Hadley, PA d: 2/5/1952, Cleveland, OH BR/TR, 5'11", 170 lbs. Deb: 8/2/1913																										
1913	Bos-A	0	0	....	1	0	0	0	0	1	1	1	1	0	0	2	0	3.000	9.00	33	7.41	.200	0	....	-1	0	-0.1
1914	Bro-F	0	0	....	1	0	0	0	0	4	7	3	3	0	0	2	1	2.250	6.75	48	8.11	.389	0	.000	-2	0	-0.2
Total	2	0	0	....	2	0	0	0	0	5	8	4	4	0	0	4	1	2.400	7.20	44	7.97	.348	0	.000	-2	0	-0.2
• CHAPIN, Darrin	Darrin John Chapin b: 2/1/1966, Warren, OH BR/TR, 6', 170 lbs. Deb: 9/21/1991																										
1991	NY-A	0	1	.000	3	0	0	0	0	5^1	3	3	3	0	0	6	5	1.688	5.06	82	3.52	.158	0	....	-1	0	-0.1
1992	Phi-N	0	0	....	1	0	0	0	0	2	2	2	2	1	0	0	1	1.000	9.00	39	4.70	.250	0	....	-1	0	-0.1
Total	2	0	1	.000	4	0	0	0	0	7^1	5	5	5	1	0	6	6	1.500	6.14	63	3.84	.185	0	....	-2	0	-0.2
• CHAPLIN, Tiny	James Bailey Chaplin b: 7/13/1905, Los Angeles, CA d: 3/25/1939, National City, CA BR/TR, 6'1", 195 lbs. Deb: 4/13/1928																										
1928	NY-N	0	2	.000	12	1	0	0	0	24	27	15	12	0	0	8	5	1.458	4.50	87	3.64	.284	0	.000	-2	0	-0.2
1930	NY-N	2	6	.250	19	8	3	0	1	73	89	45	42	8	4	16	20	1.438	5.18	91	4.87	.305	2	.105	-4	3	-0.4
1931	NY-N	3	0	1.000	16	3	1	0	1	42^1	39	17	15	2	2	16	7	1.299	3.19	116	3.26	.242	2	.182	2	3	0.2
1936	Bos-N	10	15	.400	40	31	14	0	2	231^2	273	131	106	21	3	62	86	1.446	4.12	93	4.51	.294	17	.202	-9	9	-1.0
Total	4	15	23	.395	87	43	18	0	4	371	428	208	175	31	9	102	118	1.429	4.25	94	4.38	.290	21	.176	-13	15	-1.4
• CHAPMAN, Ed	Edwin Volney Chapman b: 11/28/1905, Courtland, MS d: 5/3/2000, Clarksdale, MS BB/TR, 6'1", 185 lbs. Deb: 8/6/1933																										
1933	Was-A	0	0	....	6	1	0	0	0	9	10	9	8	2	0	2	4	1.333	8.00	52	4.67	.270	0	.000	-4	0	-0.4
• CHAPMAN, Fred	Frederick Joseph Chapman b: 11/24/1872, Little Cooley, PA d: 12/14/1957, Union City, PA BR/TR, 5'8", 165 lbs. Deb: 7/22/1887																										
1887	Phi-a	0	0	....	1	1	1	0	0	5	10	6	4	0	0	2	4	2.000	7.20	59	....	.401	0	.000	-2	0	-0.2
• CHAPPELLE, Bill	William Hogan "Big Bill" Chappelle b: 3/22/1884, Waterloo, NY d: 12/31/1944, Mineola, NY BR/TR, 6'2", 206 lbs. Deb: 8/20/1908																										
1908	Bos-N	2	4	.333	13	7	3	1	0	70^1	60	28	14	0	4	17	23	1.095	1.79	133	2.30	.233	1	.048	3	4	0.2
1909	Bos-N	1	1	.500	5	3	2	0	0	29	31	13	6	0	1	11	8	1.448	1.86	151	3.82	.279	4	.364	3	2	0.5
	Cin-N	0	0	....	1	0	0	0	1	4	5	2	1	0	1	2	0	1.750	2.25	115	5.45	.278	0	.000	0	0	0.0
	Yr.	1	1	.500	6	3	2	0	1	33	36	15	7	0	2	13	8	1.485	1.91	145	4.01	.279	4	.333	3	2	0.5
1914	Bro-F	4	2	.667	16	6	4	0	0	74^1	71	43	26	1	3	29	31	1.345	3.15	103	3.34	.255	0	.000	2	3	-0.2
Total	3	7	7	.500	35	16	9	1	1	177^2	167	86	47	1	9	59	62	1.272	2.38	120	3.05	.251	5	.089	8	9	0.6
• CHARLTON, Norm	Norman Wood Charlton b: 1/6/1963, Fort Polk, LA BB/TL, 6'3", 205 lbs. Deb: 8/19/1988																										
1988	Cin-N	4	5	.444	10	10	0	0	0	61^1	60	27	27	6	2	20	39	1.304	3.96	90	3.75	.256	0	.000	-4	3	-0.5
1989	Cin-N	8	3	.727	69	0	0	0	0	95^1	67	38	31	5	2	40	98	1.122	2.93	123	2.23	.197	0	.000	8	8	0.8
1990*	Cin-N	12	9	.571	56	16	1	1	2	154^1	131	53	47	10	4	70	117	1.302	2.74	144	3.30	.231	5	.135	18	14	1.9
1991	Cin-N	3	5	.375	39	11	0	0	1	108^1	92	37	35	6	6	34	77	1.163	2.91	131	2.88	.236	1	.043	11	8	1.0
1992	Cin-N★	4	2	.667	64	0	0	0	26	81^1	79	39	27	7	3	26	90	1.291	2.99	120	3.62	.262	1	.200	5	9	0.6
1993	Sea-A	1	3	.250	34	0	0	0	18	34^2	22	12	9	4	0	17	48	1.125	2.34	188	2.59	.179	0	....	8	7	0.8
1995	Phi-N	2	5	.286	25	0	0	0	0	22	23	19	18	2	3	15	12	1.727	7.36	57	5.85	.280	1	1.000	-8	0	-0.7
*	Sea-A	2	1	.667	30	0	0	0	14	47^2	23	12	8	2	1	16	58	.818	1.51	314	1.25	.143	0	....	18	11	1.7
1996	Sea-A	4	7	.364	70	0	0	0	20	75^2	68	37	34	7	1	38	73	1.401	4.04	122	3.95	.244	0	....	7	9	0.7
1997*	Sea-A	3	8	.273	71	0	0	0	14	69^1	89	59	56	7	4	47	55	1.962	7.27	62	7.07	.312	0	....	-21	0	-2.0
1998	Bal-A	2	1	.667	36	0	0	0	0	35	46	27	27	5	0	25	41	2.029	6.94	66	7.40	.305	0	....	-9	0	-0.8
	Atl-N	0	0	....	13	0	0	0	1	13	7	2	2	0	1	8	6	1.154	1.38	301	2.13	.167	0	.000	4	2	0.4
1999	TB-A	2	3	.400	42	0	0	0	0	50^2	49	29	25	4	1	36	45	1.678	4.44	112	5.03	.257	0	....	3	3	0.3
2000	Cin-N	0	0	....	2	0	0	0	0	3	6	9	9	1	0	6	1	4.000	27.00	17	21.95	.429	0	....	-7	0	-0.7
2001*	Sea-A	4	2	.667	44	0	0	0	1	47^2	36	19	16	4	4	11	48	.986	3.02	137	2.41	.212	0	....	5	5	0.4
Total	13	51	54	.486	605	37	1	1	97	899^1	798	419	371	70	32	409	808	1.342	3.71	112	3.72	.240	8	.092	39	79	3.8
• CHARTON, Pete	Frank Lane Charton b: 12/21/1942, Jackson, TN BL/TR, 6'2", 190 lbs. Deb: 4/19/1964																										
1964	Bos-A	0	2	.000	25	5	0	0	0	65	67	39	38	12	1	24	37	1.400	5.26	73	4.95	.275	1	.100	-9	1	-0.9
• CHASE, Ken	Kendall Fay "Lefty" Chase b: 10/6/1913, Oneonta, NY d: 1/16/1985, Oneonta, NY BL/TL, 6'2", 210 lbs. Deb: 4/23/1936																										
1936	Was-A	0	0	....	1	0	0	0	0	2^1	2	3	3	0	0	4	1	2.571	11.57	41	7.41	.250	1	1.000	-2	0	-0.1
1937	Was-A	4	3	.571	14	9	4	0	0	76^1	74	41	35	4	0	60	43	1.755	4.13	107	4.87	.257	1	.034	1	4	-0.2
1938	Was-A	9	10	.474	32	21	7	0	1	150	151	99	93	4	4	113	64	1.760	5.58	81	4.90	.268	10	.208	-18	6	-1.6
1939	Was-A	10	19	.345	32	31	15	1	0	232	215	116	98	10	1	114	118	1.418	3.80	114	3.45	.243	15	.169	12	13	0.8
1940	Was-A	15	17	.469	35	34	20	1	0	261^2	260	120	94	14	5	143	129	1.540	3.23	129	4.20	.261	15	.163	31	20	2.9
1941	Was-A	6	18	.250	33	30	8	1	0	205^2	228	136	116	11	3	115	98	1.668	5.08	80	4.81	.280	11	.149	-21	4	-2.2
1942	Bos-A	5	1	.833	13	10	4	0	0	80^1	82	37	34	5	0	41	34	1.531	3.81	98	4.21	.263	6	.182	-3	5	-0.2
1943	Bos-A	0	4	.000	7	5	0	0	0	27^1	36	25	21	0	0	30	9	2.415	6.91	48	7.55	.316	1	.091	-11	0	-1.3
	NY-N	4	12	.250	21	20	4	1	0	129^1	140	70	59	7	2	74	86	1.655	4.11	84	4.75	.275	9	.214	-8	4	-0.8
Total	8	53	84	.387	188	160	62	4	1	1165	1188	647	553	55	15	694	582	1.615	4.27	96	4.44	.265	69	.165	-18	56	-2.8
• CHAVEZ, Anthony	Anthony Francisco Chavez b: 10/22/1970, Turlock, CA BR/TR, 5'11", 180 lbs. Deb: 9/2/1997																										
1997	Ana-A	0	0	....	7	0	0	0	0	9^2	7	1	1	1	0	5	10	1.241	0.93	495	2.85	.206	0	....	4	1	0.4
• CHAVEZ, Nestor	Nestor Isais (Silva) Chavez b: 7/6/1947, Chacao, Venezuela d: 3/16/1969, Maracaibo, Venezuela BR/TR, 6', 170 lbs. Deb: 9/9/1967																										
1967	SF-N	1	0	1.000	2	0	0	0	0	5	4	2	0	0	0	3	3	1.400	0.00	....	2.64	.211	0	.000	2	1	0.2
• CHEADLE, Dave	David Baird Cheadle b: 2/19/1952, Greensboro, NC BL/TL, 6'2", 203 lbs. Deb: 9/16/1973																										
1973	Atl-N	0	1	.000	2	0	0	0	0	2	2	4	4	1	0	3	2	2.500	18.00	22	10.15	.250	0	....	-3	0	-0.3
• CHECH, Charlie	Charles William Chech b: 4/27/1878, Madison, WI d: 1/31/1938, Los Angeles, CA BR/TR, 5'11.5", 190 lbs. Deb: 4/14/1905																										
1905	Cin-N	14	14	.500	39	25	20	1	0	267^2	300	139	86	4	11	77	79	1.408	2.89	114	3.91	.288	17	.191	7	13	0.9
1906	Cin-N	1	4	.200	11	5	5	0	3	66	59	32	17	1	6	24	17	1.258	2.32	118	3.11	.243	5	.200	3	4	0.4
1908	Cle-A	11	7	.611	27	20	14	4	0	165^2	136	51	32	2	7	34	51	1.026	1.74	137	2.11	.229	5	.104	10	13	1.1
1909	Bos-A	7	5	.583	17	13	6	1	0	106^2	107	51	35	3	5	27	40	1.256	2.95	84	3.20	.260	3	.083	-7	5	-1.1
Total	4	33	30	.524	94	63	45	6	3	606	602	273	170	10	29	162	187	1.261	2.52	113	3.21	.263	30	.152	12	35	1.3
• CHECO, Robinson	Robinson (Perez) Checo b: 9/9/1971, Santiago, Dominican Republic BR/TR, 6'1", 185 lbs. Deb: 9/16/1997																										
1997	Bos-A	1	1	.500	5	2	0	0	0	13^1	12	5	5	0	0	3	14	1.125	3.38	137	2.27	.235	0	....	2	1	0.2
1998	Bos-A	0	2	.000	2	2	0	0	0	7^2	11	8	8	3	0	5	5	2.087	9.39	50	11.82	.379	0	....	-4	0	-0.4

YEAR TM-L	W	L	PCT	G	GS	CG	SH	SV	IP	H	R	ER	HR	HB	BB	SO	RAT	ERA	ERA+	CERA	OAV	BH	AVG	PR+	WS	TPW
1999 LA-N	2	2	.500	9	2	0	0	0	15^{2}	24	20	18	5	0	13	11	2.362	10.34	41	10.88	.333	1	.333	-10	0	-1.0
Total 3	3	5	.375	16	6	0	0	0	36^{2}	47	33	31	8	0	21	30	1.855	7.61	58	7.94	.309	1	.333	-13	1	-1.2

• CHEEVES, Virgil Virgil Earl "Chief" Cheeves b: 2/12/1901, Oklahoma City, OK d: 5/5/1979, Dallas, TX BR/TR, 6', 195 lbs. Deb: 9/7/1920

YEAR TM-L	W	L	PCT	G	GS	CG	SH	SV	IP	H	R	ER	HR	HB	BB	SO	RAT	ERA	ERA+	CERA	OAV	BH	AVG	PR+	WS	TPW
1920 Chi-N	0	0	....	5	2	0	0	0	18	16	7	7	0	0	7	3	1.278	3.50	92	2.78	.250	0	.000	-0	1	-0.1
1921 Chi-N	11	12	.478	37	22	9	1	0	163	192	97	84	8	9	47	39	1.466	4.64	82	4.48	.309	8	.167	-15	7	-1.7
1922 Chi-N	12	11	.522	39	22	9	1	2	182^{2}	195	99	83	9	10	76	40	1.484	4.09	103	4.28	.281	13	.210	1	12	0.2
1923 Chi-N	3	4	.429	19	8	0	0	0	71^{1}	89	54	49	8	3	37	13	1.766	6.18	65	6.20	.314	4	.174	-19	0	-1.9
1924 Cle-A	0	0	....	8	1	0	0	0	17^{1}	26	17	15	2	1	17	2	2.481	7.79	55	10.22	.388	1	.250	-7	0	-0.6
1927 NY-N	0	0	....	3	0	0	0	0	6^{1}	8	3	3	1	0	4	1	1.895	4.26	90	6.99	.333	0	....	-0	0	0.0
Total 6	26	27	.491	111	55	18	2	2	458^{2}	526	277	241	28	23	188	98	1.557	4.73	84	4.86	.300	26	.184	-41	20	-4.1

• CHELINI, Italo Italo Vincent "Chilly,Lefty" Chelini b: 10/10/1914, San Francisco, CA d: 8/25/1972, San Francisco, CA BL/TL, 5'10.5", 175 lbs. Deb: 9/12/1935

YEAR TM-L	W	L	PCT	G	GS	CG	SH	SV	IP	H	R	ER	HR	HB	BB	SO	RAT	ERA	ERA+	CERA	OAV	BH	AVG	PR+	WS	TPW
1935 Chi-A	0	0	....	2	0	0	0	0	5	7	7	7	1	1	4	1	2.200	12.60	37	10.36	.350	1	.500	-4	0	-0.4
1936 Chi-A	4	3	.571	18	6	5	0	0	83^{2}	100	51	46	8	0	30	16	1.554	4.95	105	4.82	.291	5	.156	1	5	0.0
1937 Chi-A	0	1	.000	4	0	0	0	0	8^{2}	15	10	10	2	1	0	3	1.731	10.38	44	8.86	.405	0	.000	-6	0	-0.5
Total 3	4	4	.500	24	6	5	0	0	97^{1}	122	68	63	11	2	34	20	1.603	5.83	86	5.47	.304	6	.171	-9	5	-0.9

• CHEN, Bruce Bruce Kastulo Chen b: 6/19/1977, Panama City, Panama BB/TL, 6'2", 210 lbs. Deb: 9/7/1998

YEAR TM-L	W	L	PCT	G	GS	CG	SH	SV	IP	H	R	ER	HR	HB	BB	SO	RAT	ERA	ERA+	CERA	OAV	BH	AVG	PR+	WS	TPW
1998 Atl-N	2	0	1.000	4	4	0	0	0	20^{1}	23	9	9	3	1	9	17	1.574	3.98	104	5.55	.288	1	.143	0	1	0.0
1999 Atl-N	2	2	.500	16	7	0	0	0	51	38	32	31	11	2	27	45	1.275	5.47	82	4.07	.208	0	.000	-5	1	-0.6
2000 Atl-N	4	0	1.000	22	0	0	0	0	39^{2}	35	15	11	4	1	19	32	1.361	2.50	183	3.62	.232	0	.000	9	4	0.8
Phi-N	3	4	.429	15	15	0	0	0	94^{1}	81	39	38	14	1	27	80	1.145	3.63	129	3.22	.232	1	.040	11	7	0.8
Yr.	7	4	.636	37	15	0	0	0	134	116	54	49	18	2	46	112	1.209	3.29	141	3.34	.232	1	.033	20	11	1.7
2001 Phi-N	4	5	.444	16	16	0	0	0	86^{1}	90	53	48	19	1	31	79	1.402	5.00	85	4.87	.262	3	.107	-8	2	-0.9
NY-N	3	2	.600	11	11	0	0	0	59^{2}	56	37	31	10	0	28	47	1.408	4.68	88	4.58	.255	3	.158	-4	2	-0.4
Yr.	7	7	.500	27	27	0	0	0	146	146	90	79	29	1	59	126	1.404	4.87	86	4.75	.259	6	.128	-12	4	-1.3
2002 NY-N	0	0	....	1	0	0	0	0	0^{2}	1	0	0	0	0	0	0	1.500	0.00	....	4.47	.333	0	....	0	0	0.0
Mon-N	2	3	.400	15	5	0	0	0	37^{1}	47	29	29	9	1	23	43	1.875	6.99	61	7.69	.303	5	.417	-11	0	-1.0
Cin-N	0	2	.000	39	1	0	0	0	39^{2}	37	24	19	7	1	20	37	1.437	4.31	98	4.55	.243	0	.000	-0	1	-0.1
Yr.	2	5	.286	55	6	0	0	0	77^{2}	85	53	48	16	2	43	80	1.648	5.56	76	6.06	.274	5	.333	-11	1	-1.0
2003 Hou-N	0	0	....	11	0	0	0	0	12	14	8	8	2	2	8	8	1.833	6.00	74	7.11	.311	0	.000	-2	0	-0.2
Bos-A	0	1	.000	5	2	0	0	0	12^{1}	12	8	7	4	0	2	12	1.135	5.11	89	4.40	.255	0	....	-1	0	0.0
Total 6	20	19	.513	155	61	0	0	0	453^{1}	434	254	231	83	10	194	400	1.385	4.59	95	4.57	.251	13	.117	-11	18	-1.6

• CHENEY, Larry Laurance Russell Cheney b: 5/2/1886, Belleville, KS d: 1/6/1969, Daytona Beach, FL BR/TR, 6'1.5", 185 lbs. Deb: 9/9/1911

YEAR TM-L	W	L	PCT	G	GS	CG	SH	SV	IP	H	R	ER	HR	HB	BB	SO	RAT	ERA	ERA+	CERA	OAV	BH	AVG	PR+	WS	TPW
1911 Chi-N	1	0	1.000	3	1	0	0	0	10	8	0	0	0	0	3	11	1.100	0.00	....	2.14	.229	1	.250	3	2	0.4
1912 Chi-N	**26**	10	.722	42	37	**28**	4	0	303^{1}	262	122	96	5	7	111	140	1.230	2.85	117	2.65	.234	24	.226	9	27	1.3
1913 Chi-N	21	14	.600	**54**	36	25	2	**11**	305	271	117	87	7	8	98	136	1.210	2.57	124	2.72	.241	20	.192	19	25	2.2
1914 Chi-N	20	18	.526	**50**	40	21	6	5	311^{1}	239	136	88	9	10	140	157	1.217	2.54	109	2.57	.215	18	.180	14	20	1.8
1915 Chi-N	8	9	.471	25	18	6	2	0	131^{1}	120	69	52	1	4	55	68	1.332	3.56	78	3.02	.246	6	.150	-10	4	-1.2
Bro-N	0	2	.000	5	4	1	0	0	27	16	10	5	0	2	17	11	1.222	1.67	166	2.17	.174	1	.143	3	2	0.4
Yr.	8	11	.421	30	22	7	2	0	158^{1}	136	79	57	1	6	72	79	1.314	3.24	86	2.88	.235	7	.149	-6	6	-0.9
1916* Bro-N	18	12	.600	41	32	15	5	0	253	178	91	54	5	10	105	166	1.119	1.92	139	2.09	**.198**	9	.114	17	17	1.6
1917 Bro-N	8	12	.400	35	24	14	1	2	210^{1}	185	80	55	4	5	73	102	1.227	2.35	119	2.72	.239	14	.206	8	14	1.2
1918 Bro-N	11	13	.458	32	21	15	0	1	200^{2}	177	84	67	2	10	74	83	1.251	3.00	93	2.78	.241	16	.242	-5	13	-0.3
1919 Bro-N	1	3	.250	9	4	2	0	0	39	45	21	18	1	2	14	14	1.513	4.15	71	4.35	.300	2	.182	-4	0	-0.5
Bos-N	0	2	.000	8	2	0	0	0	33	35	20	13	0	0	15	13	1.515	3.55	81	4.07	.294	2	.182	-3	0	-0.2
Phi-N	2	5	.286	9	6	5	0	0	57^{1}	69	34	29	2	1	28	25	1.692	4.55	71	5.08	.315	2	.095	-8	1	-1.1
Yr.	3	10	.231	26	12	7	0	0	129^{1}	149	75	60	3	3	57	52	1.593	4.18	73	4.60	.305	6	.140	-15	1	-1.9
Total 9	116	100	.537	313	225	132	20	19	1881^{1}	1605	784	564	36	59	733	926	1.243	2.70	109	2.75	.234	115	.186	43	125	5.4

• CHENEY, Tom Thomas Edgar Cheney b: 10/14/1934, Morgan, GA d: 11/1/2001, Rome, GA BR/TR, 5'11", 180 lbs. Deb: 4/21/1957

YEAR TM-L	W	L	PCT	G	GS	CG	SH	SV	IP	H	R	ER	HR	HB	BB	SO	RAT	ERA	ERA+	CERA	OAV	BH	AVG	PR+	WS	TPW
1957 StL-N	0	1	.000	4	3	0	0	0	9	6	6	5	0	0	15	10	2.333	5.00	79	6.65	.207	0	.000	-1	0	-0.1
1959 StL-N	0	1	.000	11	2	0	0	0	11^{2}	17	9	9	2	2	11	8	2.400	6.94	61	10.47	.354	0	....	-3	0	-0.3
1960* Pit-N	2	2	.500	11	8	1	1	0	52	44	25	23	5	0	33	35	1.481	3.98	94	4.25	.238	3	.176	-2	2	-0.2
1961 Pit-N	0	0	....	1	0	0	0	0	0	1	5	4	1	0	4	0	....	∞	....	∞	.500	0	....	-4	0	-0.4
Was-A	1	3	.250	10	7	0	0	0	29^{2}	32	30	29	8	0	26	20	1.955	8.80	45	8.03	.283	4	.500	-16	1	-1.4
1962 Was-A	7	9	.438	37	23	4	3	1	173^{1}	134	68	61	12	2	97	147	1.333	3.17	127	3.28	.213	3	.063	17	13	1.4
1963 Was-A	8	9	.471	23	21	7	4	0	136^{1}	99	51	41	14	1	40	97	1.020	2.71	137	2.27	.202	5	.109	15	9	1.3
1964 Was-A	1	3	.250	15	6	1	0	1	48^{2}	45	26	20	10	0	13	25	1.192	3.70	100	3.83	.245	3	.250	-0	2	0.0
1966 Was-A	0	1	.000	3	1	0	0	0	5^{1}	4	4	3	1	1	6	3	1.875	5.06	68	7.48	.222	0	....	-1	0	-0.1
Total 8	19	29	.396	115	71	13	8	2	466	382	224	195	53	6	245	345	1.345	3.77	105	3.75	.225	18	.135	4	27	0.2

• CHESBRO, Jack John Dwight "Happy Jack" Chesbro b: 6/5/1874, North Adams, MA d: 11/6/1931, Conway, MA BR/TR, 5'9", 180 lbs. Deb: 7/12/1899 C HOF: 1946

YEAR TM-L	W	L	PCT	G	GS	CG	SH	SV	IP	H	R	ER	HR	HB	BB	SO	RAT	ERA	ERA+	CERA	OAV	BH	AVG	PR+	WS	TPW
1899 Pit-N	6	9	.400	19	17	15	0	0	149	165	99	68	3	11	59	28	1.503	4.11	93	4.25	.280	9	.155	-6	6	-0.8
1900 Pit-N	15	13	.536	32	26	20	3	1	215^{2}	220	123	88	4	12	79	56	1.386	3.67	99	3.53	.264	15	.176	-2	14	-0.3
1901 Pit-N	21	10	.677	36	28	26	**6**	1	287^{2}	261	104	76	4	14	52	129	1.088	2.38	137	2.31	.241	25	.216	25	23	2.6
1902 Pit-N	**28**	6	.824	35	33	31	**8**	1	286^{1}	242	81	69	1	21	62	136	1.062	2.17	126	2.18	.229	20	.179	11	25	1.0
1903 NY-A	21	15	.583	40	36	33	1	0	324^{2}	300	140	100	7	9	74	147	1.152	2.77	113	2.51	.245	23	.185	14	22	1.4
1904 NY-A	**41**	12	.774	**55**	**51**	**48**	6	0	**454^{2}**	338	128	92	4	7	88	239	.937	1.82	149	**1.56**	**.208**	41	.236	35	**53**	4.6
1905 NY-A	19	15	.559	41	38	24	3	0	303^{1}	262	125	74	5	6	71	156	1.098	2.20	133	2.21	.235	21	.188	29	20	3.2
1906 NY-A	23	17	.575	**49**	**42**	24	4	1	325	314	138	107	2	10	75	152	1.197	2.96	100	2.65	.257	26	.208	2	25	0.2
1907 NY-A	10	10	.500	30	25	17	1	0	206	192	83	58	0	6	46	78	1.155	2.53	110	2.46	.250	15	.197	9	13	1.0
1908 NY-A	14	20	.412	45	31	20	3	1	288^{2}	276	134	94	6	14	67	124	1.188	2.93	84	2.79	.251	18	.176	-7	8	-0.9
1909 NY-A	0	4	.000	9	4	2	0	0	49^{2}	70	47	35	2	3	13	17	1.671	6.34	40	5.16	.347	3	.176	-20	0	-2.2
Bos-A	0	1	.000	1	1	0	0	0	6	7	4	3	1	0	4	3	1.833	4.50	55	7.16	.318	1	.500	-1	0	-0.1
Yr.	0	5	.000	10	5	2	0	0	55^{2}	77	51	38	3	3	17	20	1.689	6.14	41	5.38	.344	4	.211	-21	0	-2.4
Total 11	198	132	.600	392	332	260	35	5	2896^{2}	2647	1206	864	39	113	690	1265	1.152	2.68	110	2.54	.244	217	.197	89	209	9.6

• CHESNES, Bob Robert Vincent Chesnes b: 5/6/1921, Oakland, CA d: 5/23/1979, Everett, WA BB/TR, 6', 180 lbs. Deb: 5/6/1948

YEAR TM-L	W	L	PCT	G	GS	CG	SH	SV	IP	H	R	ER	HR	HB	BB	SO	RAT	ERA	ERA+	CERA	OAV	BH	AVG	PR+	WS	TPW
1948 Pit-N	14	6	.700	25	23	15	0	0	194^{1}	180	92	77	13	4	90	69	1.389	3.57	114	3.69	.247	25	.275	10	16	1.7
1949 Pit-N	7	13	.350	27	25	8	1	1	145^{1}	153	104	95	15	5	82	49	1.617	5.88	71	5.16	.276	17	.250	-26	3	-2.0
1950 Pit-N	3	3	.500	9	7	2	0	0	39	44	26	24	7	3	17	12	1.564	5.54	79	5.87	.293	2	.154	-5	1	-0.5
Total 3	24	22	.522	61	55	25	1	1	378^{2}	377	222	196	35	12	189	130	1.495	4.66	90	4.48	.263	44	.256	-21	20	-0.8

• CHETKOVICH, Mitch Mitchell Chetkovich b: 7/21/1917, Fairpoint, OH d: 8/24/1971, Grass Valley, CA BR/TR, 6'3.5", 208 lbs. Deb: 4/19/1945

YEAR TM-L	W	L	PCT	G	GS	CG	SH	SV	IP	H	R	ER	HR	HB	BB	SO	RAT	ERA	ERA+	CERA	OAV	BH	AVG	PR+	WS	TPW
1945 Phi-N	0	0	....	4	0	0	0	0	3	2	2	0	0	0	3	0	1.667	0.00	....	3.10	.182	0	....	1	0	0.1

• CHEVEZ, Tony Silvio Antonio Chevez b: 6/20/1954, Telica, Nicaragua BR/TR, 5'11", 177 lbs. Deb: 5/31/1977

YEAR TM-L	W	L	PCT	G	GS	CG	SH	SV	IP	H	R	ER	HR	HB	BB	SO	RAT	ERA	ERA+	CERA	OAV	BH	AVG	PR+	WS	TPW
1977 Bal-A	0	0	....	4	0	0	0	0	8	10	13	11	3	2	8	7	2.250	12.38	31	10.95	.294	0	....	-8	0	-0.8

• CHIAMPARINO, Scott Scott Michael Chiamparino b: 8/22/1966, San Mateo, CA BR/TR, 6'2", 190 lbs. Deb: 9/5/1990

YEAR TM-L	W	L	PCT	G	GS	CG	SH	SV	IP	H	R	ER	HR	HB	BB	SO	RAT	ERA	ERA+	CERA	OAV	BH	AVG	PR+	WS	TPW
1990 Tex-A	1	2	.333	6	6	0	0	0	37^{2}	36	14	11	1	2	12	19	1.274	2.63	149	3.21	.250	0	....	5	3	0.5
1991 Tex-A	1	0	1.000	5	5	0	0	0	22^{1}	26	11	10	1	0	12	8	1.701	4.03	100	5.23	.295	0	....	0	1	0.0
1992 Tex-A	0	4	.000	4	4	0	0	0	25^{1}	25	11	10	2	0	5	13	1.184	3.55	107	3.16	.260	0	....	1	1	0.1
Total 3	2	6	.250	15	15	0	0	0	85^{1}	87	36	31	4	2	29	40	1.359	3.27	120	3.72	.265	0	....	7	5	0.7

• CHIASSON, Scott Scott Christopher Chiasson b: 8/14/1977, Norwich, CT BR/TR, 6'3", 200 lbs. Deb: 9/19/2001

YEAR TM-L	W	L	PCT	G	GS	CG	SH	SV	IP	H	R	ER	HR	HB	BB	SO	RAT	ERA	ERA+	CERA	OAV	BH	AVG	PR+	WS	TPW
2001 Chi-N	1	1	.500	6	0	0	0	0	6^{2}	5	2	2	2	1	2	6	1.050	2.70	154	4.13	.200	0	....	1	1	0.1

YEAR	TM-L	W	L	PCT	G	GS	CG	SH	SV	IP	H	R	ER	HR	HB	BB	SO	RAT	ERA	ERA+	CERA	OAV	BH	AVG	PR+	WS	TPW
2002	Chi-N	0	0	....	4	0	0	0	0	4^{2}	11	12	12	2	0	6	3	3.643	23.14	17	20.56	.440	0	....	-10	0	-1.0
Total	**2**	**1**	**1**	**.500**	**10**	**0**	**0**	**0**	**0**	11^{1}	**16**	**14**	**14**	**4**	**1**	**8**	**9**	**2.118**	**11.12**	**36**	**10.89**	**.320**	**0**	**....**	**-9**	**1**	**-0.9**
• CHIFFER, Floyd					Floyd John Chiffer b: 4/20/1956, Glen Cove, NY BR/TR, 6'2", 185 lbs. Deb: 4/7/1982																						
1982	SD-N	4	3	.571	51	0	0	0	4	79^{1}	73	33	26	9	4	34	48	1.349	2.95	116	4.04	.247	0	.000	3	5	0.3
1983	SD-N	0	2	.000	15	0	0	0	1	22^{2}	17	10	8	0	0	10	15	1.191	3.18	110	2.18	.210	0	.000	0	1	0.0
1984	SD-N	1	0	1.000	15	1	0	0	0	28	42	24	24	1	0	16	20	2.071	7.71	46	7.11	.347	0	.000	-13	0	-1.5
Total	**3**	**5**	**5**	**.500**	**81**	**1**	**0**	**0**	**5**	**130**	**132**	**67**	**58**	**10**	**4**	**60**	**83**	**1.477**	**4.02**	**87**	**4.38**	**.266**	**0**	**.000**	**-10**	**6**	**-1.2**
• CHILD, Harry					Harry Stephen Patrick Child b: 5/23/1905, Baltimore, MD d: 11/8/1972, Alexandria, VA BB/TR, 5'11", 187 lbs. Deb: 7/16/1930																						
1930	Was-A	0	0	....	5	0	0	0	0	10	10	7	7	1	0	5	5	1.500	6.30	73	4.35	.263	1	.250	-2	0	-0.2
• CHILDERS, Bill					William Childers b: St. Louis, MO Deb: 7/27/1895																						
1895	Lou-N	0	0	....	1	0	0	0	0	0	2	0	0	0	5	....	....	....	....	....	∞	1.000	0	....	0	0	0.0
• CHILDERS, Matt					Matthew Wilkie Childers b: 12/3/1978, Douglas, GA BR/TR, 6'5", 195 lbs. Deb: 8/3/2002																						
2002	Mil-N	0	0	....	8	0	0	0	0	9	13	12	12	2	1	8	6	2.333	12.00	34	10.39	.342	0	.000	-8	0	-0.8
• CHILDRESS, Rocky					Rodney Osborne Childress b: 2/18/1962, Santa Rosa, CA BR/TR, 6'2", 195 lbs. Deb: 5/17/1985																						
1985	Phi-N	0	1	.000	16	1	0	0	0	33^{1}	45	23	23	3	0	9	14	1.620	6.21	59	5.33	.326	1	.167	-9	0	-0.9
1986	Phi-N	0	0	....	2	0	0	0	0	2^{2}	4	3	2	0	0	1	1	1.875	6.75	57	6.51	.364	0	....	-1	0	-0.1
1987	Hou-N	1	2	.333	32	0	0	0	0	48^{1}	46	17	16	4	0	18	26	1.324	2.98	131	3.46	.260	0	.000	5	4	0.5
1988	Hou-N	1	0	1.000	11	0	0	0	0	23^{1}	26	17	16	3	1	9	24	1.500	6.17	54	4.95	.280	1	.250	-7	0	-0.8
Total	**4**	**2**	**3**	**.400**	**61**	**1**	**0**	**0**	**0**	107^{2}	**121**	**60**	**57**	**10**	**1**	**37**	**65**	**1.467**	**4.76**	**76**	**4.44**	**.289**	**2**	**.167**	**-12**	**4**	**-1.3**
• CHIPMAN, Bob					Robert Howard "Mr. Chips" Chipman b: 10/11/1918, Brooklyn, NY d: 11/8/1973, Huntington, NY BL/TL, 6'2", 190 lbs. Deb: 9/28/1941																						
1941	Bro-N	1	0	1.000	1	0	0	0	0	5	3	0	0	0	0	1	3	.800	0.00	....	0.98	.150	0	.000	2	1	0.2
1942	Bro-N	0	0	....	2	0	0	0	0	1^{1}	1	0	0	0	0	2	1	2.250	0.00	....	6.42	.250	0	....	0	0	0.1
1943	Bro-N	0	0	....	1	0	0	0	0	1^{2}	2	0	0	0	0	2	0	2.400	0.00	....	9.26	.400	0	....	1	0	0.1
1944	Bro-N	3	1	.750	11	3	1	0	0	36^{1}	38	19	17	1	0	24	20	1.706	4.21	84	4.52	.270	2	.182	-1	1	-0.2
	Chi-N	9	9	.500	26	21	8	1	2	129	147	62	50	9	0	40	41	1.450	3.49	101	4.21	.288	5	.104	2	7	0.0
	Yr.	12	10	.545	37	24	9	1	2	165^{1}	185	81	67	10	0	64	61	1.506	3.65	97	4.28	.284	7	.119	1	8	-0.2
1945*	Chi-N	4	5	.444	25	10	3	1	0	72	63	37	28	4	1	34	29	1.347	3.50	104	3.23	.230	3	.176	0	4	0.1
1946	Chi-N	6	5	.545	34	10	5	3	2	109^{1}	103	44	38	8	1	54	42	1.436	3.13	106	3.92	.255	2	.061	4	7	0.1
1947	Chi-N	7	6	.538	32	17	5	1	0	134^{2}	135	58	55	6	0	66	51	1.493	3.68	107	3.99	.264	4	.091	5	10	0.2
1948	Chi-N	2	1	.667	34	3	0	0	4	60^{1}	73	34	24	5	0	24	16	1.608	3.58	109	4.89	.293	4	.250	3	4	0.4
1949	Chi-N	7	8	.467	38	11	3	1	1	113^{1}	110	65	50	7	2	63	46	1.526	3.97	102	4.09	.248	3	.125	3	6	0.3
1950	Bos-N	7	7	.500	27	12	4	0	1	124	127	75	61	10	4	37	40	1.323	4.43	87	3.68	.262	6	.154	-7	4	-0.8
1951	Bos-N	4	3	.571	33	0	0	0	4	52	59	29	28	5	2	19	17	1.500	4.85	76	4.67	.284	1	.100	-6	2	-0.7
1952	Bos-N	1	1	.500	29	0	0	0	0	41^{2}	28	15	13	5	0	20	16	1.152	2.81	128	2.63	.188	2	.400	4	3	0.6
Total	**12**	**51**	**46**	**.526**	**293**	**87**	**29**	**7**	**14**	880^{2}	**889**	**438**	**364**	**60**	**10**	**386**	**322**	**1.448**	**3.72**	**100**	**3.98**	**.261**	**32**	**.128**	**10**	**49**	**0.2**
• CHITREN, Steve					Stephen Vincent Chitren b: 6/8/1967, Tokyo, Japan BR/TR, 6', 180 lbs. Deb: 9/5/1990																						
1990	Oak-A	1	0	1.000	8	0	0	0	0	17^{2}	7	2	2	0	0	4	19	.623	1.02	364	0.66	.117	0	....	5	2	0.5
1991	Oak-A	1	4	.200	56	0	0	0	4	60^{1}	59	31	29	8	4	32	47	1.508	4.33	89	4.85	.258	0	....	-3	2	-0.3
Total	**2**	**2**	**4**	**.333**	**64**	**0**	**0**	**0**	**4**	**78**	**66**	**33**	**31**	**8**	**4**	**36**	**66**	**1.308**	**3.58**	**107**	**3.90**	**.228**	**0**	**....**	**2**	**4**	**0.2**
• CHITTUM, Nelson					Nelson Boyd Chittum b: 3/25/1933, Harrisonburg, VA BR/TR, 6'1", 180 lbs. Deb: 8/17/1958																						
1958	StL-N	0	1	.000	13	2	0	0	0	29^{1}	31	21	21	5	1	7	13	1.295	6.44	64	4.28	.265	1	.250	-8	0	-0.8
1959	Bos-A	3	0	1.000	21	0	0	0	0	30^{1}	29	9	4	0	0	11	12	1.319	1.19	342	3.02	.266	1	.200	10	4	1.0
1960	Bos-A	0	0	....	6	0	0	0	0	8^{1}	8	4	4	0	0	6	5	1.680	4.32	94	3.88	.242	0	.000	-0	0	0.0
Total	**3**	**3**	**1**	**.750**	**40**	**2**	**0**	**0**	**0**	**68**	**68**	**34**	**29**	**5**	**1**	**24**	**30**	**1.353**	**3.84**	**107**	**3.67**	**.263**	**2**	**.200**	**2**	**4**	**0.2**
• CHLUPSA, Bob					Robert Joseph Chlupsa b: 9/16/1945, New York, NY BR/TR, 6'7", 215 lbs. Deb: 7/16/1970																						
1970	StL-N	0	2	.000	14	0	0	0	0	16^{1}	26	16	16	2	0	9	10	2.143	8.82	47	8.10	.366	0	....	-8	0	-0.8
1971	StL-N	0	0	....	1	0	0	0	0	2	3	2	2	0	0	0	1	1.500	9.00	40	4.47	.333	0	....	-1	0	-0.1
Total	**2**	**0**	**2**	**.000**	**15**	**0**	**0**	**0**	**0**	18^{1}	**29**	**18**	**18**	**2**	**0**	**9**	**11**	**2.073**	**8.84**	**46**	**7.71**	**.363**	**0**	**....**	**-9**	**0**	**-1.0**
• CHO, Jin Ho					Jin Ho Cho b: 8/16/1975, Jun Ju City, South Korea BR/TR, 6', 220 lbs. Deb: 7/4/1998																						
1998	Bos-A	0	3	.000	4	4	0	0	0	18^{2}	28	17	17	4	1	3	15	1.661	8.20	58	7.12	.341	0	....	-7	0	-0.7
1999	Bos-A	2	3	.400	9	7	0	0	0	39^{1}	45	26	25	7	2	8	16	1.347	5.72	87	4.81	.287	0	.000	-3	1	-0.3
Total	**2**	**2**	**6**	**.250**	**13**	**11**	**0**	**0**	**0**	**58**	**73**	**43**	**42**	**11**	**3**	**11**	**31**	**1.448**	**6.52**	**75**	**5.55**	**.305**	**0**	**.000**	**-11**	**1**	**-1.0**
• CHOATE, Don					Donald Leon Choate b: 7/2/1938, Potosi, MO BR/TR, 6', 185 lbs. Deb: 9/12/1960																						
1960	SF-N	0	0	....	4	0	0	0	0	8	7	4	2	0	0	4	7	1.375	2.25	155	3.10	.233	0	....	1	0	0.1
• CHOATE, Randy					Randol Doyle Choate b: 9/5/1975, San Antonio, TX BL/TL, 6'3", 180 lbs. Deb: 7/1/2000																						
2000*	NY-A	0	1	.000	22	0	0	0	0	17	14	10	9	3	1	8	12	1.294	4.76	101	3.99	.215	0	....	0	1	0.0
2001*	NY-A	3	1	.750	37	0	0	0	0	48^{1}	34	21	18	0	9	27	35	1.262	3.35	134	3.03	.202	0	.000	7	4	0.7
2002	NY-A	0	0	....	18	0	0	0	0	22^{1}	18	18	15	1	3	15	17	1.478	6.04	72	4.13	.217	0	.000	-4	0	-0.3
2003	NY-A	0	0	....	5	0	0	0	0	3^{2}	7	3	3	0	0	1	0	2.182	7.36	59	9.72	.467	0	....	-1	0	-0.1
Total	**4**	**3**	**2**	**.600**	**82**	**0**	**0**	**0**	**0**	91^{1}	**73**	**52**	**45**	**4**	**13**	**51**	**64**	**1.358**	**4.43**	**101**	**3.75**	**.221**	**0**	**.000**	**3**	**5**	**0.2**
• CHOUINARD, Bobby					Robert William Chouinard b: 5/1/1972, Manila, Philippines BR/TR, 6'1", 188 lbs. Deb: 5/26/1996																						
1996	Oak-A	4	2	.667	13	11	0	0	0	59	75	41	40	10	3	32	32	1.814	6.10	80	7.05	.316	0	....	-9	2	-0.8
1998	Mil-N	0	0	....	1	0	0	0	0	3	5	1	1	0	0	0	1	1.667	3.00	142	6.42	.455	0	....	0	0	0.0
	Ari-N	0	2	.000	26	2	0	0	0	38^{1}	41	23	18	5	0	11	26	1.357	4.23	100	3.99	.268	0	.000	-0	2	0.0
	Yr.	0	2	.000	27	2	0	0	0	41^{1}	46	24	19	5	0	11	27	1.379	4.14	102	4.17	.280	0	.000	0	2	0.0
1999*	Ari-N	5	2	.714	32	0	0	0	1	40^{1}	31	16	12	3	0	12	23	1.066	2.68	171	2.27	.220	0	.000	8	5	0.8
2000	Col-N	2	2	.500	31	0	0	0	0	32^{2}	35	17	14	4	1	9	23	1.347	3.86	150	4.16	.273	1	.333	7	3	0.7
2001	Col-N	0	0	....	8	0	0	0	0	7^{2}	10	7	7	4	0	1	5	1.435	8.22	65	7.39	.303	0	....	-2	0	-0.2
Total	**5**	**11**	**8**	**.579**	**111**	**13**	**0**	**0**	**1**	**181**	**197**	**105**	**92**	**26**	**4**	**65**	**110**	**1.448**	**4.57**	**106**	**4.82**	**.280**	**1**	**.125**	**4**	**12**	**0.4**
• CHOUNEAU, Chief					William Chouneau b: 9/2/1888, Cloquet, MN d: 9/17/1946, Cloquet, MN BR/TR, 5'9", 150 lbs. Deb: 10/9/1910																						
1910	Chi-A	0	1	.000	1	1	0	0	0	5^{1}	7	2	2	0	0	0	1	1.313	3.38	71	3.29	.292	0	.000	-1	0	0.0
• CHRIS, Mike					Michael Chris b: 10/8/1957, Santa Monica, CA BL/TL, 6'3", 180 lbs. Deb: 7/31/1979																						
1979	Det-A	3	3	.500	13	8	0	0	0	39	46	30	30	3	0	21	31	1.718	6.92	62	5.53	.297	0	....	-12	0	-1.1
1982	SF-N	0	2	.000	9	6	0	0	0	26	23	16	14	2	1	26	10	1.885	4.85	74	5.66	.245	1	.143	-3	0	-0.4
1983	SF-N	0	0	....	7	0	0	0	0	13^{1}	16	14	12	1	2	16	5	2.400	8.10	44	8.77	.308	0	.000	-7	0	-0.7
Total	**3**	**3**	**5**	**.375**	**29**	**14**	**0**	**0**	**0**	78^{1}	**85**	**60**	**56**	**6**	**3**	**63**	**46**	**1.889**	**6.43**	**61**	**6.12**	**.282**	**1**	**.111**	**-21**	**0**	**-2.2**
• CHRISTENSON, Gary					Gary Richard Christenson b: 5/5/1953, Mineola, NY BL/TL, 6'5", 200 lbs. Deb: 9/1/1979																						
1979	KC-A	0	0	....	6	0	0	0	0	10^{2}	10	5	4	1	0	2	4	1.125	3.38	126	2.91	.250	0	....	1	1	0.1
1980	KC-A	3	0	1.000	24	0	0	0	1	31^{1}	35	23	18	4	2	18	16	1.691	5.17	78	5.79	.278	0	....	-4	1	-0.4
Total	**2**	**3**	**0**	**1.000**	**30**	**0**	**0**	**0**	**1**	**42**	**45**	**28**	**22**	**5**	**2**	**20**	**20**	**1.548**	**4.71**	**87**	**5.06**	**.271**	**0**	**....**	**-3**	**2**	**-0.3**
• CHRISTENSON, Larry					Larry Richard Christenson b: 11/10/1953, Everett, WA BR/TR, 6'4", 215 lbs. Deb: 4/13/1973																						
1973	Phi-N	1	4	.200	10	9	1	0	0	34^{1}	53	25	25	3	1	20	11	2.126	6.55	58	8.47	.366	0	.000	-11	0	-1.2
1974	Phi-N	1	1	.500	10	1	0	0	2	23	20	11	11	2	0	15	18	1.522	4.30	88	4.14	.241	0	.000	-2	1	-0.2
1975	Phi-N	11	6	.647	29	26	5	2	1	171^{2}	149	73	70	12	1	45	88	1.130	3.67	102	2.71	.236	14	.246	-4	13	0.2

YEAR	TM-L	W	L	PCT	G	GS	CG	SH	SV	IP	H	R	ER	HR	HB	BB	SO	RAT	ERA	ERA+	CERA	OAV	BH	AVG	PR+	WS	TPW
1976	Phi-N	13	8	.619	32	29	2	0	0	168^2	199	77	69	8	1	42	54	1.429	3.68	96	4.12	.297	10	.196	-5	9	-0.1
1977*	Phi-N	19	6	.760	34	34	5	1	0	219^1	229	113	99	21	7	69	118	1.359	4.06	98	4.06	.268	10	.135	-5	11	-0.5
1978*	Phi-N	13	14	.481	33	33	9	3	0	228	209	90	82	16	1	47	131	1.123	3.24	110	2.68	.244	5	.075	4	13	0.2
1979	Phi-N	5	10	.333	19	17	2	0	0	106	118	56	53	9	2	30	53	1.396	4.50	85	4.28	.291	9	.290	-9	5	-0.4
1980*	Phi-N	5	1	.833	14	14	0	0	0	73^2	62	35	33	4	3	27	49	1.208	4.03	94	2.86	.227	7	.368	-2	5	0.2
1981*	Phi-N	4	7	.364	20	15	0	0	1	106^2	108	48	42	8	1	30	70	1.294	3.54	102	3.54	.267	3	.100	0	5	-0.1
1982	Phi-N	9	10	.474	33	33	3	0	0	223	212	95	86	15	3	53	145	1.188	3.47	106	3.05	.253	5	.075	5	13	0.3
1983	Phi-N	2	4	.333	9	9	0	0	0	48^1	42	25	21	2	1	17	44	1.221	3.91	91	2.81	.233	1	.059	-1	2	-0.2
Total	11	83	71	.539	243	220	27	6	4	1402^2	1401	648	591	100	21	395	781	1.280	3.79	98	3.50	.262	64	.150	-30	77	-2.0
• CHRISTIANSEN, Clay	Clay C. Christiansen b: 6/28/1958, Wichita, KS BR/TR, 6'5", 205 lbs. Deb: 5/10/1984																										
1984	NY-A	2	4	.333	24	1	0	0	2	38^2	50	28	26	4	1	12	27	1.603	6.05	63	5.45	.309	0	....	-9	0	-1.0
• CHRISTIANSEN, Jason	Jason Samuel Christiansen b: 9/21/1969, Omaha, NE BR/TL, 6'5", 230 lbs. Deb: 4/26/1995																										
1995	Pit-N	1	3	.250	63	0	0	0	0	56^1	49	28	26	5	3	34	53	1.473	4.15	104	3.89	.234	0	.000	2	4	0.1
1996	Pit-N	3	3	.500	33	0	0	0	0	44^1	56	34	33	7	1	19	38	1.692	6.70	65	6.19	.311	0	.000	-11	0	-1.1
1997	Pit-N	3	0	1.000	39	0	0	0	0	33^2	37	11	11	2	2	17	37	1.604	2.94	146	4.80	.274	0	....	5	4	0.5
1998	Pit-N	3	3	.500	60	0	0	0	6	64^2	51	22	18	2	0	27	71	1.206	2.51	172	2.39	.216	1	.250	12	9	1.2
1999	Pit-N	2	3	.400	39	0	0	0	3	37^2	26	17	17	2	2	22	35	1.274	4.06	112	2.85	.198	0	.000	2	4	0.2
2000	Pit-N	2	8	.200	44	0	0	0	1	38	28	22	21	2	0	25	41	1.395	4.97	92	3.11	.207	0	....	-1	3	-0.1
	*StL-N	1	0	1.000	21	0	0	0	0	10	13	7	6	1	2	2	12	1.500	5.40	85	5.64	.317	0	....	-1	1	-0.1
	Yr.	3	8	.273	65	0	0	0	1	48	41	29	27	3	2	27	53	1.417	5.06	91	3.64	.233	0	....	-2	4	-0.2
2001	StL-N	1	1	.500	30	0	0	0	3	19^1	15	10	10	4	1	10	19	1.293	4.66	92	4.12	.211	0	....	-1	2	-0.1
	SF-N	1	0	1.000	25	0	0	0	0	17	14	3	3	1	0	5	12	1.118	1.59	251	2.62	.241	0	....	4	2	0.4
	Yr.	2	1	.667	55	0	0	0	3	36^1	29	13	13	5	1	15	31	1.211	3.22	130	3.42	.225	0	....	3	4	0.3
2002	SF-N	0	1	.000	6	0	0	0	0	5	6	3	3	1	0	2	1	1.600	5.40	72	6.48	.316	0	....	-1	0	-0.1
2003*	SF-N	0	0	....	40	0	0	0	0	26	25	15	15	3	1	11	22	1.385	5.19	79	4.11	.243	0	....	-4	1	-0.4
Total	9	17	22	.436	400	0	0	0	13	352	320	172	163	30	12	174	341	1.403	4.17	104	3.85	.243	1	.100	7	30	0.7
• CHRISTMAN, Tim	Timothy Arthur Christman b: 3/31/1975, Oneonta, NY BL/TL, 6', 195 lbs. Deb: 4/21/2001																										
2001	Col-N	0	0	....	1	0	0	0	0	2	1	1	1	1	0	0	2	.500	4.50	119	1.73	.143	0	....	0	0	0.0
• CHRISTOPHER, Mike	Michael Wayne Christopher b: 11/3/1963, Petersburg, VA BR/TR, 6'5", 206 lbs. Deb: 9/10/1991																										
1991	LA-N	0	0	....	3	0	0	0	0	4	2	0	0	0	0	3	2	1.250	0.00	....	2.38	.167	0	....	2	1	0.2
1992	Cle-A	0	0	....	10	0	0	0	0	18	17	8	6	2	0	10	13	1.500	3.00	130	4.38	.254	0	....	2	1	0.2
1993	Cle-A	0	0	....	9	0	0	0	0	11^2	14	6	5	3	0	2	8	1.371	3.86	112	5.13	.286	0	....	1	0	0.1
1995	Det-A	4	0	1.000	36	0	0	0	1	61^1	71	28	26	8	2	14	34	1.386	3.82	125	4.64	.292	0	....	7	6	0.7
1996	Det-A	1	1	.500	13	0	0	0	0	30	47	36	31	12	0	11	19	1.933	9.30	54	9.58	.351	0	....	-13	0	-1.2
Total	5	5	1	.833	71	0	0	0	1	125	151	78	68	25	2	40	76	1.528	4.90	97	5.76	.299	0	....	-2	8	-0.1
• CHRISTOPHER, Russ	Russell Ormand Christopher b: 9/12/1917, Richmond, CA d: 12/5/1954, Richmond, CA BR/TR, 6'3.5", 180 lbs. Deb: 4/14/1942																										
1942	Phi-A	4	13	.235	30	18	10	0	1	165	154	78	70	8	3	99	58	1.533	3.82	99	4.11	.254	5	.089	3	8	0.0
1943	Phi-A	5	8	.385	24	15	5	0	2	133	120	58	51	3	3	58	56	1.338	3.45	98	3.11	.242	7	.156	3	7	0.2
1944	Phi-A	14	14	.500	35	24	13	1	1	215^1	200	91	71	6	9	63	84	1.221	2.97	117	2.87	.245	18	.222	13	18	1.7
1945	Phi-A★	13	13	.500	33	27	17	2	2	227^1	213	92	80	9	9	75	100	1.267	3.17	108	3.15	.251	13	.171	8	15	0.8
1946	Phi-A	5	7	.417	30	13	1	0	0	119^1	119	71	57	5	3	44	79	1.366	4.30	83	3.47	.254	5	.139	-9	3	-1.0
1947	Phi-A	10	7	.588	44	0	0	0	12	80^2	70	30	26	4	0	33	33	1.277	2.90	132	3.02	.236	2	.125	6	11	0.6
1948*	Cle-A	3	2	.600	45	0	0	0	**17**	59	55	21	19	3	0	27	14	1.390	2.90	140	3.44	.247	0	.000	6	8	0.6
Total	7	54	64	.458	241	97	46	3	35	999^2	931	441	374	38	27	399	424	1.330	3.37	106	3.29	.248	50	.158	29	70	2.9
• CHULK, Vinnie	Charles Vincent Chulk b: 12/19/1978, Miami, FL BR/TR, 6'2", 195 lbs. Deb: 9/8/2003																										
2003	Tor-A	0	0	....	3	0	0	0	0	5^1	6	3	3	0	0	3	2	1.688	5.06	91	4.53	.273	0	....	-0	0	0.0
• CHURCH, Bubba	Emory Nicholas Church b: 9/12/1924, Birmingham, AL d: 9/17/2001, Birmingham, AL BR/TR, 6', 180 lbs. Deb: 4/30/1950																										
1950	Phi-N	8	6	.571	31	18	8	2	1	142	113	50	43	12	0	56	50	1.190	2.73	149	2.91	.225	8	.182	21	13	2.0
1951	Phi-N	15	11	.577	38	33	15	4	1	247	246	107	97	17	1	90	104	1.360	3.53	109	3.66	.261	22	.256	9	18	1.3
1952	Phi-N	0	0	....	2	1	0	0	0	5	11	6	6	0	1	1	3	2.400	10.80	34	10.50	.440	0	.000	-4	0	-0.4
	Cin-N	5	9	.357	29	22	5	1	0	153^1	173	85	74	21	3	48	47	1.441	4.34	87	5.02	.301	12	.240	-10	5	-0.7
	Yr.	5	9	.357	31	23	5	1	0	158^1	184	91	80	21	4	49	50	1.472	4.55	83	5.20	.307	12	.235	-14	5	-1.2
1953	Cin-N	3	3	.500	11	7	2	0	0	43^2	55	32	29	9	2	19	12	1.695	5.98	73	6.90	.318	4	.267	-9	1	-0.7
	Chi-N	4	5	.444	27	11	1	0	1	104^1	115	67	58	16	2	49	47	1.572	5.00	89	5.23	.276	7	.212	-3	5	-0.2
	Yr.	7	8	.467	38	18	3	0	1	148	170	99	87	25	4	68	59	1.608	5.29	84	5.73	.289	11	.229	-12	6	-1.0
1954	Chi-N	1	3	.250	7	3	1	0	0	14^2	21	18	16	8	0	13	8	2.318	9.82	43	12.94	.350	0	.000	-9	0	-1.0
1955	Chi-N	0	0	....	2	0	0	0	1	3^1	4	2	2	1	0	1	3	1.500	5.40	76	6.16	.286	0	.000	-1	0	-0.1
Total	6	36	37	.493	147	95	32	7	4	713^1	738	367	325	84	9	277	274	1.423	4.10	98	4.48	.272	53	.226	-6	42	0.2
• CHURCH, Len	Leonard Church b: 3/21/1942, Chicago, IL d: 4/22/1988, Richardson, TX BB/TR, 6', 190 lbs. Deb: 8/27/1966																										
1966	Chi-N	0	1	.000	4	0	0	0	0	6	10	6	5	1	0	7	3	2.833	7.50	49	11.40	.400	0	.000	-2	0	-0.3
• CHURN, Chuck	Clarence Nottingham Churn b: 2/1/1930, Bridgetown, VA BR/TR, 6'3", 205 lbs. Deb: 4/18/1957																										
1957	Pit-N	0	0	....	5	0	0	0	0	8^1	9	4	4	1	0	4	4	1.560	4.32	88	5.29	.333	0	.000	-1	0	-0.1
1958	Cle-A	0	0	....	6	0	0	0	0	8^2	12	7	6	1	0	5	4	1.962	6.23	59	7.47	.343	0	....	-3	0	-0.3
1959*	LA-N	3	2	.600	14	0	0	0	1	30^2	28	17	17	2	1	10	24	1.239	4.99	85	3.11	.255	1	.167	-3	2	-0.3
Total	3	3	2	.600	25	0	0	0	1	47^2	49	28	27	4	1	19	32	1.427	5.10	79	4.28	.285	1	.143	-6	2	-0.6
• CIARDI, Mark	Mark Thomas Ciardi b: 8/19/1961, New Brunswick, NJ BR/TR, 6', 180 lbs. Deb: 4/9/1987																										
1987	Mil-A	1	1	.500	4	3	0	0	0	16^1	26	17	17	5	0	9	8	2.143	9.37	49	10.46	.361	0	....	-9	0	-0.8
• CICOTTE, Al	Alva Warren "Bozo" Cicotte b: 12/23/1929, Melvindale, MI d: 11/29/1982, Westland, MI BR/TR, 6'3", 185 lbs. Deb: 4/22/1957																										
1957	NY-A	2	2	.500	20	2	0	0	2	65^1	57	25	22	5	1	30	36	1.332	3.03	118	3.53	.238	3	.150	3	4	0.3
1958	Was-A	0	3	.000	8	4	0	0	0	28	36	18	15	3	0	14	14	1.786	4.82	79	6.29	.316	2	.200	-2	0	-0.3
	Det-A	3	1	.750	14	2	0	0	0	43	50	19	17	1	0	15	21	1.512	3.56	113	4.30	.307	3	.176	2	3	0.1
	Yr.	3	4	.429	22	6	0	0	0	71	86	37	32	4	0	29	35	1.620	4.06	97	5.09	.310	5	.185	-1	3	-0.1
1959	Cle-A	3	1	.750	26	1	0	0	1	44	46	29	26	4	2	25	23	1.614	5.32	69	5.21	.299	1	.333	-8	1	-0.8
1961	StL-N	2	6	.250	29	7	0	0	1	75	83	47	44	16	2	34	51	1.560	5.28	83	5.91	.283	6	.286	-8	2	-0.7
1962	Hou-N	0	0	....	5	0	0	0	0	4^2	8	4	2	1	0	1	4	1.929	3.86	97	8.86	.381	0	....	0	0	0.0
Total	5	10	13	.435	102	16	0	0	4	260	280	142	126	30	5	119	149	1.535	4.36	91	5.02	.284	15	.211	-13	10	-1.3
• CICOTTE, Eddie	Edward Victor "Knuckles" Cicotte b: 6/19/1884, Springwells, MI d: 5/5/1969, Detroit, MI BB/TR, 5'9", 175 lbs. Deb: 9/3/1905																										
1905	Det-A	1	1	.500	3	1	1	0	0	18	25	8	7	0	0	5	6	1.667	3.50	78	5.50	.331	3	.429	-2	1	-0.1
1908	Bos-A	11	12	.478	39	24	17	2	2	207^1	198	73	56	0	11	59	95	1.240	2.43	101	3.01	.261	17	.236	-4	12	-0.1
1909	Bos-A	14	5	.737	27	17	10	1	1	159^2	117	63	35	3	1	56	82	1.084	1.97	126	2.16	.210	12	.235	7	14	1.1
1910	Bos-A	15	11	.577	36	30	20	3	0	250	213	94	76	4	13	86	104	1.196	2.74	93	2.71	.233	12	.141	-4	13	-0.5
1911	Bos-A	11	15	.423	35	25	16	1	0	220	236	118	69	2	4	73	106	1.405	2.82	116	3.73	.282	10	.141	11	11	0.9
1912	Bos-A	1	3	.250	9	6	2	0	0	46	58	34	29	0	1	15	20	1.587	5.67	60	4.73	.319	2	.154	-11	0	-1.1
	Chi-A	9	7	.563	20	18	13	1	0	152	159	63	48	3	0	37	70	1.289	2.84	113	3.28	.277	13	.245	9	11	1.0
	Yr.	10	10	.500	29	24	15	1	0	198	217	97	77	3	1	52	90	1.359	3.50	94	3.62	.287	15	.227	-2	11	-0.1
1913	Chi-A	18	11	.621	41	30	18	3	1	268	224	77	47	2	3	73	121	1.108	1.58	185	2.21	.226	13	.143	40	27	3.9
1914	Chi-A	11	16	.407	45	30	15	4	3	269^1	220	96	61	0	3	72	122	1.084	2.04	131	2.15	.232	14	.163	20	21	2.1
1915	Chi-A	13	12	.520	39	26	15	1	3	223^1	216	89	75	2	6	48	106	1.182	3.02	98	2.80	.261	14	.209	1	13	0.2
1916	Chi-A	15	7	.682	44	19	11	2	5	187	138	56	37	1	1	70	91	1.112	1.78	155	2.16	.218	12	.211	18	19	2.2

YEAR TM-L	W	L	PCT	G	GS	CG	SH	SV	IP	H	R	ER	HR	HB	BB	SO	RAT	ERA	ERA+	CERA	OAV	BH	AVG	PR+	WS	TPW
1917* Chi-A	**28**	12	.700	49	35	29	7	4	**346^{2}**	246	76	59	2	3	70	150	.912	**1.53**	**173**	**1.52**	.203	20	.179	**46**	35	**5.2**
1918 Chi-A	12	19	.387	38	30	24	1	2	266	275	102	82	2	2	40	104	1.184	2.77	98	2.81	.271	14	.163	2	14	0.4
1919* Chi-A	**29**	7	.806	40	35	**30**	5	1	**306^{2}**	256	77	62	5	2	49	110	.995	1.82	175	1.91	.228	20	.202	40	**32**	4.2
1920 Chi-A	21	10	.677	37	35	28	4	2	303^{1}	316	128	110	6	2	74	87	1.286	3.26	115	3.24	.275	22	.196	13	24	1.0
Total 14	209	148	.585	502	361	249	35	24	3223^{1}	2897	1154	853	32	52	827	1374	1.155	2.38	123	2.58	.246	198	.186	185	247	20.5

• CIMINO, Pete Peter William Cimino b: 10/17/1942, Philadelphia, PA BR/TR, 6'2", 195 lbs. Deb: 9/22/1965

YEAR TM-L	W	L	PCT	G	GS	CG	SH	SV	IP	H	R	ER	HR	HB	BB	SO	RAT	ERA	ERA+	CERA	OAV	BH	AVG	PR+	WS	TPW
1965 Min-A	0	0	....	1	0	0	0	0	1	0	0	0	0	0	0	0	.000	0.00	....	0.00	.000	0	....	0	0	0.0
1966 Min-A	2	5	.286	35	0	0	0	4	64^{2}	53	27	21	4	1	30	57	1.284	2.92	123	3.03	.222	0	.000	5	5	0.5
1967 Cal-A	3	3	.500	46	1	0	0	1	88^{1}	73	38	32	12	2	31	80	1.177	3.26	96	3.22	.229	5	.417	-2	5	0.0
1968 Cal-A	0	0	....	4	0	0	0	0	7	7	5	2	0	0	4	2	1.571	2.57	113	3.89	.259	0	....	0	0	0.0
Total 4	5	8	.385	86	1	0	0	5	161	133	70	55	16	3	65	139	1.230	3.07	107	3.15	.227	5	.278	4	10	0.5

• CIMORELLI, Frank Frank Thomas Cimorelli b: 8/2/1968, Poughkeepsie, NY BR/TR, 6', 175 lbs. Deb: 4/30/1994

YEAR TM-L	W	L	PCT	G	GS	CG	SH	SV	IP	H	R	ER	HR	HB	BB	SO	RAT	ERA	ERA+	CERA	OAV	BH	AVG	PR+	WS	TPW
1994 StL-N	0	0	....	11	0	0	0	1	13^{1}	20	14	13	0	2	10	1	2.250	8.78	47	7.71	.345	0	.000	-7	0	-0.7

• CIOLA, Lou Louis Alexander Ciola b: 9/6/1922, Norfolk, VA d: 10/18/1981, Austin, MN BR/TR, 5'9", 165 lbs. Deb: 7/25/1943

YEAR TM-L	W	L	PCT	G	GS	CG	SH	SV	IP	H	R	ER	HR	HB	BB	SO	RAT	ERA	ERA+	CERA	OAV	BH	AVG	PR+	WS	TPW
1943 Phi-A	1	3	.250	12	3	2	0	0	43^{2}	48	33	27	2	1	22	7	1.603	5.56	61	4.44	.273	3	.167	-9	0	-1.1

• CISCO, Galen Galen Bernard Cisco b: 3/7/1936, St. Marys, OH BR/TR, 6', 215 lbs. Deb: 6/11/1961 C

YEAR TM-L	W	L	PCT	G	GS	CG	SH	SV	IP	H	R	ER	HR	HB	BB	SO	RAT	ERA	ERA+	CERA	OAV	BH	AVG	PR+	WS	TPW
1961 Bos-A	2	4	.333	17	8	0	0	0	52^{1}	67	40	39	5	0	28	26	1.815	6.71	62	6.38	.325	1	.100	-15	0	-1.5
1962 Bos-A	4	7	.364	23	9	1	0	0	83	95	66	62	11	3	50	43	1.747	6.72	61	6.18	.292	2	.080	-24	0	-2.5
NY-N	1	1	.500	4	2	1	0	0	19^{1}	15	7	7	0	3	11	13	1.345	3.26	128	3.08	.208	0	.000	2	1	0.2
1963 NY-N	7	15	.318	51	17	1	0	0	155^{2}	165	88	75	15	7	64	81	1.471	4.34	80	4.60	.273	5	.132	-13	5	-1.3
1964 NY-N	6	19	.240	36	25	5	2	0	191^{2}	182	85	77	17	6	54	78	1.231	3.62	99	3.43	.256	6	.111	-2	7	-0.2
1965 NY-N	4	8	.333	35	17	1	1	0	112^{1}	119	63	56	12	1	51	58	1.513	4.49	79	4.66	.272	7	.259	-12	4	-1.0
1967 Bos-A	0	1	.000	11	0	0	0	1	22^{1}	21	10	9	4	0	8	8	1.299	3.63	96	4.34	.266	0	.000	-0	1	-0.1
1969 KC-A	1	1	.500	15	0	0	0	1	22^{1}	17	11	9	4	0	15	18	1.433	3.63	102	4.33	.215	0	....	0	1	0.0
Total 7	25	56	.309	192	78	9	3	2	659	681	370	334	68	20	281	325	1.460	4.56	81	4.55	.271	21	.128	-63	19	-6.4

• CITARELLA, Ralph Ralph Alexander Citarella b: 2/7/1958, East Orange, NJ BR/TR, 6', 180 lbs. Deb: 9/13/1983

YEAR TM-L	W	L	PCT	G	GS	CG	SH	SV	IP	H	R	ER	HR	HB	BB	SO	RAT	ERA	ERA+	CERA	OAV	BH	AVG	PR+	WS	TPW
1983 StL-N	0	0	....	6	0	0	0	0	11	8	2	2	0	0	3	4	1.000	1.64	221	1.62	.205	0	.000	2	1	0.2
1984 StL-N	0	1	.000	10	2	0	0	0	22^{1}	20	9	9	0	3	7	15	1.209	3.63	96	2.85	.238	1	.250	-1	1	-0.1
1987 Chi-A	0	0	....	5	0	0	0	0	11	13	9	9	4	2	4	9	1.545	7.36	62	8.21	.302	0	....	-4	0	-0.4
Total 3	0	1	.000	21	2	0	0	0	44^{1}	41	20	20	4	5	14	28	1.241	4.06	96	3.88	.247	1	.200	-2	2	-0.2

• CLANCY, Jim James Clancy b: 12/18/1955, Chicago, IL BR/TR, 6'4", 220 lbs. Deb: 7/26/1977

YEAR TM-L	W	L	PCT	G	GS	CG	SH	SV	IP	H	R	ER	HR	HB	BB	SO	RAT	ERA	ERA+	CERA	OAV	BH	AVG	PR+	WS	TPW
1977 Tor-A	4	9	.308	13	13	4	1	0	76^{2}	80	47	43	7	0	47	44	1.657	5.05	83	5.14	.280	0	....	-5	2	-0.5
1978 Tor-A	10	12	.455	31	30	7	0	0	193^{2}	199	96	88	10	1	91	106	1.497	4.09	96	4.20	.270	0	....	-2	10	-0.2
1979 Tor-A	2	7	.222	12	11	2	0	0	63^{2}	65	44	39	8	0	31	33	1.508	5.51	79	4.79	.272	0	....	-9	1	-0.8
1980 Tor-A	13	16	.448	34	34	15	2	0	250^{2}	217	108	92	19	2	128	152	1.376	3.30	130	3.60	.233	0	....	25	19	2.5
1981 Tor-A	6	12	.333	22	22	2	0	0	125	126	77	68	12	5	64	56	1.520	4.90	81	4.71	.262	0	....	-13	3	-1.3
1982 Tor-A★	16	14	.533	40	**40**	11	3	0	266^{2}	251	122	110	26	2	77	139	1.230	3.71	121	3.36	.248	0	....	25	20	2.5
1983 Tor-A	15	11	.577	34	34	11	1	0	223	238	115	97	23	1	61	99	1.341	3.91	110	3.96	.271	0	....	9	14	0.9
1984 Tor-A	13	15	.464	36	**36**	5	0	0	219^{2}	249	132	125	25	3	88	118	1.534	5.12	80	5.05	.287	0	....	-26	7	-2.6
1985* Tor-A	9	6	.600	23	23	1	0	0	128^{2}	117	54	54	15	0	37	66	1.197	3.78	111	3.28	.241	0	....	4	9	0.4
1986 Tor-A	14	14	.500	34	34	6	3	0	219^{1}	202	100	96	24	4	63	126	1.208	3.94	107	3.33	.243	0	....	7	13	0.7
1987 Tor-A	15	11	.577	37	37	5	1	0	241^{1}	234	103	95	24	1	80	180	1.301	3.54	127	3.67	.255	0	....	22	17	2.1
1988 Tor-A	11	13	.458	36	31	4	0	1	196^{1}	207	106	98	26	9	47	118	1.294	4.49	87	4.17	.272	0	....	-13	7	-1.3
1989 Hou-N	7	14	.333	33	26	1	0	0	147	155	100	83	13	0	66	91	1.503	5.08	67	4.26	.269	6	.146	-27	0	-2.9
1990 Hou-N	2	8	.200	33	10	0	0	1	76	100	58	55	4	3	33	44	1.750	6.51	57	5.69	.322	3	.214	-24	0	-2.4
1991 Hou-N	0	3	.000	30	0	0	0	5	55	37	19	17	5	0	20	33	1.036	2.78	126	2.18	.193	0	.000	4	5	0.4
*Atl-N	3	2	.600	24	0	0	0	3	34^{2}	36	23	22	3	1	14	17	1.442	5.71	68	4.23	.267	0	.000	-7	1	-0.8
Yr.	3	5	.375	54	0	0	0	8	89^{2}	73	42	39	8	1	34	50	1.193	3.91	95	2.97	.223	0	.000	-3	6	-0.4
Total 15	140	167	.456	472	381	74	11	10	2517^{1}	2513	1304	1182	244	32	947	1422	1.374	4.23	97	4.00	.261	9	.148	-29	128	-3.4

• CLARK, Bob Robert William Clark b: 8/22/1897, Newport, PA d: 5/18/1944, Carlsbad, NM BR/TR, 6'3", 188 lbs. Deb: 5/26/1920

YEAR TM-L	W	L	PCT	G	GS	CG	SH	SV	IP	H	R	ER	HR	HB	BB	SO	RAT	ERA	ERA+	CERA	OAV	BH	AVG	PR+	WS	TPW
1920 Cle-A	1	2	.333	11	2	2	1	0	42	59	19	16	0	1	13	8	1.714	3.43	111	6.04	.383	2	.200	1	3	0.0
1921 Cle-A	0	0	....	5	0	0	0	0	9^{1}	23	17	15	2	1	6	2	3.107	14.46	29	17.94	.511	0	.000	-11	0	-1.0
Total 2	1	2	.333	16	2	2	1	0	51^{1}	82	36	31	2	2	19	10	1.968	5.44	74	8.20	.412	2	.154	-10	3	-1.0

• CLARK, Bryan Bryan Donald Clark b: 7/12/1956, Madera, CA BL/TL, 6'2", 185 lbs. Deb: 4/11/1981

YEAR TM-L	W	L	PCT	G	GS	CG	SH	SV	IP	H	R	ER	HR	HB	BB	SO	RAT	ERA	ERA+	CERA	OAV	BH	AVG	PR+	WS	TPW
1981 Sea-A	2	5	.286	29	9	1	0	2	93^{1}	92	54	45	3	1	55	52	1.575	4.34	89	4.16	.261	0	....	-4	3	-0.4
1982 Sea-A	5	2	.714	37	5	1	1	0	114^{2}	104	44	35	6	0	58	70	1.413	2.75	154	3.64	.241	0	....	19	10	1.9
1983 Sea-A	7	10	.412	41	17	2	0	0	162^{1}	160	82	71	14	3	72	76	1.429	3.94	108	4.14	.261	0	....	6	9	0.6
1984 Tor-A	1	2	.333	20	3	0	0	0	45^{2}	66	33	30	6	1	22	21	1.927	5.91	69	7.39	.342	0	....	-9	0	-0.9
1985 Cle-A	3	4	.429	31	3	0	0	2	62^{2}	78	47	44	8	0	34	24	1.787	6.32	65	6.35	.311	0	....	-15	0	-1.5
1986 Chi-A	0	0	....	5	0	0	0	0	8	8	4	4	0	0	2	5	1.250	4.50	96	3.09	.276	0	....	-0	0	0.0
1987 Chi-A	0	0	....	11	0	0	0	0	18^{2}	19	5	5	1	0	8	8	1.446	2.41	190	4.20	.297	0	....	4	2	0.4
1990 Sea-A	2	0	1.000	12	0	0	0	0	11	9	4	4	0	0	10	3	1.727	3.27	121	4.51	.237	0	....	1	1	0.1
Total 8	20	23	.465	186	37	4	1	4	516^{1}	536	273	238	38	5	261	259	1.544	4.15	100	4.58	.272	0	....	2	25	0.1

• CLARK, Ed Edward C. Clark b: Cincinnati, OH Deb: 7/4/1886

YEAR TM-L	W	L	PCT	G	GS	CG	SH	SV	IP	H	R	ER	HR	HB	BB	SO	RAT	ERA	ERA+	CERA	OAV	BH	AVG	PR+	WS	TPW
1886 Phi-a	0	1	.000	1	1	1	0	0	8	10	8	6	2	2	2	2	1.500	6.75	52	....	.293	0	.000	-3	0	-0.2
1891 Col-a	0	0	....	1	0	0	0	0	2	2	0	0	0	0	0	1	1.000	0.00	....	....	.252	0	.000	1	0	0.0
Total 2	0	1	.000	2	1	1	0	0	10	12	8	6	2	2	2	3	1.400	5.40	65	....	.285	0	.000	-2	0	-0.2

• CLARK, George George Myron Clark b: 5/19/1891, Smithland, IA d: 11/14/1940, Sioux City, IA BR/TL, 6', 190 lbs. Deb: 5/16/1913

YEAR TM-L	W	L	PCT	G	GS	CG	SH	SV	IP	H	R	ER	HR	HB	BB	SO	RAT	ERA	ERA+	CERA	OAV	BH	AVG	PR+	WS	TPW
1913 NY-A	0	1	.000	11	1	0	0	0	19	22	23	19	1	3	19	5	2.158	9.00	33	7.02	.272	2	.500	-13	0	-1.2

• CLARK, Ginger Harvey Daniel Clark b: 3/7/1879, Wooster, OH d: 5/10/1943, Lake Charles, LA BR/TR, 5'11", 165 lbs. Deb: 8/11/1902

YEAR TM-L	W	L	PCT	G	GS	CG	SH	SV	IP	H	R	ER	HR	HB	BB	SO	RAT	ERA	ERA+	CERA	OAV	BH	AVG	PR+	WS	TPW
1902 Cle-A	1	0	1.000	1	0	0	0	0	6	10	6	4	0	1	3	1	2.167	6.00	57	8.24	.370	2	.500	-2	0	-0.1

• CLARK, Mark Mark Willard Clark b: 5/12/1968, Bath, IL BR/TR, 6'5", 225 lbs. Deb: 9/6/1991

YEAR TM-L	W	L	PCT	G	GS	CG	SH	SV	IP	H	R	ER	HR	HB	BB	SO	RAT	ERA	ERA+	CERA	OAV	BH	AVG	PR+	WS	TPW
1991 StL-N	1	1	.500	7	2	0	0	0	22^{1}	17	10	10	3	0	11	13	1.254	4.03	92	3.38	.215	0	.000	-1	1	-0.2
1992 StL-N	3	10	.231	20	20	1	1	0	113^{1}	117	59	56	12	0	36	44	1.350	4.45	76	3.90	.265	5	.139	-15	1	-1.7
1993 Cle-A	7	5	.583	26	15	1	0	0	109^{1}	119	55	52	18	1	25	57	1.317	4.28	101	4.46	.279	0	....	0	5	0.0
1994 Cle-A	11	3	.786	20	20	4	1	0	127^{1}	133	61	54	14	4	40	60	1.359	3.82	124	4.24	.273	0	....	13	10	1.2
1995 Cle-A	9	7	.563	22	21	2	0	0	124^{2}	143	77	73	13	4	42	68	1.484	5.27	89	4.81	.288	0	....	-8	5	-0.7
1996 NY-N	14	11	.560	32	32	2	0	0	212^{1}	217	98	81	20	3	48	142	1.248	3.43	117	3.50	.265	3	.043	12	13	0.6
1997 NY-N	8	7	.533	23	22	1	0	0	142	158	74	67	18	3	47	72	1.444	4.25	95	4.80	.289	2	.047	-6	6	-0.8
Chi-N	6	1	.857	9	9	2	0	0	63	55	22	20	6	1	12	51	1.063	2.86	151	2.56	.226	0	.000	10	6	0.8
Yr.	14	8	.636	32	31	3	0	0	205	213	96	87	24	4	59	123	1.327	3.82	107	4.11	.270	2	.030	4	12	0.0
1998* Chi-N	9	14	.391	33	33	2	1	0	213^{2}	236	116	115	23	4	48	161	1.329	4.84	91	4.02	.278	4	.065	-7	7	-1.0
1999 Tex-A	3	7	.300	15	15	0	0	0	74^{1}	103	73	71	17	1	34	44	1.843	8.60	59	7.75	.329	0	.000	-28	0	-2.6
2000 Tex-A	3	5	.375	12	8	0	0	0	44	66	42	39	10	3	24	16	2.045	7.98	63	9.14	.347	0	....	-14	0	-1.3
Total 10	74	71	.510	219	197	15	3	0	1246^{1}	1364	687	638	154	24	367	728	1.389	4.61	94	4.47	.279	14	.058	-43	54	-5.5

• CLARK, Mike Michael John Clark b: 2/12/1922, Camden, NJ d: 1/25/1996, Camden, NJ BR/TR, 6'4", 190 lbs. Deb: 7/27/1952

YEAR TM-L	W	L	PCT	G	GS	CG	SH	SV	IP	H	R	ER	HR	HB	BB	SO	RAT	ERA	ERA+	CERA	OAV	BH	AVG	PR+	WS	TPW
1952 StL-N	2	0	1.000	12	4	0	0	0	25^{1}	32	18	17	2	0	14	10	1.816	6.04	61	5.83	.311	0	.000	-7	0	-0.7

YEAR	TM-L	W	L	PCT	G	GS	CG	SH	SV	IP	H	R	ER	HR	HB	BB	SO	RAT	ERA	ERA+	CERA	OAV	BH	AVG	PR+	WS	TPW
1953	StL-N	1	0	1.000	23	2	0	0	1	35^{2}	46	21	19	2	2	21	17	1.879	4.79	89	6.28	.315	0	.000	-2	1	-0.2
Total	2	3	0	1.000	35	6	0	0	1	61	78	39	36	4	2	35	27	1.852	5.31	75	6.09	.313	0	.000	-8	1	-1.0
• CLARK, Otey	William Otis Clark b: 5/22/1915, Boscobel, WI BR/TR, 6'1.5", 190 lbs. Deb: 4/17/1945																										
1945	Bos-A	4	4	.500	12	9	4	1	0	82	86	33	28	6	1	19	20	1.280	3.07	111	3.49	.268	5	.208	2	5	0.3
• CLARK, Phil	Philip James Clark b: 10/3/1932, Albany, GA BR/TR, 6'3", 210 lbs. Deb: 4/15/1958																										
1958	StL-N	0	1	.000	7	0	0	0	1	7^{2}	11	5	3	2	0	3	1	1.826	3.52	117	8.29	.355	0	.000	1	0	0.0
1959	StL-N	0	1	.000	7	0	0	0	0	7	8	11	10	0	0	8	5	2.286	12.86	33	6.79	.286	0	....	-7	0	-0.7
Total	2	0	2	.000	14	0	0	0	1	14^{2}	19	16	13	2	0	11	6	2.045	7.98	53	7.57	.322	0	.000	-6	0	-0.6
• CLARK, Rickey	Rickey Charles Clark b: 3/21/1946, Mount Clemens, MI BR/TR, 6'2", 170 lbs. Deb: 4/22/1967																										
1967	Cal-A	12	11	.522	32	30	1	1	0	174	144	69	50	15	6	69	81	1.224	2.59	121	3.16	.224	2	.040	9	11	0.6
1968	Cal-A	1	11	.083	21	17	0	0	0	94^{1}	74	51	37	4	1	54	60	1.357	3.53	82	3.15	.217	3	.107	-8	1	-1.0
1969	Cal-A	0	0	....	6	1	0	0	0	9^{2}	12	6	6	2	0	7	6	1.966	5.59	62	7.42	.300	1	.500	-2	0	-0.2
1971	Cal-A	2	1	.667	11	7	1	1	1	44	36	15	14	6	2	28	28	1.455	2.86	113	4.30	.220	4	.267	1	4	0.2
1972	Cal-A	4	9	.308	26	15	2	0	1	109^{2}	105	59	55	10	2	55	61	1.459	4.51	64	4.24	.261	3	.097	-20	0	-2.5
Total	5	19	32	.373	96	70	4	2	2	431^{2}	371	200	162	37	11	213	236	1.353	3.38	89	3.64	.233	13	.103	-20	16	-2.9
• CLARK, Spider	Owen F. Clark b: 9/16/1867, Brooklyn, NY d: 2/8/1892, Brooklyn, NY TR, 5'10", 150 lbs. Deb: 5/2/1889 ♦																										
1890	Buf-P	0	0	....	1	0	0	0	0	4	8	4	3	0	0	2	2	2.500	6.75	61	....	.399	69	.265	-1	4	-0.4
• CLARK, Terry	Terry Lee Clark b: 10/18/1960, Los Angeles, CA BR/TR, 6'2", 196 lbs. Deb: 7/7/1988																										
1988	Cal-A	6	6	.500	15	15	2	1	0	94	120	54	53	8	0	31	39	1.606	5.07	76	5.35	.323	0	....	-12	3	-1.3
1989	Cal-A	0	2	.000	4	2	0	0	0	11	13	8	6	0	0	3	7	1.455	4.91	78	3.86	.310	0	....	-2	0	-0.2
1990	Hou-N	0	0	....	1	1	0	0	0	4	9	7	6	0	0	3	2	3.000	13.50	28	12.11	.429	1	.500	-4	0	-0.4
1995	Atl-N	0	0	....	3	0	0	0	0	3^{2}	3	2	2	0	0	5	2	2.182	4.91	87	6.15	.231	0	....	-0	0	0.0
	Bal-A	2	5	.286	38	0	0	0	1	39	40	15	15	3	1	15	18	1.410	3.46	137	3.97	.276	0	....	5	4	0.5
1996	KC-A	1	1	.500	12	0	0	0	0	17^{1}	28	15	15	3	0	7	12	2.019	7.79	64	8.21	.350	0	....	-5	0	-0.5
	Hou-N	0	2	.000	5	0	0	0	0	6^{1}	16	10	8	1	1	2	5	2.842	11.37	34	15.08	.471	0	....	-5	0	-0.5
1997	Cle-A	0	3	.000	4	4	0	0	0	26^{1}	29	21	18	3	0	13	13	1.595	6.15	76	5.09	.284	0	....	-4	0	-0.4
	Tex-A	1	4	.200	9	5	0	0	0	30^{2}	41	20	20	3	2	10	11	1.663	5.87	82	6.19	.325	1	1.000	-3	1	-0.3
	Yr.	1	7	.125	13	9	0	0	0	57	70	41	38	6	2	23	24	1.632	6.00	79	5.68	.307	1	1.000	-7	1	-0.7
Total	6	10	23	.303	91	27	2	1	1	232^{1}	299	152	143	21	4	89	109	1.670	5.54	77	5.74	.320	2	.667	-31	8	-3.0
• CLARK, Watty	William Watson "Lefty" Clark b: 5/16/1902, St. Joseph, LA d: 3/4/1972, Clearwater, FL BL/TL, 6'.5", 175 lbs. Deb: 5/28/1924																										
1924	Cle-A	1	3	.250	12	1	0	0	0	25^{2}	38	27	20	0	2	14	6	2.026	7.01	61	6.56	.345	2	.222	-8	0	-0.6
1927	Bro-N	7	2	.778	27	3	1	0	2	73^{2}	74	23	19	2	0	19	32	1.262	2.32	170	3.04	.265	3	.143	13	9	1.2
1928	Bro-N	12	9	.571	40	19	10	2	3	194^{2}	193	75	58	4	1	50	85	1.248	2.68	148	2.84	.259	10	.152	29	17	2.6
1929	Bro-N	16	19	.457	41	**36**	19	3	1	**279**	295	136	116	14	3	71	140	1.312	3.74	123	3.43	.270	16	.165	34	23	2.8
1930	Bro-N	13	13	.500	44	24	9	1	6	200	209	110	93	20	0	38	81	1.235	4.19	117	3.48	.271	14	.206	11	16	1.0
1931	Bro-N	14	10	.583	34	28	16	3	1	233^{1}	243	86	83	4	1	52	96	1.264	3.20	119	3.01	.267	21	.250	19	22	2.2
1932	Bro-N	20	12	.625	40	**36**	19	2	0	273	282	122	106	10	4	49	99	1.212	3.49	109	2.98	.264	21	.216	9	20	1.1
1933	Bro-N	2	4	.333	11	8	4	1	1	50^{2}	61	29	27	2	3	6	14	1.322	4.80	67	3.91	.303	2	.154	-8	1	-0.8
	NY-N	3	4	.429	16	5	0	0	0	44	58	25	23	3	1	11	11	1.568	4.70	68	5.04	.317	3	.273	-8	1	-0.8
	Yr.	5	8	.385	27	13	4	1	1	94^{2}	119	54	50	5	4	17	25	1.437	4.75	68	4.43	.310	5	.208	-16	2	-1.6
1934	NY-N	1	2	.333	5	4	1	0	0	18^{2}	23	15	14	5	0	5	6	1.500	6.75	57	5.99	.295	1	.167	-6	0	-0.6
	Bro-N	2	0	1.000	17	1	0	0	0	25^{1}	40	19	15	0	1	9	10	1.934	5.33	73	6.35	.345	1	.125	-4	1	-0.4
	Yr.	3	2	.600	22	5	1	0	0	44	63	34	29	5	1	14	16	1.750	5.93	66	6.20	.325	2	.143	-10	1	-1.0
1935	Bro-N	13	8	.619	33	25	11	1	0	207	215	93	76	11	1	28	35	1.174	3.30	120	2.93	.264	14	.177	13	14	1.3
1936	Bro-N	7	11	.389	33	16	1	1	2	120	162	73	59	11	0	28	28	1.583	4.43	93	5.19	.316	9	.231	-2	6	-0.2
1937	Bro-N	0	0	....	2	0	0	0	0	2^{1}	4	3	2	0	0	3	0	3.000	7.71	52	9.38	.308	0	....	-1	0	-0.1
Total	12	111	97	.534	355	206	91	14	16	1747^{1}	1897	836	711	86	17	383	643	1.305	3.66	111	3.47	.275	117	.196	92	130	8.7
• CLARKE, Dad	William H. Clarke b: 1/7/1865, Oswego, NY d: 6/3/1911, Lorian, OH BB/TR, 5'7" Deb: 4/23/1888																										
1888	Chi-N	1	0	1.000	2	2	1	0	0	16	23	17	9	2	2	6	6	1.813	5.06	59	....	.325	2	.286	-4	1	-0.2
1891	Col-a	1	2	.333	4	3	2	0	0	21	30	21	16	0	1	16	2	2.190	6.86	50	....	.325	1	.111	-9	0	-0.7
1894	NY-N	3	4	.429	15	6	5	0	1	84	114	76	46	3	3	26	15	1.667	4.93	106	5.35	.321	8	.216	2	6	0.1
1895	NY-N	18	15	.545	37	30	27	1	1	281^{2}	336	174	106	5	11	60	67	1.406	3.39	137	3.93	.292	29	.240	37	22	2.9
1896	NY-N	17	24	.415	48	40	33	1	1	351	431	246	166	9	11	60	66	1.399	4.26	99	4.00	.300	30	.204	-4	19	-0.6
1897	NY-N	2	1	.667	6	4	2	0	0	31	43	34	21	1	2	11	10	1.742	6.10	68	5.78	.326	3	.167	-7	0	-0.7
	Lou-N	2	4	.333	7	6	6	0	0	54^{2}	74	33	24	3	2	10	7	1.537	3.95	108	5.00	.321	5	.227	2	3	0.1
	Yr.	4	5	.444	13	10	8	0	0	85^{2}	117	67	45	4	4	21	17	1.611	4.73	89	5.28	.323	8	.200	-5	3	-0.6
1898	Lou-N	0	1	.000	1	1	1	0	0	9	10	7	5	1	2	2	1	1.333	5.00	71	4.87	.279	0	.000	-1	0	-0.2
Total	7	44	51	.463	120	92	77	2	3	848^{1}	1061	608	393	24	34	191	174	1.476	4.17	104	4.07	.303	78	.214	17	51	0.7
• CLARKE, Henry	Henry Tefft Clarke b: 8/28/1875, Bellevue, NE d: 3/28/1950, Colorado Springs, CO BR/TR Deb: 6/26/1897																										
1897	Cle-N	0	4	.000	5	4	3	0	0	30^{2}	32	29	21	4	3	12	3	1.435	6.16	73	4.80	.267	7	.280	-7	1	-0.7
1898	Chi-N	1	0	1.000	1	1	1	0	0	9	8	4	2	0	1	5	1	1.444	2.00	179	3.57	.237	1	.250	2	1	0.1
Total	2	1	4	.200	6	5	4	0	0	39^{2}	40	33	23	4	4	17	4	1.437	5.22	84	4.52	.260	8	.276	-6	2	-0.6
• CLARKE, Lefty	Alan Thomas Clarke b: 3/8/1896, Clarksville, MD d: 3/11/1975, Cheverly, MD BB/TL, 5'11", 180 lbs. Deb: 10/2/1921																										
1921	Cin-N	0	1	.000	1	1	1	0	0	5	7	7	3	0	0	2	1	1.800	5.40	66	5.12	.304	0	.000	-1	0	-0.1
• CLARKE, Rufe	Rufus Rivers Clarke b: 4/13/1900, Estill, SC d: 2/8/1983, Columbia, SC BR/TR, 6'1", 203 lbs. Deb: 9/3/1923																										
1923	Det-A	1	1	.500	5	0	0	0	0	6	6	3	3	0	1	6	2	2.000	4.50	86	6.68	.300	0	....	-0	0	0.0
1924	Det-A	0	0	....	2	0	0	0	0	5^{1}	3	2	2	0	1	5	1	1.500	3.38	122	3.21	.158	0	.000	0	0	0.0
Total	2	1	1	.500	7	0	0	0	0	11^{1}	9	5	5	0	2	11	3	1.765	3.97	100	5.05	.231	0	.000	0	0	0.0
• CLARKE, Stan	Stanley Martin Clarke b: 8/9/1960, Toledo, OH BL/TL, 6'1", 180 lbs. Deb: 6/7/1983																										
1983	Tor-A	1	1	.500	10	0	0	0	0	11	10	4	4	2	0	5	7	1.364	3.27	131	4.47	.256	0	....	1	1	0.1
1985	Tor-A	0	0	....	4	0	0	0	0	4	3	2	2	1	0	2	2	1.250	4.50	94	4.30	.214	0	....	-0	0	0.0
1986	Tor-A	0	1	.000	10	0	0	0	0	12^{2}	18	13	13	4	0	10	9	2.211	9.24	46	10.64	.375	0	....	-7	0	-0.7
1987	Sea-A	2	2	.500	22	0	0	0	0	23	31	14	14	7	0	10	13	1.783	5.48	86	7.95	.333	0	....	-2	1	-0.2
1989	KC-A	0	2	.000	2	2	0	0	0	7	14	12	12	2	0	4	2	2.571	15.43	25	14.07	.438	0	....	-9	0	-0.9
1990	StL-N	0	0	....	2	0	0	0	0	3^{1}	2	1	1	0	0	0	3	.600	2.70	141	0.75	.167	0	....	0	0	0.0
Total	6	3	6	.333	50	2	0	0	0	61	78	46	46	16	0	31	36	1.787	6.79	63	7.95	.328	0	....	-17	2	-1.6
• CLARKE, Webbo	Vibert Ernesto Clarke b: 6/8/1928, Colon, Panama d: 6/14/1970, Cristobal, Canal Zone BL/TL, 6', 165 lbs. Deb: 9/4/1955																										
1955	Was-A	0	0	....	7	2	0	0	0	21^{1}	17	11	11	2	0	14	9	1.453	4.64	83	3.90	.221	1	.167	-1	1	-0.2
• CLARKSON, Bill	William Henry "Blackie" Clarkson b: 9/27/1898, Portsmouth, VA d: 8/27/1971, Raleigh, NC BR/TR, 5'11", 160 lbs. Deb: 5/2/1927																										
1927	NY-N	3	9	.250	26	7	2	0	2	86^{2}	92	50	42	3	1	52	28	1.662	4.36	88	4.57	.280	1	.050	-5	3	-0.6
1928	NY-N	0	0	....	4	0	0	0	0	5^{2}	10	6	5	0	0	1	3	1.941	7.94	49	7.58	.455	0	....	-3	0	-0.3
	Bos-N	0	2	.000	19	1	0	0	0	34^{2}	53	29	26	2	1	22	8	2.163	6.75	58	7.40	.349	0	.000	-10	0	-1.0
	Yr.	0	2	.000	23	1	0	0	0	40^{1}	63	35	31	2	1	23	11	2.132	6.92	56	7.42	.362	0	.000	-12	0	-1.2
1929	Bos-N	0	1	.000	2	1	0	0	0	7	16	10	8	0	0	4	0	2.857	10.29	45	12.15	.485	1	.500	-4	0	-0.4
Total	3	3	12	.200	51	9	2	0	2	134	171	95	81	5	2	79	39	1.866	5.44	72	5.82	.319	2	.080	-21	3	-2.2
• CLARKSON, Dad	Arthur Hamilton Clarkson b: 8/31/1866, Cambridge, MA d: 2/5/1911, Somerville, MA BR/TR, 5'10", 165 lbs. Deb: 8/20/1891 U																										
1891	NY-N	1	2	.333	5	2	1	0	0	28	24	23	9	0	3	18	11	1.500	2.89	110	....	.223	4	.444	1	2	0.2

YEAR TM-L	W	L	PCT	G	GS	CG	SH	SV	IP	H	R	ER	HR	HB	BB	SO	RAT	ERA	ERA+	CERA	OAV	BH	AVG	PR+	WS	TPW
1892 Bos-N	1	0	1.000	1	1	1	0	0	7	5	1	1	0	0	3	0	1.143	1.29	273	1.99	.193	0	.000	2	1	0.1
1893 StL-N	12	9	.571	24	21	17	1	0	186^1	194	116	72	4	14	79	37	1.465	3.48	136	3.99	.260	10	.133	27	12	1.7
1894 StL-N	8	17	.320	32	32	24	1	0	233^1	318	236	165	9	11	117	46	1.864	6.36	85	6.18	.322	16	.182	-25	9	-2.1
1895 StL-N	1	6	.143	7	7	7	0	0	61	91	66	50	7	2	26	9	1.918	7.38	66	7.31	.340	1	.043	-16	0	-1.5
Bal-N	12	3	.800	20	14	10	0	0	142	169	84	61	5	4	64	23	1.641	3.87	123	4.86	.291	8	.140	5	12	0.1
Yr.	13	9	.591	27	21	17	0	0	203	260	150	111	12	6	90	32	1.724	4.92	97	5.60	.307	9	.113	-10	12	-1.4
1896 Bal-N	4	2	.667	7	4	3	0	0	47	72	40	26	1	2	18	7	1.915	4.98	86	6.60	.348	5	.278	-5	2	-0.3
Total 6	39	39	.500	96	81	63	2	0	704^2	873	566	384	26	36	325	133	1.700	4.90	100	5.17	.299	44	.161	-11	38	-1.8

• CLARKSON, John John Gibson Clarkson b: 7/1/1861, Cambridge, MA d: 2/4/1909, Belmont, MA BR/TR, 5'10", 155 lbs. Deb: 5/2/1882 U HOF: 1963

YEAR TM-L	W	L	PCT	G	GS	CG	SH	SV	IP	H	R	ER	HR	HB	BB	SO	RAT	ERA	ERA+	CERA	OAV	BH	AVG	PR+	WS	TPW
1882 Wor-N	1	2	.333	3	3	2	0	0	24	49	31	12	0	....	2	3	2.125	4.50	69	....	.399	4	.364	-3	1	-0.1
1884 Chi-N	10	3	.769	14	13	12	0	0	118	94	64	28	10	....	25	102	1.008	2.14	147	....	.207	22	.262	8	11	1.1
1885* Chi-N	**53**	16	.768	**70**	**70**	**68**	**10**	0	**623**	497	255	128	21	....	97	**308**	.953	1.85	164	....	.209	61	.216	**64**	**62**	**6.1**
1886* Chi-N	36	17	.679	55	55	50	3	0	466^2	419	248	125	20	....	86	313	1.082	2.41	150	....	.231	49	.233	44	42	4.1
1887 Chi-N	**38**	21	.644	**60**	**59**	**56**	2	0	**523**	605	283	179	20	8	92	**237**	1.157	3.08	145	....	.282	63	.279	**80**	**51**	**7.1**
1888 Bos-N	33	20	.623	54	54	53	3	0	**483^1**	448	247	148	17	10	119	223	1.173	2.76	104	....	.237	40	.195	1	32	0.3
1889 Bos-N	**49**	19	.721	**73**	**72**	**68**	**8**	1	**620**	589	280	188	16	17	203	**284**	1.277	**2.73**	**153**	....	.242	54	.206	**104**	**60**	**9.1**
1890 Bos-N	26	18	.591	44	44	43	2	0	383	370	186	139	14	16	140	138	1.332	3.27	114	....	.246	43	.249	22	33	2.3
1891 Bos-N	33	19	.635	55	51	47	3	**3**	460^2	435	244	143	18	15	154	141	1.279	2.79	131	....	.240	42	.225	45	42	4.4
1892 Bos-N	8	6	.571	16	16	15	4	0	145^2	115	65	38	4	5	60	48	1.201	2.35	149	2.57	.209	13	.228	14	16	1.5
* Cle-N	17	10	.630	29	28	27	1	1	243^1	235	132	69	4	4	72	91	1.262	2.55	133	2.93	.244	14	.139	23	17	1.7
Yr.	25	16	.610	45	44	42	5	1	389	350	197	107	8	9	132	139	1.239	2.48	139	2.80	.231	27	.171	38	33	3.2
1893 Cle-N	16	17	.485	36	35	31	0	0	295	358	240	146	11	5	95	62	1.536	4.45	110	4.50	.291	27	.206	15	16	0.9
1894 Cle-N	8	10	.444	22	18	13	1	0	150^2	173	109	74	6	0	46	28	1.454	4.42	123	4.03	.285	11	.200	18	13	1.2
Total 12	328	178	.648	531	518	485	37	5	4536^1	4387	2384	1417	161	80	1191	1978	1.209	2.81	134	0.67	.245	443	.223	436	396	39.7

• CLARKSON, Walter Walter Hamilton Clarkson b: 11/3/1878, Cambridge, MA d: 10/10/1946, Cambridge, MA BR/TR, 5'10", 150 lbs. Deb: 7/2/1904

YEAR TM-L	W	L	PCT	G	GS	CG	SH	SV	IP	H	R	ER	HR	HB	BB	SO	RAT	ERA	ERA+	CERA	OAV	BH	AVG	PR+	WS	TPW
1904 NY-A	1	2	.333	13	4	2	0	1	66^1	63	42	37	3	10	25	43	1.327	5.02	54	3.71	.251	7	.269	-18	1	-1.9
1905 NY-A	3	3	.500	9	4	3	0	0	46	40	26	20	1	2	13	35	1.152	3.91	75	2.54	.236	1	.053	-4	1	-0.7
1906 NY-A	9	4	.692	32	16	9	3	0	151	135	59	39	6	5	55	64	1.258	2.32	127	3.01	.242	8	.157	12	13	1.2
1907 NY-A	1	1	.500	5	2	0	0	0	17^1	19	12	12	1	2	8	3	1.558	6.23	45	5.30	.281	2	.286	-6	0	-0.7
Cle-A	4	6	.400	17	10	9	1	0	90^2	77	40	20	1	3	29	32	1.169	1.99	126	2.41	.233	1	.036	3	4	0.0
Yr.	5	7	.417	22	12	9	1	0	108	96	52	32	2	5	37	35	1.231	2.67	98	2.88	.241	3	.086	-3	4	-0.7
1908 Cle-A	0	0	....	2	1	0	0	0	3^1	6	4	4	0	2	2	1	2.400	10.80	22	11.66	.400	1	1.000	-3	0	-0.3
Total 5	18	16	.529	78	37	23	4	1	374^2	340	183	132	12	24	132	178	1.260	3.17	87	3.11	.244	20	.152	-17	19	-2.3

• CLARY, Marty Martin Keith Clary b: 4/3/1962, Detroit, MI BR/TR, 6'4", 190 lbs. Deb: 9/5/1987

YEAR TM-L	W	L	PCT	G	GS	CG	SH	SV	IP	H	R	ER	HR	HB	BB	SO	RAT	ERA	ERA+	CERA	OAV	BH	AVG	PR+	WS	TPW
1987 Atl-N	0	1	.000	7	1	0	0	0	14^2	20	13	10	2	1	4	7	1.636	6.14	71	6.21	.328	0	.000	-3	0	-0.3
1989 Atl-N	4	3	.571	18	17	2	1	0	108^2	103	47	38	6	1	31	30	1.233	3.15	116	3.05	.249	5	.161	7	7	0.8
1990 Atl-N	1	10	.091	33	14	0	0	0	101^2	128	72	64	9	1	39	44	1.643	5.67	71	5.35	.308	0	.000	-16	0	-1.9
Total 3	5	14	.263	58	32	2	1	0	225	251	132	112	17	3	74	81	1.444	4.48	87	4.29	.282	5	.083	-12	7	-1.4

• CLASET, Gowell Gowell Sylvester "Lefty" Claset b: 11/26/1907, Battle Creek, MI d: 3/8/1981, St. Petersburg, FL BB/TL, 6'3.5", 210 lbs. Deb: 4/12/1933

YEAR TM-L	W	L	PCT	G	GS	CG	SH	SV	IP	H	R	ER	HR	HB	BB	SO	RAT	ERA	ERA+	CERA	OAV	BH	AVG	PR+	WS	TPW
1933 Phi-A	2	0	1.000	8	1	0	0	0	11^1	23	15	12	1	0	11	1	3.000	9.53	45	12.88	.426	1	.500	-6	0	-0.5

• CLAUSEN, Fritz Frederick William Clausen b: 4/26/1869, New York, NY d: 2/11/1960, Memphis, TN BR/TL, 5'11", 190 lbs. Deb: 7/23/1892

YEAR TM-L	W	L	PCT	G	GS	CG	SH	SV	IP	H	R	ER	HR	HB	BB	SO	RAT	ERA	ERA+	CERA	OAV	BH	AVG	PR+	WS	TPW
1892 Lou-N	9	13	.409	24	24	24	2	0	200	181	120	68	3	3	87	94	1.340	3.06	100	3.06	.232	13	.155	-2	10	-0.4
1893 Lou-N	1	4	.200	5	5	3	0	0	33	41	25	22	2	1	22	4	1.909	6.00	73	6.21	.296	3	.214	-5	1	-0.5
Chi-N	6	2	.750	10	9	8	0	1	76	71	46	26	1	5	39	31	1.447	3.08	150	3.62	.240	4	.121	13	6	0.8
Yr.	7	6	.538	15	14	11	0	1	109	112	71	48	3	6	61	35	1.587	3.96	114	4.40	.258	7	.149	8	7	0.3
1894 Chi-N	0	1	.000	1	2	0	0	0	4^1	5	7	5	0	0	5	1	2.308	10.38	54	9.86	.360	0	.000	-2	0	-0.2
1896 Lou-N	0	2	.000	2	2	1	0	0	11	17	13	8	1	3	6	4	2.091	6.55	66	8.95	.350	0	.000	-2	0	-0.3
Total 4	16	22	.421	42	42	36	2	1	324^1	315	211	129	7	12	159	134	1.461	3.58	101	3.80	.247	20	.147	2	17	-0.5

• CLAUSS, Al Albert Stanley "Lefty" Clauss b: 6/24/1891, New Haven, CT d: 9/13/1952, New Haven, CT BR/TL, 5'10.5", 178 lbs. Deb: 4/22/1913

YEAR TM-L	W	L	PCT	G	GS	CG	SH	SV	IP	H	R	ER	HR	HB	BB	SO	RAT	ERA	ERA+	CERA	OAV	BH	AVG	PR+	WS	TPW
1913 Det-A	0	1	.000	5	1	0	0	0	13^1	11	9	7	0	2	12	1	1.725	4.73	62	4.43	.220	0	.000	-2	0	-0.3

• CLAUSSEN, Brandon Brandon Allen Falker Claussen b: 5/1/1979, Rapid City, SD BR/TL, 6'2", 175 lbs. Deb: 6/28/2003

YEAR TM-L	W	L	PCT	G	GS	CG	SH	SV	IP	H	R	ER	HR	HB	BB	SO	RAT	ERA	ERA+	CERA	OAV	BH	AVG	PR+	WS	TPW
2003 NY-A	1	0	1.000	1	1	0	0	0	6^1	8	2	1	1	0	1	5	1.421	1.42	307	4.89	.296	1	.250	2	1	0.2

• CLAY, Danny Danny Bruce Clay b: 10/24/1961, Sun Valley, CA BR/TR, 6'1", 190 lbs. Deb: 5/1/1988

YEAR TM-L	W	L	PCT	G	GS	CG	SH	SV	IP	H	R	ER	HR	HB	BB	SO	RAT	ERA	ERA+	CERA	OAV	BH	AVG	PR+	WS	TPW
1988 Phi-N	0	1	.000	17	0	0	0	0	24	27	17	16	5	0	21	12	2.000	6.00	59	7.81	.303	0	.000	-6	0	-0.7

• CLAY, Ken Kenneth Earl Clay b: 4/6/1954, Lynchburg, VA BR/TR, 6'3", 195 lbs. Deb: 6/7/1977

YEAR TM-L	W	L	PCT	G	GS	CG	SH	SV	IP	H	R	ER	HR	HB	BB	SO	RAT	ERA	ERA+	CERA	OAV	BH	AVG	PR+	WS	TPW
1977* NY-A	2	3	.400	21	3	0	0	1	55^2	53	32	27	6	1	24	20	1.383	4.37	90	3.99	.251	0	....	-4	2	-0.4
1978* NY-A	3	4	.429	28	6	0	0	0	75^2	89	41	36	3	2	21	32	1.454	4.28	85	4.12	.291	0	....	-6	2	-0.6
1979 NY-A	1	7	.125	32	5	0	0	2	78^1	88	49	47	12	2	25	28	1.443	5.40	75	5.00	.291	0	....	-13	1	-1.3
1980 Tex-A	2	3	.400	8	8	0	0	0	43	43	24	22	4	3	29	17	1.674	4.60	85	5.24	.256	0	....	-3	1	-0.3
1981 Sea-A	2	7	.222	22	14	0	0	0	101	116	62	52	10	3	42	32	1.564	4.63	83	5.16	.294	0	....	-7	2	-0.8
Total 5	10	24	.294	111	36	0	0	3	353^2	389	208	184	35	11	141	129	1.499	4.68	83	4.73	.281	0	....	-33	8	-3.3

• CLEAR, Mark Mark Alan Clear b: 5/27/1956, Los Angeles, CA BR/TR, 6'4", 215 lbs. Deb: 4/4/1979

YEAR TM-L	W	L	PCT	G	GS	CG	SH	SV	IP	H	R	ER	HR	HB	BB	SO	RAT	ERA	ERA+	CERA	OAV	BH	AVG	PR+	WS	TPW
1979* Cal-A★	11	5	.688	52	0	0	0	14	109	87	48	44	6	3	68	98	1.422	3.63	112	3.48	.219	0	....	6	10	0.6
1980 Cal-A	11	11	.500	58	0	0	0	9	106^1	82	51	39	2	5	65	105	1.382	3.30	119	3.09	.216	0	....	8	9	0.8
1981 Bos-A	8	3	.727	34	0	0	0	9	76^2	69	36	35	11	2	51	82	1.565	4.11	94	4.92	.239	0	....	-1	6	-0.1
1982 Bos-A★	14	9	.609	55	0	0	0	14	105	92	39	35	11	7	61	109	1.457	3.00	144	4.27	.238	0	....	17	14	1.7
1983 Bos-A	4	5	.444	48	0	0	0	4	96	101	71	67	10	3	68	81	1.760	6.28	69	5.71	.273	0	....	-20	1	-2.0
1984 Bos-A	8	3	.727	47	0	0	0	8	67	47	38	30	2	2	70	76	1.746	4.03	103	4.27	.198	0	....	3	6	0.3
1985 Bos-A	1	3	.250	41	0	0	0	3	55^2	45	26	23	1	5	50	55	1.707	3.72	115	4.30	.225	0	....	4	3	0.4
1986 Mil-A	5	5	.500	59	0	0	0	16	73^2	53	23	18	4	1	36	85	1.208	2.20	197	2.62	.201	0	....	18	13	1.8
1987 Mil-A	8	5	.615	58	1	0	0	6	78^1	70	46	39	9	5	55	81	1.596	4.48	102	4.92	.239	0	....	1	6	0.1
1988 Mil-A	1	0	1.000	25	0	0	0	0	29	23	12	9	4	0	21	26	1.517	2.79	142	4.40	.215	0	....	4	2	0.4
1990 Cal-A	0	0	....	4	0	0	0	0	7^2	5	7	5	0	2	9	6	1.826	5.87	65	5.25	.200	0	....	-2	0	-0.2
Total 11	71	49	.592	481	1	0	0	83	804^1	674	397	344	60	35	554	804	1.527	3.85	109	4.17	.228	0	....	39	70	3.8

• CLEARY, Joe Joseph Christopher "Fire" Cleary b: 12/3/1918, Cork, Ireland BR/TR, 5'9", 150 lbs. Deb: 8/4/1945

YEAR TM-L	W	L	PCT	G	GS	CG	SH	SV	IP	H	R	ER	HR	HB	BB	SO	RAT	ERA	ERA+	CERA	OAV	BH	AVG	PR+	WS	TPW
1945 Was-A	0	0	....	1	0	0	0	0	0^1	5	7	7	0	0	3	1	24.00	189.00	2	167.67	.833	0		-7	0	-0.7

• CLEMENS, Roger William Roger "Rocket" Clemens b: 8/4/1962, Dayton, OH BR/TR, 6'4", 220 lbs. Deb: 5/15/1984

YEAR TM-L	W	L	PCT	G	GS	CG	SH	SV	IP	H	R	ER	HR	HB	BB	SO	RAT	ERA	ERA+	CERA	OAV	BH	AVG	PR+	WS	TPW
1984 Bos-A	9	4	.692	21	20	5	1	0	133^1	146	67	64	13	2	29	126	1.313	4.32	96	3.81	.271	0	....	2	8	0.2
1985 Bos-A	7	5	.583	15	15	3	1	0	98^1	83	38	36	5	3	37	74	1.220	3.29	130	2.96	.228	0	....	12	8	1.2
1986* Bos-A★	**24**	4	.857	33	33	10	1	0	254	179	77	70	21	4	67	238	.969	**2.48**	**168**	**2.03**	**.195**	0	....	**50**	**29**	**4.9**
1987 Bos-A	**20**	9	.690	36	36	**18**	**7**	0	281^2	248	100	93	19	9	83	256	1.175	2.97	153	2.94	.235	0	....	**51**	**28**	**4.8**
1988* Bos-A★	18	12	.600	35	35	**14**	**8**	0	264	217	93	86	17	6	62	**291**	1.057	2.93	140	2.36	.220	0	....	38	22	3.9
1989 Bos-A	17	11	.607	35	35	8	3	0	253^1	215	101	88	20	8	93	230	1.216	3.13	131	3.13	.231	0	....	30	18	3.0
1990* Bos-A★	21	6	.778	31	31	7	**4**	0	228^1	193	59	49	7	7	54	209	1.082	**1.93**	**211**	2.33	.228	0	....	**59**	**28**	**6.0**
1991 Bos-A★	18	10	.643	35	**35**	13	**4**	0	**271^1**	219	93	79	15	5	65	**241**	1.047	**2.62**	**164**	2.23	.221	0	....	**51**	**26**	**5.1**
1992 Bos-A★	18	11	.621	32	32	11	**5**	0	246^2	203	80	66	11	9	62	208	1.074	**2.41**	**175**	2.38	.224	0	....	**49**	**26**	**5.0**
1993 Bos-A	11	14	.440	29	29	2	1	0	191^2	175	99	95	17	11	67	160	1.263	4.46	103	3.53	.244	0	....	2	11	0.2
1994 Bos-A	9	7	.563	24	24	3	1	0	170^2	124	62	54	15	4	71	168	1.143	2.85	**176**	2.72	**.203**	0	....	**40**	16	**3.7**
1995* Bos-A	10	5	.667	23	23	0	0	0	140	141	70	65	15	14	60	132	1.436	4.18	116	4.67	.259	0	....	10	10	0.9

YEAR TM-L	W	L	PCT	G	GS	CG	SH	SV	IP	H	R	ER	HR	HB	BB	SO	RAT	ERA	ERA+	CERA	OAV	BH	AVG	PR+	WS	TPW
1996 Bos-A	10	13	.435	34	34	6	2	0	242^2	216	106	98	19	4	106	**257**	1.327	3.63	140	3.52	.237	1	1.000	44	20	4.1
1997 Tor-A★	**21**	7	.750	34	34	**9**	**3**	0	**264**	204	65	60	9	12	68	**292**	1.030	**2.05**	**225**	**2.17**	.213	1	.500	**70**	**32**	**6.8**
1998 Tor-A★	**20**	6	.769	33	33	5	3	0	234^2	169	78	69	11	7	88	**271**	1.095	**2.65**	**176**	**2.27**	**.197**	0	.000	**52**	**25**	**4.9**
1999* NY-A	14	10	.583	30	30	1	1	0	187^2	185	101	96	20	9	90	163	1.465	4.60	103	4.59	.261	0	.000	4	10	0.3
2000* NY-A	13	8	.619	32	32	1	0	0	204^1	184	96	84	26	10	84	188	1.312	3.70	131	3.93	.236	0	.000	29	16	2.7
2001* NY-A★	20	3	.870	33	33	0	0	0	220^1	205	94	86	19	5	72	213	1.257	3.51	128	3.43	.246	0	.000	28	19	2.7
2002* NY-A	13	6	.684	29	29	0	0	0	180	172	94	87	18	7	63	192	1.306	4.35	100	3.72	.250	2	.667	6	11	0.7
2003* NY-A★	17	9	.654	33	33	1	1	0	211^2	199	99	92	24	5	58	190	1.214	3.91	112	3.44	.247	0	.000	16	15	1.5
Total 20	310	160	.660	607	606	117	46	0	4278^2	3677	1672	1517	321	141	1379	4099	1.182	3.19	140	3.00	.231	4	.200	644	378	62.6

• CLEMENSEN, Bill William Melville Clemensen b: 6/20/1919, New Brunswick, NJ d: 2/18/1994, Alta, CA BR/TR, 6'1", 193 lbs. Deb: 5/22/1939

YEAR TM-L	W	L	PCT	G	GS	CG	SH	SV	IP	H	R	ER	HR	HB	BB	SO	RAT	ERA	ERA+	CERA	OAV	BH	AVG	PR+	WS	TPW
1939 Pit-N	0	1	.000	12	1	0	0	0	27	32	26	22	0	3	20	13	1.926	7.33	52	5.87	.311	2	.333	-10	0	-0.9
1941 Pit-N	1	0	1.000	2	1	1	0	0	13	7	5	4	0	0	7	4	1.077	2.77	130	1.53	.159	0	.000	1	1	0.1
1946 Pit-N	0	0	....	1	0	0	0	0	2	0	0	0	0	0	0	2	.000	0.00	....	0.00	.000	0	....	1	0	0.1
Total 3	1	1	.500	15	2	1	0	0	42	39	31	26	0	3	27	19	1.571	5.57	68	4.25	.265	2	.200	-8	1	-0.7

• CLEMENT, Matt Matthew Paul Clement b: 8/12/1974, McCandless, PA BR/TR, 6'3", 195 lbs. Deb: 9/6/1998

YEAR TM-L	W	L	PCT	G	GS	CG	SH	SV	IP	H	R	ER	HR	HB	BB	SO	RAT	ERA	ERA+	CERA	OAV	BH	AVG	PR+	WS	TPW
1998 SD-N	2	0	1.000	4	2	0	0	0	13^2	15	8	7	0	0	7	13	1.610	4.61	85	4.14	.283	0	.000	-1	1	-0.1
1999 SD-N	10	12	.455	31	31	0	0	0	180^2	190	106	90	18	9	86	135	1.528	4.48	94	4.89	.273	4	.077	-7	6	-0.9
2000 SD-N	13	17	.433	34	34	0	0	0	205	194	131	117	22	16	125	170	1.556	5.14	84	4.87	.248	4	.067	-21	5	-2.3
2001 Fla-N	9	10	.474	31	31	0	0	0	169^1	172	102	95	15	15	85	134	1.518	5.05	83	4.84	.267	4	.080	-17	4	-1.8
2002 Chi-N	12	11	.522	32	32	3	2	0	205	162	84	82	18	6	85	215	1.205	3.60	112	2.96	.215	3	.049	11	11	0.8
2003* Chi-N	14	12	.538	32	32	2	1	0	201^2	169	100	92	22	14	79	171	1.230	4.11	102	3.47	.227	9	.145	2	11	0.2
Total 6	60	62	.492	164	162	5	3	0	975^1	902	531	483	95	60	467	838	1.404	4.46	94	4.17	.246	24	.084	-33	38	-4.1

• CLEMENTS, Pat Patrick Brian Clements b: 2/2/1962, McCloud, CA BR/TL, 6', 180 lbs. Deb: 4/9/1985

YEAR TM-L	W	L	PCT	G	GS	CG	SH	SV	IP	H	R	ER	HR	HB	BB	SO	RAT	ERA	ERA+	CERA	OAV	BH	AVG	PR+	WS	TPW
1985 Cal-A	5	0	1.000	41	0	0	0	1	62	47	23	23	4	2	25	19	1.161	3.34	123	2.76	.218	0	....	3	6	0.3
Pit-N	0	2	.000	27	0	0	0	2	34^1	39	14	14	2	0	15	17	1.573	3.67	97	4.54	.289	1	.333	0	2	0.0
1986 Pit-N	0	4	.000	65	0	0	0	2	61	53	20	19	1	2	32	31	1.393	2.80	137	3.32	.251	0	.000	7	4	0.7
1987 NY-A	3	3	.500	55	0	0	0	7	80	91	45	44	4	3	30	36	1.513	4.95	89	4.62	.299	0	....	-5	5	-0.5
1988 NY-A	0	0	....	6	1	0	0	0	8^1	12	8	6	1	0	4	3	1.920	6.48	61	7.06	.343	0	....	-2	0	-0.2
1989 SD-N	4	1	.800	23	1	0	0	0	39	39	17	17	4	0	15	18	1.385	3.92	89	3.84	.267	0	.000	-2	2	-0.3
1990 SD-N	0	0	....	9	0	0	0	0	13	20	9	6	1	0	7	6	2.077	4.15	92	7.79	.357	0	....	-1	0	-0.1
1991 SD-N	1	0	1.000	12	0	0	0	0	14^1	13	8	6	0	0	9	8	1.535	3.77	101	3.24	.255	0	.000	-0	1	0.0
1992 SD-N	2	1	.667	27	0	0	0	0	23^2	25	9	7	0	2	12	11	1.563	2.66	134	4.18	.281	0	.000	2	2	0.3
Bal-A	2	0	1.000	23	0	0	0	0	24^2	23	10	9	0	2	11	9	1.378	3.28	122	3.56	.258	0	....	2	2	0.2
Total 8	17	11	.607	288	2	0	0	12	360^1	362	163	151	17	11	160	158	1.449	3.77	105	4.00	.272	1	.059	4	24	0.4

• CLEMONS, Chris Christopher Hale Clemons b: 10/31/1972, Baytown, TX BR/TR, 6'4", 220 lbs. Deb: 7/23/1997

YEAR TM-L	W	L	PCT	G	GS	CG	SH	SV	IP	H	R	ER	HR	HB	BB	SO	RAT	ERA	ERA+	CERA	OAV	BH	AVG	PR+	WS	TPW
1997 Chi-A	0	2	.000	5	2	0	0	0	12^2	19	13	12	4	1	11	8	2.368	8.53	51	11.84	.345	0	....	-6	0	-0.5

• CLEMONS, Lance Lance Levis Clemons b: 7/6/1947, Philadelphia, PA BL/TL, 6'2", 205 lbs. Deb: 8/12/1971

YEAR TM-L	W	L	PCT	G	GS	CG	SH	SV	IP	H	R	ER	HR	HB	BB	SO	RAT	ERA	ERA+	CERA	OAV	BH	AVG	PR+	WS	TPW
1971 KC-A	1	0	1.000	10	3	0	0	0	24	26	16	11	2	1	12	20	1.583	4.13	83	4.73	.263	2	.286	-2	1	0.1
1972 StL-N	0	1	.000	3	1	0	0	0	5^1	8	7	6	1	1	5	2	2.438	10.13	34	11.88	.364	0	.000	-4	0	-0.4
1974 Bos-A	1	0	1.000	6	0	0	0	0	6^1	8	8	7	1	1	4	1	1.895	9.95	39	6.66	.296	0	....	-4	0	-0.4
Total 3	2	1	.667	19	4	0	0	0	35^2	42	31	24	4	3	21	23	1.766	6.06	58	6.14	.284	2	.250	-10	1	-0.8

• CLEVELAND, Reggie Reginald Leslie Cleveland b: 5/23/1948, Swift Current, Canada BR/TR, 6'1", 195 lbs. Deb: 10/1/1969

YEAR TM-L	W	L	PCT	G	GS	CG	SH	SV	IP	H	R	ER	HR	HB	BB	SO	RAT	ERA	ERA+	CERA	OAV	BH	AVG	PR+	WS	TPW
1969 StL-N	0	0	....	1	1	0	0	0	4	7	4	4	0	0	1	3	2.000	9.00	40	6.98	.368	0	.000	-2	0	-0.3
1970 StL-N	0	4	.000	16	1	0	0	0	26	31	27	22	3	0	18	22	1.885	7.62	54	5.84	.298	1	.250	-10	0	-1.0
1971 StL-N	12	12	.500	34	34	10	2	0	222	238	107	99	20	6	53	148	1.311	4.01	90	3.75	.271	14	.171	-5	9	-0.6
1972 StL-N	14	15	.483	33	33	11	3	0	230^2	229	120	101	21	5	60	153	1.253	3.94	86	3.42	.258	17	.239	-14	10	-1.2
1973 StL-N	14	10	.583	32	32	6	3	0	224	211	88	75	13	4	61	122	1.214	3.01	121	2.95	.246	17	.230	16	13	2.0
1974 Bos-A	12	14	.462	41	27	10	0	0	221^1	234	121	106	25	9	69	103	1.369	4.31	89	4.24	.271	0	....	-9	9	-1.0
1975* Bos-A	13	9	.591	31	20	3	1	0	170^2	173	90	84	19	3	52	78	1.318	4.43	92	3.92	.263	0	....	-7	10	-0.7
1976 Bos-A	10	9	.526	41	14	3	0	2	170	159	73	58	3	4	61	76	1.294	3.07	127	3.05	.246	0	....	18	12	1.9
1977 Bos-A	11	8	.579	36	27	9	1	2	190^1	211	97	90	20	4	43	85	1.335	4.26	105	4.11	.281	0	....	8	13	0.8
1978 Bos-A	0	1	.000	1	0	0	0	0	0^1	1	1	0	0	0	0	0	3.000	0.00	....	9.49	.333	0	....	0	0	0.0
Tex-A	5	7	.417	53	0	0	0	12	75^2	65	33	26	5	3	23	46	1.163	3.09	121	2.74	.236	0	....	6	8	0.6
Yr.	5	8	.385	54	0	0	0	12	76	66	34	26	5	3	23	46	1.171	3.08	122	2.77	.237	0	....	6	8	0.6
1979 Mil-A	1	5	.167	29	1	0	0	4	55	77	44	41	9	0	23	22	1.818	6.71	62	6.96	.344	0	....	-15	0	-1.5
1980 Mil-A	11	9	.550	45	13	5	2	4	154^1	150	73	64	9	5	49	54	1.289	3.73	104	3.40	.254	0	....	1	9	0.1
1981 Mil-A	2	3	.400	35	0	0	0	1	64^2	57	41	37	5	1	30	18	1.345	5.15	67	3.56	.239	0	....	-13	0	-1.4
Total 13	105	106	.498	428	203	57	12	25	1809	1843	919	807	152	44	543	930	1.319	4.01	95	3.71	.264	49	.211	-28	93	-2.3

• CLEVENGER, Tex Truman Eugene Clevenger b: 7/9/1932, Visalia, CA BR/TR, 6'1", 180 lbs. Deb: 4/18/1954

YEAR TM-L	W	L	PCT	G	GS	CG	SH	SV	IP	H	R	ER	HR	HB	BB	SO	RAT	ERA	ERA+	CERA	OAV	BH	AVG	PR+	WS	TPW
1954 Bos-A	2	4	.333	23	8	1	0	0	67^2	67	42	36	9	2	29	43	1.419	4.79	86	4.32	.262	3	.214	-4	2	-0.4
1956 Was-A	0	0	....	20	1	0	0	0	31^2	33	22	19	4	0	21	17	1.705	5.40	80	5.45	.264	0	.000	-3	1	-0.3
1957 Was-A	7	6	.538	52	9	2	0	8	139^2	139	69	65	11	4	47	75	1.332	4.19	93	3.70	.261	7	.212	-1	9	0.0
1958 Was-A	9	9	.500	**55**	4	0	0	6	124	119	65	60	12	1	50	70	1.363	4.35	88	3.76	.251	3	.136	-4	7	-0.4
1959 Was-A	8	5	.615	50	7	2	2	8	117^1	114	56	51	8	2	51	71	1.406	3.91	100	3.84	.256	4	.174	4	9	0.6
1960 Was-A	5	11	.313	53	11	1	0	7	128^2	150	77	60	10	3	49	49	1.547	4.20	94	4.75	.298	2	.091	-2	5	-0.3
1961 LA-A	2	1	.667	12	0	0	0	1	16	13	5	3	1	0	13	11	1.625	1.69	267	4.25	.220	0	.000	5	2	0.5
NY-A	1	1	.500	21	0	0	0	0	31^2	35	20	17	3	1	21	14	1.768	4.83	77	5.90	.287	1	.250	-5	1	-0.4
Yr.	3	2	.600	33	0	0	0	1	47^2	48	25	20	4	1	34	25	1.720	3.78	101	5.34	.265	1	.143	0	3	0.0
1962 NY-A	2	0	1.000	21	0	0	0	0	38	36	14	12	3	1	17	11	1.395	2.84	132	3.72	.248	0	.000	3	3	0.3
Total 8	36	37	.493	307	40	6	2	30	694^2	706	370	323	61	14	298	361	1.445	4.18	94	4.18	.265	20	.157	-6	39	-0.5

• CLIBURN, Stew Stewart Walker Cliburn b: 12/19/1956, Jackson, MS BR/TR, 6', 195 lbs. Deb: 9/17/1984

YEAR TM-L	W	L	PCT	G	GS	CG	SH	SV	IP	H	R	ER	HR	HB	BB	SO	RAT	ERA	ERA+	CERA	OAV	BH	AVG	PR+	WS	TPW
1984 Cal-A	0	0	....	1	0	0	0	0	2	3	3	3	0	0	1	1	2.000	13.50	29	5.47	.333	0	....	-2	0	-0.2
1985 Cal-A	9	3	.750	44	0	0	0	6	99	87	25	23	5	1	26	48	1.141	2.09	197	2.62	.241	0	....	19	13	1.9
1988 Cal-A	4	2	.667	40	1	0	0	0	84	83	45	38	11	6	32	42	1.369	4.07	95	4.38	.266	0	....	-2	4	-0.2
Total 3	13	5	.722	85	1	0	0	6	185	173	73	64	16	7	59	91	1.254	3.11	127	3.45	.254	0	....	15	17	1.5

• CLONINGER, Tony Tony Lee Cloninger b: 8/13/1940, Lincoln, NC BR/TR, 6', 210 lbs. Deb: 6/15/1961 C

YEAR TM-L	W	L	PCT	G	GS	CG	SH	SV	IP	H	R	ER	HR	HB	BB	SO	RAT	ERA	ERA+	CERA	OAV	BH	AVG	PR+	WS	TPW
1961 Mil-N	7	2	.778	19	10	3	0	0	84	84	49	49	16	1	33	51	1.393	5.25	71	4.71	.258	5	.167	-14	2	-1.4
1962 Mil-N	8	3	.727	24	15	4	1	0	111	113	61	53	10	1	46	69	1.432	4.30	88	4.18	.264	4	.103	-7	5	-0.8
1963 Mil-N	9	11	.450	41	18	4	2	1	145^1	131	68	61	17	2	63	100	1.335	3.78	85	3.68	.239	5	.135	-11	5	-1.3
1964 Mil-N	19	14	.576	38	34	15	3	2	242^2	206	112	96	20	3	82	163	1.187	3.56	99	2.92	.231	21	.241	-1	12	0.2
1965 Mil-N	24	11	.686	40	38	16	1	1	279	247	115	102	20	3	119	211	1.312	3.29	107	3.38	.236	17	.162	6	19	0.8
1966 Atl-N	14	11	.560	39	38	11	1	1	257^2	253	134	118	29	6	116	178	**1.432**	4.12	88	4.26	.258	26	.234	-14	11	-0.5
1967 Atl-N	4	7	.364	16	16	1	0	0	76^2	85	50	44	13	0	31	55	1.513	5.17	64	5.17	.285	5	.200	-16	0	-1.7
1968 Atl-N	1	3	.250	8	1	0	0	0	19	15	9	9	0	0	11	7	1.368	4.26	70	2.80	.227	0	.000	-3	0	-0.4
Cin-N	4	3	.571	17	17	2	2	0	91^1	81	49	41	7	3	48	65	1.412	4.04	78	3.68	.233	7	.206	-8	3	-0.6
Yr.	5	6	.455	25	18	2	2	0	110^1	96	58	50	7	3	59	72	1.405	4.08	77	3.53	.232	7	.184	-11	3	-1.0
1969 Cin-N	11	17	.393	35	34	6	2	0	189^2	184	123	106	24	5	103	103	**1.513**	5.03	75	4.67	.250	12	.167	-27	2	-2.7
1970* Cin-N	9	7	.563	30	18	0	0	1	148	136	69	63	10	4	78	56	1.446	3.83	109	4.00	.249	10	.213	5	10	0.8
1971 Cin-N	3	6	.333	28	8	1	1	0	97^1	79	42	42	12	4	49	51	1.315	3.88	84	3.77	.230	7	.259	-9	4	-0.8
1972 StL-N	0	2	.000	17	0	0	0	0	26	29	17	15	2	1	19	11	1.846	5.19	65	5.95	.293	0	.000	-5	0	-0.6
Total 12	113	97	.538	352	247	63	13	6	1767^2	1643	898	799	180	33	798	1120	1.381	4.07	87	3.92	.247	119	.192	-105	73	-9.0

• CLONTZ, Brad — John Bradley Clontz b: 4/25/1971, Stuart, VA BR/TR, 6'1", 180 lbs. Deb: 4/26/1995

YEAR TM-L	W	L	PCT	G	GS	CG	SH	SV	IP	H	R	ER	HR	HB	BB	SO	RAT	ERA	ERA+	CERA	OAV	BH	AVG	PR+	WS	TPW
1995* Atl-N	8	1	.889	59	0	0	0	4	69	71	29	28	5	4	22	55	1.348	3.65	117	3.89	.269	0	.000	6	8	0.5
1996* Atl-N	6	3	.667	**81**	0	0	0	1	80^2	78	53	51	11	2	33	49	1.376	5.69	77	4.09	.255	0	.000	-10	3	-1.0
1997 Atl-N	5	1	.833	51	0	0	0	1	48	52	24	20	3	1	18	42	1.458	3.75	112	4.32	.286	0	.000	2	4	0.2
1998 LA-N	2	0	1.000	18	0	0	0	0	20^2	15	13	13	3	2	10	14	1.210	5.66	70	3.30	.200	0	.000	-4	1	-0.4
NY-N	0	0	....	2	0	0	0	0	3	4	3	3	1	0	2	2	2.000	9.00	46	9.77	.333	0	....	-2	0	-0.2
Yr.	2	0	1.000	20	0	0	0	0	23^2	19	16	16	4	2	12	16	1.310	6.08	66	4.12	.218	0	.000	-5	1	-0.6
1999 Pit-N	1	3	.250	56	0	0	0	2	49^1	49	21	15	6	3	24	40	1.480	2.74	167	4.52	.254	0	.000	10	5	0.9
2000 Pit-N	0	0	....	5	0	0	0	0	7	7	4	4	1	0	11	8	2.571	5.14	89	9.01	.269	0	....	-0	0	0.0
Total 6	22	8	.733	272	0	0	0	8	277^2	276	147	134	30	12	120	210	1.426	4.34	99	4.28	.261	0	.000	2	21	0.1

• CLOSTER, Al — Alan Edward Closter b: 6/15/1943, Creighton, NE BL/TL, 6'2", 190 lbs. Deb: 4/19/1966

YEAR TM-L	W	L	PCT	G	GS	CG	SH	SV	IP	H	R	ER	HR	HB	BB	SO	RAT	ERA	ERA+	CERA	OAV	BH	AVG	PR+	WS	TPW
1966 Was-A	0	0	....	1	0	0	0	0	0^1	1	0	0	0	0	2	0	9.000	0.00	....	44.74	.500	0	....	0	0	0.0
1971 NY-A	2	2	.500	14	1	0	0	0	28^1	33	22	16	4	2	13	22	1.624	5.08	64	5.21	.289	0	.000	-6	0	-0.7
1972 NY-A	0	0	....	2	0	0	0	0	2^1	2	3	3	1	0	4	2	2.571	11.57	25	12.78	.250	0	.000	-2	0	-0.3
1973 Atl-N	0	0	....	4	0	0	0	0	4^1	7	7	7	1	0	4	2	2.538	14.54	27	11.30	.389	0	....	-5	0	-0.5
Total 4	2	2	.500	21	1	0	0	0	35^1	43	32	26	6	2	23	26	1.868	6.62	51	6.83	.303	0	.000	-13	0	-1.5

• CLOUDE, Ken — Kenneth Brian Cloude b: 1/9/1975, Baltimore, MD BR/TR, 6'1", 200 lbs. Deb: 8/9/1997

YEAR TM-L	W	L	PCT	G	GS	CG	SH	SV	IP	H	R	ER	HR	HB	BB	SO	RAT	ERA	ERA+	CERA	OAV	BH	AVG	PR+	WS	TPW
1997 Sea-A	4	2	.667	10	9	0	0	0	51	41	32	29	8	3	26	46	1.314	5.12	88	4.04	.218	0	.000	-3	2	-0.3
1998 Sea-A	8	10	.444	30	30	0	0	0	155^1	187	116	110	29	3	80	114	1.719	6.37	73	6.46	.296	0	.000	-28	2	-2.6
1999 Sea-A	4	4	.500	31	6	0	0	1	72^1	106	67	64	10	5	46	35	2.101	7.96	63	8.54	.346	0	.000	-24	0	-2.2
Total 3	16	16	.500	71	45	0	0	1	278^2	334	215	203	47	11	152	195	1.744	6.56	72	6.56	.297	0	.000	-54	4	-5.2

• CLOUGH, Ed — Edgar George "Big Ed,Spec" Clough b: 10/28/1906, Wiconisco, PA d: 1/30/1944, Harrisburg, PA BL/TL, 6', 188 lbs. Deb: 8/28/1924 ♦

YEAR TM-L	W	L	PCT	G	GS	CG	SH	SV	IP	H	R	ER	HR	HB	BB	SO	RAT	ERA	ERA+	CERA	OAV	BH	AVG	PR+	WS	TPW
1925 StL-N	0	1	.000	3	1	0	0	0	10	11	9	9	1	1	5	3	1.600	8.10	53	5.42	.289	1	.250	-4	0	-0.4
1926 StL-N	0	0	....	1	0	0	0	0	2	5	6	5	0	1	3	0	4.000	22.50	17	19.65	.556	0	.000	-4	0	-0.4
Total 2	0	1	.000	4	1	0	0	0	12	16	15	14	1	2	8	3	2.000	10.50	40	7.79	.340	2	.105	-8	0	-0.8

• CLOWERS, Bill — William Perry Clowers b: 8/14/1898, San Marcos, TX d: 1/13/1978, Sweeney, TX BL/TL, 5'11", 175 lbs. Deb: 7/20/1926

YEAR TM-L	W	L	PCT	G	GS	CG	SH	SV	IP	H	R	ER	HR	HB	BB	SO	RAT	ERA	ERA+	CERA	OAV	BH	AVG	PR+	WS	TPW
1926 Bos-A	0	0	....	2	0	0	0	0	1^2	2	1	0	0	0	0	0	1.200	0.00	....	2.46	.333	0	....	1	0	0.1

• CLUTTERBUCK, Bryan — Bryan Richard Clutterbuck b: 12/17/1959, Detroit, MI BR/TR, 6'4", 223 lbs. Deb: 7/18/1986

YEAR TM-L	W	L	PCT	G	GS	CG	SH	SV	IP	H	R	ER	HR	HB	BB	SO	RAT	ERA	ERA+	CERA	OAV	BH	AVG	PR+	WS	TPW
1986 Mil-A	0	1	.000	20	0	0	0	0	56^2	68	32	27	8	2	16	38	1.482	4.29	101	5.15	.296	0	....	1	2	0.1
1989 Mil-A	2	5	.286	14	11	1	0	0	67^1	73	39	31	11	0	16	29	1.322	4.14	93	4.22	.269	0	....	-3	2	-0.3
Total 2	2	6	.250	34	11	1	0	0	124	141	71	58	19	2	32	67	1.395	4.21	96	4.64	.281	0	....	-2	4	-0.2

• CLYDE, David — David Eugene Clyde b: 4/22/1955, Kansas City, KS BL/TL, 6'1.5", 185 lbs. Deb: 6/27/1973

YEAR TM-L	W	L	PCT	G	GS	CG	SH	SV	IP	H	R	ER	HR	HB	BB	SO	RAT	ERA	ERA+	CERA	OAV	BH	AVG	PR+	WS	TPW
1973 Tex-A	4	8	.333	18	18	0	0	0	93^1	106	63	52	8	4	54	74	1.714	5.01	74	5.75	.293	0	....	-11	1	-1.1
1974 Tex-A	3	9	.250	28	21	4	0	0	117	129	64	57	14	4	47	52	1.504	4.38	81	5.03	.286	0	....	-11	3	-1.2
1975 Tex-A	0	1	.000	1	1	0	0	0	7	6	3	2	0	0	6	2	1.714	2.57	146	4.79	.273	0	....	1	0	0.1
1978 Cle-A	8	11	.421	28	25	5	0	0	153^1	166	80	73	4	3	60	83	1.474	4.28	87	4.03	.280	0	....	-8	6	-0.8
1979 Cle-A	3	4	.429	9	8	1	0	0	45^2	50	33	30	7	1	13	17	1.380	5.91	72	4.67	.279	0	....	-7	1	-0.7
Total 5	18	33	.353	84	73	10	0	0	416^1	457	243	214	33	12	180	228	1.530	4.63	81	4.78	.285	0	....	-37	11	-3.8

• CLYDE, Tom — Thomas Knox Clyde b: 8/17/1923, Wachapreague, VA BR/TR, 6'3", 195 lbs. Deb: 5/31/1943

YEAR TM-L	W	L	PCT	G	GS	CG	SH	SV	IP	H	R	ER	HR	HB	BB	SO	RAT	ERA	ERA+	CERA	OAV	BH	AVG	PR+	WS	TPW
1943 Phi-A	0	0	....	4	0	0	0	0	6	7	8	6	1	1	4	0	1.833	9.00	38	6.55	.304	0	.000	-4	0	-0.4

• COAKLEY, Andy — Andrew James Coakley b: 11/20/1882, Providence, RI d: 9/27/1963, New York, NY BL/TR, 6', 165 lbs. Deb: 9/17/1902

YEAR TM-L	W	L	PCT	G	GS	CG	SH	SV	IP	H	R	ER	HR	HB	BB	SO	RAT	ERA	ERA+	CERA	OAV	BH	AVG	PR+	WS	TPW
1902 Phi-A	2	1	.667	3	3	3	0	0	27	25	15	8	0	2	9	9	1.259	2.67	137	2.96	.246	3	.375	3	3	0.4
1903 Phi-A	0	3	.000	6	3	2	0	0	37^2	48	31	23	2	2	11	20	1.566	5.50	55	4.98	.309	3	.200	-10	0	-1.1
1904 Phi-A	4	3	.571	8	8	7	2	0	62	48	19	13	1	2	23	33	1.145	1.89	142	2.29	.215	2	.087	7	5	0.5
1905* Phi-A	18	8	.692	35	31	21	3	0	255	227	93	52	2	6	73	145	1.176	1.84	144	2.50	.241	13	.138	31	21	3.0
1906 Phi-A	7	8	.467	22	16	10	0	0	149	144	78	52	0	3	44	59	1.262	3.14	87	2.84	.257	7	.143	-7	4	-0.9
1907 Cin-N	17	16	.515	37	30	21	1	1	265^1	269	97	69	1	7	79	89	1.312	2.34	111	3.31	.274	6	.071	4	13	-0.1
1908 Cin-N	8	18	.308	32	28	20	4	2	242^1	219	79	50	3	4	64	61	1.168	1.86	123	2.64	.249	7	.092	15	16	1.3
Chi-N	2	0	1.000	4	3	2	1	0	20^1	14	4	2	0	0	6	7	.984	0.89	264	1.55	.192	0	.000	3	2	0.3
Yr.	10	18	.357	36	31	22	5	2	262^2	233	83	52	3	4	70	68	1.154	1.78	128	2.56	.245	7	.085	18	18	1.6
1909 Chi-N	0	1	.000	1	1	0	0	0	2	7	7	4	0	0	3	1	5.000	18.00	14	27.17	.583	0	....	-3	0	-0.4
1911 NY-A	0	1	.000	2	1	1	0	0	11^2	20	13	7	0	0	2	4	1.886	5.40	66	6.63	.377	1	.250	-2	0	-0.2
Total 9	58	59	.496	150	124	87	11	3	1072^1	1021	436	280	9	26	314	428	1.245	2.35	112	2.94	.256	42	.117	41	64	3.0

• COATES, Jim — James Alton Coates b: 8/4/1932, Farnham, VA BR/TR, 6'4", 192 lbs. Deb: 9/21/1956

YEAR TM-L	W	L	PCT	G	GS	CG	SH	SV	IP	H	R	ER	HR	HB	BB	SO	RAT	ERA	ERA+	CERA	OAV	BH	AVG	PR+	WS	TPW
1956 NY-A	0	0	....	2	0	0	0	0	2	1	3	3	0	1	4	0	2.500	13.50	29	8.25	.167	0	....	-2	0	-0.2
1959 NY-A	6	1	.857	37	4	2	0	0	100^1	89	39	32	10	3	36	64	1.246	2.87	127	3.32	.234	2	.095	9	7	0.7
1960* NY-A★	13	3	.813	35	18	6	2	1	149^1	139	78	71	16	2	66	73	1.373	4.28	84	3.92	.248	12	.250	-16	8	-1.2
1961* NY-A	11	5	.688	43	11	4	1	5	141^1	128	60	54	15	7	53	80	1.281	3.44	108	3.73	.243	1	.029	-0	10	-0.3
1962* NY-A	7	6	.538	50	6	0	0	6	117^2	119	62	58	9	5	50	67	1.436	4.44	84	4.15	.263	4	.125	-10	5	-1.1
1963 Was-A	2	4	.333	20	2	0	0	0	44^1	51	29	26	4	3	21	31	1.624	5.28	70	5.34	.297	0	.000	-8	1	-0.9
Cin-N	0	0	....	9	0	0	0	0	16^1	21	10	10	2	0	7	11	1.714	5.51	61	5.96	.313	0	.000	-4	0	-0.5
1965 Cal-A	2	0	1.000	17	0	0	0	3	28	23	13	11	1	0	16	15	1.393	3.54	96	3.08	.228	0	.000	-1	2	-0.1
1966 Cal-A	1	1	.500	9	4	1	1	0	31^2	32	16	14	3	0	10	16	1.326	3.98	84	3.74	.258	1	.091	-2	1	-0.3
1967 Cal-A	1	2	.333	25	1	0	0	0	52^1	47	26	25	5	4	23	39	1.338	4.30	73	3.86	.244	1	.333	-7	1	-0.7
Total 9	43	22	.662	247	46	13	4	15	683^1	650	336	304	65	25	286	396	1.370	4.00	90	3.94	.252	21	.131	-41	35	-4.6

• COBB, George — George Woodworth Cobb b: 9/25/1865, Independence, IA d: 8/19/1926, Pomona, CA, 6', 168 lbs. Deb: 4/15/1892

YEAR TM-L	W	L	PCT	G	GS	CG	SH	SV	IP	H	R	ER	HR	HB	BB	SO	RAT	ERA	ERA+	CERA	OAV	BH	AVG	PR+	WS	TPW
1892 Bal-N	10	37	.213	53	47	42	0	0	394^1	495	333	213	21	19	140	159	**1.610**	4.86	71	5.10	.295	36	.209	-46	7	-3.6

• COBB, Herb — Herbert Edward Cobb b: 8/6/1904, Pinetops, NC d: 1/8/1980, Tarboro, NC BR/TR, 5'11", 150 lbs. Deb: 4/21/1929

YEAR TM-L	W	L	PCT	G	GS	CG	SH	SV	IP	H	R	ER	HR	HB	BB	SO	RAT	ERA	ERA+	CERA	OAV	BH	AVG	PR+	WS	TPW
1929 StL-A	0	0	....	1	0	0	0	0	1	3	4	4	1	0	1	0	4.000	36.00	12	31.68	.600	0	....	-4	0	-0.3

• COCANOWER, Jaime — James Stanley Cocanower b: 2/14/1957, San Juan, Puerto Rico BR/TR, 6'4", 200 lbs. Deb: 9/7/1983

YEAR TM-L	W	L	PCT	G	GS	CG	SH	SV	IP	H	R	ER	HR	HB	BB	SO	RAT	ERA	ERA+	CERA	OAV	BH	AVG	PR+	WS	TPW
1983 Mil-A	2	0	1.000	5	3	1	0	0	30	21	8	6	1	1	12	8	1.100	1.80	207	2.31	.200	0	....	6	3	0.6
1984 Mil-A	8	16	.333	33	27	1	0	0	174^2	188	99	78	13	9	78	65	1.523	4.02	96	4.75	.279	0	....	-2	6	-0.2
1985 Mil-A	6	8	.429	24	15	3	1	0	116^1	122	72	56	6	8	73	44	1.676	4.33	96	5.18	.274	0	....	-2	5	-0.2
1986 Mil-A	0	1	.000	17	2	0	0	0	44^2	40	29	22	1	2	38	22	1.746	4.43	98	4.91	.248	0	....	-0	1	0.0
Total 4	16	25	.390	79	47	5	1	0	365^2	371	208	162	21	20	201	139	1.564	3.99	101	4.70	.268	0	....	3	15	0.3

• COCHRAN, Goat — Alvah Jackson "Al,Goat" Cochran b: 1/31/1891, Concord, GA d: 5/23/1947, Atlanta, GA BR/TR, 5'10", 175 lbs. Deb: 8/25/1915

YEAR TM-L	W	L	PCT	G	GS	CG	SH	SV	IP	H	R	ER	HR	HB	BB	SO	RAT	ERA	ERA+	CERA	OAV	BH	AVG	PR+	WS	TPW
1915 Cin-N	0	0	....	1	0	0	0	0	2	5	3	2	0	0	0	1	2.500	9.00	32	10.86	.455	0	....	-1	0	-0.2

• COCO, Pasqual — Pasqual (Reynoso) Coco b: 9/8/1977, Santo Domingo, Dominican Republic BR/TR, 6'1", 160 lbs. Deb: 7/17/2000

YEAR TM-L	W	L	PCT	G	GS	CG	SH	SV	IP	H	R	ER	HR	HB	BB	SO	RAT	ERA	ERA+	CERA	OAV	BH	AVG	PR+	WS	TPW
2000 Tor-A	0	0	....	1	1	0	0	0	4	5	4	4	1	1	5	2	2.500	9.00	56	11.69	.294	0	....	-2	0	-0.2
2001 Tor-A	1	0	1.000	7	1	0	0	0	14^1	12	8	7	0	2	6	9	1.256	4.40	104	3.00	.226	0	....	0	1	0.0
2002 Tor-A	0	1	.000	2	0	0	0	0	1	4	2	2	0	0	3	0	7.000	18.00	26	34.64	.571	0	....	-1	0	-0.1
Total 3	1	1	.500	10	2	0	0	0	19^1	21	14	13	1	3	14	11	1.810	6.05	78	6.44	.273	0	....	-3	1	-0.3

• COCREHAM, Gene — Eugene Cocreham b: 11/14/1884, Luling, TX d: 12/27/1945, Luling, TX BR/TR, 6'3.5", 192 lbs. Deb: 9/25/1913

YEAR TM-L	W	L	PCT	G	GS	CG	SH	SV	IP	H	R	ER	HR	HB	BB	SO	RAT	ERA	ERA+	CERA	OAV	BH	AVG	PR+	WS	TPW
1913 Bos-N	0	1	.000	1	1	0	0	0	8^1	13	7	7	0	1	4	3	2.040	7.56	43	7.45	.371	0	.000	-4	0	-0.5
1914 Bos-N	3	4	.429	15	3	1	0	0	44^2	48	30	24	2	0	27	15	1.679	4.84	57	4.97	.296	1	.100	-12	0	-1.3

YEAR	TM-L	W	L	PCT	G	GS	CG	SH	SV	IP	H	R	ER	HR	HB	BB	SO	RAT	ERA	ERA+	CERA	OAV	BH	AVG	PR+	WS	TPW
1915	Bos-N	0	0	....	1	0	0	0	0	1^2	3	2	1	0	0	0	0	1.800	5.40	50	7.19	.429	0	....	-1	0	-0.1
Total	3	3	5	.375	17	4	1	0	0	54^2	64	39	32	2	1	31	18	1.738	5.27	54	5.41	.313	1	.071	-16	0	-1.9

• CODIROLI, Chris Christopher Allen Codiroli b: 3/26/1958, Oxnard, CA BR/TR, 6'1", 160 lbs. Deb: 9/11/1982

YEAR	TM-L	W	L	PCT	G	GS	CG	SH	SV	IP	H	R	ER	HR	HB	BB	SO	RAT	ERA	ERA+	CERA	OAV	BH	AVG	PR+	WS	TPW
1982	Oak-A	1	2	.333	3	3	0	0	0	16^2	16	8	8	1	0	4	5	1.200	4.32	90	2.92	.246	0	....	-1	1	-0.1
1983	Oak-A	12	12	.500	37	31	7	2	1	205^2	208	115	102	17	7	72	85	1.361	4.46	86	3.93	.264	0	....	-16	7	-1.6
1984	Oak-A	6	4	.600	28	14	1	0	1	89^1	111	67	58	16	3	34	44	1.623	5.84	64	6.11	.304	0	....	-21	0	-2.1
1985	Oak-A	14	14	.500	37	**37**	4	0	0	226	228	125	112	23	3	78	111	1.354	4.46	86	3.92	.259	0	....	-13	7	-1.3
1986	Oak-A	5	8	.385	16	16	1	0	0	91^2	91	54	41	15	2	38	43	1.407	4.03	96	4.50	.250	0	....	-2	3	-0.2
1987	Oak-A	0	2	.000	3	3	0	0	0	11^1	12	11	11	1	1	8	4	1.765	8.74	47	5.89	.273	0	....	-6	0	-0.5
1988	Cle-A	0	4	.000	14	2	0	0	1	19^1	32	22	20	2	3	10	12	2.172	9.31	44	9.14	.372	0	....	-11	0	-1.1
1990	KC-A	0	1	.000	6	2	0	0	0	10^1	13	11	11	1	4	17	8	2.903	9.58	40	13.11	.325	0	....	-6	0	-0.6
Total	8	38	47	.447	144	108	13	2	3	670^1	711	413	363	76	23	261	312	1.450	4.87	79	4.59	.270	0	....	-75	18	-7.5

• COFFMAN, Dick Samuel Richard Coffman b: 12/18/1906, Veto, AL d: 3/24/1972, Athens, AL BR/TR, 6'2", 195 lbs. Deb: 4/28/1927

YEAR	TM-L	W	L	PCT	G	GS	CG	SH	SV	IP	H	R	ER	HR	HB	BB	SO	RAT	ERA	ERA+	CERA	OAV	BH	AVG	PR+	WS	TPW
1927	Was-A	0	1	.000	5	2	0	0	0	16	20	9	6	0	2	2	5	1.375	3.38	120	4.05	.313	1	.333	1	1	0.1
1928	StL-A	4	5	.444	29	7	3	0	1	85^2	122	68	58	7	1	37	25	1.856	6.09	69	6.45	.359	1	.043	-18	0	-2.0
1929	StL-A	1	1	.500	27	3	1	1	1	52^2	61	40	35	3	3	14	11	1.424	5.98	74	4.16	.295	0	.000	-10	1	-1.0
1930	StL-A	8	18	.308	38	30	12	1	1	196	250	134	112	14	5	69	54	1.628	5.14	95	5.25	.311	9	.136	-8	8	-1.2
1931	StL-A	9	13	.409	32	17	11	2	1	169^1	159	81	73	10	2	51	39	1.240	3.88	119	3.00	.241	4	.078	14	13	0.8
1932	StL-A	5	3	.625	9	6	3	0	0	61	66	24	21	3	2	21	14	1.426	3.10	157	4.03	.277	1	.045	12	6	0.9
	Was-A	1	6	.143	22	9	2	1	0	76^1	92	45	41	2	1	31	17	1.611	4.83	89	4.77	.307	2	.091	-6	2	-0.7
	Yr.	6	9	.400	31	15	5	1	0	137^1	158	69	62	5	3	52	31	1.529	4.06	110	4.44	.294	3	.068	5	8	0.2
1933	StL-A	3	7	.300	21	13	3	1	1	81	114	57	53	9	2	39	19	1.889	5.89	79	6.84	.329	1	.037	-13	2	-1.4
1934	StL-A	9	10	.474	40	21	6	1	3	173	212	112	87	11	1	59	55	1.566	4.53	110	4.80	.303	11	.216	7	11	0.6
1935	StL-A	5	11	.313	41	18	5	0	2	143^2	206	116	98	14	2	46	34	1.754	6.14	78	6.13	.335	6	.146	-21	3	-2.0
1936★	NY-N	7	5	.583	42	2	0	0	7	101^2	119	53	44	7	2	23	26	1.397	3.90	100	4.16	.296	4	.200	-3	7	-0.4
1937★	NY-N	8	3	.727	42	1	0	0	3	80	93	36	27	4	4	31	30	1.550	3.04	128	4.61	.289	7	.368	6	8	0.8
1938	NY-N	8	4	.667	**51**	3	1	1	**12**	111^1	116	50	43	3	3	21	21	1.231	3.48	108	3.06	.268	2	.071	3	11	0.1
1939	NY-N	1	2	.333	28	0	0	0	3	38	50	18	13	1	3	6	9	1.474	3.08	127	4.52	.316	0	.000	4	3	0.3
1940	Bos-N	1	5	.167	31	0	0	0	3	48^1	63	33	29	4	2	11	11	1.531	5.40	69	5.17	.323	1	.083	-10	0	-1.1
1945	Phi-N	2	1	.667	14	0	0	0	0	26^1	39	18	15	0	0	2	2	1.557	5.13	75	4.82	.351	1	.250	-3	1	-0.3
Total	15	72	95	.431	472	132	47	8	38	1460^1	1782	894	755	92	35	463	372	1.537	4.65	96	4.74	.302	51	.128	-46	77	-6.3

• COFFMAN, Kevin Kevin Reese Coffman b: 1/19/1965, Austin, TX BR/TR, 6'2", 175 lbs. Deb: 9/5/1987

YEAR	TM-L	W	L	PCT	G	GS	CG	SH	SV	IP	H	R	ER	HR	HB	BB	SO	RAT	ERA	ERA+	CERA	OAV	BH	AVG	PR+	WS	TPW
1987	Atl-N	2	3	.400	5	5	0	0	0	25^1	31	14	13	2	3	22	14	2.092	4.62	94	7.89	.313	1	.100	-1	1	-0.1
1988	Atl-N	2	6	.250	18	11	0	0	0	67	62	52	43	3	4	54	24	1.731	5.78	64	5.03	.251	5	.227	-15	0	-1.4
1990	Chi-N	0	2	.000	8	2	0	0	0	18^1	26	24	23	0	0	19	9	2.455	11.29	36	8.21	.333	1	.200	-14	0	-1.5
Total	3	4	11	.267	31	18	0	0	0	110^2	119	90	79	5	7	95	47	1.934	6.42	60	6.21	.281	7	.189	-30	1	-2.9

• COFFMAN, Slick George David Coffman b: 12/11/1910, Veto, AL d: 5/8/2003, Birmingham, AL BR/TR, 6', 155 lbs. Deb: 5/21/1937

YEAR	TM-L	W	L	PCT	G	GS	CG	SH	SV	IP	H	R	ER	HR	HB	BB	SO	RAT	ERA	ERA+	CERA	OAV	BH	AVG	PR+	WS	TPW
1937	Det-A	7	5	.583	28	5	1	0	0	101	121	61	49	8	3	39	22	1.584	4.37	107	4.99	.295	5	.172	5	7	0.5
1938	Det-A	4	4	.500	39	6	1	0	2	95^2	120	70	64	6	0	48	31	1.756	6.02	83	5.54	.310	4	.167	-12	4	-1.0
1939	Det-A	2	1	.667	23	1	0	0	0	42^1	51	36	30	4	1	22	10	1.724	6.38	77	5.52	.295	0	.000	-7	1	-0.7
1940	StL-A	2	2	.500	31	4	1	0	1	74^2	108	62	52	5	0	23	26	1.754	6.27	73	5.89	.334	3	.200	-13	1	-1.3
Total	4	15	12	.556	121	16	3	0	3	313^2	400	229	195	23	4	132	89	1.696	5.60	85	5.44	.309	12	.164	-27	13	-2.5

• COGAN, Dick Richard Henry Cogan b: 12/5/1871, Paterson, NJ d: 5/2/1948, Paterson, NJ BR/TR, 5'7", 150 lbs. Deb: 5/10/1897

YEAR	TM-L	W	L	PCT	G	GS	CG	SH	SV	IP	H	R	ER	HR	HB	BB	SO	RAT	ERA	ERA+	CERA	OAV	BH	AVG	PR+	WS	TPW
1897	Bal-N	0	0	....	1	0	0	0	0	2	4	3	3	0	1	2	0	3.000	13.50	31	14.08	.411	0	.000	-2	0	-0.2
1899	Chi-N	2	3	.400	5	5	5	0	0	44	54	32	21	1	4	24	9	1.773	4.30	87	5.55	.302	5	.200	-3	2	-0.2
1900	NY-N	0	0	....	2	0	0	0	0	8	10	6	6	0	0	6	1	2.000	6.75	53	5.91	.305	1	.125	-3	0	-0.3
Total	3	2	3	.400	8	5	5	0	0	54	68	41	30	1	5	32	10	1.852	5.00	75	5.92	.307	6	.176	-8	2	-0.6

• COGAN, Tony Anthony Michael Cogan b: 12/21/1976, Chicago, IL BL/TL, 6'2", 195 lbs. Deb: 4/2/2001

YEAR	TM-L	W	L	PCT	G	GS	CG	SH	SV	IP	H	R	ER	HR	HB	BB	SO	RAT	ERA	ERA+	CERA	OAV	BH	AVG	PR+	WS	TPW
2001	KC-A	0	4	.000	39	0	0	0	0	24^2	32	17	16	7	5	13	17	1.824	5.84	84	9.09	.320	0	....	-3	0	-0.3

• COGGIN, Dave David Raymond Coggin b: 10/30/1976, Covina, CA BR/TR, 6'4", 195 lbs. Deb: 6/23/2000

YEAR	TM-L	W	L	PCT	G	GS	CG	SH	SV	IP	H	R	ER	HR	HB	BB	SO	RAT	ERA	ERA+	CERA	OAV	BH	AVG	PR+	WS	TPW
2000	Phi-N	2	0	1.000	5	5	0	0	0	27	35	20	16	2	1	12	17	1.741	5.33	87	5.95	.315	0	.000	-2	1	-0.3
2001	Phi-N	6	7	.462	17	17	0	0	0	95	99	46	44	7	5	39	62	1.453	4.17	102	4.30	.272	2	.061	-0	5	-0.2
2002	Phi-N	2	5	.286	38	7	0	0	0	77	65	42	40	4	4	51	64	1.506	4.68	83	4.05	.231	0	.000	-7	2	-0.8
Total	3	10	12	.455	60	29	0	0	0	199	199	108	100	13	10	102	143	1.513	4.52	92	4.43	.263	2	.042	-9	8	-1.2

• COHEN, Hy Hyman Cohen b: 1/29/1931, Brooklyn, NY BR/TR, 6'5", 220 lbs. Deb: 4/17/1955

YEAR	TM-L	W	L	PCT	G	GS	CG	SH	SV	IP	H	R	ER	HR	HB	BB	SO	RAT	ERA	ERA+	CERA	OAV	BH	AVG	PR+	WS	TPW
1955	Chi-N	0	0	....	7	1	0	0	0	17	28	17	15	2	1	10	4	2.235	7.94	51	9.60	.378	0	.000	-7	0	-0.7

• COHEN, Syd Sydney Harry Cohen b: 5/7/1906, Baltimore, MD d: 4/9/1988, El Paso, TX BB/TL, 5'11", 180 lbs. Deb: 9/18/1934

YEAR	TM-L	W	L	PCT	G	GS	CG	SH	SV	IP	H	R	ER	HR	HB	BB	SO	RAT	ERA	ERA+	CERA	OAV	BH	AVG	PR+	WS	TPW
1934	Was-A	1	1	.500	3	2	2	0	0	18	25	15	15	2	0	6	6	1.722	7.50	58	6.10	.333	3	.273	-6	0	-0.6
1936	Was-A	0	2	.000	19	1	0	0	1	36	44	27	21	4	3	14	21	1.611	5.25	91	5.63	.303	0	.000	-2	1	-0.3
1937	Was-A	2	4	.333	33	0	0	0	4	55	64	30	19	1	0	17	22	1.473	3.11	142	4.07	.299	2	.143	7	4	0.6
Total	3	3	7	.300	55	3	2	0	5	109	133	72	55	7	3	37	49	1.560	4.54	100	4.92	.306	5	.152	-1	5	-0.3

• COLBERT, Vince Vincent Norman Colbert b: 12/20/1945, Washington, DC BR/TR, 6'4", 200 lbs. Deb: 5/19/1970

YEAR	TM-L	W	L	PCT	G	GS	CG	SH	SV	IP	H	R	ER	HR	HB	BB	SO	RAT	ERA	ERA+	CERA	OAV	BH	AVG	PR+	WS	TPW
1970	Cle-A	1	1	.500	23	0	0	0	2	31	37	25	25	4	1	16	17	1.710	7.26	55	6.01	.298	0	.000	-11	0	-1.2
1971	Cle-A	7	6	.538	50	10	2	0	2	142^2	140	71	63	11	6	71	74	1.479	3.97	96	4.29	.265	4	.138	-3	8	-0.4
1972	Cle-A	1	7	.125	22	11	1	1	0	74^2	74	42	38	8	7	38	36	1.500	4.58	70	4.86	.267	4	.200	-12	0	-1.3
Total	3	9	14	.391	95	21	3	1	4	248^1	251	138	126	23	14	125	127	1.514	4.57	80	4.67	.270	8	.157	-27	8	-2.9

• COLBORN, Jim James William Colborn b: 5/22/1946, Santa Paula, CA BR/TR, 6', 191 lbs. Deb: 7/13/1969 C

YEAR	TM-L	W	L	PCT	G	GS	CG	SH	SV	IP	H	R	ER	HR	HB	BB	SO	RAT	ERA	ERA+	CERA	OAV	BH	AVG	PR+	WS	TPW
1969	Chi-N	1	0	1.000	6	2	0	0	0	14^2	15	6	5	2	1	9	4	1.636	3.07	131	5.74	.283	0	.000	2	1	0.1
1970	Chi-N	3	1	.750	34	5	0	0	4	72^2	88	37	29	3	1	23	50	1.528	3.59	125	4.35	.298	1	.067	7	6	0.6
1971	Chi-N	0	1	.000	14	0	0	0	0	10^1	18	8	8	1	0	3	2	2.032	6.97	56	8.30	.383	0	....	-3	0	-0.4
1972	Mil-A	7	7	.500	39	12	4	1	0	147^2	135	53	51	14	2	43	97	1.205	3.11	97	3.16	.245	3	.081	-1	8	-0.3
1973	Mil-A★	20	12	.625	43	36	22	4	1	314^1	297	133	111	21	3	87	135	1.222	3.18	118	3.15	.251	0	....	22	20	2.2
1974	Mil-A	10	13	.435	33	31	10	1	0	224	230	104	101	27	6	60	83	1.295	4.06	89	3.97	.268	0	....	-12	10	-1.3
1975	Mil-A	11	13	.458	36	29	8	1	2	206^1	215	111	98	18	5	65	79	1.357	4.27	90	3.97	.270	0	....	-9	9	-0.9
1976	Mil-A	9	15	.375	32	32	7	0	0	225^2	232	97	93	20	2	54	101	1.267	3.71	94	3.54	.268	0	....	-6	10	-0.6
1977	KC-A	18	14	.563	36	35	6	1	0	239	233	106	96	22	13	81	103	1.314	3.62	112	3.84	.255	0	....	9	16	0.9
1978	KC-A	1	2	.333	8	3	0	0	0	28^1	31	18	15	4	2	12	8	1.518	4.76	80	5.21	.282	0	....	-3	0	-0.3
	Sea-A	3	10	.231	20	19	3	0	0	114^1	125	77	68	21	6	38	26	1.426	5.35	71	5.14	.279	0	....	-19	1	-1.9
	Yr.	4	12	.250	28	22	3	0	0	142^2	156	95	83	25	8	50	34	1.444	5.24	73	5.15	.280	0	....	-22	1	-2.3
Total	10	83	88	.485	301	204	60	8	7	1597^1	1619	750	675	153	41	475	688	1.311	3.80	98	3.82	.265	4	.073	-14	81	-1.8

• COLCOLOUGH, Tom Thomas Bernard Colcolough b: 10/8/1870, Charleston, SC d: 12/10/1919, Charleston, SC BR/TR, 5'10.5", 180 lbs. Deb: 8/1/1893

YEAR	TM-L	W	L	PCT	G	GS	CG	SH	SV	IP	H	R	ER	HR	HB	BB	SO	RAT	ERA	ERA+	CERA	OAV	BH	AVG	PR+	WS	TPW
1893	Pit-N	1	0	1.000	8	3	1	0	**2**	43^2	45	30	20	1	0	32	7	1.763	4.12	110	4.75	.258	2	.143	1	3	0.1
1894	Pit-N	8	5	.615	22	14	11	0	0	150^2	213	147	117	5	5	72	29	1.892	6.99	75	6.31	.330	14	.200	-29	5	-2.4
1895	Pit-N	1	1	.500	6	6	3	0	0	43^1	54	49	22	3	5	21	16	1.731	4.57	99	5.93	.301	5	.333	-0	1	0.2
1899	NY-N	4	5	.444	11	8	7	0	0	81^2	85	49	36	1	3	41	14	1.543	3.97	95	4.05	.268	10	.270	-3	5	-0.2
Total	4	14	11	.560	47	31	22	0	2	319^1	397	275	195	10	13	166	66	1.763	5.50	86	5.47	.301	31	.228	-31	14	-2.3

YEAR TM-L	W	L	PCT	G	GS	CG	SH	SV	IP	H	R	ER	HR	HB	BB	SO	RAT	ERA	ERA+	CERA	OAV	BH	AVG	PR+	WS	TPW
• COLE, Bert	Albert George Cole b: 7/1/1896, San Francisco, CA d: 5/30/1975, San Mateo, CA BL/TL, 6'1", 180 lbs. Deb: 4/19/1921																									
1921 Det-A	7	4	.636	20	11	7	1	1	109^{2}	134	66	52	3	4	36	22	1.550	4.27	100	4.53	.305	13	.283	3	6	0.5
1922 Det-A	1	6	.143	23	5	2	1	0	79^{1}	105	60	43	4	1	39	21	1.815	4.88	79	5.71	.313	4	.160	-7	1	-0.8
1923 Det-A	13	5	.722	52	13	6	1	5	163	183	95	75	9	5	61	32	1.497	4.14	93	4.27	.284	14	.255	-3	10	-0.1
1924 Det-A	3	9	.250	28	12	2	1	2	109^{1}	135	69	57	4	4	35	16	1.555	4.69	88	4.76	.314	10	.270	-7	5	-0.6
1925 Det-A	2	3	.400	14	2	1	0	1	33^{2}	44	27	22	2	1	15	7	1.752	5.88	73	5.74	.336	3	.273	-6	1	-0.5
Cle-A	1	1	.500	13	2	0	0	1	44	55	33	30	1	1	25	9	1.818	6.14	72	5.72	.322	2	.154	-8	1	-0.8
Yr.	3	4	.429	27	4	1	0	2	77^{2}	99	60	52	3	2	40	16	1.790	6.03	73	5.73	.328	5	.208	-14	2	-1.3
1927 Chi-A	1	4	.200	27	2	0	0	0	66^{2}	79	43	35	3	3	19	12	1.470	4.73	86	4.39	.309	3	.167	-6	2	-0.7
Total 6	**28**	**32**	**.467**	**177**	**47**	**18**	**4**	**10**	**605^{2}**	**735**	**393**	**314**	**26**	**19**	**230**	**119**	**1.593**	**4.67**	**87**	**4.80**	**.305**	**49**	**.239**	**-36**	**26**	**-3.0**
• COLE, Dave	David Bruce Cole b: 8/29/1930, Williamsport, MD BR/TR, 6'2", 175 lbs. Deb: 9/9/1950																									
1950 Bos-N	0	1	.000	4	0	0	0	0	8	7	2	1	0	1	3	8	1.250	1.13	342	3.20	.259	0	.000	2	1	0.2
1951 Bos-N	2	4	.333	23	7	1	0	0	67^{2}	64	43	32	3	2	64	33	1.892	4.26	86	5.39	.254	6	.353	-4	3	0.0
1952 Bos-N	1	1	.500	22	3	0	0	0	44^{2}	38	21	20	2	3	42	22	1.791	4.03	90	4.99	.241	0	.000	-1	2	-0.2
1953 Mil-N	0	1	.000	10	0	0	0	0	14^{2}	17	14	14	1	0	14	13	2.114	8.59	46	6.56	.279	1	.500	-8	0	-0.6
1954 Chi-N	3	8	.273	18	14	2	1	0	84	74	56	50	7	1	62	37	1.619	5.36	78	4.46	.241	6	.214	-10	1	-0.8
1955 Phi-N	0	3	.000	7	3	0	0	0	18^{1}	21	15	13	3	0	14	6	1.909	6.38	62	6.98	.304	1	.200	-5	0	-0.5
Total 6	**6**	**18**	**.250**	**84**	**27**	**3**	**1**	**0**	**237^{1}**	**221**	**151**	**130**	**16**	**7**	**199**	**119**	**1.770**	**4.93**	**79**	**5.11**	**.253**	**14**	**.230**	**-25**	**7**	**-2.0**
• COLE, Ed	Edward William Cole b: 3/22/1909, Wilkes-Barre, PA d: 7/28/1999, Nashville, TN BR/TR, 5'11", 170 lbs. Deb: 4/22/1938																									
1938 StL-A	1	5	.167	36	6	1	0	3	88^{2}	116	69	51	8	5	48	26	1.850	5.18	96	6.36	.313	3	.143	-2	3	-0.3
1939 StL-A	0	2	.000	6	0	0	0	0	6^{1}	8	7	5	1	0	6	5	2.211	7.11	68	7.77	.308	0	.000	-1	0	-0.1
Total 2	**1**	**7**	**.125**	**42**	**6**	**1**	**0**	**3**	**95**	**124**	**76**	**56**	**9**	**5**	**54**	**31**	**1.874**	**5.31**	**94**	**6.45**	**.312**	**3**	**.136**	**-3**	**3**	**-0.4**
• COLE, King	Leonard Leslie Cole b: 4/15/1886, Toledo, IA d: 1/6/1916, Bay City, MI BR/TR, 6'1", 170 lbs. Deb: 10/6/1909																									
1909 Chi-N	1	0	1.000	1	1	1	1	0	9	6	0	0	0	0	3	1	1.000	0.00	....	1.61	.194	3	.750	2	3	0.5
1910* Chi-N	20	4	.833	33	29	21	4	1	239^{2}	174	64	48	2	9	130	114	1.268	1.80	**159**	2.68	**.211**	21	.231	26	25	2.9
1911 Chi-N	18	7	.720	32	27	13	2	0	221^{1}	188	87	77	3	9	99	101	1.297	3.13	105	3.02	.236	12	.152	-0	15	-0.2
1912 Chi-N	1	2	.333	8	3	0	0	0	19	36	26	23	2	2	8	9	2.316	10.89	30	10.30	.409	2	.400	-16	0	-1.5
Pit-N	2	2	.500	12	5	2	0	0	49	61	42	35	1	2	18	11	1.612	6.43	51	4.90	.330	2	.133	-18	0	-1.8
Yr.	3	4	.429	20	8	2	0	0	68	97	68	58	3	4	26	20	1.809	7.68	43	6.41	.355	4	.200	-34	0	-3.4
1914 NY-A	10	9	.526	33	15	8	2	0	141^{2}	151	63	52	3	1	51	43	1.426	3.30	83	3.93	.288	2	.048	-10	7	-1.5
1915 NY-A	2	3	.400	10	6	2	0	1	51	41	27	18	2	3	22	19	1.235	3.18	92	2.94	.224	1	.077	-2	2	-0.3
Total 6	**54**	**27**	**.667**	**129**	**86**	**47**	**9**	**2**	**730^{2}**	**657**	**309**	**253**	**13**	**26**	**331**	**298**	**1.352**	**3.12**	**98**	**3.38**	**.250**	**43**	**.173**	**-18**	**52**	**-2.0**
• COLE, Victor	Victor Alexander Cole b: 1/23/1968, Leningrad, Russia BB/TR, 5'10", 160 lbs. Deb: 6/6/1992																									
1992 Pit-N	0	2	.000	8	4	0	0	0	23	23	14	14	1	0	14	12	1.609	5.48	63	4.45	.261	0	.000	-5	0	-0.6
• COLEMAN, Joe	Joseph Howard Coleman b: 2/3/1947, Boston, MA BR/TR, 6'3", 195 lbs. Deb: 9/28/1965 C																									
1965 Was-A	2	0	1.000	2	2	2	0	0	18	9	3	3	0	0	8	7	.944	1.50	232	1.34	.153	0	.000	4	2	0.4
1966 Was-A	1	0	1.000	1	1	1	0	0	9	6	2	2	0	0	2	4	.889	2.00	173	1.34	.188	0	.000	1	1	0.1
1967 Was-A	8	9	.471	28	22	3	0	0	134	154	78	69	6	9	47	77	1.500	4.63	68	4.54	.291	2	.056	-22	1	-2.6
1968 Was-A	12	16	.429	33	33	12	2	0	223	212	98	81	18	12	51	139	1.179	3.27	89	3.20	.250	9	.129	-6	7	-0.8
1969 Was-A	12	13	.480	40	36	12	4	1	247^{2}	222	102	90	26	6	100	182	1.300	3.27	106	3.64	.243	9	.107	4	13	0.1
1970 Was-A	8	12	.400	39	29	6	1	0	218^{2}	190	98	87	25	4	89	152	1.276	3.58	99	3.52	.233	8	.119	-4	10	-0.2
1971 Det-A	20	9	.690	39	38	16	3	0	286	241	106	100	17	7	96	236	1.178	3.15	114	2.82	.229	9	.094	14	20	1.2
1972* Det-A★	19	14	.576	40	39	9	3	0	280	216	99	87	23	9	110	222	1.164	2.80	113	2.83	.214	9	.110	8	19	0.6
1973 Det-A	23	15	.605	40	40	13	2	0	288^{1}	283	125	113	32	10	93	202	1.304	3.53	116	3.90	.258	0	....	20	21	2.0
1974 Det-A	14	12	.538	41	41	11	2	0	285^{2}	272	160	137	30	12	158	177	1.505	4.32	88	4.57	.254	0	....	-15	13	-1.5
1975 Det-A	10	18	.357	31	31	6	1	0	201	234	137	124	27	9	85	125	1.587	5.55	72	5.48	.291	0	....	-30	3	-3.1
1976 Det-A	2	5	.286	12	12	1	0	0	66^{2}	80	44	36	1	5	34	38	1.710	4.86	76	5.35	.308	0	....	-8	1	-0.8
Chi-N	2	8	.200	39	4	0	0	4	79	72	43	36	9	2	35	66	1.354	4.10	94	3.79	.246	2	.154	-1	4	-0.1
1977 Oak-A	4	4	.500	43	12	2	0	2	127^{2}	114	51	42	11	2	49	55	1.277	2.96	136	3.41	.241	0	....	17	9	1.7
1978 Oak-A	3	0	1.000	10	0	0	0	0	19^{2}	12	3	3	1	0	5	4	.864	1.37	265	1.51	.185	0	....	5	3	0.5
Tor-A	2	0	1.000	31	0	0	0	0	60^{2}	67	34	31	6	1	30	28	1.599	4.60	85	5.06	.286	0	....	-4	2	-0.4
Yr.	5	0	1.000	41	0	0	0	0	80^{1}	79	37	34	7	1	35	32	1.419	3.81	102	4.19	.264	0	....	1	5	0.1
1979 SF-N	0	0	....	5	0	0	0	0	3^{2}	3	2	0	0	1	2	0	1.364	0.00	....	3.56	.231	0	....	1	0	0.2
Pit-N	0	0	....	10	0	0	0	0	20^{2}	29	17	14	1	1	9	14	1.839	6.10	64	6.15	.326	1	.200	-5	0	-0.5
Yr.	0	0	....	15	0	0	0	0	24^{1}	32	19	14	1	2	11	14	1.767	5.18	75	5.76	.314	1	.200	-4	0	-0.4
Total 15	**142**	**135**	**.513**	**484**	**340**	**94**	**18**	**7**	**2569^{1}**	**2416**	**1202**	**1055**	**233**	**90**	**1003**	**1728**	**1.331**	**3.70**	**97**	**3.79**	**.250**	**49**	**.106**	**-21**	**129**	**-3.4**
• COLEMAN, Joe	Joseph Patrick Coleman b: 7/30/1922, Medford, MA d: 4/9/1997, Fort Myers, FL BR/TR, 6'2.5", 200 lbs. Deb: 9/19/1942																									
1942 Phi-A	0	1	.000	1	0	0	0	0	6	8	5	2	0	0	1	0	1.500	3.00	126	3.98	.308	0	.000	1	0	0.0
1946 Phi-A	0	2	.000	4	2	0	0	0	13	19	8	8	1	0	8	8	2.077	5.54	64	7.46	.345	2	.400	-3	0	-0.2
1947 Phi-A	6	12	.333	32	21	9	2	1	160^{1}	171	84	77	17	0	62	65	1.453	4.32	88	4.41	.275	7	.146	-13	5	-1.4
1948 Phi-A★	14	13	.519	33	29	13	3	0	215^{2}	224	105	98	11	1	90	86	1.456	4.09	105	3.90	.269	9	.122	3	15	-0.1
1949 Phi-A	13	14	.481	33	30	18	1	1	240^{1}	249	119	103	12	3	127	109	1.564	3.86	106	4.37	.271	14	.177	1	14	0.2
1950 Phi-A	0	5	.000	15	6	2	0	0	54	74	54	51	9	0	50	12	2.296	8.50	54	8.98	.332	1	.059	-23	0	-2.2
1951 Phi-A	1	6	.143	28	9	1	0	1	96^{1}	117	69	64	12	3	59	34	1.827	5.98	72	6.45	.305	7	.259	-20	1	-1.8
1953 Phi-A	3	4	.429	21	9	2	1	0	90	85	46	40	8	1	49	18	1.489	4.00	107	4.25	.254	8	.286	3	6	0.5
1954 Bal-A	13	17	.433	33	32	15	4	0	221^{1}	184	102	86	16	3	96	103	1.265	3.50	102	3.12	.232	13	.176	4	13	0.7
1955 Bal-A	0	1	.000	6	2	0	0	0	11^{2}	19	15	14	5	1	10	4	2.486	10.80	35	13.32	.373	2	.667	-9	0	-0.8
Det-A	2	1	.667	17	0	0	0	3	25^{1}	22	9	9	1	1	14	5	1.421	3.20	120	3.71	.239	3	.750	2	3	0.3
Yr.	2	2	.500	23	2	0	0	3	37	41	24	23	6	2	24	9	1.757	5.59	68	6.74	.287	5	.714	-7	3	-0.5
Total 10	**52**	**76**	**.406**	**223**	**140**	**60**	**11**	**6**	**1134**	**1172**	**616**	**552**	**92**	**13**	**566**	**444**	**1.533**	**4.38**	**92**	**4.54**	**.271**	**66**	**.182**	**-54**	**57**	**-4.9**
• COLEMAN, John	John Coleman b: Bristol, PA TR Deb: 6/23/1890																									
1890 Phi-N	0	1	.000	1	1	0	0	0	1^{2}	4	8	4	0	0	3	2	4.200	21.60	17	....	.448	0	....	-3	0	-0.3
• COLEMAN, John	John Francis Coleman b: 3/6/1863, Saratoga Springs, NY d: 5/31/1922, Detroit, MI BL/TR, 5'9.5", 170 lbs. Deb: 5/1/1883 U ♦																									
1883 Phi-N	12	48	.200	65	61	59	3	0	538^{1}	772	510	291	17	....	48	159	1.523	4.87	63	....	.318	83	.234	-62	8	-4.5
1884 Phi-N	5	15	.250	21	19	14	1	0	154^{1}	216	147	84	9	....	22	37	1.542	4.90	61	....	.314	42	.246	-26	6	-2.4
Phi-a	0	2	.000	3	2	2	0	0	21	28	14	8	0	4	2	5	1.429	3.43	99	....	.304	22	.206	-0	2	-0.4
1885 Phi-a	2	2	.500	8	3	3	0	0	60^{1}	82	46	23	0	0	5	12	1.442	3.43	100	....	.311	119	.299	0	17	1.4
1886 Phi-a	1	1	.500	3	1	1	0	0	20^{2}	18	9	6	1	1	5	2	1.113	2.61	134	....	.224	121	.246	3	15	-0.1
1889 Phi-a	3	2	.600	5	5	4	0	0	34	38	23	11	2	1	14	6	1.529	2.91	130	....	.274	1	.053	2	2	-0.1
1890 Pit-N	0	2	.000	2	2	1	0	0	14	28	23	15	1	0	6	3	2.429	9.64	34	....	.404	2	.182	-9	0	-0.8
Total 6	**23**	**72**	**.242**	**107**	**93**	**84**	**4**	**0**	**842^{2}**	**1182**	**772**	**438**	**30**	**6**	**102**	**224**	**1.524**	**4.68**	**67**	**....**	**.314**	**676**	**.266**	**-92**	**50**	**-7.0**
• COLEMAN, Percy	Pierce D. Coleman b: 10/15/1876, Mason, OH d: 2/16/1948, Van Nuys, CA TR Deb: 7/2/1897																									
1897 StL-N	1	2	.333	13	5	3	0	0	66^{1}	108	71	52	0	8	33	10	2.126	7.06	62	7.61	.362	6	.214	-17	0	-1.5
1898 Cin-N	0	1	.000	1	1	1	0	0	9	13	7	3	0	1	3	2	1.778	3.00	128	5.95	.335	0	.000	1	0	0.0
Total 2	**1**	**3**	**.250**	**14**	**6**	**4**	**0**	**0**	**75^{1}**	**121**	**78**	**55**	**0**	**9**	**36**	**12**	**2.084**	**6.57**	**66**	**7.41**	**.359**	**6**	**.194**	**-16**	**0**	**-1.5**
• COLEMAN, Rip	Walter Gary Coleman b: 7/31/1931, Troy, NY BL/TL, 6'2", 185 lbs. Deb: 8/15/1955																									
1955* NY-A	2	1	.667	10	6	0	0	1	29	40	19	17	2	1	16	15	1.931	5.28	71	6.96	.331	2	.200	-6	0	-0.6
1956 NY-A	3	5	.375	29	9	0	0	2	88^{1}	97	42	36	6	1	42	42	1.574	3.67	106	4.77	.285	1	.042	-0	4	-0.3
1957 KC-A	0	7	.000	19	6	1	1	0	41	53	32	27	5	0	25	15	1.902	5.93	67	6.98	.325	0	.000	-9	0	-1.0

YEAR	TM-L	W	L	PCT	G	GS	CG	SH	SV	IP	H	R	ER	HR	HB	BB	SO	RAT	ERA	ERA+	CERA	OAV	BH	AVG	PR+	WS	TPW
1959	KC-A	2	10	.167	29	11	2	0	2	81	85	46	41	8	1	34	54	1.469	4.56	88	4.45	.273	2	.080	-5	2	-0.7
	Bal-A	0	0	....	3	0	0	0	0	4	4	0	0	0	0	2	4	1.500	0.00	....	3.88	.267	0	....	2	1	0.2
	Yr.	2	10	.167	32	11	2	0	2	85	89	46	41	8	1	36	58	1.471	4.34	92	4.42	.273	2	.080	-3	3	-0.5
1960	Bal-A	0	2	.000	5	1	0	0	0	4	8	5	5	0	1	5	0	3.250	11.25	34	14.84	.444	0	.000	-3	0	-0.4
Total 5		**7**	**25**	**.219**	**95**	**33**	**3**	**1**	**5**	**247^1**	**287**	**144**	**126**	**21**	**4**	**124**	**130**	**1.662**	**4.58**	**85**	**5.44**	**.296**	**5**	**.072**	**-21**	**7**	**-2.7**
• COLEMAN, Walter	Walter L. Coleman b: 6/13/1873, Lee's Summit, MO d: 11/20/1925, Bunceton, MO TL, 5'10", 174 lbs. Deb: 9/25/1895																										
1895	StL-N	0	1	.000	1	1	1	0	0	8	12	15	12	1	1	8	5	2.500	13.50	36	10.27	.341	1	.200	-7	0	-0.6
• COLLAMORE, Allan	Allan Edward Collamore b: 6/5/1887, Worcester, MA d: 8/8/1980, Battle Creek, MI BR/TR, 6', 170 lbs. Deb: 4/15/1911																										
1911	Phi-A	0	1	.000	2	0	0	0	0	2	6	9	8	0	2	3	1	4.500	36.00	9	29.39	.600	0	....	-7	0	-0.7
1914	Cle-A	3	7	.300	27	8	3	0	0	105^1	100	52	38	3	6	49	32	1.415	3.25	89	3.87	.264	3	.094	-3	3	-0.5
1915	Cle-A	2	5	.286	11	6	5	2	0	64^1	52	22	17	1	0	22	15	1.150	2.38	128	2.46	.235	4	.174	5	5	0.6
Total 3		**5**	**13**	**.278**	**40**	**14**	**8**	**2**	**0**	**171^2**	**158**	**83**	**63**	**4**	**8**	**74**	**48**	**1.351**	**3.30**	**89**	**3.64**	**.259**	**7**	**.127**	**-5**	**8**	**-0.6**
• COLLARD, Hap	Earl Clinton Collard b: 8/29/1898, Williams, AZ d: 7/9/1968, Jamestown, CA BR/TR, 6', 170 lbs. Deb: 4/23/1927																										
1927	Cle-A	0	0	....	4	0	0	0	0	5^1	8	7	3	0	0	3	2	2.063	5.06	83	6.07	.333	0	....	-0	0	0.0
1928	Cle-A	0	0	....	1	0	0	0	0	4	4	3	1	0	0	4	1	2.000	2.25	184	5.17	.250	1	1.000	1	1	0.1
1930	Phi-N	6	12	.333	30	15	4	0	0	127	188	106	96	15	3	39	25	1.787	6.80	80	6.72	.350	9	.205	-16	4	-1.5
Total 3		**6**	**12**	**.333**	**35**	**15**	**4**	**0**	**0**	**136^1**	**200**	**116**	**100**	**15**	**3**	**46**	**28**	**1.804**	**6.60**	**82**	**6.65**	**.347**	**10**	**.222**	**-15**	**5**	**-1.4**
• COLLIER, Orlin	Orlin Edward Collier b: 2/17/1907, East Prairie, MO d: 9/9/1944, Memphis, TN BR/TR, 5'11.5", 180 lbs. Deb: 9/11/1931																										
1931	Det-A	0	1	.000	2	2	0	0	0	10^1	17	12	9	0	0	7	3	2.323	7.84	58	7.92	.362	0	.000	-4	0	-0.4
• COLLIFLOWER, Harry	James Harry "Collie" Colliflower b: 3/11/1869, Petersville, MD d: 8/12/1961, Washington, DC BL/TL, 5'11.5", 175 lbs. Deb: 7/21/1899 U																										
1899	Cle-N	1	11	.083	14	12	11	0	0	98	152	122	89	6	11	41	8	1.969	8.17	45	7.51	.353	23	.303	-44	0	-4.0
• COLLINS, Don	Donald Edward Collins b: 9/15/1952, Lyons, GA BR/TL, 6'2", 195 lbs. Deb: 5/4/1977																										
1977	Atl-N	3	9	.250	40	6	0	0	2	70^2	82	43	40	8	1	41	27	1.741	5.09	87	5.78	.299	0	.000	-3	3	-0.4
1980	Cle-A	0	0	....	4	0	0	0	0	6	9	5	5	0	0	7	0	2.667	7.50	54	9.19	.346	0	....	-2	0	-0.2
Total 2		**3**	**9**	**.250**	**44**	**6**	**0**	**0**	**2**	**76^2**	**91**	**48**	**45**	**8**	**1**	**48**	**27**	**1.813**	**5.28**	**83**	**6.05**	**.303**	**0**	**.000**	**-5**	**3**	**-0.7**
• COLLINS, Phil	Philip Eugene "Fidgety Phil" Collins b: 8/27/1901, Chicago, IL d: 8/14/1948, Chicago, IL BR/TR, 5'11", 175 lbs. Deb: 10/7/1923																										
1923	Chi-N	1	0	1.000	1	1	0	0	0	5	8	2	2	0	0	1	2	1.800	3.60	111	6.37	.400	0	.000	0	1	0.0
1929	Phi-N	9	7	.563	43	11	3	0	5	153^1	172	106	98	18	4	83	61	1.663	5.75	90	5.41	.284	11	.190	-7	8	-0.6
1930	Phi-N	16	11	.593	47	25	17	1	3	239	287	148	127	22	10	86	87	1.561	4.78	114	5.00	.299	22	.253	24	16	2.5
1931	Phi-N	12	16	.429	42	27	16	2	4	240^1	268	126	103	14	5	83	73	1.460	3.86	110	4.18	.283	16	.168	13	16	1.0
1932	Phi-N	14	12	.538	43	21	6	0	3	184^1	231	117	108	21	6	65	66	**1.606**	5.27	84	5.61	.314	18	.265	-17	9	-1.4
1933	Phi-N	8	13	.381	42	13	5	1	**6**	151	178	79	69	9	6	57	40	1.556	4.11	93	4.74	.293	7	.132	-5	9	-0.7
1934	Phi-N	13	18	.419	45	32	15	0	1	254	277	138	118	30	3	87	72	1.433	4.18	113	4.38	.273	15	.170	12	14	0.8
1935	Phi-N	0	2	.000	3	3	0	0	0	14^2	24	20	19	5	0	9	4	2.250	11.66	39	10.68	.348	0	.000	-11	0	-1.2
	StL-N	7	6	.538	26	9	2	0	2	82^2	96	48	42	6	3	26	18	1.476	4.57	90	4.51	.290	4	.160	-5	4	-0.6
	Yr.	7	8	.467	29	12	2	0	2	97^1	120	68	61	11	3	35	22	1.592	5.64	75	5.44	.300	4	.129	-17	4	-1.8
Total 8		**80**	**85**	**.485**	**292**	**142**	**64**	**4**	**24**	**1324^1**	**1541**	**784**	**686**	**125**	**37**	**497**	**423**	**1.539**	**4.66**	**99**	**4.87**	**.291**	**93**	**.193**	**3**	**77**	**-0.3**
• COLLINS, Ray	Raymond Williston Collins b: 2/11/1887, Colchester, VT d: 1/9/1970, Burlington, VT BL/TL, 6'1", 185 lbs. Deb: 7/19/1909																										
1909	Bos-A	4	3	.571	12	8	4	2	0	73^2	70	29	23	2	0	18	31	1.195	2.81	89	2.98	.269	3	.130	-4	4	-0.4
1910	Bos-A	13	11	.542	35	26	18	4	1	244^2	205	73	44	1	1	41	109	1.005	1.62	157	1.88	.229	15	.179	27	18	2.9
1911	Bos-A	11	12	.478	31	24	14	0	1	194^2	184	81	52	1	4	44	86	1.171	2.40	136	2.67	.256	9	.150	19	15	1.9
1912*	Bos-A	13	8	.619	27	24	17	4	0	199^1	192	65	56	4	2	42	82	1.174	2.53	135	2.73	.256	11	.169	20	19	2.1
1913	Bos-A	19	8	.704	30	30	19	3	0	246^2	242	88	72	3	2	37	88	1.131	2.63	112	2.60	.263	12	.150	13	19	1.6
1914	Bos-A	20	13	.606	39	30	16	6	0	272^1	252	5	76	3	0	56	72	1.131	2.51	107	2.55	.258	11	.139	0	19	0.0
1915	Bos-A	4	7	.364	25	9	2	0	2	104^2	101	62	50	1	1	31	43	1.261	4.30	65	3.00	.261	8	.286	-18	3	-1.5
Total 7		**84**	**62**	**.575**	**199**	**151**	**90**	**19**	**4**	**1336**	**1246**	**403**	**373**	**15**	**10**	**269**	**511**	**1.134**	**2.51**	**115**	**2.54**	**.254**	**69**	**.165**	**56**	**97**	**6.5**
• COLLINS, Rip	Harry Warren Collins b: 2/26/1896, Weatherford, TX d: 5/27/1968, Bryan, TX BR/TR, 6'1", 205 lbs. Deb: 4/19/1920																										
1920	NY-A	14	8	.636	36	18	10	2	1	187^1	171	82	67	6	14	79	66	1.335	3.22	118	3.39	.247	8	.129	12	13	0.8
1921*	NY-A	11	5	.688	28	16	7	2	0	137^1	158	103	83	6	10	78	64	1.718	5.44	78	5.30	.293	11	.196	-20	4	-2.0
1922	Bos-A	14	11	.560	32	29	15	3	0	210^2	219	101	88	4	10	103	69	1.528	3.76	109	4.09	.274	12	.158	11	16	0.8
1923	Det-A	3	7	.300	17	14	3	1	0	92^1	104	61	50	3	10	22	25	1.365	4.87	79	3.87	.284	3	.111	-9	2	-1.1
1924	Det-A	14	7	.667	34	30	11	1	0	216	199	99	77	6	4	63	75	1.213	3.21	128	2.78	.249	11	.145	22	16	1.4
1925	Det-A	6	11	.353	26	20	5	0	0	140	149	86	71	7	6	52	33	1.436	4.56	94	4.04	.281	5	.119	-4	6	-0.8
1926	Det-A	8	8	.500	30	13	5	3	1	122	128	53	37	4	7	44	44	1.410	2.73	149	3.88	.278	6	.154	19	9	1.7
1927	Det-A	13	7	.650	30	25	10	1	0	172^2	207	116	90	5	8	59	37	1.541	4.69	90	4.56	.312	11	.204	-8	8	-0.7
1929	StL-A	11	6	.647	26	20	10	1	1	155^1	162	79	69	16	6	73	47	1.513	4.00	111	4.64	.270	17	.274	6	13	0.9
1930	StL-A	9	7	.563	35	20	6	1	2	171^2	168	90	83	11	5	63	75	1.346	4.35	112	3.58	.259	7	.130	8	13	0.6
1931	StL-A	5	5	.500	17	14	2	0	0	107	130	55	45	5	1	38	34	1.570	3.79	122	4.81	.307	5	.147	10	8	0.9
Total 11		**108**	**82**	**.568**	**311**	**219**	**84**	**15**	**5**	**1712^1**	**1795**	**925**	**760**	**73**	**81**	**674**	**569**	**1.442**	**3.99**	**106**	**4.01**	**.275**	**96**	**.165**	**47**	**108**	**2.6**
• COLLUM, Jackie	Jack Dean Collum b: 6/21/1927, Victor, IA BL/TL, 5'7.5", 163 lbs. Deb: 9/21/1951																										
1951	StL-N	2	1	.667	3	2	1	1	0	17	11	3	3	0	0	10	5	1.235	1.59	250	2.31	.204	3	.429	4	3	0.5
1952	StL-N	0	0	....	2	0	0	0	0	3	2	1	0	0	0	1	0	1.000	0.00	....	1.52	.200	0	....	1	0	0.1
1953	StL-N	0	0	....	7	0	0	0	0	11^1	15	10	8	1	0	4	5	1.676	6.35	67	5.56	.326	0	.000	-2	0	-0.2
	Cin-N	7	11	.389	30	12	4	1	3	124^2	123	57	52	8	6	39	51	1.299	3.75	116	3.64	.263	10	.278	6	10	0.8
	Yr.	7	11	.389	37	12	4	1	3	136	138	67	60	9	6	43	56	1.331	3.97	109	3.80	.269	10	.256	3	10	0.6
1954	Cin-N	7	3	.700	36	2	1	0	0	79	86	43	33	8	5	32	28	1.494	3.76	112	4.79	.283	3	.231	3	6	0.5
1955	Cin-N	9	8	.529	32	17	5	0	1	134	128	65	54	17	2	37	49	1.231	3.63	117	3.63	.254	10	.250	9	9	1.1
1956	StL-N	6	2	.750	38	1	0	0	7	60	63	29	28	6	2	27	17	1.500	4.20	90	4.64	.281	3	.214	-3	4	-0.2
1957	Chi-N	1	1	.500	9	0	0	0	1	10^2	8	8	8	0	1	9	7	1.594	6.75	57	3.60	.211	0	....	-3	0	-0.3
	Bro-N	0	0	....	3	0	0	0	0	4^1	7	4	4	1	0	1	3	1.846	8.31	50	8.00	.368	0	....	-2	0	-0.2
	Yr.	1	1	.500	12	0	0	0	1	15	15	12	12	1	1	10	10	1.667	7.20	55	4.87	.263	0	....	-5	0	-0.5
1958	LA-N	0	0	....	2	0	0	0	0	3^1	4	3	3	2	0	2	0	1.800	8.10	51	10.75	.308	0	.000	-1	0	-0.2
1962	Min-A	0	2	.000	8	3	0	0	0	15^1	29	22	19	1	0	11	5	2.609	11.15	37	11.04	.414	0	.000	-12	0	-1.3
	Cle-A	0	0	....	1	0	0	0	0	1^1	4	2	2	0	0	0	1	3.000	13.50	29	16.67	.571	0	....	-1	0	-0.1
	Yr.	0	2	.000	9	3	0	0	0	16^2	33	24	21	1	0	11	6	2.640	11.34	36	11.49	.429	0	.000	-14	0	-1.4
Total 9		**32**	**28**	**.533**	**171**	**37**	**11**	**2**	**12**	**464**	**480**	**247**	**214**	**44**	**16**	**173**	**171**	**1.407**	**4.15**	**100**	**4.32**	**.273**	**29**	**.246**	**-2**	**32**	**0.5**
• COLOME, Jesus	Jesus (De la Cruz) Colome b: 12/23/1977, San Pedro de Macoris, Dominican Republic BR/TR, 6'2", 170 lbs. Deb: 6/21/2001																										
2001	TB-A	2	3	.400	30	0	0	0	0	48^2	37	22	18	8	2	25	31	1.274	3.33	135	3.62	.208	0	....	6	4	0.6
2002	TB-A	2	7	.222	32	0	0	0	0	41^1	56	41	38	6	2	33	33	2.153	8.27	54	8.57	.341	0	....	-18	0	-1.7
2003	TB-A	3	7	.300	54	0	0	0	2	74	69	37	37	9	3	46	69	1.554	4.50	101	4.76	.247	0	....	-1	4	-0.1
Total 3		**7**	**17**	**.292**	**116**	**0**	**0**	**0**	**2**	**164**	**162**	**100**	**93**	**23**	**7**	**104**	**133**	**1.622**	**5.10**	**88**	**5.38**	**.261**	**0**	**....**	**-14**	**8**	**-1.3**
• COLON, Bartolo	Bartolo Colon b: 5/24/1973, Altamira, Dominican Republic BR/TR, 6', 185 lbs. Deb: 4/4/1997																										
1997	Cle-A	4	7	.364	19	17	1	0	0	94	107	66	59	12	3	45	66	1.617	5.65	83	5.53	.286	0	.000	-9	2	-0.9
1998*	Cle-A★	14	9	.609	31	31	6	2	0	204	205	91	84	15	3	79	158	1.392	3.71	129	3.87	.260	1	.500	25	16	2.4
1999*	Cle-A	18	5	.783	32	32	1	1	0	205	185	97	90	24	7	76	161	1.273	3.95	127	3.68	.242	1	.143	26	16	2.4
2000	Cle-A	15	8	.652	30	30	2	1	0	188	163	86	81	21	4	98	212	1.388	3.88	128	3.97	.233	0	.000	25	15	2.2
2001*	Cle-A	14	12	.538	34	34	1	0	0	222^1	220	106	101	26	2	90	201	1.394	4.09	110	4.24	.261	1	.143	15	14	1.4
2002	Cle-A	10	4	.714	16	16	4	2	0	116^1	104	37	33	11	2	31	75	1.160	2.55	172	3.09	.245	1	.167	25	13	2.4
	Mon-N	10	4	.714	17	17	4	1	0	117	115	48	43	9	0	39	74	1.316	3.31	129	3.48	.259	5	.128	12	9	1.1

YEAR TM-L	W	L	PCT	G	GS	CG	SH	SV	IP	H	R	ER	HR	HB	BB	SO	RAT	ERA	ERA+	CERA	OAV	BH	AVG	PR+	WS	TPW
2003 Chi-A	15	13	.536	34	34	**9**	0	0	242	223	107	104	30	5	67	173	1.198	3.87	116	3.47	.248	0	.000	13	17	1.2
Total 7	100	62	.617	213	211	28	7	0	1388^{2}	1322	638	595	148	26	525	1120	1.330	3.86	121	3.86	.252	9	.123	132	102	12.3
• COLPAERT, Dick	Richard Charles Colpaert b: 1/3/1944, Fraser, MI BR/TR, 5'10", 182 lbs. Deb: 7/21/1970																									
1970 Pit-N	1	0	1.000	8	0	0	0	0	10^{2}	9	7	7	3	0	8	6	1.594	5.91	66	5.77	.237	0	....	-3	0	-0.3
• COLSON, Loyd	Loyd Albert Colson b: 11/4/1947, Wellington, TX BR/TR, 6'1", 190 lbs. Deb: 9/25/1970																									
1970 NY-A	0	0	....	1	3	0	0	0	2	3	1	1	0	0	0	2	1.500	4.50	78	4.47	.333	0	....	-0	0	0.0
• COLTON, Larry	Lawrence Robert Colton b: 6/8/1942, Los Angeles, CA BL/TR, 6'3", 200 lbs. Deb: 5/6/1968																									
1968 Phi-N	0	0	....	1	0	0	0	0	2	3	1	1	0	0	0	2	1.500	4.50	67	4.47	.333	0	....	-0	0	0.0
• COLYER, Steve	Stephen Edward Colyer b: 2/22/1979, St. Louis, MO BL/TL, 6'4", 205 lbs. Deb: 4/3/2003																									
2003 LA-N	0	0	....	13	0	0	0	0	19^{2}	22	6	6	0	0	9	16	1.576	2.75	146	4.44	.297	0	....	2	2	0.3
• COMBE, Geoff	Geoffrey Wade Combe b: 2/1/1956, Melrose, MA BR/TR, 6'2", 185 lbs. Deb: 9/2/1980																									
1980 Cin-N	0	0	....	4	0	0	0	0	6^{2}	9	8	8	0	0	4	10	1.950	10.80	33	6.08	.346	0	....	-5	0	-0.6
1981 Cin-N	1	0	1.000	14	0	0	0	0	17^{2}	27	15	15	3	0	10	9	2.094	7.64	47	8.87	.370	0	....	-8	0	-0.9
Total 2	1	0	1.000	18	0	0	0	0	24^{1}	36	23	23	3	0	14	19	2.055	8.51	42	8.11	.364	0	....	-13	0	-1.4
• COMBS, Pat	Patrick Dennis Combs b: 10/29/1966, Newport, RI BL/TL, 6'3", 200 lbs. Deb: 9/5/1989																									
1989 Phi-N	4	0	1.000	6	6	1	1	0	38^{2}	36	10	9	2	0	6	30	1.086	2.09	169	2.50	.248	2	.167	6	4	0.7
1990 Phi-N	10	10	.500	32	31	3	2	0	183^{1}	179	90	83	12	4	86	108	1.445	4.07	94	3.99	.257	9	.150	-8	9	-0.7
1991 Phi-N	2	6	.250	14	13	1	0	0	64^{1}	64	41	35	7	2	43	41	1.663	4.90	75	5.20	.254	2	.133	-9	0	-0.8
1992 Phi-N	1	1	.500	4	4	0	0	0	18^{2}	20	16	16	0	0	12	11	1.714	7.71	45	4.53	.278	1	.125	-9	0	-0.9
Total 4	17	17	.500	56	54	5	3	0	305	299	157	143	21	6	147	190	1.462	4.22	88	4.09	.257	14	.147	-18	13	-1.7
• COMELLAS, Jorge	Jorge (Pous) "Pancho" Comellas b: 12/7/1916, Havana, Cuba d: 9/13/2001, Miami, FL BR/TR, 6', 190 lbs. Deb: 4/19/1945																									
1945 Chi-N	0	2	.000	7	1	0	0	0	12	11	7	6	1	0	6	6	1.417	4.50	81	3.83	.244	0	.000	-1	0	-0.2
• COMER, Steve	Steven Michael Comer b: 1/13/1954, Minneapolis, MN BB/TR, 6'3", 205 lbs. Deb: 4/15/1978 C																									
1978 Tex-A	11	5	.688	30	11	3	2	1	117^{1}	107	36	30	5	1	37	65	1.227	2.30	163	2.95	.249	0	....	19	13	2.0
1979 Tex-A	17	12	.586	36	36	6	1	0	242^{1}	230	114	99	24	8	84	86	1.296	3.68	113	3.71	.252	0	....	10	15	1.0
1980 Tex-A	2	4	.333	12	11	0	0	0	41^{2}	65	41	37	5	2	22	9	2.088	7.99	49	8.65	.367	0	....	-18	0	-1.8
1981 Tex-A	8	2	.800	36	1	0	0	6	77^{1}	70	25	22	1	1	31	22	1.306	2.56	135	2.82	.241	0	....	6	8	0.7
1982 Tex-A	1	6	.143	37	3	1	0	6	97	133	64	55	11	2	36	23	1.742	5.10	76	6.34	.342	0	....	-12	1	-1.2
1983 Phi-N	1	0	1.000	3	1	0	0	0	8^{2}	11	6	5	0	0	3	1	1.615	5.19	69	4.78	.314	0	.000	-1	0	-0.2
1984 Cle-A	4	8	.333	22	20	1	0	0	117^{1}	146	80	74	11	4	39	39	1.577	5.68	72	5.26	.309	0	....	-22	1	-2.2
Total 7	44	37	.543	176	83	11	3	13	701^{2}	762	366	322	57	18	252	245	1.445	4.13	96	4.42	.281	0	.000	-18	38	-1.8
• COMPTON, Clint	Robert Clinton Compton b: 11/1/1950, Montgomery, AL BL/TL, 5'11", 185 lbs. Deb: 10/3/1972																									
1972 Chi-N	0	0	....	1	0	0	0	0	2	2	2	2	0	0	2	0	2.000	9.00	42	6.15	.286	0	....	-1	0	-0.1
• COMPTON, Jack	Harry Leroy Compton b: 3/9/1882, Lancaster, OH d: 7/4/1974, Lancaster, OH BR/TR, 5'9", 157 lbs. Deb: 9/7/1911																									
1911 Cin-N	0	1	.000	8	3	0	0	1	25^{1}	19	11	11	0	1	15	6	1.342	3.91	84	2.70	.204	2	.333	-2	1	-0.1
• COMSTOCK, Keith	Keith Martin Comstock b: 12/23/1955, San Francisco, CA BL/TL, 6', 175 lbs. Deb: 4/3/1984																									
1984 Min-A	0	0	....	4	0	0	0	0	6^{1}	6	6	6	2	0	4	2	1.579	8.53	49	6.46	.261	0	....	-3	0	-0.3
1987 SF-N	2	0	1.000	15	0	0	0	1	20^{2}	19	8	7	1	0	10	21	1.403	3.05	126	3.53	.253	0	.000	2	2	0.1
SD-N	0	1	.000	26	0	0	0	0	36	33	22	22	4	0	21	38	1.500	5.50	72	4.32	.252	0	.000	-7	1	-0.7
Yr.	2	1	.667	41	0	0	0	1	56^{2}	52	30	29	5	0	31	59	1.465	4.61	85	4.03	.252	0	.000	-5	3	-0.5
1988 SD-N	0	0	....	7	0	0	0	0	8	8	6	6	1	0	3	9	1.375	6.75	50	3.86	.250	0	....	-3	0	-0.3
1989 Sea-A	1	2	.333	31	0	0	0	0	25^{2}	26	8	8	2	0	10	22	1.403	2.81	144	3.81	.268	0	....	3	2	0.3
1990 Sea-A	7	4	.636	60	0	0	0	2	56	40	22	18	4	0	26	50	1.179	2.89	137	2.52	.206	0	....	7	6	0.7
1991 Sea-A	0	0	....	1	0	0	0	0	0^{1}	2	2	2	0	0	1	0	9.000	54.00	8	56.02	.667	0	....	-2	0	-0.2
Total 6	10	7	.588	144	0	0	0	3	153	134	74	69	14	0	75	142	1.366	4.06	97	3.64	.241	0	.000	-3	11	-0.3
• COMSTOCK, Ralph	Ralph Remick "Commy" Comstock b: 11/24/1890, Sylvania, OH d: 9/13/1966, Toledo, OH BR/TR, 5'10", 168 lbs. Deb: 8/26/1913																									
1913 Det-A	2	5	.286	10	7	1	0	1	60^{1}	90	55	36	0	1	16	37	1.757	5.37	54	5.61	.344	5	.227	-15	0	-1.5
1915 Bos-A	1	0	1.000	3	0	0	0	0	9	10	3	2	2	0	2	1	1.333	2.00	139	5.11	.294	0	.000	1	1	0.1
Pit-F	3	3	.500	12	7	3	0	2	52^{2}	44	25	19	3	1	7	18	.968	3.25	96	2.20	.237	0	.000	-1	3	-0.3
1918 Pit-N	5	6	.455	15	8	6	0	1	81	78	33	27	0	2	14	44	1.136	3.00	96	2.45	.259	5	.192	-4	4	-0.4
Total 3	11	14	.440	40	22	10	0	4	203	222	116	84	5	4	39	100	1.286	3.72	79	3.44	.284	10	.152	-19	8	-2.1
• CONDREY, Clay	Clayton Lee Condrey b: 11/19/1975, Beaumont, TX BR/TR, 6'3", 195 lbs. Deb: 8/28/2002																									
2002 SD-N	1	2	.333	9	3	0	0	0	26^{2}	20	7	5	1	2	8	16	1.050	1.69	223	2.29	.217	0	.000	6	2	0.6
2003 SD-N	1	2	.333	9	6	0	0	0	34	43	32	32	7	3	21	25	1.882	8.47	46	7.50	.305	2	.200	-17	0	-1.7
Total 2	2	4	.333	18	9	0	0	0	60^{2}	63	39	37	8	5	29	41	1.516	5.49	71	5.21	.270	2	.125	-10	2	-1.1
• CONE, Bob	Robert Earl Cone b: 2/27/1894, Galveston, TX d: 5/24/1955, Galveston, TX BR/TR, 6'2", 172 lbs. Deb: 7/25/1915																									
1915 Phi-A	0	0	....	1	1	0	0	0	0^{2}	5	3	3	0	0	0	0	7.500	40.50	7	53.29	.714	0	....	-3	0	-0.3
• CONE, David	David Brian Cone b: 1/2/1963, Kansas City, MO BL/TR, 6'1", 190 lbs. Deb: 6/8/1986																									
1986 KC-A	0	0	....	11	0	0	0	0	22^{2}	29	14	14	2	1	13	21	1.853	5.56	76	6.48	.309	0	....	-3	0	-0.3
1987 NY-N	5	6	.455	21	13	1	0	1	99^{1}	87	46	41	11	5	44	68	1.319	3.71	102	3.87	.239	2	.065	2	5	0.0
1988★NY-N★	20	3	.870	35	28	8	4	0	231^{1}	178	67	57	10	4	80	213	1.115	2.22	145	2.34	.213	12	.150	26	19	2.9
1989 NY-N	14	8	.636	34	33	7	2	0	219^{2}	183	92	86	20	4	74	190	1.170	3.52	93	2.89	.223	18	.234	-4	11	-0.1
1990 NY-N	14	10	.583	31	30	6	2	0	211^{2}	177	84	76	21	1	65	**233**	1.143	3.23	116	2.87	.226	14	.200	15	13	1.8
1991 NY-N	14	14	.500	34	34	5	2	0	232^{2}	204	95	85	13	5	73	**241**	1.191	3.29	111	2.85	.235	9	.125	14	15	1.4
1992 NY-N★	13	7	.650	27	27	7	**5**	0	196^{2}	162	75	63	12	9	82	214	1.241	2.88	120	3.04	.223	6	.092	15	13	1.5
★Tor-A	4	3	.571	8	7	0	0	0	53	39	16	15	3	3	29	47	1.283	2.55	160	3.08	.206	0	....	9	5	0.9
1993 KC-A	11	14	.440	34	34	6	1	0	254	205	102	94	20	10	114	191	1.256	3.33	138	3.25	.223	0	....	34	21	3.3
1994 KC-A★	16	5	.762	23	23	4	3	0	171^{2}	130	60	56	15	7	54	132	1.072	2.94	170	2.57	.209	0	....	39	**20**	3.6
1995 Tor-A	9	6	.600	17	17	5	2	0	130^{1}	113	53	49	12	5	41	102	1.182	3.38	139	3.12	.232	0	....	19	11	1.8
★NY-A	9	2	.818	13	13	1	0	0	99	82	42	42	12	1	47	89	1.303	3.82	121	3.63	.223	0	....	8	8	0.8
Yr.	18	8	.692	30	30	6	2	0	**229^{1}**	195	95	91	24	6	88	191	1.234	3.57	131	3.34	.228	0	....	27	19	2.5
1996★NY-A	7	2	.778	11	11	1	0	0	72	50	25	23	3	2	34	71	1.167	2.88	172	2.48	.198	0	....	18	8	1.6
1997★NY-A★	12	6	.667	29	29	1	0	0	195	155	67	61	17	4	86	222	1.236	2.82	158	3.15	.218	0	.000	37	16	3.5
1998★NY-A	**20**	7	.741	31	31	3	0	0	207^{2}	186	89	82	20	15	59	209	1.180	3.55	123	3.31	.237	0	.000	15	17	1.4
1999★NY-A★	12	9	.571	31	31	1	1	0	193^{1}	164	84	74	21	11	90	177	1.314	3.44	137	3.76	.229	1	.333	29	15	2.7
2000★NY-A	4	14	.222	30	29	0	0	0	155	192	124	119	25	9	82	120	1.768	6.91	70	6.72	.306	1	.333	-33	0	-3.0
2001 Bos-A	9	7	.563	25	25	0	0	0	135^{2}	148	74	65	17	10	57	115	1.511	4.31	104	5.06	.275	0	.000	5	8	0.5
2003 NY-N	1	3	.250	5	4	0	0	0	18	20	13	13	4	0	13	13	1.833	6.50	64	6.98	.282	1	.250	-5	0	-0.4
Total 17	194	126	.606	450	419	56	22	1	2898^{2}	2504	1222	1115	258	106	1137	2668	1.256	3.46	119	3.39	.232	64	.155	241	205	24.0
• CONGER, Dick	Richard Conger b: 4/3/1921, Los Angeles, CA d: 2/16/1970, Los Angeles, CA BR/TR, 6', 185 lbs. Deb: 4/22/1940																									
1940 Det-A	1	0	1.000	2	0	0	0	0	3	2	1	1	0	0	3	1	1.667	3.00	159	3.36	.200	0	....	1	0	0.1
1941 Pit-N	0	0	....	2	1	0	0	0	4	3	0	0	0	0	3	2	1.500	0.00	....	3.23	.214	0	....	2	1	0.2
1942 Pit-N	0	0	....	2	1	0	0	0	8^{1}	9	3	2	0	0	5	3	1.680	2.16	157	4.38	.290	0	.000	1	1	0.1
1943 Phi-N	2	7	.222	13	10	2	0	0	54^{2}	72	46	37	3	5	24	18	1.756	6.09	55	6.06	.327	1	.063	-16	0	-1.8
Total 4	3	7	.300	19	12	2	0	0	70	86	50	40	3	5	35	24	1.729	5.14	66	5.58	.313	1	.053	-12	2	-1.5

YEAR	TM-L	W	L	PCT	G	GS	CG	SH	SV	IP	H	R	ER	HR	HB	BB	SO	RAT	ERA	ERA+	CERA	OAV	BH	AVG	PR+	WS	TPW
• CONKWRIGHT, Allen	Allen Howard "Red" Conkwright b: 12/4/1896, Sedalia, MO d: 7/30/1991, La Mesa, CA BR/TR, 5'10", 170 lbs. Deb: 9/16/1920																										
1920	Det-A	2	1	.667	5	2	0	0	1	19^1	29	16	15	0	0	16	4	2.328	6.98	53	8.85	.397	1	.200	-7	0	-0.6
• CONLEY, Bob	Robert Burns Conley b: 2/1/1934, Mousie, KY BR/TR, 6'1", 188 lbs. Deb: 9/11/1958																										
1958	Phi-N	0	0	....	2	2	0	0	0	8^1	9	7	7	0	0	1	0	1.200	7.56	52	2.62	.273	0	.000	-3	0	-0.3
• CONLEY, Ed	Edward J. Conley b: 7/10/1864, Sandwich, MA d: 10/16/1894, Cumberland, RI, 5'8", 142 lbs. Deb: 7/20/1884																										
1884	Pro-N	4	4	.500	8	8	8	1	0	71	63	47	17	4	....	22	33	1.197	2.15	131	....	.225	4	.143	3	4	0.1
• CONLEY, Gene	Donald Eugene Conley b: 11/10/1930, Muskogee, OK BR/TR, 6'8", 225 lbs. Deb: 4/17/1952																										
1952	Bos-N	0	3	.000	4	3	0	0	0	12^2	23	16	11	4	2	9	6	2.526	7.82	46	13.09	.397	2	.400	-6	0	-0.5
1954	Mil-N★	14	9	.609	28	27	12	2	0	194^1	171	73	64	17	7	79	113	1.286	2.96	126	3.44	.240	12	.156	14	14	1.1
1955	Mil-N★	11	7	.611	22	21	10	0	0	158	152	81	73	23	1	52	107	1.291	4.16	90	3.81	.254	11	.204	-7	7	-0.8
1956	Mil-N	8	9	.471	31	19	5	1	3	158^1	169	74	55	13	2	52	68	1.396	3.13	111	4.00	.276	7	.156	4	8	0.4
1957*	Mil-N	9	9	.500	35	18	6	1	1	148	133	63	52	9	2	64	61	1.331	3.16	111	3.38	.244	9	.196	3	9	0.4
1958	Mil-N	0	6	.000	26	7	0	0	2	72	89	44	39	8	4	17	53	1.472	4.88	72	5.09	.309	3	.188	-12	0	-1.1
1959	Phi-N★	12	7	.632	25	22	12	3	1	180	159	68	60	13	2	42	102	1.117	3.00	**137**	2.65	.235	16	.239	23	17	2.5
1960	Phi-N	8	14	.364	29	25	9	2	0	183^1	192	85	75	10	2	42	117	1.276	3.68	105	3.37	.272	8	.127	3	10	0.2
1961	Bos-A	11	14	.440	33	30	6	2	1	199^2	229	116	109	33	3	65	113	1.472	4.91	85	5.14	.287	16	.219	-16	9	-1.2
1962	Bos-A	15	14	.517	34	33	9	2	1	241^2	238	116	106	28	5	68	134	1.266	3.95	105	3.68	.256	18	.207	4	15	0.8
1963	Bos-A	3	4	.429	9	9	0	0	0	40^2	51	31	30	4	1	21	14	1.770	6.64	57	6.13	.305	3	.200	-13	0	-1.3
Total	**11**	**91**	**96**	**.487**	**276**	**214**	**69**	**13**	**9**	**1588^2**	**1606**	**767**	**674**	**162**	**31**	**511**	**888**	**1.333**	**3.82**	**101**	**3.90**	**.264**	**105**	**.192**	**-2**	**89**	**0.5**
• CONLEY, Snipe	James Patrick Conley b: 4/25/1894, Cressona, PA d: 1/7/1978, DeSoto, TX BR/TR, 5'11.5", 179 lbs. Deb: 5/20/1914																										
1914	Bal-F	4	6	.400	35	11	4	2	1	125	112	49	35	2	6	47	86	1.272	2.52	126	3.23	.259	4	.114	12	9	1.0
1915	Bal-F	1	4	.200	25	6	4	0	0	86	97	48	41	5	4	32	40	1.500	4.29	79	4.99	.314	6	.250	-7	3	-0.6
1918	Cin-N	2	0	1.000	5	0	0	0	1	13^2	17	10	8	2	0	5	2	1.610	5.27	51	5.78	.321	1	.250	-4	0	-0.4
Total	**3**	**7**	**10**	**.412**	**65**	**17**	**8**	**2**	**2**	**224^2**	**226**	**107**	**84**	**9**	**10**	**84**	**128**	**1.380**	**3.36**	**95**	**4.06**	**.285**	**11**	**.175**	**1**	**12**	**0.0**
• CONN, Bert	Albert Thomas Conn b: 9/22/1879, Philadelphia, PA d: 11/2/1944, Philadelphia, PA TR, 6' Deb: 9/16/1898 ♦																										
1898	Phi-N	0	1	.000	1	1	0	0	0	7	13	9	5	1	0	2	3	2.143	6.43	53	9.28	.393	1	.333	-2	0	-0.1
1900	Phi-N	0	2	.000	4	1	1	0	0	17^1	29	29	16	0	6	16	2	2.596	8.31	43	10.74	.370	3	.333	-9	0	-0.8
Total	**2**	**0**	**3**	**.000**	**5**	**2**	**1**	**0**	**0**	**24^1**	**42**	**38**	**21**	**1**	**6**	**18**	**5**	**2.466**	**7.77**	**46**	**10.32**	**.377**	**8**	**.267**	**-11**	**0**	**-0.9**
• CONNALLY, Sarge	George Walter Connally b: 8/31/1898, McGregor, TX d: 1/27/1978, Temple, TX BR/TR, 5'11", 170 lbs. Deb: 9/10/1921																										
1921	Chi-A	0	1	.000	5	2	0	0	0	22^1	29	16	16	0	1	10	6	1.746	6.45	66	5.50	.330	4	.500	-6	1	-0.4
1923	Chi-A	0	0	....	3	0	0	0	0	8^2	7	6	6	0	0	12	3	2.192	6.23	64	5.50	.241	1	.333	-2	0	-0.2
1924	Chi-A	7	13	.350	44	13	6	0	6	160	177	95	72	4	9	68	55	1.531	4.05	102	4.24	.290	11	.220	2	8	0.1
1925	Chi-A	6	7	.462	40	2	0	0	8	104^2	122	66	54	2	2	58	45	1.720	4.64	89	4.96	.310	7	.250	-6	6	-0.4
1926	Chi-A	6	5	.545	31	8	5	0	3	108^1	128	51	38	0	2	35	47	1.505	3.16	122	4.09	.300	5	.156	7	8	0.6
1927	Chi-A	10	15	.400	43	18	11	1	5	198^1	217	108	90	8	9	83	58	1.513	4.08	99	4.41	.292	22	.328	-4	13	0.0
1928	Chi-A	2	5	.286	28	5	1	0	2	74^1	89	52	40	1	4	29	28	1.587	4.84	84	4.41	.313	2	.105	-7	2	-0.8
1929	Chi-A	0	0	....	11	0	0	0	1	11^1	13	6	6	0	0	8	3	1.853	4.76	90	5.32	.317	0	....	-1	1	-0.1
1931	Cle-A	5	5	.500	17	9	5	0	1	85^2	87	56	40	7	6	50	37	1.599	4.20	110	4.67	.256	5	.185	6	5	0.7
1932	Cle-A	8	6	.571	35	7	4	1	3	112^1	119	59	54	6	3	42	32	1.433	4.33	110	3.90	.266	7	.175	7	9	0.7
1933	Cle-A	5	3	.625	41	3	1	0	1	103	112	60	56	4	3	49	30	1.563	4.89	91	4.33	.271	6	.231	-5	5	-0.4
1934	Cle-A	0	0	....	5	0	0	0	1	5^1	4	3	3	0	0	5	1	1.688	5.06	90	3.96	.222	0	.000	-0	0	0.0
Total	**12**	**49**	**60**	**.450**	**303**	**67**	**33**	**2**	**31**	**994^1**	**1104**	**578**	**475**	**32**	**39**	**449**	**345**	**1.562**	**4.30**	**98**	**4.40**	**.288**	**70**	**.233**	**-8**	**58**	**-0.3**
• CONNELLY, Bill	William Wirt "Wild Bill" Connelly b: 6/29/1925, Alberta, VA d: 11/27/1980, Richmond, VA BL/TR, 6', 175 lbs. Deb: 8/22/1945																										
1945	Phi-A	1	1	.500	2	1	0	0	0	8	7	4	4	0	0	8	0	1.875	4.50	76	5.04	.259	0	.000	-1	0	-0.1
1950	Chi-A	0	0	....	2	0	0	0	0	2^1	5	3	3	1	0	1	0	2.571	11.57	39	14.58	.455	0	....	-2	0	-0.2
	Det-A	0	0	....	2	0	0	0	0	4	4	3	3	1	0	2	1	1.500	6.75	69	5.34	.250	0	.000	-1	0	-0.1
	Yr.	0	0	....	4	0	0	0	0	6^1	9	6	6	2	0	3	1	1.895	8.53	54	8.74	.333	0	.000	-3	0	-0.2
1952	NY-N	5	0	1.000	11	4	0	0	0	31^2	22	18	16	4	0	25	22	1.484	4.55	81	4.05	.208	4	.364	-3	3	0.0
1953	NY-N	0	1	.000	8	2	0	0	0	20^1	33	26	25	4	0	17	11	2.459	11.07	39	10.86	.371	0	.000	-15	0	-1.6
Total	**4**	**6**	**2**	**.750**	**25**	**7**	**0**	**0**	**0**	**66^1**	**71**	**54**	**51**	**10**	**0**	**53**	**34**	**1.869**	**6.92**	**58**	**6.70**	**.285**	**4**	**.211**	**-22**	**3**	**-1.9**
• CONNELLY, Steve	Steven Lee Connelly b: 4/27/1974, Long Beach, CA BR/TR, 6'4" Deb: 6/28/1998																										
1998	Oak-A	0	0	....	3	0	0	0	0	4^2	10	1	1	0	1	4	1	3.000	1.93	237	13.87	.435	0	....	1	0	0.1
• CONNOLLY, Ed	Edward Joseph Connolly, Jr. b: 12/3/1939, Brooklyn, NY d: 7/1/1998, New Canaan, CT BL/TL, 6'1", 190 lbs. Deb: 4/19/1964																										
1964	Bos-A	4	11	.267	27	15	1	1	0	80^2	80	50	44	3	6	64	73	1.785	4.91	79	5.28	.261	3	.167	-8	2	-0.8
1967	Cle-A	2	1	.667	15	4	0	0	0	49^1	63	46	41	6	1	34	45	1.966	7.48	44	7.12	.315	2	.182	-23	0	-2.5
Total	**2**	**6**	**12**	**.333**	**42**	**19**	**1**	**1**	**0**	**130**	**143**	**96**	**85**	**9**	**7**	**98**	**118**	**1.854**	**5.88**	**60**	**5.98**	**.282**	**5**	**.172**	**-30**	**2**	**-3.2**
• CONNOR, John	John Connor b: 7/1861, Nashua, NH d: 11/14/1905, Nashua, NH, 6' Deb: 7/26/1884																										
1884	Bos-N	1	4	.200	7	7	7	0	0	60	70	44	21	1	....	18	29	1.467	3.15	92	....	.276	2	.080	-3	2	-0.5
1885	Buf-N	0	1	.000	1	1	1	0	0	9	14	9	4	0	....	2	0	1.778	4.00	74	....	.340	0	.000	-0	0	-0.1
	Lou-a	1	3	.250	4	4	4	0	0	35	43	27	19	0	2	12	19	1.571	4.89	66	....	.290	2	.143	-6	1	-0.7
Total	**2**	**2**	**8**	**.200**	**12**	**12**	**12**	**0**	**0**	**104**	**127**	**80**	**44**	**1**	**2**	**32**	**48**	**1.529**	**3.81**	**80**	**....**	**.287**	**4**	**.095**	**-10**	**3**	**-1.2**
• CONNORS, Bill	William Joseph Connors b: 11/2/1941, Schenectady, NY BR/TR, 6'1", 180 lbs. Deb: 5/3/1966 C																										
1966	Chi-N	0	1	.000	11	0	0	0	0	16	20	13	13	4	0	7	3	1.688	7.31	50	6.62	.308	0	....	-6	0	-0.6
1967	NY-N	0	0	....	6	1	0	0	0	13	8	9	9	3	1	5	13	1.000	6.23	54	2.96	.170	0	.000	-4	0	-0.5
1968	NY-N	0	1	.000	9	0	0	0	0	14	21	14	14	0	1	7	8	2.000	9.00	34	6.53	.339	1	1.000	-9	0	-1.0
Total	**3**	**0**	**2**	**.000**	**26**	**1**	**0**	**0**	**0**	**43**	**49**	**36**	**36**	**7**	**2**	**19**	**24**	**1.581**	**7.53**	**44**	**5.49**	**.282**	**1**	**.500**	**-20**	**0**	**-2.1**
• CONNORS, Joe	Joseph P. Connors b: 1862, Paterson, NJ d: 1/13/1891, Denver, CO Deb: 5/3/1884 ♦																										
1884	Alt-U	0	1	.000	1	1	1	0	0	9	18	14	7	0	....	5	0	2.556	7.00	47	....	.391	1	.091	-3	0	-0.4
	KC-U	0	1	.000	2	1	1	0	0	12	24	14	6	1	....	0	1	2.000	4.50	62	....	.391	1	.091	-2	0	-0.2
	Yr.	0	2	.000	3	2	2	0	0	21	42	28	13	1	....	5	1	2.238	5.57	55	....	.391	2	.091	-5	0	-0.7
• CONOVER, Ted	Theodore "Huck" Conover b: 3/10/1868, Lexington, KY d: 7/27/1910, Paris, KY BR/TR, 5'10.5", 165 lbs. Deb: 5/26/1889																										
1889	Cin-a	0	0	....	1	0	0	0	1	2	4	4	3	0	0	2	1	3.000	13.50	29	....	.403	0	....	-2	0	-0.2
• CONROY, Tim	Timothy James Conroy b: 4/3/1960, McKeesport, PA BL/TL, 6', 185 lbs. Deb: 6/23/1978																										
1978	Oak-A	0	0	....	2	2	0	0	0	4^2	3	6	4	0	1	9	0	2.571	7.71	47	7.45	.188	0	....	-2	0	-0.2
1982	Oak-A	2	2	.500	5	5	1	0	0	25^1	20	13	10	1	0	18	17	1.500	3.55	110	3.72	.222	0	....	1	1	0.1
1983	Oak-A	7	10	.412	39	18	3	1	0	162^1	141	89	71	17	2	98	112	1.472	3.94	98	4.18	.232	0	....	-3	6	-0.3
1984	Oak-A	1	6	.143	38	14	0	0	0	93	82	58	55	11	2	63	69	1.559	5.32	70	4.71	.235	0	....	-17	1	-1.7
1985	Oak-A	0	1	.000	16	2	0	0	0	25^1	22	15	12	3	1	15	8	1.461	4.26	90	4.39	.237	0	....	-1	0	-0.1
1986	StL-N	5	11	.313	25	21	1	0	0	115^1	122	72	67	15	3	56	79	1.543	5.23	70	5.00	.275	4	.138	-24	0	-2.4
1987	StL-N	3	2	.600	10	9	0	0	0	40^2	48	26	25	0	1	25	22	1.795	5.53	75	5.23	.306	0	.000	-7	0	-0.8
Total	**7**	**18**	**32**	**.360**	**135**	**71**	**5**	**1**	**0**	**466^2**	**438**	**279**	**244**	**47**	**10**	**284**	**307**	**1.547**	**4.71**	**81**	**4.60**	**.249**	**4**	**.091**	**-52**	**8**	**-5.4**
• CONSTABLE, Jim	Jimmy Lee "Sheriff" Constable b: 6/14/1933, Jonesboro, TN BB/TL, 6'1", 185 lbs. Deb: 6/24/1956																										
1956	NY-N	0	0	....	3	0	0	0	0	4^1	9	7	7	0	1	7	1	3.692	14.54	26	16.54	.429	0	....	-5	0	-0.5
1957	NY-N	1	1	.500	16	0	0	0	0	28^1	27	10	9	2	4	7	13	1.200	2.86	137	3.76	.262	0	.000	3	2	0.3

YEAR	TM-L	W	L	PCT	G	GS	CG	SH	SV	IP	H	R	ER	HR	HB	BB	SO	RAT	ERA	ERA+	CERA	OAV	BH	AVG	PR+	WS	TPW
1958	SF-N	1	0	1.000	9	0	0	0	1	8	10	6	5	1	0	3	4	1.625	5.63	68	5.83	.323	1	1.000	-2	1	-0.1
	Cle-A	0	1	.000	6	2	0	0	0	9^{1}	17	13	12	2	1	4	3	2.250	11.57	32	11.48	.415	2	1.000	-8	0	-0.8
	Was-A	0	1	.000	15	2	0	0	0	27^{2}	29	15	15	3	1	15	25	1.590	4.88	78	5.14	.271	1	.250	-3	1	-0.3
	Yr.	0	2	.000	21	4	0	0	0	37	46	28	27	5	2	19	28	1.757	6.57	57	6.74	.311	3	.500	-11	1	-1.0
1962	Mil-N	1	1	.500	3	2	1	1	1	18	14	4	4	1	0	4	12	1.000	2.00	190	2.09	.222	0	.000	4	2	0.3
1963	SF-N	0	0	....	4	0	0	0	0	2^{1}	3	1	1	0	0	1	1	1.714	3.86	83	4.93	.333	0	....	-0	0	0.0
Total	5	3	4	.429	56	6	1	1	2	98	109	56	53	9	7	41	59	1.531	4.87	78	5.34	.291	4	.235	-11	6	-0.9
• CONSUEGRA, Sandy	Sandalio Simeon (Castello) Consuegra b: 9/3/1920, Potrerillos, Cuba BR/TR, 5'11", 165 lbs. Deb: 6/10/1950																										
1950	Was-A	7	8	.467	21	18	8	2	2	124^{2}	132	71	61	6	1	57	38	1.516	4.40	102	4.14	.270	7	.175	2	8	0.1
1951	Was-A	7	8	.467	40	12	5	0	3	146	140	71	65	10	0	63	31	1.390	4.01	102	3.65	.251	10	.233	3	8	0.3
1952	Was-A	6	0	1.000	30	2	0	0	5	73^{2}	80	30	25	2	0	27	19	1.452	3.05	116	3.81	.276	3	.176	5	7	0.5
1953	Was-A	0	0	....	4	0	0	0	0	5	9	6	6	0	0	4	0	2.600	10.80	36	9.80	.391	0	....	-4	0	-0.4
	Chi-A	7	5	.583	29	13	5	1	3	124	122	39	35	9	2	28	30	1.210	2.54	158	3.19	.258	2	.057	20	12	1.6
	Yr.	7	5	.583	33	13	5	1	3	129	131	45	41	9	2	32	30	1.264	2.86	140	3.44	.264	2	.057	16	12	1.3
1954	Chi-A★	16	3	.842	39	17	3	2	3	154	142	52	46	9	0	35	31	1.149	2.69	139	2.73	.248	11	.229	16	15	1.8
1955	Chi-A	6	5	.545	44	7	3	0	7	126^{1}	120	42	37	4	2	18	35	1.092	2.64	150	2.45	.256	3	.103	16	13	1.5
1956	Chi-A	1	2	.333	28	1	0	0	3	38^{1}	45	25	22	0	1	11	7	1.461	5.17	79	3.85	.296	0	.000	-5	1	-0.5
	Bal-A	1	1	.500	4	1	0	0	0	8^{2}	10	4	4	2	0	2	1	1.385	4.15	94	5.22	.294	1	.500	-0	1	0.0
	Yr.	2	3	.400	32	2	0	0	3	47	55	29	26	2	1	13	8	1.447	4.98	82	4.10	.296	1	.167	-5	2	-0.5
1957	Bal-A	0	0	....	5	0	0	0	0	5	4	1	1	0	0	0	0	.800	1.80	200	1.21	.211	0	....	1	1	0.1
	NY-N	0	0	....	4	0	0	0	0	3^{2}	7	5	1	1	0	1	1	2.182	2.45	160	9.52	.389	0	....	1	0	0.1
Total	8	51	32	.614	248	71	24	5	26	809^{1}	811	346	303	43	6	246	193	1.306	3.37	119	3.38	.262	37	.170	55	66	5.0
• CONTRERAS, Jose	Jose Contreras b: 12/12/1971, La Martinas, Cuba BR/TR, 6'4", 224 lbs. Deb: 3/31/2003																										
2003*	NY-A	7	2	.778	18	9	0	0	0	71	52	27	26	4	5	30	72	1.155	3.30	132	2.71	.202	0	.000	10	7	0.9
• CONTRERAS, Nardi	Arnaldo Juan Contreras b: 9/19/1951, Tampa, FL BB/TR, 6'2", 193 lbs. Deb: 5/23/1980 C																										
1980	Chi-A	0	0	....	8	0	0	0	0	13^{2}	18	10	9	1	2	7	8	1.829	5.93	68	6.68	.333	0	....	-3	0	-0.3
• CONVERSE, Jim	James Daniel Converse b: 8/17/1971, San Francisco, CA BL/TR, 5'9", 180 lbs. Deb: 5/22/1993																										
1993	Sea-A	1	3	.250	4	4	0	0	0	20^{1}	23	12	12	0	0	14	10	1.820	5.31	83	5.15	.295	0	....	-2	0	-0.2
1994	Sea-A	0	5	.000	13	8	0	0	0	48^{2}	73	49	47	5	1	40	39	2.322	8.69	56	8.98	.353	0	....	-20	0	-1.8
1995	Sea-A	0	3	.000	6	1	0	0	1	11	16	9	9	2	0	8	9	2.182	7.36	64	9.16	.348	0	....	-3	0	-0.3
	KC-A	1	0	1.000	9	0	0	0	0	12^{1}	12	8	8	0	0	8	5	1.622	5.84	82	3.97	.267	0	....	-2	1	-0.2
	Yr.	1	3	.250	15	1	0	0	1	23^{1}	28	17	17	2	0	16	14	1.886	6.56	73	6.42	.308	0	....	-5	1	-0.4
1997	KC-A	0	0	....	3	0	0	0	0	5	4	2	2	2	0	5	3	1.800	3.60	131	8.00	.222	0	....	1	0	0.1
Total	4	2	11	.154	35	13	0	0	1	97^{1}	128	80	78	9	1	75	66	2.086	7.21	66	7.51	.325	0	....	-26	1	-2.4
• CONWAY, Dick	Richard Butler Conway b: 4/25/1866, Lowell, MA d: 9/9/1926, Lowell, MA BL/TR, 5'7.5", 140 lbs. Deb: 7/22/1886																										
1886	Bal-a	2	7	.222	9	9	8	0	0	76^{2}	106	91	58	6	3	43	64	1.943	6.81	50	....	.314	7	.206	-27	1	-2.4
1887	Bos-N	9	15	.375	26	26	25	0	0	222^{1}	335	161	115	10	7	86	45	1.507	4.66	84	....	.338	52	.323	-22	12	-2.0
1888	Bos-N	4	2	.667	6	6	6	0	0	53	49	31	14	2	4	8	12	1.075	2.38	121	....	.237	4	.160	2	3	0.1
Total	3	15	24	.385	41	41	39	0	0	352	490	283	187	18	14	137	121	1.537	4.78	76	....	.319	63	.286	-47	16	-4.2
• CONWAY, Jerry	Jerome Patrick Conway b: 6/7/1901, Holyoke, MA d: 4/16/1980, Holyoke, MA BL/TL, 6'2", 190 lbs. Deb: 8/31/1920																										
1920	Was-A	0	0	....	1	0	0	0	0	2	1	0	0	0	0	1	0	1.000	0.00	....	1.54	.167	0	....	1	0	0.1
• CONWAY, Jim	James P. Conway b: 10/8/1858, Clifton, PA TR Deb: 5/5/1884																										
1884	Bro-a	3	9	.250	13	13	10	0	0	105^{1}	132	84	52	4	3	15	25	1.396	4.44	75	....	.291	6	.128	-11	2	-1.5
1885	Phi-a	0	1	.000	2	2	1	0	0	12^{1}	19	16	10	0	0	2	0	1.703	7.30	47	....	.339	0	.000	-5	0	-0.5
1889	KC-a	19	19	.500	41	37	33	0	0	335	334	232	121	12	14	90	115	1.266	3.25	128	....	.252	31	.208	45	20	3.4
Total	3	22	29	.431	56	52	44	0	0	452^{2}	485	332	183	16	17	107	140	1.308	3.64	106	....	.264	37	.183	29	22	1.5
• CONWAY, Pete	Peter J. Conway b: 10/30/1866, Burmont, PA d: 1/13/1903, Clifton Heights, PA BR/TR, 5'10.5", 162 lbs. Deb: 8/10/1885																										
1885	Buf-N	10	17	.370	27	27	26	1	0	210	256	173	109	10	....	44	94	1.429	4.67	64	....	.287	10	.111	-26	4	-2.9
1886	KC-N	5	15	.250	23	20	19	0	0	180	236	185	115	6	....	61	81	1.650	5.75	65	....	.305	47	.242	-35	4	-3.5
	Det-N	6	5	.545	11	11	11	0	0	91	93	55	34	1	....	25	35	1.297	3.36	98	....	.255	8	.186	-2	6	-0.1
	Yr.	11	20	.355	34	31	30	0	0	271	329	240	149	7	....	86	116	1.531	4.95	73	....	.289	55	.232	-37	10	-3.6
1887*	Det-N	8	9	.471	17	17	16	0	0	146	179	95	47	3	5	47	40	1.226	2.90	139	....	.293	24	.247	17	10	1.2
1888	Det-N	30	14	.682	45	45	43	4	0	391	315	170	98	11	13	57	176	.951	2.26	122	....	.213	46	.275	31	29	4.5
1889	Pit-N	2	1	.667	3	3	2	0	0	22	26	16	12	1	0	16	2	1.909	4.91	76	....	.285	1	.100	-3	1	-0.2
Total	5	61	61	.500	126	123	117	5	0	1040	1105	694	415	32	18	250	428	1.258	3.59	90	....	.262	136	.226	-19	54	-1.0
• CONZELMAN, Joe	Joseph Harrison Conzelman b: 7/14/1885, Bristol, CT d: 4/17/1979, Mountain Brook, AL BR/TR, 6', 170 lbs. Deb: 5/1/1913																										
1913	Pit-N	0	1	.000	3	2	1	0	0	15	13	4	2	0	1	5	9	1.200	1.20	251	2.74	.245	0	.000	3	1	0.3
1914	Pit-N	5	6	.455	33	9	4	1	2	101	88	39	33	2	3	40	39	1.267	2.94	90	2.97	.254	3	.111	-4	6	-0.6
1915	Pit-N	1	1	.500	18	1	0	0	0	47^{1}	41	18	18	0	3	20	22	1.289	3.42	80	3.00	.248	1	.091	-3	2	-0.5
Total	3	6	8	.429	54	12	5	1	2	163^{1}	142	61	53	2	7	65	70	1.267	2.92	92	2.96	.251	4	.095	-4	9	-0.8
• COOK, Aaron	Aaron Lane Cook b: 2/8/1979, Fort Campbell, KY BR/TR, 6'3", 175 lbs. Deb: 8/10/2002																										
2002	Col-N	2	1	.667	9	5	0	0	0	35^{2}	41	18	18	4	2	13	14	1.514	4.54	105	5.31	.295	1	.091	1	2	0.1
2003	Col-N	4	6	.400	43	16	1	0	0	124	160	89	83	8	8	57	43	1.750	6.02	81	5.95	.317	5	.172	-13	3	-1.3
Total	2	6	7	.462	52	21	1	0	0	159^{2}	201	107	101	12	10	70	57	1.697	5.69	86	5.81	.313	6	.150	-12	5	-1.2
• COOK, Andy	Andrew Bernard Cook b: 8/30/1967, Memphis, TN BR/TR, 6'5", 215 lbs. Deb: 5/9/1993																										
1993	NY-A	0	1	.000	4	0	0	0	0	5^{1}	4	3	3	1	0	7	4	2.063	5.06	82	6.62	.200	0	....	-1	0	-0.1
• COOK, Dennis	Dennis Bryan Cook b: 10/4/1962, LaMarque, TX BL/TL, 6'3", 185 lbs. Deb: 9/12/1988																										
1988	SF-N	2	1	.667	4	4	1	1	0	22	9	8	7	1	0	11	13	.909	2.86	114	1.29	.125	0	.000	1	2	0.2
1989	SF-N	1	0	1.000	2	2	1	0	0	15	13	3	3	1	0	5	9	1.200	1.80	187	3.12	.245	1	.167	2	2	0.3
	Phi-N	6	8	.429	21	16	1	1	0	106	97	56	47	17	2	33	58	1.226	3.99	89	3.66	.243	8	.222	-5	4	-0.4
	Yr.	7	8	.467	23	18	2	1	0	121	110	59	50	18	2	38	67	1.223	3.72	95	3.59	.243	9	.214	-2	6	-0.1
1990	Phi-N	8	3	.727	42	13	2	1	1	141^{2}	132	61	56	13	2	54	58	1.313	3.56	107	3.57	.250	13	.310	2	11	0.7
	LA-N	1	1	.500	5	3	0	0	0	14^{1}	23	13	12	7	0	2	6	1.744	7.53	49	9.43	.365	2	.286	-6	0	-0.6
	Yr.	9	4	.692	47	16	2	1	1	156	155	74	68	20	2	56	64	1.353	3.92	97	4.11	.262	15	.306	-4	11	0.1
1991	LA-N	1	0	1.000	20	1	0	0	0	17^{2}	12	3	1	0	0	7	8	1.075	0.51	705	1.79	.203	0	.000	6	3	0.6
1992	Cle-A	5	7	.417	32	25	1	0	0	158	156	79	67	29	2	50	96	1.304	3.82	102	4.28	.255	0	....	3	7	0.3
1993	Cle-A	5	5	.500	25	6	0	0	0	54	62	36	34	9	2	16	34	1.444	5.67	76	5.21	.295	0	....	-8	1	-0.8
1994	Chi-A	3	1	.750	38	0	0	0	0	33	29	17	13	4	0	14	26	1.303	3.55	132	3.40	.230	0	....	4	3	0.4
1995	Cle-A	0	0	....	11	0	0	0	0	12^{2}	16	9	9	3	1	10	13	2.053	6.39	73	8.80	.320	0	....	-2	0	-0.2
	Tex-A	0	2	.000	35	1	0	0	2	45	47	23	20	6	1	16	40	1.400	4.00	121	4.49	.280	0	....	4	4	0.4
	Yr.	0	2	.000	46	1	0	0	2	57^{2}	63	32	29	9	2	26	53	1.543	4.53	106	5.43	.289	0	....	2	4	0.2
1996*	Tex-A	5	2	.714	60	0	0	0	0	70^{1}	53	34	32	2	7	35	64	1.251	4.09	128	2.85	.214	0	....	9	7	0.8
1997*	Fla-N	1	2	.333	59	0	0	0	0	62^{1}	64	28	27	4	2	28	63	1.476	3.90	103	4.22	.267	5	.556	1	5	0.3
1998	NY-N	8	4	.667	73	0	0	0	1	68	60	21	18	5	3	27	79	1.279	2.38	174	3.35	.240	0	.000	13	9	1.3
1999*	NY-N	10	5	.667	71	0	0	0	3	63	50	27	27	11	1	27	68	1.222	3.86	114	3.60	.216	0	.000	3	7	0.3
2000*	NY-N	6	3	.667	68	0	0	0	2	59	63	35	35	8	5	31	53	1.593	5.34	83	5.49	.270	0	....	-6	3	-0.5
2001	NY-N	1	1	.500	43	0	0	0	0	36	28	18	17	6	1	10	34	1.056	4.25	97	2.83	.207	0	.000	-1	3	-0.1
	Phi-N	0	0	....	19	0	0	0	0	9^{2}	15	6	6	2	1	4	4	1.966	5.59	76	8.88	.385	0	....	-2	0	-0.2
	Yr.	1	1	.500	62	0	0	0	0	45^{2}	43	24	23	8	2	14	38	1.248	4.53	92	4.11	.247	0	.000	-2	3	-0.2

YEAR	TM-L	W	L	PCT	G	GS	CG	SH	SV	IP	H	R	ER	HR	HB	BB	SO	RAT	ERA	ERA+	CERA	OAV	BH	AVG	PR+	WS	TPW
2002	Ana-A	1	1	.500	37	0	0	0	0	24	21	9	9	2	1	10	13	1.292	3.38	131	3.58	.241	0	....	2	2	0.2
Total	15	64	46	.582	665	71	6	3	9	1011^{2}	950	486	440	130	31	390	739	1.325	3.91	105	3.99	.250	29	.264	21	73	3.0
• COOK, Earl	Earl Davis Cook b: 12/10/1908, Stouffville, Canada d: 11/21/1996, Markham, Canada BR/TR, 6', 195 lbs. Deb: 9/12/1941																										
1941	Det-A	0	0	....	1	0	0	0	0	2	4	1	1	0	0	0	1	2.000	4.50	101	7.48	.400	0	....	0	0	0.0
• COOK, Glen	Glen Patrick Cook b: 9/8/1959, Buffalo, NY BR/TR, 5'11", 180 lbs. Deb: 6/23/1985																										
1985	Tex-A	2	3	.400	9	7	0	0	0	40	53	42	42	12	3	18	19	1.775	9.45	45	8.32	.327	0	....	-23	0	-2.2
• COOK, Mike	Michael Horace Cook b: 8/14/1963, Charleston, SC BR/TR, 6'3", 200 lbs. Deb: 7/1/1986																										
1986	Cal-A	0	2	.000	5	1	0	0	0	9	13	12	9	3	0	7	6	2.222	9.00	46	10.40	.333	0	....	-5	0	-0.5
1987	Cal-A	1	2	.333	16	1	0	0	0	34^{1}	34	21	21	7	0	18	27	1.515	5.50	78	5.44	.264	0	....	-5	1	-0.4
1988	Cal-A	0	1	.000	3	0	0	0	0	3^{2}	4	2	2	0	1	1	2	1.364	4.91	79	4.93	.308	0	....	-0	0	0.0
1989	Min-A	0	1	.000	15	0	0	0	0	21^{1}	22	12	12	1	1	17	15	1.828	5.06	82	5.48	.268	0	....	-2	1	-0.2
1993	Bal-A	0	0	....	2	0	0	0	0	3	1	0	0	0	0	2	3	1.000	0.00	....	0.87	.091	0	....	1	1	0.1
Total	5	1	6	.143	41	2	0	0	0	71^{1}	74	47	44	11	2	45	53	1.668	5.55	76	5.86	.270	0	....	-11	3	-1.1
• COOK, Rollin	Rollin Edward Cook b: 10/5/1890, Toledo, OH d: 8/11/1975, Toledo, OH BR/TR, 5'9", 152 lbs. Deb: 7/6/1915																										
1915	StL-A	0	0	....	5	0	0	0	0	13^{2}	16	14	11	0	1	9	7	1.829	7.24	39	5.14	.276	1	.250	-7	0	-0.7
• COOK, Ron	Ronald Wayne Cook b: 7/11/1947, Jefferson, TX BL/TL, 6'1", 175 lbs. Deb: 4/10/1970																										
1970	Hou-N	4	4	.500	41	7	0	0	2	82^{1}	80	37	34	4	3	42	50	1.482	3.72	104	4.21	.274	4	.235	2	6	0.4
1971	Hou-N	0	4	.000	5	4	0	0	0	25^{2}	23	14	14	2	1	8	10	1.208	4.91	68	3.02	.237	2	.250	-5	0	-0.5
Total	2	4	8	.333	46	11	0	0	2	108	103	51	48	6	4	50	60	1.417	4.00	93	3.92	.265	6	.240	-3	6	-0.1
• COOKE, Steve	Steven Montague Cooke b: 1/14/1970, Lihue-Kauai, HI BR/TL, 6'6", 229 lbs. Deb: 7/28/1992																										
1992	Pit-N	2	0	1.000	11	0	0	0	1	23	22	9	9	2	0	4	10	1.130	3.52	98	2.92	.253	1	.333	-0	2	0.0
1993	Pit-N	10	10	.500	32	32	3	1	0	210^{2}	207	101	91	22	3	59	132	1.263	3.89	104	3.58	.258	11	.155	2	12	0.1
1994	Pit-N	4	11	.267	25	23	2	0	0	134^{1}	157	79	75	21	5	46	74	1.511	5.02	86	5.38	.298	8	.190	-12	4	-1.1
1996	Pit-N	0	0	....	3	0	0	0	0	8^{1}	11	7	7	1	0	5	7	1.920	7.56	58	6.83	.314	0	.000	-3	0	-0.3
1997	Pit-N	9	15	.375	32	32	0	0	0	167^{1}	184	95	80	15	9	77	109	1.560	4.30	100	4.90	.284	3	.058	1	7	-0.2
1998	Cin-N	1	0	1.000	1	1	0	0	0	6	4	1	1	0	1	0	3	.667	1.50	286	1.23	.182	1	.500	2	1	0.2
Total	6	26	36	.419	104	88	5	1	1	549^{2}	585	292	263	61	18	191	335	1.412	4.31	97	4.41	.276	24	.140	-10	26	-1.3
• COOMBS, Bobby	Raymond Franklin Coombs b: 2/2/1908, Goodwins Mills, ME d: 10/21/1991, Ogunquit, ME BR/TR, 5'9.5", 160 lbs. Deb: 6/8/1933																										
1933	Phi-A	0	1	.000	21	0	0	0	2	31^{1}	47	30	26	4	0	20	8	2.138	7.47	57	8.13	.348	2	.400	-10	0	-0.9
1943	NY-N	0	1	.000	9	0	0	0	0	16	33	26	23	1	0	8	5	2.563	12.94	27	10.61	.423	0	.000	-17	0	-1.8
Total	2	0	2	.000	30	0	0	0	2	47^{1}	80	56	49	5	0	28	13	2.282	9.32	41	8.97	.375	2	.286	-27	0	-2.6
• COOMBS, Danny	Daniel Bernard Coombs b: 3/23/1942, Lincoln, ME BR/TL, 6'4", 210 lbs. Deb: 9/27/1963																										
1963	Hou-N	0	0	....	1	0	0	0	0	0^{1}	3	1	1	0	0	0	0	9.000	27.00	12	67.29	.750	0	....	-1	0	-0.1
1964	Hou-N	1	1	.500	7	1	0	0	0	18	21	10	10	1	1	10	14	1.722	5.00	68	5.70	.300	0	.000	-3	0	-0.4
1965	Hou-N	0	2	.000	26	3	0	0	0	47	54	26	25	3	3	23	35	1.638	4.79	70	5.18	.292	1	.111	-7	0	-0.7
1966	Hou-N	0	0	....	2	0	0	0	0	2^{2}	4	1	1	0	0	0	3	1.500	3.38	101	4.47	.333	0	.000	0	0	0.0
1967	Hou-N	3	0	1.000	6	2	0	0	0	24^{1}	21	9	9	0	0	9	23	1.233	3.33	99	2.32	.233	1	.125	0	2	0.1
1968	Hou-N	4	3	.571	40	2	0	0	2	46^{2}	52	21	17	0	1	17	29	1.479	3.28	90	3.74	.286	4	.400	-1	3	0.1
1969	Hou-N	0	1	.000	8	0	0	0	0	8	12	6	6	0	1	2	3	1.750	6.75	52	6.25	.364	0	.000	-3	0	-0.3
1970	SD-N	10	14	.417	35	27	5	1	0	188^{1}	185	83	69	12	2	76	105	1.386	3.30	121	3.62	.256	5	.096	14	11	1.3
1971	SD-N	1	6	.143	19	7	0	0	0	57^{2}	81	52	40	10	0	25	37	1.838	6.24	53	6.97	.327	3	.214	-18	0	-1.9
Total	9	19	27	.413	144	42	5	1	2	393	433	209	178	26	8	162	249	1.514	4.08	86	4.44	.280	14	.140	-17	16	-1.9
• COOMBS, Jack	John Wesley "Colby Jack" Coombs b: 11/18/1882, Le Grand, IA d: 4/15/1957, Palestine, TX BB/TR, 6', 185 lbs. Deb: 7/5/1906 M/C ♦																										
1906	Phi-A	10	10	.500	23	18	13	1	0	173	144	65	48	0	7	68	90	1.225	2.50	109	2.55	.229	16	.239	5	11	0.7
1907	Phi-A	6	9	.400	23	17	10	2	2	132^{2}	109	58	46	2	9	64	73	1.304	3.12	83	2.92	.227	8	.167	-8	6	-1.0
1908	Phi-A	7	5	.583	26	18	10	4	0	153	130	63	34	1	3	64	80	1.268	2.00	128	2.77	.233	56	.255	13	17	2.0
1909	Phi-A	12	11	.522	30	24	18	6	1	205^{2}	156	63	53	1	6	73	97	1.113	2.32	103	2.15	.213	14	.169	-0	13	0.1
1910*	Phi-A	**31**	9	.775	**45**	38	35	**13**	1	353	248	74	51	0	7	115	224	1.028	1.30	182	1.72	.201	29	.220	35	**37**	4.2
1911*	Phi-A	**28**	12	.700	47	**40**	26	1	2	336^{2}	360	166	132	8	16	119	185	1.423	3.53	89	3.96	.280	45	.319	-16	23	-0.3
1912	Phi-A	21	10	.677	40	32	23	1	2	262^{1}	227	120	96	5	10	94	120	1.224	3.29	94	2.86	.241	28	.255	-10	18	-0.4
1913	Phi-A	0	0	....	2	2	0	0	0	5^{1}	5	9	6	0	1	6	0	2.063	10.13	27	6.12	.250	1	.333	-4	0	-0.4
1914	Phi-A	0	1	.000	2	2	0	0	0	8	8	4	4	0	1	3	1	1.375	4.50	58	3.74	.267	3	.273	-2	0	-0.2
1915	Bro-N	15	10	.600	29	24	17	2	0	195^{2}	166	71	56	1	16	91	56	1.313	2.58	108	3.02	.236	21	.280	3	16	0.8
1916*	Bro-N	13	8	.619	27	20	10	3	0	159	136	54	47	3	2	44	47	1.132	2.66	101	2.38	.239	11	.180	-3	11	-0.3
1917	Bro-N	7	11	.389	31	14	9	0	0	141	147	76	62	7	8	49	34	1.390	3.96	70	3.96	.284	10	.227	-20	3	-2.0
1918	Bro-N	8	14	.364	27	20	16	2	0	189	191	97	80	10	2	49	44	1.270	3.81	73	3.25	.266	19	.168	-21	5	-2.8
1920	Det-A	0	0	....	2	0	0	0	0	5^{2}	7	5	2	0	0	2	1	1.588	3.18	117	4.66	.318	0	.000	0	0	0.0
Total	14	158	110	.590	354	269	187	35	8	2320	2034	925	717	38	88	841	1052	1.239	2.78	100	2.85	.241	261	.235	-29	160	0.3
• COONEY, Bob	Robert Daniel Cooney b: 7/12/1907, Glens Falls, NY d: 5/4/1976, Glens Falls, NY BR/TR, 5'11", 160 lbs. Deb: 9/6/1931																										
1931	StL-A	0	3	.000	5	4	1	0	0	39^{1}	46	21	18	1	1	20	13	1.678	4.12	113	4.87	.291	5	.385	2	3	0.3
1932	StL-A	1	2	.333	23	3	1	0	1	71	94	61	55	8	2	36	23	1.831	6.97	70	6.60	.324	0	.000	-17	0	-1.8
Total	2	1	5	.167	28	7	2	0	1	110^{1}	140	82	73	9	3	56	36	1.776	5.95	81	5.99	.312	5	.143	-15	3	-1.5
• COONEY, Johnny	John Walter Cooney b: 3/18/1901, Cranston, RI d: 7/8/1986, Sarasota, FL BR/TL, 5'10", 165 lbs. Deb: 4/19/1921 M/C/U ♦																										
1921	Bos-N	0	1	.000	8	1	0	0	0	20^{2}	19	12	9	3	0	10	9	1.403	3.92	93	4.11	.241	1	.200	-1	1	-0.1
1922	Bos-N	1	2	.333	4	3	1	0	0	25	19	10	6	0	1	6	7	1.000	2.16	185	1.76	.224	0	.000	5	2	0.4
1923	Bos-N	3	5	.375	23	8	5	2	0	98	92	43	36	3	3	22	23	1.163	3.31	120	2.67	.246	25	.379	8	9	1.3
1924	Bos-N	8	9	.471	34	19	12	2	2	181	176	79	64	4	4	50	67	1.249	3.18	120	2.96	.260	33	.254	14	16	1.1
1925	Bos-N	14	14	.500	31	29	20	2	0	245^{2}	267	123	95	18	3	50	65	1.290	3.48	115	3.55	.274	33	.320	11	19	1.8
1926	Bos-N	3	3	.500	19	8	3	1	0	83^{1}	106	52	37	0	7	29	23	1.620	4.00	89	4.82	.320	38	.302	-3	6	0.1
1928	Bos-N	3	7	.300	24	5	2	0	1	89^{2}	106	47	43	7	0	31	18	1.528	4.32	91	4.75	.303	7	.171	-1	3	-0.3
1929	Bos-N	2	3	.400	14	2	1	0	3	45	57	29	25	4	0	22	11	1.756	5.00	94	5.75	.315	23	.319	-1	4	-0.1
1930	Bos-N	0	0	....	2	0	0	0	0	7	16	14	14	2	1	3	1	2.714	18.00	27	14.90	.471	0	.000	-10	0	-0.9
Total	9	34	44	.436	159	75	44	7	6	795^{1}	858	409	329	41	19	223	224	1.359	3.72	106	3.76	.278	965	.286	23	60	3.3
• COOPER, Brian	Brian John Cooper b: 8/19/1974, Hollywood, CA BR/TR, 6'1", 185 lbs. Deb: 9/7/1999																										
1999	Ana-A	1	1	.500	5	5	0	0	0	27^{2}	23	15	15	3	4	18	15	1.482	4.88	99	4.79	.228	0	....	-0	2	0.0
2000	Ana-A	4	8	.333	15	15	1	1	0	87	105	66	57	18	2	35	36	1.609	5.90	86	6.17	.299	0	.000	-10	2	-1.0
2001	Ana-A	0	1	.000	7	1	0	0	0	13^{2}	10	5	4	2	0	4	7	1.024	2.63	173	2.51	.200	0	....	3	1	0.3
2002	Tor-A	0	1	.000	2	2	0	0	0	8^{1}	14	13	13	5	0	4	3	2.160	14.04	33	13.71	.400	0	....	-9	0	-0.8
Total	4	5	11	.313	29	23	1	1	0	136^{2}	152	99	89	28	6	61	61	1.559	5.86	84	5.98	.283	0	.000	-16	5	-1.5
• COOPER, Cal	Calvin Asa Cooper b: 8/11/1922, Great Falls, SC d: 7/4/1994, Clinton, SC BR/TR, 6'2.5", 180 lbs. Deb: 9/14/1948																										
1948	Was-A	0	0	....	1	0	0	0	0	1	5	5	5	1	0	1	0	6.000	45.00	10	50.46	.625	0	....	-4	0	-0.4
• COOPER, Don	Donald James Cooper b: 1/15/1956, New York, NY BR/TR, 6'1", 185 lbs. Deb: 4/9/1981 C																										
1981	Min-A	1	5	.167	27	2	0	0	0	58^{2}	61	33	28	9	1	32	33	1.585	4.30	92	5.29	.274	0	....	-2	2	-0.2
1982	Min-A	0	1	.000	6	1	0	0	0	11^{1}	14	12	12	0	0	11	5	2.206	9.53	44	6.64	.311	0	....	-7	0	-0.7
1983	Tor-A	0	0	....	4	0	0	0	0	5^{1}	8	4	4	3	0	0	5	1.500	6.75	64	8.99	.348	0	....	-1	0	-0.1
1985	NY-A	0	0	....	7	0	0	0	0	10	12	6	6	2	0	3	4	1.500	5.40	74	5.57	.300	0	....	-2	0	-0.2
Total	4	1	6	.143	44	3	0	0	0	85^{1}	95	55	50	14	1	46	47	1.652	5.27	77	5.74	.287	0	....	-12	2	-1.2

YEAR TM-L	W	L	PCT	G	GS	CG	SH	SV	IP	H	R	ER	HR	HB	BB	SO	RAT	ERA	ERA+	CERA	OAV	BH	AVG	PR+	WS	TPW
• COOPER, Guy	Guy Evans "Rebel" Cooper b: 1/28/1893, Rome, GA d: 8/2/1951, Santa Monica, CA BB/TR, 6'1", 185 lbs. Deb: 5/2/1914																									
1914 NY-A	0	0	....	1	0	0	0	0	3	3	3	3	0	0	2	3	1.667	9.00	31	4.40	.273	0	.000	-2	0	-0.2
Bos-A	1	0	1.000	9	1	0	0	0	22	23	15	13	1	3	9	5	1.455	5.32	50	4.88	.299	0	.000	-7	0	-0.9
Yr.	1	0	1.000	10	1	0	0	0	25	26	18	16	1	3	11	8	1.480	5.76	47	4.83	.296	0	.000	-9	0	-1.1
1915 Bos-A	0	0	....	1	0	0	0	0	2	0	0	0	0	0	2	0	1.000	0.00	....	0.92	.000	0	....	1	0	0.1
Total 2	1	0	1.000	11	1	0	0	0	27	26	18	16	1	3	13	8	1.444	5.33	51	4.54	.296	0	.000	-8	0	-1.0
• COOPER, Mort	Morton Cecil Cooper b: 3/2/1913, Atherton, MO d: 11/17/1958, Little Rock, AR BR/TR, 6'2", 210 lbs. Deb: 9/14/1938																									
1938 StL-N	2	1	.667	4	3	1	0	1	23^2	17	11	8	1	1	12	11	1.225	3.04	130	2.53	.195	2	.222	2	2	0.3
1939 StL-N	12	6	.667	45	26	7	2	4	210^2	208	94	76	6	2	97	130	1.448	3.25	127	3.64	.260	16	.232	18	17	2.1
1940 StL-N	11	12	.478	38	29	16	3	3	230^2	225	103	93	12	3	86	95	1.348	3.63	110	3.43	.253	13	.157	13	15	1.1
1941 StL-N	13	9	.591	29	25	12	0	0	186^2	175	88	81	15	3	69	118	1.307	3.91	96	3.40	.244	13	.186	-6	11	-0.7
1942* StL-N★	**22**	7	.759	37	35	22	**10**	0	278^2	207	73	55	9	5	68	152	.987	**1.78**	**193**	**1.81**	**.204**	19	.184	**47**	**29**	**5.0**
1943* StL-N★	**21**	8	.724	37	32	24	6	3	274	228	81	70	5	5	79	141	1.120	2.30	146	2.27	.226	17	.170	26	**28**	2.6
1944* StL-N	22	7	.759	34	33	22	**7**	1	252^1	227	74	69	6	5	60	97	1.137	2.46	143	2.48	.239	19	.202	24	24	2.6
1945 StL-N	2	0	1.000	4	3	1	0	0	23^2	20	7	4	1	1	7	14	1.141	1.52	246	2.58	.227	2	.333	5	3	0.6
Bos-N★	7	4	.636	20	11	4	1	1	78	77	35	29	4	1	27	45	1.333	3.35	114	3.46	.257	6	.231	4	6	0.5
Yr.	9	4	.692	24	14	5	1	1	101^2	97	42	33	5	2	34	59	1.289	2.92	131	3.25	.250	8	.250	9	9	1.1
1946 Bos-N★	13	11	.542	28	27	15	4	1	199	181	76	69	16	0	39	83	1.106	3.12	110	2.65	.239	14	.209	8	13	1.0
1947 Bos-N	2	5	.286	10	7	2	0	0	46^2	48	26	21	2	2	13	15	1.307	4.05	96	3.47	.271	0	.000	-0	2	-0.2
NY-N	1	5	.167	8	8	2	0	0	36^2	51	32	29	7	0	13	12	1.745	7.12	57	6.81	.323	6	.429	-13	1	-0.9
Yr.	3	10	.231	18	15	4	0	0	83^1	99	58	50	9	2	26	27	1.500	5.40	74	4.94	.296	6	.222	-13	3	-1.0
1949 Chi-N	0	0	....	1	0	0	0	0	0	2	3	3	1	0	1	0	....	∞	....	∞	1.000	0	....	-3	0	-0.3
Total 11	128	75	.631	295	239	128	33	14	1840^2	1666	703	607	85	28	571	913	1.215	2.97	125	2.87	.240	127	.194	126	151	13.8
• COOPER, Pat	Orge Patterson Cooper b: 11/26/1917, Albemarle, NC d: 3/15/1993, Charlotte, NC BR/TR, 6'3", 180 lbs. Deb: 5/11/1946 ♦																									
1946 Phi-A	0	0	....	1	0	0	0	0	1	1	0	0	0	0	1	0	2.000	0.00	....	5.17	.250	0	....	0	0	0.0
• COOPER, Wilbur	Arley Wilbur Cooper b: 2/24/1892, Bearsville, WV d: 8/7/1973, Encino, CA BR/TL, 5'11", 175 lbs. Deb: 8/29/1912																									
1912 Pit-N	3	0	1.000	6	4	3	2	0	38	32	7	7	1	0	15	30	1.237	1.66	196	2.63	.227	2	.154	6	4	0.6
1913 Pit-N	5	3	.625	30	9	3	1	0	93	98	52	34	0	2	45	39	1.538	3.29	91	3.91	.276	2	.077	-2	3	-0.4
1914 Pit-N	16	15	.516	40	34	19	0	0	266^2	246	99	63	4	5	79	102	1.219	2.13	124	2.73	.254	19	.207	15	19	1.7
1915 Pit-N	5	16	.238	38	21	11	1	4	185^2	180	92	68	4	9	52	71	1.250	3.30	83	3.04	.262	7	.117	-11	4	-1.5
1916 Pit-N	12	11	.522	42	23	16	2	2	246	189	72	51	4	4	74	111	1.069	1.87	143	2.00	.215	17	.215	28	20	3.2
1917 Pit-N	17	11	.607	40	34	23	7	1	297^2	276	96	78	4	4	54	99	1.109	2.36	120	2.45	.258	21	.204	18	22	2.3
1918 Pit-N	19	14	.576	38	29	26	2	**3**	273^1	219	86	64	2	10	65	117	1.039	2.11	136	2.00	.223	23	.242	14	23	1.9
1919 Pit-N	19	13	.594	35	32	**27**	4	1	286^2	229	97	85	10	15	74	106	1.057	2.67	113	2.25	.225	29	.287	13	25	2.1
1920 Pit-N	24	15	.615	44	36	28	3	2	327	307	113	87	4	11	52	114	1.098	2.39	134	2.41	.253	25	.221	31	31	3.3
1921 Pit-N	**22**	14	.611	38	**38**	29	2	0	**327**	341	145	118	9	10	80	134	1.287	3.25	118	3.28	.272	31	.254	20	27	2.4
1922 Pit-N	23	14	.622	41	36	**27**	4	0	294^2	330	130	104	13	7	61	129	1.327	3.18	128	3.64	.286	29	.269	**34**	**27**	**4.1**
1923 Pit-N	17	19	.472	39	**38**	26	1	0	294^2	331	136	117	11	11	71	77	1.364	3.57	112	3.80	.288	28	.262	9	21	1.2
1924 Pit-N	20	14	.588	38	35	25	**4**	1	268^2	296	116	98	13	5	40	62	1.251	3.28	117	3.39	.283	36	.346	6	24	1.5
1925 Chi-N	12	14	.462	32	26	13	0	0	212^1	249	115	101	18	4	61	41	1.460	4.28	101	4.46	.291	17	.207	-3	13	-0.2
1926 Chi-N	2	1	.667	8	8	3	2	0	55	65	32	27	6	0	21	18	1.564	4.42	87	5.14	.311	7	.389	-5	3	-0.2
Det-A	0	4	.000	8	3	0	0	0	13^2	27	18	17	0	3	9	2	2.634	11.20	36	11.25	.443	0	.000	-11	0	-1.1
Total 15	216	178	.548	517	406	279	35	14	3480	3415	1406	1119	103	100	853	1252	1.226	2.89	116	3.02	.262	293	.239	162	266	20.8
• COPELAND, Mays	Mays Copeland b: 8/31/1913, Mountain View, AR d: 11/29/1982, Indio, CA BR/TR, 6', 180 lbs. Deb: 4/27/1935																									
1935 StL-N	0	0	....	1	0	0	0	0	0^2	2	1	1	0	0	0	0	3.000	13.50	30	14.52	.667	0	....	-1	0	-0.1
• COPPINGER, Rocky	John Thomas Coppinger b: 3/19/1974, El Paso, TX BR/TR, 6'5", 245 lbs. Deb: 6/11/1996																									
1996* Bal-A	10	6	.625	23	22	0	0	0	125	126	76	72	25	2	60	104	1.488	5.18	95	5.27	.263	0	....	-4	6	-0.3
1997 Bal-A	1	1	.500	5	4	0	0	0	20	21	14	14	2	1	16	22	1.850	6.30	70	6.15	.273	0	....	-4	0	-0.4
1998 Bal-A	0	0	....	6	1	0	0	0	15^2	16	9	9	3	0	7	13	1.468	5.17	88	4.68	.246	0	....	-1	1	-0.1
1999 Bal-A	0	1	.000	11	2	0	0	0	21^2	25	21	20	8	0	19	17	2.031	8.31	56	9.55	.294	1	1.000	-9	0	-0.8
Mil-N	5	3	.625	29	0	0	0	0	36^2	35	16	15	5	0	23	39	1.582	3.68	123	4.87	.250	0	.000	4	4	0.3
2001 Mil-N	1	0	1.000	8	3	0	0	0	22^2	24	17	17	5	1	15	15	1.721	6.75	64	6.77	.282	0	.000	-6	0	-0.7
Total 5	17	11	.607	82	32	0	0	0	241^2	247	153	147	48	4	140	210	1.601	5.47	86	5.77	.265	1	.125	-20	11	-1.9
• COPPOLA, Henry	Henry Peter Coppola b: 8/4/1912, East Douglas, MA d: 7/10/1990, Norfolk, MA BR/TR, 5'11", 175 lbs. Deb: 4/19/1935																									
1935 Was-A	3	4	.429	19	5	2	1	0	59^1	72	40	39	6	1	29	19	1.702	5.92	73	5.55	.300	1	.071	-10	1	-1.0
1936 Was-A	0	0	....	6	0	0	0	1	14	17	9	7	1	0	12	2	2.071	4.50	106	6.77	.315	1	.333	0	1	0.1
Total 2	3	4	.429	25	5	2	1	1	73^1	89	49	46	7	1	41	21	1.773	5.65	78	5.78	.303	2	.118	-10	2	-0.9
• CORBETT, Doug	Douglas Mitchell Corbett b: 11/4/1952, Sarasota, FL BR/TR, 6'1", 185 lbs. Deb: 4/10/1980																									
1980 Min-A	8	6	.571	73	0	0	0	23	136^1	102	31	30	7	1	42	89	1.056	1.98	220	2.16	.213	0	....	35	24	3.5
1981 Min-A★	2	6	.250	**54**	0	0	0	17	87^2	80	29	25	5	0	34	60	1.300	2.57	154	2.96	.239	0	....	14	12	1.5
1982 Min-A	0	2	.000	10	0	0	0	3	22	27	13	13	3	0	10	15	1.682	5.32	80	5.88	.300	0	....	-3	1	-0.3
Cal-A	1	7	.125	33	0	0	0	8	57	46	32	32	8	0	25	37	1.246	5.05	80	3.37	.223	0	....	-7	3	-0.7
Yr.	1	9	.100	43	0	0	0	11	79	73	45	45	11	0	35	52	1.367	5.13	80	4.07	.247	0	....	-10	4	-1.0
1983 Cal-A	1	1	.500	11	0	0	0	0	17^1	26	10	7	1	1	4	18	1.731	3.63	110	6.11	.351	0	....	1	1	0.1
1984 Cal-A	5	1	.833	45	1	0	0	4	85	76	22	20	2	2	30	48	1.247	2.12	187	2.71	.244	0	....	17	10	1.7
1985 Cal-A	3	3	.500	30	0	0	0	0	46	49	33	25	7	1	20	24	1.500	4.89	84	4.97	.274	0	....	-5	1	-0.5
1986* Cal-A	4	2	.667	46	0	0	0	10	78^2	66	36	32	11	1	22	36	1.119	3.66	112	3.11	.231	0	....	2	7	0.2
1987 Bal-A	0	2	.000	11	0	0	0	1	23	25	20	20	5	0	13	16	1.652	7.83	56	5.98	.281	0	....	-9	0	-0.8
Total 8	24	30	.444	313	1	0	0	66	553	497	226	204	49	6	200	343	1.260	3.32	124	3.29	.242	0	....	45	59	4.7
• CORBETT, Joe	Joseph A. Corbett b: 12/4/1875, San Francisco, CA d: 5/2/1945, San Francisco, CA BR/TR, 5'10", 175 lbs. Deb: 8/23/1895																									
1895 Was-N	0	2	.000	3	3	3	0	0	19	26	22	12	3	2	9	3	1.842	5.68	84	7.39	.321	2	.133	-2	0	-0.5
1896* Bal-N	3	0	1.000	8	3	3	0	1	41	31	17	10	0	5	17	28	1.171	2.20	195	2.50	.209	6	.273	9	5	0.8
1897* Bal-N	24	8	.750	37	37	34	1	0	313	330	173	108	2	21	115	149	1.422	3.11	134	3.73	.269	37	.247	32	23	2.6
1904 StL-N	5	8	.385	14	14	12	0	0	108^2	110	75	53	2	8	51	68	1.482	4.39	61	3.66	.240	9	.209	-18	1	-1.8
Total 4	32	18	.640	62	57	52	1	1	481^2	497	287	183	7	36	192	248	1.430	3.42	106	3.75	.259	54	.235	21	29	1.1
• CORBETT, Sherman	Sherman Stanley Corbett b: 11/3/1962, New Braunfels, TX BL/TL, 6'4", 205 lbs. Deb: 5/29/1988																									
1988 Cal-A	2	1	.667	34	0	0	0	1	45^2	47	23	21	2	0	23	28	1.533	4.14	93	4.08	.273	0	....	-1	2	-0.1
1989 Cal-A	0	0	....	4	0	0	0	0	5^1	3	2	2	1	0	1	3	.750	3.38	113	1.61	.158	0	....	0	0	0.0
1990 Cal-A	0	0	....	4	0	0	0	0	5	8	5	5	0	0	3	2	2.200	9.00	42	7.52	.364	0	....	-3	0	-0.3
Total 3	2	1	.667	42	0	0	0	1	56	58	30	28	3	0	27	33	1.518	4.50	85	4.15	.272	0	....	-4	2	-0.4
• CORBIN, Archie	Archie Ray Corbin b: 12/30/1967, Beaumont, TX BR/TR, 6'4", 190 lbs. Deb: 9/10/1991																									
1991 KC-A	0	0	....	2	0	0	0	0	2^1	3	1	1	0	0	2	1	2.143	3.86	107	6.63	.300	0	....	0	0	0.0
1996 Bal-A	2	0	1.000	18	0	0	0	0	27^1	22	7	7	2	1	22	20	1.610	2.30	214	4.54	.222	0	....	8	3	0.7
1999 Fla-N	0	1	.000	17	0	0	0	0	21	25	20	17	2	1	15	30	1.905	7.29	60	6.50	.291	0	.000	-7	0	-0.7
Total 3	2	1	.667	37	0	0	0	0	50^2	50	28	25	4	2	39	51	1.757	4.44	101	5.45	.256	0	.000	1	3	0.1
• CORBIN, Ray	Alton Ray Corbin b: 2/12/1949, Live Oak, FL BR/TR, 6'2", 200 lbs. Deb: 4/6/1971																									
1971 Min-A	8	11	.421	52	11	2	0	3	140^1	141	74	64	19	3	70	83	1.504	4.10	87	4.72	.265	7	.206	-6	5	-0.6
1972 Min-A	8	9	.471	31	19	5	3	0	161^2	135	56	47	12	6	53	83	1.163	2.62	123	2.92	.230	4	.082	9	10	0.8
1973 Min-A	8	5	.615	51	7	1	0	14	148^1	124	58	50	7	5	60	83	1.240	3.03	130	2.94	.229	0	....	16	15	1.6

YEAR TM-L	W	L	PCT	G	GS	CG	SH	SV	IP	H	R	ER	HR	HB	BB	SO	RAT	ERA	ERA+	CERA	OAV	BH	AVG	PR+	WS	TPW
1974 Min-A	7	6	.538	29	15	1	0	0	112^1	133	78	66	8	3	40	50	1.540	5.29	71	4.71	.294	0	....	-18	1	-1.9
1975 Min-A	5	7	.417	18	11	3	0	0	89^2	105	59	51	13	2	38	49	1.595	5.12	75	5.49	.295	0	....	-12	2	-1.2
Total 5	**36**	**38**	**.486**	**181**	**63**	**12**	**3**	**17**	**652^1**	**638**	**325**	**278**	**59**	**19**	**261**	**348**	**1.378**	**3.84**	**95**	**3.97**	**.258**	**11**	**.133**	**-11**	**33**	**-1.3**

• CORCORAN, Larry Lawrence J. Corcoran b: 8/10/1859, Brooklyn, NY d: 10/14/1891, Newark, NJ BL/TR, 120 lbs. Deb: 5/1/1880 ♦

YEAR TM-L	W	L	PCT	G	GS	CG	SH	SV	IP	H	R	ER	HR	HB	BB	SO	RAT	ERA	ERA+	CERA	OAV	BH	AVG	PR+	WS	TPW
1880 Chi-N	43	14	.754	63	60	57	4	2	536^1	404	218	116	6	....	99	**268**	.938	1.95	124	....	.198	66	.231	18	52	1.6
1881 Chi-N	**31**	14	.689	45	44	43	4	0	396^2	380	204	102	10	....	78	150	1.155	2.31	121	....	.241	42	.222	9	30	0.6
1882 Chi-N	27	12	.692	39	39	38	3	0	355^2	281	153	77	5	....	63	170	.967	**1.95**	**140**	....	**.205**	35	.207	16	28	1.3
1883 Chi-N	34	20	.630	56	53	51	3	0	473^2	483	281	131	7	....	82	216	1.193	2.49	133	....	.249	55	.209	29	38	1.9
1884 Chi-N	35	23	.603	60	59	57	7	0	516^2	473	286	138	35	....	116	272	1.140	2.40	130	....	.230	61	.243	21	37	2.2
1885 Chi-N	5	2	.714	7	7	6	1	0	59^1	63	38	24	2	....	24	10	1.466	3.64	83	....	.260	6	.273	-6	5	-0.4
NY-N	2	1	.667	3	3	2	0	0	25	24	12	8	1	....	11	10	1.400	2.88	93	....	.241	5	.357	-2	3	-0.1
Yr.	7	3	.700	10	10	8	1	0	84^1	87	50	32	3	....	35	20	1.447	3.42	86	....	.254	11	.306	-8	8	-0.4
1886 Was-N	0	1	.000	2	1	1	0	0	14	16	11	9	0	....	4	3	1.429	5.79	56	....	.277	15	.185	-4	0	-1.0
1887 Ind-N	0	2	.000	2	2	1	0	0	15	42	31	21	3	2	19	4	2.800	12.60	33	....	.487	4	.333	-14	0	-1.2
Total 8	**177**	**89**	**.665**	**277**	**268**	**256**	**22**	**2**	**2392^1**	**2166**	**1234**	**626**	**69**	**2**	**496**	**1103**	**1.105**	**2.36**	**124**	**....**	**.229**	**289**	**.224**	**66**	**193**	**4.9**

• CORCORAN, Mike Michael Corcoran b: Brooklyn, NY Deb: 7/15/1884

YEAR TM-L	W	L	PCT	G	GS	CG	SH	SV	IP	H	R	ER	HR	HB	BB	SO	RAT	ERA	ERA+	CERA	OAV	BH	AVG	PR+	WS	TPW
1884 Chi-N	0	1	.000	1	1	1	0	0	9	16	14	4	1	....	7	2	2.556	4.00	78	....	.367	0	.000	-1	0	-0.1

• CORCORAN, Roy Roy Elliot Corcoran b: 5/11/1980, Baton Rouge, LA BR/TR, 5'10", 170 lbs. Deb: 7/30/2003

YEAR TM-L	W	L	PCT	G	GS	CG	SH	SV	IP	H	R	ER	HR	HB	BB	SO	RAT	ERA	ERA+	CERA	OAV	BH	AVG	PR+	WS	TPW
2003 Mon-N	0	0	....	5	0	0	0	0	7^1	7	2	1	0	0	3	2	1.364	1.23	412	3.20	.250	0	.000	3	1	0.3

• CORDERO, Chad Chad P. Cordero b: 3/18/1982, Upland, CA BR/TR, 6', 195 lbs. Deb: 8/30/2003

YEAR TM-L	W	L	PCT	G	GS	CG	SH	SV	IP	H	R	ER	HR	HB	BB	SO	RAT	ERA	ERA+	CERA	OAV	BH	AVG	PR+	WS	TPW
2003 Mon-N	1	0	1.000	12	0	0	0	1	11	4	2	2	1	0	3	12	.636	1.64	309	0.86	.111	0	....	4	2	0.4

• CORDERO, Francisco Francisco Javier Cordero b: 5/11/1975, Santo Domingo, Dominican Republic BR/TR, 6'2", 200 lbs. Deb: 8/2/1999

YEAR TM-L	W	L	PCT	G	GS	CG	SH	SV	IP	H	R	ER	HR	HB	BB	SO	RAT	ERA	ERA+	CERA	OAV	BH	AVG	PR+	WS	TPW
1999 Det-A	2	2	.500	20	0	0	0	0	19	19	7	7	2	0	18	19	1.947	3.32	149	6.19	.284	0	....	3	2	0.3
2000 Tex-A	1	2	.333	56	0	0	0	0	77^1	87	51	46	11	4	48	49	1.746	5.35	93	6.15	.285	0	....	-2	3	-0.1
2001 Tex-A	0	1	.000	3	0	0	0	0	2^1	3	1	1	0	0	2	1	2.143	3.86	121	5.73	.300	0	....	0	0	0.0
2002 Tex-A	2	0	1.000	39	0	0	0	10	45^1	33	12	9	2	2	13	41	1.015	1.79	264	2.11	.204	0	.000	15	8	1.5
2003 Tex-A	5	8	.385	73	0	0	0	15	82^2	70	33	27	4	2	38	90	1.306	2.94	169	3.08	.230	0	....	20	12	1.9
Total 5	**10**	**13**	**.435**	**191**	**0**	**0**	**0**	**25**	**226^2**	**212**	**104**	**90**	**19**	**8**	**119**	**200**	**1.306**	**3.57**	**139**	**4.22**	**.250**	**0**	**.000**	**37**	**25**	**3.5**

• CORDOVA, Francisco Francisco Cordova b: 4/26/1972, Veracruz, Mexico BR/TR, 5'11", 165 lbs. Deb: 4/2/1996

YEAR TM-L	W	L	PCT	G	GS	CG	SH	SV	IP	H	R	ER	HR	HB	BB	SO	RAT	ERA	ERA+	CERA	OAV	BH	AVG	PR+	WS	TPW
1996 Pit-N	4	7	.364	59	6	0	0	12	99	103	49	45	11	2	20	95	1.242	4.09	107	3.58	.263	2	.125	4	8	0.4
1997 Pit-N	11	8	.579	29	29	2	2	0	178^2	175	80	72	14	9	49	121	1.254	3.63	118	3.54	.259	5	.089	15	13	1.3
1998 Pit-N	13	14	.481	33	33	3	2	0	220^1	204	91	81	22	3	69	157	1.239	3.31	130	3.35	.245	9	.120	23	15	2.1
1999 Pit-N	8	10	.444	27	27	2	0	0	160^2	166	83	79	16	4	59	98	1.400	4.43	103	4.26	.273	8	.163	3	9	0.3
2000 Pit-N	6	8	.429	18	17	0	0	0	95	107	63	55	12	2	38	66	1.526	5.21	88	5.03	.285	4	.114	-5	3	-0.6
Total 5	**42**	**47**	**.472**	**166**	**112**	**7**	**4**	**12**	**753^2**	**755**	**366**	**332**	**75**	**20**	**235**	**537**	**1.314**	**3.96**	**111**	**3.83**	**.262**	**28**	**.121**	**40**	**48**	**3.4**

• COREY, Bryan Bryan Scott Corey b: 10/21/1973, Thousand Oaks, CA BR/TR, 6'1", 170 lbs. Deb: 5/13/1998

YEAR TM-L	W	L	PCT	G	GS	CG	SH	SV	IP	H	R	ER	HR	HB	BB	SO	RAT	ERA	ERA+	CERA	OAV	BH	AVG	PR+	WS	TPW
1998 Ari-N	0	0	....	3	0	0	0	0	4	6	4	4	1	1	2	1	2.000	9.00	47	10.40	.375	0	....	-2	0	-0.2
2002 LA-N	0	0	....	1	0	0	0	0	1	0	0	0	0	0	0	0	.000	0.00	....	0.00	.000	0	....	0	0	0.0
Total 2	**0**	**0**	**....**	**4**	**0**	**0**	**0**	**0**	**5**	**6**	**4**	**4**	**1**	**1**	**2**	**1**	**1.600**	**7.20**	**59**	**8.32**	**.375**	**0**	**....**	**-2**	**0**	**-0.2**

• COREY, Ed Edward Norman "Ike" Corey b: 7/13/1899, Chicago, IL d: 9/17/1970, Kenosha, WI BR/TR, 6', 170 lbs. Deb: 7/2/1918

YEAR TM-L	W	L	PCT	G	GS	CG	SH	SV	IP	H	R	ER	HR	HB	BB	SO	RAT	ERA	ERA+	CERA	OAV	BH	AVG	PR+	WS	TPW
1918 Chi-A	0	0	....	1	0	0	0	0	2	2	1	1	0	0	1	0	1.500	4.50	61	4.66	.333	0	.000	-0	0	-0.1

• COREY, Fred Frederick Harrison Corey b: 1857, South Kingston, RI d: 11/27/1912, Providence, RI BR/TR, 5'7" Deb: 5/1/1878 ♦

YEAR TM-L	W	L	PCT	G	GS	CG	SH	SV	IP	H	R	ER	HR	HB	BB	SO	RAT	ERA	ERA+	CERA	OAV	BH	AVG	PR+	WS	TPW
1878 Pro-N	1	2	.333	5	5	2	0	0	23	22	10	6	0	....	7	7	1.261	2.35	94	....	.239	3	.143	-1	1	-0.2
1880 Wor-N	8	9	.471	25	17	9	2	2	148^1	131	72	40	6	....	16	47	.991	2.43	107	....	.225	24	.174	-0	10	-1.2
1881 Wor-N	6	15	.286	23	21	20	1	0	188^2	231	127	78	3	....	31	33	1.389	3.72	81	....	.289	45	.222	-10	10	-1.3
1882 Wor-N	1	13	.071	21	14	12	0	0	139	180	132	55	5	....	19	36	1.432	3.56	87	....	.297	63	.247	-1	6	-1.0
1883 Phi-a	10	7	.588	18	16	15	0	0	148^1	182	106	56	3	....	24	42	1.389	3.40	102	....	.284	77	.258	6	18	0.5
1885 Phi-a	1	0	1.000	1	1	1	0	0	9	18	9	7	2	0	1	3	2.111	7.00	49	....	.399	94	.245	-4	9	-0.7
Total 6	**27**	**46**	**.370**	**93**	**74**	**59**	**3**	**2**	**656^1**	**764**	**456**	**242**	**19**	**0**	**98**	**168**	**1.313**	**3.32**	**91**	**....**	**.276**	**427**	**.246**	**-10**	**54**	**-3.9**

• COREY, Mark Mark Franklin Corey b: 11/16/1974, Coudersport, PA BR/TR, 6'2", 210 lbs. Deb: 10/2/2001

YEAR TM-L	W	L	PCT	G	GS	CG	SH	SV	IP	H	R	ER	HR	HB	BB	SO	RAT	ERA	ERA+	CERA	OAV	BH	AVG	PR+	WS	TPW
2001 NY-N	0	0	....	2	0	0	0	0	1^2	5	3	3	0	0	3	3	4.800	16.20	25	21.72	.500	0	....	-2	0	-0.2
2002 NY-N	0	3	.000	12	0	0	0	0	10	10	7	5	2	1	8	9	1.800	4.50	88	6.61	.250	0	.000	-1	0	-0.1
Col-N	0	0	....	14	0	0	0	0	12	22	16	16	7	2	8	12	2.500	12.00	40	16.43	.400	0	.000	-10	0	-1.0
Yr.	0	3	.000	26	0	0	0	0	22	32	23	21	9	3	16	21	2.182	8.59	53	11.96	.337	0	.000	-10	0	-1.0
2003 Pit-N	1	2	.333	22	0	0	0	0	30^1	29	19	18	2	1	11	27	1.319	5.34	82	3.47	.252	0	....	-3	1	-0.3
Total 3	**1**	**5**	**.167**	**50**	**0**	**0**	**0**	**0**	**54**	**66**	**45**	**42**	**11**	**4**	**30**	**51**	**1.778**	**7.00**	**63**	**7.50**	**.300**	**0**	**.000**	**-15**	**1**	**-1.6**

• CORKHILL, Pop John Stewart Corkhill b: 4/11/1858, Parkesburg, PA d: 4/3/1921, Pennsauken, NJ BL/TR, 5'10", 180 lbs. Deb: 5/1/1883 ♦

YEAR TM-L	W	L	PCT	G	GS	CG	SH	SV	IP	H	R	ER	HR	HB	BB	SO	RAT	ERA	ERA+	CERA	OAV	BH	AVG	PR+	WS	TPW
1884 Cin-a	1	0	1.000	1	0	0	0	0	5	1	1	1	0	0	2	4	.600	1.80	185	....	.061	124	.274	1	16	0.6
1885 Cin-a	1	4	.200	8	1	0	0	1	37	36	25	15	2	1	10	12	1.243	3.65	89	....	.244	111	.252	-2	13	0.1
1886 Cin-a	0	0	....	1	0	0	0	0	0^2	1	1	1	0	0	0	1	1.500	13.50	26	....	.332	143	.265	-1	13	-0.5
1887 Cin-a	1	0	1.000	5	0	0	0	0	14^2	27	15	9	0	0	5	3	1.841	5.52	79	....	.382	182	.328	-3	19	0.6
1888 Cin-a	0	0	....	2	0	0	0	**1**	5	8	6	6	1	0	0	1	1.600	10.80	29	....	.349	133	.271	-4	16	-0.9
Total 5	**3**	**4**	**.429**	**17**	**1**	**0**	**0**	**2**	**62^1**	**73**	**48**	**32**	**3**	**1**	**17**	**21**	**1.364**	**4.62**	**76**	**....**	**.281**	**1134**	**.257**	**-9**	**77**	**-0.1**

• CORKINS, Mike Michael Patrick Corkins b: 5/25/1946, Riverside, CA BR/TR, 6'1", 200 lbs. Deb: 9/8/1969

YEAR TM-L	W	L	PCT	G	GS	CG	SH	SV	IP	H	R	ER	HR	HB	BB	SO	RAT	ERA	ERA+	CERA	OAV	BH	AVG	PR+	WS	TPW
1969 SD-N	1	3	.250	6	4	0	0	0	17	27	17	16	3	0	8	13	2.059	8.47	42	8.36	.370	0	.000	-9	0	-0.9
1970 SD-N	5	6	.455	24	18	1	0	0	111	109	62	57	11	4	79	75	1.694	4.62	86	5.14	.258	8	.216	-8	4	-0.5
1971 SD-N	0	0	....	8	0	0	0	0	13	14	6	5	1	0	6	16	1.538	3.46	95	4.74	.280	0	....	-0	1	0.0
1972 SD-N	6	9	.400	47	9	2	1	6	140	125	61	55	14	4	62	108	1.336	3.54	93	3.63	.240	9	.237	-2	8	0.1
1973 SD-N	5	8	.385	47	11	2	0	3	122	130	79	61	12	11	61	82	1.566	4.50	77	5.03	.274	7	.212	-13	4	-0.9
1974 SD-N	2	2	.500	25	2	0	0	0	56^1	53	32	30	5	1	32	41	1.509	4.79	74	4.34	.255	0	.000	-6	2	-0.6
Total 6	**19**	**28**	**.404**	**157**	**44**	**5**	**1**	**9**	**459^1**	**458**	**257**	**224**	**46**	**20**	**248**	**335**	**1.537**	**4.39**	**81**	**4.66**	**.262**	**24**	**.202**	**-38**	**19**	**-2.9**

• CORMIER, Rheal Rheal Paul Cormier b: 4/23/1967, Moncton, Canada BL/TL, 5'10", 185 lbs. Deb: 8/15/1991

YEAR TM-L	W	L	PCT	G	GS	CG	SH	SV	IP	H	R	ER	HR	HB	BB	SO	RAT	ERA	ERA+	CERA	OAV	BH	AVG	PR+	WS	TPW
1991 StL-N	4	5	.444	11	10	2	0	0	67^2	74	35	31	5	2	8	38	1.212	4.12	90	3.41	.277	5	.238	-4	2	-0.3
1992 StL-N	10	10	.500	31	30	3	0	0	186	194	83	76	15	5	33	117	1.220	3.68	92	3.42	.269	6	.102	-8	7	-1.1
1993 StL-N	7	6	.538	38	21	1	0	0	145^1	163	80	70	18	4	27	75	1.307	4.33	91	4.13	.284	11	.234	-6	6	-0.4
1994 StL-N	3	2	.600	7	7	0	0	0	39^2	40	24	24	6	3	7	26	1.185	5.45	76	3.80	.256	4	.286	-6	2	-0.4
1995* Bos-A	7	5	.583	48	12	0	0	0	115	131	60	52	12	3	31	69	1.409	4.07	120	4.56	.294	0	....	10	8	0.9
1996 Mon-N	7	10	.412	33	27	1	1	0	159^2	165	80	74	16	9	41	100	1.290	4.17	104	3.93	.270	8	.186	3	8	0.4
1997 Mon-N	0	1	.000	1	1	0	0	0	1^1	4	5	5	1	0	1	0	3.750	33.75	12	27.46	.500	0	....	-4	0	-0.4
1999* Bos-A	2	0	1.000	60	0	0	0	0	63^1	61	34	26	4	5	18	39	1.247	3.69	134	3.33	.246	0	....	9	5	0.8
2000 Bos-A	3	3	.500	64	0	0	0	0	68^1	74	40	35	7	0	17	43	1.332	4.61	109	3.86	.275	0	....	3	4	0.3
2001 Phi-N	5	6	.455	60	0	0	0	1	51^1	49	26	24	5	4	17	37	1.286	4.21	101	3.67	.247	0	.000	-0	4	0.0
2002 Phi-N	5	6	.455	54	0	0	0	0	60	61	38	35	6	4	32	49	1.550	5.25	74	4.85	.265	1	.333	-9	1	-0.9
2003 Phi-N	8	0	1.000	65	0	0	0	1	84^2	54	18	16	4	1	25	67	.933	1.70	235	1.63	.182	1	.500	22	13	2.2
Total 12	**61**	**54**	**.530**	**472**	**108**	**7**	**1**	**2**	**1042^1**	**1070**	**523**	**468**	**99**	**40**	**257**	**660**	**1.273**	**4.04**	**102**	**3.74**	**.266**	**36**	**.189**	**9**	**60**	**1.0**

• CORNEJO, Mardie Nieves Mardie Cornejo b: 8/5/1951, Wellington, KS BR/TR, 6'3", 200 lbs. Deb: 4/8/1978

YEAR TM-L	W	L	PCT	G	GS	CG	SH	SV	IP	H	R	ER	HR	HB	BB	SO	RAT	ERA	ERA+	CERA	OAV	BH	AVG	PR+	WS	TPW
1978 NY-N	4	2	.667	25	0	0	0	3	36^2	37	12	10	1	3	14	17	1.391	2.45	142	3.76	.285	0	....	4	4	0.4

• CORNEJO, Nate Nathan J. Cornejo b: 9/24/1979, Wellington, KS BR/TR, 6'5", 200 lbs. Deb: 8/8/2001

YEAR	TM-L	W	L	PCT	G	GS	CG	SH	SV	IP	H	R	ER	HR	HB	BB	SO	RAT	ERA	ERA+	CERA	OAV	BH	AVG	PR+	WS	TPW
2001	Det-A	4	4	.500	10	10	0	0	0	42^2	63	38	35	10	3	28	22	2.133	7.38	59	9.48	.342	0	....	-14	0	-1.3
2002	Det-A	1	5	.167	9	9	1	0	0	50	63	33	28	6	2	18	23	1.620	5.04	85	5.69	.303	0	....	-4	1	-0.4
2003	Det-A	6	17	.261	32	32	2	0	0	194^2	236	111	101	18	3	58	46	1.510	4.67	92	4.94	.307	0	.000	-8	7	-0.8
Total	**3**	**11**	**26**	**.297**	**51**	**51**	**3**	**0**	**0**	**287^1**	**362**	**182**	**164**	**34**	**8**	**104**	**91**	**1.622**	**5.14**	**84**	**5.75**	**.312**	**0**	**.000**	**-26**	**8**	**-2.5**

• CORNELIUS, Reid Jonathan Reid Cornelius b: 6/2/1970, Thomasville, AL BR/TR, 6', 200 lbs. Deb: 4/29/1995

YEAR	TM-L	W	L	PCT	G	GS	CG	SH	SV	IP	H	R	ER	HR	HB	BB	SO	RAT	ERA	ERA+	CERA	OAV	BH	AVG	PR+	WS	TPW
1995	Mon-N	0	0	....	8	0	0	0	0	9	11	8	8	3	2	5	4	1.778	8.00	54	9.29	.306	0	....	-4	0	-0.4
	NY-N	3	7	.300	10	10	0	0	0	57^2	64	36	33	8	1	25	35	1.543	5.15	79	5.04	.284	2	.100	-7	1	-0.8
	Yr.	3	7	.300	18	10	0	0	0	66^2	75	44	41	11	3	30	39	1.575	5.54	74	5.61	.287	2	.100	-11	1	-1.2
1999	Fla-N	1	0	1.000	5	2	0	0	0	19^1	16	7	7	0	0	5	12	1.086	3.26	134	2.03	.229	1	.200	2	2	0.2
2000	Fla-N	4	10	.286	22	21	0	0	0	125	135	74	67	19	4	50	50	1.480	4.82	92	5.04	.282	5	.135	-5	4	-0.5
Total	**3**	**8**	**17**	**.320**	**45**	**33**	**0**	**0**	**0**	**211**	**226**	**125**	**115**	**30**	**7**	**85**	**101**	**1.474**	**4.91**	**88**	**4.95**	**.279**	**8**	**.129**	**-13**	**7**	**-1.5**

• CORNELL, Jeff Jeffery Ray Cornell b: 2/10/1957, Kansas City, MO BB/TR, 5'11", 170 lbs. Deb: 6/2/1984

YEAR	TM-L	W	L	PCT	G	GS	CG	SH	SV	IP	H	R	ER	HR	HB	BB	SO	RAT	ERA	ERA+	CERA	OAV	BH	AVG	PR+	WS	TPW
1984	SF-N	1	3	.250	23	0	0	0	0	38^1	51	30	26	4	1	22	19	1.904	6.10	57	6.76	.340	0	.000	-10	0	-1.1

• CORNETT, Brad Brad Byron Cornett b: 2/4/1969, Lamesa, TX BR/TR, 6'3", 190 lbs. Deb: 6/8/1994

YEAR	TM-L	W	L	PCT	G	GS	CG	SH	SV	IP	H	R	ER	HR	HB	BB	SO	RAT	ERA	ERA+	CERA	OAV	BH	AVG	PR+	WS	TPW
1994	Tor-A	1	3	.250	9	4	0	0	0	31	40	25	23	1	3	11	22	1.645	6.68	72	5.43	.331	0	....	-6	0	-0.6
1995	Tor-A	0	0	....	5	0	0	0	0	5	9	6	5	1	1	3	4	2.400	9.00	52	13.23	.429	0	....	-2	0	-0.2
Total	**2**	**1**	**3**	**.250**	**14**	**4**	**0**	**0**	**0**	**36**	**49**	**31**	**28**	**2**	**4**	**14**	**26**	**1.750**	**7.00**	**69**	**6.51**	**.345**	**0**	**....**	**-8**	**0**	**-0.8**

• CORNUTT, Terry Terry Stanton Cornutt b: 10/2/1952, Roseburg, OR BR/TR, 6'2", 195 lbs. Deb: 4/9/1977

YEAR	TM-L	W	L	PCT	G	GS	CG	SH	SV	IP	H	R	ER	HR	HB	BB	SO	RAT	ERA	ERA+	CERA	OAV	BH	AVG	PR+	WS	TPW
1977	SF-N	1	2	.333	28	1	0	0	0	44^1	38	24	19	4	0	22	23	1.353	3.86	101	3.38	.229	0	.000	1	2	0.1
1978	SF-N	0	0	....	1	0	0	0	0	3	1	0	0	0	0	0	0	.333	0.00	....	0.25	.100	0	....	1	0	0.1
Total	**2**	**1**	**2**	**.333**	**29**	**1**	**0**	**0**	**0**	**47^1**	**39**	**24**	**19**	**4**	**0**	**22**	**23**	**1.289**	**3.61**	**108**	**3.18**	**.222**	**0**	**.000**	**2**	**2**	**0.2**

• CORREA, Ed Edwin Josue (Andino) Correa b: 4/29/1966, Hato Rey, Puerto Rico BR/TR, 6'2", 192 lbs. Deb: 9/18/1985

YEAR	TM-L	W	L	PCT	G	GS	CG	SH	SV	IP	H	R	ER	HR	HB	BB	SO	RAT	ERA	ERA+	CERA	OAV	BH	AVG	PR+	WS	TPW
1985	Chi-A	1	0	1.000	5	1	0	0	0	10^1	11	9	8	2	0	11	10	2.129	6.97	62	8.21	.275	0	....	-3	0	-0.3
1986	Tex-A	12	14	.462	32	32	4	2	0	202^1	167	102	95	15	3	126	189	1.448	4.23	102	3.81	.223	0	....	2	10	0.2
1987	Tex-A	3	5	.375	15	15	0	0	0	70	83	63	59	17	4	52	61	1.929	7.59	59	8.11	.296	0	....	-23	0	-2.2
Total	**3**	**16**	**19**	**.457**	**52**	**48**	**4**	**2**	**0**	**282^2**	**261**	**174**	**162**	**34**	**7**	**189**	**260**	**1.592**	**5.16**	**85**	**5.04**	**.244**	**0**	**....**	**-24**	**10**	**-2.3**

• CORREIA, Kevin Kevin John Correia b: 8/24/1980, San Diego, CA BR/TR, 6'3", 200 lbs. Deb: 7/10/2003

YEAR	TM-L	W	L	PCT	G	GS	CG	SH	SV	IP	H	R	ER	HR	HB	BB	SO	RAT	ERA	ERA+	CERA	OAV	BH	AVG	PR+	WS	TPW
2003	SF-N	3	1	.750	10	7	0	0	0	39^1	41	16	16	6	4	18	28	1.500	3.66	112	5.46	.275	2	.154	1	3	0.1

• CORRIDON, Frank Frank J. "Fiddler" Corridon b: 11/25/1880, Newport, RI d: 2/21/1941, Syracuse, NY BR/TR, 6', 170 lbs. Deb: 4/15/1904

YEAR	TM-L	W	L	PCT	G	GS	CG	SH	SV	IP	H	R	ER	HR	HB	BB	SO	RAT	ERA	ERA+	CERA	OAV	BH	AVG	PR+	WS	TPW
1904	Chi-N	5	5	.500	12	10	9	0	0	100^1	88	43	34	2	7	37	34	1.246	3.05	87	3.01	.240	13	.224	-6	6	-0.8
	Phi-N	6	5	.545	12	11	11	1	0	94^1	88	33	23	2	8	28	44	1.230	2.19	121	3.11	.250	6	.171	7	4	0.7
	Yr.	11	10	.524	24	21	20	1	0	194^2	176	76	57	4	15	65	78	1.238	2.64	101	3.06	.245	19	.204	1	10	-0.1
1905	Phi-N	10	12	.455	35	26	18	1	1	212	203	109	82	2	16	57	79	1.226	3.48	84	3.05	.257	15	.208	-17	11	-1.3
1907	Phi-N	18	14	.563	37	32	23	3	2	274	228	107	75	0	9	89	131	1.157	2.46	98	2.40	.230	16	.165	-6	18	-0.7
1908	Phi-N	14	10	.583	27	24	18	2	1	208^1	178	69	58	0	6	48	50	1.085	2.51	96	2.26	.239	9	.123	-4	13	-0.7
1909	Phi-N	11	7	.611	27	19	11	3	0	171	147	61	40	0	6	61	69	1.216	2.11	123	2.72	.242	11	.186	6	14	0.8
1910	StL-N	6	14	.300	30	18	9	0	3	156	168	88	66	1	9	55	51	1.429	3.81	78	3.93	.283	10	.196	-10	4	-1.1
Total	**6**	**70**	**67**	**.511**	**180**	**140**	**99**	**10**	**7**	**1216**	**1100**	**510**	**378**	**7**	**61**	**375**	**458**	**1.213**	**2.80**	**95**	**2.83**	**.247**	**80**	**.180**	**-30**	**70**	**-3.0**

• CORSI, Jim James Bernard Corsi b: 9/9/1961, Newton, MA BR/TR, 6'1", 220 lbs. Deb: 6/28/1988

YEAR	TM-L	W	L	PCT	G	GS	CG	SH	SV	IP	H	R	ER	HR	HB	BB	SO	RAT	ERA	ERA+	CERA	OAV	BH	AVG	PR+	WS	TPW
1988	Oak-A	0	1	.000	11	1	0	0	0	21^1	20	10	9	1	0	6	10	1.219	3.80	100	2.84	.260	0	....	-0	1	0.0
1989	Oak-A	1	2	.333	22	0	0	0	0	38^1	26	8	8	2	1	10	21	.939	1.88	196	1.78	.194	0	....	7	4	0.7
1991	Hou-N	0	5	.000	47	0	0	0	0	77^2	76	37	32	6	0	23	53	1.275	3.71	95	3.35	.259	0	.000	-2	3	-0.2
1992*	Oak-A	4	2	.667	32	0	0	0	0	44	44	12	7	2	0	18	19	1.409	1.43	261	3.76	.273	0	....	11	5	1.1
1993	Fla-N	0	2	.000	15	0	0	0	0	20^1	28	15	15	1	0	10	7	1.869	6.64	65	5.97	.337	0	....	-5	0	-0.5
1995	Oak-A	2	4	.333	38	0	0	0	2	45	31	14	11	2	2	26	26	1.267	2.20	202	2.89	.203	0	....	11	5	1.1
1996	Oak-A	6	0	1.000	56	0	0	0	3	73^2	71	33	33	6	3	34	43	1.425	4.03	122	4.20	.269	0	....	6	7	0.6
1997	Bos-A	5	3	.625	52	0	0	0	2	57^2	56	26	22	1	4	21	40	1.335	3.43	135	3.22	.255	0	....	8	6	0.7
1998*	Bos-A	3	2	.600	59	0	0	0	0	66	58	23	19	6	1	23	49	1.227	2.59	182	3.18	.235	0	.000	15	7	1.4
1999	Bos-A	1	2	.333	23	0	0	0	0	24	25	15	14	4	2	19	14	1.833	5.25	95	6.73	.284	0	....	-1	1	-0.1
	Bal-A	0	1	.000	13	0	0	0	0	13^1	15	4	4	2	0	1	8	1.200	2.70	174	3.96	.294	0	....	3	1	0.2
	Yr.	1	3	.250	36	0	0	0	0	37^1	40	19	18	6	2	20	22	1.607	4.34	113	5.74	.288	0	....	2	2	0.2
Total	**10**	**22**	**24**	**.478**	**368**	**1**	**0**	**0**	**7**	**481^1**	**450**	**197**	**174**	**33**	**13**	**191**	**290**	**1.332**	**3.25**	**131**	**3.58**	**.254**	**0**	**.000**	**53**	**40**	**5.0**

• CORT, Barry Barry Lee Cort b: 4/15/1956, Toronto, Canada BR/TR, 6'5", 210 lbs. Deb: 4/22/1977

YEAR	TM-L	W	L	PCT	G	GS	CG	SH	SV	IP	H	R	ER	HR	HB	BB	SO	RAT	ERA	ERA+	CERA	OAV	BH	AVG	PR+	WS	TPW
1977	Mil-A	1	1	.500	7	3	1	0	0	24^1	25	9	9	1	1	9	17	1.397	3.33	122	3.93	.281	0	....	2	2	0.2

• CORTES, David David C. Cortes b: 10/15/1973, Mexicali, Mexico BR/TR, 5'11", 195 lbs. Deb: 8/30/1999

YEAR	TM-L	W	L	PCT	G	GS	CG	SH	SV	IP	H	R	ER	HR	HB	BB	SO	RAT	ERA	ERA+	CERA	OAV	BH	AVG	PR+	WS	TPW
1999	Atl-N	0	0	....	4	0	0	0	0	3^2	3	3	2	0	0	4	2	1.909	4.91	92	4.78	.214	0	....	-0	0	0.0
2003	Cle-A	0	0	....	2	0	0	0	0	3	8	5	4	1	0	0	1	2.667	12.00	37	14.61	.471	0	....	-3	0	-0.2
Total	**2**	**0**	**0**	**....**	**6**	**0**	**0**	**0**	**0**	**6^2**	**11**	**8**	**6**	**1**	**0**	**4**	**3**	**2.250**	**8.10**	**55**	**9.20**	**.355**	**0**	**....**	**-3**	**0**	**-0.3**

• CORWIN, Al Elmer Nathan Corwin b: 12/3/1926, Newburgh, NY d: 10/23/2003, Geneva, IL BR/TR, 6'1", 170 lbs. Deb: 7/25/1951

YEAR	TM-L	W	L	PCT	G	GS	CG	SH	SV	IP	H	R	ER	HR	HB	BB	SO	RAT	ERA	ERA+	CERA	OAV	BH	AVG	PR+	WS	TPW
1951*	NY-N	5	1	.833	15	8	3	1	1	59	49	27	24	7	0	21	30	1.186	3.66	107	3.02	.222	1	.050	2	4	0.0
1952	NY-N	6	1	.857	21	7	1	0	2	67^2	58	23	20	5	0	36	36	1.389	2.66	139	3.52	.237	2	.095	8	6	0.7
1953	NY-N	6	4	.600	48	7	2	1	2	106^2	122	65	59	17	3	68	49	1.781	4.98	86	6.40	.290	9	.281	-8	5	-0.4
1954	NY-N	1	3	.250	20	0	0	0	0	31^1	35	19	14	4	0	14	14	1.564	4.02	100	5.10	.297	0	.000	-0	1	-0.1
1955	NY-N	0	1	.000	13	0	0	0	0	24^2	25	11	11	3	0	17	13	1.703	4.01	100	5.21	.263	0	.000	0	1	0.0
Total	**5**	**18**	**10**	**.643**	**117**	**22**	**6**	**2**	**5**	**289^1**	**289**	**145**	**128**	**36**	**3**	**156**	**142**	**1.538**	**3.98**	**102**	**4.80**	**.263**	**12**	**.152**	**1**	**17**	**0.2**

• COSGROVE, Mike Michael John Cosgrove b: 2/17/1951, Phoenix, AZ BL/TL, 6'1", 180 lbs. Deb: 9/10/1972

YEAR	TM-L	W	L	PCT	G	GS	CG	SH	SV	IP	H	R	ER	HR	HB	BB	SO	RAT	ERA	ERA+	CERA	OAV	BH	AVG	PR+	WS	TPW
1972	Hou-N	0	1	.000	7	1	0	0	1	13^2	16	8	7	2	0	3	7	1.390	4.61	73	4.54	.286	0	.000	-2	0	-0.2
1973	Hou-N	1	1	.500	13	0	0	0	0	10	11	2	2	1	0	8	2	1.900	1.80	202	5.75	.282	0	....	2	1	0.2
1974	Hou-N	7	3	.700	45	0	0	0	2	90	76	35	35	2	1	39	47	1.278	3.50	99	2.88	.232	1	.056	-2	7	-0.3
1975	Hou-N	1	2	.333	32	3	1	0	5	71^1	62	24	24	2	0	37	32	1.388	3.03	111	3.37	.245	2	.154	2	5	0.2
1976	Hou-N	3	4	.429	22	16	1	1	0	89^2	106	63	55	6	2	58	34	1.829	5.52	58	5.93	.303	2	.087	-23	0	-2.5
Total	**5**	**12**	**11**	**.522**	**119**	**20**	**2**	**1**	**8**	**274^2**	**271**	**132**	**123**	**13**	**3**	**145**	**122**	**1.515**	**4.03**	**82**	**4.19**	**.264**	**5**	**.089**	**-23**	**13**	**-2.6**

• COSMAN, Jim James Henry Cosman b: 2/19/1943, Brockport, NY BR/TR, 6'4.5", 211 lbs. Deb: 10/2/1966

YEAR	TM-L	W	L	PCT	G	GS	CG	SH	SV	IP	H	R	ER	HR	HB	BB	SO	RAT	ERA	ERA+	CERA	OAV	BH	AVG	PR+	WS	TPW
1966	StL-N	1	0	1.000	1	1	1	1	0	9	2	0	0	0	1	2	5	.444	0.00	....	0.49	.074	0	.000	4	2	0.3
1967	StL-N	1	0	1.000	10	5	0	0	0	31^1	21	12	11	2	5	24	11	1.436	3.16	103	3.93	.198	1	.125	0	2	0.0
1970	Chi-N	0	0	....	1	0	0	0	0	1	3	3	3	1	0	1	0	4.000	27.00	17	34.20	.600	0	....	-3	0	-0.2
Total	**3**	**2**	**0**	**1.000**	**12**	**6**	**1**	**1**	**0**	**41^1**	**26**	**15**	**14**	**3**	**6**	**27**	**16**	**1.282**	**3.05**	**113**	**3.91**	**.188**	**1**	**.091**	**1**	**4**	**0.1**

• COSTELLO, John John Reilly Costello b: 12/24/1960, Bronx, NY BR/TR, 6'1", 190 lbs. Deb: 6/2/1988

YEAR	TM-L	W	L	PCT	G	GS	CG	SH	SV	IP	H	R	ER	HR	HB	BB	SO	RAT	ERA	ERA+	CERA	OAV	BH	AVG	PR+	WS	TPW
1988	StL-N	5	2	.714	36	0	0	0	1	49^2	44	15	10	3	0	25	38	1.389	1.81	192	3.43	.235	0	.000	9	6	0.9
1989	StL-N	5	4	.556	48	0	0	0	3	62^1	48	24	23	5	2	20	40	1.091	3.32	109	2.42	.213	0	.000	1	6	0.1
1990	StL-N	0	0	....	4	0	0	0	0	4^1	7	3	3	1	1	1	1	1.846	6.23	61	9.07	.368	0	....	-1	0	-0.1
	Mon-N	0	0	....	4	0	0	0	0	6^1	5	5	4	2	0	1	1	.947	5.68	64	3.06	.208	0	....	-1	0	-0.1
	Yr.	0	0	....	8	0	0	0	0	10^2	12	8	7	3	1	2	2	1.313	5.91	63	5.50	.279	0	....	-3	0	-0.3
1991	SD-N	1	0	1.000	27	0	0	0	0	35	37	15	12	2	0	17	24	1.543	3.09	123	4.22	.276	0	.000	3	2	0.3
Total	**4**	**11**	**6**	**.647**	**119**	**0**	**0**	**0**	**4**	**157^2**	**141**	**62**	**52**	**13**	**3**	**64**	**104**	**1.300**	**2.97**	**123**	**3.34**	**.239**	**0**	**.000**	**10**	**14**	**1.0**

YEAR TM-L	W	L	PCT	G	GS	CG	SH	SV	IP	H	R	ER	HR	HB	BB	SO	RAT	ERA	ERA+	CERA	OAV	BH	AVG	PR+	WS	TPW
• COTTER, Dan	Daniel Joseph Cotter b: 4/14/1867, Boston, MA d: 9/14/1935, Dorchester, MA BR/TR Deb: 7/16/1890																									
1890 Buf-P	0	1	.000	1	1	1	0	0	9	18	19	14	1	0	7	0	2.778	14.00	29	....	.399	0	.000	-10	0	-0.8
• COTTRELL, Ensign	Ensign Stover Cottrell b: 8/29/1888, Hoosick Falls, NY d: 2/27/1947, Syracuse, NY BL/TL, 5'9.5", 173 lbs. Deb: 6/21/1911																									
1911 Pit-N	0	0	....	1	0	0	0	0	1	4	4	1	0	0	1	0	5.000	9.00	38	31.22	.667	0	....	-1	0	-0.1
1912 Chi-N	0	0	....	1	0	0	0	0	4	8	4	4	0	0	1	1	2.250	9.00	37	9.47	.444	0	.000	-3	0	-0.3
1913 Phi-A	1	0	1.000	2	1	1	0	0	10	15	7	6	0	0	2	3	1.700	5.40	51	5.08	.326	1	.250	-3	0	-0.2
1914 Bos-N	0	1	.000	1	1	0	0	0	1	2	2	1	0	0	3	1	5.000	9.00	31	15.91	.333	0	....	-1	0	-0.1
1915 NY-A	0	1	.000	7	0	0	0	0	21^1	29	12	8	2	1	7	7	1.688	3.38	87	6.12	.330	0	.000	-1	0	-0.3
Total 5	**1**	**2**	**.333**	**12**	**2**	**1**	**0**	**0**	**37^1**	**58**	**29**	**20**	**2**	**1**	**14**	**12**	**1.929**	**4.82**	**61**	**7.13**	**.354**	**1**	**.083**	**-8**	**0**	**-0.9**
• COTTS, Neal	Neal James Cotts b: 3/25/1980, Belleville, IL BL/TL, 6'2", 200 lbs. Deb: 8/12/2003																									
2003 Chi-A	1	1	.500	4	4	0	0	0	13^1	15	12	12	1	0	17	10	2.400	8.10	55	8.43	.294	0	....	-6	0	-0.5
• COUCH, Johnny	John Daniel Couch b: 3/31/1891, Vaughn, MT d: 12/8/1975, San Mateo, CA BL/TR, 6', 180 lbs. Deb: 4/11/1917																									
1917 Det-A	0	0	....	3	0	0	0	0	13^1	13	6	4	0	0	1	1	1.050	2.70	98	2.17	.255	0	.000	0	0	0.0
1922 Cin-N	16	9	.640	43	34	18	2	1	264	301	132	114	13	5	56	45	1.352	3.89	103	3.78	.289	12	.132	-3	16	-0.6
1923 Cin-N	2	7	.222	19	8	1	0	0	69^1	98	60	46	2	0	15	14	1.630	5.97	65	5.19	.344	4	.174	-16	0	-1.6
Phi-N	2	4	.333	11	7	2	0	0	65	91	45	38	4	3	21	18	1.723	5.26	87	5.89	.335	6	.250	-3	3	-0.3
Yr.	4	11	.267	30	15	3	0	0	134^1	189	105	84	6	3	36	32	1.675	5.63	74	5.53	.340	10	.213	-19	3	-1.9
1924 Phi-N	4	8	.333	37	6	3	0	3	137	170	97	72	13	1	39	23	1.526	4.73	94	4.85	.306	10	.204	-1	5	-0.1
1925 Phi-N	5	6	.455	34	7	2	1	2	94^1	112	71	57	9	1	39	11	1.601	5.44	88	5.05	.298	5	.161	-3	4	-0.4
Total 5	**29**	**34**	**.460**	**147**	**62**	**26**	**3**	**6**	**643**	**785**	**411**	**331**	**41**	**10**	**171**	**112**	**1.487**	**4.63**	**91**	**4.53**	**.304**	**37**	**.167**	**-27**	**28**	**-3.0**
• COUCHEE, Mike	Michael Eugene Couchee b: 12/4/1957, San Jose, CA BR/TR, 6', 190 lbs. Deb: 4/5/1983 C																									
1983 SD-N	0	1	.000	8	0	0	0	0	14	12	8	8	1	0	6	5	1.286	5.14	68	2.86	.214	1	.500	-3	0	-0.3
• COUGHLIN, Roscoe	William Edward Coughlin b: 3/15/1868, Walpole, MA d: 3/20/1951, Chelsea, MA TR, 5'10", 160 lbs. Deb: 4/22/1890																									
1890 Chi-N	4	6	.400	11	10	10	0	0	95	102	60	45	3	4	40	29	1.495	4.26	86	....	.266	10	.256	-9	6	-0.7
1891 NY-N	3	4	.429	8	7	6	0	0	61	74	50	26	5	3	23	22	1.590	3.84	83	....	.289	3	.130	-5	2	-0.4
Total 2	**7**	**10**	**.412**	**19**	**17**	**16**	**0**	**0**	**156**	**176**	**110**	**71**	**8**	**7**	**63**	**51**	**1.532**	**4.10**	**85**	**....**	**.275**	**13**	**.210**	**-14**	**8**	**-1.1**
• COUMBE, Fritz	Frederick Nicholas Coumbe b: 12/13/1889, Antrim, PA d: 3/21/1978, Paradise, CA BL/TL, 6', 152 lbs. Deb: 4/22/1914																									
1914 Bos-A	1	2	.333	17	5	1	0	1	62^1	49	20	10	0	0	16	17	1.043	1.44	186	1.91	.222	2	.111	7	5	0.7
Cle-A	1	5	.167	14	5	2	0	0	55^1	59	31	20	0	4	16	22	1.355	3.25	89	3.75	.288	6	.261	-1	2	-0.1
Yr.	2	7	.222	31	10	3	0	1	117^2	108	51	30	0	4	32	39	1.190	2.29	123	2.77	.254	8	.195	6	7	0.7
1915 Cle-A	4	7	.364	30	12	4	1	2	114	123	63	44	1	3	37	37	1.404	3.47	88	3.89	.294	10	.270	-5	5	-0.4
1916 Cle-A	7	5	.583	29	13	7	2	0	120^1	121	36	27	1	1	27	39	1.230	2.02	149	3.08	.279	2	.057	13	9	1.1
1917 Cle-A	8	6	.571	34	10	4	1	5	134^1	119	54	32	0	3	35	30	1.146	2.14	132	2.53	.251	6	.154	7	11	0.6
1918 Cle-A	13	7	.650	30	17	9	0	3	150	164	60	51	4	1	52	41	1.440	3.06	98	4.12	.286	12	.214	2	10	0.0
1919 Cle-A	1	1	.500	8	2	0	0	1	23^2	32	15	14	2	0	9	7	1.732	5.32	63	6.37	.348	3	.500	-5	1	-0.4
1920 Cin-N	0	1	.000	3	0	0	0	0	14^2	17	13	8	0	0	4	7	1.432	4.91	62	3.65	.304	3	.231	-3	0	-0.2
1921 Cin-N	3	4	.429	28	6	3	0	1	86^2	89	42	31	2	1	21	12	1.269	3.22	111	3.18	.280	8	.320	5	6	0.6
Total 8	**38**	**38**	**.500**	**193**	**70**	**30**	**4**	**13**	**761^1**	**773**	**334**	**237**	**10**	**13**	**217**	**212**	**1.300**	**2.80**	**108**	**3.39**	**.277**	**52**	**.206**	**19**	**49**	**1.9**
• COURTNEY, Harry	Henry Seymour Courtney b: 11/19/1898, Asheville, NC d: 12/11/1954, Lyme, CT BL/TL, 6'4", 185 lbs. Deb: 9/13/1919																									
1919 Was-A	3	0	1.000	4	3	2	1	0	26^1	25	9	8	0	0	19	6	1.671	2.73	117	4.40	.269	2	.200	2	2	0.1
1920 Was-A	8	11	.421	37	24	10	1	0	188	223	128	99	6	9	77	48	1.596	4.74	78	4.84	.298	16	.232	-20	5	-1.5
1921 Was-A	6	9	.400	30	15	3	0	1	132^2	159	103	83	7	8	71	26	1.734	5.63	73	5.45	.305	14	.298	-24	2	-2.1
1922 Was-A	0	1	.000	5	0	0	0	0	10	11	4	4	0	0	9	4	2.000	3.60	107	7.50	.306	0	.000	-0	0	-0.1
Chi-A	5	6	.455	18	11	5	0	0	86^2	100	52	48	5	1	37	28	1.581	4.98	81	4.49	.299	9	.273	-10	4	-0.7
Yr.	5	7	.417	23	11	5	0	0	96^2	111	56	52	5	1	46	32	1.624	4.84	84	4.80	.300	9	.243	-10	4	-0.7
Total 4	**22**	**27**	**.449**	**94**	**53**	**20**	**2**	**1**	**443^2**	**518**	**296**	**242**	**18**	**18**	**213**	**112**	**1.648**	**4.91**	**79**	**4.99**	**.299**	**41**	**.252**	**-52**	**13**	**-4.3**
• COURTRIGHT, John	John Charles Courtright b: 5/30/1970, Marion, OH BL/TL, 6'2", 185 lbs. Deb: 5/6/1995																									
1995 Cin-N	0	0	....	1	0	0	0	0	1	2	1	1	0	0	0	0	2.000	9.00	46	7.48	.500	0	....	-1	0	-0.1
• COVELESKI, Harry	Harry Frank "The Giant Killer" Coveleski b: 4/23/1886, Shamokin, PA d: 8/4/1950, Shamokin, PA BB/TL, 6', 180 lbs. Deb: 9/10/1907																									
1907 Phi-N	1	0	1.000	4	0	0	0	0	20	10	2	0	0	1	3	6	.650	0.00	....	0.86	.147	0	.000	5	3	0.5
1908 Phi-N	4	1	.800	6	5	5	2	0	43^2	29	7	6	0	2	12	22	.939	1.24	194	1.60	.196	2	.133	5	5	0.6
1909 Phi-N	6	10	.375	24	17	8	2	1	121^2	109	51	37	0	5	49	56	1.299	2.74	95	2.95	.247	4	.108	-4	6	-0.7
1910 Cin-N	1	1	.500	7	4	2	0	0	39^1	35	41	23	1	4	42	27	1.958	5.26	55	5.69	.246	1	.063	-10	0	-1.2
1914 Det-A	22	12	.647	44	36	23	5	2	303^1	251	109	84	4	12	100	124	1.157	2.49	112	2.48	.227	23	.242	14	23	1.9
1915 Det-A	22	13	.629	**50**	38	20	1	4	312^2	271	123	85	2	20	87	150	1.145	2.45	124	2.51	.233	18	.175	26	24	2.6
1916 Det-A	21	11	.656	44	39	22	3	2	324^1	278	105	71	6	11	63	108	1.051	1.97	145	2.26	.237	25	.212	38	27	4.4
1917 Det-A	4	6	.400	16	11	2	0	0	69	70	39	20	0	2	14	15	1.217	2.61	101	2.88	.265	5	.227	1	2	0.2
1918 Det-A	0	1	.000	3	1	1	0	0	14	17	9	6	0	0	6	3	1.643	3.86	69	4.65	.315	1	.250	-1	0	-0.1
Total 9	**81**	**55**	**.596**	**198**	**151**	**83**	**13**	**9**	**1248**	**1070**	**486**	**332**	**13**	**57**	**376**	**511**	**1.159**	**2.39**	**118**	**2.57**	**.235**	**79**	**.189**	**75**	**90**	**8.2**
• COVELESKI, Stan	Stanley Anthony Coveleski b: 7/13/1889, Shamokin, PA d: 3/20/1984, South Bend, IN BR/TR, 5'11", 166 lbs. Deb: 9/10/1912 HOF: 1969																									
1912 Phi-A	2	1	.667	5	2	2	1	0	21	18	9	8	0	1	4	9	1.048	3.43	90	2.11	.231	1	.143	-1	1	-0.1
1916 Cle-A	15	13	.536	45	27	11	1	3	232	247	100	88	6	1	58	76	1.315	3.41	88	3.44	.278	13	.173	-11	11	-1.2
1917 Cle-A	19	14	.576	45	36	24	**9**	4	298^1	202	78	60	3	1	94	133	.992	1.81	156	1.64	**.194**	13	.134	26	29	2.4
1918 Cle-A	22	13	.629	38	33	25	2	1	311	261	90	63	2	4	76	87	1.084	1.82	164	2.07	.229	21	.191	**47**	29	5.0
1919 Cle-A	24	12	.667	43	34	24	4	4	286	286	99	83	2	5	60	118	1.210	2.61	128	2.89	.267	20	.213	24	27	2.9
1920* Cle-A	24	14	.632	41	38	26	3	2	315	284	110	87	6	4	65	**133**	1.108	2.49	153	**2.39**	**.243**	25	.225	40	32	**4.1**
1921 Cle-A	23	13	.639	43	**40**	28	2	2	315	341	137	118	6	4	84	99	1.349	3.37	126	3.38	.280	18	.155	31	25	2.4
1922 Cle-A	17	14	.548	35	33	21	3	2	276^2	292	120	102	14	2	64	98	1.287	3.32	120	3.36	.274	10	.101	28	22	2.0
1923 Cle-A	13	14	.481	33	31	17	**5**	2	228	251	98	70	8	2	42	54	1.285	**2.76**	**144**	3.34	.282	7	.089	33	16	2.4
1924 Cle-A	15	16	.484	37	33	18	2	0	240^1	286	140	108	6	4	73	58	1.494	4.04	106	4.12	.294	11	.134	9	12	0.4
1925* Was-A	20	5	.800	32	32	15	3	0	241	230	86	76	7	2	73	58	1.257	**2.84**	**149**	2.99	.255	9	.111	30	23	2.1
1926 Was-A	14	11	.560	36	34	11	3	1	245^1	272	112	85	1	0	81	50	1.439	3.12	124	3.63	.286	17	.207	19	16	2.0
1927 Was-A	2	1	.667	5	4	0	0	0	14^1	13	7	5	0	0	8	3	1.465	3.14	129	3.27	.250	2	.333	1	1	0.1
1928 NY-A	5	1	.833	12	8	2	0	0	58	72	41	37	5	0	20	5	1.586	5.74	65	5.11	.323	1	.053	-12	1	-1.4
Total 14	**215**	**142**	**.602**	**450**	**385**	**224**	**38**	**21**	**3082**	**3055**	**1227**	**990**	**66**	**30**	**802**	**981**	**1.251**	**2.89**	**127**	**3.00**	**.262**	**168**	**.159**	**265**	**245**	**23.2**
• COVINGTON, Chet	Chester Rogers "Chesty" Covington b: 11/6/1910, Cairo, IL d: 6/11/1976, Pembroke Park, FL BB/TL, 6'2", 195 lbs. Deb: 4/23/1944																									
1944 Phi-N	1	1	.500	19	0	0	0	0	38^2	46	22	20	2	0	8	13	1.397	4.66	78	3.93	.297	0	.000	-4	1	-0.5
• COVINGTON, Tex	William Wilkes Covington b: 3/19/1887, Henryville, TN d: 12/10/1931, Denison, TX BL/TR, 6'1", 175 lbs. Deb: 4/25/1911																									
1911 Det-A	7	1	.875	17	6	5	0	0	83^2	94	43	38	2	10	33	29	1.518	4.09	85	4.77	.297	6	.188	-5	6	-0.6
1912 Det-A	3	4	.429	14	9	2	1	0	63^1	58	33	29	0	3	30	19	1.389	4.12	80	3.41	.253	2	.133	-6	3	-0.5
Total 2	**10**	**5**	**.667**	**31**	**15**	**7**	**1**	**0**	**147**	**152**	**76**	**67**	**2**	**13**	**63**	**48**	**1.463**	**4.10**	**82**	**4.19**	**.279**	**8**	**.170**	**-10**	**9**	**-1.1**
• COWLEY, Joe	Joseph Alan Cowley b: 8/15/1958, Lexington, KY BR/TR, 6'5", 210 lbs. Deb: 4/13/1982																									
1982 Atl-N	1	2	.333	17	8	0	0	0	52^1	53	27	26	6	1	16	27	1.318	4.47	83	3.92	.265	3	.200	-4	1	-0.5
1984 NY-A	9	2	.818	16	11	3	1	0	83^1	75	34	33	12	2	31	71	1.272	3.56	106	3.73	.234	0	....	3	6	0.3
1985 NY-A	12	6	.667	30	26	1	0	0	159^2	132	75	70	29	6	85	97	1.359	3.95	101	4.37	.224	0	....	-1	9	-0.1
1986 Chi-A	11	11	.500	27	27	4	0	0	162^1	133	81	70	20	3	83	132	1.331	3.88	111	3.74	.223	0	....	4	10	0.4

YEAR	TM-L	W	L	PCT	G	GS	CG	SH	SV	IP	H	R	ER	HR	HB	BB	SO	RAT	ERA	ERA+	CERA	OAV	BH	AVG	PR+	WS	TPW
1987	Phi-N	0	4	.000	5	4	0	0	0	11^2	21	26	20	2	2	17	5	3.257	15.43	27	15.68	.389	1	.333	-15	0	-1.4
Total	5	33	25	.569	95	76	8	1	0	469^1	414	243	219	69	14	232	332	1.376	4.20	96	4.27	.235	4	.222	-13	26	-1.3
• COX, Bill	William Donald Cox b: 6/23/1913, Ashmore, IL d: 2/16/1988, Charleston, IL BR/TR, 6'1", 185 lbs. Deb: 6/6/1936																										
1936	StL-N	0	0	....	2	0	0	0	0	2^2	4	5	2	0	0	1	1	1.875	6.75	58	5.00	.333	0	....	-1	0	-0.1
1937	Chi-A	1	0	1.000	3	2	1	1	0	12^2	9	1	1	0	0	5	8	1.105	0.71	648	1.91	.200	1	.250	5	2	0.5
1938	Chi-A	0	2	.000	7	1	0	0	0	11^2	11	14	9	0	0	13	5	2.057	6.94	70	5.33	.244	0	.000	-3	0	-0.3
	StL-A	1	4	.200	22	7	1	0	0	63	81	53	49	8	0	35	16	1.841	7.00	71	6.53	.315	1	.059	-14	0	-1.4
	Yr.	1	6	.143	29	8	1	0	0	74^2	92	67	58	8	0	48	21	1.875	6.99	71	6.34	.305	1	.053	-17	0	-1.7
1939	StL-A	0	2	.000	4	2	1	0	0	9^1	10	10	10	0	0	8	8	1.929	9.64	50	4.97	.256	0	.000	-5	0	-0.4
1940	StL-A	0	1	.000	12	0	0	0	0	17^1	23	17	14	3	0	12	7	2.019	7.27	63	7.82	.333	0	.000	-5	0	-0.5
Total	5	2	9	.182	50	12	3	1	0	116^2	138	100	85	11	0	74	45	1.817	6.56	74	5.94	.296	2	.080	-22	2	-2.2
• COX, Casey	Joseph Casey Cox b: 7/3/1941, Long Beach, CA BR/TR, 6'5", 200 lbs. Deb: 4/15/1966																										
1966	Was-A	4	5	.444	66	0	0	0	7	113	104	53	44	6	4	35	46	1.230	3.50	99	2.93	.250	0	.000	-1	6	-0.3
1967	Was-A	7	4	.636	54	0	0	0	1	73	67	33	24	2	4	21	32	1.205	2.96	107	2.82	.250	0	.000	1	5	0.1
1968	Was-A	0	1	.000	4	0	0	0	0	7^2	7	2	2	0	0	0	4	.913	2.35	124	1.66	.250	0	....	1	0	0.1
1969	Was-A	12	7	.632	52	13	4	0	0	171^2	161	62	53	15	1	64	73	1.311	2.78	125	3.54	.251	5	.106	12	12	1.1
1970	Was-A	8	12	.400	37	30	1	0	1	192^1	211	108	95	27	4	44	68	1.326	4.45	80	4.33	.285	7	.121	-22	4	-2.5
1971	Was-A	5	7	.417	54	11	0	0	7	124^1	131	69	55	9	7	40	43	1.375	3.98	83	3.95	.273	2	.077	-10	4	-1.2
1972	Tex-A	3	5	.375	35	4	0	0	4	65^1	73	41	32	7	1	26	27	1.515	4.41	68	4.55	.277	1	.111	-9	1	-0.9
	NY-A	0	1	.000	5	1	0	0	0	11^2	13	6	6	0	2	3	4	1.371	4.63	64	3.92	.289	0	....	-2	0	-0.2
	Yr.	3	6	.333	40	5	0	0	4	77	86	47	38	7	3	29	31	1.494	4.44	67	4.46	.278	1	.111	-11	1	-1.2
1973	NY-A	0	0	....	1	0	0	0	0	3	5	3	2	0	2	1	0	2.000	6.00	61	9.13	.357	0	....	-1	0	-0.1
Total	8	39	42	.481	308	59	5	0	20	762	772	377	313	66	25	234	297	1.320	3.70	91	3.74	.266	15	.099	-31	32	-3.9
• COX, Danny	Danny Bradford Cox b: 9/21/1959, Northampton, England BR/TR, 6'4", 235 lbs. Deb: 8/6/1983																										
1983	StL-N	3	6	.333	12	12	0	0	0	83	92	38	30	6	0	23	36	1.386	3.25	111	4.02	.286	2	.074	4	4	0.2
1984	StL-N	9	11	.450	29	27	1	1	0	156^1	171	81	70	9	7	54	70	1.439	4.03	86	4.31	.289	7	.132	-12	5	-1.3
1985*	StL-N	18	9	.667	35	35	10	4	0	241	226	91	77	19	3	64	131	1.203	2.88	123	3.13	.251	12	.152	13	16	1.4
1986	StL-N	12	13	.480	32	32	8	0	0	220	189	85	71	14	2	60	108	1.132	2.90	125	2.66	.234	5	.077	10	15	0.8
1987*	StL-N	11	9	.550	31	31	2	0	0	199^1	224	99	86	17	3	71	101	1.480	3.88	107	4.58	.290	8	.116	5	10	0.3
1988	StL-N	3	8	.273	13	13	0	0	0	86	89	40	38	6	1	25	47	1.326	3.98	87	3.60	.272	1	.043	-6	3	-0.8
1991	Phi-N	4	6	.400	23	17	0	0	0	102^1	98	57	52	14	1	39	46	1.339	4.57	80	4.06	.258	3	.103	-10	2	-1.1
1992	Phi-N	2	2	.500	9	7	0	0	0	38^1	46	28	23	3	0	19	30	1.696	5.40	65	5.34	.299	1	.091	-8	0	-0.9
	* Pit-N	3	1	.750	16	0	0	0	3	24^1	20	9	9	2	0	8	18	1.151	3.33	103	2.67	.225	0	.000	0	3	0.0
	Yr.	5	3	.625	25	7	0	0	3	62^2	66	37	32	5	0	27	48	1.484	4.60	76	4.30	.272	1	.071	-8	3	-0.9
1993*	Tor-A	7	6	.538	44	0	0	0	2	83^2	73	31	29	8	0	29	84	1.219	3.12	138	3.05	.230	0	....	12	9	1.1
1994	Tor-A	1	1	.500	10	0	0	0	3	18^2	7	3	3	0	1	7	14	.750	1.45	333	0.88	.113	0	....	7	4	0.7
1995	Tor-A	1	3	.250	24	0	0	0	0	45	57	40	37	4	1	33	38	2.000	7.40	64	6.97	.317	0	....	-14	0	-1.3
Total	11	74	75	.497	278	174	21	5	8	1298	1292	602	525	102	19	432	723	1.328	3.64	103	3.73	.263	39	.109	1	71	-0.9
• COX, Ernie	Ernest Thompson Cox b: 2/19/1894, Birmingham, AL d: 4/29/1974, Birmingham, AL BL/TR, 6'1", 180 lbs. Deb: 5/5/1922																										
1922	Chi-A	0	0	....	1	0	0	0	0	1	1	2	2	0	0	2	0	3.000	18.00	23	8.74	.250	0	....	-2	0	-0.2
• COX, George	George Melvin Cox b: 11/15/1904, Sherman, TX d: 12/17/1995, Bedford, TX BR/TR, 6'1", 170 lbs. Deb: 4/12/1928																										
1928	Chi-A	1	2	.333	26	2	0	0	0	89	110	58	52	6	2	39	22	1.674	5.26	77	5.39	.313	2	.077	-12	1	-1.4
• COX, Glenn	Glenn Melvin Cox b: 2/3/1931, Montebello, CA BR/TR, 6'2", 210 lbs. Deb: 9/20/1955																										
1955	KC-A	0	2	.000	2	2	0	0	0	2^1	11	8	8	0	0	1	2	5.143	30.86	14	30.74	.611	0	.000	-7	0	-0.7
1956	KC-A	0	2	.000	3	3	1	0	0	23^1	15	11	11	2	0	22	6	1.586	4.24	102	4.24	.203	0	.000	-0	1	-0.1
1957	KC-A	1	0	1.000	10	0	0	0	0	14^1	18	9	8	1	0	9	8	1.884	5.02	79	6.38	.321	0	.000	-2	0	-0.1
1958	KC-A	0	0	....	2	0	0	0	0	3^2	6	4	4	1	0	3	1	2.455	9.82	40	12.03	.400	0	....	-2	0	-0.2
Total	4	1	4	.200	17	5	1	0	0	43^2	50	32	31	4	0	35	17	1.947	6.39	65	7.01	.307	0	.000	-11	1	-1.2
• COX, Les	Leslie Warren Cox b: 8/14/1905, Junction, TX d: 10/14/1934, San Angelo, TX BR/TR, 6', 164 lbs. Deb: 9/11/1926																										
1926	Chi-A	0	1	.000	2	0	0	0	0	5	6	10	3	2	0	5	3	2.200	5.40	71	9.31	.261	1	.500	-1	0	-0.1
• COX, Red	Plateau Rex Cox b: 2/16/1895, Laurel Springs, NC d: 10/15/1984, Roanoke, VA BL/TR, 6'2", 190 lbs. Deb: 4/17/1920																										
1920	Det-A	0	0	....	3	0	0	0	0	5	9	4	3	0	0	3	1	2.400	5.40	69	8.62	.375	0	.000	-1	0	-0.1
• COX, Terry	Terry Lee Cox b: 3/30/1949, Odessa, TX BR/TR, 6'5", 215 lbs. Deb: 9/7/1970																										
1970	Cal-A	0	0	....	3	0	0	0	0	2^1	4	1	1	0	0	0	3	1.714	3.86	94	6.33	.400	0	....	-0	0	0.0
• COYLE, Bill	William Claude Coyle b: 9/20/1871, KY d: 6/4/1941, San Francisco, CA TR Deb: 7/7/1893																										
1893	Bos-N	0	1	.000	2	1	0	0	0	8	14	10	8	1	0	3	2	2.125	9.00	55	8.77	.372	0	.000	-4	0	-0.4
• COZART, Charlie	Charles Rhubin Cozart b: 10/17/1919, Lenoir, NC BR/TL, 6', 190 lbs. Deb: 4/17/1945																										
1945	Bos-N	1	0	1.000	5	0	0	0	0	8	10	11	9	2	0	15	4	3.125	10.13	38	12.75	.303	0	.000	-6	0	-0.6
• CRABB, Roy	James Roy Crabb b: 8/23/1890, Monticello, IA d: 3/30/1940, Lewistown, MT BR/TR, 5'11", 160 lbs. Deb: 8/10/1912																										
1912	Chi-A	0	1	.000	2	1	0	0	0	8^2	6	2	1	0	0	4	3	1.154	1.04	310	2.23	.214	0	.000	2	1	0.2
	Phi-A	2	4	.333	7	7	3	0	0	43^1	48	22	18	0	4	17	12	1.500	3.74	83	4.29	.287	0	.000	-4	2	-0.6
	Yr.	2	5	.286	9	8	3	0	0	52	54	24	19	0	4	21	15	1.442	3.29	94	3.94	.277	0	.000	-2	3	-0.5
• CRABLE, George	George E. Crable b: 12/1885, NE BL/TL, 6'1", 190 lbs. Deb: 8/3/1910																										
1910	Bro-N	0	0	....	2	1	1	0	0	7^1	5	4	4	0	2	5	3	1.364	4.91	62	3.81	.217	0	.000	-2	0	-0.2
• CRABTREE, Tim	Timothy Lyle Crabtree b: 10/13/1969, Jackson, MI BR/TR, 6'4", 205 lbs. Deb: 6/23/1995																										
1995	Tor-A	0	2	.000	31	0	0	0	0	32	30	16	11	1	2	13	21	1.344	3.09	152	3.42	.240	0	....	6	2	0.5
1996	Tor-A	5	3	.625	53	0	0	0	1	67^1	59	26	19	4	3	22	57	1.203	2.54	197	2.90	.231	0	....	17	8	1.5
1997	Tor-A	3	3	.500	37	0	0	0	2	40^2	65	32	32	7	2	17	26	2.016	7.08	65	8.66	.374	0	....	-12	0	-1.1
1998*	Tex-A	6	1	.857	64	0	0	0	0	85^1	86	40	34	3	3	35	60	1.418	3.59	135	3.80	.264	0	.000	13	7	1.2
1999*	Tex-A	5	1	.833	68	0	0	0	0	65	71	26	25	4	1	18	54	1.369	3.46	147	3.93	.280	0	....	13	7	1.2
2000	Tex-A	2	7	.222	68	0	0	0	2	80^1	86	52	46	7	2	31	54	1.456	5.15	97	4.30	.274	0	....	0	5	0.0
2001	Tex-A	0	5	.000	21	0	0	0	4	23^1	37	18	17	3	1	14	16	2.186	6.56	71	9.03	.385	0	....	-5	0	-0.5
Total	7	21	22	.488	342	0	0	0	9	394	434	210	184	29	14	150	288	1.482	4.20	115	4.55	.281	0	.000	32	29	2.9
• CRADDOCK, Walt	Walter Anderson Craddock b: 3/25/1932, Pax, WV d: 7/6/1980, Parma Heights, OH BR/TL, 5'11.5", 176 lbs. Deb: 9/3/1955																										
1955	KC-A	0	2	.000	4	2	0	0	0	15	18	14	13	3	0	10	9	1.867	7.80	53	7.04	.300	0	.000	-6	0	-0.7
1956	KC-A	0	2	.000	2	2	0	0	0	9^1	9	7	7	1	0	10	8	2.036	6.75	64	6.81	.265	0	.000	-3	0	-0.3
1958	KC-A	0	3	.000	23	1	0	0	0	36^2	41	25	24	4	1	20	22	1.664	5.89	66	5.54	.289	0	.000	-8	0	-0.9
Total	3	0	7	.000	29	5	0	0	0	61	68	46	44	8	1	40	39	1.770	6.49	62	6.10	.288	0	.000	-17	0	-1.8
• CRAFT, Molly	Maurice Montague Craft b: 11/28/1895, Portsmouth, VA d: 10/25/1978, Los Angeles, CA BR/TR, 6'2", 165 lbs. Deb: 8/8/1916																										
1916	Was-A	0	1	.000	2	1	1	0	0	11	12	5	4	0	0	6	9	1.636	3.27	85	4.88	.316	0	.000	-1	0	-0.2
1917	Was-A	0	0	....	8	0	0	0	1	14	17	10	6	0	0	8	2	1.786	3.86	68	5.35	.315	1	.500	-2	0	-0.2
1918	Was-A	0	0	....	3	0	0	0	0	7	5	1	1	0	0	1	5	.857	1.29	212	1.40	.208	0	.000	1	1	0.1
1919	Was-A	0	3	.000	16	2	0	0	1	48^2	59	28	21	2	2	18	17	1.582	3.88	82	5.00	.309	2	.111	-3	1	-0.5
Total	4	0	4	.000	29	3	1	0	2	80^2	93	44	32	2	2	33	33	1.562	3.57	84	4.73	.303	3	.115	-5	2	-0.8

YEAR TM-L	W	L	PCT	G	GS	CG	SH	SV	IP	H	R	ER	HR	HB	BB	SO	RAT	ERA	ERA+	CERA	OAV	BH	AVG	PR+	WS	TPW
• CRAGHEAD, Howard	Howard Oliver "Judge" Craghead b: 5/25/1908, Selma, CA d: 7/15/1962, San Diego, CA BR/TR, 6'2", 200 lbs. Deb: 4/30/1931																									
1931 Cle-A	0	0	....	4	0	0	0	0	5^2	8	4	4	0	0	2	2	1.765	6.35	73	5.26	.320	0	....	-1	0	-0.1
1933 Cle-A	0	0	....	11	0	0	0	0	17^1	19	13	12	1	1	10	2	1.673	6.23	71	5.14	.292	0	.000	-3	0	-0.4
Total 2	**0**	**0**	**....**	**15**	**0**	**0**	**0**	**0**	**23**	**27**	**17**	**16**	**1**	**1**	**12**	**4**	**1.696**	**6.26**	**72**	**5.17**	**.300**	**0**	**.000**	**-4**	**0**	**-0.5**
• CRAIG, George	George McCarthy "Lefty" Craig b: 11/15/1887, Philadelphia, PA d: 4/23/1911, Indianapolis, IN TL Deb: 7/19/1907																									
1907 Phi-A	0	0	....	2	0	0	0	0	1^2	2	3	2	0	2	3	0	3.000	10.80	24	16.86	.300	0	.000	-2	0	-0.2
• CRAIG, Pete	Peter Joel Craig b: 7/10/1940, LaSalle, Canada BL/TR, 6'5", 220 lbs. Deb: 9/6/1964																									
1964 Was-A	0	0	....	2	1	0	0	0	1^2	8	9	9	1	0	4	0	7.200	48.60	8	52.33	.667	0	....	-8	0	-0.9
1965 Was-A	0	3	.000	3	3	0	0	0	14^1	18	15	13	1	0	8	2	1.814	8.16	43	5.89	.321	2	.667	-7	0	-0.7
1966 Was-A	0	0	....	1	0	0	0	0	2	2	2	1	0	0	1	1	1.500	4.50	77	2.46	.250	0	....	-0	0	0.0
Total 3	**0**	**3**	**.000**	**6**	**4**	**0**	**0**	**0**	**18**	**28**	**26**	**23**	**2**	**0**	**13**	**3**	**2.278**	**11.50**	**31**	**9.81**	**.368**	**2**	**.667**	**-16**	**0**	**-1.6**
• CRAIG, Roger	Roger Lee Craig b: 2/17/1930, Durham, NC BR/TR, 6'4", 191 lbs. Deb: 7/17/1955 M/C																									
1955* Bro-N	5	3	.625	21	10	3	0	2	90^2	81	37	28	8	1	43	48	1.368	2.78	146	3.64	.238	2	.077	12	7	1.0
1956* Bro-N	12	11	.522	35	32	8	2	1	199	169	90	82	25	4	87	109	1.286	3.71	107	3.61	.231	1	.016	2	11	-0.3
1957 Bro-N	6	9	.400	32	13	1	0	0	111^1	102	58	57	18	2	47	69	1.338	4.61	90	4.23	.249	4	.138	-5	5	-0.6
1958 LA-N	2	1	.667	9	2	1	0	0	32	30	20	16	3	0	12	16	1.313	4.50	91	3.52	.242	0	.000	-1	1	-0.2
1959* LA-N	11	5	.688	29	17	7	**4**	0	152^2	122	49	35	13	1	45	76	1.094	2.06	205	2.55	.217	3	.058	36	17	3.3
1960 LA-N	8	3	.727	21	15	6	1	0	115^2	99	48	42	8	3	43	69	1.228	3.27	121	3.07	.230	2	.056	8	9	0.6
1961 LA-N	5	6	.455	40	14	2	0	2	112^2	130	87	77	22	4	52	63	1.615	6.15	70	6.00	.288	4	.148	-23	0	-2.3
1962 NY-N	10	24	.294	42	33	13	0	3	233^1	261	133	117	35	7	70	118	1.419	4.51	93	4.91	.288	4	.053	-4	9	-0.9
1963 NY-N	5	22	.185	46	31	14	0	2	236	249	117	99	28	6	58	108	1.301	3.78	92	3.93	.267	6	.087	-5	9	-0.8
1964* StL-N	7	9	.438	39	19	3	0	5	166	180	76	60	16	4	35	84	1.295	3.25	117	3.81	.276	10	.208	10	12	1.3
1965 Cin-N	1	4	.200	40	0	0	0	3	64^1	74	33	26	6	3	25	30	1.539	3.64	103	4.77	.289	2	.182	1	3	0.1
1966 Phi-N	2	1	.667	14	0	0	0	1	22^2	31	15	14	4	0	5	13	1.588	5.56	65	5.91	.326	0	.000	-5	0	-0.6
Total 12	**74**	**98**	**.430**	**368**	**186**	**58**	**7**	**19**	**1536^1**	**1528**	**763**	**653**	**186**	**35**	**522**	**803**	**1.334**	**3.83**	**104**	**4.03**	**.259**	**38**	**.085**	**25**	**83**	**0.4**
• CRAM, Jerry	Gerald Allen Cram b: 12/9/1947, Los Angeles, CA BR/TR, 6', 180 lbs. Deb: 9/3/1969																									
1969 KC-A	0	1	.000	5	2	0	0	0	16^2	15	8	6	0	0	6	10	1.260	3.24	114	2.56	.231	0	.000	1	1	0.1
1974 NY-N	0	1	.000	10	0	0	0	0	22^1	22	4	4	1	0	4	8	1.164	1.61	221	2.88	.275	1	.333	5	3	0.5
1975 NY-N	0	1	.000	4	0	0	0	0	5	7	3	3	2	0	2	2	1.800	5.40	64	9.18	.333	0	....	-1	0	-0.1
1976 KC-A	0	0	....	4	0	0	0	0	4^1	8	3	3	0	0	1	2	2.077	6.23	56	7.89	.421	0	....	-1	0	-0.1
Total 4	**0**	**3**	**.000**	**23**	**2**	**0**	**0**	**0**	**48^1**	**52**	**18**	**16**	**3**	**0**	**13**	**22**	**1.345**	**2.98**	**120**	**3.87**	**.281**	**1**	**.167**	**3**	**4**	**0.3**
• CRAMER, Bill	William Wendell Cramer b: 5/21/1891, Bedford, IN d: 9/11/1966, Fort Wayne, IN BR/TR, 6', 175 lbs. Deb: 6/25/1912																									
1912 Cin-N	0	0	....	1	0	0	0	0	2^1	6	6	0	0	0	0	2	2.571	0.00	....	9.78	.500	0	.000	1	0	0.1
• CRANDALL, Doc	James Otis Crandall b: 10/8/1887, Wadena, IN d: 8/17/1951, Bell, CA BR/TR, 5'10.5", 180 lbs. Deb: 4/24/1908 C ♦																									
1908 NY-N	12	12	.500	32	24	13	0	0	214^2	198	83	70	3	9	59	77	1.197	2.93	82	2.80	.248	16	.222	-10	11	-0.7
1909 NY-N	6	4	.600	30	7	4	0	6	122	117	58	39	5	3	33	55	1.230	2.88	89	3.04	.252	10	.244	-3	7	-0.1
1910 NY-N	17	4	.810	42	18	13	2	5	207^2	194	86	59	10	4	43	73	1.141	2.56	116	2.74	.246	25	.342	12	19	2.3
1911* NY-N	15	5	.750	41	15	9	2	5	198^2	199	82	58	10	6	51	94	1.258	2.63	127	3.24	.256	27	.239	19	20	2.4
1912* NY-N	13	7	.650	37	10	7	0	2	162	181	85	65	7	2	35	60	1.333	3.61	94	3.61	.286	25	.313	-5	12	0.3
1913* NY-N	2	4	.333	24	2	1	0	5	55^1	61	28	19	2	1	13	28	1.337	3.09	101	3.63	.293	7	.280	-0	8	0.2
* NY-N	2	0	1.000	11	1	1	0	1	42^1	41	17	12	1	0	11	14	1.228	2.55	122	2.71	.248	8	.364	2	0	0.6
Yr.	4	4	.500	35	3	2	0	6	97^2	102	45	31	3	1	24	42	1.290	2.86	109	3.23	.273	15	.319	2	8	0.8
1914 StL-F	13	9	.591	27	21	18	1	0	196	194	94	77	8	2	52	84	1.255	3.54	98	3.11	.256	86	.309	2	26	1.7
1915 StL-F	21	15	.583	51	33	22	4	1	312^2	307	116	90	5	10	77	117	1.228	2.59	120	3.02	.263	40	.284	13	29	3.0
1916 StL-A	0	0	....	2	0	0	0	0	1^1	7	9	4	0	1	1	0	6.000	27.00	10	40.42	.636	1	.083	-4	0	-0.4
1918 Bos-N	1	2	.333	5	3	3	0	0	34	39	11	9	1	1	4	4	1.265	2.38	113	3.58	.307	8	.286	2	3	0.4
Total 10	**102**	**62**	**.622**	**302**	**134**	**91**	**9**	**25**	**1546^2**	**1538**	**669**	**502**	**52**	**39**	**379**	**606**	**1.239**	**2.92**	**103**	**3.11**	**.261**	**253**	**.285**	**29**	**135**	**9.7**
• CRANE, Ed	Edward Nicholas "Cannonball" Crane b: 5/27/1862, Boston, MA d: 9/20/1896, Rochester, NY BR/TR, 5'10.5", 204 lbs. Deb: 4/17/1884 U ♦																									
1884 Bos-U	0	2	.000	4	2	1	0	0	18	17	14	8	1	....	6	13	1.278	4.00	74	....	.233	122	.285	-2	22	2.3
1886 Was-N	1	7	.125	10	8	7	1	0	70	91	85	56	5	....	53	39	2.057	7.20	45	....	.303	50	.171	-30	1	-4.6
1888* NY-N	5	6	.455	12	11	11	2	1	92^2	70	51	25	3	2	40	58	1.187	2.43	112	....	.202	6	.162	0	5	0.2
1889* NY-N	14	10	.583	29	25	23	0	0	230	221	161	94	10	10	136	130	1.552	3.68	107	....	.245	21	.204	5	15	0.8
1890 NY-P	16	19	.457	43	35	28	0	0	330^1	323	280	170	12	10	208	116	1.607	4.63	98	....	.245	46	.315	-8	22	0.1
1891 Cin-a	14	14	.500	32	31	25	1	0	250	216	151	68	3	14	139	122	1.420	**2.45**	**168**	....	.225	17	.155	46	20	3.4
Cin-N	4	8	.333	15	13	11	1	0	116^2	134	91	53	3	3	64	51	1.697	4.09	82	....	.278	5	.109	-10	3	-1.2
1892 NY-N	16	24	.400	47	42	35	2	1	364^1	350	276	154	10	12	189	174	1.479	3.80	85	3.78	.243	40	.245	-19	14	-1.4
1893 NY-N	2	4	.333	10	7	4	0	0	68^1	84	62	45	2	6	41	11	1.829	5.93	78	5.81	.294	12	.462	-10	4	-0.4
Bro-N	0	2	.000	2	2	1	0	0	10	19	19	15	2	1	9	5	2.800	13.50	33	13.44	.391	2	.400	-10	0	-0.8
Yr.	2	6	.250	12	9	5	0	0	78^1	103	81	60	4	7	50	16	1.953	6.89	67	6.79	.308	14	.452	-20	4	-1.2
Total 8	**72**	**96**	**.429**	**204**	**176**	**146**	**7**	**2**	**1550^1**	**1525**	**1190**	**688**	**51**	**58**	**885**	**719**	**1.555**	**3.99**	**94**	**1.23**	**.248**	**335**	**.238**	**-39**	**106**	**-1.6**
• CRAWFORD, Carlos	Carlos Lamonte Crawford b: 10/4/1971, Charlotte, NC BR/TR, 6'1", 185 lbs. Deb: 6/7/1996																									
1996 Phi-N	0	1	.000	1	1	0	0	0	3^2	7	10	2	1	1	2	4	2.455	4.91	88	12.76	.389	0	.000	-0	0	0.0
• CRAWFORD, Jim	James Frederick "Catfish" Crawford b: 9/29/1950, Chicago, IL BL/TL, 6'3", 200 lbs. Deb: 4/6/1973																									
1973 Hou-N	2	4	.333	48	0	0	0	6	70	69	41	35	7	2	33	56	1.457	4.50	81	4.09	.256	3	.231	-7	3	-0.6
1975 Hou-N	3	5	.375	44	2	0	0	4	86^2	92	40	35	0	2	37	37	1.488	3.63	93	3.86	.280	5	.294	-3	5	-0.1
1976 Det-A	1	8	.111	32	5	1	0	2	109^1	115	65	55	4	0	43	68	1.445	4.53	82	3.80	.275	0	....	-9	3	-0.9
1977 Det-A	7	8	.467	37	7	0	0	1	126	156	82	67	13	1	50	91	1.635	4.79	90	5.41	.310	0	....	-7	4	-0.7
1978 Det-A	2	3	.400	20	0	0	0	0	39^1	45	24	19	3	2	19	24	1.627	4.35	89	5.12	.292	0	....	-3	1	-0.3
Total 5	**15**	**28**	**.349**	**181**	**14**	**1**	**0**	**13**	**431^1**	**477**	**252**	**211**	**27**	**7**	**182**	**276**	**1.528**	**4.40**	**86**	**4.45**	**.285**	**8**	**.267**	**-28**	**16**	**-2.6**
• CRAWFORD, Joe	Joseph Randal Crawford b: 5/2/1970, Gainesville, FL BL/TL, 6'3", 225 lbs. Deb: 4/7/1997																									
1997 NY-N	4	3	.571	19	2	0	0	0	46^1	36	18	17	7	0	13	25	1.058	3.30	122	2.79	.216	0	.000	3	3	0.2
• CRAWFORD, Larry	Charles Lowrie Crawford b: 4/27/1914, Swissvale, PA d: 12/20/1994, Hanover, PA BL/TL, 6'1", 165 lbs. Deb: 7/21/1937																									
1937 Phi-N	0	0	....	6	0	0	0	0	6	12	10	10	2	0	1	2	2.167	15.00	29	10.87	.387	0		-7	0	-0.7
• CRAWFORD, Paxton	Paxton Keith Crawford b: 8/4/1977, Little Rock, AR BR/TR, 6'3", 205 lbs. Deb: 7/1/2000																									
2000 Bos-A	2	1	.667	7	4	0	0	0	29	25	15	11	0	2	13	17	1.310	3.41	148	2.99	.240	0	....	5	2	0.5
2001 Bos-A	3	0	1.000	8	7	0	0	0	36	40	19	19	3	2	13	25	1.472	4.75	94	4.60	.276	0	....	-0	2	0.0
Total 2	**5**	**1**	**.833**	**15**	**11**	**0**	**0**	**0**	**65**	**65**	**34**	**30**	**3**	**4**	**26**	**42**	**1.400**	**4.15**	**112**	**3.88**	**.261**	**0**	**....**	**5**	**4**	**0.4**
• CRAWFORD, Steve	Steven Ray Crawford b: 4/29/1958, Pryor, OK BR/TR, 6'5", 225 lbs. Deb: 9/2/1980																									
1980 Bos-A	2	0	1.000	6	4	2	0	0	32^1	41	14	13	3	0	8	10	1.515	3.62	117	4.87	.306	0	....	2	2	0.2
1981 Bos-A	0	5	.000	14	11	0	0	0	57^2	69	38	32	10	3	18	29	1.509	4.99	78	5.63	.301	0	....	-6	0	-0.7
1982 Bos-A	1	0	1.000	5	0	0	0	0	9	14	3	2	0	0	0	2	1.556	2.00	215	4.78	.341	0	....	2	1	0.2
1984 Bos-A	5	0	1.000	35	0	0	0	1	62	69	31	23	6	1	21	21	1.452	3.34	125	4.43	.286	0	....	8	5	0.8
1985 Bos-A	6	5	.545	44	1	0	0	12	91	103	47	38	5	0	28	58	1.440	3.76	114	3.99	.289	0	....	7	7	0.7
1986* Bos-A	0	2	.000	40	0	0	0	4	57^1	69	29	25	5	0	19	32	1.535	3.92	106	4.79	.308	0	....	2	3	0.2
1987 Bos-A	5	4	.556	29	0	0	0	0	72^2	91	48	43	13	2	32	43	1.693	5.33	85	6.67	.314	0	....	-6	3	-0.6
1989 KC-A	3	1	.750	25	0	0	0	0	54	48	19	17	2	3	19	33	1.241	2.83	136	3.04	.242	0	....	7	5	0.7
1990 KC-A	5	4	.556	46	0	0	0	1	80	79	38	37	7	3	23	54	1.275	4.16	92	3.54	.254	0	....	-1	4	-0.1

YEAR	TM-L	W	L	PCT	G	GS	CG	SH	SV	IP	H	R	ER	HR	HB	BB	SO	RAT	ERA	ERA+	CERA	OAV	BH	AVG	PR+	WS	TPW
1991	KC-A	3	2	.600	33	0	0	0	1	46^2	60	31	31	3	1	18	38	1.671	5.98	69	5.24	.311	0	....	-8	1	-0.8
Total	10	30	23	.566	277	16	2	0	19	562^2	643	298	261	54	13	186	320	1.473	4.17	99	4.65	.290	0	....	7	31	0.7

• CREEK, Doug

Paul Douglas Creek b: 3/1/1969, Winchester, VA BL/TL, 5'10", 205 lbs. Deb: 9/17/1995

YEAR	TM-L	W	L	PCT	G	GS	CG	SH	SV	IP	H	R	ER	HR	HB	BB	SO	RAT	ERA	ERA+	CERA	OAV	BH	AVG	PR+	WS	TPW
1995	StL-N	0	0	....	6	0	0	0	0	6^2	2	0	0	0	0	3	10	.750	0.00	....	0.83	.095	0	....	3	1	0.3
1996	SF-N	0	2	.000	63	0	0	0	0	48^1	45	41	35	11	2	32	38	1.593	6.52	63	5.80	.243	0	.000	-13	0	-1.3
1997	SF-N	1	2	.333	3	3	0	0	0	13^1	12	12	10	1	0	14	14	1.950	6.75	60	5.94	.240	1	.333	-4	0	-0.4
1999	Chi-N	0	0	....	3	0	0	0	0	6	6	7	7	1	0	8	6	2.333	10.50	43	8.01	.261	0	....	-4	0	-0.4
2000	TB-A	1	3	.250	45	0	0	0	1	60^2	49	33	31	10	2	39	73	1.451	4.60	107	4.50	.224	0	....	1	4	0.1
2001	TB-A	2	5	.286	66	0	0	0	0	62^2	51	34	30	7	4	49	66	1.596	4.31	104	4.84	.230	0	....	1	3	0.1
2002	TB-A	2	1	.667	29	0	0	0	0	37^1	39	27	26	8	3	21	37	1.607	6.27	71	6.15	.264	0	.000	-8	1	-0.8
	Sea-A	1	1	.500	23	0	0	0	0	18^1	18	10	10	2	4	14	19	1.745	4.91	86	6.22	.257	0	....	-1	1	-0.1
	Yr.	3	2	.600	52	0	0	0	0	55^2	57	37	36	10	7	35	56	1.653	5.82	75	6.17	.261	0	.000	-9	2	-0.9
2003	Tor-A	0	0	....	21	0	0	0	0	13^2	14	6	5	2	2	12	11	1.902	3.29	139	6.57	.264	0	....	2	1	0.2
Total	8	7	14	.333	259	3	0	0	1	267	236	170	154	42	17	192	274	1.603	5.19	85	5.33	.238	1	.200	-23	11	-2.2

• CREEL, Jack

Jack Dalton "Tex" Creel b: 4/23/1916, Kyle, TX d: 8/13/2002, Houston, TX BR/TR, 6', 165 lbs. Deb: 4/22/1945

YEAR	TM-L	W	L	PCT	G	GS	CG	SH	SV	IP	H	R	ER	HR	HB	BB	SO	RAT	ERA	ERA+	CERA	OAV	BH	AVG	PR+	WS	TPW
1945	StL-N	5	4	.556	26	8	2	0	2	87	78	41	40	5	6	45	34	1.414	4.14	90	3.85	.245	2	.077	-6	4	-0.8

• CREEL, Keith

Steven Keith Creel b: 2/4/1959, Dallas, TX BR/TR, 6'2", 180 lbs. Deb: 5/25/1982

YEAR	TM-L	W	L	PCT	G	GS	CG	SH	SV	IP	H	R	ER	HR	HB	BB	SO	RAT	ERA	ERA+	CERA	OAV	BH	AVG	PR+	WS	TPW
1982	KC-A	1	4	.200	9	6	0	0	0	41^2	43	28	25	8	0	25	13	1.632	5.40	76	5.75	.267	0	....	-6	0	-0.6
1983	KC-A	2	5	.286	25	10	1	0	0	89^1	116	66	63	17	2	35	31	1.690	6.35	64	6.76	.320	0	....	-22	0	-2.2
1985	Cle-A	2	5	.286	15	8	0	0	0	62	73	35	33	7	2	23	31	1.548	4.79	86	5.17	.296	0	....	-4	2	-0.4
1987	Tex-A	0	0	....	6	0	0	0	0	9^2	12	5	5	2	0	5	5	1.759	4.66	96	6.70	.293	0	....	-0	0	0.0
Total	4	5	14	.263	55	24	1	0	0	202^2	244	134	126	34	4	88	80	1.638	5.60	73	6.06	.300	0	....	-32	2	-3.2

• CREMINS, Bob

Robert Anthony "Lefty,Crooked Arm" Cremins b: 2/15/1906, Pelham Manor, NY d: 3/27/2004, Pelham, NY BL/TL, 5'11", 178 lbs. Deb: 8/17/1927

YEAR	TM-L	W	L	PCT	G	GS	CG	SH	SV	IP	H	R	ER	HR	HB	BB	SO	RAT	ERA	ERA+	CERA	OAV	BH	AVG	PR+	WS	TPW
1927	Bos-A	0	0	....	4	0	0	0	0	5^1	5	4	3	0	0	3	0	1.500	5.06	83	3.38	.250	0	....	-0	0	0.0

• CRESS, Walker

Walker James "Foots" Cress b: 3/6/1917, Ben Hur, VA d: 4/21/1996, Baton Rouge, LA BR/TR, 6'5", 205 lbs. Deb: 4/27/1948

YEAR	TM-L	W	L	PCT	G	GS	CG	SH	SV	IP	H	R	ER	HR	HB	BB	SO	RAT	ERA	ERA+	CERA	OAV	BH	AVG	PR+	WS	TPW
1948	Cin-N	0	1	.000	30	2	1	0	0	60	60	32	30	2	1	42	33	1.700	4.50	87	4.80	.271	4	.500	-3	3	-0.1
1949	Cin-N	0	0	....	3	0	0	0	0	2	2	0	0	0	0	3	0	2.500	0.00	....	7.67	.286	0	....	1	0	0.1
Total	2	0	1	.000	33	2	1	0	0	62	62	32	30	2	1	45	33	1.726	4.35	90	4.90	.272	4	.500	-2	3	0.0

• CRESSEND, Jack

John Baptiste Cressend b: 5/13/1975, New Orleans, LA BR/TR, 6'1", 185 lbs. Deb: 8/26/2000

YEAR	TM-L	W	L	PCT	G	GS	CG	SH	SV	IP	H	R	ER	HR	HB	BB	SO	RAT	ERA	ERA+	CERA	OAV	BH	AVG	PR+	WS	TPW
2000	Min-A	0	0	....	11	0	0	0	0	13^2	20	8	8	0	0	6	6	1.902	5.27	98	6.65	.364	0	....	0	1	0.0
2001	Min-A	3	2	.600	44	0	0	0	0	56^1	50	24	23	6	1	16	40	1.172	3.67	125	3.13	.237	0	....	6	5	0.6
2002	Min-A	0	1	.000	23	0	0	0	0	32	40	25	21	6	1	19	22	1.844	5.91	76	6.92	.305	0	....	-5	0	-0.5
2003	Cle-A	2	1	.667	33	0	0	0	0	43	40	12	12	1	2	9	28	1.140	2.51	176	2.67	.252	0	....	8	4	0.8
Total	4	5	4	.556	111	0	0	0	0	145	150	69	64	13	4	50	96	1.379	3.97	115	4.17	.270	0	....	9	10	0.9

• CREWS, Tim

Stanley Timothy Crews b: 4/3/1961, Tampa, FL d: 3/23/1993, Orlando, FL BR/TR, 6', 192 lbs. Deb: 7/27/1987

YEAR	TM-L	W	L	PCT	G	GS	CG	SH	SV	IP	H	R	ER	HR	HB	BB	SO	RAT	ERA	ERA+	CERA	OAV	BH	AVG	PR+	WS	TPW
1987	LA-N	1	1	.500	20	0	0	0	3	29	30	9	8	2	2	8	20	1.310	2.48	160	3.79	.268	0	.000	5	3	0.5
1988	LA-N	4	0	1.000	42	0	0	0	0	71^2	77	29	25	3	0	16	45	1.298	3.14	106	3.26	.278	1	.200	2	5	0.2
1989	LA-N	0	1	.000	44	0	0	0	1	61^2	69	27	22	7	2	23	56	1.492	3.21	106	4.58	.284	0	....	1	2	0.1
1990	LA-N	4	5	.444	66	2	0	0	5	107^1	98	40	33	9	1	24	76	1.137	2.77	132	2.77	.238	0	.000	10	9	1.0
1991	LA-N	2	3	.400	60	0	0	0	6	76	75	30	29	7	0	19	53	1.237	3.43	105	3.13	.256	0	.000	1	6	0.2
1992	LA-N	0	3	.000	49	2	0	0	0	78	95	46	45	6	2	20	43	1.474	5.19	66	4.54	.310	2	.286	-13	0	-1.4
Total	6	11	13	.458	281	4	0	0	15	423^2	444	181	162	34	7	110	293	1.308	3.44	102	3.58	.270	3	.136	6	25	0.6

• CRIDER, Jerry

Jerry Stephen Crider b: 9/2/1941, Sioux Falls, SD BR/TR, 6'2", 200 lbs. Deb: 5/21/1969

YEAR	TM-L	W	L	PCT	G	GS	CG	SH	SV	IP	H	R	ER	HR	HB	BB	SO	RAT	ERA	ERA+	CERA	OAV	BH	AVG	PR+	WS	TPW
1969	Min-A	1	0	1.000	21	1	0	0	1	28^2	31	15	15	3	2	15	16	1.605	4.71	78	5.02	.284	4	.444	-4	1	-0.2
1970	Chi-A	4	7	.364	32	8	0	0	4	91	101	49	45	13	2	34	40	1.484	4.45	88	5.07	.288	2	.083	-4	4	-0.6
Total	2	5	7	.417	53	9	0	0	5	119^2	132	64	60	16	4	49	56	1.513	4.51	85	5.05	.287	6	.182	-8	5	-0.8

• CRIM, Chuck

Charles Robert Crim b: 7/23/1961, Van Nuys, CA BR/TR, 6', 185 lbs. Deb: 4/8/1987

YEAR	TM-L	W	L	PCT	G	GS	CG	SH	SV	IP	H	R	ER	HR	HB	BB	SO	RAT	ERA	ERA+	CERA	OAV	BH	AVG	PR+	WS	TPW
1987	Mil-A	6	8	.429	53	5	0	0	12	130	133	60	53	15	3	39	56	1.323	3.67	125	3.98	.266	0	....	14	12	1.3
1988	Mil-A	7	6	.538	**70**	0	0	0	9	105	95	38	34	11	2	28	58	1.171	2.91	137	3.17	.247	0	....	12	11	1.2
1989	Mil-A	9	7	.563	**76**	0	0	0	7	117^2	114	42	37	7	2	36	59	1.275	2.83	136	3.28	.259	0	....	13	11	1.3
1990	Mil-A	3	5	.375	67	0	0	0	11	85^2	88	39	33	7	2	23	39	1.296	3.47	112	3.55	.261	0	....	5	7	0.5
1991	Mil-A	8	5	.615	66	0	0	0	3	91^1	115	52	47	9	2	25	39	1.533	4.63	86	4.95	.305	0	....	-7	4	-0.7
1992	Cal-A	7	6	.538	57	0	0	0	1	87	100	56	50	11	6	29	30	1.483	5.17	77	5.08	.293	0	....	-12	2	-1.2
1993	Cal-A	2	2	.500	11	0	0	0	0	15^1	17	11	10	2	2	5	10	1.435	5.87	77	5.17	.298	0	....	-3	0	-0.2
1994	Chi-N	5	4	.556	49	1	0	0	2	64^1	69	36	32	9	1	24	43	1.446	4.48	93	4.54	.271	0	.000	-3	3	-0.3
Total	8	47	43	.522	449	6	0	0	45	696^1	731	334	296	71	20	209	334	1.350	3.83	107	4.03	.272	0	.000	19	50	1.9

• CRIMIAN, Jack

John Melvin Crimian b: 2/17/1926, Philadelphia, PA BR/TR, 5'10", 180 lbs. Deb: 7/3/1951

YEAR	TM-L	W	L	PCT	G	GS	CG	SH	SV	IP	H	R	ER	HR	HB	BB	SO	RAT	ERA	ERA+	CERA	OAV	BH	AVG	PR+	WS	TPW
1951	StL-N	1	0	1.000	11	0	0	0	1	17	24	17	17	3	0	8	5	1.882	9.00	44	7.47	.338	1	.333	-10	0	-1.0
1952	StL-N	0	0	....	5	0	0	0	0	8^1	15	9	9	4	0	4	4	2.280	9.72	38	13.67	.417	0	.000	-6	0	-0.6
1956	KC-A	4	8	.333	54	7	0	0	3	129	129	87	79	19	5	49	59	1.380	5.51	79	4.48	.265	5	.227	-18	4	-1.7
1957	Det-A	0	1	.000	4	0	0	0	0	5^2	9	8	8	1	0	4	1	2.294	12.71	30	9.13	.375	0	....	-6	0	-0.6
Total	4	5	9	.357	74	7	0	0	4	160	177	121	113	27	5	65	69	1.513	6.36	66	5.44	.287	6	.231	-39	4	-3.8

• CRISS, Dode

Dode Criss b: 3/12/1885, Sherman, MS d: 9/8/1955, Sherman, MS BL/TR, 6'2", 200 lbs. Deb: 4/20/1908 ♦

YEAR	TM-L	W	L	PCT	G	GS	CG	SH	SV	IP	H	R	ER	HR	HB	BB	SO	RAT	ERA	ERA+	CERA	OAV	BH	AVG	PR+	WS	TPW
1908	StL-A	0	1	.000	9	1	0	0	0	18	15	14	13	1	3	13	9	1.556	6.50	37	4.91	.250	28	.341	-9	5	-0.2
1909	StL-A	1	5	.167	11	6	3	0	0	55^1	53	33	21	0	2	32	43	1.536	3.42	71	3.96	.262	14	.292	-6	3	-0.1
1910	StL-A	2	1	.667	6	0	0	0	0	19^1	12	7	3	0	4	9	9	1.086	1.40	177	2.25	.176	21	.231	2	4	0.4
1911	StL-A	0	2	.000	4	2	0	0	0	18^1	24	21	17	0	2	10	9	1.855	8.35	40	6.28	.333	21	.253	-10	2	-1.0
Total	4	3	9	.250	30	9	3	0	0	111	104	75	54	1	11	64	70	1.514	4.38	60	4.20	.258	84	.276	-23	14	-0.8

• CRISTALL, Bill

William Arthur "Lefty" Cristall b: 9/12/1878, Odessa, Ukraine d: 1/28/1939, Buffalo, NY BL/TL, 5'7", 145 lbs. Deb: 9/3/1901

YEAR	TM-L	W	L	PCT	G	GS	CG	SH	SV	IP	H	R	ER	HR	HB	BB	SO	RAT	ERA	ERA+	CERA	OAV	BH	AVG	PR+	WS	TPW
1901	Cle-A	1	5	.167	6	6	5	1	0	48^1	54	42	26	1	4	30	12	1.738	4.84	73	5.13	.279	7	.350	-7	2	-0.4

• CRISTANTE, Leo

Dante Leo Cristante b: 12/10/1926, Detroit, MI d: 8/24/1977, Dearborn, MI BR/TR, 6'1", 195 lbs. Deb: 4/21/1951

YEAR	TM-L	W	L	PCT	G	GS	CG	SH	SV	IP	H	R	ER	HR	HB	BB	SO	RAT	ERA	ERA+	CERA	OAV	BH	AVG	PR+	WS	TPW
1951	Phi-N	1	1	.500	10	1	0	0	0	22	28	13	12	3	1	9	6	1.682	4.91	78	6.18	.318	1	.167	-3	1	-0.3
1955	Det-A	0	1	.000	20	1	0	0	0	36^2	37	15	13	1	0	14	9	1.391	3.19	120	3.42	.261	0	.000	3	2	0.2
Total	2	1	2	.333	30	2	0	0	0	58^2	65	28	25	4	1	23	15	1.500	3.84	100	4.45	.283	1	.077	0	3	-0.1

• CRITCHLEY, Morrie

Morris Arthur Critchley b: 3/26/1850, New London, CT d: 3/6/1910, Pittsburgh, PA, 6'1", 190 lbs. Deb: 5/8/1882 U

YEAR	TM-L	W	L	PCT	G	GS	CG	SH	SV	IP	H	R	ER	HR	HB	BB	SO	RAT	ERA	ERA+	CERA	OAV	BH	AVG	PR+	WS	TPW
1882	Pit-a	1	0	1.000	1	1	1	1	0	9	7	0	0	0	....	1	3	.889	0.00	....	....	.200	0	.000	3	1	0.2
	StL-a	0	4	.000	4	4	4	0	0	34	43	31	16	3	....	7	2	1.471	4.24	66	....	.289	3	.214	-5	1	-0.5
	Yr.	1	4	.200	5	5	5	1	0	43	50	31	16	3	....	8	5	1.349	3.35	84	....	.272	3	.158	-2	2	-0.3

• CROCKER, Claude

Claude Arthur Crocker b: 7/20/1924, Caroleen, NC d: 12/19/2002, Clinton, SC BR/TR, 6'2", 185 lbs. Deb: 8/1/1944

YEAR	TM-L	W	L	PCT	G	GS	CG	SH	SV	IP	H	R	ER	HR	HB	BB	SO	RAT	ERA	ERA+	CERA	OAV	BH	AVG	PR+	WS	TPW
1944	Bro-N	0	0	....	2	0	0	0	0	3^1	6	4	4	0	0	5	1	3.300	10.80	33	12.92	.400	1	1.000	-3	0	-0.2
1945	Bro-N	0	0	....	1	0	0	0	1	2	2	0	0	0	0	1	1	1.500	0.00	....	4.01	.286	0	....	1	0	0.1
Total	2	0	0	....	3	0	0	0	1	5^1	8	4	4	0	0	6	2	2.625	6.75	53	9.58	.364	1	1.000	-2	0	-0.1

• CRONE, Ray

Raymond Hayes Crone b: 8/7/1931, Memphis, TN BR/TR, 6'2", 185 lbs. Deb: 4/13/1954

YEAR	TM-L	W	L	PCT	G	GS	CG	SH	SV	IP	H	R	ER	HR	HB	BB	SO	RAT	ERA	ERA+	CERA	OAV	BH	AVG	PR+	WS	TPW
1954	Mil-N	1	0	1.000	19	2	1	0	1	49	44	11	11	6	1	19	33	1.286	2.02	184	3.75	.247	2	.200	9	5	0.8
1955	Mil-N	10	9	.526	33	15	6	1	0	140^1	117	63	54	11	0	42	76	1.133	3.46	108	2.62	.227	7	.159	5	8	0.3

YEAR	TM-L	W	L	PCT	G	GS	CG	SH	SV	IP	H	R	ER	HR	HB	BB	SO	RAT	ERA	ERA+	CERA	OAV	BH	AVG	PR+	WS	TPW
1956	Mil-N	11	10	.524	35	21	6	0	2	169^{2}	173	92	73	19	1	44	73	1.279	3.87	89	3.69	.263	6	.122	-9	6	-0.9
1957	Mil-N	3	1	.750	11	5	2	0	0	42^{1}	54	23	21	8	0	15	15	1.630	4.46	78	6.20	.312	2	.182	-5	1	-0.4
	NY-N	4	8	.333	25	17	2	0	1	120^{2}	131	68	58	11	3	40	56	1.417	4.33	91	4.25	.272	1	.025	-5	4	-0.8
	Yr.	7	9	.438	36	22	4	0	1	163	185	91	79	19	3	55	71	**1.472**	4.36	87	4.76	.282	3	.059	-10	5	-1.3
1958	SF-N	1	2	.333	14	1	0	0	0	24	35	18	18	5	0	13	7	2.000	6.75	57	8.53	.354	0	.000	-8	0	-0.8
Total	5	30	30	.500	137	61	17	1	4	546	554	275	235	60	5	173	260	1.332	3.87	95	3.95	.263	18	.115	-14	24	-1.8
• CRONIN, Jack	John J. Cronin b: 5/26/1874, West New Brighton, NY d: 7/12/1929, Middletown, NY BR/TR, 6', 200 lbs. Deb: 8/24/1895 U																										
1895	Bro-N	0	0	....	2	0	0	0	2	5	10	8	6	0	0	3	1	2.600	10.80	41	10.24	.409	1	.500	-4	0	-0.2
1898	Pit-N	2	2	.500	4	4	2	1	0	28	35	14	11	0	0	8	9	1.536	3.54	100	4.23	.304	1	.100	0	2	0.0
1899	Cin-N	2	2	.500	5	5	5	0	0	41	56	35	25	2	5	16	9	1.756	5.49	71	6.15	.325	2	.118	-7	1	-0.8
1901	Det-A	13	16	.448	30	28	21	1	0	219^{2}	261	145	95	6	11	42	62	1.379	3.89	99	3.93	.292	21	.247	-4	15	-0.2
1902	Det-A	0	0	....	4	0	0	0	0	17^{1}	26	23	18	1	3	8	5	1.962	9.35	39	7.57	.346	0	.000	-11	0	-1.2
	Bal-A	3	5	.375	10	8	8	0	0	75^{2}	66	29	22	1	0	24	20	1.189	2.62	144	2.47	.235	4	.148	14	4	1.2
	Yr.	3	5	.375	14	8	8	0	0	93	92	52	40	2	3	32	25	1.333	3.87	96	3.42	.259	4	.118	2	4	0.1
	NY-N	5	6	.455	13	12	11	0	0	114	105	49	31	3	0	18	52	1.079	2.45	115	2.29	.245	11	.169	5	8	0.5
1903	NY-N	6	4	.600	20	11	8	0	1	115^{2}	130	67	49	5	6	37	50	1.444	3.81	88	4.22	.284	9	.196	-9	6	-0.8
1904	Bro-N	12	23	.343	40	34	33	4	0	307	284	132	92	10	12	79	110	1.182	2.70	101	2.78	.245	17	.157	3	15	0.1
Total	7	43	58	.426	128	102	88	6	3	923^{1}	973	502	349	28	37	235	318	1.308	3.40	97	3.47	.270	66	.180	-12	51	-1.3
• CROSBY, George	George Washington Crosby b: 1860, Chicago, IL d: 1/9/1913, San Francisco, CA Deb: 5/22/1884																										
1884	Chi-N	1	2	.333	3	3	3	0	0	28	27	21	11	3	....	12	11	1.393	3.54	89	....	.240	4	.308	-2	2	-0.1
• CROSBY, Ken	Kenneth Stewart Crosby b: 12/15/1947, New Denver, Canada BR/TR, 6'2", 179 lbs. Deb: 8/5/1975																										
1975	Chi-N	1	0	1.000	9	0	0	0	0	8^{1}	10	3	3	0	0	7	6	2.040	3.24	119	6.04	.294	0	....	1	1	0.1
1976	Chi-N	0	0	....	7	1	0	0	0	12	20	16	16	3	0	8	5	2.333	12.00	32	10.64	.377	1	.500	-11	0	-1.1
Total	2	1	0	1.000	16	1	0	0	0	20^{1}	30	19	19	3	0	15	11	2.213	8.41	46	8.76	.345	1	.500	-10	1	-1.0
• CROSS, Lem	George Lewis Cross b: 1/9/1872, Sanbornton, NH d: 10/9/1930, Manchester, NH TR, 5'9", 155 lbs. Deb: 8/6/1893																										
1893	Cin-N	0	2	.000	3	3	2	0	0	21	24	16	13	3	0	9	7	1.571	5.57	86	5.24	.279	2	.333	-2	1	-0.1
1894	Cin-N	3	4	.429	8	7	3	0	0	53	94	73	50	8	5	21	11	2.170	8.49	65	9.69	.381	6	.231	-17	0	-1.4
Total	2	3	6	.333	11	10	5	0	0	74	118	89	63	11	5	30	18	2.000	7.66	70	8.43	.355	8	.250	-20	1	-1.5
• CROTHERS, Doug	Douglas Crothers b: 11/16/1859, Natchez, MS d: 3/29/1907, St. Louis, MO BR/TR Deb: 8/3/1884																										
1884	KC-U	1	2	.333	3	3	3	0	0	25	26	15	5	0	....	6	11	1.280	1.80	155	....	.251	2	.133	3	0	0.1
1885	NY-a	7	11	.389	18	18	18	1	0	154	192	135	87	4	2	49	40	**1.565**	5.08	58	....	.293	8	.157	-36	2	-3.1
Total	2	8	13	.381	21	21	21	1	0	179	218	150	92	4	2	55	51	1.525	4.63	64	....	.287	10	.152	-33	2	-3.0
• CROUCH, Bill	Wilmer Elmer Crouch b: 8/20/1910, Wilmington, DE d: 12/26/1980, Howell, MI BB/TR, 6'1", 180 lbs. Deb: 5/9/1939																										
1939	Bro-N	4	0	1.000	6	3	3	0	0	38^{1}	37	14	11	3	0	14	10	1.330	2.58	156	3.53	.255	2	.133	6	4	0.6
1941	Phi-N	2	3	.400	20	5	1	0	1	59	65	31	29	4	0	17	26	1.390	4.42	84	3.98	.286	1	.091	-4	3	-0.5
	StL-N	1	2	.333	18	4	0	0	6	45	45	16	15	2	0	14	15	1.311	3.00	126	3.36	.271	0	.000	3	5	0.2
	Yr.	3	5	.375	38	9	1	0	7	104	110	47	44	6	0	31	41	1.356	3.81	98	3.71	.280	1	.042	-1	8	-0.3
1945	StL-N	1	0	1.000	6	0	0	0	0	13^{1}	12	5	5	1	1	7	4	1.425	3.38	111	4.09	.255	0	.000	0	1	0.0
Total	3	8	5	.615	50	12	4	0	7	155^{2}	159	66	60	10	1	52	55	1.355	3.47	109	3.70	.272	3	.073	5	13	0.3
• CROUCH, Bill	William Henry "Skip" Crouch b: 12/3/1886, Marshallton, DE d: 12/22/1945, Highland Park, MI BL/TL, 6'1", 210 lbs. Deb: 7/12/1910																										
1910	StL-A	0	0	....	1	1	1	0	0	8	6	4	3	0	0	7	2	1.625	3.38	73	3.88	.231	0	.000	-1	0	-0.1
• CROUCH, Zach	Zachary Quinn Crouch b: 10/26/1965, Folsom, CA BL/TL, 6'3", 180 lbs. Deb: 6/4/1988																										
1988	Bos-A	0	0	....	3	0	0	0	0	1^{1}	4	1	1	0	0	2	0	4.500	6.75	61	24.59	.571	0	....	-0	0	0.0
• CROUSHORE, Rich	Richard Steven Croushore b: 8/7/1970, Lakehurst, NJ BR/TR, 6'4", 210 lbs. Deb: 5/18/1998																										
1998	StL-N	0	3	.000	41	0	0	0	8	54^{1}	44	31	30	6	4	29	47	1.344	4.97	84	3.70	.213	0	....	-4	3	-0.4
1999	StL-N	3	7	.300	59	0	0	0	3	71^{2}	68	42	33	9	3	43	88	1.549	4.14	110	4.73	.247	1	.333	4	5	0.4
2000	Col-N	2	0	1.000	6	0	0	0	0	11^{1}	15	11	11	1	1	6	11	1.853	8.74	66	6.48	.313	1	1.000	-4	1	-0.3
	Bos-A	0	1	.000	5	0	0	0	0	4^{2}	4	3	3	0	1	5	3	1.929	5.79	87	5.28	.250	0	....	-0	0	0.0
Total	3	5	11	.313	111	0	0	0	11	142	131	87	77	16	9	83	149	1.507	4.88	94	4.49	.240	2	.500	-5	9	-0.4
• CROW, Dean	Paul Dean Crow b: 8/21/1972, Garland, TX BL/TR, 6'4" Deb: 5/29/1998																										
1998	Det-A	2	2	.500	32	0	0	0	0	45^{2}	55	22	20	6	2	16	18	1.555	3.94	120	5.49	.313	0	....	3	3	0.3
• CROWDER, Alvin	Alvin Floyd "General" Crowder b: 1/11/1899, Winston-Salem, NC d: 4/3/1972, Winston-Salem, NC BL/TR, 5'10", 170 lbs. Deb: 7/24/1926																										
1926	Was-A	7	4	.636	19	12	6	0	1	100	97	52	44	3	2	60	26	1.570	3.96	98	4.05	.261	9	.237	-2	5	-0.1
1927	Was-A	4	7	.364	15	11	4	2	0	67^{1}	58	44	34	3	2	42	22	1.485	4.54	89	3.80	.232	3	.136	-4	2	-0.6
	StL-A	3	5	.375	21	8	2	1	3	73^{2}	71	44	41	3	1	42	30	1.534	5.01	87	3.94	.260	6	.261	-6	4	-0.5
	Yr.	7	12	.368	36	19	6	3	3	141	129	88	75	6	3	84	52	1.511	4.79	88	3.87	.247	9	.200	-10	6	-1.1
1928	StL-A	21	5	.808	41	31	19	1	2	244	238	113	100	11	1	91	99	1.348	3.69	114	3.27	.258	15	.188	14	20	1.2
1929	StL-A	17	15	.531	40	34	19	**4**	4	266^{2}	272	133	116	22	0	93	79	1.369	3.92	113	3.83	.271	18	.188	13	20	0.9
1930	StL-A	3	7	.300	13	10	5	1	1	77^{1}	85	43	40	11	1	27	42	1.448	4.66	105	4.65	.283	4	.160	1	5	-0.1
	Was-A	15	9	.625	27	25	20	0	1	202^{1}	191	90	81	6	1	69	65	1.285	3.60	127	3.02	.249	13	.171	16	17	1.2
	Yr.	18	16	.529	40	35	25	1	2	279^{2}	276	133	121	17	2	96	107	1.330	3.89	120	3.47	.259	17	.168	17	22	1.1
1931	Was-A	18	11	.621	44	26	13	1	2	234^{1}	255	117	101	13	1	72	85	1.395	3.88	111	3.83	.275	19	.216	8	16	0.7
1932	Was-A	**26**	13	.667	50	**39**	21	3	1	**327**	319	136	121	17	0	77	103	1.211	3.33	130	2.93	.252	27	.221	28	30	2.6
1933*	Was-A★	**24**	15	.615	**52**	35	17	0	4	299^{1}	311	140	132	14	3	81	110	1.310	3.97	105	3.39	.267	19	.186	1	21	0.1
1934	Was-A	4	10	.286	29	13	4	0	3	100^{2}	142	88	76	9	0	38	39	1.788	6.79	64	6.06	.326	7	.219	-27	0	-2.5
	*Det-A	5	1	.833	9	9	3	1	0	66^{2}	81	35	31	3	0	20	30	1.515	4.19	105	4.38	.295	4	.133	1	4	-0.1
	Yr.	9	11	.450	38	22	7	1	3	167^{1}	223	123	107	12	0	58	69	1.679	5.75	75	5.39	.314	11	.177	-26	4	-2.6
1935*	Det-A	16	10	.615	33	32	16	2	0	241	269	127	114	16	4	67	59	1.394	4.26	98	4.06	.285	17	.183	-4	12	-0.6
1936	Det-A	4	3	.571	9	7	1	0	0	44	64	42	41	5	0	21	10	1.932	8.39	59	7.16	.342	3	.150	-16	0	-1.5
Total	11	167	115	.592	402	292	150	16	22	2344^{1}	2453	1204	1072	136	16	800	799	1.388	4.12	105	3.76	.270	164	.194	21	156	0.7
• CROWELL, Billy	William Theodore Crowell b: 11/6/1865, Cincinnati, OH d: 7/24/1935, Fort Worth, TX BR/TR, 5'8.5", 160 lbs. Deb: 4/20/1887 U																										
1887	Cle-a	14	31	.311	45	45	45	1	0	389^{1}	679	350	211	9	20	138	72	1.744	4.88	89	....	.369	32	.193	-9	11	-1.6
1888	Cle-a	5	13	.278	18	18	16	0	0	150^{2}	212	148	97	8	0	61	61	1.812	5.79	53	....	.321	5	.086	-44	0	-4.5
	Lou-a	0	1	.000	1	1	1	0	0	9	12	14	6	1	0	6	5	2.000	6.00	51	....	.309	0	.000	-3	0	-0.3
	Yr.	5	14	.263	19	19	17	0	0	159^{2}	224	162	103	9	0	67	66	**1.823**	5.81	53	....	.320	5	.082	-47	0	-4.8
Total	2	19	45	.297	64	64	62	1	0	549	903	512	314	18	20	205	138	1.767	5.15	74	....	.355	37	.163	-56	11	-6.4
• CROWELL, Cap	Minot Joy Crowell b: 9/5/1892, Roxbury, MA d: 9/30/1962, Central Falls, RI BR/TR, 6'1", 178 lbs. Deb: 6/23/1915																										
1915	Phi-A	2	6	.250	10	8	4	0	0	54^{1}	56	53	33	1	5	47	15	1.896	5.47	53	6.02	.292	5	.227	-15	0	-1.6
1916	Phi-A	0	5	.000	9	6	1	0	0	39^{2}	43	33	22	0	2	34	15	1.941	4.99	57	5.75	.289	0	.000	-9	0	-1.1
Total	2	2	11	.154	19	14	5	0	0	94	99	86	55	1	7	81	30	1.915	5.27	55	5.90	.291	5	.147	-23	0	-2.7
• CROWELL, Jim	James Everette Crowell b: 5/14/1974, Minneapolis, MN BL/TL, 6'4", 220 lbs. Deb: 9/12/1997																										
1997	Cin-N	0	1	.000	2	1	0	0	0	6^{1}	12	7	7	2	0	5	3	2.684	9.95	43	13.59	.414	0	.000	-4	0	-0.4
• CROWSON, Woody	Thomas Woodrow Crowson b: 9/9/1918, Fuquay Springs, NC d: 8/14/1947, Mayodan, NC BR/TR, 6'2", 185 lbs. Deb: 4/17/1945																										
1945	Phi-A	0	0	....	1	0	0	0	0	3	2	2	2	0	0	3	2	1.667	6.00	57	3.36	.200	0	.000	-1	0	-0.1

YEAR	TM-L	W	L	PCT	G	GS	CG	SH	SV	IP	H	R	ER	HR	HB	BB	SO	RAT	ERA	ERA+	CERA	OAV	BH	AVG	PR+	WS	TPW
• CRUDALE, Mike	Michael Christopher Crudale b: 1/3/1977, San Diego, CA BR/TR, 6', 205 lbs. Deb: 4/10/2002																										
2002*	StL-N	3	0	1.000	49	1	0	0	0	52^2	43	11	11	3	1	14	47	1.082	1.88	210	2.35	.228	0	.000	11	6	1.1
2003	StL-N	0	1	.000	13	0	0	0	0	11^1	11	5	3	1	1	12	6	2.029	2.38	170	6.37	.250	0	....	2	1	0.2
	Mil-N	0	0	....	9	0	0	0	0	9^1	1	3	3	0	0	6	7	.750	2.89	147	0.67	.036	0	....	2	1	0.2
	Yr.	0	1	.000	22	0	0	0	0	20^2	12	8	6	1	1	18	13	1.452	2.61	159	3.79	.167	0	....	4	2	0.4
Total 2		3	1	.750	71	1	0	0	0	73^1	55	19	17	4	2	32	60	1.186	2.09	193	2.76	.211	0	.000	15	8	1.5
• CRUM, Cal	Calvin N. Crum b: 7/27/1890, Cooks Mills, IL d: 7/7/1945, Tulsa, OK BR/TR, 6'1", 175 lbs. Deb: 4/17/1917																										
1917	Bos-N	0	0	....	1	1	0	0	0	1	1	5	0	0	0	1	0	2.000	0.00	....	0.98	.250	0	....	0	0	0.0
1918	Bos-N	0	1	.000	1	1	0	0	0	2^1	6	4	4	0	1	3	0	3.857	15.43	17	21.56	.600	0	.000	-3	0	-0.4
Total 2		0	1	.000	2	1	0	0	0	3^1	7	9	4	0	1	4	0	3.300	10.80	25	15.38	.500	0	.000	-3	0	-0.3
• CRUMPLER, Roy	Roy Maxton Crumpler b: 7/8/1896, Clinton, NC d: 10/6/1969, Fayetteville, NC BL/TL, 6'1", 195 lbs. Deb: 9/16/1920																										
1920	Det-A	1	0	1.000	2	2	1	0	0	13	17	13	8	2	1	11	2	2.154	5.54	67	8.44	.315	3	.333	-2	1	-0.1
1925	Phi-N	0	0	....	3	1	0	0	0	4^2	8	4	4	0	0	2	1	2.143	7.71	62	7.73	.381	0	.000	-1	0	-0.2
Total 2		1	0	1.000	5	3	1	0	0	17^2	25	17	12	2	1	13	3	2.151	6.11	66	8.25	.333	3	.273	-4	1	-0.3
• CRUTCHER, Dick	Richard Louis Crutcher b: 11/25/1889, Frankfort, KY d: 6/19/1952, Frankfort, KY BR/TR, 5'9", 148 lbs. Deb: 4/14/1914																										
1914	Bos-N	5	7	.417	33	15	5	1	0	158^2	169	73	61	4	6	66	48	**1.481**	3.46	80	4.20	.293	8	.148	-19	6	-2.1
1915	Bos-N	2	2	.500	14	4	1	0	2	43^2	50	28	21	1	2	16	17	1.511	4.33	62	4.50	.309	3	.231	-9	0	-0.9
Total 2		7	9	.438	47	19	6	1	2	202^1	219	101	82	5	8	82	65	1.488	3.65	75	4.27	.297	11	.164	-27	6	-3.0
• CRUZ, Juan	Juan Carlos Cruz b: 10/15/1978, Bonao, Dominican Republic BR/TR, 6'2", 155 lbs. Deb: 8/21/2001																										
2001	Chi-N	3	1	.750	8	8	0	0	0	44^2	40	16	16	4	2	17	39	1.276	3.22	129	3.59	.244	2	.125	5	4	0.5
2002	Chi-N	3	11	.214	45	9	0	0	1	97^1	84	56	43	11	8	59	81	1.469	3.98	101	4.49	.241	2	.143	1	3	0.1
2003*	Chi-N	2	7	.222	25	6	0	0	0	61	66	44	41	7	7	28	65	1.541	6.05	70	5.23	.275	3	.250	-12	0	-1.1
Total 3		8	19	.296	78	23	0	0	1	203	190	116	100	22	17	104	185	1.448	4.43	93	4.52	.252	7	.167	-6	7	-0.6
• CRUZ, Nelson	Nelson Cruz b: 9/13/1972, Puerto Plata, Dominican Republic BR/TR, 6'1", 160 lbs. Deb: 8/1/1997																										
1997	Chi-A	0	2	.000	19	0	0	0	0	26^1	29	19	19	6	0	9	23	1.443	6.49	68	5.21	.274	0	....	-6	0	-0.6
1999	Det-A	2	5	.286	29	6	0	0	0	66^2	74	44	42	11	3	23	46	1.455	5.67	87	5.09	.281	0	....	-5	2	-0.5
2000	Det-A	5	2	.714	27	0	0	0	0	41	39	14	14	4	3	13	34	1.268	3.07	157	3.69	.253	0	.000	8	4	0.7
2001*	Hou-N	3	3	.500	66	0	0	0	2	82^1	72	41	38	11	9	24	75	1.166	4.15	110	3.59	.237	1	.167	4	6	0.3
2002	Hou-N	2	6	.250	43	5	0	0	0	78^1	90	44	39	12	6	29	61	1.519	4.48	95	5.31	.284	0	.000	-1	3	-0.2
2003	Col-N	3	5	.375	20	7	0	0	0	53^2	65	43	43	15	3	11	38	1.416	7.21	68	6.03	.301	2	.154	-13	0	-1.3
Total 6		15	23	.395	204	18	0	0	2	348^1	369	205	195	59	24	109	277	1.372	5.04	92	4.78	.271	3	.091	-14	15	-1.5
• CRUZ, Victor	Victor Manuel (Gil) Cruz b: 12/24/1957, Rancho Viejo la Vega, Dominican Republic BR/TR, 5'9", 200 lbs. Deb: 6/24/1978																										
1978	Tor-A	7	3	.700	32	0	0	0	9	47^1	28	10	9	0	1	35	51	1.331	1.71	229	2.45	.179	0	....	12	10	1.2
1979	Cle-A	3	9	.250	61	0	0	0	10	78^2	70	41	37	10	1	44	63	1.449	4.23	101	4.26	.244	0	....	2	6	0.2
1980	Cle-A	6	7	.462	55	0	0	0	12	86	71	36	33	10	3	27	88	1.140	3.45	118	2.90	.229	0	....	6	10	0.6
1981	Pit-N	1	1	.500	22	0	0	0	1	34	33	10	10	6	1	15	28	1.412	2.65	136	4.69	.264	0	.000	4	3	0.3
1983	Tex-A	1	3	.250	17	0	0	0	5	25	16	7	4	2	1	10	18	1.040	1.44	278	2.01	.184	0	....	7	4	0.7
Total 5		18	23	.439	187	0	0	0	37	271	218	104	93	28	7	131	248	1.288	3.09	132	3.36	.226	0	.000	31	33	3.1
• CUBILLAN, Darwin	Darwin Harrikson (Salom) Cubillan b: 11/15/1972, Bobures, Venezuela BR/TR, 6'2", 170 lbs. Deb: 5/20/2000																										
2000	Tor-A	1	0	1.000	7	0	0	0	0	15^2	20	14	14	5	1	11	14	1.979	8.04	63	9.56	.317	0	.000	-5	0	-0.5
	Tex-A	0	0	....	13	0	0	0	0	17^2	32	22	21	4	0	14	13	2.604	10.70	47	12.33	.400	0	....	-11	0	-1.0
	Yr.	1	0	1.000	20	0	0	0	0	33^1	52	36	35	9	1	25	27	2.310	9.45	53	11.03	.364	0	.000	-16	0	-1.5
2001	Mon-N	0	0	....	29	0	0	0	0	26^1	31	13	12	1	0	12	19	1.633	4.10	109	4.69	.295	0	....	2	2	0.2
Total 2		1	0	1.000	49	0	0	0	0	59^2	83	49	47	10	1	37	46	2.011	7.09	69	8.23	.335	0	.000	-14	2	-1.3
• CUCCURULLO, Cookie	Arthur Joseph Cuccurullo b: 2/8/1918, Asbury Park, NJ d: 1/23/1983, West Orange, NJ BL/TL, 5'10", 168 lbs. Deb: 10/3/1943																										
1943	Pit-N	0	1	.000	1	1	0	0	0	7	10	7	5	0	0	3	3	1.857	6.43	54	5.63	.323	0	....	-2	0	-0.2
1944	Pit-N	2	1	.667	32	4	0	0	4	106^1	110	65	48	5	3	44	31	1.448	4.06	91	3.96	.270	14	.368	-3	6	0.2
1945	Pit-N	1	3	.250	29	4	0	0	1	56^2	68	41	33	2	1	34	17	1.800	5.24	75	5.50	.305	3	.214	-8	1	-0.8
Total 3		3	5	.375	62	9	0	0	5	170	188	113	86	7	4	81	51	1.582	4.55	83	4.54	.284	17	.327	-13	7	-0.8
• CUELLAR, Bobby	Robert Cuellar b: 8/20/1952, Alice, TX BR/TR, 5'11", 188 lbs. Deb: 9/9/1977 C																										
1977	Tex-A	0	0	....	4	0	0	0	0	6^2	4	1	1	1	0	2	3	.900	1.35	302	2.15	.182	0	....	2	1	0.2
• CUELLAR, Charlie	Jesus Patracis Cuellar b: 9/24/1917, Ybor City, FL d: 10/11/1994, Tampa, FL BR/TR, 5'11", 183 lbs. Deb: 7/2/1950																										
1950	Chi-A	0	0	....	2	0	0	0	0	1^1	6	6	5	0	0	3	1	6.750	33.75	13	37.42	.600	0		-4	0	-0.4
• CUELLAR, Mike	Miguel Angel (Santana) Cuellar b: 5/8/1937, Las Villas, Cuba BL/TL, 6', 175 lbs. Deb: 4/18/1959																										
1959	Cin-N	0	0	....	2	0	0	0	0	4	7	8	7	1	0	4	5	2.750	15.75	26	11.75	.368	0	.000	-5	0	-0.5
1964	StL-N	5	5	.500	32	7	1	0	4	72	80	43	36	8	1	33	56	1.569	4.50	84	5.04	.288	0	.000	-6	3	-0.8
1965	Hou-N	1	4	.200	25	4	0	0	2	56	55	24	22	3	1	21	46	1.357	3.54	95	3.54	.262	0	.000	-0	3	-0.1
1966	Hou-N	12	10	.545	38	28	11	1	2	227^1	193	79	56	10	0	52	175	1.078	2.22	154	2.25	.229	8	.113	33	19	3.3
1967	Hou-N★	16	11	.593	36	32	16	3	1	246^1	233	99	83	16	1	63	203	1.202	3.03	109	2.98	.248	13	.140	13	13	1.5
1968	Hou-N	8	11	.421	28	24	11	2	1	170^2	152	60	52	8	1	45	133	1.154	2.74	108	2.59	.238	11	.193	8	12	1.1
1969*	Bal-A	23	11	.676	39	39	18	5	0	290^2	213	94	77	18	1	79	182	1.005	2.38	149	**2.02**	.204	12	.117	27	24	2.5
1970*	Bal-A★	**24**	8	.750	40	**40**	**21**	4	0	297^2	273	126	115	34	1	69	190	1.149	3.48	105	3.07	.242	10	.089	-1	18	-0.5
1971*	Bal-A★	20	9	.690	38	38	21	4	0	292^1	250	111	100	30	1	78	124	1.122	3.08	109	2.88	.234	11	.103	5	18	0.2
1972	Bal-A	18	12	.600	35	35	17	4	0	248^1	197	78	71	21	0	71	132	1.079	2.57	119	2.47	.220	11	.126	8	16	0.7
1973*	Bal-A	18	13	.581	38	38	17	2	0	267	265	120	97	29	0	84	140	1.307	3.27	114	3.75	.258	0	....	2	16	0.3
1974*	Bal-A★	22	10	.688	38	38	20	5	0	269^1	253	106	93	17	2	86	106	1.259	3.11	111	3.25	.252	0	....	7	19	0.7
1975	Bal-A	14	12	.538	36	36	17	5	0	256	229	112	104	17	1	84	105	1.223	3.66	96	3.09	.249	0	....	-12	12	-1.2
1976	Bal-A	4	13	.235	26	19	2	1	1	107	129	63	59	8	2	50	32	1.673	4.96	66	5.34	.307	0	....	-21	0	-2.3
1977	Cal-A	0	1	.000	2	1	0	0	0	3^1	9	7	7	2	0	3	3	3.600	18.90	21	24.22	.500	0	....	-6	0	-0.5
Total 15		185	130	.587	453	379	172	36	11	2808	2538	1130	979	222	12	822	1632	1.197	3.14	109	3.05	.243	76	.115	52	173	4.2
• CUETO, Bert	Dagoberto (Concepcion) Cueto b: 8/14/1937, San Luis Pinar, Cuba BR/TR, 6'4", 170 lbs. Deb: 6/18/1961																										
1961	Min-A	1	3	.250	7	5	0	0	0	21^1	27	24	17	7	1	10	5	1.734	7.17	59	7.84	.300	0	.000	-6	0	-0.7
• CULLEN, Jack	John Patrick Cullen b: 10/6/1939, Newark, NJ BR/TR, 5'11", 170 lbs. Deb: 9/9/1962																										
1962	NY-A	0	0	....	2	0	0	0	1	3	2	0	0	0	0	2	2	1.333	0.00	....	2.54	.182	0	....	1	1	0.1
1965	NY-A	3	4	.429	12	9	2	1	0	59	59	22	20	2	0	21	25	1.356	3.05	112	3.41	.262	3	.150	3	4	0.2
1966	NY-A	1	0	1.000	5	0	0	0	0	11^1	11	5	5	0	0	5	7	1.412	3.97	84	2.99	.256	0	.000	-1	1	-0.1
Total 3		4	4	.500	19	9	2	1	1	73^1	72	27	25	2	0	28	34	1.364	3.07	110	3.31	.258	3	.130	3	6	0.2
• CULLOP, Nick	Henry Nicholas "Tomato Face" Cullop b: 10/16/1900, St. Louis, MO d: 12/1/1978, Gahanna, OH BR/TR, 6', 200 lbs. Deb: 4/14/1926 ♦																										
1927	Cle-A	0	0	....	1	0	0	0	0	1	3	1	1	0	0	0	0	3.000	9.00	47	17.53	.600	16	.235	-1	1	-0.3
• CULLOP, Nick	Norman Andrew Cullop b: 9/17/1887, Chilhowie, VA d: 4/15/1961, Tazewell, VA BL/TL, 5'11.5", 172 lbs. Deb: 5/20/1913																										
1913	Cle-A	3	6	.333	23	8	4	0	0	97^2	105	58	48	3	3	35	30	1.433	4.42	69	4.15	.291	4	.129	-17	1	-1.9
1914	Cle-A	0	1	.000	1	0	0	0	0	3^1	4	3	1	0	0	1	3	1.500	2.70	107	5.00	.364	0	.000	0	0	0.0
	KC-F	14	19	.424	44	36	22	4	1	295^2	256	116	77	6	12	87	149	1.160	2.34	131	2.35	.235	14	.141	23	19	2.0
1915	KC-F	22	11	.667	44	36	22	3	2	302^1	278	105	82	8	9	67	111	1.141	2.44	120	2.68	.249	18	.188	18	25	2.0
1916	NY-A	13	6	.684	28	22	9	0	1	167	151	60	38	4	3	32	77	1.096	2.05	141	2.42	.243	6	.109	14	13	1.2
1917	NY-A	5	9	.357	30	18	5	2	1	146^1	161	70	54	2	2	31	27	1.312	3.32	81	3.72	.307	7	.159	-11	5	-1.3

YEAR TM-L	W	L	PCT	G	GS	CG	SH	SV	IP	H	R	ER	HR	HB	BB	SO	RAT	ERA	ERA+	CERA	OAV	BH	AVG	PR+	WS	TPW
1921 StL-A	0	2	.000	4	1	0	0	0	11^2	18	12	11	1	0	6	3	2.057	8.49	53	7.15	.340	0	.000	-5	0	-0.5
Total 6	57	54	.514	174	121	62	9	5	1024	973	424	311	24	29	259	400	1.203	2.73	108	2.89	.258	49	.149	22	63	1.5

• CULLOTON, Bud Bernard Aloysius Culloton b: 5/19/1896, Kingston, NY d: 11/9/1976, Kingston, NY BR/TR, 5'11", 180 lbs. Deb: 4/16/1925

YEAR TM-L	W	L	PCT	G	GS	CG	SH	SV	IP	H	R	ER	HR	HB	BB	SO	RAT	ERA	ERA+	CERA	OAV	BH	AVG	PR+	WS	TPW
1925 Pit-N	0	1	.000	9	1	0	0	0	21	19	8	6	1	0	1	3	.952	2.57	173	1.99	.241	0	.000	4	2	0.3
1926 Pit-N	0	0	....	4	0	0	0	0	3^2	3	4	3	0	0	6	1	2.455	7.36	53	5.96	.214	0	....	-1	0	-0.1
Total 2	0	1	.000	13	1	0	0	0	24^2	22	12	9	1	0	7	4	1.176	3.28	130	2.58	.237	0	.000	2	2	0.2

• CULP, Bill William Edward Culp b: 6/11/1887, Bellaire, OH d: 9/3/1969, Arnold, PA BB/TR, 6'1.5", 165 lbs. Deb: 9/8/1910

YEAR TM-L	W	L	PCT	G	GS	CG	SH	SV	IP	H	R	ER	HR	HB	BB	SO	RAT	ERA	ERA+	CERA	OAV	BH	AVG	PR+	WS	TPW
1910 Phi-N	0	0	....	4	0	0	0	1	6^2	8	6	6	0	0	4	4	1.800	8.10	38	5.71	.333	0	.000	-4	0	-0.4

• CULP, Ray Raymond Leonard Culp b: 8/6/1941, Elgin, TX BR/TR, 6', 200 lbs. Deb: 4/10/1963

YEAR TM-L	W	L	PCT	G	GS	CG	SH	SV	IP	H	R	ER	HR	HB	BB	SO	RAT	ERA	ERA+	CERA	OAV	BH	AVG	PR+	WS	TPW
1963 Phi-N★	14	11	.560	34	30	10	5	0	203^1	148	76	67	15	6	102	176	1.230	2.97	109	2.92	.206	9	.136	3	13	0.3
1964 Phi-N	8	7	.533	30	19	3	1	0	135	139	77	62	15	5	56	96	1.444	4.13	84	4.41	.263	5	.114	-11	3	-1.2
1965 Phi-N	14	10	.583	33	30	11	2	0	204^1	188	89	73	14	12	78	134	1.302	3.22	108	3.48	.243	6	.088	5	13	0.4
1966 Phi-N	7	4	.636	34	12	1	0	1	110^2	106	66	62	19	7	53	100	1.437	5.04	71	4.79	.246	2	.077	-18	2	-2.1
1967 Chi-N	8	11	.421	30	22	4	1	0	152^2	138	69	66	22	2	59	111	1.290	3.89	91	3.77	.239	5	.098	-8	6	-1.0
1968 Bos-A	16	6	.727	35	30	11	6	0	216^1	166	79	70	18	9	82	190	1.146	2.91	108	2.76	.210	8	.114	7	15	0.7
1969 Bos-A★	17	8	.680	32	32	9	2	0	227	195	103	96	25	6	79	172	1.207	3.81	100	3.24	.231	12	.152	5	14	0.6
1970 Bos-A	17	14	.548	33	33	15	1	0	251^1	211	104	85	22	11	91	197	1.202	3.04	130	3.07	.224	12	.124	31	17	2.9
1971 Bos-A	14	16	.467	35	35	12	3	0	242^1	236	108	97	21	5	67	151	1.250	3.60	103	3.38	.253	8	.118	5	13	0.4
1972 Bos-A	5	8	.385	16	16	4	1	0	105	104	60	52	8	3	53	52	1.495	4.46	72	4.30	.260	7	.212	-12	1	-1.3
1973 Bos-A	2	6	.250	10	9	0	0	0	50^1	46	32	25	9	4	32	32	1.550	4.47	90	5.56	.247	0	....	-3	1	-0.3
Total 11	122	101	.547	322	268	80	22	1	1898^1	1677	863	755	188	70	752	1411	1.280	3.58	99	3.51	.235	74	.123	5	98	-0.7

• CULVER, George George Raymond Culver b: 7/8/1943, Salinas, CA BR/TR, 6'2", 185 lbs. Deb: 9/7/1966

YEAR TM-L	W	L	PCT	G	GS	CG	SH	SV	IP	H	R	ER	HR	HB	BB	SO	RAT	ERA	ERA+	CERA	OAV	BH	AVG	PR+	WS	TPW
1966 Cle-A	0	2	.000	5	1	0	0	0	9^2	15	9	9	1	1	7	6	2.276	8.38	41	9.38	.357	0	.000	-5	0	-0.6
1967 Cle-A	7	3	.700	53	1	0	0	3	75	71	40	33	2	6	31	41	1.360	3.96	83	3.46	.258	1	.250	-5	4	-0.5
1968 Cin-N	11	16	.407	42	35	5	2	2	226^1	229	95	81	8	14	84	114	1.383	3.22	98	3.77	.264	8	.121	0	10	-0.1
1969 Cin-N	5	7	.417	32	13	0	0	4	101^1	117	55	48	8	9	52	58	1.668	4.26	88	5.53	.291	3	.097	-6	3	-0.8
1970 StL-N	3	3	.500	11	7	2	0	0	56^2	64	31	29	6	1	24	23	1.553	4.61	89	4.93	.284	3	.176	-2	2	-0.2
Hou-N	3	3	.500	32	0	0	0	3	45	44	17	16	1	3	21	31	1.444	3.20	121	3.79	.254	1	.250	3	4	0.4
Yr.	6	6	.500	43	7	2	0	3	101^2	108	48	45	7	4	45	54	1.505	3.98	101	4.42	.271	4	.190	1	6	0.2
1971 Hou-N	5	8	.385	59	0	0	0	7	95^1	89	33	28	4	2	38	57	1.332	2.64	127	3.29	.257	1	.091	7	8	0.7
1972 Hou-N	6	2	.750	45	0	0	0	2	97^1	73	33	33	7	5	43	82	1.192	3.05	110	2.90	.212	3	.158	4	8	0.4
1973 LA-N	4	4	.500	28	0	0	0	2	42	45	15	14	4	1	21	23	1.571	3.00	115	4.79	.292	0	.000	2	3	0.1
Phi-N	3	1	.750	14	0	0	0	0	18^2	26	10	10	0	0	15	7	2.196	4.82	79	6.61	.342	0	....	-2	1	-0.2
Yr.	7	5	.583	42	0	0	0	2	60^2	71	25	24	4	1	36	30	1.764	3.56	100	5.35	.309	0	.000	-1	4	-0.1
1974 Phi-N	1	0	1.000	14	0	0	0	0	21^2	20	16	16	1	1	16	9	1.662	6.65	57	4.73	.267	0	.000	-7	0	-0.8
Total 9	48	49	.495	335	57	7	2	23	789	793	354	317	42	43	352	451	1.451	3.62	96	4.10	.266	20	.124	-12	43	-1.7

• CUMBERLAND, John John Sheldon Cumberland b: 5/10/1947, Westbrook, ME BR/TL, 6', 190 lbs. Deb: 9/27/1968 C

YEAR TM-L	W	L	PCT	G	GS	CG	SH	SV	IP	H	R	ER	HR	HB	BB	SO	RAT	ERA	ERA+	CERA	OAV	BH	AVG	PR+	WS	TPW
1968 NY-A	0	0	....	1	0	0	0	0	2	3	4	2	1	0	1	1	2.000	9.00	32	10.88	.333	0	....	-1	0	-0.2
1969 NY-A	0	0	....	2	0	0	0	0	4	3	2	2	0	0	4	0	1.750	4.50	77	3.84	.231	0	....	-0	0	0.0
1970 NY-A	3	4	.429	15	8	1	0	0	64	62	31	28	9	0	15	38	1.203	3.94	89	3.43	.252	1	.059	-3	2	-0.5
SF-N	2	0	1.000	7	0	0	0	0	11	6	3	1	0	0	4	6	.909	0.82	486	1.25	.158	0	.000	4	2	0.4
1971★ SF-N	9	6	.600	45	21	5	2	2	185	153	66	60	22	0	55	65	1.124	2.92	116	2.84	.223	7	.119	11	13	0.9
1972 SF-N	0	4	.000	9	6	0	0	0	25	38	29	24	6	0	7	8	1.800	8.64	40	7.41	.336	1	.111	-14	0	-1.6
StL-N	1	1	.500	14	1	0	0	0	21^2	23	17	16	6	0	7	7	1.385	6.65	51	5.50	.291	0	.000	-8	0	-0.9
Yr.	1	5	.167	23	7	0	0	0	46^2	61	46	40	12	0	14	15	1.607	7.71	45	6.53	.318	1	.071	-22	0	-2.5
1974 Cal-A	0	1	.000	17	0	0	0	0	21^2	24	9	9	2	0	10	12	1.569	3.74	92	4.87	.289	0	....	-1	1	-0.1
Total 6	15	16	.484	110	36	6	2	2	334^1	312	161	142	46	0	103	137	1.241	3.82	90	3.61	.246	9	.099	-13	18	-1.9

• CUMMINGS, Candy William Arthur Cummings b: 10/18/1848, Ware, MA d: 5/16/1924, Toledo, OH BR/TR, 5'9", 120 lbs. Deb: 4/22/1872 HOF: 1939

YEAR TM-L	W	L	PCT	G	GS	CG	SH	SV	IP	H	R	ER	HR	HB	BB	SO	RAT	ERA	ERA+	CERA	OAV	BH	AVG	PR+	WS	TPW
1872 Mut-n	33	20	.623	**55**	**55**	**53**	**3**	0	**497**	605	347	164	2	....	30	43	1.278	2.97	137	....	.262	52	.208	30	....	1.7
1873 Bal-n	28	14	.667	42	42	42	1	0	382	475	292	113	4	....	33	34	1.330	2.66	122	....	.270	48	.250	12	....	1.1
1874 Phi-n	28	26	.519	54	54	52	3	0	482	616	386	105	4	....	18	61	1.315	1.96	106	....	.278	52	.225	16	....	1.0
1875 Har-n	35	12	.745	48	47	46	**7**	0	417	397	184	74	0	....	4	**82**	.962	1.60	162	....	.228	44	.199	**34**	....	2.5
1876 Har-N	16	8	.667	24	24	24	5	0	216	215	97	40	0	....	14	26	1.060	1.67	142	....	.238	17	.162	6	22	-0.1
1877 Cin-N	5	14	.263	19	19	16	0	0	155^2	219	144	75	2	....	13	11	1.490	4.34	61	....	.314	14	.200	-21	2	-1.7
Total 4 n	124	72	.633	199	198	193	14	0	1778	2093	1209	456	10	....	85	220	1.225	2.31	128	....	.261	196	.219	92	....	6.3
Total 2	21	22	.488	43	43	40	5	0	371^2	434	241	115	2	....	27	37	1.240	2.78	91	....	.271	31	.177	-15	24	-1.9

• CUMMINGS, John John Russell Cummings b: 5/10/1969, Torrance, CA BL/TL, 6'3", 200 lbs. Deb: 4/10/1993

YEAR TM-L	W	L	PCT	G	GS	CG	SH	SV	IP	H	R	ER	HR	HB	BB	SO	RAT	ERA	ERA+	CERA	OAV	BH	AVG	PR+	WS	TPW
1993 Sea-A	0	6	.000	10	8	1	0	0	46^1	59	34	31	6	2	16	19	1.619	6.02	73	5.91	.316	0	....	-9	0	-0.8
1994 Sea-A	2	4	.333	17	8	0	0	0	64	66	43	40	7	0	37	33	1.609	5.63	87	5.05	.270	0	....	-5	2	-0.4
1995 Sea-A	0	0	....	4	0	0	0	0	5^1	8	8	7	0	0	7	4	2.813	11.81	40	9.34	.400	0	....	-4	0	-0.4
★LA-N	3	1	.750	35	0	0	0	0	39	38	16	13	3	0	10	21	1.231	3.00	126	3.01	.250	0	.000	3	4	0.3
1996 LA-N	0	1	.000	4	0	0	0	0	5^1	12	7	4	1	0	2	5	2.625	6.75	57	12.36	.462	0	....	-2	0	-0.2
Det-A	3	3	.500	21	0	0	0	0	31^2	36	20	18	3	2	20	24	1.768	5.12	99	5.75	.283	0	....	0	1	0.0
1997 Det-A	2	0	1.000	19	0	0	0	0	24^2	32	22	15	3	0	14	8	1.865	5.47	84	6.54	.311	0	....	-3	0	-0.3
Total 5	10	15	.400	110	16	1	0	0	216^1	251	150	128	23	4	106	114	1.650	5.33	86	5.42	.292	0	.000	-18	7	-1.7

• CUMMINGS, Steve Steven Brent Cummings b: 7/15/1964, Houston, TX BB/TR, 6'2", 200 lbs. Deb: 6/24/1989

YEAR TM-L	W	L	PCT	G	GS	CG	SH	SV	IP	H	R	ER	HR	HB	BB	SO	RAT	ERA	ERA+	CERA	OAV	BH	AVG	PR+	WS	TPW
1989 Tor-A	2	0	1.000	5	2	0	0	0	21	18	9	7	1	1	11	8	1.381	3.00	121	3.62	.231	0	....	1	2	0.1
1990 Tor-A	0	0	....	6	2	0	0	0	12^1	22	7	7	4	1	5	4	2.189	5.11	80	12.72	.431	0	....	-1	0	-0.1
Total 2	2	0	1.000	11	4	0	0	0	33^1	40	16	14	5	2	16	12	1.680	3.78	102	6.99	.310	0	....	0	2	0.0

• CUNNANE, Will William Joseph Cunnane b: 4/24/1974, Suffern, NY BR/TR, 6'2", 175 lbs. Deb: 4/3/1997

YEAR TM-L	W	L	PCT	G	GS	CG	SH	SV	IP	H	R	ER	HR	HB	BB	SO	RAT	ERA	ERA+	CERA	OAV	BH	AVG	PR+	WS	TPW
1997 SD-N	6	3	.667	54	8	0	0	0	91^1	114	69	59	11	5	49	79	1.785	5.81	66	6.48	.305	5	.357	-19	2	-1.6
1998 SD-N	0	0	....	3	0	0	0	0	3	4	2	2	1	0	1	1	1.667	6.00	66	6.84	.308	0	....	-1	0	-0.1
1999 SD-N	2	1	.667	24	0	0	0	0	31	34	19	18	8	0	12	22	1.484	5.23	80	5.87	.293	0	.000	-4	1	-0.4
2000 SD-N	1	1	.500	27	3	0	0	0	38^1	35	21	18	2	1	21	34	1.461	4.23	102	3.90	.241	1	.143	-0	2	0.0
2001 Mil-N	0	3	.000	31	1	0	0	0	51^2	66	34	31	6	2	22	37	1.703	5.40	79	5.93	.320	0	.000	-7	1	-0.7
2002 Chi-N	1	1	.500	16	0	0	0	0	26^1	27	16	16	5	1	13	30	1.519	5.47	73	5.49	.270	1	.250	-4	1	-0.4
2003★ Atl-N	2	2	.500	20	0	0	0	3	20	14	6	6	2	0	6	20	1.000	2.70	156	2.00	.189	0	....	3	3	0.3
Total 7	12	11	.522	175	12	0	0	3	261^2	294	167	150	35	9	124	223	1.597	5.16	79	5.48	.286	7	.200	-31	10	-2.8

• CUNNINGHAM, Bert Ellsworth Elmer Cunningham b: 11/25/1865, Wilmington, DE d: 5/14/1952, Wilmington, DE BR/TR, 5'6", 187 lbs. Deb: 9/15/1887 U

YEAR TM-L	W	L	PCT	G	GS	CG	SH	SV	IP	H	R	ER	HR	HB	BB	SO	RAT	ERA	ERA+	CERA	OAV	BH	AVG	PR+	WS	TPW
1887 Bro-a	0	2	.000	3	3	3	0	0	23	39	22	13	0	4	13	8	1.696	5.09	85	....	.362	2	.200	-2	0	-0.2
1888 Bal-a	22	29	.431	51	51	50	0	0	453^1	412	275	171	8	30	157	186	1.255	3.39	88	....	.234	33	.186	-12	24	-1.2
1889 Bal-a	16	19	.457	39	33	29	0	1	279^1	306	245	151	11	15	141	140	1.600	4.87	78	....	.270	27	.206	-27	11	-2.6
1890 Phi-P	3	9	.250	14	11	11	0	0	108^2	133	103	63	0	7	67	33	1.840	5.22	82	....	.289	6	.115	-11	3	-1.3
Buf-P	9	15	.375	25	25	24	2	0	211	251	190	137	8	6	134	78	1.825	5.84	70	....	.283	23	.228	-38	4	-3.0
Yr.	12	24	.333	39	36	35	2	0	319^2	384	293	200	8	13	201	111	1.830	5.63	74	....	.285	29	.190	-50	7	-4.3
1891 Bal-a	11	14	.440	30	25	21	0	0	237^2	241	181	106	8	11	138	59	1.595	4.01	93	....	.254	15	.150	-4	11	-0.5
1895 Lou-N	11	16	.407	31	28	24	1	0	231	299	185	122	6	5	104	49	1.745	4.75	97	5.37	.309	30	.300	7	10	1.1
1896 Lou-N	7	14	.333	27	20	17	0	1	189^1	242	168	107	6	17	74	37	1.669	5.09	85	5.35	.308	22	.250	-12	7	-0.8
1897 Lou-N	14	13	.519	30	28	26	0	0	242^2	294	152	108	3	14	72	49	1.508	4.01	106	4.35	.297	22	.237	8	15	0.7
1898 Lou-N	28	15	.651	44	42	41	0	0	362	387	174	127	8	20	65	34	1.249	3.16	113	3.24	.272	32	.229	19	30	2.1

YEAR	TM-L	W	L	PCT	G	GS	CG	SH	SV	IP	H	R	ER	HR	HB	BB	SO	RAT	ERA	ERA+	CERA	OAV	BH	AVG	PR+	WS	TPW
1899	Lou-N	17	17	.500	39	37	33	1	0	323^2	385	188	138	4	15	75	36	1.421	3.84	100	3.96	.295	40	.260	6	21	0.8
1900	Chi-N	4	3	.571	8	7	7	0	0	64	84	53	31	0	4	21	7	1.641	4.36	83	4.96	.316	4	.148	-4	2	-0.5
1901	Chi-N	0	1	.000	1	1	1	0	0	9	11	6	5	0	0	3	2	1.556	5.00	65	4.24	.299	0	.000	-2	0	-0.1
Total	12	142	167	.460	342	311	287	4	2	2734^2	3084	1942	1279	62	148	1064	718	1.512	4.21	91	2.24	.279	256	.218	-72	138	-5.6

• CUNNINGHAM, Bruce Bruce Lee Cunningham b: 9/29/1905, San Francisco, CA d: 3/8/1984, Hayward, CA BR/TR, 5'10.5", 165 lbs. Deb: 5/7/1929

YEAR	TM-L	W	L	PCT	G	GS	CG	SH	SV	IP	H	R	ER	HR	HB	BB	SO	RAT	ERA	ERA+	CERA	OAV	BH	AVG	PR+	WS	TPW
1929	Bos-N	4	6	.400	17	8	4	0	1	91^2	100	52	46	7	2	32	22	1.440	4.52	104	4.18	.282	4	.148	2	6	0.1
1930	Bos-N	5	6	.455	36	6	2	0	0	106^2	121	73	65	7	0	41	28	1.519	5.48	90	4.39	.289	6	.194	-7	5	-0.5
1931	Bos-N	3	12	.200	33	16	6	1	1	136^2	157	74	68	7	2	54	32	1.544	4.48	85	4.54	.296	3	.071	-10	4	-1.3
1932	Bos-N	1	0	1.000	18	3	0	0	0	47	50	21	18	1	4	19	21	1.468	3.45	109	4.18	.281	2	.222	2	3	0.3
Total	4	13	24	.351	104	33	12	1	2	382	428	220	197	22	8	146	103	1.503	4.64	93	4.37	.289	15	.138	-13	18	-1.4

• CUNNINGHAM, George George Harold Cunningham b: 7/13/1894, Sturgeon Lake, MN d: 3/10/1972, Chattanooga, TN BR/TR, 5'11", 185 lbs. Deb: 4/14/1916 ♦

YEAR	TM-L	W	L	PCT	G	GS	CG	SH	SV	IP	H	R	ER	HR	HB	BB	SO	RAT	ERA	ERA+	CERA	OAV	BH	AVG	PR+	WS	TPW
1916	Det-A	7	10	.412	35	14	5	0	2	150^1	146	71	46	0	3	74	68	1.463	2.75	104	3.75	.269	11	.268	5	9	1.1
1917	Det-A	2	7	.222	44	8	4	0	4	139	113	72	45	2	4	51	49	1.180	2.91	91	2.49	.227	6	.176	-2	4	-0.1
1918	Det-A	6	7	.462	27	14	10	0	1	140	131	68	49	0	5	38	39	1.207	3.15	84	2.67	.255	25	.223	-1	7	0.0
1919	Det-A	1	1	.500	17	0	0	0	1	47^2	54	36	26	0	5	15	11	1.448	4.91	65	4.20	.292	5	.217	-8	1	-0.6
Total	4	16	25	.390	123	36	19	0	8	477	444	247	166	2	17	178	167	1.304	3.13	89	3.11	.255	47	.224	-6	21	0.4

• CUNNINGHAM, Mike Mody Cunningham b: 6/14/1882, Lancaster, SC d: 12/10/1969, Lancaster, SC BR/TR, 5'10.5", 175 lbs. Deb: 8/31/1906

YEAR	TM-L	W	L	PCT	G	GS	CG	SH	SV	IP	H	R	ER	HR	HB	BB	SO	RAT	ERA	ERA+	CERA	OAV	BH	AVG	PR+	WS	TPW
1906	Phi-A	1	0	1.000	5	1	1	0	0	28	29	15	10	1	1	9	15	1.357	3.21	85	3.58	.270	4	.333	-1	1	-0.1

• CUPPY, Nig George Joseph Cuppy b: 7/3/1869, Logansport, IN d: 7/27/1922, Elkhart, IN BR/TR, 5'7", 160 lbs. Deb: 4/16/1892

YEAR	TM-L	W	L	PCT	G	GS	CG	SH	SV	IP	H	R	ER	HR	HB	BB	SO	RAT	ERA	ERA+	CERA	OAV	BH	AVG	PR+	WS	TPW
1892*	Cle-N	28	13	.683	47	42	38	1	1	376	333	175	105	9	10	121	103	1.207	2.51	135	2.70	.228	36	.214	38	31	3.5
1893	Cle-N	17	10	.630	31	30	24	0	0	243^2	316	200	121	6	10	75	39	1.605	4.47	109	4.92	.305	27	.248	12	15	1.1
1894	Cle-N	24	15	.615	43	33	29	**3**	0	316	381	246	160	11	10	128	65	1.611	4.56	120	4.79	.295	35	.259	32	28	2.6
1895*	Cle-N	26	14	.650	47	40	36	1	2	353	384	210	139	9	8	95	91	1.357	3.54	141	3.56	.273	40	.286	56	33	5.2
1896*	Cle-N	25	14	.641	46	40	35	1	1	358	388	173	124	8	7	75	86	1.293	3.12	145	3.30	.274	38	.270	56	38	5.4
1897	Cle-N	10	6	.625	19	17	13	1	0	139^1	150	69	49	3	5	26	23	1.263	3.17	142	3.24	.273	8	.145	13	13	0.8
1898	Cle-N	9	8	.529	18	15	13	1	0	128	147	62	47	4	6	25	27	1.344	3.30	109	3.75	.286	5	.104	3	8	-0.1
1899	StL-N	11	8	.579	21	21	18	1	0	171^2	203	89	60	3	5	26	25	1.334	3.15	126	3.62	.294	13	.186	14	14	1.1
1900	Bos-N	8	4	.667	17	13	9	0	1	105^1	107	64	36	8	6	24	23	1.244	3.08	134	3.50	.263	11	.262	10	9	1.1
1901	Bos-A	4	6	.400	13	11	9	0	0	93^1	111	58	43	1	2	14	22	1.339	4.15	85	3.58	.292	10	.204	-10	4	-1.0
Total	10	162	98	.623	302	262	224	9	5	2284^1	2520	1346	884	62	69	609	504	1.370	3.48	127	3.69	.275	223	.233	225	193	19.7

• CURRAN, Sammy Simon Francis Curran b: 10/30/1874, Dorchester, MA d: 5/19/1936, Dorchester, MA TL Deb: 8/1/1902

YEAR	TM-L	W	L	PCT	G	GS	CG	SH	SV	IP	H	R	ER	HR	HB	BB	SO	RAT	ERA	ERA+	CERA	OAV	BH	AVG	PR+	WS	TPW
1902	Bos-N	0	0	....	1	0	0	0	0	6^2	6	1	1	0	0	0	3	.900	1.35	209	1.61	.241	0	.000	1	1	0.1

• CURRENCE, Lafayette Delancey Lafayette Currence b: 12/3/1951, Rock Hill, SC BB/TL, 5'11", 175 lbs. Deb: 7/24/1975

YEAR	TM-L	W	L	PCT	G	GS	CG	SH	SV	IP	H	R	ER	HR	HB	BB	SO	RAT	ERA	ERA+	CERA	OAV	BH	AVG	PR+	WS	TPW
1975	Mil-A	0	2	.000	8	1	0	0	0	18^2	25	17	16	5	0	14	7	2.089	7.71	50	8.93	.316	0	....	-8	0	-0.8

• CURRIE, Bill William Cleveland Currie b: 11/29/1928, Leary, GA BR/TR, 6', 175 lbs. Deb: 4/13/1955

YEAR	TM-L	W	L	PCT	G	GS	CG	SH	SV	IP	H	R	ER	HR	HB	BB	SO	RAT	ERA	ERA+	CERA	OAV	BH	AVG	PR+	WS	TPW
1955	Was-A	0	0	....	3	0	0	0	0	4^1	7	7	6	3	1	2	2	2.077	12.46	31	14.00	.350	0	....	-4	0	-0.4

• CURRIE, Clarence Clarence Franklin Currie b: 12/30/1878, Glencoe, Canada d: 7/15/1941, Little Chute, WI BR/TR Deb: 4/25/1902

YEAR	TM-L	W	L	PCT	G	GS	CG	SH	SV	IP	H	R	ER	HR	HB	BB	SO	RAT	ERA	ERA+	CERA	OAV	BH	AVG	PR+	WS	TPW
1902	Cin-N	3	4	.429	10	7	6	1	0	65^1	70	37	27	1	2	17	20	1.332	3.72	80	3.53	.274	2	.083	-7	2	-0.9
	StL-N	7	5	.583	15	12	10	2	0	124^2	125	54	36	0	6	35	30	1.283	2.60	105	3.22	.261	9	.196	4	6	0.5
	Yr.	10	9	.526	25	19	16	3	0	190	195	91	63	1	8	52	50	1.300	2.98	95	3.32	.265	11	.157	-2	8	-0.4
1903	StL-N	4	12	.250	22	16	13	1	1	148	155	93	66	7	0	60	52	1.453	4.01	81	4.03	.281	4	.085	-15	5	-1.7
	Chi-N	1	2	.333	6	3	2	0	1	33^1	35	25	11	1	3	9	9	1.320	2.97	105	3.28	.254	5	.417	0	2	0.2
	Yr.	5	14	.263	28	19	15	1	2	181^1	190	118	77	8	3	69	61	1.428	3.82	85	3.89	.276	9	.153	-15	7	-1.6
Total	2	15	23	.395	53	38	31	4	2	371^1	385	209	140	9	11	121	111	1.363	3.39	90	3.60	.270	20	.155	-17	15	-2.0

• CURRIE, Murphy Archibald Murphy Currie b: 8/31/1893, Fayetteville, NC d: 6/22/1939, Asheboro, NC BR/TR, 5'11.5", 185 lbs. Deb: 8/31/1916

YEAR	TM-L	W	L	PCT	G	GS	CG	SH	SV	IP	H	R	ER	HR	HB	BB	SO	RAT	ERA	ERA+	CERA	OAV	BH	AVG	PR+	WS	TPW
1916	StL-N	0	0	....	6	0	0	0	0	14^1	7	4	3	1	0	9	8	1.116	1.88	140	1.92	.149	0	.000	1	1	0.1

• CURRY, George George James "Soldier Boy" Curry b: 12/21/1888, Bridgeport, CT d: 10/5/1963, West Haven, CT BR/TR, 6', 185 lbs. Deb: 7/16/1911

YEAR	TM-L	W	L	PCT	G	GS	CG	SH	SV	IP	H	R	ER	HR	HB	BB	SO	RAT	ERA	ERA+	CERA	OAV	BH	AVG	PR+	WS	TPW
1911	StL-A	0	3	.000	3	3	0	0	0	15^2	19	15	13	0	0	24	2	2.745	7.47	45	9.51	.339	0	.000	-7	0	-0.8

• CURRY, Steve Stephen Thomas Curry b: 9/13/1965, Winter Park, FL BR/TR, 6'6", 217 lbs. Deb: 7/10/1988

YEAR	TM-L	W	L	PCT	G	GS	CG	SH	SV	IP	H	R	ER	HR	HB	BB	SO	RAT	ERA	ERA+	CERA	OAV	BH	AVG	PR+	WS	TPW
1988	Bos-A	0	1	.000	3	3	0	0	0	11	15	10	10	0	0	14	4	2.636	8.18	50	8.88	.357	0	....	-5	0	-0.5

• CURRY, Wes Wesley Curry b: 4/1/1860, Wilmington, DE d: 5/19/1933, Philadelphia, PA Deb: 8/6/1884 U

YEAR	TM-L	W	L	PCT	G	GS	CG	SH	SV	IP	H	R	ER	HR	HB	BB	SO	RAT	ERA	ERA+	CERA	OAV	BH	AVG	PR+	WS	TPW
1884	Ric-a	0	2	.000	2	2	2	0	0	16	15	14	9	2	1	3	1	1.125	5.06	65	....	.235	2	.250	-3	0	-0.3

• CURTIS, Cliff Clifton Garfield Curtis b: 7/3/1881, Delaware, OH d: 4/23/1943, Utica, OH BR/TR, 6'2", 180 lbs. Deb: 8/23/1909

YEAR	TM-L	W	L	PCT	G	GS	CG	SH	SV	IP	H	R	ER	HR	HB	BB	SO	RAT	ERA	ERA+	CERA	OAV	BH	AVG	PR+	WS	TPW
1909	Bos-N	4	5	.444	10	9	8	2	0	83	53	17	13	1	2	30	22	1.000	1.41	199	1.73	.191	1	.034	13	8	1.2
1910	Bos-N	6	24	.200	43	37	12	2	2	251	251	154	99	9	12	124	75	1.494	3.55	93	4.32	.277	12	.146	-11	8	-1.5
1911	Bos-N	1	8	.111	12	9	5	0	1	77	79	50	38	4	2	34	23	1.468	4.44	86	4.07	.265	7	.250	-4	2	-0.4
	Chi-N	1	2	.333	4	1	0	0	0	7	7	4	3	0	3	5	4	1.714	3.86	86	5.50	.241	1	.500	-1	0	0.0
	Phi-N	2	1	.667	8	5	3	1	0	45	45	19	13	0	1	15	13	1.333	2.60	132	3.18	.260	4	.267	4	4	0.4
	Yr.	4	11	.267	24	15	8	1	1	129	131	73	54	4	6	54	40	1.434	3.77	98	3.84	.262	12	.267	-0	6	0.0
1912	Phi-N	2	5	.286	10	8	2	0	0	50	55	30	18	3	4	17	20	1.440	3.24	111	4.25	.286	0	.000	2	2	0.0
	Bro-N	4	7	.364	19	9	3	0	1	80	72	44	35	4	6	37	22	1.363	3.94	85	3.58	.250	8	.308	-4	4	-0.3
	Yr.	6	12	.333	29	17	5	0	1	130	127	74	53	7	10	54	42	1.392	3.67	93	3.83	.264	8	.195	-2	6	-0.3
1913	Bro-N	8	9	.471	30	16	6	0	2	151^2	145	75	55	1	7	55	57	1.319	3.26	101	3.14	.255	6	.122	-2	7	-0.5
Total	5	28	61	.315	136	94	39	5	6	744^2	707	393	274	22	37	317	236	1.375	3.31	102	3.62	.259	39	.159	-2	35	-1.1

• CURTIS, Jack Jack Patrick Curtis b: 1/11/1937, Rhodhiss, NC BL/TL, 5'10", 175 lbs. Deb: 4/22/1961

YEAR	TM-L	W	L	PCT	G	GS	CG	SH	SV	IP	H	R	ER	HR	HB	BB	SO	RAT	ERA	ERA+	CERA	OAV	BH	AVG	PR+	WS	TPW
1961	Chi-N	10	13	.435	31	27	6	0	0	180^1	220	117	98	23	1	51	57	**1.503**	4.89	85	4.99	.303	10	.167	-11	6	-0.8
1962	Chi-N	0	2	.000	4	3	0	0	0	18	18	8	7	2	0	6	8	1.333	3.50	118	4.07	.277	1	.250	1	1	0.2
	Mil-N	4	4	.500	30	5	0	0	1	75^2	82	39	35	8	2	27	40	1.441	4.16	91	4.58	.282	4	.222	-3	4	-0.2
	Yr.	4	6	.400	34	8	0	0	1	93^2	100	47	42	10	2	33	48	1.420	4.04	95	4.48	.281	5	.227	-2	5	0.0
1963	Cle-A	0	0	....	4	0	0	0	0	5	8	10	10	0	1	5	3	2.600	18.00	20	9.30	.348	0	....	-8	0	-0.8
Total	3	14	19	.424	69	35	6	0	1	279	328	174	150	33	4	89	108	1.495	4.84	83	4.89	.297	15	.183	-21	11	-1.6

• CURTIS, John John Duffield Curtis b: 3/9/1948, Newton, MA BL/TL, 6'1", 185 lbs. Deb: 8/13/1970

YEAR	TM-L	W	L	PCT	G	GS	CG	SH	SV	IP	H	R	ER	HR	HB	BB	SO	RAT	ERA	ERA+	CERA	OAV	BH	AVG	PR+	WS	TPW
1970	Bos-A	0	0	....	1	0	0	0	0	2^1	4	4	3	1	0	1	1	2.143	11.57	34	10.52	.333	0	....	-2	0	-0.2
1971	Bos-A	2	2	.500	5	3	1	0	0	26	30	9	9	3	0	6	19	1.385	3.12	119	4.38	.291	1	.111	2	2	0.2
1972	Bos-A	11	8	.579	26	21	8	3	0	154^1	161	69	64	8	0	50	106	1.367	3.73	86	3.67	.271	5	.094	-6	7	-0.9
1973	Bos-A	13	13	.500	35	30	10	4	0	221^1	225	103	88	24	2	83	101	1.392	3.58	112	4.13	.264	0	....	10	13	1.0
1974	StL-N	10	14	.417	33	29	5	2	1	195	199	91	82	15	2	83	89	1.446	3.78	94	4.13	.267	10	.159	-8	10	-0.8
1975	StL-N	8	9	.471	39	18	4	0	1	146^2	151	70	56	13	2	65	67	1.473	3.44	109	4.31	.268	8	.211	9	9	1.1
1976	StL-N	6	11	.353	37	15	3	1	1	134	139	68	67	11	0	65	52	1.522	4.50	79	4.48	.276	7	.200	-15	5	-1.4
1977	SF-N	3	3	.500	43	9	1	1	1	77	95	48	47	5	1	48	47	1.857	5.49	71	6.02	.314	3	.231	-12	2	-1.1
1978	SF-N	4	3	.571	46	0	0	0	1	63	60	31	26	1	0	29	38	1.413	3.71	93	3.26	.262	0	.000	-2	3	-0.2
1979	SF-N	10	9	.526	27	18	3	2	0	120^2	121	62	56	15	0	42	85	1.351	4.18	84	3.91	.257	5	.147	-8	5	-0.7
1980	SD-N	10	8	.556	30	27	6	0	0	187	184	84	73	9	2	67	71	1.342	3.51	98	3.45	.262	12	.194	-4	9	-0.4
1981	SD-N	2	6	.250	28	8	0	0	0	66^2	70	41	38	11	1	30	31	1.500	5.13	63	5.08	.275	1	.077	-14	0	-1.6
1982	SD-N	8	6	.571	26	18	1	1	0	116^1	121	62	53	15	1	46	54	1.436	4.10	84	4.57	.271	11	.297	-10	4	-0.7
	Cal-A	0	1	.000	8	0	0	0	1	12	16	8	8	0	0	3	10	1.583	6.00	68	4.30	.320	0	....	-3	0	-0.3
1983	Cal-A	1	2	.333	37	3	0	0	5	90	89	44	38	5	2	40	36	1.433	3.80	106	3.73	.258	0	....	2	6	0.2

YEAR	TM-L	W	L	PCT	G	GS	CG	SH	SV	IP	H	R	ER	HR	HB	BB	SO	RAT	ERA	ERA+	CERA	OAV	BH	AVG	PR+	WS	TPW
1984	Cal-A	1	2	.333	17	0	0	0	0	28^2	30	16	14	4	0	11	18	1.430	4.40	90	4.39	.263	0	....	-1	1	-0.1
Total	15	89	97	.478	438	199	42	14	11	1641	1695	810	722	140	13	669	825	1.441	3.96	91	4.16	.270	63	.175	-62	76	-6.1
• CURTIS, Vern	Vernon Eugene “Turk” Curtis b: 5/24/1920, Cairo, IL d: 6/24/1992, Cairo, IL BR/TR, 6', 170 lbs. Deb: 9/6/1943																										
1943	Was-A	0	0	....	2	0	0	0	0	4	3	3	3	0	0	6	1	2.250	6.75	47	5.42	.200	0	....	-2	0	-0.2
1944	Was-A	0	1	.000	3	1	0	0	0	9^2	8	3	3	0	0	3	2	1.138	2.79	117	2.31	.235	0	.000	1	1	0.0
1946	Was-A	0	0	....	11	0	0	0	0	16^1	19	13	13	1	0	10	7	1.776	7.16	47	5.12	.297	0	.000	-7	0	-0.7
Total	3	0	1	.000	16	1	0	0	0	30	30	19	19	1	0	19	10	1.633	5.70	58	4.25	.265	0	.000	-8	1	-0.9
• CUSHMAN, Ed	Edgar Leander Cushman b: 3/27/1852, Eagleville, OH d: 9/26/1915, Erie, PA BR/TL, 6', 177 lbs. Deb: 7/6/1883																										
1883	Buf-N	3	3	.500	7	7	5	0	0	50^1	61	41	22	0	....	17	34	1.550	3.93	81	....	.283	5	.217	-4	2	-0.4
1884	Mil-U	4	0	1.000	4	4	4	2	0	36	10	4	4	0	....	3	47	.361	1.00	305	....	.082	1	.091	4	7	0.3
1885	Phi-a	3	7	.300	10	10	10	0	0	87	101	77	34	1	3	17	37	1.356	3.52	98	....	.278	7	.189	-0	3	-0.1
	NY-a	8	14	.364	22	22	22	0	0	191	158	105	59	2	3	33	133	1.000	2.78	106	....	.216	10	.145	5	7	0.4
	Yr.	11	21	.344	32	32	32	0	0	278	259	182	93	3	6	50	170	1.112	3.01	103	....	.236	17	.160	4	10	0.3
1886	NY-a	17	21	.447	38	38	37	2	0	325^2	278	180	113	6	1	99	167	1.158	3.12	109	....	.220	19	.151	6	23	0.0
1887	NY-a	10	15	.400	26	26	25	0	0	220	393	232	146	9	9	83	64	1.786	5.97	71	....	.375	33	.320	-35	5	-2.5
1890	Tol-a	17	21	.447	40	38	34	0	1	315^2	346	208	147	5	10	107	125	1.435	4.19	94	....	.270	13	.100	-16	17	-2.1
Total	6	62	81	.434	147	145	137	4	1	1225^2	1347	847	525	23	26	359	607	1.324	3.86	95	....	.268	88	.176	-41	64	-4.4
• CUSHMAN, Harvey	Harvey Barnes Cushman b: 7/10/1877, Rockland, ME d: 12/27/1920, Emsworth, PA Deb: 8/24/1902																										
1902	Pit-N	0	4	.000	4	4	3	0	0	25^2	30	31	21	0	2	31	12	2.377	7.36	37	7.40	.292	2	.200	-14	0	-1.5
• CVENGROS, Mike	Michael John Cvengros b: 12/1/1901, Pana, IL d: 8/2/1970, Hot Springs, AR BL/TL, 5'8", 159 lbs. Deb: 9/30/1922																										
1922	NY-N	0	1	.000	1	1	1	0	0	9	6	5	4	1	1	3	3	1.000	4.00	100	2.51	.194	0	.000	-0	0	-0.1
1923	Chi-A	12	13	.480	40	26	14	0	3	214^1	216	110	105	6	13	107	86	1.507	4.41	90	4.07	.269	15	.203	-10	11	-1.1
1924	Chi-A	3	12	.200	26	15	2	0	0	105^2	119	80	69	5	3	67	36	1.760	5.88	70	5.15	.300	6	.200	-20	1	-1.7
1925	Chi-A	3	9	.250	22	11	4	0	0	104^2	109	56	50	7	3	55	32	1.567	4.30	97	4.58	.278	5	.152	-2	5	-0.3
1927*	Pit-N	2	1	.667	23	4	0	0	1	53^2	55	25	20	3	1	24	21	1.472	3.35	122	4.02	.271	3	.158	4	4	0.4
1929	Chi-N	5	4	.556	32	4	0	0	2	64	82	39	33	2	1	29	23	1.734	4.64	99	5.37	.319	6	.400	-1	4	0.1
Total	6	25	40	.385	144	61	21	0	6	551^1	587	315	281	24	22	285	201	1.582	4.59	90	4.50	.282	35	.201	-29	25	-2.7
• CYR, Eric	Eric Cyr b: 2/11/1979, Montreal, Canada BR/TL, 6'4", 200 lbs. Deb: 6/23/2002																										
2002	SD-N	0	1	.000	5	0	0	0	0	6	6	7	7	0	0	6	4	2.000	10.50	36	5.34	.286	0	.000	-4	0	-0.5
• CZAJKOWSKI, Jim	James Mark Czajkowski b: 12/18/1963, Parma, OH BB/TR, 6'4", 215 lbs. Deb: 7/29/1994																										
1994	Col-N	0	0	....	5	0	0	0	0	8^2	9	4	4	2	3	6	2	1.731	4.15	120	8.08	.281	0	....	1	1	0.1
• DAAL, Omar	Omar Jesus (Cordero) Daal b: 3/1/1972, Maracaibo, Venezuela BL/TL, 6'3", 175 lbs. Deb: 4/23/1993																										
1993	LA-N	2	3	.400	47	0	0	0	0	35^1	36	20	20	5	0	21	19	1.613	5.09	75	5.29	.277	0	....	-5	1	-0.5
1994	LA-N	0	0	....	24	0	0	0	0	13^2	12	5	5	1	0	5	9	1.244	3.29	119	3.24	.245	0	....	1	1	0.1
1995	LA-N	4	0	1.000	28	0	0	0	0	20	29	16	16	1	1	15	11	2.200	7.20	53	7.85	.354	0	....	-8	0	-0.7
1996	Mon-N	4	5	.444	64	6	0	0	0	87^1	74	40	39	10	1	37	82	1.271	4.02	108	3.44	.228	0	.000	3	6	0.2
1997	Mon-N	1	2	.333	33	0	0	0	1	30^1	48	35	33	4	2	15	16	2.077	9.79	43	8.60	.378	1	.200	-19	0	-1.9
	Tor-A	1	1	.500	9	3	0	0	0	27	34	13	12	3	0	6	28	1.481	4.00	115	4.85	.304	0	....	1	2	0.1
1998	Ari-N	8	12	.400	33	23	3	1	0	162^2	146	60	52	12	3	51	132	1.211	2.88	146	3.12	.245	5	.109	24	12	2.3
1999*	Ari-N	16	9	.640	32	32	2	1	0	214^2	188	92	87	21	7	79	148	1.244	3.65	125	3.39	.236	16	.232	21	16	2.2
2000	Ari-N	2	10	.167	20	16	0	0	0	96	127	88	77	17	7	42	45	1.760	7.22	65	6.78	.315	7	.259	-26	1	-2.3
	Phi-N	2	9	.182	12	12	0	0	0	71	81	40	37	9	2	30	51	1.563	4.69	99	5.37	.290	5	.278	-0	4	0.2
	Yr.	4	19	.174	32	28	0	0	0	167	208	128	114	26	9	72	96	**1.677**	6.14	76	6.18	.305	12	.267	-27	5	-2.1
2001	Phi-N	13	7	.650	32	32	0	0	0	185^2	199	100	92	26	5	56	107	1.373	4.46	95	4.45	.273	13	.236	-7	11	-0.4
2002	LA-N	11	9	.550	39	23	0	0	0	161^1	142	73	70	20	4	54	105	1.215	3.90	98	3.42	.239	6	.154	-2	8	-0.1
2003	Bal-A	4	11	.267	19	17	0	0	0	93^2	134	69	66	11	2	30	53	1.751	6.34	69	6.57	.343	0	....	-20	0	-1.9
Total	11	68	78	.466	392	164	5	2	1	1198^2	1250	651	606	140	34	441	806	1.411	4.55	95	4.46	.271	53	.196	-37	62	-2.6
• D'ACQUISTO, John	John Francis D'Acquisto b: 12/24/1951, San Diego, CA BR/TR, 6'2", 205 lbs. Deb: 9/2/1973																										
1973	SF-N	1	1	.500	7	3	1	0	0	27^2	23	14	11	4	0	19	29	1.518	3.58	107	4.48	.219	0	.000	1	1	0.0
1974	SF-N	12	14	.462	38	36	5	1	0	215	182	101	90	13	6	124	167	1.423	3.77	101	3.68	.227	8	.113	2	12	0.1
1975	SF-N	2	4	.333	10	6	0	0	0	28	29	35	32	5	2	34	22	2.250	10.29	37	8.58	.264	0	.000	-20	0	-2.1
1976	SF-N	3	8	.273	28	19	0	0	0	106	93	69	63	5	3	102	53	1.840	5.35	68	5.27	.243	7	.269	-19	0	-1.8
1977	StL-N	0	0	....	3	2	0	0	0	8^1	5	4	4	0	1	10	9	1.800	4.32	89	4.64	.185	0	.000	-1	0	-0.1
	SD-N	1	2	.333	17	12	0	0	0	44	49	41	34	3	1	47	45	2.182	6.95	51	7.46	.297	0	.000	-16	0	-1.7
	Yr.	1	2	.333	20	14	0	0	0	52^1	54	45	38	3	2	57	54	2.121	6.54	55	7.01	.281	0	.000	-17	0	-1.8
1978	SD-N	4	3	.571	45	3	0	0	10	93	60	24	22	2	1	56	104	1.247	2.13	156	2.42	.185	4	.190	12	11	1.4
1979	SD-N	9	13	.409	51	11	1	1	2	133^2	140	83	73	15	3	86	97	1.691	4.92	72	5.49	.275	4	.129	-22	2	-2.1
1980	SD-N	2	3	.400	39	0	0	0	1	67	67	29	28	2	1	36	44	1.537	3.76	91	3.97	.270	0	.000	-3	3	-0.4
	Mon-N	0	2	.000	11	0	0	0	2	20^2	14	7	5	0	0	9	15	1.113	2.18	164	2.06	.206	0	....	3	2	0.3
	Yr.	2	5	.286	50	0	0	0	3	87^2	81	36	33	2	1	45	59	1.437	3.39	102	3.52	.256	0	.000	-0	5	-0.1
1981	Cal-A	0	0	....	6	0	0	0	0	19^1	26	24	23	2	1	12	8	1.966	10.71	34	7.31	.338	0	....	-15	0	-1.6
1982	Oak-A	0	1	.000	11	0	0	0	0	17	20	11	10	1	0	9	7	1.706	5.29	74	5.31	.290	0	....	-3	0	-0.3
Total	10	34	51	.400	266	92	7	2	15	779^2	708	442	395	52	19	544	600	1.606	4.56	80	4.59	.245	23	.127	-81	31	-8.3
• DAGENHARD, John	John Douglas Dagenhard b: 4/25/1917, Magnolia, OH d: 7/16/2001, Bolivar, OH BR/TR, 6'2", 195 lbs. Deb: 9/28/1943																										
1943	Bos-N	1	0	1.000	2	1	1	0	0	11	9	2	0	0	2	4	2	1.182	0.00	....	2.88	.225	0	.000	4	2	0.4
• DAGLIA, Pete	Peter George Daglia b: 2/28/1906, Napa, CA d: 3/11/1952, Willits, CA BR/TR, 6'1", 210 lbs. Deb: 6/8/1932																										
1932	Chi-A	2	4	.333	12	5	2	0	0	50	67	35	32	4	4	20	16	1.740	5.76	75	6.16	.324	1	.077	-7	1	-0.8
• DAHL, Jay	Jay Steven Dahl b: 12/6/1945, San Bernardino, CA d: 6/20/1965, Salisbury, NC BB/TL, 5'10", 183 lbs. Deb: 9/27/1963																										
1963	Hou-N	0	1	.000	1	1	0	0	0	2^2	7	7	5	0	0	0	0	2.625	16.88	19	10.98	.438	0	....	-4	0	-0.4
• DAHLKE, Jerry	Jerome Alexander “Joe” Dahlke b: 6/8/1930, Marathon, WI BR/TR, 6', 180 lbs. Deb: 5/6/1956																										
1956	Chi-A	0	0	....	5	0	0	0	0	2^1	5	5	5	0	0	6	1	4.714	19.29	21	20.52	.455	0	....	-4	0	-0.4
• DAILEY, Bill	William Garland Dailey b: 3/13/1935, Arlington, VA BR/TR, 6'3", 185 lbs. Deb: 8/17/1961																										
1961	Cle-A	1	0	1.000	12	0	0	0	0	19	16	4	2	0	0	6	7	1.158	0.95	415	2.27	.232	0	.000	6	2	0.6
1962	Cle-A	2	2	.500	27	0	0	0	1	42^2	43	18	17	0	2	17	24	1.406	3.59	108	3.41	.270	0	.000	1	3	0.1
1963	Min-A	6	3	.667	66	0	0	0	21	108^2	80	26	24	9	0	19	72	.911	1.99	183	1.80	.208	5	.238	20	17	2.3
1964	Min-A	1	2	.333	14	0	0	0	0	15^1	23	16	14	3	4	17	6	2.609	8.22	44	12.86	.377	0	....	-8	0	-0.8
Total	4	10	7	.588	119	0	0	0	22	185^2	162	64	57	12	6	59	109	1.190	2.76	134	3.13	.241	5	.192	20	22	2.2
• DAILEY, Sam	Samuel Laurence Dailey b: 3/31/1904, Oakford, IL d: 12/2/1979, Columbia, MO BL/TR, 5'11", 168 lbs. Deb: 7/4/1929																										
1929	Phi-N	2	2	.500	20	4	0	0	0	51^1	74	48	43	5	1	23	18	1.890	7.54	69	6.89	.349	1	.059	-12	0	-1.3
• DAILY, Ed	Edward M. Daily b: 9/7/1862, Providence, RI d: 10/21/1891, Washington, DC BR/TR, 5'10.5", 174 lbs. Deb: 5/4/1885 ♦																										
1885	Phi-N	26	23	.531	50	50	49	4	0	440	370	212	108	12	....	90	140	1.045	2.21	126	....	.217	38	.207	25	35	2.4
1886	Phi-N	16	9	.640	27	23	22	1	0	218	211	123	74	7	....	59	95	1.239	3.06	107	....	.245	70	.227	11	22	0.5
1887	Phi-N	0	4	.000	6	5	4	0	0	41^1	77	52	33	2	0	25	7	1.863	7.19	58	....	.387	33	.303	-13	3	-1.6
	Was-N	0	1	.000	1	1	1	0	0	7	11	6	6	0	0	6	3	1.571	7.71	52	....	.347	92	.283	-3	5	-1.4
	Yr.	0	5	.000	7	6	5	0	0	48^1	88	58	39	2	0	31	10	1.821	7.26	57	....	.382	125	.288	-15	8	-3.0
1888	Was-N	2	7	.222	9	8	8	0	0	73^2	88	69	40	7	3	19	20	1.452	4.89	57	....	.286	102	.225	-17	8	-2.9
1889	Col-a	0	0	....	2	0	0	0	1	1^2	1	7	4	0	0	4	2	3.000	21.60	17	....	.168	148	.256	-3	11	-1.7

YEAR	TM-L	W	L	PCT	G	GS	CG	SH	SV	IP	H	R	ER	HR	HB	BB	SO	RAT	ERA	ERA+	CERA	OAV	BH	AVG	PR+	WS	TPW
1890	Bro-a	10	15	.400	27	27	27	0	0	235^{2}	252	161	106	3	18	93	82	1.464	4.05	96	....	.266	94	.239	-3	13	-0.3
	NY-N	2	0	1.000	2	1	1	0	0	16	6	6	4	0	4	6	0	.750	2.25	155	....	.113	2	.133	2	1	0.1
	*Lou-a	6	3	.667	12	10	9	1	0	93	83	35	20	2	4	30	31	1.215	1.94	199	....	.232	20	.250	19	12	1.9
	Yr.	16	18	.471	39	37	36	1	0	328^{2}	335	196	126	5	22	123	113	1.394	3.45	112	....	.256	114	.241	17	25	1.5
1891	Lou-a	4	8	.333	15	14	11	0	0	111^{1}	149	109	71	6	8	48	27	1.769	5.74	64	....	.311	16	.250	-27	2	-2.2
Total	7	66	70	.485	151	139	132	6	1	1237^{2}	1248	780	466	39	37	380	407	1.290	3.39	99	....	.252	633	.244	-8	112	-5.2
• DAILY, Hugh	Hugh Ignatius "One Arm" Daily b: 1848, Ireland BR/TR, 6'2", 180 lbs. Deb: 5/1/1882																										
1882	Buf-N	15	14	.517	29	29	29	0	0	255^{2}	246	165	85	6	....	70	116	1.236	2.99	98	....	.239	18	.164	2	14	-0.3
1883	Cle-N	23	19	.548	45	43	40	4	1	378^{2}	360	193	102	5	....	99	171	1.212	2.42	130	....	.236	18	.127	16	34	0.7
1884	CP-U	27	27	.500	56	56	54	5	0	484^{2}	430	257	131	11	....	71	469	1.034	2.43	118	....	.222	43	.219	29	37	2.6
	Was-U	1	1	.500	2	2	2	0	0	16	16	11	4	0	....	1	14	1.063	2.25	133	....	.243	0	.000	2	1	0.1
	Yr.	28	28	.500	58	58	56	5	0	500^{2}	446	268	135	11	....	72	**483**	1.035	2.43	119	....	.223	43	.214	31	38	2.7
1885	StL-N	3	8	.273	11	11	10	1	0	91^{1}	92	72	40	5	....	44	31	1.489	3.94	70	....	.250	3	.086	-15	2	-1.7
1886	Was-N	0	6	.000	6	6	6	0	0	49	69	60	40	2	....	40	15	2.224	7.35	44	....	.320	2	.125	-22	0	-2.0
1887	Cle-a	4	12	.250	16	16	16	0	0	139^{2}	225	108	57	1	3	44	30	1.611	3.67	118	....	.351	7	.115	16	5	0.7
Total	6	73	87	.456	165	163	157	10	1	1415	1438	866	459	30	3	369	846	1.246	2.92	106	....	.249	91	.161	28	93	0.0
• DALCANTON, Bruce	John Bruce Dalcanton b: 6/15/1942, California, PA BR/TR, 6'2", 205 lbs. Deb: 9/3/1967 C																										
1967	Pit-N	2	1	.667	8	2	1	0	0	24	19	5	5	1	1	10	13	1.208	1.88	179	2.57	.211	2	.333	4	3	0.5
1968	Pit-N	1	1	.500	7	0	0	0	2	17	7	4	4	0	2	6	8	.765	2.12	138	1.01	.127	0	.000	1	2	0.1
1969	Pit-N	8	2	.800	57	0	0	0	5	86^{1}	79	34	32	3	0	49	56	1.483	3.34	104	3.61	.252	3	.300	2	8	0.4
1970	Pit-N	9	4	.692	41	6	1	0	1	84^{2}	94	48	43	7	1	39	53	1.571	4.57	85	4.70	.282	0	.000	-8	4	-0.9
1971	KC-A	8	6	.571	25	22	2	0	0	141^{1}	144	63	54	8	0	44	58	1.330	3.44	100	3.51	.262	4	.087	1	7	-0.2
1972	KC-A	6	6	.500	35	16	1	0	2	132^{1}	135	54	50	7	1	29	75	1.239	3.40	89	3.13	.265	4	.098	-4	6	-0.6
1973	KC-A	4	3	.571	32	3	1	0	3	97^{1}	108	60	52	8	4	46	38	1.582	4.81	85	4.80	.284	0	....	-6	4	-0.6
1974	KC-A	8	10	.444	31	22	9	2	0	175^{1}	135	71	61	5	5	82	96	1.238	3.13	122	2.69	.211	0	....	16	12	1.7
1975	KC-A	0	2	.000	4	2	0	0	0	8^{2}	23	18	15	0	1	7	5	3.462	15.58	25	16.78	.479	0	....	-11	0	-1.1
	Atl-N	2	7	.222	26	9	0	0	3	67	63	33	25	2	6	24	38	1.299	3.36	112	3.29	.248	2	.105	5	4	0.4
1976	Atl-N	3	5	.375	42	1	0	0	1	73^{1}	67	41	29	6	2	42	36	1.486	3.56	106	3.99	.244	2	.222	4	4	0.4
1977	Chi-A	0	2	.000	8	0	0	0	2	24	20	11	10	1	0	13	9	1.375	3.75	109	3.37	.230	0	....	2	2	0.2
Total	11	51	49	.510	316	83	15	2	19	931^{1}	894	442	380	48	23	391	485	1.380	3.67	99	3.63	.253	17	.113	4	56	0.1
• DALE, Carl	James Carl Dale b: 12/7/1972, Indianapolis, IN BR/TR, 6'2", 200 lbs. Deb: 9/7/1999																										
1999	Mil-N	0	1	.000	4	0	0	0	0	4	8	9	9	2	1	6	4	3.500	20.25	22	21.62	.400	0	....	-7	0	-0.7
• DALE, Gene	Emmett Eugene Dale b: 6/16/1889, St. Louis, MO d: 3/20/1958, St. Louis, MO BR/TR, 6'3", 179 lbs. Deb: 9/19/1911																										
1911	StL-N	0	2	.000	5	2	0	0	0	14^{2}	13	12	11	0	2	16	13	1.977	6.75	50	5.71	.250	2	.400	-6	0	-0.5
1912	StL-N	0	5	.000	19	3	1	0	0	61^{2}	76	58	45	4	3	51	37	2.059	6.57	52	6.71	.311	6	.273	-22	0	-2.1
1915	Cin-N	18	17	.514	49	35	20	4	3	296^{2}	256	115	81	6	6	107	104	1.224	2.46	116	2.73	.243	20	.220	7	20	1.0
1916	Cin-N	3	4	.429	17	5	2	0	0	69^{2}	80	44	40	3	2	33	23	1.622	5.17	50	4.89	.304	3	.143	-21	0	-2.4
Total	4	21	28	.429	90	45	23	4	3	442^{2}	425	229	177	13	13	207	177	1.428	3.60	82	3.72	.263	31	.223	-41	20	-4.0
• DALEY, Bill	William Daley b: 6/27/1868, Poughkeepsie, NY d: 5/4/1922, Poughkeepsie, NY TL, 5'7" Deb: 7/17/1889																										
1889	Bos-N	3	3	.500	9	7	4	0	0	48	34	29	23	1	2	43	40	1.604	4.31	97	....	.193	3	.150	-0	3	-0.1
1890	Bos-P	18	7	.720	34	25	19	2	2	235	246	178	94	7	9	167	110	1.757	3.60	122	....	.258	17	.155	18	18	1.1
1891	Bos-a	8	6	.571	19	11	10	0	**2**	126^{2}	119	76	42	6	7	81	68	1.579	2.98	117	....	.240	10	.169	4	8	0.1
Total	3	29	16	.644	62	43	33	2	4	409^{2}	399	283	159	14	18	291	218	1.684	3.49	117	....	.245	30	.159	22	29	1.0
• DALEY, Bud	Leavitt Leo Daley b: 10/7/1932, Orange, CA BL/TL, 6'1", 185 lbs. Deb: 9/10/1955																										
1955	Cle-A	0	1	.000	2	1	0	0	0	7	10	5	5	1	0	1	2	1.571	6.43	62	5.70	.333	0	.000	-2	0	-0.2
1956	Cle-A	1	0	1.000	14	0	0	0	0	20^{1}	21	15	14	2	5	14	13	1.721	6.20	68	6.18	.273	0	.000	-4	0	-0.5
1957	Cle-A	2	8	.200	34	10	1	0	2	87^{1}	99	59	43	6	10	40	54	1.592	4.43	84	5.11	.279	4	.200	-6	1	-0.6
1958	KC-A	3	2	.600	26	5	1	0	0	70^{2}	67	29	26	5	6	19	39	1.217	3.31	118	3.40	.249	2	.125	5	5	0.4
1959	KC-A★	16	13	.552	39	29	12	2	1	216^{1}	212	90	76	24	11	62	125	1.267	3.16	127	3.80	.257	23	.295	21	18	2.7
1960	KC-A★	16	16	.500	37	35	13	1	0	231	234	129	117	27	10	96	126	1.429	4.56	87	4.46	.263	12	.160	-11	10	-1.0
1961	KC-A	4	8	.333	16	10	2	0	1	63^{2}	84	46	35	6	5	22	36	1.665	4.95	83	5.93	.319	2	.111	-5	1	-0.6
	*NY-A	8	9	.471	23	17	7	0	0	129^{2}	127	63	57	17	4	51	83	1.373	3.96	94	4.21	.257	6	.133	-8	5	-0.9
	Yr.	12	17	.414	39	27	9	0	1	193^{1}	211	109	92	23	9	73	119	1.469	4.28	90	4.78	.278	8	.127	-13	6	-1.5
1962*	NY-A	7	5	.583	43	6	0	0	4	105^{1}	105	47	42	8	5	21	55	1.196	3.59	104	3.27	.258	5	.185	1	7	0.1
1963	NY-A	0	0	....	1	0	0	0	1	1	2	0	0	0	0	0	0	2.000	0.00	....	9.49	.667	0	....	0	0	0.0
1964	NY-A	3	2	.600	13	3	0	0	1	35	37	19	18	3	4	25	16	1.771	4.63	78	5.98	.274	2	.250	-4	1	-0.4
Total	10	60	64	.484	248	116	36	3	10	967^{1}	998	502	433	99	60	351	549	1.395	4.03	97	4.33	.266	56	.192	-12	48	-0.9
• DALTON, Mike	Michael Edward Dalton b: 3/27/1963, Palo Alto, CA BR/TL, 6', 215 lbs. Deb: 5/31/1991																										
1991	Det-A	0	0	....	4	0	0	0	0	8	12	3	3	2	0	2	4	1.750	3.38	123	7.48	.333	0	....	1	0	0.1
• DALY, George	George Josephs "Pecks" Daly b: 7/28/1887, Buffalo, NY d: 12/12/1957, Buffalo, NY BR/TR, 5'10.5", 175 lbs. Deb: 9/26/1909																										
1909	NY-N	0	3	.000	3	3	3	0	0	21	31	19	14	0	1	8	8	1.857	6.00	42	6.11	.341	1	.111	-8	0	-0.9
• D'AMICO, Jeff	Jeffrey Charles D'Amico b: 12/27/1975, St. Petersburg, FL BR/TR, 6'7", 250 lbs. Deb: 6/28/1996																										
1996	Mil-A	6	6	.500	17	17	0	0	0	86	88	53	52	21	0	31	53	1.384	5.44	95	5.11	.267	0	....	-4	4	-0.4
1997	Mil-A	9	7	.563	23	23	1	1	0	135^{2}	139	81	71	25	8	43	94	1.342	4.71	98	4.69	.264	0	.000	-6	6	-0.6
1999	Mil-N	0	0	....	1	0	0	0	0	1	1	0	0	0	0	0	1	1.000	0.00	....	1.95	.250	0	....	1	0	0.0
2000	Mil-N	12	7	.632	23	23	1	1	0	162^{1}	143	55	48	14	6	46	101	1.164	2.66	171	3.01	.238	4	.091	32	15	2.9
2001	Mil-N	2	4	.333	10	10	0	0	0	47^{1}	60	42	32	11	1	16	32	1.606	6.08	70	6.30	.306	1	.067	-10	0	-0.9
2002	NY-N	6	10	.375	29	22	1	1	0	145^{2}	152	84	80	20	3	37	101	1.297	4.94	80	3.96	.267	4	.108	-15	3	-1.6
2003	Pit-N	9	16	.360	29	29	2	1	0	175^{1}	204	104	93	23	7	42	100	1.403	4.77	92	4.67	.291	6	.125	-7	6	-0.6
Total	7	44	50	.468	132	124	5	4	0	753^{1}	787	419	376	114	25	215	482	1.330	4.49	99	4.33	.269	15	.101	-9	34	-1.1
• D'AMICO, Jeff	Jeffrey Michael D'Amico b: 11/9/1974, Inglewood, CA BR/TR, 6'3", 200 lbs. Deb: 6/3/2000																										
2000	KC-A	0	1	.000	7	1	0	0	0	13^{2}	19	14	14	2	0	15	9	2.488	9.22	56	10.15	.345	0	....	-7	0	-0.6
• DAMMANN, Bill	William Henry "Wee Willie" Dammann b: 8/9/1872, Chicago, IL d: 12/6/1948, Lynnhaven, VA BL/TL, 5'7", 155 lbs. Deb: 4/24/1897																										
1897	Cin-N	6	4	.600	16	11	7	1	0	95	122	65	50	2	5	37	21	1.674	4.74	96	5.16	.309	5	.161	-2	7	-0.2
1898	Cin-N	16	10	.615	35	22	16	2	2	224^{2}	277	132	90	3	7	67	51	1.531	3.61	106	4.39	.301	16	.195	3	17	0.4
1899	Cin-N	2	1	.667	9	5	3	1	1	48	74	30	26	0	1	11	2	1.771	4.88	80	5.79	.352	1	.056	-5	2	-0.6
Total	3	24	15	.615	60	38	26	4	3	367^{2}	473	227	166	5	13	115	74	1.599	4.06	99	4.77	.310	22	.168	-4	26	-0.4
• DANEKER, Pat	Patrick Rees Daneker b: 1/14/1976, Williamsport, PA BR/TR, 6'3", 195 lbs. Deb: 7/2/1999																										
1999	Chi-A	0	0	....	3	2	0	0	0	15	14	8	7	1	0	6	5	1.333	4.20	116	3.46	.255	0	.000	1	1	0.1
• DANEY, Art	Arthur Lee Daney b: 7/9/1904, Talihina, OK d: 3/11/1988, Phoenix, AZ BR/TR, 5'11", 165 lbs. Deb: 5/25/1928																										
1928	Phi-A	0	0	....	1	0	0	0	0	1	1	0	0	0	0	0	0	1.000	0.00	....	1.95	.250	0	....	0	0	0.0
• DANFORTH, Dave	David Charles "Dauntless Dave" Danforth b: 3/7/1890, Granger, TX d: 9/19/1970, Baltimore, MD BL/TL, 6', 167 lbs. Deb: 8/1/1911																										
1911	Phi-A	4	1	.800	14	2	1	0	1	33^{2}	29	18	14	1	3	17	21	1.366	3.74	84	3.56	.240	1	.167	-2	2	-0.2
1912	Phi-A	0	0	....	3	0	0	0	0	20^{1}	26	14	9	0	0	12	8	1.869	3.98	78	6.01	.338	2	.250	-2	0	-0.2
1916	Chi-A	6	5	.545	28	8	1	0	2	93^{2}	87	43	34	1	3	37	49	1.324	3.27	84	3.29	.259	2	.087	-6	4	-0.8
1917*	Chi-A	11	6	.647	**50**	9	1	1	**9**	173	155	56	51	1	3	74	79	1.324	2.65	100	3.02	.244	6	.130	1	12	0.2
1918	Chi-A	6	15	.286	39	11	5	0	2	139	148	73	53	1	5	40	48	1.353	3.43	80	3.61	.288	6	.143	-9	3	-1.2

YEAR	TM-L	W	L	PCT	G	GS	CG	SH	SV	IP	H	R	ER	HR	HB	BB	SO	RAT	ERA	ERA+	CERA	OAV	BH	AVG	PR+	WS	TPW
1919	Chi-A	1	2	.333	15	1	0	0	1	41^2	58	44	36	1	1	20	17	1.872	7.78	41	6.20	.333	1	.111	-22	0	-2.3
1922	StL-A	5	2	.714	20	10	3	0	1	79^2	93	37	29	1	1	38	48	1.644	3.28	126	4.64	.304	2	.087	6	5	0.3
1923	StL-A	16	14	.533	38	29	16	0	1	226^1	221	111	99	4	12	87	96	1.361	3.94	106	3.44	.262	15	.211	3	16	0.6
1924	StL-A	15	12	.556	41	27	12	1	4	219^2	246	126	110	16	3	69	65	1.434	4.51	100	4.22	.292	13	.171	-2	15	-0.3
1925	StL-A	7	9	.438	38	15	5	0	2	159	172	96	77	19	3	61	53	1.465	4.36	107	4.59	.284	8	.174	4	10	0.2
Total	**10**	**71**	**66**	**.518**	**286**	**112**	**44**	**2**	**23**	**1186**	**1235**	**618**	**512**	**45**	**34**	**455**	**484**	**1.425**	**3.89**	**93**	**3.91**	**.277**	**56**	**.160**	**-30**	**67**	**-3.8**

• DANIEL, Chuck

Charles Edward Daniel b: 9/17/1933, Bluffton, AR BR/TR, 6'2", 195 lbs. Deb: 9/21/1957

YEAR	TM-L	W	L	PCT	G	GS	CG	SH	SV	IP	H	R	ER	HR	HB	BB	SO	RAT	ERA	ERA+	CERA	OAV	BH	AVG	PR+	WS	TPW
1957	Det-A	0	0	....	1	0	0	0	0	2^1	3	2	2	1	0	0	2	1.286	7.71	50	6.89	.333	0	....	-1	0	-0.1

• DANIELS, Bennie

Bennie Daniels b: 6/17/1932, Tuscaloosa, AL BL/TR, 6'1.5", 193 lbs. Deb: 9/24/1957

YEAR	TM-L	W	L	PCT	G	GS	CG	SH	SV	IP	H	R	ER	HR	HB	BB	SO	RAT	ERA	ERA+	CERA	OAV	BH	AVG	PR+	WS	TPW
1957	Pit-N	0	1	.000	1	1	0	0	0	7	5	2	1	0	0	3	2	1.143	1.29	295	2.11	.208	0	.000	2	1	0.2
1958	Pit-N	0	3	.000	8	5	1	0	0	27^2	31	19	17	3	1	15	7	1.663	5.53	70	5.50	.290	1	.125	-6	0	-0.6
1959	Pit-N	7	9	.438	34	12	0	0	1	100^2	115	69	61	9	2	39	67	1.530	5.45	71	4.69	.287	9	.310	-19	3	-1.3
1960	Pit-N	1	3	.250	10	6	0	0	0	40^1	52	35	35	4	0	17	16	1.711	7.81	48	5.70	.311	3	.188	-19	0	-2.0
1961	Was-A	12	11	.522	32	28	12	1	0	212	184	90	81	14	3	80	110	1.245	3.44	114	3.09	.237	15	.197	11	14	1.4
1962	Was-A	7	16	.304	44	21	3	1	2	161^1	172	98	87	14	2	68	66	1.488	4.85	83	4.51	.280	6	.130	-14	4	-1.5
1963	Was-A	5	10	.333	35	24	6	1	1	168^2	163	90	82	19	1	58	88	1.310	4.38	85	3.64	.250	7	.152	-12	6	-1.2
1964	Was-A	8	10	.444	33	24	3	2	0	163	147	75	67	20	0	64	73	1.294	3.70	100	3.63	.245	6	.128	-1	8	0.0
1965	Was-A	5	13	.278	33	18	1	0	1	116^1	135	75	61	16	0	39	42	1.496	4.72	74	4.89	.290	4	.133	-15	1	-1.6
Total	**9**	**45**	**76**	**.372**	**230**	**139**	**26**	**5**	**5**	**997**	**1004**	**553**	**492**	**99**	**9**	**383**	**471**	**1.391**	**4.44**	**85**	**4.04**	**.264**	**51**	**.170**	**-73**	**37**	**-6.6**

• DANIELS, Charlie

Charles L. Daniels b: 7/1/1861, Roxbury, MA d: 2/9/1938, Boston, MA Deb: 4/18/1884

YEAR	TM-L	W	L	PCT	G	GS	CG	SH	SV	IP	H	R	ER	HR	HB	BB	SO	RAT	ERA	ERA+	CERA	OAV	BH	AVG	PR+	WS	TPW
1884	Bos-U	0	2	.000	2	2	2	0	0	16^2	20	14	8	0	....	2	12	1.320	4.32	69	....	.279	3	.273	-3	1	-0.2

• DANIELS, Pete

Peter J. "Smiling Pete" Daniels b: 4/8/1864, County Caven, Ireland d: 2/13/1928, Indianapolis, IN BL/TL Deb: 4/19/1890

YEAR	TM-L	W	L	PCT	G	GS	CG	SH	SV	IP	H	R	ER	HR	HB	BB	SO	RAT	ERA	ERA+	CERA	OAV	BH	AVG	PR+	WS	TPW
1890	Pit-N	1	2	.333	4	4	3	0	0	28	40	29	22	1	3	12	8	1.857	7.07	46	....	.326	4	.333	-10	0	-0.8
1898	StL-N	1	6	.143	10	6	3	0	0	54^2	62	41	22	0	3	14	13	1.390	3.62	104	3.68	.284	3	.176	3	3	0.3
Total	**2**	**2**	**8**	**.200**	**14**	**10**	**6**	**0**	**0**	**82^2**	**102**	**70**	**44**	**1**	**6**	**26**	**21**	**1.548**	**4.79**	**73**	**2.44**	**.299**	**7**	**.241**	**-7**	**3**	**-0.5**

• DARBY, George

George William "Deacon" Darby b: 2/6/1869, Kansas City, MO d: 2/25/1937, Sacramento, CA BR/TR, 5'10.5", 160 lbs. Deb: 4/28/1893

YEAR	TM-L	W	L	PCT	G	GS	CG	SH	SV	IP	H	R	ER	HR	HB	BB	SO	RAT	ERA	ERA+	CERA	OAV	BH	AVG	PR+	WS	TPW
1893	Cin-N	1	1	.500	4	3	2	0	0	29	41	32	25	2	3	18	6	2.034	7.76	62	7.47	.324	3	.300	-10	0	-0.8

• DARCY, Pat

Patrick Leonard Darcy b: 5/12/1950, Troy, OH BL/TR, 6'3", 175 lbs. Deb: 9/12/1974

YEAR	TM-L	W	L	PCT	G	GS	CG	SH	SV	IP	H	R	ER	HR	HB	BB	SO	RAT	ERA	ERA+	CERA	OAV	BH	AVG	PR+	WS	TPW
1974	Cin-N	1	0	1.000	6	2	0	0	0	17	17	7	7	2	0	8	14	1.471	3.71	94	4.48	.262	1	.333	-1	1	-0.1
1975*	Cin-N	11	5	.688	27	22	1	0	1	130^2	134	54	52	4	0	59	46	1.477	3.58	100	3.80	.269	4	.085	-4	7	-0.7
1976	Cin-N	2	3	.400	11	4	0	0	2	39	41	27	27	2	0	22	15	1.615	6.23	56	4.64	.279	2	.182	-12	0	-1.2
Total	**3**	**14**	**8**	**.636**	**44**	**28**	**1**	**0**	**3**	**186^2**	**192**	**88**	**86**	**8**	**0**	**89**	**75**	**1.505**	**4.15**	**86**	**4.03**	**.270**	**7**	**.115**	**-17**	**8**	**-2.0**

• DARENSBOURG, Vic

Victor Anthony Darensbourg b: 11/13/1970, Los Angeles, CA BL/TL, 5'10", 165 lbs. Deb: 4/1/1998

YEAR	TM-L	W	L	PCT	G	GS	CG	SH	SV	IP	H	R	ER	HR	HB	BB	SO	RAT	ERA	ERA+	CERA	OAV	BH	AVG	PR+	WS	TPW
1998	Fla-N	0	7	.000	59	0	0	0	1	71	52	29	29	5	0	30	74	1.155	3.68	111	2.47	.207	0	.000	4	3	0.3
1999	Fla-N	0	1	.000	56	0	0	0	0	34^2	50	36	34	3	5	21	16	2.048	8.83	49	7.90	.340	0	....	-17	0	-1.6
2000	Fla-N	5	3	.625	56	0	0	0	0	62	61	32	28	7	2	28	59	1.435	4.06	109	4.33	.260	2	.250	3	5	0.3
2001	Fla-N	1	2	.333	58	0	0	0	1	48^2	52	24	23	4	1	10	33	1.274	4.25	99	3.52	.277	0	....	-1	3	0.0
2002	Fla-N	1	2	.333	42	0	0	0	0	48^1	61	34	33	10	2	26	33	1.800	6.14	64	6.98	.305	0	.000	-12	0	-1.2
2003	Col-N	0	0	....	3	0	0	0	0	2^1	4	1	0	0	0	0	0	1.714	0.00	....	5.18	.333	0	....	1	0	0.1
	Mon-N	0	0	....	6	0	0	0	0	6^2	13	8	8	2	0	1	4	2.100	10.80	47	10.54	.406	0	.000	-4	0	-0.4
	Yr.	0	0	....	9	0	0	0	0	9	17	9	8	2	0	1	4	2.000	8.00	63	9.15	.386	0	.000	-3	0	-0.3
Total	**6**	**7**	**15**	**.318**	**280**	**0**	**0**	**0**	**2**	**273^2**	**293**	**164**	**155**	**31**	**10**	**116**	**219**	**1.495**	**5.10**	**83**	**4.78**	**.275**	**2**	**.111**	**-26**	**11**	**-2.5**

• DARLING, Ron

Ronald Maurice Darling b: 8/19/1960, Honolulu, HI BR/TR, 6'3", 195 lbs. Deb: 9/6/1983

YEAR	TM-L	W	L	PCT	G	GS	CG	SH	SV	IP	H	R	ER	HR	HB	BB	SO	RAT	ERA	ERA+	CERA	OAV	BH	AVG	PR+	WS	TPW
1983	NY-N	1	3	.250	5	5	1	0	0	35^1	31	11	11	0	3	17	23	1.358	2.80	129	3.41	.248	1	.100	3	3	0.2
1984	NY-N	12	9	.571	33	33	2	2	0	205^2	179	97	87	17	5	104	136	1.376	3.81	93	3.74	.235	10	.149	-6	9	-0.7
1985	NY-N★	16	6	.727	36	35	4	2	0	248	214	93	80	21	3	114	167	1.323	2.90	119	3.53	.235	13	.171	17	17	2.0
1986*	NY-N	15	6	.714	34	34	4	2	0	237	203	84	74	21	3	81	184	1.198	2.81	126	3.09	.234	8	.099	18	17	1.7
1987	NY-N	12	8	.600	32	32	2	0	0	207^2	183	111	99	24	3	96	167	1.343	4.29	88	3.79	.233	8	.123	-9	8	-0.9
1988*	NY-N	17	9	.654	34	34	7	4	0	240^2	218	97	87	24	5	60	161	1.155	3.25	99	3.12	.245	18	.220	-1	13	0.5
1989	NY-N	14	14	.500	33	33	4	0	0	217^1	214	100	85	19	3	70	153	1.307	3.52	93	3.60	.258	9	.123	-4	9	-0.4
1990	NY-N	7	9	.438	33	18	1	0	0	126	135	73	63	20	5	44	99	1.421	4.50	83	4.77	.273	4	.129	-9	2	-0.9
1991	NY-N	5	6	.455	17	17	0	0	0	102^1	96	50	44	9	6	28	58	1.212	3.87	94	3.39	.251	4	.118	-0	4	-0.1
	Mon-N	0	2	.000	3	3	0	0	0	17	25	16	14	6	1	5	11	1.765	7.41	49	8.75	.333	1	.167	-7	0	-0.7
	Yr.	5	8	.385	20	20	0	0	0	119^1	121	66	58	15	7	33	69	1.291	4.37	83	4.16	.265	5	.125	-8	4	-0.8
	Oak-A	3	7	.300	12	12	0	0	0	75	64	34	34	7	2	38	60	1.360	4.08	94	3.74	.237	0	....	-2	3	-0.2
1992*	Oak-A	15	10	.600	33	33	4	3	0	206^1	198	98	84	15	4	72	99	1.309	3.66	102	3.55	.253	0	....	0	10	0.0
1993	Oak-A	5	9	.357	31	29	3	0	0	178	198	107	102	22	5	72	95	1.517	5.16	79	4.97	.281	0	....	-21	4	-2.0
1994	Oak-A	10	11	.476	25	**25**	4	0	0	160	162	89	80	18	7	59	108	1.381	4.50	98	4.33	.267	0	.000	-3	7	-0.3
1995	Oak-A	4	7	.364	21	21	1	0	0	104	124	79	72	16	4	46	69	1.635	6.23	71	5.80	.296	0	....	-20	0	-1.9
Total	**13**	**136**	**116**	**.540**	**382**	**364**	**37**	**13**	**0**	**2360^1**	**2244**	**1139**	**1016**	**239**	**59**	**906**	**1590**	**1.335**	**3.87**	**96**	**3.86**	**.252**	**76**	**.144**	**-45**	**106**	**-3.8**

• DARNELL, Bob

Robert Jack Darnell b: 11/6/1930, Wewoka, OK d: 1/1/1995, Fredericksburg, TX BR/TR, 5'10", 175 lbs. Deb: 8/10/1954

YEAR	TM-L	W	L	PCT	G	GS	CG	SH	SV	IP	H	R	ER	HR	HB	BB	SO	RAT	ERA	ERA+	CERA	OAV	BH	AVG	PR+	WS	TPW
1954	Bro-N	0	0	....	6	1	0	0	0	14^1	15	7	5	2	0	7	5	1.535	3.14	130	5.00	.278	0	.000	1	1	0.1
1956	Bro-N	0	0	....	1	0	0	0	0	1^1	1	0	0	0	0	0	0	.750	0.00	....	1.13	.200	0	....	1	0	0.1
Total	**2**	**0**	**0**	**....**	**7**	**1**	**0**	**0**	**0**	**15^2**	**16**	**7**	**5**	**2**	**0**	**7**	**5**	**1.468**	**2.87**	**142**	**4.67**	**.271**	**0**	**.000**	**2**	**1**	**0.2**

• DARR, Mike

Michael Edward Darr b: 3/23/1956, Pomona, CA BR/TR, 6'4", 190 lbs. Deb: 9/6/1977

YEAR	TM-L	W	L	PCT	G	GS	CG	SH	SV	IP	H	R	ER	HR	HB	BB	SO	RAT	ERA	ERA+	CERA	OAV	BH	AVG	PR+	WS	TPW
1977	Tor-A	0	1	.000	1	1	0	0	0	1^1	3	5	5	1	1	4	1	5.250	33.75	12	38.11	.429	0		-4	0	-0.4

• DARROW, George

George Oliver Darrow b: 7/12/1903, Beloit, KS d: 3/24/1983, Sun City, AZ BL/TL, 6', 180 lbs. Deb: 4/22/1934

YEAR	TM-L	W	L	PCT	G	GS	CG	SH	SV	IP	H	R	ER	HR	HB	BB	SO	RAT	ERA	ERA+	CERA	OAV	BH	AVG	PR+	WS	TPW
1934	Phi-N	2	6	.250	17	8	2	0	1	49	57	37	30	4	4	28	14	1.735	5.51	86	5.85	.302	2	.133	-5	1	-0.4

• DARWIN, Danny

Daniel Wayne "Bonham Bullet,Dr. Death" Darwin b: 10/25/1955, Bonham, TX BR/TR, 6'3", 190 lbs. Deb: 9/8/1978

YEAR	TM-L	W	L	PCT	G	GS	CG	SH	SV	IP	H	R	ER	HR	HB	BB	SO	RAT	ERA	ERA+	CERA	OAV	BH	AVG	PR+	WS	TPW
1978	Tex-A	1	0	1.000	3	1	0	0	0	8^2	11	4	4	0	0	1	8	1.385	4.15	90	3.89	.324	0	....	-0	1	0.0
1979	Tex-A	4	4	.500	20	6	1	0	0	78	50	36	35	5	5	30	58	1.026	4.04	103	2.15	.186	0	....	0	4	0.0
1980	Tex-A	13	4	.765	53	2	0	0	8	109^2	98	37	32	4	2	50	104	1.350	2.63	148	3.24	.243	0	....	17	12	1.7
1981	Tex-A	9	9	.500	22	22	6	2	0	146	115	67	59	12	6	57	98	1.178	3.64	95	2.91	.218	0	....	-5	6	-0.6
1982	Tex-A	10	8	.556	56	1	0	0	7	89	95	38	34	6	2	37	61	1.483	3.44	113	4.19	.279	0	....	5	9	0.5
1983	Tex-A	8	13	.381	28	26	9	2	0	183	175	86	71	9	3	62	92	1.295	3.49	115	3.26	.250	0	....	11	10	1.1
1984	Tex-A	8	12	.400	35	32	5	1	0	223^2	249	110	98	19	4	54	123	1.355	3.94	105	4.04	.279	0	....	7	11	0.7
1985	Mil-A	8	18	.308	39	29	11	1	2	217^2	212	112	92	34	4	65	125	1.273	3.80	110	3.94	.254	0	....	9	12	0.9
1986	Mil-A	6	8	.429	27	14	5	1	0	130^1	120	62	51	13	3	35	80	1.189	3.52	123	3.23	.246	0	....	13	9	1.2
	Hou-N	5	2	.714	12	8	1	0	0	54^1	50	19	14	3	0	9	40	1.086	2.32	155	2.44	.239	1	.063	8	5	0.7
1987	Hou-N	9	10	.474	33	30	3	1	0	195^2	184	87	78	17	5	69	134	1.293	3.59	109	3.45	.246	12	.182	8	12	1.0
1988	Hou-N	8	13	.381	44	20	3	0	3	192	189	86	82	20	7	48	129	1.234	3.84	86	3.50	.259	4	.071	-10	6	-1.2
1989	Hou-N	11	4	.733	68	0	0	0	7	122	92	34	32	8	2	33	104	1.025	2.36	143	2.10	.212	2	.118	15	14	1.5
1990	Hou-N	11	4	.733	48	17	3	0	2	162^2	136	42	40	11	4	31	109	1.027	**2.21**	**168**	**2.31**	.225	5	.132	26	17	2.8
1991	Bos-A	3	6	.333	12	12	0	0	0	68	71	39	39	15	4	15	42	1.265	5.16	83	4.58	.263	0	....	-6	2	-0.6
1992	Bos-A	9	9	.500	51	15	2	0	3	161^1	159	76	71	11	5	53	124	1.314	3.96	106	3.52	.257	0	....	4	11	0.4
1993	Bos-A	15	11	.577	34	34	2	1	0	229^1	196	93	83	31	3	49	130	1.068	3.26	142	2.82	.230	0	....	33	20	3.2
1994	Bos-A	7	5	.583	13	13	0	0	0	75^2	101	54	53	13	1	24	54	1.652	6.30	80	6.09	.317	0	....	-11	3	-1.1

YEAR	TM-L	W	L	PCT	G	GS	CG	SH	SV	IP	H	R	ER	HR	HB	BB	SO	RAT	ERA	ERA+	CERA	OAV	BH	AVG	PR+	WS	TPW
1995	Tor-A	1	8	.111	13	11	1	0	0	65	91	60	55	13	3	24	36	1.769	7.62	62	7.39	.340	0	....	-21	0	-2.0
	Tex-A	2	2	.500	7	4	0	0	0	34	40	27	27	12	1	7	22	1.382	7.15	67	6.27	.292	0	....	-9	0	-0.8
	Yr.	3	10	.231	20	15	1	0	0	99	131	87	82	25	4	31	58	1.636	7.45	64	7.00	.323	0	....	-30	0	-2.8
1996	Pit-N	7	9	.438	19	19	0	0	0	122^1	117	48	41	9	6	16	69	1.087	3.02	145	2.86	.253	8	.205	20	10	2.2
	Hou-N	3	2	.600	15	6	0	0	0	42^1	43	31	28	7	6	11	27	1.276	5.95	65	4.50	.267	1	.100	-9	0	-0.9
	Yr.	10	11	.476	34	25	0	0	0	164^2	160	79	69	16	12	27	96	1.136	3.77	110	3.28	.257	9	.184	11	10	1.3
1997	Chi-A	4	8	.333	21	17	1	0	0	113^1	130	60	52	21	1	31	62	1.421	4.13	106	4.99	.286	0	.000	5	6	0.4
	SF-N	1	3	.250	10	7	0	0	0	44	51	26	24	5	1	14	30	1.477	4.91	82	4.78	.288	2	.133	-4	1	-0.4
1998	SF-N	8	10	.444	33	25	0	0	0	148^2	176	97	91	23	3	49	81	1.513	5.51	72	5.29	.297	4	.089	-25	1	-2.7
Total	21	171	182	.484	716	371	53	9	32	3016^2	2951	1431	1286	321	81	874	1942	1.268	3.84	106	3.66	.256	39	.128	79	182	8.1

• DARWIN, Jeff

Jeffrey Scott Darwin b: 7/6/1969, Sherman, TX BR/TR, 6'3", 180 lbs. Deb: 6/13/1994

YEAR	TM-L	W	L	PCT	G	GS	CG	SH	SV	IP	H	R	ER	HR	HB	BB	SO	RAT	ERA	ERA+	CERA	OAV	BH	AVG	PR+	WS	TPW
1994	Sea-A	0	0	....	2	0	0	0	0	4	7	6	6	1	1	3	1	2.500	13.50	36	12.87	.389	0	....	-4	0	-0.3
1996	Chi-A	0	1	.000	22	0	0	0	0	30^2	26	10	10	5	2	9	15	1.141	2.93	162	3.54	.232	0	....	6	3	0.6
1997	Chi-A	0	1	.000	14	0	0	0	0	13^2	17	8	8	1	0	7	9	1.756	5.27	83	5.60	.298	0	....	-1	0	-0.1
Total	3	0	2	.000	38	0	0	0	0	48^1	50	24	24	7	3	19	25	1.428	4.47	104	4.90	.267	0	....	1	3	0.1

• DASHNER, Lee

Lee Claire "Lefty" Dashner b: 4/25/1887, Renault, IL d: 12/16/1959, El Dorado, KS BB/TL, 5'11.5", 192 lbs. Deb: 8/4/1913

YEAR	TM-L	W	L	PCT	G	GS	CG	SH	SV	IP	H	R	ER	HR	HB	BB	SO	RAT	ERA	ERA+	CERA	OAV	BH	AVG	PR+	WS	TPW
1913	Cle-A	0	0	....	1	0	0	0	0	1^2	0	1	1	0	0	0	2	.000	5.40	56	0.00	.000	0	....	-0	0	0.0

• DASSO, Frank

Frank Joseph Nicholas Dasso b: 8/31/1917, Chicago, IL BR/TR, 5'11.5", 185 lbs. Deb: 4/22/1945

YEAR	TM-L	W	L	PCT	G	GS	CG	SH	SV	IP	H	R	ER	HR	HB	BB	SO	RAT	ERA	ERA+	CERA	OAV	BH	AVG	PR+	WS	TPW
1945	Cin-N	4	5	.444	16	12	6	0	0	95^2	89	50	39	9	0	53	39	1.484	3.67	102	4.12	.253	5	.161	1	5	0.1
1946	Cin-N	0	0	....	2	0	0	0	0	1	2	3	3	0	0	2	1	4.000	27.00	12	15.81	.400	0	....	-3	0	-0.3
Total	2	4	5	.444	18	12	6	0	0	96^2	91	53	42	9	0	55	40	1.510	3.91	95	4.25	.255	5	.161	-2	5	-0.2

• DAUB, Dan

Daniel William "Mickey" Daub b: 1/12/1868, Middletown, OH d: 3/25/1951, Bradenton, FL BR/TR, 5'10", 160 lbs. Deb: 8/31/1892

YEAR	TM-L	W	L	PCT	G	GS	CG	SH	SV	IP	H	R	ER	HR	HB	BB	SO	RAT	ERA	ERA+	CERA	OAV	BH	AVG	PR+	WS	TPW
1892	Cin-N	1	2	.333	4	3	2	0	0	25	23	10	8	0	2	13	7	1.440	2.88	113	3.51	.235	0	.000	1	2	0.0
1893	Bro-N	6	6	.500	12	12	12	0	0	103	104	64	44	3	5	61	25	1.602	3.84	115	4.36	.255	8	.190	8	7	0.5
1894	Bro-N	10	12	.455	34	27	15	0	0	224	291	209	152	7	18	91	45	1.705	6.11	81	5.50	.311	18	.189	-26	7	-2.5
1895	Bro-N	10	10	.500	25	21	16	0	0	184^2	212	134	88	4	11	51	36	1.424	4.29	102	4.01	.284	14	.197	-0	11	-0.2
1896	Bro-N	12	11	.522	32	24	18	0	0	225	255	120	90	4	8	63	53	1.413	3.60	114	3.83	.283	19	.226	14	16	1.4
1897	Bro-N	6	11	.353	19	16	11	0	0	137^2	180	117	93	8	10	48	19	1.656	6.08	67	5.52	.313	11	.224	-29	5	-2.2
Total	6	45	52	.464	126	103	74	0	0	899^1	1065	654	475	26	54	327	185	1.548	4.75	93	4.59	.291	70	.201	-33	48	-2.9

• DAUSS, Hooks

George August Dauss b: 9/22/1889, Indianapolis, IN d: 7/27/1963, St. Louis, MO BR/TR, 5'10.5", 168 lbs. Deb: 9/28/1912

YEAR	TM-L	W	L	PCT	G	GS	CG	SH	SV	IP	H	R	ER	HR	HB	BB	SO	RAT	ERA	ERA+	CERA	OAV	BH	AVG	PR+	WS	TPW
1912	Det-A	1	1	.500	2	2	2	0	0	17	11	7	6	0	3	9	7	1.176	3.18	103	2.52	.186	1	.250	0	1	0.1
1913	Det-A	13	12	.520	33	29	22	2	1	225	188	96	62	4	13	82	107	1.200	2.48	117	2.71	.228	14	.177	17	14	2.2
1914	Det-A	18	15	.545	45	35	22	3	3	302	286	126	96	3	18	87	150	1.235	2.86	98	3.04	.257	21	.216	2	19	0.8
1915	Det-A	24	13	.649	46	35	27	1	2	309^2	261	115	86	1	11	115	132	1.214	2.50	121	2.66	.235	15	.146	24	25	2.6
1916	Det-A	19	12	.613	39	29	18	1	4	238^2	220	102	85	2	16	90	95	1.299	3.21	89	3.29	.257	16	.222	-5	17	0.4
1917	Det-A	17	14	.548	37	31	22	6	2	270^2	243	105	73	3	7	87	102	1.219	2.43	109	2.76	.245	11	.126	11	15	1.1
1918	Det-A	12	16	.429	33	26	21	1	3	249^2	243	105	83	3	9	58	73	1.206	2.99	89	2.82	.263	14	.182	3	13	0.8
1919	Det-A	21	9	.700	34	32	22	2	0	256^1	262	125	101	9	5	63	73	1.268	3.55	90	3.27	.267	14	.144	-6	13	-0.9
1920	Det-A	13	21	.382	38	32	18	0	0	270^1	308	158	107	11	8	84	82	1.450	3.56	104	4.14	.289	14	.169	10	14	1.1
1921	Det-A	10	15	.400	32	28	16	0	1	233	275	141	112	11	13	81	68	1.528	4.33	99	4.60	.297	23	.261	4	10	0.6
1922	Det-A	13	13	.500	39	25	12	1	4	218^2	251	123	102	7	6	59	78	1.418	4.20	92	3.86	.289	15	.208	-3	12	-0.1
1923	Det-A	21	13	.618	50	39	22	4	3	316	331	140	127	10	7	78	105	1.294	3.62	107	3.28	.272	24	.231	12	25	1.6
1924	Det-A	12	11	.522	40	10	5	0	6	131^1	155	78	67	6	1	40	44	1.485	4.59	90	4.24	.302	5	.132	-7	8	-0.8
1925	Det-A	16	11	.593	35	30	16	1	1	228	238	110	80	11	4	85	58	1.417	3.16	136	3.81	.272	15	.185	29	18	2.8
1926	Det-A	12	6	.667	35	5	0	0	9	124^1	135	63	58	6	0	49	27	1.480	4.20	97	4.13	.287	10	.238	-1	11	0.3
Total	15	222	182	.550	538	388	245	22	39	3390^2	3407	1594	1245	87	121	1067	1201	1.320	3.30	102	3.39	.266	212	.189	90	215	12.6

• DAVALILLO, Vic

Victor Jose (Romero) Davalillo b: 7/31/1936, Cabimas, Venezuela BL/TL, 5'7", 155 lbs. Deb: 4/9/1963 ♦

YEAR	TM-L	W	L	PCT	G	GS	CG	SH	SV	IP	H	R	ER	HR	HB	BB	SO	RAT	ERA	ERA+	CERA	OAV	BH	AVG	PR+	WS	TPW
1969	StL-N	0	0	....	2	0	0	0	0	0	2	1	1	0	0	2	0	....	∞	....	∞	1.000	26	.265	-1	2	-0.4

• DAVENPORT, Claude

Claude Edwin "Big Dave" Davenport b: 5/28/1898, Runge, TX d: 6/13/1976, Corpus Christi, TX BR/TR, 6'6", 193 lbs. Deb: 10/2/1920

YEAR	TM-L	W	L	PCT	G	GS	CG	SH	SV	IP	H	R	ER	HR	HB	BB	SO	RAT	ERA	ERA+	CERA	OAV	BH	AVG	PR+	WS	TPW
1920	NY-N	0	0	....	1	0	0	0	0	2	2	1	1	1	0	1	0	1.500	4.50	67	7.17	.250	0	.000	-0	0	-0.1

• DAVENPORT, Dave

David W. Davenport b: 2/20/1890, DeRidder, LA d: 10/16/1954, El Dorado, AR BR/TR, 6'6", 220 lbs. Deb: 4/17/1914

YEAR	TM-L	W	L	PCT	G	GS	CG	SH	SV	IP	H	R	ER	HR	HB	BB	SO	RAT	ERA	ERA+	CERA	OAV	BH	AVG	PR+	WS	TPW
1914	Cin-N	2	2	.500	10	6	3	1	2	54	38	18	15	1	3	30	22	1.259	2.50	117	2.58	.202	2	.111	3	4	0.2
	StL-F	8	13	.381	33	26	13	2	4	215^2	204	100	83	3	7	80	142	1.317	3.46	100	3.18	.251	6	.088	4	13	-0.1
1915	StL-F	22	18	.550	**55**	**46**	**30**	**10**	1	**392^2**	300	116	96	5	5	96	**229**	1.008	2.20	141	1.82	**.215**	12	.092	**33**	**34**	2.7
1916	StL-A	12	11	.522	**59**	31	13	1	2	290^2	267	112	92	4	8	100	129	1.263	2.85	96	3.07	.256	10	.137	-10	15	-0.8
1917	StL-A	17	17	.500	47	**39**	20	2	2	280^2	273	137	96	5	8	105	100	1.347	3.08	84	3.34	.260	9	.098	-15	9	-2.3
1918	StL-A	10	11	.476	31	22	12	2	1	180	182	84	65	0	7	69	60	1.394	3.25	84	3.51	.273	7	.135	-11	8	-1.1
1919	StL-A	2	11	.154	24	16	5	0	0	123^1	135	74	54	4	2	41	37	1.427	3.94	84	3.92	.280	3	.077	-10	2	-1.4
Total	6	73	83	.468	259	186	96	18	12	1537	1399	641	501	22	40	521	719	1.249	2.93	100	2.92	.248	49	.104	-5	85	-2.7

• DAVENPORT, Joe

Joseph Jonathan Davenport b: 3/24/1976, Chicago, IL BR/TR, 6'5", 225 lbs. Deb: 7/20/1999

YEAR	TM-L	W	L	PCT	G	GS	CG	SH	SV	IP	H	R	ER	HR	HB	BB	SO	RAT	ERA	ERA+	CERA	OAV	BH	AVG	PR+	WS	TPW
1999	Chi-A	0	0	....	3	0	0	0	0	1^2	1	0	0	0	0	2	0	1.800	0.00	....	4.62	.200	0		1	0	0.1
2001	Col-N	0	0	....	7	0	0	0	0	10^1	8	7	4	1	0	7	8	1.452	3.48	153	3.98	.222	1	1.000	2	1	0.2
Total	2	0	0	....	10	0	0	0	0	12	9	7	4	1	0	9	8	1.500	3.00	178	4.07	.220	1	1.000	3	1	0.3

• DAVENPORT, Lum

Joubert Lum Davenport b: 6/27/1900, Tucson, AZ d: 4/21/1961, Dallas, TX BL/TL, 6'1", 165 lbs. Deb: 5/2/1921

YEAR	TM-L	W	L	PCT	G	GS	CG	SH	SV	IP	H	R	ER	HR	HB	BB	SO	RAT	ERA	ERA+	CERA	OAV	BH	AVG	PR+	WS	TPW
1921	Chi-A	0	3	.000	13	2	0	0	0	35^1	41	35	27	1	1	32	9	2.066	6.88	62	6.49	.318	7	.412	-10	1	-0.8
1922	Chi-A	1	1	.500	9	1	0	0	0	16^2	14	21	20	2	0	13	9	1.620	10.80	38	4.77	.233	0	.000	-13	0	-1.2
1923	Chi-A	0	0	....	2	0	0	0	0	4^1	7	4	3	0	0	4	1	2.538	6.23	64	10.54	.438	1	1.000	-1	0	-0.1
1924	Chi-A	0	0	....	1	0	0	0	0	2	1	1	0	0	0	2	1	1.500	0.00	....	2.23	.125	0	....	1	0	0.1
Total	4	1	4	.200	25	3	0	0	0	58^1	63	61	50	3	1	51	20	1.954	7.71	54	6.15	.296	8	.381	-23	1	-2.0

• DAVEY, Mike

Michael Gerard Davey b: 6/2/1952, Spokane, WA BR/TL, 6'2", 190 lbs. Deb: 8/13/1977

YEAR	TM-L	W	L	PCT	G	GS	CG	SH	SV	IP	H	R	ER	HR	HB	BB	SO	RAT	ERA	ERA+	CERA	OAV	BH	AVG	PR+	WS	TPW
1977	Atl-N	0	0	....	16	0	0	0	2	16	19	9	9	1	0	9	7	1.750	5.06	88	5.00	.302	0	.000	-1	1	-0.1
1978	Atl-N	0	0	....	3	0	0	0	0	2^2	1	0	0	0	0	1	0	.750	0.00	....	0.94	.125	0	....	1	0	0.1
Total	2	0	0	....	19	0	0	0	2	18^2	20	9	9	1	0	10	7	1.607	4.34	103	4.42	.282	0	.000	1	1	0.1

• DAVEY, Tom

Thomas Joseph Davey b: 9/11/1973, Garden City, MI BR/TR, 6'7", 230 lbs. Deb: 4/6/1999

YEAR	TM-L	W	L	PCT	G	GS	CG	SH	SV	IP	H	R	ER	HR	HB	BB	SO	RAT	ERA	ERA+	CERA	OAV	BH	AVG	PR+	WS	TPW
1999	Tor-A	1	1	.500	29	0	0	0	1	44	40	28	23	5	3	26	42	1.500	4.70	105	4.65	.241	0	....	1	2	0.1
	Sea-A	1	0	1.000	16	0	0	0	0	21	22	13	11	0	4	14	17	1.714	4.71	106	5.28	.268	0	....	1	1	0.1
	Yr.	2	1	.667	45	0	0	0	1	65	62	41	34	5	7	40	59	1.569	4.71	105	4.86	.250	0	....	2	3	0.2
2000	SD-N	2	1	.667	11	0	0	0	0	12^2	12	1	1	0	0	2	6	1.105	0.71	607	2.33	.250	0	....	5	2	0.5
2001	SD-N	2	4	.333	39	0	0	0	0	38	41	22	19	3	1	17	37	1.526	4.50	89	4.53	.272	0	....	-1	2	-0.1
2002	SD-N	1	0	1.000	19	0	0	0	0	21	23	14	13	2	3	11	21	1.619	5.57	68	5.63	.288	0	....	-4	0	-0.4
Total	4	7	6	.538	114	0	0	0	1	136^2	138	78	67	10	11	70	123	1.522	4.41	99	4.65	.262	0	....	1	7	0.1

• DAVIAULT, Ray

Raymond Joseph Robert Daviault b: 5/27/1934, Montreal, Canada BR/TR, 6'1", 170 lbs. Deb: 4/13/1962

YEAR	TM-L	W	L	PCT	G	GS	CG	SH	SV	IP	H	R	ER	HR	HB	BB	SO	RAT	ERA	ERA+	CERA	OAV	BH	AVG	PR+	WS	TPW
1962	NY-N	1	5	.167	36	3	0	0	0	81	92	64	56	14	4	48	51	1.728	6.22	67	6.46	.288	1	.067	-17	0	-1.8

• DAVIDSON, Bob

Robert Banks Davidson b: 1/6/1963, Bad Kurznach, West Germany BR/TR, 6', 185 lbs. Deb: 7/15/1989

YEAR	TM-L	W	L	PCT	G	GS	CG	SH	SV	IP	H	R	ER	HR	HB	BB	SO	RAT	ERA	ERA+	CERA	OAV	BH	AVG	PR+	WS	TPW
1989	NY-A	0	0	....	1	0	0	0	0	1	1	2	2	1	0	1	0	2.000	18.00	21	14.27	.250	0	....	-2	0	-0.2

YEAR	TM-L	W	L	PCT	G	GS	CG	SH	SV	IP	H	R	ER	HR	HB	BB	SO	RAT	ERA	ERA+	CERA	OAV	BH	AVG	PR+	WS	TPW
• DAVIDSON, Ted	Thomas Eugene Davidson b: 10/4/1939, Las Vegas, NV BR/TL, 6', 192 lbs. Deb: 7/24/1965																										
1965	Cin-N	4	3	.571	24	1	0	0	1	68^{2}	57	21	17	5	2	17	54	1.078	2.23	168	2.52	.233	0	.000	12	6	1.0
1966	Cin-N	5	4	.556	54	0	0	0	4	85^{1}	82	41	37	11	1	23	54	1.230	3.90	100	3.56	.253	0	.000	1	6	0.0
1967	Cin-N	1	0	1.000	9	0	0	0	0	13	13	6	6	0	0	3	6	1.231	4.15	90	2.59	.250	0	....	-1	1	-0.1
1968	Cin-N	1	0	1.000	23	0	0	0	0	21^{2}	27	15	15	3	0	7	7	1.569	6.23	51	5.47	.307	0	.000	-7	0	-0.9
	Atl-N	0	0	....	4	0	0	0	0	6^{2}	10	5	5	2	0	4	3	2.100	6.75	44	9.60	.345	0	....	-3	0	-0.3
	Yr.	1	0	1.000	27	0	0	0	0	28^{1}	37	20	20	5	0	11	10	1.694	6.35	49	6.44	.316	0	.000	-10	0	-1.1
Total	**4**	**11**	**7**	**.611**	**114**	**1**	**0**	**0**	**5**	**195^{1}**	**189**	**88**	**80**	**21**	**3**	**54**	**124**	**1.244**	**3.69**	**98**	**3.55**	**.256**	**0**	**.000**	**2**	**13**	**-0.2**
• DAVIE, Jerry	Gerald Lee Davie b: 2/10/1933, Detroit, MI BR/TR, 6', 180 lbs. Deb: 4/14/1959																										
1959	Det-A	2	2	.500	11	5	1	0	0	36^{2}	40	25	17	8	4	17	20	1.555	4.17	97	5.93	.265	4	.400	-0	2	0.1
• DAVIES, Chick	Lloyd Garrison Davies b: 3/6/1892, Peabody, MA d: 9/5/1973, Middletown, CT BL/TL, 5'8", 145 lbs. Deb: 7/11/1914 ◆																										
1914	Phi-A	1	0	1.000	1	1	1	0	0	9	8	4	1	0	0	3	4	1.222	1.00	261	2.70	.258	11	.239	2	2	0.2
1915	Phi-A	1	2	.333	4	2	0	0	0	15^{1}	20	16	15	0	1	12	2	2.087	8.80	33	7.11	.339	24	.182	-10	0	-1.6
1925	NY-N	0	0	....	2	1	0	0	0	7^{1}	13	8	5	0	0	4	5	2.318	6.14	66	7.80	.361	0	.000	-2	0	-0.3
1926	NY-N	2	4	.333	38	1	0	0	**6**	89	96	60	39	3	0	35	27	1.472	3.94	95	3.84	.277	4	.222	-3	4	-0.2
Total	**4**	**4**	**6**	**.400**	**45**	**5**	**1**	**0**	**6**	**120^{2}**	**137**	**88**	**60**	**3**	**1**	**54**	**38**	**1.583**	**4.48**	**78**	**4.41**	**.290**	**39**	**.193**	**-13**	**6**	**-2.0**
• DAVIES, George	George Washington Davies b: 2/22/1868, Portage, WI d: 9/22/1906, Waterloo, WI, 180 lbs. Deb: 8/18/1891																										
1891	Mil-a	7	5	.583	12	12	12	1	0	102	94	48	30	2	3	35	61	1.265	2.65	166	....	.237	9	.243	20	10	1.9
1892	Cle-N	10	16	.385	26	26	23	0	0	215^{2}	201	112	62	4	6	69	95	1.252	2.59	131	2.89	.237	12	.138	20	13	1.4
1893	Cle-N	0	2	.000	3	3	1	0	0	15	28	25	19	1	0	10	3	2.533	11.40	43	10.28	.387	2	.333	-11	0	-0.9
	NY-N	1	1	.500	5	1	1	0	0	36^{1}	41	31	25	1	0	13	7	1.486	6.19	75	4.02	.276	4	.333	-7	2	-0.4
	Yr.	1	3	.250	8	4	2	0	0	51^{1}	69	56	44	2	0	23	10	1.792	7.71	62	5.85	.313	6	.333	-17	2	-1.2
Total	**3**	**18**	**24**	**.429**	**46**	**42**	**37**	**1**	**0**	**369**	**364**	**216**	**136**	**8**	**9**	**127**	**166**	**1.331**	**3.32**	**119**	**2.51**	**.248**	**27**	**.190**	**23**	**25**	**2.0**
• DAVIS, Bob	Robert Edward Davis b: 9/11/1933, New York, NY d: 12/22/2001, New York, NY BR/TR, 6', 170 lbs. Deb: 7/26/1958																										
1958	KC-A	0	4	.000	8	4	0	0	0	31	45	28	27	5	2	12	22	1.839	7.84	50	7.75	.346	1	.167	-13	0	-1.4
1960	KC-A	0	0	....	21	0	0	0	1	32	31	15	13	1	1	22	28	1.656	3.66	109	4.58	.263	1	.250	2	2	0.2
Total	**2**	**0**	**4**	**.000**	**29**	**4**	**0**	**0**	**1**	**63**	**76**	**43**	**40**	**6**	**3**	**34**	**50**	**1.746**	**5.71**	**69**	**6.14**	**.306**	**2**	**.200**	**-12**	**2**	**-1.2**
• DAVIS, Bud	John Wilbur "Country" Davis b: 7/7/1896, Merry Point, VA d: 5/26/1967, Williamsburg, VA BL/TR, 6', 207 lbs. Deb: 4/19/1915																										
1915	Phi-A	0	2	.000	18	2	2	0	0	66^{2}	65	53	30	1	6	59	18	1.860	4.05	72	5.57	.273	8	.308	-8	2	-0.6
• DAVIS, Curt	Curtis Benton "Coonskin" Davis b: 9/7/1903, Greenfield, MO d: 10/13/1965, Covina, CA BR/TR, 6'2", 185 lbs. Deb: 4/21/1934																										
1934	Phi-N	19	17	.528	**51**	31	18	3	5	274^{1}	283	114	90	14	7	60	99	1.250	2.95	160	3.31	.269	20	.211	50	24	4.8
1935	Phi-N	16	14	.533	44	27	19	3	2	231	264	103	94	14	7	47	74	1.346	3.66	124	3.89	.285	13	.173	25	21	2.5
1936	Phi-N	2	4	.333	10	8	3	0	0	60^{1}	71	37	31	6	1	19	18	1.492	4.62	98	4.68	.291	4	.154	1	2	0.0
	Chi-N★	11	9	.550	24	20	10	0	1	153	146	60	51	11	1	31	52	1.157	3.00	133	2.91	.251	8	.151	14	12	1.1
	Yr.	13	13	.500	34	28	13	0	1	213^{1}	217	97	82	17	2	50	70	1.252	3.46	121	3.41	.263	12	.152	15	14	1.1
1937	Chi-N	10	5	.667	28	14	8	0	1	123^{2}	138	64	56	7	5	30	32	1.358	4.08	98	3.93	.286	12	.300	-2	8	0.2
1938	StL-N	12	8	.600	40	21	8	2	3	173^{1}	187	80	70	9	1	27	36	1.235	3.63	109	3.20	.272	13	.228	7	13	0.9
1939	StL-N★	22	16	.579	49	31	13	3	7	248	279	121	100	18	3	48	70	1.319	3.63	113	3.74	.280	40	.381	11	22	2.3
1940	StL-N	0	4	.000	14	7	0	0	1	54	73	34	31	4	1	19	12	1.704	5.17	77	5.84	.327	0	.000	-6	0	-0.9
	Bro-N	8	7	.533	22	18	9	0	2	137	135	62	58	13	1	19	46	1.124	3.81	105	2.98	.256	6	.128	3	9	0.3
	Yr.	8	11	.421	36	25	9	0	3	191	208	96	89	17	2	38	58	1.288	4.19	95	3.79	.277	6	.091	-3	9	-0.6
1941★	Bro-N	13	7	.650	28	16	10	5	2	154^{1}	141	58	51	6	2	27	50	1.089	2.97	123	2.43	.244	11	.186	9	12	1.1
1942	Bro-N	15	6	.714	32	26	13	5	2	206	179	62	54	10	7	51	60	1.117	2.36	138	2.55	.233	12	.176	18	18	1.9
1943	Bro-N	10	13	.435	31	21	8	2	3	164^{1}	182	85	69	8	2	39	47	1.345	3.78	89	3.64	.281	9	.164	-5	6	-0.6
1944	Bro-N	10	11	.476	31	23	12	1	4	194	207	84	72	12	5	39	49	1.268	3.34	106	3.43	.270	10	.159	11	9	1.0
1945	Bro-N	10	10	.500	24	18	10	0	0	149^{2}	171	66	54	9	3	21	39	1.283	3.25	116	3.54	.280	7	.137	9	9	0.8
1946	Bro-N	0	0	....	1	0	0	0	0	2	3	3	3	1	1	2	0	2.500	13.50	25	15.68	.375	0	....	-2	0	-0.2
Total	**13**	**158**	**131**	**.547**	**429**	**281**	**141**	**24**	**33**	**2325**	**2459**	**1033**	**884**	**142**	**47**	**479**	**684**	**1.264**	**3.42**	**115**	**3.42**	**.270**	**165**	**.203**	**143**	**165**	**15.1**
• DAVIS, Daisy	John Henry Albert Davis b: 11/28/1858, Boston, MA d: 11/5/1902, Lynn, MA TR, 5'6.5" Deb: 5/6/1884																										
1884	StL-a	10	12	.455	25	24	20	1	0	198^{1}	196	113	64	1	14	35	143	1.165	2.90	112	....	.244	15	.172	3	13	0.0
	Bos-N	1	3	.250	4	4	3	0	0	31	50	36	27	2	....	8	13	1.871	7.84	37	....	.345	0	.000	-18	0	-1.8
1885	Bos-N	5	6	.455	11	11	10	1	0	94^{1}	110	58	45	2	....	28	30	1.463	4.29	63	....	.278	7	.189	-13	4	-1.2
Total	**2**	**16**	**21**	**.432**	**40**	**39**	**33**	**2**	**0**	**323^{2}**	**356**	**207**	**136**	**5**	**14**	**71**	**186**	**1.319**	**3.78**	**79**	**....**	**.265**	**22**	**.157**	**-28**	**17**	**-3.1**
• DAVIS, Dixie	Frank Talmadge Davis b: 10/12/1890, Wilsons Mills, NC d: 2/4/1944, Raleigh, NC BR/TR, 5'11", 155 lbs. Deb: 7/12/1912																										
1912	Cin-N	0	1	.000	7	0	0	0	0	26^{2}	25	17	8	0	1	16	12	1.538	2.70	124	3.69	.258	2	.200	2	1	0.2
1915	Chi-A	0	0	....	2	0	0	0	0	3	2	0	0	0	1	2	2	1.333	0.00	....	4.43	.250	0	....	1	0	0.1
1918	Phi-N	0	2	.000	17	2	1	0	0	47	43	25	16	1	0	30	18	1.553	3.06	98	3.67	.247	0	.000	-0	1	-0.1
1920	StL-A	18	12	.600	38	31	22	0	0	269^{1}	250	117	95	10	7	149	85	1.481	3.17	123	3.83	.256	25	.266	21	22	2.4
1921	StL-A	16	16	.500	40	36	20	2	0	265^{1}	279	150	131	12	10	123	100	1.515	4.44	101	4.32	.281	20	.211	2	15	0.0
1922	StL-A	11	6	.647	25	25	7	2	0	174^{1}	162	91	79	10	8	87	65	1.428	4.08	101	3.80	**.250**	8	.136	-3	9	-0.6
1923	StL-A	4	6	.400	19	17	5	1	0	109^{1}	106	61	44	4	5	63	36	1.546	3.62	115	4.10	.259	10	.250	5	7	0.5
1924	StL-A	11	13	.458	29	24	11	5	0	160^{1}	159	84	73	9	6	72	45	1.441	4.10	110	3.86	.263	7	.152	6	11	0.4
1925	StL-A	12	7	.632	35	22	9	0	1	180^{1}	192	121	92	10	6	106	58	1.652	4.59	102	4.77	.279	11	.172	-0	10	-0.4
1926	StL-A	3	8	.273	27	7	2	0	1	83	93	56	43	7	1	40	39	1.602	4.66	92	4.88	.292	4	.167	-4	3	-0.4
Total	**10**	**75**	**71**	**.514**	**239**	**164**	**77**	**10**	**2**	**1318^{2}**	**1311**	**722**	**581**	**63**	**45**	**688**	**460**	**1.516**	**3.97**	**107**	**4.14**	**.267**	**87**	**.197**	**31**	**79**	**2.1**
• DAVIS, Doug	Douglas P. Davis b: 9/21/1975, Sacramento, CA BR/TL, 6'3", 190 lbs. Deb: 8/9/1999																										
1999	Tex-A	0	0	....	2	0	0	0	0	2^{2}	12	10	10	3	0	0	3	4.500	33.75	15	41.42	.600	0	....	-8	0	-0.8
2000	Tex-A	7	6	.538	30	13	1	0	0	98^{2}	109	61	59	14	3	58	66	1.693	5.38	93	5.93	.288	0	....	-2	5	-0.2
2001	Tex-A	11	10	.524	30	30	1	0	0	186	220	103	92	14	3	69	115	**1.554**	4.45	105	4.90	.295	0	.000	6	8	0.5
2002	Tex-A	3	5	.375	10	10	1	1	0	59^{2}	67	36	33	7	3	22	28	1.492	4.98	95	5.05	.290	0	....	-1	3	-0.1
2003	Tex-A	0	0	....	1	1	0	0	0	3	4	4	4	2	0	4	2	2.667	12.00	41	15.81	.308	0	....	-2	0	-0.2
	Tor-A	4	6	.400	12	11	0	0	0	54	70	33	30	6	1	26	25	1.778	5.00	92	6.39	.318	0	.000	-1	2	-0.1
	Yr.	4	6	.400	13	12	0	0	0	57	74	37	34	8	1	30	27	1.825	5.37	86	6.88	.318	0	.000	-4	2	-0.4
	Mil-N	3	2	.600	8	8	1	0	0	52^{1}	49	18	15	8	0	21	35	1.338	2.58	165	4.06	.247	2	.100	11	5	0.9
Total	**5**	**28**	**29**	**.491**	**93**	**73**	**4**	**1**	**0**	**456^{1}**	**531**	**265**	**243**	**54**	**10**	**200**	**274**	**1.602**	**4.79**	**99**	**5.51**	**.294**	**2**	**.083**	**1**	**23**	**0.0**
• DAVIS, George	George Allen Davis b: 3/9/1890, Lancaster, NY d: 6/4/1961, Buffalo, NY BB/TR, 5'10.5", 175 lbs. Deb: 7/16/1912																										
1912	NY-A	1	4	.200	10	7	5	0	0	54	61	43	39	3	3	28	22	1.648	6.50	56	5.23	.293	2	.111	-14	0	-1.5
1913	Bos-N	0	0	....	2	0	0	0	0	8	7	5	4	1	0	5	3	1.500	4.50	73	4.31	.241	0	.000	-1	0	-0.1
1914	Bos-N	3	3	.500	9	6	4	1	0	55^{2}	42	25	21	1	3	26	26	1.222	3.40	81	2.62	.215	3	.167	-6	3	-0.7
1915	Bos-N	3	3	.500	15	9	4	0	0	73^{1}	85	45	31	2	4	19	26	1.418	3.80	70	4.10	.304	6	.261	-10	1	-1.0
Total	**4**	**7**	**10**	**.412**	**36**	**22**	**13**	**1**	**0**	**191**	**195**	**118**	**95**	**7**	**10**	**78**	**77**	**1.429**	**4.48**	**68**	**4.00**	**.274**	**11**	**.180**	**-31**	**4**	**-3.3**
• DAVIS, Jason	Jason Thomas Davis b: 5/8/1980, Chattanooga, TN BR/TR, 6'6", 195 lbs. Deb: 9/9/2002																										
2002	Cle-A	1	0	1.000	3	2	0	0	0	14^{2}	12	3	3	1	0	4	11	1.091	1.84	239	2.40	.218	0	....	4	2	0.4
2003	Cle-A	8	11	.421	27	27	1	0	0	165^{1}	172	101	86	25	8	47	85	1.325	4.68	94	4.44	.273	0	.000	-8	5	-0.8
Total	**2**	**9**	**11**	**.450**	**30**	**29**	**1**	**0**	**0**	**180**	**184**	**104**	**89**	**26**	**8**	**51**	**96**	**1.306**	**4.45**	**99**	**4.28**	**.268**	**0**	**.000**	**-4**	**7**	**-0.4**
• DAVIS, Jim	James Bennett Davis b: 9/15/1924, Red Bluff, CA d: 11/30/1995, San Mateo, CA BB/TL, 6', 180 lbs. Deb: 4/18/1954																										
1954	Chi-N	11	7	.611	46	12	2	0	4	127^{2}	114	57	50	12	3	51	58	1.292	3.52	119	3.45	.247	2	.063	11	10	1.0
1955	Chi-N	7	11	.389	42	16	0	0	3	133^{2}	122	79	66	16	2	58	62	1.347	4.44	92	3.89	.246	1	.027	-6	6	-1.0

YEAR	TM-L	W	L	PCT	G	GS	CG	SH	SV	IP	H	R	ER	HR	HB	BB	SO	RAT	ERA	ERA+	CERA	OAV	BH	AVG	PR+	WS	TPW
1956	Chi-N	5	7	.417	46	11	2	1	2	120^1	116	56	49	11	6	59	66	1.454	3.66	103	4.35	.256	5	.179	-1	7	-0.1
1957	StL-N	0	1	.000	10	0	0	0	1	13^2	18	8	8	1	0	6	5	1.756	5.27	75	6.15	.340	0	.000	-2	0	-0.2
	NY-N	1	0	1.000	10	0	0	0	0	11	13	9	8	2	0	5	6	1.636	6.55	60	5.57	.283	1	1.000	-3	0	-0.3
	Yr.	1	1	.500	20	0	0	0	1	24^2	31	17	16	3	0	11	11	1.703	5.84	68	5.89	.313	1	.500	-5	0	-0.5
Total	4	24	26	.480	154	39	4	1	10	406^1	383	209	181	42	11	179	197	1.383	4.01	100	4.01	.253	9	.091	-1	23	-0.5

• DAVIS, Joel Joel Clark Davis b: 1/30/1965, Jacksonville, FL BL/TR, 6'5", 205 lbs. Deb: 8/11/1985

YEAR	TM-L	W	L	PCT	G	GS	CG	SH	SV	IP	H	R	ER	HR	HB	BB	SO	RAT	ERA	ERA+	CERA	OAV	BH	AVG	PR+	WS	TPW
1985	Chi-A	3	3	.500	12	11	1	0	0	71^1	71	34	33	6	1	26	37	1.360	4.16	104	3.83	.256	0	....	1	4	0.1
1986	Chi-A	4	5	.444	19	19	1	0	0	105^1	115	64	55	9	1	51	54	1.576	4.70	92	4.91	.280	0	....	-7	4	-0.7
1987	Chi-A	1	5	.167	13	9	1	0	0	55	56	35	35	7	0	29	25	1.545	5.73	80	4.90	.264	0	....	-9	1	-0.8
1988	Chi-A	0	1	.000	5	2	0	0	0	16	21	12	12	4	0	5	10	1.625	6.75	59	6.97	.328	0	....	-5	0	-0.5
Total	4	8	14	.364	49	41	3	0	0	247^2	263	145	135	26	2	111	126	1.510	4.91	89	4.73	.273	0	....	-20	9	-1.9

• DAVIS, John John Kirk Davis b: 1/5/1963, Chicago, IL BR/TR, 6'7", 215 lbs. Deb: 7/24/1987

YEAR	TM-L	W	L	PCT	G	GS	CG	SH	SV	IP	H	R	ER	HR	HB	BB	SO	RAT	ERA	ERA+	CERA	OAV	BH	AVG	PR+	WS	TPW
1987	KC-A	5	2	.714	27	0	0	0	2	43^2	29	13	11	0	2	26	24	1.260	2.27	201	2.41	.195	0	....	12	6	1.1
1988	Chi-A	2	5	.286	34	1	0	0	1	63^2	77	58	47	5	4	50	37	1.995	6.64	60	6.57	.297	0	....	-20	0	-2.0
1989	Chi-A	0	1	.000	4	0	0	0	1	6	5	4	3	2	0	2	5	1.167	4.50	85	4.31	.217	0	....	-0	0	0.0
1990	SD-N	0	1	.000	6	0	0	0	0	9^1	9	7	6	1	0	4	7	1.393	5.79	66	4.18	.257	0	.000	-2	0	-0.2
Total	4	7	9	.438	71	1	0	0	4	122^2	120	82	67	8	6	82	73	1.647	4.92	82	4.80	.258	0	.000	-11	6	-1.2

• DAVIS, Kane Kane Thomas Davis b: 6/25/1975, Ripley, WV BR/TR, 6'3", 194 lbs. Deb: 6/12/2000

YEAR	TM-L	W	L	PCT	G	GS	CG	SH	SV	IP	H	R	ER	HR	HB	BB	SO	RAT	ERA	ERA+	CERA	OAV	BH	AVG	PR+	WS	TPW
2000	Cle-A	0	3	.000	5	2	0	0	0	11	20	21	18	3	1	8	2	2.545	14.73	34	12.94	.385	0	.000	-12	0	-1.1
	Mil-N	0	0	....	3	0	0	0	0	4	7	3	3	1	1	5	2	3.000	6.75	67	16.04	.389	0	....	-1	0	-0.1
2001	Col-N	2	4	.333	57	0	0	0	0	68^1	66	36	33	11	1	32	47	1.434	4.35	123	4.50	.252	0	.000	7	5	0.6
2002	NY-N	1	1	.500	16	0	0	0	0	14	15	11	11	2	1	11	24	1.857	7.07	56	6.19	.273	0	....	-5	0	-0.5
Total	3	3	8	.273	81	2	0	0	0	97^1	108	71	65	17	4	56	75	1.685	6.01	82	6.17	.279	0	.000	-10	5	-1.0

• DAVIS, Lance Johnny Lance Davis b: 9/1/1976, Winter Haven, FL BR/TL, 6', 165 lbs. Deb: 6/16/2001

YEAR	TM-L	W	L	PCT	G	GS	CG	SH	SV	IP	H	R	ER	HR	HB	BB	SO	RAT	ERA	ERA+	CERA	OAV	BH	AVG	PR+	WS	TPW
2001	Cin-N	8	4	.667	20	20	1	0	0	106^1	124	60	56	12	1	34	53	1.486	4.74	96	4.91	.294	4	.121	-1	5	-0.1

• DAVIS, Mark Mark William Davis b: 10/19/1960, Livermore, CA BL/TL, 6'3", 205 lbs. Deb: 9/12/1980 C

YEAR	TM-L	W	L	PCT	G	GS	CG	SH	SV	IP	H	R	ER	HR	HB	BB	SO	RAT	ERA	ERA+	CERA	OAV	BH	AVG	PR+	WS	TPW
1980	Phi-N	0	0	....	2	1	0	0	0	7	4	2	2	0	0	5	5	1.286	2.57	147	2.24	.160	1	.500	1	0	0.1
1981	Phi-N	1	4	.200	9	9	0	0	0	43	49	37	37	7	0	24	29	1.698	7.74	47	6.16	.299	1	.091	-20	0	-2.2
1983	SF-N	6	4	.600	20	20	2	2	0	111	93	51	43	14	3	50	83	1.288	3.49	101	3.62	.227	4	.133	1	6	0.2
1984	SF-N	5	17	.227	46	27	1	0	0	174^2	201	113	104	25	5	54	124	1.460	5.36	65	4.90	.293	6	.130	-31	1	-3.3
1985	SF-N	5	12	.294	77	1	0	0	7	114^1	89	49	45	13	3	41	131	1.137	3.54	97	2.86	.219	3	.250	0	7	0.1
1986	SF-N	5	7	.417	67	2	0	0	4	84^1	63	33	28	6	1	34	90	1.150	2.99	118	2.52	.212	1	.125	4	6	0.4
1987	SF-N	4	5	.444	20	11	1	0	0	70^2	72	38	37	9	4	28	51	1.415	4.71	82	4.71	.273	5	.217	-8	2	-0.6
	SD-N	5	3	.625	43	0	0	0	2	62^1	51	26	22	5	2	31	47	1.316	3.18	124	3.27	.224	2	.286	5	6	0.5
	Yr.	9	8	.529	63	11	1	0	2	133	123	64	59	14	6	59	98	1.368	3.99	97	4.04	.250	7	.233	-3	8	-0.1
1988	SD-N★	5	10	.333	62	0	0	0	28	98^1	70	24	22	2	0	42	102	1.139	2.01	169	2.00	.199	2	.200	14	19	1.6
1989	SD-N★	4	3	.571	70	0	0	0	**44**	92^2	66	21	19	6	2	31	92	1.047	1.85	189	2.20	.200	0	.000	16	19	1.6
1990	KC-A	2	7	.222	53	3	0	0	6	68^2	71	43	39	9	4	52	73	1.791	5.11	75	5.97	.259	0	....	-8	1	-0.8
1991	KC-A	6	3	.667	29	5	0	0	1	62^2	55	36	31	6	1	39	47	1.500	4.45	92	4.31	.240	0	....	-0	3	0.0
1992	KC-A	1	3	.250	13	6	0	0	0	36^1	42	31	29	6	0	28	19	1.927	7.18	56	7.05	.294	0	....	-12	0	-1.2
	Atl-N	1	0	1.000	14	0	0	0	0	16^2	22	13	13	3	1	13	15	2.100	7.02	52	8.27	.314	0	.000	-6	0	-0.7
1993	Phi-N	1	2	.333	25	0	0	0	0	31^1	35	22	18	4	1	24	28	1.883	5.17	77	6.41	.273	1	.333	-4	0	-0.4
	SD-N	0	3	.000	35	0	0	0	4	38^1	44	15	15	6	0	20	42	1.670	3.52	117	5.66	.295	0	.000	3	2	0.3
	Yr.	1	5	.167	60	0	0	0	4	69^2	79	37	33	10	1	44	70	1.766	4.26	95	6.00	.285	1	.250	-1	2	-0.1
1994	SD-N	0	1	.000	20	0	0	0	0	16^1	20	18	16	4	0	13	15	2.020	8.82	47	8.16	.299	0	....	-8	0	-0.8
1997	Mil-A	0	0	....	19	0	0	0	0	16^1	21	10	10	4	1	5	14	1.592	5.51	84	7.00	.323	0	....	-2	0	-0.2
Total	15	51	84	.378	624	85	4	2	96	1145	1068	582	530	129	28	534	1007	1.399	4.17	89	4.15	.249	26	.156	-57	72	-5.4

• DAVIS, Peaches Roy Thomas Davis b: 5/31/1905, Glen Rose, TX d: 4/28/1995, Duncan, OK BL/TR, 6'3.5", 190 lbs. Deb: 7/11/1936

YEAR	TM-L	W	L	PCT	G	GS	CG	SH	SV	IP	H	R	ER	HR	HB	BB	SO	RAT	ERA	ERA+	CERA	OAV	BH	AVG	PR+	WS	TPW
1936	Cin-N	8	8	.500	26	15	5	0	5	125^2	139	62	50	7	2	36	32	1.393	3.58	107	3.87	.280	7	.163	4	8	0.3
1937	Cin-N	11	13	.458	42	24	11	1	3	218	252	105	87	5	2	51	59	1.390	3.59	104	3.81	.295	10	.128	4	10	0.0
1938	Cin-N	7	12	.368	29	19	11	1	1	167^2	193	86	74	9	1	40	28	1.390	3.97	92	3.93	.290	15	.246	-9	7	-0.7
1939	Cin-N	1	0	1.000	20	0	0	0	2	30^2	43	24	22	5	1	11	4	1.761	6.46	59	6.94	.341	1	.333	-10	0	-1.0
Total	4	27	33	.450	117	58	27	2	11	542	627	277	233	26	6	138	123	1.411	3.87	96	4.04	.293	33	.178	-10	25	-1.4

• DAVIS, Ron Ronald Gene Davis b: 8/6/1955, Houston, TX BR/TR, 6'4", 207 lbs. Deb: 7/29/1978

YEAR	TM-L	W	L	PCT	G	GS	CG	SH	SV	IP	H	R	ER	HR	HB	BB	SO	RAT	ERA	ERA+	CERA	OAV	BH	AVG	PR+	WS	TPW
1978	NY-A	0	0	....	4	0	0	0	0	2^1	3	4	3	0	0	3	0	2.571	11.57	31	9.14	.333	0	....	-2	0	-0.2
1979	NY-A	14	2	.875	44	0	0	0	9	85^1	84	29	27	5	1	28	43	1.313	2.85	143	3.35	.262	0	.000	10	12	1.0
1980*	NY-A	9	3	.750	53	0	0	0	7	131	121	50	43	9	5	32	65	1.168	2.95	133	2.96	.246	0	.000	15	12	1.5
1981*	NY-A★	4	5	.444	43	0	0	0	6	73	47	22	22	6	0	25	83	.986	2.71	132	1.92	.186	0	....	6	7	0.7
1982	Min-A	3	9	.250	63	0	0	0	22	106	106	53	52	16	1	47	89	1.443	4.42	96	4.50	.260	0	....	-3	8	-0.3
1983	Min-A	5	8	.385	66	0	0	0	30	89	89	34	33	6	3	33	84	1.371	3.34	127	3.83	.266	0	....	8	12	0.8
1984	Min-A	7	11	.389	64	0	0	0	29	83	79	44	42	11	2	41	74	1.446	4.55	92	4.32	.253	0	....	-5	9	-0.5
1985	Min-A	2	6	.250	57	0	0	0	25	64^2	55	28	25	7	4	35	72	1.392	3.48	127	3.89	.230	0	....	7	10	0.7
1986	Min-A	2	6	.250	36	0	0	0	2	38^2	55	42	39	7	4	29	30	2.172	9.08	47	9.01	.340	0	....	-20	0	-2.0
	Chi-N	0	2	.000	17	0	0	0	0	20	31	18	17	3	0	3	10	1.700	7.65	53	6.78	.356	0	.000	-8	0	-0.8
1987	Chi-N	0	0	....	21	0	0	0	0	32^1	43	23	21	8	0	12	31	1.701	5.85	73	7.28	.328	0	....	-5	0	-0.5
	LA-N	0	0	....	4	0	0	0	0	4	7	4	3	0	1	6	1	3.250	6.75	59	12.82	.412	0	....	-1	0	-0.1
	Yr.	0	0	....	25	0	0	0	0	36^1	50	27	24	8	1	18	32	1.872	5.94	71	7.89	.338	0	....	-6	0	-0.6
1988	SF-N	1	1	.500	9	0	0	0	0	17^1	15	10	9	4	1	6	15	1.212	4.67	70	4.27	.234	0	.000	-3	0	-0.3
Total	11	47	53	.470	481	0	0	0	130	746^2	735	361	336	82	22	300	597	1.386	4.05	101	4.16	.260	0	.000	-1	70	-0.2

• DAVIS, Steve Steven Kennon Davis b: 8/4/1960, San Antonio, TX BL/TL, 6'1", 195 lbs. Deb: 8/25/1985

YEAR	TM-L	W	L	PCT	G	GS	CG	SH	SV	IP	H	R	ER	HR	HB	BB	SO	RAT	ERA	ERA+	CERA	OAV	BH	AVG	PR+	WS	TPW
1985	Tor-A	2	1	.667	10	5	0	0	0	28	23	14	11	5	0	13	22	1.286	3.54	119	3.91	.223	0	....	2	2	0.2
1986	Tor-A	0	0	....	3	0	0	0	0	3^2	8	7	7	2	0	5	5	3.545	17.18	25	22.74	.471	0	....	-5	0	-0.5
1989	Cle-A	1	1	.500	12	2	0	0	0	25^2	34	24	23	2	0	14	12	1.870	8.06	49	6.41	.318	0	....	-12	0	-1.2
Total	3	3	2	.600	25	7	0	0	0	57^1	65	45	41	9	0	32	39	1.692	6.44	63	6.23	.286	0	....	-15	2	-1.5

• DAVIS, Storm George Earl Davis b: 12/26/1961, Dallas, TX BR/TR, 6'4", 207 lbs. Deb: 4/29/1982

YEAR	TM-L	W	L	PCT	G	GS	CG	SH	SV	IP	H	R	ER	HR	HB	BB	SO	RAT	ERA	ERA+	CERA	OAV	BH	AVG	PR+	WS	TPW
1982	Bal-A	8	4	.667	29	8	1	0	0	100^2	96	40	39	8	0	28	67	1.232	3.49	116	3.21	.257	0	....	6	8	0.6
1983*	Bal-A	13	7	.650	34	29	6	1	0	200^1	180	90	80	14	2	64	125	1.218	3.59	110	3.03	.238	0	....	8	13	0.8
1984	Bal-A	14	9	.609	35	31	10	2	1	225	205	86	78	7	5	71	105	1.227	3.12	124	2.91	.247	0	....	14	18	1.4
1985	Bal-A	10	8	.556	31	28	8	1	0	175	172	92	88	11	1	70	93	1.383	4.53	89	3.70	.256	0	....	-8	8	-0.8
1986	Bal-A	9	12	.429	25	25	2	0	0	154	166	70	62	16	0	49	96	1.396	3.62	114	4.24	.275	0	....	10	10	1.0
1987	SD-N	2	7	.222	21	10	0	0	0	62^2	70	48	43	5	2	36	37	1.691	6.18	64	5.19	.280	1	.063	-16	0	-1.7
	Oak-A	1	1	.500	5	5	0	0	0	30^1	28	13	11	3	0	11	28	1.286	3.26	126	3.49	.241	0	....	3	2	0.3
1988*	Oak-A	16	7	.696	33	33	1	0	0	201^2	211	86	83	16	1	91	127	1.498	3.70	102	4.48	.274	0	....	-1	11	-0.1
1989*	Oak-A	19	7	.731	31	31	1	0	0	169^1	187	91	82	19	3	68	91	1.506	4.36	84	4.95	.288	0	....	-15	7	-1.6
1990	KC-A	7	10	.412	21	20	0	0	0	112	129	66	59	9	0	35	62	1.464	4.74	81	4.34	.281	0	....	-8	3	-0.9
1991	KC-A	3	9	.250	51	9	1	1	2	114^1	140	69	63	11	1	46	53	1.627	4.96	83	5.29	.306	0	....	-7	3	-0.7
1992	Bal-A	7	3	.700	48	2	0	0	4	89^1	79	35	34	5	2	36	53	1.287	3.43	117	3.19	.244	0	....	5	8	0.5
1993	Oak-A	2	6	.250	19	8	0	0	0	62^2	68	45	43	5	2	33	37	1.612	6.18	66	4.99	.276	0	....	-14	0	-1.4
	Det-A	0	2	.000	24	0	0	0	4	35^1	25	12	12	4	1	15	36	1.132	3.06	140	2.66	.198	0	....	5	4	0.5
	Yr.	2	8	.200	43	8	0	0	4	98	93	57	55	9	3	48	73	1.439	5.05	82	4.15	.250	0	....	-9	4	-0.9

YEAR	TM-L	W	L	PCT	G	GS	CG	SH	SV	IP	H	R	ER	HR	HB	BB	SO	RAT	ERA	ERA+	CERA	OAV	BH	AVG	PR+	WS	TPW
1994	Det-A	2	4	.333	35	0	0	0	0	48	36	23	19	3	0	34	38	1.458	3.56	136	3.32	.207	0	....	8	3	0.7
Total	**13**	**113**	**96**	**.541**	**442**	**239**	**30**	**5**	**11**	**1780^2**	**1792**	**866**	**796**	**136**	**20**	**687**	**1048**	**1.392**	**4.02**	**98**	**3.93**	**.263**	**1**	**.063**	**-11**	**98**	**-1.3**
• DAVIS, Tim	Timothy Howard Davis b: 7/14/1970, Marianna, FL BL/TL, 5'11", 165 lbs. Deb: 4/4/1994																										
1994	Sea-A	2	2	.500	42	1	0	0	2	49^1	57	25	22	4	1	25	28	1.662	4.01	122	5.17	.295	0	....	5	4	0.5
1995	Sea-A	2	1	.667	5	5	0	0	0	24	30	21	17	2	0	18	19	2.000	6.38	74	6.73	.306	0	....	-4	0	-0.4
1996	Sea-A	2	2	.500	40	0	0	0	0	42^2	43	21	19	4	2	17	34	1.406	4.01	124	4.19	.259	0	....	4	3	0.4
1997	Sea-A	0	0	....	2	0	0	0	0	6^2	6	5	5	1	1	4	10	1.500	6.75	67	5.16	.231	0	....	-2	0	-0.2
Total	**4**	**6**	**5**	**.545**	**89**	**6**	**0**	**0**	**2**	**122^2**	**136**	**72**	**63**	**11**	**4**	**64**	**91**	**1.630**	**4.62**	**105**	**5.13**	**.282**	**0**	**....**	**4**	**7**	**0.4**
• DAVIS, Wiley	Wiley Anderson Davis b: 8/1/1875, Seymour, TN d: 9/22/1942, Detroit, MI BR/TR, 5'10", 165 lbs. Deb: 4/18/1896																										
1896	Cin-N	1	1	.500	2	0	0	0	0	4^1	8	4	4	0	0	2	1	2.308	8.31	55	8.60	.392	0	.000	-2	0	-0.1
• DAVIS, Woody	Woodrow Wilson "Babe" Davis b: 4/25/1913, Nicholas, GA BL/TR, 6'1", 200 lbs. Deb: 5/2/1938																										
1938	Det-A	0	0	....	2	0	0	0	0	6	3	1	1	0	0	4	1	1.167	1.50	333	1.84	.158	0	.000	2	1	0.2
• DAVISON, Mike	Michael Lynn Davison b: 8/4/1945, Galesburg, IL BL/TL, 6'1", 170 lbs. Deb: 10/1/1969																										
1969	SF-N	0	0	....	1	0	0	0	0	2	2	1	1	0	0	0	2	1.000	4.50	78	1.95	.250	0	....	-0	0	0.0
1970	SF-N	3	5	.375	31	0	0	0	1	36	46	29	26	4	0	22	21	1.889	6.50	61	6.52	.324	0	.000	-9	0	-0.9
Total	**2**	**3**	**5**	**.375**	**32**	**0**	**0**	**0**	**1**	**38**	**48**	**30**	**27**	**4**	**0**	**22**	**23**	**1.842**	**6.39**	**62**	**6.28**	**.320**	**0**	**.000**	**-10**	**0**	**-0.9**
• DAVISON, Scott	Scotty Ray Davison b: 10/16/1970, Inglewood, CA BR/TR, 6', 190 lbs. Deb: 9/4/1995																										
1995	Sea-A	0	0	....	3	0	0	0	0	4^1	7	3	3	1	0	1	3	1.846	6.23	76	8.00	.350	0	....	-1	0	-0.1
1996	Sea-A	0	0	....	5	0	0	0	0	9	11	9	9	6	0	3	9	1.556	9.00	55	9.46	.297	0	....	-4	0	-0.4
Total	**2**	**0**	**0**	**....**	**8**	**0**	**0**	**0**	**0**	**13^1**	**18**	**12**	**12**	**7**	**0**	**4**	**12**	**1.650**	**8.10**	**60**	**8.99**	**.316**	**0**	**....**	**-5**	**0**	**-0.4**
• DAWLEY, Bill	William Chester Dawley b: 2/6/1958, Norwich, CT BR/TR, 6'5", 240 lbs. Deb: 4/15/1983																										
1983	Hou-N★	6	6	.500	48	0	0	0	14	79^2	51	26	25	9	1	22	60	.916	2.82	120	1.90	.185	2	.222	4	10	0.4
1984	Hou-N	11	4	.733	60	0	0	0	5	98	82	24	21	5	0	35	47	1.194	1.93	172	2.60	.234	3	.333	14	12	1.6
1985	Hou-N	5	3	.625	49	0	0	0	2	81	76	35	32	7	0	37	48	1.395	3.56	97	3.74	.259	2	.200	-2	4	-0.1
1986	Chi-A	0	7	.000	46	0	0	0	2	97^2	91	38	36	10	1	28	66	1.218	3.32	130	3.28	.247	0	.000	9	7	0.8
1987	StL-N	5	8	.385	60	0	0	0	2	96^2	93	51	48	15	1	38	65	1.355	4.47	93	4.17	.259	2	.167	-4	5	-0.4
1988	Phi-N	0	2	.000	8	0	0	0	0	8^2	16	13	13	3	0	4	3	2.308	13.50	26	11.32	.381	0	....	-9	0	-1.0
1989	Oak-A	0	0	....	4	0	0	0	0	9	11	5	4	0	1	2	3	1.444	4.00	92	4.21	.297	0	....	-0	0	0.0
Total	**7**	**27**	**30**	**.474**	**275**	**0**	**0**	**0**	**25**	**470^2**	**420**	**192**	**179**	**49**	**4**	**166**	**292**	**1.245**	**3.42**	**110**	**3.33**	**.243**	**9**	**.214**	**11**	**38**	**1.3**
• DAWLEY, Joey	Joseph Thomas Dawley b: 9/19/1971, Riverside, CA BR/TR, 6'4", 205 lbs. Deb: 9/29/2002																										
2002	Atl-N	0	0	....	1	0	0	0	0	0^1	0	0	0	0	0	0	1	.000	0.00	....	0.00	.000	0	....	0	0	0.0
2003	Atl-N	0	0	....	5	0	0	0	0	7	15	14	14	3	1	3	8	2.571	18.00	23	15.12	.405	0	.000	-11	0	-1.1
Total	**2**	**0**	**0**	**....**	**6**	**0**	**0**	**0**	**0**	**7^1**	**15**	**14**	**14**	**3**	**1**	**3**	**9**	**2.455**	**17.18**	**25**	**14.44**	**.405**	**0**	**.000**	**-11**	**0**	**-1.0**
• DAWSON, Joe	Ralph Fenton Dawson b: 3/9/1897, Bow, WA d: 1/4/1978, Longview, TX BR/TR, 5'11", 182 lbs. Deb: 7/4/1924																										
1924	Cle-A	1	2	.333	4	4	0	0	0	20^1	24	17	15	0	1	21	7	2.213	6.64	64	6.80	.300	2	.286	-5	0	-0.5
1927*	Pit-N	3	7	.300	20	7	4	0	0	80^2	80	47	40	2	0	32	17	1.388	4.46	92	3.36	.268	5	.200	-4	3	-0.4
1928	Pit-N	7	7	.500	31	7	1	0	3	128^2	116	54	47	6	1	56	36	1.337	3.29	123	3.22	.242	12	.279	11	11	1.4
1929	Pit-N	0	1	.000	4	0	0	0	0	8^2	13	9	8	2	0	3	2	1.846	8.31	57	7.88	.342	1	.500	-4	0	-0.3
Total	**4**	**11**	**17**	**.393**	**59**	**18**	**5**	**0**	**3**	**238^1**	**233**	**127**	**110**	**10**	**2**	**112**	**62**	**1.448**	**4.15**	**100**	**3.74**	**.260**	**20**	**.260**	**-2**	**14**	**0.2**
• DAWSON, Rex	Rexford Paul Dawson b: 2/10/1889, Skagit County, WA d: 10/20/1958, Indianapolis, IN BL/TR, 6', 185 lbs. Deb: 10/3/1913																										
1913	Was-A	0	0	....	1	0	0	0	0	1	1	0	0	0	0	0	1	1.000	0.00	....	1.95	.250	0	....	0	0	0.0
• DAY, Bill	William M. Day b: 7/28/1867, Wilmington, DE d: 8/16/1923, Wilmington, DE TR, 5'8", 150 lbs. Deb: 8/20/1889																										
1889	Phi-N	0	3	.000	4	3	2	0	0	19	16	24	11	0	0	23	20	2.053	5.21	84	....	.221	0	.000	-1	0	-0.2
1890	Phi-N	1	1	.500	4	2	2	0	0	23^2	26	16	8	0	0	12	9	1.606	3.04	120	....	.271	1	.100	1	1	0.0
	Pit-N	0	6	.000	6	6	6	0	0	50	66	50	29	1	1	24	10	1.800	5.22	63	....	.309	1	.043	-8	0	-1.0
	Yr.	1	7	.125	10	8	8	0	0	73^2	92	66	37	1	1	36	19	1.738	4.52	74	....	.297	2	.061	-7	1	-1.0
Total	**2**	**1**	**10**	**.091**	**14**	**11**	**10**	**0**	**0**	**92^2**	**108**	**90**	**48**	**1**	**1**	**59**	**39**	**1.802**	**4.66**	**76**	**....**	**.283**	**2**	**.047**	**-8**	**1**	**-1.2**
• DAY, Pea Ridge	Clyde Henry Day b: 8/26/1899, Pea Ridge, AR d: 3/21/1934, Kansas City, MO BR/TR, 6', 190 lbs. Deb: 9/19/1924																										
1924	StL-N	1	1	.500	3	3	1	0	0	17^2	22	11	9	0	0	6	3	1.585	4.58	83	4.21	.306	1	.125	-2	0	-0.2
1925	StL-N	2	4	.333	17	4	1	0	1	40	53	31	28	5	3	7	13	1.500	6.30	69	5.61	.325	2	.154	-9	0	-0.9
1926	Cin-N	0	0	....	4	0	0	0	0	7^1	13	13	6	1	0	2	2	2.045	7.36	50	8.35	.406	0	.000	-3	0	-0.3
1931	Bro-N	2	2	.500	22	2	1	0	1	57^1	75	38	29	5	0	13	30	1.535	4.55	84	5.00	.315	4	.222	-4	2	-0.4
Total	**4**	**5**	**7**	**.417**	**46**	**9**	**3**	**0**	**2**	**122^1**	**163**	**93**	**72**	**11**	**3**	**28**	**48**	**1.561**	**5.30**	**75**	**5.28**	**.323**	**7**	**.171**	**-18**	**2**	**-1.9**
• DAY, Zach	Stephen Zachary Day b: 6/15/1978, Cincinnati, OH BR/TR, 6'4", 185 lbs. Deb: 6/15/2002																										
2002	Mon-N	4	1	.800	19	2	0	0	1	37^1	28	18	15	3	1	15	25	1.152	3.62	118	2.66	.207	1	.167	3	3	0.3
2003	Mon-N	9	8	.529	23	23	1	1	0	131^1	132	64	61	8	10	59	61	1.454	4.18	121	4.28	.262	2	.043	13	9	0.9
Total	**2**	**13**	**9**	**.591**	**42**	**25**	**1**	**1**	**1**	**168^2**	**160**	**82**	**76**	**11**	**11**	**74**	**86**	**1.387**	**4.06**	**120**	**3.92**	**.250**	**3**	**.057**	**16**	**12**	**1.2**
• DAYLEY, Ken	Kenneth Grant Dayley b: 2/25/1959, Jerome, ID BL/TL, 6', 175 lbs. Deb: 5/13/1982																										
1982	Atl-N	5	6	.455	20	11	0	0	0	71^1	79	39	36	9	0	25	34	1.458	4.54	82	4.60	.286	5	.250	-7	3	-0.6
1983	Atl-N	5	8	.385	24	16	0	0	0	104^2	100	59	50	12	2	39	70	1.328	4.30	90	3.97	.257	7	.219	-6	4	-0.5
1984	Atl-N	0	3	.000	4	4	0	0	0	18^2	28	18	11	5	1	6	10	1.821	5.30	73	8.03	.341	2	.500	-3	0	-0.2
	StL-N	0	2	.000	3	2	0	0	0	5	16	10	10	1	0	5	0	4.200	18.00	19	26.74	.615	0	....	-8	0	-0.9
	Yr.	0	5	.000	7	6	0	0	0	23^2	44	28	21	6	1	11	10	2.324	7.99	46	11.99	.407	2	.500	-11	0	-1.1
1985*	StL-N	4	4	.500	57	0	0	0	11	65^1	65	24	20	2	0	18	62	1.270	2.76	128	2.92	.263	2	.400	4	7	0.5
1986	StL-N	0	3	.000	31	0	0	0	5	38^2	42	19	14	1	1	11	33	1.371	3.26	112	3.46	.275	1	.200	0	2	0.1
1987*	StL-N	9	5	.643	53	0	0	0	4	61	52	21	18	2	2	33	63	1.393	2.66	156	3.30	.234	0	....	10	8	1.0
1988	StL-N	2	7	.222	54	0	0	0	5	55^1	48	20	17	2	1	19	38	1.211	2.77	126	2.66	.239	0	.000	4	6	0.4
1989	StL-N	4	3	.571	71	0	0	0	12	75^1	63	26	24	3	0	30	40	1.235	2.87	126	2.63	.228	0	.000	5	10	0.5
1990	StL-N	4	4	.500	58	0	0	0	2	73^1	63	32	29	5	0	30	51	1.268	3.56	107	2.99	.233	0	.000	2	6	0.2
1991	Tor-A	0	0	....	8	0	0	0	0	4^1	7	3	3	0	1	5	3	2.769	6.23	68	11.05	.368	0	....	-1	0	-0.1
1993	Tor-A	0	0	....	2	0	0	0	0	0^2	1	2	0	0	0	4	2	7.500	0.00	....	31.81	.333	0	....	0	0	0.0
Total	**11**	**33**	**45**	**.423**	**385**	**33**	**0**	**0**	**39**	**573^2**	**564**	**273**	**232**	**42**	**8**	**225**	**406**	**1.375**	**3.64**	**103**	**3.81**	**.261**	**17**	**.210**	**2**	**46**	**0.4**
• DE LA CRUZ, Tommy	Tomas (Rivero) de la Cruz b: 9/18/1911, Marianao, Cuba d: 9/6/1958, Havana, Cuba BR/TR, 6'1" Deb: 4/20/1944																										
1944	Cin-N	9	9	.500	34	20	9	0	1	191^1	170	73	69	9	1	45	65	1.124	3.25	107	2.52	.238	9	.155	1	13	0.0
• DE LA ROSA, Francisco	Francisco (Jimenez) de la Rosa b: 3/3/1966, La Romana, Dominican Republic BB/TR, 5'11" Deb: 9/7/1991																										
1991	Bal-A	0	0	....	2	0	0	0	0	4	6	3	2	0	0	2	1	2.000	4.50	88	6.48	.353	0	....	-0	0	0.0
• DE LOS SANTOS, Luis	Luis De Los Santos b: 11/1/1977, Santo Domingo, Dominican Republic BR/TR, 6'2", 216 lbs. Deb: 7/20/2002																										
2002	TB-A	0	3	.000	3	3	0	0	0	14	24	19	18	5	3	4	7	2.000	11.57	39	11.49	.387	0	....	-11	0	-1.1
• DE LOS SANTOS, Ramon	Ramon (Genero) de los Santos b: 1/19/1949, Santo Domingo, Dominican Republic BL/TL, 6' Deb: 8/21/1974																										
1974	Hou-N	1	1	.500	12	0	0	0	0	12^1	11	6	3	0	0	9	7	1.622	2.19	158	3.30	.234	0	....	2	1	0.2
• DE LOS SANTOS, Valerio	Valerio Lorenzo De Los Santos b: 10/6/1972, Las Matas de Farfan, Dominican Republic BL/TL, 6'4", 180 lbs. Deb: 7/31/1998																										
1998	Mil-N	0	0	....	13	0	0	0	0	21^2	11	7	7	4	0	2	18	.600	2.91	147	1.25	.151	0	....	3	2	0.3
1999	Mil-N	0	1	.000	7	0	0	0	0	8^1	12	6	6	1	1	7	5	2.280	6.48	70	9.65	.343	0	....	-2	0	-0.2
2000	Mil-N	2	3	.400	66	2	0	0	0	73^2	72	43	42	15	1	33	70	1.425	5.13	89	4.79	.254	0	.000	-6	3	-0.6

YEAR	TM-L	W	L	PCT	G	GS	CG	SH	SV	IP	H	R	ER	HR	HB	BB	SO	RAT	ERA	ERA+	CERA	OAV	BH	AVG	PR+	WS	TPW
2001	Mil-N	0	0	....	1	0	0	0	0	1	1	1	1	0	0	1	1	2.000	9.00	48	5.48	.250	0	....	-1	0	-0.1
2002	Mil-N	2	3	.400	51	0	0	0	0	57^2	42	21	20	4	2	26	38	1.179	3.12	131	2.70	.211	0	.000	6	4	0.7
2003	Mil-N	3	3	.500	45	0	0	0	1	48	38	24	22	8	4	22	35	1.250	4.13	103	3.92	.225	0	.000	2	4	0.1
	Phi-N	1	0	1.000	6	0	0	0	0	4	7	7	4	0	1	3	4	2.500	9.00	44	10.26	.389	0	....	-2	0	-0.2
	Yr.	4	3	.571	51	0	0	0	1	52	45	31	26	8	5	25	39	1.346	4.50	93	4.41	.241	0	.000	-1	4	-0.1
Total	**6**	8	10	.444	189	2	0	0	1	214^1	183	109	102	32	9	94	171	1.292	4.28	101	3.97	.234	0	.000	1	13	0.1
• DEAGLE, Ren		Lorenzo Burroughs Deagle	b: 6/26/1858, New York, NY	d: 12/24/1936, Kansas City, MO	BR/TR, 5'9", 190 lbs.	Deb: 5/17/1883																					
1883	Cin-a	10	8	.556	18	18	17	1	0	148	136	78	38	0	....	34	48	1.149	2.31	140	....	.229	9	.129	10	10	0.4
1884	Cin-a	3	1	.750	4	4	4	1	0	34	39	26	19	0	1	9	12	1.412	5.03	66	....	.273	0	.000	-7	1	-0.8
	Lou-a	4	6	.400	12	12	8	0	0	87^1	80	43	25	0	7	13	23	1.065	2.58	120	....	.231	6	.133	2	5	-0.2
	Yr.	7	7	.500	16	16	12	1	0	121^1	119	69	44	0	8	22	35	1.162	3.26	97	....	.243	6	.103	-5	6	-1.0
Total	**2**	17	15	.531	34	34	29	2	0	269^1	255	147	82	0	8	56	83	1.155	2.74	117	....	.235	15	.117	4	16	-0.6
• DEAGO, Roger		Roger I. Villarreal Deago	b: 6/21/1977, Monagrillo, Panama	BR/TL, 5'10", 180 lbs.	Deb: 5/10/2003																						
2003	SD-N	0	1	.000	2	2	0	0	0	10^1	11	9	9	0	0	8	10	1.839	7.84	50	5.10	.282	0	.000	-4	0	-0.5
• DEAL, Cot		Ellis Fergason Deal	b: 1/23/1923, Arapaho, OK	BB/TR, 5'10.5", 185 lbs.	Deb: 9/11/1947	C																					
1947	Bos-A	0	1	.000	5	2	0	0	0	12^2	20	13	13	0	0	7	6	2.132	9.24	42	7.25	.364	2	.500	-8	0	-0.7
1948	Bos-A	1	0	1.000	4	0	0	0	0	4	3	0	0	0	0	3	2	1.500	0.00	....	3.02	.200	0	....	2	1	0.2
1950	StL-N	0	0	....	3	0	0	0	0	1	3	5	2	0	0	2	1	5.000	18.00	24	20.94	.500	0	....	-2	0	-0.1
1954	StL-N	2	3	.400	33	0	0	0	1	71^2	85	56	50	14	4	36	25	1.688	6.28	66	6.32	.297	2	.100	-17	0	-1.6
Total	**4**	3	4	.429	45	2	0	0	1	89^1	111	74	65	14	4	48	34	1.780	6.55	62	6.47	.307	4	.167	-24	1	-2.3
• DEAN, Chubby		Alfred Lovill Dean	b: 8/24/1915, Mount Airy, NC	d: 12/21/1970, Riverside, NJ	BL/TL, 5'11", 181 lbs.	Deb: 4/14/1936	♦																				
1937	Phi-A	1	0	1.000	2	1	0	0	0	9	7	4	4	0	0	6	4	1.444	4.00	118	2.91	.219	81	.262	1	5	-1.5
1938	Phi-A	2	1	.667	6	1	0	0	0	23	22	10	9	3	0	15	3	1.609	3.52	137	4.93	.250	6	.300	4	3	0.5
1939	Phi-A	5	8	.385	54	1	0	0	7	116^2	132	93	68	8	0	80	39	1.817	5.25	90	5.47	.289	27	.351	-3	7	0.5
1940	Phi-A	6	13	.316	30	19	8	1	1	159^1	220	136	117	21	0	63	38	**1.776**	6.61	67	6.37	.324	26	.289	-36	2	-2.6
1941	Phi-A	2	4	.333	18	7	2	0	0	75^2	90	53	52	9	0	35	22	1.652	6.19	68	5.44	.294	9	.243	-17	1	-1.5
	Cle-A	1	4	.200	8	8	2	0	0	53^1	57	31	26	3	0	24	14	1.519	4.39	90	4.40	.282	4	.160	-3	2	-0.2
	Yr.	3	8	.273	26	15	4	0	0	129	147	84	78	12	0	59	36	1.597	5.44	75	5.01	.289	13	.210	-20	3	-1.7
1942	Cle-A	8	11	.421	27	22	8	0	1	172^2	170	83	73	7	0	66	46	1.367	3.81	91	3.44	.261	27	.267	-10	10	-0.2
1943	Cle-A	5	5	.500	17	9	3	0	0	76	83	46	38	1	1	34	29	1.539	4.50	69	4.09	.281	9	.196	-13	0	-1.3
Total	**7**	30	46	.395	162	68	23	1	9	685^2	781	456	387	52	1	323	195	1.610	5.08	79	4.88	.288	287	.274	-78	30	-6.3
• DEAN, Dizzy		Jay Hanna Dean	b: 1/16/1910, Lucas, AR	d: 7/17/1974, Reno, NV	BR/TR, 6'2", 182 lbs.	Deb: 9/28/1930	C	HOF: 1953																			
1930	StL-N	1	0	1.000	1	1	1	0	0	9	3	1	1	0	0	3	5	.667	1.00	502	0.65	.103	1	.333	4	1	0.4
1932	StL-N	18	15	.545	46	33	16	**4**	2	**286**	280	122	105	14	5	102	**191**	1.336	3.30	119	3.47	.260	25	.258	22	24	2.6
1933	StL-N	20	18	.526	**48**	34	**26**	3	4	293	279	113	99	11	5	64	**199**	1.171	3.04	114	2.74	.250	19	.181	14	22	1.5
1934*	StL-N★	**30**	7	.811	50	33	24	**7**	7	311^2	288	110	92	14	6	75	**195**	1.165	2.66	159	2.69	.241	29	.246	51	**37**	**5.3**
1935	StL-N★	**28**	12	.700	50	**36**	**29**	3	5	**325^1**	324	126	110	16	4	77	**190**	1.233	3.04	135	3.05	.256	30	.234	34	**31**	3.6
1936	StL-N★	24	13	.649	**51**	34	**28**	2	**11**	**315**	310	128	111	21	3	53	195	1.152	3.17	124	2.84	.253	27	.223	27	31	2.7
1937	StL-N★	13	10	.565	27	25	17	4	1	197^1	200	76	59	9	2	33	120	1.181	2.69	148	2.87	.259	15	.227	29	17	3.1
1938*	Chi-N	7	1	.875	13	10	3	1	0	74^2	63	20	15	2	1	8	22	.951	1.81	211	1.84	.226	5	.192	16	9	1.6
1939	Chi-N	6	4	.600	19	13	7	2	0	96^1	98	40	36	4	1	17	27	1.194	3.36	117	2.88	.261	5	.147	9	7	0.8
1940	Chi-N	3	3	.500	10	9	3	0	0	54	68	35	31	4	0	20	18	1.630	5.17	73	5.09	.306	4	.222	-8	1	-0.8
1941	Chi-N	0	0	....	1	1	0	0	0	1	3	3	2	0	0	0	1	3.000	18.00	20	12.36	.429	0	....	-2	0	-0.2
1947	StL-A	0	0	....	1	1	0	0	0	4	3	0	0	0	0	1	0	1.000	0.00	....	1.90	.231	1	1.000	2	1	0.2
Total	**12**	150	83	.644	317	230	154	26	30	1967^1	1919	774	661	95	27	453	1163	1.206	3.02	129	2.95	.253	161	.225	197	181	20.9
• DEAN, Dory		Charles Wilson Dean	b: 11/6/1852, Cincinnati, OH	d: 5/4/1935, Nashville, TN	BR/TR, 5'9"	Deb: 6/22/1876																					
1876	Cin-N	4	26	.133	30	30	26	0	0	262^2	397	268	109	1	....	24	22	**1.603**	3.73	59	....	.320	36	.257	-29	3	-2.4
• DEAN, Harry		James Harry Dean	b: 5/12/1915, Rockmart, GA	d: 6/1/1960, Rockmart, GA	BR/TR, 6'4", 185 lbs.	Deb: 4/16/1941																					
1941	Was-A	0	0	....	2	0	0	0	0	2	2	3	1	0	1	3	0	2.500	4.50	90	8.74	.250	0	....	-0	0	0.0
• DEAN, Paul		Paul Dee "Daffy" Dean	b: 8/14/1913, Lucas, AR	d: 3/17/1981, Springdale, AR	BR/TR, 6', 175 lbs.	Deb: 4/18/1934																					
1934*	StL-N	19	11	.633	39	26	16	5	2	233^1	225	96	89	19	5	52	150	1.187	3.43	123	3.07	.248	20	.241	18	22	1.9
1935	StL-N	19	12	.613	46	33	19	2	5	269^2	261	109	101	16	9	55	143	1.172	3.37	122	2.92	.249	12	.133	18	22	1.3
1936	StL-N	5	5	.500	17	14	5	0	1	92	113	57	47	3	1	20	28	1.446	4.60	86	4.07	.300	2	.059	-7	3	-1.0
1937	StL-N	0	0	....	1	0	0	0	0	0	1	3	0	0	0	2	0	....	....	....	∞	1.000	0	....	0	0	0.0
1938	StL-N	3	1	.750	5	4	2	1	0	31	37	12	9	3	0	5	14	1.355	2.61	151	4.19	.298	2	.182	5	3	0.4
1939	StL-N	0	1	.000	16	2	0	0	0	43	54	30	29	4	1	10	16	1.488	6.07	68	4.72	.310	1	.111	-10	0	-1.0
1940	NY-N	4	4	.500	27	7	2	0	0	99^1	110	50	43	8	0	29	32	1.399	3.90	100	4.06	.281	3	.115	0	5	-0.1
1941	NY-N	0	0	....	5	0	0	0	0	5^2	8	2	2	0	0	3	3	1.941	3.18	116	5.90	.320	0	....	0	0	0.0
1943	StL-A	0	0	....	3	1	0	0	0	13^1	16	5	5	0	1	3	1	1.425	3.38	99	4.04	.296	0	.000	0	1	0.0
Total	**9**	50	34	.595	159	87	44	8	8	787^1	825	364	325	53	17	179	387	1.275	3.72	109	3.43	.266	40	.156	25	56	1.4
• DEAN, Wayland		Wayland Ogden Dean	b: 6/20/1902, Richwood, WV	d: 4/10/1930, Huntington, WV	BB/TR, 6'1", 178 lbs.	Deb: 4/17/1924																					
1924*	NY-N	6	12	.333	26	20	6	0	0	125^2	139	80	70	9	5	45	39	1.464	5.01	73	4.32	.280	8	.200	-19	2	-1.8
1925	NY-N	10	7	.588	33	14	6	1	1	151^1	169	98	78	13	4	50	53	1.447	4.64	87	4.33	.282	12	.235	-10	8	-0.7
1926	Phi-N	8	16	.333	33	26	15	1	0	203^2	245	136	111	9	3	89	52	1.640	4.91	84	4.91	.307	27	.265	-11	9	-0.5
1927	Phi-N	0	1	.000	2	0	0	0	0	3	6	4	4	0	0	2	1	2.667	12.00	34	11.68	.500	2	.667	-3	1	-0.1
	Chi-N	0	0	....	2	0	0	0	0	2	0	0	0	0	1	2	2	1.000	0.00	....	1.60	.375	0	....	1	0	0.1
	Yr.	0	1	.000	4	0	0	0	0	5	6	4	4	0	1	4	3	2.000	7.20	57	7.65	.500	2	.667	-2	1	0.0
Total	**4**	24	36	.400	96	60	27	2	1	485^2	559	318	263	31	13	188	147	1.538	4.87	82	4.60	.293	49	.250	-42	20	-3.0
• DEBARR, Dennis		Dennis Lee DeBarr	b: 1/16/1953, Cheyenne, WY	BL/TL, 6'2", 190 lbs.	Deb: 5/14/1977																						
1977	Tor-A	0	1	.000	14	0	0	0	0	21^1	29	14	14	1	0	8	10	1.734	5.91	71	5.70	.337	0	....	-4	0	-0.4
• DEBERRY, Joe		Joseph Gaddy DeBerry	b: 11/29/1896, Mount Gilead, NC	d: 10/9/1944, Southern Pines, NC	BL/TR, 6'1", 175 lbs.	Deb: 8/24/1920																					
1920	StL-A	2	4	.333	10	7	3	1	0	54^2	65	35	30	2	2	20	12	1.555	4.94	79	4.44	.307	3	.167	-6	2	-0.7
1921	StL-A	0	1	.000	10	1	0	0	0	12^1	15	9	9	0	0	10	1	2.027	6.57	68	5.87	.300	0	.000	-3	0	-0.3
Total	**2**	2	5	.286	20	8	3	1	0	67	80	44	39	2	2	30	13	1.642	5.24	77	4.70	.306	3	.150	-9	2	-1.0
• DEBUSSCHERE, Dave		David Albert DeBusschere	b: 10/16/1940, Detroit, MI	d: 5/14/2003, New York, NY	BR/TR, 6'6", 225 lbs.	Deb: 4/22/1962																					
1962	Chi-A	0	0	....	12	0	0	0	0	18	5	7	4	1	1	23	8	1.556	2.00	195	3.14	.089	0	....	4	1	0.4
1963	Chi-A	3	4	.429	24	10	1	1	0	84^1	80	35	29	9	4	34	53	1.352	3.09	113	4.00	.249	1	.045	3	4	0.2
Total	**2**	3	4	.429	36	10	1	1	0	102^1	85	42	33	10	5	57	61	1.388	2.90	122	3.85	.225	1	.045	7	5	0.5
• DECATUR, Art		Arthur Rue Decatur	b: 1/14/1894, Cleveland, OH	d: 4/25/1966, Talladega, AL	BR/TR, 6'1", 190 lbs.	Deb: 4/15/1922																					
1922	Bro-N	3	4	.429	29	3	1	0	1	87^2	87	31	27	3	1	29	31	1.323	2.77	147	3.25	.265	2	.080	13	7	1.1
1923	Bro-N	3	3	.500	36	5	2	0	3	97^2	101	44	28	3	2	32	25	1.362	2.58	150	3.12	.264	0	.000	14	8	1.1
1924	Bro-N	10	9	.526	31	10	3	0	1	126^1	156	74	58	12	4	27	38	1.449	4.13	91	4.70	.308	5	.114	-2	6	-0.6
1925	Bro-N	0	0	....	1	0	0	0	0	1	3	2	2	0	0	0	0	3.000	18.00	23	14.52	.600	0	....	-2	0	-0.1
	Phi-N	4	13	.235	25	15	4	0	2	128	170	87	75	13	2	35	31	1.602	5.27	90	5.38	.316	2	.049	-2	6	-0.6
	Yr.	4	13	.235	26	15	4	0	2	129	173	89	77	13	2	35	31	1.612	5.37	88	5.45	.319	2	.049	-4	6	-0.8
1926	Phi-N	0	0	....	2	1	0	0	0	3	6	3	2	0	0	2	0	2.667	6.00	69	9.64	.375	0	.000	-1	0	-0.1

YEAR TM-L	W	L	PCT	G	GS	CG	SH	SV	IP	H	R	ER	HR	HB	BB	SO	RAT	ERA	ERA+	CERA	OAV	BH	AVG	PR+	WS	TPW
1927 Phi-N	3	5	.375	29	3	0	0	0	94^2	130	78	78	11	4	20	27	1.585	7.42	56	5.64	.334	6	.222	-33	0	-3.2
Total 6	23	34	.404	153	37	10	0	7	538^1	653	319	270	42	13	145	152	1.482	4.51	92	4.55	.302	15	.094	-11	27	-2.5
• DECKER, Joe	George Henry Decker b: 6/16/1947, Storm Lake, IA d: 3/2/2003, Fraser, MI BR/TR, 6', 180 lbs. Deb: 9/18/1969																									
1969 Chi-N	1	0	1.000	4	1	0	0	0	12^1	10	4	4	0	0	6	13	1.297	2.92	138	2.77	.222	0	.000	2	1	0.1
1970 Chi-N	2	7	.222	24	17	1	0	0	108^2	108	64	56	12	4	56	79	1.509	4.64	97	4.69	.263	6	.176	-2	5	-0.1
1971 Chi-N	3	2	.600	21	4	0	0	0	45^2	62	24	24	2	0	25	37	1.905	4.73	83	6.33	.343	2	.250	-3	2	-0.3
1972 Chi-N	1	0	1.000	5	1	0	0	0	12^2	9	3	3	1	0	4	7	1.026	2.13	179	2.06	.188	0	.000	2	1	0.2
1973 Min-A	10	10	.500	29	24	6	3	0	170^1	167	87	79	12	4	88	109	1.497	4.17	95	4.36	.260	0	....	-3	8	-0.3
1974 Min-A	16	14	.533	37	37	11	1	0	248^2	234	105	91	24	2	97	158	1.331	3.29	114	3.76	.252	0	....	15	17	1.5
1975 Min-A	1	3	.250	10	7	1	0	0	26^1	25	25	25	2	0	36	8	2.316	8.54	45	7.62	.260	0	....	-13	0	-1.4
1976 Min-A	2	7	.222	13	12	0	0	0	58	60	37	34	3	1	51	35	1.914	5.28	68	5.89	.273	0	....	-11	0	-1.2
1979 Sea-A	0	1	.000	9	2	0	0	0	27^1	27	14	13	2	0	14	12	1.500	4.28	102	4.16	.255	0	....	0	1	0.0
Total 9	36	44	.450	152	105	19	4	0	710	702	363	329	58	11	377	458	1.520	4.17	95	4.50	.262	8	.174	-14	35	-1.3
• DECKER, Marty	Dee Martin Decker b: 6/7/1957, Upland, CA BR/TR, 5'11", 168 lbs. Deb: 9/20/1983																									
1983 SD-N	0	0	....	4	0	0	0	0	8^2	5	2	2	1	1	3	9	.923	2.08	168	2.26	.167	0	....	1	1	0.1
• DEDMON, Jeff	Jeffrey Linden Dedmon b: 3/4/1960, Torrance, CA BL/TR, 6'2", 200 lbs. Deb: 9/2/1983																									
1983 Atl-N	0	0	....	5	0	0	0	0	4	10	6	6	1	0	0	3	2.500	13.50	29	12.76	.455	0	....	-4	0	-0.5
1984 Atl-N	4	3	.571	54	0	0	0	4	81	86	39	34	5	2	35	51	1.494	3.78	102	4.23	.277	0	.000	1	5	0.1
1985 Atl-N	6	3	.667	60	0	0	0	0	86	84	52	39	5	1	49	41	1.547	4.08	94	4.13	.264	1	.111	-2	4	-0.2
1986 Atl-N	6	6	.500	57	0	0	0	3	99^2	90	43	33	8	4	39	58	1.294	2.98	133	3.44	.242	2	.125	12	9	1.2
1987 Atl-N	3	4	.429	53	3	0	0	4	89^2	82	46	39	8	1	42	40	1.383	3.91	111	3.84	.246	4	.250	5	7	0.6
1988 Cle-A	1	0	1.000	21	0	0	0	1	33^2	35	20	17	3	3	21	17	1.663	4.54	90	5.40	.276	0	....	-1	1	-0.1
Total 6	20	16	.556	250	3	0	0	12	394	387	206	168	30	11	186	210	1.454	3.84	104	4.11	.261	7	.149	11	26	1.1
• DEDRICK, Jim	James Michael Dedrick b: 4/4/1968, Los Angeles, CA BB/TR, 6', 185 lbs. Deb: 8/12/1995																									
1995 Bal-A	0	0	....	6	0	0	0	0	7^2	8	2	2	1	1	6	3	1.826	2.35	202	7.14	.308	0	....	2	1	0.2
• DEEGAN, Dummy	William John Deegan b: 11/16/1874, Bronx, NY d: 5/17/1957, Bronx, NY Deb: 8/3/1901																									
1901 NY-N	0	1	.000	2	1	1	0	0	17	27	17	12	0	0	6	8	1.941	6.35	52	6.48	.357	0	.000	-5	0	-0.6
• DEERING, John	John Thomas Deering b: 6/25/1878, Lynn, MA d: 2/15/1943, Beverly, MA BR/TR, 6', 180 lbs. Deb: 5/12/1903																									
1903 Det-A	3	4	.429	10	8	5	0	0	60^2	77	38	26	3	1	24	14	1.665	3.86	75	5.36	.308	8	.333	-6	2	-0.4
NY-A	4	3	.571	9	7	6	1	0	60	59	33	25	0	1	18	14	1.283	3.75	83	2.92	.257	1	.043	-4	2	-0.7
Yr.	7	7	.500	19	15	11	1	0	120^2	136	71	51	3	2	42	28	1.475	3.80	79	4.15	.283	9	.191	-10	4	-1.1
• DEGERICK, Mike	Michael Arthur Degerick b: 4/1/1943, New York, NY BR/TR, 6'2", 178 lbs. Deb: 9/4/1961																									
1961 Chi-A	0	0	....	1	0	0	0	0	1^2	2	1	1	0	0	1	0	1.800	5.40	72	5.91	.400	0	....	-0	0	0.0
1962 Chi-A	0	0	....	1	0	0	0	0	1	1	0	0	0	0	1	0	2.000	0.00	....	5.48	.250	0	....	0	0	0.0
Total 2	0	0	....	2	0	0	0	0	2^2	3	1	1	0	0	2	0	1.875	3.38	116	5.75	.333	0	....	0	0	0.0
• DEHART, Rick	Richard Allen DeHart b: 3/21/1970, Topeka, KS BL/TL, 6'1", 180 lbs. Deb: 7/16/1997																									
1997 Mon-N	2	1	.667	23	0	0	0	0	29^1	33	21	18	7	0	14	29	1.602	5.52	76	6.05	.292	0	.000	-4	1	-0.5
1998 Mon-N	0	0	....	26	0	0	0	1	28	34	22	15	3	0	13	14	1.679	4.82	87	5.31	.291	0	....	-1	0	-0.1
1999 Mon-N	0	0	....	3	0	0	0	0	1^2	6	4	4	2	0	3	1	5.400	21.60	21	43.55	.545	0	....	-3	0	-0.3
2003 KC-A	0	2	.000	4	0	0	0	0	4	8	6	6	1	0	2	1	2.500	13.50	38	12.83	.421	0	.000	-4	0	-0.4
Total 4	2	3	.400	56	0	0	0	1	63	81	53	43	13	0	32	45	1.794	6.14	71	7.14	.312	0	.000	-13	1	-1.3
• DEJEAN, Mike	Michael Dwain DeJean b: 9/28/1970, Baton Rouge, LA BR/TR, 6'2", 205 lbs. Deb: 5/2/1997																									
1997 Col-N	5	0	1.000	55	0	0	0	2	67^2	74	34	30	4	3	24	38	1.448	3.99	130	4.29	.280	1	.333	10	7	1.0
1998 Col-N	3	1	.750	59	1	0	0	2	74^1	78	29	25	4	1	24	27	1.372	3.03	171	3.92	.285	0	.000	18	9	1.7
1999 Col-N	2	4	.333	56	0	0	0	0	61	83	61	57	13	2	32	31	1.885	8.41	69	7.77	.335	0	.000	-17	0	-1.7
2000 Col-N	4	4	.500	54	0	0	0	0	53^1	54	31	29	9	0	30	34	1.575	4.89	118	5.22	.269	0	.000	5	4	0.5
2001 Mil-N	4	2	.667	75	0	0	0	2	84^1	75	31	26	4	9	39	68	1.352	2.77	155	3.56	.236	0	.000	14	8	1.3
2002 Mil-N	1	5	.167	68	0	0	0	27	75	66	28	26	7	2	39	65	1.400	3.12	131	3.74	.237	0	.000	8	8	0.8
2003 Mil-N	4	7	.364	58	0	0	0	18	64^2	69	38	35	12	1	27	58	1.485	4.87	87	5.02	.271	0	....	-3	5	-0.3
StL-N	1	1	.500	18	0	0	0	1	18	17	8	8	1	1	12	13	1.611	4.00	102	4.89	.262	0	....	0	1	0.0
Yr.	5	8	.385	76	0	0	0	19	82^2	86	46	43	13	2	39	71	1.512	4.68	90	4.99	.269	0	....	-3	6	-0.3
Total 7	24	24	.500	443	1	0	0	52	498^1	516	260	236	54	19	227	334	1.491	4.26	115	4.67	.271	1	.063	34	42	3.3
• DEJESUS, Jose	Jose Luis DeJesus b: 1/6/1965, Brooklyn, NY BR/TR, 6'5", 195 lbs. Deb: 9/9/1988																									
1988 KC-A	0	1	.000	2	1	0	0	0	2^2	6	10	8	0	0	5	2	4.125	27.00	15	16.91	.429	0	....	-7	0	-0.7
1989 KC-A	0	0	....	3	1	0	0	0	8	7	4	4	1	0	8	2	1.875	4.50	86	6.16	.241	0	....	-0	0	0.0
1990 Phi-N	7	8	.467	22	22	3	1	0	130	97	63	54	10	2	73	87	1.308	3.74	102	3.23	.210	3	.079	-1	7	-0.1
1991 Phi-N	10	9	.526	31	29	3	0	1	181^2	147	74	69	7	4	128	118	**1.514**	3.42	107	3.81	.224	8	.129	6	11	0.5
1994 KC-A	3	1	.750	5	4	0	0	0	26^2	27	14	14	2	0	13	12	1.500	4.73	106	4.54	.276	0	....	1	2	0.1
Total 5	20	19	.513	63	57	6	1	1	349	284	165	149	20	6	227	221	1.464	3.84	100	3.80	.226	11	.110	-1	20	-0.3
• DEL TORO, Miguel	Miguel Alfonso Del Toro b: 6/22/1972, Obregon, Mexico d: 10/6/2001, Obregon, Mexico BR/TR, 6'1", 160 lbs. Deb: 4/6/1999																									
1999 SF-N	0	0	....	14	0	0	0	0	23^2	24	11	11	5	0	11	20	1.479	4.18	100	5.34	.264	0	.000	0	1	0.0
2000* SF-N	2	0	1.000	9	1	0	0	0	17^1	17	10	10	3	2	6	16	1.327	5.19	81	4.44	.250	1	.500	-2	1	-0.1
Total 2	2	0	1.000	23	1	0	0	0	41	41	21	21	8	2	17	36	1.415	4.61	91	4.96	.258	1	.167	-2	2	-0.2
• DELAMAZA, Roland	Roland Robert DeLaMaza b: 11/11/1971, Granada Hills, CA BR/TR, 6'2" Deb: 9/26/1997																									
1997 KC-A	0	0	....	1	0	0	0	0	2	1	1	1	1	0	1	1	1.000	4.50	105	3.56	.125	0	....	0	0	0.0
• DELANEY, Art	Arthur Dewey "Swede" Delaney b: 1/5/1897, Chicago, IL d: 5/2/1970, Hayward, CA BR/TR, 5'10.5", 178 lbs. Deb: 4/16/1924																									
1924 StL-N	1	0	1.000	8	1	1	0	0	20	19	4	4	0	0	6	2	1.250	1.80	210	2.74	.250	2	.286	4	2	0.4
1928 Bos-N	9	17	.346	39	22	8	0	2	192^1	197	100	81	11	1	56	45	1.315	3.79	103	3.38	.267	9	.143	9	8	0.6
1929 Bos-N	3	5	.375	20	8	3	1	0	75	103	59	51	6	1	35	17	1.840	6.12	76	6.32	.336	3	.143	-12	1	-1.0
Total 3	13	22	.371	67	31	12	1	2	287^1	319	163	136	17	2	97	64	1.448	4.26	98	4.10	.285	14	.154	2	11	0.1
• DELEON, Jose	Jose (Chestaro) DeLeon b: 12/20/1960, Rancho Viejo, Dominican Republic BR/TR, 6'3", 215 lbs. Deb: 7/23/1983																									
1983 Pit-N	7	3	.700	15	15	3	2	0	108	75	36	34	5	1	47	118	1.130	2.83	131	2.29	.196	2	.059	11	9	1.1
1984 Pit-N	7	13	.350	30	28	5	1	0	192^1	147	86	80	10	3	92	153	1.243	3.74	96	2.84	.214	5	.085	-6	7	-1.0
1985 Pit-N	2	19	.095	31	25	1	0	3	162^2	138	93	85	15	3	89	149	1.395	4.70	76	3.81	.231	2	.056	-18	2	-2.0
1986 Pit-N	1	3	.250	9	1	0	0	1	16^1	17	16	15	2	1	17	11	2.082	8.27	46	6.94	.266	0	.000	-8	0	-0.8
Chi-A	4	5	.444	13	13	1	0	0	79	49	30	26	7	4	42	68	1.152	2.96	146	2.69	.179	0	....	10	7	1.0
1987 Chi-A	11	12	.478	33	31	2	0	0	206	177	106	92	24	10	97	153	1.330	4.02	114	3.82	.230	0	....	7	12	0.7
1988 StL-N	13	10	.565	34	34	3	1	0	225^1	198	95	92	13	2	86	208	1.260	3.67	95	3.06	.237	10	.139	-7	12	-0.8
1989 StL-N	16	12	.571	36	36	5	3	0	244^2	173	96	83	16	6	80	**201**	1.034	3.05	119	2.16	**.197**	8	.096	13	15	1.0
1990 StL-N	7	19	.269	32	32	0	0	0	182^2	168	96	90	15	5	86	164	1.391	4.43	86	3.79	.246	6	.107	-12	6	-1.4
1991 StL-N	5	9	.357	28	28	1	0	0	162^2	144	57	49	15	6	61	118	1.260	2.71	137	3.47	.239	2	.043	17	11	1.3
1992 StL-N	2	7	.222	29	15	0	0	0	102^1	95	56	52	7	2	43	72	1.349	4.57	74	3.55	.245	1	.048	-15	1	-1.7
Phi-N	0	1	.000	3	3	0	0	0	15	16	7	5	0	0	5	7	1.400	3.00	116	3.57	.281	2	.400	1	1	0.2
Yr.	2	8	.200	32	18	0	0	0	117^1	111	63	57	7	2	48	79	1.355	4.37	78	3.55	.250	3	.115	-14	2	-1.5
1993 Phi-N	3	0	1.000	24	3	0	0	0	47	39	25	17	5	5	27	34	1.404	3.26	122	4.17	.229	0	.000	4	3	0.3
* Chi-A	0	0	....	11	0	0	0	0	10^1	5	2	2	2	1	3	6	.774	1.74	240	2.13	.152	0	....	3	1	0.3
1994 Chi-A	3	2	.600	42	0	0	0	2	67	48	28	25	5	6	31	67	1.179	3.36	139	2.76	.200	0	....	10	6	0.9

YEAR	TM-L	W	L	PCT	G	GS	CG	SH	SV	IP	H	R	ER	HR	HB	BB	SO	RAT	ERA	ERA+	CERA	OAV	BH	AVG	PR+	WS	TPW
1995	Chi-A	5	3	.625	38	0	0	0	0	67^2	60	41	39	10	6	28	53	1.300	5.19	86	4.11	.238	0	....	-5	3	-0.4
	Mon-N	0	1	.000	7	0	0	0	0	8^1	7	7	7	2	1	7	12	1.680	7.56	57	6.40	.233	0	....	-3	0	-0.3
Total	13	86	119	.420	415	264	21	7	6	1897^1	1556	877	793	153	62	841	1594	1.263	3.76	101	3.24	.224	38	.091	2	96	-1.7

• DELEON, Luis Luis Antonio (Tricoche) DeLeon b: 8/19/1958, Ponce, Puerto Rico BR/TR, 6'1", 153 lbs. Deb: 9/6/1981

YEAR	TM-L	W	L	PCT	G	GS	CG	SH	SV	IP	H	R	ER	HR	HB	BB	SO	RAT	ERA	ERA+	CERA	OAV	BH	AVG	PR+	WS	TPW
1981	StL-N	0	1	.000	10	0	0	0	0	15^1	11	4	4	1	0	3	8	.913	2.35	151	1.60	.200	0	.000	2	1	0.2
1982	SD-N	9	5	.643	61	0	0	0	15	102	77	25	23	10	1	16	60	.912	2.03	169	1.88	.212	1	.091	15	14	1.6
1983	SD-N	6	6	.500	63	0	0	0	13	111	89	34	33	8	1	27	90	1.045	2.68	130	2.25	.224	2	.143	8	13	0.9
1984	SD-N	2	2	.500	32	0	0	0	0	42^2	44	34	26	12	4	12	44	1.313	5.48	65	5.16	.256	0	.000	-10	0	-1.1
1985	SD-N	0	3	.000	29	0	0	0	3	38^2	39	18	18	6	3	10	31	1.267	4.19	84	4.14	.267	1	.200	-3	1	-0.4
1987	Bal-A	0	2	.000	11	0	0	0	1	20^2	19	15	11	1	2	8	13	1.306	4.79	92	3.43	.253	0	....	-1	1	-0.1
1989	Sea-A	0	0	....	1	1	0	0	0	4	5	1	1	1	1	1	2	1.500	2.25	179	7.44	.313	0	....	1	0	0.1
Total	7	17	19	.472	207	1	0	0	32	334^1	284	131	116	39	12	77	248	1.080	3.12	115	2.83	.232	4	.114	11	30	1.1

• DELHI, Flame Lee William Delhi b: 11/5/1892, Harqua Hala, AZ d: 5/9/1966, Greenbrae, CA BR/TR, 6'2.5", 198 lbs. Deb: 4/16/1912

YEAR	TM-L	W	L	PCT	G	GS	CG	SH	SV	IP	H	R	ER	HR	HB	BB	SO	RAT	ERA	ERA+	CERA	OAV	BH	AVG	PR+	WS	TPW
1912	Chi-A	0	0	....	1	0	0	0	0	3	7	6	3	0	0	3	2	3.333	9.00	36	13.31	.412	0	....	-2	0	-0.2

• DELL, Wheezer William George Dell b: 6/11/1886, Tuscarora, NV d: 8/24/1966, Independence, CA BR/TR, 6'4", 210 lbs. Deb: 4/22/1912

YEAR	TM-L	W	L	PCT	G	GS	CG	SH	SV	IP	H	R	ER	HR	HB	BB	SO	RAT	ERA	ERA+	CERA	OAV	BH	AVG	PR+	WS	TPW
1912	StL-N	0	0	....	3	0	0	0	0	2^1	3	3	3	0	0	3	0	2.571	11.57	30	7.94	.188	0	....	-2	0	-0.2
1915	Bro-N	11	10	.524	40	24	12	4	1	215	166	80	56	5	8	100	94	1.237	2.34	118	2.63	.218	10	.152	9	15	0.9
1916*	Bro-N	8	9	.471	32	16	9	2	1	155	143	52	39	2	4	43	76	1.200	2.26	118	2.75	.256	4	.091	4	10	0.2
1917	Bro-N	0	4	.000	17	4	0	0	1	58	55	35	24	3	2	25	28	1.379	3.72	75	3.66	.263	1	.063	-7	0	-0.9
Total	4	19	23	.452	92	44	21	6	3	430^1	367	170	122	10	14	171	198	1.250	2.55	108	2.84	.238	15	.119	5	25	0.0

• DELOCK, Ike Ivan Martin Delock b: 11/11/1929, Highland Park, MI BR/TR, 5'11", 175 lbs. Deb: 4/17/1952

YEAR	TM-L	W	L	PCT	G	GS	CG	SH	SV	IP	H	R	ER	HR	HB	BB	SO	RAT	ERA	ERA+	CERA	OAV	BH	AVG	PR+	WS	TPW
1952	Bos-A	4	9	.308	39	7	1	1	5	95	88	50	45	9	2	50	46	1.453	4.26	92	4.04	.245	1	.045	-4	5	-0.5
1953	Bos-A	3	1	.750	23	1	0	0	1	48^2	60	27	24	2	2	20	22	1.644	4.44	95	5.04	.308	1	.100	-2	3	-0.2
1955	Bos-A	9	7	.563	29	18	6	0	3	143^2	136	67	60	17	4	61	88	1.371	3.76	114	4.07	.247	7	.143	10	10	0.9
1956	Bos-A	13	7	.650	48	8	1	0	9	128^1	122	65	60	12	5	80	105	1.574	4.21	110	4.70	.252	3	.103	6	11	0.4
1957	Bos-A	9	8	.529	49	2	0	0	11	94	80	40	40	11	3	45	62	1.330	3.83	104	3.68	.230	1	.048	3	10	0.2
1958	Bos-A	14	8	.636	31	19	9	1	2	160	155	66	60	13	0	56	82	1.319	3.38	119	3.50	.252	3	.063	14	13	1.1
1959	Bos-A	11	6	.647	28	17	4	0	0	134^1	120	53	44	12	2	62	55	1.355	2.95	138	3.63	.236	3	.064	16	11	1.4
1960	Bos-A	9	10	.474	24	23	3	1	0	129^1	145	77	68	21	4	52	49	1.523	4.73	85	5.34	.283	5	.116	-6	5	-0.9
1961	Bos-A	6	9	.400	28	28	3	1	0	156	185	110	85	24	2	52	80	1.519	4.90	85	5.26	.293	5	.104	-12	3	-1.4
1962	Bos-A	4	5	.444	17	13	4	2	0	86^1	89	39	36	10	0	24	49	1.309	3.75	110	3.86	.268	2	.087	3	5	0.2
1963	Bos-A	1	2	.333	6	6	1	0	0	32	31	18	16	4	0	12	23	1.344	4.50	84	3.89	.246	0	.000	-2	1	-0.4
	Bal-A	1	3	.250	7	5	0	0	0	30^1	25	17	17	7	0	16	11	1.352	5.04	70	4.64	.236	0	.000	-5	0	-0.7
	Yr.	2	5	.286	13	11	1	0	0	62^1	56	35	33	11	0	28	34	1.348	4.76	77	4.25	.241	0	.000	-7	1	-1.1
Total	11	84	75	.528	329	147	32	6	31	1238	1236	629	555	142	24	530	672	1.426	4.03	102	4.30	.259	31	.086	21	77	0.2

• DELUCIA, Rich Richard Anthony DeLucia b: 10/7/1964, Reading, PA BR/TR, 6', 185 lbs. Deb: 9/8/1990

YEAR	TM-L	W	L	PCT	G	GS	CG	SH	SV	IP	H	R	ER	HR	HB	BB	SO	RAT	ERA	ERA+	CERA	OAV	BH	AVG	PR+	WS	TPW
1990	Sea-A	1	2	.333	5	5	1	0	0	36	30	9	8	2	0	9	20	1.083	2.00	198	2.38	.226	0	....	8	3	0.8
1991	Sea-A	12	13	.480	32	31	0	0	0	182	176	107	103	31	4	78	98	1.396	5.09	81	4.62	.260	0	....	-23	5	-2.3
1992	Sea-A	3	6	.333	30	11	0	0	1	83^2	100	55	51	13	2	35	66	1.614	5.49	72	5.75	.293	0	....	-14	1	-1.4
1993	Sea-A	3	6	.333	30	1	0	0	0	42^2	46	24	22	5	1	23	48	1.617	4.64	95	5.15	.272	0	....	-1	2	-0.1
1994	Cin-N	0	0	....	8	0	0	0	0	10^2	9	6	5	4	0	5	15	1.313	4.22	98	5.13	.214	0	....	-0	0	0.0
1995	StL-N	8	7	.533	56	1	0	0	0	82^1	63	38	31	9	3	36	76	1.202	3.39	124	3.13	.213	2	.200	6	6	0.6
1996	SF-N	3	6	.333	56	0	0	0	0	61^2	62	44	40	8	3	31	55	1.508	5.84	70	4.69	.259	1	.250	-12	1	-1.2
1997	SF-N	0	0	....	3	0	0	0	0	1^2	6	3	2	0	0	0	2	3.600	10.80	37	17.53	.500	0	....	-1	0	-0.1
	Ana-A	6	4	.600	33	0	0	0	3	42^1	29	18	17	5	1	27	42	1.323	3.61	128	3.56	.204	0	....	4	5	0.4
1998	Ana-A	2	6	.250	61	0	0	0	3	71^2	56	36	34	10	3	46	73	1.423	4.27	110	4.13	.221	0	....	4	5	0.4
1999	Cle-A	0	1	.000	6	0	0	0	0	9^1	13	7	7	4	0	9	7	2.357	6.75	75	11.41	.317	0	....	-2	0	-0.2
Total	10	38	51	.427	320	49	1	0	7	624	590	347	320	91	17	299	502	1.425	4.62	91	4.50	.251	3	.214	-31	28	-3.0

• DEMARAIS, Fred Frederick Demarais b: 11/1/1866, Canada d: 3/6/1919, Stamford, CT TR, 5'9", 168 lbs. Deb: 7/26/1890

YEAR	TM-L	W	L	PCT	G	GS	CG	SH	SV	IP	H	R	ER	HR	HB	BB	SO	RAT	ERA	ERA+	CERA	OAV	BH	AVG	PR+	WS	TPW
1890	Chi-N	0	0	....	1	0	0	0	0	2	1	0	0	0	0	1	1	1.000	0.00	....	....	.145	0	.000	1	0	0.0

• DEMAREE, Al Albert Wentworth Demaree b: 9/8/1884, Quincy, IL d: 4/30/1962, Los Angeles, CA BL/TR, 6', 170 lbs. Deb: 9/26/1912

YEAR	TM-L	W	L	PCT	G	GS	CG	SH	SV	IP	H	R	ER	HR	HB	BB	SO	RAT	ERA	ERA+	CERA	OAV	BH	AVG	PR+	WS	TPW
1912	NY-N	1	0	1.000	2	2	1	1	0	16	17	3	3	0	0	2	11	1.188	1.69	200	2.72	.288	0	.000	3	2	0.2
1913*	NY-N	13	4	.765	31	24	11	2	2	199^2	176	65	49	4	5	38	76	1.072	2.21	141	2.29	.243	7	.106	19	17	1.6
1914	NY-N	10	17	.370	38	30	13	2	0	224	219	97	77	3	8	77	89	1.321	3.09	86	3.21	.263	9	.132	-11	9	-1.4
1915	Phi-N	14	11	.560	32	26	13	3	1	209^2	201	84	71	4	3	58	69	1.235	3.05	90	2.91	.260	12	.176	-7	12	-0.8
1916	Phi-N	19	14	.576	39	35	25	4	1	285	252	99	83	4	8	48	130	1.053	2.62	101	2.18	.242	11	.109	1	18	-0.3
1917	Chi-N	5	9	.357	24	18	6	1	1	141^1	125	53	40	5	2	37	43	1.146	2.55	113	2.57	.244	5	.122	8	8	0.7
	NY-N	4	5	.444	15	11	1	0	0	78^1	70	33	23	1	1	17	23	1.111	2.64	96	2.25	.239	2	.111	-2	3	-0.3
	Yr.	9	14	.391	39	29	7	1	1	219^2	195	86	63	6	3	54	66	1.134	2.58	107	2.45	.242	7	.119	6	11	0.4
1918	NY-N	8	6	.571	26	14	8	2	1	142	143	56	39	5	2	25	39	1.183	2.47	106	2.84	.262	6	.128	2	8	-0.1
1919	Bos-N	6	6	.500	25	13	6	0	3	128	147	66	54	8	1	35	34	1.422	3.80	75	4.19	.300	2	.048	-13	3	-2.0
Total	8	80	72	.526	232	173	84	15	9	1424	1350	556	439	34	30	337	514	1.185	2.77	99	2.76	.256	54	.118	-1	80	-2.4

• DEMERY, Larry Lawrence Calvin Demery b: 6/4/1953, Bakersfield, CA BR/TR, 6', 170 lbs. Deb: 6/2/1974

YEAR	TM-L	W	L	PCT	G	GS	CG	SH	SV	IP	H	R	ER	HR	HB	BB	SO	RAT	ERA	ERA+	CERA	OAV	BH	AVG	PR+	WS	TPW
1974*	Pit-N	6	6	.500	19	15	2	0	0	95^1	95	47	45	12	0	51	51	1.531	4.25	81	4.73	.262	5	.152	-9	3	-0.9
1975*	Pit-N	7	5	.583	45	8	1	0	4	114^2	95	40	37	7	3	43	59	1.203	2.90	122	2.88	.230	3	.125	8	9	0.9
1976	Pit-N	10	7	.588	36	15	4	1	2	145	123	56	51	8	2	58	72	1.248	3.17	110	2.94	.234	5	.125	5	10	0.4
1977	Pit-N	6	5	.545	39	8	0	0	1	90^1	100	59	51	13	0	47	35	1.627	5.08	78	5.46	.279	3	.150	-12	2	-1.3
Total	4	29	23	.558	139	46	7	1	7	445^1	413	202	184	40	5	199	217	1.374	3.72	97	3.82	.249	16	.137	-9	24	-0.8

• DEMILLER, Harry Harry DeMiller b: 11/12/1867, Wooster, OH d: 10/19/1928, Santa Ana, CA BR/TL Deb: 8/20/1892

YEAR	TM-L	W	L	PCT	G	GS	CG	SH	SV	IP	H	R	ER	HR	HB	BB	SO	RAT	ERA	ERA+	CERA	OAV	BH	AVG	PR+	WS	TPW
1892	Chi-N	1	1	.500	4	2	2	0	0	24	29	22	17	1	1	16	15	1.875	6.38	52	5.87	.287	3	.300	-8	0	-0.6

• DEMOLA, Don Donald John DeMola b: 7/5/1952, Glen Cove, NY BR/TR, 6'2", 185 lbs. Deb: 4/13/1974

YEAR	TM-L	W	L	PCT	G	GS	CG	SH	SV	IP	H	R	ER	HR	HB	BB	SO	RAT	ERA	ERA+	CERA	OAV	BH	AVG	PR+	WS	TPW
1974	Mon-N	1	0	1.000	25	1	0	0	0	57^2	46	21	20	7	0	21	47	1.162	3.12	123	3.03	.223	0	.000	5	4	0.4
1975	Mon-N	4	7	.364	60	0	0	0	1	97^2	92	47	45	8	4	42	63	1.372	4.15	92	3.81	.251	0	.000	-4	5	-0.5
Total	2	5	7	.417	85	1	0	0	1	155^1	138	68	65	15	4	63	110	1.294	3.77	102	3.52	.241	0	.000	1	9	0.0

• DEMOTT, Ben Benyew Harrison DeMott b: 4/2/1889, Green Village, NJ d: 7/5/1963, Somerville, NJ BR/TR, 6', 192 lbs. Deb: 8/12/1910

YEAR	TM-L	W	L	PCT	G	GS	CG	SH	SV	IP	H	R	ER	HR	HB	BB	SO	RAT	ERA	ERA+	CERA	OAV	BH	AVG	PR+	WS	TPW
1910	Cle-A	0	3	.000	6	4	1	0	0	28^1	45	25	17	0	1	8	13	1.871	5.40	48	6.92	.388	3	.167	-9	0	-1.1
1911	Cle-A	0	1	.000	1	1	0	0	0	3^2	10	5	5	0	0	2	2	3.273	12.27	28	18.23	.588	0	.000	-4	0	-0.4
Total	2	0	4	.000	7	5	1	0	0	32	55	30	22	0	1	10	15	2.031	6.19	44	8.22	.414	3	.136	-13	0	-1.5

• DEMPSEY, Con Cornelius Francis Dempsey b: 9/16/1923, San Francisco, CA BR/TR, 6'4", 190 lbs. Deb: 4/28/1951

YEAR	TM-L	W	L	PCT	G	GS	CG	SH	SV	IP	H	R	ER	HR	HB	BB	SO	RAT	ERA	ERA+	CERA	OAV	BH	AVG	PR+	WS	TPW
1951	Pit-N	0	2	.000	3	2	0	0	0	7	11	7	7	2	0	4	3	2.143	9.00	47	10.59	.393	0	.000	-4	0	-0.4

• DEMPSEY, Mark Mark Steven Dempsey b: 12/17/1957, Dayton, OH BR/TR, 6'6", 220 lbs. Deb: 9/4/1982

YEAR	TM-L	W	L	PCT	G	GS	CG	SH	SV	IP	H	R	ER	HR	HB	BB	SO	RAT	ERA	ERA+	CERA	OAV	BH	AVG	PR+	WS	TPW
1982	SF-N	0	0	....	3	1	0	0	0	5^2	11	5	5	1	0	2	4	2.294	7.94	45	11.13	.440	0	.000	-3	0	-0.3

• DEMPSTER, Ryan Ryan Scott Dempster b: 5/3/1977, Sechelt, Canada BR/TR, 6'2", 201 lbs. Deb: 5/23/1998

YEAR	TM-L	W	L	PCT	G	GS	CG	SH	SV	IP	H	R	ER	HR	HB	BB	SO	RAT	ERA	ERA+	CERA	OAV	BH	AVG	PR+	WS	TPW
1998	Fla-N	1	5	.167	14	11	0	0	0	54^2	72	47	43	6	9	38	35	2.012	7.08	58	8.14	.336	0	.000	-18	0	-1.9
1999	Fla-N	7	8	.467	25	25	0	0	0	147	146	77	77	21	6	93	126	1.626	4.71	92	5.49	.262	5	.102	-5	6	-0.7
2000	Fla-N★	14	10	.583	33	33	2	1	0	226^1	210	102	92	30	5	97	209	1.356	3.66	121	4.04	.243	6	.078	21	17	1.5
2001	Fla-N	15	12	.556	34	34	2	1	0	211^1	218	123	116	21	10	112	171	1.562	4.94	85	4.91	.269	3	.049	-18	7	-2.2

YEAR	TM-L	W	L	PCT	G	GS	CG	SH	SV	IP	H	R	ER	HR	HB	BB	SO	RAT	ERA	ERA+	CERA	OAV	BH	AVG	PR+	WS	TPW
2002	Fla-N	5	8	.385	18	18	3	0	0	120^1	126	66	64	12	7	55	87	1.504	4.79	82	4.95	.281	2	.059	-12	3	-1.4
	Cin-N	5	5	.500	15	15	1	0	0	88^2	102	61	61	16	3	38	66	1.579	6.19	68	5.90	.293	6	.207	-19	1	-1.9
	Yr.	10	13	.435	33	33	4	0	0	209	228	127	125	28	10	93	153	1.536	5.38	76	5.35	.286	8	.127	-31	4	-3.2
2003	Cin-N	3	7	.300	22	20	0	0	0	115^2	134	89	84	14	5	70	84	1.764	6.54	65	6.11	.293	1	.030	-29	0	-3.1
Total	6	50	55	.476	161	156	8	2	0	964	1008	565	537	120	45	503	778	1.567	5.01	84	5.22	.273	23	.078	-81	34	-9.6
• DENEHY, Bill	William Francis Denehy b: 3/31/1946, Middletown, CT BB/TR, 6'3", 200 lbs. Deb: 4/16/1967																										
1967	NY-N	1	7	.125	15	8	0	0	0	53^2	51	38	28	8	0	29	35	1.491	4.70	72	4.56	.248	0	.000	-8	0	-0.9
1968	Was-A	0	0	....	3	0	0	0	0	2	4	3	2	0	0	4	1	4.000	9.00	32	16.46	.444	0	....	-1	0	-0.2
1971	Det-A	0	3	.000	31	1	0	0	1	49	47	25	23	4	4	28	27	1.531	4.22	85	4.63	.250	0	.000	-3	1	-0.3
Total	3	1	10	.091	49	9	0	0	1	104^2	102	66	53	12	4	61	63	1.557	4.56	76	4.82	.253	0	.000	-13	1	-1.4
• DENMAN, Brian	Brian John Denman b: 2/12/1956, Minneapolis, MN BR/TR, 6'4", 205 lbs. Deb: 8/22/1982																										
1982	Bos-A	3	4	.429	9	9	2	1	0	49	55	32	26	6	0	9	9	1.306	4.78	90	3.97	.282	0	....	-2	2	-0.2
• DENNIS, Don	Donald Ray Dennis b: 3/3/1942, Uniontown, KS BR/TR, 6'2", 190 lbs. Deb: 6/18/1965																										
1965	StL-N	2	3	.400	41	0	0	0	6	55	47	17	14	3	1	16	29	1.145	2.29	168	2.43	.236	2	.400	9	7	1.0
1966	StL-N	4	2	.667	38	1	0	0	2	59^2	73	36	33	8	1	17	25	1.508	4.98	72	4.91	.302	1	.083	-10	1	-1.1
Total	2	6	5	.545	79	1	0	0	8	114^2	120	53	47	11	2	33	54	1.334	3.69	99	3.72	.272	3	.176	-0	8	-0.1
• DENNY, John	John Allen Denny b: 11/8/1952, Prescott, AZ BR/TR, 6'3", 190 lbs. Deb: 9/12/1974																										
1974	StL-N	0	0	....	2	0	0	0	0	2	3	2	0	0	0	0	1	1.500	0.00	....	3.55	.273	0	....	1	0	0.1
1975	StL-N	10	7	.588	25	24	3	2	0	136	149	73	60	5	3	51	72	1.471	3.97	95	4.11	.280	10	.227	0	6	0.1
1976	StL-N	11	9	.550	30	30	8	3	0	207	189	71	58	11	8	74	74	1.271	**2.52**	**140**	3.30	.246	15	.224	22	18	2.6
1977	StL-N	8	8	.500	26	26	3	1	0	149^2	165	85	75	9	5	62	60	1.517	4.51	85	4.56	.281	5	.098	-14	3	-1.7
1978	StL-N	14	11	.560	33	33	11	2	0	234	200	81	77	13	6	74	103	1.171	2.96	119	2.87	.238	13	.178	12	15	1.6
1979	StL-N	8	11	.421	31	31	5	2	0	206	206	116	111	24	3	100	99	1.485	4.85	78	4.58	.264	9	.129	-30	5	-3.2
1980	Cle-A	8	6	.571	16	16	4	1	0	108^2	116	54	53	4	5	47	59	1.500	4.39	93	4.46	.284	0	....	-3	6	-0.3
1981	Cle-A	10	6	.625	19	19	6	3	0	145^2	139	62	51	9	3	66	94	1.407	3.15	115	3.86	.254	0	....	13	11	1.3
1982	Cle-A	6	11	.353	21	21	5	0	0	138^1	126	80	77	11	6	73	94	1.439	5.01	81	4.06	.240	0	....	-13	5	-1.3
	Phi-N	0	2	.000	4	4	0	0	0	22^1	18	12	10	1	0	10	19	1.254	4.03	91	2.75	.217	1	.167	-1	1	0.0
1983*	Phi-N	**19**	6	.760	36	36	7	1	0	242^2	229	77	64	9	4	53	139	1.162	2.37	150	2.75	.250	13	.169	**36**	23	**3.8**
1984	Phi-N	7	7	.500	22	22	2	0	0	154^1	122	53	42	11	4	29	94	.978	2.45	148	2.11	.214	9	.191	23	12	2.4
1985	Phi-N	11	14	.440	33	33	6	2	0	230^2	252	112	98	15	3	83	123	1.452	3.82	96	4.24	.282	10	.123	-1	10	-0.1
1986	Cin-N	11	10	.524	27	27	2	1	0	171^1	179	89	80	15	4	56	115	1.372	4.20	92	3.99	.272	12	.222	-5	8	-0.4
Total	13	123	108	.532	325	322	62	18	0	2148^2	2093	967	856	137	54	778	1146	1.336	3.59	104	3.66	.258	97	.170	40	123	4.7
• DENT, Eddie	Elliott Estill Dent b: 12/8/1887, Baltimore, MD d: 11/25/1974, Birmingham, AL BR/TR, 6'1", 190 lbs. Deb: 8/31/1909																										
1909	Bro-N	2	4	.333	6	5	4	0	0	42	47	23	20	2	0	15	17	1.476	4.29	60	4.54	.307	1	.067	-8	0	-1.0
1911	Bro-N	2	1	.667	5	3	1	0	0	31^2	30	15	13	0	2	10	3	1.263	3.69	90	3.07	.256	1	.100	-1	2	-0.2
1912	Bro-N	0	0	....	1	0	0	0	0	1	4	4	4	0	0	1	1	5.000	36.00	9	27.24	.571	0	.000	-4	0	-0.4
Total	3	4	5	.444	12	8	5	0	0	74^2	81	42	37	2	2	26	21	1.433	4.46	65	4.22	.292	2	.077	-12	2	-1.5
• DENZER, Roger	Roger "Peaceful Valley" Denzer b: 10/5/1871, Le Sueur, MN d: 9/18/1949, Le Sueur, MN BL/TR, 6', 180 lbs. Deb: 4/24/1897																										
1897	Chi-N	2	8	.200	12	10	8	0	0	94^2	125	91	54	4	2	34	17	1.680	5.13	87	5.31	.315	6	.154	-6	2	-0.8
1901	NY-N	2	6	.250	11	9	3	1	0	61^2	69	30	23	2	2	5	22	1.200	3.36	98	3.16	.281	2	.091	1	2	0.1
Total	2	4	14	.222	23	19	11	1	0	156^1	194	121	77	6	4	39	39	1.490	4.43	91	4.46	.302	8	.131	-5	4	-0.7
• DEPAULA, Jorge	Jorge DePaula b: 11/10/1978, Sabana Grande, Dominican Republic BR/TR, 6'1", 160 lbs. Deb: 9/5/2003																										
2003	NY-A	0	0	....	4	1	0	0	0	11^1	3	1	1	1	1	1	7	.353	0.79	550	0.54	.083	0	....	5	2	0.5
• DEPAULA, Sean	Sean Michael DePaula b: 11/7/1973, Newton, MA BR/TR, 6'4", 220 lbs. Deb: 8/31/1999																										
1999*	Cle-A	0	0	....	11	0	0	0	0	11^2	8	6	6	0	0	3	18	.943	4.63	109	1.50	.200	0	....	1	1	0.1
2000	Cle-A	0	0	....	13	0	0	0	0	16^2	20	11	11	3	0	14	16	2.040	5.94	84	7.49	.294	0	....	-2	1	-0.2
2002	Cle-A	1	1	.500	5	0	0	0	0	6^1	11	9	9	3	0	3	8	2.211	12.79	34	12.28	.367	0	....	-6	0	-0.6
Total	3	1	1	.500	29	0	0	0	0	34^2	39	26	26	6	0	20	42	1.702	6.75	71	6.35	.283	0	....	-7	2	-0.7
• DERBY, George	George H. "Jonah" Derby b: 7/6/1857, Webster, MA d: 7/4/1925, Philadelphia, PA BL/TR, 6', 175 lbs. Deb: 5/2/1881																										
1881	Det-N	29	26	.527	56	55	55	**9**	0	494^2	505	252	121	3	....	86	**212**	1.195	2.20	133	....	.253	44	.186	37	34	2.5
1882	Det-N	17	20	.459	40	39	38	3	0	362	386	267	131	8	....	81	182	1.290	3.26	90	....	.258	29	.195	-6	19	-1.1
1883	Buf-N	2	10	.167	14	13	12	0	1	107^2	173	120	70	3	....	15	34	**1.746**	5.85	54	....	.343	14	.237	-31	0	-2.8
Total	3	48	56	.462	110	107	105	12	1	964^1	1064	639	322	14	....	182	428	1.292	3.01	99	....	.266	87	.196	-0	53	-1.4
• DERRINGER, Paul	Samuel Paul "Duke,Oom Paul" Derringer b: 10/17/1906, Springfield, KY d: 11/17/1987, Sarasota, FL BR/TR, 6'3.5", 205 lbs. Deb: 4/16/1931																										
1931*	StL-N	18	8	.692	35	23	15	4	2	211^2	225	88	79	9	4	65	134	1.370	3.36	117	3.69	.274	7	.097	13	17	0.7
1932	StL-N	11	14	.440	39	30	14	1	0	233^1	296	133	105	6	2	67	78	1.556	4.05	97	4.54	.310	13	.178	-2	11	-0.2
1933	StL-N	0	2	.000	3	2	1	0	0	17	24	11	8	0	1	9	3	1.941	4.24	82	6.20	.353	0	.000	-1	0	-0.2
	Cin-N	7	25	.219	33	31	16	2	1	231	240	106	83	4	5	51	86	1.260	3.23	105	3.09	.271	14	.184	6	11	0.6
	Yr.	7	27	.206	36	33	17	2	1	248	264	117	91	4	6	60	89	1.306	3.30	103	3.31	.277	14	.173	5	11	0.3
1934	Cin-N	15	21	.417	47	31	18	1	4	261	297	129	104	8	4	59	122	1.364	3.59	114	3.64	.283	18	.196	21	17	2.1
1935	Cin-N★	22	13	.629	45	33	20	3	2	276^2	295	132	108	13	4	49	120	1.243	3.51	113	3.23	.271	13	.140	17	20	1.2
1936	Cin-N	19	19	.500	**51**	**37**	13	2	5	282^1	331	147	126	11	4	42	121	1.321	4.02	95	3.61	.289	18	.200	-4	17	-0.5
1937	Cin-N	10	14	.417	43	26	12	1	1	222^2	240	112	100	7	0	55	94	1.325	4.04	92	3.29	.271	16	.200	-7	9	-0.6
1938	Cin-N★	21	14	.600	41	**37**	**26**	4	3	**307**	315	110	100	20	0	49	132	1.186	2.93	124	3.02	.262	21	.176	20	25	1.9
1939*	Cin-N★	25	7	.781	38	35	28	5	0	301	321	115	98	15	3	35	128	1.183	2.93	131	3.00	.272	23	.209	22	26	2.2
1940*	Cin-N★	20	12	.625	37	**37**	26	3	0	296^2	280	110	101	17	0	48	115	1.106	3.06	124	2.55	.246	18	.167	13	24	1.1
1941	Cin-N★	12	14	.462	29	28	17	2	1	228^1	233	91	84	16	0	54	76	1.257	3.31	109	3.31	.266	13	.155	8	15	0.5
1942	Cin-N★	10	11	.476	29	27	13	1	0	208^2	203	83	71	4	4	49	68	1.208	3.06	107	2.75	.250	9	.132	4	12	0.3
1943	Chi-N	10	14	.417	32	22	10	2	3	174	184	90	69	7	0	39	75	1.282	3.57	93	3.18	.264	13	.224	-1	7	0.0
1944	Chi-N	7	13	.350	42	16	7	0	3	180	205	96	83	13	0	39	69	1.356	4.15	85	3.85	.284	9	.158	-10	6	-1.2
1945*	Chi-N	16	11	.593	35	30	15	1	4	213^2	223	99	82	8	1	51	86	1.282	3.45	106	3.21	.265	15	.200	1	14	0.1
Total	15	223	212	.513	579	445	251	32	29	3645	3912	1652	1401	158	32	761	1507	1.282	3.46	107	3.32	.272	220	.175	101	231	8.0
• DERRINGTON, Jim	Charles James "Blackie" Derrington b: 11/29/1939, Compton, CA BL/TL, 6'3", 190 lbs. Deb: 9/30/1956																										
1956	Chi-A	0	1	.000	1	1	0	0	0	6	9	6	5	2	0	6	3	2.500	7.50	55	12.72	.375	1	.500	-2	0	-0.2
1957	Chi-A	0	1	.000	20	5	0	0	0	37	29	21	20	4	1	29	14	1.568	4.86	77	4.54	.216	0	.000	-5	0	-0.6
Total	2	0	2	.000	21	6	0	0	0	43	38	27	25	6	1	35	17	1.698	5.23	73	5.68	.241	1	.167	-8	0	-0.8
• DES JARDIEN, Shorty	Paul Raymond Des Jardien b: 8/24/1893, Coffeyville, KS d: 3/7/1956, Monrovia, CA BR/TR, 6'4.5", 205 lbs. Deb: 5/20/1916																										
1916	Cle-A	0	0	....	1	0	0	0	0	1	1	2	2	0	0	1	0	2.000	18.00	17	4.22	.200	0	....	-2	0	-0.2
• DESHAIES, Jim	James Joseph Deshaies b: 6/23/1960, Massena, NY BL/TL, 6'4", 220 lbs. Deb: 8/7/1984																										
1984	NY-A	0	1	.000	2	2	0	0	0	7	14	9	9	1	0	7	5	3.000	11.57	33	14.29	.438	0	....	-6	0	-0.6
1985	Hou-N	0	0	....	2	0	0	0	0	3	1	0	0	0	0	0	2	.333	0.00	....	0.25	.100	0	....	1	0	0.1
1986	Hou-N	12	5	.706	26	26	1	1	0	144	124	58	52	16	2	59	128	1.271	3.25	111	3.51	.234	2	.047	5	10	0.4
1987	Hou-N	11	6	.647	26	25	1	0	0	152	149	81	78	22	0	57	104	1.355	4.62	85	4.11	.257	5	.094	-11	6	-1.1
1988	Hou-N	11	14	.440	31	31	3	2	0	207	164	77	69	20	2	72	127	1.140	3.00	111	2.75	.218	3	.048	8	11	0.4
1989	Hou-N	15	10	.600	34	34	6	3	0	225^2	180	80	73	15	4	79	153	1.148	2.91	116	2.60	.217	9	.120	13	15	1.2
1990	Hou-N	7	12	.368	34	34	2	0	0	209^1	186	93	88	21	8	84	119	1.290	3.78	98	3.59	.245	4	.063	-3	8	-0.6
1991	Hou-N	5	12	.294	28	28	1	0	0	161	156	90	89	19	1	72	98	1.416	4.98	70	4.27	.259	4	.098	-27	1	-2.9
1992	SD-N	4	7	.364	15	15	0	0	0	96	92	40	35	6	1	33	46	1.302	3.28	109	3.49	.258	6	.207	3	6	0.5

YEAR	TM-L	W	L	PCT	G	GS	CG	SH	SV	IP	H	R	ER	HR	HB	BB	SO	RAT	ERA	ERA+	CERA	OAV	BH	AVG	PR+	WS	TPW
1993	Min-A	11	13	.458	27	27	1	0	0	167^{1}	159	85	82	24	6	51	80	1.255	4.41	99	3.93	.254	0	....	0	10	0.0
	SF-N	2	2	.500	5	4	0	0	0	17	24	9	8	2	1	6	5	1.765	4.24	92	7.03	.348	0	.000	-1	1	-0.2
1994	Min-A	6	12	.333	25	**25**	0	0	0	130^{1}	170	109	107	30	2	54	78	1.719	7.39	66	7.15	.321	0	....	-34	0	-3.2
1995	Phi-N	0	1	.000	2	2	0	0	0	5^{1}	15	12	12	3	0	1	6	3.000	20.25	21	20.23	.484	0	.000	-10	0	-0.9
Total	12	84	95	.469	257	253	15	6	0	1525	1434	743	702	179	27	575	951	1.317	4.14	92	3.92	.251	33	.088	-59	68	-6.9
• DESHONG, Jimmie	James Brooklyn DeShong b: 11/30/1909, Harrisburg, PA d: 10/16/1993, Lower Paxton Township, PA BR/TR, 5'11", 165 lbs. Deb: 4/12/1932																										
1932	Phi-A	0	0	....	6	0	0	0	0	10	17	14	13	3	1	9	5	2.600	11.70	39	12.92	.378	0	.000	-8	0	-0.8
1934	NY-A	6	7	.462	31	12	6	0	3	133^{2}	126	71	61	6	2	56	40	1.362	4.11	99	3.34	.243	8	.190	-3	8	-0.1
1935	NY-A	4	1	.800	29	3	0	0	3	69	64	30	25	6	2	33	30	1.406	3.26	124	3.78	.242	1	.071	5	6	0.4
1936	Was-A	18	10	.643	34	31	16	2	2	223^{2}	255	135	115	11	3	96	59	1.569	4.63	103	4.53	.285	15	.190	1	14	0.3
1937	Was-A	14	15	.483	37	34	20	0	1	264^{1}	290	161	144	15	3	124	86	1.566	4.90	90	4.51	.280	19	.202	-18	11	-1.5
1938	Was-A	5	8	.385	31	14	1	0	0	131^{1}	160	104	96	11	1	83	41	1.850	6.58	69	6.14	.310	12	.261	-30	2	-2.5
1939	Was-A	0	3	.000	7	6	1	0	0	40^{2}	56	45	39	7	0	31	12	2.139	8.63	50	8.26	.337	3	.200	-20	0	-1.8
Total	7	47	44	.516	175	100	44	2	9	872^{2}	968	560	493	59	12	432	273	1.604	5.08	87	4.79	.281	58	.198	-73	41	-6.0
• DESILVA, John	John Reed DeSilva b: 9/30/1967, Fort Bragg, CA BR/TR, 6', 193 lbs. Deb: 8/15/1993																										
1993	Det-A	0	0	....	1	0	0	0	0	1	2	1	1	0	0	0	0	2.000	9.00	48	9.49	.667	0	....	-1	0	-0.1
	LA-N	0	0	....	3	0	0	0	0	5^{1}	6	4	4	0	0	1	6	1.313	6.75	56	3.17	.273	0	....	-2	0	-0.2
1995	Bal-A	1	0	1.000	2	2	0	0	0	8^{2}	8	7	7	3	1	7	1	1.731	7.27	65	7.85	.258	0	....	-3	0	-0.2
Total	2	1	0	1.000	6	2	0	0	0	15	16	12	12	3	1	8	7	1.600	7.20	60	6.29	.286	0	....	-5	0	-0.5
• DESSAU, Rube	Frank Rolland Dessau b: 3/29/1883, New Galilee, PA d: 5/6/1952, York, PA BB/TR, 5'11", 175 lbs. Deb: 9/22/1907																										
1907	Bos-N	0	1	.000	2	2	1	0	0	9^{1}	13	11	11	0	1	10	1	2.464	10.61	24	9.83	.394	0	.000	-8	0	-1.0
1910	Bro-N	2	3	.400	19	0	0	0	1	51^{1}	67	48	33	0	5	29	24	1.870	5.79	52	6.21	.328	1	.067	-16	0	-1.8
Total	2	2	4	.333	21	2	1	0	1	60^{2}	80	59	44	0	6	39	25	1.962	6.53	44	6.77	.337	1	.053	-25	0	-2.8
• DESSENS, Elmer	Elmer Dessens b: 1/13/1971, Hermosillo, Mexico BR/TR, 6', 190 lbs. Deb: 6/24/1996																										
1996	Pit-N	0	2	.000	15	3	0	0	0	25	40	23	23	2	0	4	13	1.760	8.28	53	6.77	.385	2	.400	-11	1	-1.0
1997	Pit-N	0	0	....	3	0	0	0	0	3^{1}	2	0	0	0	1	0	2	.600	0.00	....	1.31	.167	0	....	2	1	0.2
1998	Pit-N	2	6	.250	43	5	0	0	0	74^{2}	90	50	47	10	0	25	43	1.540	5.67	76	5.19	.300	0	.000	-12	1	-1.2
2000	Cin-N	11	5	.688	40	16	1	0	1	147^{1}	170	73	70	10	3	43	85	1.446	4.28	110	4.31	.296	4	.100	5	10	0.5
2001	Cin-N	10	14	.417	34	34	1	1	0	205	221	103	102	32	1	56	128	1.351	4.48	102	4.49	.279	11	.193	5	10	0.6
2002	Cin-N	7	8	.467	30	30	0	0	0	178	173	70	60	24	7	49	93	1.247	3.03	140	3.82	.257	9	.200	24	15	2.5
2003	Ari-N	8	8	.500	34	30	0	0	0	175^{2}	212	107	99	22	4	57	113	1.531	5.07	92	5.19	.299	9	.196	-6	7	-0.5
Total	7	38	43	.469	199	118	2	1	1	809	908	426	401	100	16	234	477	1.412	4.46	101	4.58	.287	35	.174	7	45	1.1
• DETTMER, John	John Franklin Dettmer b: 3/4/1970, Cahokia, IL BR/TR, 6', 185 lbs. Deb: 6/16/1994																										
1994	Tex-A	0	6	.000	11	9	0	0	0	54	63	42	26	10	3	20	27	1.537	4.33	111	5.52	.286	0	....	4	1	0.4
1995	Tex-A	0	0	....	1	0	0	0	0	0^{1}	2	1	1	0	0	0	0	6.000	27.00	18	29.60	.667	0	....	-1	0	-0.1
Total	2	0	6	.000	12	9	0	0	0	54^{1}	65	43	27	10	3	20	27	1.564	4.47	108	5.66	.291	0	....	4	1	0.3
• DETTORE, Tom	Thomas Anthony Dettore b: 11/17/1947, Canonsburg, PA BL/TR, 6'4", 200 lbs. Deb: 6/11/1973																										
1973	Pit-N	0	1	.000	12	1	0	0	0	22^{2}	33	19	15	1	3	14	13	2.074	5.96	59	7.48	.340	0	.000	-6	0	-0.7
1974	Chi-N	3	5	.375	16	9	0	0	0	64^{2}	64	39	30	4	6	31	43	1.469	4.18	91	4.25	.255	5	.250	1	3	0.2
1975	Chi-N	5	4	.556	36	5	0	0	0	85^{1}	88	57	51	8	9	31	46	1.395	5.38	71	4.43	.270	6	.250	-12	2	-1.1
1976	Chi-N	0	1	.000	4	0	0	0	0	7	11	8	8	3	0	2	4	1.857	10.29	38	9.94	.355	0	....	-5	0	-0.5
Total	4	8	11	.421	68	15	0	0	0	179^{2}	196	123	104	16	18	78	106	1.525	5.21	73	4.97	.278	11	.229	-22	5	-2.1
• DEUTSCH, Mel	Melvin Elliott Deutsch b: 7/26/1915, Caldwell, TX d: 11/18/2001, Austin, TX BR/TR, 6'4", 215 lbs. Deb: 4/21/1946																										
1946	Bos-A	0	0	....	3	0	0	0	0	6^{1}	7	5	4	1	0	3	2	1.579	5.68	64	5.37	.280	0	.000	-1	0	-0.2
• DEVENS, Charlie	Charles Devens b: 1/1/1910, Milton, MA d: 8/13/2003, Milton, MA BR/TR, 6'1", 180 lbs. Deb: 9/24/1932																										
1932	NY-A	1	0	1.000	1	1	1	0	0	9	6	2	2	0	0	7	4	1.444	2.00	204	2.87	.200	0	.000	2	1	0.2
1933	NY-A	3	3	.500	14	8	2	0	0	62	59	39	30	1	0	50	23	1.758	4.35	89	4.45	.250	2	.095	-2	2	-0.3
1934	NY-A	1	0	1.000	1	1	1	0	0	11	9	3	2	0	0	5	4	1.273	1.64	249	2.53	.225	1	.500	3	2	0.4
Total	3	5	3	.625	16	10	4	0	0	82	74	44	34	1	0	62	31	1.659	3.73	105	4.02	.242	3	.120	2	5	0.3
• DEVINE, Adrian	Paul Adrian Devine b: 12/2/1951, Galveston, TX BR/TR, 6'4", 205 lbs. Deb: 6/27/1973																										
1973	Atl-N	2	3	.400	24	1	0	0	4	32^{1}	45	24	23	6	2	12	15	1.763	6.40	61	7.12	.338	1	.250	-9	0	-0.9
1975	Atl-N	1	0	1.000	5	2	0	0	0	16^{1}	19	8	8	2	1	7	8	1.592	4.41	86	5.32	.284	0	.000	-1	1	-0.1
1976	Atl-N	5	6	.455	48	1	0	0	9	73	72	30	26	3	1	26	48	1.342	3.21	118	3.23	.255	0	.000	7	8	0.5
1977	Tex-A	11	6	.647	56	2	0	0	15	105^{2}	102	43	42	8	4	31	67	1.259	3.58	114	3.30	.259	0	....	5	12	0.5
1978	Atl-N	5	4	.556	31	6	0	0	3	65^{1}	84	45	43	3	0	25	26	1.668	5.92	68	5.18	.323	1	.091	-13	1	-1.4
1979	Atl-N	1	2	.333	40	0	0	0	0	66^{2}	84	28	24	8	2	25	22	1.635	3.24	125	5.68	.311	0	.000	8	5	0.7
1980	Tex-A	1	1	.500	13	0	0	0	0	28	49	22	15	4	1	9	8	2.071	4.82	81	8.73	.377	0	....	-2	0	-0.2
Total	7	26	22	.542	217	12	0	0	31	387^{1}	455	200	181	34	11	135	194	1.523	4.21	95	4.81	.296	2	.049	-5	27	-0.9
• DEVINEY, Hal	Harold John Deviney b: 4/11/1893, Newton, MA d: 1/4/1933, Westwood, MA BR/TR Deb: 7/30/1920																										
1920	Bos-A	0	0	....	1	0	0	0	0	3	7	5	5	0	0	2	0	3.000	15.00	24	14.24	.500	2	1.000	-4	1	-0.2
• DEVLIN, Jim	James Alexander Devlin b: 1849, Philadelphia, PA d: 10/10/1883, Philadelphia, PA BR/TR, 5'11", 175 lbs. Deb: 4/21/1873 ♦																										
1875	Chi-n	7	16	.304	28	24	24	0	0	224	254	....	48	0	....	11	10	1.183	1.93	87	....	.260	92	.289	-13	....	0.3
1876	Lou-N	30	35	.462	**68**	**68**	**66**	5	0	**622**	566	309	108	3	....	37	**122**	.969	1.56	174	....	.223	94	.314	**54**	53	**5.3**
1877	Lou-N	35	25	.583	**61**	**61**	**61**	4	0	**559**	617	288	140	4	....	41	141	1.177	2.25	**147**	....	.264	72	.269	40	**60**	**3.8**
Total	2	65	60	.520	129	129	127	9	0	1181	1183	597	248	7	....	78	263	1.068	1.89	160	....	.242	166	.293	94	113	9.1
• DEVLIN, Jim	James H. Devlin b: 4/16/1866, Troy, NY d: 12/14/1900, Troy, NY TL, 5'7", 135 lbs. Deb: 6/28/1886																										
1886	NY-N	0	0	....	1	0	0	0	1	2	3	5	4	0	....	4	2	3.500	18.00	18	....	.334	0	.000	-3	0	-0.3
1887	Phi-N	0	2	.000	2	2	2	0	0	18	30	19	12	0	3	10	6	1.667	6.00	70	....	.361	3	.429	-3	0	-0.2
1888*	StL-a	6	5	.545	11	11	10	0	0	90^{1}	82	54	32	3	8	20	45	1.129	3.19	102	....	.233	11	.297	-2	7	0.0
1889	StL-a	5	3	.625	9	8	5	0	0	60	56	38	16	0	7	24	37	1.333	2.40	176	....	.240	5	.192	11	6	0.8
Total	4	11	10	.524	23	21	17	0	1	170^{1}	171	116	64	3	18	58	90	1.286	3.38	107	....	.253	19	.268	3	13	0.3
• DEWALD, Charlie	Charles H. "Carl" Dewald b: 9/1867, Newark, NJ d: 8/22/1904, Cleveland, OH TL Deb: 9/2/1890																										
1890	Cle-P	2	0	1.000	2	2	2	0	0	14	13	7	1	0	0	5	6	1.286	0.64	618	....	.236	3	.375	5	1	0.5
• DEWEY, Mark	Mark Alan Dewey b: 1/3/1965, Grand Rapids, MI BR/TR, 6', 207 lbs. Deb: 8/24/1990																										
1990	SF-N	1	1	.500	14	0	0	0	0	22^{2}	22	7	7	1	0	5	11	1.191	2.78	131	2.85	.259	0	.000	2	2	0.2
1992	NY-N	1	0	1.000	20	0	0	0	0	33^{1}	37	16	16	2	0	10	24	1.410	4.32	80	3.94	.280	0	.000	-3	1	-0.3
1993	Pit-N	1	2	.333	21	0	0	0	7	26^{2}	14	8	7	0	3	10	14	.900	2.36	171	1.41	.157	0	....	5	6	0.5
1994	Pit-N	2	1	.667	45	0	0	0	1	51^{1}	61	22	21	4	3	19	30	1.558	3.68	117	5.14	.303	1	1.000	3	5	0.4
1995	SF-N	1	0	1.000	27	0	0	0	0	31^{2}	30	12	11	2	0	17	32	1.484	3.13	131	3.78	.254	0	.000	3	2	0.3
1996	SF-N	6	3	.667	78	0	0	0	0	83^{1}	79	40	39	9	5	41	57	1.440	4.21	97	4.35	.257	0	.000	-2	5	-0.2
Total	6	12	7	.632	205	0	0	0	8	249	243	105	101	18	11	102	168	1.386	3.65	109	3.94	.261	1	.091	9	21	0.9
• DEWITT, Matt	Matthew Brian DeWitt b: 9/4/1977, San Bernardino, CA BR/TR, 6'4", 220 lbs. Deb: 6/20/2000																										
2000	Tor-A	1	0	1.000	8	0	0	0	0	13^{2}	20	13	13	4	2	9	6	2.122	8.56	59	10.93	.351	0	....	-5	0	-0.5
2001	Tor-A	0	2	.000	16	0	0	0	0	19	22	8	8	2	1	10	13	1.684	3.79	121	5.34	.293	0	....	2	1	0.2

YEAR	TM-L	W	L	PCT	G	GS	CG	SH	SV	IP	H	R	ER	HR	HB	BB	SO	RAT	ERA	ERA+	CERA	OAV	BH	AVG	PR+	WS	TPW
2002	SD-N	0	1	.000	5	0	0	0	0	7^1	6	2	1	1	0	3	5	1.227	1.23	307	3.43	.231	0	....	2	1	0.2
Total	3	1	3	.250	29	0	0	0	0	40	48	23	22	7	3	22	24	1.750	4.95	97	6.90	.304	0	....	-2	2	-0.1
• DIAZ, Carlos	Carlos Antonio Diaz b: 1/7/1958, Kaneohe, HI BR/TL, 6', 170 lbs. Deb: 6/30/1982																										
1982	Atl-N	3	2	.600	19	0	0	0	1	25^1	31	15	13	3	0	9	16	1.579	4.62	81	5.21	.307	0	.000	-3	1	-0.3
	NY-N	0	0	....	4	0	0	0	0	3^2	6	2	0	0	0	4	0	2.727	0.00	....	9.24	.353	0	....	2	0	0.2
	Yr.	3	2	.600	23	0	0	0	1	29	37	17	13	3	0	13	16	1.724	4.03	92	5.72	.314	0	.000	-1	1	-0.1
1983	NY-N	3	1	.750	54	0	0	0	2	83^1	62	22	19	1	1	35	64	1.164	2.05	177	2.08	.211	0	.000	14	9	1.4
1984	LA-N	1	0	1.000	37	0	0	0	1	41	47	26	25	4	0	24	36	1.732	5.49	64	5.39	.285	0	.000	-9	0	-0.9
1985*	LA-N	6	3	.667	46	0	0	0	0	79^1	70	28	23	7	0	18	73	1.109	2.61	133	2.56	.230	0	.000	7	6	0.7
1986	LA-N	0	0	....	19	0	0	0	0	25^1	33	14	12	2	0	7	18	1.579	4.26	81	5.04	.317	0	.000	-2	1	-0.2
Total	5	13	6	.684	179	0	0	0	4	258	249	107	92	17	1	97	207	1.341	3.21	111	3.45	.253	0	.000	10	17	0.9
• DIBBLE, Rob	Robert Keith "Nasty Boy,Officer" Dibble b: 1/24/1964, Bridgeport, CT BL/TR, 6'4", 230 lbs. Deb: 6/29/1988																										
1988	Cin-N	1	1	.500	37	0	0	0	0	59^1	43	12	12	2	1	21	59	1.079	1.82	197	2.06	.207	0	.000	11	7	1.1
1989	Cin-N	10	5	.667	74	0	0	0	2	99	62	23	23	4	3	39	141	1.020	2.09	172	1.71	.176	0	.000	18	14	1.8
1990*	Cin-N★	8	3	.727	68	0	0	0	11	98	62	22	19	3	1	34	136	.980	1.74	226	1.64	.183	0	.000	22	17	2.2
1991	Cin-N★	3	5	.375	67	0	0	0	31	82^1	67	32	29	5	0	25	124	1.117	3.17	120	2.45	.223	0	.000	6	13	0.6
1992	Cin-N	3	5	.375	63	0	0	0	25	70^1	48	26	24	3	2	31	110	1.123	3.07	117	2.28	.193	2	.400	4	12	0.5
1993	Cin-N	1	4	.200	45	0	0	0	19	41^2	34	33	30	8	2	42	49	1.824	6.48	62	6.50	.225	1	1.000	-11	0	-1.1
1995	Chi-A	0	1	.000	16	0	0	0	1	14^1	7	10	10	1	3	27	16	2.372	6.28	71	7.17	.156	0	....	-3	0	-0.3
	Mil-A	1	1	.500	15	0	0	0	0	12	9	11	11	1	0	19	10	2.333	8.25	60	6.91	.225	0	....	-5	0	-0.4
	Yr.	1	2	.333	31	0	0	0	1	26^1	16	21	21	2	3	46	26	2.354	7.18	66	7.05	.188	0	....	-7	0	-0.7
Total	7	27	25	.519	385	0	0	0	89	477	332	169	158	27	12	238	645	1.195	2.98	130	2.67	.197	3	.120	42	63	4.5
• DIBUT, Pedro	Pedro (Villafana) Dibut b: 11/18/1892, Cienfuegos, Cuba d: 12/4/1979, Hialeah, FL BR/TR, 5'8", 190 lbs. Deb: 5/1/1924																										
1924	Cin-N	3	0	1.000	7	2	2	0	0	36^2	24	9	9	1	0	12	15	.982	2.21	170	1.63	.180	3	.273	6	5	0.8
1925	Cin-N	0	0	....	1	0	0	0	0	0	3	0	0	0	0	0	0		....	....	∞	1.000	0	....	0	0	0.0
Total	2	3	0	1.000	8	2	2	0	0	36^2	27	9	9	1	0	12	15	1.064	2.21	170	1.63	.198	3	.273	6	5	0.8
• DICKERMAN, Leo	Leo Louis Dickerman b: 10/31/1896, DeSoto, MO d: 4/30/1982, Atkins, AR BR/TR, 6'4", 192 lbs. Deb: 4/21/1923																										
1923	Bro-N	8	12	.400	35	20	7	1	0	159^2	180	95	66	4	2	72	58	1.578	3.72	104	4.17	.283	13	.250	3	8	0.6
1924	Bro-N	0	0	....	7	2	0	0	0	19^2	20	16	12	0	2	16	9	1.831	5.49	68	5.04	.263	1	.167	-3	0	-0.3
	StL-N	7	4	.636	18	13	8	1	0	119^2	108	43	32	6	0	51	28	1.329	2.41	157	3.33	.249	9	.231	18	10	1.9
	Yr.	7	4	.636	25	15	8	1	0	139^1	128	59	44	6	2	67	37	1.400	2.84	133	3.57	.251	10	.222	15	10	1.6
1925	StL-N	4	11	.267	29	20	7	2	1	130^2	135	95	81	10	2	79	40	1.638	5.58	77	4.89	.273	5	.114	-19	2	-2.1
Total	3	19	27	.413	89	55	22	4	1	429^2	443	249	191	20	6	218	135	1.538	4.00	101	4.20	.270	28	.199	-1	20	0.1
• DICKERSON, George	George Clark Dickerson b: 12/1/1892, Renner, TX d: 7/9/1938, Los Angeles, CA BR/TR, 6'1", 170 lbs. Deb: 8/2/1917																										
1917	Cle-A	0	0	....	1	0	0	0	0	1	0	0	0	0	0	0	0	.000	0.00	....	0.00	.000	0	....	0	0	0.0
• DICKEY, R.A.	Robert Alan Dickey b: 10/29/1974, Nashville, TN BR/TR, 6'3", 205 lbs. Deb: 4/22/2001																										
2001	Tex-A	0	1	.000	4	0	0	0	0	12	13	9	9	3	0	7	4	1.667	6.75	69	6.57	.283	0	....	-3	0	-0.3
2003	Tex-A	9	8	.529	38	13	1	1	1	116^2	135	68	66	16	5	38	94	1.483	5.09	97	5.09	.292	1	1.000	-0	7	0.0
Total	2	9	9	.500	42	13	1	1	1	128^2	148	77	75	19	5	45	98	1.500	5.25	94	5.23	.291	1	1.000	-3	7	-0.2
• DICKMAN, Emerson	George Emerson Dickman b: 11/12/1914, Buffalo, NY d: 4/27/1981, New York, NY BR/TR, 6'2", 175 lbs. Deb: 6/27/1936																										
1936	Bos-A	0	0	....	1	0	0	0	0	1	2	2	1	0	0	1	2	3.000	9.00	59	11.63	.400	0	....	-0	0	0.0
1938	Bos-A	5	5	.500	32	11	3	1	0	104	117	74	61	9	4	54	22	1.644	5.28	93	5.25	.288	10	.286	-5	5	-0.1
1939	Bos-A	8	3	.727	48	1	0	0	5	113^2	126	70	56	10	3	43	46	1.487	4.43	107	4.46	.282	2	.056	4	9	0.0
1940	Bos-A	8	6	.571	35	9	2	0	3	100	121	74	67	15	4	38	40	1.590	6.03	75	5.56	.291	3	.107	-16	3	-1.7
1941	Bos-A	1	1	.500	9	3	1	0	0	31	37	23	22	4	0	17	16	1.742	6.39	65	5.97	.301	1	.091	-7	0	-0.8
Total	5	22	15	.595	125	24	6	1	8	349^2	403	243	207	38	11	153	126	1.590	5.33	87	5.16	.288	16	.145	-25	17	-2.6
• DICKSON, Jason	Jason Royce Dickson b: 3/30/1973, London, Canada BL/TR, 6', 190 lbs. Deb: 8/21/1996																										
1996	Cal-A	1	4	.200	7	7	0	0	0	43^1	52	22	22	6	1	18	20	1.615	4.57	107	5.80	.306	0	....	2	2	0.1
1997	Ana-A★	13	9	.591	33	32	2	1	0	203^2	236	111	97	32	7	56	115	1.434	4.29	108	5.03	.289	0	.000	6	12	0.6
1998	Ana-A	10	10	.500	27	18	0	0	0	122	147	89	82	17	6	41	61	1.541	6.05	78	5.52	.303	0	.000	-17	2	-1.7
2000	Ana-A	2	2	.500	6	6	0	0	0	28	39	20	19	5	1	7	18	1.643	6.11	83	6.72	.336	0	....	-4	1	-0.4
Total	4	26	25	.510	73	63	2	1	0	397	474	242	220	60	15	122	214	1.501	4.99	94	5.38	.299	0	.000	-13	17	-1.3
• DICKSON, Jim	James Edward Dickson b: 4/20/1938, Portland, OR BL/TR, 6'1", 185 lbs. Deb: 7/2/1963																										
1963	Hou-N	0	1	.000	13	0	0	0	2	14^2	22	13	10	0	0	2	6	1.636	6.14	51	4.92	.344	0	.000	-5	0	-0.5
1964	Cin-N	1	0	1.000	4	0	0	0	0	5	8	4	4	0	0	5	6	2.600	7.20	50	9.90	.444	0	....	-2	0	-0.2
1965	KC-A	3	2	.600	68	0	0	0	0	85^2	68	40	33	6	2	47	54	1.342	3.47	101	3.25	.220	0	.000	1	4	0.1
1966	KC-A	1	0	1.000	24	1	0	0	1	37	37	28	22	4	0	23	20	1.622	5.35	63	4.90	.264	1	.250	-8	0	-0.9
Total	4	5	3	.625	109	1	0	0	3	142^1	135	85	69	10	2	77	86	1.489	4.36	78	4.09	.254	1	.143	-14	4	-1.5
• DICKSON, Lance	Lance Michael Dickson b: 10/19/1969, Fullerton, CA BR/TL, 6', 185 lbs. Deb: 8/9/1990																										
1990	Chi-N	0	3	.000	3	3	0	0	0	13^2	20	12	11	2	0	4	4	1.756	7.24	56	6.93	.370	0	.000	-4	0	-0.5
• DICKSON, Murry	Murry Monroe Dickson b: 8/21/1916, Tracy, MO d: 9/21/1989, Kansas City, KS BR/TR, 5'10.5", 157 lbs. Deb: 9/30/1939																										
1939	StL-N	0	0	....	1	0	0	0	0	3^2	1	0	0	0	0	1	2	.545	0.00	....	0.49	.091	0	.000	2	1	0.1
1940	StL-N	0	0	....	1	1	0	0	0	1^2	5	4	3	0	0	1	0	3.600	16.20	25	17.29	.500	0	....	-2	0	-0.2
1942	StL-N	6	3	.667	36	7	2	0	2	120^2	91	41	39	1	1	61	66	1.260	2.91	118	2.56	.216	8	.190	5	9	0.6
1943*	StL-N	8	2	.800	31	7	2	0	0	115^2	119	51	46	4	1	49	44	1.452	3.58	94	3.85	.269	9	.265	-6	8	-0.5
1946*	StL-N	15	6	.714	47	19	12	2	1	184^1	160	71	59	8	4	56	82	1.172	2.88	120	2.66	.234	18	.277	9	16	1.4
1947	StL-N	13	16	.448	47	25	11	4	3	231^2	211	101	79	16	2	88	111	1.291	3.07	135	3.27	.243	17	.213	27	18	2.7
1948	StL-N	12	16	.429	42	29	11	1	1	252^1	257	121	116	39	0	85	113	1.355	4.14	99	4.29	.265	27	.281	-0	15	0.4
1949	Pit-N	12	14	.462	44	20	11	2	0	224^1	216	97	82	17	6	80	89	1.319	3.29	128	3.58	.255	17	.202	24	19	2.5
1950	Pit-N	10	15	.400	51	22	8	0	3	225	227	104	95	20	2	83	76	1.378	3.80	115	3.88	.260	21	.256	16	16	1.8
1951	Pit-N	20	16	.556	45	35	19	3	2	288^2	294	151	129	32	6	101	112	1.368	4.02	105	4.05	.263	30	.273	11	18	1.6
1952	Pit-N	14	21	.400	43	34	21	2	2	277^2	278	128	110	26	1	76	112	1.275	3.57	112	3.52	.261	24	.224	15	17	1.9
1953	Pit-N★	10	19	.345	45	26	10	1	4	200^2	240	121	101	27	3	58	88	1.485	4.53	99	5.03	.298	7	.115	-0	11	-0.3
1954	Phi-N	10	20	.333	40	31	12	4	3	226^1	256	107	95	31	2	73	64	1.454	3.78	107	4.74	.286	15	.190	6	13	0.5
1955	Phi-N	12	11	.522	36	28	12	4	0	216	190	98	84	27	4	82	92	1.259	3.50	113	3.53	.238	18	.220	9	14	0.9
1956	Phi-N	0	3	.000	3	3	0	0	0	23	20	15	13	1	0	12	1	1.391	5.09	73	3.43	.241	3	.333	-3	0	-0.2
	StL-N	13	8	.619	28	27	12	3	0	196^1	175	75	67	20	1	57	109	1.182	3.07	123	3.11	.240	19	.247	16	15	2.0
	Yr.	13	11	.542	31	30	12	3	0	219^1	195	90	80	21	1	69	110	1.204	3.28	115	3.14	.240	22	.256	13	15	1.8
1957	StL-N	5	3	.625	14	13	3	1	0	74	87	41	34	8	1	25	29	1.514	4.14	96	4.97	.296	6	.222	-1	3	-0.1
1958	KC-A	9	5	.643	27	9	3	0	1	99	99	42	36	12	2	31	46	1.313	3.27	119	3.86	.258	9	.257	7	9	1.0
	*NY-A	1	2	.333	6	2	0	0	1	20^1	18	17	13	4	1	12	9	1.475	5.75	61	5.10	.237	2	.286	-5	0	-0.5
	Yr.	10	7	.588	33	11	3	0	2	119^1	117	59	49	16	3	43	55	1.341	3.70	103	4.07	.255	11	.262	2	9	0.4
1959	KC-A	2	1	.667	38	0	0	0	0	71	85	46	39	9	0	27	36	1.577	4.94	81	5.17	.290	3	.176	-7	2	-0.8
Total	18	172	181	.487	625	338	149	27	23	3052^1	3029	1431	1240	302	37	1058	1281	1.339	3.66	110	3.83	.260	253	.231	122	204	14.9
• DICKSON, Walt	Walter R. "Hickory" Dickson b: 12/3/1878, New Summerfield, TX d: 12/9/1918, Ardmore, OK BR/TR, 5'11.5", 175 lbs. Deb: 4/26/1910																										
1910	NY-N	1	0	1.000	12	1	0	0	0	29^2	31	19	18	1	0	9	9	1.348	5.46	54	3.52	.272	1	.250	-8	0	-0.8
1912	Bos-N	3	19	.136	36	20	9	1	1	189	233	123	81	2	3	61	47	1.556	3.86	92	4.51	.320	10	.167	-4	7	-0.5
1913	Bos-N	6	7	.462	19	15	8	0	0	128	118	71	46	4	1	45	47	1.273	3.23	101	2.98	.249	8	.178	3	5	0.2

YEAR	TM-L	W	L	PCT	G	GS	CG	SH	SV	IP	H	R	ER	HR	HB	BB	SO	RAT	ERA	ERA+	CERA	OAV	BH	AVG	PR+	WS	TPW
1914	Pit-F	9	19	.321	40	32	19	3	1	256^2	262	117	90	5	2	74	63	1.309	3.16	98	3.76	.273	7	.084	-1	12	-0.9
1915	Pit-F	7	5	.583	27	11	4	0	0	96^2	115	51	45	5	2	33	36	1.531	4.19	74	4.95	.316	4	.129	-12	3	-1.3
Total	5	26	50	.342	134	79	40	4	2	700	759	381	280	17	8	222	202	1.401	3.60	90	3.97	.288	30	.135	-22	27	-3.3

• DIEHL, George George Krause Diehl b: 2/25/1918, Emmaus, PA d: 8/24/1986, Kingsport, TN BR/TR, 6'2", 196 lbs. Deb: 4/19/1942

YEAR	TM-L	W	L	PCT	G	GS	CG	SH	SV	IP	H	R	ER	HR	HB	BB	SO	RAT	ERA	ERA+	CERA	OAV	BH	AVG	PR+	WS	TPW
1942	Bos-N	0	0	....	1	0	0	0	0	3^2	2	2	1	0	1	2	0	1.091	2.45	136	2.43	.167	0	.000	0	0	0.0
1943	Bos-N	0	0	....	1	0	0	0	0	4	4	2	2	0	0	3	1	1.750	4.50	76	4.32	.267	0	.000	-1	0	-0.1
Total	2	0	0	....	2	0	0	0	0	7^2	6	4	3	0	1	5	1	1.435	3.52	96	3.42	.222	0	.000	-0	0	0.0

• DIERKER, Larry Lawrence Edward Dierker b: 9/22/1946, Hollywood, CA BR/TR, 6'4", 215 lbs. Deb: 9/22/1964 M

YEAR	TM-L	W	L	PCT	G	GS	CG	SH	SV	IP	H	R	ER	HR	HB	BB	SO	RAT	ERA	ERA+	CERA	OAV	BH	AVG	PR+	WS	TPW
1964	Hou-N	0	1	.000	3	1	0	0	0	9	7	4	2	1	0	3	5	1.111	2.00	171	2.76	.219	0	.000	2	1	0.1
1965	Hou-N	7	8	.467	26	19	1	0	0	146^2	135	69	57	16	3	37	109	1.173	3.50	96	3.13	.240	5	.100	0	6	-0.1
1966	Hou-N	10	8	.556	29	28	8	2	0	187	173	73	66	17	1	45	108	1.166	3.18	108	2.98	.240	10	.149	7	12	0.8
1967	Hou-N	6	5	.545	15	15	4	0	0	99	95	44	37	4	1	25	68	1.212	3.36	98	2.94	.252	7	.226	1	5	0.4
1968	Hou-N	12	15	.444	32	32	10	1	0	233^2	206	95	86	14	8	89	161	1.262	3.31	89	3.15	.240	5	.068	-5	10	-0.9
1969	Hou-N★	20	13	.606	39	37	20	4	0	305^1	240	97	79	18	1	72	232	1.022	2.33	152	2.11	.214	17	.144	45	25	4.6
1970	Hou-N	16	12	.571	37	36	17	2	1	269^2	263	124	116	31	6	82	191	1.279	3.87	100	3.75	.254	16	.174	0	15	0.0
1971	Hou-N★	12	6	.667	24	23	6	2	0	159	150	50	48	8	2	33	91	1.151	2.72	124	2.78	.248	4	.074	10	12	0.8
1972	Hou-N	15	8	.652	31	31	12	5	0	214^2	209	87	81	14	5	51	115	1.211	3.40	99	3.19	.256	13	.167	-0	13	-0.1
1973	Hou-N	1	1	.500	14	3	0	0	0	27	27	14	13	3	2	13	18	1.481	4.33	84	4.79	.265	0	.000	-2	1	-0.3
1974	Hou-N	11	10	.524	33	33	7	3	0	223^2	189	76	72	18	6	82	150	1.212	2.90	120	3.13	.232	14	.197	11	17	1.2
1975	Hou-N	14	16	.467	34	34	14	2	0	232	225	109	103	24	7	91	127	1.362	4.00	84	4.05	.260	7	.092	-18	9	-2.4
1976	Hou-N	13	14	.481	28	28	7	4	0	187^2	171	85	77	9	6	72	112	1.295	3.69	86	3.27	.243	9	.141	-11	6	-1.2
1977	StL-N	2	6	.250	11	9	0	0	0	39^1	40	21	20	7	2	16	6	1.424	4.58	84	5.08	.267	0	.000	-4	1	-0.5
Total	14	139	123	.531	356	329	106	25	1	2333^2	2130	948	857	184	50	711	1493	1.217	3.31	103	3.18	.243	107	.136	37	133	2.5

• DIETRICH, Bill William John "Bullfrog" Dietrich b: 3/29/1910, Philadelphia, PA d: 6/20/1978, Philadelphia, PA BR/TR, 6', 185 lbs. Deb: 4/13/1933

YEAR	TM-L	W	L	PCT	G	GS	CG	SH	SV	IP	H	R	ER	HR	HB	BB	SO	RAT	ERA	ERA+	CERA	OAV	BH	AVG	PR+	WS	TPW
1933	Phi-A	0	1	.000	8	1	0	0	0	17	13	11	11	1	0	19	4	1.882	5.82	74	5.16	.236	1	.333	-2	1	-0.2
1934	Phi-A	11	12	.478	39	23	14	4	3	207^2	201	121	108	12	3	114	88	1.517	4.68	94	4.05	.255	15	.208	-9	12	-0.5
1935	Phi-A	7	13	.350	43	15	8	1	3	185^1	203	128	111	7	1	101	59	1.640	5.39	84	4.54	.276	5	.083	-15	5	-1.9
1936	Phi-A	4	6	.400	21	4	0	0	3	71^2	91	55	52	4	0	40	34	1.828	6.53	78	5.68	.305	3	.111	-11	2	-1.2
	Was-A	0	1	.000	5	0	0	0	0	8^1	13	11	9	0	0	6	4	2.280	9.72	49	7.54	.351	0	....	-5	0	-0.4
	Chi-A	4	4	.500	14	11	6	1	0	82^2	93	50	43	8	1	36	39	1.560	4.68	111	4.86	.284	8	.267	4	5	0.4
	Yr.	8	11	.421	40	15	6	1	3	162^2	197	116	104	12	1	82	77	1.715	5.75	89	5.36	.297	11	.193	-12	7	-1.2
1937	Chi-A	8	10	.444	29	20	7	1	1	143^1	162	93	78	15	0	72	62	1.633	4.90	94	5.11	.285	8	.182	-8	7	-0.6
1938	Chi-A	2	4	.333	8	7	1	0	0	48	49	33	29	7	0	31	11	1.667	5.44	90	5.24	.259	1	.063	-3	1	-0.4
1939	Chi-A	7	8	.467	25	19	2	0	0	127^2	134	81	74	14	2	56	43	1.488	5.22	91	4.55	.272	8	.216	-8	7	-0.6
1940	Chi-A	10	6	.625	23	17	6	1	0	149^2	154	78	67	10	0	65	43	1.463	4.03	110	4.03	.266	12	.240	3	11	0.6
1941	Chi-A	5	8	.385	19	15	4	1	0	109^1	114	73	65	7	4	50	26	1.500	5.35	77	4.17	.263	3	.088	-17	1	-1.6
1942	Chi-A	6	11	.353	26	23	6	0	0	160	173	92	87	16	5	70	39	1.519	4.89	74	4.69	.277	5	.104	-24	2	-2.6
1943	Chi-A	12	10	.545	26	26	12	2	0	186^2	180	72	58	4	2	53	52	1.248	2.80	119	2.87	.253	8	.143	10	14	1.1
1944	Chi-A	16	17	.485	36	36	15	2	0	246	269	132	99	15	2	68	70	1.370	3.62	95	3.77	.279	9	.117	-5	11	-0.8
1945	Chi-A	7	10	.412	18	16	6	3	0	122^1	136	61	57	4	0	36	43	1.406	4.19	79	3.70	.279	6	.167	-10	4	-1.0
1946	Chi-A	3	3	.500	11	9	3	0	1	62	63	21	18	4	0	24	20	1.403	2.61	131	3.79	.267	1	.053	5	5	0.3
1947	Phi-A	5	2	.714	11	9	2	1	0	60^2	48	24	21	0	2	40	18	1.451	3.12	123	3.23	.223	1	.063	3	5	0.2
1948	Phi-A	1	2	.333	4	2	0	0	0	15^1	21	10	10	0	0	9	5	1.957	5.87	73	6.42	.356	0	.000	-3	0	-0.3
Total	16	108	128	.458	366	253	92	17	11	2003^2	2117	1146	997	128	22	890	660	1.501	4.48	92	4.22	.271	94	.150	-94	93	-9.4

• DIETZ, Dutch Lloyd Arthur Dietz b: 2/12/1912, Cincinnati, OH d: 10/29/1972, Beaumont, TX BR/TR, 5'11.5", 180 lbs. Deb: 4/26/1940

YEAR	TM-L	W	L	PCT	G	GS	CG	SH	SV	IP	H	R	ER	HR	HB	BB	SO	RAT	ERA	ERA+	CERA	OAV	BH	AVG	PR+	WS	TPW
1940	Pit-N	0	1	.000	4	2	0	0	0	15^1	22	11	10	2	0	4	8	1.696	5.87	65	6.69	.355	1	.143	-3	0	-0.3
1941	Pit-N	7	2	.778	33	6	4	1	1	100^1	88	28	26	6	2	33	22	1.206	2.33	155	2.88	.233	4	.160	15	10	1.5
1942	Pit-N	6	9	.400	40	13	3	0	3	134^1	139	67	59	8	1	57	35	1.459	3.95	86	3.97	.268	7	.200	-7	6	-0.7
1943	Pit-N	0	3	.000	8	0	0	0	0	9	12	6	6	0	1	4	4	1.778	6.00	58	5.54	.324	0	....	-3	0	-0.3
	Phi-N	1	1	.500	21	0	0	0	2	36	42	29	26	2	0	15	10	1.583	6.50	52	4.62	.292	1	.167	-12	0	-1.3
	Yr.	1	4	.200	29	0	0	0	2	45	54	35	32	2	1	19	14	1.622	6.40	53	4.81	.298	1	.167	-15	0	-1.5
Total	4	14	16	.467	106	21	7	1	6	295	303	141	127	18	4	113	79	1.410	3.87	89	3.87	.266	13	.178	-9	16	-1.0

• DIGGINS, Ben Benjamin Howard Diggins b: 6/13/1979, Leoti, KS BR/TR, 6'7", 230 lbs. Deb: 9/2/2002

YEAR	TM-L	W	L	PCT	G	GS	CG	SH	SV	IP	H	R	ER	HR	HB	BB	SO	RAT	ERA	ERA+	CERA	OAV	BH	AVG	PR+	WS	TPW
2002	Mil-N	0	4	.000	5	5	0	0	0	24	28	24	23	4	1	18	15	1.917	8.63	47	7.08	.298	1	.143	-12	0	-1.2

• DIGGS, Reese Reese Wilson "Diggsy" Diggs b: 9/22/1915, Mathews, VA d: 10/30/1978, Baltimore, MD BB/TR, 6'2", 180 lbs. Deb: 9/15/1934

YEAR	TM-L	W	L	PCT	G	GS	CG	SH	SV	IP	H	R	ER	HR	HB	BB	SO	RAT	ERA	ERA+	CERA	OAV	BH	AVG	PR+	WS	TPW
1934	Was-A	1	2	.333	4	3	2	0	0	21^1	26	17	16	3	0	15	2	1.922	6.75	64	7.12	.313	2	.250	-6	0	-0.5

• DILAURO, Jack Jack Edward DiLauro b: 3/3/1943, Akron, OH BB/TL, 6'2", 185 lbs. Deb: 5/15/1969

YEAR	TM-L	W	L	PCT	G	GS	CG	SH	SV	IP	H	R	ER	HR	HB	BB	SO	RAT	ERA	ERA+	CERA	OAV	BH	AVG	PR+	WS	TPW
1969	NY-N	1	4	.200	23	4	0	0	1	63^2	50	19	17	4	0	18	27	1.068	2.40	152	2.18	.216	0	.000	7	6	0.6
1970	Hou-N	1	3	.250	42	0	0	0	3	33^2	34	23	16	4	0	17	23	1.515	4.28	91	4.48	.262	0	.000	-1	1	-0.2
Total	2	2	7	.222	65	4	0	0	4	97^1	84	42	33	8	0	35	50	1.223	3.05	123	2.97	.232	0	.000	6	7	0.5

• DILLARD, Gordon Gordon Lee Dillard b: 5/20/1964, Salinas, CA BL/TL, 6'1", 190 lbs. Deb: 8/12/1988

YEAR	TM-L	W	L	PCT	G	GS	CG	SH	SV	IP	H	R	ER	HR	HB	BB	SO	RAT	ERA	ERA+	CERA	OAV	BH	AVG	PR+	WS	TPW
1988	Bal-A	0	0	....	2	1	0	0	0	3	3	2	2	1	0	4	2	2.333	6.00	65	10.69	.273	0	....	-1	0	-0.1
1989	Phi-N	0	0	....	5	0	0	0	0	4	7	3	3	0	0	0	2	1.750	6.75	53	5.92	.368	0	....	-1	0	-0.1
Total	2	0	0	....	7	1	0	0	0	7	10	5	5	1	0	4	4	2.000	6.43	57	7.96	.333	0	....	-2	0	-0.2

• DILLINGER, Harley Harley Hugh "Hoke,Lefty" Dillinger b: 10/30/1894, Pomeroy, OH d: 1/8/1959, Cleveland, OH BR/TL, 5'11", 175 lbs. Deb: 8/16/1914

YEAR	TM-L	W	L	PCT	G	GS	CG	SH	SV	IP	H	R	ER	HR	HB	BB	SO	RAT	ERA	ERA+	CERA	OAV	BH	AVG	PR+	WS	TPW
1914	Cle-A	0	1	.000	11	2	1	0	0	33^2	41	28	17	0	1	25	11	1.960	4.54	63	6.67	.325	0	.000	-6	0	-0.8

• DILLMAN, Bill William Howard Dillman b: 5/25/1945, Trenton, NJ BR/TR, 6'2", 180 lbs. Deb: 4/14/1967

YEAR	TM-L	W	L	PCT	G	GS	CG	SH	SV	IP	H	R	ER	HR	HB	BB	SO	RAT	ERA	ERA+	CERA	OAV	BH	AVG	PR+	WS	TPW
1967	Bal-A	5	9	.357	32	15	2	1	3	124	115	61	60	13	3	33	69	1.194	4.35	72	3.35	.249	5	.161	-19	2	-2.1
1970	Mon-N	2	3	.400	18	0	0	0	0	30^2	28	18	18	4	1	18	17	1.500	5.28	78	4.53	.255	0	.000	-4	1	-0.4
Total	2	7	12	.368	50	15	2	1	3	154^2	143	79	78	17	4	51	86	1.254	4.54	73	3.58	.250	5	.152	-23	3	-2.6

• DILLON, Steve Stephen Edward Dillon b: 3/20/1943, Yonkers, NY BL/TL, 5'10", 160 lbs. Deb: 9/5/1963

YEAR	TM-L	W	L	PCT	G	GS	CG	SH	SV	IP	H	R	ER	HR	HB	BB	SO	RAT	ERA	ERA+	CERA	OAV	BH	AVG	PR+	WS	TPW
1963	NY-N	0	0	....	1	0	0	0	0	1^2	3	2	2	0	0	0	1	1.800	10.80	32	7.19	.429	0	....	-1	0	-0.1
1964	NY-N	0	0	....	2	0	0	0	0	3	4	3	3	1	0	2	2	2.000	9.00	40	9.08	.333	0	....	-2	0	-0.2
Total	2	0	0	....	3	0	0	0	0	4^2	7	5	5	1	0	2	3	1.929	9.64	37	8.40	.368	0	....	-3	0	-0.3

• DIMICHELE, Frank Frank Lawrence DiMichele b: 2/16/1965, Philadelphia, PA BR/TL, 6'3", 205 lbs. Deb: 4/8/1988

YEAR	TM-L	W	L	PCT	G	GS	CG	SH	SV	IP	H	R	ER	HR	HB	BB	SO	RAT	ERA	ERA+	CERA	OAV	BH	AVG	PR+	WS	TPW
1988	Cal-A	0	0	....	4	0	0	0	0	4^2	5	5	5	2	0	2	1	1.500	9.64	40	6.89	.263	0	....	-3	0	-0.3

• DINEEN, Bill William Henry "Big Bill" Dineen b: 4/5/1876, Syracuse, NY d: 1/13/1955, Syracuse, NY BR/TR, 6'1", 190 lbs. Deb: 4/22/1898 U

YEAR	TM-L	W	L	PCT	G	GS	CG	SH	SV	IP	H	R	ER	HR	HB	BB	SO	RAT	ERA	ERA+	CERA	OAV	BH	AVG	PR+	WS	TPW
1898	Was-N	9	16	.360	29	27	22	0	0	218^1	238	140	97	6	16	88	83	1.493	4.00	91	4.22	.276	8	.100	-4	9	-0.7
1899	Was-N	14	20	.412	37	35	30	0	0	291	350	191	127	6	11	106	91	1.567	3.93	99	4.54	.297	36	.303	11	13	1.5
1900	Bos-N	20	14	.588	40	37	33	1	0	320^2	304	161	111	11	9	105	107	1.275	3.12	132	3.11	.250	35	.280	29	27	2.9
1901	Bos-N	15	18	.455	37	34	31	0	0	309^1	295	136	101	8	6	77	141	1.203	2.94	123	2.72	.250	31	.211	19	27	1.7
1902	Bos-A	21	21	.500	42	42	39	2	0	371^1	348	155	121	9	8	99	136	1.204	2.93	122	2.78	.249	18	.128	16	27	0.8
1903*	Bos-A	21	13	.618	37	34	32	6	**2**	299	255	98	75	6	4	66	148	1.074	2.26	134	2.21	.230	17	.160	17	27	1.7
1904	Bos-A	23	14	.622	37	37	37	5	0	335^2	283	115	82	8	2	63	153	1.031	2.20	122	2.02	.230	25	.208	17	26	1.8
1905	Bos-A	12	14	.462	31	29	23	2	1	243^2	235	117	101	7	7	50	97	1.170	3.73	72	2.76	.256	13	.148	-27	8	-3.3
1906	Bos-A	8	19	.296	28	27	22	1	0	218^2	209	101	71	4	1	52	60	1.194	2.92	94	2.67	.255	7	.111	-2	10	-0.3

YEAR	TM-L	W	L	PCT	G	GS	CG	SH	SV	IP	H	R	ER	HR	HB	BB	SO	RAT	ERA	ERA+	CERA	OAV	BH	AVG	PR+	WS	TPW
1907	Bos-A	0	4	.000	5	5	3	0	0	32^2	42	25	19	5	2	8	8	1.531	5.23	49	5.93	.314	0	.000	-11	0	-1.3
	StL-A	7	10	.412	24	16	15	2	4	155^1	153	67	42	3	5	33	38	1.197	2.43	103	2.76	.260	10	.204	1	9	0.3
	Yr.	7	14	.333	29	21	18	2	**4**	188	195	92	61	8	7	41	46	1.255	2.92	87	3.31	.270	10	.169	-10	9	-1.0
1908	StL-A	14	7	.667	27	16	11	1	0	167	133	52	39	2	4	53	39	1.114	2.10	114	2.36	.231	12	.203	-2	13	-0.2
1909	StL-A	6	7	.462	17	13	8	3	0	112	112	53	43	3	1	29	26	1.259	3.46	70	3.24	.267	7	.194	-13	4	-1.3
Total	12	170	177	.490	391	352	306	23	7	3074^2	2957	1411	1029	78	76	829	1127	1.231	3.01	105	2.96	.254	219	.192	50	200	3.6
• DINGMAN, Craig	Craig Allen Dingman b: 3/12/1974, Wichita, KS BR/TR, 6'4", 215 lbs. Deb: 6/30/2000																										
2000	NY-A	0	0	....	10	0	0	0	0	11	18	8	8	1	0	3	8	1.909	6.55	74	7.60	.375	0	....	-2	0	-0.2
2001	Col-N	0	0	....	7	0	0	0	1	7^1	11	11	11	4	2	3	2	1.909	13.50	40	12.04	.355	0	....	-7	0	-0.7
Total	2	0	0	....	17	0	0	0	1	18^1	29	19	19	5	2	6	10	1.909	9.33	55	9.38	.367	0	....	-9	0	-0.8
• DIORIO, Ron	Ronald Michael Diorio b: 7/15/1946, Waterbury, CT BR/TR, 6'6", 212 lbs. Deb: 8/9/1973																										
1973	Phi-N	0	0	....	23	0	0	0	1	19^1	18	5	5	1	0	6	11	1.241	2.33	163	2.79	.257	0	....	3	2	0.3
1974	Phi-N	0	0	....	2	0	0	0	0	1	2	2	2	1	0	1	0	3.000	18.00	21	23.01	.400	0	....	-2	0	-0.2
Total	2	0	0	....	25	0	0	0	1	20^1	20	7	7	2	0	7	11	1.328	3.10	122	3.78	.267	0	....	1	2	0.1
• DIPINO, Frank	Frank Michael DiPino b: 10/22/1956, Syracuse, NY BL/TL, 5'10", 180 lbs. Deb: 9/14/1981																										
1981	Mil-A	0	0	....	2	0	0	0	0	2^1	0	0	0	0	0	3	3	1.286	0.00	....	1.46	.000	0	....	1	0	0.1
1982	Hou-N	2	2	.500	6	6	0	0	0	28^1	32	20	19	1	0	11	25	1.518	6.04	55	4.34	.302	0	.000	-9	0	-1.0
1983	Hou-N	3	4	.429	53	0	0	0	20	71^1	52	21	21	2	1	20	67	1.009	2.65	128	1.81	.205	1	.167	5	12	0.6
1984	Hou-N	4	9	.308	57	0	0	0	14	75^1	74	32	28	3	1	36	65	1.460	3.35	99	3.65	.260	0	.000	-1	5	-0.2
1985	Hou-N	3	7	.300	54	0	0	0	6	76	69	44	34	7	2	43	49	1.474	4.03	86	4.20	.248	2	.167	-6	2	-0.6
1986	Hou-N	1	3	.250	31	0	0	0	3	40^1	27	18	16	5	2	16	27	1.066	3.57	101	2.56	.189	1	.200	0	3	0.0
	Chi-N	2	4	.333	30	0	0	0	0	40	47	27	23	6	0	14	43	1.525	5.18	78	5.01	.297	0	.000	-4	1	-0.5
	Yr.	3	7	.300	61	0	0	0	3	80^1	74	45	39	11	2	30	70	1.295	4.37	88	3.78	.246	1	.167	-4	4	-0.5
1987	Chi-N	3	3	.500	69	0	0	0	4	80	75	31	28	7	1	34	61	1.363	3.15	136	3.75	.252	1	.500	12	9	1.2
1988	Chi-N	2	3	.400	63	0	0	0	6	90^1	102	54	50	6	0	32	69	1.483	4.98	72	4.22	.285	1	.100	-12	2	-1.3
1989	StL-N	9	0	1.000	67	0	0	0	0	88^1	73	26	24	6	0	20	44	1.053	2.45	148	2.27	.227	1	.077	11	9	1.0
1990	StL-N	5	2	.714	62	0	0	0	3	81	92	45	41	8	1	31	49	1.519	4.56	84	4.55	.294	1	.250	-6	4	-0.6
1992	StL-N	0	0	....	9	0	0	0	0	11	9	2	2	0	0	3	8	1.091	1.64	207	2.00	.220	1	1.000	2	1	0.3
1993	KC-A	1	1	.500	11	0	0	0	0	15^2	21	12	12	2	2	6	5	1.723	6.89	66	6.83	.328	0	....	-4	0	-0.4
Total	12	35	38	.479	514	6	0	0	56	700	673	332	298	53	10	269	515	1.346	3.83	96	3.62	.257	9	.125	-12	48	-1.5
• DIPOTO, Jerry	Gerard Peter Dipoto b: 5/24/1968, Jersey City, NJ BR/TR, 6'2", 200 lbs. Deb: 5/11/1993																										
1993	Cle-A	4	4	.500	46	0	0	0	11	56^1	57	21	15	0	1	30	41	1.544	2.40	180	3.83	.270	0	....	12	6	1.2
1994	Cle-A	0	0	....	7	0	0	0	0	15^2	26	14	14	1	1	10	9	2.298	8.04	59	9.57	.406	0	....	-6	0	-0.5
1995	NY-N	4	6	.400	58	0	0	0	2	78^2	77	41	33	2	4	29	49	1.347	3.78	107	3.44	.267	0	.000	2	5	0.1
1996	NY-N	7	2	.778	57	0	0	0	0	77^1	91	44	36	5	3	45	52	1.759	4.19	96	5.50	.298	0	.000	-2	4	-0.2
1997	Col-N	5	3	.625	74	0	0	0	16	95^2	108	56	50	6	4	33	74	1.474	4.70	110	4.39	.288	1	.111	6	10	0.6
1998	Col-N	3	4	.429	68	0	0	0	19	71^1	61	31	28	8	3	25	49	1.206	3.53	146	3.31	.232	0	.000	13	13	1.3
1999	Col-N	4	5	.444	63	0	0	0	1	86^2	91	44	41	10	3	44	69	1.558	4.26	136	5.12	.279	0	.000	15	9	1.4
2000	Col-N	0	0	....	17	0	0	0	0	13^2	16	6	6	1	0	5	9	1.537	3.95	147	4.60	.314	0	.000	3	1	0.2
Total	8	27	24	.529	390	0	0	0	49	495^1	527	257	223	33	19	221	352	1.510	4.05	118	4.49	.280	1	.045	43	48	4.1
• DISCH, George	George Charles Disch b: 3/15/1879, Lincoln, MO d: 8/25/1950, Rapid City, SD TR, 5'11" Deb: 8/8/1905																										
1905	Det-A	0	2	.000	8	3	1	0	0	47^2	43	19	14	1	2	8	14	1.070	2.64	103	2.33	.243	2	.105	-0	2	-0.1
• DISHMAN, Glenn	Glenelg Edward Dishman b: 11/5/1970, Baltimore, MD BR/TL, 6'1", 195 lbs. Deb: 6/22/1995																										
1995	SD-N	4	8	.333	19	16	0	0	0	97	104	60	54	11	4	34	43	1.423	5.01	80	4.56	.278	6	.200	-12	2	-1.2
1996	SD-N	0	0	....	3	0	0	0	0	2^1	3	2	2	0	0	1	0	1.714	7.71	51	4.93	.300	0	....	-1	0	-0.1
	Phi-N	0	0	....	4	1	0	0	0	7	9	6	6	2	0	2	3	1.571	7.71	56	6.77	.321	0	....	-3	0	-0.3
	Yr.	0	0	....	7	1	0	0	0	9^1	12	8	8	2	0	3	3	1.607	7.71	55	6.31	.316	0	....	-4	0	-0.4
1997	Det-A	1	2	.333	7	4	0	0	0	29	30	18	17	4	2	8	20	1.310	5.28	87	4.29	.268	0	....	-3	1	-0.2
Total	3	5	10	.333	33	21	0	0	0	135^1	146	86	79	17	6	45	66	1.411	5.25	79	4.63	.279	6	.200	-19	3	-1.8
• DISTASO, Alec	Alec John Distaso b: 12/23/1948, Los Angeles, CA BR/TR, 6'2", 200 lbs. Deb: 4/20/1969																										
1969	Chi-N	0	0	....	2	0	0	0	0	4^2	6	2	2	0	0	1	1	1.500	3.86	104	4.11	.316	0	....	0	0	0.0
• DITMAR, Art	Arthur John Ditmar b: 4/3/1929, Winthrop, MA BR/TR, 6'2", 196 lbs. Deb: 4/19/1954																										
1954	Phi-A	1	4	.200	14	5	0	0	0	39^1	50	35	28	4	1	36	14	2.186	6.41	61	7.76	.314	1	.125	-10	0	-1.0
1955	KC-A	12	12	.500	35	22	7	1	1	175^1	180	109	98	23	7	86	79	1.517	5.03	83	5.00	.270	13	.210	-16	7	-1.6
1956	KC-A	12	22	.353	44	34	14	2	1	254^1	254	141	125	30	7	108	126	1.423	4.42	98	4.40	.262	13	.143	-6	11	-1.0
1957*	NY-A	8	3	.727	46	11	0	0	6	127^1	128	55	46	9	2	35	64	1.280	3.25	110	3.50	.261	7	.200	3	8	0.3
1958*	NY-A	9	8	.529	38	13	4	0	4	139^2	124	71	53	14	5	38	52	1.160	3.42	104	3.10	.237	11	.250	-1	7	0.1
1959	NY-A	13	9	.591	38	25	7	1	1	202	156	75	65	17	8	52	96	1.030	2.90	126	**2.39**	.211	15	.197	17	14	1.8
1960*	NY-A	15	9	.625	34	28	8	1	0	200	195	77	68	25	1	56	65	1.255	3.06	117	3.70	.256	11	.159	6	14	0.6
1961	NY-A	2	3	.400	12	8	1	0	0	54^1	59	33	28	9	2	14	24	1.344	4.64	80	4.65	.285	1	.053	-7	1	-0.9
	KC-A	0	5	.000	20	5	0	0	1	54	60	34	34	6	2	23	19	1.537	5.67	73	5.01	.286	2	.167	-9	1	-0.9
	Yr.	2	8	.200	32	13	1	0	1	108^1	119	67	62	15	4	37	43	1.440	5.15	76	4.83	.285	3	.097	-16	2	-1.8
1962	KC-A	0	2	.000	6	5	0	0	0	21^2	31	19	16	1	2	13	13	2.031	6.65	63	7.03	.323	1	.167	-6	0	-0.6
Total	9	72	77	.483	287	156	41	5	14	1268	1237	649	561	138	37	461	552	1.339	3.98	98	4.00	.256	75	.178	-29	63	-3.2
• DIVEN, Jim	Frank Robert Diven b: 8/29/1859, Brooklyn, NY d: 5/30/1914, Nutley, NJ TL Deb: 5/9/1883 U ♦																										
1883	Bal-a	1	1	.500	2	2	1	0	0	11	15	15	9	0	....	1	3	1.455	7.36	47	....	.305	2	.222	-4	0	-0.4
• DIXON, Ken	Kenneth John Dixon b: 10/17/1960, Monroe, VA BB/TR, 5'11", 166 lbs. Deb: 9/22/1984																										
1984	Bal-A	0	1	.000	2	2	0	0	0	13	14	6	6	1	0	4	8	1.385	4.15	93	3.96	.269	0	....	-1	1	-0.1
1985	Bal-A	8	4	.667	34	18	3	1	1	162	144	68	66	20	2	64	108	1.284	3.67	110	3.59	.237	0	....	8	10	0.8
1986	Bal-A	11	13	.458	35	33	2	0	0	202^1	194	111	103	33	1	83	170	1.369	4.58	90	4.26	.249	0	....	-9	9	-0.9
1987	Bal-A	7	10	.412	34	15	0	0	5	105	128	81	75	31	1	27	91	1.476	6.43	68	6.04	.292	0	....	-24	1	-2.3
Total	4	26	28	.481	105	68	5	1	6	482^1	480	266	250	85	4	178	377	1.364	4.66	89	4.42	.256	0	....	-25	21	-2.4
• DIXON, Sonny	John Craig Dixon b: 11/5/1924, Charlotte, NC BB/TR, 6'2.5", 205 lbs. Deb: 4/20/1953																										
1953	Was-A	5	8	.385	43	6	3	0	3	120	123	57	50	13	2	31	40	1.283	3.75	104	3.73	.267	4	.154	1	6	0.1
1954	Was-A	1	2	.333	16	0	0	0	1	29^2	26	15	10	3	0	12	7	1.281	3.03	117	3.32	.236	0	.000	2	2	0.1
	Phi-A	5	7	.417	38	6	1	0	4	107^1	136	63	58	8	3	27	42	1.519	4.86	80	4.79	.308	7	.250	-10	5	-0.8
	Yr.	6	9	.400	**54**	6	1	0	5	137	162	78	68	11	3	39	49	1.467	4.47	86	4.47	.293	7	.206	-8	7	-0.7
1955	KC-A	0	0	....	2	0	0	0	0	1^2	6	3	3	1	0	0	0	3.600	16.20	26	26.38	.545	0	....	-2	0	-0.2
1956	NY-A	0	1	.000	3	0	0	0	1	4^1	5	3	1	0	0	5	1	2.308	2.08	186	6.51	.294	0	.000	1	0	0.1
Total	4	11	18	.379	102	12	4	0	9	263	296	141	122	25	5	75	90	1.411	4.17	93	4.31	.284	11	.180	-8	13	-0.7
• DIXON, Steve	Steven Ross Dixon b: 8/3/1969, Cincinnati, OH BL/TL, 6', 190 lbs. Deb: 9/7/1993																										
1993	StL-N	0	0	....	4	0	0	0	0	2^2	7	10	10	1	0	5	2	4.500	33.75	12	25.89	.538	0	....	-9	0	-0.9
1994	StL-N	0	0	....	2	0	0	0	0	2^1	3	6	6	0	0	8	1	4.714	23.14	18	17.90	.333	0	....	-5	0	-0.5
Total	2	0	0	....	6	0	0	0	0	5	10	16	16	1	0	13	3	4.600	28.80	14	22.16	.455	0	....	-14	0	-1.4
• DIXON, Tom	Thomas Earl Dixon b: 4/23/1955, Orlando, FL BR/TR, 5'11", 175 lbs. Deb: 7/30/1977																										
1977	Hou-N	1	0	1.000	9	4	1	0	0	30^1	40	12	11	0	1	7	15	1.549	3.26	109	4.63	.320	0	.000	1	2	0.0
1978	Hou-N	7	11	.389	30	19	3	2	1	140	140	70	62	8	1	40	66	1.286	3.99	83	3.32	.265	4	.100	-8	4	-1.0
1979	Hou-N	1	2	.333	19	1	0	0	0	25^2	39	23	19	2	0	15	9	2.104	6.66	53	7.64	.348	1	1.000	-9	0	-0.9

YEAR	TM-L	W	L	PCT	G	GS	CG	SH	SV	IP	H	R	ER	HR	HB	BB	SO	RAT	ERA	ERA+	CERA	OAV	BH	AVG	PR+	WS	TPW
1983	Mon-N	0	1	.000	4	0	0	0	0	3^2	6	4	4	1	1	1	4	1.909	9.82	37	10.05	.375	0	....	-3	0	-0.3
Total	**4**	**9**	**14**	**.391**	**62**	**24**	**4**	**2**	**1**	**199^2**	**225**	**109**	**96**	**11**	**3**	**63**	**94**	**1.442**	**4.33**	**78**	**4.19**	**.288**	**5**	**.104**	**-18**	**6**	**-2.1**

• DOAK, Bill William Leopold "Spittin' Bill" Doak b: 1/28/1891, Pittsburgh, PA d: 11/26/1954, Bradenton, FL BR/TR, 6'.5", 165 lbs. Deb: 9/1/1912

YEAR	TM-L	W	L	PCT	G	GS	CG	SH	SV	IP	H	R	ER	HR	HB	BB	SO	RAT	ERA	ERA+	CERA	OAV	BH	AVG	PR+	WS	TPW
1912	Cin-N	0	0	....	1	1	0	0	0	2	4	2	1	0	0	1	0	2.500	4.50	74	10.56	.444	0	....	-0	0	0.0
1913	StL-N	2	8	.200	15	12	5	1	1	93	79	42	32	4	5	39	51	1.269	3.10	104	3.09	.236	1	.032	1	5	-0.2
1914	StL-N	19	6	.760	36	33	16	7	1	256	193	79	49	2	7	87	118	1.094	**1.72**	**162**	**2.07**	.216	10	.118	29	24	2.8
1915	StL-N	16	18	.471	38	36	19	3	1	276	263	103	81	4	8	85	124	1.261	2.64	105	2.96	.261	15	.174	7	17	0.9
1916	StL-N	12	8	.600	29	26	11	2	0	192	177	76	56	5	3	55	82	1.208	2.63	100	2.76	.251	8	.129	1	10	-0.1
1917	StL-N	16	20	.444	44	37	16	3	2	281^1	257	123	97	6	9	85	111	1.216	3.10	87	2.82	.250	12	.126	-16	13	-2.3
1918	StL-N	9	15	.375	31	23	16	1	1	211	191	76	57	3	4	60	74	1.190	2.43	111	2.60	.249	12	.182	6	12	0.7
1919	StL-N	13	14	.481	31	29	13	3	0	202^2	182	87	70	5	2	55	69	1.169	3.11	90	2.57	.246	7	.109	-10	9	-1.5
1920	StL-N	20	12	.625	39	37	20	5	1	270	256	94	76	7	6	80	90	1.244	2.53	121	2.95	.253	10	.114	15	18	1.0
1921	StL-N	15	6	.714	32	28	13	1	1	208^2	224	85	60	3	4	37	83	1.251	**2.59**	141	3.10	.278	10	.143	24	16	2.1
1922	StL-N	11	13	.458	37	29	8	2	2	180^1	222	127	111	12	3	69	73	1.614	5.54	70	5.15	.311	7	.130	-30	5	-3.1
1923	StL-N	8	13	.381	30	26	7	2	0	185	199	85	67	4	3	69	53	1.449	3.26	120	3.82	.279	3	.045	15	11	0.6
1924	StL-N	2	1	.667	11	1	0	0	3	22	25	8	8	0	0	14	7	1.773	3.27	116	5.07	.313	1	.200	1	2	0.1
	Bro-N	11	5	.688	21	16	8	2	0	149^1	130	58	51	8	3	35	32	1.105	3.07	122	2.54	.239	10	.179	15	13	1.5
	Yr.	13	6	.684	32	17	8	2	3	171^1	155	66	59	8	3	49	39	1.191	3.10	121	2.86	.248	11	.180	16	15	1.6
1927	Bro-N	11	8	.579	27	20	6	1	0	145	153	73	56	6	3	40	32	1.331	3.48	114	3.47	.271	6	.128	7	9	0.5
1928	Bro-N	3	8	.273	28	12	4	1	3	99^1	104	51	36	1	5	35	12	1.399	3.26	122	3.47	.271	3	.111	8	6	0.6
1929	StL-N	1	2	.333	3	2	0	0	0	9	17	15	12	1	0	5	3	2.444	12.00	39	10.13	.415	0	.000	-7	0	-0.7
Total	**16**	**169**	**157**	**.518**	**453**	**368**	**162**	**34**	**16**	**2782^2**	**2676**	**1184**	**920**	**71**	**65**	**851**	**1014**	**1.267**	**2.98**	**107**	**3.07**	**.259**	**115**	**.127**	**67**	**170**	**2.8**

• DOANE, Walt Walter Rudolph Doane b: 3/12/1887, Bellevue, ID d: 10/19/1935, West Brandywine, PA BL/TR, 6', 165 lbs. Deb: 9/20/1909 ♦

YEAR	TM-L	W	L	PCT	G	GS	CG	SH	SV	IP	H	R	ER	HR	HB	BB	SO	RAT	ERA	ERA+	CERA	OAV	BH	AVG	PR+	WS	TPW
1909	Cle-A	0	1	.000	1	1	0	0	0	5	10	7	3	0	0	1	2	2.200	5.40	47	8.31	.400	1	.111	-2	0	-0.2
1910	Cle-A	0	0	....	6	0	0	0	0	17^2	31	21	11	1	1	8	7	2.208	5.60	46	9.47	.413	2	.286	-6	0	-0.6
Total	**2**	**0**	**1**	**.000**	**7**	**1**	**0**	**0**	**0**	**22^2**	**41**	**28**	**14**	**1**	**1**	**9**	**9**	**2.206**	**5.56**	**46**	**9.21**	**.410**	**3**	**.188**	**-8**	**0**	**-0.8**

• DOBB, John John Kenneth "Lefty" Dobb b: 11/15/1901, Muskegon, MI d: 7/31/1991, Muskegon, MI BR/TL, 6'2", 180 lbs. Deb: 8/13/1924

YEAR	TM-L	W	L	PCT	G	GS	CG	SH	SV	IP	H	R	ER	HR	HB	BB	SO	RAT	ERA	ERA+	CERA	OAV	BH	AVG	PR+	WS	TPW
1924	Chi-A	0	0	....	2	0	0	0	0	2	4	2	2	0	0	1	2	2.500	9.00	46	9.55	.400	0	....	-1	0	-0.1

• DOBENS, Ray Raymond Joseph "Lefty" Dobens b: 7/28/1906, Nashua, NH d: 4/21/1980, Stuart, FL BL/TL, 5'8", 175 lbs. Deb: 7/7/1929

YEAR	TM-L	W	L	PCT	G	GS	CG	SH	SV	IP	H	R	ER	HR	HB	BB	SO	RAT	ERA	ERA+	CERA	OAV	BH	AVG	PR+	WS	TPW
1929	Bos-A	0	0	....	11	1	0	0	0	28^1	32	12	12	0	1	9	4	1.447	3.81	112	3.90	.302	3	.375	2	2	0.2

• DOBERNIC, Jess Andrew Joseph Dobernic b: 11/20/1917, Mount Olive, IL d: 7/16/1998, St. Louis, MO BR/TR, 5'10", 170 lbs. Deb: 7/2/1939

YEAR	TM-L	W	L	PCT	G	GS	CG	SH	SV	IP	H	R	ER	HR	HB	BB	SO	RAT	ERA	ERA+	CERA	OAV	BH	AVG	PR+	WS	TPW
1939	Chi-A	0	1	.000	4	0	0	0	0	3^1	3	6	5	0	1	6	1	2.700	13.50	35	8.02	.231	0	.000	-3	0	-0.3
1948	Chi-N	7	2	.778	54	0	0	0	1	85^2	67	33	30	8	1	40	48	1.249	3.15	124	2.98	.213	2	.200	8	8	0.8
1949	Chi-N	0	0	....	4	0	0	0	0	4	9	9	9	2	0	4	0	3.250	20.25	20	19.14	.450	0	....	-7	0	-0.7
	Cin-N	0	0	....	14	0	0	0	0	19^1	28	22	21	7	0	16	6	2.276	9.78	43	10.79	.329	0	.000	-12	0	-1.2
	Yr.	0	0	....	18	0	0	0	0	23^1	37	31	30	9	0	20	6	2.443	11.57	36	12.22	.352	0	.000	-19	0	-1.9
Total	**3**	**7**	**3**	**.700**	**76**	**0**	**0**	**0**	**1**	**112^1**	**107**	**70**	**65**	**17**	**2**	**66**	**55**	**1.540**	**5.21**	**78**	**5.05**	**.247**	**2**	**.154**	**-15**	**8**	**-1.4**

• DOBSON, Chuck Charles Thomas Dobson b: 1/10/1944, Kansas City, MO BR/TR, 6'4", 200 lbs. Deb: 4/19/1966

YEAR	TM-L	W	L	PCT	G	GS	CG	SH	SV	IP	H	R	ER	HR	HB	BB	SO	RAT	ERA	ERA+	CERA	OAV	BH	AVG	PR+	WS	TPW
1966	KC-A	4	6	.400	14	14	1	0	0	83^2	71	41	38	7	2	50	61	1.446	4.09	83	4.07	.234	3	.115	-7	2	-0.9
1967	KC-A	10	10	.500	32	29	4	1	0	197^2	172	83	81	17	3	75	110	1.250	3.69	86	3.22	.233	13	.181	-11	8	-1.2
1968	Oak-A	12	14	.462	35	34	11	3	0	225^1	197	91	75	20	4	80	168	1.229	3.00	94	3.15	.234	15	.200	-5	9	-0.4
1969	Oak-A	15	13	.536	35	35	11	1	0	235^1	244	111	101	16	1	80	137	1.377	3.86	89	3.87	.270	8	.101	-11	9	-1.5
1970	Oak-A	16	15	.516	41	**40**	13	**5**	0	267	230	122	111	32	5	92	149	1.206	3.74	95	3.26	.229	11	.118	-8	11	-1.3
1971	Oak-A	15	5	.750	30	30	7	1	0	189	185	84	80	24	1	71	100	1.354	3.81	87	4.09	.259	13	.197	-13	9	-1.2
1973	Oak-A	0	1	.000	1	1	0	0	0	2^1	6	4	2	1	0	2	3	3.429	7.71	46	19.24	.429	0	....	-1	0	-0.1
1974	Cal-A	2	3	.400	5	5	2	0	0	30	39	19	19	3	0	13	16	1.733	5.70	60	6.00	.315	0	....	-7	0	-0.8
1975	Cal-A	0	2	.000	9	2	0	0	0	28	30	26	21	5	2	13	14	1.536	6.75	53	5.45	.275	0	....	-10	0	-1.0
Total	**9**	**74**	**69**	**.517**	**202**	**190**	**49**	**11**	**0**	**1258^1**	**1174**	**581**	**528**	**125**	**18**	**476**	**758**	**1.311**	**3.78**	**87**	**3.67**	**.247**	**63**	**.153**	**-74**	**48**	**-8.2**

• DOBSON, Joe Joseph Gordon "Burrhead" Dobson b: 1/20/1917, Durant, OK d: 6/23/1994, Jacksonville, FL BR/TR, 6'2", 197 lbs. Deb: 4/26/1939

YEAR	TM-L	W	L	PCT	G	GS	CG	SH	SV	IP	H	R	ER	HR	HB	BB	SO	RAT	ERA	ERA+	CERA	OAV	BH	AVG	PR+	WS	TPW
1939	Cle-A	2	3	.400	35	3	0	0	1	78	87	56	51	3	1	51	27	1.769	5.88	75	5.16	.290	1	.056	-13	1	-1.3
1940	Cle-A	3	7	.300	40	7	2	1	3	100	101	60	55	8	0	48	57	1.490	4.95	85	4.26	.268	3	.125	-11	2	-1.1
1941	Bos-A	12	5	.706	27	18	7	1	0	134^1	136	70	67	8	2	67	69	1.511	4.49	93	4.15	.262	7	.149	-3	8	-0.3
1942	Bos-A	11	9	.550	30	23	10	3	0	182^2	155	73	67	9	2	68	72	1.221	3.30	113	2.82	.231	10	.145	4	12	0.3
1943	Bos-A	7	11	.389	25	20	9	3	0	164^1	144	63	57	4	0	57	63	1.223	3.12	106	2.67	.239	5	.096	3	9	0.0
1946★	Bos-A	13	7	.650	32	24	9	1	0	166^2	148	72	60	11	1	68	91	1.296	3.24	113	3.15	.234	5	.100	7	11	0.5
1947	Bos-A	18	8	.692	33	31	15	1	1	228^2	203	84	75	15	1	73	110	1.207	2.95	132	2.92	.238	16	.208	23	20	2.6
1948	Bos-A★	16	10	.615	38	32	16	5	2	245^1	237	115	97	14	1	92	116	1.341	3.56	123	3.42	.253	17	.202	21	20	2.2
1949	Bos-A	14	12	.538	33	27	12	2	2	212^2	219	103	91	12	2	97	87	1.486	3.85	113	4.12	.269	10	.147	8	15	0.7
1950	Bos-A	15	10	.600	39	27	12	1	4	206^2	217	103	96	15	0	81	81	1.442	4.18	117	4.11	.275	15	.214	17	17	1.7
1951	Chi-A	7	6	.538	28	21	6	0	3	146^2	136	68	59	17	0	51	67	1.275	3.62	111	3.54	.248	3	.065	4	8	-0.1
1952	Chi-A	14	10	.583	29	25	11	3	1	200^2	164	66	56	11	0	60	101	1.116	2.51	145	2.42	.222	12	.190	24	18	2.5
1953	Chi-A	5	5	.500	23	15	3	1	1	100^2	96	46	41	10	0	37	50	1.321	3.67	110	3.62	.249	2	.069	4	6	0.1
1954	Bos-A	0	0	....	2	0	0	0	0	2^2	5	2	2	0	0	1	1	2.250	6.75	61	8.21	.385	0	....	-1	0	-0.1
Total	**14**	**137**	**103**	**.571**	**414**	**273**	**112**	**22**	**18**	**2170**	**2048**	**981**	**874**	**137**	**10**	**851**	**992**	**1.336**	**3.62**	**112**	**3.45**	**.250**	**106**	**.152**	**89**	**147**	**7.6**

• DOBSON, Pat Patrick Edward Dobson b: 2/12/1942, Depew, NY BR/TR, 6'3", 190 lbs. Deb: 5/31/1967 C

YEAR	TM-L	W	L	PCT	G	GS	CG	SH	SV	IP	H	R	ER	HR	HB	BB	SO	RAT	ERA	ERA+	CERA	OAV	BH	AVG	PR+	WS	TPW
1967	Det-A	1	2	.333	28	1	0	0	0	49^1	38	20	16	6	2	27	34	1.318	2.92	112	3.68	.216	0	.000	1	3	0.1
1968★	Det-A	5	8	.385	47	10	2	1	7	125	89	39	37	13	2	48	93	1.096	2.66	113	2.55	.200	4	.143	4	9	0.5
1969	Det-A	5	10	.333	49	9	1	0	9	105	100	48	42	10	1	39	64	1.324	3.60	104	3.58	.253	2	.091	1	7	0.0
1970	SD-N	14	15	.483	40	34	8	1	1	251	257	126	105	28	4	78	185	1.335	3.76	106	3.90	.265	10	.141	6	12	0.6
1971★	Bal-A	20	8	.714	38	37	18	4	1	282^1	248	104	91	24	2	63	187	1.102	2.90	115	2.70	.235	10	.110	11	19	0.8
1972	Bal-A★	16	18	.471	38	36	13	3	0	268^1	220	89	79	13	4	69	161	1.077	2.65	116	2.34	.224	12	.141	6	15	0.5
1973	Atl-N	3	7	.300	12	10	1	1	0	57^2	73	33	32	1	1	19	23	1.595	4.99	79	4.58	.315	1	.067	-6	1	-0.8
	NY-A	9	8	.529	22	21	6	1	0	142^1	150	72	66	22	2	34	70	1.293	4.17	88	4.04	.266	0	....	-10	6	-1.0
1974	NY-A	19	15	.559	39	39	12	2	0	281	282	111	96	23	4	75	157	1.270	3.07	113	3.52	.262	0	....	8	19	0.8
1975	NY-A	11	14	.440	33	30	7	1	0	207^2	205	105	94	21	1	83	129	1.387	4.07	89	3.99	.261	0	....	-16	9	-1.6
1976	Cle-A	16	12	.571	35	35	6	0	0	217^1	226	98	84	13	2	65	117	1.339	3.48	100	3.64	.272	0	....	-1	12	-0.1
1977	Cle-A	3	12	.200	33	17	0	0	1	133^1	155	94	91	23	1	65	81	1.650	6.14	64	6.02	.299	0	....	-33	0	-3.3
Total	**11**	**122**	**129**	**.486**	**414**	**279**	**74**	**14**	**19**	**2120^1**	**2043**	**939**	**833**	**197**	**26**	**665**	**1301**	**1.277**	**3.54**	**100**	**3.54**	**.255**	**39**	**.123**	**-28**	**112**	**-3.4**

• DOCKINS, George George Woodrow "Lefty" Dockins b: 5/5/1917, Clyde, KS d: 1/22/1997, Clyde, KS BL/TL, 6', 175 lbs. Deb: 5/5/1945

YEAR	TM-L	W	L	PCT	G	GS	CG	SH	SV	IP	H	R	ER	HR	HB	BB	SO	RAT	ERA	ERA+	CERA	OAV	BH	AVG	PR+	WS	TPW
1945	StL-N	8	6	.571	31	12	5	2	0	126^1	132	53	45	4	0	38	33	1.346	3.21	117	3.33	.269	6	.176	5	9	0.5
1947	Bro-N	0	0	....	4	0	0	0	0	5^1	10	7	7	2	0	2	1	2.250	11.81	35	11.74	.400	0	.000	-5	0	-0.5
Total	**2**	**8**	**6**	**.571**	**35**	**12**	**5**	**2**	**0**	**131^2**	**142**	**60**	**52**	**6**	**0**	**40**	**34**	**1.382**	**3.55**	**107**	**3.67**	**.275**	**6**	**.171**	**-0**	**9**	**0.1**

• DODD, Robert Robert Wayne Dodd b: 3/14/1973, Kansas City, KS BL/TL, 6'3" Deb: 5/28/1998

YEAR	TM-L	W	L	PCT	G	GS	CG	SH	SV	IP	H	R	ER	HR	HB	BB	SO	RAT	ERA	ERA+	CERA	OAV	BH	AVG	PR+	WS	TPW
1998	Phi-N	1	0	1.000	4	0	0	0	0	5	7	6	4	1	1	1	4	1.600	7.20	60	6.82	.333	0	....	-2	0	-0.2

• DODGE, Sam Samuel Edward Dodge b: 12/9/1899, Neath, PA d: 4/5/1966, Utica, NY BR/TR, 6'1", 170 lbs. Deb: 9/24/1921

YEAR	TM-L	W	L	PCT	G	GS	CG	SH	SV	IP	H	R	ER	HR	HB	BB	SO	RAT	ERA	ERA+	CERA	OAV	BH	AVG	PR+	WS	TPW
1921	Bos-A	0	0	....	1	0	0	0	0	1	1	1	1	0	0	1	0	2.000	9.00	47	6.60	.500	0	....	-1	0	-0.1
1922	Bos-A	0	0	....	3	0	0	0	0	6	11	6	3	0	0	3	3	2.333	4.50	91	8.17	.379	0	.000	-0	0	0.0
Total	**2**	**0**	**0**	**....**	**4**	**0**	**0**	**0**	**0**	**7**	**12**	**7**	**4**	**0**	**0**	**4**	**3**	**2.286**	**5.14**	**80**	**7.94**	**.387**	**0**	**.000**	**-1**	**0**	**-0.1**

YEAR TM-L	W	L	PCT	G	GS	CG	SH	SV	IP	H	R	ER	HR	HB	BB	SO	RAT	ERA	ERA+	CERA	OAV	BH	AVG	PR+	WS	TPW
• DOE, Fred	Alfred George "Count" Doe b: 4/18/1864, Gloucester, MA d: 10/4/1938, Quincy, MA BR/TR, 5'10", 165 lbs. Deb: 8/23/1890																									
1890 Buf-P	0	1	.000	1	1	1	0	0	6	10	10	8	0	0	7	2	2.833	12.00	34	....	.356	0	.000	-5	0	-0.4
Pit-P	0	0	....	1	0	0	0	0	4	4	2	2	0	0	2	2	1.500	4.50	87	....	.249	1	.500	-0	1	0.0
Yr.	0	1	.000	2	1	1	0	0	10	14	12	10	0	0	9	4	2.300	9.00	45	....	.317	1	.250	-5	1	-0.4
• DOHENY, Ed	Edwin Richard Doheny b: 11/24/1873, Northfield, VT d: 12/29/1916, Worcester, MA BL/TL, 5'10.5", 165 lbs. Deb: 9/16/1895																									
1895 NY-N	0	3	.000	3	3	3	0	0	25^2	37	29	19	2	3	19	9	2.182	6.66	70	8.28	.332	1	.100	-6	0	-0.5
1896 NY-N	6	7	.462	17	15	9	0	0	108^1	112	78	54	3	6	59	39	1.578	4.49	94	4.35	.265	6	.150	-4	5	-0.5
1897 NY-N	4	4	.500	10	10	10	0	0	85	69	45	20	0	8	45	37	1.341	2.12	196	3.03	.221	7	.200	19	7	1.5
1898 NY-N	7	19	.269	28	27	23	0	0	213	238	164	87	1	20	101	96	1.592	3.68	95	4.52	.281	14	.163	-5	6	-0.5
1899 NY-N	14	17	.452	36	34	31	1	0	277^2	291	207	133	2	37	158	120	1.617	4.31	87	4.62	.269	27	.241	-20	10	-1.7
1900 NY-N	4	14	.222	20	18	12	0	0	133^2	148	134	81	2	22	96	44	1.825	5.45	66	5.67	.280	12	.222	-28	1	-2.5
1901 NY-N	2	5	.286	10	6	6	0	0	74	88	53	37	1	6	17	36	1.419	4.50	73	4.08	.293	10	.345	-8	2	-0.4
Pit-N	6	2	.750	11	10	6	1	0	76^2	68	36	17	1	5	22	28	1.174	2.00	163	2.65	.236	3	.115	10	6	1.0
Yr.	8	7	.533	21	16	12	1	0	150^2	156	89	54	2	11	39	64	1.294	3.23	102	3.35	.265	13	.236	2	8	0.6
1902 Pit-N	16	4	.800	22	21	19	2	0	188^1	161	68	53	0	15	61	88	1.179	2.53	108	2.57	.231	12	.156	-0	14	-0.2
1903 Pit-N	16	8	.667	27	25	22	2	2	222^2	209	122	79	1	19	89	75	1.338	3.19	101	3.36	.252	19	.209	-8	15	-0.8
Total 9	75	83	.475	184	169	141	6	2	1405	1421	936	580	13	141	667	572	1.486	3.72	95	4.04	.262	111	.198	-50	66	-4.8
• DOHERTY, John	John Harold Doherty b: 6/11/1967, Bronx, NY BR/TR, 6'4", 210 lbs. Deb: 4/8/1992																									
1992 Det-A	7	4	.636	47	11	0	0	3	116	131	61	50	4	4	25	37	1.345	3.88	102	3.73	.287	0	....	2	6	0.2
1993 Det-A	14	11	.560	32	31	3	2	0	184^2	205	104	91	19	5	48	63	1.370	4.44	97	4.29	.286	0	....	-3	9	-0.3
1994 Det-A	6	7	.462	18	17	2	0	0	101^1	139	75	73	13	3	26	28	1.628	6.48	75	6.01	.337	0	....	-17	2	-1.6
1995 Det-A	5	9	.357	48	2	0	0	6	113	130	66	64	10	6	37	46	1.478	5.10	93	4.63	.288	0	....	-3	7	-0.2
1996 Bos-A	0	0	....	3	0	0	0	0	6^1	8	10	4	1	1	4	3	1.895	5.68	89	7.14	.276	0	....	-0	0	0.0
Total 5	32	31	.508	148	61	5	2	9	521^1	613	316	282	47	19	140	177	1.444	4.87	92	4.61	.296	0	....	-20	24	-1.9
• DOLAN, Cozy	Patrick Henry Dolan b: 12/3/1872, Cambridge, MA d: 3/29/1907, Louisville, KY BL/TL, 5'10", 160 lbs. Deb: 4/26/1895 ♦																									
1895 Bos-N	11	7	.611	25	21	18	3	1	198^1	215	142	94	11	14	67	47	1.422	4.27	117	4.16	.272	20	.241	15	14	1.1
1896 Bos-N	1	4	.200	6	5	3	0	0	41	55	44	22	1	3	27	14	2.000	4.83	94	6.63	.319	2	.143	-2	1	-0.3
1905 Bos-N	0	1	.000	2	0	0	0	0	4	7	5	4	2	0	1	1	2.000	9.00	34	11.30	.368	119	.275	-3	10	-0.3
1906 Bos-N	0	1	.000	2	0	0	0	0	12	12	6	6	1	0	6	7	1.500	4.50	60	4.93	.300	136	.248	-2	11	-1.0
Total 4	12	13	.480	35	26	21	3	1	255^1	289	197	126	15	17	101	69	1.527	4.44	104	4.71	.283	855	.269	7	36	-0.5
• DOLAN, John	John Dolan b: 9/12/1867, Newport, KY d: 5/8/1948, Springfield, OH TR, 5'10", 170 lbs. Deb: 9/5/1890																									
1890 Cin-N	1	1	.500	2	2	2	0	0	18	17	13	9	3	1	10	9	1.500	4.50	79	....	.242	1	.125	-2	1	-0.3
1891 Col-a	12	11	.522	27	24	19	0	0	203^1	216	131	94	8	0	84	68	1.475	4.16	83	....	.263	7	.090	-22	9	-2.2
1892 Was-N	2	2	.500	5	4	3	0	0	37	39	26	18	0	1	15	8	1.459	4.38	74	3.67	.260	3	.231	-5	2	-0.4
1893 StL-N	0	1	.000	3	1	1	0	1	17^1	26	22	8	1	1	7	1	1.904	4.15	114	6.87	.337	1	.143	1	0	0.1
1895 Chi-N	0	1	.000	2	2	1	0	0	11	16	12	8	0	1	6	1	2.000	6.55	78	6.75	.334	0	.000	-2	0	-0.2
Total 5	15	16	.484	39	33	26	0	1	286^2	314	204	137	12	4	122	87	1.521	4.30	83	1.15	.269	12	.110	-29	12	-2.9
• DOLL, Art	Arthur James "Moose" Doll b: 5/7/1913, Chicago, IL d: 4/28/1978, Calumet City, IL BR/TR, 6'1", 190 lbs. Deb: 9/21/1935 ♦																									
1936 Bos-N	0	1	.000	1	1	0	0	0	8	11	3	3	1	1	2	2	1.625	3.38	114	6.71	.355	0	.000	0	0	0.0
1938 Bos-N	0	0	....	3	0	0	0	0	4	4	1	1	0	0	3	1	1.750	2.25	152	4.90	.286	1	1.000	1	1	0.1
Total 2	0	1	.000	4	1	0	0	0	12	15	4	4	1	1	5	3	1.667	3.00	124	6.11	.333	2	.154	1	1	0.1
• DOMINGUEZ, Juan	Juan Ramon Dominguez b: 5/18/1980, Sanchez Ramirez, Dominican Republic BR/TR, 6'2", 180 lbs. Deb: 8/12/2003																									
2003 Tex-A	0	2	.000	6	3	0	0	0	16^1	16	14	13	5	0	12	13	1.714	7.16	69	7.22	.271	0	....	-4	0	-0.4
• DONAHUE, Deacon	John Stephen Michael Donahue b: 6/23/1920, Chicago, IL BR/TR, 6', 180 lbs. Deb: 9/16/1943																									
1943 Phi-N	0	0	....	2	0	0	0	0	4	4	3	2	0	1	1	1	1.250	4.50	75	3.29	.235	0	....	-0	0	0.0
1944 Phi-N	0	2	.000	6	0	0	0	0	9^1	18	8	8	0	0	2	2	2.143	7.71	47	8.46	.429	0	.000	-4	0	-0.4
Total 2	0	2	.000	8	0	0	0	0	13^1	22	11	10	0	1	3	3	1.875	6.75	53	6.91	.373	0	.000	-5	0	-0.5
• DONAHUE, Red	Francis Rostell Donahue b: 1/23/1873, Waterbury, CT d: 8/25/1913, Philadelphia, PA BR/TR, 6', 187 lbs. Deb: 5/6/1893 U																									
1893 NY-N	0	0	....	2	0	0	0	1	5	8	10	5	1	2	3	1	2.200	9.00	52	11.23	.351	0	.000	-2	0	-0.2
1895 StL-N	0	1	.000	1	1	1	0	0	8	9	6	6	2	1	3	2	1.500	6.75	72	6.27	.280	0	.000	-1	0	-0.2
1896 StL-N	7	24	.226	32	32	28	0	0	267	376	235	172	6	13	98	70	1.775	5.80	75	5.81	.329	17	.159	-36	7	-3.6
1897 StL-N	10	35	.222	46	42	**38**	1	1	348	485	306	237	16	22	106	64	1.698	6.13	72	5.74	.327	33	.213	-53	4	-4.8
1898 Phi-N	16	17	.485	35	35	33	1	0	284^1	327	165	112	7	14	80	57	1.431	3.55	97	4.02	.286	16	.143	-2	13	-0.8
1899 Phi-N	21	8	.724	35	31	27	4	0	279	292	147	105	6	11	63	51	1.272	3.39	109	3.22	.269	20	.180	5	19	0.1
1900 Phi-N	15	10	.600	32	24	21	2	0	240	299	144	96	6	9	50	41	1.454	3.60	100	4.25	.304	20	.222	2	14	0.1
1901 Phi-N	20	13	.606	34	33	33	1	1	295	299	111	88	2	9	59	88	1.214	2.68	127	2.75	.261	11	.097	23	24	1.4
1902 StL-A	22	11	.667	35	34	33	2	0	316^1	322	134	97	7	8	65	63	1.223	2.76	128	2.92	.264	11	.093	22	30	1.3
1903 StL-A	8	7	.533	16	15	14	0	0	131	145	59	40	0	0	22	51	1.275	2.75	106	2.95	.280	8	.157	2	8	0.0
Cle-A	7	9	.438	16	15	14	4	0	136^2	142	61	37	3	6	12	45	1.127	2.44	117	2.67	.267	8	.151	5	7	0.4
Yr.	15	16	.484	32	30	28	4	0	267^2	287	120	77	3	6	34	96	1.199	2.59	111	2.81	.273	16	.154	7	15	0.4
1904 Cle-A	19	14	.576	35	32	30	6	0	277	281	96	74	2	5	49	127	1.191	2.40	106	2.69	.264	17	.168	3	18	0.2
1905 Cle-A	6	12	.333	20	18	14	1	0	137^2	132	68	52	2	5	25	45	1.140	3.40	77	2.59	.254	4	.075	-12	4	-1.8
1906 Det-A	13	14	.481	28	28	26	3	0	241	260	96	73	1	8	54	82	1.303	2.73	101	3.24	.278	10	.123	1	17	-0.4
Total 13	164	175	.484	367	340	312	25	3	2966	3377	1638	1194	61	113	689	787	1.371	3.62	97	3.74	.286	175	.152	-44	165	-8.5
• DONALD, Atley	Richard Atley "Swampy" Donald b: 8/19/1910, Morton, MS d: 10/19/1992, West Monroe, LA BL/TR, 6'1", 186 lbs. Deb: 4/21/1938																									
1938 NY-A	0	1	.000	2	2	0	0	0	12	7	8	7	0	1	14	6	1.750	5.25	86	3.92	.175	1	.167	-1	0	-0.1
1939 NY-A	13	3	.813	24	20	11	2	1	153	144	74	63	12	0	60	55	1.333	3.71	118	3.43	.247	15	.250	5	11	0.6
1940 NY-A	8	3	.727	24	11	6	1	0	118^2	113	49	40	11	2	59	60	1.449	3.03	133	4.07	.249	6	.146	12	10	0.9
1941* NY-A	9	5	.643	22	20	10	0	0	159	141	69	63	11	3	69	71	1.321	3.57	110	3.36	.237	5	.081	0	10	-0.4
1942* NY-A	11	3	.786	20	19	10	1	0	147^2	133	58	51	6	0	45	53	1.205	3.11	111	2.74	.239	9	.148	-1	9	-0.2
1943 NY-A	6	4	.600	22	15	2	0	0	119^1	134	69	61	10	0	38	57	1.441	4.60	70	4.16	.276	6	.128	-20	1	-2.5
1944 NY-A	13	10	.565	30	19	9	0	0	159	173	77	59	13	2	59	48	1.459	3.34	104	4.29	.280	10	.182	-0	10	0.0
1945 NY-A	5	4	.556	9	9	6	2	0	63^2	62	29	21	3	0	25	19	1.366	2.97	117	3.37	.248	5	.208	2	4	0.2
Total 8	65	33	.663	153	115	54	6	1	932^1	907	433	365	66	8	369	369	1.369	3.52	105	3.63	.253	57	.160	-3	55	-1.5
• DONALDS, Ed	Edward Alexander "Erston,Skipper" Donalds b: 6/22/1885, Bidwell, OH d: 7/3/1950, Columbus, OH BR/TR, 5'11", 180 lbs. Deb: 9/1/1912																									
1912 Cin-N	1	0	1.000	1	0	0	0	0	4	7	2	2	0	0	0	1	1.750	4.50	74	6.68	.438	0	.000	-0	0	-0.1
• DONNELLY, Blix	Sylvester Urban Donnelly b: 1/21/1914, Olivia, MN d: 6/20/1976, Olivia, MN BR/TR, 5'10", 178 lbs. Deb: 5/6/1944																									
1944* StL-N	2	1	.667	27	4	2	1	2	76^1	61	26	18	2	2	34	45	1.245	2.12	166	2.64	.218	1	.063	10	6	1.0
1945 StL-N	8	10	.444	31	23	9	4	2	166^1	157	79	65	10	6	87	76	1.467	3.52	106	3.95	.250	7	.130	0	9	-0.2
1946 StL-N	1	2	.333	13	0	0	0	0	13^2	17	7	6	1	1	10	11	1.976	3.95	87	7.24	.347	0	....	-1	1	-0.1
Phi-N	3	4	.429	12	8	2	0	1	76^1	64	31	25	7	2	24	38	1.153	2.95	117	2.80	.220	7	.280	4	6	0.7
Yr.	4	6	.400	25	8	2	0	1	90	81	38	31	8	3	34	49	1.278	3.10	111	3.47	.238	7	.280	3	7	0.6
1947 Phi-N	4	6	.400	38	10	5	1	5	120^2	113	44	40	6	3	46	31	1.318	2.98	134	3.51	.265	2	.063	13	11	1.1
1948 Phi-N	5	7	.417	26	19	8	1	2	131^2	125	65	54	13	0	49	46	1.322	3.69	107	3.76	.261	10	.222	4	8	0.6
1949 Phi-N	2	1	.667	23	10	1	0	0	78^1	84	50	44	7	1	40	36	1.583	5.06	78	5.03	.294	4	.174	-11	1	-1.1
1950 Phi-N	2	4	.333	14	1	0	0	0	21	30	13	10	5	0	10	10	1.905	4.29	94	7.92	.330	1	.200	-1	1	-0.1
1951 Bos-N	0	1	.000	6	0	0	0	0	7^1	8	6	6	1	1	6	3	1.909	7.36	50	6.56	.286	0	.000	-3	0	-0.3
Total 8	27	36	.429	190	75	27	7	12	691^2	659	321	268	52	16	306	296	1.395	3.49	109	3.90	.257	32	.159	17	43	1.6

YEAR	TM-L	W	L	PCT	G	GS	CG	SH	SV	IP	H	R	ER	HR	HB	BB	SO	RAT	ERA	ERA+	CERA	OAV	BH	AVG	PR+	WS	TPW
• DONNELLY, Brendan	Brendan Kevin Donnelly b: 7/4/1971, Washington, DC BR/TR, 6'3", 205 lbs. Deb: 4/9/2002																										
2002*	Ana-A	1	1	.500	46	0	0	0	1	49^2	32	13	12	2	2	19	54	1.027	2.17	204	1.89	.184	0	....	11	6	1.0
2003	Ana-A★	2	2	.500	63	0	0	0	3	74	55	14	13	2	4	24	79	1.068	1.58	273	2.12	.200	0	....	21	11	2.0
Total	2	3	3	.500	109	0	0	0	4	123^2	87	27	25	4	6	43	133	1.051	1.82	240	2.03	.194	0	....	32	17	3.1
• DONNELLY, Ed	Edward Vincent Donnelly b: 12/10/1932, Allen, MI d: 12/25/1992, Houston, TX BR/TR, 6', 175 lbs. Deb: 8/1/1959																										
1959	Chi-N	1	1	.500	9	0	0	0	0	14^1	18	7	5	1	0	9	6	1.884	3.14	126	6.08	.305	0	....	1	1	0.1
• DONNELLY, Ed	Edward "Big Ed,Ned" Donnelly b: 7/29/1880, Hampton, NY d: 11/28/1957, Rutland, VT BR/TR, 6'1", 205 lbs. Deb: 9/19/1911																										
1911	Bos-N	3	2	.600	5	4	4	1	0	36^2	33	15	10	0	2	9	16	1.145	2.45	155	2.45	.236	1	.071	6	2	0.5
1912	Bos-N	5	10	.333	37	18	10	0	0	184^1	225	127	89	10	5	72	67	**1.611**	4.35	82	4.94	.304	19	.275	-13	7	-1.0
Total	2	8	12	.400	42	22	14	1	0	221	258	142	99	10	7	81	83	1.534	4.03	89	4.52	.293	20	.241	-7	9	-0.5
• DONNELLY, Frank	Franklin Marion Donnelly b: 10/7/1869, Tamaroa, IL d: 2/3/1953, Canton, IL, 5'6", 180 lbs. Deb: 8/15/1893																										
1893	Chi-N	3	1	.750	7	5	3	0	**2**	42	51	42	25	1	0	17	6	1.619	5.36	86	4.64	.291	8	.444	-3	3	0.1
1894	Chi-N	0	0	....	1	0	0	0	0	4^2	6	8	8	0	....	0	1	1.286	15.43	36	3.42	.309	0	.000	-5	0	-0.4
Total	2	3	1	.750	8	5	3	0	2	46^2	57	50	33	1	0	17	7	1.586	6.36	76	4.52	.293	8	.421	-8	3	-0.3
• DONOHUE, Jim	James Thomas Donohue b: 10/31/1938, St. Louis, MO BR/TR, 6'4", 190 lbs. Deb: 4/11/1961																										
1961	Det-A	1	1	.500	14	0	0	0	1	20^1	23	10	8	2	0	15	20	1.869	3.54	116	5.94	.288	0	.000	1	1	0.1
	LA-A	4	6	.400	38	7	0	0	5	100^1	93	48	48	16	0	50	79	1.425	4.31	105	4.42	.246	4	.148	3	7	0.3
	Yr.	5	7	.417	52	7	0	0	6	120^2	116	58	56	18	0	65	99	1.500	4.18	106	4.67	.253	4	.143	5	8	0.4
1962	LA-A	1	0	1.000	12	1	0	0	0	24^1	24	14	10	4	2	11	14	1.438	3.70	104	5.05	.258	1	.250	1	1	0.1
	Min-A	0	1	.000	6	1	0	0	1	10^1	12	8	8	2	0	6	3	1.742	6.97	59	6.82	.324	0	.000	-3	0	-0.4
	Yr.	1	1	.500	18	2	0	0	1	34^2	36	22	18	6	2	17	17	1.529	4.67	85	5.58	.277	1	.167	-3	1	-0.3
Total	2	6	8	.429	70	9	0	0	7	155^1	152	80	74	24	2	82	116	1.506	4.29	101	4.87	.259	5	.147	2	9	0.1
• DONOHUE, Pete	Peter Joseph Donohue b: 11/5/1900, Athens, TX d: 2/23/1988, Fort Worth, TX BR/TR, 6'2", 185 lbs. Deb: 7/1/1921																										
1921	Cin-N	7	6	.538	21	11	7	0	1	118^1	117	48	44	5	0	26	44	1.208	3.35	107	2.92	.263	8	.211	5	9	0.5
1922	Cin-N	18	9	.667	33	30	18	2	1	242	257	110	84	7	5	43	66	1.240	3.12	128	3.14	.276	16	.182	18	19	1.4
1923	Cin-N	21	15	.583	42	36	19	2	3	274^1	304	138	103	3	10	68	84	1.356	3.38	114	3.44	.278	24	.250	14	21	1.6
1924	Cin-N	16	9	.640	35	31	16	3	0	222^1	248	100	89	9	9	36	72	1.277	3.60	105	3.51	.285	14	.192	4	15	0.4
1925	Cin-N	21	14	.600	42	**38**	**27**	3	2	**301**	310	122	103	3	2	49	78	1.193	3.08	133	2.75	.268	32	.294	29	**28**	3.4
1926	Cin-N	**20**	14	.588	47	**36**	17	**5**	2	**285^2**	298	133	107	6	9	39	73	1.180	3.37	110	2.83	.268	33	.311	9	21	1.8
1927	Cin-N	6	16	.273	33	24	12	1	1	190^2	253	111	87	3	1	32	48	1.495	4.11	92	4.34	.328	16	.250	-6	7	-0.5
1928	Cin-N	7	11	.389	23	18	8	0	0	150	180	84	79	10	3	32	37	1.413	4.74	83	4.24	.309	7	.146	-14	5	-1.4
1929	Cin-N	10	13	.435	32	24	7	0	0	177^2	243	123	107	12	4	51	30	1.655	5.42	84	5.49	.331	20	.333	-18	7	-1.2
1930	Cin-N	1	3	.250	8	5	2	0	1	34^1	53	24	24	0	1	13	4	1.922	6.29	77	6.58	.363	1	.100	-5	1	-0.6
	NY-N	7	6	.538	18	11	4	0	1	86^2	135	65	59	6	2	18	26	1.765	6.13	77	6.46	.360	9	.273	-14	3	-1.2
	Yr.	8	9	.471	26	16	6	0	2	121	188	89	83	6	3	31	30	1.810	6.17	77	6.50	.361	10	.233	-19	4	-1.7
1931	NY-N	0	1	.000	4	1	0	0	0	11^1	14	7	7	1	0	4	4	1.588	5.56	66	5.04	.311	0	.000	-2	0	-0.3
	Cle-A	0	0	....	2	0	0	0	0	5^1	9	6	5	1	0	5	4	2.625	8.44	55	12.95	.429	0	.000	-2	0	-0.2
1932	Bos-A	0	1	.000	4	2	0	0	0	12^2	18	11	11	2	0	6	1	1.895	7.82	58	7.35	.340	0	.000	-4	0	-0.5
Total	12	134	118	.532	344	267	137	16	12	2112^1	2439	1082	909	68	46	422	571	1.354	3.87	103	3.74	.293	180	.246	13	136	3.3
• DONOSO, Lino	Lino (Galeta) Donoso b: 9/23/1922, Havana, Cuba d: 10/13/1990, Veracruz, Mexico BL/TL, 5'11", 160 lbs. Deb: 6/18/1955																										
1955	Pit-N	4	6	.400	25	9	3	0	1	95	106	58	56	16	1	35	38	1.484	5.31	78	5.10	.287	5	.185	-12	2	-1.3
1956	Pit-N	0	0	....	3	0	0	0	0	1^2	2	0	0	0	0	1	1	1.800	0.00	....	4.47	.250	0	....	1	0	0.1
Total	2	4	6	.400	28	9	3	0	1	96^2	108	58	56	16	1	36	39	1.490	5.21	79	5.09	.286	5	.185	-11	2	-1.2
• DONOVAN, Bill	William Edward "Wild Bill" Donovan b: 10/13/1876, Lawrence, MA d: 12/9/1923, Forsyth, NY BR/TR, 5'11", 190 lbs. Deb: 4/22/1898 M/U ♦																										
1898	Was-N	1	6	.143	17	7	6	0	0	88	88	74	42	0	7	69	36	1.784	4.30	85	4.79	.259	17	.165	-4	2	-1.1
1899	Bro-N	1	2	.333	5	2	2	0	1	25	35	22	12	0	0	13	11	1.920	4.32	91	6.18	.330	3	.231	-2	1	-0.1
1900	Bro-N	1	2	.333	5	4	2	0	0	31	36	23	23	0	3	18	13	1.742	6.68	57	5.09	.290	0	.000	-10	0	-1.1
1901	Bro-N	**25**	15	.625	**45**	38	36	2	**3**	351	324	151	108	1	8	152	226	1.356	2.77	121	3.01	.244	23	.170	20	27	1.9
1902	Bro-N	17	15	.531	35	33	30	4	1	297^2	250	122	92	1	7	111	170	1.213	2.78	99	2.44	.228	28	.174	-1	18	-0.3
1903	Det-A	17	16	.515	35	34	**34**	4	0	307	247	104	78	3	5	95	187	1.114	2.29	127	2.17	.220	30	.242	22	22	2.7
1904	Det-A	17	16	.515	34	34	30	3	0	293	251	111	80	5	10	94	137	1.177	2.46	104	2.53	.232	38	.271	-1	19	0.3
1905	Det-A	18	15	.545	34	32	27	5	0	280^2	236	111	81	2	10	101	135	1.201	2.60	105	2.49	.230	25	.192	1	20	0.4
1906	Det-A	9	15	.375	25	25	22	0	0	211^2	221	92	74	4	8	72	85	1.384	3.15	88	3.53	.272	11	.121	-9	11	-1.8
1907*	Det-A	25	4	.862	32	28	27	3	1	271	222	96	66	3	8	82	123	1.122	2.19	119	2.24	.226	29	.266	13	23	2.2
1908*	Det-A	18	7	.720	29	28	25	6	0	242^2	210	78	56	2	6	53	141	1.084	2.08	116	2.12	.231	13	.159	13	18	1.5
1909*	Det-A	8	7	.533	21	17	13	4	2	140^1	121	50	36	0	6	60	76	1.290	2.31	109	2.80	.235	9	.200	3	10	0.4
1910	Det-A	17	7	.708	26	23	20	3	0	206^2	184	74	56	4	7	61	107	1.185	2.44	108	2.64	.243	10	.145	5	15	0.3
1911	Det-A	10	9	.526	20	19	15	1	0	168^1	160	83	62	4	3	64	81	1.331	3.31	104	3.12	.250	12	.200	5	14	0.8
1912	Det-A	1	0	1.000	3	1	0	0	0	10	5	2	1	0	1	2	6	.700	0.90	364	1.02	.147	1	.077	3	1	0.0
1915	NY-A	0	3	.000	9	1	0	0	0	33^2	35	18	18	1	1	10	17	1.337	4.81	61	3.43	.278	1	.083	-7	0	-0.9
1916	NY-A	0	0	....	1	0	0	0	0	1	1	0	0	0	0	1	0	2.000	0.00	....	5.17	.250	0	....	0	0	0.0
1918	Det-A	1	0	1.000	2	1	0	0	0	6	5	1	1	0	0	1	1	1.000	1.50	177	1.81	.227	1	.500	1	1	0.2
Total	18	186	139	.572	378	327	289	35	8	2964^2	2631	1212	886	30	90	1059	1552	1.245	2.69	106	2.73	.239	251	.193	51	202	5.4
• DONOVAN, Bill	Willard Earl Donovan b: 7/6/1916, Maywood, IL d: 9/25/1997, Maywood, IL BB/TL, 6'2", 198 lbs. Deb: 4/19/1942 C																										
1942	Bos-N	3	6	.333	31	10	2	0	0	89^1	97	43	34	2	0	32	23	1.444	3.43	97	3.80	.283	6	.240	-0	4	0.1
1943	Bos-N	1	0	1.000	7	0	0	0	0	14^2	17	4	3	0	0	9	1	1.773	1.84	185	4.82	.304	1	.333	2	2	0.3
Total	2	4	6	.400	38	10	2	0	0	104	114	47	37	2	0	41	24	1.490	3.20	104	3.94	.286	7	.250	2	6	0.4
• DONOVAN, Dick	Richard Edward Donovan b: 12/7/1927, Boston, MA d: 1/6/1997, Weymouth, MA BL/TR, 6'3", 205 lbs. Deb: 4/24/1950																										
1950	Bos-N	0	2	.000	10	3	0	0	0	29^2	28	28	27	4	2	34	9	2.090	8.19	47	7.12	.255	1	.167	-14	0	-1.3
1951	Bos-N	0	0	....	8	2	0	0	0	13^2	17	11	8	0	0	11	4	2.049	5.27	70	5.91	.298	1	.333	-2	0	-0.1
1952	Bos-N	0	2	.000	7	2	0	0	1	13	18	10	8	1	2	12	6	2.308	5.54	65	8.68	.346	0	.000	-3	0	-0.3
1954	Det-A	0	0	....	2	0	0	0	0	6	9	7	7	1	0	5	2	2.333	10.50	35	9.20	.360	0	.000	-5	0	-0.5
1955	Chi-A★	15	9	.625	29	24	11	5	0	187	186	77	69	17	3	48	88	1.251	3.32	119	3.49	.261	17	.224	10	15	1.5
1956	Chi-A	12	10	.545	34	31	14	3	0	234^2	212	99	95	22	6	59	120	1.155	3.64	113	3.00	.240	20	.222	11	18	1.8
1957	Chi-A	16	6	.727	28	28	**16**	2	0	220^2	203	76	68	17	8	45	88	1.124	2.77	135	2.87	.247	12	.145	19	18	2.2
1958	Chi-A	15	14	.517	34	34	16	4	0	248	240	92	83	23	7	53	127	1.181	3.01	121	3.19	.251	9	.113	14	18	1.3
1959*	Chi-A	9	10	.474	31	29	5	1	0	179^2	171	84	73	15	5	58	71	1.275	3.66	103	3.43	.247	8	.131	-1	9	-0.1
1960	Chi-A	6	1	.857	33	8	0	0	3	78^2	87	49	47	13	0	25	30	1.424	5.38	70	4.76	.283	3	.130	-15	2	-1.5
1961	Was-A★	10	10	.500	23	22	11	2	0	168^2	138	60	45	10	3	35	62	1.026	**2.40**	**163**	**2.21**	.224	10	.179	28	15	3.0
1962	Cle-A★	20	10	.667	34	34	16	**5**	0	250^2	255	109	100	23	2	47	94	1.205	3.59	108	3.31	.263	16	.180	6	20	1.2
1963	Cle-A	11	13	.458	30	30	7	3	0	206	211	106	97	27	5	28	84	1.160	4.24	85	3.46	.265	9	.130	-13	7	-1.5
1964	Cle-A	7	9	.438	30	23	5	0	1	158^1	181	86	80	19	2	29	83	1.326	4.55	79	4.16	.290	7	.146	-13	5	-1.0
1965	Cle-A	1	3	.250	12	3	0	0	0	22^2	32	15	15	6	0	6	12	1.676	5.96	58	7.39	.333	0	.000	-6	0	-0.7
Total	15	122	99	.552	345	273	101	25	5	2017^1	1988	909	822	198	45	495	880	1.231	3.67	103	3.46	.258	113	.163	16	127	3.9
• DOPSON, John	John Robert Dopson b: 7/14/1963, Baltimore, MD BL/TR, 6'4", 225 lbs. Deb: 9/4/1985																										
1985	Mon-N	0	2	.000	4	3	0	0	0	13	25	17	16	4	0	4	4	2.231	11.08	31	10.89	.379	0	.000	-11	0	-1.2
1988	Mon-N	3	11	.214	26	26	1	0	0	168^2	150	69	57	15	1	58	101	1.233	3.04	118	3.17	.235	3	.059	8	7	0.6
1989	Bos-A	12	8	.600	29	28	2	0	0	169^1	166	84	75	14	2	69	95	1.388	3.99	103	3.93	.257	0	....	4	9	0.4
1990	Bos-A	0	0	....	4	4	0	0	0	17^2	13	7	4	2	0	9	9	1.245	2.04	200	3.09	.200	0	....	4	2	0.4
1991	Bos-A	0	0	....	1	0	0	0	0	1	2	2	2	0	0	1	0	3.000	18.00	24	12.01	.500	0	....	-2	0	-0.2

YEAR	TM-L	W	L	PCT	G	GS	CG	SH	SV	IP	H	R	ER	HR	HB	BB	SO	RAT	ERA	ERA+	CERA	OAV	BH	AVG	PR+	WS	TPW
1992	Bos-A	7	11	.389	25	25	0	0	0	141^{1}	159	78	64	17	2	38	55	1.394	4.08	103	4.53	.287	0	....	2	7	0.2
1993	Bos-A	7	11	.389	34	28	1	1	0	155^{2}	170	93	86	16	2	59	89	1.471	4.97	93	4.47	.281	0	....	-7	6	-0.7
1994	Cal-A	1	4	.200	21	5	0	0	1	58^{2}	67	41	40	6	3	26	33	1.585	6.14	80	5.24	.288	0	....	-8	2	-0.8
Total	**8**	**30**	**47**	**.390**	**144**	**119**	**4**	**1**	**1**	**725^{1}**	**752**	**391**	**344**	**74**	**10**	**264**	**386**	**1.401**	**4.27**	**98**	**4.21**	**.268**	**3**	**.055**	**-11**	**33**	**-1.2**
• DORAN, John	John F. Doran b: 1867, Chicago, IL TL, 5'11", 160 lbs. Deb: 4/11/1891																										
1891	Lou-a	5	10	.333	15	14	12	1	0	126	160	111	76	3	13	75	55	1.865	5.43	67	....	.299	10	.189	-26	2	-2.4
• DORISH, Harry	Harry "Fritz" Dorish b: 7/13/1921, Swoyersville, PA d: 12/31/2000, Wilkes-Barre, PA BR/TR, 5'11", 206 lbs. Deb: 4/15/1947 C																										
1947	Bos-A	7	8	.467	41	9	2	0	2	136	149	80	71	6	1	54	50	1.493	4.70	83	4.19	.283	5	.143	-12	4	-1.4
1948	Bos-A	0	1	.000	9	0	0	0	0	14^{1}	18	13	9	1	0	6	5	1.674	5.65	78	4.83	.281	1	.250	-2	0	-0.2
1949	Bos-A	0	0	....	5	0	0	0	0	7^{2}	7	2	2	1	0	1	5	1.043	2.35	186	2.80	.241	0	....	2	1	0.2
1950	StL-A	4	9	.308	29	13	4	0	0	109	162	90	78	13	9	36	36	1.817	6.44	77	7.00	.337	5	.161	-15	2	-1.3
1951	Chi-A	5	6	.455	32	4	2	1	0	96^{2}	101	50	38	6	0	31	29	1.366	3.54	114	3.74	.272	8	.258	4	5	0.4
1952	Chi-A	8	4	.667	39	1	1	0	**11**	91	66	28	25	4	1	42	47	1.187	2.47	147	2.45	.208	2	.091	11	12	1.0
1953	Chi-A	10	6	.625	55	6	2	0	18	145^{2}	140	59	55	9	6	52	69	1.318	3.40	118	3.49	.254	7	.171	10	14	0.8
1954	Chi-A	6	4	.600	37	6	2	1	6	109	88	35	33	9	1	29	48	1.073	2.72	137	2.52	.228	3	.111	11	10	1.0
1955	Chi-A	2	0	1.000	13	0	0	0	1	17	16	4	3	0	0	9	6	1.471	1.59	248	3.49	.258	1	.333	4	2	0.4
	Bal-A	3	3	.500	35	1	0	0	6	65^{2}	58	25	23	5	1	28	22	1.310	3.15	121	3.36	.238	0	.000	6	6	0.4
	Yr.	5	3	.625	48	1	0	0	7	82^{2}	74	29	26	5	1	37	28	1.343	2.83	135	3.39	.242	1	.077	10	8	0.9
1956	Bal-A	0	0	....	13	0	0	0	0	19^{2}	22	10	9	3	0	3	4	1.271	4.12	95	4.13	.297	0	....	-0	1	0.0
	Bos-A	0	2	.000	15	0	0	0	0	22^{2}	23	10	9	1	0	10	11	1.456	3.57	129	3.83	.277	0	....	3	2	0.3
	Yr.	0	2	.000	28	0	0	0	0	42^{1}	45	20	18	4	0	13	15	1.370	3.83	111	3.97	.287	0	....	2	3	0.2
Total	**10**	**45**	**43**	**.511**	**323**	**40**	**13**	**2**	**44**	**834^{1}**	**850**	**406**	**355**	**58**	**19**	**301**	**332**	**1.380**	**3.83**	**107**	**3.88**	**.267**	**32**	**.157**	**21**	**59**	**1.5**
• DORNER, Gus	Augustus Dorner b: 8/18/1876, Chambersburg, PA d: 5/4/1956, Chambersburg, PA BR/TR, 5'10", 176 lbs. Deb: 9/17/1902																										
1902	Cle-A	3	1	.750	4	4	4	1	0	36	33	13	5	1	1	13	5	1.278	1.25	275	2.88	.245	5	.385	9	4	1.0
1903	Cle-A	3	5	.375	12	8	4	2	0	73^{2}	83	51	37	4	1	24	28	1.452	4.52	63	4.07	.283	2	.080	-14	0	-1.7
1906	Cin-N	0	1	.000	2	1	1	0	0	15	16	5	2	0	1	4	5	1.333	1.20	229	3.49	.276	0	.000	2	1	0.2
	Bos-N	8	25	.242	34	32	29	0	0	273^{1}	264	152	111	5	16	103	104	1.343	3.65	73	3.49	.260	14	.140	-27	6	-3.4
	Yr.	8	26	.235	36	33	30	0	0	288^{1}	280	157	113	5	17	107	109	1.342	3.53	76	3.49	.261	14	.133	-25	7	-3.2
1907	Bos-N	12	16	.429	36	31	24	2	0	271^{1}	253	120	94	4	15	92	85	1.271	3.12	82	3.17	.255	12	.130	-20	9	-2.5
1908	Bos-N	8	19	.296	38	28	14	3	0	216^{1}	176	120	85	3	15	77	41	1.169	3.54	68	2.58	.224	12	.179	-33	3	-3.9
1909	Bos-N	1	2	.333	5	2	0	0	1	24^{2}	17	11	7	1	2	17	7	1.378	2.55	110	3.25	.198	1	.167	1	2	0.1
Total	**6**	**35**	**69**	**.337**	**131**	**106**	**76**	**8**	**1**	**910^{1}**	**842**	**472**	**341**	**18**	**51**	**330**	**275**	**1.287**	**3.37**	**77**	**3.19**	**.250**	**46**	**.149**	**-82**	**25**	**-10.3**
• DORR, Bert	Charles Albert Dorr b: 2/2/1862, New York, NY d: 6/16/1914, Dickinson, NY Deb: 8/24/1882																										
1882	StL-a	2	6	.250	8	8	8	0	0	66	53	39	19	0	....	1	34	.818	2.59	108	....	.205	4	.154	3	3	0.1
• DORSETT, Cal	Calvin Leavelle "Preacher" Dorsett b: 6/10/1913, Lone Oak, TX d: 10/22/1970, Elk City, OK BR/TR, 6', 180 lbs. Deb: 8/19/1940																										
1940	Cle-A	0	0	....	1	0	0	0	0	1	1	1	1	1	0	0	0	1.000	9.00	47	7.45	.250	0	....	-1	0	-0.1
1941	Cle-A	0	1	.000	5	2	0	0	0	11^{1}	21	15	13	0	0	10	5	2.735	10.32	38	10.12	.382	0	.000	-8	0	-0.8
1947	Cle-A	0	0	....	2	0	0	0	0	1^{1}	3	4	4	1	0	3	1	4.500	27.00	13	31.93	.500	0	....	-4	0	-0.4
Total	**3**	**0**	**1**	**.000**	**8**	**2**	**0**	**0**	**0**	**13^{2}**	**25**	**20**	**18**	**2**	**0**	**13**	**6**	**2.780**	**11.85**	**32**	**12.05**	**.385**	**0**	**.000**	**-12**	**0**	**-1.2**
• DORSEY, Jim	James Edward Dorsey b: 8/2/1955, Chicago, IL BR/TR, 6'7", 190 lbs. Deb: 9/2/1980																										
1980	Cal-A	1	2	.333	4	4	0	0	0	15^{2}	25	16	16	2	1	8	8	2.106	9.19	43	8.92	.368	0	....	-9	0	-0.9
1984	Bos-A	0	0	....	2	0	0	0	0	2^{2}	6	3	3	0	0	2	4	3.000	10.13	41	13.52	.462	0	....	-2	0	-0.2
1985	Bos-A	0	1	.000	2	1	0	0	0	5^{1}	12	12	12	2	0	10	2	4.125	20.25	21	22.85	.444	0	....	-9	0	-0.9
Total	**3**	**1**	**3**	**.250**	**8**	**5**	**0**	**0**	**0**	**23^{2}**	**43**	**31**	**31**	**4**	**1**	**20**	**14**	**2.662**	**11.79**	**35**	**12.58**	**.398**	**0**	**....**	**-20**	**0**	**-2.0**
• DOSCHER, Jack	John Henry Doscher, Jr. b: 7/27/1880, Troy, NY d: 5/27/1971, Park Ridge, NJ BL/TL, 6'1", 205 lbs. Deb: 7/2/1903																										
1903	Chi-N	0	1	.000	1	1	0	0	0	3	6	5	4	0	1	2	5	2.667	12.00	26	12.35	.429	0	.000	-3	0	-0.3
	Bro-N	0	0	....	3	0	0	0	0	7	8	8	6	1	1	9	4	2.429	7.71	41	9.53	.296	0	.000	-3	0	-0.3
	Yr.	0	1	.000	4	1	0	0	0	10	14	13	10	1	2	11	9	2.500	9.00	35	10.37	.341	0	.000	-6	0	-0.6
1904	Bro-N	0	0	....	2	0	0	0	0	6^{1}	1	1	0	0	0	1	2	.316	0.00	....	0.17	.053	1	.500	2	1	0.2
1905	Bro-N	1	5	.167	12	7	6	0	0	71	60	34	25	1	3	30	33	1.268	3.17	91	2.88	.232	2	.083	-0	3	-0.2
1906	Bro-N	0	1	.000	2	1	1	0	0	14	12	3	2	0	0	4	10	1.143	1.29	195	2.47	.250	0	.000	2	1	0.2
1908	Cin-N	1	3	.250	7	4	3	0	0	44^{1}	31	19	9	1	3	22	7	1.195	1.83	125	2.48	.196	2	.133	3	2	0.3
Total	**5**	**2**	**10**	**.167**	**27**	**13**	**10**	**0**	**0**	**145^{2}**	**118**	**70**	**46**	**3**	**8**	**68**	**61**	**1.277**	**2.84**	**98**	**3.11**	**.225**	**5**	**.100**	**1**	**7**	**-0.1**
• DOTEL, Octavio	Octavio Eduardo (Diaz) Dotel b: 11/25/1973, Santo Domingo, Dominican Republic BR/TR, 6', 175 lbs. Deb: 6/26/1999																										
1999★	NY-N	8	3	.727	19	14	0	0	0	85^{1}	69	52	51	12	6	49	85	1.383	5.38	82	4.30	.226	3	.125	-10	3	-0.9
2000	Hou-N	3	7	.300	50	16	0	0	16	125	127	80	75	26	7	61	142	1.504	5.40	90	5.47	.265	1	.031	-5	7	-0.8
2001★	Hou-N	7	5	.583	61	4	0	0	2	105	79	35	31	5	2	47	145	1.200	2.66	172	2.62	.205	1	.091	22	12	2.1
2002	Hou-N	6	4	.600	83	0	0	0	6	97^{1}	58	21	20	7	4	27	118	.873	1.85	230	1.61	.173	0	.000	27	17	2.7
2003	Hou-N	6	4	.600	76	0	0	0	4	87	53	25	24	9	3	31	97	.966	2.48	179	2.02	.172	0	.000	17	12	1.6
Total	**5**	**30**	**23**	**.566**	**289**	**34**	**0**	**0**	**28**	**499^{2}**	**386**	**213**	**201**	**59**	**22**	**215**	**587**	**1.203**	**3.62**	**126**	**3.32**	**.213**	**5**	**.068**	**50**	**51**	**4.7**
• DOTSON, Richard	Richard Elliott "Rich" Dotson b: 1/10/1959, Cincinnati, OH BR/TR, 6'1", 204 lbs. Deb: 9/4/1979																										
1979	Chi-A	2	0	1.000	5	5	1	1	0	24^{1}	28	13	10	0	0	6	13	1.397	3.70	115	3.51	.286	0	....	1	2	0.1
1980	Chi-A	12	10	.545	33	32	8	0	0	198	185	105	94	20	6	87	109	1.374	4.27	94	3.93	.247	0	....	-4	10	-0.4
1981	Chi-A	9	8	.529	24	24	5	**4**	0	141	145	67	59	13	4	49	73	1.376	3.77	95	4.15	.270	0	....	-4	6	-0.5
1982	Chi-A	11	15	.423	34	31	3	1	0	196^{2}	219	97	84	19	5	73	109	1.485	3.84	105	4.65	.282	0	....	6	10	0.6
1983★	Chi-A	22	7	.759	35	35	8	1	0	240	209	92	86	19	8	106	137	1.313	3.23	130	3.61	.240	0	....	25	21	2.5
1984	Chi-A★	14	15	.483	32	32	14	1	0	245^{2}	216	110	98	24	7	103	120	1.299	3.59	116	3.58	.238	0	....	14	18	1.4
1985	Chi-A	3	4	.429	9	9	0	0	0	52^{1}	53	30	26	5	3	17	33	1.338	4.47	97	4.00	.261	0	....	-1	2	-0.1
1986	Chi-A	10	17	.370	34	34	3	1	0	197	226	125	120	24	2	69	110	1.497	5.48	79	4.95	.289	0	....	-30	4	-2.9
1987	Chi-A	11	12	.478	31	31	7	2	0	211^{1}	201	109	98	24	0	86	114	1.358	4.17	110	3.92	.249	0	....	4	12	0.3
1988	NY-A	12	9	.571	32	29	4	0	0	171	178	103	95	27	4	72	77	1.462	5.00	79	4.85	.266	0	....	-19	5	-1.9
1989	NY-A	2	5	.286	11	9	1	0	0	51^{2}	69	33	32	8	1	17	14	1.665	5.57	69	6.21	.317	0	....	-10	1	-1.0
	Chi-A	3	7	.300	17	17	1	0	0	99^{2}	112	51	43	8	0	41	55	1.535	3.88	98	4.58	.282	0	....	-1	3	-0.1
	Yr.	5	12	.294	28	26	2	0	0	151^{1}	181	84	75	16	1	58	69	1.579	4.46	86	5.13	.294	0	....	-11	4	-1.1
1990	KC-A	0	4	.000	8	7	0	0	0	28^{2}	43	29	27	3	0	14	9	1.988	8.48	45	7.50	.355	0	....	-14	0	-1.4
Total	**12**	**111**	**113**	**.496**	**305**	**295**	**55**	**11**	**0**	**1857^{1}**	**1884**	**964**	**872**	**194**	**40**	**740**	**973**	**1.413**	**4.23**	**97**	**4.28**	**.264**	**0**	**....**	**-33**	**94**	**-3.3**
• DOTTER, Gary	Gary Richard Dotter b: 8/7/1942, St. Louis, MO BL/TL, 6'1", 180 lbs. Deb: 9/10/1961																										
1961	Min-A	0	0	....	2	0	0	0	0	6	6	6	6	0	0	4	2	1.667	9.00	47	3.93	.273	0	.000	-3	0	-0.3
1963	Min-A	0	0	....	2	0	0	0	0	2	0	0	0	0	0	0	2	.000	0.00	....	0.00	.000	0	....	1	0	0.1
1964	Min-A	0	0	....	3	0	0	0	0	4^{1}	3	2	1	1	0	3	6	1.385	2.08	172	4.10	.188	0	....	1	0	0.1
Total	**3**	**0**	**0**	**....**	**7**	**0**	**0**	**0**	**0**	**12^{1}**	**9**	**8**	**7**	**1**	**0**	**7**	**10**	**1.297**	**5.11**	**81**	**3.35**	**.237**	**0**	**.000**	**-1**	**0**	**-0.1**
• DOTY, Babe	Elmer L. Doty b: 12/17/1867, Lyons, NY d: 11/20/1929, Toledo, OH BL/TR, 6', 160 lbs. Deb: 8/18/1890																										
1890	Tol-a	1	0	1.000	1	1	1	0	0	9	9	1	1	0	0	1	4	1.111	1.00	394	....	.253	0	.000	3	1	0.2
• DOUGHERTY, Jim	James E. Dougherty b: 3/8/1968, Brentwood, NY BR/TR, 6', 210 lbs. Deb: 4/27/1995																										
1995	Hou-N	8	4	.667	56	0	0	0	0	67^{2}	76	37	37	7	3	25	49	1.493	4.92	79	4.95	.292	1	.125	-6	3	-0.7
1996	Hou-N	0	2	.000	12	0	0	0	0	13	14	14	13	2	1	11	6	1.923	9.00	43	6.94	.280	0	....	-7	0	-0.7
1998	Oak-A	0	2	.000	9	0	0	0	0	12	17	11	11	2	1	7	3	2.000	8.25	55	8.45	.340	0	....	-5	0	-0.5

YEAR	TM-L	W	L	PCT	G	GS	CG	SH	SV	IP	H	R	ER	HR	HB	BB	SO	RAT	ERA	ERA+	CERA	OAV	BH	AVG	PR+	WS	TPW
1999	Pit-N	0	0	....	2	0	0	0	0	2	3	3	2	0	0	3	1	3.000	9.00	51	10.76	.333	0	....	-1	0	-0.1
Total	**4**	**8**	**8**	**.500**	**79**	**0**	**0**	**0**	**0**	**94^2**	**110**	**65**	**63**	**11**	**5**	**46**	**59**	**1.648**	**5.99**	**67**	**5.79**	**.298**	**1**	**.125**	**-19**	**3**	**-1.9**
• DOUGHERTY, Tom	Thomas James "Sugar Boy" Dougherty b: 5/30/1881, Chicago, IL d: 11/6/1953, Milwaukee, WI BL/TR, 195 lbs. Deb: 4/24/1904																										
1904	Chi-A	1	0	1.000	1	0	0	0	0	2	0	0	0	0	0	0	0	.000	0.00	....	0.00	.000	0	.000	0	0	0.0
• DOUGLAS, Larry	Lawrence Howard Douglas b: 6/5/1890, Jellico, TN d: 11/4/1949, Jellico, TN BR/TR, 6'3", 175 lbs. Deb: 6/17/1915																										
1915	Bal-F	1	0	1.000	2	0	0	0	0	3	3	1	1	0	0	2	1	1.667	3.00	113	4.17	.273	0	....	0	0	0.0
• DOUGLAS, Phil	Phillip Brooks "Shufflin' Phil" Douglas b: 6/17/1890, Cedartown, GA d: 8/2/1952, Sequatchie, TN BR/TR, 6'3", 190 lbs. Deb: 8/30/1912																										
1912	Chi-A	0	1	.000	3	1	0	0	0	12^1	21	17	10	0	0	6	7	2.189	7.30	44	7.94	.382	0	.000	-5	0	-0.6
1914	Cin-N	11	18	.379	45	25	13	0	1	239^1	186	111	68	7	11	92	121	1.162	2.56	114	2.50	.223	10	.137	11	12	0.9
1915	Cin-N	1	5	.167	8	7	0	0	0	46^2	53	35	28	0	0	23	29	1.629	5.40	53	4.27	.299	2	.118	-14	0	-1.7
	Bro-N	5	5	.500	20	13	5	1	0	116^2	104	45	34	1	5	17	63	1.037	2.62	106	2.12	.241	6	.154	1	7	0.0
	Chi-N	1	1	.500	4	4	2	1	0	25	17	9	6	0	1	7	18	.960	2.16	128	1.51	.187	0	.000	2	2	0.1
	Yr.	7	11	.389	32	24	7	2	0	188^1	174	89	68	1	6	47	110	1.173	3.25	86	2.57	.249	8	.125	-11	9	-1.5
1917	Chi-N	14	20	.412	**51**	37	20	5	1	293^1	269	123	83	13	6	50	151	1.088	2.55	113	2.52	.250	11	.126	16	15	1.4
1918*	Chi-N	10	9	.526	25	19	11	2	2	156^2	145	57	37	2	1	31	51	1.123	2.13	131	2.32	.246	14	.255	15	12	1.8
1919	Chi-N	10	6	.625	25	19	8	4	0	161^2	133	52	36	0	2	34	63	1.033	2.00	143	1.87	.230	8	.157	17	13	1.7
	NY-N	2	4	.333	8	6	4	0	0	51^1	53	22	12	0	1	6	21	1.149	2.10	133	2.48	.264	0	.000	3	2	0.1
	Yr.	12	10	.545	33	25	12	4	0	213	186	74	48	0	3	40	84	1.061	2.03	141	2.02	.239	8	.121	20	15	1.8
1920	NY-N	14	10	.583	46	21	10	3	2	226	225	84	68	6	2	55	71	1.239	2.71	111	2.96	.263	11	.151	4	14	0.0
1921*	NY-N	15	10	.600	40	27	13	**3**	2	221^2	266	119	104	17	2	55	55	1.448	4.22	87	4.46	.308	16	.198	-20	10	-2.0
1922	NY-N	11	4	.733	24	21	9	1	0	157^2	154	56	46	6	4	35	33	1.199	**2.63**	**152**	**2.91**	**.257**	12	.207	19	15	1.9
Total	**9**	**94**	**93**	**.503**	**299**	**200**	**95**	**20**	**8**	**1708^1**	**1626**	**730**	**532**	**52**	**35**	**411**	**683**	**1.192**	**2.80**	**110**	**2.83**	**.256**	**90**	**.161**	**49**	**102**	**3.7**
• DOUGLAS, Whammy	Charles William Douglas b: 2/17/1935, Carrboro, NC BR/TR, 6'2", 185 lbs. Deb: 7/29/1957																										
1957	Pit-N	3	3	.500	11	8	0	0	0	47	48	23	17	5	3	30	28	1.660	3.26	116	5.50	.270	1	.063	2	2	0.1
• DOUGLASS, Sean	Sean R. Douglass b: 4/28/1979, Lancaster, CA BR/TR, 6'6", 200 lbs. Deb: 7/18/2001																										
2001	Bal-A	2	1	.667	4	4	0	0	0	20^1	21	12	12	3	1	11	17	1.574	5.31	81	5.27	.259	0	....	-3	1	-0.2
2002	Bal-A	0	5	.000	15	8	0	0	0	53^1	58	41	36	10	2	35	44	1.744	6.08	70	6.56	.283	0	....	-11	0	-1.1
2003	Bal-A	0	0	....	3	0	0	0	0	8	14	12	12	2	1	6	3	2.500	13.50	33	12.56	.378	0	....	-8	0	-0.8
Total	**3**	**2**	**6**	**.250**	**22**	**12**	**0**	**0**	**0**	**81^2**	**93**	**65**	**60**	**15**	**4**	**52**	**64**	**1.776**	**6.61**	**65**	**6.83**	**.288**	**0**	**....**	**-22**	**1**	**-2.1**
• DOWD, Kip	James Joseph Dowd b: 2/16/1889, Holyoke, MA d: 12/20/1960, Holyoke, MA BR/TR, 5'10.5", 160 lbs. Deb: 7/5/1910																										
1910	Pit-N	0	0	....	1	0	0	0	0	2	4	4	0	0	1	2	1	3.000	0.00	....	13.72	.400	0	....	1	0	0.1
• DOWLING, Dave	David Barclay Dowling b: 8/23/1942, Baton Rouge, LA BR/TL, 6'2", 181 lbs. Deb: 10/3/1964																										
1964	StL-N	0	0	....	1	0	0	0	0	1	2	0	0	0	0	0	0	2.000	0.00	....	7.48	.400	0	....	0	0	0.0
1966	Chi-N	1	0	1.000	1	1	1	0	0	9	10	2	2	0	0	0	3	1.111	2.00	184	2.46	.270	0	.000	2	1	0.2
Total	**2**	**1**	**0**	**1.000**	**2**	**1**	**1**	**0**	**0**	**10**	**12**	**2**	**2**	**0**	**0**	**0**	**3**	**1.200**	**1.80**	**204**	**2.96**	**.286**	**0**	**.000**	**2**	**1**	**0.2**
• DOWLING, Pete	Henry Peter Dowling b: St. Louis, MO d: 6/30/1905, Hot Lake, OR BL/TL, 5'11" Deb: 7/17/1897																										
1897	Lou-N	1	2	.333	4	4	2	0	0	26	39	30	17	0	6	8	3	1.808	5.88	72	6.65	.343	2	.200	-5	0	-0.4
1898	Lou-N	13	20	.394	36	32	30	0	0	285^2	284	176	132	7	22	120	84	1.414	4.16	86	3.75	.258	21	.196	-17	15	-1.4
1899	Lou-N	13	17	.433	35	33	30	0	0	298^1	329	166	100	6	17	95	89	1.421	3.02	128	3.89	.280	27	.233	32	20	2.9
1901	Mil-A	1	3	.250	10	4	3	0	1	49^2	71	49	31	1	15	14	25	1.711	5.62	64	5.72	.331	4	.211	-10	1	-0.8
	Cle-A	11	22	.333	33	30	28	2	0	256^1	269	160	110	1	19	104	99	1.455	3.86	92	3.81	.267	16	.162	-8	11	-1.0
	Yr.	12	25	.324	43	34	31	2	1	306	340	209	141	2	34	118	124	1.497	4.15	86	4.12	.278	20	.169	-18	12	-1.9
Total	**4**	**39**	**64**	**.379**	**118**	**103**	**93**	**2**	**1**	**916**	**992**	**581**	**390**	**15**	**79**	**341**	**300**	**1.455**	**3.83**	**96**	**4.00**	**.274**	**70**	**.199**	**-7**	**47**	**-0.7**
• DOWNING, Al	Alphonso Erwin Downing b: 6/28/1941, Trenton, NJ BR/TL, 5'11", 177 lbs. Deb: 7/19/1961																										
1961	NY-A	0	1	.000	5	1	0	0	0	9	7	8	8	0	1	12	12	2.111	8.00	46	5.86	.212	0	.000	-5	0	-0.5
1962	NY-A	0	0	....	1	0	0	0	0	1	0	0	0	0	0	0	1	.000	0.00	....	0.00	.000	0	....	0	0	0.0
1963*	NY-A	13	5	.722	24	22	10	4	0	175^2	114	52	50	7	0	80	171	1.104	2.56	137	**2.09**	**.184**	6	.103	16	16	1.4
1964*	NY-A	13	8	.619	37	35	11	1	2	244	201	104	94	18	0	120	**217**	1.316	3.47	104	3.23	.223	15	.176	2	13	0.4
1965	NY-A	12	14	.462	35	32	8	2	0	212	185	92	80	16	2	105	179	1.368	3.40	100	3.63	.237	8	.108	2	10	0.1
1966	NY-A	10	11	.476	30	30	1	0	0	200	178	90	79	23	1	79	152	1.285	3.56	93	3.54	.235	7	.100	-4	8	-0.7
1967	NY-A★	14	10	.583	31	28	10	4	0	201^2	158	65	59	13	6	61	171	1.086	2.63	119	2.49	.217	8	.121	13	16	1.6
1968	NY-A	3	3	.500	15	12	1	0	0	61^1	54	24	24	7	1	20	40	1.207	3.52	82	3.23	.237	3	.176	-4	2	-0.4
1969	NY-A	7	5	.583	30	15	5	1	0	130^2	117	57	49	12	0	49	85	1.270	3.38	103	3.27	.240	6	.136	1	7	0.0
1970	Oak-A	3	3	.500	10	6	1	0	0	41	39	19	18	5	1	22	26	1.488	3.95	90	4.63	.252	2	.182	-2	2	-0.2
	Mil-A	2	10	.167	17	16	1	0	0	94^1	79	47	35	8	3	59	53	1.463	3.34	113	4.02	.232	2	.083	7	4	0.5
	Yr.	5	13	.278	27	22	2	0	0	135^1	118	66	53	13	4	81	79	1.470	3.52	105	4.21	.238	4	.114	5	6	0.3
1971	LA-N	20	9	.690	37	36	12	**5**	0	262^1	245	93	78	16	3	84	136	1.254	2.68	121	3.18	.247	16	.174	16	19	1.8
1972	LA-N	9	9	.500	31	30	7	4	0	202^2	196	81	67	13	7	67	117	1.298	2.98	112	3.46	.254	8	.121	7	10	0.6
1973	LA-N	9	9	.500	30	28	5	2	0	193	155	87	71	19	1	68	124	1.155	3.31	104	2.83	.219	5	.088	0	9	-0.1
1974*	LA-N	5	6	.455	21	16	1	1	0	98^1	94	52	40	7	3	45	63	1.414	3.66	93	3.97	.255	5	.172	-2	3	-0.3
1975	LA-N	2	1	.667	22	6	0	0	1	74^2	59	31	24	6	2	28	39	1.165	2.89	118	2.78	.215	0	.000	3	4	0.2
1976	LA-N	1	2	.333	17	3	0	0	0	46^2	43	21	20	3	0	18	30	1.307	3.86	88	3.33	.250	0	.000	-3	2	-0.4
1977	LA-N	0	1	.000	12	1	0	0	0	20	22	15	15	4	0	16	23	1.900	6.75	57	6.92	.278	0	.000	-7	0	-0.7
Total	**17**	**123**	**107**	**.535**	**405**	**317**	**73**	**24**	**3**	**2268^1**	**1946**	**938**	**811**	**177**	**31**	**933**	**1639**	**1.269**	**3.22**	**106**	**3.24**	**.232**	**91**	**.127**	**41**	**125**	**3.5**
• DOWNS, Dave	David Ralph Downs b: 6/21/1952, Logan, UT BR/TR, 6'5", 220 lbs. Deb: 9/2/1972																										
1972	Phi-N	1	1	.500	4	4	1	1	0	23	25	7	7	1	1	3	5	1.217	2.74	131	3.60	.294	2	.250	2	2	0.2
• DOWNS, Kelly	Kelly Robert Downs b: 10/25/1960, Ogden, UT BR/TR, 6'4", 200 lbs. Deb: 7/29/1986																										
1986	SF-N	4	4	.500	14	14	1	0	0	88^1	78	29	27	5	3	30	64	1.223	2.75	128	2.90	.236	5	.172	6	6	0.6
1987*	SF-N	12	9	.571	41	28	4	3	1	186	185	83	75	14	4	67	137	1.355	3.63	106	3.71	.258	8	.143	2	11	0.1
1988	SF-N	13	9	.591	27	26	6	3	0	168	140	67	62	11	3	47	118	1.113	3.32	98	2.51	.225	9	.167	-1	9	0.1
1989*	SF-N	4	8	.333	18	15	0	0	0	82^2	82	47	44	7	1	26	49	1.306	4.79	70	3.57	.261	2	.091	-15	0	-1.7
1990	SF-N	3	2	.600	13	9	0	0	0	63	56	26	24	2	2	20	31	1.206	3.43	106	2.70	.233	0	.000	1	4	0.0
1991	SF-N	10	4	.714	45	11	0	0	0	111^2	99	59	52	12	3	53	62	1.361	4.19	85	3.77	.239	2	.087	-9	4	-1.0
1992	SF-N	1	2	.333	19	7	0	0	0	62^1	65	27	24	4	3	24	33	1.428	3.47	95	4.20	.275	0	.000	-2	2	-0.4
	* Oak-A	5	5	.500	18	13	0	0	0	82	72	36	30	4	4	46	38	1.439	3.29	114	3.73	.237	0	....	3	5	0.3
1993	Oak-A	5	10	.333	42	12	0	0	0	119^2	135	80	75	14	2	60	66	1.630	5.64	72	5.36	.287	0	....	-20	1	-2.0
Total	**8**	**57**	**53**	**.518**	**237**	**135**	**11**	**6**	**1**	**963^2**	**912**	**454**	**413**	**73**	**25**	**373**	**598**	**1.333**	**3.86**	**94**	**3.59**	**.250**	**26**	**.123**	**-35**	**42**	**-4.0**
• DOWNS, Scott	Scott Jeremy Downs b: 3/17/1976, Louisville, KY BL/TL, 6'2", 190 lbs. Deb: 4/9/2000																										
2000	Chi-N	4	3	.571	18	18	0	0	0	94	117	59	54	13	5	37	63	1.638	5.17	88	6.07	.310	2	.077	-6	3	-0.7
	Mon-N	0	0	....	1	1	0	0	0	3	5	3	3	0	0	3	0	2.667	9.00	53	10.34	.385	0	.000	-1	0	-0.2
	Yr.	4	3	.571	19	19	0	0	0	97	122	62	57	13	5	40	63	1.670	5.29	86	6.20	.312	2	.071	-8	3	-0.9
2003	Mon-N	0	1	.000	1	1	0	0	0	3	5	5	5	2	0	3	4	2.667	15.00	34	15.01	.357	0	.000	-3	0	-0.3
Total	**2**	**4**	**4**	**.500**	**20**	**20**	**0**	**0**	**0**	**100**	**127**	**67**	**62**	**15**	**5**	**43**	**67**	**1.700**	**5.58**	**82**	**6.46**	**.314**	**2**	**.069**	**-11**	**3**	**-1.2**
• DOYLE, Carl	William Carl Doyle b: 7/30/1912, Knoxville, TN d: 9/4/1951, Knoxville, TN BR/TR, 6'1", 185 lbs. Deb: 8/5/1935																										
1935	Phi-A	2	7	.222	14	9	3	0	0	79^2	86	63	53	3	2	72	34	1.983	5.99	76	5.93	.282	4	.133	-12	1	-1.3
1936	Phi-A	0	3	.000	8	6	1	0	0	38^2	66	53	47	4	5	29	12	2.457	10.94	47	10.28	.369	4	.267	-25	0	-2.1
1939	Bro-N	1	2	.333	5	1	1	1	1	17^2	8	5	2	1	0	7	7	.849	1.02	395	1.26	.136	1	.167	6	3	0.6

YEAR	TM-L	W	L	PCT	G	GS	CG	SH	SV	IP	H	R	ER	HR	HB	BB	SO	RAT	ERA	ERA+	CERA	OAV	BH	AVG	PR+	WS	TPW
1940	Bro-N	0	0	....	3	0	0	0	1	5^2	18	17	17	3	4	6	4	4.235	27.00	15	31.97	.545	1	1.000	-14	0	-1.4
	StL-N	3	3	.500	21	5	1	0	0	81	99	57	53	7	6	41	44	1.728	5.89	68	5.71	.294	6	.200	-16	1	-1.4
	Yr.	3	3	.500	24	5	1	0	1	86^2	117	74	70	10	10	47	48	1.892	7.27	55	7.43	.316	7	.226	-30	1	-2.8
Total	4	6	15	.286	51	21	6	1	2	222^2	277	195	172	18	17	155	101	1.940	6.95	64	6.90	.303	16	.195	-61	5	-5.6

• DOYLE, Jess

Jesse Herbert Doyle b: 4/14/1898, Knoxville, TN d: 4/15/1961, Belleville, IL BR/TR, 5'11", 175 lbs. Deb: 4/14/1925

YEAR	TM-L	W	L	PCT	G	GS	CG	SH	SV	IP	H	R	ER	HR	HB	BB	SO	RAT	ERA	ERA+	CERA	OAV	BH	AVG	PR+	WS	TPW
1925	Det-A	4	7	.364	45	3	0	0	8	118^1	158	83	78	6	5	50	31	1.758	5.93	73	5.91	.340	8	.242	-22	4	-1.7
1926	Det-A	0	0	....	2	0	0	0	1	4^1	6	3	2	0	0	1	2	1.615	4.15	98	4.66	.316	1	1.000	-0	1	0.0
1927	Det-A	0	0	....	7	0	0	0	0	12^1	16	11	11	0	0	5	5	1.703	8.03	52	4.88	.314	1	.333	-5	0	-0.5
1931	StL-A	0	0	....	1	0	0	0	0	1	3	3	3	0	0	1	0	4.000	27.00	17	19.12	.500	0	....	-2	0	-0.2
Total	4	4	7	.364	55	3	0	0	9	136	183	100	94	6	5	57	38	1.765	6.22	69	5.87	.338	10	.270	-29	5	-2.4

• DOYLE, John

John Aloysius Doyle b: 1858, Canada d: 12/24/1915, Providence, RI Deb: 7/26/1882

YEAR	TM-L	W	L	PCT	G	GS	CG	SH	SV	IP	H	R	ER	HR	HB	BB	SO	RAT	ERA	ERA+	CERA	OAV	BH	AVG	PR+	WS	TPW
1882	StL-a	0	3	.000	3	3	3	0	0	24	41	33	7	0	....	3	5	1.833	2.63	107	....	.355	2	.182	1	0	0.1

• DOYLE, Paul

Paul Sinnott Doyle b: 10/2/1939, Philadelphia, PA BL/TL, 5'11", 172 lbs. Deb: 5/28/1969

YEAR	TM-L	W	L	PCT	G	GS	CG	SH	SV	IP	H	R	ER	HR	HB	BB	SO	RAT	ERA	ERA+	CERA	OAV	BH	AVG	PR+	WS	TPW
1969*	Atl-N	2	0	1.000	36	0	0	0	4	39	31	9	9	4	0	16	25	1.205	2.08	174	3.08	.231	0	.000	7	5	0.7
1970	Cal-A	3	1	.750	40	0	0	0	5	42	43	25	24	7	1	21	34	1.524	5.14	70	5.18	.267	0	.000	-8	1	-0.9
	SD-N	0	2	.000	9	0	0	0	2	7	9	5	5	0	0	6	2	2.143	6.43	62	7.19	.360	0	.000	-2	0	-0.2
1972	Cal-A	0	0	....	2	0	0	0	0	2^1	2	0	0	0	0	3	4	2.143	0.00	....	5.73	.250	0	....	1	0	0.1
Total	3	5	3	.625	87	0	0	0	11	90^1	85	39	38	11	1	46	65	1.450	3.79	97	4.44	.259	0	.000	-3	6	-0.3

• DOYLE, Slow Joe

Judd Bruce Doyle b: 9/15/1881, Clay Center, KS d: 11/21/1947, Tannersville, NY BR/TR, 5'8", 150 lbs. Deb: 8/25/1906

YEAR	TM-L	W	L	PCT	G	GS	CG	SH	SV	IP	H	R	ER	HR	HB	BB	SO	RAT	ERA	ERA+	CERA	OAV	BH	AVG	PR+	WS	TPW
1906	NY-A	2	1	.667	9	6	3	2	0	45^1	34	15	12	1	1	13	28	1.037	2.38	124	1.94	.212	3	.214	3	4	0.3
1907	NY-A	11	11	.500	29	23	15	1	1	193^2	169	86	57	2	6	67	94	1.219	2.65	105	2.68	.237	8	.138	6	11	0.6
1908	NY-A	1	1	.500	12	4	2	1	0	48	42	24	14	1	2	14	20	1.167	2.63	94	2.62	.235	3	.214	0	1	0.1
1909	NY-A	8	6	.571	17	15	8	3	0	125^2	103	49	36	3	2	37	57	1.114	2.58	98	2.35	.232	7	.167	3	7	0.4
1910	NY-A	0	2	.000	3	2	1	0	0	12^1	19	13	11	0	1	5	6	1.946	8.03	33	7.01	.365	1	.250	-7	0	-0.8
	Cin-N	0	0	....	5	0	0	0	0	11^1	16	19	8	0	0	11	4	2.382	6.35	46	7.69	.327	0	.000	-4	0	-0.5
Total	5	22	21	.512	75	50	29	7	1	436^1	383	206	138	7	12	147	209	1.215	2.85	94	2.75	.240	22	.163	1	23	0.1

• DOZIER, Buzz

William Joseph Dozier b: 8/31/1927, Waco, TX BR/TR, 6'3", 185 lbs. Deb: 9/12/1947

YEAR	TM-L	W	L	PCT	G	GS	CG	SH	SV	IP	H	R	ER	HR	HB	BB	SO	RAT	ERA	ERA+	CERA	OAV	BH	AVG	PR+	WS	TPW
1947	Was-A	0	0	....	2	0	0	0	0	4^2	2	0	0	0	0	1	2	.643	0.00	....	0.73	.133	0	.000	2	1	0.2
1949	Was-A	0	0	....	2	0	0	0	0	6^1	12	8	8	0	0	6	1	2.842	11.37	37	11.67	.429	0	.000	-5	0	-0.5
Total	2	0	0	....	4	0	0	0	0	11	14	8	8	0	0	7	3	1.909	6.55	65	7.03	.326	0	.000	-3	1	-0.3

• DOZIER, Tom

Thomas Dean Dozier b: 9/5/1961, San Pablo, CA BR/TR, 6'2", 190 lbs. Deb: 5/17/1986

YEAR	TM-L	W	L	PCT	G	GS	CG	SH	SV	IP	H	R	ER	HR	HB	BB	SO	RAT	ERA	ERA+	CERA	OAV	BH	AVG	PR+	WS	TPW
1986	Oak-A	0	0	....	4	0	0	0	0	6^1	6	6	4	1	0	5	4	1.737	5.68	68	5.37	.261	0	....	-1	0	-0.1

• DRABEK, Doug

Douglas Dean Drabek b: 7/25/1962, Victoria, TX BR/TR, 6'1", 185 lbs. Deb: 5/30/1986

YEAR	TM-L	W	L	PCT	G	GS	CG	SH	SV	IP	H	R	ER	HR	HB	BB	SO	RAT	ERA	ERA+	CERA	OAV	BH	AVG	PR+	WS	TPW
1986	NY-A	7	8	.467	27	21	0	0	0	131^2	126	64	60	13	3	50	76	1.337	4.10	100	3.84	.251	0	....	-1	7	-0.1
1987	Pit-N	11	12	.478	29	28	1	1	0	176^1	165	86	76	22	0	46	120	1.197	3.88	106	3.36	.247	7	.119	1	10	0.0
1988	Pit-N	15	7	.682	33	32	3	1	0	219^1	194	83	75	21	6	50	127	1.112	3.08	111	2.90	.239	13	.171	7	15	1.0
1989	Pit-N	14	12	.538	35	34	8	5	0	244^1	215	83	76	21	3	69	123	1.162	2.80	120	2.95	.238	8	.104	15	14	1.3
1990*	Pit-N	**22**	6	.786	33	33	9	3	0	231^1	190	78	71	15	3	56	131	1.063	2.76	131	2.40	.225	18	.214	19	**20**	2.5
1991*	Pit-N	15	14	.517	35	35	5	2	0	234^2	245	92	80	16	3	62	142	1.308	3.07	116	3.65	.274	15	.179	11	14	1.2
1992*	Pit-N	15	11	.577	34	34	10	4	0	256^2	218	84	79	17	6	54	177	1.060	2.77	124	2.44	.231	14	.157	17	20	1.9
1993	Hou-N	9	18	.333	34	34	7	2	0	237^2	242	108	100	18	3	60	157	1.271	3.79	102	3.44	.267	6	.085	0	10	-0.2
1994	Hou-N★	12	6	.667	23	23	6	2	0	164^2	132	58	52	14	2	45	121	1.075	2.84	139	2.52	.220	14	.241	19	13	2.2
1995	Hou-N	10	9	.526	31	**31**	2	1	0	185	205	104	98	18	8	54	143	1.400	4.77	81	4.42	.282	14	.233	-15	6	-1.1
1996	Hou-N	7	9	.438	30	30	1	0	0	175^1	208	102	89	21	7	60	137	1.529	4.57	85	5.16	.298	10	.179	-11	6	-1.0
1997	Chi-A	12	11	.522	31	31	0	0	0	169^1	170	109	108	30	4	69	85	1.411	5.74	76	4.76	.261	0	.000	-23	5	-2.2
1998	Bal-A	6	11	.353	23	21	1	0	0	108^2	138	90	88	20	5	29	55	1.537	7.29	62	5.94	.312	0	.000	-32	0	-3.0
Total	13	155	134	.536	398	387	53	21	0	2535	2448	1141	1052	246	53	704	1594	1.243	3.73	103	3.51	.255	119	.166	8	140	2.6

• DRABOWSKY, Moe

Myron Walter Drabowsky b: 7/21/1935, Ozanna, Poland BR/TR, 6'3", 200 lbs. Deb: 8/7/1956 C

YEAR	TM-L	W	L	PCT	G	GS	CG	SH	SV	IP	H	R	ER	HR	HB	BB	SO	RAT	ERA	ERA+	CERA	OAV	BH	AVG	PR+	WS	TPW
1956	Chi-N	2	4	.333	9	7	3	0	0	51	37	19	14	1	2	39	36	1.490	2.47	153	3.42	.207	4	.250	6	4	0.7
1957	Chi-N	13	15	.464	36	33	12	2	0	239^2	214	103	94	22	10	94	170	1.285	3.53	110	3.55	.242	15	.183	13	15	1.5
1958	Chi-N	9	11	.450	22	20	4	1	0	125^2	118	73	63	19	5	73	77	1.520	4.51	87	4.86	.245	7	.156	-7	4	-0.8
1959	Chi-N	5	10	.333	31	23	3	1	0	141^2	138	78	65	21	3	75	70	1.504	4.13	96	4.81	.251	5	.111	-4	5	-0.5
1960	Chi-N	3	1	.750	32	7	0	0	1	50^1	71	44	36	3	1	23	26	1.868	6.44	59	6.44	.338	0	.000	-15	0	-1.6
1961	Mil-N	0	2	.000	16	0	0	0	2	25^1	26	15	13	4	1	18	5	1.737	4.62	81	5.91	.277	1	.250	-2	1	-0.2
1962	Cin-N	2	6	.250	23	10	1	0	1	83	84	49	46	13	6	31	56	1.386	4.99	81	4.71	.267	0	.000	-9	2	-1.1
	KC-A	1	1	.500	10	3	0	0	0	28	29	20	16	8	1	10	19	1.393	5.14	81	5.42	.266	1	.167	-3	1	-0.3
1963	KC-A	7	13	.350	26	22	9	2	0	174^1	135	62	59	16	8	64	109	1.141	3.05	126	2.90	.214	10	.161	17	14	1.9
1964	KC-A	5	13	.278	53	21	1	0	1	168^1	176	103	99	24	8	72	119	1.473	5.29	72	4.94	.273	1	.023	-25	3	-3.0
1965	KC-A	1	5	.167	14	5	0	0	0	38^2	44	22	19	5	3	18	25	1.603	4.42	79	5.53	.291	1	.091	-4	1	-0.5
1966*	Bal-A	6	0	1.000	44	3	0	0	7	96	62	31	30	10	1	29	98	.948	2.81	118	1.90	.181	8	.364	5	10	0.9
1967	Bal-A	7	5	.583	43	0	0	0	12	95^1	66	21	17	7	2	25	96	.955	1.60	196	1.90	.194	7	.350	15	13	1.9
1968	Bal-A	4	4	.500	45	0	0	0	7	61^1	35	17	13	3	4	25	46	.978	1.91	153	1.76	.166	2	.286	6	7	0.7
1969	KC-A	11	9	.550	52	0	0	0	11	98	68	33	32	10	2	30	76	1.000	2.94	125	2.14	.190	4	.235	9	13	1.0
1970	KC-A	1	2	.333	24	0	0	0	2	35^2	28	13	13	3	2	12	38	1.121	3.28	114	2.62	.217	1	.250	2	3	0.2
	*Bal-A	4	2	.667	21	0	0	0	1	33^1	30	17	14	7	1	15	21	1.350	3.78	96	4.36	.233	0	.000	-1	2	-0.2
	Yr.	5	4	.556	45	0	0	0	3	69	58	30	27	10	3	27	59	1.232	3.52	105	3.46	.225	1	.111	0	5	0.0
1971	StL-N	6	1	.857	51	0	0	0	8	60^1	45	23	23	2	2	33	49	1.293	3.43	105	2.72	.207	1	.167	2	7	0.3
1972	StL-N	1	1	.500	30	0	0	0	2	27^2	29	13	8	4	1	14	22	1.554	2.60	131	4.84	.259	0	.000	2	2	0.3
	Chi-A	0	0	....	7	0	0	0	0	7^1	6	2	2	0	0	2	4	1.091	2.45	127	2.28	.240	0	.000	1	1	0.1
Total	17	88	105	.456	589	154	33	6	55	1641	1441	758	676	182	63	702	1162	1.306	3.71	101	3.73	.236	68	.162	8	108	1.1

• DRAGO, Dick

Richard Anthony Drago b: 6/25/1945, Toledo, OH BR/TR, 6'1", 190 lbs. Deb: 4/11/1969

YEAR	TM-L	W	L	PCT	G	GS	CG	SH	SV	IP	H	R	ER	HR	HB	BB	SO	RAT	ERA	ERA+	CERA	OAV	BH	AVG	PR+	WS	TPW
1969	KC-A	11	13	.458	41	26	10	2	1	200^2	190	95	84	19	2	65	108	1.271	3.77	98	3.42	.248	3	.058	1	10	-0.2
1970	KC-A	9	15	.375	35	34	7	1	0	240	239	110	100	20	7	72	127	1.296	3.75	100	3.69	.266	4	.053	-2	10	-0.8
1971	KC-A	17	11	.607	35	34	15	4	0	241^1	251	84	80	14	9	46	109	1.231	2.98	115	3.47	.276	10	.130	13	18	1.5
1972	KC-A	12	17	.414	34	33	11	2	0	239^1	230	88	80	22	6	51	135	1.174	3.01	101	3.21	.254	4	.059	4	12	0.2
1973	KC-A	12	14	.462	37	33	10	1	0	212^2	252	116	100	16	7	76	98	1.542	4.23	97	4.91	.300	0	....	-0	11	0.0
1974	Bos-A	7	10	.412	33	18	8	0	3	175^2	165	71	68	17	5	56	90	1.258	3.48	110	3.49	.251	0	....	9	13	0.9
1975*	Bos-A	2	2	.500	40	2	0	0	15	72^2	69	31	31	5	0	31	43	1.376	3.84	106	3.59	.247	0	....	2	8	0.2
1976	Cal-A	7	8	.467	43	0	0	0	6	79^1	80	42	39	7	5	31	43	1.399	4.42	75	4.09	.264	0	....	-9	3	-1.0
1977	Cal-A	0	1	.000	13	0	0	0	2	21	22	8	7	3	0	3	15	1.190	3.00	130	3.44	.272	0	....	2	2	0.2
	Bal-A	6	3	.667	36	0	0	0	3	39^2	49	19	16	2	1	15	20	1.613	3.63	104	4.82	.308	0	....	-0	4	0.0
	Yr.	6	4	.600	49	0	0	0	5	60^2	71	27	23	5	1	18	35	1.467	3.41	112	4.34	.296	0	....	2	6	0.2
1978	Bos-A	4	4	.500	37	1	0	0	7	77^1	71	30	26	5	4	32	42	1.332	3.03	136	3.51	.246	0	....	9	8	0.9
1979	Bos-A	10	6	.625	53	1	0	0	13	89	85	33	30	6	3	21	67	1.191	3.03	145	3.03	.254	0	....	14	13	1.4
1980	Bos-A	7	7	.500	43	7	1	0	3	132^2	127	67	61	17	5	44	63	1.289	4.14	102	3.82	.251	0	.000	1	8	0.1
1981	Sea-A	4	6	.400	39	0	0	0	5	53^2	71	33	33	4	0	15	27	1.602	5.53	70	5.13	.324	0	....	-9	1	-1.0
Total	13	108	117	.480	519	189	62	10	58	1875	1901	827	755	157	54	558	987	1.311	3.62	103	3.74	.266	21	.077	33	121	2.3

• DRAHMAN, Brian

Brian Stacy Drahman b: 11/7/1966, Kenton, KY BR/TR, 6'3", 205 lbs. Deb: 4/16/1991

YEAR	TM-L	W	L	PCT	G	GS	CG	SH	SV	IP	H	R	ER	HR	HB	BB	SO	RAT	ERA	ERA+	CERA	OAV	BH	AVG	PR+	WS	TPW
1991	Chi-A	3	2	.600	28	0	0	0	0	30^2	21	12	11	4	0	13	18	1.109	3.23	123	2.63	.193	0	....	2	2	0.2
1992	Chi-A	0	0	....	5	0	0	0	0	7	6	3	2	0	0	2	1	1.143	2.57	150	2.21	.222	0	....	1	1	0.1

YEAR TM-L	W	L	PCT	G	GS	CG	SH	SV	IP	H	R	ER	HR	HB	BB	SO	RAT	ERA	ERA+	CERA	OAV	BH	AVG	PR+	WS	TPW
1993 Chi-A	0	0	....	5	0	0	0	1	5^1	7	0	0	0	0	2	3	1.688	0.00	....	5.34	.333	0	....	2	1	0.2
1994 Fla-N	0	0	....	9	0	0	0	0	13	15	9	9	2	0	6	7	1.615	6.23	70	5.46	.300	0	....	-3	0	-0.3
Total 4	3	2	.600	47	0	0	0	1	56	49	24	22	6	0	23	29	1.286	3.54	116	3.49	.237	0	....	2	4	0.2

• DRAKE, Logan Logan Gaffney "L.G." Drake b: 12/26/1900, Spartanburg, SC d: 6/1/1940, Columbia, SC BR/TR, 5'10.5", 165 lbs. Deb: 9/21/1922

YEAR TM-L	W	L	PCT	G	GS	CG	SH	SV	IP	H	R	ER	HR	HB	BB	SO	RAT	ERA	ERA+	CERA	OAV	BH	AVG	PR+	WS	TPW
1922 Cle-A	0	0	....	1	0	0	0	0	3	4	1	1	0	0	2	1	2.000	3.00	133	6.41	.364	0	.000	0	0	0.0
1923 Cle-A	0	0	....	4	0	0	0	0	4^1	2	2	2	0	1	4	2	1.385	4.15	95	2.63	.133	0	....	-0	0	0.0
1924 Cle-A	0	1	.000	5	1	0	0	0	11^1	18	15	13	0	1	10	8	2.471	10.32	41	9.33	.400	0	.000	-7	0	-0.7
Total 3	0	1	.000	10	1	0	0	0	18^2	24	18	16	0	2	16	11	2.143	7.71	55	7.30	.338	0	.000	-7	0	-0.7

• DRAKE, Tom Thomas Kendall Drake b: 8/7/1912, Birmingham, AL d: 7/2/1988, Birmingham, AL BR/TR, 6'1", 185 lbs. Deb: 4/24/1939

YEAR TM-L	W	L	PCT	G	GS	CG	SH	SV	IP	H	R	ER	HR	HB	BB	SO	RAT	ERA	ERA+	CERA	OAV	BH	AVG	PR+	WS	TPW
1939 Cle-A	0	1	.000	8	1	0	0	0	15	23	18	15	2	2	19	1	2.800	9.00	49	11.89	.377	0	.000	-8	0	-0.7
1941 Bro-N	1	1	.500	10	2	0	0	0	24^2	26	13	12	2	0	9	12	1.419	4.38	84	4.13	.280	2	.400	-2	1	-0.2
Total 2	1	2	.333	18	3	0	0	0	39^2	49	31	27	4	2	28	13	1.941	6.13	66	7.06	.318	2	.286	-10	1	-0.9

• DRAPER, Mike Michael Anthony Draper b: 9/14/1966, Hagerstown, MD BR/TR, 6'2", 180 lbs. Deb: 4/10/1993

YEAR TM-L	W	L	PCT	G	GS	CG	SH	SV	IP	H	R	ER	HR	HB	BB	SO	RAT	ERA	ERA+	CERA	OAV	BH	AVG	PR+	WS	TPW
1993 NY-N	1	1	.500	29	1	0	0	0	42^1	53	22	20	2	0	14	16	1.583	4.25	94	4.88	.327	2	.667	-1	2	-0.1

• DRAVECKY, Dave David Francis Dravecky b: 2/14/1956, Youngstown, OH BR/TL, 6'1", 195 lbs. Deb: 6/15/1982

YEAR TM-L	W	L	PCT	G	GS	CG	SH	SV	IP	H	R	ER	HR	HB	BB	SO	RAT	ERA	ERA+	CERA	OAV	BH	AVG	PR+	WS	TPW
1982 SD-N	5	3	.625	31	10	0	0	2	105	86	37	30	8	1	33	59	1.133	2.57	133	2.65	.225	3	.130	9	7	0.9
1983 SD-N★	14	10	.583	28	28	9	1	0	183^2	181	78	73	18	3	44	74	1.225	3.58	97	3.43	.262	6	.098	-5	10	-0.7
1984* SD-N	9	8	.529	50	14	3	2	8	156^2	125	53	51	12	4	51	71	1.123	2.93	122	2.71	.222	4	.098	8	12	0.8
1985 SD-N	13	11	.542	34	31	7	2	0	214^2	200	79	70	18	1	57	105	1.197	2.93	120	3.11	.249	8	.116	11	14	1.1
1986 SD-N	9	11	.450	26	26	3	1	0	161^1	149	68	55	17	1	54	87	1.258	3.07	119	3.39	.246	7	.140	11	10	1.1
1987 SD-N	3	7	.300	30	10	1	0	0	79	71	39	33	10	3	31	60	1.291	3.76	105	3.74	.240	3	.167	1	4	0.1
* SF-N	7	5	.583	18	18	4	3	0	112^1	115	43	40	8	2	33	78	1.318	3.20	120	3.72	.272	5	.132	6	8	0.7
Yr.	10	12	.455	48	28	5	3	0	191^1	186	82	73	18	5	64	138	1.307	3.43	113	3.73	.259	8	.143	7	12	0.8
1988 SF-N	2	2	.500	7	7	1	0	0	37	33	19	13	4	0	8	19	1.108	3.16	103	2.82	.243	1	.100	0	1	0.0
1989 SF-N	2	0	1.000	2	2	0	0	0	13	8	5	5	2	1	4	5	.923	3.46	97	2.43	.182	1	.333	-0	1	0.1
Total 8	64	57	.529	226	146	28	9	10	1062^2	968	421	370	97	16	315	558	1.207	3.13	115	3.20	.245	38	.121	41	67	4.0

• DREES, Tom Thomas Kent Drees b: 6/17/1963, Des Moines, IA BB/TL, 6'6", 210 lbs. Deb: 9/3/1991

YEAR TM-L	W	L	PCT	G	GS	CG	SH	SV	IP	H	R	ER	HR	HB	BB	SO	RAT	ERA	ERA+	CERA	OAV	BH	AVG	PR+	WS	TPW
1991 Chi-A	0	0	....	4	0	0	0	0	7^1	10	10	10	4	0	6	2	2.182	12.27	32	12.34	.345	0	....	-7	0	-0.7

• DREIFORT, Darren Darren James Dreifort b: 5/3/1972, Wichita, KS BR/TR, 6'2", 205 lbs. Deb: 4/7/1994

YEAR TM-L	W	L	PCT	G	GS	CG	SH	SV	IP	H	R	ER	HR	HB	BB	SO	RAT	ERA	ERA+	CERA	OAV	BH	AVG	PR+	WS	TPW
1994 LA-N	0	5	.000	27	0	0	0	6	29	45	21	20	0	4	15	22	2.069	6.21	63	7.39	.357	1	1.000	-7	0	-0.7
1996* LA-N	1	4	.200	19	0	0	0	0	23^2	23	13	13	2	0	12	24	1.479	4.94	78	3.84	.256	0	.000	-3	0	-0.3
1997 LA-N	5	2	.714	48	0	0	0	4	63	45	21	20	3	1	34	63	1.254	2.86	135	2.72	.202	1	.143	8	7	0.7
1998 LA-N	8	12	.400	32	26	1	1	0	180	171	84	80	12	10	57	168	1.267	4.00	99	3.50	.256	11	.224	-0	9	0.3
1999 LA-N	13	13	.500	30	29	1	1	0	178^2	177	105	95	20	7	76	140	1.416	4.79	90	4.39	.260	13	.210	-9	8	-0.4
2000 LA-N	12	9	.571	32	32	1	1	0	192^2	175	105	89	31	12	87	164	1.360	4.16	104	4.40	.238	11	.162	5	9	0.8
2001 LA-N	4	7	.364	16	16	0	0	0	94^2	89	62	54	11	6	47	91	1.437	5.13	78	4.50	.251	5	.152	-11	1	-0.9
2003 LA-N	4	4	.500	10	10	0	0	0	60^1	58	29	27	6	0	25	67	1.376	4.03	100	3.87	.250	2	.133	-1	3	-0.1
Total 8	47	56	.456	214	113	3	3	10	822	783	440	398	85	40	353	739	1.382	4.36	94	4.13	.252	44	.185	-19	37	-0.6

• DREISEWERD, Clem Clemens Johann "Steamboat" Dreisewerd b: 1/24/1916, Old Monroe, MO d: 9/11/2001, Ocean Springs, MS BL/TL, 6'1.5", 195 lbs. Deb: 8/29/1944

YEAR TM-L	W	L	PCT	G	GS	CG	SH	SV	IP	H	R	ER	HR	HB	BB	SO	RAT	ERA	ERA+	CERA	OAV	BH	AVG	PR+	WS	TPW
1944 Bos-A	2	4	.333	7	7	3	0	0	48^2	52	25	22	2	0	9	9	1.253	4.07	84	3.10	.268	3	.188	-4	2	-0.4
1945 Bos-A	0	1	.000	2	2	0	0	0	9^2	13	5	5	0	1	2	3	1.552	4.66	73	4.96	.325	0	.000	-1	0	-0.2
1946* Bos-A	4	1	.800	20	1	0	0	0	47^1	50	22	22	3	0	15	19	1.373	4.18	88	3.74	.276	0	.000	-3	3	-0.4
1948 StL-A	0	2	.000	13	0	0	0	1	22^1	28	15	14	6	0	8	6	1.612	5.64	81	6.88	.318	0	.000	-2	0	-0.3
NY-N	0	0	....	4	0	0	0	1	12^2	17	8	8	3	0	5	2	1.737	5.68	69	7.17	.321	1	.250	-2	0	-0.2
Total 4	6	8	.429	46	10	3	0	2	140^2	160	75	71	14	1	39	39	1.415	4.54	82	4.41	.288	4	.105	-13	5	-1.5

• DRESE, Ryan Ryan Thomas Drese b: 4/5/1976, San Francisco, CA BR/TR, 6'3", 220 lbs. Deb: 7/29/2001

YEAR TM-L	W	L	PCT	G	GS	CG	SH	SV	IP	H	R	ER	HR	HB	BB	SO	RAT	ERA	ERA+	CERA	OAV	BH	AVG	PR+	WS	TPW
2001 Cle-A	1	2	.333	9	4	0	0	0	36^2	32	15	14	2	1	15	24	1.282	3.44	131	3.27	.242	0	....	5	3	0.5
2002 Cle-A	10	9	.526	26	26	1	0	0	137^1	176	104	100	15	6	62	102	1.733	6.55	67	6.26	.317	0	.000	-31	2	-3.0
2003 Tex-A	2	4	.333	11	8	0	0	0	46	61	42	35	8	5	24	26	1.848	6.85	72	7.60	.314	0	....	-9	0	-0.9
Total 3	13	15	.464	46	38	1	0	0	220	269	161	149	25	12	101	152	1.682	6.10	74	6.04	.305	0	.000	-35	5	-3.4

• DRESSENDORFER, Kirk Kirk Richard Dressendorfer b: 4/8/1969, Houston, TX BR/TR, 5'11", 190 lbs. Deb: 4/13/1991

YEAR TM-L	W	L	PCT	G	GS	CG	SH	SV	IP	H	R	ER	HR	HB	BB	SO	RAT	ERA	ERA+	CERA	OAV	BH	AVG	PR+	WS	TPW
1991 Oak-A	3	3	.500	7	7	0	0	0	34^2	33	28	21	5	0	21	17	1.558	5.45	70	4.80	.244	0	....	-6	0	-0.6

• DRESSER, Bob Robert Nicholson Dresser b: 10/4/1878, Newton, MA d: 7/27/1924, Duxbury, MA BL/TL Deb: 8/13/1902

YEAR TM-L	W	L	PCT	G	GS	CG	SH	SV	IP	H	R	ER	HR	HB	BB	SO	RAT	ERA	ERA+	CERA	OAV	BH	AVG	PR+	WS	TPW
1902 Bos-N	0	1	.000	1	1	1	0	0	9	12	6	3	0	0	0	8	1.333	3.00	94	3.36	.319	1	.250	-0	0	0.0

• DRESSLER, Rob Robert Anthony Dressler b: 2/2/1954, Portland, OR BR/TR, 6'3", 180 lbs. Deb: 9/7/1975

YEAR TM-L	W	L	PCT	G	GS	CG	SH	SV	IP	H	R	ER	HR	HB	BB	SO	RAT	ERA	ERA+	CERA	OAV	BH	AVG	PR+	WS	TPW
1975 SF-N	1	0	1.000	3	2	1	0	0	16^1	17	3	2	0	0	4	6	1.286	1.10	345	2.91	.274	0	.000	5	2	0.5
1976 SF-N	3	10	.231	25	19	0	0	0	107^2	125	68	53	8	2	35	33	1.486	4.43	82	4.45	.291	4	.129	-8	1	-0.9
1978 StL-N	0	1	.000	3	2	0	0	0	13	12	3	3	0	0	4	4	1.231	2.08	169	2.85	.267	0	.000	2	1	0.2
1979 Sea-A	3	2	.600	21	11	2	0	0	104	134	61	57	11	0	22	36	1.500	4.93	88	4.96	.312	0	....	-6	4	-0.6
1980 Sea-A	4	10	.286	30	14	3	0	0	149^1	161	75	66	14	3	33	50	1.299	3.98	104	3.82	.280	0	....	4	8	0.4
Total 5	11	23	.324	82	48	6	0	0	390^1	449	210	181	33	5	98	129	1.401	4.17	96	4.23	.291	4	.105	-4	16	-0.5

• DREW, Tim Timothy Andrew Drew b: 8/31/1978, Valdosta, GA BR/TR, 6'1", 195 lbs. Deb: 5/24/2000

YEAR TM-L	W	L	PCT	G	GS	CG	SH	SV	IP	H	R	ER	HR	HB	BB	SO	RAT	ERA	ERA+	CERA	OAV	BH	AVG	PR+	WS	TPW
2000 Cle-A	1	0	1.000	3	3	0	0	0	9	17	12	10	1	1	8	5	2.778	10.00	50	12.94	.425	0	....	-5	0	-0.5
2001 Cle-A	0	2	.000	8	6	0	0	0	35	51	39	31	9	4	16	15	1.914	7.97	57	8.95	.340	0	....	-13	0	-1.2
2002 Mon-N	1	0	1.000	7	1	0	0	2	16	12	8	5	1	0	2	10	.875	2.81	152	1.57	.200	0	.000	3	2	0.2
2003 Mon-N	0	2	.000	6	1	0	0	0	8^2	12	12	12	3	0	8	3	2.308	12.46	41	10.57	.343	0	.000	-7	0	-0.7
Total 4	2	4	.333	24	11	0	0	2	68^2	92	71	58	14	5	34	33	1.835	7.60	61	7.96	.323	0	.000	-22	2	-2.2

• DREWS, Karl Karl August Drews b: 2/22/1920, Staten Island, NY d: 8/15/1963, Dania, FL BR/TR, 6'4.5", 198 lbs. Deb: 9/8/1946

YEAR TM-L	W	L	PCT	G	GS	CG	SH	SV	IP	H	R	ER	HR	HB	BB	SO	RAT	ERA	ERA+	CERA	OAV	BH	AVG	PR+	WS	TPW
1946 NY-A	0	1	.000	3	1	0	0	0	6^1	6	6	6	0	1	6	4	1.895	8.53	40	5.42	.250	0	.000	-4	0	-0.4
1947* NY-A	6	6	.500	30	10	0	0	1	91^2	92	57	50	6	5	55	45	1.604	4.91	72	4.67	.264	1	.037	-15	1	-1.7
1948 NY-A	2	3	.400	19	2	0	0	1	38	35	17	16	3	0	31	11	1.737	3.79	108	4.87	.248	0	.000	1	2	0.0
StL-A	3	2	.600	20	2	0	0	2	38	43	35	34	3	0	38	11	2.132	8.05	57	6.89	.289	0	.000	-14	0	-1.4
Yr.	5	5	.500	39	4	0	0	3	76	78	52	50	6	0	69	22	1.934	5.92	74	5.88	.269	0	.000	-13	2	-1.4
1949 StL-A	4	12	.250	31	23	3	1	0	139^2	180	113	103	11	9	66	35	1.761	6.64	68	6.05	.317	0	.000	-28	0	-3.2
1951 Phi-N	1	0	1.000	5	3	1	0	0	23	29	16	16	2	4	7	13	1.565	6.26	61	5.49	.296	2	.250	-6	0	-0.6
1952 Phi-N	14	15	.483	33	30	15	5	0	228^2	213	79	69	13	4	52	96	1.159	2.72	134	2.86	.252	9	.110	20	18	1.9
1953 Phi-N	9	10	.474	47	27	6	0	3	185^1	218	116	93	26	10	50	72	1.446	4.52	93	4.99	.293	7	.119	-6	7	-0.8
1954 Phi-N	1	0	1.000	8	0	0	0	0	16	18	10	10	2	0	8	6	1.625	5.63	72	5.37	.300	0	.000	-3	0	-0.3
Cin-N	4	4	.500	22	9	1	1	0	60	79	44	40	6	2	19	29	1.633	6.00	70	5.69	.326	2	.167	-13	1	-1.1
Yr.	5	4	.556	30	9	1	1	0	76	97	54	50	8	2	27	35	1.632	5.92	70	5.62	.321	2	.125	-16	1	-1.5
Total 8	44	53	.454	218	107	26	7	7	826^2	913	493	437	72	35	332	322	1.506	4.76	86	4.70	.284	21	.083	-67	29	-7.7

• DREYER, Steve Steven William Dreyer b: 11/19/1969, Ames, IA BR/TR, 6'3", 180 lbs. Deb: 8/8/1993

YEAR TM-L	W	L	PCT	G	GS	CG	SH	SV	IP	H	R	ER	HR	HB	BB	SO	RAT	ERA	ERA+	CERA	OAV	BH	AVG	PR+	WS	TPW
1993 Tex-A	3	3	.500	10	6	0	0	0	41	48	26	26	7	1	20	23	1.659	5.71	73	6.11	.291	0	....	-6	1	-0.6
1994 Tex-A	1	1	.500	5	3	0	0	0	17^1	19	15	11	1	1	8	11	1.558	5.71	84	4.66	.271	0	....	-1	0	-0.1
Total 2	4	4	.500	15	9	0	0	0	58^1	67	41	37	8	2	28	34	1.629	5.71	76	5.68	.285	0	....	-8	1	-0.7

YEAR TM-L	W	L	PCT	G	GS	CG	SH	SV	IP	H	R	ER	HR	HB	BB	SO	RAT	ERA	ERA+	CERA	OAV	BH	AVG	PR+	WS	TPW
• DRISCOLL, Denny	John F. Driscoll b: 11/19/1855, Lowell, MA d: 7/11/1886, Lowell, MA BL/TL, 5'10.5", 160 lbs. Deb: 7/1/1880 ♦																									
1880 Buf-N	1	3	.250	6	4	4	0	0	41^2	48	33	18	1	....	9	17	1.368	3.89	63	....	.275	10	.154	-5	0	-0.9
1882 Pit-a	13	9	.591	23	23	23	0	0	201	162	73	27	0	....	12	59	.866	**1.21**	**216**	....	.206	11	.138	32	17	2.8
1883 Pit-a	18	21	.462	41	40	35	1	0	336^1	427	239	149	3	....	39	79	1.386	3.99	80	....	.290	27	.182	-23	10	-2.4
1884 Lou-a	6	6	.500	13	13	10	0	0	102	110	69	39	3	2	7	16	1.147	3.44	89	....	.261	9	.188	-8	4	-0.8
Total 4	38	39	.494	83	80	72	1	0	681	747	414	233	7	2	67	171	1.195	3.08	98		.262	57	.167	-3	31	-1.4
• DRISCOLL, Michael	Michael Columbus Driscoll b: 10/19/1892, North Abington, MA d: 3/22/1953, Foxboro, MA BR/TR, 5'11", 160 lbs. Deb: 7/6/1916																									
1916 Phi-A	0	1	.000	1	0	0	0	0	5	6	5	3	0	0	2	0	1.600	5.40	53	4.03	.273	0	.000	-1	0	-0.2
• DRISKILL, Travis	Travis Corey Driskill b: 8/1/1971, Omaha, NE BR/TR, 6', 225 lbs. Deb: 4/26/2002																									
2002 Bal-A	8	8	.500	29	19	0	0	0	132^2	150	78	73	21	8	48	78	1.492	4.95	86	5.36	.284	0	.000	-11	5	-1.1
2003 Bal-A	3	5	.375	20	0	0	0	1	48	62	35	32	8	1	9	33	1.479	6.00	73	5.30	.310	0	.000	-8	1	-0.8
Total 2	11	13	.458	49	19	0	0	1	180^2	212	113	105	29	9	57	111	1.489	5.23	83	5.35	.291	0	.000	-20	6	-1.9
• DROHAN, Tom	Thomas F. Drohan b: 8/26/1887, Fall River, MA d: 9/17/1926, Kewanee, IL BR/TR, 5'10", 175 lbs. Deb: 5/1/1913																									
1913 Was-A	0	0	....	2	0	0	0	0	2	5	2	2	1	0	0	2	2.500	9.00	33	17.50	.500	0	....	-1	0	-0.1
• DROTT, Dick	Richard Fred "Hummer" Drott b: 7/1/1936, Cincinnati, OH d: 8/16/1985, Glendale Heights, IL BR/TR, 6', 185 lbs. Deb: 4/16/1957																									
1957 Chi-N	15	11	.577	38	32	7	3	0	229	200	107	91	22	7	129	170	1.437	3.58	108	4.06	.234	8	.100	11	13	0.7
1958 Chi-N	7	11	.389	39	31	4	0	0	167^1	156	118	101	23	6	99	127	**1.524**	5.43	72	4.70	.245	15	.273	-27	2	-2.4
1959 Chi-N	1	2	.333	8	6	1	1	0	27^1	25	19	18	5	0	26	15	1.866	5.93	67	6.49	.245	1	.125	-6	0	-0.7
1960 Chi-N	0	6	.000	23	9	0	0	0	55^1	63	49	44	7	3	42	32	1.898	7.16	53	6.80	.296	1	.100	-21	0	-2.2
1961 Chi-N	1	4	.200	35	8	0	0	0	98	75	54	46	13	1	51	48	1.286	4.22	99	3.52	.215	6	.273	1	5	0.3
1962 Hou-N	1	0	1.000	6	1	0	0	0	13	12	12	11	1	0	9	10	1.615	7.62	49	4.50	.240	0	.000	-5	0	-0.6
1963 Hou-N	2	12	.143	27	14	2	1	0	97^2	95	61	54	13	6	49	58	1.474	4.98	63	4.75	.257	3	.130	-18	0	-2.0
Total 7	27	46	.370	176	101	14	5	0	687^2	626	420	365	84	23	405	460	1.499	4.78	79	4.56	.243	34	.168	-64	20	-6.9
• DRUCKE, Louis	Louis Frank Drucke b: 12/3/1888, Waco, TX d: 9/22/1955, Waco, TX BR/TR, 6'1", 188 lbs. Deb: 9/25/1909																									
1909 NY-N	2	1	.667	3	3	2	0	0	24	20	9	6	0	0	13	8	1.375	2.25	113	2.93	.227	1	.125	1	2	0.1
1910 NY-N	12	10	.545	34	27	15	0	0	215^1	174	73	59	3	11	82	151	1.189	2.47	120	2.64	.228	15	.214	15	16	1.9
1911 NY-N	4	4	.500	15	10	4	0	0	75^2	83	39	34	1	8	41	42	1.639	4.04	83	4.85	.281	2	.087	-5	3	-0.6
1912 NY-N	0	0	....	1	0	0	0	1	2	5	4	3	0	0	1	0	3.000	13.50	25	12.03	.417	0	....	-2	0	-0.2
Total 4	18	15	.545	53	40	21	0	1	317	282	125	102	4	19	137	201	1.322	2.90	105	3.25	.243	18	.178	9	21	1.2
• DRUHOT, Carl	Carl A. "Collie" Druhot b: 9/1/1882, OH d: 2/11/1918, Portland, OR BL/TL, 5'7", 150 lbs. Deb: 4/18/1906																									
1906 Cin-N	2	2	.500	4	3	1	0	0	25	27	17	12	0	2	7	14	1.360	4.32	64	3.53	.270	2	.222	-5	1	-0.5
StL-N	6	7	.462	15	13	12	1	0	130^1	117	55	38	1	5	46	45	1.251	2.62	100	2.81	.238	13	.232	1	7	0.3
Yr.	8	9	.471	19	16	13	1	0	155^1	144	72	50	1	7	53	59	1.268	2.90	91	2.92	.243	15	.231	-3	8	-0.2
1907 StL-N	0	1	.000	1	1	0	0	0	2^1	3	5	4	0	1	4	1	3.000	15.43	16	11.22	.600	0	....	-3	0	-0.4
Total 2	8	10	.444	20	17	13	1	0	157^2	147	77	54	1	8	57	60	1.294	3.08	85	3.05	.246	15	.231	-7	8	-0.6
• DRUMMOND, Tim	Timothy Darnell Drummond b: 12/24/1964, La Plata, MD BR/TR, 6'3", 170 lbs. Deb: 9/12/1987																									
1987 Pit-N	0	0	....	6	0	0	0	0	6	5	3	3	0	0	3	5	1.333	4.50	91	2.79	.227	0	.000	-0	0	0.0
1989 Min-A	0	0	....	8	0	0	0	1	16^1	16	7	7	0	2	8	9	1.469	3.86	107	3.82	.246	0	....	1	1	0.1
1990 Min-A	3	5	.375	35	4	0	0	1	91	104	46	44	8	1	36	49	1.538	4.35	95	4.89	.295	0	....	-2	4	-0.2
Total 3	3	5	.375	49	4	0	0	2	113^1	125	56	54	8	3	47	63	1.518	4.29	97	4.62	.284	0	.000	-2	5	-0.2
• DRYSDALE, Don	Donald Scott Drysdale b: 7/23/1936, Van Nuys, CA d: 7/3/1993, Montreal, Canada BR/TR, 6'5", 216 lbs. Deb: 4/17/1956 HOF: 1984																									
1956* Bro-N	5	5	.500	25	12	2	0	0	99	95	35	29	9	3	31	55	1.273	2.64	150	3.57	.255	5	.192	13	9	1.4
1957 Bro-N	17	9	.654	34	29	9	4	0	221	197	76	66	17	7	61	148	1.167	2.69	155	2.97	.236	9	.123	**37**	21	**3.7**
1958 LA-N	12	13	.480	44	29	6	1	0	211^2	214	107	98	21	14	72	131	1.351	4.17	98	4.12	.263	15	.227	-2	14	0.6
1959* LA-N★	17	13	.567	44	36	15	**4**	2	270^2	237	113	104	26	18	93	**242**	1.219	3.46	122	3.34	.233	15	.165	22	22	2.6
1960 LA-N	15	14	.517	41	36	15	5	2	269	214	93	85	27	10	72	**246**	1.063	2.84	140	**2.62**	.215	13	.157	31	**25**	3.4
1961 LA-N★	13	10	.565	40	37	10	3	0	244	236	111	100	29	20	83	182	1.307	3.69	118	4.02	.254	16	.193	16	19	2.0
1962 LA-N★	**25**	9	.735	43	**41**	19	2	1	**314^1**	272	122	99	21	11	78	**232**	1.113	2.83	128	2.63	.230	22	.198	28	24	3.2
1963* LA-N★	19	17	.528	42	**42**	17	3	0	315^1	287	114	92	25	10	57	251	1.091	2.63	115	2.73	.242	16	.167	17	21	2.3
1964 LA-N★	18	16	.529	40	**40**	21	5	0	**321^1**	242	91	78	15	10	68	237	.965	2.18	148	1.89	.207	19	.173	**38**	**26**	**4.4**
1965* LA-N★	23	12	.657	44	**42**	20	7	1	308^1	270	113	95	30	12	66	210	1.090	2.77	118	2.76	.232	39	.300	12	27	3.5
1966* LA-N	13	16	.448	40	40	11	3	0	273^2	279	114	104	21	17	45	177	1.184	3.42	96	3.32	.265	20	.189	-4	13	-0.1
1967 LA-N★	13	16	.448	38	38	9	3	0	282	269	101	86	19	8	60	196	1.167	2.74	113	2.94	.251	12	.129	14	18	1.5
1968 LA-N★	14	12	.538	31	31	12	8	0	239	201	68	57	11	12	56	155	1.075	2.15	129	2.45	.231	14	.177	14	18	1.8
1969 LA-N	5	4	.556	12	12	1	1	0	62^2	71	34	31	9	2	13	24	1.340	4.45	75	4.51	.291	3	.136	-8	1	-0.8
Total 14	209	166	.557	518	465	167	49	6	3432	3084	1292	1124	280	154	855	2486	1.148	2.95	121	2.98	.239	218	.186	228	258	29.6
• DUBIEL, Monk	Walter John Dubiel b: 2/12/1918, Hartford, CT d: 10/23/1969, Hartford, CT BR/TR, 6', 190 lbs. Deb: 4/19/1944																									
1944 NY-A	13	13	.500	30	28	19	3	0	232	217	93	87	12	1	86	79	1.306	3.38	103	3.19	.248	15	.181	-1	14	-0.4
1945 NY-A	10	9	.526	26	20	9	1	0	151^1	157	88	78	9	0	62	45	1.447	4.64	75	3.88	.266	16	.276	-23	5	-2.1
1948 Phi-N	8	10	.444	37	17	6	2	4	150^1	139	84	65	13	1	58	42	1.310	3.89	101	3.50	.248	7	.167	1	8	0.2
1949 Chi-N	6	9	.400	32	20	3	1	4	147^2	142	75	68	16	1	54	52	1.327	4.14	97	3.72	.250	10	.286	1	10	0.4
1950 Chi-N	6	10	.375	39	12	4	2	2	142^2	152	79	66	12	1	67	51	1.535	4.16	101	4.49	.270	9	.200	4	8	0.5
1951 Chi-N	2	2	.500	22	0	0	0	1	54^2	46	17	14	3	0	22	19	1.244	2.30	178	2.94	.232	0	.000	11	6	1.0
1952 Chi-N	0	0	....	1	0	0	0	0	0^2	1	0	0	0	0	0	1	1.500	0.00	....	4.47	.333	0	....	0	0	0.0
Total 7	45	53	.459	187	97	41	9	11	879^1	854	436	378	65	4	349	289	1.368	3.87	98	3.65	.254	57	.207	-6	51	-0.3
• DUBOIS, Brian	Brian Andrew Dubois b: 4/18/1965, Joliet, IL BL/TL, 5'10", 195 lbs. Deb: 8/17/1989																									
1989 Det-A	0	4	.000	6	5	0	0	1	36	29	14	7	2	2	17	13	1.278	1.75	218	3.07	.218	0	....	9	3	0.9
1990 Det-A	3	5	.375	12	11	0	0	0	58^1	70	37	33	9	1	22	34	1.577	5.09	78	5.77	.310	0	....	-9	1	-0.9
Total 2	3	9	.250	18	16	0	0	1	94^1	99	51	40	11	3	39	47	1.463	3.82	103	4.74	.276	0	....	-0	4	0.0
• DUBOSE, Eric	Eric Ladell DuBose b: 5/15/1976, Bradenton, FL BL/TL, 6'3", 231 lbs. Deb: 9/19/2002																									
2002 Bal-A	0	0	....	4	0	0	0	0	6	7	2	2	1	1	1	4	1.333	3.00	143	5.59	.304	0	....	1	1	0.1
2003 Bal-A	3	6	.333	17	10	1	0	0	73^2	60	33	31	6	5	25	44	1.154	3.79	116	2.95	.222	0	....	5	5	0.5
Total 2	3	6	.333	21	10	1	0	0	79^2	67	35	33	7	6	26	48	1.167	3.73	118	3.15	.229	0	....	6	6	0.6
• DUBUC, Jean	Jean Joseph Octave Arthur "Chauncey" Dubuc b: 9/15/1888, St. Johnsbury, VT d: 8/28/1958, Fort Myers, FL BR/TR, 5'10.5", 185 lbs. Deb: 6/25/1908 C																									
1908 Cin-N	5	6	.455	15	9	7	1	0	85^1	62	34	26	2	5	41	32	1.207	2.74	83	2.57	.205	4	.138	-3	4	-0.4
1909 Cin-N	2	5	.286	19	5	2	0	1	71^1	72	58	29	0	4	46	19	1.654	3.66	71	4.18	.269	3	.167	-9	0	-1.0
1912 Det-A	17	10	.630	37	26	23	2	3	250	217	107	77	2	7	109	97	1.304	2.77	118	2.93	.235	29	.269	16	19	2.2
1913 Det-A	15	14	.517	36	28	22	1	2	242^2	228	113	78	1	8	91	73	1.315	2.89	101	2.80	.252	36	.267	8	15	1.7
1914 Det-A	12	14	.462	36	27	15	2	1	224	216	124	86	3	6	76	70	1.304	3.46	81	3.18	.257	28	.226	-14	9	-0.7
1915 Det-A	17	12	.586	39	33	22	5	2	258	231	116	92	6	10	88	74	1.236	3.21	94	2.96	.245	23	.205	-0	16	0.0
1916 Det-A	10	10	.500	36	16	8	1	1	170^1	134	66	56	1	5	84	40	1.280	2.96	97	2.89	.233	20	.256	1	11	0.7
1918* Bos-A	0	1	.000	2	1	1	0	0	10^2	11	5	5	1	0	5	1	1.500	4.22	63	4.46	.268	1	.167	-2	0	-0.2
1919 NY-N	6	4	.600	36	5	1	0	3	132	119	49	39	4	2	37	32	1.182	2.66	105	2.64	.246	6	.143	0	7	-0.2
Total 9	84	76	.525	256	150	101	12	13	1444^1	1290	672	488	20	47	577	438	1.293	3.04	95	2.97	.244	150	.230	-3	81	2.2
• DUCHSCHERER, Justin	Justin Craig Duchscherer b: 11/19/1977, Aberdeen, SD BR/TR, 6'3", 164 lbs. Deb: 7/25/2001																									
2001 Tex-A	1	1	.500	5	2	0	0	0	14^2	24	20	20	5	4	4	11	1.909	12.27	38	10.68	.353	0	....	-12	0	-1.2

YEAR	TM-L	W	L	PCT	G	GS	CG	SH	SV	IP	H	R	ER	HR	HB	BB	SO	RAT	ERA	ERA+	CERA	OAV	BH	AVG	PR+	WS	TPW
2003	Oak-A	1	1	.500	4	3	0	0	0	16^1	17	7	6	1	2	3	15	1.224	3.31	137	3.58	.262	0	....	2	1	0.2
Total	**2**	**2**	**2**	**.500**	**9**	**5**	**0**	**0**	**0**	**31**	**41**	**27**	**26**	**6**	**6**	**7**	**26**	**1.548**	**7.55**	**61**	**6.94**	**.308**	**0**	**....**	**-10**	**1**	**-1.0**
• DUCKWORTH, Brandon	Brandon J. Duckworth b: 1/23/1976, Salt Lake City, UT BB/TR, 6'2", 185 lbs. Deb: 8/7/2001																										
2001	Phi-N	3	2	.600	11	11	0	0	0	69	57	29	27	2	6	29	40	1.246	3.52	121	2.98	.234	5	.227	5	5	0.6
2002	Phi-N	8	9	.471	30	29	0	0	0	163	167	103	98	26	7	69	167	1.448	5.41	72	4.80	.261	9	.188	-28	2	-2.6
2003	Phi-N	4	7	.364	24	18	0	0	0	93	98	58	51	12	10	44	68	1.527	4.94	81	5.25	.272	5	.185	-10	2	-0.9
Total	**3**	**15**	**18**	**.455**	**65**	**58**	**0**	**0**	**0**	**325**	**322**	**190**	**176**	**40**	**23**	**142**	**275**	**1.428**	**4.87**	**82**	**4.54**	**.259**	**19**	**.196**	**-33**	**9**	**-2.9**
• DUCKWORTH, Jim	James Raymond Duckworth b: 5/24/1939, National City, CA BR/TR, 6'4", 194 lbs. Deb: 4/13/1963																										
1963	Was-A	4	12	.250	37	15	2	0	0	120^2	131	89	81	13	10	67	66	1.641	6.04	61	5.49	.278	0	.000	-31	0	-3.6
1964	Was-A	1	6	.143	30	2	0	0	3	56	52	37	27	9	3	25	56	1.375	4.34	85	4.35	.244	2	.222	-4	1	-0.4
1965	Was-A	2	2	.500	17	8	0	0	0	64	45	30	28	11	2	36	74	1.266	3.94	88	3.60	.202	0	.000	-3	2	-0.5
1966	Was-A	0	3	.000	5	4	0	0	0	14^1	14	12	8	2	1	10	14	1.674	5.02	69	5.65	.259	0	.000	-3	0	-0.3
	KC-A	0	2	.000	8	0	0	0	1	12	14	12	12	2	1	10	10	2.000	9.00	38	7.92	.292	0	.000	-8	0	-0.8
	Yr.	0	5	.000	13	4	0	0	1	26^1	28	24	20	4	2	20	24	1.823	6.84	50	6.69	.275	0	.000	-10	0	-1.1
Total	**4**	**7**	**25**	**.219**	**97**	**29**	**2**	**0**	**4**	**267**	**256**	**180**	**156**	**37**	**17**	**148**	**220**	**1.513**	**5.26**	**69**	**4.91**	**.253**	**2**	**.034**	**-48**	**3**	**-5.6**
• DUDLEY, Clise	Elzie Clise Dudley b: 8/8/1903, Graham, NC d: 1/12/1989, Moncks Corner, SC BL/TR, 6'1", 195 lbs. Deb: 4/18/1929																										
1929	Bro-N	6	14	.300	35	21	8	1	0	156^2	202	130	99	9	10	64	33	1.698	5.69	81	5.45	.315	5	.098	-15	2	-1.5
1930	Bro-N	2	4	.333	21	7	2	0	1	66^2	103	62	47	3	2	27	18	1.950	6.35	77	6.95	.371	5	.208	-12	0	-1.1
1931	Phi-N	8	14	.364	30	24	8	0	0	179	206	95	70	10	6	56	50	1.464	3.52	121	4.27	.287	18	.214	17	12	1.7
1932	Phi-N	1	1	.500	13	0	0	0	1	17^2	23	14	14	3	0	8	5	1.755	7.13	62	6.71	.329	4	.286	-5	1	-0.2
1933	Pit-N	0	0	....	1	0	0	0	0	0^1	6	5	5	0	0	1	0	21.00	135.00	2	168.99	.857	0	....	-5	0	-0.5
Total	**5**	**17**	**33**	**.340**	**100**	**52**	**18**	**1**	**2**	**420^1**	**540**	**306**	**235**	**25**	**18**	**156**	**106**	**1.656**	**5.03**	**89**	**5.37**	**.315**	**32**	**.185**	**-21**	**15**	**-1.6**
• DUES, Hal	Hal Joseph Dues b: 9/22/1954, LaMarque, TX BR/TR, 6'3", 180 lbs. Deb: 9/9/1977																										
1977	Mon-N	1	1	.500	6	4	0	0	0	23	26	14	11	2	0	9	9	1.522	4.30	88	4.31	.265	0	.000	-1	1	-0.2
1978	Mon-N	5	6	.455	25	12	1	0	1	99	85	29	26	5	4	42	36	1.283	2.36	149	3.26	.240	6	.194	10	8	1.0
1980	Mon-N	0	1	.000	6	1	0	0	0	12^1	17	9	9	1	0	4	2	1.703	6.57	54	5.65	.333	0	.000	-4	0	-0.5
Total	**3**	**6**	**8**	**.429**	**37**	**17**	**1**	**0**	**1**	**134^1**	**128**	**52**	**46**	**8**	**4**	**55**	**47**	**1.362**	**3.08**	**117**	**3.66**	**.254**	**6**	**.154**	**4**	**9**	**0.4**
• DUFF, Larry	Cecil Elba Duff b: 5/6/1895, Radersburg, MT d: 11/10/1969, Bend, OR BL/TR, 6'1", 175 lbs. Deb: 9/5/1922																										
1922	Chi-A	1	1	.500	3	1	0	0	0	12^2	16	7	7	1	0	3	7	1.500	4.97	82	4.98	.340	2	.400	-1	1	-0.1
• DUFF, Matt	Matthew Clark Duff b: 10/6/1974, Clarksdale, MS BR/TR, 6'1", 192 lbs. Deb: 7/30/2002																										
2002	StL-N	0	0	....	7	0	0	0	0	5^2	3	3	3	0	0	8	4	1.941	4.76	83	3.63	.150	0	....	-1	0	-0.1
• DUFFALO, Jim	James Francis Duffalo b: 11/25/1935, Helvetia, PA BR/TR, 6'1", 175 lbs. Deb: 4/12/1961																										
1961	SF-N	5	1	.833	24	4	1	0	1	61^2	59	31	29	9	2	32	37	1.476	4.23	90	4.60	.257	5	.294	-2	4	0.0
1962	SF-N	1	2	.333	24	2	0	0	0	42	42	27	17	3	0	23	29	1.548	3.64	104	4.21	.256	0	.000	1	1	0.0
1963	SF-N	4	2	.667	34	5	0	0	2	75^1	56	26	24	3	2	37	55	1.235	2.87	112	2.63	.209	2	.111	4	5	0.4
1964	SF-N	5	1	.833	35	3	1	0	3	74	57	25	24	9	2	31	55	1.189	2.92	122	3.03	.209	1	.071	5	7	0.4
1965	SF-N	0	1	.000	2	0	0	0	0	0^1	1	1	1	0	0	2	0	9.000	27.00	13	44.74	.500	0	....	-1	0	-0.1
	Cin-N	0	1	.000	22	0	0	0	0	44^1	33	21	17	3	5	30	34	1.421	3.45	109	3.83	.212	0	.000	1	2	0.1
	Yr.	0	2	.000	24	0	0	0	0	44^2	34	22	18	3	5	32	34	1.478	3.63	103	4.14	.215	0	.000	1	2	0.0
Total	**5**	**15**	**8**	**.652**	**141**	**14**	**2**	**0**	**6**	**297^2**	**248**	**131**	**112**	**27**	**11**	**155**	**210**	**1.354**	**3.39**	**106**	**3.59**	**.227**	**8**	**.127**	**8**	**19**	**0.9**
• DUFFIE, John	John Brown Duffie b: 10/4/1945, Greenwood, SC BR/TR, 6'7", 210 lbs. Deb: 9/18/1967																										
1967	LA-N	0	2	.000	2	2	0	0	0	9^2	11	6	3	1	0	4	6	1.552	2.79	111	4.65	.282	0	.000	0	0	0.0
• DUFFY, Bernie	Bernard Allen Duffy b: 8/18/1893, Vinson, OK d: 2/9/1962, Abilene, TX BR/TR, 5'11", 180 lbs. Deb: 9/20/1913																										
1913	Pit-N	0	0	....	3	2	0	0	0	11^1	18	8	7	0	0	3	8	1.853	5.56	54	6.09	.360	1	.250	-3	0	-0.3
• DUGAN, Dan	Daniel Phillip Dugan b: 2/22/1907, Plainfield, NJ d: 6/25/1968, Green Brook, NJ BL/TL, 6'1.5", 187 lbs. Deb: 9/5/1928																										
1928	Chi-A	0	0	....	1	0	0	0	0	0^1	0	0	0	0	0	0	0	.000	0.00	....	0.00	.000	0	....	0	0	0.0
1929	Chi-A	1	4	.200	19	2	0	0	1	65	77	51	48	8	2	19	15	1.477	6.65	64	4.81	.300	3	.150	-18	0	-1.8
Total	**2**	**1**	**4**	**.200**	**20**	**2**	**0**	**0**	**1**	**65^1**	**77**	**51**	**48**	**8**	**2**	**19**	**15**	**1.469**	**6.61**	**65**	**4.78**	**.300**	**3**	**.150**	**-18**	**0**	**-1.8**
• DUGAN, Ed	Edward John Dugan b: 1864, Brooklyn, NY TR Deb: 8/5/1884																										
1884	Ric-a	5	14	.263	20	20	20	0	0	166^1	196	137	83	5	2	15	60	1.269	4.49	74	....	.278	8	.114	-21	3	-2.3
• DUGGLEBY, Bill	William James "Frosty Bill" Duggleby b: 3/16/1874, Utica, NY d: 8/30/1944, Redfield, NY TR Deb: 4/21/1898 U																										
1898	Phi-N	3	3	.500	9	5	4	0	0	54	70	39	33	4	6	18	12	1.630	5.50	62	5.68	.311	5	.238	-12	2	-0.9
1901	Phi-N	20	12	.625	35	28	26	5	0	284^2	302	120	88	9	10	41	95	1.205	2.78	122	3.08	.270	19	.165	19	22	1.5
1902	Phi-A	1	1	.500	2	2	2	0	0	17	19	9	6	0	0	4	4	1.353	3.18	115	3.41	.283	0	.000	1	1	0.0
	Phi-N	11	17	.393	33	28	25	0	1	258^2	282	130	97	2	12	57	60	1.311	3.38	83	3.36	.277	17	.173	-9	14	-1.1
1903	Phi-N	13	16	.448	36	30	28	3	2	264^1	318	162	110	4	12	79	57	1.502	3.75	87	4.42	.303	24	.231	-18	10	-1.5
1904	Phi-N	12	13	.480	32	27	22	2	1	223^2	265	138	94	3	11	53	55	1.422	3.78	70	3.99	.292	14	.171	-23	4	-2.4
1905	Phi-N	18	17	.514	38	36	27	1	0	289^1	270	116	79	10	13	83	75	1.220	2.46	118	3.08	.253	11	.109	10	20	0.9
1906	Phi-N	13	19	.406	42	30	22	5	2	280^1	241	93	70	5	12	66	83	1.095	2.25	116	2.30	.227	14	.141	14	16	1.4
1907	Phi-N	0	2	.000	5	2	2	0	0	29	43	27	24	2	5	11	8	1.862	7.45	32	7.83	.371	1	.111	-17	0	-1.8
	Pit-N	2	2	.500	9	3	1	1	0	40^1	34	17	12	0	2	12	4	1.140	2.68	91	2.50	.239	2	.154	-0	2	-0.1
	Yr.	2	4	.333	14	5	3	1	0	69^1	77	44	36	2	7	23	12	1.442	4.67	52	4.73	.298	3	.136	-17	2	-1.9
Total	**8**	**93**	**102**	**.477**	**241**	**191**	**159**	**17**	**6**	**1741^1**	**1844**	**851**	**613**	**39**	**83**	**424**	**453**	**1.302**	**3.17**	**92**	**3.46**	**.272**	**107**	**.165**	**-36**	**91**	**-3.9**
• DUKE, Martin	Martin F. "Duck" Duke b: 1867, Zanesville, OH d: 12/31/1898, Minneapolis, MN TL, 5'8" Deb: 8/24/1891 U																										
1891	Was-a	0	3	.000	4	3	2	0	0	23	36	33	19	0	0	19	5	2.391	7.43	50	....	.345	1	.111	-8	0	-0.8
• DUKES, Jan	Noble Jan Dukes b: 8/16/1945, Cheyenne, WY BL/TL, 5'11", 175 lbs. Deb: 9/6/1969																										
1969	Was-A	0	2	.000	8	0	0	0	0	11	8	3	3	0	0	4	3	1.091	2.45	141	1.92	.216	0	.000	1	1	0.1
1970	Was-A	0	0	....	5	0	0	0	0	6^2	6	3	2	0	1	1	4	1.050	2.70	132	2.46	.240	0	.000	1	0	0.0
1972	Tex-A	0	0	....	3	0	0	0	0	2^1	1	2	1	0	0	5	0	2.571	3.86	78	5.42	.167	0	....	-0	0	0.0
Total	**3**	**0**	**2**	**.000**	**16**	**0**	**0**	**0**	**0**	**20**	**15**	**8**	**6**	**0**	**1**	**10**	**7**	**1.250**	**2.70**	**126**	**2.51**	**.221**	**0**	**.000**	**2**	**1**	**0.2**
• DUKES, Tom	Thomas Earl Dukes b: 8/31/1942, Knoxville, TN BR/TR, 6'2", 185 lbs. Deb: 8/15/1967																										
1967	Hou-N	0	2	.000	17	0	0	0	1	23^2	25	14	14	2	2	11	23	1.521	5.32	62	4.78	.275	1	.500	-5	0	-0.5
1968	Hou-N	2	2	.500	43	0	0	0	4	52^2	62	31	25	3	2	28	37	1.709	4.27	69	4.87	.291	0	.000	-7	0	-0.8
1969	SD-N	1	0	1.000	13	0	0	0	1	22^1	26	18	18	2	0	10	15	1.612	7.25	49	4.96	.295	0	.000	-9	0	-1.0
1970	SD-N	1	6	.143	53	0	0	0	10	69	62	39	31	7	2	25	56	1.261	4.04	98	3.33	.246	0	.000	-0	4	-0.1
1971*	Bal-A	1	5	.167	28	0	0	0	4	38^1	40	15	15	4	1	8	30	1.252	3.52	95	3.51	.263	1	.143	-1	2	-0.1
1972	Cal-A	0	1	.000	7	0	0	0	1	11	11	3	2	1	1	0	8	1.000	1.64	178	2.93	.262	0	....	1	1	0.2
Total	**6**	**5**	**16**	**.238**	**161**	**0**	**0**	**0**	**21**	**217**	**226**	**120**	**105**	**19**	**8**	**82**	**169**	**1.419**	**4.35**	**78**	**4.04**	**.270**	**2**	**.095**	**-21**	**7**	**-2.3**
• DULIBA, Bob	Robert John Duliba b: 1/9/1935, Glen Lyon, PA BR/TR, 5'10", 185 lbs. Deb: 8/11/1959																										
1959	StL-N	0	1	.000	11	0	0	0	1	22^2	19	7	7	2	0	12	14	1.368	2.78	152	3.67	.238	0	.000	4	2	0.3
1960	StL-N	4	4	.500	27	0	0	0	0	40^2	49	20	19	6	0	16	23	1.598	4.20	97	5.59	.310	1	.200	-0	3	0.0
1962	StL-N	2	0	1.000	28	0	0	0	2	39^1	33	11	9	3	0	17	22	1.271	2.06	207	3.28	.239	0	.000	9	5	0.9
1963	LA-A	1	1	.500	6	0	0	0	1	7^2	3	1	1	0	0	6	4	1.174	1.17	292	1.73	.125	0	.000	2	1	0.2
1964	LA-A	6	4	.600	58	0	0	0	9	72^2	80	35	29	5	1	22	33	1.404	3.59	91	4.13	.287	0	.000	-3	4	-0.4
1965	Bos-A	4	2	.667	39	0	0	0	1	64^1	60	31	27	6	0	22	27	1.275	3.78	99	3.20	.248	0	.000	1	4	0.0

YEAR TM-L	W	L	PCT	G	GS	CG	SH	SV	IP	H	R	ER	HR	HB	BB	SO	RAT	ERA	ERA+	CERA	OAV	BH	AVG	PR+	WS	TPW
1967 KC-A	0	0	....	7	0	0	0	0	9^2	13	7	7	3	0	1	6	1.448	6.52	49	6.74	.342	0	....	-4	0	-0.4
Total 7	17	12	.586	176	0	0	0	14	257	257	112	99	25	1	96	129	1.374	3.47	106	3.98	.268	1	.038	9	19	0.6
• DUMONT, George	George Henry "Pea Soup" Dumont b: 11/13/1895, Minneapolis, MN d: 10/13/1956, Minneapolis, MN BR/TR, 5'11", 163 lbs. Deb: 9/14/1915																									
1915 Was-A	2	1	.667	6	4	3	2	0	40	23	17	9	0	2	12	18	.875	2.03	146	1.35	.169	2	.167	4	3	0.4
1916 Was-A	2	3	.400	17	5	2	0	1	53	37	25	18	0	1	17	21	1.019	3.06	91	1.67	.194	1	.071	-2	2	-0.2
1917 Was-A	5	14	.263	37	23	8	2	2	204^2	171	76	58	3	6	76	65	1.207	2.55	103	2.59	.227	2	.034	-1	10	-0.6
1918 Was-A	1	1	.500	4	1	1	0	0	14	18	12	8	0	0	6	12	1.714	5.14	53	4.65	.295	1	.333	-4	0	-0.4
1919 Bos-A	0	4	.000	13	2	0	0	0	35^1	45	21	17	1	1	19	12	1.811	4.33	70	5.96	.326	0	.000	-6	0	-0.6
Total 5	10	23	.303	77	35	14	4	3	347	294	151	110	4	10	130	128	1.222	2.85	96	2.73	.230	6	.064	-9	15	-1.5
• DUMOULIN, Dan	Daniel Lynn Dumoulin b: 8/20/1953, Kokomo, IN BR/TR, 6', 175 lbs. Deb: 9/5/1977																									
1977 Cin-N	0	0	....	5	0	0	0	0	5^1	12	8	8	0	0	3	5	2.813	13.50	29	10.93	.462	0	....	-6	0	-0.6
1978 Cin-N	1	0	1.000	3	0	0	0	0	5	7	1	1	0	1	3	2	2.000	1.80	197	7.62	.368	0	....	1	1	0.1
Total 2	1	0	1.000	8	0	0	0	0	10^1	19	9	9	0	1	6	7	2.419	7.84	50	9.33	.422	0	....	-5	1	-0.5
• DUMOVICH, Nick	Nicholas Dumovich b: 1/2/1902, Sacramento, CA d: 12/12/1979, Laguna Hills, CA BL/TL, 6', 170 lbs. Deb: 4/20/1923																									
1923 Chi-N	3	5	.375	28	8	1	0	1	94	118	60	48	4	3	45	23	1.734	4.60	87	5.45	.319	7	.241	-9	4	-0.7
• DUNBAR, Matt	Matthew Marshall Dunbar b: 10/15/1968, Tallahassee, FL BL/TL, 6', 170 lbs. Deb: 4/25/1995																									
1995 Fla-N	0	1	.000	8	0	0	0	0	7	12	9	9	0	1	11	5	3.286	11.57	36	12.09	.387	0	....	-6	0	-0.6
• DUNCAN, Courtney	Courtney Demond Duncan b: 10/9/1974, Mobile, AL BL/TR, 6', 185 lbs. Deb: 4/2/2001																									
2001 Chi-N	3	3	.500	36	0	0	0	0	42^2	42	24	24	5	2	25	49	1.570	5.06	82	4.91	.259	0	.000	-4	2	-0.3
2002 Chi-N	0	0	....	2	0	0	0	0	2^1	2	0	0	0	0	1	1	1.286	0.00	....	2.67	.222	0	....	1	0	0.1
Total 2	3	3	.500	38	0	0	0	0	45	44	24	24	5	2	26	50	1.556	4.80	86	4.80	.257	0	.000	-3	2	-0.2
• DUNDON, Ed	Edward Joseph "Dummy" Dundon b: 7/10/1859, Columbus, OH d: 8/18/1893, Columbus, OH TR, 6' Deb: 6/2/1883 ♦																									
1883 Col-a	3	16	.158	20	19	16	0	0	166^2	213	153	83	7	....	38	31	1.506	4.48	69	....	.292	15	.161	-27	2	-2.7
1884 Col-a	6	4	.600	11	9	7	0	0	81	85	55	34	9	0	15	37	1.235	3.78	80	....	.256	12	.140	-9	5	-1.0
Total 2	9	20	.310	31	28	23	0	0	247^2	298	208	117	16	0	53	68	1.417	4.25	72	....	.281	27	.151	-35	7	-3.8
• DUNEGAN, Jim	James William Dunegan b: 8/6/1947, Burlington, IA BR/TR, 6'1", 205 lbs. Deb: 5/28/1970																									
1970 Chi-N	0	2	.000	7	0	0	0	0	13^1	13	7	7	2	0	12	3	1.875	4.73	95	6.29	.277	1	.250	-0	1	0.0
• DUNHAM, Wiley	Henry Huston Dunham b: 1/30/1877, Piketon, OH d: 1/16/1934, Cleveland, OH, 6'1", 180 lbs. Deb: 5/24/1902																									
1902 StL-N	2	3	.400	7	5	3	0	1	38	47	31	24	1	3	13	15	1.579	5.68	48	4.85	.303	1	.083	-12	0	-1.4
• DUNKLE, Davey	Edward Perks Dunkle b: 8/30/1872, Phillipsburg, PA d: 11/19/1941, Lock Haven, PA BB/TR, 6'2", 220 lbs. Deb: 8/28/1897																									
1897 Phi-N	5	2	.714	7	7	7	0	0	62	72	41	24	0	1	23	9	1.532	3.48	120	4.09	.288	4	.174	6	4	0.5
1898 Phi-N	1	4	.200	12	7	4	0	0	68^1	83	70	53	1	9	38	21	1.771	6.98	49	5.60	.298	6	.214	-26	0	-2.5
1899 Was-N	0	2	.000	4	2	2	0	0	26	46	34	29	3	1	14	9	2.308	10.04	39	9.70	.384	3	.273	-17	0	-1.5
1903 Chi-A	4	4	.500	12	7	6	0	1	82	96	58	37	1	3	31	26	1.549	4.06	69	4.28	.291	10	.303	-10	2	-0.8
Was-A	5	9	.357	14	13	10	0	0	108^1	111	60	51	4	4	33	51	1.329	4.24	74	3.42	.264	4	.098	-12	4	-1.6
Yr.	9	13	.409	26	20	16	0	1	190^1	207	118	88	5	7	64	77	1.424	4.16	72	3.79	.276	14	.189	-22	6	-2.4
1904 Was-A	2	9	.182	12	11	7	0	0	74^1	95	56	41	1	3	23	23	1.587	4.96	54	4.74	.311	4	.143	-17	0	-2.1
Total 5	17	30	.362	61	47	36	0	1	421	503	319	235	10	21	162	139	1.580	5.02	64	4.66	.295	31	.189	-76	10	-8.1
• DUNLEAVY, Jack	John Francis Dunleavy b: 9/14/1879, Harrison, NJ d: 4/11/1944, South Norwalk, CT BL/TL, 5'6", 167 lbs. Deb: 5/30/1903 ♦																									
1903 StL-N	6	8	.429	14	13	9	0	0	102	101	59	46	2	8	57	51	1.549	4.06	80	4.31	.264	48	.249	-11	7	-0.8
1904 StL-N	1	4	.200	7	5	5	0	0	55	63	32	27	4	1	23	28	1.564	4.42	61	4.59	.275	40	.233	-9	6	-1.0
Total 2	7	12	.368	21	18	14	0	0	157	164	91	73	6	9	80	79	1.554	4.18	72	4.41	.268	193	.241	-21	13	-1.7
• DUNN, Jack	John Joseph Dunn b: 10/6/1872, Meadville, PA d: 10/22/1928, Towson, MD BR/TR, 5'9" Deb: 5/6/1897 ♦																									
1897 Bro-N	14	9	.609	25	21	21	0	0	216^2	251	147	110	6	9	66	26	1.463	4.57	90	4.15	.288	29	.221	-9	13	-1.4
1898 Bro-N	16	21	.432	41	37	31	0	0	322^2	352	180	129	10	15	82	66	1.345	3.60	99	3.64	.276	41	.246	3	17	0.2
1899 Bro-N	23	13	.639	41	34	29	2	2	299^1	323	161	123	8	18	86	48	1.366	3.70	106	3.71	.275	30	.246	2	24	0.1
1900 Bro-N	3	4	.429	10	7	5	0	0	63	88	48	39	1	4	28	6	1.841	5.57	69	6.04	.329	6	.231	-13	2	-1.2
Phi-N	5	5	.500	10	9	9	1	0	80	87	50	43	2	5	29	12	1.450	4.84	75	4.01	.276	10	.303	-10	4	-0.8
Yr.	8	9	.471	20	16	14	1	0	143	175	98	82	3	9	57	18	1.622	5.16	72	4.90	.301	16	.271	-23	6	-2.0
1901 Phi-N	0	1	.000	2	2	0	0	0	4^2	11	16	11	0	2	7	1	3.857	21.21	16	18.71	.451	1	1.000	-9	0	-0.8
Bal-A	3	3	.500	9	6	6	0	0	59^2	74	45	24	2	1	21	5	1.592	3.62	107	4.73	.301	90	.249	4	8	-1.4
1902 NY-N	0	3	.000	3	2	2	0	0	26^2	28	14	11	0	0	12	6	1.500	3.71	75	3.71	.270	72	.211	-2	3	-2.9
1904 NY-N	0	0	....	1	0	0	0	1	4	3	3	2	1	0	3	1	1.500	4.50	60	4.08	.167	56	.309	-1	9	0.5
Total 7	64	59	.520	142	118	103	3	3	1076^2	1217	664	492	30	54	334	171	1.441	4.11	92	4.06	.283	397	.245	-37	80	-7.7
• DUNN, Jim	James William "Bill" Dunn b: 2/25/1931, Valdosta, GA d: 1/6/1999, Gadsden, AL BR/TR, 6'.5", 185 lbs. Deb: 8/26/1952																									
1952 Pit-N	0	0	....	3	0	0	0	0	5^1	4	2	2	0	0	3	2	1.313	3.38	118	2.34	.190	0	.000	0	0	0.0
• DUNNE, Mike	Michael Dennis Dunne b: 10/27/1962, South Bend, IN BR/TR, 6'4", 200 lbs. Deb: 6/5/1987																									
1987 Pit-N	13	6	.684	23	23	5	1	0	163^1	143	66	55	10	1	68	72	1.292	3.03	136	3.19	.240	5	.094	17	13	1.6
1988 Pit-N	7	11	.389	30	28	1	0	0	170	163	88	74	15	5	88	70	1.476	3.92	87	4.29	.255	5	.109	-11	4	-1.2
1989 Pit-N	1	1	.500	3	3	0	0	0	14^1	21	12	12	1	1	9	4	2.093	7.53	45	7.47	.328	1	.250	-7	0	-0.7
Sea-A	2	9	.182	15	15	1	0	0	85^1	104	61	50	7	2	37	38	1.652	5.27	76	5.48	.307	0	....	-12	0	-1.2
1990 SD-N	0	3	.000	10	6	0	0	0	28^2	28	21	18	4	0	17	15	1.570	5.65	68	4.77	.241	0	.000	-6	0	-0.7
1992 Chi-A	2	0	1.000	4	1	0	0	0	12^2	12	7	6	0	1	6	6	1.421	4.26	91	3.63	.255	0	....	-1	1	-0.1
Total 5	25	30	.455	85	76	7	1	0	474^1	471	255	215	37	10	225	205	1.467	4.08	92	4.23	.261	11	.101	-19	18	-2.2
• DUNNING, Andy	Andrew Jackson Dunning b: 8/12/1871, New York, NY d: 6/21/1952, New York, NY BR/TR, 6', 175 lbs. Deb: 5/23/1889																									
1889 Pit-N	0	2	.000	2	2	2	0	0	18	20	19	14	1	0	16	4	2.000	7.00	54	....	.272	0	.000	-7	0	-0.7
1891 NY-N	0	1	.000	1	1	0	0	0	2	3	5	1	1	0	3	1	3.000	4.50	71	....	.334	0	....	-0	0	0.0
Total 2	0	3	.000	3	3	2	0	0	20	23	24	15	2	0	19	5	2.100	6.75	55	....	.279	0	.000	-7	0	-0.7
• DUNNING, Steve	Steven John Dunning b: 5/15/1949, Denver, CO BR/TR, 6'2", 205 lbs. Deb: 6/14/1970																									
1970 Cle-A	4	9	.308	19	17	0	0	0	94^1	93	55	52	16	4	54	77	1.558	4.96	80	5.39	.261	5	.161	-11	3	-1.2
1971 Cle-A	8	14	.364	31	29	3	1	1	184	173	98	92	25	5	109	132	**1.533**	4.50	85	4.90	.254	10	.182	-15	7	-1.4
1972 Cle-A	6	4	.600	16	16	1	0	0	105	98	39	38	16	0	43	52	1.343	3.26	99	4.05	.248	9	.273	-2	9	0.4
1973 Cle-A	0	2	.000	4	3	0	0	0	18	17	15	13	2	0	13	10	1.667	6.50	60	5.07	.250	0	....	-5	0	-0.5
Tex-A	2	6	.250	23	12	2	0	0	94^1	101	63	56	11	1	52	38	1.622	5.34	70	5.24	.275	0	....	-15	1	-1.5
Yr.	2	8	.200	27	15	2	0	0	112^1	118	78	69	13	1	65	48	1.629	5.53	68	5.22	.271	0	....	-20	1	-2.0
1974 Tex-A	0	0	....	1	0	0	0	0	2^1	3	5	5	2	0	3	1	2.571	19.29	18	17.49	.333	0	....	-4	0	-0.4
1976 Cal-A	0	0	....	4	0	0	0	0	6	9	9	5	2	0	6	4	2.500	7.50	44	10.23	.310	0	....	-3	0	-0.3
Mon-N	2	6	.250	32	7	1	0	0	91^1	93	50	42	6	2	33	72	1.380	4.14	90	3.84	.274	2	.133	-4	3	-0.4
1977 Oak-A	1	0	1.000	6	0	0	0	0	18^1	17	8	8	2	0	10	4	1.473	3.93	102	4.35	.254	0	....	0	1	0.0
Total 7	23	41	.359	136	84	7	1	1	613^2	604	342	311	82	12	323	390	1.511	4.56	82	4.81	.261	26	.194	-58	24	-5.3
• DUPEE, Frank	Frank Oliver Dupee b: 4/29/1877, Monkton, VT d: 8/14/1956, Portland, ME TL, 6'1", 200 lbs. Deb: 8/24/1901																									
1901 Chi-A	0	1	.000	1	1	0	0	0	0	0	0	0	0	0	3	0	....	....	....	∞	-1.000	0		0	0	0.0
• DUPREE, Mike	Michael Dennis Dupree b: 5/29/1953, Kansas City, KS BR/TR, 6'1", 185 lbs. Deb: 4/13/1976																									
1976 SD-N	0	0	....	12	0	0	0	0	15^2	18	17	16	4	0	7	5	1.596	9.19	36	6.28	.286	1	1.000	-10	0	-1.0

YEAR	TM-L	W	L	PCT	G	GS	CG	SH	SV	IP	H	R	ER	HR	HB	BB	SO	RAT	ERA	ERA+	CERA	OAV	BH	AVG	PR+	WS	TPW
• DURAN, Roberto	Roberto Alejandro Duran b: 3/6/1973, Moca, Dominican Republic BL/TL, 6', 167 lbs. Deb: 7/6/1997																										
1997	Det-A	0	0	....	13	0	0	0	0	10^{2}	7	9	9	0	3	15	11	2.063	7.59	60	6.18	.189	0	....	-4	0	-0.4
1998	Det-A	0	1	.000	18	0	0	0	0	15^{1}	9	10	10	0	2	17	12	1.696	5.87	80	4.04	.170	0	....	-2	0	-0.2
Total	2	0	1	.000	31	0	0	0	0	26	16	19	19	0	5	32	23	1.846	6.58	71	4.92	.178	0	....	-6	0	-0.6
• DURBIN, Chad	Chad Griffin Durbin b: 12/3/1977, Spring Valley, IL BR/TR, 6'1", 200 lbs. Deb: 9/26/1999																										
1999	KC-A	0	0	....	1	0	0	0	0	2^{1}	1	0	0	0	0	1	3	.857	0.00	....	1.08	.125	0	....	1	0	0.1
2000	KC-A	2	5	.286	16	16	0	0	0	72^{1}	91	71	66	14	0	43	37	1.853	8.21	62	7.05	.301	0	....	-26	0	-2.4
2001	KC-A	9	16	.360	29	29	2	0	0	179	201	109	98	26	11	58	95	1.447	4.93	99	5.15	.288	0	.000	-5	8	-0.5
2002	KC-A	0	1	.000	2	2	0	0	0	8^{1}	13	11	11	3	1	4	5	2.040	11.88	42	10.58	.342	0	....	-6	0	-0.6
2003	Cle-A	0	1	.000	3	1	0	0	0	8^{2}	18	12	7	2	0	3	8	2.423	7.27	61	12.37	.429	0	....	-3	0	-0.3
Total	5	11	23	.324	51	48	2	0	0	270^{2}	324	203	182	45	12	109	148	1.600	6.05	82	6.02	.298	0	.000	-39	8	-3.7
• DURBIN, Kid	Blaine Alphonsus Durbin b: 9/10/1886, Lamar, MO d: 9/11/1943, Kirkwood, MO BL/TL, 5'8", 155 lbs. Deb: 4/24/1907 ♦																										
1907	Chi-N	0	1	.000	5	1	1	0	1	16^{2}	14	13	10	0	1	10	5	1.440	5.40	46	3.41	.233	6	.333	-6	1	-0.5
• DUREN, Ryne	Rinold George Duren b: 2/22/1929, Cazenovia, WI BR/TR, 6'2", 195 lbs. Deb: 9/25/1954																										
1954	Bal-A	0	0	....	1	0	0	0	0	2	3	3	2	0	0	1	2	2.000	9.00	40	5.70	.333	0	....	-1	0	-0.1
1957	KC-A	0	3	.000	14	6	0	0	1	42^{2}	37	26	25	4	2	30	37	1.570	5.27	75	4.60	.236	1	.071	-6	0	-0.8
1958*	NY-A★	6	4	.600	44	1	0	0	**20**	75^{2}	40	20	17	4	7	43	87	1.097	2.02	175	2.30	.157	1	.077	11	12	1.2
1959	NY-A★	3	6	.333	41	0	0	0	14	76^{2}	49	18	16	6	3	43	96	1.200	1.88	194	2.70	.181	0	.000	15	10	1.4
1960*	NY-A	3	4	.429	42	1	0	0	9	49	27	29	27	3	7	49	67	1.551	4.96	72	3.99	.160	0	.000	-9	2	-1.0
1961	NY-A	0	1	.000	4	0	0	0	0	5	2	3	3	2	0	4	7	1.200	5.40	69	4.25	.125	0	....	-1	0	-0.1
	LA-A★	6	12	.333	40	14	1	1	2	99	87	70	57	13	3	75	108	1.636	5.18	87	5.05	.233	1	.040	-6	3	-0.8
	Yr.	6	13	.316	44	14	1	1	2	104	89	73	60	15	3	79	115	1.615	5.19	86	5.01	.229	1	.040	-7	3	-0.9
1962	LA-A	2	9	.182	42	3	0	0	8	71^{1}	53	38	35	1	6	57	74	1.542	4.42	87	3.73	.206	1	.067	-4	3	-0.5
1963	Phi-N	6	2	.750	33	7	1	0	2	87^{1}	65	33	32	6	5	52	84	1.340	3.30	98	3.45	.210	3	.143	-2	6	-0.2
1964	Phi-N	0	0	....	2	0	0	0	0	3	5	3	2	0	1	1	5	2.000	6.00	58	7.72	.357	0	....	-1	0	-0.1
	Cin-N	0	2	.000	26	0	0	0	1	43^{2}	41	17	14	1	3	15	39	1.282	2.89	125	3.18	.248	0	.000	3	3	0.3
	Yr.	0	2	.000	28	0	0	0	1	46^{2}	46	20	16	1	4	16	44	1.329	3.09	116	3.47	.257	0	.000	2	3	0.2
1965	Phi-N	0	0	....	6	0	0	0	0	11	10	7	4	0	1	4	6	1.273	3.27	106	3.18	.270	0	.000	0	0	0.0
	Was-A	1	1	.500	16	0	0	0	0	23	24	17	17	0	3	18	18	1.826	6.65	52	5.26	.286	0	....	-8	0	-0.9
Total	10	27	44	.380	311	32	2	1	57	589^{1}	443	284	251	40	41	392	630	1.417	3.83	98	3.72	.209	7	.061	-9	39	-1.4
• DURHAM, Bull	Louis Raphael Durham b: 6/27/1877, New Oxford, PA d: 6/28/1960, Bentley, KS BR/TR, 5'10" Deb: 9/15/1904																										
1904	Bro-N	2	0	1.000	2	2	1	0	0	11	10	5	4	0	0	5	1	1.364	3.27	84	3.13	.250	1	.250	-1	1	-0.1
1907	Was-A	0	0	....	2	0	0	0	0	5	10	9	7	0	1	4	1	2.800	12.60	19	11.63	.416	0	.000	-5	0	-0.6
1908	NY-N	0	0	....	1	0	0	0	0	2	2	2	2	0	0	1	2	1.500	9.00	27	3.50	.250	0	....	-1	0	-0.2
1909	NY-N	0	0	....	4	0	0	0	1	11	15	8	4	0	0	2	2	1.545	3.27	78	4.57	.326	0	.000	-1	0	-0.1
Total	4	2	0	1.000	9	2	1	0	1	29	37	24	17	0	1	12	6	1.690	5.28	48	5.17	.313	1	.143	-8	1	-1.0
• DURHAM, Don	Donald Gary Durham b: 3/21/1949, Yosemite, KY BR/TR, 6', 170 lbs. Deb: 7/16/1972																										
1972	StL-N	2	7	.222	10	8	1	0	0	47^{2}	42	28	23	1	0	22	35	1.343	4.34	78	2.88	.240	7	.500	-5	2	-0.1
1973	Tex-A	0	4	.000	15	4	0	0	1	40^{1}	49	35	34	7	1	23	23	1.785	7.59	49	6.79	.304	0	....	-16	0	-1.7
Total	2	2	11	.154	25	12	1	0	1	88	91	63	57	8	1	45	58	1.545	5.83	61	4.67	.271	7	.500	-21	2	-1.7
• DURHAM, Ed	Edward Fant "Bull" Durham b: 8/17/1907, Chester, SC d: 4/27/1976, Chester, SC BL/TR, 5'11", 170 lbs. Deb: 4/19/1929																										
1929	Bos-A	1	0	1.000	14	1	0	0	0	22^{1}	34	24	23	2	0	14	6	2.149	9.27	46	8.31	.374	0	.000	-12	0	-1.2
1930	Bos-A	4	15	.211	33	12	6	1	1	140	144	81	73	9	2	43	28	1.336	4.69	98	3.58	.270	4	.098	-3	6	-0.6
1931	Bos-A	8	10	.444	38	15	7	2	0	165^{1}	175	91	78	9	4	50	53	1.361	4.25	101	3.67	.266	3	.056	1	10	-0.4
1932	Bos-A	6	13	.316	34	22	4	0	0	175^{1}	187	90	74	13	4	49	52	1.346	3.80	118	3.81	.274	7	.123	17	11	1.2
1933	Chi-A	10	6	.625	24	21	6	0	0	138^{2}	137	74	69	12	5	46	65	1.320	4.48	95	3.67	.256	10	.217	-2	8	-0.2
Total	5	29	44	.397	143	71	23	3	1	641^{2}	677	360	317	45	15	202	204	1.370	4.45	99	3.85	.271	24	.119	1	35	-1.2
• DURHAM, John	John Garfield Durham b: 10/7/1881, Douglass, KS d: 5/7/1949, Coffeyville, KS BR/TR, 6', 175 lbs. Deb: 9/15/1902																										
1902	Chi-A	1	1	.500	3	3	3	0	0	20	21	15	13	0	0	16	3	1.850	5.85	58	4.94	.270	1	.067	-6	0	-0.8
• DURNING, Rich	Richard Knott Durning b: 10/10/1892, Louisville, KY d: 9/23/1948, Castle Point, NY BL/TL, 6'2", 178 lbs. Deb: 4/16/1917																										
1917	Bro-N	0	0	....	1	0	0	0	0	1	0	0	0	0	0	0	0	.000	0.00	....	0.00	.000	0	....	0	0	0.0
1918	Bro-N	0	0	....	1	0	0	0	0	2	3	5	3	0	0	4	0	3.500	13.50	21	12.16	.375	0	....	-2	0	-0.3
Total	2	0	0	....	2	0	0	0	0	3	3	5	3	0	0	4	0	2.333	9.00	31	8.11	.375	0	....	-2	0	-0.2
• DUROCHER, Jayson	Jayson Paul Durocher b: 8/18/1974, Hartford, CT BR/TR, 6'3", 195 lbs. Deb: 6/11/2002																										
2002	Mil-N	1	1	.500	39	0	0	0	0	48	27	13	10	3	2	21	44	1.000	1.88	218	1.88	.164	0	.000	12	4	1.2
2003	Mil-N	2	0	1.000	6	0	0	0	0	7^{1}	9	9	9	4	1	2	7	1.500	11.05	38	9.04	.300	0	....	-5	0	-0.5
Total	2	3	1	.750	45	0	0	0	0	55^{1}	36	22	19	7	3	23	51	1.066	3.09	135	2.83	.185	0	.000	7	4	0.6
• DURYEA, Jesse	James Newton "Cyclone Jim" Duryea b: 9/7/1859, Osage, IA d: 8/19/1942, Algona, IA BR/TR, 5'10", 175 lbs. Deb: 4/20/1889																										
1889	Cin-a	32	19	.627	53	48	38	2	1	401	372	208	114	9	16	127	183	1.244	2.56	152	....	.239	44	.272	55	37	5.3
1890	Cin-N	16	12	.571	33	32	29	2	0	274	270	148	89	11	8	60	108	1.204	2.92	121	....	.250	15	.152	15	23	1.5
1891	Cin-N	1	9	.100	10	10	8	0	0	77	101	67	46	4	7	25	23	1.636	5.38	63	....	.305	1	.031	-18	0	-2.0
	StL-a	1	1	.500	3	3	2	0	0	24	19	13	9	0	0	10	13	1.208	3.38	125	....	.210	4	.364	2	2	0.3
1892	Cin-N	2	5	.286	9	7	5	0	0	68	55	37	27	3	3	26	21	1.191	3.57	91	2.71	.213	3	.111	-4	4	-0.4
	Was-N	3	11	.214	18	15	13	1	2	127	102	59	34	6	6	45	48	1.157	2.41	135	2.62	.211	6	.120	12	9	0.9
	Yr.	5	16	.238	27	22	18	1	2	195	157	96	61	9	9	71	69	1.169	2.82	116	2.65	.212	9	.117	9	13	0.6
1893	Was-N	4	10	.286	17	15	9	0	0	117	182	137	98	8	9	56	20	2.034	7.54	61	7.71	.345	13	.277	-35	1	-2.7
Total	5	59	67	.468	143	130	104	5	3	1088	1101	669	417	41	49	349	416	1.333	3.45	110	1.30	.254	86	.201	28	76	3.0
• DUSAK, Erv	Ervin Frank "Four Sack" Dusak b: 7/29/1920, Chicago, IL d: 11/6/1994, Glendale Heights, IL BR/TR, 6'2", 185 lbs. Deb: 9/18/1941 ♦																										
1948	StL-N	0	0	....	1	0	0	0	0	1	0	0	0	0	0	1	0	1.000	0.00	....	0.80	.000	65	.209	0	7	-1.5
1950	StL-N	0	2	.000	14	2	0	0	1	36^{1}	27	17	15	2	1	27	16	1.486	3.72	116	3.53	.211	1	.083	3	2	0.1
1951	StL-N	0	0	....	5	0	0	0	0	10	14	8	8	0	0	7	8	2.100	7.20	55	6.75	.333	1	.500	-4	0	-0.2
	Pit-N	0	1	.000	3	1	0	0	0	6^{2}	10	10	9	2	1	9	2	2.850	12.15	35	14.22	.357	12	.308	-6	1	-0.6
	Yr.	0	1	.000	8	1	0	0	0	16^{2}	24	18	17	2	1	16	10	2.400	9.18	45	9.74	.343	13	.317	-10	1	-0.9
Total	3	0	3	.000	23	3	0	0	1	54	51	35	32	4	2	44	26	1.759	5.33	79	5.40	.258	251	.243	-6	10	-2.3
• DUSER, Carl	Carl Robert Duser b: 7/22/1932, Hazleton, PA BL/TL, 6'1", 175 lbs. Deb: 9/15/1956																										
1956	KC-A	1	1	.500	2	2	0	0	0	6	14	6	6	0	0	2	5	2.667	9.00	48	11.63	.452	0	.000	-3	0	-0.4
1958	KC-A	0	0	....	1	0	0	0	0	2	5	1	1	0	0	1	0	3.000	4.50	87	12.01	.500	0	....	-0	0	0.0
Total	2	1	1	.500	3	2	0	0	0	8	19	7	7	0	0	3	5	2.750	7.88	54	11.72	.463	0	.000	-3	0	-0.4
• DUSTAL, Bob	Robert Andrew Dustal b: 9/28/1935, Sayreville, NJ BR/TR, 6', 172 lbs. Deb: 4/9/1963																										
1963	Det-A	0	1	.000	7	0	0	0	0	6	10	9	6	0	0	5	4	2.500	9.00	42	8.06	.357	0	....	-4	0	-0.4
• DUVALL, Mike	Michael Alan Duvall b: 10/11/1974, Warrenton, VA BR/TL, 6', 200 lbs. Deb: 9/22/1998																										
1998	TB-A	0	0	....	3	0	0	0	0	4	4	3	3	0	0	2	1	1.500	6.75	71	3.88	.267	0	....	-1	0	-0.1
1999	TB-A	1	1	.500	40	0	0	0	0	40	46	21	18	5	2	27	18	1.825	4.05	123	6.56	.293	0	....	4	3	0.4
2000	TB-A	0	0	....	2	0	0	0	0	2^{1}	5	2	2	0	0	1	0	2.571	7.71	64	11.29	.455	0	....	-1	0	-0.1
2001	Min-A	0	0	....	8	0	0	0	0	4^{2}	7	4	4	1	0	2	4	1.929	7.71	60	8.42	.368	0	....	-2	0	-0.2
Total	4	1	1	.500	53	0	0	0	0	51	62	30	27	6	2	32	23	1.843	4.76	103	6.73	.307	0	....	1	3	0.1

YEAR	TM-L	W	L	PCT	G	GS	CG	SH	SV	IP	H	R	ER	HR	HB	BB	SO	RAT	ERA	ERA+	CERA	OAV	BH	AVG	PR+	WS	TPW
• DUZEN, Bill	William George Duzen b: 2/21/1870, Buffalo, NY d: 3/11/1944, Buffalo, NY BR/TR, 5'11", 165 lbs. Deb: 9/21/1890																										
1890	Buf-P	0	2	.000	2	2	2	0	0	13	20	24	20	2	0	14	5	2.615	13.85	30	....	.338	1	.250	-14	0	-1.0
• DWYER, Frank	John Francis Dwyer b: 3/25/1868, Lee, MA d: 2/4/1943, Pittsfield, MA BR/TR, 5'8", 145 lbs. Deb: 9/20/1888 M																										
1888	Chi-N	4	1	.800	5	5	5	1	0	42	32	20	5	1	0	9	17	.976	1.07	281	....	.203	4	.190	8	4	0.8
1889	Chi-N	16	13	.552	32	30	27	0	0	276	307	177	110	14	7	72	63	1.373	3.59	116	....	.273	27	.200	16	16	1.1
1890	Chi-P	3	6	.333	12	6	6	0	1	69^1	98	71	48	4	0	25	17	1.774	6.23	70	....	.319	14	.264	-15	2	-1.3
1891	Cin-a	13	19	.406	35	31	29	1	0	289	332	225	145	10	10	124	101	1.578	4.52	91	....	.279	40	.284	-14	16	-0.8
	Mil-a	6	4	.600	10	10	10	0	0	86	92	41	21	2	4	21	27	1.314	2.20	200	....	.265	9	.225	22	8	1.8
	Yr.	19	23	.452	45	41	39	1	0	375	424	266	166	12	14	145	128	1.517	3.98	104	....	.276	49	.271	8	24	0.9
1892	StL-N	2	8	.200	10	10	6	0	0	64	90	58	40	1	2	24	16	1.781	5.63	57	5.70	.319	2	.080	-15	0	-1.5
	Cin-N	20	10	.667	34	28	25	3	1	268^1	262	101	67	6	5	49	47	1.159	2.25	145	2.68	.246	21	.159	25	26	1.8
	Yr.	22	18	.550	44	38	31	3	1	332^1	352	159	107	7	7	73	63	1.279	2.90	112	3.26	.261	23	.146	10	26	0.3
1893	Cin-N	18	15	.545	37	30	28	1	**2**	287^1	332	187	132	17	7	93	53	1.479	4.13	116	4.37	.281	24	.200	16	22	1.0
1894	Cin-N	19	22	.463	45	39	34	1	1	348	471	282	196	27	15	106	49	1.658	5.07	109	5.56	.320	46	.267	18	23	1.4
1895	Cin-N	18	15	.545	37	31	23	2	0	280^1	355	191	132	10	14	74	46	1.530	4.24	117	4.71	.304	30	.265	22	21	1.9
1896	Cin-N	24	11	.686	36	34	30	3	1	288^2	321	144	101	8	11	60	57	1.320	3.15	146	3.58	.280	29	.264	40	30	3.8
1897	Cin-N	18	13	.581	37	31	22	0	0	247^1	315	142	104	5	11	56	41	1.500	3.78	120	4.46	.308	25	.266	21	23	1.8
1898	Cin-N	16	10	.615	31	28	24	0	0	240	257	117	81	3	16	42	29	1.246	3.04	126	3.21	.272	12	.141	18	21	1.4
1899	Cin-N	0	5	.000	5	5	2	0	0	32^2	48	26	20	1	1	9	2	1.745	5.51	71	5.83	.341	4	.364	-6	1	-0.5
Total	**12**	**177**	**152**	**.538**	**366**	**318**	**271**	**12**	**6**	**2819**	**3312**	**1782**	**1202**	**109**	**103**	**764**	**565**	**1.446**	**3.84**	**115**	**3.08**	**.287**	**287**	**.229**	**155**	**213**	**12.7**
• DYER, Eddie	Edwin Hawley Dyer b: 10/11/1900, Morgan City, LA d: 4/20/1964, Houston, TX BL/TL, 5'11.5", 168 lbs. Deb: 7/8/1922 M ♦																										
1922	StL-N	0	0	....	2	0	0	0	0	3^2	7	2	1	0	0	0	3	1.909	2.45	157	7.34	.412	1	.333	1	1	0.1
1923	StL-N	2	1	.667	4	3	2	1	0	22	30	10	10	0	1	5	7	1.591	4.09	95	4.96	.333	12	.267	-0	3	0.1
1924	StL-N	8	11	.421	29	15	7	1	0	136^2	174	82	70	6	4	51	23	1.646	4.61	82	5.36	.331	18	.237	-13	5	-1.0
1925	StL-N	4	3	.571	27	5	1	0	3	82^1	93	52	38	4	7	24	25	1.421	4.15	104	4.13	.278	3	.097	1	4	-0.1
1926	StL-N	1	0	1.000	6	0	0	0	0	9^1	7	14	12	0	1	14	4	2.250	11.57	34	5.91	.219	1	.500	-8	0	-0.8
1927	StL-N	0	0	....	1	0	0	0	0	2	5	4	4	1	0	2	1	3.500	18.00	22	23.01	.500	0	....	-3	0	-0.3
Total	**6**	**15**	**15**	**.500**	**69**	**23**	**10**	**2**	**3**	**256**	**316**	**164**	**135**	**11**	**13**	**96**	**63**	**1.609**	**4.75**	**83**	**5.12**	**.313**	**35**	**.223**	**-22**	**13**	**-2.0**
• DYER, Mike	Michael Lawrence Dyer b: 9/8/1966, Upland, CA BR/TR, 6'3", 195 lbs. Deb: 6/29/1989																										
1989	Min-A	4	7	.364	16	12	1	0	0	71	74	43	38	2	2	37	37	1.563	4.82	86	4.38	.273	0	....	-5	2	-0.5
1994	Pit-N	1	1	.500	14	0	0	0	4	15^1	15	12	10	1	3	12	13	1.761	5.87	74	5.47	.268	0	.000	-3	1	-0.3
1995	Pit-N	4	5	.444	55	0	0	0	0	74^2	81	40	36	9	5	30	53	1.487	4.34	99	5.01	.281	4	.571	1	5	0.2
1996	Mon-N	5	5	.500	70	1	0	0	2	75^2	79	40	37	7	5	34	51	1.493	4.40	98	4.69	.277	0	.000	-0	5	-0.1
Total	**4**	**14**	**18**	**.438**	**155**	**13**	**1**	**0**	**6**	**236^2**	**249**	**135**	**121**	**19**	**15**	**113**	**154**	**1.530**	**4.60**	**93**	**4.75**	**.277**	**4**	**.267**	**-8**	**13**	**-0.7**
• DYGERT, Jimmy	James Henry "Sunny Jim" Dygert b: 7/5/1884, Utica, NY d: 2/8/1936, New Orleans, LA BR/TR, 5'10", 158 lbs. Deb: 9/8/1905																										
1905	Phi-A	1	4	.200	6	3	2	0	0	35^1	41	20	17	2	2	11	24	1.472	4.33	61	4.45	.292	4	.267	-6	0	-0.6
1906	Phi-A	11	13	.458	35	25	15	4	0	213^2	175	88	64	1	10	91	106	1.245	2.70	101	2.64	.227	13	.176	1	10	0.1
1907	Phi-A	21	8	.724	42	28	18	5	1	261^2	200	98	68	2	18	85	151	1.089	2.34	111	2.15	**.214**	12	.128	6	20	0.3
1908	Phi-A	11	15	.423	41	28	15	5	1	238^2	184	95	76	3	11	97	164	1.177	2.87	89	2.52	.220	6	.080	-3	12	-1.0
1909	Phi-A	9	5	.643	32	13	6	1	0	137^1	117	60	37	1	11	50	79	1.216	2.42	99	3.12	.242	9	.205	-2	6	-0.2
1910	Phi-A	4	4	.500	19	8	6	1	0	99^1	81	44	28	0	3	49	59	1.309	2.54	93	2.89	.231	3	.083	-4	3	-0.6
Total	**6**	**57**	**49**	**.538**	**175**	**105**	**62**	**16**	**2**	**986**	**798**	**405**	**290**	**9**	**55**	**383**	**583**	**1.198**	**2.65**	**97**	**2.64**	**.227**	**47**	**.139**	**-7**	**51**	**-1.9**
• DYKHOFF, Radhames	Radhames Alviro Dykhoff b: 9/27/1974, Paradera, Aruba BL/TL, 6' Deb: 6/7/1998																										
1998	Bal-A	0	0	....	1	0	0	0	0	1	2	2	2	0	0	1	1	3.000	18.00	25	12.01	.400	0	....	-1	0	-0.1
• EARLEY, Arnold	Arnold Carl Earley b: 6/4/1933, Lincoln Park, MI d: 9/29/1999, Flint, MI BL/TL, 6'1", 200 lbs. Deb: 9/27/1960																										
1960	Bos-A	0	1	.000	2	0	0	0	0	4	9	8	7	1	0	4	5	3.250	15.75	26	16.68	.429	0	.000	-5	0	-0.5
1961	Bos-A	2	4	.333	33	0	0	0	7	49^2	42	31	22	3	0	34	44	1.530	3.99	105	3.86	.226	0	.000	1	4	0.0
1962	Bos-A	4	5	.444	38	3	0	0	5	68^1	76	53	44	8	1	46	59	1.785	5.80	71	5.81	.281	2	.200	-13	1	-1.3
1963	Bos-A	3	7	.300	53	4	0	0	1	115^2	124	73	61	13	8	43	97	1.444	4.75	80	4.50	.270	5	.278	-12	3	-1.1
1964	Bos-A	1	1	.500	25	3	1	0	1	50^1	51	17	15	3	1	18	45	1.371	2.68	144	3.74	.266	1	.111	8	4	0.8
1965	Bos-A	0	1	.000	57	0	0	0	0	74^1	79	42	30	5	3	29	47	1.453	3.63	103	4.05	.271	0	.000	2	3	0.2
1966	Chi-N	2	1	.667	13	0	0	0	0	17^2	14	11	7	1	0	9	12	1.302	3.57	103	3.10	.226	0	.000	0	1	0.0
1967	Hou-N	0	0	....	2	0	0	0	0	1^1	5	5	4	1	0	1	1	4.500	27.00	12	38.09	.625	0	....	-3	0	-0.4
Total	**8**	**12**	**20**	**.375**	**223**	**10**	**1**	**0**	**14**	**381^1**	**400**	**240**	**190**	**35**	**13**	**184**	**310**	**1.531**	**4.48**	**87**	**4.64**	**.269**	**8**	**.157**	**-22**	**16**	**-2.2**
• EARLEY, Bill	William Albert Earley b: 1/30/1956, Cincinnati, OH BR/TL, 6'4", 200 lbs. Deb: 9/22/1986																										
1986	StL-N	0	0	....	3	0	0	0	0	3	0	0	0	0	0	2	2	.667	0.00	....	0.46	.000	0	....	1	0	0.1
• EARLEY, Tom	Thomas Francis Aloysius Earley b: 2/19/1917, Boston, MA d: 4/5/1988, Nantucket, MA BR/TR, 6', 180 lbs. Deb: 9/27/1938																										
1938	Bos-N	1	0	1.000	2	1	1	0	0	11	8	9	4	2	1	1	4	.818	3.27	105	2.07	.186	0	.000	0	0	0.0
1939	Bos-N	1	4	.200	14	2	0	0	1	40	49	28	21	1	2	19	9	1.700	4.73	78	5.04	.304	3	.300	-5	0	-0.5
1940	Bos-N	2	0	1.000	4	1	1	1	0	16^1	16	7	7	1	2	3	5	1.163	3.86	96	3.48	.267	2	.400	-1	2	0.1
1941	Bos-N	6	8	.429	33	13	6	1	3	138^2	120	52	39	9	3	46	54	1.197	2.53	141	2.89	.233	11	.234	15	12	1.6
1942	Bos-N	6	11	.353	27	18	6	0	1	112^2	120	65	59	10	1	55	28	1.553	4.71	71	4.66	.276	4	.118	-16	1	-1.8
1945	Bos-N	2	1	.667	11	2	1	0	0	41	36	22	21	4	0	19	4	1.341	4.61	83	3.44	.235	3	.214	-4	2	-0.3
Total	**6**	**18**	**24**	**.429**	**91**	**37**	**15**	**2**	**5**	**359^2**	**349**	**183**	**151**	**27**	**9**	**143**	**104**	**1.368**	**3.78**	**93**	**3.75**	**.256**	**23**	**.202**	**-11**	**17**	**-1.0**
• EARNSHAW, George	George Livingston "Moose" Earnshaw b: 2/15/1900, New York, NY d: 12/1/1976, Little Rock, AR BR/TR, 6'4", 210 lbs. Deb: 6/3/1928 C																										
1928	Phi-A	7	7	.500	26	22	7	3	1	158^1	143	81	67	7	1	100	117	1.535	3.81	105	3.72	.240	14	.246	4	9	0.5
1929*	Phi-A	**24**	8	.750	44	33	13	3	1	254^2	233	110	93	8	5	125	149	1.406	3.29	129	3.37	**.241**	15	.172	26	23	2.2
1930*	Phi-A	22	13	.629	49	**39**	20	**3**	2	296	299	162	146	20	1	139	193	1.480	4.44	105	4.06	.266	26	.228	7	21	0.6
1931*	Phi-A	21	7	.750	43	30	23	3	6	281^2	255	130	115	16	3	75	152	1.172	3.67	122	2.71	.236	30	.263	18	29	2.2
1932	Phi-A	19	13	.594	36	33	21	1	0	245^1	262	147	130	28	4	94	109	1.451	4.77	95	4.41	.270	26	.286	-8	15	-0.4
1933	Phi-A	5	10	.333	21	18	4	0	0	117^2	153	93	78	8	1	58	37	1.793	5.97	72	5.78	.311	8	.182	-19	1	-1.8
1934	Chi-A	14	11	.560	33	30	16	2	0	227	242	128	114	28	4	104	97	1.524	4.52	105	4.75	.270	16	.203	12	15	1.1
1935	Chi-A	1	2	.333	3	3	0	0	0	18	26	19	18	2	0	11	8	2.056	9.00	51	7.67	.342	2	.286	-9	0	-0.8
	Bro-N	8	12	.400	25	22	6	2	0	166	175	87	76	14	0	53	72	1.373	4.12	96	3.84	.270	13	.217	-4	7	-0.4
1936	Bro-N	4	9	.308	19	13	4	1	1	93	113	63	55	7	3	30	40	1.538	5.32	78	4.81	.297	8	.242	-11	2	-1.0
	StL-N	2	1	.667	20	6	1	0	1	57^2	80	43	41	4	3	20	28	1.734	6.40	62	6.07	.333	4	.222	-16	0	-1.6
	Yr.	6	10	.375	39	19	5	1	2	150^2	193	106	96	11	6	50	68	1.613	5.73	71	5.29	.311	12	.235	-27	2	-2.6
Total	**9**	**127**	**93**	**.577**	**319**	**249**	**115**	**18**	**12**	**1915^1**	**1981**	**1063**	**933**	**142**	**25**	**809**	**1002**	**1.457**	**4.38**	**100**	**4.09**	**.265**	**162**	**.230**	**0**	**122**	**0.7**
• EASLEY, Logan	Kenneth Logan Easley b: 11/4/1961, Salt Lake City, UT BR/TR, 6'1", 185 lbs. Deb: 4/9/1987																										
1987	Pit-N	1	1	.500	17	0	0	0	1	26^1	23	17	16	5	1	17	21	1.519	5.47	75	4.87	.242	0	.000	-4	1	-0.5
1989	Pit-N	1	0	1.000	10	0	0	0	1	12^1	8	6	6	1	1	7	6	1.216	4.38	77	2.94	.190	0	.000	-1	1	-0.2
Total	**2**	**2**	**1**	**.667**	**27**	**0**	**0**	**0**	**2**	**38^2**	**31**	**23**	**22**	**6**	**2**	**24**	**27**	**1.422**	**5.12**	**76**	**4.26**	**.226**	**0**	**.000**	**-6**	**2**	**-0.6**
• EASON, Mal	Malcolm Wayne "Kid" Eason b: 3/13/1879, Brookville, PA d: 4/16/1970, Douglas, AZ BR/TR, 6', 175 lbs. Deb: 10/1/1900 U																										
1900	Chi-N	1	0	1.000	1	1	1	0	0	9	9	2	1	0	0	3	2	1.333	1.00	360	3.06	.260	0	.000	3	1	0.2
1901	Chi-N	8	17	.320	27	25	23	1	0	220^2	246	136	88	9	13	60	68	1.387	3.59	90	3.95	.280	12	.138	-6	8	-1.1
1902	Chi-N	1	1	.500	2	2	2	0	0	18	21	7	2	0	0	2	4	1.278	1.00	270	3.45	.291	1	.200	3	1	0.4
	Bos-N	9	12	.429	27	27	20	2	0	213^1	249	100	63	4	12	61	51	1.453	2.66	106	4.11	.291	6	.083	2	10	-0.4
	Yr.	10	13	.435	29	29	22	2	0	231^1	270	107	65	4	12	63	55	1.439	2.53	111	4.06	.291	7	.091	6	11	0.0
1903	Det-A	2	5	.286	7	6	6	1	0	56^1	60	33	21	1	3	19	21	1.402	3.36	87	3.55	.272	2	.100	-3	1	-0.4

YEAR	TM-L	W	L	PCT	G	GS	CG	SH	SV	IP	H	R	ER	HR	HB	BB	SO	RAT	ERA	ERA+	CERA	OAV	BH	AVG	PR+	WS	TPW
1905	Bro-N	5	21	.192	27	27	20	3	0	207	230	128	99	5	5	72	64	1.459	4.30	67	4.16	.292	14	.173	-27	4	-3.1
1906	Bro-N	10	17	.370	34	26	18	3	1	227	212	109	82	1	9	74	64	1.260	3.25	77	3.01	.256	8	.091	-16	6	-2.2
Total	6	36	73	.330	125	114	90	10	1	951^1	1027	515	356	20	42	291	274	1.385	3.37	85	3.77	.279	43	.121	-44	31	-6.7
• EAST, Carl	Carlton William East b: 8/27/1894, Marietta, GA d: 1/15/1953, Whitesburg, GA BL/TR, 6'2", 178 lbs. Deb: 8/24/1915 ♦																										
1915	StL-A	0	0	....	1	1	0	0	0	3^1	6	6	6	0	0	2	1	2.400	16.20	18	9.16	.400	0	.000	-5	0	-0.5
• EAST, Hugh	Gordon Hugh East b: 7/7/1919, Birmingham, AL d: 11/2/1981, Charleston, SC BR/TR, 6'2", 185 lbs. Deb: 9/13/1941																										
1941	NY-N	1	1	.500	2	2	0	0	0	15^2	19	12	6	0	0	9	4	1.787	3.45	107	4.98	.297	2	.222	0	1	0.1
1942	NY-N	0	2	.000	4	1	0	0	0	7^1	15	16	8	1	0	7	2	3.000	9.82	34	12.95	.429	1	.500	-5	1	-0.4
1943	NY-N	1	3	.250	13	5	1	0	0	40^1	51	27	24	4	0	25	21	1.884	5.36	64	6.24	.298	1	.077	-8	0	-1.0
Total	3	2	6	.250	19	8	1	0	0	63^1	85	55	38	5	0	41	27	1.989	5.40	64	6.71	.315	4	.167	-13	2	-1.3
• EASTERLY, Jamie	James Morris Easterly b: 2/17/1953, Houston, TX BL/TL, 5'9", 180 lbs. Deb: 4/6/1974																										
1974	Atl-N	0	0	....	3	0	0	0	0	2^2	6	7	5	0	0	4	0	3.750	16.88	22	15.32	.400	0	....	-4	0	-0.4
1975	Atl-N	2	9	.182	21	13	0	0	0	68^2	73	47	38	5	2	42	34	1.675	4.98	76	5.08	.275	1	.056	-8	0	-0.9
1976	Atl-N	1	1	.500	4	4	0	0	0	22	23	12	12	0	0	13	11	1.636	4.91	77	4.41	.280	1	.111	-2	1	-0.3
1977	Atl-N	2	4	.333	22	5	0	0	1	58^2	72	46	40	5	3	30	37	1.739	6.14	72	5.82	.303	4	.267	-9	1	-0.8
1978	Atl-N	3	6	.333	37	6	0	0	1	78	91	52	49	9	2	45	42	1.744	5.65	72	6.02	.299	4	.211	-13	1	-1.3
1979	Atl-N	0	0	....	4	0	0	0	0	2^2	7	6	4	0	0	3	3	3.750	13.50	30	17.25	.467	0	....	-3	0	-0.3
1981*	Mil-A	3	3	.500	44	0	0	0	4	62	46	23	22	0	0	34	31	1.290	3.19	107	2.57	.219	0	....	1	5	0.1
1982	Mil-A	0	2	.000	28	0	0	0	2	30^2	39	19	16	6	0	15	16	1.761	4.70	81	6.88	.312	0	....	-4	0	-0.4
1983	Mil-A	0	1	.000	12	0	0	0	1	11^2	14	7	5	0	2	10	6	2.057	3.86	97	7.25	.350	0	.000	-0	0	0.0
	Cle-A	4	2	.667	41	0	0	0	3	57	69	25	23	4	2	22	39	1.596	3.63	117	5.20	.309	0	....	4	5	0.4
	Yr.	4	3	.571	53	0	0	0	4	68^2	83	32	28	4	4	32	45	1.675	3.67	113	5.55	.316	0	.000	4	5	0.4
1984	Cle-A	3	1	.750	26	1	0	0	2	69^1	74	31	26	3	1	23	42	1.399	3.38	121	3.75	.273	0	....	5	5	0.5
1985	Cle-A	4	1	.800	50	7	0	0	0	98^2	96	52	43	9	4	53	58	1.510	3.92	105	4.54	.264	0	....	3	5	0.3
1986	Cle-A	0	2	.000	13	0	0	0	0	17^2	27	16	15	3	0	12	9	2.208	7.64	54	9.31	.365	0	....	-7	0	-0.7
1987	Cle-A	1	1	.500	16	0	0	0	0	31^2	26	17	16	4	1	13	22	1.232	4.55	99	3.26	.218	0	....	0	2	0.0
Total	13	23	33	.411	321	36	0	0	14	611^1	663	360	314	48	17	319	350	1.606	4.62	87	5.02	.283	10	.161	-36	25	-3.8
• EASTON, Jack	John S. Easton b: 2/28/1867, Bridgeport, OH d: 11/28/1903, Steubenville, OH Deb: 9/23/1889 U																										
1889	Col-a	1	0	1.000	4	1	1	0	1	18	13	8	7	0	3	21	7	1.889	3.50	103	....	.196	0	.000	0	1	-0.1
1890	Col-a	15	14	.517	37	29	23	0	1	255^2	213	148	100	4	20	125	147	1.322	3.52	102	....	.220	19	.178	-8	15	-0.8
1891	Col-a	5	10	.333	18	16	13	0	0	135^1	145	111	68	3	15	59	52	1.507	4.52	76	....	.265	15	.238	-20	0	-1.7
	StL-a	3	2	.600	7	6	4	0	0	47^2	48	38	27	3	4	23	22	1.490	5.10	82	....	.253	5	.179	-5	2	-0.5
	Col-a	0	2	.000	2	2	2	0	0	15	15	8	6	2	2	4	13	1.267	3.60	96	....	.252	0	.000	-1	5	-0.2
	Yr.	8	14	.364	27	24	19	0	0	198	208	157	101	8	21	86	87	1.485	4.59	79	....	.261	20	.196	-26	7	-2.5
1892	StL-N	2	0	1.000	5	2	2	0	0	31	38	31	22	2	3	26	4	2.065	6.39	50	7.06	.290	3	.176	-10	0	-1.0
1894	Pit-N	0	1	.000	3	1	1	0	0	19^2	26	16	9	0	3	4	1	1.525	4.12	127	4.89	.315	0	.000	2	1	0.1
Total	5	26	29	.473	76	57	46	0	2	522^1	498	360	239	14	50	262	246	1.455	4.12	88	0.60	.243	42	.176	-41	24	-4.2
• EASTWICK, Rawly	Rawlins Jackson Eastwick b: 10/24/1950, Camden, NJ BR/TR, 6'3", 180 lbs. Deb: 9/12/1974																										
1974	Cin-N	0	0	....	8	0	0	0	2	17^2	12	5	4	1	0	5	14	.962	2.04	171	1.71	.188	0	.000	3	2	0.2
1975*	Cin-N	5	3	.625	58	0	0	0	**22**	90	77	26	26	6	2	25	61	1.133	2.60	138	2.66	.229	1	.067	7	13	0.6
1976*	Cin-N	11	5	.688	71	0	0	0	**26**	107^2	93	30	25	3	2	27	70	1.115	2.09	168	2.36	.232	0	.000	16	17	1.5
1977	Cin-N	2	2	.500	23	0	0	0	7	43^1	40	14	14	3	0	8	17	1.108	2.91	135	2.68	.244	1	.167	5	5	0.4
	StL-N	3	7	.300	41	1	0	0	4	53^2	74	34	28	6	0	21	30	1.770	4.70	82	6.34	.332	2	.400	-6	1	-0.5
	Yr.	5	9	.357	64	1	0	0	11	97	114	48	42	9	0	29	47	1.474	3.90	99	4.71	.295	3	.273	-1	6	0.0
1978	NY-A	2	1	.667	8	0	0	0	0	24^2	22	9	9	2	1	4	13	1.054	3.28	110	2.59	.232	0	....	1	2	0.1
*	Phi-N	2	1	.667	22	0	0	0	0	40^1	31	21	18	5	0	18	14	1.215	4.02	89	3.03	.209	0	.000	-3	2	-0.3
1979	Phi-N	3	6	.333	51	0	0	0	6	82^2	90	46	45	8	1	25	47	1.391	4.90	78	4.25	.284	0	.000	-11	3	-1.2
1980	KC-A	0	1	.000	14	0	0	0	0	22	37	14	13	2	2	8	5	2.045	5.32	76	7.99	.363	0	....	-3	0	-0.3
1981	Chi-N	0	1	.000	30	0	0	0	1	43^1	43	16	11	2	0	15	24	1.338	2.28	162	3.37	.264	0	.000	8	4	0.8
Total	8	28	27	.509	326	1	0	0	68	525^1	519	215	193	38	8	156	295	1.285	3.31	113	3.50	.258	4	.071	16	49	1.4
• EATON, Adam	Adam Thomas Eaton b: 11/23/1977, Seattle, WA BR/TR, 6'2", 190 lbs. Deb: 5/30/2000																										
2000	SD-N	7	4	.636	22	22	0	0	0	135	134	63	62	14	2	61	90	1.444	4.13	104	4.34	.260	11	.289	1	9	0.7
2001	SD-N	8	5	.615	17	17	2	0	0	116^2	108	61	56	20	5	40	109	1.269	4.32	93	4.01	.241	4	.105	-2	5	-0.2
2002	SD-N	1	1	.500	6	6	0	0	0	33^1	28	20	20	5	2	17	25	1.350	5.40	70	4.28	.235	1	.111	-6	0	-0.6
2003	SD-N	9	12	.429	31	31	1	0	0	183	173	91	83	20	7	68	146	1.317	4.08	96	3.78	.246	11	.196	-2	7	0.3
Total	4	25	22	.532	76	76	3	0	0	468	443	235	221	59	16	186	370	1.344	4.25	95	4.03	.248	27	.191	-9	21	0.2
• EATON, Craig	Craig Eaton b: 9/7/1954, Cincinnati, OH BR/TR, 5'11", 175 lbs. Deb: 9/5/1979																										
1979	KC-A	0	0	....	5	0	0	0	0	10	8	3	3	0	0	3	4	1.100	2.70	158	1.73	.222	0	....	2	1	0.2
• EATON, Zeb	Zebulon Vance "Red" Eaton b: 2/2/1920, Cooleemee, NC d: 12/17/1989, West Palm Beach, FL BR/TR, 5'10", 185 lbs. Deb: 4/18/1944																										
1944	Det-A	0	0	....	6	0	0	0	0	15^2	19	12	10	2	0	8	4	1.723	5.74	62	6.26	.322	1	.100	-4	0	-0.4
1945*	Det-A	4	2	.667	17	3	0	0	0	53^1	48	28	24	0	3	40	15	1.650	4.05	87	4.22	.247	8	.250	-3	3	-0.2
Total	2	4	2	.667	23	3	0	0	0	69	67	40	34	2	3	48	19	1.667	4.43	80	4.68	.265	9	.214	-7	3	-0.6
• EAVE, Gary	Gary Louis Eave b: 7/22/1963, Monroe, LA BR/TR, 6'4", 200 lbs. Deb: 4/12/1988																										
1988	Atl-N	0	0	....	5	0	0	0	0	5	7	5	5	0	0	3	0	2.000	9.00	41	6.56	.333	0	....	-3	0	-0.3
1989	Atl-N	2	0	1.000	3	3	0	0	0	20^2	15	3	3	0	1	12	9	1.306	1.31	279	2.77	.200	0	.000	6	3	0.5
1990	Sea-A	0	3	.000	8	5	0	0	0	30	27	16	14	5	2	20	16	1.567	4.20	94	5.38	.241	0	....	-1	1	-0.1
Total	3	2	3	.400	16	8	0	0	0	55^2	49	24	22	5	3	35	25	1.509	3.56	108	4.52	.236	0	.000	2	4	0.1
• EAVES, Vallie	Vallie Ennis "Chief,Tom" Eaves b: 9/6/1911, Allen, OK d: 4/19/1960, Norman, OK BR/TR, 6'2.5", 180 lbs. Deb: 9/12/1935																										
1935	Phi-A	1	2	.333	3	3	1	0	0	14	12	9	8	0	0	15	6	1.929	5.14	88	4.68	.240	0	.000	-1	1	-0.1
1939	Chi-A	0	1	.000	2	1	1	0	0	11^2	11	7	6	1	1	8	5	1.629	4.63	102	4.87	.250	2	.333	0	1	0.0
1940	Chi-A	0	2	.000	5	3	0	0	0	18^2	22	16	14	2	1	24	11	2.464	6.75	65	9.00	.301	0	.000	-5	0	-0.6
1941	Chi-N	3	3	.500	12	7	4	0	0	58^2	56	27	23	4	3	21	24	1.313	3.53	99	3.62	.253	2	.100	1	3	0.0
1942	Chi-N	0	0	....	2	0	0	0	0	3	4	3	3	0	1	2	0	2.000	9.00	36	7.17	.308	0	....	-2	0	-0.2
Total	5	4	8	.333	24	14	6	0	0	106	105	62	54	7	6	70	46	1.651	4.58	86	4.94	.262	4	.114	-6	5	-0.9
• EAYRS, Eddie	Edwin Eayrs b: 11/10/1890, Blackstone, MA d: 11/30/1969, Warwick, RI BL/TL, 5'7", 160 lbs. Deb: 6/30/1913 ♦																										
1913	Pit-N	0	0	....	2	0	0	0	0	8	8	6	2	0	0	6	5	1.750	2.25	134	4.60	.267	1	.167	1	0	0.1
1920	Bos-N	1	2	.333	7	3	0	0	0	26^1	36	18	16	1	2	12	7	1.823	5.47	56	6.40	.346	80	.328	-7	11	0.3
1921	Bos-N	0	0	....	2	0	0	0	0	4^2	9	10	9	0	0	9	1	3.857	17.36	21	14.98	.391	1	.067	-7	0	-0.9
Total	3	1	2	.333	11	3	0	0	0	39	53	34	27	1	2	27	13	2.051	6.23	52	7.06	.338	83	.306	-14	11	-0.5
• EBERT, Derrin	Derrin Lee Ebert b: 8/21/1976, Anaheim, CA BR/TL, 6'3", 200 lbs. Deb: 4/6/1999																										
1999	Atl-N	0	1	.000	5	0	0	0	1	8	9	5	5	2	0	5	4	1.750	5.63	80	7.17	.300	0	.000	-1	0	-0.1
• ECCLES, Harry	Harry Josiah "Bugs" Eccles b: 7/9/1893, Kennedy, NY d: 6/2/1955, Jamestown, NY BL/TL, 6'2", 170 lbs. Deb: 9/13/1915																										
1915	Phi-A	0	1	.000	5	1	0	0	1	21	18	16	11	2	0	6	13	1.143	4.71	62	2.98	.240	1	.167	-4	0	-0.5
• ECKENSTAHLER, Eric	Eric Ryan Eckenstahler b: 12/17/1976, Waukegan, IL BL/TL, 6'7", 220 lbs. Deb: 9/9/2002																										
2002	Det-A	1	0	1.000	7	0	0	0	0	8	14	5	5	1	0	2	13	2.000	5.63	77	8.30	.378	0	....	-1	0	-0.1
2003	Det-A	0	0	....	20	0	0	0	0	15^2	9	6	5	0	2	15	12	1.532	2.87	150	3.44	.167	0	....	2	1	0.2
Total	2	1	0	1.000	27	0	0	0	0	23^2	23	11	10	1	2	17	25	1.690	3.80	113	5.08	.253	0	....	1	1	0.1

YEAR	TM-L	W	L	PCT	G	GS	CG	SH	SV	IP	H	R	ER	HR	HB	BB	SO	RAT	ERA	ERA+	CERA	OAV	BH	AVG	PR+	WS	TPW
• ECKERSLEY, Dennis	Dennis Lee Eckersley b: 10/3/1954, Oakland, CA BR/TR, 6'2", 190 lbs. Deb: 4/12/1975 HOF: 2004																										
1975	Cle-A	13	7	.650	34	24	6	2	2	186^2	147	61	54	16	7	90	152	1.270	2.60	145	3.19	.215	0	....	23	17	2.4
1976	Cle-A	13	12	.520	36	30	9	3	1	199^1	155	82	76	13	5	78	200	1.169	3.43	102	2.72	.214	0	....	1	11	0.1
1977	Cle-A★	14	13	.519	33	33	12	3	0	247^1	214	100	97	31	7	54	191	1.084	3.53	112	2.85	.231	0	....	11	18	1.1
1978	Bos-A	20	8	.714	35	35	16	3	0	268^1	258	99	89	30	7	71	162	1.226	2.99	138	3.47	.251	0	....	32	24	3.2
1979	Bos-A	17	10	.630	33	33	17	2	0	246^2	234	89	82	29	6	59	150	1.188	2.99	**147**	3.37	.250	0	....	**41**	**24**	**4.0**
1980	Bos-A	12	14	.462	30	30	8	0	0	197^2	188	101	94	25	2	44	121	1.174	4.28	99	3.26	.248	0	....	-2	10	-0.2
1981	Bos-A	9	8	.529	23	23	8	2	0	154	160	82	73	9	3	35	79	1.266	4.27	91	3.38	.267	0	....	-4	6	-0.4
1982	Bos-A★	13	13	.500	33	33	11	3	0	224^1	228	101	93	31	2	43	127	1.208	3.73	115	3.63	.261	0	....	19	17	1.9
1983	Bos-A	9	13	.409	28	28	2	0	0	176^1	223	119	110	27	6	39	77	1.486	5.61	77	5.31	.303	0	....	-24	3	-2.4
1984	Bos-A	4	4	.500	9	9	2	0	0	64^2	71	38	36	10	1	13	33	1.299	5.01	83	4.28	.284	0	....	-4	3	-0.4
	*Chi-N	10	8	.556	24	24	2	0	0	160^1	152	59	54	11	4	36	81	1.173	3.03	129	2.94	.250	6	.109	18	13	1.6
1985	Chi-N	11	7	.611	25	25	6	2	0	169^1	145	61	58	15	3	19	117	.969	3.08	129	2.23	.229	7	.125	19	15	2.1
1986	Chi-N	6	11	.353	33	32	1	0	0	201	226	109	102	21	3	43	137	1.338	4.57	88	4.07	.285	11	.159	-8	8	-0.7
1987	Oak-A	6	8	.429	54	2	0	0	16	115^2	99	41	39	11	3	17	113	1.003	3.03	136	2.40	.228	0	....	15	13	1.5
1988*	Oak-A★	4	2	.667	60	0	0	0	**45**	72^2	52	20	19	5	1	11	70	.867	2.35	161	1.62	.198	0	....	11	15	1.1
1989*	Oak-A	4	0	1.000	51	0	0	0	33	57^2	32	10	10	5	1	3	55	.607	1.56	236	1.03	.162	0	....	13	14	1.3
1990*	Oak-A★	4	2	.667	63	0	0	0	48	73^1	41	9	5	2	0	4	73	.614	0.61	605	0.83	.160	0	....	24	19	2.4
1991	Oak-A★	5	4	.556	67	0	0	0	43	76	60	26	25	11	1	9	87	.908	2.96	129	2.15	.208	0	....	7	14	0.7
1992*	Oak-A★	7	1	.875	69	0	0	0	**51**	80	62	17	17	5	1	11	93	.913	1.91	196	1.73	.211	0	....	16	18	1.6
1993	Oak-A	2	4	.333	64	0	0	0	36	67	67	32	31	7	2	13	80	1.194	4.16	98	3.35	.261	0	....	-0	9	0.0
1994	Oak-A	5	4	.556	45	0	0	0	19	44^1	49	26	21	5	1	13	47	1.398	4.26	104	4.32	.275	0	....	0	5	0.0
1995	Oak-A	4	6	.400	52	0	0	0	29	50^1	53	29	27	5	1	11	40	1.272	4.83	92	3.72	.269	0	....	-2	6	-0.2
1996*	StL-N	0	6	.000	63	0	0	0	30	60	65	26	22	8	4	6	49	1.183	3.30	127	3.77	.274	0	.000	5	8	0.4
1997	StL-N	1	5	.167	57	0	0	0	36	53	49	24	23	9	2	8	45	1.075	3.91	106	3.22	.238	0	....	1	8	0.1
1998*	Bos-A	4	1	.800	50	0	0	0	1	39^2	46	21	21	6	2	8	22	1.361	4.76	99	4.64	.291	0	....	-1	3	-0.1
Total	**24**	**197**	**171**	**.535**	**1071**	**361**	**100**	**20**	**390**	3285^2	**3076**	**1382**	**1278**	**347**	**75**	**738**	**2401**	**1.161**	**3.50**	**116**	**3.18**	**.246**	**24**	**.133**	**209**	**301**	**21.1**
• ECKERT, Al	Albert George "Obbie" Eckert b: 5/17/1906, Milwaukee, WI d: 4/20/1974, Milwaukee, WI BL/TL, 5'10", 174 lbs. Deb: 4/21/1930																										
1930	Cin-N	0	1	.000	2	1	0	0	0	5	7	6	4	0	0	4	1	2.200	7.20	67	6.57	.304	0	.000	-1	0	-0.1
1931	Cin-N	0	1	.000	14	1	0	0	0	18^2	26	20	19	3	0	9	5	1.875	9.16	41	7.06	.325	1	.333	-11	0	-1.1
1935	StL-N	0	0	....	2	0	0	0	0	3	7	4	4	0	0	1	1	2.667	12.00	34	11.15	.467	0	....	-3	0	-0.3
Total	**3**	**0**	**2**	**.000**	**18**	**2**	**0**	**0**	**0**	26^2	**40**	**30**	**27**	**3**	**0**	**14**	**7**	**2.025**	**9.11**	**43**	**7.43**	**.339**	**1**	**.250**	**-15**	**0**	**-1.5**
• ECKERT, Charlie	Charles William "Buzz" Eckert b: 8/8/1897, Philadelphia, PA d: 8/22/1986, Trevose, PA BR/TR, 5'10.5", 165 lbs. Deb: 9/18/1919																										
1919	Phi-A	0	1	.000	2	1	1	0	0	16	17	9	7	1	0	3	6	1.250	3.94	87	3.34	.270	1	.167	-0	0	-0.1
1920	Phi-A	0	0	....	2	0	0	0	0	5^2	8	3	3	0	1	1	1	1.588	4.76	84	6.92	.421	0	.000	-0	0	-0.1
1922	Phi-A	0	2	.000	21	0	0	0	0	50	61	33	26	7	1	23	15	1.680	4.68	91	5.98	.319	1	.091	-2	2	-0.3
Total	**3**	**0**	**3**	**.000**	**25**	**1**	**1**	**0**	**0**	71^2	**86**	**45**	**36**	**8**	**2**	**27**	**22**	**1.577**	**4.52**	**89**	**5.47**	**.315**	**2**	**.111**	**-3**	**2**	**-0.4**
• EDDY, Chris	Christopher Mark Eddy b: 11/27/1969, Dallas, TX BL/TL, 6'3", 200 lbs. Deb: 4/26/1995																										
1995	Oak-A	0	0	....	6	0	0	0	0	3^2	7	3	3	0	2	2	2	2.455	7.36	60	11.78	.438	0	....	-1	0	-0.1
• EDDY, Don	Donald Eugene Eddy b: 10/25/1946, Mason City, IA BR/TL, 5'11", 170 lbs. Deb: 9/7/1970																										
1970	Chi-A	0	0	....	7	0	0	0	0	11^2	10	4	3	0	0	6	9	1.371	2.31	168	3.18	.244	0	....	2	1	0.2
1971	Chi-A	0	2	.000	22	0	0	0	0	22^2	19	6	6	3	0	19	14	1.676	2.38	151	5.02	.232	1	1.000	3	2	0.5
Total	**2**	**0**	**2**	**.000**	**29**	**0**	**0**	**0**	**0**	34^1	**29**	**10**	**9**	**3**	**0**	**25**	**23**	**1.573**	**2.36**	**156**	**4.39**	**.236**	**1**	**1.000**	**6**	**3**	**0.7**
• EDDY, Steve	Steven Allen Eddy b: 8/21/1957, Sterling, IL BR/TR, 6'2", 185 lbs. Deb: 6/13/1979																										
1979	Cal-A	1	1	.500	7	4	0	0	0	32^1	36	19	17	1	2	20	7	1.732	4.73	86	5.28	.290	0	....	-2	1	-0.2
• EDELEN, Ed	Edward Joseph "Doc" Edelen b: 3/16/1912, Bryantown, MD d: 2/1/1982, La Plata, MD BR/TR, 6', 191 lbs. Deb: 8/20/1932																										
1932	Was-A	0	0	....	2	0	0	0	0	1	0	3	3	0	0	6	0	6.000	27.00	16	14.83	.000	0	....	-3	0	-0.2
• EDELEN, Joe	Benny Joe Edelen b: 9/16/1955, Durant, OK BR/TR, 6', 165 lbs. Deb: 4/18/1981																										
1981	StL-N	1	0	1.000	13	0	0	0	0	17^1	29	18	18	2	1	3	10	1.846	9.35	38	7.29	.367	1	.333	-11	0	-1.2
	Cin-N	1	0	1.000	5	0	0	0	0	12^2	5	1	1	1	0	0	5	.395	0.71	500	0.53	.128	0	.000	4	2	0.4
	Yr.	2	0	1.000	18	0	0	0	0	30	34	19	19	3	1	3	15	1.233	5.70	62	4.44	.288	1	.200	-8	2	-0.8
1982	Cin-N	0	0	....	9	0	0	0	0	15^1	22	15	15	2	0	8	11	1.957	8.80	42	7.12	.344	1	.500	-9	0	-0.9
Total	**2**	**2**	**0**	**1.000**	**27**	**0**	**0**	**0**	**0**	45^1	**56**	**34**	**34**	**5**	**1**	**11**	**26**	**1.478**	**6.75**	**54**	**5.34**	**.308**	**2**	**.286**	**-16**	**2**	**-1.7**
• EDELMAN, John	John Rogers Edelman b: 7/27/1935, Philadelphia, PA BR/TR, 6'3", 185 lbs. Deb: 6/2/1955																										
1955	Mil-N	0	0	....	5	0	0	0	0	5^2	7	7	7	0	0	8	3	2.647	11.12	34	8.89	.304	0	....	-5	0	-0.5
• EDEN, Charlie	Charles M. Eden b: 1/18/1855, Lexington, KY d: 9/17/1920, Cincinnati, OH BL/TL, 168 lbs. Deb: 8/17/1877 ♦																										
1884	Pit-a	0	1	.000	2	1	1	0	0	12	12	9	8	1	1	3	3	1.250	6.00	56	....	.247	33	.270	-3	5	-0.2
1885	Pit-a	1	2	.333	4	1	0	0	0	15^2	22	13	9	0	0	3	5	1.596	5.17	62	....	.318	103	.254	-4	8	-1.9
Total	**2**	**1**	**3**	**.250**	**6**	**2**	**1**	**0**	**0**	27^2	**34**	**22**	**17**	**1**	**1**	**6**	**8**	**1.446**	**5.53**	**59**	**....**	**.289**	**244**	**.261**	**-7**	**13**	**-2.1**
• EDENFIELD, Ken	Kenneth Edward Edenfield b: 3/18/1967, Jesup, GA BR/TR, 6'1", 165 lbs. Deb: 5/11/1995																										
1995	Cal-A	0	0	....	7	0	0	0	0	12^2	15	7	6	1	0	5	6	1.579	4.26	110	5.02	.300	0	....	1	1	0.0
1996	Cal-A	0	0	....	2	0	0	0	0	4^1	10	5	5	2	1	2	4	2.769	10.38	47	17.86	.435	0	....	-3	0	-0.2
Total	**2**	**0**	**0**	**....**	**9**	**0**	**0**	**0**	**0**	**17**	**25**	**12**	**11**	**3**	**1**	**7**	**10**	**1.882**	**5.82**	**82**	**8.29**	**.342**	**0**	**....**	**-2**	**1**	**-0.2**
• EDENS, Tom	Thomas Patrick Edens b: 6/9/1961, Ontario, OR BR/TR, 6'3", 188 lbs. Deb: 6/2/1987																										
1987	NY-N	0	0	....	2	2	0	0	0	8	15	6	6	2	0	4	4	2.375	6.75	56	11.59	.417	0	.000	-3	0	-0.3
1990	Mil-A	4	5	.444	35	6	0	0	2	89	89	52	44	8	4	33	40	1.371	4.45	87	3.98	.262	0	....	-5	3	-0.5
1991	Min-A	2	2	.500	8	6	0	0	0	33	34	15	15	2	0	10	19	1.333	4.09	104	3.46	.256	0	....	0	2	0.0
1992	Min-A	6	3	.667	52	0	0	0	3	76^1	65	26	24	1	2	36	57	1.323	2.83	143	3.07	.236	0	....	10	8	1.0
1993	Hou-N	1	1	.500	38	0	0	0	0	49	47	17	17	4	0	19	21	1.347	3.12	124	3.56	.263	0	.000	4	4	0.4
1994	Hou-N	4	1	.800	39	0	0	0	1	50	55	25	25	3	2	17	38	1.440	4.50	88	4.24	.289	0	.000	-3	3	-0.4
	Phi-N	1	0	1.000	3	0	0	0	0	4	4	1	1	0	0	1	1	1.250	2.25	191	2.77	.267	0	....	1	1	0.1
	Yr.	5	1	.833	42	0	0	0	1	54	59	26	26	3	2	18	39	1.426	4.33	92	4.13	.288	0	.000	-2	4	-0.3
1995	Chi-N	1	0	1.000	5	0	0	0	0	3	6	3	2	0	0	3	2	3.000	6.00	68	12.01	.400	0	....	-1	0	-0.1
Total	**7**	**19**	**12**	**.613**	**182**	**14**	**0**	**0**	**6**	312^1	**315**	**145**	**134**	**20**	**8**	**123**	**182**	**1.402**	**3.86**	**103**	**3.94**	**.266**	**0**	**.000**	**3**	**21**	**0.3**
• EDGE, Butch	Claude Lee Edge b: 7/18/1956, Houston, TX BR/TR, 6'3", 203 lbs. Deb: 8/13/1979																										
1979	Tor-A	3	4	.429	9	9	1	0	0	51^2	60	32	30	6	1	24	19	1.626	5.23	83	5.31	.283	0	....	-5	2	-0.5
• EDGERTON, Bill	William Albert Edgerton b: 8/16/1941, South Bend, IN BL/TL, 6'2", 185 lbs. Deb: 9/3/1966																										
1966	KC-A	0	1	.000	6	1	0	0	0	8^1	10	3	3	0	0	7	3	2.040	3.24	105	5.70	.303	0	....	0	0	0.0
1967	KC-A	1	0	1.000	7	0	0	0	0	8^1	11	4	2	1	1	3	6	1.680	2.16	147	6.49	.324	0	....	1	1	0.1
1969	Sea-A	0	1	.000	4	0	0	0	0	4	10	7	6	1	1	0	2	2.500	13.50	27	14.69	.455	0	....	-4	0	-0.4
Total	**3**	**1**	**2**	**.333**	**17**	**1**	**0**	**0**	**0**	20^2	**31**	**14**	**11**	**2**	**2**	**10**	**11**	**1.984**	**4.79**	**73**	**7.76**	**.348**	**0**	**....**	**-3**	**1**	**-0.3**
• EDMONDSON, Brian	Brian Christopher Edmondson b: 1/29/1973, Fontana, CA BR/TR, 6'2", 175 lbs. Deb: 4/2/1998																										
1998	Atl-N	0	1	.000	10	0	0	0	0	16^2	14	10	8	2	0	8	8	1.320	4.32	96	3.42	.215	0	.000	-0	0	-0.1
	Fla-N	4	3	.571	43	0	0	0	0	59^1	62	28	25	8	3	29	32	1.534	3.79	108	5.15	.281	0	.000	2	3	0.1
	Yr.	4	4	.500	53	0	0	0	0	76	76	38	33	10	3	37	40	1.487	3.91	105	4.77	.266	0	.000	2	3	0.1

YEAR	TM-L	W	L	PCT	G	GS	CG	SH	SV	IP	H	R	ER	HR	HB	BB	SO	RAT	ERA	ERA+	CERA	OAV	BH	AVG	PR+	WS	TPW
1999	Fla-N	5	8	.385	68	0	0	0	1	94	106	65	61	11	6	44	58	1.596	5.84	75	5.39	.290	4	.364	-15	3	-1.3
Total	**2**	9	12	.429	121	0	0	0	1	170	182	103	94	21	9	81	98	1.547	4.98	86	5.11	.280	4	.174	-13	6	-1.2
• EDMONDSON, George	George Henderson "Big Ed" Edmondson b: 5/18/1896, Waxahachie, TX d: 7/11/1973, Waco, TX BR/TR, 6'1", 179 lbs. Deb: 8/15/1922																										
1922	Cle-A	0	0	....	2	0	0	0	0	2	4	2	2	0	0	0	0	2.000	9.00	44	8.38	.444	0	....	-1	0	-0.1
1923	Cle-A	0	0	....	1	0	0	0	0	4	8	5	5	0	1	3	0	2.750	11.25	35	12.74	.444	0	.000	-3	0	-0.3
1924	Cle-A	0	0	....	5	1	0	0	0	8	10	8	8	1	0	5	3	1.875	9.00	47	6.36	.294	1	.333	-4	0	-0.4
Total	**3**	0	0	....	8	1	0	0	0	14	22	15	15	1	1	8	3	2.143	9.64	43	8.47	.360	1	.250	-8	0	-0.8
• EDMONDSON, Paul	Paul Michael Edmondson b: 2/12/1943, Kansas City, KS d: 2/13/1970, Santa Barbara, CA BR/TR, 6'5", 195 lbs. Deb: 6/20/1969																										
1969	Chi-A	1	6	.143	14	13	1	0	0	87^2	72	36	36	5	4	39	46	1.266	3.70	104	3.10	.227	5	.172	3	5	0.3
• EDMONSTON, Sam	Samuel Sherwood "Big Sam" Edmonston b: 8/30/1883, Washington, DC d: 4/12/1979, Corpus Christi, TX BL/TL, 5'11.5", 185 lbs. Deb: 9/15/1906																										
1907	Was-A	0	0	....	1	0	0	0	0	3	8	3	3	0	0	1	0	3.000	9.00	27	13.56	.488	0	.000	-2	0	-0.3
• EDMUNDSON, Bob	Robert E. Edmundson b: 4/30/1879, Paris, KY d: 8/14/1931, Lawrence, KS BR/TR, 5'11", 185 lbs. Deb: 7/30/1908 ♦																										
1906	Was-A	0	1	.000	2	1	1	0	0	10	10	8	5	0	0	2	0	1.200	4.50	59	2.64	.263	1	.333	-2	0	-0.2
• EDWARDS,	Edwards Deb: 9/11/1875																										
1875	Atl-n	0	1	.000	1	1	0	0	0	2	4	6	1	0	....	0	0	2.000	4.50	26	....	.383	1	.200	-1	....	-0.1
• EDWARDS, Foster	Foster Hamilton "Eddie" Edwards b: 9/1/1903, Holstein, IA d: 1/4/1980, Orleans, MA BR/TR, 6'3", 175 lbs. Deb: 7/2/1925																										
1925	Bos-N	0	0	....	1	0	0	0	0	2	6	5	2	0	0	1	1	3.500	9.00	44	15.59	.545	0	....	-1	0	-0.1
1926	Bos-N	2	0	1.000	3	3	1	0	0	25	20	4	2	0	0	13	4	1.320	0.72	492	2.73	.230	0	.000	8	3	0.7
1927	Bos-N	2	8	.200	29	11	1	0	0	92	95	59	51	2	3	45	37	1.522	4.99	74	3.97	.274	1	.045	-11	1	-1.3
1928	Bos-N	2	1	.667	21	3	2	0	0	49^1	67	36	31	2	2	23	17	1.824	5.66	69	5.82	.327	1	.091	-8	1	-0.9
1930	NY-A	0	0	....	2	0	0	0	0	1^2	5	4	4	0	0	2	1	4.200	21.60	20	20.02	.500	0	....	-3	0	-0.3
Total	**5**	6	9	.400	56	17	4	0	0	170	193	108	90	4	5	84	60	1.629	4.76	80	4.62	.293	2	.048	-15	5	-1.9
• EDWARDS, Jim Joe	James Corbette "Little Joe" Edwards b: 12/14/1894, Banner, MS d: 1/19/1965, Serepta, MS BR/TL, 6'2", 185 lbs. Deb: 5/14/1922																										
1922	Cle-A	3	8	.273	25	7	0	0	0	92^2	113	56	46	1	5	40	44	1.651	4.47	89	4.76	.313	2	.087	-3	4	-0.5
1923	Cle-A	10	10	.500	38	21	7	1	1	179^1	200	101	74	5	5	75	68	1.533	3.71	107	4.20	.286	7	.119	7	9	0.2
1924	Cle-A	4	3	.571	10	7	5	1	0	57	64	29	18	3	0	34	15	1.719	2.84	150	5.14	.305	3	.150	10	4	0.8
1925	Cle-A	0	3	.000	13	3	1	0	0	36	60	44	33	0	1	23	12	2.306	8.25	54	8.02	.382	1	.111	-15	0	-1.5
	Chi-A	1	2	.333	9	4	1	1	0	45^1	46	25	20	4	1	23	20	1.522	3.97	105	4.41	.263	3	.176	1	2	0.0
	Yr.	1	5	.167	22	7	2	1	0	81^1	106	69	53	4	2	46	32	1.869	5.86	74	6.00	.319	4	.154	-14	2	-1.5
1926	Chi-A	6	9	.400	32	16	8	3	1	142	140	76	66	4	1	63	41	1.430	4.18	92	3.57	.264	5	.109	-6	6	-1.0
1928	Cin-N	2	2	.500	18	1	0	0	2	32	43	29	27	1	0	20	11	1.969	7.59	52	6.34	.347	3	.300	-13	0	-1.2
Total	**6**	26	37	.413	145	59	22	6	4	584^1	666	360	284	18	13	278	211	1.616	4.37	92	4.59	.295	24	.130	-20	25	-3.2
• EDWARDS, Sherman	Sherman Stanley Edwards b: 7/25/1909, Mount Ida, AR d: 3/8/1992, El Dorado, AR BR/TR, 6', 165 lbs. Deb: 9/21/1934																										
1934	Cin-N	0	0	....	1	0	0	0	0	3	4	1	1	0	0	1	1	1.667	3.00	136	5.14	.333	0	.000	0	0	0.0
• EDWARDS, Wayne	Wayne Maurice Edwards b: 3/7/1964, Burbank, CA BL/TL, 6'5", 185 lbs. Deb: 9/11/1989																										
1989	Chi-A	0	0	....	7	0	0	0	0	7^1	7	3	3	1	0	3	9	1.364	3.68	103	4.33	.269	0	....	0	0	0.0
1990	Chi-A	5	3	.625	42	5	0	0	2	95	81	39	34	6	3	41	63	1.284	3.22	119	3.29	.234	0	....	4	7	0.4
1991	Chi-A	0	2	.000	13	0	0	0	0	23^1	22	14	10	2	0	17	12	1.671	3.86	103	4.73	.259	0	....	-0	1	0.0
Total	**3**	5	5	.500	62	5	0	0	2	125^2	110	56	47	9	3	61	84	1.361	3.37	114	3.62	.241	0	....	4	8	0.4
• EELLS, Harry	Harry Archibald "Slippery" Eells b: 2/14/1881, Ida Grove, IA d: 10/15/1940, Los Angeles, CA BR/TR, 6'1", 195 lbs. Deb: 4/22/1906																										
1906	Cle-A	4	5	.444	14	8	6	1	0	86^1	77	39	25	1	3	48	35	1.448	2.61	101	3.42	.242	6	.188	-2	4	-0.1
• EGAN, Dick	Richard Wallis Egan b: 3/24/1937, Berkeley, CA BL/TL, 6'4", 193 lbs. Deb: 4/9/1963 C																										
1963	Det-A	0	1	.000	20	0	0	0	0	21	25	12	12	4	0	3	16	1.333	5.14	73	4.58	.287	0	....	-3	0	-0.3
1964	Det-A	0	0	....	23	0	0	0	2	34^1	33	22	17	4	1	17	21	1.456	4.46	82	4.22	.246	0	.000	-3	1	-0.4
1966	Cal-A	0	0	....	11	0	0	0	0	14^1	17	7	7	2	0	6	11	1.605	4.40	76	5.43	.309	0	.000	-2	0	-0.2
1967	LA-N	1	1	.500	20	0	0	0	0	31^2	34	25	22	3	4	15	20	1.547	6.25	50	4.91	.272	0	.000	-11	0	-1.2
Total	**4**	1	2	.333	74	0	0	0	2	101^1	109	66	58	13	5	41	68	1.480	5.15	66	4.68	.272	0	.000	-19	1	-2.1
• EGAN, Jim	James K. "Troy Terrier" Egan b: 1858, Derby, CT d: 9/26/1884, New Haven, CT TL Deb: 5/15/1882 ♦																										
1882	Tro-N	4	6	.400	12	10	10	0	0	100	133	79	46	2	....	24	20	**1.570**	4.14	68	....	.302	23	.200	-14	3	-2.3
• EGAN, Rip	John Joseph Egan b: 7/9/1871, Philadelphia, PA d: 12/22/1950, Cranston, RI TR, 5'11", 168 lbs. Deb: 4/30/1894 U																										
1894	Was-N	0	0	....	1	0	0	0	0	5	8	6	6	1	0	2	2	2.000	10.80	49	8.54	.357	0	.000	-3	0	-0.3
• EGAN, Wish	Aloysius Jerome Egan b: 6/16/1881, Evart, MI d: 4/13/1951, Detroit, MI BR/TR, 6'3", 185 lbs. Deb: 9/3/1902																										
1902	Det-A	0	2	.000	3	3	2	0	0	22	23	12	7	0	0	6	0	1.318	2.86	127	3.10	.270	2	.250	2	1	0.2
1905	StL-N	6	15	.286	23	19	18	0	0	171^1	189	93	68	2	9	39	29	1.331	3.57	83	4.01	.285	6	.102	-6	5	-0.9
1906	StL-N	2	9	.182	16	12	7	0	0	86^1	97	45	44	3	2	27	23	1.436	4.59	57	3.94	.278	2	.069	-18	0	-2.2
Total	**3**	8	26	.235	42	34	27	0	0	279^2	309	150	119	5	11	72	52	1.362	3.83	75	3.91	.282	10	.104	-22	6	-2.9
• EGLOFF, Bruce	Bruce Edward Egloff b: 4/10/1965, Denver, CO BR/TR, 6'2", 215 lbs. Deb: 4/13/1991																										
1991	Cle-A	0	0	....	6	0	0	0	0	5^2	8	3	3	0	0	4	8	2.118	4.76	87	6.67	.333	0	....	-0	0	0.0
• EHMKE, Howard	Howard Jonathan "Bob" Ehmke b: 4/24/1894, Silver Creek, NY d: 3/17/1959, Philadelphia, PA BR/TR, 6'3", 190 lbs. Deb: 4/12/1915																										
1915	Buf-F	0	2	.000	18	2	0	0	0	53^2	69	46	33	2	5	25	18	1.752	5.53	55	6.04	.325	0	.000	-15	0	-1.8
1916	Det-A	3	1	.750	5	4	4	0	0	37^1	34	16	13	0	0	15	15	1.313	3.13	91	2.99	.252	2	.143	-0	2	-0.1
1917	Det-A	10	15	.400	35	25	13	4	2	206	174	84	68	3	5	88	90	1.272	2.97	89	2.99	.243	17	.246	-4	10	-0.2
1919	Det-A	17	10	.630	33	31	20	2	0	248^2	255	114	88	5	6	107	79	1.456	3.18	100	3.92	.274	23	.253	4	16	0.8
1920	Det-A	15	18	.455	38	33	23	2	3	268^1	250	132	97	8	13	124	98	1.394	3.25	114	3.58	.253	25	.238	19	18	2.1
1921	Det-A	13	14	.481	30	22	13	1	0	196^1	220	123	99	15	13	81	68	1.533	4.54	94	4.74	.286	21	.284	-1	8	0.1
1922	Det-A	17	17	.500	45	29	16	1	1	279^2	299	146	131	12	23	101	108	1.430	4.22	92	4.10	.281	16	.157	-5	14	-0.9
1923	Bos-A	20	17	.541	43	39	28	2	3	316^2	318	155	133	12	20	119	121	1.380	3.78	109	3.84	.272	25	.223	13	25	1.2
1924	Bos-A	19	17	.528	45	36	26	4	4	**315**	324	139	121	9	11	81	119	1.286	3.46	126	3.13	.265	28	.222	36	25	3.2
1925	Bos-A	9	20	.310	34	31	**22**	0	1	260^2	285	141	108	8	11	85	95	1.419	3.73	122	3.89	.285	13	.148	31	14	2.4
1926	Bos-A	3	10	.231	14	14	7	1	0	97^1	115	69	59	3	4	45	38	1.644	5.46	75	4.73	.303	5	.147	-13	1	-1.4
	Phi-A	12	4	.750	20	18	10	1	0	147^1	125	54	46	1	4	50	55	1.188	2.81	148	2.44	.232	7	.152	22	15	2.0
	Yr.	15	14	.517	34	32	17	2	0	244^2	240	123	105	4	8	95	93	1.369	3.86	106	3.35	.261	12	.150	9	16	0.6
1927	Phi-A	12	10	.545	30	27	10	1	0	189^2	200	103	89	13	14	60	68	1.371	4.22	101	4.07	.281	14	.206	3	11	0.1
1928	Phi-A	9	8	.529	23	18	5	1	0	139^1	135	65	56	6	4	44	34	1.285	3.62	111	3.17	.254	11	.239	7	10	0.8
1929*	Phi-A	7	2	.778	11	8	2	0	0	54^2	48	24	20	2	1	15	20	1.152	3.29	128	2.48	.233	2	.105	6	5	0.4
1930	Phi-A	0	1	.000	3	1	0	0	0	10	22	13	13	4	3	2	4	2.400	11.70	40	15.66	.458	1	.333	-8	0	-0.7
Total	**15**	166	166	.500	427	338	199	20	14	2820^2	2873	1424	1174	103	137	1042	1030	1.388	3.75	103	3.76	.270	210	.208	94	174	8.0
• EHRET, Red	Philip Sydney Ehret b: 8/31/1868, Louisville, KY d: 7/28/1940, Cincinnati, OH BR/TR, 6', 175 lbs. Deb: 7/7/1888 U ♦																										
1888	KC-a	3	2	.600	7	6	5	0	0	52	58	30	23	1	3	22	12	1.538	3.98	86	....	.272	12	.190	-3	3	-0.8
1889	Lou-a	10	29	.256	45	38	35	1	0	364	441	287	194	11	18	115	135	1.527	4.80	80	....	.290	65	.252	-33	11	-3.1
1890*	Lou-a	25	14	.641	43	38	35	4	2	359	351	182	101	5	17	79	174	1.198	2.53	152	....	.248	31	.212	50	34	4.3
1891	Lou-a	13	13	.500	26	24	23	2	0	220^2	225	150	85	2	11	70	76	1.337	3.47	105	....	.255	22	.242	3	13	0.4
1892	Pit-N	16	20	.444	39	36	32	0	0	316	290	183	93	7	22	83	101	1.180	2.65	124	2.80	.234	34	.258	13	20	1.5
1893	Pit-N	18	18	.500	39	35	32	**4**	0	314^1	322	203	120	3	23	115	70	1.390	3.44	132	3.60	.257	24	.176	30	24	2.0
1894	Pit-N	19	21	.475	46	38	31	1	0	346^2	441	269	198	12	10	128	102	1.641	5.14	102	5.03	.307	23	.170	4	21	-0.4

YEAR	TM-L	W	L	PCT	G	GS	CG	SH	SV	IP	H	R	ER	HR	HB	BB	SO	RAT	ERA	ERA+	CERA	OAV	BH	AVG	PR+	WS	TPW
1895	StL-N	6	19	.240	37	32	18	0	0	231^2	360	223	155	11	10	88	55	**1.934**	6.02	80	6.97	.349	21	.219	-24	7	-2.1
1896	Cin-N	18	14	.563	34	33	29	2	0	276^2	298	147	105	5	9	74	60	1.345	3.42	135	3.48	.273	20	.196	30	24	2.4
1897	Cin-N	8	10	.444	34	19	11	0	2	184^1	256	135	98	3	13	47	43	1.644	4.78	95	5.30	.326	13	.197	-5	11	-0.6
1898	Lou-N	3	7	.300	12	10	9	0	0	89	130	72	57	3	3	20	20	1.685	5.76	62	5.62	.338	9	.225	-21	1	-1.9
Total	11	139	167	.454	362	309	260	14	4	2754^1	3172	1881	1229	63	139	841	848	1.457	4.02	105	2.84	.282	274	.217	45	169	1.6
• EHRHARDT, Rube	Welton Claude Ehrhardt b: 11/20/1894, Beecher, IL d: 4/27/1980, Chicago, IL BR/TR, 6'2", 190 lbs. Deb: 7/18/1924																										
1924	Bro-N	5	3	.625	15	9	6	2	0	83^2	71	27	21	5	1	17	13	1.052	2.26	166	2.38	.232	4	.138	16	8	1.4
1925	Bro-N	10	14	.417	36	25	12	0	1	207^2	239	134	116	10	3	62	47	1.449	5.03	83	4.09	.293	15	.211	-13	8	-1.1
1926	Bro-N	2	5	.286	44	1	0	0	4	97	101	52	42	5	0	35	25	1.402	3.90	98	3.63	.275	6	.250	1	6	0.1
1927	Bro-N	3	7	.300	46	3	2	0	2	95^2	90	46	38	3	3	37	22	1.328	3.57	111	3.28	.264	6	.250	4	6	0.5
1928	Bro-N	1	3	.250	28	2	1	0	2	54	74	36	28	1	1	27	12	1.870	4.67	85	5.95	.352	4	.286	-4	1	-0.3
1929	Cin-N	1	2	.333	24	1	1	1	1	49^1	58	29	26	2	1	22	9	1.622	4.74	96	4.85	.305	2	.182	-1	2	-0.2
Total	6	22	34	.393	193	41	22	3	10	587^1	633	324	271	26	9	200	128	1.418	4.15	98	3.87	.284	37	.214	3	31	0.5
• EIBEL, Hack	Henry Hack Eibel b: 12/6/1893, Brooklyn, NY d: 10/16/1945, Macon, GA BL/TL, 5'11", 220 lbs. Deb: 6/13/1912 ♦																										
1920	Bos-A	0	0	....	3	0	0	0	0	10^1	10	4	4	0	0	3	5	1.258	3.48	104	3.01	.270	8	.186	0	0	-0.4
• EICHELBERGER, Juan	Juan Tyrone Eichelberger b: 10/21/1953, St. Louis, MO BR/TR, 6'2", 205 lbs. Deb: 9/7/1978																										
1978	SD-N	0	0	....	3	0	0	0	0	3^1	4	4	4	0	0	2	2	1.800	10.80	31	4.76	.267	0	....	-3	0	-0.3
1979	SD-N	1	1	.500	3	3	1	0	0	21	15	10	8	1	0	11	12	1.238	3.43	103	2.77	.211	2	.400	0	1	0.1
1980	SD-N	4	2	.667	15	13	0	0	0	88^2	73	41	36	8	1	55	43	1.444	3.65	94	3.96	.233	3	.111	-3	4	-0.4
1981	SD-N	8	8	.500	25	24	3	1	0	141^1	136	60	55	5	3	74	81	1.486	3.50	93	3.95	.259	4	.087	-4	6	-0.8
1982	SD-N	7	14	.333	31	24	8	0	0	177^2	171	98	83	23	2	72	74	1.368	4.20	81	4.04	.251	5	.091	-17	2	-2.0
1983	Cle-A	4	11	.267	28	15	2	0	0	134	132	80	73	10	2	59	56	1.425	4.90	86	4.03	.259	0	....	-9	4	-0.9
1988	Atl-N	2	0	1.000	20	0	0	0	0	37^1	44	19	16	3	0	10	13	1.446	3.86	95	4.25	.297	0	.000	-0	2	0.0
Total	7	26	36	.419	125	79	14	1	0	603^1	575	312	275	50	8	283	281	1.422	4.10	87	3.98	.254	14	.103	-37	19	-4.2
• EICHHORN, Mark	Mark Anthony Eichhorn b: 11/21/1960, San Jose, CA BR/TR, 6'4", 210 lbs. Deb: 8/30/1982																										
1982	Tor-A	0	3	.000	7	7	0	0	0	38	40	28	23	4	0	14	16	1.421	5.45	82	4.06	.260	0	....	-4	0	-0.4
1986	Tor-A	14	6	.700	69	0	0	0	10	157	105	32	30	8	7	45	166	.955	1.72	245	1.77	.191	0	....	44	21	4.3
1987	Tor-A	10	6	.625	**89**	0	0	0	4	127^2	110	47	45	14	6	52	96	1.269	3.17	142	3.44	.234	0	....	17	12	1.6
1988	Tor-A	0	3	.000	37	0	0	0	1	66^2	79	32	31	3	6	27	28	1.590	4.19	94	5.04	.304	0	....	-2	2	-0.2
1989	Atl-N	5	5	.500	45	0	0	0	0	68^1	70	36	33	6	1	19	49	1.302	4.35	84	3.57	.275	0	.000	-4	3	-0.5
1990	Cal-A	2	5	.286	60	0	0	0	13	84^2	98	36	29	2	6	23	69	1.429	3.08	124	4.15	.289	0	....	7	8	0.7
1991	Cal-A	3	3	.500	70	0	0	0	1	81^2	63	21	18	2	2	13	49	.931	1.98	207	1.74	.219	0	....	18	10	1.8
1992	Cal-A	2	4	.333	42	0	0	0	2	56^2	51	19	15	2	0	18	42	1.218	2.38	167	2.56	.238	0	....	10	6	1.0
	*Tor-A	2	0	1.000	23	0	0	0	0	31	35	15	15	1	2	7	19	1.355	4.35	94	3.85	.285	0	....	-1	2	-0.1
	Yr.	4	4	.500	65	0	0	0	2	87^2	86	34	30	3	2	25	61	1.266	3.08	131	3.01	.255	0	....	9	8	0.9
1993*	Tor-A	3	1	.750	54	0	0	0	0	72^2	76	26	22	3	3	22	47	1.349	2.72	158	3.58	.272	0	....	13	7	1.3
1994	Bal-A	6	5	.545	43	0	0	0	1	71	62	19	17	1	5	19	35	1.141	2.15	232	2.56	.240	0	....	22	10	2.0
1996	Cal-A	1	2	.333	24	0	0	0	0	30^1	36	17	17	3	2	11	24	1.549	5.04	97	5.16	.308	0	....	-0	2	0.0
Total	11	48	43	.527	563	7	0	0	32	885^2	825	328	295	49	40	270	640	1.236	3.00	139	3.17	.249	0	.000	119	83	11.5
• EILAND, Dave	David William Eiland b: 7/5/1966, Dade City, FL BR/TR, 6'3", 205 lbs. Deb: 8/3/1988																										
1988	NY-A	0	0	....	3	3	0	0	0	12^2	15	9	9	6	2	4	7	1.500	6.39	62	8.54	.294	0	....	-3	0	-0.3
1989	NY-A	1	3	.250	6	6	0	0	0	34^1	44	25	22	5	2	13	11	1.660	5.77	67	6.37	.328	0	....	-7	0	-0.7
1990	NY-A	2	1	.667	5	5	0	0	0	30^1	31	14	12	2	0	5	16	1.187	3.56	111	3.00	.254	0	....	1	2	0.1
1991	NY-A	2	5	.286	18	13	0	0	0	72^2	87	51	43	10	3	23	18	1.514	5.33	78	5.43	.302	0	....	-9	1	-0.9
1992	SD-N	0	2	.000	7	7	0	0	0	27	33	21	17	1	0	5	10	1.407	5.67	63	3.88	.287	1	.111	-6	0	-0.6
1993	SD-N	0	3	.000	10	9	0	0	0	48^1	58	33	28	5	1	17	14	1.552	5.21	79	5.08	.297	1	.083	-6	0	-0.6
1995	NY-A	1	1	.500	4	1	0	0	0	10	16	10	7	1	1	3	6	1.900	6.30	73	7.20	.348	0	....	-2	0	-0.2
1998	TB-A	0	1	.000	1	1	0	0	0	2^2	6	6	6	0	0	3	1	3.375	20.25	24	14.42	.429	0	....	-5	0	-0.4
1999	TB-A	4	8	.333	21	15	0	0	0	80^1	98	59	50	8	3	27	53	1.556	5.60	89	5.08	.294	0	.000	-5	2	-0.5
2000	TB-A	2	3	.400	17	10	0	0	0	54^2	77	46	44	8	4	18	17	1.738	7.24	68	6.83	.326	0	....	-15	0	-1.4
Total	10	12	27	.308	92	70	0	0	0	373	465	274	238	46	16	118	153	1.563	5.74	76	5.51	.303	2	.091	-57	5	-5.6
• EILERS, Dave	David Louis Eilers b: 12/3/1936, Oldenburg, TX BR/TR, 5'11", 188 lbs. Deb: 7/27/1964																										
1964	Mil-N	0	0	....	6	0	0	0	0	7^2	11	5	4	1	1	1	1	1.565	4.70	75	5.75	.333	0	....	-1	0	-0.1
1965	Mil-N	0	0	....	6	0	0	0	0	3^2	8	5	5	1	0	0	1	2.182	12.27	29	10.61	.421	0	....	-4	0	-0.4
	NY-N	1	1	.500	11	0	0	0	2	18	20	11	8	2	2	4	9	1.333	4.00	88	4.14	.274	1	1.000	-1	1	0.0
	Yr.	1	1	.500	17	0	0	0	2	21^2	28	16	13	3	2	4	10	1.477	5.40	65	5.23	.304	1	1.000	-4	1	-0.4
1966	NY-N	1	1	.500	23	0	0	0	0	34^2	39	18	18	7	1	7	14	1.327	4.67	78	4.75	.287	0	.000	-4	1	-0.4
1967	Hou-N	6	4	.600	35	0	0	0	1	59^1	68	29	26	3	3	17	27	1.433	3.94	84	4.14	.296	0	.000	-3	2	-0.4
Total	4	8	6	.571	81	0	0	0	3	123^1	146	68	61	14	7	29	52	1.419	4.45	78	4.61	.297	1	.111	-13	4	-1.4
• EINERTSON, Darrell	Darrell Lee Einertson b: 9/4/1972, Rhinelander, WI BR/TR, 6'2", 196 lbs. Deb: 4/15/2000																										
2000	NY-A	0	0	....	11	0	0	0	0	12^2	16	9	5	1	0	4	3	1.579	3.55	136	4.97	.302	0	....	2	1	0.2
• EISCHEN, Joey	Joseph Raymond Eischen b: 5/25/1970, West Covina, CA BL/TL, 6'1", 190 lbs. Deb: 6/19/1994																										
1994	Mon-N	0	0	....	1	0	0	0	0	0^2	4	4	4	0	1	0	1	6.000	54.00	8	47.92	.667	0	....	-4	0	-0.4
1995	LA-N	0	0	....	17	0	0	0	0	20^1	19	9	7	1	2	11	15	1.475	3.10	122	3.97	.232	0	.000	2	1	0.1
1996	LA-N	0	1	.000	28	0	0	0	0	43^1	48	25	23	4	4	20	36	1.569	4.78	81	5.07	.282	0	.000	-4	1	-0.5
	Det-A	1	1	.500	24	0	0	0	0	25	27	11	9	3	0	14	15	1.640	3.24	156	5.30	.284	0	....	6	2	0.5
1997	Cin-N	0	0	....	1	0	0	0	0	1^1	2	2	1	0	0	1	2	2.250	6.75	64	7.52	.333	0	.000	-0	0	0.0
2001	Mon-N	0	1	.000	24	0	0	0	0	29^2	29	17	16	4	1	16	19	1.517	4.85	92	4.89	.257	0	....	-1	1	-0.1
2002	Mon-N	6	1	.857	59	0	0	0	2	53^2	43	11	8	1	2	18	51	1.137	1.34	318	2.31	.224	1	.125	17	9	1.8
2003	Mon-N	2	2	.500	70	0	0	0	1	53	57	27	18	7	3	13	40	1.321	3.06	165	4.44	.282	1	.250	12	6	1.2
Total	7	9	6	.600	224	0	0	0	3	227	229	106	86	20	13	93	179	1.419	3.41	128	4.31	.264	2	.100	28	20	2.7
• EISENHART, Jake	Jacob Henry Eisenhart b: 10/3/1922, Perkasie, PA d: 12/20/1987, Huntingdon, PA BL/TL, 6'3.5", 195 lbs. Deb: 6/10/1944																										
1944	Cin-N	0	0	....	1	0	0	0	0	0^1	0	0	0	0	0	1	0	3.000	0.00	....	5.85	.000	0	....	0	0	0.0
• EISENSTAT, Harry	Harry Eisenstat b: 10/10/1915, Brooklyn, NY d: 3/21/2003, Beachwood, OH BL/TL, 5'11", 185 lbs. Deb: 5/19/1935																										
1935	Bro-N	0	1	.000	2	0	0	0	0	4^2	9	8	7	0	0	2	2	2.357	13.50	29	8.78	.429	0	.000	-5	0	-0.5
1936	Bro-N	1	2	.333	5	2	1	0	0	14^1	22	17	9	1	0	6	5	1.953	5.65	73	6.84	.344	1	.333	-2	0	-0.2
1937	Bro-N	3	3	.500	13	5	0	0	0	47^2	61	28	21	2	1	11	12	1.510	3.97	102	4.51	.308	0	.000	2	3	0.1
1938	Det-A	9	6	.600	32	9	5	0	4	125^1	131	60	52	7	1	29	37	1.277	3.73	134	3.34	.266	5	.139	17	13	1.4
1939	Det-A	2	2	.500	10	2	1	0	0	29^2	39	24	23	3	0	9	6	1.618	6.98	70	5.39	.315	3	.375	-7	1	-0.6
	Cle-A	6	7	.462	26	11	4	1	2	103^2	109	45	38	8	0	23	38	1.273	3.30	133	3.36	.262	8	.250	13	9	1.2
	Yr.	8	9	.471	36	13	5	1	2	133^1	148	69	61	11	0	32	44	1.350	4.12	111	3.81	.274	11	.275	6	10	0.6
1940	Cle-A	1	4	.200	27	3	0	0	4	71^2	78	25	25	6	0	12	27	1.256	3.14	134	3.61	.282	6	.273	7	6	0.7
1941	Cle-A	1	1	.500	21	0	0	0	2	34	43	16	16	2	2	16	11	1.735	4.24	93	5.76	.312	2	.333	-1	2	-0.1
1942	Cle-A	2	1	.667	29	1	0	0	2	47^2	58	19	13	1	0	6	19	1.343	2.45	140	3.70	.304	1	.250	4	4	0.5
Total	8	25	27	.481	165	33	11	1	14	478^2	550	242	204	30	4	114	157	1.387	3.84	114	3.99	.286	26	.211	27	38	2.6
• EITELJORGE, Ed	Edward Henry Eiteljorge b: 10/14/1871, Berlin, Germany d: 12/5/1942, Greencastle, IN BR/TR, 6'2", 190 lbs. Deb: 5/2/1890																										
1890	Chi-N	0	1	.000	1	1	0	0	0	2	5	7	5	0	0	1	1	3.000	22.50	16	....	.458	0	.000	-4	0	-0.4
1891	Was-a	1	5	.167	8	7	6	0	0	61^1	79	67	42	3	9	41	23	1.957	6.16	61	....	.302	5	.192	-13	0	-1.2
Total	2	1	6	.143	9	8	6	0	0	63^1	84	74	47	3	9	42	24	1.989	6.68	56	....	.309	5	.185	-17	0	-1.6

YEAR TM-L	W	L	PCT	G	GS	CG	SH	SV	IP	H	R	ER	HR	HB	BB	SO	RAT	ERA	ERA+	CERA	OAV	BH	AVG	PR+	WS	TPW
• ELARTON, Scott	Vincent Scott Elarton b: 2/23/1976, Lamar, CO BR/TR, 6'7", 240 lbs. Deb: 6/20/1998																									
1998★ Hou-N	2	1	.667	28	2	0	0	2	57	40	21	21	5	1	20	56	1.053	3.32	122	2.35	.196	0	.000	4	5	0.4
1999★ Hou-N	9	5	.643	42	15	0	0	1	124	111	55	48	8	4	43	121	1.242	3.48	127	3.16	.238	5	.192	12	10	1.1
2000 Hou-N	17	7	.708	30	30	2	0	0	192^{2}	198	117	103	29	6	84	131	1.464	4.81	101	4.82	.263	10	.159	4	11	0.4
2001 Hou-N	4	8	.333	20	20	0	0	0	109^{2}	126	88	87	26	6	49	76	1.596	7.14	64	6.42	.290	2	.067	-32	0	-3.2
Col-N	0	2	.000	4	4	0	0	0	23	20	17	17	8	0	10	11	1.304	6.65	80	5.18	.233	1	.125	-3	0	-0.4
Yr.	4	10	.286	24	24	0	0	0	132^{2}	146	105	104	34	6	59	87	1.545	7.06	66	6.20	.280	3	.079	-35	0	-3.5
2003 Col-N	4	4	.500	11	10	0	0	0	51^{2}	73	46	36	13	4	20	20	1.800	6.27	78	7.79	.329	1	.071	-7	0	-0.7
Total 5	36	27	.571	135	81	2	0	3	558	568	344	312	89	21	226	415	1.423	5.03	93	4.80	.262	19	.128	-22	26	-2.4
• ELDER, Dave	David Matthew Elder b: 9/23/1975, Atlanta, GA BR/TR, 6', 180 lbs. Deb: 7/24/2002																									
2002 Cle-A	0	2	.000	15	0	0	0	0	23	18	10	8	1	1	14	23	1.391	3.13	140	3.22	.220	0	....	3	2	0.3
2003 Cle-A	1	1	.500	4	0	0	0	0	2^{1}	5	5	5	2	0	4	3	3.857	19.29	23	27.02	.417	0	....	-4	0	-0.4
Total 2	1	3	.250	19	0	0	0	0	25^{1}	23	15	13	3	1	18	26	1.618	4.62	95	5.41	.245	0	....	-0	2	0.0
• ELDER, Heinie	Henry Knox Elder b: 8/23/1890, Seattle, WA d: 11/13/1958, Long Beach, CA BL/TL, 6'2", 200 lbs. Deb: 7/7/1913																									
1913 Det-A	0	0	....	1	0	0	0	0	3^{1}	4	3	3	0	0	5	0	2.700	8.10	36	8.19	.286	0	.000	-2	0	-0.2
• ELDRED, Cal	Calvin John Eldred b: 11/24/1967, Cedar Rapids, IA BR/TR, 6'4", 235 lbs. Deb: 9/24/1991																									
1991 Mil-A	2	0	1.000	3	3	0	0	0	16	20	9	8	2	0	6	10	1.625	4.50	88	5.57	.299	0	....	-1	1	-0.1
1992 Mil-A	11	2	.846	14	14	2	1	0	100^{1}	76	21	20	4	2	23	62	.987	1.79	214	1.94	.207	0	....	21	11	2.1
1993 Mil-A	16	16	.500	36	**36**	8	1	0	**258**	232	120	115	32	10	91	180	1.252	4.01	106	3.62	.239	0	....	9	16	0.8
1994 Mil-A	11	11	.500	25	**25**	6	0	0	179	158	96	93	23	4	84	98	1.352	4.68	108	3.97	.236	0	....	2	11	0.2
1995 Mil-A	1	1	.500	4	4	0	0	0	23^{2}	24	10	9	4	1	10	18	1.437	3.42	146	4.91	.261	0	....	4	2	0.3
1996 Mil-A	4	4	.500	15	15	0	0	0	84^{2}	82	43	42	8	4	38	50	1.417	4.46	116	4.33	.259	0	....	5	5	0.5
1997 Mil-A	13	15	.464	34	34	1	1	0	202	207	118	112	31	9	89	122	1.465	4.99	93	5.00	.266	0	.000	-15	9	-1.4
1998 Mil-N	4	8	.333	23	23	0	0	0	133	157	82	71	14	4	61	86	1.639	4.80	89	5.54	.297	4	.125	-9	3	-1.0
1999 Mil-N	2	8	.200	20	15	0	0	0	82	101	75	71	19	1	46	60	1.793	7.79	58	7.13	.297	2	.083	-29	0	-2.8
2000 Chi-A	10	2	.833	20	20	2	1	0	112	103	61	57	12	5	59	97	1.446	4.58	109	4.36	.243	1	.250	3	7	0.4
2001 Chi-A	0	1	.000	2	2	0	0	0	6	12	9	9	1	3	3	6	2.500	13.50	34	14.25	.429	0	....	-6	0	-0.6
2003 StL-N	7	4	.636	62	0	0	0	8	67^{1}	62	32	28	9	4	31	67	1.381	3.74	108	4.25	.248	1	.500	2	6	0.3
Total 12	81	72	.529	258	191	19	4	8	1264	1234	676	635	159	47	541	856	1.404	4.52	101	4.43	.256	8	.123	-14	71	-1.3
• ELLER, Hod	Horace Owen Eller b: 7/5/1894, Muncie, IN d: 7/18/1961, Indianapolis, IN BR/TR, 5'11.5", 185 lbs. Deb: 4/16/1917																									
1917 Cin-N	10	5	.667	37	11	7	1	1	152^{1}	131	60	40	2	3	37	77	1.103	2.36	110	2.24	.239	6	.133	5	8	0.3
1918 Cin-N	16	12	.571	37	22	14	0	1	217^{2}	205	71	57	1	6	59	84	1.213	2.36	113	2.70	.253	11	.157	6	14	0.4
1919★ Cin-N	19	9	.679	38	30	16	7	2	248^{1}	216	80	66	7	4	50	137	1.071	2.39	116	2.26	.238	26	.280	6	23	1.4
1920 Cin-N	13	12	.520	35	23	15	1	0	210^{1}	208	79	69	6	5	52	76	1.236	2.95	103	3.04	.266	22	.253	1	12	0.1
1921 Cin-N	2	2	.500	13	3	0	0	1	34^{1}	46	23	19	3	0	15	7	1.777	4.98	72	6.06	.322	3	.231	-5	1	-0.5
Total 5	60	40	.600	160	89	52	9	5	863	806	313	251	19	18	213	381	1.181	2.62	108	2.71	.253	68	.221	13	58	1.8
• ELLINGSEN, Bruce	Harold Bruce Ellingsen b: 4/26/1949, Pocatello, ID BL/TL, 6', 180 lbs. Deb: 7/4/1974																									
1974 Cle-A	1	1	.500	16	2	0	0	0	42	45	21	15	5	0	17	16	1.476	3.21	112	4.45	.278	0	....	2	2	0.2
• ELLIOTT, Claude	Claud Judson "Chaucer,Old Pardee" Elliott b: 11/17/1876, Pardeeville, WI d: 6/21/1923, Pardeeville, WI BR/TR, 6', 190 lbs. Deb: 4/16/1904																									
1904 Cin-N	3	1	.750	9	6	4	1	0	57^{2}	53	25	19	1	4	23	19	1.318	2.97	98	3.28	.247	5	.208	-2	4	-0.1
NY-N	0	1	.000	3	1	1	0	0	15	21	14	5	2	0	3	8	1.600	3.00	91	5.84	.328	1	.200	-1	0	-0.1
Yr.	3	2	.600	12	7	5	1	0	72^{2}	74	39	24	3	4	26	27	1.376	2.97	97	3.81	.266	6	.207	-3	4	-0.1
1905 NY-N	0	1	.000	10	2	2	0	**6**	38	41	39	17	3	1	12	20	1.395	4.03	73	4.04	.270	3	.188	-4	1	-0.5
Total 2	3	3	.500	22	9	7	1	6	110^{2}	115	78	41	6	5	38	47	1.383	3.33	87	3.89	.267	9	.200	-7	5	-0.6
• ELLIOTT, Donnie	Donald Glenn Elliott b: 9/20/1968, Pasadena, TX BR/TR, 6'4", 190 lbs. Deb: 4/23/1994																									
1994 SD-N	0	1	.000	30	1	0	0	0	33	31	12	12	3	1	21	24	1.576	3.27	126	4.63	.250	0	.000	4	2	0.4
1995 SD-N	0	0	....	1	0	0	0	0	2	2	0	0	0	0	1	3	1.500	0.00	....	3.63	.250	0	....	1	0	0.1
Total 2	0	1	.000	31	1	0	0	0	35	33	12	12	3	1	22	27	1.571	3.09	133	4.57	.250	0	.000	5	2	0.5
• ELLIOTT, Glenn	Herbert Glenn "Lefty" Elliott b: 11/11/1919, Sapulpa, OK d: 7/27/1969, Portland, OR BB/TL, 5'10", 170 lbs. Deb: 4/17/1947																									
1947 Bos-N	0	1	.000	11	0	0	0	1	19	18	10	10	4	0	11	8	1.526	4.74	82	5.47	.269	1	.500	-2	1	-0.1
1948 Bos-N	1	0	1.000	1	1	0	0	0	3	5	1	1	0	0	1	2	2.000	3.00	128	6.71	.357	0	.000	0	0	0.0
1949 Bos-N	3	4	.429	22	6	1	0	0	68^{1}	70	35	30	7	0	27	15	1.420	3.95	96	4.19	.269	1	.059	-1	3	-0.2
Total 3	4	5	.444	34	7	1	0	1	90^{1}	93	46	41	11	0	39	25	1.461	4.08	93	4.54	.273	2	.095	-2	4	-0.3
• ELLIOTT, Hal	Harold William Elliott b: 5/29/1899, Mount Clemens, MI d: 4/25/1963, Honolulu, HI BR/TR, 6'1.5", 170 lbs. Deb: 4/19/1929																									
1929 Phi-N	3	7	.300	40	8	2	0	2	114^{1}	146	94	77	5	0	59	32	1.793	6.06	86	6.93	.313	5	.167	-9	4	-0.8
1930 Phi-N	6	11	.353	**48**	11	2	0	0	117^{1}	191	120	100	7	1	58	37	2.122	7.67	71	7.99	.382	3	.094	-26	1	-2.5
1931 Phi-N	0	2	.000	16	4	0	0	2	33	46	36	35	5	1	19	8	1.970	9.55	44	7.82	.338	1	.111	-19	0	-1.9
1932 Phi-N	2	4	.333	16	7	0	0	0	57^{2}	70	45	37	5	0	38	13	1.873	5.77	76	6.09	.297	3	.167	-9	1	-0.9
Total 4	11	24	.314	120	30	4	0	4	322^{1}	453	295	249	22	2	174	90	1.945	6.95	72	7.25	.339	12	.135	-62	6	-6.2
• ELLIOTT, Jumbo	James Thomas Elliott b: 10/22/1900, St. Louis, MO d: 1/7/1970, Terre Haute, IN BR/TL, 6'3", 235 lbs. Deb: 4/21/1923																									
1923 StL-A	0	0	....	1	0	0	0	0	1	1	3	3	0	0	3	0	4.000	27.00	15	12.51	.333	0	....	-3	0	-0.2
1925 Bro-N	0	2	.000	3	1	0	0	0	10^{2}	17	14	10	0	1	9	3	2.438	8.44	49	8.93	.362	0	.000	-5	0	-0.5
1927 Bro-N	6	13	.316	30	21	12	2	3	188^{1}	188	82	69	5	1	60	99	1.317	3.30	120	3.23	.269	9	.141	13	13	1.2
1928 Bro-N	9	14	.391	41	21	7	2	1	192	194	106	83	8	6	64	74	1.344	3.89	102	3.53	.268	12	.176	3	9	0.5
1929 Bro-N	1	2	.333	6	3	0	0	0	19	21	17	14	2	1	16	7	1.947	6.63	70	6.41	.280	1	.250	-4	0	-0.3
1930 Bro-N	10	7	.588	35	21	6	2	1	198^{1}	204	100	87	16	5	70	59	1.382	3.95	124	3.95	.271	10	.147	16	15	1.3
1931 Phi-N	**19**	14	.576	**52**	30	12	2	5	249	288	138	118	15	4	83	99	**1.490**	4.27	99	4.37	.287	11	.122	2	16	-0.3
1932 Phi-N	11	10	.524	39	22	8	0	0	166	210	115	100	14	2	47	62	1.548	5.42	81	4.86	.300	12	.197	-18	5	-1.9
1933 Phi-N	6	10	.375	35	21	6	0	2	161^{2}	188	89	69	8	3	49	43	1.466	3.84	99	4.26	.295	12	.231	-0	9	0.0
1934 Phi-N	0	1	.000	3	1	0	0	0	5^{1}	8	7	6	0	1	4	1	2.250	10.13	47	8.00	.333	0	.000	-3	0	-0.3
Bos-N	1	1	.500	7	3	0	0	0	15^{1}	19	16	10	2	1	9	6	1.826	5.87	65	6.26	.284	1	.250	-3	0	-0.3
Yr.	1	2	.333	10	4	0	0	0	20^{2}	27	23	16	2	2	13	7	1.935	6.97	59	6.71	.297	1	.200	-7	0	-0.6
Total 10	63	74	.460	252	144	51	8	12	1206^{2}	1338	687	569	70	25	414	453	1.452	4.24	100	4.16	.283	68	.163	-2	67	-0.9
• ELLIS, Dock	Dock Phillip Ellis b: 3/11/1945, Los Angeles, CA BB/TR, 6'3", 210 lbs. Deb: 6/18/1968																									
1968 Pit-N	6	5	.545	26	10	2	0	0	104	82	35	29	4	1	38	52	1.154	2.51	117	2.41	.213	2	.069	3	6	0.2
1969 Pit-N	11	17	.393	35	33	8	2	0	218^{2}	206	101	87	14	4	76	173	1.290	3.58	97	3.36	.250	6	.088	-1	9	-0.5
1970★ Pit-N	13	10	.565	30	30	9	4	0	201^{2}	194	81	72	9	10	87	128	1.393	3.21	121	3.76	.257	7	.100	10	14	0.7
1971★ Pit-N★	19	9	.679	31	31	11	2	0	226^{2}	207	93	77	15	2	63	137	1.191	3.06	112	2.89	.239	16	.203	7	14	1.0
1972★ Pit-N	15	7	.682	25	25	4	1	0	163^{1}	156	60	49	6	3	33	96	1.157	2.70	123	2.74	.253	9	.153	9	11	0.8
1973 Pit-N	12	14	.462	28	28	3	1	0	192	176	86	65	7	6	55	122	1.203	3.05	115	2.81	.240	7	.108	10	8	0.8
1974 Pit-N	12	9	.571	26	26	9	0	0	176^{2}	163	71	62	13	7	41	91	1.155	3.16	109	2.94	.242	12	.214	5	12	0.8
1975★ Pit-N	8	9	.471	27	24	5	2	0	140	163	69	59	9	3	43	69	1.471	3.79	93	4.30	.292	4	.111	-4	5	-0.4
1976★ NY-A	17	8	.680	32	32	8	1	0	211^{2}	195	83	75	14	4	76	65	1.280	3.19	107	3.35	.247	0	....	-2	13	-0.2
1977 NY-A	1	1	.500	3	3	1	0	0	19^{2}	18	9	4	1	0	8	5	1.322	1.83	215	3.22	.237	0	....	4	2	0.4
Oak-A	1	5	.167	7	7	0	0	0	26	35	33	28	5	1	14	11	1.885	9.69	42	7.51	.315	0	....	-16	0	-1.6
Tex-A	10	6	.625	23	22	7	1	1	167^{1}	158	60	54	13	0	42	90	1.195	2.90	141	3.07	.254	0	....	20	15	2.0
Yr.	12	12	.500	33	32	8	1	1	213	211	102	86	19	1	64	106	1.291	3.63	112	3.63	.260	0	....	8	17	0.8
1978 Tex-A	9	7	.563	22	22	3	0	0	141^{1}	131	81	66	15	2	46	45	1.252	4.20	89	3.48	.245	0	....	-7	5	-0.7

YEAR TM-L	W	L	PCT	G	GS	CG	SH	SV	IP	H	R	ER	HR	HB	BB	SO	RAT	ERA	ERA+	CERA	OAV	BH	AVG	PR+	WS	TPW
1979 Tex-A	1	5	.167	10	9	0	0	0	46^{2}	64	34	31	5	0	16	10	1.714	5.98	69	6.01	.323	0	....	-10	0	-1.0
NY-N	3	7	.300	17	14	1	0	0	85	110	60	57	9	1	34	41	1.694	6.04	60	5.68	.320	2	.077	-24	0	-2.6
Pit-N	0	0	....	3	1	0	0	0	7	9	2	2	1	0	2	1	1.571	2.57	151	6.08	.346	0	.000	1	1	0.1
Yr.	3	7	.300	20	15	1	0	0	92	119	62	59	10	1	36	42	1.685	5.77	63	5.71	.322	2	.074	-23	1	-2.5
Total 12	138	119	.537	345	317	71	14	1	2127^{2}	2067	958	817	140	44	674	1136	1.288	3.46	104	3.42	.255	65	.133	6	115	0.0
• ELLIS, Jim	James Russell Ellis b: 3/25/1945, Tulare, CA BR/TL, 6'2", 185 lbs. Deb: 8/11/1967																									
1967 Chi-N	1	1	.500	8	1	0	0	0	16^{2}	20	7	6	1	0	9	8	1.740	3.24	109	5.55	.313	1	.200	0	1	0.1
1969 StL-N	0	0	....	2	1	0	0	0	5^{1}	7	1	1	0	0	3	0	1.875	1.69	212	5.47	.318	0	....	1	1	0.1
Total 2	1	1	.500	10	2	0	0	0	22	27	8	7	1	0	12	8	1.773	2.86	124	5.53	.314	1	.200	1	2	0.2
• ELLIS, Robert	Robert Randolph Ellis b: 12/15/1970, Baton Rouge, LA BR/TR, 6'5", 220 lbs. Deb: 9/12/1996																									
1996 Cal-A	0	0	....	3	0	0	0	0	5	0	0	0	0	0	4	5	.800	0.00	....	0.64	.000	0	....	3	1	0.2
2001 Ari-N	6	5	.545	19	17	0	0	0	92	106	61	59	12	4	34	41	1.522	5.77	79	5.17	.293	4	.154	-14	2	-1.3
2002 LA-N	0	1	.000	3	0	0	0	0	2^{2}	6	3	3	1	0	0	0	2.250	10.13	38	13.68	.462	0	....	-2	0	-0.2
2003 Tex-A	1	1	.500	4	4	0	0	0	18^{1}	26	17	17	7	1	10	8	1.964	8.35	59	10.11	.342	0	....	-7	0	-0.6
Total 4	7	7	.500	29	21	0	0	0	118	138	81	79	20	5	48	54	1.576	6.03	77	5.94	.306	4	.154	-19	3	-1.9
• ELLIS, Sammy	Samuel Joseph Ellis b: 2/11/1941, Youngstown, OH BL/TR, 6'1", 180 lbs. Deb: 4/14/1962 C																									
1962 Cin-N	2	2	.500	8	4	0	0	0	28	29	25	21	6	1	29	27	2.071	6.75	60	8.09	.269	2	.200	-9	0	-0.9
1964 Cin-N	10	3	.769	52	5	2	0	14	122^{1}	101	38	35	9	1	28	125	1.054	2.57	140	2.38	.223	2	.083	13	16	1.3
1965 Cin-N★	22	10	.688	44	39	15	2	2	263^{2}	222	119	111	22	6	104	183	1.236	3.79	99	3.16	.226	12	.125	-1	14	-0.2
1966 Cin-N	12	19	.387	41	36	7	0	0	221	226	135	130	35	3	78	154	1.376	5.29	74	4.37	.264	8	.114	-31	4	-3.5
1967 Cin-N	8	11	.421	32	27	8	1	0	175^{2}	197	86	75	18	4	67	80	**1.503**	3.84	98	4.79	.286	4	.082	-1	7	-0.3
1968 Cal-A	9	10	.474	42	24	3	0	2	164	150	80	72	22	6	56	93	1.256	3.95	74	3.69	.244	2	.045	-21	4	-2.7
1969 Chi-A	0	3	.000	10	5	0	0	0	29^{1}	42	20	19	6	1	16	15	1.977	5.83	66	8.24	.336	1	.167	-6	0	-0.6
Total 7	63	58	.521	229	140	35	3	18	1004	967	503	463	118	22	378	677	1.340	4.15	87	3.99	.253	31	.104	-57	45	-6.9
• ELLISON, George	George Russell Ellison b: 1/24/1895, CA d: 1/20/1978, San Francisco, CA BR/TR, 6'3", 185 lbs. Deb: 8/21/1920																									
1920 Cle-A	0	0	....	1	0	0	0	0	1	0	0	0	0	0	2	1	2.000	0.00	....	1.88	.000	0	....	0	0	0.0
• ELLSWORTH, Dick	Richard Clark Ellsworth b: 3/22/1940, Lusk, WY BL/TL, 6'3.5", 195 lbs. Deb: 6/22/1958																									
1958 Chi-N	0	1	.000	1	1	0	0	0	2^{1}	4	4	4	0	1	3	0	3.000	15.43	25	13.24	.364	0	.000	-3	0	-0.3
1960 Chi-N	7	13	.350	31	27	6	0	0	176^{2}	170	83	73	12	2	72	94	1.370	3.72	102	3.72	.257	2	.042	2	8	-0.1
1961 Chi-N	10	11	.476	37	31	7	1	0	186^{2}	213	90	80	23	3	48	91	1.398	3.86	108	4.55	.292	2	.036	10	11	0.5
1962 Chi-N	9	20	.310	37	33	6	0	1	208^{2}	241	131	118	23	5	77	113	1.524	5.09	81	5.01	.291	7	.113	-22	7	-2.1
1963 Chi-N	22	10	.688	37	37	19	4	0	290^{2}	223	75	68	14	2	75	185	1.025	2.11	**167**	2.02	.210	9	.096	41	**32**	**4.2**
1964 Chi-N★	14	18	.438	37	36	16	1	0	256^{2}	267	129	107	34	3	71	148	1.317	3.75	99	4.01	.266	4	.046	1	13	-0.4
1965 Chi-N	14	15	.483	36	34	8	0	1	222^{1}	227	108	94	22	4	57	130	1.277	3.81	97	3.66	.265	7	.096	-1	10	-0.2
1966 Chi-N	8	22	.267	38	37	9	0	0	269^{1}	321	150	119	28	5	51	144	1.381	3.98	92	4.35	.294	14	.156	-5	9	-0.6
1967 Phi-N	6	7	.462	32	21	3	1	0	125^{1}	152	75	61	6	5	36	45	1.500	4.38	78	4.53	.306	4	.108	-13	1	-1.6
1968 Bos-A	16	7	.696	31	28	10	1	0	196	196	74	66	16	7	37	106	1.189	3.03	104	3.27	.260	4	.056	4	13	-0.1
1969 Bos-A	0	0	....	2	2	0	0	0	12	16	5	5	1	0	4	4	1.667	3.75	101	5.71	.320	0	.000	0	1	0.0
Cle-A	6	9	.400	34	22	3	1	0	135	162	73	62	10	5	40	48	1.496	4.13	91	4.68	.301	6	.133	-5	4	-0.6
Yr.	6	9	.400	36	24	3	1	0	147	178	78	67	11	5	44	52	1.510	4.10	92	4.76	.302	6	.125	-5	5	-0.6
1970 Cle-A	3	3	.500	29	1	0	0	2	43^{2}	49	23	22	4	1	14	13	1.443	4.53	87	4.56	.299	0	.000	-3	3	-0.3
Mil-A	0	0	....	14	0	0	0	1	15^{2}	11	3	3	0	1	3	9	.894	1.72	220	1.54	.196	0	....	4	2	0.4
Yr.	3	3	.500	43	1	0	0	3	59^{1}	60	26	25	4	2	17	22	1.298	3.79	104	3.76	.273	0	.000	1	5	0.1
1971 Mil-A	0	1	.000	11	0	0	0	0	14^{2}	22	10	8	1	1	7	10	1.977	4.91	71	7.35	.361	0	.000	-2	0	-0.3
Total 13	115	137	.456	407	310	87	9	5	2155^{2}	2274	1033	890	194	45	595	1140	1.331	3.72	100	3.91	.272	59	.088	7	114	-1.5
• ELLSWORTH, Steve	Steven Clark Ellsworth b: 7/30/1960, Chicago, IL BR/TR, 6'8", 220 lbs. Deb: 4/7/1988																									
1988 Bos-A	1	6	.143	8	7	0	0	0	36	47	29	27	7	1	16	16	1.750	6.75	61	6.92	.315	0	....	-10	0	-1.0
• ELSTON, Don	Donald Ray Elston b: 4/6/1929, Campbellstown, OH d: 1/2/1995, Arlington Heights, IL BR/TR, 6', 170 lbs. Deb: 9/17/1953																									
1953 Chi-N	0	1	.000	2	1	0	0	0	5	11	8	8	1	0	0	2	2.200	14.40	31	11.11	.458	0	.000	-5	0	-0.5
1957 Bro-N	0	0	....	1	0	0	0	0	1	1	0	0	0	0	0	1	1.000	0.00	....	1.95	.250	0	....	0	0	0.0
Chi-N	6	7	.462	39	14	2	0	8	144	139	61	57	15	5	55	102	1.347	3.56	109	4.01	.259	4	.108	7	10	0.5
Yr.	6	7	.462	40	14	2	0	8	145	140	61	57	15	5	55	103	1.345	3.54	109	4.00	.259	4	.108	8	10	0.6
1958 Chi-N	9	8	.529	**69**	0	0	0	10	97	75	35	31	9	1	39	84	1.175	2.88	136	2.71	.214	5	.357	12	12	1.3
1959 Chi-N★	10	8	.556	**65**	0	0	0	13	97^{2}	77	40	36	11	3	46	82	1.259	3.32	119	3.27	.218	4	.211	6	11	0.6
1960 Chi-N	8	9	.471	60	0	0	0	11	127	109	57	48	17	4	55	85	1.291	3.40	111	3.62	.231	3	.125	6	9	0.5
1961 Chi-N	6	7	.462	58	0	0	0	8	93^{1}	108	64	58	11	6	45	59	1.639	5.59	75	5.61	.297	2	.182	-13	3	-1.3
1962 Chi-N	4	8	.333	57	0	0	0	8	66^{1}	57	25	18	6	1	32	37	1.342	2.44	170	3.56	.247	0	.000	12	9	1.2
1963 Chi-N	4	1	.800	51	0	0	0	4	70	57	26	22	6	2	21	41	1.114	2.83	124	2.73	.226	0	.000	4	7	0.4
1964 Chi-N	2	5	.286	48	0	0	0	1	54^{1}	68	38	32	4	3	34	26	1.877	5.30	70	6.11	.330	1	.167	-9	0	-1.0
Total 9	49	54	.476	450	15	2	0	63	755^{2}	702	354	310	80	25	327	519	1.362	3.69	106	3.92	.251	19	.153	20	61	1.7
• ELVIRA, Narciso	Narciso Chicho (Delgado) Elvira b: 10/29/1967, Vera Cruz, Mexico BL/TL, 5'10", 160 lbs. Deb: 9/9/1990																									
1990 Mil-A	0	0	....	4	0	0	0	0	5	6	3	3	0	0	5	6	2.200	5.40	72	6.97	.300	0	....	-1	0	-0.1
• ELY, Harry	Harry Ely Deb: 9/24/1892																									
1892 Bal-N	0	1	.000	1	1	1	0	0	7	14	9	6	0	2	7	0	3.000	7.71	44	13.13	.400	0	.000	-3	0	-0.3
• EMBREE, Alan	Alan Duane Embree b: 1/23/1970, Vancouver, WA BL/TL, 6'2", 185 lbs. Deb: 9/15/1992																									
1992 Cle-A	0	2	.000	4	4	0	0	0	18	19	14	14	3	1	8	12	1.500	7.00	56	5.25	.271	0	....	-6	0	-0.6
1995* Cle-A	3	2	.600	23	0	0	0	1	24^{2}	23	16	14	2	0	16	23	1.581	5.11	92	4.51	.253	0	....	-1	1	-0.1
1996* Cle-A	1	1	.500	24	0	0	0	0	31	30	26	22	10	0	21	33	1.645	6.39	77	6.58	.259	0	....	-5	0	-0.5
1997* Atl-N	3	1	.750	66	0	0	0	0	46	36	13	13	1	2	20	45	1.217	2.54	165	2.66	.221	0	....	8	6	0.8
1998 Atl-N	1	0	1.000	20	0	0	0	0	18^{2}	23	14	9	2	0	10	19	1.768	4.34	96	6.06	.307	0	.000	-1	0	-0.1
Ari-N	3	2	.600	35	0	0	0	1	35	33	18	16	5	1	13	24	1.314	4.11	102	4.03	.248	0	....	0	3	0.1
Yr.	4	2	.667	55	0	0	0	1	53^{2}	56	32	25	7	1	23	43	1.472	4.19	100	4.73	.269	0	.000	-0	3	0.0
1999 SF-N	3	2	.600	68	0	0	0	0	58^{2}	42	22	22	6	3	26	53	1.159	3.38	124	2.86	.200	0	....	5	6	0.5
2000* SF-N	3	5	.375	63	0	0	0	2	60	62	34	33	4	3	25	49	1.450	4.95	85	4.24	.274	0	....	-5	3	-0.5
2001 SF-N	0	2	.000	22	0	0	0	0	20	34	26	25	7	2	10	25	2.200	11.25	35	11.29	.374	0	.000	-16	0	-1.6
Chi-A	1	2	.333	39	0	0	0	0	34	31	21	19	7	1	7	34	1.118	5.03	92	3.61	.242	0	....	-2	2	-0.2
2002 SD-N	3	4	.429	36	0	0	0	0	28^{2}	23	7	3	2	0	9	38	1.116	0.94	400	2.38	.211	0	....	9	3	0.9
Bos-A	1	2	.333	32	0	0	0	2	33^{1}	24	12	11	4	1	11	43	1.050	2.97	151	2.56	.203	0	....	5	4	0.5
2003* Bos-A	4	1	.800	65	0	0	0	1	55	49	26	26	5	0	16	45	1.182	4.25	107	3.01	.241	0	....	3	5	0.3
Total 10	26	26	.500	497	4	0	0	7	463	429	249	227	58	14	192	443	1.341	4.41	98	4.05	.248	0	.000	-4	33	-0.4
• EMBREE, Red	Charles Willard Embree b: 8/30/1917, El Monte, CA d: 9/24/1996, Eugene, OR BR/TR, 6', 165 lbs. Deb: 9/10/1941																									
1941 Cle-A	0	1	.000	1	1	0	0	0	4	7	3	3	0	1	3	4	2.500	6.75	58	10.89	.438	0	.000	-1	0	-0.1
1942 Cle-A	3	4	.429	19	6	2	0	0	63	58	31	27	0	2	31	44	1.413	3.86	89	3.23	.242	2	.133	-4	2	-0.4
1944 Cle-A	0	1	.000	3	1	0	0	0	3^{1}	2	5	5	0	0	5	4	2.100	13.50	24	4.56	.167	0	....	-4	0	-0.4
1945 Cle-A	4	4	.500	8	8	5	1	0	70	56	17	15	3	0	26	42	1.171	1.93	168	2.41	.215	3	.143	11	7	1.1
1946 Cle-A	8	12	.400	28	26	8	0	0	200	170	86	77	15	2	79	87	1.245	3.47	95	2.99	.227	13	.186	-3	8	-0.2
1947 Cle-A	8	10	.444	27	21	6	0	0	162^{2}	137	65	57	13	1	67	56	1.254	3.15	111	3.11	.233	9	.173	3	8	0.2
1948 NY-A	5	3	.625	20	8	4	0	0	76^{2}	77	37	32	6	1	30	25	1.396	3.76	109	3.89	.261	4	.148	2	4	0.1

YEAR	TM-L	W	L	PCT	G	GS	CG	SH	SV	IP	H	R	ER	HR	HB	BB	SO	RAT	ERA	ERA+	CERA	OAV	BH	AVG	PR+	WS	TPW
1949	StL-A	3	13	.188	35	19	4	0	1	127^{1}	146	90	76	13	3	89	24	1.846	5.37	84	6.11	.294	6	.162	-8	3	-0.8
Total	8	31	48	.392	141	90	29	1	1	707	653	334	292	50	10	330	286	1.390	3.72	99	3.69	.246	37	.166	-4	32	-0.7
• EMBREY, Slim	Charles Akin Embrey b: 8/17/1901, Columbia, TN d: 10/10/1947, Nashville, TN BR/TR, 6'2", 184 lbs. Deb: 10/1/1923																										
1923	Chi-A	0	0	....	1	0	0	0	0	2^{2}	7	6	3	0	0	2	1	3.375	10.13	39	14.24	.500	0	....	-2	0	-0.1
• EMIG, Charlie	Charles Henry Emig b: 4/5/1875, Cincinnati, OH d: 10/2/1975, Oklahoma City, OK TL Deb: 9/4/1896																										
1896	Lou-N	0	1	.000	1	1	1	0	0	8	12	17	7	1	3	7	1	2.375	7.88	55	10.81	.344	0	.000	-3	0	-0.3
• EMMERICH, Slim	William Peter Emmerich b: 9/29/1919, Allentown, PA d: 9/17/1998, Allentown, PA BR/TR, 6'1", 170 lbs. Deb: 5/14/1945																										
1945	NY-N	4	4	.500	31	7	1	0	0	100	111	55	54	8	1	33	27	1.440	4.86	80	4.15	.278	3	.120	-11	4	-1.2
1946	NY-N	0	0	....	2	0	0	0	0	4	6	2	2	1	0	0	1	1.500	4.50	77	7.16	.400	0	....	-0	0	0.0
Total	2	4	4	.500	33	7	1	0	0	104	117	57	56	9	1	33	28	1.442	4.85	80	4.27	.282	3	.120	-11	4	-1.3
• EMSLIE, Bob	Robert Daniel Emslie b: 1/27/1859, Guelph, Canada d: 4/26/1943, St. Thomas, Canada BR/TR, 5'11" Deb: 7/25/1883 U																										
1883	Bal-a	9	13	.409	24	23	21	1	0	201^{1}	188	149	71	3	....	41	62	1.137	3.17	110	....	.231	16	.165	17	10	1.2
1884	Bal-a	32	17	.653	50	50	50	4	0	455^{1}	419	241	139	5	14	88	264	1.113	2.75	126	....	.231	37	.190	45	31	3.8
1885	Bal-a	3	10	.231	13	13	11	0	0	107	131	87	51	0	5	30	27	1.505	4.29	76	....	.289	12	.235	-10	4	-0.9
	Phi-a	0	4	.000	4	4	3	0	0	28^{2}	37	30	20	1	0	6	9	1.500	6.28	55	....	.300	1	.083	-9	0	-0.9
	Yr.	3	14	.176	17	17	14	0	0	135^{2}	168	117	71	1	5	36	36	1.504	4.71	70	....	.292	13	.206	-19	4	-1.8
Total	3	44	44	.500	91	90	85	5	0	792^{1}	775	507	281	9	19	165	362	1.186	3.19	107	....	.242	66	.186	43	45	3.2
• ENCARNACION, Luis	Luis Martin Lora Encarnacion b: 10/20/1963, Santo Domingo, Dominican Republic BR/TR, 5'10", 178 lbs. Deb: 7/27/1990																										
1990	KC-A	0	0	....	4	0	0	0	0	10^{1}	14	10	9	1	0	4	8	1.742	7.84	49	5.94	.311	0	....	-4	0	-0.4
• ENDERS, Trevor	Trevor Hale Enders b: 12/22/1974, Milwaukee, WI BR/TL, 6'1", 214 lbs. Deb: 9/2/2000																										
2000	TB-A	0	1	.000	9	0	0	0	0	9^{1}	14	13	11	2	0	5	5	2.036	10.61	47	8.73	.359	0	....	-6	0	-0.6
• ENGEL, Joe	Joseph William Engel b: 3/12/1893, Washington, DC d: 6/12/1969, Chattanooga, TN BR/TL, 6'1.5", 183 lbs. Deb: 5/30/1912																										
1912	Was-A	2	5	.286	17	10	2	0	1	75	70	41	33	2	4	50	29	1.600	3.96	85	4.33	.253	1	.059	-8	2	-0.9
1913	Was-A	8	9	.471	36	24	6	2	0	164^{2}	124	75	56	2	11	85	70	1.269	3.06	96	2.71	.207	3	.061	-5	9	-1.0
1914	Was-A	7	5	.583	35	15	1	0	3	124^{1}	108	53	41	2	5	75	41	1.472	2.97	95	3.85	.254	3	.107	-3	7	-0.2
1915	Was-A	0	3	.000	11	3	0	0	0	33^{2}	30	15	12	0	3	19	9	1.455	3.21	92	3.90	.261	0	.000	-1	1	-0.2
1917	Cin-N	0	1	.000	1	1	1	0	0	8	12	8	5	0	0	6	2	2.250	5.63	46	7.28	.353	0	.000	-3	0	-0.3
1919	Cle-A	0	0	....	1	0	0	0	0	0	0	3	0	0	0	3	0		....	....	∞	.000	0	....	0	0	0.0
1920	Was-A	0	0	....	1	0	0	0	0	1^{2}	0	4	4	0	1	4	0	2.400	21.60	17	6.57	.000	0	.000	-3	0	-0.3
Total	7	17	23	.425	102	53	10	2	4	407^{1}	344	199	151	6	24	242	151	1.439	3.34	90	3.56	.237	7	.067	-23	19	-2.9
• ENGEL, Steve	Steven Michael Engel b: 12/31/1961, Cincinnati, OH BR/TL, 6'3", 216 lbs. Deb: 7/30/1985																										
1985	Chi-N	1	5	.167	11	8	1	0	1	51^{2}	61	36	32	10	0	26	29	1.684	5.57	72	6.25	.298	3	.188	-9	0	-0.7
• ENGLE, Rick	Richard Douglas Engle b: 4/7/1957, Corbin, KY BR/TL, 5'11.5", 181 lbs. Deb: 9/2/1981																										
1981	Mon-N	0	0	....	1	0	0	0	0	2	6	4	4	0	0	1	2	3.500	18.00	19	17.04	.500	0	....	-3	0	-0.3
• ENNIS, John	John Wayne Ennis b: 10/17/1979, Montrose, CO BR/TR, 6'5", 220 lbs. Deb: 4/10/2002																										
2002	Atl-N	0	0	....	1	1	0	0	0	4	5	2	2	0	0	3	1	2.000	4.50	91	6.70	.385	0	.000	-0	0	0.0
• ENRIGHT, Jack	Jackson Percy Enright b: 11/29/1895, Fort Worth, TX d: 8/17/1975, Pompano Beach, FL BR/TR, 5'11", 177 lbs. Deb: 9/26/1917																										
1917	NY-A	0	1	.000	1	1	0	0	0	5	5	5	3	0	0	3	1	1.600	5.40	50	4.49	.294	0	.000	-2	0	-0.2
• ENYART, Terry	Terry Gene Enyart b: 10/10/1950, Ironton, OH BR/TL, 6'2", 190 lbs. Deb: 6/17/1974																										
1974	Mon-N	0	0	....	2	0	0	0	0	1^{2}	4	6	3	0	0	4	2	4.800	16.20	24	21.73	.444	0	....	-2	0	-0.2
• ENZMANN, Johnny	John "Gentleman John" Enzmann b: 3/4/1890, Brooklyn, NY d: 3/14/1984, Riverhead, NY BR/TR, 5'10", 165 lbs. Deb: 7/10/1914																										
1914	Bro-N	1	0	1.000	7	1	0	0	0	19	21	16	10	1	3	8	5	1.526	4.74	60	5.06	.300	0	.000	-4	0	-0.5
1918	Cle-A	5	7	.417	30	14	8	0	2	136^{2}	130	44	36	2	5	29	38	1.163	2.37	126	2.73	.263	7	.149	12	10	1.1
1919	Cle-A	3	2	.600	14	4	2	0	0	55^{1}	67	29	14	0	2	8	13	1.355	2.28	147	3.87	.312	2	.133	7	4	0.7
1920	Phi-N	2	3	.400	16	2	1	0	0	58^{2}	79	40	25	1	5	16	35	1.619	3.84	89	5.16	.320	4	.167	-3	2	-0.2
Total	4	11	12	.478	67	21	11	0	2	269^{2}	297	129	85	4	15	61	91	1.328	2.84	111	3.66	.289	13	.141	12	16	1.1
• EPPERLY, Al	Albert Paul "Tub,Pard" Epperly b: 5/7/1918, Glidden, IA d: 4/14/2003, McFarland, WI BL/TR, 6'2", 194 lbs. Deb: 4/25/1938																										
1938	Chi-N	2	0	1.000	9	4	1	0	0	27	28	11	11	1	0	15	10	1.593	3.67	104	4.24	.264	2	.250	0	2	0.1
1950	Bro-N	0	0	....	5	0	0	0	0	9	14	8	5	1	0	5	3	2.111	5.00	82	8.27	.378	0	....	-1	0	-0.1
Total	2	2	0	1.000	14	4	1	0	0	36	42	19	16	2	0	20	13	1.722	4.00	98	5.25	.294	2	.250	-1	2	0.0
• ERARDI, Greg	Joseph Gregory Erardi b: 5/31/1954, Syracuse, NY BR/TR, 6'1", 190 lbs. Deb: 9/6/1977																										
1977	Sea-A	0	1	.000	5	0	0	0	0	9	12	8	6	3	0	6	5	2.000	6.00	69	8.65	.300	0	....	-2	0	-0.2
• ERAUTT, Eddie	Edward Lorenz Sebastian Erautt b: 9/26/1924, Portland, OR BR/TR, 5'11.5", 186 lbs. Deb: 4/16/1947																										
1947	Cin-N	4	9	.308	36	10	2	0	0	119	146	78	67	5	2	53	43	1.672	5.07	81	5.15	.307	2	.069	-11	2	-1.2
1948	Cin-N	0	0	....	2	0	0	0	0	3	3	2	2	0	0	1	0	1.333	6.00	65	2.97	.250	0	....	-1	0	-0.1
1949	Cin-N	4	11	.267	39	9	1	0	1	112^{2}	99	53	42	9	3	61	43	1.420	3.36	125	3.85	.247	4	.174	11	7	1.1
1950	Cin-N	4	2	.667	33	2	1	0	1	65^{1}	82	48	41	9	6	22	35	1.592	5.65	75	5.89	.307	2	.154	-9	2	-0.9
1951	Cin-N	0	0	....	30	0	0	0	0	39^{1}	50	31	25	4	3	23	20	1.856	5.72	71	6.65	.314	0	.000	-7	0	-0.7
1953	Cin-N	0	0	....	4	0	0	0	0	4^{2}	11	3	3	1	0	3	1	3.000	5.79	75	16.89	.500	0	.000	-1	0	-0.1
	StL-N	3	1	.750	20	1	0	0	0	35^{2}	43	25	25	6	2	16	15	1.654	6.31	67	6.21	.299	1	.167	-8	1	-0.8
	Yr.	3	1	.750	24	1	0	0	0	40^{1}	54	28	28	7	2	19	16	1.810	6.25	68	7.44	.325	1	.143	-9	1	-0.9
Total	6	15	23	.395	164	22	4	0	2	379^{2}	434	240	205	34	16	179	157	1.615	4.86	86	5.28	.293	9	.120	-26	12	-2.7
• ERDOS, Todd	Todd Michael Erdos b: 11/21/1973, Washington, PA BR/TR, 6'1", 205 lbs. Deb: 6/8/1997																										
1997	SD-N	2	0	1.000	11	0	0	0	0	13^{2}	17	9	8	1	2	4	13	1.537	5.27	73	5.31	.293	0	.000	-2	0	-0.2
1998	NY-A	0	0	....	2	0	0	0	0	2	5	2	2	0	0	1	0	3.000	9.00	49	13.15	.500	0	....	-1	0	-0.1
1999	NY-A	0	0	....	4	0	0	0	0	7	5	4	3	2	0	4	4	1.286	3.86	123	4.18	.192	0	....	1	0	0.1
2000	NY-A	0	0	....	14	0	0	0	1	25	31	14	14	2	1	11	18	1.680	5.04	96	5.72	.304	0	.000	-0	1	0.0
	SD-N	0	0	....	22	0	0	0	1	29^{2}	32	24	22	5	6	17	16	1.652	6.67	65	6.33	.271	0	.000	-8	0	-0.8
2001	Bos-A	0	0	....	10	0	0	0	0	16^{1}	15	9	9	2	3	8	7	1.408	4.96	90	4.94	.263	0	....	-1	1	-0.1
Total	5	2	0	1.000	63	0	0	0	2	93^{2}	105	62	58	12	12	45	58	1.601	5.57	79	5.76	.283	0	.000	-11	2	-1.1
• ERICKS, John	John Edward Ericks b: 9/16/1967, Tinley Park, IL BR/TR, 6'7", 220 lbs. Deb: 6/24/1995																										
1995	Pit-N	3	9	.250	19	18	1	0	0	106	108	59	54	7	2	50	80	1.491	4.58	94	4.18	.263	3	.097	-2	4	-0.4
1996	Pit-N	4	5	.444	28	4	0	0	8	46^{2}	56	35	30	11	0	19	46	1.607	5.79	75	6.16	.292	0	.000	-7	1	-0.7
1997	Pit-N	1	0	1.000	10	0	0	0	6	9^{1}	7	3	2	1	0	4	6	1.179	1.93	223	2.84	.200	0	....	3	2	0.3
Total	3	8	14	.364	57	22	1	0	14	162	171	97	86	19	2	73	132	1.506	4.78	90	4.67	.268	3	.083	-6	7	-0.8
• ERICKSON, Don	Don Lee Erickson b: 12/13/1931, Springfield, IL BR/TR, 6', 175 lbs. Deb: 9/1/1958																										
1958	Phi-N	0	1	.000	9	0	0	0	1	11^{2}	11	7	6	3	0	9	9	1.714	4.63	86	6.20	.244	0	.000	-1	0	-0.1
• ERICKSON, Eric	Eric George Adolph Erickson b: 3/13/1895, Goteborg, Sweden d: 5/19/1965, Jamestown, NY BR/TR, 6'2", 190 lbs. Deb: 10/6/1914																										
1914	NY-N	0	1	.000	1	1	0	0	0	5	8	7	0	0	0	3	3	2.200	0.00	....	6.77	.364	0	.000	1	0	0.1
1916	Det-A	0	0	....	8	0	0	0	0	16	13	6	5	0	1	8	7	1.313	2.81	102	2.86	.220	0	.000	0	1	0.0
1918	Det-A	4	5	.444	12	9	8	0	1	94^{1}	81	32	26	2	3	29	48	1.166	2.48	107	2.62	.240	4	.121	7	5	0.5

YEAR	TM-L	W	L	PCT	G	GS	CG	SH	SV	IP	H	R	ER	HR	HB	BB	SO	RAT	ERA	ERA+	CERA	OAV	BH	AVG	PR+	WS	TPW
1919	Det-A	0	2	.000	3	2	0	0	0	14^{2}	17	17	11	0	1	10	4	1.841	6.75	47	5.47	.293	1	.200	-6	0	-0.6
	Was-A	6	11	.353	20	15	7	1	0	132	130	69	58	7	7	63	86	1.462	3.95	81	4.03	.254	7	.146	-10	3	-1.2
	Yr.	6	13	.316	23	17	7	1	0	146^{2}	147	86	69	7	8	73	90	1.500	4.23	76	4.17	.258	8	.151	-15	3	-1.8
1920	Was-A	12	16	.429	39	27	12	0	1	239^{1}	231	142	102	13	11	128	87	1.500	3.84	97	4.27	.264	23	.277	-1	11	0.3
1921	Was-A	8	10	.444	32	22	9	3	0	179	181	90	72	7	9	65	71	1.374	3.62	114	3.66	.269	9	.150	7	12	0.3
1922	Was-A	4	12	.250	30	17	6	2	2	141^{2}	144	95	78	8	3	73	61	1.532	4.96	78	4.30	.279	6	.133	-21	1	-2.3
Total	7	34	57	.374	145	93	42	6	4	822	805	458	352	37	35	379	367	1.440	3.85	93	3.92	.264	50	.179	-22	33	-2.8

• ERICKSON, Hal Harold James Erickson b: 7/17/1919, Portland, OR BR/TR, 6'5", 230 lbs. Deb: 4/14/1953

YEAR	TM-L	W	L	PCT	G	GS	CG	SH	SV	IP	H	R	ER	HR	HB	BB	SO	RAT	ERA	ERA+	CERA	OAV	BH	AVG	PR+	WS	TPW
1953	Det-A	0	1	.000	18	0	0	0	1	32^{1}	43	23	17	4	2	10	19	1.639	4.73	86	6.01	.323	0	.000	-1	1	-0.2

• ERICKSON, Paul Paul Walford "Li'L Abner" Erickson b: 12/14/1915, Zion, IL d: 4/5/2002, Fond du Lac, WI BR/TR, 6'2", 200 lbs. Deb: 6/29/1941

YEAR	TM-L	W	L	PCT	G	GS	CG	SH	SV	IP	H	R	ER	HR	HB	BB	SO	RAT	ERA	ERA+	CERA	OAV	BH	AVG	PR+	WS	TPW
1941	Chi-N	5	7	.417	32	15	7	1	1	141	126	70	58	2	2	64	85	1.348	3.70	95	2.97	.234	7	.152	1	6	0.1
1942	Chi-N	1	6	.143	18	7	1	0	0	63	70	40	38	4	0	41	26	1.762	5.43	59	5.33	.288	3	.143	-14	0	-1.6
1943	Chi-N	1	3	.250	15	4	0	0	0	42^{2}	47	32	29	4	2	22	24	1.617	6.12	55	5.10	.280	3	.200	-12	0	-1.3
1944	Chi-N	5	9	.357	33	15	5	3	1	124^{1}	113	59	49	5	0	67	82	1.448	3.55	100	3.50	.243	2	.056	2	6	0.0
1945*	Chi-N	7	4	.636	28	9	3	0	3	108^{1}	94	41	40	5	7	48	53	1.311	3.32	110	3.24	.233	5	.156	2	9	0.3
1946	Chi-N	9	7	.563	32	14	5	1	0	137	119	46	37	2	3	65	70	1.343	2.43	137	2.95	.232	2	.050	16	11	1.3
1947	Chi-N	7	12	.368	40	20	6	0	1	174	179	90	84	17	5	93	82	1.563	4.34	91	4.74	.268	15	.250	-7	10	-0.4
1948	Chi-N	0	0	....	3	0	0	0	0	5^{2}	7	5	4	0	0	6	4	2.294	6.35	61	6.55	.292	0	.000	-1	0	-0.2
	Phi-N	2	0	1.000	4	2	0	0	0	17^{1}	19	10	10	2	0	17	5	2.077	5.19	76	7.14	.288	1	.143	-2	1	-0.3
	NY-N	0	0	....	2	0	0	0	0	1	0	0	0	0	0	2	1	2.000	0.00	....	2.86	.000	0	....	0	0	0.0
	Yr.	2	0	1.000	9	2	0	0	0	24	26	15	14	2	0	25	10	2.125	5.25	75	6.82	.289	1	.125	-3	1	-0.4
Total	8	37	48	.435	207	86	27	5	6	814^{1}	774	393	349	41	19	425	432	1.472	3.86	92	3.87	.251	38	.147	-17	43	-2.0

• ERICKSON, Ralph Ralph Lief Erickson b: 6/25/1902, DuBois, ID d: 6/27/2002, Chandler, AZ BL/TL, 6'1", 175 lbs. Deb: 9/11/1929

YEAR	TM-L	W	L	PCT	G	GS	CG	SH	SV	IP	H	R	ER	HR	HB	BB	SO	RAT	ERA	ERA+	CERA	OAV	BH	AVG	PR+	WS	TPW
1929	Pit-N	0	0	....	1	0	0	0	0	1	2	3	3	0	0	2	0	4.000	27.00	18	18.54	.500	0	....	-2	0	-0.2
1930	Pit-N	1	0	1.000	7	0	0	0	0	14	21	12	11	1	0	10	2	2.214	7.07	70	8.04	.375	1	.250	-3	0	-0.3
Total	2	1	0	1.000	8	0	0	0	0	15	23	15	14	1	0	12	2	2.333	8.40	59	8.74	.383	1	.250	-6	0	-0.5

• ERICKSON, Roger Roger Farrell Erickson b: 8/30/1956, Springfield, IL BR/TR, 6'3", 190 lbs. Deb: 4/6/1978

YEAR	TM-L	W	L	PCT	G	GS	CG	SH	SV	IP	H	R	ER	HR	HB	BB	SO	RAT	ERA	ERA+	CERA	OAV	BH	AVG	PR+	WS	TPW
1978	Min-A	14	13	.519	37	37	14	0	0	265^{2}	268	129	117	19	8	79	121	1.306	3.96	96	3.67	.263	0	....	-5	12	-0.5
1979	Min-A	3	10	.231	24	21	0	0	0	123	154	86	77	17	1	48	47	1.642	5.63	78	5.86	.310	0	....	-17	2	-1.7
1980	Min-A	7	13	.350	32	27	7	0	0	191^{1}	198	83	69	13	4	56	97	1.328	3.25	134	3.73	.268	0	....	23	14	2.3
1981	Min-A	3	8	.273	14	14	1	0	0	91^{1}	93	48	39	7	0	31	44	1.358	3.84	103	3.61	.262	0	....	2	4	0.2
1982	Min-A	4	3	.571	7	7	2	0	0	40^{2}	56	29	22	6	1	12	12	1.672	4.87	87	6.26	.326	0	....	-3	1	-0.3
	NY-A	4	5	.444	16	11	0	0	1	70^{2}	86	36	35	5	0	17	37	1.458	4.46	89	4.43	.301	0	....	-3	3	-0.3
	Yr.	8	8	.500	23	18	2	0	1	111^{1}	142	65	57	11	1	29	49	1.536	4.61	88	5.10	.310	0	....	-7	4	-0.7
1983	NY-A	0	1	.000	5	0	0	0	0	16^{2}	13	8	8	1	0	8	7	1.260	4.32	90	2.87	.213	0	....	-1	1	-0.1
Total	6	35	53	.398	135	117	24	0	1	799^{1}	868	419	367	68	14	251	365	1.400	4.13	99	4.20	.277	0	....	-5	37	-0.5

• ERICKSON, Scott Scott Gavin Erickson b: 2/2/1968, Long Beach, CA BR/TR, 6'4", 224 lbs. Deb: 6/25/1990

YEAR	TM-L	W	L	PCT	G	GS	CG	SH	SV	IP	H	R	ER	HR	HB	BB	SO	RAT	ERA	ERA+	CERA	OAV	BH	AVG	PR+	WS	TPW
1990	Min-A	8	4	.667	19	17	1	0	0	113	108	49	36	9	5	51	53	1.407	2.87	145	4.07	.256	0	....	16	9	1.6
1991*	Min-A	**20**	8	.714	32	32	5	3	0	204	189	80	72	13	6	71	108	1.275	3.18	134	3.36	.248	0	....	22	18	2.3
1992	Min-A	13	12	.520	32	32	5	3	0	212	197	86	80	18	8	83	101	1.321	3.40	119	3.75	.252	0	....	14	14	1.4
1993	Min-A	8	19	.296	34	34	1	0	0	218^{2}	266	138	126	17	10	71	116	1.541	5.19	84	5.05	.305	0	....	-18	7	-1.8
1994	Min-A	8	11	.421	23	23	2	1	0	144	173	95	87	15	9	59	104	1.611	5.44	90	5.61	.299	0	....	-7	6	-0.6
1995	Min-A	4	6	.400	15	15	0	0	0	87^{2}	102	61	58	11	4	32	45	1.529	5.95	80	5.29	.291	0	....	-11	2	-1.1
	Bal-A	9	4	.692	17	16	7	2	0	108^{2}	111	47	47	7	1	35	61	1.344	3.89	122	3.84	.273	0	....	9	9	0.8
	Yr.	13	10	.565	32	31	7	2	0	196^{1}	213	108	105	18	5	67	106	1.426	4.81	99	4.49	.281	0	....	-2	11	-0.2
1996*	Bal-A	13	12	.520	34	34	6	0	0	222^{1}	262	137	124	21	11	66	100	1.475	5.02	98	4.90	.297	0	....	-2	10	-0.2
1997*	Bal-A	16	7	.696	34	33	3	2	0	221^{2}	218	100	91	16	5	61	131	1.259	3.69	119	3.40	.257	0	.000	17	16	1.6
1998	Bal-A	16	13	.552	36	**36**	**11**	2	0	**251^{1}**	284	125	112	23	13	69	186	1.405	4.01	114	4.40	.281	0	.000	17	15	1.7
1999	Bal-A	15	12	.556	34	34	6	**3**	0	230^{1}	244	127	123	27	11	99	106	1.489	4.81	97	4.97	.280	0	.000	-8	12	-0.8
2000	Bal-A	5	8	.385	16	16	1	0	0	92^{2}	127	81	81	14	5	48	41	1.888	7.87	60	7.50	.330	2	.400	-32	0	-2.8
2002	Bal-A	5	12	.294	29	28	3	1	0	160^{2}	192	109	99	20	8	68	74	1.618	5.55	77	5.80	.303	0	.000	-24	2	-2.4
Total	12	140	128	.522	355	350	51	17	0	2267	2473	1235	1136	211	96	813	1226	1.449	4.51	100	4.61	.281	2	.105	-7	120	-0.2

• ERRICKSON, Dick Richard Merriwell "Lief" Errickson b: 3/5/1912, Vineland, NJ d: 11/28/1999, Vineland, NJ BL/TR, 6'1", 175 lbs. Deb: 4/27/1938

YEAR	TM-L	W	L	PCT	G	GS	CG	SH	SV	IP	H	R	ER	HR	HB	BB	SO	RAT	ERA	ERA+	CERA	OAV	BH	AVG	PR+	WS	TPW
1938	Bos-N	9	7	.563	34	10	6	1	6	122^{2}	113	53	43	1	2	56	40	1.378	3.15	109	3.17	.246	4	.114	3	9	0.2
1939	Bos-N	6	9	.400	28	11	3	0	1	128^{1}	143	63	57	6	1	54	33	1.535	4.00	92	4.42	.293	10	.227	-6	6	-0.6
1940	Bos-N	12	13	.480	34	29	17	3	4	236^{1}	241	91	83	8	1	90	34	1.401	3.16	118	3.65	.270	13	.157	9	18	0.7
1941	Bos-N	6	12	.333	38	23	5	2	1	165^{2}	192	100	88	12	4	62	45	1.533	4.78	75	4.64	.287	8	.178	-24	3	-2.5
1942	Bos-N	2	5	.286	21	4	0	0	1	59^{1}	76	34	33	8	0	20	15	1.618	5.01	67	5.68	.309	2	.125	-11	0	-1.2
	Chi-N	1	1	.500	13	0	0	0	0	24	39	12	11	1	1	8	9	1.958	4.13	77	7.67	.411	0	.000	-2	1	-0.3
	Yr.	3	6	.333	34	4	0	0	1	83^{1}	115	46	44	9	1	28	24	1.716	4.75	69	6.25	.337	2	.095	-13	1	-1.5
Total	5	36	47	.434	168	77	31	6	13	736^{1}	804	353	315	36	9	290	176	1.486	3.85	93	4.22	.282	37	.162	-30	37	-3.7

• ERSKINE, Carl Carl Daniel "Oisk" Erskine b: 12/13/1926, Anderson, IN BR/TR, 5'10", 165 lbs. Deb: 7/25/1948

YEAR	TM-L	W	L	PCT	G	GS	CG	SH	SV	IP	H	R	ER	HR	HB	BB	SO	RAT	ERA	ERA+	CERA	OAV	BH	AVG	PR+	WS	TPW
1948	Bro-N	6	3	.667	17	9	3	0	0	64	51	28	23	5	1	35	29	1.344	3.23	123	3.45	.231	2	.095	4	5	0.2
1949*	Bro-N	8	1	.889	22	3	2	0	0	79^{2}	68	44	41	6	2	51	49	1.494	4.63	89	3.99	.235	3	.115	-6	4	-0.8
1950	Bro-N	7	6	.538	22	13	3	0	1	103	109	56	54	15	1	35	50	1.398	4.72	87	4.48	.273	9	.243	-9	6	-0.8
1951	Bro-N	16	12	.571	46	19	7	0	4	189^{2}	206	105	94	23	2	78	95	**1.497**	4.46	88	4.75	.280	8	.131	-15	8	-1.8
1952*	Bro-N	14	6	.700	33	26	10	4	2	206^{2}	167	72	62	17	2	71	131	1.152	2.70	135	2.72	.220	10	.152	20	17	2.0
1953*	Bro-N	20	6	.769	39	33	16	4	3	246^{2}	213	106	97	21	3	95	187	1.249	3.54	120	3.14	.230	20	.215	16	20	1.6
1954	Bro-N★	18	15	.545	38	37	12	2	1	260^{1}	239	128	120	31	4	92	166	1.271	4.15	98	3.54	.243	14	.159	-2	16	-0.3
1955*	Bro-N	11	8	.579	31	29	7	2	1	194^{2}	185	89	82	29	0	64	84	1.279	3.79	107	3.88	.253	15	.203	5	12	0.4
1956*	Bro-N	13	11	.542	31	28	8	1	0	186^{1}	189	92	88	25	1	57	95	1.320	4.25	93	4.00	.264	8	.121	-10	9	-1.3
1957	Bro-N	5	3	.625	15	7	1	0	0	66	62	27	26	8	0	20	26	1.242	3.55	117	3.50	.248	2	.091	5	5	0.3
1958	LA-N	4	4	.500	31	9	2	1	0	98^{1}	115	61	56	14	0	35	54	1.525	5.13	80	5.13	.297	1	.037	-11	3	-1.4
1959	LA-N	0	3	.000	10	3	0	0	1	23^{1}	33	22	20	5	0	13	15	1.971	7.71	55	7.90	.320	0	.000	-9	0	-1.0
Total	12	122	78	.610	335	216	71	14	13	1718^{2}	1637	830	763	199	16	646	981	1.328	4.00	101	3.83	.252	92	.156	-14	105	-2.8

• ESCARREGA, Chico Ernesto (Acosta) Escarrega b: 12/27/1949, Los Mochis, Mexico BR/TR, 5'11", 185 lbs. Deb: 4/26/1982

YEAR	TM-L	W	L	PCT	G	GS	CG	SH	SV	IP	H	R	ER	HR	HB	BB	SO	RAT	ERA	ERA+	CERA	OAV	BH	AVG	PR+	WS	TPW
1982	Chi-A	1	3	.250	38	2	0	0	1	73^{2}	73	33	30	3	0	16	33	1.208	3.67	110	2.95	.263	0	....	4	4	0.4

• ESCOBAR, Kelvim Kelvim Jose (Bolivar) Escobar b: 4/11/1976, La Guaira, Venezuela BB/TR, 6'1", 205 lbs. Deb: 6/29/1997

YEAR	TM-L	W	L	PCT	G	GS	CG	SH	SV	IP	H	R	ER	HR	HB	BB	SO	RAT	ERA	ERA+	CERA	OAV	BH	AVG	PR+	WS	TPW
1997	Tor-A	3	2	.600	27	0	0	0	14	31	28	12	10	1	0	19	36	1.516	2.90	158	3.68	.237	0	....	5	6	0.5
1998	Tor-A	7	3	.700	22	10	0	0	0	79^{2}	72	37	33	5	0	35	72	1.343	3.73	125	3.41	.237	0	....	8	7	0.8
1999	Tor-A	14	11	.560	33	30	1	0	0	174	203	118	110	19	10	81	129	1.632	5.69	87	5.62	.293	0	.000	-15	7	-1.4
2000	Tor-A	10	15	.400	43	24	3	1	2	180	186	118	107	26	3	85	142	1.506	5.35	95	4.94	.267	0	.000	-6	8	-0.6
2001	Tor-A	6	8	.429	59	11	1	1	0	126	93	51	49	8	3	52	121	1.151	3.50	131	2.54	.204	0	....	15	11	1.4
2002	Tor-A	5	7	.417	76	0	0	0	38	78	75	39	37	10	5	44	85	1.526	4.27	108	4.77	.246	0	....	4	9	0.3
2003	Tor-A	13	9	.591	41	26	1	1	4	180^{1}	189	94	86	15	9	78	159	1.481	4.29	107	4.53	.270	1	.167	9	12	0.9
Total	7	58	55	.513	301	101	6	3	58	849	846	469	432	84	30	394	744	1.461	4.58	105	4.43	.258	1	.071	20	60	1.9

• ESHELMAN, Vaughn Vaughn Michael Eshelman b: 5/22/1969, Philadelphia, PA BL/TL, 6'3", 205 lbs. Deb: 5/2/1995

YEAR	TM-L	W	L	PCT	G	GS	CG	SH	SV	IP	H	R	ER	HR	HB	BB	SO	RAT	ERA	ERA+	CERA	OAV	BH	AVG	PR+	WS	TPW
1995	Bos-A	6	3	.667	23	14	0	0	0	81^{2}	86	47	44	3	1	36	41	1.494	4.85	100	4.17	.272	0	....	-0	5	0.0
1996	Bos-A	6	3	.667	39	10	0	0	0	87^{2}	112	79	69	13	2	58	59	1.939	7.08	72	7.21	.311	0	....	-18	1	-1.6

YEAR	TM-L	W	L	PCT	G	GS	CG	SH	SV	IP	H	R	ER	HR	HB	BB	SO	RAT	ERA	ERA+	CERA	OAV	BH	AVG	PR+	WS	TPW
1997	Bos-A	3	3	.500	21	6	0	0	0	42^2	58	32	30	3	2	17	18	1.758	6.33	73	6.00	.330	1	.250	-8	1	-0.7
Total	3	15	9	.625	83	30	0	0	0	212	256	158	143	19	5	111	118	1.731	6.07	81	5.79	.300	1	.250	-26	7	-2.4
• ESPER, Duke	Charles H. Esper b: 7/28/1868, Salem, NJ d: 8/31/1910, Philadelphia, PA TL, 5'11.5", 185 lbs. Deb: 4/18/1890																										
1890	Phi-a	8	9	.471	18	16	14	1	0	143^2	176	99	78	1	5	67	61	1.691	4.89	78	....	.293	18	.295	-9	7	-0.4
	Pit-N	0	2	.000	2	2	2	0	0	17	18	16	10	0	1	10	9	1.647	5.29	62	....	.264	1	.143	-3	0	-0.3
	Phi-N	5	0	1.000	5	5	4	0	0	41	40	22	14	1	0	16	18	1.366	3.07	119	....	.248	3	.158	2	3	0.1
	Yr.	5	2	.714	7	7	6	0	0	58	58	38	24	1	1	26	27	1.448	3.72	94	....	.253	4	.154	-1	3	-0.2
1891	Phi-N	20	15	.571	39	36	25	1	1	296	302	185	117	8	7	121	108	1.429	3.56	96	....	.255	27	.220	-7	17	-0.5
1892	Phi-N	11	6	.647	21	18	14	0	1	160^1	171	84	61	2	1	60	45	1.441	3.42	95	3.59	.263	17	.243	-6	11	-0.3
	Pit-N	2	0	1.000	3	3	1	0	0	18^1	18	13	11	0	12	12	5	1.636	5.40	61	6.31	.247	0	.000	-5	1	-0.6
	Yr.	13	6	.684	24	21	15	0	1	178^2	189	97	72	2	13	72	50	1.461	3.63	90	3.87	.261	17	.215	-11	12	-0.9
1893	Was-N	12	28	.300	42	36	34	0	0	334^1	442	277	175	14	12	156	78	1.789	4.71	98	5.79	.309	41	.287	5	11	1.1
1894	Was-N	5	10	.333	18	14	7	0	0	116	177	132	96	8	2	39	24	1.862	7.45	71	6.70	.347	14	.259	-25	3	-1.8
	*Bal-N	10	2	.833	16	9	8	0	2	101	107	56	44	1	1	36	25	1.416	3.92	139	3.55	.269	10	.222	14	11	1.0
	Yr.	15	12	.556	34	23	15	0	2	217	284	188	140	9	3	75	49	1.654	5.81	92	5.23	.313	24	.242	-11	14	-0.8
1895*	Bal-N	10	12	.455	34	25	16	1	1	218^1	248	132	95	2	0	79	39	1.498	3.92	121	3.94	.282	16	.178	7	18	0.1
1896	Bal-N	14	5	.737	20	18	14	1	0	155^2	168	80	62	3	2	39	19	1.330	3.58	119	3.37	.274	13	.197	9	13	0.6
1897	StL-N	1	6	.143	8	8	7	0	0	61^1	95	51	36	5	1	12	8	1.745	5.28	83	6.37	.351	8	.320	-4	1	-0.2
1898	StL-N	3	5	.375	10	8	6	0	0	64^2	86	49	43	1	0	22	14	1.670	5.98	63	5.00	.317	10	.370	-14	2	-1.1
Total	9	101	100	.502	236	198	152	4	5	1727^2	2048	1196	842	46	44	669	453	1.573	4.39	95	3.39	.288	178	.241	-35	98	-2.3
• ESPINOSA, Nino	Arnulfo Acevedo Espinosa b: 8/15/1953, Villa Altagracia, Dominican Republic d: 12/24/1987, Santo Domingo, Dominican Republic BR/TR, 6'1", 192 lbs. Deb: 9/13/1974																										
1974	NY-N	0	0	....	2	1	0	0	0	9	12	5	5	1	0	0	2	1.333	5.00	71	4.32	.324	1	.500	-1	0	-0.1
1975	NY-N	0	1	.000	2	0	0	0	0	3	8	6	6	0	0	1	2	3.000	18.00	19	13.68	.471	0	....	-5	0	-0.5
1976	NY-N	4	4	.500	12	5	0	0	0	41^2	41	21	17	3	0	13	30	1.296	3.67	90	3.35	.265	0	.000	-2	2	-0.3
1977	NY-N	10	13	.435	32	29	7	1	0	200	188	82	76	17	5	55	105	1.215	3.42	109	3.26	.249	8	.129	7	12	0.5
1978	NY-N	11	15	.423	32	32	6	1	0	203^2	230	117	107	24	3	75	76	**1.498**	4.73	74	4.86	.292	14	.209	-30	3	-2.9
1979	Phi-N	14	12	.538	33	33	8	3	0	212	211	94	86	20	3	65	88	1.302	3.65	105	3.72	.262	14	.194	2	14	0.3
1980	Phi-N	3	5	.375	12	12	1	0	0	76^1	73	36	32	9	2	19	13	1.205	3.77	100	3.43	.250	3	.115	0	3	-0.1
1981	Phi-N	2	5	.286	14	14	2	0	0	73^2	98	52	50	11	1	24	22	1.656	6.11	59	6.30	.333	4	.200	-21	0	-2.3
	Tor-A	0	0	....	1	0	0	0	0	1	4	1	1	0	0	0	0	4.000	9.00	44	26.25	.667	0	....	-1	0	-0.1
Total	8	44	55	.444	140	126	24	5	0	820^1	865	414	380	85	14	252	338	1.362	4.17	87	4.15	.275	44	.171	-51	34	-5.4
• ESSER, Mark	Mark Gerald Esser b: 4/1/1956, Erie, PA BR/TL, 6'1", 190 lbs. Deb: 4/22/1979																										
1979	Chi-A	0	0	....	2	0	0	0	0	1^2	2	3	3	0	0	4	1	3.600	16.20	26	12.62	.286	0	....	-2	0	-0.2
• ESSICK, Bill	William Earl "Vinegar Bill" Essick b: 12/18/1880, Grand Ridge, IL d: 10/12/1951, Los Angeles, CA TR, 5'10", 175 lbs. Deb: 9/12/1906																										
1906	Cin-N	2	2	.500	6	4	3	0	0	39^1	39	18	13	1	2	16	16	1.398	2.97	92	3.86	.273	1	.077	-1	2	-0.2
1907	Cin-N	0	2	.000	3	2	2	0	0	21^2	23	15	7	0	1	8	7	1.431	2.91	89	3.72	.274	0	.000	-1	0	-0.2
Total	2	2	4	.333	9	6	5	0	0	61	62	33	20	1	3	24	23	1.410	2.95	91	3.81	.273	1	.048	-2	2	-0.5
• ESTELLE, Dick	Richard Henry Estelle b: 1/18/1942, Lakewood, NJ BB/TL, 6'2", 170 lbs. Deb: 9/4/1964																										
1964	SF-N	1	2	.333	6	6	0	0	0	41^2	39	15	14	3	0	23	23	1.488	3.02	118	4.06	.247	1	.067	2	3	0.2
1965	SF-N	0	0	....	6	1	0	0	0	11^1	12	6	5	0	1	8	6	1.765	3.97	91	4.77	.261	0	.000	-0	0	0.0
Total	2	1	2	.333	12	7	0	0	0	53	51	21	19	3	1	31	29	1.547	3.23	111	4.21	.250	1	.063	2	3	0.2
• ESTES, Shawn	Aaron Shawn Estes b: 2/18/1973, San Bernardino, CA BB/TL, 6'2", 185 lbs. Deb: 9/16/1995																										
1995	SF-N	0	3	.000	3	3	0	0	0	17^1	16	14	13	2	1	5	14	1.212	6.75	60	3.37	.229	0	.000	-5	0	-0.6
1996	SF-N	3	5	.375	11	11	0	0	0	70	63	30	28	3	2	39	60	1.457	3.60	114	3.78	.243	3	.158	3	4	0.3
1997*	SF-N★	19	5	.792	32	32	3	2	0	201	162	80	71	12	8	100	181	1.303	3.18	127	3.28	.223	10	.147	20	16	2.0
1998	SF-N	7	12	.368	25	25	1	1	0	149^1	150	89	84	14	5	80	136	1.540	5.06	78	4.71	.269	8	.190	-18	3	-1.7
1999	SF-N	11	11	.500	32	32	1	1	0	203	209	121	111	21	5	112	159	1.581	4.92	85	4.96	.268	10	.164	-16	6	-1.4
2000*	SF-N	15	6	.714	30	30	4	2	0	190^1	194	99	90	11	3	108	136	1.587	4.26	99	4.75	.275	14	.206	-1	10	0.3
2001	SF-N	9	8	.529	27	27	0	0	0	159	151	78	71	11	5	77	109	1.434	4.02	99	3.96	.253	3	.071	-1	7	-0.3
2002	NY-N	4	9	.308	23	23	1	1	0	132^2	133	70	67	12	5	66	92	1.500	4.55	87	4.51	.267	3	.086	-8	4	-0.8
	Cin-N	1	3	.250	6	6	0	0	0	28	38	24	24	1	4	17	17	1.964	7.71	55	7.52	.345	0	.000	-11	0	-1.2
	Yr.	5	12	.294	29	29	1	1	0	160^2	171	94	91	13	9	83	109	1.581	5.10	79	5.04	.281	3	.070	-18	4	-2.0
2003	Chi-N	8	11	.421	29	28	1	1	0	152^1	182	113	97	20	1	83	103	1.740	5.73	73	6.15	.305	7	.179	-26	1	-2.4
Total	9	77	73	.513	218	217	11	8	0	1303	1298	718	656	107	39	687	1007	1.523	4.53	91	4.58	.265	58	.150	-62	51	-5.7
• ESTOCK, George	George John Estock b: 11/2/1924, Stirling, NJ BR/TR, 6', 185 lbs. Deb: 4/21/1951																										
1951	Bos-N	0	1	.000	37	1	0	0	3	60^1	56	33	29	2	0	37	11	1.541	4.33	85	3.92	.258	2	.286	-4	2	-0.3
• ESTRADA, Chuck	Charles Leonard Estrada b: 2/15/1938, San Luis Obispo, CA BR/TR, 6'1", 185 lbs. Deb: 4/21/1960 C																										
1960	Bal-A★	**18**	11	.621	36	25	12	1	2	208^2	162	87	83	18	15	101	144	1.260	3.58	106	3.35	**.218**	9	.141	1	15	0.1
1961	Bal-A	15	9	.625	33	31	6	1	0	212	159	91	87	19	10	132	160	1.373	3.69	106	3.64	**.207**	8	.114	2	13	-0.1
1962	Bal-A	9	17	.346	34	33	6	0	0	223^1	199	112	95	24	10	121	165	1.433	3.83	98	4.15	.240	10	.152	-4	8	-0.4
1963	Bal-A	3	2	.600	8	7	0	0	0	31^1	26	17	16	2	1	19	16	1.436	4.60	77	3.76	.226	1	.100	-4	1	-0.5
1964	Bal-A	3	2	.600	17	6	0	0	0	54^2	62	34	32	8	2	21	32	1.518	5.27	68	5.04	.282	2	.143	-12	0	-1.3
1966	Chi-N	1	1	.500	9	1	0	0	0	12^1	16	12	10	2	1	5	3	1.703	7.30	50	6.55	.314	0	.000	-5	0	-0.5
1967	NY-N	1	2	.333	9	2	0	0	0	22	28	24	23	5	1	17	15	2.045	9.41	36	8.85	.326	0	.000	-15	0	-1.7
Total	7	50	44	.532	146	105	24	2	2	764^1	652	377	346	78	40	416	535	1.397	4.07	92	4.01	.232	30	.129	-35	37	-4.3
• ESTRADA, Horacio	Horacio (Jimenez) Estrada b: 10/19/1975, San Joaquin, Venezuela BL/TL, 6'1", 160 lbs. Deb: 5/4/1999																										
1999	Mil-N	0	0	....	4	0	0	0	0	7^1	10	6	6	4	0	4	5	1.909	7.36	62	10.50	.313	0	.000	-2	0	-0.2
2000	Mil-N	3	0	1.000	7	4	0	0	0	24^1	30	18	17	5	2	20	13	2.055	6.29	72	8.17	.300	1	.143	-5	1	-0.5
2001	Col-N	1	1	.500	4	0	0	0	0	4^1	8	7	7	1	1	1	4	2.077	14.54	37	11.24	.400	0	....	-4	0	-0.4
Total	3	4	1	.800	15	4	0	0	0	36	48	31	30	10	3	25	22	2.028	7.50	63	9.01	.316	1	.111	-12	1	-1.2
• ESTRADA, Oscar	Oscar Estrada b: 2/15/1904, Havana, Cuba d: 1/2/1978, Havana, Cuba BL/TL, 5'8", 160 lbs. Deb: 4/21/1929																										
1929	StL-A	0	0	....	1	0	0	0	0	1	1	0	0	0	0	1	0	2.000	0.00	....	5.17	.250	0	....	0	0	0.0
• ESTRELLA, Leo	Leoncio (Ramirez) Estrella b: 2/20/1975, Puerto Plata, Dominican Republic BR/TR, 6'1", 185 lbs. Deb: 7/18/2000																										
2000	Tor-A	0	0	....	2	0	0	0	0	4^2	9	3	3	1	0	0	3	1.929	5.79	88	9.77	.450	0	....	-0	0	0.0
2003	Mil-N	7	3	.700	58	0	0	0	3	66	75	32	32	10	3	21	25	1.455	4.36	97	4.97	.290	0	....	0	5	0.0
Total	2	7	3	.700	60	0	0	0	3	70^2	84	35	35	11	3	21	28	1.486	4.46	97	5.29	.301	0	....	0	5	0.0
• ETHERTON, Seth	Seth Michael Etherton b: 10/17/1976, Laguna Beach, CA BR/TR, 6'1", 200 lbs. Deb: 5/26/2000																										
2000	Ana-A	5	1	.833	11	11	0	0	0	60^1	68	38	37	16	1	22	32	1.492	5.52	92	5.87	.278	0	.000	-4	3	-0.4
2003	Cin-N	2	4	.333	7	7	0	0	0	30	39	23	23	4	3	15	17	1.800	6.90	62	6.85	.322	1	.143	-9	0	-0.9
Total	2	7	5	.583	18	18	0	0	0	90^1	107	61	60	20	4	37	49	1.594	5.98	79	6.20	.292	1	.111	-13	3	-1.3
• ETTLES, Mark	Mark Edward Ettles b: 10/30/1966, Perth, Australia BR/TR, 6', 178 lbs. Deb: 6/5/1993																										
1993	SD-N	1	0	1.000	14	0	0	0	0	18	23	16	13	4	0	4	9	1.500	6.50	64	5.63	.307	0	.000	-5	0	-0.5
• EUBANK, John	John Franklin "Honest John" Eubank b: 9/9/1872, Servia, IN d: 11/3/1958, Bellevue, MI BR/TR, 6'2", 215 lbs. Deb: 9/19/1905																										
1905	Det-A	1	0	1.000	3	2	0	0	0	17^1	13	12	4	0	1	3	1	.923	2.08	131	1.62	.211	5	.357	1	1	0.3
1906	Det-A	4	10	.286	24	12	7	1	2	135	147	69	53	0	8	35	38	1.348	3.53	78	3.47	.280	13	.206	-12	6	-1.4

YEAR	TM-L	W	L	PCT	G	GS	CG	SH	SV	IP	H	R	ER	HR	HB	BB	SO	RAT	ERA	ERA+	CERA	OAV	BH	AVG	PR+	WS	TPW
1907	Det-A	3	3	.500	15	8	4	1	0	81	88	40	24	0	0	20	17	1.333	2.67	98	3.18	.279	4	.129	-0	3	-0.2
Total	3	8	13	.381	42	22	11	2	2	233^1	248	121	81	0	9	58	56	1.311	3.12	87	3.23	.275	22	.204	-11	10	-1.3
• EUBANKS, Uel	Uel Melvin "Poss" Eubanks b: 2/14/1903, Quinlan, TX d: 11/21/1954, Dallas, TX BR/TR, 6'3", 175 lbs. Deb: 7/20/1922																										
1922	Chi-N	0	0	....	2	0	0	0	0	1^2	5	9	5	0	0	4	1	5.400	27.00	16	22.17	.556	1	1.000	-4	0	-0.3
• EUFEMIA, Frank	Frank Anthony Eufemia b: 12/23/1959, Bronx, NY BR/TR, 5'11", 185 lbs. Deb: 5/21/1985																										
1985	Min-A	4	2	.667	39	0	0	0	2	61^2	56	27	26	7	0	21	30	1.249	3.79	116	3.37	.250	0	....	4	6	0.4
• EVANS, Art	William Arthur Evans b: 8/3/1911, Elvins, MO d: 1/8/1952, Wichita, KS BB/TL, 6'1.5", 181 lbs. Deb: 6/20/1932																										
1932	Chi-A	0	0	....	7	0	0	0	0	18	19	9	6	1	0	10	6	1.611	3.00	144	4.34	.257	0	.000	3	1	0.3
• EVANS, Bart	Bart Steven Evans b: 12/30/1970, Springfield, MO BR/TR, 6'2" Deb: 6/16/1998																										
1998	KC-A	0	0	....	8	0	0	0	0	9	7	3	2	1	0	0	7	.778	2.00	241	1.58	.206	0	....	3	1	0.3
• EVANS, Bill	William James Evans b: 2/10/1894, Reidsville, NC d: 12/21/1946, Burlington, NC BR/TR, 6', 175 lbs. Deb: 8/13/1916																										
1916	Pit-N	2	5	.286	13	7	3	0	0	63	57	27	21	2	3	16	21	1.159	3.00	89	2.77	.249	3	.150	-1	2	-0.2
1917	Pit-N	0	4	.000	8	2	1	0	0	26^2	24	14	10	0	1	14	5	1.425	3.38	84	3.07	.231	1	.111	-1	0	-0.2
1919	Pit-N	0	4	.000	7	3	2	0	0	36^2	41	25	23	1	0	18	15	1.609	5.65	53	4.39	.297	0	.000	-10	0	-1.3
Total	3	2	13	.133	28	12	6	0	0	126^1	122	66	54	3	4	48	41	1.346	3.85	74	3.30	.259	4	.100	-13	2	-1.7
• EVANS, Bill	William Lawrence Evans b: 3/25/1919, Quanah, TX d: 11/30/1983, Grand Junction, CO BR/TR, 6'2", 180 lbs. Deb: 4/21/1949																										
1949	Chi-A	0	1	.000	4	0	0	0	0	6^1	6	6	5	0	0	8	1	2.211	7.11	59	6.18	.261	0	.000	-2	0	-0.2
1951	Bos-A	0	0	....	9	0	0	0	0	15^1	15	8	7	0	0	8	3	1.500	4.11	109	3.64	.268	0	.000	1	1	0.0
Total	2	0	1	.000	13	0	0	0	0	21^2	21	14	12	0	0	16	4	1.708	4.98	87	4.39	.266	0	.000	-2	1	-0.2
• EVANS, Chick	Charles Franklin Evans b: 10/15/1889, Arlington, VT d: 9/2/1916, Schenectady, NY BR/TR Deb: 9/19/1909																										
1909	Bos-N	0	3	.000	4	3	1	0	0	21^2	25	16	11	0	0	14	11	1.800	4.57	61	5.27	.305	0	.000	-4	0	-0.6
1910	Bos-N	1	1	.500	13	1	0	0	2	31	28	20	18	1	3	27	12	1.774	5.23	63	5.56	.275	1	.100	-7	1	-0.8
Total	2	1	4	.200	17	4	1	0	2	52^2	53	36	29	1	3	41	23	1.785	4.96	63	5.44	.288	1	.053	-11	1	-1.4
• EVANS, Red	Russell Edison Evans b: 11/12/1906, Chicago, IL d: 6/14/1982, Lakeview, AR BR/TR, 5'11", 168 lbs. Deb: 4/24/1936																										
1936	Chi-A	0	3	.000	17	0	0	0	1	47^1	70	46	40	4	0	22	19	1.944	7.61	68	6.67	.338	2	.133	-13	0	-1.3
1939	Bro-N	1	8	.111	24	6	0	0	1	64^1	74	43	37	4	0	26	28	1.554	5.18	78	4.39	.284	4	.308	-8	1	-0.7
Total	2	1	11	.083	41	6	0	0	2	111^2	144	89	77	8	0	48	47	1.719	6.21	73	5.36	.308	6	.214	-21	1	-2.0
• EVANS, Roy	Roy Evans b: 3/19/1874, Knoxville, TN d: 8/15/1915, Galveston, TX BR/TR, 6', 180 lbs. Deb: 5/15/1897																										
1897	StL-N	0	0	....	3	0	0	0	0	13	33	27	14	1	0	13	4	3.538	9.69	45	16.92	.470	0	.000	-7	0	-0.6
	Lou-N	5	4	.556	9	8	6	0	0	59^1	66	40	27	4	8	24	20	1.517	4.10	104	4.89	.280	3	.130	1	3	0.0
	Yr.	5	4	.556	12	8	6	0	0	72^1	99	67	41	5	8	37	24	1.880	5.10	84	7.05	.323	3	.115	-6	3	-0.6
1898	Was-N	3	3	.500	7	6	4	0	0	50^2	50	27	19	0	7	25	11	1.480	3.38	108	3.98	.256	1	.053	3	3	0.1
1899	Was-N	3	4	.429	7	7	6	0	0	54	60	40	34	1	0	25	27	1.574	5.67	69	4.22	.281	4	.200	-8	1	-0.8
1902	NY-N	8	13	.381	23	17	17	0	0	176	186	87	62	2	9	58	48	1.386	3.17	88	3.59	.271	8	.148	-6	9	-0.7
	Bro-N	5	6	.455	13	11	11	2	0	97^1	91	42	29	0	2	33	35	1.274	2.68	103	2.82	.248	9	.265	1	6	0.3
	Yr.	13	19	.406	36	28	28	2	0	273^1	277	129	91	2	11	91	83	1.346	3.00	93	3.32	.263	17	.193	-5	15	-0.4
1903	Bro-N	5	9	.357	15	12	9	0	0	110	121	75	40	1	7	41	42	1.473	3.27	97	4.31	.297	5	.172	13	5	1.3
	StL-A	0	4	.000	7	7	4	0	0	54	66	30	25	1	3	14	24	1.481	4.17	70	4.28	.300	2	.105	-8	0	-0.9
Total	5	29	43	.403	84	68	57	2	0	614^1	673	368	250	10	36	233	211	1.475	3.66	88	4.15	.281	32	.159	-11	27	-1.3
• EVERITT, Leon	Edward Leon Everitt b: 1/12/1947, Marshall, TX BL/TR, 6'1.5", 195 lbs. Deb: 4/21/1969																										
1969	SD-N	0	1	.000	5	0	0	0	0	15^2	18	14	14	4	1	12	11	1.915	8.04	44	8.13	.300	0	.000	-8	0	-0.8
• EVERSGERD, Bryan	Bryan David Eversgerd b: 2/11/1969, Centralia, IL BR/TL, 6'1", 190 lbs. Deb: 4/30/1994																										
1994	StL-N	2	3	.400	40	1	0	0	0	67^2	75	36	34	8	2	20	47	1.404	4.52	92	4.69	.295	0	.000	-3	3	-0.3
1995	Mon-N	0	0	....	25	0	0	0	0	21	22	13	12	2	1	9	8	1.476	5.14	83	4.34	.268	0	.000	-2	1	-0.2
1997	Tex-A	0	2	.000	3	0	0	0	0	1^1	5	3	3	0	0	3	2	6.000	20.25	24	32.13	.556	0	....	-2	0	-0.2
1998	StL-N	0	0	....	8	0	0	0	0	6	9	7	6	1	1	2	4	1.833	9.00	47	7.67	.346	0	....	-3	0	-0.3
Total	4	2	5	.286	76	1	0	0	0	96	111	59	55	11	4	34	61	1.510	5.16	82	5.18	.299	0	.000	-10	4	-1.1
• EWING, Bob	George Lemuel "Long Bob" Ewing b: 4/24/1873, New Hampshire, OH d: 6/20/1947, Wapakoneta, OH BR/TR, 6'1.5", 170 lbs. Deb: 4/19/1902																										
1902	Cin-N	5	6	.455	15	12	10	0	0	117^2	126	67	39	1	3	47	44	1.470	2.98	100	3.80	.274	12	.169	-2	4	-0.5
1903	Cin-N	14	13	.519	29	28	27	1	1	246^2	254	127	76	3	10	64	104	1.289	2.77	128	3.22	.265	24	.253	22	18	2.5
1904	Cin-N	11	13	.458	26	24	22	0	0	212	198	85	58	3	4	58	99	1.208	2.46	119	2.81	.253	25	.258	5	17	1.1
1905	Cin-N	20	11	.645	40	34	30	4	0	311^2	284	125	87	5	11	79	164	1.165	2.51	131	2.67	.246	32	.262	21	23	2.7
1906	Cin-N	13	14	.481	33	32	26	2	0	287^2	248	98	76	4	2	60	145	1.071	2.38	115	2.22	.238	14	.139	9	21	0.7
1907	Cin-N	17	19	.472	41	37	32	2	0	332^2	279	104	64	2	7	85	147	1.094	1.73	150	2.22	.231	19	.154	**28**	21	3.1
1908	Cin-N	17	15	.531	37	32	23	4	3	293^2	247	105	72	5	5	57	95	1.035	2.21	104	2.20	.241	14	.149	7	20	0.8
1909	Cin-N	11	12	.478	31	29	14	2	0	218^1	195	94	59	1	6	63	86	1.182	2.43	106	2.54	.238	8	.110	2	9	-0.1
1910	Phi-N	16	14	.533	34	32	20	4	0	255^1	235	110	85	5	7	86	102	1.257	3.00	104	3.02	.251	20	.222	1	15	0.4
1911	Phi-N	0	1	.000	4	3	1	0	0	24	29	25	21	2	0	14	12	1.792	7.88	44	6.00	.309	2	.333	-12	0	-1.2
1912	StL-N	0	0	....	1	1	0	0	0	1^1	2	0	0	0	0	1	0	2.250	0.00	....	7.28	.333	0	....	0	0	0.0
Total	11	124	118	.512	291	264	205	19	4	2301	2097	940	637	31	55	614	998	1.178	2.49	116	2.68	.247	170	.195	83	148	9.7
• EWING, John	John "Long John" Ewing b: 6/1/1863, Cincinnati, OH d: 4/23/1895, Denver, CO TR, 6'1" Deb: 6/18/1883 U ♦																										
1888	Lou-a	8	13	.381	21	21	21	2	0	191	175	105	60	3	8	34	87	1.094	2.83	109	....	.235	16	.203	10	6	0.9
1889	Lou-a	6	30	.167	40	39	37	1	0	331	407	296	179	6	14	147	155	1.674	4.87	79	....	.293	23	.172	-32	7	-3.1
1890	NY-P	18	12	.600	35	31	27	1	2	267^1	294	196	126	6	16	104	145	1.489	4.24	107	....	.268	24	.211	5	19	0.3
1891	NY-N	21	8	.724	33	30	28	5	0	269^1	237	118	68	2	11	105	138	1.270	**2.27**	141	....	.228	23	.204	24	21	2.0
Total	4	53	63	.457	129	121	113	9	2	1058^2	1113	715	433	17	49	390	525	1.420	3.68	102	....	.261	87	.192	7	53	0.1
• EYRE, Scott	Scott Alan Eyre b: 5/30/1972, Inglewood, CA BL/TL, 6'1", 160 lbs. Deb: 8/1/1997																										
1997	Chi-A	4	4	.500	11	11	0	0	0	60^2	62	36	34	11	1	31	36	1.533	5.04	87	5.37	.267	1	.500	-4	2	-0.3
1998	Chi-A	3	8	.273	33	17	0	0	0	107	114	78	64	24	2	64	73	1.664	5.38	85	6.31	.271	0	.000	-10	2	-1.0
1999	Chi-A	1	1	.500	21	0	0	0	0	25	38	22	21	6	1	15	17	2.120	7.56	64	9.23	.339	0	....	-7	0	-0.7
2000	Chi-A	1	1	.500	13	1	0	0	0	19	29	15	14	3	1	12	16	2.158	6.63	75	9.49	.372	0	....	-4	0	-0.3
2001	Tor-A	1	2	.333	17	0	0	0	2	15^2	15	6	6	1	1	7	16	1.404	3.45	133	3.96	.263	0	....	2	2	0.2
2002	Tor-A	2	4	.333	49	3	0	0	0	63^1	69	37	35	4	0	29	51	1.547	4.97	93	4.32	.278	0	....	-2	3	-0.2
*	SF-N	0	0	....	21	0	0	0	0	11^1	11	4	2	0	0	7	7	1.588	1.59	244	3.91	.256	0	....	3	1	0.3
2003*	SF-N	2	1	.667	74	0	0	0	1	57	60	23	21	4	1	26	35	1.509	3.32	124	4.37	.268	1	.500	4	5	0.4
Total	7	14	21	.400	239	32	0	0	3	359	398	221	197	53	7	191	251	1.641	4.94	92	5.69	.281	2	.286	-19	15	-1.6
• EYRICH, George	George Lincoln Eyrich b: 3/3/1925, Reading, PA BR/TR, 5'11", 175 lbs. Deb: 6/13/1943																										
1943	Phi-N	0	0	....	9	0	0	0	0	18^2	27	8	7	1	0	9	5	1.929	3.38	100	6.55	.342	0	.000	0	1	0.0
• FABER, Red	Urban Charles Faber b: 9/6/1888, Cascade, IA d: 9/25/1976, Chicago, IL BB/TR, 6'2", 180 lbs. Deb: 4/17/1914 C HOF: 1964																										
1914	Chi-A	10	9	.526	40	19	11	2	**4**	181^1	154	77	54	3	12	64	88	1.202	2.68	100	2.76	.239	8	.145	0	12	0.2
1915	Chi-A	24	14	.632	**50**	32	21	2	2	299^2	264	118	85	3	11	99	182	1.211	2.55	116	2.63	.240	11	.131	17	21	2.0
1916	Chi-A	17	9	.654	35	25	15	3	1	205^1	167	67	46	1	5	61	87	1.110	2.02	137	2.20	.228	6	.095	14	17	1.3
1917*	Chi-A	16	13	.552	41	29	16	3	3	248	224	92	53	1	10	85	84	1.246	1.92	138	2.74	.247	4	.058	22	16	2.0
1918	Chi-A	4	1	.800	11	9	5	1	1	80^2	70	23	11	3	0	23	26	1.153	1.23	222	2.58	.245	1	.042	15	7	1.4
1919	Chi-A	11	9	.550	25	20	9	0	0	162^1	185	92	69	7	8	45	45	1.417	3.83	83	4.01	.287	10	.185	-15	6	-1.6

YEAR	TM-L	W	L	PCT	G	GS	CG	SH	SV	IP	H	R	ER	HR	HB	BB	SO	RAT	ERA	ERA+	CERA	OAV	BH	AVG	PR+	WS	TPW
1920	Chi-A	23	13	.639	40	**39**	28	2	1	319	332	136	106	8	4	88	108	1.317	2.99	126	3.29	.277	11	.106	23	25	1.9
1921	Chi-A	25	15	.625	43	39	**32**	4	1	330^{2}	293	107	91	10	7	87	124	1.149	**2.48**	**171**	**2.53**	**.242**	16	.148	**64**	**37**	**5.7**
1922	Chi-A	21	17	.553	43	38	**31**	4	2	**352**	334	128	110	10	6	83	148	1.185	**2.81**	**144**	**2.69**	.252	25	.200	**45**	**31**	**4.2**
1923	Chi-A	14	11	.560	32	31	15	2	0	232^{1}	233	114	88	6	6	62	91	1.270	3.41	116	3.02	.259	15	.217	15	16	1.8
1924	Chi-A	9	11	.450	21	20	9	0	0	161^{1}	173	78	69	5	2	58	47	1.432	3.85	107	3.68	.282	8	.148	5	9	0.3
1925	Chi-A	12	11	.522	34	32	16	1	0	238	266	117	100	8	2	59	71	1.366	3.78	110	3.68	.289	8	.104	9	15	0.5
1926	Chi-A	15	9	.625	27	25	13	1	0	184^{2}	203	84	73	3	2	57	65	1.408	3.56	108	3.63	.281	9	.150	4	13	0.4
1927	Chi-A	4	7	.364	18	15	6	0	0	110^{2}	131	64	56	2	5	41	39	1.554	4.55	89	4.54	.312	10	.270	-8	5	-0.6
1928	Chi-A	13	9	.591	27	27	16	2	0	201^{1}	223	98	84	11	4	68	43	1.445	3.75	108	3.90	.286	8	.114	6	13	0.2
1929	Chi-A	13	13	.500	31	31	15	1	0	234	241	119	101	10	9	61	68	1.291	3.88	110	3.41	.273	10	.128	7	15	0.4
1930	Chi-A	8	13	.381	29	26	10	0	1	169	188	101	79	7	5	49	62	1.402	4.21	110	3.83	.283	2	.041	12	10	0.7
1931	Chi-A	10	14	.417	44	19	5	1	1	184	210	96	78	11	3	57	49	1.451	3.82	112	4.18	.285	4	.075	12	11	0.8
1932	Chi-A	2	11	.154	42	5	0	0	6	106	123	61	44	0	1	38	26	1.519	3.74	116	3.98	.290	4	.222	8	6	1.0
1933	Chi-A	3	4	.429	36	2	0	0	5	86^{1}	92	41	33	2	1	28	18	1.390	3.44	123	3.51	.275	0	.000	8	7	0.5
Total	20	254	213	.544	669	483	273	29	28	4086^{2}	4106	1813	1430	111	103	1213	1471	1.302	3.15	119	3.23	.266	170	.134	264	292	23.3

• FACE, Roy — Elroy Leon Face b: 2/20/1928, Stephentown, NY BR/TR, 5'8", 155 lbs. Deb: 4/16/1953

YEAR	TM-L	W	L	PCT	G	GS	CG	SH	SV	IP	H	R	ER	HR	HB	BB	SO	RAT	ERA	ERA+	CERA	OAV	BH	AVG	PR+	WS	TPW
1953	Pit-N	6	8	.429	41	13	2	0	0	119	145	90	87	19	2	30	56	1.471	6.58	68	5.15	.297	4	.133	-27	1	-2.7
1955	Pit-N	5	7	.417	42	10	4	0	5	125^{2}	128	58	50	10	0	40	84	1.337	3.58	115	3.75	.268	3	.115	9	9	0.7
1956	Pit-N	12	13	.480	**68**	3	0	0	6	135^{1}	131	57	53	16	1	42	96	1.278	3.52	107	3.53	.256	5	.192	5	11	0.4
1957	Pit-N	4	6	.400	59	1	0	0	10	93^{2}	97	41	32	9	1	24	53	1.292	3.07	123	3.64	.270	2	.125	6	7	0.6
1958	Pit-N	5	2	.714	57	0	0	0	**20**	84	77	30	27	6	0	22	47	1.179	2.89	134	2.85	.244	0	.000	7	12	0.7
1959	Pit-N★	18	1	.947	57	0	0	0	10	93^{1}	91	29	28	5	1	25	69	1.243	2.70	143	3.12	.266	3	.231	11	15	1.2
1960★	Pit-N★	10	8	.556	**68**	0	0	0	24	114^{2}	93	39	37	11	0	29	72	1.064	2.90	129	2.43	.226	7	.412	9	17	1.2
1961	Pit-N★	6	12	.333	62	0	0	0	**17**	92	94	44	39	12	1	10	55	1.130	3.82	104	3.25	.267	3	.273	1	10	0.2
1962	Pit-N	8	7	.533	63	0	0	0	**28**	91	74	23	19	7	1	18	45	1.011	1.88	209	2.25	.231	1	.083	20	20	1.9
1963	Pit-N	3	9	.250	56	0	0	0	16	69^{2}	75	33	25	6	3	19	41	1.349	3.23	102	3.84	.285	2	.250	0	5	0.0
1964	Pit-N	3	3	.500	55	0	0	0	4	79^{2}	82	48	46	11	1	27	63	1.368	5.20	67	4.10	.269	0	.000	-14	1	-1.5
1965	Pit-N	5	2	.714	16	0	0	0	0	20^{1}	20	6	6	1	0	7	19	1.328	2.66	132	3.08	.263	0	.000	2	3	0.1
1966	Pit-N	6	6	.500	54	0	0	0	18	70	68	24	21	9	1	24	67	1.314	2.70	132	3.86	.262	0	.000	5	8	0.4
1967	Pit-N	7	5	.583	61	0	0	0	17	74^{1}	62	23	20	5	0	22	41	1.130	2.42	139	2.43	.230	0	.000	7	10	0.7
1968	Pit-N	2	4	.333	43	0	0	0	13	52	46	17	15	3	2	7	34	1.019	2.60	113	2.33	.238	0	.000	1	6	0.1
	Det-A	0	0	....	2	0	0	0	0	1	2	0	0	0	0	1	1	3.000	0.00	....	11.50	.500	0	....	0	0	0.0
1969	Mon-N	4	2	.667	44	0	0	0	5	59^{1}	62	29	26	11	0	15	34	1.298	3.94	93	4.19	.263	1	.500	-1	4	-0.1
Total	16	104	95	.523	848	27	6	0	193	1375	1347	591	531	141	14	362	877	1.243	3.48	110	3.42	.260	31	.160	42	139	3.9

• FAETH, Tony — Anthony Joseph Faeth b: 7/9/1893, Aberdeen, SD d: 12/22/1982, St. Paul, MN BR/TR, 6', 180 lbs. Deb: 8/10/1919

YEAR	TM-L	W	L	PCT	G	GS	CG	SH	SV	IP	H	R	ER	HR	HB	BB	SO	RAT	ERA	ERA+	CERA	OAV	BH	AVG	PR+	WS	TPW
1919	Cle-A	0	0	....	6	0	0	0	0	18^{1}	13	4	1	0	0	10	7	1.255	0.49	680	2.64	.224	0	.000	6	2	0.6
1920	Cle-A	0	0	....	13	0	0	0	0	25	31	19	12	0	1	20	14	2.040	4.32	88	6.76	.333	0	.000	-2	0	-0.2
Total	2	0	0	....	19	0	0	0	0	43^{1}	44	23	13	0	1	30	21	1.708	2.70	139	5.02	.291	0	.000	4	2	0.3

• FAGAN, Bill — William A. "Clinkers" Fagan b: 2/15/1869, Troy, NY d: 3/21/1930, Troy, NY TL, 5'11", 165 lbs. Deb: 9/15/1887

YEAR	TM-L	W	L	PCT	G	GS	CG	SH	SV	IP	H	R	ER	HR	HB	BB	SO	RAT	ERA	ERA+	CERA	OAV	BH	AVG	PR+	WS	TPW
1887	NY-a	1	4	.200	6	6	6	0	0	45	79	34	20	1	2	24	12	1.756	4.00	106	....	.371	3	.143	3	1	0.1
1888	KC-a	5	11	.313	17	17	15	0	0	142^{1}	179	148	90	4	1	75	49	1.785	5.69	60	....	.297	14	.215	-36	2	-3.4
Total	2	6	15	.286	23	23	21	0	0	187^{1}	258	182	110	5	3	99	61	1.778	5.28	67	....	.316	17	.198	-33	3	-3.4

• FAGAN, Everett — Everett Joseph Fagan b: 1/13/1918, Pottersville, NJ d: 2/16/1983, Morristown, NJ BR/TR, 6', 195 lbs. Deb: 4/24/1943

YEAR	TM-L	W	L	PCT	G	GS	CG	SH	SV	IP	H	R	ER	HR	HB	BB	SO	RAT	ERA	ERA+	CERA	OAV	BH	AVG	PR+	WS	TPW
1943	Phi-A	2	6	.250	18	2	0	0	3	37^{1}	41	28	26	4	2	14	9	1.473	6.27	54	4.70	.283	0	.000	-11	0	-1.2
1946	Phi-A	0	1	.000	20	0	0	0	0	45	47	27	24	2	3	24	12	1.578	4.80	74	4.41	.264	4	.286	-6	1	-0.5
Total	2	2	7	.222	38	2	0	0	3	82^{1}	88	55	50	6	5	38	21	1.530	5.47	63	4.54	.272	4	.190	-17	1	-1.7

• FAHR, Jerry — Gerald Warren Fahr b: 12/9/1924, Marmaduke, AR BR/TR, 6'5", 185 lbs. Deb: 4/29/1951

YEAR	TM-L	W	L	PCT	G	GS	CG	SH	SV	IP	H	R	ER	HR	HB	BB	SO	RAT	ERA	ERA+	CERA	OAV	BH	AVG	PR+	WS	TPW
1951	Cle-A	0	0	....	5	0	0	0	0	5^{2}	11	3	3	0	0	2	0	2.294	4.76	79	10.37	.500	0	....	-1	0	-0.1

• FAHRER, Pete — Clarence Willie Fahrer b: 3/10/1890, Holgate, OH d: 6/10/1967, Fremont, MI BL/TR, 6', 190 lbs. Deb: 8/17/1914

YEAR	TM-L	W	L	PCT	G	GS	CG	SH	SV	IP	H	R	ER	HR	HB	BB	SO	RAT	ERA	ERA+	CERA	OAV	BH	AVG	PR+	WS	TPW
1914	Cin-N	0	0	....	5	0	0	0	0	8	8	3	1	0	0	4	2	1.500	1.13	260	3.87	.308	0	.000	2	1	0.2

• FAIRBANK, Jim — James Lee "Lee,Smokey" Fairbank b: 3/17/1881, Deansboro, NY d: 12/27/1955, Utica, NY BR/TR, 5'10", 175 lbs. Deb: 9/18/1903

YEAR	TM-L	W	L	PCT	G	GS	CG	SH	SV	IP	H	R	ER	HR	HB	BB	SO	RAT	ERA	ERA+	CERA	OAV	BH	AVG	PR+	WS	TPW
1903	Phi-A	1	1	.500	4	1	1	0	0	24	33	14	13	1	0	12	10	1.875	4.88	63	6.16	.325	1	.100	-5	0	-0.5
1904	Phi-A	0	1	.000	3	1	1	0	0	17	19	14	12	0	2	13	6	1.882	6.35	42	5.59	.283	0	.000	-7	0	-0.8
Total	2	1	2	.333	7	2	2	0	0	41	52	28	25	1	2	25	16	1.878	5.49	52	5.92	.309	1	.063	-11	0	-1.4

• FAIRCLOTH, Rags — James Lamar Faircloth b: 8/19/1892, Kenton, TN d: 10/5/1953, Tucson, AZ BR/TR, 5'11", 160 lbs. Deb: 5/6/1919

YEAR	TM-L	W	L	PCT	G	GS	CG	SH	SV	IP	H	R	ER	HR	HB	BB	SO	RAT	ERA	ERA+	CERA	OAV	BH	AVG	PR+	WS	TPW
1919	Phi-N	0	0	....	2	0	0	0	0	2	5	2	2	0	0	0	0	2.500	9.00	36	12.01	.625	0	....	-1	0	-0.1

• FAJARDO, Hector — Hector (Nabaratte) Fajardo b: 11/16/1970, Sahuayo, Mexico BR/TR, 6'4", 185 lbs. Deb: 8/10/1991

YEAR	TM-L	W	L	PCT	G	GS	CG	SH	SV	IP	H	R	ER	HR	HB	BB	SO	RAT	ERA	ERA+	CERA	OAV	BH	AVG	PR+	WS	TPW
1991	Pit-N	0	0	....	2	2	0	0	0	6^{1}	10	7	7	0	0	7	8	2.684	9.95	36	9.86	.357	0	.000	-5	0	-0.5
	Tex-A	0	2	.000	4	3	0	0	0	19	25	13	12	2	1	4	15	1.526	5.68	71	5.46	.329	0	....	-3	0	-0.3
1993	Tex-A	0	0	....	1	0	0	0	0	0^{2}	0	0	0	0	0	0	1	.000	0.00	....	0.00	.000	0	....	0	0	0.0
1994	Tex-A	5	7	.417	18	12	0	0	0	83^{1}	95	67	64	15	2	26	45	1.452	6.91	70	5.13	.284	0	....	-17	1	-1.6
1995	Tex-A	0	0	....	5	0	0	0	0	15	19	13	13	2	1	5	9	1.600	7.80	62	6.04	.311	0	....	-5	0	-0.5
Total	4	5	9	.357	30	17	0	0	0	124^{1}	149	100	96	19	4	42	78	1.536	6.95	66	5.50	.299	0	.000	-29	1	-2.8

• FALCONE, Pete — Peter Frank Falcone b: 10/1/1953, Brooklyn, NY BL/TL, 6'2", 185 lbs. Deb: 4/13/1975

YEAR	TM-L	W	L	PCT	G	GS	CG	SH	SV	IP	H	R	ER	HR	HB	BB	SO	RAT	ERA	ERA+	CERA	OAV	BH	AVG	PR+	WS	TPW
1975	SF-N	12	11	.522	34	32	3	1	0	190	171	97	88	16	4	111	131	1.484	4.17	91	4.15	.244	4	.062	-8	8	-1.3
1976	StL-N	12	16	.429	32	32	9	2	0	212	173	87	76	12	2	93	138	1.255	3.23	110	2.95	.222	8	.129	6	13	0.5
1977	StL-N	4	8	.333	27	22	1	1	1	124	130	79	75	19	3	61	75	1.540	5.44	71	5.19	.273	10	.244	-24	1	-2.2
1978	StL-N	2	7	.222	19	14	0	0	0	75	94	52	48	9	2	48	28	1.893	5.76	61	6.99	.319	5	.238	-19	0	-1.9
1979	NY-N	6	14	.300	33	31	1	1	0	184	194	91	85	24	1	76	113	1.467	4.16	88	4.64	.276	9	.173	-13	6	-1.3
1980	NY-N	7	10	.412	37	23	1	0	1	157^{1}	163	89	79	16	2	58	109	1.405	4.52	79	4.10	.269	6	.146	-17	3	-1.9
1981	NY-N	5	3	.625	35	9	3	1	1	95^{1}	84	32	27	3	0	36	56	1.259	2.55	137	2.84	.241	4	.182	11	7	1.3
1982	NY-N	8	10	.444	40	23	3	0	2	171	159	82	73	24	1	71	101	1.345	3.84	94	4.08	.252	6	.113	-2	8	-0.4
1983	Atl-N	9	4	.692	33	15	2	0	0	106^{2}	102	47	43	14	1	60	59	1.519	3.63	107	4.78	.256	3	.115	2	7	0.1
1984	Atl-N	5	7	.417	35	16	2	1	2	120	115	61	55	15	0	57	55	1.433	4.13	93	4.26	.252	7	.212	-3	6	-0.2
Total	10	70	90	.438	325	217	25	7	7	1435^{1}	1385	717	649	152	16	671	865	1.432	4.07	90	4.23	.257	62	.149	-67	59	-7.5

• FALK, Chet — Chester Emanuel "Spot" Falk b: 5/15/1905, Austin, TX d: 1/7/1982, Austin, TX BL/TL, 6'2", 170 lbs. Deb: 4/20/1925

YEAR	TM-L	W	L	PCT	G	GS	CG	SH	SV	IP	H	R	ER	HR	HB	BB	SO	RAT	ERA	ERA+	CERA	OAV	BH	AVG	PR+	WS	TPW
1925	StL-A	0	0	....	13	0	0	0	0	25	38	26	23	2	0	17	7	2.200	8.28	56	8.01	.362	5	.625	-10	1	-0.7
1926	StL-A	4	4	.500	18	8	3	0	0	74	95	53	44	1	6	27	7	1.649	5.35	80	5.43	.338	6	.194	-9	2	-1.0
1927	StL-A	1	0	1.000	9	0	0	0	0	15^{2}	25	18	10	1	0	10	2	2.234	5.74	76	7.95	.352	1	.200	-3	0	-0.3
Total	3	5	4	.556	40	8	3	0	0	114^{2}	158	97	77	4	6	54	16	1.849	6.04	73	6.33	.346	12	.273	-22	3	-2.0

• FALKENBERG, Cy — Frederick Peter Falkenberg b: 12/17/1879, Chicago, IL d: 4/15/1961, San Francisco, CA BR/TR, 6'5", 180 lbs. Deb: 4/21/1903

YEAR	TM-L	W	L	PCT	G	GS	CG	SH	SV	IP	H	R	ER	HR	HB	BB	SO	RAT	ERA	ERA+	CERA	OAV	BH	AVG	PR+	WS	TPW
1903	Pit-N	1	5	.167	10	6	3	0	0	56	65	43	24	0	2	32	24	1.732	3.86	84	5.00	.295	4	.190	-6	1	-0.6
1905	Was-A	7	2	.778	12	10	6	2	0	75^{1}	71	41	32	1	5	31	35	1.354	3.82	69	3.33	.251	4	.125	-12	3	-1.5
1906	Was-A	14	20	.412	40	36	30	2	1	298^{2}	277	136	95	1	13	108	178	1.289	2.86	92	2.95	.249	18	.170	-3	9	-0.1
1907	Was-A	6	17	.261	32	24	17	1	1	233^{2}	195	105	61	0	8	77	108	1.164	2.35	103	2.29	.229	12	.140	10	6	0.8
1908	Was-A	6	2	.750	17	8	5	1	0	82^{2}	70	29	18	2	2	21	34	1.101	1.96	116	2.40	.236	6	.222	3	6	0.3
	Cle-A	2	4	.333	8	7	2	0	0	46^{1}	52	25	20	1	2	10	17	1.338	3.88	61	3.68	.284	2	.118	-8	0	-1.1
	Yr.	8	6	.571	25	15	7	1	0	129	122	54	38	3	4	31	51	1.186	2.65	88	2.86	.254	8	.182	-5	6	-0.7
1909	Cle-A	10	9	.526	24	18	13	2	0	165	135	56	44	0	5	50	82	1.121	2.40	106	**1.51**	.231	9	.173	2	11	0.1

YEAR	TM-L	W	L	PCT	G	GS	CG	SH	SV	IP	H	R	ER	HR	HB	BB	SO	RAT	ERA	ERA+	CERA	OAV	BH	AVG	PR+	WS	TPW
1910	Cle-A	14	13	.519	37	29	18	3	1	256^2	246	114	84	3	8	75	107	1.251	2.95	88	3.05	.261	15	.183	-12	14	-1.3
1911	Cle-A	8	5	.615	15	13	7	0	1	106^2	117	56	39	0	3	24	46	1.322	3.29	104	3.38	.282	7	.175	-0	7	-0.1
1913	Cle-A	23	10	.697	39	36	23	6	0	276	238	85	68	2	5	88	166	1.181	2.22	137	2.48	.235	10	.119	21	25	2.0
1914	Ind-F	25	16	.610	**49**	**43**	33	**9**	3	**377^1**	332	127	93	5	5	89	**236**	1.116	2.22	156	2.33	.236	21	.168	**48**	34	4.8
1915	New-F	9	11	.450	25	21	14	0	1	172	175	78	62	6	9	47	76	1.291	3.24	88	2.72	.268	3	.053	-8	7	-1.6
	Bro-F	3	3	.500	7	7	5	1	0	48	31	15	8	1	1	12	20	.896	1.50	198	1.46	.189	1	.067	8	4	0.7
	Yr.	12	14	.462	32	28	19	1	1	220	206	93	70	7	10	59	96	1.205	2.86	100	2.44	.252	4	.056	-1	11	-0.9
1917	Phi-A	2	6	.250	15	8	4	0	0	80^2	86	53	30	1	0	26	35	1.388	3.35	82	3.77	.293	5	.185	-4	1	-0.4
Total	**12**	**130**	**123**	**.514**	**330**	**266**	**180**	**27**	**8**	**2275**	**2090**	**963**	**678**	**23**	**68**	**690**	**1164**	**1.222**	**2.68**	**104**	**2.69**	**.248**	**117**	**.152**	**38**	**128**	**2.0**
• FALKENBORG, Brian		Brian Thomas Falkenborg b: 1/18/1978, Newport Beach, CA BR/TR, 6'6", 195 lbs. Deb: 10/1/1999																									
1999	Bal-A	0	0	....	2	0	0	0	0	3	2	0	0	0	0	2	1	1.333	0.00	....	2.79	.200	0	....	2	0	0.1
• FALLENSTEIN, Ed		Edward Joseph "Ace" Fallenstein b: 12/22/1908, Newark, NJ d: 11/24/1971, Orange, NJ BR/TR, 6'3", 180 lbs. Deb: 4/16/1931																									
1931	Phi-N	0	0	....	24	0	0	0	0	41^2	56	37	33	2	0	26	15	1.968	7.13	60	6.47	.333	1	.200	-13	0	-1.3
1933	Bos-N	2	1	.667	9	4	1	1	0	35	43	23	14	1	1	13	5	1.600	3.60	85	4.77	.305	3	.375	-2	1	-0.1
Total	**2**	**2**	**1**	**.667**	**33**	**4**	**1**	**1**	**0**	**76^2**	**99**	**60**	**47**	**3**	**1**	**39**	**20**	**1.800**	**5.52**	**69**	**5.70**	**.320**	**4**	**.308**	**-15**	**1**	**-1.3**
• FALLON, Bob		Robert Joseph Fallon b: 2/18/1960, Bronx, NY BL/TL, 6'3", 200 lbs. Deb: 4/26/1984																									
1984	Chi-A	0	0	....	3	3	0	0	0	14^2	12	7	6	0	0	11	10	1.568	3.68	113	3.89	.235	0	....	1	1	0.1
1985	Chi-A	0	0	....	10	0	0	0	0	16	25	11	11	5	0	9	17	2.125	6.19	70	10.11	.362	0	....	-3	0	-0.3
Total	**2**	**0**	**0**	**....**	**13**	**3**	**0**	**0**	**0**	**30^2**	**37**	**18**	**17**	**5**	**0**	**20**	**27**	**1.859**	**4.99**	**85**	**7.13**	**.308**	**0**	**....**	**-3**	**1**	**-0.3**
• FALTEISEK, Steve		Steven James Falteisek b: 1/28/1972, Mineola, NY BR/TR, 6'2", 200 lbs. Deb: 7/21/1997																									
1997	Mon-N	0	0	....	5	0	0	0	0	8	8	4	3	0	1	3	2	1.375	3.38	124	3.88	.286	0	.000	1	0	0.0
1999	Mil-N	0	0	....	10	0	0	0	0	12	18	10	10	3	0	3	5	1.750	7.50	60	8.26	.375	0	.000	-4	0	-0.4
Total	**2**	**0**	**0**	**....**	**15**	**0**	**0**	**0**	**0**	**20**	**26**	**14**	**13**	**3**	**1**	**6**	**7**	**1.600**	**5.85**	**76**	**6.51**	**.342**	**0**	**.000**	**-3**	**0**	**-0.3**
• FANNIN, Cliff		Clifford Bryson "Mule" Fannin b: 5/13/1924, Louisa, KY d: 12/11/1966, Sandusky, OH BL/TR, 6', 170 lbs. Deb: 9/2/1945																									
1945	StL-A	0	0	....	5	0	0	0	0	10^1	8	3	3	0	0	5	5	1.258	2.61	135	2.56	.222	0	.000	1	1	0.1
1946	StL-A	5	2	.714	27	7	4	1	2	86^2	76	37	29	4	1	42	52	1.362	3.01	124	3.25	.236	5	.161	7	7	0.7
1947	StL-A	6	8	.429	26	18	6	2	1	145^2	134	70	58	10	1	77	77	1.449	3.58	108	3.78	.245	9	.196	7	9	0.7
1948	StL-A	10	14	.417	34	29	10	3	1	213^2	198	106	99	14	1	104	102	1.413	4.17	109	3.67	.245	11	.169	13	14	1.3
1949	StL-A	8	14	.364	30	25	5	0	1	143	177	106	98	15	0	93	57	1.888	6.17	73	6.40	.308	9	.164	-21	2	-2.2
1950	StL-A	5	9	.357	25	16	3	0	1	102	116	82	74	18	0	58	42	1.706	6.53	76	5.94	.280	6	.176	-15	2	-1.5
1951	StL-A	0	2	.000	7	1	0	0	0	15^1	20	16	11	7	0	5	11	1.630	6.46	68	8.21	.317	1	.250	-3	0	-0.3
1952	StL-A	0	2	.000	10	2	0	0	0	16^1	34	25	23	5	0	9	6	2.633	12.67	31	14.62	.453	0	.000	-16	0	-1.6
Total	**8**	**34**	**51**	**.400**	**164**	**98**	**28**	**6**	**6**	**733**	**763**	**445**	**395**	**73**	**3**	**393**	**352**	**1.577**	**4.85**	**90**	**4.81**	**.269**	**41**	**.173**	**-27**	**35**	**-3.0**
• FANNING, Jack		John Jacob Fanning b: 1863, South Orange, NJ d: 6/10/1917, Aberdeen, WA TR, 5'9", 163 lbs. Deb: 9/20/1889																									
1889	Ind-N	0	1	.000	1	1	0	0	0	1	3	3	2	0	0	2	0	5.000	18.00	23	....	.503	0	.000	-2	0	-0.1
1894	Phi-N	1	3	.250	6	4	2	0	0	34^1	54	52	29	4	2	22	7	2.214	7.60	67	8.88	.354	2	.154	-9	0	-0.8
Total	**2**	**1**	**4**	**.200**	**7**	**5**	**2**	**0**	**0**	**35^1**	**57**	**55**	**31**	**4**	**2**	**24**	**7**	**2.292**	**7.90**	**64**	**8.63**	**.359**	**2**	**.143**	**-11**	**0**	**-0.9**
• FANOK, Harry		Harry Michael "The Flame Thrower" Fanok b: 5/11/1940, Whippany, NJ BB/TR, 6', 180 lbs. Deb: 4/16/1963																									
1963	StL-N	2	1	.667	12	0	0	0	1	25^2	24	16	15	3	1	21	25	1.753	5.26	67	5.56	.255	2	.400	-5	1	-0.4
1964	StL-N	0	0	....	4	0	0	0	0	7^2	5	6	5	0	0	3	10	1.043	5.87	65	1.55	.179	0	.000	-2	0	-0.2
Total	**2**	**2**	**1**	**.667**	**16**	**0**	**0**	**0**	**1**	**33^1**	**29**	**22**	**20**	**3**	**1**	**24**	**35**	**1.590**	**5.40**	**67**	**4.64**	**.238**	**2**	**.333**	**-7**	**1**	**-0.6**
• FANOVICH, Frank		Frank Joseph "Lefty" Fanovich b: 1/11/1922, New York, NY BL/TL, 5'11", 180 lbs. Deb: 4/25/1949																									
1949	Cin-N	0	2	.000	29	1	0	0	0	43^1	44	31	26	2	2	28	27	1.662	5.40	77	4.61	.257	0	.000	-6	0	-0.6
1953	Phi-A	0	3	.000	26	3	0	0	0	61^2	62	41	38	5	6	37	37	1.605	5.55	77	4.98	.273	2	.182	-8	1	-0.9
Total	**2**	**0**	**5**	**.000**	**55**	**4**	**0**	**0**	**0**	**105**	**106**	**72**	**64**	**7**	**8**	**65**	**64**	**1.629**	**5.49**	**77**	**4.83**	**.266**	**2**	**.133**	**-14**	**1**	**-1.5**
• FANSLER, Stan		Stanley Robert Fansler b: 2/12/1965, Elkins, WV BR/TR, 5'11", 180 lbs. Deb: 9/6/1986																									
1986	Pit-N	0	3	.000	5	5	0	0	0	24	20	12	10	2	0	15	13	1.458	3.75	102	4.16	.247	1	.167	0	1	0.0
• FANWELL, Harry		Harry Clayton Fanwell b: 10/16/1886, Patapsco, MD d: 7/15/1965, Baltimore, MD BB/TR, 6', 175 lbs. Deb: 7/23/1910																									
1910	Cle-A	2	9	.182	17	11	5	1	0	92	87	52	37	0	6	38	30	1.359	3.62	71	3.44	.260	1	.033	-11	1	-1.6
• FARMER, Ed		Edward Joseph Farmer b: 10/18/1949, Evergreen Park, IL BR/TR, 6'5", 210 lbs. Deb: 6/9/1971																									
1971	Cle-A	5	4	.556	43	4	0	0	4	78^2	77	42	38	9	3	41	48	1.500	4.35	88	4.68	.263	1	.071	-5	4	-0.6
1972	Cle-A	2	5	.286	46	1	0	0	7	61^1	51	32	30	10	1	27	33	1.272	4.40	73	3.67	.231	1	.143	-9	2	-1.0
1973	Cle-A	0	2	.000	16	0	0	0	0	17^1	25	12	9	4	0	5	10	1.731	4.67	84	6.95	.325	0	....	-1	0	-0.1
	Det-A	3	0	1.000	24	0	0	0	2	45	52	26	25	3	2	27	28	1.756	5.00	82	5.77	.292	0	....	-4	2	-0.4
	Yr.	3	2	.600	40	0	0	0	3	62^1	77	38	34	7	2	32	38	1.749	4.91	82	6.10	.302	0	....	-6	2	-0.6
1974	Phi-N	2	1	.667	14	3	0	0	0	31	41	32	29	5	0	27	20	2.194	8.42	45	8.52	.323	1	.111	-17	0	-1.8
1977	Bal-A	0	0	....	1	0	0	0	0	0	1	1	0	0	0	1	0	....	....	....	∞	1.000	0	....	0	0	0.0
1978	Mil-A	1	0	1.000	3	0	0	0	1	11	7	1	1	1	0	4	6	1.000	0.82	459	1.94	.175	0	....	4	2	0.4
1979	Tex-A	2	0	1.000	11	2	0	0	0	33	30	21	16	2	2	19	25	1.485	4.36	95	4.18	.252	0	....	-1	1	-0.1
	Chi-A	3	7	.300	42	3	0	0	14	81^1	66	36	22	2	1	34	48	1.230	2.43	175	2.46	.219	0	....	16	10	1.6
	Yr.	5	7	.417	53	5	0	0	14	114^1	96	57	38	4	3	53	73	1.303	2.99	141	2.95	.229	0	....	15	11	1.5
1980	Chi-A★	7	9	.438	64	0	0	0	30	99^2	92	37	37	6	1	56	54	1.485	3.34	120	3.84	.244	0	....	8	14	0.8
1981	Chi-A	3	3	.500	42	0	0	0	10	52^2	53	33	27	5	1	34	42	1.652	4.61	78	5.04	.262	0	....	-7	1	-0.7
1982	Phi-N	2	6	.250	47	4	0	0	6	76	66	44	41	2	0	50	58	1.526	4.86	76	3.55	.234	0	.000	-10	2	-1.2
1983	Phi-N	0	6	.000	12	3	0	0	0	26^2	35	22	18	2	1	20	16	2.063	6.08	59	6.51	.307	1	.167	-7	0	-0.7
	Oak-A	0	0	....	5	1	0	0	0	10^1	15	4	4	1	0	0	7	1.452	3.48	111	5.41	.366	0	....	0	1	0.0
Total	**11**	**30**	**43**	**.411**	**370**	**21**	**0**	**0**	**75**	**624**	**611**	**343**	**297**	**52**	**12**	**345**	**395**	**1.532**	**4.28**	**88**	**4.40**	**.257**	**4**	**.085**	**-33**	**39**	**-3.9**
• FARMER, Howard		Howard Earl Farmer b: 11/18/1966, Gary, IN BR/TR, 6'3", 185 lbs. Deb: 7/2/1990																									
1990	Mon-N	0	3	.000	6	4	0	0	0	23	26	18	18	9	0	10	14	1.565	7.04	52	7.42	.302	2	.400	-9	0	-0.8
• FARMER, Mike		Michael Anthony Farmer b: 7/3/1968, Gary, IN BB/TL, 6'1", 193 lbs. Deb: 5/4/1996																									
1996	Col-N	0	1	.000	7	4	0	0	0	28	32	25	24	8	0	13	16	1.607	7.71	68	6.57	.286	4	.400	-7	1	-0.6
• FARNSWORTH, Jeff		Jeffrey Ellis Farnsworth b: 10/6/1975, Wichita, KS BR/TR, 6'2", 190 lbs. Deb: 4/3/2002																									
2002	Det-A	2	3	.400	44	0	0	0	0	70	100	47	45	6	2	29	28	1.843	5.79	74	6.52	.338	0	....	-11	1	-1.1
• FARNSWORTH, Kyle		Kyle Lynn Farnsworth b: 4/14/1976, Wichita, KS BR/TR, 6'4", 220 lbs. Deb: 4/29/1999																									
1999	Chi-N	5	9	.357	27	21	1	1	0	130	140	80	73	28	3	52	70	1.477	5.05	89	5.39	.271	3	.086	-6	5	-0.7
2000	Chi-N	2	9	.182	46	5	0	0	1	77	90	58	55	14	4	50	74	1.818	6.43	71	6.72	.291	1	.071	-16	0	-1.6
2001	Chi-N	4	6	.400	76	0	0	0	2	82	65	26	25	8	1	29	107	1.146	2.74	151	2.76	.213	0	.000	14	9	1.4
2002	Chi-N	4	6	.400	45	0	0	0	1	46^2	53	47	38	9	1	24	46	1.650	7.33	55	5.89	.293	0	.000	-17	0	-1.7
2003★	Chi-N	3	2	.600	77	0	0	0	0	76^1	53	31	28	6	0	36	92	1.166	3.30	127	2.58	.196	0	.000	8	7	0.7
Total	**5**	**18**	**32**	**.360**	**271**	**26**	**1**	**1**	**4**	**412**	**401**	**242**	**219**	**65**	**9**	**191**	**389**	**1.437**	**4.78**	**91**	**4.65**	**.253**	**4**	**.075**	**-17**	**21**	**-1.9**
• FARR, Jim		James Alfred Farr b: 5/18/1956, Waverly, NY BR/TR, 6'1", 195 lbs. Deb: 9/7/1982																									
1982	Tex-A	0	0	....	5	0	0	0	0	18	20	8	5	0	0	7	6	1.500	2.50	155	3.68	.278	0	....	3	1	0.3
• FARR, Steve		Steven Michael Farr b: 12/12/1956, Cheverly, MD BR/TR, 5'10", 200 lbs. Deb: 5/16/1984																									
1984	Cle-A	3	11	.214	31	16	0	0	1	116	106	61	59	14	5	46	83	1.310	4.58	89	3.92	.245	0	....	-7	4	-0.7
1985★	KC-A	2	1	.667	16	3	0	0	1	37^2	34	15	13	2	2	20	36	1.434	3.11	134	3.76	.245	0	....	5	3	0.5

YEAR	TM-L	W	L	PCT	G	GS	CG	SH	SV	IP	H	R	ER	HR	HB	BB	SO	RAT	ERA	ERA+	CERA	OAV	BH	AVG	PR+	WS	TPW
1986	KC-A	8	4	.667	56	0	0	0	8	109^1	90	39	38	10	4	39	83	1.180	3.13	136	3.01	.228	0	....	15	12	1.5
1987	KC-A	4	3	.571	47	0	0	0	1	91	97	47	42	9	2	44	88	1.549	4.15	110	4.77	.270	0	....	5	6	0.5
1988	KC-A	5	4	.556	62	1	0	0	20	82^2	74	25	23	5	2	30	72	1.258	2.50	159	3.11	.240	0	....	15	13	1.5
1989	KC-A	2	5	.286	51	2	0	0	18	63^1	75	35	29	5	1	22	56	1.532	4.12	93	4.73	.296	0	....	-1	4	-0.1
1990	KC-A	13	7	.650	57	6	1	1	1	127	99	32	28	6	5	48	94	1.157	1.98	193	2.57	.220	0	....	29	13	3.0
1991	NY-A	5	5	.500	60	0	0	0	23	70	57	19	17	4	5	20	60	1.100	2.19	189	2.61	.219	0	....	15	13	1.5
1992	NY-A	2	2	.500	50	0	0	0	30	52	34	10	9	2	2	19	37	1.019	1.56	251	1.95	.186	0	....	13	10	1.4
1993	NY-A	2	2	.500	49	0	0	0	25	47	44	22	22	8	2	28	39	1.532	4.21	99	5.03	.253	0	....	-0	5	0.0
1994	Cle-A	1	1	.500	19	0	0	0	4	15^1	17	12	9	3	2	15	12	2.087	5.28	89	8.35	.279	0	....	-1	0	-0.1
	Bos-A	1	0	1.000	11	0	0	0	0	13	24	9	9	2	0	3	8	2.077	6.23	81	9.19	.407	0	....	-2	0	-0.2
	Yr.	2	1	.667	30	0	0	0	4	28^1	41	21	18	5	2	18	20	2.082	5.72	85	8.73	.342	0	....	-3	0	-0.3
Total	11	48	45	.516	509	28	1	1	132	824^1	751	326	298	70	32	334	668	1.316	3.25	128	3.65	.244	0	....	87	83	8.8

• FARRELL, John John Edward Farrell b: 8/4/1962, Monmouth Beach, NJ BR/TR, 6'4", 210 lbs. Deb: 8/18/1987

YEAR	TM-L	W	L	PCT	G	GS	CG	SH	SV	IP	H	R	ER	HR	HB	BB	SO	RAT	ERA	ERA+	CERA	OAV	BH	AVG	PR+	WS	TPW
1987	Cle-A	5	1	.833	10	9	1	0	0	69	68	29	26	7	5	22	28	1.304	3.39	133	3.93	.256	0	....	10	6	0.9
1988	Cle-A	14	10	.583	31	30	4	0	0	210^1	216	106	99	15	9	67	92	1.345	4.24	97	3.89	.269	0	....	1	12	0.1
1989	Cle-A	9	14	.391	31	31	7	2	0	208	196	97	84	14	7	71	132	1.284	3.63	109	3.34	.244	0	....	9	12	0.9
1990	Cle-A	4	5	.444	17	17	1	0	0	96^2	108	49	46	10	1	33	44	1.459	4.28	91	4.61	.286	0	....	-2	4	-0.2
1993	Cal-A	3	12	.200	21	17	0	0	0	90^2	110	74	74	22	7	44	45	1.699	7.35	61	7.18	.301	0	....	-30	0	-2.9
1994	Cal-A	1	2	.333	3	3	0	0	0	13	16	14	13	2	1	8	10	1.846	9.00	54	7.33	.308	0	....	-6	0	-0.6
1995	Cle-A	0	0	....	1	0	0	0	0	4^2	7	4	2	0	0	0	4	1.500	3.86	122	4.47	.368	0	....	0	0	0.0
1996	Det-A	0	2	.000	2	2	0	0	0	6^1	11	10	10	2	1	5	0	2.526	14.21	36	14.47	.407	0	....	-6	0	-0.6
Total	8	36	46	.439	116	109	13	2	0	698^2	732	383	354	72	31	250	355	1.406	4.56	92	4.42	.270	0	....	-24	34	-2.3

• FARRELL, Turk Richard Joseph Farrell b: 4/8/1934, Boston, MA d: 6/10/1977, Great Yarmouth, England BR/TR, 6'4", 220 lbs. Deb: 9/21/1956

YEAR	TM-L	W	L	PCT	G	GS	CG	SH	SV	IP	H	R	ER	HR	HB	BB	SO	RAT	ERA	ERA+	CERA	OAV	BH	AVG	PR+	WS	TPW
1956	Phi-N	0	1	.000	1	1	0	0	0	4^1	6	6	6	0	1	3	0	2.077	12.46	30	8.28	.353	0	.000	-4	0	-0.4
1957	Phi-N	10	2	.833	52	0	0	0	10	83^1	74	29	22	2	2	36	54	1.320	2.38	160	3.00	.242	1	.111	14	12	1.4
1958	Phi-N★	8	9	.471	54	0	0	0	11	94	84	41	35	7	0	40	73	1.319	3.35	118	3.28	.244	5	.208	8	10	0.8
1959	Phi-N	1	6	.143	38	0	0	0	6	57	61	30	30	9	0	25	31	1.509	4.74	87	4.84	.288	1	.167	-4	3	-0.4
1960	Phi-N	10	6	.625	59	0	0	0	11	103^1	88	36	31	3	4	29	70	1.132	2.70	144	2.51	.239	3	.200	13	15	1.4
1961	Phi-N	2	1	.667	5	0	0	0	0	9^2	10	8	7	3	1	6	10	1.655	6.52	62	6.96	.270	1	.500	-3	0	-0.2
	LA-N	6	6	.500	50	0	0	0	10	89	107	56	50	12	1	43	80	1.685	5.06	86	5.55	.296	0	.000	-8	4	-1.0
	Yr.	8	7	.533	55	0	0	0	10	98^2	117	64	57	15	2	49	90	1.682	5.20	83	5.69	.294	1	.050	-10	4	-1.2
1962	Hou-N★	10	20	.333	43	29	11	2	4	241^2	210	91	81	21	5	55	203	1.097	3.02	124	2.70	.233	14	.179	23	19	2.5
1963	Hou-N	14	13	.519	34	26	12	0	1	202^1	161	76	68	12	2	35	141	.969	3.02	104	1.98	.219	9	.143	7	15	1.0
1964	Hou-N★	11	10	.524	32	27	7	0	0	198^1	196	80	72	21	3	52	117	1.250	3.27	104	3.58	.261	5	.072	6	12	0.3
1965	Hou-N★	11	11	.500	33	29	8	3	1	208^1	202	94	81	18	3	35	122	1.138	3.50	96	2.91	.252	10	.135	0	10	-0.1
1966	Hou-N	6	10	.375	32	21	3	0	2	152^2	167	84	78	23	0	28	101	1.277	4.60	74	4.01	.278	7	.146	-18	3	-2.0
1967	Hou-N	1	0	1.000	7	0	0	0	0	11^2	11	7	6	0	1	7	10	1.543	4.63	71	3.92	.244	0	.000	-1	0	-0.2
	Phi-N	9	6	.600	50	1	0	0	12	92	76	26	21	6	1	15	68	.989	2.05	166	2.08	.228	2	.105	14	13	1.5
	Yr.	10	6	.625	57	1	0	0	12	103^2	87	33	27	6	2	22	78	1.051	2.34	144	2.29	.230	2	.100	12	13	1.3
1968	Phi-N	4	6	.400	54	0	0	0	12	83	83	40	32	7	2	32	57	1.386	3.47	87	3.90	.271	1	.167	-3	4	-0.4
1969	Phi-N	3	4	.429	46	0	0	0	3	74^1	92	33	33	8	1	27	40	1.601	4.00	89	5.31	.307	0	.000	-4	4	-0.4
Total	14	106	111	.488	590	134	41	5	83	1705	1628	737	653	152	27	468	1177	1.229	3.45	103	3.30	.254	59	.135	40	124	3.9

• FASS, Frederick Frederick Peter Fass b: 10/30/1859, Milwaukee, WI d: 7/5/1930, Burnt Mill, CO Deb: 7/11/1887

YEAR	TM-L	W	L	PCT	G	GS	CG	SH	SV	IP	H	R	ER	HR	HB	BB	SO	RAT	ERA	ERA+	CERA	OAV	BH	AVG	PR+	WS	TPW
1887	Ind-N	0	1	.000	4	2	1	0	**1**	15^2	33	22	18	1	2	8	0	2.106	10.34	40	....	.416	2	.182	-11	0	-1.0

• FASSERO, Jeff Jeffrey Joseph Fassero b: 1/5/1963, Springfield, IL BL/TL, 6'1", 195 lbs. Deb: 5/4/1991

YEAR	TM-L	W	L	PCT	G	GS	CG	SH	SV	IP	H	R	ER	HR	HB	BB	SO	RAT	ERA	ERA+	CERA	OAV	BH	AVG	PR+	WS	TPW
1991	Mon-N	2	5	.286	51	0	0	0	8	55^1	39	17	15	1	1	17	42	1.012	2.44	148	1.75	.196	0	.000	7	7	0.7
1992	Mon-N	8	7	.533	70	0	0	0	1	85^2	81	35	27	1	2	34	63	1.342	2.84	122	3.10	.249	1	.143	6	7	0.7
1993	Mon-N	12	5	.706	56	15	1	0	1	149^2	119	50	38	7	0	54	140	1.156	2.29	182	2.48	.216	2	.063	31	15	2.9
1994	Mon-N	8	6	.571	21	21	1	0	0	138^2	119	54	46	13	1	40	119	1.147	2.99	141	2.82	.229	3	.068	19	10	1.7
1995	Mon-N	13	14	.481	30	30	1	0	0	189	207	102	91	15	2	74	164	1.487	4.33	99	4.43	.283	4	.070	1	8	-0.2
1996	Mon-N	15	11	.577	34	34	5	1	0	231^2	217	95	85	20	3	55	222	1.174	3.30	131	3.00	.244	6	.094	27	18	2.6
1997*	Sea-A	16	9	.640	35	**35**	2	1	0	234^1	226	108	94	21	3	84	189	1.323	3.61	125	3.60	.249	1	.200	26	17	2.4
1998	Sea-A	13	12	.520	32	32	7	0	0	224^2	223	115	99	33	10	66	176	1.286	3.97	117	4.10	.259	0	.000	20	14	1.8
1999	Sea-A	4	14	.222	30	24	0	0	0	139	188	123	114	34	4	73	101	1.878	7.38	68	8.02	.321	0	.000	-37	0	-3.5
	*Tex-A	1	0	1.000	7	3	0	0	0	17^1	20	12	11	1	0	10	13	1.731	5.71	89	5.21	.286	0	....	-1	1	-0.1
	Yr.	5	14	.263	37	27	0	0	0	156^1	208	135	125	35	4	83	114	1.861	7.20	69	7.71	.318	0	.000	-38	1	-3.5
2000	Bos-A	8	8	.500	38	23	0	0	0	130	153	72	69	16	1	50	97	1.562	4.78	105	5.25	.296	0	.000	4	8	0.3
2001	Chi-N	4	4	.500	82	0	0	0	12	73^2	66	31	28	6	1	23	79	1.208	3.42	121	2.97	.235	0	.000	7	10	0.7
2002	Chi-N	5	6	.455	57	0	0	0	0	51	65	37	35	5	3	22	44	1.706	6.18	65	5.79	.313	1	.333	-12	0	-1.2
	*StL-N	3	0	1.000	16	0	0	0	0	18	16	6	6	4	0	5	12	1.167	3.00	132	3.70	.232	0	....	2	2	0.2
	Yr.	8	6	.571	73	0	0	0	0	69	81	43	41	9	3	27	56	1.565	5.35	75	5.25	.292	1	.333	-10	2	-1.0
2003	StL-N	1	7	.125	62	6	0	0	3	77^2	93	51	49	17	2	34	55	1.635	5.68	72	6.34	.296	0	.000	-14	0	-1.5
Total	13	113	108	.511	621	223	17	2	25	1815^2	1832	908	807	194	33	641	1516	1.362	4.00	110	4.07	.261	18	.076	86	117	7.7

• FAST, Darcy Darcy Rae Fast b: 3/10/1947, Dallas, OR BL/TL, 6'3", 195 lbs. Deb: 6/15/1968

YEAR	TM-L	W	L	PCT	G	GS	CG	SH	SV	IP	H	R	ER	HR	HB	BB	SO	RAT	ERA	ERA+	CERA	OAV	BH	AVG	PR+	WS	TPW
1968	Chi-N	0	1	.000	8	1	0	0	0	10	8	6	6	1	0	8	10	1.600	5.40	59	4.40	.216	0	.000	-2	0	-0.3

• FASZHOLZ, Jack John Edward "Preacher" Faszholz b: 4/11/1927, St. Louis, MO BR/TR, 6'3", 205 lbs. Deb: 4/25/1953

YEAR	TM-L	W	L	PCT	G	GS	CG	SH	SV	IP	H	R	ER	HR	HB	BB	SO	RAT	ERA	ERA+	CERA	OAV	BH	AVG	PR+	WS	TPW
1953	StL-N	0	0	....	4	1	0	0	0	11^2	16	9	9	3	1	1	7	1.457	6.94	61	6.56	.327	0	.000	-3	0	-0.4

• FAUL, Bill William Alvan Faul b: 4/21/1940, Cincinnati, OH d: 2/21/2002, Cincinnati, OH BR/TR, 5'10", 190 lbs. Deb: 9/19/1962

YEAR	TM-L	W	L	PCT	G	GS	CG	SH	SV	IP	H	R	ER	HR	HB	BB	SO	RAT	ERA	ERA+	CERA	OAV	BH	AVG	PR+	WS	TPW
1962	Det-A	0	0	....	1	0	0	0	0	1^2	4	6	6	1	1	3	2	4.200	32.40	13	29.85	.444	0	....	-5	0	-0.5
1963	Det-A	5	6	.455	28	10	2	0	1	97	93	55	50	14	4	48	64	1.454	4.64	81	4.61	.251	4	.148	-10	3	-1.0
1964	Det-A	0	0	....	1	1	0	0	0	5	5	6	6	2	0	2	1	1.400	10.80	34	6.08	.250	0	.000	-4	0	-0.4
1965	Chi-N	6	6	.500	17	16	5	3	0	96^2	83	43	38	12	3	18	59	1.045	3.54	104	2.83	.232	3	.100	3	5	0.2
1966	Chi-N	1	4	.200	17	6	1	0	0	51^1	47	31	29	12	4	18	32	1.266	5.08	72	4.59	.242	0	.000	-7	1	-0.9
1970	SF-N	0	0	....	7	0	0	0	1	9^2	15	9	8	1	0	6	6	2.172	7.45	53	7.99	.357	0	....	-4	0	-0.4
Total	6	12	16	.429	71	33	8	3	2	261^1	247	150	137	42	12	95	164	1.309	4.72	79	4.26	.249	7	.097	-27	9	-3.1

• FAULKNER, Jim James Leroy "Lefty" Faulkner b: 7/27/1899, Beatrice, NE d: 6/1/1962, West Palm Beach, FL BB/TL, 6'3", 190 lbs. Deb: 9/15/1927

YEAR	TM-L	W	L	PCT	G	GS	CG	SH	SV	IP	H	R	ER	HR	HB	BB	SO	RAT	ERA	ERA+	CERA	OAV	BH	AVG	PR+	WS	TPW
1927	NY-N	1	0	1.000	3	1	0	0	0	9^2	13	4	4	0	1	5	2	1.862	3.72	103	5.98	.317	1	.500	0	1	0.1
1928	NY-N	9	8	.529	38	8	3	0	2	117^1	131	61	46	5	3	41	32	1.466	3.53	111	4.11	.289	9	.231	4	8	0.4
1930	Bro-N	0	0	....	2	1	0	0	1	0^1	2	3	3	1	0	1	0	9.000	81.00	6	103.77	.667	0	....	-3	0	-0.2
Total	3	10	8	.556	43	10	3	0	3	127^1	146	68	53	6	4	47	34	1.516	3.75	105	4.51	.294	10	.244	1	9	0.3

• FAUST, Charlie Charles Victor "Victory" Faust b: 10/9/1880, Marion, KS d: 6/18/1915, Fort Steilacoom, WA BR/TR, 6'2" Deb: 10/7/1911

YEAR	TM-L	W	L	PCT	G	GS	CG	SH	SV	IP	H	R	ER	HR	HB	BB	SO	RAT	ERA	ERA+	CERA	OAV	BH	AVG	PR+	WS	TPW
1911	NY-N	0	0	....	2	0	0	0	0	2	2	1	1	0	0	0	0	1.000	4.50	74	1.95	.250	0	....	-0	0	0.0

• FAUVER, Clay Clayton King "Cayt,Pop" Fauver b: 8/1/1872, North Eaton, OH d: 3/3/1942, Chatsworth, GA BB/TR, 5'10" Deb: 9/7/1899

YEAR	TM-L	W	L	PCT	G	GS	CG	SH	SV	IP	H	R	ER	HR	HB	BB	SO	RAT	ERA	ERA+	CERA	OAV	BH	AVG	PR+	WS	TPW
1899	Lou-N	1	0	1.000	1	1	1	0	0	9	11	4	0	0	0	2	1	1.444	0.00	....	3.85	.301	0	.000	4	1	0.3

• FEAR, Vern Luvern Carl Fear b: 8/21/1924, Everly, IA d: 9/6/1976, Spencer, IA BB/TR, 6', 170 lbs. Deb: 8/3/1952

YEAR	TM-L	W	L	PCT	G	GS	CG	SH	SV	IP	H	R	ER	HR	HB	BB	SO	RAT	ERA	ERA+	CERA	OAV	BH	AVG	PR+	WS	TPW
1952	Chi-N	0	0	....	4	0	0	0	0	8	9	7	7	1	1	3	4	1.500	7.88	49	5.29	.290	0	.000	-4	0	-0.4

• FEE, Jack John Fee b: 12/23/1867, Carbondale, PA d: 3/3/1913, Carbondale, PA Deb: 9/14/1889

YEAR	TM-L	W	L	PCT	G	GS	CG	SH	SV	IP	H	R	ER	HR	HB	BB	SO	RAT	ERA	ERA+	CERA	OAV	BH	AVG	PR+	WS	TPW
1889	Ind-N	2	2	.500	7	3	2	0	0	40	39	29	19	2	6	31	10	1.750	4.28	98	....	.247	3	.143	-1	2	-0.2

YEAR TM-L	W	L	PCT	G	GS	CG	SH	SV	IP	H	R	ER	HR	HB	BB	SO	RAT	ERA	ERA+	CERA	OAV	BH	AVG	PR+	WS	TPW
• FELDMAN, Harry	Harry Feldman b: 11/10/1919, New York, NY d: 3/16/1962, Fort Smith, AR BR/TR, 6', 175 lbs. Deb: 9/10/1941																									
1941 NY-N	1	1	.500	3	3	1	1	0	20^1	21	10	9	0	0	6	9	1.328	3.98	93	3.14	.280	1	.167	-1	1	-0.1
1942 NY-N	7	1	.875	31	6	2	1	0	114	100	46	40	5	1	73	49	1.518	3.16	106	3.78	.236	11	.282	1	8	0.5
1943 NY-N	4	5	.444	31	10	1	0	0	104^2	114	59	50	7	4	58	49	1.643	4.30	80	4.96	.279	4	.133	-9	3	-1.0
1944 NY-N	11	13	.458	40	27	8	1	2	205^1	214	120	95	18	2	91	70	1.485	4.16	88	4.26	.266	15	.205	-13	9	-1.3
1945 NY-N	12	13	.480	35	30	10	3	1	217^2	213	92	79	14	1	69	74	1.296	3.27	120	3.27	.251	7	.097	15	16	1.3
1946 NY-N	0	2	.000	3	2	0	0	0	4	9	8	8	1	0	3	3	3.000	18.00	19	15.10	.474	0	.000	-6	0	-0.7
Total 6	35	35	.500	143	78	22	6	3	666	671	335	281	45	8	300	254	1.458	3.80	96	3.99	.260	38	.172	-12	37	-1.3
• FELICIANO, Pedro	Pedro Juan (Molina) Feliciano b: 8/25/1976, Rio Piedras, Puerto Rico BL/TL, 5'11", 185 lbs. Deb: 9/4/2002																									
2002 NY-N	0	0	....	6	0	0	0	0	6	9	5	5	0	0	1	4	1.667	7.50	53	5.56	.360	0	....	-2	0	-0.2
2003 NY-N	0	0	....	23	0	0	0	0	48^1	52	21	18	5	3	21	43	1.510	3.35	124	4.77	.269	0	.000	5	3	0.5
Total 2	0	0	....	29	0	0	0	0	54^1	61	26	23	5	3	22	47	1.528	3.81	108	4.85	.280	0	.000	2	3	0.2
• FELIX, Harry	Harry Felix b: 1870, Brooklyn, NY d: 10/17/1961, Miami, FL BR/TR, 5'7.5", 160 lbs. Deb: 10/5/1901																									
1901 NY-N	0	0	....	1	0	0	0	0	2	3	0	0	0	0	0	0	1.500	0.00	....	4.60	.344	0	.000	1	0	0.1
1902 Phi-N	1	3	.250	9	5	3	0	0	45	61	37	28	1	0	11	10	1.600	5.60	50	4.85	.323	5	.135	-13	0	-1.6
Total 2	1	3	.250	10	5	3	0	0	47	64	37	28	1	0	11	10	1.596	5.36	52	4.84	.324	5	.132	-12	0	-1.6
• FELLER, Bob	Robert William Andrew "Rapid Robert" Feller b: 11/3/1918, Van Meter, IA BR/TR, 6', 185 lbs. Deb: 7/19/1936 HOF: 1962																									
1936 Cle-A	5	3	.625	14	8	5	0	1	62	52	29	23	1	4	47	76	1.597	3.34	151	3.98	.229	3	.136	12	6	0.9
1937 Cle-A	9	7	.563	26	19	9	0	1	148^2	116	68	56	4	2	106	150	1.493	3.39	136	3.41	.218	9	.170	22	13	1.9
1938 Cle-A★	17	11	.607	39	36	20	2	1	277^2	225	136	126	13	7	208	**240**	1.559	4.08	114	3.84	**.220**	17	.181	16	22	1.6
1939 Cle-A★	**24**	9	.727	39	35	**24**	4	1	**296^2**	227	105	94	13	3	142	**246**	1.244	2.85	154	2.66	**.210**	21	.212	**51**	**32**	**5.2**
1940 Cle-A★	**27**	11	.711	**43**	**37**	**31**	**4**	4	**320^1**	245	102	93	13	5	118	**261**	1.133	**2.61**	161	**2.32**	**.210**	18	.157	49	**34**	4.7
1941 Cle-A★	**25**	13	.658	**44**	**40**	28	**6**	2	**343**	284	129	120	15	5	194	**260**	1.394	3.15	125	3.32	.226	18	.150	28	30	2.9
1945 Cle-A	5	3	.625	9	9	7	1	0	72	50	21	20	1	2	35	59	1.181	2.50	130	2.19	.192	4	.160	7	7	0.7
1946 Cle-A★	**26**	15	.634	**48**	**42**	**36**	**10**	4	**371^1**	277	101	90	11	3	153	**348**	1.158	2.18	151	2.29	.208	16	.129	47	32	4.7
1947 Cle-A★	**20**	11	.645	42	**37**	20	**5**	3	**299**	230	97	89	17	4	127	**196**	1.194	2.68	130	2.66	.215	18	.184	22	23	2.4
1948* Cle-A★	19	15	.559	44	**38**	18	2	3	280^1	255	123	111	20	2	116	**164**	1.323	3.56	114	3.38	.241	9	.095	9	15	0.1
1949 Cle-A	15	14	.517	36	28	15	0	0	211	198	104	88	18	1	84	108	1.336	3.75	106	3.57	.248	17	.236	3	14	0.7
1950 Cle-A★	16	11	.593	35	34	16	3	0	247	230	105	94	20	5	103	119	1.348	3.43	126	3.61	.247	10	.120	24	19	2.0
1951 Cle-A	**22**	8	.733	33	32	16	4	0	249^2	239	105	97	22	7	95	111	1.338	3.50	108	3.72	.253	10	.123	8	18	0.4
1952 Cle-A	9	13	.409	30	30	11	0	0	191^2	219	124	101	13	3	83	81	**1.576**	4.74	70	4.67	.288	7	.117	-28	1	-2.9
1953 Cle-A	10	7	.588	25	25	10	1	0	175^2	163	78	70	16	3	60	60	1.269	3.59	105	3.47	.251	6	.107	3	10	0.1
1954 Cle-A	13	3	.813	19	19	9	1	0	140	127	53	48	13	3	39	59	1.186	3.09	119	3.07	.239	9	.188	7	11	0.8
1955 Cle-A	4	4	.500	25	11	2	1	0	83	71	43	32	7	1	31	25	1.229	3.47	115	3.16	.235	1	.048	5	4	0.3
1956 Cle-A	0	4	.000	19	4	2	0	1	58	63	34	32	7	0	23	18	1.483	4.97	85	4.61	.280	0	.000	-5	1	-0.7
Total 18	266	162	.621	570	484	279	44	21	3827	3271	1557	1384	224	60	1764	2581	1.316	3.25	121	3.21	.231	193	.151	281	292	25.9
• FELTON, Terry	Terry Lane Felton b: 10/29/1957, Texarkana, AR BR/TR, 6'1", 180 lbs. Deb: 9/28/1979																									
1979 Min-A	0	0	....	1	0	0	0	0	2	0	0	0	0	0	0	1	.000	0.00	....	0.00	.000	0	....	1	0	0.1
1980 Min-A	0	3	.000	5	4	0	0	0	17^2	20	18	14	2	1	9	14	1.642	7.13	61	5.38	.286	0	....	-6	0	-0.6
1981 Min-A	0	0	....	1	0	0	0	0	1^1	4	6	6	1	0	2	1	4.500	40.50	10	31.96	.500	0	....	-5	0	-0.6
1982 Min-A	0	13	.000	48	6	0	0	3	117^1	99	71	65	18	4	76	92	1.491	4.99	85	4.62	.230	0	....	-11	2	-1.1
Total 4	0	16	.000	55	10	0	0	3	138^1	123	95	85	21	5	87	108	1.518	5.53	77	4.91	.242	0	....	-21	2	-2.1
• FENNER, Hod	Horace Alfred Fenner b: 7/12/1897, Martin, MI d: 11/20/1954, Detroit, MI BR/TR, 5'10.5", 165 lbs. Deb: 9/9/1921																									
1921 Chi-A	0	0	....	2	1	0	0	0	7	14	6	6	0	0	3	1	2.429	7.71	55	10.41	.452	0	.000	-3	0	-0.3
• FERENS, Stan	Stanley "Lefty" Ferens b: 3/5/1915, Wendel, PA d: 10/7/1994, Hempfield Township, PA BB/TL, 5'11", 170 lbs. Deb: 6/10/1942																									
1942 StL-A	3	4	.429	19	3	1	0	0	69	76	31	29	2	0	21	23	1.406	3.78	98	3.66	.279	3	.143	0	4	0.0
1946 StL-A	2	9	.182	34	6	1	0	0	88	100	60	44	3	3	38	28	1.568	4.50	83	4.46	.293	4	.167	-7	1	-0.8
Total 2	5	13	.278	53	9	2	0	0	157	176	91	73	5	3	59	51	1.497	4.18	89	4.11	.287	7	.156	-7	5	-0.9
• FERGUSON, Alex	James Alexander Ferguson b: 2/16/1897, Montclair, NJ d: 4/26/1976, Sepulveda, CA BR/TR, 6', 180 lbs. Deb: 8/16/1918																									
1918 NY-A	0	0	....	1	0	0	0	0	1^2	2	0	0	0	0	2	1	2.400	0.00	....	8.04	.333	0	.000	0	0	0.0
1921 NY-A	3	1	.750	17	4	1	0	1	56^1	64	40	37	4	4	27	9	1.615	5.91	72	5.09	.296	4	.211	-11	1	-1.1
1922 Bos-A	9	16	.360	39	27	10	1	2	198^1	201	108	95	5	6	62	44	1.326	4.31	95	3.30	.265	6	.092	-1	10	-0.7
1923 Bos-A	9	13	.409	34	27	11	0	0	198^1	229	115	89	5	9	67	72	1.492	4.04	102	4.27	.297	6	.097	3	10	-0.3
1924 Bos-A	14	17	.452	41	32	15	0	2	237^2	259	114	100	6	6	108	78	1.544	3.79	115	4.10	.286	12	.140	18	15	1.2
1925 Bos-A	0	2	.000	5	4	0	0	1	15^2	22	22	19	6	1	5	5	1.723	10.91	42	8.23	.314	0	.000	-11	0	-1.0
NY-A	4	2	.667	21	5	0	0	1	54^1	83	57	47	3	2	42	20	2.301	7.79	55	8.53	.358	2	.133	-21	0	-2.1
*Was-A	5	1	.833	7	6	3	0	0	55^1	52	22	20	2	2	23	24	1.355	3.25	130	3.45	.256	1	.050	4	5	0.2
Yr.	9	5	.643	33	15	3	0	2	125^1	157	101	86	11	5	70	49	1.811	6.18	70	6.25	.311	3	.077	-27	5	-2.9
1926 Was-A	3	4	.429	19	4	0	0	1	47^2	69	51	41	4	3	18	16	1.825	7.74	50	6.50	.343	2	.182	-21	0	-2.0
1927 Phi-N	8	16	.333	31	31	16	0	0	227	280	132	122	15	6	65	73	1.520	4.84	85	4.77	.313	7	.100	-14	8	-1.8
1928 Phi-N	5	10	.333	34	19	5	1	2	134^2	168	91	83	14	6	52	51	1.634	5.55	77	5.75	.314	1	.026	-17	3	-2.1
1929 Phi-N	1	2	.333	5	4	1	0	0	12^2	19	18	17	2	0	10	3	2.289	12.08	43	8.93	.345	0	.000	-9	0	-0.9
Bro-N	0	1	.000	3	3	0	0	0	2	7	7	5	2	0	1	1	4.000	22.50	20	31.07	.583	1	1.000	-4	0	-0.3
Yr.	1	3	.250	8	7	1	0	0	14^2	26	25	22	4	0	11	4	2.523	13.50	37	11.95	.388	1	.200	-13	0	-1.2
Total 10	61	85	.418	257	166	62	2	10	1241^2	1455	777	675	68	45	482	397	1.560	4.89	86	4.75	.299	42	.106	-83	52	-11.0
• FERGUSON, Bob	Robert Lester Ferguson b: 4/18/1919, Birmingham, AL BR/TR, 6'1.5", 180 lbs. Deb: 4/29/1944																									
1944 Cin-N	0	3	.000	9	2	0	0	1	16	24	17	16	3	2	10	9	2.125	9.00	39	9.28	.358	1	.333	-10	0	-1.0
• FERGUSON, Charlie	Charles J. Ferguson b: 4/17/1863, Charlottesville, VA d: 4/29/1888, Philadelphia, PA BB/TR, 6', 165 lbs. Deb: 5/1/1884 U ♦																									
1884 Phi-N	21	25	.457	50	47	46	2	1	416^2	443	297	164	13	....	93	194	1.286	3.54	84	....	.258	50	.246	-8	16	0.2
1885 Phi-N	26	20	.565	48	45	45	5	0	405	345	197	100	5	....	81	197	1.052	2.22	125	....	.220	72	.306	22	41	3.9
1886 Phi-N	30	9	.769	48	45	43	4	**2**	395^2	317	145	87	11	....	69	212	.976	1.98	165	....	.211	66	.253	**68**	49	**7.3**
1887 Phi-N	22	10	.688	37	33	31	2	**1**	297^1	344	154	99	13	11	47	125	1.157	3.00	140	....	.282	123	.413	47	36	5.6
Total 4	99	64	.607	183	170	165	13	4	1514^2	1449	793	450	42	11	290	728	1.117	2.67	119	....	.241	311	.312	129	142	17.0
• FERGUSON, Charlie	Charles Augustus Ferguson b: 5/10/1875, Okemos, MI d: 5/17/1931, Sault Ste. Marie, MI TR, 5'11" Deb: 9/20/1901 U																									
1901 Chi-N	0	0	....	1	0	0	0	0	2	1	0	0	0	0	2	0	1.500	0.00	....	2.62	.149	0	.000	1	0	0.1
• FERGUSON, George	George Cecil "Cecil" Ferguson b: 8/19/1886, Ellsworth, IN d: 9/5/1943, Orlando, FL BR/TR, 5'10", 165 lbs. Deb: 4/19/1906																									
1906 NY-N	2	0	1.000	22	1	1	1	**7**	52^1	43	22	15	1	2	24	32	1.280	2.58	101	2.92	.229	5	.333	-0	5	0.2
1907 NY-N	3	2	.600	15	5	4	0	1	64	63	32	15	2	5	20	37	1.297	2.11	117	3.56	.266	1	.056	5	3	0.4
1908 Bos-N	11	11	.500	37	21	13	3	0	208	168	72	57	1	8	84	98	1.212	2.47	97	2.63	.230	11	.169	-7	12	-0.6
1909 Bos-N	5	23	.179	36	30	19	3	0	226^2	235	121	94	2	12	83	87	1.403	3.73	75	3.85	.282	15	.205	-23	6	-2.4
1910 Bos-N	7	7	.500	26	14	10	1	0	123	110	56	52	3	7	58	40	1.366	3.80	87	3.58	.254	7	.175	-9	7	-0.9
1911 Bos-N	1	3	.250	6	3	0	0	0	24	40	29	26	3	0	12	4	2.167	9.75	39	9.23	.388	2	.286	-15	0	-1.5
Total 6	29	46	.387	142	74	47	8	8	698	659	332	259	12	34	281	298	1.347	3.34	85	3.53	.261	41	.188	-49	33	-4.7
• FERMIN, Ramon	Ramon Antonio (Ventura) Fermin b: 11/25/1972, San Francisco de Macoris, Dominican Republic BR/TR, 6'3", 180 lbs. Deb: 8/6/1995																									
1995 Oak-A	0	0	....	1	0	0	0	0	1^1	4	2	2	0	0	1	0	3.750	13.50	33	18.29	.500	0	....	-1	0	-0.1
• FERNANDEZ, Alex	Alexander Fernandez b: 8/13/1969, Miami Beach, FL BR/TR, 6'2", 215 lbs. Deb: 8/2/1990																									
1990 Chi-A	5	5	.500	13	13	3	0	0	87^2	89	40	37	6	3	34	61	1.403	3.80	101	4.05	.265	0	....	-2	5	-0.2
1991 Chi-A	9	13	.409	34	32	2	0	0	191^2	186	100	96	16	2	88	145	1.430	4.51	88	4.08	.259	0	....	-17	7	-1.7

YEAR	TM-L	W	L	PCT	G	GS	CG	SH	SV	IP	H	R	ER	HR	HB	BB	SO	RAT	ERA	ERA+	CERA	OAV	BH	AVG	PR+	WS	TPW
1992	Chi-A	8	11	.421	29	29	4	2	0	187^2	199	100	89	21	8	50	95	1.327	4.27	90	4.11	.270	0	....	-8	6	-0.9
1993*	Chi-A	18	9	.667	34	34	3	1	0	247^1	221	95	86	27	6	67	169	1.164	3.13	133	3.18	.240	0	....	28	20	2.8
1994	Chi-A	11	7	.611	24	24	4	3	0	170^1	163	83	73	25	1	50	122	1.250	3.86	121	3.72	.250	0	....	16	11	1.5
1995	Chi-A	12	8	.600	30	30	5	2	0	203^2	200	98	86	19	0	65	159	1.301	3.80	117	3.57	.255	0	....	17	12	1.6
1996	Chi-A	16	10	.615	35	35	6	1	0	258	248	110	99	34	7	72	200	1.240	3.45	138	3.72	.253	0	....	39	19	3.5
1997*	Fla-N	17	12	.586	32	32	5	1	0	220^2	193	93	88	25	4	69	183	1.187	3.59	112	3.24	.238	10	.152	9	16	1.2
1999	Fla-N	7	8	.467	24	24	1	0	0	141	135	60	53	10	4	41	91	1.248	3.38	129	3.33	.252	10	.233	16	10	1.9
2000	Fla-N	4	4	.500	8	8	0	0	0	52^1	59	25	24	7	0	16	27	1.433	4.13	107	4.75	.292	2	.118	2	4	0.2
Total	**10**	**107**	**87**	**.552**	**263**	**261**	**33**	**10**	**0**	**1760^1**	**1693**	**804**	**731**	**190**	**35**	**552**	**1252**	**1.275**	**3.74**	**113**	**3.66**	**.254**	**22**	**.175**	**101**	**110**	**10.0**
• FERNANDEZ, Jared	Jared Wade Fernandez b: 2/2/1972, Salt Lake City, UT BR/TR, 6'2", 223 lbs. Deb: 9/19/2001																										
2001	Cin-N	0	1	.000	5	2	0	0	0	12^1	13	9	6	1	2	6	5	1.541	4.38	104	5.21	.265	0	.000	0	0	0.0
2002	Cin-N	1	3	.250	14	8	0	0	0	50^2	59	31	25	5	3	24	36	1.638	4.44	95	5.57	.294	2	.200	-1	2	-0.1
2003	Hou-N	3	3	.500	12	6	0	0	0	38^1	37	17	17	2	2	12	19	1.278	3.99	111	3.38	.259	0	.000	1	2	0.0
Total	**3**	**4**	**7**	**.364**	**31**	**16**	**0**	**0**	**0**	**101^1**	**109**	**57**	**48**	**8**	**7**	**42**	**60**	**1.490**	**4.26**	**102**	**4.70**	**.277**	**2**	**.095**	**0**	**4**	**-0.1**
• FERNANDEZ, Osvaldo	Osvaldo (Guerra) Fernandez b: 11/4/1968, Holguin, Cuba BR/TR, 6'2", 190 lbs. Deb: 4/5/1996																										
1996	SF-N	7	13	.350	30	28	2	0	0	171^2	193	95	88	20	10	57	106	1.456	4.61	89	4.82	.286	5	.088	-11	6	-1.4
1997	SF-N	3	4	.429	11	11	0	0	0	56^1	74	39	31	9	0	15	31	1.580	4.95	82	5.66	.314	0	.000	-5	1	-0.6
2000	Cin-N	4	3	.571	15	14	1	0	0	79^2	69	33	32	6	2	31	36	1.255	3.62	130	3.28	.238	2	.091	9	6	0.7
2001	Cin-N	5	6	.455	20	14	0	0	0	79^1	103	62	61	8	0	33	35	1.714	6.92	66	5.82	.316	1	.053	-20	0	-2.0
Total	**4**	**19**	**26**	**.422**	**76**	**67**	**3**	**0**	**0**	**387**	**439**	**229**	**212**	**43**	**12**	**136**	**208**	**1.486**	**4.93**	**87**	**4.83**	**.287**	**8**	**.070**	**-28**	**13**	**-3.4**
• FERNANDEZ, Sid	Charles Sidney Fernandez b: 10/12/1962, Honolulu, HI BL/TL, 6'1", 230 lbs. Deb: 9/20/1983																										
1983	LA-N	0	1	.000	2	1	0	0	0	6	7	4	4	0	1	7	9	2.333	6.00	60	7.83	.280	1	1.000	-1	0	-0.1
1984	NY-N	6	6	.500	15	15	0	0	0	90	74	40	35	8	0	34	62	1.200	3.50	101	2.92	.226	5	.179	0	5	0.0
1985	NY-N	9	9	.500	26	26	3	0	0	170^1	108	56	53	14	2	80	180	1.104	2.80	123	2.36	**.181**	11	.212	13	12	1.6
1986*	NY-N★	16	6	.727	32	31	2	1	1	204^1	161	82	80	13	2	91	200	1.233	3.52	100	2.88	.216	11	.162	-0	12	0.1
1987	NY-N★	12	8	.600	28	27	3	1	0	156	130	75	66	16	8	67	134	1.263	3.81	99	3.38	.224	7	.163	1	8	0.2
1988*	NY-N	12	10	.545	31	31	1	1	0	187	127	69	63	15	6	70	189	1.053	3.03	106	2.31	**.191**	14	.250	4	11	1.0
1989	NY-N	14	5	.737	35	32	6	2	0	219^1	157	73	69	21	6	75	198	1.058	2.83	115	2.43	.198	15	.211	13	16	1.8
1990	NY-N	9	14	.391	30	30	2	1	0	179^1	130	79	69	18	5	67	181	1.099	3.46	108	2.57	**.200**	11	.190	8	9	0.9
1991	NY-N	1	3	.250	8	8	0	0	0	44	36	18	14	4	0	9	31	1.023	2.86	127	2.30	.222	2	.154	5	3	0.5
1992	NY-N	14	11	.560	32	32	5	2	0	214^2	162	67	65	12	4	67	193	1.067	2.73	127	2.24	.210	15	.203	21	16	2.5
1993	NY-N	5	6	.455	18	18	1	1	0	119^2	82	42	39	17	3	36	81	.986	2.93	137	2.45	.192	3	.094	14	9	1.3
1994	Bal-A	6	6	.500	19	19	2	0	0	115^1	109	66	66	27	2	46	95	1.344	5.15	97	4.73	.248	0	....	-3	6	-0.3
1995	Bal-A	0	4	.000	8	7	0	0	0	28	36	26	23	9	0	17	31	1.893	7.39	64	8.22	.305	0	....	-9	0	-0.8
	Phi-N	6	1	.857	11	11	0	0	0	64^2	48	25	24	11	1	21	79	1.067	3.34	127	2.88	.200	1	.043	6	6	0.4
1996	Phi-N	3	6	.333	11	11	0	0	0	63	50	25	24	5	1	26	77	1.206	3.43	126	2.86	.215	2	.105	6	4	0.6
1997	Hou-N	1	0	1.000	1	1	0	0	0	5	4	2	2	1	0	2	3	1.200	3.60	111	3.57	.211	0	.000	0	0	0.0
Total	**15**	**114**	**96**	**.543**	**307**	**300**	**25**	**9**	**1**	**1866^2**	**1421**	**749**	**696**	**191**	**41**	**715**	**1743**	**1.144**	**3.36**	**111**	**2.83**	**.209**	**98**	**.182**	**77**	**117**	**9.6**
• FERRARESE, Don	Donald Hugh Ferrarese b: 6/19/1929, Oakland, CA BR/TL, 5'9", 170 lbs. Deb: 4/11/1955																										
1955	Bal-A	0	0	....	6	0	0	0	0	9	8	3	3	0	0	11	5	2.111	3.00	127	6.11	.276	0	.000	1	1	0.1
1956	Bal-A	4	10	.286	36	14	3	1	2	102	86	60	57	8	3	64	81	1.471	5.03	78	4.03	.229	1	.036	-12	3	-1.5
1957	Bal-A	1	1	.500	8	2	0	0	0	19	14	13	10	1	0	12	13	1.368	4.74	76	3.04	.200	0	.000	-3	0	-0.3
1958	Cle-A	3	4	.429	28	10	2	0	1	94^2	91	45	39	4	1	46	62	1.447	3.71	98	3.78	.254	3	.115	-1	4	-0.3
1959	Cle-A	5	3	.625	15	10	4	0	0	76	58	29	27	6	1	51	45	1.434	3.20	115	3.79	.219	7	.259	4	6	0.6
1960	Chi-A	0	1	.000	5	0	0	0	0	4	8	8	8	2	0	9	4	4.250	18.00	21	24.32	.400	1	.500	-6	0	-0.6
1961	Phi-N	5	12	.294	42	14	3	1	1	138^2	120	64	58	14	1	68	89	1.356	3.76	108	3.72	.234	6	.171	3	8	0.2
1962	Phi-N	0	1	.000	5	0	0	0	0	6^2	9	8	6	1	0	3	6	1.800	8.10	48	6.40	.310	1	1.000	-3	0	-0.3
	StL-N	1	4	.200	38	0	0	0	1	56^2	55	19	17	2	1	31	45	1.518	2.70	158	4.06	.270	1	.200	9	5	1.0
	Yr.	1	5	.167	43	0	0	0	1	63^1	64	27	23	3	1	34	51	1.547	3.27	127	4.31	.275	2	.333	6	5	0.7
Total	**8**	**19**	**36**	**.345**	**183**	**50**	**12**	**2**	**5**	**506^2**	**449**	**249**	**225**	**38**	**7**	**295**	**350**	**1.468**	**4.00**	**97**	**4.06**	**.241**	**20**	**.156**	**-9**	**27**	**-1.2**
• FERRARI, Anthony	Anthony Michael Ferrari b: 6/22/1978, San Francisco, CA BL/TL, 5'9", 165 lbs. Deb: 6/7/2003																										
2003	Mon-N	0	0	....	4	0	0	0	0	4	4	3	3	1	1	5	1	2.250	6.75	75	9.84	.267	0	....	-1	0	-0.1
• FERRAZZI, Bill	William Joseph Ferrazzi b: 4/19/1907, West Quincy, MA d: 8/10/1993, Gainesville, FL BR/TR, 6'2.5", 200 lbs. Deb: 9/7/1935																										
1935	Phi-A	1	2	.333	3	2	0	0	0	7	7	5	4	0	0	5	0	1.714	5.14	88	4.21	.269	0	.000	-0	0	0.0
• FERREIRA, Tony	Anthony Ross Ferreira b: 10/4/1962, Riverside, CA BL/TL, 6'1", 160 lbs. Deb: 9/17/1985																										
1985	KC-A	0	0	....	2	0	0	0	0	5^2	6	5	5	0	0	2	5	1.412	7.94	52	3.58	.273	0	....	-2	0	-0.2
• FERRELL, Wes	Wesley Cheek Ferrell b: 2/2/1908, Greensboro, NC d: 12/9/1976, Sarasota, FL BR/TR, 6'2", 195 lbs. Deb: 9/9/1927																										
1927	Cle-A	0	0	....	1	0	0	0	0	1	3	3	3	0	0	2	0	5.000	27.00	16	23.63	.600	0	....	-3	0	-0.2
1928	Cle-A	0	2	.000	2	2	1	0	0	16	15	5	4	0	0	5	4	1.250	2.25	184	2.65	.242	1	.250	3	2	0.4
1929	Cle-A	21	10	.677	43	25	18	1	5	242^2	256	112	97	7	3	109	100	1.504	3.60	123	4.02	.279	22	.237	25	25	2.8
1930	Cle-A	25	13	.658	43	35	25	1	3	296^2	299	141	109	14	0	106	143	1.365	3.31	146	3.48	.262	35	.297	55	32	5.8
1931	Cle-A	22	12	.647	40	35	**27**	2	3	276^1	276	134	115	9	3	130	123	1.469	3.75	123	3.71	.255	37	.319	35	28	4.9
1932	Cle-A	23	13	.639	38	34	26	3	1	287^2	299	141	117	17	0	104	105	1.401	3.66	130	3.75	.264	31	.242	40	26	4.2
1933	Cle-A★	11	12	.478	28	26	16	1	0	201	225	108	94	8	2	70	41	1.468	4.21	106	4.02	.282	38	.271	5	18	1.6
1934	Bos-A	14	5	.737	26	23	17	3	1	181	205	87	73	4	0	49	67	1.403	3.63	132	3.66	.282	22	.282	25	18	3.1
1935	Bos-A	**25**	14	.641	41	**38**	**31**	3	0	**322^1**	336	149	126	16	3	108	110	1.377	3.52	135	3.63	.267	52	.347	43	**35**	**6.0**
1936	Bos-A	20	15	.571	39	**38**	**28**	3	0	**301**	330	160	140	11	6	119	106	1.492	4.19	127	4.05	.274	36	.267	37	27	4.3
1937	Bos-A	3	6	.333	12	11	5	0	0	73^1	111	66	62	14	1	34	31	1.977	7.61	62	8.21	.348	12	.364	-22	1	-1.5
	Was-A★	11	13	.458	25	24	21	0	0	207^2	214	111	91	11	2	88	92	1.454	3.94	112	3.91	.265	27	.255	8	13	1.2
	Yr.	14	19	.424	37	35	**26**	0	0	**281**	325	177	153	25	3	122	123	1.591	4.90	93	5.04	.289	39	.281	-14	14	-0.2
1938	Was-A	13	8	.619	23	22	9	0	0	149	193	111	98	12	1	68	36	1.752	5.92	76	5.77	.311	11	.224	-24	6	-1.5
	NY-A	2	2	.500	5	4	1	0	0	30	52	33	27	6	0	18	7	2.333	8.10	56	10.53	.388	2	.167	-12	0	-1.1
	Yr.	15	10	.600	28	26	10	0	0	179	245	144	125	18	1	86	43	**1.849**	6.28	72	6.57	.325	13	.213	-36	6	-2.6
1939	NY-A	1	2	.333	3	3	1	0	0	19^1	14	10	10	2	0	17	6	1.603	4.66	94	4.30	.219	1	.125	-1	1	-0.2
1940	Bro-N	0	0	....	1	0	0	0	0	4	4	3	3	0	1	4	4	2.000	6.75	59	6.04	.250	0	.000	-1	0	-0.1
1941	Bos-N	2	1	.667	4	3	1	0	0	14	13	8	8	1	1	9	10	1.571	5.14	69	4.46	.241	2	.500	-3	1	-0.1
Total	**15**	**193**	**128**	**.601**	**374**	**323**	**227**	**17**	**13**	**2623**	**2845**	**1382**	**1177**	**132**	**23**	**1040**	**985**	**1.481**	**4.04**	**116**	**4.12**	**.275**	**329**	**.280**	**212**	**233**	**29.6**
• FERRICK, Tom	Thomas Jerome Ferrick b: 1/6/1915, New York, NY d: 10/15/1996, Lima, PA BR/TR, 6'2.5", 220 lbs. Deb: 4/19/1941 C																										
1941	Phi-A	8	10	.444	36	4	2	1	7	119^1	130	61	50	8	0	33	30	1.366	3.77	111	3.78	.275	9	.205	5	9	0.6
1942	Cle-A	3	2	.600	31	2	2	0	3	81^1	56	20	18	3	0	32	28	1.082	1.99	173	2.05	.200	4	.211	12	9	1.2
1946	Cle-A	0	0	....	9	0	0	0	1	18	25	12	10	3	0	4	9	1.611	5.00	66	5.93	.321	2	.667	-3	0	-0.2
	StL-A	4	1	.800	25	1	0	0	5	32^1	26	13	10	1	0	5	13	.959	2.78	134	1.78	.224	0	.000	4	5	0.3
	Yr.	4	1	.800	34	1	0	0	6	50^1	51	25	20	4	0	9	22	1.192	3.58	98	3.26	.263	2	.286	0	5	0.1
1947	Was-A	1	7	.125	31	0	0	0	9	60	57	24	21	1	0	20	23	1.283	3.15	118	2.91	.256	1	.100	5	7	0.4
1948	Was-A	2	5	.286	37	0	0	0	10	73^2	75	37	34	3	0	38	34	1.534	4.15	105	4.01	.261	1	.067	3	6	0.2
1949	StL-A	6	4	.600	50	0	0	0	6	104^1	102	51	45	9	1	41	34	1.371	3.88	117	3.77	.258	3	.143	11	8	1.0
1950	StL-A	1	3	.250	16	0	0	0	2	24	24	15	11	2	0	7	6	1.292	4.13	120	3.43	.267	1	.250	3	2	0.3
	*NY-A	8	4	.667	30	0	0	0	9	56^2	49	26	23	5	0	22	20	1.253	3.65	118	3.17	.233	2	.143	3	7	0.3
	Yr.	9	7	.563	46	0	0	0	11	80^2	73	41	34	7	0	29	26	1.264	3.79	118	3.25	.243	3	.167	6	9	0.6

YEAR	TM-L	W	L	PCT	G	GS	CG	SH	SV	IP	H	R	ER	HR	HB	BB	SO	RAT	ERA	ERA+	CERA	OAV	BH	AVG	PR+	WS	TPW
1951	NY-A	1	1	.500	9	0	0	0	1	12	21	12	10	4	0	7	3	2.333	7.50	51	11.62	.389	1	1.000	-5	0	-0.4
	Was-A	2	0	1.000	22	0	0	0	2	41^{2}	36	16	11	3	0	7	17	1.032	2.38	172	2.34	.234	2	.286	8	4	0.9
	Yr.	3	1	.750	31	0	0	0	3	53^{2}	57	28	21	7	0	14	20	1.323	3.52	113	4.41	.274	3	.375	3	4	0.4
1952	Was-A	4	3	.571	27	0	0	0	1	50^{2}	53	19	17	2	0	11	28	1.263	3.02	118	3.25	.273	1	.200	3	5	0.4
Total	**9**	40	40	.500	323	7	4	1	56	674	654	306	260	44	1	227	245	1.307	3.47	117	3.43	.256	27	.184	48	62	5.0
• FERRIS, Bob	Robert Eugene Ferris b: 5/7/1955, Arlington, VA BR/TR, 6'6", 225 lbs. Deb: 9/12/1979																										
1979	Cal-A	0	0	....	2	0	0	0	0	6	5	2	1	1	0	3	2	1.333	1.50	271	3.51	.217	0	....	2	1	0.2
1980	Cal-A	0	2	.000	5	3	0	0	0	15^{1}	23	13	10	2	0	9	4	2.087	5.87	67	8.48	.354	0	....	-3	0	-0.3
Total	**2**	0	2	.000	7	3	0	0	0	21^{1}	28	15	11	3	0	12	6	1.875	4.64	85	7.08	.318	0	....	-2	1	-0.2
• FERRISS, Dave	David Meadow "Boo" Ferriss b: 12/5/1921, Shaw, MS BL/TR, 6'2", 208 lbs. Deb: 4/29/1945 C																										
1945	Bos-A★	21	10	.677	35	31	26	5	2	264^{2}	263	101	87	6	7	85	94	1.315	2.96	115	3.29	.264	32	.267	11	24	2.4
1946*	Bos-A★	25	6	.806	40	35	26	6	3	274	274	109	99	14	3	71	106	1.259	3.25	113	3.20	.259	24	.209	11	23	1.4
1947	Bos-A	12	11	.522	33	28	14	1	0	218^{1}	241	106	98	14	7	92	64	**1.525**	4.04	96	4.58	.287	27	.273	-4	13	0.3
1948	Bos-A	7	3	.700	31	9	1	0	3	115^{1}	127	71	67	7	7	61	30	1.630	5.23	84	5.06	.286	9	.243	-11	6	-0.9
1949	Bos-A	0	0	....	4	0	0	0	0	6^{2}	7	3	3	1	1	4	1	1.650	4.05	108	6.50	.292	1	1.000	0	1	0.1
1950	Bos-A	0	0	....	1	0	0	0	0	1	2	2	2	0	0	1	1	3.000	18.00	27	11.63	.500	0	....	-1	0	-0.1
Total	**6**	65	30	.684	144	103	67	12	8	880	914	392	356	42	25	314	296	1.395	3.64	104	3.85	.272	93	.250	5	67	3.1
• FERRY, Cy	Alfred Joseph Ferry b: 9/27/1878, Hudson, NY d: 9/27/1938, Pittsfield, MA BR/TR, 6'1", 170 lbs. Deb: 5/12/1904																										
1904	Det-A	0	1	.000	3	1	1	0	0	13	12	9	9	0	1	11	4	1.769	6.23	41	4.56	.246	2	.333	-5	0	-0.5
1905	Cle-A	0	0	....	1	1	0	0	0	2	3	3	3	1	2	0	2	1.500	13.50	19	13.59	.348	0	.000	-2	0	-0.3
Total	**2**	0	1	.000	4	2	1	0	0	15	15	12	12	1	3	11	6	1.733	7.20	36	5.76	.261	2	.286	-8	0	-0.8
• FERRY, Jack	John Francis Ferry b: 4/7/1887, Pittsfield, MA d: 8/29/1954, Pittsfield, MA BR/TR, 5'11", 175 lbs. Deb: 9/4/1910																										
1910	Pit-N	1	2	.333	6	3	2	0	0	31	26	10	8	0	1	8	12	1.097	2.32	135	2.21	.230	3	.333	3	3	0.4
1911	Pit-N	6	4	.600	26	8	4	1	3	85^{2}	83	35	30	3	2	27	32	1.284	3.15	109	3.29	.260	9	.310	1	7	0.4
1912	Pit-N	2	0	1.000	11	3	1	1	1	39	33	21	13	1	1	23	10	1.436	3.00	108	3.36	.234	1	.077	1	2	0.0
1913	Pit-N	1	0	1.000	4	0	0	0	0	5	4	3	3	0	0	2	2	1.200	5.40	56	2.37	.286	0	....	-1	0	-0.1
Total	**4**	10	6	.625	47	14	7	2	4	160^{2}	146	69	54	4	4	60	56	1.282	3.02	109	3.07	.249	13	.255	3	12	0.6
• FERSON, Alex	Alexander "Colonel" Ferson b: 7/14/1866, Philadelphia, PA d: 12/5/1957, Boston, MA BR/TR, 5'9", 165 lbs. Deb: 5/4/1889																										
1889	Was-N	17	17	.500	36	34	28	1	0	288^{1}	319	199	125	9	12	105	85	1.471	3.90	101	....	.272	13	.114	6	11	0.2
1890	Buf-P	1	7	.125	10	10	7	0	0	71	88	66	43	5	1	40	13	1.803	5.45	75	....	.292	7	.219	-10	1	-0.7
1892	Bal-N	0	1	.000	2	1	1	0	0	9	17	13	11	1	0	6	8	2.556	11.00	31	10.90	.387	0	.000	-7	0	-0.7
Total	**3**	18	25	.419	48	45	36	1	0	368^{1}	424	278	179	15	13	151	106	1.561	4.37	90	0.27	.279	20	.133	-10	12	-1.2
• FETTE, Lou	Louis Henry William Fette b: 3/15/1907, Alma, MO d: 1/3/1981, Warrensburg, MO BR/TR, 6'1.5", 200 lbs. Deb: 4/26/1937																										
1937	Bos-N	20	10	.667	35	33	23	**5**	0	259	243	93	83	5	4	81	70	1.251	2.88	124	2.88	.251	22	.239	14	23	1.7
1938	Bos-N	11	13	.458	33	32	17	3	1	239^{2}	235	95	84	11	4	79	83	1.310	3.15	109	3.32	.258	16	.188	6	16	0.6
1939	Bos-N★	10	10	.500	27	26	11	**6**	0	146	123	62	48	7	1	61	35	1.260	2.96	125	2.89	.229	3	.061	10	10	0.5
1940	Bos-N	0	5	.000	7	5	0	0	0	32^{1}	38	23	20	0	1	18	2	1.732	5.57	67	5.03	.302	3	.375	-7	0	-0.6
	Bro-N	0	0	....	2	0	0	0	0	3	3	0	0	0	0	2	0	1.667	0.00	....	4.82	.300	0	....	1	1	0.1
	Yr.	0	5	.000	9	5	0	0	0	35^{1}	41	23	20	0	1	20	2	1.726	5.09	73	5.01	.301	3	.375	-6	1	-0.5
1945	Bos-N	0	2	.000	5	1	0	0	0	11	16	10	7	1	1	7	4	2.091	5.73	67	8.37	.356	0	.000	-2	0	-0.3
Total	**5**	41	40	.506	109	97	51	14	1	691	658	283	242	24	11	248	194	1.311	3.15	113	3.23	.253	44	.186	21	50	2.1
• FETTERS, Mike	Michael Lee Fetters b: 12/19/1964, Van Nuys, CA BR/TR, 6'4", 212 lbs. Deb: 9/1/1989																										
1989	Cal-A	0	0	....	1	0	0	0	0	3^{1}	5	4	3	1	0	1	4	1.800	8.10	47	8.14	.333	0	....	-2	0	-0.2
1990	Cal-A	1	1	.500	26	2	0	0	1	67^{2}	77	33	31	9	2	20	35	1.433	4.12	93	4.88	.287	0	....	-2	3	-0.2
1991	Cal-A	2	5	.286	19	4	0	0	0	44^{2}	53	29	24	4	3	28	24	1.813	4.84	85	6.44	.305	0	....	-4	1	-0.4
1992	Mil-A	5	1	.833	50	0	0	0	2	62^{2}	38	15	13	3	7	24	43	.989	1.87	206	2.13	.185	0	....	12	8	1.3
1993	Mil-A	3	3	.500	45	0	0	0	0	59^{1}	59	29	22	4	2	22	23	1.365	3.34	127	3.89	.278	0	....	6	4	0.6
1994	Mil-A	1	4	.200	42	0	0	0	17	46	41	16	13	0	1	27	31	1.478	2.54	198	3.36	.243	0	....	11	8	1.0
1995	Mil-A	0	3	.000	40	0	0	0	22	34^{2}	40	16	13	3	0	20	33	1.731	3.38	148	5.27	.286	0	....	6	5	0.5
1996	Mil-A	3	3	.500	61	0	0	0	32	61^{1}	65	28	23	4	1	26	53	1.484	3.38	154	4.24	.274	0	....	11	10	1.0
1997	Mil-A	1	5	.167	51	0	0	0	6	70^{1}	62	30	27	4	1	33	62	1.351	3.45	134	3.41	.244	0	....	7	7	0.7
1998	Oak-A	1	6	.143	48	0	0	0	5	47^{1}	48	26	21	3	1	21	34	1.458	3.99	114	3.93	.258	0	....	4	4	0.3
	Ana-A	1	2	.333	12	0	0	0	0	11^{1}	14	8	7	2	0	4	9	1.588	5.56	84	5.95	.304	0	....	-1	0	-0.1
	Yr.	2	8	.200	60	0	0	0	5	58^{2}	62	34	28	5	1	25	43	1.483	4.30	107	4.32	.267	0	....	3	4	0.2
1999	Bal-A	1	0	1.000	27	0	0	0	0	31	35	23	20	5	2	22	22	1.839	5.81	81	6.66	.278	0	....	-4	1	-0.4
2000	LA-N	6	2	.750	51	0	0	0	5	50	35	18	18	7	2	25	40	1.200	3.24	134	3.34	.205	0	....	6	7	0.6
2001	LA-N	2	1	.667	34	0	0	0	1	29^{2}	33	23	20	6	1	13	26	1.551	6.07	66	5.53	.273	0	....	-7	0	-0.6
	Pit-N	1	1	.500	20	0	0	0	8	17^{2}	16	9	9	1	3	13	11	1.642	4.58	98	5.01	.235	0	....	-0	2	0.0
	Yr.	3	2	.600	54	0	0	0	9	47^{1}	49	32	29	7	4	26	37	1.585	5.51	75	5.34	.259	0	....	-7	2	-0.7
2002	Pit-N	1	0	1.000	32	0	0	0	0	30^{1}	25	13	11	3	1	18	29	1.418	3.26	128	3.86	.219	0	....	3	3	0.3
	*Ari-N	2	3	.400	33	0	0	0	0	24^{2}	28	18	14	1	2	19	24	1.905	5.11	87	5.91	.292	0	....	-2	1	-0.2
	Yr.	3	3	.500	65	0	0	0	0	55	53	31	25	4	3	37	53	1.636	4.09	105	4.78	.252	0	....	1	4	0.1
2003	Min-A	0	0	....	5	0	0	0	0	6	2	0	0	0	1	1	1	.500	0.00	....	0.69	.100	0	....	3	1	0.3
Total	**15**	31	40	.437	597	6	0	0	99	698	676	338	289	60	30	337	504	1.451	3.73	117	4.29	.258	0	....	48	65	4.5
• FICK, John	John Ralph Fick b: 5/18/1921, Baltimore, MD d: 6/9/1958, Somers Point, NJ BL/TL, 5'10", 150 lbs. Deb: 7/29/1944																										
1944	Phi-N	0	0	....	4	0	0	0	0	5^{1}	3	2	2	0	1	3	2	1.125	3.38	107	2.02	.150	0	....	0	0	0.0
• FIDRYCH, Mark	Mark Steven "The Bird" Fidrych b: 8/14/1954, Worcester, MA BR/TR, 6'3", 175 lbs. Deb: 4/20/1976																										
1976	Det-A★	19	9	.679	31	29	**24**	4	0	250^{1}	217	76	65	12	3	53	97	1.079	**2.34**	**159**	2.41	.235	0	....	**41**	**27**	**4.3**
1977	Det-A★	6	4	.600	11	11	7	1	0	81	82	29	26	2	1	12	42	1.160	2.89	148	2.76	.269	0	....	13	7	1.3
1978	Det-A	2	0	1.000	3	3	2	0	0	22	17	6	6	1	0	5	10	1.000	2.45	157	2.01	.213	0	....	3	2	0.3
1979	Det-A	0	3	.000	4	4	0	0	0	14^{2}	23	17	17	3	1	9	5	2.182	10.43	41	9.84	.371	0	....	-10	0	-1.0
1980	Det-A	2	3	.400	9	9	1	0	0	44^{1}	58	35	28	5	1	20	16	1.759	5.68	72	5.98	.309	0	....	-7	0	-0.7
Total	**5**	29	19	.604	58	56	34	5	0	412^{1}	397	163	142	23	6	99	170	1.203	3.10	128	3.11	.255	0	....	40	36	4.2
• FIEBER, Clarence	Clarence Thomas "Lefty" Fieber b: 9/4/1913, San Francisco, CA d: 8/20/1985, Redwood City, CA BL/TL, 6'4", 187 lbs. Deb: 5/18/1932																										
1932	Chi-A	1	0	1.000	3	0	0	0	0	5^{1}	6	1	1	0	0	3	1	1.688	1.69	256	4.38	.273	0	....	2	1	0.1
• FIELD, Nate	Nathan Patrick Field b: 12/11/1975, Denver, CO BR/TR, 6'2", 200 lbs. Deb: 4/12/2002																										
2002	KC-A	0	0	....	5	0	0	0	0	5	8	5	5	2	0	3	3	2.200	9.00	56	10.82	.364	0	....	-2	0	-0.2
2003	KC-A	1	1	.500	19	0	0	0	0	21^{2}	19	10	10	3	1	14	19	1.523	4.15	124	4.74	.235	0	....	2	2	0.2
Total	**2**	1	1	.500	24	0	0	0	0	26^{2}	27	15	15	5	1	17	22	1.650	5.06	101	5.88	.262	0	....	0	2	0.0
• FIENE, Lou	Louis Henry "Big Finn" Fiene b: 12/29/1884, Fort Dodge, IA d: 12/22/1964, Chicago, IL BR/TR, 6', 175 lbs. Deb: 5/7/1906																										
1906	Chi-A	1	1	.500	6	2	1	0	0	31	35	17	10	0	4	9	12	1.419	2.90	87	4.03	.288	2	.200	-2	1	-0.2
1907	Chi-A	0	1	.000	6	1	1	0	1	26	30	17	12	0	2	7	15	1.423	4.15	58	3.91	.292	2	.182	-5	0	-0.6
1908	Chi-A	0	1	.000	1	1	1	0	0	9	9	7	4	0	0	1	3	1.111	4.00	58	2.36	.257	0	.000	-2	0	-0.2
1909	Chi-A	2	5	.286	13	6	4	0	0	72	75	37	33	1	5	18	24	1.292	4.13	57	3.59	.284	2	.069	-14	0	-1.8
Total	**4**	3	8	.273	26	10	7	0	1	138	149	78	59	1	11	35	54	1.333	3.85	62	3.67	.285	6	.113	-22	1	-2.8
• FIFE, Danny	Danny Wayne Fife b: 10/5/1949, Harrisburg, IL BR/TR, 6'3", 175 lbs. Deb: 8/18/1973																										
1973	Min-A	3	2	.600	10	7	1	0	0	51^{2}	54	26	25	2	3	29	18	1.606	4.35	91	4.74	.270	0	....	-2	3	-0.2

YEAR	TM-L	W	L	PCT	G	GS	CG	SH	SV	IP	H	R	ER	HR	HB	BB	SO	RAT	ERA	ERA+	CERA	OAV	BH	AVG	PR+	WS	TPW
1974	Min-A	0	0	....	4	0	0	0	0	4^{2}	10	11	9	0	1	4	3	3.000	17.36	22	13.38	.417	0	....	-7	0	-0.7
Total	2	3	2	.600	14	7	1	0	0	56^{1}	64	37	34	2	4	33	21	1.722	5.43	72	5.45	.286	0	....	-9	3	-0.9
• FIFIELD, Jack	John Proctor Fifield b: 10/5/1871, Enfield, NH d: 11/27/1939, Syracuse, NY BR/TR, 5'11", 160 lbs. Deb: 4/28/1897																										
1897	Phi-N	5	18	.217	27	26	21	0	0	210^{2}	263	163	129	8	9	80	38	1.628	5.51	76	5.01	.303	18	.234	-26	7	-2.0
1898	Phi-N	11	9	.550	21	21	18	2	0	171^{1}	170	91	63	2	18	60	31	1.342	3.31	104	3.50	.257	7	.109	4	9	0.0
1899	Phi-N	3	8	.273	14	11	9	1	1	92^{2}	110	64	42	0	4	36	8	1.576	4.08	90	4.39	.295	9	.257	-5	4	-0.4
	Was-N	2	4	.333	6	6	6	0	0	47	73	44	32	1	2	17	12	1.915	6.13	64	6.65	.353	4	.200	-10	1	-0.9
	Yr.	5	12	.294	20	17	15	1	1	139^{2}	183	108	74	1	6	53	20	1.690	4.77	79	5.15	.316	13	.236	-15	5	-1.3
Total	3	21	39	.350	68	64	54	3	1	521^{2}	616	362	266	11	33	193	89	1.551	4.59	84	4.56	.292	38	.194	-38	21	-3.3
• FIGGEMEIER, Frank	Frank Y. Figgemeier b: 4/22/1873, St. Louis, MO d: 4/15/1915, St. Louis, MO Deb: 9/25/1894																										
1894	Phi-N	0	1	.000	1	1	1	0	0	8	12	14	10	1	3	4	2	2.000	11.25	45	9.21	.343	1	.333	-5	0	-0.4
• FIGUEROA, Ed	Eduardo (Padilla) Figueroa b: 10/14/1948, Ciales, Puerto Rico BR/TR, 6'1", 190 lbs. Deb: 4/9/1974																										
1974	Cal-A	2	8	.200	25	12	5	1	0	105^{1}	119	46	43	3	4	36	49	1.472	3.67	93	4.26	.294	0	....	-2	4	-0.2
1975	Cal-A	16	13	.552	33	32	16	2	0	244^{2}	213	96	79	14	5	84	139	1.214	2.91	122	2.93	.233	0	....	18	18	1.9
1976*	NY-A	19	10	.655	34	34	14	4	0	256^{2}	237	101	86	13	3	94	119	1.290	3.02	113	3.24	.246	0	....	3	16	0.3
1977*	NY-A	16	11	.593	32	32	12	2	0	239^{1}	228	102	95	19	3	75	104	1.266	3.57	110	3.40	.252	0	....	6	15	0.6
1978*	NY-A	20	9	.690	35	35	12	2	0	253	233	96	84	22	3	77	92	1.225	2.99	121	3.26	.248	0	....	16	19	1.6
1979	NY-A	4	6	.400	16	16	4	1	0	104^{2}	109	49	48	6	0	35	42	1.376	4.13	99	3.84	.275	0	....	-2	5	-0.2
1980	NY-A	3	3	.500	15	9	0	0	1	58	90	47	45	3	1	24	16	1.966	6.98	56	7.25	.363	0	....	-19	0	-1.9
	Tex-A	0	7	.000	8	8	0	0	0	39^{2}	62	29	26	9	0	12	9	1.866	5.90	66	8.28	.365	0	....	-8	0	-0.8
	Yr.	3	10	.231	23	17	0	0	1	97^{2}	152	76	71	12	1	36	25	1.925	6.54	60	7.67	.364	0	....	-28	0	-2.8
1981	Oak-A	0	0	....	2	1	0	0	0	8^{1}	8	5	5	1	0	6	1	1.680	5.40	64	5.46	.258	0	....	-2	0	-0.2
Total	8	80	67	.544	200	179	63	12	1	1309^{2}	1299	571	511	90	19	443	571	1.330	3.51	105	3.69	.261	0	....	9	77	1.0
• FIGUEROA, Nelson	Nelson Walter Figueroa b: 5/18/1974, Brooklyn, NY BB/TR, 6'1", 155 lbs. Deb: 6/3/2000																										
2000	Ari-N	0	1	.000	3	3	0	0	0	15^{2}	17	13	13	4	0	5	7	1.404	7.47	63	5.31	.283	1	.333	-5	0	-0.4
2001	Phi-N	4	5	.444	19	13	0	0	0	89	95	40	39	8	7	37	61	1.483	3.94	108	4.76	.275	6	.250	2	6	0.3
2002	Mil-N	1	7	.125	30	11	0	0	0	93	96	59	52	18	4	37	51	1.430	5.03	81	4.94	.270	2	.133	-9	1	-1.0
2003	Pit-N	2	1	.667	12	3	0	0	0	35^{1}	28	13	13	8	2	13	23	1.160	3.31	132	3.80	.220	0	.000	4	3	0.3
Total	4	7	14	.333	64	30	0	0	0	233	236	125	117	38	13	92	142	1.408	4.52	94	4.72	.266	9	.184	-8	10	-0.7
• FIKAC, Jeremy	Jeremy Joseph Fikac b: 4/8/1975, Shiner, TX BR/TR, 6'2", 185 lbs. Deb: 8/16/2001																										
2001	SD-N	2	0	1.000	23	0	0	0	0	26^{1}	15	6	4	2	1	5	19	.759	1.37	292	1.33	.165	0	....	8	3	0.8
2002	SD-N	4	7	.364	65	0	0	0	0	69	74	50	42	13	3	34	66	1.565	5.48	69	5.39	.267	0	.000	-12	0	-1.3
2003	Oak-A	0	1	.000	14	0	0	0	0	16	14	8	8	4	3	11	9	1.563	4.50	100	6.69	.246	0	....	0	1	0.0
Total	3	6	8	.429	102	0	0	0	0	111^{1}	103	64	54	19	7	50	94	1.374	4.37	89	4.62	.242	0	.000	-4	4	-0.5
• FILE, Bob	Robert Michael File b: 1/28/1977, Philadelphia, PA BR/TR, 6'4", 215 lbs. Deb: 4/14/2001																										
2001	Tor-A	5	3	.625	60	0	0	0	0	74^{1}	57	28	27	6	7	29	38	1.157	3.27	140	2.98	.220	0	....	10	7	1.0
2002	Tor-A	0	1	.000	5	0	0	0	0	3^{1}	8	7	7	0	0	2	2	3.000	18.90	24	13.02	.471	0	....	-5	0	-0.5
Total	2	5	4	.556	65	0	0	0	0	77^{2}	65	35	34	6	7	31	40	1.236	3.94	117	3.41	.236	0	....	5	7	0.5
• FILER, Tom	Thomas Carson Filer b: 12/1/1956, Philadelphia, PA BR/TR, 6'1", 198 lbs. Deb: 6/8/1982																										
1982	Chi-N	1	2	.333	8	8	0	0	0	40^{2}	50	25	25	5	0	18	15	1.672	5.53	68	5.64	.301	1	.083	-8	0	-0.9
1985	Tor-A	7	0	1.000	11	9	0	0	0	48^{2}	38	21	21	6	0	18	24	1.151	3.88	108	3.06	.222	0	....	1	4	0.1
1988	Mil-A	5	8	.385	19	16	2	1	0	101^{2}	108	54	50	8	1	33	39	1.387	4.43	90	4.02	.281	0	....	-6	4	-0.6
1989	Mil-A	7	3	.700	13	13	0	0	0	72^{1}	74	30	29	6	4	23	20	1.341	3.61	106	4.10	.271	0	....	2	5	0.2
1990	Mil-A	2	3	.400	7	4	0	0	0	22	26	17	15	2	0	9	8	1.591	6.14	63	5.08	.289	0	....	-5	0	-0.5
1992	NY-N	0	1	.000	9	1	0	0	0	22	18	8	5	2	0	6	9	1.091	2.05	170	2.48	.222	0	.000	4	1	0.4
Total	6	22	17	.564	67	51	2	1	0	307^{1}	314	155	145	29	5	107	115	1.370	4.25	92	4.07	.269	1	.067	-13	14	-1.4
• FILES, Eddie	Charles Edward Files b: 5/19/1883, Portland, ME d: 5/10/1954, Cornish, ME BR/TR Deb: 10/3/1908																										
1908	Phi-A	0	0	....	2	0	0	0	0	9	8	7	6	0	2	3	6	1.222	6.00	43	3.90	.286	0	.000	-3	0	-0.4
• FILLEY, Marc	Marcus Lucius Filley b: 2/28/1912, Lansingburgh, NY d: 1/20/1995, Yarmouth, ME BR/TR, 5'11", 172 lbs. Deb: 4/19/1934																										
1934	Was-A	0	0	....	1	0	0	0	0	0^{1}	2	1	1	0	0	0	0	6.000	27.00	16	39.65	.667	0	....	-1	0	-0.1
• FILLINGIM, Dana	Dana Fillingim b: 11/6/1893, Columbus, GA d: 2/3/1961, Tuskegee, AL BL/TR, 5'10", 175 lbs. Deb: 8/2/1915																										
1915	Phi-A	0	5	.000	8	4	1	0	0	39^{1}	42	25	15	0	1	32	17	1.881	3.43	85	5.87	.313	2	.167	-2	1	-0.2
1918	Bos-N	7	6	.538	14	13	10	4	0	113	99	37	28	0	5	28	29	1.124	2.23	120	2.36	.243	9	.214	8	8	0.9
1919	Bos-N	6	13	.316	32	18	9	0	2	186^{1}	185	80	70	2	2	39	50	1.202	3.38	84	2.70	.270	16	.246	-11	8	-1.0
1920	Bos-N	12	21	.364	37	31	22	2	0	272	292	123	94	8	3	79	66	1.364	3.11	98	3.60	.287	16	.174	-5	14	-0.7
1921	Bos-N	15	10	.600	44	23	11	**3**	1	239^{2}	249	108	92	10	2	56	54	1.273	3.45	106	3.23	.272	21	.247	4	16	0.8
1922	Bos-N	5	9	.357	25	12	5	1	2	117	143	74	59	6	1	37	25	1.538	4.54	88	4.57	.311	6	.158	-6	5	-0.7
1923	Bos-N	1	9	.100	35	12	1	0	0	100^{1}	141	74	58	6	1	36	27	1.764	5.20	76	5.98	.345	7	.226	-13	1	-1.1
1925	Phi-N	1	0	1.000	5	1	0	0	0	8^{2}	19	12	10	0	0	6	2	2.885	10.38	46	11.94	.432	0	.000	-5	0	-0.5
Total	8	47	73	.392	200	114	59	10	5	1076^{1}	1170	533	426	32	15	313	270	1.378	3.56	94	3.71	.287	77	.209	-29	53	-2.4
• FILSON, Pete	William Peter Filson b: 9/28/1958, Darby, PA BB/TL, 6'2", 195 lbs. Deb: 5/15/1982																										
1982	Min-A	0	2	.000	5	3	0	0	0	12^{1}	17	12	12	2	0	8	10	2.027	8.76	48	7.49	.321	0	....	-6	0	-0.6
1983	Min-A	4	1	.800	26	8	0	0	1	90	87	34	34	9	1	29	49	1.289	3.40	125	3.65	.252	0	....	7	7	0.7
1984	Min-A	6	5	.545	55	7	0	0	1	118^{2}	106	56	54	14	3	54	59	1.348	4.10	103	3.78	.238	0	....	-1	7	-0.1
1985	Min-A	4	5	.444	40	6	1	0	2	95^{2}	93	42	39	13	0	30	42	1.286	3.67	120	3.72	.251	0	....	8	8	0.8
1986	Min-A	0	0	....	4	0	0	0	0	6^{1}	13	4	4	1	1	2	4	2.368	5.68	76	11.55	.406	0	....	-1	0	-0.1
	Chi-A	0	1	.000	3	1	0	0	0	11^{2}	14	9	8	4	0	5	4	1.629	6.17	70	7.10	.286	0	....	-3	0	-0.3
	Yr.	0	1	.000	7	1	0	0	0	18	27	13	12	5	1	7	8	1.889	6.00	72	8.66	.333	0	....	-4	0	-0.4
1987	NY-A	1	0	1.000	7	2	0	0	0	22	26	10	8	2	1	9	10	1.591	3.27	134	5.24	.299	0	....	3	2	0.2
1990	KC-A	0	4	.000	8	7	0	0	0	35	42	31	23	6	2	13	9	1.571	5.91	65	5.66	.282	0	....	-7	0	-0.7
Total	7	15	18	.455	148	34	1	0	4	391^{2}	398	198	182	51	8	150	187	1.399	4.18	101	4.33	.260	0	....	-1	24	-0.1
• FINCH, Joel	Joel D. Finch b: 8/20/1956, South Bend, IN BR/TR, 6'2", 175 lbs. Deb: 6/12/1979																										
1979	Bos-A	0	3	.000	15	7	0	0	0	57^{1}	65	31	31	5	1	25	25	1.570	4.87	91	4.96	.289	0	.000	-2	2	-0.3
• FINCHER, Bill	William Allen Fincher b: 5/26/1894, Atlanta, GA d: 5/7/1946, Shreveport, LA BR/TR, 6'1", 180 lbs. Deb: 4/23/1916																										
1916	StL-A	0	1	.000	12	1	0	0	0	21	22	11	5	0	0	7	5	1.381	2.14	128	3.52	.282	1	.250	1	1	0.1
• FINE, Tommy	Thomas Morgan Fine b: 10/10/1914, Cleburne, TX BB/TR, 6', 180 lbs. Deb: 4/26/1947																										
1947	Bos-A	1	2	.333	9	7	1	0	0	36	41	24	22	0	1	19	10	1.667	5.50	71	4.46	.285	3	.333	-7	1	-0.6
1950	StL-A	0	1	.000	14	0	0	0	0	36^{2}	53	38	33	6	0	25	6	2.127	8.10	61	8.51	.342	4	.333	-12	0	-1.0
Total	2	1	3	.250	23	7	1	0	0	72^{2}	94	62	55	6	1	44	16	1.899	6.81	65	6.50	.314	7	.333	-18	1	-1.5
• FINGERS, Rollie	Roland Glen Fingers b: 8/25/1946, Steubenville, OH BR/TR, 6'4", 195 lbs. Deb: 9/15/1968 HOF: 1992																										
1968	Oak-A	0	0	....	1	0	0	0	0	1^{1}	4	4	4	1	1	1	0	3.750	27.00	10	35.58	.571	0	....	-4	0	-0.4
1969	Oak-A	6	7	.462	60	8	1	1	12	119	116	60	49	13	4	41	61	1.319	3.71	93	3.89	.257	5	.200	-4	6	-0.4
1970	Oak-A	7	9	.438	45	19	1	0	2	148	137	65	60	13	2	48	79	1.250	3.65	97	3.37	.250	4	.103	-3	7	-0.4
1971*	Oak-A	4	6	.400	48	8	2	1	17	129^{1}	94	46	43	14	8	30	98	.959	2.99	111	2.34	.207	7	.212	3	12	0.3
1972*	Oak-A	11	9	.550	65	0	0	0	21	111^{1}	85	35	31	8	1	32	113	1.051	2.51	113	2.26	.212	6	.316	3	13	0.6
1973*	Oak-A★	7	8	.467	62	2	0	0	22	126^{2}	107	41	27	5	4	39	110	1.153	1.92	185	2.56	.226	0	.000	20	14	2.0

YEAR TM-L	W	L	PCT	G	GS	CG	SH	SV	IP	H	R	ER	HR	HB	BB	SO	RAT	ERA	ERA+	CERA	OAV	BH	AVG	PR+	WS	TPW
1974* Oak-A★	9	5	.643	**76**	0	0	0	18	119	104	41	35	5	1	29	95	1.118	2.65	125	2.42	.240	0	....	7	14	0.7
1975* Oak-A★	10	6	.625	**75**	0	0	0	24	126^2	95	43	42	13	6	33	115	1.011	2.98	122	2.47	.213	0	.000	9	15	0.9
1976 Oak-A★	13	11	.542	70	0	0	0	20	134^2	118	40	37	3	7	40	113	1.173	2.47	136	2.59	.243	0	....	15	17	1.6
1977 SD-N	8	9	.471	**78**	0	0	0	**35**	132^1	123	47	44	12	1	36	113	1.202	2.99	118	3.06	.248	1	.050	9	12	0.7
1978 SD-N★	6	13	.316	67	0	0	0	**37**	107^1	84	33	30	4	1	29	72	1.053	2.52	132	1.94	.212	2	.167	9	17	1.0
1979 SD-N	9	9	.500	54	0	0	0	13	83^2	91	47	42	7	1	37	65	1.530	4.52	78	4.50	.281	1	.083	-10	5	-1.1
1980 SD-N	11	9	.550	66	0	0	0	23	103	101	35	32	3	0	32	69	1.291	2.80	123	2.99	.263	5	.278	6	15	0.8
1981* Mil-A★	6	3	.667	47	0	0	0	**28**	78	55	9	9	3	1	13	61	.872	1.04	330	1.48	.198	0	....	20	17	2.1
1982 Mil-A★	5	6	.455	50	0	0	0	29	79^2	63	23	23	5	1	20	71	1.042	2.60	146	2.17	.220	0	....	9	12	0.9
1984 Mil-A	1	2	.333	33	0	0	0	23	46	38	13	10	5	0	13	40	1.109	1.96	197	2.58	.213	0	....	10	8	1.0
1985 Mil-A	1	6	.143	47	0	0	0	17	55^1	59	33	31	9	0	19	24	1.410	5.04	83	4.48	.272	0	....	-5	4	-0.5
Total 17	114	118	.491	944	37	4	2	341	1701^1	1474	615	549	123	39	492	1299	1.156	2.90	119	2.82	.235	31	.172	94	188	9.9

• FINK, Herman Herman Adam Fink b: 8/22/1911, Concord, NC d: 8/24/1980, Salisbury, NC BR/TR, 6'2", 198 lbs. Deb: 9/16/1935

YEAR TM-L	W	L	PCT	G	GS	CG	SH	SV	IP	H	R	ER	HR	HB	BB	SO	RAT	ERA	ERA+	CERA	OAV	BH	AVG	PR+	WS	TPW
1935 Phi-A	0	3	.000	5	3	0	0	0	15^2	18	19	16	0	1	10	2	1.787	9.19	49	5.14	.290	1	.200	-8	0	-0.8
1936 Phi-A	8	16	.333	34	24	9	0	3	188^2	222	126	113	18	0	78	53	1.590	5.39	95	4.99	.294	8	.125	-6	9	-0.9
1937 Phi-A	2	1	.667	28	3	1	0	1	80	82	43	36	6	1	35	18	1.463	4.05	116	4.09	.263	5	.208	6	5	0.5
Total 3	10	20	.333	67	30	10	0	4	284^1	322	188	165	24	2	123	73	1.565	5.22	95	4.74	.285	14	.151	-8	14	-1.1

• FINLAYSON, Pembroke Pembroke Finlayson b: 7/31/1888, Cheraw, SC d: 3/6/1912, Brooklyn, NY BR/TR, 5'6", 140 lbs. Deb: 6/6/1908

YEAR TM-L	W	L	PCT	G	GS	CG	SH	SV	IP	H	R	ER	HR	HB	BB	SO	RAT	ERA	ERA+	CERA	OAV	BH	AVG	PR+	WS	TPW
1908 Bro-N	0	0	....	1	0	0	0	0	0^1	0	5	5	0	0	4	0	12.00	135.00	2	40.48	.000	0	....	-5	0	-0.6
1909 Bro-N	0	0	....	1	0	0	0	0	7	7	4	4	0	0	4	2	1.571	5.14	50	4.53	.212	0	.000	-2	0	-0.3
Total 2	0	0	....	2	0	0	0	0	7^1	7	9	9	0	0	8	2	2.045	11.05	22	6.16	.212	0	.000	-7	0	-0.8

• FINLEY, Chuck Charles Edward Finley b: 11/26/1962, Monroe, LA BL/TL, 6'6", 214 lbs. Deb: 5/29/1986

YEAR TM-L	W	L	PCT	G	GS	CG	SH	SV	IP	H	R	ER	HR	HB	BB	SO	RAT	ERA	ERA+	CERA	OAV	BH	AVG	PR+	WS	TPW
1986* Cal-A	3	1	.750	25	0	0	0	0	46^1	40	17	17	2	1	23	37	1.360	3.30	124	3.36	.235	0	....	3	4	0.3
1987 Cal-A	2	7	.222	35	3	0	0	0	90^2	102	54	47	7	3	43	63	1.599	4.67	92	5.07	.287	0	....	-4	3	-0.4
1988 Cal-A	9	15	.375	31	31	2	0	0	194^1	191	95	90	15	6	82	111	1.405	4.17	93	4.03	.263	0	....	-6	8	-0.6
1989 Cal-A★	16	9	.640	29	29	9	1	0	199^2	171	64	57	13	2	82	156	1.267	2.57	148	3.19	.233	0	....	24	19	2.5
1990 Cal-A★	18	9	.667	32	32	7	2	0	236	210	77	63	17	2	81	177	1.233	2.40	159	3.17	.243	0	....	37	23	3.8
1991 Cal-A	18	9	.667	34	34	4	2	0	227^1	205	102	96	23	8	101	171	1.346	3.80	108	3.94	.244	0	....	4	14	0.4
1992 Cal-A	7	12	.368	31	31	4	1	0	204^1	212	99	90	24	3	98	124	1.517	3.96	101	4.91	.277	0	....	-1	11	-0.1
1993 Cal-A	16	14	.533	35	35	**13**	2	0	251^1	243	108	88	22	6	82	187	1.293	3.15	143	3.60	.253	0	....	35	19	3.4
1994 Cal-A	10	10	.500	25	**25**	7	2	0	**183**^{1}	178	95	88	21	3	71	148	1.358	4.32	113	4.10	.260	0	....	11	14	1.0
1995 Cal-A★	15	12	.556	32	32	2	1	0	203	192	106	95	20	7	93	195	1.404	4.21	111	4.13	.249	0	....	9	12	0.9
1996 Cal-A★	15	16	.484	35	35	4	1	0	238	241	124	110	27	11	94	215	1.408	4.16	118	4.38	.263	0	....	20	16	1.8
1997 Ana-A	13	6	.684	25	25	3	1	0	164	152	79	77	20	5	65	155	1.323	4.23	109	3.99	.248	0	.000	6	11	0.5
1998 Ana-A	11	9	.550	34	34	1	1	0	223^1	210	97	84	20	6	109	212	1.428	3.39	139	4.10	.246	0	.000	34	17	3.2
1999 Ana-A	12	11	.522	33	33	1	0	0	213^1	197	117	105	23	8	94	200	1.364	4.43	109	4.03	.246	0	.000	8	14	0.7
2000 Cle-A★	16	11	.593	34	34	3	0	0	218	211	108	101	23	2	101	189	1.431	4.17	119	4.26	.256	0	.000	21	16	1.9
2001* Cle-A	8	7	.533	22	22	1	0	0	113^2	131	78	70	14	2	35	96	1.460	5.54	82	4.85	.290	0	....	-11	3	-1.0
2002 Cle-A	4	11	.267	18	18	1	0	0	105^1	114	56	52	6	0	48	91	1.538	4.44	99	4.49	.284	0	.000	1	5	0.0
*StL-N	7	4	.636	14	14	1	1	0	85^1	69	41	36	7	1	30	83	1.160	3.80	104	2.74	.219	3	.107	0	4	-0.1
Total 17	200	173	.536	524	467	63	15	0	3197^1	3069	1517	1366	304	76	1332	2610	1.376	3.85	115	4.01	.255	3	.057	193	213	18.2

• FINNERAN, Happy Joseph Ignatius "Smokey Joe" Finneran b: 10/29/1891, East Orange, NJ d: 2/3/1942, Orange, NJ BR/TR, 5'10.5", 169 lbs. Deb: 8/20/1912

YEAR TM-L	W	L	PCT	G	GS	CG	SH	SV	IP	H	R	ER	HR	HB	BB	SO	RAT	ERA	ERA+	CERA	OAV	BH	AVG	PR+	WS	TPW
1912 Phi-N	0	2	.000	14	4	0	0	1	46^1	50	27	13	2	1	10	10	1.295	2.53	143	3.47	.282	2	.200	5	3	0.6
1913 Phi-N	0	0	....	3	0	0	0	0	5	12	7	4	0	0	2	0	2.800	7.20	46	12.36	.462	2	.667	-2	1	-0.1
1914 Bro-F	12	11	.522	27	23	13	2	1	175^1	153	77	62	6	6	60	54	1.215	3.18	102	2.87	.237	7	.127	3	10	-0.1
1915 Bro-F	10	12	.455	37	24	12	1	2	215^1	197	90	67	2	9	87	68	1.319	2.80	106	3.18	.249	11	.149	3	11	0.0
1918 Det-A	0	2	.000	5	2	0	0	1	13^2	22	17	15	0	0	8	2	2.195	9.88	27	8.20	.393	0	.000	-10	0	-1.2
NY-A	3	6	.333	23	13	4	0	0	114^1	134	52	48	7	2	35	34	1.478	3.78	75	5.17	.305	9	.231	-16	3	-1.6
Yr.	3	8	.273	28	15	4	0	1	128	156	69	63	7	2	43	36	1.555	4.43	63	5.49	.315	9	.214	-26	3	-2.8
Total 5	25	33	.431	109	66	29	3	5	570	568	270	209	17	18	202	168	1.351	3.30	92	3.71	.266	31	.168	-17	28	-2.5

• FINNVOLD, Gar Anders Gar Finnvold b: 3/11/1968, Boynton Beach, FL BR/TR, 6'5", 195 lbs. Deb: 5/10/1994

YEAR TM-L	W	L	PCT	G	GS	CG	SH	SV	IP	H	R	ER	HR	HB	BB	SO	RAT	ERA	ERA+	CERA	OAV	BH	AVG	PR+	WS	TPW
1994 Bos-A	0	4	.000	8	8	0	0	0	36^1	45	27	24	4	3	15	17	1.651	5.94	85	5.99	.304	0	....	-4	1	-0.4

• FIORE, Tony Anthony James Fiore b: 10/12/1971, Oak Park, IL BR/TR, 6'4", 210 lbs. Deb: 8/27/2000

YEAR TM-L	W	L	PCT	G	GS	CG	SH	SV	IP	H	R	ER	HR	HB	BB	SO	RAT	ERA	ERA+	CERA	OAV	BH	AVG	PR+	WS	TPW
2000 TB-A	1	1	.500	11	0	0	0	0	15	21	16	14	3	2	9	8	2.000	8.40	59	8.74	.333	0	....	-6	0	-0.5
2001 TB-A	0	0	....	3	0	0	0	0	3^1	4	2	2	0	1	1	3	1.500	5.40	83	5.47	.308	0	....	-0	0	0.0
Min-A	0	1	.000	4	0	0	0	0	6^1	5	4	4	0	0	2	5	1.105	5.68	81	2.01	.208	0	....	-1	0	-0.1
Yr.	0	1	.000	7	0	0	0	0	9^2	9	6	6	0	1	3	8	1.241	5.59	82	3.20	.243	0	....	-1	0	-0.1
2002* Min-A	10	3	.769	48	2	0	0	0	91	74	32	32	10	5	43	55	1.286	3.16	142	3.57	.224	0	.000	13	9	1.3
2003 Min-A	1	1	.500	21	0	0	0	0	36	32	25	22	5	3	21	23	1.472	5.50	83	4.73	.242	0	.000	-3	1	-0.3
Total 4	12	6	.667	87	2	0	0	0	151^2	136	79	74	18	11	76	94	1.398	4.39	105	4.33	.242	0	.000	3	10	0.3

• FIREOVID, Steve Stephen John Fireovid b: 6/6/1957, Bryan, OH BB/TR, 6'2", 195 lbs. Deb: 9/6/1981

YEAR TM-L	W	L	PCT	G	GS	CG	SH	SV	IP	H	R	ER	HR	HB	BB	SO	RAT	ERA	ERA+	CERA	OAV	BH	AVG	PR+	WS	TPW
1981 SD-N	0	1	.000	5	4	0	0	0	26^1	30	8	8	2	0	7	11	1.405	2.73	119	4.30	.294	1	.143	1	1	0.1
1983 SD-N	0	0	....	3	0	0	0	0	5	4	2	1	0	0	2	1	1.200	1.80	194	2.46	.235	0	....	1	0	0.1
1984 Phi-N	0	0	....	6	0	0	0	0	5^2	4	1	1	0	0	0	3	.706	1.59	229	1.06	.200	0	....	1	1	0.1
1985 Chi-A	0	0	....	4	0	0	0	0	7	17	4	4	0	0	2	2	2.714	5.14	84	12.37	.472	0	....	-1	0	-0.1
1986 Sea-A	2	0	1.000	10	1	0	0	0	21	28	11	10	1	1	4	10	1.524	4.29	99	5.24	.333	0	....	-0	2	0.0
1992 Tex-A	1	0	1.000	3	0	0	0	0	6^2	10	5	3	0	0	4	0	2.100	4.05	94	6.93	.370	0	....	-0	0	0.0
Total 6	3	1	.750	31	5	0	0	0	71^2	93	31	27	3	1	19	27	1.563	3.39	112	5.23	.325	1	.143	3	4	0.3

• FIRTH, Ted John E. Firth b: 5/6/1855, Lowell, MA d: 6/23/1902, Tewksbury, MA Deb: 8/15/1884

YEAR TM-L	W	L	PCT	G	GS	CG	SH	SV	IP	H	R	ER	HR	HB	BB	SO	RAT	ERA	ERA+	CERA	OAV	BH	AVG	PR+	WS	TPW
1884 Ric-a	0	1	.000	1	1	1	0	0	9	14	13	8	0	0	5	0	2.111	8.00	41	....	.337	1	.333	-5	0	-0.4

• FISCHER, Bill William Charles Fischer b: 10/11/1930, Wausau, WI BR/TR, 6', 190 lbs. Deb: 4/21/1956 C

YEAR TM-L	W	L	PCT	G	GS	CG	SH	SV	IP	H	R	ER	HR	HB	BB	SO	RAT	ERA	ERA+	CERA	OAV	BH	AVG	PR+	WS	TPW
1956 Chi-A	0	0	....	3	0	0	0	0	1^2	6	4	4	0	0	1	2	4.200	21.60	19	22.31	.545	0	....	-3	0	-0.3
1957 Chi-A	7	8	.467	33	11	3	1	1	124	139	50	48	1	3	35	48	1.403	3.48	107	3.74	.291	6	.150	1	7	-0.1
1958 Chi-A	2	3	.400	17	3	0	0	0	36^1	43	28	27	6	0	13	16	1.541	6.69	54	5.42	.301	1	.143	-13	0	-1.3
Det-A	2	4	.333	22	0	0	0	2	30^2	46	34	26	6	0	13	16	1.924	7.63	53	8.00	.362	0	.000	-13	0	-1.3
Was-A	0	3	.000	3	3	0	0	0	21	24	9	9	1	1	5	10	1.381	3.86	99	4.23	.320	1	.200	0	1	0.1
Yr.	4	10	.286	42	6	0	0	2	88	113	71	62	13	1	31	42	1.636	6.34	60	6.04	.328	2	.154	-25	1	-2.5
1959 Was-A	9	11	.450	34	29	6	1	0	187^1	211	98	89	16	4	43	62	1.356	4.28	92	4.01	.281	7	.130	-1	8	-0.3
1960 Was-A	3	5	.375	20	7	1	0	0	77	85	45	42	7	0	17	31	1.325	4.91	80	3.86	.281	3	.158	-7	2	-0.6
Det-A	5	3	.625	20	6	1	0	0	55	50	23	21	6	0	18	24	1.236	3.44	120	3.29	.244	4	.364	4	5	0.7
Yr.	8	8	.500	40	13	2	0	0	132	135	68	63	13	0	35	55	1.288	4.30	93	3.62	.266	7	.233	-3	7	0.0
1961 Det-A	3	2	.600	26	1	0	0	3	46^2	54	28	26	10	0	17	18	1.521	5.01	82	5.66	.292	0	.000	-5	2	-0.6
KC-A	1	0	1.000	15	0	0	0	2	21	26	9	9	1	0	6	12	1.524	3.86	107	4.81	.321	0	.000	1	2	0.1
Yr.	4	2	.667	41	1	0	0	5	67^2	80	37	35	11	0	23	30	1.522	4.66	88	5.40	.301	0	.000	-4	4	-0.5
1962 KC-A	4	12	.250	34	16	5	0	2	127^2	150	61	56	16	1	8	38	1.238	3.95	105	3.87	.293	4	.105	4	7	0.2
1963 KC-A	9	6	.600	45	2	0	0	3	95^2	86	44	38	13	3	29	34	1.202	3.57	108	3.43	.242	1	.067	4	8	0.4
1964 Min-A	0	1	.000	9	0	0	0	0	7^1	16	6	6	2	0	5	2	2.864	7.36	49	14.45	.471	0	....	-3	0	-0.3
Total 9	45	58	.437	281	78	16	2	13	831^1	936	439	401	85	12	210	313	1.379	4.34	91	4.27	.287	27	.136	-30	42	-3.5

• FISCHER, Carl Charles William Fischer b: 11/5/1905, Medina, NY d: 12/10/1963, Medina, NY BR/TL, 6', 180 lbs. Deb: 7/19/1930

YEAR TM-L	W	L	PCT	G	GS	CG	SH	SV	IP	H	R	ER	HR	HB	BB	SO	RAT	ERA	ERA+	CERA	OAV	BH	AVG	PR+	WS	TPW
1930 Was-A	1	1	.500	8	4	1	0	1	33^1	37	22	18	0	2	18	21	1.650	4.86	94	4.42	.285	0	.000	-2	1	-0.3

YEAR	TM-L	W	L	PCT	G	GS	CG	SH	SV	IP	H	R	ER	HR	HB	BB	SO	RAT	ERA	ERA+	CERA	OAV	BH	AVG	PR+	WS	TPW
1931	Was-A	13	9	.591	46	23	7	0	3	191	207	98	93	12	2	80	96	1.503	4.38	98	4.25	.273	8	.121	-4	10	-0.8
1932	Was-A	3	2	.600	12	7	1	1	1	50^2	57	30	28	4	0	31	23	1.737	4.97	87	5.30	.282	3	.200	-5	3	-0.4
	StL-A	3	7	.300	24	11	4	0	0	97	122	65	60	12	0	45	35	1.722	5.57	87	5.95	.310	9	.265	-8	4	-0.7
	Yr.	6	9	.400	36	18	5	1	1	147^2	179	95	88	16	0	76	58	1.727	5.36	87	5.73	.300	12	.245	-13	7	-1.1
1933	Det-A	11	15	.423	35	22	9	0	3	182^2	176	88	72	5	3	84	93	1.423	3.55	121	3.49	.251	9	.145	14	13	1.0
1934	Det-A	6	4	.600	20	15	4	1	1	95	107	50	46	5	1	38	39	1.526	4.36	101	4.39	.288	2	.065	-0	5	-0.3
1935	Det-A	0	1	.000	3	1	0	0	0	12	16	8	8	2	1	5	7	1.750	6.00	70	6.99	.320	0	.000	-3	0	-0.3
	Chi-A	5	5	.500	24	11	3	1	0	88^2	102	67	61	7	2	39	31	1.590	6.19	75	4.82	.283	4	.190	-16	2	-1.6
	Yr.	5	6	.455	27	12	3	1	0	100^2	118	75	69	9	3	44	38	1.609	6.17	74	5.08	.287	4	.174	-19	2	-1.8
1937	Cle-A	0	1	.000	2	0	0	0	0	0^2	2	2	2	0	0	1	1	4.500	27.00	17	21.38	.667	0	....	-2	0	-0.2
	Was-A	4	5	.444	17	11	2	0	2	72	74	43	35	6	0	31	30	1.458	4.38	101	4.23	.270	3	.136	-1	4	-0.1
	Yr.	4	6	.400	19	11	2	0	2	72^2	76	45	37	6	0	32	31	1.486	4.58	97	4.39	.274	3	.136	-2	4	-0.3
Total	7	46	50	.479	191	105	31	3	11	823	900	473	423	53	11	372	376	1.546	4.63	96	4.48	.277	38	.145	-27	42	-3.6

• FISCHER, Hank — Henry William "Bulldog" Fischer b: 1/11/1940, Yonkers, NY BR/TR, 6', 190 lbs. Deb: 4/16/1962

YEAR	TM-L	W	L	PCT	G	GS	CG	SH	SV	IP	H	R	ER	HR	HB	BB	SO	RAT	ERA	ERA+	CERA	OAV	BH	AVG	PR+	WS	TPW
1962	Mil-N	2	3	.400	29	0	0	0	4	37^1	43	27	22	4	0	20	29	1.688	5.30	72	5.45	.291	0	.000	-6	0	-0.6
1963	Mil-N	4	3	.571	31	6	1	0	0	74^1	74	46	41	8	5	28	72	1.372	4.96	65	4.19	.262	2	.105	-16	0	-1.7
1964	Mil-N	11	10	.524	37	28	9	5	2	168^1	177	95	75	17	3	39	99	1.283	4.01	88	3.67	.265	8	.154	-9	5	-0.9
1965	Mil-N	8	9	.471	31	19	2	0	0	122^2	126	61	53	18	3	39	79	1.345	3.89	91	4.33	.270	4	.108	-6	5	-0.7
1966	Atl-N	2	3	.400	14	8	0	0	0	48^1	55	23	21	3	1	14	22	1.428	3.91	93	4.31	.296	0	.000	-2	2	-0.3
	Cin-N	0	6	.000	11	9	0	0	0	38	53	31	28	3	3	15	24	1.789	6.63	59	6.60	.331	1	.091	-11	0	-1.2
	Yr.	2	9	.182	25	17	0	0	0	86^1	108	54	49	6	4	29	46	1.587	5.11	74	5.32	.312	1	.042	-13	2	-1.6
	Bos-A	2	3	.400	6	5	1	0	0	31	35	12	10	4	1	11	26	1.484	2.90	131	5.00	.287	2	.222	3	3	0.4
1967	Bos-A	1	2	.333	9	2	1	0	1	26^2	24	15	7	3	1	8	18	1.200	2.36	148	3.27	.229	1	.143	3	1	0.4
Total	6	30	39	.435	168	77	14	5	7	546^2	587	310	257	60	17	174	369	1.392	4.23	84	4.33	.275	18	.118	-43	16	-4.8

• FISCHER, Jeff — Jeffrey Thomas Fischer b: 8/17/1963, West Palm Beach, FL BR/TR, 6'3", 185 lbs. Deb: 6/19/1987

YEAR	TM-L	W	L	PCT	G	GS	CG	SH	SV	IP	H	R	ER	HR	HB	BB	SO	RAT	ERA	ERA+	CERA	OAV	BH	AVG	PR+	WS	TPW
1987	Mon-N	0	1	.000	4	2	0	0	0	13^2	21	14	13	3	0	5	6	1.902	8.56	49	8.15	.362	1	.200	-6	0	-0.6
1989	LA-N	0	0	....	2	0	0	0	0	3^1	7	5	5	1	0	0	2	2.100	13.50	25	10.85	.438	0	....	-4	0	-0.4
Total	2	0	1	.000	6	2	0	0	0	17	28	19	18	4	0	5	8	1.941	9.53	41	8.68	.378	1	.200	-10	0	-1.0

• FISCHER, Rube — Reuben Walter Fischer b: 9/19/1916, Carlock, SD d: 7/16/1997, Green Bay, WI BR/TR, 6'4", 190 lbs. Deb: 9/12/1941

YEAR	TM-L	W	L	PCT	G	GS	CG	SH	SV	IP	H	R	ER	HR	HB	BB	SO	RAT	ERA	ERA+	CERA	OAV	BH	AVG	PR+	WS	TPW
1941	NY-N	1	0	1.000	2	1	1	0	0	11	10	3	3	0	0	6	9	1.455	2.45	151	3.19	.238	1	.333	1	1	0.2
1943	NY-N	5	10	.333	22	17	4	0	1	130^2	140	69	67	4	2	59	47	1.523	4.61	75	4.20	.281	11	.256	-15	4	-1.3
1944	NY-N	6	14	.300	38	18	2	1	2	128^2	128	83	74	7	6	87	39	1.671	5.18	71	4.78	.266	5	.125	-23	2	-2.5
1945	NY-N	3	8	.273	31	4	0	0	1	76^2	90	55	48	6	1	49	27	1.813	5.63	69	5.61	.288	4	.211	-15	1	-1.3
1946	NY-N	1	2	.333	15	1	0	0	0	35^2	48	32	25	3	0	21	14	1.935	6.31	55	6.46	.316	1	.111	-11	0	-1.2
Total	5	16	34	.320	108	41	7	1	4	382^2	416	242	217	20	9	222	136	1.667	5.10	71	4.86	.280	22	.193	-62	8	-6.2

• FISCHER, Todd — Todd Richard Fischer b: 9/15/1960, Columbus, OH BR/TR, 5'10", 170 lbs. Deb: 5/29/1986

YEAR	TM-L	W	L	PCT	G	GS	CG	SH	SV	IP	H	R	ER	HR	HB	BB	SO	RAT	ERA	ERA+	CERA	OAV	BH	AVG	PR+	WS	TPW
1986	Cal-A	0	0	....	9	0	0	0	0	17	18	8	8	4	0	8	7	1.529	4.24	97	5.71	.286	0	....	-1	1	-0.1

• FISHEL, Leo — Leo Fishel b: 12/13/1877, Babylon, NY d: 5/19/1960, Hempstead, NY BR/TR, 6', 175 lbs. Deb: 5/3/1899

YEAR	TM-L	W	L	PCT	G	GS	CG	SH	SV	IP	H	R	ER	HR	HB	BB	SO	RAT	ERA	ERA+	CERA	OAV	BH	AVG	PR+	WS	TPW
1899	NY-N	0	1	.000	1	1	1	0	0	9	9	7	6	0	2	6	6	1.667	6.00	63	4.93	.260	1	.250	-2	0	-0.2

• FISHER, Brian — Brian Kevin Fisher b: 3/18/1962, Honolulu, HI BR/TR, 6'4", 210 lbs. Deb: 5/7/1985

YEAR	TM-L	W	L	PCT	G	GS	CG	SH	SV	IP	H	R	ER	HR	HB	BB	SO	RAT	ERA	ERA+	CERA	OAV	BH	AVG	PR+	WS	TPW
1985	NY-A	4	4	.500	55	0	0	0	14	98^1	77	32	26	4	0	29	85	1.078	2.38	168	2.18	.216	0	....	16	12	1.6
1986	NY-A	9	5	.643	62	0	0	0	6	96^2	105	61	53	14	1	37	67	1.469	4.93	83	4.83	.277	0	....	-10	4	-1.0
1987	Pit-N	11	9	.550	37	26	6	3	0	185^1	185	99	93	27	4	72	117	1.387	4.52	91	4.42	.262	11	.190	-12	9	-0.7
1988	Pit-N	8	10	.444	33	22	1	1	1	146^1	157	78	75	13	5	57	66	1.462	4.61	74	4.44	.277	2	.048	-21	2	-2.5
1989	Pit-N	0	3	.000	9	3	0	0	1	17	25	17	15	2	0	10	8	2.059	7.94	42	7.17	.329	0	.000	-9	0	-1.0
1990	Hou-N	0	0	....	4	0	0	0	0	5	9	5	4	1	0	0	1	1.800	7.20	52	7.87	.409	0	....	-2	0	-0.2
1992	Sea-A	4	3	.571	22	14	0	0	1	91^1	80	49	46	9	1	47	26	1.391	4.53	88	3.83	.234	0	....	-5	4	-0.6
Total	7	36	34	.514	222	65	7	4	23	640	638	341	312	70	11	252	370	1.391	4.39	88	4.16	.261	13	.124	-42	31	-4.3

• FISHER, Chauncey — Chauncey Burr "Peach,Whoa Bill" Fisher b: 1/8/1872, Anderson, IN d: 4/27/1939, Los Angeles, CA BR/TR, 5'11", 175 lbs. Deb: 9/20/1893

YEAR	TM-L	W	L	PCT	G	GS	CG	SH	SV	IP	H	R	ER	HR	HB	BB	SO	RAT	ERA	ERA+	CERA	OAV	BH	AVG	PR+	WS	TPW
1893	Cle-N	0	2	.000	2	2	2	0	0	18	26	18	11	0	0	9	9	1.944	5.50	89	6.16	.328	2	.250	-1	0	-0.1
1894	Cle-N	0	2	.000	3	2	0	0	0	11	22	17	14	0	0	5	0	2.455	11.45	48	9.62	.410	0	.000	-7	0	-0.6
	Cin-N	2	8	.200	12	12	11	0	0	100^1	153	123	74	4	1	46	17	1.983	6.64	84	6.90	.347	10	.233	-12	2	-1.0
	Yr.	2	10	.167	15	14	11	0	0	111^1	175	140	88	4	1	51	17	2.030	7.11	78	7.16	.353	10	.213	-20	2	-1.6
1896	Cin-N	10	7	.588	27	15	13	2	2	159^2	199	111	79	9	0	36	25	1.472	4.45	103	4.41	.303	14	.246	-1	11	0.0
1897	Bro-N	9	7	.563	20	13	11	1	1	149	184	96	70	5	2	43	31	1.523	4.23	97	4.46	.301	12	.203	-1	10	-0.1
1901	NY-N	0	0	....	1	1	0	0	0	4	11	9	7	0	0	2	1	3.250	15.75	21	15.32	.490	0	.000	-5	0	-0.6
	StL-N	0	0	....	1	0	0	0	0	3	7	5	5	0	0	1	0	2.667	15.00	21	11.45	.449	0	.000	-4	0	-0.4
	Yr.	0	0	....	2	1	0	0	0	7	18	14	12	0	0	3	1	3.000	15.43	21	13.66	.473	0	.000	-9	0	-1.0
Total	5	21	26	.447	66	45	37	3	3	445	602	379	260	18	3	142	83	1.672	5.26	88	5.33	.320	38	.218	-32	23	-2.8

• FISHER, Cherokee — William Charles Fisher b: 12/1845, Philadelphia, PA d: 9/26/1912, New York, NY BR/TR, 5'9", 164 lbs. Deb: 5/6/1871 U ♦

YEAR	TM-L	W	L	PCT	G	GS	CG	SH	SV	IP	H	R	ER	HR	HB	BB	SO	RAT	ERA	ERA+	CERA	OAV	BH	AVG	PR+	WS	TPW
1871	Rok-n	4	16	.200	24	24	22	**1**	0	213	295	257	103	3	....	31	15	1.531	4.35	94	....	.288	28	.228	2	....	-0.1
1872	Bal-n	10	1	.909	19	11	9	1	1	110^1	93	78	22	0	....	11	20	.943	**1.79**	148	....	**.198**	52	.231	16	....	0.3
1873	Ath-n	3	4	.429	13	5	5	0	1	84^1	90	73	17	1	....	10	14	1.186	**1.81**	**188**	....	**.241**	66	.261	13	....	0.8
1874	Har-n	13	23	.361	39	35	31	0	0	322	416	277	83	1	....	13	25	1.332	2.32	105	....	.280	54	.228	17	....	0.6
1875	Phi-n	22	19	.537	41	41	36	2	0	358	345	189	79	6	....	9	18	.989	1.99	132	....	.230	41	.232	21	....	1.7
1876	Cin-N	4	20	.167	28	24	22	0	0	229^1	294	206	77	6	....	6	29	1.308	3.02	73	....	.290	32	.248	-7	2	-0.9
1878	Pro-N	0	1	.000	1	1	1	0	0	9	14	12	4	0	....	0	2	1.556	4.00	55	....	.338	0	.000	-2	0	-0.2
Total	5 n	52	63	.452	136	116	103	4	2	1087^2	1239	874	304	11	....	74	92	1.207	2.52	118	....	.255	241	.237	68	....	3.3
Total	2	4	21	.160	29	25	23	0	0	238^1	308	218	81	6	....	6	31	1.317	3.06	72	....	.291	32	.235	-9	2	-1.1

• FISHER, Clarence — Clarence Henry Fisher b: 8/27/1898, Letart, WV d: 11/2/1965, Point Pleasant, WV BR/TR, 6', 174 lbs. Deb: 9/14/1919

YEAR	TM-L	W	L	PCT	G	GS	CG	SH	SV	IP	H	R	ER	HR	HB	BB	SO	RAT	ERA	ERA+	CERA	OAV	BH	AVG	PR+	WS	TPW
1919	Was-A	0	0	....	2	0	0	0	0	4	8	6	6	0	0	3	1	2.750	13.50	24	11.10	.421	0	....	-5	0	-0.5
1920	Was-A	0	1	.000	2	0	0	0	0	3^2	5	4	4	0	0	5	0	2.727	9.82	38	9.72	.714	0	.000	-2	0	-0.3
Total	2	0	1	.000	4	0	0	0	0	7^2	13	10	10	0	0	8	1	2.739	11.74	29	10.44	.500	0	.000	-7	0	-0.7

• FISHER, Don — Donald Raymond Fisher b: 2/6/1916, Cleveland, OH d: 7/29/1973, Mayfield Heights, OH BR/TR, 6', 210 lbs. Deb: 8/25/1945

YEAR	TM-L	W	L	PCT	G	GS	CG	SH	SV	IP	H	R	ER	HR	HB	BB	SO	RAT	ERA	ERA+	CERA	OAV	BH	AVG	PR+	WS	TPW
1945	NY-N	1	0	1.000	2	1	1	1	0	18	12	4	4	0	2	7	4	1.056	2.00	195	1.95	.190	1	.143	4	2	0.4

• FISHER, Ed — Edward Fredrick Fisher b: 10/31/1876, Wayne, MI d: 7/24/1951, Spokane, WA BR/TR, 6'2", 200 lbs. Deb: 9/5/1902

YEAR	TM-L	W	L	PCT	G	GS	CG	SH	SV	IP	H	R	ER	HR	HB	BB	SO	RAT	ERA	ERA+	CERA	OAV	BH	AVG	PR+	WS	TPW
1902	Det-A	0	0	....	1	0	0	0	0	4	4	0	0	0	0	1	0	1.250	0.00	....	2.79	.261	0	.000	2	0	0.1

• FISHER, Eddie — Eddie Gene Fisher b: 7/16/1936, Shreveport, LA BR/TR, 6'2.5", 200 lbs. Deb: 6/22/1959

YEAR	TM-L	W	L	PCT	G	GS	CG	SH	SV	IP	H	R	ER	HR	HB	BB	SO	RAT	ERA	ERA+	CERA	OAV	BH	AVG	PR+	WS	TPW
1959	SF-N	2	6	.250	17	5	0	0	1	40	57	37	35	8	1	8	15	1.625	7.88	48	6.68	.339	0	.000	-18	0	-1.9
1960	SF-N	1	0	1.000	3	1	1	0	0	12^2	11	5	5	2	0	2	7	1.026	3.55	98	2.82	.244	3	.600	0	1	0.1
1961	SF-N	0	2	.000	15	1	0	0	1	33^2	36	23	20	7	0	9	16	1.337	5.35	71	4.44	.267	1	.143	-5	0	-0.5
1962	Chi-A	9	5	.643	57	12	2	1	5	182^2	169	74	63	17	1	45	88	1.172	3.10	126	3.07	.245	6	.130	17	14	1.7
1963	Chi-A	9	8	.529	33	15	2	1	0	120^2	114	57	53	14	2	28	67	1.177	3.95	89	3.22	.244	5	.139	-7	5	-0.8
1964	Chi-A	6	3	.667	59	2	0	0	9	125	86	43	42	13	3	32	74	.944	3.02	114	2.03	.192	3	.167	3	10	0.2
1965	Chi-A★	15	7	.682	**82**	0	0	0	24	165^1	118	51	44	13	2	43	90	.974	2.40	133	**1.97**	.205	4	.138	13	20	1.3
1966	Chi-A	1	3	.250	23	0	0	0	6	35^1	27	11	9	1	1	17	18	1.245	2.29	138	2.72	.214	0	.000	3	4	0.3
	Bal-A	5	3	.625	44	0	0	0	13	71^2	60	26	21	4	2	19	39	1.102	2.64	126	2.52	.226	2	.154	5	8	0.6
	Yr.	6	6	.500	**67**	0	0	0	19	107	87	37	30	5	3	36	57	1.150	2.52	130	2.58	.222	2	.133	9	12	0.9
1967	Bal-A	4	3	.571	46	0	0	0	1	89^2	82	40	36	7	4	26	53	1.204	3.61	87	3.19	.245	1	.200	-6	4	-0.6

YEAR	TM-L	W	L	PCT	G	GS	CG	SH	SV	IP	H	R	ER	HR	HB	BB	SO	RAT	ERA	ERA+	CERA	OAV	BH	AVG	PR+	WS	TPW
1968	Cle-A	4	2	.667	54	0	0	0	4	94^2	87	36	30	8	2	17	42	1.099	2.85	104	2.77	.248	0	.000	0	6	-0.1
1969	Cal-A	3	2	.600	52	1	0	0	2	96^2	100	46	39	9	1	28	47	1.324	3.63	96	3.86	.272	0	.000	-3	5	-0.5
1970	Cal-A	4	4	.500	67	2	0	0	8	130^1	117	51	44	15	2	35	74	1.166	3.04	119	3.19	.239	1	.091	5	10	0.5
1971	Cal-A	10	8	.556	57	3	0	0	3	119	92	46	36	11	2	50	82	1.193	2.72	119	2.89	.211	1	.063	5	10	0.5
1972	Cal-A	4	5	.444	43	1	0	0	4	81^1	73	35	34	6	0	31	32	1.279	3.76	77	3.26	.247	2	.118	-8	3	-1.0
	Chi-A	0	1	.000	6	4	0	0	0	22^1	31	13	11	1	0	9	10	1.791	4.43	70	6.09	.348	0	.000	-3	0	-0.4
	Yr.	4	6	.400	49	5	0	0	4	103^2	104	48	45	7	0	40	42	1.389	3.91	76	3.87	.271	2	.083	-11	3	-1.4
1973	Chi-A	6	7	.462	26	16	2	0	0	110^2	135	64	60	12	3	38	57	1.563	4.88	81	5.31	.301	0	....	-10	4	-1.0
	StL-N	2	1	.667	6	0	0	0	0	7	3	1	1	1	1	1	1	.571	1.29	283	1.28	.125	1	1.000	2	2	0.2
Total	**15**	**85**	**70**	**.548**	**690**	**63**	**7**	**2**	**81**	**1538^2**	**1398**	**659**	**583**	**149**	**27**	**438**	**812**	**1.193**	**3.41**	**101**	**3.21**	**.243**	**30**	**.122**	**-7**	**106**	**-1.3**
• FISHER, Fritz	Frederick Brown Fisher b: 11/28/1941, Adrian, MI BL/TL, 6'1", 180 lbs. Deb: 4/19/1964																										
1964	Det-A	0	0	....	1	0	0	0	0	0^1	2	4	4	0	0	2	1	12.00	108.00	3	71.88	.667	0	....	-4	0	-0.4
• FISHER, Harry	Harry Devereux Fisher b: 1/3/1926, Newbury, Canada d: 9/20/1981, Waterloo, Canada BL/TR, 6', 180 lbs. Deb: 9/16/1951																										
1952	Pit-N	1	2	.333	8	3	0	0	0	18^1	17	14	14	4	2	13	5	1.636	6.87	58	6.23	.266	5	.333	-6	0	-0.4
• FISHER, J.	J. Fisher b: Philadelphia, PA Deb: 7/17/1884																										
1884	Phi-U	1	7	.125	8	8	8	0	0	70^2	76	49	28	0	....	13	42	1.259	3.57	81	....	.257	8	.222	-2	2	-0.2
1885	Buf-N	0	1	.000	1	1	1	0	0	9	10	9	5	0	....	2	4	1.333	5.00	60	....	.269	0	.000	-1	0	-0.2
Total	**2**	**1**	**8**	**.111**	**9**	**9**	**9**	**0**	**0**	**79^2**	**86**	**58**	**33**	**0**	**....**	**15**	**46**	**1.268**	**3.73**	**78**	**....**	**.258**	**8**	**.200**	**-3**	**2**	**-0.4**
• FISHER, Jack	John Howard "Fat Jack" Fisher b: 3/4/1939, Frostburg, MD BR/TR, 6'2", 215 lbs. Deb: 4/14/1959																										
1959	Bal-A	1	6	.143	27	7	1	1	2	88^2	76	36	30	7	1	38	52	1.286	3.05	124	3.28	.230	3	.130	7	6	0.6
1960	Bal-A	12	11	.522	40	20	8	3	2	197^2	174	87	75	13	2	78	99	1.275	3.41	111	3.21	.241	11	.183	5	13	0.7
1961	Bal-A	10	13	.435	36	25	10	1	1	196	205	104	85	17	4	75	118	1.429	3.90	100	4.23	.270	5	.089	-3	8	-0.5
1962	Bal-A	7	9	.438	32	25	4	0	1	152	173	101	86	23	2	56	81	1.507	5.09	74	5.13	.284	5	.102	-24	0	-2.5
1963	SF-N	6	10	.375	36	12	2	0	1	116	132	77	59	12	5	38	57	1.466	4.58	70	4.67	.284	3	.103	-16	0	-1.6
1964	NY-N	10	17	.370	40	34	8	1	0	227^2	256	124	107	23	10	56	115	1.370	4.23	84	4.34	.283	12	.158	-18	6	-1.8
1965	NY-N	8	24	.250	43	36	10	0	1	253^2	252	121	111	22	4	68	116	1.261	3.94	90	3.50	.259	12	.154	-11	11	-1.1
1966	NY-N	11	14	.440	38	33	10	2	0	230	229	108	94	26	8	54	127	1.230	3.68	99	3.63	.260	6	.090	-2	11	-0.3
1967	NY-N	9	18	.333	39	30	7	1	0	220^1	251	121	115	21	4	64	117	1.430	4.70	72	4.39	.287	7	.100	-33	3	-3.8
1968	Chi-A	8	13	.381	35	28	2	0	0	180^2	176	68	60	14	7	48	80	1.240	2.99	101	3.42	.257	6	.113	2	7	0.0
1969	Cin-N	4	4	.500	34	15	0	0	1	113	137	77	69	15	5	30	55	1.478	5.50	68	5.10	.295	4	.121	-22	0	-2.4
Total	**11**	**86**	**139**	**.382**	**400**	**265**	**62**	**9**	**9**	**1975^2**	**2061**	**1024**	**891**	**193**	**52**	**605**	**1017**	**1.349**	**4.06**	**88**	**4.02**	**.269**	**74**	**.125**	**-115**	**65**	**-12.7**
• FISHER, Maurice	Maurice Wayne Fisher b: 2/16/1931, Uniondale, IN BR/TR, 6'5", 210 lbs. Deb: 4/16/1955																										
1955	Cin-N	0	0	....	1	0	0	0	0	2^2	5	2	2	1	0	2	1	2.625	6.75	63	13.85	.385	0	.000	-1	0	-0.1
• FISHER, Ray	Ray Lyle "Pick,Chic" Fisher b: 10/4/1887, Middlebury, VT d: 11/3/1982, Ann Arbor, MI BR/TR, 5'11.5", 180 lbs. Deb: 7/2/1910																										
1910	NY-A	5	3	.625	17	7	3	0	1	92^1	95	41	30	0	3	18	42	1.224	2.92	91	3.01	.274	3	.103	-0	5	-0.2
1911	NY-A	10	11	.476	29	22	8	2	0	171^2	178	85	62	3	5	55	99	1.357	3.25	110	3.50	.269	7	.119	10	12	0.7
1912	NY-A	2	8	.200	17	13	5	0	0	90^1	107	70	59	2	2	32	47	1.539	5.88	62	4.68	.312	2	.065	-18	0	-2.1
1913	NY-A	12	16	.429	43	31	14	1	1	246^1	244	113	87	3	8	71	92	1.279	3.18	94	2.80	.261	22	.278	-5	14	-0.2
1914	NY-A	10	12	.455	29	26	17	2	1	209	177	65	53	2	4	61	86	1.139	2.28	121	2.48	.241	9	.138	9	15	0.7
1915	NY-A	18	11	.621	30	28	20	4	0	247^2	219	82	58	7	5	62	97	1.135	2.11	139	2.59	.243	9	.108	19	21	1.6
1916	NY-A	11	8	.579	31	21	9	1	2	179	191	81	63	4	4	51	56	1.352	3.17	91	3.69	.285	11	.177	-8	9	-0.7
1917	NY-A	8	9	.471	23	18	12	3	0	144	126	49	35	3	2	43	64	1.174	2.19	123	2.63	.243	9	.180	7	11	0.8
1919*	Cin-N	14	5	.737	26	20	12	5	1	174^1	141	55	42	5	1	38	41	1.027	2.17	128	2.00	.226	16	.271	8	17	1.3
1920	Cin-N	10	11	.476	33	21	10	1	1	201	189	86	61	5	8	50	56	1.189	2.73	111	2.72	.249	17	.243	6	10	0.8
Total	**10**	**100**	**94**	**.515**	**278**	**207**	**110**	**19**	**7**	**1755^2**	**1667**	**727**	**550**	**34**	**42**	**481**	**680**	**1.223**	**2.82**	**106**	**2.90**	**.257**	**105**	**.179**	**30**	**114**	**2.6**
• FISHER, Tom	Thomas Chalmers "Red" Fisher b: 11/1/1880, Anderson, IN d: 9/3/1972, Anderson, IN BR/TR, 5'10.5", 185 lbs. Deb: 4/17/1904																										
1904	Bos-N	6	16	.273	31	21	19	2	0	214	257	165	101	5	10	82	84	**1.584**	4.25	65	4.78	.302	21	.212	-30	3	-3.0
• FISHER, Tom	Thomas Gene Fisher b: 4/4/1942, Cleveland, OH BR/TR, 6', 180 lbs. Deb: 9/20/1967																										
1967	Bal-A	0	0	....	2	0	0	0	0	3^1	2	0	0	0	0	2	1	1.200	0.00	....	2.23	.182	0	....	1	0	0.1
• FISKE, Max	Maximilian Patrick "Ski" Fiske b: 10/12/1888, Chicago, IL d: 5/25/1928, Chicago, IL BR/TR, 5'11", 185 lbs. Deb: 4/19/1914																										
1914	Chi-F	12	12	.500	38	22	7	0	0	198	161	84	69	7	7	59	87	1.111	3.14	94	2.53	.231	16	.235	-9	10	-0.8
• FITTERY, Paul	Paul Clarence Fittery b: 10/10/1887, Lebanon, PA d: 1/28/1974, Cartersville, GA BR/TL, 5'8.5", 156 lbs. Deb: 9/5/1914																										
1914	Cin-N	0	2	.000	8	4	2	0	0	43^2	41	20	15	0	1	12	21	1.214	3.09	95	2.60	.246	1	.059	-1	2	-0.3
1917	Phi-N	1	1	.500	17	2	1	0	0	55^2	69	36	28	1	5	27	13	1.725	4.53	62	5.48	.317	2	.091	-11	0	-1.4
Total	**2**	**1**	**3**	**.250**	**25**	**6**	**3**	**0**	**0**	**99^1**	**110**	**56**	**43**	**1**	**6**	**39**	**34**	**1.500**	**3.90**	**73**	**4.22**	**.286**	**3**	**.077**	**-12**	**2**	**-1.7**
• FITZGERALD, Brian	Brian Michael Fitzgerald b: 12/26/1974, Woodbridge, VA BL/TL, 5'11", 175 lbs. Deb: 4/17/2002																										
2002	Sea-A	0	0	....	6	0	0	0	0	6^1	11	8	6	2	1	2	3	2.053	8.53	50	9.86	.344	0	....	-3	0	-0.3
• FITZGERALD, John	John H. Fitzgerald b: 5/30/1870, Natick, MA d: 3/31/1921, Boston, MA Deb: 7/18/1891																										
1891	Bos-a	1	1	.500	6	3	2	0	1	32	49	32	20	2	2	11	16	1.875	5.63	62	....	.340	1	.071	-8	0	-0.8
• FITZGERALD, John	Warren B. Fitzgerald b: 1866, d: 12/20/1892, Waterbury, CT Deb: 4/18/1890																										
1890	Roc-a	3	8	.273	11	11	8	1	0	78	77	51	35	0	6	45	35	1.564	4.04	88	....	.250	6	.194	-5	3	-0.4
• FITZGERALD, John	John Francis Fitzgerald b: 9/15/1933, Brooklyn, NY BL/TL, 6'3", 190 lbs. Deb: 9/28/1958																										
1958	SF-N	0	0	....	1	1	0	0	0	3	1	1	1	1	0	1	3	.667	3.00	127	1.91	.111	0	.000	0	0	0.0
• FITZGERALD, Warren	Warren B. Fitzgerald b: 4/1872, PA d: 11/7/1930, Phoenix, AZ TL, 5'9" Deb: 6/4/1891																										
1891	Lou-a	14	17	.452	32	31	28	3	0	267	265	157	110	5	12	89	110	1.326	3.71	98	....	.250	19	.170	-4	16	-0.2
1892	Lou-N	1	3	.250	4	4	4	0	0	34	45	27	16	2	1	11	3	1.647	4.24	72	5.36	.306	2	.133	-5	1	-0.5
Total	**2**	**15**	**20**	**.429**	**36**	**35**	**32**	**3**	**0**	**301**	**310**	**184**	**126**	**7**	**13**	**100**	**113**	**1.362**	**3.77**	**95**	**0.61**	**.257**	**21**	**.165**	**-8**	**17**	**-0.7**
• FITZKE, Paul	Paul Frederick Herman "Bob" Fitzke b: 7/30/1900, La Crosse, WI d: 6/30/1950, Sacramento, CA BR/TR, 5'11.5", 185 lbs. Deb: 9/1/1924																										
1924	Cle-A	0	0	....	1	0	0	0	0	4	5	2	2	0	0	3	1	2.000	4.50	95	6.08	.313	0	.000	-0	0	0.0
• FITZMORRIS, Al	Alan James Fitzmorris b: 3/21/1946, Buffalo, NY BB/TR, 6'2", 190 lbs. Deb: 9/8/1969																										
1969	KC-A	1	1	.500	7	0	0	0	2	10^2	9	5	5	1	0	4	3	1.219	4.22	87	3.03	.237	0	.000	-1	1	-0.1
1970	KC-A	8	5	.615	43	11	2	0	1	117^2	112	60	58	14	0	52	47	1.394	4.44	84	4.06	.254	9	.290	-10	6	-0.6
1971	KC-A	7	5	.583	36	15	2	1	0	127^1	112	61	59	6	1	55	53	1.312	4.17	82	3.27	.245	11	.250	-10	5	-0.9
1972	KC-A	2	5	.286	38	2	0	0	3	101	99	46	42	10	1	28	51	1.257	3.74	81	3.41	.252	4	.174	-7	3	-0.6
1973	KC-A	8	3	.727	15	13	3	1	0	89	88	29	28	5	0	25	26	1.270	2.83	145	3.27	.259	0	....	14	9	1.4
1974	KC-A	13	6	.684	34	27	9	4	1	190	189	73	59	8	0	63	53	1.326	2.79	136	3.30	.260	0	....	24	16	2.5
1975	KC-A	16	12	.571	35	35	11	3	0	242	239	104	96	16	5	76	78	1.302	3.57	108	3.54	.262	0	....	11	16	1.1
1976	KC-A	15	11	.577	35	33	8	2	0	220^1	227	89	75	6	2	56	80	1.284	3.06	114	3.26	.273	0	....	10	14	1.1
1977	Cle-A	6	10	.375	29	21	1	0	0	133	164	87	80	12	1	53	54	1.632	5.41	73	5.34	.306	0	....	-22	2	-2.2
1978	Cle-A	0	1	.000	7	0	0	0	0	14^1	19	10	10	3	1	7	5	1.814	6.28	60	7.76	.333	0	....	-4	0	-0.4
	Cal-A	1	0	1.000	9	2	0	0	0	31^2	26	9	6	2	0	14	8	1.263	1.71	212	3.00	.236	0	....	7	3	0.7
	Yr.	1	1	.500	16	2	0	0	0	46	45	19	16	5	1	21	13	1.435	3.13	118	4.48	.269	0	....	3	3	0.3
Total	**10**	**77**	**59**	**.566**	**288**	**159**	**36**	**11**	**7**	**1277**	**1284**	**573**	**518**	**83**	**11**	**433**	**458**	**1.345**	**3.65**	**100**	**3.66**	**.265**	**24**	**.242**	**13**	**75**	**2.1**

• FITZSIMMONS, Freddie
Frederick Landis "Fat Freddie" Fitzsimmons b: 7/26/1901, Mishawaka, IN d: 11/18/1979, Yucca Valley, CA BR/TR, 5'11", 185 lbs. Deb: 8/12/1925 M/C/U

YEAR	TM-L	W	L	PCT	G	GS	CG	SH	SV	IP	H	R	ER	HR	HB	BB	SO	RAT	ERA	ERA+	CERA	OAV	BH	AVG	PR+	WS	TPW
1925	NY-N	6	3	.667	10	8	6	1	0	74^2	70	25	22	4	0	18	17	1.179	2.65	152	2.81	.248	9	.310	12	9	1.3
1926	NY-N	14	10	.583	37	26	12	0	0	219	224	90	70	7	4	58	48	1.288	2.88	130	3.29	.272	11	.128	18	17	1.2
1927	NY-N	17	10	.630	42	31	14	1	3	244^2	260	127	101	15	4	67	78	1.337	3.72	104	3.65	.275	18	.207	5	15	0.4
1928	NY-N	20	9	.690	40	32	16	1	1	261^1	264	119	107	13	4	65	67	1.259	3.68	106	3.24	.268	18	.191	4	18	0.4
1929	NY-N	15	11	.577	37	31	14	4	1	221^2	242	122	101	14	2	66	55	1.389	4.10	112	3.90	.285	15	.183	9	13	0.6
1930	NY-N	19	7	.731	41	29	17	1	1	224^1	230	125	106	26	1	59	76	1.288	4.25	111	3.73	.266	22	.265	10	18	1.3
1931	NY-N	18	11	.621	35	33	19	4	0	253^2	242	111	86	16	0	62	78	1.198	3.05	121	2.94	.251	21	.228	16	18	2.4
1932	NY-N	11	11	.500	35	31	11	0	0	237^2	287	132	117	18	3	83	65	1.557	4.43	84	4.84	.299	19	.221	-15	9	-1.1
1933*	NY-N	16	11	.593	36	**35**	13	1	0	251^2	243	106	81	14	2	72	65	1.252	2.90	111	3.76	.251	19	.200	5	15	0.8
1934	NY-N	18	14	.563	38	37	14	3	1	263^1	266	114	89	12	1	51	73	1.204	3.04	127	2.97	.261	22	.232	22	20	2.6
1935	NY-N	4	8	.333	18	15	6	**4**	0	94	104	43	42	7	1	22	23	1.340	4.02	96	3.83	.281	8	.258	-2	6	-0.1
1936*	NY-N	10	7	.588	28	17	7	0	2	141	147	58	52	6	0	39	35	1.319	3.32	117	3.43	.274	7	.149	4	11	0.2
1937	NY-N	2	2	.500	6	4	1	1	0	27^1	28	14	14	3	0	8	13	1.317	4.61	84	3.97	.272	3	.300	-3	2	-0.1
	Bro-N	4	8	.333	13	13	4	0	0	90^2	91	47	43	2	1	32	29	1.357	4.27	95	3.30	.263	5	.167	-0	5	-0.1
	Yr.	6	10	.375	19	17	5	1	0	118	119	61	57	5	1	40	42	1.347	4.35	92	3.45	.265	8	.200	-3	7	-0.2
1938	Bro-N	11	8	.579	27	26	12	3	0	202^2	205	83	68	8	3	43	38	1.224	3.02	129	3.02	.261	12	.171	22	14	2.1
1939	Bro-N	7	9	.438	27	20	5	0	3	151^1	178	79	65	6	3	28	44	1.361	3.87	104	3.78	.293	11	.234	3	10	0.6
1940	Bro-N	16	2	.889	20	18	11	4	1	134^1	120	43	42	5	1	25	35	1.079	2.81	142	2.30	.233	5	.106	18	15	1.7
1941*	Bro-N	6	1	.857	13	12	3	1	0	82^2	78	33	19	3	2	26	19	1.258	2.07	177	2.98	.245	4	.143	13	7	1.4
1942	Bro-N	0	0	....	1	1	0	0	0	3	6	5	5	1	0	1	0	2.333	15.00	22	12.07	.400	1	.500	-4	0	-0.4
1943	Bro-N	3	4	.429	9	7	1	0	0	44^2	50	29	27	6	1	21	12	1.590	5.44	62	5.28	.281	1	.071	-10	0	-1.1
Total	19	217	146	.598	513	426	186	29	13	3223^2	3335	1505	1257	186	33	846	870	1.297	3.51	111	3.49	.268	231	.200	126	222	14.0

• FLAHERTY, Patsy
Patrick Joseph Flaherty b: 6/29/1876, Mansfield, PA d: 1/23/1968, Alexandria, LA BL/TL, 5'8", 165 lbs. Deb: 9/8/1899 U ♦

YEAR	TM-L	W	L	PCT	G	GS	CG	SH	SV	IP	H	R	ER	HR	HB	BB	SO	RAT	ERA	ERA+	CERA	OAV	BH	AVG	PR+	WS	TPW
1899	Lou-N	2	3	.400	5	4	4	0	0	39	41	21	10	0	1	5	5	1.179	2.31	167	2.74	.270	5	.208	7	3	0.7
1900	Pit-N	0	0	....	4	1	0	0	0	22	30	16	15	0	5	9	5	1.773	6.14	59	6.18	.324	1	.111	-6	0	-0.6
1903	Chi-A	11	25	.306	40	34	29	2	1	293^2	338	173	122	9	14	50	65	1.321	3.74	75	3.61	.288	14	.137	-25	7	-2.9
1904	Chi-A	1	2	.333	5	5	4	0	0	43	36	19	10	1	1	10	14	1.070	2.09	117	2.13	.228	4	.333	1	3	0.4
	Pit-N	19	9	.679	29	28	28	5	0	242	210	81	55	3	11	59	54	1.112	2.05	133	2.38	.232	22	.212	17	22	2.4
1905	Pit-N	10	10	.500	27	20	15	0	1	187^2	197	87	73	2	6	49	44	1.311	3.50	85	3.34	.272	15	.197	-14	11	-1.3
1907	Bos-N	12	15	.444	27	25	23	0	0	217	197	90	65	4	7	59	34	1.180	2.70	94	2.75	.248	22	.191	-5	10	-0.4
1908	Bos-N	12	18	.400	31	31	21	0	0	244	221	109	88	6	8	81	50	1.238	3.25	74	2.83	.236	12	.140	-29	8	-3.3
1910	Phi-N	0	0	....	1	0	0	0	0	0^1	1	4	0	0	0	1	0	6.000	0.00	....	20.93	.333	1	.500	0	0	0.0
1911	Bos-N	0	2	.000	4	2	1	0	0	14	21	15	11	0	3	8	0	2.071	7.07	54	7.75	.350	27	.287	-5	2	-0.5
Total	9	67	84	.444	173	150	125	7	2	1302^2	1292	615	449	25	56	331	271	1.246	3.10	88	3.07	.258	123	.197	-59	66	-5.5

• FLANAGAN, Mike
Michael Kendall Flanagan b: 12/16/1951, Manchester, NH BL/TL, 6', 195 lbs. Deb: 9/5/1975 C

YEAR	TM-L	W	L	PCT	G	GS	CG	SH	SV	IP	H	R	ER	HR	HB	BB	SO	RAT	ERA	ERA+	CERA	OAV	BH	AVG	PR+	WS	TPW
1975	Bal-A	0	1	.000	2	1	0	0	0	9^2	9	4	3	0	0	6	7	1.552	2.79	126	3.71	.250	0	....	0	1	0.0
1976	Bal-A	3	5	.375	20	10	4	0	0	85	83	41	39	7	0	33	56	1.365	4.13	79	3.84	.260	0	....	-9	2	-1.0
1977	Bal-A	15	10	.600	36	33	15	2	1	235	235	100	95	17	2	70	149	1.298	3.64	104	3.56	.266	0	....	-2	16	-0.2
1978	Bal-A★	19	15	.559	40	**40**	17	2	0	281^1	271	128	126	22	3	87	167	1.273	4.03	87	3.48	.257	0	....	-21	14	-2.1
1979*	Bal-A	**23**	9	.719	39	38	16	**5**	0	265^2	245	107	91	23	3	70	190	1.186	3.08	130	3.12	.245	0	....	23	23	2.2
1980	Bal-A	16	13	.552	37	37	12	2	0	251^1	278	121	115	27	2	71	128	1.389	4.12	96	4.35	.287	0	....	-10	12	-1.0
1981	Bal-A	9	6	.600	20	20	3	2	0	116	108	55	54	11	2	37	72	1.250	4.19	86	3.43	.244	0	....	-7	6	-0.7
1982	Bal-A	15	11	.577	36	35	11	1	0	236	233	110	104	24	4	76	103	1.309	3.97	102	3.79	.259	0	....	1	14	0.1
1983*	Bal-A	12	4	.750	20	20	3	1	0	125^1	135	53	46	10	2	31	50	1.324	3.30	120	3.84	.278	0	....	9	10	0.9
1984	Bal-A	13	13	.500	34	34	10	2	0	226^2	213	103	89	24	1	81	115	1.297	3.53	110	3.64	.250	0	....	4	14	0.4
1985	Bal-A	4	5	.444	15	15	1	0	0	86	101	49	49	14	2	28	42	1.500	5.13	79	5.37	.297	0	....	-10	3	-1.0
1986	Bal-A	7	11	.389	29	28	2	0	0	172	179	95	81	15	1	66	96	1.424	4.24	97	4.12	.270	0	....	-1	8	-0.1
1987	Bal-A	3	6	.333	16	16	4	0	0	94^2	102	57	52	9	0	36	50	1.458	4.94	89	4.42	.278	0	....	-6	4	-0.5
	Tor-A	3	2	.600	7	7	0	0	0	49^1	46	15	13	3	0	15	43	1.236	2.37	189	2.92	.237	0	....	11	5	1.0
	Yr.	6	8	.429	23	23	4	0	0	144	148	72	65	12	0	51	93	1.382	4.06	109	3.91	.264	0	....	5	9	0.5
1988	Tor-A	13	13	.500	34	34	2	1	0	211	220	106	98	23	6	80	99	1.422	4.18	94	4.42	.271	0	....	-7	10	-0.7
1989*	Tor-A	8	10	.444	30	30	1	1	0	171^2	186	82	75	10	5	47	47	1.357	3.93	92	3.93	.283	0	....	-6	7	-0.6
1990	Tor-A	2	2	.500	5	5	0	0	0	20^1	28	14	12	3	0	8	5	1.770	5.31	77	6.74	.329	0	....	-3	0	-0.3
1991	Bal-A	2	7	.222	64	1	0	0	3	98^1	84	27	26	6	3	25	55	1.108	2.38	166	2.61	.236	0	....	17	9	1.7
1992	Bal-A	0	0	....	42	0	0	0	0	34^2	50	34	31	3	5	23	17	2.106	8.05	50	8.25	.338	0	....	-16	0	-1.6
Total	18	167	143	.539	526	404	101	19	4	2770	2806	1301	1199	251	41	890	1491	1.334	3.90	99	3.87	.266	0	....	-31	158	-3.3

• FLANIGAN, Ray
Raymond Arthur Flanigan b: 1/8/1923, Morgantown, WV d: 3/28/1993, Baltimore, MD BR/TR, 6', 190 lbs. Deb: 9/20/1946

YEAR	TM-L	W	L	PCT	G	GS	CG	SH	SV	IP	H	R	ER	HR	HB	BB	SO	RAT	ERA	ERA+	CERA	OAV	BH	AVG	PR+	WS	TPW
1946	Cle-A	0	1	.000	3	1	0	0	0	9	11	12	11	1	0	8	2	2.111	11.00	30	6.77	.289	1	.500	-8	0	-0.7

• FLANIGAN, Tom
Thomas Anthony Flanigan b: 9/6/1934, Cincinnati, OH BR/TR, 6'3", 175 lbs. Deb: 4/14/1954

YEAR	TM-L	W	L	PCT	G	GS	CG	SH	SV	IP	H	R	ER	HR	HB	BB	SO	RAT	ERA	ERA+	CERA	OAV	BH	AVG	PR+	WS	TPW
1954	Chi-A	0	0	....	2	0	0	0	0	1^2	1	0	0	0	0	1	0	1.200	0.00	....	1.90	.200	0	....	1	0	0.1
1958	StL-N	0	0	....	1	0	0	0	0	1	2	1	1	1	0	1	0	3.000	9.00	46	27.72	.500	0	....	-1	0	-0.1
Total	2	0	0	....	3	0	0	0	0	2^2	3	1	1	1	0	2	0	1.875	3.38	122	11.58	.333	0	....	0	0	0.0

• FLATER, Jack
John William Flater b: 9/22/1880, Sandymount, MD d: 3/20/1970, Westminster, MD BR/TR, 5'10", 175 lbs. Deb: 9/18/1908

YEAR	TM-L	W	L	PCT	G	GS	CG	SH	SV	IP	H	R	ER	HR	HB	BB	SO	RAT	ERA	ERA+	CERA	OAV	BH	AVG	PR+	WS	TPW
1908	Phi-A	1	3	.250	5	3	3	0	0	39^1	35	15	9	0	2	12	8	1.195	2.06	124	2.79	.252	2	.133	3	2	0.3

• FLAVIN, John
John Thomas Flavin b: 5/7/1942, Albany, CA BL/TL, 6'2", 208 lbs. Deb: 8/25/1964

YEAR	TM-L	W	L	PCT	G	GS	CG	SH	SV	IP	H	R	ER	HR	HB	BB	SO	RAT	ERA	ERA+	CERA	OAV	BH	AVG	PR+	WS	TPW
1964	Chi-N	0	1	.000	5	1	0	0	0	4^2	11	7	7	0	0	3	5	3.000	13.50	27	12.85	.500	0	.000	-5	0	-0.5

• FLEET, Frank
Frank H. Fleet b: 1848, New York, NY d: 6/13/1900, New York, NY Deb: 10/18/1871 ♦

YEAR	TM-L	W	L	PCT	G	GS	CG	SH	SV	IP	H	R	ER	HR	HB	BB	SO	RAT	ERA	ERA+	CERA	OAV	BH	AVG	PR+	WS	TPW
1871	Mut-n	0	1	.000	1	1	1	0	0	9	20	21	10	0	....	3	0	2.556	10.00	38	....	.393	2	.333	-6	....	-0.4
1873	Res-n	0	3	.000	3	3	2	0	0	24	57	47	15	0	....	0	1	2.375	5.63	60	....	.414	23	.256	-3	....	-0.5
1875	StL-n	2	1	.667	3	3	3	0	0	27	33	17	10	0	....	3	3	1.333	3.33	95	....	.275	1	.063	-1	....	-0.3
	Atl-n	0	1	.000	2	1	1	0	0	15^1	24	370	8	1	....	0	0	1.565	4.70	49	....	.327	25	.225	-3	....	-1.1
	Yr.	2	2	.500	5	4	4	0	0	42^1	57	387	18	1	....	3	3	1.417	3.83	71	....	.295	26	.205	-4	....	-1.3
Total	3 n	2	6	.250	9	8	7	0	0	75^1	134	455	43	1	....	6	4	1.858	5.14	61	....	.351	86	.231	-13	....	-2.2

• FLEMING, Bill
Leslie Fletchard Fleming b: 7/31/1913, Rowland, CA BR/TR, 6', 190 lbs. Deb: 8/21/1940

YEAR	TM-L	W	L	PCT	G	GS	CG	SH	SV	IP	H	R	ER	HR	HB	BB	SO	RAT	ERA	ERA+	CERA	OAV	BH	AVG	PR+	WS	TPW
1940	Bos-A	1	2	.333	10	6	1	0	0	46^1	53	27	25	4	2	20	24	1.576	4.86	93	5.06	.290	0	.000	-1	2	-0.3
1941	Bos-A	1	1	.500	16	1	0	0	1	41^1	32	21	18	4	0	24	20	1.355	3.92	106	3.30	.212	2	.222	2	3	0.2
1942	Chi-N	5	6	.455	33	14	4	2	2	134^1	117	51	45	9	3	63	59	1.340	3.01	106	3.32	.230	2	.051	5	9	0.2
1943	Chi-N	0	1	.000	11	0	0	0	0	32^1	41	24	23	2	3	12	12	1.639	6.40	52	5.45	.311	0	.000	-10	0	-1.2
1944	Chi-N	9	10	.474	39	18	9	1	0	158^1	163	74	55	6	1	62	42	1.421	3.13	113	3.67	.269	9	.170	9	9	0.9
1946	Chi-N	0	1	.000	14	1	0	0	0	29^1	37	23	20	2	1	12	10	1.670	6.14	54	5.14	.301	0	.000	-9	0	-1.0
Total	6	16	21	.432	123	40	14	3	3	442	443	220	186	27	10	193	167	1.439	3.79	94	3.90	.260	13	.104	-4	23	-1.2

• FLEMING, Dave
David Anthony Fleming b: 11/7/1969, Jackson Heights, NY BL/TL, 6'3", 200 lbs. Deb: 8/6/1991

YEAR	TM-L	W	L	PCT	G	GS	CG	SH	SV	IP	H	R	ER	HR	HB	BB	SO	RAT	ERA	ERA+	CERA	OAV	BH	AVG	PR+	WS	TPW
1991	Sea-A	1	0	1.000	9	3	0	0	0	17^2	19	13	13	3	3	3	11	1.245	6.62	62	5.01	.284	0	....	-5	0	-0.5
1992	Sea-A	17	10	.630	33	33	7	4	0	228^1	225	95	86	13	4	60	112	1.248	3.39	117	3.26	.257	0	....	15	16	1.6
1993	Sea-A	12	5	.706	26	26	1	1	0	167^1	189	84	81	15	6	67	75	1.530	4.36	101	4.89	.290	0	....	0	10	0.0
1994	Sea-A	7	11	.389	23	23	0	0	0	117	152	93	84	17	1	65	65	**1.855**	6.46	76	6.79	.311	0	....	-19	2	-1.8
1995	Sea-A	1	5	.167	16	7	1	0	0	48	57	44	40	15	0	34	26	1.896	7.50	63	8.06	.294	0	....	-14	0	-1.3
	KC-A	0	1	.000	9	5	0	0	0	32	27	17	13	4	2	19	14	1.438	3.66	131	4.34	.229	0	....	4	2	0.3
	Yr.	1	6	.143	25	12	1	0	0	80	84	61	53	19	2	53	40	1.713	5.96	80	6.57	.269	0	....	-10	2	-0.9
Total	5	38	32	.543	116	97	9	5	0	610^1	669	346	317	67	16	248	303	1.502	4.67	95	4.87	.279	0	....	-19	30	-1.7

YEAR TM-L	W	L	PCT	G	GS	CG	SH	SV	IP	H	R	ER	HR	HB	BB	SO	RAT	ERA	ERA+	CERA	OAV	BH	AVG	PR+	WS	TPW
• FLENER, Huck				Gregory Alan Flener b: 2/25/1969, Austin, TX BB/TL, 5'11", 185 lbs. Deb: 9/14/1993																						
1993 Tor-A	0	0	....	6	0	0	0	0	6^{2}	7	3	3	0	0	4	2	1.650	4.05	107	4.14	.269	0	....	0	0	0.0
1996 Tor-A	3	2	.600	15	11	0	0	0	70^{2}	68	40	36	9	1	33	44	1.429	4.58	109	4.33	.251	0	....	2	4	0.2
1997 Tor-A	0	1	.000	8	1	0	0	0	17^{1}	40	19	19	3	0	6	9	2.654	9.87	47	13.07	.444	0	....	-10	0	-1.0
Total 3	3	3	.500	29	12	0	0	0	94^{2}	115	62	58	12	1	43	55	1.669	5.51	88	5.92	.297	0	....	-8	4	-0.8
• FLETCHER, Paul				Edward Paul Fletcher b: 1/14/1967, Gallipolis, OH BR/TR, 6'1", 185 lbs. Deb: 7/11/1993																						
1993 Phi-N	0	0	....	1	0	0	0	0	0^{1}	0	0	0	0	0	0	0	.000	0.00	....	0.00	.000	0	....	0	0	0.0
1995 Phi-N	1	0	1.000	10	0	0	0	0	13^{1}	15	8	8	2	1	9	10	1.800	5.40	78	6.33	.288	0	....	-2	1	-0.2
1996 Oak-A	0	0	....	1	0	0	0	0	1^{1}	6	3	3	0	0	1	0	5.250	20.25	24	33.75	.667	0	....	-2	0	-0.2
Total 3	1	0	1.000	12	0	0	0	0	15	21	11	11	2	1	10	10	2.067	6.60	67	8.62	.344	0	....	-4	1	-0.4
• FLETCHER, Sam				Samuel S. Fletcher b: Altoona, PA TR, 6'2", 210 lbs. Deb: 10/6/1909																						
1909 Bro-N	0	1	.000	1	1	1	0	0	9	13	8	8	0	0	2	5	1.667	8.00	32	5.39	.351	0	.000	-5	0	-0.6
1912 Cin-N	0	0	....	2	0	0	0	0	9^{2}	15	15	13	1	0	11	3	2.690	12.10	28	10.59	.366	2	.500	-9	0	-0.8
Total 2	0	1	.000	3	1	1	0	0	18^{2}	28	23	21	1	0	13	8	2.196	10.13	30	8.09	.359	2	.286	-15	0	-1.5
• FLETCHER, Tom				Thomas Wayne Fletcher b: 6/28/1942, Elmira, NY BB/TL, 6', 170 lbs. Deb: 9/12/1962																						
1962 Det-A	0	0	....	1	0	0	0	0	2	2	0	0	0	0	2	1	2.000	0.00	....	5.48	.250	0	....	1	0	0.1
• FLETCHER, Van				Alfred Vanoide Fletcher b: 8/6/1924, East Bend, NC BR/TR, 6'2", 185 lbs. Deb: 4/12/1955																						
1955 Det-A	0	0	....	9	0	0	0	0	12	13	10	4	1	0	2	4	1.250	3.00	128	3.09	.260	0	....	1	0	0.1
• FLINN, John				John Richard Flinn b: 9/2/1954, Merced, CA BR/TR, 6', 175 lbs. Deb: 5/6/1978																						
1978 Bal-A	1	1	.500	13	0	0	0	0	15^{2}	24	18	14	3	0	13	8	2.362	8.04	43	9.49	.348	0	....	-8	0	-0.8
1979 Bal-A	0	0	....	4	0	0	0	0	2^{2}	2	0	0	0	0	1	0	1.125	0.00	....	2.01	.222	0	....	1	0	0.1
1980 Mil-A	2	1	.667	20	1	0	0	2	37	31	20	16	3	0	20	15	1.378	3.89	99	3.38	.220	0	....	-0	2	0.0
1982 Bal-A	2	0	1.000	5	0	0	0	0	13^{2}	13	3	2	1	0	3	13	1.171	1.32	306	3.04	.260	0	....	4	2	0.4
Total 4	5	2	.714	42	1	0	0	2	69	70	41	32	7	0	37	36	1.551	4.17	89	4.65	.260	0	....	-3	4	-0.4
• FLITCRAFT, Hilly				Hildreth Milton Flitcraft b: 8/21/1923, Woodstown, NJ d: 4/2/2003, Boulder, CO BL/TL, 6'2", 180 lbs. Deb: 8/31/1942																						
1942 Phi-N	0	0	....	3	0	0	0	0	3^{1}	6	4	3	0	0	2	1	2.400	8.10	41	9.16	.429	0	....	-2	0	-0.2
• FLOHR, Mort				Moritz Herman "Dutch" Flohr b: 8/15/1911, Canisteo, NY d: 6/2/1994, Hornell, NY BL/TL, 6', 173 lbs. Deb: 6/8/1934																						
1934 Phi-A	0	2	.000	14	3	0	0	0	30^{2}	34	21	20	3	1	33	6	2.185	5.87	75	7.46	.296	4	.333	-5	1	-0.4
• FLORENCE, Don				Donald Emery Florence b: 3/16/1967, Manchester, NH BR/TL, 6', 195 lbs. Deb: 8/8/1995																						
1995 NY-N	3	0	1.000	14	0	0	0	0	12	17	3	2	0	0	6	5	1.917	1.50	270	6.20	.340	0	.000	3	2	0.3
• FLORES, Jesse				Jesse Sandoval Flores b: 11/2/1914, Guadalajara, Mexico d: 12/17/1991, Orange, CA BR/TR, 5'10", 175 lbs. Deb: 4/16/1942																						
1942 Chi-N	0	1	.000	4	0	0	0	0	5^{1}	5	5	2	1	0	2	6	1.313	3.38	95	3.86	.227	0	....	-0	0	0.0
1943 Phi-A	12	14	.462	31	27	13	0	0	231^{1}	208	88	80	13	5	70	113	1.202	3.11	109	2.88	.240	14	.175	13	15	1.4
1944 Phi-A	9	11	.450	27	25	11	2	0	185^{2}	172	75	70	8	4	49	65	1.190	3.39	103	2.79	.245	11	.172	2	12	0.2
1945 Phi-A	7	10	.412	29	24	9	4	1	191^{1}	180	79	73	6	4	63	52	1.270	3.43	100	3.03	.250	9	.148	1	10	-0.1
1946 Phi-A	9	7	.563	29	15	8	4	1	155	147	51	40	8	1	38	48	1.194	2.32	153	2.86	.249	11	.250	22	15	2.7
1947 Phi-A	4	13	.235	28	20	4	0	0	151^{1}	139	72	57	10	0	59	41	1.308	3.39	113	3.30	.244	10	.227	3	8	0.4
1950 Cle-A	3	3	.500	28	2	1	1	4	53	53	24	22	3	1	25	27	1.472	3.74	116	4.02	.261	0	.000	3	4	0.1
Total 7	44	59	.427	176	113	46	11	6	973	904	394	344	49	15	306	352	1.244	3.18	112	3.02	.246	55	.181	45	64	4.8
• FLORES, Randy				Randy Alan Flores b: 7/31/1975, Bellflower, CA BL/TL, 6', 180 lbs. Deb: 4/23/2002																						
2002 Tex-A	0	0	....	20	0	0	0	1	12	11	7	6	2	0	8	7	1.583	4.50	105	5.07	.268	0	....	0	1	0.0
Col-N	0	2	.000	8	2	0	0	0	17	29	19	18	5	3	8	7	2.176	9.53	50	11.52	.382	0	.000	-9	0	-0.9
• FLORIE, Bryce				Bryce Bettencourt Florie b: 5/21/1970, Charleston, SC BR/TR, 6', 185 lbs. Deb: 7/17/1994																						
1994 SD-N	0	0	....	9	0	0	0	0	9^{1}	8	1	1	0	0	3	8	1.179	0.96	426	2.48	.242	0	....	3	1	0.3
1995 SD-N	2	2	.500	47	0	0	0	1	68^{2}	49	30	23	8	4	38	68	1.267	3.01	133	3.39	.202	0	.000	6	5	0.6
1996 SD-N	2	2	.500	39	0	0	0	0	49^{1}	45	24	22	1	6	27	51	1.459	4.01	99	3.90	.239	0	.000	-0	3	0.0
Mil-A	0	1	.000	15	0	0	0	0	19	20	16	14	3	0	13	12	1.737	6.63	78	5.66	.270	0	....	-3	0	-0.3
1997 Mil-A	4	4	.500	32	8	0	0	0	75	74	43	36	4	3	42	53	1.547	4.32	107	4.45	.262	0	....	0	4	0.0
1998 Det-A	8	9	.471	42	16	0	0	0	133	141	80	71	16	4	59	97	1.504	4.80	98	4.88	.275	1	.333	-3	7	-0.2
1999 Det-A	2	1	.667	27	3	0	0	0	51^{1}	61	31	26	6	1	20	40	1.578	4.56	108	5.18	.292	0	.000	2	3	0.2
Bos-A	2	0	1.000	14	2	0	0	0	30	33	19	16	2	1	15	25	1.600	4.80	103	4.82	.282	0	....	1	2	0.1
Yr.	4	1	.800	41	5	0	0	0	81^{1}	94	50	42	8	2	35	65	1.586	4.65	106	5.05	.288	0	.000	3	5	0.2
2000 Bos-A	0	4	.000	29	0	0	0	1	49^{1}	57	30	25	5	1	19	34	1.541	4.56	110	4.71	.294	0	....	3	2	0.2
2001 Bos-A	0	1	.000	7	0	0	0	0	8^{2}	12	11	11	1	0	7	7	2.192	11.42	39	7.37	.316	0	....	-7	0	-0.6
Total 8	20	24	.455	261	29	0	0	2	493^{2}	500	285	245	46	20	243	395	1.505	4.47	104	4.55	.265	1	.111	2	27	0.3
• FLOWERS, Ben				Bennett Flowers b: 6/15/1927, Wilson, NC BR/TR, 6'4", 195 lbs. Deb: 9/29/1951																						
1951 Bos-A	0	0	....	1	0	0	0	0	3	2	0	0	0	0	1	2	1.000	0.00	....	1.66	.200	0	.000	1	1	0.1
1953 Bos-A	1	4	.200	32	6	1	1	3	79^{1}	87	39	34	6	1	24	36	1.399	3.86	109	4.00	.280	3	.158	3	5	0.2
1955 Det-A	0	0	....	4	0	0	0	0	6	5	4	4	1	0	2	2	1.167	6.00	64	3.44	.238	0	.000	-1	0	-0.2
StL-N	1	0	1.000	4	4	0	0	0	27^{1}	27	12	11	1	0	12	19	1.427	3.62	112	3.65	.255	1	.100	2	2	0.1
1956 StL-N	1	1	.500	3	3	0	0	0	11^{2}	15	9	9	1	0	5	5	1.714	6.94	54	5.68	.341	0	.000	-4	0	-0.5
Phi-N	0	2	.000	32	0	0	0	0	41	54	29	26	9	1	10	22	1.561	5.71	65	6.33	.331	0	.000	-8	0	-0.8
Yr.	1	3	.250	35	3	0	0	0	52^{2}	69	38	35	10	1	15	27	1.595	5.98	63	6.19	.333	0	.000	-12	0	-1.3
Total 4	3	7	.300	76	13	1	1	3	168^{1}	190	93	84	18	2	54	86	1.450	4.49	88	4.56	.290	4	.111	-8	8	-1.0
• FLOWERS, Wes				Charles Wesley Flowers b: 8/13/1913, Vanndale, AR d: 12/31/1988, Wynne, AR BL/TL, 6'1.5", 190 lbs. Deb: 8/8/1940																						
1940 Bro-N	1	1	.500	5	2	0	0	0	21	23	10	8	2	3	10	8	1.571	3.43	117	5.35	.299	1	.200	1	1	0.1
1944 Bro-N	1	1	.500	9	1	0	0	0	17^{1}	26	17	15	3	1	13	3	2.250	7.79	46	9.05	.333	3	.600	-8	1	-0.7
Total 2	2	2	.500	14	3	0	0	0	38^{1}	49	27	23	5	4	23	11	1.878	5.40	68	7.02	.316	4	.400	-6	2	-0.5
• FLYNN, Carney				Cornelius Francis Xavier Flynn b: 1/23/1875, Cincinnati, OH d: 2/10/1947, Cincinnati, OH BL/TL, 5'11", 165 lbs. Deb: 7/17/1894																						
1894 Cin-N	0	2	.000	2	1	0	0	0	7^{2}	16	15	15	4	1	10	4	3.391	17.61	32	20.81	.421	0	.000	-10	0	-0.8
1896 NY-N	0	2	.000	3	2	1	0	0	10^{2}	18	22	14	0	5	8	4	2.438	11.81	36	10.63	.371	2	.500	-9	0	-0.6
Was-N	0	1	.000	4	1	1	0	0	20	43	31	19	0	24	10	3	2.650	8.55	51	16.09	.429	2	.250	-9	0	-0.8
Yr.	0	3	.000	7	3	2	0	0	30^{2}	61	53	33	0	29	18	7	2.576	9.68	45	14.19	.410	4	.333	-18	0	-1.4
Total 2	0	5	.000	9	4	2	0	0	38^{1}	77	68	48	4	30	28	11	2.739	11.27	41	15.51	.412	4	.267	-28	0	-2.2
• FLYNN, Jocko				John A. Flynn b: 6/30/1864, Lawrence, MA d: 12/30/1907, Lawrence, MA BR/TR, 5'6.5", 143 lbs. Deb: 5/1/1886 U ♦																						
1886 Chi-N	23	6	.793	32	29	28	2	1	257	207	127	64	9	....	63	146	1.051	2.24	161	....	.212	41	.200	29	27	2.6
• FLYTHE, Stu				Stuart McGuire Flythe b: 12/5/1911, Conway, NC d: 10/18/1963, Durham, NC BR/TR, 6'2", 175 lbs. Deb: 5/31/1936																						
1936 Phi-A	0	0	....	17	3	0	0	0	39^{1}	49	63	57	4	3	61	14	2.797	13.04	39	10.16	.302	4	.267	-35	0	-3.0
• FODGE, Gene				Gene Arlan "Suds" Fodge b: 7/9/1931, South Bend, IN BR/TR, 6', 175 lbs. Deb: 4/20/1958																						
1958 Chi-N	1	1	.500	16	4	1	0	0	39^{2}	47	22	21	5	0	11	15	1.462	4.76	82	4.64	.296	0	.000	-3	1	-0.4
• FOGG, Josh				Joshua Smith Fogg b: 12/13/1976, Lynn, MA BR/TR, 6'2", 205 lbs. Deb: 9/2/2001																						
2001 Chi-A	0	0	....	11	0	0	0	0	13^{1}	10	3	3	0	1	3	17	.975	2.03	227	1.73	.208	0	....	4	2	0.4
2002 Pit-N	12	12	.500	33	33	0	0	0	194^{1}	199	102	94	28	8	69	113	1.379	4.35	96	4.46	.267	7	.121	-5	10	-0.7

YEAR TM-L	W	L	PCT	G	GS	CG	SH	SV	IP	H	R	ER	HR	HB	BB	SO	RAT	ERA	ERA+	CERA	OAV	BH	AVG	PR+	WS	TPW
2003 Pit-N	10	9	.526	26	26	1	0	0	142	166	90	83	22	9	40	71	1.451	5.26	83	5.25	.293	8	.190	-14	4	-1.3
Total 3	**22**	**21**	**.512**	**70**	**59**	**1**	**0**	**0**	**349^{2}**	**375**	**195**	**180**	**50**	**18**	**112**	**201**	**1.393**	**4.63**	**92**	**4.68**	**.276**	**15**	**.150**	**-15**	**16**	**-1.6**
• FOLEY, Curry	Charles Joseph Foley b: 1/14/1856, Milltown, Ireland d: 10/20/1898, New York, NY TL, 5'10", 160 lbs. Deb: 5/13/1879 ♦																									
1879 Bos-N	9	9	.500	21	16	16	1	0	161^{2}	175	111	45	1	....	15	57	1.175	2.51	99	....	.259	46	.315	-7	12	-0.4
1880 Bos-N	14	14	.500	36	28	21	1	0	238	264	150	103	1	....	40	68	1.277	3.89	58	....	.267	97	.292	-38	18	-2.7
1881 Buf-N	3	4	.429	10	6	2	0	0	41	70	48	24	1	....	5	2	1.829	5.27	53	....	.362	96	.256	-10	7	-1.7
1882 Buf-N	0	0	....	1	0	0	0	0	1	2	2	2	0	....	0	0	2.000	18.00	16	....	.394	104	.305	-2	12	0.6
1883 Buf-N	1	0	1.000	1	0	0	0	0	1	0	0	0	0	....	4	0	4.000	0.00	....	....	.000	30	.270	0	3	-0.2
Total 5	**27**	**27**	**.500**	**69**	**50**	**39**	**2**	**0**	**442^{2}**	**511**	**311**	**174**	**3**	**....**	**64**	**127**	**1.299**	**3.54**	**68**	**....**	**.274**	**373**	**.286**	**-56**	**52**	**-4.5**
• FOLEY, John	John J. Foley b: 10/25/1857, Brattleboro, VT TL Deb: 9/18/1885																									
1885 Pro-N	0	1	.000	1	1	1	0	0	8	6	7	4	0	....	5	2	1.375	4.50	59	....	.199	0	.000	-2	0	-0.1
• FOLKERS, Rich	Richard Nevin Folkers b: 10/17/1946, Waterloo, IA BL/TL, 6'2", 180 lbs. Deb: 6/10/1970																									
1970 NY-N	0	2	.000	16	1	0	0	2	29^{1}	36	21	21	6	0	25	15	2.080	6.44	62	8.04	.313	2	.333	-8	0	-0.8
1972 StL-N	1	0	1.000	9	0	0	0	0	13^{1}	12	5	5	0	0	5	7	1.275	3.38	101	2.76	.240	0	.000	0	1	0.0
1973 StL-N	4	4	.500	34	9	1	0	3	82^{1}	74	34	33	10	3	34	44	1.312	3.61	101	3.79	.239	2	.100	0	4	-0.1
1974 StL-N	6	2	.750	55	0	0	0	2	90	65	31	30	4	2	38	57	1.144	3.00	119	2.31	.207	1	.100	4	8	0.4
1975 SD-N	6	11	.353	45	15	4	0	0	142	155	70	66	8	1	39	87	1.366	4.18	83	3.74	.278	6	.167	-9	6	-0.9
1976 SD-N	2	3	.400	33	3	0	0	0	59^{2}	67	39	35	10	2	25	26	1.542	5.28	62	5.15	.279	0	.000	-13	0	-1.5
1977 Mil-A	0	1	.000	3	0	0	0	0	6^{1}	7	7	3	2	0	4	6	1.737	4.26	95	6.69	.269	0	....	-0	0	0.0
Total 7	**19**	**23**	**.452**	**195**	**28**	**5**	**0**	**7**	**423**	**416**	**207**	**193**	**40**	**8**	**170**	**242**	**1.385**	**4.11**	**86**	**3.95**	**.258**	**11**	**.143**	**-26**	**19**	**-2.8**
• FONTENOT, Joe	Joseph Daniel Fontenot b: 3/20/1977, Scott, LA BR/TR, 6'2", 185 lbs. Deb: 5/23/1998																									
1998 Fla-N	0	7	.000	8	8	0	0	0	42^{2}	56	34	30	5	5	20	24	1.781	6.33	65	6.83	.320	0	.000	-10	0	-1.1
• FONTENOT, Ray	Silton Ray Fontenot b: 8/8/1957, Lake Charles, LA BL/TL, 6', 175 lbs. Deb: 6/30/1983																									
1983 NY-A	8	2	.800	15	15	3	1	0	97^{1}	101	41	36	3	1	25	27	1.295	3.33	117	3.32	.266	0	....	7	7	0.7
1984 NY-A	8	9	.471	35	24	0	0	0	169^{1}	189	77	68	8	3	58	85	1.459	3.61	105	4.29	.291	0	....	4	9	0.4
1985 Chi-N	6	10	.375	38	23	0	0	0	154^{2}	177	86	75	23	0	45	70	1.435	4.36	91	4.85	.294	2	.049	-5	6	-0.8
1986 Chi-N	3	5	.375	42	0	0	0	2	56	57	30	24	5	0	21	24	1.393	3.86	105	3.91	.266	1	.167	2	4	0.2
Min-A	0	0	....	15	0	0	0	0	16^{1}	27	19	18	3	2	4	10	1.898	9.92	43	8.61	.360	0	.000	-10	0	-1.0
Total 4	**25**	**26**	**.490**	**145**	**62**	**3**	**1**	**2**	**493^{2}**	**551**	**253**	**221**	**42**	**6**	**153**	**216**	**1.426**	**4.03**	**98**	**4.37**	**.287**	**3**	**.063**	**-2**	**26**	**-0.5**
• FOOR, Jim	James Emerson Foor b: 1/13/1949, St. Louis, MO BL/TL, 6'2", 170 lbs. Deb: 4/9/1971																									
1971 Det-A	0	0	....	3	0	0	0	0	1	2	2	2	0	0	4	2	6.000	18.00	20	26.28	.400	0	....	-2	0	-0.2
1972 Det-A	1	0	1.000	7	0	0	0	0	3^{2}	6	6	6	1	0	6	2	3.273	14.73	21	14.74	.353	0	....	-5	0	-0.5
1973 Pit-N	0	0	....	3	0	0	0	0	1^{1}	2	0	0	0	0	1	1	2.250	0.00	....	5.09	.286	0	....	1	0	0.1
Total 3	**1**	**0**	**1.000**	**13**	**0**	**0**	**0**	**0**	**6**	**10**	**8**	**8**	**1**	**0**	**11**	**5**	**3.500**	**12.00**	**27**	**14.52**	**.345**	**0**	**....**	**-6**	**0**	**-0.7**
• FOPPERT, Jesse	Jesse W. Foppert b: 7/10/1980, Reading, PA BR/TR, 6'6", 210 lbs. Deb: 4/14/2003																									
2003 SF-N	8	9	.471	23	21	0	0	0	111	103	69	62	16	3	69	101	1.550	5.03	82	4.89	.249	3	.081	-14	2	-1.5
• FORCE, Davy	David W. "Wee Davy,Tom Thumb" Force b: 7/27/1849, New York, NY d: 6/21/1918, Englewood, NJ BR/TR, 5'4", 130 lbs. Deb: 5/5/1871 U ♦																									
1873 Bal-n	1	1	.500	3	1	1	0	0	18	23	20	7	0	....	0	0	1.278	3.50	93	....	.275	86	.368	-1	....	1.5
1874 Chi-n	0	0	....	1	0	0	0	0	7	22	24	12	4	....	0	0	3.143	15.43	12	....	.486	92	.313	-17	....	-0.3
Total 2 n	**1**	**1**	**.500**	**4**	**1**	**1**	**0**	**0**	**25**	**45**	**44**	**19**	**4**	**....**	**0**	**0**	**1.800**	**6.84**	**33**	**....**	**.349**	**437**	**.336**	**-18**	**....**	**1.2**
• FORD, Ben	Benjamin Cooper Ford b: 8/15/1975, Cedar Rapids, IA BR/TR, 6'7", 200 lbs. Deb: 8/20/1998																									
1998 Ari-N	0	0	....	8	0	0	0	0	10	13	12	11	2	2	3	5	1.600	9.90	43	6.78	.295	0	....	-6	0	-0.6
2000 NY-A	0	1	.000	4	2	0	0	0	11	14	11	11	1	3	7	5	1.909	9.00	54	8.38	.333	0	....	-5	0	-0.4
Total 2	**0**	**1**	**.000**	**12**	**2**	**0**	**0**	**0**	**21**	**27**	**23**	**22**	**3**	**5**	**10**	**10**	**1.762**	**9.43**	**48**	**7.62**	**.314**	**0**	**....**	**-11**	**0**	**-1.1**
• FORD, Bill	William Brown Ford b: 10/14/1915, Buena Vista, PA d: 4/6/1994, Jefferson, PA BR/TR, 6'2", 200 lbs. Deb: 9/27/1936																									
1936 Bos-N	0	0	....	1	0	0	0	0	0	0	2	2	0	0	3	0	....	∞	....	∞	1.000	0	....	-2	0	-0.2
• FORD, Dave	David Alan Ford b: 12/29/1956, Cleveland, OH BR/TR, 6'4", 190 lbs. Deb: 9/2/1978																									
1978 Bal-A	1	0	1.000	2	1	0	0	0	15	10	0	0	0	0	2	5	.800	0.00	....	1.25	.196	0	....	6	2	0.6
1979 Bal-A	2	1	.667	9	2	0	0	2	30	23	7	7	2	0	7	7	1.000	2.10	191	2.12	.219	0	....	6	4	0.6
1980 Bal-A	1	3	.250	25	3	1	0	1	69^{2}	66	34	33	11	2	13	22	1.134	4.26	93	3.46	.251	0	....	-4	3	-0.4
1981 Bal-A	1	2	.333	15	2	0	0	0	40	61	33	29	2	0	10	12	1.775	6.53	56	6.13	.359	0	....	-13	0	-1.3
Total 4	**5**	**6**	**.455**	**51**	**8**	**1**	**0**	**3**	**154^{2}**	**160**	**74**	**69**	**15**	**2**	**32**	**46**	**1.241**	**4.02**	**95**	**3.68**	**.272**	**0**	**....**	**-5**	**9**	**-0.6**
• FORD, Gene	Eugene Matthew Ford b: 6/23/1912, Fort Dodge, IA d: 9/7/1970, Emmetsburg, IA BR/TR, 6'2", 195 lbs. Deb: 6/17/1936																									
1936 Bos-N	0	0	....	1	0	0	0	0	2	2	1	1	0	0	0	0	1.000	4.50	85	1.95	.250	0	....	-0	0	0.0
1938 Chi-A	0	0	....	4	0	0	0	0	14	21	16	16	1	0	12	2	2.357	10.29	48	8.50	.350	1	.167	-8	0	-0.8
Total 2	**0**	**0**	**....**	**5**	**0**	**0**	**0**	**0**	**16**	**23**	**17**	**17**	**1**	**0**	**12**	**2**	**2.188**	**9.56**	**50**	**7.68**	**.338**	**1**	**.167**	**-9**	**0**	**-0.8**
• FORD, Gene	Eugene Wyman Ford b: 4/16/1881, Milton, Canada d: 8/23/1973, Dunedin, FL BR/TR, 6', 170 lbs. Deb: 5/5/1905																									
1905 Det-A	0	1	.000	7	1	1	0	0	35	51	30	22	0	2	14	20	1.857	5.66	48	5.80	.342	0	.000	-12	0	-1.4
• FORD, Matt	Matthew Lee Ford b: 4/8/1981, Plantation, FL BB/TL, 6'1", 170 lbs. Deb: 4/2/2003																									
2003 Mil-N	0	3	.000	25	4	0	0	0	43^{2}	46	23	21	5	1	21	26	1.534	4.33	98	4.84	.264	1	.143	0	2	0.1
• FORD, Russ	Russell William Ford b: 4/25/1883, Brandon, Canada d: 1/24/1960, Rockingham, NC BR/TR, 5'11", 175 lbs. Deb: 4/28/1909																									
1909 NY-A	0	0	....	1	0	0	0	0	3	4	4	3	0	3	4	2	2.667	9.00	28	12.30	.333	0	.000	-2	0	-0.3
1910 NY-A	26	6	.813	36	33	29	8	1	299^{2}	194	69	55	4	8	70	209	.881	1.65	161	1.41	.188	20	.208	41	35	5.1
1911 NY-A	22	11	.667	37	33	26	1	0	281^{1}	251	119	71	3	4	76	158	1.162	2.27	158	2.38	.237	20	.196	47	28	4.4
1912 NY-A	13	21	.382	36	35	30	0	0	291^{2}	317	165	115	10	5	79	112	1.358	3.55	102	3.53	.280	32	.286	18	16	2.4
1913 NY-A	12	18	.400	33	28	15	1	2	237	244	108	70	9	4	58	72	1.274	2.66	112	3.33	.275	12	.162	9	14	1.0
1914 Buf-F	21	6	.778	35	26	19	5	**6**	247^{1}	190	63	50	11	7	41	123	.934	1.82	**183**	1.83	.214	10	.128	38	29	3.7
1915 Buf-F	5	9	.357	21	15	7	0	0	127^{1}	140	74	64	7	3	48	34	1.476	4.52	68	4.21	.285	12	.279	-20	3	-1.8
Total 7	**99**	**71**	**.582**	**199**	**170**	**126**	**15**	**9**	**1487^{1}**	**1340**	**602**	**428**	**44**	**34**	**376**	**710**	**1.154**	**2.59**	**124**	**2.65**	**.244**	**106**	**.209**	**131**	**125**	**14.6**
• FORD, Tom	Thomas Walter Ford b: 1866, Chattanooga, TN d: 5/27/1917, Chattanooga, TN, 5'10.5", 155 lbs. Deb: 5/6/1890																									
1890 Col-a	0	0	....	1	0	0	0	0	2	0	0	0	0	0	3	0	1.500	0.00	....	....	.000	0	.000	1	0	0.0
Bro-a	0	6	.000	7	6	6	0	0	49	70	60	28	2	0	32	12	2.082	5.14	76	....	.326	1	.033	-7	0	-1.2
Yr.	0	6	.000	8	6	6	0	0	51	70	60	28	2	0	35	12	2.059	4.94	79	....	.326	1	.032	-6	0	-1.2
• FORD, Wenty	Percival Edmund Wentworth Ford b: 11/25/1946, Nassau, Bahamas d: 7/8/1980, Nassau, Bahamas BR/TR, 5'11", 165 lbs. Deb: 9/10/1973																									
1973 Atl-N	1	2	.333	4	2	1	0	0	16^{1}	17	10	10	3	1	8	4	1.531	5.51	71	5.68	.279	2	.400	-3	1	-0.2
• FORD, Whitey	Edward Charles "The Chairman of the Board" Ford b: 10/21/1926, New York, NY BL/TL, 5'10", 181 lbs. Deb: 7/1/1950 C HOF: 1974																									
1950★NY-A	9	1	.900	20	12	7	2	1	112	87	39	35	7	2	52	59	1.241	2.81	153	2.85	.216	7	.194	17	11	1.6
1953★NY-A	18	6	.750	32	30	11	3	0	207	187	77	69	13	4	110	110	1.435	3.00	123	3.81	.245	20	.267	10	17	1.6
1954 NY-A★	16	8	.667	34	28	11	3	1	210^{2}	170	72	66	10	1	101	125	1.286	2.82	122	2.94	.227	10	.161	9	16	1.1
1955★NY-A★	**18**	7	.720	39	33	**18**	5	2	253^{2}	188	83	74	20	1	113	137	1.187	2.63	142	2.77	.208	14	.163	21	22	2.2
1956★NY-A★	19	6	.760	31	30	18	2	1	225^{2}	187	70	62	13	4	84	141	1.201	**2.47**	157	2.88	.228	17	.218	30	22	3.2
1957★NY-A	11	5	.688	24	17	5	0	0	129^{1}	114	46	37	10	1	53	84	1.291	2.57	139	3.35	.237	6	.143	13	10	1.2
1958★NY-A★	14	7	.667	30	29	15	**7**	1	219^{1}	174	62	49	14	3	62	145	1.076	**2.01**	**176**	**2.40**	.217	15	.205	**33**	20	**3.6**
1959 NY-A★	16	10	.615	35	29	9	2	1	204	194	82	69	13	1	89	114	1.387	3.04	120	3.67	.250	15	.231	14	16	2.0

YEAR TM-L	W	L	PCT	G	GS	CG	SH	SV	IP	H	R	ER	HR	HB	BB	SO	RAT	ERA	ERA+	CERA	OAV	BH	AVG	PR+	WS	TPW
1960* NY-A★	12	9	.571	33	29	8	**4**	0	192^2	168	76	66	15	1	65	85	1.209	3.08	116	2.98	.235	8	.151	5	14	0.7
1961* NY-A★	**25**	4	.862	39	**39**	11	3	0	**283**	242	108	101	23	1	92	209	1.180	3.21	116	2.90	.229	17	.177	7	**22**	0.9
1962* NY-A	17	8	.680	38	37	7	0	0	257^2	243	90	83	22	4	69	160	1.211	2.90	129	3.21	.246	10	.118	22	20	2.1
1963* NY-A	**24**	7	.774	38	**37**	13	3	1	**269^1**	240	94	82	26	2	56	189	1.099	2.74	128	2.82	.241	13	.141	18	23	1.9
1964* NY-A★	17	6	.739	39	36	12	8	1	244^2	212	67	58	10	2	57	172	1.099	2.13	170	2.37	.230	8	.119	39	24	4.1
1965 NY-A	16	13	.552	37	36	9	2	1	244^1	241	97	88	22	1	50	162	1.191	3.24	105	3.21	.258	15	.183	6	16	0.8
1966 NY-A	2	5	.286	22	9	0	0	0	73	79	33	20	8	0	24	43	1.411	2.47	135	4.15	.277	0	.000	7	4	0.6
1967 NY-A	2	4	.333	7	7	2	1	0	44	40	11	8	2	0	9	21	1.114	1.64	191	2.60	.247	2	.154	8	4	0.8
Total 16	236	106	.690	498	438	156	45	10	3170^1	2766	1107	967	228	28	1086	1956	1.215	2.75	132	3.01	.235	177	.173	259	261	28.7

• FORDHAM, Tom Thomas James Fordham b: 2/20/1974, San Diego, CA BL/TL, 6'2", 210 lbs. Deb: 8/19/1997

YEAR TM-L	W	L	PCT	G	GS	CG	SH	SV	IP	H	R	ER	HR	HB	BB	SO	RAT	ERA	ERA+	CERA	OAV	BH	AVG	PR+	WS	TPW
1997 Chi-A	0	1	.000	7	1	0	0	0	17^1	17	13	12	2	1	10	10	1.558	6.23	70	4.83	.266	0	....	-3	0	-0.3
1998 Chi-A	1	2	.333	29	5	0	0	0	48	51	36	36	7	1	42	23	1.938	6.75	67	7.03	.279	0	.000	-12	0	-1.1
Total 2	1	3	.250	36	6	0	0	0	65^1	68	49	48	9	2	52	33	1.837	6.61	68	6.44	.275	0	.000	-15	0	-1.4

• FOREMAN, Brownie John Davis Foreman b: 8/6/1875, Baltimore, MD d: 10/10/1926, Baltimore, MD BL/TL, 5'8", 150 lbs. Deb: 7/18/1895 U

YEAR TM-L	W	L	PCT	G	GS	CG	SH	SV	IP	H	R	ER	HR	HB	BB	SO	RAT	ERA	ERA+	CERA	OAV	BH	AVG	PR+	WS	TPW
1895 Pit-N	8	6	.571	19	16	12	0	2	139^2	131	83	50	0	19	64	54	1.396	3.22	140	3.59	**.245**	3	.065	20	11	1.2
1896 Pit-N	3	3	.500	9	9	5	0	0	61^2	73	55	45	4	8	35	18	1.751	6.57	64	5.89	.292	3	.150	-16	1	-1.3
Cin-N	1	3	.250	4	4	3	1	0	23	41	30	29	2	2	16	9	2.478	11.35	41	10.40	.383	2	.200	-18	0	-1.5
Yr.	4	6	.400	13	13	8	1	0	84^2	114	85	74	6	10	51	27	1.949	7.87	55	7.11	.320	5	.167	-34	1	-2.9
Total 2	12	12	.500	32	29	20	1	2	224^1	245	168	124	6	29	115	81	1.605	4.97	89	4.92	.275	8	.105	-14	12	-1.7

• FOREMAN, Frank Francis Isaiah "Monkey" Foreman b: 5/1/1863, Baltimore, MD d: 11/19/1957, Baltimore, MD BL/TL, 6', 160 lbs. Deb: 5/15/1884 U

YEAR TM-L	W	L	PCT	G	GS	CG	SH	SV	IP	H	R	ER	HR	HB	BB	SO	RAT	ERA	ERA+	CERA	OAV	BH	AVG	PR+	WS	TPW
1884 CP-U	1	2	.333	3	3	1	0	0	18	23	17	8	0	....	2	10	1.389	4.00	72	....	.291	1	.091	-2	0	-0.3
KC-U	0	1	.000	1	1	1	0	0	8	17	12	5	0	....	2	5	2.375	5.63	50	....	.406	0	.000	-3	0	-0.3
Yr.	1	3	.250	4	4	2	0	0	26	40	29	13	0	....	4	15	1.692	4.50	63	....	.331	1	.071	-5	0	-0.6
1885 Bal-a	2	1	.667	3	3	2	0	0	27	33	32	18	0	1	9	11	1.556	6.00	54	....	.289	4	.286	-8	0	-0.6
1889 Bal-a	23	21	.523	51	48	43	5	0	414	364	257	162	8	40	137	180	1.210	3.52	108	....	.229	26	.144	21	28	1.0
1890 Cin-N	13	10	.565	25	24	20	0	0	198^1	201	139	87	6	20	89	57	1.462	3.95	90	....	.255	10	.133	-12	11	-1.0
1891 Was-a	18	20	.474	43	41	39	1	1	345^1	381	245	143	9	43	142	170	1.514	3.73	100	....	.271	34	.222	20	17	2.8
1892 Was-N	2	4	.333	11	7	4	0	0	60	53	39	22	3	5	37	16	1.500	3.30	98	4.04	.228	13	.464	-0	5	0.7
Bal-N	0	3	.000	4	3	2	0	0	25	40	29	19	4	6	11	5	2.040	6.84	50	9.41	.348	4	.174	-8	0	-0.9
Yr.	2	7	.222	15	10	6	0	0	85	93	68	41	7	11	48	21	1.659	4.34	77	5.62	.267	17	.333	-9	5	-0.2
1893 NY-N	0	1	.000	2	1	0	0	0	5^2	19	17	17	1	1	10	0	5.118	27.00	17	29.48	.531	0	.000	-14	0	-1.2
1895 Cin-N	11	14	.440	32	27	19	0	1	219	253	142	100	11	15	92	55	1.575	4.11	121	4.82	.285	29	.309	20	18	2.0
1896 Cin-N	14	7	.667	27	22	17	0	1	185^2	212	105	82	2	8	62	33	1.476	3.97	116	4.03	.285	18	.243	9	17	0.7
1901 Bos-A	0	1	.000	1	1	1	0	0	8	8	9	8	1	2	2	1	1.250	9.00	39	4.55	.257	0	.000	-5	0	-0.5
Bal-A	12	6	.667	24	22	18	1	1	191^1	225	120	78	2	6	58	41	1.479	3.67	105	4.07	.290	26	.325	10	15	1.4
Yr.	12	7	.632	25	23	19	1	1	199^1	233	129	86	3	8	60	42	1.470	3.88	99	4.09	.288	26	.310	5	15	0.9
1902 Bal-A	0	2	.000	2	2	2	0	0	16^1	28	18	11	0	0	6	2	2.082	6.06	62	6.87	.377	3	.429	-3	0	-0.2
Total 11	96	93	.508	229	205	169	7	4	1721^2	1857	1181	760	47	147	659	586	1.461	3.97	98	1.96	.269	169	.224	25	111	3.5

• FOREMAN, Happy August G. Foreman b: 7/20/1897, Memphis, TN d: 2/13/1953, New York, NY BL/TL, 5'7", 160 lbs. Deb: 9/3/1924

YEAR TM-L	W	L	PCT	G	GS	CG	SH	SV	IP	H	R	ER	HR	HB	BB	SO	RAT	ERA	ERA+	CERA	OAV	BH	AVG	PR+	WS	TPW
1924 Chi-A	0	0	....	3	0	0	0	0	4	7	3	1	0	0	4	1	2.750	2.25	183	11.47	.467	0	.000	1	0	0.0
1926 Bos-A	0	0	....	3	0	0	0	0	7^1	3	3	3	0	0	5	3	1.091	3.68	111	1.45	.130	0	.000	0	1	0.0
Total 2	0	0	....	6	0	0	0	0	11^1	10	6	4	0	0	9	4	1.676	3.18	128	4.99	.263	0	.000	1	1	0.1

• FORMAN, Bill William Orange Forman b: 10/10/1886, Venango, PA d: 10/2/1958, Uniontown, PA BB/TR, 5'11", 180 lbs. Deb: 9/20/1909

YEAR TM-L	W	L	PCT	G	GS	CG	SH	SV	IP	H	R	ER	HR	HB	BB	SO	RAT	ERA	ERA+	CERA	OAV	BH	AVG	PR+	WS	TPW
1909 Was-A	0	2	.000	2	2	1	0	0	11	8	8	6	0	2	7	2	1.364	4.91	49	3.35	.211	1	.333	-3	0	-0.3
1910 Was-A	0	0	....	1	0	0	0	0	0^2	1	1	1	0	0	0	0	1.500	13.50	18	4.47	.333	0	....	-1	0	-0.1
Total 2	0	2	.000	3	2	1	0	0	11^2	9	9	7	0	2	7	2	1.371	5.40	45	3.41	.220	1	.333	-4	0	-0.4

• FORNIELES, Mike Jose Miguel (Torres) Fornieles b: 1/18/1932, Havana, Cuba d: 2/11/1998, St. Petersburg, FL BR/TR, 5'11", 172 lbs. Deb: 9/2/1952

YEAR TM-L	W	L	PCT	G	GS	CG	SH	SV	IP	H	R	ER	HR	HB	BB	SO	RAT	ERA	ERA+	CERA	OAV	BH	AVG	PR+	WS	TPW
1952 Was-A	2	2	.500	4	2	2	1	0	26^1	13	4	4	1	0	11	12	.911	1.37	260	1.31	.143	0	.000	7	3	0.5
1953 Chi-A	8	7	.533	39	16	5	0	3	153	160	68	61	8	2	61	72	1.444	3.59	112	3.95	.270	4	.098	7	9	0.4
1954 Chi-A	1	2	.333	15	6	0	0	1	42	41	24	20	4	0	14	18	1.310	4.29	87	3.54	.252	3	.273	-3	1	-0.3
1955 Chi-A	6	3	.667	26	9	2	0	2	86^1	84	37	37	12	2	29	23	1.309	3.86	102	4.00	.255	3	.103	-0	6	-0.2
1956 Chi-A	0	1	.000	6	0	0	0	0	15^2	22	9	8	1	0	6	6	1.787	4.60	89	5.51	.306	1	.200	-1	0	-0.1
Bal-A	4	7	.364	30	11	1	1	1	111	109	59	49	7	0	25	53	1.207	3.97	99	3.15	.266	5	.167	0	6	-0.1
Yr.	4	8	.333	36	11	1	1	1	126^2	131	68	57	8	0	31	59	1.279	4.05	97	3.44	.272	6	.171	-1	6	-0.2
1957 Bal-A	2	6	.250	15	4	1	1	0	57	57	30	27	4	0	17	43	1.298	4.26	84	3.42	.257	5	.278	-5	1	-0.5
Bos-A	8	7	.533	25	18	7	1	2	125^1	136	61	49	7	3	38	64	1.388	3.52	113	3.79	.271	6	.136	8	9	0.7
Yr.	10	13	.435	40	22	8	2	2	182^1	193	91	76	11	3	55	107	1.360	3.75	102	3.68	.267	11	.177	3	10	0.2
1958 Bos-A	4	6	.400	37	7	1	0	1	110^2	123	62	61	10	6	33	49	1.410	4.96	81	4.47	.284	6	.207	-10	3	-1.1
1959 Bos-A	5	3	.625	46	0	0	0	11	82	77	29	28	6	1	29	54	1.293	3.07	132	3.42	.254	3	.158	9	9	0.8
1960 Bos-A	10	5	.667	**70**	0	0	0	**14**	109	86	38	32	6	6	49	64	1.239	2.64	153	2.91	.219	6	.400	20	16	2.2
1961 Bos-A★	9	8	.529	57	2	1	0	15	119^1	121	65	62	18	2	54	70	1.466	4.68	89	4.68	.265	5	.156	-6	9	-0.6
1962 Bos-A	3	6	.333	42	1	0	0	5	82^1	96	57	49	14	8	37	36	1.615	5.36	77	6.23	.303	3	.188	-12	1	-1.2
1963 Bos-A	0	0	....	9	0	0	0	0	14	16	10	10	0	0	5	5	1.500	6.43	59	3.87	.286	1	.333	-4	0	-0.4
Min-A	1	1	.500	11	0	0	0	0	22^2	24	14	12	0	2	13	7	1.632	4.76	77	4.58	.273	1	.167	-3	1	-0.2
Yr.	1	1	.500	20	0	0	0	0	36^2	40	24	22	0	2	18	12	1.582	5.40	69	4.31	.278	2	.222	-7	1	-0.6
Total 12	63	64	.496	432	76	20	4	55	1156^2	1165	567	509	98	32	421	576	1.371	3.96	100	3.94	.263	52	.169	6	74	0.0

• FORSCH, Bob Robert Herbert Forsch b: 1/13/1950, Sacramento, CA BR/TR, 6'4", 200 lbs. Deb: 7/7/1974

YEAR TM-L	W	L	PCT	G	GS	CG	SH	SV	IP	H	R	ER	HR	HB	BB	SO	RAT	ERA	ERA+	CERA	OAV	BH	AVG	PR+	WS	TPW
1974 StL-N	7	4	.636	19	14	5	2	0	100	84	38	33	5	1	34	39	1.180	2.97	120	2.68	.230	7	.241	5	9	0.7
1975 StL-N	15	10	.600	34	34	7	4	0	230	213	89	73	14	3	70	108	1.230	2.86	131	3.04	.244	24	.308	29	21	4.0
1976 StL-N	8	10	.444	33	32	2	0	0	194	209	112	85	17	3	71	76	1.443	3.94	90	4.29	.277	11	.177	-10	6	-0.9
1977 StL-N	20	7	.741	35	35	8	2	0	217^1	210	97	84	20	3	69	95	1.284	3.48	111	3.56	.251	12	.167	5	14	0.5
1978 StL-N	11	17	.393	34	34	7	3	0	233^2	205	110	96	15	5	97	114	1.292	3.70	95	3.27	.238	15	.181	-7	8	-0.4
1979 StL-N	11	11	.500	33	32	7	1	0	218^2	215	102	93	16	3	52	92	1.221	3.83	98	3.29	.262	8	.110	-7	12	-0.7
1980 StL-N	11	10	.524	31	31	8	0	0	214^2	225	102	90	12	4	33	87	1.202	3.77	98	3.17	.273	23	.295	-5	12	0.4
1981 StL-N	10	5	.667	20	20	1	0	0	124^1	106	47	44	7	4	29	41	1.086	3.18	112	2.50	.232	5	.122	3	8	0.2
1982* StL-N	15	9	.625	36	34	6	2	1	233	238	95	90	16	4	54	69	1.253	3.48	104	3.40	.268	15	.205	-2	16	0.1
1983 StL-N	10	12	.455	34	30	6	2	0	187	190	104	89	23	3	54	56	1.305	4.28	84	3.94	.266	13	.241	-13	7	-0.9
1984 StL-N	2	5	.286	16	11	1	0	0	52^1	64	38	35	6	0	19	21	1.586	6.02	58	5.37	.303	4	.250	-16	0	-1.5
1985* StL-N	9	6	.600	34	19	3	1	2	136	132	63	59	11	2	47	48	1.316	3.90	90	3.65	.258	11	.244	-8	7	-0.5
1986 StL-N	14	10	.583	33	33	3	0	0	230	211	91	83	19	2	68	104	1.213	3.25	112	3.13	.247	13	.171	2	16	0.5
1987* StL-N	11	7	.611	33	30	2	1	0	179	189	90	86	15	4	45	89	1.307	4.32	96	3.77	.273	17	.298	-5	11	0.4
1988 StL-N	9	4	.692	30	12	1	1	0	108^2	111	51	45	8	1	38	40	1.371	3.73	93	3.76	.270	7	.280	-4	7	-0.2
Hou-N	1	4	.200	6	6	0	0	0	27^2	42	22	20	2	2	6	14	1.735	6.51	51	6.25	.359	1	.143	-10	0	-1.0
Yr.	10	8	.556	36	18	1	1	0	136^1	153	73	65	10	3	44	54	1.445	4.29	80	4.26	.290	8	.250	-14	7	-1.2
1989 Hou-N	4	5	.444	37	15	0	0	0	108^1	133	68	64	10	1	46	40	1.652	5.32	64	5.37	.303	4	.167	-22	0	-2.4
Total 16	168	136	.553	498	422	67	19	3	2794^2	2777	1319	1169	216	45	832	1133	1.291	3.76	97	3.55	.261	190	.213	-64	154	-1.7

• FORSCH, Ken Kenneth Roth Forsch b: 9/8/1946, Sacramento, CA BR/TR, 6'4", 210 lbs. Deb: 9/7/1970

YEAR TM-L	W	L	PCT	G	GS	CG	SH	SV	IP	H	R	ER	HR	HB	BB	SO	RAT	ERA	ERA+	CERA	OAV	BH	AVG	PR+	WS	TPW
1970 Hou-N	1	2	.333	4	4	1	0	0	24	28	15	15	1	0	5	13	1.375	5.63	69	4.00	.298	0	.000	-5	0	-0.5
1971 Hou-N	8	8	.500	33	23	7	2	0	188^1	162	60	53	8	4	53	131	1.142	2.53	133	2.56	.230	8	.136	16	14	1.6
1972 Hou-N	6	8	.429	30	24	1	0	0	156^1	163	75	68	19	0	62	113	1.439	3.91	86	4.51	.273	6	.146	-9	5	-1.1
1973 Hou-N	9	12	.429	46	26	5	0	4	201^1	197	101	94	18	4	74	149	1.346	4.20	86	3.78	.257	4	.065	-13	8	-1.7
1974 Hou-N	8	7	.533	70	0	0	0	10	103^1	98	38	32	3	4	37	48	1.306	2.79	124	3.13	.255	0	.000	6	10	0.6

YEAR	TM-L	W	L	PCT	G	GS	CG	SH	SV	IP	H	R	ER	HR	HB	BB	SO	RAT	ERA	ERA+	CERA	OAV	BH	AVG	PR+	WS	TPW
1975	Hou-N	4	8	.333	34	9	2	0	2	109	114	42	39	9	2	30	54	1.321	3.22	105	3.87	.277	1	.045	1	6	0.0
1976	Hou-N★	4	3	.571	52	0	0	0	19	92	76	23	22	5	2	26	49	1.109	2.15	148	2.42	.226	1	.091	11	11	1.1
1977	Hou-N	5	8	.385	42	5	0	0	8	86	80	32	26	2	2	28	45	1.256	2.72	131	2.85	.246	1	.077	8	8	0.8
1978	Hou-N	10	6	.625	52	6	4	2	7	133^1	136	44	40	2	1	37	71	1.298	2.70	122	3.00	.268	5	.185	12	13	1.2
1979	Hou-N	11	6	.647	26	24	10	2	0	177^2	155	67	60	14	0	35	58	1.069	3.04	115	2.54	.236	8	.138	10	12	1.0
1980*	Hou-N	12	13	.480	32	32	6	3	0	222^1	230	90	79	15	7	41	84	1.219	3.20	103	3.33	.266	18	.234	2	13	0.6
1981	Cal-A★	11	7	.611	20	20	10	**4**	0	153	143	54	49	7	4	27	55	1.111	2.88	127	2.65	.250	0	....	12	10	1.3
1982	Cal-A	13	11	.542	37	35	12	4	0	228	225	108	98	25	11	57	73	1.237	3.87	105	3.67	.258	0	....	1	13	0.1
1983	Cal-A	11	12	.478	31	31	11	1	0	219^1	226	107	99	21	4	61	81	1.309	4.06	99	3.81	.266	0	....	-1	12	-0.1
1984	Cal-A	1	1	.500	2	2	1	0	0	16^1	14	4	4	2	0	3	10	1.041	2.20	180	2.79	.237	0	....	3	2	0.3
1986	Cal-A	0	1	.000	10	0	0	0	1	17	24	21	18	4	2	10	13	2.000	9.53	43	9.15	.343	0	....	-11	0	-1.0
Total	16	114	113	.502	521	241	70	18	51	2127^1	2071	881	796	155	47	586	1047	1.249	3.37	107	3.35	.257	52	.136	44	137	4.2

• FORSTER, Scott Scott Christian Forster b: 10/27/1971, Philadelphia, PA BR/TL, 6'1", 194 lbs. Deb: 6/18/2000

YEAR	TM-L	W	L	PCT	G	GS	CG	SH	SV	IP	H	R	ER	HR	HB	BB	SO	RAT	ERA	ERA+	CERA	OAV	BH	AVG	PR+	WS	TPW
2000	Mon-N	0	1	.000	42	0	0	0	0	32	28	31	28	5	2	25	23	1.656	7.88	61	5.27	.230	0	....	-11	0	-1.0

• FORSTER, Terry Terry Jay Forster b: 1/14/1952, Sioux Falls, SD BL/TL, 6'3", 210 lbs. Deb: 4/11/1971

YEAR	TM-L	W	L	PCT	G	GS	CG	SH	SV	IP	H	R	ER	HR	HB	BB	SO	RAT	ERA	ERA+	CERA	OAV	BH	AVG	PR+	WS	TPW
1971	Chi-A	2	3	.400	45	3	0	0	1	49^2	46	23	22	5	1	23	48	1.389	3.99	90	3.80	.241	2	.400	-1	3	0.0
1972	Chi-A	6	5	.545	62	0	0	0	29	100	75	31	25	0	3	44	104	1.190	2.25	139	2.28	.208	10	.526	12	19	1.8
1973	Chi-A	6	11	.353	51	12	4	0	16	172^2	174	69	62	7	0	78	120	1.459	3.23	122	3.88	.266	0	.000	16	15	1.7
1974	Chi-A	7	8	.467	59	1	0	0	**24**	134^1	120	57	54	6	8	48	105	1.251	3.62	103	3.20	.245	0	....	3	13	0.3
1975	Chi-A	3	3	.500	17	1	0	0	4	37	30	12	9	0	0	24	32	1.459	2.19	177	3.23	.236	0	....	7	4	0.8
1976	Chi-A	2	12	.143	29	16	1	0	1	111^1	126	61	54	7	1	41	70	1.500	4.37	82	4.45	.288	0	....	-9	3	-0.9
1977	Pit-N	6	4	.600	33	6	0	0	1	87^1	90	47	43	7	2	32	58	1.397	4.43	90	4.00	.269	9	.346	-6	5	-0.3
1978*	LA-N	5	4	.556	47	0	0	0	22	65^1	56	19	14	2	0	23	46	1.209	1.93	182	2.63	.233	4	.500	11	12	1.4
1979	LA-N	1	2	.333	17	0	0	0	2	16^1	18	11	10	0	0	11	8	1.776	5.51	66	4.70	.295	0	....	-3	0	-0.3
1980	LA-N	0	0	....	9	0	0	0	0	11^2	10	4	4	0	0	4	2	1.200	3.09	113	2.40	.222	0	....	0	1	0.0
1981*	LA-N	0	1	.000	21	0	0	0	0	30^2	37	14	14	1	0	15	17	1.696	4.11	81	5.06	.308	0	.000	-3	1	-0.3
1982	LA-N	5	6	.455	56	0	0	0	3	83	66	38	28	3	4	31	52	1.169	3.04	114	2.44	.221	0	.000	5	6	0.5
1983	Atl-N	3	2	.600	56	0	0	0	13	79^1	60	19	19	3	2	31	54	1.147	2.16	180	2.37	.217	4	.500	14	12	1.7
1984	Atl-N	2	0	1.000	25	0	0	0	5	26^2	30	9	8	1	0	7	10	1.388	2.70	143	3.66	.297	2	.667	4	4	0.5
1985	Atl-N	2	3	.400	46	0	0	0	1	59^1	49	22	15	7	0	28	37	1.298	2.28	169	3.38	.222	0	.000	11	5	1.1
1986	Cal-A	4	1	.800	41	0	0	0	5	41	47	18	16	2	3	17	28	1.561	3.51	117	4.94	.297	0	....	2	4	0.2
Total	16	54	65	.454	614	39	5	0	127	1105^2	1034	454	397	51	24	457	791	1.349	3.23	114	3.44	.251	31	.397	64	107	8.0

• FORTUGNO, Tim Timothy Shawn Fortugno b: 4/11/1962, Clinton, MA BL/TL, 6'1", 195 lbs. Deb: 7/20/1992

YEAR	TM-L	W	L	PCT	G	GS	CG	SH	SV	IP	H	R	ER	HR	HB	BB	SO	RAT	ERA	ERA+	CERA	OAV	BH	AVG	PR+	WS	TPW
1992	Cal-A	1	1	.500	14	5	1	1	1	41^2	37	24	24	5	0	19	31	1.344	5.18	77	3.83	.236	0	....	-6	1	-0.6
1994	Cin-N	1	0	1.000	25	0	0	0	0	30	32	14	14	2	3	14	29	1.533	4.20	99	5.02	.288	1	.333	-0	1	0.0
1995	Chi-A	1	3	.250	37	0	0	0	0	38^2	30	24	24	7	0	19	24	1.267	5.59	80	3.65	.213	0	....	-4	1	-0.4
Total	3	3	4	.429	76	5	1	1	1	110^1	99	62	62	14	3	52	84	1.369	5.06	83	4.09	.242	1	.333	-10	3	-1.0

• FORTUNE, Gary Garrett Reese Fortune b: 10/11/1894, High Point, NC d: 9/23/1955, Washington, DC BB/TR, 5'11.5", 176 lbs. Deb: 10/5/1916

YEAR	TM-L	W	L	PCT	G	GS	CG	SH	SV	IP	H	R	ER	HR	HB	BB	SO	RAT	ERA	ERA+	CERA	OAV	BH	AVG	PR+	WS	TPW
1916	Phi-N	0	1	.000	1	1	0	0	0	5	2	2	2	0	0	4	3	1.200	3.60	73	1.59	.118	0	.000	-1	0	-0.1
1918	Phi-N	0	2	.000	5	2	1	0	0	31	41	30	28	2	1	19	10	1.935	8.13	37	6.50	.333	2	.200	-18	0	-1.9
1920	Bos-A	0	2	.000	14	3	1	0	0	41^2	46	32	27	0	0	23	10	1.656	5.83	62	4.35	.282	2	.167	-11	0	-1.1
Total	3	0	5	.000	20	6	2	0	0	77^2	89	64	57	2	1	46	23	1.738	6.61	49	5.03	.294	4	.167	-29	0	-3.1

• FOSNOW, Jerry Gerald Eugene Fosnow b: 9/21/1940, Deshler, OH BR/TL, 6'4", 195 lbs. Deb: 6/29/1964

YEAR	TM-L	W	L	PCT	G	GS	CG	SH	SV	IP	H	R	ER	HR	HB	BB	SO	RAT	ERA	ERA+	CERA	OAV	BH	AVG	PR+	WS	TPW
1964	Min-A	0	1	.000	7	0	0	0	0	10^2	13	13	13	3	0	8	9	1.969	10.97	33	8.08	.302	0	....	-9	0	-0.9
1965	Min-A	3	3	.500	29	0	0	0	2	46^2	33	29	23	7	1	25	35	1.243	4.44	80	3.24	.193	0	.000	-5	1	-0.6
Total	2	3	4	.429	36	0	0	0	2	57^1	46	42	36	10	1	33	44	1.378	5.65	63	4.14	.215	0	.000	-14	1	-1.5

• FOSS, Larry Larry Curtis Foss b: 4/18/1936, Castleton, KS BR/TR, 6'2", 187 lbs. Deb: 9/18/1961

YEAR	TM-L	W	L	PCT	G	GS	CG	SH	SV	IP	H	R	ER	HR	HB	BB	SO	RAT	ERA	ERA+	CERA	OAV	BH	AVG	PR+	WS	TPW
1961	Pit-N	1	1	.500	3	3	0	0	0	15^1	15	11	10	3	2	11	9	1.696	5.87	68	6.80	.273	1	.167	-3	0	-0.3
1962	NY-N	0	1	.000	5	1	0	0	0	11^2	17	6	6	2	1	7	3	2.057	4.63	90	9.03	.362	0	.000	-0	1	0.0
Total	2	1	2	.333	8	4	0	0	0	27	32	17	16	5	3	18	12	1.852	5.33	76	7.77	.314	1	.143	-4	1	-0.4

• FOSSAS, Tony Emilio Antonio (Morejon) Fossas b: 9/23/1957, Havana, Cuba BL/TL, 6', 187 lbs. Deb: 5/15/1988

YEAR	TM-L	W	L	PCT	G	GS	CG	SH	SV	IP	H	R	ER	HR	HB	BB	SO	RAT	ERA	ERA+	CERA	OAV	BH	AVG	PR+	WS	TPW
1988	Tex-A	0	0	....	5	0	0	0	0	5^2	11	3	3	0	0	2	0	2.294	4.76	86	9.33	.423	0	....	-0	0	0.0
1989	Mil-A	2	2	.500	51	0	0	0	1	61	57	27	24	3	1	22	42	1.295	3.54	108	3.13	.256	0	....	2	4	0.2
1990	Mil-A	2	3	.400	32	0	0	0	0	29^1	44	23	21	5	0	10	24	1.841	6.44	60	6.91	.331	0	....	-8	0	-0.8
1991	Bos-A	3	2	.600	64	0	0	0	1	57	49	27	22	3	3	28	29	1.351	3.47	124	3.29	.236	0	....	5	5	0.5
1992	Bos-A	1	2	.333	60	0	0	0	2	29^2	31	9	8	1	1	14	19	1.517	2.43	174	4.18	.279	0	....	6	4	0.6
1993	Bos-A	1	1	.500	71	0	0	0	0	40	38	28	23	4	2	15	39	1.325	5.18	89	3.65	.242	0	....	-3	2	-0.3
1994	Bos-A	2	0	1.000	44	0	0	0	1	34	35	18	18	6	1	15	31	1.471	4.76	105	5.00	.263	0	....	1	3	0.1
1995	StL-N	3	0	1.000	58	0	0	0	0	36^2	28	6	6	1	1	10	40	1.036	1.47	285	1.96	.214	0	....	11	7	1.0
1996*	StL-N	0	4	.000	65	0	0	0	2	47	43	19	14	7	0	21	36	1.362	2.68	156	3.85	.231	0	.000	7	4	0.7
1997	StL-N	2	7	.222	71	0	0	0	0	51^2	62	32	22	7	1	26	41	1.703	3.83	108	5.91	.298	0	....	2	2	0.2
1998	Sea-A	0	3	.000	23	0	0	0	0	11^1	19	11	11	1	0	6	10	2.206	8.74	53	9.20	.404	0	....	-5	0	-0.5
	Chi-N	0	0	....	8	0	0	0	0	4	8	4	4	0	0	6	6	3.500	9.00	49	14.34	.421	0	....	-2	0	-0.2
	Tex-A	1	0	1.000	10	0	0	0	0	7^1	3	0	0	0	0	4	7	.955	0.00	....	1.24	.120	0	....	4	1	0.4
	Yr.	1	3	.250	33	0	0	0	0	18^2	22	11	11	1	0	10	17	1.714	5.30	87	6.07	.306	0	....	-1	1	-0.1
1999	NY-A	0	0	....	5	0	0	0	0	1	6	4	4	1	0	1	0	7.000	36.00	13	57.05	.667	0	....	-3	0	-0.3
Total	12	17	24	.415	567	0	0	0	7	415^2	434	211	180	39	10	180	324	1.477	3.90	109	4.47	.269	0	.000	15	32	1.5

• FOSSUM, Casey Casey Paul Fossum b: 1/6/1978, Cherry Hill, NJ BB/TL, 6'1", 160 lbs. Deb: 7/28/2001

YEAR	TM-L	W	L	PCT	G	GS	CG	SH	SV	IP	H	R	ER	HR	HB	BB	SO	RAT	ERA	ERA+	CERA	OAV	BH	AVG	PR+	WS	TPW
2001	Bos-A	3	2	.600	13	7	0	0	0	44^1	44	26	24	4	6	20	26	1.444	4.87	92	4.70	.259	0	....	-1	2	-0.1
2002	Bos-A	5	4	.556	43	12	0	0	1	106^2	113	56	41	12	4	30	101	1.341	3.46	130	4.14	.268	0	....	11	6	1.0
2003	Bos-A	6	5	.545	19	14	0	0	1	79	82	55	48	9	4	34	63	1.468	5.47	83	4.77	.270	0	....	-6	3	-0.6
Total	3	14	11	.560	75	33	0	0	2	230	239	137	113	25	14	84	190	1.404	4.42	102	4.46	.267	0	....	3	11	0.3

• FOSTER, Alan Alan Benton Foster b: 12/8/1946, Pasadena, CA BR/TR, 6', 180 lbs. Deb: 4/25/1967

YEAR	TM-L	W	L	PCT	G	GS	CG	SH	SV	IP	H	R	ER	HR	HB	BB	SO	RAT	ERA	ERA+	CERA	OAV	BH	AVG	PR+	WS	TPW
1967	LA-N	0	1	.000	4	2	0	0	0	16^2	10	4	4	0	0	3	15	.780	2.16	143	1.09	.169	0	.000	2	1	0.2
1968	LA-N	1	1	.500	3	3	0	0	0	15^2	11	4	3	1	0	2	10	.830	1.72	160	1.56	.200	1	.250	2	2	0.2
1969	LA-N	3	9	.250	24	15	2	2	0	102^2	119	55	50	11	4	29	59	1.442	4.38	76	4.64	.290	2	.074	-13	1	-1.4
1970	LA-N	10	13	.435	33	33	7	1	0	198^2	200	104	94	22	2	81	83	1.414	4.26	90	4.26	.264	7	.109	-13	6	-1.5
1971	Cle-A	8	12	.400	36	26	3	0	0	181^2	158	93	84	19	4	82	97	1.321	4.16	92	3.62	.232	2	.039	-8	7	-1.3
1972	Cal-A	0	1	.000	8	0	0	0	0	12^2	12	8	7	3	2	6	11	1.421	4.97	58	5.62	.245	0	....	-3	0	-0.3
1973	StL-N	13	9	.591	35	29	6	2	0	203^2	195	82	71	17	5	63	106	1.267	3.14	116	3.46	.254	13	.191	11	11	1.3
1974	StL-N	7	10	.412	31	25	5	1	0	162^1	167	81	70	16	3	61	78	1.405	3.88	92	4.17	.268	8	.167	-8	7	-0.9
1975	SD-N	3	1	.750	17	4	1	0	0	44^2	41	14	12	1	0	21	20	1.388	2.42	144	3.14	.244	1	.091	6	5	0.5
1976	SD-N	3	6	.333	26	11	2	0	0	86^2	75	36	31	9	1	35	22	1.269	3.22	102	3.44	.235	1	.056	1	4	0.0
Total	10	48	63	.432	217	148	26	6	0	1025^1	988	481	426	99	21	383	501	1.337	3.74	96	3.82	.254	35	.119	-24	44	-3.3

• FOSTER, Ed Edward Lee "Slim" Foster b: 1885, GA d: 3/1/1929, Montgomery, AL BR/TR, 6'1" Deb: 7/31/1908

YEAR	TM-L	W	L	PCT	G	GS	CG	SH	SV	IP	H	R	ER	HR	HB	BB	SO	RAT	ERA	ERA+	CERA	OAV	BH	AVG	PR+	WS	TPW
1908	Cle-A	1	0	1.000	6	1	1	0	2	21	16	5	5	1	2	12	11	1.333	2.14	111	3.62	.229	0	.000	0	2	0.0

• FOSTER, John John Norman Foster b: 5/17/1978, Stockton, CA BL/TL, 6', 200 lbs. Deb: 4/24/2002

YEAR	TM-L	W	L	PCT	G	GS	CG	SH	SV	IP	H	R	ER	HR	HB	BB	SO	RAT	ERA	ERA+	CERA	OAV	BH	AVG	PR+	WS	TPW
2002	Atl-N	1	0	1.000	5	0	0	0	0	5	6	6	6	3	1	6	6	2.400	10.80	38	14.44	.286	0	....	-4	0	-0.4

YEAR TM-L	W	L	PCT	G	GS	CG	SH	SV	IP	H	R	ER	HR	HB	BB	SO	RAT	ERA	ERA+	CERA	OAV	BH	AVG	PR+	WS	TPW
2003 Mil-N	2	0	1.000	23	0	0	0	0	21	30	11	11	5	1	8	16	1.810	4.71	90	7.82	.341	0	....	-1	1	-0.1
Total 2	3	0	1.000	28	0	0	0	0	26	36	17	17	8	2	14	22	1.923	5.88	71	9.09	.330	0	....	-5	1	-0.4
• FOSTER, Kevin	Kevin Christopher Foster b: 1/13/1969, Evanston, IL BR/TR, 6'1", 170 lbs. Deb: 9/12/1993																									
1993 Phi-N	0	1	.000	2	1	0	0	0	6^{2}	13	11	11	3	0	7	6	3.000	14.85	27	16.83	.394	0	.000	-8	0	-0.8
1994 Chi-N	3	4	.429	13	13	0	0	0	81	70	31	26	7	1	35	75	1.296	2.89	144	3.46	.234	2	.074	11	6	0.9
1995 Chi-N	12	11	.522	30	28	0	0	0	167^{2}	149	90	84	32	6	65	146	1.276	4.51	91	4.18	.240	15	.250	-9	9	-0.3
1996 Chi-N	7	6	.538	17	16	1	0	0	87	98	63	60	16	2	35	53	1.529	6.21	70	5.50	.288	8	.296	-19	3	-1.4
1997 Chi-N	10	7	.588	26	25	1	0	0	146^{1}	141	79	75	27	2	66	118	1.415	4.61	93	4.67	.255	6	.128	-5	7	-0.6
1998 Chi-N	0	0	....	3	0	0	0	0	3^{1}	8	6	6	1	0	2	3	3.000	16.20	27	16.31	.500	0	....	-4	0	-0.4
2001 Tex-A	0	1	.000	9	0	0	0	0	17^{2}	21	14	13	2	3	10	16	1.755	6.62	70	6.96	.309	0	....	-4	0	-0.4
Total 7	32	30	.516	100	83	2	0	0	509^{2}	500	294	275	88	14	220	417	1.413	4.86	87	4.77	.259	31	.190	-38	25	-3.0
• FOSTER, Kris	John Kristian Foster b: 8/30/1974, Riverdale, NJ BR/TR, 6'1", 200 lbs. Deb: 8/3/2001																									
2001 Bal-A	0	0	....	7	0	0	0	0	10	9	4	3	1	0	8	8	1.700	2.70	159	4.97	.231	0	....	2	1	0.2
• FOSTER, Larry	Larry Lynn Foster b: 12/24/1937, Lansing, MI BL/TR, 6', 185 lbs. Deb: 9/18/1963																									
1963 Det-A	0	0	....	1	0	0	0	0	2	4	3	3	0	0	1	1	2.500	13.50	28	8.87	.364	0	....	-2	0	-0.2
• FOSTER, Rube	George Foster b: 1/5/1888, Lehigh, OK d: 3/1/1976, Bokoshe, OK BR/TR, 5'7.5", 170 lbs. Deb: 4/10/1913																									
1913 Bos-A	3	4	.429	19	8	4	1	0	68^{1}	64	35	24	1	4	28	36	1.346	3.16	93	3.34	.249	2	.095	-0	3	-0.2
1914 Bos-A	14	8	.636	32	27	17	5	0	211^{2}	164	68	40	2	7	52	89	1.020	1.70	158	1.96	.218	11	.175	19	18	2.2
1915* Bos-A	19	8	.704	37	33	21	5	1	255^{1}	217	83	60	3	10	86	82	1.187	2.11	131	2.67	.237	23	.277	17	25	2.6
1916* Bos-A	14	7	.667	33	19	9	3	2	182^{1}	173	73	62	0	4	86	53	1.420	3.06	90	3.54	.263	11	.177	-4	10	-0.4
1917 Bos-A	8	7	.533	17	16	9	1	0	124^{2}	108	43	35	0	4	53	34	1.291	2.53	102	2.88	.243	11	.268	-0	9	0.2
Total 5	58	34	.630	138	103	60	15	3	842^{1}	726	302	221	6	29	305	294	1.224	2.36	116	2.76	.240	58	.215	32	65	4.3
• FOSTER, Steve	Steven Eugene Foster b: 8/16/1966, Dallas, TX BR/TR, 6', 180 lbs. Deb: 8/22/1991																									
1991 Cin-N	0	0	....	11	0	0	0	0	14	7	5	3	1	0	4	11	.786	1.93	197	1.25	.143	0	....	3	1	0.3
1992 Cin-N	1	1	.500	31	1	0	0	2	50	52	16	16	4	0	13	34	1.300	2.88	125	3.61	.275	1	.200	4	4	0.4
1993 Cin-N	2	2	.500	17	0	0	0	0	25^{2}	23	8	5	1	1	5	16	1.091	1.75	229	2.38	.235	0	....	7	3	0.7
Total 3	3	3	.500	59	1	0	0	2	89^{2}	82	29	24	6	1	22	61	1.160	2.41	154	2.89	.244	1	.200	13	8	1.4
• FOUCAULT, Steve	Steven Raymond Foucault b: 10/3/1949, Duluth, MN BL/TR, 6', 205 lbs. Deb: 4/7/1973																									
1973 Tex-A	2	4	.333	32	0	0	0	8	55^{2}	54	26	24	6	3	31	28	1.527	3.88	96	4.79	.262	0	....	0	3	0.0
1974 Tex-A	8	9	.471	69	0	0	0	12	144^{1}	123	51	36	8	5	40	106	1.129	2.24	159	2.66	.234	0	....	21	15	2.2
1975 Tex-A	8	4	.667	59	0	0	0	10	107	96	57	49	10	4	55	56	1.411	4.12	91	3.84	.249	0	....	-4	7	-0.4
1976 Tex-A	8	8	.500	46	0	0	0	5	75^{2}	68	31	28	9	4	25	41	1.229	3.33	108	3.45	.249	0	....	2	6	0.2
1977 Det-A	7	7	.500	44	0	0	0	13	74^{1}	64	29	26	7	0	17	58	1.090	3.15	136	2.54	.226	0	....	10	10	1.0
1978 Det-A	2	4	.333	24	0	0	0	4	37^{1}	48	18	13	1	1	21	18	1.848	3.13	123	5.75	.324	0	....	2	2	0.3
KC-A	0	0	....	3	0	0	0	0	2^{1}	5	1	1	0	0	1	0	2.571	3.86	99	9.38	.417	0	....	-0	0	0.0
Yr.	2	4	.333	27	0	0	0	4	39^{2}	53	19	14	1	1	22	18	1.891	3.18	122	5.96	.331	0	....	2	2	0.3
Total 6	35	36	.493	277	0	0	0	52	496^{2}	458	213	177	41	17	190	307	1.305	3.21	117	3.52	.250	0	....	31	43	3.2
• FOULKE, Keith	Keith Charles Foulke b: 10/19/1972, San Diego, CA BR/TR, 6', 195 lbs. Deb: 5/21/1997																									
1997 SF-N	1	5	.167	11	8	0	0	0	44^{2}	60	41	41	9	4	18	33	1.746	8.26	49	7.41	.324	2	.154	-21	0	-2.1
Chi-A	3	0	1.000	16	0	0	0	3	28^{2}	28	11	11	4	0	5	21	1.151	3.45	127	3.27	.255	0	....	3	4	0.3
1998 Chi-A	3	2	.600	54	0	0	0	1	65^{1}	51	31	30	9	4	20	57	1.087	4.13	110	2.95	.213	0	....	3	5	0.3
1999 Chi-A	3	3	.500	67	0	0	0	9	105^{1}	72	28	26	11	3	21	123	.883	2.22	219	1.80	.188	0	.000	32	16	2.9
2000* Chi-A	3	1	.750	72	0	0	0	34	88	66	31	29	9	2	22	91	1.000	2.97	168	2.28	.207	0	....	18	16	1.7
2001 Chi-A	4	9	.308	72	0	0	0	42	81	57	21	21	3	8	22	75	.975	2.33	197	2.06	.199	0	....	20	17	1.9
2002 Chi-A	2	4	.333	65	0	0	0	11	77^{2}	65	26	25	7	2	13	58	1.004	2.90	157	2.38	.225	0	.000	14	10	1.3
2003* Oak-A★	9	1	.900	72	0	0	0	**43**	86^{2}	57	21	20	10	7	20	88	.888	2.08	217	2.07	.184	0	....	23	21	2.2
Total 7	28	25	.528	429	8	0	0	143	577^{1}	456	210	203	62	30	141	546	1.034	3.16	143	2.67	.215	2	.125	93	89	8.6
• FOURNIER, Henry	Julius Henry "Frenchy" Fournier b: 8/8/1865, Syracuse, NY d: 12/8/1945, Eloise, MI TL Deb: 8/22/1894																									
1894 Cin-N	1	3	.250	6	4	4	0	0	45	71	51	27	4	2	20	5	2.022	5.40	103	7.77	.354	2	.105	1	1	-0.2
• FOUTZ, Dave	David Luther "Scissors" Foutz b: 9/7/1856, Carroll County, MD d: 3/5/1897, Waverly, MD BR/TR, 6'2", 161 lbs. Deb: 7/29/1884 M ♦																									
1884 StL-a	15	6	.714	25	25	19	2	0	206^{2}	167	100	50	7	9	36	95	.982	2.18	149	....	.209	27	.227	19	19	1.6
1885* StL-a	33	14	.702	47	46	46	2	0	407^{2}	351	200	119	8	18	92	147	1.087	2.63	124	....	.223	59	.248	17	37	1.8
1886* StL-a	**41**	16	.719	59	57	55	11	**1**	504	418	216	118	5	10	144	283	1.115	**2.11**	**163**	....	.215	116	.280	**71**	**62**	7.0
1887* StL-a	25	12	.676	40	38	36	1	0	339^{1}	459	244	146	7	10	90	94	1.353	3.87	117	....	.312	174	.390	17	43	3.0
1888 Bro-a	12	7	.632	23	19	19	0	0	176	146	85	49	3	5	35	73	1.028	2.51	119	....	.218	156	.277	9	33	1.8
1889* Bro-a	3	0	1.000	12	4	3	0	0	59^{2}	70	50	29	2	0	19	21	1.492	4.37	85	....	.284	152	.275	-4	24	-0.2
1890* Bro-N	2	1	.667	5	2	2	0	**2**	29	29	10	6	0	1	6	4	1.207	1.86	184	....	.253	154	.303	5	27	2.0
1891 Bro-N	3	2	.600	6	5	5	0	0	52	51	24	19	1	1	16	14	1.288	3.29	100	....	.247	134	.257	1	16	-1.1
1892 Bro-N	13	8	.619	27	20	17	0	1	203	210	119	77	3	4	63	56	1.345	3.41	93	3.33	.257	41	.186	-6	13	-1.6
1893 Bro-N	0	0	....	6	0	0	0	0	18	28	17	15	2	0	8	3	2.000	7.50	59	7.64	.345	137	.246	-6	10	-3.4
1894 Bro-N	0	0	....	1	0	0	0	0	2	4	3	3	0	0	1	0	2.500	13.50	37	9.81	.410	90	.303	-2	6	-0.8
Total 11	147	66	.690	251	216	202	16	4	1997^{1}	1933	1068	631	38	58	510	790	1.178	2.84	124	0.42	.244	1276	.280	122	290	10.1
• FOWLER, Art	John Arthur Fowler b: 7/3/1922, Converse, SC BR/TR, 5'11", 180 lbs. Deb: 4/17/1954 C																									
1954 Cin-N	12	10	.545	40	29	8	1	0	227^{2}	256	112	97	20	4	85	93	1.498	3.83	109	4.59	.286	6	.100	7	14	0.5
1955 Cin-N	11	10	.524	46	28	8	3	2	207^{2}	198	96	90	20	1	63	94	1.257	3.90	109	3.42	.250	12	.200	8	13	0.7
1956 Cin-N	11	11	.500	45	23	8	0	1	177^{2}	191	92	80	15	0	35	86	1.272	4.05	98	3.60	.278	7	.146	0	10	0.1
1957 Cin-N	3	0	1.000	33	7	1	0	0	87^{2}	111	65	63	11	2	24	45	1.540	6.47	64	5.33	.310	3	.176	-23	0	-2.3
1959 LA-N	3	4	.429	36	0	0	0	2	61	70	39	36	8	0	23	47	1.525	5.31	80	4.84	.294	1	.083	-8	1	-0.8
1961 LA-A	5	8	.385	53	3	0	0	11	89	68	42	36	12	0	29	78	1.090	3.64	124	2.70	.209	1	.077	10	10	0.8
1962 LA-A	4	3	.571	48	0	0	0	5	77	67	25	24	6	1	25	38	1.195	2.81	137	2.93	.234	3	.273	10	8	1.0
1963 LA-A	5	3	.625	57	0	0	0	10	89^{1}	70	26	24	5	0	19	53	.996	2.42	142	1.95	.219	2	.222	10	11	1.1
1964 LA-A	0	2	.000	4	0	0	0	1	7	8	8	8	2	1	5	5	1.857	10.29	32	7.94	.296	0	.000	-5	0	-0.6
Total 9	54	51	.514	362	90	25	4	32	1024	1039	505	458	99	9	308	539	1.315	4.03	102	3.76	.265	35	.152	8	67	0.6
• FOWLER, Dick	Richard John Fowler b: 3/30/1921, Toronto, Canada d: 5/22/1972, Oneonta, NY BR/TR, 6'4.5", 215 lbs. Deb: 9/13/1941																									
1941 Phi-A	1	2	.333	4	3	1	0	0	24	26	11	9	4	0	8	8	1.417	3.38	124	4.82	.289	0	.000	2	2	0.1
1942 Phi-A	6	11	.353	31	17	4	0	1	140	159	90	77	13	0	45	38	1.457	4.95	76	4.44	.287	8	.160	-15	3	-1.7
1945 Phi-A	1	2	.333	7	3	2	1	0	37^{1}	41	21	20	1	0	18	21	1.580	4.82	71	4.28	.283	8	.444	-6	2	-0.2
1946 Phi-A	9	16	.360	32	28	14	1	0	205^{2}	213	101	75	16	2	75	89	1.400	3.28	108	3.86	.263	13	.183	7	11	0.7
1947 Phi-A	12	11	.522	36	31	16	3	0	227^{1}	210	77	71	12	3	85	75	1.298	2.81	136	3.26	.249	14	.171	19	18	1.7
1948 Phi-A	15	8	.652	29	26	16	2	2	204^{2}	221	93	86	15	4	76	50	1.451	3.78	113	4.28	.281	14	.171	10	17	0.8
1949 Phi-A	15	11	.577	31	28	15	4	1	213^{2}	210	108	89	13	2	115	43	1.521	3.75	110	4.21	.263	18	.234	4	14	0.6
1950 Phi-A	1	5	.167	11	9	2	0	0	66^{2}	75	52	48	7	3	56	15	1.965	6.48	70	6.84	.300	5	.192	-14	0	-1.4
1951 Phi-A	5	11	.313	22	22	4	0	0	125	141	89	78	11	1	72	29	1.704	5.62	76	5.38	.291	8	.190	-21	2	-2.0
1952 Phi-A	1	2	.333	18	3	1	0	0	58^{2}	71	43	42	4	4	28	14	1.688	6.44	61	5.48	.302	0	.000	-15	0	-1.8
Total 10	66	79	.455	221	170	75	11	4	1303	1367	685	595	96	19	578	382	1.493	4.11	97	4.34	.273	88	.186	-28	69	-3.4
• FOWLER, Jesse	Jesse Peter "Pete" Fowler b: 10/30/1898, Spartanburg, SC d: 9/23/1973, Columbia, SC BR/TL, 5'10.5", 158 lbs. Deb: 7/29/1924																									
1924 StL-N	1	1	.500	13	3	0	0	0	32^{2}	28	21	16	0	2	18	5	1.408	4.41	86	3.11	.226	2	.222	-2	1	-0.2

YEAR TM-L	W	L	PCT	G	GS	CG	SH	SV	IP	H	R	ER	HR	HB	BB	SO	RAT	ERA	ERA+	CERA	OAV	BH	AVG	PR+	WS	TPW
• FOWLKES, Alan	Alan Kim Fowlkes b: 8/8/1958, Brawley, CA BR/TR, 6'2", 190 lbs. Deb: 4/7/1982																									
1982 SF-N	4	2	.667	21	15	1	0	0	85	111	55	49	12	5	24	50	1.588	5.19	69	5.87	.321	3	.115	-13	0	-1.5
1985 Cal-A	0	0	....	2	0	0	0	0	7	8	7	7	4	0	4	5	1.714	9.00	46	9.23	.276	0	....	-4	0	-0.4
Total 2	**4**	**2**	**.667**	**23**	**15**	**1**	**0**	**0**	**92**	**119**	**62**	**56**	**16**	**5**	**28**	**55**	**1.598**	**5.48**	**67**	**6.13**	**.317**	**3**	**.115**	**-17**	**0**	**-1.9**
• FOX, Chad	Chad Douglas Fox b: 9/3/1970, Coronado, CA BR/TR, 6'2", 175 lbs. Deb: 7/13/1997																									
1997 Atl-N	0	1	.000	30	0	0	0	0	27^{1}	24	12	10	4	0	16	28	1.463	3.29	128	4.44	.231	0	....	3	2	0.3
1998 Mil-N	1	4	.200	49	0	0	0	0	57	56	27	25	4	1	20	64	1.333	3.95	108	3.66	.260	0	.000	1	4	0.1
1999 Mil-N	0	0	....	6	0	0	0	0	6^{2}	11	8	8	1	1	4	12	2.250	10.80	42	9.96	.355	0	.000	-5	0	-0.4
2001 Mil-N	5	2	.714	65	0	0	0	2	66^{2}	44	16	14	6	5	36	80	1.200	1.89	227	2.75	.181	0	.000	17	9	1.7
2002 Mil-N	1	0	1.000	3	0	0	0	0	4^{2}	6	3	3	0	0	5	3	2.357	5.79	71	7.03	.316	0	....	-1	0	-0.1
2003 Bos-A	1	2	.333	17	0	0	0	3	18	19	10	9	2	1	17	19	2.000	4.50	101	6.42	.264	0	....	0	1	0.0
*Fla-N	2	1	.667	21	0	0	0	0	25^{1}	16	6	6	1	0	14	27	1.184	2.13	192	2.18	.190	0	....	5	4	0.5
Total 6	**10**	**10**	**.500**	**191**	**0**	**0**	**0**	**5**	**205^{2}**	**176**	**82**	**75**	**18**	**8**	**112**	**233**	**1.400**	**3.28**	**131**	**3.81**	**.229**	**0**	**.000**	**22**	**20**	**2.1**
• FOX, Henry	Henry Fox b: 11/18/1874, Scranton, PA d: 6/6/1927, Scranton, PA Deb: 9/4/1902																									
1902 Phi-N	0	0	....	1	0	0	0	1	1	2	3	2	0	0	1	1	3.000	18.00	16	11.94	.413	0	....	-2	0	-0.2
• FOX, Howie	Howard Francis Fox b: 3/1/1921, Coburg, OR d: 10/9/1955, San Antonio, TX BR/TR, 6'3", 210 lbs. Deb: 9/28/1944																									
1944 Cin-N	0	0	....	2	0	0	0	0	2^{1}	2	0	0	0	0	0	0	.857	0.00	....	1.44	.222	0	.000	1	0	0.1
1945 Cin-N	8	13	.381	45	15	7	0	0	164^{1}	169	102	90	6	6	77	54	1.497	4.93	76	4.03	.268	13	.283	-21	4	-1.8
1946 Cin-N	0	0	....	4	0	0	0	0	5	12	13	10	2	0	5	1	3.400	18.00	19	19.84	.462	0	....	-8	0	-0.9
1948 Cin-N	6	9	.400	34	24	5	0	1	171	185	100	86	11	1	62	63	1.444	4.53	86	4.11	.280	12	.200	-9	7	-0.7
1949 Cin-N	6	19	.240	38	30	9	0	0	215	221	120	95	13	4	77	60	1.386	3.98	105	3.76	.265	17	.236	5	9	0.7
1950 Cin-N	11	8	.579	34	22	10	1	1	187	196	97	90	14	2	85	64	1.503	4.33	98	4.32	.269	11	.175	0	12	0.0
1951 Cin-N	9	14	.391	40	30	9	4	2	228	239	105	97	16	2	69	57	1.351	3.83	107	3.78	.272	8	.114	7	13	0.5
1952 Phi-N	2	7	.222	13	11	2	0	0	62	70	41	35	8	0	26	16	1.548	5.08	72	5.02	.287	1	.048	-11	0	-1.3
1954 Bal-A	1	2	.333	38	0	0	0	2	73^{2}	80	33	30	2	2	34	27	1.548	3.67	98	4.37	.289	4	.250	-0	4	0.1
Total 9	**43**	**72**	**.374**	**248**	**132**	**42**	**5**	**6**	**1108^{1}**	**1174**	**611**	**533**	**72**	**17**	**435**	**342**	**1.452**	**4.33**	**91**	**4.13**	**.274**	**66**	**.189**	**-36**	**49**	**-3.3**
• FOX, John	John Joseph Fox b: 2/7/1859, Roxbury, MA d: 4/18/1893, Boston, MA Deb: 6/2/1881 ◆																									
1881 Bos-N	6	8	.429	17	16	12	0	0	124^{1}	144	90	46	0	....	39	30	**1.472**	3.33	80	....	.278	21	.178	-9	4	-1.8
1883 Bal-a	6	13	.316	20	19	18	0	0	165^{1}	209	140	74	2	....	32	49	1.458	4.03	86	....	.290	14	.152	-1	6	-0.6
1884 Pit-a	1	6	.143	7	7	7	0	0	59	76	59	37	2	3	16	22	1.559	5.64	60	....	.297	6	.240	-13	1	-1.2
1886 Was-N	0	1	.000	1	1	1	0	0	8	11	13	8	0	....	11	3	2.750	9.00	36	....	.315	1	.333	-5	0	-0.4
Total 4	**13**	**28**	**.317**	**45**	**43**	**38**	**0**	**0**	**356^{2}**	**440**	**302**	**165**	**4**	**3**	**98**	**104**	**1.508**	**4.16**	**76**	**....**	**.287**	**42**	**.176**	**-29**	**11**	**-4.0**
• FOX, Terry	Terrence Edward Fox b: 7/31/1935, Chicago, IL BR/TR, 6', 175 lbs. Deb: 9/4/1960																									
1960 Mil-N	0	0	....	5	0	0	0	0	8^{1}	6	5	4	0	0	6	5	1.440	4.32	79	3.06	.200	0	.000	-1	0	-0.1
1961 Det-A	5	2	.714	39	0	0	0	12	57^{1}	42	12	9	6	3	16	32	1.012	1.41	291	2.41	.200	2	.167	17	11	1.7
1962 Det-A	3	1	.750	44	0	0	0	16	58	48	13	11	2	1	16	23	1.103	1.71	238	2.24	.227	2	.250	16	12	1.8
1963 Det-A	8	6	.571	46	0	0	0	11	80^{1}	81	37	32	9	2	20	35	1.257	3.59	104	3.64	.263	1	.091	1	7	0.1
1964 Det-A	4	3	.571	32	0	0	0	5	61	77	26	23	4	1	16	28	1.525	3.39	108	4.82	.316	3	.250	2	5	0.3
1965 Det-A	6	4	.600	42	0	0	0	10	77^{2}	59	26	24	7	3	31	34	1.159	2.78	125	2.87	.214	0	.000	6	9	0.6
1966 Det-A	0	1	.000	4	0	0	0	1	10	9	8	7	3	0	2	6	1.100	6.30	55	3.91	.243	0	.000	-3	0	-0.4
Phi-N	3	2	.600	36	0	0	0	4	44^{1}	57	22	22	3	2	17	22	1.669	4.47	80	5.36	.322	0	.000	-4	2	-0.5
Total 7	**29**	**19**	**.604**	**248**	**0**	**0**	**0**	**59**	**397**	**379**	**149**	**132**	**34**	**12**	**124**	**185**	**1.267**	**2.99**	**123**	**3.48**	**.254**	**8**	**.123**	**34**	**46**	**3.5**
• FOXEN, Bill	William Aloysius Foxen b: 5/31/1884, Tenafly, NJ d: 4/17/1937, Brooklyn, NY BL/TL, 5'11.5", 165 lbs. Deb: 5/5/1908																									
1908 Phi-N	7	7	.500	22	16	10	2	0	147^{1}	126	45	32	2	8	53	52	1.215	1.95	123	2.84	.240	5	.094	6	10	0.4
1909 Phi-N	3	7	.300	18	7	5	1	0	83^{1}	65	40	31	0	4	32	37	1.164	3.35	77	2.38	.219	5	.208	-8	4	-0.5
1910 Phi-N	5	5	.500	16	9	5	0	0	77^{2}	73	30	22	2	3	40	33	1.455	2.55	122	4.00	.268	4	.174	4	5	0.4
Chi-N	0	0	....	2	0	0	0	0	5	7	5	5	0	0	3	2	2.000	9.00	32	6.67	.350	0	.000	-3	0	-0.4
Yr.	5	5	.500	18	9	5	0	0	82^{2}	80	35	27	2	3	43	35	1.488	2.94	104	4.16	.274	4	.160	1	5	0.0
1911 Chi-N	1	1	.500	3	1	0	0	0	13	12	6	3	0	0	12	6	1.846	2.08	159	4.82	.255	1	.250	2	1	0.2
Total 4	**16**	**20**	**.444**	**61**	**33**	**20**	**3**	**0**	**326^{1}**	**283**	**126**	**93**	**4**	**15**	**140**	**130**	**1.296**	**2.56**	**104**	**3.14**	**.244**	**15**	**.142**	**-0**	**20**	**0.1**
• FOXX, Jimmie	James Emory "Beast,Double X" Foxx b: 10/22/1907, Sudlersville, MD d: 7/21/1967, Miami, FL BR/TR, 6', 195 lbs. Deb: 5/1/1925 C HOF: 1951 ◆																									
1939 Bos-A★	0	0	....	1	0	0	0	0	1	0	0	0	0	0	0	1	.000	0.00	....	0.00	.000	168	.360	1	30	4.5
1945 Phi-N	1	0	1.000	9	2	0	0	0	22^{2}	13	4	4	0	1	14	10	1.191	1.59	241	2.00	.171	60	.268	6	8	0.7
Total 2	**1**	**0**	**1.000**	**10**	**2**	**0**	**0**	**0**	**23^{2}**	**13**	**4**	**4**	**0**	**1**	**14**	**11**	**1.141**	**1.52**	**252**	**1.92**	**.171**	**2646**	**.325**	**7**	**38**	**5.3**
• FOYTACK, Paul	Paul Eugene Foytack b: 11/16/1930, Scranton, PA BR/TR, 5'11", 180 lbs. Deb: 4/21/1953																									
1953 Det-A	0	0	....	6	0	0	0	0	9^{2}	15	12	12	1	1	9	7	2.483	11.17	36	10.37	.375	0	.000	-7	0	-0.8
1955 Det-A	0	1	.000	22	1	0	0	0	49^{2}	48	29	29	4	0	36	38	1.691	5.26	73	4.93	.259	1	.091	-8	1	-0.9
1956 Det-A	15	13	.536	43	33	16	1	1	256	211	114	102	24	2	142	184	1.379	3.59	115	3.68	.226	11	.122	15	15	0.9
1957 Det-A	14	11	.560	38	27	8	1	1	212	175	79	74	19	4	104	118	1.316	3.14	123	3.37	.226	14	.222	15	18	1.6
1958 Det-A	15	13	.536	39	33	16	2	1	230	198	98	88	23	3	77	135	1.196	3.44	117	3.15	.233	18	.240	13	16	1.6
1959 Det-A	14	14	.500	39	**37**	11	2	1	240^{1}	239	137	124	34	2	64	110	1.261	4.64	88	3.84	.259	9	.111	-16	9	-1.9
1960 Det-A	2	11	.154	28	13	1	0	2	96^{2}	108	70	66	11	0	49	38	1.624	6.14	67	5.26	.286	7	.280	-21	0	-1.9
1961 Det-A	11	10	.524	32	20	6	0	0	169^{2}	152	81	74	27	2	56	89	1.226	3.93	105	3.70	.238	12	.222	3	10	0.5
1962 Det-A	10	7	.588	29	21	5	1	0	143^{2}	145	80	70	18	1	86	63	1.608	4.39	93	5.07	.259	6	.143	-4	6	-0.5
1963 Det-A	0	1	.000	9	0	0	0	1	17^{2}	18	18	17	4	0	8	7	1.472	8.66	43	5.27	.265	0	.000	-10	0	-1.0
LA-A	5	5	.500	25	8	0	0	0	70^{1}	68	35	29	9	0	29	37	1.379	3.71	92	4.03	.255	4	.267	-2	3	-0.1
Yr.	5	6	.455	34	8	0	0	1	88	86	53	46	13	0	37	44	1.398	4.70	75	4.28	.257	4	.211	-12	3	-1.1
1964 LA-A	0	1	.000	2	0	0	0	0	2^{1}	4	4	4	2	0	2	1	2.571	15.43	21	17.09	.364	0	....	-3	0	-0.3
Total 11	**86**	**87**	**.497**	**312**	**193**	**63**	**7**	**7**	**1498**	**1381**	**757**	**689**	**176**	**15**	**662**	**827**	**1.364**	**4.14**	**97**	**3.96**	**.246**	**82**	**.178**	**-24**	**78**	**-2.8**
• FRAILING, Ken	Kenneth Douglas Frailing b: 1/19/1948, Madison, WI BL/TL, 6', 190 lbs. Deb: 9/1/1972																									
1972 Chi-A	1	0	1.000	4	0	0	0	0	3	3	1	1	1	0	1	1	1.333	3.00	104	5.31	.250	0	....	0	0	0.0
1973 Chi-A	0	0	....	10	0	0	0	0	18^{1}	18	6	4	1	1	7	15	1.364	1.96	201	3.75	.254	0	....	4	2	0.4
1974 Chi-N	6	9	.400	55	16	1	0	1	125^{1}	150	65	54	11	1	43	71	1.540	3.88	98	4.79	.296	8	.258	5	7	0.7
1975 Chi-N	2	5	.286	41	0	0	0	1	53	61	37	32	6	2	26	39	1.642	5.43	71	5.47	.293	1	.143	-8	1	-0.8
1976 Chi-N	1	2	.333	6	3	0	0	0	18^{2}	20	7	5	0	0	5	10	1.339	2.41	160	3.28	.274	0	.000	3	2	0.3
Total 5	**10**	**16**	**.385**	**116**	**19**	**1**	**0**	**2**	**218^{1}**	**252**	**116**	**96**	**19**	**4**	**82**	**136**	**1.530**	**3.96**	**97**	**4.74**	**.290**	**9**	**.220**	**5**	**12**	**0.6**
• FRANCE, Ossie	Osman Beverly "O. B." France b: 10/4/1858, Greensburg, OH d: 5/2/1947, Akron, OH BL/TL, 5'8", 155 lbs. Deb: 7/14/1890																									
1890 Chi-N	0	0	....	1	0	0	0	0	2	3	3	3	0	0	2	0	2.500	13.50	27	....	.337	0	.000	-2	0	-0.2
• FRANCIS, Earl	Earl Coleman Francis b: 7/14/1935, Slab Fork, WV d: 7/3/2002, Pittsburgh, PA BR/TR, 6'2", 215 lbs. Deb: 6/30/1960																									
1960 Pit-N	1	0	1.000	7	0	0	0	0	18	14	5	4	0	1	4	8	1.000	2.00	188	1.98	.222	0	.000	3	2	0.3
1961 Pit-N	2	8	.200	23	15	0	0	0	102^{2}	110	60	48	4	1	47	53	1.529	4.21	95	4.15	.274	3	.107	-3	3	-0.4
1962 Pit-N	9	8	.529	36	23	5	1	0	176	153	68	60	8	2	83	121	1.341	3.07	128	3.24	.235	10	.164	15	13	1.6
1963 Pit-N	4	6	.400	33	13	0	0	0	97^{1}	107	59	49	6	4	43	72	1.541	4.53	73	4.53	.284	8	.308	-14	1	-1.2
1964 Pit-N	0	1	.000	2	1	0	0	0	6^{1}	7	7	6	2	1	1	6	1.263	8.53	41	5.75	.269	0	.000	-3	0	-0.4
1965 StL-N	0	0	....	2	0	0	0	0	5^{1}	7	4	3	1	0	3	3	1.875	5.06	76	6.46	.318	0	.000	-1	0	-0.1
Total 6	**16**	**23**	**.410**	**103**	**52**	**5**	**1**	**0**	**405^{2}**	**398**	**203**	**170**	**21**	**9**	**181**	**263**	**1.427**	**3.77**	**99**	**3.80**	**.258**	**21**	**.172**	**-3**	**19**	**-0.1**
• FRANCIS, Ray	Ray James Francis b: 3/8/1893, Sherman, TX d: 7/6/1934, Atlanta, GA BL/TL, 6'1.5", 182 lbs. Deb: 4/18/1922																									
1922 Was-A	7	18	.280	39	26	15	2	2	225	265	136	107	7	6	66	64	1.471	4.28	90	4.20	.303	13	.167	-17	6	-1.8

YEAR	TM-L	W	L	PCT	G	GS	CG	SH	SV	IP	H	R	ER	HR	HB	BB	SO	RAT	ERA	ERA+	CERA	OAV	BH	AVG	PR+	WS	TPW
1923	Det-A	5	8	.385	33	6	0	0	1	79^1	95	51	39	2	4	28	27	1.550	4.42	87	4.55	.308	3	.143	-4	3	-0.6
1925	NY-A	0	0	....	4	0	0	0	0	4^2	5	4	4	0	1	3	1	1.714	7.71	55	5.09	.278	0	....	-2	0	-0.2
	Bos-A	0	2	.000	6	4	0	0	0	28	44	29	24	3	1	13	4	2.036	7.71	59	7.85	.373	1	.125	-9	0	-0.8
	Yr.	0	2	.000	10	4	0	0	0	32^2	49	33	28	3	2	16	5	1.990	7.71	58	7.45	.360	1	.125	-11	0	-1.0
Total	3	12	28	.300	82	36	15	2	3	337	409	220	174	12	12	110	96	1.540	4.65	85	4.60	.310	17	.159	-32	9	-3.4

• FRANCO, John John Anthony Franco b: 9/17/1960, Brooklyn, NY BL/TL, 5'10", 185 lbs. Deb: 4/24/1984

YEAR	TM-L	W	L	PCT	G	GS	CG	SH	SV	IP	H	R	ER	HR	HB	BB	SO	RAT	ERA	ERA+	CERA	OAV	BH	AVG	PR+	WS	TPW
1984	Cin-N	6	2	.750	54	0	0	0	4	79^1	74	28	23	3	2	36	55	1.387	2.61	145	3.58	.256	0	.000	11	9	1.1
1985	Cin-N	12	3	.800	67	0	0	0	12	99	83	27	24	5	1	40	61	1.242	2.18	173	2.86	.234	2	.333	17	16	1.8
1986	Cin-N★	6	6	.500	74	0	0	0	29	101	90	40	33	7	2	44	84	1.327	2.94	131	3.30	.242	0	.000	11	15	1.1
1987	Cin-N★	8	5	.615	68	0	0	0	32	82	76	26	23	6	0	27	61	1.256	2.52	168	3.10	.245	0	.000	15	15	1.5
1988	Cin-N	6	6	.500	70	0	0	0	**39**	86	60	18	15	3	0	27	46	1.012	1.57	228	1.82	.198	0	.000	18	20	1.9
1989	Cin-N★	4	8	.333	60	0	0	0	32	80^2	77	35	28	3	0	36	60	1.401	3.12	115	3.42	.258	1	.333	5	10	0.6
1990	NY-N★	5	3	.625	55	0	0	0	**33**	67^2	66	22	19	4	0	21	56	1.286	2.53	148	3.24	.252	0	.000	10	11	1.0
1991	NY-N	5	9	.357	52	0	0	0	30	55^1	61	27	18	2	1	18	45	1.428	2.93	124	3.73	.271	0	.000	6	8	0.6
1992	NY-N	6	2	.750	31	0	0	0	15	33	24	6	6	1	0	11	20	1.061	1.64	212	2.00	.209	0	.000	7	8	0.8
1993	NY-N	4	3	.571	35	0	0	0	10	36^1	46	24	21	6	1	19	29	1.789	5.20	77	6.62	.313	0	.000	-5	1	-0.5
1994	NY-N	1	4	.200	47	0	0	0	**30**	50	47	20	15	2	1	19	42	1.320	2.70	155	3.27	.244	0	.000	8	8	0.8
1995	NY-N	5	3	.625	48	0	0	0	29	51^2	48	17	14	4	0	17	41	1.258	2.44	166	3.26	.251	0	....	9	10	0.9
1996	NY-N	4	3	.571	51	0	0	0	28	54	54	15	11	2	0	21	48	1.389	1.83	219	3.53	.260	0	.000	13	10	1.2
1997	NY-N	5	3	.625	59	0	0	0	36	60	49	18	17	3	1	20	53	1.150	2.55	158	2.57	.226	0	....	9	12	0.9
1998	NY-N	0	8	.000	61	0	0	0	38	64^2	66	28	26	4	4	29	59	1.469	3.62	114	4.11	.267	0	.000	4	8	0.3
1999*	NY-N	0	2	.000	46	0	0	0	19	40^2	40	14	13	1	2	19	41	1.451	2.88	152	3.77	.255	0	....	7	6	0.6
2000*	NY-N	5	4	.556	62	0	0	0	4	55^2	46	24	21	6	2	26	56	1.293	3.40	130	3.36	.221	0	.000	7	7	0.6
2001	NY-N	6	2	.750	58	0	0	0	2	53^1	55	25	24	8	2	19	50	1.388	4.05	102	4.50	.264	0	....	0	5	0.0
2003	NY-N	0	3	.000	38	0	0	0	2	34^1	35	11	10	5	1	13	16	1.398	2.62	158	4.48	.265	0	....	6	3	0.6
Total	19	88	79	.527	1036	0	0	0	424	1184^2	1097	425	361	75	20	462	923	1.316	2.74	144	3.37	.247	3	.088	156	182	15.7

• FRANKHOUSE, Fred Frederick Meloy Frankhouse b: 4/9/1904, Port Royal, PA d: 8/17/1989, Port Royal, PA BR/TR, 5'11", 175 lbs. Deb: 9/11/1927

YEAR	TM-L	W	L	PCT	G	GS	CG	SH	SV	IP	H	R	ER	HR	HB	BB	SO	RAT	ERA	ERA+	CERA	OAV	BH	AVG	PR+	WS	TPW
1927	StL-N	5	1	.833	6	6	5	1	0	50	41	18	15	2	1	16	20	1.140	2.70	146	2.33	.218	5	.250	6	5	0.6
1928	StL-N	3	2	.600	21	10	1	0	1	84	91	47	37	6	5	36	29	1.512	3.96	101	4.57	.277	5	.185	-0	4	0.0
1929	StL-N	7	2	.778	30	12	6	0	1	133^1	149	70	61	9	4	43	37	1.440	4.12	113	4.29	.289	15	.288	8	11	1.1
1930	StL-N	2	3	.400	8	1	0	0	0	19^2	31	16	16	1	0	11	4	2.136	7.32	69	8.00	.373	0	.000	-5	0	-0.5
	Bos-N	7	6	.538	27	11	3	1	0	110^2	138	72	69	13	2	43	30	1.636	5.61	88	5.70	.313	14	.359	-8	7	-0.4
	Yr.	9	9	.500	35	12	3	1	0	130^1	169	88	85	14	2	54	34	1.711	5.87	84	6.04	.323	14	.318	-13	7	-0.9
1931	Bos-N	8	8	.500	26	15	6	0	1	127^1	125	64	57	4	3	43	50	1.319	4.03	94	3.24	.252	6	.150	-3	8	-0.3
1932	Bos-N	4	6	.400	37	6	3	0	0	108^2	113	56	43	7	3	45	35	1.454	3.56	106	4.11	.278	3	.100	2	5	0.1
1933	Bos-N	16	15	.516	43	30	14	2	2	244^2	249	97	86	12	3	77	83	1.332	3.16	97	3.48	.267	19	.238	-1	16	0.3
1934	Bos-N★	17	9	.654	37	31	13	2	1	233^2	239	102	83	10	4	77	78	1.352	3.20	120	3.49	.262	17	.200	16	18	1.7
1935	Bos-N	11	15	.423	40	29	10	1	0	230^2	278	147	122	12	6	81	64	1.556	4.76	80	4.60	.293	20	.263	-17	7	-1.0
1936	Bro-N	13	10	.565	41	31	9	1	2	234^1	236	112	95	18	3	89	84	1.387	3.65	113	3.75	.257	13	.143	16	16	1.1
1937	Bro-N	10	13	.435	33	26	9	1	0	179^1	214	104	85	8	4	78	64	1.628	4.27	95	4.84	.297	11	.190	-0	9	0.0
1938	Bro-N	3	5	.375	30	8	2	1	0	93^2	92	48	42	6	4	44	32	1.452	4.04	97	3.97	.256	4	.154	-1	4	-0.1
1939	Bos-N	0	2	.000	23	0	0	0	4	38	37	16	11	3	1	18	12	1.447	2.61	142	4.05	.253	0	.000	4	3	0.3
Total	13	106	97	.522	402	216	81	10	12	1888	2033	969	822	111	43	701	622	1.448	3.92	100	4.09	.275	132	.208	17	113	2.9

• FRANKLIN, Jack James Wilford Franklin b: 10/20/1919, Paris, IL d: 11/15/1991, Panama City, FL BR/TR, 5'11.5", 170 lbs. Deb: 6/12/1944

YEAR	TM-L	W	L	PCT	G	GS	CG	SH	SV	IP	H	R	ER	HR	HB	BB	SO	RAT	ERA	ERA+	CERA	OAV	BH	AVG	PR+	WS	TPW
1944	Bro-N	0	0	....	1	0	0	0	0	2	2	3	3	1	2	4	0	3.000	13.50	26	18.80	.250	0	....	-2	0	-0.2

• FRANKLIN, Jay John William Franklin b: 3/16/1953, Arlington, VA BR/TR, 6'2", 180 lbs. Deb: 9/4/1971

YEAR	TM-L	W	L	PCT	G	GS	CG	SH	SV	IP	H	R	ER	HR	HB	BB	SO	RAT	ERA	ERA+	CERA	OAV	BH	AVG	PR+	WS	TPW
1971	SD-N	0	1	.000	3	1	0	0	0	5^2	5	5	4	3	0	4	4	1.588	6.35	52	7.46	.250	0	.000	-2	0	-0.2

• FRANKLIN, Ryan Ryan Ray Franklin b: 3/5/1973, Fort Smith, AR BR/TR, 6'3", 165 lbs. Deb: 5/15/1999

YEAR	TM-L	W	L	PCT	G	GS	CG	SH	SV	IP	H	R	ER	HR	HB	BB	SO	RAT	ERA	ERA+	CERA	OAV	BH	AVG	PR+	WS	TPW
1999	Sea-A	0	0	....	6	0	0	0	0	11^1	10	6	6	2	1	8	6	1.588	4.76	105	5.52	.238	0	....	0	1	0.0
2001	Sea-A	5	1	.833	38	0	0	0	0	78^1	76	32	31	13	4	24	60	1.277	3.56	116	4.08	.250	0	....	3	5	0.3
2002	Sea-A	7	5	.583	41	12	0	0	0	118^2	117	62	53	14	5	22	65	1.171	4.02	105	3.40	.255	0	....	4	6	0.3
2003	Sea-A	11	13	.458	32	32	2	1	0	212	199	93	84	34	9	61	99	1.226	3.57	121	3.90	.251	1	.250	12	13	1.2
Total	4	23	19	.548	117	44	2	1	0	420^1	402	193	174	63	19	115	230	1.230	3.73	115	3.84	.252	1	.250	19	25	1.8

• FRANKLIN, Wayne Gary Wayne Franklin b: 3/9/1974, Wilmington, DE BL/TL, 6'2", 195 lbs. Deb: 7/24/2000

YEAR	TM-L	W	L	PCT	G	GS	CG	SH	SV	IP	H	R	ER	HR	HB	BB	SO	RAT	ERA	ERA+	CERA	OAV	BH	AVG	PR+	WS	TPW
2000	Hou-N	0	0	....	25	0	0	0	0	21^1	24	14	13	2	4	12	21	1.688	5.48	88	6.01	.282	0	.000	-1	1	-0.1
2001	Hou-N	0	0	....	11	0	0	0	0	12	17	9	9	4	0	9	9	2.167	6.75	68	10.43	.333	0	....	-3	0	-0.3
2002	Mil-N	2	1	.667	4	4	0	0	0	24	16	8	7	1	0	17	17	1.375	2.63	156	2.96	.188	0	.000	4	2	0.4
2003	Mil-N	10	13	.435	36	34	1	1	0	194^2	201	129	119	36	10	94	116	1.515	5.50	77	5.43	.268	10	.169	-23	4	-2.3
Total	4	12	14	.462	76	38	1	1	0	252	258	160	148	43	14	132	163	1.548	5.29	81	5.48	.265	10	.149	-24	7	-2.4

• FRASCATORE, John John Vincent Frascatore b: 2/4/1970, Ozone Park, NY BR/TR, 6'1", 200 lbs. Deb: 7/21/1994

YEAR	TM-L	W	L	PCT	G	GS	CG	SH	SV	IP	H	R	ER	HR	HB	BB	SO	RAT	ERA	ERA+	CERA	OAV	BH	AVG	PR+	WS	TPW
1994	StL-N	0	1	.000	1	1	0	0	0	3^1	7	6	6	2	0	2	2	2.700	16.20	26	18.10	.438	0	.000	-4	0	-0.5
1995	StL-N	1	1	.500	14	4	0	0	0	32^2	39	19	16	3	2	16	21	1.684	4.41	95	5.72	.298	0	.000	-1	1	-0.2
1997	StL-N	5	2	.714	59	0	0	0	0	80	74	25	22	5	6	33	58	1.338	2.48	168	3.60	.247	0	.000	15	8	1.4
1998	StL-N	3	4	.429	69	0	0	0	0	95^2	95	48	44	11	3	36	49	1.369	4.14	101	4.09	.256	1	.167	1	5	0.1
1999	Ari-N	1	4	.200	26	0	0	0	0	33	31	16	15	6	1	12	15	1.303	4.09	112	4.23	.256	0	....	2	2	0.2
	Tor-A	7	1	.875	33	0	0	0	1	37	42	16	14	5	1	9	22	1.378	3.41	145	4.35	.292	0	....	6	5	0.6
2000	Tor-A	2	4	.333	60	0	0	0	0	73	87	51	44	14	7	33	30	1.644	5.42	94	6.58	.301	0	....	-3	3	-0.3
2001	Tor-A	1	0	1.000	12	0	0	0	0	16^1	16	4	4	4	0	4	9	1.224	2.20	208	4.12	.246	0	....	4	2	0.4
Total	7	20	17	.541	274	5	0	0	1	371	391	185	165	50	20	145	206	1.445	4.00	112	4.78	.272	1	.059	19	26	1.7

• FRASER, Chick Charles Carrolton Fraser b: 3/17/1871, Chicago, IL d: 5/8/1940, Wendell, ID BR/TR, 5'10.5", 188 lbs. Deb: 4/19/1896 C

YEAR	TM-L	W	L	PCT	G	GS	CG	SH	SV	IP	H	R	ER	HR	HB	BB	SO	RAT	ERA	ERA+	CERA	OAV	BH	AVG	PR+	WS	TPW
1896	Lou-N	12	27	.308	43	38	36	0	1	349^1	396	282	189	9	29	166	91	1.609	4.87	89	4.45	.283	22	.151	-14	12	-1.9
1897	Lou-N	15	19	.441	36	34	32	0	0	294^1	334	226	130	11	22	139	70	1.607	3.98	107	4.83	.284	18	.161	11	14	0.6
1898	Lou-N	7	17	.292	26	26	20	1	0	203	230	157	120	4	23	100	58	1.626	5.32	67	4.86	.283	13	.167	-38	3	-3.7
	Cle-N	2	3	.400	6	6	6	0	0	42	49	34	26	2	6	12	19	1.452	5.57	65	4.64	.289	4	.250	-9	1	-0.9
	Yr.	9	20	.310	32	32	26	1	0	245	279	191	146	6	29	112	77	1.596	5.36	67	4.83	.284	17	.181	-47	4	-4.6
1899	Phi-N	21	12	.636	35	33	29	4	0	270^2	278	146	101	1	22	85	68	1.341	3.36	110	3.43	.266	21	.179	6	19	0.3
1900	Phi-N	15	9	.625	29	26	22	1	0	223^1	250	117	78	7	11	93	58	1.536	3.14	115	4.38	.282	22	.259	13	17	1.5
1901	Phi-A	22	16	.579	40	37	35	2	0	331	344	210	140	6	32	132	110	1.438	3.81	99	3.88	.265	26	.187	-2	19	-0.5
1902	Phi-N	12	13	.480	27	26	24	3	0	224	238	115	85	2	15	74	97	1.393	3.42	82	3.66	.272	15	.174	-9	13	-0.8
1903	Phi-N	12	17	.414	31	29	26	1	1	250	260	160	125	8	16	97	104	1.428	4.50	73	3.94	.267	19	.204	-38	9	-3.2
1904	Phi-N	14	24	.368	42	36	32	2	1	302	287	164	109	5	11	100	127	1.281	3.25	82	3.01	.246	17	.155	-14	7	-1.5
1905	Bos-N	14	21	.400	39	38	35	2	0	334^1	320	174	122	8	15	149	130	1.403	3.28	94	3.45	.254	35	.224	1	19	0.5
1906	Cin-N	10	20	.333	31	28	25	2	0	236	221	92	70	1	8	80	58	1.275	2.67	103	3.09	.259	14	.171	0	14	-0.1
1907	Chi-N	8	5	.615	22	15	9	2	1	138^1	112	51	35	1	3	46	41	1.142	2.28	109	2.37	.229	3	.067	-0	9	-0.3
1908	Chi-N	11	9	.550	26	17	11	2	2	162^2	141	71	41	4	6	61	66	1.242	2.27	103	3.00	.244	6	.120	-0	8	-0.2
1909	Chi-N	0	0	....	1	0	0	0	0	3	2	1	0	0	0	4	1	2.000	0.00	....	6.20	.222	0	.000	1	0	0.1
Total	14	175	212	.452	434	389	342	22	6	3364	3462	2000	1371	69	219	1338	1098	1.427	3.67	92	3.80	.266	235	.179	-93	164	-10.2

• FRASER, Willie William Patrick Fraser b: 5/26/1964, New York, NY BR/TR, 6'1", 206 lbs. Deb: 9/10/1986

YEAR	TM-L	W	L	PCT	G	GS	CG	SH	SV	IP	H	R	ER	HR	HB	BB	SO	RAT	ERA	ERA+	CERA	OAV	BH	AVG	PR+	WS	TPW
1986	Cal-A	0	0	....	1	1	0	0	0	4^1	6	4	4	0	0	1	2	1.615	8.31	49	4.72	.353	0	....	-2	0	-0.2
1987	Cal-A	10	10	.500	36	23	5	1	1	176^2	160	85	77	26	6	63	106	1.262	3.92	110	3.82	.240	0	....	7	11	0.7
1988	Cal-A	12	13	.480	34	32	2	0	0	194^2	203	129	117	33	9	80	86	1.454	5.41	71	4.98	.267	0	....	-33	3	-3.3

YEAR	TM-L	W	L	PCT	G	GS	CG	SH	SV	IP	H	R	ER	HR	HB	BB	SO	RAT	ERA	ERA+	CERA	OAV	BH	AVG	PR+	WS	TPW
1989	Cal-A	4	7	.364	44	0	0	0	2	91^2	80	33	33	6	5	23	46	1.124	3.24	118	2.76	.235	0	....	4	7	0.4
1990	Cal-A	5	4	.556	45	0	0	0	2	76	69	29	26	4	0	24	32	1.224	3.08	124	2.89	.241	0	....	6	7	0.6
1991	Tor-A	0	2	.000	13	1	0	0	0	26^1	33	20	18	4	3	11	12	1.671	6.15	68	6.41	.303	0	....	-6	0	-0.6
	StL-N	3	3	.500	35	0	0	0	0	49^1	44	28	27	9	3	21	25	1.318	4.93	75	4.34	.242	0	.000	-7	1	-0.8
1994	Fla-N	2	0	1.000	9	0	0	0	0	12^1	20	9	8	1	0	6	7	2.108	5.84	75	7.41	.370	0	....	-2	1	-0.2
1995	Mon-N	2	1	.667	22	0	0	0	2	25^2	25	17	16	6	3	9	12	1.325	5.61	77	4.99	.248	0	.000	-4	1	-0.4
Total	**8**	**38**	**40**	**.487**	**239**	**57**	**7**	**1**	**7**	**657**	**640**	**354**	**326**	**89**	**29**	**238**	**328**	**1.336**	**4.47**	**89**	**4.17**	**.254**	**0**	**.000**	**-36**	**31**	**-3.7**

• FRASIER, Vic Victor Patrick Frasier b: 8/5/1904, Ruston, LA d: 1/10/1977, Jacksonville, TX BR/TR, 6', 182 lbs. Deb: 4/18/1931

YEAR	TM-L	W	L	PCT	G	GS	CG	SH	SV	IP	H	R	ER	HR	HB	BB	SO	RAT	ERA	ERA+	CERA	OAV	BH	AVG	PR+	WS	TPW
1931	Chi-A	13	15	.464	46	29	13	2	4	254	258	156	126	11	5	127	87	1.516	4.46	95	4.01	.259	18	.209	-1	13	0.0
1932	Chi-A	3	13	.188	29	21	4	0	0	146	180	121	101	14	4	70	33	1.712	6.23	69	5.57	.297	4	.091	-29	0	-3.0
1933	Chi-A	1	1	.500	10	1	0	0	0	20^1	32	22	20	2	0	11	4	2.115	8.85	48	8.08	.368	0	.000	-10	0	-1.0
	Det-A	5	5	.500	20	14	4	0	0	104^1	129	85	77	9	1	59	26	1.802	6.64	65	5.97	.312	7	.189	-28	0	-2.7
	Yr.	6	6	.500	30	15	4	0	0	124^2	161	107	97	11	1	70	30	1.853	7.00	61	6.31	.322	7	.171	-38	0	-3.7
1934	Det-A	1	3	.250	8	2	0	0	0	22^2	30	19	15	0	1	12	11	1.853	5.96	74	5.54	.313	2	.286	-4	0	-0.4
1937	Bos-N	0	0	....	3	0	0	0	0	8	12	7	5	1	0	1	2	1.625	5.63	64	5.89	.364	0	.000	-2	0	-0.2
1939	Chi-A	0	1	.000	10	1	0	0	0	23^2	45	27	27	0	0	11	7	2.366	10.27	46	8.97	.405	2	.286	-15	0	-1.4
Total	**6**	**23**	**38**	**.377**	**126**	**68**	**21**	**2**	**4**	**579**	**686**	**437**	**371**	**37**	**11**	**291**	**170**	**1.687**	**5.77**	**75**	**5.19**	**.293**	**33**	**.177**	**-90**	**13**	**-8.6**

• FRAZIER, George George Allen Frazier b: 10/13/1954, Oklahoma City, OK BR/TR, 6'5", 205 lbs. Deb: 5/25/1978

YEAR	TM-L	W	L	PCT	G	GS	CG	SH	SV	IP	H	R	ER	HR	HB	BB	SO	RAT	ERA	ERA+	CERA	OAV	BH	AVG	PR+	WS	TPW
1978	StL-N	0	3	.000	14	0	0	0	0	22	22	14	10	2	0	6	8	1.273	4.09	86	3.22	.250	1	.333	-2	0	-0.1
1979	StL-N	2	4	.333	25	0	0	0	0	32^1	35	19	16	3	1	12	14	1.454	4.45	84	4.35	.278	0	.000	-3	1	-0.3
1980	StL-N	1	4	.200	22	0	0	0	3	23	24	10	7	2	0	7	11	1.348	2.74	135	3.73	.273	0	....	2	2	0.2
1981*	NY-A	0	1	.000	16	0	0	0	3	27^2	26	7	5	1	0	11	17	1.337	1.63	220	3.20	.245	0	....	6	3	0.6
1982	NY-A	4	4	.500	63	0	0	0	1	111^2	103	51	43	7	5	39	69	1.272	3.47	115	3.36	.252	0	....	7	6	0.7
1983	NY-A	4	4	.500	61	0	0	0	8	115^1	94	44	44	5	3	45	78	1.205	3.43	113	2.72	.227	0	....	7	10	0.7
1984	Cle-A	3	2	.600	22	0	0	0	1	44^1	45	19	18	3	0	14	24	1.331	3.65	112	3.42	.259	0	....	2	3	0.2
	*Chi-N	6	3	.667	37	0	0	0	3	63^2	53	30	29	4	1	26	58	1.241	4.10	95	2.74	.221	2	.286	-1	5	-0.1
1985	Chi-N	7	8	.467	51	0	0	0	2	76	88	57	54	11	3	52	46	1.842	6.39	62	6.60	.299	0	.000	-19	0	-2.1
1986	Chi-N	2	4	.333	35	0	0	0	0	51^2	63	36	31	5	1	34	41	1.877	5.40	75	6.46	.310	0	.000	-7	1	-0.8
	Min-A	1	1	.500	15	0	0	0	6	26^2	23	13	13	2	0	16	25	1.463	4.39	98	3.75	.232	0	....	0	3	0.0
1987*	Min-A	5	5	.500	54	0	0	0	2	81^1	77	49	45	9	2	51	58	1.574	4.98	93	4.81	.258	0	....	-4	4	-0.3
Total	**10**	**35**	**43**	**.449**	**415**	**0**	**0**	**0**	**29**	**675^2**	**653**	**349**	**315**	**54**	**16**	**313**	**449**	**1.430**	**4.20**	**96**	**4.04**	**.257**	**3**	**.143**	**-12**	**38**	**-1.4**

• FREDERICK, Kevin Kevin Albert Francis Frederick b: 11/4/1976, Evanston, IL BL/TR, 6'1", 208 lbs. Deb: 7/15/2002

YEAR	TM-L	W	L	PCT	G	GS	CG	SH	SV	IP	H	R	ER	HR	HB	BB	SO	RAT	ERA	ERA+	CERA	OAV	BH	AVG	PR+	WS	TPW
2002	Min-A	0	0	....	8	0	0	0	0	11^2	13	13	13	3	0	10	5	1.971	10.03	45	8.14	.283	0	....	-7	0	-0.7

• FREDRICKSON, Scott Scott Eric Fredrickson b: 8/19/1967, Manchester, NH BR/TR, 6'3", 215 lbs. Deb: 4/29/1993

YEAR	TM-L	W	L	PCT	G	GS	CG	SH	SV	IP	H	R	ER	HR	HB	BB	SO	RAT	ERA	ERA+	CERA	OAV	BH	AVG	PR+	WS	TPW
1993	Col-N	0	1	.000	25	0	0	0	0	29	33	25	20	3	1	17	20	1.724	6.21	77	5.58	.287	0	.000	-4	0	-0.4

• FREEMAN, Buck John Frank Freeman b: 10/30/1871, Catasauqua, PA d: 6/25/1949, Wilkes-Barre, PA BL/TL, 5'9", 169 lbs. Deb: 6/27/1891 U ♦

YEAR	TM-L	W	L	PCT	G	GS	CG	SH	SV	IP	H	R	ER	HR	HB	BB	SO	RAT	ERA	ERA+	CERA	OAV	BH	AVG	PR+	WS	TPW
1891	Was-a	3	2	.600	5	4	4	0	0	44	35	32	19	0	4	33	28	1.545	3.89	96	....	.211	4	.222	2	2	0.2
1899	Was-N	0	0	....	2	0	0	0	0	7	15	13	6	3	3	3	0	2.571	7.71	51	17.20	.430	187	.318	-3	25	0.9
Total	**2**	**3**	**2**	**.600**	**7**	**4**	**4**	**0**	**0**	**51**	**50**	**45**	**25**	**3**	**7**	**36**	**28**	**1.686**	**4.41**	**86**	**2.36**	**.249**	**1235**	**.293**	**-1**	**27**	**1.1**

• FREEMAN, Buck Alexander Vernon Freeman b: 7/5/1896, Mart, TX d: 2/21/1953, Fort Sam Houston, TX BB/TR, 5'10", 167 lbs. Deb: 4/13/1921

YEAR	TM-L	W	L	PCT	G	GS	CG	SH	SV	IP	H	R	ER	HR	HB	BB	SO	RAT	ERA	ERA+	CERA	OAV	BH	AVG	PR+	WS	TPW
1921	Chi-N	9	10	.474	38	20	6	0	3	177^1	189	96	81	12	8	70	42	1.461	4.11	93	4.32	.281	11	.208	-6	10	-0.6
1922	Chi-N	0	1	.000	11	1	0	0	1	25^2	47	28	25	0	2	10	10	2.221	8.77	48	8.63	.412	1	.125	-13	0	-1.3
Total	**2**	**9**	**11**	**.450**	**49**	**21**	**6**	**0**	**4**	**203**	**236**	**124**	**106**	**12**	**10**	**80**	**52**	**1.557**	**4.70**	**83**	**4.86**	**.300**	**12**	**.197**	**-19**	**10**	**-1.9**

• FREEMAN, Harvey Harvey Bayard "Buck" Freeman b: 12/22/1897, Mottville, MI d: 1/10/1970, Kalamazoo, MI BR/TR, 5'10", 160 lbs. Deb: 7/10/1921

YEAR	TM-L	W	L	PCT	G	GS	CG	SH	SV	IP	H	R	ER	HR	HB	BB	SO	RAT	ERA	ERA+	CERA	OAV	BH	AVG	PR+	WS	TPW
1921	Phi-A	1	4	.200	18	4	2	0	0	48	65	50	41	2	5	35	5	2.083	7.69	58	7.52	.346	1	.083	-16	0	-1.7

• FREEMAN, Hersh Hershell Baskin "Buster" Freeman b: 7/1/1928, Gadsden, AL BR/TR, 6'3", 220 lbs. Deb: 9/10/1952

YEAR	TM-L	W	L	PCT	G	GS	CG	SH	SV	IP	H	R	ER	HR	HB	BB	SO	RAT	ERA	ERA+	CERA	OAV	BH	AVG	PR+	WS	TPW
1952	Bos-A	1	0	1.000	4	1	1	0	0	13^2	13	5	5	1	1	5	5	1.317	3.29	120	3.87	.260	2	.500	1	2	0.2
1953	Bos-A	1	4	.200	18	2	0	0	0	39	50	31	24	2	0	17	15	1.718	5.54	76	5.38	.316	1	.091	-6	0	-0.7
1955	Bos-A	0	0	....	2	0	0	0	0	1^2	1	0	0	0	0	1	1	1.200	0.00	....	1.51	.200	0	....	1	0	0.1
	Cin-N	7	4	.636	52	0	0	0	11	91^2	94	31	22	3	2	30	37	1.353	2.16	196	3.51	.276	3	.167	21	12	2.1
1956	Cin-N	14	5	.737	64	0	0	0	18	108^2	112	44	41	2	1	34	50	1.344	3.40	117	3.25	.274	1	.056	8	15	0.8
1957	Cin-N	7	2	.778	52	0	0	0	8	83^2	90	49	42	14	3	14	36	1.243	4.52	91	4.07	.277	2	.200	-4	7	-0.4
1958	Cin-N	0	0	....	3	0	0	0	0	7^2	4	3	3	0	0	5	7	1.174	3.52	118	1.84	.154	0	.000	1	1	0.0
	Chi-N	0	1	.000	9	0	0	0	0	13	23	13	12	3	0	3	7	2.000	8.31	47	8.49	.354	0	.000	-6	0	-0.6
	Yr.	0	1	.000	12	0	0	0	0	20^2	27	16	15	3	0	8	14	1.694	6.53	61	6.02	.297	0	.000	-6	1	-0.6
Total	**6**	**30**	**16**	**.652**	**204**	**3**	**1**	**0**	**37**	**359**	**387**	**176**	**149**	**25**	**7**	**109**	**158**	**1.382**	**3.74**	**109**	**3.91**	**.281**	**9**	**.143**	**15**	**37**	**1.5**

• FREEMAN, Jimmy Jimmy Lee Freeman b: 6/29/1951, Carlsbad, NM BL/TL, 6'4", 180 lbs. Deb: 9/1/1972

YEAR	TM-L	W	L	PCT	G	GS	CG	SH	SV	IP	H	R	ER	HR	HB	BB	SO	RAT	ERA	ERA+	CERA	OAV	BH	AVG	PR+	WS	TPW
1972	Atl-N	2	2	.500	6	6	1	0	0	36	40	26	24	5	0	22	18	1.722	6.00	63	5.81	.278	1	.077	-8	0	-0.9
1973	Atl-N	0	2	.000	13	5	0	0	1	37^1	50	33	32	7	0	25	20	2.009	7.71	51	8.02	.327	2	.154	-15	0	-1.6
Total	**2**	**2**	**4**	**.333**	**19**	**11**	**1**	**0**	**1**	**73^1**	**90**	**59**	**56**	**12**	**0**	**47**	**38**	**1.868**	**6.87**	**56**	**6.94**	**.303**	**3**	**.115**	**-24**	**0**	**-2.6**

• FREEMAN, Julie Julius Benjamin Freeman b: 11/7/1868, MO d: 6/10/1921, St. Louis, MO BR Deb: 10/10/1888

YEAR	TM-L	W	L	PCT	G	GS	CG	SH	SV	IP	H	R	ER	HR	HB	BB	SO	RAT	ERA	ERA+	CERA	OAV	BH	AVG	PR+	WS	TPW
1888	StL-a	0	1	.000	1	1	0	0	0	6^1	7	5	3	0	1	4	1	1.737	4.26	76	....	.270	1	.333	-1	0	-0.1

• FREEMAN, Mark Mark Price Freeman b: 12/7/1930, Memphis, TN BR/TR, 6'4", 220 lbs. Deb: 4/18/1959

YEAR	TM-L	W	L	PCT	G	GS	CG	SH	SV	IP	H	R	ER	HR	HB	BB	SO	RAT	ERA	ERA+	CERA	OAV	BH	AVG	PR+	WS	TPW
1959	KC-A	0	0	....	3	0	0	0	0	3^2	6	6	4	0	0	3	1	2.455	9.82	41	8.70	.375	0	....	-2	0	-0.2
	NY-A	0	0	....	1	1	0	0	0	7	6	2	2	0	1	2	4	1.143	2.57	142	2.78	.240	0	.000	1	0	0.1
	Yr.	0	0	....	4	1	0	0	0	10^2	12	8	6	0	1	5	5	1.594	5.06	77	4.82	.293	0	.000	-2	0	-0.2
1960	Chi-N	3	3	.500	30	8	1	0	1	76^2	70	51	48	10	5	33	50	1.343	5.63	67	4.08	.240	3	.150	-16	1	-1.6
Total	**2**	**3**	**3**	**.500**	**34**	**9**	**1**	**0**	**1**	**87^1**	**82**	**59**	**54**	**10**	**6**	**38**	**55**	**1.374**	**5.56**	**68**	**4.17**	**.246**	**3**	**.136**	**-17**	**1**	**-1.8**

• FREEMAN, Marvin Marvin Freeman b: 4/10/1963, Chicago, IL BR/TR, 6'7", 222 lbs. Deb: 9/16/1986

YEAR	TM-L	W	L	PCT	G	GS	CG	SH	SV	IP	H	R	ER	HR	HB	BB	SO	RAT	ERA	ERA+	CERA	OAV	BH	AVG	PR+	WS	TPW
1986	Phi-N	2	0	1.000	3	3	0	0	0	16	6	4	4	0	0	10	8	1.000	2.25	171	1.36	.120	0	.000	3	2	0.2
1988	Phi-N	2	3	.400	11	11	0	0	0	51^2	55	36	35	2	1	43	37	1.897	6.10	58	5.66	.276	3	.214	-14	0	-1.5
1989	Phi-N	0	0	....	1	1	0	0	0	3	2	2	2	0	0	5	0	2.333	6.00	59	6.05	.182	0	.000	-1	0	-0.1
1990	Phi-N	0	2	.000	16	3	0	0	1	32^1	34	21	20	5	3	14	26	1.485	5.57	69	5.10	.264	0	.000	-7	0	-0.8
	Atl-N	1	0	1.000	9	0	0	0	0	15^2	7	3	3	0	2	3	12	.638	1.72	234	0.92	.130	0	....	4	2	0.5
	Yr.	1	2	.333	25	3	0	0	1	48	41	24	23	5	5	17	38	1.208	4.31	89	3.73	.224	0	.000	-2	2	-0.3
1991	Atl-N	1	0	1.000	34	0	0	0	1	48	37	19	16	2	2	13	34	1.042	3.00	129	2.21	.214	0	.000	5	4	0.4
1992*	Atl-N	7	5	.583	58	0	0	0	3	64^1	61	26	23	7	1	29	41	1.399	3.22	114	3.97	.251	2	.500	3	6	0.4
1993	Atl-N	2	0	1.000	21	0	0	0	0	23^2	24	16	16	1	1	10	25	1.437	6.08	66	3.87	.261	0	....	-6	0	-0.6
1994	Col-N	10	2	.833	19	18	0	0	0	112^2	113	39	35	10	5	23	67	1.207	2.80	178	3.44	.262	4	.111	31	13	3.0
1995	Col-N	3	7	.300	22	18	0	0	0	94^2	122	64	62	15	2	41	61	1.722	5.89	91	6.49	.318	2	.087	-3	4	-0.3
1996	Col-N	7	9	.438	26	23	0	0	0	129^2	151	100	87	21	6	57	71	1.604	6.04	87	5.87	.294	5	.122	-9	4	-1.0
	Chi-A	0	0	....	1	1	0	0	0	2	4	3	3	0	0	1	1	2.500	13.50	35	8.87	.364	0	.000	-2	0	-0.2
Total	**10**	**35**	**28**	**.556**	**221**	**78**	**0**	**0**	**5**	**593^2**	**616**	**333**	**306**	**63**	**23**	**249**	**383**	**1.457**	**4.64**	**98**	**4.63**	**.269**	**16**	**.114**	**5**	**35**	**0.1**

• FREEZE, Jake Carl Alexander Freeze b: 4/25/1900, Huntington, AR d: 4/9/1983, San Angelo, TX BR/TR, 5'8", 150 lbs. Deb: 7/1/1925

YEAR	TM-L	W	L	PCT	G	GS	CG	SH	SV	IP	H	R	ER	HR	HB	BB	SO	RAT	ERA	ERA+	CERA	OAV	BH	AVG	PR+	WS	TPW
1925	Chi-A	0	0	....	2	0	0	0	0	3^2	5	7	1	1	0	3	1	2.182	2.45	169	9.21	.333	0	.000	1	0	0.0

• FREISLEBEN, Dave David James Freisleben b: 10/31/1951, Coraopolis, PA BR/TR, 5'11", 200 lbs. Deb: 4/26/1974

YEAR	TM-L	W	L	PCT	G	GS	CG	SH	SV	IP	H	R	ER	HR	HB	BB	SO	RAT	ERA	ERA+	CERA	OAV	BH	AVG	PR+	WS	TPW
1974	SD-N	9	14	.391	33	31	6	2	0	211^2	194	100	86	13	7	112	130	1.446	3.66	97	3.87	.241	11	.172	4	10	0.6

YEAR	TM-L	W	L	PCT	G	GS	CG	SH	SV	IP	H	R	ER	HR	HB	BB	SO	RAT	ERA	ERA+	CERA	OAV	BH	AVG	PR+	WS	TPW
1975	SD-N	5	14	.263	36	27	4	1	0	181	206	102	86	11	7	82	77	**1.591**	4.28	81	4.81	.289	4	.083	-14	3	-1.6
1976	SD-N	10	13	.435	34	24	6	3	1	172	163	73	67	10	5	66	81	1.331	3.51	93	3.47	.248	7	.189	-4	8	-0.3
1977	SD-N	7	9	.438	33	23	1	0	0	138^2	140	86	71	21	2	71	72	1.522	4.61	77	4.98	.266	5	.135	-16	2	-1.6
1978	SD-N	0	3	.000	12	4	0	0	0	26^2	41	22	18	3	0	15	16	2.100	6.08	55	8.07	.363	0	.000	-8	0	-0.9
	Cle-A	1	4	.200	12	10	0	0	0	44^1	52	37	35	4	2	31	19	1.872	7.11	53	6.42	.299	0	....	-16	0	-1.7
1979	Tor-A	2	3	.400	42	2	0	0	3	91	101	57	50	5	2	53	35	1.692	4.95	88	5.28	.294	0	....	-7	4	-0.6
Total	6	34	60	.362	202	121	17	6	4	865^1	897	477	413	67	25	430	430	1.534	4.30	83	4.57	.269	27	.141	-61	27	-6.1

• FREITAS, Tony — Antonio Freitas b: 5/5/1908, Mill Valley, CA d: 3/14/1994, Orangevale, CA BR/TL, 5'8", 161 lbs. Deb: 5/31/1932

YEAR	TM-L	W	L	PCT	G	GS	CG	SH	SV	IP	H	R	ER	HR	HB	BB	SO	RAT	ERA	ERA+	CERA	OAV	BH	AVG	PR+	WS	TPW
1932	Phi-A	12	5	.706	23	18	10	1	0	150^1	150	68	64	11	4	48	31	1.317	3.83	118	3.66	.263	8	.148	11	12	1.0
1933	Phi-A	2	4	.333	19	9	2	0	1	64^1	90	56	52	8	2	24	15	1.772	7.27	59	6.68	.337	1	.063	-19	0	-1.9
1934	Cin-N	6	12	.333	30	18	5	0	1	152^2	194	80	68	6	3	25	37	1.434	4.01	102	4.28	.311	9	.191	5	8	0.6
1935	Cin-N	5	10	.333	31	18	5	0	2	143^2	174	95	73	6	2	38	51	1.476	4.57	87	4.19	.295	6	.130	-8	4	-0.8
1936	Cin-N	0	2	.000	4	0	0	0	0	7	6	2	1	0	0	2	1	1.143	1.29	297	2.25	.240	0	.000	2	1	0.2
Total	5	25	33	.431	107	63	22	1	4	518	614	301	258	31	11	137	135	1.450	4.48	94	4.34	.296	24	.145	-9	25	-1.0

• FRENCH, Larry — Lawrence Herbert French b: 11/1/1907, Visalia, CA d: 2/9/1987, San Diego, CA BR/TL, 6'1", 195 lbs. Deb: 4/18/1929

YEAR	TM-L	W	L	PCT	G	GS	CG	SH	SV	IP	H	R	ER	HR	HB	BB	SO	RAT	ERA	ERA+	CERA	OAV	BH	AVG	PR+	WS	TPW
1929	Pit-N	7	5	.583	30	13	6	0	1	123	130	78	67	10	3	62	49	1.561	4.90	97	4.62	.276	8	.190	-4	6	-0.4
1930	Pit-N	17	18	.486	42	35	21	3	1	274^2	325	163	133	20	6	89	90	1.507	4.36	114	4.54	.295	22	.242	19	19	1.8
1931	Pit-N	15	13	.536	39	33	20	1	1	275^2	301	127	100	9	1	70	73	1.346	3.26	118	3.51	.278	17	.179	13	19	1.2
1932	Pit-N	18	16	.529	**47**	33	19	3	4	274^1	301	127	92	17	1	62	72	1.323	3.02	126	3.61	.276	19	.207	22	22	2.2
1933	Pit-N	18	13	.581	47	**35**	21	5	1	291^1	290	106	88	9	5	55	88	1.184	2.72	122	2.79	.257	15	.149	18	21	1.7
1934	Pit-N	12	18	.400	49	34	16	3	1	263^2	299	135	105	8	3	59	103	1.358	3.58	115	3.58	.281	16	.190	18	15	1.8
1935*	Chi-N	17	10	.630	42	30	16	**4**	2	246^1	279	94	81	10	2	44	90	1.311	2.96	133	3.53	.286	12	.141	18	19	1.3
1936	Chi-N	18	9	.667	43	28	16	**4**	3	252^1	262	103	95	16	6	54	104	1.252	3.39	117	3.36	.266	18	.212	11	21	1.1
1937	Chi-N	16	10	.615	42	28	11	4	0	208	229	106	92	17	1	65	100	1.413	3.98	100	4.05	.274	9	.127	-1	12	-0.5
1938*	Chi-N	10	19	.345	43	27	10	3	0	201^1	210	95	85	17	1	62	83	1.351	3.80	101	3.82	.271	13	.210	-1	11	0.1
1939	Chi-N	15	8	.652	36	21	10	2	1	194	205	80	71	7	1	50	98	1.314	3.29	119	3.32	.269	14	.192	19	16	2.0
1940	Chi-N★	14	14	.500	40	33	18	3	2	246	240	93	90	12	4	64	107	1.236	3.29	114	3.07	.256	14	.165	13	18	1.4
1941	Chi-N	5	14	.263	26	18	6	1	0	138	161	88	71	10	2	43	60	1.478	4.63	76	4.32	.285	9	.191	-13	1	-1.3
	*Bro-N	0	0	....	6	1	0	0	0	15^2	16	6	6	1	1	4	8	1.277	3.45	106	3.53	.267	1	.250	0	1	0.0
	Yr.	5	14	.263	32	19	6	1	0	153^2	177	94	77	11	3	47	68	1.458	4.51	78	4.24	.283	10	.196	-13	2	-1.3
1942	Bro-N	15	4	.789	38	14	8	4	0	147^2	127	39	30	1	5	36	62	1.104	1.83	178	2.25	.233	12	.300	22	17	2.7
Total	14	197	171	.535	570	383	198	40	17	3152	3375	1440	1206	164	42	819	1187	1.331	3.44	114	3.57	.273	199	.188	154	218	15.3

• FREY, Benny — Benjamin Rudolph Frey b: 4/6/1906, Dexter, MI d: 11/1/1937, Spring Arbor Township, MI BR/TR, 5'10", 165 lbs. Deb: 9/18/1929

YEAR	TM-L	W	L	PCT	G	GS	CG	SH	SV	IP	H	R	ER	HR	HB	BB	SO	RAT	ERA	ERA+	CERA	OAV	BH	AVG	PR+	WS	TPW
1929	Cin-N	1	2	.333	3	3	2	0	0	24	29	12	11	2	0	8	1	1.542	4.13	111	4.87	.302	3	.375	1	2	0.2
1930	Cin-N	11	18	.379	44	28	14	2	1	245	295	145	128	15	3	62	43	1.457	4.70	103	4.39	.305	25	.284	5	16	0.9
1931	Cin-N	8	12	.400	34	17	7	1	2	133^2	166	76	73	2	2	36	19	1.511	4.92	76	4.47	.319	14	.318	-19	5	-1.5
1932	StL-N	0	2	.000	2	0	0	0	0	3	6	5	4	0	0	2	0	2.667	12.00	33	14.74	.600	0	.000	-3	0	-0.3
	Cin-N	4	10	.286	28	15	5	0	0	131^1	159	72	63	10	1	30	27	1.439	4.32	89	4.39	.299	9	.205	-6	4	-0.6
	Yr.	4	12	.250	30	15	5	0	0	134^1	165	77	67	10	1	32	27	1.467	4.49	86	4.62	.305	9	.200	-9	4	-0.9
1933	Cin-N	6	4	.600	37	9	1	1	0	132	144	67	56	4	0	21	12	1.250	3.82	89	3.15	.281	11	.262	-5	7	-0.1
1934	Cin-N	11	16	.407	39	30	12	2	2	245^1	288	118	96	10	2	42	33	1.345	3.52	116	3.66	.289	14	.171	21	16	2.1
1935	Cin-N	6	10	.375	38	13	3	1	3	114^1	164	100	87	6	4	32	24	1.714	6.85	58	5.75	.335	11	.344	-35	1	-3.1
1936	Cin-N	10	8	.556	31	12	5	0	0	131^1	164	73	62	5	0	30	20	1.477	4.25	90	4.17	.296	11	.250	-5	7	-0.4
Total	8	57	82	.410	256	127	49	7	8	1160	1415	668	580	54	12	263	179	1.447	4.50	90	4.25	.303	98	.255	-46	58	-2.8

• FREY, Steve — Steven Francis Frey b: 7/29/1963, Meadowbrook, PA BR/TL, 5'9", 170 lbs. Deb: 5/10/1989

YEAR	TM-L	W	L	PCT	G	GS	CG	SH	SV	IP	H	R	ER	HR	HB	BB	SO	RAT	ERA	ERA+	CERA	OAV	BH	AVG	PR+	WS	TPW
1989	Mon-N	3	2	.600	20	0	0	0	0	21^1	29	15	13	4	1	11	15	1.875	5.48	64	7.56	.326	0	....	-5	0	-0.5
1990	Mon-N	8	2	.800	51	0	0	0	9	55^2	44	15	13	4	1	29	29	1.311	2.10	174	3.11	.219	0	.000	9	9	1.0
1991	Mon-N	0	1	.000	31	0	0	0	1	39^2	43	31	22	3	1	23	21	1.664	4.99	72	5.00	.281	0	.000	-6	0	-0.7
1992	Cal-A	4	2	.667	51	0	0	0	4	45^1	39	18	18	6	2	22	24	1.346	3.57	111	3.98	.238	0	....	2	5	0.2
1993	Cal-A	2	3	.400	55	0	0	0	13	48^1	41	20	16	1	3	26	22	1.386	2.98	151	3.37	.230	0	....	8	7	0.7
1994	SF-N	1	0	1.000	44	0	0	0	0	31	37	17	17	6	2	15	20	1.645	4.94	81	6.74	.322	0	....	-4	1	-0.4
1995	SF-N	0	1	.000	9	0	0	0	0	6^1	7	6	3	1	0	2	5	1.421	4.26	96	4.46	.280	0	....	-0	0	0.0
	Sea-A	0	3	.000	13	0	0	0	0	11^1	16	7	6	0	1	6	7	1.941	4.76	99	6.36	.356	0	....	0	0	0.0
	Phi-N	0	0	....	9	0	0	0	1	10^2	3	1	1	1	0	2	2	.469	0.84	501	0.56	.091	0	.000	4	2	0.4
	Yr.	0	1	.000	18	0	0	0	1	17	10	7	4	2	0	4	7	.824	2.12	194	2.01	.172	0	.000	4	2	0.4
1996	Phi-N	0	1	.000	31	0	0	0	0	34^1	38	19	18	4	0	18	12	1.631	4.72	91	5.33	.295	0	....	-2	1	-0.2
Total	8	18	15	.545	314	0	0	0	28	304	297	149	127	30	11	154	157	1.484	3.76	105	4.52	.262	0	.000	6	25	0.5

• FRICANO, Marion — Marion John Fricano b: 7/15/1923, Brant, NY d: 5/18/1976, Tijuana, Mexico BR/TR, 6', 170 lbs. Deb: 9/6/1952

YEAR	TM-L	W	L	PCT	G	GS	CG	SH	SV	IP	H	R	ER	HR	HB	BB	SO	RAT	ERA	ERA+	CERA	OAV	BH	AVG	PR+	WS	TPW
1952	Phi-A	1	0	1.000	2	0	0	0	0	5	5	1	1	0	0	1	0	1.200	1.80	220	2.29	.238	0	....	1	1	0.1
1953	Phi-A	9	12	.429	39	23	10	0	1	211	206	105	91	21	6	90	67	1.403	3.88	110	4.07	.257	10	.145	10	14	0.8
1954	Phi-A	5	11	.313	37	20	4	0	1	151^2	163	98	87	17	4	64	43	1.497	5.16	76	4.66	.275	4	.098	-19	4	-2.3
1955	KC-A	0	0	....	10	0	0	0	0	20	19	9	7	2	0	9	5	1.400	3.15	132	4.11	.253	2	.667	2	2	0.3
Total	4	15	23	.395	88	43	14	0	1	387^2	393	213	186	40	10	164	115	1.437	4.32	95	4.28	.264	16	.142	-5	21	-1.0

• FRIDAY, Skipper — Grier William Friday b: 10/26/1897, Gastonia, NC d: 8/25/1962, Gastonia, NC BR/TR, 5'11", 170 lbs. Deb: 6/17/1923

YEAR	TM-L	W	L	PCT	G	GS	CG	SH	SV	IP	H	R	ER	HR	HB	BB	SO	RAT	ERA	ERA+	CERA	OAV	BH	AVG	PR+	WS	TPW
1923	Was-A	0	1	.000	7	2	1	0	0	30	35	27	23	2	2	22	9	1.900	6.90	55	6.39	.313	2	.222	-11	0	-1.1

• FRIED, Cy — Arthur Edwin Fried b: 7/23/1897, San Antonio, TX d: 10/10/1970, San Antonio, TX BL/TL, 5'11.5", 150 lbs. Deb: 9/17/1920

YEAR	TM-L	W	L	PCT	G	GS	CG	SH	SV	IP	H	R	ER	HR	HB	BB	SO	RAT	ERA	ERA+	CERA	OAV	BH	AVG	PR+	WS	TPW
1920	Det-A	0	0	....	2	0	0	0	0	1^2	3	4	3	0	0	4	0	4.200	16.20	23	19.29	.500	0	....	-2	0	-0.2

• FRIEDRICHS, Bob — Robert George Friedrichs b: 8/30/1906, Cincinnati, OH d: 4/15/1997, Jasper, IN BR/TR, 5'11.5", 165 lbs. Deb: 5/17/1932

YEAR	TM-L	W	L	PCT	G	GS	CG	SH	SV	IP	H	R	ER	HR	HB	BB	SO	RAT	ERA	ERA+	CERA	OAV	BH	AVG	PR+	WS	TPW
1932	Was-A	0	0	....	2	0	0	0	0	4	4	5	5	0	1	7	2	2.750	11.25	38	8.74	.250	0	.000	-3	0	-0.3

• FRIEND, Bob — Robert Bartmess "Warrior" Friend b: 11/24/1930, Lafayette, IN BR/TR, 6', 190 lbs. Deb: 4/28/1951

YEAR	TM-L	W	L	PCT	G	GS	CG	SH	SV	IP	H	R	ER	HR	HB	BB	SO	RAT	ERA	ERA+	CERA	OAV	BH	AVG	PR+	WS	TPW
1951	Pit-N	6	10	.375	34	22	3	1	0	149^2	173	94	71	12	0	68	41	1.610	4.27	99	4.99	.293	4	.091	1	5	-0.1
1952	Pit-N	7	17	.292	35	23	6	1	0	185	186	96	86	15	3	84	75	1.459	4.18	95	4.07	.258	3	.058	-3	7	-0.6
1953	Pit-N	8	11	.421	32	24	8	0	0	170^2	193	103	93	18	3	57	66	1.465	4.90	91	4.58	.286	7	.135	-7	8	-0.9
1954	Pit-N	7	12	.368	35	20	4	2	2	170^1	204	106	96	16	1	58	73	1.538	5.07	83	4.85	.302	14	.275	-13	7	-0.7
1955	Pit-N	14	9	.609	44	20	9	2	2	200^1	178	80	63	18	2	52	98	1.148	**2.83**	**145**	**2.91**	.242	10	.164	**30**	19	2.8
1956	Pit-N★	17	17	.500	49	**42**	19	4	3	**314^1**	310	137	121	25	2	85	166	1.257	3.46	109	3.29	.258	16	.165	13	20	1.3
1957	Pit-N	14	18	.438	40	**38**	17	3	0	**277**	273	121	104	28	1	68	143	1.231	3.38	112	3.38	.257	16	.184	9	16	1.1
1958	Pit-N★	**22**	14	.611	38	**38**	16	1	0	274	299	120	112	25	4	61	135	1.314	3.68	105	3.88	.281	10	.106	0	16	-0.4
1959	Pit-N	8	19	.296	35	35	7	2	0	234^2	267	129	105	19	7	52	104	1.359	4.03	96	4.03	.283	12	.164	-6	9	-0.6
1960*	Pit-N★	18	12	.600	38	37	16	4	1	275^2	266	97	92	18	0	45	183	1.128	3.00	125	2.72	.251	6	.068	18	20	1.4
1961	Pit-N	14	19	.424	41	35	10	1	1	236	271	119	101	16	3	45	108	1.339	3.85	103	3.85	.289	11	.139	3	12	0.0
1962	Pit-N	18	14	.563	39	36	13	**5**	1	261^2	280	99	89	23	2	53	144	1.273	3.06	128	3.58	.273	11	.121	23	21	1.9
1963	Pit-N	17	16	.515	39	38	12	4	0	268^2	236	87	70	13	5	44	144	1.042	2.34	141	2.25	.233	9	.105	27	21	2.6
1964	Pit-N	13	18	.419	35	35	13	3	0	240^1	253	98	89	10	4	50	128	1.261	3.33	105	3.22	.271	5	.070	8	13	0.5
1965	Pit-N	8	12	.400	34	34	8	2	0	222	221	89	80	17	8	47	74	1.207	3.24	108	3.29	.260	3	.042	2	11	-0.4
1966	NY-A	1	4	.200	12	8	0	0	0	44^2	61	25	24	2	0	9	22	1.567	4.84	69	4.99	.330	0	.000	-7	0	-0.9
	NY-N	5	8	.385	22	12	2	1	1	86	101	52	42	11	1	16	30	1.360	4.40	83	4.27	.289	1	.034	-8	2	-1.1
Total	16	197	230	.461	602	497	163	36	11	3611	3772	1652	1438	286	46	894	1734	1.292	3.58	107	3.59	.269	138	.121	92	207	5.8

• FRIEND, Danny — Daniel Sebastian Friend b: 4/18/1873, Cincinnati, OH d: 6/1/1942, Chillicothe, OH BL/TL, 5'9", 175 lbs. Deb: 9/10/1895

YEAR	TM-L	W	L	PCT	G	GS	CG	SH	SV	IP	H	R	ER	HR	HB	BB	SO	RAT	ERA	ERA+	CERA	OAV	BH	AVG	PR+	WS	TPW
1895	Chi-N	2	2	.500	5	5	5	0	0	41	50	27	24	5	3	14	10	1.561	5.27	96	5.48	.296	4	.235	-1	3	-0.1

YEAR	TM-L	W	L	PCT	G	GS	CG	SH	SV	IP	H	R	ER	HR	HB	BB	SO	RAT	ERA	ERA+	CERA	OAV	BH	AVG	PR+	WS	TPW
1896	Chi-N	18	14	.563	36	33	28	1	0	290^2	298	196	153	11	39	139	86	1.503	4.74	96	4.42	.263	30	.238	-11	21	-1.0
1897	Chi-N	12	11	.522	24	24	23	0	0	203	244	144	102	5	17	86	58	1.626	4.52	98	4.95	.295	25	.284	1	12	0.2
1898	Chi-N	0	2	.000	2	2	2	0	0	17	20	15	10	1	1	10	4	1.765	5.29	68	5.60	.291	2	.286	-3	0	-0.3
Total	**4**	**32**	**29**	**.525**	**67**	**64**	**58**	**1**	**0**	**551^2**	**612**	**382**	**289**	**22**	**60**	**249**	**158**	**1.561**	**4.71**	**95**	**4.73**	**.279**	**61**	**.256**	**-14**	**36**	**-1.1**
• FRIES, Pete					Peter Martin Fries b: 10/30/1857, Scranton, PA d: 7/30/1937, Chicago, IL BL/TL, 5'8", 160 lbs. Deb: 8/10/1883 ♦																						
1883	Col-a	0	3	.000	3	3	3	0	0	25	34	31	18	1	....	14	7	1.920	6.48	47	....	.305	3	.300	-10	0	-0.7
• FRILL, John					John Edmond Frill b: 4/3/1879, Reading, PA d: 9/28/1918, Westerly, RI BR/TL, 5'10.5", 170 lbs. Deb: 4/16/1910																						
1910	NY-A	2	2	.500	10	5	3	1	1	48^1	55	33	24	1	1	5	27	1.241	4.47	59	3.31	.289	2	.111	-8	0	-1.1
1912	StL-A	0	1	.000	3	3	0	0	0	4^1	16	11	10	1	1	1	2	3.923	20.77	16	25.94	.571	1	.500	-8	0	-0.8
	Cin-N	1	0	1.000	3	2	0	0	0	15	19	11	10	0	2	1	4	1.333	6.00	56	4.11	.345	1	.250	-4	0	-0.4
Total	**2**	**3**	**3**	**.500**	**16**	**10**	**3**	**1**	**1**	**67^2**	**90**	**55**	**44**	**2**	**4**	**7**	**33**	**1.433**	**5.85**	**50**	**4.93**	**.329**	**4**	**.167**	**-21**	**0**	**-2.3**
• FRISELLA, Danny					Daniel Vincent "Bear" Frisella b: 3/4/1946, San Francisco, CA d: 1/1/1977, Phoenix, AZ BL/TR, 6', 195 lbs. Deb: 7/27/1967																						
1967	NY-N	1	6	.143	14	11	0	0	0	74	68	32	28	6	0	33	51	1.365	3.41	99	3.66	.249	2	.087	-0	3	-0.1
1968	NY-N	2	4	.333	19	4	0	0	2	50^2	53	23	22	5	0	17	47	1.382	3.91	77	4.10	.270	1	.083	-6	1	-0.7
1969	NY-N	0	0	....	3	0	0	0	0	4^2	8	4	4	1	0	3	5	2.357	7.71	47	10.98	.381	0	.000	-2	0	-0.2
1970	NY-N	8	3	.727	30	1	0	0	1	65^2	49	23	22	4	0	34	54	1.264	3.02	133	2.60	.204	4	.308	6	7	0.7
1971	NY-N	8	5	.615	53	0	0	0	12	90^2	76	28	20	6	3	30	93	1.169	1.99	172	2.69	.227	3	.231	13	12	1.5
1972	NY-N	5	8	.385	39	0	0	0	9	67^1	63	31	25	8	0	20	46	1.233	3.34	101	3.28	.243	2	.286	1	6	0.1
1973	Atl-N	1	2	.333	42	0	0	0	8	45	40	27	21	5	1	23	27	1.400	4.20	94	3.91	.241	1	.500	-1	3	-0.1
1974	Atl-N	3	4	.429	36	1	0	0	6	41^2	37	26	24	4	0	28	27	1.560	5.18	73	4.12	.240	0	.000	-7	1	-0.7
1975	SD-N	1	6	.143	65	0	0	0	9	97^2	86	36	34	7	2	51	67	1.403	3.13	111	3.51	.242	1	.200	5	8	0.5
1976	StL-N	0	0	....	18	0	0	0	1	22^2	19	10	10	3	0	13	11	1.412	3.97	89	4.06	.232	0	.000	-1	1	-0.1
	Mil-A	5	2	.714	32	0	0	0	9	49^1	30	16	15	4	1	34	43	1.297	2.74	128	2.83	.175	0	....	4	6	0.4
Total	**10**	**34**	**40**	**.459**	**351**	**17**	**0**	**0**	**57**	**609^1**	**529**	**256**	**225**	**53**	**7**	**286**	**471**	**1.338**	**3.32**	**106**	**3.43**	**.235**	**14**	**.179**	**12**	**48**	**1.4**
• FRISK, Emil					John Emil Frisk b: 10/15/1874, Kalkaska, MI d: 1/27/1922, Seattle, WA BL/TR, 6'1", 190 lbs. Deb: 9/2/1899 ♦																						
1899	Cin-N	3	6	.333	9	9	9	0	0	68^1	81	52	30	1	6	17	17	1.434	3.95	99	4.01	.294	7	.280	-1	4	0.1
1901	Det-A	5	4	.556	11	7	6	0	0	74^2	94	60	36	1	2	26	22	1.607	4.34	89	4.53	.304	15	.313	-5	5	-0.2
Total	**2**	**8**	**10**	**.444**	**20**	**16**	**15**	**0**	**0**	**143**	**175**	**112**	**66**	**2**	**8**	**43**	**39**	**1.524**	**4.15**	**93**	**4.28**	**.299**	**135**	**.267**	**-5**	**9**	**-0.1**
• FRITZ, Charlie					Charles Cornelius Fritz b: 6/18/1882, Mobile, AL d: 7/30/1943, Mobile, AL TL Deb: 10/5/1907																						
1907	Phi-A	0	0	....	1	1	0	0	0	3	0	1	1	0	1	3	1	1.000	3.00	87	1.32	.000	0	.000	-0	0	0.0
• FROATS, Bill					William John Froats b: 10/20/1930, New York, NY d: 2/9/1998, Minneapolis, MN BL/TL, 6', 180 lbs. Deb: 4/22/1955																						
1955	Det-A	0	0	....	1	0	0	0	0	2	0	0	0	0	0	2	0	1.000	0.00	....	1.08	.000	0	....	1	0	0.1
• FROCK, Sam					Samuel William Frock b: 12/23/1882, Baltimore, MD d: 11/3/1925, Baltimore, MD BR/TR, 6', 168 lbs. Deb: 9/21/1907																						
1907	Bos-N	1	2	.333	5	3	3	1	0	33^1	28	17	11	1	2	11	12	1.170	2.97	86	2.89	.243	1	.071	-2	1	-0.3
1909	Pit-N	2	1	.667	8	4	3	0	1	36^1	44	19	10	0	3	4	11	1.321	2.48	104	3.74	.299	2	.143	-0	2	-0.1
1910	Pit-N	0	0	....	1	0	0	0	0	2	2	4	1	0	1	2	1	2.000	4.50	70	9.73	.400	0	....	-0	0	0.0
	Bos-N	12	19	.387	45	29	13	2	2	255^1	245	133	91	8	4	91	170	1.316	3.21	103	3.38	.262	16	.190	-1	14	-0.4
	Yr.	12	19	.387	46	29	13	2	2	257^1	247	137	92	8	5	93	171	1.321	3.22	103	3.43	.263	16	.190	-2	14	-0.4
1911	Bos-N	0	1	.000	4	1	1	0	0	16	29	18	10	0	1	5	8	2.125	5.63	68	8.82	.426	1	.200	-3	0	-0.3
Total	**4**	**15**	**23**	**.395**	**63**	**37**	**20**	**3**	**3**	**343**	**348**	**191**	**123**	**9**	**11**	**113**	**202**	**1.344**	**3.23**	**99**	**3.66**	**.274**	**20**	**.171**	**-6**	**17**	**-1.1**
• FROHWIRTH, Todd					Todd Gerard Frohwirth b: 9/28/1962, Milwaukee, WI BR/TR, 6'4", 205 lbs. Deb: 8/10/1987																						
1987	Phi-N	1	0	1.000	10	0	0	0	0	11	12	0	0	0	0	2	9	1.273	0.00	....	3.31	.293	0	.000	5	2	0.5
1988	Phi-N	1	2	.333	12	0	0	0	0	12	16	11	11	2	0	11	11	2.250	8.25	43	7.79	.327	0	....	-6	0	-0.7
1989	Phi-N	1	0	1.000	45	0	0	0	0	62^2	56	26	25	4	3	18	39	1.181	3.59	99	3.04	.240	0	.000	0	3	0.0
1990	Phi-N	0	1	.000	5	0	0	0	0	1	3	2	2	0	0	6	1	9.000	18.00	21	37.18	.500	0	....	-2	0	-0.2
1991	Bal-A	7	3	.700	51	0	0	0	3	96^1	64	24	20	2	1	29	77	.965	1.87	211	1.62	.190	0	....	22	11	2.2
1992	Bal-A	4	3	.571	65	0	0	0	4	106	97	33	29	4	3	41	58	1.302	2.46	163	3.23	.247	0	....	18	11	1.8
1993	Bal-A	6	7	.462	70	0	0	0	3	96^1	91	47	41	7	3	44	50	1.401	3.83	117	3.85	.256	0	....	5	8	0.5
1994	Bos-A	0	3	.000	22	0	0	0	1	26^2	40	36	32	3	2	17	13	2.138	10.80	47	8.13	.339	0	....	-17	0	-1.6
1996	Cal-A	0	0	....	4	0	0	0	0	5^2	10	11	7	1	1	4	1	2.471	11.12	44	11.29	.370	0	....	-4	0	-0.4
Total	**9**	**20**	**19**	**.513**	**284**	**0**	**0**	**0**	**11**	**417^2**	**389**	**190**	**167**	**23**	**13**	**172**	**259**	**1.343**	**3.60**	**116**	**3.61**	**.250**	**0**	**.000**	**21**	**35**	**2.2**
• FROMME, Art					Arthur Henry Fromme b: 9/3/1883, Quincy, IL d: 8/24/1956, Los Angeles, CA BR/TR, 6', 178 lbs. Deb: 9/14/1906																						
1906	StL-N	1	2	.333	3	3	3	1	0	25	19	6	4	0	1	10	11	1.160	1.44	182	2.38	.221	2	.222	4	2	0.4
1907	StL-N	5	13	.278	23	16	13	2	0	145^2	138	73	47	3	4	67	67	1.407	2.90	86	3.57	.256	10	.182	-6	4	-0.6
1908	StL-N	5	13	.278	20	14	9	2	0	116	102	59	35	1	2	50	62	1.310	2.72	86	2.68	.218	5	.139	-2	3	-0.3
1909	Cin-N	19	13	.594	37	34	22	4	2	279^1	195	84	59	2	3	101	126	1.060	1.90	136	1.88	.201	18	.191	19	19	2.4
1910	Cin-N	3	4	.429	11	5	1	0	0	49^1	44	22	16	2	1	39	40	1.682	2.92	100	4.79	.260	2	.133	0	2	0.0
1911	Cin-N	10	11	.476	38	26	11	1	0	208	190	111	80	8	16	79	107	1.293	3.46	95	3.41	.248	14	.189	-3	8	-0.4
1912	Cin-N	16	18	.471	43	37	23	3	0	296	285	126	90	7	11	88	120	1.260	2.74	122	3.06	.260	9	.087	24	20	1.5
1913	Cin-N	1	4	.200	9	7	2	0	0	56	55	30	26	1	2	21	24	1.357	4.18	78	3.43	.274	3	.143	-6	1	-0.6
	NY-N	11	6	.647	26	12	3	0	0	112^1	112	58	50	5	3	29	50	1.255	4.01	78	3.18	.260	6	.171	-12	5	-1.2
	Yr.	12	10	.545	35	19	5	0	0	168^1	167	88	76	6	5	50	74	1.289	4.06	78	3.26	.264	9	.161	-18	6	-1.9
1914	NY-N	9	5	.643	38	12	3	1	2	138	142	57	49	7	7	44	57	1.348	3.20	83	3.86	.283	7	.226	-8	6	-0.8
1915	NY-N	0	1	.000	4	1	0	0	0	12^1	15	11	8	1	0	2	4	1.378	5.84	44	4.07	.306	1	.333	-4	1	-0.4
Total	**10**	**80**	**90**	**.471**	**252**	**167**	**90**	**14**	**4**	**1438**	**1297**	**637**	**464**	**37**	**50**	**530**	**638**	**1.271**	**2.90**	**100**	**3.06**	**.246**	**77**	**.162**	**6**	**73**	**-0.2**
• FROST, Dave					Carl David Frost b: 11/17/1952, Long Beach, CA BR/TR, 6'6", 235 lbs. Deb: 9/11/1977																						
1977	Chi-A	1	1	.500	4	3	0	0	0	23^2	30	9	8	0	1	3	15	1.394	3.04	134	4.02	.323	0	....	3	2	0.3
1978	Cal-A	5	4	.556	11	10	2	1	0	80^1	71	24	23	6	2	24	30	1.183	2.58	140	2.96	.240	0	....	10	7	1.0
1979★	Cal-A	16	10	.615	36	33	12	2	1	239^1	226	108	95	17	5	77	107	1.266	3.57	114	3.35	.251	0	....	14	15	1.4
1980	Cal-A	4	8	.333	15	15	2	0	0	78^1	97	53	46	8	2	21	28	1.506	5.29	74	5.08	.308	0	....	-12	1	-1.2
1981	Cal-A	1	8	.111	12	9	0	0	0	47^1	44	30	29	3	1	19	16	1.331	5.51	66	3.56	.250	0	....	-10	0	-1.1
1982	KC-A	6	6	.500	21	14	0	0	0	81^2	103	53	50	7	3	30	26	1.629	5.51	74	5.57	.313	0	....	-13	1	-1.3
Total	**6**	**33**	**37**	**.471**	**99**	**84**	**16**	**3**	**1**	**550^2**	**571**	**277**	**251**	**41**	**14**	**174**	**222**	**1.353**	**4.10**	**96**	**3.91**	**.271**	**0**	**....**	**-7**	**26**	**-0.8**
• FRY, Johnson					Johnson "Jay" Fry b: 11/21/1901, Huntington, WV d: 4/7/1959, Carmi, IL BR/TR, 6'1", 150 lbs. Deb: 8/24/1923																						
1923	Cle-A	0	0	....	1	0	0	0	0	3^2	6	5	5	0	0	4	0	2.727	12.27	32	9.49	.353	1	1.000	-3	0	-0.2
• FRYE, Charlie					Charles Andrew Frye b: 7/17/1914, Hickory, NC d: 5/25/1945, Hickory, NC BR/TR, 6'1", 175 lbs. Deb: 7/28/1940																						
1940	Phi-N	0	6	.000	15	5	1	0	0	50^1	58	32	26	3	0	26	18	1.669	4.65	84	5.00	.291	5	.263	-4	1	-0.3
• FRYMAN, Woodie					Woodrow Thompson Fryman b: 4/15/1940, Ewing, KY BR/TL, 6'3", 205 lbs. Deb: 4/15/1966																						
1966	Pit-N	12	9	.571	36	28	9	3	1	181^2	182	86	77	13	1	47	105	1.261	3.81	94	3.33	.261	10	.159	-8	8	-1.0
1967	Pit-N	3	8	.273	28	18	3	1	1	113^1	121	67	51	12	4	44	74	1.456	4.05	83	4.56	.276	4	.118	-10	1	-1.2
1968	Phi-N★	12	14	.462	34	32	10	5	0	213^2	198	78	66	12	6	64	151	1.226	2.78	108	3.09	.246	6	.085	8	13	0.6
1969	Phi-N	12	15	.444	36	35	10	1	0	228^1	243	123	112	15	11	89	150	1.454	4.41	80	4.29	.270	9	.118	-22	6	-2.5
1970	Phi-N	8	6	.571	27	20	4	3	0	127^2	122	61	58	11	1	43	97	1.292	4.09	98	3.55	.253	5	.128	-0	8	-0.2
1971	Phi-N	10	7	.588	37	17	3	2	2	149^1	133	61	56	7	3	46	104	1.199	3.38	104	2.87	.242	7	.189	1	11	0.1
1972	Phi-N	4	10	.286	23	17	3	2	1	119^2	131	64	58	15	2	39	69	1.421	4.36	82	4.46	.279	5	.152	-12	3	-1.2
	★Det-A	10	3	.769	16	14	6	1	0	113^2	93	31	26	6	7	31	72	1.091	2.06	153	2.50	.220	5	.125	12	11	1.2
1973	Det-A	6	13	.316	34	29	1	0	0	169^2	200	106	101	23	3	64	119	**1.556**	5.36	76	5.35	.294	0	....	-23	2	-2.3
1974	Det-A	6	9	.400	27	22	4	1	0	141^2	120	73	68	16	4	67	92	1.320	4.32	88	3.74	.233	0	....	-7	7	-0.8

YEAR	TM-L	W	L	PCT	G	GS	CG	SH	SV	IP	H	R	ER	HR	HB	BB	SO	RAT	ERA	ERA+	CERA	OAV	BH	AVG	PR+	WS	TPW
1975	Mon-N	9	12	.429	38	20	7	3	3	157	141	69	58	10	5	68	118	1.331	3.32	115	3.44	.239	10	.204	8	12	1.0
1976	Mon-N★	13	13	.500	34	32	4	2	2	216^1	218	89	81	14	9	76	123	1.359	3.37	110	3.78	.263	7	.109	9	14	0.6
1977	Cin-N	5	5	.500	17	12	0	0	1	75^1	83	45	45	13	2	45	57	1.699	5.38	73	6.22	.292	7	.318	-13	2	-1.1
1978	Chi-N	2	4	.333	13	9	0	0	0	55^2	64	37	32	6	0	37	28	1.814	5.17	78	6.10	.309	1	.063	-7	1	-0.8
	Mon-N	5	7	.417	19	17	4	3	1	94^2	93	39	38	4	3	37	53	1.373	3.61	97	3.70	.260	2	.059	-4	4	-0.7
	Yr.	7	11	.389	32	26	4	3	1	150^1	157	76	70	10	3	74	81	1.537	4.19	89	4.59	.278	3	.060	-11	5	-1.5
1979	Mon-N	3	6	.333	44	0	0	0	10	58	52	25	18	4	3	22	44	1.276	2.79	131	3.40	.248	0	.000	5	6	0.5
1980	Mon-N	7	4	.636	61	0	0	0	17	80	61	23	20	1	2	30	59	1.138	2.25	159	2.08	.209	2	.167	12	13	1.3
1981*	Mon-N	5	3	.625	35	0	0	0	7	43	38	16	9	1	1	14	25	1.209	1.88	186	2.84	.247	2	.667	8	6	0.9
1982	Mon-N	9	4	.692	60	0	0	0	12	69^2	66	36	29	3	1	26	46	1.321	3.75	97	3.30	.259	2	.222	-1	6	-0.1
1983	Mon-N	0	3	.000	6	0	0	0	0	3	8	7	7	1	0	1	1	3.000	21.00	17	19.59	.571	0	....	-6	0	-0.6
Total	**18**	**141**	**155**	**.476**	**625**	**322**	**68**	**27**	**58**	**2411^1**	**2367**	**1136**	**1010**	**187**	**68**	**890**	**1587**	**1.351**	**3.77**	**96**	**3.81**	**.259**	**84**	**.138**	**-50**	**134**	**-6.1**

• FUCHS, Charlie Charles Thomas Fuchs b: 11/18/1913, Union City, NJ d: 6/10/1969, Weehawken, NJ BB/TR, 5'8", 168 lbs. Deb: 4/17/1942

YEAR	TM-L	W	L	PCT	G	GS	CG	SH	SV	IP	H	R	ER	HR	HB	BB	SO	RAT	ERA	ERA+	CERA	OAV	BH	AVG	PR+	WS	TPW
1942	Det-A	3	3	.500	9	4	1	1	0	36^2	43	27	27	5	1	19	15	1.691	6.63	60	5.64	.285	1	.077	-10	0	-1.2
1943	Phi-N	2	7	.222	17	9	4	1	1	77^2	76	40	37	4	3	34	12	1.416	4.29	79	3.83	.266	2	.091	-7	2	-0.9
	StL-A	0	0	....	13	0	0	0	0	35^2	42	22	16	4	1	11	9	1.486	4.04	82	4.85	.294	0	.000	-2	0	-0.4
1944	Bro-N	1	0	1.000	8	0	0	0	0	15^2	25	16	10	2	1	9	5	2.170	5.74	62	8.43	.347	0	.000	-3	0	-0.3
Total	**3**	**6**	**10**	**.375**	**47**	**13**	**5**	**2**	**1**	**165^2**	**186**	**105**	**90**	**15**	**6**	**73**	**41**	**1.563**	**4.89**	**72**	**4.88**	**.285**	**3**	**.070**	**-23**	**2**	**-2.8**

• FUENTES, Brian Brian Christopher Fuentes b: 8/9/1975, Merced, CA BL/TL, 6'4", 220 lbs. Deb: 6/2/2001

YEAR	TM-L	W	L	PCT	G	GS	CG	SH	SV	IP	H	R	ER	HR	HB	BB	SO	RAT	ERA	ERA+	CERA	OAV	BH	AVG	PR+	WS	TPW
2001	Sea-A	1	1	.500	10	0	0	0	0	11^2	6	6	6	2	3	8	10	1.200	4.63	90	4.39	.171	0	....	-1	1	-0.1
2002	Col-N	2	0	1.000	31	0	0	0	0	26^2	25	14	14	4	3	13	38	1.425	4.73	101	4.91	.250	0	....	0	2	0.0
2003	Col-N	3	3	.500	75	0	0	0	4	75^1	64	24	23	7	6	34	82	1.301	2.75	179	3.71	.231	0	.000	19	10	1.9
Total	**3**	**6**	**4**	**.600**	**116**	**0**	**0**	**0**	**4**	**113^2**	**95**	**44**	**43**	**13**	**12**	**55**	**130**	**1.320**	**3.40**	**139**	**4.06**	**.231**	**0**	**.000**	**19**	**13**	**1.9**

• FUENTES, Miguel Miguel (Pinet) Fuentes b: 5/10/1946, Loiza Aldea, Puerto Rico d: 1/29/1970, Loiza Aldea, Puerto Rico BR/TR, 6', 160 lbs. Deb: 9/1/1969

YEAR	TM-L	W	L	PCT	G	GS	CG	SH	SV	IP	H	R	ER	HR	HB	BB	SO	RAT	ERA	ERA+	CERA	OAV	BH	AVG	PR+	WS	TPW
1969	Sea-A	1	3	.250	8	4	1	0	0	26	29	15	15	1	0	16	14	1.731	5.19	70	5.15	.284	2	.333	-4	1	-0.3

• FUHR, Oscar Oscar Lawrence Fuhr b: 8/22/1893, Defiance, MO d: 3/27/1975, Dallas, TX BL/TL, 6'.5", 176 lbs. Deb: 4/19/1921

YEAR	TM-L	W	L	PCT	G	GS	CG	SH	SV	IP	H	R	ER	HR	HB	BB	SO	RAT	ERA	ERA+	CERA	OAV	BH	AVG	PR+	WS	TPW
1921	Chi-N	0	0	....	1	0	0	0	0	4	11	9	4	1	0	0	2	2.750	9.00	42	16.01	.500	0	.000	-2	0	-0.2
1924	Bos-A	3	6	.333	23	10	4	1	0	80^1	100	71	53	1	5	39	30	1.730	5.94	74	5.16	.310	4	.182	-13	0	-1.3
1925	Bos-A	0	6	.000	39	5	0	0	0	91^1	138	83	67	7	3	30	27	1.839	6.60	69	6.70	.364	5	.250	-18	0	-1.7
Total	**3**	**3**	**12**	**.200**	**63**	**15**	**4**	**1**	**0**	**175^2**	**249**	**163**	**124**	**9**	**8**	**69**	**59**	**1.810**	**6.35**	**70**	**6.21**	**.344**	**9**	**.209**	**-34**	**0**	**-3.2**

• FULGHAM, John John Thomas Fulgham b: 6/9/1956, St. Louis, MO BR/TR, 6'2", 205 lbs. Deb: 6/19/1979

YEAR	TM-L	W	L	PCT	G	GS	CG	SH	SV	IP	H	R	ER	HR	HB	BB	SO	RAT	ERA	ERA+	CERA	OAV	BH	AVG	PR+	WS	TPW
1979	StL-N	10	6	.625	20	19	10	2	0	146	123	47	41	10	3	26	75	1.021	2.53	149	2.31	.227	6	.143	17	14	1.9
1980	StL-N	4	6	.400	15	14	4	1	0	85^1	66	33	32	7	1	32	48	1.148	3.38	109	2.80	.219	0	.000	2	4	-0.2
Total	**2**	**14**	**12**	**.538**	**35**	**33**	**14**	**3**	**0**	**231^1**	**189**	**80**	**73**	**17**	**4**	**58**	**123**	**1.068**	**2.84**	**131**	**2.49**	**.224**	**6**	**.087**	**19**	**18**	**1.7**

• FULLERTON, Curt Curtis Hooper Fullerton b: 9/13/1898, Ellsworth, ME d: 1/2/1975, Winthrop, MA BL/TR, 6', 162 lbs. Deb: 4/14/1921

YEAR	TM-L	W	L	PCT	G	GS	CG	SH	SV	IP	H	R	ER	HR	HB	BB	SO	RAT	ERA	ERA+	CERA	OAV	BH	AVG	PR+	WS	TPW
1921	Bos-A	0	1	.000	4	1	1	0	0	15^1	22	17	15	3	1	10	4	2.087	8.80	48	8.90	.355	0	.000	-8	0	-0.8
1922	Bos-A	1	4	.200	31	3	0	0	0	64^1	70	40	39	4	5	35	17	1.632	5.46	75	5.06	.290	2	.250	-9	2	-0.7
1923	Bos-A	2	15	.118	37	15	6	0	1	143^1	167	108	81	9	6	71	37	1.660	5.09	81	5.16	.300	11	.297	-15	3	-1.3
1924	Bos-A	7	12	.368	33	20	9	0	2	152	166	93	73	1	6	73	33	1.572	4.32	101	4.19	.283	3	.071	3	7	0.0
1925	Bos-A	0	3	.000	4	2	0	0	0	22^2	22	11	8	1	2	9	3	1.368	3.18	143	3.66	.259	2	.200	4	1	0.4
1933	Bos-A	0	2	.000	6	2	2	0	0	25^1	36	24	24	1	1	13	10	1.934	8.53	51	6.99	.364	2	.222	-12	0	-1.1
Total	**6**	**10**	**37**	**.213**	**115**	**43**	**18**	**0**	**3**	**423**	**483**	**293**	**240**	**19**	**21**	**211**	**104**	**1.641**	**5.11**	**83**	**4.96**	**.296**	**20**	**.182**	**-36**	**13**	**-3.5**

• FULMER, Chick Charles John Fulmer b: 2/12/1851, Philadelphia, PA d: 2/15/1940, Philadelphia, PA BR/TR, 6', 158 lbs. Deb: 8/23/1871 U

YEAR	TM-L	W	L	PCT	G	GS	CG	SH	SV	IP	H	R	ER	HR	HB	BB	SO	RAT	ERA	ERA+	CERA	OAV	BH	AVG	PR+	WS	TPW
1873	Phi-n	0	0	....	2	0	0	0	0	5	7	4	2	0	....	1	0	1.600	3.60	92	....	.294	66	.280	-0	....	0.8

• FULTON, Bill William David Fulton b: 10/22/1963, Pittsburgh, PA BR/TR, 6'3", 195 lbs. Deb: 9/12/1987

YEAR	TM-L	W	L	PCT	G	GS	CG	SH	SV	IP	H	R	ER	HR	HB	BB	SO	RAT	ERA	ERA+	CERA	OAV	BH	AVG	PR+	WS	TPW
1987	NY-A	1	0	1.000	3	0	0	0	0	4^2	9	6	6	4	1	1	2	2.143	11.57	38	17.95	.409	0	....	-4	0	-0.4

• FULTZ, Aaron Richard Aaron Fultz b: 9/4/1973, Memphis, TN BL/TL, 6', 196 lbs. Deb: 4/5/2000

YEAR	TM-L	W	L	PCT	G	GS	CG	SH	SV	IP	H	R	ER	HR	HB	BB	SO	RAT	ERA	ERA+	CERA	OAV	BH	AVG	PR+	WS	TPW
2000*	SF-N	5	2	.714	58	0	0	0	1	69^1	67	38	36	8	3	28	62	1.370	4.67	90	4.19	.263	2	.333	-4	3	-0.3
2001	SF-N	3	1	.750	66	0	0	0	1	71	70	40	36	9	1	21	67	1.282	4.56	87	3.75	.258	2	.400	-5	3	-0.4
2002*	SF-N	2	2	.500	43	0	0	0	0	41^1	47	22	22	4	3	19	31	1.597	4.79	81	5.36	.294	0	.000	-5	1	-0.5
2003	Tex-A	1	3	.250	64	0	0	0	0	67^1	75	43	39	9	2	27	53	1.515	5.21	95	4.99	.287	0	....	-1	3	-0.1
Total	**4**	**11**	**8**	**.579**	**231**	**0**	**0**	**0**	**2**	**249**	**259**	**143**	**133**	**30**	**9**	**95**	**213**	**1.422**	**4.81**	**89**	**4.47**	**.273**	**4**	**.333**	**-14**	**10**	**-1.2**

• FUNK, Frank Franklin Ray Funk b: 8/30/1935, Washington, DC BR/TR, 6', 175 lbs. Deb: 9/3/1960 C

YEAR	TM-L	W	L	PCT	G	GS	CG	SH	SV	IP	H	R	ER	HR	HB	BB	SO	RAT	ERA	ERA+	CERA	OAV	BH	AVG	PR+	WS	TPW
1960	Cle-A	4	2	.667	9	0	0	0	1	31^2	27	8	7	3	0	9	18	1.137	1.99	188	2.87	.248	1	.111	6	4	0.6
1961	Cle-A	11	11	.500	56	0	0	0	11	92^1	79	35	34	9	4	31	64	1.191	3.31	119	3.12	.234	1	.059	6	11	0.5
1962	Cle-A	2	1	.667	47	0	0	0	6	80^2	62	35	29	11	4	32	49	1.165	3.24	120	3.21	.212	1	.067	5	7	0.4
1963	Mil-N	3	3	.500	25	0	0	0	0	43^2	42	14	13	3	1	13	19	1.260	2.68	120	3.33	.258	0	.000	2	3	0.2
Total	**4**	**20**	**17**	**.541**	**137**	**0**	**0**	**0**	**18**	**248^1**	**210**	**92**	**83**	**26**	**9**	**85**	**150**	**1.188**	**3.01**	**125**	**3.15**	**.233**	**3**	**.067**	**19**	**25**	**1.7**

• FUNK, Tom Thomas James Funk b: 3/13/1962, Kansas City, MO BL/TL, 6'2", 210 lbs. Deb: 7/24/1986

YEAR	TM-L	W	L	PCT	G	GS	CG	SH	SV	IP	H	R	ER	HR	HB	BB	SO	RAT	ERA	ERA+	CERA	OAV	BH	AVG	PR+	WS	TPW
1986	Hou-N	0	0	....	8	0	0	0	0	8^1	10	6	6	1	0	6	2	1.920	6.48	56	6.59	.286	0	.000	-3	0	-0.3

• FUSSELL, Chris Christopher Wren Fussell b: 5/19/1976, Oregon, OH BR/TR, 6'2", 200 lbs. Deb: 9/15/1998

YEAR	TM-L	W	L	PCT	G	GS	CG	SH	SV	IP	H	R	ER	HR	HB	BB	SO	RAT	ERA	ERA+	CERA	OAV	BH	AVG	PR+	WS	TPW
1998	Bal-A	0	1	.000	3	2	0	0	0	9^2	11	9	9	1	0	9	8	2.069	8.38	54	7.05	.306	0	....	-4	0	-0.4
1999	KC-A	0	5	.000	17	8	0	0	2	56	72	51	46	9	5	36	37	1.929	7.39	68	7.92	.329	0	....	-16	0	-1.5
2000	KC-A	5	3	.625	20	9	0	0	0	70	76	52	49	18	2	44	46	1.714	6.30	81	6.96	.286	0	.000	-11	2	-1.0
Total	**3**	**5**	**9**	**.357**	**40**	**19**	**0**	**0**	**2**	**135^2**	**159**	**112**	**104**	**28**	**7**	**89**	**91**	**1.828**	**6.90**	**73**	**7.36**	**.305**	**0**	**.000**	**-31**	**2**	**-2.9**

• FUSSELL, Fred Frederick Morris "Moonlight Ace" Fussell b: 10/7/1895, Sheridan, MO d: 10/23/1966, Syracuse, NY BL/TL, 5'10", 155 lbs. Deb: 9/23/1922

YEAR	TM-L	W	L	PCT	G	GS	CG	SH	SV	IP	H	R	ER	HR	HB	BB	SO	RAT	ERA	ERA+	CERA	OAV	BH	AVG	PR+	WS	TPW
1922	Chi-N	1	1	.500	3	2	1	0	0	19	24	11	10	0	0	8	4	1.684	4.74	89	5.17	.333	0	.000	-1	1	-0.2
1923	Chi-N	3	5	.375	28	2	1	0	3	76^1	90	51	47	2	3	31	38	1.585	5.54	72	4.55	.298	4	.200	-15	2	-1.4
1928	Pit-N	8	9	.471	28	20	9	2	1	159^2	183	79	64	6	1	41	43	1.403	3.61	112	3.84	.295	7	.121	8	9	0.4
1929	Pit-N	2	2	.500	21	3	0	0	1	39^2	68	42	38	8	1	8	18	1.916	8.62	55	8.66	.389	4	.250	-18	0	-1.4
Total	**4**	**14**	**17**	**.452**	**80**	**27**	**11**	**2**	**5**	**294^2**	**365**	**183**	**159**	**16**	**5**	**88**	**103**	**1.537**	**4.86**	**86**	**4.76**	**.312**	**15**	**.150**	**-26**	**12**	**-2.6**

• FYHRIE, Mike Michael Edwin Fyhrie b: 12/9/1969, Long Beach, CA BR/TR, 6'2", 190 lbs. Deb: 9/14/1996

YEAR	TM-L	W	L	PCT	G	GS	CG	SH	SV	IP	H	R	ER	HR	HB	BB	SO	RAT	ERA	ERA+	CERA	OAV	BH	AVG	PR+	WS	TPW
1996	NY-N	0	1	.000	2	0	0	0	0	2^1	4	4	4	0	0	3	0	3.000	15.43	26	11.30	.364	0	....	-3	0	-0.3
1999	Ana-A	0	4	.000	16	7	0	0	0	51^2	61	32	29	8	0	21	26	1.587	5.05	96	5.45	.286	0	....	-2	2	-0.2
2000	Ana-A	0	0	....	32	0	0	0	0	52^2	54	14	14	4	0	15	43	1.310	2.39	212	3.53	.269	0	....	14	6	1.3
2001	Chi-N	0	2	.000	15	0	0	0	0	15	16	7	7	1	0	7	6	1.533	4.20	99	4.67	.281	0	.000	0	1	0.0
	Oak-A	0	0	....	3	0	0	0	0	5	2	0	0	0	0	1	5	.600	0.00	....	0.67	.125	0	....	2	1	0.2
2002	Oak-A	2	4	.333	16	4	0	0	0	48^2	46	25	24	3	4	20	29	1.356	4.44	99	3.81	.246	0	....	0	3	0.0
Total	**5**	**2**	**11**	**.154**	**84**	**11**	**0**	**0**	**0**	**175^1**	**183**	**82**	**78**	**16**	**4**	**67**	**109**	**1.426**	**4.00**	**115**	**4.29**	**.267**	**0**	**.000**	**13**	**13**	**1.1**

• GABLER, Frank Frank Harold "The Great Gabbo" Gabler b: 11/6/1911, East Highland, CA d: 11/1/1967, Long Beach, CA BR/TR, 6'1", 175 lbs. Deb: 4/19/1935

YEAR	TM-L	W	L	PCT	G	GS	CG	SH	SV	IP	H	R	ER	HR	HB	BB	SO	RAT	ERA	ERA+	CERA	OAV	BH	AVG	PR+	WS	TPW
1935	NY-N	2	1	.667	26	1	0	0	0	60	79	43	38	6	0	20	24	1.650	5.70	68	5.49	.315	2	.125	-13	0	-1.3
1936*	NY-N	9	8	.529	43	14	5	0	6	161^2	170	62	56	11	3	34	46	1.262	3.12	125	3.48	.274	10	.208	9	15	1.0
1937	NY-N	0	0	....	6	0	0	0	0	9	20	14	10	1	0	2	3	2.444	10.00	39	11.23	.455	0	....	-6	0	-0.6
	Bos-N	4	7	.364	19	9	2	1	2	76	84	45	43	7	0	16	19	1.316	5.09	70	3.87	.283	4	.182	-14	1	-1.4
	Yr.	4	7	.364	25	9	2	1	2	85	104	59	53	8	0	18	22	1.435	5.61	65	4.65	.305	4	.182	-21	1	-2.0

YEAR TM-L	W	L	PCT	G	GS	CG	SH	SV	IP	H	R	ER	HR	HB	BB	SO	RAT	ERA	ERA+	CERA	OAV	BH	AVG	PR+	WS	TPW
1938 Bos-N	0	0	....	1	0	0	0	0	0^1	3	3	3	0	0	1	0	12.00	81.00	4	102.74	1.000	0	....	-3	0	-0.3
Chi-A	1	7	.125	18	7	3	0	0	69^1	101	74	70	12	1	34	17	1.947	9.09	54	7.91	.348	5	.238	-32	0	-2.9
Total 4	16	23	.410	113	31	10	1	8	376^1	457	241	220	37	4	107	109	1.499	5.26	77	4.97	.303	21	.196	-60	16	-5.5
• GABLER, John	John Richard Gabler b: 10/2/1930, Kansas City, MO BB/TR, 6'2", 165 lbs. Deb: 9/18/1959																									
1959 NY-A	1	1	.500	3	1	0	0	0	19^1	21	6	6	1	1	10	11	1.603	2.79	131	5.06	.284	0	.000	2	1	0.1
1960 NY-A	3	3	.500	21	4	0	0	1	52	46	27	24	2	0	32	19	1.500	4.15	86	3.80	.242	1	.091	-5	2	-0.5
1961 Was-A	3	8	.273	29	9	0	0	4	92^2	104	61	50	5	1	37	33	1.522	4.86	81	4.41	.283	5	.200	-10	2	-0.9
Total 3	7	12	.368	53	14	0	0	5	164	171	94	80	8	2	79	63	1.524	4.39	86	4.29	.271	6	.143	-13	5	-1.3
• GABLES, Ken	Kenneth Harlin "Coral" Gables b: 1/31/1919, Walnut Grove, MO d: 1/2/1960, Walnut Grove, MO BR/TR, 5'11", 210 lbs. Deb: 4/18/1945																									
1945 Pit-N	11	7	.611	29	16	6	0	1	138^2	139	69	64	5	4	46	49	1.334	4.15	95	3.36	.256	4	.103	-2	8	-0.4
1946 Pit-N	2	4	.333	32	7	0	0	1	100^2	113	64	59	3	1	52	39	1.639	5.27	67	4.53	.281	6	.250	-18	1	-1.8
1947 Pit-N	0	0	....	1	0	0	0	0	0^1	3	2	2	1	0	0	0	9.000	54.00	8	116.77	.750	0	....	-2	0	-0.2
Total 3	13	11	.542	62	23	6	0	2	239^2	255	135	125	9	5	98	88	1.473	4.69	80	4.01	.269	10	.159	-22	9	-2.4
• GADDY, John	John Wilson "Sheriff" Gaddy b: 2/5/1914, Wadesboro, NC d: 5/3/1966, Albemarle, NC BR/TR, 6'.5", 182 lbs. Deb: 9/27/1938																									
1938 Bro-N	2	0	1.000	2	2	1	0	0	13	13	3	1	0	1	4	3	1.308	0.69	563	3.13	.255	0	.000	5	2	0.4
• GAFF, Brent	Brent Allen Gaff b: 10/5/1958, Fort Wayne, IN BR/TR, 6'2", 200 lbs. Deb: 7/7/1982																									
1982 NY-N	0	3	.000	7	5	0	0	0	31^2	41	22	16	3	1	10	14	1.611	4.55	80	5.61	.323	0	.000	-3	0	-0.3
1983 NY-N	1	0	1.000	4	0	0	0	0	10^1	18	9	7	0	0	1	4	1.839	6.10	59	5.72	.360	0	.000	-3	0	-0.3
1984 NY-N	3	2	.600	47	0	0	0	1	84^1	77	39	34	4	1	36	42	1.340	3.63	97	3.19	.247	0	.000	-1	4	-0.2
Total 3	4	5	.444	58	5	0	0	1	126^1	136	70	57	7	2	47	60	1.449	4.06	88	4.00	.278	0	.000	-7	4	-0.8
• GAGNE, Eric	Eric Serge Gagne b: 1/7/1976, Montreal, Canada BR/TR, 6'2", 195 lbs. Deb: 9/7/1999																									
1999 LA-N	1	1	.500	5	5	0	0	0	30	18	8	7	3	0	15	30	1.100	2.10	204	2.42	.175	2	.200	7	3	0.7
2000 LA-N	4	6	.400	20	19	0	0	0	101^1	106	62	58	20	3	60	79	1.638	5.15	84	5.97	.270	4	.143	-9	2	-0.9
2001 LA-N	6	7	.462	33	24	0	0	0	151^2	144	90	80	24	16	46	130	1.253	4.75	84	4.22	.251	6	.136	-12	4	-1.0
2002 LA-N★	4	1	.800	77	0	0	0	52	82^1	55	18	18	6	2	16	114	.862	1.97	194	1.60	.189	0	.000	16	19	1.6
2003 LA-N★	2	3	.400	77	0	0	0	**55**	82^1	37	12	11	2	3	20	137	.692	1.20	334	0.93	.133	0	....	24	25	2.4
Total 5	17	18	.486	212	48	0	0	107	447^2	360	190	174	55	24	157	490	1.155	3.50	117	3.41	.220	12	.145	28	53	2.8
• GAGUS, Charlie	Charles Frederick Gagus b: 3/25/1862, San Francisco, CA d: 1/16/1917, San Francisco, CA Deb: 8/7/1884																									
1884 Was-U	10	9	.526	23	21	19	0	0	177^1	143	100	50	2	....	38	156	1.021	2.54	118	....	.206	38	.247	14	15	1.5
• GAILLARD, Eddie	Julian Edward Gaillard b: 8/13/1970, Camden, NJ BR/TR, 6'1", 180 lbs. Deb: 8/11/1997																									
1997 Det-A	1	0	1.000	16	0	0	0	1	20^1	16	12	12	2	0	10	12	1.279	5.31	86	3.00	.211	0	....	-2	1	-0.2
1998 TB-A	0	0	....	6	0	0	0	0	7^2	4	5	5	3	0	3	5	.913	5.87	82	3.13	.148	0	....	-1	0	-0.1
1999 TB-A	1	0	1.000	8	0	0	0	0	8^2	12	9	2	1	1	4	7	1.846	2.08	239	7.10	.324	0	....	3	0	0.3
Total 3	2	0	1.000	30	0	0	0	1	36^2	32	26	19	6	1	17	24	1.336	4.66	100	4.00	.229	0	....	-0	1	0.0
• GAINES, Nemo	Willard Roland Gaines b: 12/23/1897, Alexandria, VA d: 1/28/1979, Warrenton, VA BL/TL, 6', 180 lbs. Deb: 6/26/1921																									
1921 Was-A	0	0	....	4	0	0	0	0	4^2	5	0	0	0	0	2	1	1.500	0.00	....	4.08	.294	0	.000	2	1	0.2
• GAISER, Fred	Frederick Jacob Gaiser b: 8/31/1885, Stuttgart, Germany d: 10/9/1918, Trenton, NJ Deb: 9/3/1908																									
1908 StL-N	0	0	....	1	0	0	0	0	2^1	4	2	2	0	0	3	2	3.000	7.71	30	12.70	.444	0	.000	-1	0	-0.2
• GAJKOWSKI, Steve	Stephen Robert Gajkowski b: 12/30/1969, Seattle, WA BR/TR, 6'2" Deb: 5/25/1998																									
1998 Sea-A	0	0	....	9	0	0	0	0	8^2	14	8	7	3	2	4	3	2.077	7.27	64	12.46	.389	0	....	-2	0	-0.2
• GAKELER, Dan	Daniel Michael Gakeler b: 5/1/1964, Mount Holly, NJ BR/TR, 6'6", 215 lbs. Deb: 6/9/1991																									
1991 Det-A	1	4	.200	31	7	0	0	2	73^2	73	52	47	5	1	39	43	1.520	5.74	72	4.14	.256	0	....	-13	1	-1.3
• GALASSO, Bob	Robert Joseph Galasso b: 1/13/1952, Connellsville, PA BL/TR, 6'1", 205 lbs. Deb: 7/24/1977																									
1977 Sea-A	0	6	.000	11	7	0	0	0	35	57	36	35	8	3	8	21	1.857	9.00	46	8.63	.365	0	....	-20	0	-1.9
1979 Mil-A	3	1	.750	31	0	0	0	3	51^1	64	30	25	5	0	26	28	1.753	4.38	95	5.71	.299	0	....	-1	3	-0.1
1981 Sea-A	1	1	.500	13	1	0	0	1	31^2	32	19	17	2	0	13	14	1.421	4.83	80	3.89	.264	0	....	-3	1	-0.3
Total 3	4	8	.333	55	8	0	0	4	118	153	85	77	15	3	47	63	1.695	5.87	69	6.09	.312	0	....	-24	4	-2.4
• GALE, Rich	Richard Blackwell Gale b: 1/19/1954, Littleton, NH BR/TR, 6'7", 225 lbs. Deb: 4/30/1978 C																									
1978 KC-A	14	8	.636	31	30	9	3	0	192^1	171	78	66	10	3	100	88	1.409	3.09	124	3.68	.244	0	....	14	13	1.5
1979 KC-A	9	10	.474	34	31	2	1	0	181^2	197	131	114	19	4	99	103	1.629	5.65	75	5.20	.278	0	....	-30	3	-2.9
1980* KC-A	13	9	.591	32	28	6	1	1	190^2	169	90	83	16	2	78	97	1.295	3.92	103	3.43	.239	0	....	3	11	0.3
1981 KC-A	6	6	.500	19	15	2	0	0	101^2	107	63	61	14	2	38	47	1.426	5.40	67	4.65	.270	0	....	-20	1	-2.1
1982 SF-N	7	14	.333	33	29	2	0	0	170^1	193	91	80	9	5	81	102	**1.609**	4.23	85	4.83	.294	6	.125	-9	4	-0.8
1983 Cin-N	4	6	.400	33	7	0	0	1	89^2	103	64	58	8	1	43	53	1.628	5.82	65	5.04	.286	3	.150	-20	0	-2.0
1984 Bos-A	2	3	.400	13	4	0	0	0	43^2	57	27	27	6	1	18	28	1.718	5.56	75	6.41	.315	0	....	-5	1	-0.5
Total 7	55	56	.495	195	144	21	5	2	970	997	544	489	82	18	457	518	1.499	4.54	86	4.47	.269	9	.132	-66	33	-6.5
• GALEHOUSE, Denny	Dennis Ward Galehouse b: 12/7/1911, Marshallville, OH d: 12/12/1998, Doylestown, OH BR/TR, 6'1", 195 lbs. Deb: 4/30/1934																									
1934 Cle-A	0	0	....	1	0	0	0	0	1	2	3	2	0	0	1	0	3.000	18.00	25	9.89	.500	0	....	-1	0	-0.1
1935 Cle-A	1	0	1.000	5	1	1	0	0	13	16	14	13	1	1	9	8	1.923	9.00	50	6.60	.314	1	.250	-6	0	-0.6
1936 Cle-A	8	7	.533	36	15	5	0	1	148^1	161	86	80	5	2	68	71	1.544	4.85	104	4.27	.280	8	.170	4	10	0.4
1937 Cle-A	9	14	.391	36	29	7	0	3	200^2	238	114	102	11	1	83	78	1.600	4.57	101	4.85	.302	15	.208	3	12	0.1
1938 Cle-A	7	8	.467	36	12	5	1	3	114	119	62	55	12	1	65	66	1.614	4.34	107	5.04	.275	6	.154	3	8	0.2
1939 Bos-A	9	10	.474	30	18	6	1	0	146^2	160	84	74	6	1	52	68	1.445	4.54	104	3.91	.276	3	.064	3	9	0.0
1940 Bos-A	6	6	.500	25	20	5	0	0	120	155	77	69	10	0	41	53	1.633	5.18	87	5.32	.313	3	.077	-8	4	-1.1
1941 StL-A	9	10	.474	30	24	11	2	0	190^1	183	85	77	10	4	68	61	1.319	3.64	118	3.39	.253	13	.191	17	14	1.6
1942 StL-A	12	12	.500	32	28	12	3	1	192^1	193	91	77	5	4	79	75	1.414	3.60	103	3.63	.262	14	.194	4	11	0.5
1943 StL-A	11	11	.500	31	28	14	2	1	224	217	80	69	8	1	74	114	1.299	2.77	120	3.13	.255	9	.125	17	15	1.5
1944* StL-A	9	10	.474	24	19	6	2	0	153	162	64	53	6	1	44	80	1.346	3.12	116	3.42	.266	3	.063	11	10	0.7
1946 StL-A	8	12	.400	30	24	11	2	0	180	194	82	73	9	0	52	90	1.367	3.65	102	3.65	.273	5	.091	2	9	-0.1
1947 StL-A	1	3	.250	9	4	0	0	1	32^1	42	26	22	3	0	16	11	1.794	6.12	63	5.88	.311	0	.000	-8	0	-0.9
Bos-A	11	7	.611	21	21	11	3	0	149	150	60	55	7	0	34	38	1.235	3.32	117	3.05	.260	5	.096	9	10	0.5
Yr.	12	10	.545	30	25	11	3	1	181^1	192	86	77	10	0	50	49	1.335	3.82	102	3.55	.269	5	.083	1	10	-0.4
1948 Bos-A	8	8	.500	27	15	6	1	3	137^1	152	68	61	10	2	46	38	1.442	4.00	110	4.22	.282	7	.167	5	10	0.5
1949 Bos-A	0	0	....	2	0	0	0	0	2	4	3	3	1	0	3	0	3.500	13.50	32	19.64	.400	0	....	-2	0	-0.2
Total 15	109	118	.480	375	258	100	17	13	2004	2148	999	885	104	18	735	851	1.439	3.97	105	3.98	.275	92	.138	53	122	3.0
• GALLAGHER, Bill	William John Gallagher b: Philadelphia, PA TL Deb: 5/2/1883 ♦																									
1883 Bal-a	0	5	.000	7	5	4	0	0	51^2	79	57	31	0	....	6	19	1.645	5.40	64	....	.330	10	.164	-8	1	-1.1
1884 Phi-U	1	2	.333	3	3	3	0	0	25	32	29	9	3	....	4	12	1.440	3.24	89	....	.292	1	.091	0	0	-0.1
Total 2	1	7	.125	10	8	7	0	0	76^2	111	86	40	3	....	10	31	1.578	4.70	71	....	.318	11	.138	-8	1	-1.2
• GALLAGHER, Doug	Douglas Eugene Gallagher b: 2/21/1940, Fremont, OH BR/TL, 6'3.5", 195 lbs. Deb: 4/9/1962																									
1962 Det-A	0	4	.000	9	2	0	0	1	25	31	18	13	2	0	15	14	1.840	4.68	87	5.71	.290	2	.333	-1	0	0.0
• GALLAGHER, Ed	Edward Michael "Lefty" Gallagher b: 11/28/1910, Dorchester, MA d: 12/22/1981, Hyannis, MA BB/TL, 6'2", 197 lbs. Deb: 7/8/1932																									
1932 Bos-A	0	3	.000	9	3	0	0	0	23^2	30	36	33	3	0	28	6	2.451	12.55	36	9.07	.323	0	.000	-21	0	-2.0

YEAR	TM-L	W	L	PCT	G	GS	CG	SH	SV	IP	H	R	ER	HR	HB	BB	SO	RAT	ERA	ERA+	CERA	OAV	BH	AVG	PR+	WS	TPW
• GALLIA, Bert		Melvin Allys Gallia b: 10/14/1891, Beeville, TX d: 3/19/1976, Devine, TX BR/TR, 6', 165 lbs. Deb: 9/4/1912																									
1912	Was-A	0	0	....	2	0	0	0	0	2	0	0	0	0	0	3	0	1.500	0.00	....	1.60	.000	0	....	1	0	0.1
1913	Was-A	1	5	.167	31	4	0	0	3	96	85	66	44	2	7	46	46	1.365	4.13	71	3.15	.222	2	.087	-14	0	-1.7
1914	Was-A	0	0	....	2	0	0	0	0	6	3	4	3	0	0	4	4	1.167	4.50	62	1.43	.120	0	.000	-1	0	-0.2
1915	Was-A	17	11	.607	43	29	14	3	1	259^{2}	220	90	66	2	4	64	130	1.094	2.29	130	2.24	.234	14	.165	17	22	1.6
1916	Was-A	17	13	.567	49	31	13	1	2	283^{2}	278	109	87	3	8	99	120	1.329	2.76	101	3.35	.266	18	.194	-1	18	0.0
1917	Was-A	9	13	.409	42	23	9	1	1	207^{2}	191	92	69	1	4	93	84	1.368	2.99	88	3.34	.258	14	.209	-11	9	-1.0
1918	StL-A	8	6	.571	19	17	10	1	0	124	126	63	48	1	6	61	48	1.508	3.48	78	3.89	.268	6	.130	-11	4	-1.6
1919	StL-A	12	14	.462	34	25	14	1	1	222^{1}	220	106	89	10	8	92	83	1.403	3.60	92	3.86	.264	11	.153	-9	11	-1.1
1920	StL-A	0	1	.000	2	1	0	0	0	3^{2}	8	7	3	0	0	3	0	3.000	7.36	53	11.60	.400	0	.000	-1	0	-0.2
	Phi-N	2	6	.250	18	5	1	0	2	72	79	48	36	2	3	29	35	1.500	4.50	76	4.15	.287	4	.174	-9	1	-1.0
Total	9	66	69	.489	242	135	61	7	10	1277	1210	585	445	21	40	494	550	1.334	3.14	94	3.31	.256	69	.167	-39	65	-4.9
• GALLIVAN, Phil		Philip Joseph Gallivan b: 5/29/1907, Seattle, WA d: 11/24/1969, St. Paul, MN BR/TR, 6', 170 lbs. Deb: 4/21/1931																									
1931	Bro-N	0	1	.000	6	1	0	0	0	15^{1}	23	11	9	2	0	7	1	1.957	5.28	72	7.51	.354	0	.000	-2	0	-0.2
1932	Chi-A	1	3	.250	13	3	1	0	0	33^{1}	49	32	28	4	1	24	12	2.190	7.56	57	8.26	.338	3	.375	-12	0	-1.0
1934	Chi-A	4	7	.364	35	7	3	0	1	126^{2}	155	97	79	14	1	64	55	1.729	5.61	84	5.65	.295	9	.225	-9	4	-0.7
Total	3	5	11	.313	54	11	4	0	1	175^{1}	227	140	116	20	2	95	68	1.837	5.95	76	6.31	.309	12	.235	-23	4	-2.0
• GALLO, Mike		Michael Dwain Gallo b: 4/2/1977, Long Beach, CA BL/TL, 6', 175 lbs. Deb: 7/2/2003																									
2003	Hou-N	1	0	1.000	32	0	0	0	0	30	28	10	10	3	1	10	16	1.267	3.00	148	3.66	.267	0	.000	4	3	0.4
• GALVEZ, Balvino		Balvino (Jerez) Galvez b: 3/31/1964, San Pedro de Macoris, Dominican Republic BR/TR, 6', 170 lbs. Deb: 5/7/1986																									
1986	LA-N	0	1	.000	10	0	0	0	0	20^{2}	19	10	9	3	0	12	11	1.500	3.92	88	4.51	.241	0	.000	-1	1	-0.1
• GALVIN, Lou		Louis J. Galvin b: 4/1862, St. Paul, MN d: 6/17/1895, Deb: 10/1/1884																									
1884	StP-U	0	2	.000	3	3	3	0	0	25	21	18	8	0	....	10	17	1.240	2.88	106	....	.213	2	.222	-1	1	-0.1
• GALVIN, Pud		James Francis "Pud,Gentle Jeems,The Little Steam Engine" Galvin b: 12/25/1856, St. Louis, MO d: 3/7/1902, Pittsburgh, PA BR/TR, 5'8", 190 lbs. Deb: 5/22/1875 M/U HOF: 1965																									
1875	StL-n	4	2	.667	8	7	7	1	1	62	53	....	8	0	....	1	7	.871	**1.16**	**102**	....	.210	6	.130	-1	....	-0.2
1879	Buf-N	37	27	.578	66	66	65	6	0	593	585	299	150	3	....	31	136	1.039	2.28	115	....	.241	66	.249	8	**61**	1.4
1880	Buf-N	20	35	.364	58	54	46	5	0	458^{2}	528	281	138	5	....	32	128	1.221	2.71	91	....	.274	51	.212	10	14	0.3
1881	Buf-N	28	24	.538	56	53	48	5	0	474	546	250	125	4	....	46	136	1.249	2.37	117	....	.276	50	.212	**39**	36	**3.3**
1882	Buf-N	28	23	.549	52	51	48	3	0	445^{1}	476	255	157	8	....	40	162	1.159	3.17	92	....	.258	44	.214	-5	29	-0.8
1883	Buf-N	46	29	.613	**76**	**75**	**72**	**5**	0	**656^{1}**	676	367	198	9	....	50	279	1.106	2.72	117	....	.251	71	.220	37	47	2.9
1884	Buf-N	46	22	.676	72	72	71	**12**	0	636^{1}	566	254	141	23	....	63	369	.988	1.99	158	....	.225	49	.179	**92**	57	7.2
1885	Buf-N	13	19	.406	33	32	31	3	1	284	356	204	129	8	....	37	93	1.384	4.09	73	....	.293	23	.189	-17	8	-1.7
	Pit-a	3	7	.300	11	11	9	0	0	88^{1}	97	64	36	2	0	7	27	1.177	3.67	88	....	.267	4	.105	-5	4	-0.7
1886	Pit-a	29	21	.580	50	50	49	2	0	434^{2}	457	229	129	3	7	75	72	1.224	2.67	126	....	.258	49	.253	30	32	2.8
1887	Pit-N	28	21	.571	49	48	47	2	0	440^{2}	557	259	161	12	11	67	76	1.264	3.29	117	....	.300	43	.221	33	33	2.7
1888	Pit-N	23	25	.479	50	50	49	6	0	437^{1}	446	190	128	9	8	53	107	1.141	2.63	101	....	.255	25	.143	3	30	-0.1
1889	Pit-N	23	16	.590	41	40	38	4	0	341	392	230	158	19	10	78	77	1.378	4.17	90	....	.279	28	.187	-16	16	-1.4
1890	Pit-P	12	13	.480	26	25	23	1	0	217	275	192	105	3	9	49	35	1.493	4.35	90	....	.296	20	.206	-5	10	-0.4
1891	Pit-N	15	14	.517	33	30	23	2	0	246^{2}	256	143	79	10	13	62	46	1.289	2.88	114	....	.258	18	.165	13	15	0.8
1892	Pit-N	5	6	.455	12	12	10	0	0	96	104	51	28	0	3	28	29	1.375	2.63	125	3.47	.266	5	.122	4	6	0.2
	StL-N	5	6	.455	12	12	10	0	0	92	102	47	33	4	0	26	27	1.391	3.23	99	3.55	.270	2	.051	3	5	-0.2
	Yr.	10	12	.455	24	24	20	0	0	188	206	98	61	4	3	54	56	1.383	2.92	111	3.51	.268	7	.088	7	11	0.0
Total	14	361	308	.540	697	681	639	56	1	5941^{1}	6419	3315	1895	122	61	744	1799	1.194	2.87	107	0.11	.263	548	.203	223	403	16.4
• GAMBLE, Bob		Robert J. Gamble b: 2/6/1867, Philadelphia, PA TR, 5'10", 155 lbs. Deb: 5/2/1888																									
1888	Phi-a	0	1	.000	1	1	1	0	0	9	10	10	8	0	0	3	2	1.444	8.00	37	....	.271	1	.333	-5	0	-0.5
• GANDARILLAS, Gus		Gustavo Gandarillas b: 7/19/1971, Coral Gables, FL BR/TR, 6', 183 lbs. Deb: 7/17/2001																									
2001	Mil-N	0	0	....	16	0	0	0	0	19^{2}	25	13	12	2	0	10	7	1.780	5.49	78	5.90	.321	0	....	-3	0	-0.3
• GANNON, Gussie		James Edward Gannon b: 11/26/1873, Erie, PA d: 4/12/1966, Erie, PA BL/TL, 5'11", 154 lbs. Deb: 6/15/1895																									
1895	Pit-N	0	0	....	1	0	0	0	0	5	7	4	1	0	0	2	0	1.800	1.80	251	5.51	.326	0	.000	1	0	0.1
• GANNON, Joe		Michael Joseph Gannon b: 2/22/1877, St. Louis, MO d: 3/19/1931, St. Louis, MO Deb: 8/28/1898																									
1898	StL-N	0	1	.000	1	1	1	0	0	9	13	13	11	0	1	5	2	2.000	11.00	34	6.80	.335	0	.000	-7	0	-0.7
• GARAGOZZO, Keith		Keith John Garagozzo b: 10/25/1969, Camden, NJ BL/TL, 6', 170 lbs. Deb: 4/5/1994																									
1994	Min-A	0	0	....	7	0	0	0	0	9^{1}	9	10	10	3	0	13	3	2.357	9.64	50	9.84	.273	0	....	-5	0	-0.4
• GARBER, Bob		Robert Mitchell Garber b: 9/10/1928, Hunker, PA d: 6/7/1999, Redwood City, CA BR/TR, 6'1", 190 lbs. Deb: 5/13/1956																									
1956	Pit-N	0	0	....	2	0	0	0	0	4	3	1	1	1	0	3	3	1.500	2.25	168	4.63	.200	0	....	1	0	0.1
• GARBER, Gene		Henry Eugene Garber b: 11/13/1947, Lancaster, PA BR/TR, 5'10", 175 lbs. Deb: 6/17/1969																									
1969	Pit-N	0	0	....	2	1	0	0	0	5	6	3	3	3	0	1	3	1.400	5.40	65	8.63	.333	0	.000	-1	0	-0.1
1970	Pit-N	0	3	.000	14	0	0	0	0	22^{1}	22	13	13	4	2	10	7	1.433	5.24	74	5.34	.275	2	.667	-4	0	-0.3
1972	Pit-N	0	0	....	4	0	0	0	0	6^{1}	7	5	5	3	0	3	3	1.579	7.11	47	7.69	.269	0	.000	-3	0	-0.3
1973	KC-A	9	9	.500	48	8	4	0	11	152^{2}	164	78	72	14	2	49	60	1.395	4.24	97	4.12	.283	0	....	-0	11	0.0
1974	KC-A	1	2	.333	17	0	0	0	1	28	35	21	15	3	1	13	14	1.714	4.82	79	5.31	.313	0	....	-3	0	-0.3
	Phi-N	4	0	1.000	34	0	0	0	4	48	39	15	11	1	1	31	27	1.458	2.06	183	3.05	.236	0	.000	8	7	0.8
1975	Phi-N	10	12	.455	**71**	0	0	0	14	110	104	48	44	13	2	27	69	1.191	3.60	104	3.28	.254	2	.167	-1	10	-0.2
1976*	Phi-N	9	3	.750	59	0	0	0	11	92^{2}	78	33	29	4	4	30	92	1.165	2.82	126	2.60	.228	2	.286	6	11	0.8
1977*	Phi-N	8	6	.571	64	0	0	0	19	103^{1}	82	30	27	6	2	23	78	1.016	2.35	170	2.10	.220	0	.000	17	15	1.6
1978	Phi-N	2	1	.667	22	0	0	0	3	38^{2}	26	6	6	1	3	11	24	.957	1.40	255	1.75	.191	0	.000	9	6	0.9
	Atl-N	4	4	.500	43	0	0	0	22	78^{1}	58	26	22	11	2	13	61	.906	2.53	160	2.17	.204	1	.091	14	16	1.5
	Yr.	6	5	.545	65	0	0	0	25	117	84	32	28	12	5	24	85	.923	2.15	183	2.03	.200	1	.071	23	22	2.4
1979	Atl-N	6	16	.273	68	0	0	0	25	106	121	66	51	10	5	24	56	1.368	4.33	94	4.16	.283	3	.300	-0	9	0.1
1980	Atl-N	5	5	.500	68	0	0	0	7	82^{1}	95	42	35	6	0	24	51	1.445	3.83	98	4.20	.288	1	.500	-1	6	0.0
1981	Atl-N	4	6	.400	35	0	0	0	2	58^{2}	49	23	17	2	0	20	34	1.176	2.61	137	2.21	.214	0	.000	6	5	0.6
1982*	Atl-N	8	10	.444	69	0	0	0	30	119^{1}	100	40	31	4	2	32	68	1.106	2.34	160	2.21	.231	2	.133	18	19	1.9
1983	Atl-N	4	5	.444	43	0	0	0	9	60^{2}	72	37	31	8	2	23	45	1.566	4.60	84	5.16	.300	0	.000	-5	2	-0.5
1984	Atl-N	3	6	.333	62	0	0	0	11	106	103	45	36	7	2	24	55	1.198	3.06	126	2.94	.254	2	.143	10	10	1.0
1985	Atl-N	6	6	.500	59	0	0	0	1	97^{1}	98	41	39	8	2	25	66	1.264	3.61	107	3.39	.263	1	.200	3	7	0.4
1986	Atl-N	5	5	.500	61	0	0	0	24	78	76	23	22	3	1	20	56	1.231	2.54	156	2.95	.260	1	.167	13	15	1.4
1987	Atl-N	8	10	.444	49	0	0	0	10	69^{1}	87	39	34	7	1	28	48	1.659	4.41	98	5.32	.311	0	.000	-0	5	0.0
	KC-A	0	0	....	13	0	0	0	8	14^{1}	13	5	4	1	1	1	3	.977	2.51	181	2.54	.245	0	....	3	3	0.3
1988	KC-A	0	4	.000	26	0	0	0	6	32^{2}	29	15	13	4	2	13	20	1.286	3.58	111	3.78	.238	0	....	2	3	0.2
Total	19	96	113	.459	931	9	4	0	218	1510	1464	654	560	123	37	445	940	1.264	3.34	117	3.37	.257	17	.148	93	160	9.7
• GARCES, Rich		Richard Aron (Mendoza) "El Guapo" Garces b: 5/18/1971, Maracay, Venezuela BR/TR, 6', 250 lbs. Deb: 9/18/1990																									
1990	Min-A	0	0	....	5	0	0	0	2	5^{2}	4	2	1	0	0	4	1	1.412	1.59	261	2.99	.200	0	....	2	1	0.2
1993	Min-A	0	0	....	3	0	0	0	0	4	4	2	0	0	0	2	3	1.500	0.00	....	3.63	.250	0	....	2	0	0.2
1995	Chi-N	0	0	....	7	0	0	0	0	11	11	6	4	0	0	3	6	1.273	3.27	125	2.92	.256	0	.000	1	1	0.1
	Fla-N	0	2	.000	11	0	0	0	0	13^{1}	14	9	8	1	0	8	16	1.650	5.40	78	4.58	.264	0	....	-2	0	-0.2
	Yr.	0	2	.000	18	0	0	0	0	24^{1}	25	15	12	1	0	11	22	1.479	4.44	94	3.83	.260	0	.000	-1	1	-0.1
1996	Bos-A	3	2	.600	37	0	0	0	0	44	42	26	24	5	0	33	55	1.705	4.91	103	5.04	.251	0	....	2	3	0.2

YEAR	TM-L	W	L	PCT	G	GS	CG	SH	SV	IP	H	R	ER	HR	HB	BB	SO	RAT	ERA	ERA+	CERA	OAV	BH	AVG	PR+	WS	TPW
1997	Bos-A	0	1	.000	12	0	0	0	0	13^2	14	9	7	2	1	9	12	1.683	4.61	101	5.70	.255	0	....	0	0	0.0
1998	Bos-A	1	1	.500	30	0	0	0	1	46	36	19	17	6	2	27	34	1.370	3.33	142	3.83	.213	0	....	7	4	0.6
1999*	Bos-A	5	1	.833	30	0	0	0	2	40^2	25	9	7	1	0	18	33	1.057	1.55	320	1.75	.171	0	....	15	7	1.4
2000	Bos-A	8	1	.889	64	0	0	0	1	74^2	64	28	27	7	1	23	69	1.165	3.25	155	2.85	.229	0	....	15	10	1.4
2001	Bos-A	6	1	.857	62	0	0	0	1	67	55	32	29	6	4	25	51	1.194	3.90	115	3.09	.219	0	.000	6	6	0.5
2002	Bos-A	0	1	.000	26	0	0	0	0	21^1	21	20	18	4	3	12	16	1.547	7.59	59	5.78	.273	0	....	-8	0	-0.7
Total	10	23	10	.697	287	0	0	0	7	341^1	290	162	142	32	11	164	296	1.330	3.74	126	3.56	.227	0	.000	40	32	3.6

• GARCIA, Freddy Freddy Antonio Garcia b: 6/10/1976, Caracas, Venezuela BR/TR, 6'4", 235 lbs. Deb: 4/7/1999

YEAR	TM-L	W	L	PCT	G	GS	CG	SH	SV	IP	H	R	ER	HR	HB	BB	SO	RAT	ERA	ERA+	CERA	OAV	BH	AVG	PR+	WS	TPW
1999	Sea-A	17	8	.680	33	33	2	1	0	201^1	205	96	91	18	10	90	170	1.465	4.07	123	4.46	.263	1	.250	21	16	2.0
2000*	Sea-A	9	5	.643	21	20	0	0	0	124^1	112	62	54	16	2	64	79	1.416	3.91	116	4.20	.241	2	.667	8	8	0.8
2001*	Sea-A★	18	6	.750	34	34	4	3	0	**238^2**	199	88	81	16	5	69	163	1.123	**3.05**	136	**2.61**	**.225**	1	.143	22	18	2.1
2002	Sea-A★	16	10	.615	34	34	1	0	0	223^2	227	110	109	30	6	63	181	1.297	4.39	96	3.98	.260	2	.333	-2	11	-0.1
2003	Sea-A	12	14	.462	33	33	1	0	0	201^1	196	109	101	31	11	71	144	1.326	4.51	96	4.33	.255	1	.200	-10	8	-0.9
Total	5	72	43	.626	155	154	8	4	0	989^1	939	465	436	111	34	357	737	1.310	3.97	111	3.85	.249	7	.280	39	61	3.8

• GARCIA, Miguel Miguel Angel (Sifontes) Garcia b: 4/3/1967, Caracas, Venezuela BL/TL, 5'11", 173 lbs. Deb: 4/30/1987

YEAR	TM-L	W	L	PCT	G	GS	CG	SH	SV	IP	H	R	ER	HR	HB	BB	SO	RAT	ERA	ERA+	CERA	OAV	BH	AVG	PR+	WS	TPW
1987	Cal-A	0	0	....	1	0	0	0	0	1^2	3	4	3	0	0	3	0	3.600	16.20	27	14.26	.375	0	....	-2	0	-0.2
	Pit-N	0	0	....	1	0	0	0	0	0^2	0	0	0	0	0	0	0	.000	0.00	....	0.00	.000	0	....	0	0	0.0
1988	Pit-N	0	0	....	1	0	0	0	0	2	3	2	1	1	1	2	2	2.500	4.50	76	16.26	.375	0	....	-0	0	0.0
1989	Pit-N	0	2	.000	11	0	0	0	0	16	25	15	15	2	0	7	9	2.000	8.44	40	7.53	.357	1	1.000	-9	0	-0.9
Total	3	0	2	.000	14	0	0	0	0	20^1	31	21	19	3	1	12	11	2.115	8.41	41	8.69	.360	1	1.000	-11	0	-1.1

• GARCIA, Mike Michael R. Garcia b: 5/11/1968, Riverside, CA BR/TR, 6'2", 220 lbs. Deb: 9/10/1999

YEAR	TM-L	W	L	PCT	G	GS	CG	SH	SV	IP	H	R	ER	HR	HB	BB	SO	RAT	ERA	ERA+	CERA	OAV	BH	AVG	PR+	WS	TPW
1999	Pit-N	1	0	1.000	7	0	0	0	0	7	2	1	1	1	0	3	9	.714	1.29	355	1.23	.091	0	....	3	1	0.2
2000	Pit-N	0	2	.000	13	0	0	0	0	11^1	21	15	14	1	0	7	9	2.471	11.12	41	10.47	.429	1	.333	-8	0	-0.7
Total	2	1	2	.333	20	0	0	0	0	18^1	23	16	15	2	0	10	18	1.800	7.36	62	6.94	.324	1	.333	-6	1	-0.5

• GARCIA, Mike Edward Miguel "The Big Bear" Garcia b: 11/17/1923, San Gabriel, CA d: 1/13/1986, Fairview Park, OH BR/TR, 6'1", 200 lbs. Deb: 10/3/1948

YEAR	TM-L	W	L	PCT	G	GS	CG	SH	SV	IP	H	R	ER	HR	HB	BB	SO	RAT	ERA	ERA+	CERA	OAV	BH	AVG	PR+	WS	TPW
1948	Cle-A	0	0	....	1	0	0	0	0	2	3	0	0	0	0	0	1	1.500	0.00	....	4.47	.333	0	....	1	0	0.1
1949	Cle-A	14	5	.737	41	20	8	5	2	175^2	154	51	46	6	2	60	94	1.218	**2.36**	**169**	2.77	.241	12	.235	30	21	3.2
1950	Cle-A	11	11	.500	33	29	11	0	0	184	191	88	79	15	0	74	76	1.440	3.86	112	4.04	.266	13	.200	9	12	0.7
1951	Cle-A	20	13	.606	47	30	15	1	6	254	239	101	89	10	3	82	118	1.264	3.15	120	3.01	.246	18	.212	18	22	1.8
1952	Cle-A★	22	11	.667	46	**36**	19	**6**	4	292^1	284	93	77	9	7	87	143	1.269	2.37	141	3.05	.253	13	.137	34	23	3.3
1953	Cle-A★	18	9	.667	38	35	21	3	0	271^2	260	106	98	18	3	81	134	1.255	3.25	116	3.20	.250	24	.250	15	21	1.9
1954*	Cle-A★	19	8	.704	45	34	13	**5**	5	258^2	220	85	76	6	2	71	129	1.125	**2.64**	**139**	**2.30**	.229	11	.136	26	**24**	2.4
1955	Cle-A	11	13	.458	38	31	6	2	3	210^2	230	101	94	17	3	56	120	1.358	4.02	99	3.97	.278	15	.217	-1	12	0.1
1956	Cle-A	11	12	.478	35	30	8	4	0	197^2	213	93	83	18	5	74	119	1.452	3.78	111	4.36	.272	7	.115	10	11	0.7
1957	Cle-A	12	8	.600	38	27	9	1	0	211^1	221	98	88	14	6	73	110	1.391	3.75	99	3.94	.269	12	.160	2	12	0.1
1958	Cle-A	1	0	1.000	6	1	0	0	0	8	15	10	8	2	1	7	2	2.750	9.00	41	14.13	.395	0	.000	-5	0	-0.5
1959	Cle-A	3	6	.333	29	8	1	0	1	72	72	39	32	4	0	31	49	1.431	4.00	92	3.84	.265	1	.071	-3	2	-0.4
1960	Chi-A	0	0	....	15	0	0	0	2	17^2	23	9	9	2	0	10	8	1.868	4.58	82	6.86	.338	1	.333	-2	0	-0.2
1961	Was-A	0	1	.000	16	0	0	0	0	19	23	14	10	1	1	13	14	1.895	4.74	83	5.64	.288	0	....	-2	0	-0.2
Total	14	142	97	.594	428	281	111	27	23	2174^2	2148	888	789	122	33	719	1117	1.318	3.27	117	3.45	.257	127	.182	132	160	12.9

• GARCIA, Ralph Ralph Garcia b: 12/14/1948, Los Angeles, CA BR/TR, 6', 195 lbs. Deb: 9/26/1972

YEAR	TM-L	W	L	PCT	G	GS	CG	SH	SV	IP	H	R	ER	HR	HB	BB	SO	RAT	ERA	ERA+	CERA	OAV	BH	AVG	PR+	WS	TPW
1972	SD-N	0	0	....	3	0	0	0	0	5	4	1	1	0	0	3	3	1.400	1.80	183	2.32	.211	0	....	1	0	0.1
1974	SD-N	0	0	....	8	0	0	0	0	10^1	15	8	7	1	0	7	9	2.129	6.10	58	7.39	.357	0	....	-3	0	-0.3
Total	2	0	0	....	11	0	0	0	0	15^1	19	9	8	1	0	10	12	1.891	4.70	75	5.74	.311	0	....	-2	0	-0.2

• GARCIA, Ramon Ramon (Garcia) Garcia b: 3/5/1924, La Esperanza, Cuba BR/TR, 5'10", 170 lbs. Deb: 4/19/1948

YEAR	TM-L	W	L	PCT	G	GS	CG	SH	SV	IP	H	R	ER	HR	HB	BB	SO	RAT	ERA	ERA+	CERA	OAV	BH	AVG	PR+	WS	TPW
1948	Was-A	0	0	....	4	0	0	0	0	3^2	11	7	7	0	1	4	2	4.091	17.18	25	21.59	.524	1	1.000	-5	0	-0.5

• GARCIA, Ramon Ramon Antonio (Fortunato) Garcia b: 2/9/1969, Guanare, Venezuela BR/TR, 6'2", 200 lbs. Deb: 5/31/1991

YEAR	TM-L	W	L	PCT	G	GS	CG	SH	SV	IP	H	R	ER	HR	HB	BB	SO	RAT	ERA	ERA+	CERA	OAV	BH	AVG	PR+	WS	TPW
1991	Chi-A	4	4	.500	16	15	0	0	0	78^1	79	50	47	13	2	31	40	1.404	5.40	74	4.76	.269	0	....	-15	1	-1.5
1996	Mil-A	4	4	.500	37	2	0	0	4	75^2	84	58	56	17	6	21	40	1.388	6.66	78	5.47	.287	0	....	-14	2	-1.3
1997*	Hou-N	9	8	.529	42	20	1	1	1	158^2	155	71	65	20	9	52	120	1.305	3.69	108	4.15	.262	4	.111	4	9	0.3
Total	3	17	16	.515	95	37	1	1	5	312^2	318	179	168	50	17	104	200	1.350	4.84	89	4.62	.270	4	.111	-25	12	-2.4

• GARCIA, Reynaldo Reynaldo Garcia b: 4/15/1974, Nagua, Dominican Republic BR/TR, 6'3", 170 lbs. Deb: 7/19/2002

YEAR	TM-L	W	L	PCT	G	GS	CG	SH	SV	IP	H	R	ER	HR	HB	BB	SO	RAT	ERA	ERA+	CERA	OAV	BH	AVG	PR+	WS	TPW
2002	Tex-A	0	0	....	3	0	0	0	0	2	7	7	7	3	0	1	2	4.000	31.50	15	39.83	.538	0	....	-6	0	-0.6
2003	Tex-A	0	0	....	17	0	0	0	0	18	19	18	18	6	2	14	15	1.833	9.00	55	8.46	.275	0	....	-8	0	-0.8
Total	2	0	0	....	20	0	0	0	0	20	26	25	25	9	2	15	17	2.050	11.25	43	11.60	.317	0	....	-14	0	-1.3

• GARCIA, Rosman Rosman J. Garcia b: 1/3/1979, Maracay, Venezuela BR/TR, 6'2", 160 lbs. Deb: 4/19/2003

YEAR	TM-L	W	L	PCT	G	GS	CG	SH	SV	IP	H	R	ER	HR	HB	BB	SO	RAT	ERA	ERA+	CERA	OAV	BH	AVG	PR+	WS	TPW
2003	Tex-A	1	2	.333	46	0	0	0	0	46^1	63	33	31	4	2	23	25	1.856	6.02	82	6.62	.320	0	....	-5	1	-0.5

• GARDINER, Art Arthur Cecil Gardiner b: 12/26/1899, Brooklyn, NY d: 10/21/1954, Copiague, NY BR/TR Deb: 9/25/1923

YEAR	TM-L	W	L	PCT	G	GS	CG	SH	SV	IP	H	R	ER	HR	HB	BB	SO	RAT	ERA	ERA+	CERA	OAV	BH	AVG	PR+	WS	TPW
1923	Phi-N	0	0	....	1	0	0	0	0	0	1	0	0	0	0	1	0	....	....	....	∞	1.000	0	....	0	0	0.0

• GARDINER, Mike Michael James Gardiner b: 10/19/1965, Sarnia, Canada BB/TR, 6', 200 lbs. Deb: 9/8/1990

YEAR	TM-L	W	L	PCT	G	GS	CG	SH	SV	IP	H	R	ER	HR	HB	BB	SO	RAT	ERA	ERA+	CERA	OAV	BH	AVG	PR+	WS	TPW
1990	Sea-A	0	2	.000	5	3	0	0	0	12^2	22	17	15	1	2	5	6	2.132	10.66	37	9.10	.379	0	....	-9	0	-1.0
1991	Bos-A	9	10	.474	22	22	0	0	0	130	140	79	70	18	0	47	91	1.438	4.85	89	4.64	.274	0	....	-8	5	-0.8
1992	Bos-A	4	10	.286	28	18	0	0	0	130^2	126	78	69	12	2	58	79	1.408	4.75	89	4.02	.253	0	....	-8	4	-0.8
1993	Mon-N	2	3	.400	24	2	0	0	0	38	40	28	22	3	1	19	21	1.553	5.21	80	4.54	.268	0	.000	-4	0	-0.5
	Det-A	0	0	....	10	0	0	0	0	11^1	12	5	5	0	0	7	4	1.676	3.97	108	4.40	.279	0	....	0	1	0.0
1994	Det-A	2	2	.500	38	1	0	0	5	58^2	53	35	27	10	0	23	31	1.295	4.14	117	3.74	.233	0	....	5	4	0.5
1995	Det-A	0	0	....	9	0	0	0	0	12^1	27	20	20	5	0	2	7	2.351	14.59	33	13.21	.458	0	....	-13	0	-1.2
Total	6	17	27	.386	136	46	0	0	5	393^2	420	262	228	49	5	161	239	1.476	5.21	83	4.70	.272	0	.000	-37	14	-3.7

• GARDNER, Bill William A. Gardner b: 9/1868, Baltimore, MD Deb: 8/9/1887

YEAR	TM-L	W	L	PCT	G	GS	CG	SH	SV	IP	H	R	ER	HR	HB	BB	SO	RAT	ERA	ERA+	CERA	OAV	BH	AVG	PR+	WS	TPW
1887	Bal-a	0	1	.000	3	2	1	0	0	13	33	20	16	0	1	10	3	2.538	11.08	37	....	.460	4	.333	-10	0	-0.8

• GARDNER, Chris Christopher John Gardner b: 3/30/1969, Long Beach, CA BR/TR, 6', 175 lbs. Deb: 9/10/1991

YEAR	TM-L	W	L	PCT	G	GS	CG	SH	SV	IP	H	R	ER	HR	HB	BB	SO	RAT	ERA	ERA+	CERA	OAV	BH	AVG	PR+	WS	TPW
1991	Hou-N	1	2	.333	5	4	0	0	0	24^2	19	12	11	5	0	14	12	1.338	4.01	87	4.20	.218	0	.000	-1	1	-0.2

• GARDNER, Gid Franklin Washington Gardner b: 5/6/1859, Boston, MA d: 8/1/1914, Cambridge, MA, 165 lbs. Deb: 8/23/1879 ♦

YEAR	TM-L	W	L	PCT	G	GS	CG	SH	SV	IP	H	R	ER	HR	HB	BB	SO	RAT	ERA	ERA+	CERA	OAV	BH	AVG	PR+	WS	TPW
1879	Tro-N	0	2	.000	2	2	2	0	0	14	27	21	9	0	....	0	3	1.929	5.79	43	....	.383	1	.167	-5	0	-0.5
1880	Cle-N	1	8	.111	9	9	9	0	0	77	80	53	22	2	....	20	21	1.299	2.57	91	....	.254	6	.188	-3	2	-0.3
1883	Bal-a	1	0	1.000	2	0	0	0	0	7	9	7	4	1	....	1	2	1.429	5.14	68	....	.293	44	.273	-1	5	0.2
1884	CP-U	0	1	.000	1	1	0	0	0	6	10	8	4	0	....	1	4	1.833	6.00	48	....	.349	38	.255	-2	5	0.1
1885	Bal-a	0	1	.000	1	1	1	0	0	9	16	13	10	2	1	6	3	2.444	10.00	33	....	.371	37	.218	-7	3	-0.7
Total	5	2	12	.143	15	13	12	0	0	113	142	102	49	5	1	28	33	1.504	3.90	68	....	.291	190	.245	-17	15	-1.2

• GARDNER, Glenn Miles Glenn Gardner b: 1/25/1916, Burnsville, NC d: 7/7/1964, Rochester, NY BR/TR, 5'11", 180 lbs. Deb: 7/19/1945

YEAR	TM-L	W	L	PCT	G	GS	CG	SH	SV	IP	H	R	ER	HR	HB	BB	SO	RAT	ERA	ERA+	CERA	OAV	BH	AVG	PR+	WS	TPW
1945	StL-N	3	1	.750	17	4	2	1	1	54^2	50	21	20	2	0	27	20	1.409	3.29	114	3.37	.242	7	.333	1	5	0.3

• GARDNER, Harry Harry Ray Gardner b: 9/20/1888, Portland, OR d: 8/2/1961, Barlow, OR BR/TR, 6'2", 180 lbs. Deb: 4/17/1911

YEAR	TM-L	W	L	PCT	G	GS	CG	SH	SV	IP	H	R	ER	HR	HB	BB	SO	RAT	ERA	ERA+	CERA	OAV	BH	AVG	PR+	WS	TPW
1911	Pit-N	1	1	.500	13	3	2	0	2	42	39	25	21	2	2	20	24	1.405	4.50	76	3.67	.244	3	.214	-6	1	-0.6
1912	Pit-N	0	0	....	1	0	0	0	0	0^1	3	6	0	0	0	1	0	12.00	0.00	....	58.47	.500	0	....	0	0	0.0
Total	2	1	1	.500	14	3	2	0	2	42^1	42	31	21	2	2	21	24	1.488	4.46	77	4.10	.253	3	.214	-6	1	-0.6

YEAR TM-L	W	L	PCT	G	GS	CG	SH	SV	IP	H	R	ER	HR	HB	BB	SO	RAT	ERA	ERA+	CERA	OAV	BH	AVG	PR+	WS	TPW
• GARDNER, Jim	James Anderson Gardner b: 10/4/1874, Pittsburgh, PA d: 4/24/1905, Pittsburgh, PA TR Deb: 6/20/1895 U																									
1895 Pit-N	8	2	.800	11	10	8	0	0	85^1	99	53	25	1	6	27	31	1.477	2.64	171	4.18	.286	9	.265	18	8	1.5
1897 Pit-N	5	5	.500	14	11	8	0	0	95^1	115	72	55	4	9	32	35	1.542	5.19	80	4.83	.296	12	.158	-9	5	-1.3
1898 Pit-N	10	13	.435	25	22	19	1	0	185^1	179	96	66	3	8	48	41	1.225	3.21	111	2.90	.252	14	.154	7	13	0.2
1899 Pit-N	1	0	1.000	6	3	0	0	0	32^1	52	37	27	1	0	13	2	2.010	7.52	51	7.08	.361	3	.231	-13	0	-1.2
1902 Chi-N	1	2	.333	3	3	2	0	0	25	23	12	8	0	0	10	6	1.320	2.88	94	2.87	.245	2	.200	-1	1	-0.1
Total 5	**25**	**22**	**.532**	**59**	**49**	**37**	**1**	**0**	**423^1**	**468**	**270**	**181**	**9**	**23**	**130**	**115**	**1.413**	**3.85**	**99**	**3.91**	**.278**	**40**	**.179**	**2**	**27**	**-0.8**
• GARDNER, Lee	Terrence Lee Gardner b: 1/16/1975, Hartland, MI BR/TR, 6', 219 lbs. Deb: 5/24/2002																									
2002 TB-A	1	1	.500	12	0	0	0	0	13^1	12	11	6	3	3	8	8	1.500	4.05	110	5.86	.235	0	....	0	0	0.0
• GARDNER, Mark	Mark Allan Gardner b: 3/1/1962, Los Angeles, CA BR/TR, 6'1", 205 lbs. Deb: 5/16/1989 C																									
1989 Mon-N	0	3	.000	7	4	0	0	0	26^1	26	16	15	2	2	11	21	1.405	5.13	69	4.07	.250	1	.167	-5	0	-0.5
1990 Mon-N	7	9	.438	27	26	3	3	0	152^2	129	62	58	13	9	61	135	1.245	3.42	107	3.32	.230	5	.114	4	8	0.3
1991 Mon-N	9	11	.450	27	27	0	0	0	168^1	139	78	72	17	4	75	107	1.271	3.85	94	3.49	.230	5	.091	-6	6	-0.9
1992 Mon-N	12	10	.545	33	30	0	0	0	179^2	179	91	87	15	9	60	132	1.330	4.36	79	3.82	.259	7	.140	-18	5	-1.8
1993 KC-A	4	6	.400	17	16	0	0	0	91^2	92	65	63	17	4	36	54	1.396	6.19	74	5.02	.271	0	....	-17	1	-1.6
1994 Fla-N	4	4	.500	20	14	0	0	0	92^1	97	53	50	14	1	30	57	1.375	4.87	90	4.51	.276	1	.040	-6	4	-0.8
1995 Fla-N	5	5	.500	39	11	1	1	1	102^1	109	60	51	14	5	43	87	1.485	4.49	94	4.89	.272	4	.190	-3	3	-0.3
1996 SF-N	12	7	.632	30	28	4	1	0	179^1	200	105	88	28	8	57	145	1.433	4.42	93	4.99	.283	11	.162	-8	7	-0.7
1997 SF-N	12	9	.571	30	30	2	1	0	180^1	188	92	86	28	1	57	136	1.359	4.29	94	4.38	.272	7	.115	-4	8	-0.6
1998 SF-N	13	6	.684	33	33	4	2	0	212	203	106	102	29	6	65	151	1.264	4.33	92	3.83	.253	12	.164	-8	9	-0.7
1999 SF-N	5	11	.313	29	21	1	0	0	139	142	103	100	27	8	57	86	1.432	6.47	65	5.12	.267	4	.103	-35	0	-3.3
2000* SF-N	11	7	.611	30	20	0	0	0	149	155	72	67	16	5	42	92	1.322	4.05	104	4.01	.270	5	.116	3	8	0.1
2001 SF-N	5	5	.500	23	15	0	0	0	91^2	93	57	55	17	3	34	53	1.385	5.40	74	4.71	.263	0	.000	-15	1	-1.6
Total 13	**99**	**93**	**.516**	**345**	**275**	**15**	**8**	**1**	**1764^2**	**1752**	**960**	**894**	**237**	**65**	**628**	**1256**	**1.349**	**4.56**	**87**	**4.25**	**.261**	**62**	**.123**	**-118**	**60**	**-12.6**
• GARDNER, Rob	Richard Frank Gardner b: 12/19/1944, Binghamton, NY BR/TL, 6'1", 176 lbs. Deb: 9/1/1965																									
1965 NY-N	0	2	.000	5	4	0	0	0	28	23	13	10	4	0	7	19	1.071	3.21	110	2.74	.217	0	.000	1	1	0.0
1966 NY-N	4	8	.333	41	17	3	0	1	133^2	147	82	76	15	3	64	74	1.579	5.12	71	5.14	.285	7	.171	-22	2	-2.4
1967 Chi-N	0	2	.000	18	5	0	0	0	31^2	33	14	14	2	0	6	16	1.232	3.98	89	3.14	.260	0	.000	-2	1	-0.2
1968 Cle-A	0	0	....	5	0	0	0	0	2^2	5	3	2	0	0	2	6	2.625	6.75	44	10.00	.417	0	....	-1	0	-0.1
1970 NY-A	1	0	1.000	1	1	0	0	0	7^1	8	4	4	2	0	4	6	1.636	4.91	72	6.61	.276	1	.333	-1	1	-0.1
1971 Oak-A	0	0	....	4	1	0	0	0	7^2	8	2	2	1	0	3	5	1.435	2.35	142	4.40	.267	1	.500	1	0	0.1
NY-A	0	0	....	2	0	0	0	0	3	3	1	1	0	0	2	2	1.667	3.00	108	4.60	.273	0	....	0	0	0.0
Yr.	0	0	....	6	1	0	0	0	10^2	11	3	3	1	0	5	7	1.500	2.53	130	4.46	.268	1	.500	1	0	0.1
1972 NY-A	8	5	.615	20	14	1	0	0	97	91	43	33	9	0	28	58	1.227	3.06	96	3.16	.243	3	.107	-1	4	-0.3
1973 Oak-A	0	0	....	3	0	0	0	0	7^1	10	4	4	2	0	4	2	1.909	4.91	72	9.26	.370	0	....	-1	0	-0.1
Mil-A	1	1	.500	10	0	0	0	1	12^2	17	14	14	0	1	13	5	2.368	9.95	38	8.26	.327	0	....	-9	0	-0.9
Yr.	1	1	.500	13	0	0	0	1	20	27	18	18	2	1	17	7	2.200	8.10	46	8.63	.342	0	....	-10	0	-1.0
Total 8	**14**	**18**	**.438**	**109**	**42**	**4**	**0**	**2**	**331**	**345**	**180**	**160**	**35**	**4**	**133**	**193**	**1.444**	**4.35**	**79**	**4.43**	**.269**	**12**	**.138**	**-36**	**9**	**-4.0**
• GARDNER, Wes	Wesley Brian Gardner b: 4/29/1961, Benton, AR BR/TR, 6'4", 197 lbs. Deb: 7/29/1984																									
1984 NY-N	1	1	.500	21	0	0	0	1	25^1	34	19	18	0	0	8	19	1.658	6.39	55	4.76	.321	0	.000	-8	0	-0.9
1985 NY-N	0	2	.000	9	0	0	0	0	12	18	14	7	1	0	8	11	2.167	5.25	66	7.72	.375	0	....	-2	0	-0.2
1986 Bos-A	0	0	....	1	0	0	0	0	1	1	1	1	0	0	0	1	1.000	9.00	46	1.95	.333	0	....	-1	0	-0.1
1987 Bos-A	3	6	.333	49	1	0	0	10	89^2	98	55	54	17	2	42	70	1.561	5.42	84	5.54	.279	0	....	-8	4	-0.8
1988* Bos-A	8	6	.571	36	18	1	0	2	149	119	61	58	17	3	64	106	1.228	3.50	117	3.26	.220	0	....	12	11	1.2
1989 Bos-A	3	7	.300	22	16	0	0	0	86	97	64	57	10	1	47	81	1.674	5.97	69	5.45	.287	0	....	-17	0	-1.7
1990 Bos-A	3	7	.300	34	9	0	0	0	77^1	77	43	42	6	2	35	58	1.448	4.89	83	4.18	.259	0	....	-5	3	-0.6
1991 SD-N	0	1	.000	14	0	0	0	1	20^1	27	16	16	1	0	12	9	1.918	7.08	54	6.20	.310	0	.000	-7	0	-0.8
KC-A	0	0	....	3	0	0	0	0	5^2	5	4	1	0	0	2	3	1.235	1.59	259	2.31	.208	0	....	2	0	0.2
Total 8	**18**	**30**	**.375**	**189**	**44**	**1**	**0**	**14**	**466^1**	**476**	**277**	**254**	**52**	**8**	**218**	**358**	**1.488**	**4.90**	**84**	**4.57**	**.265**	**0**	**.000**	**-35**	**18**	**-3.6**
• GARFIELD, Bill	William Milton Garfield b: 10/26/1867, Sheffield, OH d: 12/16/1941, Danville, IL BR/TR, 5'11.5", 160 lbs. Deb: 7/10/1889																									
1889 Pit-N	0	2	.000	4	2	2	0	0	29	45	35	25	2	1	17	4	2.138	7.76	48	....	.343	0	.000	-13	0	-1.3
1890 Cle-N	1	7	.125	9	8	7	0	0	70	91	64	38	3	8	35	16	1.800	4.89	73	....	.305	4	.154	-10	1	-1.0
Total 2	**1**	**9**	**.100**	**13**	**10**	**9**	**0**	**0**	**99**	**136**	**99**	**63**	**5**	**9**	**52**	**20**	**1.899**	**5.73**	**64**	**....**	**.317**	**4**	**.103**	**-23**	**1**	**-2.3**
• GARIBALDI, Bob	Robert Roy Garibaldi b: 3/3/1942, Stockton, CA BL/TR, 6'4", 210 lbs. Deb: 7/15/1962																									
1962 SF-N	0	0	....	9	0	0	0	1	12^1	13	7	7	1	0	5	9	1.459	5.11	74	4.16	.265	0	.000	-2	0	-0.2
1963 SF-N	0	1	.000	4	0	0	0	1	8	8	2	1	0	1	4	4	1.500	1.13	284	4.01	.276	0	.000	2	1	0.2
1966 SF-N	0	0	....	1	0	0	0	0	1	1	0	0	0	0	0	0	1.000	0.00	....	1.95	.250	0	....	0	0	0.0
1969 SF-N	0	1	.000	1	1	0	0	0	5	6	4	1	0	0	2	1	1.600	1.80	195	4.56	.316	0	.000	1	0	0.1
Total 4	**0**	**2**	**.000**	**15**	**1**	**0**	**0**	**2**	**26^1**	**28**	**13**	**9**	**1**	**1**	**11**	**14**	**1.481**	**3.08**	**120**	**4.11**	**.277**	**0**	**.000**	**2**	**1**	**0.1**
• GARIBAY, Daniel	Daniel (Bravo) Garibay b: 2/14/1973, Maniadero, Mexico BL/TL, 5'8", 160 lbs. Deb: 4/9/2000																									
2000 Chi-N	2	8	.200	30	8	0	0	0	74^2	88	54	50	9	1	39	46	1.701	6.03	75	5.80	.299	2	.133	-12	0	-1.2
• GARLAND, Jon	Jon Steven Garland b: 9/27/1979, Valencia, CA BR/TR, 6'6", 205 lbs. Deb: 7/4/2000																									
2000 Chi-A	4	8	.333	15	13	0	0	0	69^2	82	55	50	10	1	40	42	1.751	6.46	77	6.26	.292	0	....	-13	1	-1.1
2001 Chi-A	6	7	.462	35	16	0	0	1	117	123	59	48	16	4	55	61	1.521	3.69	125	5.16	.277	0	.000	11	8	1.1
2002 Chi-A	12	12	.500	33	33	1	1	0	192^2	188	109	98	23	9	83	112	1.407	4.58	100	4.46	.258	0	.000	-2	9	-0.2
2003 Chi-A	12	13	.480	32	32	0	0	0	191^2	188	103	96	28	4	74	108	1.367	4.51	99	4.38	.260	0	.000	-3	10	-0.3
Total 4	**34**	**40**	**.459**	**115**	**94**	**1**	**1**	**1**	**571**	**581**	**326**	**292**	**77**	**18**	**252**	**323**	**1.459**	**4.60**	**100**	**4.79**	**.267**	**0**	**.000**	**-6**	**28**	**-0.6**
• GARLAND, Lou	Louis Lyman Garland b: 7/16/1905, Archie, MO d: 8/30/1990, Idaho Falls, ID BR/TR, 6'2.5", 200 lbs. Deb: 8/31/1931																									
1931 Chi-A	0	2	.000	7	2	0	0	0	16^2	30	24	19	2	1	14	4	2.640	10.26	41	11.46	.400	0	.000	-11	0	-1.1
• GARLAND, Wayne	Marcus Wayne Garland b: 10/26/1950, Nashville, TN BR/TR, 6', 195 lbs. Deb: 9/13/1973																									
1973 Bal-A	0	1	.000	4	1	0	0	0	16	14	8	7	1	0	7	10	1.313	3.94	95	3.26	.233	0	....	-1	0	-0.1
1974* Bal-A	5	5	.500	20	6	0	0	1	91	68	37	30	5	3	26	40	1.033	2.97	116	2.18	.211	0	....	4	6	0.4
1975 Bal-A	2	5	.286	29	1	0	0	4	87^1	80	37	36	7	1	31	46	1.271	3.71	95	3.33	.252	0	....	-5	4	-0.5
1976 Bal-A	20	7	.741	38	25	14	4	1	232^1	224	81	69	10	6	64	113	1.240	2.67	122	3.04	.255	0	....	13	20	1.4
1977 Cle-A	13	19	.406	38	38	21	1	0	282^2	281	130	113	23	2	88	118	1.305	3.60	110	3.59	.261	0	....	10	17	1.0
1978 Cle-A	2	3	.400	6	6	0	0	0	29^2	43	27	26	6	1	16	13	1.989	7.89	47	8.50	.347	0	....	-13	0	-1.4
1979 Cle-A	4	10	.286	18	14	2	0	0	94^2	120	70	55	11	3	34	40	1.627	5.23	81	5.69	.318	0	....	-8	2	-0.8
1980 Cle-A	6	9	.400	25	20	4	1	0	150^1	163	85	77	18	6	48	55	1.404	4.61	88	4.49	.276	0	....	-8	6	-0.8
1981 Cle-A	3	7	.300	12	10	2	1	0	56	89	40	36	8	0	14	15	1.839	5.79	63	7.39	.374	0	....	-12	0	-1.2
Total 9	**55**	**66**	**.455**	**190**	**121**	**43**	**7**	**6**	**1040**	**1082**	**515**	**449**	**89**	**22**	**328**	**450**	**1.356**	**3.89**	**97**	**3.98**	**.272**	**0**	**....**	**-20**	**55**	**-2.0**
• GARMAN, Mike	Michael Douglas Garman b: 9/16/1949, Caldwell, ID BR/TR, 6'3", 215 lbs. Deb: 9/22/1969																									
1969 Bos-A	1	0	1.000	2	2	0	0	0	12^1	13	6	6	0	0	10	10	1.865	4.38	87	5.36	.277	2	.400	-1	1	0.0
1971 Bos-A	1	1	.500	3	3	0	0	0	18^2	15	8	8	3	1	9	6	1.286	3.86	96	3.83	.217	2	.333	-0	1	0.0
1972 Bos-A	0	1	.000	3	1	0	0	0	3^1	4	4	4	1	0	2	1	1.800	10.80	30	7.57	.286	0	....	-3	0	-0.3
1973 Bos-A	0	0	....	12	0	0	0	0	22	32	15	13	1	0	15	9	2.136	5.32	76	7.36	.352	0	....	-3	0	-0.3
1974 StL-N	7	2	.778	64	0	0	0	6	81^2	66	26	24	4	2	27	45	1.139	2.64	135	2.44	.227	1	.100	7	10	0.7
1975 StL-N	3	8	.273	66	0	0	0	10	79	73	31	21	3	1	48	48	1.532	2.39	157	3.46	.245	0	.000	14	8	1.4
1976 Chi-N	2	4	.333	47	2	0	0	1	76^1	79	48	42	7	3	35	37	1.493	4.95	78	4.41	.273	0	.000	-8	2	-0.9
1977* LA-N	4	4	.500	49	0	0	0	12	62^2	60	20	19	7	2	22	29	1.309	2.73	140	3.77	.254	0	.000	7	7	0.6

YEAR	TM-L	W	L	PCT	G	GS	CG	SH	SV	IP	H	R	ER	HR	HB	BB	SO	RAT	ERA	ERA+	CERA	OAV	BH	AVG	PR+	WS	TPW
1978	LA-N	0	1	.000	10	0	0	0	0	16^{1}	15	8	8	3	0	3	5	1.102	4.41	80	3.50	.259	0	....	-2	0	-0.2
	Mon-N	4	6	.400	47	0	0	0	13	61^{1}	54	32	30	5	0	31	23	1.386	4.40	80	3.49	.238	0	.000	-8	4	-0.9
	Yr.	4	7	.364	57	0	0	0	13	77^{2}	69	40	38	8	0	34	28	1.326	4.40	80	3.49	.242	0	.000	-10	4	-1.1
Total	**9**	**22**	**27**	**.449**	**303**	**8**	**0**	**0**	**42**	**433^{2}**	**411**	**198**	**175**	**34**	**9**	**202**	**213**	**1.414**	**3.63**	**102**	**3.79**	**.254**	**5**	**.119**	**4**	**33**	**0.1**
• GARONI, Willie	William Garoni b: 7/28/1877, Fort Lee, NJ d: 9/9/1914, Fort Lee, NJ BR/TR, 6'1", 165 lbs. Deb: 9/7/1899																										
1899	NY-N	0	1	.000	3	1	1	0	0	10	12	7	5	0	0	2	2	1.400	4.50	83	3.66	.297	0	.000	-1	0	-0.1
• GARRELTS, Scott	Scott William Garrelts b: 10/30/1961, Champaign, IL BR/TR, 6'4", 195 lbs. Deb: 10/2/1982																										
1982	SF-N	0	0	....	1	0	0	0	0	2	3	3	3	0	0	2	4	2.500	13.50	27	8.58	.333	0	....	-2	0	-0.2
1983	SF-N	2	2	.500	5	5	1	1	0	35^{2}	33	11	10	4	2	19	16	1.458	2.52	140	4.41	.254	2	.222	4	3	0.5
1984	SF-N	2	3	.400	21	3	0	0	0	43	45	33	27	6	1	34	32	1.837	5.65	62	6.26	.274	1	.100	-9	0	-1.0
1985	SF-N★	9	6	.600	74	0	0	0	13	105^{2}	76	37	27	2	3	58	106	1.268	2.30	149	2.45	.198	2	.222	15	13	1.6
1986	SF-N	13	9	.591	53	18	2	0	10	173^{2}	144	65	60	17	2	74	125	1.255	3.11	113	3.24	.231	8	.178	5	13	0.7
1987*	SF-N	11	7	.611	64	0	0	0	12	106^{1}	70	41	38	10	0	55	127	1.176	3.22	120	2.68	.192	2	.200	6	12	0.6
1988	SF-N	5	9	.357	65	0	0	0	13	98	80	42	39	3	2	46	86	1.286	3.58	91	2.80	.226	1	.077	-4	7	-0.5
1989*	SF-N	14	5	.737	30	29	2	1	0	193^{1}	149	58	49	11	0	46	119	1.009	**2.28**	**148**	**2.02**	.212	9	.136	19	15	2.1
1990	SF-N	12	11	.522	31	31	4	2	0	182	190	91	84	16	3	70	80	1.429	4.15	88	4.20	.272	4	.061	-12	7	-1.5
1991	SF-N	1	1	.500	8	3	0	0	0	19^{2}	25	14	14	5	0	9	8	1.729	6.41	56	7.25	.313	0	.000	-6	0	-0.7
Total	**10**	**69**	**53**	**.566**	**352**	**89**	**9**	**4**	**48**	**959^{1}**	**815**	**395**	**351**	**74**	**13**	**413**	**703**	**1.280**	**3.29**	**107**	**3.25**	**.232**	**29**	**.125**	**16**	**70**	**1.6**
• GARRETT, Clarence	Clarence Raymond "Laz" Garrett b: 3/6/1891, Reader, WV d: 2/11/1977, Moundsville, WV BR/TR, 6'5.5", 185 lbs. Deb: 9/13/1915																										
1915	Cle-A	2	2	.500	4	4	2	0	0	23^{1}	19	13	6	1	1	6	5	1.071	2.31	131	2.38	.224	0	.000	2	1	0.2
• GARRETT, Greg	Gregory Garrett b: 3/12/1947, Atascadero, CA d: 6/7/2003, Newhall, CA BB/TL, 6', 200 lbs. Deb: 4/24/1970																										
1970	Cal-A	5	6	.455	32	7	0	0	0	74^{2}	48	23	22	6	1	44	53	1.232	2.65	136	2.70	.190	1	.067	6	6	0.5
1971	Cin-N	0	1	.000	2	1	0	0	0	8^{2}	7	1	1	0	0	10	2	1.962	1.04	313	5.51	.250	1	.333	2	1	0.2
Total	**2**	**5**	**7**	**.417**	**34**	**8**	**0**	**0**	**0**	**83^{1}**	**55**	**24**	**23**	**6**	**1**	**54**	**55**	**1.308**	**2.48**	**145**	**2.99**	**.196**	**2**	**.111**	**8**	**7**	**0.8**
• GARRISON, Cliff	Clifford William Garrison b: 8/13/1906, Belmont, OK d: 8/25/1994, Woodland, CA BR/TR, 6', 180 lbs. Deb: 4/16/1928																										
1928	Bos-A	0	0	....	6	0	0	0	0	16	22	15	14	2	0	6	0	1.750	7.88	52	6.41	.361	0	.000	-7	0	-0.7
• GARRY, Jim	James Thomas Garry b: 9/21/1869, Great Barrington, MA d: 1/15/1917, Pittsfield, MA BL/TL, 5'10" Deb: 5/2/1893																										
1893	Bos-N	0	1	.000	1	0	0	0	0	1	5	8	7	0	0	4	2	9.000	63.00	8	51.26	.628	0	.000	-6	0	-0.5
• GARVER, Ned	Ned Franklin Garver b: 12/25/1925, Ney, OH BR/TR, 5'10.5", 180 lbs. Deb: 4/28/1948																										
1948	StL-A	7	11	.389	38	24	7	0	5	198	200	92	75	14	1	95	75	1.490	3.41	134	4.25	.268	19	.288	29	18	3.2
1949	StL-A	12	17	.414	41	32	16	1	3	223^{2}	245	126	99	14	3	102	70	1.551	3.98	114	4.43	.277	14	.187	21	13	2.3
1950	StL-A	13	18	.419	37	31	**22**	2	0	260	264	120	98	18	4	108	85	1.431	3.39	**146**	3.98	.264	26	.286	**53**	**25**	**5.6**
1951	StL-A★	20	12	.625	33	30	**24**	1	0	246	237	114	102	17	5	96	84	1.354	3.73	118	3.64	.255	29	.305	24	22	3.1
1952	StL-A	7	10	.412	21	21	7	2	0	148^{2}	130	67	61	14	4	55	60	1.244	3.69	106	3.31	.235	9	.184	3	8	0.4
	Det-A	1	0	1.000	1	1	1	0	0	9	9	2	2	1	0	3	3	1.333	2.00	190	3.95	.265	0	.000	2	1	0.2
	Yr.	8	10	.444	22	22	8	2	0	157^{2}	139	69	63	15	4	58	63	1.249	3.60	109	3.34	.237	9	.176	5	9	0.6
1953	Det-A	11	11	.500	30	26	13	0	1	198^{1}	228	107	98	16	2	66	69	1.482	4.45	91	4.49	.290	11	.153	-2	7	-0.3
1954	Det-A	14	11	.560	35	32	16	3	1	246^{1}	216	93	77	20	4	62	93	1.129	2.81	131	2.74	.236	13	.165	23	20	2.4
1955	Det-A	12	16	.429	33	32	16	1	0	230^{2}	251	115	102	21	5	67	83	1.379	3.98	97	4.09	.279	17	.224	-3	11	0.2
1956	Det-A	0	2	.000	6	3	1	0	0	17^{2}	15	10	8	2	1	13	6	1.585	4.08	101	4.88	.234	0	.000	0	1	0.0
1957	KC-A	6	13	.316	24	23	6	1	0	145^{1}	120	72	62	13	5	55	61	1.204	3.84	103	3.04	.223	8	.182	3	7	0.3
1958	KC-A	12	11	.522	31	28	10	3	1	201	192	97	90	24	2	66	72	1.284	4.03	97	3.57	.244	12	.174	-2	12	-0.2
1959	KC-A	10	13	.435	32	30	9	2	1	201^{1}	214	94	83	22	3	42	61	1.272	3.71	108	3.78	.270	20	.282	8	14	1.5
1960	KC-A	4	9	.308	28	15	5	2	0	122^{1}	110	57	52	15	2	35	50	1.185	3.83	104	3.24	.240	2	.074	4	6	0.3
1961	LA-A	0	3	.000	12	2	0	0	0	29	40	18	18	2	0	16	9	1.931	5.59	81	7.03	.348	0	.000	-3	1	-0.4
Total	**14**	**129**	**157**	**.451**	**402**	**330**	**153**	**18**	**12**	**2477^{1}**	**2471**	**1184**	**1027**	**213**	**41**	**881**	**881**	**1.353**	**3.73**	**111**	**3.80**	**.260**	**180**	**.218**	**159**	**166**	**18.5**
• GARVIN, Jerry	Theodore Jared Garvin b: 10/21/1955, Oakland, CA BL/TL, 6'3", 195 lbs. Deb: 4/10/1977																										
1977	Tor-A	10	18	.357	34	34	12	1	0	244^{2}	247	127	114	33	4	85	127	1.357	4.19	100	4.21	.264	0	....	6	13	0.6
1978	Tor-A	4	12	.250	26	22	3	0	0	144^{2}	189	92	89	20	4	48	67	1.638	5.54	71	6.00	.319	0	....	-25	1	-2.6
1979	Tor-A	0	1	.000	8	1	0	0	0	22^{2}	15	9	7	2	2	10	14	1.103	2.78	156	2.78	.197	0	....	4	2	0.4
1980	Tor-A	4	7	.364	61	0	0	0	8	82^{2}	70	23	21	6	0	27	52	1.173	2.29	188	2.71	.233	0	....	18	11	1.8
1981	Tor-A	1	2	.333	35	4	0	0	0	53	46	20	20	3	0	23	25	1.302	3.40	116	3.12	.240	0	....	4	4	0.4
1982	Tor-A	1	1	.500	32	4	0	0	0	58^{1}	81	48	47	10	1	26	35	1.834	7.25	62	7.28	.335	0	....	-18	0	-1.8
Total	**6**	**20**	**41**	**.328**	**196**	**65**	**15**	**1**	**8**	**606**	**648**	**319**	**298**	**74**	**11**	**219**	**320**	**1.431**	**4.43**	**94**	**4.58**	**.277**	**0**	**....**	**-11**	**31**	**-1.2**
• GARVIN, Ned	Virgil Lee Garvin b: 1/1/1874, Navasota, TX d: 6/16/1908, Fresno, CA BR/TR, 6'3.5", 160 lbs. Deb: 7/13/1896																										
1896	Phi-N	0	1	.000	2	1	1	0	0	13	19	13	11	0	0	7	4	2.000	7.62	56	6.41	.338	0	.000	-5	0	-0.5
1899	Chi-N	9	13	.409	24	23	22	4	0	199	202	101	63	1	12	42	69	1.226	2.85	131	2.97	.263	11	.155	19	12	1.4
1900	Chi-N	10	18	.357	30	28	25	1	0	246^{1}	225	126	66	4	18	63	107	1.169	2.41	149	2.73	.243	14	.154	**37**	17	**3.0**
1901	Mil-A	8	20	.286	37	27	22	1	2	257^{1}	258	155	99	4	14	90	122	1.352	3.46	104	3.42	.258	10	.108	8	12	-0.1
1902	Chi-A	10	10	.500	23	19	16	2	0	175^{1}	169	68	43	3	8	43	55	1.209	2.21	153	2.86	.254	9	.153	20	14	1.7
	Bro-N	1	1	.500	2	2	2	1	0	18	15	3	2	0	0	4	7	1.056	1.00	276	1.87	.227	1	.143	4	2	0.3
1903	Bro-N	15	18	.455	38	34	30	2	2	298	1277	163	102	2	13	84	154	**4.567**	3.08	103	49.85	.248	8	.075	42	17	3.3
1904	Bro-N	5	15	.250	23	22	16	2	0	181^{2}	141	81	34	6	6	78	86	1.206	1.68	162	2.67	.218	8	.127	22	10	2.0
	NY-A	0	1	.000	2	2	0	0	0	12	14	4	3	0	0	2	8	1.333	2.25	120	3.34	.292	0	.000	0	1	0.0
Total	**7**	**58**	**97**	**.374**	**181**	**158**	**134**	**13**	**4**	**1400^{2}**	**2320**	**714**	**423**	**20**	**71**	**413**	**612**	**1.951**	**2.72**	**125**	**12.95**	**.249**	**61**	**.122**	**148**	**85**	**11.0**
• GASPAR, Harry	Harry Lambert Gaspar b: 4/28/1883, Kingsley, IA d: 5/14/1940, Orange, CA BR/TR, 6', 180 lbs. Deb: 4/21/1909																										
1909	Cin-N	19	11	.633	44	29	19	4	2	260	228	97	58	0	9	57	65	1.096	2.01	129	2.32	.242	10	.122	15	15	1.3
1910	Cin-N	15	17	.469	48	31	16	4	**7**	275	257	103	79	6	15	75	74	1.207	2.59	112	3.01	.255	10	.115	13	18	1.0
1911	Cin-N	11	17	.393	44	32	11	2	4	253^{2}	272	112	93	9	14	69	76	1.344	3.30	100	3.85	.283	13	.153	1	13	-0.2
1912	Cin-N	1	3	.250	7	6	2	0	0	36^{2}	38	21	17	0	1	16	13	1.473	4.17	80	3.70	.277	3	.250	-3	1	-0.3
Total	**4**	**46**	**48**	**.489**	**143**	**98**	**48**	**10**	**13**	**825^{1}**	**795**	**333**	**247**	**15**	**39**	**217**	**228**	**1.226**	**2.69**	**111**	**3.08**	**.261**	**36**	**.135**	**25**	**47**	**1.9**
• GASSAWAY, Charlie	Charles Cason "Sheriff" Gassaway b: 8/12/1918, Gassaway, TN d: 1/15/1992, Miami, FL BL/TL, 6'2.5", 210 lbs. Deb: 9/25/1944																										
1944	Chi-N	0	1	.000	2	2	0	0	0	11^{2}	20	11	10	3	0	10	7	2.571	7.71	46	12.29	.385	1	.250	-5	0	-0.5
1945	Phi-A	4	7	.364	24	11	4	0	0	118	114	59	49	4	2	55	50	1.432	3.74	92	3.61	.252	6	.154	-4	4	-0.6
1946	Cle-A	1	1	.500	13	6	0	0	0	50^{2}	54	25	22	2	4	26	23	1.579	3.91	85	4.51	.273	1	.067	-3	1	-0.4
Total	**3**	**5**	**9**	**.357**	**39**	**19**	**4**	**0**	**0**	**180^{1}**	**188**	**95**	**81**	**9**	**6**	**91**	**80**	**1.547**	**4.04**	**84**	**4.42**	**.268**	**8**	**.138**	**-12**	**5**	**-1.5**
• GASTON, Milt	Nathaniel Milton Gaston b: 1/27/1896, Ridgefield Park, NJ d: 4/26/1996, Barnstable, MA BR/TR, 6'1", 185 lbs. Deb: 4/20/1924																										
1924	NY-A	5	3	.625	29	2	0	0	1	86	92	48	43	3	6	44	24	1.581	4.50	92	4.50	.286	6	.222	-4	4	-0.4
1925	StL-A	15	14	.517	42	29	16	0	1	238^{2}	284	146	117	8	5	101	84	1.613	4.41	106	4.79	.305	21	.263	5	16	0.7
1926	StL-A	10	18	.357	32	28	14	1	0	214^{1}	227	116	103	13	4	101	39	1.530	4.33	99	4.38	.283	13	.167	-3	11	-0.4
1927	StL-A	13	17	.433	37	30	21	0	1	254	275	177	141	18	3	100	77	1.476	5.00	87	4.24	.281	25	.260	-20	12	-1.3
1928	Was-A	6	12	.333	28	22	8	3	0	148^{2}	179	102	91	3	0	53	45	1.561	5.51	73	4.34	.302	7	.143	-27	1	-2.9
1929	Bos-A	12	19	.387	39	28	20	1	2	243^{2}	265	121	101	15	3	81	83	1.420	3.73	115	4.11	.289	15	.192	16	18	1.6
1930	Bos-A	13	20	.394	38	34	20	2	2	273	272	138	119	15	0	98	99	1.355	3.92	117	3.46	.259	20	.204	18	20	1.3
1931	Bos-A	2	13	.133	23	18	4	0	0	119	137	76	59	4	0	41	33	1.496	4.46	96	4.10	.291	6	.158	-2	4	-0.3
1932	Chi-A	7	17	.292	28	25	7	1	1	166^{2}	183	101	74	10	1	73	44	1.536	4.00	108	4.38	.279	14	.233	8	6	0.9
1933	Chi-A	8	12	.400	30	25	7	1	0	167	177	106	90	9	1	60	39	1.419	4.85	87	3.85	.272	8	.154	-10	6	-0.9

YEAR TM-L	W	L	PCT	G	GS	CG	SH	SV	IP	H	R	ER	HR	HB	BB	SO	RAT	ERA	ERA+	CERA	OAV	BH	AVG	PR+	WS	TPW
1934 Chi-A	6	19	.240	29	28	10	1	0	194	247	146	126	16	1	84	48	**1.706**	5.85	81	5.56	.313	10	.147	-19	4	-2.0
Total 11	97	164	.372	355	269	127	10	8	2105	2338	1277	1064	114	24	836	615	1.508	4.55	96	4.31	.286	145	.200	-37	102	-3.9
• GASTON, Welcome	Welcome Thornburg Gaston b: 12/19/1872, Guernsey County, OH d: 12/13/1944, Columbus, OH TL Deb: 10/6/1898																									
1898 Bro-N	1	1	.500	2	2	2	0	0	16	17	9	5	0	0	9	0	1.625	2.81	127	4.10	.271	1	.125	2	1	0.1
1899 Bro-N	0	0	....	1	0	0	0	0	3	3	1	1	0	1	4	0	2.333	3.00	130	8.03	.260	1	1.000	0	1	0.1
Total 2	1	1	.500	3	2	2	0	0	19	20	10	6	0	1	13	0	1.737	2.84	128	4.72	.269	2	.222	2	2	0.3
• GASTRIGHT, Hank	Henry Carl Gastright b: 3/29/1865, Covington, KY d: 10/9/1937, Cold Spring, KY BR/TR, 6'2", 190 lbs. Deb: 4/19/1889																									
1889 Col-a	10	16	.385	32	26	21	0	0	222^2	255	175	113	8	5	104	115	1.612	4.57	79	....	.279	17	.181	-23	8	-2.3
1890 Col-a	30	14	.682	48	45	41	4	0	401^1	312	204	131	8	18	135	199	1.114	2.94	122	....	.208	36	.213	13	30	1.5
1891 Col-a	12	19	.387	35	33	28	1	0	283^2	280	196	119	7	11	136	109	1.467	3.78	92	....	.249	23	.197	-18	14	-1.3
1892 Was-N	3	3	.500	11	8	6	0	0	79^2	94	54	45	3	3	38	32	1.657	5.08	64	4.95	.283	4	.138	-16	3	-1.4
1893 Pit-N	3	1	.750	9	5	3	0	0	59	74	54	41	3	3	39	12	1.915	6.25	73	6.25	.298	1	.042	-13	2	-1.3
Bos-N	12	4	.750	19	18	16	0	0	156	179	117	89	9	9	76	27	1.635	5.13	96	5.04	.280	13	.191	-5	9	-0.7
Yr.	15	5	.750	28	23	19	0	0	215	253	171	130	12	12	115	39	1.712	5.44	88	5.37	.285	14	.152	-18	11	-2.0
1894 Bro-N	2	6	.250	16	8	6	1	2	93	135	85	66	1	12	55	20	2.043	6.39	77	7.15	.335	7	.171	-14	4	-1.3
1896 Cin-N	0	0	....	1	0	0	0	0	6	8	6	3	0	0	1	0	1.500	4.50	102	4.27	.317	0	.000	-0	0	0.0
Total 7	72	63	.533	171	143	121	6	2	1301^1	1337	891	607	39	61	584	514	1.476	4.20	92	1.72	.258	101	.186	-76	70	-6.8
• GATEWOOD, Aubrey	Aubrey Lee Gatewood b: 11/17/1938, Little Rock, AR BR/TR, 6'1", 170 lbs. Deb: 9/11/1963																									
1963 LA-A	1	1	.500	4	3	1	0	0	24	12	5	4	0	0	16	13	1.167	1.50	228	1.79	.148	0	.000	5	2	0.4
1964 LA-A	3	3	.500	15	7	0	0	0	60^1	59	18	15	4	1	12	25	1.177	2.24	147	3.05	.258	2	.100	7	5	0.6
1965 Cal-A	4	5	.444	46	3	0	0	0	92	91	41	35	5	1	37	37	1.391	3.42	99	3.73	.266	3	.214	-1	4	0.0
1970 Atl-N	0	0	....	3	0	0	0	0	2	4	6	1	0	1	2	0	3.000	4.50	95	12.01	.364	0	....	0	0	0.0
Total 4	8	9	.471	68	13	1	0	0	178^1	166	70	55	9	3	67	75	1.307	2.78	122	3.33	.250	5	.119	11	11	1.0
• GAUDIN, Chad	Chad Edward Gaudin b: 3/24/1983, Metairie, LA BR/TR, 5'10", 165 lbs. Deb: 8/1/2003																									
2003 TB-A	2	0	1.000	15	3	0	0	0	40	37	18	16	4	1	16	23	1.325	3.60	126	3.70	.240	0	....	3	3	0.3
• GAW, Chippy	George Joseph Gaw b: 3/13/1892, West Newton, MA d: 5/26/1968, Boston, MA BR/TR, 5'11", 180 lbs. Deb: 4/20/1920																									
1920 Chi-N	1	1	.500	6	1	0	0	0	13	16	9	7	1	1	3	4	1.462	4.85	66	4.74	.320	1	.250	-2	0	-0.2
• GEAR, Dale	Dale Dudley Gear b: 2/2/1872, Lone Elm, KS d: 9/23/1951, Topeka, KS BR/TR, 5'11", 165 lbs. Deb: 8/15/1896 ♦																									
1896 Cle-N	0	2	.000	3	2	2	0	0	23	35	23	14	1	2	6	6	1.783	5.48	83	6.43	.347	6	.400	-2	1	-0.1
1901 Was-A	4	11	.267	24	16	14	1	1	163	199	100	73	9	4	22	35	1.356	4.03	91	4.02	.297	47	.236	-6	9	-1.2
Total 2	4	13	.235	27	18	16	1	1	186	234	123	87	10	6	28	41	1.409	4.21	90	4.32	.304	57	.239	-9	10	-1.3
• GEARIN, Dinty	Dennis John Gearin b: 10/15/1897, Providence, RI d: 3/11/1959, Providence, RI BL/TL, 5'4", 148 lbs. Deb: 8/6/1923																									
1923* NY-N	1	1	.500	6	2	1	0	0	24	23	11	9	1	0	10	9	1.375	3.38	113	3.47	.260	2	.286	1	2	0.1
1924 NY-N	1	2	.333	6	3	2	0	0	29	30	9	8	3	0	16	4	1.586	2.48	148	4.80	.270	3	.333	4	2	0.4
Bos-N	0	1	.000	1	1	0	0	0	0	3	5	0	0	0	2	0	....	....	....	∞	1.000	0	....	0	0	0.0
Yr.	1	3	.250	7	4	2	0	0	29	33	14	8	3	0	18	4	1.759	2.48	148	4.80	.289	3	.333	4	2	0.4
Total 2	2	4	.333	13	6	3	0	0	53	56	25	17	4	0	28	13	1.585	2.89	130	4.20	.276	5	.313	5	4	0.5
• GEARY, Bob	Robert Norton "Speed" Geary b: 5/10/1891, Cincinnati, OH d: 1/3/1980, Cincinnati, OH BR/TR, 5'11", 168 lbs. Deb: 4/25/1918																									
1918 Phi-A	2	5	.286	16	7	6	2	4	87	94	37	26	0	3	31	22	1.437	2.69	109	3.80	.289	4	.148	-0	6	-0.1
1919 Phi-A	0	3	.000	9	2	1	0	0	32^1	32	22	17	1	0	18	9	1.546	4.73	72	4.12	.264	5	.500	-3	1	-0.1
1921 Cin-N	1	1	.500	10	1	0	0	0	29	38	17	14	1	0	2	10	1.379	4.34	82	4.03	.333	2	.250	-2	1	-0.2
Total 3	3	9	.250	35	10	7	2	4	148^1	164	76	57	2	3	51	41	1.449	3.46	93	3.91	.293	11	.244	-6	8	-0.4
• GEARY, Geoff	Geoffrey Michael Geary b: 8/26/1976, Buffalo, NY BR/TR, 6', 170 lbs. Deb: 8/27/2003																									
2003 Phi-N	0	0	....	5	0	0	0	0	6	8	3	3	0	0	3	3	1.833	4.50	89	5.70	.333	0	....	-0	0	0.0
• GEBHARD, Bob	Robert Henry Gebhard b: 1/3/1943, Lamberton, MN BR/TR, 6'2", 210 lbs. Deb: 8/2/1971 C																									
1971 Min-A	1	2	.333	17	0	0	0	0	18	17	6	6	0	1	11	13	1.556	3.00	118	3.54	.243	0	....	1	1	0.2
1972 Min-A	0	1	.000	13	0	0	0	1	21	36	29	20	3	2	13	13	2.333	8.57	37	9.77	.371	0	....	-13	0	-1.4
1974 Mon-N	0	0	....	1	0	0	0	0	2	5	1	1	1	0	0	0	2.500	4.50	85	15.86	.500	0	....	-0	0	0.0
Total 3	1	3	.250	31	0	0	0	1	41	58	36	27	4	3	24	26	2.000	5.93	56	7.33	.328	0	....	-11	1	-1.3
• GEBRIAN, Pete	Peter "Gabe" Gebrian b: 8/10/1923, Bayonne, NJ BR/TR, 6', 170 lbs. Deb: 5/6/1947																									
1947 Chi-A	2	3	.400	27	4	0	0	5	66^1	61	40	33	7	2	33	17	1.417	4.48	82	4.05	.247	0	.000	-6	2	-0.8
• GEDDES, Jim	James Lee Geddes b: 3/23/1949, Columbus, OH BR/TR, 6'2", 200 lbs. Deb: 4/28/1972																									
1972 Chi-A	0	0	....	5	1	0	0	0	10^1	12	9	8	1	1	10	3	2.129	6.97	45	7.92	.293	0	.000	-4	0	-0.5
1973 Chi-A	0	0	....	6	1	0	0	0	15^2	14	6	5	0	3	14	7	1.787	2.87	138	5.58	.255	0	....	2	1	0.2
Total 2	0	0	....	11	2	0	0	0	26	26	15	13	1	4	24	10	1.923	4.50	76	6.51	.271	0	.000	-2	1	-0.3
• GEE, Johnny	John Alexander "Whiz" Gee b: 12/7/1915, Syracuse, NY d: 1/23/1988, Cortland, NY BL/TL, 6'9", 225 lbs. Deb: 9/17/1939																									
1939 Pit-N	1	2	.333	3	3	1	0	0	19^2	20	17	9	0	0	10	16	1.525	4.12	93	3.40	.253	0	.000	-0	0	-0.1
1941 Pit-N	0	2	.000	3	2	0	0	0	7^1	10	10	5	0	0	5	2	2.045	6.14	59	5.52	.294	1	.333	-2	0	-0.2
1943 Pit-N	4	4	.500	15	10	2	0	0	82	89	42	39	5	0	27	18	1.415	4.28	81	3.95	.280	3	.115	-7	2	-0.8
1944 Pit-N	0	0	....	4	0	0	0	0	11^1	20	10	9	0	0	5	3	2.206	7.15	52	7.76	.377	1	.500	-4	0	-0.4
NY-N	0	0	....	4	0	0	0	0	4^2	5	1	0	0	0	0	3	1.071	0.00	....	2.27	.263	0	....	2	1	0.2
Yr.	0	0	....	8	0	0	0	0	16	25	11	9	0	0	5	6	1.875	5.06	73	6.16	.347	1	.500	-2	1	-0.2
1945 NY-N	0	0	....	2	0	0	0	1	3	5	3	3	0	0	2	1	2.333	9.00	43	8.59	.385	0	.000	-2	0	-0.2
1946 NY-N	2	4	.333	13	6	1	0	0	47^1	60	27	21	3	2	15	22	1.585	3.99	86	5.03	.308	3	.231	-2	1	-0.2
Total 6	7	12	.368	44	21	4	0	1	175^1	209	110	86	8	2	64	65	1.557	4.41	80	4.53	.294	8	.157	-16	4	-1.7
• GEHRING, Henry	Henry Gehring b: 1/24/1881, St. Paul, MN d: 4/18/1912, Kansas City, MO BR/TR Deb: 7/16/1907																									
1907 Was-A	3	7	.300	15	9	8	2	0	87	92	44	32	1	1	14	31	1.218	3.31	73	2.79	.274	9	.205	-6	2	-0.3
1908 Was-A	0	1	.000	3	1	0	0	0	5	9	8	8	0	2	2	0	2.200	14.40	16	11.09	.450	3	.600	-7	1	-0.5
Total 2	3	8	.273	18	10	8	2	0	92	101	52	40	1	3	16	31	1.272	3.91	61	3.24	.284	12	.245	-12	3	-0.8
• GEHRMAN, Paul	Paul Arthur "Dutch" Gehrman b: 5/3/1912, Marquam, OR d: 10/23/1986, Bend, OR BR/TR, 6', 195 lbs. Deb: 9/15/1937																									
1937 Cin-N	0	1	.000	2	1	0	0	0	9^1	11	8	3	0	0	5	1	1.714	2.89	129	4.58	.282	0	.000	1	0	0.0
• GEIS, Emil	Emil Michael Geis b: 3/1861, Villmar, Germany BR/TR, 5'11", 170 lbs. Deb: 7/19/1882																									
1882 Bal-a	4	9	.308	13	13	10	1	0	95^2	84	73	51	2	....	22	10	1.108	4.80	57	....	.220	6	.146	-20	2	-2.0
• GEISEL, Dave	John David Geisel b: 1/18/1955, Windber, PA BL/TL, 6'3", 210 lbs. Deb: 6/13/1978																									
1978 Chi-N	1	0	1.000	18	1	0	0	0	23^1	27	12	11	0	0	11	15	1.629	4.24	95	4.02	.278	0	.000	-0	1	-0.1
1979 Chi-N	0	0	....	7	0	0	0	0	15	10	1	1	0	1	4	5	.933	0.60	686	1.56	.189	0	.000	6	2	0.6
1981 Chi-N	2	0	1.000	11	2	0	0	0	16	11	3	1	0	0	10	7	1.313	0.56	657	2.54	.204	0	.000	6	2	0.6
1982 Tor-A	1	1	.500	16	2	0	0	0	31^2	32	15	14	6	2	17	22	1.547	3.98	113	5.56	.260	0	....	2	2	0.2
1983 Tor-A	0	3	.000	47	0	0	0	5	52^1	47	28	27	4	2	31	50	1.490	4.64	93	4.10	.240	0	....	-2	3	-0.2
1984 Sea-A	1	1	.500	20	3	0	0	3	43^1	47	22	20	2	2	9	28	1.292	4.15	96	3.47	.273	0	....	0	3	0.0
1985 Sea-A	0	0	....	12	0	0	0	0	27	35	21	19	3	0	15	17	1.852	6.33	67	6.36	.310	0	....	-6	0	-0.6
Total 7	5	5	.500	131	8	0	0	8	208^2	209	102	93	15	7	97	144	1.466	4.01	105	4.17	.259	0	.000	5	13	0.6

YEAR TM-L	W	L	PCT	G	GS	CG	SH	SV	IP	H	R	ER	HR	HB	BB	SO	RAT	ERA	ERA+	CERA	OAV	BH	AVG	PR+	WS	TPW
• GEISHERT, Vern	Vernon William Geishert b: 1/10/1946, Madison, WI BR/TR, 6'1", 215 lbs. Deb: 8/26/1969																									
1969 Cal-A	1	1	.500	11	3	0	0	1	31	32	18	16	4	1	7	18	1.258	4.65	75	3.76	.267	0	.000	-4	1	-0.5
• GEISS, Emil	Emil August Geiss b: 3/20/1867, Chicago, IL d: 10/4/1911, Chicago, IL BR/TR, 5'11", 170 lbs. Deb: 5/18/1887 ♦																									
1887 Chi-N	0	1	.000	1	1	1	0	0	9	20	11	8	0	0	3	4	2.222	8.00	56	....	.430	1	.083	-4	0	-0.6
• GELNAR, John	John Richard Gelnar b: 6/25/1943, Granite, OK BR/TR, 6'2", 190 lbs. Deb: 8/4/1964																									
1964 Pit-N	0	0	....	7	0	0	0	0	9	11	5	5	2	0	1	4	1.333	5.00	70	5.04	.314	0	....	-1	0	-0.1
1967 Pit-N	0	1	.000	10	1	0	0	0	19	30	18	17	4	2	11	5	2.158	8.05	42	9.62	.375	1	.167	-10	0	-1.1
1969 Sea-A	3	10	.231	39	10	0	0	3	108^2	103	49	40	7	5	26	69	1.187	3.31	110	3.03	.250	1	.053	7	6	0.6
1970 Mil-A	4	3	.571	53	0	0	0	4	92^1	98	46	43	7	5	23	48	1.310	4.19	90	3.79	.277	1	.083	-2	5	-0.3
1971 Mil-A	0	0	....	2	0	0	0	0	1^1	3	2	2	0	0	1	0	3.000	13.50	26	12.64	.429	0	....	-1	0	-0.2
Total 5	**7**	**14**	**.333**	**111**	**11**	**0**	**0**	**7**	**230^1**	**245**	**120**	**107**	**20**	**12**	**62**	**126**	**1.333**	**4.18**	**87**	**4.01**	**.276**	**3**	**.081**	**-8**	**11**	**-1.1**
• GENEWICH, Joe	Joseph Edward Genewich b: 1/15/1897, Elmira, NY d: 12/21/1985, Lockport, NY BR/TR, 6', 174 lbs. Deb: 9/3/1922																									
1922 Bos-N	0	2	.000	6	2	1	0	0	23	29	19	18	2	0	11	4	1.739	7.04	57	5.60	.319	1	.167	-8	0	-0.7
1923 Bos-N	13	14	.481	43	24	12	1	1	227^1	272	110	94	15	7	46	54	1.399	3.72	107	4.27	.303	19	.247	9	15	1.1
1924 Bos-N	10	19	.345	34	27	11	2	1	200^1	258	136	116	4	8	65	43	1.612	5.21	73	5.01	.329	10	.167	-29	4	-3.1
1925 Bos-N	12	10	.545	34	21	10	0	0	169	185	87	75	4	6	41	34	1.337	3.99	100	3.50	.279	15	.273	-2	11	-0.1
1926 Bos-N	8	16	.333	37	26	12	2	2	216	239	114	93	6	6	63	59	1.398	3.88	91	3.72	.288	11	.164	-5	9	-0.6
1927 Bos-N	11	8	.579	40	19	7	0	1	181	199	93	77	7	2	54	38	1.398	3.83	97	3.69	.279	11	.193	1	10	0.0
1928 Bos-N	3	7	.300	13	11	4	0	0	80^2	88	43	37	14	3	18	15	1.314	4.13	95	4.48	.280	1	.038	1	3	-0.2
NY-N	11	4	.733	26	18	10	2	3	158^1	136	62	56	10	1	54	37	1.200	3.18	123	2.80	.232	13	.203	11	14	1.0
Yr.	14	11	.560	39	29	14	2	3	239	224	105	93	24	4	72	52	1.238	3.50	112	3.36	.249	14	.156	12	17	0.8
1929 NY-N	3	7	.300	21	9	1	0	1	85	133	70	64	9	1	30	19	1.918	6.78	68	7.23	.359	12	.375	-22	1	-1.8
1930 NY-N	2	5	.286	18	9	3	0	3	61	71	44	38	6	1	20	13	1.492	5.61	84	4.68	.297	3	.150	-6	2	-0.7
Total 9	**73**	**92**	**.442**	**272**	**166**	**71**	**7**	**12**	**1401^2**	**1610**	**778**	**668**	**77**	**35**	**402**	**316**	**1.435**	**4.29**	**92**	**4.19**	**.293**	**96**	**.207**	**-50**	**69**	**-5.1**
• GENTRY, Gary	Gary Edward Gentry b: 10/6/1946, Phoenix, AZ BR/TR, 6', 183 lbs. Deb: 4/10/1969																									
1969* NY-N	13	12	.520	35	35	6	3	0	233^2	192	94	89	24	5	81	154	1.168	3.43	107	2.98	.222	6	.081	-0	14	-0.4
1970 NY-N	9	9	.500	32	29	5	2	1	188^1	155	88	77	19	9	86	134	1.280	3.68	109	3.46	.224	4	.068	4	10	0.1
1971 NY-N	12	11	.522	32	31	8	3	0	203^1	167	84	73	16	6	82	155	1.225	3.23	105	3.03	.224	5	.074	2	11	-0.3
1972 NY-N	7	10	.412	32	26	3	0	0	164	153	82	73	20	6	75	120	1.390	4.01	84	4.17	.250	5	.104	-11	4	-1.2
1973 Atl-N	4	6	.400	16	14	3	0	1	86^2	74	37	33	7	1	35	42	1.258	3.43	115	3.18	.231	7	.233	6	6	0.7
1974 Atl-N	0	0	....	3	1	0	0	0	6^2	4	1	1	1	1	2	0	.900	1.35	280	2.45	.167	0	.000	2	1	0.2
1975 Atl-N	1	1	.500	7	2	0	0	0	20	25	14	11	3	0	8	10	1.650	4.95	76	5.90	.313	0	.000	-2	0	-0.3
Total 7	**46**	**49**	**.484**	**157**	**138**	**25**	**8**	**2**	**902^2**	**770**	**400**	**357**	**90**	**28**	**369**	**615**	**1.262**	**3.56**	**102**	**3.39**	**.231**	**27**	**.095**	**1**	**46**	**-1.3**
• GENTRY, Rufe	James Ruffus Gentry b: 5/18/1918, Daisy Station, NC d: 7/3/1997, Winston-Salem, NC BR/TR, 6'1", 180 lbs. Deb: 9/10/1943																									
1943 Det-A	1	3	.250	4	4	2	0	0	29^1	30	12	12	2	2	12	8	1.432	3.68	96	4.27	.268	0	.000	-0	1	-0.2
1944 Det-A	12	14	.462	37	30	10	3	0	203^2	211	104	96	9	4	108	68	1.566	4.24	84	4.36	.273	15	.197	-15	8	-1.6
1946 Det-A	0	0	....	2	0	0	0	0	3	4	5	5	0	0	7	1	3.667	15.00	24	12.97	.333	0	....	-4	0	-0.4
1947 Det-A	0	0	....	1	0	0	0	0	0^1	1	3	3	0	0	2	0	9.000	81.00	5	41.30	.500	0	....	-3	0	-0.3
1948 Det-A	0	0	....	4	0	0	0	0	6^2	5	2	2	0	1	5	1	1.500	2.70	162	3.62	.208	1	1.000	1	1	0.2
Total 5	**13**	**17**	**.433**	**48**	**34**	**12**	**3**	**0**	**243**	**251**	**126**	**118**	**11**	**7**	**134**	**78**	**1.584**	**4.37**	**82**	**4.49**	**.272**	**16**	**.184**	**-20**	**10**	**-2.3**
• GEORGE, Bill	William M. George b: 1/27/1865, Bellaire, OH d: 8/23/1916, Wheeling, WV BR/TL, 5'8", 165 lbs. Deb: 5/11/1887 U ♦																									
1887 NY-N	3	9	.250	13	13	10	0	0	108	215	112	63	1	14	89	49	1.991	5.25	71	....	.403	10	.185	-20	2	-2.0
1888* NY-N	2	1	.667	4	3	3	1	0	33^2	18	9	5	0	1	11	26	.861	1.34	203	....	.152	9	.231	4	4	0.5
1889 Col-a	0	0	....	2	0	0	0	0	8	11	13	7	1	0	3	3	1.750	7.88	46	....	.317	4	.235	-4	0	-0.5
Total 3	**5**	**10**	**.333**	**19**	**16**	**13**	**1**	**0**	**149^2**	**244**	**134**	**75**	**2**	**15**	**103**	**78**	**1.724**	**4.51**	**81**	**....**	**.355**	**27**	**.216**	**-20**	**6**	**-2.0**
• GEORGE, Chris	Christopher Sean George b: 9/24/1966, Pittsburgh, PA BR/TR, 6'2", 200 lbs. Deb: 10/1/1991																									
1991 Mil-A	0	0	....	2	1	0	0	0	6	8	2	2	0	0	0	2	1.333	3.00	132	3.73	.333	0	....	1	0	0.1
• GEORGE, Chris	Christopher Coleman George b: 9/16/1979, Houston, TX BL/TL, 6'2", 165 lbs. Deb: 7/26/2001																									
2001 KC-A	4	8	.333	13	13	1	0	0	74	83	48	46	14	0	18	32	1.365	5.59	88	4.82	.288	0	....	-8	2	-0.7
2002 KC-A	0	4	.000	6	6	0	0	0	27^1	37	17	17	2	1	8	13	1.646	5.60	90	5.30	.325	0	....	-2	1	-0.2
2003 KC-A	9	6	.600	18	18	0	0	0	93^2	120	75	74	22	3	44	39	1.751	7.11	73	7.19	.309	1	1.000	-20	2	-1.9
Total 3	**13**	**18**	**.419**	**37**	**37**	**1**	**0**	**0**	**195**	**240**	**140**	**137**	**38**	**4**	**70**	**84**	**1.590**	**6.32**	**80**	**6.08**	**.304**	**1**	**1.000**	**-29**	**5**	**-2.8**
• GEORGE, Lefty	Thomas Edward George b: 8/13/1886, Pittsburgh, PA d: 5/13/1955, York, PA BL/TL, 6', 155 lbs. Deb: 4/14/1911																									
1911 StL-A	4	9	.308	27	13	6	1	0	116^1	136	81	54	3	9	51	23	1.607	4.18	81	4.26	.256	5	.114	-11	2	-1.4
1912 Cle-A	0	5	.000	11	5	2	0	0	44^1	69	38	24	1	2	18	18	1.962	4.87	70	7.29	.373	3	.214	-8	0	-0.7
1915 Cin-N	2	2	.500	5	3	2	1	0	28	24	12	12	1	5	8	11	1.143	3.86	74	3.07	.242	4	.333	-4	2	-0.2
1918 Bos-N	1	5	.167	9	5	4	0	0	54^1	56	23	14	0	3	21	22	1.417	2.32	116	3.66	.281	2	.091	3	2	0.2
Total 4	**7**	**21**	**.250**	**52**	**26**	**14**	**2**	**0**	**243**	**285**	**154**	**104**	**5**	**19**	**98**	**74**	**1.576**	**3.85**	**83**	**4.54**	**.281**	**14**	**.152**	**-20**	**6**	**-2.1**
• GEORGY, Oscar	Oscar John Georgy b: 11/25/1916, New Orleans, LA d: 1/15/1999, New Orleans, LA BR/TR, 6'3.5", 180 lbs. Deb: 6/4/1938																									
1938 NY-N	0	0	....	1	0	0	0	0	1	2	2	2	0	0	1	0	3.000	18.00	21	11.63	.400	0	....	-2	0	-0.2
• GERARD, Dave	David Frederick Gerard b: 8/6/1936, New York, NY d: 10/10/2001, Newtown, PA BR/TR, 6'2", 205 lbs. Deb: 4/10/1962																									
1962 Chi-N	2	3	.400	39	0	0	0	3	58^2	67	40	32	10	1	28	30	1.619	4.91	84	5.68	.289	3	.375	-5	2	-0.4
• GERBERMAN, George	George Alois Gerberman b: 3/8/1942, El Campo, TX BR/TR, 6', 180 lbs. Deb: 9/23/1962																									
1962 Chi-N	0	0	....	1	1	0	0	0	5^1	3	1	1	1	0	5	1	1.500	1.69	246	4.27	.158	0	.000	1	1	0.2
• GERHARDT, Rusty	Allen Russell Gerhardt b: 8/13/1950, Baltimore, MD BB/TL, 5'9", 175 lbs. Deb: 7/27/1974																									
1974 SD-N	2	1	.667	23	1	0	0	1	35^2	44	28	28	1	2	17	22	1.710	7.07	50	5.17	.308	1	.167	-13	0	-1.4
• GERHEAUSER, Al	Albert "Lefty" Gerheauser b: 6/24/1917, St. Louis, MO d: 5/28/1972, Springfield, MO BL/TL, 6'3", 190 lbs. Deb: 4/24/1943																									
1943 Phi-N	10	19	.345	38	31	11	2	0	215	222	108	86	10	2	70	92	1.358	3.60	94	3.47	.263	8	.113	-3	7	-0.6
1944 Phi-N	8	16	.333	30	29	10	2	0	182^2	210	102	93	8	1	65	66	1.505	4.58	79	4.23	.285	15	.231	-19	6	-1.6
1945 Pit-N	5	10	.333	32	14	5	0	1	140^1	170	72	61	5	1	54	55	1.596	3.91	101	4.68	.304	12	.250	2	8	0.5
1946 Pit-N	2	2	.500	35	3	1	0	0	81^2	92	42	36	2	1	25	32	1.433	3.97	89	3.82	.286	7	.333	-3	4	-0.1
1948 StL-A	0	3	.000	14	2	0	0	0	23^1	32	23	19	0	1	10	10	1.800	7.33	62	5.35	.317	2	.333	-7	0	-0.6
Total 5	**25**	**50**	**.333**	**149**	**79**	**27**	**4**	**1**	**643**	**726**	**347**	**295**	**25**	**6**	**224**	**255**	**1.477**	**4.13**	**88**	**4.06**	**.283**	**44**	**.209**	**-30**	**25**	**-2.5**
• GERKIN, Steve	Stephen Paul "Splinter" Gerkin b: 11/19/1912, Grafton, WV d: 11/8/1978, Bay Pines, FL BR/TR, 6'1", 162 lbs. Deb: 5/13/1945																									
1945 Phi-A	0	12	.000	21	12	3	0	0	102	112	49	41	4	3	27	25	1.363	3.62	95	3.76	.285	2	.059	-2	2	-0.6
• GERMAN, Franklyn	Franklyn Miguel (Made) German b: 1/20/1980, San Cristobal, Dominican Republic BR/TR, 6'6", 170 lbs. Deb: 9/7/2002																									
2002 Det-A	1	0	1.000	7	0	0	0	1	6^2	3	0	0	0	1	2	6	.750	0.00	....	1.09	.150	0	....	3	2	0.3
2003 Det-A	2	4	.333	45	0	0	0	5	44^2	47	32	30	5	2	45	41	2.060	6.04	71	7.06	.273	0	....	-9	1	-0.8
Total 2	**3**	**4**	**.429**	**52**	**0**	**0**	**0**	**6**	**51^1**	**50**	**32**	**30**	**5**	**3**	**47**	**47**	**1.890**	**5.26**	**82**	**6.29**	**.260**	**0**	**....**	**-5**	**3**	**-0.5**
• GERMAN, Les	Lester Stanley German b: 6/1/1869, Baltimore, MD d: 6/10/1934, Germantown, MD BR/TR, 5'8", 165 lbs. Deb: 8/27/1890 U																									
1890 Bal-a	5	11	.313	17	16	15	0	0	132^1	147	95	71	2	13	54	37	1.519	4.83	88	....	.273	6	.118	-8	6	-0.9
1893 NY-N	8	8	.500	20	18	14	0	0	152	162	109	70	6	9	70	35	1.526	4.14	112	4.34	.265	23	.311	7	10	0.7
1894 NY-N	9	8	.529	24	16	11	0	1	143^1	186	139	86	7	12	68	21	1.772	5.40	97	5.91	.311	17	.298	-4	7	-0.3
1895 NY-N	7	11	.389	25	18	16	0	0	178^1	243	159	118	7	9	78	36	1.800	5.96	78	5.95	.320	29	.261	-27	7	-2.2

YEAR	TM-L	W	L	PCT	G	GS	CG	SH	SV	IP	H	R	ER	HR	HB	BB	SO	RAT	ERA	ERA+	CERA	OAV	BH	AVG	PR+	WS	TPW
1896	NY-N	0	0	....	1	0	0	0	0	2^2	9	6	4	0	0	1	0	3.750	13.50	31	19.69	.541	0	.000	-3	0	-0.3
	Was-N	2	20	.091	28	20	14	0	1	166^2	240	174	117	6	5	74	20	1.884	6.32	70	6.35	.334	16	.229	-32	2	-2.8
	Yr.	2	20	.091	29	20	14	0	1	169^1	249	180	121	6	5	75	20	1.913	6.43	68	6.56	.339	16	.225	-35	2	-3.0
1897	Was-N	3	5	.375	15	5	4	0	0	83^2	117	74	52	2	7	33	2	1.793	5.59	78	6.00	.328	15	.341	-13	3	-0.9
Total	6	34	63	.351	130	93	74	0	2	859	1104	756	518	30	55	378	151	1.725	5.43	84	4.87	.307	106	.260	-81	35	-6.6

• GERNER, Ed Edwin Frederick "Lefty" Gerner b: 7/22/1897, Philadelphia, PA d: 5/15/1970, Philadelphia, PA BL/TL, 5'8.5", 175 lbs. Deb: 5/14/1919

YEAR	TM-L	W	L	PCT	G	GS	CG	SH	SV	IP	H	R	ER	HR	HB	BB	SO	RAT	ERA	ERA+	CERA	OAV	BH	AVG	PR+	WS	TPW
1919	Cin-N	1	0	1.000	5	1	0	0	0	17	22	10	6	0	2	3	2	1.471	3.18	87	4.65	.333	1	.167	-1	0	-0.1

• GERVAIS, Lefty Lucien Edward Gervais b: 7/6/1890, Grover, WI d: 10/19/1950, Los Angeles, CA BL/TL, 5'10", 165 lbs. Deb: 4/17/1913

YEAR	TM-L	W	L	PCT	G	GS	CG	SH	SV	IP	H	R	ER	HR	HB	BB	SO	RAT	ERA	ERA+	CERA	OAV	BH	AVG	PR+	WS	TPW
1913	Bos-N	0	1	.000	5	2	1	0	0	15^2	18	11	10	0	0	4	1	1.404	5.74	57	4.32	.383	0	.000	-4	0	-0.5

• GESSNER, Charlie Charles R. Gessner b: 12/1863, Philadelphia, PA d: 5/25/1922, Washington, DC, 5'8" Deb: 7/19/1886

YEAR	TM-L	W	L	PCT	G	GS	CG	SH	SV	IP	H	R	ER	HR	HB	BB	SO	RAT	ERA	ERA+	CERA	OAV	BH	AVG	PR+	WS	TPW
1886	Phi-a	0	1	.000	1	1	1	0	0	8	13	14	8	0	2	5	0	2.250	9.00	39	....	.350	1	.250	-5	0	-0.4

• GETTEL, Al Allen Jones Gettel b: 9/17/1917, Norfolk, VA BR/TR, 6'3.5", 200 lbs. Deb: 4/20/1945

YEAR	TM-L	W	L	PCT	G	GS	CG	SH	SV	IP	H	R	ER	HR	HB	BB	SO	RAT	ERA	ERA+	CERA	OAV	BH	AVG	PR+	WS	TPW
1945	NY-A	9	8	.529	27	17	9	0	3	154^2	141	70	67	11	7	53	67	1.254	3.90	89	3.26	.243	16	.281	-11	9	-1.0
1946	NY-A	6	7	.462	26	11	5	2	0	103	89	40	34	6	2	40	54	1.252	2.97	116	2.97	.229	4	.125	2	6	0.1
1947	Cle-A	11	10	.524	31	21	9	2	0	149	122	54	53	12	3	62	64	1.235	3.20	109	3.07	.229	15	.294	2	10	0.6
1948	Cle-A	0	1	.000	5	2	0	0	0	7^2	15	15	15	2	1	10	4	3.261	17.61	23	15.84	.385	0	.000	-12	0	-1.2
	Chi-A	8	10	.444	22	19	7	0	1	148	154	76	66	7	4	60	49	1.446	4.01	106	3.94	.268	13	.241	2	10	0.3
	Yr.	8	11	.421	27	21	7	0	1	155^2	169	91	81	9	5	70	53	1.535	4.68	90	4.53	.276	13	.228	-9	10	-0.9
1949	Chi-A	2	5	.286	19	7	1	1	1	63	69	48	45	12	2	26	22	1.508	6.43	65	5.47	.283	3	.167	-16	0	-1.6
	Was-A	0	2	.000	16	1	0	0	1	34^2	43	24	21	4	0	24	7	1.933	5.45	78	6.69	.314	0	.000	-3	0	-0.4
	Yr.	2	7	.222	35	8	1	1	2	97^2	112	72	66	16	2	50	29	1.659	6.08	69	5.90	.294	3	.115	-19	0	-2.0
1951	NY-N	1	2	.333	30	1	0	0	0	57^1	52	37	31	12	0	25	36	1.343	4.87	80	4.32	.240	1	.083	-6	1	-0.7
1955	StL-N	1	0	1.000	8	0	0	0	0	17	26	18	17	6	0	10	7	2.118	9.00	45	10.37	.361	3	.500	-9	1	-0.8
Total	7	38	45	.458	184	79	31	5	6	734^1	711	382	349	72	19	310	310	1.390	4.28	89	4.05	.255	55	.228	-51	37	-4.7

• GETTIG, Charlie Charles Henry Gettig b: 12/1870, Baltimore, MD d: 4/11/1935, Baltimore, MD BR, 5'10", 172 lbs. Deb: 8/5/1896 ♦

YEAR	TM-L	W	L	PCT	G	GS	CG	SH	SV	IP	H	R	ER	HR	HB	BB	SO	RAT	ERA	ERA+	CERA	OAV	BH	AVG	PR+	WS	TPW
1896	NY-N	1	0	1.000	4	1	1	0	1	14	20	17	15	0	0	8	5	2.000	9.64	44	6.33	.333	3	.333	-9	0	-0.7
1897	NY-N	1	1	.500	3	2	2	0	0	19	23	23	11	0	2	9	7	1.684	5.21	80	5.05	.297	15	.200	-2	0	-1.1
1898	NY-N	6	3	.667	17	8	7	0	0	115	141	72	49	1	8	39	14	1.565	3.83	91	4.60	.300	49	.250	-5	8	-0.8
1899	NY-N	7	8	.467	18	15	12	0	0	128	161	102	63	3	4	54	25	1.680	4.43	85	5.06	.307	24	.247	-11	5	-1.3
Total	4	15	12	.556	42	26	22	0	1	276	345	214	138	4	14	110	51	1.649	4.50	83	4.93	.305	91	.241	-26	13	-3.9

• GETZEIN, Charlie Charles H. "Pretzels" Getzein b: 2/14/1864, Germany d: 6/19/1932, Chicago, IL BR/TR, 5'10", 172 lbs. Deb: 8/13/1884

YEAR	TM-L	W	L	PCT	G	GS	CG	SH	SV	IP	H	R	ER	HR	HB	BB	SO	RAT	ERA	ERA+	CERA	OAV	BH	AVG	PR+	WS	TPW
1884	Det-N	5	12	.294	17	17	17	1	0	147^1	118	73	32	2	....	25	107	.971	1.95	148	....	.207	6	.109	21	7	1.6
1885	Det-N	12	25	.324	37	37	37	1	0	330	360	222	111	8	....	92	110	1.370	3.03	94	....	.265	29	.212	-2	13	-0.3
1886	Det-N	30	11	.732	43	43	42	1	0	386^2	388	203	130	6	....	85	172	1.223	3.03	109	....	.251	29	.176	7	32	0.4
1887*	Det-N	29	13	.690	43	42	41	2	0	366^2	479	217	152	24	2	106	135	1.306	3.73	108	....	.307	39	.235	9	25	0.6
1888	Det-N	19	25	.432	46	46	45	2	0	404	411	225	137	13	8	54	202	1.151	3.05	90	....	.254	41	.246	-4	20	0.6
1889	Ind-N	18	22	.450	45	44	36	0	1	349	395	256	176	27	9	100	139	1.418	4.54	92	....	.276	25	.180	-19	20	-1.3
1890	Bos-N	23	17	.575	40	40	39	4	0	350	342	201	124	5	3	82	140	1.211	3.19	117	....	.248	34	.231	24	29	2.6
1891	Bos-N	4	5	.444	11	9	7	0	0	89	112	62	38	4	0	23	29	1.517	3.84	95	....	.296	7	.171	-2	6	-0.1
	Cle-N	0	1	.000	1	1	1	0	0	9	12	9	8	1	0	4	4	1.778	8.00	43	....	.309	0	.000	-4	0	-0.5
	Yr.	4	6	.400	12	10	8	0	0	98	124	71	46	5	0	27	33	1.541	4.22	86	....	.297	7	.156	-6	6	-0.5
1892	StL-N	5	8	.385	13	13	12	0	0	108	159	87	68	5	6	31	32	1.759	5.67	56	6.12	.329	9	.200	-26	2	-2.3
Total	9	145	139	.511	296	292	277	11	1	2539^2	2776	1555	976	95	28	602	1070	1.288	3.46	98	0.26	.268	219	.205	3	154	1.3

• GEYER, Rube Jacob Bowman Geyer b: 3/22/1884, Allegheny, PA d: 10/12/1962, Wahkon, MN BR/TR, 5'10", 170 lbs. Deb: 4/24/1910

YEAR	TM-L	W	L	PCT	G	GS	CG	SH	SV	IP	H	R	ER	HR	HB	BB	SO	RAT	ERA	ERA+	CERA	OAV	BH	AVG	PR+	WS	TPW
1910	StL-N	0	1	.000	4	0	0	0	0	4	5	3	2	0	0	3	5	2.000	4.50	66	5.75	.294	0	.000	-1	0	-0.1
1911	StL-N	9	6	.600	29	11	7	1	0	148^2	141	80	54	7	6	56	46	1.325	3.27	103	3.58	.259	13	.228	1	8	0.2
1912	StL-N	7	14	.333	41	18	5	0	0	181	191	110	66	4	4	84	61	1.519	3.28	104	4.13	.288	11	.208	2	8	0.2
1913	StL-N	1	5	.167	30	4	2	0	1	78^2	83	57	46	6	2	38	21	1.538	5.26	61	4.54	.282	2	.091	-18	0	-2.1
Total	4	17	26	.395	104	33	14	1	1	412^1	420	250	168	17	12	181	133	1.458	3.67	91	4.03	.277	26	.195	-16	16	-1.7

• GHELFI, Tony Anthony Paul Ghelfi b: 8/23/1961, La Crosse, WI BR/TR, 6'3", 185 lbs. Deb: 9/1/1983

YEAR	TM-L	W	L	PCT	G	GS	CG	SH	SV	IP	H	R	ER	HR	HB	BB	SO	RAT	ERA	ERA+	CERA	OAV	BH	AVG	PR+	WS	TPW
1983	Phi-N	1	1	.500	3	3	0	0	0	14^1	15	5	5	2	0	6	14	1.465	3.14	114	4.76	.268	1	.250	1	1	0.1

• GIALLOMBARDO, Bob Robert Paul Giallombardo b: 5/20/1937, Brooklyn, NY BL/TL, 6', 175 lbs. Deb: 6/21/1958

YEAR	TM-L	W	L	PCT	G	GS	CG	SH	SV	IP	H	R	ER	HR	HB	BB	SO	RAT	ERA	ERA+	CERA	OAV	BH	AVG	PR+	WS	TPW
1958	LA-N	1	1	.500	6	5	0	0	0	26^1	29	14	11	3	0	15	14	1.671	3.76	109	5.47	.284	1	.167	1	1	0.1

• GIARD, Joe Joseph Oscar "Peco" Giard b: 10/7/1898, Ware, MA d: 7/10/1956, Worcester, MA BL/TL, 5'10.5", 170 lbs. Deb: 4/18/1925

YEAR	TM-L	W	L	PCT	G	GS	CG	SH	SV	IP	H	R	ER	HR	HB	BB	SO	RAT	ERA	ERA+	CERA	OAV	BH	AVG	PR+	WS	TPW
1925	StL-A	10	5	.667	30	21	9	4	0	160^2	179	96	90	13	5	87	43	1.656	5.04	93	5.24	.295	3	.057	-8	9	-1.3
1926	StL-A	3	10	.231	22	15	2	0	0	90	113	81	70	7	1	67	18	2.000	7.00	61	6.68	.318	8	.276	-28	0	-2.7
1927	NY-A	0	0	....	16	0	0	0	0	27	38	25	24	1	0	19	10	2.111	8.00	48	7.08	.352	2	.286	-13	0	-1.2
Total	3	13	15	.464	68	36	11	4	0	277^2	330	202	184	21	6	173	71	1.812	5.96	74	5.89	.308	13	.146	-49	9	-5.1

• GIBBON, Joe Joseph Charles Gibbon b: 4/10/1935, Hickory, MS BR/TL, 6'4", 210 lbs. Deb: 4/17/1960

YEAR	TM-L	W	L	PCT	G	GS	CG	SH	SV	IP	H	R	ER	HR	HB	BB	SO	RAT	ERA	ERA+	CERA	OAV	BH	AVG	PR+	WS	TPW
1960*	Pit-N	4	2	.667	27	9	0	0	0	80^1	87	40	36	5	0	31	60	1.469	4.03	93	4.11	.277	4	.211	-4	4	-0.3
1961	Pit-N	13	10	.565	30	29	7	3	0	195^1	185	85	72	16	4	57	145	1.239	3.32	120	3.30	.251	8	.136	14	13	1.2
1962	Pit-N	3	4	.429	19	8	0	0	0	57	53	29	23	4	0	24	26	1.351	3.63	108	3.50	.250	3	.176	1	3	0.1
1963	Pit-N	5	12	.294	37	22	5	0	1	147^1	147	61	54	7	5	54	110	1.364	3.30	100	3.49	.258	4	.093	-1	6	-0.3
1964	Pit-N	10	7	.588	28	24	3	0	0	146^2	145	66	60	10	6	54	97	1.357	3.68	95	3.72	.262	12	.255	-1	9	0.2
1965	Pit-N	4	9	.308	31	15	1	0	1	105^2	85	57	53	7	4	34	63	1.126	4.51	78	2.56	.221	3	.115	-14	2	-1.5
1966	SF-N	4	6	.400	37	10	1	0	1	81	86	41	33	4	2	16	48	1.259	3.67	100	3.34	.275	3	.200	-0	4	0.0
1967	SF-N	6	2	.750	28	10	3	1	1	82	65	31	28	4	3	33	63	1.195	3.07	107	2.72	.220	1	.042	2	5	0.1
1968	SF-N	1	2	.333	29	0	0	0	1	40	33	10	7	3	2	19	22	1.300	1.58	187	3.32	.234	0	.000	6	4	0.7
1969	SF-N	1	3	.250	16	0	0	0	2	20	15	10	8	1	1	13	9	1.400	3.60	97	3.08	.211	0	.000	-0	1	0.0
	Pit-N	5	1	.833	35	0	0	0	9	51^1	38	14	11	5	2	17	35	1.071	1.93	181	2.57	.208	0	.000	9	8	0.9
	Yr.	6	4	.600	51	0	0	0	11	71^1	53	24	19	6	3	30	44	1.164	2.40	146	2.71	.209	0	.000	9	9	0.9
1970*	Pit-N	0	1	.000	41	0	0	0	5	41	44	25	22	2	2	24	26	1.659	4.83	80	4.62	.280	0	.000	-5	1	-0.6
1971	Cin-N	5	6	.455	50	0	0	0	11	64^1	54	25	21	3	1	32	34	1.337	2.94	111	3.03	.239	0	.000	1	7	0.1
1972	Cin-N	0	0	....	2	0	0	0	0	0^1	3	2	2	1	0	1	1	12.00	54.00	6	124.59	.750	0	....	-2	0	-0.2
	Hou-N	0	0	....	9	0	0	0	0	7^1	13	9	8	2	1	5	4	2.455	9.82	34	11.75	.394	0	....	-5	0	-0.6
	Yr.	0	0	....	11	0	0	0	0	7^2	16	11	10	3	1	6	5	2.870	11.74	28	16.66	.432	0	....	-7	0	-0.8
Total	13	61	65	.484	419	127	20	4	32	1119^2	1053	505	438	74	33	414	743	1.310	3.52	102	3.43	.251	38	.144	1	67	-0.2

• GIBSON, Bob Robert Louis Gibson b: 6/19/1957, Philadelphia, PA BR/TR, 6', 195 lbs. Deb: 4/13/1983

YEAR	TM-L	W	L	PCT	G	GS	CG	SH	SV	IP	H	R	ER	HR	HB	BB	SO	RAT	ERA	ERA+	CERA	OAV	BH	AVG	PR+	WS	TPW
1983	Mil-A	3	4	.429	27	7	0	0	2	80^2	71	40	35	6	1	46	46	1.450	3.90	96	3.83	.237	0	....	-1	4	-0.1
1984	Mil-A	2	5	.286	18	9	1	1	0	69	61	43	38	10	0	47	54	1.565	4.96	78	4.76	.236	0	....	-8	1	-0.8
1985	Mil-A	6	7	.462	41	1	0	0	11	92^1	86	44	40	10	1	49	53	1.462	3.90	107	4.40	.260	0	....	3	8	0.3
1986	Mil-A	1	2	.333	11	1	0	0	0	26^2	23	18	14	3	0	23	11	1.725	4.73	91	5.16	.232	0	....	-1	1	-0.1
1987	NY-N	0	0	....	1	0	0	0	0	1	0	0	0	0	0	1	2	1.000	0.00	....	0.95	.000	0	....	0	0	0.0
Total	5	12	18	.400	98	18	1	1	13	269^2	241	145	127	29	2	166	166	1.509	4.24	93	4.39	.244	0	....	-7	14	-0.7

• GIBSON, Bob Robert "Hoot,Gibby" Gibson b: 11/9/1935, Omaha, NE BR/TR, 6'1", 195 lbs. Deb: 4/15/1959 C HOF: 1981

YEAR	TM-L	W	L	PCT	G	GS	CG	SH	SV	IP	H	R	ER	HR	HB	BB	SO	RAT	ERA	ERA+	CERA	OAV	BH	AVG	PR+	WS	TPW
1959	StL-N	3	5	.375	13	9	2	1	0	75^2	77	35	28	4	1	39	48	1.533	3.33	127	4.33	.273	3	.115	8	5	0.8
1960	StL-N	3	6	.333	27	12	2	0	0	86^2	97	61	54	7	1	48	69	1.673	5.61	73	5.12	.284	5	.179	-14	0	-1.5
1961	StL-N	13	12	.520	35	27	10	2	1	211^1	186	91	76	13	6	119	166	1.443	3.24	136	3.86	.239	13	.197	26	18	2.8

YEAR	TM-L	W	L	PCT	G	GS	CG	SH	SV	IP	H	R	ER	HR	HB	BB	SO	RAT	ERA	ERA+	CERA	OAV	BH	AVG	PR+	WS	TPW
1962	StL-N★	15	13	.536	32	30	15	**5**	1	233^2	174	84	74	15	10	95	208	1.151	2.85	**150**	2.60	.204	20	.263	35	21	**4.1**
1963	StL-N	18	9	.667	36	33	14	2	0	254^2	224	110	96	19	13	96	204	1.257	3.39	105	3.30	.233	18	.207	3	17	1.2
1964*	StL-N	19	12	.613	40	36	17	2	1	287^1	250	106	96	25	9	86	245	1.169	3.01	126	2.96	.232	15	.156	25	24	2.7
1965	StL-N★	20	12	.625	38	36	20	6	1	299	243	110	102	34	11	103	270	1.157	3.07	125	3.06	.222	25	.240	24	26	3.6
1966	StL-N★	21	12	.636	35	35	20	**5**	0	280^1	210	90	76	20	5	78	225	1.027	2.44	148	2.19	.207	20	.200	34	26	3.8
1967*	StL-N★	13	7	.650	24	24	10	2	0	175^1	151	62	58	10	3	40	147	1.089	2.98	109	2.49	.231	8	.133	5	12	0.6
1968*	StL-N★	22	9	.710	34	34	28	**13**	0	304^2	198	49	38	11	7	62	**268**	.853	**1.12**	**258**	**1.44**	**.184**	16	.170	**57**	**36**	**7.0**
1969	StL-N★	20	13	.606	35	35	**28**	4	0	314	251	84	76	12	10	95	269	1.102	2.18	164	2.37	.219	29	.246	46	**33**	**5.6**
1970	StL-N★	**23**	7	.767	34	34	23	3	0	294	262	111	102	13	4	88	274	1.190	3.12	132	2.75	.237	33	.303	37	**28**	**4.8**
1971	StL-N	16	13	.552	31	31	20	**5**	0	245^2	215	96	83	14	7	76	185	1.185	3.04	118	2.79	.232	15	.172	21	17	2.5
1972	StL-N★	19	11	.633	34	34	23	4	0	278	226	83	76	14	3	88	208	1.129	2.46	138	2.48	.224	20	.194	29	29	3.8
1973	StL-N	12	10	.545	25	25	13	1	0	195	159	71	60	12	3	57	142	1.108	2.77	131	2.47	.224	12	.185	19	12	2.2
1974	StL-N	11	13	.458	33	33	9	1	0	240	236	111	102	24	5	104	129	1.417	3.83	93	4.11	.259	17	.210	-10	12	-0.9
1975	StL-N	3	10	.231	22	14	1	0	2	109	120	66	61	10	4	62	60	1.670	5.04	75	5.35	.287	5	.179	-13	1	-1.3
Total	**17**	**251**	**174**	**.591**	**528**	**482**	**255**	**56**	**6**	**3884^1**	**3279**	**1420**	**1258**	**257**	**102**	**1336**	**3117**	**1.188**	**2.91**	**128**	**2.90**	**.228**	**274**	**.206**	**332**	**317**	**41.9**

• GIBSON, Norwood Norwood Ringold "Gibby" Gibson b: 3/11/1877, Peoria, IL d: 7/7/1959, Peoria, IL BR/TR, 5'10", 165 lbs. Deb: 4/29/1903

YEAR	TM-L	W	L	PCT	G	GS	CG	SH	SV	IP	H	R	ER	HR	HB	BB	SO	RAT	ERA	ERA+	CERA	OAV	BH	AVG	PR+	WS	TPW
1903	Bos-A	13	9	.591	24	21	17	2	0	183^1	166	95	65	2	7	65	76	1.260	3.19	95	2.91	.241	17	.266	-9	12	-0.4
1904	Bos-A	17	14	.548	33	32	29	1	0	273	216	111	67	8	4	81	112	1.088	2.21	121	2.14	.219	6	.065	13	16	0.8
1905	Bos-A	4	7	.364	23	17	9	0	0	134	118	77	55	9	5	55	67	1.291	3.69	73	3.29	.239	4	.095	-14	2	-1.8
1906	Bos-A	0	2	.000	5	2	1	0	0	18^2	25	21	11	2	0	7	3	1.714	5.30	52	5.94	.324	1	.200	-5	0	-0.5
Total	**4**	**34**	**32**	**.515**	**85**	**72**	**56**	**3**	**0**	**609**	**525**	**304**	**198**	**21**	**16**	**208**	**258**	**1.204**	**2.93**	**95**	**2.74**	**.234**	**28**	**.138**	**-15**	**30**	**-2.0**

• GIBSON, Paul Paul Marshall Gibson b: 1/4/1960, Southampton, NY BR/TL, 6', 185 lbs. Deb: 4/8/1988

YEAR	TM-L	W	L	PCT	G	GS	CG	SH	SV	IP	H	R	ER	HR	HB	BB	SO	RAT	ERA	ERA+	CERA	OAV	BH	AVG	PR+	WS	TPW
1988	Det-A	4	2	.667	40	1	0	0	0	92	83	33	30	6	2	34	50	1.272	2.93	130	3.11	.240	0	....	8	7	0.8
1989	Det-A	4	8	.333	45	13	0	0	0	132	129	71	68	11	6	57	77	1.409	4.64	82	4.00	.259	0	....	-11	5	-1.1
1990	Det-A	5	4	.556	61	0	0	0	3	97^1	99	36	33	10	1	44	56	1.469	3.05	130	4.28	.269	0	....	8	7	0.8
1991	Det-A	5	7	.417	68	0	0	0	8	96	112	51	49	10	3	48	52	1.667	4.59	90	5.58	.297	0	....	-5	5	-0.5
1992	NY-N	0	1	.000	43	1	0	0	0	62	70	37	36	7	0	25	49	1.532	5.23	66	4.96	.287	0	.000	-11	0	-1.2
1993	NY-N	1	1	.500	8	0	0	0	0	8^2	14	6	5	1	0	2	12	1.846	5.19	77	7.04	.350	0	....	-1	0	-0.1
	NY-A	2	0	1.000	20	0	0	0	0	35^1	31	15	12	4	0	9	25	1.132	3.06	136	2.99	.238	0	....	4	3	0.4
1994	NY-A	1	1	.500	30	0	0	0	0	29	26	17	16	5	1	17	21	1.483	4.97	92	4.66	.236	0	....	-2	1	-0.2
1996	NY-A	0	0	....	4	0	0	0	0	4^1	6	3	3	1	0	0	3	1.385	6.23	79	5.44	.316	0	....	-1	0	0.0
Total	**8**	**22**	**24**	**.478**	**319**	**15**	**0**	**0**	**11**	**556^2**	**570**	**269**	**252**	**55**	**13**	**236**	**345**	**1.448**	**4.07**	**96**	**4.31**	**.267**	**0**	**.000**	**-10**	**28**	**-1.1**

• GIBSON, Robert Robert Murray Gibson b: 8/20/1869, Duncansville, PA d: 12/19/1949, Pittsburgh, PA BR/TR, 6'3", 185 lbs. Deb: 6/4/1890

YEAR	TM-L	W	L	PCT	G	GS	CG	SH	SV	IP	H	R	ER	HR	HB	BB	SO	RAT	ERA	ERA+	CERA	OAV	BH	AVG	PR+	WS	TPW
1890	Chi-N	1	0	1.000	1	1	1	0	0	9	6	1	0	0	0	2	1	.889	0.00	....	....	.184	0	.000	3	1	0.3
	Pit-N	0	3	.000	3	3	2	0	0	12	24	38	23	0	3	23	3	3.917	17.25	19	....	.404	3	.231	-18	0	-1.7
	Yr.	1	3	.250	4	4	3	0	0	21	30	39	23	0	3	25	4	2.619	9.86	33	....	.326	3	.176	-15	1	-1.5

• GIBSON, Sam Samuel Braxton Gibson b: 8/5/1899, King, NC d: 1/31/1983, High Point, NC BL/TR, 6'2", 198 lbs. Deb: 4/19/1926

YEAR	TM-L	W	L	PCT	G	GS	CG	SH	SV	IP	H	R	ER	HR	HB	BB	SO	RAT	ERA	ERA+	CERA	OAV	BH	AVG	PR+	WS	TPW
1926	Det-A	12	9	.571	35	24	16	2	2	196^1	199	94	76	6	6	75	61	1.396	3.48	116	3.61	.269	18	.250	14	14	1.6
1927	Det-A	11	12	.478	33	26	11	0	0	184^2	201	113	78	9	8	86	76	1.554	3.80	111	4.47	.285	14	.212	10	10	0.9
1928	Det-A	5	8	.385	20	18	5	1	0	119^2	155	83	72	4	7	52	29	1.730	5.42	76	5.45	.322	12	.286	-17	3	-1.5
1930	NY-A	0	1	.000	2	2	0	0	0	6	14	11	10	1	0	6	3	3.333	15.00	29	15.54	.424	1	.333	-7	0	-0.6
1932	NY-N	4	8	.333	41	5	1	1	3	81^2	107	51	44	7	2	30	39	1.678	4.85	77	5.74	.322	5	.263	-9	2	-0.8
Total	**5**	**32**	**38**	**.457**	**131**	**75**	**33**	**4**	**5**	**588^1**	**676**	**352**	**280**	**27**	**23**	**249**	**208**	**1.572**	**4.28**	**95**	**4.67**	**.295**	**50**	**.248**	**-9**	**29**	**-0.5**

• GICK, George George Edward Gick b: 10/18/1915, Dunnington, IN BB/TR, 6', 190 lbs. Deb: 10/3/1937

YEAR	TM-L	W	L	PCT	G	GS	CG	SH	SV	IP	H	R	ER	HR	HB	BB	SO	RAT	ERA	ERA+	CERA	OAV	BH	AVG	PR+	WS	TPW
1937	Chi-A	0	0	....	1	0	0	0	1	2	0	0	0	0	0	0	1	.000	0.00	....	0.00	.000	0	....	1	1	0.1
1938	Chi-A	0	0	....	1	0	0	0	0	1	0	0	0	0	1	0	1	.000	0.00	....	0.80	.000	0	....	1	0	0.0
Total	**2**	**0**	**0**	**....**	**2**	**0**	**0**	**0**	**1**	**3**	**0**	**0**	**0**	**0**	**1**	**0**	**2**	**.000**	**0.00**	**....**	**0.27**	**....**	**0**	**....**	**2**	**1**	**0.1**

• GIDEON, Brett Byron Brett Gideon b: 8/8/1963, Ozona, TX BR/TR, 6'2", 200 lbs. Deb: 7/5/1987

YEAR	TM-L	W	L	PCT	G	GS	CG	SH	SV	IP	H	R	ER	HR	HB	BB	SO	RAT	ERA	ERA+	CERA	OAV	BH	AVG	PR+	WS	TPW
1987	Pit-N	1	5	.167	29	0	0	0	3	36^2	34	22	19	6	1	10	31	1.200	4.66	88	3.56	.243	1	1.000	-3	2	-0.2
1989	Mon-N	0	0	....	4	0	0	0	0	4^2	5	1	1	1	0	5	2	2.143	1.93	183	8.44	.294	0	....	1	0	0.1
1990	Mon-N	0	0	....	1	0	0	0	0	1	2	1	1	0	0	4	0	6.000	9.00	41	25.86	.500	0	....	-1	0	-0.1
Total	**3**	**1**	**5**	**.167**	**34**	**0**	**0**	**0**	**3**	**42^1**	**41**	**24**	**21**	**7**	**1**	**19**	**33**	**1.417**	**4.46**	**91**	**4.63**	**.255**	**1**	**1.000**	**-3**	**2**	**-0.2**

• GIDEON, Jim James Leslie Gideon b: 9/26/1953, Taylor, TX BR/TR, 6'3", 190 lbs. Deb: 9/14/1975

YEAR	TM-L	W	L	PCT	G	GS	CG	SH	SV	IP	H	R	ER	HR	HB	BB	SO	RAT	ERA	ERA+	CERA	OAV	BH	AVG	PR+	WS	TPW
1975	Tex-A	0	0	....	1	1	0	0	0	5^2	7	6	5	1	0	5	2	2.118	7.94	47	8.02	.292	0	....	-3	0	-0.3

• GIEBELL, Floyd Floyd George Giebell b: 12/10/1909, Pennsboro, WV BL/TR, 6'2.5", 172 lbs. Deb: 4/21/1939

YEAR	TM-L	W	L	PCT	G	GS	CG	SH	SV	IP	H	R	ER	HR	HB	BB	SO	RAT	ERA	ERA+	CERA	OAV	BH	AVG	PR+	WS	TPW
1939	Det-A	1	1	.500	9	0	0	0	0	15^1	19	7	5	1	0	12	9	2.022	2.93	167	6.66	.317	0	.000	3	1	0.3
1940	Det-A	2	0	1.000	2	2	2	1	0	18	14	2	2	2	0	4	11	1.000	1.00	476	2.20	.206	0	.000	8	3	0.7
1941	Det-A	0	0	....	17	2	0	0	0	34^1	45	29	23	3	0	26	10	2.068	6.03	75	7.01	.313	2	.333	-5	0	-0.4
Total	**3**	**3**	**1**	**.750**	**28**	**4**	**2**	**1**	**0**	**67^2**	**78**	**38**	**30**	**6**	**0**	**42**	**30**	**1.773**	**3.99**	**116**	**5.65**	**.287**	**2**	**.143**	**6**	**4**	**0.5**

• GIEL, Paul Paul Robert Giel b: 9/29/1932, Winona, MN d: 5/22/2002, Minneapolis, MN BR/TR, 5'11", 185 lbs. Deb: 7/10/1954

YEAR	TM-L	W	L	PCT	G	GS	CG	SH	SV	IP	H	R	ER	HR	HB	BB	SO	RAT	ERA	ERA+	CERA	OAV	BH	AVG	PR+	WS	TPW
1954	NY-N	0	0	....	6	0	0	0	0	4^1	8	4	4	0	0	2	4	2.308	8.31	49	8.77	.421	0	....	-2	0	-0.2
1955	NY-N	4	4	.500	34	2	0	0	0	82^1	70	36	31	8	2	50	47	1.457	3.39	119	4.02	.233	1	.053	6	6	0.4
1958	SF-N	4	5	.444	29	9	0	0	0	92	89	56	48	12	2	55	55	1.565	4.70	81	4.96	.259	2	.074	-8	2	-1.0
1959	Pit-N	0	0	....	4	0	0	0	0	7^2	17	12	12	0	0	6	3	3.000	14.09	27	12.51	.472	0	....	-9	0	-0.9
1960	Pit-N	2	0	1.000	16	0	0	0	0	33	35	25	21	3	0	15	21	1.515	5.73	66	4.51	.276	0	.000	-8	0	-0.9
1961	Min-A	1	0	1.000	12	0	0	0	0	19^1	24	27	21	6	0	17	14	2.121	9.78	43	8.88	.289	1	.500	-11	0	-1.1
	KC-A	0	0	....	1	0	0	0	0	1^2	6	7	7	1	0	3	1	5.400	37.80	11	39.91	.600	0	....	-6	0	-0.6
	Yr.	1	0	1.000	13	0	0	0	0	21	30	34	28	7	0	20	15	2.381	12.00	35	11.34	.323	1	.500	-18	0	-1.7
Total	**6**	**11**	**9**	**.550**	**102**	**11**	**0**	**0**	**0**	**240^1**	**249**	**167**	**144**	**30**	**4**	**148**	**145**	**1.652**	**5.39**	**73**	**5.44**	**.271**	**4**	**.073**	**-39**	**8**	**-4.3**

• GIGGIE, Bob Robert Thomas Giggie b: 8/13/1933, Dorchester, MA BR/TR, 6'1", 200 lbs. Deb: 4/18/1959

YEAR	TM-L	W	L	PCT	G	GS	CG	SH	SV	IP	H	R	ER	HR	HB	BB	SO	RAT	ERA	ERA+	CERA	OAV	BH	AVG	PR+	WS	TPW
1959	Mil-N	1	0	1.000	13	0	0	0	1	20	24	10	9	2	0	10	15	1.700	4.05	87	5.92	.316	0	.000	-1	1	-0.1
1960	Mil-N	0	0	....	3	0	0	0	0	4^1	5	2	2	0	0	4	5	2.077	4.15	82	5.61	.278	0	....	-0	0	0.0
	KC-A	1	0	1.000	10	0	0	0	0	18^2	24	12	12	1	0	15	8	2.089	5.79	69	6.91	.333	0	.000	-3	0	-0.4
1962	KC-A	1	1	.500	4	2	0	0	0	14^1	17	11	10	5	1	3	4	1.395	6.28	66	6.33	.293	0	.000	-3	0	-0.4
Total	**3**	**3**	**1**	**.750**	**30**	**2**	**0**	**0**	**1**	**57^1**	**70**	**35**	**33**	**8**	**1**	**32**	**32**	**1.779**	**5.18**	**75**	**6.32**	**.313**	**0**	**.000**	**-8**	**1**	**-0.9**

• GILBERT, Bill Alfred Gideon Gilbert b: 3/13/1868, Havre de Grace, MD, 6', 180 lbs. Deb: 9/15/1892

YEAR	TM-L	W	L	PCT	G	GS	CG	SH	SV	IP	H	R	ER	HR	HB	BB	SO	RAT	ERA	ERA+	CERA	OAV	BH	AVG	PR+	WS	TPW
1892	Bal-N	0	1	.000	2	1	1	0	0	14	14	15	9	1	0	17	5	2.214	5.79	59	6.76	.250	2	.333	-3	0	-0.2

• GILBERT, Joe Joe Dennis Gilbert b: 4/20/1952, Jasper, TX BR/TL, 6'1", 167 lbs. Deb: 4/30/1972

YEAR	TM-L	W	L	PCT	G	GS	CG	SH	SV	IP	H	R	ER	HR	HB	BB	SO	RAT	ERA	ERA+	CERA	OAV	BH	AVG	PR+	WS	TPW
1972	Mon-N	0	1	.000	22	0	0	0	0	33	41	31	31	3	0	18	25	1.788	8.45	42	5.87	.306	0	.000	-18	0	-1.9
1973	Mon-N	1	2	.333	21	0	0	0	1	29	30	18	16	1	0	19	17	1.690	4.97	77	4.63	.270	0	.000	-4	1	-0.4
Total	**2**	**1**	**3**	**.250**	**43**	**0**	**0**	**0**	**1**	**62**	**71**	**49**	**47**	**4**	**0**	**37**	**42**	**1.742**	**6.82**	**53**	**5.29**	**.290**	**0**	**.000**	**-22**	**1**	**-2.3**

• GILBRETH, Bill William Freeman Gilbreth b: 9/3/1947, Abilene, TX BL/TL, 6', 180 lbs. Deb: 6/25/1971

YEAR	TM-L	W	L	PCT	G	GS	CG	SH	SV	IP	H	R	ER	HR	HB	BB	SO	RAT	ERA	ERA+	CERA	OAV	BH	AVG	PR+	WS	TPW
1971	Det-A	2	1	.667	9	5	2	0	0	30	28	17	16	4	2	21	14	1.633	4.80	75	5.58	.264	2	.182	-4	1	-0.4
1972	Det-A	0	0	....	2	0	0	0	0	5	10	9	9	1	0	4	2	2.800	16.20	19	14.24	.476	0	.000	-7	0	-0.8
1974	Cal-A	0	0	....	3	0	0	0	0	1^1	2	2	2	0	0	1	0	2.250	13.50	25	7.52	.400	0	....	-1	0	-0.2
Total	**3**	**2**	**1**	**.667**	**14**	**5**	**2**	**0**	**0**	**36^1**	**40**	**28**	**27**	**5**	**2**	**26**	**16**	**1.817**	**6.69**	**51**	**6.84**	**.303**	**2**	**.167**	**-13**	**1**	**-1.4**

YEAR	TM-L	W	L	PCT	G	GS	CG	SH	SV	IP	H	R	ER	HR	HB	BB	SO	RAT	ERA	ERA+	CERA	OAV	BH	AVG	PR+	WS	TPW
• GILFILLAN, Jason					Jason Edward Gilfillan b: 8/31/1976, Shelby, NC BR/TR, 6'5", 220 lbs. Deb: 5/16/2003																						
2003	KC-A	2	0	1.000	13	0	0	0	0	16^1	22	14	14	3	1	10	12	1.959	7.71	67	7.66	.310	0	....	-5	0	-0.4
• GILKS, Bob					Robert James Gilks b: 7/2/1864, Cincinnati, OH d: 8/21/1944, Brunswick, GA BR/TR, 5'8", 178 lbs. Deb: 8/25/1887 ♦																						
1887	Cle-a	7	5	.583	13	13	12	1	0	108	146	66	37	1	9	42	28	1.352	3.08	140	....	.312	29	.337	19	7	1.7
1888	Cle-a	0	2	.000	4	2	2	0	**1**	21	26	23	19	1	1	8	3	1.619	8.14	38	....	.293	111	.229	-12	6	-3.1
1890	Cle-N	2	2	.500	4	3	3	0	0	31^2	34	17	15	0	4	9	5	1.358	4.26	84	....	.266	116	.213	-2	4	-3.4
Total	**3**	**9**	**9**	**.500**	**21**	**18**	**17**	**1**	**1**	**160^2**	**206**	**106**	**71**	**2**	**14**	**59**	**36**	**1.388**	**3.98**	**94**	**....**	**.301**	**323**	**.233**	**5**	**17**	**-4.8**
• GILL, Ed					Edward James Gill b: 8/7/1895, Somerville, MA d: 10/10/1995, Brockton, MA BL/TR, 5'10", 165 lbs. Deb: 7/5/1919																						
1919	Was-A	1	1	.500	16	2	0	0	0	37^1	38	25	20	0	2	21	7	1.580	4.82	66	4.08	.260	0	.000	-6	0	-0.7
• GILL, George					George Lloyd Gill b: 2/13/1909, Catchings, MS d: 2/21/1999, Jackson, MS BR/TR, 6'1", 185 lbs. Deb: 5/4/1937																						
1937	Det-A	11	4	.733	31	10	4	1	1	127^2	146	74	64	11	1	42	40	1.473	4.51	104	4.41	.285	7	.140	4	9	0.1
1938	Det-A	12	9	.571	24	23	13	1	0	164	195	82	75	15	2	50	30	1.494	4.12	122	4.70	.296	6	.105	15	14	1.0
1939	Det-A	0	1	.000	3	1	0	0	0	8^2	14	8	8	1	0	3	1	1.962	8.31	59	7.64	.368	0	.000	-3	0	-0.3
	StL-A	1	12	.077	27	11	5	0	0	95	139	89	75	10	3	34	24	1.821	7.11	68	6.70	.343	4	.154	-21	0	-2.1
	Yr.	1	13	.071	30	12	5	0	0	103^2	153	97	83	11	3	37	25	1.833	7.21	68	6.78	.345	4	.143	-25	0	-2.4
Total	**3**	**24**	**26**	**.480**	**85**	**45**	**22**	**2**	**1**	**395^1**	**494**	**253**	**222**	**37**	**6**	**129**	**95**	**1.576**	**5.05**	**96**	**5.15**	**.306**	**17**	**.126**	**-6**	**23**	**-1.4**
• GILL, Haddie					Harold Edward Gill b: 1/23/1899, Brockton, MA d: 8/1/1932, Brockton, MA BL/TL, 5'11", 165 lbs. Deb: 8/16/1923																						
1923	Cin-N	0	0	....	1	0	0	0	0	1	1	0	0	0	0	1	1	2.000	0.00	....	6.60	.333	0	....	0	0	0.0
• GILLENWATER, Claral					Claral Lewis Gillenwater b: 5/20/1900, Sims, IN d: 2/26/1978, Bradenton, FL BR/TR, 6', 187 lbs. Deb: 8/20/1923																						
1923	Chi-A	1	3	.250	5	3	1	1	0	21^1	28	15	13	2	1	6	2	1.594	5.48	72	5.51	.337	0	.000	-4	0	-0.4
• GILLES, Tom					Thomas Bradford Gilles b: 7/2/1962, Peoria, IL BR/TR, 6'1", 185 lbs. Deb: 6/7/1990																						
1990	Tor-A	1	0	1.000	2	0	0	0	0	1^1	2	1	1	0	0	0	1	1.500	6.75	61	4.47	.333	0	....	-0	0	0.0
• GILLESPIE, Bob					Robert William "Bunch" Gillespie b: 10/8/1919, Columbus, OH d: 11/4/2001, Winston-Salem, NC BR/TR, 6'4", 187 lbs. Deb: 5/11/1944																						
1944	Det-A	0	1	.000	7	0	0	0	0	11	7	8	8	0	0	12	4	1.727	6.55	55	3.73	.194	0	.000	-4	0	-0.4
1947	Chi-A	5	8	.385	25	17	1	0	0	118	133	71	62	4	1	53	36	1.576	4.73	77	4.41	.291	2	.061	-14	2	-1.7
1948	Chi-A	0	4	.000	25	6	1	0	0	72	81	45	41	3	1	33	19	1.583	5.13	83	4.57	.287	0	.000	-8	2	-1.0
1950	Bos-A	0	0	....	1	0	0	0	0	1^1	2	3	3	1	0	4	0	4.500	20.25	24	26.08	.333	0	....	-2	0	-0.2
Total	**4**	**5**	**13**	**.278**	**58**	**23**	**2**	**0**	**0**	**202^1**	**223**	**127**	**114**	**8**	**2**	**102**	**59**	**1.606**	**5.07**	**76**	**4.57**	**.286**	**2**	**.039**	**-27**	**4**	**-3.3**
• GILLESPIE, Duke					John Patrick "Silent John" Gillespie b: 2/25/1900, Oakland, CA d: 2/15/1954, Vallejo, CA BR/TR, 5'11.5", 172 lbs. Deb: 4/12/1922																						
1922	Cin-N	3	3	.500	31	4	1	0	0	77^2	84	43	39	2	4	29	21	1.455	4.52	88	4.06	.294	2	.133	-6	3	-0.7
• GILLIFORD, Paul					Paul Gant "Gorilla" Gilliford b: 1/12/1945, Bryn Mawr, PA BR/TL, 5'11", 210 lbs. Deb: 9/20/1967																						
1967	Bal-A	0	0	....	2	0	0	0	0	3	6	4	4	1	0	1	2	2.333	12.00	26	13.03	.429	0	....	-3	0	-0.3
• GILLIGAN, Jack					John Patrick Gilligan b: 10/18/1885, Chicago, IL d: 11/19/1980, Modesto, CA BB/TR, 6', 190 lbs. Deb: 9/16/1909																						
1909	StL-A	1	2	.333	3	3	3	0	0	23	28	19	14	1	2	9	4	1.609	5.48	44	5.38	.315	1	.111	-8	0	-1.0
1910	StL-A	0	3	.000	9	5	2	0	0	39^1	37	21	16	0	1	28	10	1.653	3.66	67	4.20	.253	3	.200	-5	1	-0.6
Total	**2**	**1**	**5**	**.167**	**12**	**8**	**5**	**0**	**0**	**62^1**	**65**	**40**	**30**	**1**	**3**	**37**	**14**	**1.636**	**4.33**	**56**	**4.63**	**.276**	**4**	**.167**	**-13**	**1**	**-1.5**
• GILLPATRICK, George					George F. Gillpatrick b: 2/28/1875, Holden, MO d: 12/15/1941, Kansas City, MO BR/TR, 6', 210 lbs. Deb: 5/22/1898																						
1898	StL-N	0	2	.000	7	3	1	0	0	35	42	38	27	0	2	19	12	1.743	6.94	54	5.07	.295	2	.125	-11	0	-1.2
• GILMORE, Frank					Frank T. "Shadow" Gilmore b: 4/27/1864, Webster, MA d: 7/21/1929, Hartford, CT BR Deb: 9/11/1886																						
1886	Was-N	4	4	.500	9	9	9	1	0	75	57	35	21	3	....	22	75	1.053	2.52	129	....	.203	0	.000	6	4	0.2
1887	Was-N	7	20	.259	28	27	27	1	0	234^2	339	172	101	7	13	92	114	1.445	3.87	104	....	.329	13	.130	9	11	-0.2
1888	Was-N	1	9	.100	12	11	10	0	0	95^2	131	101	70	4	7	29	23	1.672	6.59	42	....	.315	1	.024	-40	0	-4.4
Total	**3**	**12**	**33**	**.267**	**49**	**47**	**46**	**2**	**0**	**405^1**	**527**	**308**	**192**	**14**	**20**	**143**	**212**	**1.426**	**4.26**	**80**	**....**	**.305**	**14**	**.082**	**-25**	**15**	**-4.4**
• GILMORE, Len					Leonard Preston "Meow" Gilmore b: 11/3/1917, Fairview Park, IN BR/TR, 6'3", 175 lbs. Deb: 10/1/1944																						
1944	Pit-N	0	1	.000	1	1	1	0	0	8	13	7	7	2	0	0	0	1.625	7.88	47	7.32	.361	0	.000	-4	0	-0.4
• GILROY, John					John M. Gilroy b: 10/26/1869, Washington, DC d: 8/4/1897, Norfolk, VA Deb: 8/30/1895																						
1895	Was-N	1	4	.200	8	4	2	0	0	41^1	63	48	30	3	4	24	2	2.105	6.53	73	8.04	.345	7	.241	-7	1	-0.7
1896	Was-N	0	0	....	1	0	0	0	0	2	0	0	0	0	0	1	0	.500	0.00	....	0.23	.000	0	.000	1	0	0.1
Total	**2**	**1**	**4**	**.200**	**9**	**4**	**2**	**0**	**0**	**43^1**	**63**	**48**	**30**	**3**	**4**	**25**	**2**	**2.031**	**6.23**	**77**	**7.68**	**.345**	**7**	**.233**	**-6**	**1**	**-0.7**
• GILSON, Hal					Harold "Lefty" Gilson b: 2/9/1942, Los Angeles, CA BR/TL, 6'5", 195 lbs. Deb: 4/14/1968																						
1968	StL-N	0	2	.000	13	0	0	0	2	21^2	27	11	11	1	0	11	19	1.754	4.57	63	5.41	.310	0	.000	-4	0	-0.5
	Hou-N	0	0	....	2	0	0	0	0	3^2	7	4	3	0	1	1	1	2.182	7.36	40	9.18	.412	0	....	-2	0	-0.2
	Yr.	0	2	.000	15	0	0	0	2	25^1	34	15	14	1	1	12	20	1.816	4.97	58	5.96	.327	0	.000	-6	0	-0.7
• GING, Billy					William Joseph Ging b: 11/7/1872, Elmira, NY d: 9/14/1950, Elmira, NY BR/TR, 5'10", 170 lbs. Deb: 9/25/1899																						
1899	Bos-N	1	0	1.000	1	1	1	0	0	8	5	1	1	0	0	5	2	1.250	1.13	369	2.14	.180	0	.000	2	1	0.2
• GINGRAS, Joe					Joseph Elzead John Gingras b: 1/10/1893, New York, NY d: 9/6/1947, Jersey City, NJ BR/TR, 6'2", 188 lbs. Deb: 6/18/1915																						
1915	KC-F	0	0	....	2	0	0	0	0	4	6	3	3	0	0	1	2	1.750	6.75	43	5.54	.353	0	.000	-2	0	-0.2
• GINTER, Matt					Matthew Shane Ginter b: 12/24/1977, Lexington, KY BR/TR, 6'1", 220 lbs. Deb: 9/1/2000																						
2000	Chi-A	1	0	1.000	7	0	0	0	0	9^1	18	14	14	5	0	7	6	2.679	13.50	37	16.24	.409	0	....	-9	0	-0.8
2001	Chi-A	1	0	1.000	20	0	0	0	0	39^2	34	23	23	2	7	14	24	1.210	5.22	88	3.44	.238	0	....	-3	2	-0.3
2002	Chi-A	1	0	1.000	33	0	0	0	1	54^1	59	34	27	6	1	21	37	1.472	4.47	102	4.72	.278	0	....	0	2	0.0
2003	Chi-A	0	0	....	3	0	0	0	0	3^1	2	5	5	1	2	1	0	.900	13.50	33	5.16	.182	0	....	-3	0	-0.3
Total	**4**	**3**	**0**	**1.000**	**63**	**0**	**0**	**0**	**1**	**106^2**	**113**	**76**	**69**	**14**	**10**	**43**	**67**	**1.463**	**5.82**	**80**	**5.27**	**.276**	**0**	**....**	**-15**	**4**	**-1.4**
• GIRARD, Charlie					Charles August Girard b: 12/16/1884, Brooklyn, NY d: 8/6/1936, Brooklyn, NY BR/TR, 5'10", 175 lbs. Deb: 9/14/1910																						
1910	Phi-N	1	2	.333	7	1	0	0	1	26^2	33	26	19	2	2	12	11	1.688	6.41	49	5.78	.308	1	.125	-10	0	-1.1
• GIUSTI, Dave					David John Giusti b: 11/27/1939, Seneca Falls, NY BR/TR, 5'11", 195 lbs. Deb: 4/13/1962																						
1962	Hou-N	2	3	.400	22	5	0	0	0	73^2	82	49	46	7	0	30	43	1.520	5.62	66	4.67	.280	7	.292	-14	1	-1.2
1964	Hou-N	0	0	....	8	0	0	0	0	25^2	24	10	9	1	0	8	16	1.247	3.16	108	2.95	.253	2	.286	1	2	0.2
1965	Hou-N	8	7	.533	38	13	4	1	3	131^1	132	67	63	13	1	46	92	1.355	4.32	78	3.76	.259	6	.171	-12	5	-1.0
1966	Hou-N	15	14	.517	34	33	9	4	0	210	215	112	98	23	5	54	131	1.281	4.20	81	3.75	.260	17	.230	-16	9	-1.2
1967	Hou-N	11	15	.423	37	33	8	1	1	221^2	231	114	103	20	3	58	157	1.304	4.18	79	3.66	.265	13	.155	-17	6	-1.5
1968	Hou-N	11	14	.440	37	34	12	2	1	251	226	95	89	15	4	67	186	1.167	3.19	93	2.80	.239	15	.183	-1	13	0.0
1969	StL-N	3	7	.300	22	12	2	1	0	99^2	96	46	40	7	1	37	62	1.334	3.61	99	3.56	.255	5	.200	-1	4	0.0
1970*	Pit-N	9	3	.750	66	1	0	0	26	103	98	38	35	7	0	39	85	1.330	3.06	127	3.45	.259	3	.188	7	15	0.9
1971*	Pit-N	5	6	.455	58	0	0	0	**30**	86	79	31	28	5	1	31	55	1.279	2.93	116	3.06	.241	1	.059	4	10	0.3
1972*	Pit-N	7	4	.636	54	0	0	0	22	74^2	59	18	16	3	0	20	54	1.058	1.93	172	2.06	.219	0	.000	10	13	1.0
1973	Pit-N★	9	2	.818	67	0	0	0	20	98^2	89	31	26	9	0	37	64	1.277	2.37	148	3.17	.241	4	.308	13	12	1.4
1974*	Pit-N	7	5	.583	64	2	0	0	12	105^2	101	43	39	2	0	40	53	1.334	3.32	104	3.05	.258	1	.111	1	9	0.1
1975*	Pit-N	5	4	.556	61	0	0	0	17	91^2	79	38	30	3	0	42	38	1.320	2.95	120	2.79	.237	3	.300	6	10	0.7
1976	Pit-N	5	4	.556	40	0	0	0	6	58^1	59	31	28	5	0	27	24	1.474	4.32	81	3.99	.267	0	.000	-6	3	-0.6

YEAR	TM-L	W	L	PCT	G	GS	CG	SH	SV	IP	H	R	ER	HR	HB	BB	SO	RAT	ERA	ERA+	CERA	OAV	BH	AVG	PR+	WS	TPW
1977	Oak-A	3	3	.500	40	0	0	0	6	60^1	54	22	20	4	0	20	28	1.227	2.98	135	3.01	.245	0	....	8	6	0.8
	Chi-N	0	2	.000	20	0	0	0	1	25^1	30	19	17	2	0	14	15	1.737	6.04	73	5.52	.297	0	.000	-4	0	-0.4
Total	15	100	93	.518	668	133	35	9	145	1716^2	1654	764	687	126	15	570	1103	1.296	3.60	95	3.37	.253	77	.187	-22	118	-0.4

• GIVENS, Brian Brian Allen Givens b: 11/6/1965, Lompoc, CA BR/TL, 6'6" Deb: 6/24/1995

YEAR	TM-L	W	L	PCT	G	GS	CG	SH	SV	IP	H	R	ER	HR	HB	BB	SO	RAT	ERA	ERA+	CERA	OAV	BH	AVG	PR+	WS	TPW
1995	Mil-A	5	7	.417	19	19	0	0	0	107^1	116	71	59	11	3	54	73	1.584	4.95	101	5.12	.275	0	....	-2	4	-0.2
1996	Mil-A	1	3	.250	4	4	0	0	0	14	32	22	20	3	0	7	10	2.786	12.86	40	13.99	.438	0	....	-12	0	-1.1
Total	2	6	10	.375	23	23	0	0	0	121^1	148	93	79	14	3	61	83	1.723	5.86	86	6.14	.299	0	....	-14	4	-1.3

• GLADDING, Fred Fred Earl Gladding b: 6/28/1936, Flat Rock, MI BL/TR, 6'1", 225 lbs. Deb: 7/1/1961 C

YEAR	TM-L	W	L	PCT	G	GS	CG	SH	SV	IP	H	R	ER	HR	HB	BB	SO	RAT	ERA	ERA+	CERA	OAV	BH	AVG	PR+	WS	TPW
1961	Det-A	1	0	1.000	8	0	0	0	0	16^1	18	7	6	1	2	11	11	1.776	3.31	124	5.77	.286	0	.000	1	1	0.1
1962	Det-A	0	0	....	6	0	0	0	0	5	3	0	0	0	0	2	4	1.000	0.00	....	1.51	.176	0	....	2	1	0.2
1963	Det-A	1	1	.500	22	0	0	0	7	27^1	19	6	6	1	0	14	24	1.207	1.98	189	2.42	.198	0	.000	5	5	0.5
1964	Det-A	7	4	.636	42	0	0	0	7	67^1	57	23	23	7	2	27	59	1.248	3.07	119	3.32	.233	0	.000	4	7	0.3
1965	Det-A	6	2	.750	46	0	0	0	5	70	63	22	22	6	4	29	43	1.314	2.83	123	3.57	.239	0	.000	5	8	0.5
1966	Det-A	5	0	1.000	51	0	0	0	2	74	62	33	27	6	1	29	57	1.230	3.28	106	3.02	.230	0	.000	1	5	0.1
1967	Det-A	6	4	.600	42	1	0	0	12	77	62	20	17	6	4	19	64	1.052	1.99	164	2.62	.227	0	.000	10	10	0.9
1968	Hou-N	0	0	....	7	0	0	0	2	4^1	8	7	7	0	1	3	2	2.538	14.54	20	10.46	.421	0	....	-5	0	-0.6
1969	Hou-N	4	8	.333	57	0	0	0	**29**	72^2	83	39	34	2	1	27	40	1.514	4.21	84	4.18	.289	1	.100	-5	6	-0.5
1970	Hou-N	7	4	.636	63	0	0	0	18	71	84	39	32	4	3	24	46	1.521	4.06	96	4.40	.293	0	.000	-1	7	-0.2
1971	Hou-N	4	5	.444	48	0	0	0	12	51^1	51	17	12	0	7	22	17	1.422	2.10	160	3.70	.268	0	.000	7	6	0.7
1972	Hou-N	5	6	.455	42	0	0	0	14	48^2	38	16	15	1	2	12	18	1.027	2.77	121	1.97	.222	0	.000	3	8	0.3
1973	Hou-N	2	0	1.000	16	0	0	0	1	16	18	8	8	4	0	4	9	1.375	4.50	81	5.27	.290	0	....	-2	1	-0.2
Total	13	48	34	.585	450	1	0	0	109	601	566	237	209	38	27	223	394	1.313	3.13	113	3.49	.252	1	.016	27	65	2.2

• GLADE, Fred Frederick Monroe "Lucky" Glade b: 1/25/1876, Dubuque, IA d: 11/21/1934, Grand Island, NE BR/TR, 5'10", 190 lbs. Deb: 5/27/1902

YEAR	TM-L	W	L	PCT	G	GS	CG	SH	SV	IP	H	R	ER	HR	HB	BB	SO	RAT	ERA	ERA+	CERA	OAV	BH	AVG	PR+	WS	TPW
1902	Chi-N	0	1	.000	1	1	1	0	0	8	13	11	8	0	1	3	3	2.000	9.00	30	6.42	.364	1	.333	-6	0	-0.5
1904	StL-A	18	15	.545	35	34	30	6	1	289	248	101	73	2	13	58	156	1.059	2.27	109	2.13	.233	19	.186	11	21	1.4
1905	StL-A	6	25	.194	32	32	28	2	0	275	257	109	86	3	11	58	127	1.145	2.81	90	2.55	.250	9	.092	-4	9	-1.1
1906	StL-A	15	14	.517	35	32	28	4	1	266^2	215	91	70	4	10	59	96	1.028	2.36	109	2.00	.224	13	.137	6	16	0.3
1907	StL-A	13	9	.591	24	22	18	2	0	202	187	81	60	2	9	45	71	1.149	2.67	94	2.55	.248	15	.205	-4	12	-0.2
1908	NY-A	0	4	.000	5	5	2	0	0	32	30	18	15	0	4	14	11	1.375	4.22	59	3.91	.275	0	.000	-5	0	-0.8
Total	6	52	68	.433	132	126	107	14	2	1072^2	950	411	312	11	48	237	464	1.107	2.62	97	2.37	.240	57	.150	-2	58	-0.8

• GLAISER, John John Burke "Bert" Glaiser b: 7/28/1894, Yoakum, TX d: 3/7/1959, Houston, TX BL/TR, 5'8", 165 lbs. Deb: 4/20/1920

YEAR	TM-L	W	L	PCT	G	GS	CG	SH	SV	IP	H	R	ER	HR	HB	BB	SO	RAT	ERA	ERA+	CERA	OAV	BH	AVG	PR+	WS	TPW
1920	Det-A	0	0	....	9	1	0	0	1	17	23	15	12	1	1	8	3	1.824	6.35	58	6.86	.354	0	.000	-5	0	-0.5

• GLASS, Tom Thomas Joseph Glass b: 4/29/1898, Greensboro, NC d: 12/15/1981, Greensboro, NC BR/TR, 6'3", 170 lbs. Deb: 6/12/1925

YEAR	TM-L	W	L	PCT	G	GS	CG	SH	SV	IP	H	R	ER	HR	HB	BB	SO	RAT	ERA	ERA+	CERA	OAV	BH	AVG	PR+	WS	TPW
1925	Phi-A	1	0	1.000	2	0	0	0	0	5	9	4	3	0	0	0	2	1.800	5.40	86	5.95	.409	0	.000	-0	0	-0.1

• GLAUBER, Keith Keith Harris Glauber b: 1/18/1972, Brooklyn, NY BR/TR, 6'2", 190 lbs. Deb: 9/8/1998

YEAR	TM-L	W	L	PCT	G	GS	CG	SH	SV	IP	H	R	ER	HR	HB	BB	SO	RAT	ERA	ERA+	CERA	OAV	BH	AVG	PR+	WS	TPW
1998	Cin-N	0	0	....	3	0	0	0	0	7^2	6	2	2	0	0	1	4	.913	2.35	183	1.44	.214	0	.000	2	1	0.1
2000	Cin-N	0	0	....	4	0	0	0	0	7^1	5	3	3	0	1	2	4	.955	3.68	128	1.82	.185	0	.000	1	1	0.1
Total	2	0	0	....	7	0	0	0	0	15	11	5	5	0	1	3	8	.933	3.00	151	1.63	.200	0	.000	2	2	0.2

• GLAVENICH, Luke Luke Frank Glavenich b: 1/17/1893, Jackson, CA d: 5/22/1935, Stockton, CA BR/TR, 5'9.5", 189 lbs. Deb: 4/12/1913

YEAR	TM-L	W	L	PCT	G	GS	CG	SH	SV	IP	H	R	ER	HR	HB	BB	SO	RAT	ERA	ERA+	CERA	OAV	BH	AVG	PR+	WS	TPW
1913	Cle-A	0	0	....	1	0	0	0	0	1	3	5	1	0	0	3	1	6.000	9.00	34	28.10	.500	0	....	-1	0	-0.1

• GLAVINE, Tom Thomas Michael Glavine b: 3/25/1966, Concord, MA BL/TL, 6', 190 lbs. Deb: 8/17/1987

YEAR	TM-L	W	L	PCT	G	GS	CG	SH	SV	IP	H	R	ER	HR	HB	BB	SO	RAT	ERA	ERA+	CERA	OAV	BH	AVG	PR+	WS	TPW
1987	Atl-N	2	4	.333	9	9	0	0	0	50^1	55	34	31	5	3	33	20	1.748	5.54	78	5.70	.279	2	.125	-6	1	-0.7
1988	Atl-N	7	17	.292	34	34	1	0	0	195^1	201	111	99	12	8	63	84	1.352	4.56	81	3.74	.270	11	.183	-17	4	-1.6
1989	Atl-N	14	8	.636	29	29	6	4	0	186	172	88	76	20	2	40	90	1.140	3.68	99	2.99	.243	10	.149	2	10	0.2
1990	Atl-N	10	12	.455	33	33	1	0	0	214^1	232	111	102	18	1	78	129	1.446	4.28	94	4.24	.281	7	.113	-1	10	0.0
1991*	Atl-N★	**20**	11	.645	34	34	**9**	1	0	246^2	201	83	70	17	2	69	192	1.095	2.55	**152**	2.47	.222	17	.230	**37**	**23**	**4.3**
1992*	Atl-N★	**20**	8	.714	33	33	7	**5**	0	225	197	81	69	6	2	70	129	1.187	2.76	132	2.61	.235	19	.247	22	19	2.8
1993*	Atl-N★	**22**	6	.786	36	**36**	4	2	0	239^1	236	91	85	16	2	90	120	1.362	3.20	126	3.70	.259	14	.173	20	20	2.0
1994	Atl-N	13	9	.591	25	25	2	0	0	165^1	173	76	73	10	1	70	140	1.470	3.97	107	4.02	.268	10	.179	7	12	0.8
1995*	Atl-N	16	7	.696	29	29	3	1	0	198^2	182	76	68	9	5	66	127	1.248	3.08	138	3.14	.246	14	.222	29	20	3.1
1996*	Atl-N★	15	10	.600	36	**36**	1	0	0	235^1	222	91	78	14	0	85	181	1.305	2.98	148	3.29	.249	22	.289	40	22	4.6
1997*	Atl-N★	14	7	.667	33	33	5	2	0	240	197	86	79	20	4	79	152	1.150	2.96	142	2.80	.226	14	.222	32	21	3.5
1998*	Atl-N★	**20**	6	.769	33	33	4	3	0	229^1	202	67	63	13	2	74	157	1.203	2.47	168	2.93	.238	17	.239	41	23	4.3
1999*	Atl-N	14	11	.560	35	**35**	2	0	0	234	259	115	107	18	4	83	138	1.462	4.12	109	4.31	.287	9	.138	12	14	1.1
2000*	Atl-N★	**21**	9	.700	35	**35**	4	2	0	241	222	101	91	24	4	65	152	1.191	3.40	135	3.19	.244	10	.147	33	21	3.2
2001*	Atl-N	16	7	.696	35	**35**	1	1	0	219^1	213	92	87	24	2	97	116	1.413	3.57	123	4.21	.261	8	.140	19	16	1.9
2002*	Atl-N★	18	11	.621	36	**36**	2	1	0	224^2	210	85	74	21	8	78	127	1.282	2.96	138	3.61	.252	7	.103	24	18	2.2
2003	NY-N	9	14	.391	32	32	0	0	0	183^1	205	94	92	21	2	66	82	1.478	4.52	92	4.77	.288	8	.151	-6	7	-0.6
Total	17	251	157	.615	537	537	52	22	0	3528	3379	1482	1344	268	52	1206	2136	1.300	3.43	120	3.50	.254	199	.185	286	261	31.1

• GLAZE, Ralph Daniel Ralph Glaze b: 3/13/1881, Denver, CO d: 10/31/1968, Atascadero, CA BR/TR, 5'9", 165 lbs. Deb: 6/1/1906

YEAR	TM-L	W	L	PCT	G	GS	CG	SH	SV	IP	H	R	ER	HR	HB	BB	SO	RAT	ERA	ERA+	CERA	OAV	BH	AVG	PR+	WS	TPW
1906	Bos-A	4	6	.400	19	10	7	0	0	123	110	58	49	4	5	32	56	1.154	3.59	77	2.65	.242	10	.182	-10	5	-1.1
1907	Bos-A	9	13	.409	32	21	11	1	0	182^1	150	75	47	4	4	48	68	1.086	2.32	111	2.16	.227	11	.180	-3	10	-0.3
1908	Bos-A	2	2	.500	10	3	2	0	0	34^2	43	24	13	1	0	5	13	1.385	3.38	73	3.20	.253	1	.077	-4	0	-0.6
Total	3	15	21	.417	61	34	20	1	0	340	303	157	109	9	9	85	137	1.141	2.89	91	2.45	.236	22	.171	-17	15	-2.0

• GLAZNER, Whitey Charles Franklin Glazner b: 9/17/1893, Sycamore, AL d: 6/6/1989, Orlando, FL BR/TR, 5'9", 165 lbs. Deb: 9/26/1920

YEAR	TM-L	W	L	PCT	G	GS	CG	SH	SV	IP	H	R	ER	HR	HB	BB	SO	RAT	ERA	ERA+	CERA	OAV	BH	AVG	PR+	WS	TPW
1920	Pit-N	0	0	....	2	0	0	0	0	8^2	9	3	3	0	0	2	1	1.269	3.12	103	3.25	.300	0	.000	0	1	0.0
1921	Pit-N	14	5	.737	36	25	15	0	1	234	214	88	72	5	12	58	88	1.162	2.77	138	2.71	**.250**	10	.132	27	21	2.3
1922	Pit-N	11	12	.478	34	26	10	1	1	193	238	118	94	9	2	52	77	1.503	4.38	93	4.49	.309	16	.246	-4	10	-0.1
1923	Pit-N	2	1	.667	7	4	1	1	1	30	29	18	11	5	0	11	8	1.333	3.30	121	4.11	.250	4	.333	2	3	0.3
	Phi-N	7	14	.333	28	23	12	2	1	161^1	195	104	84	11	6	63	51	1.599	4.69	98	5.07	.304	9	.170	3	8	0.3
	Yr.	9	15	.375	35	27	13	3	2	191^1	224	122	95	16	6	74	59	1.557	4.47	101	4.92	.296	13	.200	5	11	0.6
1924	Phi-N	7	16	.304	35	24	8	2	0	156^2	210	108	103	14	4	63	41	**1.743**	5.92	75	6.26	.339	8	.157	-22	3	-2.5
Total	5	41	48	.461	142	102	46	6	4	783^2	895	439	367	44	24	249	266	1.460	4.21	100	4.40	.295	47	.181	6	46	0.4

• GLEASON, Bill William Gleason b: 1868, Cleveland, OH d: 12/2/1893, Cleveland, OH Deb: 4/24/1890

YEAR	TM-L	W	L	PCT	G	GS	CG	SH	SV	IP	H	R	ER	HR	HB	BB	SO	RAT	ERA	ERA+	CERA	OAV	BH	AVG	PR+	WS	TPW
1890	Cle-P	0	1	.000	1	1	0	0	0	4	14	16	12	1	0	6	0	5.000	27.00	15	....	.538	0	.000	-10	0	-0.8

• GLEASON, Joe Joseph Paul Gleason b: 7/9/1895, Phelps, NY d: 9/8/1990, Phelps, NY BR/TR, 5'10.5", 175 lbs. Deb: 9/11/1920

YEAR	TM-L	W	L	PCT	G	GS	CG	SH	SV	IP	H	R	ER	HR	HB	BB	SO	RAT	ERA	ERA+	CERA	OAV	BH	AVG	PR+	WS	TPW
1920	Was-A	0	0	....	3	0	0	0	0	8	14	13	12	2	1	6	2	2.500	13.50	28	10.71	.326	0	.000	-9	0	-0.8
1922	Was-A	2	2	.500	8	5	3	0	0	40^2	53	26	21	3	1	18	12	1.746	4.65	83	5.78	.319	2	.143	-5	1	-0.5
Total	2	2	2	.500	11	5	3	0	0	48^2	67	39	33	5	2	24	14	1.870	6.10	62	6.59	.320	2	.125	-13	1	-1.3

• GLEASON, Kid William J. Gleason b: 10/26/1866, Camden, NJ d: 1/2/1933, Philadelphia, PA BB/TR, 5'7", 158 lbs. Deb: 4/20/1888 M/C/U ♦

YEAR	TM-L	W	L	PCT	G	GS	CG	SH	SV	IP	H	R	ER	HR	HB	BB	SO	RAT	ERA	ERA+	CERA	OAV	BH	AVG	PR+	WS	TPW
1888	Phi-N	7	16	.304	24	23	23	0	0	199^2	199	112	63	11	12	53	89	1.262	2.84	104	....	.250	17	.205	5	13	0.6
1889	Phi-N	9	15	.375	29	21	15	0	1	205	242	177	127	8	9	97	64	1.654	5.58	78	....	.285	25	.253	-20	8	-1.6
1890	Phi-N	38	17	.691	60	55	54	6	**2**	506	479	253	148	8	15	167	222	1.277	2.63	138	....	.243	47	.210	50	45	4.0
1891	Phi-N	24	22	.522	53	44	40	1	1	418	431	237	163	10	13	165	100	1.426	3.51	97	....	.257	53	.248	-8	29	-0.4
1892	StL-N	20	24	.455	47	45	43	2	0	400	389	244	148	11	16	151	133	1.350	3.33	96	3.34	.245	50	.215	8	25	1.5
1893	StL-N	21	22	.488	48	45	37	1	1	380^1	436	276	195	18	10	187	86	1.638	4.61	102	4.85	.279	51	.256	6	22	0.6

YEAR TM-L	W	L	PCT	G	GS	CG	SH	SV	IP	H	R	ER	HR	HB	BB	SO	RAT	ERA	ERA+	CERA	OAV	BH	AVG	PR+	WS	TPW
1894 StL-N	2	6	.250	8	8	6	0	0	58	75	50	39	2	3	21	9	1.655	6.05	89	5.21	.310	7	.250	-4	3	-0.3
*Bal-N	15	5	.750	21	20	19	0	0	172	224	111	85	3	3	44	35	1.558	4.45	123	4.61	.312	30	.349	14	16	1.4
Yr.	17	11	.607	29	28	25	0	0	230	299	161	124	5	6	65	44	1.583	4.85	112	4.76	.311	37	.325	10	19	1.1
1895* Bal-N	2	4	.333	9	5	3	0	1	50^1	77	51	39	4	3	21	6	1.947	6.97	68	7.32	.346	130	.309	-15	12	-1.7
Total 8	138	131	.513	299	266	240	10	6	2389^1	2552	1511	1007	75	78	906	744	1.447	3.79	103	1.94	.265	1946	.261	35	173	4.1
• GLEATON, Jerry Don	Jerry Don Gleaton b: 9/14/1957, Brownwood, TX BL/TL, 6'3", 210 lbs. Deb: 7/11/1979																									
1979 Tex-A	0	1	.000	5	2	0	0	0	9^2	15	7	7	0	1	2	2	1.759	6.52	64	6.31	.375	0	....	-3	0	-0.3
1980 Tex-A	0	0	....	5	0	0	0	0	7	5	2	2	0	0	4	2	1.286	2.57	151	2.46	.208	0	....	1	1	0.1
1981 Sea-A	4	7	.364	20	13	1	0	0	85^1	88	50	45	10	2	38	31	1.477	4.75	81	4.71	.273	0	....	-7	2	-0.8
1982 Sea-A	0	0	....	3	0	0	0	0	4^2	7	7	7	3	1	2	1	1.929	13.50	31	12.96	.333	0	....	-5	0	-0.5
1984 Chi-A	1	2	.333	11	1	0	0	2	18^1	20	12	7	2	1	6	4	1.418	3.44	121	4.54	.286	0	....	1	1	0.1
1985 Chi-A	1	0	1.000	31	0	0	0	1	29^2	37	19	19	3	0	13	22	1.685	5.76	75	5.54	.316	0	....	-5	1	-0.5
1987 KC-A	4	4	.500	48	0	0	0	5	50^2	38	28	24	4	0	28	44	1.303	4.26	107	3.14	.216	0	....	2	5	0.2
1988 KC-A	0	4	.000	42	0	0	0	3	38	33	17	15	2	3	17	29	1.316	3.55	112	3.45	.232	0	....	2	3	0.2
1989 KC-A	0	0	....	15	0	0	0	0	14^1	20	10	9	0	0	6	9	1.814	5.65	68	5.80	.345	0	....	-3	0	-0.3
1990 Det-A	1	3	.250	57	0	0	0	13	82^2	62	27	27	5	3	25	56	1.052	2.94	135	2.34	.213	0	....	7	9	0.8
1991 Det-A	3	2	.600	47	0	0	0	2	75^1	74	37	34	7	0	39	47	1.500	4.06	102	4.40	.269	0	....	1	4	0.1
1992 Pit-N	1	0	1.000	23	0	0	0	0	31^2	34	16	15	4	0	19	18	1.674	4.26	81	5.46	.283	0	.000	-3	1	-0.3
Total 12	15	23	.395	307	16	1	0	26	447^1	433	232	211	40	11	199	265	1.413	4.25	95	4.15	.261	0	.000	-10	27	-1.0
• GLENDON, Martin	Martin J. Glendon b: 2/8/1877, Milwaukee, WI d: 11/6/1950, Chicago, IL BR/TR, 5'8", 165 lbs. Deb: 4/18/1902																									
1902 Cin-N	0	1	.000	1	1	0	0	0	3	5	5	4	0	0	4	0	3.000	12.00	25	10.96	.370	0	.000	-3	0	-0.3
1903 Cle-A	1	2	.333	3	3	3	0	0	27^2	20	9	3	0	0	7	9	.976	0.98	292	1.51	.202	0	.000	5	2	0.5
Total 2	1	3	.250	4	4	3	0	0	30^2	25	14	7	0	0	11	9	1.174	2.05	143	2.43	.222	0	.000	2	2	0.1
• GLENN, Bob	Burdette Glenn b: 6/16/1894, West Sunbury, PA d: 6/3/1977, Richmond, CA BR/TR Deb: 7/27/1920																									
1920 StL-N	0	0	....	2	0	0	0	0	2	2	0	0	0	0	0	0	1.000	0.00	....	1.68	.222	0	....	1	0	0.1
• GLIATTO, Sal	Salvador Michael Gliatto b: 5/7/1902, Chicago, IL d: 11/2/1995, Tyler, TX BB/TR, 5'8.5", 150 lbs. Deb: 4/19/1930																									
1930 Cle-A	0	0	....	8	0	0	0	2	15	21	15	11	1	2	9	7	2.000	6.60	73	7.30	.328	0	.000	-3	0	-0.3
• GLINATSIS, George	George Glinatsis b: 6/29/1969, Youngstown, OH BR/TR, 6'4", 195 lbs. Deb: 7/18/1994																									
1994 Sea-A	0	1	.000	2	2	0	0	0	5^1	9	8	8	2	0	6	1	2.813	13.50	36	15.98	.429	0	....	-5	0	-0.5
• GLOVER, Gary	John Gary Glover b: 12/3/1976, Cleveland, OH BR/TR, 6'5", 205 lbs. Deb: 9/30/1999																									
1999 Tor-A	0	0	....	1	0	0	0	0	1	0	0	0	0	0	1	0	1.000	0.00	....	0.97	.000	0	....	1	0	0.1
2001 Chi-A	5	5	.500	46	11	0	0	0	100^1	98	61	55	16	4	32	63	1.296	4.93	93	4.12	.252	0	....	-4	4	-0.4
2002 Chi-A	7	8	.467	41	22	0	0	1	138^1	136	86	80	21	7	52	70	1.359	5.20	88	4.39	.253	0	.000	-11	5	-1.1
2003 Chi-A	1	0	1.000	24	0	0	0	0	35^2	43	18	18	3	2	14	23	1.598	4.54	98	5.32	.305	0	....	-1	2	-0.1
Ana-A	1	0	1.000	18	0	0	0	0	27	34	15	15	3	1	8	14	1.556	5.00	86	5.44	.315	0	....	-2	1	-0.2
Yr.	2	0	1.000	42	0	0	0	0	62^2	77	33	33	6	3	22	37	1.580	4.74	93	5.37	.309	0	....	-3	3	-0.3
Total 4	14	13	.519	130	33	0	0	1	302^1	311	180	168	43	14	107	170	1.383	5.00	91	4.49	.265	0	.000	-18	12	-1.7
• GLYNN, Ed	Edward Paul Glynn b: 6/3/1953, New York, NY BR/TL, 6'2", 180 lbs. Deb: 9/19/1975																									
1975 Det-A	0	2	.000	3	1	0	0	0	14^2	11	8	7	1	0	8	8	1.295	4.30	93	3.24	.220	0	....	-0	0	0.0
1976 Det-A	1	3	.250	5	4	1	0	0	23^2	22	18	16	3	0	20	17	1.775	6.08	61	5.73	.265	0	....	-6	0	-0.6
1977 Det-A	2	1	.667	8	3	0	0	0	27^1	36	17	16	3	0	12	13	1.756	5.27	81	6.02	.316	0	....	-3	1	-0.3
1978 Det-A	0	0	....	10	0	0	0	0	14^2	11	5	5	3	0	4	9	1.023	3.07	126	2.79	.208	0	....	1	1	0.1
1979 NY-N	1	4	.200	46	0	0	0	7	60	57	22	20	3	2	40	32	1.617	3.00	121	4.35	.259	0	.000	4	5	0.3
1980 NY-N	3	3	.500	38	0	0	0	1	52^1	49	26	24	5	0	23	32	1.376	4.13	86	3.65	.246	0	.000	-3	2	-0.4
1981 Cle-A	0	0	....	4	0	0	0	0	7^2	5	1	1	0	0	4	4	1.174	1.17	309	2.20	.192	0	....	2	1	0.2
1982 Cle-A	5	2	.714	47	0	0	0	4	49^2	43	27	23	6	0	30	54	1.470	4.17	98	4.07	.232	0	....	-0	4	0.0
1983 Cle-A	0	2	.000	11	0	0	0	0	12^1	22	11	8	2	0	6	13	2.270	5.84	72	9.60	.373	0	....	-2	0	-0.2
1985 Mon-N	0	0	....	3	0	0	0	0	2^1	5	5	5	0	0	4	2	3.857	19.29	18	16.42	.455	0	....	-4	0	-0.4
Total 10	12	17	.414	175	8	1	0	12	264^2	261	140	125	26	2	151	184	1.557	4.25	90	4.60	.261	0	.000	-12	14	-1.3
• GLYNN, Ryan	Ryan David Glynn b: 11/1/1974, Portsmouth, VA BR/TR, 6'3", 200 lbs. Deb: 5/16/1999																									
1999 Tex-A	2	4	.333	13	10	0	0	0	54^2	71	46	44	10	1	35	39	1.939	7.24	70	7.77	.316	0	.000	-12	0	-1.2
2000 Tex-A	5	7	.417	16	16	0	0	0	88^2	107	65	55	15	3	41	33	1.669	5.58	90	6.12	.293	0	.000	-4	3	-0.4
2001 Tex-A	1	5	.167	12	9	0	0	0	46	59	38	36	7	0	26	15	1.848	7.04	66	6.81	.309	0	....	-12	0	-1.1
Total 3	8	16	.333	41	35	0	0	0	189^1	237	149	135	32	4	102	87	1.790	6.42	77	6.77	.303	0	.000	-28	3	-2.7
• GOAR, Jot	Joshua Mercer Goar b: 1/31/1870, New Lisbon, IN d: 4/4/1947, New Castle, IN BR/TR, 5'9", 160 lbs. Deb: 4/18/1896																									
1896 Pit-N	0	1	.000	3	0	0	0	0	13^1	36	33	25	1	0	8	3	3.300	16.88	25	16.29	.485	1	.167	-19	0	-1.6
1898 Cin-N	0	0	....	1	0	0	0	0	2	4	3	2	0	1	1	0	2.500	9.00	43	11.94	.411	0	....	-1	0	-0.1
Total 2	0	1	.000	4	0	0	0	0	15^1	40	36	27	1	1	9	3	3.196	15.85	26	15.72	.476	1	.167	-20	0	-1.7
• GOBBLE, Jimmy	Billy James Gobble b: 7/19/1981, Bristol, TN BL/TL, 6'3", 190 lbs. Deb: 8/3/2003																									
2003 KC-A	4	5	.444	9	9	0	0	0	52^2	56	32	27	8	4	15	31	1.348	4.61	112	4.61	.271	0		3	3	0.3
• GOETZ, George	George Burt Goetz b: 1865, Greencastle, PA, 6'2", 180 lbs. Deb: 6/17/1889																									
1889 Bal-a	1	0	1.000	1	1	0	0	0	9	12	6	4	0	0	0	2	1.333	4.00	95	....	.310	0	.000	-0	1	-0.1
• GOETZ, John	John Hardy Goetz b: 10/24/1937, Goetzville, MI BR/TR, 6', 185 lbs. Deb: 4/16/1960																									
1960 Chi-N	0	0	....	4	0	0	0	0	6^1	10	9	9	2	0	4	6	2.211	12.79	30	10.47	.370	0	.000	-6	0	-0.7
• GOGOLEWSKI, Bill	William Joseph Gogolewski b: 10/26/1947, Oshkosh, WI BL/TR, 6'4", 190 lbs. Deb: 9/3/1970																									
1970 Was-A	2	2	.500	8	5	0	0	0	33^2	33	18	18	2	1	25	19	1.723	4.81	74	5.11	.260	0	.000	-5	1	-0.6
1971 Was-A	6	5	.545	27	17	4	1	0	124^1	112	39	38	5	2	39	70	1.214	2.75	120	2.82	.241	5	.156	7	9	0.8
1972 Tex-A	4	11	.267	36	21	2	1	2	150^2	136	74	71	9	6	58	95	1.288	4.24	71	3.26	.239	5	.125	-18	3	-2.1
1973 Tex-A	3	6	.333	49	1	0	0	6	123^2	139	67	58	10	1	48	77	1.512	4.22	88	4.41	.286	0	....	-4	5	-0.4
1974 Cle-A	0	0	....	5	0	0	0	0	13^2	15	7	7	1	1	2	3	1.244	4.61	78	3.86	.283	0	....	-2	0	-0.2
1975 Chi-A	0	0	....	19	0	0	0	2	55	61	35	32	5	1	28	37	1.618	5.24	74	5.15	.292	0	....	-8	1	-0.8
Total 6	15	24	.385	144	44	6	2	10	501	496	240	224	32	12	200	301	1.389	4.02	84	3.78	.260	10	.127	-28	19	-3.2
• GOHR, Greg	Gregory James Gohr b: 10/29/1967, Santa Clara, CA BR/TR, 6'3", 205 lbs. Deb: 4/7/1993																									
1993 Det-A	0	0	....	16	0	0	0	0	22^2	26	15	15	1	2	14	23	1.765	5.96	72	5.51	.289	0	....	-4	0	-0.4
1994 Det-A	2	2	.500	8	6	0	0	0	34	36	19	17	3	0	21	21	1.676	4.50	108	5.01	.263	0	....	2	2	0.2
1995 Det-A	1	0	1.000	10	0	0	0	0	10^1	9	1	1	0	0	3	12	1.161	0.87	546	2.43	.243	0	....	5	2	0.4
1996 Det-A	4	8	.333	17	16	0	0	0	91^2	129	76	73	24	3	34	60	1.778	7.17	71	7.79	.328	0	....	-19	1	-1.8
Cal-A	1	1	.500	15	0	0	0	1	24	34	20	20	7	0	10	15	1.833	7.50	65	8.38	.337	0	....	-7	0	-0.6
Yr.	5	9	.357	32	16	0	0	1	115^2	163	96	93	31	3	44	75	1.790	7.24	69	7.91	.330	0	....	-26	1	-2.4
Total 4	8	11	.421	66	22	0	0	1	182^2	234	131	126	35	5	82	131	1.730	6.21	79	6.76	.309	0	....	-24	5	-2.2
• GOLDEN, Jim	James Edward Golden b: 3/20/1936, Eldon, MO BL/TR, 6', 175 lbs. Deb: 9/30/1960																									
1960 LA-N	1	0	1.000	1	1	0	0	0	7	6	5	5	1	0	4	4	1.429	6.43	62	4.32	.240	1	.333	-2	0	-0.2
1961 LA-N	1	1	.500	28	0	0	0	0	42	52	30	27	7	0	20	18	1.714	5.79	75	6.05	.306	0	.000	-7	0	-0.7
1962 Hou-N	7	11	.389	37	18	5	2	1	152^2	163	84	69	13	0	50	88	1.395	4.07	92	3.98	.270	12	.222	-3	7	0.1
1963 Hou-N	0	1	.000	3	1	0	0	0	6^1	12	4	4	0	0	2	5	2.211	5.68	56	9.07	.429	0	....	-2	0	-0.2
Total 4	9	13	.409	69	20	5	2	1	208	233	123	105	21	0	76	115	1.486	4.54	85	4.57	.282	13	.217	-14	7	-1.0

• GOLDEN, Mike Michael Henry Golden b: 9/11/1851, Shirley, MA d: 1/11/1929, Rockford, IL BR/TR, 5'7", 168 lbs. Deb: 5/5/1875 ♦

YEAR	TM-L	W	L	PCT	G	GS	CG	SH	SV	IP	H	R	ER	HR	HB	BB	SO	RAT	ERA	ERA+	CERA	OAV	BH	AVG	PR+	WS	TPW
1875	Wes-n	1	12	.077	13	13	13	0	0	112	110	....	23	0	....	14	10	1.107	1.85	96	....	.233	6	.130	-2	....	-0.4
	Chi-n	6	7	.462	14	14	12	1	0	119	129	....	25	0	....	11	10	1.176	1.89	87	....	.252	40	.258	-6	....	-0.4
	Yr.	7	19	.269	27	27	25	1	0	231	239	....	48	0	....	25	20	1.143	1.87	91	....	.243	46	.229	-8	....	-0.9
1878	Mil-N	3	13	.188	22	18	15	0	0	161	217	171	74	1	....	33	52	1.553	4.14	63	....	.307	44	.206	-18	2	-3.0

• GOLDEN, Roy Roy Kramer Golden b: 7/12/1888, Madisonville, OH d: 10/4/1961, Norwood, OH BR/TR, 6'1", 195 lbs. Deb: 9/7/1910

YEAR	TM-L	W	L	PCT	G	GS	CG	SH	SV	IP	H	R	ER	HR	HB	BB	SO	RAT	ERA	ERA+	CERA	OAV	BH	AVG	PR+	WS	TPW
1910	StL-N	2	3	.400	7	6	3	0	0	42^{2}	44	28	21	3	2	33	31	1.805	4.43	67	5.89	.286	4	.267	-6	1	-0.5
1911	StL-N	4	9	.308	30	25	6	0	0	148^{2}	127	90	83	6	5	129	81	1.722	5.02	67	4.69	.240	5	.114	-28	2	-2.9
Total	2	6	12	.333	37	31	9	0	0	191^{1}	171	118	104	9	7	162	112	1.740	4.89	67	4.95	.250	9	.153	-34	3	-3.5

• GOLDSMITH, Fred Fredrick Ernest Goldsmith b: 5/15/1852, New Haven, CT d: 3/28/1939, Berkley, MI BR/TR, 6'1", 195 lbs. Deb: 10/23/1875 U ♦

YEAR	TM-L	W	L	PCT	G	GS	CG	SH	SV	IP	H	R	ER	HR	HB	BB	SO	RAT	ERA	ERA+	CERA	OAV	BH	AVG	PR+	WS	TPW
1879	Tro-N	2	4	.333	8	7	7	0	0	63	61	38	11	0	....	1	31	.984	1.57	159	....	.238	9	.237	8	2	0.8
1880	Chi-N	21	3	.875	26	24	22	4	1	210^{1}	189	80	41	2	....	18	90	.984	1.75	138	....	.228	37	.261	11	24	1.2
1881	Chi-N	24	13	.649	39	39	37	5	0	330	328	166	95	4	....	44	76	1.127	2.59	108	....	.248	38	.241	-3	25	-0.1
1882	Chi-N	28	17	.622	45	45	45	4	0	405	377	192	109	7	....	38	109	1.025	2.42	113	....	.233	42	.230	-4	29	-0.5
1883	Chi-N	25	19	.568	46	45	40	2	0	383^{1}	456	256	134	14	....	39	82	1.291	3.15	105	....	.279	52	.221	-5	27	-0.8
1884	Chi-N	9	11	.450	21	21	20	1	0	188	245	140	89	11	....	29	34	1.457	4.26	74	....	.299	11	.136	-31	7	-2.9
	Bal-a	3	1	.750	4	4	3	0	0	30	29	12	9	0	1	2	11	1.033	2.70	128	....	.240	2	.143	3	2	0.2
Total	6	112	68	.622	189	185	174	16	1	1609^{2}	1685	884	488	38	1	171	433	1.153	2.73	107	....	.255	191	.224	-20	116	-2.1

• GOLDSMITH, Hal Harold Eugene Goldsmith b: 8/18/1898, Peconic, NY d: 10/20/1985, Riverhead, NY BR/TR, 6', 174 lbs. Deb: 6/23/1926

YEAR	TM-L	W	L	PCT	G	GS	CG	SH	SV	IP	H	R	ER	HR	HB	BB	SO	RAT	ERA	ERA+	CERA	OAV	BH	AVG	PR+	WS	TPW
1926	Bos-N	5	7	.417	19	15	5	0	0	101	135	62	49	2	1	28	16	1.614	4.37	81	4.93	.333	8	.211	-8	3	-0.7
1927	Bos-N	1	3	.250	22	5	1	0	1	71^{2}	83	34	28	4	0	26	13	1.521	3.52	105	4.35	.289	5	.238	3	4	0.3
1928	Bos-N	0	0	....	4	0	0	0	0	8^{1}	14	5	3	2	0	1	1	1.800	3.24	121	7.94	.359	0	.000	1	0	0.1
1929	StL-N	0	0	....	2	0	0	0	0	4	3	3	3	1	0	1	0	1.000	6.75	69	3.20	.214	0	.000	-1	0	-0.1
Total	4	6	10	.375	47	20	6	0	1	185	235	104	83	9	1	56	30	1.573	4.04	90	4.80	.315	13	.210	-5	7	-0.5

• GOLDSTEIN, Izzy Isidore Goldstein b: 6/6/1908, Odessa, Ukraine d: 9/24/1993, Delray Beach, FL BB/TR, 6', 160 lbs. Deb: 4/24/1932

YEAR	TM-L	W	L	PCT	G	GS	CG	SH	SV	IP	H	R	ER	HR	HB	BB	SO	RAT	ERA	ERA+	CERA	OAV	BH	AVG	PR+	WS	TPW
1932	Det-A	3	2	.600	16	6	2	0	0	56^{1}	63	42	28	2	3	41	14	1.846	4.47	105	5.44	.276	5	.294	1	2	0.1

• GOLTZ, Dave David Allan Goltz b: 6/23/1949, Pelican Rapids, MN BR/TR, 6'4", 215 lbs. Deb: 7/18/1972

YEAR	TM-L	W	L	PCT	G	GS	CG	SH	SV	IP	H	R	ER	HR	HB	BB	SO	RAT	ERA	ERA+	CERA	OAV	BH	AVG	PR+	WS	TPW
1972	Min-A	3	3	.500	15	11	2	0	1	91	75	30	27	5	0	26	38	1.110	2.67	120	2.40	.224	3	.103	5	6	0.4
1973	Min-A	6	4	.600	32	10	1	0	1	106^{1}	138	68	62	11	2	32	65	1.599	5.25	75	5.53	.318	0	....	-15	2	-1.5
1974	Min-A	10	10	.500	28	24	5	1	1	174^{1}	192	81	63	14	7	45	89	1.359	3.25	115	4.12	.282	0	....	11	11	1.2
1975	Min-A	14	14	.500	32	32	15	1	0	243	235	112	99	18	6	72	128	1.263	3.67	105	3.43	.255	0	....	7	15	0.7
1976	Min-A	14	14	.500	36	35	13	4	0	249^{1}	239	113	93	14	5	91	133	1.324	3.36	107	3.49	.254	0	....	6	13	0.7
1977	Min-A	**20**	11	.645	39	**39**	19	2	0	303	284	129	113	23	2	91	186	1.238	3.36	119	3.22	.247	0	....	21	22	2.1
1978	Min-A	15	10	.600	29	29	13	2	0	220^{1}	209	72	61	12	1	67	116	1.253	2.49	153	3.16	.253	0	....	32	19	3.3
1979	Min-A	14	13	.519	36	35	12	1	0	250^{2}	282	124	116	22	1	69	132	1.400	4.16	105	4.28	.288	0	....	6	16	0.6
1980	LA-N	7	11	.389	35	27	2	2	1	171^{1}	198	91	82	12	0	59	91	1.500	4.31	81	4.59	.299	6	.128	-17	3	-1.8
1981*	LA-N	2	7	.222	26	8	0	0	1	77	83	35	35	4	0	25	48	1.403	4.09	81	3.98	.288	1	.059	-6	2	-0.8
1982	LA-N	0	1	.000	2	1	0	0	0	3^{2}	6	4	2	0	0	0	3	1.636	4.91	71	5.25	.353	0	.000	-1	0	-0.1
	*Cal-A	8	5	.615	28	7	1	0	3	86	82	43	39	4	1	32	49	1.326	4.08	99	3.37	.252	0	....	-2	6	-0.2
1983	Cal-A	0	6	.000	15	6	0	0	0	63^{2}	81	48	44	10	1	37	27	1.853	6.22	64	6.99	.315	0	....	-16	0	-1.5
Total	12	113	109	.509	353	264	83	13	8	2039^{2}	2104	950	836	149	26	646	1105	1.348	3.69	104	3.83	.269	10	.106	32	115	3.1

• GOMES, Wayne Wayne Maurice Gomes b: 1/15/1973, Hampton, VA BR/TR, 6'2", 215 lbs. Deb: 6/13/1997

YEAR	TM-L	W	L	PCT	G	GS	CG	SH	SV	IP	H	R	ER	HR	HB	BB	SO	RAT	ERA	ERA+	CERA	OAV	BH	AVG	PR+	WS	TPW
1997	Phi-N	5	1	.833	37	0	0	0	0	42^{2}	45	26	25	4	1	24	24	1.617	5.27	81	5.16	.274	0	.000	-5	2	-0.5
1998	Phi-N	9	6	.600	71	0	0	0	1	93^{1}	94	48	44	9	3	35	86	1.382	4.24	102	4.00	.258	0	.000	1	7	0.0
1999	Phi-N	5	5	.500	73	0	0	0	19	74	70	38	35	5	2	56	58	1.703	4.26	111	5.00	.255	0	.000	3	8	0.2
2000	Phi-N	4	6	.400	65	0	0	0	7	73^{2}	72	41	36	6	3	35	49	1.452	4.40	106	4.20	.262	0	....	2	6	0.2
2001	Phi-N	4	3	.571	42	0	0	0	1	48	51	23	23	4	1	22	35	1.521	4.31	98	4.43	.276	1	1.000	-1	4	0.0
	SF-N	2	0	1.000	13	0	0	0	0	15	21	14	14	3	0	7	17	1.867	8.40	47	7.50	.350	0	....	-7	0	-0.7
	Yr.	6	3	.667	55	0	0	0	1	63	72	37	37	7	1	29	52	1.603	5.29	78	5.16	.294	1	1.000	-8	4	-0.7
2002	Bos-A	1	2	.333	20	0	0	0	1	21^{1}	20	11	11	2	3	12	15	1.500	4.64	97	4.59	.241	0	....	-1	1	-0.1
Total	6	30	23	.566	321	0	0	0	29	368	373	201	188	33	13	191	284	1.533	4.60	96	4.61	.265	1	.167	-8	28	-0.8

• GOMEZ, Lefty Vernon Louis "Goofy" Gomez b: 11/26/1908, Rodeo, CA d: 2/17/1989, Greenbrae, CA BL/TL, 6'2", 173 lbs. Deb: 4/29/1930 HOF: 1972

YEAR	TM-L	W	L	PCT	G	GS	CG	SH	SV	IP	H	R	ER	HR	HB	BB	SO	RAT	ERA	ERA+	CERA	OAV	BH	AVG	PR+	WS	TPW
1930	NY-A	2	5	.286	15	6	2	0	1	60	66	41	37	12	1	28	22	1.567	5.55	77	5.54	.280	3	.150	-8	1	-0.9
1931	NY-A	21	9	.700	40	26	17	1	3	243	206	88	72	7	4	85	150	1.198	2.67	149	2.56	.226	11	.133	34	20	2.8
1932*	NY-A	24	7	.774	37	31	21	1	1	265^{1}	266	140	124	23	2	105	176	1.398	4.21	97	3.89	.259	18	.173	-3	17	-0.5
1933	NY-A★	16	10	.615	35	30	14	4	2	234^{2}	218	108	83	16	0	106	**163**	1.381	3.18	122	3.47	.240	9	.113	21	16	1.7
1934	NY-A★	**26**	5	.839	38	33	**25**	**6**	1	**281^{2}**	223	86	73	12	0	96	**158**	1.133	**2.33**	174	**2.33**	**.215**	13	.131	50	**31**	4.3
1935	NY-A★	12	15	.444	34	30	15	2	1	246	223	104	87	18	2	86	138	1.256	3.18	127	3.14	.242	10	.120	20	16	1.2
1936*	NY-A★	13	7	.650	31	30	10	0	0	188^{2}	184	104	92	6	1	122	105	1.622	4.39	106	4.20	.254	10	.145	4	11	0.1
1937*	NY-A★	**21**	11	.656	34	34	25	**6**	0	278^{1}	233	88	72	10	1	93	**194**	1.171	**2.33**	191	2.47	**.223**	21	.200	**61**	**29**	**5.5**
1938*	NY-A★	18	12	.600	32	32	20	**4**	0	239	239	110	89	7	1	99	129	1.414	3.35	135	3.53	.260	13	.151	30	19	2.4
1939*	NY-A★	12	8	.600	26	26	14	2	0	198	173	80	75	11	3	84	102	1.298	3.41	128	3.16	.235	11	.151	13	13	1.0
1940	NY-A	3	3	.500	9	5	0	0	0	27^{1}	37	20	20	2	1	18	14	2.012	6.59	61	7.04	.325	0	.000	-8	0	-0.9
1941	NY-A	15	5	.750	23	23	8	2	0	156^{1}	151	76	65	10	1	103	76	1.625	3.74	105	4.44	.250	9	.153	-3	10	-0.4
1942	NY-A	6	4	.600	13	13	2	0	0	80	67	42	38	4	2	65	41	1.650	4.28	80	4.38	.237	5	.152	-11	2	-1.2
1943	Was-A	0	1	.000	1	1	0	0	0	4^{2}	4	4	3	0	0	5	0	1.929	5.79	55	4.60	.250	0	.000	-1	0	-0.2
Total	14	189	102	.649	368	320	173	28	9	2503	2290	1091	930	138	19	1095	1468	1.352	3.34	124	3.37	.242	133	.147	199	185	15.0

• GOMEZ, Pat Patrick Alexander Gomez b: 3/17/1968, Roseville, CA BL/TL, 6', 185 lbs. Deb: 4/6/1993

YEAR	TM-L	W	L	PCT	G	GS	CG	SH	SV	IP	H	R	ER	HR	HB	BB	SO	RAT	ERA	ERA+	CERA	OAV	BH	AVG	PR+	WS	TPW
1993	SD-N	1	2	.333	27	1	0	0	0	31^{2}	35	19	18	2	0	19	26	1.705	5.12	81	5.02	.292	0	.000	-3	1	-0.4
1994	SF-N	0	1	.000	26	0	0	0	0	33^{1}	23	14	14	2	0	20	14	1.290	3.78	106	3.04	.211	0	.000	-0	2	-0.1
1995	SF-N	0	0	....	18	0	0	0	0	14	16	8	8	2	0	12	15	2.000	5.14	79	6.88	.276	0	.000	-2	0	-0.2
Total	3	1	3	.250	71	1	0	0	0	79	74	41	40	6	0	51	55	1.582	4.56	90	4.51	.258	0	.000	-6	3	-0.6

• GOMEZ, Ruben Ruben (Colon) Gomez b: 7/13/1927, Arroyo, Puerto Rico BR/TR, 6', 175 lbs. Deb: 4/17/1953

YEAR	TM-L	W	L	PCT	G	GS	CG	SH	SV	IP	H	R	ER	HR	HB	BB	SO	RAT	ERA	ERA+	CERA	OAV	BH	AVG	PR+	WS	TPW
1953	NY-N	13	11	.542	29	26	13	3	0	204	166	89	77	17	4	101	113	1.309	3.40	126	3.24	.218	15	.208	20	14	1.9
1954*	NY-N	17	9	.654	37	32	10	4	0	221^{2}	202	85	71	20	7	109	106	1.403	2.88	140	3.85	.244	14	.173	26	19	2.5
1955	NY-N	9	10	.474	33	31	9	3	1	185^{1}	207	103	94	20	7	63	79	1.457	4.56	88	4.69	.285	18	.300	-11	9	-0.7
1956	NY-N	7	17	.292	40	31	4	2	0	196^{1}	191	108	100	19	9	77	76	1.365	4.58	82	4.02	.259	11	.183	-17	5	-1.7
1957	NY-N	15	13	.536	38	36	16	1	0	238^{1}	233	110	100	28	5	71	92	1.276	3.78	104	3.66	.254	16	.184	5	14	0.7
1958	SF-N	10	12	.455	42	30	8	1	1	207^{2}	204	107	101	21	8	77	112	1.353	4.38	87	4.05	.261	14	.200	-11	9	-1.0
1959	Phi-N	3	8	.273	20	12	2	1	1	72^{1}	90	55	49	12	0	24	37	1.576	6.10	67	5.61	.300	3	.176	-16	0	-1.6
1960	Phi-N	0	3	.000	22	1	0	0	1	52^{1}	68	37	31	7	1	9	24	1.471	5.33	73	5.06	.321	1	.083	-9	0	-0.9
1962	Cle-A	1	2	.333	15	4	0	0	1	45^{1}	50	23	22	5	2	25	21	1.654	4.37	89	5.46	.292	3	.231	-3	2	-0.3
	Min-A	1	1	.500	6	2	1	0	0	19^{1}	17	11	10	3	0	11	8	1.448	4.66	88	4.42	.254	0	.000	-1	1	-0.2
	Yr.	2	3	.400	21	6	1	0	1	64^{2}	67	34	32	8	2	36	29	1.593	4.45	88	5.15	.282	3	.167	-4	3	-0.4
1967	Phi-N	0	0	....	7	0	0	0	0	11^{1}	8	6	5	2	0	7	9	1.324	3.97	86	3.43	.211	0	....	-1	0	-0.1
Total	10	76	86	.469	289	205	63	15	5	1454	1436	734	660	154	43	574	677	1.382	4.09	97	4.08	.259	95	.199	-17	73	-1.4

• GONZALES, Joe Joe Madrid "Smokey" Gonzales b: 3/19/1915, San Francisco, CA d: 11/16/1996, Torrance, CA BR/TR, 5'9", 175 lbs. Deb: 8/25/1937

YEAR	TM-L	W	L	PCT	G	GS	CG	SH	SV	IP	H	R	ER	HR	HB	BB	SO	RAT	ERA	ERA+	CERA	OAV	BH	AVG	PR+	WS	TPW
1937	Bos-A	1	2	.333	8	2	2	0	0	31	37	16	15	1	0	11	11	1.548	4.35	109	4.32	.291	0	.000	2	2	0.0

YEAR TM-L	W	L	PCT	G	GS	CG	SH	SV	IP	H	R	ER	HR	HB	BB	SO	RAT	ERA	ERA+	CERA	OAV	BH	AVG	PR+	WS	TPW
• GONZALES, Vince	Wenceslao (O'Reilly) Gonzales b: 9/28/1925, Quivican, Cuba d: 3/11/1981, Ciudad del Carmen, Mexico BL/TL, 6'1", 165 lbs. Deb: 4/13/1955																									
1955 Was-A	0	0	....	1	0	0	0	0	2	6	6	6	0	0	3	1	4.500	27.00	14	22.07	.500	0	....	-5	0	-0.5
• GONZALEZ, Dicky	Dicky Angel Gonzalez b: 12/21/1978, Bayamon, Puerto Rico BR/TR, 5'11", 170 lbs. Deb: 5/1/2001																									
2001 NY-N	3	2	.600	16	7	0	0	0	59	72	33	32	4	1	17	31	1.508	4.88	85	4.63	.306	2	.100	-5	2	-0.6
• GONZALEZ, Edgar	Edgar Gerardo Gonzalez b: 2/23/1983, Monterrey, Mexico BR/TR, 6', 215 lbs. Deb: 6/1/2003																									
2003 Ari-N	2	1	.667	9	2	0	0	0	18^1	28	10	10	3	0	7	14	1.909	4.91	95	7.81	.368	1	.250	-0	1	0.0
• GONZALEZ, Gabe	Gabriel Gonzalez b: 5/24/1972, Long Beach, CA BL/TL, 6'1" Deb: 4/1/1998																									
1998 Fla-N	0	0	....	3	0	0	0	0	1	1	1	1	0	0	1	0	2.000	9.00	45	5.48	.250	0	....	-1	0	-0.1
• GONZALEZ, German	German Jose (Caraballo) Gonzalez b: 3/7/1962, Rio Caribe, Venezuela BR/TR, 6', 170 lbs. Deb: 8/5/1988																									
1988 Min-A	0	0	....	16	0	0	0	1	21^1	20	8	8	4	1	8	19	1.313	3.38	121	4.31	.244	0	....	2	2	0.2
1989 Min-A	3	2	.600	22	0	0	0	0	29	32	17	15	2	4	11	25	1.483	4.66	89	4.72	.274	0	....	-2	1	-0.2
Total 2	**3**	**2**	**.600**	**38**	**0**	**0**	**0**	**1**	**50^1**	**52**	**25**	**23**	**6**	**5**	**19**	**44**	**1.411**	**4.11**	**100**	**4.54**	**.261**	**0**	**....**	**0**	**3**	**0.0**
• GONZALEZ, Jeremi	Geremis Segundo (Acosta) Gonzalez b: 1/8/1975, Maracaibo, Venezuela BR/TR, 6'2", 200 lbs. Deb: 5/27/1997																									
1997 Chi-N	11	9	.550	23	23	1	1	0	144	126	73	68	16	2	69	93	1.354	4.25	101	3.79	.236	4	.100	1	9	0.0
1998 Chi-N	7	7	.500	20	20	1	1	0	110	124	72	65	13	3	41	70	1.500	5.32	83	4.80	.281	6	.188	-9	2	-0.9
2003 TB-A	6	11	.353	25	25	2	0	0	156^1	131	71	68	18	12	69	97	1.279	3.91	116	3.74	.228	0	.000	7	8	0.6
Total 3	**24**	**27**	**.471**	**68**	**68**	**4**	**2**	**0**	**410^1**	**381**	**216**	**201**	**47**	**17**	**179**	**260**	**1.365**	**4.41**	**100**	**4.04**	**.246**	**10**	**.128**	**-1**	**19**	**-0.3**
• GONZALEZ, Julio	Julio Enrique (Herrera) Gonzalez b: 12/20/1920, Banes, Cuba d: 2/15/1991, Banes, Cuba BR/TR, 5'11", 150 lbs. Deb: 8/9/1949																									
1949 Was-A	0	0	....	13	0	0	0	0	34^1	33	20	18	3	1	27	5	1.748	4.72	90	5.15	.256	1	.200	-1	1	0.0
• GONZALEZ, Lariel	Lariel Alfonso Gonzalez b: 5/25/1976, San Cristobal, Dominican Republic BR/TR, 6'4" Deb: 9/22/1998																									
1998 Col-N	0	0	....	1	0	0	0	0	1	0	0	0	0	0	0	0	.000	0.00	....	0.00	.000	0	....	1	0	0.1
• GONZALEZ, Mike	Michael Vela Gonzalez b: 5/23/1978, Corpus Christi, TX BR/TL, 6'2", 213 lbs. Deb: 8/11/2003																									
2003 Pit-N	0	1	.000	16	0	0	0	0	8^1	7	7	7	4	0	6	6	1.560	7.56	58	7.18	.233	0	....	-3	0	-0.3
• GOOD, Andrew	Andrew Richard Good b: 9/19/1979, San Diego, CA BR/TR, 6'3", 209 lbs. Deb: 4/18/2003																									
2003 Ari-N	4	2	.667	16	10	0	0	0	66^1	74	42	39	15	3	16	42	1.357	5.29	88	5.04	.281	2	.125	-4	2	-0.5
• GOOD, Ralph	Ralph Nelson "Holy" Good b: 4/25/1886, Monticello, ME d: 11/24/1965, Waterville, ME BR/TR, 6', 165 lbs. Deb: 7/1/1910																									
1910 Bos-N	0	0	....	2	0	0	0	0	9	6	4	2	0	2	2	4	.889	2.00	166	1.83	.188	0	.000	1	1	0.1
• GOODALL, Herb	Herbert Frank Goodall b: 3/10/1870, Mansfield, PA d: 1/20/1938, Mansfield, PA BR/TR, 5'9", 180 lbs. Deb: 4/29/1890																									
1890 Lou-a	8	5	.615	18	13	8	1	**4**	109	94	73	41	2	10	51	46	1.330	3.39	113	....	.226	19	.422	5	11	1.0
• GOODELL, John	John Henry William "Lefty" Goodell b: 4/5/1907, Muskogee, OK d: 9/21/1993, Mesquite, TX BR/TL, 5'10", 165 lbs. Deb: 4/19/1928																									
1928 Chi-A	0	0	....	2	0	0	0	0	3	6	6	6	0	1	2	0	2.667	18.00	22	11.63	.500	0	....	-5	0	-0.5
• GOODEN, Dwight	Dwight Eugene "Doc,Dr. K." Gooden b: 11/16/1964, Tampa, FL BR/TR, 6'2", 210 lbs. Deb: 4/7/1984																									
1984 NY-N★	17	9	.654	31	31	7	3	0	218	161	72	63	7	2	73	**276**	1.073	2.60	136	**2.08**	**.202**	14	.200	23	18	2.5
1985 NY-N★	**24**	4	.857	35	35	**16**	8	0	**276^2**	198	51	47	13	2	69	**268**	.965	**1.53**	**226**	**1.83**	.201	21	.226	**61**	**33**	**7.0**
1986* NY-N★	17	6	.739	33	33	12	2	0	250	197	92	79	17	4	80	200	1.108	2.84	124	2.48	.215	7	.086	19	17	1.6
1987 NY-N	15	7	.682	25	25	7	3	0	179^2	162	68	64	11	2	53	148	1.197	3.21	118	2.98	.244	14	.219	14	14	1.5
1988* NY-N★	18	9	.667	34	34	10	3	0	248^1	242	98	88	8	6	57	175	1.204	3.19	101	2.93	.256	16	.178	1	13	0.3
1989 NY-N	9	4	.692	19	17	0	0	1	118^1	93	42	38	9	2	47	101	1.183	2.89	113	2.75	.211	8	.200	6	8	0.8
1990 NY-N	19	7	.731	34	34	2	1	0	232^2	229	106	99	10	7	70	223	1.285	3.83	98	3.31	.258	14	.187	1	13	0.4
1991 NY-N	13	7	.650	27	27	3	1	0	190	185	80	76	12	3	56	150	1.268	3.60	101	3.36	.257	15	.238	5	13	0.9
1992 NY-N	10	13	.435	31	31	3	0	0	206	197	93	84	11	3	70	145	1.296	3.67	95	3.32	.255	19	.264	-2	11	0.5
1993 NY-N	12	15	.444	29	29	7	2	0	208^2	188	89	80	16	9	61	149	1.193	3.45	116	3.14	.242	14	.200	12	14	1.6
1994 NY-N	3	4	.429	7	7	0	0	0	41^1	46	32	29	9	1	15	40	1.476	6.31	66	5.51	.282	2	.167	-10	0	-1.0
1996 NY-A	11	7	.611	29	29	1	1	0	170^2	169	101	95	19	9	88	126	1.506	5.01	99	4.77	.259	0	....	2	9	0.2
1997* NY-A	9	5	.643	20	19	0	0	0	106^1	116	61	58	14	7	53	66	1.589	4.91	91	5.65	.283	0	.000	-4	5	-0.4
1998* Cle-A	8	6	.571	23	23	0	0	0	134	135	59	56	13	9	51	83	1.388	3.76	127	4.32	.262	0	.000	15	10	1.4
1999 Cle-A	3	4	.429	26	22	0	0	0	115	127	90	80	18	9	67	88	1.687	6.26	80	6.21	.282	1	.500	-15	3	-1.2
2000 Hou-N	0	0	....	1	1	0	0	0	4	6	4	4	1	0	3	1	2.250	9.00	54	10.40	.353	0	.000	-2	0	-0.2
TB-A	2	3	.400	8	8	0	0	0	36^2	47	32	27	14	3	20	23	1.827	6.63	74	9.33	.315	0	....	-7	0	-0.7
* NY-A	4	2	.667	18	5	0	0	2	64^1	66	28	24	8	0	21	31	1.352	3.36	144	4.03	.266	0	.000	12	6	1.1
Yr.	6	5	.545	26	13	0	0	2	101	113	60	51	22	3	41	54	1.525	4.54	108	5.95	.285	0	.000	4	6	0.4
Total 16	**194**	**112**	**.634**	**430**	**410**	**68**	**24**	**3**	**2800^2**	**2564**	**1198**	**1091**	**210**	**78**	**954**	**2293**	**1.256**	**3.51**	**111**	**3.39**	**.244**	**145**	**.196**	**129**	**187**	**16.3**
• GOODWIN, Art	Arthur Ingram Goodwin b: 2/27/1876, Greene County, PA d: 6/19/1943, Greene County, PA TR, 5'8", 195 lbs. Deb: 10/7/1905																									
1905 NY-A	0	0	....	1	0	0	0	0	0^1	2	4	3	0	0	2	0	12.00	81.00	4	69.98	.681	0	....	-3	0	-0.3
• GOODWIN, Clyde	Clyde Samuel Goodwin b: 11/12/1886, Shade, OH d: 10/12/1963, Dayton, OH BR/TR, 5'11", 145 lbs. Deb: 9/18/1906																									
1906 Was-A	0	2	.000	4	3	1	0	0	22^1	20	16	11	0	1	13	9	1.478	4.43	59	3.47	.243	1	.200	-4	0	-0.5
• GOODWIN, Jim	James Patrick Goodwin b: 8/15/1926, St. Louis, MO BL/TL, 6'1", 170 lbs. Deb: 4/24/1948																									
1948 Chi-A	0	0	....	8	1	0	0	1	10^1	9	11	10	0	1	12	3	2.032	8.71	49	5.31	.237	1	.500	-5	0	-0.5
• GOODWIN, Marv	Marvin Mardo Goodwin b: 1/16/1891, Gordonsville, VA d: 10/21/1925, Houston, TX BR/TR, 5'11", 168 lbs. Deb: 9/7/1916																									
1916 Was-A	0	0	....	3	0	0	0	0	5^2	5	4	2	0	0	3	1	1.412	3.18	88	2.87	.217	0	.000	-0	0	0.0
1917 StL-N	6	4	.600	14	12	6	3	0	85^1	70	33	21	1	0	19	38	1.043	2.21	121	1.92	.222	4	.174	3	7	0.4
1919 StL-N	11	9	.550	33	17	7	0	0	179	163	66	50	3	8	33	48	1.095	2.51	111	2.39	.245	12	.200	3	11	0.6
1920 StL-N	3	8	.273	32	12	3	0	1	116^1	153	79	64	1	5	28	23	1.556	4.95	62	4.56	.314	7	.200	-25	0	-2.7
1921 StL-N	1	2	.333	14	4	1	0	1	36^1	47	21	15	1	1	9	7	1.541	3.72	98	4.52	.315	0	.000	-0	1	-0.1
1922 StL-N	0	0	....	2	0	0	0	0	4	3	1	1	0	0	3	0	1.500	2.25	172	3.02	.250	0	....	1	0	0.1
1925 Cin-N	0	2	.000	4	3	2	0	0	20^2	26	14	11	2	1	5	4	1.500	4.79	86	5.01	.317	1	.250	-2	0	-0.2
Total 7	**21**	**25**	**.457**	**102**	**48**	**19**	**3**	**2**	**447^1**	**467**	**218**	**164**	**8**	**15**	**100**	**121**	**1.268**	**3.30**	**91**	**3.17**	**.269**	**24**	**.186**	**-20**	**19**	**-2.0**
• GORDINIER, Ray	Raymond Cornelius "Gordy" Gordinier b: 4/11/1892, Rochester, NY d: 11/15/1960, Rochester, NY BB/TR, 5'8.5", 170 lbs. Deb: 9/17/1921																									
1921 Bro-N	1	0	1.000	3	3	0	0	0	12	10	8	7	0	0	8	4	1.500	5.25	74	3.25	.227	1	.250	-2	1	-0.1
1922 Bro-N	0	0	....	5	0	0	0	0	11^1	13	11	11	3	0	8	5	1.853	8.74	47	7.51	.289	0	.000	-6	0	-0.6
Total 2	**1**	**0**	**1.000**	**8**	**3**	**0**	**0**	**0**	**23^1**	**23**	**19**	**18**	**3**	**0**	**16**	**9**	**1.671**	**6.94**	**57**	**5.32**	**.258**	**1**	**.167**	**-8**	**1**	**-0.7**
• GORDON, Don	Donald Thomas Gordon b: 10/10/1959, New York, NY BR/TR, 6'1", 175 lbs. Deb: 4/10/1986																									
1986 Tor-A	0	1	.000	14	0	0	0	1	21^2	28	20	17	1	1	8	13	1.662	7.06	60	5.20	.311	0	....	-7	0	-0.7
1987 Tor-A	0	0	....	5	0	0	0	0	11	8	5	5	2	0	3	3	1.000	4.09	110	2.68	.200	0	....	0	1	0.0
Cle-A	0	3	.000	21	0	0	0	1	39^2	49	31	18	3	4	12	20	1.538	4.08	111	4.97	.295	0	....	3	1	0.2
Yr.	0	3	.000	26	0	0	0	1	50^2	57	36	23	5	4	15	23	1.421	4.09	111	4.47	.277	0	....	3	2	0.3
1988 Cle-A	3	4	.429	38	0	0	0	1	59^1	65	33	29	5	3	19	20	1.416	4.40	93	4.27	.284	0	....	-1	3	-0.1
Total 3	**3**	**8**	**.273**	**78**	**0**	**0**	**0**	**3**	**131^2**	**150**	**89**	**69**	**11**	**8**	**42**	**56**	**1.458**	**4.72**	**90**	**4.50**	**.286**	**0**	**....**	**-5**	**5**	**-0.5**
• GORDON, Tom	Thomas "Flash" Gordon b: 11/18/1967, Sebring, FL BR/TR, 5'9", 180 lbs. Deb: 9/8/1988																									
1988 KC-A	0	2	.000	5	2	0	0	0	15^2	16	9	9	1	0	7	18	1.468	5.17	77	4.22	.267	0	....	-2	0	-0.2
1989 KC-A	17	9	.654	49	16	1	1	1	163	122	67	66	10	1	86	153	1.276	3.64	106	2.97	.210	0	....	6	13	0.6
1990 KC-A	12	11	.522	32	32	6	1	0	195^1	192	99	81	17	3	99	175	1.490	3.73	103	4.37	.257	0	....	7	9	0.7
1991 KC-A	9	14	.391	45	14	1	0	1	158	129	76	68	16	4	87	167	1.367	3.87	106	3.67	.221	0	....	9	9	0.9

YEAR	TM-L	W	L	PCT	G	GS	CG	SH	SV	IP	H	R	ER	HR	HB	BB	SO	RAT	ERA	ERA+	CERA	OAV	BH	AVG	PR+	WS	TPW
1992	KC-A	6	10	.375	40	11	0	0	0	117^2	116	67	60	9	4	55	98	1.453	4.59	88	4.17	.258	0	....	-5	4	-0.5
1993	KC-A	12	6	.667	48	14	2	0	1	155^2	125	65	62	11	1	77	143	1.298	3.58	128	3.18	.223	0	....	16	14	1.6
1994	KC-A	11	7	.611	24	24	0	0	0	155^1	136	79	75	15	3	87	126	1.436	4.35	115	4.04	.237	0	....	11	12	1.0
1995	KC-A	12	12	.500	31	31	2	0	0	189	204	110	93	12	4	89	119	1.550	4.43	108	4.59	.279	0	....	5	11	0.5
1996	Bos-A	12	9	.571	34	34	4	1	0	215^2	249	143	134	28	4	105	171	1.641	5.59	91	5.50	.284	0	....	-7	10	-0.7
1997	Bos-A	6	10	.375	42	25	2	1	11	182^2	155	85	76	10	3	78	159	1.276	3.74	124	3.08	.226	0	....	18	15	1.7
1998*	Bos-A★	7	4	.636	73	0	0	0	**46**	79^1	55	24	24	2	0	25	78	1.008	2.72	173	1.72	.191	0	....	17	17	1.6
1999*	Bos-A	0	2	.000	21	0	0	0	11	17^2	17	11	11	2	1	12	24	1.642	5.60	89	5.04	.246	0	....	-1	2	-0.1
2001	Chi-N	1	2	.333	47	0	0	0	27	45^1	32	18	17	4	1	16	67	1.059	3.38	123	2.27	.188	0	....	5	8	0.5
2002	Chi-N	1	1	.500	19	0	0	0	0	23^2	27	12	9	1	1	10	31	1.563	3.42	117	4.75	.293	0	....	2	1	0.2
	Hou-N	0	2	.000	15	0	0	0	0	19	15	7	7	2	0	6	17	1.105	3.32	128	2.53	.217	0	.000	2	2	0.2
	Yr.	1	3	.250	34	0	0	0	0	42^2	42	19	16	3	1	16	48	1.359	3.38	122	3.76	.261	0	.000	4	3	0.4
2003	Chi-A	7	6	.538	66	0	0	0	12	74	57	29	26	4	4	31	91	1.189	3.16	141	2.74	.213	0	....	10	11	0.9
Total	**15**	**113**	**107**	**.514**	**591**	**203**	**18**	**4**	**110**	**1807**	**1647**	**901**	**818**	**144**	**34**	**870**	**1637**	**1.393**	**4.07**	**109**	**3.82**	**.242**	**0**	**.000**	**93**	**138**	**8.9**

• GORECKI, Rick

Richard John Gorecki b: 8/27/1973, Evergreen Park, IL BR/TR, 6'3", 167 lbs. Deb: 9/10/1997

YEAR	TM-L	W	L	PCT	G	GS	CG	SH	SV	IP	H	R	ER	HR	HB	BB	SO	RAT	ERA	ERA+	CERA	OAV	BH	AVG	PR+	WS	TPW
1997	LA-N	1	0	1.000	4	1	0	0	0	6	9	10	10	3	0	6	6	2.500	15.00	26	13.63	.346	0	....	-7	0	-0.7
1998	TB-A	1	2	.333	3	3	0	0	0	16^2	15	9	9	1	0	10	7	1.500	4.86	99	4.22	.259	0	....	-1	1	-0.1
Total	**2**	**2**	**2**	**.500**	**7**	**4**	**0**	**0**	**0**	**22^2**	**24**	**19**	**19**	**4**	**0**	**16**	**13**	**1.765**	**7.54**	**56**	**6.71**	**.286**	**0**	**....**	**-8**	**1**	**-0.8**

• GORIN, Charlie

Charles Perry Gorin b: 2/6/1928, Waco, TX BL/TL, 5'10", 165 lbs. Deb: 5/29/1954

YEAR	TM-L	W	L	PCT	G	GS	CG	SH	SV	IP	H	R	ER	HR	HB	BB	SO	RAT	ERA	ERA+	CERA	OAV	BH	AVG	PR+	WS	TPW
1954	Mil-N	0	1	.000	5	0	0	0	0	9^2	5	3	2	0	0	6	12	1.138	1.86	200	1.62	.152	0	.000	2	1	0.1
1955	Mil-N	0	0	....	2	0	0	0	0	0^1	1	2	2	0	0	3	0	12.00	54.00	7	59.85	.500	0	....	-2	0	-0.2
Total	**2**	**0**	**1**	**.000**	**7**	**0**	**0**	**0**	**0**	**10**	**6**	**5**	**4**	**0**	**0**	**9**	**12**	**1.500**	**3.60**	**104**	**3.56**	**.171**	**0**	**.000**	**0**	**1**	**0.0**

• GORMAN, Tom

Thomas David "Big Tom" Gorman b: 3/16/1916, New York, NY d: 8/11/1986, Closter, NJ BR/TR, 6'2", 200 lbs. Deb: 9/14/1939 U

YEAR	TM-L	W	L	PCT	G	GS	CG	SH	SV	IP	H	R	ER	HR	HB	BB	SO	RAT	ERA	ERA+	CERA	OAV	BH	AVG	PR+	WS	TPW
1939	NY-N	0	0	....	4	0	0	0	0	5	7	4	4	0	0	1	2	1.600	7.20	55	4.87	.350	0	.000	-2	0	-0.2

• GORMAN, Tom

Thomas Patrick Gorman b: 12/16/1957, Portland, OR BL/TL, 6'4", 200 lbs. Deb: 9/2/1981

YEAR	TM-L	W	L	PCT	G	GS	CG	SH	SV	IP	H	R	ER	HR	HB	BB	SO	RAT	ERA	ERA+	CERA	OAV	BH	AVG	PR+	WS	TPW
1981	Mon-N	0	0	....	9	0	0	0	0	15	12	7	7	0	1	6	13	1.200	4.20	83	2.37	.222	0	....	-1	0	-0.1
1982	Mon-N	1	0	1.000	5	0	0	0	0	7	8	4	4	0	0	4	6	1.714	5.14	71	4.66	.286	0	....	-1	0	-0.1
	NY-N	0	1	.000	3	1	0	0	0	9^1	8	1	1	0	0	0	7	.857	0.96	376	1.44	.235	0	.000	3	1	0.3
	Yr.	1	1	.500	8	1	0	0	0	16^1	16	5	5	0	0	4	13	1.224	2.76	132	2.82	.258	0	.000	2	1	0.2
1983	NY-N	1	4	.200	25	4	0	0	0	49^1	45	29	27	3	0	15	30	1.216	4.93	74	2.86	.245	1	.250	-8	0	-0.8
1984	NY-N	6	0	1.000	36	0	0	0	0	57^2	51	20	19	6	1	13	40	1.110	2.97	119	2.87	.238	0	.000	4	5	0.3
1985	NY-N	4	4	.500	34	2	0	0	0	52^2	56	32	30	8	0	18	32	1.405	5.13	67	4.51	.277	0	.000	-9	0	-1.1
1986	Phi-N	0	1	.000	8	0	0	0	0	11^2	21	10	10	0	0	5	8	2.229	7.71	50	7.89	.382	0	.000	-5	0	-0.5
1987	SD-N	0	0	....	6	0	0	0	0	11	11	5	5	1	0	5	8	1.455	4.09	97	4.32	.262	0	....	-0	1	0.0
Total	**7**	**12**	**10**	**.545**	**126**	**7**	**0**	**0**	**0**	**213^2**	**212**	**108**	**103**	**18**	**2**	**66**	**144**	**1.301**	**4.34**	**83**	**3.58**	**.261**	**1**	**.071**	**-18**	**7**	**-2.1**

• GORMAN, Tom

Thomas Aloysius Gorman b: 1/4/1925, New York, NY d: 12/26/1992, Valley Stream, NY BR/TR, 6'1", 190 lbs. Deb: 7/16/1952

YEAR	TM-L	W	L	PCT	G	GS	CG	SH	SV	IP	H	R	ER	HR	HB	BB	SO	RAT	ERA	ERA+	CERA	OAV	BH	AVG	PR+	WS	TPW
1952*	NY-A	6	2	.750	12	6	1	1	1	60^2	63	34	31	8	2	22	31	1.401	4.60	72	4.49	.272	2	.087	-11	2	-1.2
1953*	NY-A	4	5	.444	40	1	0	0	6	77	65	32	29	5	6	32	38	1.260	3.39	109	3.20	.226	2	.133	1	5	0.0
1954	NY-A	0	0	....	23	0	0	0	2	36^2	30	14	9	1	1	14	31	1.200	2.21	155	2.53	.222	0	.000	4	3	0.4
1955	KC-A	7	6	.538	57	0	0	0	18	109	98	48	43	11	4	36	46	1.229	3.55	117	3.38	.246	2	.083	8	12	0.7
1956	KC-A	9	10	.474	52	13	1	0	3	171^1	168	83	73	23	2	68	56	1.377	3.83	113	4.20	.258	2	.051	7	11	0.4
1957	KC-A	5	9	.357	38	12	3	1	3	124^2	125	59	53	18	1	33	66	1.267	3.83	103	3.80	.261	4	.121	2	7	0.1
1958	KC-A	4	4	.500	50	1	0	0	8	89^2	86	41	35	8	3	20	44	1.182	3.51	111	3.38	.258	2	.118	4	8	0.3
1959	KC-A	1	0	1.000	17	0	0	0	1	20^1	24	21	16	3	1	14	9	1.869	7.08	57	6.71	.293	0	....	-7	0	-0.7
Total	**8**	**36**	**36**	**.500**	**289**	**33**	**5**	**2**	**42**	**689^1**	**659**	**332**	**289**	**77**	**20**	**239**	**321**	**1.303**	**3.77**	**104**	**3.79**	**.254**	**14**	**.090**	**9**	**48**	**-0.1**

• GORMLEY, Joe

Joseph Gormley b: 12/20/1866, Summit Hill, PA d: 7/2/1950, Summit Hill, PA BL/TL Deb: 6/16/1891

YEAR	TM-L	W	L	PCT	G	GS	CG	SH	SV	IP	H	R	ER	HR	HB	BB	SO	RAT	ERA	ERA+	CERA	OAV	BH	AVG	PR+	WS	TPW
1891	Phi-N	0	1	.000	1	1	1	0	0	8	10	8	5	0	0	5	2	1.875	5.63	60	....	.295	0	.000	-2	0	-0.2

• GORNICKI, Hank

Henry Frank Gornicki b: 1/14/1911, Niagara Falls, NY d: 2/16/1996, Riviera Beach, FL BR/TR, 6'1", 145 lbs. Deb: 4/17/1941

YEAR	TM-L	W	L	PCT	G	GS	CG	SH	SV	IP	H	R	ER	HR	HB	BB	SO	RAT	ERA	ERA+	CERA	OAV	BH	AVG	PR+	WS	TPW
1941	StL-N	1	0	1.000	4	1	1	1	0	11^1	6	4	4	0	1	9	6	1.324	3.18	119	2.41	.158	1	.250	1	1	0.1
	Chi-N	0	0	....	1	0	0	0	0	2	3	1	1	0	0	0	2	1.500	4.50	78	5.09	.375	0	....	-0	0	0.0
	Yr.	1	0	1.000	5	1	1	1	0	13^1	9	5	5	0	1	9	8	1.350	3.38	110	2.81	.196	1	.250	0	1	0.0
1942	Pit-N	5	6	.455	25	14	7	2	2	112	89	45	32	2	1	40	48	1.152	2.57	132	2.23	.215	4	.114	11	8	1.2
1943	Pit-N	9	13	.409	42	19	4	1	4	147	165	86	65	10	2	47	63	1.442	3.98	87	4.20	.286	7	.175	-8	4	-0.9
1946	Pit-N	0	0	....	7	0	0	0	0	12^2	12	10	5	0	0	11	4	1.816	3.55	99	4.35	.255	0	.000	0	0	0.0
Total	**4**	**15**	**19**	**.441**	**79**	**34**	**12**	**4**	**6**	**285**	**275**	**146**	**107**	**12**	**4**	**107**	**123**	**1.340**	**3.38**	**102**	**3.36**	**.254**	**12**	**.146**	**4**	**13**	**0.2**

• GORSICA, Johnny

John Joseph Perry Gorsica b: 3/29/1915, Bayonne, NJ d: 12/16/1998, Charlottesville, VA BR/TR, 6'2", 180 lbs. Deb: 4/22/1940

YEAR	TM-L	W	L	PCT	G	GS	CG	SH	SV	IP	H	R	ER	HR	HB	BB	SO	RAT	ERA	ERA+	CERA	OAV	BH	AVG	PR+	WS	TPW
1940*	Det-A	7	7	.500	29	20	5	2	0	160	170	85	77	10	4	57	68	1.419	4.33	110	4.01	.272	12	.194	10	10	1.0
1941	Det-A	9	11	.450	33	21	8	1	2	171	193	98	85	14	2	55	59	1.450	4.47	102	4.28	.281	17	.298	6	12	1.0
1942	Det-A	3	2	.600	28	0	0	0	4	53	63	31	28	2	3	26	19	1.679	4.75	83	5.19	.310	1	.100	-4	2	-0.4
1943	Det-A	4	5	.444	35	4	1	0	5	96^1	88	43	36	3	2	40	45	1.329	3.36	105	3.20	.247	4	.174	2	6	0.2
1944	Det-A	6	14	.300	34	19	8	1	4	162	192	88	74	5	4	32	47	1.383	4.11	87	3.88	.296	7	.135	-9	5	-1.1
1946	Det-A	0	0	....	14	0	0	0	1	23^2	28	13	12	5	0	11	14	1.648	4.56	80	6.32	.301	2	.667	-2	1	-0.1
1947	Det-A	2	0	1.000	31	0	0	0	1	57^2	44	27	24	5	2	26	20	1.214	3.75	101	2.91	.208	2	.200	1	4	0.2
Total	**7**	**31**	**39**	**.443**	**204**	**64**	**22**	**4**	**17**	**723^2**	**778**	**385**	**336**	**44**	**17**	**247**	**272**	**1.416**	**4.18**	**97**	**4.01**	**.276**	**45**	**.207**	**5**	**40**	**0.8**

• GOSSAGE, Rich

Richard Michael "Goose" Gossage b: 7/5/1951, Colorado Springs, CO BR/TR, 6'3", 217 lbs. Deb: 4/16/1972

YEAR	TM-L	W	L	PCT	G	GS	CG	SH	SV	IP	H	R	ER	HR	HB	BB	SO	RAT	ERA	ERA+	CERA	OAV	BH	AVG	PR+	WS	TPW
1972	Chi-A	7	1	.875	36	1	0	0	2	80	72	44	38	2	4	44	57	1.450	4.28	73	3.68	.247	0	.000	-9	3	-1.2
1973	Chi-A	0	4	.000	20	4	1	0	0	49^2	57	44	41	9	3	37	33	1.893	7.43	53	7.54	.311	0	....	-18	0	-1.9
1974	Chi-A	4	6	.400	39	3	0	0	1	89^1	92	45	41	4	2	47	64	1.556	4.13	90	4.31	.272	0	....	-3	4	-0.3
1975	Chi-A★	9	8	.529	62	0	0	0	**26**	141^2	99	32	29	3	5	70	130	1.193	1.84	210	2.32	.201	0	....	34	23	3.5
1976	Chi-A★	9	17	.346	31	29	15	0	1	224	214	104	98	16	9	90	135	1.357	3.94	90	3.81	.254	0	....	-7	10	-0.7
1977	Pit-N★	11	9	.550	72	0	0	0	26	133	78	27	24	9	2	49	151	.955	1.62	245	1.68	.170	5	.217	33	26	3.4
1978*	NY-A★	10	11	.476	63	0	0	0	**27**	134^1	87	41	30	9	2	59	122	1.087	2.01	180	2.16	.187	0	....	23	20	2.4
1979	NY-A	5	3	.625	36	0	0	0	18	58^1	48	18	17	5	0	19	41	1.149	2.62	155	2.72	.227	0	....	8	11	0.8
1980*	NY-A★	6	2	.750	64	0	0	0	**33**	99	74	29	25	5	1	37	103	1.121	2.27	172	2.35	.211	0	....	19	18	1.9
1981*	NY-A★	3	2	.600	32	0	0	0	20	46^2	22	6	4	2	1	14	48	.771	0.77	463	1.15	.141	0	....	14	12	1.5
1982	NY-A★	4	5	.444	56	0	0	0	30	93	63	23	23	5	0	28	102	.978	2.23	179	1.80	.196	0	....	19	17	1.9
1983	NY-A	13	5	.722	57	0	0	0	22	87^1	82	27	22	5	1	25	90	1.225	2.27	172	2.94	.248	0	....	16	16	1.6
1984*	SD-N★	10	6	.625	62	0	0	0	25	102^1	75	34	33	6	1	36	84	1.085	2.90	123	2.24	.204	4	.182	5	15	0.6
1985	SD-N★	5	3	.625	50	0	0	0	26	79	64	21	16	1	1	17	52	1.025	1.82	194	1.97	.226	0	.000	14	15	1.4
1986	SD-N	5	7	.417	45	0	0	0	21	64^2	69	36	32	8	2	20	63	1.376	4.45	82	4.35	.273	0	.000	-6	5	-0.7
1987	SD-N	5	4	.556	40	0	0	0	11	52	47	18	18	4	0	19	44	1.269	3.12	127	3.10	.244	0	.000	4	7	0.4
1988	Chi-N	4	4	.500	46	0	0	0	13	43^2	50	23	21	3	3	15	30	1.489	4.33	83	4.53	.291	0	.000	-3	4	-0.3
1989	SF-N	2	1	.667	31	0	0	0	4	43^2	32	16	13	2	0	27	24	1.351	2.68	126	3.05	.212	0	.000	2	4	0.2
	NY-A	1	0	1.000	11	0	0	0	1	14^1	14	6	6	0	1	3	6	1.186	3.77	103	2.94	.275	0	....	0	1	0.0
1991	Tex-A	4	2	.667	44	0	0	0	1	40^1	33	16	16	4	3	16	28	1.215	3.57	113	3.38	.228	0	....	3	3	0.3
1992	Oak-A	0	2	.000	30	0	0	0	0	38	32	13	12	5	2	19	26	1.342	2.84	132	3.87	.230	0	....	3	2	0.4
1993	Oak-A	4	5	.444	39	0	0	0	1	47^2	49	24	24	6	1	26	40	1.573	4.53	90	5.06	.266	0	....	-2	3	-0.2
1994	Sea-A	3	0	1.000	36	0	0	0	1	47^1	44	23	22	6	3	15	29	1.246	4.18	117	3.83	.251	0	....	4	4	0.4
Total	**22**	**124**	**107**	**.537**	**1002**	**37**	**16**	**0**	**310**	**1809^1**	**1497**	**670**	**605**	**119**	**47**	**732**	**1502**	**1.232**	**3.01**	**124**	**3.05**	**.228**	**9**	**.106**	**156**	**223**	**15.3**

YEAR	TM-L	W	L	PCT	G	GS	CG	SH	SV	IP	H	R	ER	HR	HB	BB	SO	RAT	ERA	ERA+	CERA	OAV	BH	AVG	PR+	WS	TPW
• GOTT, Jim	James William Gott b: 8/3/1959, Hollywood, CA BR/TR, 6'4", 220 lbs. Deb: 4/9/1982																										
1982	Tor-A	5	10	.333	30	23	1	1	0	136	134	76	67	15	3	66	82	1.471	4.43	101	4.48	.255	0	....	2	6	0.2
1983	Tor-A	9	14	.391	34	30	6	1	0	176^2	195	103	93	15	5	68	121	1.489	4.74	91	4.59	.280	0	....	-9	7	-0.9
1984	Tor-A	7	6	.538	35	12	1	1	2	109^2	93	54	49	7	3	49	73	1.295	4.02	102	3.25	.233	0	....	0	7	0.0
1985	SF-N	7	10	.412	26	26	2	0	0	148^1	144	73	64	10	1	51	78	1.315	3.88	88	3.46	.254	10	.196	-5	6	-0.1
1986	SF-N	0	0	....	9	2	0	0	1	13	16	12	11	0	0	13	9	2.231	7.62	46	6.75	.314	0	.000	-6	0	-0.6
1987	SF-N	1	0	1.000	30	3	0	0	0	56	53	32	28	4	2	32	63	1.518	4.50	85	4.15	.244	1	.100	-5	1	-0.4
	Pit-N	0	2	.000	25	0	0	0	13	31	28	11	5	0	0	8	27	1.161	1.45	283	2.25	.233	0	.000	9	6	0.8
	Yr.	1	2	.333	55	3	0	0	13	87	81	43	33	4	2	40	90	1.391	3.41	114	3.47	.240	1	.091	4	7	0.4
1988	Pit-N	6	6	.500	67	0	0	0	34	77^1	68	30	30	9	2	22	76	1.164	3.49	97	3.14	.243	0	.000	-1	11	-0.1
1989	Pit-N	0	0	....	1	0	0	0	0	0^2	1	0	0	0	0	1	1	3.000	0.00	....	10.76	.333	0	....	0	0	0.0
1990	LA-N	3	5	.375	50	0	0	0	3	62	59	27	20	5	0	34	44	1.500	2.90	126	4.10	.257	0	.000	5	4	0.5
1991	LA-N	4	3	.571	55	0	0	0	2	76	63	28	25	5	1	32	73	1.250	2.96	121	2.87	.223	1	.500	5	6	0.6
1992	LA-N	3	3	.500	68	0	0	0	6	88	72	27	24	4	1	41	75	1.284	2.45	140	2.80	.225	1	.500	12	9	1.3
1993	LA-N	4	8	.333	62	0	0	0	25	77^2	71	23	20	6	1	17	67	1.133	2.32	164	2.78	.248	0	.000	13	14	1.3
1994	LA-N	5	3	.625	37	0	0	0	2	36^1	46	24	24	3	3	20	29	1.817	5.94	66	6.33	.322	0	....	-8	1	-0.8
1995	Pit-N	2	4	.333	25	0	0	0	3	31^1	38	26	21	2	1	12	19	1.596	6.03	71	4.77	.288	0	.000	-6	1	-0.6
Total	14	56	74	.431	554	96	10	3	91	1120	1081	546	481	85	23	466	837	1.381	3.87	101	3.79	.254	13	.178	6	79	1.2
• GOULAIT, Ted	Theodore Lee Goulait b: 8/12/1889, St. Clair, MI d: 7/15/1936, St. Clair, MI BR/TR, 5'9.5", 172 lbs. Deb: 9/28/1912																										
1912	NY-N	0	0	....	1	1	1	0	0	7	11	6	5	0	0	4	6	2.143	6.43	53	7.49	.367	1	.500	-2	0	-0.2
• GOULD, Al	Albert Frank "Pudgy" Gould b: 1/20/1893, Muscantine, IA d: 8/8/1982, San Jose, CA BR/TR, 5'6.5", 160 lbs. Deb: 7/11/1916																										
1916	Cle-A	5	6	.455	30	9	6	1	1	106^2	101	37	30	0	3	40	41	1.322	2.53	118	3.14	.256	3	.103	5	7	0.4
1917	Cle-A	4	4	.500	27	7	1	0	0	94	95	44	38	1	3	52	24	1.564	3.64	78	4.29	.281	5	.208	-11	4	-1.1
Total	2	9	10	.474	57	16	7	1	1	200^2	196	81	68	1	6	92	65	1.435	3.05	95	3.68	.268	8	.151	-6	11	-0.7
• GOWELL, Larry	Lawrence Clyde Gowell b: 5/2/1948, Lewiston, ME BR/TR, 6'2", 182 lbs. Deb: 9/21/1972																										
1972	NY-A	0	1	.000	2	1	0	0	0	7	3	1	1	0	0	2	7	.714	1.29	229	0.90	.143	1	1.000	1	1	0.2
• GOZZO, Mauro	Mauro Paul Gozzo b: 3/7/1966, New Britain, CT BR/TR, 6'2", 212 lbs. Deb: 8/8/1989																										
1989	Tor-A	4	1	.800	9	3	0	0	0	31^2	35	19	17	1	1	9	10	1.389	4.83	75	3.92	.289	0	....	-4	1	-0.4
1990	Cle-A	0	0	....	2	0	0	0	0	3	2	0	0	0	0	2	2	1.333	0.00	....	2.54	.182	0	....	1	0	0.1
1991	Cle-A	0	0	....	2	2	0	0	0	4^2	9	10	10	0	0	7	3	3.429	19.29	22	14.84	.450	0	....	-8	0	-0.8
1992	Min-A	0	0	....	2	0	0	0	0	1^2	7	5	5	2	0	0	1	4.200	27.00	15	39.46	.583	0	....	-4	0	-0.4
1993	NY-N	0	1	.000	10	0	0	0	1	14	11	5	4	1	0	5	6	1.143	2.57	156	2.50	.212	0	....	2	1	0.2
1994	NY-N	3	5	.375	23	8	0	0	0	69	86	48	37	5	1	28	33	1.652	4.83	87	4.96	.304	4	.250	-5	2	-0.4
Total	6	7	7	.500	48	13	0	0	1	124	150	87	73	9	2	51	55	1.621	5.30	76	5.19	.301	4	.250	-18	4	-1.7
• GRABOW, John	John Grabow b: 11/4/1978, Arcadia, CA BL/TL, 6'2", 185 lbs. Deb: 9/14/2003																										
2003	Pit-N	0	0	....	5	0	0	0	0	5	6	3	2	0	0	0	9	1.200	3.60	122	2.73	.273	0	....	0	0	0.0
• GRABOWSKI, Al	Alfons Francis Grabowski b: 9/6/1901, Syracuse, NY d: 10/29/1966, Memphis, TN BL/TL, 5'11.5", 175 lbs. Deb: 9/11/1929																										
1929	StL-N	3	2	.600	6	6	4	2	0	50	44	18	14	0	0	8	22	1.040	2.52	185	1.87	.227	4	.250	12	6	1.2
1930	StL-N	6	4	.600	33	8	1	0	1	107	120	66	57	7	3	49	43	1.579	4.79	105	4.75	.295	12	.364	2	7	0.4
Total	2	9	6	.600	39	14	5	2	1	157	164	84	71	7	3	57	65	1.408	4.07	121	3.83	.273	16	.327	14	13	1.6
• GRABOWSKI, Reggie	Reginald John Grabowski b: 7/16/1907, Syracuse, NY d: 4/2/1955, Syracuse, NY BR/TR, 6'.5", 185 lbs. Deb: 4/15/1932																										
1932	Phi-N	2	2	.500	14	2	0	0	0	34^1	38	18	14	2	2	22	15	1.748	3.67	120	5.26	.273	0	.000	3	2	0.2
1933	Phi-N	1	3	.250	10	5	4	1	0	48	38	13	13	4	1	10	9	1.000	2.44	156	2.26	.220	2	.125	7	5	0.7
1934	Phi-N	1	3	.250	27	5	0	0	0	65^1	114	72	67	13	3	23	13	2.097	9.23	51	9.52	.384	1	.056	-34	0	-3.5
Total	3	4	8	.333	51	12	4	1	0	147^2	190	103	94	19	6	55	37	1.659	5.73	79	6.17	.312	3	.075	-23	7	-2.5
• GRACE, Mike	Michael James Grace b: 6/20/1970, Joliet, IL BR/TR, 6'4", 210 lbs. Deb: 9/1/1995																										
1995	Phi-N	1	1	.500	2	2	0	0	0	11^1	10	4	4	0	0	4	7	1.235	3.18	133	2.61	.238	0	.000	1	1	0.1
1996	Phi-N	7	2	.778	12	12	1	1	0	80	72	33	31	9	1	16	49	1.100	3.49	124	2.89	.238	4	.138	7	6	0.7
1997	Phi-N	3	2	.600	6	6	1	1	0	39	32	16	15	3	1	10	26	1.077	3.46	123	2.64	.230	1	.083	4	3	0.3
1998	Phi-N	4	7	.364	21	15	0	0	0	90^1	116	61	55	10	8	30	46	1.616	5.48	79	5.85	.312	2	.087	-12	2	-1.2
1999	Phi-N	1	4	.200	27	5	0	0	0	55	80	48	47	5	6	30	28	2.000	7.69	61	7.90	.346	0	.000	-19	0	-1.8
Total	5	16	16	.500	68	40	2	2	0	275^2	310	162	152	27	16	90	156	1.451	4.96	89	4.82	.285	7	.096	-19	12	-2.0
• GRAFF, John	John F. Graff b: 11/1866, Washington, DC Deb: 7/19/1893																										
1893	Was-N	0	1	.000	2	1	1	0	0	12	21	21	15	2	1	13	4	2.833	11.25	41	12.71	.372	1	.200	-9	0	-0.7
• GRAHAM, Bill	William Albert Graham b: 1/21/1937, Flemingsburg, KY BR/TR, 6'3", 217 lbs. Deb: 10/2/1966																										
1966	Det-A	0	0	....	1	0	0	0	0	2	2	0	0	0	0	0	2	1.000	0.00	....	1.95	.250	0	....	1	0	0.1
1967	NY-N	1	2	.333	5	3	1	0	0	27^1	20	10	8	3	0	11	14	1.134	2.63	129	2.73	.200	1	.125	2	2	0.2
Total	2	1	2	.333	6	3	1	0	0	29^1	22	10	8	3	0	11	16	1.125	2.45	138	2.68	.204	1	.125	3	2	0.3
• GRAHAM, Oscar	Oscar M. Graham b: 7/20/1878, Plattsmouth, NE d: 10/15/1931, Moline, IL BL/TL, 6'.5", 180 lbs. Deb: 4/16/1907																										
1907	Was-A	4	9	.308	20	14	6	0	0	104	116	66	46	3	10	29	44	1.394	3.98	61	4.06	.285	11	.229	-14	2	-1.2
• GRAHAM, Peaches	George Frederick Graham b: 3/23/1877, Aledo, IL d: 7/25/1939, Long Beach, CA BR/TR, 5'9", 180 lbs. Deb: 9/14/1902 ♦																										
1903	Chi-N	0	1	.000	1	1	0	0	0	5	9	6	3	0	1	3	4	2.400	5.40	58	10.63	.429	0	.000	-1	0	-0.2
• GRAHAM, Skinny	Kyle Graham b: 8/14/1899, Oak Grove, AL d: 12/1/1973, Oak Grove, AL BR/TR, 6'2", 172 lbs. Deb: 9/3/1924																										
1924	Bos-N	0	4	.000	5	4	1	0	0	33	33	14	14	0	0	11	15	1.333	3.82	100	3.27	.287	0	.000	0	2	-0.1
1925	Bos-N	7	12	.368	34	23	5	0	1	157	177	90	77	6	3	62	32	1.522	4.41	91	4.39	.296	6	.136	-9	7	-1.1
1926	Bos-N	3	3	.500	15	4	1	0	0	36^1	54	32	32	3	2	19	7	2.009	7.93	45	7.54	.370	2	.167	-17	0	-1.8
1929	Det-A	1	3	.250	13	6	2	0	1	51^2	70	41	32	2	3	33	7	1.994	5.57	77	6.72	.340	2	.105	-6	1	-0.6
Total	4	11	22	.333	67	37	9	0	2	278	334	177	155	11	8	125	61	1.651	5.02	78	5.10	.314	10	.122	-32	10	-3.6
• GRAHAME, Bill	William James Grahame b: 7/22/1883, Owosso, MI d: 2/15/1936, Holt, MI TL, 6' Deb: 4/18/1908																										
1908	StL-A	6	7	.462	21	13	7	0	0	117^1	104	46	30	0	12	32	47	1.159	2.30	104	2.70	.240	5	.119	-4	6	-0.8
1909	StL-A	8	14	.364	34	21	13	3	1	187^1	171	78	65	3	5	60	82	1.233	3.12	77	2.99	.256	10	.159	-15	7	-1.7
1910	StL-A	0	8	.000	9	6	1	0	0	43	46	31	17	2	4	13	12	1.372	3.56	69	4.37	.297	2	.154	-5	0	-0.6
Total	3	14	29	.326	64	40	21	3	1	347^2	321	155	112	5	21	105	141	1.225	2.90	83	3.06	.256	17	.144	-24	13	-3.0
• GRAHE, Joe	Joseph Milton Grahe b: 8/14/1967, West Palm Beach, FL BR/TR, 6'1", 200 lbs. Deb: 8/4/1990																										
1990	Cal-A	3	4	.429	8	8	0	0	0	43^1	51	30	24	3	3	23	25	1.708	4.98	77	5.70	.293	0	....	-6	1	-0.6
1991	Cal-A	3	7	.300	18	10	1	0	0	73	84	43	39	2	3	33	40	1.603	4.81	85	4.77	.288	0	....	-7	2	-0.7
1992	Cal-A	5	6	.455	46	7	0	0	21	94^2	85	37	37	5	6	39	39	1.310	3.52	113	3.51	.246	0	....	4	12	0.4
1993	Cal-A	4	1	.800	45	0	0	0	11	56^2	54	22	18	5	2	25	31	1.394	2.86	158	3.89	.251	0	....	10	7	0.9
1994	Cal-A	2	5	.286	40	0	0	0	13	43^1	68	33	32	5	6	18	26	1.985	6.65	73	8.15	.362	0	....	-9	0	-0.8
1995	Col-N	4	3	.571	17	9	0	0	0	56^2	69	42	32	6	3	27	27	1.694	5.08	106	5.81	.301	5	.417	4	3	0.5
1999	Phi-N	1	4	.200	13	5	0	0	0	32^2	40	16	14	1	3	17	16	1.745	3.86	122	5.74	.308	1	.143	3	2	0.3
Total	7	22	30	.423	187	39	1	0	45	400^1	451	223	196	27	26	182	204	1.581	4.41	100	5.04	.287	6	.316	-1	27	0.1
• GRAMLY, Tommy	Bert Thomas Gramly b: 4/19/1945, Dallas, TX BR/TR, 6'3", 175 lbs. Deb: 4/18/1968																										
1968	Cle-A	0	1	.000	3	0	0	0	0	3^1	3	1	1	0	0	2	1	1.500	2.70	110	2.46	.250	0	....	0	0	0.0

YEAR TM-L	W	L	PCT	G	GS	CG	SH	SV	IP	H	R	ER	HR	HB	BB	SO	RAT	ERA	ERA+	CERA	OAV	BH	AVG	PR+	WS	TPW
• GRAMPP, Hank				Henry Erchardt Grampp b: 9/28/1903, New York, NY d: 3/24/1986, New York, NY BR/TR, 6'1", 185 lbs. Deb: 6/21/1927																						
1927 Chi-N	0	0	....	2	0	0	0	0	3	4	3	3	0	0	1	3	1.667	9.00	43	5.14	.333	0	....	-2	0	-0.2
1929 Chi-N	0	1	.000	1	1	0	0	0	2	4	6	6	0	1	3	0	3.500	27.00	17	17.07	.500	0	....	-5	0	-0.5
Total 2	0	1	.000	3	1	0	0	0	5	8	9	9	0	1	4	3	2.400	16.20	27	9.92	.400	0	....	-7	0	-0.6
• GRANGER, Jeff				Jeffery Adam Granger b: 12/16/1971, San Pedro, CA BR/TL, 6'4", 200 lbs. Deb: 9/16/1993																						
1993 KC-A	0	0	....	1	0	0	0	0	1	3	3	3	0	0	2	1	5.000	27.00	17	24.59	.500	0	....	-2	0	-0.2
1994 KC-A	0	1	.000	2	2	0	0	0	9^{1}	13	8	7	2	0	6	3	2.036	6.75	74	8.31	.325	0	....	-2	0	-0.2
1996 KC-A	0	0	....	15	0	0	0	0	16^{1}	21	13	12	3	2	10	11	1.898	6.61	76	7.96	.313	0	....	-3	0	-0.3
1997 Pit-N	0	0	....	9	0	0	0	0	5	10	10	10	3	0	8	4	3.600	18.00	24	22.14	.417	0	....	-8	0	-0.7
Total 4	0	1	.000	27	2	0	0	0	31^{2}	47	34	32	8	2	26	19	2.305	9.09	52	10.83	.343	0	....	-15	0	-1.4
• GRANGER, Wayne				Wayne Allan Granger b: 3/15/1944, Springfield, MA BR/TR, 6'2", 165 lbs. Deb: 6/5/1968																						
1968* StL-N	4	2	.667	34	0	0	0	4	44	40	14	11	2	2	12	27	1.182	2.25	129	2.79	.238	1	.200	3	4	0.3
1969 Cin-N	9	6	.600	**90**	0	0	0	27	144^{2}	143	64	45	10	7	40	68	1.265	2.80	134	3.36	.262	2	.095	15	15	1.6
1970* Cin-N	6	5	.545	67	0	0	0	**35**	84^{2}	79	33	25	5	1	27	38	1.252	2.66	157	3.05	.252	1	.100	14	15	1.3
1971 Cin-N	7	6	.538	**70**	0	0	0	11	100	94	39	37	8	1	28	51	1.220	3.33	97	3.12	.251	1	.143	-3	9	-0.2
1972 Min-A	4	6	.400	63	0	0	0	19	89^{2}	83	42	30	7	2	28	45	1.238	3.01	106	3.14	.243	2	.200	1	8	0.2
1973 StL-N	2	4	.333	33	0	0	0	5	46^{2}	50	29	22	3	2	21	14	1.521	4.24	86	4.44	.284	0	.000	-3	1	-0.3
NY-A	0	1	.000	7	0	0	0	0	15^{1}	19	7	3	1	1	3	10	1.435	1.76	208	4.19	.279	0	....	3	1	0.3
1974 Chi-A	0	0	....	5	0	0	0	0	7^{2}	16	8	7	1	0	3	4	2.478	8.22	45	11.70	.432	0	....	-4	0	-0.4
1975 Hou-N	2	5	.286	55	0	0	0	5	74	76	39	30	7	4	23	30	1.338	3.65	92	3.83	.264	0	.000	-3	3	-0.4
1976 Mon-N	1	0	1.000	27	0	0	0	2	32	32	15	13	3	2	16	16	1.500	3.66	102	4.45	.264	0	.000	0	2	0.0
Total 9	35	35	.500	451	0	0	0	108	638^{2}	632	290	223	47	22	201	303	1.304	3.14	111	3.52	.260	7	.103	24	58	2.4
• GRANT, George				George Addison Grant b: 1/6/1903, East Tallassee, AL d: 3/25/1986, Montgomery, AL BR/TR, 5'11.5", 175 lbs. Deb: 9/17/1923																						
1923 StL-A	0	0	....	4	0	0	0	0	8^{2}	15	7	5	0	0	3	2	2.077	5.19	80	7.34	.395	0	.000	-1	0	-0.1
1924 StL-A	1	2	.333	22	2	0	0	0	51^{1}	69	43	36	4	1	25	11	1.831	6.31	71	6.10	.325	0	.000	-11	0	-1.2
1925 StL-A	0	2	.000	12	0	0	0	0	16^{1}	26	15	11	2	0	8	7	2.082	6.06	77	8.39	.400	1	.250	-3	0	-0.3
1927 Cle-A	4	6	.400	25	3	2	0	1	74^{2}	85	46	37	1	0	40	19	1.674	4.46	94	4.66	.300	2	.095	-2	3	-0.4
1928 Cle-A	10	8	.556	28	18	6	1	0	155^{1}	196	102	87	7	2	76	39	**1.751**	5.04	82	5.39	.319	11	.183	-15	6	-1.6
1929 Cle-A	0	2	.000	12	0	0	0	0	24	41	29	28	2	0	23	5	2.667	10.50	42	10.99	.414	0	.000	-16	0	-1.5
1931 Pit-N	0	0	....	11	0	0	0	0	17	28	16	14	0	1	7	6	2.059	7.41	52	7.04	.364	0	.000	-7	0	-0.7
Total 7	15	20	.429	114	23	8	1	1	347^{1}	460	258	218	16	4	182	89	1.848	5.65	75	5.99	.331	14	.135	-54	9	-5.9
• GRANT, Jim				James Ronald Grant b: 8/4/1894, Coalville, IA d: 11/30/1985, Des Moines, IA BR/TL, 5'11", 180 lbs. Deb: 4/21/1923																						
1923 Phi-N	0	0	....	2	0	0	0	0	4	10	8	6	0	1	4	0	3.500	13.50	34	19.32	.588	0	.000	-4	0	-0.4
• GRANT, Mark				Mark Andrew Grant b: 10/24/1963, Aurora, IL BR/TR, 6'2", 205 lbs. Deb: 4/27/1984																						
1984 SF-N	1	4	.200	11	10	0	0	1	53^{2}	56	40	38	6	1	19	32	1.398	6.37	55	4.32	.272	0	.000	-16	0	-1.8
1986 SF-N	0	1	.000	4	1	0	0	0	10	6	4	4	0	0	5	5	1.100	3.60	98	1.85	.176	0	.000	-0	0	0.0
1987 SF-N	1	2	.333	16	8	0	0	1	61	66	29	24	6	1	21	32	1.426	3.54	109	4.25	.282	1	.083	1	3	0.1
SD-N	6	7	.462	17	17	2	1	0	102^{1}	104	59	53	16	0	52	58	1.524	4.66	85	4.94	.263	3	.094	-9	3	-1.0
Yr.	7	9	.438	33	25	2	1	1	163^{1}	170	88	77	22	1	73	90	1.488	4.24	92	4.68	.270	4	.091	-8	6	-0.9
1988 SD-N	2	8	.200	33	11	0	0	0	97^{2}	97	41	40	14	2	36	61	1.362	3.69	92	4.31	.268	0	.000	-5	3	-0.6
1989 SD-N	8	2	.800	50	0	0	0	2	116^{1}	105	45	43	11	3	32	69	1.178	3.33	105	3.17	.248	1	.050	1	8	0.1
1990 SD-N	1	1	.500	26	0	0	0	0	39	47	23	21	5	0	19	29	1.692	4.85	79	5.44	.305	1	.500	-5	1	-0.4
Atl-N	1	2	.333	33	1	0	0	3	52^{1}	61	30	27	4	1	18	40	1.510	4.64	87	4.61	.293	1	.250	-2	3	-0.2
Yr.	2	3	.400	59	1	0	0	3	91^{1}	108	53	48	9	1	37	69	1.588	4.73	83	4.97	.298	2	.333	-7	4	-0.6
1992 Sea-A	2	4	.333	23	10	0	0	0	81	100	39	35	6	2	22	42	1.506	3.89	102	4.87	.311	0	....	1	4	0.1
1993 Hou-N	0	0	....	6	0	0	0	0	11	11	4	1	0	0	5	6	1.455	0.82	473	3.41	.275	0	....	4	1	0.4
Col-N	0	1	.000	14	0	0	0	1	14^{1}	23	20	20	4	0	6	8	2.023	12.56	38	9.69	.377	0	....	-12	0	-1.2
Yr.	0	1	.000	20	0	0	0	1	25^{1}	34	24	21	4	0	11	14	1.776	7.46	63	6.96	.337	0	....	-8	1	-0.8
Total 8	22	32	.407	233	58	2	1	8	638^{2}	676	334	306	72	10	235	382	1.426	4.31	87	4.43	.277	7	.067	-42	26	-4.6
• GRANT, Mudcat				James Timothy "Jim" Grant b: 8/13/1935, Lacoochee, FL BR/TR, 6'1", 186 lbs. Deb: 4/17/1958																						
1958 Cle-A	10	11	.476	44	28	11	1	4	204	173	93	87	20	1	104	111	1.358	3.84	95	3.58	.228	5	.076	-5	9	-1.0
1959 Cle-A	10	7	.588	38	19	6	1	3	165^{1}	140	80	76	23	2	81	85	1.337	4.14	89	3.90	.232	11	.200	-10	8	-0.9
1960 Cle-A	9	8	.529	33	19	5	0	0	159^{2}	147	88	78	26	2	78	75	1.409	4.40	85	4.40	.243	16	.281	-12	6	-0.9
1961 Cle-A	15	9	.625	35	35	11	3	0	244^{2}	207	118	105	32	3	109	146	1.292	3.86	102	3.63	.227	15	.170	2	14	0.3
1962 Cle-A	7	10	.412	26	23	6	1	0	149^{2}	128	75	71	24	0	81	90	1.396	4.27	91	4.26	.233	8	.151	-8	7	-0.8
1963 Cle-A★	13	14	.481	38	32	10	2	1	229^{1}	213	107	94	30	4	87	157	1.308	3.69	98	3.82	.243	13	.188	-0	13	0.3
1964 Cle-A	3	4	.429	13	9	1	0	0	62	82	41	41	11	1	25	43	1.726	5.95	61	6.72	.324	6	.273	-15	1	-1.1
Min-A	11	9	.550	26	23	10	1	1	166	162	73	52	21	0	36	75	1.193	2.82	127	3.34	.248	10	.167	16	10	1.7
Yr.	14	13	.519	39	32	11	1	1	228	244	114	93	32	1	61	118	1.338	3.67	98	4.26	.270	16	.195	1	11	0.6
1965* Min-A★	**21**	7	.750	41	39	14	**6**	0	270^{1}	252	107	99	34	0	61	142	1.158	3.30	108	3.22	.247	15	.155	5	17	0.7
1966 Min-A	13	13	.500	35	35	10	3	0	249	248	104	90	23	6	49	110	1.193	3.25	110	3.29	.260	15	.192	11	16	1.4
1967 Min-A	5	6	.455	27	14	2	0	0	95^{1}	121	56	50	10	1	17	50	1.448	4.72	73	4.88	.315	5	.179	-12	1	-1.3
1968 LA-N	6	4	.600	37	4	1	0	3	94^{2}	77	29	22	1	6	19	35	1.014	2.09	132	2.03	.226	4	.129	6	8	0.7
1969 Mon-N	1	6	.143	11	10	1	0	0	50^{2}	64	33	27	7	1	14	20	1.539	4.80	77	5.30	.299	2	.125	-6	0	-0.7
StL-N	7	5	.583	30	3	1	0	7	63^{1}	62	31	29	9	2	22	35	1.326	4.12	87	3.93	.252	5	.294	-4	5	-0.3
Yr.	8	11	.421	41	13	2	0	7	114	126	64	56	16	3	36	55	1.421	4.42	82	4.54	.274	7	.212	-10	5	-1.0
1970 Oak-A	6	2	.750	72	0	0	0	24	123^{1}	104	26	25	8	3	30	54	1.086	1.82	194	2.53	.235	2	.222	22	20	2.5
Pit-N	2	1	.667	8	0	0	0	0	12	8	3	3	2	0	2	4	.833	2.25	173	1.99	.190	0	.000	2	2	0.2
1971 Pit-N	5	3	.625	42	0	0	0	7	75	79	32	30	8	1	28	22	1.427	3.60	95	4.24	.274	2	.250	-2	5	-0.2
* Oak-A	1	0	1.000	15	0	0	0	3	27^{1}	25	9	6	3	0	6	13	1.134	1.98	169	2.99	.243	1	.333	4	3	0.4
Total 14	145	119	.549	571	293	89	18	53	2441^{2}	2292	1105	985	292	33	849	1267	1.286	3.63	100	3.71	.248	135	.178	-7	145	1.1
• GRAPENTHIN, Rick				Richard Ray Grapenthin b: 4/16/1958, Linn Grove, IA BR/TR, 6'2", 205 lbs. Deb: 5/3/1983																						
1983 Mon-N	0	1	.000	1	0	0	0	0	4	4	4	4	2	0	1	3	1.250	9.00	40	6.41	.267	0	.000	-2	0	-0.3
1984 Mon-N	1	2	.333	13	1	0	0	2	23	19	9	9	3	0	7	9	1.130	3.52	97	3.03	.235	1	.200	-1	2	-0.1
1985 Mon-N	0	0	....	5	0	0	0	0	7	13	11	11	0	1	8	4	3.000	14.14	24	11.57	.394	1	1.000	-8	0	-0.8
Total 3	1	3	.250	19	1	0	0	2	34	36	24	24	5	1	16	16	1.529	6.35	54	5.19	.279	2	.286	-11	2	-1.2
• GRASMICK, Lou				Louis Junior Grasmick b: 9/11/1924, Baltimore, MD BR/TR, 6', 195 lbs. Deb: 4/22/1948																						
1948 Phi-N	0	0	....	2	0	0	0	0	5	3	4	4	1	0	8	2	2.200	7.20	55	7.04	.176	1	1.000	-2	0	-0.1
• GRATE, Don				Donald "Buckeye" Grate b: 8/27/1923, Greenfield, OH BR/TR, 6'2.5", 180 lbs. Deb: 7/6/1945																						
1945 Phi-N	0	1	.000	4	2	0	0	0	8^{1}	18	16	16	0	0	12	6	3.600	17.28	22	15.22	.439	0	.000	-12	0	-1.3
1946 Phi-N	1	0	1.000	3	0	0	0	0	8	4	1	1	0	0	2	2	.750	1.13	305	1.02	.160	0	.000	2	1	0.2
Total 2	1	1	.500	7	2	0	0	0	16^{1}	22	17	17	0	0	14	8	2.204	9.37	41	8.26	.333	0	.000	-10	1	-1.0
• GRATER, Mark				Mark Anthony Grater b: 1/19/1964, Rochester, PA BR/TR, 5'10", 205 lbs. Deb: 6/12/1991																						
1991 StL-N	0	0	....	3	0	0	0	0	3	5	0	0	0	0	2	0	2.333	0.00	....	8.83	.385	0	....	1	1	0.1
1993 Det-A	0	0	....	6	0	0	0	0	5	6	3	3	0	0	4	4	2.000	5.40	79	5.47	.286	0	....	-1	0	-0.1
Total 2	0	0	....	9	0	0	0	0	8	11	3	3	0	0	6	4	2.125	3.38	127	6.73	.324	0	....	1	1	0.1
• GRATEROL, Beiker				Beiker Graterol b: 11/9/1974, Lara, Venezuela BR/TR, 6'2", 165 lbs. Deb: 4/9/1999																						
1999 Det-A	0	1	.000	1	1	0	0	0	4	4	7	7	3	0	4	2	2.000	15.75	31	11.57	.250	0	....	-5	0	-0.4

• GRAVES, Danny — Daniel Peter "Baby-faced Assassin" Graves b: 8/7/1973, Saigon, South Vietnam BR/TR, 5'11", 200 lbs. Deb: 7/13/1996

YEAR	TM-L	W	L	PCT	G	GS	CG	SH	SV	IP	H	R	ER	HR	HB	BB	SO	RAT	ERA	ERA+	CERA	OAV	BH	AVG	PR+	WS	TPW
1996	Cle-A	2	0	1.000	15	0	0	0	0	29^2	29	18	15	2	0	10	22	1.315	4.55	108	3.37	.246	0	....	1	2	0.1
1997	Cle-A	0	0	....	5	0	0	0	0	11^1	15	8	6	2	0	9	4	2.118	4.76	98	8.52	.326	0	....	0	0	0.0
	Cin-N	0	0	....	10	0	0	0	0	14^2	26	14	10	0	0	11	7	2.523	6.14	70	9.52	.413	0	.000	-3	0	-0.3
1998	Cin-N	2	1	.667	62	0	0	0	8	81^1	76	31	30	6	2	28	44	1.279	3.32	129	3.38	.251	0	.000	9	8	0.8
1999	Cin-N	8	7	.533	75	0	0	0	27	111	90	42	38	10	2	49	69	1.252	3.08	151	3.25	.227	0	.000	16	16	1.5
2000	Cin-N★	10	5	.667	66	0	0	0	30	91^1	81	31	26	8	3	42	53	1.347	2.56	184	3.64	.243	1	.500	21	18	2.1
2001	Cin-N	6	5	.545	66	0	0	0	32	80^1	83	41	37	7	4	18	49	1.257	4.15	110	3.59	.268	1	.250	5	11	0.6
2002	Cin-N	7	3	.700	68	4	0	0	32	98^2	99	37	35	7	3	25	58	1.257	3.19	133	3.33	.264	0	.000	11	17	1.1
2003	Cin-N	4	15	.211	30	26	2	1	2	169	204	108	100	30	7	41	60	1.450	5.33	80	5.32	.298	6	.111	-19	3	-2.1
Total	8	39	36	.520	397	30	2	1	131	687^1	703	330	297	72	21	233	366	1.362	3.89	114	4.10	.268	8	.105	41	75	3.7

• GRAY, Charlie — Charles A. Gray b: 6/1864, Indianapolis, IN d: 6/1/1900, Indianapolis, IN Deb: 4/23/1890

YEAR	TM-L	W	L	PCT	G	GS	CG	SH	SV	IP	H	R	ER	HR	HB	BB	SO	RAT	ERA	ERA+	CERA	OAV	BH	AVG	PR+	WS	TPW
1890	Pit-N	1	4	.200	5	4	3	0	0	31	48	35	26	0	1	24	10	2.323	7.55	44	....	.344	3	.200	-13	0	-1.2

• GRAY, Chummy — George Edward Gray b: 7/17/1873, Rockland, ME d: 8/14/1913, Rockland, ME TR, 5'11.5", 163 lbs. Deb: 9/14/1899

YEAR	TM-L	W	L	PCT	G	GS	CG	SH	SV	IP	H	R	ER	HR	HB	BB	SO	RAT	ERA	ERA+	CERA	OAV	BH	AVG	PR+	WS	TPW
1899	Pit-N	3	3	.500	9	7	6	0	0	70^2	85	35	27	1	4	24	9	1.542	3.44	111	4.47	.297	1	.038	3	4	0.0

• GRAY, Dave — David Alexander Gray b: 1/7/1943, Ogden, UT BR/TR, 6'1", 190 lbs. Deb: 6/14/1964

YEAR	TM-L	W	L	PCT	G	GS	CG	SH	SV	IP	H	R	ER	HR	HB	BB	SO	RAT	ERA	ERA+	CERA	OAV	BH	AVG	PR+	WS	TPW
1964	Bos-A	0	0	....	9	1	0	0	0	13	18	20	13	3	0	20	17	2.923	9.00	43	12.64	.321	1	1.000	-7	0	-0.7

• GRAY, Dolly — Samuel David "Sad Sam" Gray b: 10/15/1897, Van Alstyne, TX d: 4/16/1953, McKinney, TX BR/TR, 5'10", 175 lbs. Deb: 4/19/1924

YEAR	TM-L	W	L	PCT	G	GS	CG	SH	SV	IP	H	R	ER	HR	HB	BB	SO	RAT	ERA	ERA+	CERA	OAV	BH	AVG	PR+	WS	TPW
1924	Phi-A	8	7	.533	34	19	8	2	2	151^2	169	95	67	5	6	89	54	1.701	3.98	108	4.87	.284	10	.175	7	9	0.4
1925	Phi-A	16	8	.667	32	28	14	4	3	203^2	199	90	74	11	3	63	80	1.286	3.27	142	3.30	.260	12	.179	33	19	2.9
1926	Phi-A	11	12	.478	38	18	5	0	0	150^2	164	81	61	9	4	50	82	1.420	3.64	114	4.01	.279	11	.216	9	10	1.0
1927	Phi-A	9	6	.600	37	13	3	1	3	133^1	153	79	68	4	4	51	49	1.530	4.59	93	4.39	.295	8	.190	-3	7	-0.4
1928	StL-A	20	12	.625	35	31	21	2	3	262^2	256	119	93	11	1	86	102	1.302	3.19	132	3.11	.260	19	.188	29	23	2.7
1929	StL-A	18	15	.545	43	**37**	23	**4**	1	**305**	336	142	126	18	1	96	109	1.416	3.72	119	3.98	.285	19	.184	21	24	1.8
1930	StL-A	4	15	.211	27	24	7	0	0	167^2	215	133	117	17	4	52	51	1.592	6.28	78	5.37	.316	11	.204	-28	3	-2.7
1931	StL-A	11	24	.314	43	**37**	13	0	2	258	323	187	146	20	4	54	88	1.461	5.09	91	4.46	.297	14	.177	-14	10	-1.4
1932	StL-A	7	12	.368	52	18	7	3	4	206^2	250	126	104	9	1	53	79	1.466	4.53	107	4.15	.294	13	.210	6	13	0.6
1933	StL-A	7	4	.636	38	6	0	0	4	112	131	55	51	7	1	45	36	1.571	4.10	113	4.82	.301	7	.219	5	10	0.6
Total	10	111	115	.491	379	231	101	16	22	1951^1	2196	1107	907	111	29	639	730	1.453	4.18	108	4.14	.286	124	.191	65	128	5.6

• GRAY, Dolly — William Denton Gray b: 12/3/1878, Houghton, MI d: 4/3/1956, Yuba City, CA BL/TL, 6'2", 160 lbs. Deb: 4/13/1909

YEAR	TM-L	W	L	PCT	G	GS	CG	SH	SV	IP	H	R	ER	HR	HB	BB	SO	RAT	ERA	ERA+	CERA	OAV	BH	AVG	PR+	WS	TPW
1909	Was-A	5	19	.208	36	26	19	0	0	218	210	123	87	1	9	77	87	**1.317**	3.59	68	3.22	.258	13	.146	-26	3	-3.1
1910	Was-A	8	19	.296	34	29	21	3	0	229	216	106	67	3	10	65	84	1.227	2.63	94	2.89	.249	21	.247	-8	10	-0.5
1911	Was-A	2	13	.133	28	15	6	0	0	121	160	90	68	4	3	40	42	1.653	5.06	65	5.43	.331	10	.227	-24	1	-2.3
Total	3	15	51	.227	98	70	46	3	0	568	586	319	222	8	22	182	213	1.352	3.52	76	3.56	.271	44	.202	-58	14	-5.9

• GRAY, Jeff — Jeffrey Edward Gray b: 4/10/1963, Richmond, VA BR/TR, 6'1", 175 lbs. Deb: 6/21/1988

YEAR	TM-L	W	L	PCT	G	GS	CG	SH	SV	IP	H	R	ER	HR	HB	BB	SO	RAT	ERA	ERA+	CERA	OAV	BH	AVG	PR+	WS	TPW
1988	Cin-N	0	0	....	5	0	0	0	0	9^1	12	4	4	0	0	4	5	1.714	3.86	93	4.42	.333	0	.000	-0	0	-0.1
1990*	Bos-A	2	4	.333	41	0	0	0	9	50^2	53	27	25	3	1	15	50	1.342	4.44	92	3.61	.268	0	....	-1	4	-0.1
1991	Bos-A	2	3	.400	50	0	0	0	1	61^2	39	17	16	7	1	10	41	.795	2.34	184	1.53	.181	0	....	14	8	1.4
Total	3	4	7	.364	96	0	0	0	10	121^2	104	48	45	10	2	29	96	1.093	3.33	123	2.62	.231	0	.000	12	12	1.2

• GRAY, Johnny — John Leonard Gray b: 12/11/1927, West Palm Beach, FL BR/TR, 6'4", 226 lbs. Deb: 7/18/1954

YEAR	TM-L	W	L	PCT	G	GS	CG	SH	SV	IP	H	R	ER	HR	HB	BB	SO	RAT	ERA	ERA+	CERA	OAV	BH	AVG	PR+	WS	TPW
1954	Phi-A	3	12	.200	18	16	5	0	0	105	111	83	76	10	0	91	51	1.924	6.51	60	6.06	.273	1	.029	-29	0	-3.4
1955	KC-A	0	3	.000	8	5	0	0	0	26^2	28	23	19	2	1	24	11	1.950	6.41	65	6.40	.277	1	.125	-7	0	-0.7
1957	Cle-A	1	3	.250	7	3	1	1	0	20	21	17	13	1	0	13	3	1.700	5.85	64	4.99	.288	0	.000	-4	0	-0.5
1958	Phi-N	0	0	....	15	0	0	0	0	17^1	12	9	8	3	0	14	10	1.500	4.15	95	4.41	.222	0	.000	-0	1	0.0
Total	4	4	18	.182	48	24	6	1	0	169	172	132	116	16	1	142	75	1.858	6.18	64	5.82	.271	2	.043	-40	1	-4.6

• GRAY, Ted — Ted Glenn Gray b: 12/31/1924, Detroit, MI BB/TL, 5'11", 175 lbs. Deb: 5/15/1946

YEAR	TM-L	W	L	PCT	G	GS	CG	SH	SV	IP	H	R	ER	HR	HB	BB	SO	RAT	ERA	ERA+	CERA	OAV	BH	AVG	PR+	WS	TPW
1946	Det-A	0	2	.000	3	2	0	0	1	11^2	17	12	11	4	0	5	5	1.886	8.49	43	9.05	.340	0	.000	-6	0	-0.6
1948	Det-A	6	2	.750	26	11	3	1	0	85^1	73	43	40	2	3	72	60	1.699	4.22	104	4.30	.236	7	.241	3	6	0.4
1949	Det-A	10	10	.500	34	27	8	3	1	195	163	83	76	11	5	103	96	1.364	3.51	119	3.30	.227	8	.127	16	14	1.3
1950	Det-A★	10	7	.588	27	21	7	0	1	149^1	139	85	73	22	2	72	102	1.413	4.40	107	4.31	.248	7	.140	4	9	0.2
1951	Det-A	7	14	.333	34	28	9	1	1	197^1	194	103	89	17	6	95	131	1.465	4.06	103	4.14	.256	9	.143	4	11	0.2
1952	Det-A	12	17	.414	35	32	13	2	0	224	212	118	103	21	3	101	138	1.397	4.14	92	3.87	.249	13	.171	-4	9	-0.6
1953	Det-A	10	15	.400	30	28	8	0	0	176	166	102	90	25	7	76	115	1.375	4.60	88	4.26	.252	14	.230	-5	6	-0.3
1954	Det-A	3	5	.375	19	10	2	0	0	72	70	48	43	8	2	56	29	1.750	5.38	69	5.48	.268	1	.045	-14	0	-1.7
1955	Chi-A	0	0	....	2	1	0	0	0	3	9	6	6	0	0	2	1	3.667	18.00	22	17.87	.500	0	....	-5	0	-0.5
	Cle-A	0	0	....	2	0	0	0	0	2	5	4	4	1	0	2	1	3.500	18.00	22	21.61	.455	0	....	-3	0	-0.3
	NY-A	0	0	....	1	1	0	0	0	3	3	1	1	0	0	0	1	1.000	3.00	125	2.18	.300	0	.000	0	0	0.0
	Bal-A	1	2	.333	9	1	0	0	0	15^1	21	19	14	3	0	11	8	2.087	8.22	46	8.32	.344	0	.000	-7	0	-0.8
	Yr.	1	2	.333	14	3	0	0	0	23^1	38	30	25	4	0	15	11	2.271	9.64	40	9.90	.380	0	.000	-15	0	-1.5
Total	9	59	74	.444	222	162	50	7	4	1134	1072	624	550	114	28	595	687	1.470	4.37	94	4.25	.251	59	.159	-16	55	-2.7

• GRBA, Eli — Eli Grba b: 8/9/1934, Chicago, IL BR/TR, 6'2", 207 lbs. Deb: 7/10/1959

YEAR	TM-L	W	L	PCT	G	GS	CG	SH	SV	IP	H	R	ER	HR	HB	BB	SO	RAT	ERA	ERA+	CERA	OAV	BH	AVG	PR+	WS	TPW
1959	NY-A	2	5	.286	19	6	0	0	0	50^1	52	44	36	6	0	39	23	1.808	6.44	57	5.85	.269	3	.214	-16	0	-1.5
1960*	NY-A	6	4	.600	24	9	1	0	1	80^2	65	45	33	9	2	46	32	1.376	3.68	97	3.80	.226	5	.238	-3	4	-0.1
1961	LA-A	11	13	.458	40	30	8	0	2	211^2	197	119	100	26	7	114	105	1.469	4.25	106	4.41	.242	15	.234	8	13	1.3
1962	LA-A	8	9	.471	40	29	1	0	1	176^1	185	101	89	19	2	75	90	1.474	4.54	85	4.45	.267	12	.207	-12	6	-0.9
1963	LA-A	1	2	.333	12	1	0	0	0	17^1	14	9	9	2	1	10	5	1.385	4.67	73	3.84	.222	0	.000	-2	0	-0.3
Total	5	28	33	.459	135	75	10	0	4	536^1	513	318	267	62	12	284	255	1.486	4.48	89	4.45	.250	35	.219	-25	23	-1.5

• GREASON, Bill — William Henry "Booster" Greason b: 9/3/1924, Atlanta, GA BR/TR, 5'10", 170 lbs. Deb: 5/31/1954

YEAR	TM-L	W	L	PCT	G	GS	CG	SH	SV	IP	H	R	ER	HR	HB	BB	SO	RAT	ERA	ERA+	CERA	OAV	BH	AVG	PR+	WS	TPW
1954	StL-N	0	1	.000	3	2	0	0	0	4	8	8	6	4	0	4	2	3.000	13.50	30	22.62	.421	0	.000	-4	0	-0.4

• GREASON, John — John R. Greason TL Deb: 8/27/1873

YEAR	TM-L	W	L	PCT	G	GS	CG	SH	SV	IP	H	R	ER	HR	HB	BB	SO	RAT	ERA	ERA+	CERA	OAV	BH	AVG	PR+	WS	TPW
1873	Was-n	1	6	.143	7	7	7	0	0	63	112	....	38	3	....	7	3	**1.889**	5.43	62	....	.346	4	.143	-14	....	-1.1

• GREEN, Chris — Christopher De Wayne Green b: 9/5/1960, Los Angeles, CA BL/TL, 6'2", 214 lbs. Deb: 4/17/1984

YEAR	TM-L	W	L	PCT	G	GS	CG	SH	SV	IP	H	R	ER	HR	HB	BB	SO	RAT	ERA	ERA+	CERA	OAV	BH	AVG	PR+	WS	TPW
1984	Pit-N	0	0	....	4	0	0	0	0	3	5	2	2	0	0	1	3	2.000	6.00	60	7.34	.417	0	....	-1	0	-0.1

• GREEN, Dallas — George Dallas Green b: 8/4/1934, Newport, DE BL/TR, 6'5", 210 lbs. Deb: 6/18/1960 M

YEAR	TM-L	W	L	PCT	G	GS	CG	SH	SV	IP	H	R	ER	HR	HB	BB	SO	RAT	ERA	ERA+	CERA	OAV	BH	AVG	PR+	WS	TPW
1960	Phi-N	3	6	.333	23	10	5	1	0	108^2	100	54	49	10	2	44	51	1.325	4.06	96	3.61	.248	7	.206	-3	5	-0.2
1961	Phi-N	2	4	.333	42	10	1	1	1	128	160	77	69	8	2	47	51	1.617	4.85	84	5.21	.315	5	.152	-13	4	-1.2
1962	Phi-N	6	6	.500	37	10	2	0	1	129^1	145	58	55	10	5	43	58	1.454	3.83	101	4.49	.289	2	.063	-0	8	-0.1
1963	Phi-N	7	5	.583	40	14	4	0	2	120	134	53	43	10	2	38	68	1.433	3.23	100	4.27	.286	3	.086	-2	6	-0.4
1964	Phi-N	2	1	.667	25	0	0	0	0	42	63	31	27	4	2	14	21	1.833	5.79	60	7.14	.362	0	.000	-11	0	-1.2
1965	Was-A	0	0	....	6	2	0	0	0	14^1	14	6	5	0	0	3	6	1.186	3.14	111	2.47	.241	0	.000	1	1	0.0
1966	NY-N	0	0	....	4	0	0	0	0	5	6	3	3	2	0	2	1	1.600	5.40	67	7.77	.333	0	....	-1	0	-0.1
1967	Phi-N	0	0	....	8	0	0	0	0	15	25	16	15	2	1	6	12	2.067	9.00	38	8.44	.362	0	.000	-9	0	-1.0
Total	8	20	22	.476	185	46	12	2	4	562^1	647	298	266	46	14	197	268	1.501	4.26	87	4.72	.294	17	.120	-38	24	-4.2

• GREEN, Ed — Edward M. Green b: 1850, Philadelphia, PA Deb: 4/22/1890

YEAR	TM-L	W	L	PCT	G	GS	CG	SH	SV	IP	H	R	ER	HR	HB	BB	SO	RAT	ERA	ERA+	CERA	OAV	BH	AVG	PR+	WS	TPW
1890	Phi-a	7	15	.318	25	22	20	1	1	191	267	184	123	4	6	94	56	**1.890**	5.80	66	....	.321	15	.119	-31	3	-3.7

YEAR	TM-L	W	L	PCT	G	GS	CG	SH	SV	IP	H	R	ER	HR	HB	BB	SO	RAT	ERA	ERA+	CERA	OAV	BH	AVG	PR+	WS	TPW
• GREEN, Fred	Fred Allen Green b: 9/14/1933, Titusville, NJ d: 12/22/1996, Titusville, NJ BR/TL, 6'4", 190 lbs. Deb: 4/15/1959																										
1959	Pit-N	1	2	.333	17	1	0	0	1	37^1	37	16	13	2	0	15	20	1.393	3.13	123	3.34	.259	0	.000	3	3	0.2
1960*	Pit-N	8	4	.667	45	0	0	0	3	70	61	26	25	4	1	33	49	1.343	3.21	117	3.19	.243	3	.375	3	7	0.6
1961	Pit-N	0	0	....	13	0	0	0	0	20^2	27	16	11	2	0	9	4	1.742	4.79	83	5.87	.321	0	.000	-2	0	-0.2
1962	Was-A	0	1	.000	5	0	0	0	0	7	7	6	5	3	0	6	2	1.857	6.43	63	8.01	.250	0	....	-2	0	-0.2
1964	Pit-N	0	0	....	8	0	0	0	0	7^1	10	1	1	1	0	0	2	1.364	1.23	286	4.66	.323	0	....	2	1	0.2
Total	**5**	**9**	**7**	**.563**	**88**	**1**	**0**	**0**	**4**	**142^1**	**142**	**65**	**55**	**12**	**1**	**63**	**77**	**1.440**	**3.48**	**111**	**3.93**	**.264**	**3**	**.176**	**4**	**11**	**0.6**
• GREEN, Harvey	Harvey George "Buck" Green b: 2/9/1915, Kenosha, WI d: 7/24/1970, Franklin, LA BB/TR, 6'2.5", 185 lbs. Deb: 9/12/1935																										
1935	Bro-N	0	0	....	2	0	0	0	0	1	2	1	1	0	1	3	0	5.000	9.00	44	24.24	.400	0	....	-1	0	-0.1
• GREEN, Jason	David Jason Green b: 6/5/1975, Port Hope, Canada BR/TR, 6'1", 190 lbs. Deb: 7/23/2000																										
2000	Hou-N	1	1	.500	14	0	0	0	0	17^2	15	16	13	3	1	20	19	1.981	6.62	73	6.88	.234	0	.000	-3	0	-0.3
• GREEN, Steve	Steve Green b: 1/26/1978, Greenfield Park, Canada BR/TR, 6'2", 195 lbs. Deb: 4/7/2001																										
2001	Ana-A	0	0	....	1	1	0	0	0	6	4	2	2	0	0	6	4	1.667	3.00	152	3.79	.190	0	....	1	0	0.1
• GREEN, Tyler	Tyler Scott Green b: 2/18/1970, Springfield, OH BR/TR, 6'5", 185 lbs. Deb: 4/9/1993																										
1993	Phi-N	0	0	....	3	2	0	0	0	7^1	16	9	6	1	0	5	7	2.864	7.36	54	13.97	.444	0	.000	-3	0	-0.3
1995	Phi-N★	8	9	.471	26	25	4	2	0	140^2	157	86	83	15	4	66	85	1.585	5.31	80	5.26	.290	8	.182	-18	5	-1.6
1997	Phi-N	4	4	.500	14	14	0	0	0	76^2	72	50	42	8	1	45	58	1.526	4.93	86	4.47	.247	8	.308	-6	3	-0.3
1998	Phi-N	6	12	.333	27	27	0	0	0	159^1	142	97	89	23	9	85	113	1.425	5.03	86	4.53	.239	6	.146	-13	5	-1.3
Total	**4**	**18**	**25**	**.419**	**70**	**68**	**4**	**2**	**0**	**384**	**387**	**242**	**220**	**47**	**14**	**201**	**263**	**1.531**	**5.16**	**83**	**4.96**	**.265**	**22**	**.195**	**-39**	**13**	**-3.5**
• GREENE, June	Julius Foust Greene b: 6/25/1899, Ramseur, NC d: 3/19/1974, Glendora, CA BL/TR, 6'2.5", 185 lbs. Deb: 4/20/1928																										
1928	Phi-N	0	0	....	1	0	0	0	0	2	5	2	2	0	0	0	0	2.500	9.00	47	13.40	.556	3	.500	-1	0	0.1
1929	Phi-N	0	0	....	5	0	0	0	0	13^2	33	32	30	2	3	9	4	3.073	19.76	26	15.98	.465	4	.211	-22	0	-2.0
Total	**2**	**0**	**0**	**....**	**6**	**0**	**0**	**0**	**0**	**15^2**	**38**	**34**	**32**	**2**	**3**	**9**	**4**	**3.000**	**18.38**	**28**	**15.65**	**.475**	**7**	**.280**	**-23**	**0**	**-1.9**
• GREENE, Nelson	Nelson George "Lefty" Greene b: 9/20/1900, Philadelphia, PA d: 4/6/1983, Lebanon, PA BL/TL, 6', 185 lbs. Deb: 4/28/1924																										
1924	Bro-N	0	1	.000	4	1	0	0	0	9	14	6	4	1	0	2	3	1.778	4.00	94	6.69	.350	0	.000	-0	0	0.0
1925	Bro-N	2	0	1.000	11	0	0	0	1	22	45	28	26	4	0	7	4	2.364	10.64	39	10.96	.417	2	.286	-15	0	-1.4
Total	**2**	**2**	**1**	**.667**	**15**	**1**	**0**	**0**	**1**	**31**	**59**	**34**	**30**	**5**	**0**	**9**	**7**	**2.194**	**8.71**	**47**	**9.72**	**.399**	**2**	**.250**	**-15**	**0**	**-1.4**
• GREENE, Rick	Richard Douglas Greene b: 1/2/1971, Fort Knox, KY BR/TR, 6'5", 200 lbs. Deb: 6/19/1999																										
1999	Cin-N	0	0	....	1	0	0	0	0	5^2	7	4	3	2	0	1	3	1.412	4.76	98	6.18	.292	0	.000	-0	0	0.0
• GREENE, Tommy	Ira Thomas Greene b: 4/6/1967, Lumberton, NC BR/TR, 6'5", 227 lbs. Deb: 9/10/1989																										
1989	Atl-N	1	2	.333	4	4	1	1	0	26^1	22	12	12	5	0	6	17	1.063	4.10	89	3.12	.234	1	.100	-1	1	-0.2
1990	Atl-N	1	0	1.000	5	2	0	0	0	12^1	14	11	11	3	1	9	4	1.865	8.03	50	7.64	.286	0	.000	-5	0	-0.5
	Phi-N	2	3	.400	10	7	0	0	0	39	36	20	18	5	0	17	17	1.359	4.15	92	3.96	.247	2	.182	-2	2	-0.2
	Yr.	3	3	.500	15	9	0	0	0	51^1	50	31	29	8	1	26	21	1.481	5.08	77	4.85	.256	2	.167	-7	2	-0.7
1991	Phi-N	13	7	.650	36	27	3	2	0	207^2	177	85	78	19	3	66	154	1.170	3.38	108	2.93	.230	19	.268	7	17	1.6
1992	Phi-N	3	3	.500	13	12	0	0	0	64^1	75	39	38	5	0	34	39	1.694	5.32	66	5.27	.291	3	.125	-13	0	-1.4
1993*	Phi-N	16	4	.800	31	30	7	2	0	200	175	84	76	12	3	62	167	1.185	3.42	116	2.80	.233	16	.222	14	16	1.9
1994	Phi-N	2	0	1.000	7	7	0	0	0	35^2	37	20	18	5	0	22	28	1.654	4.54	95	5.42	.272	5	.385	-1	1	0.1
1995	Phi-N	0	5	.000	11	6	0	0	0	33^2	45	32	31	6	3	20	24	1.931	8.29	51	7.91	.319	0	.000	-15	0	-1.5
1997	Hou-N	0	1	.000	2	2	0	0	0	9	10	7	7	2	0	5	11	1.667	7.00	57	6.51	.286	1	.333	-3	0	-0.2
Total	**8**	**38**	**25**	**.603**	**119**	**97**	**11**	**5**	**0**	**628**	**591**	**310**	**289**	**62**	**10**	**241**	**461**	**1.325**	**4.14**	**93**	**3.75**	**.249**	**47**	**.221**	**-19**	**37**	**-0.5**
• GREENFIELD, Kent	Kent Greenfield b: 7/1/1902, Guthrie, KY d: 3/14/1978, Guthrie, KY BR/TR, 6'1", 180 lbs. Deb: 9/28/1924																										
1924	NY-N	0	1	.000	1	1	0	0	0	3	9	8	5	1	0	1	1	3.333	15.00	24	19.92	.500	0	....	-4	0	-0.4
1925	NY-N	12	8	.600	29	20	12	0	0	171^2	195	86	74	4	2	64	66	1.509	3.88	104	4.08	.288	5	.081	3	12	-0.3
1926	NY-N	13	12	.520	39	28	8	1	1	222^2	206	111	98	17	5	82	74	1.293	3.96	95	3.39	.251	6	.092	-8	12	-1.3
1927	NY-N	2	2	.500	12	1	0	0	0	20	39	25	21	3	2	13	4	2.600	9.45	41	11.92	.411	0	.000	-12	0	-1.3
	Bos-N	11	14	.440	27	26	11	1	0	190	203	92	81	3	5	59	59	1.379	3.84	97	3.53	.282	11	.172	1	10	-0.1
	Yr.	13	16	.448	39	27	11	1	0	210	242	117	102	6	7	72	63	1.495	4.37	85	4.33	.297	11	.167	-11	10	-1.3
1928	Bos-N	3	11	.214	32	20	5	0	0	143^2	173	100	85	6	5	60	30	1.622	5.32	73	4.87	.307	2	.053	-18	2	-2.1
1929	Bos-N	0	0	....	6	2	0	0	0	15^2	33	19	19	1	2	15	7	3.064	10.91	43	14.07	.465	0	.000	-11	0	-1.1
	Bro-N	0	0	....	6	0	0	0	0	8^2	13	8	8	1	0	3	1	1.846	8.31	56	6.71	.382	0	.000	-3	0	-0.3
	Yr.	0	0	....	12	2	0	0	0	24^1	46	27	27	2	2	18	8	2.630	9.99	47	11.45	.438	0	.000	-14	0	-1.4
Total	**6**	**41**	**48**	**.461**	**152**	**98**	**36**	**2**	**1**	**775^1**	**871**	**449**	**391**	**36**	**21**	**297**	**242**	**1.506**	**4.54**	**86**	**4.39**	**.290**	**24**	**.101**	**-52**	**36**	**-6.8**
• GREENING, John	John A. Greening b: 1848, Philadelphia, PA d: 7/28/1913, Philadelphia, PA Deb: 5/9/1888																										
1888	Was-N	0	1	.000	1	1	1	0	0	9	17	13	11	2	0	4	2	2.333	11.00	25	....	.388	0	.000	-8	0	-0.8
• GREENWOOD, Bob	Robert Chandler "Greenie" Greenwood b: 3/13/1928, Cananea, Mexico d: 9/1/1994, Hayward, CA BR/TR, 6'5", 200 lbs. Deb: 4/21/1954																										
1954	Phi-N	1	2	.333	11	4	0	0	0	36^2	28	16	13	2	0	18	9	1.255	3.19	127	2.70	.209	0	.000	3	2	0.3
1955	Phi-N	0	0	....	1	0	0	0	0	2^1	7	4	4	1	0	0	0	3.000	15.43	26	19.23	.500	0	.000	-3	0	-0.3
Total	**2**	**1**	**2**	**.333**	**12**	**4**	**0**	**0**	**0**	**39**	**35**	**20**	**17**	**3**	**0**	**18**	**9**	**1.359**	**3.92**	**103**	**3.69**	**.236**	**0**	**.000**	**0**	**2**	**0.0**
• GREER, Kenny	Kenneth William Greer b: 5/12/1967, Boston, MA BR/TR, 6'3", 210 lbs. Deb: 9/29/1993																										
1993	NY-N	1	0	1.000	1	0	0	0	0	1	0	0	0	0	0	0	2	.000	0.00	....	0.00	.000	0	....	0	0	0.0
1995	SF-N	0	2	.000	8	0	0	0	0	12	15	12	7	3	1	5	7	1.667	5.25	78	6.24	.288	0	.000	-2	0	-0.2
Total	**2**	**1**	**2**	**.333**	**9**	**0**	**0**	**0**	**0**	**13**	**15**	**12**	**7**	**3**	**1**	**5**	**9**	**1.538**	**4.85**	**84**	**5.76**	**.288**	**0**	**.000**	**-1**	**0**	**-0.1**
• GREGG, Dave	David Charles "Highpockets" Gregg b: 3/14/1891, Chehalis, WA d: 11/12/1965, Clarkston, WA BR/TR, 6'1", 185 lbs. Deb: 6/15/1913																										
1913	Cle-A	0	0	....	1	0	0	0	0	1	2	2	2	0	1	0	0	2.000	18.00	17	11.63	.400	0	....	-2	0	-0.2
• GREGG, Hal	Harold Dana "Skeets" Gregg b: 7/11/1921, Anaheim, CA d: 5/13/1991, Bishop, CA BR/TR, 6'3.5", 195 lbs. Deb: 8/18/1943																										
1943	Bro-N	0	3	.000	5	4	0	0	0	18^2	21	21	20	2	0	21	7	2.250	9.64	35	7.69	.304	0	.000	-13	0	-1.3
1944	Bro-N	9	16	.360	39	31	6	0	2	197^2	201	142	120	12	9	137	92	**1.710**	5.46	65	4.87	.258	14	.206	-35	2	-3.7
1945	Bro-N★	18	13	.581	42	34	13	2	2	254^1	221	116	98	5	8	120	139	1.341	3.47	108	3.06	.232	20	.220	9	17	1.3
1946	Bro-N	6	4	.600	26	16	4	1	2	117^1	103	46	39	3	1	44	54	1.253	2.99	113	2.78	.236	4	.125	4	8	0.3
1947*	Bro-N	4	5	.444	37	16	2	1	1	104^1	115	79	68	6	4	55	59	1.629	5.87	70	4.73	.272	9	.265	-22	0	-2.0
1948	Pit-N	2	4	.333	22	8	1	0	1	74^1	72	40	38	3	3	34	25	1.426	4.60	88	3.76	.255	6	.273	-5	4	-0.3
1949	Pit-N	1	1	.500	8	1	0	0	0	18^2	20	10	7	1	1	8	9	1.500	3.38	125	4.58	.303	0	.000	2	1	0.1
1950	Pit-N	0	1	.000	5	1	0	0	0	5^1	10	10	8	2	1	7	3	3.188	13.50	32	17.72	.400	0	.000	-5	0	-0.5
1952	NY-N	0	1	.000	16	4	1	0	1	36^1	42	22	19	7	2	17	13	1.624	4.71	79	5.93	.286	1	.125	-4	0	-0.4
Total	**9**	**40**	**48**	**.455**	**200**	**115**	**27**	**4**	**9**	**827**	**805**	**486**	**417**	**41**	**29**	**443**	**401**	**1.509**	**4.54**	**82**	**4.08**	**.253**	**54**	**.205**	**-69**	**32**	**-6.6**
• GREGG, Kevin	Kevin Marschall Gregg b: 6/20/1978, Corvallis, OR BR/TR, 6'6", 220 lbs. Deb: 8/9/2003																										
2003	Ana-A	2	0	1.000	5	3	0	0	0	24^2	18	9	9	3	1	8	14	1.054	3.28	131	2.74	.205	0	....	2	2	0.2
• GREGG, Vean	Sylveanus Augustus Gregg b: 4/13/1885, Chehalis, WA d: 7/29/1964, Aberdeen, WA BR/TL, 6'1", 185 lbs. Deb: 4/12/1911																										
1911	Cle-A	23	7	.767	34	26	22	5	0	244^2	172	67	49	2	10	86	125	1.054	**1.80**	**189**	**1.99**	**.205**	14	.165	40	28	3.6
1912	Cle-A	20	13	.606	37	34	26	1	2	271^1	242	99	78	4	10	90	184	1.224	2.59	133	2.87	.246	17	.175	21	23	1.8
1913	Cle-A	20	13	.606	44	34	23	3	3	285^2	258	103	71	2	13	124	166	1.337	2.24	136	3.19	.246	13	.131	21	23	1.8
1914	Cle-A	9	3	.750	17	12	6	1	0	96^2	88	46	33	0	3	48	56	1.407	3.07	94	3.39	.251	6	.176	-1	5	0.0
	Bos-A	3	4	.429	12	9	4	0	0	68^1	71	39	30	0	0	37	24	1.580	3.95	68	4.74	.283	4	.211	-11	1	-1.2
	Yr.	12	7	.632	29	21	10	1	0	165	159	85	63	0	3	85	80	1.479	3.44	81	3.95	.264	10	.189	-12	6	-1.2

YEAR	TM-L	W	L	PCT	G	GS	CG	SH	SV	IP	H	R	ER	HR	HB	BB	SO	RAT	ERA	ERA+	CERA	OAV	BH	AVG	PR+	WS	TPW
1915	Bos-A	4	2	.667	18	9	3	1	3	75	71	37	28	2	5	32	43	1.373	3.36	83	3.69	.260	7	.350	-5	5	-0.4
1916	Bos-A	2	5	.286	21	7	3	0	0	77^2	71	30	26	0	3	30	41	1.300	3.01	92	3.17	.259	2	.111	-1	3	-0.2
1918	Phi-A	9	14	.391	30	25	17	3	2	199^1	180	85	69	4	5	67	63	1.239	3.12	94	2.86	.251	12	.169	-11	11	-1.5
1925	Was-A	2	2	.500	26	5	1	0	2	74^1	87	41	34	3	2	38	18	1.682	4.12	103	5.25	.318	3	.214	-1	4	-0.1
Total	**8**	**92**	**63**	**.594**	**239**	**161**	**105**	**14**	**12**	**1393**	**1240**	**547**	**418**	**17**	**51**	**552**	**720**	**1.286**	**2.70**	**115**	**3.10**	**.247**	**78**	**.171**	**52**	**103**	**3.8**

• GREGORY, Frank Frank Ernst Gregory b: 7/25/1888, Spring Valley Twp., WI d: 11/5/1955, Beloit, WI BR/TR, 5'11", 185 lbs. Deb: 9/5/1912

YEAR	TM-L	W	L	PCT	G	GS	CG	SH	SV	IP	H	R	ER	HR	HB	BB	SO	RAT	ERA	ERA+	CERA	OAV	BH	AVG	PR+	WS	TPW
1912	Cin-N	2	0	1.000	4	2	1	0	0	15^2	19	12	8	0	0	7	4	1.660	4.60	73	4.39	.297	1	.200	-2	1	-0.2

• GREGORY, Howie Howard Watterson Gregory b: 11/18/1886, Hannibal, MO d: 5/30/1970, Tulsa, OK BL/TR, 6', 175 lbs. Deb: 4/16/1911

YEAR	TM-L	W	L	PCT	G	GS	CG	SH	SV	IP	H	R	ER	HR	HB	BB	SO	RAT	ERA	ERA+	CERA	OAV	BH	AVG	PR+	WS	TPW
1911	StL-A	0	1	.000	3	1	0	0	0	7	11	5	4	0	0	4	1	2.143	5.14	66	7.99	.393	0	.000	-1	0	-0.2

• GREGORY, Lee Grover Leroy Gregory b: 6/2/1938, Bakersfield, CA BL/TL, 6'1", 180 lbs. Deb: 4/17/1964

YEAR	TM-L	W	L	PCT	G	GS	CG	SH	SV	IP	H	R	ER	HR	HB	BB	SO	RAT	ERA	ERA+	CERA	OAV	BH	AVG	PR+	WS	TPW
1964	Chi-N	0	0	....	11	0	0	0	0	18	23	8	7	3	0	5	8	1.556	3.50	106	5.83	.333	1	.077	1	1	0.0

• GREGORY, Paul Paul Edwin "Pop" Gregory b: 6/9/1908, Tomnolen, MS d: 9/16/1999, Southaven, MS BR/TR, 6'2", 180 lbs. Deb: 4/20/1932

YEAR	TM-L	W	L	PCT	G	GS	CG	SH	SV	IP	H	R	ER	HR	HB	BB	SO	RAT	ERA	ERA+	CERA	OAV	BH	AVG	PR+	WS	TPW
1932	Chi-A	5	3	.625	33	9	3	0	0	117^2	125	75	59	8	2	51	39	1.496	4.51	96	4.29	.273	3	.079	-1	4	-0.4
1933	Chi-A	4	11	.267	23	17	5	0	0	103^2	124	75	57	10	1	47	18	1.650	4.95	86	5.27	.296	5	.143	-7	2	-0.8
Total	**2**	**9**	**14**	**.391**	**56**	**26**	**8**	**0**	**0**	**221^1**	**249**	**150**	**116**	**18**	**3**	**98**	**57**	**1.568**	**4.72**	**91**	**4.74**	**.284**	**8**	**.110**	**-8**	**6**	**-1.2**

• GREIF, Bill William Briley Greif b: 4/25/1950, Fort Stockton, TX BR/TR, 6'4", 205 lbs. Deb: 7/19/1971

YEAR	TM-L	W	L	PCT	G	GS	CG	SH	SV	IP	H	R	ER	HR	HB	BB	SO	RAT	ERA	ERA+	CERA	OAV	BH	AVG	PR+	WS	TPW
1971	Hou-N	1	1	.500	7	3	0	0	0	16	18	10	9	1	2	8	14	1.625	5.06	66	5.27	.290	1	.333	-3	0	-0.3
1972	SD-N	5	16	.238	34	22	2	1	2	125^1	143	86	78	18	8	47	91	1.516	5.60	59	5.25	.287	1	.030	-30	0	-3.5
1973	SD-N	10	17	.370	36	31	9	3	1	199^1	181	88	71	20	5	62	120	1.219	3.21	108	3.27	.246	6	.098	7	12	0.6
1974	SD-N	9	19	.321	43	35	7	1	1	226	244	126	117	17	14	95	137	1.500	4.66	76	4.59	.279	4	.071	-21	6	-2.3
1975	SD-N	4	6	.400	59	1	0	0	9	72	74	44	31	7	5	38	43	1.556	3.88	90	4.49	.269	0	.000	-2	3	-0.3
1976	SD-N	1	3	.250	5	5	0	0	0	22^1	27	20	20	2	0	11	5	1.701	8.06	41	5.51	.297	0	.000	-12	0	-1.4
	StL-N	1	5	.167	47	0	0	0	6	54^2	60	28	25	5	2	26	32	1.573	4.12	86	4.91	.290	0	.000	-4	2	-0.4
	Yr.	2	8	.200	52	5	0	0	6	77	87	48	45	7	2	37	37	1.610	5.26	65	5.08	.292	0	.000	-16	2	-1.7
Total	**6**	**31**	**67**	**.316**	**231**	**97**	**18**	**5**	**19**	**715^2**	**747**	**402**	**351**	**70**	**36**	**287**	**442**	**1.445**	**4.41**	**78**	**4.40**	**.272**	**12**	**.072**	**-65**	**23**	**-7.6**

• GREISINGER, Seth Seth Adam Greisinger b: 7/29/1975, Kansas City, KS BR/TR, 6'4", 200 lbs. Deb: 6/3/1998

YEAR	TM-L	W	L	PCT	G	GS	CG	SH	SV	IP	H	R	ER	HR	HB	BB	SO	RAT	ERA	ERA+	CERA	OAV	BH	AVG	PR+	WS	TPW
1998	Det-A	6	9	.400	21	21	0	0	0	130	142	79	74	17	4	48	66	1.462	5.12	92	4.89	.282	1	.250	-8	6	-0.7
2002	Det-A	2	2	.500	8	8	0	0	0	37^2	46	26	26	4	1	13	14	1.566	6.21	69	5.23	.303	0	....	-8	1	-0.7
Total	**2**	**8**	**11**	**.421**	**29**	**29**	**0**	**0**	**0**	**167^2**	**188**	**105**	**100**	**21**	**5**	**61**	**80**	**1.485**	**5.37**	**86**	**4.97**	**.287**	**1**	**.250**	**-16**	**7**	**-1.5**

• GREVELL, Bill William J. Grevell b: 3/5/1898, Williamstown, NJ d: 6/21/1923, Philadelphia, PA BR/TR, 5'11", 170 lbs. Deb: 5/14/1919

YEAR	TM-L	W	L	PCT	G	GS	CG	SH	SV	IP	H	R	ER	HR	HB	BB	SO	RAT	ERA	ERA+	CERA	OAV	BH	AVG	PR+	WS	TPW
1919	Phi-A	0	0	....	5	2	0	0	0	12	15	20	19	0	1	18	3	2.750	14.25	24	9.11	.306	0	.000	-14	0	-1.5

• GRIFFETH, Lee Leon Clifford Griffeth b: 5/20/1925, Carmel, NY BB/TL, 5'11.5", 180 lbs. Deb: 6/25/1946

YEAR	TM-L	W	L	PCT	G	GS	CG	SH	SV	IP	H	R	ER	HR	HB	BB	SO	RAT	ERA	ERA+	CERA	OAV	BH	AVG	PR+	WS	TPW
1946	Phi-A	0	0	....	10	0	0	0	0	15^1	13	7	5	1	2	6	4	1.239	2.93	121	3.44	.232	0	.000	1	1	0.1

• GRIFFIN, Hank James Linton "Pepper" Griffin b: 7/11/1886, Whitehouse, TX d: 2/11/1950, Terrell, TX BR/TR, 6', 165 lbs. Deb: 5/5/1911

YEAR	TM-L	W	L	PCT	G	GS	CG	SH	SV	IP	H	R	ER	HR	HB	BB	SO	RAT	ERA	ERA+	CERA	OAV	BH	AVG	PR+	WS	TPW
1911	Chi-N	0	0	....	1	1	0	0	0	1	1	2	2	1	0	3	1	4.000	18.00	18	25.08	.250	0	....	-2	0	-0.2
	Bos-N	0	6	.000	15	6	1	0	0	82^2	96	70	48	3	6	34	30	1.573	5.23	73	5.01	.305	7	.233	-11	1	-1.1
	Yr.	0	6	.000	16	7	1	0	0	83^2	97	72	50	4	6	37	31	1.602	5.38	70	5.25	.304	7	.233	-13	1	-1.3
1912	Bos-N	0	0	....	3	0	0	0	0	1^2	3	5	5	0	1	3	0	3.600	27.00	13	19.29	.750	0	....	-4	0	-0.4
Total	**2**	**0**	**6**	**.000**	**19**	**7**	**1**	**0**	**0**	**85^1**	**100**	**77**	**55**	**4**	**7**	**40**	**31**	**1.641**	**5.80**	**65**	**5.52**	**.310**	**7**	**.233**	**-17**	**1**	**-1.7**

• GRIFFIN, Marty Martin John Griffin b: 9/2/1901, San Francisco, CA d: 11/19/1951, Los Angeles, CA BR/TR, 6'2", 200 lbs. Deb: 7/25/1928

YEAR	TM-L	W	L	PCT	G	GS	CG	SH	SV	IP	H	R	ER	HR	HB	BB	SO	RAT	ERA	ERA+	CERA	OAV	BH	AVG	PR+	WS	TPW
1928	Bos-A	0	3	.000	11	3	0	0	0	37^2	42	21	21	0	0	17	9	1.566	5.02	82	4.03	.300	4	.308	-4	1	-0.3

• GRIFFIN, Mike Michael Leroy Griffin b: 6/26/1957, Colusa, CA BR/TR, 6'4", 197 lbs. Deb: 9/17/1979

YEAR	TM-L	W	L	PCT	G	GS	CG	SH	SV	IP	H	R	ER	HR	HB	BB	SO	RAT	ERA	ERA+	CERA	OAV	BH	AVG	PR+	WS	TPW
1979	NY-A	0	0	....	3	0	0	0	1	4^1	5	2	2	0	0	2	5	1.615	4.15	98	4.57	.313	0	....	-0	0	0.0
1980	NY-A	2	4	.333	13	9	0	0	0	54	64	36	29	6	1	23	25	1.611	4.83	81	5.22	.287	0	....	-5	1	-0.5
1981	NY-A	0	0	....	2	0	0	0	0	4^1	5	1	1	0	0	0	4	1.154	2.08	172	2.66	.278	0	....	1	0	0.1
	Chi-N	2	5	.286	16	9	0	0	1	52	64	27	26	4	0	9	20	1.404	4.50	82	4.22	.302	2	.154	-3	2	-0.4
1982	SD-N	0	1	.000	7	0	0	0	0	10^1	9	4	4	0	0	3	4	1.161	3.48	98	2.43	.237	0	.000	-0	0	0.0
1987	Bal-A	3	5	.375	23	6	1	0	1	74^1	78	39	36	9	3	33	42	1.493	4.36	101	4.76	.269	0	....	0	4	0.0
1989	Cin-N	0	0	....	3	0	0	0	0	4^1	10	6	6	0	0	3	1	3.000	12.46	29	11.62	.500	1	1.000	-4	0	-0.4
Total	**6**	**7**	**15**	**.318**	**67**	**24**	**1**	**0**	**3**	**203^2**	**235**	**115**	**104**	**19**	**4**	**73**	**101**	**1.512**	**4.60**	**86**	**4.72**	**.288**	**3**	**.200**	**-12**	**7**	**-1.3**

• GRIFFIN, Pat Patrick Richard Griffin b: 5/6/1893, Niles, OH d: 6/7/1927, Youngstown, OH BR/TR, 6'2", 180 lbs. Deb: 7/23/1914

YEAR	TM-L	W	L	PCT	G	GS	CG	SH	SV	IP	H	R	ER	HR	HB	BB	SO	RAT	ERA	ERA+	CERA	OAV	BH	AVG	PR+	WS	TPW
1914	Cin-N	0	0	....	1	0	0	0	0	1	3	3	1	0	0	2	0	5.000	9.00	33	31.70	.750	0	....	-1	0	-0.1

• GRIFFIN, Tom Thomas James Griffin b: 2/22/1948, Los Angeles, CA BR/TR, 6'3", 210 lbs. Deb: 4/10/1969

YEAR	TM-L	W	L	PCT	G	GS	CG	SH	SV	IP	H	R	ER	HR	HB	BB	SO	RAT	ERA	ERA+	CERA	OAV	BH	AVG	PR+	WS	TPW
1969	Hou-N	11	10	.524	31	31	6	3	0	188^1	156	80	74	19	7	93	200	1.322	3.54	100	3.58	.220	9	.145	2	11	0.5
1970	Hou-N	3	13	.188	23	20	2	1	0	111^1	118	72	71	9	3	72	72	1.707	5.74	68	5.40	.275	2	.061	-23	0	-2.5
1971	Hou-N	0	6	.000	10	6	0	0	0	37^2	44	22	20	4	2	20	29	1.699	4.78	70	5.74	.288	1	.111	-6	0	-0.7
1972	Hou-N	5	4	.556	39	5	1	1	3	94^1	92	39	34	7	3	38	83	1.378	3.24	104	3.78	.258	7	.280	1	7	0.5
1973	Hou-N	4	6	.400	25	12	4	0	0	99^2	83	51	46	10	2	46	69	1.294	4.15	87	3.42	.229	3	.107	-6	4	-0.6
1974	Hou-N	14	10	.583	34	34	8	3	0	211	202	97	83	14	5	89	110	1.379	3.54	98	3.68	.250	20	.294	-5	14	0.4
1975	Hou-N	3	8	.273	17	13	3	1	0	79^1	89	52	47	11	2	46	56	1.702	5.33	63	5.88	.288	3	.136	-18	0	-1.9
1976	Hou-N	5	3	.625	20	2	0	0	0	41^2	44	29	28	4	1	37	33	1.944	6.05	53	6.41	.278	0	.000	-13	0	-1.4
	SD-N	4	3	.571	11	11	2	0	0	70^1	56	27	23	0	1	42	36	1.393	2.94	111	3.03	.222	2	.077	3	4	0.1
	Yr.	9	6	.600	31	13	2	0	0	112	100	56	51	4	2	79	69	1.598	4.10	79	4.28	.244	2	.065	-11	4	-1.3
1977	SD-N	6	9	.400	38	20	0	0	0	151^1	144	88	75	17	5	88	79	1.533	4.46	79	4.68	.254	6	.133	-15	3	-1.4
1978	Cal-A	3	4	.429	24	4	0	0	0	56	63	39	25	8	1	31	35	1.679	4.02	90	5.50	.279	0	....	-2	1	-0.2
1979	SF-N	5	6	.455	59	3	0	0	2	94^1	83	46	41	9	4	46	82	1.367	3.91	89	3.75	.237	1	.071	-3	4	-0.4
1980	SF-N	5	1	.833	42	4	0	0	0	107^2	80	35	33	8	8	49	79	1.198	2.76	128	2.96	.212	2	.111	12	9	1.2
1981	SF-N	8	8	.500	22	22	3	1	0	129^1	121	62	54	8	7	57	83	1.376	3.76	91	3.74	.249	8	.195	-4	6	-0.2
1982	Pit-N	1	3	.250	6	4	0	0	0	22^1	32	23	22	5	1	15	8	2.104	8.87	42	8.99	.330	2	.222	-13	0	-1.3
Total	**14**	**77**	**94**	**.450**	**401**	**191**	**29**	**10**	**5**	**1494^2**	**1407**	**762**	**676**	**133**	**52**	**769**	**1054**	**1.456**	**4.07**	**86**	**4.21**	**.249**	**66**	**.163**	**-89**	**63**	**-7.9**

• GRIFFITH, Clark Clark Calvin "The Old Fox" Griffith
b: 11/20/1869, Clear Creek, MO d: 10/27/1955, Washington, DC BR/TR, 5'6.5", 156 lbs. Deb: 4/11/1891 M/U HOF: 1946

YEAR	TM-L	W	L	PCT	G	GS	CG	SH	SV	IP	H	R	ER	HR	HB	BB	SO	RAT	ERA	ERA+	CERA	OAV	BH	AVG	PR+	WS	TPW
1891	StL-a	11	8	.579	27	17	12	0	0	186^1	195	122	69	8	15	58	68	1.358	3.33	126	....	.260	12	.156	16	13	1.2
	Bos-a	3	1	.750	7	4	3	0	0	40	47	33	25	3	5	15	20	1.550	5.63	62	....	.283	4	.174	-10	2	-0.6
	Yr.	14	9	.609	34	21	15	0	0	226^1	242	155	94	11	20	73	88	1.392	3.74	107	....	.265	16	.160	5	15	0.5
1893	Chi-N	1	2	.333	4	2	2	0	0	19^2	24	14	11	1	1	5	9	1.475	5.03	92	4.52	.292	2	.182	-1	1	-0.1
1894	Chi-N	21	14	.600	36	30	28	0	0	261^1	328	193	143	12	14	85	71	1.580	4.92	114	4.95	.304	33	.232	25	19	1.7
1895	Chi-N	26	14	.650	42	41	39	0	0	353	434	228	154	11	22	91	79	1.487	3.93	129	4.47	.298	46	.319	46	34	4.3
1896	Chi-N	23	11	.676	36	35	35	0	0	317^2	370	189	125	3	12	70	81	1.385	3.54	128	3.74	.289	36	.267	30	30	2.9
1897	Chi-N	21	18	.538	41	38	**38**	1	1	343^2	410	231	142	3	17	86	102	1.443	3.72	120	4.03	.294	38	.235	32	22	2.9
1898	Chi-N	24	10	.706	38	38	36	4	0	325^2	305	105	68	1	20	64	97	1.133	**1.88**	**190**	2.53	.246	20	.164	**60**	32	5.5
1899	Chi-N	22	14	.611	38	38	35	0	0	319^2	329	163	99	5	14	65	73	1.233	2.79	134	3.04	.266	31	.258	33	25	3.6
1900	Chi-N	14	13	.519	30	30	27	**4**	0	248	245	126	84	6	16	51	61	1.194	3.05	118	2.96	.258	24	.253	20	19	2.3
1901	Chi-A	24	7	.774	35	30	26	**5**	1	266^2	275	114	79	4	4	50	67	1.219	2.67	131	2.90	.263	27	.303	24	27	3.4
1902	Chi-A	15	9	.625	28	24	20	3	0	213	247	117	99	11	16	47	51	1.380	4.18	81	4.15	.291	20	.217	-22	11	-2.0
1903	NY-A	14	11	.560	25	24	22	2	0	213	201	92	64	3	6	33	69	1.099	2.70	115	2.33	.249	11	.159	11	16	1.4
1904	NY-A	7	5	.583	16	11	8	1	0	100^1	91	40	32	3	4	16	36	1.066	2.87	94	2.41	.243	6	.143	-4	7	-0.5

YEAR	TM-L	W	L	PCT	G	GS	CG	SH	SV	IP	H	R	ER	HR	HB	BB	SO	RAT	ERA	ERA+	CERA	OAV	BH	AVG	PR+	WS	TPW
1905	NY-A	9	6	.600	25	7	4	2	1	101^{2}	82	30	19	1	1	15	46	.954	1.68	174	1.68	.223	7	.219	15	10	1.8
1906	NY-A	2	2	.500	17	2	1	0	2	59^{2}	58	30	20	0	4	15	16	1.223	3.02	98	2.87	.258	2	.111	0	4	0.0
1907	NY-A	0	0	....	4	0	0	0	0	8^{1}	15	16	8	0	0	6	5	2.520	8.64	32	8.51	.391	0	.000	-5	0	-0.6
1909	Cin-N	0	1	.000	1	1	1	0	0	6	11	8	4	0	0	2	3	2.167	6.00	43	7.77	.370	0	.000	-2	0	-0.3
1912	Was-A	0	0	....	1	0	0	0	0	0	1	1	1	1	0	0	0	....	∞	....	∞	1.000	0	.000	-1	0	-0.1
1913	Was-A	0	0	....	1	0	0	0	0	1	1	0	0	0	0	0	0	1.000	0.00	....	1.95	.250	1	1.000	0	1	0.1
1914	Was-A	0	0	....	1	0	0	0	1	1	1	0	0	0	0	0	1	1.000	0.00	....	1.95	.250	1	1.000	0	0	0.1
Total	20	237	146	.619	453	372	337	22	6	3385^{2}	3670	1852	1246	76	171	774	955	1.313	3.31	121	3.23	.274	321	.233	266	273	26.6
• GRIFFITH, Frank	Frank Wesley Griffith b: 11/18/1872, Gilman, IL d: 12/8/1908, Waterman, IL BL/TL Deb: 8/13/1892																										
1892	Chi-N	0	1	.000	1	1	0	0	0	4	3	5	5	1	0	6	3	2.250	11.25	30	7.99	.200	0	.000	-3	0	-0.3
1894	Cle-N	1	2	.333	7	6	3	0	0	42^{1}	64	62	47	5	9	37	15	2.386	9.99	55	10.12	.345	8	.333	-21	0	-1.6
Total	2	1	3	.250	8	7	3	0	0	46^{1}	67	67	52	6	9	43	18	2.374	10.10	51	9.94	.334	8	.320	-25	0	-1.9
• GRIFFITHS, Jeremy	Jeremy Richard Griffiths b: 3/22/1978, Fairview, OH BR/TR, 6'6", 240 lbs. Deb: 6/5/2003																										
2003	NY-N	1	4	.200	9	6	0	0	0	41	57	34	32	5	2	19	25	1.854	7.02	59	6.88	.328	0	.000	-13	0	-1.3
• GRIGGS, Hal	Harold Lloyd Griggs b: 8/24/1928, Shannon, GA BR/TR, 6', 170 lbs. Deb: 4/18/1956																										
1956	Was-A	1	6	.143	34	12	1	0	1	98^{2}	120	82	66	14	1	76	48	1.986	6.02	72	7.29	.307	0	.000	-16	0	-1.6
1957	Was-A	0	1	.000	2	2	0	0	0	13^{2}	11	5	5	1	0	7	12	1.317	3.29	118	3.46	.229	1	.250	1	1	0.1
1958	Was-A	3	11	.214	32	21	3	0	0	137	138	91	84	20	2	74	69	1.547	5.52	69	5.08	.262	5	.122	-22	0	-2.5
1959	Was-A	2	8	.200	37	10	2	1	2	97^{2}	103	63	57	8	1	52	43	1.587	5.25	75	4.70	.270	1	.056	-11	1	-1.3
Total	4	6	26	.188	105	45	6	1	3	347	372	241	212	43	4	209	172	1.674	5.50	73	5.54	.276	7	.089	-48	2	-5.3
• GRILLI, Guido	Guido John Grilli b: 1/9/1939, Memphis, TN BL/TL, 6', 188 lbs. Deb: 4/12/1966																										
1966	Bos-A	0	1	.000	6	0	0	0	0	4^{2}	5	6	4	1	0	9	4	3.000	7.71	49	12.51	.278	1	.500	-2	0	-0.2
	KC-A	0	1	.000	16	0	0	0	1	15^{2}	19	15	12	0	3	11	8	1.915	6.89	49	6.04	.302	0	....	-6	0	-0.7
	Yr.	0	2	.000	22	0	0	0	1	20^{1}	24	21	16	1	3	20	12	2.164	7.08	49	7.53	.296	1	.500	-8	0	-0.8
• GRILLI, Jason	Jason Michael Grilli b: 11/11/1976, Royal Oak, MI BR/TR, 6'4", 185 lbs. Deb: 5/11/2000																										
2000	Fla-N	1	0	1.000	1	1	0	0	0	6^{2}	11	4	4	0	2	2	3	1.950	5.40	82	7.84	.379	1	.500	-1	0	0.0
2001	Fla-N	2	2	.500	6	5	0	0	0	26^{2}	30	18	18	6	2	11	17	1.538	6.08	69	6.44	.297	2	.286	-6	1	-0.4
Total	2	3	2	.600	7	6	0	0	0	33^{1}	41	22	22	6	4	13	20	1.620	5.94	72	6.72	.315	3	.333	-6	1	-0.4
• GRILLI, Steve	Stephen Joseph Grilli b: 5/2/1949, Brooklyn, NY BR/TR, 6'2", 170 lbs. Deb: 9/19/1975																										
1975	Det-A	0	0	....	3	0	0	0	0	6^{2}	3	2	1	0	0	6	5	1.350	1.35	297	2.02	.136	0	....	2	1	0.2
1976	Det-A	3	1	.750	36	0	0	0	3	66	63	43	34	5	5	41	36	1.576	4.64	80	4.65	.258	0	....	-6	2	-0.6
1977	Det-A	1	2	.333	30	2	0	0	0	72^{2}	71	42	39	8	3	49	49	1.651	4.83	89	5.37	.265	0	....	-4	3	-0.4
1979	Tor-A	0	0	....	1	0	0	0	0	2^{1}	1	0	0	0	0	0	1	.429	0.00	....	0.40	.143	0	....	1	0	0.1
Total	4	4	3	.571	70	2	0	0	3	147^{2}	138	87	74	13	8	96	91	1.585	4.51	89	4.82	.255	0	....	-7	6	-0.7
• GRIM, Bob	Robert Anton Grim b: 3/8/1930, New York, NY d: 10/23/1996, Shawnee, KS BR/TR, 6'1", 185 lbs. Deb: 4/18/1954																										
1954	NY-A	20	6	.769	37	20	8	1	0	199	175	78	72	9	3	85	108	1.307	3.26	105	3.18	.244	10	.143	-1	13	-0.2
1955*	NY-A	7	5	.583	26	11	1	1	4	92^{1}	81	49	43	9	3	42	63	1.332	4.19	89	3.67	.238	3	.120	-8	4	-0.9
1956	NY-A	6	1	.857	26	6	1	0	5	74^{2}	64	27	23	3	2	31	48	1.272	2.77	140	3.12	.235	1	.063	7	7	0.7
1957*	NY-A★	12	8	.600	46	0	0	0	**19**	72	60	22	21	5	0	36	52	1.333	2.63	137	3.32	.239	1	.111	7	11	0.8
1958	NY-A	0	1	.000	11	0	0	0	0	16^{1}	12	10	10	3	1	10	11	1.347	5.51	64	4.31	.211	0	.000	-4	0	-0.4
	KC-A	7	6	.538	26	14	5	1	0	113^{2}	118	54	45	7	3	41	54	1.399	3.56	110	3.92	.269	6	.188	5	8	0.4
	Yr.	7	7	.500	37	14	5	1	0	130	130	64	55	10	4	51	65	1.392	3.81	101	3.97	.263	6	.182	1	8	0.0
1959	KC-A	6	10	.375	40	9	3	1	4	125^{1}	124	69	57	10	3	57	65	1.444	4.09	98	4.10	.260	3	.094	-1	6	-0.2
1960	Cle-A	0	1	.000	3	0	0	0	0	2^{1}	6	3	3	0	0	1	2	3.000	11.57	32	13.44	.500	0	....	-2	0	-0.2
	Cin-N	2	2	.500	26	0	0	0	2	30^{1}	32	18	15	3	0	10	22	1.385	4.45	86	3.90	.274	0	.000	-2	1	-0.2
	StL-N	1	0	1.000	15	0	0	0	0	20^{2}	22	7	7	1	0	9	15	1.500	3.05	134	4.06	.272	0	.000	2	2	0.2
	Yr.	3	2	.600	41	0	0	0	2	51	54	25	22	4	0	19	37	1.431	3.88	101	3.96	.273	0	.000	0	3	0.0
1962	KC-A	0	1	.000	12	0	0	0	3	13	14	9	9	0	0	8	3	1.692	6.23	67	4.43	.292	0	.000	-3	1	-0.3
Total	8	61	41	.598	268	60	18	4	37	759^{2}	708	346	305	50	15	330	443	1.366	3.61	104	3.64	.252	24	.127	0	53	-0.4
• GRIMES, Burleigh	Burleigh Arland "Ol' Stubblebeard" Grimes b: 8/18/1893, Emerald, WI d: 12/6/1985, Clear Lake, WI BR/TR, 5'10", 175 lbs. Deb: 9/10/1916 M/C HOF: 1964																										
1916	Pit-N	2	3	.400	6	5	4	0	0	45^{2}	40	19	12	1	0	10	20	1.095	2.36	113	2.25	.241	3	.176	3	2	0.3
1917	Pit-N	3	16	.158	37	17	8	1	0	194	186	101	76	5	6	70	72	**1.320**	3.53	80	3.22	.260	16	.232	-13	4	-1.3
1918	Bro-N	19	9	.679	**40**	30	19	7	1	269^{2}	210	94	64	3	4	76	113	1.061	2.14	130	1.95	.216	18	.200	19	25	2.2
1919	Bro-N	10	11	.476	25	21	13	1	0	181^{1}	179	97	70	2	7	60	82	1.318	3.47	85	3.09	.256	17	.246	-6	6	-0.5
1920*	Bro-N	23	11	.676	40	33	25	5	2	303^{2}	271	101	75	5	4	67	131	1.113	2.22	144	2.28	.238	34	.306	37	32	5.1
1921	Bro-N	**22**	13	.629	37	35	**30**	2	0	302^{1}	313	120	95	6	5	76	**136**	1.287	2.83	137	3.21	.274	27	.237	**37**	**29**	**3.8**
1922	Bro-N	17	14	.548	36	34	18	1	1	259	324	159	137	17	7	84	99	1.575	4.76	85	5.03	.308	22	.237	-18	11	-1.3
1923	Bro-N	21	18	.538	39	**38**	**33**	2	0	**327**	356	165	130	9	11	100	119	1.394	3.58	108	3.72	.280	30	.238	12	21	1.5
1924	Bro-N	22	13	.629	38	**36**	**30**	1	1	**310^{2}**	351	161	132	15	6	91	135	1.423	3.82	98	4.02	.287	37	.298	6	21	1.2
1925	Bro-N	12	19	.387	33	31	19	0	0	246^{2}	305	164	138	15	7	102	73	**1.650**	5.04	83	5.18	.309	24	.250	-16	9	-1.0
1926	Bro-N	12	13	.480	30	29	18	1	0	225^{1}	238	114	93	4	5	88	64	1.447	3.71	103	3.68	.276	18	.222	7	15	0.8
1927	NY-N	19	8	.704	39	34	15	2	2	259^{2}	274	116	102	12	4	87	102	1.390	3.54	109	3.78	.276	18	.188	10	19	1.0
1928	Pit-N	**25**	14	.641	**48**	**37**	**28**	**4**	3	**330^{2}**	311	146	110	11	9	77	97	1.173	2.99	136	2.70	.248	42	.321	38	30	4.8
1929	Pit-N	17	7	.708	33	29	18	2	2	232^{2}	245	108	81	11	4	70	62	1.354	3.13	**152**	3.57	.269	26	.286	**38**	23	**4.0**
1930	Bos-N	3	5	.375	11	9	1	0	0	49	72	53	40	4	3	22	15	1.918	7.35	67	7.05	.353	3	.188	-13	0	-1.2
	*StL-N	13	6	.684	22	19	10	1	0	152^{1}	174	66	51	5	4	43	58	1.425	3.01	167	3.99	.293	15	.263	33	16	3.1
	Yr.	16	11	.593	33	28	11	1	0	201^{1}	246	119	91	9	7	65	73	1.545	4.07	122	4.73	.308	18	.247	20	16	2.0
1931*	StL-N	17	9	.654	29	28	17	3	0	212^{1}	240	97	86	11	10	59	67	1.408	3.65	108	4.14	.286	14	.184	6	15	0.4
1932*	Chi-N	6	11	.353	30	18	5	1	1	141^{1}	174	89	75	8	1	50	36	1.585	4.78	79	4.75	.297	11	.250	-18	4	-1.7
1933	Chi-N	3	6	.333	17	7	3	1	3	69^{2}	71	29	27	2	1	29	12	1.435	3.49	94	3.78	.277	3	.150	-3	3	-0.4
	StL-N	0	1	.000	4	3	0	0	1	13^{2}	15	13	8	1	1	8	4	1.683	5.27	66	4.98	.263	1	.200	-3	0	-0.3
	Yr.	3	7	.300	21	10	3	1	4	83^{1}	86	42	35	3	2	37	16	1.476	3.78	88	3.98	.274	4	.160	-6	3	-0.7
1934	StL-N	2	1	.667	4	0	0	0	0	7^{2}	5	3	3	1	0	2	1	.913	3.52	120	1.90	.179	0	....	1	1	0.0
	Pit-N	1	2	.333	8	4	0	0	0	27^{1}	36	24	22	0	1	10	9	1.683	7.24	57	4.85	.310	1	.143	-9	0	-0.9
	Yr.	3	3	.500	12	4	0	0	0	35	41	27	25	1	1	12	10	1.514	6.43	64	4.20	.285	1	.143	-9	1	-0.9
	NY-A	1	2	.333	10	0	0	0	1	18	22	11	11	0	1	14	5	2.000	5.50	74	6.34	.319	0	.000	-3	0	-0.3
Total	19	270	212	.560	616	497	314	35	18	4179^{2}	4412	2050	1638	148	101	1295	1512	1.365	3.53	107	3.63	.273	380	.248	144	286	19.2
• GRIMES, John	John Thomas Grimes b: 4/17/1869, Woodstock, MD d: 1/17/1964, San Francisco, CA BR/TR, 5'11", 160 lbs. Deb: 7/28/1897																										
1897	StL-N	0	2	.000	3	1	1	0	0	19^{2}	24	23	13	0	6	8	4	1.627	5.95	74	5.59	.299	2	.286	-3	0	-0.1
• GRIMSLEY, Jason	Jason Alan Grimsley b: 8/7/1967, Cleveland, TX BR/TR, 6'3", 180 lbs. Deb: 9/8/1989																										
1989	Phi-N	1	3	.250	4	4	0	0	0	18^{1}	19	13	12	2	0	19	7	2.073	5.89	60	6.86	.268	0	.000	-5	0	-0.6
1990	Phi-N	3	2	.600	11	11	0	0	0	57^{1}	47	21	21	1	2	43	41	1.570	3.30	116	3.98	.227	3	.188	3	4	0.3
1991	Phi-N	1	7	.125	12	12	0	0	0	61	54	34	33	4	3	41	42	1.557	4.87	75	4.39	.242	1	.059	-8	0	-0.9
1993	Cle-A	3	4	.429	10	6	0	0	0	42^{1}	52	26	25	3	1	20	27	1.701	5.31	81	5.57	.302	0	....	-5	1	-0.5
1994	Cle-A	5	2	.714	14	13	1	0	0	82^{2}	91	47	42	7	6	34	59	1.512	4.57	103	4.89	.283	0	....	1	5	0.1
1995	Cle-A	0	0	....	15	2	0	0	1	34	37	24	23	4	2	32	25	2.029	6.09	77	7.37	.289	0	....	-5	0	-0.5
1996	Cal-A	5	7	.417	35	20	2	1	0	130^{1}	150	110	99	14	13	74	82	1.719	6.84	72	5.98	.286	0	....	-28	1	-2.6
1999*	NY-A	7	2	.778	55	0	0	0	1	75	66	39	30	7	4	40	49	1.413	3.60	131	3.87	.231	0	....	10	6	0.9
2000*	NY-A	3	2	.600	63	4	0	0	1	96^{1}	100	58	54	10	5	42	53	1.474	5.04	96	4.63	.268	0	.000	-1	5	0.0

YEAR	TM-L	W	L	PCT	G	GS	CG	SH	SV	IP	H	R	ER	HR	HB	BB	SO	RAT	ERA	ERA+	CERA	OAV	BH	AVG	PR+	WS	TPW
2001	KC-A	1	5	.167	73	0	0	0	0	80^1	71	32	27	8	2	28	61	1.232	3.02	162	3.34	.241	0	....	15	8	1.4
2002	KC-A	4	7	.364	70	0	0	0	1	71^1	64	32	31	4	1	37	59	1.416	3.91	128	3.51	.236	0	....	9	7	0.9
2003	KC-A	2	6	.250	76	0	0	0	0	75	88	47	43	6	5	36	58	1.653	5.16	100	5.40	.299	0	....	0	4	0.0
Total	12	35	47	.427	438	72	3	1	4	824	839	483	440	70	44	446	563	1.559	4.81	96	4.79	.265	4	.103	-13	41	-1.3

• GRIMSLEY, Ross — Ross Albert Ii Grimsley b: 1/7/1950, Topeka, KS BL/TL, 6'3", 200 lbs. Deb: 5/16/1971

YEAR	TM-L	W	L	PCT	G	GS	CG	SH	SV	IP	H	R	ER	HR	HB	BB	SO	RAT	ERA	ERA+	CERA	OAV	BH	AVG	PR+	WS	TPW
1971	Cin-N	10	7	.588	26	26	6	3	0	161^1	151	67	64	15	2	43	67	1.202	3.57	91	3.24	.250	6	.118	-10	8	-1.2
1972*	Cin-N	14	8	.636	30	28	4	1	1	197^2	194	73	67	18	0	50	79	1.234	3.05	105	3.32	.260	8	.121	-0	11	-0.3
1973*	Cin-N	13	10	.565	38	36	8	1	1	242^1	245	96	87	24	0	68	90	1.292	3.23	105	3.64	.266	5	.061	-1	14	-0.8
1974*	Bal-A	18	13	.581	40	39	17	4	1	295^2	267	111	101	26	3	76	158	1.160	3.07	112	2.96	.244	0	....	9	21	0.9
1975	Bal-A	10	13	.435	35	32	8	1	0	197	210	95	89	29	1	47	89	1.305	4.07	86	4.20	.276	0	....	-18	7	-1.9
1976	Bal-A	8	7	.533	28	19	2	0	0	136^2	143	66	60	8	1	35	41	1.302	3.95	83	3.48	.270	0	....	-12	5	-1.2
1977	Bal-A	14	10	.583	34	34	11	2	0	218^1	230	105	96	24	1	74	53	1.392	3.96	96	4.29	.277	0	....	-10	12	-1.0
1978	Mon-N★	20	11	.645	36	36	19	3	0	263	237	103	89	17	2	67	84	1.156	3.05	116	2.79	.243	13	.144	6	16	0.5
1979	Mon-N	10	9	.526	32	27	2	0	0	151^1	199	102	90	18	3	41	42	1.586	5.35	68	5.63	.322	11	.200	-29	0	-2.9
1980	Mon-N	2	4	.333	11	7	0	0	0	41^1	61	31	29	5	1	12	11	1.766	6.31	56	6.60	.351	2	.222	-12	0	-1.3
	Cle-A	4	5	.444	14	11	2	0	0	74^2	103	63	56	11	1	24	18	1.701	6.75	60	6.45	.331	0	....	-22	0	-2.2
1982	Bal-A	1	2	.333	21	0	0	0	0	60	65	35	35	7	0	22	18	1.450	5.25	77	4.48	.283	0	....	-8	1	-0.8
Total	11	124	99	.556	345	295	79	15	3	2039^1	2105	947	863	202	15	559	750	1.306	3.81	93	3.82	.270	45	.127	-108	95	-12.1

• GRIMSLEY, Ross — Ross Albert I Grimsley b: 6/4/1922, Americus, KS d: 2/6/1994, Memphis, TN BL/TL, 6', 175 lbs. Deb: 9/3/1951

YEAR	TM-L	W	L	PCT	G	GS	CG	SH	SV	IP	H	R	ER	HR	HB	BB	SO	RAT	ERA	ERA+	CERA	OAV	BH	AVG	PR+	WS	TPW
1951	Chi-A	0	0	....	7	0	0	0	0	14	12	8	6	1	0	10	8	1.571	3.86	105	4.22	.235	0	.000	0	1	0.0

• GRINER, Dan — Donald Dexter "Rusty" Griner b: 3/7/1888, Centerville, TN d: 6/3/1950, Bishopville, SC BL/TR, 6', 200 lbs. Deb: 8/17/1912

YEAR	TM-L	W	L	PCT	G	GS	CG	SH	SV	IP	H	R	ER	HR	HB	BB	SO	RAT	ERA	ERA+	CERA	OAV	BH	AVG	PR+	WS	TPW
1912	StL-N	3	4	.429	12	7	2	0	0	54	59	35	19	3	3	15	20	1.370	3.17	108	3.93	.278	1	.077	1	2	0.1
1913	StL-N	10	22	.313	34	34	18	1	0	225	279	150	127	12	10	66	79	1.533	5.08	63	4.84	.312	21	.259	-47	4	-4.3
1914	StL-N	9	13	.409	37	16	11	2	2	179	163	66	50	3	3	57	74	1.229	2.51	111	2.80	.254	14	.255	5	13	1.0
1915	StL-N	5	11	.313	37	18	9	3	3	150^1	137	59	47	4	8	46	46	1.217	2.81	99	2.97	.259	14	.269	1	9	0.5
1916	StL-N	0	0	....	4	0	0	0	1	11	15	5	5	0	1	3	3	1.636	4.09	64	5.36	.341	1	.250	-2	0	-0.2
1918	Bro-N	1	5	.167	11	6	3	1	0	54^1	47	16	13	0	7	15	22	1.141	2.15	129	2.95	.267	1	.071	4	4	0.3
Total	6	28	55	.337	135	81	43	7	6	673^2	700	331	261	22	32	202	244	1.339	3.49	87	3.66	.280	52	.237	-38	32	-2.6

• GRISSOM, Lee — Lee Theo Grissom b: 10/23/1907, Sherman, TX d: 10/4/1998, Corning, CA BB/TL, 6'3", 200 lbs. Deb: 9/2/1934

YEAR	TM-L	W	L	PCT	G	GS	CG	SH	SV	IP	H	R	ER	HR	HB	BB	SO	RAT	ERA	ERA+	CERA	OAV	BH	AVG	PR+	WS	TPW
1934	Cin-N	0	1	.000	4	1	0	0	0	7	13	12	12	0	0	7	4	2.857	15.43	26	10.37	.382	0	.000	-9	0	-0.9
1935	Cin-N	1	1	.500	3	3	1	0	0	21	31	10	9	0	0	4	13	1.667	3.86	103	5.09	.333	0	.000	1	1	0.0
1936	Cin-N	1	1	.500	6	4	0	0	0	24^1	33	18	17	1	0	9	13	1.726	6.29	61	5.43	.320	0	.000	-7	0	-0.7
1937	Cin-N★	12	17	.414	50	30	14	**5**	6	223^2	193	89	81	7	4	93	149	1.279	3.26	114	2.90	.232	7	.109	13	14	0.9
1938	Cin-N	2	3	.400	14	7	0	0	0	51	60	38	30	4	2	22	16	1.608	5.29	69	5.12	.300	3	.188	-10	0	-1.1
1939*	Cin-N	9	7	.563	33	21	3	0	0	153^2	145	77	70	14	1	56	53	1.308	4.10	93	3.52	.249	4	.085	-9	7	-1.1
1940	NY-A	0	0	....	5	0	0	0	0	4^2	4	0	0	0	0	2	1	1.286	0.00	....	2.74	.250	0	....	2	1	0.2
	Bro-N	2	5	.286	14	10	3	1	0	73^2	59	30	23	3	0	34	56	1.262	2.81	142	2.71	.215	5	.217	10	6	1.0
1941	Bro-N	0	0	....	4	1	0	0	1	11^1	10	3	3	2	0	8	5	1.588	2.38	154	4.90	.238	1	.500	1	1	0.2
	Phi-N	2	13	.133	29	18	2	0	0	131^1	120	69	58	4	2	70	74	1.447	3.97	93	3.52	.242	6	.167	-3	5	-0.4
	Yr.	2	13	.133	33	19	2	0	1	142^2	130	72	61	6	2	78	79	1.458	3.85	96	3.63	.242	7	.184	-2	6	-0.2
Total	8	29	48	.377	162	95	23	6	7	701^2	668	346	303	35	9	305	384	1.387	3.89	97	3.55	.250	26	.127	-11	35	-1.8

• GRISSOM, Marv — Marvin Edward Grissom b: 3/31/1918, Los Molinas, CA BR/TR, 6'3", 195 lbs. Deb: 9/10/1946 C

YEAR	TM-L	W	L	PCT	G	GS	CG	SH	SV	IP	H	R	ER	HR	HB	BB	SO	RAT	ERA	ERA+	CERA	OAV	BH	AVG	PR+	WS	TPW
1946	NY-N	0	2	.000	4	3	0	0	0	18^2	17	11	9	1	1	13	9	1.607	4.34	79	4.44	.254	1	.200	-2	0	-0.2
1949	Det-A	2	4	.333	27	2	0	0	0	39^1	56	32	28	6	1	34	17	2.288	6.41	65	8.92	.335	2	.222	-9	0	-0.9
1952	Chi-A	12	10	.545	28	24	7	1	0	166	156	79	69	6	3	79	97	1.416	3.74	97	3.55	.250	8	.151	-3	8	-0.4
1953	Bos-A	2	6	.250	13	11	1	1	0	59^1	61	34	31	5	1	30	31	1.534	4.70	89	4.48	.266	0	.000	-4	2	-0.6
	NY-N	4	2	.667	21	7	3	0	0	84^1	83	40	37	6	1	31	46	1.352	3.95	109	3.58	.255	2	.074	3	5	0.2
1954*	NY-N★	10	7	.588	56	3	1	1	19	122^1	100	37	32	13	7	50	64	1.226	2.35	171	3.29	.226	5	.156	21	17	2.1
1955	NY-N	5	4	.556	55	0	0	0	8	89^1	76	35	29	6	6	41	49	1.310	2.92	138	3.42	.237	2	.154	11	9	1.0
1956	NY-N	1	1	.500	43	2	0	0	7	80^2	71	15	14	3	1	16	49	1.079	1.56	242	2.31	.241	1	.091	20	13	2.0
1957	NY-N	4	4	.500	55	0	0	0	14	82^2	74	36	24	6	2	23	51	1.173	2.61	150	2.88	.243	2	.167	12	10	1.3
1958	SF-N	7	5	.583	51	0	0	0	10	65^1	71	34	29	11	5	26	46	1.485	3.99	95	5.34	.287	0	.000	-1	5	-0.2
1959	StL-N	0	0	....	3	0	0	0	0	2	6	5	5	2	0	0	0	3.000	22.50	19	25.51	.500	0	....	-4	0	-0.4
Total	10	47	45	.511	356	52	12	3	58	810	771	358	307	65	28	343	459	1.375	3.41	115	3.86	.254	23	.122	46	69	3.9

• GROB, Connie — Conrad George Grob b: 11/9/1932, Cross Plains, WI d: 9/28/1997, Madison, WI BL/TR, 6'.5", 180 lbs. Deb: 4/22/1956

YEAR	TM-L	W	L	PCT	G	GS	CG	SH	SV	IP	H	R	ER	HR	HB	BB	SO	RAT	ERA	ERA+	CERA	OAV	BH	AVG	PR+	WS	TPW
1956	Was-A	4	5	.444	37	1	0	0	1	79^1	121	79	69	14	1	26	27	1.853	7.83	55	7.57	.353	6	.333	-28	0	-2.6

• GRODZICKI, Johnny — John "Grod" Grodzicki b: 2/26/1917, Nanticoke, PA d: 5/2/1998, Daytona Beach, FL BR/TR, 6'1.5", 200 lbs. Deb: 4/18/1941 C

YEAR	TM-L	W	L	PCT	G	GS	CG	SH	SV	IP	H	R	ER	HR	HB	BB	SO	RAT	ERA	ERA+	CERA	OAV	BH	AVG	PR+	WS	TPW
1941	StL-N	2	1	.667	5	1	0	0	0	13^1	6	7	2	0	0	11	10	1.275	1.35	279	1.80	.130	0	.000	3	1	0.4
1946	StL-N	0	0	....	3	0	0	0	0	4	4	5	4	1	0	4	2	2.000	9.00	38	7.37	.250	0	....	-3	0	-0.3
1947	StL-N	0	1	.000	16	0	0	0	0	23^1	21	17	14	5	0	19	8	1.714	5.40	77	5.88	.253	0	.000	-3	0	-0.3
Total	3	2	2	.500	24	1	0	0	0	40^2	31	29	20	6	0	34	20	1.598	4.43	89	4.69	.214	0	.000	-2	1	-0.2

• GROMEK, Steve — Stephen Joseph Gromek b: Hamtramck, MI d: 3/12/2002, Clinton Twp, MI BB/TR, 6'2", 180 lbs. Deb: 8/18/1941

YEAR	TM-L	W	L	PCT	G	GS	CG	SH	SV	IP	H	R	ER	HR	HB	BB	SO	RAT	ERA	ERA+	CERA	OAV	BH	AVG	PR+	WS	TPW
1941	Cle-A	1	1	.500	9	2	1	0	2	23^1	25	12	11	0	0	11	19	1.543	4.24	93	3.78	.266	1	.167	-1	2	-0.1
1942	Cle-A	2	0	1.000	14	0	0	0	0	44^1	46	24	18	2	0	23	14	1.556	3.65	94	4.22	.267	5	.333	-2	3	0.1
1943	Cle-A	0	0	....	3	0	0	0	0	4	6	4	4	0	0	0	4	1.500	9.00	35	4.76	.353	2	1.000	-3	1	-0.2
1944	Cle-A	10	9	.526	35	21	12	2	1	203^2	160	74	58	5	3	70	115	1.129	2.56	129	2.27	**.219**	19	.260	14	17	2.0
1945	Cle-A★	19	9	.679	33	30	21	3	1	251	229	80	71	6	4	66	101	1.175	2.55	127	2.61	.243	21	.231	22	24	2.7
1946	Cle-A	5	15	.250	29	21	5	2	4	153^2	159	79	74	20	3	47	75	1.341	4.33	76	4.07	.264	11	.196	-17	3	-1.7
1947	Cle-A	3	5	.375	29	7	0	0	4	84^1	77	43	35	8	1	36	39	1.340	3.74	93	3.52	.240	7	.318	-4	4	-0.2
1948*	Cle-A	9	3	.750	38	9	4	1	2	130	109	52	41	10	6	51	50	1.231	2.84	143	3.09	.226	6	.146	15	10	1.3
1949	Cle-A	4	6	.400	27	12	3	0	0	92	86	41	34	8	2	40	22	1.370	3.33	120	3.79	.250	4	.167	6	6	0.6
1950	Cle-A	10	7	.588	31	13	4	1	0	113^1	94	50	46	10	3	36	43	1.147	3.65	119	2.81	.226	6	.158	8	8	0.6
1951	Cle-A	7	4	.636	27	8	4	0	1	107^1	98	41	33	6	4	29	40	1.183	2.77	137	2.85	.238	8	.296	12	11	1.5
1952	Cle-A	7	7	.500	29	13	3	1	1	122^2	109	55	50	14	2	28	65	1.117	3.67	91	2.88	.232	3	.100	-3	5	-0.4
1953	Cle-A	1	1	.500	5	1	0	0	0	11	11	4	4	0	1	3	8	1.273	3.27	115	3.22	.268	0	.000	1	1	0.0
	Det-A	6	8	.429	19	17	6	1	1	125^2	138	70	63	17	8	36	59	1.385	4.51	90	4.59	.276	3	.073	-2	4	-0.7
	Yr.	7	9	.438	24	18	6	1	1	136^2	149	74	67	17	9	39	67	1.376	4.41	92	4.48	.275	3	.070	-2	5	-0.6
1954	Det-A	18	16	.529	36	32	17	4	1	252^2	236	85	77	26	12	57	102	1.160	2.74	135	3.17	.246	15	.190	**26**	**24**	2.8
1955	Det-A	13	10	.565	28	25	8	2	0	181	183	89	80	26	9	37	73	1.215	3.98	97	3.80	.261	9	.167	-2	10	0.2
1956	Det-A	8	6	.571	40	13	4	0	4	141	142	74	67	25	9	47	64	1.340	4.28	96	4.55	.263	4	.148	-2	8	0.0
1957	Det-A	0	1	.000	15	1	0	0	1	23^2	32	16	16	3	1	13	11	1.901	6.08	63	7.06	.333	0	.000	-6	0	-0.7
Total	17	123	108	.532	447	225	92	17	23	2064^2	1940	893	782	186	68	630	904	1.245	3.41	108	3.38	.247	124	.197	60	141	7.7

• GROOM, Bob — Robert Groom b: 9/12/1884, Belleville, IL d: 2/19/1948, Belleville, IL BR/TR, 6'2", 175 lbs. Deb: 4/13/1909 U

YEAR	TM-L	W	L	PCT	G	GS	CG	SH	SV	IP	H	R	ER	HR	HB	BB	SO	RAT	ERA	ERA+	CERA	OAV	BH	AVG	PR+	WS	TPW
1909	Was-A	7	26	.212	44	31	17	1	0	260^2	218	114	83	2	13	105	131	1.239	2.87	85	2.74	.229	8	.091	-10	7	-1.9
1910	Was-A	12	17	.414	34	30	22	3	0	257^2	244	117	79	8	9	77	98	1.246	2.76	90	3.19	.260	11	.120	-13	10	-2.1
1911	Was-A	13	17	.433	37	32	20	2	2	254^2	280	148	108	9	8	67	135	1.363	3.82	86	3.79	.282	11	.134	-16	11	-1.9
1912	Was-A	24	13	.649	43	40	28	2	1	316	287	133	92	3	5	94	179	1.206	2.62	128	2.70	.246	12	.117	15	23	0.8
1913	Was-A	16	16	.500	37	36	17	4	0	264^1	258	118	95	8	5	81	156	1.282	3.23	91	3.14	.254	15	.163	-13	15	-1.3
1914	StL-F	13	20	.394	42	34	23	1	1	280^2	281	141	101	9	4	75	167	1.268	3.24	107	3.18	.262	15	.160	12	17	1.1
1915	StL-F	11	11	.500	37	26	11	4	2	209	200	93	76	6	2	73	111	1.306	3.27	95	3.29	.261	10	.152	-7	11	-1.0
1916	StL-A	13	9	.591	41	26	8	1	4	217^1	174	82	62	1	3	98	92	1.252	2.57	107	2.64	.226	7	.111	-1	13	-0.3

YEAR	TM-L	W	L	PCT	G	GS	CG	SH	SV	IP	H	R	ER	HR	HB	BB	SO	RAT	ERA	ERA+	CERA	OAV	BH	AVG	PR+	WS	TPW
1917	StL-A	8	19	.296	38	28	11	4	3	232^2	193	80	76	3	5	95	82	1.238	2.94	88	2.71	.233	8	.111	-9	9	-1.4
1918	Cle-A	2	2	.500	14	5	0	0	0	43^1	70	42	34	0	1	18	8	2.031	7.06	42	7.38	.380	1	.083	-19	0	-2.2
Total	10	119	150	.442	367	288	157	22	13	2336^1	2205	1068	806	49	55	783	1159	1.279	3.10	94	3.12	.254	98	.128	-60	116	-10.1

• GROOM, Buddy

Wedsel Gary Groom b: 7/10/1965, Dallas, TX BL/TL, 6'2", 200 lbs. Deb: 6/20/1992

YEAR	TM-L	W	L	PCT	G	GS	CG	SH	SV	IP	H	R	ER	HR	HB	BB	SO	RAT	ERA	ERA+	CERA	OAV	BH	AVG	PR+	WS	TPW
1992	Det-A	0	5	.000	12	7	0	0	1	38^2	48	28	25	4	0	22	15	1.810	5.82	68	6.20	.320	0	....	-8	0	-0.8
1993	Det-A	0	2	.000	19	3	0	0	0	36^2	48	25	25	4	2	13	15	1.664	6.14	70	5.72	.322	0	....	-7	0	-0.7
1994	Det-A	0	1	.000	40	0	0	0	1	32	31	14	14	4	2	13	27	1.375	3.94	123	4.25	.256	0	....	4	3	0.3
1995	Det-A	1	3	.250	23	4	0	0	1	40^2	55	35	34	6	2	26	23	1.992	7.52	63	7.54	.322	0	....	-12	0	-1.1
	Fla-N	1	2	.333	14	0	0	0	0	15	26	12	12	2	0	6	12	2.133	7.20	59	9.52	.400	0	....	-5	0	-0.5
1996	Oak-A	5	0	1.000	72	1	0	0	2	77^1	85	37	33	8	3	34	57	1.539	3.84	128	5.00	.281	0	....	8	7	0.7
1997	Oak-A	2	2	.500	78	0	0	0	3	64^2	75	38	37	9	0	24	45	1.531	5.15	87	5.18	.292	0	....	-3	3	-0.3
1998	Oak-A	3	1	.750	75	0	0	0	0	57^1	62	30	27	4	1	20	36	1.430	4.24	108	4.12	.274	0	....	3	4	0.3
1999	Oak-A	3	2	.600	**76**	0	0	0	0	46	48	29	26	1	1	18	32	1.435	5.09	91	3.71	.274	0	....	-2	3	-0.2
2000	Bal-A	6	3	.667	70	0	0	0	4	59^1	63	37	32	5	0	21	44	1.416	4.85	97	4.01	.275	0	....	-1	6	-0.1
2001	Bal-A	1	4	.200	70	0	0	0	11	66	64	28	26	4	1	9	54	1.106	3.55	121	2.75	.252	0	....	5	8	0.5
2002	Bal-A	3	2	.600	70	0	0	0	2	62	44	11	11	4	2	12	48	.903	1.60	268	1.73	.196	0	....	18	10	1.7
2003	Bal-A	1	3	.250	60	0	0	0	1	45^1	58	27	27	7	3	14	34	1.588	5.36	82	5.93	.309	0	....	-5	1	-0.5
Total	12	26	30	.464	679	15	0	0	26	641	707	351	329	62	17	232	442	1.465	4.62	97	4.62	.282	0	....	-6	45	-0.6

• GROSS, Don

Donald John Gross b: 6/30/1931, Weidman, MI BL/TL, 5'11", 186 lbs. Deb: 7/21/1955

YEAR	TM-L	W	L	PCT	G	GS	CG	SH	SV	IP	H	R	ER	HR	HB	BB	SO	RAT	ERA	ERA+	CERA	OAV	BH	AVG	PR+	WS	TPW
1955	Cin-N	4	5	.444	17	11	2	1	0	67^1	79	33	31	11	1	16	33	1.411	4.14	102	5.01	.298	3	.158	1	3	0.0
1956	Cin-N	3	0	1.000	19	7	2	0	0	69^1	69	25	15	4	1	20	47	1.284	1.95	204	3.30	.257	2	.105	16	7	1.6
1957	Cin-N	7	9	.438	43	16	5	0	1	148^1	152	75	71	21	3	33	73	1.247	4.31	95	3.81	.264	5	.109	-4	8	-0.6
1958	Pit-N	5	7	.417	40	3	0	0	7	74^2	67	37	33	5	1	38	59	1.406	3.98	97	3.58	.241	1	.056	-2	5	-0.4
1959	Pit-N	1	1	.500	21	0	0	0	2	33	28	16	13	3	1	10	15	1.152	3.55	109	2.81	.228	0	.000	1	3	0.1
1960	Pit-N	0	0	....	5	0	0	0	0	5^1	5	2	2	1	0	0	3	.938	3.38	111	2.67	.238	0	....	0	0	0.0
Total	6	20	22	.476	145	37	9	1	10	398	400	188	165	45	7	117	230	1.299	3.73	108	3.78	.261	11	.106	12	26	0.7

• GROSS, Kevin

Kevin Frank Gross b: 6/8/1961, Downey, CA BR/TR, 6'5", 215 lbs. Deb: 6/25/1983

YEAR	TM-L	W	L	PCT	G	GS	CG	SH	SV	IP	H	R	ER	HR	HB	BB	SO	RAT	ERA	ERA+	CERA	OAV	BH	AVG	PR+	WS	TPW
1983	Phi-N	4	6	.400	17	17	1	1	0	96	100	46	38	13	3	35	66	1.406	3.56	100	4.49	.265	3	.091	1	4	0.0
1984	Phi-N	8	5	.615	44	14	1	0	1	129	140	66	59	8	5	44	84	1.426	4.12	88	4.13	.277	2	.067	-5	5	-0.7
1985	Phi-N	15	13	.536	38	31	6	2	0	205^2	194	86	78	11	7	81	151	1.337	3.41	108	3.53	.251	9	.138	9	13	1.0
1986	Phi-N	12	12	.500	37	36	7	2	0	241^2	240	115	108	28	8	94	154	1.382	4.02	96	4.25	.259	15	.188	-4	12	-0.1
1987	Phi-N	9	16	.360	34	33	3	1	0	200^2	205	107	97	26	10	87	110	1.455	4.35	97	4.73	.267	12	.190	-5	9	-0.3
1988	Phi-N★	12	14	.462	33	33	5	1	0	231^2	209	101	95	18	11	89	162	1.286	3.69	97	3.45	.239	13	.173	-0	11	0.1
1989	Mon-N	11	12	.478	31	31	4	3	0	201^1	188	105	98	20	6	88	158	1.371	4.38	81	3.92	.247	9	.141	-18	6	-1.8
1990	Mon-N	9	12	.429	31	26	2	1	0	163^1	171	86	83	9	4	65	111	1.445	4.57	80	4.04	.272	10	.200	-17	5	-1.4
1991	LA-N	10	11	.476	46	10	0	0	3	115^2	123	55	46	10	2	50	95	1.496	3.58	100	4.46	.275	7	.280	-0	7	0.3
1992	LA-N	8	13	.381	34	30	4	3	0	204^2	182	82	72	11	3	77	158	1.265	3.17	109	3.07	.241	6	.095	11	10	1.1
1993	LA-N	13	13	.500	33	32	3	0	0	202^1	224	110	93	15	5	74	150	1.473	4.14	92	4.38	.281	13	.203	-7	9	-0.2
1994	LA-N	9	7	.563	25	23	1	0	1	157^1	162	64	63	11	2	43	124	1.303	3.60	109	3.57	.263	7	.149	6	11	0.7
1995	Tex-A	9	15	.375	31	30	4	0	0	183^2	200	124	113	27	8	89	106	1.574	5.54	87	5.42	.279	0	....	-14	7	-1.3
1996	Tex-A	11	8	.579	28	19	1	0	0	129^1	151	78	75	19	4	50	78	1.554	5.22	101	5.45	.293	0	....	0	8	0.0
1997	Ana-A	2	1	.667	12	3	0	0	0	25^1	30	20	19	4	1	20	20	1.974	6.75	68	7.60	.313	0	.000	-6	0	-0.6
Total	15	142	158	.473	474	368	42	14	5	2487^2	2519	1245	1137	230	79	986	1727	1.409	4.11	95	4.18	.264	106	.161	-48	117	-3.2

• GROSS, Kip

Kip Lee Gross b: 8/24/1964, Scottsbluff, NE BR/TR, 6'2", 195 lbs. Deb: 4/21/1990

YEAR	TM-L	W	L	PCT	G	GS	CG	SH	SV	IP	H	R	ER	HR	HB	BB	SO	RAT	ERA	ERA+	CERA	OAV	BH	AVG	PR+	WS	TPW
1990	Cin-N	0	0	....	5	0	0	0	0	6^1	6	3	3	0	0	2	3	1.263	4.26	93	3.00	.273	0	....	-0	0	0.0
1991	Cin-N	6	4	.600	29	9	1	0	0	85^2	93	43	33	8	0	40	40	1.553	3.47	110	4.75	.279	2	.091	3	5	0.2
1992	LA-N	1	1	.500	16	1	0	0	0	23^2	32	14	11	1	0	10	14	1.775	4.18	82	5.77	.323	2	1.000	-1	1	0.0
1993	LA-N	0	0	....	10	0	0	0	0	15	13	1	1	0	0	4	12	1.133	0.60	635	2.34	.236	0	....	5	2	0.5
1999	Bos-A	0	2	.000	11	1	0	0	0	12^2	15	11	11	3	3	8	9	1.816	7.82	64	7.85	.294	0	....	-4	0	-0.4
2000	Hou-N	0	1	.000	2	1	0	0	0	4^1	9	8	5	2	0	2	3	2.538	10.38	47	15.39	.429	0	.000	-3	0	-0.3
Total	6	7	8	.467	73	12	1	0	0	147^2	168	80	64	14	3	66	81	1.585	3.90	102	5.17	.289	4	.160	0	8	0.1

• GROSSMAN, Harley

Harley Joseph Grossman b: 5/5/1930, Evansville, IN BR/TR, 6', 170 lbs. Deb: 4/22/1952

YEAR	TM-L	W	L	PCT	G	GS	CG	SH	SV	IP	H	R	ER	HR	HB	BB	SO	RAT	ERA	ERA+	CERA	OAV	BH	AVG	PR+	WS	TPW
1952	Was-A	0	0	....	1	0	0	0	0	0^1	2	2	2	1	0	0	0	6.000	54.00	7	83.63	.667	0	....	-2	0	-0.2

• GROTH, Ernest

Ernest William Groth b: 5/3/1922, Beaver Falls, PA BR/TR, 5'9", 185 lbs. Deb: 9/11/1947

YEAR	TM-L	W	L	PCT	G	GS	CG	SH	SV	IP	H	R	ER	HR	HB	BB	SO	RAT	ERA	ERA+	CERA	OAV	BH	AVG	PR+	WS	TPW
1947	Cle-A	0	0	....	2	0	0	0	0	1^1	0	0	0	0	0	1	1	.750	0.00	....	0.49	.000	0	....	0	0	0.1
1948	Cle-A	0	0	....	1	0	0	0	0	1	1	1	1	0	0	2	0	3.000	9.00	45	8.74	.250	0	....	-1	0	-0.1
1949	Chi-A	0	1	.000	3	0	0	0	0	5	2	3	3	2	1	3	1	1.000	5.40	77	4.08	.125	0	....	-1	0	-0.1
Total	3	0	1	.000	6	0	0	0	0	7^1	3	4	4	2	1	6	2	1.227	4.91	84	4.06	.150	0	....	-1	0	-0.1

• GROTH, Ernie

Ernest John "Dango" Groth b: 12/24/1884, Cedarburg, WI d: 5/23/1950, Milwaukee, WI BR/TR, 5'11", 175 lbs. Deb: 9/6/1904

YEAR	TM-L	W	L	PCT	G	GS	CG	SH	SV	IP	H	R	ER	HR	HB	BB	SO	RAT	ERA	ERA+	CERA	OAV	BH	AVG	PR+	WS	TPW
1904	Chi-N	0	2	.000	3	2	2	0	1	16	22	13	10	1	1	6	9	1.750	5.63	47	5.79	.310	0	.000	-6	0	-0.7

• GROTT, Matt

Matthew Allen Grott b: 12/5/1967, La Porte, IN BL/TL, 6'1", 210 lbs. Deb: 5/4/1995

YEAR	TM-L	W	L	PCT	G	GS	CG	SH	SV	IP	H	R	ER	HR	HB	BB	SO	RAT	ERA	ERA+	CERA	OAV	BH	AVG	PR+	WS	TPW
1995	Cin-N	0	0	....	2	0	0	0	0	1^2	6	4	4	1	0	0	2	3.600	21.60	19	26.38	.545	0	....	-3	0	-0.3

• GROVE, Lefty

Robert Moses Grove b: 3/6/1900, Lonaconing, MD d: 5/22/1975, Norwalk, OH BL/TL, 6'3", 190 lbs. Deb: 4/14/1925 HOF: 1947

YEAR	TM-L	W	L	PCT	G	GS	CG	SH	SV	IP	H	R	ER	HR	HB	BB	SO	RAT	ERA	ERA+	CERA	OAV	BH	AVG	PR+	WS	TPW
1925	Phi-A	10	12	.455	45	18	5	0	1	197	207	120	104	11	5	131	**116**	1.716	4.75	98	5.01	.278	8	.123	-0	9	-0.6
1926	Phi-A	13	13	.500	45	33	20	1	6	258	227	97	72	6	6	101	**194**	1.271	**2.51**	**166**	**2.91**	.244	8	.099	**48**	25	**4.1**
1927	Phi-A	20	13	.606	51	28	14	1	9	262^1	251	116	93	6	2	79	**174**	1.258	3.19	134	2.87	.252	10	.125	34	24	3.0
1928	Phi-A	**24**	8	.750	39	31	24	4	4	261^2	228	93	75	10	1	64	**183**	1.116	2.58	155	2.35	.229	15	.170	**42**	**27**	**4.2**
1929*	Phi-A	20	6	.769	42	**37**	19	2	4	275^1	278	104	86	8	3	81	**170**	1.304	**2.81**	**150**	3.19	.262	22	.216	**43**	**28**	**4.1**
1930*	Phi-A	**28**	5	.848	**50**	32	22	2	**9**	291	273	101	82	8	5	60	**209**	1.144	**2.54**	**184**	**2.56**	**.247**	22	.200	**68**	**37**	**6.1**
1931*	Phi-A	**31**	4	.886	41	30	**27**	**4**	5	288^2	249	84	66	10	1	62	**175**	1.077	**2.06**	**218**	**2.23**	.229	23	.200	**70**	**42**	**6.3**
1932	Phi-A	25	10	.714	44	30	**27**	**4**	7	291^2	269	101	92	13	1	79	188	1.193	**2.84**	**159**	**2.74**	.241	18	.168	**54**	**33**	**4.9**
1933	Phi-A★	**24**	8	.750	45	28	**21**	2	6	275^1	280	113	98	12	4	83	114	1.318	3.20	134	3.36	.261	9	.086	41	23	3.3
1934	Bos-A	8	8	.500	22	12	5	0	0	109^1	149	84	79	5	1	32	43	1.655	6.50	74	5.19	.320	6	.162	-20	2	-1.8
1935	Bos-A★	20	12	.625	35	30	23	2	1	273	269	105	82	6	3	65	121	1.223	**2.70**	**175**	**2.83**	.257	7	.079	**61**	29	5.3
1936	Bos-A★	17	12	.586	35	30	22	**6**	2	253^1	237	90	79	14	4	65	130	1.192	**2.81**	**189**	**2.88**	.246	11	.138	**70**	**29**	**6.0**
1937	Bos-A★	17	9	.654	32	32	21	3	0	262	269	101	88	9	1	83	153	1.344	3.02	157	3.34	.261	13	.143	56	27	4.9
1938	Bos-A★	14	4	.778	24	21	12	1	1	163^2	169	65	56	8	1	52	99	1.350	**3.08**	**160**	3.48	.263	8	.148	32	17	2.8
1939	Bos-A★	15	4	.789	23	23	17	2	0	191	180	63	54	8	1	58	81	1.246	**2.54**	**186**	2.95	.249	9	.134	47	23	4.2
1940	Bos-A	7	6	.538	22	21	9	1	0	153^1	159	73	68	20	1	50	62	1.363	3.99	113	4.18	.269	8	.151	10	11	0.8
1941	Bos-A	7	7	.500	21	21	10	0	0	134	155	84	65	8	2	42	54	1.470	4.37	96	4.21	.287	5	.111	-1	5	-0.2
Total	17	300	141	.680	616	457	298	35	55	3940^2	3849	1594	1339	162	42	1187	2266	1.278	3.06	148	3.14	.255	202	.148	654	391	57.3

• GROVE, Orval

Orval Leroy Grove b: 8/29/1919, Mineral, KS d: 4/20/1992, Carmichael, CA BR/TR, 6'3", 196 lbs. Deb: 5/28/1940

YEAR	TM-L	W	L	PCT	G	GS	CG	SH	SV	IP	H	R	ER	HR	HB	BB	SO	RAT	ERA	ERA+	CERA	OAV	BH	AVG	PR+	WS	TPW
1940	Chi-A	0	0	....	3	0	0	0	0	6	4	2	2	0	0	4	1	1.333	3.00	147	2.38	.182	0	.000	1	0	0.1
1941	Chi-A	0	0	....	2	0	0	0	0	7	9	8	8	2	0	5	5	2.000	10.29	40	8.34	.321	0	.000	-5	0	-0.5
1942	Chi-A	4	6	.400	12	8	4	0	0	66^1	77	47	38	1	1	33	21	1.658	5.16	70	4.54	.283	5	.227	-12	0	-1.1
1943	Chi-A	15	9	.625	32	25	18	3	2	216^1	192	84	66	9	4	72	76	1.220	2.75	122	2.86	.239	12	.182	13	18	1.6
1944	Chi-A★	14	15	.483	34	33	11	2	0	234^2	237	112	97	11	8	71	105	1.313	3.72	92	3.40	.263	8	.104	-7	12	-1.1
1945	Chi-A	14	12	.538	33	30	16	4	1	217	233	100	83	12	5	68	54	1.387	3.44	96	3.85	.273	7	.099	-0	11	-0.5
1946	Chi-A	8	13	.381	33	26	10	1	0	205^1	213	96	69	10	3	78	60	1.417	3.02	113	3.84	.272	7	.108	7	10	0.4
1947	Chi-A	6	8	.429	25	19	6	1	0	135^2	158	78	67	10	4	70	33	1.681	4.44	82	5.31	.296	7	.146	-12	3	-1.2

YEAR TM-L	W	L	PCT	G	GS	CG	SH	SV	IP	H	R	ER	HR	HB	BB	SO	RAT	ERA	ERA+	CERA	OAV	BH	AVG	PR+	WS	TPW
1948 Chi-A	2	10	.167	32	11	1	0	1	87^{2}	110	64	60	6	3	42	18	1.734	6.16	69	5.70	.315	2	.095	-19	0	-2.1
1949 Chi-A	0	0	....	1	0	0	0	0	0^{2}	4	4	4	1	1	1	1	7.500	54.00	8	79.03	.667	0	....	-4	0	-0.4
Total 10	63	73	.463	207	152	66	11	4	1176^{2}	1237	595	494	62	29	444	374	1.429	3.78	94	3.98	.272	48	.129	-38	54	-4.7
• GROVER, Charlie	Charles Byrd "Bugs" Grover b: 6/20/1890, Gallipolis, OH d: 5/24/1971, Emmett Township, Calhoun Cty, MI BL/TR, 6'1.5", 185 lbs. Deb: 9/9/1913																									
1913 Det-A	0	0	....	2	1	0	0	0	10^{2}	9	4	4	0	0	7	2	1.500	3.38	86	3.84	.265	0	.000	-0	0	0.0
• GRUBBS, Tom	Thomas Dillard "Judge" Grubbs b: 2/22/1894, Mount Sterling, KY d: 1/28/1986, Lexington, KY BR/TR, 6'2", 165 lbs. Deb: 10/3/1920																									
1920 NY-N	0	1	.000	1	1	0	0	0	5	9	4	4	0	0	0	0	1.800	7.20	42	6.52	.409	0	.000	-2	0	-0.3
• GRUBER, Henry	Henry John Gruber b: 12/14/1863, Hamden, CT d: 9/26/1932, New Haven, CT BR/TR, 5'9", 155 lbs. Deb: 7/28/1887 U																									
1887 Det-N	4	3	.571	7	7	7	0	0	62^{1}	84	29	19	3	0	21	12	1.348	2.74	146	....	.313	10	.333	8	5	0.8
1888 Det-N	11	14	.440	27	25	25	3	0	240	196	121	61	8	4	41	71	.988	2.29	120	....	.215	13	.141	18	12	1.7
1889 Cle-N	7	16	.304	25	23	23	0	1	205	198	125	83	6	8	94	74	1.424	3.64	111	....	.246	7	.101	2	13	0.2
1890 Cle-P	22	23	.489	48	44	39	1	0	383^{1}	464	352	182	15	15	204	110	1.743	4.27	93	....	.287	36	.221	-14	16	-0.5
1891 Cle-N	17	22	.436	44	40	35	1	0	348^{2}	407	258	160	10	7	119	79	1.509	4.13	84	....	.281	23	.163	-22	16	-1.8
Total 5	61	78	.439	151	139	129	5	1	1239^{1}	1349	885	505	42	34	479	346	1.458	3.67	99	....	.267	89	.180	-7	62	0.4
• GRUNDT, Ken	Kenneth Allan Grundt b: 8/26/1969, Melrose Park, IL BL/TL, 6'4", 195 lbs. Deb: 8/8/1996																									
1996 Bos-A	0	0	....	1	0	0	0	0	0^{1}	1	1	1	0	0	0	0	3.000	27.00	19	14.52	.500	0	....	-1	0	-0.1
1997 Bos-A	0	0	....	2	0	0	0	0	3	5	3	3	0	0	0	0	1.667	9.00	52	5.42	.357	0	....	-1	0	-0.1
Total 2	0	0	....	3	0	0	0	0	3^{1}	6	4	4	0	0	0	0	1.800	10.80	44	6.33	.375	0	....	-2	0	-0.2
• GRUNWALD, Al	Alfred Henry "Stretch" Grunwald b: 2/13/1930, Los Angeles, CA BL/TL, 6'4", 210 lbs. Deb: 4/18/1955																									
1955 Pit-N	0	0	....	3	0	0	0	0	7^{2}	7	4	4	1	0	7	2	1.826	4.70	88	5.91	.241	2	.500	-0	1	0.0
1959 KC-A	0	1	.000	6	1	0	0	1	11^{1}	18	14	10	1	0	11	9	2.559	7.94	50	9.90	.360	0	.000	-5	0	-0.6
Total 2	0	1	.000	9	1	0	0	1	19	25	18	14	2	0	18	11	2.263	6.63	61	8.29	.316	2	.250	-5	1	-0.5
• GRYBOSKI, Kevin	Kevin John Gryboski b: 11/15/1973, Wilkes-Barre, PA BR/TR, 6'5", 235 lbs. Deb: 4/13/2002																									
2002* Atl-N	2	1	.667	57	0	0	0	0	51^{2}	50	20	20	6	5	37	33	1.684	3.48	117	5.58	.256	0	....	3	4	0.3
2003* Atl-N	6	4	.600	64	0	0	0	0	44^{1}	44	22	19	3	2	23	32	1.511	3.86	109	4.36	.272	0	.000	2	3	0.2
Total 2	8	5	.615	121	0	0	0	0	96	94	42	39	9	7	60	65	1.604	3.66	114	5.02	.263	0	.000	5	7	0.4
• GRZANICH, Mike	Michael Edward Grzanich b: 8/24/1972, Canton, IL BR/TR, 6'1" Deb: 5/14/1998																									
1998 Hou-N	0	0	....	1	0	0	0	0	1	1	2	2	0	0	2	1	3.000	18.00	23	9.51	.333	0	....	-2	0	-0.2
• GRZENDA, Joe	Joseph Charles Grzenda b: 6/8/1937, Scranton, PA BR/TL, 6'2", 180 lbs. Deb: 4/26/1961																									
1961 Det-A	1	0	1.000	4	0	0	0	0	5^{2}	9	5	5	2	0	2	0	1.941	7.94	52	9.11	.375	1	1.000	-2	0	-0.2
1964 KC-A	0	2	.000	20	0	0	0	0	25	34	15	15	2	1	13	17	1.880	5.40	71	6.52	.324	0	.000	-4	0	-0.4
1966 KC-A	0	2	.000	21	0	0	0	0	22	28	8	8	1	0	12	14	1.818	3.27	104	5.85	.337	0	.000	0	1	0.0
1967 NY-N	0	0	....	11	0	0	0	0	16^{2}	14	4	4	0	1	8	9	1.320	2.16	157	2.71	.237	0	.000	2	2	0.2
1969* Min-A	4	1	.800	38	0	0	0	3	48^{2}	52	23	21	4	1	17	24	1.418	3.88	94	4.17	.281	0	.000	-2	3	-0.2
1970 Was-A	3	6	.333	49	3	0	0	6	84^{2}	86	52	47	8	3	34	38	1.417	5.00	71	4.13	.267	0	.000	-15	1	-1.7
1971 Was-A	5	2	.714	46	0	0	0	5	70^{1}	54	19	15	2	1	17	56	1.009	1.92	172	1.85	.217	1	.143	11	9	1.1
1972 StL-N	1	0	1.000	30	0	0	0	0	35	46	24	22	1	3	17	15	1.800	5.66	60	5.67	.326	0	.000	-9	0	-1.0
Total 8	14	13	.519	219	3	0	0	14	308	323	150	137	20	10	120	173	1.438	4.00	89	4.12	.277	2	.067	-19	16	-2.1
• GUANTE, Cecilio	Cecilio (Magallane) Guante b: 2/1/1960, Villa Mella, Dominican Republic BR/TR, 6'3", 205 lbs. Deb: 5/1/1982																									
1982 Pit-N	0	0	....	10	0	0	0	0	27	28	16	10	1	2	5	26	1.222	3.33	111	3.19	.264	0	.000	1	1	0.1
1983 Pit-N	2	6	.250	49	0	0	0	9	100^{1}	90	45	37	5	2	46	82	1.355	3.32	112	3.35	.241	2	.091	5	7	0.4
1984 Pit-N	2	3	.400	27	0	0	0	2	41^{1}	32	12	12	3	2	16	30	1.161	2.61	138	2.85	.224	0	.000	4	4	0.4
1985 Pit-N	4	6	.400	63	0	0	0	5	109	84	34	33	5	5	40	92	1.138	2.72	131	2.46	.214	1	.059	12	10	1.1
1986 Pit-N	5	2	.714	52	0	0	0	4	78	65	32	29	11	3	29	63	1.205	3.35	115	3.41	.225	0	.000	4	6	0.4
1987 NY-A	3	2	.600	23	0	0	0	1	44	42	30	28	8	1	20	46	1.409	5.73	77	4.61	.247	0	....	-7	1	-0.6
1988 NY-A	5	6	.455	56	0	0	0	11	75	59	25	24	10	5	22	61	1.080	2.88	137	2.93	.213	0	....	9	9	1.0
Tex-A	0	0	....	7	0	0	0	1	4^{2}	8	1	1	1	0	4	4	2.571	1.93	212	12.03	.400	0	....	1	0	0.1
Yr.	5	6	.455	63	0	0	0	12	79^{2}	67	26	25	11	5	26	65	1.167	2.82	140	3.46	.226	0	....	11	9	1.1
1989 Tex-A	6	6	.500	50	0	0	0	2	69	66	35	30	7	4	36	69	1.478	3.91	101	4.22	.249	0	....	1	4	0.1
1990 Cle-A	2	3	.400	26	1	0	0	0	46^{2}	38	26	26	10	3	18	30	1.200	5.01	78	3.85	.220	0	....	-5	1	-0.5
Total 9	29	34	.460	363	1	0	0	35	595	512	256	230	61	27	236	503	1.257	3.48	111	3.40	.232	3	.061	26	43	2.5
• GUARDADO, Eddie	Edward Adrian "Everyday Eddie" Guardado b: 10/2/1970, Stockton, CA BR/TL, 6', 193 lbs. Deb: 6/13/1993																									
1993 Min-A	3	8	.273	19	16	0	0	0	94^{2}	123	68	65	13	1	36	46	1.680	6.18	70	6.18	.319	0	....	-18	1	-1.8
1994 Min-A	0	2	.000	4	4	0	0	0	17	26	16	16	3	0	4	8	1.765	8.47	57	7.01	.351	0	....	-7	0	-0.6
1995 Min-A	4	9	.308	51	5	0	0	2	91^{1}	99	54	52	13	0	45	71	1.577	5.12	93	5.20	.280	0	....	-3	4	-0.3
1996 Min-A	6	5	.545	**83**	0	0	0	4	73^{2}	61	45	43	12	3	33	74	1.276	5.25	97	3.81	.228	0	....	-2	6	-0.2
1997 Min-A	0	4	.000	69	0	0	0	1	46	45	23	20	7	2	17	54	1.348	3.91	119	4.23	.251	0	....	4	3	0.4
1998 Min-A	3	1	.750	79	0	0	0	0	65^{2}	66	34	33	10	0	28	53	1.431	4.52	105	4.42	.265	0	....	3	5	0.3
1999 Min-A	2	5	.286	63	0	0	0	2	48	37	25	25	6	2	25	50	1.292	4.69	108	3.63	.222	0	....	2	4	0.2
2000 Min-A	7	4	.636	70	0	0	0	9	61^{2}	55	27	27	14	1	25	52	1.297	3.94	131	4.34	.238	0	....	9	8	0.8
2001 Min-A	7	1	.875	67	0	0	0	12	66^{2}	47	27	26	5	1	23	67	1.050	3.51	131	2.13	.197	0	....	8	12	0.8
2002* Min-A★	1	3	.250	68	0	0	0	**45**	67^{2}	53	22	22	9	1	18	70	1.049	2.93	153	2.66	.215	0	....	12	14	1.1
2003* Min-A★	3	5	.375	66	0	0	0	41	65^{1}	50	22	21	7	0	14	60	.980	2.89	157	2.14	.207	0	....	13	14	1.3
Total 11	36	47	.434	639	25	0	0	116	697^{2}	662	363	350	99	11	268	605	1.333	4.52	105	4.08	.252	0	....	22	71	2.0
• GUBICZA, Mark	Mark Steven Gubicza b: 8/14/1962, Philadelphia, PA BR/TR, 6'6", 220 lbs. Deb: 4/6/1984																									
1984 KC-A	10	14	.417	29	29	4	2	0	189	172	90	85	13	5	75	111	1.307	4.05	100	3.47	.243	0	....	-2	10	-0.2
1985* KC-A	14	10	.583	29	28	0	0	0	177^{1}	160	88	80	14	5	77	99	1.336	4.06	102	3.62	.238	0	....	4	12	0.4
1986 KC-A	12	6	.667	35	24	3	2	0	180^{2}	155	77	73	8	5	84	118	1.323	3.64	117	3.28	.233	0	....	14	14	1.4
1987 KC-A	13	18	.419	35	35	10	2	0	241^{2}	231	114	107	18	6	120	166	1.452	3.98	114	4.20	.259	0	....	19	16	1.8
1988 KC-A★	20	8	.714	35	35	8	4	0	269^{2}	237	94	81	11	6	83	183	1.187	2.70	147	2.77	.234	0	....	**43**	24	**4.3**
1989 KC-A★	15	11	.577	36	**36**	8	2	0	255	252	100	86	10	5	63	173	1.235	3.04	127	3.06	.259	0	....	27	19	2.8
1990 KC-A	4	7	.364	16	16	2	0	0	94	101	48	47	5	4	38	71	1.479	4.50	85	4.34	.283	0	....	-5	3	-0.5
1991 KC-A	9	12	.429	26	26	0	0	0	133	168	90	84	10	6	42	89	1.579	5.68	72	5.24	.308	0	....	-19	2	-1.9
1992 KC-A	7	6	.538	18	18	2	1	0	111^{1}	110	47	46	8	1	36	81	1.311	3.72	109	3.52	.259	0	....	6	7	0.6
1993 KC-A	5	8	.385	49	6	0	0	2	104^{1}	128	61	54	2	2	43	80	1.639	4.66	98	4.75	.307	0	....	-2	5	-0.2
1994 KC-A	7	9	.438	22	22	0	0	0	130	158	74	65	11	0	26	59	1.415	4.50	111	4.32	.301	0	....	7	8	0.7
1995 KC-A	12	14	.462	33	**33**	3	2	0	213^{1}	222	97	89	21	6	62	81	1.331	3.75	127	4.02	.272	0	....	22	16	2.0
1996 KC-A	4	12	.250	19	19	2	1	0	119^{1}	132	70	68	22	7	34	55	1.391	5.13	98	5.15	.284	0	....	-2	5	-0.1
1997 Ana-A	0	1	.000	2	2	0	0	0	4^{2}	13	13	13	2	0	3	5	3.429	25.07	18	21.13	.481	0	....	-11	0	-1.0
Total 14	132	136	.493	384	329	42	16	2	2223^{1}	2239	1063	978	155	58	786	1371	1.361	3.96	109	3.85	.264	0	....	102	141	10.1
• GUDAT, Marv	Marvin John Gudat b: 8/27/1903, Goliad, TX d: 3/1/1954, Los Angeles, CA BL/TL, 5'11", 162 lbs. Deb: 5/21/1929 ♦																									
1929 Cin-N	1	1	.500	7	2	2	0	0	26^{2}	29	12	10	0	0	4	0	1.238	3.38	135	2.88	.282	2	.200	3	2	0.3
1932* Chi-N	0	0	....	1	0	0	0	0	1	1	0	0	0	0	0	2	1.000	0.00	....	1.95	.250	24	.255	0	3	-0.2
Total 2	1	1	.500	8	2	2	0	0	27^{2}	30	12	10	0	0	4	2	1.229	3.25	140	2.85	.281	26	.250	4	5	0.1
• GUESE, Whitey	Theodore Guese b: 1/24/1872, New Bremen, OH d: 4/8/1951, Wapakoneta, OH BR/TR, 6'.5", 200 lbs. Deb: 7/13/1901																									
1901 Cin-N	1	4	.200	6	5	4	0	0	44^{1}	62	48	30	5	3	14	11	1.714	6.09	52	6.39	.328	3	.200	-13	0	-1.2

YEAR	TM-L	W	L	PCT	G	GS	CG	SH	SV	IP	H	R	ER	HR	HB	BB	SO	RAT	ERA	ERA+	CERA	OAV	BH	AVG	PR+	WS	TPW
• GUETTERMAN, Lee	Arthur Lee Guetterman b: 11/22/1958, Chattanooga, TN BL/TL, 6'8", 227 lbs. Deb: 9/12/1984																										
1984	Sea-A	0	0	....	3	0	0	0	0	4^1	9	2	2	0	0	2	2	2.538	4.15	96	11.04	.450	0	....	0	0	0.0
1986	Sea-A	0	4	.000	41	4	1	0	0	76	108	67	62	7	4	30	38	1.816	7.34	58	6.83	.347	0	....	-26	0	-2.6
1987	Sea-A	11	4	.733	25	17	2	1	0	113^1	117	60	48	13	2	35	42	1.341	3.81	124	4.05	.267	0	....	11	9	1.0
1988	NY-A	1	2	.333	20	2	0	0	0	40^2	49	21	21	2	1	14	15	1.549	4.65	85	4.88	.306	0	....	-3	1	-0.3
1989	NY-A	5	5	.500	70	0	0	0	13	103	98	31	28	6	0	26	51	1.204	2.45	158	2.95	.258	0	....	16	13	1.6
1990	NY-A	11	7	.611	64	0	0	0	2	93	80	37	35	6	0	26	48	1.140	3.39	117	2.57	.236	0	....	6	10	0.6
1991	NY-A	3	4	.429	64	0	0	0	6	88	91	42	36	6	3	25	35	1.318	3.68	112	3.62	.268	0	....	5	6	0.5
1992	NY-A	1	1	.500	15	0	0	0	0	22^2	35	24	24	5	0	13	5	2.118	9.53	41	8.95	.354	0	....	-14	0	-1.4
	NY-N	3	4	.429	43	0	0	0	2	43^1	57	28	28	5	1	14	15	1.638	5.82	60	5.66	.324	0	.000	-11	0	-1.2
1993	StL-N	3	3	.500	40	0	0	0	1	46	41	18	15	1	2	16	19	1.239	2.93	135	2.78	.240	1	.500	5	4	0.6
1995	Sea-A	0	0	....	23	0	0	0	1	17	21	13	13	1	3	11	11	1.882	6.88	69	6.79	.300	0	....	-4	0	-0.3
1996	Sea-A	0	2	.000	17	0	0	0	0	11	11	8	5	0	0	10	6	1.909	4.09	121	5.20	.275	0	....	1	0	0.1
Total	11	38	36	.514	425	23	3	1	25	658^1	717	351	317	52	16	222	287	1.426	4.33	95	4.31	.282	1	.250	-14	43	-1.4
• GUIDRY, Ron	Ronald Ames "Louisiana Lightning,Gator" Guidry b: 8/28/1950, Lafayette, LA BL/TL, 5'11", 162 lbs. Deb: 7/27/1975																										
1975	NY-A	0	1	.000	10	1	0	0	0	15^2	15	6	6	0	1	9	15	1.532	3.45	106	4.09	.259	0	....	-0	1	0.0
1976*	NY-A	0	0	....	7	0	0	0	0	16	20	12	10	1	0	4	12	1.500	5.63	61	4.51	.294	0	....	-4	0	-0.5
1977*	NY-A	16	7	.696	31	25	9	5	1	210^2	174	72	66	12	0	65	176	1.134	2.82	140	2.55	.224	0	....	22	18	2.2
1978*	NY-A★	**25**	3	.893	35	35	16	**9**	0	273^2	187	61	53	13	1	72	248	.946	**1.74**	**208**	**1.71**	**.193**	0	....	**55**	**31**	**5.7**
1979	NY-A★	18	8	.692	33	30	15	2	2	236^1	203	83	73	20	0	71	201	1.159	**2.78**	146	2.92	.236	0	....	30	22	2.9
1980*	NY-A	17	10	.630	37	29	5	3	1	219^2	215	97	87	19	1	80	166	1.343	3.56	110	3.77	.260	0	....	10	15	1.0
1981*	NY-A	11	5	.688	23	21	0	0	0	127	100	41	39	12	1	26	104	.992	2.76	129	2.27	.214	0	....	11	10	1.1
1982	NY-A★	14	8	.636	34	33	6	1	0	222	216	104	94	22	1	69	162	1.284	3.81	105	3.56	.254	0	....	6	12	0.6
1983	NY-A★	21	9	.700	31	31	**21**	3	0	250^1	232	99	95	26	2	60	156	1.166	3.42	114	3.11	.244	0	....	15	19	1.4
1984	NY-A	10	11	.476	29	28	5	1	0	195^2	223	102	98	24	2	44	127	1.365	4.51	84	4.32	.287	0	....	-14	7	-1.4
1985	NY-A	**22**	6	.786	34	33	11	2	0	259	243	104	94	28	0	42	143	1.100	3.27	123	2.91	.248	0	....	18	18	1.8
1986	NY-A	9	12	.429	30	30	5	0	0	192^1	202	94	85	28	1	38	140	1.248	3.98	103	3.83	.265	0	....	1	10	0.1
1987	NY-A	5	8	.385	22	17	2	0	0	117^2	111	50	48	14	1	38	96	1.266	3.67	119	3.59	.248	0	....	9	9	0.8
1988	NY-A	2	3	.400	12	10	0	0	0	56	57	28	26	7	2	15	32	1.286	4.18	94	3.85	.259	0	....	-1	2	-0.1
Total	14	170	91	.651	368	323	95	26	4	2392	2198	953	874	226	13	633	1778	1.184	3.29	119	3.13	.244	0	....	156	174	15.6
• GUINN, Skip	Drannon Eugene Guinn b: 10/25/1944, St. Charles, MO BR/TL, 5'10", 180 lbs. Deb: 5/7/1968																										
1968	Atl-N	0	0	....	3	0	0	0	0	5	3	2	2	0	0	3	4	1.200	3.60	83	2.03	.167	0	....	-0	0	0.0
1969	Hou-N	1	2	.333	28	0	0	0	0	27	34	22	20	3	1	21	33	2.037	6.67	53	7.20	.304	0	.000	-9	0	-1.0
1971	Hou-N	0	0	....	4	0	0	0	1	4^2	1	0	0	0	0	3	3	.857	0.00	....	0.72	.067	0	....	2	1	0.2
Total	3	1	2	.333	35	0	0	0	1	36^2	38	24	22	3	1	27	40	1.773	5.40	65	5.67	.262	0	.000	-8	1	-0.8
• GUISE, Lefty	Witt Orison Guise b: 9/18/1909, Driggs, AR d: 8/13/1968, Little Rock, AR BL/TL, 6'2", 172 lbs. Deb: 9/3/1940																										
1940	Cin-N	0	0	....	2	0	0	0	0	7^2	8	2	1	0	1	5	1	1.696	1.17	323	5.14	.296	1	.333	2	1	0.2
• GULLETT, Don	Donald Edward Gullett b: 1/6/1951, Lynn, KY BR/TL, 6', 190 lbs. Deb: 4/10/1970 C																										
1970*	Cin-N	5	2	.714	44	2	0	0	6	77^2	54	23	21	4	0	44	76	1.262	2.43	171	2.65	.196	4	.211	15	10	1.6
1971	Cin-N	16	6	.727	35	31	4	3	0	217^2	196	73	64	14	2	64	107	1.194	2.65	123	2.93	.242	9	.120	10	17	0.8
1972*	Cin-N	9	10	.474	31	16	2	0	2	134^2	127	61	59	15	1	43	96	1.262	3.94	81	3.54	.250	8	.211	-14	5	-1.3
1973*	Cin-N	18	8	.692	45	30	7	4	2	228^1	198	95	89	24	3	69	153	1.169	3.51	97	3.01	.232	12	.188	-8	15	-0.5
1974	Cin-N	17	11	.607	36	35	10	3	0	243	201	93	82	22	2	88	183	1.189	3.04	115	2.90	.222	19	.238	8	18	1.1
1975*	Cin-N	15	4	.789	22	22	8	3	0	159^2	127	49	43	11	2	56	98	1.146	2.42	148	2.64	.218	14	.226	16	15	1.9
1976*	Cin-N	11	3	.786	23	20	4	0	1	126	119	48	42	8	0	48	64	1.325	3.00	117	3.45	.253	8	.182	6	8	0.6
1977*	NY-A	14	4	.778	22	22	7	1	0	158^1	137	67	63	14	1	69	116	1.301	3.58	110	3.42	.232	0	....	4	11	0.3
1978	NY-A	4	2	.667	8	8	2	0	0	44^2	46	19	18	3	1	20	28	1.478	3.63	100	4.30	.269	0	....	-0	3	0.0
Total	9	109	50	.686	266	186	44	14	11	1390	1205	528	481	115	12	501	921	1.227	3.11	112	3.09	.233	74	.194	36	102	4.6
• GULLICKSON, Bill	William Lee Gullickson b: 2/20/1959, Marshall, MN BR/TR, 6'3", 215 lbs. Deb: 9/26/1979																										
1979	Mon-N	0	0	....	1	0	0	0	0	1	2	0	0	0	0	0	0	2.000	0.00	....	9.49	.500	0	....	0	0	0.0
1980	Mon-N	10	5	.667	24	19	5	2	0	141	127	53	47	6	2	50	120	1.255	3.00	119	3.00	.238	7	.175	10	10	1.1
1981*	Mon-N	7	9	.438	22	22	3	2	0	157^1	142	54	49	3	4	34	115	1.119	2.80	125	2.42	.239	7	.152	12	10	1.2
1982	Mon-N	12	14	.462	34	34	6	0	0	236^2	231	101	94	25	4	61	155	1.234	3.57	102	3.47	.254	10	.122	1	11	-0.2
1983	Mon-N	17	12	.586	34	34	10	1	0	242^1	230	108	101	19	4	59	120	1.193	3.75	96	3.14	.251	11	.134	-8	13	-0.7
1984	Mon-N	12	9	.571	32	32	3	0	0	226^2	230	100	91	27	1	37	100	1.178	3.61	95	3.38	.265	8	.110	-8	10	-1.1
1985	Mon-N	14	12	.538	29	29	4	1	0	181^1	187	78	71	8	1	47	68	1.290	3.52	96	3.29	.271	12	.188	-4	9	-0.3
1986	Cin-N	15	12	.556	37	37	6	2	0	244^2	245	103	92	24	2	60	121	1.247	3.38	114	3.46	.264	6	.076	15	16	1.1
1987	Cin-N	10	11	.476	27	27	3	1	0	165	172	99	89	33	2	39	89	1.279	4.85	87	4.31	.267	11	.208	-12	6	-1.0
	NY-A	4	2	.667	8	8	1	0	0	48	46	29	26	7	1	11	28	1.188	4.88	90	3.54	.253	0	....	-3	2	-0.3
1990	Hou-N	10	14	.417	32	32	2	1	0	193^1	221	100	82	21	2	61	73	1.459	3.82	97	4.53	.287	9	.158	-3	7	-0.1
1991	Det-A	**20**	9	.690	35	**35**	4	0	0	226^1	256	109	98	22	4	44	91	1.325	3.90	107	3.99	.288	0	....	7	14	0.7
1992	Det-A	14	13	.519	34	34	4	1	0	221^2	228	109	107	35	0	50	64	1.254	4.34	91	3.93	.267	0	....	-7	10	-0.7
1993	Det-A	13	9	.591	28	28	2	0	0	159^1	186	106	95	28	3	44	70	1.444	5.37	80	5.10	.291	0	....	-19	5	-1.8
1994	Det-A	4	5	.444	21	19	1	0	0	115^1	156	79	76	24	4	25	65	1.569	5.93	82	6.31	.322	0	....	-12	3	-1.1
Total	14	162	136	.544	398	390	54	11	0	2560	2659	1228	1118	282	34	622	1279	1.282	3.93	98	3.78	.268	81	.141	-32	126	-3.2
• GUMBERT, Ad	Addison Courtney Gumbert b: 10/10/1868, Pittsburgh, PA d: 4/23/1925, Pittsburgh, PA BR/TR, 5'10", 200 lbs. Deb: 9/15/1888 U																										
1888	Chi-N	3	3	.500	6	6	5	0	0	48^2	44	24	17	0	5	10	16	1.110	3.14	96	....	.233	8	.333	-2	4	0.0
1889	Chi-N	16	13	.552	31	28	25	2	0	246^1	258	148	99	16	14	76	91	1.356	3.62	115	....	.261	44	.288	13	19	2.0
1890	Bos-P	23	12	.657	39	33	27	1	0	277^1	338	189	122	18	11	86	81	1.529	3.96	111	....	.288	35	.241	10	25	1.2
1891	Chi-N	17	11	.607	32	31	24	1	0	256^1	282	149	102	5	10	90	73	1.451	3.58	93	....	.269	32	.305	-12	23	0.2
1892	Chi-N	22	19	.537	46	45	39	0	0	382^2	399	220	145	11	14	107	118	1.322	3.41	97	3.43	.258	42	.236	1	24	0.2
1893	Pit-N	11	7	.611	22	20	16	2	0	162^2	207	119	93	5	5	78	40	1.752	5.15	88	5.42	.301	21	.221	-15	11	-1.2
1894	Pit-N	15	14	.517	38	32	26	0	0	271^1	376	245	180	13	6	85	67	1.699	5.97	88	5.58	.325	33	.292	-22	15	-1.2
1895	Bro-N	11	16	.407	33	26	20	0	1	234	288	183	132	11	12	69	45	1.526	5.08	86	4.70	.298	35	.361	-21	16	-0.8
1896	Bro-N	0	4	.000	5	4	2	0	0	31	34	18	13	2	0	11	3	1.452	3.77	109	4.11	.277	2	.182	1	2	0.1
	Phi-N	5	3	.625	11	10	7	1	0	77^1	99	55	39	0	4	23	14	1.578	4.54	95	4.62	.309	9	.265	-1	5	0.0
	Yr.	5	7	.417	16	14	9	1	0	108^1	133	73	52	2	4	34	17	1.542	4.32	98	4.48	.300	11	.244	0	7	0.1
Total	9	123	102	.547	263	235	191	7	1	1987^2	2325	1350	942	81	81	635	548	1.489	4.27	97	2.66	.284	261	.273	-48	144	0.4
• GUMBERT, Billy	William Skeen Gumbert b: 8/8/1865, Pittsburgh, PA d: 4/13/1946, Pittsburgh, PA BR/TR, 6'1.5", 200 lbs. Deb: 6/19/1890																										
1890	Pit-N	4	6	.400	10	10	8	0	0	79^1	96	71	46	0	8	31	18	1.601	5.22	63	....	.290	9	.243	-13	2	-0.9
1892	Pit-N	3	2	.600	6	3	2	0	0	39^2	30	15	6	0	1	23	3	1.336	1.36	242	2.70	.202	2	.111	7	4	0.6
1893	Lou-N	0	0	....	1	1	0	0	0	0^2	2	6	2	0	0	5	0	10.50	27.00	16	49.07	.504	1	1.000	-2	0	-0.1
Total	3	7	8	.467	17	14	10	0	0	119^2	128	92	54	0	9	59	21	1.563	4.06	82	1.17	.265	12	.214	-7	6	-0.4
• GUMBERT, Harry	Harry Edwards "Gunboat" Gumbert b: 11/5/1909, Elizabeth, PA d: 1/4/1995, Wimberley, TX BR/TR, 6'2", 185 lbs. Deb: 9/12/1935																										
1935	NY-N	1	2	.333	6	3	1	0	0	23^2	35	27	16	1	0	10	11	1.901	6.08	63	6.21	.330	0	.000	-6	0	-0.7
1936*	NY-N	11	3	.786	39	15	3	0	0	140^2	157	77	61	7	2	54	52	1.500	3.90	100	4.25	.281	11	.250	-5	9	-0.3
1937*	NY-N	10	11	.476	34	24	10	1	1	200^1	194	92	82	11	4	62	65	1.278	3.68	105	3.23	.257	13	.181	0	12	-0.1
1938	NY-N	15	13	.536	38	33	14	1	0	235^2	238	114	105	13	7	84	84	1.366	4.01	94	3.66	.261	13	.155	-7	12	-1.0
1939	NY-N	18	11	.621	36	34	14	2	0	243^2	257	132	117	21	1	81	81	1.387	4.32	91	3.95	.271	18	.200	-11	13	-1.1
1940	NY-N	12	14	.462	35	30	14	2	2	237	230	110	99	17	3	81	77	1.312	3.76	103	3.45	.252	17	.195	4	14	0.6

YEAR TM-L	W	L	PCT	G	GS	CG	SH	SV	IP	H	R	ER	HR	HB	BB	SO	RAT	ERA	ERA+	CERA	OAV	BH	AVG	PR+	WS	TPW
1941 NY-N	1	1	.500	5	5	1	0	0	32^1	34	20	16	3	0	18	9	1.608	4.45	83	4.71	.266	2	.167	-3	1	-0.3
StL-N	11	5	.688	33	17	8	3	1	144^1	139	52	44	7	1	30	53	1.171	2.74	137	2.77	.251	17	.321	14	16	2.0
Yr.	12	6	.667	38	22	9	3	1	176^2	173	72	60	10	1	48	62	1.251	3.06	123	3.12	.254	19	.292	11	17	1.7
1942* StL-N	9	5	.643	38	19	5	0	5	163	156	67	59	3	1	59	52	1.319	3.26	105	3.04	.250	6	.111	1	10	-0.2
1943 StL-N	10	5	.667	21	19	7	3	0	133	115	46	42	4	0	32	40	1.105	2.84	118	2.35	.237	7	.156	4	11	0.3
1944 StL-N	4	2	.667	10	7	3	0	1	61^1	60	23	17	1	0	19	16	1.288	2.49	141	3.01	.258	4	.190	6	5	0.6
Cin-N	10	8	.556	24	19	11	2	2	155^1	157	61	57	7	2	40	40	1.268	3.30	106	3.19	.262	5	.096	-0	11	-0.3
Yr.	14	10	.583	34	26	14	2	3	216^2	217	84	74	8	2	59	56	1.274	3.07	114	3.14	.261	9	.123	5	16	0.3
1946 Cin-N	6	8	.429	36	10	5	0	4	119	112	48	43	8	1	42	44	1.294	3.25	103	3.28	.248	8	.250	-2	8	-0.1
1947 Cin-N	10	10	.500	46	0	0	0	10	90^1	88	42	39	3	0	47	43	1.494	3.89	106	3.80	.260	6	.273	3	9	0.4
1948 Cin-N	10	8	.556	**61**	0	0	0	**17**	106^1	123	50	41	5	0	34	25	1.476	3.47	113	4.19	.291	1	.040	7	13	0.5
1949 Cin-N	4	3	.571	29	0	0	0	2	40^2	58	28	25	5	1	8	12	1.623	5.53	76	5.99	.341	0	.000	-6	1	-0.6
Pit-N	1	4	.200	16	0	0	0	3	27^2	30	20	18	5	0	18	5	1.735	5.86	72	5.81	.270	1	.250	-5	0	-0.5
Yr.	5	7	.417	45	0	0	0	5	68^1	88	48	43	10	1	26	17	1.668	5.66	74	5.92	.313	1	.167	-11	1	-1.1
1950 Pit-N	0	0	....	1	0	0	0	0	1^2	3	3	1	0	0	2	0	3.000	5.40	81	10.00	.333	1	1.000	-0	0	0.0
Total 15	143	113	.559	508	235	96	14	48	2156	2186	1012	882	121	23	721	709	1.348	3.68	102	3.56	.263	130	.184	-5	145	-0.7

• GUMPERT, Dave David Lawrence Gumpert b: 5/5/1958, South Haven, MI BR/TR, 6'1", 190 lbs. Deb: 7/25/1982

YEAR TM-L	W	L	PCT	G	GS	CG	SH	SV	IP	H	R	ER	HR	HB	BB	SO	RAT	ERA	ERA+	CERA	OAV	BH	AVG	PR+	WS	TPW
1982 Det-A	0	0	....	5	1	0	0	1	2	7	6	6	1	0	2	0	4.500	27.00	15	34.90	.700	0	....	-5	0	-0.5
1983 Det-A	0	2	.000	26	0	0	0	2	44^1	43	16	13	1	0	7	14	1.128	2.64	148	2.43	.257	0	....	6	3	0.6
1985 Chi-N	1	0	1.000	9	0	0	0	0	10^1	12	7	4	0	0	7	4	1.839	3.48	115	4.77	.279	0	.000	1	1	0.1
1986 Chi-N	2	0	1.000	38	0	0	0	2	59^2	60	32	29	4	1	28	45	1.475	4.37	92	4.06	.267	0	.000	-1	3	-0.2
1987 KC-A	0	0	....	8	0	0	0	0	19^1	27	16	13	3	0	6	13	1.707	6.05	75	6.57	.333	0	....	-3	0	-0.3
Total 5	3	2	.600	86	1	0	0	5	135^2	149	77	65	9	1	50	76	1.467	4.31	95	4.39	.283	0	.000	-3	7	-0.3

• GUMPERT, Randy Randall Pennington Gumpert b: 1/23/1918, Monocacy, PA BR/TR, 6'3", 205 lbs. Deb: 6/13/1936

YEAR TM-L	W	L	PCT	G	GS	CG	SH	SV	IP	H	R	ER	HR	HB	BB	SO	RAT	ERA	ERA+	CERA	OAV	BH	AVG	PR+	WS	TPW
1936 Phi-A	1	2	.333	22	3	2	0	2	62^1	74	42	33	2	0	32	9	1.701	4.76	107	4.94	.295	6	.273	2	4	0.2
1937 Phi-A	0	0	....	10	1	0	0	0	12	16	17	16	1	1	15	5	2.583	12.00	39	9.75	.333	1	.333	-10	0	-0.9
1938 Phi-A	0	2	.000	4	2	0	0	0	12^1	24	18	15	1	0	10	1	2.757	10.95	44	11.16	.393	1	.250	-8	0	-0.7
1946 NY-A	11	3	.786	33	12	4	0	1	132^2	113	44	34	8	0	32	63	1.093	2.31	150	2.42	.229	6	.128	13	12	1.1
1947 NY-A	4	1	.800	24	6	2	0	0	56^1	71	36	34	4	0	28	25	1.757	5.43	65	5.72	.311	1	.071	-12	0	-1.4
1948 NY-A	1	0	1.000	15	0	0	0	0	25	27	10	8	0	1	6	12	1.320	2.88	142	3.20	.267	0	....	3	2	0.3
Chi-A	2	6	.250	16	11	6	1	0	97^1	103	43	41	6	2	13	31	1.192	3.79	112	3.16	.275	4	.138	4	7	0.2
Yr.	3	6	.333	31	11	6	1	0	122^1	130	53	49	6	3	19	43	1.218	3.60	117	3.17	.273	4	.138	7	9	0.5
1949 Chi-A	13	16	.448	34	32	18	3	1	234	223	111	99	22	1	83	78	1.308	3.81	110	3.57	.253	16	.190	8	14	0.7
1950 Chi-A	5	12	.294	40	17	6	1	0	155^1	165	87	82	15	4	58	48	1.436	4.75	94	4.34	.275	3	.071	-8	7	-1.1
1951 Chi-A★	9	8	.529	33	16	7	1	2	141^2	156	74	68	20	1	34	45	1.341	4.32	93	4.16	.272	15	.333	-7	8	-0.4
1952 Bos-A	1	0	1.000	10	1	0	0	1	19^2	15	11	9	1	1	5	6	1.017	4.12	96	2.06	.205	0	.000	-0	1	-0.1
Was-A	4	9	.308	20	12	2	0	0	104	112	55	49	12	5	30	29	1.365	4.24	84	4.26	.273	7	.206	-7	3	-0.7
Yr.	5	9	.357	30	13	2	0	1	123^2	127	66	58	13	6	35	35	1.310	4.22	85	3.91	.262	7	.179	-8	4	-0.8
Total 10	51	59	.464	261	113	47	6	7	1052^2	1099	548	488	92	16	346	352	1.373	4.17	98	3.97	.268	60	.182	-22	58	-2.8

• GUNDERSON, Eric Eric Andrew Gunderson b: 3/29/1966, Portland, OR BR/TL, 6', 195 lbs. Deb: 4/11/1990

YEAR TM-L	W	L	PCT	G	GS	CG	SH	SV	IP	H	R	ER	HR	HB	BB	SO	RAT	ERA	ERA+	CERA	OAV	BH	AVG	PR+	WS	TPW
1990 SF-N	1	2	.333	7	4	0	0	0	19^2	24	14	12	2	0	11	14	1.780	5.49	66	5.79	.293	0	.000	-4	0	-0.5
1991 SF-N	0	0	....	2	0	0	0	1	3^1	6	4	2	0	0	1	2	2.100	5.40	66	7.06	.353	0	....	-1	0	-0.1
1992 Sea-A	2	1	.667	9	0	0	0	0	9^1	12	12	9	1	1	5	2	1.821	8.68	46	6.20	.324	0	....	-5	0	-0.5
1994 NY-N	0	0	....	14	0	0	0	0	9	5	0	0	0	0	4	4	1.000	0.00	....	1.71	.185	0	....	4	2	0.4
1995 NY-N	1	1	.500	30	0	0	0	0	24^1	25	10	10	2	1	8	19	1.356	3.70	109	3.86	.269	0	....	1	2	0.1
Bos-A	2	1	.667	19	0	0	0	0	12^1	13	7	7	0	2	9	9	1.784	5.11	95	5.52	.295	0	....	-0	1	0.0
1996 Bos-A	0	1	.000	28	0	0	0	0	17^1	21	17	16	5	2	8	7	1.673	8.31	61	7.32	.300	0	....	-6	0	-0.5
1997 Tex-A	2	1	.667	60	0	0	0	1	49^2	45	19	18	5	2	15	31	1.208	3.26	147	3.22	.241	0	....	9	5	0.9
1998 Tex-A	0	3	.000	68	1	0	0	0	67^2	88	43	39	13	1	19	41	1.581	5.19	93	6.03	.315	0	....	-2	3	-0.2
1999 Tex-A	0	0	....	11	0	0	0	0	10	20	8	8	1	0	2	6	2.200	7.20	70	9.50	.417	0	....	-2	0	-0.2
2000 Tor-A	0	1	.000	6	0	0	0	0	6^1	15	6	5	0	1	2	2	2.684	7.11	71	11.80	.455	0	....	-1	0	-0.1
Total 10	8	11	.421	254	5	0	0	2	229	274	140	126	29	10	84	137	1.563	4.95	92	5.40	.299	0	.000	-7	13	-0.7

• GUNKEL, Red Woodward William Gunkel b: 4/15/1894, Sheffield, IL d: 4/19/1954, Chicago, IL BB/TR, 5'8", 158 lbs. Deb: 6/18/1916

YEAR TM-L	W	L	PCT	G	GS	CG	SH	SV	IP	H	R	ER	HR	HB	BB	SO	RAT	ERA	ERA+	CERA	OAV	BH	AVG	PR+	WS	TPW
1916 Cle-A	0	0	....	1	0	0	0	0	1	0	2	0	0	1	1	1	1.000	0.00	....	3.72	.000	0	....	0	0	0.0

• GURA, Larry Lawrence Cyril Gura b: 11/26/1947, Joliet, IL BB/TL, 6', 185 lbs. Deb: 4/30/1970

YEAR TM-L	W	L	PCT	G	GS	CG	SH	SV	IP	H	R	ER	HR	HB	BB	SO	RAT	ERA	ERA+	CERA	OAV	BH	AVG	PR+	WS	TPW
1970 Chi-N	1	3	.250	20	3	1	0	1	38	35	18	16	6	1	23	21	1.526	3.79	119	4.92	.254	0	.000	3	2	0.2
1971 Chi-N	0	0	....	6	0	0	0	0	3	6	3	2	0	0	1	2	2.333	6.00	66	7.26	.400	0	.000	-1	0	-0.1
1972 Chi-N	0	0	....	7	0	0	0	0	12^1	11	5	5	3	0	3	13	1.135	3.65	104	3.76	.250	0	.000	0	1	0.0
1973 Chi-N	2	4	.333	21	7	0	0	0	64^2	79	39	35	10	1	11	43	1.392	4.87	81	4.80	.296	3	.200	-5	2	-0.5
1974 NY-A	5	1	.833	8	8	4	2	0	56	54	17	15	2	0	12	17	1.179	2.41	145	2.73	.248	0	....	6	6	0.6
1975 NY-A	7	8	.467	26	20	5	0	0	151^1	173	65	59	13	3	41	65	1.414	3.51	104	4.46	.295	0	....	-2	9	-0.2
1976* KC-A	4	0	1.000	20	2	1	1	1	62^2	47	20	16	4	1	20	22	1.069	2.30	152	2.28	.213	0	....	8	6	0.9
1977* KC-A	8	5	.615	52	6	1	1	10	106^1	108	43	37	8	1	28	46	1.279	3.13	129	3.46	.265	0	....	10	11	1.0
1978* KC-A	16	4	.800	35	26	8	2	0	221^2	183	73	67	13	4	60	81	1.096	2.72	140	2.49	.229	0	....	26	19	2.6
1979 KC-A	13	12	.520	39	33	7	1	0	233^2	226	137	116	29	7	73	85	1.280	4.47	95	3.79	.253	0	....	-8	10	-0.7
1980* KC-A★	18	10	.643	36	36	16	4	0	283^1	272	107	93	20	5	76	113	1.228	2.95	137	3.21	.255	0	....	35	22	3.5
1981* KC-A	11	8	.579	23	23	12	2	0	172^1	139	61	52	11	4	35	61	1.010	2.72	133	**2.23**	.223	0	....	18	13	1.9
1982 KC-A	18	12	.600	37	37	8	3	0	248	251	124	111	31	6	64	98	1.270	4.03	101	3.85	.261	0	....	2	13	0.2
1983 KC-A	11	18	.379	34	31	5	0	0	200^1	220	119	109	23	8	76	57	1.478	4.90	83	4.80	.284	0	....	-17	6	-1.7
1984 KC-A	12	9	.571	31	25	3	0	0	168^2	175	102	97	26	4	67	68	1.435	5.18	78	4.77	.269	0	....	-23	5	-2.3
1985 KC-A	0	0	....	3	0	0	0	1	4^1	7	6	6	1	0	4	2	2.538	12.46	33	11.86	.368	0	....	-4	0	-0.4
Chi-N	0	3	.000	5	4	0	0	0	20^1	34	19	19	4	1	6	7	1.967	8.41	47	8.63	.370	0	.000	-10	0	-1.1
Total 16	126	97	.565	403	261	71	16	14	2047	2020	958	855	204	46	600	801	1.280	3.76	106	3.70	.260	3	.091	38	125	3.8

• GUTH, Charlie Charles J. Guth b: 1856, Chicago, IL d: 7/5/1883, Cambridge, MA Deb: 9/30/1880

YEAR TM-L	W	L	PCT	G	GS	CG	SH	SV	IP	H	R	ER	HR	HB	BB	SO	RAT	ERA	ERA+	CERA	OAV	BH	AVG	PR+	WS	TPW
1880 Chi-N	1	0	1.000	1	1	1	0	0	9	12	8	5	0	....	1	7	1.444	5.00	48	....	.305	1	.250	-3	0	-0.2

• GUTHRIE, Mark Mark Andrew Guthrie b: 9/22/1965, Buffalo, NY BR/TL, 6'4", 206 lbs. Deb: 7/25/1989

YEAR TM-L	W	L	PCT	G	GS	CG	SH	SV	IP	H	R	ER	HR	HB	BB	SO	RAT	ERA	ERA+	CERA	OAV	BH	AVG	PR+	WS	TPW
1989 Min-A	2	4	.333	13	8	0	0	0	57^1	66	32	29	7	1	21	38	1.517	4.55	91	5.02	.292	0	....	-2	2	-0.2
1990 Min-A	7	9	.438	24	21	3	1	0	144^2	154	65	61	8	1	39	101	1.334	3.79	109	3.69	.276	0	....	6	9	0.6
1991* Min-A	7	5	.583	41	12	0	0	2	98	116	52	47	11	1	41	72	1.602	4.32	99	5.45	.303	0	....	-2	5	-0.2
1992 Min-A	2	3	.400	54	0	0	0	5	75	59	27	24	7	0	23	76	1.093	2.88	141	2.43	.215	0	....	9	8	0.9
1993 Min-A	2	1	.667	22	0	0	0	0	21	20	11	11	2	0	16	15	1.714	4.71	92	5.20	.267	0	....	-1	1	-0.1
1994 Min-A	4	2	.667	50	2	0	0	1	51^1	65	43	35	8	2	18	38	1.617	6.14	79	5.95	.316	0	....	-6	2	-0.6
1995 Min-A	5	3	.625	36	0	0	0	0	42^1	47	22	21	5	1	16	48	1.488	4.46	107	4.89	.290	0	....	2	3	0.1
*LA-N	0	2	.000	24	0	0	0	0	19^2	19	11	8	1	1	9	19	1.424	3.66	104	3.54	.241	0	.000	0	1	0.0
1996* LA-N	2	3	.400	66	0	0	0	1	73	65	21	18	3	1	22	56	1.192	2.22	174	2.73	.240	0	.000	14	8	1.3
1997 LA-N	1	4	.200	62	0	0	0	1	69^1	71	44	41	12	0	30	42	1.457	5.32	72	4.69	.271	1	.250	-10	1	-1.0
1998 LA-N	2	1	.667	53	0	0	0	0	54	56	26	21	3	2	24	45	1.481	3.50	113	4.20	.267	0	.000	3	3	0.3
1999 Bos-A	1	1	.500	46	0	0	0	2	46^1	50	32	30	9	2	20	36	1.511	5.83	85	5.42	.275	0	....	-4	2	-0.4
Chi-N	0	2	.000	11	0	0	0	0	12^1	7	6	5	1	0	4	9	.892	3.65	124	1.46	.171	0	....	1	1	0.1
2000 Chi-N	2	3	.400	19	0	0	0	0	18^2	17	11	10	1	1	10	17	1.446	4.82	94	3.61	.258	0	.000	-1	1	-0.1
TB-A	1	1	.500	34	0	0	0	0	32	33	18	16	4	0	18	26	1.594	4.50	110	4.77	.262	0	....	1	2	0.1
Tor-A	0	2	.000	23	0	0	0	0	20^2	20	12	11	3	1	9	20	1.403	4.79	106	4.68	.263	0	....	1	1	0.1
Yr.	1	3	.250	57	0	0	0	0	52^2	53	30	27	7	1	27	46	1.519	4.61	108	4.73	.262	0	....	2	3	0.2

YEAR TM-L	W	L	PCT	G	GS	CG	SH	SV	IP	H	R	ER	HR	HB	BB	SO	RAT	ERA	ERA+	CERA	OAV	BH	AVG	PR+	WS	TPW
2001* Oak-A	6	2	.750	54	0	0	0	1	52^{1}	49	29	26	7	4	20	52	1.318	4.47	99	4.17	.249	0	....	-0	3	0.0
2002 NY-N	5	3	.625	68	0	0	0	1	48	35	13	13	3	1	19	44	1.125	2.44	162	2.48	.207	0	.000	9	6	0.8
2003* Chi-N	2	3	.400	65	0	0	0	0	42^{2}	40	14	13	6	3	22	24	1.453	2.74	153	4.65	.260	0	.000	7	4	0.7
Total 15	51	54	.486	765	43	3	1	14	978^{2}	989	489	440	101	22	381	778	1.400	4.05	106	4.19	.266	1	.071	25	63	2.5

• GUZMAN, Domingo Domingo Serrano Guzman b: 4/5/1975, San Cristobal, Dominican Republic BR/TR, 6', 210 lbs. Deb: 9/9/1999

YEAR TM-L	W	L	PCT	G	GS	CG	SH	SV	IP	H	R	ER	HR	HB	BB	SO	RAT	ERA	ERA+	CERA	OAV	BH	AVG	PR+	WS	TPW
1999 SD-N	0	1	.000	7	0	0	0	0	5	13	12	12	1	0	3	4	3.200	21.60	19	14.73	.464	0	....	-10	0	-0.9
2000 SD-N	0	0	....	1	0	0	0	0	1	1	1	1	0	2	1	0	2.000	9.00	48	16.22	.333	0	....	-1	0	-0.1
Total 2	0	1	.000	8	0	0	0	0	6	14	13	13	1	2	4	4	3.000	19.50	22	14.98	.452	0	....	-10	0	-1.0

• GUZMAN, Geraldo Geraldo Moreno Guzman b: 11/28/1972, Tenares, Dominican Republic BR/TR, 6'2", 186 lbs. Deb: 7/6/2000

YEAR TM-L	W	L	PCT	G	GS	CG	SH	SV	IP	H	R	ER	HR	HB	BB	SO	RAT	ERA	ERA+	CERA	OAV	BH	AVG	PR+	WS	TPW
2000 Ari-N	5	4	.556	13	10	0	0	0	60^{1}	66	36	36	8	2	22	52	1.459	5.37	88	4.97	.286	0	.000	-4	2	-0.6
2001 Ari-N	0	0	....	4	0	0	0	0	9^{1}	7	4	3	2	0	3	4	1.071	2.89	158	3.04	.206	0	.000	2	1	0.1
Total 2	5	4	.556	17	10	0	0	0	69^{2}	73	40	39	10	2	25	56	1.407	5.04	93	4.71	.275	0	.000	-3	3	-0.5

• GUZMAN, Johnny Dionini Ramon (Estrella) Guzman b: 1/21/1971, Hatillo Palma, Dominican Republic BR/TL, 5'10", 155 lbs. Deb: 6/8/1991

YEAR TM-L	W	L	PCT	G	GS	CG	SH	SV	IP	H	R	ER	HR	HB	BB	SO	RAT	ERA	ERA+	CERA	OAV	BH	AVG	PR+	WS	TPW
1991 Oak-A	1	0	1.000	5	0	0	0	0	5	11	5	5	0	0	2	3	2.600	9.00	43	12.51	.500	0	....	-3	0	-0.3
1992 Oak-A	0	0	....	2	0	0	0	0	3	8	4	4	0	1	0	0	2.667	12.00	31	13.68	.471	0	....	-3	0	-0.3
Total 2	1	0	1.000	7	0	0	0	0	8	19	9	9	0	1	2	3	2.625	10.13	37	12.95	.487	0	....	-6	0	-0.6

• GUZMAN, Jose Jose Alberto (Mirabal) Guzman b: 4/9/1963, Santa Isabel, Puerto Rico BR/TR, 6'2", 195 lbs. Deb: 9/10/1985

YEAR TM-L	W	L	PCT	G	GS	CG	SH	SV	IP	H	R	ER	HR	HB	BB	SO	RAT	ERA	ERA+	CERA	OAV	BH	AVG	PR+	WS	TPW
1985 Tex-A	3	2	.600	5	5	0	0	0	32^{2}	27	13	10	3	0	14	24	1.255	2.76	154	3.05	.214	0	....	6	3	0.6
1986 Tex-A	9	15	.375	29	29	2	0	0	172^{1}	199	101	87	23	6	60	87	1.503	4.54	95	5.19	.293	0	....	-4	6	-0.4
1987 Tex-A	14	14	.500	37	30	6	0	0	208^{1}	196	115	108	30	3	82	143	1.334	4.67	96	4.13	.251	0	....	-2	10	-0.2
1988 Tex-A	11	13	.458	30	30	6	2	0	206^{2}	180	99	85	20	5	82	157	1.268	3.70	110	3.38	.231	0	....	8	12	0.8
1991 Tex-A	13	7	.650	25	25	5	1	0	169^{2}	152	67	58	10	4	84	125	1.391	3.08	131	3.68	.239	0	....	21	12	2.1
1992 Tex-A	16	11	.593	33	33	5	0	0	224	229	103	91	17	4	73	179	1.348	3.66	104	3.86	.268	0	....	7	14	0.7
1993 Chi-N	12	10	.545	30	30	2	1	0	191	188	98	92	25	3	74	163	1.372	4.34	92	4.18	.258	7	.111	-10	9	-1.2
1994 Chi-N	2	2	.500	4	4	0	0	0	19^{2}	22	20	20	1	1	13	11	1.780	9.15	45	5.61	.289	0	.000	-11	0	-1.1
Total 8	80	74	.519	193	186	26	4	0	1224^{1}	1193	616	551	129	26	482	889	1.368	4.05	102	4.04	.256	7	.099	15	66	1.2

• GUZMAN, Juan Juan Andres (Correa) Guzman b: 10/28/1966, Santo Domingo, Dominican Republic BR/TR, 5'11", 195 lbs. Deb: 6/7/1991

YEAR TM-L	W	L	PCT	G	GS	CG	SH	SV	IP	H	R	ER	HR	HB	BB	SO	RAT	ERA	ERA+	CERA	OAV	BH	AVG	PR+	WS	TPW
1991* Tor-A	10	3	.769	23	23	1	0	0	138^{2}	98	53	46	6	4	66	123	1.183	2.99	141	2.54	.197	0	....	19	12	1.9
1992* Tor-A★	16	5	.762	28	28	1	0	0	180^{2}	135	56	53	6	1	72	165	1.146	2.64	155	**2.34**	.207	0	....	30	17	3.0
1993* Tor-A	14	3	.824	33	33	2	1	0	221	211	107	98	17	3	110	194	1.452	3.99	108	4.09	.252	0	....	10	15	0.9
1994 Tor-A	12	11	.522	25	**25**	2	0	0	147^{1}	165	102	93	20	3	76	124	1.636	5.68	85	5.59	.282	0	....	-13	5	-1.2
1995 Tor-A	4	14	.222	24	24	3	0	0	135^{1}	151	101	95	13	3	73	94	1.655	6.32	74	5.28	.281	0	....	-24	1	-2.3
1996 Tor-A	11	8	.579	27	27	4	1	0	187^{2}	158	68	61	20	7	53	165	1.124	**2.93**	**171**	**3.00**	**.228**	0	....	39	17	3.6
1997 Tor-A	3	6	.333	13	13	0	0	0	60	48	42	33	14	2	31	52	1.317	4.95	93	4.39	.213	0	....	-3	1	-0.3
1998 Tor-A	6	12	.333	22	22	2	0	0	145	133	83	71	19	6	65	113	1.366	4.41	106	4.13	.239	0	.000	4	7	0.4
Bal-A	4	4	.500	11	11	0	0	0	66	60	34	31	4	2	33	55	1.409	4.23	108	3.78	.241	0	....	3	4	0.3
Yr.	10	16	.385	33	33	2	0	0	211	193	117	102	23	8	98	168	1.379	4.35	106	4.02	.240	0	.000	7	11	0.6
1999 Bal-A	5	9	.357	21	21	1	1	0	122^{2}	124	63	57	18	3	65	95	1.541	4.18	112	5.11	.264	1	.167	4	7	0.4
Cin-N	6	3	.667	12	12	1	0	0	77^{1}	70	33	26	10	1	21	60	1.177	3.03	154	3.23	.238	3	.115	12	6	1.0
2000 TB-A	0	1	.000	1	1	0	0	0	1^{2}	7	8	8	2	0	2	3	5.400	43.20	11	47.43	.636	0	....	-7	0	-0.7
Total 10	91	79	.535	240	240	17	3	0	1483^{1}	1360	750	672	149	35	667	1243	1.367	4.08	112	3.94	.243	4	.118	73	92	7.1

• GUZMAN, Santiago Santiago Donovan Guzman b: 7/25/1949, San Pedro de Macoris, Dominican Republic BR/TR, 6'2", 180 lbs. Deb: 9/30/1969

YEAR TM-L	W	L	PCT	G	GS	CG	SH	SV	IP	H	R	ER	HR	HB	BB	SO	RAT	ERA	ERA+	CERA	OAV	BH	AVG	PR+	WS	TPW
1969 StL-N	0	1	.000	1	1	0	0	0	7^{1}	9	4	4	2	0	3	7	1.636	4.91	73	7.07	.321	1	.333	-1	0	-0.1
1970 StL-N	1	1	.500	8	3	1	0	0	13^{2}	14	12	11	1	0	13	9	1.976	7.24	57	6.49	.275	1	.200	-5	0	-0.5
1971 StL-N	0	0	....	2	1	0	0	0	10	6	1	0	0	0	2	13	.800	0.00	....	1.08	.162	0	.000	4	1	0.4
1972 StL-N	0	0	....	1	0	0	0	0	1	1	1	1	1	0	0	0	1.000	9.00	38	7.45	.250	0	....	-1	0	-0.1
Total 4	1	2	.333	12	5	1	0	0	32	30	18	16	4	0	18	29	1.500	4.50	87	4.96	.250	2	.222	-2	1	-0.2

• HAAS, Bruno Bruno Philip "Boon" Haas b: 5/5/1891, Worcester, MA d: 6/5/1952, Sarasota, FL BB/TL, 5'10", 180 lbs. Deb: 6/23/1915

YEAR TM-L	W	L	PCT	G	GS	CG	SH	SV	IP	H	R	ER	HR	HB	BB	SO	RAT	ERA	ERA+	CERA	OAV	BH	AVG	PR+	WS	TPW
1915 Phi-A	0	1	.000	6	2	1	0	0	14^{1}	23	27	19	0	0	28	7	3.558	11.93	24	14.13	.404	1	.056	-14	0	-1.8

• HAAS, Dave Robert David Haas b: 10/19/1965, Independence, MO BR/TR, 6'1", 200 lbs. Deb: 9/8/1991

YEAR TM-L	W	L	PCT	G	GS	CG	SH	SV	IP	H	R	ER	HR	HB	BB	SO	RAT	ERA	ERA+	CERA	OAV	BH	AVG	PR+	WS	TPW
1991 Det-A	1	0	1.000	11	0	0	0	0	10^{2}	8	8	8	1	1	12	6	1.875	6.75	62	5.46	.242	0	....	-3	0	-0.3
1992 Det-A	5	3	.625	12	11	1	1	0	61^{2}	68	30	27	8	1	16	29	1.362	3.94	100	4.35	.276	0	....	1	3	0.1
1993 Det-A	1	2	.333	20	0	0	0	0	28	45	20	19	9	0	8	17	1.893	6.11	70	9.05	.375	0	....	-6	0	-0.5
Total 3	7	5	.583	43	11	1	1	0	100^{1}	121	58	54	18	2	36	52	1.565	4.84	85	5.78	.303	0	....	-8	3	-0.8

• HAAS, Moose Bryan Edmund Haas b: 4/22/1956, Baltimore, MD BR/TR, 6', 180 lbs. Deb: 9/8/1976

YEAR TM-L	W	L	PCT	G	GS	CG	SH	SV	IP	H	R	ER	HR	HB	BB	SO	RAT	ERA	ERA+	CERA	OAV	BH	AVG	PR+	WS	TPW
1976 Mil-A	0	1	.000	5	2	0	0	0	16	12	8	7	0	0	12	9	1.500	3.94	89	3.16	.207	0	....	-1	0	-0.1
1977 Mil-A	10	12	.455	32	32	6	0	0	197^{2}	195	104	95	21	2	84	113	1.411	4.33	94	4.18	.261	0	....	-7	10	-0.7
1978 Mil-A	2	3	.400	7	6	2	0	1	30^{2}	33	22	21	6	0	8	32	1.337	6.16	61	4.58	.273	0	....	-8	0	-0.9
1979 Mil-A	11	11	.500	29	28	8	1	0	184^{2}	198	112	98	26	0	59	95	1.392	4.78	87	4.46	.275	0	....	-12	7	-1.1
1980 Mil-A	16	15	.516	33	33	14	3	0	252^{1}	246	96	87	25	1	56	146	1.197	3.10	125	3.29	.258	0	....	19	17	1.9
1981* Mil-A	11	7	.611	24	22	5	0	0	137^{1}	146	69	68	10	1	40	64	1.354	4.46	77	3.82	.275	0	....	-17	5	-1.8
1982* Mil-A	11	8	.579	32	27	3	0	1	193^{1}	232	101	96	15	3	39	104	1.402	4.47	85	4.34	.302	0	....	-17	6	-1.7
1983 Mil-A	13	3	.813	25	25	7	3	0	179	170	66	65	12	1	42	75	1.184	3.27	114	2.97	.251	0	....	9	14	0.9
1984 Mil-A	9	11	.450	31	30	4	0	0	189^{1}	205	91	84	15	0	43	84	1.310	3.99	96	3.72	.279	0	....	-1	9	-0.1
1985 Mil-A	8	8	.500	27	26	6	1	0	161^{2}	165	85	69	21	1	25	78	1.175	3.84	108	3.41	.260	0	....	6	9	0.6
1986 Oak-A	7	2	.778	12	12	1	0	0	72^{1}	58	23	22	4	1	19	40	1.065	2.74	141	2.29	.218	0	....	9	6	0.9
1987 Oak-A	2	2	.500	9	9	0	0	0	40^{2}	57	29	26	7	0	9	13	1.623	5.75	72	6.36	.335	0	....	-7	1	-0.7
Total 12	100	83	.546	266	252	56	8	2	1655	1717	806	738	162	10	436	853	1.301	4.01	97	3.77	.269	0	....	-27	84	-2.8

• HABENICHT, Bob Robert Julius "Hobby" Habenicht b: 2/13/1926, St. Louis, MO d: 12/24/1980, Richmond, VA BR/TR, 6'2", 185 lbs. Deb: 4/17/1951

YEAR TM-L	W	L	PCT	G	GS	CG	SH	SV	IP	H	R	ER	HR	HB	BB	SO	RAT	ERA	ERA+	CERA	OAV	BH	AVG	PR+	WS	TPW
1951 StL-N	0	0	....	3	0	0	0	0	5	5	4	4	0	0	9	1	2.800	7.20	55	8.64	.278	0	.000	-2	0	-0.2
1953 StL-A	0	0	....	1	0	0	0	0	1^{2}	1	1	1	0	1	1	1	1.200	5.40	78	3.63	.167	0	....	-0	0	0.0
Total 2	0	0	....	4	0	0	0	0	6^{2}	6	5	5	0	1	10	2	2.400	6.75	59	7.39	.250	0	.000	-2	0	-0.2

• HABYAN, John John Gabriel Habyan b: 1/29/1964, Bay Shore, NY BR/TR, 6'1", 195 lbs. Deb: 9/29/1985

YEAR TM-L	W	L	PCT	G	GS	CG	SH	SV	IP	H	R	ER	HR	HB	BB	SO	RAT	ERA	ERA+	CERA	OAV	BH	AVG	PR+	WS	TPW
1985 Bal-A	1	0	1.000	2	0	0	0	0	2^{2}	3	1	0	0	0	0	2	1.125	0.00	....	2.27	.250	0	....	1	0	0.1
1986 Bal-A	1	3	.250	6	5	0	0	0	26^{1}	24	17	13	3	0	18	14	1.595	4.44	93	4.73	.250	0	....	-1	1	-0.1
1987 Bal-A	6	7	.462	27	13	0	0	1	116^{1}	110	67	62	20	2	40	64	1.289	4.80	92	4.08	.248	0	....	-5	6	-0.5
1988 Bal-A	1	0	1.000	7	0	0	0	0	14^{2}	22	10	7	2	0	4	4	1.773	4.30	91	6.88	.355	0	....	-1	1	-0.1
1990 NY-A	0	0	....	6	0	0	0	0	8^{2}	10	2	2	0	1	2	4	1.385	2.08	191	4.13	.294	0	....	2	1	0.2
1991 NY-A	4	2	.667	66	0	0	0	2	90	73	28	23	2	2	20	70	1.033	2.30	180	2.10	.225	0	....	19	10	1.9
1992 NY-A	5	6	.455	56	0	0	0	7	72^{2}	84	32	31	6	2	21	44	1.445	3.84	103	4.41	.295	0	....	0	5	0.0
1993 NY-A	2	1	.667	36	0	0	0	1	42^{1}	45	20	19	5	0	16	29	1.441	4.04	103	4.48	.276	0	....	1	3	0.1
KC-A	0	0	....	12	0	0	0	0	14	14	7	7	1	0	4	10	1.286	4.50	102	3.27	.259	0	....	0	1	0.0
Yr.	2	1	.667	48	0	0	0	1	56^{1}	59	27	26	6	0	20	39	1.402	4.15	103	4.18	.272	0	....	1	4	0.1
1994 StL-N	1	0	1.000	52	0	0	0	1	47^{1}	50	17	17	2	0	20	46	1.479	3.23	129	3.84	.275	0	....	5	5	0.5
1995 StL-N	3	2	.600	31	0	0	0	0	40^{2}	32	18	13	0	1	15	35	1.156	2.88	146	2.17	.222	0	.000	5	3	0.5
Cal-A	1	2	.333	28	0	0	0	0	32^{2}	36	16	15	2	1	12	25	1.469	4.13	114	4.28	.279	0	....	2	2	0.2
1996 Col-N	1	1	.500	19	0	0	0	0	24	34	19	19	4	1	14	25	2.000	7.13	73	8.25	.347	0	.000	-5	1	-0.4
Total 11	26	24	.520	348	18	0	0	12	532^{1}	537	254	228	47	10	186	372	1.358	3.85	111	3.94	.265	0	.000	24	39	2.4

YEAR	TM-L	W	L	PCT	G	GS	CG	SH	SV	IP	H	R	ER	HR	HB	BB	SO	RAT	ERA	ERA+	CERA	OAV	BH	AVG	PR+	WS	TPW
• HACKER, Warren	Warren Louis Hacker b: 11/21/1924, Marissa, IL d: 5/22/2002, Lenzburg, IL BR/TR, 6'1", 185 lbs. Deb: 9/24/1948																										
1948	Chi-N	0	1	.000	3	1	0	0	0	3	7	7	7	0	0	3	0	3.333	21.00	19	14.04	.438	0	....	-6	0	-0.6
1949	Chi-N	5	8	.385	30	12	3	0	0	125^{2}	141	68	59	7	4	53	40	1.544	4.23	95	4.53	.283	7	.184	-0	6	-0.1
1950	Chi-N	0	1	.000	5	3	1	0	1	15^{1}	20	11	9	3	0	8	5	1.826	5.28	80	6.97	.313	0	.000	-1	0	-0.2
1951	Chi-N	0	0	....	2	0	0	0	0	1^{1}	3	2	2	0	1	0	2	2.250	13.50	30	12.35	.500	0	....	-1	0	-0.1
1952	Chi-N	15	9	.625	33	20	12	5	1	185	144	56	53	17	1	31	84	.946	2.58	149	**2.02**	**.212**	7	.121	27	18	2.5
1953	Chi-N	12	19	.387	39	32	9	0	2	221^{2}	225	123	108	35	3	54	106	1.259	4.38	102	3.80	.254	17	.218	8	14	0.8
1954	Chi-N	6	13	.316	39	18	4	1	2	158^{2}	157	89	75	28	4	37	80	1.223	4.25	99	3.86	.257	13	.236	1	7	0.2
1955	Chi-N	11	15	.423	35	30	13	0	3	213	202	112	101	38	2	43	80	1.150	4.27	96	3.45	.245	18	.250	-5	13	-0.3
1956	Chi-N	3	13	.188	34	24	4	0	0	168	190	103	87	28	1	44	65	1.393	4.66	81	4.64	.285	8	.148	-20	2	-2.2
1957	Cin-N	3	2	.600	15	6	0	0	0	43^{1}	50	26	25	5	3	13	18	1.454	5.19	79	4.85	.294	1	.125	-5	2	-0.5
	Phi-N	4	4	.500	20	10	1	0	0	74	72	40	37	10	1	18	33	1.216	4.50	85	3.60	.257	6	.261	-5	3	-0.4
	Yr.	7	6	.538	35	16	1	0	0	117^{1}	122	66	62	15	4	31	51	1.304	4.76	82	4.06	.271	7	.226	-11	5	-1.0
1958	Phi-N	0	1	.000	9	1	0	0	0	17	24	17	14	2	0	8	4	1.882	7.41	53	6.89	.329	0	.000	-6	0	-0.6
1961	Chi-A	3	3	.500	42	0	0	0	8	57^{1}	62	26	24	8	1	8	40	1.221	3.77	104	3.70	.272	1	.111	1	5	0.1
Total	12	62	89	.411	306	157	47	6	17	1283^{1}	1297	680	601	181	21	320	557	1.260	4.21	96	3.81	.259	78	.195	-14	70	-1.5
• HACKETT, Jim	James Joseph "Sunny Jim" Hackett b: 10/1/1877, Jacksonville, IL d: 3/28/1961, Douglas, MI BR/TR, 6'2", 185 lbs. Deb: 9/14/1902 ♦																										
1902	StL-N	0	3	.000	4	3	3	0	0	30^{1}	46	26	21	0	1	16	7	2.044	6.23	44	6.56	.348	6	.286	-11	1	-1.1
1903	StL-N	1	3	.250	7	6	5	0	1	48^{1}	47	28	20	0	3	18	21	1.345	3.72	87	3.21	.249	80	.228	-3	5	-2.2
Total	2	1	6	.143	11	9	8	0	1	78^{2}	93	54	41	0	4	34	28	1.614	4.69	63	4.50	.290	86	.231	-15	6	-3.3
• HACKMAN, Luther	Luther Gean Hackman b: 10/10/1974, Columbus, MS BR/TR, 6'4", 195 lbs. Deb: 9/1/1999																										
1999	Col-N	1	2	.333	5	3	0	0	0	16	26	19	19	5	0	12	10	2.375	10.69	54	11.65	.371	1	.200	-9	0	-0.8
2000	StL-N	0	0	....	1	0	0	0	0	2^{2}	4	3	3	0	1	4	0	3.000	10.13	45	11.43	.400	0	....	-2	0	-0.2
2001	StL-N	1	2	.333	35	0	0	0	1	35^{2}	28	18	17	7	2	14	24	1.178	4.29	99	3.71	.212	0	.000	-1	2	-0.1
2002	StL-N	5	4	.556	43	6	0	0	0	81	90	42	37	7	4	39	46	1.593	4.11	96	5.09	.287	1	.063	-3	3	-0.4
2003	SD-N	2	2	.500	65	0	0	0	0	76^{2}	78	51	44	7	8	36	48	1.487	5.17	76	4.71	.261	0	.000	-10	1	-1.0
Total	5	9	10	.474	149	9	0	0	1	212	226	133	120	26	15	105	128	1.561	5.09	83	5.30	.274	2	.083	-24	6	-2.4
• HADDIX, Harvey	Harvey "Kitten" Haddix b: 9/18/1925, Medway, OH d: 1/8/1994, Springfield, OH BL/TL, 5'9.5", 170 lbs. Deb: 8/20/1952 C																										
1952	StL-N	2	2	.500	7	6	3	0	0	42	31	18	13	4	2	10	31	.976	2.79	133	2.20	.201	3	.214	4	3	0.5
1953	StL-N★	20	9	.690	36	33	19	**6**	1	253	220	97	86	24	4	69	163	1.142	3.06	139	2.87	.232	28	.289	37	27	4.5
1954	StL-N★	18	13	.581	43	35	13	3	4	259^{2}	247	114	103	26	3	77	184	1.248	3.57	115	3.38	.249	18	.194	17	17	2.0
1955	StL-N★	12	16	.429	37	30	9	2	1	208	216	111	103	27	5	62	150	1.337	4.46	91	4.14	.268	12	.164	-7	10	-0.6
1956	StL-N	1	0	1.000	4	4	1	1	0	23^{2}	28	15	14	3	0	10	16	1.606	5.32	71	5.47	.298	2	.222	-4	1	-0.3
	Phi-N	12	8	.600	31	26	11	2	2	206^{2}	196	98	80	23	6	55	154	1.215	3.48	107	3.35	.247	22	.237	10	13	1.5
	Yr.	13	8	.619	35	30	12	3	2	230^{1}	224	113	94	26	6	65	170	1.255	3.67	102	3.57	.253	24	.235	6	14	1.2
1957	Phi-N	10	13	.435	27	25	8	1	0	170^{2}	176	84	77	18	1	39	136	1.260	4.06	94	3.56	.264	21	.309	-4	10	0.3
1958	Cin-N	8	7	.533	29	26	8	1	0	184	191	79	72	28	7	43	110	1.272	3.52	118	4.10	.268	11	.180	12	13	1.5
1959	Pit-N	12	12	.500	31	29	14	2	0	224^{1}	189	88	78	26	2	49	149	1.061	3.13	124	**2.62**	.228	12	.145	16	17	1.6
1960*	Pit-N	11	10	.524	29	28	4	0	1	172^{1}	189	87	76	13	1	38	101	1.317	3.97	95	3.66	.277	17	.254	-7	9	-0.3
1961	Pit-N	10	6	.625	29	22	5	2	0	156	159	72	71	15	2	41	99	1.282	4.10	97	3.68	.266	8	.143	-2	9	-0.2
1962	Pit-N	9	6	.600	28	20	4	0	0	141^{1}	146	74	66	17	2	42	101	1.330	4.20	94	3.96	.264	13	.250	-6	8	-0.1
1963	Pit-N	3	4	.429	49	1	0	0	1	70	67	27	26	7	4	20	70	1.243	3.34	99	3.49	.256	2	.182	-1	4	0.0
1964	Bal-A	5	5	.500	49	0	0	0	10	89^{2}	68	26	23	4	2	23	90	1.015	2.31	155	1.95	.211	0	.000	10	11	0.8
1965	Bal-A	3	2	.600	24	0	0	0	1	33^{2}	31	22	13	5	2	23	21	1.604	3.48	100	4.99	.248	0	.000	-1	1	-0.1
Total	14	136	113	.546	453	285	99	20	21	2235	2154	1012	901	240	43	601	1575	1.233	3.63	108	3.44	.252	169	.212	76	153	11.1
• HADDOCK, George	George Silas "Gentleman George" Haddock b: 12/25/1866, Portsmouth, NH d: 4/18/1926, Boston, MA BR/TR, 5'11", 155 lbs. Deb: 9/27/1888 U																										
1888	Was-N	0	2	.000	2	2	2	0	0	16	9	8	4	0	1	2	3	.688	2.25	124	....	.159	1	.200	1	1	0.1
1889	Was-N	11	19	.367	33	31	30	0	0	276^{1}	299	203	129	10	9	123	106	1.527	4.20	94	....	.267	25	.223	-3	11	0.5
1890	Buf-P	9	26	.257	35	34	31	0	0	290^{2}	366	307	186	15	14	149	123	1.772	5.76	71	....	.295	36	.247	-50	7	-3.1
1891	Bos-a	34	11	.756	51	47	37	**5**	1	379^{2}	330	172	105	8	14	137	169	1.230	2.49	140	....	.226	45	.243	34	34	3.5
1892	Bro-N	29	13	.690	46	44	39	3	1	381^{1}	340	190	133	11	14	163	153	1.319	3.14	101	3.14	.229	28	.177	0	27	0.0
1893	Bro-N	8	9	.471	23	20	12	0	0	151	193	145	94	10	7	89	37	1.868	5.60	79	6.24	.302	24	.282	-18	6	-1.3
1894	Phi-N	4	3	.571	10	7	5	0	0	56	63	46	36	0	1	34	7	1.732	5.79	88	4.72	.281	5	.172	-4	3	-0.3
	Was-N	0	4	.000	4	4	4	0	0	29	50	40	28	2	1	17	1	2.310	8.69	61	9.11	.375	3	.188	-10	0	-0.9
	Yr.	4	7	.364	14	11	9	0	0	85	113	86	64	2	2	51	8	1.929	6.78	76	6.22	.316	8	.178	-14	3	-1.2
Total	7	95	87	.522	204	189	160	8	2	1580	1650	1111	715	56	61	714	599	1.496	4.07	95	1.69	.260	167	.227	-50	89	-1.4
• HADLEY, Bump	Irving Darius Hadley b: 7/5/1904, Lynn, MA d: 2/15/1963, Lynn, MA BR/TR, 5'11", 190 lbs. Deb: 4/20/1926																										
1926	Was-A	0	0	....	1	0	0	0	0	3	6	5	4	0	0	2	0	2.667	12.00	32	10.24	.429	0	....	-3	0	-0.3
1927	Was-A	14	6	.700	30	27	13	0	0	198^{2}	177	72	63	2	9	86	60	1.324	2.85	142	3.06	.244	19	.271	24	19	2.5
1928	Was-A	12	13	.480	33	31	16	3	0	231^{2}	236	105	91	4	8	100	80	1.450	3.54	113	3.67	.268	17	.210	9	16	1.0
1929	Was-A	6	16	.273	37	27	7	1	0	195^{1}	196	139	122	10	5	85	98	1.439	5.62	75	3.87	.263	6	.097	-33	2	-3.5
1930	Was-A	15	11	.577	42	34	15	1	2	260^{1}	242	123	108	6	6	105	162	1.333	3.73	123	3.14	**.247**	21	.226	17	21	1.6
1931	Was-A	11	10	.524	**55**	11	2	1	8	179^{2}	145	81	61	4	1	92	124	1.319	3.06	140	2.79	**.218**	9	.167	23	16	2.0
1932	Chi-A	1	1	.500	3	2	1	0	1	18^{2}	17	8	8	2	0	8	13	1.339	3.86	112	3.89	.262	1	.167	1	1	0.1
	StL-A	13	20	.394	40	33	12	1	1	229^{2}	244	160	141	21	8	163	132	1.772	5.53	88	5.54	.274	22	.282	-18	11	-1.2
	Yr.	14	21	.400	43	35	13	1	2	248^{1}	261	168	149	23	8	171	145	**1.740**	5.40	89	5.42	.273	23	.274	-17	12	-1.1
1933	StL-A	15	20	.429	45	36	19	2	3	**316^{2}**	309	152	138	17	3	141	149	1.421	3.92	119	3.73	.256	17	.156	20	23	1.6
1934	StL-A	10	16	.385	39	32	7	2	1	213	212	120	103	14	6	127	79	1.592	4.35	115	4.47	.257	13	.203	13	14	1.1
1935	Was-A	10	15	.400	35	32	13	0	0	230^{1}	268	143	126	18	4	102	77	1.606	4.92	88	5.01	.292	15	.195	-15	7	-1.2
1936*	NY-A	14	4	.778	31	17	8	1	1	173^{2}	194	97	84	12	1	89	74	1.630	4.35	107	4.89	.283	16	.235	5	11	0.5
1937*	NY-A	11	8	.579	29	25	6	0	0	178^{1}	199	122	105	16	3	83	70	1.581	5.30	84	4.85	.281	11	.169	-20	6	-1.8
1938	NY-A	9	8	.529	29	17	8	1	1	167^{1}	165	79	67	13	3	66	61	1.380	3.60	126	3.74	.254	5	.093	16	13	1.3
1939*	NY-A	12	6	.667	26	18	7	1	2	154	132	62	51	10	3	85	65	1.409	2.98	146	3.62	.237	11	.177	18	12	1.6
1940	NY-A	3	5	.375	25	2	0	0	2	80	88	62	51	4	1	52	39	1.750	5.74	70	4.97	.276	3	.111	-16	0	-1.6
1941	NY-N	1	0	1.000	3	2	0	0	0	13	19	10	9	1	0	9	4	2.154	6.23	59	7.90	.345	0	.000	-4	0	-0.4
	Phi-A	4	6	.400	25	9	1	0	3	102^{1}	131	69	57	13	2	47	31	1.739	5.01	84	6.09	.308	4	.129	-10	3	-1.0
Total	16	161	165	.494	528	355	135	14	25	2945^{2}	2980	1609	1389	167	63	1442	1318	1.501	4.24	105	4.15	.263	190	.189	27	175	2.3
• HAEFNER, Mickey	Milton Arnold Haefner b: 10/9/1912, Lenzberg, IL d: 1/3/1995, New Athens, IL BL/TL, 5'8", 160 lbs. Deb: 4/22/1943																										
1943	Was-A	11	5	.688	36	13	8	1	6	165^{1}	126	56	42	4	4	60	65	1.125	2.29	140	2.20	.208	6	.133	17	14	1.9
1944	Was-A	12	15	.444	31	28	18	3	1	228	221	94	77	7	4	71	86	1.281	3.04	107	3.03	.251	11	.157	8	12	0.8
1945	Was-A	16	14	.533	37	28	19	1	3	238^{1}	226	103	92	10	7	69	83	1.238	3.47	89	2.97	.247	20	.244	-9	14	-0.5
1946	Was-A	14	11	.560	33	27	17	2	1	227^{2}	220	86	72	10	5	80	85	1.318	2.85	118	3.30	.251	15	.203	17	17	2.2
1947	Was-A	10	14	.417	31	28	14	4	1	193	195	86	78	8	4	85	77	1.451	3.64	102	3.86	.264	8	.136	5	13	0.4
1948	Was-A	5	13	.278	28	20	4	0	0	147^{2}	151	86	66	7	6	61	45	1.436	4.02	108	3.90	.265	7	.163	8	7	0.6
1949	Was-A	5	5	.500	19	12	4	1	0	91^{2}	85	51	45	7	2	53	23	1.505	4.42	96	4.08	.249	5	.200	2	5	0.3
	Chi-A	4	6	.400	14	12	4	1	1	80^{1}	84	40	39	9	5	41	17	1.556	4.37	95	5.04	.275	6	.261	-2	5	-0.1
	Yr.	9	11	.450	33	24	8	2	1	172	169	91	84	16	7	94	40	1.529	4.40	96	4.53	.261	11	.229	-0	10	0.2
1950	Chi-A	1	6	.143	24	9	2	0	0	70^{2}	83	49	45	11	2	45	17	1.811	5.73	78	6.56	.299	4	.200	-11	1	-1.0
	Bos-N	0	2	.000	8	2	1	0	0	24	23	15	15	3	0	12	10	1.458	5.63	68	4.23	.247	2	.286	-5	0	-0.4
Total	8	78	91	.462	261	179	91	13	13	1466^{2}	1414	666	571	76	39	577	508	1.358	3.50	103	3.53	.252	84	.188	30	88	4.2
• HAFFORD, Leo	Leo Edgar Hafford b: 9/17/1883, Somerville, MA d: 10/2/1911, Willimantic, CT TR, 6', 170 lbs. Deb: 4/15/1906																										
1906	Cin-N	1	1	.500	3	1	1	0	0	19	13	9	2	0	1	11	5	1.263	0.95	290	2.43	.191	2	.222	4	2	0.4

YEAR	TM-L	W	L	PCT	G	GS	CG	SH	SV	IP	H	R	ER	HR	HB	BB	SO	RAT	ERA	ERA+	CERA	OAV	BH	AVG	PR+	WS	TPW
• HAFNER, Frank	Francis R. Hafner b: 8/14/1867, Hannibal, MO d: 3/2/1957, Hannibal, MO TR Deb: 5/5/1888																										
1888	KC-a	0	2	.000	2	2	2	0	0	18	24	23	14	2	1	16	5	2.222	7.00	49	....	.309	0	.000	-7	0	-0.7
• HAGAN, Art	Arthur Charles Hagan b: 3/17/1863, Providence, RI d: 3/25/1936, Providence, RI TR Deb: 6/30/1883																										
1883	Phi-N	1	14	.067	17	16	15	0	0	137	207	151	83	2	....	33	39	1.752	5.45	57	....	.329	6	.102	-25	1	-2.6
	Buf-N	0	2	.000	2	2	1	0	0	15	17	12	6	0	....	6	7	1.533	3.60	88	....	.269	0	.000	-1	0	-0.2
	Yr.	1	16	.059	19	18	16	0	0	152	224	163	89	2	....	39	46	1.730	5.27	59	....	.324	6	.091	-25	1	-2.8
1884	Buf-N	1	2	.333	3	3	3	0	0	26	53	38	17	1	....	4	4	2.192	5.88	54	....	.400	4	.308	-7	0	-0.6
Total	**2**	**2**	**18**	**.100**	**22**	**21**	**19**	**0**	**0**	**178**	**277**	**201**	**106**	**3**	**....**	**43**	**50**	**1.798**	**5.36**	**58**	**....**	**.336**	**10**	**.127**	**-33**	**1**	**-3.4**
• HAGEMAN, Casey	Kurt Moritz Hageman b: 5/12/1887, Mount Olive, PA d: 4/1/1964, New Bedford, PA BR/TR, 5'10.5", 186 lbs. Deb: 9/18/1911																										
1911	Bos-A	0	2	.000	2	2	2	0	0	17	16	8	4	2	1	5	8	1.235	2.12	154	3.89	.262	0	.000	2	1	0.2
1912	Bos-A	0	0	....	2	1	0	0	0	1^{1}	5	5	4	0	0	3	1	6.000	27.00	13	28.56	.500	0	....	-3	0	-0.3
1914	StL-N	2	4	.333	12	7	2	0	0	55^{1}	43	24	15	0	5	20	21	1.139	2.44	114	2.26	.215	2	.125	2	3	0.1
	Chi-N	1	1	.500	16	1	0	0	1	46^{2}	44	26	18	0	3	12	17	1.200	3.47	80	2.76	.254	7	.467	-3	3	0.0
	Yr.	3	5	.375	28	8	2	0	1	102	87	50	33	0	8	32	38	1.167	2.91	96	2.49	.233	9	.290	-1	6	0.1
Total	**3**	**3**	**7**	**.300**	**32**	**11**	**4**	**0**	**1**	**120^{1}**	**108**	**63**	**41**	**2**	**9**	**40**	**47**	**1.230**	**3.07**	**94**	**2.97**	**.243**	**9**	**.257**	**-2**	**7**	**0.0**
• HAGEN, Kevin	Kevin Eugene Hagen b: 3/8/1960, Renton, WA BR/TR, 6'2", 185 lbs. Deb: 6/4/1983																										
1983	StL-N	2	2	.500	9	4	0	0	0	22^{1}	34	15	12	0	0	7	7	1.836	4.84	75	6.16	.362	0	.000	-3	0	-0.4
1984	StL-N	1	0	1.000	4	0	0	0	0	7^{1}	9	2	2	0	0	1	2	1.364	2.45	141	3.64	.300	0	....	1	1	0.1
Total	**2**	**3**	**2**	**.600**	**13**	**4**	**0**	**0**	**0**	**29^{2}**	**43**	**17**	**14**	**0**	**0**	**8**	**9**	**1.719**	**4.25**	**85**	**5.54**	**.347**	**0**	**.000**	**-2**	**1**	**-0.3**
• HAGERMAN, Rip	Zerah Zequiel Hagerman b: 6/20/1888, Lyndon, KS d: 1/30/1930, Albuquerque, NM BR/TR, 6'2", 200 lbs. Deb: 4/16/1909																										
1909	Chi-N	4	4	.500	13	7	4	1	0	79	64	29	16	0	2	28	32	1.165	1.82	139	2.35	.225	3	.130	6	5	0.6
1914	Cle-A	9	15	.375	37	26	12	3	0	198	189	98	68	3	5	118	112	**1.551**	3.09	93	4.14	.265	1	.016	-2	7	-0.8
1915	Cle-A	6	14	.300	29	22	7	0	0	151	156	85	59	4	6	77	69	1.543	3.52	87	4.37	.277	4	.105	-7	5	-1.0
1916	Cle-A	0	0	....	2	0	0	0	0	3^{2}	5	6	5	1	2	2	1	1.909	12.27	24	10.98	.333	0	.000	-4	0	-0.4
Total	**4**	**19**	**33**	**.365**	**81**	**55**	**23**	**4**	**0**	**431^{2}**	**414**	**218**	**148**	**8**	**15**	**225**	**214**	**1.480**	**3.09**	**94**	**3.95**	**.263**	**8**	**.065**	**-7**	**17**	**-1.6**
• HAHN, Fred	Frederick Aloys Hahn b: 2/16/1929, Nyack, NY d: 8/16/1984, Valhalla, NY BR/TL, 6'3", 174 lbs. Deb: 4/19/1952																										
1952	StL-N	0	0	....	1	0	0	0	0	2	2	2	0	0	0	1	0	1.500	0.00	....	3.50	.250	0	....	1	0	0.1
• HAHN, Noodles	Frank George Hahn b: 4/29/1879, Nashville, TN d: 2/6/1960, Candler, NC BL/TL, 5'9", 160 lbs. Deb: 4/18/1899																										
1899	Cin-N	23	8	.742	38	34	32	4	0	309	280	128	92	3	10	68	**145**	1.126	2.68	146	**2.41**	.242	16	.147	41	29	3.4
1900	Cin-N	16	20	.444	39	37	29	**4**	0	311^{1}	306	145	113	4	7	89	**132**	1.269	3.27	112	2.98	.257	24	.209	13	21	1.3
1901	Cin-N	22	19	.537	42	42	**41**	2	0	**375^{1}**	370	159	113	12	9	69	**239**	1.170	2.71	118	2.76	.256	24	.170	29	26	2.8
1902	Cin-N	23	12	.657	36	36	35	6	0	321	282	97	63	2	6	58	142	1.059	1.77	169	2.07	.236	22	.185	37	29	4.0
1903	Cin-N	22	12	.647	34	34	34	5	0	296	297	125	83	3	8	47	127	1.162	2.52	141	2.73	.262	18	.161	34	24	3.2
1904	Cin-N	16	18	.471	35	34	33	2	0	297^{2}	258	101	68	3	7	35	98	.984	2.06	142	1.94	.234	17	.172	21	25	2.4
1905	Cin-N	5	3	.625	13	8	5	1	0	77	85	44	24	0	2	9	17	1.221	2.81	117	2.92	.272	4	.167	3	4	0.2
1906	NY-A	3	2	.600	6	6	3	1	0	42	38	22	18	0	3	6	17	1.048	3.86	77	2.23	.245	4	.333	-4	3	-0.3
Total	**8**	**130**	**94**	**.580**	**243**	**231**	**212**	**25**	**0**	**2029^{1}**	**1916**	**821**	**574**	**27**	**52**	**381**	**917**	**1.132**	**2.55**	**132**	**2.50**	**.249**	**129**	**.176**	**175**	**161**	**16.9**
• HAID, Hal	Harold Augustine Haid b: 12/21/1897, Barberton, OH d: 8/13/1952, Los Angeles, CA BR/TR, 5'10.5", 150 lbs. Deb: 9/5/1919																										
1919	StL-A	0	0	....	1	0	0	0	0	2	5	5	4	0	0	3	1	4.000	18.00	18	20.47	.556	0	....	-3	0	-0.3
1928	StL-N	2	2	.500	27	0	0	0	**5**	47	39	24	12	1	1	11	21	1.064	2.30	174	1.96	.218	3	.375	9	5	0.9
1929	StL-N	9	9	.500	38	14	8	0	4	154^{2}	171	90	70	8	5	66	41	1.532	4.07	114	4.44	.284	4	.082	11	10	0.6
1930	StL-N	3	2	.600	20	0	0	0	2	33	38	17	15	1	3	14	13	1.576	4.09	123	4.74	.297	0	.000	3	3	0.3
1931	Bos-N	0	2	.000	27	0	0	0	1	56	59	36	28	3	3	16	20	1.339	4.50	84	3.63	.263	1	.125	-4	1	-0.5
1933	Chi-A	0	0	....	6	0	0	0	0	14^{2}	18	15	13	2	2	13	7	2.114	7.98	53	8.00	.310	1	.250	-6	0	-0.6
Total	**6**	**14**	**15**	**.483**	**119**	**14**	**8**	**0**	**12**	**307^{1}**	**330**	**187**	**142**	**15**	**14**	**123**	**103**	**1.474**	**4.16**	**104**	**4.22**	**.275**	**9**	**.125**	**9**	**19**	**0.5**
• HAINES, Jesse	Jesse Joseph "Pop" Haines b: 7/22/1893, Clayton, OH d: 8/5/1978, Dayton, OH BR/TR, 6', 190 lbs. Deb: 7/20/1918 C HOF: 1970																										
1918	Cin-N	0	0	....	1	0	0	0	0	5	5	1	1	0	0	1	2	1.200	1.80	148	2.71	.294	1	1.000	0	1	0.1
1920	StL-N	13	20	.394	**47**	37	19	4	2	301^{2}	303	136	100	9	9	80	120	1.270	2.98	103	3.18	.270	19	.176	2	14	0.1
1921	StL-N	18	12	.600	37	29	13	**3**	0	244^{1}	261	112	95	15	8	56	84	1.297	3.50	104	3.68	.286	17	.181	4	14	0.1
1922	StL-N	11	9	.550	29	26	11	2	0	183	207	103	78	10	4	45	62	1.377	3.84	101	3.81	.284	12	.167	5	11	0.2
1923	StL-N	20	13	.606	37	36	23	1	0	266	283	125	92	7	5	75	73	1.346	3.11	125	3.46	.275	20	.202	25	20	2.2
1924	StL-N	8	19	.296	35	31	16	1	0	222^{2}	275	129	109	14	5	66	69	1.531	4.41	86	4.78	.309	14	.189	-15	7	-1.8
1925	StL-N	13	14	.481	29	25	15	0	0	207	234	116	105	11	1	52	63	1.382	4.57	95	3.86	.290	13	.176	-7	11	-0.8
1926*	StL-N	13	4	.765	33	20	14	3	1	183	186	76	66	10	2	48	46	1.279	3.25	120	3.31	.265	13	.213	12	14	1.1
1927	StL-N	24	10	.706	38	36	**25**	**6**	1	300^{2}	273	114	91	11	5	77	89	1.164	2.72	145	2.65	.245	23	.202	36	**28**	3.4
1928*	StL-N	20	8	.714	33	28	20	1	0	240^{1}	238	98	85	14	6	72	77	1.290	3.18	126	3.40	.266	16	.184	20	19	1.9
1929	StL-N	13	10	.565	28	25	12	0	0	179^{2}	230	123	114	21	2	73	59	1.686	5.71	82	5.83	.313	11	.159	-20	6	-2.1
1930*	StL-N	13	8	.619	29	24	14	0	1	182	215	107	87	15	1	54	68	1.478	4.30	117	4.58	.298	16	.246	14	13	1.3
1931	StL-N	12	3	.800	19	17	8	2	0	122^{1}	134	48	41	2	0	28	27	1.324	3.02	130	3.34	.278	6	.133	12	11	1.0
1932	StL-N	3	5	.375	20	10	4	1	0	85^{1}	116	51	45	4	1	16	27	1.547	4.75	83	4.85	.326	5	.185	-7	3	-0.7
1933	StL-N	9	6	.600	32	10	5	0	1	115^{1}	113	46	32	3	1	37	37	1.301	2.50	139	3.03	.252	2	.067	12	9	1.1
1934*	StL-N	4	4	.500	37	6	0	0	1	90	86	42	35	6	4	19	17	1.167	3.50	121	3.10	.262	3	.158	6	7	0.5
1935	StL-N	6	5	.545	30	11	3	0	2	115^{1}	110	49	46	4	1	28	24	1.197	3.59	114	2.81	.252	9	.273	5	9	0.6
1936	StL-N	7	5	.583	25	9	4	0	1	99^{1}	110	44	43	4	1	21	19	1.319	3.90	101	3.53	.284	5	.167	0	7	0.0
1937	StL-N	3	3	.500	16	6	2	0	0	65^{2}	81	36	33	5	1	23	18	1.584	4.52	88	4.99	.303	4	.182	-4	3	-0.4
Total	**19**	**210**	**158**	**.571**	**555**	**386**	**208**	**24**	**10**	**3208^{2}**	**3460**	**1556**	**1298**	**165**	**57**	**871**	**981**	**1.350**	**3.64**	**108**	**3.71**	**.280**	**209**	**.186**	**100**	**207**	**7.7**
• HAISLIP, Jim	James Clifton "Slim" Haislip b: 8/4/1891, Farmersville, TX d: 1/22/1970, Dallas, TX BR/TR, 6'1", 186 lbs. Deb: 8/27/1913																										
1913	Phi-N	0	0	....	1	0	0	0	0	3	4	4	2	0	0	3	0	2.333	6.00	55	7.17	.400	0	.000	-1	0	-0.1
• HALAMA, John	John Thadeuz Halama b: 2/22/1972, Brooklyn, NY BL/TL, 6'5", 210 lbs. Deb: 4/2/1998																										
1998	Hou-N	1	1	.500	6	6	0	0	0	32^{1}	37	21	21	0	2	13	21	1.546	5.85	69	4.34	.296	0	.000	-7	0	-0.7
1999	Sea-A	11	10	.524	38	24	1	1	0	179	193	88	84	20	7	56	105	1.391	4.22	118	4.47	.281	1	.200	16	13	1.5
2000*	Sea-A	14	9	.609	30	30	1	1	0	166^{2}	206	108	94	19	2	56	87	1.572	5.08	89	5.42	.308	1	.500	-11	6	-1.0
2001*	Sea-A	10	7	.588	31	17	0	0	0	110^{1}	132	69	58	18	6	26	50	1.432	4.73	88	5.21	.296	0	.000	-10	4	-1.0
2002	Sea-A	6	5	.545	31	10	0	0	0	101	112	45	40	9	1	33	70	1.436	3.56	118	4.29	.281	0	....	8	6	0.8
2003	Oak-A	3	5	.375	35	13	0	0	0	108^{2}	117	68	51	18	2	36	51	1.408	4.22	107	4.61	.268	0	....	3	4	0.3
Total	**6**	**45**	**37**	**.549**	**171**	**100**	**2**	**2**	**0**	**698**	**797**	**399**	**348**	**84**	**20**	**220**	**384**	**1.457**	**4.49**	**100**	**4.80**	**.289**	**2**	**.111**	**-1**	**33**	**-0.1**
• HALBRITER, Ed	Edward L. Halbriter b: 2/2/1860, Auburn, NY d: 8/9/1936, Los Angeles, CA Deb: 5/23/1882																										
1882	Phi-a	0	1	.000	1	1	1	0	0	8	17	12	7	1	....	4	4	2.625	7.88	38	....	.406	0	.000	-4	0	-0.5
• HALE, Dad	Ray Luther Hale b: 2/18/1880, Allegan, MI d: 2/1/1946, Allegan, MI BR/TR, 5'10", 180 lbs. Deb: 4/21/1902																										
1902	Bos-N	1	4	.200	8	6	3	0	0	47	69	44	33	1	1	18	12	1.851	6.32	45	6.12	.341	0	.000	-19	0	-2.1
	Bal-A	0	1	.000	3	2	1	0	0	14	21	14	7	0	1	6	6	1.929	4.50	84	6.50	.346	0	.000	-0	0	-0.1
• HALICKI, Ed	Edward Louis Halicki b: 10/4/1950, Kearny, NJ BR/TR, 6'7", 220 lbs. Deb: 7/8/1974																										
1974	SF-N	1	8	.111	16	11	2	0	0	74^{1}	84	49	35	6	2	31	40	1.547	4.24	90	4.43	.275	6	.240	-3	1	-0.2
1975	SF-N	9	13	.409	24	23	7	2	0	159^{2}	143	76	62	6	3	59	153	1.265	3.49	109	2.93	.240	6	.113	5	8	0.4
1976	SF-N	12	14	.462	32	31	8	4	0	186^{1}	171	86	75	10	2	61	130	1.245	3.62	100	3.06	.246	9	.170	3	11	0.4
1977	SF-N	16	12	.571	37	37	7	2	0	257^{2}	241	105	95	27	7	70	168	1.207	3.32	118	3.32	.244	15	.176	21	20	2.4
1978	SF-N	9	10	.474	29	28	9	4	1	199	166	74	63	11	7	45	105	1.060	2.85	121	**2.29**	.221	9	.136	14	13	1.2
1979	SF-N	5	8	.385	33	19	3	1	0	125^{2}	134	82	64	12	3	47	81	1.440	4.58	76	4.19	.266	7	.206	-14	2	-1.3

YEAR	TM-L	W	L	PCT	G	GS	CG	SH	SV	IP	H	R	ER	HR	HB	BB	SO	RAT	ERA	ERA+	CERA	OAV	BH	AVG	PR+	WS	TPW
1980	SF-N	0	0	....	11	2	0	0	0	25	29	15	15	5	0	10	14	1.560	5.40	66	5.78	.293	1	.167	-5	0	-0.5
	Cal-A	3	1	.750	10	6	0	0	0	35^{1}	39	22	19	5	0	11	16	1.415	4.84	81	4.60	.279	0	....	-3	1	-0.3
Total	7	55	66	.455	192	157	36	13	1	1063	1007	509	428	82	24	334	707	1.262	3.62	102	3.30	.247	53	.165	17	56	2.1

• HALL, Bert Herbert Ernest Hall b: 10/15/1888, Portland, OR d: 7/18/1948, Seattle, WA BR/TR, 5'10", 178 lbs. Deb: 8/21/1911

YEAR	TM-L	W	L	PCT	G	GS	CG	SH	SV	IP	H	R	ER	HR	HB	BB	SO	RAT	ERA	ERA+	CERA	OAV	BH	AVG	PR+	WS	TPW
1911	Phi-N	0	1	.000	7	1	0	0	0	18	19	11	8	0	1	13	8	1.778	4.00	86	5.34	.297	1	.333	-1	1	-0.1

• HALL, Bill William Bernard "Beanie" Hall b: 2/22/1894, Charleston, WV d: 8/15/1947, Newport, KY BR/TR, 6'2", 250 lbs. Deb: 7/4/1913

YEAR	TM-L	W	L	PCT	G	GS	CG	SH	SV	IP	H	R	ER	HR	HB	BB	SO	RAT	ERA	ERA+	CERA	OAV	BH	AVG	PR+	WS	TPW
1913	Bro-N	0	0	....	3	0	0	0	0	4^{2}	4	3	3	0	1	5	3	1.929	5.79	57	5.85	.267	0	.000	-1	0	-0.2

• HALL, Bob Robert Lewis Hall b: 12/22/1923, Swissvale, PA d: 3/12/1983, St. Petersburg, FL BR/TR, 6'2", 195 lbs. Deb: 4/23/1949

YEAR	TM-L	W	L	PCT	G	GS	CG	SH	SV	IP	H	R	ER	HR	HB	BB	SO	RAT	ERA	ERA+	CERA	OAV	BH	AVG	PR+	WS	TPW
1949	Bos-N	6	4	.600	31	6	2	0	0	74^{1}	77	40	36	7	1	41	43	1.587	4.36	87	4.76	.272	8	.364	-4	5	-0.2
1950	Bos-N	0	2	.000	21	4	0	0	0	50^{1}	58	43	39	8	2	33	22	1.808	6.97	55	6.52	.293	1	.083	-17	0	-1.7
1953	Pit-N	3	12	.200	37	17	6	1	1	152	172	99	91	17	1	72	68	1.605	5.39	83	5.13	.286	6	.158	-15	5	-1.4
Total	3	9	18	.333	89	27	8	1	1	276^{2}	307	182	166	32	4	146	133	1.637	5.40	77	5.29	.284	15	.208	-36	10	-3.3

• HALL, Charley Carlos Clolo "Sea Lion" Hall b: 7/27/1885, Ventura, CA d: 12/6/1943, Ventura, CA BL/TR, 6'1", 187 lbs. Deb: 7/12/1906

YEAR	TM-L	W	L	PCT	G	GS	CG	SH	SV	IP	H	R	ER	HR	HB	BB	SO	RAT	ERA	ERA+	CERA	OAV	BH	AVG	PR+	WS	TPW
1906	Cin-N	4	8	.333	14	9	9	1	1	95	86	56	35	1	8	50	49	1.432	3.32	83	3.86	.258	6	.128	-7	2	-1.0
1907	Cin-N	4	2	.667	11	8	5	0	0	68	51	22	19	0	4	43	25	1.382	2.51	103	3.21	.226	7	.269	-0	4	0.1
1909	Bos-A	6	4	.600	11	7	3	0	0	59^{2}	59	24	17	0	3	17	27	1.274	2.56	97	3.22	.271	3	.158	-1	4	-0.2
1910	Bos-A	12	9	.571	35	16	13	0	2	188^{2}	142	68	40	6	9	73	95	1.140	1.91	134	2.39	.207	17	.207	14	14	2.0
1911	Bos-A	8	7	.533	32	10	6	0	**4**	146^{1}	149	79	61	3	5	72	83	1.510	3.75	87	4.22	.279	9	.141	-8	7	-0.9
1912*	Bos-A	15	8	.652	34	20	9	2	2	191	178	85	64	3	4	70	83	1.298	3.02	113	3.18	.257	20	.267	9	17	1.4
1913	Bos-A	5	4	.556	35	4	2	0	2	105	97	67	40	1	5	46	48	1.362	3.43	86	3.12	.235	9	.214	-4	4	-0.3
1916	StL-N	0	4	.000	10	5	2	0	1	42^{2}	45	27	26	1	0	14	15	1.383	5.48	48	3.54	.280	2	.143	-13	0	-1.6
1918	Det-A	0	1	.000	6	1	0	0	0	13^{1}	14	10	10	1	0	6	2	1.500	6.75	39	4.07	.269	0	.000	-5	0	-0.6
Total	9	54	47	.535	188	80	49	3	12	909^{2}	821	438	312	16	38	391	427	1.332	3.09	94	3.28	.248	73	.197	-16	52	-1.1

• HALL, Darren Michael Darren Hall b: 7/14/1964, Marysville, OH BR/TR, 6'3", 205 lbs. Deb: 4/30/1994

YEAR	TM-L	W	L	PCT	G	GS	CG	SH	SV	IP	H	R	ER	HR	HB	BB	SO	RAT	ERA	ERA+	CERA	OAV	BH	AVG	PR+	WS	TPW
1994	Tor-A	2	3	.400	30	0	0	0	17	31^{2}	26	12	12	3	1	14	28	1.263	3.41	141	3.37	.226	0	....	5	6	0.5
1995	Tor-A	0	2	.000	17	0	0	0	3	16^{1}	21	9	8	2	0	9	11	1.837	4.41	107	6.61	.309	0	....	1	1	0.0
1996	LA-N	0	2	.000	9	0	0	0	0	12	13	9	8	2	0	5	12	1.500	6.00	64	5.10	.271	0	....	-3	0	-0.3
1997	LA-N	3	2	.600	63	0	0	0	2	54^{2}	58	15	14	3	0	26	39	1.537	2.30	167	4.35	.283	0	....	10	6	1.0
1998	LA-N	0	3	.000	11	0	0	0	0	11^{1}	17	14	13	2	1	5	8	1.941	10.32	38	8.32	.347	0	....	-8	0	-0.8
Total	5	5	12	.294	130	0	0	0	22	126	135	59	55	12	2	59	98	1.540	3.93	106	4.83	.278	0	....	5	13	0.5

• HALL, Dick Richard Wallace Hall b: 9/27/1930, St. Louis, MO BR/TR, 6'6", 200 lbs. Deb: 4/15/1952 ♦

YEAR	TM-L	W	L	PCT	G	GS	CG	SH	SV	IP	H	R	ER	HR	HB	BB	SO	RAT	ERA	ERA+	CERA	OAV	BH	AVG	PR+	WS	TPW
1955	Pit-N	6	6	.500	15	13	4	0	1	94^{1}	92	43	41	8	2	28	46	1.272	3.91	105	3.41	.253	7	.175	3	7	0.4
1956	Pit-N	0	7	.000	19	9	1	0	1	62^{1}	64	36	33	8	0	21	27	1.364	4.76	79	4.09	.270	10	.345	-6	2	-0.2
1957	Pit-N	0	0	....	8	0	0	0	0	10	17	12	12	4	1	5	7	2.200	10.80	35	11.77	.362	0	.000	-8	0	-0.8
1959	Pit-N	0	0	....	2	1	0	0	0	8^{2}	12	5	3	1	0	1	3	1.500	3.12	124	4.93	.333	0	.000	1	0	0.0
1960	KC-A	8	13	.381	29	28	9	1	0	182^{1}	183	96	82	28	3	38	79	1.212	4.05	98	3.73	.261	6	.107	2	8	0.0
1961	Bal-A	7	5	.583	29	13	4	2	4	122^{1}	102	47	42	10	0	30	92	1.079	3.09	126	2.47	.227	5	.139	9	10	0.9
1962	Bal-A	6	6	.500	43	6	1	0	6	118^{1}	102	31	30	9	0	19	71	1.023	2.28	165	2.30	.230	4	.167	18	13	2.0
1963	Bal-A	5	5	.500	47	3	0	0	12	111^{2}	91	39	37	12	4	16	74	.958	2.98	118	2.29	.224	13	.464	7	13	1.3
1964	Bal-A	9	1	.900	45	0	0	0	7	87^{2}	58	19	18	8	0	16	52	.844	1.85	193	1.57	.188	2	.125	15	13	1.5
1965	Bal-A	11	8	.579	48	0	0	0	12	93^{2}	84	34	32	8	0	11	79	1.014	3.07	113	2.31	.243	5	.333	3	12	0.5
1966	Bal-A	6	2	.750	32	0	0	0	7	66	59	30	29	8	3	8	44	1.015	3.95	84	2.62	.233	2	.167	-5	5	-0.5
1967	Phi-N	10	8	.556	48	1	1	0	8	86	83	28	21	5	2	12	49	1.105	2.20	155	2.61	.255	1	.071	12	10	1.2
1968	Phi-N	4	1	.800	32	0	0	0	0	46	53	26	25	6	1	5	31	1.261	4.89	61	3.98	.296	1	.333	-9	1	-1.0
1969*	Bal-A	5	2	.714	39	0	0	0	6	65^{2}	49	14	14	3	1	9	31	.883	1.92	186	1.59	.213	2	.286	10	9	1.1
1970*	Bal-A	10	5	.667	32	0	0	0	3	61^{1}	51	25	21	8	0	6	30	.929	3.08	118	2.28	.229	1	.083	3	6	0.2
1971*	Bal-A	6	6	.500	27	0	0	0	1	43^{1}	52	27	24	4	1	11	26	1.454	4.98	67	4.20	.302	2	.400	-8	1	-0.8
Total	16	93	75	.554	495	74	20	3	68	1259^{2}	1152	512	464	130	18	236	741	1.102	3.32	110	2.86	.244	150	.210	44	110	5.6

• HALL, Drew Andrew Clark Hall b: 3/27/1963, Louisville, KY BL/TL, 6'4", 205 lbs. Deb: 9/14/1986

YEAR	TM-L	W	L	PCT	G	GS	CG	SH	SV	IP	H	R	ER	HR	HB	BB	SO	RAT	ERA	ERA+	CERA	OAV	BH	AVG	PR+	WS	TPW
1986	Chi-N	1	2	.333	5	4	1	0	1	23^{2}	24	12	12	3	0	10	21	1.437	4.56	89	4.53	.267	1	.143	-1	1	-0.1
1987	Chi-N	1	1	.500	21	0	0	0	0	32^{2}	40	31	25	4	0	14	20	1.653	6.89	62	5.74	.308	0	.000	-9	0	-0.9
1988	Chi-N	1	1	.500	19	0	0	0	1	22^{1}	26	20	19	4	1	9	22	1.567	7.66	47	5.54	.295	0	.000	-10	0	-1.0
1989	Tex-A	2	1	.667	38	0	0	0	0	58^{1}	42	24	24	3	3	33	45	1.286	3.70	107	3.11	.207	0	....	2	4	0.2
1990	Mon-N	4	7	.364	42	0	0	0	3	58^{1}	52	35	33	6	0	29	40	1.389	5.09	72	3.68	.242	0	.000	-9	1	-1.0
Total	5	9	12	.429	125	4	1	0	5	195^{1}	184	122	113	20	4	95	148	1.428	5.21	74	4.17	.253	1	.063	-27	6	-2.8

• HALL, Herb Herbert Silas "Iron Duke" Hall b: 6/5/1893, Steeleville, IL d: 7/1/1970, Fresno, CA BB/TR, 6'4", 220 lbs. Deb: 4/28/1918

YEAR	TM-L	W	L	PCT	G	GS	CG	SH	SV	IP	H	R	ER	HR	HB	BB	SO	RAT	ERA	ERA+	CERA	OAV	BH	AVG	PR+	WS	TPW
1918	Det-A	0	0	....	3	0	0	0	0	6	12	11	10	0	2	7	1	3.167	15.00	18	16.31	.500	0	.000	-8	0	-0.9

• HALL, John John Sylvester Hall b: 1/9/1924, Muskogee, OK d: 1/17/1995, Midwest City, CA BR/TR, 6'2.5", 170 lbs. Deb: 4/21/1948

YEAR	TM-L	W	L	PCT	G	GS	CG	SH	SV	IP	H	R	ER	HR	HB	BB	SO	RAT	ERA	ERA+	CERA	OAV	BH	AVG	PR+	WS	TPW
1948	Bro-N	0	0	....	3	0	0	0	0	4^{1}	4	3	3	1	0	2	2	1.385	6.23	64	4.60	.267	0	....	-1	0	-0.1

• HALL, Josh Joshua Alan Hall b: 12/16/1980, Lynchburg, VA BR/TR, 6'2", 190 lbs. Deb: 8/2/2003

YEAR	TM-L	W	L	PCT	G	GS	CG	SH	SV	IP	H	R	ER	HR	HB	BB	SO	RAT	ERA	ERA+	CERA	OAV	BH	AVG	PR+	WS	TPW
2003	Cin-N	0	2	.000	6	5	0	0	0	24^{2}	33	22	18	4	0	15	18	1.946	6.57	65	7.32	.314	1	.167	-6	0	-0.6

• HALL, Marc Marcus Hall b: 8/12/1887, Joplin, MO d: 2/24/1915, Joplin, MO BR/TR, 6'1.5", 190 lbs. Deb: 8/20/1910

YEAR	TM-L	W	L	PCT	G	GS	CG	SH	SV	IP	H	R	ER	HR	HB	BB	SO	RAT	ERA	ERA+	CERA	OAV	BH	AVG	PR+	WS	TPW
1910	StL-A	1	7	.125	8	7	5	0	0	46^{1}	50	33	22	0	3	31	25	1.748	4.27	58	5.12	.289	1	.067	-9	0	-1.2
1913	Det-A	10	12	.455	30	21	8	1	0	165	154	79	60	1	2	79	69	1.412	3.27	89	3.43	.255	4	.089	-2	7	-0.5
1914	Det-A	4	6	.400	25	8	1	0	0	90^{1}	88	38	27	1	0	27	18	1.273	2.69	104	3.08	.267	1	.043	2	4	0.0
Total	3	15	25	.375	63	36	14	1	0	301^{2}	292	150	109	2	5	137	112	1.422	3.25	86	3.59	.264	6	.072	-9	11	-1.6

• HALL, Tom Tom Edward Hall b: 11/23/1947, Thomasville, NC BL/TL, 6', 155 lbs. Deb: 6/9/1968

YEAR	TM-L	W	L	PCT	G	GS	CG	SH	SV	IP	H	R	ER	HR	HB	BB	SO	RAT	ERA	ERA+	CERA	OAV	BH	AVG	PR+	WS	TPW
1968	Min-A	2	1	.667	8	4	0	0	0	29^{2}	27	15	8	1	1	12	18	1.315	2.43	127	3.14	.239	0	.000	3	2	0.2
1969*	Min-A	8	7	.533	31	18	5	2	0	140^{2}	129	63	52	12	0	50	92	1.273	3.33	110	3.35	.243	8	.186	3	8	0.5
1970*	Min-A	11	6	.647	52	11	1	0	4	155^{1}	94	46	44	11	2	66	184	1.030	2.55	146	1.98	.173	8	.182	19	14	2.0
1971	Min-A	4	7	.364	48	11	0	0	9	129^{2}	104	54	48	13	0	58	137	1.249	3.33	107	3.08	.216	9	.265	5	10	0.8
1972*	Cin-N	10	1	.909	47	7	1	1	8	124^{1}	77	43	36	13	2	56	134	1.070	2.61	123	2.31	.173	3	.100	6	11	0.5
1973*	Cin-N	8	5	.615	54	7	0	0	8	103^{2}	74	43	40	13	0	48	96	1.177	3.47	98	2.83	.202	1	.045	-3	8	-0.5
1974	Cin-N	3	1	.750	40	1	0	0	1	64	54	32	29	9	0	30	48	1.313	4.08	85	3.79	.232	0	.000	-5	3	-0.6
1975	Cin-N	0	0	....	2	0	0	0	0	2	2	0	0	0	0	2	3	2.000	0.00	....	5.48	.250	0	....	1	0	0.1
	NY-N	4	3	.571	34	4	0	0	1	60^{2}	58	39	32	10	3	31	48	1.467	4.75	73	4.79	.254	2	.400	-10	1	-0.9
	Yr.	4	3	.571	36	4	0	0	1	62^{2}	60	39	32	10	3	33	51	1.484	4.60	75	4.81	.254	2	.400	-9	1	-0.9
1976	NY-N	1	1	.500	5	0	0	0	0	4^{2}	5	3	3	0	0	5	2	2.143	5.79	57	5.04	.250	0	....	-1	0	-0.1
	*KC-A	1	1	.500	31	0	0	0	1	30^{1}	28	19	15	4	0	18	25	1.516	4.45	79	4.59	.246	0	....	-3	0	-0.3
1977	KC-A	0	0	....	6	0	0	0	0	7^{2}	4	3	3	2	0	6	10	1.304	3.52	115	4.10	.154	0	....	0	0	0.0
Total	10	52	33	.612	358	63	7	3	32	852^{2}	656	360	310	88	8	382	797	1.217	3.27	107	3.04	.211	31	.161	15	57	1.5

• HALLA, John John Arthur Halla b: 5/13/1884, St. Louis, MO d: 9/30/1947, El Segundo, CA BL/TL, 5'11", 175 lbs. Deb: 8/18/1905

YEAR	TM-L	W	L	PCT	G	GS	CG	SH	SV	IP	H	R	ER	HR	HB	BB	SO	RAT	ERA	ERA+	CERA	OAV	BH	AVG	PR+	WS	TPW
1905	Cle-A	0	0	....	3	0	0	0	0	12^{2}	12	6	4	0	1	0	4	.947	2.84	92	2.02	.252	1	.200	-0	0	0.0

• HALLADAY, Roy Harry Leroy Halladay b: 5/14/1977, Denver, CO BR/TR, 6'6", 225 lbs. Deb: 9/20/1998

YEAR	TM-L	W	L	PCT	G	GS	CG	SH	SV	IP	H	R	ER	HR	HB	BB	SO	RAT	ERA	ERA+	CERA	OAV	BH	AVG	PR+	WS	TPW
1998	Tor-A	1	0	1.000	2	2	1	0	0	14	9	4	3	2	0	2	13	.786	1.93	242	1.61	.176	0	....	4	2	0.4
1999	Tor-A	8	7	.533	36	18	1	1	1	149^{1}	156	76	65	19	4	79	82	1.574	3.92	126	5.19	.270	0	.000	16	10	1.5
2000	Tor-A	4	7	.364	19	13	0	0	0	67^{2}	107	87	80	14	2	42	44	2.202	10.64	48	9.70	.357	0	....	-42	0	-3.8

YEAR	TM-L	W	L	PCT	G	GS	CG	SH	SV	IP	H	R	ER	HR	HB	BB	SO	RAT	ERA	ERA+	CERA	OAV	BH	AVG	PR+	WS	TPW
2001	Tor-A	5	3	.625	17	16	1	1	0	105^1	97	41	37	3	1	25	96	1.158	3.16	145	2.61	.241	0	.000	16	9	1.5
2002	Tor-A★	19	7	.731	34	34	2	1	0	**239^1**	223	93	78	10	7	62	168	1.191	2.93	157	2.85	.244	0	.000	**47**	21	4.4
2003	Tor-A★	**22**	7	.759	36	**36**	**9**	**2**	0	**266**	253	111	96	26	9	32	204	1.071	3.25	141	2.86	.247	1	.111	45	**23**	4.3
Total	**6**	**59**	**31**	**.656**	**144**	**119**	**14**	**5**	**1**	**841^2**	**845**	**412**	**359**	**74**	**23**	**242**	**607**	**1.291**	**3.84**	**124**	**3.77**	**.258**	**1**	**.056**	**86**	**65**	**8.3**

• HALLAHAN, Bill William Anthony "Wild Bill" Hallahan b: 8/4/1902, Binghamton, NY d: 7/8/1981, Binghamton, NY BR/TL, 5'10.5", 170 lbs. Deb: 4/16/1925

YEAR	TM-L	W	L	PCT	G	GS	CG	SH	SV	IP	H	R	ER	HR	HB	BB	SO	RAT	ERA	ERA+	CERA	OAV	BH	AVG	PR+	WS	TPW
1925	StL-N	1	0	1.000	6	0	0	0	0	15^1	14	6	6	0	0	11	8	1.630	3.52	123	4.01	.259	1	.333	1	1	0.1
1926*	StL-N	1	4	.200	19	3	0	0	0	56^2	45	27	23	1	1	32	28	1.359	3.65	107	3.44	.260	4	.250	1	3	0.1
1929	StL-N	4	4	.500	20	12	5	0	0	93^2	94	51	46	6	0	60	52	1.644	4.42	105	4.67	.269	4	.154	3	6	0.2
1930*	StL-N	15	9	.625	35	32	13	2	2	237^1	233	135	123	15	0	126	**177**	1.513	4.66	108	4.09	.260	10	.123	8	15	0.2
1931*	StL-N	**19**	9	.679	37	30	16	3	4	248^2	242	102	91	10	1	112	**159**	1.424	3.29	119	3.66	.259	8	.099	17	21	1.3
1932	StL-N	12	7	.632	25	22	13	1	1	176^1	169	79	61	10	0	69	108	1.350	3.11	126	3.45	.253	12	.214	17	15	1.9
1933	StL-N★	16	13	.552	36	32	16	2	0	244^1	245	114	95	6	0	98	93	1.404	3.50	99	3.43	.260	12	.150	-1	13	-0.1
1934*	StL-N	8	12	.400	32	26	10	2	0	162^2	195	93	77	2	0	66	70	1.605	4.26	99	4.42	.294	10	.182	-2	8	-0.4
1935	StL-N	15	8	.652	40	23	8	2	1	181^1	196	91	69	7	1	57	73	1.395	3.42	120	3.67	.275	8	.143	11	13	0.9
1936	StL-N	2	2	.500	9	6	1	0	0	37	58	28	26	4	0	17	16	2.027	6.32	62	7.81	.360	5	.556	-10	1	-0.7
	Cin-N	5	9	.357	23	19	5	2	0	135	150	78	65	3	1	57	32	1.533	4.33	88	4.13	.287	9	.191	-7	5	-0.6
	Yr.	7	11	.389	32	25	6	2	0	172	208	106	91	7	1	74	48	1.640	4.76	81	4.93	.305	14	.250	-17	6	-1.3
1937	Cin-N	3	9	.250	21	9	2	0	0	63	90	52	43	3	2	29	18	1.889	6.14	61	6.55	.345	2	.095	-17	0	-1.8
1938	Phi-N	1	8	.111	21	10	1	0	0	89	107	59	54	4	2	45	22	1.708	5.46	73	5.13	.295	5	.192	-12	1	-1.2
Total	**12**	**102**	**94**	**.520**	**324**	**224**	**90**	**14**	**8**	**1740^1**	**1838**	**915**	**779**	**71**	**8**	**779**	**856**	**1.504**	**4.03**	**101**	**4.09**	**.274**	**90**	**.162**	**10**	**102**	**0.1**

• HALLETT, Jack Jack Price Hallett b: 11/13/1914, Toledo, OH d: 6/11/1982, Toledo, OH BR/TR, 6'4", 215 lbs. Deb: 9/13/1940

YEAR	TM-L	W	L	PCT	G	GS	CG	SH	SV	IP	H	R	ER	HR	HB	BB	SO	RAT	ERA	ERA+	CERA	OAV	BH	AVG	PR+	WS	TPW
1940	Chi-A	1	1	.500	2	2	1	0	0	14	15	10	10	1	1	6	9	1.500	6.43	69	4.50	.273	2	.400	-3	0	-0.3
1941	Chi-A	5	5	.500	22	6	3	0	0	74^2	96	57	50	7	3	38	25	1.795	6.03	68	6.00	.306	4	.154	-17	0	-1.6
1942	Pit-N	0	1	.000	3	3	2	0	0	22^1	23	12	12	0	0	8	16	1.388	4.84	70	3.32	.274	3	.375	-3	1	-0.2
1943	Pit-N	1	2	.333	9	4	2	1	0	47^2	36	11	9	0	1	11	11	.986	1.70	205	1.69	.212	4	.286	9	5	1.2
1946	Pit-N	5	7	.417	35	9	3	1	0	115	107	48	42	0	0	39	64	1.270	3.29	107	2.98	.267	6	.231	5	8	0.5
1948	NY-N	0	0	....	2	0	0	0	0	4	3	3	2	0	0	4	3	1.750	4.50	87	4.03	.214	0	.000	-0	0	0.0
Total	**6**	**12**	**16**	**.429**	**73**	**24**	**11**	**2**	**0**	**277^2**	**280**	**141**	**125**	**8**	**5**	**106**	**128**	**1.390**	**4.05**	**93**	**3.69**	**.270**	**19**	**.238**	**-10**	**14**	**-0.4**

• HALLSTROM, Charlie Charles E. "Swedish Wonder" Hallstrom b: 1/22/1864, Jonkoping, Sweden d: 5/6/1949, Chicago, IL Deb: 9/23/1885

YEAR	TM-L	W	L	PCT	G	GS	CG	SH	SV	IP	H	R	ER	HR	HB	BB	SO	RAT	ERA	ERA+	CERA	OAV	BH	AVG	PR+	WS	TPW
1885	Pro-N	0	1	.000	1	1	1	0	0	9	18	16	11	3	....	6	0	2.667	11.00	24	....	.398	0	.000	-8	0	-0.8

• HALTER, Shane Shane David Halter b: 11/8/1969, La Plata, MD BR/TR, 5'10", 160 lbs. Deb: 4/6/1997 ♦

YEAR	TM-L	W	L	PCT	G	GS	CG	SH	SV	IP	H	R	ER	HR	HB	BB	SO	RAT	ERA	ERA+	CERA	OAV	BH	AVG	PR+	WS	TPW
1998	KC-A	0	0	....	1	0	0	0	0	1	1	0	0	0	0	0	0	1.000	0.00	....	2.02	.333	45	.221	1	3	-0.9
2000	Det-A	0	0	....	1	0	0	0	0	0	0	0	0	0	0	1	0	....	....	....	∞	1.000	62	.261	0	3	-0.5
Total	**2**	**0**	**0**	**....**	**2**	**0**	**0**	**0**	**0**	**1**	**1**	**0**	**0**	**0**	**0**	**1**	**0**	**2.000**	**0.00**	**....**	**2.02**	**.333**	**445**	**.249**	**1**	**6**	**-1.4**

• HAMANN, Doc Elmer Joseph Hamann b: 12/21/1900, New Ulm, MN d: 1/11/1973, Milwaukee, WI BR/TR, 6'1", 180 lbs. Deb: 9/21/1922

YEAR	TM-L	W	L	PCT	G	GS	CG	SH	SV	IP	H	R	ER	HR	HB	BB	SO	RAT	ERA	ERA+	CERA	OAV	BH	AVG	PR+	WS	TPW
1922	Cle-A	0	0	....	1	0	0	0	0	0	3	0	0	0	1	3	0	....	....	....	∞	1.000	0	....	0	0	0.0

• HAMBRIGHT, Roger Roger Dee Hambright b: 3/26/1949, Sunnyside, WA BR/TR, 5'10", 180 lbs. Deb: 7/19/1971

YEAR	TM-L	W	L	PCT	G	GS	CG	SH	SV	IP	H	R	ER	HR	HB	BB	SO	RAT	ERA	ERA+	CERA	OAV	BH	AVG	PR+	WS	TPW
1971	NY-A	3	1	.750	18	0	0	0	2	26^2	22	13	13	5	0	10	14	1.200	4.39	74	3.49	.224	1	.500	-3	2	-0.3

• HAMILL, John John Alexander Charles Hamill b: 12/18/1860, New York, NY d: 12/6/1911, Bristol, RI BR/TR, 5'8", 158 lbs. Deb: 5/1/1884

YEAR	TM-L	W	L	PCT	G	GS	CG	SH	SV	IP	H	R	ER	HR	HB	BB	SO	RAT	ERA	ERA+	CERA	OAV	BH	AVG	PR+	WS	TPW
1884	Was-a	2	17	.105	19	19	18	1	0	156^2	197	158	78	8	5	43	50	**1.532**	4.48	67	....	.292	7	.099	-16	1	-1.9

• HAMILTON, Dave David Edward Hamilton b: 12/13/1947, Seattle, WA BL/TL, 6', 190 lbs. Deb: 5/29/1972

YEAR	TM-L	W	L	PCT	G	GS	CG	SH	SV	IP	H	R	ER	HR	HB	BB	SO	RAT	ERA	ERA+	CERA	OAV	BH	AVG	PR+	WS	TPW
1972*	Oak-A	6	6	.500	25	14	1	0	0	101^1	94	34	33	7	1	31	55	1.234	2.93	97	3.15	.249	4	.154	-2	5	0.0
1973	Oak-A	6	4	.600	16	11	1	0	0	69^2	74	37	34	8	1	24	34	1.407	4.39	81	4.46	.274	0	....	-8	2	-0.9
1974	Oak-A	7	4	.636	29	18	1	1	0	117	104	45	41	10	5	48	69	1.299	3.15	105	3.60	.241	0	....	0	7	0.0
1975	Oak-A	1	2	.333	11	4	0	0	0	35^2	42	19	16	4	0	18	20	1.682	4.04	90	5.48	.290	0	....	-2	1	-0.2
	Chi-A	6	5	.545	30	1	0	0	6	69^2	63	23	22	4	0	29	51	1.321	2.84	136	3.32	.246	0	....	9	7	0.9
	Yr.	7	7	.500	41	5	0	0	6	105^1	105	42	38	8	0	47	71	1.443	3.25	116	4.05	.262	0	....	7	8	0.7
1976	Chi-A	6	6	.500	45	1	0	0	10	90^1	81	38	36	4	4	45	62	1.395	3.59	99	3.52	.243	0	....	1	8	0.1
1977	Chi-A	4	5	.444	55	0	0	0	9	67^1	71	33	27	6	0	33	45	1.545	3.61	113	4.43	.270	0	....	6	5	0.6
1978	StL-N	0	0	....	13	0	0	0	0	14	16	13	10	5	0	6	8	1.571	6.43	55	7.07	.296	0	.000	-5	0	-0.5
	Pit-N	0	2	.000	16	0	0	0	1	26^1	23	16	10	2	0	12	15	1.329	3.42	108	3.11	.221	0	.000	1	1	0.1
	Yr.	0	2	.000	29	0	0	0	1	40^1	39	29	20	7	0	18	23	1.413	4.46	81	4.48	.247	0	.000	-3	1	-0.4
1979	Oak-A	3	4	.429	40	7	1	0	5	82^2	80	42	34	5	1	43	52	1.488	3.70	109	4.12	.261	0	....	6	6	0.5
1980	Oak-A	0	3	.000	21	1	0	0	0	30	44	39	38	6	3	28	23	2.400	11.40	33	10.42	.344	0	....	-26	0	-2.6
Total	**9**	**39**	**41**	**.488**	**301**	**57**	**4**	**1**	**31**	**704**	**692**	**339**	**301**	**61**	**15**	**317**	**434**	**1.433**	**3.85**	**93**	**4.16**	**.259**	**4**	**.121**	**-20**	**42**	**-1.9**

• HAMILTON, Earl Earl Andrew Hamilton b: 7/19/1891, Gibson, IL d: 11/17/1968, Anaheim, CA BL/TL, 5'8", 160 lbs. Deb: 4/14/1911

YEAR	TM-L	W	L	PCT	G	GS	CG	SH	SV	IP	H	R	ER	HR	HB	BB	SO	RAT	ERA	ERA+	CERA	OAV	BH	AVG	PR+	WS	TPW
1911	StL-A	5	12	.294	32	17	10	1	0	177	191	103	78	4	4	69	55	1.469	3.97	85	4.08	.284	6	.107	-13	6	-1.4
1912	StL-A	11	14	.440	41	26	17	1	2	249^2	228	117	90	2	9	86	139	1.258	3.24	103	2.94	.248	13	.178	-1	16	0.0
1913	StL-A	13	12	.520	31	24	19	3	1	217^1	197	95	62	3	9	83	101	1.288	2.57	114	3.01	.241	10	.135	5	13	0.4
1914	StL-A	16	18	.471	44	35	20	5	2	302^1	265	111	84	5	10	100	111	1.207	2.50	108	2.74	.239	15	.176	10	22	1.6
1915	StL-A	9	17	.346	35	28	13	1	0	204	203	98	65	4	12	69	63	1.333	2.87	100	3.64	.274	7	.113	-3	8	-0.5
1916	StL-A	0	0	....	1	0	0	0	0	4	4	5	4	0	0	4	0	2.000	9.00	30	5.17	.250	0	....	-3	0	-0.3
	Det-A	1	2	.333	5	5	3	0	0	37^1	34	14	11	0	4	22	7	1.500	2.65	108	3.99	.254	1	.077	2	2	0.1
	StL-A	5	7	.417	22	12	3	0	0	91^1	97	44	31	2	2	26	25	1.347	3.05	90	3.66	.284	0	.000	-5	2	-0.7
	Yr.	6	9	.400	28	17	6	0	0	132^2	135	63	46	2	6	52	32	1.410	3.12	89	3.80	.275	1	.027	-7	4	-1.0
1917	StL-A	0	9	.000	27	8	2	0	1	83	86	46	29	1	2	41	19	1.530	3.14	82	4.09	.274	7	.368	-5	3	-0.2
1918	Pit-N	6	0	1.000	6	6	6	1	0	54	47	7	5	0	0	13	20	1.111	0.83	345	2.23	.242	6	.286	10	8	1.2
1919	Pit-N	8	11	.421	28	19	9	1	1	160^1	167	73	59	3	5	49	39	1.347	3.31	91	3.48	.280	7	.135	-4	6	-0.7
1920	Pit-N	10	13	.435	39	23	12	0	3	230^1	223	99	83	2	2	69	74	1.268	3.24	99	2.85	.258	10	.149	-0	13	-0.3
1921	Pit-N	13	15	.464	35	30	12	2	0	225	237	103	84	5	8	58	59	1.311	3.36	114	3.30	.272	12	.160	11	16	1.0
1922	Pit-N	11	7	.611	33	14	9	1	2	160	183	84	71	6	1	40	34	1.394	3.99	102	3.82	.296	9	.155	4	10	0.2
1923	Pit-N	7	9	.438	28	15	5	0	1	141	148	67	59	6	1	42	42	1.348	3.77	106	3.45	.271	9	.173	1	9	0.0
1924	Phi-N	0	1	.000	3	0	0	0	0	6	9	9	7	0	1	2	2	1.833	10.50	42	7.39	.391	0	.000	-4	0	-0.4
Total	**14**	**115**	**147**	**.439**	**410**	**262**	**140**	**16**	**13**	**2342^2**	**2319**	**1075**	**822**	**43**	**70**	**773**	**790**	**1.320**	**3.16**	**102**	**3.31**	**.264**	**112**	**.153**	**6**	**134**	**0.0**

• HAMILTON, Jack Jack Edwin Hamilton b: 12/25/1938, Burlington, IA BR/TR, 6', 200 lbs. Deb: 4/13/1962

YEAR	TM-L	W	L	PCT	G	GS	CG	SH	SV	IP	H	R	ER	HR	HB	BB	SO	RAT	ERA	ERA+	CERA	OAV	BH	AVG	PR+	WS	TPW
1962	Phi-N	9	12	.429	41	26	4	1	2	182	185	115	103	18	5	107	101	1.604	5.09	76	4.97	.268	3	.056	-26	4	-3.0
1963	Phi-N	2	1	.667	19	1	0	0	1	30	22	19	18	3	0	17	23	1.300	5.40	60	3.10	.200	0	.000	-8	0	-0.9
1964	Det-A	0	1	.000	5	1	0	0	0	15	24	17	14	2	1	8	5	2.133	8.40	44	8.89	.364	0	.000	-8	0	-0.9
1965	Det-A	1	1	.500	4	1	0	0	0	4^1	6	7	7	1	0	4	3	2.308	14.54	24	8.90	.316	0	....	-5	0	-0.6
1966	NY-N	6	13	.316	57	13	3	1	13	148^2	138	89	65	13	5	88	93	1.520	3.93	92	4.42	.248	5	.132	-5	6	-0.7
1967	NY-N	2	0	1.000	17	1	0	0	1	31^1	24	15	13	2	1	16	22	1.277	3.73	91	2.79	.205	1	.200	-1	2	0.0
	Cal-A	9	6	.600	26	20	0	0	0	119^1	104	47	43	6	1	63	74	1.399	3.24	97	3.55	.239	6	.158	-2	7	-0.3
1968	Cal-A	3	1	.750	21	2	1	0	2	38	34	15	14	0	0	15	18	1.289	3.32	88	2.83	.246	1	.143	-2	2	-0.3
1969	Cle-A	0	2	.000	20	0	0	0	1	30^2	37	17	15	2	0	23	13	1.957	4.40	86	6.44	.316	0	.000	-2	0	-0.2
	Chi-A	0	3	.000	8	0	0	0	0	12^1	23	16	16	1	0	7	5	2.432	11.68	33	9.67	.411	0	....	-11	0	-1.1
	Yr.	0	5	.000	28	0	0	0	1	43	60	33	31	3	0	30	18	2.093	6.49	59	7.37	.347	0	.000	-13	0	-1.3
Total	**8**	**32**	**40**	**.444**	**218**	**65**	**8**	**2**	**20**	**611^2**	**597**	**357**	**308**	**48**	**13**	**348**	**357**	**1.545**	**4.53**	**79**	**4.52**	**.259**	**16**	**.107**	**-71**	**21**	**-8.0**

• HAMILTON, Joey Johns Joseph Hamilton b: 9/9/1970, Statesboro, GA BR/TR, 6'4", 220 lbs. Deb: 5/24/1994

YEAR	TM-L	W	L	PCT	G	GS	CG	SH	SV	IP	H	R	ER	HR	HB	BB	SO	RAT	ERA	ERA+	CERA	OAV	BH	AVG	PR+	WS	TPW
1994	SD-N	9	6	.600	16	16	1	1	0	108^2	98	40	36	7	6	29	61	1.169	2.98	138	3.00	.241	0	.000	16	8	1.2
1995	SD-N	6	9	.400	31	30	2	2	0	204^1	189	89	70	17	11	56	123	1.199	3.08	130	3.25	.246	7	.108	18	12	1.5

YEAR TM-L	W	L	PCT	G	GS	CG	SH	SV	IP	H	R	ER	HR	HB	BB	SO	RAT	ERA	ERA+	CERA	OAV	BH	AVG	PR+	WS	TPW
1996* SD-N	15	9	.625	34	33	3	1	0	211^2	206	100	98	19	9	83	184	1.365	4.17	95	3.99	.256	11	.162	-4	11	-0.3
1997 SD-N	12	7	.632	31	29	1	0	0	192^2	199	100	91	22	12	69	124	1.391	4.25	90	4.48	.271	7	.130	-6	6	-0.5
1998* SD-N	13	13	.500	34	34	0	0	0	217^1	220	113	103	15	8	106	147	1.500	4.27	92	4.36	.267	10	.141	-9	8	-0.9
1999 Tor-A	7	8	.467	22	18	0	0	0	98	118	73	71	13	3	39	56	1.602	6.52	76	5.69	.298	0	.000	-18	2	-1.6
2000 Tor-A	2	1	.667	6	6	0	0	0	33	28	13	13	3	2	12	15	1.212	3.55	143	3.38	.233	0	....	6	3	0.5
2001 Tor-A	5	8	.385	22	22	0	0	0	122^1	170	88	80	17	3	38	82	1.700	5.89	78	6.55	.339	1	.333	-18	2	-1.7
Cin-N	1	2	.333	4	4	0	0	0	17^1	23	12	12	3	1	6	10	1.673	6.23	73	6.72	.329	0	.000	-3	0	-0.3
2002 Cin-N	4	10	.286	39	17	0	0	1	124^2	136	78	73	11	6	50	85	1.492	5.27	80	4.67	.279	7	.250	-14	3	-1.3
2003 Cin-N	0	0	....	3	0	0	0	0	10^2	21	15	15	3	0	5	7	2.438	12.66	34	12.37	.404	0	.000	-10	0	-1.0
Total 10	74	73	.503	242	209	7	4	1	1340^2	1408	721	662	130	61	493	894	1.418	4.44	94	4.44	.273	43	.127	-42	55	-4.4

• HAMILTON, Steve Steven Absher Hamilton b: 11/30/1935, Columbia, KY d: 12/2/1997, Morehead, KY BL/TL, 6'6", 195 lbs. Deb: 4/23/1961 C

YEAR TM-L	W	L	PCT	G	GS	CG	SH	SV	IP	H	R	ER	HR	HB	BB	SO	RAT	ERA	ERA+	CERA	OAV	BH	AVG	PR+	WS	TPW
1961 Cle-A	0	0	....	2	0	0	0	0	3	2	1	1	0	0	3	4	1.667	3.00	131	3.35	.200	1	1.000	0	1	0.1
1962 Was-A	3	8	.273	41	10	1	0	2	107^1	103	51	45	10	3	39	83	1.323	3.77	107	3.62	.248	2	.077	3	6	0.2
1963 Was-A	0	1	.000	3	0	0	0	0	2	5	3	3	0	0	2	1	3.500	13.50	27	15.69	.556	0	....	-2	0	-0.2
* NY-A	5	1	.833	34	0	0	0	5	62^1	49	19	18	3	1	24	63	1.171	2.60	135	2.58	.220	4	.286	5	8	0.7
Yr.	5	2	.714	37	0	0	0	5	64^1	54	22	21	3	1	26	64	1.244	2.94	121	2.99	.233	4	.286	3	8	0.5
1964* NY-A	7	2	.778	30	3	1	0	3	60^1	55	24	22	6	0	15	49	1.160	3.28	110	3.03	.246	4	.200	2	6	0.3
1965 NY-A	3	1	.750	46	1	0	0	5	58^1	47	12	9	2	0	16	51	1.080	1.39	245	2.01	.214	1	.167	13	8	1.5
1966 NY-A	8	3	.727	44	3	1	1	3	90	69	32	30	8	3	22	57	1.011	3.00	111	2.34	.218	1	.053	4	7	0.2
1967 NY-A	2	4	.333	44	0	0	0	4	62	57	25	24	7	1	23	55	1.290	3.48	90	3.58	.250	1	.111	-2	3	-0.2
1968 NY-A	2	2	.500	40	0	0	0	11	50^2	37	13	12	0	1	13	42	.987	2.13	136	1.64	.211	0	.000	5	8	0.6
1969 NY-A	3	4	.429	38	0	0	0	2	57	39	22	21	7	0	21	39	1.053	3.32	105	2.37	.194	0	.000	1	4	0.0
1970 NY-A	4	3	.571	35	0	0	0	3	45^1	36	16	14	3	1	16	33	1.147	2.78	126	2.51	.222	0	.000	4	4	0.3
Chi-A	0	0	....	3	0	0	0	0	3	4	2	2	0	0	1	3	1.667	6.00	65	4.83	.333	0	....	-1	0	-0.1
Yr.	4	3	.571	38	0	0	0	3	48^1	40	18	16	3	1	17	36	1.179	2.98	119	2.65	.230	0	.000	3	4	0.2
1971* SF-N	2	2	.500	39	0	0	0	4	44^2	29	15	15	4	1	11	38	.896	3.02	112	1.63	.186	0	.000	2	5	0.2
1972 Chi-N	1	0	1.000	22	0	0	0	0	17	24	9	9	1	1	8	13	1.882	4.76	80	6.22	.333	0	.000	-2	1	-0.2
Total 12	40	31	.563	421	17	3	1	42	663	556	244	225	51	12	214	531	1.161	3.05	115	2.79	.229	14	.125	33	61	3.3

• HAMLIN, Luke Luke Daniel "Hot Potato" Hamlin b: 7/3/1904, Ferris Center, MI d: 2/18/1978, Clare, MI BL/TR, 6'2", 168 lbs. Deb: 9/18/1933

YEAR TM-L	W	L	PCT	G	GS	CG	SH	SV	IP	H	R	ER	HR	HB	BB	SO	RAT	ERA	ERA+	CERA	OAV	BH	AVG	PR+	WS	TPW
1933 Det-A	1	0	1.000	3	3	0	0	0	16^2	20	11	9	3	0	10	10	1.800	4.86	89	6.41	.294	2	.400	-1	1	0.0
1934 Det-A	2	3	.400	20	5	1	0	1	75^1	87	48	45	11	0	44	30	1.739	5.38	82	5.96	.289	6	.231	-9	2	-0.8
1937 Bro-N	11	13	.458	39	25	11	1	1	185^2	183	96	74	4	0	48	93	1.244	3.59	112	2.81	.252	11	.186	14	13	1.3
1938 Bro-N	12	15	.444	44	30	10	3	6	237^1	243	111	97	14	2	65	97	1.298	3.68	106	3.03	.263	11	.141	8	14	0.5
1939 Bro-N	20	13	.606	40	**36**	19	2	0	269^2	255	115	109	27	0	54	88	1.146	3.64	111	2.97	.248	13	.126	13	19	0.8
1940 Bro-N	9	8	.529	33	25	9	2	0	182^1	183	77	62	17	2	34	91	1.190	3.06	131	3.19	.256	5	.086	20	13	1.6
1941 Bro-N	8	8	.500	30	20	5	1	1	136	139	75	64	14	2	41	58	1.324	4.24	87	3.79	.261	6	.146	-11	4	-1.2
1942 Pit-N	4	4	.500	23	14	6	1	0	112	128	58	49	3	1	19	38	1.313	3.94	86	3.37	.281	9	.243	-6	4	-0.5
1944 Phi-A	6	12	.333	29	23	9	2	0	190	204	94	79	13	3	38	58	1.274	3.74	93	3.44	.271	13	.232	-5	9	-0.2
Total 9	73	76	.490	261	181	70	12	9	1405	1442	685	588	106	10	353	563	1.278	3.77	102	3.43	.262	76	.164	23	79	1.5

• HAMM, Pete Peter Whitfield Hamm b: 9/20/1947, Buffalo, NY BR/TR, 6'5", 210 lbs. Deb: 7/29/1970

YEAR TM-L	W	L	PCT	G	GS	CG	SH	SV	IP	H	R	ER	HR	HB	BB	SO	RAT	ERA	ERA+	CERA	OAV	BH	AVG	PR+	WS	TPW
1970 Min-A	0	2	.000	10	0	0	0	0	16^1	17	10	10	3	0	7	3	1.469	5.51	68	4.89	.262	0	.000	-3	0	-0.4
1971 Min-A	2	4	.333	13	8	1	0	0	44	55	33	33	7	1	18	16	1.659	6.75	53	6.11	.309	3	.273	-15	0	-1.5
Total 2	2	6	.250	23	8	1	0	0	60^1	72	43	43	10	1	25	19	1.608	6.41	56	5.78	.296	3	.250	-18	0	-1.9

• HAMMAKER, Atlee Charlton Atlee Hammaker b: 1/24/1958, Carmel, CA BB/TL, 6'3", 200 lbs. Deb: 8/13/1981

YEAR TM-L	W	L	PCT	G	GS	CG	SH	SV	IP	H	R	ER	HR	HB	BB	SO	RAT	ERA	ERA+	CERA	OAV	BH	AVG	PR+	WS	TPW
1981 KC-A	1	3	.250	10	6	0	0	0	39	44	24	24	2	0	12	11	1.436	5.54	65	4.04	.286	0	....	-8	0	-0.9
1982 SF-N	12	8	.600	29	27	4	1	0	175	189	86	80	16	2	28	102	1.240	4.11	87	3.52	.278	4	.068	-7	7	-1.1
1983 SF-N★	10	9	.526	23	23	8	3	0	172^1	147	57	43	9	3	32	127	1.039	**2.25**	**157**	**2.16**	.228	6	.102	26	13	2.6
1984 SF-N	2	0	1.000	6	6	0	0	0	33	32	10	8	2	0	9	24	1.242	2.18	161	3.07	.256	2	.182	6	2	0.7
1985 SF-N	5	12	.294	29	29	1	1	0	170^2	161	81	71	17	0	47	100	1.219	3.74	92	3.21	.247	4	.085	-4	6	-0.7
1987* SF-N	10	10	.500	31	27	2	0	0	168^1	159	73	67	22	3	57	107	1.283	3.58	107	3.74	.248	7	.123	3	9	0.1
1988 SF-N	9	9	.500	43	17	3	1	5	144^2	136	68	60	11	3	41	65	1.224	3.73	87	3.10	.248	4	.121	-8	6	-0.9
1989* SF-N	6	6	.500	28	9	0	0	0	76^2	78	34	32	5	1	23	30	1.317	3.76	90	3.59	.271	7	.368	-5	4	-0.3
1990 SF-N	4	5	.444	25	6	0	0	0	67^1	69	33	32	7	0	21	28	1.337	4.28	85	3.86	.273	1	.059	-5	3	-0.6
SD-N	0	4	.000	9	1	0	0	0	19^1	16	11	10	1	0	6	16	1.138	4.66	82	2.36	.213	1	.500	-2	0	-0.2
Yr.	4	9	.308	34	7	0	0	0	86^2	85	44	42	8	0	27	44	1.292	4.36	84	3.53	.259	2	.105	-7	3	-0.8
1991 SD-N	0	1	.000	1	1	0	0	0	4^2	8	7	3	0	0	3	1	2.357	5.79	66	7.78	.364	0	.000	-1	0	-0.1
1994 Chi-A	0	0	....	2	0	0	0	0	1^1	1	0	0	0	0	0	1	.750	0.00	....	1.13	.200	0	....	1	0	0.1
1995 Chi-A	0	0	....	13	0	0	0	0	6^1	11	9	9	2	1	8	3	3.000	12.79	35	15.63	.393	0	....	-6	0	-0.5
Total 12	59	67	.468	249	152	18	6	5	1078^2	1051	493	439	94	13	287	615	1.240	3.66	97	3.33	.255	36	.118	-10	50	-1.8

• HAMMOND, Chris Christopher Andrew Hammond b: 1/21/1966, Atlanta, GA BL/TL, 6'1", 195 lbs. Deb: 7/16/1990

YEAR TM-L	W	L	PCT	G	GS	CG	SH	SV	IP	H	R	ER	HR	HB	BB	SO	RAT	ERA	ERA+	CERA	OAV	BH	AVG	PR+	WS	TPW
1990 Cin-N	0	2	.000	3	3	0	0	0	11^1	13	9	8	2	0	12	4	2.206	6.35	62	8.50	.302	0	.000	-3	0	-0.4
1991 Cin-N	7	7	.500	20	18	0	0	0	99^2	92	51	45	4	2	48	50	1.405	4.06	94	3.63	.250	12	.353	-3	6	0.2
1992 Cin-N	7	10	.412	28	26	0	0	0	147^1	149	75	69	13	3	55	79	1.385	4.21	85	4.02	.266	6	.136	-10	5	-0.9
1993 Fla-N	11	12	.478	32	32	1	0	0	191	207	106	99	18	1	66	108	1.429	4.66	93	4.31	.277	12	.190	-4	8	0.1
1994 Fla-N	4	4	.500	13	13	1	1	0	73^1	79	30	25	5	1	23	40	1.391	3.07	143	4.03	.281	3	.136	10	6	1.0
1995 Fla-N	9	6	.600	25	24	3	2	0	161	157	73	68	17	9	47	126	1.267	3.80	111	3.75	.256	13	.271	7	10	1.3
1996 Fla-N	5	8	.385	38	9	0	0	0	81	104	65	59	14	4	27	50	1.617	6.56	62	6.21	.315	1	.067	-24	0	-2.4
1997 Bos-A	3	4	.429	29	8	0	0	1	65^1	81	45	43	5	2	27	48	1.653	5.92	78	5.47	.310	0	....	-9	2	-0.9
1998 Fla-N	0	2	.000	3	3	0	0	0	13^2	20	11	10	3	1	8	8	2.049	6.59	62	9.33	.357	1	.200	-4	0	-0.4
2002* Atl-N	7	2	.778	63	0	0	0	0	76	53	15	8	1	1	31	63	1.105	0.95	432	1.85	.195	0	.000	25	13	2.6
2003* NY-A	3	2	.600	62	0	0	0	1	63	65	23	20	5	2	11	45	1.206	2.86	153	3.36	.270	0	....	12	7	1.2
Total 11	56	59	.487	316	136	5	3	2	982^2	1020	503	454	87	26	355	621	1.399	4.16	99	4.19	.270	48	.204	-3	57	1.4

• HAMNER, Ralph Ralph Conant "Bruz" Hamner b: 9/12/1916, Gibsland, LA d: 5/22/2001, Little Rock, AR BR/TR, 6'3", 165 lbs. Deb: 4/28/1946

YEAR TM-L	W	L	PCT	G	GS	CG	SH	SV	IP	H	R	ER	HR	HB	BB	SO	RAT	ERA	ERA+	CERA	OAV	BH	AVG	PR+	WS	TPW
1946 Chi-A	2	7	.222	25	7	1	0	1	71^1	80	47	35	2	5	39	29	1.668	4.42	77	4.79	.276	3	.167	-9	0	-0.9
1947 Chi-N	1	2	.333	3	3	2	0	0	25	24	10	7	0	0	16	14	1.600	2.52	157	3.94	.267	1	.125	4	2	0.4
1948 Chi-N	5	9	.357	27	17	5	0	0	111^1	110	63	58	12	5	69	53	1.608	4.69	83	4.95	.259	6	.182	-9	3	-0.8
1949 Chi-N	0	2	.000	6	1	0	0	0	12^1	22	13	12	1	1	8	3	2.432	8.76	46	10.33	.407	0	.000	-6	0	-0.6
Total 4	8	20	.286	61	28	8	0	1	220	236	133	112	15	11	132	99	1.673	4.58	82	5.08	.275	10	.164	-20	5	-2.0

• HAMPTON, Mike Michael William Hampton b: 9/9/1972, Brooksville, FL BR/TL, 5'10", 180 lbs. Deb: 4/17/1993

YEAR TM-L	W	L	PCT	G	GS	CG	SH	SV	IP	H	R	ER	HR	HB	BB	SO	RAT	ERA	ERA+	CERA	OAV	BH	AVG	PR+	WS	TPW
1993 Sea-A	1	3	.250	13	3	0	0	1	17	28	20	18	3	0	17	8	2.647	9.53	46	11.09	.368	0	....	-10	0	-1.0
1994 Hou-N	2	1	.667	44	0	0	0	0	41^1	46	19	17	4	2	16	24	1.500	3.70	107	4.88	.282	0	.000	1	3	0.1
1995 Hou-N	9	8	.529	24	24	0	0	0	150^2	141	73	56	13	4	49	115	1.261	3.35	116	3.37	.247	7	.146	12	8	1.2
1996 Hou-N	10	10	.500	27	27	2	1	0	160^1	175	79	64	12	3	49	101	1.397	3.59	108	4.11	.280	10	.238	8	11	1.1
1997* Hou-N	15	10	.600	34	34	7	2	0	223	217	105	95	16	2	77	139	1.318	3.83	104	3.56	.257	10	.137	1	11	0.2
1998* Hou-N	11	7	.611	32	32	1	1	0	211^2	227	92	79	18	5	81	137	1.455	3.36	121	4.45	.278	16	.262	16	15	2.2
1999* Hou-N★	**22**	4	.846	34	34	3	2	0	239	206	86	77	12	5	101	177	1.285	2.90	152	3.25	.241	23	.311	38	**26**	4.6
2000* NY-N	15	10	.600	33	33	3	1	0	217^2	194	89	76	10	8	99	151	1.346	3.14	140	3.44	.241	20	.274	32	19	3.5
2001 Col-N★	14	13	.519	32	32	2	1	0	203	236	138	122	31	8	85	122	**1.581**	5.41	99	5.69	.296	23	.291	-3	11	0.6
2002 Col-N	7	15	.318	30	30	0	0	0	178^2	228	135	122	24	7	91	74	**1.785**	6.15	78	6.61	.313	22	.344	-25	5	-1.8
2003* Atl-N	14	8	.636	31	31	1	0	0	190	186	91	81	14	1	78	110	1.389	3.84	110	3.77	.255	11	.183	9	11	1.3
Total 11	120	89	.574	334	280	19	8	1	1832^1	1884	927	807	157	45	743	1158	1.434	3.96	110	4.30	.269	142	.247	78	120	12.0

YEAR	TM-L	W	L	PCT	G	GS	CG	SH	SV	IP	H	R	ER	HR	HB	BB	SO	RAT	ERA	ERA+	CERA	OAV	BH	AVG	PR+	WS	TPW
• HANCOCK, Josh	Joshua Morgan Hancock b: 4/11/1978, Cleveland, MS BR/TR, 6'3", 217 lbs. Deb: 9/10/2002																										
2002	Bos-A	0	1	.000	3	1	0	0	0	7^{1}	5	3	3	1	0	2	6	.955	3.68	122	2.25	.200	0	....	1	0	0.1
2003	Phi-N	0	0	....	2	0	0	0	0	3	2	1	1	0	0	0	4	.667	3.00	133	0.91	.182	0	....	0	0	0.0
Total	2	0	1	.000	5	1	0	0	0	10^{1}	7	4	4	1	0	2	10	.871	3.48	125	1.86	.194	0	....	1	0	0.1
• HANCOCK, Lee	Leland David Hancock b: 6/27/1967, North Hollywood, CA BL/TL, 6'4", 215 lbs. Deb: 9/3/1995																										
1995	Pit-N	0	0	....	11	0	0	0	0	14	10	3	3	0	0	2	6	.857	1.93	223	1.32	.192	0	....	4	2	0.4
1996	Pit-N	0	0	....	13	0	0	0	0	18^{1}	21	18	13	5	2	10	13	1.691	6.38	68	6.85	.276	0	....	-4	0	-0.4
Total	2	0	0	....	24	0	0	0	0	32^{1}	31	21	16	5	2	12	19	1.330	4.45	98	4.45	.242	0	....	-0	2	0.0
• HANCOCK, Ryan	Ryan Lee Hancock b: 11/11/1971, Santa Clara, CA BR/TR, 6'2", 220 lbs. Deb: 6/8/1996																										
1996	Cal-A	4	1	.800	11	4	0	0	0	27^{2}	34	23	23	2	2	17	19	1.843	7.48	65	6.46	.306	1	1.000	-8	1	-0.7
• HAND, Rich	Richard Allen Hand b: 7/10/1948, Bellevue, WA BR/TR, 6'1", 195 lbs. Deb: 4/9/1970																										
1970	Cle-A	6	13	.316	35	25	3	1	3	159^{2}	132	71	68	27	4	69	110	1.259	3.83	103	3.84	.228	6	.146	2	11	0.1
1971	Cle-A	2	6	.250	15	12	0	0	0	60^{2}	74	43	39	6	4	38	26	1.846	5.79	66	6.75	.311	2	.125	-14	0	-1.5
1972	Tex-A	10	14	.417	30	28	2	1	0	170^{2}	139	66	63	12	3	103	109	**1.418**	3.32	91	3.60	.226	8	.154	-2	8	-0.1
1973	Tex-A	2	3	.400	8	7	1	0	0	41^{2}	49	29	25	2	2	19	14	1.632	5.40	69	4.76	.290	0	....	-7	1	-0.7
	Cal-A	4	3	.571	16	6	0	0	0	54^{2}	58	29	22	5	1	21	19	1.445	3.62	98	4.36	.274	0	....	0	3	0.0
	Yr.	6	6	.500	24	13	1	0	0	96^{1}	107	58	47	7	3	40	33	1.526	4.39	83	4.53	.281	0	....	-7	4	-0.7
Total	4	24	39	.381	104	78	6	2	3	487^{1}	452	238	217	52	14	250	278	1.440	4.01	88	4.25	.249	16	.147	-21	23	-2.2
• HANDIBOE, Jim	James Edward "Nick" Handiboe b: 7/17/1866, Columbus, OH d: 11/8/1942, Columbus, OH BR/TR, 5'11", 160 lbs. Deb: 5/28/1886																										
1886	Pit-a	7	7	.500	14	14	12	1	0	114	82	65	42	1	12	33	83	1.009	3.32	102	....	.192	5	.114	-0	6	-0.2
• HANDRAHAN, Vern	James Vernon Handrahan b: 11/27/1938, Charlottetown, Canada BL/TR, 6'2", 185 lbs. Deb: 4/14/1964																										
1964	KC-A	0	1	.000	18	1	0	0	0	35^{2}	33	24	24	9	2	25	18	1.626	6.06	63	6.40	.252	2	.222	-8	0	-0.9
1966	KC-A	0	1	.000	16	1	0	0	1	25^{1}	20	12	12	5	1	15	18	1.382	4.26	80	4.62	.227	0	.000	-3	1	-0.3
Total	2	0	2	.000	34	2	0	0	1	61	53	36	36	14	3	40	36	1.525	5.31	69	5.66	.242	2	.167	-11	1	-1.2
• HANDS, Bill	William Alfred "Froggy" Hands b: 5/6/1940, Hackensack, NJ BR/TR, 6'2", 185 lbs. Deb: 6/3/1965																										
1965	SF-N	0	2	.000	4	2	0	0	0	6	13	11	11	0	0	6	5	3.167	16.50	22	12.71	.433	0	.000	-9	0	-0.9
1966	Chi-N	8	13	.381	41	26	0	0	2	159	168	91	81	17	5	59	93	1.428	4.58	80	4.36	.272	2	.041	-14	5	-1.8
1967	Chi-N	7	8	.467	49	11	3	1	6	150	134	46	41	9	2	48	84	1.213	2.46	144	2.86	.239	4	.105	16	13	1.7
1968	Chi-N	16	10	.615	38	34	11	4	0	258^{2}	221	91	83	26	6	36	148	.994	2.89	110	2.46	.231	5	.061	8	18	0.4
1969	Chi-N	20	14	.588	41	41	18	3	0	300	268	102	83	21	6	73	181	1.137	2.49	162	2.77	.237	9	.092	**51**	28	5.0
1970	Chi-N	18	15	.545	39	38	12	2	1	265	278	121	109	20	4	76	170	1.336	3.70	122	3.75	.269	10	.133	23	21	2.4
1971	Chi-N	12	18	.400	36	35	14	1	0	242^{1}	248	112	92	27	2	50	128	1.230	3.42	115	3.47	.260	6	.083	18	15	1.7
1972	Chi-N	11	8	.579	32	28	6	3	0	189	168	73	63	12	2	47	96	1.138	3.00	127	2.67	.237	1	.018	17	13	1.4
1973	Min-A	7	10	.412	39	15	3	1	2	142	138	69	55	14	2	41	78	1.261	3.49	114	3.49	.252	0	....	8	8	0.8
1974	Min-A	4	5	.444	35	10	0	0	3	115^{1}	130	57	57	9	4	25	74	1.344	4.45	84	4.07	.284	0	....	-8	5	-0.8
	Tex-A	2	0	1.000	2	2	1	1	0	14	11	3	3	0	0	3	4	1.000	1.93	185	1.68	.208	0	....	2	2	0.3
	Yr.	6	5	.545	37	12	1	1	3	129^{1}	141	60	60	9	4	28	78	1.307	4.18	90	3.81	.276	0	....	-6	7	-0.6
1975	Tex-A	6	7	.462	18	18	4	1	0	109^{2}	118	58	49	12	3	28	67	1.331	4.02	93	4.08	.271	0	....	-3	5	-0.3
Total	11	111	110	.502	374	260	72	17	14	1951	1895	834	727	167	36	492	1128	1.223	3.35	114	3.30	.253	37	.078	111	133	9.8
• HANEY, Chris	Christopher Deane Haney b: 11/16/1968, Baltimore, MD BL/TL, 6'3", 195 lbs. Deb: 6/21/1991																										
1991	Mon-N	3	7	.300	16	16	0	0	0	84^{2}	94	49	38	6	1	43	51	1.618	4.04	90	4.89	.280	2	.074	-5	1	-0.7
1992	Mon-N	2	3	.400	9	6	1	1	0	38	40	25	23	6	4	10	27	1.316	5.45	64	4.65	.270	2	.222	-8	0	-0.9
	KC-A	2	3	.400	7	7	1	1	0	42	35	18	18	5	0	16	27	1.214	3.86	105	3.15	.226	0	....	2	2	0.2
1993	KC-A	9	9	.500	23	23	1	1	0	124	141	87	83	13	3	53	65	1.565	6.02	76	5.08	.286	0	....	-21	3	-2.0
1994	KC-A	2	2	.500	6	6	0	0	0	28^{1}	36	25	23	2	1	11	18	1.659	7.31	68	5.59	.333	0	....	-7	0	-0.7
1995	KC-A	3	4	.429	16	13	1	0	0	81^{1}	78	35	33	7	2	33	31	1.365	3.65	131	4.02	.262	0	....	9	6	0.9
1996	KC-A	10	14	.417	35	35	4	1	0	228	267	136	119	29	6	51	115	1.395	4.70	107	4.63	.291	0	....	8	12	0.7
1997	KC-A	1	2	.333	8	3	0	0	0	24^{2}	29	16	12	1	2	5	16	1.378	4.38	108	3.93	.290	0	....	1	1	0.1
1998	KC-A	6	6	.500	33	12	0	0	0	97^{1}	125	78	76	18	5	36	51	1.654	7.03	69	6.49	.316	0	....	-23	1	-2.1
	Chi-N	0	0	....	5	0	0	0	0	5	3	4	4	2	0	1	4	.800	7.20	61	2.77	.167	0	....	-1	0	-0.1
1999	Cle-A	0	2	.000	13	4	0	0	0	40^{1}	43	22	21	3	3	16	22	1.463	4.69	107	4.57	.270	0	....	2	2	0.2
2000	Cle-A	0	0	....	1	0	0	0	0	1	1	1	1	0	0	1	0	2.000	9.00	55	5.48	.333	0	....	-0	0	0.0
2002	Bos-A	0	0	....	24	0	0	0	1	30	32	14	14	2	4	10	15	1.400	4.20	107	4.32	.274	0	....	1	2	0.0
Total	11	38	52	.422	196	125	8	4	1	824^{2}	924	510	465	94	31	286	442	1.467	5.07	90	4.80	.284	4	.111	-44	30	-4.5
• HANKINS, Don	Donald Wayne Hankins b: 2/9/1902, Pendleton, IN d: 5/16/1963, Winston-Salem, NC BR/TR, 6'3", 183 lbs. Deb: 4/23/1927																										
1927	Det-A	2	1	.667	20	1	0	0	2	42^{2}	67	39	30	1	0	13	10	1.875	6.33	66	6.55	.383	1	.143	-10	0	-1.0
• HANKINSON, Frank	Frank Edward Hankinson b: 4/29/1856, New York, NY d: 4/5/1911, Palisades Park, NJ BR/TR, 5'11", 168 lbs. Deb: 5/1/1878 ♦																										
1878	Chi-N	0	1	.000	1	1	1	0	0	9	11	9	6	0	....	0	4	1.222	6.00	40	....	.287	64	.267	-4	5	0.5
1879	Chi-N	15	10	.600	26	25	25	2	0	230^{2}	248	134	64	0	....	27	69	1.192	2.50	103	....	.257	31	.181	-7	16	-1.3
1880	Cle-N	1	1	.500	4	2	2	0	1	25	20	10	3	0	....	3	8	.920	1.08	218	....	.208	55	.209	3	6	-1.5
1885	NY-a	0	0	....	1	0	0	0	0	2	2	1	1	1	0	1	0	1.500	4.50	66	....	.249	81	.224	-0	7	0.8
Total	4	16	12	.571	32	28	28	2	1	266^{2}	281	154	74	1	0	31	81	1.170	2.50	102	....	.254	785	.237	-9	34	-1.6
• HANLEY, Jim	James Patrick Hanley b: 10/13/1885, Providence, RI d: 5/1/1961, Elmhurst, NY BR/TL, 5'11", 165 lbs. Deb: 7/3/1913																										
1913	NY-A	0	0	....	1	0	0	0	0	4	5	3	3	0	0	4	2	2.250	6.75	44	7.02	.313	0	.000	-2	0	-0.2
• HANNA, Preston	Preston Lee Hanna b: 9/10/1954, Pensacola, FL BR/TR, 6'1", 195 lbs. Deb: 9/13/1975																										
1975	Atl-N	0	0	....	4	0	0	0	0	5^{2}	7	1	1	0	2	5	2	2.118	1.59	238	8.14	.304	0	....	2	1	0.2
1976	Atl-N	0	0	....	5	0	0	0	0	8	11	5	4	0	0	4	3	1.875	4.50	84	6.07	.333	0	.000	-0	0	-0.1
1977	Atl-N	2	6	.250	17	9	1	0	1	60	69	40	33	6	2	34	37	1.717	4.95	90	5.66	.285	1	.071	-2	2	-0.2
1978	Atl-N	7	13	.350	29	28	0	0	0	140^{1}	132	89	80	10	3	93	90	1.603	5.13	79	4.56	.251	9	.184	-15	3	-1.4
1979	Atl-N	1	1	.500	6	4	0	0	0	24^{1}	27	11	8	1	0	15	15	1.726	2.96	137	5.05	.284	0	.000	4	2	0.3
1980	Atl-N	2	0	1.000	32	2	0	0	0	79^{1}	63	28	28	3	3	44	35	1.349	3.18	118	3.21	.224	2	.143	5	6	0.5
1981	Atl-N	2	1	.667	20	1	0	0	0	35^{1}	45	27	25	2	0	23	22	1.925	6.37	56	6.51	.341	1	.250	-11	0	-1.1
1982	Atl-N	3	0	1.000	20	1	0	0	0	36	36	15	15	3	0	28	17	1.778	3.75	99	5.73	.277	2	.400	-0	3	0.1
	Oak-A	0	4	.000	23	2	1	0	0	48^{1}	54	34	30	3	1	33	32	1.800	5.59	70	5.63	.287	0	....	-9	0	-0.9
Total	8	17	25	.405	156	47	2	0	1	437^{1}	444	250	224	28	11	279	253	1.653	4.61	86	4.94	.269	15	.161	-27	17	-2.6
• HANNAHS, Gerry	Gerald Ellis Hannahs b: 3/6/1953, Binghamton, NY BL/TL, 6'3", 210 lbs. Deb: 9/8/1976																										
1976	Mon-N	2	0	1.000	3	3	0	0	0	16	20	14	12	2	0	12	10	2.000	6.75	55	7.48	.323	3	.375	-5	0	-0.5
1977	Mon-N	1	5	.167	8	7	0	0	0	37	43	27	20	7	0	17	21	1.622	4.86	78	5.85	.291	0	.000	-4	0	-0.5
1978	LA-N	0	0	....	1	0	0	0	0	2	3	2	2	0	0	0	5	1.500	9.00	39	4.47	.333	0	....	-1	0	-0.1
1979	LA-N	0	2	.000	4	2	0	0	1	16	10	8	6	2	0	13	6	1.438	3.38	108	3.59	.175	1	.250	1	1	0.1
Total	4	3	7	.300	16	12	0	0	1	71	76	51	40	11	0	42	42	1.662	5.07	74	5.67	.275	4	.211	-10	1	-1.0
• HANNAN, Jim	James John Hannan b: 1/7/1940, Jersey City, NJ BR/TR, 6'3", 205 lbs. Deb: 4/17/1962																										
1962	Was-A	2	4	.333	42	3	0	0	4	68	56	27	25	6	0	49	39	1.544	3.31	122	4.12	.230	1	.091	6	6	0.5
1963	Was-A	2	2	.500	13	2	0	0	0	27^{2}	23	18	15	2	0	17	14	1.446	4.88	76	3.72	.228	0	.000	-4	1	-0.4
1964	Was-A	4	7	.364	49	7	0	0	3	106	108	60	49	13	0	45	67	1.443	4.16	89	4.39	.266	3	.150	-6	4	-0.7
1965	Was-A	1	1	.500	4	1	1	1	0	14^{2}	18	8	8	0	1	6	5	1.636	4.91	71	5.44	.340	0	.000	-2	0	-0.3
1966	Was-A	3	9	.250	30	18	2	0	0	114	125	58	54	9	3	59	68	1.614	4.26	81	5.03	.288	2	.067	-11	2	-1.4
1967	Was-A	1	1	.500	8	2	0	0	0	21^{2}	28	14	13	3	1	7	14	1.615	5.40	59	6.01	.315	0	.000	-5	0	-0.6

YEAR	TM-L	W	L	PCT	G	GS	CG	SH	SV	IP	H	R	ER	HR	HB	BB	SO	RAT	ERA	ERA+	CERA	OAV	BH	AVG	PR+	WS	TPW
1968	Was-A	10	6	.625	25	22	4	1	0	140^1	147	53	47	4	4	50	75	1.404	3.01	97	3.81	.272	3	.064	0	6	-0.2
1969	Was-A	7	6	.538	35	28	1	1	0	158^1	138	73	64	17	2	91	72	1.446	3.64	95	4.17	.238	6	.115	-4	6	-0.6
1970	Was-A	9	11	.450	42	17	1	1	0	128	119	65	57	17	1	54	61	1.352	4.01	89	3.99	.250	4	.129	-8	5	-0.9
1971	Det-A	1	0	1.000	7	0	0	0	0	11	7	4	4	1	1	7	6	1.273	3.27	110	3.37	.189	0	.000	0	1	0.0
	Mil-A	1	1	.500	21	1	0	0	0	32^1	38	23	18	7	1	21	17	1.825	5.01	69	6.99	.295	0	.000	-6	0	-0.7
	Yr.	2	1	.667	28	1	0	0	0	43^1	45	27	22	8	2	28	23	1.685	4.57	76	6.07	.271	0	.000	-5	1	-0.6
Total	10	41	48	.461	276	101	9	4	7	822	807	403	354	79	14	406	438	1.476	3.88	89	4.38	.261	19	.091	-40	31	-5.3
• HANNING, Loy	Loy Vernon Hanning b: 10/18/1917, Bunker, MO d: 6/24/1986, Anaconda, MO BR/TR, 6'2", 175 lbs. Deb: 9/20/1939																										
1939	StL-A	0	1	.000	4	1	0	0	0	10	6	5	4	1	0	4	8	1.000	3.60	135	1.75	.158	0	.000	2	1	0.1
1942	StL-A	1	1	.500	11	0	0	0	0	17^1	26	15	15	2	1	12	9	2.192	7.79	48	8.77	.356	1	.250	-8	0	-0.8
Total	2	1	2	.333	15	1	0	0	0	27^1	32	20	19	3	1	16	17	1.756	6.26	62	6.20	.288	1	.200	-6	1	-0.6
• HANSELL, Greg	Gregory Michael Hansell b: 3/12/1971, Bellflower, CA BR/TR, 6'5", 215 lbs. Deb: 4/28/1995																										
1995	LA-N	0	1	.000	20	0	0	0	0	19^1	29	17	16	5	2	6	13	1.810	7.45	51	8.43	.349	0	....	-8	0	-0.8
1996	Min-A	3	0	1.000	50	0	0	0	3	74^1	83	48	47	14	2	31	46	1.534	5.69	90	5.62	.285	0	....	-5	4	-0.5
1997	Mil-A	0	0	....	3	0	0	0	0	4^2	5	5	5	1	1	1	5	1.286	9.64	48	5.32	.263	0	....	-3	0	-0.3
1999	Pit-N	1	3	.250	33	0	0	0	0	39^1	42	20	17	5	3	11	34	1.347	3.89	117	4.42	.280	0	.000	3	3	0.3
Total	4	4	4	.500	106	0	0	0	3	137^2	159	90	85	25	8	49	98	1.511	5.56	84	5.66	.293	0	.000	-13	7	-1.3
• HANSEN, Andy	Andrew Viggo "Swede" Hansen b: 11/12/1924, Lake Worth, FL d: 2/2/2002, Lake Worth, FL BR/TR, 6'3", 190 lbs. Deb: 6/30/1944																										
1944	NY-N	3	3	.500	23	4	0	0	1	52^2	63	39	38	3	3	32	15	1.804	6.49	56	5.78	.301	2	.167	-17	0	-1.7
1945	NY-N	4	3	.571	23	13	4	0	3	92^2	98	52	48	7	2	28	37	1.360	4.66	84	3.85	.273	0	.000	-8	4	-1.1
1947	NY-N	1	5	.167	27	9	1	0	0	82^1	78	45	40	8	0	38	18	1.409	4.37	93	3.86	.248	4	.190	-3	3	-0.3
1948	NY-N	5	3	.625	36	9	3	0	1	100	96	40	33	4	0	36	27	1.320	2.97	133	3.24	.255	1	.050	11	8	1.1
1949	NY-N	2	6	.250	33	2	0	0	1	66^1	58	35	34	7	0	28	26	1.296	4.61	86	3.41	.234	0	.000	-4	2	-0.5
1950	NY-N	0	1	.000	31	1	0	0	3	57	64	37	35	8	1	26	19	1.579	5.53	74	5.22	.279	0	.000	-11	1	-1.1
1951	Phi-N	3	1	.750	24	0	0	0	0	39	34	14	11	4	1	7	11	1.051	2.54	152	2.62	.228	1	.333	6	4	0.7
1952	Phi-N	5	6	.455	43	0	0	0	4	77^1	76	36	28	6	3	27	18	1.332	3.26	112	3.71	.259	2	.182	2	5	0.3
1953	Phi-N	0	2	.000	30	1	0	0	3	51^1	60	30	23	6	1	24	17	1.636	4.03	104	5.48	.296	2	.286	1	3	0.1
Total	9	23	30	.434	270	39	8	0	16	618^2	627	328	290	53	11	246	188	1.411	4.22	93	4.04	.263	12	.102	-23	30	-2.6
• HANSEN, Roy	Roy Inglof "Ing" Hansen b: 3/6/1898, Beloit, WI d: 2/9/1977, Beloit, WI BR/TR, 6', 165 lbs. Deb: 5/28/1918																										
1918	Was-A	1	0	1.000	5	0	0	0	0	9	10	4	3	0	1	3	2	1.444	3.00	91	4.01	.278	0	....	-1	1	-0.1
• HANSEN, Snipe	Roy Emil Frederick Hansen b: 2/21/1907, Chicago, IL d: 9/11/1978, Chicago, IL BB/TL, 6'3", 195 lbs. Deb: 7/5/1930																										
1930	Phi-N	0	7	.000	22	9	1	0	0	84^1	123	76	63	8	2	38	25	1.909	6.72	81	7.19	.364	3	.111	-10	1	-1.0
1932	Phi-N	10	10	.500	39	23	5	0	2	191	215	103	79	13	6	51	56	1.393	3.72	118	4.01	.278	8	.127	15	13	1.2
1933	Phi-N	6	14	.300	32	22	8	0	1	168^1	199	103	83	12	4	30	47	1.360	4.44	86	4.03	.294	9	.155	-11	6	-1.5
1934	Phi-N	6	12	.333	50	16	5	2	3	151	194	112	91	15	3	61	40	1.689	5.42	87	5.59	.307	10	.233	-14	4	-1.3
1935	Phi-N	0	1	.000	2	1	0	0	0	4^1	8	7	6	0	0	5	0	3.000	12.46	36	11.66	.421	0	.000	-4	0	-0.4
	StL-A	0	1	.000	10	0	0	0	0	26^2	44	28	26	2	1	9	8	1.988	8.78	55	7.49	.364	1	.143	-12	0	-1.1
Total	5	22	45	.328	155	71	19	2	6	625^2	783	429	348	50	16	194	176	1.562	5.01	90	5.03	.306	31	.155	-36	24	-4.2
• HANSFORD, F.C.	Frank Cicero Hansford b: 12/26/1874, DuQuoin, IL d: 12/14/1952, Fort Scott, KS TL, 6', 180 lbs. Deb: 6/9/1898																										
1898	Bro-N	0	0	....	1	0	0	0	0	7	10	4	3	0	0	5	0	2.143	3.86	93	6.88	.333	0	.000	-0	0	-0.1
• HANSKI, Don	Donald Thomas Hanski b: 2/27/1916, La Porte, IN d: 9/2/1957, Worth, IL BL/TL, 5'11", 180 lbs. Deb: 5/6/1943 ♦																										
1943	Chi-A	0	0	....	1	0	0	0	0	1	1	0	0	0	0	1	0	2.000	0.00	....	6.60	.333	5	.238	0	0	-0.2
1944	Chi-A	0	0	....	2	0	0	0	0	3	5	4	4	0	0	2	0	2.333	12.00	29	8.02	.357	0	.000	-3	0	-0.3
Total	2	0	0	....	3	0	0	0	0	4	6	4	4	0	0	3	0	2.250	9.00	38	7.66	.353	5	.227	-2	0	-0.5
• HANSON, Erik	Erik Brian Hanson b: 5/18/1965, Kinnelon, NJ BR/TR, 6'6", 210 lbs. Deb: 9/5/1988																										
1988	Sea-A	2	3	.400	6	6	0	0	0	41^2	35	17	15	4	1	12	36	1.128	3.24	128	2.87	.230	0	....	4	3	0.4
1989	Sea-A	9	5	.643	17	17	1	0	0	113^1	103	44	40	7	5	32	75	1.191	3.18	127	3.08	.243	0	....	10	9	1.1
1990	Sea-A	18	9	.667	33	33	5	1	0	236	205	88	85	15	2	68	211	1.157	3.24	122	2.72	.232	0	....	19	18	1.9
1991	Sea-A	8	8	.500	27	27	2	1	0	174^2	182	82	74	16	2	56	143	1.363	3.81	108	3.99	.269	0	....	3	9	0.3
1992	Sea-A	8	17	.320	31	30	6	1	0	186^2	209	110	100	14	7	57	112	1.425	4.82	82	4.37	.287	0	....	-17	5	-1.8
1993	Sea-A	11	12	.478	31	30	7	0	0	215	215	91	83	17	5	60	163	1.279	3.47	127	3.55	.263	0	....	21	15	2.1
1994	Cin-N	5	5	.500	22	21	0	0	0	122^2	137	60	56	10	3	23	101	1.304	4.11	101	3.83	.283	6	.154	0	5	0.0
1995*	Bos-A★	15	5	.750	29	29	1	1	0	186^2	187	94	88	17	1	59	139	1.318	4.24	115	3.67	.258	0	....	12	13	1.1
1996	Tor-A	13	17	.433	35	35	4	1	0	214^2	243	143	129	26	2	102	156	1.607	5.41	93	5.41	.289	0	....	-14	8	-1.3
1997	Tor-A	0	0	....	3	2	0	0	0	15	15	13	13	3	0	6	18	1.400	7.80	59	4.76	.254	0	....	-6	0	-0.5
1998	Tor-A	0	3	.000	11	8	0	0	0	49	73	34	34	10	1	29	21	2.082	6.24	75	8.95	.348	0	....	-9	0	-0.8
Total	11	89	84	.514	245	238	26	5	0	1555^1	1604	776	717	139	29	504	1175	1.355	4.15	105	3.99	.267	6	.154	25	85	2.5
• HANSON, Ollie	Earl Sylvester Hanson b: 1/19/1896, Holbrook, MA d: 8/19/1951, Clifton, NJ BR/TR, 5'11", 178 lbs. Deb: 4/27/1921																										
1921	Chi-N	0	2	.000	2	2	1	0	0	9	9	7	7	0	1	6	2	1.667	7.00	55	4.54	.265	0	.000	-3	0	-0.4
• HANYZEWSKI, Ed	Edward Michael Hanyzewski b: 9/18/1920, Union Mills, IN d: 10/8/1991, Fargo, ND BR/TR, 6'1", 200 lbs. Deb: 5/12/1942																										
1942	Chi-N	1	1	.500	6	1	0	0	0	19	17	9	8	2	0	8	6	1.316	3.79	84	3.70	.254	1	.200	-1	1	-0.1
1943	Chi-N	8	7	.533	33	16	3	0	0	130	120	54	37	2	2	45	55	1.269	2.56	130	2.79	.243	2	.049	14	8	1.0
1944	Chi-N	2	5	.286	14	7	3	0	0	58^1	61	33	29	6	1	20	19	1.389	4.47	79	4.01	.262	1	.059	-5	1	-0.6
1945	Chi-N	0	0	....	2	1	0	0	0	4^2	7	4	3	1	0	1	0	1.714	5.79	63	6.97	.350	0	.000	-1	0	-0.1
1946	Chi-N	1	0	1.000	3	0	0	0	0	6	8	3	3	0	1	5	1	2.167	4.50	74	7.97	.348	0	.000	-1	0	-0.1
Total	5	12	13	.480	58	25	6	0	0	218	213	103	80	11	4	79	81	1.339	3.30	103	3.42	.254	4	.062	6	10	0.1
• HARANG, Aaron	Aaron Michael Harang b: 5/9/1978, San Diego, CA BR/TR, 6'7", 240 lbs. Deb: 5/25/2002																										
2002	Oak-A	5	4	.556	16	15	0	0	0	78^1	78	44	42	7	3	45	64	1.570	4.83	91	4.76	.261	0	.000	-3	4	-0.3
2003	Oak-A	1	3	.250	7	6	0	0	0	30^1	41	19	18	5	0	9	16	1.648	5.34	85	6.32	.331	0	.000	-3	1	-0.3
	Cin-N	4	3	.571	9	9	0	0	0	46	48	28	27	6	1	10	26	1.261	5.28	81	3.94	.271	1	.059	-5	2	-0.6
Total	2	10	10	.500	32	30	0	0	0	154^2	167	91	87	18	4	64	106	1.494	5.06	86	4.82	.278	1	.048	-11	7	-1.2
• HARDEN, Rich	James Richard Harden b: 11/30/1981, Victoria, Canada BL/TR, 6'1", 180 lbs. Deb: 7/21/2003																										
2003*	Oak-A	5	4	.556	15	13	0	0	0	74^2	72	38	37	5	1	40	67	1.500	4.46	101	4.28	.259	0	....	0	4	0.0
• HARDER, Mel	Melvin Leroy "Chief" Harder b: 10/15/1909, Beemer, NE d: 10/20/2002, Chardon, OH BR/TR, 6'1", 195 lbs. Deb: 4/24/1928 M/C																										
1928	Cle-A	0	2	.000	23	1	0	0	1	49	64	42	36	4	0	32	15	1.959	6.61	63	6.50	.335	0	.000	-13	0	-1.4
1929	Cle-A	1	0	1.000	11	0	0	0	0	17^2	24	15	11	2	3	5	4	1.642	5.60	79	6.33	.333	0	.000	-2	0	-0.2
1930	Cle-A	11	10	.524	36	19	7	0	2	175^1	205	108	82	9	4	68	45	1.557	4.21	115	4.55	.295	9	.143	15	12	1.0
1931	Cle-A	13	14	.481	40	24	9	0	1	194	229	119	94	8	6	72	63	1.552	4.36	106	4.50	.289	19	.253	11	12	1.2
1932	Cle-A	15	13	.536	39	32	17	1	0	254^2	277	125	106	9	3	68	90	1.355	3.75	127	3.50	.272	17	.181	33	21	3.0
1933	Cle-A	15	17	.469	43	31	14	2	4	253	254	113	83	10	3	67	81	1.269	**2.95**	**151**	3.11	.259	16	.190	**41**	**24**	**3.9**
1934	Cle-A★	20	12	.625	44	29	17	**6**	4	255^1	246	97	74	6	7	81	91	1.281	2.61	**174**	3.08	.254	14	.161	**56**	27	**5.1**
1935	Cle-A★	22	11	.667	42	35	17	4	2	287^1	313	120	105	6	0	53	95	1.274	3.29	137	3.14	.275	21	.206	43	27	3.9
1936	Cle-A★	15	15	.500	36	30	13	0	1	224^2	294	155	129	13	6	71	84	1.625	5.17	98	5.16	.313	11	.138	-1	12	-0.5
1937	Cle-A★	15	12	.556	38	30	13	0	2	233^2	269	127	111	9	4	86	95	1.519	4.28	108	4.30	.288	15	.174	11	16	0.9
1938	Cle-A	17	10	.630	38	29	15	2	4	240	257	115	102	16	5	62	102	1.329	3.83	121	3.68	.271	10	.114	21	20	1.5
1939	Cle-A	15	9	.625	29	26	12	1	1	208	213	89	81	15	3	64	67	1.332	3.50	126	3.67	.269	10	.139	21	17	1.8
1940	Cle-A	12	11	.522	31	25	5	0	0	186^1	200	96	84	16	5	59	76	1.390	4.06	104	4.13	.278	11	.177	-1	10	-0.2
1941	Cle-A	5	4	.556	15	10	1	0	1	68^2	76	43	40	8	2	37	21	1.646	5.24	75	5.29	.279	2	.080	-10	2	-1.2

YEAR	TM-L	W	L	PCT	G	GS	CG	SH	SV	IP	H	R	ER	HR	HB	BB	SO	RAT	ERA	ERA+	CERA	OAV	BH	AVG	PR+	WS	TPW
1942	Cle-A	13	14	.481	29	29	13	4	0	198^2	179	83	76	8	3	82	74	1.314	3.44	100	3.13	.240	8	.119	-3	11	-0.6
1943	Cle-A	8	7	.533	19	18	6	1	0	135^1	126	57	46	7	1	61	40	1.382	3.06	102	3.54	.254	10	.213	-2	6	-0.1
1944	Cle-A	12	10	.545	30	27	12	2	0	196^1	211	95	81	5	3	69	64	1.426	3.71	89	3.78	.278	16	.216	-12	9	-1.2
1945	Cle-A	3	7	.300	11	11	2	0	0	76	93	37	31	3	0	23	16	1.526	3.67	88	4.45	.303	2	.080	-3	2	-0.6
1946	Cle-A	5	4	.556	13	12	4	1	0	92^1	85	37	35	4	0	31	21	1.256	3.41	97	2.98	.249	3	.086	-1	4	-0.3
1947	Cle-A	6	4	.600	15	15	4	1	0	80	91	41	40	3	1	27	17	1.475	4.50	77	4.14	.289	5	.179	-10	2	-1.1
Total	**20**	**223**	**186**	**.545**	**582**	**433**	**181**	**25**	**23**	**3426^1**	**3706**	**1714**	**1447**	**161**	**59**	**1118**	**1161**	**1.408**	**3.80**	**111**	**3.85**	**.276**	**199**	**.165**	**193**	**234**	**14.9**

• HARDIN, Jim James Warren Hardin b: 8/6/1943, Morris Chapel, TN d: 3/9/1991, Key West, FL BR/TR, 6', 175 lbs. Deb: 6/23/1967

YEAR	TM-L	W	L	PCT	G	GS	CG	SH	SV	IP	H	R	ER	HR	HB	BB	SO	RAT	ERA	ERA+	CERA	OAV	BH	AVG	PR+	WS	TPW
1967	Bal-A	8	3	.727	19	14	5	2	0	111	85	30	28	5	3	27	64	1.009	2.27	139	2.10	.211	5	.135	9	8	1.0
1968	Bal-A	18	13	.581	35	35	16	2	0	244	188	79	68	20	10	70	160	1.057	2.51	117	2.49	.212	7	.085	7	16	0.4
1969	Bal-A	6	7	.462	30	20	3	1	1	137^2	128	62	55	18	6	43	64	1.242	3.60	99	3.66	.248	7	.156	-6	6	-0.4
1970	Bal-A	6	5	.545	36	19	3	2	1	145^1	150	60	57	13	1	26	78	1.211	3.53	103	3.35	.267	3	.067	-1	8	-0.3
1971	Bal-A	0	0	....	6	0	0	0	0	5^2	12	5	3	0	0	3	3	2.647	4.76	70	10.60	.480	0	....	-1	0	-0.1
	NY-A	0	2	.000	12	3	0	0	0	28^1	35	19	16	3	1	9	14	1.553	5.08	64	5.15	.313	0	.000	-6	0	-0.7
	Yr.	0	2	.000	18	3	0	0	0	34	47	24	19	3	1	12	17	1.735	5.03	65	6.06	.343	0	.000	-7	0	-0.8
1972	Atl-N	5	2	.714	26	9	1	0	2	79^2	93	47	39	11	2	24	25	1.469	4.41	86	4.84	.287	2	.095	-4	4	-0.3
Total	**6**	**43**	**32**	**.573**	**164**	**100**	**28**	**7**	**4**	**751^2**	**691**	**302**	**266**	**70**	**23**	**202**	**408**	**1.188**	**3.18**	**105**	**3.22**	**.244**	**24**	**.103**	**-2**	**42**	**-0.5**

• HARDING, Charlie Charles Harold "Slim" Harding b: 1/3/1891, Nashville, TN d: 10/30/1971, Bold Spring, TN BR/TR, 6'2.5", 172 lbs. Deb: 9/18/1913

YEAR	TM-L	W	L	PCT	G	GS	CG	SH	SV	IP	H	R	ER	HR	HB	BB	SO	RAT	ERA	ERA+	CERA	OAV	BH	AVG	PR+	WS	TPW
1913	Det-A	0	0	....	1	0	0	0	0	2	3	1	1	0	0	1	0	2.000	4.50	65	7.09	.375	0	....	-0	0	0.0

• HARDY, Alex David Alexander "Dooney" Hardy b: 9/29/1877, Toronto, Canada d: 4/22/1940, Toronto, Canada BR/TL, 5'10.5", 175 lbs. Deb: 9/4/1902

YEAR	TM-L	W	L	PCT	G	GS	CG	SH	SV	IP	H	R	ER	HR	HB	BB	SO	RAT	ERA	ERA+	CERA	OAV	BH	AVG	PR+	WS	TPW
1902	Chi-N	2	2	.500	4	4	4	1	0	35	29	19	14	0	0	12	12	1.171	3.60	75	2.37	.226	3	.214	-4	1	-0.3
1903	Chi-N	1	1	.500	3	3	1	0	0	12^2	21	10	9	0	1	7	4	2.211	6.39	49	8.08	.375	1	.167	-5	0	-0.4
Total	**2**	**3**	**3**	**.500**	**7**	**7**	**5**	**1**	**0**	**47^2**	**50**	**29**	**23**	**0**	**1**	**19**	**16**	**1.448**	**4.34**	**66**	**3.89**	**.271**	**4**	**.200**	**-8**	**1**	**-0.8**

• HARDY, Harry Harry Hardy b: 11/5/1875, Steubenville, OH d: 9/4/1943, Steubenville, OH BL/TL, 5'6", 155 lbs. Deb: 9/26/1905

YEAR	TM-L	W	L	PCT	G	GS	CG	SH	SV	IP	H	R	ER	HR	HB	BB	SO	RAT	ERA	ERA+	CERA	OAV	BH	AVG	PR+	WS	TPW
1905	Was-A	1	1	.500	3	2	2	0	0	24	20	9	5	0	0	6	10	1.083	1.88	141	2.01	.229	1	.111	1	2	0.1
1906	Was-A	0	3	.000	5	3	2	0	0	20	35	27	20	0	0	12	4	2.350	9.00	29	8.52	.385	0	.000	-14	0	-1.6
Total	**2**	**1**	**4**	**.200**	**8**	**5**	**4**	**0**	**0**	**44**	**55**	**36**	**25**	**0**	**0**	**18**	**14**	**1.659**	**5.11**	**52**	**4.97**	**.308**	**1**	**.067**	**-12**	**2**	**-1.5**

• HARDY, Jack John Graydon Hardy b: 10/8/1959, St. Petersburg, FL BR/TR, 6'2", 175 lbs. Deb: 5/23/1989

YEAR	TM-L	W	L	PCT	G	GS	CG	SH	SV	IP	H	R	ER	HR	HB	BB	SO	RAT	ERA	ERA+	CERA	OAV	BH	AVG	PR+	WS	TPW
1989	Chi-A	0	0	....	5	0	0	0	0	12^1	14	9	9	1	1	5	4	1.541	6.57	58	5.03	.286	0	....	-4	0	-0.4

• HARDY, Larry Howard Lawrence Hardy b: 1/10/1948, Goose Creek, TX BR/TR, 5'10", 180 lbs. Deb: 4/28/1974 C

YEAR	TM-L	W	L	PCT	G	GS	CG	SH	SV	IP	H	R	ER	HR	HB	BB	SO	RAT	ERA	ERA+	CERA	OAV	BH	AVG	PR+	WS	TPW
1974	SD-N	9	4	.692	76	1	0	0	2	101^2	129	58	53	9	0	44	57	1.702	4.69	76	5.42	.317	0	.000	-10	4	-1.1
1975	SD-N	0	0	....	3	0	0	0	0	2^2	8	6	4	3	0	2	3	3.750	13.50	26	32.04	.500	0	....	-3	0	-0.3
1976	Hou-N	0	0	....	15	0	0	0	3	21^2	34	19	17	2	0	10	10	2.031	7.06	45	7.60	.362	0	.000	-9	0	-1.0
Total	**3**	**9**	**4**	**.692**	**94**	**1**	**0**	**0**	**5**	**126**	**171**	**83**	**74**	**14**	**0**	**56**	**70**	**1.802**	**5.29**	**65**	**6.36**	**.331**	**0**	**.000**	**-22**	**4**	**-2.5**

• HARDY, Red Francis Joseph Hardy b: 1/6/1923, Marmarth, ND d: 8/15/2003, Phoenix, AZ BR/TR, 5'11", 175 lbs. Deb: 6/20/1951

YEAR	TM-L	W	L	PCT	G	GS	CG	SH	SV	IP	H	R	ER	HR	HB	BB	SO	RAT	ERA	ERA+	CERA	OAV	BH	AVG	PR+	WS	TPW
1951	NY-N	0	0	....	2	0	0	0	0	1^1	4	1	1	0	1	1	0	3.750	6.75	58	21.38	.571	0	....	-0	0	0.0

• HAREN, Danny Daniel John Haren b: 9/17/1980, Monterey Park, CA BR/TR, 6'5", 220 lbs. Deb: 6/30/2003

YEAR	TM-L	W	L	PCT	G	GS	CG	SH	SV	IP	H	R	ER	HR	HB	BB	SO	RAT	ERA	ERA+	CERA	OAV	BH	AVG	PR+	WS	TPW
2003	StL-N	3	7	.300	14	14	0	0	0	72^2	84	44	41	9	5	22	43	1.459	5.08	80	5.07	.293	2	.080	-8	1	-0.8

• HARGAN, Steve Steven Lowell Hargan b: 9/8/1942, Fort Wayne, IN BR/TR, 6'3", 180 lbs. Deb: 8/3/1965

YEAR	TM-L	W	L	PCT	G	GS	CG	SH	SV	IP	H	R	ER	HR	HB	BB	SO	RAT	ERA	ERA+	CERA	OAV	BH	AVG	PR+	WS	TPW
1965	Cle-A	4	3	.571	17	8	1	0	2	60^1	55	26	23	2	1	28	37	1.376	3.43	101	3.36	.246	1	.053	0	4	-0.1
1966	Cle-A	13	10	.565	38	21	7	3	0	192	173	60	53	9	1	45	132	1.135	2.48	138	2.57	.241	7	.121	23	18	2.3
1967	Cle-A★	14	13	.519	30	29	15	**6**	0	223	180	79	65	9	3	72	141	1.130	2.62	125	2.43	.224	11	.164	18	16	2.2
1968	Cle-A	8	15	.348	32	27	4	2	0	158^1	139	81	73	11	5	81	78	1.389	4.15	71	3.71	.241	9	.176	-23	1	-2.5
1969	Cle-A	5	14	.263	32	23	1	1	0	143^2	145	95	91	14	3	81	76	1.573	5.70	66	4.71	.265	7	.159	-30	0	-3.3
1970	Cle-A	11	3	.786	23	19	8	1	0	142^2	101	47	46	14	3	53	72	1.079	2.90	136	2.56	.201	5	.111	16	15	1.5
1971	Cle-A	1	13	.071	37	16	1	0	1	113^1	138	83	78	18	6	56	52	1.712	6.19	62	6.39	.304	2	.063	-31	0	-3.6
1972	Cle-A	0	3	.000	12	1	0	0	0	20	23	16	13	1	0	15	10	1.900	5.85	55	5.68	.291	0	.000	-6	0	-0.7
1974	Tex-A	12	9	.571	37	27	8	2	0	186^2	202	103	82	15	5	48	98	1.339	3.95	90	3.87	.275	0	....	-9	7	-0.9
1975	Tex-A	9	10	.474	33	26	8	1	0	189^1	203	96	80	17	6	62	93	1.400	3.80	99	4.18	.275	0	....	-0	9	0.0
1976	Tex-A	8	8	.500	35	8	2	1	1	124^1	127	63	50	8	3	38	63	1.327	3.62	99	3.58	.261	0	....	-1	6	-0.1
1977	Tor-A	1	3	.250	6	5	1	0	0	29^1	36	17	17	2	0	14	11	1.705	5.22	80	5.37	.308	0	....	-3	1	-0.3
	Tex-A	1	0	1.000	6	0	0	0	0	12^1	22	13	12	2	0	5	10	2.189	8.76	47	9.37	.393	0	....	-7	0	-0.7
	Yr.	2	3	.400	12	5	1	0	0	41^2	58	30	29	4	0	19	21	1.848	6.26	66	6.56	.335	0	....	-9	1	-0.9
	Atl-N	0	3	.000	16	5	0	0	0	36^2	49	31	28	3	0	16	18	1.773	6.87	65	5.98	.325	0	.000	-9	0	-1.0
Total	**12**	**87**	**107**	**.448**	**354**	**215**	**56**	**17**	**4**	**1632**	**1593**	**810**	**711**	**125**	**36**	**614**	**891**	**1.352**	**3.92**	**91**	**3.77**	**.257**	**42**	**.129**	**-59**	**77**	**-7.2**

• HARGESHEIMER, Alan Alan Robert Hargesheimer b: 11/21/1954, Chicago, IL BR/TR, 6'3", 195 lbs. Deb: 7/14/1980

YEAR	TM-L	W	L	PCT	G	GS	CG	SH	SV	IP	H	R	ER	HR	HB	BB	SO	RAT	ERA	ERA+	CERA	OAV	BH	AVG	PR+	WS	TPW
1980	SF-N	4	6	.400	15	13	0	0	0	75	82	38	36	3	0	32	40	1.520	4.32	82	4.31	.285	4	.182	-5	2	-0.4
1981	SF-N	1	2	.333	6	3	0	0	0	18^2	20	9	9	1	1	9	6	1.554	4.34	79	4.73	.299	1	.200	-2	0	-0.2
1983	Chi-N	0	0	....	5	0	0	0	0	4	6	4	4	0	0	2	5	2.000	9.00	42	6.85	.375	0	....	-2	0	-0.2
1986	KC-A	0	1	.000	5	1	0	0	0	13	18	9	9	1	1	7	4	1.923	6.23	68	7.09	.340	0	....	-3	0	-0.3
Total	**4**	**5**	**9**	**.357**	**31**	**17**	**0**	**0**	**0**	**110^2**	**126**	**60**	**58**	**5**	**2**	**50**	**55**	**1.590**	**4.72**	**77**	**4.80**	**.297**	**5**	**.185**	**-12**	**2**	**-1.1**

• HARIKKALA, Tim Timothy Allan Harikkala b: 7/15/1971, West Palm Beach, FL BR/TR, 6'2", 185 lbs. Deb: 5/27/1995

YEAR	TM-L	W	L	PCT	G	GS	CG	SH	SV	IP	H	R	ER	HR	HB	BB	SO	RAT	ERA	ERA+	CERA	OAV	BH	AVG	PR+	WS	TPW
1995	Sea-A	0	0	....	1	0	0	0	0	3^1	7	6	6	1	0	1	1	2.400	16.20	29	12.43	.412	0	....	-4	0	-0.4
1996	Sea-A	0	1	.000	1	1	0	0	0	4^1	4	6	6	1	1	2	1	1.385	12.46	40	5.68	.250	0	....	-4	0	-0.3
1999	Bos-A	1	1	.500	7	0	0	0	0	13	15	9	9	0	1	6	7	1.615	6.23	80	4.72	.306	0	....	-2	0	-0.2
Total	**3**	**1**	**2**	**.333**	**9**	**1**	**0**	**0**	**0**	**20^2**	**26**	**21**	**21**	**2**	**2**	**9**	**9**	**1.694**	**9.15**	**54**	**6.17**	**.317**	**0**	**....**	**-10**	**0**	**-0.9**

• HARKEY, Mike Michael Anthony Harkey b: 10/25/1966, San Diego, CA BR/TR, 6'5", 220 lbs. Deb: 9/5/1988

YEAR	TM-L	W	L	PCT	G	GS	CG	SH	SV	IP	H	R	ER	HR	HB	BB	SO	RAT	ERA	ERA+	CERA	OAV	BH	AVG	PR+	WS	TPW
1988	Chi-N	0	3	.000	5	5	0	0	0	34^2	33	14	10	0	2	15	18	1.385	2.60	139	3.18	.248	1	.091	5	2	0.4
1990	Chi-N	12	6	.667	27	27	2	1	0	173^2	153	71	63	14	7	59	94	1.221	3.26	125	3.14	.234	14	.250	21	15	2.5
1991	Chi-N	0	2	.000	4	4	0	0	0	18^2	21	11	11	3	0	6	15	1.446	5.30	73	4.64	.273	2	.400	-3	0	-0.2
1992	Chi-N	4	0	1.000	7	7	0	0	0	38	34	13	8	4	1	15	21	1.289	1.89	190	3.66	.243	4	.267	7	4	0.8
1993	Chi-N	10	10	.500	28	28	1	0	0	157^1	187	100	92	17	3	43	67	1.462	5.26	76	4.84	.305	5	.093	-24	3	-2.6
1994	Col-N	1	6	.143	24	13	0	0	0	91^2	125	61	59	10	1	35	39	1.745	5.79	86	6.37	.336	4	.182	-6	3	-0.6
1995	Oak-A	4	6	.400	14	12	0	0	0	66	75	46	46	12	3	31	28	1.606	6.27	71	6.07	.292	0	....	-13	1	-1.2
	Cal-A	4	3	.571	12	8	1	0	0	61^1	80	32	31	12	1	16	28	1.565	4.55	103	5.97	.311	0	....	0	4	0.0
	Yr.	8	9	.471	26	20	1	0	0	127^1	155	78	77	24	4	47	56	1.586	5.44	83	6.02	.302	0	....	-13	5	-1.2
1997	LA-N	1	0	1.000	10	0	0	0	0	14^2	12	8	7	3	0	5	6	1.159	4.30	90	3.40	.211	0	.000	-1	1	-0.1
Total	**8**	**36**	**36**	**.500**	**131**	**104**	**4**	**1**	**0**	**656**	**720**	**356**	**327**	**75**	**18**	**225**	**316**	**1.441**	**4.49**	**95**	**4.64**	**.281**	**30**	**.183**	**-13**	**33**	**-0.9**

• HARKINS, John John Joseph "Pa" Harkins b: 4/12/1859, New Brunswick, NJ d: 11/20/1940, New Brunswick, NJ BR/TR, 6'1", 205 lbs. Deb: 5/2/1884

YEAR	TM-L	W	L	PCT	G	GS	CG	SH	SV	IP	H	R	ER	HR	HB	BB	SO	RAT	ERA	ERA+	CERA	OAV	BH	AVG	PR+	WS	TPW
1884	Cle-N	12	32	.273	46	45	42	3	0	391	399	300	160	7	....	108	192	1.297	3.68	85	....	.250	47	.205	-26	17	-3.0
1885	Bro-a	14	20	.412	34	34	33	1	0	293	303	224	122	7	7	56	141	1.225	3.75	88	....	.256	42	.264	-13	16	-0.8
1886	Bro-a	15	16	.484	34	33	33	0	0	292^1	286	203	117	6	5	114	118	1.368	3.60	97	....	.245	32	.225	-2	19	0.1
1887	Bro-a	10	14	.417	24	24	22	0	0	199	339	184	133	6	5	77	36	1.704	6.02	71	....	.364	30	.286	-38	7	-3.2
1888	Bal-a	0	1	.000	1	1	1	0	0	8	12	12	6	0	0	3	2	1.875	6.75	44	....	.335	0	.000	-3	0	-0.3
Total	**5**	**51**	**83**	**.381**	**139**	**137**	**131**	**4**	**0**	**1183^1**	**1339**	**923**	**538**	**26**	**17**	**358**	**489**	**1.369**	**4.09**	**85**	**....**	**.272**	**151**	**.237**	**-82**	**59**	**-7.2**

• HARKNESS, Spec Frederick Harvey Harkness b: 12/13/1887, Los Angeles, CA d: 5/18/1952, Compton, CA BR/TR, 5'11", 180 lbs. Deb: 6/13/1910

YEAR	TM-L	W	L	PCT	G	GS	CG	SH	SV	IP	H	R	ER	HR	HB	BB	SO	RAT	ERA	ERA+	CERA	OAV	BH	AVG	PR+	WS	TPW
1910	Cle-A	10	7	.588	26	16	6	1	1	136^1	132	61	46	2	3	55	60	1.372	3.04	85	3.54	.268	7	.140	-8	7	-1.0

YEAR	TM-L	W	L	PCT	G	GS	CG	SH	SV	IP	H	R	ER	HR	HB	BB	SO	RAT	ERA	ERA+	CERA	OAV	BH	AVG	PR+	WS	TPW
1911	Cle-A	2	2	.500	12	6	3	0	0	53^{1}	62	36	25	1	0	21	25	1.556	4.22	81	4.57	.310	6	.316	-6	2	-0.4
Total	**2**	**12**	**9**	**.571**	**38**	**22**	**9**	**1**	**1**	**189^{2}**	**194**	**97**	**71**	**3**	**3**	**76**	**85**	**1.424**	**3.37**	**84**	**3.83**	**.280**	**13**	**.188**	**-13**	**9**	**-1.4**
• HARLEY, Dick	Henry Risk Harley b: 8/18/1874, Springfield, OH d: 5/16/1961, Springfield, OH BR/TR Deb: 4/15/1905																										
1905	Bos-N	2	5	.286	9	4	4	1	0	65^{2}	72	45	34	5	1	19	19	1.386	4.66	66	4.17	.286	1	.045	-10	0	-1.3
• HARMAN, Bill	William Bell Harman b: 1/2/1919, Bridgewater, VA BR/TR, 6'4", 200 lbs. Deb: 6/17/1941																										
1941	Phi-N	0	0	....	5	0	0	0	0	13	15	8	7	0	0	8	3	1.769	4.85	76	5.18	.319	1	.071	-2	0	-0.4
• HARMON, Bob	Robert Green "Hickory Bob" Harmon b: 10/15/1887, Liberal, MO d: 11/27/1961, Monroe, LA BB/TR, 6', 187 lbs. Deb: 6/23/1909																										
1909	StL-N	6	11	.353	21	17	10	0	0	159	155	85	65	6	4	65	48	1.384	3.68	69	3.71	.265	13	.255	-17	4	-1.4
1910	StL-N	13	15	.464	43	33	15	0	2	236	227	128	117	1	7	133	87	**1.525**	4.46	67	3.87	.258	14	.184	-32	6	-3.2
1911	StL-N	23	16	.590	51	**41**	28	2	4	348	290	155	121	10	7	181	144	1.353	3.13	108	3.24	.235	17	.153	8	23	0.9
1912	StL-N	18	18	.500	43	34	15	3	0	268	284	156	117	4	3	116	73	1.493	3.93	87	3.87	.281	23	.232	-17	12	-1.5
1913	StL-N	8	21	.276	42	27	16	1	2	273^{1}	291	135	119	6	6	99	66	1.427	3.92	82	3.86	.286	24	.261	-22	12	-1.7
1914	Pit-N	13	17	.433	37	30	19	2	3	245	226	84	69	3	7	55	61	1.147	2.53	104	2.54	.252	12	.140	2	16	0.1
1915	Pit-N	16	17	.485	37	32	25	5	1	269^{2}	242	106	75	6	3	62	86	1.127	2.50	109	2.44	.247	14	.147	8	15	1.0
1916	Pit-N	8	11	.421	31	17	10	2	0	172^{2}	175	78	54	4	1	39	62	1.239	2.81	95	2.92	.267	6	.109	1	7	-0.2
1918	Pit-N	2	7	.222	16	9	5	0	0	82^{1}	76	30	24	3	0	12	7	1.069	2.62	110	2.37	.254	4	.148	-0	4	-0.1
Total	**9**	**107**	**133**	**.446**	**321**	**240**	**143**	**15**	**12**	**2054**	**1966**	**957**	**761**	**43**	**38**	**762**	**634**	**1.328**	**3.33**	**90**	**3.26**	**.260**	**127**	**.184**	**-69**	**99**	**-6.1**
• HARNISCH, Pete	Peter Thomas Harnisch b: 9/23/1966, Commack, NY BB/TR, 6'1", 207 lbs. Deb: 9/13/1988																										
1988	Bal-A	0	2	.000	2	2	0	0	0	13	13	8	8	1	0	9	10	1.692	5.54	70	4.79	.260	0	....	-2	0	-0.2
1989	Bal-A	5	9	.357	18	17	2	0	0	103^{1}	97	55	53	10	5	64	70	1.558	4.62	82	4.68	.249	0	....	-10	3	-1.0
1990	Bal-A	11	11	.500	31	31	3	0	0	188^{2}	189	96	91	17	1	86	122	1.458	4.34	87	4.23	.261	0	....	-13	7	-1.3
1991	Hou-N★	12	9	.571	33	33	4	2	0	216^{2}	169	71	65	14	5	83	172	1.163	2.70	130	2.65	**.212**	6	.097	19	16	1.8
1992	Hou-N	9	10	.474	34	34	0	0	0	206^{2}	182	92	85	18	5	64	164	1.190	3.70	91	3.06	.233	11	.164	-7	7	-0.6
1993	Hou-N	16	9	.640	33	33	5	**4**	0	217^{2}	171	84	72	20	6	79	185	1.149	2.98	130	2.80	**.214**	7	.104	20	16	1.8
1994	Hou-N	8	5	.615	17	17	1	0	0	95	100	59	57	13	3	39	62	1.463	5.40	73	4.78	.269	6	.171	-16	2	-1.5
1995	NY-N	2	8	.200	18	18	0	0	0	110	111	55	45	13	3	24	82	1.227	3.68	110	3.56	.261	3	.091	4	4	0.2
1996	NY-N	8	12	.400	31	31	2	1	0	194^{2}	195	103	91	30	7	61	114	1.315	4.21	96	4.17	.260	5	.091	-6	7	-0.8
1997	NY-N	0	1	.000	6	5	0	0	0	25^{2}	35	24	23	5	1	11	12	1.792	8.06	50	7.27	.327	0	.000	-12	0	-1.3
	Mil-A	1	1	.500	4	3	0	0	0	14	13	9	8	1	0	12	10	1.786	5.14	90	5.30	.245	0	....	-1	1	-0.1
1998	Cin-N	14	7	.667	32	32	2	1	0	209	176	79	73	24	6	64	157	1.148	3.14	136	3.09	.228	7	.106	27	16	2.3
1999	Cin-N	16	10	.615	33	33	2	2	0	198^{1}	190	86	81	25	5	57	120	1.245	3.68	127	3.65	.252	10	.152	16	14	1.5
2000	Cin-N	8	6	.571	22	22	3	1	0	131	133	76	69	23	1	46	71	1.366	4.74	99	4.51	.261	8	.186	-2	7	-0.1
2001	Cin-N	1	3	.250	7	7	0	0	0	35^{1}	48	29	25	9	1	17	17	1.840	6.37	71	7.81	.318	3	.273	-7	0	-0.6
Total	**14**	**111**	**103**	**.519**	**321**	**318**	**24**	**11**	**0**	**1959**	**1822**	**926**	**846**	**223**	**49**	**716**	**1368**	**1.296**	**3.89**	**102**	**3.73**	**.245**	**66**	**.129**	**8**	**100**	**0.1**
• HARPER, Bill	William Homer "Blue Sleeve" Harper b: 6/14/1889, Bertrand, MO d: 6/17/1951, Somerville, TN BB/TR, 6'1", 180 lbs. Deb: 6/10/1911																										
1911	StL-A	0	0	....	2	0	0	0	0	8	9	9	6	0	1	4	6	1.625	6.75	50	5.03	.300	0	.000	-3	0	-0.4
• HARPER, George	George B. Harper b: 8/17/1866, Milwaukee, WI d: 12/11/1931, Stockton, CA BR/TR, 5'10", 165 lbs. Deb: 7/11/1894																										
1894	Phi-N	6	6	.500	12	9	7	0	0	86^{1}	128	84	51	3	0	49	24	2.050	5.32	96	6.97	.340	6	.150	-1	3	-0.4
1896	Bro-N	4	8	.333	16	11	7	0	0	86	106	72	53	4	0	39	22	1.686	5.55	74	5.11	.301	6	.162	-13	2	-1.1
Total	**2**	**10**	**14**	**.417**	**28**	**20**	**14**	**0**	**0**	**172^{1}**	**234**	**156**	**104**	**7**	**0**	**88**	**46**	**1.868**	**5.43**	**84**	**6.04**	**.321**	**12**	**.156**	**-14**	**5**	**-1.4**
• HARPER, Harry	Harry Clayton Harper b: 4/24/1895, Hackensack, NJ d: 4/23/1963, Layton, NJ BL/TL, 6'2", 165 lbs. Deb: 6/27/1913																										
1913	Was-A	0	0	....	4	0	0	0	0	12^{2}	10	11	5	1	1	5	9	1.184	3.55	83	2.84	.204	1	.250	-1	0	-0.1
1914	Was-A	2	1	.667	23	3	1	0	2	57	45	29	22	1	5	35	50	1.404	3.47	81	3.24	.211	3	.250	-5	2	-0.5
1915	Was-A	4	4	.500	19	10	5	2	2	86^{1}	66	26	17	1	1	40	54	1.228	1.77	167	2.60	.222	0	.000	11	8	0.8
1916	Was-A	14	10	.583	36	34	13	2	0	249^{2}	209	82	68	4	8	101	149	1.242	2.45	114	2.83	.235	18	.207	8	19	1.0
1917	Was-A	11	12	.478	31	31	10	4	0	179^{1}	145	85	60	1	5	106	99	1.400	3.01	87	3.17	.230	7	.117	-10	6	-1.5
1918	Was-A	11	10	.524	35	32	14	3	1	244	182	77	59	1	8	104	78	1.172	2.18	125	2.27	.212	11	.134	7	16	0.3
1919	Was-A	6	21	.222	35	31	8	0	0	208	220	119	86	3	8	97	87	**1.524**	3.72	86	4.29	.284	11	.169	-10	4	-1.2
1920	Bos-A	5	14	.263	27	22	11	1	0	162^{2}	163	73	55	9	2	66	71	1.408	3.04	120	3.84	.275	6	.120	9	10	0.6
1921*	NY-A	4	3	.571	8	7	4	0	0	52^{2}	52	23	22	3	2	25	22	1.462	3.76	113	3.93	.263	2	.125	2	4	0.1
1923	Bro-N	0	1	.000	1	1	0	0	0	3^{2}	8	6	6	2	0	3	4	3.000	14.73	26	18.15	.421	0	.000	-4	0	-0.4
Total	**10**	**57**	**76**	**.429**	**219**	**171**	**66**	**12**	**5**	**1256**	**1100**	**531**	**400**	**26**	**40**	**582**	**623**	**1.339**	**2.87**	**105**	**3.24**	**.243**	**59**	**.147**	**7**	**69**	**-1.1**
• HARPER, Jack	John Wesley Harper b: 8/5/1893, Hendricks, WV d: 6/18/1927, Halstead, KS BR/TR, 5'11", 180 lbs. Deb: 4/17/1915																										
1915	Phi-A	0	0	....	3	0	0	0	0	8^{2}	5	4	3	0	0	1	3	.692	3.12	94	0.88	.161	0	.000	-0	0	0.0
• HARPER, Jack	Charles William Harper b: 4/2/1878, Galloway, PA d: 9/30/1950, Jamestown, NY BR/TR, 6', 178 lbs. Deb: 9/18/1899																										
1899	Cle-N	1	4	.200	5	5	5	0	0	37	44	33	16	3	3	12	14	1.514	3.89	95	4.95	.295	2	.182	1	2	0.2
1900	StL-N	0	1	.000	1	1	0	0	0	3	4	7	4	0	0	2	0	2.000	12.00	30	6.11	.319	0	.000	-3	0	-0.3
1901	StL-N	23	13	.639	39	37	28	1	0	308^{2}	294	158	124	7	16	99	128	1.273	3.62	88	3.11	.250	20	.172	-22	16	-2.0
1902	StL-A	15	11	.577	29	26	20	2	0	222^{1}	224	131	102	8	8	81	74	1.372	4.13	85	3.58	.262	17	.205	-18	13	-1.7
1903	Cin-N	8	9	.471	17	15	13	0	0	135	143	87	65	2	10	70	45	1.578	4.33	82	5.27	.271	14	.250	-11	6	-0.9
1904	Cin-N	23	9	.719	35	35	31	6	0	293^{2}	262	113	75	2	9	85	125	1.182	2.30	127	2.52	.234	18	.159	13	24	1.2
1905	Cin-N	9	13	.409	26	23	15	1	1	179^{1}	189	116	77	2	8	69	70	1.439	3.86	85	3.80	.271	10	.167	-15	5	-1.4
1906	Cin-N	1	4	.200	5	5	3	0	0	36^{2}	38	23	17	1	2	20	10	1.582	4.17	66	4.70	.286	3	.273	-6	1	-0.5
	Chi-N	0	0	....	1	1	0	0	0	1	0	0	0	0	0	0	0	.000	0.00	....	0.00	.275	0	....	0	0	0.0
	Yr.	1	4	.200	6	6	3	0	0	37^{2}	38	23	17	1	2	20	10	1.540	4.06	68	4.57	.286	3	.273	-6	1	-0.5
Total	**8**	**80**	**64**	**.556**	**158**	**148**	**115**	**10**	**1**	**1216^{2}**	**1198**	**668**	**480**	**25**	**56**	**438**	**466**	**1.345**	**3.55**	**92**	**3.50**	**.256**	**84**	**.186**	**-61**	**67**	**-5.5**
• HARPER, Travis	Travis Boyd Harper b: 5/21/1976, Harrisonburg, VA BL/TR, 6'4", 190 lbs. Deb: 8/4/2000																										
2000	TB-A	1	2	.333	6	5	1	1	0	32	30	17	17	5	1	15	14	1.406	4.78	103	4.46	.244	0	....	0	2	0.0
2001	TB-A	0	2	.000	2	2	0	0	0	7	15	11	6	5	0	3	2	2.571	7.71	58	19.14	.455	0	....	-3	0	-0.2
2002	TB-A	5	9	.357	37	7	0	0	1	85^{2}	101	54	52	14	9	27	60	1.494	5.46	82	5.49	.289	0	....	-11	3	-1.0
2003	TB-A	4	8	.333	61	0	0	0	1	93	86	45	39	9	6	31	64	1.258	3.77	120	3.56	.252	0	....	6	6	0.5
Total	**4**	**10**	**21**	**.323**	**106**	**14**	**1**	**1**	**2**	**217^{2}**	**232**	**127**	**114**	**33**	**16**	**76**	**140**	**1.415**	**4.71**	**97**	**4.95**	**.274**	**0**	**....**	**-8**	**11**	**-0.7**
• HARRELL, Ray	Raymond James "Cowboy" Harrell b: 2/16/1912, Petrolia, TX d: 1/28/1984, Alexandria, LA BR/TR, 6'1", 185 lbs. Deb: 4/16/1935																										
1935	StL-N	1	1	.500	11	1	0	0	0	29^{2}	39	26	22	4	0	11	13	1.685	6.67	61	5.97	.320	0	.000	-9	0	-0.9
1937	StL-N	3	7	.300	35	15	1	1	1	96^{2}	99	73	63	7	2	59	41	1.634	5.87	68	4.63	.263	1	.045	-20	0	-2.1
1938	StL-N	2	3	.400	32	3	1	0	2	63	78	37	34	6	3	29	32	1.698	4.86	81	5.71	.308	0	.000	-6	2	-0.7
1939	Chi-N	0	2	.000	4	2	0	0	0	17^{1}	29	16	16	2	0	6	5	2.019	8.31	47	8.33	.387	0	.000	-8	0	-0.9
	Phi-N	3	7	.300	22	10	4	0	0	94^{2}	101	77	57	6	4	56	35	1.658	5.42	73	4.80	.270	3	.115	-15	1	-1.6
	Yr.	3	9	.250	26	12	4	0	0	112	130	93	73	8	4	62	40	1.714	5.87	67	5.35	.290	3	.097	-23	1	-2.5
1940	Pit-N	0	0	....	3	0	0	0	0	3^{1}	5	5	3	0	0	2	3	2.100	8.10	47	6.71	.333	0	....	-1	0	-0.2
1945	NY-N	0	0	....	12	0	0	0	0	25^{1}	34	22	14	1	1	14	7	1.895	4.97	79	6.40	.343	1	.200	-3	0	-0.2
Total	**6**	**9**	**20**	**.310**	**119**	**31**	**6**	**1**	**3**	**330**	**385**	**256**	**209**	**26**	**10**	**177**	**136**	**1.703**	**5.70**	**70**	**5.36**	**.293**	**5**	**.069**	**-63**	**3**	**-6.7**
• HARRELL, Slim	Oscar Martin Harrell b: 7/31/1890, Grandview, TX d: 4/30/1971, Hillsboro, TX BR/TR, 6'3", 180 lbs. Deb: 6/21/1912																										
1912	Phi-A	0	0	....	1	0	0	0	0	3	4	0	0	0	0	0	1	1.333	0.00	....	4.31	.364	0	.000	1	1	0.1
• HARRELSON, Bill	William Charles Harrelson b: 11/17/1945, Tahlequah, OK BB/TR, 6'5", 215 lbs. Deb: 7/31/1968																										
1968	Cal-A	1	6	.143	10	5	1	0	0	33^{2}	28	23	19	4	1	26	22	1.604	5.08	57	4.80	.226	1	.100	-9	0	-1.0

YEAR TM-L	W	L	PCT	G	GS	CG	SH	SV	IP	H	R	ER	HR	HB	BB	SO	RAT	ERA	ERA+	CERA	OAV	BH	AVG	PR+	WS	TPW
• HARRIGER, Denny	Dennis Scott Harriger b: 7/21/1969, Kittanning, PA BR/TR, 5'11" Deb: 6/16/1998																									
1998 Det-A	0	3	.000	4	2	0	0	0	12	17	12	9	1	0	8	3	2.083	6.75	70	7.06	.327	0	....	-3	0	-0.3
• HARRINGTON, Andy	Andrew Francis Harrington b: 11/13/1888, Wakefield, MA d: 11/12/1938, Malden, MA BR/TR, 6', 193 lbs. Deb: 9/8/1913																									
1913 Cin-N	0	0	....	1	0	0	0	0	4	6	5	4	0	0	1	1	1.750	9.00	36	5.09	.353	1	.500	-3	0	-0.2
• HARRINGTON, Bill	William Womble Harrington b: 10/3/1927, Sanford, NC BR/TR, 5'11", 160 lbs. Deb: 4/16/1953																									
1953 Phi-A	0	0	....	1	0	0	0	0	2	5	3	3	0	0	0	0	2.500	13.50	32	10.86	.500	0	....	-2	0	-0.2
1955 KC-A	3	3	.500	34	1	0	0	2	76^2	69	41	35	6	2	41	26	1.435	4.11	101	3.88	.246	2	.118	1	4	0.0
1956 KC-A	2	2	.500	23	1	0	0	1	37^2	40	27	27	3	0	26	14	1.752	6.45	67	5.46	.274	0	.000	-9	1	-1.0
Total 3	5	5	.500	58	2	0	0	3	116^1	114	71	65	9	2	67	40	1.556	5.03	84	4.51	.261	2	.083	-10	5	-1.1
• HARRIS, Ben	Ben Franklin Harris b: 12/17/1889, Donelson, TN d: 4/1/1927, St. Louis, MO BR/TR, 6', 220 lbs. Deb: 4/19/1914																									
1914 KC-F	7	7	.500	31	14	5	0	1	154	179	89	70	7	6	41	40	1.429	4.09	75	4.40	.303	9	.200	-18	4	-1.7
1915 KC-F	0	0	....	1	0	0	0	0	2	1	0	0	0	0	0	0	.500	0.00	....	0.55	.143	0	....	1	0	0.1
Total 2	7	7	.500	32	14	5	0	1	156	180	89	70	7	6	41	40	1.417	4.04	76	4.35	.301	9	.200	-17	4	-1.7
• HARRIS, Bill	William Milton Harris b: 6/23/1900, Wylie, TX d: 8/21/1965, Charlotte, NC BR/TR, 6'1", 180 lbs. Deb: 4/22/1923																									
1923 Cin-N	3	2	.600	22	3	1	0	0	69^2	79	42	40	3	3	18	18	1.392	5.17	75	3.97	.292	6	.353	-10	2	-0.8
1924 Cin-N	0	0	....	3	0	0	0	0	7	10	7	7	0	0	2	5	1.714	9.00	42	5.11	.323	1	1.000	-4	0	-0.4
1931 Pit-N	2	2	.500	4	4	3	1	0	31	21	6	3	0	0	9	10	.968	0.87	442	1.50	.194	1	.091	10	4	0.9
1932 Pit-N	10	9	.526	37	17	4	0	2	168	178	84	68	6	6	38	63	1.286	3.64	105	3.33	.271	10	.182	2	11	0.1
1933 Pit-N	4	4	.500	31	0	0	0	5	58^2	68	28	21	1	1	14	19	1.398	3.22	103	3.68	.289	0	.000	0	4	-0.1
1934 Pit-N	0	0	....	11	2	0	0	0	19	28	15	14	2	1	7	8	1.842	6.63	62	6.93	.350	1	.500	-5	0	-0.5
1938 Bos-A	5	5	.500	13	11	5	1	1	80^1	83	39	36	5	1	21	26	1.295	4.03	122	3.44	.268	6	.214	7	7	0.6
Total 7	24	22	.522	121	37	13	2	8	433^2	467	221	189	17	12	109	149	1.328	3.92	101	3.56	.276	25	.203	-0	28	-0.2
• HARRIS, Bill	William Thomas Harris b: 12/3/1931, Duguayville, Canada BL/TR, 5'8", 187 lbs. Deb: 9/27/1957																									
1957 Bro-N	0	1	.000	1	1	0	0	0	7	9	3	3	1	0	1	3	1.429	3.86	108	5.04	.321	1	.500	0	0	0.1
1959 LA-N	0	0	....	1	0	0	0	0	1^2	0	0	0	0	0	3	0	1.800	0.00	....	1.71	.000	0	....	1	0	0.1
Total 2	0	1	.000	2	1	0	0	0	8^2	9	3	3	1	0	4	3	1.500	3.12	134	4.40	.321	1	.500	1	0	0.1
• HARRIS, Bob	Robert Arthur Harris b: 5/1/1917, Gillette, WY d: 8/9/1989, North Platte, NE BR/TR, 6', 185 lbs. Deb: 9/19/1938																									
1938 Det-A	1	0	1.000	3	1	1	0	0	10	14	9	8	0	0	4	7	1.800	7.20	69	5.36	.318	1	.333	-3	0	-0.2
1939 Det-A	1	1	.500	5	1	0	0	0	18	18	8	8	4	0	8	9	1.444	4.00	122	5.20	.269	2	.400	2	2	0.2
StL-A	3	12	.200	28	16	6	0	0	126	162	88	80	5	0	71	48	1.849	5.71	85	5.83	.321	7	.189	-9	3	-0.8
Yr.	4	13	.235	33	17	6	0	0	144	180	96	88	9	0	79	57	1.799	5.50	88	5.75	.315	9	.214	-7	5	-0.6
1940 StL-A	11	15	.423	35	28	8	1	1	193^2	225	120	106	24	3	85	49	1.601	4.93	93	5.27	.290	15	.250	-6	11	-0.3
1941 StL-A	12	14	.462	34	29	9	2	1	186^2	237	117	108	18	2	85	57	1.725	5.21	83	5.85	.312	7	.115	-16	7	-1.8
1942 StL-A	1	5	.167	6	6	0	0	0	33^2	37	24	21	2	0	17	9	1.604	5.61	66	4.43	.268	0	.000	-7	0	-0.8
Phi-A	1	5	.167	16	8	2	1	0	78	77	31	25	5	0	24	26	1.295	2.88	131	3.26	.253	7	.269	9	5	1.1
Yr.	2	10	.167	22	14	2	1	0	111^2	114	55	46	7	0	41	35	1.388	3.71	101	3.62	.258	7	.194	3	5	0.3
Total 5	30	52	.366	127	89	26	4	2	646	770	397	356	58	5	294	205	1.647	4.96	90	5.26	.297	39	.193	-29	28	-2.6
• HARRIS, Bubba	Charles Harris b: 2/15/1926, Sulligent, AL BR/TR, 6'4", 204 lbs. Deb: 4/29/1948																									
1948 Phi-A	5	2	.714	45	0	0	0	5	93^2	89	51	43	2	1	35	32	1.324	4.13	104	3.10	.249	3	.125	1	8	0.0
1949 Phi-A	1	1	.500	37	0	0	0	3	84^1	92	57	51	12	1	42	18	1.589	5.44	75	5.33	.286	3	.125	-14	1	-1.6
1951 Phi-A	0	0	....	3	0	0	0	0	4	4	4	4	0	1	5	2	2.250	9.00	48	6.92	.250	0	....	-2	0	-0.2
Cle-A	0	0	....	2	0	0	0	0	4	5	2	2	0	0	4	1	2.250	4.50	84	7.02	.333	0	....	-0	0	0.0
Yr.	0	0	....	5	0	0	0	0	8	9	6	6	0	1	9	3	2.250	6.75	61	6.97	.290	0	....	-2	0	-0.2
Total 3	6	3	.667	87	0	0	0	8	186	190	114	100	14	3	86	53	1.484	4.84	86	4.28	.267	6	.125	-16	9	-1.8
• HARRIS, Buddy	Walter Francis Harris b: 12/5/1948, Philadelphia, PA BR/TR, 6'7", 245 lbs. Deb: 9/10/1970																									
1970 Hou-N	0	0	....	2	0	0	0	0	6^1	6	4	4	3	0	0	2	.947	5.68	68	4.23	.240	0	.000	-1	0	-0.1
1971 Hou-N	1	1	.500	20	0	0	0	0	30^2	33	22	22	3	0	16	21	1.598	6.46	52	4.92	.275	0	.000	-11	0	-1.2
Total 2	1	1	.500	22	0	0	0	0	37	39	26	26	6	0	16	23	1.486	6.32	54	4.80	.269	0	.000	-12	0	-1.3
• HARRIS, Gene	Tyrone Eugene Harris b: 12/5/1964, Sebring, FL BR/TR, 5'11", 190 lbs. Deb: 4/5/1989																									
1989 Mon-N	1	1	.500	11	0	0	0	0	20	16	11	11	1	0	10	11	1.300	4.95	71	3.05	.242	0	.000	-3	0	-0.3
Sea-A	1	4	.200	10	6	0	0	1	33^1	47	27	24	3	1	15	14	1.860	6.48	62	7.08	.353	0	....	-9	0	-0.9
1990 Sea-A	1	2	.333	25	0	0	0	0	38	31	25	20	5	1	30	43	1.605	4.74	83	4.56	.217	0	....	-3	1	-0.3
1991 Sea-A	0	0	....	8	0	0	0	1	13^1	15	8	6	1	0	10	6	1.875	4.05	102	5.35	.273	0	....	-0	0	0.0
1992 Sea-A	0	0	....	8	0	0	0	0	9	8	7	7	3	0	6	6	1.556	7.00	57	6.31	.235	0	....	-3	0	-0.3
SD-N	0	2	.000	14	1	0	0	0	21^1	15	8	7	0	1	9	19	1.125	2.95	121	2.06	.195	1	.333	2	1	0.2
1993 SD-N	6	6	.500	59	0	0	0	23	59^1	57	27	20	3	1	37	39	1.584	3.03	136	4.14	.254	0	.000	7	8	0.7
1994 SD-N	1	1	.500	13	0	0	0	0	12^1	21	11	11	2	0	8	9	2.351	8.03	51	9.92	.389	0	.000	-5	0	-0.5
Det-A	0	0	....	11	0	0	0	1	11^1	13	10	9	1	1	4	10	1.500	7.15	68	4.62	.271	0	....	-3	0	-0.3
1995 Phi-N	2	2	.500	21	0	0	0	0	19	19	9	9	2	0	8	9	1.421	4.26	99	4.21	.260	0	....	-0	2	0.0
Bal-A	0	0	....	3	0	0	0	0	4	4	2	2	0	0	1	4	1.250	4.50	106	2.77	.267	0	....	0	0	0.0
Total 7	12	18	.400	183	7	0	0	26	241	246	145	126	21	5	138	170	1.593	4.71	86	4.79	.267	1	.167	-18	12	-1.8
• HARRIS, Greg	Gregory Wade Harris b: 12/1/1963, Greensboro, NC BR/TR, 6'3", 187 lbs. Deb: 9/19/1988																									
1988 SD-N	2	0	1.000	3	1	1	0	0	18	13	3	3	0	0	3	15	.889	1.50	226	1.43	.200	0	.000	4	2	0.3
1989 SD-N	8	9	.471	56	8	0	0	6	135	106	43	39	8	2	52	106	1.170	2.60	134	2.58	.215	1	.053	12	13	1.2
1990 SD-N	8	8	.500	73	0	0	0	9	117^1	92	35	30	6	4	49	97	1.202	2.30	166	2.63	.220	1	.083	19	14	2.0
1991 SD-N	9	5	.643	20	20	3	2	0	133	116	42	33	16	1	27	95	1.075	2.23	170	2.72	.233	3	.083	23	12	2.2
1992 SD-N	4	8	.333	20	20	1	0	0	118	113	62	54	13	2	35	66	1.254	4.12	87	3.54	.252	4	.129	-7	4	-0.6
1993 SD-N	10	9	.526	22	22	4	0	0	152	151	65	62	18	3	39	83	1.250	3.67	113	3.60	.257	9	.170	8	9	1.0
Col-N	1	8	.111	13	13	0	0	0	73^1	88	62	53	15	4	30	40	1.609	6.50	73	6.23	.299	1	.050	-12	0	-1.3
Yr.	11	17	.393	35	35	4	0	0	225^1	239	127	115	33	7	69	123	1.367	4.59	96	4.46	.271	10	.137	-3	9	-0.3
1994 Col-N	3	12	.200	29	19	1	0	1	130	154	99	96	22	5	52	82	1.585	6.65	75	5.79	.300	7	.175	-20	1	-1.9
1995 Min-A	0	5	.000	7	6	0	0	0	32^2	50	35	32	5	0	16	21	2.020	8.82	54	8.19	.355	0	....	-15	0	-1.4
Total 8	45	64	.413	243	109	10	2	16	909^1	883	446	402	103	21	303	605	1.304	3.98	105	3.83	.255	26	.119	12	55	1.5
• HARRIS, Greg	Greg Allen Harris b: 11/2/1955, Lynwood, CA BB/TR, 6', 175 lbs. Deb: 5/20/1981																									
1981 NY-N	3	5	.375	16	14	0	0	1	68^2	65	36	34	8	2	28	54	1.354	4.46	78	3.92	.245	4	.182	-7	1	-0.7
1982 Cin-N	2	6	.250	34	10	1	0	1	91^1	96	56	49	12	2	37	67	1.456	4.83	77	4.72	.274	3	.167	-12	1	-1.3
1983 Cin-N	0	0	....	1	0	0	0	0	1	2	3	3	0	1	3	1	5.000	27.00	14	19.56	.500	0	.000	-3	0	-0.3
1984 Mon-N	0	1	.000	15	0	0	0	2	17^2	10	4	4	0	2	7	15	.962	2.04	168	1.67	.172	0	.000	3	2	0.3
*SD-N	2	1	.667	19	1	0	0	1	36^2	28	14	11	3	2	18	30	1.255	2.70	132	3.15	.209	3	.375	3	3	0.4
Yr.	2	2	.500	34	1	0	0	3	54^1	38	18	15	3	4	25	45	1.160	2.48	142	2.67	.198	3	.333	5	5	0.7
1985 Tex-A	5	4	.556	58	0	0	0	11	113	74	35	31	7	5	43	111	1.035	2.47	171	2.14	.186	0	....	24	16	2.4
1986 Tex-A	10	8	.556	73	0	0	0	20	111^1	103	40	35	12	1	42	95	1.302	2.83	152	3.66	.251	0	....	18	14	1.8
1987 Tex-A	5	10	.333	42	19	0	0	0	140^2	157	92	76	18	4	56	106	1.514	4.86	92	4.99	.281	0	....	-5	5	-0.4
1988 Phi-N	4	6	.400	66	1	0	0	1	107	80	34	28	7	4	52	71	1.234	2.36	151	2.77	.209	3	.333	16	10	1.8
1989 Phi-N	2	2	.500	44	0	0	0	1	75^1	64	34	30	7	2	43	51	1.420	3.58	99	3.86	.234	1	.167	0	4	0.1
Bos-A	2	2	.500	15	0	0	0	0	28	21	12	8	1	0	15	25	1.286	2.57	159	2.69	.208	0	....	5	2	0.5
1990* Bos-A	13	9	.591	34	30	1	0	0	184^1	186	90	82	13	6	77	117	1.427	4.00	102	4.05	.265	0	....	5	12	0.5
1991 Bos-A	11	12	.478	53	21	1	0	2	173	157	79	74	13	5	69	127	1.306	3.85	112	3.48	.243	0	....	9	12	0.9
1992 Bos-A	4	9	.308	70	2	1	0	4	107^2	82	38	30	6	4	60	73	1.319	2.51	168	3.05	.215	0	....	20	12	2.0

YEAR TM-L	W	L	PCT	G	GS	CG	SH	SV	IP	H	R	ER	HR	HB	BB	SO	RAT	ERA	ERA+	CERA	OAV	BH	AVG	PR+	WS	TPW
1993 Bos-A	6	7	.462	**80**	0	0	0	8	112^1	95	55	47	7	10	60	103	1.380	3.77	123	3.58	.232	0	....	10	10	1.0
1994 Bos-A	3	4	.429	35	0	0	0	2	45^2	60	44	42	8	1	23	44	1.818	8.28	61	6.88	.321	0	....	-17	0	-1.6
NY-A	0	1	.000	3	0	0	0	0	5	4	5	3	1	2	3	4	1.400	5.40	85	5.37	.222	0	....	-1	0	-0.1
Yr.	3	5	.375	38	0	0	0	2	50^2	64	49	45	9	3	26	48	1.776	7.99	62	6.73	.312	0	....	-17	0	-1.6
1995 Mon-N	2	3	.400	45	0	0	0	0	48^1	45	18	14	6	1	16	47	1.262	2.61	165	3.62	.245	1	.333	9	4	1.0
Total 15	74	90	.451	703	98	4	0	54	1467	1329	689	601	129	54	652	1141	1.350	3.69	112	3.73	.243	15	.221	79	108	8.4
• HARRIS, Herb	Herbert Benjamin "Hub,Lefty" Harris b: 4/24/1913, Chicago, IL d: 1/18/1991, Crystal Lake, IL BL/TL, 6'1", 175 lbs. Deb: 7/21/1936																									
1936 Phi-N	0	0	....	4	0	0	0	0	7	14	8	8	0	1	5	0	2.714	10.29	44	11.63	.438	0	.000	-4	0	-0.4
• HARRIS, Joe	Joseph White Harris b: 2/1/1882, Melrose, MA d: 4/12/1966, Melrose, MA BR/TR, 6'1", 198 lbs. Deb: 9/22/1905 U																									
1905 Bos-A	1	2	.333	3	3	3	0	0	23	16	6	6	0	0	8	14	1.043	2.35	115	1.64	.198	1	.111	1	2	0.0
1906 Bos-A	2	21	.087	30	24	20	1	2	235	211	130	92	5	7	67	99	1.183	3.52	78	2.64	.243	13	.160	-18	6	-2.1
1907 Bos-A	0	7	.000	12	5	3	0	0	59	57	28	20	0	1	13	24	1.186	3.05	84	2.59	.256	4	.190	-6	1	-0.6
Total 3	3	30	.091	45	32	26	1	2	317	284	164	118	5	8	88	137	1.174	3.35	81	2.56	.243	18	.162	-22	9	-2.8
• HARRIS, Lum	Chalmer Luman Harris b: 1/17/1915, New Castle, AL d: 11/11/1996, Pell City, AL BR/TR, 6'1", 180 lbs. Deb: 4/19/1941 M/C																									
1941 Phi-A	4	4	.500	33	10	5	0	2	131^2	134	77	70	16	2	51	49	1.405	4.78	88	4.22	.260	11	.275	-10	6	-0.7
1942 Phi-A	11	15	.423	26	20	10	1	0	166	146	80	69	14	1	70	60	1.301	3.74	101	3.29	.234	10	.161	4	9	0.3
1943 Phi-A	7	21	.250	32	27	15	1	1	216^1	241	122	101	17	3	63	55	1.405	4.20	81	4.09	.279	12	.171	-14	5	-1.5
1944 Phi-A	10	9	.526	23	22	12	2	0	174^1	193	70	64	8	0	26	33	1.256	3.30	105	3.30	.281	10	.169	4	12	0.4
1946 Phi-A	3	14	.176	34	12	4	0	0	125^1	153	78	73	11	0	48	33	1.604	5.24	68	5.17	.308	8	.222	-23	1	-2.2
1947 Was-A	0	0	....	3	0	0	0	0	6^1	7	2	2	0	0	7	2	2.211	2.84	131	6.16	.318	0	.000	1	1	0.1
Total 6	35	63	.357	151	91	46	4	3	820	874	429	379	66	6	265	232	1.389	4.16	87	3.96	.273	51	.190	-37	34	-3.8
• HARRIS, Mickey	Maurice Charles Harris b: 1/30/1917, New York, NY d: 4/15/1971, Farmington, MI BL/TL, 6', 195 lbs. Deb: 4/23/1940																									
1940 Bos-A	4	2	.667	13	9	3	0	0	68^1	83	40	38	8	2	26	36	1.595	5.00	90	5.30	.292	6	.273	-3	4	-0.1
1941 Bos-A	8	14	.364	35	22	11	1	1	194	189	86	70	6	2	86	111	1.418	3.25	128	3.46	.250	6	.109	22	14	2.4
1946★ Bos-A★	17	9	.654	34	30	15	0	0	222^2	236	105	90	18	3	76	131	1.401	3.64	101	3.95	.268	18	.231	-1	14	0.3
1947 Bos-A	5	4	.556	15	6	1	0	0	51^2	42	20	14	3	0	23	35	1.258	2.44	159	2.89	.225	5	.417	8	6	1.1
1948 Bos-A	7	10	.412	20	17	6	1	0	113^2	120	73	67	10	1	59	42	1.575	5.30	83	4.72	.273	2	.063	-12	4	-1.3
1949 Bos-A	2	3	.400	7	6	2	0	0	37^2	53	26	21	3	1	20	14	1.938	5.02	87	6.56	.323	1	.083	-3	1	-0.4
Was-A	2	12	.143	23	19	4	0	0	129	151	82	74	8	0	55	54	1.597	5.16	82	4.73	.292	8	.205	-8	3	-0.6
Yr.	4	15	.211	30	25	6	0	0	166^2	204	108	95	11	1	75	68	1.674	5.13	83	5.15	.299	9	.176	-12	4	-1.0
1950 Was-A	5	9	.357	**53**	0	0	0	**15**	98	93	56	52	10	1	46	41	1.418	4.78	94	3.94	.247	4	.235	-3	9	-0.2
1951 Was-A	6	8	.429	41	0	0	0	4	87^1	87	45	37	6	1	43	47	1.489	3.81	107	4.09	.260	3	.188	4	5	0.4
1952 Was-A	0	0	....	1	0	0	0	0	1	1	1	1	1	0	0	0	1.000	9.00	39	7.45	.250	0	....	-1	0	-0.1
Cle-A	3	0	1.000	29	0	0	0	1	46^2	42	26	24	6	1	21	23	1.350	4.63	72	3.95	.249	1	.200	-6	1	-0.7
Yr.	3	0	1.000	30	0	0	0	1	47^2	43	27	25	7	1	21	23	1.343	4.72	71	4.03	.249	1	.200	-7	1	-0.7
Total 9	59	71	.454	271	109	42	2	21	1050	1097	560	488	79	12	455	534	1.478	4.18	98	4.18	.267	54	.188	-3	61	0.9
• HARRIS, Pep	Hernando Petrocelli Harris b: 9/23/1972, Lancaster, SC BR/TR, 6'2", 185 lbs. Deb: 8/14/1996																									
1996 Cal-A	2	0	1.000	11	3	0	0	0	32^1	31	16	14	4	3	17	20	1.485	3.90	126	4.74	.254	0	....	4	2	0.3
1997 Ana-A	5	4	.556	61	0	0	0	0	79^2	82	33	32	7	2	38	56	1.506	3.62	128	4.53	.274	0	....	8	7	0.8
1998 Ana-A	3	1	.750	49	0	0	0	0	60	55	32	29	7	0	23	34	1.300	4.35	108	3.50	.239	0	....	3	4	0.3
Total 3	10	5	.667	121	3	0	0	0	172	168	81	75	18	5	78	110	1.430	3.92	120	4.21	.258	0	....	15	13	1.4
• HARRIS, Reggie	Reginald Allen Harris b: 8/12/1968, Waynesboro, VA BR/TR, 6'1", 180 lbs. Deb: 7/4/1990																									
1990 Oak-A	1	0	1.000	16	1	0	0	0	41^1	25	16	16	5	2	21	31	1.113	3.48	107	2.70	.176	0	....	0	2	0.0
1991 Oak-A	0	0	....	2	0	0	0	0	3	5	4	4	0	0	3	2	2.667	12.00	32	10.17	.455	0	....	-3	0	-0.3
1996 Bos-A	0	0	....	4	0	0	0	0	4^1	7	6	6	2	1	5	4	2.769	12.46	41	17.51	.389	0	....	-3	0	-0.3
1997 Phi-N	1	3	.250	50	0	0	0	0	54^1	55	33	32	1	5	43	45	1.804	5.30	80	5.27	.263	0	....	-6	2	-0.6
1998 Hou-N	0	0	....	6	0	0	0	0	6	6	4	4	1	0	2	2	1.333	6.00	68	4.18	.261	0	....	-1	0	-0.1
1999 Mil-N	0	0	....	8	0	0	0	0	12	8	4	4	1	2	7	11	1.250	3.00	151	3.39	.186	0	.000	2	1	0.2
Total 6	2	3	.400	86	1	0	0	0	121	106	67	66	10	10	81	95	1.545	4.91	84	4.71	.238	0	.000	-11	5	-1.1
• HARRISON, Bob	Robert Lee Harrison b: 9/22/1930, St. Louis, MO BL/TR, 5'11", 178 lbs. Deb: 9/23/1955																									
1955 Bal-A	0	0	....	1	0	0	0	0	2	3	2	2	0	0	4	0	3.500	9.00	42	15.45	.500	0	....	-1	0	-0.1
1956 Bal-A	0	0	....	1	1	0	0	0	1^2	3	3	3	0	0	5	0	4.800	16.20	24	19.88	.375	0	....	-2	0	-0.2
Total 2	0	0	....	2	1	0	0	0	3^2	6	5	5	0	0	9	0	4.091	12.27	32	17.46	.429	0	....	-3	0	-0.3
• HARRISON, Roric	Roric Edward Harrison b: 9/20/1946, Los Angeles, CA BR/TR, 6'3", 195 lbs. Deb: 4/18/1972																									
1972 Bal-A	3	4	.429	39	2	0	0	4	94	68	24	24	2	4	34	62	1.085	2.30	134	2.09	.209	2	.118	6	8	0.8
1973 Atl-N	11	8	.579	38	22	3	0	5	177^1	161	90	82	15	3	98	130	1.461	4.16	94	4.05	.242	3	.056	-3	10	-0.5
1974 Atl-N	6	11	.353	20	20	3	0	0	126	148	70	66	12	3	49	46	1.563	4.71	80	5.11	.294	7	.184	-15	3	-1.4
1975 Atl-N	3	4	.429	15	7	2	0	1	54^2	58	33	29	7	0	19	22	1.409	4.77	79	4.30	.266	3	.200	-5	2	-0.4
Cle-A	7	7	.500	19	19	4	0	0	126	137	71	67	9	4	46	52	1.452	4.79	79	4.24	.274	0	....	-15	4	-1.5
1978 Min-A	0	1	.000	9	0	0	0	0	12	18	10	10	0	0	11	7	2.417	7.50	51	8.37	.346	0	....	-5	0	-0.5
Total 5	30	35	.462	140	70	12	0	10	590	590	298	278	45	14	257	319	1.436	4.24	88	4.12	.261	15	.121	-37	27	-3.5
• HARRISON, Tom	Thomas James Harrison b: 1/18/1945, Trail, Canada BR/TR, 6'3", 200 lbs. Deb: 5/7/1965																									
1965 KC-A	0	0	....	1	0	0	0	0	1	2	1	1	0	0	1	0	3.000	9.00	39	18.30	.667	0	....	-1	0	-0.1
• HARRISS, Slim	William Jennings Bryan Harriss b: 12/11/1896, Brownwood, TX d: 9/19/1963, Temple, TX BR/TR, 6'6", 180 lbs. Deb: 4/19/1920																									
1920 Phi-A	9	14	.391	31	25	11	1	0	192	226	111	87	5	5	57	60	1.474	4.08	98	4.32	.305	7	.106	2	8	-0.4
1921 Phi-A	11	16	.407	39	28	14	0	2	227^2	258	136	108	16	9	73	92	1.454	4.27	104	4.41	.290	12	.148	9	12	0.2
1922 Phi-A	9	20	.310	47	32	13	0	3	229^2	262	148	128	19	3	94	102	1.550	5.02	85	4.73	.290	13	.176	-18	8	-2.1
1923 Phi-A	10	16	.385	46	28	9	0	6	209^1	221	114	93	9	2	95	89	1.510	4.00	103	4.15	.280	4	.066	8	12	0.0
1924 Phi-A	6	10	.375	36	12	4	1	2	123	138	78	64	5	3	62	45	1.626	4.68	91	4.59	.291	7	.167	-4	6	-0.6
1925 Phi-A	19	12	.613	46	**33**	15	2	1	252^2	263	118	98	8	6	95	95	1.417	3.49	133	3.68	.268	18	.205	35	21	3.0
1926 Phi-A	3	5	.375	12	10	2	0	0	57	66	34	26	0	0	22	13	1.544	4.11	101	3.92	.289	1	.059	0	2	-0.1
Bos-A	6	10	.375	21	18	6	1	0	113	135	66	56	0	2	33	34	1.487	4.46	91	4.03	.311	7	.206	-3	6	-0.3
Yr.	9	15	.375	33	28	8	1	0	170	201	100	82	0	2	55	47	1.506	4.34	94	3.99	.303	8	.157	-3	8	-0.4
1927 Bos-A	14	21	.400	44	27	11	1	1	217^2	253	127	101	8	9	66	77	1.466	4.18	101	4.20	.298	8	.121	3	12	-0.1
1928 Bos-A	8	11	.421	27	15	4	1	1	128^1	141	74	66	5	2	33	37	1.356	4.63	89	3.50	.287	5	.139	-8	6	-1.0
Total 9	95	135	.413	349	228	89	7	16	1750^1	1963	1006	827	75	41	630	644	1.481	4.25	100	4.19	.289	82	.145	25	93	-1.4
• HARRIST, Earl	Earl "Irish" Harrist b: 4/20/1919, Dubach, LA d: 9/1/1998, Simsboro, LA BR/TR, 6', 178 lbs. Deb: 8/18/1945																									
1945 Cin-N	2	4	.333	14	5	1	0	0	62^1	60	30	25	2	1	27	15	1.396	3.61	104	3.39	.249	0	.000	1	3	-0.1
1947 Chi-A	3	8	.273	33	4	0	0	5	93^2	85	48	37	3	3	49	55	1.431	3.56	103	3.56	.248	5	.208	1	5	0.1
1948 Chi-A	1	3	.250	11	1	0	0	0	23	23	17	15	4	3	13	14	1.565	5.87	73	5.64	.267	0	.000	-4	0	-0.5
Was-A	3	3	.500	23	4	0	0	0	60^2	70	35	31	1	3	37	21	1.764	4.60	94	5.21	.293	3	.167	-1	3	-0.2
Yr.	4	6	.400	34	5	0	0	0	83^2	93	52	46	5	6	50	35	1.709	4.95	87	5.32	.286	3	.136	-5	3	-0.6
1952 StL-A	2	8	.200	36	9	1	0	5	116^2	119	61	52	7	10	47	49	1.423	4.01	97	4.19	.269	3	.097	-2	5	-0.5
1953 Chi-A	1	0	1.000	7	0	0	0	0	8^1	9	7	7	1	0	5	1	1.680	7.56	53	5.69	.290	0	.000	-3	0	-0.3
Det-A	0	2	.000	8	1	0	0	0	18^2	25	19	18	2	0	15	7	2.143	8.68	47	7.55	.333	0	.000	-9	0	-0.9
Yr.	1	2	.333	15	1	0	0	0	27	34	26	25	3	0	20	8	2.000	8.33	49	6.97	.321	0	.000	-12	0	-1.3
Total 5	12	28	.300	132	24	2	0	10	383^1	391	217	185	20	20	193	162	1.523	4.34	91	4.35	.268	11	.115	-17	16	-2.4

• HARSHMAN, Jack John Elvin Harshman b: 7/12/1927, San Diego, CA BL/TL, 6'2", 185 lbs. Deb: 9/16/1948 ♦

YEAR	TM-L	W	L	PCT	G	GS	CG	SH	SV	IP	H	R	ER	HR	HB	BB	SO	RAT	ERA	ERA+	CERA	OAV	BH	AVG	PR+	WS	TPW
1952	NY-N	0	2	.000	2	2	0	0	0	6^1	12	10	10	2	0	6	6	2.842	14.21	26	14.46	.429	0	.000	-7	0	-0.8
1954	Chi-A	14	8	.636	35	21	9	4	1	177	157	61	58	7	5	96	134	1.429	2.95	127	3.53	.238	8	.143	14	15	1.7
1955	Chi-A	11	7	.611	32	23	9	0	0	179^1	144	74	67	16	4	97	116	1.344	3.36	117	3.56	.224	11	.183	9	13	1.2
1956	Chi-A	15	11	.577	34	30	15	4	0	226^2	183	85	78	14	3	102	143	1.257	3.10	132	2.99	.221	12	.169	24	20	2.9
1957	Chi-A	8	8	.500	30	26	6	0	1	151^1	142	78	69	16	5	82	83	1.480	4.10	91	4.44	.250	10	.222	-9	7	-0.4
1958	Bal-A	12	15	.444	34	29	17	3	4	236^1	204	89	76	20	3	75	161	1.181	2.89	124	2.96	.231	16	.195	19	**22**	3.1
1959	Bal-A	0	6	.000	14	8	0	0	0	47^1	58	39	36	6	2	28	24	1.817	6.85	55	6.51	.319	2	.200	-16	1	-1.5
	Bos-A	2	3	.400	8	2	0	0	0	24^2	29	19	18	2	0	10	14	1.581	6.57	62	4.79	.284	1	.143	-7	0	-0.7
	Cle-A	5	1	.833	13	6	5	1	1	66	46	21	19	6	0	13	35	.894	2.59	142	1.60	.179	7	.206	8	7	0.9
	Yr.	7	10	.412	35	16	5	1	1	138	133	79	73	14	2	51	73	1.333	4.76	80	3.85	.246	10	.196	-16	8	-1.3
1960	Cle-A	2	4	.333	15	8	0	0	0	54^1	50	32	24	7	0	30	25	1.472	3.98	94	4.33	.243	3	.176	-2	1	-0.2
Total	**8**	**69**	**65**	**.515**	**217**	**155**	**61**	**12**	**7**	**1169^1**	**1025**	**508**	**455**	**96**	**22**	**539**	**741**	**1.338**	**3.50**	**109**	**3.57**	**.235**	**76**	**.179**	**32**	**86**	**6.4**

• HARSTAD, Oscar Oscar Theander Harstad b: 5/24/1892, Parkland, WA d: 11/14/1985, Corvallis, OR BR/TR, 6', 174 lbs. Deb: 4/23/1915

YEAR	TM-L	W	L	PCT	G	GS	CG	SH	SV	IP	H	R	ER	HR	HB	BB	SO	RAT	ERA	ERA+	CERA	OAV	BH	AVG	PR+	WS	TPW
1915	Cle-A	3	5	.375	32	7	4	0	1	82	81	45	31	1	1	35	35	1.415	3.40	89	3.64	.270	2	.125	-3	4	-0.4

• HART, Bill William Franklin Hart b: 7/19/1865, Louisville, KY d: 9/19/1936, Cincinnati, OH TR, 5'10", 163 lbs. Deb: 7/26/1886 U

YEAR	TM-L	W	L	PCT	G	GS	CG	SH	SV	IP	H	R	ER	HR	HB	BB	SO	RAT	ERA	ERA+	CERA	OAV	BH	AVG	PR+	WS	TPW
1886	Phi-a	9	13	.409	22	22	22	2	0	186	183	144	66	7	7	66	78	1.339	3.19	109	....	.246	10	.137	11	9	0.6
1887	Phi-a	1	2	.333	3	3	3	0	0	26	45	22	13	1	1	17	4	1.731	4.50	95	....	.367	1	.077	-1	1	-0.2
1892	Bro-N	9	12	.429	28	23	16	2	1	195	188	109	71	3	7	96	65	1.456	3.28	96	3.63	.243	24	.192	-3	12	-0.3
1895	Pit-N	14	17	.452	36	29	24	0	1	261^2	293	186	138	4	15	135	85	1.636	4.75	95	4.64	.279	25	.236	-7	16	-0.7
1896	StL-N	12	29	.293	42	41	37	0	0	336	411	271	191	11	15	141	65	1.643	5.12	85	4.98	.299	30	.186	-20	14	-2.3
1897	StL-N	9	27	.250	39	38	31	0	0	294^2	395	292	205	10	16	148	67	**1.843**	6.26	70	6.04	.319	39	.250	-50	3	-4.5
1898	Pit-N	5	9	.357	16	15	13	1	1	125	141	81	67	4	7	44	19	1.480	4.82	74	4.23	.282	12	.240	-18	5	-1.6
1901	Cle-A	7	11	.389	20	19	16	0	0	157^2	180	109	66	3	10	57	48	1.503	3.77	94	4.26	.284	14	.219	-3	7	-0.4
Total	**8**	**66**	**120**	**.355**	**206**	**190**	**162**	**5**	**3**	**1582**	**1836**	**1214**	**817**	**43**	**78**	**704**	**431**	**1.595**	**4.65**	**87**	**4.15**	**.285**	**155**	**.207**	**-90**	**67**	**-9.5**

• HART, Billy Robert Lee Hart b: 5/16/1866, Palmyra, MO d: 5/14/1944, Hannibal, MO, 5'8" Deb: 7/13/1890

YEAR	TM-L	W	L	PCT	G	GS	CG	SH	SV	IP	H	R	ER	HR	HB	BB	SO	RAT	ERA	ERA+	CERA	OAV	BH	AVG	PR+	WS	TPW
1890	StL-a	12	8	.600	26	24	20	0	0	201^1	188	111	82	6	16	66	95	1.262	3.67	117	....	.240	15	.192	14	18	1.2

• HARTENSTEIN, Chuck Charles Oscar "Twiggy" Hartenstein b: 5/26/1942, Seguin, TX BR/TR, 5'11", 165 lbs. Deb: 9/11/1965 C

YEAR	TM-L	W	L	PCT	G	GS	CG	SH	SV	IP	H	R	ER	HR	HB	BB	SO	RAT	ERA	ERA+	CERA	OAV	BH	AVG	PR+	WS	TPW
1966	Chi-N	0	0	....	5	0	0	0	0	9^1	8	2	2	0	1	3	4	1.179	1.93	191	2.67	.222	0	....	2	1	0.2
1967	Chi-N	9	5	.643	45	0	0	0	10	73	74	27	25	4	1	17	20	1.247	3.08	115	3.27	.278	1	.063	3	8	0.2
1968	Chi-N	2	4	.333	28	0	0	0	1	35^2	41	19	18	3	1	11	17	1.458	4.54	70	4.47	.291	0	.000	-5	1	-0.6
1969	Pit-N	5	4	.556	56	0	0	0	10	95^2	84	42	42	9	4	27	44	1.160	3.95	88	3.10	.241	1	.071	-4	7	-0.5
1970	Pit-N	1	1	.500	17	0	0	0	1	23^2	25	15	12	3	0	8	14	1.394	4.56	85	4.01	.278	0	.000	-2	1	-0.2
	StL-N	0	0	....	6	0	0	0	0	13^1	24	13	13	1	0	5	9	2.175	8.78	47	8.28	.375	0	.000	-7	0	-0.7
	Yr.	1	1	.500	23	0	0	0	1	37	49	28	25	4	0	13	23	1.676	6.08	66	5.55	.318	0	.000	-9	1	-0.9
	Bos-A	0	3	.000	17	0	0	0	1	19	21	17	17	6	1	12	12	1.737	8.05	49	7.24	.288	0	.000	-8	0	-0.8
1977	Tor-A	0	2	.000	13	0	0	0	0	27^1	40	22	20	8	1	6	15	1.683	6.59	64	8.01	.348	0	....	-7	0	-0.7
Total	**6**	**17**	**19**	**.472**	**187**	**0**	**0**	**0**	**23**	**297**	**317**	**157**	**149**	**34**	**9**	**89**	**135**	**1.367**	**4.52**	**81**	**4.31**	**.280**	**2**	**.054**	**-29**	**18**	**-3.2**

• HARTER, Frank Franklin Pierce "Chief" Harter b: 9/19/1886, Keyesport, IL d: 4/14/1959, Breese, IL BR/TR, 5'11", 165 lbs. Deb: 8/31/1912

YEAR	TM-L	W	L	PCT	G	GS	CG	SH	SV	IP	H	R	ER	HR	HB	BB	SO	RAT	ERA	ERA+	CERA	OAV	BH	AVG	PR+	WS	TPW
1912	Cin-N	1	2	.333	6	3	1	0	0	29^1	25	16	10	1	0	11	12	1.227	3.07	109	2.66	.234	1	.091	1	1	0.0
1913	Cin-N	1	1	.500	17	2	0	0	0	46^2	47	23	20	3	0	19	10	1.414	3.86	84	3.87	.272	2	.143	-3	2	-0.4
1914	Ind-F	1	2	.333	6	1	1	0	0	24^2	33	12	11	0	0	7	8	1.622	4.01	86	4.72	.330	0	.000	-2	1	-0.3
Total	**3**	**3**	**5**	**.375**	**29**	**6**	**2**	**0**	**0**	**100^2**	**105**	**51**	**41**	**4**	**0**	**37**	**30**	**1.411**	**3.67**	**91**	**3.72**	**.277**	**3**	**.091**	**-4**	**4**	**-0.7**

• HARTGRAVES, Dean Dean Charles Hartgraves b: 8/12/1966, Bakersfield, CA BR/TL, 6', 185 lbs. Deb: 5/3/1995

YEAR	TM-L	W	L	PCT	G	GS	CG	SH	SV	IP	H	R	ER	HR	HB	BB	SO	RAT	ERA	ERA+	CERA	OAV	BH	AVG	PR+	WS	TPW
1995	Hou-N	2	0	1.000	40	0	0	0	0	36^1	30	14	13	2	0	16	24	1.266	3.22	120	2.95	.227	0	.000	3	3	0.3
1996	Hou-N	0	0	....	19	0	0	0	0	19	18	11	11	1	1	16	16	1.789	5.21	74	5.10	.257	0	....	-2	0	-0.2
	Atl-N	1	0	1.000	20	0	0	0	0	18^2	16	10	9	3	1	7	14	1.232	4.34	102	3.84	.232	0	.000	0	1	0.0
	Yr.	1	0	1.000	39	0	0	0	0	37^2	34	21	20	4	2	23	30	1.513	4.78	86	4.48	.245	0	.000	-2	1	-0.2
1998	SF-N	0	0	....	5	0	0	0	0	5^2	10	7	6	1	0	4	4	2.471	9.53	42	10.46	.385	0	....	-3	0	-0.3
Total	**3**	**3**	**0**	**1.000**	**84**	**0**	**0**	**0**	**0**	**79^2**	**74**	**42**	**39**	**7**	**2**	**43**	**58**	**1.469**	**4.41**	**91**	**4.21**	**.249**	**0**	**.000**	**-2**	**4**	**-0.3**

• HARTLEY, Mike Michael Edward Hartley b: 8/31/1961, Hawthorne, CA BR/TR, 6'1", 197 lbs. Deb: 9/10/1989

YEAR	TM-L	W	L	PCT	G	GS	CG	SH	SV	IP	H	R	ER	HR	HB	BB	SO	RAT	ERA	ERA+	CERA	OAV	BH	AVG	PR+	WS	TPW
1989	LA-N	0	1	.000	5	0	0	0	0	6	2	1	1	0	0	0	4	.333	1.50	228	0.25	.100	0	.000	1	0	0.1
1990	LA-N	6	3	.667	32	6	1	1	1	79^1	58	32	26	7	2	30	76	1.109	2.95	124	2.54	.200	1	.077	6	6	0.5
1991	LA-N	2	0	1.000	40	0	0	0	1	57	53	29	28	7	3	37	44	1.579	4.42	81	4.83	.245	0	.000	-5	2	-0.6
	Phi-N	2	1	.667	18	0	0	0	1	26^1	21	11	11	4	3	10	19	1.177	3.76	97	3.66	.219	0	.000	-0	2	0.0
	Yr.	4	1	.800	58	0	0	0	2	83^1	74	40	39	11	6	47	63	1.452	4.21	86	4.46	.237	0	.000	-6	4	-0.6
1992	Phi-N	7	6	.538	46	0	0	0	0	55	54	23	21	5	2	23	53	1.400	3.44	102	3.86	.255	0	.000	1	4	0.0
1993	Min-A	1	2	.333	53	0	0	0	1	81	86	38	36	4	7	36	57	1.506	4.00	109	4.56	.281	0	....	4	5	0.4
1995	Bos-A	0	0	....	5	0	0	0	0	7	8	7	7	1	2	2	2	1.429	9.00	54	5.81	.308	0	....	-3	0	-0.3
	Bal-A	1	0	1.000	3	0	0	0	0	7	5	1	1	0	0	1	4	.857	1.29	370	1.42	.217	0	....	3	1	0.2
	Yr.	1	0	1.000	8	0	0	0	0	14	13	8	8	1	2	3	6	1.143	5.14	94	3.61	.265	0	....	-1	1	-0.1
Total	**6**	**19**	**13**	**.594**	**202**	**6**	**1**	**1**	**4**	**318^2**	**287**	**142**	**131**	**28**	**19**	**139**	**259**	**1.337**	**3.70**	**104**	**3.79**	**.241**	**1**	**.043**	**6**	**20**	**0.4**

• HARTMAN, Bob Robert Louis Hartman b: 8/28/1937, Kenosha, WI BR/TL, 5'11", 185 lbs. Deb: 4/26/1959

YEAR	TM-L	W	L	PCT	G	GS	CG	SH	SV	IP	H	R	ER	HR	HB	BB	SO	RAT	ERA	ERA+	CERA	OAV	BH	AVG	PR+	WS	TPW
1959	Mil-N	0	0	....	3	0	0	0	0	1^2	6	5	5	0	0	2	1	4.800	27.00	13	25.43	.545	0	....	-4	0	-0.4
1962	Cle-A	0	1	.000	8	2	0	0	0	17^1	14	10	6	1	0	8	11	1.269	3.12	124	2.83	.209	0	.000	1	1	0.1
Total	**2**	**0**	**1**	**.000**	**11**	**2**	**0**	**0**	**0**	**19**	**20**	**15**	**11**	**1**	**0**	**10**	**12**	**1.579**	**5.21**	**71**	**4.81**	**.256**	**0**	**.000**	**-3**	**1**	**-0.4**

• HARTMAN, Charlie Charles Otto Hartman b: 8/10/1888, Los Angeles, CA d: 10/22/1960, Los Angeles, CA TL Deb: 6/24/1908

YEAR	TM-L	W	L	PCT	G	GS	CG	SH	SV	IP	H	R	ER	HR	HB	BB	SO	RAT	ERA	ERA+	CERA	OAV	BH	AVG	PR+	WS	TPW
1908	Bos-A	0	0	....	1	0	0	0	0	2	1	1	1	0	0	2	1	1.500	4.50	55	2.54	.143	0	....	-0	0	-0.1

• HARTRANFT, Ray Raymond Joseph Hartranft b: 9/19/1890, Quakertown, PA d: 2/10/1955, Spring City, PA BL/TL, 6'1", 195 lbs. Deb: 6/16/1913

YEAR	TM-L	W	L	PCT	G	GS	CG	SH	SV	IP	H	R	ER	HR	HB	BB	SO	RAT	ERA	ERA+	CERA	OAV	BH	AVG	PR+	WS	TPW
1913	Phi-N	0	0	....	1	0	0	0	0	1	3	1	1	0	0	1	1	4.000	9.00	37	19.12	.500	0	....	-1	0	-0.1

• HARTSOCK, Jeff Jeffrey Roger Hartsock b: 11/19/1966, Fairfield, OH BR/TR, 6', 190 lbs. Deb: 9/12/1992

YEAR	TM-L	W	L	PCT	G	GS	CG	SH	SV	IP	H	R	ER	HR	HB	BB	SO	RAT	ERA	ERA+	CERA	OAV	BH	AVG	PR+	WS	TPW
1992	Chi-N	0	0	....	4	0	0	0	0	9^1	15	7	7	2	0	4	6	2.036	6.75	53	8.95	.375	0	.000	-3	0	-0.4

• HARTUNG, Clint Clinton Clarence "Floppy,The Hondo Hurricane" Hartung b: 8/10/1922, Hondo, TX BR/TR, 6'5", 215 lbs. Deb: 4/15/1947 ♦

YEAR	TM-L	W	L	PCT	G	GS	CG	SH	SV	IP	H	R	ER	HR	HB	BB	SO	RAT	ERA	ERA+	CERA	OAV	BH	AVG	PR+	WS	TPW
1947	NY-N	9	7	.563	23	20	8	1	0	138	140	76	70	15	2	69	54	1.514	4.57	89	4.57	.263	29	.309	-8	10	0.1
1948	NY-N	8	8	.500	36	19	6	2	1	153^1	146	89	81	15	5	72	42	1.422	4.75	83	4.16	.258	10	.179	-13	5	-1.1
1949	NY-N	9	11	.450	33	25	8	0	0	154^2	156	98	86	16	4	86	48	1.565	5.00	80	4.73	.260	12	.190	-17	5	-1.3
1950	NY-N	3	3	.500	20	8	1	0	0	65^1	87	56	48	10	2	44	23	2.005	6.61	62	7.78	.326	13	.302	-20	2	-1.5
Total	**4**	**29**	**29**	**.500**	**112**	**72**	**23**	**3**	**1**	**511^1**	**529**	**319**	**285**	**56**	**13**	**271**	**167**	**1.565**	**5.02**	**80**	**4.91**	**.269**	**90**	**.238**	**-59**	**22**	**-3.8**

• HARTZELL, Paul Paul Franklin Hartzell b: 11/2/1953, Bloomsburg, PA BR/TR, 6'5", 200 lbs. Deb: 4/10/1976

YEAR	TM-L	W	L	PCT	G	GS	CG	SH	SV	IP	H	R	ER	HR	HB	BB	SO	RAT	ERA	ERA+	CERA	OAV	BH	AVG	PR+	WS	TPW
1976	Cal-A	7	4	.636	37	15	7	2	2	166	166	64	51	6	10	43	51	1.259	2.77	120	3.33	.266	0	....	11	12	1.2
1977	Cal-A	8	12	.400	41	23	6	0	4	189^1	200	92	75	14	4	38	79	1.257	3.57	110	3.47	.274	0	....	9	10	0.9
1978	Cal-A	6	10	.375	54	12	5	0	6	157	168	67	60	8	5	41	55	1.331	3.44	105	3.68	.278	0	....	4	10	0.4
1979	Min-A	6	10	.375	28	26	4	0	0	163	193	102	97	18	4	44	44	1.454	5.36	82	4.81	.301	0	....	-18	5	-1.7
1980	Bal-A	0	2	.000	6	0	0	0	0	17^2	22	14	13	3	0	9	5	1.755	6.62	60	6.51	.310	0	....	-6	0	-0.6
1984	Mil-A	0	1	.000	4	1	0	0	0	10^1	17	11	9	0	0	6	3	2.226	7.84	49	7.73	.370	0	....	-4	0	-0.5
Total	**6**	**27**	**39**	**.409**	**170**	**77**	**22**	**2**	**12**	**703^1**	**766**	**350**	**305**	**49**	**23**	**181**	**237**	**1.346**	**3.90**	**99**	**3.94**	**.282**	**0**	**....**	**-4**	**37**	**-0.2**

YEAR TM-L	W	L	PCT	G	GS	CG	SH	SV	IP	H	R	ER	HR	HB	BB	SO	RAT	ERA	ERA+	CERA	OAV	BH	AVG	PR+	WS	TPW
• HARVEY, Bryan	Bryan Stanley Harvey b: 6/2/1963, Soddy-Daisy, TN BR/TR, 6'3", 212 lbs. Deb: 5/16/1987																									
1987 Cal-A	0	0	....	3	0	0	0	0	5	6	0	0	0	0	2	3	1.600	0.00	....	4.56	.300	0	....	2	1	0.2
1988 Cal-A	7	5	.583	50	0	0	0	17	76	59	22	18	4	1	20	67	1.039	2.13	181	2.07	.214	0	....	15	13	1.5
1989 Cal-A	3	3	.500	51	0	0	0	25	55	36	21	21	6	0	41	78	1.400	3.44	111	3.41	.183	0	....	1	8	0.1
1990 Cal-A	4	4	.500	54	0	0	0	25	64^{1}	45	24	23	4	0	35	82	1.244	3.22	119	2.64	.201	0	....	4	11	0.4
1991 Cal-A★	2	4	.333	67	0	0	0	**46**	78^{2}	51	20	14	6	1	17	101	.864	1.60	256	1.53	.178	0	....	21	18	2.1
1992 Cal-A	0	4	.000	25	0	0	0	13	28^{2}	22	12	9	4	0	11	34	1.151	2.83	141	2.83	.208	0	....	4	5	0.4
1993 Fla-N★	1	5	.167	59	0	0	0	45	69	45	14	13	4	0	13	73	.841	1.70	255	1.42	.186	0	....	21	18	2.1
1994 Fla-N	0	0	....	12	0	0	0	6	10^{1}	12	6	6	1	0	4	10	1.548	5.23	84	4.80	.279	0	....	-1	1	-0.1
1995 Fla-N	0	0	....	1	0	0	0	0	0	2	3	3	1	0	1	0	....	∞	....	∞	1.000	0	....	-3	0	-0.3
Total 9	17	25	.405	322	0	0	0	177	387	278	122	107	30	2	144	448	1.090	2.49	164	2.29	.199	0	....	64	75	6.5
• HARVEY, Zaza	Ervin King Harvey b: 1/5/1879, Saratoga, CA d: 6/3/1954, Santa Monica, CA BL/TL, 6', 190 lbs. Deb: 5/3/1900 ♦																									
1900 Chi-N	0	0	....	1	0	0	0	0	4	3	0	0	0	0	1	0	1.000	0.00	....	1.66	.209	0	.000	2	1	0.1
1901 Chi-A	3	7	.300	16	9	5	0	1	92	91	59	37	2	5	34	27	1.359	3.62	96	3.46	.255	10	.250	-2	5	0.1
Total 2	3	7	.300	17	9	5	0	1	96	94	59	37	2	5	35	27	1.344	3.47	100	3.38	.254	86	.332	0	6	0.2
• HARVILLE, Chad	Chad Ashley Harville b: 9/16/1976, Selmer, TN BR/TR, 5'9", 180 lbs. Deb: 6/23/1999																									
1999 Oak-A	0	2	.000	15	0	0	0	0	14^{1}	18	11	11	2	0	10	15	1.953	6.91	67	7.09	.310	0	....	-4	0	-0.3
2001 Oak-A	0	0	....	3	0	0	0	0	3	2	0	0	0	0	0	2	.667	0.00	....	0.91	.182	0	....	1	1	0.1
2003 Oak-A	1	0	1.000	21	0	0	0	1	21^{2}	25	15	14	3	1	17	18	1.938	5.82	78	7.13	.294	0	....	-3	0	-0.3
Total 3	1	2	.333	39	0	0	0	1	39	45	26	25	5	1	27	35	1.846	5.77	79	6.64	.292	0	....	-5	1	-0.5
• HASEGAWA, Shigetoshi	Shigetoshi Hasegawa b: 8/1/1968, Kobe, Japan BR/TR, 5'11", 160 lbs. Deb: 4/5/1997																									
1997 Ana-A	3	7	.300	50	7	0	0	0	116^{2}	118	60	51	14	3	46	83	1.406	3.93	117	4.37	.269	0	....	8	7	0.8
1998 Ana-A	8	3	.727	61	0	0	0	5	97^{1}	86	37	34	14	2	32	73	1.212	3.14	149	3.54	.241	0	....	17	11	1.6
1999 Ana-A	4	6	.400	64	1	0	0	2	77	80	45	42	14	2	34	44	1.481	4.91	99	5.25	.276	0	....	-1	5	-0.1
2000 Ana-A	10	6	.625	66	0	0	0	9	95^{2}	100	43	38	11	2	38	59	1.443	3.57	142	4.44	.270	0	.000	14	11	1.2
2001 Ana-A	5	6	.455	46	0	0	0	0	55^{2}	52	28	25	5	2	20	41	1.293	4.04	113	3.50	.248	0	....	3	5	0.3
2002 Sea-A	8	3	.727	53	0	0	0	1	70^{1}	60	26	25	4	2	30	39	1.280	3.20	132	3.13	.238	0	....	9	7	0.8
2003 Sea-A★	2	4	.333	63	0	0	0	16	73	62	12	12	5	0	18	32	1.096	1.48	292	2.57	.235	0	....	21	13	2.0
Total 7	40	35	.533	403	8	0	0	33	585^{2}	558	251	227	67	13	218	371	1.325	3.49	134	3.90	.256	0	.000	71	59	6.7
• HASH, Herb	Herbert Howard Hash b: 2/13/1911, Woolwine, VA BR/TR, 6'1", 180 lbs. Deb: 4/19/1940																									
1940 Bos-A	7	7	.500	34	12	3	1	3	120	123	68	66	11	5	84	36	1.725	4.95	91	5.33	.266	7	.175	-5	7	-0.5
1941 Bos-A	1	0	1.000	4	0	0	0	1	8^{1}	7	5	5	1	0	7	3	1.680	5.40	77	4.71	.226	0	.000	-1	1	-0.1
Total 2	8	7	.533	38	12	3	1	4	128^{1}	130	73	71	12	5	91	39	1.722	4.98	90	5.28	.264	7	.167	-6	8	-0.6
• HASSLER, Andy	Andrew Earl Hassler b: 10/18/1951, Texas City, TX BL/TL, 6'5", 220 lbs. Deb: 5/30/1971																									
1971 Cal-A	0	3	.000	6	4	0	0	0	18^{2}	25	10	8	0	1	15	13	2.143	3.86	84	7.12	.333	0	.000	-2	0	-0.2
1973 Cal-A	0	4	.000	7	4	1	0	0	31^{2}	33	23	13	0	3	19	19	1.642	3.69	96	4.57	.262	0	....	-0	0	0.0
1974 Cal-A	7	11	.389	23	22	10	2	1	162	132	64	47	10	9	79	76	1.302	2.61	132	3.37	.225	0	....	16	9	1.7
1975 Cal-A	3	12	.200	30	18	6	1	0	133^{1}	158	94	88	12	6	53	82	1.583	5.94	60	5.30	.303	0	....	-35	0	-3.6
1976 Cal-A	0	6	.000	14	4	0	0	0	47^{1}	50	31	27	3	0	17	16	1.415	5.13	65	4.00	.284	0	....	-9	0	-1.0
*KC-A	5	6	.455	19	14	4	1	0	99^{2}	89	37	32	2	0	39	45	1.284	2.89	121	2.96	.242	0	....	7	6	0.7
Yr.	5	12	.294	33	18	4	1	0	147	139	68	59	5	0	56	61	1.327	3.61	95	3.30	.256	0	....	-3	6	-0.3
1977*KC-A	9	6	.600	29	27	3	1	0	156^{1}	166	88	73	7	5	75	83	1.542	4.20	96	4.40	.270	0	....	-4	7	-0.4
1978 KC-A	1	4	.200	11	9	1	0	0	58^{1}	76	36	28	1	2	24	26	1.714	4.32	88	5.38	.317	0	....	-4	1	-0.4
Bos-A	2	1	.667	13	2	0	0	1	30	38	13	10	0	0	13	23	1.700	3.00	137	4.79	.302	0	....	3	2	0.4
Yr.	3	5	.375	24	11	1	0	1	88^{1}	114	49	38	1	2	37	49	1.709	3.87	101	5.18	.311	0	....	-0	3	0.0
1979 Bos-A	1	2	.333	8	0	0	0	0	15^{1}	23	17	15	0	1	7	7	1.957	8.80	50	7.06	.365	0	....	-7	0	-0.7
NY-N	4	5	.444	29	8	1	0	4	80^{1}	74	35	33	5	0	42	53	1.444	3.70	98	3.76	.252	0	.000	-1	5	-0.4
1980 Pit-N	0	0	....	6	0	0	0	0	11^{2}	9	6	5	2	0	4	4	1.114	3.86	94	3.27	.243	0	.000	-0	0	-0.1
Cal-A	5	1	.833	41	0	0	0	10	83	67	25	23	8	1	37	75	1.253	2.49	157	3.02	.214	0	....	14	10	1.4
1981 Cal-A	4	3	.571	42	0	0	0	5	75^{2}	72	29	27	8	0	33	44	1.388	3.21	114	3.96	.262	0	....	3	5	0.3
1982*Cal-A	2	1	.667	54	0	0	0	4	71^{1}	58	24	22	5	4	40	38	1.374	2.78	146	3.65	.232	0	....	9	7	0.9
1983 Cal-A	0	5	.000	42	0	0	0	4	36^{1}	42	22	22	2	0	17	20	1.624	5.45	74	4.63	.302	0	....	-6	1	-0.6
1984 StL-N	1	0	1.000	3	0	0	0	0	2^{1}	4	3	3	2	0	2	1	2.571	11.57	30	17.09	.364	0	....	-2	0	-0.2
1985 StL-N	0	1	.000	10	0	0	0	0	10	9	5	2	0	0	4	5	1.300	1.80	196	2.64	.225	0	....	2	0	0.2
Total 14	44	71	.383	387	112	26	5	29	1123^{1}	1125	562	478	67	32	520	630	1.464	3.83	97	4.14	.264	0	.000	-17	53	-2.0
• HASTINGS, Charlie	Charles Morton Hastings b: 11/11/1870, Ironton, OH d: 8/3/1934, Parkersburg, WV, 5'11", 179 lbs. Deb: 5/3/1893																									
1893 Cle-N	4	5	.444	15	9	6	0	1	92	128	81	48	5	5	33	14	1.750	4.70	104	5.97	.320	7	.179	2	5	0.2
1896 Pit-N	5	10	.333	17	13	9	0	1	104	126	86	68	1	7	44	19	1.635	5.88	71	4.82	.297	8	.216	-20	2	-1.7
1897 Pit-N	5	4	.556	16	10	9	0	0	118	138	84	60	3	7	47	42	1.568	4.58	91	4.59	.290	10	.233	-3	8	0.0
1898 Pit-N	4	10	.286	19	13	12	0	0	137^{1}	142	76	52	2	10	52	40	1.413	3.41	104	3.73	.265	10	.233	2	9	0.4
Total 4	18	29	.383	67	45	36	0	2	451^{1}	534	327	228	11	29	176	115	1.573	4.55	91	4.66	.291	35	.216	-18	24	-1.0
• HASTY, Bob	Robert Keller Hasty b: 5/3/1896, Canton, GA d: 5/28/1972, Dallas, GA BR/TR, 6'3", 210 lbs. Deb: 9/11/1919																									
1919 Phi-A	0	2	.000	2	2	1	0	0	12	15	10	7	1	0	4	5	1.583	5.25	65	5.11	.306	1	.333	-2	0	-0.2
1920 Phi-A	1	3	.250	19	4	1	0	0	71^{2}	91	53	40	5	0	28	12	1.660	5.02	80	5.57	.323	6	.250	-7	2	-0.6
1921 Phi-A	5	16	.238	35	22	9	0	0	179^{1}	238	120	97	8	2	40	46	1.550	4.87	92	4.79	.331	20	.294	-5	8	-0.2
1922 Phi-A	9	14	.391	28	26	14	1	0	192^{1}	225	110	91	20	3	41	33	1.383	4.26	100	4.29	.298	15	.200	1	10	0.0
1923 Phi-A	13	15	.464	44	36	10	1	1	243^{1}	274	146	120	11	9	72	56	1.422	4.44	93	4.02	.291	17	.193	-3	11	-0.5
1924 Phi-A	1	3	.250	18	4	0	0	0	52^{2}	57	36	33	4	1	30	15	1.652	5.64	76	4.83	.282	1	.077	-7	1	-0.8
Total 6	29	53	.354	146	94	35	2	1	751^{1}	900	475	388	49	15	215	167	1.484	4.65	91	4.49	.305	60	.221	-22	32	-2.3
• HATFIELD, Gil	Gilbert "Colonel" Hatfield b: 1/27/1855, Hoboken, NJ d: 5/26/1921, Hoboken, NJ TR, 5'9.5", 168 lbs. Deb: 9/24/1885 U ♦																									
1889 NY-N	2	4	.333	6	5	5	0	0	52	53	43	23	2	1	25	28	1.500	3.98	99	....	.256	23	.184	-1	3	-0.7
1890 NY-P	1	1	.500	3	0	0	0	1	7^{2}	8	8	3	1	1	4	3	1.565	3.52	129	....	.257	80	.279	1	7	-1.4
1891 Was-a	0	0	....	4	0	0	0	0	18	29	28	22	1	0	14	3	2.389	11.00	34	....	.352	128	.256	-14	14	-1.5
Total 3	3	5	.375	13	5	5	0	1	77^{2}	90	79	48	4	2	43	34	1.712	5.56	70	....	.280	295	.248	-13	24	-3.5
• HATHAWAY, Hilly	Hillary Houston Hathaway b: 9/12/1969, Jacksonville, FL BL/TL, 6'4", 195 lbs. Deb: 9/8/1992																									
1992 Cal-A	0	0	....	2	1	0	0	0	5^{2}	8	5	5	1	0	3	1	1.941	7.94	50	7.31	.333	0	....	-3	0	-0.3
1993 Cal-A	4	3	.571	11	11	0	0	0	57^{1}	71	35	32	6	5	26	11	1.692	5.02	90	6.45	.326	0	....	-4	2	-0.4
Total 2	4	3	.571	13	12	0	0	0	63	79	40	37	7	5	29	12	1.714	5.29	84	6.53	.326	0	....	-6	2	-0.6
• HATHAWAY, Ray	Ray Wilson Hathaway b: 10/13/1916, Greenville, OH BR/TR, 6', 165 lbs. Deb: 4/20/1945																									
1945 Bro-N	0	1	.000	4	1	0	0	0	9	11	7	4	1	0	6	3	1.889	4.00	94	6.39	.297	0	.000	-0	0	0.0
• HATTEN, Joe	Joseph Hilarian Hatten b: 11/17/1916, Bancroft, IA d: 12/16/1988, Redding, CA BR/TL, 6', 176 lbs. Deb: 4/21/1946																									
1946 Bro-N	14	11	.560	42	30	13	1	2	222	207	79	70	10	7	110	85	1.428	2.84	119	3.75	.253	6	.076	11	15	0.5
1947*Bro-N	17	8	.680	42	32	11	3	0	225^{1}	211	95	91	9	5	105	76	1.402	3.63	114	3.54	.252	17	.205	8	17	0.8
1948 Bro-N	13	10	.565	42	30	11	1	0	208^{2}	228	93	83	9	3	94	73	1.543	3.58	112	4.38	.283	13	.206	5	14	0.6
1949*Bro-N	12	8	.600	37	29	11	2	2	187^{1}	194	102	87	15	2	69	58	1.404	4.18	98	4.05	.271	12	.179	-5	9	-0.6
1950 Bro-N	2	2	.500	23	8	2	1	0	68^{2}	82	45	35	10	0	31	29	1.646	4.59	89	5.67	.294	2	.111	-5	2	-0.6
1951 Bro-N	1	0	1.000	11	6	0	0	0	49^{1}	55	25	25	3	0	21	22	1.541	4.56	86	4.45	.281	2	.133	-5	2	-0.6
Chi-N	2	6	.250	23	6	1	0	0	75^{1}	82	48	43	8	1	37	23	1.580	5.14	80	4.98	.281	4	.235	-8	1	-0.8
Yr.	3	6	.333	34	12	1	0	0	124^{2}	137	73	68	11	1	58	45	1.564	4.91	82	4.77	.281	6	.188	-13	3	-1.4

YEAR	TM-L	W	L	PCT	G	GS	CG	SH	SV	IP	H	R	ER	HR	HB	BB	SO	RAT	ERA	ERA+	CERA	OAV	BH	AVG	PR+	WS	TPW
1952	Chi-N	4	4	.500	13	8	2	0	0	50^{1}	65	35	34	6	1	25	15	1.788	6.08	63	6.34	.314	1	.067	-12	0	-1.4
Total	7	65	49	.570	233	149	51	8	4	1087	1124	522	468	70	19	492	381	1.487	3.87	102	4.24	.271	57	.160	-11	60	-2.0

• HATTER, Clyde Clyde Melno Hatter b: 8/7/1908, Poplar Hill, KY d: 10/16/1937, Yosemite, KY BR/TL, 5'11", 170 lbs. Deb: 4/23/1935

YEAR	TM-L	W	L	PCT	G	GS	CG	SH	SV	IP	H	R	ER	HR	HB	BB	SO	RAT	ERA	ERA+	CERA	OAV	BH	AVG	PR+	WS	TPW
1935	Det-A	0	0	....	8	2	0	0	0	33^{1}	44	33	28	2	1	30	15	2.220	7.56	55	7.53	.319	3	.300	-13	0	-1.2
1937	Det-A	1	0	1.000	3	0	0	0	0	9^{1}	17	12	12	0	1	11	4	3.000	11.57	40	12.22	.415	0	.000	-7	0	-0.7
Total	2	1	0	1.000	11	2	0	0	0	42^{2}	61	45	40	2	2	41	19	2.391	8.44	51	8.56	.341	3	.231	-20	0	-1.8

• HAUGHEY, Chris Christopher Francis "Bud" Haughey b: 10/3/1925, Astoria, NY BR/TR, 6'1", 180 lbs. Deb: 10/3/1943

YEAR	TM-L	W	L	PCT	G	GS	CG	SH	SV	IP	H	R	ER	HR	HB	BB	SO	RAT	ERA	ERA+	CERA	OAV	BH	AVG	PR+	WS	TPW
1943	Bro-N	0	1	.000	1	0	0	0	0	7	5	6	3	0	0	10	0	2.143	3.86	87	5.48	.238	0	.000	-0	0	-0.1

• HAUGHT, Gary Gary Allen Haught b: 9/29/1970, Tacoma, WA BB/TR, 6'1", 190 lbs. Deb: 7/16/1997

YEAR	TM-L	W	L	PCT	G	GS	CG	SH	SV	IP	H	R	ER	HR	HB	BB	SO	RAT	ERA	ERA+	CERA	OAV	BH	AVG	PR+	WS	TPW
1997	Oak-A	0	0	....	6	0	0	0	0	11^{1}	12	9	9	3	2	6	11	1.588	7.15	63	7.14	.279	0	....	-3	0	-0.3

• HAUGSTAD, Phil Philip Donald Haugstad b: 2/23/1924, Black River Falls, WI d: 10/21/1998, Black River Falls, WI BR/TR, 6'2", 165 lbs. Deb: 9/1/1947

YEAR	TM-L	W	L	PCT	G	GS	CG	SH	SV	IP	H	R	ER	HR	HB	BB	SO	RAT	ERA	ERA+	CERA	OAV	BH	AVG	PR+	WS	TPW
1947	Bro-N	1	0	1.000	6	1	0	0	0	12^{2}	14	4	4	1	0	4	4	1.421	2.84	145	4.35	.298	0	.000	2	1	0.1
1948	Bro-N	0	0	....	1	0	0	0	0	1	1	0	0	0	0	0	0	1.000	0.00	....	1.95	.333	0	....	0	0	0.0
1951	Bro-N	0	1	.000	21	1	0	0	0	30^{2}	28	25	22	4	3	24	22	1.696	6.46	61	5.32	.233	0	.000	-9	0	-0.9
1952	Cin-N	0	0	....	9	0	0	0	0	12	8	9	9	1	1	13	2	1.750	6.75	56	4.48	.190	0	.000	-4	0	-0.4
Total	4	1	1	.500	37	2	0	0	0	56^{1}	51	38	35	6	4	41	28	1.633	5.59	70	4.86	.241	0	.000	-11	1	-1.2

• HAUSMAN, Tom Thomas Matthew Hausman b: 3/31/1953, Mobridge, SD BR/TR, 6'4", 200 lbs. Deb: 4/26/1975

YEAR	TM-L	W	L	PCT	G	GS	CG	SH	SV	IP	H	R	ER	HR	HB	BB	SO	RAT	ERA	ERA+	CERA	OAV	BH	AVG	PR+	WS	TPW
1975	Mil-A	3	6	.333	29	9	1	0	0	112	110	57	51	7	6	47	46	1.402	4.10	93	3.85	.258	0	....	-3	5	-0.3
1976	Mil-A	0	0	....	3	0	0	0	0	3^{1}	3	2	2	0	0	3	1	1.800	5.40	65	4.27	.250	0	....	-1	0	-0.1
1978	NY-N	3	3	.500	10	10	0	0	0	51^{2}	58	28	27	6	1	9	16	1.297	4.70	74	4.07	.287	3	.176	-7	1	-0.7
1979	NY-N	2	6	.250	19	10	1	0	2	78^{2}	65	25	24	6	4	19	33	1.068	2.75	132	2.62	.226	3	.115	7	6	0.6
1980	NY-N	6	5	.545	55	4	0	0	1	122	125	63	54	12	3	26	53	1.238	3.98	89	3.44	.266	1	.063	-6	5	-0.8
1981	NY-N	0	1	.000	20	0	0	0	0	33	28	8	8	2	0	7	13	1.061	2.18	160	2.34	.235	0	.000	5	3	0.6
1982	NY-N	1	2	.333	21	0	0	0	0	36^{2}	44	26	18	4	2	6	16	1.364	4.42	82	4.39	.295	0	.000	-3	0	-0.3
	Atl-N	0	0	....	3	0	0	0	0	3^{2}	6	2	2	0	0	4	2	2.727	4.91	76	9.54	.500	0	....	-0	0	-0.1
	Yr.	1	2	.333	24	0	0	0	0	40^{1}	50	28	20	4	2	10	18	1.488	4.46	82	4.86	.311	0	.000	-3	0	-0.4
Total	7	15	23	.395	160	33	2	0	3	441	439	211	186	37	16	121	180	1.270	3.80	96	3.53	.262	7	.111	-8	20	-1.1

• HAUSMANN, Clem Clemens Raymond Hausmann b: 8/17/1919, Houston, TX d: 8/29/1972, Baytown, TX BR/TR, 5'9", 165 lbs. Deb: 4/28/1944

YEAR	TM-L	W	L	PCT	G	GS	CG	SH	SV	IP	H	R	ER	HR	HB	BB	SO	RAT	ERA	ERA+	CERA	OAV	BH	AVG	PR+	WS	TPW
1944	Bos-A	4	7	.364	32	12	3	0	2	137	139	55	52	6	3	69	43	1.518	3.42	100	4.14	.266	3	.079	-1	7	-0.3
1945	Bos-A	5	7	.417	31	13	4	2	2	125	131	77	70	5	2	60	30	1.528	5.04	67	4.11	.270	4	.103	-24	1	-2.8
1949	Phi-A	0	0	....	1	0	0	0	0	1	0	1	1	0	0	2	0	2.000	9.00	46	3.72	.000	0	....	-1	0	-0.1
Total	3	9	14	.391	64	25	7	2	4	263	270	133	123	11	5	131	73	1.525	4.21	81	4.13	.268	7	.091	-25	8	-3.2

• HAVENS, Brad Bradley David Havens b: 11/17/1959, Highland Park, MI BL/TL, 6'1", 196 lbs. Deb: 6/5/1981

YEAR	TM-L	W	L	PCT	G	GS	CG	SH	SV	IP	H	R	ER	HR	HB	BB	SO	RAT	ERA	ERA+	CERA	OAV	BH	AVG	PR+	WS	TPW
1981	Min-A	3	6	.333	14	12	1	1	0	78	76	33	31	6	1	24	43	1.282	3.58	110	3.46	.257	0	....	4	5	0.4
1982	Min-A	10	14	.417	33	32	4	1	0	208^{2}	201	112	100	32	0	80	129	1.347	4.31	98	4.13	.250	0	....	-4	9	-0.4
1983	Min-A	5	8	.385	16	14	1	0	0	80^{1}	110	75	73	11	0	38	40	1.842	8.18	52	6.87	.333	0	....	-36	0	-3.6
1985	Bal-A	0	1	.000	8	1	0	0	0	14^{1}	20	14	14	4	0	10	19	2.093	8.79	46	9.44	.333	0	....	-7	0	-0.7
1986	Bal-A	3	3	.500	46	0	0	0	1	71	64	37	36	7	0	29	57	1.310	4.56	91	3.62	.248	0	....	-3	3	-0.3
1987	LA-N	0	0	....	31	1	0	0	1	35^{1}	30	18	17	2	1	23	23	1.500	4.33	92	3.44	.227	0	.000	-1	1	-0.1
1988	LA-N	0	0	....	9	0	0	0	0	9^{2}	15	5	5	1	0	4	8	1.966	4.66	72	7.51	.357	0	.000	-1	0	-0.2
	Cle-A	2	3	.400	28	0	0	0	1	57^{1}	62	22	20	7	0	17	30	1.378	3.14	131	4.15	.273	0	....	7	5	0.7
1989	Cle-A	0	0	....	7	0	0	0	0	13^{1}	18	6	6	3	0	7	6	1.875	4.05	98	7.94	.353	0	....	-0	1	0.0
	Det-A	1	2	.333	13	1	0	0	0	22^{2}	28	14	14	3	3	14	15	1.853	5.56	69	7.07	.308	0	....	-4	0	-0.4
	Yr.	1	2	.333	20	1	0	0	0	36	46	20	20	6	3	21	21	1.861	5.00	77	7.40	.324	0	....	-4	1	-0.4
Total	8	24	37	.393	205	61	6	2	3	590^{2}	624	336	316	76	5	246	370	1.473	4.81	86	4.69	.272	0	.000	-46	24	-4.6

• HAWBLITZEL, Ryan Ryan Wade Hawblitzel b: 4/30/1971, West Palm Beach, FL BR/TR, 6'2", 170 lbs. Deb: 6/9/1996

YEAR	TM-L	W	L	PCT	G	GS	CG	SH	SV	IP	H	R	ER	HR	HB	BB	SO	RAT	ERA	ERA+	CERA	OAV	BH	AVG	PR+	WS	TPW
1996	Col-N	0	1	.000	8	0	0	0	0	15	18	12	10	2	0	6	7	1.600	6.00	87	5.36	.290	0	.000	-1	0	-0.1

• HAWK, Ed Edward Hawk b: 2/22/1888, Neosho, MO d: 3/26/1936, Neosho, MO BL/TR, 5'11", 175 lbs. Deb: 9/7/1911

YEAR	TM-L	W	L	PCT	G	GS	CG	SH	SV	IP	H	R	ER	HR	HB	BB	SO	RAT	ERA	ERA+	CERA	OAV	BH	AVG	PR+	WS	TPW
1911	StL-A	0	4	.000	5	4	4	0	0	37^{2}	38	18	14	1	4	8	14	1.221	3.35	101	3.17	.253	2	.154	-0	1	-0.1

• HAWKE, Bill William Victor "Dick" Hawke b: 4/28/1870, Elsmere, DE d: 12/11/1902, Wilmington, DE BR/TR, 5'8.5", 169 lbs. Deb: 7/28/1892

YEAR	TM-L	W	L	PCT	G	GS	CG	SH	SV	IP	H	R	ER	HR	HB	BB	SO	RAT	ERA	ERA+	CERA	OAV	BH	AVG	PR+	WS	TPW
1892	StL-N	5	5	.500	14	11	10	1	0	97^{1}	108	59	40	2	8	45	55	1.572	3.70	86	4.52	.270	4	.089	-2	4	-0.6
1893	StL-N	0	1	.000	1	1	0	0	0	5^{1}	9	9	3	0	0	3	1	2.250	5.06	93	7.95	.363	1	.333	-0	0	0.0
	Bal-N	11	16	.407	29	29	22	1	0	225	248	175	119	8	9	108	69	1.582	4.76	100	4.51	.272	16	.172	4	13	0.0
	Yr.	11	17	.393	30	30	22	1	0	230^{1}	257	184	122	8	9	111	70	1.598	4.77	99	4.59	.274	17	.177	4	13	0.0
1894*	Bal-N	16	9	.640	32	25	17	0	3	206	264	174	133	9	12	78	68	1.660	5.81	94	5.31	.308	28	.304	-14	13	-0.9
Total	3	32	31	.508	76	66	49	2	3	533^{2}	629	417	295	19	29	234	193	1.617	4.98	95	4.85	.287	49	.210	-13	30	-1.5

• HAWKINS, Andy Melton Andrew Hawkins b: 1/21/1960, Waco, TX BR/TR, 6'4", 223 lbs. Deb: 7/17/1982

YEAR	TM-L	W	L	PCT	G	GS	CG	SH	SV	IP	H	R	ER	HR	HB	BB	SO	RAT	ERA	ERA+	CERA	OAV	BH	AVG	PR+	WS	TPW
1982	SD-N	2	5	.286	15	10	1	0	0	63^{2}	66	33	29	4	2	27	25	1.461	4.10	84	4.13	.274	0	.000	-5	1	-0.7
1983	SD-N	5	7	.417	21	19	4	1	0	119^{2}	106	50	39	8	5	48	59	1.287	2.93	119	3.39	.244	2	.065	5	7	0.5
1984*	SD-N	8	9	.471	36	22	2	1	0	146	143	90	76	13	2	72	77	1.473	4.68	76	4.21	.254	8	.195	-21	1	-2.2
1985	SD-N	18	8	.692	33	33	5	2	0	228^{2}	229	88	80	18	4	65	69	1.286	3.15	112	3.55	.267	6	.078	6	15	0.2
1986	SD-N	10	8	.556	37	35	3	1	0	209^{1}	218	111	100	24	5	75	117	1.400	4.30	85	4.30	.268	10	.149	-15	6	-1.6
1987	SD-N	3	10	.231	24	20	0	0	0	117^{2}	131	71	66	16	2	49	51	1.530	5.05	78	5.18	.287	5	.156	-15	2	-1.6
1988	SD-N	14	11	.560	33	33	4	2	0	217^{2}	196	88	81	16	6	76	91	1.250	3.35	101	3.27	.244	7	.113	-2	12	-0.4
1989	NY-A	15	15	.500	34	34	5	2	0	208^{1}	238	127	111	23	6	76	98	1.507	4.80	81	4.99	.290	0	....	-22	7	-2.2
1990	NY-A	5	12	.294	28	26	2	1	0	157^{2}	156	101	94	20	2	82	74	1.510	5.37	74	4.15	.260	0	....	-25	2	-2.5
1991	NY-A	0	2	.000	4	3	0	0	0	12^{2}	23	15	14	5	0	6	5	2.289	9.95	42	12.32	.383	0	....	-8	0	-0.8
	Oak-A	4	4	.500	15	14	1	0	0	77	68	41	41	5	5	36	40	1.351	4.79	80	3.69	.237	0	....	-8	3	-0.8
	Yr.	4	6	.400	19	17	1	0	0	89^{2}	91	56	55	10	5	42	45	1.483	5.52	71	4.91	.262	0	....	-16	3	-1.6
Total	10	84	91	.480	280	249	27	10	0	1558^{1}	1574	815	731	152	39	612	706	1.403	4.22	87	4.20	.265	38	.117	-110	56	-12.2

• HAWKINS, La Troy La Troy Hawkins b: 12/21/1972, Gary, IN BR/TR, 6'5", 195 lbs. Deb: 4/29/1995

YEAR	TM-L	W	L	PCT	G	GS	CG	SH	SV	IP	H	R	ER	HR	HB	BB	SO	RAT	ERA	ERA+	CERA	OAV	BH	AVG	PR+	WS	TPW
1995	Min-A	2	3	.400	6	6	1	0	0	27	39	29	26	3	1	12	9	1.889	8.67	55	7.14	.339	0	....	-12	0	-1.1
1996	Min-A	1	1	.500	7	6	0	0	0	26^{1}	42	24	24	8	0	9	24	1.937	8.20	62	9.49	.372	0	....	-9	0	-0.8
1997	Min-A	6	12	.333	20	20	0	0	0	103^{1}	134	71	67	19	4	47	58	1.752	5.84	80	7.01	.317	0	.000	-14	2	-1.3
1998	Min-A	7	14	.333	33	33	0	0	0	190^{1}	227	126	111	27	5	61	105	1.513	5.25	91	5.31	.299	0	.000	-7	6	-0.7
1999	Min-A	10	14	.417	33	33	1	0	0	175^{1}	238	136	129	29	1	60	103	1.700	6.62	77	6.51	.323	0	.000	-29	3	-2.7
2000	Min-A	2	5	.286	66	0	0	0	14	87^{2}	85	34	33	7	1	32	59	1.335	3.39	152	3.70	.256	0	.000	19	12	1.7
2001	Min-A	1	5	.167	62	0	0	0	28	51^{1}	59	34	34	3	1	39	36	1.909	5.96	77	6.02	.291	0	....	-8	3	-0.7
2002*	Min-A	6	0	1.000	65	0	0	0	0	80^{1}	63	23	19	5	0	15	63	.971	2.13	211	1.99	.217	0	....	21	11	2.0
2003*	Min-A	9	3	.750	74	0	0	0	2	77^{1}	69	20	16	4	1	15	75	1.086	1.86	244	2.48	.239	0	....	25	13	2.4
Total	9	44	57	.436	366	98	2	0	44	819	956	497	459	105	14	290	532	1.521	5.04	96	5.25	.293	0	.000	-14	50	-1.3

• HAWKINS, Wynn Wynn Firth "Hawk" Hawkins b: 2/20/1936, East Palestine, OH BR/TR, 6'3", 195 lbs. Deb: 4/22/1960

YEAR	TM-L	W	L	PCT	G	GS	CG	SH	SV	IP	H	R	ER	HR	HB	BB	SO	RAT	ERA	ERA+	CERA	OAV	BH	AVG	PR+	WS	TPW
1960	Cle-A	4	4	.500	15	9	1	0	0	66	68	32	31	10	1	39	39	1.621	4.23	88	5.47	.269	2	.100	-4	3	-0.5
1961	Cle-A	7	9	.438	30	21	3	1	1	133	139	72	60	16	2	59	51	1.489	4.06	97	4.70	.270	4	.108	-2	6	-0.4
1962	Cle-A	1	0	1.000	3	0	0	0	0	3^{2}	9	5	3	1	0	1	0	2.727	7.36	53	14.01	.429	0	.000	-1	0	-0.1
Total	3	12	13	.480	48	30	4	1	1	202^{2}	216	109	94	27	3	99	90	1.554	4.17	93	5.12	.274	6	.105	-7	9	-0.9

YEAR	TM-L	W	L	PCT	G	GS	CG	SH	SV	IP	H	R	ER	HR	HB	BB	SO	RAT	ERA	ERA+	CERA	OAV	BH	AVG	PR+	WS	TPW
• HAWLEY, Pink	Emerson P. Hawley b: 12/5/1872, Beaver Dam, WI d: 9/19/1938, Beaver Dam, WI BL/TR, 5'10", 185 lbs. Deb: 8/13/1892																										
1892	StL-N	6	14	.300	20	20	18	0	0	166^1	160	116	59	4	11	63	63	1.341	3.19	100	3.40	.243	12	.169	6	7	0.4
1893	StL-N	5	17	.227	31	24	21	0	1	227	249	184	116	6	20	103	73	1.551	4.60	103	4.49	.271	26	.286	4	11	0.9
1894	StL-N	19	27	.413	53	41	36	0	0	392^2	481	306	214	14	21	149	120	1.604	4.90	110	4.90	.299	43	.264	22	29	1.9
1895	Pit-N	31	22	.585	**56**	50	44	**4**	1	**444**^{1}	449	242	157	7	33	122	142	1.285	3.18	142	3.28	.259	57	.308	65	**44**	**6.4**
1896	Pit-N	22	21	.512	49	43	37	2	0	378	382	197	150	2	28	157	137	1.426	3.57	117	3.67	.261	39	.239	25	27	2.4
1897	Pit-N	18	18	.500	40	39	33	0	0	311^1	362	221	166	7	26	94	88	1.465	4.80	87	4.27	.289	30	.231	-16	19	-1.4
1898	Cin-N	27	11	.711	43	37	32	3	0	331	357	163	124	5	22	91	69	1.353	3.37	114	3.60	.273	24	.185	13	28	0.9
1899	Cin-N	14	17	.452	34	29	25	0	1	250^1	289	161	118	7	20	65	46	1.414	4.24	92	4.10	.289	22	.218	-10	14	-1.0
1900	NY-N	18	18	.500	41	38	**34**	2	0	329^1	377	204	129	7	20	89	80	1.415	3.53	102	3.97	.287	25	.203	2	18	0.1
1901	Mil-A	7	14	.333	26	23	17	0	0	182^1	228	133	93	3	9	41	50	1.475	4.59	78	4.31	.302	19	.260	-18	7	-1.3
Total	10	167	179	.483	393	344	297	11	3	3012^2	3334	1927	1326	62	210	974	868	1.430	3.96	106	3.98	.277	297	.241	94	204	9.2
• HAWLEY, Scott	Marvin Hiram Hawley b: Painesville, OH d: 4/28/1904, Alliance, OH Deb: 9/22/1894																										
1894	Bos-N	0	1	.000	1	1	1	0	0	7	10	6	6	0	0	7	1	2.429	7.71	77	7.99	.332	0	.000	-2	0	-0.2
• HAYDEL, Hal	John Harold Haydel b: 7/9/1944, Houma, LA BR/TR, 6', 190 lbs. Deb: 9/7/1970																										
1970	Min-A	2	0	1.000	4	0	0	0	0	9	7	3	3	2	0	4	4	1.222	3.00	124	3.88	.226	2	.667	1	2	0.3
1971	Min-A	4	2	.667	31	0	0	0	1	40	33	19	19	3	2	20	29	1.325	4.28	83	3.64	.243	1	.333	-3	2	-0.2
Total	2	6	2	.750	35	0	0	0	1	49	40	22	22	5	2	24	33	1.306	4.04	88	3.68	.240	3	.500	-2	4	0.0
• HAYDEN, Lefty	Eugene Franklin Hayden b: 4/14/1935, San Francisco, CA BL/TL, 6'2", 175 lbs. Deb: 6/26/1958																										
1958	Cin-N	0	0	....	3	0	0	0	0	3^2	5	2	2	0	0	1	3	1.636	4.91	84	4.76	.313	0	....	-0	0	0.0
• HAYES, Ben	Ben Joseph Hayes b: 8/4/1957, Niagara Falls, NY BR/TR, 6'1", 180 lbs. Deb: 6/25/1982																										
1982	Cin-N	2	0	1.000	26	0	0	0	2	45^2	37	12	10	3	0	22	38	1.292	1.97	188	2.87	.219	0	.000	9	5	0.8
1983	Cin-N	4	6	.400	60	0	0	0	7	69^1	82	53	50	8	1	37	44	1.716	6.49	59	5.76	.301	0	.000	-21	0	-2.2
Total	2	6	6	.500	86	0	0	0	9	115	119	65	60	11	1	59	82	1.548	4.70	81	4.61	.270	0	.000	-12	5	-1.4
• HAYES, Jim	James Millard "Whitey" Hayes b: 2/11/1913, Montevallo, AL d: 11/27/1993, Decatur, GA BL/TR, 6'1", 168 lbs. Deb: 7/13/1935																										
1935	Was-A	2	4	.333	7	4	1	0	0	28	38	28	26	0	0	23	9	2.179	8.36	52	6.76	.322	2	.250	-12	0	-1.2
• HAYNER, Fred	Fred Ames Hayner b: 11/3/1871, Janesville, WI d: 1/14/1929, Lake Forest, IL, 6' Deb: 8/19/1890																										
1890	Pit-N	0	0	....	1	0	0	0	0	4	7	9	6	2	0	5	1	3.000	13.50	24	....	.372	0	.000	-4	0	-0.4
• HAYNES, Heath	Heath Burnett Haynes b: 11/30/1968, Wheeling, WV BR/TR, 6', 175 lbs. Deb: 6/1/1994																										
1994	Mon-N	0	0	....	4	0	0	0	0	3^2	3	1	0	0	0	3	1	1.636	0.00	....	3.80	.231	0	....	2	0	0.2
• HAYNES, Jimmy	Jimmy Wayne Haynes b: 9/5/1972, La Grange, GA BR/TR, 6'4", 185 lbs. Deb: 9/13/1995																										
1995	Bal-A	2	1	.667	4	3	0	0	0	24	11	6	6	2	0	12	22	.958	2.25	211	1.61	.136	0	....	6	3	0.6
1996	Bal-A	3	6	.333	26	11	0	0	1	89	122	84	82	14	2	58	65	2.022	8.29	59	8.05	.333	0	....	-33	0	-3.0
1997	Oak-A	3	6	.333	13	13	0	0	0	73^1	74	38	36	7	2	40	65	1.555	4.42	102	4.75	.262	0	.000	2	4	0.2
1998	Oak-A	11	9	.550	33	33	1	1	0	194^1	229	124	110	25	5	88	134	1.631	5.09	90	5.69	.298	0	.000	-9	7	-0.9
1999	Oak-A	7	12	.368	30	25	0	0	0	142	158	112	100	21	2	80	93	1.676	6.34	73	5.79	.282	0	.000	-26	1	-2.4
2000	Mil-N	12	13	.480	33	33	0	0	0	199^1	228	128	118	21	7	100	88	1.645	5.33	85	5.54	.295	8	.125	-20	6	-2.0
2001	Mil-N	8	17	.320	31	29	0	0	0	172^2	182	98	93	20	4	78	112	1.506	4.85	88	4.69	.279	8	.154	-11	6	-1.1
2002	Cin-N	15	10	.600	34	34	0	0	0	196^2	210	97	90	21	3	81	126	1.480	4.12	103	4.66	.278	10	.164	2	12	0.2
2003	Cin-N	2	12	.143	18	18	1	0	0	94^1	118	74	66	14	3	57	49	1.855	6.30	68	6.94	.311	6	.261	-21	0	-1.9
Total	9	63	86	.423	222	199	2	1	1	1185^2	1332	761	701	145	28	594	754	1.624	5.32	85	5.50	.288	32	.153	-110	39	-10.3
• HAYNES, Joe	Joseph Walton Haynes b: 9/21/1917, Lincolnton, GA d: 1/6/1967, Hopkins, MN BR/TR, 6'2.5", 190 lbs. Deb: 4/24/1939 C																										
1939	Was-A	8	12	.400	27	20	10	1	0	173	186	118	103	10	1	78	64	1.526	5.36	81	4.28	.276	14	.209	-21	4	-1.9
1940	Was-A	3	6	.333	22	7	1	0	0	63^1	85	50	46	4	1	34	23	1.879	6.54	64	6.38	.327	2	.105	-16	0	-1.6
1941	Chi-A	0	0	....	8	0	0	0	0	28	30	13	12	0	0	11	18	1.464	3.86	106	3.69	.280	3	.273	0	2	0.1
1942	Chi-A	8	5	.615	**40**	1	1	0	6	103	88	37	30	6	3	47	35	1.311	2.62	137	3.25	.234	5	.179	11	11	1.1
1943	Chi-A	7	2	.778	35	2	1	0	3	109^1	114	51	36	2	2	32	37	1.335	2.96	113	3.27	.263	9	.265	4	8	0.6
1944	Chi-A	5	6	.455	33	12	8	0	2	154^1	148	55	44	5	0	43	44	1.238	2.57	134	2.89	.254	10	.200	15	14	1.7
1945	Chi-A	5	5	.500	14	13	8	1	1	104	92	44	41	5	1	29	34	1.163	3.55	93	2.64	.237	7	.175	-1	6	-0.4
1946	Chi-A	7	9	.438	32	23	9	0	2	177^1	203	80	74	14	4	60	60	1.483	3.76	91	4.54	.289	14	.246	-8	9	-0.6
1947	Chi-A	14	6	.700	29	22	7	2	0	182	174	65	49	5	2	61	50	1.291	**2.42**	**151**	3.05	.250	17	.262	25	18	2.8
1948	Chi-A★	9	10	.474	27	22	6	0	0	149^2	167	79	66	13	2	52	40	1.463	3.97	107	4.40	.284	8	.160	3	10	0.2
1949	Was-A	2	9	.182	37	10	0	0	2	96^1	106	77	67	6	3	55	19	1.671	6.26	68	4.99	.283	6	.240	-18	0	-1.6
1950	Was-A	7	5	.583	27	10	1	1	0	101^2	124	73	66	14	5	46	15	1.672	5.84	77	6.00	.305	7	.200	-15	3	-1.3
1951	Was-A	1	4	.200	26	3	1	0	2	73	85	46	37	9	1	37	18	1.671	4.56	90	5.57	.290	7	.333	-3	2	-0.1
1952	Was-A	0	3	.000	22	2	0	0	3	66	70	35	33	2	1	35	18	1.591	4.50	79	4.33	.275	2	.105	-6	1	-0.7
Total	14	76	82	.481	379	147	53	5	21	1581	1672	823	704	95	26	620	475	1.450	4.01	97	4.09	.272	111	.213	-30	88	-1.8
• HAYWARD, Ray	Raymond Alton Hayward b: 4/27/1961, Enid, OK BL/TL, 6'1", 190 lbs. Deb: 9/20/1986																										
1986	SD-N	0	2	.000	3	3	0	0	0	10	16	12	10	1	0	4	6	2.000	9.00	41	7.40	.340	0	.000	-6	0	-0.7
1987	SD-N	0	0	....	4	0	0	0	0	6	12	11	11	3	0	3	2	2.500	16.50	24	15.71	.444	0	.000	-8	0	-0.8
1988	Tex-A	4	6	.400	12	12	1	1	0	62^2	63	44	38	6	0	35	37	1.564	5.46	75	4.87	.276	0	....	-10	1	-1.0
Total	3	4	8	.333	19	15	1	1	0	78^2	91	67	59	10	0	42	45	1.691	6.75	59	6.02	.301	0	.000	-24	1	-2.5
• HAYWOOD, Bill	William Kiernan Haywood b: 4/21/1937, Colon, Panama BR/TR, 6'3", 205 lbs. Deb: 7/28/1968																										
1968	Was-A	0	0	....	14	0	0	0	0	23	27	16	12	1	2	12	10	1.696	4.70	62	5.50	.314	0	....	-4	0	-0.5
• HEAD, Ed	Edward Marvin Head b: 1/25/1918, Selma, LA d: 1/31/1980, Bastrop, LA BR/TR, 6'1", 175 lbs. Deb: 7/27/1940																										
1940	Bro-N	1	2	.333	13	5	2	0	0	39^1	40	21	18	0	0	18	13	1.475	4.12	97	3.45	.260	2	.182	-0	2	-0.1
1942	Bro-N	10	6	.625	36	15	5	1	4	136^2	118	60	54	11	3	47	78	1.207	3.56	92	2.97	.231	13	.333	-6	9	-0.2
1943	Bro-N	9	10	.474	47	18	7	3	6	169^2	166	75	69	8	0	66	83	1.367	3.66	92	3.36	.250	7	.152	-3	8	-0.5
1944	Bro-N	4	3	.571	9	8	5	1	0	63^1	54	21	19	2	0	19	17	1.153	2.70	132	2.86	.266	5	.263	8	4	0.9
1946	Bro-N	3	2	.600	13	7	3	1	1	56	56	24	20	3	0	24	17	1.429	3.21	105	3.79	.267	5	.313	0	4	0.2
Total	5	27	23	.540	118	53	22	6	11	465	434	201	180	24	3	174	208	1.308	3.48	98	3.24	.249	32	.244	-1	27	0.3
• HEAD, Ralph	Ralph Head b: 8/30/1893, Tallapoosa, GA d: 10/8/1962, Muscadine, AL BR/TR, 5'10", 175 lbs. Deb: 4/18/1923																										
1923	Phi-N	2	9	.182	35	13	5	0	0	132^1	185	111	98	13	1	57	24	1.829	6.66	69	6.47	.341	3	.071	-27	1	-3.0
• HEALEY, Tom	Thomas F. Healey b: 1853, Cranston, RI d: 2/6/1891, Lewiston, ME TR Deb: 6/13/1878																										
1878	Pro-N	0	3	.000	3	3	3	0	0	24	27	17	8	1	....	7	2	1.417	3.00	73	....	.270	2	.222	-2	1	-0.2
	Ind-N	6	4	.600	11	10	9	0	1	89	98	50	22	1	....	13	18	1.247	2.22	91	....	.266	8	.178	-1	4	-0.3
	Yr.	6	7	.462	14	13	12	0	**1**	113	125	67	30	2	....	20	20	1.283	2.39	87	....	.267	10	.185	-4	5	-0.5
• HEALY, John	John J. "Egyptian,Long John" Healy b: 10/27/1866, Cairo, IL d: 3/16/1899, St. Louis, MO BR/TR, 6'2", 158 lbs. Deb: 9/11/1885 U																										
1885	StL-N	1	7	.125	8	8	8	0	0	66	54	37	22	0	....	20	32	1.121	3.00	91	....	.213	1	.042	-4	3	-0.6
1886	StL-N	17	23	.425	43	41	39	3	0	353^2	315	213	113	5	....	118	213	1.224	2.88	111	....	.230	14	.097	4	16	-0.6
1887	Ind-N	12	29	.293	41	41	40	3	0	341	523	292	196	24	15	108	75	1.534	5.17	80	....	.342	28	.197	-43	9	-3.8
1888	Ind-N	12	24	.333	37	37	36	1	0	321^1	347	199	139	13	15	87	124	1.351	3.89	76	....	.266	30	.229	-29	11	-2.4
1889	Was-N	1	11	.083	13	12	10	0	0	101	139	111	70	2	5	38	49	1.752	6.24	63	....	.317	10	.222	-24	0	-1.9
	Chi-N	1	4	.200	5	5	5	0	0	46	48	35	23	4	4	18	22	1.435	4.50	93	....	.260	2	.100	-2	1	-0.3
	Yr.	2	15	.118	18	17	15	0	0	147	187	146	93	6	9	56	71	1.653	5.69	70	....	.300	12	.185	-26	1	-2.3
1890	Tol-a	22	21	.512	46	46	44	2	0	389	326	201	125	5	24	127	225	1.165	2.89	136	....	.221	34	.218	36	34	3.9

YEAR	TM-L	W	L	PCT	G	GS	CG	SH	SV	IP	H	R	ER	HR	HB	BB	SO	RAT	ERA	ERA+	CERA	OAV	BH	AVG	PR+	WS	TPW
1891	Bal-a	8	10	.444	23	22	19	0	0	170^{1}	179	124	71	6	5	57	54	1.386	3.75	100	....	.261	9	.141	2	8	0.1
1892	Bal-N	3	6	.333	9	8	5	0	0	68^{1}	82	51	36	4	2	21	24	1.507	4.74	72	4.58	.286	6	.222	-7	2	-0.6
	Lou-N	1	1	.500	2	2	2	0	0	18^{1}	15	7	4	0	0	5	4	1.091	1.96	156	2.01	.215	2	.286	2	2	0.3
	Yr.	4	7	.364	11	10	7	0	0	86^{2}	97	58	40	4	2	26	28	1.419	4.15	82	4.03	.272	8	.235	-5	4	-0.3
Total	**8**	**78**	**136**	**.364**	**227**	**222**	**208**	**9**	**0**	**1875**	**2028**	**1270**	**799**	**63**	**70**	**599**	**822**	**1.343**	**3.84**	**93**	**0.19**	**.267**	**136**	**.179**	**-65**	**86**	**-6.1**

• HEARD, Charlie — Charles Heard b: 1/30/1872, Philadelphia, PA d: 2/20/1945, Philadelphia, PA BR/TR, 6'2", 190 lbs. Deb: 7/14/1890 ♦

YEAR	TM-L	W	L	PCT	G	GS	CG	SH	SV	IP	H	R	ER	HR	HB	BB	SO	RAT	ERA	ERA+	CERA	OAV	BH	AVG	PR+	WS	TPW
1890	Pit-N	0	6	.000	6	6	5	0	0	44	75	65	41	5	2	32	13	2.432	8.39	39	....	.366	8	.186	-23	0	-2.4

• HEARD, Jay — Jehosie Heard b: 1/17/1920, Athens, GA d: 11/18/1999, Birmingham, AL BL/TL, 5'7", 155 lbs. Deb: 4/24/1954

YEAR	TM-L	W	L	PCT	G	GS	CG	SH	SV	IP	H	R	ER	HR	HB	BB	SO	RAT	ERA	ERA+	CERA	OAV	BH	AVG	PR+	WS	TPW
1954	Bal-A	0	0	....	2	0	0	0	0	3^{1}	6	5	5	1	0	3	2	2.700	13.50	27	12.96	.375	0	....	-4	0	-0.4

• HEARN, Bunny — Elmer Lafayette Hearn b: 1/13/1904, Brooklyn, NY d: 3/31/1974, Venice, FL BL/TL, 5'8", 160 lbs. Deb: 4/13/1926

YEAR	TM-L	W	L	PCT	G	GS	CG	SH	SV	IP	H	R	ER	HR	HB	BB	SO	RAT	ERA	ERA+	CERA	OAV	BH	AVG	PR+	WS	TPW
1926	Bos-N	4	9	.308	34	12	3	0	2	117^{1}	121	63	55	2	0	56	40	1.509	4.22	84	3.87	.276	3	.100	-7	4	-0.9
1927	Bos-N	0	2	.000	8	0	0	0	0	12^{2}	16	9	6	0	0	9	5	1.974	4.26	87	6.11	.327	2	.400	-1	0	0.0
1928	Bos-N	1	0	1.000	7	0	0	0	0	10	6	8	7	0	1	8	8	1.400	6.30	62	2.73	.167	0	.000	-2	0	-0.2
1929	Bos-N	2	0	1.000	10	1	0	0	0	18^{1}	18	10	9	2	0	9	12	1.473	4.42	106	4.48	.277	0	.000	1	1	0.1
Total	**4**	**7**	**11**	**.389**	**59**	**13**	**3**	**0**	**2**	**158^{1}**	**161**	**90**	**77**	**4**	**1**	**82**	**65**	**1.535**	**4.38**	**84**	**4.05**	**.274**	**5**	**.132**	**-10**	**5**	**-1.1**

• HEARN, Bunny — Charles Bunn Hearn b: 5/21/1891, Chapel Hill, NC d: 10/19/1959, Wilson, NC BL/TL, 5'11", 190 lbs. Deb: 9/17/1910

YEAR	TM-L	W	L	PCT	G	GS	CG	SH	SV	IP	H	R	ER	HR	HB	BB	SO	RAT	ERA	ERA+	CERA	OAV	BH	AVG	PR+	WS	TPW
1910	StL-N	1	3	.250	5	5	4	0	0	39	49	22	22	2	1	16	14	1.667	5.08	59	5.54	.322	2	.133	-8	0	-0.8
1911	StL-N	0	0	....	2	0	0	0	0	2^{2}	7	4	4	1	0	0	1	2.625	13.50	25	18.09	.538	0	.000	-3	0	-0.3
1913	NY-N	1	1	.500	2	2	1	0	0	13	13	6	4	0	0	7	8	1.538	2.77	112	3.85	.277	2	.400	0	1	0.1
1915	Pit-F	6	11	.353	29	17	8	1	0	175^{2}	187	74	66	6	2	37	49	1.275	3.38	92	3.48	.285	10	.189	-5	8	-0.5
1918	Bos-N	5	6	.455	17	12	9	1	0	126^{1}	119	43	35	2	0	29	30	1.172	2.49	108	2.58	.256	8	.178	6	7	0.5
1920	Bos-N	0	3	.000	11	4	2	0	0	43	54	34	27	3	1	11	9	1.512	5.65	54	4.80	.329	2	.143	-13	0	-1.5
Total	**6**	**13**	**24**	**.351**	**66**	**40**	**24**	**2**	**0**	**399^{2}**	**429**	**183**	**158**	**14**	**4**	**100**	**111**	**1.324**	**3.56**	**84**	**3.65**	**.287**	**24**	**.180**	**-23**	**16**	**-2.6**

• HEARN, Jim — James Tolbert Hearn b: 4/11/1921, Atlanta, GA d: 6/10/1998, Boca Grande, FL BR/TR, 6'3", 205 lbs. Deb: 4/17/1947

YEAR	TM-L	W	L	PCT	G	GS	CG	SH	SV	IP	H	R	ER	HR	HB	BB	SO	RAT	ERA	ERA+	CERA	OAV	BH	AVG	PR+	WS	TPW
1947	StL-N	12	7	.632	37	21	4	1	1	162	151	67	58	9	1	63	57	1.321	3.22	128	3.32	.248	8	.145	16	13	1.5
1948	StL-N	8	6	.571	34	13	3	0	1	89^{2}	92	44	42	9	2	35	27	1.416	4.22	97	4.24	.271	5	.200	-1	5	-0.1
1949	StL-N	1	3	.250	17	4	0	0	0	42	48	27	24	3	2	23	18	1.690	5.14	81	5.25	.294	1	.100	-5	1	-0.5
1950	StL-N	0	1	.000	6	0	0	0	0	9	12	11	10	1	0	6	4	2.000	10.00	43	6.92	.333	1	1.000	-6	0	-0.5
	NY-N	11	3	.786	16	16	11	5	0	125	72	33	27	8	0	38	54	.880	**1.94**	211	1.50	.169	6	.136	26	15	2.5
	Yr.	11	4	.733	22	16	11	**5**	0	134	84	44	37	9	0	44	58	.955	2.49	167	1.86	.182	7	.156	20	15	2.0
1951*	NY-N	17	9	.654	34	34	11	0	0	211^{1}	204	102	85	21	2	82	66	1.353	3.62	108	3.78	.251	12	.162	7	14	0.6
1952	NY-N★	14	7	.667	37	34	11	1	1	223^{2}	208	113	94	16	5	97	89	1.364	3.78	98	3.59	.245	14	.182	-1	12	0.3
1953	NY-N	9	12	.429	36	32	6	0	0	196^{2}	206	111	99	22	3	84	77	1.475	4.53	95	4.45	.266	9	.136	-5	8	-0.5
1954	NY-N	8	8	.500	29	18	3	2	1	130	137	71	60	10	2	66	45	1.562	4.15	97	4.57	.272	5	.111	-3	6	-0.4
1955	NY-N	14	16	.467	39	33	11	1	0	226^{2}	225	107	94	27	3	66	86	1.284	3.73	108	3.76	.260	12	.156	7	14	0.9
1956	NY-N	5	11	.313	30	19	2	0	1	129^{1}	124	74	57	17	3	44	66	1.299	3.97	95	3.83	.254	4	.098	-2	5	-0.5
1957	Phi-N	5	1	.833	36	4	1	0	3	74	79	35	30	7	2	18	46	1.311	3.65	104	3.84	.274	0	.000	2	5	-0.1
1958	Phi-N	5	3	.625	39	1	0	0	0	73^{1}	88	45	34	6	0	27	33	1.568	4.17	95	4.69	.292	0	.000	-0	3	-0.2
1959	Phi-N	0	2	.000	6	0	0	0	0	11	15	7	7	2	0	6	1	1.909	5.73	70	7.36	.333	0	.000	-2	0	-0.2
Total	**13**	**109**	**89**	**.551**	**396**	**229**	**63**	**10**	**8**	**1703^{2}**	**1661**	**847**	**721**	**158**	**25**	**655**	**669**	**1.359**	**3.81**	**105**	**3.82**	**.255**	**77**	**.141**	**32**	**101**	**2.8**

• HEATH, Spencer — Spencer Paul Heath b: 11/15/1894, Chicago, IL d: 1/25/1930, Chicago, IL BB/TR, 6', 170 lbs. Deb: 5/4/1920

YEAR	TM-L	W	L	PCT	G	GS	CG	SH	SV	IP	H	R	ER	HR	HB	BB	SO	RAT	ERA	ERA+	CERA	OAV	BH	AVG	PR+	WS	TPW
1920	Chi-A	0	0	....	4	0	0	0	0	7	19	12	12	1	0	2	0	3.000	15.43	24	15.26	.475	0	.000	-9	0	-0.9

• HEATHCOCK, Jeff — Ronald Jeffrey Heathcock b: 11/18/1959, Covina, CA BR/TR, 6'4", 205 lbs. Deb: 9/3/1983

YEAR	TM-L	W	L	PCT	G	GS	CG	SH	SV	IP	H	R	ER	HR	HB	BB	SO	RAT	ERA	ERA+	CERA	OAV	BH	AVG	PR+	WS	TPW
1983	Hou-N	2	1	.667	6	3	0	0	1	28	19	14	10	1	1	4	12	.821	3.21	106	1.38	.181	0	.000	0	2	-0.1
1985	Hou-N	3	1	.750	14	7	1	0	1	56^{1}	50	25	21	9	1	13	25	1.118	3.36	103	3.32	.239	1	.063	0	3	0.0
1987	Hou-N	4	2	.667	19	2	0	0	1	42^{2}	44	15	15	4	1	9	15	1.242	3.16	124	3.63	.277	0	.000	4	4	0.3
1988	Hou-N	0	5	.000	17	1	0	0	0	31	33	25	20	2	1	16	12	1.581	5.81	57	4.30	.275	0	.000	-8	0	-0.9
Total	**4**	**9**	**9**	**.500**	**56**	**13**	**1**	**0**	**3**	**158**	**146**	**79**	**66**	**16**	**4**	**42**	**64**	**1.190**	**3.76**	**93**	**3.25**	**.246**	**1**	**.029**	**-4**	**9**	**-0.7**

• HEATHCOTT, Mike — Michael Joseph Heathcott b: 5/16/1969, Chicago, IL BR/TR, 6'3" Deb: 8/28/1998

YEAR	TM-L	W	L	PCT	G	GS	CG	SH	SV	IP	H	R	ER	HR	HB	BB	SO	RAT	ERA	ERA+	CERA	OAV	BH	AVG	PR+	WS	TPW
1998	Chi-A	0	0	....	1	0	0	0	0	3	2	1	1	0	0	1	3	1.000	3.00	152	1.57	.182	0		1	0	0.0

• HEATON, Neal — Neal Heaton b: 3/3/1960, South Ozone Park, NY BL/TL, 6'1", 205 lbs. Deb: 9/3/1982

YEAR	TM-L	W	L	PCT	G	GS	CG	SH	SV	IP	H	R	ER	HR	HB	BB	SO	RAT	ERA	ERA+	CERA	OAV	BH	AVG	PR+	WS	TPW
1982	Cle-A	0	2	.000	8	4	0	0	0	31	32	21	18	1	0	16	14	1.548	5.23	78	4.07	.260	0	....	-4	0	-0.4
1983	Cle-A	11	7	.611	39	16	4	3	7	149^{1}	157	79	69	11	1	44	75	1.346	4.16	102	3.68	.269	0	....	2	11	0.2
1984	Cle-A	12	15	.444	38	34	4	1	0	198^{2}	231	128	115	21	0	75	75	1.540	5.21	78	4.93	.293	0	....	-26	4	-2.6
1985	Cle-A	9	17	.346	36	33	5	1	0	207^{2}	244	119	113	19	7	80	82	1.560	4.90	84	5.15	.298	0	....	-17	7	-1.7
1986	Cle-A	3	6	.333	12	12	2	0	0	74^{1}	73	42	35	8	1	34	24	1.439	4.24	98	4.22	.254	0	....	-0	3	0.0
	Min-A	4	9	.308	21	17	3	0	1	124^{1}	128	60	55	18	1	47	66	1.408	3.98	108	4.56	.273	0	....	6	7	0.6
	Yr.	7	15	.318	33	29	5	0	1	198^{2}	201	102	90	26	2	81	90	1.419	4.08	104	4.44	.266	0	....	6	10	0.5
1987	Mon-N	13	10	.565	32	32	3	1	0	193^{1}	207	103	97	25	3	37	105	1.262	4.52	93	3.90	.273	14	.209	-4	10	-0.2
1988	Mon-N	3	10	.231	32	11	0	0	2	97^{1}	98	54	54	14	3	43	43	1.449	4.99	72	4.79	.271	3	.143	-17	0	-1.8
1989	Pit-N	6	7	.462	42	18	1	0	0	147^{1}	127	55	50	12	6	55	67	1.235	3.05	110	3.12	.233	9	.214	5	8	0.5
1990	Pit-N★	12	9	.571	30	24	0	0	0	146	143	66	56	17	2	38	68	1.240	3.45	105	3.64	.263	2	.047	1	8	-0.1
1991	Pit-N	3	3	.500	42	1	0	0	0	68^{2}	72	37	33	6	4	21	34	1.354	4.33	83	4.12	.275	4	.286	-6	2	-0.5
1992	KC-A	3	1	.750	31	0	0	0	0	41	43	21	19	5	1	22	29	1.585	4.17	97	5.08	.274	0	....	0	2	0.0
	Mil-A	0	0	....	1	0	0	0	0	1	0	0	0	0	0	1	2	1.000	0.00	....	0.95	.000	0	....	0	0	0.0
	Yr.	3	1	.750	32	0	0	0	0	42	43	21	19	5	1	23	31	1.571	4.07	100	4.98	.274	0	....	0	2	0.0
1993	NY-A	1	0	1.000	18	0	0	0	0	27	34	19	18	6	3	11	15	1.667	6.00	69	6.93	.301	0	....	-6	0	-0.5
Total	**12**	**80**	**96**	**.455**	**382**	**202**	**22**	**6**	**10**	**1507**	**1589**	**804**	**732**	**163**	**32**	**524**	**699**	**1.402**	**4.37**	**91**	**4.31**	**.274**	**32**	**.171**	**-65**	**62**	**-6.5**

• HEAVERLO, Dave — David Wallace Heaverlo b: 8/25/1950, Ellensburg, WA BR/TR, 6'2", 210 lbs. Deb: 4/14/1975

YEAR	TM-L	W	L	PCT	G	GS	CG	SH	SV	IP	H	R	ER	HR	HB	BB	SO	RAT	ERA	ERA+	CERA	OAV	BH	AVG	PR+	WS	TPW
1975	SF-N	3	1	.750	42	0	0	0	1	64	62	18	17	2	1	31	35	1.453	2.39	159	3.76	.262	2	.500	10	7	1.1
1976	SF-N	4	4	.500	61	0	0	0	1	75	85	45	37	2	2	15	40	1.333	4.44	82	3.53	.289	1	.333	-6	3	-0.6
1977	SF-N	5	1	.833	56	0	0	0	1	98^{2}	92	36	28	10	3	21	58	1.145	2.55	153	3.06	.251	0	.000	16	9	1.6
1978	Oak-A	3	6	.333	69	0	0	0	10	130	141	56	47	11	3	41	71	1.400	3.25	112	4.06	.281	0	....	8	10	0.8
1979	Oak-A	4	11	.267	62	0	0	0	9	85^{2}	97	42	40	7	4	42	40	1.623	4.20	96	4.85	.294	0	.000	1	6	0.1
1980	Sea-A	6	3	.667	60	0	0	0	4	78^{2}	75	37	34	9	5	35	42	1.398	3.89	106	4.13	.253	0	....	3	6	0.3
1981	Oak-A	1	0	1.000	6	0	0	0	0	5^{2}	7	1	1	0	0	3	2	1.765	1.59	219	4.70	.292	0	....	1	1	0.1
Total	**7**	**26**	**26**	**.500**	**356**	**0**	**0**	**0**	**26**	**537^{2}**	**559**	**235**	**204**	**41**	**18**	**188**	**288**	**1.389**	**3.41**	**112**	**3.91**	**.273**	**3**	**.231**	**33**	**42**	**3.4**

• HEBERT, Wally — Wallace Andrew "Preacher" Hebert b: 8/21/1907, Lake Charles, LA d: 12/8/1999, Westlake, LA BL/TL, 6'1", 195 lbs. Deb: 5/1/1931

YEAR	TM-L	W	L	PCT	G	GS	CG	SH	SV	IP	H	R	ER	HR	HB	BB	SO	RAT	ERA	ERA+	CERA	OAV	BH	AVG	PR+	WS	TPW
1931	StL-A	6	7	.462	23	13	5	0	0	103	128	70	58	11	3	43	26	1.660	5.07	91	5.71	.306	9	.209	-5	4	-0.6
1932	StL-A	1	12	.077	35	15	2	0	1	108^{1}	145	99	78	6	2	45	29	1.754	6.48	75	5.74	.322	12	.353	-20	1	-1.6
1933	StL-A	4	6	.400	33	10	3	0	0	88^{1}	114	58	52	4	1	35	19	1.687	5.30	88	5.20	.308	9	.391	-8	4	-0.4
1943	Pit-N	10	11	.476	34	23	12	1	0	184	197	75	61	3	2	45	41	1.315	2.98	116	3.24	.272	13	.220	10	11	1.2
Total	**4**	**21**	**36**	**.368**	**125**	**61**	**22**	**1**	**1**	**483^{2}**	**584**	**302**	**249**	**24**	**8**	**168**	**115**	**1.555**	**4.63**	**94**	**4.68**	**.297**	**43**	**.270**	**-23**	**20**	**-1.5**

• HEBSON, Bryan — Bryan McCall Hebson b: 3/12/1976, Columbus, GA BR/TR, 6'5", 210 lbs. Deb: 7/6/2003

YEAR	TM-L	W	L	PCT	G	GS	CG	SH	SV	IP	H	R	ER	HR	HB	BB	SO	RAT	ERA	ERA+	CERA	OAV	BH	AVG	PR+	WS	TPW
2003	Mon-N	0	0	....	2	0	0	0	0	2	4	3	3	1	1	1	1	2.500	13.50	37	17.51	.444	0	....	-2	0	-0.2

• HECKER, Guy — Guy Jackson Hecker b: 4/3/1856, Youngsville, PA d: 12/3/1938, Wooster, OH BR/TR, 6', 190 lbs. Deb: 5/2/1882 M/U ♦

YEAR	TM-L	W	L	PCT	G	GS	CG	SH	SV	IP	H	R	ER	HR	HB	BB	SO	RAT	ERA	ERA+	CERA	OAV	BH	AVG	PR+	WS	TPW
1882	Lou-a	6	6	.500	13	11	10	0	0	104	75	49	15	0	....	5	33	.769	1.30	191	....	**.188**	94	.276	13	17	2.0
1883	Lou-a	26	23	.531	53	52	51	3	0	469	526	298	167	4	....	75	164	1.281	3.20	93	....	.266	90	.271	-3	36	1.1

YEAR	TM-L	W	L	PCT	G	GS	CG	SH	SV	IP	H	R	ER	HR	HB	BB	SO	RAT	ERA	ERA+	CERA	OAV	BH	AVG	PR+	WS	TPW
1884	Lou-a	**52**	20	.722	**75**	**73**	**72**	6	0	**670^2**	526	230	134	4	16	56	**385**	.868	**1.80**	**171**	....	.204	94	.297	**71**	**74**	**9.1**
1885	Lou-a	30	23	.566	53	53	51	2	0	480	454	252	116	6	18	54	209	1.058	2.18	148	....	.239	81	.273	**57**	42	**5.8**
1886	Lou-a	26	23	.531	49	48	45	2	0	420^2	390	273	134	6	10	118	133	1.208	2.87	127	....	.235	117	.341	29	39	4.8
1887	Lou-a	18	12	.600	34	32	32	2	1	285^1	375	214	132	9	10	50	58	1.314	4.16	105	....	.306	149	.372	2	30	0.9
1888	Lou-a	8	17	.320	26	25	25	0	0	223^1	251	154	84	5	10	43	63	1.316	3.39	91	....	.274	48	.227	-2	9	-0.8
1889	Lou-a	5	13	.278	19	16	15	0	0	151^1	215	145	94	7	5	47	33	1.731	5.59	69	....	.324	93	.284	-27	7	-2.6
1890	Pit-N	2	9	.182	14	12	11	0	0	119^2	160	111	68	9	3	44	32	1.705	5.11	64	....	.311	77	.226	-18	5	-2.3
Total	9	173	146	.542	336	322	312	15	1	2924	2972	1726	944	50	72	492	1110	1.168	2.91	116	....	.251	843	.290	121	259	18.0

• HEDGPETH, Harry Harry Malcolm Hedgpeth b: 9/4/1888, Fayetteville, NC d: 7/30/1966, Richmond, VA BL/TL, 6'1.5", 194 lbs. Deb: 10/3/1913

YEAR	TM-L	W	L	PCT	G	GS	CG	SH	SV	IP	H	R	ER	HR	HB	BB	SO	RAT	ERA	ERA+	CERA	OAV	BH	AVG	PR+	WS	TPW
1913	Was-A	0	0	....	1	0	0	0	1	1	1	0	0	0	0	0	0	1.000	0.00	....	1.95	.250	0	....	0	0	0.0

• HEDLUND, Mike Michael David "Red" Hedlund b: 8/11/1946, Dallas, TX BR/TR, 6'1", 190 lbs. Deb: 5/8/1965

YEAR	TM-L	W	L	PCT	G	GS	CG	SH	SV	IP	H	R	ER	HR	HB	BB	SO	RAT	ERA	ERA+	CERA	OAV	BH	AVG	PR+	WS	TPW
1965	Cle-A	0	0	....	6	0	0	0	0	5^1	6	4	3	0	0	5	4	2.063	5.06	69	5.59	.286	0	.000	-1	0	-0.1
1968	Cle-A	0	0	....	3	0	0	0	0	1^2	6	2	2	0	1	2	0	4.800	10.80	27	28.54	.545	0	....	-1	0	-0.2
1969	KC-A	3	6	.333	34	16	1	0	2	125	123	53	45	8	1	40	74	1.304	3.24	114	3.41	.259	5	.152	8	8	0.8
1970	KC-A	2	3	.400	9	0	0	0	0	15	18	13	12	6	0	7	5	1.667	7.20	52	7.85	.300	0	.000	-6	0	-0.7
1971	KC-A	15	8	.652	32	30	7	1	0	205^2	168	68	62	15	1	72	76	1.167	2.71	126	2.79	.227	6	.088	18	16	1.5
1972	KC-A	5	7	.417	29	16	1	0	0	113	119	67	60	10	4	41	52	1.416	4.78	63	4.31	.275	6	.188	-21	0	-2.3
Total	6	25	24	.510	113	62	9	1	2	465^2	440	207	184	39	7	167	211	1.304	3.56	94	3.61	.253	17	.123	-4	24	-1.0

• HEFFNER, Bob Robert Frederic Heffner b: 9/13/1938, Allentown, PA BR/TR, 6'4", 205 lbs. Deb: 6/19/1963

YEAR	TM-L	W	L	PCT	G	GS	CG	SH	SV	IP	H	R	ER	HR	HB	BB	SO	RAT	ERA	ERA+	CERA	OAV	BH	AVG	PR+	WS	TPW
1963	Bos-A	4	9	.308	20	19	3	1	0	124^2	131	61	59	15	2	36	77	1.340	4.26	89	4.07	.267	5	.116	-6	4	-0.7
1964	Bos-A	7	9	.438	55	10	1	1	6	158^2	152	81	72	20	3	44	112	1.235	4.08	94	3.57	.251	7	.159	-0	8	0.0
1965	Bos-A	0	2	.000	27	1	0	0	0	49	59	42	39	9	1	18	42	1.571	7.16	52	5.82	.304	0	.000	-18	0	-2.0
1966	Cle-A	0	1	.000	5	1	0	0	0	13	12	6	5	1	0	3	7	1.154	3.46	99	2.81	.240	0	.000	0	0	0.0
1968	Cal-A	0	0	....	7	0	0	0	0	8	6	2	2	0	0	6	3	1.500	2.25	129	3.33	.240	0	....	0	1	0.1
Total	5	11	21	.344	114	31	4	2	6	353^1	360	192	177	45	6	107	241	1.322	4.51	84	4.02	.264	12	.128	-24	13	-2.6

• HEFLIN, Bronson Bronson Wayne Heflin b: 8/29/1971, Clarksville, TN BR/TR, 6'3", 195 lbs. Deb: 8/1/1996

YEAR	TM-L	W	L	PCT	G	GS	CG	SH	SV	IP	H	R	ER	HR	HB	BB	SO	RAT	ERA	ERA+	CERA	OAV	BH	AVG	PR+	WS	TPW
1996	Phi-N	0	0	....	3	0	0	0	0	6^2	11	7	5	1	0	3	4	2.100	6.75	64	8.56	.367	0	....	-2	0	-0.2

• HEFLIN, Randy Randolph Rutherford Heflin b: 9/11/1918, Fredericksburg, VA d: 8/17/1999, Fredericksburg, VA BL/TR, 6', 185 lbs. Deb: 6/9/1945

YEAR	TM-L	W	L	PCT	G	GS	CG	SH	SV	IP	H	R	ER	HR	HB	BB	SO	RAT	ERA	ERA+	CERA	OAV	BH	AVG	PR+	WS	TPW
1945	Bos-A	4	10	.286	20	14	6	2	0	102	102	52	46	3	4	61	39	1.598	4.06	84	4.41	.272	3	.086	-8	3	-1.2
1946	Bos-A	0	1	.000	5	1	0	0	0	14^2	16	5	4	0	1	12	6	1.909	2.45	149	5.47	.296	2	.667	2	1	0.3
Total	2	4	11	.267	25	15	6	2	0	116^2	118	57	50	3	5	73	45	1.637	3.86	89	4.54	.275	5	.132	-6	4	-0.9

• HEHL, Jake Herman Jacob Hehl b: 12/8/1899, Brooklyn, NY d: 7/4/1961, Brooklyn, NY BR/TR, 5'11", 180 lbs. Deb: 6/20/1918

YEAR	TM-L	W	L	PCT	G	GS	CG	SH	SV	IP	H	R	ER	HR	HB	BB	SO	RAT	ERA	ERA+	CERA	OAV	BH	AVG	PR+	WS	TPW
1918	Bro-N	0	0	....	1	0	0	0	0	1	0	0	0	0	1	0	0	.000	0.00	....	0.80	.000	0	....	0	0	0.0

• HEILMAN, Aaron Aaron Michael Heilman b: 11/12/1978, Logansport, IN BR/TR, 6'5", 220 lbs. Deb: 6/26/2003

YEAR	TM-L	W	L	PCT	G	GS	CG	SH	SV	IP	H	R	ER	HR	HB	BB	SO	RAT	ERA	ERA+	CERA	OAV	BH	AVG	PR+	WS	TPW
2003	NY-N	2	7	.222	14	13	0	0	0	65^1	79	53	49	13	3	41	51	1.837	6.75	62	7.16	.300	1	.045	-18	0	-2.0

• HEIMACH, Fred Frederick Amos "Lefty" Heimach b: 1/27/1901, Camden, NJ d: 6/1/1973, Fort Myers, FL BL/TL, 6', 175 lbs. Deb: 10/1/1920

YEAR	TM-L	W	L	PCT	G	GS	CG	SH	SV	IP	H	R	ER	HR	HB	BB	SO	RAT	ERA	ERA+	CERA	OAV	BH	AVG	PR+	WS	TPW
1920	Phi-A	0	1	.000	1	1	0	0	0	5	13	9	8	0	0	1	0	2.800	14.40	28	14.56	.542	0	.000	-6	0	-0.6
1921	Phi-A	1	0	1.000	1	1	1	1	0	9	7	0	0	0	0	1	1	.889	0.00	....	1.56	.226	1	.250	5	2	0.4
1922	Phi-A	7	11	.389	37	19	7	0	1	171^2	220	117	96	18	3	63	47	**1.649**	5.03	84	5.58	.316	15	.250	-13	7	-1.0
1923	Phi-A	6	12	.333	40	19	10	0	0	208^1	238	120	100	14	6	69	63	1.474	4.32	95	4.36	.292	30	.254	0	11	0.0
1924	Phi-A	14	12	.538	40	26	10	0	0	198	243	122	104	2	4	60	60	1.530	4.73	91	4.23	.306	29	.322	-8	13	-0.1
1925	Phi-A	0	1	.000	10	0	0	0	0	20^1	24	10	9	2	1	9	6	1.623	3.98	117	5.60	.312	1	.167	2	1	0.1
1926	Phi-A	1	0	1.000	13	1	0	0	0	31^2	28	14	10	1	0	5	8	1.042	2.84	147	2.15	.239	1	.100	5	3	0.4
	Bos-A	2	9	.182	20	13	6	0	0	102	119	72	64	5	0	42	17	1.578	5.65	72	4.65	.303	13	.295	-16	2	-1.3
	Yr.	3	9	.250	33	14	6	0	0	133^2	147	86	74	6	0	47	25	1.451	4.98	82	4.06	.288	14	.259	-11	5	-0.9
1928	NY-A	2	3	.400	13	9	5	0	0	68	66	30	25	3	1	16	25	1.206	3.31	113	2.59	.250	5	.167	4	4	0.3
1929	NY-A	11	6	.647	35	10	3	3	4	134^2	141	72	60	4	3	29	26	1.262	4.01	96	3.17	.272	9	.184	-4	9	-0.3
1930	Bro-N	0	2	.000	9	0	0	0	1	7^1	14	5	4	0	0	3	1	2.318	4.91	100	8.57	.424	1	.250	-0	0	0.0
1931	Bro-N	9	7	.563	31	10	7	1	1	135^1	145	66	52	6	1	23	43	1.241	3.46	110	3.18	.274	12	.197	7	10	0.8
1932	Bro-N	9	4	.692	36	15	7	0	0	167^2	203	85	74	7	6	28	30	1.378	3.97	96	4.00	.299	9	.164	-3	9	-0.3
1933	Bro-N	0	1	.000	10	3	0	0	0	29^2	49	33	33	2	2	11	7	2.022	10.01	32	7.80	.374	2	.200	-22	0	-2.3
Total	13	62	69	.473	296	127	56	5	7	1288^2	1510	755	639	64	27	360	334	1.451	4.46	90	4.23	.296	128	.236	-49	71	-3.9

• HEIMUELLER, Gorman Gorman John Heimueller b: 9/24/1955, Los Angeles, CA BL/TL, 6'4", 195 lbs. Deb: 7/12/1983

YEAR	TM-L	W	L	PCT	G	GS	CG	SH	SV	IP	H	R	ER	HR	HB	BB	SO	RAT	ERA	ERA+	CERA	OAV	BH	AVG	PR+	WS	TPW
1983	Oak-A	3	5	.375	16	14	2	1	0	83^2	93	43	41	8	1	29	31	1.458	4.41	87	4.52	.286	0	....	-6	3	-0.6
1984	Oak-A	0	1	.000	6	0	0	0	0	14^2	21	14	10	2	0	7	3	1.909	6.14	61	7.01	.344	0	....	-4	0	-0.4
Total	2	3	6	.333	22	14	2	1	0	98^1	114	57	51	10	1	36	34	1.525	4.67	82	4.89	.295	0	....	-10	3	-1.0

• HEINKEL, Don Donald Elliott Heinkel b: 10/20/1959, Racine, WI BL/TR, 6', 185 lbs. Deb: 4/7/1988

YEAR	TM-L	W	L	PCT	G	GS	CG	SH	SV	IP	H	R	ER	HR	HB	BB	SO	RAT	ERA	ERA+	CERA	OAV	BH	AVG	PR+	WS	TPW
1988	Det-A	0	0	....	21	0	0	0	1	36^1	30	17	16	4	1	12	30	1.156	3.96	96	2.97	.219	0	....	-1	2	-0.1
1989	StL-N	1	1	.500	7	5	0	0	0	26^1	40	19	17	2	0	7	16	1.785	5.81	62	6.31	.348	0	.000	-7	0	-0.7
Total	2	1	1	.500	28	5	0	0	1	62^2	70	36	33	6	1	19	46	1.420	4.74	78	4.37	.278	0	.000	-8	2	-0.8

• HEINTZELMAN, Ken Kenneth Alphonse Heintzelman b: 10/14/1915, Peruque, MO d: 8/14/2000, St. Peters, MO BR/TL, 5'11.5", 185 lbs. Deb: 10/3/1937

YEAR	TM-L	W	L	PCT	G	GS	CG	SH	SV	IP	H	R	ER	HR	HB	BB	SO	RAT	ERA	ERA+	CERA	OAV	BH	AVG	PR+	WS	TPW
1937	Pit-N	1	0	1.000	1	1	1	0	0	9	6	3	2	0	1	3	4	1.000	2.00	193	1.97	.207	0	.000	2	1	0.1
1938	Pit-N	0	0	....	1	0	0	0	0	2	1	2	2	0	0	3	1	2.000	9.00	42	4.52	.167	0	....	-1	0	-0.1
1939	Pit-N	1	1	.500	17	2	1	1	0	35^2	35	23	20	2	0	18	18	1.486	5.05	76	3.80	.250	2	.222	-4	1	-0.4
1940	Pit-N	8	8	.500	39	16	5	2	3	165	193	86	82	7	4	65	71	**1.564**	4.47	85	4.55	.292	9	.167	-7	6	-0.8
1941	Pit-N	11	11	.500	35	24	13	2	0	196	206	91	75	8	1	83	81	1.474	3.44	105	3.96	.272	8	.127	6	11	0.4
1942	Pit-N	8	11	.421	27	18	5	3	0	130	143	69	66	9	0	63	39	1.585	4.57	74	4.63	.281	3	.086	-16	3	-1.9
1946	Pit-N	8	12	.400	32	24	6	2	1	157^2	165	84	66	7	0	86	57	**1.592**	3.77	94	4.34	.271	6	.136	-2	7	-0.3
1947	Pit-N	0	0	....	2	1	0	0	0	4	9	11	9	2	0	6	2	3.750	20.25	21	20.88	.409	0	....	-7	0	-0.7
	Phi-N	7	10	.412	24	19	8	0	1	136	144	72	61	12	2	46	55	1.397	4.04	99	4.18	.277	5	.116	-1	7	-0.4
	Yr.	7	10	.412	26	20	8	0	1	140	153	83	70	14	2	52	57	1.464	4.50	90	4.66	.282	5	.116	-9	7	-1.0
1948	Phi-N	6	11	.353	27	16	5	2	2	130	117	66	62	10	1	45	57	1.246	4.29	92	3.17	.241	5	.135	-5	6	-0.6
1949	Phi-N	17	10	.630	33	32	15	**5**	0	250	239	96	84	19	1	93	65	1.328	3.02	130	3.56	.255	13	.157	23	23	2.2
1950*	Phi-N	3	9	.250	23	17	4	1	0	125^1	122	66	57	10	0	54	39	1.404	4.09	99	3.75	.250	2	.053	-1	5	-0.4
1951	Phi-N	6	12	.333	35	12	3	0	2	118^1	119	61	55	13	4	53	55	1.454	4.18	92	4.41	.267	3	.107	-4	5	-0.6
1952	Phi-N	1	3	.250	23	1	0	0	1	42^2	41	16	15	1	0	12	20	1.242	3.16	115	2.99	.266	0	.000	2	3	0.1
Total	13	77	98	.440	319	183	66	18	10	1501^2	1540	746	656	100	14	630	564	1.445	3.93	96	4.03	.267	56	.127	-16	78	-3.3

• HEISE, Clarence Clarence Edward "Lefty" Heise b: 8/7/1907, Topeka, KS d: 5/30/1999, Winter Park, FL BL/TL, 5'10", 172 lbs. Deb: 4/22/1934

YEAR	TM-L	W	L	PCT	G	GS	CG	SH	SV	IP	H	R	ER	HR	HB	BB	SO	RAT	ERA	ERA+	CERA	OAV	BH	AVG	PR+	WS	TPW
1934	StL-N	0	0	....	1	0	0	0	0	2	3	3	1	1	0	0	1	1.500	4.50	94	7.26	.300	0	....	-0	0	0.0

• HEISE, Jim James Edward Heise b: 10/2/1932, Scottdale, PA BR/TR, 6'1", 185 lbs. Deb: 6/29/1957

YEAR	TM-L	W	L	PCT	G	GS	CG	SH	SV	IP	H	R	ER	HR	HB	BB	SO	RAT	ERA	ERA+	CERA	OAV	BH	AVG	PR+	WS	TPW
1957	Was-A	0	3	.000	8	2	0	0	0	19	25	19	17	2	0	16	8	2.158	8.05	48	7.78	.329	0	.000	-8	0	-0.9

• HEISER, Roy Le Roy Barton Heiser b: 6/22/1942, Baltimore, MD BR/TR, 6'4", 190 lbs. Deb: 9/2/1961

YEAR	TM-L	W	L	PCT	G	GS	CG	SH	SV	IP	H	R	ER	HR	HB	BB	SO	RAT	ERA	ERA+	CERA	OAV	BH	AVG	PR+	WS	TPW
1961	Was-A	0	0	....	3	0	0	0	0	5^2	6	5	4	1	1	9	1	2.647	6.35	62	10.79	.261	0	.000	-2	0	-0.2

• HEISERMAN, Rick Richard Michael Heiserman b: 2/22/1973, Atlantic, IA BR/TR, 6'7", 225 lbs. Deb: 5/23/1999

YEAR	TM-L	W	L	PCT	G	GS	CG	SH	SV	IP	H	R	ER	HR	HB	BB	SO	RAT	ERA	ERA+	CERA	OAV	BH	AVG	PR+	WS	TPW
1999	StL-N	0	0	....	3	0	0	0	0	4^1	8	4	4	2	0	4	4	2.769	8.31	55	16.12	.400	0	.000	-2	0	-0.2

• HEISMANN, Crese Christian Ernest Heismann b: 4/16/1880, Cincinnati, OH d: 11/19/1951, Cincinnati, OH BR/TL, 6'2", 150 lbs. Deb: 9/25/1901

YEAR	TM-L	W	L	PCT	G	GS	CG	SH	SV	IP	H	R	ER	HR	HB	BB	SO	RAT	ERA	ERA+	CERA	OAV	BH	AVG	PR+	WS	TPW
1901	Cin-N	0	1	.000	3	2	1	0	0	13^{2}	18	9	9	1	3	6	6	1.756	5.93	54	6.63	.315	2	.400	-4	0	-0.3
1902	Cin-N	2	1	.667	5	3	2	0	0	33	33	18	9	1	5	10	15	1.303	2.45	122	3.68	.260	3	.214	1	2	0.2
	Bal-A	0	3	.000	3	3	2	0	0	16	20	17	15	1	2	12	2	2.000	8.44	45	6.95	.306	1	.143	-7	0	-0.8
Total	**2**	**2**	**5**	**.286**	**11**	**8**	**5**	**0**	**0**	**62^{2}**	**71**	**44**	**33**	**3**	**10**	**28**	**23**	**1.580**	**4.74**	**71**	**5.16**	**.285**	**6**	**.231**	**-10**	**2**	**-0.8**

• HEITMANN, Harry Henry Anton Heitmann b: 10/6/1896, Albany, NY d: 12/15/1958, Brooklyn, NY BR/TR, 6', 175 lbs. Deb: 7/27/1918

YEAR	TM-L	W	L	PCT	G	GS	CG	SH	SV	IP	H	R	ER	HR	HB	BB	SO	RAT	ERA	ERA+	CERA	OAV	BH	AVG	PR+	WS	TPW
1918	Bro-N	0	1	.000	1	1	0	0	0	0^{1}	4	4	4	0	0	0	0	12.00	108.00	3	120.07	1.000	0	....	-4	0	-0.4

• HELD, Mel Melvin Nicholas "Country" Held b: 4/12/1929, Edon, OH BR/TR, 6'1", 178 lbs. Deb: 4/27/1956

YEAR	TM-L	W	L	PCT	G	GS	CG	SH	SV	IP	H	R	ER	HR	HB	BB	SO	RAT	ERA	ERA+	CERA	OAV	BH	AVG	PR+	WS	TPW
1956	Bal-A	0	0	....	4	0	0	0	0	7	7	4	4	1	0	3	4	1.429	5.14	76	4.49	.318	0	....	-1	0	-0.1

• HELLING, Rick Ricky Allen Helling b: 12/15/1970, Devils Lake, ND BR/TR, 6'3", 215 lbs. Deb: 4/10/1994

YEAR	TM-L	W	L	PCT	G	GS	CG	SH	SV	IP	H	R	ER	HR	HB	BB	SO	RAT	ERA	ERA+	CERA	OAV	BH	AVG	PR+	WS	TPW
1994	Tex-A	3	2	.600	9	9	1	1	0	52	62	34	34	14	0	18	25	1.538	5.88	82	6.33	.295	0	....	-5	2	-0.4
1995	Tex-A	0	2	.000	3	3	0	0	0	12^{1}	17	11	9	2	2	8	5	2.027	6.57	73	8.81	.340	0	....	-2	0	-0.2
1996	Tex-A	1	2	.333	6	2	0	0	0	20^{1}	23	17	17	7	0	9	16	1.574	7.52	70	6.80	.280	0	....	-5	0	-0.5
	Fla-N	2	1	.667	5	4	0	0	0	27^{2}	14	6	6	2	0	7	26	.759	1.95	209	1.18	.143	1	.111	6	3	0.6
1997	Fla-N	2	6	.250	31	8	0	0	0	76	61	38	37	12	4	48	53	1.434	4.38	92	4.62	.232	1	.091	-3	3	-0.4
	Tex-A	3	3	.500	10	8	0	0	0	55	47	29	28	5	2	21	46	1.236	4.58	105	3.37	.235	0	.000	2	3	0.2
1998*	Tex-A	**20**	7	.741	33	33	4	2	0	216^{1}	209	109	106	27	1	78	164	1.327	4.41	109	3.86	.253	1	.200	13	15	1.2
1999*	Tex-A	13	11	.542	35	**35**	3	0	0	219^{1}	228	127	118	41	6	85	131	1.427	4.84	105	5.03	.272	0	.000	9	12	0.8
2000	Tex-A	16	13	.552	35	**35**	0	0	0	217	212	122	108	29	9	99	146	1.433	4.48	112	4.50	.252	0	.000	17	15	1.5
2001	Tex-A	12	11	.522	34	34	2	1	0	215^{2}	256	134	124	38	4	63	154	1.479	5.17	90	5.39	.297	0	.000	-10	7	-1.0
2002*	Ari-N	10	12	.455	30	30	0	0	0	175^{2}	180	94	88	31	6	48	120	1.298	4.51	98	4.29	.264	2	.043	1	8	-0.1
2003	Bal-A	7	8	.467	24	24	0	0	0	138^{2}	156	90	88	30	12	40	86	1.413	5.71	77	5.63	.286	0	.000	-20	3	-1.9
	*Fla-N	1	0	1.000	11	0	0	0	0	16^{1}	11	1	1	1	0	5	12	.980	0.55	743	1.93	.193	1	.500	6	3	0.7
Total	**10**	**90**	**78**	**.536**	**266**	**225**	**10**	**4**	**0**	**1442^{1}**	**1476**	**812**	**764**	**239**	**46**	**529**	**984**	**1.390**	**4.77**	**99**	**4.71**	**.266**	**6**	**.068**	**7**	**74**	**0.4**

• HELMBOLD, Horace Horace Willing Helmbold b: 8/27/1867, Philadelphia, PA Deb: 10/11/1890

YEAR	TM-L	W	L	PCT	G	GS	CG	SH	SV	IP	H	R	ER	HR	HB	BB	SO	RAT	ERA	ERA+	CERA	OAV	BH	AVG	PR+	WS	TPW
1890	Phi-a	0	1	.000	1	1	1	0	0	7	17	15	11	0	0	6	3	3.286	14.14	27	....	.451	0	.000	-8	0	-0.7

• HEMAN, Russ Russell Frederick Heman b: 2/10/1933, Olive, CA BR/TR, 6'4", 200 lbs. Deb: 4/20/1961

YEAR	TM-L	W	L	PCT	G	GS	CG	SH	SV	IP	H	R	ER	HR	HB	BB	SO	RAT	ERA	ERA+	CERA	OAV	BH	AVG	PR+	WS	TPW
1961	Cle-A	0	0	....	6	0	0	0	1	10	8	4	4	0	1	8	4	1.600	3.60	109	4.09	.216	0	.000	0	1	0.0
	LA-A	0	0	....	6	0	0	0	0	10	4	3	2	1	1	2	2	.600	1.80	250	1.07	.125	0	.000	3	1	0.3
	Yr.	0	0	....	12	0	0	0	1	20	12	7	6	1	2	10	6	1.100	2.70	152	2.58	.174	0	.000	3	2	0.3

• HEMMING, George George Earl "Old Wax Figger" Hemming b: 12/15/1868, Carrollton, OH d: 6/3/1930, Springfield, MA BR/TR, 5'11", 170 lbs. Deb: 4/21/1890 U

YEAR	TM-L	W	L	PCT	G	GS	CG	SH	SV	IP	H	R	ER	HR	HB	BB	SO	RAT	ERA	ERA+	CERA	OAV	BH	AVG	PR+	WS	TPW
1890	Cle-P	0	1	.000	3	1	1	0	0	21	25	23	16	1	2	19	3	2.095	6.86	58	....	.283	2	.182	-7	0	-0.6
	Bro-P	8	4	.667	19	11	11	0	3	123	117	86	52	3	3	59	32	1.431	3.80	117	....	.240	9	.158	8	10	0.3
	Yr.	8	5	.615	22	12	12	0	**3**	144	142	109	68	4	5	78	35	1.528	4.25	102	....	.247	11	.162	1	10	-0.3
1891	Bro-N	8	15	.348	27	22	19	1	1	199^{2}	231	173	110	11	11	84	83	1.578	4.96	67	....	.279	13	.159	-32	5	-2.9
1892	Cin-N	0	1	.000	1	0	0	0	0	6	10	6	5	1	0	2	0	2.000	7.50	44	8.40	.357	1	.333	-3	0	-0.3
	Lou-N	2	2	.500	4	4	4	0	0	35	36	25	18	1	0	17	12	1.514	4.63	66	3.93	.256	1	.077	-6	1	-0.7
	Yr.	2	3	.400	5	4	4	0	0	41	46	31	23	2	0	19	12	1.585	5.05	62	4.58	.272	2	.125	-9	1	-0.9
1893	Lou-N	18	17	.514	41	32	32	1	1	332	369	245	188	7	15	175	79	1.639	5.10	86	4.63	.273	32	.203	-21	18	-1.9
1894	Lou-N	13	19	.406	35	32	32	1	1	294^{1}	358	213	143	7	9	133	66	1.668	4.37	116	4.93	.297	33	.252	24	16	2.0
	*Bal-N	4	0	1.000	6	6	4	0	0	45^{1}	48	22	18	0	2	26	4	1.632	3.57	153	4.32	.269	6	.286	8	5	0.7
	Yr.	17	19	.472	41	38	36	1	1	339^{2}	406	235	161	7	11	159	70	1.663	4.27	120	4.85	.294	39	.257	32	21	2.7
1895	Bal-N	20	13	.606	34	31	26	1	0	262^{1}	288	155	118	10	6	96	43	1.464	4.05	117	4.04	.275	33	.282	5	24	0.6
1896	Bal-N	15	6	.714	25	21	20	3	0	202	233	113	94	9	3	54	33	1.421	4.19	102	4.01	.287	25	.258	-2	16	0.1
1897	Lou-N	3	4	.429	9	8	7	0	0	67	80	59	38	5	1	25	7	1.567	5.10	83	4.86	.294	5	.179	-6	2	-0.6
Total	**8**	**91**	**82**	**.526**	**204**	**168**	**156**	**7**	**6**	**1587^{2}**	**1795**	**1120**	**800**	**55**	**52**	**690**	**362**	**1.565**	**4.53**	**95**	**3.51**	**.279**	**160**	**.223**	**-33**	**97**	**-3.3**

• HENDERSON, Bernie Bernard "Barnyard" Henderson b: 4/12/1899, Douglasville, TX d: 6/4/1966, Linden, TX BR/TR, 5'9", 175 lbs. Deb: 9/5/1921

YEAR	TM-L	W	L	PCT	G	GS	CG	SH	SV	IP	H	R	ER	HR	HB	BB	SO	RAT	ERA	ERA+	CERA	OAV	BH	AVG	PR+	WS	TPW
1921	Cle-A	0	1	.000	2	1	0	0	0	3	5	5	3	0	0	0	1	1.667	9.00	47	5.02	.333	0	.000	-2	0	-0.1

• HENDERSON, Bill William Maxwell Henderson b: 11/4/1901, Pensacola, FL d: 10/6/1966, Pensacola, FL BR/TR, 6', 190 lbs. Deb: 6/20/1930

YEAR	TM-L	W	L	PCT	G	GS	CG	SH	SV	IP	H	R	ER	HR	HB	BB	SO	RAT	ERA	ERA+	CERA	OAV	BH	AVG	PR+	WS	TPW
1930	NY-A	0	0	....	3	0	0	0	0	8	7	6	4	1	0	4	2	1.375	4.50	95	3.74	.250	1	.500	-0	0	0.0

• HENDERSON, Ed Edward J. Henderson b: 12/25/1884, Newark, NJ d: 1/15/1964, New York, NY BL/TL, 5'9", 168 lbs. Deb: 5/15/1914

YEAR	TM-L	W	L	PCT	G	GS	CG	SH	SV	IP	H	R	ER	HR	HB	BB	SO	RAT	ERA	ERA+	CERA	OAV	BH	AVG	PR+	WS	TPW
1914	Pit-F	0	1	.000	6	1	1	0	0	16	14	8	7	2	0	8	4	1.375	3.94	78	3.85	.241	0	.000	-1	0	-0.2
	Ind-F	1	0	1.000	2	1	1	0	0	10	8	7	5	0	3	4	1	1.200	4.50	77	3.21	.229	0	.000	-1	0	-0.2
	Yr.	1	1	.500	8	2	2	0	0	26	22	15	12	2	3	12	5	1.308	4.15	78	3.60	.236	0	.000	-3	0	-0.4

• HENDERSON, Hardie James Harding Henderson b: 10/31/1862, Philadelphia, PA d: 2/6/1903, Philadelphia, PA BR/TR Deb: 5/2/1883 U

YEAR	TM-L	W	L	PCT	G	GS	CG	SH	SV	IP	H	R	ER	HR	HB	BB	SO	RAT	ERA	ERA+	CERA	OAV	BH	AVG	PR+	WS	TPW
1883	Phi-N	0	1	.000	1	1	1	0	0	9	26	24	19	0	....	2	2	3.111	19.00	16	....	.484	2	.250	-15	0	-1.3
	Bal-a	10	32	.238	45	42	38	0	0	358^{1}	383	315	160	4	....	87	145	1.312	4.02	86	....	.256	31	.162	-3	12	-1.0
1884	Bal-a	27	23	.540	52	52	50	4	0	439^{1}	382	235	128	9	16	116	346	1.134	2.62	132	....	.222	46	.227	49	32	4.9
1885	Bal-a	25	35	.417	61	61	59	0	0	539^{1}	539	311	191	7	19	117	263	1.216	3.19	102	....	.249	51	.223	16	36	1.9
1886	Bal-a	3	15	.167	19	19	19	0	0	171^{1}	188	147	88	0	9	66	88	1.482	4.62	74	....	.266	16	.235	-19	5	-1.4
	Bro-a	10	4	.714	14	14	14	0	0	124	112	82	40	2	0	51	49	1.315	2.90	120	....	.230	9	.180	9	9	0.7
	Yr.	13	19	.406	33	33	33	0	0	295^{1}	300	229	128	2	9	117	137	1.412	3.90	88	....	.252	25	.212	-10	14	-0.7
1887	Bro-a	5	8	.385	13	12	12	0	0	111^{2}	190	85	49	3	5	63	28	1.701	3.95	109	....	.363	11	.234	4	6	0.2
1888	Pit-N	1	3	.250	5	5	4	0	0	35^{1}	43	31	21	0	2	20	9	1.783	5.35	50	....	.290	5	.278	-10	0	-1.0
Total	**6**	**81**	**121**	**.401**	**210**	**206**	**197**	**4**	**0**	**1788^{1}**	**1863**	**1230**	**696**	**25**	**51**	**522**	**930**	**1.298**	**3.50**	**97**	**....**	**.255**	**171**	**.210**	**31**	**100**	**3.0**

• HENDERSON, Joe Joseph Lee Henderson b: 7/4/1946, Lake Cormorant, MS BL/TR, 6'2", 195 lbs. Deb: 6/7/1974

YEAR	TM-L	W	L	PCT	G	GS	CG	SH	SV	IP	H	R	ER	HR	HB	BB	SO	RAT	ERA	ERA+	CERA	OAV	BH	AVG	PR+	WS	TPW
1974	Chi-A	1	0	1.000	5	3	0	0	0	15	21	15	14	2	0	11	12	2.133	8.40	44	8.16	.328	0	.000	-8	0	-0.8
1976	Cin-N	2	0	1.000	4	0	0	0	0	11	9	1	0	0	0	8	7	1.545	0.00	....	3.16	.225	0	....	4	2	0.4
1977	Cin-N	0	2	.000	7	0	0	0	0	9	17	13	12	2	0	6	8	2.556	12.00	33	11.97	.386	0	.000	-8	0	-0.8
Total	**3**	**3**	**2**	**.600**	**16**	**3**	**0**	**0**	**0**	**35**	**47**	**29**	**26**	**4**	**0**	**25**	**27**	**2.057**	**6.69**	**57**	**7.57**	**.318**	**0**	**.000**	**-12**	**2**	**-1.2**

• HENDERSON, Rod Rodney Wood Henderson b: 3/11/1971, Greensburg, KY BR/TR, 6'4", 195 lbs. Deb: 4/19/1994

YEAR	TM-L	W	L	PCT	G	GS	CG	SH	SV	IP	H	R	ER	HR	HB	BB	SO	RAT	ERA	ERA+	CERA	OAV	BH	AVG	PR+	WS	TPW
1994	Mon-N	0	1	.000	3	2	0	0	0	6^{2}	9	9	7	1	0	7	3	2.400	9.45	45	9.02	.333	0	.000	-4	0	-0.4
1998	Mil-N	0	0	....	2	0	0	0	0	3^{2}	5	4	4	2	1	0	1	1.364	9.82	43	9.00	.313	0	....	-2	0	-0.2
Total	**2**	**0**	**1**	**.000**	**5**	**2**	**0**	**0**	**0**	**10^{1}**	**14**	**13**	**11**	**3**	**1**	**7**	**4**	**2.032**	**9.58**	**44**	**9.01**	**.326**	**0**	**.000**	**-6**	**0**	**-0.6**

• HENDLEY, Bob Charles Robert Hendley b: 4/30/1939, Macon, GA BR/TL, 6'2", 190 lbs. Deb: 6/23/1961

YEAR	TM-L	W	L	PCT	G	GS	CG	SH	SV	IP	H	R	ER	HR	HB	BB	SO	RAT	ERA	ERA+	CERA	OAV	BH	AVG	PR+	WS	TPW
1961	Mil-N	5	7	.417	19	13	3	0	0	97	96	46	42	8	0	39	44	1.392	3.90	96	3.92	.262	1	.032	-2	4	-0.4
1962	Mil-N	11	13	.458	35	29	7	2	1	200	188	90	80	17	0	59	112	1.235	3.60	105	3.22	.247	7	.119	4	13	0.5
1963	Mil-N	9	9	.500	41	24	7	3	3	169^{1}	153	80	74	16	1	64	105	1.281	3.93	82	3.44	.244	5	.106	-16	6	-1.9
1964	SF-N	10	11	.476	30	29	4	1	0	163^{1}	161	71	66	18	2	59	104	1.347	3.64	98	3.89	.258	5	.106	-3	8	-0.4
1965	SF-N	0	0	....	8	2	0	0	0	15	27	22	21	6	1	13	8	2.667	12.60	29	14.01	.397	0	.000	-15	0	-1.6
	Chi-N	4	4	.500	18	10	2	0	0	62	59	39	30	9	1	25	38	1.355	4.35	85	4.07	.244	0	.000	-4	2	-0.6
	Yr.	4	4	.500	26	12	2	0	0	77	86	61	51	15	2	38	46	1.610	5.96	61	6.01	.277	0	.000	-19	2	-2.2
1966	Chi-N	4	5	.444	43	6	0	0	7	89^{2}	98	46	39	10	0	39	65	1.528	3.91	94	4.76	.285	3	.167	-1	5	-0.1
1967	Chi-N	2	0	1.000	7	0	0	0	1	12^{1}	17	10	9	4	0	3	10	1.622	6.57	54	7.23	.315	0	.000	-4	0	-0.5
	NY-N	3	3	.500	15	13	2	0	0	70^{2}	65	35	27	11	1	28	36	1.316	3.44	98	3.91	.241	2	.111	-1	3	-0.1
	Yr.	5	3	.625	22	13	2	0	1	83	82	45	36	15	1	31	46	1.361	3.90	88	4.40	.253	2	.083	-5	3	-0.6
Total	**7**	**48**	**52**	**.480**	**216**	**126**	**25**	**6**	**12**	**879^{1}**	**864**	**439**	**388**	**99**	**6**	**329**	**522**	**1.357**	**3.97**	**90**	**3.97**	**.257**	**23**	**.095**	**-42**	**41**	**-5.1**

YEAR TM-L	W	L	PCT	G	GS	CG	SH	SV	IP	H	R	ER	HR	HB	BB	SO	RAT	ERA	ERA+	CERA	OAV	BH	AVG	PR+	WS	TPW
• HENDRICKS, Ed	Edward "Big Ed" Hendricks b: 6/20/1885, Zeeland, MI d: 11/28/1930, Jackson, MI BL/TL, 6'3", 200 lbs. Deb: 9/15/1910																									
1910 NY-N	0	1	.000	4	1	1	0	1	12	12	7	5	0	0	4	2	1.333	3.75	79	3.11	.261	0	.000	-1	0	-0.2
• HENDRICKSON, Don	Donald William Hendrickson b: 7/14/1913, Kewanna, IN d: 1/19/1977, Norfolk, VA BR/TR, 6'2", 204 lbs. Deb: 7/4/1945																									
1945 Bos-N	4	8	.333	37	2	1	0	5	73^{1}	74	46	40	8	1	39	14	1.541	4.91	78	4.55	.261	3	.167	-9	3	-0.9
1946 Bos-N	0	1	.000	2	0	0	0	0	2	4	2	1	0	0	2	2	3.000	4.50	76	10.69	.364	0	.000	-0	0	0.0
Total 2	4	9	.308	39	2	1	0	5	75^{1}	78	48	41	8	1	41	16	1.580	4.90	78	4.71	.265	3	.158	-9	3	-1.0
• HENDRICKSON, Mark	Mark Allan Hendrickson b: 6/23/1974, Mount Vernon, WA BL/TL, 6'9", 230 lbs. Deb: 8/6/2002																									
2002 Tor-A	3	0	1.000	16	4	0	0	0	36^{2}	25	11	10	1	2	12	21	1.009	2.45	188	1.90	.202	0	....	9	4	0.9
2003 Tor-A	9	9	.500	30	30	1	1	0	158^{1}	207	111	97	24	0	40	76	1.560	5.51	83	5.64	.317	1	.250	-13	5	-1.2
Total 2	12	9	.571	46	34	1	1	0	195	232	122	107	25	2	52	97	1.456	4.94	93	4.94	.298	1	.250	-4	9	-0.3
• HENDRIX, Claude	Claude Raymond Hendrix b: 4/13/1889, Olathe, KS d: 3/22/1944, Allentown, PA BR/TR, 6', 195 lbs. Deb: 6/7/1911																									
1911 Pit-N	4	6	.400	22	12	6	1	1	118^{2}	85	52	36	1	1	53	57	1.163	2.73	125	2.19	.204	4	.098	7	7	0.6
1912 Pit-N	24	9	.727	39	32	25	4	1	288^{2}	256	110	83	6	9	105	176	1.251	2.59	125	2.90	.246	39	.322	18	29	3.3
1913 Pit-N	14	15	.483	42	25	17	2	3	241	216	95	76	3	5	89	138	1.266	2.84	106	2.86	.248	27	.273	7	18	1.6
1914 Chi-F	**29**	10	.744	**49**	37	**34**	6	5	362	262	91	68	6	5	77	189	.936	**1.69**	174	**1.62**	**.203**	30	.231	42	**37**	**4.9**
1915 Chi-F	16	15	.516	40	31	26	5	4	285	256	120	95	7	2	84	107	1.193	3.00	93	2.67	.241	30	.265	-6	18	0.6
1916 Chi-N	8	16	.333	36	24	15	3	2	218	193	81	65	4	6	67	117	1.193	2.68	108	2.63	.242	16	.200	8	15	1.3
1917 Chi-N	10	12	.455	40	21	13	1	1	215	202	94	62	3	4	72	81	1.274	2.60	111	2.95	.257	22	.256	10	13	1.6
1918* Chi-N	20	7	.741	32	27	21	3	0	233	229	87	72	2	5	54	86	1.215	2.78	100	2.76	.259	24	.264	6	18	1.6
1919 Chi-N	10	14	.417	33	25	15	2	0	206^{1}	208	79	60	3	9	42	69	1.212	2.62	110	2.91	.266	15	.192	8	12	0.8
1920 Chi-N	9	12	.429	27	23	12	0	0	203^{2}	216	101	81	6	3	54	72	1.326	3.58	89	3.36	.273	15	.181	-6	7	-0.8
Total 10	144	116	.554	360	257	184	27	17	2371^{1}	2123	910	698	41	49	697	1092	1.189	2.65	112	2.64	.243	222	.241	93	174	15.5
• HENION, Lafayette	Lafayette Marion Henion b: 6/7/1899, Eureka, CA d: 7/22/1955, San Luis Obispo, CA BR/TR, 5'11", 154 lbs. Deb: 9/10/1919																									
1919 Bro-N	0	0	....	1	0	0	0	0	3	2	2	2	0	0	2	2	1.333	6.00	49	2.62	.200	0	.000	-1	0	-0.1
• HENKE, Tom	Thomas Anthony "The Terminator" Henke b: 12/21/1957, Kansas City, MO BR/TR, 6'5", 215 lbs. Deb: 9/10/1982																									
1982 Tex-A	1	0	1.000	8	0	0	0	0	15^{2}	14	2	2	0	1	8	9	1.404	1.15	337	3.30	.246	0	....	5	2	0.5
1983 Tex-A	1	0	1.000	8	0	0	0	1	16	16	6	6	1	0	4	17	1.250	3.38	119	3.34	.262	0	....	1	2	0.1
1984 Tex-A	1	1	.500	25	0	0	0	2	28^{1}	36	21	20	0	1	20	25	1.976	6.35	65	5.97	.313	0	....	-7	0	-0.7
1985* Tor-A	3	3	.500	28	0	0	0	13	40	29	12	9	4	0	8	42	.925	2.03	208	1.92	.206	0	....	9	9	0.9
1986 Tor-A	9	5	.643	63	0	0	0	27	91^{1}	63	39	34	6	1	32	118	1.040	3.35	126	2.03	.191	0	....	9	15	0.9
1987 Tor-A★	0	6	.000	72	0	0	0	**34**	94	62	27	26	10	0	25	128	.926	2.49	180	1.87	.188	0	....	20	18	1.9
1988 Tor-A	4	4	.500	52	0	0	0	25	68	60	23	22	6	2	24	66	1.235	2.91	135	3.22	.237	0	....	7	10	0.7
1989* Tor-A	8	3	.727	64	0	0	0	20	89	66	20	19	5	2	25	116	1.022	1.92	188	2.05	.205	0	....	17	15	1.7
1990 Tor-A	2	4	.333	61	0	0	0	32	74^{2}	58	18	18	8	1	19	75	1.031	2.17	189	2.43	.213	0	....	16	14	1.6
1991* Tor-A	0	2	.000	49	0	0	0	32	50^{1}	33	13	13	4	0	11	53	.874	2.32	181	1.60	.184	0	....	11	12	1.1
1992* Tor-A	3	2	.600	57	0	0	0	34	55^{2}	40	19	14	5	0	22	46	1.114	2.26	180	2.43	.197	0	....	11	11	1.2
1993 Tex-A	5	5	.500	66	0	0	0	40	74^{1}	55	25	24	7	1	27	79	1.103	2.91	143	2.52	.205	0	....	12	14	1.1
1994 Tex-A	3	6	.333	37	0	0	0	15	38	33	16	16	6	0	12	39	1.184	3.79	127	3.42	.232	0	....	5	6	0.5
1995 StL-N★	1	1	.500	52	0	0	0	36	54^{1}	42	11	11	2	0	18	48	1.104	1.82	230	2.22	.209	0	.000	14	12	1.3
Total 14	41	42	.494	642	0	0	0	311	789^{2}	607	252	234	64	9	255	861	1.092	2.67	156	2.47	.211	0	.000	130	140	12.9
• HENLEY, Weldon	Weldon Henley b: 10/25/1880, Jasper, GA d: 11/16/1960, Palatka, FL BR/TR, 6', 175 lbs. Deb: 4/23/1903																									
1903 Phi-A	12	10	.545	29	21	13	1	0	186^{1}	186	108	81	3	12	67	86	1.358	3.91	78	3.43	.259	9	.132	-16	6	-2.0
1904 Phi-A	15	17	.469	36	34	31	5	0	295^{2}	245	126	83	3	19	76	130	1.086	2.53	106	2.19	.227	24	.222	12	16	1.6
1905 Phi-A	4	11	.267	25	19	13	1	0	183^{2}	155	74	53	4	9	67	82	1.209	2.60	102	2.69	.231	11	.169	7	10	0.6
1907 Bro-N	1	5	.167	7	7	5	0	0	56	54	31	19	2	1	21	11	1.339	3.05	76	3.64	.273	4	.200	-4	1	-0.4
Total 4	32	43	.427	97	81	62	7	0	721^{2}	640	339	236	12	41	231	309	1.207	2.94	94	2.75	.240	48	.184	-1	33	-0.2
• HENNEMAN, Mike	Michael Alan Henneman b: 12/11/1961, St. Charles, MO BR/TR, 6'4", 195 lbs. Deb: 5/11/1987																									
1987* Det-A	11	3	.786	55	0	0	0	7	96^{2}	86	36	32	8	3	30	75	1.200	2.98	142	3.09	.238	0	.000	13	12	1.2
1988 Det-A	9	6	.600	65	0	0	0	22	91^{1}	72	23	19	7	2	24	58	1.051	1.87	204	2.26	.218	0	....	19	17	1.9
1989 Det-A★	11	4	.733	60	0	0	0	8	90	84	46	37	4	5	51	69	1.500	3.70	103	3.86	.251	0	....	2	8	0.2
1990 Det-A	8	6	.571	69	0	0	0	22	94^{1}	90	36	32	4	3	33	50	1.304	3.05	130	3.17	.253	0	....	7	12	0.7
1991 Det-A	10	2	.833	60	0	0	0	21	84^{1}	81	29	27	2	0	34	61	1.364	2.88	144	3.21	.258	0	....	12	13	1.2
1992 Det-A	2	6	.250	60	0	0	0	24	77^{1}	75	36	34	6	0	20	58	1.228	3.96	100	3.02	.256	0	....	1	8	0.1
1993 Det-A	5	3	.625	63	0	0	0	24	71^{2}	69	28	21	4	2	32	58	1.409	2.64	163	3.59	.251	0	....	13	11	1.3
1994 Det-A	1	3	.250	30	0	0	0	8	34^{2}	43	27	20	5	2	17	27	1.731	5.19	93	5.89	.297	0	....	-1	2	-0.1
1995 Det-A	0	1	.000	29	0	0	0	18	29^{1}	24	5	5	0	0	9	24	1.125	1.53	310	2.12	.222	0	....	11	7	1.0
Hou-N	0	1	.000	21	0	0	0	8	21	21	7	7	1	2	4	19	1.190	3.00	129	3.26	.266	0	....	2	3	0.2
1996* Tex-A	0	7	.000	49	0	0	0	31	42	41	28	27	6	0	17	34	1.381	5.79	91	4.03	.258	0	....	-3	5	-0.2
Total 10	57	42	.576	561	0	0	0	193	732^{2}	686	301	261	47	19	271	533	1.306	3.21	130	3.30	.249	0	.000	77	98	7.6
• HENNESSEY, George	George "Three Star" Hennessey b: 10/28/1907, Slatington, PA d: 1/15/1988, Princeton, NJ BR/TR, 5'10", 168 lbs. Deb: 9/2/1937																									
1937 StL-A	0	1	.000	5	0	0	0	0	7	15	8	8	2	0	6	4	3.000	10.29	47	16.84	.500	0	....	-4	0	-0.4
1942 Phi-N	1	1	.500	5	1	0	0	0	17	11	5	5	1	0	10	2	1.235	2.65	125	2.49	.180	0	.000	1	2	0.1
1945 Chi-N	0	0	....	2	0	0	0	0	3^{2}	7	3	3	0	0	1	2	2.182	7.36	50	9.02	.438	0	....	-2	0	-0.2
Total 3	1	2	.333	12	1	0	0	0	27^{2}	33	16	16	3	0	17	8	1.807	5.20	77	6.99	.308	0	.000	-4	2	-0.5
• HENNIGAN, Phil	Phillip Winston Hennigan b: 4/10/1946, Jasper, TX BR/TR, 5'11.5", 185 lbs. Deb: 9/2/1969																									
1969 Cle-A	2	1	.667	9	0	0	0	0	16^{1}	14	6	6	0	1	4	10	1.102	3.31	114	2.28	.241	0	.000	1	1	0.1
1970 Cle-A	6	3	.667	42	1	0	0	3	71^{2}	69	34	32	7	4	44	43	1.577	4.02	98	4.91	.263	1	.143	-1	6	0.0
1971 Cle-A	4	3	.571	57	0	0	0	14	82	80	45	45	13	3	51	69	1.598	4.94	77	5.34	.261	0	.000	-11	4	-1.2
1972 Cle-A	5	3	.625	38	1	0	0	6	67^{1}	54	20	20	8	2	18	44	1.069	2.67	120	2.73	.226	1	.083	3	8	0.4
1973 NY-N	0	4	.000	30	0	0	0	3	43^{1}	50	30	30	6	1	16	22	1.523	6.23	58	4.91	.289	1	.333	-13	0	-1.3
Total 5	17	14	.548	176	2	0	0	26	280^{2}	267	135	133	34	11	133	188	1.425	4.26	87	4.36	.257	3	.100	-20	19	-2.0
• HENNING, Pete	Ernest Herman Henning b: 12/28/1887, Crown Point, IN d: 11/4/1939, Dyer, IN BR/TR, 5'11", 185 lbs. Deb: 4/17/1914																									
1914 KC-F	5	10	.333	28	14	7	0	2	138	153	88	74	5	7	58	45	1.529	4.83	64	4.59	.291	8	.182	-27	2	-2.8
1915 KC-F	9	15	.375	40	20	15	1	2	207	181	88	73	5	3	76	73	1.242	3.17	92	2.80	.235	14	.206	-5	10	-0.6
Total 2	14	25	.359	68	34	22	1	4	345	334	176	147	10	10	134	118	1.357	3.83	78	3.51	.258	22	.196	-32	12	-3.3
• HENNINGER, Rick	Richard Lee Henninger b: 1/11/1948, Hastings, NE BR/TR, 6'6", 225 lbs. Deb: 9/3/1973																									
1973 Tex-A	1	0	1.000	6	2	0	0	0	23	23	8	7	1	0	11	6	1.478	2.74	136	3.91	.261	0	....	3	2	0.3
• HENNIS, Randy	Randall Philip Hennis b: 12/16/1965, Clearlake, CA BR/TR, 6'6", 220 lbs. Deb: 9/17/1990																									
1990 Hou-N	0	0	....	3	1	0	0	0	9^{2}	1	0	0	0	1	3	4	.414	0.00	....	0.34	.033	0	.000	4	1	0.4
• HENRIQUEZ, Oscar	Oscar Eduardo Henriquez b: 1/28/1974, La Guaira, Venezuela BR/TR, 6'6", 220 lbs. Deb: 9/7/1997																									
1997 Hou-N	0	1	.000	4	0	0	0	0	4	2	2	2	0	1	3	3	1.250	4.50	89	2.99	.167	0	....	-0	0	0.0
1998 Fla-N	0	0	....	15	0	0	0	0	20	26	22	19	4	1	12	19	1.900	8.55	48	7.53	.306	0	.000	-10	0	-1.0
2002 Det-A	1	1	.500	30	0	0	0	2	28	19	14	14	5	1	15	23	1.214	4.50	96	3.37	.196	0	....	-0	2	0.0
Total 3	1	2	.333	49	0	0	0	2	52	47	38	35	9	3	30	45	1.481	6.06	69	4.94	.242	0	.000	-10	2	-1.0
• HENRY, Bill	William Francis Henry b: 2/15/1942, Long Beach, CA BL/TL, 6'3", 195 lbs. Deb: 9/13/1966																									
1966 NY-A	0	0	....	2	0	0	0	0	3	0	0	0	0	0	2	3	.667	0.00	....	0.46	.000	0	....	1	0	0.1

• HENRY, Bill

William Rodman Henry b: 10/15/1927, Alice, TX BL/TL, 6'2", 180 lbs. Deb: 4/17/1952

YEAR TM-L	W	L	PCT	G	GS	CG	SH	SV	IP	H	R	ER	HR	HB	BB	SO	RAT	ERA	ERA+	CERA	OAV	BH	AVG	PR+	WS	TPW
1952 Bos-A	5	4	.556	13	10	5	0	0	76^2	75	40	33	7	2	36	23	1.448	3.87	102	4.12	.254	8	.258	0	5	0.2
1953 Bos-A	5	5	.500	21	12	4	1	1	85^2	86	39	31	4	4	33	56	1.389	3.26	129	3.73	.260	6	.188	9	7	0.8
1954 Bos-A	3	7	.300	24	13	3	1	0	95^2	104	56	48	9	1	49	38	1.599	4.52	91	4.75	.270	4	.118	-3	2	-0.5
1955 Bos-A	2	4	.333	17	7	0	0	0	59^2	56	28	22	7	0	21	23	1.291	3.32	129	3.57	.247	2	.105	7	4	0.6
1958 Chi-N	5	4	.556	44	0	0	0	6	81^1	63	27	26	8	1	17	58	.984	2.88	136	2.20	.214	4	.235	10	9	1.1
1959 Chi-N	9	8	.529	**65**	0	0	0	12	134^1	111	42	40	19	1	26	115	1.020	2.68	147	2.67	.227	6	.194	18	16	1.8
1960 Cin-N★	1	5	.167	51	0	0	0	17	67^2	62	25	24	8	4	20	58	1.212	3.19	120	3.53	.247	0	.000	5	8	0.4
1961* Cin-N	2	1	.667	47	0	0	0	16	53^1	50	18	13	8	0	15	53	1.219	2.19	185	3.43	.244	0	.000	11	10	1.0
1962 Cin-N	4	2	.667	40	0	0	0	11	37^1	40	21	19	5	1	20	35	1.607	4.58	88	5.20	.280	1	.333	-3	3	-0.2
1963 Cin-N	1	3	.250	47	0	0	0	14	52	55	30	24	4	1	11	45	1.269	4.15	81	3.56	.279	1	.167	-5	4	-0.5
1964 Cin-N	2	2	.500	37	0	0	0	6	52	31	9	5	2	3	12	28	.827	0.87	417	1.35	.170	3	.500	15	9	1.7
1965 Cin-N	2	0	1.000	3	0	0	0	0	5	3	0	0	0	0	1	5	.800	0.00	....	1.17	.176	0	....	2	1	0.2
SF-N	2	2	.500	35	0	0	0	4	42	40	18	17	2	1	8	35	1.143	3.64	99	2.65	.248	1	.200	0	3	0.0
Yr.	4	2	.667	38	0	0	0	4	47	43	18	17	2	1	9	40	1.106	3.26	111	2.49	.242	1	.200	2	4	0.3
1966 SF-N	1	1	.500	35	0	0	0	1	22	15	6	6	3	1	10	15	1.136	2.45	149	2.71	.190	0	.000	3	2	0.3
1967 SF-N	2	0	1.000	28	1	0	0	2	21^2	16	5	5	1	2	9	23	1.154	2.08	158	2.33	.198	0	.000	3	3	0.3
1968 SF-N	0	2	.000	7	1	0	0	0	5	4	3	3	0	1	3	0	1.400	5.40	54	3.66	.250	0	....	-1	0	-0.2
Pit-N	0	0	....	10	0	0	0	0	16^2	29	18	15	2	2	3	9	1.920	8.10	36	8.40	.382	0	.000	-10	0	-1.2
Yr.	0	2	.000	17	1	0	0	0	21^2	33	21	18	2	3	6	9	1.800	7.48	39	7.30	.359	0	.000	-11	0	-1.3
1969 Hou-N	0	0	....	3	0	0	0	0	5	2	1	0	0	0	2	2	.800	0.00	....	0.91	.111	0	....	2	1	0.2
Total 16	46	50	.479	527	44	12	2	90	913	842	386	331	89	25	296	621	1.246	3.26	118	3.40	.244	36	.177	63	87	6.3

• HENRY, Butch

Floyd Bluford Henry b: 10/7/1968, El Paso, TX BL/TL, 6'1", 205 lbs. Deb: 4/9/1992

YEAR TM-L	W	L	PCT	G	GS	CG	SH	SV	IP	H	R	ER	HR	HB	BB	SO	RAT	ERA	ERA+	CERA	OAV	BH	AVG	PR+	WS	TPW
1992 Hou-N	6	9	.400	28	28	2	1	0	165^2	185	81	74	16	1	41	96	1.364	4.02	84	4.05	.285	8	.148	-12	4	-1.2
1993 Col-N	2	8	.200	20	15	1	0	0	84^2	117	66	62	14	1	24	39	1.665	6.59	72	6.32	.331	2	.091	-14	1	-1.5
Mon-N	1	1	.500	10	1	0	0	0	18^1	18	10	8	1	0	4	8	1.200	3.93	106	2.92	.250	0	.000	0	1	0.0
Yr.	3	9	.250	30	16	1	0	0	103	135	76	70	15	1	28	47	1.583	6.12	77	5.71	.317	2	.083	-14	2	-1.5
1994 Mon-N	8	3	.727	24	15	0	0	1	107^1	97	30	29	10	2	20	70	1.090	2.43	174	2.77	.241	9	.290	22	12	2.4
1995 Mon-N	7	9	.438	21	21	1	1	0	126^2	133	47	40	11	2	28	60	1.271	2.84	151	3.65	.275	2	.048	22	10	1.8
1997 Bos-A	7	3	.700	36	5	0	0	6	84^1	89	36	33	6	0	19	51	1.281	3.52	132	3.57	.277	0	....	11	9	1.0
1998 Bos-A	0	0	....	2	2	0	0	0	9	8	4	4	2	1	3	6	1.222	4.00	118	4.51	.235	0	....	1	0	0.1
1999 Sea-A	2	0	1.000	7	4	0	0	0	25	30	15	14	1	2	10	15	1.600	5.04	99	5.20	.303	0	....	-0	1	0.0
Total 7	33	33	.500	148	91	4	2	7	621	677	289	264	61	9	149	345	1.330	3.83	108	4.01	.280	21	.139	29	38	2.5

• HENRY, Doug

Richard Douglas Henry b: 12/10/1963, Sacramento, CA BR/TR, 6'4", 205 lbs. Deb: 7/15/1991

YEAR TM-L	W	L	PCT	G	GS	CG	SH	SV	IP	H	R	ER	HR	HB	BB	SO	RAT	ERA	ERA+	CERA	OAV	BH	AVG	PR+	WS	TPW
1991 Mil-A	2	1	.667	32	0	0	0	15	36	16	4	4	1	0	14	28	.833	1.00	397	1.13	.133	0	....	12	9	1.2
1992 Mil-A	1	4	.200	68	0	0	0	29	65	64	34	29	6	0	24	52	1.354	4.02	96	3.72	.256	0	....	-3	6	-0.3
1993 Mil-A	4	4	.500	54	0	0	0	17	55	67	37	34	7	3	25	38	1.673	5.56	76	5.61	.300	0	....	-8	3	-0.7
1994 Mil-A	2	3	.400	25	0	0	0	0	31^1	32	17	16	7	1	23	20	1.755	4.60	109	6.83	.271	0	.000	1	2	0.0
1995 NY-N	3	6	.333	51	0	0	0	4	67	48	23	22	7	1	25	62	1.090	2.96	137	2.42	.198	1	1.000	8	7	0.8
1996 NY-N	2	8	.200	58	0	0	0	9	75	82	48	39	7	1	36	58	1.573	4.68	86	4.69	.273	0	.000	-6	3	-0.7
1997* SF-N	4	5	.444	75	0	0	0	3	70^2	70	45	37	5	1	41	69	1.571	4.71	86	4.41	.261	0	.000	-5	3	-0.5
1998* Hou-N	8	2	.800	59	0	0	0	2	71	55	25	24	9	0	35	59	1.268	3.04	133	3.30	.216	0	.000	8	7	0.7
1999* Hou-N	2	3	.400	35	0	0	0	2	40^2	45	24	21	8	3	24	36	1.697	4.65	95	6.64	.281	0	.000	-1	2	-0.1
2000 Hou-N	1	3	.250	45	0	0	0	1	53	39	26	26	10	3	28	46	1.264	4.42	110	3.89	.204	0	.000	4	4	0.3
* SF-N	3	1	.750	27	0	0	0	0	25^1	18	10	7	2	1	21	16	1.539	2.49	170	4.19	.214	0	....	5	2	0.5
Yr.	4	4	.500	72	0	0	0	1	78^1	57	36	33	12	4	49	62	1.353	3.79	124	3.99	.207	0	.000	8	6	0.8
2001 KC-A	2	2	.500	53	0	0	0	0	75^2	75	53	51	14	3	45	57	1.586	6.07	81	5.59	.262	0	....	-12	2	-1.1
Total 11	34	42	.447	582	0	0	0	82	665^2	611	346	310	83	17	341	541	1.430	4.19	103	4.31	.245	1	.059	2	50	0.1

• HENRY, Dutch

Frank John Henry b: 5/12/1902, Cleveland, OH d: 8/23/1968, Cleveland, OH BL/TL, 6'1", 175 lbs. Deb: 9/15/1921

YEAR TM-L	W	L	PCT	G	GS	CG	SH	SV	IP	H	R	ER	HR	HB	BB	SO	RAT	ERA	ERA+	CERA	OAV	BH	AVG	PR+	WS	TPW
1921 StL-A	0	0	....	1	0	0	0	0	2	2	1	1	0	0	0	1	1.000	4.50	99	1.68	.250	1	1.000	0	0	0.0
1922 StL-A	0	0	....	4	0	0	0	0	5	7	3	3	0	0	5	3	2.400	5.40	77	6.54	.280	0	....	-1	0	-0.1
1923 Bro-N	4	6	.400	17	9	5	2	0	94^1	105	55	41	9	2	28	28	1.410	3.91	99	4.23	.281	8	.229	-0	5	0.1
1924 Bro-N	1	2	.333	16	4	0	0	0	46	69	33	29	0	0	15	11	1.826	5.67	66	5.85	.352	5	.250	-9	0	-0.8
1927 NY-N	11	6	.647	45	15	7	1	4	163^2	184	93	77	6	0	31	40	1.314	4.23	91	3.35	.278	13	.236	-6	9	-0.5
1928 NY-N	3	6	.333	17	8	4	0	1	64	82	36	27	4	1	25	23	1.672	3.80	103	5.44	.325	3	.158	0	3	0.0
1929 NY-N	5	6	.455	27	9	4	0	1	101^1	129	52	43	10	1	31	27	1.579	3.82	120	5.29	.316	7	.250	7	7	0.8
Chi-A	1	0	1.000	2	1	1	0	0	15	20	12	10	1	0	7	2	1.800	6.00	71	5.68	.308	1	.143	-3	0	-0.3
1930 Chi-A	2	17	.105	35	16	4	0	0	155	211	116	84	12	4	48	35	**1.671**	4.88	95	5.71	.331	12	.235	-0	5	0.1
Total 8	27	43	.386	164	62	25	3	6	646^1	809	401	315	42	8	190	170	1.546	4.39	94	4.80	.308	50	.231	-12	29	-0.7

• HENRY, Dwayne

Dwayne Allen Henry b: 2/16/1962, Elkton, MD BR/TR, 6'3", 205 lbs. Deb: 9/7/1984

YEAR TM-L	W	L	PCT	G	GS	CG	SH	SV	IP	H	R	ER	HR	HB	BB	SO	RAT	ERA	ERA+	CERA	OAV	BH	AVG	PR+	WS	TPW
1984 Tex-A	0	1	.000	3	0	0	0	0	4^1	5	4	4	0	0	7	2	2.769	8.31	50	8.92	.294	0	....	-2	0	-0.2
1985 Tex-A	2	2	.500	16	0	0	0	3	21	16	7	6	0	0	7	20	1.095	2.57	165	1.94	.211	0	....	4	3	0.4
1986 Tex-A	1	0	1.000	19	0	0	0	0	19^1	14	11	10	1	1	22	17	1.862	4.66	92	5.17	.209	0	....	-1	1	-0.1
1987 Tex-A	0	0	....	5	0	0	0	0	10	12	10	10	2	0	9	7	2.100	9.00	50	8.26	.293	0	....	-5	0	-0.5
1988 Tex-A	0	1	.000	11	0	0	0	1	10^1	15	10	10	1	3	9	10	2.323	8.71	47	9.55	.326	0	....	-5	0	-0.5
1989 Atl-N	0	2	.000	12	0	0	0	1	12^2	12	6	6	2	0	5	16	1.342	4.26	86	3.95	.250	0	....	-1	1	-0.1
1990 Atl-N	2	2	.500	34	0	0	0	0	38^1	41	26	24	3	0	25	34	1.722	5.63	72	5.35	.273	0	....	-6	1	-0.6
1991 Hou-N	3	2	.600	52	0	0	0	2	67^2	51	25	24	7	2	39	51	1.330	3.19	110	3.48	.219	0	.000	2	5	0.2
1992 Cin-N	3	3	.500	60	0	0	0	0	83^2	59	31	31	4	1	44	72	1.231	3.33	108	2.54	.199	1	.250	2	6	0.3
1993 Cin-N	0	1	.000	3	0	0	0	0	4^2	6	8	2	0	0	4	2	2.143	3.86	104	5.66	.273	0	.000	0	0	0.0
Sea-A	2	1	.667	31	1	0	0	2	54	56	40	40	6	2	35	35	1.685	6.67	66	5.40	.273	0	....	-14	0	-1.3
1995 Det-A	1	0	1.000	10	0	0	0	5	8^2	11	6	6	0	0	10	9	2.423	6.23	76	7.22	.306	0	....	-1	1	-0.1
Total 11	14	15	.483	256	1	0	0	14	334^2	298	184	173	26	9	216	275	1.536	4.65	86	4.31	.241	1	.167	-26	18	-2.5

• HENRY, Earl

Earl Clifford "Hook" Henry b: 6/10/1917, Roseville, OH d: 12/10/2002, Zanesville, OH BL/TL, 5'11", 172 lbs. Deb: 9/23/1944

YEAR TM-L	W	L	PCT	G	GS	CG	SH	SV	IP	H	R	ER	HR	HB	BB	SO	RAT	ERA	ERA+	CERA	OAV	BH	AVG	PR+	WS	TPW
1944 Cle-A	1	1	.500	2	2	1	0	0	17^2	18	9	9	0	0	3	5	1.189	4.58	72	2.68	.269	0	.000	-3	1	-0.3
1945 Cle-A	0	3	.000	15	1	0	0	0	21^2	20	13	13	0	1	20	10	1.846	5.40	60	4.89	.253	2	.500	-5	0	-0.5
Total 2	1	4	.200	17	3	1	0	0	39^1	38	22	22	0	1	23	15	1.551	5.03	65	3.90	.260	2	.222	-8	1	-0.8

• HENRY, Jim

James Francis Henry b: 6/26/1910, Danville, VA d: 8/15/1976, Memphis, TN BR/TR, 6'2", 175 lbs. Deb: 4/23/1936

YEAR TM-L	W	L	PCT	G	GS	CG	SH	SV	IP	H	R	ER	HR	HB	BB	SO	RAT	ERA	ERA+	CERA	OAV	BH	AVG	PR+	WS	TPW
1936 Bos-A	5	1	.833	21	8	2	0	0	76^1	75	43	39	10	2	40	36	1.507	4.60	116	4.64	.255	3	.115	6	5	0.4
1937 Bos-A	1	0	1.000	3	2	1	0	0	15^1	15	9	9	2	0	11	8	1.696	5.28	90	5.30	.263	0	.000	-1	1	-0.1
1939 Phi-N	0	1	.000	9	1	0	0	1	23	24	13	13	3	1	8	7	1.391	5.09	77	4.45	.276	0	.000	-3	1	-0.4
Total 3	6	2	.750	33	11	3	0	1	114^2	114	65	61	15	3	59	51	1.509	4.79	102	4.69	.260	3	.083	2	7	0.0

• HENRY, John

John Michael Henry b: 9/2/1863, Springfield, MA d: 6/11/1939, Hartford, CT TL Deb: 8/13/1884 ♦

YEAR TM-L	W	L	PCT	G	GS	CG	SH	SV	IP	H	R	ER	HR	HB	BB	SO	RAT	ERA	ERA+	CERA	OAV	BH	AVG	PR+	WS	TPW
1884 Cle-N	1	4	.200	5	5	5	1	0	42	46	39	17	2	....	26	23	1.714	3.64	86	....	.264	4	.154	-3	1	-0.4
1885 Bal-a	2	7	.222	9	9	9	0	0	71	71	55	34	0	2	13	31	1.183	4.31	75	....	.249	9	.265	-7	3	-0.4
1886 Was-N	1	3	.250	4	4	4	0	0	27^2	35	27	13	1	....	15	19	1.807	4.23	77	....	.297	5	.357	-3	1	-0.2
Total 3	4	14	.222	18	18	18	1	0	140^2	152	121	64	3	2	54	73	1.464	4.09	79	....	.264	53	.243	-12	5	-1.0

• HENSHAW, Roy

Roy Knikelbine Henshaw b: 7/29/1911, Chicago, IL d: 6/8/1993, La Grange, IL BR/TL, 5'8", 155 lbs. Deb: 4/15/1933

YEAR TM-L	W	L	PCT	G	GS	CG	SH	SV	IP	H	R	ER	HR	HB	BB	SO	RAT	ERA	ERA+	CERA	OAV	BH	AVG	PR+	WS	TPW
1933 Chi-N	2	1	.667	21	0	0	0	0	38^2	32	22	18	0	2	20	16	1.345	4.19	78	3.00	.230	2	.200	-5	1	-0.5
1935* Chi-N	13	5	.722	31	18	7	3	1	142^2	135	60	52	6	4	68	53	1.423	3.28	120	3.64	.249	13	.255	5	12	0.6
1936 Chi-N	6	5	.545	39	14	6	2	1	129^1	152	67	57	8	5	56	69	1.608	3.97	100	4.97	.296	6	.136	-2	6	-0.5
1937 Bro-N	5	12	.294	42	16	5	0	2	156^1	176	110	88	14	4	69	98	1.567	5.07	80	4.76	.278	8	.167	-14	3	-1.6

YEAR	TM-L	W	L	PCT	G	GS	CG	SH	SV	IP	H	R	ER	HR	HB	BB	SO	RAT	ERA	ERA+	CERA	OAV	BH	AVG	PR+	WS	TPW
1938	StL-N	5	11	.313	27	15	4	0	0	130	132	63	58	7	1	48	34	1.385	4.02	98	3.70	.266	9	.220	-0	6	0.0
1942	Det-A	2	4	.333	23	2	0	0	1	61^2	63	32	28	3	1	27	24	1.459	4.09	97	3.97	.269	1	.083	-0	3	-0.1
1943	Det-A	0	2	.000	26	3	0	0	2	71^1	75	35	30	2	3	33	33	1.514	3.79	93	4.08	.276	2	.111	-2	2	-0.3
1944	Det-A	0	0	....	7	1	0	0	0	12^1	17	12	12	0	0	6	10	1.865	8.76	41	5.55	.315	0	.000	-7	0	-0.8
Total	8	33	40	.452	216	69	22	5	7	742^1	782	401	343	40	20	327	337	1.494	4.16	93	4.19	.271	41	.179	-26	33	-3.2

• HENSIEK, Phil Philip Frank "Sid" Hensiek b: 10/13/1901, St. Louis, MO d: 2/21/1972, St. Louis, MO BR/TR, 6', 160 lbs. Deb: 8/15/1935

YEAR	TM-L	W	L	PCT	G	GS	CG	SH	SV	IP	H	R	ER	HR	HB	BB	SO	RAT	ERA	ERA+	CERA	OAV	BH	AVG	PR+	WS	TPW
1935	Was-A	0	3	.000	6	1	0	0	1	13	21	15	14	2	0	9	6	2.308	9.69	45	9.12	.356	2	.667	-8	0	-0.6

• HENSLEY, Chuck Charles Floyd Hensley b: 3/11/1959, Tulare, CA BL/TL, 6'3", 190 lbs. Deb: 5/10/1986

YEAR	TM-L	W	L	PCT	G	GS	CG	SH	SV	IP	H	R	ER	HR	HB	BB	SO	RAT	ERA	ERA+	CERA	OAV	BH	AVG	PR+	WS	TPW
1986	SF-N	0	0	....	11	0	0	0	1	7^1	5	2	2	2	0	2	6	.955	2.45	143	2.76	.179	0	....	1	1	0.1

• HENTGEN, Pat Patrick George Hentgen b: 11/13/1968, Detroit, MI BR/TR, 6'2", 200 lbs. Deb: 9/3/1991

YEAR	TM-L	W	L	PCT	G	GS	CG	SH	SV	IP	H	R	ER	HR	HB	BB	SO	RAT	ERA	ERA+	CERA	OAV	BH	AVG	PR+	WS	TPW
1991	Tor-A	0	0	....	3	1	0	0	0	7^1	5	2	2	1	2	3	3	1.091	2.45	171	3.87	.208	0	....	1	1	0.1
1992	Tor-A	5	2	.714	28	2	0	0	0	50^1	49	30	30	7	0	32	39	1.609	5.36	76	4.94	.254	0	....	-7	2	-0.7
1993*	Tor-A★	19	9	.679	34	32	3	0	0	216^1	215	103	93	27	7	74	122	1.336	3.87	112	4.11	.258	0	....	12	16	1.2
1994	Tor-A★	13	8	.619	24	24	6	3	0	174^2	158	74	66	21	3	59	147	1.242	3.40	142	3.52	.240	0	....	29	15	2.7
1995	Tor-A	10	14	.417	30	30	2	0	0	200^2	236	129	114	24	5	90	135	1.625	5.11	92	5.49	.290	0	....	-9	7	-0.9
1996	Tor-A	20	10	.667	35	35	**10**	**3**	0	**265^2**	238	105	95	20	5	94	177	1.250	3.22	156	3.26	.241	0	....	**47**	**24**	**4.3**
1997	Tor-A★	15	10	.600	35	**35**	**9**	**3**	0	**264**	253	116	108	31	7	71	160	1.227	3.68	125	3.61	.254	0	.000	22	19	2.0
1998	Tor-A	12	11	.522	29	29	0	0	0	177^2	208	109	102	28	5	69	94	1.559	5.17	90	5.58	.293	0	.000	-10	8	-1.0
1999	Tor-A	11	12	.478	34	34	1	0	0	199	225	115	106	32	3	65	118	1.457	4.79	103	5.04	.286	1	.167	2	10	0.2
2000*	StL-N	15	12	.556	33	33	1	1	0	194^1	202	107	102	24	3	89	118	1.497	4.72	98	4.81	.276	8	.133	-5	10	-0.5
2001	Bal-A	2	3	.400	9	9	1	0	0	62^1	51	25	24	7	0	19	33	1.123	3.47	124	2.77	.221	0	....	5	4	0.5
2002	Bal-A	0	4	.000	4	4	0	0	0	22	31	20	19	6	0	10	11	1.864	7.77	55	8.38	.337	0	....	-9	0	-0.8
2003	Bal-A	7	8	.467	28	22	1	0	1	160^2	150	74	73	25	5	58	100	1.295	4.09	108	4.09	.247	0	.000	6	10	0.5
Total	13	129	103	.556	326	290	34	10	1	1995	2021	1009	934	253	45	733	1257	1.380	4.21	110	4.33	.264	9	.108	85	126	7.6

• HEPLER, Bill William Lewis Hepler b: 9/25/1945, Covington, VA BL/TL, 6', 160 lbs. Deb: 4/23/1966

YEAR	TM-L	W	L	PCT	G	GS	CG	SH	SV	IP	H	R	ER	HR	HB	BB	SO	RAT	ERA	ERA+	CERA	OAV	BH	AVG	PR+	WS	TPW
1966	NY-N	3	3	.500	37	3	0	0	0	69	71	30	27	3	3	51	25	1.768	3.52	103	5.26	.274	3	.214	1	4	0.1

• HERBEL, Ron Ronald Samuel Herbel b: 1/16/1938, Denver, CO d: 1/20/2000, Tacoma, WA BR/TR, 6'1", 195 lbs. Deb: 9/10/1963

YEAR	TM-L	W	L	PCT	G	GS	CG	SH	SV	IP	H	R	ER	HR	HB	BB	SO	RAT	ERA	ERA+	CERA	OAV	BH	AVG	PR+	WS	TPW
1963	SF-N	0	0	....	2	0	0	0	0	1^1	1	1	1	0	0	1	1	1.500	6.75	47	3.21	.200	0	....	-1	0	-0.1
1964	SF-N	9	9	.500	40	22	7	2	1	161	162	65	55	7	3	61	98	1.385	3.07	116	3.58	.259	0	.000	8	10	0.4
1965	SF-N	12	9	.571	47	21	1	0	1	170^2	172	80	73	16	3	47	106	1.283	3.85	93	3.60	.261	1	.020	-2	8	-0.7
1966	SF-N	4	5	.444	32	18	0	0	1	129^2	149	70	60	15	2	39	55	1.450	4.16	88	4.63	.291	1	.026	-7	3	-1.1
1967	SF-N	4	5	.444	42	11	1	1	1	125^2	125	54	43	10	2	35	52	1.273	3.08	107	3.47	.268	3	.107	3	6	0.3
1968	SF-N	0	0	....	28	2	0	0	0	42^2	55	26	16	5	1	15	18	1.641	3.38	87	5.41	.309	0	.000	-2	0	-0.2
1969	SF-N	4	1	.800	39	4	2	0	1	87^1	92	43	39	7	1	23	34	1.317	4.02	87	3.67	.275	0	.000	-4	4	-0.6
1970	SD-N	7	5	.583	64	1	0	0	9	111	114	69	61	14	4	39	53	1.378	4.95	80	4.28	.266	0	.000	-12	4	-1.3
	NY-N	2	2	.500	12	0	0	0	1	13	14	3	2	1	0	2	8	1.231	1.38	291	3.26	.275	0	....	4	2	0.4
	Yr.	9	7	.563	**76**	1	0	0	10	124	128	72	63	15	4	41	61	1.363	4.57	87	4.17	.267	0	.000	-8	6	-0.9
1971	Atl-N	0	1	.000	25	0	0	0	1	51^2	61	31	30	6	4	23	22	1.626	5.23	71	5.76	.300	1	.091	-8	1	-1.0
Total	9	42	37	.532	331	79	11	3	16	894	945	442	380	81	20	285	447	1.376	3.83	94	4.02	.273	6	.029	-23	38	-4.0

• HERBERT, Ernie Ernie Albert "Tex" Herbert b: 1/30/1887, Hale, MO d: 1/13/1968, Dallas, TX BR/TR, 5'10", 165 lbs. Deb: 7/27/1913

YEAR	TM-L	W	L	PCT	G	GS	CG	SH	SV	IP	H	R	ER	HR	HB	BB	SO	RAT	ERA	ERA+	CERA	OAV	BH	AVG	PR+	WS	TPW
1913	Cin-N	0	0	....	6	0	0	0	0	17^1	12	12	4	0	1	5	5	.981	2.08	156	1.56	.179	1	.250	2	1	0.2
1914	StL-F	1	0	1.000	18	1	0	0	1	50^1	56	33	21	2	4	27	24	1.649	3.75	92	5.20	.293	7	.538	-1	3	0.2
1915	StL-F	1	0	1.000	11	1	1	0	0	48	48	21	18	1	3	18	23	1.375	3.38	92	3.49	.253	5	.278	-2	3	-0.1
Total	3	2	0	1.000	35	2	1	0	1	115^2	116	66	43	3	8	50	52	1.435	3.35	98	3.94	.259	13	.371	-1	7	0.3

• HERBERT, Fred Frederick Herbert b: 3/4/1887, La Grange, IL d: 5/29/1963, Tice, FL BR/TR, 6', 185 lbs. Deb: 9/25/1915

YEAR	TM-L	W	L	PCT	G	GS	CG	SH	SV	IP	H	R	ER	HR	HB	BB	SO	RAT	ERA	ERA+	CERA	OAV	BH	AVG	PR+	WS	TPW
1915	NY-N	1	1	.500	2	2	1	0	0	17	12	5	2	0	0	4	6	.941	1.06	241	1.50	.197	1	.167	3	1	0.3

• HERBERT, Ray Raymond Ernest Herbert b: 12/15/1929, Detroit, MI BR/TR, 5'11", 185 lbs. Deb: 8/27/1950

YEAR	TM-L	W	L	PCT	G	GS	CG	SH	SV	IP	H	R	ER	HR	HB	BB	SO	RAT	ERA	ERA+	CERA	OAV	BH	AVG	PR+	WS	TPW
1950	Det-A	1	2	.333	8	3	1	0	1	22^1	20	11	9	1	0	12	5	1.433	3.63	129	3.53	.244	2	.286	2	2	0.2
1951	Det-A	4	0	1.000	5	0	0	0	0	12^2	8	2	2	0	0	9	9	1.342	1.42	294	2.57	.190	0	.000	4	3	0.4
1953	Det-A	4	6	.400	43	3	0	0	6	87^2	109	58	51	5	0	46	37	1.768	5.24	78	5.55	.308	3	.158	-9	2	-0.9
1954	Det-A	3	6	.333	42	4	0	0	0	84^1	114	64	55	6	2	50	44	1.945	5.87	63	6.79	.334	3	.176	-21	0	-2.0
1955	KC-A	1	8	.111	23	11	2	0	0	87^2	99	65	61	10	1	40	30	1.586	6.26	67	4.99	.292	4	.190	-20	0	-2.0
1958	KC-A	8	8	.500	42	16	5	0	3	175	161	76	68	20	4	55	108	1.234	3.50	112	3.53	.248	10	.192	8	13	1.0
1959	KC-A	11	11	.500	37	26	10	2	1	183^2	196	108	99	24	1	62	99	1.405	4.85	83	4.40	.275	12	.211	-16	7	-1.5
1960	KC-A	14	15	.483	37	33	14	0	1	252^2	256	106	92	17	7	72	122	1.298	3.28	121	3.57	.267	13	.171	24	18	2.6
1961	KC-A	3	6	.333	13	12	1	0	0	83^2	103	56	50	10	2	30	34	1.590	5.38	77	5.42	.303	3	.107	-11	2	-1.2
	Chi-A	9	6	.600	21	20	4	0	0	137^2	142	69	62	15	0	36	50	1.293	4.05	97	3.70	.265	12	.226	-1	9	0.3
	Yr.	12	12	.500	34	32	5	0	0	221^1	245	125	112	25	2	66	84	1.405	4.55	88	4.35	.280	15	.185	-12	11	-0.9
1962	Chi-A★	20	9	.690	35	35	12	2	0	236^2	228	90	86	13	1	74	115	1.276	3.27	119	3.26	.255	16	.195	18	20	2.3
1963	Chi-A	13	10	.565	33	33	14	**7**	0	224^2	230	86	81	12	2	35	105	1.180	3.24	108	3.00	.265	14	.222	5	15	1.1
1964	Chi-A	6	7	.462	20	19	1	1	0	111^2	117	50	43	14	2	17	40	1.200	3.47	100	3.64	.275	5	.139	-3	4	-0.4
1965	Phi-N	5	8	.385	25	19	4	1	1	130^2	162	60	56	13	1	19	51	1.385	3.86	90	4.52	.309	11	.268	-6	6	-0.3
1966	Phi-N	2	5	.286	23	2	0	0	2	50^1	55	26	24	7	1	14	15	1.371	4.29	84	4.55	.293	1	.077	-4	2	-0.5
Total	14	104	107	.493	407	236	68	13	15	1881^1	2000	927	839	167	24	571	864	1.367	4.01	96	4.02	.276	109	.192	-29	103	-0.9

• HEREDIA, Felix Felix (Perez) Heredia b: 6/18/1975, Barahona, Dominican Republic BL/TL, 6', 160 lbs. Deb: 8/9/1996

YEAR	TM-L	W	L	PCT	G	GS	CG	SH	SV	IP	H	R	ER	HR	HB	BB	SO	RAT	ERA	ERA+	CERA	OAV	BH	AVG	PR+	WS	TPW
1996	Fla-N	1	1	.500	21	0	0	0	0	16^2	21	8	8	1	0	10	10	1.860	4.32	94	6.08	.313	0	....	-1	1	-0.1
1997*	Fla-N	5	3	.625	56	0	0	0	0	56^2	53	30	27	3	5	30	54	1.465	4.29	94	4.06	.241	1	.500	-2	3	-0.2
1998	Fla-N	0	3	.000	41	2	0	0	2	41	38	25	25	1	1	32	38	1.707	5.49	75	4.44	.241	0	.000	-6	1	-0.6
	*Chi-N	3	0	1.000	30	0	0	0	0	17^2	19	8	8	1	0	6	16	1.415	4.08	108	3.99	.279	0	....	1	2	0.1
	Yr.	3	3	.500	71	2	0	0	2	58^2	57	33	33	2	1	38	54	1.619	5.06	82	4.31	.252	0	.000	-5	3	-0.5
1999	Chi-N	3	1	.750	69	0	0	0	1	52	56	35	28	7	1	25	50	1.558	4.85	93	5.01	.272	2	.500	-1	3	0.0
2000	Chi-N	7	3	.700	74	0	0	0	2	58^2	46	31	31	6	2	33	52	1.347	4.76	95	3.59	.220	0	.000	-1	4	-0.1
2001	Chi-N	2	2	.500	48	0	0	0	0	35	45	27	24	6	2	16	28	1.743	6.17	67	6.75	.315	0	.000	-7	0	-0.7
2002	Tor-A	1	2	.333	53	0	0	0	0	52^1	51	29	21	5	2	26	31	1.471	3.61	128	4.31	.256	0	....	6	3	0.6
2003	Cin-N	5	2	.714	57	0	0	0	1	72	61	27	24	9	2	28	41	1.236	3.00	142	3.35	.228	1	.333	10	7	1.0
	*NY-A	0	1	.000	12	0	0	0	0	15	13	5	2	1	0	5	4	1.200	1.20	364	2.69	.228	0	....	6	2	0.5
Total	8	27	18	.600	461	2	0	0	6	417	403	225	198	40	15	211	324	1.472	4.27	101	4.31	.253	4	.267	5	26	0.5

• HEREDIA, Gil Gilbert Heredia b: 10/26/1965, Nogales, AZ BR/TR, 6'1", 190 lbs. Deb: 9/1/1991

YEAR	TM-L	W	L	PCT	G	GS	CG	SH	SV	IP	H	R	ER	HR	HB	BB	SO	RAT	ERA	ERA+	CERA	OAV	BH	AVG	PR+	WS	TPW
1991	SF-N	0	2	.000	7	4	0	0	0	33	27	14	14	4	0	7	13	1.030	3.82	94	2.58	.233	3	.429	-1	2	0.0
1992	SF-N	2	3	.400	13	4	0	0	0	30	32	20	18	3	1	16	15	1.600	5.40	61	5.23	.278	1	.167	-8	0	-0.8
	Mon-N	0	0	....	7	1	0	0	0	14^2	12	3	3	1	0	4	7	1.091	1.84	188	2.67	.250	0	.000	3	1	0.3
	Yr.	2	3	.400	20	5	0	0	0	44^2	44	23	21	4	1	20	22	1.433	4.23	79	4.39	.270	1	.111	-5	1	-0.6
1993	Mon-N	4	2	.667	20	9	1	0	2	57^1	66	28	25	4	2	14	40	1.395	3.92	106	4.22	.293	2	.154	1	3	0.1
1994	Mon-N	6	3	.667	39	3	0	0	0	75^1	85	34	29	7	2	13	62	1.301	3.46	122	3.81	.281	5	.313	6	6	0.7
1995	Mon-N	5	6	.455	40	18	0	0	1	119	137	60	57	7	5	21	74	1.328	4.31	100	3.90	.291	6	.182	1	6	0.1
1996	Tex-A	2	5	.286	44	0	0	0	1	73^1	91	50	48	12	1	14	43	1.432	5.89	89	5.06	.301	0	....	-5	3	-0.5
1998	Oak-A	3	3	.500	8	6	0	0	0	42^2	43	14	13	4	3	3	27	1.078	2.74	167	3.05	.256	0	....	9	4	0.9
1999	Oak-A	13	8	.619	33	33	1	0	0	200^1	228	119	107	22	8	34	117	1.308	4.81	97	4.13	.283	0	.000	-3	10	-0.3
2000*	Oak-A	15	11	.577	32	32	2	0	0	198^2	214	106	91	24	4	66	101	1.409	4.12	115	4.44	.274	1	.500	17	13	1.6

YEAR TM-L	W	L	PCT	G	GS	CG	SH	SV	IP	H	R	ER	HR	HB	BB	SO	RAT	ERA	ERA+	CERA	OAV	BH	AVG	PR+	WS	TPW
2001 Oak-A	7	8	.467	24	18	0	0	0	109^{2}	144	75	68	27	2	29	48	1.578	5.58	79	6.50	.316	1	.333	-14	2	-1.4
Total 10	**57**	**51**	**.528**	**267**	**128**	**4**	**0**	**4**	**954**	**1079**	**523**	**473**	**115**	**28**	**221**	**547**	**1.363**	**4.46**	**100**	**4.40**	**.285**	**19**	**.213**	**6**	**50**	**0.7**

• HEREDIA, Ubaldo
Ubaldo Jose (Martinez) Heredia b: 5/4/1956, Ciudad Bolivar, Venezuela BR/TR, 6'2", 180 lbs. Deb: 5/12/1987

YEAR TM-L	W	L	PCT	G	GS	CG	SH	SV	IP	H	R	ER	HR	HB	BB	SO	RAT	ERA	ERA+	CERA	OAV	BH	AVG	PR+	WS	TPW
1987 Mon-N	0	1	.000	2	2	0	0	0	10	10	6	6	2	1	3	6	1.300	5.40	78	4.76	.263	0	.000	-1	0	-0.1

• HEREDIA, Wilson
Wilson Heredia b: 3/30/1972, La Romana, Dominican Republic BR/TR, 6', 175 lbs. Deb: 4/27/1995

YEAR TM-L	W	L	PCT	G	GS	CG	SH	SV	IP	H	R	ER	HR	HB	BB	SO	RAT	ERA	ERA+	CERA	OAV	BH	AVG	PR+	WS	TPW
1995 Tex-A	0	1	.000	6	0	0	0	0	12	9	5	5	2	0	15	6	2.000	3.75	129	6.34	.225	0	....	1	1	0.1
1997 Tex-A	1	0	1.000	10	0	0	0	0	19^{2}	14	9	7	2	0	16	8	1.525	3.20	150	3.99	.197	0	....	4	2	0.4
Total 2	**1**	**1**	**.500**	**16**	**0**	**0**	**0**	**0**	31^{2}	**23**	**14**	**12**	**4**	**0**	**31**	**14**	**1.705**	**3.41**	**141**	**4.88**	**.207**	**0**	**....**	**5**	**3**	**0.5**

• HERGES, Matt
Matthew Tyler Herges b: 4/1/1970, Champaign, IL BL/TR, 6', 200 lbs. Deb: 8/3/1999

YEAR TM-L	W	L	PCT	G	GS	CG	SH	SV	IP	H	R	ER	HR	HB	BB	SO	RAT	ERA	ERA+	CERA	OAV	BH	AVG	PR+	WS	TPW
1999 LA-N	0	2	.000	17	0	0	0	0	24^{1}	24	13	11	5	1	8	18	1.315	4.07	105	4.61	.255	0	.000	1	1	0.1
2000 LA-N	11	3	.786	59	4	0	0	1	110^{2}	100	43	39	7	6	40	75	1.265	3.17	136	3.35	.249	1	.077	15	10	1.3
2001 LA-N	9	8	.529	75	0	0	0	1	99^{1}	97	39	38	8	8	46	76	1.440	3.44	116	4.20	.259	4	.444	7	9	0.8
2002 Mon-N	2	5	.286	62	0	0	0	6	64^{2}	80	33	29	10	2	26	50	1.639	4.04	106	5.74	.305	0	.000	2	4	0.2
2003 SD-N	2	2	.500	40	0	0	0	3	44	40	16	14	2	2	20	40	1.364	2.86	137	3.45	.244	0	.000	6	3	0.5
*SF-N	1	0	1.000	27	0	0	0	0	35	28	11	9	1	1	9	28	1.057	2.31	177	2.18	.219	1	.500	6	4	0.6
Yr.	3	2	.600	67	0	0	0	3	79	68	27	23	3	3	29	68	1.228	2.62	153	2.89	.233	1	.333	12	7	1.2
Total 5	**25**	**20**	**.556**	**280**	**4**	**0**	**0**	**11**	**378**	**369**	**155**	**140**	**33**	**20**	**149**	**287**	**1.370**	**3.33**	**125**	**3.97**	**.259**	**6**	**.222**	**36**	**31**	**3.5**

• HERMAN, Art
Arthur Herman b: 5/11/1871, Louisville, KY d: 9/20/1955, Los Angeles, CA Deb: 6/29/1896

YEAR TM-L	W	L	PCT	G	GS	CG	SH	SV	IP	H	R	ER	HR	HB	BB	SO	RAT	ERA	ERA+	CERA	OAV	BH	AVG	PR+	WS	TPW
1896 Lou-N	4	6	.400	14	12	9	0	0	94^{1}	122	73	59	4	20	36	13	1.675	5.63	77	5.96	.311	5	.139	-12	3	-1.3
1897 Lou-N	0	1	.000	3	2	1	0	0	18	23	14	8	1	0	5	4	1.556	4.00	106	4.78	.308	2	.333	1	1	0.2
Total 2	**4**	**7**	**.364**	**17**	**14**	**10**	**0**	**0**	112^{1}	**145**	**87**	**67**	**5**	**20**	**41**	**17**	**1.656**	**5.37**	**80**	**5.77**	**.310**	**7**	**.167**	**-11**	**4**	**-1.1**

• HERMANSON, Dustin
Dustin Michael Hermanson b: 12/21/1972, Springfield, OH BR/TR, 6'3", 195 lbs. Deb: 5/8/1995

YEAR TM-L	W	L	PCT	G	GS	CG	SH	SV	IP	H	R	ER	HR	HB	BB	SO	RAT	ERA	ERA+	CERA	OAV	BH	AVG	PR+	WS	TPW
1995 SD-N	3	1	.750	26	0	0	0	0	31^{2}	35	26	24	8	1	22	19	1.800	6.82	59	7.19	.280	0	....	-10	0	-1.0
1996 SD-N	1	0	1.000	8	0	0	0	0	13^{2}	18	15	13	3	0	4	11	1.610	8.56	46	6.37	.340	0	....	-7	0	-0.7
1997 Mon-N	8	8	.500	32	28	1	1	0	158^{1}	134	68	65	15	1	66	136	1.263	3.69	114	3.32	.234	5	.104	9	10	0.8
1998 Mon-N	14	11	.560	32	30	1	0	0	187	163	80	65	21	3	56	154	1.171	3.13	135	3.12	.234	6	.115	25	13	2.7
1999 Mon-N	9	14	.391	34	34	0	0	0	216^{1}	225	110	101	20	7	69	145	1.359	4.20	107	4.03	.271	3	.047	11	12	0.6
2000 Mon-N	12	14	.462	38	30	2	1	4	198	226	128	105	26	4	75	94	1.520	4.77	100	5.10	.290	8	.145	2	9	0.1
2001* StL-N	14	13	.519	33	33	0	0	0	192^{1}	195	106	95	34	8	73	123	1.393	4.45	96	4.80	.264	5	.081	-8	8	-1.1
2002 Bos-A	1	1	.500	12	1	0	0	0	22	35	19	19	3	0	7	13	1.909	7.77	58	7.52	.354	0	....	-8	0	-0.8
2003 StL-N	1	2	.333	23	0	0	0	1	29^{2}	35	18	18	4	1	14	12	1.652	5.46	74	6.04	.315	0	....	-5	1	-0.4
*SF-N	2	1	.667	9	6	0	0	0	39	35	14	13	5	2	10	27	1.154	3.00	137	3.25	.238	0	.000	4	3	0.3
Yr.	3	3	.500	32	6	0	0	1	68^{2}	70	32	31	9	3	24	39	1.369	4.06	100	4.46	.271	0	.000	-1	4	-0.2
Total 9	**65**	**65**	**.500**	**247**	**162**	**4**	**2**	**5**	**1088**	**1101**	**584**	**518**	**139**	**27**	**396**	**734**	**1.376**	**4.28**	**102**	**4.32**	**.265**	**27**	**.092**	**12**	**56**	**0.5**

• HERNAIZ, Jesus
Jesus Rafael (Rodriguez) Hernaiz b: 1/8/1945, Santurce, Puerto Rico BR/TR, 6'2", 175 lbs. Deb: 6/14/1974

YEAR TM-L	W	L	PCT	G	GS	CG	SH	SV	IP	H	R	ER	HR	HB	BB	SO	RAT	ERA	ERA+	CERA	OAV	BH	AVG	PR+	WS	TPW
1974 Phi-N	2	3	.400	27	0	0	0	1	41^{1}	53	31	27	6	0	25	16	1.887	5.88	64	7.16	.323	0	.000	-10	0	-1.1

• HERNANDEZ, Adrian
Adrian "El Duquecito" Hernandez b: 3/25/1975, Havana, Cuba BR/TR, 6'1", 185 lbs. Deb: 4/21/2001

YEAR TM-L	W	L	PCT	G	GS	CG	SH	SV	IP	H	R	ER	HR	HB	BB	SO	RAT	ERA	ERA+	CERA	OAV	BH	AVG	PR+	WS	TPW
2001 NY-A	0	3	.000	6	3	0	0	0	22	15	10	9	7	2	10	10	1.136	3.68	122	4.30	.190	0	....	2	1	0.2
2002 NY-A	0	1	.000	2	1	0	0	0	6	10	8	8	2	0	6	9	2.667	12.00	36	13.15	.357	0	....	-5	0	-0.5
Total 2	**0**	**4**	**.000**	**8**	**4**	**0**	**0**	**0**	**28**	**25**	**18**	**17**	**9**	**2**	**16**	**19**	**1.464**	**5.46**	**81**	**6.19**	**.234**	**0**	**....**	**-2**	**1**	**-0.2**

• HERNANDEZ, Carlos
Carlos E. Hernandez b: 4/22/1980, Guacara, Venezuela BB/TL, 5'10", 145 lbs. Deb: 8/18/2001

YEAR TM-L	W	L	PCT	G	GS	CG	SH	SV	IP	H	R	ER	HR	HB	BB	SO	RAT	ERA	ERA+	CERA	OAV	BH	AVG	PR+	WS	TPW
2001 Hou-N	1	0	1.000	3	3	0	0	0	17^{2}	11	2	2	1	0	7	17	1.019	1.02	448	1.88	.177	1	.200	7	2	0.7
2002 Hou-N	7	5	.583	23	21	0	0	0	111	112	56	54	11	3	61	93	1.559	4.38	97	4.77	.261	6	.171	-0	6	0.0
Total 2	**8**	**5**	**.615**	**26**	**24**	**0**	**0**	**0**	128^{2}	**123**	**58**	**56**	**12**	**3**	**68**	**110**	**1.484**	**3.92**	**109**	**4.38**	**.251**	**7**	**.175**	**6**	**8**	**0.6**

• HERNANDEZ, Evelio
Gregorio Evelio (Lopez) Hernandez b: 12/24/1931, Guanabacoa, Cuba BR/TR, 6'1", 195 lbs. Deb: 9/12/1956

YEAR TM-L	W	L	PCT	G	GS	CG	SH	SV	IP	H	R	ER	HR	HB	BB	SO	RAT	ERA	ERA+	CERA	OAV	BH	AVG	PR+	WS	TPW
1956 Was-A	1	1	.500	4	4	1	0	0	22^{2}	24	12	12	2	0	8	9	1.412	4.76	91	4.18	.276	2	.182	-0	1	-0.1
1957 Was-A	0	0	....	14	2	0	0	0	36	38	18	17	2	0	20	15	1.611	4.25	92	4.57	.268	0	.000	-1	1	-0.1
Total 2	**1**	**1**	**.500**	**18**	**6**	**1**	**0**	**0**	58^{2}	**62**	**30**	**29**	**4**	**0**	**28**	**24**	**1.534**	**4.45**	**91**	**4.42**	**.271**	**2**	**.118**	**-1**	**2**	**-0.2**

• HERNANDEZ, Fernando
Fernando Hernandez b: 6/16/1971, Santiago, Dominican Republic BR/TR, 6'2", 185 lbs. Deb: 4/3/1997

YEAR TM-L	W	L	PCT	G	GS	CG	SH	SV	IP	H	R	ER	HR	HB	BB	SO	RAT	ERA	ERA+	CERA	OAV	BH	AVG	PR+	WS	TPW
1997 Det-A	0	0	....	2	0	0	0	0	1^{1}	5	6	6	0	1	3	2	6.000	40.50	11	33.39	.556	0	....	-5	0	-0.5

• HERNANDEZ, Jeremy
Jeremy Stuart Hernandez b: 7/6/1966, Burbank, CA BR/TR, 6'5", 195 lbs. Deb: 9/2/1991

YEAR TM-L	W	L	PCT	G	GS	CG	SH	SV	IP	H	R	ER	HR	HB	BB	SO	RAT	ERA	ERA+	CERA	OAV	BH	AVG	PR+	WS	TPW
1991 SD-N	0	0	....	9	0	0	0	2	14^{1}	8	1	0	0	0	5	9	.907	0.00	....	1.28	.157	0	.000	6	3	0.6
1992 SD-N	1	4	.200	26	0	0	0	1	36^{2}	39	17	17	4	1	11	25	1.364	4.17	86	4.01	.291	0	.000	-2	2	-0.3
1993 SD-N	0	2	.000	21	0	0	0	0	34^{1}	41	19	18	2	0	7	26	1.398	4.72	88	4.10	.301	0	.000	-2	1	-0.2
Cle-A	6	5	.545	49	0	0	0	8	77^{1}	75	33	27	12	0	27	44	1.319	3.14	138	4.06	.261	0	....	10	7	1.0
1994 Fla-N	3	3	.500	21	0	0	0	9	23^{1}	16	9	7	0	2	14	13	1.286	2.70	162	2.64	.205	0	.000	4	5	0.4
1995 Fla-N	0	0	....	7	0	0	0	0	7	12	9	9	2	1	3	5	2.143	11.57	36	10.85	.400	0	.000	-6	0	-0.6
Total 5	**10**	**14**	**.417**	**133**	**0**	**0**	**0**	**20**	**193**	**191**	**88**	**78**	**20**	**4**	**67**	**122**	**1.337**	**3.64**	**112**	**3.92**	**.267**	**0**	**.000**	**10**	**18**	**0.9**

• HERNANDEZ, Livan
Eisler Livan (Carrera) Hernandez b: 2/20/1975, Villa Clara, Cuba BR/TR, 6'2", 220 lbs. Deb: 9/24/1996

YEAR TM-L	W	L	PCT	G	GS	CG	SH	SV	IP	H	R	ER	HR	HB	BB	SO	RAT	ERA	ERA+	CERA	OAV	BH	AVG	PR+	WS	TPW
1996 Fla-N	0	0	....	1	0	0	0	0	3	3	0	0	0	0	2	2	1.667	0.00	....	4.60	.273	1	1.000	1	1	0.2
1997* Fla-N	9	3	.750	17	17	0	0	0	96^{1}	81	39	34	5	3	38	72	1.235	3.18	127	2.96	.229	5	.172	9	8	0.9
1998 Fla-N	10	12	.455	33	33	9	0	0	234^{1}	265	133	123	37	6	104	162	1.575	4.72	87	5.58	.289	16	.195	-15	6	-1.3
1999 Fla-N	5	9	.357	20	20	2	0	0	136	161	78	72	17	2	55	97	1.588	4.76	91	5.37	.294	13	.289	-6	6	0.0
SF-N	3	3	.500	10	10	0	0	0	63^{2}	66	32	31	6	0	21	47	1.366	4.38	96	3.88	.267	4	.222	-1	3	0.0
Yr.	8	12	.400	30	30	2	0	0	199^{2}	227	110	103	23	2	76	144	1.518	4.64	93	4.90	.286	17	.270	-7	9	-0.1
2000* SF-N	17	11	.607	33	33	5	2	0	240	254	114	100	22	4	73	165	1.363	3.75	113	4.01	.273	21	.236	12	14	1.6
2001 SF-N	13	15	.464	34	34	2	0	0	226^{2}	266	143	132	24	3	85	138	1.549	5.24	76	5.03	.297	24	.296	-32	5	-2.3
2002* SF-N	12	16	.429	33	33	5	3	0	216	233	113	105	19	4	71	134	1.407	4.38	89	4.26	.283	15	.234	-14	7	-1.1
2003 Mon-N	15	10	.600	33	33	**8**	0	0	$\mathbf{233^{1}}$	225	92	83	27	10	57	178	1.209	3.20	158	3.55	.253	14	.189	**48**	**23**	**4.8**
Total 8	**84**	**79**	**.515**	**214**	**213**	**31**	**5**	**0**	1449^{1}	**1554**	**744**	**680**	**157**	**32**	**506**	**995**	**1.421**	**4.22**	**99**	**4.44**	**.277**	**113**	**.234**	**2**	**73**	**2.7**

• HERNANDEZ, Manny
Manuel Antonio (Montas) Hernandez b: 5/7/1961, La Romana, Dominican Republic BR/TR, 6', 150 lbs. Deb: 6/5/1986

YEAR TM-L	W	L	PCT	G	GS	CG	SH	SV	IP	H	R	ER	HR	HB	BB	SO	RAT	ERA	ERA+	CERA	OAV	BH	AVG	PR+	WS	TPW
1986 Hou-N	2	3	.400	9	4	0	0	0	27^{2}	33	15	12	2	0	12	9	1.627	3.90	92	4.92	.306	0	.000	-1	1	-0.2
1987 Hou-N	0	4	.000	6	3	0	0	0	21^{2}	25	15	13	1	1	5	12	1.385	5.40	73	3.94	.301	0	.000	-3	0	-0.4
1989 NY-N	0	0	....	1	0	0	0	0	1	0	0	0	0	0	0	1	.000	0.00	....	0.00	.000	0	....	0	0	0.0
Total 3	**2**	**7**	**.222**	**16**	**7**	**0**	**0**	**0**	50^{1}	**58**	**30**	**25**	**3**	**1**	**17**	**22**	**1.490**	**4.47**	**84**	**4.40**	**.304**	**0**	**.000**	**-4**	**1**	**-0.5**

• HERNANDEZ, Orlando
Orlando (Pedroso) "El Duque" Hernandez b: 10/11/1965, Villa Clara, Cuba BR/TR, 6'2", 220 lbs. Deb: 6/3/1998

YEAR TM-L	W	L	PCT	G	GS	CG	SH	SV	IP	H	R	ER	HR	HB	BB	SO	RAT	ERA	ERA+	CERA	OAV	BH	AVG	PR+	WS	TPW
1998* NY-A	12	4	.750	21	21	3	1	0	141	113	53	49	11	6	52	131	1.170	3.13	140	2.96	.222	0	.000	17	13	1.5
1999* NY-A	17	9	.654	33	33	2	1	0	214^{1}	187	108	98	24	8	87	157	1.278	4.12	115	3.60	.233	1	.333	16	14	1.5
2000* NY-A	12	13	.480	29	29	3	0	0	195^{2}	186	104	98	34	6	51	141	1.211	4.51	107	3.82	.247	0	.000	11	12	0.9
2001* NY-A	4	7	.364	17	16	0	0	0	94^{2}	90	51	51	19	5	42	77	1.394	4.85	93	4.87	.248	0	....	-2	4	-0.2
2002* NY-A	8	5	.615	24	22	0	0	1	146	131	63	59	17	8	36	113	1.144	3.64	120	3.20	.236	0	....	16	11	1.6
Total 5	**53**	**38**	**.582**	**124**	**121**	**8**	**2**	**1**	791^{2}	**707**	**379**	**355**	**105**	**33**	**268**	**619**	**1.232**	**4.04**	**114**	**3.62**	**.237**	**1**	**.053**	**58**	**54**	**5.4**

• HERNANDEZ, Ramon
Ramon (Gonzalez) Hernandez b: 8/31/1940, Carolina, Puerto Rico BB/TL, 5'11", 170 lbs. Deb: 4/11/1967

YEAR TM-L	W	L	PCT	G	GS	CG	SH	SV	IP	H	R	ER	HR	HB	BB	SO	RAT	ERA	ERA+	CERA	OAV	BH	AVG	PR+	WS	TPW
1967 Atl-N	0	2	.000	46	0	0	0	5	51^{2}	60	27	24	5	2	14	28	1.432	4.18	79	4.55	.296	0	.000	-5	2	-0.6
1968 Chi-N	0	0	....	8	0	0	0	0	9	14	11	9	1	1	0	3	1.556	9.00	35	6.10	.350	0	....	-6	0	-0.7
1971 Pit-N	0	1	.000	10	0	0	0	4	12^{1}	5	1	1	0	0	2	7	.568	0.73	467	0.54	.122	1	.500	4	3	0.4

YEAR	TM-L	W	L	PCT	G	GS	CG	SH	SV	IP	H	R	ER	HR	HB	BB	SO	RAT	ERA	ERA+	CERA	OAV	BH	AVG	PR+	WS	TPW
1972*	Pit-N	5	0	1.000	53	0	0	0	14	70	50	14	13	3	3	22	47	1.029	1.67	199	2.01	.194	2	.167	12	11	1.3
1973	Pit-N	4	5	.444	59	0	0	0	11	89^2	71	27	24	5	4	25	64	1.071	2.41	146	2.31	.218	1	.125	11	9	1.2
1974*	Pit-N	5	2	.714	58	0	0	0	2	68^2	68	21	21	3	2	18	33	1.252	2.75	125	3.04	.258	1	.250	5	6	0.6
1975*	Pit-N	7	2	.778	46	0	0	0	5	64	62	21	21	0	0	28	43	1.406	2.95	120	2.92	.252	0	.000	4	7	0.4
1976	Pit-N	2	2	.500	37	0	0	0	3	43	42	17	17	3	1	16	17	1.349	3.56	98	3.53	.263	0	.000	-1	3	-0.1
	Chi-N	0	0	....	2	0	0	0	0	1^2	2	0	0	0	0	0	1	1.200	0.00	....	2.89	.333	0	....	1	0	0.1
	Yr.	2	2	.500	39	0	0	0	3	44^2	44	17	17	3	1	16	18	1.343	3.43	102	3.51	.265	0	.000	0	3	0.0
1977	Chi-N	0	0	....	6	0	0	0	1	7^2	11	9	7	1	0	3	4	1.826	8.22	53	6.36	.306	0	.000	-3	0	-0.3
	Bos-A	0	1	.000	12	0	0	0	1	12^2	14	10	8	2	1	7	8	1.658	5.68	79	6.03	.280	0	....	-1	0	-0.1
Total	**9**	**23**	**15**	**.605**	**337**	**0**	**0**	**0**	**46**	**430^1**	**399**	**158**	**145**	**23**	**14**	**135**	**255**	**1.241**	**3.03**	**116**	**3.07**	**.245**	**5**	**.125**	**20**	**41**	**2.1**

• HERNANDEZ, Roberto Roberto Manuel (Rodriguez) Hernandez b: 11/11/1964, Santurce, Puerto Rico BR/TR, 6'4", 235 lbs. Deb: 9/2/1991

YEAR	TM-L	W	L	PCT	G	GS	CG	SH	SV	IP	H	R	ER	HR	HB	BB	SO	RAT	ERA	ERA+	CERA	OAV	BH	AVG	PR+	WS	TPW
1991	Chi-A	1	0	1.000	9	3	0	0	0	15	18	15	13	1	0	7	6	1.667	7.80	51	5.19	.290	0	....	-7	0	-0.7
1992	Chi-A	7	3	.700	43	0	0	0	12	71	45	15	13	4	4	20	68	.915	1.65	234	1.74	.180	0	....	17	13	1.8
1993*	Chi-A	3	4	.429	70	0	0	0	38	78^2	66	21	20	6	0	20	71	1.093	2.29	183	2.54	.228	0	....	16	16	1.6
1994	Chi-A	4	4	.500	45	0	0	0	14	47^2	44	29	26	5	1	19	50	1.322	4.91	95	3.66	.238	0	....	-1	5	-0.1
1995	Chi-A	3	7	.300	60	0	0	0	32	59^2	63	30	26	9	3	28	84	1.525	3.92	114	5.04	.266	0	....	4	6	0.4
1996	Chi-A★	6	5	.545	72	0	0	0	38	84^2	65	21	18	2	0	38	85	1.217	1.91	248	2.40	.208	0	....	27	17	2.5
1997	Chi-A	5	1	.833	46	0	0	0	27	48	38	15	13	5	1	24	47	1.292	2.44	180	3.30	.216	0	....	11	10	1.1
	*SF-N	5	2	.714	28	0	0	0	4	32^2	29	9	9	2	0	14	35	1.316	2.48	163	3.29	.238	1	.500	6	5	0.6
1998	TB-A	2	6	.250	67	0	0	0	26	71^1	55	33	32	5	5	41	55	1.346	4.04	119	3.43	.212	0	....	3	10	0.3
1999	TB-A★	2	3	.400	72	0	0	0	43	73^1	68	27	25	1	4	33	69	1.377	3.07	162	3.40	.244	0	....	16	14	1.5
2000	TB-A	4	7	.364	68	0	0	0	32	73^1	76	33	26	9	3	23	61	1.350	3.19	155	4.24	.272	0	....	13	12	1.2
2001	KC-A	5	6	.455	63	0	0	0	28	67^2	69	34	31	7	1	26	46	1.404	4.12	119	4.23	.266	0	....	4	9	0.4
2002	KC-A	1	3	.250	53	0	0	0	26	52	62	29	25	6	3	12	39	1.423	4.33	116	4.79	.300	0	....	4	7	0.4
2003*	Atl-N	5	3	.625	66	0	0	0	0	60	61	36	29	10	3	43	45	1.733	4.35	97	5.95	.263	0	....	-1	3	-0.1
Total	**13**	**53**	**54**	**.495**	**762**	**3**	**0**	**0**	**320**	**835**	**759**	**347**	**306**	**72**	**28**	**348**	**761**	**1.326**	**3.30**	**139**	**3.65**	**.241**	**1**	**.500**	**114**	**127**	**10.8**

• HERNANDEZ, Rudy Rudolph Albert (Fuentes) Hernandez b: 12/10/1931, Santiago, Dominican Republic BR/TR, 6'3", 185 lbs. Deb: 7/3/1960

YEAR	TM-L	W	L	PCT	G	GS	CG	SH	SV	IP	H	R	ER	HR	HB	BB	SO	RAT	ERA	ERA+	CERA	OAV	BH	AVG	PR+	WS	TPW
1960	Was-A	4	1	.800	21	0	0	0	0	34^2	34	24	17	2	1	21	22	1.587	4.41	89	4.36	.262	1	.167	-1	1	-0.2
1961	Was-A	0	1	.000	7	0	0	0	0	9	8	5	3	0	0	3	4	1.222	3.00	131	2.60	.250	0	....	1	0	0.1
Total	**2**	**4**	**2**	**.667**	**28**	**0**	**0**	**0**	**0**	**43^2**	**42**	**29**	**20**	**2**	**1**	**24**	**26**	**1.511**	**4.12**	**96**	**4.00**	**.259**	**1**	**.167**	**-0**	**1**	**-0.1**

• HERNANDEZ, Runelvys Runelvys Antonio Hernandez b: 4/27/1978, Santo Domingo, Dominican Republic BR/TR, 6'3", 205 lbs. Deb: 7/15/2002

YEAR	TM-L	W	L	PCT	G	GS	CG	SH	SV	IP	H	R	ER	HR	HB	BB	SO	RAT	ERA	ERA+	CERA	OAV	BH	AVG	PR+	WS	TPW
2002	KC-A	4	4	.500	12	12	0	0	0	74^1	79	36	36	8	1	22	45	1.359	4.36	115	4.16	.273	0	....	6	5	0.6
2003	KC-A	7	5	.583	16	16	0	0	0	91^2	87	51	47	9	6	37	48	1.353	4.61	112	4.05	.249	0	....	6	6	0.5
Total	**2**	**11**	**9**	**.550**	**28**	**28**	**0**	**0**	**0**	**166**	**166**	**87**	**83**	**17**	**7**	**59**	**93**	**1.355**	**4.50**	**113**	**4.09**	**.260**	**0**	**....**	**11**	**11**	**1.1**

• HERNANDEZ, Willie Guillermo (Villanueva) Hernandez b: 11/14/1954, Aguada, Puerto Rico BL/TL, 6'3", 180 lbs. Deb: 4/9/1977

YEAR	TM-L	W	L	PCT	G	GS	CG	SH	SV	IP	H	R	ER	HR	HB	BB	SO	RAT	ERA	ERA+	CERA	OAV	BH	AVG	PR+	WS	TPW
1977	Chi-N	8	7	.533	67	1	0	0	4	110	94	42	37	11	1	28	78	1.109	3.03	145	2.73	.234	1	.063	19	11	1.8
1978	Chi-N	8	2	.800	54	0	0	0	3	59^2	57	26	25	6	1	35	38	1.542	3.77	107	4.46	.263	0	.000	2	6	0.2
1979	Chi-N	4	4	.500	51	2	0	0	0	79	85	50	44	8	4	39	53	1.570	5.01	82	4.80	.281	2	.250	-7	2	-0.6
1980	Chi-N	1	9	.100	53	7	0	0	0	108^1	115	58	53	8	2	45	75	1.477	4.40	89	4.34	.276	4	.211	-4	3	-0.4
1981	Chi-N	0	0	....	12	0	0	0	2	13^2	14	7	6	0	0	8	13	1.610	3.95	94	3.88	.280	0	....	-0	1	0.0
1982	Chi-N	4	6	.400	75	0	0	0	10	75	74	26	25	3	1	24	54	1.307	3.00	125	3.16	.268	0	.000	7	8	0.7
1983	Chi-N	1	0	1.000	11	1	0	0	1	19^2	16	8	7	0	0	6	18	1.119	3.20	118	2.04	.222	1	.500	2	2	0.2
	*Phi-N	8	4	.667	63	0	0	0	7	95^2	93	39	35	9	1	26	75	1.244	3.29	108	3.33	.254	5	.385	4	9	0.6
	Yr.	9	4	.692	74	1	0	0	8	115^1	109	47	42	9	1	32	93	1.223	3.28	110	3.11	.249	6	.400	6	11	0.8
1984*	Det-A★	9	3	.750	**80**	0	0	0	32	140^1	96	30	30	6	4	36	112	.941	1.92	204	1.67	.194	0	....	30	24	3.0
1985	Det-A★	8	10	.444	74	0	0	0	31	106^2	82	38	32	13	1	14	76	.900	2.70	151	2.02	.210	0	.000	16	19	1.6
1986	Det-A★	8	7	.533	64	0	0	0	24	88^2	87	35	35	13	5	21	77	1.218	3.55	116	3.80	.251	0	....	5	11	0.5
1987*	Det-A	3	4	.429	45	0	0	0	8	49	53	27	20	8	0	20	30	1.490	3.67	115	4.76	.276	0	....	3	4	0.3
1988	Det-A	6	5	.545	63	0	0	0	10	67^2	50	24	23	8	4	31	59	1.197	3.06	125	3.09	.208	0	....	5	8	0.5
1989	Det-A	2	2	.500	32	0	0	0	15	31^1	36	21	20	4	1	16	30	1.660	5.74	66	5.74	.293	0	....	-6	1	-0.7
Total	**13**	**70**	**63**	**.526**	**744**	**11**	**0**	**0**	**147**	**1044^2**	**952**	**431**	**392**	**97**	**25**	**349**	**788**	**1.245**	**3.38**	**117**	**3.32**	**.245**	**13**	**.206**	**75**	**109**	**7.7**

• HERNANDEZ, Xavier Francis Xavier Hernandez b: 8/16/1965, Port Arthur, TX BL/TR, 6'2", 185 lbs. Deb: 6/4/1989

YEAR	TM-L	W	L	PCT	G	GS	CG	SH	SV	IP	H	R	ER	HR	HB	BB	SO	RAT	ERA	ERA+	CERA	OAV	BH	AVG	PR+	WS	TPW
1989	Tor-A	1	0	1.000	7	0	0	0	0	22^2	25	15	12	2	1	8	7	1.456	4.76	76	4.50	.278	0	....	-3	0	-0.3
1990	Hou-N	2	1	.667	34	1	0	0	0	62^1	60	34	32	8	4	24	24	1.348	4.62	80	4.15	.256	1	.333	-7	2	-0.6
1991	Hou-N	2	7	.222	32	6	0	0	3	63	66	34	33	6	0	32	55	1.556	4.71	74	4.47	.263	0	.000	-9	1	-0.9
1992	Hou-N	9	1	.900	77	0	0	0	7	111	81	31	26	5	3	42	96	1.108	2.11	159	2.23	.200	0	.000	16	11	1.6
1993	Hou-N	4	5	.444	72	0	0	0	9	96^2	75	37	28	6	1	28	101	1.066	2.61	149	2.25	.212	0	.000	13	12	1.2
1994	NY-A	4	4	.500	31	0	0	0	6	40	48	27	26	7	2	21	37	1.725	5.85	78	6.44	.300	0	....	-6	1	-0.6
1995*	Cin-N	7	2	.778	59	0	0	0	3	90	95	47	46	8	4	31	84	1.400	4.60	90	4.25	.273	0	.000	-7	5	-0.8
1996	Cin-N	0	0	....	3	0	0	0	0	3^1	8	6	5	2	0	2	3	3.000	13.50	31	20.67	.471	0	....	-3	0	-0.3
	Hou-N	5	5	.500	58	0	0	0	6	74^2	69	39	35	11	2	26	78	1.272	4.22	92	3.70	.245	0	.000	-2	5	-0.2
	Yr.	5	5	.500	61	0	0	0	6	78	77	45	40	13	2	28	81	1.346	4.62	85	4.42	.258	0	.000	-5	5	-0.5
1997	Tex-A	0	4	.000	44	0	0	0	0	49^1	51	27	25	7	2	22	36	1.480	4.56	105	4.72	.262	0	....	2	3	0.2
1998	Tex-A	6	6	.500	46	0	0	0	1	58	43	27	23	5	1	30	41	1.259	3.57	135	3.08	.207	0	....	9	6	0.8
Total	**10**	**40**	**35**	**.533**	**463**	**7**	**0**	**0**	**35**	**671**	**621**	**324**	**291**	**67**	**20**	**266**	**562**	**1.322**	**3.90**	**102**	**3.73**	**.244**	**1**	**.027**	**3**	**46**	**0.1**

• HERNDON, Junior Harry Francis Herndon b: 9/11/1978, Liberal, KS BR/TR, 6'1", 190 lbs. Deb: 8/2/2001

YEAR	TM-L	W	L	PCT	G	GS	CG	SH	SV	IP	H	R	ER	HR	HB	BB	SO	RAT	ERA	ERA+	CERA	OAV	BH	AVG	PR+	WS	TPW
2001	SD-N	2	6	.250	12	8	0	0	0	42^2	55	34	30	5	3	25	14	1.875	6.33	63	6.98	.322	0	.000	-10	0	-1.1

• HERRELL, Walt Walter William "Reds" Herrell b: 2/19/1889, Rockville, MD d: 1/23/1949, Front Royal, VA Deb: 6/10/1911

YEAR	TM-L	W	L	PCT	G	GS	CG	SH	SV	IP	H	R	ER	HR	HB	BB	SO	RAT	ERA	ERA+	CERA	OAV	BH	AVG	PR+	WS	TPW
1911	Was-A	0	0	....	1	0	0	0	0	2	5	4	4	0	0	2	0	3.500	18.00	18	18.15	.556	0	.000	-3	0	-0.3

• HERRERA, Alex Alexander J. Herrera b: 11/5/1979, Maracaibo, Venezuela BL/TL, 5'11", 175 lbs. Deb: 9/13/2002

YEAR	TM-L	W	L	PCT	G	GS	CG	SH	SV	IP	H	R	ER	HR	HB	BB	SO	RAT	ERA	ERA+	CERA	OAV	BH	AVG	PR+	WS	TPW
2002	Cle-A	0	0	....	5	0	0	0	0	5^1	3	0	0	0	0	1	5	.750	0.00	....	0.99	.158	0	....	3	1	0.3
2003	Cle-A	0	0	....	10	0	0	0	0	7	7	7	7	3	0	8	6	2.143	9.00	49	9.65	.250	0	....	-4	0	-0.4
Total	**2**	**0**	**0**	**....**	**15**	**0**	**0**	**0**	**0**	**12^1**	**10**	**7**	**7**	**3**	**0**	**9**	**11**	**1.541**	**5.11**	**86**	**5.91**	**.213**	**0**	**....**	**-1**	**1**	**-0.1**

• HERRERA, Bobby Procopio Rodriguez "Tito" Herrera b: 7/26/1926, Nuevo Laredo, Mexico BR/TR, 6', 184 lbs. Deb: 4/19/1951

YEAR	TM-L	W	L	PCT	G	GS	CG	SH	SV	IP	H	R	ER	HR	HB	BB	SO	RAT	ERA	ERA+	CERA	OAV	BH	AVG	PR+	WS	TPW
1951	StL-A	0	0	....	3	0	0	0	0	2^1	6	7	7	2	1	4	1	4.286	27.00	16	32.35	.462	0	....	-6	0	-0.6

• HERRIAGE, Troy William Troy "Dutch" Herriage b: 12/20/1930, Tipton, OK BR/TR, 6'1", 170 lbs. Deb: 4/25/1956

YEAR	TM-L	W	L	PCT	G	GS	CG	SH	SV	IP	H	R	ER	HR	HB	BB	SO	RAT	ERA	ERA+	CERA	OAV	BH	AVG	PR+	WS	TPW
1956	KC-A	1	13	.071	31	16	1	0	0	103	135	83	76	16	6	64	59	1.932	6.64	65	7.51	.321	3	.120	-28	0	-2.8

• HERRIN, Tom Thomas Edward Herrin b: 9/12/1929, Shreveport, LA d: 11/29/1999, Homer, LA BR/TR, 6'3", 190 lbs. Deb: 4/13/1954

YEAR	TM-L	W	L	PCT	G	GS	CG	SH	SV	IP	H	R	ER	HR	HB	BB	SO	RAT	ERA	ERA+	CERA	OAV	BH	AVG	PR+	WS	TPW
1954	Bos-A	1	2	.333	14	1	0	0	0	28^1	34	23	23	2	0	22	8	1.976	7.31	56	6.46	.315	1	.125	-10	0	-1.1

• HERRING, Art Arthur L. "Red,Sandy" Herring b: 3/10/1906, Altus, OK d: 12/2/1995, Marion, IN BR/TR, 5'7", 168 lbs. Deb: 9/12/1929

YEAR	TM-L	W	L	PCT	G	GS	CG	SH	SV	IP	H	R	ER	HR	HB	BB	SO	RAT	ERA	ERA+	CERA	OAV	BH	AVG	PR+	WS	TPW
1929	Det-A	2	1	.667	4	4	2	0	0	32	38	17	17	0	1	19	15	1.781	4.78	90	5.20	.302	3	.214	-1	2	0.0
1930	Det-A	3	3	.500	23	6	1	0	0	77^2	97	54	46	2	3	36	16	1.712	5.33	90	5.22	.315	3	.130	-5	3	-0.6
1931	Det-A	7	13	.350	35	16	9	0	1	165	186	95	79	8	8	67	64	1.533	4.31	106	4.47	.281	11	.200	5	10	0.4
1932	Det-A	1	2	.333	12	0	0	0	2	22^1	25	18	13	2	1	15	12	1.791	5.24	90	5.80	.284	0	.000	-2	1	-0.2
1933	Det-A	1	2	.333	24	3	1	0	0	61	61	34	26	6	1	20	20	1.328	3.84	112	3.79	.264	1	.077	3	3	0.2
1934	Bro-N	2	4	.333	14	4	2	0	0	49^1	63	36	34	2	0	29	15	1.865	6.20	63	5.72	.307	2	.143	-12	0	-1.1
1939	Chi-A	0	0	....	7	0	0	0	0	14^1	13	9	9	2	1	5	8	1.256	5.65	84	3.87	.250	0	.000	-2	1	-0.2
1944	Bro-N	3	4	.429	12	6	3	1	1	55^1	59	28	21	3	1	17	19	1.373	3.42	104	3.74	.277	3	.200	3	2	0.3
1945	Bro-N	7	4	.636	22	15	7	2	2	124	103	60	48	11	3	43	34	1.177	3.48	108	2.85	.222	4	.095	4	7	0.2

YEAR TM-L	W	L	PCT	G	GS	CG	SH	SV	IP	H	R	ER	HR	HB	BB	SO	RAT	ERA	ERA+	CERA	OAV	BH	AVG	PR+	WS	TPW
1946 Bro-N	7	2	.778	35	2	0	0	5	86	91	39	32	2	1	29	34	1.395	3.35	101	3.54	.277	4	.182	-1	6	0.0
1947 Pit-N	1	3	.250	11	0	0	0	2	10^{2}	18	11	10	3	0	4	6	2.063	8.44	50	9.34	.360	0	.000	-5	0	-0.5
Total 11	34	38	.472	199	56	25	3	13	697^{2}	754	401	335	41	20	284	243	1.488	4.32	96	4.26	.276	31	.149	-12	35	-1.5
• HERRING, Bill	William Francis "Smoke" Herring b: 10/31/1893, New York, NY d: 9/10/1962, Honesdale, PA BR/TR, 6'3", 185 lbs. Deb: 6/26/1915																									
1915 Bro-F	0	0	....	3	0	0	0	0	3	5	6	5	1	1	2	3	2.333	15.00	20	13.13	.385	0	....	-4	0	-0.4
• HERRING, Herb	Herbert Lee Herring b: 7/22/1891, Danville, AR d: 4/22/1964, Tucson, AZ BR/TR, 5'11", 178 lbs. Deb: 9/4/1912																									
1912 Was-A	0	0	....	1	0	0	0	0	1	1	0	0	0	0	1	0	2.000	0.00	....	5.17	.250	0	....	0	0	0.0
• HERRING, Lefty	Silas Clarke Herring b: 3/4/1880, Philadelphia, PA d: 2/11/1965, Massapequa, NY BL/TL, 5'11", 160 lbs. Deb: 5/16/1899 ♦																									
1899 Was-N	0	0	....	2	0	0	0	0	2	0	0	0	0	0	2	0	1.000	0.00	....	0.82	.000	1	1.000	1	1	0.2
• HERRMANN, Leroy	Leroy George Herrmann b: 2/27/1906, Steward, IL d: 7/3/1972, Livermore, CA BR/TR, 5'10", 185 lbs. Deb: 7/30/1932																									
1932 Chi-N	2	1	.667	7	0	0	0	0	12^{2}	18	9	9	0	0	9	5	2.132	6.39	59	6.98	.346	1	.500	-4	0	-0.4
1933 Chi-N	0	1	.000	9	1	0	0	1	21	26	19	13	3	4	8	4	1.619	5.57	59	6.09	.299	1	.167	-6	0	-0.6
1935 Cin-N	3	5	.375	29	8	2	0	0	108	124	53	43	9	8	31	30	1.435	3.58	111	4.64	.297	8	.267	6	7	0.7
Total 3	5	7	.417	45	9	2	0	1	141^{2}	168	81	65	12	12	48	39	1.525	4.13	92	5.06	.302	10	.263	-4	7	-0.3
• HERRMANN, Marty	Martin John "Lefty" Herrmann b: 1/10/1893, Oldenburg, IN d: 9/11/1956, Cincinnati, OH BL/TL, 5'10", 150 lbs. Deb: 7/10/1918																									
1918 Bro-N	0	0	....	1	0	0	0	0	1	0	0	0	0	0	1	0	1.000	0.00	....	0.80	.000	0	....	0	0	0.0
• HERSHEY, Frank	Frank Hershey b: 12/13/1877, Gorham, NY d: 12/15/1949, Canandaigua, NY TR, 5'10", 175 lbs. Deb: 4/20/1905																									
1905 Bos-N	0	1	.000	1	1	0	0	0	4	5	4	3	0	0	2	1	1.750	6.75	46	5.16	.313	0	.000	-2	0	-0.2
• HERSHISER, Orel	Orel Leonard "Bulldog" Hershiser b: 9/16/1958, Buffalo, NY BR/TR, 6'3", 192 lbs. Deb: 9/1/1983 C																									
1983 LA-N	0	0	....	8	0	0	0	1	8	7	6	3	1	0	6	5	1.625	3.38	106	4.82	.233	0	....	0	0	0.0
1984 LA-N	11	8	.579	45	20	8	**4**	2	189^{2}	160	65	56	9	4	50	150	1.107	2.66	133	2.42	.225	10	.200	20	18	2.3
1985* LA-N	19	3	.864	36	34	9	5	0	239^{2}	179	72	54	8	6	68	157	1.031	2.03	171	2.01	.206	15	.197	38	23	4.3
1986 LA-N	14	14	.500	35	35	8	1	0	231^{1}	213	112	99	13	5	86	153	1.293	3.85	90	3.20	.243	17	.239	-5	12	-0.2
1987 LA-N★	16	16	.500	37	35	10	1	1	**264^{2}**	247	105	90	17	9	74	190	1.213	3.06	130	3.15	.247	19	.211	**29**	**21**	**3.2**
1988* LA-N★	**23**	8	.742	35	34	**15**	**8**	1	**267**	208	73	67	18	4	73	178	1.052	2.26	147	2.26	.213	11	.129	**34**	**25**	**3.7**
1989 LA-N★	15	15	.500	35	33	8	4	0	**256^{2}**	226	75	66	9	3	77	178	1.181	2.31	147	2.63	.240	14	.182	**29**	**21**	**3.5**
1990 LA-N	1	1	.500	4	4	0	0	0	25^{1}	26	12	12	1	1	4	16	1.184	4.26	86	3.00	.260	0	.000	-2	1	-0.3
1991 LA-N	7	2	.778	21	21	0	0	0	112	112	43	43	3	5	32	73	1.286	3.46	104	3.23	.259	8	.258	2	8	0.5
1992 LA-N	10	15	.400	33	33	1	0	0	210^{2}	209	101	86	15	8	69	130	1.320	3.67	94	3.55	.257	15	.221	-0	8	0.4
1993 LA-N	12	14	.462	33	33	5	1	0	215^{2}	201	106	86	17	7	72	141	1.266	3.59	106	3.32	.246	26	.356	6	13	1.5
1994 LA-N	6	6	.500	21	21	1	0	0	135^{1}	146	67	57	15	2	42	72	1.389	3.79	104	4.30	.279	9	.205	3	7	0.4
1995* Cle-A	16	6	.727	26	26	1	1	0	167^{1}	151	76	72	21	5	51	111	1.207	3.87	121	3.53	.244	0	....	16	13	1.5
1996* Cle-A	15	9	.625	33	33	1	0	0	206	238	115	97	21	12	58	125	1.437	4.24	116	4.69	.287	0	....	16	14	1.4
1997* Cle-A	14	6	.700	32	32	1	0	0	195^{1}	199	105	97	26	11	69	107	1.372	4.47	105	4.57	.272	0	.000	6	11	0.6
1998 SF-N	11	10	.524	34	34	0	0	0	202	200	105	99	22	13	85	126	1.411	4.41	90	4.35	.259	10	.152	-10	7	-0.9
1999* NY-N	13	12	.520	32	32	0	0	0	179	175	92	91	14	11	77	89	1.408	4.58	96	4.17	.260	9	.145	-5	8	-0.6
2000 LA-N	1	5	.167	10	6	0	0	0	24^{2}	42	36	36	5	11	14	13	2.270	13.14	33	12.48	.389	0	.000	-24	0	-2.3
Total 18	204	150	.576	510	466	68	25	5	3130^{1}	2939	1366	1211	235	117	1007	2014	1.261	3.48	112	3.42	.248	163	.201	153	210	19.1
• HESKETH, Joe	Joseph Thomas Hesketh b: 2/15/1959, Lackawanna, NY BR/TL, 6'2", 170 lbs. Deb: 8/7/1984																									
1984 Mon-N	2	2	.500	11	5	1	1	1	45	38	12	9	2	0	15	32	1.178	1.80	190	2.59	.233	1	.100	8	4	0.8
1985 Mon-N	10	5	.667	25	25	2	1	0	155^{1}	125	52	43	10	0	45	113	1.094	2.49	136	2.44	.222	4	.091	14	11	1.4
1986 Mon-N	6	5	.545	15	15	0	0	0	82^{2}	92	46	46	11	2	31	67	1.488	5.01	74	4.92	.283	0	.000	-12	2	-1.5
1987 Mon-N	0	0	....	18	0	0	0	1	28^{2}	23	12	10	2	2	15	31	1.326	3.14	134	3.21	.211	0	.000	4	2	0.3
1988 Mon-N	4	3	.571	60	0	0	0	9	72^{2}	63	30	23	1	0	35	64	1.349	2.85	126	2.93	.242	0	.000	5	7	0.6
1989 Mon-N	6	4	.600	43	0	0	0	3	48^{1}	54	34	31	5	0	26	44	1.655	5.77	61	5.14	.292	1	.500	-12	0	-1.2
1990 Mon-N	1	0	1.000	2	0	0	0	0	3	2	0	0	0	0	2	3	1.333	0.00	....	2.23	.200	0	....	1	1	0.1
Atl-N	0	2	.000	31	0	0	0	5	31	30	23	20	5	1	12	21	1.355	5.81	69	4.34	.248	0	.000	-5	1	-0.6
Yr.	1	2	.333	33	0	0	0	5	34	32	23	20	5	1	14	24	1.353	5.29	76	4.16	.244	0	.000	-4	2	-0.4
Bos-A	0	4	.000	12	2	0	0	0	25^{2}	37	12	10	2	0	11	26	1.870	3.51	116	6.59	.333	0	....	2	1	0.2
1991 Bos-A	12	4	.750	39	17	0	0	0	153^{1}	142	59	56	19	0	53	104	1.272	3.29	131	3.67	.250	0	....	17	13	1.8
1992 Bos-A	8	9	.471	30	25	1	0	1	148^{2}	162	84	72	15	2	58	104	1.480	4.36	97	4.46	.276	0	....	-3	7	-0.3
1993 Bos-A	3	4	.429	28	5	0	0	1	53^{1}	62	35	30	4	0	29	34	1.706	5.06	91	5.25	.294	0	....	-3	2	-0.3
1994 Bos-A	8	5	.615	25	20	0	0	0	114	117	70	54	9	2	46	83	1.430	4.26	118	4.12	.267	0	....	9	7	0.8
Total 11	60	47	.561	339	114	4	2	21	961^{2}	947	469	404	85	9	378	726	1.378	3.78	107	3.89	.259	6	.070	25	58	2.2
• HESS, Otto	Otto C. Hess b: 10/10/1878, Berne, Switzerland d: 2/25/1926, Tucson, AZ BL/TL, 6'1", 170 lbs. Deb: 8/3/1902 ♦																									
1902 Cle-A	2	4	.333	7	4	4	0	0	43^{2}	67	42	29	0	1	23	13	2.061	5.98	58	6.91	.351	1	.071	-12	0	-1.3
1904 Cle-A	8	7	.533	21	16	15	4	0	151^{1}	134	60	28	2	5	31	64	1.090	1.67	152	2.21	.238	12	.120	14	9	0.9
1905 Cle-A	10	15	.400	26	25	22	4	0	213^{2}	179	97	75	1	9	72	109	1.175	3.16	83	2.44	.230	44	.254	-13	14	-0.8
1906 Cle-A	20	17	.541	43	36	33	7	**3**	333^{2}	274	104	68	4	24	85	167	1.076	1.83	143	2.25	.227	31	.201	22	24	2.5
1907 Cle-A	6	6	.500	17	14	7	0	1	93^{1}	84	37	30	1	12	37	36	1.296	2.89	87	3.17	.243	4	.133	-6	5	-0.7
1908 Cle-A	0	0	....	4	0	0	0	0	7	11	6	4	0	0	1	2	1.714	5.14	46	6.47	.407	0	.000	-2	0	-0.6
1912 Bos-N	12	17	.414	33	31	21	0	0	254	270	142	106	3	15	90	80	1.417	3.76	95	3.81	.283	23	.245	-2	14	0.2
1913 Bos-N	7	17	.292	29	27	19	2	0	218^{1}	231	123	93	13	7	70	80	1.379	3.83	85	3.87	.279	26	.313	-10	9	-0.1
1914 Bos-N	5	6	.455	14	11	7	1	1	89	89	39	30	2	5	33	24	1.371	3.03	91	3.63	.271	11	.234	-6	6	-0.6
1915 Bos-N	0	1	.000	4	1	1	0	0	14	16	13	6	0	2	6	5	1.571	3.86	69	4.58	.286	2	.400	-2	0	-0.1
Total 10	70	90	.438	198	165	129	18	5	1418	1355	663	469	26	80	448	580	1.272	2.98	99	3.14	.257	154	.216	-17	81	-0.7
• HESSELBACHER, George	George Edward Hesselbacher b: 1/18/1895, Philadelphia, PA d: 2/18/1980, Rydal, PA BR/TR, 6'2", 175 lbs. Deb: 6/29/1916																									
1916 Phi-A	0	4	.000	6	4	2	0	0	26	37	33	21	3	0	22	6	2.269	7.27	39	8.87	.349	1	.125	-12	0	-1.4
• HESTERFER, Larry	Lawrence Hesterfer b: 6/9/1878, Newark, NJ d: 9/22/1943, Cedar Grove, NJ BR/TL, 5'8", 145 lbs. Deb: 9/5/1901																									
1901 NY-N	0	1	.000	1	1	1	0	0	6	15	15	5	0	0	3	2	3.000	7.50	44	11.13	.466	0	.000	-3	0	-0.3
• HETKI, Johnny	John Edward Hetki b: 5/12/1922, Leavenworth, KS BR/TR, 6'1", 205 lbs. Deb: 9/14/1945																									
1945 Cin-N	1	2	.333	5	2	2	0	0	32^{2}	28	13	13	1	0	11	9	1.194	3.58	105	2.54	.235	1	.091	1	2	0.0
1946 Cin-N	6	6	.500	32	11	4	0	1	126^{1}	121	44	42	3	1	31	41	1.203	2.99	112	2.73	.253	11	.333	2	10	0.5
1947 Cin-N	3	4	.429	37	5	2	0	0	96	110	72	62	7	1	48	33	1.646	5.81	71	5.00	.287	6	.222	-17	0	-1.6
1948 Cin-N	0	1	.000	3	0	0	0	0	6^{2}	8	7	7	0	0	3	3	1.650	9.45	41	4.10	.286	0	.000	-4	0	-0.4
1950 Cin-N	1	2	.333	22	1	0	0	0	53	53	33	30	9	3	27	21	1.509	5.09	83	5.21	.265	2	.222	-4	2	-0.4
1952 StL-A	0	1	.000	3	1	0	0	0	9^{1}	15	7	4	2	0	2	4	1.821	3.86	101	7.67	.357	0	.000	-0	0	0.0
1953 Pit-N	3	6	.333	54	2	0	0	3	118^{1}	120	60	52	9	1	33	37	1.293	3.95	113	3.49	.266	5	.208	8	10	0.9
1954 Pit-N	4	4	.500	58	1	0	0	9	83	102	53	46	11	0	30	27	1.590	4.99	84	5.22	.297	2	.222	-5	4	-0.5
Total 8	18	26	.409	214	23	8	0	13	525^{1}	557	289	256	42	6	185	175	1.412	4.39	92	4.05	.272	27	.235	-21	28	-1.5
• HETZEL, Eric	Eric Paul Hetzel b: 9/25/1963, Crowley, LA BR/TR, 6'3", 175 lbs. Deb: 7/1/1989																									
1989 Bos-A	2	3	.400	12	11	0	0	0	50^{1}	61	39	35	7	2	28	33	1.768	6.26	66	6.35	.296	0	....	-12	0	-1.2
1990 Bos-A	1	4	.200	9	8	0	0	0	35	39	28	23	3	1	21	20	1.714	5.91	69	5.52	.281	0	....	-6	0	-0.7
Total 2	3	7	.300	21	19	0	0	0	85^{1}	100	67	58	10	3	49	53	1.746	6.12	67	6.01	.290	0	....	-18	0	-1.8
• HEUSSER, Ed	Edward Burlton "The Wild Elk Of The Wasatch" Heusser b: 5/7/1909, Salt Lake County, UT d: 3/1/1956, Aurora, CO BB/TR, 6'.5", 187 lbs. Deb: 4/25/1935																									
1935 StL-N	5	5	.500	33	11	2	0	2	123^{1}	125	50	40	5	2	27	39	1.232	2.92	140	3.08	.263	4	.118	15	10	1.3
1936 StL-N	7	3	.700	42	3	0	0	3	104^{1}	130	73	63	6	4	38	26	1.610	5.43	73	5.08	.310	7	.269	-17	4	-1.4

YEAR	TM-L	W	L	PCT	G	GS	CG	SH	SV	IP	H	R	ER	HR	HB	BB	SO	RAT	ERA	ERA+	CERA	OAV	BH	AVG	PR+	WS	TPW
1938	Phi-N	0	0	....	1	0	0	0	0	1	2	3	3	1	0	1	0	3.000	27.00	15	22.62	.400	0	....	-3	0	-0.3
1940	Phi-A	6	13	.316	41	6	2	0	5	110	144	84	61	11	2	42	39	1.691	4.99	89	5.63	.308	5	.167	-5	4	-0.4
1943	Cin-N	4	3	.571	26	10	2	1	0	91	97	40	35	4	0	23	28	1.319	3.46	96	3.47	.275	5	.185	-4	4	-0.5
1944	Cin-N	13	11	.542	30	23	17	4	2	192^{2}	165	59	51	9	1	42	42	1.074	**2.38**	**146**	**2.30**	.231	15	.217	19	20	2.0
1945	Cin-N	11	16	.407	31	30	18	4	1	223	248	105	92	10	3	60	56	1.381	3.71	101	3.75	.280	19	.247	1	14	0.6
1946	Cin-N	7	14	.333	29	21	9	1	2	167^{2}	167	68	60	11	1	39	47	1.229	3.22	104	3.17	.260	11	.208	-2	10	-0.1
1948	Phi-N	3	2	.600	33	0	0	0	3	74	89	46	41	9	0	28	22	1.581	4.99	79	5.25	.299	3	.158	-8	2	-0.9
Total	9	56	67	.455	266	104	50	10	18	1087	1167	528	446	66	13	300	299	1.350	3.69	102	3.74	.274	69	.206	-4	68	0.4

• HEVING, Joe Joseph William Heving b: 9/2/1900, Covington, KY d: 4/11/1970, Covington, KY BR/TR, 6'1", 185 lbs. Deb: 4/29/1930

YEAR	TM-L	W	L	PCT	G	GS	CG	SH	SV	IP	H	R	ER	HR	HB	BB	SO	RAT	ERA	ERA+	CERA	OAV	BH	AVG	PR+	WS	TPW
1930	NY-N	7	5	.583	41	2	0	0	6	89^{2}	109	57	52	7	1	27	37	1.517	5.22	91	4.70	.309	5	.227	-6	6	-0.5
1931	NY-N	1	6	.143	22	0	0	0	3	42^{1}	48	27	23	4	2	11	26	1.394	4.89	75	4.19	.277	1	.125	-6	0	-0.7
1933	Chi-A	7	5	.583	40	6	3	1	6	118	113	50	35	6	2	27	47	1.186	2.67	159	2.85	.249	8	.211	22	13	2.1
1934	Chi-A	1	7	.125	33	2	0	0	4	88	133	85	71	12	3	48	40	2.057	7.26	65	7.93	.343	5	.185	-22	0	-2.0
1937	Cle-A	8	4	.667	40	0	0	0	5	72^{2}	92	53	39	6	2	30	35	1.679	4.83	95	5.48	.311	5	.263	-1	5	-0.1
1938	Cle-A	1	1	.500	3	0	0	0	0	6	10	8	6	0	0	5	0	2.500	9.00	52	8.96	.370	0	.000	-3	0	-0.3
	Bos-A	8	1	.889	16	11	7	1	2	82	94	35	34	5	1	22	34	1.415	3.73	132	4.06	.283	4	.133	10	8	0.8
	Yr.	9	2	.818	19	11	7	1	2	88	104	43	40	5	1	27	34	1.489	4.09	119	4.40	.290	4	.129	7	8	0.5
1939	Bos-A	11	3	.786	46	5	1	0	7	107	124	65	44	8	2	34	43	1.477	3.70	128	4.44	.295	6	.188	12	11	1.1
1940	Bos-A	12	7	.632	39	7	4	0	3	119	129	63	53	7	3	42	55	1.437	4.01	112	4.02	.272	8	.200	7	10	0.7
1941	Cle-A	5	2	.714	27	3	2	1	5	70^{2}	63	21	18	2	1	31	18	1.330	2.29	172	3.11	.240	0	.000	13	9	1.1
1942	Cle-A	5	3	.625	27	2	0	0	3	46^{1}	52	28	25	4	2	25	13	1.662	4.86	71	5.17	.278	0	.000	-8	1	-0.9
1943	Cle-A	1	1	.500	30	1	0	0	9	72	58	23	22	1	2	34	34	1.278	2.75	113	2.79	.230	1	.071	1	5	0.1
1944	Cle-A	8	3	.727	**63**	1	0	0	10	119^{2}	106	42	26	2	2	41	46	1.228	1.96	169	2.67	.239	4	.182	16	13	1.6
1945	Bos-N	1	0	1.000	3	0	0	0	0	5^{1}	5	2	2	0	1	3	1	1.500	3.38	113	4.61	.294	0	.000	0	1	0.0
Total	13	76	48	.613	430	40	17	3	63	1038^{2}	1136	559	450	64	24	380	429	1.460	3.90	109	4.21	.279	47	.170	36	82	3.2

• HEWITT, Jake Charles Jacob Hewitt b: 6/6/1870, Madisonville, WV d: 5/18/1959, Morgantown, WV BL/TL, 5'7", 150 lbs. Deb: 8/6/1895

YEAR	TM-L	W	L	PCT	G	GS	CG	SH	SV	IP	H	R	ER	HR	HB	BB	SO	RAT	ERA	ERA+	CERA	OAV	BH	AVG	PR+	WS	TPW
1895	Pit-N	1	0	1.000	4	2	1	0	2	13	13	6	6	0	1	2	4	1.154	4.15	109	2.73	.257	1	.167	0	2	0.0

• HEYDEMAN, Greg Gregory George Heydeman b: 1/2/1952, Carmel, CA BR/TR, 6', 180 lbs. Deb: 9/2/1973

YEAR	TM-L	W	L	PCT	G	GS	CG	SH	SV	IP	H	R	ER	HR	HB	BB	SO	RAT	ERA	ERA+	CERA	OAV	BH	AVG	PR+	WS	TPW
1973	LA-N	0	0	....	1	0	0	0	0	2	2	1	1	0	1	1	1	1.500	4.50	76	4.93	.222	0	....	-0	0	0.0

• HIBBARD, Greg James Gregory Hibbard b: 9/13/1964, New Orleans, LA BL/TL, 6', 190 lbs. Deb: 5/31/1989

YEAR	TM-L	W	L	PCT	G	GS	CG	SH	SV	IP	H	R	ER	HR	HB	BB	SO	RAT	ERA	ERA+	CERA	OAV	BH	AVG	PR+	WS	TPW
1989	Chi-A	6	7	.462	23	23	2	0	0	137^{1}	142	58	49	5	2	41	55	1.333	3.21	119	3.51	.268	0	....	9	8	0.9
1990	Chi-A	14	9	.609	33	33	3	1	0	211	202	80	74	11	6	55	92	1.218	3.16	121	3.12	.255	0	....	11	16	1.2
1991	Chi-A	11	11	.500	32	29	5	0	0	194	196	107	93	23	2	57	71	1.304	4.31	92	3.95	.266	0	....	-13	7	-1.3
1992	Chi-A	10	7	.588	31	28	0	0	1	176	187	92	86	17	7	57	69	1.386	4.40	88	4.29	.277	0	....	-10	7	-1.1
1993	Chi-N	15	11	.577	31	31	1	0	0	191	209	96	84	19	3	47	82	1.340	3.96	101	4.06	.286	6	.092	-2	11	-0.4
1994	Sea-A	1	5	.167	15	14	0	0	0	80^{2}	115	78	60	11	2	31	39	1.810	6.69	73	6.74	.328	0	....	-15	0	-1.4
Total	6	57	50	.533	165	158	11	1	1	990	1051	511	446	86	22	288	408	1.353	4.05	99	4.02	.275	6	.092	-20	49	-2.1

• HIBBARD, John John Denison Hibbard b: 12/2/1864, Chicago, IL d: 11/17/1937, Hollywood, CA TL Deb: 7/31/1884

YEAR	TM-L	W	L	PCT	G	GS	CG	SH	SV	IP	H	R	ER	HR	HB	BB	SO	RAT	ERA	ERA+	CERA	OAV	BH	AVG	PR+	WS	TPW
1884	Chi-N	1	1	.500	2	2	2	1	0	17	18	10	5	1	....	9	4	1.588	2.65	118	....	.257	0	.000	0	1	-0.1

• HICKERSON, Bryan Bryan David Hickerson b: 10/13/1963, Bemidji, MN BL/TL, 6'2", 203 lbs. Deb: 7/25/1991

YEAR	TM-L	W	L	PCT	G	GS	CG	SH	SV	IP	H	R	ER	HR	HB	BB	SO	RAT	ERA	ERA+	CERA	OAV	BH	AVG	PR+	WS	TPW
1991	SF-N	2	2	.500	17	6	0	0	0	50	53	20	20	3	0	17	43	1.400	3.60	99	3.86	.275	0	.000	-1	2	-0.2
1992	SF-N	5	3	.625	61	1	0	0	0	87^{1}	74	31	30	7	1	21	68	1.088	3.09	107	2.62	.236	0	.000	0	7	0.0
1993	SF-N	7	5	.583	47	15	0	0	0	120^{1}	137	58	57	14	1	39	69	1.463	4.26	92	4.68	.291	4	.143	-8	5	-0.8
1994	SF-N	4	8	.333	28	14	0	0	1	98^{1}	118	60	59	20	1	38	59	1.586	5.40	74	6.00	.301	5	.185	-19	1	-1.8
1995	Chi-N	2	3	.400	38	0	0	0	1	31^{2}	36	28	24	3	0	15	28	1.611	6.82	60	4.85	.283	1	.500	-10	0	-0.9
	Col-N	1	0	1.000	18	0	0	0	0	16^{2}	33	24	22	5	1	13	12	2.760	11.88	45	14.50	.407	1	1.000	-12	0	-1.1
	Yr.	3	3	.500	56	0	0	0	1	48^{1}	69	52	46	8	1	28	40	2.007	8.57	54	8.17	.332	2	.667	-21	0	-1.9
Total	5	21	21	.500	209	36	0	0	2	404^{1}	451	221	212	52	4	143	279	1.469	4.72	83	4.87	.286	11	.149	-49	15	-4.8

• HICKEY, Jack John William Hickey b: 11/3/1881, Minneapolis, MN d: 12/28/1941, Seattle, WA BR/TL, 5'10", 170 lbs. Deb: 4/16/1904

YEAR	TM-L	W	L	PCT	G	GS	CG	SH	SV	IP	H	R	ER	HR	HB	BB	SO	RAT	ERA	ERA+	CERA	OAV	BH	AVG	PR+	WS	TPW
1904	Cle-A	0	1	.000	2	2	1	0	0	12^{1}	14	13	10	0	0	11	5	2.027	7.30	35	5.78	.286	0	.000	-7	0	-0.8

• HICKEY, Jim James Robert "Sid" Hickey b: 10/22/1920, North Abington, MA d: 9/20/1997, Manchester, CT BR/TR, 6'1", 204 lbs. Deb: 4/25/1942

YEAR	TM-L	W	L	PCT	G	GS	CG	SH	SV	IP	H	R	ER	HR	HB	BB	SO	RAT	ERA	ERA+	CERA	OAV	BH	AVG	PR+	WS	TPW
1942	Bos-N	0	1	.000	1	1	0	0	0	1^{1}	4	4	3	1	0	2	0	4.500	20.25	16	28.38	.500	0	.000	-2	0	-0.3
1944	Bos-N	0	0	....	8	0	0	0	0	9^{1}	15	9	5	0	1	5	3	2.143	4.82	79	7.89	.366	0	.000	-1	0	-0.1
Total	2	0	1	.000	9	1	0	0	0	10^{2}	19	13	8	1	1	7	3	2.438	6.75	54	10.45	.388	0	.000	-4	0	-0.4

• HICKEY, Kevin Kevin John Hickey b: 2/25/1956, Chicago, IL BL/TL, 6'1", 200 lbs. Deb: 4/14/1981

YEAR	TM-L	W	L	PCT	G	GS	CG	SH	SV	IP	H	R	ER	HR	HB	BB	SO	RAT	ERA	ERA+	CERA	OAV	BH	AVG	PR+	WS	TPW
1981	Chi-A	0	2	.000	41	0	0	0	3	44^{1}	38	22	18	3	1	18	17	1.263	3.65	98	2.99	.232	0	....	-1	2	-0.1
1982	Chi-A	4	4	.500	60	0	0	0	6	78	73	32	26	4	2	30	38	1.321	3.00	134	3.36	.256	0	....	10	7	1.0
1983	Chi-A	1	2	.333	23	0	0	0	5	20^{2}	23	14	12	5	0	11	8	1.645	5.23	80	5.93	.264	0	....	-2	1	-0.2
1989	Bal-A	2	3	.400	51	0	0	0	2	49^{1}	38	16	16	3	1	23	28	1.236	2.92	130	2.91	.220	0	....	4	5	0.5
1990	Bal-A	1	3	.250	37	0	0	0	1	26^{1}	26	16	15	3	0	13	17	1.481	5.13	74	4.46	.265	0	....	-4	0	-0.4
1991	Bal-A	1	0	1.000	19	0	0	0	0	14	15	14	14	3	0	6	10	1.500	9.00	44	5.42	.278	0	....	-8	0	-0.8
Total	6	9	14	.391	231	0	0	0	17	232^{2}	213	114	101	21	4	101	118	1.350	3.91	99	3.67	.247	0	....	-1	15	-0.1

• HICKMAN, Charlie Charles Taylor "Piano Legs,Cheerful Charlie" Hickman
b: 5/4/1876, Taylortown, PA d: 4/19/1934, Morgantown, WV BR/TR, 5'9", 215 lbs. Deb: 9/8/1897 U ♦

YEAR	TM-L	W	L	PCT	G	GS	CG	SH	SV	IP	H	R	ER	HR	HB	BB	SO	RAT	ERA	ERA+	CERA	OAV	BH	AVG	PR+	WS	TPW
1897*	Bos-N	0	0	....	2	0	0	0	1	7^{2}	10	5	5	0	0	5	0	1.957	5.87	76	5.88	.313	2	.667	-1	1	0.0
1898	Bos-N	1	2	.333	6	3	3	1	2	33	22	8	8	0	0	13	9	1.061	2.18	169	1.69	.189	15	.259	5	5	0.1
1899	Bos-N	6	0	1.000	11	9	5	2	1	66^{1}	52	38	33	3	8	40	14	1.387	4.48	93	3.55	.216	25	.397	-5	9	0.1
1901	NY-N	3	5	.375	9	9	6	0	0	65	76	42	33	1	3	26	11	1.569	4.57	72	4.47	.290	113	.278	-7	12	-1.0
1902	Cle-A	0	1	.000	1	1	1	0	0	8	11	8	7	0	1	5	1	2.000	7.88	44	6.86	.327	161	.378	-4	19	2.7
1907	Was-A	0	0	....	1	0	0	0	0	5	4	4	2	0	0	5	2	1.800	3.60	67	4.26	.222	55	.278	-0	6	0.4
Total	6	10	8	.556	30	22	15	3	4	185	175	105	88	4	12	94	37	1.454	4.28	85	3.80	.249	1176	.295	-14	52	2.3

• HICKMAN, Ernie Ernest P. Hickman b: 1856, East St. Louis, IL d: 11/19/1891, East St. Louis, IL Deb: 6/7/1884

YEAR	TM-L	W	L	PCT	G	GS	CG	SH	SV	IP	H	R	ER	HR	HB	BB	SO	RAT	ERA	ERA+	CERA	OAV	BH	AVG	PR+	WS	TPW
1884	KC-U	4	13	.235	17	17	15	0	0	137^{1}	172	146	69	5	....	36	68	1.515	4.52	62	....	.287	12	.167	-27	1	-2.7

• HICKMAN, Jesse Jesse Owens Hickman b: 2/18/1939, Lecompte, LA BR/TR, 6'2", 186 lbs. Deb: 6/5/1965

YEAR	TM-L	W	L	PCT	G	GS	CG	SH	SV	IP	H	R	ER	HR	HB	BB	SO	RAT	ERA	ERA+	CERA	OAV	BH	AVG	PR+	WS	TPW
1965	KC-A	0	1	.000	12	0	0	0	0	15^{1}	9	10	10	3	0	8	16	1.109	5.87	59	3.14	.184	0	....	-4	0	-0.4
1966	KC-A	0	0	....	1	0	0	0	0	1	0	0	0	0	0	1	0	1.000	0.00	....	0.97	.000	0	....	0	0	0.0
Total	2	0	1	.000	13	0	0	0	0	16^{1}	9	10	10	3	0	9	16	1.102	5.51	63	3.00	.184	0	....	-4	0	-0.4

• HIGBE, Kirby Walter Kirby Higbe b: 4/8/1915, Columbia, SC d: 5/6/1985, Columbia, SC BR/TR, 5'11", 190 lbs. Deb: 10/3/1937

YEAR	TM-L	W	L	PCT	G	GS	CG	SH	SV	IP	H	R	ER	HR	HB	BB	SO	RAT	ERA	ERA+	CERA	OAV	BH	AVG	PR+	WS	TPW
1937	Chi-N	1	0	1.000	1	0	0	0	0	5	4	3	3	1	0	1	2	1.000	5.40	74	2.33	.182	0	.000	-1	0	-0.1
1938	Chi-N	0	0	....	2	2	0	0	0	10	10	6	6	1	0	6	4	1.600	5.40	71	4.71	.263	0	.000	-2	0	-0.2
1939	Chi-N	2	1	.667	9	2	0	0	0	22^{2}	12	9	8	0	0	22	16	1.500	3.18	124	2.63	.158	2	.286	3	2	0.3
	Phi-N	10	14	.417	34	26	14	1	2	187^{1}	208	113	101	10	10	101	79	1.649	4.85	81	4.93	.283	11	.167	-19	6	-2.1
	Yr.	12	15	.444	43	28	14	1	2	210	220	122	109	10	10	123	95	**1.633**	4.67	84	4.68	.272	13	.178	-16	8	-1.8
1940	Phi-N★	14	19	.424	41	36	20	1	1	283	242	126	117	12	3	121	**137**	1.283	3.72	105	2.93	.232	17	.165	5	21	0.4
1941*	Bro-N	**22**	9	.710	**48**	**39**	19	2	3	298	244	123	104	17	6	132	121	1.262	3.14	117	2.90	.220	21	.188	12	21	1.3
1942	Bro-N	16	11	.593	38	32	13	2	0	221^{2}	180	89	80	17	2	106	115	1.290	3.25	100	3.14	.223	8	.104	-2	12	-0.7
1943	Bro-N	13	10	.565	35	27	8	1	0	185	189	81	76	4	5	95	108	**1.535**	3.70	91	4.02	.264	9	.138	-4	9	-0.6
1946	Bro-N★	17	8	.680	42	29	11	3	1	210^{2}	178	82	71	6	1	107	134	1.353	3.03	112	3.02	.229	10	.130	6	14	0.2

YEAR	TM-L	W	L	PCT	G	GS	CG	SH	SV	IP	H	R	ER	HR	HB	BB	SO	RAT	ERA	ERA+	CERA	OAV	BH	AVG	PR+	WS	TPW
1947	Bro-N	2	0	1.000	4	3	0	0	0	15^2	18	9	9	0	1	12	10	1.915	5.17	80	5.60	.295	1	.200	-2	1	-0.2
	Pit-N	11	17	.393	46	30	10	1	5	225	204	108	93	22	3	110	99	1.396	3.72	114	3.80	.240	10	.139	14	13	1.3
	Yr.	13	17	.433	50	33	10	1	5	240^2	222	117	102	22	4	122	109	1.429	3.81	111	3.92	.243	11	.143	12	14	1.1
1948	Pit-N	8	7	.533	56	8	3	0	10	158	140	75	59	11	3	83	86	1.411	3.36	121	3.68	.240	10	.208	12	14	1.2
1949	Pit-N	0	2	.000	7	1	0	0	0	15^1	25	24	23	2	0	12	5	2.413	13.50	31	9.77	.379	0	.000	-16	0	-1.6
	NY-N	2	0	1.000	37	2	0	0	2	80^1	72	42	31	12	1	41	38	1.407	3.47	115	4.25	.242	1	.067	5	5	0.4
	Yr.	2	2	.500	44	3	0	0	2	95^2	97	66	54	14	1	53	43	1.568	5.08	80	5.14	.266	1	.056	-11	5	-1.2
1950	NY-N	0	3	.000	18	1	0	0	0	34^2	37	19	19	2	0	30	17	1.933	4.93	83	5.78	.285	1	.250	-4	1	-0.4
Total	**12**	**118**	**101**	**.539**	**418**	**238**	**98**	**11**	**24**	**1952^1**	**1763**	**909**	**800**	**117**	**35**	**979**	**971**	**1.404**	**3.69**	**102**	**3.60**	**.241**	**101**	**.153**	**7**	**119**	**-0.8**

• HIGGINBOTHAM, Irv — Irving Clinton Higginbotham b: 4/26/1882, Homer, NE d: 6/12/1959, Seattle, WA BR/TR, 6'1", 196 lbs. Deb: 8/11/1906

YEAR	TM-L	W	L	PCT	G	GS	CG	SH	SV	IP	H	R	ER	HR	HB	BB	SO	RAT	ERA	ERA+	CERA	OAV	BH	AVG	PR+	WS	TPW
1906	StL-N	1	4	.200	7	6	4	0	0	47^1	50	23	17	1	1	11	14	1.289	3.23	81	3.21	.266	4	.222	-3	2	-0.3
1908	StL-N	3	8	.273	19	11	7	1	0	107	113	51	38	0	3	33	38	1.364	3.20	73	3.40	.270	5	.132	-8	3	-1.0
1909	StL-N	1	0	1.000	3	1	1	0	0	11^1	5	3	2	0	0	2	2	.618	1.59	159	0.72	.143	0	.000	1	1	0.1
	Chi-N	5	2	.714	19	6	4	0	1	78	64	32	19	0	10	20	32	1.077	2.19	116	2.25	.213	6	.231	2	5	0.3
	Yr.	6	2	.750	22	7	5	0	1	89^1	69	35	21	0	10	22	34	1.019	2.12	120	2.05	.206	6	.207	4	6	0.5
Total	**3**	**10**	**14**	**.417**	**48**	**24**	**16**	**1**	**1**	**243^2**	**232**	**109**	**76**	**1**	**14**	**66**	**86**	**1.223**	**2.81**	**87**	**2.87**	**.246**	**15**	**.176**	**-6**	**11**	**-0.8**

• HIGGINS, Dennis — Dennis Dean Higgins b: 8/4/1939, Jefferson City, MO BR/TR, 6'3", 190 lbs. Deb: 4/12/1966

YEAR	TM-L	W	L	PCT	G	GS	CG	SH	SV	IP	H	R	ER	HR	HB	BB	SO	RAT	ERA	ERA+	CERA	OAV	BH	AVG	PR+	WS	TPW
1966	Chi-A	1	0	1.000	42	1	0	0	5	93	66	27	26	9	5	33	86	1.065	2.52	126	2.54	.202	3	.176	6	8	0.7
1967	Chi-A	1	2	.333	9	0	0	0	0	12^1	13	9	8	0	3	10	8	1.865	5.84	53	6.11	.271	0	.000	-4	0	-0.4
1968	Was-A	4	4	.500	59	0	0	0	13	99^2	81	40	36	9	3	46	66	1.274	3.25	90	3.17	.226	2	.133	-3	5	-0.3
1969	Was-A	10	9	.526	55	0	0	0	16	85^1	79	42	33	7	3	56	71	1.582	3.48	100	4.55	.252	1	.091	-1	6	-0.1
1970	Cle-A	4	6	.400	58	0	0	0	11	90^1	82	43	40	8	2	54	82	1.506	3.99	99	4.24	.248	3	.250	-1	8	0.0
1971	StL-N	1	0	1.000	3	0	0	0	0	7	6	3	3	0	0	2	6	1.143	3.86	93	2.21	.240	0	.000	-0	1	0.0
1972	StL-N	1	2	.333	15	1	0	0	1	22^2	19	14	10	0	0	22	20	1.809	3.97	86	4.54	.226	0	.000	-1	1	-0.2
Total	**7**	**22**	**23**	**.489**	**241**	**2**	**0**	**0**	**46**	**410^1**	**346**	**178**	**156**	**33**	**16**	**223**	**339**	**1.387**	**3.42**	**98**	**3.70**	**.233**	**9**	**.155**	**-3**	**29**	**-0.3**

• HIGGINS, Eddie — Thomas Edward "Doc,Irish" Higgins b: 3/18/1888, Nevada, IL d: 2/14/1959, Elgin, IL BR/TR, 6'.5", 174 lbs. Deb: 5/14/1909

YEAR	TM-L	W	L	PCT	G	GS	CG	SH	SV	IP	H	R	ER	HR	HB	BB	SO	RAT	ERA	ERA+	CERA	OAV	BH	AVG	PR+	WS	TPW
1909	StL-N	3	3	.500	16	5	5	0	0	66	68	36	33	4	1	17	15	1.288	4.50	56	3.58	.273	4	.190	-13	1	-1.5
1910	StL-N	0	1	.000	2	0	0	0	0	10^1	15	8	5	0	0	7	1	2.129	4.35	68	7.13	.349	2	.400	-1	0	0.0
Total	**2**	**3**	**4**	**.429**	**18**	**5**	**5**	**0**	**0**	**76^1**	**83**	**44**	**38**	**4**	**1**	**24**	**16**	**1.402**	**4.48**	**57**	**4.06**	**.284**	**6**	**.231**	**-14**	**1**	**-1.5**

• HIGH, Ed — Edward Thomas "Lefty" High b: 12/26/1876, Baltimore, MD d: 2/20/1926, Baltimore, MD TL Deb: 7/4/1901

YEAR	TM-L	W	L	PCT	G	GS	CG	SH	SV	IP	H	R	ER	HR	HB	BB	SO	RAT	ERA	ERA+	CERA	OAV	BH	AVG	PR+	WS	TPW
1901	Det-A	1	0	1.000	4	1	1	0	0	18	21	9	7	0	1	6	4	1.500	3.50	110	4.13	.288	0	.000	0	1	0.0

• HIGUERA, Teddy — Teodoro (Valenzuela) Higuera b: 11/9/1958, Los Mochis, Mexico BB/TL, 5'10", 178 lbs. Deb: 4/23/1985

YEAR	TM-L	W	L	PCT	G	GS	CG	SH	SV	IP	H	R	ER	HR	HB	BB	SO	RAT	ERA	ERA+	CERA	OAV	BH	AVG	PR+	WS	TPW
1985	Mil-A	15	8	.652	32	30	7	2	0	212^1	186	105	92	22	3	63	127	1.173	3.90	107	3.09	.235	0	....	7	14	0.7
1986	Mil-A★	20	11	.645	34	34	15	4	0	248^1	226	84	77	26	3	74	207	1.208	2.79	155	3.23	.241	0	....	44	25	4.3
1987	Mil-A	18	10	.643	35	35	14	3	0	261^2	236	120	112	24	2	87	240	1.234	3.85	119	3.27	.241	0	....	23	20	2.2
1988	Mil-A	16	9	.640	31	31	8	1	0	227^1	168	66	62	15	6	59	192	.999	2.45	162	**2.10**	.207	0	....	37	22	3.7
1989	Mil-A	9	6	.600	22	22	2	1	0	135^1	125	56	52	9	4	48	91	1.278	3.46	111	3.38	.248	0	....	5	9	0.5
1990	Mil-A	11	10	.524	27	27	4	1	0	170	167	80	71	16	3	50	129	1.276	3.76	103	3.55	.256	0	....	4	8	0.4
1991	Mil-A	3	2	.600	7	6	0	0	0	36^1	37	18	18	2	1	10	33	1.294	4.46	89	3.51	.262	0	....	-2	2	-0.2
1993	Mil-A	1	3	.250	8	8	0	0	0	30	43	24	24	4	1	16	27	1.967	7.20	59	7.49	.333	0	....	-10	0	-0.9
1994	Mil-A	1	5	.167	17	12	0	0	0	58^2	74	55	46	13	2	36	35	1.875	7.06	71	7.77	.311	0	....	-15	0	-1.4
Total	**9**	**94**	**64**	**.595**	**213**	**205**	**50**	**12**	**0**	**1380**	**1262**	**608**	**554**	**131**	**25**	**443**	**1081**	**1.236**	**3.61**	**117**	**3.38**	**.243**	**0**	**....**	**93**	**100**	**9.3**

• HILCHER, Whitey — Walter Frank Hilcher b: 2/28/1909, Chicago, IL d: 11/21/1962, Minneapolis, MN BR/TR, 6', 174 lbs. Deb: 9/17/1931

YEAR	TM-L	W	L	PCT	G	GS	CG	SH	SV	IP	H	R	ER	HR	HB	BB	SO	RAT	ERA	ERA+	CERA	OAV	BH	AVG	PR+	WS	TPW
1931	Cin-N	0	1	.000	2	1	0	0	0	12	16	5	4	0	1	4	5	1.667	3.00	124	5.24	.320	0	.000	1	1	0.0
1932	Cin-N	0	3	.000	11	2	0	0	0	18^2	24	19	16	3	0	10	4	1.821	7.71	50	6.77	.316	1	.333	-8	0	-0.7
1935	Cin-N	2	0	1.000	4	2	1	1	0	19^1	19	6	6	0	0	5	9	1.241	2.79	142	2.74	.264	1	.167	3	2	0.2
1936	Cin-N	1	2	.333	14	1	0	0	0	35	44	31	24	3	1	14	10	1.657	6.17	62	5.36	.299	0	.000	-9	0	-1.0
Total	**4**	**3**	**6**	**.333**	**31**	**6**	**1**	**1**	**0**	**85**	**103**	**61**	**50**	**6**	**2**	**33**	**28**	**1.600**	**5.29**	**73**	**5.05**	**.299**	**2**	**.095**	**-13**	**3**	**-1.4**

• HILDEBRAND, Oral — Oral Clyde Hildebrand b: 4/7/1907, Indianapolis, IN d: 9/8/1977, Southport, IN BR/TR, 6'3", 175 lbs. Deb: 9/8/1931

YEAR	TM-L	W	L	PCT	G	GS	CG	SH	SV	IP	H	R	ER	HR	HB	BB	SO	RAT	ERA	ERA+	CERA	OAV	BH	AVG	PR+	WS	TPW
1931	Cle-A	2	1	.667	5	2	2	0	0	26^2	25	16	13	0	3	13	6	1.425	4.39	105	3.50	.243	2	.182	1	2	0.1
1932	Cle-A	8	6	.571	27	15	7	0	0	129^1	124	69	53	7	0	62	49	1.438	3.69	129	3.66	.249	7	.146	18	10	1.4
1933	Cle-A★	16	11	.593	36	31	15	**6**	0	220^1	205	110	92	8	1	88	90	1.330	3.76	118	3.17	.245	16	.190	16	17	1.4
1934	Cle-A	11	9	.550	33	28	10	1	1	198	225	112	99	14	3	99	72	1.636	4.50	101	4.87	.282	13	.171	2	11	0.1
1935	Cle-A	9	8	.529	34	20	8	0	5	171^1	171	85	75	12	3	63	49	1.366	3.94	114	3.70	.263	9	.164	13	13	1.0
1936	Cle-A	10	11	.476	36	21	9	0	4	174^2	197	107	95	10	4	83	65	1.603	4.90	103	4.69	.283	12	.190	4	12	0.4
1937	StL-A	8	17	.320	30	27	12	1	1	201^1	228	127	115	18	4	87	75	1.565	5.14	94	4.81	.284	14	.200	-5	10	-0.5
1938	StL-A	8	10	.444	23	23	10	0	0	163	194	104	103	18	3	73	66	1.638	5.69	87	5.46	.297	15	.254	-13	9	-1.0
1939*	NY-A	10	4	.714	21	15	7	1	2	126^2	102	44	43	11	1	41	50	1.129	3.06	143	2.63	.219	8	.182	13	11	1.1
1940	NY-A	1	1	.500	13	0	0	0	0	19^1	19	7	4	1	1	14	5	1.707	1.86	217	4.98	.268	0	.000	4	2	0.4
Total	**10**	**83**	**78**	**.516**	**258**	**182**	**80**	**9**	**13**	**1430^2**	**1490**	**781**	**692**	**99**	**22**	**623**	**527**	**1.477**	**4.35**	**108**	**4.17**	**.267**	**96**	**.187**	**55**	**97**	**4.4**

• HILGENDORF, Tom — Thomas Eugene Hilgendorf b: 3/10/1942, Clinton, IA BB/TL, 6'1.5", 190 lbs. Deb: 8/15/1969

YEAR	TM-L	W	L	PCT	G	GS	CG	SH	SV	IP	H	R	ER	HR	HB	BB	SO	RAT	ERA	ERA+	CERA	OAV	BH	AVG	PR+	WS	TPW
1969	StL-N	0	0	....	6	0	0	0	2	6^1	3	1	1	0	0	2	2	.789	1.42	251	0.95	.150	1	1.000	1	2	0.2
1970	StL-N	0	4	.000	23	0	0	0	3	20^2	22	11	9	0	0	13	13	1.694	3.92	105	4.01	.272	0	.000	1	1	0.1
1972	Cle-A	3	1	.750	19	5	1	0	0	47	51	16	14	4	2	21	25	1.532	2.68	120	4.62	.283	1	.077	2	4	0.2
1973	Cle-A	5	3	.625	48	1	1	0	6	94^2	87	38	33	9	3	36	58	1.299	3.14	125	3.53	.242	0	....	9	9	0.9
1974	Cle-A	4	3	.571	35	0	0	0	3	48^1	58	26	26	6	1	17	23	1.552	4.84	75	5.03	.302	0	....	-7	2	-0.7
1975	Phi-N	7	3	.700	53	0	0	0	0	96^2	81	32	23	6	1	38	52	1.231	2.14	174	2.91	.230	3	.250	14	10	1.6
Total	**6**	**19**	**14**	**.576**	**184**	**6**	**2**	**0**	**14**	**313^2**	**302**	**124**	**106**	**25**	**7**	**127**	**173**	**1.368**	**3.04**	**122**	**3.71**	**.255**	**5**	**.185**	**21**	**28**	**2.2**

• HILJUS, Erik — Erik Kristian Hiljus b: 12/25/1972, Panorama City, CA BR/TR, 6'5", 230 lbs. Deb: 9/10/1999

YEAR	TM-L	W	L	PCT	G	GS	CG	SH	SV	IP	H	R	ER	HR	HB	BB	SO	RAT	ERA	ERA+	CERA	OAV	BH	AVG	PR+	WS	TPW
1999	Det-A	0	0	....	6	0	0	0	0	8^2	7	5	4	2	0	5	1	1.385	4.15	119	4.96	.241	0	....	1	0	0.1
2000	Det-A	0	0	....	3	0	0	0	0	3^2	5	3	3	1	0	1	2	1.636	7.36	65	7.34	.333	0	....	-1	0	-0.1
2001*	Oak-A	5	0	1.000	16	11	0	0	0	66	70	29	25	7	0	21	67	1.379	3.41	130	4.00	.263	0	....	7	5	0.7
2002	Oak-A	3	3	.500	9	9	0	0	0	45^2	52	36	33	11	0	21	29	1.599	6.50	68	6.16	.284	0	....	-10	0	-1.0
Total	**4**	**8**	**3**	**.727**	**34**	**20**	**0**	**0**	**0**	**124**	**134**	**73**	**65**	**21**	**0**	**48**	**99**	**1.468**	**4.72**	**94**	**4.96**	**.272**	**0**	**....**	**-3**	**5**	**-0.3**

• HILL, Bill — William Cicero "Still Bill" Hill b: 8/2/1874, Chattanooga, TN d: 1/28/1938, Cincinnati, OH BL/TL, 6'1", 201 lbs. Deb: 4/18/1896

YEAR	TM-L	W	L	PCT	G	GS	CG	SH	SV	IP	H	R	ER	HR	HB	BB	SO	RAT	ERA	ERA+	CERA	OAV	BH	AVG	PR+	WS	TPW
1896	Lou-N	9	28	.243	43	39	32	0	2	319^2	353	229	153	14	18	155	104	1.589	4.31	100	4.66	.278	24	.207	7	13	0.3
1897	Lou-N	7	17	.292	27	26	20	1	0	199	209	127	80	6	17	69	55	1.397	3.62	118	3.87	.268	7	.095	15	11	0.7
1898	Cin-N	13	14	.481	33	32	26	2	0	262	261	146	116	3	17	119	75	1.450	3.98	96	3.74	.258	13	.133	-7	16	-1.3
1899	Cle-N	3	6	.333	11	10	7	0	0	72^1	96	67	56	0	4	39	26	1.866	6.97	53	5.80	.318	4	.129	-23	2	-2.3
	Bal-N	3	4	.429	8	7	6	0	0	61	64	35	22	1	3	18	17	1.344	3.25	122	3.47	.270	7	.292	5	5	0.5
	Bro-N	1	0	1.000	2	1	1	0	1	11	11	3	1	0	0	6	3	1.545	0.82	478	3.76	.260	3	.600	4	2	0.5
	Yr.	7	10	.412	21	18	14	0	1	144^1	171	105	79	1	7	63	46	1.621	4.93	76	4.66	.294	14	.233	-15	9	-1.3
Total	**4**	**36**	**69**	**.343**	**124**	**115**	**92**	**3**	**3**	**925**	**994**	**607**	**428**	**24**	**59**	**406**	**280**	**1.514**	**4.16**	**97**	**4.23**	**.273**	**58**	**.167**	**1**	**49**	**-1.7**

• HILL, Carmen — Carmen Proctor "Specs,Bunker" Hill b: 10/1/1895, Royalton, MN d: 1/1/1990, Indianapolis, IN BR/TR, 6'1", 180 lbs. Deb: 8/24/1915

YEAR	TM-L	W	L	PCT	G	GS	CG	SH	SV	IP	H	R	ER	HR	HB	BB	SO	RAT	ERA	ERA+	CERA	OAV	BH	AVG	PR+	WS	TPW
1915	Pit-N	2	1	.667	8	3	2	1	0	47	42	8	6	0	2	13	24	1.170	1.15	237	2.61	.255	2	.154	8	5	1.0
1916	Pit-N	0	0	....	2	0	0	0	0	6^1	11	10	6	0	1	5	5	2.526	8.53	31	14.68	.611	0	....	-4	0	-0.4
1918	Pit-N	2	3	.400	6	4	3	0	0	43^2	24	11	6	0	0	17	15	.939	1.24	232	1.30	.160	2	.167	7	4	0.8
1919	Pit-N	0	0	....	4	0	0	0	0	5	12	6	5	0	0	1	1	2.600	9.00	34	11.47	.480	0	....	-3	0	-0.4
1922	NY-N	2	1	.667	8	4	0	0	0	28^1	33	15	15	0	0	5	6	1.341	4.76	84	3.35	.295	2	.182	-3	1	-0.3

YEAR TM-L	W	L	PCT	G	GS	CG	SH	SV	IP	H	R	ER	HR	HB	BB	SO	RAT	ERA	ERA+	CERA	OAV	BH	AVG	PR+	WS	TPW
1926 Pit-N	3	3	.500	6	6	4	1	0	39^2	42	17	15	2	2	9	8	1.286	3.40	116	3.62	.288	3	.176	2	3	0.1
1927* Pit-N	22	11	.667	43	31	22	2	3	277^2	260	125	100	12	4	80	95	1.224	3.24	127	2.88	.249	22	.212	25	22	2.6
1928 Pit-N	16	10	.615	36	31	16	1	2	237	229	110	93	16	4	81	73	1.308	3.53	115	3.41	.259	20	.233	13	17	1.5
1929 Pit-N	2	3	.400	27	3	0	0	3	79	94	45	35	4	0	35	28	1.633	3.99	120	4.80	.297	1	.036	6	5	0.2
StL-N	0	0	....	3	1	0	0	0	8^2	10	10	8	2	1	8	1	2.077	8.31	56	8.77	.303	0	.000	-3	0	-0.4
Yr.	2	3	.400	30	4	0	0	3	87^2	104	55	43	6	1	43	29	1.677	4.41	108	5.20	.298	1	.032	2	5	-0.2
1930 StL-N	0	1	.000	4	2	0	0	0	14^2	12	12	12	2	0	13	8	1.705	7.36	68	5.04	.240	1	.333	-4	0	-0.3
Total 10	49	33	.598	147	85	47	5	8	787	769	369	301	38	14	267	264	1.316	3.44	117	3.44	.261	53	.191	43	57	4.3
• HILL, Dave	David Burnham Hill b: 11/11/1937, New Orleans, LA BR/TL, 6'2", 170 lbs. Deb: 8/22/1957																									
1957 KC-A	0	0	....	2	0	0	0	0	2^1	6	7	7	3	0	3	1	3.857	27.00	15	33.53	.462	0	....	-6	0	-0.6
• HILL, Garry	Garry Alton Hill b: 11/3/1946, Rutherfordton, NC BR/TR, 6'2", 195 lbs. Deb: 6/12/1969																									
1969 Atl-N	0	1	.000	1	1	0	0	0	2^1	6	4	4	1	0	1	2	3.000	15.43	23	18.16	.462	0	....	-3	0	-0.3
• HILL, Herbert	Herbert Lee Hill b: 8/19/1892, Dallas, TX d: 9/2/1970, Farmer's Branch, TX BR/TR, 5'11.5", 175 lbs. Deb: 7/17/1915																									
1915 Cle-A	0	0	....	1	0	0	0	0	2	1	0	0	0	0	2	0	1.500	0.00	....	2.62	.250	0	....	1	0	0.1
• HILL, Jeremy	Jeremy Dee Hill b: 8/8/1977, Dallas, TX BR/TR, 5'10", 185 lbs. Deb: 9/7/2002																									
2002 KC-A	0	1	.000	10	0	0	0	0	9^1	8	4	4	1	0	8	7	1.714	3.86	130	4.93	.235	0	....	1	1	0.1
2003 KC-A	0	0	....	1	0	0	0	0	1	1	0	0	0	0	0	0	1.000	0.00	....	1.95	.250	0	....	1	0	0.1
Total 2	0	1	.000	11	0	0	0	0	10^1	9	4	4	1	0	8	7	1.645	3.48	144	4.64	.237	0	....	2	1	0.2
• HILL, Ken	Kenneth Wade Hill b: 12/14/1965, Lynn, MA BR/TR, 6'4", 175 lbs. Deb: 9/3/1988																									
1988 StL-N	0	1	.000	4	1	0	0	0	14	16	9	8	0	0	6	6	1.571	5.14	68	4.28	.286	0	.000	-3	0	-0.3
1989 StL-N	7	15	.318	33	33	2	1	0	196^2	186	92	83	9	5	99	112	1.449	3.80	95	3.82	.252	9	.153	-6	7	-0.7
1990 StL-N	5	6	.455	17	14	1	0	0	78^2	79	49	48	7	1	33	58	1.424	5.49	69	4.11	.264	4	.211	-14	2	-1.4
1991 StL-N	11	10	.524	30	30	0	0	0	181^1	147	76	72	15	6	67	121	1.180	3.57	104	2.96	.224	5	.100	1	10	0.0
1992 Mon-N	16	9	.640	33	33	3	3	0	218	187	76	65	13	3	75	150	1.202	2.68	129	2.84	.230	11	.177	19	17	2.6
1993 Mon-N	9	7	.563	28	28	2	0	0	183^2	163	84	66	7	6	74	90	1.290	3.23	129	3.10	.238	6	.115	19	11	1.8
1994 Mon-N★	**16**	5	.762	23	23	2	1	0	154^2	145	61	57	12	6	44	85	1.222	3.32	127	3.22	.248	7	.146	16	12	1.5
1995 StL-N	6	7	.462	18	18	0	0	0	110^1	125	71	62	16	0	45	50	1.541	5.06	83	5.11	.286	6	.194	-12	3	-1.1
*Cle-A	4	1	.800	12	11	1	0	0	74^2	77	36	33	5	1	32	48	1.460	3.98	118	4.22	.268	0	....	6	5	0.6
1996* Tex-A	16	10	.615	35	35	7	**3**	0	250^2	250	110	101	19	6	95	170	1.376	3.63	145	3.96	.263	0	....	45	22	4.1
1997 Tex-A	5	8	.385	19	19	0	0	0	111	129	69	64	11	2	56	68	1.667	5.19	92	5.57	.298	0	....	-3	4	-0.3
Ana-A	4	4	.500	12	12	1	0	0	79	65	34	32	8	1	39	38	1.316	3.65	127	3.54	.223	1	.500	8	6	0.8
Yr.	9	12	.429	31	31	1	0	0	190	194	103	96	19	3	95	106	1.521	4.55	104	4.73	.268	1	.500	5	10	0.5
1998 Ana-A	9	6	.600	19	19	0	0	0	103	123	60	57	6	3	47	57	1.650	4.98	94	5.38	.311	0	.000	-3	5	-0.2
1999 Ana-A	4	11	.267	26	22	0	0	0	128^1	129	72	68	14	4	76	76	1.597	4.77	102	5.17	.270	0	.000	-0	7	0.0
2000 Ana-A	5	7	.417	16	16	0	0	0	78^2	102	59	57	16	2	53	50	1.970	6.52	78	8.10	.323	1	.333	-15	1	-1.3
Chi-A	0	1	.000	2	1	0	0	0	3	5	8	8	0	0	6	0	3.667	24.00	21	14.98	.455	0	....	-6	0	-0.6
Yr.	5	8	.385	18	17	0	0	0	81^2	107	67	65	16	2	59	50	2.033	7.16	71	8.35	.327	1	.333	-21	1	-1.9
2001 TB-A	0	1	.000	5	0	0	0	0	7^1	10	11	10	4	1	5	2	2.045	12.27	37	11.42	.333	0	....	-6	0	-0.6
Total 14	117	109	.518	332	315	19	8	0	1973	1938	977	891	162	47	852	1181	1.414	4.06	105	4.11	.260	50	.150	45	112	4.8
• HILL, Milt	Milton Giles Hill b: 8/22/1965, Atlanta, GA BR/TR, 6', 180 lbs. Deb: 8/1/1991																									
1991 Cin-N	1	1	.500	22	0	0	0	0	33^1	36	14	14	1	0	8	20	1.320	3.78	101	3.43	.295	0	.000	0	2	0.0
1992 Cin-N	0	0	....	14	0	0	0	1	20	15	9	7	1	1	5	10	1.000	3.15	114	1.97	.211	0	....	1	1	0.1
1993 Cin-N	3	0	1.000	19	0	0	0	0	28^2	34	18	18	5	0	9	23	1.500	5.65	71	5.34	.301	0	.000	-5	1	-0.5
1994 Atl-N	0	0	....	10	0	0	0	0	11^1	18	10	10	3	0	6	10	2.118	7.94	53	9.73	.367	0	....	-5	0	-0.4
Sea-A	1	0	1.000	13	0	0	0	0	23^2	30	19	17	4	0	11	16	1.732	6.46	76	6.15	.306	0	....	-4	1	-0.4
Total 4	5	1	.833	78	0	0	0	1	117	133	70	66	14	1	39	79	1.470	5.08	82	4.81	.294	0	.000	-12	5	-1.2
• HILL, Red	Clifford Joseph Hill b: 1/20/1893, Marshall, TX d: 8/11/1938, El Paso, TX BB/TL Deb: 4/21/1917																									
1917 Phi-A	0	0	....	1	0	0	0	0	2^2	5	4	2	0	0	1	0	2.250	6.75	41	8.21	.385	0	....	-1	0	-0.1
• HILLEBRAND, Homer	Homer Hiller Henry Hillebrand b: 10/10/1879, Freeport, IL d: 1/20/1974, Elsinore, CA BR/TL, 5'8", 165 lbs. Deb: 4/24/1905 ♦																									
1905 Pit-N	5	2	.714	10	6	4	0	1	60^2	43	20	19	0	2	19	37	1.022	2.82	106	1.75	.198	26	.236	0	7	-0.4
1906 Pit-N	3	2	.600	7	5	4	1	0	53	42	19	13	1	1	21	32	1.189	2.21	121	2.49	.220	5	.238	2	4	0.4
1908 Pit-N	0	0	....	1	0	0	0	0	1	1	0	0	0	0	0	1	1.000	0.00	....	2.02	.333	0	....	0	0	0.0
Total 3	8	4	.667	18	11	8	1	1	114^2	86	39	32	1	3	40	70	1.099	2.51	113	2.10	.209	31	.237	3	11	0.0
• HILLEGAS, Shawn	Shawn Patrick Hillegas b: 8/21/1964, Dos Palos, CA BR/TR, 6'3", 208 lbs. Deb: 8/9/1987																									
1987 LA-N	4	3	.571	12	10	0	0	0	58	52	27	23	5	0	31	51	1.431	3.57	111	3.92	.241	0	.000	3	4	0.2
1988 LA-N	3	4	.429	11	10	0	0	0	56^2	54	26	26	5	3	17	30	1.253	4.13	81	3.53	.250	2	.133	-4	2	-0.5
Chi-A	3	2	.600	6	6	0	0	0	40	30	16	14	4	1	18	26	1.200	3.15	126	3.02	.207	0	....	3	3	0.3
1989 Chi-A	7	11	.389	50	13	0	0	3	119^2	132	67	63	12	3	51	76	1.529	4.74	80	4.81	.279	0	....	-13	3	-1.3
1990 Chi-A	0	0	....	7	0	0	0	0	11^1	4	1	1	0	0	5	5	.794	0.79	481	0.84	.111	0	....	4	2	0.4
1991 Cle-A	3	4	.429	51	3	0	0	7	83	67	42	40	7	2	46	66	1.361	4.34	96	3.43	.223	0	....	-0	5	0.0
1992 NY-A	1	8	.111	21	9	1	1	0	78^1	96	52	48	12	0	33	46	1.647	5.51	71	5.96	.306	0	....	-14	0	-1.4
Oak-A	0	0	....	5	0	0	0	0	7^2	8	5	2	1	0	4	3	1.565	2.35	159	4.85	.276	0	....	1	0	0.1
Yr.	1	8	.111	26	9	1	1	0	86	104	57	50	13	0	37	49	1.640	5.23	75	5.86	.303	0	....	-13	0	-1.3
1993 Oak-A	3	6	.333	18	11	0	0	0	60^2	78	48	47	8	4	33	29	1.830	6.97	58	6.95	.317	0	....	-19	0	-1.9
Total 7	24	38	.387	181	62	1	1	10	515^1	521	284	264	54	13	238	332	1.473	4.61	84	4.55	.264	2	.069	-40	19	-4.1
• HILLER, Frank	Frank Walter "Dutch" Hiller b: 7/13/1920, Irvington, NJ d: 1/10/1987, West Chester, PA BR/TR, 6', 200 lbs. Deb: 5/25/1946																									
1946 NY-A	0	2	.000	3	1	0	0	0	11^1	13	7	6	2	0	6	4	1.676	4.76	72	6.16	.295	1	.250	-2	0	-0.2
1948 NY-A	5	2	.714	22	5	1	0	0	62^1	59	29	28	8	1	30	25	1.428	4.04	101	4.16	.244	6	.375	-1	5	0.1
1949 NY-A	0	2	.000	4	0	0	0	1	7^2	9	5	5	0	0	7	3	2.087	5.87	69	6.05	.290	1	.500	-2	0	-0.1
1950 Chi-N	12	5	.706	38	17	9	2	1	153	153	68	60	16	4	32	55	1.209	3.53	119	3.41	.258	5	.114	15	13	1.3
1951 Chi-N	6	12	.333	24	21	6	2	1	141^1	147	83	76	17	9	31	50	1.259	4.84	85	3.95	.268	6	.125	-10	4	-1.2
1952 Cin-N	5	8	.385	28	15	6	1	1	124^1	129	67	64	7	6	37	50	1.335	4.63	81	3.76	.271	5	.167	-12	4	-1.2
1953 NY-N	2	1	.667	19	1	0	0	0	33^2	43	29	23	6	4	15	10	1.723	6.15	70	6.73	.303	2	.500	-7	0	-0.6
Total 7	30	32	.484	138	60	22	5	4	533^2	553	288	262	56	24	158	197	1.332	4.42	91	4.02	.266	26	.176	-18	26	-2.0
• HILLER, John	John Frederick Hiller b: 4/8/1943, Toronto, Canada BR/TL, 6'1", 195 lbs. Deb: 9/6/1965																									
1965 Det-A	0	0	....	5	0	0	0	1	6	5	0	0	0	0	1	4	1.000	0.00	....	1.84	.227	0	....	2	1	0.3
1966 Det-A	0	0	....	1	0	0	0	0	2	2	2	2	0	0	2	1	2.000	9.00	39	5.48	.286	0	....	-1	0	-0.1
1967 Det-A	4	3	.571	23	6	2	2	3	65	57	20	19	4	0	9	49	1.015	2.63	124	2.24	.233	2	.133	4	6	0.4
1968* Det-A	9	6	.600	39	12	4	1	2	128	92	37	34	9	0	51	78	1.117	2.39	126	2.37	.200	3	.081	8	11	0.7
1969 Det-A	4	4	.500	40	8	1	1	4	99^1	97	50	44	13	1	44	74	1.419	3.99	94	4.34	.257	6	.286	-3	5	-0.2
1970 Det-A	6	6	.500	47	5	1	1	3	104	82	39	35	12	2	46	89	1.231	3.03	123	3.23	.219	0	.000	11	10	0.9
1972* Det-A	1	2	.333	24	3	1	0	3	44^1	39	13	10	4	3	13	26	1.173	2.03	155	3.11	.232	0	.000	5	4	0.5
1973 Det-A	10	5	.667	**65**	0	0	0	**38**	125^1	89	21	20	7	0	39	124	1.021	1.44	285	1.92	.198	0	....	38	31	3.9
1974 Det-A★	17	14	.548	59	0	0	0	13	150	127	51	44	10	3	62	134	1.260	2.64	144	2.94	.231	0	....	20	20	2.1
1975 Det-A	2	3	.400	36	0	0	0	14	70^2	52	20	17	6	0	36	87	1.245	2.17	185	2.88	.205	0	....	16	12	1.6
1976 Det-A	12	8	.600	56	1	1	1	13	121	93	37	32	7	2	67	117	1.322	2.38	156	3.09	.219	0	.000	19	17	2.0
1977 Det-A	8	14	.364	45	8	3	0	7	124	120	59	49	15	1	61	115	1.460	3.56	121	4.36	.258	0	....	10	9	1.0
1978 Det-A	9	4	.692	51	0	0	0	15	92^1	64	27	24	6	0	35	74	1.072	2.34	165	2.19	.202	0	....	14	15	1.5
1979 Det-A	4	7	.364	43	0	0	0	9	79^1	83	47	46	14	0	55	46	1.739	5.22	83	5.91	.274	0	....	-9	3	-0.8

YEAR	TM-L	W	L	PCT	G	GS	CG	SH	SV	IP	H	R	ER	HR	HB	BB	SO	RAT	ERA	ERA+	CERA	OAV	BH	AVG	PR+	WS	TPW
1980	Det-A	1	0	1.000	11	0	0	0	0	30^2	38	15	15	3	0	14	18	1.696	4.40	93	5.66	.309	0	....	-1	2	-0.1
Total	15	87	76	.534	545	43	13	6	125	1242	1040	438	391	110	12	535	1036	1.268	2.83	134	3.24	.229	11	.109	135	146	13.8
• HILLMAN, Dave	Darius Dutton Hillman b: 9/14/1927, Dungannon, VA BR/TR, 5'11", 168 lbs. Deb: 4/30/1955																										
1955	Chi-N	0	0	....	25	3	0	0	0	57^2	63	36	34	10	1	25	23	1.526	5.31	77	5.30	.283	1	.100	-8	1	-0.8
1956	Chi-N	0	2	.000	2	2	0	0	0	12^1	11	7	3	0	0	5	6	1.297	2.19	172	2.59	.216	0	.000	2	0	0.1
1957	Chi-N	6	11	.353	32	14	1	0	1	103^1	115	52	50	13	0	37	53	1.471	4.35	89	4.72	.280	0	.000	-4	4	-0.6
1958	Chi-N	4	8	.333	31	16	3	0	1	125^2	132	57	44	12	0	31	65	1.297	3.15	124	3.59	.265	6	.146	12	7	1.1
1959	Chi-N	8	11	.421	39	24	4	1	0	191	178	84	75	17	1	43	88	1.157	3.53	112	2.97	.248	9	.150	7	12	0.8
1960	Bos-A	0	3	.000	16	3	0	0	0	36^2	41	27	23	6	0	12	14	1.445	5.65	72	4.82	.281	0	.000	-6	0	-0.6
1961	Bos-A	3	2	.600	28	1	0	0	0	78	70	26	24	8	0	23	39	1.192	2.77	151	3.14	.242	0	.000	12	7	1.1
1962	Cin-N	0	0	....	2	0	0	0	0	3^2	8	4	4	0	0	1	0	2.455	9.82	41	9.93	.421	0	....	-2	0	-0.2
	NY-N	0	0	....	13	1	0	0	1	15^2	21	12	11	5	1	8	8	1.851	6.32	66	8.67	.333	0	.000	-3	0	-0.4
	Yr.	0	0	....	15	1	0	0	1	19^1	29	16	15	5	1	9	8	1.966	6.98	59	8.91	.354	0	.000	-6	0	-0.6
Total	8	21	37	.362	188	64	8	1	3	624	639	305	268	71	3	185	296	1.321	3.87	103	3.91	.264	16	.098	10	31	0.5
• HILLMAN, Eric	John Eric Hillman b: 4/27/1966, Gary, IN BL/TL, 6'10", 225 lbs. Deb: 5/18/1992																										
1992	NY-N	2	2	.500	11	8	0	0	0	52^1	67	31	31	9	2	10	16	1.471	5.33	65	5.57	.318	1	.077	-10	0	-1.2
1993	NY-N	2	9	.182	27	22	3	1	0	145	173	83	64	12	4	24	60	1.359	3.97	101	4.16	.299	7	.159	-0	4	0.0
1994	NY-N	0	3	.000	11	6	0	0	0	34^2	45	30	30	9	2	11	20	1.615	7.79	54	6.95	.321	0	.000	-14	0	-1.5
Total	3	4	14	.222	49	36	3	1	0	232	285	144	125	30	8	45	96	1.422	4.85	80	4.89	.306	8	.123	-24	4	-2.7
• HILSEY, Charlie	Charles T. Hilsey b: 3/23/1864, Philadelphia, PA d: 10/31/1918, Philadelphia, PA, 5'7", 180 lbs. Deb: 9/27/1883																										
1883	Phi-N	0	3	.000	3	3	3	0	0	26	36	26	16	1	....	4	8	1.538	5.54	56	....	.310	1	.100	-5	0	-0.5
1884	Phi-a	2	1	.667	3	3	3	0	0	27	29	19	14	0	0	5	10	1.259	4.67	72	....	.260	5	.208	-4	1	-0.5
Total	2	2	4	.333	6	6	6	0	0	53	65	45	30	1	0	9	18	1.396	5.09	63	....	.286	6	.176	-9	1	-1.0
• HILTON, Howard	Howard James Hilton b: 1/3/1964, Oxnard, CA BR/TR, 6'3", 230 lbs. Deb: 4/9/1990																										
1990	StL-N	0	0	....	2	0	0	0	0	3	2	0	0	0	0	3	2	1.667	0.00	....	3.63	.182	0	....	1	1	0.1
• HINCHLIFFE, Brett	Brett Hinchliffe b: 7/21/1974, Detroit, MI BR/TR, 6'5", 190 lbs. Deb: 4/5/1999																										
1999	Sea-A	0	4	.000	11	4	0	0	0	30^2	41	31	30	10	4	21	14	2.022	8.80	57	10.10	.323	0	....	-13	0	-1.2
2000	Ana-A	0	0	....	2	0	0	0	0	1^2	1	1	1	0	0	1	0	1.200	5.40	94	2.03	.167	0	....	-0	0	0.0
2001	NY-N	0	1	.000	1	1	0	0	0	2	9	8	8	2	1	1	2	5.000	36.00	11	46.20	.643	0	.000	-7	0	-0.7
Total	3	0	5	.000	14	5	0	0	0	34^1	51	40	39	12	5	23	16	2.155	10.22	47	11.81	.347	0	.000	-20	0	-1.9
• HINDS, Sam	Samuel Russell Hinds b: 7/11/1953, Frederick, MD BR/TR, 6'6", 215 lbs. Deb: 5/21/1977																										
1977	Mil-A	0	3	.000	29	1	0	0	2	72^1	72	42	38	5	2	40	46	1.548	4.73	86	4.45	.266	0	....	-6	2	-0.6
• HINRICHS, Dutch	William Louis Hinrichs b: 4/27/1889, Orange, CA d: 4/18/1972, Kingsburg, CA BR/TR, 6'3", 195 lbs. Deb: 6/25/1910																										
1910	Was-A	0	1	.000	3	0	0	0	1	7	10	7	2	0	0	3	5	1.857	2.57	97	6.23	.357	0	.000	-0	0	-0.1
• HINRICHS, Paul	Paul Edwin "Herky" Hinrichs b: 8/31/1925, Marengo, IA BR/TR, 6', 180 lbs. Deb: 5/16/1951																										
1951	Bos-A	0	0	....	4	0	0	0	0	3^1	7	8	8	1	0	4	1	3.300	21.60	21	16.64	.412	0	....	-6	0	-0.6
• HINSLEY, Jerry	Jerry Dean Hinsley b: 4/9/1944, Hugo, OK BR/TR, 5'11", 165 lbs. Deb: 4/18/1964																										
1964	NY-N	0	2	.000	9	2	0	0	0	15^1	21	17	14	0	0	7	11	1.826	8.22	43	5.36	.313	0	.000	-8	0	-0.9
1967	NY-N	0	0	....	2	0	0	0	0	5	6	2	2	0	0	4	3	2.000	3.60	94	6.44	.316	0	....	-0	0	0.0
Total	2	0	2	.000	11	2	0	0	0	20^1	27	19	16	0	0	11	14	1.869	7.08	50	5.63	.314	0	.000	-8	0	-0.9
• HINTON, Rich	Richard Michael Hinton b: 5/22/1947, Tucson, AZ BL/TL, 6'2", 185 lbs. Deb: 7/17/1971																										
1971	Chi-A	3	4	.429	18	2	0	0	0	24^1	27	12	12	1	1	6	15	1.356	4.44	81	3.92	.310	0	.000	-2	1	-0.2
1972	NY-A	1	0	1.000	7	3	0	0	0	16^2	20	11	9	2	0	8	13	1.680	4.86	61	5.29	.299	0	.000	-4	0	-0.4
	Tex-A	0	1	.000	5	0	0	0	0	11^1	7	10	3	1	0	10	4	1.500	2.38	126	3.41	.171	1	.500	1	0	0.2
	Yr.	1	1	.500	12	3	0	0	0	28	27	21	12	3	0	18	17	1.607	3.86	77	4.53	.250	1	.200	-3	0	-0.2
1975	Chi-A	1	0	1.000	15	0	0	0	0	37^1	41	22	20	2	0	15	30	1.500	4.82	80	4.09	.270	0	....	-3	1	-0.3
1976	Cin-N	1	2	.333	12	1	0	0	0	17^2	30	15	15	4	0	11	8	2.321	7.64	46	10.28	.380	0	.000	-8	0	-0.9
1978	Chi-A	2	6	.250	29	4	2	0	1	80^2	78	38	36	5	2	28	48	1.314	4.02	95	3.56	.261	0	....	-1	4	-0.1
1979	Chi-A	1	2	.333	16	2	0	0	2	41^2	57	30	28	4	2	8	27	1.560	6.05	70	5.48	.331	0	....	-8	0	-0.8
	Sea-A	0	2	.000	14	1	0	0	0	20	23	14	12	4	2	5	7	1.400	5.40	81	5.26	.284	0	....	-2	0	-0.2
	Yr.	1	4	.200	30	3	0	0	2	61^2	80	44	40	8	4	13	34	1.508	5.84	73	5.41	.316	0	....	-11	0	-1.0
Total	6	9	17	.346	116	13	2	0	3	249^2	283	152	135	23	7	91	152	1.498	4.87	78	4.72	.289	1	.143	-28	6	-2.8
• HIPPAUF, Herb	Herbert August Hippauf b: 5/9/1939, New York, NY d: 7/17/1995, Santa Clara, CA BR/TL, 6', 180 lbs. Deb: 4/27/1966																										
1966	Atl-N	0	1	.000	3	0	0	0	0	2^2	6	5	4	0	0	1	1	2.625	13.50	27	10.88	.462	0	....	-3	0	-0.3
• HISNER, Harley	Harley Parnell Hisner b: 11/6/1926, Maples, IN BR/TR, 6'1", 185 lbs. Deb: 9/30/1951																										
1951	Bos-A	0	1	.000	1	1	0	0	0	6	7	3	3	0	0	4	3	1.833	4.50	99	5.17	.292	1	.500	-0	0	0.0
• HITCHCOCK, Sterling	Sterling Alex Hitchcock b: 4/29/1971, Fayetteville, NC BL/TL, 6'1", 192 lbs. Deb: 9/11/1992																										
1992	NY-A	0	2	.000	3	3	0	0	0	13	23	12	12	2	1	6	6	2.231	8.31	47	9.98	.377	0	....	-6	0	-0.6
1993	NY-A	1	2	.333	6	6	0	0	0	31	32	18	16	4	1	14	26	1.484	4.65	89	4.83	.271	0	....	-2	1	-0.2
1994	NY-A	4	1	.800	23	5	1	0	2	49^1	48	24	23	3	0	29	37	1.561	4.20	109	4.38	.265	0	....	1	4	0.1
1995*	NY-A	11	10	.524	27	27	4	1	0	168^1	155	91	88	22	5	68	121	1.325	4.70	98	3.97	.245	0	....	-3	9	-0.2
1996	Sea-A	13	9	.591	35	35	0	0	0	196^2	245	131	117	27	7	73	132	1.617	5.35	93	5.86	.309	0	....	-9	8	-0.9
1997	SD-N	10	11	.476	32	28	1	0	0	161	172	102	93	24	4	55	106	1.410	5.20	74	4.71	.276	5	.100	-22	3	-2.4
1998*	SD-N	9	7	.563	39	27	2	1	1	176^1	169	83	77	29	9	48	158	1.231	3.93	100	3.95	.251	7	.140	-1	9	-0.2
1999	SD-N	12	14	.462	33	33	1	0	0	205^2	202	99	94	29	5	76	194	1.352	4.11	102	4.14	.254	5	.082	1	10	-0.2
2000	SD-N	1	6	.143	11	11	0	0	0	65^2	69	38	36	12	5	26	61	1.447	4.93	87	5.22	.267	0	.000	-5	1	-0.8
2001	SD-N	2	1	.667	3	3	0	0	0	19	22	9	7	1	1	3	15	1.316	3.32	121	3.68	.275	1	.125	2	1	0.1
	*NY-A	4	4	.500	10	9	1	0	0	51^1	67	37	37	5	2	18	28	1.656	6.49	69	5.74	.315	0	....	-10	1	-1.0
2002	NY-A	1	2	.333	20	2	0	0	0	39^1	57	29	24	4	1	15	31	1.831	5.49	79	6.43	.326	0	....	-4	1	-0.4
2003	NY-A	1	3	.250	27	1	0	0	0	49^2	57	33	30	6	0	18	36	1.510	5.44	80	4.77	.285	0	....	-5	1	-0.5
	StL-N	5	1	.833	8	6	0	0	0	38	34	17	16	8	1	14	32	1.263	3.79	107	4.12	.238	1	.083	1	3	0.0
Total	12	74	73	.503	277	196	10	2	3	1264^1	1352	723	670	176	42	463	983	1.436	4.77	90	4.73	.273	19	.094	-63	52	-7.0
• HITT, Bruce	Bruce Smith Hitt b: 3/14/1897, Comanche, TX d: 11/10/1973, Portland, OR BR/TR, 6'1", 190 lbs. Deb: 9/23/1917																										
1917	StL-N	0	0	....	2	0	0	0	0	4	7	6	4	1	0	1	1	2.000	9.00	30	9.10	.368	0	.000	-3	0	-0.3
• HITT, Roy	Roy Wesley "Rhino" Hitt b: 6/22/1884, Carleton, NE d: 2/8/1956, Pomona, CA BL/TL, 5'10", 200 lbs. Deb: 4/27/1907																										
1907	Cin-N	6	10	.375	21	18	14	2	0	153^1	143	76	58	2	12	56	63	1.298	3.40	76	3.36	.258	10	.179	-16	3	-1.7
• HITTLE, Lloyd	Lloyd Eldon "Red" Hittle b: 2/21/1924, Lodi, CA BR/TL, 5'10.5", 164 lbs. Deb: 6/12/1949																										
1949	Was-A	5	7	.417	36	9	3	2	0	109	123	62	51	2	0	57	32	1.651	4.21	101	4.46	.285	4	.143	5	5	0.3
1950	Was-A	2	4	.333	11	4	1	0	0	43^1	60	27	24	1	0	17	9	1.777	4.98	90	5.52	.326	1	.077	-2	2	-0.3
Total	2	7	11	.389	47	13	4	2	0	152^1	183	89	75	3	0	74	41	1.687	4.43	98	4.76	.298	5	.122	2	7	0.0
• HOBAUGH, Ed	Edward Russell Hobaugh b: 6/27/1934, Kittanning, PA BR/TR, 6', 176 lbs. Deb: 4/19/1961																										
1961	Was-A	7	9	.438	26	18	3	0	0	126^1	142	68	62	12	1	64	67	1.631	4.42	89	5.14	.281	4	.098	-7	5	-0.9
1962	Was-A	2	1	.667	26	2	0	0	1	69^1	66	36	29	9	0	25	37	1.313	3.76	107	3.85	.258	2	.167	2	4	0.3

YEAR	TM-L	W	L	PCT	G	GS	CG	SH	SV	IP	H	R	ER	HR	HB	BB	SO	RAT	ERA	ERA+	CERA	OAV	BH	AVG	PR+	WS	TPW
1963	Was-A	0	0	....	9	1	0	0	0	16	20	13	11	3	2	6	11	1.625	6.19	60	6.20	.308	1	.500	-4	1	-0.3
Total	3	9	10	.474	61	21	3	0	1	211^{2}	228	117	102	24	3	95	115	1.526	4.34	91	4.80	.276	7	.127	-9	10	-1.0

• HOBBIE, Glen Glen Frederick Hobbie b: 4/24/1936, Witt, IL BR/TR, 6'2", 195 lbs. Deb: 9/20/1957

YEAR	TM-L	W	L	PCT	G	GS	CG	SH	SV	IP	H	R	ER	HR	HB	BB	SO	RAT	ERA	ERA+	CERA	OAV	BH	AVG	PR+	WS	TPW
1957	Chi-N	0	0	....	2	0	0	0	0	4^{1}	6	5	5	0	0	5	3	2.538	10.38	37	8.48	.333	0	.000	-3	0	-0.3
1958	Chi-N	10	6	.625	55	16	2	1	2	168^{1}	163	80	70	13	7	93	91	1.521	3.74	105	4.38	.252	7	.146	5	10	0.3
1959	Chi-N	16	13	.552	46	33	10	3	0	234	204	105	96	15	6	106	138	1.325	3.69	107	3.45	.236	9	.114	5	14	0.2
1960	Chi-N	16	20	.444	46	36	16	4	1	258^{2}	253	130	114	27	9	101	134	1.369	3.97	95	4.03	.256	13	.151	-5	12	-0.4
1961	Chi-N	7	13	.350	36	29	7	2	2	198^{2}	207	113	94	26	6	54	103	1.314	4.26	98	4.07	.268	11	.167	1	9	0.4
1962	Chi-N	5	14	.263	42	23	5	0	0	162	198	112	94	18	3	62	87	**1.605**	5.22	79	5.36	.304	6	.122	-20	3	-2.1
1963	Chi-N	7	10	.412	36	24	4	1	0	165^{1}	172	80	72	17	6	49	94	1.337	3.92	90	4.08	.270	4	.080	-10	6	-1.4
1964	Chi-N	0	3	.000	8	4	0	0	0	27^{1}	39	29	24	4	1	10	14	1.793	7.90	47	6.85	.325	0	.000	-12	0	-1.3
	StL-N	1	2	.333	13	5	1	0	1	44^{1}	41	23	21	4	1	15	18	1.263	4.26	89	3.36	.241	2	.154	-2	2	-0.2
	Yr.	1	5	.167	21	9	1	0	1	71^{2}	80	52	45	8	2	25	32	1.465	5.65	66	4.69	.276	2	.111	-15	2	-1.5
Total	8	62	81	.434	284	170	45	11	6	1263	1283	677	590	124	39	495	682	1.408	4.20	93	4.20	.264	52	.131	-41	56	-4.8

• HOBBS, John John Douglas Hobbs b: 11/11/1955, Philadelphia, PA BR/TL, 6'3", 190 lbs. Deb: 8/31/1981

YEAR	TM-L	W	L	PCT	G	GS	CG	SH	SV	IP	H	R	ER	HR	HB	BB	SO	RAT	ERA	ERA+	CERA	OAV	BH	AVG	PR+	WS	TPW
1981	Min-A	0	0	....	4	0	0	0	0	5^{2}	5	2	2	0	2	6	1	1.941	3.18	124	6.21	.238	0	....	1	0	0.1

• HOCH, Harry Harry Keller Hoch b: 1/9/1887, Woodside, DE d: 10/26/1981, Lewes, DE BR/TR, 5'10.5", 165 lbs. Deb: 4/16/1908

YEAR	TM-L	W	L	PCT	G	GS	CG	SH	SV	IP	H	R	ER	HR	HB	BB	SO	RAT	ERA	ERA+	CERA	OAV	BH	AVG	PR+	WS	TPW
1908	Phi-N	2	1	.667	3	3	2	0	0	26	20	10	8	0	2	13	4	1.269	2.77	87	2.69	.211	1	.200	-1	2	-0.1
1914	StL-A	0	2	.000	15	2	1	0	0	54	55	31	18	1	2	27	13	1.519	3.00	90	4.31	.284	1	.056	-1	1	-0.3
1915	StL-A	0	4	.000	12	3	1	0	0	40	52	49	32	2	3	26	9	1.950	7.20	40	6.58	.311	2	.200	-20	0	-2.1
Total	3	2	7	.222	30	8	4	0	0	120	127	90	58	3	7	66	26	1.608	4.35	63	4.72	.279	4	.121	-22	3	-2.5

• HOCKENBERY, Chuck Charles Marion Hockenbery b: 12/15/1950, La Crosse, WI BB/TR, 6'1", 195 lbs. Deb: 7/4/1975

YEAR	TM-L	W	L	PCT	G	GS	CG	SH	SV	IP	H	R	ER	HR	HB	BB	SO	RAT	ERA	ERA+	CERA	OAV	BH	AVG	PR+	WS	TPW
1975	Cal-A	0	5	.000	16	4	0	0	1	41	48	27	24	3	3	19	15	1.634	5.27	67	5.43	.296	0	....	-8	0	-0.8

• HOCKETTE, George George Edward "Lefty" Hockette b: 4/7/1908, Perth, MS d: 1/20/1974, Plantation, FL BL/TL, 6', 174 lbs. Deb: 9/17/1934

YEAR	TM-L	W	L	PCT	G	GS	CG	SH	SV	IP	H	R	ER	HR	HB	BB	SO	RAT	ERA	ERA+	CERA	OAV	BH	AVG	PR+	WS	TPW
1934	Bos-A	2	1	.667	3	3	3	2	0	27^{1}	22	5	5	3	0	6	14	1.024	1.65	292	2.41	.218	3	.273	10	4	1.0
1935	Bos-A	2	3	.400	23	4	0	0	0	61	83	43	35	6	1	12	11	1.557	5.16	92	5.35	.329	2	.143	-3	2	-0.3
Total	2	4	4	.500	26	7	3	2	0	88^{1}	105	48	40	9	1	18	25	1.392	4.08	117	4.44	.297	5	.200	7	6	0.6

• HODGE, Ed Ed Oliver Hodge b: 4/19/1958, Bellflower, CA BL/TL, 6'2", 192 lbs. Deb: 5/1/1984

YEAR	TM-L	W	L	PCT	G	GS	CG	SH	SV	IP	H	R	ER	HR	HB	BB	SO	RAT	ERA	ERA+	CERA	OAV	BH	AVG	PR+	WS	TPW
1984	Min-A	4	3	.571	25	15	0	0	0	100	116	59	53	13	1	29	59	1.450	4.77	88	4.84	.291	0	....	-9	4	-0.9

• HODGE, Shovel Clarence Clemet Hodge b: 7/6/1893, Mount Andrew, AL d: 12/31/1967, Fort Walton Beach, FL BL/TR, 6'4", 190 lbs. Deb: 9/6/1920

YEAR	TM-L	W	L	PCT	G	GS	CG	SH	SV	IP	H	R	ER	HR	HB	BB	SO	RAT	ERA	ERA+	CERA	OAV	BH	AVG	PR+	WS	TPW
1920	Chi-A	1	1	.500	4	2	1	0	0	19^{2}	15	14	5	0	0	12	5	1.373	2.29	164	2.95	.224	0	.000	3	1	0.2
1921	Chi-A	6	8	.429	36	10	5	0	2	142^{2}	191	118	104	7	5	54	25	1.717	6.56	65	5.66	.335	17	.327	-37	2	-3.2
1922	Chi-A	7	6	.538	35	8	2	0	1	139	154	73	64	3	2	65	37	1.576	4.14	98	4.43	.300	12	.207	-3	7	-0.4
Total	3	14	15	.483	75	20	8	0	3	301^{1}	360	205	173	10	7	131	67	1.629	5.17	80	4.92	.313	29	.250	-37	10	-3.4

• HODGES, Kevin Kevin Jon Hodges b: 6/24/1973, Houston, TX BR/TR, 6'4", 200 lbs. Deb: 4/24/2000

YEAR	TM-L	W	L	PCT	G	GS	CG	SH	SV	IP	H	R	ER	HR	HB	BB	SO	RAT	ERA	ERA+	CERA	OAV	BH	AVG	PR+	WS	TPW
2000	Sea-A	0	0	....	13	0	0	0	0	17^{1}	18	10	10	4	2	12	7	1.731	5.19	87	8.02	.310	0	....	-1	1	-0.1

• HODGES, Trey Trey Alan Hodges b: 6/29/1978, Houston, TX BR/TR, 6'3", 187 lbs. Deb: 9/10/2002

YEAR	TM-L	W	L	PCT	G	GS	CG	SH	SV	IP	H	R	ER	HR	HB	BB	SO	RAT	ERA	ERA+	CERA	OAV	BH	AVG	PR+	WS	TPW
2002	Atl-N	2	0	1.000	4	0	0	0	0	11^{2}	16	7	7	2	1	2	6	1.543	5.40	76	6.20	.348	0	.000	-2	1	-0.2
2003	Atl-N	3	3	.500	52	1	0	0	0	65^{2}	69	38	34	11	3	31	66	1.523	4.66	91	5.12	.268	0	.000	-3	2	-0.4
Total	2	5	3	.625	56	1	0	0	0	77^{1}	85	45	41	13	4	33	72	1.526	4.77	88	5.28	.281	0	.000	-5	3	-0.6

• HODKEY, Eli Aloysius Joseph Hodkey b: 11/3/1917, Lorain, OH BL/TL, 6'4", 185 lbs. Deb: 9/12/1946

YEAR	TM-L	W	L	PCT	G	GS	CG	SH	SV	IP	H	R	ER	HR	HB	BB	SO	RAT	ERA	ERA+	CERA	OAV	BH	AVG	PR+	WS	TPW
1946	Phi-N	0	1	.000	2	1	0	0	0	4^{1}	9	6	6	0	0	5	0	3.231	12.46	28	12.35	.391	0	.000	-4	0	-0.5

• HODNETT, Charlie Charles Hodnett b: 1861, St. Louis, MO d: 4/25/1890, St. Louis, MO Deb: 5/3/1883

YEAR	TM-L	W	L	PCT	G	GS	CG	SH	SV	IP	H	R	ER	HR	HB	BB	SO	RAT	ERA	ERA+	CERA	OAV	BH	AVG	PR+	WS	TPW
1883	StL-a	2	2	.500	4	4	3	0	0	32	28	10	5	1	....	7	6	1.094	1.41	247	....	.220	2	.182	5	4	0.4
1884	StL-U	12	2	.857	14	14	12	1	0	121	121	56	27	0	....	16	41	1.132	2.01	148	....	.243	12	.207	7	13	0.7
Total	2	14	4	.778	18	18	15	1	0	153	149	66	32	1	....	23	47	1.124	1.88	162	....	.239	14	.203	13	17	1.1

• HODSON, George George S. Hodson b: 6/1870, PA d: 1/9/1924, San Rafael, CA TR, 5'7" Deb: 8/9/1894

YEAR	TM-L	W	L	PCT	G	GS	CG	SH	SV	IP	H	R	ER	HR	HB	BB	SO	RAT	ERA	ERA+	CERA	OAV	BH	AVG	PR+	WS	TPW
1894	Bos-N	4	4	.500	12	11	8	0	0	74	103	66	48	4	5	35	12	1.865	5.84	101	6.47	.326	3	.100	-2	4	-0.4
1895	Phi-N	1	2	.333	4	2	1	0	0	17	27	23	18	4	0	9	6	2.118	9.53	50	9.37	.354	0	.000	-9	0	-0.8
Total	2	5	6	.455	16	13	9	0	0	91	130	89	66	8	5	44	18	1.912	6.53	85	7.01	.332	3	.086	-11	4	-1.2

• HOEFT, Billy William Frederick Hoeft b: 5/17/1932, Oshkosh, WI BL/TL, 6'3", 205 lbs. Deb: 4/18/1952

YEAR	TM-L	W	L	PCT	G	GS	CG	SH	SV	IP	H	R	ER	HR	HB	BB	SO	RAT	ERA	ERA+	CERA	OAV	BH	AVG	PR+	WS	TPW
1952	Det-A	2	7	.222	34	10	1	0	4	125	123	66	60	14	5	63	67	1.488	4.32	88	4.51	.260	6	.150	-5	4	-0.6
1953	Det-A	9	14	.391	29	27	9	0	2	197^{2}	223	113	106	24	4	58	90	1.422	4.83	84	4.51	.283	11	.172	-11	6	-1.0
1954	Det-A	7	15	.318	34	25	10	4	1	175	180	93	89	22	4	59	114	1.366	4.58	81	4.17	.266	10	.192	-18	6	-1.4
1955	Det-A★	16	7	.696	32	29	17	**7**	0	220	187	75	73	17	6	75	133	1.191	2.99	129	3.01	.230	17	.207	21	18	2.5
1956	Det-A	20	14	.588	38	34	18	4	0	248	276	127	112	22	5	104	172	1.532	4.06	101	4.76	.287	20	.250	2	15	0.7
1957	Det-A	9	11	.450	34	28	10	1	1	207	188	85	80	15	5	69	111	1.242	3.48	111	3.20	.244	10	.149	7	14	0.9
1958	Det-A	10	9	.526	36	21	6	0	3	143	148	70	66	15	1	49	94	1.378	4.15	97	4.07	.268	12	.273	-3	9	0.0
1959	Det-A	1	1	.500	2	2	0	0	0	9	6	5	5	0	1	4	2	1.111	5.00	81	2.26	.188	1	.333	-1	0	-0.1
	Bos-A	0	3	.000	5	3	0	0	0	17^{2}	22	12	11	1	1	8	8	1.698	5.60	72	5.43	.319	0	.000	-3	0	-0.4
	Bal-A	1	1	.500	16	3	0	0	0	41	50	29	26	6	0	19	30	1.683	5.71	66	5.91	.307	3	.250	-9	0	-0.9
	Yr.	2	5	.286	23	8	0	0	0	67^{2}	78	46	42	7	2	31	40	1.611	5.59	70	5.30	.295	4	.222	-13	0	-1.3
1960	Bal-A	2	1	.667	19	0	0	0	0	18^{2}	18	10	9	2	0	14	14	1.714	4.34	88	5.03	.240	0	.000	-1	1	-0.2
1961	Bal-A	7	4	.636	35	12	3	1	3	138	106	37	31	7	1	55	100	1.167	2.02	193	2.56	.216	7	.179	27	16	2.7
1962	Bal-A	4	8	.333	57	4	0	0	7	113^{2}	103	62	58	7	1	43	73	1.284	4.59	82	3.18	.243	3	.158	-11	5	-0.9
1963	SF-N	2	0	1.000	23	0	0	0	4	24^{1}	26	12	12	5	0	10	8	1.479	4.44	72	5.08	.271	1	1.000	-3	2	-0.2
1964	Mil-N	4	0	1.000	42	0	0	0	4	73^{1}	76	35	31	9	1	18	47	1.282	3.80	92	3.83	.271	2	.222	-2	4	-0.1
1965	Chi-N	2	2	.500	29	2	1	0	1	51^{1}	41	21	16	3	0	20	44	1.188	2.81	131	2.56	.215	3	.273	6	4	0.6
1966	Chi-N	1	2	.333	36	0	0	0	3	41	43	28	21	4	1	14	30	1.390	4.61	80	4.00	.264	1	.250	-4	1	-0.4
	SF-N	0	2	.000	4	0	0	0	0	3^{2}	4	3	3	0	0	3	3	1.909	7.36	50	4.49	.250	0	....	-2	0	-0.2
	Yr.	1	4	.200	40	0	0	0	3	44^{2}	47	31	24	4	1	17	33	1.433	4.84	76	4.04	.263	1	.250	-5	1	-0.5
Total	15	97	101	.490	505	200	75	17	33	1847^{1}	1820	883	809	173	36	685	1140	1.356	3.94	98	3.87	.259	107	.202	-10	105	1.3

• HOERNER, Joe Joseph Walter Hoerner b: 11/12/1936, Dubuque, IA d: 10/4/1996, Hermann, MO BR/TL, 6'1", 200 lbs. Deb: 9/27/1963

YEAR	TM-L	W	L	PCT	G	GS	CG	SH	SV	IP	H	R	ER	HR	HB	BB	SO	RAT	ERA	ERA+	CERA	OAV	BH	AVG	PR+	WS	TPW
1963	Hou-N	0	0	....	1	0	0	0	0	3	2	0	0	0	0	0	2	.667	0.00	....	0.91	.182	0	.000	1	0	0.1
1964	Hou-N	0	0	....	7	0	0	0	0	11	13	11	6	3	0	6	4	1.727	4.91	70	7.10	.310	0	.000	-2	0	-0.2
1966	StL-N	5	1	.833	57	0	0	0	13	76	57	16	13	5	4	21	63	1.026	1.54	234	2.18	.212	1	.125	17	13	1.8
1967*	StL-N	4	4	.500	57	0	0	0	15	66	52	25	19	5	1	20	50	1.091	2.59	125	2.36	.225	2	.182	5	9	0.5
1968*	StL-N	8	2	.800	47	0	0	0	17	48^{2}	34	9	8	2	0	12	42	.945	1.48	196	1.56	.192	0	.000	7	12	0.8
1969	StL-N	2	3	.400	45	0	0	0	15	53^{1}	44	18	17	5	1	9	35	.994	2.87	125	2.29	.230	0	.000	4	8	0.3
1970	Phi-N★	9	5	.643	44	0	0	0	9	57^{2}	53	20	17	5	1	20	39	1.266	2.65	150	3.18	.247	2	.200	9	10	1.0
1971	Phi-N	4	5	.444	49	0	0	0	9	73	57	19	16	6	1	21	57	1.068	1.97	179	2.37	.215	1	.100	12	11	1.2
1972	Phi-N	0	2	.000	15	0	0	0	3	21^{2}	21	6	5	2	1	5	12	1.200	2.08	173	2.96	.259	0	.000	3	3	0.4
	Atl-N	1	3	.250	25	0	0	0	2	23^{1}	34	18	17	4	1	8	19	1.800	6.56	58	7.16	.351	0	.000	-7	0	-0.8
	Yr.	1	5	.167	40	0	0	0	5	45	55	24	22	6	2	13	31	1.511	4.40	85	5.14	.309	0	.000	-3	3	-0.4
1973	Atl-N	2	2	.500	20	0	0	0	2	12^{2}	17	9	9	1	0	4	10	1.658	6.39	61	5.75	.333	0	....	-3	0	-0.3
	KC-A	2	0	1.000	22	0	0	0	4	19^{1}	28	11	11	0	0	13	15	2.121	5.12	80	6.26	.329	0	....	-2	1	-0.2
1974	KC-A	2	3	.400	30	0	0	0	2	35^{1}	32	15	15	3	4	12	24	1.245	3.82	100	3.37	.244	0	....	0	3	0.1

YEAR	TM-L	W	L	PCT	G	GS	CG	SH	SV	IP	H	R	ER	HR	HB	BB	SO	RAT	ERA	ERA+	CERA	OAV	BH	AVG	PR+	WS	TPW
1975	Phi-N	0	0	....	25	0	0	0	0	21	25	6	6	3	1	8	20	1.571	2.57	145	5.39	.298	0	.000	2	2	0.2
1976	Tex-A	0	4	.000	41	0	0	0	8	35	41	22	20	3	0	19	15	1.714	5.14	70	5.23	.315	0	....	-6	0	-0.7
1977	Cin-N	0	0	....	8	0	0	0	0	5^{2}	9	8	8	3	3	3	5	2.118	12.71	31	14.47	.375	0	....	-6	0	-0.6
Total	**14**	**39**	**34**	**.534**	**493**	**0**	**0**	**0**	**99**	**562^{2}**	**519**	**213**	**187**	**50**	**18**	**181**	**412**	**1.244**	**2.99**	**121**	**3.34**	**.249**	**6**	**.102**	**35**	**72**	**3.6**

• HOERST, Lefty

Frank Joseph Hoerst b: 8/11/1917, Philadelphia, PA d: 2/18/2000, Maple Shade, NJ BL/TL, 6'3", 192 lbs. Deb: 4/26/1940

YEAR	TM-L	W	L	PCT	G	GS	CG	SH	SV	IP	H	R	ER	HR	HB	BB	SO	RAT	ERA	ERA+	CERA	OAV	BH	AVG	PR+	WS	TPW
1940	Phi-N	1	0	1.000	6	0	0	0	0	12	12	7	7	1	0	8	3	1.667	5.25	74	4.90	.267	0	.000	-2	1	-0.2
1941	Phi-N	3	10	.231	37	11	1	0	0	105^{2}	111	70	61	7	1	50	33	1.524	5.20	71	4.33	.275	4	.182	-17	1	-1.7
1942	Phi-N	4	16	.200	33	22	5	0	1	150^{2}	162	99	87	11	1	78	52	1.593	5.20	64	4.60	.271	7	.152	-32	0	-3.4
1946	Phi-N	1	6	.143	18	7	2	0	0	68^{1}	77	42	35	4	1	36	17	1.654	4.61	74	4.95	.288	1	.059	-9	0	-1.1
1947	Phi-N	1	1	.500	4	1	0	0	0	11^{1}	19	12	10	1	0	3	0	1.941	7.94	50	7.27	.358	2	.500	-5	0	-0.4
Total	**5**	**10**	**33**	**.233**	**98**	**41**	**8**	**0**	**1**	**348**	**381**	**230**	**200**	**24**	**3**	**175**	**105**	**1.598**	**5.17**	**67**	**4.69**	**.279**	**14**	**.154**	**-64**	**2**	**-6.8**

• HOFF, Chet

Chester Cornelius "Red" Hoff b: 5/8/1891, Ossining, NY d: 9/17/1998, Daytona Beach, FL BL/TL, 5'9", 162 lbs. Deb: 9/6/1911

YEAR	TM-L	W	L	PCT	G	GS	CG	SH	SV	IP	H	R	ER	HR	HB	BB	SO	RAT	ERA	ERA+	CERA	OAV	BH	AVG	PR+	WS	TPW
1911	NY-A	0	1	.000	5	1	0	0	0	20^{2}	21	8	5	0	0	7	10	1.355	2.18	165	3.19	.262	2	.286	4	2	0.4
1912	NY-A	0	1	.000	5	1	0	0	0	15^{2}	20	14	12	0	0	6	14	1.660	6.89	52	4.67	.303	1	.200	-5	0	-0.5
1913	NY-A	0	0	....	2	0	0	0	0	3	0	0	0	0	0	1	2	.333	0.00	....	0.11	.000	0	.000	1	0	0.1
1915	StL-A	2	2	.500	11	3	2	0	0	43^{2}	26	16	6	0	1	24	23	1.145	1.24	231	1.84	.169	3	.176	7	3	0.7
Total	**4**	**2**	**4**	**.333**	**23**	**5**	**2**	**0**	**0**	**83**	**67**	**38**	**23**	**0**	**1**	**38**	**49**	**1.265**	**2.49**	**135**	**2.65**	**.223**	**6**	**.200**	**7**	**5**	**0.7**

• HOFFER, Bill

William Leopold "Chick,Wizard" Hoffer b: 11/8/1870, Cedar Rapids, IA d: 7/21/1959, Cedar Rapids, IA BR/TR, 5'9", 155 lbs. Deb: 4/26/1895 U

YEAR	TM-L	W	L	PCT	G	GS	CG	SH	SV	IP	H	R	ER	HR	HB	BB	SO	RAT	ERA	ERA+	CERA	OAV	BH	AVG	PR+	WS	TPW
1895*	Bal-N	31	6	.838	41	38	32	**4**	0	314	296	146	112	9	19	124	80	1.338	3.21	148	3.37	.246	27	.214	35	35	2.6
1896*	Bal-N	25	7	.781	35	35	32	3	0	309	317	151	116	1	12	95	93	1.333	3.38	126	3.34	.264	38	.304	25	31	3.0
1897*	Bal-N	22	11	.667	38	33	29	1	0	303^{1}	350	188	145	5	17	104	62	1.497	4.30	97	4.22	.287	33	.237	-9	18	-0.8
1898	Bal-N	0	4	.000	4	4	4	0	0	34^{1}	62	44	28	0	1	16	5	2.272	7.34	49	8.46	.387	5	.208	-15	0	-1.5
	Pit-N	3	0	1.000	4	3	3	0	0	31	26	7	6	0	0	15	11	1.323	1.74	204	2.73	.226	1	.091	6	4	0.5
	Yr.	3	4	.429	8	7	7	0	0	65^{1}	88	51	34	0	1	31	16	1.821	4.68	76	5.75	.320	6	.171	-9	4	-1.0
1899	Pit-N	8	10	.444	23	19	15	2	0	163^{2}	169	98	66	5	10	64	44	1.424	3.63	105	3.85	.267	18	.198	3	9	0.0
1901	Cle-A	3	8	.273	16	10	10	0	**3**	99	113	78	50	2	1	35	19	1.495	4.55	78	4.06	.284	6	.136	-10	3	-1.1
Total	**6**	**92**	**46**	**.667**	**161**	**142**	**125**	**10**	**3**	**1254^{1}**	**1333**	**712**	**523**	**22**	**60**	**453**	**314**	**1.424**	**3.75**	**110**	**3.81**	**.270**	**128**	**.229**	**33**	**100**	**2.7**

• HOFFMAN, Bill

William Joseph Hoffman b: 3/3/1918, Philadelphia, PA BL/TL, 5'9", 170 lbs. Deb: 8/13/1939

YEAR	TM-L	W	L	PCT	G	GS	CG	SH	SV	IP	H	R	ER	HR	HB	BB	SO	RAT	ERA	ERA+	CERA	OAV	BH	AVG	PR+	WS	TPW
1939	Phi-N	0	0	....	3	0	0	0	0	6	8	9	9	2	3	7	1	2.500	13.50	29	14.19	.333	0	.000	-6	0	-0.7

• HOFFMAN, Frank

Frank J. "The Texas Wonder" Hoffman b: Houston, TX TR, 5'9.5" Deb: 8/13/1888

YEAR	TM-L	W	L	PCT	G	GS	CG	SH	SV	IP	H	R	ER	HR	HB	BB	SO	RAT	ERA	ERA+	CERA	OAV	BH	AVG	PR+	WS	TPW
1888	KC-a	3	9	.250	12	12	12	0	0	104	102	71	32	3	6	42	38	1.385	2.77	124	....	.248	6	.154	7	6	0.7

• HOFFMAN, Guy

Guy Alan Hoffman b: 7/9/1956, Ottawa, IL BL/TL, 5'9", 185 lbs. Deb: 7/4/1979

YEAR	TM-L	W	L	PCT	G	GS	CG	SH	SV	IP	H	R	ER	HR	HB	BB	SO	RAT	ERA	ERA+	CERA	OAV	BH	AVG	PR+	WS	TPW
1979	Chi-A	0	5	.000	24	0	0	0	2	30^{1}	30	18	18	0	1	23	18	1.747	5.34	80	4.42	.261	0	....	-4	1	-0.4
1980	Chi-A	1	0	1.000	23	1	0	0	1	37^{2}	38	12	11	1	0	17	24	1.460	2.63	153	3.79	.268	0	....	6	4	0.6
1983	Chi-A	1	0	1.000	11	0	0	0	0	6	14	5	5	1	0	2	2	2.667	7.50	56	13.84	.483	0	....	-2	0	-0.2
1986	Chi-N	6	2	.750	32	8	1	0	0	84	92	37	36	6	2	29	47	1.440	3.86	105	4.27	.288	1	.067	3	6	0.3
1987	Cin-N	9	10	.474	36	22	0	0	0	158^{2}	160	83	77	20	4	49	87	1.317	4.37	97	4.04	.265	5	.111	-3	7	-0.5
1988	Tex-A	0	0	....	11	0	0	0	0	22^{1}	22	14	13	5	1	8	9	1.343	5.24	78	4.72	.247	0	....	-3	0	-0.3
Total	**6**	**17**	**17**	**.500**	**137**	**31**	**1**	**0**	**3**	**339**	**356**	**169**	**160**	**33**	**8**	**128**	**187**	**1.428**	**4.25**	**98**	**4.32**	**.274**	**6**	**.100**	**-3**	**18**	**-0.4**

• HOFFMAN, Trevor

Trevor William Hoffman b: 10/13/1967, Bellflower, CA BR/TR, 6'1", 205 lbs. Deb: 4/6/1993

YEAR	TM-L	W	L	PCT	G	GS	CG	SH	SV	IP	H	R	ER	HR	HB	BB	SO	RAT	ERA	ERA+	CERA	OAV	BH	AVG	PR+	WS	TPW
1993	Fla-N	2	2	.500	28	0	0	0	2	35^{2}	24	13	13	5	0	19	26	1.206	3.28	132	2.71	.185	0	.000	5	4	0.5
	SD-N	2	4	.333	39	0	0	0	3	54^{1}	56	30	26	5	1	20	53	1.399	4.31	96	3.88	.264	1	.200	-1	3	-0.1
	Yr.	4	6	.400	67	0	0	0	5	90	80	43	39	10	1	39	79	1.322	3.90	108	3.41	.234	1	.143	4	7	0.4
1994	SD-N	4	4	.500	47	0	0	0	20	56	39	16	16	4	0	20	68	1.054	2.57	160	2.02	.193	0	.000	11	11	1.0
1995	SD-N	7	4	.636	55	0	0	0	31	53^{1}	48	25	23	10	0	14	52	1.163	3.88	103	3.48	.235	1	.500	-0	9	0.1
1996*	SD-N	9	5	.643	70	0	0	0	42	88	50	23	22	6	2	31	111	.920	2.25	176	1.58	.161	0	.000	17	20	1.6
1997	SD-N	6	4	.600	70	0	0	0	37	81^{1}	59	25	24	9	0	24	111	1.020	2.66	145	2.27	.200	1	.333	12	11	1.2
1998*	SD-N★	4	2	.667	66	0	0	0	**53**	73	41	12	12	2	1	21	86	.849	1.48	266	1.32	.165	0	.000	20	20	1.9
1999	SD-N★	2	3	.400	64	0	0	0	40	67^{1}	48	23	16	5	0	15	73	.936	2.14	196	1.78	.197	1	.333	15	14	1.5
2000	SD-N★	4	7	.364	70	0	0	0	43	72^{1}	61	29	24	7	0	11	85	.995	2.99	144	2.18	.224	0	....	10	13	0.9
2001	SD-N	3	4	.429	62	0	0	0	43	60^{1}	48	25	23	10	1	21	63	1.144	3.43	116	3.20	.216	0	.000	5	9	0.4
2002	SD-N★	2	5	.286	61	0	0	0	38	59^{1}	52	20	18	2	1	18	69	1.180	2.73	138	2.63	.234	0	....	7	8	0.7
2003	SD-N	0	0	....	9	0	0	0	0	9	7	2	2	1	0	3	11	1.111	2.00	197	2.76	.212	0	....	2	1	0.2
Total	**11**	**45**	**44**	**.506**	**641**	**0**	**0**	**0**	**352**	**710**	**533**	**243**	**219**	**66**	**6**	**217**	**808**	**1.056**	**2.78**	**146**	**2.36**	**.205**	**4**	**.121**	**102**	**123**	**9.9**

• HOFFORD, John

John William Hofford b: 5/25/1863, Philadelphia, PA d: 12/16/1915, Philadelphia, PA Deb: 9/26/1885

YEAR	TM-L	W	L	PCT	G	GS	CG	SH	SV	IP	H	R	ER	HR	HB	BB	SO	RAT	ERA	ERA+	CERA	OAV	BH	AVG	PR+	WS	TPW
1885	Pit-a	0	3	.000	3	3	3	0	0	25	28	16	10	1	0	9	21	1.480	3.60	89	....	.271	1	.125	-1	1	-0.2
1886	Pit-a	3	6	.333	9	9	9	0	0	81	88	66	39	1	2	40	25	1.580	4.33	78	....	.264	10	.294	-9	3	-0.5
Total	**2**	**3**	**9**	**.250**	**12**	**12**	**12**	**0**	**0**	**106**	**116**	**82**	**49**	**2**	**2**	**49**	**46**	**1.557**	**4.16**	**80**	**....**	**.266**	**11**	**.262**	**-11**	**4**	**-0.7**

• HOGAN, Eddie

Robert Edward Hogan b: 4/6/1862, St. Louis, MO d: 1/22/1932, Yucaipa, CA BR, 5'7", 153 lbs. Deb: 7/5/1882

YEAR	TM-L	W	L	PCT	G	GS	CG	SH	SV	IP	H	R	ER	HR	HB	BB	SO	RAT	ERA	ERA+	CERA	OAV	BH	AVG	PR+	WS	TPW
1882	StL-a	0	1	.000	1	1	1	0	0	8	10	7	1	0	....	0	4	1.250	1.13	249	....	.287	1	.333	2	1	0.2

• HOGAN, George

George A. Hogan b: 9/25/1885, Marion, OH d: 2/22/1922, Bartlesville, OK BR/TR, 6', 160 lbs. Deb: 4/18/1914

YEAR	TM-L	W	L	PCT	G	GS	CG	SH	SV	IP	H	R	ER	HR	HB	BB	SO	RAT	ERA	ERA+	CERA	OAV	BH	AVG	PR+	WS	TPW
1914	KC-F	0	1	.000	4	1	0	0	0	13	12	9	6	1	1	7	7	1.462	4.15	74	4.17	.255	0	.000	-2	0	-0.2

• HOGG, Bill

William Johnston "Buffalo Bill" Hogg b: 9/11/1881, Port Huron, MI d: 12/8/1909, New Orleans, LA BR/TR, 6', 200 lbs. Deb: 4/25/1905

YEAR	TM-L	W	L	PCT	G	GS	CG	SH	SV	IP	H	R	ER	HR	HB	BB	SO	RAT	ERA	ERA+	CERA	OAV	BH	AVG	PR+	WS	TPW
1905	NY-A	9	13	.409	39	22	9	3	1	205	178	104	73	1	13	101	125	**1.361**	3.20	91	3.11	.236	4	.060	-4	7	-1.0
1906	NY-A	14	13	.519	28	25	15	3	0	206	171	77	67	5	12	72	107	1.180	2.93	101	2.61	.229	9	.125	2	16	-0.2
1907	NY-A	10	8	.556	25	21	13	0	0	166^{2}	173	84	57	3	6	83	64	**1.536**	3.08	91	4.07	.270	11	.183	-3	9	-0.3
1908	NY-A	4	16	.200	24	21	6	0	0	152^{1}	155	89	51	4	4	63	72	1.431	3.01	82	3.56	.262	4	.093	-5	2	-0.9
Total	**4**	**37**	**50**	**.425**	**116**	**89**	**43**	**6**	**1**	**730**	**677**	**354**	**248**	**13**	**35**	**319**	**368**	**1.364**	**3.06**	**92**	**3.28**	**.248**	**28**	**.116**	**-9**	**34**	**-2.4**

• HOGG, Brad

Carter Bradley Hogg b: 3/26/1889, Buena Vista, GA d: 4/2/1935, Buena Vista, GA BR/TR, 6', 185 lbs. Deb: 9/1/1911

YEAR	TM-L	W	L	PCT	G	GS	CG	SH	SV	IP	H	R	ER	HR	HB	BB	SO	RAT	ERA	ERA+	CERA	OAV	BH	AVG	PR+	WS	TPW
1911	Bos-N	0	3	.000	8	3	2	0	1	25^{2}	33	20	19	0	1	14	8	1.831	6.66	57	5.99	.337	4	.444	-8	1	-0.6
1912	Bos-N	1	1	.500	10	1	0	0	1	31	37	32	24	2	2	16	12	1.710	6.97	51	5.43	.308	1	.091	-11	0	-1.2
1915	Chi-N	1	0	1.000	2	2	1	1	0	13	12	3	3	1	1	6	0	1.385	2.08	133	3.86	.245	0	.000	1	1	0.1
1918	Phi-N	13	13	.500	29	25	17	3	1	228	201	83	64	3	6	61	81	1.149	2.53	119	2.46	.245	18	.228	12	19	1.8
1919	Phi-N	5	12	.294	22	19	13	0	0	150^{1}	163	85	74	7	5	55	48	1.450	4.43	73	4.15	.292	17	.283	-19	4	-1.8
Total	**5**	**20**	**29**	**.408**	**71**	**50**	**33**	**4**	**3**	**448**	**446**	**223**	**184**	**13**	**15**	**152**	**149**	**1.335**	**3.70**	**87**	**3.48**	**.271**	**40**	**.247**	**-25**	**25**	**-1.8**

• HOGSETT, Chief

Elon Chester Hogsett b: 11/2/1903, Brownell, KS d: 7/17/2001, Hays, KS BL/TL, 6', 190 lbs. Deb: 9/18/1929

YEAR	TM-L	W	L	PCT	G	GS	CG	SH	SV	IP	H	R	ER	HR	HB	BB	SO	RAT	ERA	ERA+	CERA	OAV	BH	AVG	PR+	WS	TPW
1929	Det-A	1	2	.333	4	4	2	1	0	28^{2}	34	10	9	0	1	9	9	1.500	2.83	152	4.32	.312	2	.200	6	2	0.5
1930	Det-A	9	8	.529	33	17	4	0	1	146	174	102	88	9	9	63	54	1.623	5.42	88	5.11	.300	17	.293	-10	7	-0.7
1931	Det-A	3	9	.250	22	12	5	0	2	112^{1}	150	80	74	8	5	33	47	1.629	5.93	77	5.55	.324	11	.234	-17	3	-1.6
1932	Det-A	11	9	.550	47	15	7	0	7	178	201	97	70	8	5	66	56	1.500	3.54	133	4.28	.286	14	.246	20	14	2.2
1933	Det-A	6	10	.375	45	2	0	0	9	116	137	78	58	7	4	56	39	1.664	4.50	96	5.15	.296	8	.211	-3	5	-0.4
1934*	Det-A	3	2	.600	26	0	0	0	3	50^{1}	61	34	24	4	1	19	23	1.589	4.29	102	5.02	.303	3	.231	0	3	0.0
1935*	Det-A	6	6	.500	40	0	0	0	5	96^{2}	109	45	38	1	5	49	39	1.634	3.54	118	4.57	.288	6	.261	6	7	0.7
1936	Det-A	0	1	.000	3	0	0	0	0	4	8	7	4	1	0	1	1	2.250	9.00	55	10.35	.400	0	....	-2	0	-0.1
	StL-A	13	15	.464	39	29	10	0	1	215^{1}	278	153	132	15	15	90	67	1.709	5.52	97	5.74	.310	10	.143	1	13	-0.1
	Yr.	13	16	.448	42	29	10	0	1	219^{1}	286	160	136	16	15	91	68	1.719	5.58	96	5.82	.312	10	.143	-1	13	-0.2
1937	StL-A	6	19	.240	37	26	8	1	2	177^{1}	245	144	124	19	5	75	68	**1.805**	6.29	77	6.45	.328	13	.210	-27	4	-2.5
1938	Was-A	5	6	.455	31	9	1	0	3	91	107	73	61	12	8	36	33	1.571	6.03	75	5.50	.292	7	.304	-16	3	-1.1

YEAR	TM-L	W	L	PCT	G	GS	CG	SH	SV	IP	H	R	ER	HR	HB	BB	SO	RAT	ERA	ERA+	CERA	OAV	BH	AVG	PR+	WS	TPW
1944	Det-A	0	0	....	3	0	0	0	0	6^1	7	6	0	1	2	4	5	1.737	0.00	....	6.56	.250	0	.000	3	0	0.2
Total	11	63	87	.420	330	114	37	2	33	1222	1511	829	682	85	60	501	441	1.646	5.02	94	5.33	.305	91	.226	-40	61	-2.7
• HOGUE, Bobby		Robert Clinton Hogue b: 4/5/1921, Miami, FL d: 12/22/1987, Miami, FL BR/TR, 5'10", 195 lbs. Deb: 4/24/1948																									
1948	Bos-N	8	2	.800	40	1	0	0	2	86^1	88	34	31	4	2	19	43	1.239	3.23	119	3.18	.265	2	.095	5	7	0.4
1949	Bos-N	2	2	.500	33	0	0	0	3	72	78	30	25	4	2	25	23	1.431	3.13	121	4.03	.280	6	.286	6	6	0.7
1950	Bos-N	3	5	.375	36	1	0	0	7	62^2	69	35	35	8	4	31	15	1.596	5.03	77	5.40	.280	3	.231	-8	2	-0.7
1951	Bos-N	0	0	....	3	0	0	0	0	5	4	3	3	1	0	3	0	1.400	5.40	68	4.69	.235	1	.500	-1	0	-0.1
	StL-A	1	1	.500	18	0	0	0	1	29^2	31	17	17	1	0	23	11	1.820	5.16	85	5.18	.279	2	.667	-2	2	0.0
	*NY-A	1	0	1.000	7	0	0	0	0	7^1	4	0	0	0	0	3	2	.955	0.00	....	1.46	.174	0	....	3	1	0.3
	Yr.	2	1	.667	25	0	0	0	1	37	35	17	17	1	0	26	13	1.649	4.14	106	4.44	.261	2	.667	1	3	0.3
1952	NY-A	3	5	.375	27	0	0	0	4	47^1	52	30	28	6	1	25	12	1.627	5.32	62	5.51	.294	3	.273	-12	0	-1.2
	StL-A	0	1	.000	8	1	0	0	0	16^1	10	5	5	1	0	13	2	1.408	2.76	142	3.02	.179	0	.000	2	1	0.2
	Yr.	3	6	.333	35	1	0	0	4	63^2	62	35	33	7	1	38	14	1.571	4.66	73	4.87	.266	3	.231	-10	1	-1.0
Total	5	18	16	.529	172	3	0	0	17	326^2	336	154	144	25	9	142	108	1.463	3.97	95	4.29	.271	17	.233	-7	19	-0.4
• HOGUE, Cal		Calvin Grey Hogue b: 10/24/1927, Dayton, OH BR/TR, 6', 185 lbs. Deb: 7/15/1952																									
1952	Pit-N	1	8	.111	19	12	3	0	0	83^2	79	56	45	7	4	68	34	1.757	4.84	82	5.33	.258	6	.250	-7	1	-0.6
1953	Pit-N	1	1	.500	3	2	2	0	0	19	19	13	11	4	1	16	10	1.842	5.21	86	6.60	.250	0	.000	-1	1	-0.2
1954	Pit-N	0	1	.000	3	2	0	0	0	11	11	6	6	1	0	12	7	2.091	4.91	85	6.83	.282	0	.000	-1	0	-0.1
Total	3	2	10	.167	25	16	5	0	0	113^2	109	75	62	12	5	96	51	1.804	4.91	83	5.69	.259	6	.188	-9	2	-0.9
• HOLBOROW, Wally		Walter Albert Holborow b: 11/30/1913, New York, NY d: 7/14/1986, Fort Lauderdale, FL BR/TR, 5'11", 187 lbs. Deb: 9/27/1944																									
1944	Was-A	0	0	....	1	0	0	0	0	3	0	0	0	0	0	2	1	.667	0.00	....	0.39	.000	0	....	1	0	0.1
1945	Was-A	1	1	.500	15	1	1	1	0	31^1	20	9	8	0	0	16	14	1.149	2.30	135	1.94	.189	0	.000	3	2	0.3
1948	Phi-A	1	2	.333	5	1	1	0	0	17^1	32	12	11	1	0	7	3	2.250	5.71	75	8.99	.421	2	.500	-3	1	-0.2
Total	3	2	3	.400	21	2	2	1	0	51^2	52	21	19	1	0	25	18	1.490	3.31	112	4.21	.286	2	.333	1	3	0.2
• HOLCOMBE, Ken		Kenneth Edward Holcombe b: 8/23/1918, Burnsville, NC BR/TR, 5'11.5", 169 lbs. Deb: 4/27/1945																									
1945	NY-A	3	3	.500	23	2	0	0	0	55^1	43	19	11	2	0	27	20	1.265	1.79	193	2.74	.226	2	.133	9	5	0.9
1948	Cin-N	0	0	....	2	0	0	0	0	2^1	3	2	2	0	0	0	2	1.286	7.71	51	3.32	.300	0	....	-1	0	-0.1
1950	Chi-A	3	10	.231	24	15	5	0	1	96	122	68	49	10	0	45	37	1.740	4.59	98	5.79	.307	5	.156	-3	2	-0.5
1951	Chi-A	11	12	.478	28	23	12	2	0	159^1	142	69	67	9	1	68	39	1.318	3.78	107	3.24	.241	11	.250	2	10	0.3
1952	Chi-A	0	5	.000	7	7	1	0	0	35	38	24	24	3	2	18	12	1.600	6.17	59	5.14	.286	0	.000	-10	0	-1.2
	StL-A	0	2	.000	12	1	0	0	0	21	20	10	9	1	0	9	7	1.381	3.86	101	3.50	.263	1	.333	-0	1	0.0
	Yr.	0	7	.000	19	8	1	0	0	56	58	34	33	4	2	27	19	1.518	5.30	70	4.53	.278	1	.077	-10	1	-1.2
1953	Bos-A	1	0	1.000	3	0	0	0	1	6	9	4	4	0	0	3	1	2.000	6.00	70	6.33	.333	0	.000	-1	0	-0.2
Total	6	18	32	.360	99	48	18	2	2	375	377	196	166	25	3	170	118	1.459	3.98	101	4.06	.265	19	.179	-5	18	-0.7
• HOLDRIDGE, David		David Allen Holdridge b: 2/5/1969, Wayne, MI BR/TR, 6'3" Deb: 8/8/1998																									
1998	Sea-A	0	0	....	7	0	0	0	0	6^2	6	3	3	0	0	4	6	1.500	4.05	114	3.33	.231	0	....	1	0	0.0
• HOLDSWORTH, Fred		Frederick William Holdsworth b: 5/29/1952, Detroit, MI BR/TR, 6'1", 190 lbs. Deb: 7/27/1972																									
1972	Det-A	0	1	.000	2	2	0	0	0	7	13	10	10	0	0	2	5	2.143	12.86	24	8.31	.419	1	.333	-8	0	-0.8
1973	Det-A	0	1	.000	5	2	0	0	0	14^2	13	11	11	3	0	6	9	1.295	6.75	61	4.18	.236	0	....	-4	0	-0.4
1974	Det-A	0	3	.000	8	5	0	0	0	35^2	40	20	17	4	1	14	16	1.514	4.29	89	4.81	.286	0	....	-2	1	-0.2
1976	Bal-A	4	1	.800	16	0	0	0	2	39^2	24	9	9	0	0	13	24	.933	2.04	160	1.42	.179	0	....	5	5	0.5
1977	Bal-A	0	1	.000	12	0	0	0	0	14^1	17	11	10	0	1	16	4	2.302	6.28	60	7.45	.333	0	....	-4	0	-0.4
	Mon-N	3	3	.500	14	6	0	0	0	42^1	35	17	15	6	0	18	21	1.252	3.19	119	3.60	.230	0	.000	3	3	0.2
1978	Mon-N	0	0	....	6	0	0	0	0	8^2	16	10	7	3	0	8	3	2.769	7.27	48	13.40	.381	0	....	-4	0	-0.4
1980	Mil-A	0	0	....	9	0	0	0	0	19^2	24	12	10	2	0	9	12	1.678	4.58	85	5.40	.286	0	....	-2	0	-0.2
Total	7	7	10	.412	72	15	0	0	2	182	182	100	89	18	2	86	94	1.473	4.40	83	4.55	.264	1	.077	-16	9	-1.8
• HOLLAND, Al		Alfred Willis Holland b: 8/16/1952, Roanoke, VA BR/TL, 5'11", 207 lbs. Deb: 9/5/1977																									
1977	Pit-N	0	0	....	2	0	0	0	0	2^1	4	2	2	0	0	0	1	1.714	7.71	52	6.33	.400	0	....	-1	0	-0.1
1979	SF-N	0	0	....	3	0	0	0	0	7	3	0	0	0	0	5	7	1.143	0.00	....	1.64	.125	0	....	3	1	0.3
1980	SF-N	5	3	.625	54	0	0	0	7	82^1	71	21	16	2	1	34	65	1.275	1.75	202	2.74	.233	1	.200	18	11	2.0
1981	SF-N	7	5	.583	47	3	0	0	7	100^2	87	31	27	4	2	44	78	1.301	2.41	142	2.93	.233	1	.063	12	10	1.2
1982	SF-N	7	3	.700	58	7	0	0	5	129^2	115	56	48	12	1	40	97	1.195	3.33	108	2.96	.231	2	.059	6	8	0.4
1983*	Phi-N	8	4	.667	68	0	0	0	25	91^2	63	26	23	8	0	30	100	1.015	2.26	158	1.90	.188	0	.000	15	18	1.4
1984	Phi-N★	5	10	.333	68	0	0	0	29	98^1	82	38	37	14	1	30	61	1.139	3.39	107	3.02	.225	0	.000	4	12	0.4
1985	Phi-N	0	1	.000	3	0	0	0	1	4	5	2	2	0	0	4	1	2.250	4.50	82	5.91	.333	0	....	-0	0	0.0
	Pit-N	1	3	.250	38	0	0	0	4	58^2	48	22	22	5	0	17	47	1.108	3.38	106	2.49	.227	2	.400	2	5	0.4
	Yr.	1	4	.200	41	0	0	0	5	62^2	53	24	24	5	0	21	48	1.181	3.45	104	2.71	.235	2	.400	2	5	0.4
	Cal-A	0	1	.000	15	0	0	0	0	24^1	17	4	4	4	0	10	14	1.110	1.48	278	2.85	.193	0	....	6	3	0.6
1986	NY-A	1	0	1.000	25	1	0	0	0	40^2	44	29	23	5	0	9	37	1.303	5.09	80	3.77	.268	0	....	-5	1	-0.5
1987	NY-A	0	0	....	3	0	0	0	0	6^1	9	10	10	1	0	9	5	2.842	14.21	31	11.56	.321	0	....	-7	0	-0.7
Total	10	34	30	.531	384	11	0	0	78	646	548	241	214	55	5	232	513	1.207	2.98	123	2.89	.227	6	.083	54	69	5.5
• HOLLAND, Bill		William David "Dutch" Holland b: 6/4/1915, Varina, NC d: 4/5/1997, Goldsboro, NC BL/TL, 6'1", 190 lbs. Deb: 9/17/1939																									
1939	Was-A	0	1	.000	3	0	0	0	0	4	6	5	5	1	0	5	2	2.750	11.25	39	13.02	.400	0		-3	0	-0.3
• HOLLAND, Mul		Howard Arthur Holland b: 1/6/1903, Franklin, VA d: 2/16/1969, Winchester, VA BR/TR, 6'4", 185 lbs. Deb: 5/25/1926																									
1926	Cin-N	0	0	....	3	0	0	0	0	6^2	3	1	1	0	0	5	0	1.200	1.35	274	1.66	.136	1	.500	2	1	0.2
1927	NY-N	1	0	1.000	2	0	0	0	0	2	0	0	0	0	0	3	0	1.500	0.00	....	1.60	.000	0	....	1	1	0.1
1929	StL-N	0	1	.000	8	0	0	0	0	14^1	13	15	15	3	1	7	5	1.395	9.42	49	4.64	.232	1	.250	-8	0	-0.7
Total	3	1	1	.500	13	0	0	0	0	23	16	16	16	3	1	15	5	1.348	6.26	73	3.51	.205	2	.333	-5	2	-0.4
• HOLLEY, Ed		Edward Edgar Holley b: 7/23/1899, Benton, KY d: 10/26/1986, Paducah, KY BR/TR, 6'1.5", 195 lbs. Deb: 5/24/1928																									
1928	Chi-N	0	0	....	13	1	0	0	0	31	31	15	13	1	2	16	10	1.516	3.77	102	4.18	.265	0	.000	-1	2	-0.1
1932	Phi-N	11	14	.440	34	30	16	2	0	228	247	114	100	15	6	55	87	1.325	3.95	112	3.70	.273	12	.132	12	14	0.7
1933	Phi-N	13	15	.464	30	28	12	3	0	206^2	219	93	81	18	13	62	56	1.360	3.53	108	4.07	.273	12	.162	7	15	0.6
1934	Phi-N	1	8	.111	15	13	2	0	0	72^2	85	62	58	10	4	31	14	1.596	7.18	66	5.60	.294	5	.208	-21	0	-2.1
	Pit-N	0	3	.000	5	4	0	0	0	9^1	20	16	16	1	2	6	2	2.786	15.43	27	13.47	.426	2	1.000	-12	1	-1.0
	Yr.	1	11	.083	20	17	2	0	0	82	105	78	74	11	6	37	16	1.732	8.12	56	6.50	.313	7	.269	-33	1	-3.1
Total	4	25	40	.385	97	76	30	5	0	547^2	602	300	268	45	27	170	169	1.410	4.40	96	4.29	.279	31	.158	-15	32	-2.0
• HOLLING, Carl		Carl Holling b: 7/9/1896, Dana, CA d: 7/18/1962, Santa Rosa, CA BR/TR, 6'1", 172 lbs. Deb: 4/19/1921																									
1921	Det-A	3	7	.300	35	11	4	0	4	136	162	95	65	8	4	58	38	1.618	4.30	99	4.96	.305	13	.271	3	5	0.4
1922	Det-A	1	1	.500	5	1	0	0	0	9^1	21	16	16	1	2	5	2	2.786	15.43	25	15.22	.525	0	.000	-12	0	-1.2
Total	2	4	8	.333	40	12	4	0	4	145^1	183	111	81	9	6	63	40	1.693	5.02	83	5.62	.320	13	.260	-9	5	-0.8
• HOLLINGSWORTH, Al		Albert Wayne "Boots" Hollingsworth b: 2/25/1908, St. Louis, MO d: 4/28/1996, Austin, TX BL/TL, 6', 174 lbs. Deb: 4/16/1935 C																									
1935	Cin-N	6	13	.316	38	22	8	0	0	173^1	165	90	75	5	1	76	89	1.390	3.89	102	3.26	.243	8	.148	3	8	0.1
1936	Cin-N	9	10	.474	29	25	9	0	0	184	204	97	85	4	5	66	76	1.467	4.16	92	3.95	.281	23	.315	-6	11	0.1
1937	Cin-N	9	15	.375	43	24	11	1	5	202^1	224	108	88	8	2	73	74	1.468	3.91	95	3.98	.278	19	.250	-3	9	0.0
1938	Cin-N	2	2	.500	9	4	1	0	0	34	43	28	27	2	0	12	13	1.618	7.15	51	4.88	.307	3	.250	-14	0	-1.3
	Phi-N	5	16	.238	24	21	11	1	0	174^1	177	89	74	4	0	77	80	1.457	3.82	105	3.68	.264	15	.224	9	8	0.9
	Yr.	7	18	.280	33	25	12	1	0	208^1	220	117	101	6	0	89	93	1.483	4.36	89	3.87	.272	18	.228	-5	8	-0.4

YEAR	TM-L	W	L	PCT	G	GS	CG	SH	SV	IP	H	R	ER	HR	HB	BB	SO	RAT	ERA	ERA+	CERA	OAV	BH	AVG	PR+	WS	TPW
1939	Phi-N	1	9	.100	15	10	3	0	0	60	78	48	39	2	0	27	24	1.750	5.85	67	5.27	.317	2	.100	-13	0	-1.4
	Bro-N	1	2	.333	8	5	1	0	0	27^1	33	17	16	1	1	11	11	1.610	5.27	76	4.91	.311	1	.125	-4	0	-0.4
	Yr.	2	11	.154	23	15	4	0	0	87^1	111	65	55	3	1	38	35	1.706	5.67	70	5.16	.315	3	.107	-16	0	-1.8
1940	Was-A	1	0	1.000	3	2	0	0	0	18	18	12	11	0	0	11	7	1.611	5.50	76	3.97	.261	1	.167	-2	1	-0.2
1942	StL-A	10	6	.625	33	18	7	1	4	161	173	70	53	4	2	52	60	1.398	2.96	125	3.57	.272	10	.179	15	12	1.5
1943	StL-A	6	13	.316	35	20	9	1	3	154	169	81	72	7	2	51	63	1.429	4.21	79	3.92	.281	7	.140	-13	4	-1.5
1944*	StL-A	5	7	.417	26	10	3	2	1	92^2	108	51	46	3	1	37	22	1.565	4.47	81	4.38	.291	2	.071	-7	2	-0.9
1945	StL-A	12	9	.571	26	22	15	1	1	173^1	164	60	52	4	0	68	64	1.338	2.70	130	3.13	.251	12	.197	16	16	1.9
1946	StL-A	0	0	....	5	0	0	0	0	11	23	8	8	1	0	4	3	2.455	6.55	57	10.50	.411	0	.000	-3	0	-0.4
	Chi-A	3	2	.600	21	2	0	0	1	55	63	29	28	2	0	22	22	1.545	4.58	74	4.27	.288	0	.000	-8	1	-0.9
	Yr.	3	2	.600	26	2	0	0	1	66	86	37	36	3	0	26	25	1.697	4.91	71	5.30	.313	0	.000	-11	1	-1.3
Total	**11**	**70**	**104**	**.402**	**315**	**185**	**78**	**7**	**15**	**1520^1**	**1642**	**788**	**674**	**47**	**14**	**587**	**608**	**1.466**	**3.99**	**93**	**3.88**	**.275**	**103**	**.196**	**-29**	**72**	**-2.6**

• HOLLINGSWORTH, Bonnie John Burnette Hollingsworth b: 12/26/1895, Jacksboro, TN d: 1/4/1990, Knoxville, TN BR/TR, 5'10", 170 lbs. Deb: 5/30/1922

YEAR	TM-L	W	L	PCT	G	GS	CG	SH	SV	IP	H	R	ER	HR	HB	BB	SO	RAT	ERA	ERA+	CERA	OAV	BH	AVG	PR+	WS	TPW
1922	Pit-N	0	0	....	9	0	0	0	0	13^2	17	14	12	0	1	8	7	1.829	7.90	52	5.76	.315	0	....	-6	0	-0.5
1923	Was-A	3	7	.300	17	8	1	0	0	72^2	72	43	33	3	3	50	26	1.679	4.09	92	4.69	.272	2	.091	-5	2	-0.6
1924	Bro-N	1	0	1.000	3	1	1	0	0	8^2	8	6	6	0	0	10	7	2.077	6.23	60	6.00	.267	0	.000	-2	0	-0.3
1928	Bos-N	0	2	.000	7	2	0	0	0	22^1	30	19	13	2	0	13	10	1.925	5.24	75	6.73	.341	1	.167	-3	0	-0.3
Total	**4**	**4**	**9**	**.308**	**36**	**11**	**2**	**0**	**0**	**117^1**	**127**	**82**	**64**	**5**	**4**	**81**	**50**	**1.773**	**4.91**	**78**	**5.30**	**.291**	**3**	**.097**	**-15**	**2**	**-1.7**

• HOLLINS, Jessie Jessie Edward Hollins b: 1/27/1970, Conroe, TX BR/TR, 6'3", 190 lbs. Deb: 9/19/1992

YEAR	TM-L	W	L	PCT	G	GS	CG	SH	SV	IP	H	R	ER	HR	HB	BB	SO	RAT	ERA	ERA+	CERA	OAV	BH	AVG	PR+	WS	TPW
1992	Chi-N	0	0	....	4	0	0	0	0	4^2	8	7	7	1	0	5	0	2.786	13.50	27	12.61	.400	0	....	-5	0	-0.6

• HOLLISON, John John Henry "Swede" Hollison b: 5/3/1870, Chicago, IL d: 8/19/1969, Chicago, IL BR/TL, 5'8", 162 lbs. Deb: 8/13/1892

YEAR	TM-L	W	L	PCT	G	GS	CG	SH	SV	IP	H	R	ER	HR	HB	BB	SO	RAT	ERA	ERA+	CERA	OAV	BH	AVG	PR+	WS	TPW
1892	Chi-N	0	0	....	1	0	0	0	0	4	1	1	1	1	0	0	2	.250	2.25	148	0.47	.077	0	.000	1	0	0.0

• HOLLOMAN, Bobo Alva Lee Holloman b: 3/7/1925, Thomaston, GA d: 5/1/1987, Athens, GA BR/TR, 6'2", 207 lbs. Deb: 4/18/1953

YEAR	TM-L	W	L	PCT	G	GS	CG	SH	SV	IP	H	R	ER	HR	HB	BB	SO	RAT	ERA	ERA+	CERA	OAV	BH	AVG	PR+	WS	TPW
1953	StL-A	3	7	.300	22	10	1	1	0	65^1	69	41	38	2	1	50	25	1.821	5.23	80	5.19	.275	2	.105	-7	2	-0.9

• HOLLOWAY, Jim James Madison Holloway b: 9/22/1908, Plaquemine, LA d: 4/15/1997, Baton Rouge, LA BR/TR, 6'1", 165 lbs. Deb: 5/17/1929

YEAR	TM-L	W	L	PCT	G	GS	CG	SH	SV	IP	H	R	ER	HR	HB	BB	SO	RAT	ERA	ERA+	CERA	OAV	BH	AVG	PR+	WS	TPW
1929	Phi-N	0	0	....	3	0	0	0	0	4^2	10	7	7	2	0	5	1	3.214	13.50	38	19.19	.455	1	1.000	-4	0	-0.3

• HOLLOWAY, Ken Kenneth Eugene Holloway b: 8/8/1897, Thomas County, GA d: 9/25/1968, Thomasville, GA BR/TR, 6', 185 lbs. Deb: 8/27/1922

YEAR	TM-L	W	L	PCT	G	GS	CG	SH	SV	IP	H	R	ER	HR	HB	BB	SO	RAT	ERA	ERA+	CERA	OAV	BH	AVG	PR+	WS	TPW
1922	Det-A	0	0	....	1	0	0	0	0	1	1	1	0	0	0	0	1	1.000	0.00	....	1.51	.250	0	....	0	0	0.0
1923	Det-A	11	10	.524	42	24	7	1	1	194	232	117	96	12	10	75	55	1.582	4.45	87	4.94	.302	8	.123	-11	7	-1.5
1924	Det-A	14	6	.700	49	13	5	0	3	181^1	209	105	82	6	6	61	46	1.489	4.07	101	4.25	.299	11	.190	1	11	-0.1
1925	Det-A	13	4	.765	38	14	6	0	2	157^2	170	90	81	8	2	67	29	1.503	4.62	93	4.18	.282	11	.229	-6	10	-0.6
1926	Det-A	4	6	.400	36	12	3	0	2	139	192	94	79	2	8	42	43	1.683	5.12	79	5.44	.343	11	.239	-15	4	-1.4
1927	Det-A	11	12	.478	36	23	11	1	6	183^1	210	103	83	10	4	61	36	1.478	4.07	103	4.31	.299	8	.129	5	11	-0.1
1928	Det-A	4	8	.333	30	11	5	0	2	120^1	137	67	58	2	5	32	32	1.404	4.34	95	3.64	.291	4	.121	-3	5	-0.5
1929	Cle-A	6	5	.545	25	11	6	2	0	119	118	52	40	2	2	37	32	1.303	3.03	147	3.16	.264	7	.171	20	11	1.7
1930	Cle-A	1	1	.500	12	2	0	0	2	30	49	32	28	5	0	14	8	2.100	8.40	57	8.71	.374	0	.000	-11	0	-1.2
	NY-A	0	0	....	16	0	0	0	0	34^1	52	23	20	3	0	8	11	1.748	5.24	82	6.42	.374	3	.231	-3	1	-0.3
	Yr.	1	1	.500	28	2	0	0	2	64^1	101	55	48	8	0	22	19	1.912	6.72	68	7.49	.374	3	.120	-15	1	-1.6
Total	**9**	**64**	**52**	**.552**	**285**	**110**	**43**	**4**	**18**	**1160**	**1370**	**684**	**567**	**50**	**37**	**397**	**293**	**1.523**	**4.40**	**94**	**4.51**	**.303**	**63**	**.167**	**-24**	**60**	**-4.0**

• HOLLY, Jeff Jeffrey Owen Holly b: 3/1/1953, San Pedro, CA BL/TL, 6'5", 210 lbs. Deb: 5/1/1977

YEAR	TM-L	W	L	PCT	G	GS	CG	SH	SV	IP	H	R	ER	HR	HB	BB	SO	RAT	ERA	ERA+	CERA	OAV	BH	AVG	PR+	WS	TPW
1977	Min-A	2	3	.400	18	5	0	0	0	48^1	57	37	37	8	1	12	32	1.428	6.89	58	5.14	.300	0	....	-16	0	-1.5
1978	Min-A	1	1	.500	15	1	0	0	0	35^1	28	15	14	1	0	18	12	1.302	3.57	107	2.73	.222	0	....	1	2	0.1
1979	Min-A	0	0	....	6	0	0	0	0	6^1	10	7	5	0	0	3	5	2.053	7.11	62	7.10	.385	0	....	-2	0	-0.2
Total	**3**	**3**	**4**	**.429**	**39**	**6**	**0**	**0**	**0**	**90**	**95**	**59**	**56**	**9**	**1**	**33**	**49**	**1.422**	**5.60**	**71**	**4.33**	**.278**	**0**	**....**	**-17**	**2**	**-1.6**

• HOLMAN, Brad Bradley Thomas Holman b: 2/9/1968, Kansas City, MO BR/TR, 6'5", 200 lbs. Deb: 7/4/1993

YEAR	TM-L	W	L	PCT	G	GS	CG	SH	SV	IP	H	R	ER	HR	HB	BB	SO	RAT	ERA	ERA+	CERA	OAV	BH	AVG	PR+	WS	TPW
1993	Sea-A	1	3	.250	19	0	0	0	3	36^1	27	17	15	1	5	16	17	1.183	3.72	118	2.82	.208	0	....	3	3	0.3

• HOLMAN, Brian Brian Scott Holman b: 1/25/1965, Denver, CO BR/TR, 6'4", 185 lbs. Deb: 6/25/1988

YEAR	TM-L	W	L	PCT	G	GS	CG	SH	SV	IP	H	R	ER	HR	HB	BB	SO	RAT	ERA	ERA+	CERA	OAV	BH	AVG	PR+	WS	TPW
1988	Mon-N	4	8	.333	18	16	1	1	0	100^1	101	39	36	3	0	34	58	1.346	3.23	111	3.40	.264	3	.107	3	5	0.2
1989	Mon-N	1	2	.333	10	3	0	0	0	31^2	34	18	17	2	1	15	23	1.547	4.83	73	4.52	.270	1	.125	-4	0	-0.5
	Sea-A	8	10	.444	23	22	6	2	0	159^2	160	68	61	9	6	62	82	1.390	3.44	117	3.84	.261	0	....	10	10	1.0
1990	Sea-A	11	11	.500	28	28	3	0	0	189^2	188	92	85	17	6	66	121	1.339	4.03	98	3.90	.260	0	.000	-1	10	-0.1
1991	Sea-A	13	14	.481	30	30	5	3	0	195^1	199	86	80	16	10	77	108	1.413	3.69	112	4.31	.268	0	....	6	12	0.6
Total	**4**	**37**	**45**	**.451**	**109**	**99**	**15**	**6**	**0**	**676^2**	**682**	**303**	**279**	**47**	**23**	**254**	**392**	**1.383**	**3.71**	**106**	**3.96**	**.263**	**4**	**.108**	**13**	**37**	**1.2**

• HOLMAN, Scott Randy Scott Holman b: 9/18/1958, Santa Paula, CA BR/TR, 6'1", 190 lbs. Deb: 9/20/1980

YEAR	TM-L	W	L	PCT	G	GS	CG	SH	SV	IP	H	R	ER	HR	HB	BB	SO	RAT	ERA	ERA+	CERA	OAV	BH	AVG	PR+	WS	TPW
1980	NY-N	0	0	....	4	0	0	0	0	7	6	2	1	0	0	1	3	1.000	1.29	276	1.76	.250	0	....	2	1	0.2
1982	NY-N	2	1	.667	4	4	1	0	0	26^2	23	10	7	2	0	7	11	1.125	2.36	154	2.70	.232	2	.222	4	2	0.4
1983	NY-N	1	7	.125	35	10	0	0	0	101	90	48	42	7	1	52	44	1.406	3.74	97	3.59	.242	5	.217	-2	4	-0.2
Total	**3**	**3**	**8**	**.273**	**43**	**14**	**1**	**0**	**0**	**134^2**	**119**	**60**	**50**	**9**	**1**	**60**	**58**	**1.329**	**3.34**	**108**	**3.32**	**.240**	**7**	**.219**	**3**	**7**	**0.4**

• HOLMAN, Shawn Shawn Leroy Holman b: 11/10/1964, Sewickley, PA BR/TR, 6'2", 185 lbs. Deb: 9/5/1989

YEAR	TM-L	W	L	PCT	G	GS	CG	SH	SV	IP	H	R	ER	HR	HB	BB	SO	RAT	ERA	ERA+	CERA	OAV	BH	AVG	PR+	WS	TPW
1989	Det-A	0	0	....	5	0	0	0	0	10	8	2	2	0	0	11	9	1.900	1.80	212	4.41	.211	0	....	2	1	0.2

• HOLMES, Chick Elwood Marter Holmes b: 3/22/1896, Beverly, NJ d: 4/15/1954, Camden, NJ TR Deb: 6/27/1918

YEAR	TM-L	W	L	PCT	G	GS	CG	SH	SV	IP	H	R	ER	HR	HB	BB	SO	RAT	ERA	ERA+	CERA	OAV	BH	AVG	PR+	WS	TPW
1918	Phi-A	0	0	....	2	0	0	0	0	2	4	5	3	0	1	1	0	2.500	13.50	22	11.63	.400	0	....	-2	0	-0.3

• HOLMES, Darren Darren Lee Holmes b: 4/25/1966, Asheville, NC BR/TR, 6', 199 lbs. Deb: 9/1/1990

YEAR	TM-L	W	L	PCT	G	GS	CG	SH	SV	IP	H	R	ER	HR	HB	BB	SO	RAT	ERA	ERA+	CERA	OAV	BH	AVG	PR+	WS	TPW
1990	LA-N	0	1	.000	14	0	0	0	0	17^1	15	10	10	1	0	11	19	1.500	5.19	70	3.59	.238	0	....	-3	0	-0.3
1991	Mil-A	1	4	.200	40	0	0	0	3	76^1	90	43	40	6	1	27	59	1.533	4.72	84	4.71	.295	0	....	-6	2	-0.6
1992	Mil-A	4	4	.500	41	0	0	0	6	42^1	35	12	12	1	2	11	31	1.087	2.55	150	2.19	.224	0	....	5	6	0.5
1993	Col-N	3	3	.500	62	0	0	0	25	66^2	56	31	30	6	2	20	60	1.140	4.05	118	2.86	.222	0	....	8	12	0.7
1994	Col-N	0	3	.000	29	0	0	0	3	28^1	35	25	20	5	1	24	33	2.082	6.35	78	7.90	.313	0	.000	-3	0	-0.4
1995*	Col-N	6	1	.857	68	0	0	0	14	66^2	59	26	24	3	1	28	61	1.305	3.24	166	3.09	.237	0	.000	18	12	1.7
1996	Col-N	5	4	.556	62	0	0	0	1	77	78	41	34	8	1	28	73	1.377	3.97	132	4.01	.259	0	.000	12	7	1.2
1997	Col-N	9	2	.818	42	6	0	0	3	89^1	113	58	53	12	0	36	70	1.668	5.34	97	5.87	.314	3	.158	-1	5	0.0
1998	NY-A	0	3	.000	34	0	0	0	2	51^1	53	19	19	4	2	14	31	1.305	3.33	132	3.73	.270	0	....	5	4	0.5
1999*	Ari-N	4	3	.571	44	0	0	0	0	48^2	50	21	20	3	1	25	35	1.541	3.70	124	4.14	.262	0	.000	5	4	0.4
2000	Ari-N	0	0	....	4	0	0	0	1	2^1	5	3	3	0	0	1	2	2.571	11.57	41	10.38	.455	0	....	-2	0	-0.2
	StL-N	0	1	.000	5	0	0	0	0	8^1	12	9	9	2	1	3	5	1.800	9.72	47	8.54	.364	0	.000	-5	0	-0.5
	Bal-A	0	0	....	5	0	0	0	0	4^2	13	13	13	3	0	5	6	3.857	25.07	19	26.18	.481	0	....	-11	0	-1.0
	Ari-N	0	0	....	4	0	0	0	0	4	7	3	3	1	1	0	3	1.750	6.75	70	9.69	.389	0	....	-1	0	-0.1
	Yr.	0	1	.000	13	0	0	0	1	14^2	24	15	15	3	2	4	10	1.909	9.20	50	9.14	.387	0	.000	-7	0	-0.7
2002*	Atl-N	2	2	.500	55	0	0	0	1	54^2	41	12	11	3	2	12	47	.970	1.81	226	1.92	.210	0	.000	13	7	1.3
2003	Atl-N	1	2	.333	48	0	0	0	0	42	47	22	20	5	0	11	46	1.381	4.29	98	4.33	.280	0	....	-0	2	0.0
Total	**13**	**35**	**33**	**.515**	**557**	**6**	**0**	**0**	**59**	**680**	**709**	**348**	**321**	**63**	**15**	**256**	**581**	**1.419**	**4.25**	**109**	**4.27**	**.269**	**3**	**.107**	**34**	**61**	**3.4**

• HOLMES, Jim James Scott Holmes b: 8/2/1882, Lawrenceburg, KY d: 3/10/1960, Jacksonville, FL Deb: 9/8/1906

YEAR	TM-L	W	L	PCT	G	GS	CG	SH	SV	IP	H	R	ER	HR	HB	BB	SO	RAT	ERA	ERA+	CERA	OAV	BH	AVG	PR+	WS	TPW
1906	Phi-A	0	1	.000	3	1	0	0	0	9	10	11	4	0	1	8	1	2.000	4.00	68	5.98	.284	3	.600	-1	0	0.0
1908	Bro-N	1	4	.200	13	1	1	0	0	40	37	19	15	0	3	20	10	1.425	3.38	69	3.85	.270	1	.077	-5	0	-0.7
Total	**2**	**1**	**5**	**.167**	**16**	**2**	**1**	**0**	**0**	**49**	**47**	**30**	**19**	**0**	**4**	**28**	**11**	**1.531**	**3.49**	**69**	**4.24**	**.273**	**4**	**.222**	**-6**	**0**	**-0.7**

YEAR TM-L	W	L	PCT	G	GS	CG	SH	SV	IP	H	R	ER	HR	HB	BB	SO	RAT	ERA	ERA+	CERA	OAV	BH	AVG	PR+	WS	TPW
• HOLSHOUSER, Herm				Herman Alexander Holshouser b: 1/20/1907, Rockwell, NC d: 7/26/1994, Concord, NC BR/TR, 6', 170 lbs. Deb: 4/15/1930																						
1930 StL-A	0	1	.000	25	1	0	0	1	62^1	103	63	54	8	3	28	37	2.102	7.80	62	8.64	.376	2	.125	-21	0	-1.9
• HOLT, Chris				Christopher Michael Holt b: 9/18/1971, Dallas, TX BR/TR, 6'4", 205 lbs. Deb: 9/1/1996																						
1996 Hou-N	0	1	.000	4	0	0	0	0	4^2	5	3	3	0	0	3	0	1.714	5.79	67	4.14	.263	0	.000	-1	0	-0.1
1997 Hou-N	8	12	.400	33	32	0	0	0	209^2	211	98	82	17	8	61	95	1.297	3.52	114	3.71	.263	6	.090	9	10	0.5
1999* Hou-N	5	13	.278	32	26	0	0	1	164	193	92	85	12	8	57	115	1.524	4.66	95	4.96	.303	3	.067	-6	6	-0.8
2000 Hou-N	8	16	.333	34	32	3	1	0	207	247	131	123	22	8	75	136	1.556	5.35	91	5.31	.303	6	.100	-8	8	-0.9
2001 Det-A	7	9	.438	30	22	1	0	0	151^1	197	102	97	18	8	57	80	1.678	5.77	75	6.11	.319	1	.250	-22	3	-2.0
Total 5	**28**	**51**	**.354**	**133**	**112**	**4**	**1**	**1**	736^2	**853**	**426**	**390**	**69**	**32**	**253**	**426**	**1.501**	**4.76**	**93**	**4.93**	**.295**	**16**	**.090**	**-27**	**27**	**-3.3**
• HOLTGRAVE, Vern				Lavern George "Woody" Holtgrave b: 10/18/1942, Aviston, IL BR/TR, 6'1", 183 lbs. Deb: 9/26/1965																						
1965 Det-A	0	0	....	1	0	0	0	0	3	4	2	2	0	0	2	2	2.000	6.00	58	6.15	.308	0	....	-1	0	-0.1
• HOLTON, Brian				Brian John Holton b: 11/29/1959, McKeesport, PA BR/TR, 6'2", 193 lbs. Deb: 9/9/1985																						
1985 LA-N	1	1	.500	3	0	0	0	0	4	9	7	4	0	0	1	1	2.500	9.00	39	10.81	.450	0	....	-2	0	-0.3
1986 LA-N	2	3	.400	12	3	0	0	0	24^1	28	13	12	1	1	6	24	1.397	4.44	78	3.90	.292	0	.000	-2	1	-0.3
1987 LA-N	3	2	.600	53	1	0	0	2	83^1	87	39	36	11	0	32	58	1.428	3.89	102	4.29	.269	1	.200	1	5	0.1
1988* LA-N	7	3	.700	45	0	0	0	1	84^2	69	19	16	1	1	26	49	1.122	1.70	196	2.17	.228	0	.000	16	10	1.7
1989 Bal-A	5	7	.417	39	12	0	0	0	116^1	140	63	52	11	1	39	51	1.539	4.02	94	5.00	.300	0	....	-4	4	-0.4
1990 Bal-A	2	3	.400	33	0	0	0	0	58	68	31	29	7	0	21	27	1.534	4.50	84	4.89	.292	0	....	-5	2	-0.5
Total 6	**20**	**19**	**.513**	**185**	**16**	**0**	**0**	**3**	370^2	**401**	**172**	**149**	**31**	**3**	**125**	**210**	**1.419**	**3.62**	**103**	**4.17**	**.278**	**1**	**.050**	**4**	**22**	**0.4**
• HOLTZ, Mike				Michael James Holtz b: 10/10/1972, Arlington, VA BL/TL, 5'9", 172 lbs. Deb: 7/11/1996																						
1996 Cal-A	3	3	.500	30	0	0	0	0	29^1	21	11	8	1	3	19	31	1.364	2.45	200	3.29	.204	0	....	8	3	0.7
1997 Ana-A	3	4	.429	66	0	0	0	2	43^1	38	21	16	7	2	15	40	1.223	3.32	139	3.52	.228	0	.000	6	5	0.6
1998 Ana-A	2	2	.500	53	0	0	0	1	30^1	38	16	16	0	1	15	29	1.747	4.75	99	5.39	.322	0	....	0	2	0.0
1999 Ana-A	2	3	.400	28	0	0	0	0	22^1	26	20	20	3	2	15	17	1.836	8.06	60	6.85	.295	0	....	-8	0	-0.8
2000 Ana-A	3	3	.500	61	0	0	0	0	41	37	26	23	4	2	18	40	1.341	5.05	100	3.79	.248	0	....	-1	3	-0.1
2001 Ana-A	1	2	.333	63	0	0	0	0	37	40	24	20	5	2	15	38	1.486	4.86	94	4.77	.274	0	....	-1	2	-0.1
2002 Oak-A	0	0	....	16	0	0	0	0	14	24	11	10	3	1	9	7	2.357	6.43	68	10.72	.358	0	....	-3	0	-0.3
SD-N	2	2	.500	33	0	0	0	0	21	18	14	11	2	1	21	19	1.857	4.71	80	5.49	.237	0	.000	-2	1	-0.2
Total 7	**16**	**19**	**.457**	**350**	**0**	**0**	**0**	**3**	238^1	**242**	**143**	**124**	**25**	**14**	**127**	**221**	**1.548**	**4.68**	**99**	**4.88**	**.265**	**0**	**.000**	**-2**	**16**	**-0.2**
• HOLTZMAN, Ken				Kenneth Dale Holtzman b: 11/3/1945, St. Louis, MO BR/TL, 6'2", 175 lbs. Deb: 9/4/1965																						
1965 Chi-N	0	0	....	3	0	0	0	0	4	2	4	1	1	0	3	3	1.250	2.25	164	3.41	.143	0	....	1	0	0.1
1966 Chi-N	11	16	.407	34	33	9	0	0	220^2	194	104	93	27	4	68	171	1.187	3.79	97	3.24	.235	9	.123	0	10	-0.3
1967 Chi-N	9	0	1.000	12	12	3	0	0	92^2	76	31	26	11	2	44	62	1.295	2.53	140	3.48	.222	7	.200	9	8	1.1
1968 Chi-N	11	14	.440	34	32	6	3	1	215	201	89	80	17	6	76	151	1.288	3.35	94	3.46	.248	10	.125	-4	10	-0.7
1969 Chi-N	17	13	.567	39	39	12	6	0	261^1	248	117	104	18	5	93	176	1.305	3.58	112	3.42	.247	15	.150	13	17	1.3
1970 Chi-N	17	11	.607	39	38	15	1	0	287^2	271	125	108	30	3	94	202	1.269	3.38	133	3.51	.248	21	.200	35	23	3.7
1971 Chi-N	9	15	.375	30	29	9	3	0	195	213	108	97	18	2	64	143	1.421	4.48	88	4.22	.276	9	.130	-8	7	-1.0
1972* Oak-A★	19	11	.633	39	37	16	4	0	265^1	232	83	74	23	4	52	134	1.070	2.51	113	2.61	.236	16	.178	7	16	0.9
1973* Oak-A★	21	13	.618	40	40	16	4	0	297^1	275	109	98	22	4	66	157	1.147	2.97	119	2.87	.243	0	....	11	19	1.2
1974* Oak-A	19	17	.528	39	38	9	3	0	255^1	273	111	87	14	3	51	117	1.269	3.07	108	3.39	.272	0	....	3	15	0.3
1975* Oak-A	18	14	.563	39	38	13	2	0	266^1	217	111	93	16	7	108	122	1.220	3.14	115	2.93	.222	0	.000	13	15	1.4
1976 Bal-A	5	4	.556	13	13	6	1	0	97^2	100	34	31	4	1	35	25	1.382	2.86	114	3.69	.271	0	....	3	7	0.4
NY-A	9	7	.563	21	21	10	2	0	149	165	74	69	14	0	35	41	1.342	4.17	82	4.03	.283	0	....	-17	5	-1.9
Yr.	14	11	.560	34	34	16	3	0	246^2	265	108	100	18	1	70	66	1.358	3.65	92	3.90	.278	0	....	-14	12	-1.5
1977 NY-A	2	3	.400	18	11	0	0	0	71^2	105	55	46	7	1	24	14	1.800	5.78	68	6.88	.362	0	....	-16	0	-1.6
1978 NY-A	1	0	1.000	5	3	0	0	0	17^2	21	8	8	2	0	9	3	1.698	4.08	89	5.98	.313	0	....	-1	1	-0.1
Chi-N	0	3	.000	23	6	0	0	2	53	61	40	36	10	1	35	36	1.811	6.11	66	6.76	.286	2	.200	-12	0	-1.2
1979 Chi-N	6	9	.400	23	20	3	2	0	117^2	133	70	60	15	6	53	44	1.581	4.59	90	5.39	.287	10	.233	-4	4	-0.2
Total 15	**174**	**150**	**.537**	**451**	**410**	**127**	**31**	**3**	2867^1	**2787**	**1273**	**1111**	**249**	**49**	**910**	**1601**	**1.289**	**3.49**	**104**	**3.58**	**.255**	**99**	**.163**	**33**	**157**	**3.4**
• HOLZEMER, Mark				Mark Harold Holzemer b: 8/20/1969, Littleton, CO BL/TL, 6', 165 lbs. Deb: 8/21/1993																						
1993 Cal-A	0	3	.000	5	4	0	0	0	23^1	34	24	23	2	3	13	10	2.014	8.87	51	7.98	.340	0	....	-12	0	-1.1
1995 Cal-A	0	1	.000	12	0	0	0	0	8^1	11	6	5	1	1	7	5	2.160	5.40	87	7.94	.306	0	....	-1	0	-0.1
1996 Cal-A	1	0	1.000	25	0	0	0	0	24^2	35	28	24	7	3	8	20	1.743	8.76	56	8.16	.327	0	....	-11	0	-1.0
1997 Sea-A	0	0	....	14	0	0	0	1	9	9	6	6	0	0	8	7	1.889	6.00	75	5.05	.250	0	....	-1	0	-0.1
1998 Oak-A	1	0	1.000	13	0	0	0	0	9^2	13	6	6	1	1	3	3	1.655	5.59	82	6.35	.333	0	....	-1	0	-0.1
2000 Phi-N	0	1	.000	25	0	0	0	0	25^2	36	23	22	4	1	8	19	1.714	7.71	60	6.54	.336	0	.000	-9	0	-0.8
Total 6	**2**	**5**	**.286**	**94**	**4**	**0**	**0**	**1**	100^2	**138**	**93**	**86**	**15**	**9**	**47**	**64**	**1.838**	**7.69**	**61**	**7.24**	**.325**	**0**	**.000**	**-34**	**0**	**-3.2**
• HONEYCUTT, Rick				Frederick Wayne Honeycutt b: 6/29/1954, Chattanooga, TN BL/TL, 6'1", 190 lbs. Deb: 8/24/1977																						
1977 Sea-A	0	1	.000	10	3	0	0	0	29	26	16	14	7	3	11	17	1.276	4.34	95	4.69	.239	0	....	-1	1	-0.1
1978 Sea-A	5	11	.313	26	24	4	1	0	134^1	150	81	73	12	3	49	50	1.481	4.89	78	4.52	.285	0	....	-15	4	-1.6
1979 Sea-A	11	12	.478	33	28	8	1	0	194	201	103	87	22	6	67	83	1.381	4.04	108	4.22	.268	0	....	8	11	0.7
1980 Sea-A★	10	17	.370	30	30	9	1	0	203^1	221	99	89	22	3	60	79	1.382	3.94	105	4.23	.280	0	....	6	12	0.6
1981 Tex-A	11	6	.647	20	20	8	2	0	127^2	120	49	47	12	0	17	40	1.073	3.31	105	2.71	.246	0	....	-0	8	0.0
1982 Tex-A	5	17	.227	30	26	4	1	0	164	201	103	96	20	3	54	64	1.555	5.27	74	5.33	.305	0	....	-24	2	-2.4
1983 Tex-A★	14	8	.636	25	25	5	2	0	174^2	168	59	47	9	6	37	56	1.174	**2.42**	**165**	3.09	.262	0	....	31	16	3.1
*LA-N	2	3	.400	9	7	1	0	0	39	46	26	25	6	2	13	18	1.513	5.77	62	5.35	.297	1	.083	-9	0	-1.0
1984 LA-N	10	9	.526	29	28	6	2	0	183^2	180	72	58	11	2	51	75	1.258	2.84	124	3.21	.258	8	.143	16	13	1.6
1985* LA-N	8	12	.400	31	25	1	0	1	142	141	71	54	9	1	49	67	1.338	3.42	101	3.55	.261	5	.132	0	5	0.1
1986 LA-N	11	9	.550	32	28	0	0	0	171	164	71	63	9	3	45	100	1.222	3.32	104	3.04	.249	3	.070	6	11	0.7
1987 LA-N	2	12	.143	27	20	1	1	0	115^2	133	74	59	10	2	45	92	1.539	4.59	86	4.70	.278	7	.233	-7	1	-0.5
Oak-A	1	4	.200	7	4	0	0	0	23^2	25	17	14	3	2	9	10	1.437	5.32	78	4.79	.275	0	....	-3	0	-0.3
1988* Oak-A	3	2	.600	55	0	0	0	7	79^2	74	36	31	6	3	25	47	1.243	3.50	108	3.35	.253	0	....	1	6	0.1
1989* Oak-A	2	2	.500	64	0	0	0	12	76^2	56	26	20	5	1	26	52	1.070	2.35	157	2.26	.207	0	....	10	10	1.0
1990* Oak-A	2	2	.500	63	0	0	0	7	63^1	46	23	19	2	1	22	38	1.074	2.70	137	2.05	.204	0	.000	6	8	0.6
1991 Oak-A	2	4	.333	43	0	0	0	0	37^2	37	16	15	3	2	20	26	1.513	3.58	107	4.45	.261	0	....	1	2	0.1
1992* Oak-A	1	4	.200	54	0	0	0	3	39	41	19	16	2	3	10	32	1.308	3.69	101	3.59	.272	0	....	-0	3	0.0
1993 Oak-A	1	4	.200	52	0	0	0	1	41^2	30	18	13	2	1	20	21	1.200	2.81	145	2.40	.211	0	....	6	4	0.6
1994 Tex-A	1	2	.333	42	0	0	0	1	25	37	21	20	4	2	9	18	1.840	7.20	67	7.47	.349	0	....	-6	0	-0.6
1995 Oak-A	5	1	.833	49	0	0	0	2	44^2	37	13	12	5	1	9	21	1.030	2.42	184	2.66	.231	0	....	10	6	1.0
NY-A	0	0	....	3	0	0	0	0	1	2	3	3	1	0	1	0	3.000	27.00	17	23.01	.400	0	....	-2	0	-0.2
Yr.	5	1	.833	52	0	0	0	2	45^2	39	16	15	6	1	10	21	1.073	2.96	151	3.10	.236	0	....	8	6	0.7
1996* StL-N	2	1	.667	61	0	0	0	4	47^1	42	15	15	3	0	7	30	1.035	2.85	147	2.21	.240	0	.000	6	7	0.6
1997 StL-N	0	0	....	2	0	0	0	0	2	5	3	3	0	0	1	2	3.000	13.50	31	14.52	.500	0	....	-2	0	-0.2
Total 21	**109**	**143**	**.433**	**797**	**268**	**47**	**11**	**38**	**2160**	**2183**	**1034**	**893**	**185**	**50**	**657**	**1038**	**1.315**	**3.72**	**104**	**3.75**	**.264**	**24**	**.132**	**38**	**130**	**4.0**
• HOOD, Don				Donald Harris Hood b: 10/16/1949, Florence, SC BL/TL, 6'2", 180 lbs. Deb: 7/16/1973																						
1973 Bal-A	3	2	.600	8	4	1	1	1	32^1	31	17	14	1	1	6	18	1.144	3.90	96	2.72	.256	0	....	-2	2	-0.2
1974 Bal-A	1	1	.500	20	2	0	0	1	57^1	47	26	22	1	0	20	26	1.169	3.45	100	2.39	.223	0	....	-1	3	-0.1
1975 Cle-A	6	10	.375	29	19	2	0	0	135^1	136	76	66	16	0	57	51	1.426	4.39	86	4.37	.268	0	....	-10	4	-1.0
1976 Cle-A	3	5	.375	33	6	0	0	1	77^2	89	46	42	5	4	41	32	1.674	4.87	72	5.44	.296	0	....	-12	1	-1.3
1977 Cle-A	2	1	.667	41	5	1	0	0	105	87	42	35	3	4	49	62	1.295	3.00	131	2.93	.224	0	....	11	8	1.1
1978 Cle-A	5	6	.455	36	19	1	0	0	154^2	166	82	77	13	1	77	73	1.571	4.48	83	4.76	.278	0	....	-12	5	-1.2

YEAR	TM-L	W	L	PCT	G	GS	CG	SH	SV	IP	H	R	ER	HR	HB	BB	SO	RAT	ERA	ERA+	CERA	OAV	BH	AVG	PR+	WS	TPW
1979	Cle-A	1	0	1.000	13	0	0	0	1	22	13	9	9	1	1	14	7	1.227	3.68	116	2.53	.169	0	....	2	2	0.2
	NY-A	3	1	.750	27	6	0	0	1	67^1	62	24	23	3	2	30	22	1.366	3.07	132	3.54	.252	0	....	6	6	0.6
	Yr.	4	1	.800	40	6	0	0	2	89^1	75	33	32	4	3	44	29	1.332	3.22	128	3.29	.232	0	....	8	8	0.8
1980	StL-N	4	6	.400	33	8	1	0	0	82^1	90	39	31	2	2	34	35	1.506	3.39	109	4.15	.288	4	.200	2	4	0.2
1982	KC-A	4	0	1.000	30	3	0	0	1	66^2	71	31	26	7	2	22	31	1.395	3.51	116	4.31	.276	0	....	4	4	0.4
1983	KC-A	2	3	.400	27	0	0	0	0	47^2	48	20	12	5	2	14	17	1.301	2.27	180	3.91	.273	0	....	10	4	1.0
Total	10	34	35	.493	297	72	6	1	6	848^1	840	412	357	57	19	364	374	1.419	3.79	100	4.00	.263	4	.200	-1	43	-0.3

• HOOD, Wally Wallace James Hood, Jr. b: 9/24/1925, Los Angeles, CA d: 6/16/2001, Glendale, CA BR/TR, 6'1", 190 lbs. Deb: 9/23/1949

YEAR	TM-L	W	L	PCT	G	GS	CG	SH	SV	IP	H	R	ER	HR	HB	BB	SO	RAT	ERA	ERA+	CERA	OAV	BH	AVG	PR+	WS	TPW
1949	NY-A	0	0	....	2	0	0	0	0	2^1	0	0	0	0	0	1	2	.429	0.00	....	0.18	.000	0	....	1	0	0.1

• HOOK, Chris Christopher Wayne Hook b: 8/4/1968, San Diego, CA BR/TR, 6'5", 230 lbs. Deb: 4/30/1995

YEAR	TM-L	W	L	PCT	G	GS	CG	SH	SV	IP	H	R	ER	HR	HB	BB	SO	RAT	ERA	ERA+	CERA	OAV	BH	AVG	PR+	WS	TPW
1995	SF-N	5	1	.833	45	0	0	0	0	52^1	55	33	32	7	3	29	40	1.605	5.50	74	5.37	.274	0	.000	-9	2	-0.9
1996	SF-N	0	1	.000	10	0	0	0	0	13^1	16	13	11	3	2	14	4	2.250	7.43	55	9.49	.308	1	.500	-5	0	-0.5
Total	2	5	2	.714	55	0	0	0	0	65^2	71	46	43	10	5	43	44	1.736	5.89	69	6.21	.281	1	.200	-14	2	-1.3

• HOOK, Jay James Wesley Hook b: 11/18/1936, Waukegan, IL BL/TR, 6'2", 182 lbs. Deb: 9/3/1957

YEAR	TM-L	W	L	PCT	G	GS	CG	SH	SV	IP	H	R	ER	HR	HB	BB	SO	RAT	ERA	ERA+	CERA	OAV	BH	AVG	PR+	WS	TPW
1957	Cin-N	0	1	.000	3	2	0	0	0	10	6	7	5	0	0	8	6	1.400	4.50	91	2.57	.176	0	.000	-0	0	-0.1
1958	Cin-N	0	1	.000	1	1	0	0	0	3	3	4	4	2	0	2	5	1.667	12.00	35	9.47	.250	0	.000	-3	0	-0.3
1959	Cin-N	5	5	.500	17	15	4	0	0	79	79	46	45	10	3	39	37	1.494	5.13	79	4.92	.266	3	.125	-10	2	-1.0
1960	Cin-N	11	18	.379	36	33	10	2	0	222	222	119	111	31	5	73	103	1.329	4.50	85	4.15	.263	6	.083	-17	7	-2.1
1961	Cin-N	1	3	.250	22	5	0	0	0	62^2	83	55	54	14	5	22	36	1.676	7.76	52	7.09	.322	2	.133	-26	0	-2.6
1962	NY-N	8	19	.296	37	34	13	0	0	213^2	230	137	115	31	8	71	113	1.409	4.84	86	4.64	.273	14	.203	-12	7	-0.9
1963	NY-N	4	14	.222	41	20	3	0	1	152^2	168	104	93	21	9	53	89	1.448	5.48	64	4.94	.281	9	.237	-32	0	-3.2
1964	NY-N	0	1	.000	3	2	0	0	0	9^2	17	10	10	2	0	7	5	2.483	9.31	38	11.62	.395	0	.000	-6	0	-0.7
Total	8	29	62	.319	160	112	30	2	1	752^2	808	482	437	111	30	275	394	1.439	5.23	74	4.87	.276	34	.151	-105	16	-10.9

• HOOKER, Buck William Edward Hooker b: 8/28/1880, Richmond, VA d: 7/2/1929, Richmond, VA TR, 5'6" Deb: 9/5/1902

YEAR	TM-L	W	L	PCT	G	GS	CG	SH	SV	IP	H	R	ER	HR	HB	BB	SO	RAT	ERA	ERA+	CERA	OAV	BH	AVG	PR+	WS	TPW
1902	Cin-N	0	1	.000	1	1	1	0	0	8	11	5	4	1	0	0	0	1.375	4.50	66	6.19	.326	0	.000	-1	0	-0.2
1903	Cin-N	0	0	....	1	0	0	0	0	2^1	2	0	0	0	0	2	0	1.714	0.00	....	4.35	.250	0	.000	1	0	0.1
Total	2	0	1	.000	2	1	1	0	0	10^1	13	5	4	1	0	2	0	1.452	3.48	86	5.78	.312	0	.000	-1	0	-0.1

• HOOPER, Bob Robert Nelson Hooper b: 5/30/1922, Leamington, Canada d: 3/17/1980, Brunswick, NJ BR/TR, 5'11", 195 lbs. Deb: 4/19/1950

YEAR	TM-L	W	L	PCT	G	GS	CG	SH	SV	IP	H	R	ER	HR	HB	BB	SO	RAT	ERA	ERA+	CERA	OAV	BH	AVG	PR+	WS	TPW
1950	Phi-A	15	10	.600	45	20	3	0	5	170^1	181	108	95	15	1	91	58	1.597	5.02	91	4.78	.272	7	.125	-8	9	-1.0
1951	Phi-A	12	10	.545	38	23	9	0	5	189	192	98	92	13	3	61	64	1.339	4.38	98	3.71	.267	15	.208	-5	11	-0.6
1952	Phi-A	8	15	.348	43	14	4	0	6	144^1	158	100	83	13	4	68	40	1.566	5.18	76	4.80	.279	8	.195	-17	3	-1.6
1953	Cle-A	5	4	.556	43	0	0	0	7	69^1	50	37	31	4	2	38	16	1.269	4.02	93	2.87	.206	1	.083	-2	5	-0.3
1954	Cle-A	0	0	....	17	0	0	0	2	34^2	39	22	19	3	1	16	12	1.587	4.93	74	4.97	.289	0	.000	-5	0	-0.6
1955	Cin-N	0	2	.000	8	0	0	0	0	13	20	12	11	2	0	6	6	2.000	7.62	56	7.91	.357	0	.000	-5	0	-0.5
Total	6	40	41	.494	194	57	16	0	25	620^2	640	377	331	50	11	280	196	1.482	4.80	87	4.32	.268	31	.166	-43	28	-4.6

• HOOTEN, Leon Michael Leon Hooten b: 4/4/1948, Downey, CA BR/TR, 5'11", 180 lbs. Deb: 4/13/1974

YEAR	TM-L	W	L	PCT	G	GS	CG	SH	SV	IP	H	R	ER	HR	HB	BB	SO	RAT	ERA	ERA+	CERA	OAV	BH	AVG	PR+	WS	TPW
1974	Oak-A	0	0	....	6	0	0	0	0	8^1	6	3	3	1	1	4	1	1.200	3.24	102	3.49	.207	0	....	-0	0	0.0

• HOOTON, Burt Burt Carlton Hooton b: 2/7/1950, Greenville, TX BR/TR, 6'1", 210 lbs. Deb: 6/17/1971 C

YEAR	TM-L	W	L	PCT	G	GS	CG	SH	SV	IP	H	R	ER	HR	HB	BB	SO	RAT	ERA	ERA+	CERA	OAV	BH	AVG	PR+	WS	TPW
1971	Chi-N	2	0	1.000	3	3	2	1	0	21^1	8	5	5	2	0	10	22	.844	2.11	186	1.35	.111	0	.000	5	3	0.5
1972	Chi-N	11	14	.440	33	31	9	3	0	218^1	201	78	68	13	1	81	132	1.292	2.80	136	3.24	.246	9	.125	24	16	2.6
1973	Chi-N	14	17	.452	42	34	9	2	0	239^2	248	107	98	12	4	73	134	1.339	3.68	107	3.60	.270	9	.129	12	16	1.3
1974	Chi-N	7	11	.389	48	21	3	1	1	176^1	214	112	94	16	3	51	94	**1.503**	4.80	79	4.71	.299	3	.060	-11	4	-1.5
1975	Chi-N	0	2	.000	3	3	0	0	0	11	18	12	10	2	0	4	5	2.000	8.18	47	8.52	.383	0	.000	-5	0	-0.6
	LA-N	18	7	.720	31	30	12	4	0	223^2	172	76	70	16	0	64	148	1.055	2.82	121	2.26	.210	9	.129	12	17	1.3
	Yr.	18	9	.667	34	33	12	4	0	234^2	190	88	80	18	0	68	153	1.099	3.07	112	2.55	.219	9	.123	7	17	0.8
1976	LA-N	11	15	.423	33	33	8	4	0	226^2	203	93	82	16	1	60	116	1.160	3.26	104	2.80	.241	6	.097	-1	12	-0.3
1977*	LA-N	12	7	.632	32	31	6	2	1	223^1	184	74	65	14	3	60	153	1.093	2.62	146	2.46	.225	11	.164	28	19	2.8
1978*	LA-N	19	10	.655	32	32	10	3	0	236	196	74	71	17	0	61	104	1.089	2.71	129	2.48	.226	10	.149	19	19	2.2
1979	LA-N	11	10	.524	29	29	12	1	0	212	191	85	70	11	2	63	129	1.198	2.97	122	2.85	.244	11	.147	18	14	1.8
1980	LA-N	14	8	.636	34	33	4	2	1	206^2	194	90	84	22	0	64	118	1.248	3.66	96	3.44	.249	4	.063	-6	10	-1.0
1981*	LA-N★	11	6	.647	23	23	5	4	0	142^1	124	42	36	3	2	33	74	1.103	2.28	146	2.33	.237	8	.190	17	13	2.1
1982	LA-N	4	7	.364	21	21	2	2	0	120^2	130	57	54	5	2	33	51	1.351	4.03	86	3.65	.275	3	.086	-6	4	-0.8
1983	LA-N	9	8	.529	33	27	2	0	0	160	156	86	75	21	2	59	87	1.344	4.22	85	4.03	.254	8	.160	-8	5	-0.7
1984	LA-N	3	6	.333	54	6	0	0	4	110	109	43	42	5	0	43	62	1.382	3.44	103	3.59	.263	1	.071	2	7	0.1
1985	Tex-A	5	8	.385	29	20	2	0	0	124	149	78	72	18	0	40	62	1.524	5.23	81	5.26	.297	0	....	-12	5	-1.1
Total	15	151	136	.526	480	377	86	29	7	2652	2497	1112	996	193	20	799	1491	1.243	3.38	108	3.24	.250	92	.123	89	164	8.5

• HOOVER, Dick Richard Lloyd Hoover b: 12/11/1925, Columbus, OH d: 4/12/1981, Lake Placid, FL BL/TL, 6', 170 lbs. Deb: 4/16/1952

YEAR	TM-L	W	L	PCT	G	GS	CG	SH	SV	IP	H	R	ER	HR	HB	BB	SO	RAT	ERA	ERA+	CERA	OAV	BH	AVG	PR+	WS	TPW
1952	Bos-N	0	0	....	2	0	0	0	0	4^2	8	4	4	1	0	3	0	2.357	7.71	47	9.89	.348	0	....	-2	0	-0.2

• HOOVER, John John Nicklaus Hoover b: 12/22/1962, Fresno, CA BR/TR, 6'2", 190 lbs. Deb: 5/23/1990

YEAR	TM-L	W	L	PCT	G	GS	CG	SH	SV	IP	H	R	ER	HR	HB	BB	SO	RAT	ERA	ERA+	CERA	OAV	BH	AVG	PR+	WS	TPW
1990	Tex-A	0	0	....	2	0	0	0	0	4^2	8	6	6	0	0	3	0	2.357	11.57	34	8.10	.364	0	....	-4	0	-0.4

• HOPE, John John Alan Hope b: 12/21/1970, Fort Lauderdale, FL BR/TR, 6'3", 195 lbs. Deb: 8/29/1993

YEAR	TM-L	W	L	PCT	G	GS	CG	SH	SV	IP	H	R	ER	HR	HB	BB	SO	RAT	ERA	ERA+	CERA	OAV	BH	AVG	PR+	WS	TPW
1993	Pit-N	0	2	.000	7	7	0	0	0	38	47	19	17	2	2	8	8	1.447	4.03	101	4.43	.313	1	.077	-0	2	-0.1
1994	Pit-N	0	0	....	9	0	0	0	0	14	18	12	9	1	2	4	6	1.571	5.79	75	5.69	.310	1	.333	-2	0	-0.2
1995	Pit-N	0	0	....	3	0	0	0	0	2^1	8	8	8	0	3	4	2	5.143	30.86	14	34.86	.615	0	....	-7	0	-0.7
1996	Pit-N	1	3	.250	5	4	0	0	0	19^1	17	18	15	5	2	11	13	1.448	6.98	63	5.60	.243	1	.200	-5	0	-0.5
Total	4	1	5	.167	24	11	0	0	0	73^2	90	57	49	8	9	27	29	1.588	5.99	71	5.94	.309	3	.143	-15	2	-1.5

• HOPE, Sam Samuel Hope b: 12/4/1878, Brooklyn, NY d: 6/30/1946, Greenport, NY BR/TR, 5'10" Deb: 8/5/1907

YEAR	TM-L	W	L	PCT	G	GS	CG	SH	SV	IP	H	R	ER	HR	HB	BB	SO	RAT	ERA	ERA+	CERA	OAV	BH	AVG	PR+	WS	TPW
1907	Phi-A	0	0	....	1	0	0	0	0	0^1	3	1	0	0	0	0	0	9.000	0.00	....	67.29	.763	0	....	0	0	0.0

• HOPKINS, Paul Paul Henry Hopkins b: 9/25/1904, Chester, PA BR/TR, 6', 175 lbs. Deb: 9/29/1927

YEAR	TM-L	W	L	PCT	G	GS	CG	SH	SV	IP	H	R	ER	HR	HB	BB	SO	RAT	ERA	ERA+	CERA	OAV	BH	AVG	PR+	WS	TPW
1927	Was-A	1	0	1.000	2	1	0	0	0	9	13	6	5	1	0	4	5	1.889	5.00	81	7.08	.361	2	.667	-1	1	0.0
1929	Was-A	0	1	.000	7	0	0	0	0	16^1	15	5	4	1	0	9	5	1.469	2.20	192	3.87	.250	0	.000	3	1	0.3
	StL-A	0	0	....	2	0	0	0	0	2	0	0	0	0	0	2	1	1.000	0.00	....	0.92	.231	0	....	1	0	0.1
	Yr.	0	1	.000	9	0	0	0	0	18^1	15	5	4	1	0	11	6	1.418	1.96	216	3.55	.250	0	.000	4	1	0.4
Total	2	1	1	.500	11	1	0	0	0	27^1	28	11	9	2	0	15	11	1.573	2.96	140	4.71	.292	2	.333	3	2	0.4

• HOPPER, Bill William Booth "Bird Dog" Hopper b: 10/26/1890, Jackson, TN d: 1/14/1965, Allen Park, MI BR/TR, 6', 175 lbs. Deb: 9/11/1913

YEAR	TM-L	W	L	PCT	G	GS	CG	SH	SV	IP	H	R	ER	HR	HB	BB	SO	RAT	ERA	ERA+	CERA	OAV	BH	AVG	PR+	WS	TPW
1913	StL-N	0	3	.000	3	3	2	0	0	24	20	14	10	2	3	8	3	1.167	3.75	86	3.14	.230	3	.375	-1	1	0.0
1914	StL-N	0	0	....	3	0	0	0	0	5	6	3	2	0	0	5	1	2.200	3.60	78	6.35	.286	0	....	-0	0	-0.1
1915	Was-A	0	1	.000	13	0	0	0	1	31^1	39	23	16	0	1	16	8	1.755	4.60	65	5.88	.348	1	.200	-6	0	-0.6
Total	3	0	4	.000	19	3	2	0	1	60^1	65	40	28	2	4	29	12	1.558	4.18	73	4.83	.295	4	.308	-8	1	-0.7

• HOPPER, Jim James McDaniel Hopper b: 9/1/1919, Charlotte, NC d: 1/23/1982, Charlotte, NC BR/TR, 6'1", 175 lbs. Deb: 4/21/1946

YEAR	TM-L	W	L	PCT	G	GS	CG	SH	SV	IP	H	R	ER	HR	HB	BB	SO	RAT	ERA	ERA+	CERA	OAV	BH	AVG	PR+	WS	TPW
1946	Pit-N	0	1	.000	2	1	0	0	0	4	6	5	5	1	0	3	1	2.250	11.25	31	9.17	.316	0	....	-3	0	-0.4

• HOPPER, Lefty Clarence F. Hopper b: 5/27/1875, Jersey City, NJ d: 9/27/1959, San Diego, CA TL Deb: 10/10/1898

YEAR	TM-L	W	L	PCT	G	GS	CG	SH	SV	IP	H	R	ER	HR	HB	BB	SO	RAT	ERA	ERA+	CERA	OAV	BH	AVG	PR+	WS	TPW
1898	Bro-N	0	2	.000	2	2	2	0	0	11	14	11	6	0	0	5	5	1.727	4.91	73	4.63	.308	0	.000	-1	0	-0.2

• HORAN, John Patrick J. Horan, 5'10.5", 160 lbs. Deb: 5/17/1884

YEAR	TM-L	W	L	PCT	G	GS	CG	SH	SV	IP	H	R	ER	HR	HB	BB	SO	RAT	ERA	ERA+	CERA	OAV	BH	AVG	PR+	WS	TPW
1884	CP-U	3	6	.333	13	10	9	0	0	98	94	73	38	0	....	24	55	1.204	3.49	83	....	.236	6	.088	-6	3	-1.3

• HORLEN, Joe Joel Edward Horlen b: 8/14/1937, San Antonio, TX BR/TR, 6', 175 lbs. Deb: 9/4/1961

YEAR	TM-L	W	L	PCT	G	GS	CG	SH	SV	IP	H	R	ER	HR	HB	BB	SO	RAT	ERA	ERA+	CERA	OAV	BH	AVG	PR+	WS	TPW
1961	Chi-A	1	3	.250	5	4	0	0	0	17^2	25	15	13	2	0	13	11	2.151	6.62	59	8.26	.338	0	.000	-5	0	-0.6
1962	Chi-A	7	6	.538	20	19	5	1	0	108^2	108	62	59	10	2	43	63	1.390	4.89	80	4.06	.262	2	.053	-11	3	-1.4
1963	Chi-A	11	7	.611	33	21	3	0	0	124	122	50	45	10	2	55	61	1.427	3.27	107	4.03	.261	9	.225	2	8	0.3
1964	Chi-A	13	9	.591	32	28	9	2	0	210^2	142	54	44	11	4	55	138	.935	1.88	184	**1.72**	**.190**	11	.159	31	19	3.2
1965	Chi-A	13	13	.500	34	34	7	4	0	219	203	88	70	16	3	39	125	1.105	2.88	111	2.66	.245	9	.132	5	11	0.5
1966	Chi-A	10	13	.435	37	29	4	2	1	211	185	64	57	14	6	53	124	1.128	2.43	130	2.66	.233	4	.067	16	15	1.4
1967	Chi-A★	19	7	.731	35	35	13	**6**	0	258	188	66	59	13	4	58	103	.953	**2.06**	**151**	**1.84**	.203	14	.169	**29**	**23**	3.2
1968	Chi-A	12	14	.462	35	35	4	1	0	223^2	197	75	59	16	14	70	102	1.194	2.37	127	3.12	.238	7	.104	17	13	1.8
1969	Chi-A	13	16	.448	36	35	7	2	0	235^2	237	105	99	20	5	77	121	1.332	3.78	102	3.75	.261	14	.182	6	15	0.6
1970	Chi-A	6	16	.273	28	26	4	0	0	172^1	198	99	93	18	4	41	77	1.387	4.86	80	4.37	.287	6	.115	-15	4	-1.8
1971	Chi-A	8	9	.471	34	18	3	0	2	137^1	150	72	65	12	5	30	82	1.311	4.26	84	3.98	.284	4	.100	-8	5	-1.1
1972*	Oak-A	3	4	.429	32	6	0	0	1	84	74	33	28	3	4	20	58	1.119	3.00	95	2.57	.236	3	.176	-2	3	-0.3
Total	**12**	**116**	**117**	**.498**	**361**	**290**	**59**	**18**	**4**	**2002**	**1829**	**783**	**691**	**145**	**53**	**554**	**1065**	**1.190**	**3.11**	**111**	**3.08**	**.243**	**83**	**.134**	**65**	**119**	**5.9**

• HORNE, Trader Berlyn Dale "Sonny" Horne b: 4/12/1899, Bachman, OH d: 2/3/1983, Franklin, OH BB/TR, 5'9", 155 lbs. Deb: 4/24/1929

YEAR	TM-L	W	L	PCT	G	GS	CG	SH	SV	IP	H	R	ER	HR	HB	BB	SO	RAT	ERA	ERA+	CERA	OAV	BH	AVG	PR+	WS	TPW
1929	Chi-N	1	1	.500	11	1	0	0	0	23	24	20	13	3	0	21	6	1.957	5.09	91	6.44	.273	2	.400	-2	1	-0.1

• HORNER, Jack William Frank Horner b: 9/21/1863, Baltimore, MD d: 7/14/1910, New Orleans, LA BR Deb: 5/7/1894

YEAR	TM-L	W	L	PCT	G	GS	CG	SH	SV	IP	H	R	ER	HR	HB	BB	SO	RAT	ERA	ERA+	CERA	OAV	BH	AVG	PR+	WS	TPW
1894	Bal-N	0	1	.000	2	1	1	0	1	11	15	12	11	0	0	7	2	2.000	9.00	61	6.18	.322	1	.167	-5	0	-0.4

• HORSEY, Hanson Hanson Horsey b: 11/26/1889, Galena, MD d: 12/1/1949, Millington, MD BR/TR, 5'11", 165 lbs. Deb: 4/27/1912

YEAR	TM-L	W	L	PCT	G	GS	CG	SH	SV	IP	H	R	ER	HR	HB	BB	SO	RAT	ERA	ERA+	CERA	OAV	BH	AVG	PR+	WS	TPW
1912	Cin-N	0	0	....	1	0	0	0	0	4	14	10	10	0	0	3	0	4.250	22.50	15	23.61	.609	0	.000	-8	0	-0.9

• HORSMAN, Vince Vincent Stanley Joseph Horsman b: 3/9/1967, Halifax, Canada BR/TL, 6'2", 180 lbs. Deb: 9/5/1991

YEAR	TM-L	W	L	PCT	G	GS	CG	SH	SV	IP	H	R	ER	HR	HB	BB	SO	RAT	ERA	ERA+	CERA	OAV	BH	AVG	PR+	WS	TPW
1991	Tor-A	0	0	....	4	0	0	0	0	4	2	0	0	0	0	3	2	1.250	0.00	....	1.80	.167	0	....	2	1	0.2
1992	Oak-A	2	1	.667	58	0	0	0	1	43^1	39	13	12	3	0	21	18	1.385	2.49	150	3.62	.252	0	....	6	4	0.6
1993	Oak-A	2	0	1.000	40	0	0	0	0	25	25	15	15	2	3	15	17	1.600	5.40	75	5.09	.255	0	....	-4	1	-0.3
1994	Oak-A	0	1	.000	33	0	0	0	0	29^1	29	17	16	2	1	11	20	1.364	4.91	90	3.69	.266	0	....	-2	1	-0.2
1995	Min-A	0	0	....	6	0	0	0	0	9	12	8	7	2	0	4	4	1.778	7.00	68	6.87	.333	0	....	-2	0	-0.2
Total	**5**	**4**	**2**	**.667**	**141**	**0**	**0**	**0**	**1**	**110^2**	**107**	**53**	**50**	**9**	**4**	**54**	**61**	**1.455**	**4.07**	**103**	**4.17**	**.261**	**0**	**....**	**-0**	**7**	**0.0**

• HORSTMANN, Oscar Oscar Theodore Horstmann b: 6/2/1891, Alma, MO d: 5/11/1977, Salina, KS BR/TR, 5'11", 165 lbs. Deb: 4/18/1917

YEAR	TM-L	W	L	PCT	G	GS	CG	SH	SV	IP	H	R	ER	HR	HB	BB	SO	RAT	ERA	ERA+	CERA	OAV	BH	AVG	PR+	WS	TPW
1917	StL-N	9	4	.692	35	11	4	1	1	138^2	111	67	53	5	4	54	50	1.190	3.44	78	2.61	.225	9	.196	-13	6	-1.4
1918	StL-N	0	2	.000	9	2	0	0	0	23	29	18	14	0	0	14	6	1.870	5.48	49	5.88	.349	0	.000	-7	0	-0.8
1919	StL-N	0	1	.000	6	2	0	0	0	15	14	6	5	0	0	12	5	1.733	3.00	93	4.41	.264	1	.500	-1	1	0.0
Total	**3**	**9**	**7**	**.563**	**50**	**15**	**4**	**1**	**1**	**176^2**	**154**	**91**	**72**	**5**	**4**	**80**	**61**	**1.325**	**3.67**	**74**	**3.19**	**.245**	**10**	**.192**	**-21**	**7**	**-2.3**

• HORTON, Elmer Elmer E. "Herky Jerky" Horton b: 9/4/1869, Hamilton, OH d: 8/12/1920, Vienna, OH Deb: 9/24/1896

YEAR	TM-L	W	L	PCT	G	GS	CG	SH	SV	IP	H	R	ER	HR	HB	BB	SO	RAT	ERA	ERA+	CERA	OAV	BH	AVG	PR+	WS	TPW
1896	Pit-N	0	2	.000	2	2	2	0	0	15	22	18	16	0	1	9	3	2.067	9.60	44	6.94	.338	0	.000	-9	0	-0.9
1898	Bro-N	0	1	.000	1	1	1	0	0	9	16	13	10	0	0	6	0	2.444	10.00	36	8.56	.383	1	.250	-6	0	-0.6
Total	**2**	**0**	**3**	**.000**	**3**	**3**	**3**	**0**	**0**	**24**	**38**	**31**	**26**	**0**	**1**	**15**	**3**	**2.208**	**9.75**	**40**	**7.55**	**.356**	**1**	**.091**	**-15**	**0**	**-1.5**

• HORTON, Ricky Ricky Neal Horton b: 7/30/1959, Poughkeepsie, NY BL/TL, 6'2", 195 lbs. Deb: 4/7/1984

YEAR	TM-L	W	L	PCT	G	GS	CG	SH	SV	IP	H	R	ER	HR	HB	BB	SO	RAT	ERA	ERA+	CERA	OAV	BH	AVG	PR+	WS	TPW
1984	StL-N	9	4	.692	37	18	1	1	1	125^2	140	53	48	14	1	39	76	1.424	3.44	101	4.53	.285	2	.065	-1	7	-0.3
1985*	StL-N	3	2	.600	49	3	0	0	1	89^2	84	30	29	5	3	34	59	1.316	2.91	121	3.24	.251	1	.063	4	6	0.4
1986	StL-N	4	3	.571	42	9	1	0	3	100^1	77	25	25	7	1	26	49	1.027	2.24	162	2.20	.218	1	.056	12	11	1.3
1987*	StL-N	8	3	.727	67	6	0	0	7	125	127	58	53	15	0	42	55	1.352	3.82	109	3.92	.263	5	.172	4	9	0.4
1988	Chi-A	6	10	.375	52	9	1	0	2	109^1	120	64	59	6	5	36	28	1.427	4.86	82	4.21	.291	0	....	-12	4	-1.3
	*LA-N	1	1	.500	12	0	0	0	0	9	11	7	5	2	0	2	8	1.444	5.00	67	5.24	.306	0	....	-2	0	-0.2
1989	LA-N	0	0	....	23	0	0	0	0	26^2	35	15	15	1	1	11	12	1.725	5.06	67	5.67	.343	0	.000	-5	0	-0.6
	StL-N	0	3	.000	11	8	0	0	0	45^2	50	24	24	2	3	10	14	1.314	4.73	77	3.72	.282	3	.273	-6	1	-0.6
	Yr.	0	3	.000	34	8	0	0	0	72^1	85	39	39	3	4	21	26	1.465	4.85	73	4.44	.305	3	.250	-11	1	-1.1
1990	StL-N	1	1	.500	32	0	0	0	1	42	52	25	23	3	1	22	18	1.762	4.93	77	5.63	.315	0	.000	-5	1	-0.6
Total	**7**	**32**	**27**	**.542**	**325**	**53**	**3**	**1**	**15**	**673^1**	**696**	**301**	**281**	**55**	**15**	**222**	**319**	**1.363**	**3.76**	**100**	**3.91**	**.273**	**12**	**.109**	**-12**	**39**	**-1.3**

• HOSKINS, Dave David Taylor Hoskins b: 8/3/1925, Greenwood, MS d: 4/2/1970, Flint, MI BL/TR, 6'1", 180 lbs. Deb: 4/18/1953

YEAR	TM-L	W	L	PCT	G	GS	CG	SH	SV	IP	H	R	ER	HR	HB	BB	SO	RAT	ERA	ERA+	CERA	OAV	BH	AVG	PR+	WS	TPW
1953	Cle-A	9	3	.750	26	7	3	0	1	112^2	102	57	50	9	4	38	55	1.243	3.99	94	3.28	.243	15	.259	-3	7	0.1
1954	Cle-A	0	1	.000	14	1	0	0	0	26^2	29	10	9	3	0	10	9	1.463	3.04	121	4.53	.284	0	.000	1	1	0.1
Total	**2**	**9**	**4**	**.692**	**40**	**8**	**3**	**0**	**1**	**139^1**	**131**	**67**	**59**	**12**	**4**	**48**	**64**	**1.285**	**3.81**	**98**	**3.52**	**.251**	**15**	**.227**	**-2**	**8**	**0.1**

• HOST, Gene Eugene Earl "Twinkles,Slick" Host b: 1/1/1933, Leeper, PA d: 8/20/1998, Nashville, TN BB/TL, 5'11", 190 lbs. Deb: 9/16/1956

YEAR	TM-L	W	L	PCT	G	GS	CG	SH	SV	IP	H	R	ER	HR	HB	BB	SO	RAT	ERA	ERA+	CERA	OAV	BH	AVG	PR+	WS	TPW
1956	Det-A	0	0	....	1	1	0	0	0	4^2	9	4	4	2	0	2	5	2.357	7.71	53	13.63	.409	0	.000	-2	0	-0.2
1957	KC-A	0	2	.000	11	2	0	0	0	23^2	29	19	19	5	0	14	9	1.817	7.23	55	7.31	.315	0	.000	-8	0	-0.9
Total	**2**	**0**	**2**	**.000**	**12**	**3**	**0**	**0**	**0**	**28^1**	**38**	**23**	**23**	**7**	**0**	**16**	**14**	**1.906**	**7.31**	**55**	**8.35**	**.333**	**0**	**.000**	**-10**	**0**	**-1.2**

• HOUCK, Byron Byron Simon "Duke" Houck b: 8/28/1891, Prosper, MN d: 6/17/1969, Santa Cruz, CA BR/TR, 6', 175 lbs. Deb: 5/15/1912

YEAR	TM-L	W	L	PCT	G	GS	CG	SH	SV	IP	H	R	ER	HR	HB	BB	SO	RAT	ERA	ERA+	CERA	OAV	BH	AVG	PR+	WS	TPW
1912	Phi-A	8	8	.500	30	17	10	0	1	180^2	148	79	59	1	12	74	75	1.229	2.94	105	2.83	.234	4	.065	0	10	-0.7
1913	Phi-A	14	6	.700	41	19	4	1	0	176	147	93	81	3	6	122	71	**1.528**	4.14	67	3.44	.214	5	.083	-27	4	-3.3
1914	Phi-A	0	0	....	3	3	0	0	0	11	14	9	4	0	0	6	4	1.818	3.27	80	5.49	.318	1	.333	-1	0	-0.1
	Bro-F	2	6	.250	17	9	3	0	0	92	95	48	32	4	2	43	45	1.500	3.13	103	4.21	.272	7	.233	2	5	0.5
1918	StL-A	2	4	.333	27	2	0	0	2	71^2	58	24	19	0	0	29	29	1.214	2.39	115	2.39	.225	3	.150	2	5	0.2
Total	**4**	**26**	**24**	**.520**	**118**	**50**	**17**	**1**	**3**	**531^1**	**462**	**253**	**195**	**8**	**20**	**274**	**224**	**1.385**	**3.30**	**88**	**3.27**	**.234**	**20**	**.114**	**-23**	**24**	**-3.4**

• HOUGH, Charlie Charles Oliver Hough b: 1/5/1948, Honolulu, HI BR/TR, 6'2", 190 lbs. Deb: 8/12/1970 C

YEAR	TM-L	W	L	PCT	G	GS	CG	SH	SV	IP	H	R	ER	HR	HB	BB	SO	RAT	ERA	ERA+	CERA	OAV	BH	AVG	PR+	WS	TPW
1970	LA-N	0	0	....	8	0	0	0	2	17	18	11	10	7	0	11	8	1.706	5.29	72	7.87	.265	1	.333	-3	0	-0.3
1971	LA-N	0	0	....	4	0	0	0	0	4^1	3	3	2	1	0	3	4	1.385	4.15	78	4.34	.200	0	....	-0	0	0.0
1972	LA-N	0	0	....	2	0	0	0	0	2^2	2	1	1	0	1	2	4	1.500	3.38	99	4.52	.200	0	....	-0	0	0.0
1973	LA-N	4	2	.667	37	0	0	0	5	71^2	52	24	22	3	6	45	70	1.353	2.76	124	3.33	.207	3	.214	4	7	0.5
1974*	LA-N	9	4	.692	49	0	0	0	1	96	65	45	40	12	4	40	63	1.094	3.75	91	2.74	.196	0	.000	-3	5	-0.4
1975	LA-N	3	7	.300	38	0	0	0	4	61	43	25	20	3	8	34	34	1.262	2.95	115	3.16	.195	2	.333	2	4	0.3
1976	LA-N	12	8	.600	77	0	0	0	18	142^2	102	43	35	6	8	77	81	1.255	2.21	153	2.87	.200	6	.286	16	20	1.9
1977*	LA-N	6	12	.333	70	1	0	0	22	127^1	98	53	47	10	7	70	105	1.319	3.32	115	3.34	.213	4	.182	6	12	0.7
1978*	LA-N	5	5	.500	55	0	0	0	7	93^1	69	38	34	6	5	48	66	1.254	3.28	107	3.03	.205	4	.333	2	8	0.3
1979	LA-N	7	5	.583	42	14	0	0	0	151^1	152	88	80	16	8	66	76	1.441	4.76	76	4.50	.264	6	.158	-17	4	-1.8
1980	LA-N	1	3	.250	19	1	0	0	1	32^1	37	21	20	4	2	21	25	1.794	5.57	63	6.29	.291	1	.500	-8	0	-0.8
	Tex-A	2	2	.500	16	2	2	1	0	61^1	54	30	27	2	3	37	47	1.484	3.96	98	3.86	.240	0	....	0	3	0.0
1981	Tex-A	4	1	.800	21	5	2	0	1	82	61	30	27	4	3	31	69	1.122	2.96	117	2.49	.207	0	....	3	6	0.3
1982	Tex-A	16	13	.552	34	34	12	2	0	228	217	111	100	21	7	72	128	1.268	3.95	98	3.54	.251	0	....	0	15	0.0
1983	Tex-A	15	13	.536	34	33	11	3	0	252	219	96	89	22	3	95	152	1.246	3.18	126	3.32	.238	0	....	24	18	2.4
1984	Tex-A	16	14	.533	36	**36**	**17**	1	0	266	260	127	111	26	9	94	164	1.331	3.76	110	3.88	.255	0	....	14	15	1.4
1985	Tex-A	14	16	.467	34	34	14	1	0	250^1	198	102	92	23	7	83	141	1.123	3.31	128	2.77	.215	0	....	30	21	3.0
1986	Tex-A★	17	10	.630	33	33	7	2	0	230^1	188	115	97	32	9	89	146	1.203	3.79	113	3.43	.221	0	....	14	14	1.3
1987	Tex-A	18	13	.581	40	**40**	13	0	0	**285^1**	238	159	120	36	19	124	223	1.269	3.79	118	3.67	.223	0	....	25	17	2.4
1988	Tex-A	15	16	.484	34	34	10	0	0	252	202	111	93	20	12	126	174	1.302	3.32	123	3.44	.221	0	....	20	17	2.0
1989	Tex-A	10	13	.435	30	30	5	1	0	182	168	97	88	28	6	95	94	1.445	4.35	91	4.65	.245	0	....	-7	8	-0.7
1990	Tex-A	12	12	.500	32	32	5	0	0	218^2	190	108	99	24	11	119	114	1.413	4.07	96	4.19	.235	0	....	-5	12	-0.5
1991	Chi-A	9	10	.474	31	29	4	1	0	199^1	167	98	89	21	11	94	107	1.309	4.02	99	3.69	.229	0	....	-7	9	-0.7
1992	Chi-A	7	12	.368	27	27	4	0	0	176^1	160	88	77	19	7	66	76	1.282	3.93	98	3.63	.239	0	....	-1	7	-0.1
1993	Fla-N	9	16	.360	34	34	0	0	0	204^1	202	109	97	20	8	71	126	1.336	4.27	101	3.93	.259	2	.032	5	8	0.0

YEAR	TM-L	W	L	PCT	G	GS	CG	SH	SV	IP	H	R	ER	HR	HB	BB	SO	RAT	ERA	ERA+	CERA	OAV	BH	AVG	PR+	WS	TPW
1994	Fla-N	5	9	.357	21	21	1	1	0	113^2	118	74	65	17	10	52	65	1.496	5.15	85	5.18	.274	4	.121	-11	3	-1.2
Total	**25**	**216**	**216**	**.500**	**858**	**440**	**107**	**13**	**61**	**3801^1**	**3283**	**1807**	**1582**	**383**	**174**	**1665**	**2362**	**1.302**	**3.75**	**106**	**3.66**	**.233**	**33**	**.146**	**104**	**233**	**10.0**
• HOUSE, Craig					Craig Michael House b: 7/8/1977, Okinawa, Japan BR/TR, 6'2", 221 lbs. Deb: 8/6/2000																						
2000	Col-N	1	1	.500	16	0	0	0	0	13^2	13	11	11	3	2	17	8	2.195	7.24	80	9.36	.265	0	....	-2	0	-0.2
• HOUSE, Fred					Willard Edwin House b: 10/3/1890, Cabool, MO d: 11/16/1923, Kansas City, MO BR/TR, 6'3", 190 lbs. Deb: 4/22/1913																						
1913	Det-A	1	2	.333	19	2	0	0	0	53^2	64	40	31	1	2	17	16	1.509	5.20	56	5.07	.325	0	.000	-12	0	-1.4
• HOUSE, Pat					Patrick Lory House b: 9/1/1940, Boise, ID BL/TL, 6'3", 185 lbs. Deb: 9/6/1967																						
1967	Hou-N	1	0	1.000	6	0	0	0	1	4	3	2	2	0	1	0	2	.750	4.50	74	1.79	.214	0	....	-0	0	0.0
1968	Hou-N	1	1	.500	18	0	0	0	0	16^1	21	15	14	0	2	6	6	1.653	7.71	38	5.03	.323	0	....	-8	0	-1.0
Total	**2**	**2**	**1**	**.667**	**24**	**0**	**0**	**0**	**1**	**20^1**	**24**	**17**	**16**	**0**	**3**	**6**	**8**	**1.475**	**7.08**	**42**	**4.40**	**.304**	**0**	**....**	**-9**	**0**	**-1.0**
• HOUSE, Tom					Thomas Ross House b: 4/29/1947, Seattle, WA BL/TL, 5'11", 190 lbs. Deb: 6/23/1971 C																						
1971	Atl-N	1	0	1.000	11	1	0	0	0	20^2	20	8	7	2	1	3	11	1.113	3.05	122	3.20	.263	2	.400	2	2	0.2
1972	Atl-N	0	0	....	8	0	0	0	2	9^1	7	3	3	1	1	6	7	1.393	2.89	131	4.48	.226	0	.000	1	1	0.1
1973	Atl-N	4	2	.667	52	0	0	0	4	67^1	58	37	35	13	2	31	42	1.322	4.68	84	4.23	.243	2	.200	-5	4	-0.5
1974	Atl-N	6	2	.750	56	0	0	0	11	102^2	74	26	22	5	3	27	64	.984	1.93	196	1.86	.203	4	.400	19	15	2.1
1975	Atl-N	7	7	.500	58	0	0	0	11	79^1	79	39	28	2	2	36	36	1.450	3.18	119	3.55	.262	1	.111	7	8	0.7
1976	Bos-A	1	3	.250	36	0	0	0	4	43^2	39	22	21	4	2	19	27	1.328	4.33	90	3.62	.241	0	....	-2	2	-0.2
1977	Bos-A	1	0	1.000	8	0	0	0	0	7^2	15	11	11	0	0	6	6	2.739	12.91	35	10.97	.405	0	....	-7	0	-0.7
	Sea-A	4	5	.444	26	11	1	0	1	89^1	94	42	39	12	4	19	39	1.265	3.93	105	4.01	.268	0	....	0	6	0.0
	Yr.	5	5	.500	34	11	1	0	1	97	109	53	50	12	4	25	45	1.381	4.64	90	4.56	.281	0	....	-7	6	-0.7
1978	Sea-A	5	4	.556	34	9	3	0	0	116	130	70	60	10	5	35	29	1.422	4.66	82	4.42	.289	0	....	-10	4	-1.0
Total	**8**	**29**	**23**	**.558**	**289**	**21**	**4**	**0**	**33**	**536**	**516**	**258**	**226**	**49**	**20**	**182**	**261**	**1.302**	**3.79**	**103**	**3.69**	**.256**	**9**	**.257**	**6**	**42**	**0.8**
• HOUSEMAN, Frank					Frank Houseman b: Baltimore, MD Deb: 9/2/1886																						
1886	Bal-a	0	1	.000	1	1	1	0	0	8	6	3	3	0	1	1	5	.875	3.38	101	....	.199	1	.250	0	0	0.0
• HOUSER, Joe					Joseph William Houser b: 7/3/1891, Steubenville, OH d: 1/3/1953, Orlando, FL BL/TL, 5'9.5", 160 lbs. Deb: 4/24/1914																						
1914	Buf-F	0	1	.000	7	2	0	0	0	23	21	16	14	1	0	20	6	1.783	5.48	61	4.74	.250	1	.143	-6	0	-0.7
• HOUTTEMAN, Art					Arthur Joseph Houtteman b: 8/7/1927, Detroit, MI d: 5/6/2003, Rochester Hills, MI BR/TR, 6'2", 188 lbs. Deb: 4/29/1945																						
1945	Det-A	0	2	.000	13	0	0	0	0	25^1	27	17	15	1	1	11	9	1.500	5.33	66	4.01	.270	0	.000	-5	0	-0.6
1946	Det-A	0	1	.000	1	1	0	0	0	8	15	8	8	1	0	0	2	1.875	9.00	41	7.54	.385	1	.500	-5	0	-0.5
1947	Det-A	7	2	.778	23	9	7	2	0	110^2	106	51	42	6	1	36	58	1.283	3.42	110	3.18	.247	12	.300	7	8	0.9
1948	Det-A	2	16	.111	43	20	4	0	10	164^1	186	101	85	11	2	52	74	1.448	4.66	94	4.22	.287	11	.196	-1	7	-0.4
1949	Det-A	15	10	.600	34	25	13	2	0	203^2	227	101	84	19	5	59	85	1.404	3.71	112	4.28	.282	19	.244	12	14	1.3
1950	Det-A★	19	12	.613	41	34	21	**4**	4	274^2	257	112	108	29	8	99	88	1.296	3.54	132	3.69	.251	14	.151	33	**25**	2.9
1952	Det-A	8	20	.286	35	28	10	2	1	221	218	116	107	19	5	65	109	1.281	4.36	87	3.45	.253	7	.101	-9	7	-1.4
1953	Det-A	2	6	.250	16	9	3	1	1	68^2	87	50	45	11	4	29	28	1.689	5.90	69	6.39	.309	3	.158	-12	1	-1.2
	Cle-A	7	7	.500	22	13	6	1	3	109	113	56	46	4	5	25	40	1.266	3.80	99	3.32	.269	5	.147	-1	6	-0.2
	Yr.	9	13	.409	38	22	9	2	4	177^2	200	106	91	15	9	54	68	1.430	4.61	85	4.51	.285	8	.151	-13	7	-1.3
1954*	Cle-A	15	7	.682	32	25	11	1	0	188	198	80	70	14	3	59	68	1.367	3.35	110	3.84	.273	18	.277	4	14	0.9
1955	Cle-A	10	6	.625	35	12	3	1	0	124^1	126	63	55	15	2	44	53	1.367	3.98	100	4.21	.265	6	.158	-0	7	-0.1
1956	Cle-A	2	2	.500	22	4	0	0	1	46^2	60	39	34	5	4	31	19	1.950	6.56	64	7.09	.317	2	.167	-12	0	-1.2
1957	Cle-A	0	0	....	3	0	0	0	0	4	6	3	3	1	0	3	3	2.250	6.75	55	10.40	.353	0	....	-1	0	-0.1
	Bal-A	0	0	....	5	1	0	0	0	6^2	20	13	13	0	0	3	3	3.450	17.55	20	17.20	.513	1	.500	-10	0	-1.0
	Yr.	0	0	....	8	1	0	0	0	10^2	26	16	16	1	0	6	6	3.000	13.50	27	14.65	.464	1	.500	-12	0	-1.2
Total	**12**	**87**	**91**	**.489**	**325**	**181**	**78**	**14**	**20**	**1555**	**1646**	**810**	**715**	**136**	**40**	**516**	**639**	**1.390**	**4.14**	**98**	**4.11**	**.272**	**99**	**.193**	**-1**	**89**	**-0.8**
• HOVLIK, Ed					Edward Charles Hovlik b: 8/20/1891, Cleveland, OH d: 3/19/1955, Painesville, OH BR/TR, 6', 180 lbs. Deb: 7/14/1918																						
1918	Was-A	2	1	.667	8	2	1	0	0	28	25	10	4	0	0	10	10	1.250	1.29	212	2.91	.272	1	.125	4	2	0.3
1919	Was-A	0	0	....	3	0	0	0	0	5^2	12	10	8	0	0	9	3	3.706	12.71	25	16.78	.480	0	.000	-6	0	-0.7
Total	**2**	**2**	**1**	**.667**	**11**	**2**	**1**	**0**	**0**	**33^2**	**37**	**20**	**12**	**0**	**0**	**19**	**13**	**1.663**	**3.21**	**94**	**5.24**	**.316**	**1**	**.100**	**-2**	**2**	**-0.3**
• HOVLIK, Joe					Joseph Hovlik b: 8/16/1884, Czechoslovakia d: 11/3/1951, Oxford Junction, IA BR/TR, 5'10.5", 194 lbs. Deb: 7/10/1909																						
1909	Was-A	0	0	....	3	0	0	0	0	6	13	10	3	0	1	3	1	2.667	4.50	54	11.40	.419	0	.000	-1	0	-0.1
1910	Was-A	0	0	....	1	0	0	0	0	1^2	6	5	3	0	1	0	0	3.600	16.20	15	20.31	.500	0	....	-3	0	-0.3
1911	Chi-A	2	0	1.000	12	3	1	1	0	47	47	21	16	1	0	20	24	1.426	3.06	106	3.51	.257	1	.077	1	3	0.1
Total	**3**	**2**	**0**	**1.000**	**16**	**3**	**1**	**1**	**0**	**54^2**	**66**	**36**	**22**	**1**	**2**	**23**	**25**	**1.628**	**3.62**	**82**	**4.89**	**.292**	**1**	**.067**	**-3**	**3**	**-0.3**
• HOWARD, Ben					Benjamin Richard Howard b: 1/15/1979, Danville, IL BR/TR, 6'2", 190 lbs. Deb: 4/28/2002																						
2002	SD-N	0	1	.000	3	2	0	0	0	10^2	13	11	11	4	0	14	10	2.531	9.28	41	11.84	.302	0	.000	-6	0	-0.7
2003	SD-N	1	3	.250	6	6	0	0	0	34^2	31	17	14	10	0	15	24	1.327	3.63	108	4.84	.235	1	.091	1	1	0.1
Total	**2**	**1**	**4**	**.200**	**9**	**8**	**0**	**0**	**0**	**45^1**	**44**	**28**	**25**	**14**	**0**	**29**	**34**	**1.610**	**4.96**	**78**	**6.49**	**.251**	**1**	**.067**	**-5**	**1**	**-0.6**
• HOWARD, Bruce					Bruce Ernest Howard b: 3/23/1943, Salisbury, MD BB/TR, 6'2", 180 lbs. Deb: 9/4/1963																						
1963	Chi-A	2	1	.667	7	0	0	0	1	17	12	7	5	0	0	14	9	1.529	2.65	132	3.39	.207	1	.250	1	2	0.2
1964	Chi-A	2	1	.667	3	3	1	1	0	22^1	10	2	2	0	1	8	17	.806	0.81	429	1.10	.139	0	.000	6	3	0.5
1965	Chi-A	9	8	.529	30	22	1	1	0	148	123	61	57	13	1	72	120	1.318	3.47	92	3.38	.224	6	.146	-6	7	-0.5
1966	Chi-A	9	5	.643	27	21	4	2	0	149	110	48	38	14	1	44	85	1.034	2.30	138	2.30	.202	3	.070	14	11	1.4
1967	Chi-A	3	10	.231	30	17	1	0	0	112^2	102	55	43	9	3	52	76	1.367	3.43	90	3.71	.240	5	.179	-4	2	-0.4
1968	Bal-A	0	2	.000	10	5	0	0	0	31	30	16	13	2	2	26	19	1.806	3.77	77	5.59	.268	2	.286	-3	1	-0.2
	Was-A	1	4	.200	13	7	0	0	0	48^2	62	30	29	7	0	23	23	1.747	5.36	54	6.45	.330	0	.000	-13	0	-1.6
	Yr.	1	6	.143	23	12	0	0	0	79^2	92	46	42	9	2	49	42	1.770	4.74	61	6.12	.307	2	.087	-16	1	-1.8
Total	**6**	**26**	**31**	**.456**	**120**	**75**	**7**	**4**	**1**	**528^2**	**449**	**219**	**187**	**45**	**8**	**239**	**349**	**1.301**	**3.18**	**98**	**3.46**	**.231**	**17**	**.116**	**-6**	**26**	**-0.6**
• HOWARD, Chris					Christian Howard b: 11/18/1965, Lynn, MA BR/TL, 6', 185 lbs. Deb: 9/21/1993																						
1993	Chi-A	1	0	1.000	3	0	0	0	0	2^1	2	0	0	0	0	3	1	2.143	0.00	....	5.91	.286	0	....	1	1	0.1
1994	Bos-A	1	0	1.000	37	0	0	0	1	39^2	35	17	16	5	0	12	22	1.185	3.63	138	3.02	.233	0	....	6	4	0.5
1995	Tex-A	0	0	....	4	0	0	0	0	4	3	0	0	0	0	1	2	1.000	0.00	....	1.79	.231	0	....	2	1	0.2
Total	**3**	**2**	**0**	**1.000**	**44**	**0**	**0**	**0**	**1**	**46**	**40**	**17**	**16**	**5**	**0**	**16**	**25**	**1.217**	**3.13**	**161**	**3.06**	**.235**	**0**	**....**	**9**	**6**	**0.8**
• HOWARD, Earl					Earl Nycum Howard b: 6/25/1896, Everett, PA d: 4/4/1937, Everett, PA BR/TR, 6'1", 160 lbs. Deb: 4/18/1918																						
1918	StL-N	0	0	....	1	0	0	0	0	2	0	0	0	0	0	2	0	1.000	0.00	....	0.92	.000	0	....	1	0	0.1
• HOWARD, Fred					Fred Irving Howard b: 9/2/1956, Portland, ME BR/TR, 6'3", 190 lbs. Deb: 5/26/1979																						
1979	Chi-A	1	5	.167	28	6	0	0	0	68	73	34	27	5	1	32	36	1.544	3.57	119	4.60	.283	0	....	5	3	0.5
• HOWARD, Lee					Lee Vincent Howard b: 11/11/1923, Staten Island, NY BL/TL, 6'2", 175 lbs. Deb: 9/22/1946																						
1946	Pit-N	0	1	.000	3	2	1	0	0	13^1	14	3	3	0	0	9	6	1.725	2.03	174	4.51	.286	0	.000	2	1	0.2
1947	Pit-N	0	0	....	2	0	0	0	0	2^2	4	1	1	1	0	0	2	1.500	3.38	125	7.21	.333	0	....	0	0	0.0
Total	**2**	**0**	**1**	**.000**	**5**	**2**	**1**	**0**	**0**	**16**	**18**	**4**	**4**	**1**	**0**	**9**	**8**	**1.688**	**2.25**	**164**	**4.96**	**.295**	**0**	**.000**	**3**	**1**	**0.2**
• HOWE, Cal					Calvin Earl Howe b: 11/27/1924, Rock Falls, IL BL/TL, 6'3", 230 lbs. Deb: 9/26/1952																						
1952	Chi-N	0	0	....	1	0	0	0	0	2	0	0	0	0	0	1	2	.500	0.00	....	0.23	.000	0	....	1	0	0.1
• HOWE, Les					Lester Curtis "Lucky" Howe b: 8/24/1895, Brooklyn, NY d: 7/26/1976, Woodmere, NY BR/TR, 5'11.5", 170 lbs. Deb: 8/18/1923																						
1923	Bos-A	1	0	1.000	12	2	0	0	0	30	23	10	8	0	1	7	7	1.000	2.40	171	1.69	.211	0	.000	6	3	0.5

YEAR TM-L	W	L	PCT	G	GS	CG	SH	SV	IP	H	R	ER	HR	HB	BB	SO	RAT	ERA	ERA+	CERA	OAV	BH	AVG	PR+	WS	TPW
1924 Bos-A	1	0	1.000	4	0	0	0	0	7^1	11	6	6	1	1	2	3	1.773	7.36	59	8.39	.423	1	.500	-2	0	-0.2
Total 2	2	0	1.000	16	2	0	0	0	37^1	34	16	14	1	2	9	10	1.152	3.38	125	3.01	.252	1	.125	4	3	0.3

• HOWE, Steve Steven Roy Howe b: 3/10/1958, Pontiac, MI BL/TL, 6'1", 180 lbs. Deb: 4/11/1980

YEAR TM-L	W	L	PCT	G	GS	CG	SH	SV	IP	H	R	ER	HR	HB	BB	SO	RAT	ERA	ERA+	CERA	OAV	BH	AVG	PR+	WS	TPW
1980 LA-N	7	9	.438	59	0	0	0	17	84^2	83	33	25	1	2	22	39	1.240	2.66	132	2.70	.256	1	.091	7	11	0.7
1981★ LA-N	5	3	.625	41	0	0	0	8	54	51	17	15	2	0	18	32	1.278	2.50	133	2.89	.254	0	.000	5	7	0.6
1982 LA-N★	7	5	.583	66	0	0	0	13	99^1	87	27	23	3	0	17	49	1.047	2.08	166	2.03	.240	0	.000	16	14	1.6
1983 LA-N	4	7	.364	46	0	0	0	18	68^2	55	15	11	2	1	12	52	.976	1.44	249	1.71	.217	1	.125	18	14	1.9
1985 LA-N	1	1	.500	19	0	0	0	3	22	30	17	12	2	1	5	11	1.591	4.91	71	5.19	.319	0	....	-4	0	-0.4
Min-A	2	3	.400	13	0	0	0	0	19	28	16	13	1	0	7	10	1.842	6.16	72	5.88	.333	0	....	-4	0	-0.4
1987 Tex-A	3	3	.500	24	0	0	0	1	31^1	33	15	15	2	3	8	19	1.309	4.31	104	4.01	.280	0	....	1	2	0.1
1991 NY-A	3	1	.750	37	0	0	0	3	48^1	39	12	9	1	3	7	34	.952	1.68	247	1.88	.222	0	....	13	7	1.3
1992 NY-A	3	0	1.000	20	0	0	0	6	22	9	7	6	1	0	3	12	.545	2.45	160	0.63	.122	0	....	4	5	0.4
1993 NY-A	3	5	.375	51	0	0	0	4	50^2	58	31	28	7	3	10	19	1.342	4.97	83	4.54	.297	0	....	-5	2	-0.5
1994 NY-A	3	0	1.000	40	0	0	0	15	40	28	8	8	2	0	7	18	.875	1.80	254	1.54	.194	0	....	12	10	1.1
1995★ NY-A	6	3	.667	56	0	0	0	2	49	66	29	27	7	4	17	28	1.694	4.96	93	6.45	.324	0	....	-2	3	-0.2
1996 NY-A	0	1	.000	25	0	0	0	1	17	19	12	12	1	1	6	5	1.471	6.35	78	4.13	.284	0	....	-2	1	-0.2
Total 12	47	41	.534	497	0	0	0	91	606	586	239	204	32	18	139	328	1.196	3.03	131	3.03	.255	2	.074	59	76	6.0

• HOWELL, Dixie Millard Howell b: 1/7/1920, Bowman, KY d: 3/18/1960, Hollywood, FL BR/TR, 6'2", 210 lbs. Deb: 9/14/1940

YEAR TM-L	W	L	PCT	G	GS	CG	SH	SV	IP	H	R	ER	HR	HB	BB	SO	RAT	ERA	ERA+	CERA	OAV	BH	AVG	PR+	WS	TPW
1940 Cle-A	0	0	....	3	0	0	0	0	5	2	1	1	0	0	4	2	1.200	1.80	234	1.79	.143	0	....	1	1	0.1
1949 Cin-N	0	1	.000	5	1	0	0	0	13^1	21	12	12	3	0	8	7	2.175	8.10	52	9.70	.362	1	.111	-6	3	-0.6
1955 Chi-A	8	3	.727	35	0	0	0	9	73^2	70	27	24	1	0	25	25	1.290	2.93	135	2.83	.250	8	.381	7	10	0.9
1956 Chi-A	5	6	.455	34	1	0	0	4	64^1	79	39	33	3	2	36	28	1.788	4.62	89	5.55	.309	4	.235	-4	3	-0.2
1957 Chi-A	6	5	.545	37	0	0	0	6	68^1	64	25	25	6	0	30	37	1.376	3.29	113	3.81	.255	5	.185	2	7	0.6
1958 Chi-A	0	0	....	1	0	0	0	0	1^2	0	0	0	0	0	0	0	.000	0.00	....	0.00	.000	0	....	1	0	0.1
Total 6	19	15	.559	115	2	0	0	19	226^1	236	104	95	13	2	103	99	1.498	3.78	105	4.26	.275	18	.243	1	24	0.9

• HOWELL, Harry Henry Harry Howell b: 11/14/1876, NJ d: 5/22/1956, Spokane, WA BR/TR, 5'9" Deb: 10/10/1898 U ♦

YEAR TM-L	W	L	PCT	G	GS	CG	SH	SV	IP	H	R	ER	HR	HB	BB	SO	RAT	ERA	ERA+	CERA	OAV	BH	AVG	PR+	WS	TPW
1898 Bro-N	2	0	1.000	2	2	2	0	0	18	15	11	10	0	1	11	2	1.444	5.00	72	3.43	.225	2	.250	-3	1	-0.2
1899 Bal-N	13	8	.619	28	25	21	0	1	209^1	248	126	91	1	10	69	58	1.514	3.91	101	4.23	.294	12	.146	0	14	-0.3
1900★ Bro-N	6	5	.545	21	10	7	2	0	110^1	131	69	46	4	3	36	26	1.514	3.75	102	4.40	.294	12	.286	-0	9	0.4
1901 Bal-A	14	21	.400	37	34	32	1	0	294^2	333	188	120	5	7	79	93	1.398	3.67	105	3.62	.282	41	.218	16	19	1.2
1902 Bal-A	9	15	.375	26	23	19	1	0	199	243	136	91	5	7	48	33	1.462	4.12	92	4.22	.301	93	.268	3	13	-0.1
1903 NY-A	9	6	.600	25	15	13	0	0	155^2	140	79	61	4	6	44	62	1.182	3.53	88	2.70	.240	23	.217	-6	9	-0.9
1904 StL-A	13	21	.382	34	33	32	2	0	299^2	254	99	73	1	13	60	122	1.048	2.19	113	2.09	.231	25	.221	14	22	2.2
1905 StL-A	15	22	.405	38	37	**35**	4	0	323	252	109	71	2	12	101	198	1.093	1.98	128	2.11	.217	26	.193	26	20	3.1
1906 StL-A	15	14	.517	35	33	30	6	1	276^2	233	98	65	1	10	61	140	1.063	2.11	122	2.09	.232	13	.126	14	18	1.2
1907 StL-A	16	15	.516	42	35	26	2	3	316^1	258	112	68	3	8	88	118	1.094	1.93	130	2.15	.225	27	.237	20	23	2.9
1908 StL-A	18	18	.500	41	32	27	2	1	324^1	279	103	68	1	17	70	117	1.076	1.89	127	2.22	.240	22	.183	3	23	0.6
1909 StL-A	1	1	.500	10	3	0	0	0	37^1	42	21	13	0	3	8	16	1.339	3.13	77	3.63	.294	6	.176	-3	1	-0.3
1910 StL-A	0	0	....	1	0	0	0	0	3^1	7	7	4	0	0	2	1	2.700	10.80	23	11.97	.467	0	.000	-3	0	-0.4
Total 13	131	146	.473	340	282	244	20	6	2567^2	2435	1158	781	27	97	677	986	1.212	2.74	111	2.81	.252	302	.217	80	172	9.4

• HOWELL, Jay Jay Canfield Howell b: 11/26/1955, Miami, FL BR/TR, 6'3", 205 lbs. Deb: 8/10/1980

YEAR TM-L	W	L	PCT	G	GS	CG	SH	SV	IP	H	R	ER	HR	HB	BB	SO	RAT	ERA	ERA+	CERA	OAV	BH	AVG	PR+	WS	TPW
1980 Cin-N	0	0	....	5	0	0	0	0	3^1	8	5	5	0	1	0	1	2.400	13.50	27	11.58	.471	0	....	-4	0	-0.4
1981 Chi-N	2	0	1.000	10	2	0	0	0	22^1	23	13	12	3	2	10	10	1.478	4.84	76	5.06	.277	0	.000	-2	1	-0.2
1982 NY-A	2	3	.400	6	6	0	0	0	28	42	25	24	1	0	13	21	1.964	7.71	52	6.70	.341	0	....	-11	0	-1.1
1983 NY-A	1	5	.167	19	12	2	0	0	82	89	53	49	7	3	35	61	1.512	5.38	72	4.66	.275	0	....	-13	1	-1.3
1984 NY-A	9	4	.692	61	1	0	0	7	103^2	86	33	31	5	0	34	109	1.158	2.69	141	2.51	.223	0	....	13	11	1.3
1985 Oak-A★	9	8	.529	63	0	0	0	29	98	98	32	31	5	1	31	68	1.316	2.85	135	3.42	.261	0	....	12	12	1.2
1986 Oak-A	3	6	.333	38	0	0	0	16	53^1	53	23	20	3	1	23	42	1.425	3.38	115	3.83	.262	0	....	3	6	0.3
1987 Oak-A★	3	4	.429	36	0	0	0	16	44^1	48	30	29	6	1	21	35	1.556	5.89	70	5.13	.277	0	....	-8	2	-0.8
1988★ LA-N	5	3	.625	50	0	0	0	21	65	44	16	15	1	1	21	70	1.000	2.08	160	1.64	.188	0	.000	10	13	1.0
1989 LA-N★	5	3	.625	56	0	0	0	28	79^2	60	15	14	3	0	22	55	1.029	1.58	216	1.91	.211	0	.000	16	16	1.6
1990 LA-N	5	5	.500	45	0	0	0	16	66	59	17	16	5	6	20	59	1.197	2.18	168	3.33	.242	0	.000	10	10	1.1
1991 LA-N	6	5	.545	44	0	0	0	16	51	39	19	18	3	1	11	40	.980	3.18	113	1.93	.213	0	....	2	9	0.2
1992 LA-N	1	3	.250	41	0	0	0	4	46^2	41	9	8	2	1	18	36	1.264	1.54	223	2.78	.230	0	....	11	6	1.2
1993 Atl-N	3	3	.500	54	0	0	0	0	58^1	48	16	15	3	0	16	37	1.097	2.31	173	2.31	.229	0	....	10	6	1.0
1994 Tex-A	4	1	.800	40	0	0	0	2	43	44	29	26	10	1	16	22	1.395	5.44	88	4.98	.262	0	....	-2	2	-0.2
Total 15	58	53	.523	568	21	2	0	155	844^2	782	335	313	57	19	291	666	1.270	3.34	116	3.32	.246	0	.000	47	95	5.0

• HOWELL, Ken Kenneth Howell b: 11/28/1960, Detroit, MI BR/TR, 6'3", 228 lbs. Deb: 6/25/1984

YEAR TM-L	W	L	PCT	G	GS	CG	SH	SV	IP	H	R	ER	HR	HB	BB	SO	RAT	ERA	ERA+	CERA	OAV	BH	AVG	PR+	WS	TPW
1984 LA-N	5	5	.500	32	1	0	0	6	51^1	51	21	19	1	1	9	54	1.169	3.33	106	2.68	.267	0	.000	2	6	0.1
1985★ LA-N	4	7	.364	56	0	0	0	12	86	66	41	36	8	0	35	85	1.174	3.77	92	2.74	.208	0	.000	-3	6	-0.4
1986 LA-N	6	12	.333	62	0	0	0	12	97^2	86	48	42	7	3	63	104	1.526	3.87	89	4.09	.239	0	.000	-2	6	-0.3
1987 LA-N	3	4	.429	40	2	0	0	1	55	54	32	30	7	0	29	60	1.509	4.91	81	4.70	.265	1	.250	-5	2	-0.5
1988 LA-N	0	1	.000	4	1	0	0	0	12^2	16	10	9	0	0	4	12	1.579	6.39	52	4.49	.320	0	.000	-4	0	-0.5
1989 Phi-N	12	12	.500	33	32	1	1	0	204	155	84	78	11	2	86	164	1.181	3.44	103	2.63	.215	6	.092	3	11	0.2
1990 Phi-N	8	7	.533	18	18	2	0	0	106^2	106	60	55	12	3	49	70	1.453	4.64	82	4.39	.260	2	.067	-11	3	-1.3
Total 7	38	48	.442	245	54	3	1	31	613^1	534	296	269	46	9	275	549	1.319	3.95	91	3.41	.237	9	.079	-21	34	-2.6

• HOWELL, Roland Roland Boatner "Billiken" Howell b: 1/3/1892, Napoleonville, LA d: 3/31/1973, Baton Rouge, LA BR/TR, 6'4", 210 lbs. Deb: 6/14/1912

YEAR TM-L	W	L	PCT	G	GS	CG	SH	SV	IP	H	R	ER	HR	HB	BB	SO	RAT	ERA	ERA+	CERA	OAV	BH	AVG	PR+	WS	TPW
1912 StL-N	0	0	....	3	0	0	0	0	1^2	5	5	5	0	0	5	0	6.000	27.00	13	30.14	.556	0	....	-4	0	-0.4

• HOWRY, Bobby Bobby Dean Howry b: 8/4/1973, Phoenix, AZ BL/TR, 6'5", 220 lbs. Deb: 6/21/1998

YEAR TM-L	W	L	PCT	G	GS	CG	SH	SV	IP	H	R	ER	HR	HB	BB	SO	RAT	ERA	ERA+	CERA	OAV	BH	AVG	PR+	WS	TPW
1998 Chi-A	0	3	.000	44	0	0	0	9	54^1	37	20	19	7	2	19	51	1.031	3.15	145	2.50	.194	0	....	8	7	0.8
1999 Chi-A	5	3	.625	69	0	0	0	28	67^2	58	34	27	8	3	38	80	1.419	3.59	136	4.11	.229	0	....	10	10	0.9
2000★ Chi-A	2	4	.333	65	0	0	0	7	71	54	26	25	6	4	29	60	1.169	3.17	157	2.96	.216	0	....	13	9	1.2
2001 Chi-A	4	5	.444	69	0	0	0	5	78^2	85	41	41	11	4	30	64	1.462	4.69	98	4.78	.279	0	....	-1	5	-0.1
2002 Chi-A	2	2	.500	47	0	0	0	0	50^2	45	22	22	7	3	17	31	1.224	3.91	117	3.72	.245	0	....	3	3	0.3
Bos-A	1	3	.250	20	0	0	0	0	18	22	15	10	2	2	4	14	1.444	5.00	90	4.79	.306	0	....	-1	0	-0.1
Yr.	3	5	.375	67	0	0	0	0	68^2	67	37	32	9	5	21	45	1.282	4.19	108	4.00	.262	0	....	2	3	0.2
2003 Bos-A	0	0	....	4	0	0	0	0	4^1	11	6	6	1	0	3	4	3.231	12.46	37	16.51	.478	0	....	-4	0	-0.4
Total 6	14	20	.412	318	0	0	0	49	344^2	312	164	150	42	18	140	304	1.311	3.92	120	3.91	.244	0	....	29	34	2.6

• HOY, Peter Peter Alexander Hoy b: 6/29/1966, Brockville, Canada BL/TR, 6'7", 220 lbs. Deb: 4/11/1992

YEAR TM-L	W	L	PCT	G	GS	CG	SH	SV	IP	H	R	ER	HR	HB	BB	SO	RAT	ERA	ERA+	CERA	OAV	BH	AVG	PR+	WS	TPW
1992 Bos-A	0	0	....	5	0	0	0	0	3^2	8	3	3	0	0	2	2	2.727	7.36	57	11.71	.471	0	....	-1	0	-0.1

• HOYLE, Tex Roland Edison Hoyle b: 7/17/1921, Carbondale, PA d: 7/4/1994, Carbondale, PA BR/TR, 6'4", 170 lbs. Deb: 4/18/1952

YEAR TM-L	W	L	PCT	G	GS	CG	SH	SV	IP	H	R	ER	HR	HB	BB	SO	RAT	ERA	ERA+	CERA	OAV	BH	AVG	PR+	WS	TPW
1952 Phi-A	0	0	....	3	0	0	0	0	2^1	9	7	7	2	0	1	1	4.286	27.00	15	34.41	.563	0	....	-6	0	-0.6

• HOYT, La Marr Dewey La Marr Hoyt b: 1/1/1955, Columbia, SC BR/TR, 6'3", 222 lbs. Deb: 9/14/1979

YEAR TM-L	W	L	PCT	G	GS	CG	SH	SV	IP	H	R	ER	HR	HB	BB	SO	RAT	ERA	ERA+	CERA	OAV	BH	AVG	PR+	WS	TPW
1979 Chi-A	0	0	....	2	0	0	0	0	3	2	0	0	0	0	0	0	.667	0.00	....	1.01	.200	0	....	1	0	0.1
1980 Chi-A	9	3	.750	24	13	3	1	0	112^1	123	66	57	8	2	41	55	1.460	4.57	88	4.25	.281	0	....	-6	5	-0.6
1981 Chi-A	9	3	.750	43	1	0	0	10	90^2	80	40	36	10	3	28	60	1.191	3.57	100	3.32	.240	0	....	-1	7	-0.1
1982 Chi-A	**19**	15	.559	39	32	14	2	0	239^2	248	104	94	17	2	48	124	1.235	3.53	114	3.32	.266	0	....	16	16	1.6
1983★ Chi-A	**24**	10	.706	36	36	11	1	0	260^2	236	115	106	27	1	31	148	1.024	3.66	114	2.53	.238	0	....	14	20	1.4
1984 Chi-A	13	18	.419	34	34	11	1	0	235^2	244	127	117	31	5	43	126	1.218	4.47	93	3.71	.266	0	....	-10	11	-1.0
1985 SD-N★	16	8	.667	31	31	8	3	0	210^1	210	85	81	20	2	20	83	1.094	3.47	102	2.93	.261	4	.063	-2	12	-0.7

YEAR TM-L	W	L	PCT	G	GS	CG	SH	SV	IP	H	R	ER	HR	HB	BB	SO	RAT	ERA	ERA+	CERA	OAV	BH	AVG	PR+	WS	TPW
1986 SD-N	8	11	.421	35	25	1	0	0	159	170	100	91	27	3	68	85	1.497	5.15	71	5.12	.276	6	.130	-26	1	-2.8
Total 8	98	68	.590	244	172	48	8	10	1311^1	1313	637	582	140	18	279	681	1.214	3.99	98	3.46	.260	10	.091	-13	72	-1.9

• HOYT, Waite — Waite Charles "Schoolboy" Hoyt b: 9/9/1899, Brooklyn, NY d: 8/25/1984, Cincinnati, OH BR/TR, 6', 180 lbs. Deb: 7/24/1918 HOF: 1969

YEAR TM-L	W	L	PCT	G	GS	CG	SH	SV	IP	H	R	ER	HR	HB	BB	SO	RAT	ERA	ERA+	CERA	OAV	BH	AVG	PR+	WS	TPW
1918 NY-N	0	0	....	1	0	0	0	0	1	0	0	0	0	0	0	2	.000	0.00	....	0.00	.000	0	.000	0	0	0.0
1919 Bos-A	4	6	.400	13	11	6	1	0	105^1	99	42	38	1	0	22	28	1.149	3.25	93	2.46	.262	5	.132	-4	5	-0.7
1920 Bos-A	6	6	.500	22	11	6	2	1	121^1	123	72	59	2	1	47	45	1.401	4.38	83	3.26	.270	5	.116	-11	4	-1.4
1921* NY-A	19	13	.594	43	32	21	1	3	282^1	301	121	97	3	5	81	102	1.353	3.09	137	3.39	.276	22	.222	33	24	2.8
1922* NY-A	19	12	.613	37	31	17	3	0	265	271	114	101	13	9	76	95	1.309	3.43	116	3.50	.269	20	.217	15	21	1.5
1923* NY-A	17	9	.654	37	28	19	1	1	238^2	227	97	80	9	4	66	60	1.228	3.02	131	**2.92**	.253	16	.190	22	21	1.9
1924 NY-A	18	13	.581	46	32	14	2	4	247	295	117	104	8	3	76	71	1.502	3.79	110	4.24	.300	10	.133	9	17	0.3
1925 NY-A	11	14	.440	46	30	17	1	6	243	283	124	108	14	1	78	86	1.486	4.00	107	4.28	.292	24	.304	8	17	1.2
1926* NY-A	16	12	.571	40	28	12	1	4	217^2	224	112	93	4	2	62	79	1.314	3.85	100	3.11	.264	16	.211	4	13	0.3
1927* NY-A	**22**	7	.759	36	32	23	3	1	256^1	242	90	75	10	4	54	86	1.155	2.63	146	2.69	.251	22	.222	34	23	3.2
1928* NY-A	23	7	.767	42	31	19	3	**8**	273	279	118	102	16	1	60	67	1.242	3.36	112	3.13	.272	28	.257	16	22	1.6
1929 NY-A	10	9	.526	30	25	12	0	1	201^2	219	115	95	9	3	69	57	1.428	4.24	91	3.86	.279	17	.224	-11	9	-1.0
1930 NY-A	2	2	.500	8	7	2	0	0	47^2	64	27	24	7	0	9	10	1.531	4.53	95	5.45	.317	1	.063	-1	2	-0.2
Det-A	9	8	.529	26	20	8	1	4	135^2	176	89	72	7	2	47	25	1.644	4.78	100	5.07	.313	9	.196	0	8	-0.2
Yr.	11	10	.524	34	27	10	1	4	183^1	240	116	96	14	2	56	35	1.615	4.71	99	5.17	.314	10	.161	-0	10	-0.4
1931 Det-A	3	8	.273	16	12	5	0	0	92	124	70	60	2	2	32	10	1.696	5.87	78	5.19	.319	4	.133	-13	1	-1.4
* Phi-A	10	5	.667	16	14	9	2	0	111	130	60	52	9	0	37	30	1.505	4.22	107	4.66	.298	13	.302	0	9	0.3
Yr.	13	13	.500	32	26	14	2	0	203	254	130	112	11	2	69	40	1.591	4.97	91	4.90	.308	17	.233	-13	10	-1.2
1932 Bro-N	1	3	.250	8	4	0	0	1	26^2	38	27	23	3	0	12	7	1.875	7.76	49	6.75	.342	0	.000	-12	0	-1.2
NY-N	5	7	.417	18	12	3	0	0	97^1	103	43	37	6	5	25	29	1.315	3.42	109	3.66	.275	3	.097	5	5	0.3
Yr.	6	10	.375	26	16	3	0	1	124	141	70	60	9	5	37	36	1.435	4.35	86	4.32	.290	3	.081	-7	5	-1.0
1933 Pit-N	5	7	.417	36	8	4	1	4	117	118	45	38	3	1	19	44	1.171	2.92	113	2.74	.262	5	.156	4	8	0.3
1934 Pit-N	15	6	.714	48	17	8	3	5	190^2	184	75	62	6	2	43	105	1.191	2.93	141	2.77	.252	10	.179	27	18	2.6
1935 Pit-N	7	11	.389	39	11	5	0	6	164	187	72	62	8	1	27	63	1.305	3.40	121	3.55	.285	14	.259	14	13	1.6
1936 Pit-N	7	5	.583	22	9	6	0	1	116^2	115	44	35	5	3	20	37	1.157	2.70	150	2.78	.255	6	.154	18	10	1.7
1937 Pit-N	1	2	.333	11	0	0	0	2	28	31	14	14	3	0	6	21	1.321	4.50	86	3.84	.270	1	.083	-2	1	-0.3
Bro-N	7	7	.500	27	19	10	1	0	167	180	83	60	5	0	30	44	1.257	3.23	125	3.08	.270	4	.083	19	11	1.7
Yr.	8	9	.471	38	19	10	1	2	195	211	97	74	8	0	36	65	1.267	3.42	117	3.19	.270	5	.083	17	12	1.4
1938 Bro-N	0	3	.000	6	1	0	0	0	16^1	24	9	9	1	0	5	3	1.776	4.96	79	5.92	.333	0	.000	-2	0	-0.2
Total 21	237	182	.566	674	425	226	26	52	3762^1	4037	1780	1500	154	49	1003	1206	1.340	3.59	111	3.53	.276	255	.198	172	262	14.6

• HRABOSKY, Al — Alan Thomas "The Mad Hungarian,Hungo" Hrabosky b: 7/21/1949, Oakland, CA BR/TL, 5'11", 185 lbs. Deb: 6/16/1970

YEAR TM-L	W	L	PCT	G	GS	CG	SH	SV	IP	H	R	ER	HR	HB	BB	SO	RAT	ERA	ERA+	CERA	OAV	BH	AVG	PR+	WS	TPW
1970 StL-N	2	1	.667	16	1	0	0	0	19	22	10	10	2	0	7	12	1.526	4.74	87	4.74	.286	0	.000	-1	1	-0.1
1971 StL-N	0	0	....	1	0	0	0	0	2	2	0	0	0	0	0	2	1.000	0.00	....	1.95	.250	0	....	1	0	0.1
1972 StL-N	1	0	1.000	5	0	0	0	0	7	2	0	0	0	0	3	9	.714	0.00	....	0.70	.087	0	.000	3	1	0.3
1973 StL-N	2	4	.333	44	0	0	0	5	56	45	15	13	2	2	21	57	1.179	2.09	174	2.46	.220	0	.000	10	6	1.0
1974 StL-N	8	1	.889	65	0	0	0	9	88^1	71	34	29	3	1	38	82	1.234	2.95	121	2.62	.221	4	.308	5	11	0.6
1975 StL-N	13	3	.813	65	0	0	0	**22**	97^1	72	27	18	3	1	33	82	1.079	1.66	226	1.99	.205	3	.200	25	19	2.7
1976 StL-N	8	6	.571	68	0	0	0	13	95^1	89	42	35	5	4	39	73	1.343	3.30	107	3.44	.252	0	.000	2	9	0.2
1977 StL-N	6	5	.545	65	0	0	0	10	86^1	82	44	42	12	3	41	68	1.425	4.38	88	4.41	.256	0	.000	-7	5	-0.8
1978* KC-A	8	7	.533	58	0	0	0	20	75	52	24	24	6	1	35	60	1.160	2.88	133	2.59	.200	0	....	7	12	0.8
1979 KC-A	9	4	.692	58	0	0	0	11	65	67	31	27	3	1	41	39	1.662	3.74	114	4.58	.272	0	....	3	7	0.3
1980 Atl-N	4	2	.667	45	0	0	0	3	59^2	50	27	24	8	0	31	31	1.358	3.62	103	3.65	.223	0	.000	1	5	0.1
1981 Atl-N	1	1	.500	24	0	0	0	1	33^2	24	5	4	1	0	9	13	.980	1.07	335	1.71	.207	0	.000	9	5	1.0
1982 Atl-N	2	1	.667	31	0	0	0	3	37^1	41	25	23	5	0	17	20	1.554	5.54	67	5.03	.285	1	.333	-8	1	-0.8
Total 13	64	35	.646	545	1	0	0	97	722	619	284	249	50	13	315	548	1.294	3.10	122	3.22	.234	8	.143	50	82	5.3

• HUBBELL, Bill — Wilbert William Hubbell b: 6/17/1897, Henderson, CO d: 8/3/1980, Lakewood, CO BR/TR, 6'1.5", 195 lbs. Deb: 9/24/1919

YEAR TM-L	W	L	PCT	G	GS	CG	SH	SV	IP	H	R	ER	HR	HB	BB	SO	RAT	ERA	ERA+	CERA	OAV	BH	AVG	PR+	WS	TPW
1919 NY-N	1	1	.500	2	2	2	0	0	18^1	19	4	4	0	2	2	3	1.145	1.96	143	2.79	.260	1	.125	1	1	0.1
1920 NY-N	0	1	.000	14	0	0	0	2	30	26	12	7	2	1	15	8	1.367	2.10	143	3.46	.239	1	.200	3	2	0.3
Phi-N	9	9	.500	24	20	9	1	2	150	176	77	64	3	4	42	26	1.453	3.84	89	4.00	.301	7	.132	-7	8	-1.1
Yr.	9	10	.474	38	20	9	1	4	180	202	89	71	5	5	57	34	1.439	3.55	95	3.91	.291	8	.138	-4	10	-0.8
1921 Phi-N	9	16	.360	36	30	15	1	2	220^1	269	146	106	18	3	38	43	1.393	4.33	98	4.28	.306	12	.160	2	10	0.1
1922 Phi-N	7	15	.318	35	24	11	1	1	189	257	136	105	14	4	41	33	1.577	5.00	93	5.08	.317	12	.171	-6	8	-0.7
1923 Phi-N	1	6	.143	22	5	1	0	0	55	102	70	51	13	2	17	8	2.164	8.35	55	10.26	.394	4	.235	-21	0	-2.0
1924 Phi-N	10	9	.526	36	22	9	2	2	179	233	103	96	9	2	45	30	1.553	4.83	92	4.92	.324	13	.220	-3	10	-0.3
1925 Phi-N	0	0	....	2	0	0	0	0	2^2	5	4	0	0	0	1	0	2.250	0.00	....	8.21	.385	0	.000	2	0	0.1
Bro-N	3	6	.333	33	5	3	0	1	86^2	120	59	51	8	2	24	16	1.662	5.30	79	5.84	.337	3	.150	-8	2	-0.7
Yr.	3	6	.333	35	5	3	0	1	89^1	125	63	51	8	2	25	16	1.679	5.14	81	5.91	.339	3	.143	-6	2	-0.6
Total 7	40	63	.388	204	108	50	5	10	931	1207	611	484	67	20	225	167	1.538	4.68	90	4.97	.317	53	.172	-39	41	-4.3

• HUBBELL, Carl — Carl Owen "King Carl,Meal Ticket" Hubbell b: 6/22/1903, Carthage, MO d: 11/21/1988, Scottsdale, AZ BR/TL, 6', 170 lbs. Deb: 7/26/1928 HOF: 1947

YEAR TM-L	W	L	PCT	G	GS	CG	SH	SV	IP	H	R	ER	HR	HB	BB	SO	RAT	ERA	ERA+	CERA	OAV	BH	AVG	PR+	WS	TPW
1928 NY-N	10	6	.625	20	14	8	1	1	124	117	49	39	7	3	21	37	1.113	2.83	138	2.63	.248	5	.106	14	11	1.1
1929 NY-N	18	11	.621	39	35	19	1	1	268	273	128	110	17	6	67	106	1.269	3.69	124	3.36	.265	12	.129	23	19	1.5
1930 NY-N	17	12	.586	37	32	17	3	2	241^2	263	120	104	11	11	58	117	1.328	3.87	122	3.65	.278	13	.151	21	18	1.4
1931 NY-N	14	12	.538	36	30	21	4	3	248	211	88	73	14	4	67	155	1.121	2.65	139	2.52	**.227**	20	.241	26	20	3.0
1932 NY-N	18	11	.621	40	32	22	0	2	284	260	96	79	20	4	40	137	1.056	2.50	148	2.45	.238	26	.241	**43**	25	**4.7**
1933* NY-N★	**23**	12	.657	45	33	22	**10**	5	**308^2**	256	69	57	6	3	47	156	.982	**1.66**	**193**	**1.84**	.227	20	.183	**48**	**33**	**5.1**
1934 NY-N★	21	12	.636	49	35	**25**	5	**8**	313	286	100	80	17	2	37	118	1.032	**2.30**	**168**	**2.27**	.239	23	.197	**51**	32	4.9
1935 NY-N★	23	12	.657	42	35	24	1	0	302^2	314	125	110	27	3	49	150	1.199	3.27	118	3.24	.263	26	.239	18	26	2.2
1936* NY-N★	**26**	6	.813	42	34	25	3	3	304	265	81	78	7	5	57	123	1.059	**2.31**	**169**	**2.20**	.236	25	.227	**43**	**37**	**4.3**
1937* NY-N★	**22**	8	.733	39	32	18	4	4	261^2	261	108	93	18	3	55	**159**	1.208	3.20	121	3.10	.257	21	.216	15	23	1.5
1938 NY-N★	13	10	.565	24	22	13	1	1	179	171	70	61	16	2	33	104	1.140	3.07	123	2.93	.249	9	.155	14	15	1.2
1939 NY-N	11	9	.550	29	18	10	0	2	154	150	60	47	11	2	24	62	1.130	2.75	143	2.77	.249	8	.151	20	14	1.9
1940 NY-N★	11	12	.478	31	28	11	2	0	214^1	220	102	87	22	2	59	86	1.302	3.65	106	3.67	.259	15	.185	6	12	0.6
1941 NY-N★	11	9	.550	26	22	11	1	1	164	169	73	65	10	2	53	75	1.354	3.57	104	3.61	.266	8	.140	1	11	0.0
1942 NY-N★	11	8	.579	24	20	11	0	0	157^1	158	75	69	17	1	34	61	1.220	3.95	85	3.36	.259	11	.183	-12	7	-1.3
1943 NY-N	4	4	.500	12	11	3	0	0	66	87	36	36	7	0	24	31	1.682	4.91	70	5.80	.322	4	.200	-10	2	-1.1
Total 16	253	154	.622	535	433	260	36	33	3590^1	3461	1380	1188	227	53	725	1677	1.166	2.98	130	2.90	.251	246	.191	323	305	30.9

• HUCKLEBERRY, Earl — Earl Eugene Huckleberry b: 5/23/1910, Konawa, OK d: 2/25/1999, Seminole, OK BR/TR, 5'11", 165 lbs. Deb: 9/13/1935

YEAR TM-L	W	L	PCT	G	GS	CG	SH	SV	IP	H	R	ER	HR	HB	BB	SO	RAT	ERA	ERA+	CERA	OAV	BH	AVG	PR+	WS	TPW
1935 Phi-A	1	0	1.000	1	1	0	0	0	6^2	8	7	7	1	0	4	2	1.800	9.45	48	6.16	.296	0	.000	-4	0	-0.3

• HUDEK, John — John Raymond Hudek b: 8/8/1966, Tampa, FL BB/TR, 6'1", 200 lbs. Deb: 4/23/1994

YEAR TM-L	W	L	PCT	G	GS	CG	SH	SV	IP	H	R	ER	HR	HB	BB	SO	RAT	ERA	ERA+	CERA	OAV	BH	AVG	PR+	WS	TPW
1994 Hou-N★	0	2	.000	42	0	0	0	16	39^1	24	14	13	5	1	18	39	1.068	2.97	133	2.44	.174	0	....	4	6	0.4
1995 Hou-N	2	2	.500	19	0	0	0	7	20	19	12	12	3	0	5	29	1.200	5.40	72	3.52	.247	1	1.000	-3	2	-0.2
1996 Hou-N	2	0	1.000	15	0	0	0	2	16	12	5	5	2	0	5	14	1.063	2.81	138	2.38	.207	0	....	2	2	0.2
1997 Hou-N	1	3	.250	40	0	0	0	4	40^2	38	27	27	8	3	33	36	1.746	5.98	67	6.50	.252	0	....	-9	0	-0.9
1998 NY-N	1	4	.200	28	0	0	0	0	27	23	13	12	2	2	19	28	1.556	4.00	103	4.29	.237	0	....	0	1	0.0
Cin-N	4	2	.667	30	0	0	0	0	37	27	14	10	6	2	28	40	1.486	2.43	176	4.54	.206	0	.000	8	4	0.7
Yr.	5	6	.455	58	0	0	0	0	64	50	27	22	8	4	47	68	1.516	3.09	136	4.43	.219	0	.000	8	5	0.8

YEAR TM-L	W	L	PCT	G	GS	CG	SH	SV	IP	H	R	ER	HR	HB	BB	SO	RAT	ERA	ERA+	CERA	OAV	BH	AVG	PR+	WS	TPW
1999 Cin-N	0	1	.000	2	0	0	0	0	1	4	3	3	1	0	3	0	7.000	27.00	17	59.58	.667	0	....	-3	0	-0.2
Atl-N	0	1	.000	15	0	0	0	0	16^2	21	14	12	1	1	11	18	1.920	6.48	69	6.36	.296	0	.000	-4	0	-0.3
Yr.	0	2	.000	17	0	0	0	0	17^2	25	17	15	2	1	14	18	2.208	7.64	59	9.37	.325	0	.000	-6	0	-0.6
Tor-A	0	0	....	3	0	0	0	0	3^2	8	5	5	1	0	1	2	2.455	12.27	40	13.32	.471	0	....	-3	0	-0.3
Total 6	**10**	**15**	**.400**	**194**	**0**	**0**	**0**	**29**	**201^1**	**176**	**107**	**99**	**29**	**9**	**123**	**206**	**1.485**	**4.43**	**93**	**4.80**	**.236**	**1**	**.200**	**-7**	**15**	**-0.7**

• HUDLIN, Willis George Willis "Ace" Hudlin b: 5/23/1906, Wagoner, OK d: 8/5/2002, Little Rock, AR BR/TR, 6', 190 lbs. Deb: 8/15/1926 C

YEAR TM-L	W	L	PCT	G	GS	CG	SH	SV	IP	H	R	ER	HR	HB	BB	SO	RAT	ERA	ERA+	CERA	OAV	BH	AVG	PR+	WS	TPW
1926 Cle-A	1	3	.250	8	2	1	0	0	32^1	25	13	10	1	2	13	6	1.175	2.78	146	2.60	.227	1	.125	4	2	0.4
1927 Cle-A	18	12	.600	43	30	18	1	0	264^2	291	132	118	3	11	83	65	1.413	4.01	105	3.71	.283	24	.250	7	19	0.9
1928 Cle-A	14	14	.500	42	26	10	0	7	220^1	231	114	99	7	7	90	62	1.457	4.04	102	3.83	.279	14	.194	4	16	0.4
1929 Cle-A	17	15	.531	40	33	22	2	1	280^1	299	122	104	7	1	73	60	1.327	3.34	133	3.29	.272	19	.196	37	25	3.2
1930 Cle-A	13	16	.448	37	33	13	1	1	216^2	255	133	110	12	1	76	60	1.528	4.57	106	4.46	.293	16	.219	10	14	0.8
1931 Cle-A	15	14	.517	44	34	15	1	4	254^1	313	155	130	14	1	88	83	1.577	4.60	100	4.76	.301	20	.200	8	15	0.8
1932 Cle-A	12	8	.600	33	21	12	0	2	181^2	204	108	95	10	1	59	65	1.448	4.71	101	4.03	.278	13	.203	4	12	0.5
1933 Cle-A	5	13	.278	34	17	6	0	1	147^1	161	85	65	7	3	61	44	1.507	3.97	112	4.17	.275	6	.146	7	8	0.6
1934 Cle-A	15	10	.600	36	26	15	1	4	195	210	109	103	8	5	65	58	1.410	4.75	96	3.87	.277	14	.206	-3	13	-0.1
1935 Cle-A	15	11	.577	36	29	14	3	5	231^2	252	107	95	8	3	61	45	1.351	3.69	122	3.55	.277	24	.279	24	21	2.8
1936 Cle-A	1	5	.167	27	7	1	0	0	64	112	74	64	1	2	31	20	2.234	9.00	56	8.43	.397	2	.111	-28	0	-2.5
1937 Cle-A	12	11	.522	35	23	10	2	2	175^2	213	106	80	8	2	43	31	1.457	4.10	112	4.17	.295	10	.169	12	11	1.0
1938 Cle-A	8	8	.500	29	15	8	0	1	127	158	80	69	13	2	45	27	1.598	4.89	95	5.26	.303	5	.116	-4	6	-0.5
1939 Cle-A	9	10	.474	27	20	7	0	3	143	175	85	78	6	1	42	28	1.517	4.91	90	4.36	.303	9	.188	-8	7	-0.7
1940 Cle-A	2	1	.667	4	4	2	0	0	23^2	31	13	13	3	0	2	8	1.394	4.94	85	4.82	.316	1	.125	-2	1	-0.3
Was-A	1	2	.333	8	6	1	0	0	37^1	50	33	27	9	2	5	9	1.473	6.51	64	6.04	.314	1	.100	-9	0	-0.9
StL-A	0	1	.000	6	1	0	0	0	11^1	19	16	14	0	0	8	4	2.382	11.12	41	8.24	.358	1	.500	-8	0	-0.7
Yr.	3	4	.429	18	11	3	0	0	72^1	100	62	54	12	2	15	21	1.590	6.72	64	5.99	.323	3	.150	-20	1	-1.9
NY-N	0	1	.000	1	1	0	0	0	5	9	6	6	1	0	1	1	2.000	10.80	36	9.59	.409	0	.000	-4	0	-0.4
1944 StL-A	0	1	.000	1	0	0	0	0	2	3	2	1	0	0	0	1	1.500	4.50	80	3.96	.300	0	....	-0	0	0.0
Total 16	**158**	**156**	**.503**	**491**	**328**	**155**	**11**	**31**	**2613^1**	**3011**	**1493**	**1281**	**118**	**44**	**846**	**677**	**1.476**	**4.41**	**102**	**4.20**	**.289**	**180**	**.201**	**50**	**170**	**5.3**

• HUDSON, Charles Charles Lynn Hudson b: 3/16/1959, Ennis, TX BB/TR, 6'3", 185 lbs. Deb: 5/31/1983

YEAR TM-L	W	L	PCT	G	GS	CG	SH	SV	IP	H	R	ER	HR	HB	BB	SO	RAT	ERA	ERA+	CERA	OAV	BH	AVG	PR+	WS	TPW
1983* Phi-N	8	8	.500	26	26	3	0	0	169^1	158	73	63	13	0	53	101	1.246	3.35	107	3.19	.248	5	.093	6	9	0.5
1984 Phi-N	9	11	.450	30	30	1	1	0	173^2	181	101	78	12	2	52	94	1.342	4.04	90	3.66	.265	5	.089	-5	5	-0.8
1985 Phi-N	8	13	.381	38	26	3	0	0	193	188	92	81	23	1	74	122	1.358	3.78	97	3.92	.252	8	.140	1	8	0.0
1986 Phi-N	7	10	.412	33	23	0	0	0	144	165	87	79	20	0	58	82	1.549	4.94	78	5.23	.291	2	.047	-17	2	-2.1
1987 NY-A	11	7	.611	35	16	6	2	0	154^2	137	63	62	19	3	57	100	1.254	3.61	122	3.60	.239	0	....	13	13	1.2
1988 NY-A	6	6	.500	28	12	1	0	2	106^1	93	53	53	9	4	36	58	1.213	4.49	88	3.12	.235	0	....	-6	5	-0.6
1989 Det-A	1	5	.167	18	7	0	0	0	66^2	75	49	47	14	2	31	23	1.590	6.35	60	6.06	.288	0	....	-18	0	-1.8
Total 7	**50**	**60**	**.455**	**208**	**140**	**14**	**3**	**2**	**1007^2**	**997**	**518**	**463**	**110**	**12**	**361**	**580**	**1.348**	**4.14**	**92**	**3.95**	**.258**	**20**	**.095**	**-26**	**42**	**-3.7**

• HUDSON, Charlie Charles Hudson b: 8/18/1949, Ada, OK BL/TL, 6'3", 185 lbs. Deb: 5/21/1972

YEAR TM-L	W	L	PCT	G	GS	CG	SH	SV	IP	H	R	ER	HR	HB	BB	SO	RAT	ERA	ERA+	CERA	OAV	BH	AVG	PR+	WS	TPW
1972 StL-N	1	0	1.000	12	0	0	0	0	12^1	10	8	7	0	1	7	4	1.378	5.11	67	3.25	.233	0	....	-2	0	-0.3
1973 Tex-A	4	2	.667	25	4	1	1	1	62^1	59	35	32	3	0	31	34	1.444	4.62	81	3.71	.254	0	....	-5	2	-0.5
1975 Cal-A	0	1	.000	3	1	0	0	0	5^2	7	6	6	0	0	4	0	1.941	9.53	37	5.50	.304	0	....	-4	0	-0.4
Total 3	**5**	**3**	**.625**	**40**	**5**	**1**	**1**	**1**	**80^1**	**76**	**49**	**45**	**3**	**1**	**42**	**38**	**1.469**	**5.04**	**72**	**3.77**	**.255**	**0**	**....**	**-11**	**2**	**-1.1**

• HUDSON, Hal Hal Campbell "Bud,Lefty" Hudson b: 5/4/1927, Grosse Pointe, MI BL/TL, 5'10", 175 lbs. Deb: 4/20/1952

YEAR TM-L	W	L	PCT	G	GS	CG	SH	SV	IP	H	R	ER	HR	HB	BB	SO	RAT	ERA	ERA+	CERA	OAV	BH	AVG	PR+	WS	TPW
1952 StL-A	0	0	....	3	0	0	0	0	5^2	9	8	8	0	0	6	0	2.647	12.71	31	9.05	.360	0	.000	-6	0	-0.6
Chi-A	0	0	....	2	0	0	0	0	4	7	2	1	0	0	1	4	2.000	2.25	162	7.30	.389	0	....	1	0	0.1
Yr.	0	0	....	5	0	0	0	0	9^2	16	10	9	0	0	7	4	2.379	8.38	46	8.32	.372	0	.000	-5	0	-0.5
1953 Chi-A	0	0	....	1	0	0	0	0	0^2	0	0	0	0	0	0	0	.000	0.00	....	0.00	.000	0	....	0	0	0.0
Total 2	**0**	**0**	**....**	**6**	**0**	**0**	**0**	**0**	**10^1**	**16**	**10**	**9**	**0**	**0**	**7**	**4**	**2.226**	**7.84**	**49**	**7.79**	**.372**	**0**	**.000**	**-5**	**0**	**-0.5**

• HUDSON, Jesse Jesse James Hudson b: 7/22/1948, Mansfield, LA BL/TL, 6'2", 165 lbs. Deb: 9/19/1969

YEAR TM-L	W	L	PCT	G	GS	CG	SH	SV	IP	H	R	ER	HR	HB	BB	SO	RAT	ERA	ERA+	CERA	OAV	BH	AVG	PR+	WS	TPW
1969 NY-N	0	0	....	1	0	0	0	0	2	2	1	1	0	0	2	3	2.000	4.50	81	5.48	.250	0	....	-0	0	0.0

• HUDSON, Joe Joseph Paul Hudson b: 9/29/1970, Philadelphia, PA BR/TR, 6'1", 175 lbs. Deb: 6/10/1995

YEAR TM-L	W	L	PCT	G	GS	CG	SH	SV	IP	H	R	ER	HR	HB	BB	SO	RAT	ERA	ERA+	CERA	OAV	BH	AVG	PR+	WS	TPW
1995* Bos-A	0	1	.000	39	0	0	0	1	46	53	21	21	2	2	23	29	1.652	4.11	118	5.21	.301	0	....	4	3	0.3
1996 Bos-A	3	5	.375	36	0	0	0	1	45	57	35	27	4	0	32	19	1.978	5.40	94	6.85	.318	0	....	-1	2	-0.1
1997 Bos-A	3	1	.750	26	0	0	0	0	35^2	39	16	14	1	4	14	14	1.486	3.53	131	4.57	.289	0	....	4	3	0.4
1998 Mil-N	0	0	....	1	0	0	0	0	0^1	2	6	6	0	0	4	0	18.00	162.00	3	90.02	1.000	0	....	-6	0	-0.6
Total 4	**6**	**7**	**.462**	**102**	**0**	**0**	**0**	**2**	**127**	**151**	**78**	**68**	**7**	**6**	**73**	**62**	**1.764**	**4.82**	**100**	**5.84**	**.307**	**0**	**....**	**2**	**8**	**0.1**

• HUDSON, Luke Luke Stephen Hudson b: 5/2/1977, Fountain Valley, CA BR/TR, 6'3", 195 lbs. Deb: 7/1/2002

YEAR TM-L	W	L	PCT	G	GS	CG	SH	SV	IP	H	R	ER	HR	HB	BB	SO	RAT	ERA	ERA+	CERA	OAV	BH	AVG	PR+	WS	TPW
2002 Cin-N	0	0	....	3	0	0	0	0	6	5	5	3	1	0	6	7	1.833	4.50	94	6.15	.227	0	....	-0	0	0.0

• HUDSON, Nat Nathaniel P. Hudson b: 1/12/1869, Chicago, IL d: 3/14/1928, Chicago, IL BR/TR Deb: 4/18/1886

YEAR TM-L	W	L	PCT	G	GS	CG	SH	SV	IP	H	R	ER	HR	HB	BB	SO	RAT	ERA	ERA+	CERA	OAV	BH	AVG	PR+	WS	TPW
1886* StL-a	16	10	.615	29	27	25	0	**1**	234^1	224	122	79	3	2	62	100	1.220	3.03	113	....	.240	35	.233	9	22	0.7
1887 StL-a	4	4	.500	9	9	7	0	0	67	111	57	37	2	4	20	15	1.657	4.97	91	....	.357	16	.308	-5	4	-0.4
1888 StL-a	25	10	.714	39	37	36	5	0	333	283	155	94	8	15	59	130	1.027	2.54	128	....	.222	50	.255	18	36	2.0
1889 StL-a	3	2	.600	9	5	4	0	0	60	71	47	28	2	4	15	13	1.433	4.20	100	....	.286	13	.250	-1	4	-0.2
Total 4	**48**	**26**	**.649**	**86**	**78**	**72**	**5**	**1**	**694^1**	**689**	**381**	**238**	**15**	**25**	**156**	**258**	**1.188**	**3.08**	**116**	**....**	**.249**	**114**	**.253**	**21**	**66**	**2.1**

• HUDSON, Rex Rex Haughton Hudson b: 8/11/1953, Tulsa, OK BB/TR, 5'11", 165 lbs. Deb: 7/27/1974

YEAR TM-L	W	L	PCT	G	GS	CG	SH	SV	IP	H	R	ER	HR	HB	BB	SO	RAT	ERA	ERA+	CERA	OAV	BH	AVG	PR+	WS	TPW
1974 LA-N	0	0	....	1	0	0	0	0	2	6	5	5	2	0	0	0	3.000	22.50	15	25.51	.500	0	....	-4	0	-0.4

• HUDSON, Sid Sidney Charles Hudson b: 1/3/1915, Coalfield, TN BR/TR, 6'4", 180 lbs. Deb: 4/18/1940 C

YEAR TM-L	W	L	PCT	G	GS	CG	SH	SV	IP	H	R	ER	HR	HB	BB	SO	RAT	ERA	ERA+	CERA	OAV	BH	AVG	PR+	WS	TPW
1940 Was-A	17	16	.515	38	31	19	3	1	252	272	149	128	20	3	81	96	1.401	4.57	91	4.02	.274	22	.237	-8	13	-0.5
1941 Was-A★	13	14	.481	33	33	17	3	0	249^2	242	124	96	12	1	97	108	1.358	3.46	117	3.40	.253	16	.186	19	17	1.9
1942 Was-A★	10	17	.370	35	31	19	1	2	239^1	266	140	116	9	5	70	72	1.404	4.36	84	3.78	.276	19	.213	-9	7	-0.8
1946 Was-A	8	11	.421	31	15	6	1	1	142^1	160	75	57	9	4	37	35	1.384	3.60	93	3.98	.280	12	.279	-1	7	0.1
1947 Was-A	6	9	.400	20	17	5	1	0	106	113	66	66	8	1	58	37	1.613	5.60	66	4.75	.272	12	.308	-20	2	-1.9
1948 Was-A	4	16	.200	39	29	4	0	1	182	217	128	119	11	6	107	53	**1.780**	5.88	74	5.60	.299	14	.237	-28	2	-2.5
1949 Was-A	8	17	.320	40	27	11	2	1	209	234	117	98	11	5	91	54	1.555	4.22	101	4.51	.283	16	.239	9	10	1.0
1950 Was-A	14	14	.500	30	30	17	0	0	237^2	261	129	108	17	6	98	75	1.511	4.09	110	4.47	.284	20	.215	11	15	1.0
1951 Was-A	5	12	.294	23	19	8	0	0	138^2	168	90	79	8	4	52	43	1.587	5.13	80	4.91	.302	12	.273	-14	3	-1.2
1952 Was-A	3	4	.429	7	7	6	0	0	62^2	59	22	19	4	0	29	24	1.404	2.73	130	3.71	.257	4	.167	6	5	0.6
Bos-A	7	9	.438	21	18	7	0	0	134^1	145	64	54	9	7	36	50	1.347	3.62	109	3.89	.276	8	.174	4	8	0.4
Yr.	10	13	.435	28	25	13	0	0	197	204	86	73	13	7	65	74	1.365	3.34	115	3.83	.270	12	.171	10	13	1.0
1953 Bos-A	6	9	.400	30	17	4	0	2	156	164	65	61	13	4	49	60	1.365	3.52	119	3.96	.269	7	.140	11	11	0.9
1954 Bos-A	3	4	.429	33	5	0	0	5	71^1	83	43	35	5	2	30	27	1.584	4.42	93	4.89	.296	2	.154	-2	3	-0.2
Total 12	**104**	**152**	**.406**	**380**	**279**	**123**	**11**	**13**	**2181**	**2384**	**1212**	**1036**	**136**	**48**	**835**	**734**	**1.476**	**4.28**	**94**	**4.25**	**.278**	**164**	**.220**	**-22**	**103**	**-1.3**

• HUDSON, Tim Timothy Adam Hudson b: 7/14/1975, Columbus, GA BR/TR, 6', 160 lbs. Deb: 6/8/1999

YEAR TM-L	W	L	PCT	G	GS	CG	SH	SV	IP	H	R	ER	HR	HB	BB	SO	RAT	ERA	ERA+	CERA	OAV	BH	AVG	PR+	WS	TPW
1999 Oak-A	11	2	.846	21	21	1	0	0	136^1	121	56	49	8	4	62	132	1.342	3.23	143	3.50	.237	1	.250	22	12	2.1
2000* Oak-A★	**20**	6	.769	32	32	2	2	0	202^1	169	100	93	24	7	82	169	1.241	4.14	115	3.43	.227	0	.000	17	15	1.5
2001* Oak-A	18	9	.667	35	**35**	3	0	0	235	216	100	88	20	6	71	181	1.221	3.37	131	3.22	.245	0	.000	27	17	2.5
2002* Oak-A	15	9	.625	34	34	4	2	0	238^1	237	87	79	19	8	62	152	1.255	2.98	147	3.51	.263	1	.200	39	23	3.8
2003* Oak-A	16	7	.696	34	34	3	**2**	0	240	197	84	72	15	10	61	162	1.075	2.70	167	2.47	.223	1	.333	48	**23**	4.6
Total 5	**80**	**33**	**.708**	**156**	**156**	**13**	**6**	**0**	**1052**	**940**	**427**	**381**	**86**	**35**	**338**	**796**	**1.215**	**3.26**	**139**	**3.19**	**.239**	**3**	**.130**	**152**	**90**	**14.5**

YEAR TM-L	W	L	PCT	G	GS	CG	SH	SV	IP	H	R	ER	HR	HB	BB	SO	RAT	ERA	ERA+	CERA	OAV	BH	AVG	PR+	WS	TPW
• HUENKE, Al				Albert Alfred Huenke b: 6/26/1891, New Bremen, OH d: 9/20/1974, St. Marys, OH BR/TR, 6', 175 lbs. Deb: 10/6/1914																						
1914 NY-N	0	0	....	1	0	0	0	0	2	2	1	1	0	0	0	2	1.000	4.50	59	1.95	.250	0	.000	-0	0	-0.1
• HUFFMAN, Phil				Phillip Lee Huffman b: 6/20/1958, Freeport, TX BR/TR, 6'2", 180 lbs. Deb: 4/10/1979																						
1979 Tor-A	6	18	.250	31	31	2	1	0	173	220	130	111	25	0	68	56	1.665	5.77	75	5.88	.304	0	....	-28	2	-2.8
1985 Bal-A	0	0	....	2	1	0	0	0	4^2	7	8	8	1	0	5	2	2.571	15.43	26	10.57	.350	0	....	-6	0	-0.6
Total 2	6	18	.250	33	32	2	1	0	177^2	227	138	119	26	0	73	58	1.689	6.03	72	6.01	.305	0	....	-34	2	-3.4
• HUGHES, Bill				William Nesbert Hughes b: 11/18/1896, Philadelphia, PA d: 2/25/1963, Birmingham, AL BR/TR, 5'10.5", 155 lbs. Deb: 9/15/1921																						
1921 Pit-N	0	0	....	1	0	0	0	0	2	3	1	1	0	1	1	2	2.000	4.50	85	8.24	.375	0	....	-0	0	0.0
• HUGHES, Dick				Richard Henry Hughes b: 2/13/1938, Stephens, AR BR/TR, 6'3", 195 lbs. Deb: 9/11/1966																						
1966 StL-N	2	1	.667	6	2	1	1	1	21	12	4	4	0	2	7	20	.905	1.71	210	1.33	.162	2	.400	4	3	0.5
1967* StL-N	16	6	.727	37	27	12	3	3	222^1	164	72	66	22	5	48	161	.954	2.67	121	**2.09**	**.203**	10	.128	14	18	1.3
1968* StL-N	2	2	.500	25	5	0	0	4	64	45	25	25	7	0	21	49	1.031	3.52	82	2.33	.202	0	.000	-5	3	-0.7
Total 3	20	9	.690	68	34	13	4	8	307^1	221	101	95	29	7	76	230	.966	2.78	113	2.09	.200	12	.122	13	24	1.1
• HUGHES, Jay				James Jay Hughes b: 1/22/1874, Sacramento, CA d: 6/2/1924, Sacramento, CA BR/TR, 185 lbs. Deb: 4/18/1898																						
1898 Bal-N	23	12	.657	38	35	31	5	0	300^2	268	152	107	4	18	100	81	1.224	3.20	112	2.80	.237	37	.226	4	22	0.7
1899 Bro-N	**28**	6	.824	35	35	30	3	0	291^2	250	121	87	6	14	119	99	1.265	2.68	146	2.88	.232	27	.252	34	33	3.6
1901 Bro-N	17	12	.586	31	29	24	0	0	250^2	265	125	91	3	12	102	96	1.464	3.27	102	3.85	.270	16	.176	1	15	0.0
1902 Bro-N	15	10	.600	31	29	26	0	0	245	223	114	81	3	9	51	92	1.118	2.98	93	2.42	.243	19	.209	-6	15	-0.1
Total 4	83	40	.675	135	128	111	8	0	1088	1006	512	366	16	53	372	368	1.267	3.03	111	2.98	.245	99	.219	34	85	4.2
• HUGHES, Jim				James Michael Hughes b: 8/11/1951, Los Angeles, CA BR/TR, 6'3", 190 lbs. Deb: 9/14/1974																						
1974 Min-A	0	2	.000	2	2	1	0	0	10^1	8	8	6	2	0	4	8	1.161	5.23	72	3.44	.216	0	....	-2	0	-0.2
1975 Min-A	16	14	.533	37	34	12	2	0	249^2	241	119	106	17	13	127	130	1.474	3.82	101	4.28	.255	0	....	3	14	0.3
1976 Min-A	9	14	.391	37	26	3	0	0	177	190	113	98	17	8	73	87	**1.486**	4.98	72	4.77	.281	0	....	-28	1	-2.9
1977 Min-A	0	0	....	2	0	0	0	0	4^1	4	1	1	0	0	1	1	1.154	2.08	192	2.34	.250	0	....	1	0	0.1
Total 4	25	30	.455	78	62	16	2	0	441^1	443	241	211	36	21	205	226	1.468	4.30	87	4.44	.265	0	....	-25	15	-2.7
• HUGHES, Jim				James Robert Hughes b: 3/21/1923, Chicago, IL d: 8/13/2001, Palos Heights, IL BR/TR, 6'1", 200 lbs. Deb: 9/13/1952																						
1952 Bro-N	2	1	.667	6	0	0	0	0	18^2	16	4	3	0	0	11	8	1.446	1.45	251	3.25	.235	0	.000	4	2	0.4
1953* Bro-N	4	3	.571	48	0	0	0	9	85^2	80	33	33	6	1	41	49	1.412	3.47	123	3.71	.245	4	.286	6	9	0.6
1954 Bro-N	8	4	.667	**60**	0	0	0	**24**	86^2	76	36	31	7	0	44	58	1.385	3.22	127	3.55	.239	3	.188	8	14	0.8
1955 Bro-N	0	2	.000	24	0	0	0	6	42^2	41	22	20	10	0	19	20	1.406	4.22	96	5.02	.256	0	.000	-1	2	-0.2
1956 Bro-N	0	0	....	5	0	0	0	0	12	10	7	7	3	0	4	8	1.167	5.25	76	3.85	.233	0	.000	-2	0	-0.2
Chi-N	1	3	.250	25	1	0	0	0	45^1	43	35	26	4	4	30	20	1.610	5.16	73	4.93	.259	2	.286	-8	0	-0.7
Yr.	1	3	.250	30	1	0	0	0	57^1	53	42	33	7	4	34	28	1.517	5.18	74	4.71	.254	2	.222	-10	0	-1.0
1957 Chi-A	0	0	....	4	0	0	0	0	5	12	6	6	0	0	3	2	3.000	10.80	35	13.48	.462	0	....	-4	0	-0.4
Total 6	15	13	.536	172	1	0	0	39	296	278	143	126	30	5	152	165	1.453	3.83	105	4.18	.251	9	.170	4	27	0.2
• HUGHES, Mickey				Michael J. Hughes b: 10/25/1866, New York, NY d: 4/10/1931, Jersey City, NJ TR, 5'6", 165 lbs. Deb: 4/22/1888																						
1888 Bro-a	25	13	.658	40	40	40	2	0	363	281	163	86	5	6	98	159	1.044	2.13	140	....	.206	19	.137	34	33	2.6
1889* Bro-a	9	8	.529	20	17	13	0	0	153	172	120	74	6	7	86	54	1.686	4.35	85	....	.275	12	.176	-11	6	-1.2
1890 Bro-N	4	4	.500	9	8	6	0	0	66^1	77	47	38	1	4	30	22	1.613	5.16	67	....	.282	1	.038	-13	2	-1.5
Phi-a	1	3	.250	6	5	4	0	0	41^1	64	56	25	0	5	21	15	2.056	5.44	70	....	.344	2	.125	-5	0	-0.5
Total 3	39	28	.582	75	70	63	2	0	623^2	594	386	223	12	22	235	250	1.329	3.22	104	....	.243	34	.137	5	41	-0.6
• HUGHES, Tom				Thomas L. "Salida Tom" Hughes b: 1/28/1884, Coal Creek, CO d: 11/1/1961, Los Angeles, CA BR/TR, 6'2", 175 lbs. Deb: 9/18/1906																						
1906 NY-A	1	0	1.000	3	1	1	0	0	15	11	8	7	2	0	1	5	.800	4.20	71	1.73	.208	1	.200	-2	1	-0.2
1907 NY-A	2	0	1.000	4	3	2	0	0	27	16	10	8	0	2	11	10	1.000	2.67	105	1.56	.175	1	.143	1	2	0.1
1909 NY-A	7	8	.467	24	15	9	2	2	118^2	109	42	35	3	4	37	69	1.230	2.65	95	2.97	.249	5	.128	1	7	0.2
1910 NY-A	7	9	.438	23	15	11	0	1	151^2	153	77	59	2	3	37	64	1.253	3.50	76	3.13	.271	9	.164	-10	5	-1.2
1914 Bos-N	2	0	1.000	2	2	1	0	0	17	14	7	5	0	0	4	11	1.059	2.65	104	1.93	.226	0	.000	-0	1	-0.1
1915 Bos-N	16	14	.533	**50**	25	17	4	**9**	280^1	208	88	66	4	11	58	171	.949	2.12	126	1.73	.213	9	.100	14	22	1.2
1916 Bos-N	16	3	.842	40	13	7	1	5	161	121	46	42	2	8	51	97	1.068	2.35	104	2.11	.215	10	.192	2	14	0.4
1917 Bos-N	5	3	.625	11	8	6	2	0	74	54	21	16	1	3	30	40	1.135	1.95	131	2.22	.216	0	.000	6	6	0.4
1918 Bos-N	0	2	.000	3	3	1	0	0	18^1	17	10	7	0	0	6	9	1.255	3.44	78	2.64	.250	2	.333	-1	1	0.0
Total 9	56	39	.589	160	85	55	9	17	863	703	309	245	14	31	235	476	1.087	2.56	102	2.28	.229	37	.130	10	59	0.8
• HUGHES, Tom				Thomas James "Long Tom" Hughes b: 11/29/1878, Chicago, IL d: 2/8/1956, Chicago, IL BR/TR, 6'1", 175 lbs. Deb: 9/7/1900																						
1900 Chi-N	1	1	.500	3	3	3	0	0	21	31	14	12	0	1	7	12	1.810	5.14	70	5.99	.342	0	.000	-3	1	-0.3
1901 Chi-N	10	23	.303	37	35	32	1	0	308^1	309	166	111	4	17	115	225	1.375	3.24	100	3.48	.259	14	.119	3	14	-0.5
1902 Bal-A	7	5	.583	13	13	12	1	0	108^1	120	57	47	2	2	32	45	1.403	3.90	96	3.69	.281	6	.140	4	5	0.2
Bos-A	3	3	.500	9	8	4	0	0	49^1	51	31	18	0	1	24	15	1.520	3.28	109	3.81	.267	11	.367	0	4	0.2
Yr.	10	8	.556	22	21	16	1	0	157^2	171	88	65	2	3	56	60	1.440	3.71	100	3.73	.277	17	.233	4	9	0.4
1903* Bos-A	20	7	.741	33	31	25	5	0	244^2	232	95	70	5	9	60	112	1.193	2.57	118	2.80	.250	26	.280	5	23	1.2
1904 NY-A	7	11	.389	19	18	12	1	0	136^1	141	72	56	3	5	48	75	1.386	3.70	73	3.61	.268	13	.241	-18	5	-1.9
Was-A	3	12	.200	16	14	14	0	0	124^1	133	67	48	4	6	34	48	1.343	3.47	77	3.57	.274	13	.228	-8	3	-0.5
Yr.	10	23	.303	35	32	26	1	0	260^2	274	139	104	7	11	82	123	1.366	3.59	75	3.59	.271	26	.234	-26	8	-2.4
1905 Was-A	17	20	.459	39	35	26	6	0	291^1	239	113	76	3	11	79	149	1.092	2.35	113	2.19	.226	22	.212	2	22	0.7
1906 Was-A	7	17	.292	30	24	18	1	0	204	230	118	82	5	4	81	90	**1.525**	3.62	73	4.20	.287	14	.212	-19	4	-1.7
1907 Was-A	7	14	.333	34	23	18	2	**4**	211	206	104	73	1	12	47	102	1.199	3.11	78	2.66	.258	19	.238	-9	6	-0.5
1908 Was-A	18	15	.545	43	31	24	3	4	276^1	224	91	68	3	6	77	165	1.089	2.21	103	2.21	.227	17	.195	1	19	0.4
1909 Was-A	4	7	.364	22	13	7	2	1	120^1	113	56	36	1	5	33	77	1.213	2.69	90	2.77	.246	3	.083	-2	4	-0.4
1911 Was-A	11	17	.393	34	27	17	2	0	223	251	128	86	7	4	77	86	1.471	3.47	94	4.16	.288	15	.185	-5	10	-0.6
1912 Was-A	13	10	.565	31	26	11	1	0	196	201	99	64	8	6	78	108	1.423	2.94	114	3.93	.270	13	.194	2	12	0.3
1913 Was-A	4	12	.250	36	12	4	0	6	129^2	129	81	62	6	14	61	59	1.465	4.30	69	4.14	.253	4	.111	-22	2	-2.4
Total 13	132	174	.431	399	313	227	25	15	2644	2610	1292	909	52	103	853	1368	1.310	3.09	92	3.27	.259	190	.198	-69	134	-5.9
• HUGHES, Tom				Thomas Edward Hughes b: 9/13/1934, Ancon, Panama BL/TR, 6'2", 180 lbs. Deb: 9/13/1959																						
1959 StL-N	0	2	.000	2	2	0	0	0	4	9	9	7	2	0	2	2	2.750	15.75	27	16.00	.409	0	.000	-5	0	-0.5
• HUGHES, Tommy				Thomas Owen Hughes b: 10/7/1919, Wilkes-Barre, PA d: 11/28/1990, Wilkes-Barre, PA BR/TR, 6'1", 190 lbs. Deb: 4/19/1941																						
1941 Phi-N	9	14	.391	34	24	5	2	0	170	187	106	84	12	4	82	59	1.582	4.45	83	4.71	.280	11	.200	-13	5	-1.3
1942 Phi-N	12	18	.400	40	31	19	0	1	253	224	105	86	8	0	99	77	1.277	3.06	108	2.84	.238	8	.100	7	18	0.2
1946 Phi-N	6	9	.400	29	13	3	2	1	111	123	64	54	5	1	44	34	1.505	4.38	78	4.18	.281	3	.097	-11	3	-1.3
1947 Phi-N	4	11	.267	29	15	4	1	1	127	121	52	49	5	0	59	44	1.417	3.47	115	3.75	.265	2	.050	7	9	0.3
1948 Cin-N	0	4	.000	12	4	0	0	0	27	43	28	27	3	0	24	7	2.481	9.00	43	9.58	.364	1	.143	-15	0	-1.5
Total 5	31	56	.356	144	87	31	5	3	688	698	355	300	33	5	308	221	1.462	3.92	91	3.95	.266	25	.117	-25	35	-3.6
• HUGHES, Vern				Vernon Alexander "Lefty" Hughes b: 4/15/1893, Etna, PA d: 9/26/1961, Sewickley, PA BL/TL, 5'10", 155 lbs. Deb: 7/6/1914																						
1914 Bal-F	0	0	....	3	0	0	0	0	5^2	5	4	2	0	0	3	0	1.412	3.18	100	3.09	.250	0	.000	0	0	0.0
• HUGHEY, Jim				James Ulysses "Coldwater Jim" Hughey b: 3/8/1869, Wakeshma, MI d: 3/29/1945, Coldwater, MI TR, 6' Deb: 9/29/1891																						
1891 Mil-a	1	0	1.000	2	1	1	0	0	15	18	6	5	0	0	3	9	1.400	3.00	146	....	.288	1	.143	2	1	0.2
1893 Chi-N	0	1	.000	2	2	1	0	0	9	14	16	11	0	1	3	4	1.889	11.00	42	6.63	.345	0	.000	-6	0	-0.5
1896 Pit-N	6	8	.429	25	14	11	0	0	155	171	108	86	3	7	67	48	1.535	4.99	84	4.24	.278	14	.215	-14	6	-1.3
1897 Pit-N	6	10	.375	25	17	13	0	1	149^1	193	115	84	3	7	45	38	1.594	5.06	82	4.85	.311	8	.127	-12	7	-1.4
1898 StL-N	7	24	.226	35	33	31	0	0	283^2	325	169	124	2	11	71	74	1.396	3.93	96	3.72	.286	11	.113	5	15	0.0

YEAR	TM-L	W	L	PCT	G	GS	CG	SH	SV	IP	H	R	ER	HR	HB	BB	SO	RAT	ERA	ERA+	CERA	OAV	BH	AVG	PR+	WS	TPW
1899	Cle-N	4	30	.118	36	34	32	0	0	283	403	244	170	9	22	88	54	1.735	5.41	68	5.88	.334	18	.162	-40	9	-4.1
1900	StL-N	5	7	.417	20	12	11	0	0	112^2	147	90	65	4	6	40	23	1.660	5.19	70	5.27	.314	7	.171	-18	2	-1.6
Total	7	29	80	.266	145	113	100	0	1	1007^2	1271	748	545	21	54	317	250	1.576	4.87	79	4.72	.306	59	.153	-83	40	-8.7

• HUGHSON, Tex Cecil Carlton Hughson b: 2/9/1916, Buda, TX d: 8/6/1993, San Marcos, TX BR/TR, 6'3", 198 lbs. Deb: 4/16/1941

YEAR	TM-L	W	L	PCT	G	GS	CG	SH	SV	IP	H	R	ER	HR	HB	BB	SO	RAT	ERA	ERA+	CERA	OAV	BH	AVG	PR+	WS	TPW
1941	Bos-A	5	3	.625	12	8	4	0	0	61	70	30	28	3	1	13	22	1.361	4.13	101	3.83	.289	1	.059	1	4	0.0
1942	Bos-A★	**22**	6	.786	38	30	**22**	4	4	**281**	258	92	81	10	1	75	**113**	1.185	2.59	144	2.68	.245	18	.176	29	**28**	3.1
1943	Bos-A★	12	15	.444	35	32	**20**	4	2	266	242	87	78	23	2	73	114	1.184	2.64	125	3.04	.247	9	.105	19	20	1.6
1944	Bos-A★	18	5	.783	28	23	19	2	5	203^1	172	57	51	4	2	41	112	1.048	2.26	151	**2.04**	.225	10	.152	25	20	2.6
1946*	Bos-A	20	11	.645	39	35	21	6	3	278	252	89	85	15	2	51	172	1.090	2.75	133	2.45	.238	12	.132	27	25	2.6
1947	Bos-A	12	11	.522	29	26	13	3	0	189^1	173	86	70	17	2	71	119	1.289	3.33	117	3.39	.244	2	.033	11	12	0.6
1948	Bos-A	3	1	.750	15	0	0	0	0	19^1	21	14	11	0	0	7	6	1.448	5.12	86	3.60	.276	0	.000	-2	1	-0.2
1949	Bos-A	4	2	.667	29	2	0	0	3	77^2	82	49	46	5	1	41	35	1.584	5.33	82	4.54	.268	1	.045	-10	3	-1.2
Total	8	96	54	.640	225	156	99	19	17	1375^2	1270	504	450	77	11	372	693	1.194	2.94	126	2.87	.245	53	.119	100	113	9.1

• HUISMAN, Rick Richard Allen Huisman b: 5/17/1969, Oak Park, IL BR/TR, 6'3", 200 lbs. Deb: 9/4/1995

YEAR	TM-L	W	L	PCT	G	GS	CG	SH	SV	IP	H	R	ER	HR	HB	BB	SO	RAT	ERA	ERA+	CERA	OAV	BH	AVG	PR+	WS	TPW
1995	KC-A	0	0	....	7	0	0	0	0	9^2	14	8	8	2	0	1	12	1.552	7.45	64	6.13	.333	0	....	-3	0	-0.3
1996	KC-A	2	1	.667	22	0	0	0	1	29^1	25	15	15	4	0	18	23	1.466	4.60	109	4.17	.231	0	....	1	2	0.1
Total	2	2	1	.667	29	0	0	0	1	39	39	23	23	6	0	19	35	1.487	5.31	93	4.66	.260	0	....	-2	2	-0.2

• HUISMANN, Mark Mark Lawrence Huismann b: 5/11/1958, Lincoln, NE BR/TR, 6'3", 195 lbs. Deb: 8/16/1983

YEAR	TM-L	W	L	PCT	G	GS	CG	SH	SV	IP	H	R	ER	HR	HB	BB	SO	RAT	ERA	ERA+	CERA	OAV	BH	AVG	PR+	WS	TPW
1983	KC-A	2	1	.667	13	0	0	0	0	30^2	29	20	19	1	0	17	20	1.500	5.58	73	3.71	.250	0	....	-5	1	-0.5
1984*	KC-A	3	3	.500	38	0	0	0	3	75	84	38	35	7	1	21	54	1.400	4.20	96	4.21	.286	0	....	-2	4	-0.2
1985	KC-A	1	0	1.000	9	0	0	0	0	18^2	14	4	4	1	0	3	9	.911	1.93	216	1.75	.219	0	....	5	2	0.5
1986	KC-A	0	1	.000	10	0	0	0	1	17^1	18	8	8	1	0	6	13	1.385	4.15	102	3.80	.269	0	....	0	1	0.0
	Sea-A	3	3	.500	36	1	0	0	4	80	80	39	33	18	1	19	59	1.238	3.71	114	4.31	.256	0	....	5	6	0.5
	Yr.	3	4	.429	46	1	0	0	5	97^1	98	47	41	19	1	25	72	1.264	3.79	112	4.22	.259	0	....	5	7	0.5
1987	Sea-A	0	0	....	6	0	0	0	0	14^2	10	10	8	1	2	4	15	.955	4.91	96	2.17	.196	0	....	-0	0	0.0
	Cle-A	2	3	.400	20	0	0	0	2	35^1	38	22	20	6	0	8	23	1.302	5.09	89	4.22	.271	0	....	-2	2	-0.2
	Yr.	2	3	.400	26	0	0	0	2	50	48	32	28	7	2	12	38	1.200	5.04	91	3.62	.251	0	....	-2	2	-0.2
1988	Det-A	1	0	1.000	5	0	0	0	0	5^1	6	3	3	0	0	2	6	1.500	5.06	75	3.70	.286	0	....	-1	0	-0.1
1989	Bal-A	0	0	....	8	0	0	0	1	11^1	13	8	8	0	0	0	13	1.147	6.35	60	2.56	.277	0	....	-3	0	-0.3
1990	Pit-N	1	0	1.000	2	0	0	0	0	3	6	5	3	2	1	1	2	2.333	9.00	40	19.77	.462	0	....	-2	0	-0.2
1991	Pit-N	0	0	....	5	0	0	0	0	5	7	6	4	0	0	2	5	1.800	7.20	50	4.87	.304	0	....	-2	0	-0.2
Total	9	13	11	.542	152	1	0	0	11	296^1	305	163	145	37	5	83	219	1.309	4.40	94	4.00	.266	0	....	-7	16	-0.7

• HULIHAN, Harry Harry Joseph Hulihan b: 4/18/1899, Rutland, VT d: 9/11/1980, Rutland, VT BR/TL, 5'11", 170 lbs. Deb: 8/16/1922

YEAR	TM-L	W	L	PCT	G	GS	CG	SH	SV	IP	H	R	ER	HR	HB	BB	SO	RAT	ERA	ERA+	CERA	OAV	BH	AVG	PR+	WS	TPW
1922	Bos-N	2	3	.400	7	6	2	0	0	40	40	23	14	0	4	26	16	1.650	3.15	127	4.68	.274	2	.154	4	2	0.4

• HULVEY, Hank James Hensel Hulvey b: 7/18/1897, Mount Sidney, VA d: 4/9/1982, Mount Sidney, VA BB/TR, 6', 180 lbs. Deb: 9/5/1923

YEAR	TM-L	W	L	PCT	G	GS	CG	SH	SV	IP	H	R	ER	HR	HB	BB	SO	RAT	ERA	ERA+	CERA	OAV	BH	AVG	PR+	WS	TPW
1923	Phi-A	0	1	.000	1	1	0	0	0	7	10	6	6	1	0	2	2	1.714	7.71	53	6.69	.357	1	.500	-3	0	-0.2

• HUME, Tom Thomas Hubert Hume b: 3/29/1953, Cincinnati, OH BR/TR, 6'1", 185 lbs. Deb: 5/25/1977 C

YEAR	TM-L	W	L	PCT	G	GS	CG	SH	SV	IP	H	R	ER	HR	HB	BB	SO	RAT	ERA	ERA+	CERA	OAV	BH	AVG	PR+	WS	TPW
1977	Cin-N	3	3	.500	14	5	0	0	0	43	54	36	34	5	0	17	22	1.651	7.12	55	5.50	.305	2	.200	-16	0	-1.5
1978	Cin-N	8	11	.421	42	23	3	0	1	174	198	89	80	12	4	50	90	1.425	4.14	86	4.23	.289	3	.067	-9	6	-1.2
1979*	Cin-N	10	9	.526	57	12	2	0	17	163	162	54	50	12	0	33	80	1.196	2.76	**135**	3.04	.262	8	.174	17	18	1.8
1980	Cin-N	9	10	.474	78	0	0	0	25	137	121	44	39	6	3	38	68	1.161	2.56	140	2.61	.240	3	.188	17	19	1.9
1981	Cin-N	9	4	.692	51	0	0	0	13	67^2	63	27	26	7	1	31	27	1.389	3.46	103	3.95	.259	0	.000	-0	8	-0.1
1982	Cin-N★	2	6	.250	46	0	0	0	17	63^2	57	24	22	2	1	21	22	1.225	3.11	119	2.68	.245	0	.000	4	8	0.3
1983	Cin-N	3	5	.375	48	0	0	0	9	66	66	40	35	8	3	41	34	1.621	4.77	80	5.01	.264	0	.000	-7	2	-0.8
1984	Cin-N	4	13	.235	54	8	0	0	3	113^1	142	83	71	14	1	41	59	1.615	5.64	67	5.40	.309	3	.136	-22	0	-2.4
1985	Cin-N	3	5	.375	56	0	0	0	3	80	65	33	29	7	3	35	50	1.250	3.26	116	3.23	.224	0	.000	4	6	0.4
1986	Phi-N	4	1	.800	48	1	0	0	4	94^1	89	37	29	5	3	34	51	1.304	2.77	139	3.31	.252	0	.000	12	8	1.1
1987	Phi-N	1	4	.200	38	6	0	0	0	70^2	75	48	44	10	4	41	29	1.642	5.60	76	5.58	.277	3	.200	-12	0	-1.1
	Cin-N	1	0	1.000	11	0	0	0	0	13^1	14	6	6	0	1	2	4	1.200	4.05	105	3.12	.292	0	....	0	1	0.0
	Yr.	2	4	.333	49	6	0	0	0	84	89	54	50	10	5	43	33	1.571	5.36	79	5.19	.279	3	.200	-11	1	-1.1
Total	11	57	71	.445	543	55	5	0	92	1086	1106	521	465	88	24	384	536	1.372	3.85	98	3.88	.268	22	.120	-11	76	-1.6

• HUMPHREY, Bill Byron William Humphrey b: 6/17/1911, Vienna, MO d: 2/13/1992, Springfield, MO BR/TR, 6', 180 lbs. Deb: 4/24/1938

YEAR	TM-L	W	L	PCT	G	GS	CG	SH	SV	IP	H	R	ER	HR	HB	BB	SO	RAT	ERA	ERA+	CERA	OAV	BH	AVG	PR+	WS	TPW
1938	Bos-A	0	0	....	2	0	0	0	0	2	5	2	2	0	0	1	0	3.000	9.00	55	13.07	.500	0	....	-1	0	-0.1

• HUMPHREYS, Bob Robert William Humphreys b: 8/18/1935, Covington, VA BR/TR, 5'11", 170 lbs. Deb: 9/8/1962

YEAR	TM-L	W	L	PCT	G	GS	CG	SH	SV	IP	H	R	ER	HR	HB	BB	SO	RAT	ERA	ERA+	CERA	OAV	BH	AVG	PR+	WS	TPW
1962	Det-A	0	1	.000	4	0	0	0	1	5	8	4	4	3	0	2	3	2.000	7.20	57	12.48	.381	0	....	-2	0	-0.2
1963	StL-N	0	1	.000	9	0	0	0	0	10^2	11	8	6	4	1	7	8	1.688	5.06	70	8.12	.282	0	....	-2	0	-0.2
1964*	StL-N	2	0	1.000	28	0	0	0	2	42^2	32	14	12	3	1	15	36	1.102	2.53	150	2.44	.213	1	.250	6	5	0.7
1965	Chi-N	2	0	1.000	41	0	0	0	0	65^2	59	25	23	6	2	27	38	1.310	3.15	117	3.54	.244	0	.000	5	5	0.4
1966	Was-A	7	3	.700	58	1	0	0	3	111^2	91	38	35	6	4	28	88	1.066	2.82	123	2.41	.229	2	.167	7	10	0.9
1967	Was-A	6	2	.750	48	2	0	0	4	105^2	93	54	49	13	2	41	54	1.268	4.17	76	3.60	.238	2	.133	-12	5	-1.3
1968	Was-A	5	7	.417	56	0	0	0	2	92^2	78	40	38	13	0	30	56	1.165	3.69	79	3.17	.233	2	.400	-7	3	-0.7
1969	Was-A	3	3	.500	47	0	0	0	5	79^2	69	37	27	3	1	38	43	1.343	3.05	114	3.20	.233	1	.077	3	5	0.3
1970	Was-A	0	0	....	5	0	0	0	0	6^2	4	2	1	1	0	9	6	1.950	1.35	263	6.43	.200	0	....	2	1	0.2
	Mil-A	2	4	.333	23	1	0	0	3	45^2	37	18	16	3	2	22	32	1.292	3.15	120	3.13	.222	0	.000	4	4	0.4
	Yr.	2	4	.333	28	1	0	0	3	52^1	41	20	17	4	2	31	38	1.376	2.92	129	3.55	.219	0	.000	6	5	0.5
Total	9	27	21	.563	319	4	0	0	20	566	482	240	211	55	13	219	364	1.239	3.36	100	3.30	.234	8	.131	4	38	0.5

• HUMPHRIES, Bert Albert Humphries b: 9/26/1880, California, PA d: 9/21/1945, Orlando, FL BR/TR, 5'11.5", 182 lbs. Deb: 4/16/1910

YEAR	TM-L	W	L	PCT	G	GS	CG	SH	SV	IP	H	R	ER	HR	HB	BB	SO	RAT	ERA	ERA+	CERA	OAV	BH	AVG	PR+	WS	TPW
1910	Phi-N	0	0	....	5	0	0	0	2	9^2	13	8	5	0	1	3	3	1.655	4.66	67	5.22	.317	0	.000	-2	0	-0.2
1911	Phi-N	3	1	.750	11	5	2	0	1	41	56	25	19	1	6	10	13	1.610	4.17	82	5.78	.339	5	.333	-3	3	-0.1
	Cin-N	4	3	.571	14	7	3	0	0	65	62	25	17	3	6	18	16	1.231	2.35	140	3.52	.266	1	.063	7	4	0.6
	Yr.	7	4	.636	25	12	5	0	1	106	118	50	36	4	12	28	29	1.377	3.06	110	4.39	.296	6	.194	4	7	0.6
1912	Cin-N	9	11	.450	30	15	9	2	2	158^2	162	77	57	6	8	36	58	1.248	3.23	104	3.22	.270	7	.137	4	10	0.3
1913	Chi-N	16	4	.800	28	10	13	2	1	181	169	70	54	10	2	24	61	1.066	2.69	118	2.51	.250	12	.194	9	14	1.0
1914	Chi-N	10	11	.476	34	21	8	2	0	171	162	80	51	5	2	37	62	1.164	2.68	103	2.61	.250	13	.236	5	9	0.7
1915	Chi-N	8	13	.381	31	22	10	4	3	171^2	183	69	44	6	5	23	45	1.200	2.31	120	3.10	.280	8	.174	11	12	1.3
Total	6	50	43	.538	153	80	45	10	9	798	807	354	247	31	30	151	258	1.201	2.79	110	3.08	.267	46	.186	31	52	3.7

• HUMPHRIES, Johnny John William Humphries b: 6/23/1915, Clifton Forge, VA d: 6/24/1965, New Orleans, LA BR/TR, 6'1", 185 lbs. Deb: 5/8/1938

YEAR	TM-L	W	L	PCT	G	GS	CG	SH	SV	IP	H	R	ER	HR	HB	BB	SO	RAT	ERA	ERA+	CERA	OAV	BH	AVG	PR+	WS	TPW
1938	Cle-A	9	8	.529	**45**	6	1	0	6	103^1	105	69	60	6	1	63	56	1.626	5.23	89	4.52	.264	3	.103	-7	6	-0.7
1939	Cle-A	2	4	.333	15	1	0	0	2	28^1	30	30	26	0	1	32	12	2.188	8.26	53	6.28	.294	0	.000	-12	0	-1.2
1940	Cle-A	0	2	.000	19	1	1	0	1	33^2	35	35	31	5	2	29	17	1.901	8.29	51	6.46	.269	0	.000	-16	0	-1.6
1941	Chi-A	4	2	.667	14	6	4	4	1	73^1	63	18	15	2	1	22	25	1.159	1.84	223	2.47	.230	2	.087	17	9	1.6
1942	Chi-A	12	12	.500	28	28	17	2	0	228^1	227	85	68	9	7	59	71	1.253	2.68	134	3.11	.257	18	.225	22	20	2.7
1943	Chi-A	11	11	.500	28	27	8	2	0	188^1	198	86	69	7	6	54	51	1.338	3.30	101	3.50	.268	20	.290	-0	13	0.6
1944	Chi-A	8	10	.444	30	20	8	0	1	169	170	75	69	9	4	57	42	1.343	3.67	93	3.61	.267	10	.189	-5	9	-0.5
1945	Chi-A	6	14	.300	22	21	10	1	1	153	172	83	72	11	3	48	33	1.438	4.24	78	4.20	.282	8	.148	-14	3	-1.7
1946	Phi-N	0	0	....	10	1	0	0	0	24^2	24	17	11	1	1	9	10	1.338	4.01	86	3.53	.258	2	.250	-2	0	-0.1
Total	9	52	63	.452	211	111	49	9	12	1002	1024	498	421	50	26	373	317	1.394	3.78	97	3.74	.265	63	.191	-16	60	-1.0

• HUNT, Ben Benjamin Franklin "High Pockets" Hunt b: 11/10/1888, Eufaula, OK d: 9/27/1927, Greybull, WY BL/TL, 6'5", 190 lbs. Deb: 8/24/1910

YEAR	TM-L	W	L	PCT	G	GS	CG	SH	SV	IP	H	R	ER	HR	HB	BB	SO	RAT	ERA	ERA+	CERA	OAV	BH	AVG	PR+	WS	TPW
1910	Bos-A	2	3	.400	7	7	3	0	0	46^2	45	22	21	4	0	20	19	1.393	4.05	63	4.05	.266	1	.056	-8	1	-1.0

YEAR TM-L	W	L	PCT	G	GS	CG	SH	SV	IP	H	R	ER	HR	HB	BB	SO	RAT	ERA	ERA+	CERA	OAV	BH	AVG	PR+	WS	TPW
1913 StL-N	0	1	.000	2	1	0	0	0	8	6	5	3	0	1	9	6	1.875	3.38	95	4.73	.240	0	.000	-0	0	0.0
Total 2	**2**	**4**	**.333**	**9**	**8**	**3**	**0**	**0**	**54^2**	**51**	**27**	**24**	**4**	**1**	**29**	**25**	**1.463**	**3.95**	**66**	**4.15**	**.263**	**1**	**.050**	**-8**	**1**	**-1.1**
• HUNT, Ken	Kenneth Raymond Hunt b: 12/14/1938, Ogden, UT BR/TR, 6'4", 200 lbs. Deb: 4/16/1961																									
1961* Cin-N	9	10	.474	29	22	4	0	0	136^1	130	70	60	13	6	66	75	1.438	3.96	102	4.37	.257	7	.179	2	8	0.2
• HUNTER, Catfish	James Augustus "Jim" Hunter b: 4/8/1946, Hertford, NC d: 9/9/1999, Hertford, NC BR/TR, 6', 195 lbs. Deb: 5/13/1965 HOF: 1987																									
1965 KC-A	8	8	.500	32	20	3	2	0	133	124	68	63	21	2	46	82	1.278	4.26	82	3.83	.246	6	.150	-11	4	-1.2
1966 KC-A★	9	11	.450	30	25	4	0	0	176^2	158	87	79	17	2	64	103	1.257	4.02	84	3.34	.239	9	.153	-13	5	-1.3
1967 KC-A★	13	17	.433	35	35	13	5	0	259^2	209	91	81	16	2	84	196	1.128	2.81	113	2.52	.219	18	.196	11	17	1.6
1968 Oak-A	13	13	.500	36	34	11	2	1	234	210	99	87	29	4	69	172	1.192	3.35	84	3.27	.238	19	.232	-14	10	-1.1
1969 Oak-A	12	15	.444	38	35	10	3	0	247	210	99	92	34	5	85	150	1.194	3.35	103	3.45	.234	19	.224	2	13	0.6
1970 Oak-A★	18	14	.563	40	**40**	9	1	0	262^1	253	124	111	32	9	74	178	1.247	3.81	93	3.63	.250	18	.200	-10	12	-0.7
1971* Oak-A	21	11	.656	37	37	16	4	0	273^2	225	103	90	27	4	80	181	1.114	2.96	113	2.74	.223	36	.350	6	22	2.0
1972* Oak-A★	21	7	.750	38	37	16	5	0	295^1	200	74	67	21	3	70	191	.914	2.04	139	1.70	.189	23	.219	23	24	2.9
1973* Oak-A★	21	5	.808	36	36	11	3	0	256^1	222	105	95	39	1	69	124	1.135	3.34	106	3.20	.232	1	1.000	-1	15	0.0
1974* Oak-A★	**25**	12	.676	41	41	23	6	0	318^1	268	97	88	25	4	46	143	.986	**2.49**	133	2.25	.229	0	....	25	27	2.6
1975 NY-A★	**23**	14	.622	39	39	**30**	7	0	**328**	248	107	94	25	5	83	177	1.009	2.58	141	**2.18**	**.208**	0	....	29	29	3.0
1976* NY-A★	17	15	.531	36	36	21	2	0	298^2	268	126	117	28	3	68	173	1.125	3.53	97	2.86	.241	0	.000	-14	15	-1.5
1977* NY-A	9	9	.500	22	22	8	1	0	143^1	137	83	75	29	3	47	52	1.284	4.71	84	4.27	.250	0	....	-15	4	-1.5
1978* NY-A	12	6	.667	21	20	5	1	0	118	98	49	47	16	1	35	56	1.127	3.58	101	3.05	.226	0	....	-0	8	0.0
1979 NY-A	2	9	.182	19	19	1	0	0	105	128	68	62	15	1	34	34	1.543	5.31	77	5.49	.312	0	....	-16	1	-1.6
Total 15	**224**	**166**	**.574**	**500**	**476**	**181**	**42**	**1**	**3449^1**	**2958**	**1380**	**1248**	**374**	**49**	**954**	**2012**	**1.134**	**3.26**	**104**	**2.97**	**.231**	**149**	**.226**	**2**	**206**	**3.8**
• HUNTER, George	George Henry Hunter b: 7/8/1887, Buffalo, NY d: 1/11/1968, Harrisburg, PA BB/TL, 5'8.5", 165 lbs. Deb: 5/4/1909																									
1909 Bro-N	4	10	.286	16	13	10	0	0	113^1	104	48	31	2	3	38	43	1.253	2.46	105	3.03	.254	28	.228	3	7	0.0
• HUNTER, Jim	James Mac Gregor Hunter b: 6/22/1964, Jersey City, NJ BR/TR, 6'3", 205 lbs. Deb: 5/17/1991																									
1991 Mil-A	0	5	.000	8	6	0	0	0	31	45	26	25	3	4	17	14	2.000	7.26	55	8.18	.349	0	....	-11	0	-1.1
• HUNTER, Rich	Richard Thomas Hunter b: 9/25/1974, Pasadena, CA BR/TR, 6'1", 185 lbs. Deb: 4/6/1996																									
1996 Phi-N	3	7	.300	14	14	0	0	0	69^1	84	54	50	10	5	33	32	1.688	6.49	66	6.25	.303	3	.167	-17	0	-1.6
• HUNTER, Willard	Willard Mitchell Hunter b: 3/8/1934, Newark, NJ BR/TL, 6'2", 180 lbs. Deb: 4/16/1962																									
1962 LA-N	0	0	....	1	0	0	0	0	2	6	10	9	1	0	4	1	5.000	40.50	9	29.58	.545	0	....	-8	0	-0.8
NY-N	1	6	.143	27	6	1	0	0	63	67	41	39	9	1	34	40	1.603	5.57	75	5.35	.270	3	.231	-9	1	-0.8
Yr.	1	6	.143	28	6	1	0	0	65	73	51	48	10	1	38	41	1.708	6.65	61	6.10	.282	3	.231	-17	1	-1.6
1964 NY-N	3	3	.500	41	0	0	0	5	49	54	25	24	4	2	9	22	1.286	4.41	81	3.87	.284	1	1.000	-5	3	-0.5
Total 2	**4**	**9**	**.308**	**69**	**6**	**1**	**0**	**5**	**114**	**127**	**76**	**72**	**14**	**3**	**47**	**63**	**1.526**	**5.68**	**68**	**5.14**	**.283**	**4**	**.286**	**-22**	**4**	**-2.1**
• HUNTZINGER, Walt	Walter Henry "Shakes" Huntzinger b: 2/6/1899, Pottsville, PA d: 8/11/1981, Upper Darby, PA BR/TR, 6', 150 lbs. Deb: 9/29/1923																									
1923 NY-N	0	1	.000	2	1	0	0	0	8	9	7	7	0	0	1	2	1.250	7.88	48	3.03	.290	0	.000	-4	0	-0.4
1924 NY-N	1	1	.500	12	2	0	0	1	32^1	41	19	16	3	0	9	6	1.546	4.45	82	5.03	.318	4	.500	-3	1	-0.2
1925 NY-N	5	1	.833	26	1	0	0	0	64^1	68	30	25	3	0	17	19	1.321	3.50	115	3.46	.281	1	.091	4	6	0.3
1926 StL-N	0	4	.000	9	4	2	0	0	34	35	19	16	4	0	14	9	1.441	4.24	92	4.31	.267	0	.000	-2	1	-0.2
Chi-N	1	1	.500	11	0	0	0	2	28^2	26	8	3	0	3	8	4	1.186	0.94	408	2.81	.260	1	.143	9	4	0.8
Yr.	1	5	.167	20	4	2	0	2	62^2	61	27	19	4	3	22	13	1.324	2.73	143	3.62	.264	1	.067	7	5	0.6
Total 4	**7**	**8**	**.467**	**60**	**8**	**2**	**0**	**3**	**167^1**	**179**	**83**	**67**	**10**	**3**	**49**	**40**	**1.363**	**3.60**	**108**	**3.80**	**.283**	**6**	**.167**	**4**	**12**	**0.3**
• HURD, Tom	Thomas Carr "Whitey" Hurd b: 5/27/1924, Danville, VA d: 9/5/1982, Waterloo, IA BR/TR, 5'9", 155 lbs. Deb: 7/30/1954																									
1954 Bos-A	2	0	1.000	16	0	0	0	1	29^2	21	11	10	2	0	12	14	1.112	3.03	135	2.30	.198	1	.333	4	3	0.4
1955 Bos-A	8	6	.571	43	0	0	0	5	80^2	72	32	27	7	1	38	48	1.364	3.01	142	3.54	.242	1	.071	12	9	1.1
1956 Bos-A	3	4	.429	40	0	0	0	5	76	84	52	45	5	3	47	34	1.724	5.33	87	5.43	.289	6	.500	-6	4	-0.4
Total 3	**13**	**10**	**.565**	**99**	**0**	**0**	**0**	**11**	**186^1**	**177**	**95**	**82**	**14**	**4**	**97**	**96**	**1.470**	**3.96**	**112**	**4.11**	**.255**	**8**	**.276**	**10**	**16**	**1.2**
• HURST, Bill	William Hansel Hurst b: 4/28/1970, Miami Beach, FL BR/TR, 6'7", 220 lbs. Deb: 9/18/1996																									
1996 Fla-N	0	0	....	2	0	0	0	0	2	3	0	0	0	0	1	1	2.000	0.00	....	6.48	.333	0	....	1	0	0.1
• HURST, Bruce	Bruce Vee Hurst b: 3/24/1958, St. George, UT BL/TL, 6'4", 215 lbs. Deb: 4/12/1980																									
1980 Bos-A	2	2	.500	12	7	0	0	0	30^2	39	33	31	4	2	16	16	1.793	9.10	46	6.66	.307	0	....	-17	0	-1.7
1981 Bos-A	2	0	1.000	5	5	0	0	0	23	23	11	11	1	1	12	11	1.522	4.30	90	4.09	.258	0	....	-1	1	-0.1
1982 Bos-A	3	7	.300	28	19	0	0	0	117	161	87	75	16	3	40	53	1.718	5.77	75	6.53	.333	0	....	-17	1	-1.7
1983 Bos-A	12	12	.500	33	32	6	2	0	211^1	241	102	96	22	3	62	115	1.434	4.09	106	4.59	.290	0	....	7	13	0.7
1984 Bos-A	12	12	.500	33	33	9	2	0	218	232	106	95	25	6	88	136	1.468	3.92	106	4.65	.271	0	....	14	14	1.4
1985 Bos-A	11	13	.458	35	31	6	1	0	229^1	243	123	115	31	3	70	189	1.365	4.51	95	4.36	.273	0	....	-2	10	-0.2
1986* Bos-A	13	8	.619	25	25	11	4	0	174^1	169	63	58	18	3	50	167	1.256	2.99	139	3.59	.256	0	....	24	16	2.4
1987 Bos-A★	15	13	.536	33	33	15	3	0	238^2	239	124	117	35	1	76	190	1.320	4.41	103	4.12	.262	0	....	5	15	0.5
1988* Bos-A	18	6	.750	33	32	7	1	0	216^2	222	98	88	21	2	65	166	1.325	3.66	112	3.82	.264	0	....	14	15	1.4
1989 SD-N	15	11	.577	33	33	**10**	2	0	244^2	214	84	73	16	0	66	179	1.144	2.69	130	2.68	.237	5	.071	19	18	1.9
1990 SD-N	11	9	.550	33	33	9	**4**	0	223^2	188	85	78	21	1	63	162	1.122	3.14	122	2.75	.228	6	.090	16	14	1.4
1991 SD-N	15	8	.652	31	31	4	0	0	221^2	201	89	81	17	3	59	141	1.173	3.29	116	2.95	.241	9	.134	12	15	1.2
1992 SD-N	14	9	.609	32	32	6	4	0	217^1	223	96	93	22	0	51	131	1.261	3.85	93	3.59	.267	11	.159	-6	12	-0.5
1993 SD-N	0	1	.000	2	2	0	0	0	4^1	9	7	6	0	0	3	3	2.769	12.46	33	10.69	.409	0	....	-4	0	-0.4
Col-N	0	1	.000	3	3	0	0	0	8^2	6	5	5	1	0	3	6	1.038	5.19	92	2.42	.194	0	.000	-0	0	0.0
Yr.	0	2	.000	5	5	0	0	0	13	15	12	11	1	0	6	9	1.615	7.62	58	5.17	.283	0	.000	-4	0	-0.4
1994 Tex-A	2	1	.667	8	8	0	0	0	38	53	30	30	8	0	16	24	1.816	7.11	68	7.58	.342	0	....	-9	0	-0.8
Total 15	**145**	**113**	**.562**	**379**	**359**	**83**	**23**	**0**	**2417^1**	**2463**	**1143**	**1052**	**258**	**28**	**740**	**1689**	**1.325**	**3.92**	**104**	**3.95**	**.265**	**31**	**.113**	**55**	**144**	**5.5**
• HURST, James	James Lavon Hurst b: 6/1/1967, Plantation, FL BL/TL, 6', 160 lbs. Deb: 4/4/1994																									
1994 Tex-A	0	0	....	8	0	0	0	0	10^2	17	12	12	1	0	8	5	2.344	10.13	48	8.99	.362	0	....	-6	0	-0.6
• HURST, Jonathan	Jonathan Hurst b: 10/20/1966, New York, NY BR/TR, 6'3", 175 lbs. Deb: 6/9/1992																									
1992 Mon-N	1	1	.500	3	3	0	0	0	16^1	18	10	10	1	1	7	4	1.531	5.51	63	4.82	.281	0	.000	-4	0	-0.4
1994 NY-N	0	1	.000	7	0	0	0	0	10	15	14	14	5	0	5	6	2.000	12.60	33	10.88	.341	0	....	-9	0	-0.9
Total 2	**1**	**2**	**.333**	**10**	**3**	**0**	**0**	**0**	**26^1**	**33**	**24**	**24**	**6**	**1**	**12**	**10**	**1.709**	**8.20**	**47**	**7.12**	**.306**	**0**	**.000**	**-13**	**0**	**-1.4**
• HURTADO, Edwin	Edwin Amilgar Hurtado b: 2/1/1970, Barquisimeto, Venezuela BR/TR, 6'3", 215 lbs. Deb: 5/22/1995																									
1995 Tor-A	5	2	.714	14	10	1	0	0	77^2	81	50	47	11	5	40	33	1.558	5.45	86	5.40	.275	0	....	-7	3	-0.6
1996 Sea-A	2	5	.286	16	4	0	0	2	47^2	61	42	41	10	0	30	36	1.909	7.74	64	7.74	.324	0	....	-15	0	-1.4
1997 Sea-A	1	2	.333	13	1	0	0	0	19	25	19	19	5	2	15	10	2.105	9.00	50	9.95	.329	0	....	-9	0	-0.9
Total 3	**8**	**9**	**.471**	**43**	**15**	**1**	**0**	**2**	**144^1**	**167**	**111**	**107**	**26**	**7**	**85**	**79**	**1.746**	**6.67**	**71**	**6.77**	**.299**	**0**	**....**	**-31**	**3**	**-2.9**
• HUSTED, Bill	William J. Husted b: 10/11/1866, Gloucester, NJ d: 5/17/1941, Gloucester, NJ Deb: 4/29/1890																									
1890 Phi-P	5	10	.333	18	17	12	0	0	129	148	105	70	2	5	67	33	1.667	4.88	87	....	.276	6	.107	-9	6	-1.1
• HUSTING, Bert	Berthold Juneau "Pete" Husting b: 3/6/1878, Fond du Lac, WI d: 9/3/1948, Milwaukee, WI BR/TR, 5'10.5" Deb: 8/16/1900																									
1900 Pit-N	0	0	....	2	0	0	0	0	8	10	5	5	2	1	5	7	1.875	5.63	64	8.17	.305	0	.000	-2	0	-0.2
1901 Mil-A	9	15	.375	34	26	19	0	1	217^1	234	151	103	5	13	95	67	1.514	4.27	84	4.19	.272	19	.202	-13	9	-1.4

YEAR	TM-L	W	L	PCT	G	GS	CG	SH	SV	IP	H	R	ER	HR	HB	BB	SO	RAT	ERA	ERA+	CERA	OAV	BH	AVG	PR+	WS	TPW
1902	Bos-A	0	1	.000	1	1	1	0	0	8	15	15	8	0	0	8	4	2.875	9.00	40	11.05	.398	1	.250	-5	0	-0.4
	Phi-A	14	5	.737	32	27	17	1	0	204	240	126	86	7	9	91	44	1.623	3.79	97	4.82	.294	13	.159	-2	11	-0.5
	Yr.	14	6	.700	33	28	18	1	0	212	255	141	94	7	9	99	48	**1.670**	3.99	92	5.05	.298	14	.163	-7	11	-0.9
Total	3	23	21	.523	69	54	37	1	1	437^{1}	499	297	202	14	23	199	122	1.596	4.16	87	4.68	.285	33	.180	-22	20	-2.5

• HUTCHINGS, Johnny John Richard Joseph Hutchings b: 4/14/1916, Chicago, IL d: 4/27/1963, Indianapolis, IN BB/TR, 6'2", 250 lbs. Deb: 4/26/1940

YEAR	TM-L	W	L	PCT	G	GS	CG	SH	SV	IP	H	R	ER	HR	HB	BB	SO	RAT	ERA	ERA+	CERA	OAV	BH	AVG	PR+	WS	TPW
1940*	Cin-N	2	1	.667	19	4	0	0	0	54	53	21	21	3	1	18	18	1.315	3.50	108	3.42	.260	2	.154	-0	4	0.0
1941	Cin-N	0	0	....	8	0	0	0	0	11	12	6	5	0	0	4	5	1.455	4.09	88	3.61	.279	0	....	-1	0	-0.1
	Bos-N	1	6	.143	36	7	1	1	2	95^{2}	110	59	44	6	4	22	36	1.380	4.14	86	4.03	.287	4	.148	-7	2	-0.7
	Yr.	1	6	.143	44	7	1	1	2	106^{2}	122	65	49	6	4	26	41	1.388	4.13	86	3.98	.286	4	.148	-7	2	-0.7
1942	Bos-N	1	0	1.000	20	3	0	0	0	65^{2}	66	33	32	2	2	34	27	1.523	4.39	76	4.04	.260	1	.050	-7	2	-1.0
1944	Bos-N	1	4	.200	14	7	1	0	1	56^{2}	55	30	25	3	1	26	26	1.429	3.97	96	3.76	.252	1	.067	-1	2	-0.2
1945	Bos-N	7	6	.538	57	12	3	2	3	185	173	87	77	21	4	75	99	1.341	3.75	102	3.77	.244	13	.241	1	13	0.4
1946	Bos-N	0	1	.000	1	1	0	0	0	3	5	3	3	1	0	1	1	2.000	9.00	38	9.64	.357	0	.000	-2	0	-0.2
Total	6	12	18	.400	155	34	5	3	6	471	474	239	207	36	12	180	212	1.389	3.96	93	3.85	.260	21	.162	-16	23	-1.8

• HUTCHINSON, Chad Chad Martin Hutchinson b: 2/21/1977, Boulder, CO BR/TR, 6'5", 230 lbs. Deb: 4/4/2001

YEAR	TM-L	W	L	PCT	G	GS	CG	SH	SV	IP	H	R	ER	HR	HB	BB	SO	RAT	ERA	ERA+	CERA	OAV	BH	AVG	PR+	WS	TPW
2001	StL-N	0	0	....	3	0	0	0	0	4	9	11	11	3	1	6	2	3.750	24.75	17	27.84	.450	0	.000	-9	0	-0.9

• HUTCHINSON, Fred Frederick Charles Hutchinson b: 8/12/1919, Seattle, WA d: 11/12/1964, Bradenton, FL BL/TR, 6'2", 200 lbs. Deb: 5/2/1939 M

YEAR	TM-L	W	L	PCT	G	GS	CG	SH	SV	IP	H	R	ER	HR	HB	BB	SO	RAT	ERA	ERA+	CERA	OAV	BH	AVG	PR+	WS	TPW
1939	Det-A	3	6	.333	13	12	3	0	0	84^{2}	95	56	49	9	0	51	22	1.724	5.21	94	5.49	.287	13	.382	-3	4	0.0
1940*	Det-A	3	7	.300	17	10	1	0	0	76	85	52	48	6	2	26	32	1.461	5.68	84	4.35	.281	8	.267	-7	2	-0.6
1946	Det-A	14	11	.560	28	26	16	3	2	207	184	78	71	14	0	66	138	1.208	3.09	118	2.89	.236	28	.315	16	19	2.5
1947	Det-A	18	10	.643	33	25	18	3	2	219^{2}	211	84	74	14	2	61	113	1.238	3.03	124	3.13	.251	32	.302	23	22	3.5
1948	Det-A	13	11	.542	33	28	15	0	0	221	223	119	106	32	1	48	92	1.226	4.32	101	3.64	.258	23	.205	6	14	1.1
1949	Det-A	15	7	.682	33	21	9	4	1	188^{2}	167	70	62	18	1	52	54	1.161	2.96	141	2.96	.237	18	.247	27	19	3.1
1950	Det-A	17	8	.680	39	26	10	1	0	231^{2}	269	119	102	18	5	48	71	1.368	3.96	118	4.12	.290	31	.326	17	21	2.6
1951	Det-A★	10	10	.500	31	20	9	2	2	188^{1}	204	84	77	12	2	27	53	1.227	3.68	113	3.30	.275	16	.188	12	14	1.0
1952	Det-A	2	1	.667	12	1	0	0	0	37^{1}	40	16	14	4	1	9	12	1.313	3.38	113	3.99	.276	1	.056	3	2	0.2
1953	Det-A	0	0	....	3	0	0	0	0	9^{2}	9	3	3	0	0	0	4	.931	2.79	146	1.72	.243	1	.167	2	1	0.2
Total	10	95	71	.572	242	169	81	13	7	1464	1487	681	606	127	14	388	591	1.281	3.73	114	3.54	.262	171	.263	96	118	13.6

• HUTCHINSON, Ira Ira Kendall Hutchinson b: 8/31/1910, Chicago, IL d: 8/21/1973, Chicago, IL BR/TR, 5'10.5", 180 lbs. Deb: 9/24/1933

YEAR	TM-L	W	L	PCT	G	GS	CG	SH	SV	IP	H	R	ER	HR	HB	BB	SO	RAT	ERA	ERA+	CERA	OAV	BH	AVG	PR+	WS	TPW
1933	Chi-A	0	0	....	1	1	0	0	0	4	7	6	6	1	0	3	2	2.500	13.50	31	11.39	.368	1	.500	-4	0	-0.4
1937	Bos-N	4	6	.400	31	8	1	0	0	91^{2}	99	44	38	4	1	35	29	1.462	3.73	96	4.06	.286	3	.115	-4	4	-0.5
1938	Bos-N	9	8	.529	36	12	4	1	4	151	150	58	46	3	4	61	38	1.397	2.74	125	3.46	.258	9	.173	11	12	1.0
1939	Bro-N	5	2	.714	41	1	0	0	1	105^{2}	103	54	51	9	1	51	46	1.457	4.34	93	4.09	.265	1	.037	-3	5	-0.7
1940	StL-N	4	2	.667	20	2	1	0	1	63^{1}	68	27	22	3	0	19	19	1.374	3.13	128	3.60	.271	4	.222	7	5	0.7
1941	StL-N	1	5	.167	29	0	0	0	5	46^{2}	32	23	20	3	2	19	19	1.093	3.86	98	2.37	.198	2	.250	-1	4	-0.1
1944	Bos-N	9	7	.563	40	8	1	1	1	119^{2}	136	59	56	8	3	53	22	1.579	4.21	91	4.85	.296	4	.138	-6	6	-0.7
1945	Bos-N	2	3	.400	11	0	0	0	1	28^{2}	33	18	16	2	1	8	4	1.430	5.02	76	4.14	.277	0	.000	-4	1	-0.5
Total	8	34	33	.507	209	32	7	2	13	610^{2}	628	289	255	33	12	249	179	1.436	3.76	100	3.95	.270	24	.140	-4	37	-1.1

• HUTCHISON, Bill William Forrest "Wild Bill" Hutchison b: 12/17/1859, New Haven, CT d: 3/19/1926, Kansas City, MO BR/TR, 5'9", 175 lbs. Deb: 6/10/1884

YEAR	TM-L	W	L	PCT	G	GS	CG	SH	SV	IP	H	R	ER	HR	HB	BB	SO	RAT	ERA	ERA+	CERA	OAV	BH	AVG	PR+	WS	TPW
1884	KC-U	1	1	.500	2	2	2	0	0	17	14	11	5	0	....	1	5	.882	2.65	105	....	.209	2	.250	0	0	0.0
1889	Chi-N	16	17	.485	37	36	33	3	0	318	306	206	125	11	8	117	136	1.330	3.54	118	....	.245	21	.158	20	17	1.3
1890	Chi-N	**42**	25	.627	**71**	**66**	**65**	5	**2**	**603**	505	315	181	20	13	199	289	1.167	2.70	135	....	.221	53	.203	48	**54**	4.1
1891	Chi-N	**44**	19	.698	**66**	**58**	**56**	4	1	**561**	508	283	175	26	7	178	261	1.223	2.81	119	....	.233	45	.185	22	**49**	2.0
1892	Chi-N	**36**	36	.500	**75**	**70**	**67**	5	1	**622**	571	316	191	11	13	190	**314**	1.223	2.76	120	2.75	.235	57	.217	46	45	4.5
1893	Chi-N	16	24	.400	44	40	38	2	0	348^{1}	420	266	184	9	13	156	80	1.654	4.75	97	4.90	.290	41	.253	-4	20	-0.3
1894	Chi-N	14	16	.467	37	34	28	0	0	279	374	257	187	9	18	140	60	1.842	6.03	93	6.06	.318	42	.309	-7	16	-0.1
1895	Chi-N	13	21	.382	38	35	30	2	0	291	371	218	153	13	13	129	85	1.718	4.73	107	5.47	.306	25	.198	12	19	0.5
1897	StL-N	1	4	.200	6	5	2	0	0	40	55	41	27	5	2	22	5	1.925	6.08	72	7.23	.324	5	.278	-6	1	-0.4
Total	9	183	163	.529	376	346	321	21	4	3079^{1}	3124	1913	1228	104	87	1132	1235	1.382	3.59	114	2.27	.255	291	.216	130	221	11.6

• HUTSON, Herb George Herbert Hutson b: 7/17/1949, Savannah, GA BR/TR, 6'2", 205 lbs. Deb: 4/10/1974

YEAR	TM-L	W	L	PCT	G	GS	CG	SH	SV	IP	H	R	ER	HR	HB	BB	SO	RAT	ERA	ERA+	CERA	OAV	BH	AVG	PR+	WS	TPW
1974	Chi-N	0	2	.000	20	2	0	0	0	28^{2}	24	15	11	3	1	15	22	1.360	3.45	110	3.68	.233	0	.000	3	1	0.2

• HUTTON, Mark Mark Steven Hutton b: 2/6/1970, South Adelaide, Australia BR/TR, 6'6", 240 lbs. Deb: 7/23/1993

YEAR	TM-L	W	L	PCT	G	GS	CG	SH	SV	IP	H	R	ER	HR	HB	BB	SO	RAT	ERA	ERA+	CERA	OAV	BH	AVG	PR+	WS	TPW
1993	NY-A	1	1	.500	7	4	0	0	0	22	24	17	14	2	1	17	12	1.864	5.73	72	6.34	.293	0	....	-4	0	-0.4
1994	NY-A	0	0	....	2	0	0	0	0	3^{2}	4	3	2	0	0	0	1	1.091	4.91	93	2.18	.250	0	....	-0	0	0.0
1996	NY-A	0	2	.000	12	2	0	0	0	30^{1}	32	19	17	3	1	18	25	1.648	5.04	98	5.18	.269	0	....	0	1	0.0
	Fla-N	5	1	.833	13	9	0	0	0	56^{1}	47	23	23	6	3	18	31	1.154	3.67	111	3.10	.222	6	.316	2	4	0.4
1997	Fla-N	3	1	.750	32	0	0	0	0	47^{2}	50	24	20	7	2	19	29	1.448	3.78	107	4.90	.286	0	....	1	3	0.1
	Col-N	0	1	.000	8	1	0	0	0	12^{2}	22	10	10	3	4	7	10	2.289	7.11	73	12.56	.407	0	.000	-3	0	-0.3
	Yr.	3	2	.600	40	1	0	0	0	60^{1}	72	34	30	10	6	26	39	1.624	4.48	97	6.51	.314	0	.000	-2	3	-0.2
1998	Cin-N	0	1	.000	10	2	0	0	0	17	24	14	14	2	1	17	3	2.412	7.41	58	10.12	.348	1	1.000	-6	0	-0.5
Total	5	9	7	.563	84	18	0	0	0	189^{2}	203	110	100	23	12	96	111	1.576	4.75	91	5.51	.279	7	.304	-10	8	-0.7

• HYDE, Dick Richard Elde Hyde b: 8/3/1928, Hindsboro, IL BR/TR, 5'11", 170 lbs. Deb: 4/23/1955

YEAR	TM-L	W	L	PCT	G	GS	CG	SH	SV	IP	H	R	ER	HR	HB	BB	SO	RAT	ERA	ERA+	CERA	OAV	BH	AVG	PR+	WS	TPW
1955	Was-A	0	0	....	3	0	0	0	0	2	2	1	1	0	0	1	1	1.500	4.50	85	2.79	.286	0	....	-0	0	0.0
1957	Was-A	4	3	.571	52	2	0	0	1	109^{1}	104	54	50	4	7	56	46	1.463	4.12	95	3.93	.261	3	.167	-0	5	0.0
1958	Was-A	10	3	.769	53	0	0	0	18	103	82	26	20	1	2	35	49	1.136	1.75	218	2.21	.220	0	.000	26	19	2.5
1959	Was-A	2	5	.286	37	0	0	0	4	54^{1}	56	34	30	5	2	27	29	1.528	4.97	79	4.53	.269	0	.000	-4	2	-0.5
1960	Was-A	0	1	.000	9	0	0	0	0	8^{2}	11	4	4	2	1	5	4	1.846	4.15	95	8.48	.355	0	....	-0	0	0.0
1961	Bal-A	1	2	.333	15	0	0	0	0	21	18	14	13	1	1	13	15	1.476	5.57	70	3.54	.228	1	1.000	-4	0	-0.3
Total	6	17	14	.548	169	2	0	0	23	298^{1}	273	133	118	13	13	137	144	1.374	3.56	109	3.54	.249	4	.093	17	26	1.6

• HYNES, Pat Patrick J. Hynes b: 3/12/1884, St. Louis, MO d: 3/12/1907, St. Louis, MO TL Deb: 9/27/1903 ♦

YEAR	TM-L	W	L	PCT	G	GS	CG	SH	SV	IP	H	R	ER	HR	HB	BB	SO	RAT	ERA	ERA+	CERA	OAV	BH	AVG	PR+	WS	TPW
1903	StL-N	0	1	.000	1	1	1	0	0	9	10	6	4	0	0	6	1	1.778	4.00	81	5.05	.294	0	.000	-1	0	-0.1
1904	StL-A	1	0	1.000	5	2	1	0	0	26	35	21	18	1	0	7	6	1.615	6.23	40	4.97	.322	60	.236	-10	1	-3.4
Total	2	1	1	.500	6	3	2	0	0	35	45	27	22	1	0	13	7	1.657	5.66	46	4.99	.316	60	.233	-11	1	-3.6

• IBURG, Ham Herman Edward Iburg b: 10/29/1877, San Francisco, CA d: 2/11/1945, San Francisco, CA BR/TR, 5'11", 165 lbs. Deb: 4/17/1902

YEAR	TM-L	W	L	PCT	G	GS	CG	SH	SV	IP	H	R	ER	HR	HB	BB	SO	RAT	ERA	ERA+	CERA	OAV	BH	AVG	PR+	WS	TPW
1902	Phi-N	11	18	.379	30	30	20	1	0	236	286	141	102	1	11	62	106	1.475	3.89	72	4.13	.299	12	.138	-22	8	-2.7

• IGNASIAK, Gary Gary Raymond Ignasiak b: 9/1/1949, Mount Clemens, MI BR/TL, 5'11", 185 lbs. Deb: 9/20/1973

YEAR	TM-L	W	L	PCT	G	GS	CG	SH	SV	IP	H	R	ER	HR	HB	BB	SO	RAT	ERA	ERA+	CERA	OAV	BH	AVG	PR+	WS	TPW
1973	Det-A	0	0	....	3	0	0	0	0	4^{2}	5	2	2	0	0	3	4	1.714	3.86	106	4.53	.278	0	....	0	0	0.0

• IGNASIAK, Mike Michael James Ignasiak b: 3/12/1966, Anchorville, MI BB/TR, 5'11", 175 lbs. Deb: 8/22/1991

YEAR	TM-L	W	L	PCT	G	GS	CG	SH	SV	IP	H	R	ER	HR	HB	BB	SO	RAT	ERA	ERA+	CERA	OAV	BH	AVG	PR+	WS	TPW
1991	Mil-A	2	1	.667	4	1	0	0	0	12^{2}	7	8	8	2	0	8	10	1.184	5.68	70	3.03	.163	0	....	-2	0	-0.2
1993	Mil-A	1	1	.500	27	0	0	0	0	37	32	17	15	2	2	21	28	1.432	3.65	116	3.78	.241	0	....	3	2	0.3
1994	Mil-A	3	1	.750	23	5	0	0	0	47^{2}	51	25	24	5	1	13	24	1.343	4.53	111	4.07	.276	0	....	1	3	0.1
1995	Mil-A	4	1	.800	25	0	0	0	0	39^{2}	51	27	26	5	2	23	26	1.866	5.90	84	7.00	.325	0	....	-5	2	-0.5
Total	4	10	4	.714	79	6	0	0	0	137	141	77	73	14	5	65	88	1.504	4.80	98	4.74	.272	0	....	-3	7	-0.3

• ILSLEY, Blaise Blaise Francis Ilsley b: 4/9/1964, Alpena, MI BL/TL, 6'1", 195 lbs. Deb: 4/4/1994

YEAR	TM-L	W	L	PCT	G	GS	CG	SH	SV	IP	H	R	ER	HR	HB	BB	SO	RAT	ERA	ERA+	CERA	OAV	BH	AVG	PR+	WS	TPW
1994	Chi-N	0	0	....	10	0	0	0	0	15	25	13	13	2	0	9	9	2.267	7.80	53	9.57	.385	0	.000	-6	0	-0.6

• IMLAY, Doc Harry Miller Imlay b: 1/12/1889, Allentown, NJ d: 10/7/1948, Bordentown, NJ BR/TR, 5'11", 168 lbs. Deb: 7/7/1913

YEAR	TM-L	W	L	PCT	G	GS	CG	SH	SV	IP	H	R	ER	HR	HB	BB	SO	RAT	ERA	ERA+	CERA	OAV	BH	AVG	PR+	WS	TPW
1913	Phi-N	0	0	....	9	0	0	0	0	13^{2}	19	13	11	1	0	7	7	1.902	7.24	46	6.78	.358	0	.000	-6	0	-0.7

YEAR	TM-L	W	L	PCT	G	GS	CG	SH	SV	IP	H	R	ER	HR	HB	BB	SO	RAT	ERA	ERA+	CERA	OAV	BH	AVG	PR+	WS	TPW
• INGERSOLL, Bob	Robert Randolph Ingersoll b: 1/8/1883, Rapid City, SD d: 1/13/1927, Minneapolis, MN BR/TR, 5'11.5", 175 lbs. Deb: 4/23/1914																										
1914	Cin-N	0	0	....	4	0	0	0	0	6	5	2	2	0	1	5	2	1.667	3.00	98	4.79	.250	1	1.000	-0	1	0.0
• INKS, Bert	Albert John Inks b: 1/27/1871, Ligonier, IN d: 10/3/1941, Ligonier, IN BL/TL, 6'3", 175 lbs. Deb: 9/2/1891																										
1891	Bro-N	3	10	.231	13	13	11	1	0	96^1	99	70	43	2	6	43	47	1.474	4.02	82	....	.256	10	.286	-5	4	-0.3
1892	Bro-N	4	2	.667	9	8	4	1	0	58	48	34	25	0	4	33	25	1.397	3.88	81	3.16	.216	10	.400	-5	4	-0.1
	Was-N	1	2	.333	3	3	3	0	0	21	29	27	12	0	2	10	11	1.857	5.14	63	6.04	.315	3	.300	-4	0	-0.3
	Yr.	5	4	.556	12	11	7	1	0	79	77	61	37	0	6	43	36	1.519	4.22	76	3.92	.245	13	.371	-9	4	-0.5
1894	Bal-N	9	4	.692	22	14	10	0	1	133	181	108	82	4	11	54	30	1.767	5.55	98	5.87	.321	18	.316	-5	9	-0.3
	Lou-N	2	6	.250	8	8	8	0	0	59^2	87	70	43	2	1	34	8	2.028	6.49	78	6.88	.336	12	.444	-9	2	-0.5
	Yr.	11	10	.524	30	22	18	0	1	192^2	268	178	125	6	12	88	38	1.848	5.84	91	6.18	.326	30	.357	-15	11	-0.7
1895	Lou-N	7	20	.259	28	27	21	0	0	205^1	294	197	146	3	15	78	42	1.812	6.40	72	6.03	.331	21	.250	-31	4	-2.5
1896	Phi-N	0	1	.000	3	1	0	0	0	10^1	21	13	9	1	1	5	2	2.516	7.84	55	11.40	.415	1	.200	-4	0	-0.4
	Cin-N	1	1	.500	3	3	2	0	0	20	21	13	10	0	1	9	2	1.500	4.50	102	3.87	.268	0	.000	-0	1	-0.1
	Yr.	1	2	.333	6	4	2	0	0	30^1	42	26	19	1	2	14	4	1.846	5.64	79	6.44	.326	1	.083	-4	1	-0.4
Total	**5**	**27**	**46**	**.370**	**89**	**77**	**59**	**2**	**1**	**603^2**	**780**	**532**	**370**	**12**	**41**	**266**	**167**	**1.733**	**5.52**	**80**	**4.86**	**.307**	**75**	**.300**	**-65**	**24**	**-4.4**
• INNIS, Jeff	Jeffrey David Innis b: 7/5/1962, Decatur, IL BR/TR, 6'1", 170 lbs. Deb: 5/16/1987																										
1987	NY-N	0	1	.000	17	1	0	0	0	25^2	29	9	9	5	1	4	28	1.286	3.16	120	4.56	.279	0	.000	2	2	0.2
1988	NY-N	1	1	.500	12	0	0	0	0	19	19	6	4	0	0	2	14	1.105	1.89	170	2.15	.250	0	....	3	2	0.3
1989	NY-N	0	1	.000	29	0	0	0	0	39^2	38	16	14	2	1	8	16	1.160	3.18	103	2.93	.255	0	.000	1	2	0.1
1990	NY-N	1	3	.250	18	0	0	0	1	26^1	19	9	7	4	1	10	12	1.101	2.39	156	2.94	.209	0	....	4	2	0.4
1991	NY-N	0	2	.000	69	0	0	0	0	84^2	66	30	25	2	0	23	47	1.051	2.66	137	1.92	.219	0	.000	11	7	1.1
1992	NY-N	6	9	.400	76	0	0	0	1	88	85	32	28	4	6	36	39	1.375	2.86	121	3.83	.266	0	.000	7	7	0.7
1993	NY-N	2	3	.400	67	0	0	0	3	76^2	81	39	35	5	6	38	36	1.552	4.11	98	4.57	.278	0	....	-1	4	-0.1
Total	**7**	**10**	**20**	**.333**	**288**	**1**	**0**	**0**	**5**	**360**	**337**	**141**	**122**	**22**	**15**	**121**	**192**	**1.272**	**3.05**	**120**	**3.34**	**.253**	**0**	**.000**	**27**	**26**	**2.7**
• IOTT, Hooks	Clarence Eugene Iott b: 12/3/1919, Mountain Grove, MO d: 4/17/1980, St. Petersburg, FL BB/TL, 6'2", 200 lbs. Deb: 9/6/1941																										
1941	StL-A	0	0	....	2	0	0	0	0	2	2	2	2	0	0	1	1	1.500	9.00	48	3.50	.250	0	....	-1	0	-0.1
1947	StL-A	0	1	.000	4	0	0	0	0	8^1	15	16	15	4	0	14	6	3.480	16.20	24	18.68	.375	0	.000	-11	0	-1.2
	NY-N	3	8	.273	20	9	2	1	0	71^1	67	50	47	3	1	52	46	1.668	5.93	69	4.39	.251	3	.143	-15	1	-1.4
Total	**2**	**3**	**9**	**.250**	**26**	**9**	**2**	**1**	**0**	**81^2**	**84**	**68**	**64**	**7**	**1**	**67**	**53**	**1.849**	**7.05**	**57**	**5.83**	**.267**	**3**	**.130**	**-27**	**1**	**-2.7**
• IRABU, Hideki	Hideki Irabu b: 5/5/1969, Hyogo, Japan BR/TR, 6'4", 240 lbs. Deb: 7/10/1997																										
1997	NY-A	5	4	.556	13	9	0	0	0	53^1	69	47	42	15	1	20	56	1.669	7.09	63	7.19	.311	0	.000	-15	0	-1.4
1998	NY-A	13	9	.591	29	28	2	1	0	173	148	78	78	27	9	76	126	1.295	4.06	108	4.05	.233	1	.250	3	12	0.3
1999*	NY-A	11	7	.611	32	27	2	1	0	169^1	180	98	91	26	6	46	133	1.335	4.84	98	4.38	.267	0	.000	-1	8	-0.1
2000	Mon-N	2	5	.286	11	11	0	0	0	54^2	77	45	44	9	1	14	42	1.665	7.24	66	6.58	.339	2	.125	-14	0	-1.4
2001	Mon-N	0	2	.000	3	3	0	0	0	16^2	22	9	9	3	0	3	18	1.500	4.86	92	5.57	.314	0	.000	-0	1	-0.1
2002	Tex-A	3	8	.273	38	2	0	0	16	47	51	30	30	11	1	16	30	1.426	5.74	82	5.33	.279	0	....	-5	3	-0.5
Total	**6**	**34**	**35**	**.493**	**126**	**80**	**4**	**2**	**16**	**514**	**547**	**307**	**294**	**91**	**18**	**175**	**405**	**1.405**	**5.15**	**89**	**4.92**	**.272**	**3**	**.107**	**-32**	**24**	**-3.2**
• IRVINE, Daryl	Daryl Keith Irvine b: 11/15/1964, Harrisonburg, VA BR/TR, 6'3", 195 lbs. Deb: 4/28/1990																										
1990	Bos-A	1	1	.500	11	0	0	0	0	17^1	15	10	9	0	0	10	9	1.442	4.67	87	3.02	.246	0	....	-1	1	-0.1
1991	Bos-A	0	0	....	9	0	0	0	0	18	25	13	12	2	2	9	8	1.889	6.00	72	7.12	.321	0	....	-3	0	-0.3
1992	Bos-A	3	4	.429	21	0	0	0	0	28	31	20	19	1	2	14	10	1.607	6.11	69	4.74	.287	0	....	-6	0	-0.6
Total	**3**	**4**	**5**	**.444**	**41**	**0**	**0**	**0**	**0**	**63^1**	**71**	**43**	**40**	**3**	**4**	**33**	**27**	**1.642**	**5.68**	**74**	**4.95**	**.287**	**0**	**....**	**-10**	**1**	**-1.0**
• IRWIN, Bill	William Franklin "Phil" Irwin b: 9/16/1859, Neville, OH d: 8/7/1933, Fort Thomas, KY BR/TR, 6', 195 lbs. Deb: 8/30/1886																										
1886	Cin-a	0	2	.000	2	2	2	0	0	17	18	19	11	2	0	8	6	1.529	5.82	60	....	.259	0	.000	-4	0	-0.4
• ISHII, Kazuhisa	Kazuhisa Ishii b: 9/9/1973, Chiba, Japan BL/TL, 6', 190 lbs. Deb: 4/6/2002																										
2002	LA-N	14	10	.583	28	28	0	0	0	154	137	82	73	20	4	106	143	1.578	4.27	89	4.90	.240	5	.100	-9	6	-1.1
2003	LA-N	9	7	.563	27	27	0	0	0	147	129	72	63	16	6	101	140	1.565	3.86	104	4.75	.238	1	.029	0	7	-0.2
Total	**2**	**23**	**17**	**.575**	**55**	**55**	**0**	**0**	**0**	**301**	**266**	**154**	**136**	**36**	**10**	**207**	**283**	**1.571**	**4.07**	**96**	**4.82**	**.239**	**6**	**.071**	**-8**	**13**	**-1.3**
• ISRINGHAUSEN, Jason	Jason Derik Isringhausen b: 9/7/1972, Brighton, IL BR/TR, 6'3", 195 lbs. Deb: 7/17/1995																										
1995	NY-N	9	2	.818	14	14	1	0	0	93	88	29	29	6	2	31	55	1.280	2.81	144	3.40	.254	4	.148	13	8	1.3
1996	NY-N	6	14	.300	27	27	2	1	0	171^2	190	103	91	13	8	73	114	1.532	4.77	84	4.75	.284	13	.255	-16	6	-1.0
1997	NY-N	2	2	.500	6	6	0	0	0	29^2	40	27	25	3	1	22	25	2.090	7.58	53	7.99	.336	1	.143	-12	0	-1.2
1999	NY-N	1	3	.250	13	5	0	0	1	39^1	43	29	28	7	2	22	31	1.653	6.41	68	6.07	.279	1	.083	-9	0	-0.9
	Oak-A	0	1	.000	20	0	0	0	8	25^1	21	6	6	2	1	12	20	1.303	2.13	218	3.33	.223	0	....	7	4	0.7
2000*	Oak-A★	6	4	.600	66	0	0	0	33	69	67	34	29	6	3	32	57	1.435	3.78	125	4.09	.252	0	....	8	10	0.8
2001*	Oak-A	4	3	.571	65	0	0	0	34	71^1	54	24	21	5	0	23	74	1.079	2.65	167	2.18	.203	0	....	14	14	1.3
2002*	StL-N	3	2	.600	60	0	0	0	32	65^1	46	22	18	0	1	18	68	.980	2.48	159	1.61	.199	0	....	10	13	1.0
2003	StL-N	0	1	.000	40	0	0	0	22	42	31	14	11	2	0	18	41	1.167	2.36	172	2.40	.200	1	.500	8	7	0.9
Total	**8**	**31**	**32**	**.492**	**311**	**52**	**3**	**1**	**130**	**606^2**	**580**	**288**	**258**	**44**	**18**	**251**	**485**	**1.370**	**3.83**	**109**	**3.85**	**.252**	**20**	**.202**	**22**	**62**	**2.7**
• IZQUIERDO, Hansel	Hansel Izquierdo b: 1/2/1977, Havana, Cuba BR/TR, 6'2", 205 lbs. Deb: 4/21/2002																										
2002	Fla-N	2	0	1.000	20	2	0	0	0	29^2	33	17	15	2	5	21	20	1.820	4.55	87	6.23	.289	0	.000	-2	1	-0.2
• JACKSON, Al	Alvin Neill Jackson b: 12/26/1935, Waco, TX BL/TL, 5'10", 169 lbs. Deb: 6/1/1959 C																										
1959	Pit-N	0	0	....	8	3	0	0	0	18	30	14	13	1	0	8	13	2.111	6.50	60	8.21	.405	1	.200	-5	0	-0.5
1961	Pit-N	1	0	1.000	3	2	1	0	0	23^2	20	10	9	2	0	4	15	1.014	3.42	116	2.34	.233	0	.000	1	2	0.1
1962	NY-N	8	20	.286	36	33	12	4	0	231^1	244	132	113	16	5	78	118	1.392	4.40	95	3.97	.273	5	.068	-1	9	-0.5
1963	NY-N	13	17	.433	37	34	11	0	1	227	237	128	100	25	12	84	142	1.414	3.96	88	4.44	.267	16	.203	-10	9	-0.9
1964	NY-N	11	16	.407	40	31	11	3	1	213^1	229	115	101	18	4	60	112	1.355	4.26	84	3.95	.272	11	.153	-18	7	-1.6
1965	NY-N	8	20	.286	37	31	7	3	1	205^1	217	111	99	17	8	61	120	1.354	4.34	81	3.98	.271	7	.117	-18	6	-2.0
1966	StL-N	13	15	.464	36	30	11	3	0	232^2	222	82	65	18	3	45	90	1.148	2.51	143	2.88	.250	13	.176	26	19	3.0
1967	StL-N	9	4	.692	38	11	1	1	1	107	117	61	47	7	1	29	43	1.364	3.95	82	3.79	.279	8	.258	-9	4	-0.7
1968	NY-N	3	7	.300	25	9	0	0	3	92^2	88	42	38	5	2	17	59	1.133	3.69	82	2.70	.249	7	.250	-8	3	-0.7
1969	NY-N	0	0	....	9	0	0	0	0	11	18	13	13	1	1	4	10	2.000	10.64	34	7.66	.353	0	.000	-9	0	-0.9
	Cin-N	1	0	1.000	33	0	0	0	3	27^1	27	17	16	5	3	17	16	1.610	5.27	71	5.81	.260	1	.250	-5	1	-0.5
	Yr.	1	0	1.000	42	0	0	0	3	38^1	45	30	29	6	4	21	26	1.722	6.81	55	6.34	.290	1	.200	-13	1	-1.4
Total	**10**	**67**	**99**	**.404**	**302**	**184**	**54**	**14**	**10**	**1389^1**	**1449**	**725**	**614**	**115**	**39**	**407**	**738**	**1.336**	**3.98**	**90**	**3.86**	**.268**	**69**	**.159**	**-55**	**60**	**-5.4**
• JACKSON, Charlie	Charles Bernard Jackson b: 8/4/1876, Versailles, OH d: 11/23/1957, Scottsbluff, NE TR Deb: 8/11/1905																										
1905	Det-A	0	2	.000	2	2	1	0	0	11	14	12	7	1	0	7	3	1.909	5.73	48	6.43	.312	1	.250	-4	0	-0.4
• JACKSON, Danny	Danny Lynn Jackson b: 1/5/1962, San Antonio, TX BR/TL, 6', 205 lbs. Deb: 9/11/1983																										
1983	KC-A	1	1	.500	4	3	0	0	0	19	26	12	11	1	0	6	9	1.684	5.21	78	5.51	.325	0	....	-2	0	-0.2
1984	KC-A	2	6	.250	15	11	1	0	0	76	84	41	36	4	5	35	40	1.566	4.26	95	4.91	.285	0	....	-3	3	-0.3
1985*	KC-A	14	12	.538	32	32	4	3	0	208	209	94	79	7	6	76	114	1.370	3.42	122	3.60	.261	0	....	20	16	1.9
1986	KC-A	11	12	.478	32	27	4	1	1	185^2	177	83	66	13	4	79	115	1.379	3.20	133	3.84	.256	0	....	24	14	2.4
1987	KC-A	9	18	.333	36	34	11	2	0	224	219	115	100	11	7	109	152	1.464	4.02	113	4.05	.258	0	....	16	13	1.6
1988	Cin-N★	**23**	8	.742	35	35	**15**	6	0	260^2	206	86	79	13	2	71	161	1.063	2.73	131	2.23	.218	13	.144	20	22	2.1
1989	Cin-N	6	11	.353	20	20	1	0	0	115^2	122	78	72	10	1	57	70	1.548	5.60	64	4.55	.271	8	.222	-24	0	-2.5
1990*	Cin-N	6	6	.500	22	21	0	0	0	117^1	119	54	47	11	2	40	76	1.355	3.61	109	3.92	.266	2	.054	2	6	0.0
1991	Chi-N	1	5	.167	17	14	0	0	0	70^2	89	59	53	8	1	48	31	1.939	6.75	57	6.74	.309	2	.087	-21	0	-2.4

YEAR TM-L	W	L	PCT	G	GS	CG	SH	SV	IP	H	R	ER	HR	HB	BB	SO	RAT	ERA	ERA+	CERA	OAV	BH	AVG	PR+	WS	TPW
1992 Chi-N	4	9	.308	19	19	0	0	0	113	117	59	53	5	3	48	51	1.460	4.22	85	3.97	.270	3	.083	-8	2	-1.1
*Pit-N	4	4	.500	15	15	0	0	0	88^1	94	40	33	1	1	29	46	1.392	3.36	102	3.49	.276	2	.083	0	4	-0.1
Yr.	8	13	.381	34	34	0	0	0	201^1	211	99	86	6	4	77	97	1.430	3.84	92	3.76	.272	5	.083	-8	6	-1.2
1993* Phi-N	12	11	.522	32	32	2	1	0	210^1	214	105	88	12	4	80	120	1.398	3.77	105	3.80	.263	5	.077	6	11	0.4
1994 Phi-N★	14	6	.700	25	25	4	1	0	179^1	183	71	65	13	2	46	129	1.277	3.26	132	3.47	.266	9	.158	22	14	2.2
1995 StL-N	2	12	.143	19	19	2	1	0	100^2	120	82	66	10	6	48	52	1.669	5.90	71	5.71	.303	5	.161	-20	0	-2.0
1996* StL-N	1	1	.500	13	4	0	0	0	36^1	33	18	18	3	1	16	27	1.349	4.46	94	3.71	.243	3	.333	-2	2	-0.1
1997 StL-N	1	2	.333	4	4	0	0	0	18^2	26	17	16	3	2	8	13	1.821	7.71	54	7.61	.347	1	.143	-7	0	-0.7
SD-N	1	7	.125	13	9	0	0	0	49	72	47	41	8	3	20	19	1.878	7.53	51	7.81	.353	1	.077	-19	0	-2.0
Yr.	2	9	.182	17	13	0	0	0	67^2	98	64	57	11	5	28	32	1.862	7.58	52	7.75	.351	2	.100	-27	0	-2.8
Total 15	112	131	.461	353	324	44	15	1	2072^2	2110	1061	923	133	50	816	1225	1.412	4.01	99	4.01	.266	54	.126	2	107	-0.8

• JACKSON, Darrell
Darrell Preston Jackson b: 4/3/1956, Los Angeles, CA BB/TL, 5'10", 150 lbs. Deb: 6/16/1978

YEAR TM-L	W	L	PCT	G	GS	CG	SH	SV	IP	H	R	ER	HR	HB	BB	SO	RAT	ERA	ERA+	CERA	OAV	BH	AVG	PR+	WS	TPW
1978 Min-A	4	6	.400	19	15	1	1	0	92^1	89	53	46	9	2	48	54	1.484	4.48	85	4.43	.256	0	....	-7	2	-0.7
1979 Min-A	4	4	.500	24	8	1	0	0	69^1	89	36	33	5	1	26	43	1.659	4.28	102	5.58	.319	0	....	1	4	0.1
1980 Min-A	9	9	.500	32	25	1	0	1	172	161	81	74	15	2	69	90	1.337	3.87	112	3.72	.250	0	....	8	12	0.8
1981 Min-A	3	3	.500	14	5	0	0	0	32^2	35	16	16	1	1	19	26	1.653	4.41	90	4.83	.282	0	....	-1	2	-0.1
1982 Min-A	0	5	.000	13	7	0	0	0	44^2	51	33	31	6	1	24	16	1.679	6.25	68	5.80	.297	0	....	-10	0	-1.0
Total 5	20	27	.426	102	60	3	1	1	411	425	219	200	36	7	186	229	1.487	4.38	95	4.51	.272	0	....	-10	20	-1.0

• JACKSON, Edwin
Edwin Jackson b: 9/9/1983, Neu-Ulm, West Germany BR/TR, 6'3", 190 lbs. Deb: 9/9/2003

YEAR TM-L	W	L	PCT	G	GS	CG	SH	SV	IP	H	R	ER	HR	HB	BB	SO	RAT	ERA	ERA+	CERA	OAV	BH	AVG	PR+	WS	TPW
2003 LA-N	2	1	.667	4	3	0	0	0	22	17	6	6	2	1	11	19	1.273	2.45	164	3.36	.221	0	.000	3	2	0.3

• JACKSON, Grant
Grant Dwight "Buck" Jackson b: 9/28/1942, Fostoria, OH BB/TL, 6', 190 lbs. Deb: 9/3/1965 C

YEAR TM-L	W	L	PCT	G	GS	CG	SH	SV	IP	H	R	ER	HR	HB	BB	SO	RAT	ERA	ERA+	CERA	OAV	BH	AVG	PR+	WS	TPW
1965 Phi-N	1	1	.500	6	2	0	0	0	13^2	17	11	11	4	0	5	15	1.610	7.24	48	6.94	.304	0	.000	-6	0	-0.7
1966 Phi-N	0	0	....	2	0	0	0	0	1^2	2	1	1	0	0	3	0	3.000	5.40	67	11.18	.333	0	....	-0	0	0.0
1967 Phi-N	2	3	.400	43	4	0	0	1	84^1	86	40	36	3	2	43	83	1.530	3.84	89	4.08	.267	2	.133	-4	3	-0.4
1968 Phi-N	1	6	.143	33	6	1	0	1	61	59	28	20	4	0	20	49	1.295	2.95	102	3.20	.248	3	.300	1	3	0.2
1969 Phi-N★	14	18	.438	38	35	13	4	1	253	237	114	94	16	5	92	180	1.300	3.34	106	3.39	.249	12	.140	6	14	0.5
1970 Phi-N	5	15	.250	32	23	1	0	0	149^2	170	94	88	17	1	61	104	1.543	5.29	75	4.95	.288	4	.091	-20	2	-2.2
1971* Bal-A	4	3	.571	29	9	0	0	0	77^2	72	31	27	7	2	20	51	1.185	3.13	107	3.11	.249	2	.091	1	4	0.1
1972 Bal-A	1	1	.500	32	0	0	0	8	41	33	14	12	1	0	9	34	1.024	2.63	117	1.98	.217	0	.000	1	4	0.1
1973* Bal-A	8	0	1.000	45	0	0	0	9	80^1	54	18	17	5	0	24	47	.971	1.90	196	1.84	.198	0	....	13	12	1.3
1974* Bal-A	6	4	.600	49	0	0	0	12	66^2	48	19	19	7	1	22	56	1.050	2.57	135	2.31	.198	0	....	6	10	0.6
1975 Bal-A	4	3	.571	41	0	0	0	7	48^1	42	18	18	3	1	21	39	1.303	3.35	105	3.17	.241	0	....	-1	5	-0.1
1976 Bal-A	1	1	.500	13	0	0	0	3	19^1	19	11	11	1	2	9	14	1.448	5.12	64	4.27	.268	0	....	-4	1	-0.4
*NY-A	6	0	1.000	21	2	1	1	1	58^2	38	11	11	1	1	16	25	.920	1.69	202	1.52	.186	0	....	9	7	1.0
Yr.	7	1	.875	34	2	1	1	4	78	57	22	22	2	3	25	39	1.051	2.54	132	2.20	.207	0	....	5	8	0.5
1977 Pit-N	5	3	.625	49	2	0	0	4	91	81	44	39	11	1	39	41	1.319	3.86	103	3.64	.240	6	.333	-0	6	0.2
1978 Pit-N	7	5	.583	60	0	0	0	5	77^1	89	32	28	5	1	32	45	1.565	3.26	114	4.57	.298	3	.250	5	6	0.6
1979* Pit-N	8	5	.615	72	0	0	0	14	82	67	32	27	9	2	35	39	1.244	2.96	131	3.30	.230	0	.000	7	10	0.7
1980 Pit-N	8	4	.667	61	0	0	0	9	71	71	24	23	4	0	20	31	1.282	2.92	125	3.38	.275	0	.000	5	8	0.4
1981 Pit-N	1	2	.333	35	0	0	0	4	32^1	30	10	9	1	0	10	17	1.237	2.51	144	2.73	.248	0	.000	4	3	0.4
Mon-N	1	0	1.000	10	0	0	0	0	10^2	14	9	9	2	0	9	4	2.156	7.59	46	8.22	.333	0	....	-5	0	-0.5
Yr.	2	2	.500	45	0	0	0	4	43	44	19	18	3	0	19	21	1.465	3.77	94	4.09	.270	0	.000	-1	3	-0.1
1982 KC-A	3	1	.750	20	0	0	0	0	38^1	42	27	22	7	2	21	15	1.643	5.17	79	5.77	.271	0	....	-5	1	-0.5
Pit-N	0	0	....	1	0	0	0	0	0^2	1	1	1	1	0	0	0	1.500	13.50	27	15.46	.333	0	....	-1	0	-0.1
Total 18	86	75	.534	692	83	16	5	79	1358^2	1272	589	523	109	21	511	889	1.312	3.46	105	3.54	.251	32	.136	13	99	1.2

• JACKSON, John
John Lewis Jackson b: 7/15/1909, Philadelphia, PA d: 10/22/1956, Somers Point, NJ BR/TR, 6'2", 180 lbs. Deb: 6/20/1933

YEAR TM-L	W	L	PCT	G	GS	CG	SH	SV	IP	H	R	ER	HR	HB	BB	SO	RAT	ERA	ERA+	CERA	OAV	BH	AVG	PR+	WS	TPW
1933 Phi-N	2	2	.500	10	7	1	0	0	54	74	42	36	3	5	35	11	2.019	6.00	64	7.20	.329	3	.143	-13	0	-1.5

• JACKSON, Larry
Lawrence Curtis Jackson b: 6/2/1931, Nampa, ID d: 8/28/1990, Boise, ID BR/TR, 6'1.5", 190 lbs. Deb: 4/17/1955

YEAR TM-L	W	L	PCT	G	GS	CG	SH	SV	IP	H	R	ER	HR	HB	BB	SO	RAT	ERA	ERA+	CERA	OAV	BH	AVG	PR+	WS	TPW
1955 StL-N	9	14	.391	37	25	4	1	2	177^1	189	93	85	25	9	72	88	1.472	4.31	94	4.95	.277	3	.053	-3	9	-0.9
1956 StL-N	2	2	.500	51	1	0	0	9	85^1	75	44	39	5	1	45	50	1.406	4.11	92	3.53	.240	1	.091	-3	5	-0.3
1957 StL-N★	15	9	.625	41	22	6	2	1	210^1	196	84	81	21	4	57	96	1.203	3.47	114	3.27	.248	13	.181	12	16	1.2
1958 StL-N★	13	13	.500	49	23	11	1	8	198	211	93	81	21	10	51	124	1.323	3.68	112	4.04	.272	9	.150	10	16	0.7
1959 StL-N	14	13	.519	40	37	12	3	0	256	271	103	94	13	4	64	145	1.309	3.30	128	3.53	.270	9	.113	29	21	2.6
1960 StL-N★	18	13	.581	43	**38**	14	3	0	**282**	277	123	109	22	3	70	171	1.230	3.48	118	3.27	.257	20	.211	21	21	2.3
1961 StL-N	14	11	.560	33	28	12	3	0	211	203	99	88	20	4	56	113	1.227	3.75	117	3.35	.252	13	.176	14	15	1.5
1962 StL-N	16	11	.593	36	35	11	2	0	252^1	267	121	105	25	6	64	112	1.312	3.75	114	3.86	.269	15	.169	12	16	1.5
1963 Chi-N★	14	18	.438	37	37	13	4	0	275	256	102	78	11	6	54	153	1.127	2.55	137	2.61	.245	17	.195	25	22	3.0
1964 Chi-N	**24**	11	.686	40	38	19	3	0	297^2	265	114	104	17	1	58	148	1.085	3.14	118	2.43	.235	20	.175	22	25	2.3
1965 Chi-N	14	21	.400	39	39	12	4	0	257^1	268	126	110	28	5	57	131	1.263	3.85	96	3.70	.267	11	.128	-2	11	-0.1
1966 Chi-N	0	2	.000	3	2	0	0	0	8	14	13	12	3	0	4	5	2.250	13.50	27	11.31	.368	0	.000	-9	0	-0.9
Phi-N	15	13	.536	35	33	12	5	0	247	243	93	82	22	5	58	107	1.219	2.99	120	3.37	.259	13	.146	16	19	1.7
Yr.	15	15	.500	38	35	12	**5**	0	255	257	106	94	25	5	62	112	1.251	3.32	109	3.62	.264	13	.141	8	19	0.8
1967 Phi-N	13	15	.464	40	37	11	4	0	261^2	242	111	90	17	6	54	139	1.131	3.10	110	2.71	.241	14	.161	9	14	1.0
1968 Phi-N	13	17	.433	34	34	12	2	0	243^2	229	86	75	9	4	60	127	1.186	2.77	109	2.75	.248	12	.141	9	15	0.9
Total 14	194	183	.515	558	429	149	37	20	3262^2	3206	1405	1233	259	68	824	1709	1.235	3.40	112	3.33	.256	170	.156	162	225	16.6

• JACKSON, Mike
Michael Ray Jackson b: 12/22/1964, Houston, TX BR/TR, 6'1", 200 lbs. Deb: 8/11/1986

YEAR TM-L	W	L	PCT	G	GS	CG	SH	SV	IP	H	R	ER	HR	HB	BB	SO	RAT	ERA	ERA+	CERA	OAV	BH	AVG	PR+	WS	TPW
1986 Phi-N	0	0	....	9	0	0	0	0	13^1	12	5	5	2	2	4	3	1.200	3.38	114	4.19	.250	0	....	1	1	0.1
1987 Phi-N	3	10	.231	55	7	0	0	1	109^1	88	55	51	16	3	56	93	1.317	4.20	101	3.76	.219	2	.118	-1	5	-0.1
1988 Sea-A	6	5	.545	62	0	0	0	4	99^1	74	37	29	10	2	43	76	1.178	2.63	158	2.76	.209	0	....	17	10	1.7
1989 Sea-A	4	6	.400	65	0	0	0	7	99^1	81	43	35	8	6	54	94	1.359	3.17	127	3.60	.223	0	....	9	8	0.9
1990 Sea-A	5	7	.417	63	0	0	0	3	77^1	64	42	39	8	2	44	69	1.397	4.54	87	3.61	.229	0	....	-5	4	-0.5
1991 Sea-A	7	7	.500	72	0	0	0	14	88^2	64	35	32	5	6	34	74	1.105	3.25	127	2.35	.201	0	....	7	11	0.7
1992 SF-N	6	6	.500	67	0	0	0	2	82	76	35	34	7	4	33	80	1.329	3.73	89	3.64	.252	0	.000	-6	5	-0.6
1993 SF-N	6	6	.500	**81**	0	0	0	1	77^1	58	28	26	7	3	24	70	1.060	3.03	129	2.36	.204	2	.667	5	9	0.7
1994 SF-N	3	2	.600	36	0	0	0	4	42^1	23	8	7	4	2	11	51	.803	1.49	269	1.55	.164	0	.000	10	8	1.0
1995* Cin-N	6	1	.857	40	0	0	0	2	49	38	13	13	5	1	19	41	1.163	2.39	172	2.92	.213	1	.250	8	7	0.8
1996 Sea-A	1	1	.500	73	0	0	0	6	72	61	32	29	11	6	24	70	1.181	3.63	137	3.59	.225	0	....	10	7	0.9
1997* Cle-A	2	5	.286	71	0	0	0	15	75	59	33	27	3	4	29	74	1.173	3.24	145	2.58	.215	0	....	13	11	1.2
1998* Cle-A	1	1	.500	69	0	0	0	40	64	43	11	11	4	4	13	55	.875	1.55	308	1.82	.195	0	....	23	16	2.2
1999* Cle-A	3	4	.429	72	0	0	0	39	68^2	60	32	31	11	2	26	55	1.252	4.06	124	3.76	.232	0	....	8	11	0.7
2001* Hou-N	5	3	.625	67	0	0	0	4	69	68	36	36	14	2	22	46	1.304	4.70	97	4.45	.260	0	.000	-1	6	-0.1
2002* Min-A	2	3	.400	58	0	0	0	0	55	59	20	20	5	4	13	29	1.309	3.27	137	4.05	.284	0	....	7	5	0.7
Total 16	60	67	.472	960	7	0	0	142	1141^2	928	465	425	120	53	449	980	1.206	3.35	126	3.18	.223	5	.179	107	124	10.4

• JACKSON, Mike
Michael Warren Jackson b: 3/27/1946, Paterson, NJ BL/TL, 6'3", 190 lbs. Deb: 5/10/1970

YEAR TM-L	W	L	PCT	G	GS	CG	SH	SV	IP	H	R	ER	HR	HB	BB	SO	RAT	ERA	ERA+	CERA	OAV	BH	AVG	PR+	WS	TPW
1970 Phi-N	1	1	.500	5	0	0	0	0	6^1	6	1	1	0	0	4	4	1.579	1.42	281	4.52	.286	1	1.000	2	1	0.2
1971 StL-N	0	0	....	1	0	0	0	0	0^2	1	0	0	0	0	1	0	3.000	0.00	....	10.76	.333	0	.000	0	0	0.0
1972 KC-A	1	2	.333	7	3	0	0	0	19^2	24	14	14	0	0	14	15	1.932	6.41	47	5.88	.320	0	.000	-7	0	-0.9
1973 KC-A	0	0	....	9	0	0	0	0	22^1	25	17	17	3	1	20	13	2.015	6.85	60	7.56	.301	0	....	-7	0	-0.7
Cle-A	0	0	....	1	0	0	0	0	0^2	1	0	0	0	0	0	1	1.500	0.00	....	4.47	.333	0	....	0	0	0.0
Yr.	0	0	....	10	0	0	0	0	23	26	17	17	3	1	20	14	2.000	6.65	62	7.47	.302	0	....	-6	0	-0.6
Total 4	2	3	.400	23	3	0	0	0	49^2	57	32	32	3	1	39	33	1.933	5.80	61	6.51	.308	1	.143	-11	1	-1.3

YEAR	TM-L	W	L	PCT	G	GS	CG	SH	SV	IP	H	R	ER	HR	HB	BB	SO	RAT	ERA	ERA+	CERA	OAV	BH	AVG	PR+	WS	TPW
• JACKSON, Roy Lee	Roy Lee Jackson b: 5/1/1954, Opelika, AL BR/TR, 6'2", 194 lbs. Deb: 9/13/1977
1977	NY-N	0	2	.000	4	4	0	0	0	24	25	16	16	2	3	15	13	1.667	6.00	62	5.32	.263	0	.000	-6	0	-0.7
1978	NY-N	0	0	....	4	2	0	0	0	12^2	21	13	13	2	2	6	6	2.132	9.24	38	10.53	.429	2	.667	-8	0	-0.8
1979	NY-N	1	0	1.000	8	0	0	0	0	16^1	11	4	4	1	1	5	10	.980	2.20	165	2.22	.200	1	1.000	2	2	0.3
1980	NY-N	1	7	.125	24	8	1	0	1	70^2	78	37	33	4	0	20	58	1.387	4.20	85	3.86	.287	3	.188	-5	1	-0.6
1981	Tor-A	1	2	.333	39	0	0	0	7	62	65	23	18	5	1	25	27	1.452	2.61	151	4.18	.275	0	....	10	6	1.0
1982	Tor-A	8	8	.500	48	2	0	0	6	97	77	37	33	7	2	31	71	1.113	3.06	146	2.53	.218	0	....	16	11	1.6
1983	Tor-A	8	3	.727	49	0	0	0	7	92	92	48	46	6	3	41	48	1.446	4.50	96	4.10	.267	0	....	-2	7	-0.2
1984	Tor-A	7	8	.467	54	0	0	0	10	86	73	40	34	12	1	31	58	1.209	3.56	115	3.36	.230	0	....	5	9	0.5
1985	SD-N	2	3	.400	22	2	0	0	2	40	32	13	12	4	1	13	28	1.125	2.70	131	2.79	.224	0	.000	3	4	0.3
1986	Min-A	0	1	.000	28	0	0	0	1	58^1	57	29	25	7	3	16	32	1.251	3.86	112	3.74	.256	0	....	4	4	0.3
Total	**10**	**28**	**34**	**.452**	**280**	**18**	**1**	**0**	**34**	**559**	**531**	**260**	**234**	**50**	**17**	**203**	**351**	**1.313**	**3.77**	**106**	**3.71**	**.254**	**6**	**.194**	**18**	**44**	**1.8**
• JACOBS, Art	Arthur Edward Jacobs b: 8/28/1902, Luckey, OH d: 6/8/1967, Inglewood, CA BL/TL, 5'10", 170 lbs. Deb: 6/18/1939
1939	Cin-N	0	0	....	1	0	0	0	1	1	2	1	1	0	0	1	0	3.000	9.00	43	11.63	.400	0	....	-1	0	-0.1
• JACOBS, Bucky	Newton Smith Jacobs b: 3/21/1913, Altavista, VA d: 6/15/1990, Richmond, VA BR/TR, 5'11", 155 lbs. Deb: 6/27/1937
1937	Was-A	1	1	.500	11	1	0	0	0	22^1	26	12	12	0	0	11	8	1.657	4.84	92	4.50	.295	0	.000	-1	1	-0.2
1939	Was-A	0	0	....	2	0	0	0	0	3	1	0	0	0	0	0	1	.333	0.00	....	0.25	.100	0	....	1	1	0.1
1940	Was-A	0	1	.000	9	0	0	0	0	15	16	11	10	1	2	9	6	1.667	6.00	70	5.19	.271	0	.000	-3	0	-0.3
Total	**3**	**1**	**2**	**.333**	**22**	**1**	**0**	**0**	**0**	**40^1**	**43**	**23**	**22**	**1**	**2**	**20**	**15**	**1.562**	**4.91**	**88**	**4.44**	**.274**	**0**	**.000**	**-3**	**2**	**-0.3**
• JACOBS, Elmer	William Elmer Jacobs b: 8/10/1892, Salem, MO d: 2/10/1958, Salem, MO BR/TR, 6', 165 lbs. Deb: 4/23/1914
1914	Phi-N	1	3	.250	14	7	1	0	0	50^2	65	38	27	2	3	20	17	1.678	4.80	61	5.58	.342	0	.000	-9	0	-1.1
1916	Pit-N	6	10	.375	34	17	8	0	0	153	151	70	50	2	4	38	46	1.235	2.94	91	2.84	.258	3	.075	-1	5	-0.3
1917	Pit-N	6	19	.240	38	25	10	1	2	227^1	214	87	71	3	5	76	58	1.276	2.81	101	2.98	.262	12	.179	2	11	0.2
1918	Pit-N	0	1	.000	8	4	0	0	0	23^1	31	18	15	0	0	14	2	1.929	5.79	50	5.89	.344	2	.286	-8	0	-0.9
	Phi-N	9	5	.643	18	14	12	4	1	123	91	39	33	3	4	42	33	1.081	2.41	124	2.09	.210	6	.158	8	11	0.8
	Yr.	9	6	.600	26	18	12	4	1	146^1	122	57	48	3	4	56	35	1.216	2.95	100	2.70	.233	8	.178	-0	11	-0.1
1919	Phi-N	6	10	.375	17	15	13	0	0	128^2	150	66	55	5	6	44	37	1.508	3.85	84	4.55	.304	8	.178	-8	4	-1.0
	StL-N	3	6	.333	17	8	4	1	1	85^1	81	30	24	2	5	25	31	1.242	2.53	110	3.15	.264	8	.348	1	6	0.5
	Yr.	9	16	.360	34	23	17	1	1	214	231	96	79	7	11	69	68	**1.402**	3.32	92	3.99	.289	16	.235	-7	10	-0.5
1920	StL-N	4	8	.333	23	9	1	0	1	77^2	91	56	45	2	5	33	21	1.597	5.21	59	4.63	.296	5	.192	-19	0	-2.0
1924	Chi-N	11	12	.478	38	22	13	1	1	190^1	181	93	79	9	2	72	50	1.329	3.74	104	3.39	.258	6	.111	1	12	-0.3
1925	Chi-N	2	3	.400	18	4	1	1	1	55^2	63	37	32	9	1	22	19	1.527	5.17	84	5.07	.274	3	.231	-6	2	-0.6
1927	Chi-A	2	4	.333	25	8	2	1	0	74^1	105	49	38	3	4	37	22	1.910	4.60	88	6.66	.354	3	.150	-6	2	-0.7
Total	**9**	**50**	**81**	**.382**	**250**	**133**	**65**	**9**	**7**	**1189^1**	**1223**	**583**	**469**	**40**	**39**	**423**	**336**	**1.384**	**3.55**	**90**	**3.72**	**.275**	**56**	**.161**	**-45**	**53**	**-5.4**
• JACOBS, Tony	Anthony Robert Jacobs b: 8/5/1925, Dixmoor, IL d: 12/21/1980, Nashville, TN BB/TR, 5'9", 150 lbs. Deb: 9/19/1948
1948	Chi-N	0	0	....	1	0	0	0	0	2	3	1	1	1	0	0	2	1.500	4.50	87	8.13	.333	0	....	-0	0	0.0
1955	StL-N	0	0	....	1	0	0	0	0	2	6	4	4	1	0	1	1	3.500	18.00	23	22.96	.500	0	.000	-3	0	-0.3
Total	**2**	**0**	**0**	**....**	**2**	**0**	**0**	**0**	**0**	**4**	**9**	**5**	**5**	**2**	**0**	**1**	**3**	**2.500**	**11.25**	**36**	**15.54**	**.429**	**0**	**.000**	**-3**	**0**	**-0.3**
• JACOBSON, Beany	Albert L. Jacobson b: 6/5/1881, Port Washington, WI d: 1/31/1933, Decatur, IL BL/TL, 6', 170 lbs. Deb: 4/30/1904
1904	Was-A	5	23	.179	33	30	23	1	0	253^2	276	135	100	6	3	57	75	1.313	3.55	75	3.27	.278	8	.091	-18	4	-2.6
1905	Was-A	7	8	.467	22	17	12	0	0	144^1	139	83	53	1	5	35	50	1.206	3.30	80	2.75	.255	7	.159	-15	5	-1.5
1906	StL-A	9	9	.500	24	15	12	0	0	155	146	68	43	3	4	27	53	1.116	2.50	103	2.48	.252	5	.091	1	7	-0.3
1907	StL-A	1	6	.143	7	7	6	0	0	57^1	55	28	19	1	0	26	16	1.413	2.98	84	3.71	.255	4	.222	-3	1	-0.4
	Bos-A	0	0	....	2	1	0	0	0	2	2	3	2	0	0	3	1	2.500	9.00	29	6.92	.263	0	....	-2	0	-0.2
	Yr.	1	6	.143	9	8	6	0	0	59^1	57	31	21	1	0	29	17	1.449	3.19	79	3.82	.255	4	.222	-5	1	-0.5
Total	**4**	**22**	**46**	**.324**	**88**	**70**	**53**	**1**	**0**	**612^1**	**618**	**317**	**217**	**11**	**12**	**148**	**195**	**1.251**	**3.19**	**82**	**3.00**	**.264**	**24**	**.117**	**-36**	**17**	**-4.9**
• JACOBUS, Larry	Stuart Louis Jacobus b: 12/18/1893, Cincinnati, OH d: 8/19/1965, North College Hill, OH BB/TR, 6'2", 186 lbs. Deb: 7/15/1918
1918	Cin-N	0	1	.000	5	0	0	0	0	17^1	25	12	11	0	0	1	8	1.500	5.71	47	4.62	.368	0	.000	-6	0	-0.8
• JACOME, Jason	Jason James Jacome b: 11/24/1970, Tulsa, OK BL/TL, 6'1", 155 lbs. Deb: 7/2/1994
1994	NY-N	4	3	.571	8	8	1	1	0	54	54	17	16	3	0	17	30	1.315	2.67	157	3.49	.269	1	.063	9	5	0.8
1995	NY-N	0	4	.000	5	5	0	0	0	21	33	24	24	3	1	15	11	2.286	10.29	39	9.59	.359	0	.000	-15	0	-1.5
	KC-A	4	6	.400	15	14	1	0	0	84	101	52	50	15	1	21	39	1.452	5.36	89	5.26	.300	0	....	-6	3	-0.6
1996	KC-A	0	4	.000	49	2	0	0	1	47^2	67	27	25	5	2	22	32	1.867	4.72	106	6.87	.337	0	....	2	2	0.1
1997	KC-A	0	0	....	7	0	0	0	0	6^2	13	7	7	2	1	5	3	2.700	9.45	50	15.71	.448	0	....	-4	0	-0.3
	Cle-A	2	0	1.000	21	4	0	0	0	42^2	45	26	25	8	0	15	24	1.406	5.27	89	4.69	.269	0	....	-2	2	-0.2
	Yr.	2	0	1.000	28	4	0	0	0	49^1	58	33	32	10	1	20	27	1.581	5.84	80	6.18	.296	0	....	-6	2	-0.6
1998	Cle-A	0	1	.000	1	1	0	0	0	5	10	8	8	2	0	3	2	2.600	14.40	33	15.40	.435	0	....	-5	0	-0.5
Total	**5**	**10**	**18**	**.357**	**106**	**34**	**2**	**1**	**1**	**261**	**323**	**161**	**155**	**38**	**5**	**98**	**141**	**1.613**	**5.34**	**86**	**5.90**	**.308**	**1**	**.043**	**-22**	**12**	**-2.3**
• JACQUEZ, Pat	Patrick Thomas Jacquez b: 4/23/1947, Stockton, CA BR/TR, 6', 200 lbs. Deb: 4/18/1971
1971	Chi-A	0	0	....	2	0	0	0	0	2	4	1	1	0	0	2	1	3.000	4.50	80	12.01	.444	0	.000	-0	0	0.0
• JACQUEZ, Tom	Thomas Patrick Jacquez b: 12/29/1975, Stockton, CA BL/TL, 6'2", 195 lbs. Deb: 9/9/2000
2000	Phi-N	0	0	....	9	0	0	0	1	7^1	10	9	9	2	0	3	6	1.773	11.05	42	7.50	.333	0	....	-5	0	-0.5
• JAECKEL, Jake	Paul Henry Jaeckel b: 4/1/1942, East Los Angeles, CA BR/TR, 5'10", 170 lbs. Deb: 9/19/1964
1964	Chi-N	1	0	1.000	4	0	0	0	1	8	4	0	0	0	0	3	2	.875	0.00	....	1.30	.160	0	.000	3	2	0.3
• JAEGER, Charlie	Charles Thomas Jaeger b: 4/17/1875, Ottawa, IL d: 9/27/1942, Ottawa, IL BR/TR, 6'1" Deb: 9/9/1904
1904	Det-A	3	3	.500	8	6	5	0	0	49	49	29	14	0	6	15	13	1.306	2.57	99	3.14	.261	1	.059	-1	1	-0.3
• JAEGER, Joe	Joseph Peter "Zip" Jaeger b: 3/3/1895, St. Cloud, MN d: 12/13/1963, Hampton, IA BR/TR, 6'1", 190 lbs. Deb: 7/28/1920
1920	Chi-N	0	0	....	2	0	0	0	0	3	6	6	4	0	0	4	0	3.333	12.00	27	13.78	.500	0	.000	-3	0	-0.3
• JAKUCKI, Sig	Sigmund "Jack" Jakucki b: 8/20/1909, Camden, NJ d: 5/29/1979, Galveston, TX BR/TR, 6'2.5", 198 lbs. Deb: 8/30/1936
1936	StL-A	0	3	.000	7	2	0	0	0	20^2	32	22	20	2	1	12	9	2.129	8.71	62	7.93	.348	0	.000	-7	0	-0.7
1944*	StL-A	13	9	.591	35	24	12	4	3	198	211	89	78	17	3	54	67	1.338	3.55	102	3.79	.268	11	.151	5	12	0.3
1945	StL-A	12	10	.545	30	24	15	1	2	192^1	188	84	75	9	1	65	55	1.315	3.51	100	3.28	.257	13	.186	1	13	0.2
Total	**3**	**25**	**22**	**.532**	**72**	**50**	**27**	**5**	**5**	**411**	**431**	**195**	**173**	**28**	**5**	**131**	**131**	**1.367**	**3.79**	**98**	**3.76**	**.268**	**24**	**.161**	**-2**	**25**	**-0.2**
• JAMERSON, Lefty	Charles Dewey "Charlie" Jamerson b: 1/26/1900, Enfield, IL d: 8/4/1980, Mockville, NC BL/TL, 6'1", 195 lbs. Deb: 8/16/1924
1924	Bos-A	0	0	....	1	0	0	0	0	1	1	2	2	0	0	3	0	4.000	18.00	24	8.59	.250	0	....	-2	0	-0.1
• JAMES, Bill	William Henry "Big Bill" James b: 1/20/1887, Detroit, MI d: 5/25/1942, Venice, CA BB/TR, 6'4", 195 lbs. Deb: 6/12/1911
1911	Cle-A	2	4	.333	8	6	4	0	0	51^2	58	37	28	1	2	32	21	1.742	4.88	70	5.05	.284	1	.059	-9	1	-1.0
1912	Cle-A	0	0	....	3	0	0	0	0	13^2	15	11	7	0	0	9	5	1.756	4.61	74	4.89	.288	0	.000	-2	0	-0.2
1914	StL-A	15	14	.517	44	35	20	3	1	284	269	121	90	4	6	109	109	1.331	2.85	95	3.26	.257	10	.112	-2	15	-0.6
1915	StL-A	6	10	.375	34	22	8	0	1	170^1	155	89	68	2	7	92	58	1.450	3.59	80	3.71	.255	8	.190	-16	6	-1.6
	Det-A	7	3	.700	11	9	3	1	0	67	57	26	18	1	0	33	24	1.343	2.42	125	3.13	.243	6	.286	6	6	0.8
	Yr.	13	13	.500	45	31	11	1	1	237^1	212	115	86	3	7	125	82	1.420	3.26	89	3.54	.252	14	.222	-10	12	-0.8
1916	Det-A	8	12	.400	30	20	8	0	1	151^2	141	76	62	1	11	79	61	1.451	3.68	78	3.77	.255	3	.068	-11	4	-1.6
1917	Det-A	13	10	.565	34	23	10	2	1	198	163	71	46	2	12	96	62	1.308	2.09	126	2.98	.229	12	.211	16	13	2.0
1918	Det-A	6	11	.353	19	18	8	1	0	122	127	68	51	3	5	68	42	1.598	3.76	71	4.41	.279	5	.109	-9	2	-1.3

YEAR TM-L	W	L	PCT	G	GS	CG	SH	SV	IP	H	R	ER	HR	HB	BB	SO	RAT	ERA	ERA+	CERA	OAV	BH	AVG	PR+	WS	TPW
1919 Det-A	1	0	1.000	2	1	0	0	0	9^1	12	6	6	0	0	7	3	2.036	5.79	55	6.74	.324	1	.250	-3	0	-0.3
Bos-A	3	5	.375	13	7	4	0	0	72^2	74	42	33	2	3	39	12	1.555	4.09	74	4.49	.280	3	.143	-10	1	-1.1
*Chi-A	3	2	.600	5	5	3	2	0	39^1	39	12	11	0	2	14	11	1.347	2.52	126	3.59	.281	2	.143	2	3	0.1
Yr.	7	7	.500	20	13	7	2	0	121^1	125	60	50	2	5	60	26	1.525	3.71	83	4.37	.284	6	.154	-10	4	-1.2
Total 8	64	71	.474	203	146	68	9	4	1179^2	1110	559	420	16	48	578	408	1.431	3.20	89	3.67	.258	51	.142	-37	51	-4.7
• JAMES, Bill	William Lawrence "Seattle Bill" James b: 3/12/1892, Iowa Hill, CA d: 3/10/1971, Oroville, CA BR/TR, 6'3", 196 lbs. Deb: 4/17/1913																									
1913 Bos-N	6	10	.375	24	14	10	1	0	135^2	134	75	42	4	7	57	73	1.408	2.79	118	3.67	.264	12	.255	10	6	1.2
1914* Bos-N	26	7	.788	46	37	30	4	2	332^1	261	91	70	7	13	118	156	1.140	1.90	145	2.43	.225	33	.256	19	**36**	2.5
1915 Bos-N	5	4	.556	13	10	4	0	0	68^1	68	28	23	3	2	22	23	1.317	3.03	88	3.44	.269	1	.048	-3	3	-0.6
1919 Bos-N	0	0	....	1	1	0	0	0	5^1	6	2	2	0	0	2	1	1.500	3.38	85	3.74	.273	0	.000	-0	0	-0.1
Total 4	37	21	.638	84	61	44	5	2	541^2	469	196	137	14	22	199	253	1.233	2.28	127	2.88	.241	46	.231	25	45	3.0
• JAMES, Bob	Robert Harvey James b: 8/18/1958, Glendale, CA BR/TR, 6'4", 230 lbs. Deb: 9/7/1978																									
1978 Mon-N	0	1	.000	4	1	0	0	0	4	4	4	4	1	0	4	3	2.000	9.00	39	8.11	.267	0	....	-3	0	-0.3
1979 Mon-N	0	0	....	2	0	0	0	0	2	2	3	3	0	0	3	1	2.500	13.50	27	6.30	.250	0	....	-2	0	-0.2
1982 Mon-N	0	0	....	7	0	0	0	0	9	10	6	6	0	0	8	11	2.000	6.00	61	5.61	.294	0	....	-2	0	-0.3
Det-A	0	2	.000	12	1	0	0	0	19^2	22	13	11	4	0	8	20	1.525	5.03	81	5.57	.278	0	....	-3	0	-0.3
1983 Det-A	0	0	....	4	0	0	0	0	4	5	5	5	2	0	3	4	2.000	11.25	35	10.95	.313	0	....	-3	0	-0.3
Mon-N	1	0	1.000	27	0	0	0	7	50	37	17	16	3	3	23	56	1.200	2.88	125	2.83	.210	2	.286	3	5	0.4
1984 Mon-N	6	6	.500	62	0	0	0	10	96	92	47	39	6	4	45	91	1.427	3.66	94	3.77	.251	2	.143	-4	5	-0.4
1985 Chi-A	8	7	.533	69	0	0	0	32	110	90	31	26	5	2	23	88	1.027	2.13	203	2.13	.226	0	....	26	22	2.6
1986 Chi-A	5	4	.556	49	0	0	0	14	58^1	61	36	34	8	4	23	32	1.440	5.25	82	4.66	.268	0	....	-7	4	-0.7
1987 Chi-A	4	6	.400	43	0	0	0	10	54	54	32	28	10	4	17	34	1.315	4.67	98	4.33	.256	0	....	-2	4	-0.2
Total 8	24	26	.480	279	2	0	0	73	407	377	194	172	39	17	157	340	1.312	3.80	104	3.67	.246	4	.190	3	40	0.3
• JAMES, Delvin	Delvin DeWayne James b: 1/3/1978, Nacogdoches, TX BR/TR, 6'4", 240 lbs. Deb: 4/16/2002																									
2002 TB-A	0	3	.000	8	6	0	0	0	34^1	40	25	25	5	1	15	17	1.602	6.55	68	5.83	.301	0	....	-9	0	-0.8
• JAMES, Jeff	Jeffrey Lynn "Jesse" James b: 9/29/1941, Indianapolis, IN BR/TR, 6'3", 195 lbs. Deb: 4/13/1968																									
1968 Phi-N	4	4	.500	29	13	1	1	0	116	112	61	55	8	4	46	83	1.362	4.27	70	3.80	.256	4	.121	-15	1	-1.8
1969 Phi-N	2	2	.500	6	5	1	0	0	31^2	36	20	19	5	0	14	21	1.579	5.40	66	5.41	.288	2	.182	-7	0	-0.7
Total 2	6	6	.500	35	18	2	1	0	147^2	148	81	74	13	4	60	104	1.409	4.51	69	4.14	.263	6	.136	-22	1	-2.5
• JAMES, Johnny	John Phillip James b: 7/23/1933, Bonner's Ferry, ID BL/TR, 5'10", 160 lbs. Deb: 9/6/1958																									
1958 NY-A	0	0	....	1	0	0	0	0	3	2	0	0	0	0	4	1	2.000	0.00	....	6.15	.250	0	.000	1	0	0.1
1960 NY-A	5	1	.833	28	0	0	0	2	43^1	38	22	21	3	3	26	29	1.477	4.36	82	4.22	.248	0	.000	-5	3	-0.5
1961 NY-A	0	0	....	1	0	0	0	0	1^1	1	0	0	0	0	0	2	.750	0.00	....	1.16	.250	0	....	1	0	0.1
LA-A	0	2	.000	36	3	0	0	0	71^1	66	44	42	12	2	54	41	1.682	5.30	85	5.68	.246	0	.000	-5	2	-0.7
Yr.	0	2	.000	37	3	0	0	0	72^2	67	44	42	12	2	54	43	1.665	5.20	87	5.60	.246	0	.000	-5	2	-0.6
Total 3	5	3	.625	66	3	0	0	2	119	107	66	63	15	5	84	73	1.605	4.76	87	5.11	.247	0	.000	-9	5	-1.1
• JAMES, Lefty	William A. James b: 7/1/1889, Glen Roy, OH d: 5/3/1933, Glen Roy, OH BL/TL, 5'11.5", 175 lbs. Deb: 4/13/1912																									
1912 Cle-A	0	1	.000	3	1	0	0	1	6	8	9	5	0	2	4	2	2.000	7.50	46	7.97	.348	0	.000	-3	0	-0.3
1913 Cle-A	2	2	.500	11	4	3	0	0	39	42	27	13	0	3	9	18	1.308	3.00	101	3.39	.273	3	.231	-0	1	0.0
1914 Cle-A	0	3	.000	17	6	1	0	0	50^2	44	23	18	0	2	32	16	1.500	3.20	90	3.77	.251	0	.000	-1	2	-0.2
Total 3	2	6	.250	31	11	4	0	1	95^2	94	59	36	0	7	45	36	1.453	3.39	89	3.88	.267	3	.107	-4	3	-0.6
• JAMES, Mike	Michael Elmo James b: 8/15/1967, Fort Walton Beach, FL BR/TR, 6'4", 215 lbs. Deb: 4/29/1995																									
1995 Cal-A	3	0	1.000	46	0	0	0	1	55^2	49	27	24	6	3	26	36	1.347	3.88	121	3.94	.238	0	....	5	4	0.4
1996 Cal-A	5	5	.500	69	0	0	0	1	81	62	27	24	7	10	42	65	1.284	2.67	184	3.44	.214	0	....	20	9	1.8
1997 Ana-A	5	5	.500	58	0	0	0	7	62^2	69	32	30	3	5	28	57	1.548	4.31	107	4.63	.283	0	....	2	6	0.2
1998 Ana-A	0	0	....	11	0	0	0	0	14	10	3	3	0	0	7	12	1.214	1.93	243	2.44	.208	0	....	4	2	0.4
2000* StL-N	2	2	.500	51	0	0	0	2	51^1	40	22	18	7	3	24	41	1.247	3.16	146	3.62	.219	0	.000	8	5	0.7
2001 StL-N	1	2	.333	40	0	0	0	0	38	43	24	22	5	5	17	26	1.579	5.21	82	5.80	.293	0	.000	-5	1	-0.5
2002 Col-N	0	0	....	13	0	0	0	0	11^1	12	9	7	2	1	5	10	1.500	5.56	86	5.51	.267	0	....	-1	0	-0.1
Total 7	16	14	.533	288	0	0	0	11	314	285	144	128	30	27	149	247	1.382	3.67	126	4.11	.245	0	.000	33	27	3.0
• JAMES, Rick	Richard Lee James b: 10/11/1947, Sheffield, AL BR/TR, 6'2.5", 205 lbs. Deb: 9/20/1967																									
1967 Chi-N	0	1	.000	3	1	0	0	0	4^2	9	8	7	1	0	2	2	2.357	13.50	26	13.19	.529	0	.000	-5	0	-0.6
• JAMIESON, Charlie	Charles Devine "Cuckoo" Jamieson b: 2/7/1893, Paterson, NJ d: 10/27/1969, Paterson, NJ BL/TL, 5'8.5", 165 lbs. Deb: 9/20/1915 ♦																									
1916 Was-A	0	0	....	1	0	0	0	0	4	2	2	2	0	0	3	2	1.250	4.50	62	1.86	.143	36	.248	-1	3	-0.8
1917 Was-A	0	0	....	1	0	0	0	0	2^1	10	10	10	0	0	2	1	5.143	38.57	7	30.60	.625	6	.171	-9	0	-1.3
1918 Phi-A	2	1	.667	5	2	1	0	0	23	24	17	11	0	2	13	2	1.609	4.30	68	4.19	.261	84	.202	-4	4	-3.0
1919 Cle-A	0	0	....	4	1	0	0	0	13	12	9	8	0	0	8	0	1.538	5.54	60	3.69	.250	6	.353	-3	1	-0.2
1922 Cle-A	0	0	....	2	0	0	0	0	5^2	7	3	2	0	0	4	2	1.941	3.18	126	5.97	.318	183	.323	1	19	0.4
Total 5	2	1	.667	13	3	1	0	0	48	55	41	33	0	2	30	7	1.771	6.19	48	5.36	.287	1990	.303	-17	27	-4.8
• JANESKI, Jerry	Gerad Joseph Janeski b: 4/18/1946, Pasadena, CA BR/TR, 6'4", 205 lbs. Deb: 4/10/1970																									
1970 Chi-A	10	17	.370	35	35	4	1	0	205^2	247	125	109	22	5	63	79	**1.507**	4.77	82	4.94	.300	5	.076	-16	5	-2.1
1971 Was-A	1	5	.167	23	10	0	0	1	61^2	72	38	34	5	3	34	19	1.719	4.96	67	5.73	.304	3	.214	-12	0	-1.2
1972 Tex-A	0	1	.000	4	1	0	0	0	12^2	11	5	4	0	0	7	7	1.421	2.84	106	3.01	.229	0	.000	0	1	0.0
Total 3	11	23	.324	62	46	4	1	1	280	330	168	147	27	8	104	105	1.550	4.73	79	5.03	.298	8	.098	-28	6	-3.3
• JANSEN, Larry	Lawrence Joseph Jansen b: 7/16/1920, Verboort, OR BR/TR, 6'2", 190 lbs. Deb: 4/17/1947 C																									
1947 NY-N	21	5	.808	42	30	20	1	1	248	241	102	87	23	1	57	104	1.202	3.16	129	3.33	.262	16	.186	24	20	2.4
1948 NY-N	18	12	.600	42	36	15	4	2	277	283	125	111	25	3	54	126	1.217	3.61	109	3.37	.265	13	.137	11	17	0.9
1949 NY-N	15	16	.484	37	35	17	3	0	259^2	271	130	111	36	2	62	113	1.282	3.85	104	3.88	.263	16	.165	5	14	0.4
1950 NY-N★	19	13	.594	40	35	21	**5**	3	275	238	106	92	31	1	55	161	1.065	3.01	136	2.68	.232	16	.167	25	25	2.4
1951* NY-N★	**23**	11	.676	39	34	18	3	0	278^2	254	102	94	26	3	56	145	1.112	3.04	129	2.79	.239	9	.094	27	24	2.2
1952 NY-N	11	11	.500	34	27	8	1	2	167^1	183	91	76	16	6	47	74	1.375	4.09	91	4.20	.281	8	.178	-7	8	-0.3
1953 NY-N	11	16	.407	36	26	6	0	1	184^2	185	96	85	24	2	55	88	1.300	4.14	104	3.83	.256	8	.133	3	9	0.1
1954 NY-N	2	2	.500	13	7	0	0	0	40^2	57	32	27	5	1	15	15	1.770	5.98	68	6.58	.337	4	.286	-9	0	-0.8
1956 Cin-N	2	3	.400	8	7	2	0	1	34^2	39	20	20	5	1	9	16	1.385	5.19	77	4.56	.281	0	.000	-4	1	-0.5
Total 9	122	89	.578	291	237	107	17	10	1765^2	1751	804	703	191	20	410	842	1.224	3.58	112	3.46	.258	90	.150	74	118	6.7
• JANZEN, Marty	Martin Thomas Janzen b: 5/31/1973, Homestead, FL BR/TR, 6'3", 197 lbs. Deb: 5/12/1996																									
1996 Tor-A	4	6	.400	15	11	0	0	0	73^2	95	65	60	16	2	38	47	1.805	7.33	68	7.40	.317	0	....	-21	0	-1.9
1997 Tor-A	2	1	.667	12	0	0	0	0	25	23	11	10	4	0	13	17	1.440	3.60	128	4.72	.250	0	....	2	2	0.2
Total 2	6	7	.462	27	11	0	0	0	98^2	118	76	70	20	2	51	64	1.713	6.39	77	6.72	.301	0	....	-18	2	-1.7
• JARVIS, Kevin	Kevin Thomas Jarvis b: 8/1/1969, Lexington, KY BL/TR, 6'2", 200 lbs. Deb: 4/6/1994																									
1994 Cin-N	1	1	.500	6	3	0	0	0	17^2	22	14	14	4	0	5	10	1.528	7.13	58	5.91	.301	1	.250	-6	0	-0.6
1995 Cin-N	3	4	.429	19	11	1	1	0	79	91	56	50	13	3	32	33	1.557	5.70	72	5.60	.292	3	.143	-16	0	-1.5
1996 Cin-N	8	9	.471	24	20	2	1	0	120^1	152	93	80	17	2	43	63	1.620	5.98	70	5.68	.305	6	.167	-25	0	-2.5
1997 Cin-N	0	1	.000	9	0	0	0	1	13^1	21	16	15	4	1	7	12	2.100	10.13	43	9.98	.344	0	.000	-9	0	-0.9
Min-A	0	0	....	6	2	0	0	0	13	23	18	18	4	0	8	9	2.385	12.46	37	11.86	.371	0	....	-11	0	-1.1
Det-A	0	3	.000	17	3	0	0	0	41^2	55	28	25	9	0	14	27	1.656	5.40	85	6.64	.318	0	....	-4	1	-0.4
Yr.	0	3	.000	23	5	0	0	0	54^2	78	46	43	13	0	22	36	1.829	7.08	65	7.84	.332	0	....	-16	1	-1.5

YEAR	TM-L	W	L	PCT	G	GS	CG	SH	SV	IP	H	R	ER	HR	HB	BB	SO	RAT	ERA	ERA+	CERA	OAV	BH	AVG	PR+	WS	TPW
1999	Oak-A	0	1	.000	4	1	0	0	0	14	28	19	18	6	1	6	11	2.429	11.57	40	14.40	.418	0	....	-11	0	-1.0
2000	Col-N	3	4	.429	24	19	0	0	0	115	138	83	76	26	4	33	60	1.487	5.95	97	5.86	.300	3	.088	-2	4	-0.3
2001	SD-N	12	11	.522	32	32	1	1	0	193^{1}	189	107	103	37	5	49	133	1.231	4.79	83	4.05	.254	11	.180	-14	7	-1.0
2002	SD-N	2	4	.333	7	7	0	0	0	35	36	19	17	5	1	10	24	1.314	4.37	86	4.24	.269	3	.333	-2	1	0.0
2003	SD-N	4	8	.333	16	16	0	0	0	92	113	65	60	15	2	32	49	1.576	5.87	67	5.68	.304	3	.136	-19	0	-1.8
Total	9	33	46	.418	164	114	4	3	1	734^{1}	868	518	476	140	19	239	431	1.507	5.83	74	5.61	.294	30	.160	-120	13	-11.1

• JARVIS, Pat Robert Patrick Jarvis b: 3/18/1941, Carlyle, IL BR/TR, 5'10.5", 180 lbs. Deb: 8/4/1966

YEAR	TM-L	W	L	PCT	G	GS	CG	SH	SV	IP	H	R	ER	HR	HB	BB	SO	RAT	ERA	ERA+	CERA	OAV	BH	AVG	PR+	WS	TPW
1966	Atl-N	6	2	.750	10	9	3	1	0	62^{1}	46	16	16	1	1	12	41	.930	2.31	157	1.61	.206	0	.000	9	6	0.7
1967	Atl-N	15	10	.600	32	30	7	1	0	194	195	86	79	15	4	62	118	1.325	3.66	91	3.59	.260	6	.085	-9	10	-1.3
1968	Atl-N	16	12	.571	34	34	14	1	0	256	202	82	74	15	2	50	157	.984	2.60	115	1.97	.214	12	.141	10	19	1.2
1969*	Atl-N	13	11	.542	37	33	4	1	0	217^{1}	204	113	107	25	1	73	123	1.275	4.43	81	3.53	.246	8	.113	-19	8	-2.3
1970	Atl-N	16	16	.500	36	34	11	1	0	254	240	110	102	21	0	72	173	1.228	3.61	119	3.16	.247	15	.183	25	19	2.5
1971	Atl-N	6	14	.300	35	23	3	3	1	162^{1}	162	81	74	16	3	51	68	1.312	4.10	90	3.70	.261	5	.106	-6	7	-0.9
1972	Atl-N	11	7	.611	37	6	0	0	2	98^{2}	94	50	45	7	0	44	56	1.399	4.10	92	3.69	.260	3	.125	-2	6	-0.2
1973	Mon-N	2	1	.667	28	0	0	0	0	39^{1}	37	21	14	6	1	16	19	1.347	3.20	119	4.09	.250	0	.000	3	2	0.2
Total	8	85	73	.538	249	169	42	8	3	1284	1180	559	511	106	12	380	755	1.215	3.58	101	3.11	.243	49	.121	11	77	0.1

• JARVIS, Ray Raymond Arnold Jarvis b: 5/10/1946, Providence, RI BR/TR, 6'2", 198 lbs. Deb: 4/15/1969

YEAR	TM-L	W	L	PCT	G	GS	CG	SH	SV	IP	H	R	ER	HR	HB	BB	SO	RAT	ERA	ERA+	CERA	OAV	BH	AVG	PR+	WS	TPW
1969	Bos-A	5	6	.455	29	12	2	0	1	100^{1}	105	59	53	8	3	43	36	1.475	4.75	80	4.45	.274	2	.069	-8	3	-1.1
1970	Bos-A	0	1	.000	15	0	0	0	0	16	17	12	7	1	2	14	8	1.938	3.94	101	6.19	.274	0	....	0	0	0.0
Total	2	5	7	.417	44	12	2	0	1	116^{1}	122	71	60	9	5	57	44	1.539	4.64	82	4.69	.274	2	.069	-8	3	-1.0

• JASPER, Hi Henry W. Jasper b: 11/15/1880, St. Louis, MO d: 5/22/1937, St. Louis, MO BR/TR, 5'11", 180 lbs. Deb: 4/19/1914

YEAR	TM-L	W	L	PCT	G	GS	CG	SH	SV	IP	H	R	ER	HR	HB	BB	SO	RAT	ERA	ERA+	CERA	OAV	BH	AVG	PR+	WS	TPW
1914	Chi-A	1	0	1.000	16	0	0	0	0	32^{1}	22	22	12	0	1	20	19	1.299	3.34	80	2.72	.210	0	.000	-2	0	-0.3
1915	Chi-A	0	1	.000	3	2	1	0	0	15^{2}	8	8	8	2	0	9	15	1.085	4.60	65	2.39	.157	2	.286	-3	0	-0.3
1916	StL-N	5	6	.455	21	9	2	0	1	107	97	54	39	0	7	42	37	1.299	3.28	80	3.07	.254	7	.212	-7	4	-0.7
1919	Cle-A	4	5	.444	12	10	5	0	0	82^{2}	83	41	33	1	0	28	25	1.343	3.59	93	3.77	.269	3	.103	-2	4	-0.4
Total	4	10	12	.455	52	21	8	0	1	237^{2}	210	125	92	3	8	99	96	1.300	3.48	83	3.22	.248	12	.162	-14	8	-1.8

• JASTER, Larry Larry Edward Jaster b: 1/13/1944, Midland, MI BL/TL, 6'3", 205 lbs. Deb: 9/17/1965

YEAR	TM-L	W	L	PCT	G	GS	CG	SH	SV	IP	H	R	ER	HR	HB	BB	SO	RAT	ERA	ERA+	CERA	OAV	BH	AVG	PR+	WS	TPW
1965	StL-N	3	0	1.000	4	3	3	0	0	28	21	5	5	1	0	7	10	1.000	1.61	239	1.88	.206	2	.200	7	4	0.8
1966	StL-N	11	5	.688	26	21	6	**5**	0	151^{2}	124	57	55	17	5	45	92	1.114	3.26	110	2.93	.227	8	.178	4	11	0.6
1967*	StL-N	9	7	.563	34	23	2	1	3	152^{1}	141	57	51	12	2	44	87	1.214	3.01	108	3.08	.244	5	.100	4	10	0.3
1968*	StL-N	9	13	.409	31	21	3	1	0	154^{1}	153	63	60	13	6	38	70	1.238	3.50	83	3.44	.262	6	.140	-12	5	-1.3
1969	Mon-N	1	6	.143	24	11	1	0	0	77	95	60	47	17	2	28	39	1.597	5.49	67	6.11	.302	8	.421	-15	1	-1.3
1970	Atl-N	1	1	.500	14	0	0	0	0	22^{1}	33	18	17	5	0	8	9	1.836	6.85	63	7.87	.359	0	.000	-6	0	-0.6
1972	Atl-N	1	1	.500	5	1	0	0	0	12^{1}	12	7	7	4	0	8	6	1.622	5.11	74	7.06	.267	0	.000	-2	0	-0.2
Total	7	35	33	.515	138	80	15	7	3	598	579	267	242	69	15	178	313	1.266	3.64	93	3.73	.256	29	.170	-19	31	-1.7

• JAVERY, Al Alva William "Beartracks" Javery b: 6/5/1918, Worcester, MA d: 8/16/1977, Putnam, CT BR/TR, 6'3", 183 lbs. Deb: 4/23/1940

YEAR	TM-L	W	L	PCT	G	GS	CG	SH	SV	IP	H	R	ER	HR	HB	BB	SO	RAT	ERA	ERA+	CERA	OAV	BH	AVG	PR+	WS	TPW
1940	Bos-N	2	4	.333	29	4	1	0	1	83^{1}	99	62	51	2	2	36	42	1.620	5.51	67	4.65	.293	2	.087	-19	0	-2.0
1941	Bos-N	10	11	.476	34	23	9	1	1	160^{2}	181	88	77	5	6	65	54	1.531	4.31	83	4.30	.283	6	.103	-14	6	-1.9
1942	Bos-N	12	16	.429	42	**37**	19	5	0	261	251	106	88	8	3	78	85	1.261	3.03	110	2.94	.251	9	.105	11	16	0.6
1943	Bos-N★	17	16	.515	41	35	19	5	0	**303**	288	130	108	13	4	99	134	1.277	3.21	106	3.07	.248	17	.163	3	20	0.1
1944	Bos-N★	10	19	.345	40	33	11	3	3	254	248	119	100	12	2	118	137	1.441	3.54	108	3.79	.262	12	.152	7	12	0.4
1945	Bos-N	2	7	.222	17	14	2	1	0	77^{1}	92	59	54	4	0	51	18	1.849	6.28	61	5.56	.295	6	.207	-21	0	-2.2
1946	Bos-N	0	1	.000	2	1	0	0	0	3^{1}	5	5	5	0	0	5	0	3.000	13.50	25	11.38	.417	0	.000	-4	0	-0.4
Total	7	53	74	.417	205	147	61	15	5	1142^{2}	1164	569	483	44	17	452	470	1.414	3.80	94	3.68	.264	52	.137	-37	54	-5.2

• JAY, Joey Joseph Richard Jay b: 8/15/1935, Middletown, CT BB/TR, 6'4", 228 lbs. Deb: 7/21/1953

YEAR	TM-L	W	L	PCT	G	GS	CG	SH	SV	IP	H	R	ER	HR	HB	BB	SO	RAT	ERA	ERA+	CERA	OAV	BH	AVG	PR+	WS	TPW
1953	Mil-N	1	0	1.000	3	1	1	1	0	10	6	0	0	0	0	5	4	1.100	0.00	....	1.87	.188	0	.000	4	2	0.4
1954	Mil-N	1	0	1.000	15	1	0	0	0	18	21	13	13	2	1	16	13	2.056	6.50	57	7.30	.304	0	....	-6	0	-0.6
1955	Mil-N	0	0	....	12	1	0	0	0	19	23	11	10	2	0	13	3	1.895	4.74	79	6.72	.324	2	.667	-2	1	-0.1
1957	Mil-N	0	0	....	1	0	0	0	1	0^{2}	0	0	0	0	0	0	0	.000	0.00	....	0.00	.000	0	....	0	0	0.0
1958	Mil-N	7	5	.583	18	12	6	3	0	96^{2}	60	25	23	8	1	43	74	1.066	2.14	164	2.18	.177	3	.094	14	9	1.3
1959	Mil-N	6	11	.353	34	19	4	1	0	136^{1}	130	71	62	11	5	64	88	1.423	4.09	86	3.97	.248	3	.086	-8	4	-0.9
1960	Mil-N	9	8	.529	32	11	3	0	1	133^{1}	128	60	48	10	6	59	90	1.403	3.24	106	3.95	.254	7	.156	5	7	0.5
1961*	Cin-N★	**21**	10	.677	34	34	14	**4**	0	247^{1}	217	102	97	25	5	92	157	1.249	3.53	115	3.39	.236	8	.090	15	20	1.0
1962	Cin-N	21	14	.600	39	37	16	4	0	273	269	121	114	26	4	100	155	1.352	3.76	107	3.87	.260	15	.167	6	19	0.9
1963	Cin-N	7	18	.280	30	22	4	1	1	170	172	91	81	19	3	73	116	**1.441**	4.29	78	4.45	.266	8	.160	-18	3	-1.9
1964	Cin-N	11	11	.500	34	23	10	0	2	183	167	75	69	17	3	36	134	1.109	3.39	106	2.83	.245	3	.057	2	11	-0.1
1965	Cin-N	9	8	.529	37	24	4	1	1	155^{2}	150	83	73	21	4	63	102	1.368	4.22	89	4.22	.252	2	.041	-8	5	-1.2
1966	Cin-N	6	2	.750	12	10	1	1	0	73^{2}	78	33	32	8	3	23	44	1.371	3.91	100	4.34	.275	3	.115	1	5	0.0
	Atl-N	0	4	.000	9	8	0	0	1	29^{2}	39	29	26	4	1	20	19	1.989	7.89	46	7.24	.315	1	.125	-14	0	-1.5
	Yr.	6	6	.500	21	18	1	1	1	103^{1}	117	62	58	12	4	43	63	1.548	5.05	75	5.17	.287	4	.118	-13	5	-1.5
Total	13	99	91	.521	310	203	63	16	7	1546^{1}	1460	714	648	153	36	607	999	1.337	3.77	98	3.83	.251	55	.114	-8	86	-2.1

• JEAN, Domingo Domingo (Luisa) Jean b: 1/9/1969, San Pedro de Macoris, Dominican Republic BR/TR, 6'2", 175 lbs. Deb: 8/8/1993

YEAR	TM-L	W	L	PCT	G	GS	CG	SH	SV	IP	H	R	ER	HR	HB	BB	SO	RAT	ERA	ERA+	CERA	OAV	BH	AVG	PR+	WS	TPW
1993	NY-A	1	1	.500	10	6	0	0	0	40^{1}	37	20	20	7	0	19	20	1.388	4.46	93	4.30	.237	0	....	-1	2	-0.1

• JEFFCOAT, George George Edward Jeffcoat b: 12/24/1913, New Brookfield, SC d: 10/13/1978, Leesville, SC BR/TR, 5'11.5", 175 lbs. Deb: 4/20/1936

YEAR	TM-L	W	L	PCT	G	GS	CG	SH	SV	IP	H	R	ER	HR	HB	BB	SO	RAT	ERA	ERA+	CERA	OAV	BH	AVG	PR+	WS	TPW
1936	Bro-N	5	6	.455	40	5	3	0	3	95^{2}	84	58	48	7	8	63	46	1.537	4.52	91	4.32	.239	3	.130	-3	5	-0.4
1937	Bro-N	1	3	.250	21	3	1	1	0	54^{1}	58	33	31	4	1	27	29	1.564	5.13	79	4.59	.274	0	.000	-5	2	-0.7
1939	Bro-N	0	0	....	1	0	0	0	0	2	2	0	0	0	0	0	1	1.000	0.00	....	1.95	.286	0	....	1	0	0.1
1943	Bos-N	1	2	.333	8	1	0	0	0	17^{2}	15	10	6	1	0	10	10	1.415	3.06	112	3.30	.217	2	.500	0	1	0.1
Total	4	7	11	.389	70	9	4	1	3	169^{2}	159	101	85	12	9	100	86	1.527	4.51	89	4.27	.248	5	.128	-7	8	-0.9

• JEFFCOAT, Hal Harold Bentley Jeffcoat b: 9/6/1924, West Columbia, SC BR/TR, 5'10.5", 185 lbs. Deb: 4/20/1948 ♦

YEAR	TM-L	W	L	PCT	G	GS	CG	SH	SV	IP	H	R	ER	HR	HB	BB	SO	RAT	ERA	ERA+	CERA	OAV	BH	AVG	PR+	WS	TPW
1954	Chi-N	5	6	.455	43	3	1	0	7	104	110	63	60	12	4	58	35	1.615	5.19	81	5.13	.276	8	.258	-10	4	-0.7
1955	Chi-N	8	6	.571	50	1	0	0	6	100^{2}	107	46	33	5	4	53	32	1.589	2.95	138	4.52	.276	4	.174	12	10	1.3
1956	Cin-N	8	2	.800	38	16	2	0	2	171	189	79	73	12	5	55	55	1.427	3.84	104	4.23	.281	8	.148	4	11	0.3
1957	Cin-N	12	13	.480	37	31	10	1	0	207	236	117	104	29	7	46	63	1.362	4.52	91	4.62	.294	14	.203	-10	11	-0.4
1958	Cin-N	6	8	.429	49	0	0	0	9	75	76	34	31	8	2	26	35	1.360	3.72	111	3.89	.268	5	.556	3	8	0.5
1959	Cin-N	0	1	.000	17	0	0	0	1	21^{2}	21	8	8	3	0	10	12	1.431	3.32	122	4.32	.253	1	1.000	2	2	0.2
	StL-N	0	1	.000	11	0	0	0	0	17^{2}	33	18	18	4	0	9	7	2.377	9.17	46	11.33	.402	0	.000	-10	0	-1.0
	Yr.	0	2	.000	28	0	0	0	1	39^{1}	54	26	26	7	0	19	19	1.856	5.95	70	7.47	.327	1	.250	-8	2	-0.7
Total	6	39	37	.513	245	51	13	1	25	697	772	365	327	73	22	257	239	1.476	4.22	97	4.67	.285	487	.248	-8	46	0.3

• JEFFCOAT, Mike James Michael Jeffcoat b: 8/3/1959, Pine Bluff, AR BL/TL, 6'2", 187 lbs. Deb: 8/21/1983

YEAR	TM-L	W	L	PCT	G	GS	CG	SH	SV	IP	H	R	ER	HR	HB	BB	SO	RAT	ERA	ERA+	CERA	OAV	BH	AVG	PR+	WS	TPW
1983	Cle-A	1	3	.250	11	2	0	0	0	32^{2}	32	13	12	1	1	13	9	1.378	3.31	128	3.56	.256	0	....	4	2	0.4
1984	Cle-A	5	2	.714	63	1	0	0	1	75^{1}	82	28	25	7	1	24	41	1.407	2.99	137	4.08	.281	0	....	9	6	0.9
1985	Cle-A	0	0	....	9	0	0	0	0	9^{2}	8	5	3	1	0	6	4	1.448	2.79	148	3.64	.235	0	....	1	1	0.1
	SF-N	0	2	.000	19	1	0	0	0	22	27	13	13	4	2	6	10	1.500	5.32	65	5.62	.307	0	.000	-4	0	-0.4
1987	Tex-A	0	1	.000	2	2	0	0	0	7	11	10	10	4	0	4	1	2.143	12.86	35	12.83	.355	0	....	-6	0	-0.6
1988	Tex-A	0	2	.000	5	2	0	0	0	10	19	13	13	1	2	5	5	2.400	11.70	35	11.60	.432	0	....	-9	0	-0.9
1989	Tex-A	9	6	.600	22	22	2	2	0	130^{2}	139	65	52	7	4	33	64	1.316	3.58	111	3.63	.270	0	....	6	8	0.6
1990	Tex-A	5	6	.455	44	12	1	0	5	110^{2}	122	57	55	12	2	28	58	1.355	4.47	88	4.20	.283	0	....	-7	6	-0.7
1991	Tex-A	5	3	.625	70	0	0	0	1	79^{2}	104	46	41	8	4	25	43	1.619	4.63	87	5.66	.320	1	1.000	-4	3	-0.3
1992	Tex-A	0	1	.000	6	3	0	0	0	19^{2}	28	17	16	2	0	5	6	1.678	7.32	52	6.05	.350	0	....	-7	0	-0.8

YEAR TM-L	W	L	PCT	G	GS	CG	SH	SV	IP	H	R	ER	HR	HB	BB	SO	RAT	ERA	ERA+	CERA	OAV	BH	AVG	PR+	WS	TPW
1994 Fla-N	0	0	....	4	0	0	0	0	2^2	4	3	3	2	0	0	1	1.500	10.13	43	9.96	.364	0	....	-2	0	-0.2
Total 10	25	26	.490	255	45	3	2	7	500	576	270	243	49	16	149	242	1.450	4.37	91	4.65	.292	1	.500	-20	26	-1.9
• JEFFERSON, Jesse	Jesse Harrison Jefferson b: 3/3/1949, Midlothian, VA BR/TR, 6'3", 195 lbs. Deb: 6/23/1973																									
1973 Bal-A	6	5	.545	18	15	3	0	0	100^2	104	53	46	15	0	46	52	1.490	4.11	91	4.88	.267	0	....	-9	4	-0.9
1974 Bal-A	1	0	1.000	20	2	0	0	0	57^1	55	30	28	2	0	38	31	1.622	4.40	79	4.43	.261	0	....	-7	1	-0.7
1975 Bal-A	0	2	.000	4	0	0	0	0	7^2	5	3	2	0	0	8	4	1.696	2.35	149	3.58	.227	0	....	1	0	0.1
Chi-A	5	9	.357	22	21	1	0	0	107^2	100	69	61	11	2	94	67	1.802	5.10	76	5.66	.249	0	....	-13	2	-1.3
Yr.	5	11	.313	26	21	1	0	0	115^1	105	72	63	11	2	102	71	1.795	4.92	78	5.52	.248	0	....	-12	2	-1.3
1976 Chi-A	2	5	.286	19	9	0	0	0	62^1	86	62	59	4	2	42	30	2.053	8.52	42	7.42	.339	0	....	-34	0	-3.6
1977 Tor-A	9	17	.346	33	33	8	0	0	217	224	123	104	23	1	83	114	1.415	4.31	97	4.22	.269	0	....	3	10	0.3
1978 Tor-A	7	16	.304	31	30	9	2	0	211^2	214	109	103	28	3	86	97	1.417	4.38	89	4.48	.267	0	....	-9	9	-1.0
1979 Tor-A	2	10	.167	34	10	2	0	1	116	150	75	71	19	2	45	43	1.681	5.51	79	6.57	.328	0	....	-16	3	-1.5
1980 Tor-A	4	13	.235	29	18	2	2	0	121^2	130	78	74	12	2	52	53	1.496	5.47	79	4.62	.281	0	....	-17	2	-1.7
Pit-N	1	0	1.000	1	1	0	0	0	6^2	3	1	1	0	0	2	4	.750	1.35	270	0.98	.143	0	.000	2	1	0.2
1981 Cal-A	2	4	.333	26	5	0	0	0	77	80	39	31	4	2	24	27	1.351	3.62	101	3.59	.269	0	....	-0	3	0.0
Total 9	39	81	.325	237	144	25	4	1	1085^2	1151	642	580	118	14	520	522	1.539	4.81	82	4.90	.277	0	.000	-99	35	-10.2
• JENKINS, Fergie	Ferguson Arthur Jenkins b: 12/13/1942, Chatham, Canada BR/TR, 6'5", 210 lbs. Deb: 9/10/1965 C HOF: 1991																									
1965 Phi-N	2	1	.667	7	0	0	0	1	12^1	7	3	3	2	0	2	10	.730	2.19	158	1.48	.159	0	.000	2	2	0.2
1966 Phi-N	0	0	....	1	0	0	0	0	2^1	3	2	1	0	0	1	2	1.714	3.86	93	3.75	.273	0	....	-0	0	0.0
Chi-N	6	8	.429	60	12	2	1	5	182	147	75	67	24	3	51	148	1.088	3.31	111	2.76	.219	7	.137	10	12	1.1
Yr.	6	8	.429	61	12	2	1	5	184^1	150	77	68	24	3	52	150	1.096	3.32	111	2.77	.220	7	.137	10	12	1.1
1967 Chi-N★	20	13	.606	38	38	**20**	3	0	289^1	230	101	90	30	4	83	236	1.082	2.80	127	2.63	.217	14	.151	21	21	2.4
1968 Chi-N	20	15	.571	40	**40**	20	3	0	308	255	96	90	26	3	65	260	1.039	2.63	120	2.37	.222	16	.160	18	25	2.4
1969 Chi-N	21	15	.583	43	**42**	23	7	1	311^1	284	122	111	27	8	71	**273**	1.140	3.21	126	2.89	.242	15	.139	29	25	3.0
1970 Chi-N	22	16	.579	40	39	**24**	3	0	313	265	128	118	30	7	60	274	1.038	3.39	133	2.48	.224	14	.124	**38**	26	3.5
1971 Chi-N★	**24**	13	.649	39	**39**	**30**	3	0	**325**	304	114	100	29	5	37	263	1.049	2.77	142	2.62	.246	28	.243	48	**37**	**6.3**
1972 Chi-N★	20	12	.625	36	36	23	5	0	289^1	253	111	103	32	7	62	184	1.089	3.20	119	2.81	.234	20	.183	19	22	2.3
1973 Chi-N	14	16	.467	38	38	7	2	0	271	267	133	117	35	4	57	170	1.196	3.89	101	3.45	.259	10	.119	8	15	0.7
1974 Tex-A	**25**	12	.676	41	41	**29**	6	0	328^1	286	117	103	27	8	45	225	1.008	2.82	126	2.38	.232	1	.500	26	26	2.7
1975 Tex-A	17	18	.486	37	37	22	4	0	270	261	130	118	37	9	56	157	1.174	3.93	95	3.46	.251	0	....	-5	15	-0.5
1976 Bos-A	12	11	.522	30	29	12	2	0	209	201	85	76	20	5	43	142	1.167	3.27	119	3.15	.253	0	....	17	14	1.8
1977 Bos-A	10	10	.500	28	28	11	1	0	193	190	91	79	30	0	36	105	1.171	3.68	122	3.50	.257	0	....	20	14	2.0
1978 Tex-A	18	8	.692	34	30	16	4	0	249	228	92	84	21	3	41	157	1.080	3.04	123	2.71	.245	0	....	20	21	2.1
1979 Tex-A	16	14	.533	37	37	10	3	0	259	252	127	117	40	3	81	164	1.286	4.07	102	3.97	.256	0	....	-0	14	0.0
1980 Tex-A	12	12	.500	29	29	12	0	0	198	190	90	83	22	4	52	129	1.222	3.77	103	3.40	.250	0	....	5	12	0.5
1981 Tex-A	5	8	.385	19	16	1	0	0	106	122	55	53	14	0	40	63	1.528	4.50	77	5.05	.290	0	....	-14	2	-1.5
1982 Chi-N	14	15	.483	34	34	4	1	0	217^1	221	92	76	19	5	68	134	1.330	3.15	119	3.79	.264	10	.149	16	14	1.6
1983 Chi-N	6	9	.400	33	29	1	1	0	167^1	176	89	80	19	6	46	96	1.327	4.30	88	4.12	.275	13	.245	-7	6	-0.4
Total 19	284	226	.557	664	594	267	49	7	4500^2	4142	1853	1669	484	84	997	3192	1.142	3.34	115	3.06	.243	148	.165	271	323	30.3
• JENKINS, Jack	Warren Washington Jenkins b: 12/22/1942, Covington, VA d: 6/18/2002, Tampa, FL BR/TR, 6'2", 195 lbs. Deb: 9/13/1962																									
1962 Was-A	0	1	.000	3	1	1	0	0	13^1	12	6	6	4	0	7	10	1.425	4.05	100	5.65	.245	0	.000	-0	1	-0.1
1963 Was-A	0	2	.000	4	2	0	0	0	12^1	16	8	8	2	0	12	5	2.270	5.84	64	9.31	.340	1	.333	-3	0	-0.3
1969 LA-N	0	0	....	1	0	0	0	0	1	0	0	0	0	0	0	1	.000	0.00	....	0.00	.000	0	....	0	0	0.0
Total 3	0	3	.000	8	3	1	0	0	26^2	28	14	14	6	0	19	16	1.763	4.73	81	7.13	.292	1	.143	-3	1	-0.3
• JENNINGS, Jason	Jason Ryan Jennings b: 7/17/1978, Dallas, TX BR/TR, 6'2", 242 lbs. Deb: 8/23/2001																									
2001 Col-N	4	1	.800	7	7	1	1	0	39^1	42	21	20	2	1	19	26	1.551	4.58	117	4.58	.276	4	.267	3	3	0.5
2002 Col-N	16	8	.667	32	32	0	0	0	185^1	201	102	93	26	8	70	127	1.462	4.52	106	4.98	.280	19	.306	7	14	1.3
2003 Col-N	12	13	.480	32	32	1	0	0	181^1	212	115	103	20	5	88	119	**1.654**	5.11	96	5.60	.299	12	.222	-1	8	0.2
Total 3	32	22	.593	71	71	2	1	0	406	455	238	216	48	14	177	272	1.557	4.79	102	5.22	.288	35	.267	9	25	1.9
• JENSEN, Ryan	Larry Ryan Jensen b: 9/17/1975, Salt Lake City, UT BR/TR, 6', 205 lbs. Deb: 5/19/2001																									
2001 SF-N	1	2	.333	10	7	0	0	0	42^1	44	21	20	5	4	25	26	1.630	4.25	94	5.68	.268	2	.167	-1	2	-0.1
2002 SF-N	13	8	.619	32	30	1	0	0	171^2	183	93	86	21	5	66	105	1.450	4.51	86	4.69	.278	6	.107	-14	5	-1.6
2003 SF-N	0	0	....	6	2	0	0	0	13^1	21	16	16	6	1	5	3	1.950	10.80	38	11.25	.404	2	.400	-10	0	-0.9
Total 3	14	10	.583	48	39	1	0	0	227^1	248	130	122	32	10	96	134	1.513	4.83	81	5.26	.284	10	.137	-26	7	-2.6
• JENSEN, Willie	William Christian Jensen b: 11/23/1888, New Haven, CT d: 3/27/1917, Philadelphia, PA BL/TR, 5'11.5", 170 lbs. Deb: 9/10/1912																									
1912 Det-A	1	2	.333	5	4	1	0	0	33	43	23	15	1	2	18	8	1.848	4.09	80	8.89	.339	0	.000	-3	0	-0.5
1914 Phi-A	0	1	.000	1	1	1	0	0	9	7	4	2	1	0	2	1	1.000	2.00	130	2.41	.226	0	.000	1	0	0.1
Total 2	1	3	.250	6	5	2	0	0	42	50	27	17	2	2	20	9	1.667	3.64	87	7.50	.317	0	.000	-2	0	-0.4
• JERZEMBECK, Mike	Michael Joseph Jerzembeck b: 5/18/1972, Queens, NY BR/TR, 6'1" Deb: 8/8/1998																									
1998 NY-A	0	1	.000	3	2	0	0	0	6^1	9	9	9	2	0	4	1	2.053	12.79	34	9.68	.346	0	....	-6	0	-0.6
• JESTER, Virgil	Virgil Milton Jester b: 7/23/1927, Denver, CO BR/TR, 5'11", 188 lbs. Deb: 6/18/1952																									
1952 Bos-N	3	5	.375	19	8	4	1	0	73	80	31	27	5	1	23	25	1.411	3.33	108	4.08	.283	4	.211	4	5	0.5
1953 Mil-N	0	0	....	2	0	0	0	0	2	4	5	5	1	0	4	0	4.000	22.50	17	22.10	.400	0	....	-4	0	-0.4
Total 2	3	5	.375	21	8	4	1	0	75	84	36	32	6	1	27	25	1.480	3.84	95	4.56	.287	4	.211	-1	5	0.1
• JIMENEZ, German	German (Camarena) Jimenez b: 12/5/1962, Santiago, Mexico BL/TL, 5'11", 200 lbs. Deb: 6/28/1988																									
1988 Atl-N	1	6	.143	15	9	0	0	0	55^2	65	39	31	4	1	12	26	1.383	5.01	73	4.13	.294	1	.059	-8	0	-0.9
• JIMENEZ, Jason	Jason Jon Jimenez b: 1/10/1976, Modesto, CA BR/TL, 6'2", 208 lbs. Deb: 6/3/2002																									
2002 TB-A	0	0	....	5	0	0	0	0	6^2	9	4	4	2	0	1	5	1.500	5.40	83	6.65	.333	0	....	-1	0	-0.1
Det-A	0	0	....	1	0	0	0	0	0^2	3	4	2	0	0	1	0	6.000	27.00	16	29.61	.500	0	....	-2	0	-0.2
Yr.	0	0	....	6	0	0	0	0	7^1	12	8	6	2	0	2	5	1.909	7.36	60	8.74	.364	0	....	-2	0	-0.2
• JIMENEZ, Jose	Jose Jimenez b: 7/7/1973, San Pedro de Macoris, Dominican Republic BR/TR, 6'3", 228 lbs. Deb: 9/9/1998																									
1998 StL-N	3	0	1.000	4	3	0	0	0	21^1	22	8	7	0	0	8	12	1.406	2.95	142	3.35	.262	0	.000	3	2	0.2
1999 StL-N	5	14	.263	29	28	2	2	0	163	173	114	106	16	11	71	113	1.497	5.85	78	4.81	.275	5	.094	-23	2	-2.4
2000 Col-N	5	2	.714	72	0	0	0	24	70^2	63	27	25	4	3	28	44	1.288	3.18	182	3.18	.239	2	.500	20	15	2.0
2001 Col-N	6	1	.857	56	0	0	0	17	55	56	27	25	6	0	22	37	1.418	4.09	130	4.14	.264	0	.000	7	8	0.7
2002 Col-N	2	10	.167	74	0	0	0	41	73^1	76	34	29	7	3	11	47	1.186	3.56	134	3.31	.265	0	....	11	13	1.1
2003 Col-N	2	10	.167	63	7	0	0	20	101^2	137	62	59	7	6	32	45	1.662	5.22	94	5.64	.322	3	.176	-2	6	-0.2
Total 6	23	37	.383	298	38	2	2	102	485	527	272	251	40	23	172	298	1.441	4.66	104	4.38	.277	10	.123	17	46	1.4
• JIMENEZ, Juan	Juan Antonio (Martes) Jimenez b: 3/8/1949, La Torre, Dominican Republic BR/TR, 6'1", 165 lbs. Deb: 9/9/1974																									
1974 Pit-N	0	0	....	4	0	0	0	0	4	6	4	3	0	0	2	2	2.000	6.75	51	6.85	.353	0	....	-1	0	-0.2
• JIMENEZ, Miguel	Miguel Anthony Jimenez b: 8/19/1969, New York, NY BR/TR, 6'2", 205 lbs. Deb: 9/12/1993																									
1993 Oak-A	1	0	1.000	5	4	0	0	0	27	27	12	12	5	1	16	13	1.593	4.00	102	5.78	.262	0	....	0	2	0.0
1994 Oak-A	1	4	.200	8	7	0	0	0	34	38	33	28	9	1	32	22	2.059	7.41	60	8.33	.275	0	....	-12	0	-1.1
Total 2	2	4	.333	13	11	0	0	0	61	65	45	40	14	2	48	35	1.852	5.90	73	7.20	.270	0	....	-11	2	-1.0
• JODIE, Brett	Brett P. Jodie b: 3/25/1977, Columbia, SC BR/TR, 6'4", 208 lbs. Deb: 7/20/2001																									
2001 NY-A	0	1	.000	1	1	0	0	0	2	7	6	6	3	0	1	0	4.000	27.00	17	42.94	.583	0	....	-5	0	-0.5
SD-N	0	1	.000	7	2	0	0	0	23^1	19	12	12	7	0	12	13	1.329	4.63	86	4.98	.229	0	.000	-1	1	-0.2

• JOHN, Tommy Thomas Edward John b: 5/22/1943, Terre Haute, IN BR/TL, 6'3", 185 lbs. Deb: 9/6/1963

YEAR	TM-L	W	L	PCT	G	GS	CG	SH	SV	IP	H	R	ER	HR	HB	BB	SO	RAT	ERA	ERA+	CERA	OAV	BH	AVG	PR+	WS	TPW
1963	Cle-A	0	2	.000	6	3	0	0	0	20^1	23	10	5	1	0	6	9	1.426	2.21	164	3.80	.284	0	.000	3	1	0.3
1964	Cle-A	2	9	.182	25	14	2	1	0	94^1	97	53	41	10	0	35	65	1.399	3.91	92	4.03	.262	5	.208	-1	2	-0.1
1965	Chi-A	14	7	.667	39	27	6	1	3	183^2	162	67	63	12	2	58	126	1.198	3.09	103	2.92	.237	10	.169	-0	12	0.2
1966	Chi-A	14	11	.560	34	33	10	**5**	0	223	195	76	65	13	7	57	138	1.130	2.62	121	2.71	.235	10	.145	13	15	1.5
1967	Chi-A	10	13	.435	31	29	9	**6**	0	178^1	143	62	49	12	5	47	110	1.065	2.47	126	2.39	.219	8	.157	12	11	1.3
1968	Chi-A★	10	5	.667	25	25	5	1	0	177^1	135	45	39	10	12	49	117	1.038	1.98	153	2.36	.212	12	.194	21	15	2.7
1969	Chi-A	9	11	.450	33	33	6	2	0	232^1	230	91	84	16	1	90	128	1.377	3.25	119	3.75	.261	9	.114	19	17	1.9
1970	Chi-A	12	17	.414	37	37	10	3	0	269^1	253	117	98	19	9	101	138	1.314	3.27	119	3.53	.251	17	.202	23	17	2.5
1971	Chi-A	13	16	.448	38	35	10	3	0	229^1	244	115	92	17	5	58	131	1.317	3.61	99	3.72	.274	10	.145	3	10	0.2
1972	LA-N	11	5	.688	29	29	4	1	0	186^2	172	68	60	14	3	40	117	1.136	2.89	115	2.82	.244	10	.159	9	11	0.8
1973	LA-N	16	7	.696	36	31	4	2	0	218	202	88	75	16	4	50	116	1.156	3.10	111	2.94	.246	15	.203	6	15	0.8
1974	LA-N	13	3	.813	22	22	5	3	0	153	133	51	44	4	1	42	78	1.144	2.59	131	2.51	.235	6	.118	15	11	1.4
1976	LA-N	10	10	.500	31	31	6	2	0	207	207	76	71	7	0	61	91	1.295	3.09	109	3.20	.261	7	.109	3	13	0.1
1977*	LA-N	20	7	.741	31	31	11	3	0	220^1	225	82	68	12	3	50	123	1.248	2.78	138	3.31	.267	14	.177	24	19	2.5
1978*	LA-N★	17	10	.630	33	30	7	0	1	213	230	95	78	11	5	53	124	1.329	3.30	106	3.61	.271	8	.121	4	12	0.3
1979	NY-A★	21	9	.700	37	36	17	3	0	276^1	268	109	91	9	4	65	111	1.205	2.96	137	2.97	.260	0	....	29	23	2.9
1980*	NY-A★	22	9	.710	36	36	16	**6**	0	265^1	270	115	101	13	6	56	78	1.229	3.43	114	3.24	.268	0	....	16	19	1.6
1981*	NY-A	9	8	.529	20	20	7	0	0	140^1	135	50	41	10	3	39	50	1.240	2.63	136	3.31	.256	0	....	14	10	1.4
1982	NY-A	10	10	.500	30	26	9	2	0	186^2	190	84	76	11	3	34	54	1.200	3.66	109	3.14	.266	0	....	8	10	0.8
	*Cal-A	4	2	.667	7	7	1	0	0	35	49	18	15	4	0	5	14	1.543	3.86	105	5.59	.336	0	....	0	2	0.0
	Yr.	14	12	.538	37	33	10	2	0	221^2	239	102	91	15	3	39	68	1.254	3.69	108	3.53	.278	0	....	8	12	0.8
1983	Cal-A	11	13	.458	34	34	9	0	0	234^2	287	126	113	20	2	49	65	1.432	4.33	93	4.51	.304	0	....	-8	10	-0.8
1984	Cal-A	7	13	.350	32	29	4	1	0	181^1	223	97	91	15	4	56	47	1.539	4.52	88	5.04	.306	0	....	-12	7	-1.2
1985	Cal-A	2	4	.333	12	6	0	0	0	38^1	51	22	20	3	1	15	17	1.722	4.70	88	5.94	.329	0	....	-4	1	-0.4
	Oak-A	2	6	.250	11	11	0	0	0	48	66	37	33	6	1	13	8	1.646	6.19	62	5.97	.332	0	....	-12	0	-1.2
	Yr.	4	10	.286	23	17	0	0	0	86^1	117	59	53	9	2	28	25	1.680	5.53	71	5.96	.331	0	....	-16	1	-1.6
1986	NY-A	5	3	.625	13	10	1	0	0	70^2	73	27	23	8	2	15	28	1.245	2.93	140	3.79	.275	0	....	9	6	0.9
1987	NY-A	13	6	.684	33	33	3	1	0	187^2	212	95	84	12	6	47	63	1.380	4.03	109	4.07	.288	0	....	7	13	0.6
1988	NY-A	9	8	.529	35	32	0	0	0	176^1	221	96	88	11	6	46	81	**1.514**	4.49	88	4.84	.308	0	....	-9	7	-0.9
1989	NY-A	2	7	.222	10	10	0	0	0	63^2	87	45	41	6	3	22	18	1.712	5.80	67	6.25	.336	0	....	-14	0	-1.4
Total	**26**	**288**	**231**	**.555**	**760**	**700**	**162**	**46**	**4**	**4710^1**	**4783**	**2017**	**1749**	**302**	**98**	**1259**	**2245**	**1.283**	**3.34**	**111**	**3.51**	**.265**	**141**	**.157**	**177**	**289**	**18.6**

• JOHNS, Augie Augustus Francis "Lefty" Johns b: 9/10/1899, St. Louis, MO d: 9/12/1975, San Antonio, TX BL/TL, 5'8.5", 170 lbs. Deb: 4/16/1926

YEAR	TM-L	W	L	PCT	G	GS	CG	SH	SV	IP	H	R	ER	HR	HB	BB	SO	RAT	ERA	ERA+	CERA	OAV	BH	AVG	PR+	WS	TPW
1926	Det-A	6	4	.600	35	14	3	1	1	112^2	117	77	67	6	5	69	40	1.651	5.35	76	4.69	.271	4	.143	-15	3	-1.5
1927	Det-A	0	0	....	1	0	0	0	0	1	1	1	1	0	0	1	1	2.000	9.00	47	5.17	.333	0	....	-1	0	0.0
Total	**2**	**6**	**4**	**.600**	**36**	**14**	**3**	**1**	**1**	**113^2**	**118**	**78**	**68**	**6**	**5**	**70**	**41**	**1.654**	**5.38**	**75**	**4.69**	**.271**	**4**	**.143**	**-16**	**3**	**-1.6**

• JOHNS, Doug Douglas Alan Johns b: 12/19/1967, South Bend, IN BR/TL, 6'2", 185 lbs. Deb: 7/8/1995

YEAR	TM-L	W	L	PCT	G	GS	CG	SH	SV	IP	H	R	ER	HR	HB	BB	SO	RAT	ERA	ERA+	CERA	OAV	BH	AVG	PR+	WS	TPW
1995	Oak-A	5	3	.625	11	9	1	1	0	54^2	44	32	28	5	5	26	25	1.280	4.61	96	3.65	.226	0	....	-1	3	-0.1
1996	Oak-A	6	12	.333	40	23	1	0	1	158	187	112	105	21	6	69	71	1.620	5.98	82	5.73	.297	0	....	-21	4	-1.9
1998	Bal-A	3	3	.500	31	10	0	0	1	86^2	108	46	44	9	4	32	34	1.615	4.57	100	5.77	.321	2	1.000	1	4	0.1
1999	Bal-A	6	4	.600	32	5	0	0	0	86^2	81	45	43	9	8	25	50	1.223	4.47	105	3.62	.248	0	.000	0	5	0.0
Total	**4**	**20**	**22**	**.476**	**114**	**47**	**2**	**1**	**2**	**386**	**420**	**235**	**220**	**44**	**23**	**152**	**180**	**1.482**	**5.13**	**92**	**4.97**	**.282**	**2**	**.667**	**-21**	**16**	**-1.8**

• JOHNS, Ollie Oliver Tracy Johns b: 8/21/1879, Trenton, OH d: 6/17/1961, Hamilton, OH BL/TL Deb: 9/24/1905

YEAR	TM-L	W	L	PCT	G	GS	CG	SH	SV	IP	H	R	ER	HR	HB	BB	SO	RAT	ERA	ERA+	CERA	OAV	BH	AVG	PR+	WS	TPW
1905	Cin-N	1	0	1.000	4	1	1	0	1	18	31	22	7	1	0	4	8	1.944	3.50	94	7.19	.369	1	.200	-1	0	-0.1

• JOHNSON, Abe Abraham Johnson b: Chicago, IL Deb: 7/16/1893

YEAR	TM-L	W	L	PCT	G	GS	CG	SH	SV	IP	H	R	ER	HR	HB	BB	SO	RAT	ERA	ERA+	CERA	OAV	BH	AVG	PR+	WS	TPW
1893	Chi-N	0	0	....	1	0	0	0	1	1	2	4	4	0	1	2	0	4.000	36.00	13	20.55	.404	0	....	-3	0	-0.3

• JOHNSON, Adam Adam Bryant Johnson b: 7/12/1979, San Jose, CA BR/TR, 6'2", 210 lbs. Deb: 7/16/2001

YEAR	TM-L	W	L	PCT	G	GS	CG	SH	SV	IP	H	R	ER	HR	HB	BB	SO	RAT	ERA	ERA+	CERA	OAV	BH	AVG	PR+	WS	TPW
2001	Min-A	1	2	.333	7	4	0	0	0	25	32	25	23	6	5	13	17	1.800	8.28	55	8.59	.323	0	.000	-10	0	-1.0
2003	Min-A	0	1	.000	2	0	0	0	0	1^1	8	8	7	1	0	1	0	6.750	47.25	10	55.23	.667	0	....	-6	0	-0.6
Total	**2**	**1**	**3**	**.250**	**9**	**4**	**0**	**0**	**0**	**26^1**	**40**	**33**	**30**	**7**	**5**	**14**	**17**	**2.051**	**10.25**	**45**	**10.95**	**.360**	**0**	**.000**	**-16**	**0**	**-1.6**

• JOHNSON, Art Arthur Gilbert Johnson b: 2/15/1897, Warren, PA d: 6/7/1982, Sarasota, FL BB/TL, 6'1", 167 lbs. Deb: 9/18/1927

YEAR	TM-L	W	L	PCT	G	GS	CG	SH	SV	IP	H	R	ER	HR	HB	BB	SO	RAT	ERA	ERA+	CERA	OAV	BH	AVG	PR+	WS	TPW
1927	NY-N	0	0	....	1	0	0	0	0	3	1	1	0	0	0	1	0	.667	0.00	....	0.65	.125	0	....	1	0	0.1

• JOHNSON, Art Arthur Henry "Lefty" Johnson b: 7/16/1916, Winchester, MA BL/TL, 6'2", 185 lbs. Deb: 9/22/1940

YEAR	TM-L	W	L	PCT	G	GS	CG	SH	SV	IP	H	R	ER	HR	HB	BB	SO	RAT	ERA	ERA+	CERA	OAV	BH	AVG	PR+	WS	TPW
1940	Bos-N	0	1	.000	2	1	0	0	0	6	10	7	7	0	1	3	1	2.167	10.50	35	7.76	.345	0	.000	-5	0	-0.5
1941	Bos-N	7	15	.318	43	18	6	0	1	183^1	189	92	72	7	5	71	70	1.418	3.53	101	3.78	.270	8	.145	-1	8	-0.3
1942	Bos-N	0	0	....	4	0	0	0	0	6^1	4	1	1	0	1	5	0	1.421	1.42	235	3.29	.190	0	.000	1	1	0.1
Total	**3**	**7**	**16**	**.304**	**49**	**19**	**6**	**0**	**1**	**195^2**	**203**	**100**	**80**	**7**	**7**	**79**	**71**	**1.441**	**3.68**	**97**	**3.88**	**.271**	**8**	**.140**	**-4**	**9**	**-0.6**

• JOHNSON, Bart Clair Barth Johnson b: 1/3/1950, Torrance, CA BR/TR, 6'5", 215 lbs. Deb: 9/8/1969

YEAR	TM-L	W	L	PCT	G	GS	CG	SH	SV	IP	H	R	ER	HR	HB	BB	SO	RAT	ERA	ERA+	CERA	OAV	BH	AVG	PR+	WS	TPW
1969	Chi-A	1	3	.250	4	3	0	0	0	22^1	22	11	8	2	0	6	18	1.254	3.22	120	3.51	.259	1	.167	2	2	0.3
1970	Chi-A	4	7	.364	18	15	2	1	0	89^2	92	53	48	11	2	46	71	1.539	4.82	81	5.00	.268	8	.276	-8	3	-0.6
1971	Chi-A	12	10	.545	53	16	4	0	14	178	148	67	58	9	6	111	153	1.455	2.93	122	3.70	.227	11	.193	16	16	1.8
1972	Chi-A	0	3	.000	9	0	0	0	1	13^2	18	20	14	2	1	13	9	2.268	9.22	34	8.85	.327	0	.000	-9	0	-1.0
1973	Chi-A	3	3	.500	22	9	0	0	0	80^2	76	39	37	6	2	40	56	1.438	4.13	96	4.04	.252	0	....	-0	4	0.0
1974	Chi-A	10	4	.714	18	18	8	2	0	121^2	105	42	37	6	1	32	76	1.126	2.74	136	2.53	.229	0	....	15	11	1.5
1976	Chi-A	9	16	.360	32	32	8	3	0	211^1	231	115	111	19	1	62	91	1.386	4.73	75	4.15	.282	0	....	-25	5	-2.6
1977	Chi-A	4	5	.444	29	4	0	0	2	92	114	48	41	5	2	38	46	1.652	4.01	102	5.11	.302	0	....	3	5	0.3
Total	**8**	**43**	**51**	**.457**	**185**	**97**	**22**	**6**	**17**	**809^1**	**806**	**395**	**354**	**60**	**15**	**348**	**520**	**1.426**	**3.94**	**94**	**4.06**	**.261**	**20**	**.215**	**-6**	**46**	**-0.3**

• JOHNSON, Ben Benjamin Franklin Johnson b: 5/15/1931, Greenwood, SC BR/TR, 6'2", 190 lbs. Deb: 9/6/1959

YEAR	TM-L	W	L	PCT	G	GS	CG	SH	SV	IP	H	R	ER	HR	HB	BB	SO	RAT	ERA	ERA+	CERA	OAV	BH	AVG	PR+	WS	TPW
1959	Chi-N	0	0	....	4	2	0	0	0	16^2	17	5	4	1	0	4	6	1.260	2.16	183	3.33	.262	0	.000	3	1	0.3
1960	Chi-N	2	1	.667	17	0	0	0	1	29^1	39	21	16	3	1	11	9	1.705	4.91	77	6.37	.355	0	.000	-4	1	-0.4
Total	**2**	**2**	**1**	**.667**	**21**	**2**	**0**	**0**	**1**	**46**	**56**	**26**	**20**	**4**	**1**	**15**	**15**	**1.543**	**3.91**	**97**	**5.27**	**.320**	**0**	**.000**	**-0**	**2**	**-0.1**

• JOHNSON, Bill William Charles Johnson b: 10/6/1960, Wilmington, DE BR/TR, 6'5", 205 lbs. Deb: 9/6/1983

YEAR	TM-L	W	L	PCT	G	GS	CG	SH	SV	IP	H	R	ER	HR	HB	BB	SO	RAT	ERA	ERA+	CERA	OAV	BH	AVG	PR+	WS	TPW
1983	Chi-N	1	0	1.000	10	0	0	0	0	12^1	17	6	6	0	0	3	4	1.622	4.38	87	4.78	.347	0	....	-1	1	-0.1
1984	Chi-N	0	0	....	4	0	0	0	0	5^1	4	1	1	0	0	1	3	.938	1.69	232	1.49	.235	0	....	1	1	0.1
Total	**2**	**1**	**0**	**1.000**	**14**	**0**	**0**	**0**	**0**	**17^2**	**21**	**7**	**7**	**0**	**0**	**4**	**7**	**1.415**	**3.57**	**107**	**3.78**	**.318**	**0**	**....**	**1**	**2**	**0.1**

• JOHNSON, Bob Robert Dale Johnson b: 4/25/1943, Aurora, IL BL/TR, 6'4", 220 lbs. Deb: 9/19/1969

YEAR	TM-L	W	L	PCT	G	GS	CG	SH	SV	IP	H	R	ER	HR	HB	BB	SO	RAT	ERA	ERA+	CERA	OAV	BH	AVG	PR+	WS	TPW
1969	NY-N	0	0	....	2	0	0	0	1	1^2	1	0	0	0	0	1	1	1.200	0.00	....	2.03	.167	0	....	1	1	0.1
1970	KC-A	8	13	.381	40	26	10	1	4	214	178	82	73	18	11	82	206	1.215	3.07	122	3.17	.228	6	.105	14	14	1.4
1971*	Pit-N	9	10	.474	31	27	7	1	0	174^2	170	73	67	19	7	55	101	1.288	3.45	99	3.79	.259	3	.063	-3	7	-0.4
1972*	Pit-N	4	4	.500	31	11	1	0	3	115^2	98	40	38	14	4	46	79	1.245	2.96	112	3.43	.231	5	.143	3	7	0.3
1973	Pit-N	4	2	.667	50	2	0	0	4	92	98	41	37	12	5	34	68	1.435	3.62	97	4.66	.276	0	.000	-1	4	-0.2
1974	Cle-A	3	4	.429	14	10	0	0	0	72	75	42	35	12	3	37	36	1.556	4.38	83	5.33	.273	0	....	-6	2	-0.7
1977	Atl-N	0	1	.000	15	0	0	0	0	22^1	24	18	18	7	2	14	16	1.701	7.25	61	7.39	.270	1	.333	-6	0	-0.6
Total	**7**	**28**	**34**	**.452**	**183**	**76**	**18**	**2**	**12**	**692^1**	**644**	**296**	**268**	**82**	**32**	**269**	**507**	**1.319**	**3.48**	**103**	**3.93**	**.249**	**15**	**.096**	**2**	**35**	**-0.2**

• JOHNSON, Chet Chester Lillis "Chesty Chet" Johnson b: 8/1/1917, Redmond, WA d: 4/10/1983, Seattle, WA BL/TL, 6', 175 lbs. Deb: 9/12/1946

YEAR	TM-L	W	L	PCT	G	GS	CG	SH	SV	IP	H	R	ER	HR	HB	BB	SO	RAT	ERA	ERA+	CERA	OAV	BH	AVG	PR+	WS	TPW
1946	StL-A	0	0	....	5	3	0	0	0	18	20	12	10	0	0	13	8	1.833	5.00	75	5.04	.286	0	.000	-2	0	-0.3

• JOHNSON, Chief George Howard "Murphy,Big Murph" Johnson b: 3/30/1886, Winnebago, NE d: 6/12/1922, Des Moines, IA BR/TR, 5'11.5", 190 lbs. Deb: 4/16/1913

YEAR	TM-L	W	L	PCT	G	GS	CG	SH	SV	IP	H	R	ER	HR	HB	BB	SO	RAT	ERA	ERA+	CERA	OAV	BH	AVG	PR+	WS	TPW
1913	Cin-N	14	16	.467	44	31	13	3	0	269	251	137	90	8	7	86	107	1.253	3.01	108	3.02	.256	10	.114	6	13	0.4

YEAR	TM-L	W	L	PCT	G	GS	CG	SH	SV	IP	H	R	ER	HR	HB	BB	SO	RAT	ERA	ERA+	CERA	OAV	BH	AVG	PR+	WS	TPW
1914	Cin-N	0	0	....	1	1	0	0	0	4	6	4	3	0	0	2	1	2.000	6.75	43	6.33	.333	0	....	-2	0	-0.1
	KC-F	9	10	.474	20	19	12	2	0	134	157	76	47	2	4	33	78	1.418	3.16	97	4.02	.298	6	.122	-2	5	-0.3
1915	KC-F	17	17	.500	46	34	19	4	2	281^1	253	121	86	5	8	71	118	1.152	2.75	106	2.57	.242	11	.126	7	17	0.6
Total	**3**	**40**	**43**	**.482**	**111**	**85**	**44**	**9**	**2**	**688^1**	**667**	**338**	**226**	**15**	**19**	**192**	**304**	**1.248**	**2.95**	**104**	**3.05**	**.259**	**27**	**.121**	**9**	**35**	**0.5**

• JOHNSON, Connie Clifford Johnson b: 12/27/1922, Stone Mountain, GA BR/TR, 6'4", 200 lbs. Deb: 4/17/1953

YEAR	TM-L	W	L	PCT	G	GS	CG	SH	SV	IP	H	R	ER	HR	HB	BB	SO	RAT	ERA	ERA+	CERA	OAV	BH	AVG	PR+	WS	TPW
1953	Chi-A	4	4	.500	14	10	2	1	0	60^2	55	27	24	4	2	38	44	1.533	3.56	113	4.11	.238	1	.050	3	3	0.1
1955	Chi-A	7	4	.636	17	16	5	2	0	99	95	40	38	5	1	52	72	1.485	3.45	114	4.01	.251	5	.152	4	7	0.3
1956	Chi-A	0	1	.000	5	2	0	0	0	12^1	11	5	5	1	0	7	6	1.459	3.65	112	3.81	.234	0	.000	1	1	0.0
	Bal-A	9	10	.474	26	25	9	2	0	183^2	165	79	70	12	1	62	130	1.236	3.43	114	3.05	.239	15	.259	11	16	1.5
	Yr.	9	11	.450	31	27	9	2	0	196	176	84	75	13	1	69	136	1.250	3.44	114	3.09	.239	15	.246	12	17	1.5
1957	Bal-A	14	11	.560	35	30	14	3	0	242	212	93	86	17	3	66	177	1.149	3.20	112	2.79	.235	12	.135	7	15	0.2
1958	Bal-A	6	9	.400	26	17	4	0	1	118^1	116	58	51	13	0	32	68	1.251	3.88	93	3.54	.260	7	.206	-3	6	-0.3
Total	**5**	**40**	**39**	**.506**	**123**	**100**	**34**	**8**	**1**	**716**	**654**	**302**	**274**	**52**	**7**	**257**	**497**	**1.272**	**3.44**	**109**	**3.28**	**.243**	**40**	**.169**	**22**	**48**	**1.9**

• JOHNSON, Dane Dane Edward Johnson b: 2/10/1963, Coral Gables, FL BR/TR, 6'5", 205 lbs. Deb: 5/30/1994

YEAR	TM-L	W	L	PCT	G	GS	CG	SH	SV	IP	H	R	ER	HR	HB	BB	SO	RAT	ERA	ERA+	CERA	OAV	BH	AVG	PR+	WS	TPW
1994	Chi-A	2	1	.667	15	0	0	0	0	12^1	16	9	9	2	0	11	7	2.189	6.57	71	8.60	.327	0	....	-3	0	-0.2
1996	Tor-A	0	0	....	10	0	0	0	0	9	5	3	3	0	0	5	7	1.111	3.00	167	1.77	.161	0	....	2	1	0.2
1997	Oak-A	4	1	.800	38	0	0	0	2	45^2	49	28	23	4	2	31	43	1.752	4.53	99	5.45	.272	0	....	1	3	0.1
Total	**3**	**6**	**2**	**.750**	**63**	**0**	**0**	**0**	**2**	**67**	**70**	**40**	**35**	**6**	**2**	**47**	**57**	**1.746**	**4.70**	**97**	**5.54**	**.269**	**0**	**....**	**0**	**4**	**0.0**

• JOHNSON, Dave David Wayne Johnson b: 10/24/1959, Baltimore, MD BR/TR, 5'10", 183 lbs. Deb: 5/29/1987

YEAR	TM-L	W	L	PCT	G	GS	CG	SH	SV	IP	H	R	ER	HR	HB	BB	SO	RAT	ERA	ERA+	CERA	OAV	BH	AVG	PR+	WS	TPW
1987	Pit-N	0	0	....	5	0	0	0	0	6^1	13	7	7	1	0	2	4	2.368	9.95	41	11.87	.448	0	....	-4	0	-0.4
1989	Bal-A	4	7	.364	14	14	4	0	0	89^1	90	44	42	11	4	28	26	1.321	4.23	90	4.15	.265	0	....	-5	4	-0.5
1990	Bal-A	13	9	.591	30	29	3	0	0	180	196	83	82	30	3	43	68	1.328	4.10	92	4.50	.280	0	....	-8	9	-0.8
1991	Bal-A	4	8	.333	22	14	0	0	0	84	127	68	66	18	4	24	38	1.798	7.07	56	7.88	.349	0	....	-29	0	-2.9
1993	Det-A	1	1	.500	6	0	0	0	0	8^1	13	13	12	3	2	5	7	2.160	12.96	33	11.28	.342	0	....	-8	0	-0.8
Total	**5**	**22**	**25**	**.468**	**77**	**57**	**7**	**0**	**0**	**368**	**439**	**215**	**209**	**63**	**13**	**102**	**143**	**1.470**	**5.11**	**76**	**5.47**	**.298**	**0**	**....**	**-54**	**13**	**-5.4**

• JOHNSON, Dave David Charles Johnson b: 10/4/1948, Abilene, TX BR/TR, 6'1", 183 lbs. Deb: 7/2/1974

YEAR	TM-L	W	L	PCT	G	GS	CG	SH	SV	IP	H	R	ER	HR	HB	BB	SO	RAT	ERA	ERA+	CERA	OAV	BH	AVG	PR+	WS	TPW
1974	Bal-A	2	2	.500	11	0	0	0	2	15^1	17	5	5	1	0	5	6	1.435	2.93	118	3.79	.274	0	....	1	2	0.1
1975	Bal-A	0	1	.000	6	0	0	0	0	8^2	8	4	4	0	0	7	4	1.731	4.15	84	4.11	.250	0	....	-1	0	-0.1
1977	Min-A	2	5	.286	30	6	0	0	0	72^2	86	42	37	7	5	23	33	1.500	4.58	87	5.10	.299	0	....	-5	2	-0.5
1978	Min-A	0	2	.000	6	1	0	0	0	12	15	11	10	1	0	9	7	2.000	7.50	51	6.96	.313	0	....	-5	0	-0.5
Total	**4**	**4**	**10**	**.286**	**53**	**7**	**0**	**0**	**2**	**108^2**	**126**	**62**	**56**	**9**	**5**	**44**	**50**	**1.564**	**4.64**	**83**	**5.04**	**.293**	**0**	**....**	**-10**	**4**	**-1.0**

• JOHNSON, Don Donald Roy Johnson b: 11/12/1926, Portland, OR BR/TR, 6'3", 200 lbs. Deb: 4/20/1947

YEAR	TM-L	W	L	PCT	G	GS	CG	SH	SV	IP	H	R	ER	HR	HB	BB	SO	RAT	ERA	ERA+	CERA	OAV	BH	AVG	PR+	WS	TPW
1947	NY-A	4	3	.571	15	8	2	0	0	54^1	57	26	22	2	1	23	16	1.472	3.64	97	3.95	.270	0	.000	-1	2	-0.3
1950	NY-A	1	0	1.000	8	0	0	0	0	18	35	21	20	2	0	12	9	2.611	10.00	43	11.11	.398	0	.000	-12	0	-1.1
	StL-A	5	6	.455	25	12	4	1	1	96	126	72	65	14	1	55	31	1.885	6.09	81	7.00	.325	2	.069	-9	3	-1.1
	Yr.	6	6	.500	33	12	4	1	1	114	161	93	85	16	1	67	40	2.000	6.71	71	7.65	.338	2	.063	-21	3	-2.3
1951	StL-A	0	1	.000	6	3	0	0	0	15	27	26	21	4	1	18	8	3.000	12.60	35	14.29	.391	1	.333	-13	0	-1.3
	Was-A	7	11	.389	21	20	8	1	0	143^2	138	67	63	9	2	58	52	1.364	3.95	104	3.62	.255	4	.085	4	7	-0.1
	Yr.	7	12	.368	27	23	8	1	0	158^2	165	93	84	13	3	76	60	1.519	4.76	87	4.63	.270	5	.100	-9	7	-1.4
1952	Was-A	0	5	.000	29	6	0	0	2	69	80	41	34	4	4	33	37	1.638	4.43	80	5.02	.287	1	.077	-6	0	-0.8
1954	Chi-A	8	7	.533	46	16	3	3	7	144	129	53	50	14	0	43	68	1.194	3.13	119	3.12	.243	1	.029	8	11	0.5
1955	Bal-A	2	4	.333	31	5	0	0	1	68	89	46	44	4	0	35	27	1.824	5.82	65	6.09	.333	0	.000	-14	0	-1.6
1958	SF-N	0	1	.000	17	0	0	0	1	23	31	19	16	2	2	8	14	1.696	6.26	61	6.06	.323	0	.000	-6	0	-0.6
Total	**7**	**27**	**38**	**.415**	**198**	**70**	**17**	**5**	**12**	**631**	**712**	**371**	**335**	**55**	**11**	**285**	**262**	**1.580**	**4.78**	**85**	**5.02**	**.288**	**9**	**.058**	**-49**	**23**	**-6.4**

• JOHNSON, Earl Earl Douglas "Lefty" Johnson b: 4/2/1919, Redmond, WA d: 12/3/1994, Seattle, WA BL/TL, 6'3", 190 lbs. Deb: 7/20/1940

YEAR	TM-L	W	L	PCT	G	GS	CG	SH	SV	IP	H	R	ER	HR	HB	BB	SO	RAT	ERA	ERA+	CERA	OAV	BH	AVG	PR+	WS	TPW
1940	Bos-A	6	2	.750	17	10	2	0	0	70^1	69	33	32	0	2	39	26	1.536	4.09	110	3.84	.260	2	.074	4	5	0.1
1941	Bos-A	4	5	.444	17	12	4	0	0	93^2	90	57	47	4	3	51	46	1.505	4.52	92	3.92	.247	10	.294	-3	4	0.0
1946*	Bos-A	5	4	.556	29	5	0	0	3	80	78	39	33	5	2	39	40	1.463	3.71	99	3.91	.250	5	.227	-1	5	0.1
1947	Bos-A	12	11	.522	45	17	6	3	8	142^1	129	63	47	7	2	62	65	1.342	2.97	131	3.36	.246	12	.273	14	13	1.6
1948	Bos-A	10	4	.714	35	3	1	0	5	91^1	98	49	46	7	0	42	45	1.533	4.53	97	4.47	.276	3	.097	-2	7	-0.5
1949	Bos-A	3	6	.333	19	3	0	0	0	49^1	65	45	41	1	4	29	20	1.905	7.48	58	6.28	.327	0	.000	-18	0	-1.9
1950	Bos-A	0	0	....	11	0	0	0	0	13^2	18	11	11	0	1	8	6	1.902	7.24	68	6.11	.333	0	.000	-4	0	-0.4
1951	Det-A	0	0	....	6	0	0	0	1	5^2	9	5	4	0	0	2	2	1.941	6.35	66	6.83	.375	0	....	-1	0	-0.1
Total	**8**	**40**	**32**	**.556**	**179**	**50**	**13**	**3**	**17**	**546^1**	**556**	**302**	**261**	**24**	**14**	**272**	**250**	**1.516**	**4.30**	**97**	**4.15**	**.265**	**32**	**.187**	**-10**	**34**	**-1.1**

• JOHNSON, Ernie Ernest Thorwald Johnson b: 6/16/1924, Brattleboro, VT BR/TR, 6'3.5", 195 lbs. Deb: 4/28/1950

YEAR	TM-L	W	L	PCT	G	GS	CG	SH	SV	IP	H	R	ER	HR	HB	BB	SO	RAT	ERA	ERA+	CERA	OAV	BH	AVG	PR+	WS	TPW
1950	Bos-N	2	0	1.000	16	1	0	0	0	20^2	37	21	16	1	0	13	15	2.419	6.97	55	9.33	.394	1	.500	-7	0	-0.7
1952	Bos-N	6	3	.667	29	10	2	1	1	92	100	53	42	8	2	31	45	1.424	4.11	88	4.16	.270	2	.091	-3	3	-0.4
1953	Mil-N	4	3	.571	36	1	0	0	0	81	79	34	24	4	3	22	36	1.247	2.67	147	3.28	.263	1	.071	10	6	0.9
1954	Mil-N	5	2	.714	40	4	1	0	2	99^1	77	34	31	11	1	34	68	1.117	2.81	133	2.79	.219	3	.231	9	9	0.9
1955	Mil-N	5	7	.417	40	2	0	0	4	92	81	38	35	5	2	55	43	1.478	3.42	110	3.79	.240	2	.100	3	6	0.2
1956	Mil-N	4	3	.571	36	0	0	0	6	51	54	21	21	9	1	21	26	1.471	3.71	93	5.04	.270	1	.250	-2	3	-0.2
1957*	Mil-N	7	3	.700	30	0	0	0	4	65	67	29	28	9	1	26	44	1.431	3.88	90	4.44	.265	6	.353	-4	5	-0.1
1958	Mil-N	3	1	.750	15	0	0	0	1	23^1	35	21	21	4	1	10	13	1.929	8.10	43	7.74	.357	0	.000	-12	0	-1.2
1959	Bal-A	4	1	.800	31	1	0	0	1	50^1	57	32	23	6	3	19	29	1.510	4.11	92	4.94	.286	2	.333	-2	2	-0.2
Total	**9**	**40**	**23**	**.635**	**273**	**19**	**3**	**1**	**19**	**574^2**	**587**	**283**	**241**	**57**	**14**	**231**	**319**	**1.423**	**3.77**	**97**	**4.25**	**.266**	**18**	**.180**	**-8**	**34**	**-0.7**

• JOHNSON, Fred Frederick Edward "Deacon,Cactus" Johnson b: 3/10/1894, Tolar, TX d: 6/14/1973, Kerrville, TX BR/TR, 6', 185 lbs. Deb: 9/27/1922

YEAR	TM-L	W	L	PCT	G	GS	CG	SH	SV	IP	H	R	ER	HR	HB	BB	SO	RAT	ERA	ERA+	CERA	OAV	BH	AVG	PR+	WS	TPW
1922	NY-N	0	2	.000	2	2	1	0	0	18	20	8	8	3	0	1	8	1.167	4.00	100	3.84	.294	0	.000	-1	1	-0.1
1923	NY-N	2	0	1.000	3	2	1	0	0	17	11	8	8	2	0	7	5	1.059	4.24	90	2.27	.177	0	.000	-1	1	-0.2
1938	StL-A	3	7	.300	17	6	3	0	3	69	91	50	43	7	1	27	24	1.710	5.61	89	5.86	.316	6	.240	-5	3	-0.4
1939	StL-A	0	1	.000	5	2	1	0	0	14	23	12	10	0	0	9	2	2.286	6.43	76	8.25	.383	0	.000	-2	0	-0.2
Total	**4**	**5**	**10**	**.333**	**27**	**12**	**6**	**0**	**3**	**118**	**145**	**78**	**69**	**12**	**1**	**44**	**39**	**1.602**	**5.26**	**89**	**5.32**	**.303**	**6**	**.154**	**-8**	**5**	**-1.0**

• JOHNSON, Hank Henry Ward Johnson b: 5/21/1906, Bradenton, FL d: 8/20/1982, Bradenton, FL BR/TR, 5'11.5", 175 lbs. Deb: 4/17/1925

YEAR	TM-L	W	L	PCT	G	GS	CG	SH	SV	IP	H	R	ER	HR	HB	BB	SO	RAT	ERA	ERA+	CERA	OAV	BH	AVG	PR+	WS	TPW
1925	NY-A	1	3	.250	24	4	2	1	0	67	88	58	51	3	8	37	25	1.866	6.85	62	6.32	.319	1	.059	-19	0	-1.9
1926	NY-A	0	0	....	1	0	0	0	1	1	2	2	2	0	0	2	0	4.000	18.00	21	15.81	.400	0	....	-2	0	-0.2
1928	NY-A	14	9	.609	31	22	10	1	0	199	188	107	95	16	12	104	110	1.467	4.30	87	3.87	.250	19	.241	-9	9	-0.8
1929	NY-A	3	3	.500	12	8	2	0	0	42^2	37	28	24	5	0	39	24	1.781	5.06	76	5.16	.237	1	.071	-6	1	-0.7
1930	NY-A	14	11	.560	44	15	7	1	2	175^1	177	112	91	12	2	104	115	1.603	4.67	92	4.53	.265	17	.266	-5	9	-0.1
1931	NY-A	13	8	.619	40	23	8	0	4	196^1	176	114	103	13	1	102	106	1.416	4.72	84	3.54	.234	15	.195	-18	9	-1.5
1932	NY-A	2	2	.500	5	4	2	0	0	31^1	34	18	17	7	0	15	27	1.564	4.88	83	5.52	.266	3	.231	-3	1	-0.2
1933	Bos-A	8	6	.571	25	21	7	0	1	155^1	156	84	70	13	3	74	65	1.481	4.06	108	4.22	.263	12	.231	6	10	0.9
1934	Bos-A	6	8	.429	31	14	7	1	1	124^1	162	95	74	12	5	53	66	1.729	5.36	90	5.95	.316	10	.233	-7	4	-0.5
1935	Bos-A	2	1	.667	13	2	0	0	1	31	41	21	19	3	0	14	14	1.774	5.52	86	6.16	.331	0	.000	-3	1	-0.4
1936	Phi-A	0	2	.000	3	3	0	0	0	11^2	16	16	10	4	1	10	6	2.229	7.71	66	9.97	.296	1	.250	-3	0	-0.3
1939	Cin-N	0	3	.000	20	0	0	0	1	31^1	30	10	7	1	0	13	10	1.372	2.01	191	3.35	.268	2	.400	6	3	0.6
Total	**12**	**63**	**56**	**.529**	**249**	**116**	**45**	**4**	**11**	**1066^1**	**1107**	**665**	**563**	**89**	**32**	**567**	**568**	**1.570**	**4.75**	**88**	**4.60**	**.268**	**81**	**.215**	**-63**	**47**	**-5.1**

• JOHNSON, Jason Jason Michael Johnson b: 10/27/1973, Santa Barbara, CA BR/TR, 6'6", 220 lbs. Deb: 8/27/1997

YEAR	TM-L	W	L	PCT	G	GS	CG	SH	SV	IP	H	R	ER	HR	HB	BB	SO	RAT	ERA	ERA+	CERA	OAV	BH	AVG	PR+	WS	TPW
1997	Pit-N	0	0	....	3	0	0	0	0	6	10	4	4	2	0	1	3	1.833	6.00	72	9.59	.400	0	.000	-1	0	-0.1
1998	TB-A	2	5	.286	13	13	0	0	0	60	74	38	38	9	3	27	36	1.683	5.70	84	6.35	.306	0	.000	-8	2	-0.8
1999	Bal-A	8	7	.533	22	21	0	0	0	115^1	120	74	70	16	3	55	71	1.517	5.46	86	4.99	.266	0	.000	-12	4	-1.2
2000	Bal-A	1	10	.091	25	13	0	0	0	107^2	119	95	84	21	4	61	79	1.672	7.02	67	6.18	.278	0	.000	-27	0	-2.5

YEAR	TM-L	W	L	PCT	G	GS	CG	SH	SV	IP	H	R	ER	HR	HB	BB	SO	RAT	ERA	ERA+	CERA	OAV	BH	AVG	PR+	WS	TPW
2001	Bal-A	10	12	.455	32	32	2	0	0	196	194	109	89	28	13	77	114	1.383	4.09	105	4.53	.257	1	.333	2	9	0.3
2002	Bal-A	5	14	.263	22	22	1	0	0	131^1	141	68	67	19	6	41	97	1.386	4.59	93	4.70	.276	0	.000	-6	5	-0.6
2003	Bal-A	10	10	.500	32	32	0	0	0	189^2	216	100	88	22	10	80	118	**1.561**	4.18	105	5.21	.283	1	.200	5	11	0.5
Total	7	36	58	.383	149	133	3	0	0	806	874	488	440	117	39	342	518	1.509	4.91	91	5.18	.275	2	.105	-48	31	-4.4

• JOHNSON, Jeff William Jeffrey Johnson b: 8/4/1966, Durham, NC BR/TL, 6'3", 200 lbs. Deb: 6/5/1991

YEAR	TM-L	W	L	PCT	G	GS	CG	SH	SV	IP	H	R	ER	HR	HB	BB	SO	RAT	ERA	ERA+	CERA	OAV	BH	AVG	PR+	WS	TPW
1991	NY-A	6	11	.353	23	23	0	0	0	127	156	89	84	15	6	33	62	1.488	5.95	70	5.15	.305	0	....	-25	1	-2.5
1992	NY-A	2	3	.400	13	8	0	0	0	52^2	71	44	39	4	2	23	14	1.785	6.66	59	6.34	.329	0	....	-16	0	-1.7
1993	NY-A	0	2	.000	2	2	0	0	0	2^2	12	10	9	1	0	2	0	5.250	30.38	14	35.88	.600	0	....	-8	0	-0.8
Total	3	8	16	.333	38	33	0	0	0	182^1	239	143	132	20	8	58	76	1.629	6.52	62	5.94	.320	0	....	-49	1	-4.9

• JOHNSON, Jerry Jerry Michael Johnson b: 12/3/1943, Miami, FL BR/TR, 6'3", 200 lbs. Deb: 7/17/1968

YEAR	TM-L	W	L	PCT	G	GS	CG	SH	SV	IP	H	R	ER	HR	HB	BB	SO	RAT	ERA	ERA+	CERA	OAV	BH	AVG	PR+	WS	TPW
1968	Phi-N	4	4	.500	16	11	2	0	0	80^2	82	33	29	5	2	29	40	1.376	3.24	93	3.83	.264	2	.080	-1	4	-0.2
1969	Phi-N	6	13	.316	33	21	4	2	1	147^1	151	76	70	18	3	57	82	1.412	4.28	83	4.31	.268	9	.209	-12	5	-1.1
1970	StL-N	2	0	1.000	7	0	0	0	1	11^1	6	4	4	1	0	3	5	.794	3.18	130	1.32	.146	0	.000	1	2	0.2
	SF-N	3	4	.429	33	1	0	0	3	65^1	67	39	31	5	1	38	44	1.607	4.27	93	4.76	.266	1	.067	-1	3	-0.2
	Yr.	5	4	.556	40	1	0	0	4	76^2	73	43	35	6	1	41	49	1.487	4.11	97	4.25	.249	1	.063	1	5	0.0
1971*	SF-N	12	9	.571	67	0	0	0	18	109	93	42	36	9	1	48	85	1.294	2.97	114	3.15	.230	2	.154	6	12	0.6
1972	SF-N	8	6	.571	48	0	0	0	8	73^1	73	40	36	4	0	40	57	1.541	4.42	79	3.96	.261	0	.000	-8	4	-0.9
1973	Cle-A	5	6	.455	39	1	0	0	5	59^2	70	48	41	7	0	39	45	1.827	6.18	63	6.03	.299	0	....	-15	0	-1.5
1974	Hou-N	2	1	.667	34	0	0	0	0	45	47	26	24	2	0	24	32	1.578	4.80	72	4.17	.276	0	.000	-7	1	-0.8
1975	SD-N	3	1	.750	21	4	0	0	0	54	60	37	31	3	0	31	18	1.685	5.17	67	4.90	.282	1	.083	-9	0	-1.0
1976	SD-N	1	3	.250	24	1	0	0	0	39	39	27	23	0	0	26	27	1.667	5.31	62	4.03	.260	0	.000	-9	0	-1.0
1977	Tor-A	2	4	.333	43	0	0	0	5	86	91	50	44	9	0	54	54	1.686	4.60	91	5.31	.279	0	....	-2	4	-0.2
Total	10	48	51	.485	365	39	6	2	41	770^2	779	422	369	63	7	389	489	1.516	4.31	83	4.32	.265	15	.123	-56	35	-6.1

• JOHNSON, Jim James Brian Johnson b: 11/3/1945, Muskegon, MI d: 12/6/1987, North Muskegon, MI BL/TL, 5'11", 175 lbs. Deb: 4/13/1970

YEAR	TM-L	W	L	PCT	G	GS	CG	SH	SV	IP	H	R	ER	HR	HB	BB	SO	RAT	ERA	ERA+	CERA	OAV	BH	AVG	PR+	WS	TPW
1970	SF-N	1	0	1.000	3	0	0	0	0	6^2	8	6	6	0	0	5	2	1.950	8.10	49	5.38	.320	0	.000	-3	0	-0.3

• JOHNSON, Jing Russell Conwell Johnson b: 10/9/1894, Parker Ford, PA d: 12/6/1950, Pottstown, PA BR/TR, 5'9", 172 lbs. Deb: 6/27/1916

YEAR	TM-L	W	L	PCT	G	GS	CG	SH	SV	IP	H	R	ER	HR	HB	BB	SO	RAT	ERA	ERA+	CERA	OAV	BH	AVG	PR+	WS	TPW
1916	Phi-A	2	9	.182	12	12	8	0	0	84^1	90	46	35	3	0	39	25	1.530	3.74	76	4.40	.288	2	.074	-6	1	-0.8
1917	Phi-A	9	12	.429	34	23	13	0	0	191	184	76	59	3	5	56	55	1.257	2.78	99	2.92	.260	12	.203	2	9	0.5
1919	Phi-A	9	15	.375	34	25	12	0	0	202	222	106	81	8	3	62	67	1.406	3.61	95	4.04	.291	14	.194	5	8	0.5
1927	Phi-A	4	2	.667	17	3	2	0	0	51^2	42	20	20	2	4	16	16	1.123	3.48	122	2.67	.235	2	.167	5	4	0.4
1928	Phi-A	0	0	....	3	0	0	0	0	10^2	13	8	6	1	0	5	3	1.688	5.06	79	5.43	.310	2	.500	-1	0	0.0
Total	5	24	38	.387	100	63	35	0	0	539^2	551	256	201	17	12	178	166	1.351	3.35	94	3.60	.275	32	.184	4	22	0.7

• JOHNSON, Joe Joseph Richard Johnson b: 10/30/1961, Brookline, MA BR/TR, 6'2", 195 lbs. Deb: 7/25/1985

YEAR	TM-L	W	L	PCT	G	GS	CG	SH	SV	IP	H	R	ER	HR	HB	BB	SO	RAT	ERA	ERA+	CERA	OAV	BH	AVG	PR+	WS	TPW
1985	Atl-N	4	4	.500	15	14	1	0	0	85^2	95	44	39	9	3	24	34	1.389	4.10	94	4.34	.285	1	.043	-2	4	-0.2
1986	Atl-N	6	7	.462	17	15	2	0	0	87	101	58	48	8	2	35	49	1.563	4.97	80	4.96	.289	3	.115	-9	2	-1.0
	Tor-A	7	2	.778	16	15	0	0	0	88	94	39	38	3	3	22	39	1.318	3.89	108	3.60	.281	0	....	3	6	0.3
1987	Tor-A	3	5	.375	14	14	0	0	0	66^2	77	44	38	10	2	18	27	1.425	5.13	88	4.95	.289	0	....	-6	2	-0.5
Total	3	20	18	.526	62	58	3	0	0	327^1	367	185	163	30	10	99	149	1.424	4.48	92	4.43	.286	4	.082	-13	14	-1.4

• JOHNSON, John John Louis Johnson b: 11/18/1869, Pekin, IL d: 1/28/1941, Kansas City, MO TL, 5'10", 165 lbs. Deb: 9/11/1894

YEAR	TM-L	W	L	PCT	G	GS	CG	SH	SV	IP	H	R	ER	HR	HB	BB	SO	RAT	ERA	ERA+	CERA	OAV	BH	AVG	PR+	WS	TPW
1894	Phi-N	1	1	.500	4	3	2	0	0	32^2	44	30	22	3	1	15	10	1.806	6.06	84	6.32	.319	3	.188	-3	1	-0.3

• JOHNSON, John Henry John Henry Johnson b: 8/21/1956, Houston, TX BL/TL, 6'2", 190 lbs. Deb: 4/10/1978

YEAR	TM-L	W	L	PCT	G	GS	CG	SH	SV	IP	H	R	ER	HR	HB	BB	SO	RAT	ERA	ERA+	CERA	OAV	BH	AVG	PR+	WS	TPW
1978	Oak-A	11	10	.524	33	30	7	2	0	186	164	81	70	18	0	82	91	1.323	3.39	107	3.51	.238	0	....	8	13	0.9
1979	Oak-A	2	8	.200	14	13	1	0	0	84^2	89	45	41	13	1	36	50	1.476	4.36	93	4.91	.269	0	....	-1	4	0.0
	Tex-A	2	6	.250	17	12	1	0	0	82^1	79	50	45	12	1	36	46	1.397	4.92	84	4.29	.255	0	....	-8	2	-0.8
	Yr.	4	14	.222	31	25	2	0	0	167	168	95	86	25	2	72	96	1.437	4.63	88	4.60	.262	0	....	-8	6	-0.8
1980	Tex-A	2	2	.500	33	0	0	0	4	38^2	27	12	10	2	1	15	44	1.086	2.33	167	2.15	.199	0	....	7	5	0.7
1981	Tex-A	3	1	.750	24	0	0	0	2	23^2	19	7	7	2	1	6	8	1.056	2.66	130	2.54	.232	0	....	2	3	0.2
1983	Bos-A	3	2	.600	34	1	0	0	1	53^1	58	28	22	3	1	20	51	1.463	3.71	117	4.09	.283	0	....	4	3	0.4
1984	Bos-A	1	2	.333	30	3	0	0	1	63^2	64	26	25	7	0	27	57	1.429	3.53	118	4.26	.260	0	....	7	5	0.7
1986	Mil-A	2	1	.667	19	0	0	0	1	44	43	15	13	2	0	10	42	1.205	2.66	163	2.85	.251	0	....	8	4	0.8
1987	Mil-A	0	1	.000	10	2	0	0	0	26^1	42	30	28	1	0	18	18	2.278	9.57	48	8.45	.365	0	....	-14	0	-1.4
Total	8	26	33	.441	214	61	9	2	9	602^2	585	294	261	60	5	250	407	1.386	3.90	103	3.99	.256	0	....	14	39	1.5

• JOHNSON, Johnny John Clifford "Swede" Johnson b: 9/29/1914, Belmore, OH d: 6/26/1991, Iron Mountain, MI BL/TL, 6', 182 lbs. Deb: 4/19/1944

YEAR	TM-L	W	L	PCT	G	GS	CG	SH	SV	IP	H	R	ER	HR	HB	BB	SO	RAT	ERA	ERA+	CERA	OAV	BH	AVG	PR+	WS	TPW
1944	NY-A	0	2	.000	22	1	0	0	3	26^2	25	14	12	0	1	24	11	1.838	4.05	86	4.45	.243	3	.500	-2	2	-0.1
1945	Chi-A	3	0	1.000	29	0	0	0	4	69^2	85	39	33	2	1	35	38	1.722	4.26	78	5.10	.306	4	.286	-6	3	-0.5
Total	2	3	2	.600	51	1	0	0	7	96^1	110	53	45	2	2	59	49	1.754	4.20	80	4.92	.289	7	.350	-9	5	-0.6

• JOHNSON, Jonathan Jonathan Kent Johnson b: 7/16/1974, LaGrange, GA BR/TR, 6', 180 lbs. Deb: 9/27/1998

YEAR	TM-L	W	L	PCT	G	GS	CG	SH	SV	IP	H	R	ER	HR	HB	BB	SO	RAT	ERA	ERA+	CERA	OAV	BH	AVG	PR+	WS	TPW
1998	Tex-A	0	0	....	1	1	0	0	0	4^1	5	4	4	0	0	5	3	2.308	8.31	58	7.36	.313	0	....	-2	0	-0.2
1999	Tex-A	0	0	....	1	0	0	0	0	3	9	5	5	0	1	2	3	3.667	15.00	34	19.55	.529	0	....	-3	0	-0.3
2000	Tex-A	1	1	.500	15	0	0	0	0	29	34	23	20	3	6	19	23	1.828	6.21	81	6.84	.291	0	....	-3	1	-0.3
2001	Tex-A	0	0	....	5	0	0	0	0	10^1	13	11	11	2	1	7	11	1.935	9.58	49	7.49	.317	0	....	-6	0	-0.5
2002	SD-N	1	2	.333	16	0	0	0	0	15^1	15	8	7	2	1	5	21	1.304	4.11	92	3.94	.250	0	....	-0	1	0.0
2003	Hou-N	0	1	.000	4	3	0	0	0	15^1	20	11	10	2	0	15	7	2.283	5.87	76	8.38	.323	0	.000	-3	0	-0.3
Total	6	2	4	.333	42	4	0	0	0	77^1	96	62	57	9	9	53	68	1.927	6.63	70	7.18	.307	0	.000	-17	2	-1.7

• JOHNSON, Ken Kenneth Travis Johnson b: 6/16/1933, West Palm Beach, FL BR/TR, 6'4", 210 lbs. Deb: 9/13/1958

YEAR	TM-L	W	L	PCT	G	GS	CG	SH	SV	IP	H	R	ER	HR	HB	BB	SO	RAT	ERA	ERA+	CERA	OAV	BH	AVG	PR+	WS	TPW
1958	KC-A	0	0	....	2	0	0	0	0	2^1	6	7	7	1	0	3	1	3.857	27.00	14	21.54	.429	0	....	-6	0	-0.6
1959	KC-A	1	1	.500	2	2	0	0	0	11	11	6	5	2	0	5	8	1.455	4.09	98	5.00	.268	0	.000	-0	1	0.0
1960	KC-A	5	10	.333	42	6	2	0	3	120^1	120	68	57	16	7	45	83	1.371	4.26	93	4.31	.263	5	.167	-2	5	-0.2
1961	KC-A	0	4	.000	6	1	0	0	0	9^1	11	11	11	2	0	7	4	1.929	10.61	39	7.58	.297	0	.000	-7	0	-0.7
*	Cin-N	6	2	.750	15	11	3	1	1	83	71	33	30	11	2	22	42	1.120	3.25	125	3.04	.229	6	.240	8	8	0.8
1962	Hou-N	7	16	.304	33	31	5	1	0	197	195	100	84	18	7	46	178	1.223	3.84	97	3.43	.257	4	.077	1	8	-0.2
1963	Hou-N	11	17	.393	37	32	6	1	1	224	204	86	66	12	8	50	148	1.134	2.65	119	2.73	.242	5	.068	17	15	1.5
1964	Hou-N	11	16	.407	35	35	7	1	0	218	209	100	88	15	7	44	117	1.161	3.63	94	2.93	.250	6	.079	-2	10	-0.4
1965	Hou-N	3	2	.600	8	8	1	0	0	51^2	52	25	24	4	4	11	28	1.219	4.18	80	3.55	.267	2	.111	-4	2	-0.4
	Mil-N	13	8	.619	29	26	8	1	2	179^2	165	75	64	15	3	37	123	1.124	3.21	110	2.79	.240	7	.115	5	12	0.4
	Yr.	16	10	.615	37	34	9	1	2	231^1	217	100	88	19	7	48	151	1.146	3.42	101	2.96	.246	9	.114	2	14	-0.1
1966	Atl-N	14	8	.636	32	31	11	2	0	215^2	213	89	79	24	0	46	105	1.201	3.30	110	3.39	.262	10	.143	8	12	0.8
1967	Atl-N	13	9	.591	29	29	6	0	0	210^1	191	78	64	19	7	38	85	1.089	2.74	121	2.80	.244	9	.127	12	15	1.3
1968	Atl-N	5	8	.385	31	16	1	0	0	135	145	58	52	10	9	25	57	1.259	3.47	86	3.65	.279	7	.175	-8	4	-0.9
1969	Atl-N	0	1	.000	9	2	0	0	1	29	32	17	16	4	0	9	20	1.414	4.97	73	4.49	.283	0	.000	-4	0	-0.5
	NY-A	1	2	.333	12	0	0	0	0	26	19	11	10	1	0	11	21	1.154	3.46	100	2.20	.202	0	.000	-0	1	0.0
	Chi-N	1	2	.333	9	1	0	0	1	19	17	8	6	2	0	13	18	1.579	2.84	142	4.25	.230	0	.000	3	2	0.2
	Yr.	1	3	.250	18	3	0	0	2	48	49	25	22	6	0	22	38	1.479	4.13	90	4.40	.262	0	.000	-2	2	-0.3
1970	Mon-N	0	0	....	3	0	0	0	0	6	9	6	5	1	2	1	4	1.667	7.50	55	7.67	.321	0	....	-2	0	-0.2
Total	13	91	106	.462	334	231	50	7	9	1737^1	1670	778	668	157	56	413	1042	1.199	3.46	101	3.27	.253	61	.114	19	95	0.8

• JOHNSON, Ken Kenneth Wandersee "Hook" Johnson b: 1/14/1923, Topeka, KS BL/TL, 6'1", 185 lbs. Deb: 9/18/1947

YEAR	TM-L	W	L	PCT	G	GS	CG	SH	SV	IP	H	R	ER	HR	HB	BB	SO	RAT	ERA	ERA+	CERA	OAV	BH	AVG	PR+	WS	TPW
1947	StL-N	1	0	1.000	2	1	1	0	0	10	2	1	0	0	1	5	8	.700	0.00	....	0.72	.063	2	.500	5	2	0.5
1948	StL-N	2	4	.333	13	4	0	0	0	45^1	43	27	24	1	1	30	20	1.610	4.76	86	4.28	.262	6	.300	-3	2	-0.2
1949	StL-N	0	1	.000	14	2	0	0	0	33^2	29	28	24	1	3	35	18	1.901	6.42	65	5.36	.250	2	.250	-9	0	-0.8

YEAR	TM-L	W	L	PCT	G	GS	CG	SH	SV	IP	H	R	ER	HR	HB	BB	SO	RAT	ERA	ERA+	CERA	OAV	BH	AVG	PR+	WS	TPW
1950	StL-N	0	0	....	2	0	0	0	0	2	1	1	0	0	0	3	1	2.000	0.00	....	4.02	.167	0	....	1	0	0.1
	*Phi-N	4	1	.800	14	8	3	1	0	60^2	61	32	27	3	1	43	32	1.714	4.01	101	4.76	.260	3	.158	0	3	0.0
	Yr.	4	1	.800	16	8	3	1	0	62^2	62	33	27	3	1	46	33	1.723	3.88	104	4.74	.257	3	.158	1	3	0.1
1951	Phi-N	5	8	.385	20	18	4	3	0	106^1	103	56	54	8	3	68	58	1.608	4.57	84	4.67	.259	5	.143	-8	3	-0.9
1952	Det-A	0	0	....	9	1	0	0	0	11^1	12	11	8	1	0	11	10	2.029	6.35	60	6.44	.273	1	.333	-3	0	-0.3
Total	6	12	14	.462	74	34	8	4	0	269^1	251	156	137	14	9	195	147	1.656	4.58	87	4.63	.252	19	.213	-17	10	-1.6

• JOHNSON, Lloyd Lloyd William "Eppa" Johnson b: 12/24/1910, Santa Rosa, CA d: 10/8/1980, Stockton, CA BL/TL, 6'4", 204 lbs. Deb: 4/21/1934

YEAR	TM-L	W	L	PCT	G	GS	CG	SH	SV	IP	H	R	ER	HR	HB	BB	SO	RAT	ERA	ERA+	CERA	OAV	BH	AVG	PR+	WS	TPW
1934	Pit-N	0	0	....	1	0	0	0	0	1	1	0	0	0	0	0	0	1.000	0.00	....	2.02	.333	0	....	0	0	0.0

• JOHNSON, Mark J. Mark J. Johnson b: 5/2/1975, Dayton, OH BR/TR, 6'3", 226 lbs. Deb: 4/7/2000

YEAR	TM-L	W	L	PCT	G	GS	CG	SH	SV	IP	H	R	ER	HR	HB	BB	SO	RAT	ERA	ERA+	CERA	OAV	BH	AVG	PR+	WS	TPW
2000	Det-A	0	1	.000	9	3	0	0	0	24	25	23	20	3	1	16	11	1.708	7.50	64	5.44	.266	0	....	-7	0	-0.6

• JOHNSON, Mike Michael Keith Johnson b: 10/3/1975, Edmonton, Canada BL/TR, 6'2", 175 lbs. Deb: 4/6/1997

YEAR	TM-L	W	L	PCT	G	GS	CG	SH	SV	IP	H	R	ER	HR	HB	BB	SO	RAT	ERA	ERA+	CERA	OAV	BH	AVG	PR+	WS	TPW
1997	Bal-A	0	1	.000	14	5	0	0	2	39^2	52	36	35	12	1	16	29	1.714	7.94	55	7.64	.317	0	....	-16	0	-1.5
	Mon-N	2	5	.286	11	11	0	0	0	50	54	34	33	8	0	21	28	1.500	5.94	71	4.99	.277	1	.077	-10	0	-1.0
1998	Mon-N	0	2	.000	2	2	0	0	0	7^1	16	12	12	4	1	2	4	2.455	14.73	29	16.53	.432	1	.333	-8	0	-0.8
1999	Mon-N	0	0	....	3	1	0	0	0	8^1	12	8	8	2	0	7	6	2.280	8.64	52	9.54	.324	1	.250	-4	0	-0.3
2000	Mon-N	5	6	.455	41	13	0	0	0	101^1	107	73	72	18	9	53	70	1.579	6.39	75	5.81	.269	4	.182	-17	2	-1.6
2001	Mon-N	0	0	....	10	0	0	0	0	11^1	13	6	6	3	2	4	10	1.500	4.76	94	7.05	.295	0	.000	-0	1	0.0
Total	5	7	14	.333	81	32	0	0	2	218	254	169	166	47	13	103	147	1.638	6.85	66	6.52	.290	7	.163	-55	3	-5.3

• JOHNSON, Mike Michael Norton Johnson b: 3/2/1951, Slayton, MN BR/TR, 6'1", 185 lbs. Deb: 7/25/1974

YEAR	TM-L	W	L	PCT	G	GS	CG	SH	SV	IP	H	R	ER	HR	HB	BB	SO	RAT	ERA	ERA+	CERA	OAV	BH	AVG	PR+	WS	TPW
1974	SD-N	0	2	.000	18	0	0	0	0	21^1	29	13	11	1	1	15	15	2.063	4.64	77	6.58	.326	0	....	-2	0	-0.2

• JOHNSON, Randy Randall David "Big Unit" Johnson b: 9/10/1963, Walnut Creek, CA BR/TL, 6'10", 225 lbs. Deb: 9/15/1988

YEAR	TM-L	W	L	PCT	G	GS	CG	SH	SV	IP	H	R	ER	HR	HB	BB	SO	RAT	ERA	ERA+	CERA	OAV	BH	AVG	PR+	WS	TPW
1988	Mon-N	3	0	1.000	4	4	1	0	0	26	23	8	7	3	0	7	25	1.154	2.42	148	2.96	.225	1	.111	3	2	0.3
1989	Mon-N	0	4	.000	7	6	0	0	0	29^2	29	25	22	2	0	26	26	1.854	6.67	53	5.42	.264	1	.143	-10	0	-1.1
	Sea-A	7	9	.438	22	22	2	0	0	131	118	75	64	11	3	70	104	1.435	4.40	92	4.01	.244	0	....	-6	5	-0.6
1990	Sea-A★	14	11	.560	33	33	5	2	0	219^2	174	103	89	26	5	120	194	1.338	3.65	108	3.68	.216	0	....	8	13	0.8
1991	Sea-A	13	10	.565	33	33	2	1	0	201^1	151	96	89	15	12	152	228	1.505	3.98	104	4.15	.213	0	....	-0	11	0.0
1992	Sea-A	12	14	.462	31	31	6	2	0	210^1	154	104	88	13	18	144	**241**	1.417	3.77	106	3.75	**.206**	0	....	5	11	0.5
1993	Sea-A★	19	8	.704	35	34	10	3	1	255^1	185	97	92	22	16	99	**308**	1.112	3.24	136	2.73	**.203**	0	....	32	22	3.1
1994	Sea-A★	13	6	.684	23	23	**9**	**4**	0	172	132	65	61	14	6	72	**204**	1.186	3.19	153	2.99	.216	0	....	34	15	3.2
1995*	Sea-A★	18	2	.900	30	30	6	3	0	214^1	159	65	59	12	6	65	**294**	1.045	**2.48**	**191**	**2.18**	**.201**	0	....	**59**	**22**	**5.5**
1996	Sea-A	5	0	1.000	14	8	0	0	1	61^1	48	27	25	8	2	25	85	1.190	3.67	135	3.24	.211	0	....	9	5	0.8
1997*	Sea-A★	20	4	.833	30	29	5	2	0	213	147	60	54	20	10	77	291	1.052	2.28	197	2.47	**.194**	0	....	55	23	5.2
1998	Sea-A	9	10	.474	23	23	6	2	0	160	146	90	77	19	11	60	213	1.288	4.33	107	3.88	.240	1	.143	8	8	0.7
	*Hou-N	10	1	.909	11	11	4	4	0	84^1	57	12	12	4	3	26	116	.984	1.28	317	1.93	.191	2	.063	26	11	2.3
1999*	Ari-N★	17	9	.654	35	**35**	**12**	2	0	**271^2**	207	86	75	30	9	70	**364**	1.020	**2.48**	**184**	2.49	.208	12	.124	**62**	**26**	**5.6**
2000	Ari-N★	19	7	.731	35	**35**	**8**	**3**	0	248^2	202	89	73	23	6	76	**347**	1.118	2.64	**178**	2.80	.224	13	.157	**58**	**26**	**5.4**
2001*	Ari-N★	21	6	.778	35	34	3	2	0	249^2	181	74	69	19	18	71	**372**	1.009	**2.49**	**184**	**2.35**	.203	8	.100	**54**	**26**	**5.0**
2002*	Ari-N★	**24**	5	.828	35	35	**8**	4	0	**260**	197	78	67	26	13	71	**334**	1.031	**2.32**	**191**	2.54	**.208**	12	.135	**64**	**29**	**6.3**
2003	Ari-N	6	8	.429	18	18	1	1	0	114	125	61	54	16	8	27	125	1.333	4.26	109	4.52	.280	7	.194	6	6	0.7
Total	16	230	114	.669	454	444	88	35	2	3122^1	2435	1215	1077	283	146	1258	3871	1.183	3.10	141	3.05	.215	57	.130	466	261	43.6

• JOHNSON, Rankin Adam Rankin "Tex" Johnson, Sr. b: 2/4/1888, Burnet, TX d: 7/2/1972, Williamsport, PA BR/TR, 6'1.5", 185 lbs. Deb: 4/20/1914

YEAR	TM-L	W	L	PCT	G	GS	CG	SH	SV	IP	H	R	ER	HR	HB	BB	SO	RAT	ERA	ERA+	CERA	OAV	BH	AVG	PR+	WS	TPW
1914	Bos-A	3	9	.250	16	13	4	2	0	99^1	92	41	34	2	3	34	24	1.268	3.08	87	3.25	.265	4	.133	-6	4	-0.8
	Chi-F	9	5	.643	16	14	12	2	0	120	88	29	21	5	4	29	60	.975	1.58	187	1.96	.209	4	.108	15	11	1.3
1915	Chi-F	2	4	.333	11	6	3	0	1	57	58	34	28	2	2	23	19	1.421	4.42	63	3.76	.270	1	.045	-10	0	-1.4
	Bal-F	7	11	.389	23	19	12	2	1	150^2	143	68	56	3	0	58	62	1.334	3.35	101	3.11	.255	8	.157	3	8	0.2
	Yr.	9	15	.375	34	25	15	2	2	207^2	201	102	84	5	2	81	81	1.358	3.64	87	3.29	.259	9	.123	-7	8	-1.1
1918	StL-N	1	1	.500	6	1	0	0	0	23	20	10	7	0	0	7	4	1.174	2.74	99	2.45	.263	1	.250	-0	1	0.0
Total	3	22	30	.423	72	53	31	6	2	450	401	182	146	12	9	151	169	1.227	2.92	102	2.88	.248	18	.125	2	24	-0.6

• JOHNSON, Rankin Adam Rankin Johnson, Jr. b: 3/1/1917, Hayden, AZ BR/TR, 6'3", 177 lbs. Deb: 4/17/1941

YEAR	TM-L	W	L	PCT	G	GS	CG	SH	SV	IP	H	R	ER	HR	HB	BB	SO	RAT	ERA	ERA+	CERA	OAV	BH	AVG	PR+	WS	TPW
1941	Phi-A	1	0	1.000	7	0	0	0	0	10	14	10	4	0	0	3	0	1.700	3.60	116	4.99	.326	0	.000	1	0	0.0

• JOHNSON, Roy Roy J. "Hardrock" Johnson b: 10/1/1895, Madill, OK d: 1/10/1986, Scottsdale, AZ BR/TR, 6', 185 lbs. Deb: 8/7/1918 M

YEAR	TM-L	W	L	PCT	G	GS	CG	SH	SV	IP	H	R	ER	HR	HB	BB	SO	RAT	ERA	ERA+	CERA	OAV	BH	AVG	PR+	WS	TPW
1918	Phi-A	1	5	.167	10	8	3	0	0	50	47	32	19	0	2	34	12	1.620	3.42	86	4.00	.254	1	.067	-4	1	-0.7

• JOHNSON, Si Silas Kenneth Johnson b: 10/5/1906, Danway, IL d: 5/12/1994, Sheridan, IL BR/TR, 5'11.5", 185 lbs. Deb: 5/2/1928

YEAR	TM-L	W	L	PCT	G	GS	CG	SH	SV	IP	H	R	ER	HR	HB	BB	SO	RAT	ERA	ERA+	CERA	OAV	BH	AVG	PR+	WS	TPW
1928	Cin-N	0	0	....	3	0	0	0	0	10^1	9	5	5	0	0	5	1	1.355	4.35	91	3.05	.250	1	.250	-0	0	0.0
1929	Cin-N	0	0	....	1	0	0	0	0	2	2	1	1	0	0	1	0	1.500	4.50	101	3.50	.250	0	....	0	0	0.0
1930	Cin-N	3	1	.750	35	3	0	0	0	78^1	86	54	43	5	4	31	47	1.494	4.94	98	4.47	.286	4	.235	-0	4	0.0
1931	Cin-N	11	19	.367	42	33	14	0	0	262^1	273	131	110	5	6	74	95	1.323	3.77	99	3.30	.269	13	.149	-3	12	-0.7
1932	Cin-N	13	15	.464	42	27	14	2	2	245	246	109	89	8	2	57	94	1.237	3.27	118	2.97	.259	10	.125	17	16	1.2
1933	Cin-N	7	18	.280	34	28	14	4	1	211^1	212	101	82	7	3	54	51	1.259	3.49	97	3.06	.263	3	.042	-0	9	-0.8
1934	Cin-N	7	22	.241	46	31	9	0	3	215^2	264	150	125	15	7	84	89	**1.614**	5.22	78	5.03	.297	10	.139	-22	3	-2.4
1935	Cin-N	5	11	.313	30	20	4	1	0	130	155	106	90	14	3	59	40	1.646	6.23	64	5.34	.293	1	.024	-31	0	-3.4
1936	Cin-N	0	0	....	2	0	0	0	0	4	7	6	6	1	0	0	2	1.750	13.50	28	7.95	.368	0	....	-4	0	-0.4
	StL-N	5	3	.625	12	9	3	1	0	61^2	82	30	30	4	1	11	21	1.508	4.38	90	4.78	.314	4	.190	-3	4	-0.3
	Yr.	5	3	.625	14	9	3	1	0	65^2	89	36	36	5	1	11	23	1.523	4.93	79	4.97	.318	4	.190	-7	4	-0.7
1937	StL-N	12	12	.500	38	21	12	1	1	192^1	222	92	71	14	1	43	64	1.378	3.32	120	4.03	.292	9	.138	15	12	1.2
1938	StL-N	0	3	.000	6	3	0	0	0	15^2	27	17	13	0	0	6	4	2.106	7.47	53	7.36	.380	0	.000	-6	0	-0.6
1940	Phi-N	5	14	.263	37	14	5	0	1	138^1	145	81	75	13	2	42	58	1.352	4.88	80	3.88	.268	6	.140	-15	4	-1.7
1941	Phi-N	5	12	.294	39	21	6	1	2	163^1	207	91	82	8	1	54	80	**1.598**	4.52	82	4.86	.309	7	.149	-14	5	-1.6
1942	Phi-N	8	19	.296	39	26	10	1	0	195^1	198	96	80	6	1	72	78	1.382	3.69	90	3.49	.266	6	.103	-8	9	-1.3
1943	Phi-N	8	3	.727	21	14	9	1	2	113	110	48	41	4	0	25	46	1.195	3.27	103	2.73	.252	6	.182	3	7	0.3
1946	Phi-N	0	0	....	1	0	0	0	0	3	7	4	1	1	0	0	2	2.333	3.00	114	12.91	.538	1	1.000	0	0	0.1
	Bos-N	6	5	.545	28	12	5	1	1	127	134	47	39	8	4	35	41	1.331	2.76	124	3.67	.272	5	.135	10	8	0.9
	Yr.	6	5	.545	29	12	5	1	1	130	141	51	40	9	4	35	43	1.354	2.77	124	3.88	.279	6	.158	10	8	1.0
1947	Bos-N	6	8	.429	36	10	3	0	2	112^2	124	57	53	7	1	34	27	1.402	4.23	92	3.88	.275	1	.033	-3	6	-0.6
Total	17	101	165	.380	492	272	108	13	15	2281^1	2510	1226	1036	120	36	687	840	1.401	4.09	93	3.90	.279	87	.123	-66	99	-10.2

• JOHNSON, Syl Sylvester Johnson b: 12/31/1900, Portland, OR d: 2/20/1985, Portland, OR BR/TR, 5'11", 180 lbs. Deb: 4/24/1922 C/U

YEAR	TM-L	W	L	PCT	G	GS	CG	SH	SV	IP	H	R	ER	HR	HB	BB	SO	RAT	ERA	ERA+	CERA	OAV	BH	AVG	PR+	WS	TPW
1922	Det-A	7	3	.700	29	8	3	0	1	97	99	52	40	7	4	30	29	1.330	3.71	104	3.80	.273	8	.222	4	6	0.4
1923	Det-A	12	7	.632	37	18	7	0	0	176^1	181	82	78	12	3	47	93	1.293	3.98	97	3.54	.274	10	.161	-1	11	-0.1
1924	Det-A	5	4	.556	29	9	2	0	3	104	117	63	57	8	5	42	55	1.529	4.93	83	4.68	.287	7	.206	-9	5	-0.9
1925	Det-A	0	2	.000	6	0	0	0	0	13	11	7	5	1	0	10	5	1.615	3.46	124	4.41	.250	0	.000	1	1	0.1
1926	StL-N	0	3	.000	19	6	1	0	1	49	54	27	23	3	2	15	10	1.408	4.22	93	4.19	.297	0	.000	-2	2	-0.4
1927	StL-N	0	0	....	2	0	0	0	0	3	3	2	2	1	0	0	2	1.000	6.00	66	3.79	.250	0	....	-1	0	-0.1
1928*	StL-N	8	4	.667	34	6	2	0	3	120	117	53	52	6	4	33	66	1.250	3.90	102	3.17	.259	6	.158	0	8	0.0
1929	StL-N	13	7	.650	42	19	12	3	3	182^1	186	88	73	11	7	56	80	1.327	3.60	129	3.61	.265	7	.117	22	16	1.8
1930*	StL-N	12	10	.545	32	24	9	2	2	187^2	215	105	97	13	4	38	92	1.348	4.65	108	3.98	.293	15	.214	7	13	0.6
1931*	StL-N	11	9	.550	32	24	12	2	2	186	186	73	62	9	2	29	82	1.156	3.00	131	2.79	.255	14	.233	19	17	2.1
1932	StL-N	5	14	.263	32	22	7	0	2	164^2	199	103	90	14	4	35	70	1.421	4.92	80	4.41	.299	10	.196	-17	4	-1.8
1933	StL-N	3	3	.500	35	1	0	0	3	84	89	45	40	7	3	16	28	1.250	4.29	81	3.54	.271	5	.238	-8	3	-0.8
1934	Cin-N	0	0	....	2	0	0	0	0	6^2	9	6	2	2	0	0	0	1.350	2.70	151	5.70	.310	1	.500	1	1	0.2
	Phi-N	5	9	.357	42	10	4	3	3	133^2	122	58	52	14	1	24	54	1.092	3.50	135	2.80	.242	8	.195	16	11	1.6
	Yr.	5	9	.357	44	10	4	3	3	140^1	131	64	54	16	1	24	54	1.105	3.46	136	2.94	.245	9	.209	17	12	1.8

YEAR	TM-L	W	L	PCT	G	GS	CG	SH	SV	IP	H	R	ER	HR	HB	BB	SO	RAT	ERA	ERA+	CERA	OAV	BH	AVG	PR+	WS	TPW
1935	Phi-N	10	8	.556	37	18	8	1	6	174^2	182	79	69	15	3	31	89	1.219	3.56	127	3.31	.265	14	.241	21	18	2.3
1936	Phi-N	5	7	.417	39	8	1	0	7	111	129	60	53	10	3	29	48	1.423	4.30	105	4.38	.288	9	.250	7	7	0.7
1937	Phi-N	4	10	.286	32	15	4	0	3	138	155	81	77	19	2	22	46	1.283	5.02	86	4.14	.288	7	.146	-8	6	-1.0
1938	Phi-N	2	7	.222	22	6	2	0	0	83	87	43	39	4	0	11	21	1.181	4.23	95	2.93	.267	1	.034	0	3	-0.2
1939	Phi-N	8	8	.500	22	13	6	0	2	111	112	50	47	10	1	15	37	1.144	3.81	103	3.04	.264	5	.152	2	7	0.1
1940	Phi-N	2	2	.500	17	2	2	0	2	40^2	37	22	19	6	0	5	13	1.033	4.20	93	2.73	.236	0	.000	-1	3	-0.2
Total	19	112	117	.489	542	209	82	11	43	2165^2	2290	1099	977	172	48	488	920	1.283	4.06	103	3.61	.273	127	.181	53	142	4.0

• JOHNSON, Tom

Thomas Raymond Johnson b: 4/2/1951, St. Paul, MN BR/TR, 6'1", 185 lbs. Deb: 9/10/1974

YEAR	TM-L	W	L	PCT	G	GS	CG	SH	SV	IP	H	R	ER	HR	HB	BB	SO	RAT	ERA	ERA+	CERA	OAV	BH	AVG	PR+	WS	TPW
1974	Min-A	2	0	1.000	4	0	0	0	1	7	4	1	0	0	0	0	4	.571	0.00	....	0.72	.167	0	....	3	2	0.3
1975	Min-A	1	2	.333	18	0	0	0	3	38^2	40	23	18	4	2	21	17	1.578	4.19	92	4.77	.263	0	....	-1	2	-0.1
1976	Min-A	3	1	.750	18	1	0	0	0	48^1	44	14	14	2	0	8	37	1.076	2.61	138	2.38	.243	0	....	5	4	0.6
1977	Min-A	16	7	.696	71	0	0	0	15	146^2	152	57	51	11	5	47	87	1.357	3.13	127	3.84	.272	0	....	14	16	1.4
1978	Min-A	1	4	.200	18	0	0	0	3	32^2	42	22	20	2	2	17	21	1.806	5.51	69	5.97	.318	0	....	-6	0	-0.6
Total	5	23	14	.622	129	1	0	0	22	273^1	282	117	103	19	9	93	166	1.372	3.39	114	3.89	.269	0	....	15	24	1.5

• JOHNSON, Vic

Victor Oscar Johnson b: 8/3/1920, Eau Claire, WI BR/TL, 6', 160 lbs. Deb: 5/3/1944

YEAR	TM-L	W	L	PCT	G	GS	CG	SH	SV	IP	H	R	ER	HR	HB	BB	SO	RAT	ERA	ERA+	CERA	OAV	BH	AVG	PR+	WS	TPW
1944	Bos-A	0	3	.000	7	5	0	0	0	27^1	42	22	19	0	0	15	7	2.085	6.26	54	6.95	.362	0	.000	-9	0	-1.1
1945	Bos-A	6	4	.600	26	9	4	1	2	85^1	90	41	38	4	2	46	21	1.594	4.01	85	4.48	.276	5	.167	-6	4	-0.8
1946	Cle-A	0	1	.000	9	1	0	0	0	13^2	20	14	14	1	0	8	3	2.049	9.22	36	7.67	.357	0	.000	-9	0	-1.0
Total	3	6	8	.429	42	15	4	1	2	126^1	152	77	71	5	2	69	31	1.749	5.06	67	5.36	.305	5	.119	-24	4	-2.8

• JOHNSON, Walt

Ellis Walter Johnson b: 12/8/1892, Minneapolis, MN d: 1/14/1965, Minneapolis, MN BR/TR, 6'.5", 180 lbs. Deb: 7/6/1912

YEAR	TM-L	W	L	PCT	G	GS	CG	SH	SV	IP	H	R	ER	HR	HB	BB	SO	RAT	ERA	ERA+	CERA	OAV	BH	AVG	PR+	WS	TPW
1912	Chi-A	0	0	....	3	0	0	0	0	11^2	11	6	5	0	1	7	7	1.543	3.86	83	3.37	.262	0	.000	-1	0	-0.1
1915	Chi-A	0	0	....	1	0	0	0	0	2	3	2	2	0	0	0	3	1.500	9.00	33	4.47	.333	0	....	-1	0	-0.1
1917	Phi-A	0	2	.000	4	2	0	0	0	13^2	15	12	11	0	0	5	8	1.463	7.24	38	3.94	.294	0	.000	-7	0	-0.7
Total	3	0	2	.000	8	2	0	0	0	27^1	29	20	18	0	1	12	18	1.500	5.93	49	3.73	.284	0	.000	-9	0	-0.9

• JOHNSON, Walter

Walter Perry "Barney,The Big Train" Johnson
b: 11/6/1887, Humboldt, KS d: 12/10/1946, Washington, DC BR/TR, 6'1", 200 lbs. Deb: 8/2/1907 M HOF: 1936

YEAR	TM-L	W	L	PCT	G	GS	CG	SH	SV	IP	H	R	ER	HR	HB	BB	SO	RAT	ERA	ERA+	CERA	OAV	BH	AVG	PR+	WS	TPW
1907	Was-A	5	9	.357	14	12	11	2	0	110^1	100	35	23	1	2	20	71	1.088	1.88	129	2.25	.244	4	.111	11	4	1.0
1908	Was-A	14	14	.500	36	30	23	6	1	256^1	194	75	47	0	11	53	160	.964	1.65	138	1.66	.211	13	.165	17	20	2.3
1909	Was-A	13	25	.342	40	36	27	4	1	296^1	247	112	73	1	15	84	164	1.117	2.22	109	2.16	.221	13	.129	10	12	0.9
1910	Was-A	25	17	.595	**45**	**42**	**38**	8	1	**370**	262	92	56	1	13	76	**313**	.914	1.36	183	1.54	.205	24	.175	39	36	4.5
1911	Was-A	25	13	.658	40	37	**36**	**6**	1	322^1	292	119	68	8	8	70	207	1.123	1.90	173	2.40	.238	30	.234	**48**	**31**	**5.1**
1912	Was-A	33	12	.733	50	37	34	7	2	369	259	89	57	2	16	76	**303**	.908	**1.39**	**241**	**1.52**	**.196**	38	.264	**67**	**47**	**7.6**
1913	Was-A	**36**	7	.837	48	36	**29**	**11**	2	**346**	232	56	44	9	9	38	**243**	.780	**1.14**	**258**	**1.27**	**.187**	35	.261	**64**	**54**	**8.0**
1914	Was-A	**28**	18	.609	**51**	**40**	**33**	**9**	1	**371^2**	287	88	71	3	11	74	**225**	.971	1.72	163	1.75	.217	30	.221	**43**	**38**	**5.6**
1915	Was-A	**27**	13	.675	47	**39**	**35**	**7**	4	**336^2**	258	83	58	1	19	56	**203**	.933	1.55	**191**	**1.67**	.214	34	.231	**50**	**42**	**5.9**
1916	Was-A	**25**	20	.556	48	38	**36**	3	1	**369^2**	290	105	78	0	9	82	**228**	1.006	1.90	147	1.79	.220	32	.225	34	36	4.7
1917	Was-A	23	16	.590	47	34	30	8	3	326	248	105	80	3	14	68	**188**	.969	2.21	119	1.73	.211	33	.254	11	29	2.3
1918	Was-A	**23**	13	.639	39	29	29	8	3	326	241	71	46	2	8	70	**162**	.954	**1.27**	**214**	**1.63**	.210	40	.267	42	38	**5.8**
1919	Was-A	20	14	.588	39	29	27	**7**	2	290^1	235	73	48	0	7	51	**147**	.985	**1.49**	**215**	**1.72**	**.219**	24	.192	**58**	27	**6.3**
1920	Was-A	8	10	.444	21	15	12	4	3	143^2	135	68	50	5	5	27	78	1.128	3.13	119	2.58	.245	17	.266	11	10	1.5
1921	Was-A	17	14	.548	35	32	25	1	1	264	265	122	103	7	2	92	**143**	1.352	3.51	117	3.35	.263	30	.270	14	23	1.7
1922	Was-A	15	16	.484	41	31	23	4	4	280	283	115	93	8	7	99	105	1.364	2.99	129	3.48	.267	22	.204	19	21	1.8
1923	Was-A	17	12	.586	42	34	18	3	4	261^1	263	112	101	9	20	73	**130**	1.286	3.48	108	3.46	.269	18	.194	-1	17	0.0
1924*	Was-A	**23**	7	.767	38	**38**	20	**6**	0	277^2	233	97	84	10	10	77	**158**	1.116	**2.72**	148	**2.39**	**.224**	32	.283	34	**29**	**3.8**
1925*	Was-A	20	7	.741	30	29	16	3	0	229	217	95	78	7	7	78	108	1.288	3.07	138	3.12	**.250**	42	.433	23	**26**	**3.6**
1926	Was-A	15	16	.484	33	33	22	2	0	260^2	259	120	105	13	5	73	125	1.274	3.63	107	3.22	.263	20	.194	6	15	0.6
1927	Was-A	5	6	.455	18	15	7	1	0	107^2	113	70	61	7	7	26	48	1.291	5.10	80	3.66	.278	16	.348	-14	5	-0.7
Total	21	417	279	.599	802	666	531	110	34	5914^2	4913	1902	1424	97	205	1363	3509	1.061	2.17	149	2.18	.227	547	.235	587	560	72.1

• JOHNSON, Youngy

John Godfred Johnson b: 7/22/1877, San Francisco, CA d: 8/28/1936, Berkeley, CA TR Deb: 4/29/1897

YEAR	TM-L	W	L	PCT	G	GS	CG	SH	SV	IP	H	R	ER	HR	HB	BB	SO	RAT	ERA	ERA+	CERA	OAV	BH	AVG	PR+	WS	TPW
1897	Phi-N	1	2	.333	5	2	1	0	0	29	39	24	15	0	2	12	7	1.759	4.66	90	5.49	.319	1	.077	-1	1	-0.2
1899	NY-N	0	0	....	1	0	0	0	0	2	0	0	0	0	0	2	1	1.000	0.00	....	0.82	.000	0	.000	1	0	0.1
Total	2	1	2	.333	6	2	1	0	0	31	39	24	15	0	2	14	8	1.710	4.35	96	5.19	.319	1	.071	-0	1	-0.2

• JOHNSTON, Joel

Joel Raymond Johnston b: 3/8/1967, West Chester, PA BR/TR, 6'5", 220 lbs. Deb: 9/5/1991

YEAR	TM-L	W	L	PCT	G	GS	CG	SH	SV	IP	H	R	ER	HR	HB	BB	SO	RAT	ERA	ERA+	CERA	OAV	BH	AVG	PR+	WS	TPW
1991	KC-A	1	0	1.000	13	0	0	0	0	22^1	9	1	1	0	0	9	21	.806	0.40	1022	0.86	.120	0	....	10	4	1.0
1992	KC-A	0	0	....	5	0	0	0	0	2^2	3	4	4	2	0	2	0	1.875	13.50	30	11.59	.273	0	....	-3	0	-0.3
1993	Pit-N	2	4	.333	33	0	0	0	2	53^1	38	20	20	7	0	19	31	1.069	3.38	120	2.53	.203	2	.333	4	6	0.4
1994	Pit-N	0	0	....	4	0	0	0	0	3^1	14	12	11	0	2	4	5	5.400	29.70	15	33.64	.583	0	....	-9	0	-0.9
1995	Bos-A	0	1	.000	4	0	0	0	0	4	2	5	5	1	1	3	4	1.250	11.25	43	4.63	.143	0	....	-3	0	-0.3
Total	5	3	5	.375	59	0	0	0	2	85^2	66	42	41	10	3	37	61	1.202	4.31	98	3.68	.212	2	.333	-2	10	-0.1

• JOHNSTONE, John

John William Johnstone b: 11/25/1968, Liverpool, NY BR/TR, 6'3", 195 lbs. Deb: 9/3/1993

YEAR	TM-L	W	L	PCT	G	GS	CG	SH	SV	IP	H	R	ER	HR	HB	BB	SO	RAT	ERA	ERA+	CERA	OAV	BH	AVG	PR+	WS	TPW
1993	Fla-N	0	2	.000	7	0	0	0	0	10^2	16	8	7	1	0	7	5	2.156	5.91	73	8.15	.340	0	....	-2	0	-0.2
1994	Fla-N	1	2	.333	17	0	0	0	0	21^1	23	20	14	4	1	16	23	1.828	5.91	74	6.22	.264	0	....	-4	0	-0.4
1995	Fla-N	0	0	....	4	0	0	0	0	4^2	7	2	2	1	0	2	3	1.929	3.86	109	7.61	.333	0	....	0	0	0.0
1996	Hou-N	1	0	1.000	9	0	0	0	0	13	17	8	8	2	0	5	5	1.692	5.54	70	6.21	.321	0	....	-2	0	-0.2
1997	SF-N	0	0	....	10	0	0	0	0	16^1	12	4	4	0	4	6	14	1.102	2.20	183	2.73	.218	0	.000	3	0	0.3
	Oak-A	0	0	....	5	0	0	0	0	6^1	7	2	2	0	0	7	4	2.211	2.84	158	6.74	.292	0	....	1	1	0.1
	SF-N	0	0	....	3	0	0	0	0	2	3	3	3	1	0	1	1	2.000	13.50	30	10.88	.333	0	....	-2	0	-0.2
	Yr.	0	0	....	13	0	0	0	0	18^1	15	7	7	1	4	7	15	1.200	3.44	118	3.62	.234	0	.000	1	0	0.1
1998	SF-N	6	5	.545	70	0	0	0	0	88	72	32	30	10	1	38	86	1.250	3.07	129	3.19	.224	0	.000	9	7	0.9
1999	SF-N	4	6	.400	62	0	0	0	3	65^2	48	24	19	8	1	20	56	1.036	2.60	161	2.40	.203	0	....	12	8	1.1
2000	SF-N	3	4	.429	47	0	0	0	0	50	64	35	35	11	2	13	37	1.540	6.30	67	6.21	.322	0	.000	-12	0	-1.1
Total	8	15	19	.441	234	0	0	0	3	278	269	138	124	38	9	115	234	1.381	4.01	103	4.29	.255	0	.000	4	16	0.3

• JOINER, Roy

Roy Merrill "Pop" Joiner b: 10/30/1906, Red Bluff, CA d: 12/26/1989, Red Bluff, CA BL/TL, 6', 170 lbs. Deb: 4/30/1934

YEAR	TM-L	W	L	PCT	G	GS	CG	SH	SV	IP	H	R	ER	HR	HB	BB	SO	RAT	ERA	ERA+	CERA	OAV	BH	AVG	PR+	WS	TPW
1934	Chi-N	0	1	.000	20	2	0	0	0	34	61	33	31	3	0	8	9	2.029	8.21	47	8.01	.391	2	.200	-17	0	-1.6
1935	Chi-N	0	0	....	2	0	0	0	0	3^1	6	4	2	0	0	2	0	2.400	5.40	73	8.62	.429	0	.000	-1	0	-0.1
1940	NY-N	3	2	.600	30	2	0	0	1	53	66	26	20	8	5	17	25	1.566	3.40	114	5.84	.308	3	.273	3	4	0.4
Total	3	3	3	.500	52	4	0	0	1	90^1	133	63	53	11	5	27	34	1.771	5.28	73	6.76	.346	5	.227	-14	4	-1.3

• JOLLY, Dave

David "Gabby" Jolly b: 10/14/1924, Stony Point, NC d: 5/27/1963, Durham, NC BR/TR, 6', 165 lbs. Deb: 5/9/1953

YEAR	TM-L	W	L	PCT	G	GS	CG	SH	SV	IP	H	R	ER	HR	HB	BB	SO	RAT	ERA	ERA+	CERA	OAV	BH	AVG	PR+	WS	TPW
1953	Mil-N	0	1	.000	24	0	0	0	0	38^1	34	16	15	4	1	27	23	1.591	3.52	111	4.61	.239	1	.500	1	2	0.2
1954	Mil-N	11	6	.647	47	1	0	0	10	111^1	87	36	30	6	2	64	62	1.356	2.43	154	3.14	.215	9	.290	15	14	1.8
1955	Mil-N	2	3	.400	36	0	0	0	1	58^1	58	42	37	6	1	51	23	1.869	5.71	66	5.72	.258	1	.167	-13	0	-1.2
1956	Mil-N	2	3	.400	29	0	0	0	7	45^2	39	21	19	7	0	35	20	1.620	3.74	92	4.88	.228	0	.000	-2	2	-0.2
1957	Mil-N	1	1	.500	23	0	0	0	1	37^2	37	22	21	4	3	21	27	1.540	5.02	70	4.97	.264	3	.600	-7	1	-0.6
Total	5	16	14	.533	159	1	0	0	19	291^1	255	137	122	27	7	198	155	1.555	3.77	97	4.36	.236	14	.292	-5	19	-0.1

• JONES, Al

Alfornia Jones b: 2/10/1959, Charleston, MS BR/TR, 6'4", 210 lbs. Deb: 8/6/1983

YEAR	TM-L	W	L	PCT	G	GS	CG	SH	SV	IP	H	R	ER	HR	HB	BB	SO	RAT	ERA	ERA+	CERA	OAV	BH	AVG	PR+	WS	TPW
1983	Chi-A	0	0	....	2	0	0	0	0	2^1	3	1	1	0	0	2	2	2.143	3.86	109	8.06	.375	0	....	0	0	0.0
1984	Chi-A	1	1	.500	20	0	0	0	5	20^1	23	10	10	3	1	11	15	1.672	4.43	94	6.06	.299	0	....	-1	1	-0.1
1985	Chi-A	1	0	1.000	5	0	0	0	0	6	3	2	1	0	0	3	2	1.000	1.50	288	1.62	.167	0	....	2	1	0.2
Total	3	2	1	.667	27	0	0	0	5	28^2	29	13	12	3	1	16	19	1.570	3.77	111	5.29	.282	0	....	1	2	0.1

• JONES, Alex Alexander H. Jones b: 12/25/1869, Bradford, PA d: 4/4/1941, Woodville, PA BL/TL, 5'6", 135 lbs. Deb: 9/25/1889

YEAR	TM-L	W	L	PCT	G	GS	CG	SH	SV	IP	H	R	ER	HR	HB	BB	SO	RAT	ERA	ERA+	CERA	OAV	BH	AVG	PR+	WS	TPW
1889	Pit-N	1	0	1.000	1	1	1	0	0	9	7	5	3	0	0	1	10	.889	3.00	125	....	.208	1	.200	1	1	0.1
1892	Lou-N	5	11	.313	18	16	13	1	0	146^{2}	130	90	54	3	3	56	44	1.268	3.31	92	2.85	.228	8	.145	-5	7	-0.6
	Was-N	0	3	.000	4	4	3	0	0	27	33	23	12	0	0	14	7	1.741	4.00	81	4.90	.290	3	.273	-2	1	-0.2
	Yr.	5	14	.263	22	20	16	1	0	173^{2}	163	113	66	3	3	70	51	1.342	3.42	91	3.17	.239	11	.167	-7	8	-0.7
1894	Phi-N	1	0	1.000	1	1	1	0	0	9	10	4	2	0	0	0	2	1.111	2.00	255	2.54	.279	1	.250	3	1	0.2
1903	Det-A	0	1	.000	2	2	0	0	0	8^{2}	19	15	12	0	0	6	2	2.885	12.46	23	12.46	.435	0	.000	-9	0	-1.0
Total	**4**	**7**	**15**	**.318**	**26**	**24**	**18**	**1**	**0**	**200^{1}**	**199**	**137**	**83**	**3**	**3**	**77**	**65**	**1.378**	**3.73**	**84**	**3.40**	**.250**	**13**	**.165**	**-13**	**10**	**-1.4**

• JONES, Art Arthur Lennox Jones b: 2/7/1906, Kershaw, SC d: 11/25/1980, Columbia, SC BR/TR, 6', 165 lbs. Deb: 4/23/1932

YEAR	TM-L	W	L	PCT	G	GS	CG	SH	SV	IP	H	R	ER	HR	HB	BB	SO	RAT	ERA	ERA+	CERA	OAV	BH	AVG	PR+	WS	TPW
1932	Bro-N	0	0	....	1	0	0	0	0	1	2	2	2	0	0	1	0	3.000	18.00	21	14.07	.667	0	....	-2	0	-0.2

• JONES, Barry Barry Louis Jones b: 2/15/1963, Centerville, IN BR/TR, 6'4", 225 lbs. Deb: 7/18/1986

YEAR	TM-L	W	L	PCT	G	GS	CG	SH	SV	IP	H	R	ER	HR	HB	BB	SO	RAT	ERA	ERA+	CERA	OAV	BH	AVG	PR+	WS	TPW
1986	Pit-N	3	4	.429	26	0	0	0	3	37^{1}	29	16	12	3	0	21	29	1.339	2.89	132	3.26	.215	1	.200	4	3	0.4
1987	Pit-N	2	4	.333	32	0	0	0	1	43^{1}	55	34	27	6	0	23	28	1.800	5.61	73	6.27	.314	0	.000	-8	0	-0.8
1988	Pit-N	1	1	.500	42	0	0	0	2	56^{1}	57	21	19	3	1	21	31	1.385	3.04	112	3.63	.271	0	.000	2	4	0.2
	Chi-A	2	2	.500	17	0	0	0	1	26	15	7	7	3	0	17	17	1.231	2.42	164	2.89	.170	0	....	4	3	0.4
1989	Chi-A	3	2	.600	22	0	0	0	1	30^{1}	22	12	8	2	1	8	17	.989	2.37	160	2.06	.208	0	....	5	3	0.5
1990	Chi-A	11	4	.733	65	0	0	0	1	74	62	20	19	2	1	33	45	1.284	2.31	165	2.80	.235	0	....	11	11	1.1
1991	Mon-N	4	9	.308	**77**	0	0	0	13	88^{2}	76	35	33	8	1	33	46	1.229	3.35	108	3.20	.246	0	.000	2	8	0.2
1992	Phi-N	5	6	.455	44	0	0	0	0	54^{1}	65	30	28	3	2	24	19	1.638	4.64	75	5.16	.305	0	.000	-7	1	-0.7
	NY-N	2	0	1.000	17	0	0	0	1	15^{1}	20	16	16	0	0	11	11	2.022	9.39	37	5.86	.317	0	....	-10	0	-1.1
	Yr.	7	6	.538	61	0	0	0	1	69^{2}	85	46	44	3	2	35	30	1.722	5.68	61	5.32	.308	0	.000	-16	1	-1.8
1993	Chi-A	0	1	.000	6	0	0	0	0	7^{1}	14	8	7	2	0	3	7	2.318	8.59	49	11.63	.412	0	....	-4	0	-0.4
Total	**8**	**33**	**33**	**.500**	**348**	**0**	**0**	**0**	**23**	**433**	**415**	**199**	**176**	**32**	**6**	**194**	**250**	**1.406**	**3.66**	**101**	**3.89**	**.260**	**1**	**.063**	**-1**	**33**	**-0.2**

• JONES, Bobby Robert Mitchell Jones b: 4/11/1972, Orange, NJ BR/TL, 6', 185 lbs. Deb: 5/18/1997

YEAR	TM-L	W	L	PCT	G	GS	CG	SH	SV	IP	H	R	ER	HR	HB	BB	SO	RAT	ERA	ERA+	CERA	OAV	BH	AVG	PR+	WS	TPW
1997	Col-N	1	1	.500	4	4	0	0	0	19^{1}	30	18	18	2	0	12	5	2.172	8.38	62	8.63	.380	1	.200	-7	0	-0.6
1998	Col-N	7	8	.467	35	20	1	0	0	141^{1}	153	87	82	12	6	66	109	1.550	5.22	99	4.91	.282	8	.178	-1	7	-0.2
1999	Col-N	6	10	.375	30	20	0	0	0	112^{1}	132	91	79	24	6	77	74	1.861	6.33	92	7.41	.292	4	.148	-6	4	-0.6
2000	NY-N	0	1	.000	11	1	0	0	0	21^{2}	18	11	10	2	3	14	20	1.477	4.15	106	4.43	.222	1	.500	1	0	0.1
2002	NY-N	0	0	....	12	0	0	0	0	17	20	11	10	3	1	11	11	1.824	5.29	75	6.82	.299	0	....	-2	0	-0.2
	SD-N	0	0	....	4	2	0	0	0	9^{2}	10	7	7	1	0	7	7	1.759	6.52	58	5.61	.270	0	.000	-3	0	-0.3
	Yr.	0	0	....	16	2	0	0	0	26^{2}	30	18	17	4	1	18	18	1.800	5.74	68	6.38	.288	0	.000	-5	0	-0.5
Total	**5**	**14**	**20**	**.412**	**96**	**47**	**1**	**0**	**0**	**321^{1}**	**363**	**225**	**206**	**44**	**16**	**187**	**226**	**1.712**	**5.77**	**90**	**6.10**	**.288**	**14**	**.173**	**-18**	**11**	**-1.8**

• JONES, Bobby Robert Joseph Jones b: 2/10/1970, Fresno, CA BR/TR, 6'4", 225 lbs. Deb: 8/14/1993

YEAR	TM-L	W	L	PCT	G	GS	CG	SH	SV	IP	H	R	ER	HR	HB	BB	SO	RAT	ERA	ERA+	CERA	OAV	BH	AVG	PR+	WS	TPW
1993	NY-N	2	4	.333	9	9	0	0	0	61^{2}	61	35	25	6	2	22	35	1.346	3.65	110	3.87	.262	1	.050	2	2	0.1
1994	NY-N	12	7	.632	24	24	1	1	0	160	157	75	56	10	4	56	80	1.331	3.15	133	3.51	.257	5	.109	18	11	1.6
1995	NY-N	10	10	.500	30	30	3	1	0	195^{2}	209	107	91	20	7	53	127	1.339	4.19	97	4.05	.274	9	.161	-4	7	-0.4
1996	NY-N	12	8	.600	31	31	3	1	0	195^{2}	219	102	96	26	3	46	116	1.354	4.42	91	4.40	.288	7	.117	-11	8	-1.1
1997	NY-N★	15	9	.625	30	30	2	1	0	193^{1}	177	88	78	24	2	63	125	1.241	3.63	111	3.51	.242	8	.129	5	11	0.5
1998	NY-N	9	9	.500	30	30	0	0	0	195^{1}	192	88	88	23	8	53	115	1.254	4.05	102	3.84	.262	9	.188	1	11	0.2
1999	NY-N	3	3	.500	12	9	0	0	0	59^{1}	69	37	37	3	2	11	31	1.348	5.61	78	3.95	.295	5	.313	-9	2	-0.6
2000*	NY-N	11	6	.647	27	27	1	0	0	154^{2}	171	90	87	25	5	49	85	1.422	5.06	87	4.88	.281	2	.045	-10	0	-1.2
2001	SD-N	8	19	.296	33	33	1	0	0	195	250	137	111	37	4	38	113	1.477	5.12	78	5.41	.305	8	.140	-21	2	-2.0
2002	SD-N	7	8	.467	19	18	0	0	0	108	134	68	66	20	1	21	60	1.435	5.50	68	5.21	.300	5	.152	-20	1	-2.0
Total	**10**	**89**	**83**	**.517**	**245**	**241**	**11**	**4**	**0**	**1518^{2}**	**1639**	**827**	**735**	**194**	**38**	**412**	**887**	**1.351**	**4.36**	**94**	**4.27**	**.276**	**59**	**.133**	**-47**	**55**	**-5.1**

• JONES, Broadway Jesse Frank Jones b: 11/15/1898, Millsboro, DE d: 9/7/1977, Lewes, DE BR/TR, 5'9", 154 lbs. Deb: 7/4/1923

YEAR	TM-L	W	L	PCT	G	GS	CG	SH	SV	IP	H	R	ER	HR	HB	BB	SO	RAT	ERA	ERA+	CERA	OAV	BH	AVG	PR+	WS	TPW
1923	Phi-N	0	0	....	3	0	0	0	0	8	5	8	8	0	0	7	1	1.500	9.00	51	2.88	.185	1	.500	-4	0	-0.3

• JONES, Bumpus Charles Leander Jones b: 1/1/1870, Cedarville, OH d: 6/25/1938, Xenia, OH BR/TR Deb: 10/15/1892

YEAR	TM-L	W	L	PCT	G	GS	CG	SH	SV	IP	H	R	ER	HR	HB	BB	SO	RAT	ERA	ERA+	CERA	OAV	BH	AVG	PR+	WS	TPW
1892	Cin-N	1	0	1.000	1	1	1	0	0	9	0	1	0	0	0	4	3	.444	0.00	....	0.19	.000	0	.000	3	1	0.3
1893	Cin-N	1	3	.250	6	5	2	0	0	28^{2}	37	37	32	1	5	23	6	2.093	10.05	48	7.35	.304	4	.250	-17	0	-1.4
	NY-N	0	1	.000	1	1	0	0	0	4	5	5	5	0	1	10	1	3.750	11.25	41	13.69	.297	0	....	-3	0	-0.2
	Yr.	1	4	.200	7	6	2	0	0	32^{2}	42	42	37	1	6	33	7	2.296	10.19	47	8.13	.303	4	.250	-20	0	-1.6
Total	**2**	**2**	**4**	**.333**	**8**	**7**	**3**	**0**	**0**	**41^{2}**	**42**	**43**	**37**	**1**	**6**	**37**	**10**	**1.896**	**7.99**	**60**	**6.41**	**.303**	**4**	**.222**	**-17**	**1**	**-1.3**

• JONES, Calvin Calvin Douglas Jones b: 9/26/1963, Compton, CA BR/TR, 6'3", 185 lbs. Deb: 6/14/1991

YEAR	TM-L	W	L	PCT	G	GS	CG	SH	SV	IP	H	R	ER	HR	HB	BB	SO	RAT	ERA	ERA+	CERA	OAV	BH	AVG	PR+	WS	TPW
1991	Sea-A	2	2	.500	27	0	0	0	2	46^{1}	33	14	13	0	1	29	42	1.338	2.53	163	2.65	.209	0	....	7	4	0.7
1992	Sea-A	3	5	.375	38	1	0	0	0	61^{2}	50	39	39	8	2	47	49	1.573	5.69	70	4.81	.226	0	....	-12	1	-1.2
Total	**2**	**5**	**7**	**.417**	**65**	**1**	**0**	**0**	**2**	**108**	**83**	**53**	**52**	**8**	**3**	**76**	**91**	**1.472**	**4.33**	**92**	**3.88**	**.219**	**0**	**....**	**-4**	**5**	**-0.4**

• JONES, Cowboy Albert Edward "Bronco" Jones b: 8/23/1874, Golden, CO d: 2/9/1958, Inglewood, CA BL/TL, 5'11", 160 lbs. Deb: 6/24/1898

YEAR	TM-L	W	L	PCT	G	GS	CG	SH	SV	IP	H	R	ER	HR	HB	BB	SO	RAT	ERA	ERA+	CERA	OAV	BH	AVG	PR+	WS	TPW
1898	Cle-N	4	4	.500	9	9	7	0	0	72	76	44	24	0	4	29	26	1.458	3.00	120	3.76	.269	2	.071	4	4	0.2
1899	StL-N	6	5	.545	12	12	9	0	0	85^{1}	111	51	34	1	6	22	28	1.559	3.59	111	4.76	.314	5	.172	3	6	0.3
1900	StL-N	13	19	.406	39	36	29	3	0	292^{2}	334	185	116	10	19	82	68	1.421	3.57	102	4.09	.286	21	.179	7	13	0.4
1901	StL-N	2	6	.250	10	9	7	0	0	76^{1}	97	51	38	4	3	22	25	1.559	4.48	71	4.90	.307	4	.148	-13	1	-1.2
Total	**4**	**25**	**34**	**.424**	**70**	**66**	**52**	**3**	**0**	**526^{1}**	**618**	**331**	**212**	**15**	**32**	**155**	**147**	**1.469**	**3.63**	**99**	**4.27**	**.292**	**32**	**.159**	**1**	**24**	**-0.3**

• JONES, Dale Dale Eldon "Nubs" Jones b: 12/17/1918, Marquette, NE d: 11/8/1980, Orlando, FL BR/TR, 6'1", 172 lbs. Deb: 9/7/1941

YEAR	TM-L	W	L	PCT	G	GS	CG	SH	SV	IP	H	R	ER	HR	HB	BB	SO	RAT	ERA	ERA+	CERA	OAV	BH	AVG	PR+	WS	TPW
1941	Phi-N	0	1	.000	2	1	0	0	0	8^{1}	13	11	7	0	0	6	2	2.280	7.56	49	7.36	.342	1	.333	-4	0	-0.3

• JONES, Deacon Carroll Elmer Jones b: 12/20/1892, Arcadia, KS d: 12/28/1952, Pittsburg, KS BR/TR, 6'1", 174 lbs. Deb: 9/23/1916

YEAR	TM-L	W	L	PCT	G	GS	CG	SH	SV	IP	H	R	ER	HR	HB	BB	SO	RAT	ERA	ERA+	CERA	OAV	BH	AVG	PR+	WS	TPW
1916	Det-A	0	0	....	1	0	0	0	0	7	7	3	2	0	0	5	2	1.714	2.57	111	4.51	.269	0	.000	0	0	0.0
1917	Det-A	4	4	.500	24	6	2	0	0	77	69	34	25	0	6	26	28	1.234	2.92	90	3.05	.256	0	.000	-1	3	-0.2
1918	Det-A	3	2	.600	21	4	1	0	0	67	60	35	23	0	1	38	15	1.463	3.09	86	3.36	.244	5	.185	0	2	-0.2
Total	**3**	**7**	**6**	**.538**	**46**	**10**	**3**	**0**	**0**	**151**	**136**	**72**	**50**	**0**	**7**	**69**	**45**	**1.358**	**2.98**	**89**	**3.25**	**.251**	**5**	**.114**	**-1**	**5**	**-0.4**

• JONES, Dick Decatur Poindexter Jones b: 5/22/1902, Meadville, MS d: 8/2/1994, Burlingame, CA BL/TR, 6', 184 lbs. Deb: 9/11/1926

YEAR	TM-L	W	L	PCT	G	GS	CG	SH	SV	IP	H	R	ER	HR	HB	BB	SO	RAT	ERA	ERA+	CERA	OAV	BH	AVG	PR+	WS	TPW
1926	Was-A	2	1	.667	4	3	1	0	0	21	20	10	10	0	0	11	3	1.476	4.29	90	3.46	.263	2	.200	-1	1	-0.1
1927	Was-A	0	0	....	2	0	0	0	0	3^{1}	8	11	8	0	0	5	1	3.900	21.60	19	15.98	.444	0	....	-7	0	-0.6
Total	**2**	**2**	**1**	**.667**	**6**	**3**	**1**	**0**	**0**	**24^{1}**	**28**	**21**	**18**	**0**	**0**	**16**	**4**	**1.808**	**6.66**	**59**	**5.18**	**.298**	**2**	**.200**	**-8**	**1**	**-0.8**

• JONES, Doug Douglas Reid Jones b: 6/24/1957, Covina, CA BR/TR, 6'3", 195 lbs. Deb: 4/9/1982

YEAR	TM-L	W	L	PCT	G	GS	CG	SH	SV	IP	H	R	ER	HR	HB	BB	SO	RAT	ERA	ERA+	CERA	OAV	BH	AVG	PR+	WS	TPW
1982	Mil-A	0	0	....	4	0	0	0	0	2^{2}	5	3	3	1	0	1	1	2.250	10.13	37	11.86	.385	0	....	-2	0	-0.2
1986	Cle-A	1	0	1.000	11	0	0	0	1	18	18	5	5	0	1	6	12	1.333	2.50	166	3.15	.257	0	....	3	2	0.3
1987	Cle-A	6	5	.545	49	0	0	0	8	91^{1}	101	45	32	4	6	24	87	1.369	3.15	143	3.85	.281	0	....	15	9	1.5
1988	Cle-A★	3	4	.429	51	0	0	0	37	83^{1}	69	26	21	1	2	16	72	1.020	2.27	181	1.88	.218	0	....	19	18	1.9
1989	Cle-A★	7	10	.412	59	0	0	0	32	80^{2}	76	25	21	4	1	13	65	1.103	2.34	169	2.48	.251	0	....	15	16	1.5
1990	Cle-A★	5	5	.500	66	0	0	0	43	84^{1}	66	26	24	5	2	22	55	1.043	2.56	153	2.26	.218	0	....	14	15	1.4
1991	Cle-A	4	8	.333	36	4	0	0	7	63^{1}	87	42	39	7	0	17	48	1.642	5.54	75	5.54	.320	0	....	-9	1	-0.9
1992	Hou-N★	11	8	.579	80	0	0	0	36	111^{2}	96	29	23	5	5	17	93	1.012	1.85	181	2.23	.235	0	.000	19	18	2.0
1993	Hou-N	4	10	.286	71	0	0	0	26	85^{1}	102	46	43	7	5	21	66	1.441	4.54	85	4.48	.298	0	....	-7	6	-0.7
1994	Phi-N★	2	4	.333	47	0	0	0	27	54	55	14	13	2	0	6	38	1.130	2.17	198	2.57	.255	1	1.000	13	10	1.3
1995	Bal-A	0	4	.000	52	0	0	0	22	46^{2}	55	30	26	6	2	16	42	1.521	5.01	95	5.11	.286	0	....	-2	4	-0.2
1996	Chi-N	2	2	.500	28	0	0	0	2	32^{1}	41	20	18	4	1	7	26	1.485	5.01	87	4.95	.306	0	....	-3	1	-0.3
	Mil-A	5	0	1.000	24	0	0	0	1	31^{2}	31	13	12	3	2	13	34	1.389	3.41	152	4.07	.254	0	....	6	4	0.5
1997	Mil-A	6	6	.500	75	0	0	0	36	80^{1}	62	20	18	4	3	9	82	.884	2.02	229	1.74	.215	0	....	21	19	2.0

YEAR TM-L	W	L	PCT	G	GS	CG	SH	SV	IP	H	R	ER	HR	HB	BB	SO	RAT	ERA	ERA+	CERA	OAV	BH	AVG	PR+	WS	TPW
1998 Mil-N	3	4	.429	46	0	0	0	12	54	65	32	31	15	4	11	43	1.407	5.17	83	5.97	.298	0	.000	-6	3	-0.6
*Cle-A	1	2	.333	23	0	0	0	1	31^{1}	34	12	12	2	0	6	28	1.277	3.45	138	3.29	.279	0	....	5	3	0.4
1999 Oak-A	5	5	.500	70	0	0	0	10	104	106	43	41	10	3	24	63	1.250	3.55	131	3.62	.267	0	....	13	11	1.2
2000* Oak-A	4	2	.667	54	0	0	0	2	73^{1}	86	34	32	6	2	18	54	1.418	3.93	121	4.32	.292	0	....	8	6	0.7
Total 16	**69**	**79**	**.466**	**846**	**4**	**0**	**0**	**303**	**1128^{1}**	**1155**	**465**	**414**	**86**	**39**	**247**	**909**	**1.243**	**3.30**	**129**	**3.45**	**.264**	**1**	**.143**	**122**	**146**	**12.0**

• JONES, Earl — Earl Leslie "Lefty" Jones b: 6/11/1919, Fresno, CA d: 1/24/1989, Fresno, CA BL/TL, 5'10.5", 190 lbs. Deb: 7/6/1945

YEAR TM-L	W	L	PCT	G	GS	CG	SH	SV	IP	H	R	ER	HR	HB	BB	SO	RAT	ERA	ERA+	CERA	OAV	BH	AVG	PR+	WS	TPW
1945 StL-A	0	0	....	10	0	0	0	1	28^{1}	18	10	8	0	0	18	13	1.271	2.54	138	2.17	.184	2	.200	3	3	0.4

• JONES, Elijah — Elijah Albert "Bumpus" Jones b: 1/27/1882, Oxford, MI d: 4/29/1943, Pontiac, MI BR/TR, 5'11.5" Deb: 4/13/1907

YEAR TM-L	W	L	PCT	G	GS	CG	SH	SV	IP	H	R	ER	HR	HB	BB	SO	RAT	ERA	ERA+	CERA	OAV	BH	AVG	PR+	WS	TPW
1907 Det-A	0	1	.000	4	1	1	0	1	16	23	15	9	0	1	4	9	1.688	5.06	51	5.41	.339	0	.000	-4	0	-0.5
1909 Det-A	1	1	.500	2	2	0	0	0	10	10	3	3	0	0	0	2	1.000	2.70	93	2.23	.278	1	.250	-0	1	0.0
Total 2	**1**	**2**	**.333**	**6**	**3**	**1**	**0**	**1**	**26**	**33**	**18**	**12**	**0**	**1**	**4**	**11**	**1.423**	**4.15**	**62**	**4.19**	**.318**	**1**	**.125**	**-5**	**1**	**-0.6**

• JONES, Gary — Gareth Howell Jones b: 6/12/1945, Huntington Park, CA BL/TL, 6', 191 lbs. Deb: 9/25/1970

YEAR TM-L	W	L	PCT	G	GS	CG	SH	SV	IP	H	R	ER	HR	HB	BB	SO	RAT	ERA	ERA+	CERA	OAV	BH	AVG	PR+	WS	TPW
1970 NY-A	0	0	....	2	0	0	0	0	2	3	0	0	0	0	1	2	2.000	0.00	....	7.26	.375	0	....	1	0	0.1
1971 NY-A	0	0	....	12	0	0	0	0	14	19	14	14	1	0	7	10	1.857	9.00	36	5.99	.317	0	.000	-9	0	-1.0
Total 2	**0**	**0**	**....**	**14**	**0**	**0**	**0**	**0**	**16**	**22**	**14**	**14**	**1**	**0**	**8**	**12**	**1.875**	**7.88**	**41**	**6.15**	**.324**	**0**	**.000**	**-8**	**0**	**-0.9**

• JONES, Gordon — Gordon Bassett Jones b: 4/2/1930, Portland, OR d: 4/25/1994, Lodi, CA BR/TR, 6', 190 lbs. Deb: 8/6/1954 C

YEAR TM-L	W	L	PCT	G	GS	CG	SH	SV	IP	H	R	ER	HR	HB	BB	SO	RAT	ERA	ERA+	CERA	OAV	BH	AVG	PR+	WS	TPW
1954 StL-N	4	4	.500	11	10	4	2	0	81	78	25	18	3	1	19	48	1.198	2.00	206	2.79	.248	3	.125	19	7	1.9
1955 StL-N	1	4	.200	15	9	0	0	0	57	66	38	37	10	1	28	46	1.649	5.84	69	5.83	.286	1	.071	-11	0	-1.2
1956 StL-N	0	2	.000	5	1	0	0	0	11^{1}	14	9	7	2	0	5	6	1.676	5.56	68	6.08	.311	0	.000	-2	0	-0.3
1957 NY-N	0	1	.000	10	0	0	0	0	11^{2}	16	9	8	1	1	3	5	1.629	6.17	64	5.39	.320	1	.500	-3	0	-0.3
1958 SF-N	3	1	.750	11	1	0	0	1	30^{1}	33	11	8	2	1	5	8	1.253	2.37	161	3.56	.284	0	.000	5	3	0.4
1959 SF-N	3	2	.600	31	0	0	0	2	43^{2}	45	23	21	6	1	19	29	1.466	4.33	88	4.56	.280	0	.000	-2	2	-0.3
1960 Bal-A	1	1	.500	29	0	0	0	2	55	59	28	27	9	1	13	30	1.309	4.42	86	4.43	.281	2	.400	-5	3	-0.4
1961 Bal-A	0	0	....	3	0	0	0	1	5	5	3	3	3	0	0	4	1.000	5.40	72	5.25	.250	0	....	-1	0	-0.1
1962 KC-A	3	2	.600	21	0	0	0	6	32^{2}	31	23	23	10	0	14	28	1.378	6.34	66	5.23	.252	0	.000	-8	1	-0.8
1964 Hou-N	0	1	.000	34	0	0	0	0	50	58	24	23	3	0	14	28	1.440	4.14	82	4.08	.290	1	.250	-3	2	-0.3
1965 Hou-N	0	0	....	1	0	0	0	0	1	0	0	0	0	0	0	0	.000	0.00	....	0.00	.000	0	....	0	0	0.0
Total 11	**15**	**18**	**.455**	**171**	**21**	**4**	**2**	**12**	**378^{2}**	**405**	**193**	**175**	**49**	**6**	**120**	**232**	**1.386**	**4.16**	**93**	**4.34**	**.275**	**8**	**.119**	**-10**	**18**	**-1.3**

• JONES, Greg — Greg Alan Jones b: 11/15/1976, Clearwater, FL BR/TR, 6'2", 195 lbs. Deb: 7/30/2003

YEAR TM-L	W	L	PCT	G	GS	CG	SH	SV	IP	H	R	ER	HR	HB	BB	SO	RAT	ERA	ERA+	CERA	OAV	BH	AVG	PR+	WS	TPW
2003 Ana-A	0	0	....	18	0	0	0	0	27^{2}	29	15	15	3	2	14	28	1.554	4.88	88	5.05	.261	0	....	-2	1	-0.2

• JONES, Henry — Henry Jones b: Pittsburgh, PA TR Deb: 4/22/1890

YEAR TM-L	W	L	PCT	G	GS	CG	SH	SV	IP	H	R	ER	HR	HB	BB	SO	RAT	ERA	ERA+	CERA	OAV	BH	AVG	PR+	WS	TPW
1890 Pit-N	2	1	.667	5	4	2	0	0	31	35	25	12	1	0	14	13	1.581	3.48	94	....	.276	2	.222	1	1	0.1

• JONES, Jack (DA) — Daniel Albion "Jumping Jack" Jones b: 10/23/1860, Litchfield, CT d: 10/19/1936, Wallingford, CT TR Deb: 7/9/1883

YEAR TM-L	W	L	PCT	G	GS	CG	SH	SV	IP	H	R	ER	HR	HB	BB	SO	RAT	ERA	ERA+	CERA	OAV	BH	AVG	PR+	WS	TPW
1883 Det-N	6	5	.545	12	12	9	1	0	92^{2}	103	63	36	0	....	19	33	1.317	3.50	89	....	.265	8	.190	-2	4	-0.4
Phi-a	5	2	.714	7	7	7	0	0	65	58	38	19	1	....	6	28	.985	2.63	132	....	.223	6	.240	8	5	0.7

• JONES, Jeff — Jeffrey Allen Jones b: 7/29/1956, Detroit, MI BR/TR, 6'3", 210 lbs. Deb: 4/10/1980

YEAR TM-L	W	L	PCT	G	GS	CG	SH	SV	IP	H	R	ER	HR	HB	BB	SO	RAT	ERA	ERA+	CERA	OAV	BH	AVG	PR+	WS	TPW
1980 Oak-A	1	3	.250	35	0	0	0	5	44^{1}	32	21	14	2	1	26	34	1.308	2.84	133	2.85	.204	0	....	4	3	0.4
1981* Oak-A	4	1	.800	33	0	0	0	3	61	51	27	23	7	3	40	43	1.492	3.39	103	4.23	.233	0	....	-0	4	0.0
1982 Oak-A	3	1	.750	18	2	0	0	0	37	44	29	21	6	1	26	18	1.892	5.11	76	7.09	.306	0	....	-5	1	-0.5
1983 Oak-A	1	1	.500	13	1	0	0	0	29^{2}	43	19	19	7	2	8	14	1.719	5.76	67	7.62	.339	0	....	-7	0	-0.7
1984 Oak-A	0	3	.000	13	0	0	0	0	33	31	14	13	4	0	12	19	1.303	3.55	106	3.83	.258	0	....	1	1	0.1
Total 5	**9**	**9**	**.500**	**112**	**3**	**0**	**0**	**8**	**205**	**201**	**110**	**90**	**26**	**7**	**112**	**128**	**1.527**	**3.95**	**94**	**4.87**	**.262**	**0**	**....**	**-7**	**9**	**-0.7**

• JONES, Jimmy — James Condia Jones b: 4/20/1964, Dallas, TX BR/TR, 6'2", 190 lbs. Deb: 9/21/1986

YEAR TM-L	W	L	PCT	G	GS	CG	SH	SV	IP	H	R	ER	HR	HB	BB	SO	RAT	ERA	ERA+	CERA	OAV	BH	AVG	PR+	WS	TPW
1986 SD-N	2	0	1.000	3	3	1	1	0	18	10	6	5	1	0	3	15	.722	2.50	146	1.15	.164	1	.167	2	2	0.2
1987 SD-N	9	7	.563	30	22	2	1	0	145^{2}	154	85	67	14	5	54	51	1.428	4.14	96	4.34	.270	8	.163	-4	6	-0.3
1988 SD-N	9	14	.391	29	29	3	0	0	179	192	98	82	14	3	44	82	1.318	4.12	82	3.76	.277	9	.164	-17	4	-1.6
1989 NY-A	2	1	.667	11	6	0	0	0	48	56	29	28	7	2	16	25	1.500	5.25	74	5.30	.293	0	....	-7	1	-0.8
1990 NY-A	1	2	.333	17	7	0	0	0	50	72	42	35	8	1	23	25	1.900	6.30	63	7.67	.344	0	....	-13	0	-1.3
1991 Hou-N	6	8	.429	26	22	1	1	0	135^{1}	143	73	66	9	3	51	88	1.433	4.39	80	4.09	.270	7	.184	-14	3	-1.3
1992 Hou-N	10	6	.625	25	23	0	0	0	139^{1}	135	64	63	13	5	39	69	1.249	4.07	82	3.54	.258	6	.167	-11	5	-0.9
1993 Mon-N	4	1	.800	12	6	0	0	0	39^{2}	47	34	28	6	0	9	21	1.412	6.35	66	4.68	.285	1	.111	-10	0	-0.9
Total 8	**43**	**39**	**.524**	**153**	**118**	**7**	**3**	**0**	**755**	**809**	**431**	**374**	**72**	**19**	**239**	**376**	**1.388**	**4.46**	**82**	**4.23**	**.275**	**32**	**.166**	**-74**	**21**	**-6.9**

• JONES, Johnny — John Paul "Admiral" Jones b: 8/25/1892, Arcadia, LA d: 6/5/1980, Ruston, LA BR/TR, 6'1", 151 lbs. Deb: 4/24/1919

YEAR TM-L	W	L	PCT	G	GS	CG	SH	SV	IP	H	R	ER	HR	HB	BB	SO	RAT	ERA	ERA+	CERA	OAV	BH	AVG	PR+	WS	TPW
1919 NY-N	0	0	....	2	0	0	0	1	6^{2}	9	4	4	0	1	3	3	1.800	5.40	52	5.43	.310	0	.000	-2	0	-0.3
1920 Bos-N	1	0	1.000	3	1	0	0	0	9^{2}	16	7	7	1	0	5	6	2.172	6.52	47	8.68	.372	1	.250	-4	0	-0.3
Total 2	**1**	**0**	**1.000**	**5**	**1**	**0**	**0**	**1**	**16^{1}**	**25**	**11**	**11**	**1**	**1**	**8**	**9**	**2.020**	**6.06**	**49**	**7.36**	**.347**	**1**	**.143**	**-6**	**0**	**-0.6**

• JONES, Ken — Kenneth Frederick "Broadway" Jones b: 4/13/1903, Dover, NJ d: 5/15/1991, Hartford, CT BR/TR, 6'3", 193 lbs. Deb: 5/19/1924

YEAR TM-L	W	L	PCT	G	GS	CG	SH	SV	IP	H	R	ER	HR	HB	BB	SO	RAT	ERA	ERA+	CERA	OAV	BH	AVG	PR+	WS	TPW
1924 Det-A	0	0	....	1	0	0	0	0	2	1	0	0	0	0	1	0	1.000	0.00	....	1.34	.143	0	....	1	0	0.1
1930 Bos-N	0	1	.000	8	1	0	0	0	19^{2}	28	16	13	1	0	4	4	1.627	5.95	83	5.17	.359	1	.200	-2	0	-0.2
Total 2	**0**	**1**	**.000**	**9**	**1**	**0**	**0**	**0**	**21^{2}**	**29**	**16**	**13**	**1**	**0**	**5**	**4**	**1.569**	**5.40**	**91**	**4.82**	**.341**	**1**	**.200**	**-1**	**0**	**-0.1**

• JONES, Marcus — Marcus Ray Jones b: 3/29/1975, Bellflower, CA BR/TR, 6'5", 235 lbs. Deb: 7/17/2000

YEAR TM-L	W	L	PCT	G	GS	CG	SH	SV	IP	H	R	ER	HR	HB	BB	SO	RAT	ERA	ERA+	CERA	OAV	BH	AVG	PR+	WS	TPW
2000 Oak-A	0	0	....	1	1	0	0	0	2^{1}	5	4	4	1	0	3	1	3.429	15.43	31	19.41	.417	0	.000	-3	0	-0.3

• JONES, Mike — Michael Carl Jones b: 7/30/1959, Rochester, NY BL/TL, 6'6", 215 lbs. Deb: 9/6/1980

YEAR TM-L	W	L	PCT	G	GS	CG	SH	SV	IP	H	R	ER	HR	HB	BB	SO	RAT	ERA	ERA+	CERA	OAV	BH	AVG	PR+	WS	TPW
1980 KC-A	0	1	.000	3	1	0	0	0	4^{2}	6	7	6	0	0	5	2	2.357	11.57	35	7.34	.333	0	....	-4	0	-0.4
1981* KC-A	6	3	.667	12	11	0	0	0	75^{2}	74	30	27	7	2	28	29	1.348	3.21	112	3.90	.256	0	....	4	5	0.4
1984* KC-A	2	3	.400	23	12	0	0	0	81	86	48	44	10	1	36	43	1.506	4.89	82	4.79	.270	0	....	-8	2	-0.8
1985 KC-A	3	3	.500	33	1	0	0	0	64	62	40	34	6	0	39	32	1.578	4.78	87	4.51	.257	0	....	-4	2	-0.4
Total 4	**11**	**10**	**.524**	**71**	**25**	**0**	**0**	**0**	**225^{1}**	**228**	**125**	**111**	**23**	**3**	**108**	**106**	**1.491**	**4.43**	**89**	**4.47**	**.263**	**0**	**....**	**-12**	**9**	**-1.2**

• JONES, Mike — Michael Jones b: 7/6/1865, Hamilton, Canada d: 3/24/1894, Hamilton, Canada BL/TL, 5'11.5", 168 lbs. Deb: 8/1/1890

YEAR TM-L	W	L	PCT	G	GS	CG	SH	SV	IP	H	R	ER	HR	HB	BB	SO	RAT	ERA	ERA+	CERA	OAV	BH	AVG	PR+	WS	TPW
1890 Lou-a	2	0	1.000	3	3	2	0	0	22	21	12	8	2	0	9	6	1.364	3.27	117	....	.244	4	.444	1	2	0.3

• JONES, Odell — Odell Jones b: 1/13/1953, Tulare, CA BR/TR, 6'3", 175 lbs. Deb: 9/11/1975

YEAR TM-L	W	L	PCT	G	GS	CG	SH	SV	IP	H	R	ER	HR	HB	BB	SO	RAT	ERA	ERA+	CERA	OAV	BH	AVG	PR+	WS	TPW
1975 Pit-N	0	0	....	2	0	0	0	0	3	1	0	0	0	0	0	2	.333	0.00	....	0.25	.100	0	....	1	0	0.1
1977 Pit-N	3	7	.300	34	15	1	0	0	108	118	63	61	14	3	31	66	1.380	5.08	78	4.44	.278	4	.143	-15	2	-1.6
1978 Pit-N	2	0	1.000	3	1	0	0	0	9	7	3	2	0	0	4	10	1.222	2.00	185	2.35	.206	0	.000	2	1	0.2
1979 Sea-A	3	11	.214	25	19	3	0	0	118^{2}	151	90	80	16	3	58	72	1.761	6.07	72	6.34	.317	0	....	-22	0	-2.2
1981 Pit-N	4	5	.444	13	8	0	0	0	54^{1}	51	23	20	3	0	23	30	1.362	3.31	109	3.34	.250	2	.200	2	3	0.2
1983 Tex-A	3	6	.333	42	0	0	0	10	67	56	28	23	4	2	22	50	1.164	3.09	130	2.70	.223	0	....	7	7	0.7
1984 Tex-A	2	4	.333	33	0	0	0	2	59^{1}	62	28	24	7	2	23	28	1.433	3.64	114	4.57	.281	0	....	4	3	0.4
1986 Bal-A	2	2	.500	21	0	0	0	0	49^{1}	58	22	21	4	0	23	32	1.642	3.83	108	5.11	.305	0	....	2	3	0.2
1988 Mil-A	5	0	1.000	28	2	0	0	1	80^{2}	75	47	39	8	1	29	48	1.289	4.35	91	3.47	.251	0	....	-4	4	-0.4
Total 9	**24**	**35**	**.407**	**201**	**45**	**4**	**0**	**13**	**549^{1}**	**579**	**304**	**270**	**56**	**11**	**213**	**338**	**1.442**	**4.42**	**92**	**4.41**	**.275**	**6**	**.154**	**-23**	**23**	**-2.3**

• JONES, Oscar — Oscar Lafayette "Flip Flap" Jones b: 10/22/1879, Carter County, MO d: 3/16/1953, Fort Worth, TX BR/TR, 5'7", 163 lbs. Deb: 4/20/1903

YEAR TM-L	W	L	PCT	G	GS	CG	SH	SV	IP	H	R	ER	HR	HB	BB	SO	RAT	ERA	ERA+	CERA	OAV	BH	AVG	PR+	WS	TPW
1903 Bro-N	19	14	.576	38	36	31	4	0	324^{1}	320	159	106	4	19	77	95	1.224	2.94	108	2.95	.260	32	.256	**51**	23	**5.2**
1904 Bro-N	17	25	.405	46	41	38	0	0	377	387	175	115	7	17	92	96	1.271	2.75	100	3.16	.270	24	.175	2	18	0.2

YEAR TM-L	W	L	PCT	G	GS	CG	SH	SV	IP	H	R	ER	HR	HB	BB	SO	RAT	ERA	ERA+	CERA	OAV	BH	AVG	PR+	WS	TPW
1905 Bro-N	8	15	.348	29	20	14	0	1	174	197	121	90	6	9	56	66	1.454	4.66	62	4.20	.285	13	.200	-30	3	-3.1
Total 3	44	54	.449	113	97	83	4	1	875^1	904	455	311	17	45	225	257	1.290	3.20	91	3.29	.269	69	.211	23	44	2.2

• JONES, Percy Percy Lee Jones b: 10/28/1899, Harwood, TX d: 3/18/1979, Dallas, TX BR/TL, 5'11.5", 175 lbs. Deb: 8/6/1920

YEAR TM-L	W	L	PCT	G	GS	CG	SH	SV	IP	H	R	ER	HR	HB	BB	SO	RAT	ERA	ERA+	CERA	OAV	BH	AVG	PR+	WS	TPW
1920 Chi-N	0	0	....	4	0	0	0	0	7	15	10	9	1	1	3	0	2.571	11.57	28	13.37	.455	0	.000	-6	0	-0.7
1921 Chi-N	3	5	.375	32	3	1	0	0	98^2	116	57	50	2	4	39	46	1.571	4.56	84	4.48	.295	6	.222	-8	4	-0.8
1922 Chi-N	8	9	.471	44	24	7	2	1	162	197	104	86	10	5	68	45	**1.636**	4.78	88	5.16	.310	4	.085	-12	6	-1.5
1925 Chi-N	6	6	.500	28	13	6	1	0	124	123	74	64	12	5	71	60	1.565	4.65	93	4.70	.263	6	.154	-7	6	-0.9
1926 Chi-N	12	7	.632	30	20	10	2	2	160^1	151	64	55	3	5	90	80	1.503	3.09	125	3.78	.256	13	.260	10	14	1.3
1927 Chi-N	7	8	.467	30	11	5	1	0	112^2	123	67	51	3	6	72	37	1.731	4.07	95	4.96	.285	14	.350	-5	6	-0.2
1928 Chi-N	10	6	.625	39	19	9	1	3	154	167	80	69	4	7	56	41	1.448	4.03	95	3.99	.288	11	.196	-9	9	-0.9
1929 Bos-N	7	15	.318	35	22	11	1	0	188^1	219	112	97	15	4	84	69	1.609	4.64	101	5.01	.298	9	.148	2	9	-0.1
1930 Pit-N	0	1	.000	9	2	0	0	0	19	26	20	14	3	3	11	3	1.947	6.63	75	7.93	.329	0	.000	-3	0	-0.3
Total 9	53	57	.482	251	114	49	8	6	1026	1137	588	495	53	40	494	381	1.590	4.34	95	4.71	.288	63	.194	-38	54	-4.2

• JONES, Randy Randall Leo Jones b: 1/12/1950, Fullerton, CA BR/TL, 6', 178 lbs. Deb: 6/16/1973

YEAR TM-L	W	L	PCT	G	GS	CG	SH	SV	IP	H	R	ER	HR	HB	BB	SO	RAT	ERA	ERA+	CERA	OAV	BH	AVG	PR+	WS	TPW
1973 SD-N	7	6	.538	20	19	6	1	0	139^2	129	58	49	13	1	37	77	1.189	3.16	110	2.99	.241	8	.167	6	9	0.6
1974 SD-N	8	22	.267	40	34	4	1	2	208^1	217	118	103	16	5	78	124	1.416	4.45	80	4.02	.270	10	.154	-15	6	-1.7
1975 SD-N★	20	12	.625	37	36	18	6	0	285	242	94	71	17	0	56	103	1.046	**2.24**	**155**	2.27	.232	11	.133	**43**	**28**	**4.4**
1976 SD-N★	**22**	14	.611	40	**40**	**25**	5	0	**315^1**	274	109	96	15	4	50	93	1.027	2.74	119	**2.19**	.234	6	.058	19	**21**	1.3
1977 SD-N	6	12	.333	27	25	1	0	0	147^1	173	85	75	12	0	36	44	1.419	4.58	77	4.16	.291	5	.116	-16	3	-1.8
1978 SD-N	13	14	.481	37	36	7	2	0	253	263	104	81	6	0	64	71	1.292	2.88	115	3.10	.272	15	.183	12	14	1.4
1979 SD-N	11	12	.478	39	39	6	0	0	263	257	120	106	17	3	64	112	1.221	3.63	97	3.11	.259	15	.174	-5	13	-0.5
1980 SD-N	5	13	.278	24	24	4	3	0	154^1	165	71	67	14	0	29	53	1.257	3.91	88	3.55	.276	3	.067	-10	4	-1.4
1981 NY-N	1	8	.111	13	12	0	0	0	59^1	65	48	32	8	1	38	14	1.736	4.85	72	5.74	.274	2	.118	-8	0	-1.0
1982 NY-N	7	10	.412	28	20	2	1	0	107^2	130	68	55	11	4	51	44	1.681	4.60	79	5.75	.304	4	.148	-10	2	-1.1
Total 10	100	123	.448	305	285	73	19	2	1933	1915	875	735	129	18	503	735	1.251	3.42	101	3.27	.260	79	.132	15	100	0.3

• JONES, Rick Thomas Frederick Jones b: 4/16/1955, Jacksonville, FL BL/TL, 6'5", 190 lbs. Deb: 4/18/1976

YEAR TM-L	W	L	PCT	G	GS	CG	SH	SV	IP	H	R	ER	HR	HB	BB	SO	RAT	ERA	ERA+	CERA	OAV	BH	AVG	PR+	WS	TPW
1976 Bos-A	5	3	.625	24	14	1	0	0	104^1	133	48	39	6	1	26	45	1.524	3.36	116	4.73	.311	0	....	7	6	0.8
1977 Sea-A	1	4	.200	10	10	0	0	0	42^1	47	25	24	10	0	37	16	1.984	5.10	81	7.93	.283	0	....	-5	1	-0.5
1978 Sea-A	0	2	.000	3	2	0	0	0	12^1	17	8	8	1	0	7	11	1.946	5.84	65	6.72	.315	0	....	-3	0	-0.3
Total 3	6	9	.400	37	26	1	0	0	159	197	81	71	17	1	70	72	1.679	4.02	99	5.74	.304	0	....	-1	7	0.0

• JONES, Sam Samuel Pond "Sad Sam" Jones b: 7/26/1892, Woodsfield, OH d: 7/6/1966, Barnesville, OH BR/TR, 6', 170 lbs. Deb: 6/13/1914

YEAR TM-L	W	L	PCT	G	GS	CG	SH	SV	IP	H	R	ER	HR	HB	BB	SO	RAT	ERA	ERA+	CERA	OAV	BH	AVG	PR+	WS	TPW
1914 Cle-A	0	0	....	1	0	0	0	0	3^1	2	1	1	0	0	2	0	1.200	2.70	107	2.31	.200	1	.500	0	0	0.0
1915 Cle-A	4	9	.308	48	9	2	0	4	145^2	131	78	59	0	1	63	42	1.332	3.65	83	3.09	.252	5	.156	-9	7	-0.9
1916 Bos-A	0	1	.000	12	0	0	0	1	27	25	14	11	0	0	10	7	1.296	3.67	75	3.18	.272	2	.333	-2	1	-0.2
1917 Bos-A	0	1	.000	9	1	0	0	1	16^1	15	9	8	1	0	6	5	1.286	4.41	58	3.43	.259	0	.000	-3	0	-0.4
1918* Bos-A	16	5	.762	24	21	16	5	0	184	151	66	46	1	8	70	44	1.201	2.25	119	2.55	.230	10	.175	8	14	1.1
1919 Bos-A	12	20	.375	35	31	21	5	1	245	258	120	102	4	7	95	67	1.441	3.75	80	3.89	.278	11	.136	-23	8	-2.5
1920 Bos-A	13	16	.448	37	33	21	3	0	274	302	143	120	9	4	79	86	1.391	3.94	92	3.83	.288	20	.217	-13	15	-1.1
1921 Bos-A	23	16	.590	40	38	25	**5**	1	298^2	318	122	107	1	6	78	98	1.326	3.22	131	3.27	.279	24	.240	27	29	3.0
1922* NY-A	13	13	.500	45	28	20	0	**8**	260	270	132	106	16	3	76	81	1.331	3.67	109	3.63	.275	23	.264	7	20	1.5
1923* NY-A	21	8	.724	39	27	18	3	4	243	239	114	98	11	6	69	68	1.267	3.63	108	3.18	.257	19	.224	6	20	0.8
1924 NY-A	9	6	.600	36	21	8	3	3	178^2	187	85	72	6	1	76	53	1.472	3.63	115	3.88	.276	9	.176	9	13	0.9
1925 NY-A	15	21	.417	43	31	14	1	2	246^2	267	147	127	14	3	104	92	1.504	4.63	92	4.26	.281	13	.163	-10	11	-1.2
1926* NY-A	9	8	.529	39	23	6	1	5	161	186	104	89	6	4	80	69	1.652	4.98	77	4.82	.298	10	.204	-17	5	-1.6
1927 StL-A	8	14	.364	30	26	11	0	0	189^2	211	121	91	13	3	102	72	1.650	4.32	101	4.87	.282	6	.109	-1	9	-0.2
1928 Was-A	17	7	.708	30	27	19	4	0	224^2	209	89	71	5	3	78	63	1.277	2.84	141	2.96	.252	20	.253	26	22	3.1
1929 Was-A	9	9	.500	24	24	8	1	0	153^2	156	80	67	5	3	49	36	1.334	3.92	108	3.34	.264	8	.157	3	10	0.4
1930 Was-A	15	7	.682	25	25	14	1	0	183^1	195	95	83	4	3	61	60	1.396	4.07	113	3.61	.277	9	.148	5	13	0.3
1931 Was-A	9	10	.474	25	24	8	1	1	148	185	88	71	10	4	47	58	1.568	4.32	99	4.92	.304	15	.313	-2	8	0.2
1932 Chi-A	10	15	.400	30	28	10	0	0	200^1	217	123	94	9	3	75	64	1.458	4.22	102	3.90	.270	11	.193	4	8	0.6
1933 Chi-A	10	12	.455	27	25	11	2	0	176^2	181	80	66	13	4	65	60	1.392	3.36	126	3.91	.265	9	.155	19	13	1.8
1934 Chi-A	8	12	.400	27	26	11	1	0	183^1	217	120	104	16	2	60	60	1.511	5.11	93	4.63	.289	12	.200	-3	9	-0.1
1935 Chi-A	8	7	.533	21	19	7	0	0	140	162	77	63	8	1	51	38	1.521	4.05	114	4.34	.284	8	.167	8	10	0.7
Total 22	229	217	.513	647	487	250	36	31	3883	4084	2008	1656	152	69	1396	1223	1.411	3.84	103	3.79	.274	245	.197	40	245	6.0

• JONES, Sam Samuel "Toothpick Sam" Jones b: 12/14/1925, Stewartsville, OH d: 11/5/1971, Morgantown, WV BR/TR, 6'4", 200 lbs. Deb: 9/22/1951

YEAR TM-L	W	L	PCT	G	GS	CG	SH	SV	IP	H	R	ER	HR	HB	BB	SO	RAT	ERA	ERA+	CERA	OAV	BH	AVG	PR+	WS	TPW
1951 Cle-A	0	1	.000	2	1	0	0	0	8^2	4	2	2	0	0	5	4	1.038	2.08	182	1.41	.143	0	.000	2	1	0.1
1952 Cle-A	2	3	.400	14	4	0	0	1	36	38	30	29	6	4	37	28	2.083	7.25	46	7.66	.270	1	.100	-15	0	-1.7
1955 Chi-N★	14	20	.412	36	34	12	4	0	241^2	175	118	110	22	14	185	**198**	1.490	4.10	100	4.10	**.206**	14	.182	-1	14	-0.3
1956 Chi-N	9	14	.391	33	28	8	2	0	188^2	155	93	82	21	8	115	**176**	**1.431**	3.91	96	4.06	.221	10	.175	-6	9	-0.6
1957 StL-N	12	9	.571	28	27	10	2	0	182^2	164	77	73	17	6	71	154	1.286	3.60	110	3.58	.239	10	.159	8	12	0.7
1958 StL-N	14	13	.519	35	35	14	2	0	250	204	95	80	23	6	107	**225**	1.244	2.88	143	3.22	.223	9	.100	**34**	23	2.9
1959 SF-N★	**21**	15	.583	50	35	16	**4**	4	270^2	232	99	85	18	8	109	209	1.260	**2.83**	135	3.13	**.228**	11	.129	**31**	22	2.9
1960 SF-N	18	14	.563	39	35	13	3	0	234	200	112	83	18	4	91	190	1.244	3.19	109	3.13	.230	16	.200	10	12	1.1
1961 SF-N	8	8	.500	37	17	2	0	1	128^1	134	72	64	12	8	57	105	1.488	4.49	85	4.54	.264	5	.139	-9	5	-0.9
1962 Det-A	2	4	.333	30	6	1	0	1	81^1	77	39	33	13	2	35	73	1.377	3.65	111	4.40	.254	2	.095	5	4	0.4
1963 StL-N	2	0	1.000	11	0	0	0	2	11	15	12	11	0	0	5	8	1.818	9.00	39	5.42	.319	0	.000	-7	0	-0.7
1964 Bal-A	0	0	....	7	0	0	0	0	10^1	5	3	3	1	0	5	6	.968	2.61	137	1.92	.152	0	....	1	1	0.1
Total 12	102	101	.502	322	222	76	17	9	1643^1	1403	752	655	151	60	822	1376	1.354	3.59	107	3.71	.230	78	.149	51	103	4.0

• JONES, Sheldon Sheldon Leslie "Available" Jones b: 2/2/1922, Tecumseh, NE d: 4/18/1991, Greenville, NC BR/TR, 6', 180 lbs. Deb: 9/9/1946

YEAR TM-L	W	L	PCT	G	GS	CG	SH	SV	IP	H	R	ER	HR	HB	BB	SO	RAT	ERA	ERA+	CERA	OAV	BH	AVG	PR+	WS	TPW
1946 NY-N	1	2	.333	6	4	1	0	0	28	21	10	10	4	1	17	24	1.357	3.21	107	3.73	.208	2	.250	1	2	0.1
1947 NY-N	2	2	.500	15	6	0	0	0	55^2	51	27	24	2	3	29	24	1.437	3.88	105	3.75	.250	2	.125	1	3	0.0
1948 NY-N	16	8	.667	55	21	8	1	5	201^1	204	89	75	16	6	90	82	1.460	3.35	117	4.21	.263	13	.203	14	15	1.5
1949 NY-N	15	12	.556	42	27	11	1	0	207^1	198	93	77	19	10	88	79	1.379	3.34	119	3.91	.248	8	.121	15	14	1.2
1950 NY-N	13	16	.448	40	28	11	2	2	199	188	114	102	26	7	90	97	1.397	4.61	89	4.24	.249	6	.105	-18	8	-1.9
1951* NY-N	6	11	.353	41	12	2	0	4	120^1	119	77	57	12	4	52	58	1.421	4.26	92	4.17	.260	3	.097	-5	4	-0.6
1952 Bos-N	1	4	.200	39	1	0	0	1	70	81	45	37	7	1	31	40	1.600	4.76	76	5.00	.286	1	.125	-8	0	-0.8
1953 Chi-N	0	2	.000	22	2	0	0	0	38^1	47	24	23	3	5	16	9	1.643	5.40	82	5.67	.299	0	.000	-3	1	-0.4
Total 8	54	57	.486	260	101	33	4	12	920	909	479	405	89	37	413	413	1.437	3.96	100	4.22	.258	35	.136	-2	47	-0.9

• JONES, Sherman Sherman Jarvis "Roadblock" Jones b: 2/10/1935, Winton, NC BL/TR, 6'4", 205 lbs. Deb: 8/2/1960

YEAR TM-L	W	L	PCT	G	GS	CG	SH	SV	IP	H	R	ER	HR	HB	BB	SO	RAT	ERA	ERA+	CERA	OAV	BH	AVG	PR+	WS	TPW
1960 SF-N	1	1	.500	16	0	0	0	1	32	37	17	11	3	1	11	10	1.500	3.09	112	4.72	.291	2	.286	2	1	0.2
1961* Cin-N	1	1	.500	24	2	0	0	2	55	51	32	27	6	2	27	32	1.418	4.42	92	4.07	.256	2	.182	-2	2	-0.2
1962 NY-N	0	4	.000	8	3	0	0	0	23^1	31	22	20	3	2	8	11	1.671	7.71	54	6.12	.326	3	.429	-9	0	-0.8
Total 3	2	6	.250	48	5	0	0	3	110^1	119	71	58	12	5	46	53	1.495	4.73	84	4.69	.283	7	.280	-9	3	-0.8

• JONES, Stacy Joseph Stacy Jones b: 5/26/1967, Gadsden, AL BR/TR, 6'6", 225 lbs. Deb: 7/30/1991

YEAR TM-L	W	L	PCT	G	GS	CG	SH	SV	IP	H	R	ER	HR	HB	BB	SO	RAT	ERA	ERA+	CERA	OAV	BH	AVG	PR+	WS	TPW
1991 Bal-A	0	0	....	4	1	0	0	0	11	11	6	5	1	0	5	10	1.455	4.09	97	4.12	.256	0	....	-0	0	0.0
1996 Chi-A	0	0	....	2	0	0	0	0	2	0	0	0	0	0	1	1	.500	0.00	....	0.27	.000	0	....	1	0	0.1
Total 2	0	0	....	6	1	0	0	0	13	11	6	5	1	0	6	11	1.308	3.46	114	3.53	.256	0	....	1	0	0.1

• JONES, Steve Steven Howell Jones b: 4/22/1941, Huntington Park, CA BL/TL, 5'10", 175 lbs. Deb: 8/15/1967

YEAR TM-L	W	L	PCT	G	GS	CG	SH	SV	IP	H	R	ER	HR	HB	BB	SO	RAT	ERA	ERA+	CERA	OAV	BH	AVG	PR+	WS	TPW
1967 Chi-A	2	2	.500	11	3	0	0	0	25^2	21	13	12	1	0	12	17	1.286	4.21	74	2.93	.223	1	.250	-3	1	-0.3
1968 Was-A	1	2	.333	7	0	0	0	0	10^2	8	8	7	3	0	7	11	1.406	5.91	49	4.99	.205	0	.000	-3	0	-0.4

YEAR	TM-L	W	L	PCT	G	GS	CG	SH	SV	IP	H	R	ER	HR	HB	BB	SO	RAT	ERA	ERA+	CERA	OAV	BH	AVG	PR+	WS	TPW
1969	KC-A	2	3	.400	20	4	0	0	0	44^2	45	25	21	3	3	24	31	1.545	4.23	87	4.56	.260	1	.125	-2	1	-0.2
Total	3	5	7	.417	38	7	0	0	0	81	74	46	40	7	3	43	59	1.444	4.44	75	4.10	.242	2	.154	-9	2	-0.9
• JONES, Tim	Timmothy Byron Jones b: 1/24/1954, Sacramento, CA BB/TR, 6'5", 220 lbs. Deb: 9/4/1977																										
1977	Pit-N	1	0	1.000	3	1	0	0	0	10	4	0	0	0	0	3	5	.700	0.00	....	0.79	.118	0	.000	4	2	0.4
• JONES, Todd	Todd Barton Givin Jones b: 4/24/1968, Marietta, GA BL/TR, 6'3", 200 lbs. Deb: 7/7/1993																										
1993	Hou-N	1	2	.333	27	0	0	0	2	37^1	28	14	13	4	1	15	25	1.152	3.13	124	2.90	.214	0	....	3	3	0.3
1994	Hou-N	5	2	.714	48	0	0	0	5	72^2	52	23	22	3	1	26	63	1.073	2.72	145	2.10	.202	2	.400	9	9	1.0
1995	Hou-N	6	5	.545	68	0	0	0	15	99^2	89	38	34	8	6	52	96	1.415	3.07	126	3.70	.237	1	.200	11	9	1.1
1996	Hou-N	6	3	.667	51	0	0	0	17	57^1	61	30	28	5	5	32	44	1.622	4.40	88	5.16	.274	0	.000	-2	5	-0.2
1997	Det-A	5	4	.556	68	0	0	0	31	70	60	29	24	3	1	35	70	1.357	3.09	149	3.27	.231	0	....	11	13	1.0
1998	Det-A	1	4	.200	65	0	0	0	28	63^1	58	38	35	7	2	36	57	1.484	4.97	95	4.37	.249	0	....	-3	7	-0.3
1999	Det-A	4	4	.500	65	0	0	0	30	66^1	64	30	28	7	1	35	64	1.492	3.80	130	4.55	.259	0	....	8	10	0.8
2000	Det-A★	2	4	.333	67	0	0	0	**42**	64	67	28	25	6	1	25	67	1.438	3.52	137	4.43	.276	0	....	10	10	0.9
2001	Det-A	4	5	.444	45	0	0	0	11	48^2	60	31	25	6	0	22	39	1.685	4.62	94	5.74	.303	0	....	-1	3	-0.1
	Min-A	1	0	1.000	24	0	0	0	2	19^1	27	8	7	3	0	7	15	1.759	3.26	141	6.80	.333	0	....	3	2	0.3
	Yr.	5	5	.500	69	0	0	0	13	68	87	39	32	9	0	29	54	1.706	4.24	104	6.04	.312	0	....	2	5	0.2
2002	Col-N	1	4	.200	79	0	0	0	1	82^1	84	43	43	10	3	28	73	1.360	4.70	101	4.22	.269	0	.000	2	6	0.1
2003	Col-N	1	4	.200	33	1	0	0	0	39^1	61	39	36	8	1	18	28	2.008	8.24	60	8.77	.361	0	.000	-14	0	-1.4
	*Bos-A	2	1	.667	26	0	0	0	0	29^1	32	19	18	2	0	13	31	1.534	5.52	83	4.30	.269	0	....	-3	1	-0.2
Total	11	39	42	.481	666	1	0	0	184	749^2	743	370	338	72	22	344	672	1.450	4.06	110	4.33	.261	3	.188	34	78	3.3
• JONNARD, Claude	Claude Alfred Jonnard b: 11/23/1897, Nashville, TN d: 8/27/1959, Nashville, TN BR/TR, 6'1", 165 lbs. Deb: 10/1/1921																										
1921	NY-N	0	0	....	1	0	0	0	1	4	4	0	0	0	0	0	7	1.000	0.00	....	2.12	.267	0	.000	2	1	0.1
1922	NY-N	6	1	.857	33	0	0	0	**5**	96	96	45	41	7	3	28	44	1.292	3.84	104	3.56	.272	1	.042	-1	7	-0.4
1923*	NY-N	4	3	.571	**45**	1	1	0	**5**	96	105	45	35	6	0	35	45	1.458	3.28	116	4.07	.279	1	.038	4	7	0.2
1924*	NY-N	3	5	.375	34	3	1	0	5	89^2	80	33	24	2	2	24	40	1.160	2.41	152	2.40	.229	1	.045	12	7	0.9
1926	StL-A	0	2	.000	12	3	0	0	1	36	46	29	24	1	0	24	13	1.944	6.00	71	5.85	.313	0	.000	-7	0	-0.8
1929	Chi-N	0	1	.000	12	2	0	0	0	27^2	41	27	23	4	1	11	11	1.880	7.48	62	6.88	.320	2	.200	-9	0	-0.8
Total	6	13	12	.520	137	9	2	0	17	349^1	372	179	147	20	6	122	160	1.414	3.79	106	3.89	.272	5	.056	1	22	-0.7
• JORDAN, Charlie	Charles T. "Kid" Jordan b: 10/4/1871, Baltimore, MD d: 6/1/1928, Hazleton, PA Deb: 7/31/1896																										
1896	Phi-N	0	0	....	2	0	0	0	0	4^2	9	4	4	0	0	2	3	2.357	7.71	56	9.02	.402	1	.500	-2	0	-0.1
• JORDAN, Harry	Harry J. Jordan b: 2/14/1873, Titusville, PA d: 3/1/1920, Pittsburgh, PA Deb: 9/25/1894																										
1894	Pit-N	1	0	1.000	1	1	1	0	0	9	10	7	4	0	1	2	1	1.333	4.00	131	3.64	.279	0	.000	1	1	0.1
1895	Pit-N	0	2	.000	2	2	2	0	0	17	24	15	8	0	1	6	4	1.765	4.24	107	5.63	.328	2	.286	0	1	0.0
Total	2	1	2	.333	3	3	3	0	0	26	34	22	12	0	2	8	5	1.615	4.15	114	4.94	.312	2	.200	2	2	0.1
• JORDAN, Milt	Milton Mignot Jordan b: 5/24/1927, Mineral Springs, PA d: 5/13/1993, Ithaca, NY BR/TR, 6'2.5", 207 lbs. Deb: 4/16/1953																										
1953	Det-A	0	1	.000	8	1	0	0	0	17	26	13	11	3	0	5	4	1.824	5.82	70	7.59	.366	1	.500	-3	0	-0.2
• JORDAN, Niles	Niles Chapman Jordan b: 12/1/1925, Lyman, WA BL/TL, 5'11", 180 lbs. Deb: 8/26/1951																										
1951	Phi-N	2	3	.400	5	5	2	1	0	36^2	35	15	13	4	0	8	11	1.173	3.19	121	3.17	.250	1	.077	3	2	0.2
1952	Cin-N	0	1	.000	3	1	0	0	0	6^1	14	7	7	1	0	3	2	2.684	9.95	38	13.30	.452	0	.000	-4	0	-0.5
Total	2	2	4	.333	8	6	2	1	0	43	49	22	20	5	0	11	13	1.395	4.19	91	4.66	.287	1	.071	-2	2	-0.3
• JORDAN, Ricardo	Ricardo Jordan b: 6/27/1970, Boynton Beach, FL BL/TL, 6', 165 lbs. Deb: 6/23/1995																										
1995	Tor-A	1	0	1.000	15	0	0	0	1	15	18	11	11	3	2	13	10	2.067	6.60	71	8.63	.305	0	....	-3	0	-0.3
1996	Phi-N	2	2	.500	26	0	0	0	0	25	18	6	5	0	0	12	17	1.200	1.80	240	2.25	.202	0	.000	7	3	0.7
1997	NY-N	1	2	.333	22	0	0	0	0	27	31	17	16	1	2	15	19	1.704	5.33	76	5.35	.304	0	.000	-4	0	-0.4
1998	Cin-N	1	0	1.000	6	0	0	0	0	3^1	4	9	9	2	0	7	1	3.300	24.30	18	18.21	.308	0	....	-7	0	-0.7
Total	4	5	4	.556	69	0	0	0	1	70^1	71	43	41	6	4	47	47	1.678	5.25	82	5.56	.270	0	.000	-8	3	-0.8
• JORDAN, Rip	Raymond Willis "Lanky" Jordan b: 9/28/1889, Portland, ME d: 6/5/1960, Meridan, CT BL/TR, 6', 172 lbs. Deb: 6/25/1912																										
1912	Chi-A	0	0	....	4	0	0	0	0	12^1	13	8	7	2	1	3	1	1.297	5.11	63	6.22	.289	0	.000	-2	0	-0.3
1919	Was-A	0	0	....	1	1	0	0	0	4	6	5	5	1	0	2	2	2.000	11.25	28	9.00	.353	0	.000	-4	0	-0.4
Total	2	0	0	....	5	1	0	0	0	16^1	19	13	12	3	1	5	3	1.469	6.61	49	6.90	.307	0	.000	-6	0	-0.7
• JORGENS, Orville	Orville Edward Jorgens b: 6/4/1908, Rockford, IL d: 1/11/1992, Colorado Springs, CO BR/TR, 6'1", 180 lbs. Deb: 4/19/1935																										
1935	Phi-N	10	15	.400	**53**	24	6	0	2	188^1	216	129	101	12	8	96	57	1.657	4.83	94	5.01	.283	6	.097	-4	8	-0.8
1936	Phi-N	8	8	.500	39	21	4	0	0	167^1	196	110	89	16	7	69	58	1.584	4.79	95	5.06	.290	12	.200	1	7	0.0
1937	Phi-N	3	4	.429	52	9	1	0	3	140^2	159	83	69	12	5	68	34	1.614	4.41	98	5.21	.298	5	.143	1	8	0.0
Total	3	21	27	.438	144	54	11	0	5	496^1	571	322	259	40	20	233	149	1.620	4.70	95	5.09	.290	23	.146	-2	23	-0.8
• JOSEPH, Kevin	Kevin John Joseph b: 8/1/1976, Camp Hill, PA BR/TR, 6'4", 200 lbs. Deb: 8/1/2002																										
2002	StL-N	0	1	.000	11	0	0	0	0	11	16	7	6	1	2	6	2	2.000	4.91	81	8.80	.364	0	....	-1	0	-0.1
• JOSS, Addie	Adrian Joss b: 4/12/1880, Woodland, WI d: 4/14/1911, Toledo, OH BR/TR, 6'3", 185 lbs. Deb: 4/26/1902 HOF: 1978																										
1902	Cle-A	17	13	.567	32	29	28	**5**	0	269^1	225	120	83	2	13	75	106	1.114	2.77	124	2.24	.228	12	.117	19	17	1.3
1903	Cle-A	18	13	.581	32	31	31	3	0	283^2	232	105	69	3	9	37	120	.948	2.19	130	**1.69**	.223	22	.193	18	20	1.8
1904	Cle-A	14	10	.583	25	24	20	5	0	192^1	160	51	34	0	7	30	83	.988	**1.59**	159	1.82	.227	10	.132	19	16	1.6
1905	Cle-A	20	12	.625	33	32	31	3	0	286	246	90	64	4	11	46	132	1.021	2.01	130	1.97	.234	13	.134	20	25	2.1
1906	Cle-A	21	9	.700	34	31	28	9	1	282	220	81	54	3	3	43	106	.933	1.72	152	1.60	.218	21	.210	22	23	2.8
1907	Cle-A	**27**	11	.711	42	38	34	6	2	338^2	279	100	69	3	7	54	127	.983	1.83	137	1.80	.227	13	.114	19	28	1.5
1908	Cle-A	24	11	.686	42	35	29	9	2	325	232	77	42	2	2	30	130	.806	**1.16**	**205**	**1.23**	**.197**	15	.155	41	35	5.0
1909	Cle-A	14	13	.519	33	28	24	4	0	242^2	198	71	46	0	4	31	67	.944	1.71	150	1.65	.226	8	.100	21	20	2.1
1910	Cle-A	5	5	.500	13	12	9	1	0	107^1	96	35	27	2	2	18	49	1.062	2.26	114	2.24	.245	4	.111	3	7	0.2
Total	9	160	97	.623	286	260	234	45	5	2327	1888	730	488	19	58	364	920	.968	1.89	143	1.76	.223	118	.144	182	191	18.4
• JOURNELL, Jimmy	James Richard Journell b: 12/29/1977, Springfield, OH BR/TR, 6'4", 205 lbs. Deb: 6/29/2003																										
2003	StL-N	0	0	....	7	0	0	0	0	9	10	7	6	0	0	11	8	2.333	6.00	68	7.02	.278	0	....	-2	0	-0.2
• JOYCE, Bob	Robert Emmett Joyce b: 1/14/1915, Stockton, CA d: 12/10/1981, San Francisco, CA BR/TR, 6'1", 180 lbs. Deb: 5/4/1939																										
1939	Phi-A	3	5	.375	30	6	1	0	0	107^2	156	91	80	13	1	37	25	1.793	6.69	70	6.47	.337	3	.086	-20	1	-2.1
1946	NY-N	3	4	.429	14	7	2	0	0	60^2	79	43	36	3	0	20	24	1.632	5.34	65	5.05	.315	3	.158	-12	0	-1.2
Total	2	6	9	.400	44	13	3	0	0	168^1	235	134	116	16	1	57	49	1.735	6.20	68	5.96	.329	6	.111	-32	1	-3.4
• JOYCE, Dick	Richard Edward Joyce b: 11/18/1943, Portland, ME BL/TL, 6'5", 225 lbs. Deb: 9/3/1965																										
1965	KC-A	0	1	.000	5	3	0	0	0	13	12	7	4	0	0	4	7	1.231	2.77	126	2.59	.240	0	.000	1	0	0.1
• JOYCE, Mike	Michael Lewis Joyce b: 2/12/1941, Detroit, MI BR/TR, 6'2", 193 lbs. Deb: 7/2/1962																										
1962	Chi-A	2	1	.667	25	1	0	0	2	43^1	40	17	16	2	0	14	9	1.246	3.32	117	2.91	.247	3	.429	3	4	0.4
1963	Chi-A	0	0	....	6	0	0	0	0	10^2	13	10	10	1	0	8	7	1.969	8.44	42	6.23	.289	0	....	-6	0	-0.6
Total	2	2	1	.667	31	1	0	0	2	54	53	27	26	3	0	22	16	1.389	4.33	86	3.57	.256	3	.429	-3	4	-0.2
• JUDD, Mike	Michael Galen Judd b: 6/30/1975, San Diego, CA BR/TR, 6'2", 200 lbs. Deb: 9/28/1997																										
1997	LA-N	0	0	....	1	0	0	0	0	2^2	4	0	0	0	0	0	4	1.500	0.00	....	4.92	.364	0	.000	1	0	0.1
1998	LA-N	0	0	....	7	0	0	0	0	11^1	19	19	19	4	1	9	14	2.471	15.09	26	12.61	.373	0	.000	-14	0	-1.4
1999	LA-N	3	1	.750	7	4	0	0	0	28	30	17	17	4	1	12	22	1.500	5.46	78	5.26	.280	0	.000	-3	1	-0.4

YEAR	TM-L	W	L	PCT	G	GS	CG	SH	SV	IP	H	R	ER	HR	HB	BB	SO	RAT	ERA	ERA+	CERA	OAV	BH	AVG	PR+	WS	TPW
2000	LA-N	0	1	.000	1	1	0	0	0	4	4	7	7	2	1	3	5	1.750	15.75	27	9.87	.250	1	1.000	-5	0	-0.4
2001	TB-A	1	0	1.000	8	2	0	0	0	20	19	14	9	2	1	10	11	1.450	4.05	111	4.28	.250	0	....	1	1	0.1
	Tex-A	0	1	.000	4	1	0	0	0	9	15	10	8	2	0	5	5	2.222	8.00	58	9.84	.357	0	.000	-3	0	-0.3
	Yr.	1	1	.500	12	3	0	0	0	29	34	24	17	4	1	15	16	1.690	5.28	87	6.01	.288	0	.000	-2	1	-0.2
Total	5	4	3	.571	28	8	0	0	0	75	91	67	60	14	4	39	61	1.733	7.20	59	6.89	.300	1	.111	-24	2	-2.3

• JUDD, Oscar Thomas William Oscar "Ossie" Judd b: 2/14/1908, London, Canada d: 12/27/1995, Ingersoll, Canada BL/TL, 6'.5", 180 lbs. Deb: 4/16/1941

YEAR	TM-L	W	L	PCT	G	GS	CG	SH	SV	IP	H	R	ER	HR	HB	BB	SO	RAT	ERA	ERA+	CERA	OAV	BH	AVG	PR+	WS	TPW
1941	Bos-A	0	0	....	7	0	0	0	1	12^1	15	12	12	1	0	10	5	2.027	8.76	48	6.72	.300	2	.500	-6	1	-0.4
1942	Bos-A	8	10	.444	31	19	11	0	2	150^1	135	72	65	3	2	90	70	1.497	3.89	96	3.57	.239	18	.269	-6	10	0.0
1943	Bos-A★	11	6	.647	23	20	8	1	0	155^1	131	58	50	2	3	69	53	1.288	2.90	114	2.78	.230	14	.259	6	13	1.1
1944	Bos-A	1	1	.500	9	6	1	0	0	30	30	16	12	1	0	15	9	1.500	3.60	94	3.85	.261	2	.182	-1	1	0.0
1945	Bos-A	0	1	.000	2	1	0	0	0	6^1	10	8	6	1	0	3	5	2.053	8.53	40	7.61	.333	1	.500	-4	0	-0.4
	Phi-N	5	4	.556	23	9	3	1	2	82^2	80	47	35	3	1	40	36	1.452	3.81	101	3.63	.254	8	.267	2	4	0.5
1946	Phi-N	11	12	.478	30	24	12	1	2	173^1	169	86	68	6	1	90	65	1.494	3.53	97	3.82	.260	25	.316	-1	12	0.7
1947	Phi-N	4	15	.211	32	19	8	1	0	146^2	155	86	75	6	3	69	54	1.527	4.60	87	4.28	.279	12	.188	-11	5	-0.8
1948	Phi-N	0	2	.000	4	1	0	0	0	14^1	19	14	11	1	0	11	7	2.093	6.91	57	6.89	.317	1	.167	-5	0	-0.4
Total	8	40	51	.440	161	99	43	4	7	771^1	744	399	334	24	10	397	304	1.479	3.90	94	3.76	.256	83	.262	-25	46	0.3

• JUDD, Ralph Ralph Wesley Judd b: 12/7/1901, Perrysburg, OH d: 5/6/1957, Lapeer, MI BL/TR, 5'10", 170 lbs. Deb: 10/2/1927

YEAR	TM-L	W	L	PCT	G	GS	CG	SH	SV	IP	H	R	ER	HR	HB	BB	SO	RAT	ERA	ERA+	CERA	OAV	BH	AVG	PR+	WS	TPW
1927	Was-A	0	0	....	1	0	0	0	1	4	8	3	3	0	0	2	2	2.500	6.75	60	9.55	.400	0	.000	-1	0	-0.1
1929	NY-N	3	0	1.000	18	0	0	0	0	50^2	49	19	15	4	0	11	21	1.184	2.66	172	3.07	.261	0	.000	10	5	0.7
1930	NY-N	0	0	....	2	0	0	0	0	7^2	13	8	5	0	0	3	0	2.087	5.87	81	7.12	.390	0	.000	-1	0	-0.1
Total	3	3	0	1.000	21	0	0	0	1	62^1	70	30	23	4	0	16	23	1.380	3.32	137	3.98	.290	0	.000	8	5	0.4

• JUDEN, Jeff Jeffrey Daniel Juden b: 1/19/1971, Salem, MA BR/TR, 6'7", 265 lbs. Deb: 9/15/1991

YEAR	TM-L	W	L	PCT	G	GS	CG	SH	SV	IP	H	R	ER	HR	HB	BB	SO	RAT	ERA	ERA+	CERA	OAV	BH	AVG	PR+	WS	TPW
1991	Hou-N	0	2	.000	4	3	0	0	0	18	19	14	12	3	0	7	11	1.444	6.00	58	4.56	.275	0	.000	-5	0	-0.6
1993	Hou-N	0	1	.000	2	0	0	0	0	5	4	3	3	1	0	4	7	1.600	5.40	72	4.82	.222	0	....	-1	0	-0.1
1994	Phi-N	1	4	.200	6	5	0	0	0	27^2	29	25	19	4	1	12	22	1.482	6.18	69	5.02	.276	1	.111	-6	0	-0.6
1995	Phi-N	2	4	.333	13	10	1	0	0	62^2	53	31	28	6	5	31	47	1.340	4.02	105	3.87	.235	1	.056	1	3	0.0
1996	SF-N	4	0	1.000	36	0	0	0	0	41^2	39	23	19	7	1	20	35	1.416	4.10	100	4.57	.250	0	.000	-0	2	-0.1
	Mon-N	1	0	1.000	22	0	0	0	0	32^2	22	12	8	1	4	14	26	1.102	2.20	196	2.40	.188	0	....	8	3	0.8
	Yr.	5	0	1.000	58	0	0	0	0	74^1	61	35	27	8	5	34	61	1.278	3.27	127	3.62	.223	0	.000	7	5	0.7
1997	Mon-N	11	5	.688	22	22	3	0	0	130	125	64	61	17	9	57	107	1.400	4.22	99	4.52	.255	6	.140	-1	8	0.0
	*Cle-A	0	1	.000	8	5	0	0	0	31^1	32	21	19	6	1	15	29	1.500	5.46	86	5.24	.264	0	....	-2	1	-0.2
1998	Mil-N	7	11	.389	24	24	2	0	0	138^1	149	91	85	20	10	66	109	1.554	5.53	77	5.44	.277	5	.122	-21	2	-2.2
	Ana-A	1	3	.250	8	6	0	0	0	40	33	32	30	7	2	18	39	1.275	6.75	70	3.96	.217	0	....	-9	0	-0.8
1999	NY-A	0	1	.000	2	1	0	0	0	5^2	5	9	1	1	1	3	9	1.412	1.59	298	4.50	.200	0	....	2	0	0.2
Total	8	27	32	.458	147	76	6	0	0	533	510	325	285	73	34	247	441	1.420	4.81	89	4.59	.253	13	.109	-34	19	-3.6

• JUDSON, Howie Howard Kolls Judson b: 2/16/1926, Hebron, IL BR/TR, 6'1", 195 lbs. Deb: 4/22/1948

YEAR	TM-L	W	L	PCT	G	GS	CG	SH	SV	IP	H	R	ER	HR	HB	BB	SO	RAT	ERA	ERA+	CERA	OAV	BH	AVG	PR+	WS	TPW
1948	Chi-A	4	5	.444	40	5	1	0	8	107^1	102	60	57	7	3	56	38	1.472	4.78	89	4.06	.255	3	.103	-7	7	-0.9
1949	Chi-A	1	14	.067	26	12	3	0	1	108	114	65	55	13	1	70	36	1.704	4.58	91	5.43	.274	2	.065	-6	2	-0.8
1950	Chi-A	2	3	.400	46	3	1	0	0	112	105	53	49	10	2	63	34	1.500	3.94	114	4.28	.252	2	.100	4	8	0.4
1951	Chi-A	5	6	.455	27	14	3	0	1	121^2	124	67	51	9	2	55	43	1.471	3.77	107	4.14	.264	4	.121	2	5	-0.1
1952	Chi-A	0	1	.000	21	0	0	0	1	34	30	17	16	4	0	22	15	1.529	4.24	86	4.27	.244	0	.000	-3	1	-0.3
1953	Cin-N	0	1	.000	10	6	0	0	0	38^2	58	28	24	8	0	11	11	1.784	5.59	78	7.30	.341	1	.111	-6	1	-0.5
1954	Cin-N	5	7	.417	37	8	0	0	3	93^1	86	47	41	9	3	42	27	1.371	3.95	106	3.88	.251	2	.083	1	6	0.0
Total	7	17	37	.315	207	48	8	0	14	615	619	337	293	60	11	319	204	1.525	4.29	98	4.54	.265	14	.093	-14	30	-2.2

• JULIO, Jorge Jorge Dandys Julio b: 3/3/1979, Caracas, Venezuela BR/TR, 6'1", 190 lbs. Deb: 4/26/2001

YEAR	TM-L	W	L	PCT	G	GS	CG	SH	SV	IP	H	R	ER	HR	HB	BB	SO	RAT	ERA	ERA+	CERA	OAV	BH	AVG	PR+	WS	TPW
2001	Bal-A	1	1	.500	18	0	0	0	0	21^1	25	13	9	2	1	9	22	1.594	3.80	113	5.17	.287	0	....	1	1	0.1
2002	Bal-A	5	6	.455	67	0	0	0	25	68	55	22	15	5	2	27	55	1.206	1.99	216	2.83	.213	0	....	17	13	1.6
2003	Bal-A	0	7	.000	64	0	0	0	36	61^2	60	36	30	10	2	34	52	1.524	4.38	101	5.05	.256	0	....	0	6	0.0
Total	3	6	14	.300	149	0	0	0	61	151	140	71	54	17	5	70	129	1.391	3.22	135	4.07	.242	0	....	18	20	1.7

• JUNGE, Eric Eric DeBari Junge b: 1/5/1977, Manhasset, NY BR/TR, 6'5", 215 lbs. Deb: 9/11/2002

YEAR	TM-L	W	L	PCT	G	GS	CG	SH	SV	IP	H	R	ER	HR	HB	BB	SO	RAT	ERA	ERA+	CERA	OAV	BH	AVG	PR+	WS	TPW
2002	Phi-N	2	0	1.000	4	1	0	0	0	12^2	14	3	2	0	0	5	11	1.500	1.42	274	3.88	.286	0	.000	3	2	0.3
2003	Phi-N	0	0	....	6	0	0	0	0	7^2	5	3	3	1	0	1	5	.783	3.52	113	1.62	.185	0	....	0	1	0.0
Total	2	2	0	1.000	10	1	0	0	0	20^1	19	6	5	1	0	6	16	1.230	2.21	179	3.03	.250	0	.000	4	3	0.3

• JUNGELS, Ken Kenneth Peter "Curly" Jungels b: 6/23/1916, Aurora, IL d: 9/9/1975, West Bend, WI BR/TR, 6'1", 180 lbs. Deb: 9/15/1937

YEAR	TM-L	W	L	PCT	G	GS	CG	SH	SV	IP	H	R	ER	HR	HB	BB	SO	RAT	ERA	ERA+	CERA	OAV	BH	AVG	PR+	WS	TPW
1937	Cle-A	0	0	....	2	0	0	0	0	3	3	1	0	0	0	1	0	1.333	0.00	....	3.27	.273	0	....	2	0	0.1
1938	Cle-A	1	0	1.000	9	0	0	0	0	15^1	21	16	15	1	2	18	7	2.543	8.80	53	9.58	.339	0	.000	-7	0	-0.7
1940	Cle-A	0	0	....	2	0	0	0	0	3^1	3	1	1	0	0	1	1	1.200	2.70	156	2.62	.273	0	.000	0	0	0.0
1941	Cle-A	0	0	....	6	0	0	0	0	13^2	17	12	11	4	1	8	6	1.829	7.24	54	7.88	.293	0	.000	-5	0	-0.5
1942	Pit-N	0	0	....	6	0	0	0	0	13^2	12	11	10	0	0	4	7	1.171	6.59	51	2.27	.235	1	.500	-5	0	-0.5
Total	5	1	0	1.000	25	0	0	0	0	49	56	41	37	5	3	32	21	1.796	6.80	59	6.21	.290	1	.100	-15	0	-1.5

• JUREWICZ, Mike Michael Allen Jurewicz b: 9/20/1945, Buffalo, NY BB/TL, 6'3", 205 lbs. Deb: 9/7/1965

YEAR	TM-L	W	L	PCT	G	GS	CG	SH	SV	IP	H	R	ER	HR	HB	BB	SO	RAT	ERA	ERA+	CERA	OAV	BH	AVG	PR+	WS	TPW
1965	NY-A	0	0	....	2	0	0	0	0	2^1	5	2	2	0	0	1	2	2.571	7.71	44	10.38	.417	0		-1	0	-0.1

• JURISICH, Al Alvin Joseph Jurisich b: 8/25/1921, New Orleans, LA d: 11/3/1981, New Orleans, LA BR/TR, 6'2", 193 lbs. Deb: 4/26/1944

YEAR	TM-L	W	L	PCT	G	GS	CG	SH	SV	IP	H	R	ER	HR	HB	BB	SO	RAT	ERA	ERA+	CERA	OAV	BH	AVG	PR+	WS	TPW
1944*	StL-N	7	9	.438	30	14	5	2	1	130	102	53	49	7	5	65	53	1.285	3.39	104	3.06	.221	8	.178	-1	7	-0.2
1945	StL-N	3	3	.500	27	6	1	0	0	71^2	61	45	41	7	1	41	42	1.423	5.15	73	3.79	.232	2	.087	-13	0	-1.5
1946	Phi-N	4	3	.571	13	10	2	1	1	68^1	71	30	28	9	1	31	34	1.493	3.69	93	4.62	.263	3	.130	-2	4	-0.2
1947	Phi-N	1	7	.125	34	12	5	0	3	118^1	110	69	65	15	1	52	48	1.369	4.94	81	4.13	.258	1	.032	-13	3	-1.6
Total	4	15	22	.405	104	42	13	3	5	388^1	344	197	183	38	8	189	177	1.373	4.24	88	3.80	.242	14	.115	-29	14	-3.5

• JUSTIS, Walt Walter Newton "Smoke" Justis b: 8/17/1883, Moores Hill, IN d: 10/4/1941, Greendale, IN BR/TR, 5'11.5", 195 lbs. Deb: 8/1/1905

YEAR	TM-L	W	L	PCT	G	GS	CG	SH	SV	IP	H	R	ER	HR	HB	BB	SO	RAT	ERA	ERA+	CERA	OAV	BH	AVG	PR+	WS	TPW
1905	Det-A	0	0	....	2	0	0	0	0	3^1	4	3	3	0	1	6	0	3.000	8.10	34	10.74	.299	0	....	-2	0	-0.2

• JUUL, Herb Herbert Victor Juul b: 2/2/1886, Chicago, IL d: 11/14/1928, Chicago, IL BL/TL, 5'11", 150 lbs. Deb: 7/11/1911

YEAR	TM-L	W	L	PCT	G	GS	CG	SH	SV	IP	H	R	ER	HR	HB	BB	SO	RAT	ERA	ERA+	CERA	OAV	BH	AVG	PR+	WS	TPW
1911	Cin-N	0	0	....	1	0	0	0	0	4	3	2	2	0	0	4	2	1.750	4.50	73	4.30	.231	0	.000	-1	0	-0.1

• JUUL, Herold Earl Herold Juul b: 5/21/1893, Chicago, IL d: 1/4/1942, Chicago, IL BR/TR, 5'9.5", 150 lbs. Deb: 4/24/1914

YEAR	TM-L	W	L	PCT	G	GS	CG	SH	SV	IP	H	R	ER	HR	HB	BB	SO	RAT	ERA	ERA+	CERA	OAV	BH	AVG	PR+	WS	TPW
1914	Bro-F	0	3	.000	9	3	0	0	0	29	26	24	20	0	1	31	16	1.966	6.21	52	5.07	.248	2	.222	-9	0	-1.0

• KAAT, Jim James Lee "Kitty" Kaat b: 11/7/1938, Zeeland, MI BL/TL, 6'4.5", 217 lbs. Deb: 8/2/1959 C

YEAR	TM-L	W	L	PCT	G	GS	CG	SH	SV	IP	H	R	ER	HR	HB	BB	SO	RAT	ERA	ERA+	CERA	OAV	BH	AVG	PR+	WS	TPW
1959	Was-A	0	2	.000	3	2	0	0	0	5	7	9	7	1	2	4	2	2.200	12.60	31	10.43	.350	0	.000	-5	0	-0.5
1960	Was-A	1	5	.167	13	9	0	0	0	50	48	39	31	8	5	31	25	1.580	5.58	71	5.55	.255	2	.143	-8	0	-0.9
1961	Min-A	9	17	.346	36	29	8	1	0	200^2	188	105	87	12	11	82	122	1.346	3.90	109	3.68	.248	15	.238	12	11	1.5
1962	Min-A★	18	14	.563	39	35	16	**5**	1	269	243	106	94	23	18	75	173	1.182	3.14	130	3.25	.243	18	.180	27	22	3.0
1963	Min-A	10	10	.500	31	27	7	1	1	178^1	195	96	83	24	9	38	105	1.307	4.19	87	4.27	.274	8	.131	-10	5	-1.1
1964	Min-A	17	11	.607	36	34	13	0	1	243	231	100	87	23	9	60	171	1.198	3.22	111	3.29	.251	14	.169	13	15	1.9
1965*	Min-A	18	11	.621	45	**42**	7	2	2	264^1	267	121	83	25	5	63	154	1.248	2.83	126	3.47	.258	23	.247	18	17	2.6
1966	Min-A★	**25**	13	.658	41	**41**	**19**	3	0	**304^2**	271	114	93	29	3	55	205	1.070	2.75	131	2.64	.235	23	.195	**30**	**26**	**3.7**
1967	Min-A	16	13	.552	42	38	13	2	0	263^1	269	110	89	21	9	42	211	1.181	3.04	114	3.21	.260	17	.172	16	17	2.1
1968	Min-A	14	12	.538	30	29	9	2	0	208	192	78	68	16	3	40	130	1.115	2.94	105	2.75	.243	12	.156	7	13	0.8
1969	Min-A	14	13	.519	40	32	10	0	1	242^1	252	114	94	23	9	75	139	1.349	3.49	105	3.92	.265	18	.207	1	13	0.8
1970*	Min-A	14	10	.583	45	34	4	1	0	230^1	244	110	91	26	3	58	120	1.311	3.56	105	3.92	.273	15	.197	3	12	0.7
1971	Min-A	13	14	.481	39	38	15	4	0	260^1	275	104	96	16	6	47	137	1.237	3.32	107	3.27	.268	15	.161	11	15	1.2

YEAR	TM-L	W	L	PCT	G	GS	CG	SH	SV	IP	H	R	ER	HR	HB	BB	SO	RAT	ERA	ERA+	CERA	OAV	BH	AVG	PR+	WS	TPW
1972	Min-A	10	2	.833	15	15	5	0	0	113^1	94	36	26	6	0	20	64	1.006	2.06	155	2.09	.227	13	.289	13	12	2.1
1973	Min-A	11	12	.478	29	28	7	2	0	181^2	206	101	89	26	4	39	93	1.349	4.41	90	4.47	.282	0	....	-8	7	-0.8
	Chi-A	4	1	.800	7	7	3	1	0	42^2	44	23	20	4	0	4	16	1.125	4.22	94	3.02	.260	0	....	-1	2	-0.1
	Yr.	15	13	.536	36	35	10	3	0	224^1	250	124	109	30	4	43	109	1.306	4.37	91	4.19	.278	0	....	-9	9	-0.9
1974	Chi-A	21	13	.618	42	39	15	3	0	277^1	263	106	90	18	6	63	142	1.175	2.92	128	2.99	.250	0	.000	28	21	2.9
1975	Chi-A★	20	14	.588	43	41	12	1	0	303^2	321	121	105	20	9	77	142	1.311	3.11	124	3.74	.274	0	....	30	22	3.1
1976*	Phi-N	12	14	.462	38	35	7	1	0	227^2	241	95	88	21	0	32	83	1.199	3.48	102	3.37	.274	14	.177	-2	12	0.0
1977	Phi-N	6	11	.353	35	27	2	0	0	160^1	211	100	96	20	2	40	55	1.565	5.39	74	5.54	.320	10	.189	-27	2	-2.7
1978	Phi-N	8	5	.615	26	24	2	1	0	140^1	150	67	64	9	5	32	48	1.297	4.10	87	3.67	.280	7	.146	-11	5	-1.3
1979	Phi-N	1	0	1.000	3	1	0	0	0	8^1	9	4	4	1	0	5	2	1.680	4.32	88	5.23	.281	0	.000	-1	1	0.0
	NY-A	2	3	.400	40	1	0	0	2	58^1	64	29	25	4	2	14	23	1.337	3.86	106	3.86	.287	0	....	0	3	0.0
1980	NY-A	0	1	.000	4	0	0	0	0	5	8	5	4	0	0	4	1	2.400	7.20	54	7.48	.381	0	....	-2	0	-0.2
	StL-N	8	7	.533	49	14	6	1	4	129^2	140	61	55	6	0	33	36	1.334	3.82	97	3.47	.281	5	.143	-4	7	-0.3
1981	StL-N	6	6	.500	41	1	0	0	4	53	60	25	20	2	0	17	8	1.453	3.40	105	3.83	.299	3	.375	0	4	0.2
1982*	StL-N	5	3	.625	62	2	0	0	2	75	79	40	34	6	2	23	35	1.360	4.08	89	3.79	.276	0	.000	-6	3	-0.7
1983	StL-N	0	0	....	24	0	0	0	0	34^2	48	19	15	5	0	10	19	1.673	3.89	93	5.92	.327	0	.000	-1	1	-0.1
Total	**25**	**283**	**237**	**.544**	**898**	**625**	**180**	**31**	**18**	**4530^1**	**4620**	**2038**	**1738**	**395**	**122**	**1083**	**2461**	**1.259**	**3.45**	**107**	**3.56**	**.264**	**232**	**.185**	**125**	**268**	**18.0**

• KAHLER, George

George Runnells "Krum" Kahler b: 9/6/1889, Athens, OH d: 2/7/1924, Battle Creek, MI BR/TR, 6', 183 lbs. Deb: 8/13/1910

YEAR	TM-L	W	L	PCT	G	GS	CG	SH	SV	IP	H	R	ER	HR	HB	BB	SO	RAT	ERA	ERA+	CERA	OAV	BH	AVG	PR+	WS	TPW
1910	Cle-A	6	4	.600	12	12	8	2	0	95^1	80	35	17	0	4	46	38	1.322	1.60	161	3.02	.237	5	.143	10	7	0.9
1911	Cle-A	9	8	.529	30	17	10	0	1	154^1	153	78	56	1	13	66	97	1.419	3.27	104	3.86	.270	9	.167	0	10	-0.2
1912	Cle-A	12	19	.387	41	32	17	3	1	246^1	263	135	101	1	11	121	104	1.559	3.69	93	4.44	.291	9	.113	-11	11	-1.7
1913	Cle-A	5	11	.313	24	15	5	0	0	117^2	118	56	41	1	2	32	43	1.275	3.14	97	3.11	.266	2	.061	-3	5	-0.7
1914	Cle-A	0	1	.000	2	1	1	0	0	14	17	10	6	0	0	7	3	1.714	3.86	75	4.99	.309	0	.000	-1	0	-0.2
Total	**5**	**32**	**43**	**.427**	**109**	**77**	**41**	**5**	**2**	**627^2**	**631**	**314**	**221**	**3**	**30**	**272**	**285**	**1.439**	**3.17**	**102**	**3.85**	**.274**	**25**	**.121**	**-6**	**33**	**-1.8**

• KAINER, Don

Donald Wayne Kainer b: 9/3/1955, Houston, TX BR/TR, 6'3", 205 lbs. Deb: 9/6/1980

YEAR	TM-L	W	L	PCT	G	GS	CG	SH	SV	IP	H	R	ER	HR	HB	BB	SO	RAT	ERA	ERA+	CERA	OAV	BH	AVG	PR+	WS	TPW
1980	Tex-A	0	0	....	4	3	0	0	0	19^2	22	7	4	0	3	9	10	1.576	1.83	213	4.69	.289	0	....	5	2	0.5

• KAISER, Bob

Robert Thomas "Chisel" Kaiser b: 4/29/1950, Cincinnati, OH BB/TL, 5'10", 175 lbs. Deb: 9/3/1971

YEAR	TM-L	W	L	PCT	G	GS	CG	SH	SV	IP	H	R	ER	HR	HB	BB	SO	RAT	ERA	ERA+	CERA	OAV	BH	AVG	PR+	WS	TPW
1971	Cle-A	0	0	....	5	0	0	0	0	6	8	3	3	2	2	3	4	1.833	4.50	85	10.62	.333	0	....	-0	0	-0.1

• KAISER, Don

Clyde Donald "Tiger" Kaiser b: 2/3/1935, Byng, OK BR/TR, 6'5", 195 lbs. Deb: 7/20/1955

YEAR	TM-L	W	L	PCT	G	GS	CG	SH	SV	IP	H	R	ER	HR	HB	BB	SO	RAT	ERA	ERA+	CERA	OAV	BH	AVG	PR+	WS	TPW
1955	Chi-N	0	0	....	11	0	0	0	0	18^1	20	11	11	2	1	5	11	1.364	5.40	76	4.38	.274	0	.000	-3	0	-0.3
1956	Chi-N	4	9	.308	27	22	5	1	0	150^1	144	69	60	15	1	52	74	1.304	3.59	105	3.54	.247	2	.043	0	7	-0.4
1957	Chi-N	2	6	.250	20	13	1	0	0	72	91	48	40	4	0	28	23	1.653	5.00	77	5.25	.316	2	.105	-8	0	-0.9
Total	**3**	**6**	**15**	**.286**	**58**	**35**	**6**	**1**	**0**	**240^2**	**255**	**128**	**111**	**21**	**2**	**85**	**108**	**1.413**	**4.15**	**92**	**4.12**	**.270**	**4**	**.059**	**-10**	**7**	**-1.6**

• KAISER, Jeff

Jeffrey Patrick Kaiser b: 7/24/1960, Wyandotte, MI BR/TL, 6'3", 195 lbs. Deb: 4/11/1985

YEAR	TM-L	W	L	PCT	G	GS	CG	SH	SV	IP	H	R	ER	HR	HB	BB	SO	RAT	ERA	ERA+	CERA	OAV	BH	AVG	PR+	WS	TPW
1985	Oak-A	0	0	....	15	0	0	0	0	16^2	25	32	27	6	1	20	10	2.700	14.58	26	13.07	.342	0	....	-20	0	-1.9
1987	Cle-A	0	0	....	2	0	0	0	0	3^1	4	6	6	1	1	3	2	2.100	16.20	28	10.42	.286	0	....	-4	0	-0.4
1988	Cle-A	0	0	....	3	0	0	0	0	2^2	2	0	0	0	0	1	0	1.125	0.00	....	2.01	.286	0	....	1	0	0.1
1989	Cle-A	0	1	.000	6	0	0	0	0	3^2	5	5	3	1	0	5	4	2.727	7.36	54	11.52	.313	0	....	-1	0	-0.1
1990	Cle-A	0	0	....	5	0	0	0	0	12^2	16	5	5	2	0	7	9	1.816	3.55	110	6.55	.308	0	....	1	1	0.1
1991	Det-A	0	1	.000	10	0	0	0	2	5	6	5	5	1	0	5	4	2.200	9.00	46	7.68	.286	0	....	-3	0	-0.3
1993	Cin-N	0	0	....	3	0	0	0	0	3^1	4	1	1	0	0	2	4	1.800	2.70	149	4.53	.286	0	....	1	0	0.1
	NY-N	0	0	....	6	0	0	0	0	4^2	6	6	6	1	0	3	5	1.929	11.57	35	8.39	.353	0	....	-4	0	-0.4
	Yr.	0	0	....	9	0	0	0	0	8	10	7	7	1	0	5	9	1.875	7.88	51	6.78	.323	0	....	-3	0	-0.3
Total	**7**	**0**	**2**	**.000**	**50**	**0**	**0**	**0**	**2**	**52**	**68**	**60**	**53**	**12**	**2**	**46**	**38**	**2.192**	**9.17**	**43**	**9.15**	**.318**	**0**	**....**	**-29**	**1**	**-2.9**

• KAISERLING, George

George Kaiserling b: 5/12/1893, Steubenville, OH d: 3/2/1918, Steubenville, OH BR/TR, 6', 175 lbs. Deb: 4/20/1914

YEAR	TM-L	W	L	PCT	G	GS	CG	SH	SV	IP	H	R	ER	HR	HB	BB	SO	RAT	ERA	ERA+	CERA	OAV	BH	AVG	PR+	WS	TPW
1914	Ind-F	17	10	.630	37	33	20	1	0	275^1	288	119	95	8	17	72	75	1.308	3.11	112	3.58	.274	11	.112	8	17	0.3
1915	New-F	15	15	.500	41	29	16	5	2	261^1	246	90	65	1	9	73	75	1.221	2.24	127	2.88	.257	12	.152	17	19	1.6
Total	**2**	**32**	**25**	**.561**	**78**	**62**	**36**	**6**	**2**	**536^2**	**534**	**209**	**160**	**9**	**26**	**145**	**150**	**1.265**	**2.68**	**119**	**3.24**	**.266**	**23**	**.130**	**25**	**36**	**1.9**

• KALFASS, Bill

William Philip "Lefty" Kalfass b: 3/3/1916, New York, NY d: 9/8/1968, Brooklyn, NY BR/TL, 6'3.5", 190 lbs. Deb: 9/15/1937

YEAR	TM-L	W	L	PCT	G	GS	CG	SH	SV	IP	H	R	ER	HR	HB	BB	SO	RAT	ERA	ERA+	CERA	OAV	BH	AVG	PR+	WS	TPW
1937	Phi-A	1	0	1.000	3	1	1	0	0	12	10	4	4	0	0	10	9	1.667	3.00	157	3.86	.233	0	.000	2	1	0.2

• KALLIO, Rudy

Rudolph Kallio b: 12/14/1892, Portland, OR d: 4/6/1979, Newport, OR BR/TR, 5'10", 160 lbs. Deb: 4/25/1918

YEAR	TM-L	W	L	PCT	G	GS	CG	SH	SV	IP	H	R	ER	HR	HB	BB	SO	RAT	ERA	ERA+	CERA	OAV	BH	AVG	PR+	WS	TPW
1918	Det-A	8	13	.381	30	22	10	2	0	181^1	178	91	73	0	1	76	70	1.401	3.62	73	3.24	.261	9	.161	-10	5	-1.3
1919	Det-A	0	0	....	12	1	0	0	1	22^1	28	15	14	0	1	8	3	1.612	5.64	57	5.02	.326	0	.000	-6	0	-0.7
1925	Bos-A	1	4	.200	7	4	0	0	0	18^2	28	18	16	0	1	9	2	1.982	7.71	59	6.77	.364	2	.333	-6	0	-0.5
Total	**3**	**9**	**17**	**.346**	**49**	**27**	**10**	**2**	**1**	**222^1**	**234**	**124**	**103**	**0**	**3**	**93**	**75**	**1.471**	**4.17**	**70**	**3.71**	**.277**	**11**	**.167**	**-22**	**5**	**-2.5**

• KAMIENIECKI, Scott

Scott Andrew Kamieniecki b: 4/19/1964, Mount Clemens, MI BR/TR, 6', 195 lbs. Deb: 6/18/1991

YEAR	TM-L	W	L	PCT	G	GS	CG	SH	SV	IP	H	R	ER	HR	HB	BB	SO	RAT	ERA	ERA+	CERA	OAV	BH	AVG	PR+	WS	TPW
1991	NY-A	4	4	.500	9	9	0	0	0	55^1	54	24	24	8	3	22	34	1.373	3.90	106	4.46	.256	0	....	2	3	0.2
1992	NY-A	6	14	.300	28	28	4	0	0	188	193	100	91	13	5	74	88	1.420	4.36	90	4.08	.269	0	....	-10	6	-1.0
1993	NY-A	10	7	.588	30	20	2	0	1	154^1	163	73	70	17	3	59	72	1.438	4.08	102	4.51	.277	0	....	1	9	0.1
1994	NY-A	8	6	.571	22	16	1	0	0	117^1	115	53	49	13	3	59	71	1.483	3.76	122	4.56	.261	0	....	9	8	0.8
1995*	NY-A	7	6	.538	17	16	1	0	0	89^2	83	43	40	8	3	49	43	1.472	4.01	115	4.32	.246	0	....	5	6	0.5
1996	NY-A	1	2	.333	7	5	0	0	0	22^2	36	30	28	6	2	19	15	2.426	11.12	44	11.90	.364	0	....	-15	0	-1.4
1997*	Bal-A	10	6	.625	30	30	0	0	0	179^1	179	83	80	20	4	67	109	1.372	4.01	110	4.16	.261	0	.000	7	12	0.7
1998	Bal-A	2	6	.250	12	11	0	0	0	54^2	67	41	41	7	4	26	25	1.701	6.75	67	6.41	.313	0	....	-13	0	-1.2
1999	Bal-A	2	4	.333	43	3	0	0	2	56^1	52	32	31	4	4	29	39	1.438	4.95	95	4.11	.250	0	....	-3	3	-0.3
2000	Cle-A	1	3	.250	26	0	0	0	0	33^1	42	22	21	6	1	20	29	1.860	5.67	88	7.08	.311	0	....	-2	1	-0.2
	Atl-N	2	1	.667	26	0	0	0	2	24^2	22	18	15	3	0	22	17	1.784	5.47	84	5.59	.239	0	....	-2	1	-0.2
Total	**10**	**53**	**59**	**.473**	**250**	**138**	**8**	**0**	**5**	**975^2**	**1006**	**519**	**490**	**105**	**32**	**446**	**542**	**1.488**	**4.52**	**97**	**4.72**	**.270**	**0**	**.000**	**-21**	**49**	**-2.0**

• KAMMEYER, Bob

Robert Lynn Kammeyer b: 12/2/1950, Kansas City, KS d: 1/27/2003, Sacramento, CA BR/TR, 6'4", 210 lbs. Deb: 7/3/1978

YEAR	TM-L	W	L	PCT	G	GS	CG	SH	SV	IP	H	R	ER	HR	HB	BB	SO	RAT	ERA	ERA+	CERA	OAV	BH	AVG	PR+	WS	TPW
1978	NY-A	0	0	....	7	0	0	0	0	21^2	24	15	14	1	2	6	11	1.385	5.82	62	4.01	.276	0	....	-5	0	-0.6
1979	NY-A	0	0	....	1	0	0	0	0	0	7	8	8	2	1	0	0		∞	....	∞	1.000	0	....	-8	0	-0.8
Total	**2**	**0**	**0**	**....**	**8**	**0**	**0**	**0**	**0**	**21^2**	**31**	**23**	**22**	**3**	**3**	**6**	**11**	**1.708**	**9.14**	**62**	**4.01**	**.330**	**0**	**....**	**-13**	**0**	**-1.3**

• KAMP, Ike

Alphonse Francis Kamp b: 9/5/1900, Roxbury, MA d: 2/25/1955, Boston, MA BB/TL, 6', 170 lbs. Deb: 9/16/1924

YEAR	TM-L	W	L	PCT	G	GS	CG	SH	SV	IP	H	R	ER	HR	HB	BB	SO	RAT	ERA	ERA+	CERA	OAV	BH	AVG	PR+	WS	TPW
1924	Bos-N	0	1	.000	1	1	0	0	0	7	9	5	4	0	0	5	4	2.000	5.14	74	6.43	.360	0	.000	-1	0	-0.1
1925	Bos-N	2	4	.333	24	4	1	0	0	58^1	68	38	33	0	0	35	20	1.766	5.09	79	4.89	.301	2	.167	-8	1	-0.8
Total	**2**	**2**	**5**	**.286**	**25**	**5**	**1**	**0**	**0**	**65^1**	**77**	**43**	**37**	**0**	**0**	**40**	**24**	**1.791**	**5.10**	**78**	**5.05**	**.307**	**2**	**.154**	**-9**	**1**	**-0.9**

• KANE, Harry

Harry "Klondike" Kane b: 7/27/1883, Hamburg, AR d: 9/15/1932, Portland, OR BL/TL Deb: 8/8/1902

YEAR	TM-L	W	L	PCT	G	GS	CG	SH	SV	IP	H	R	ER	HR	HB	BB	SO	RAT	ERA	ERA+	CERA	OAV	BH	AVG	PR+	WS	TPW
1902	StL-A	0	1	.000	4	1	1	0	0	23	34	21	14	2	0	16	7	2.174	5.48	64	7.95	.343	1	.111	-5	0	-0.6
1903	Det-A	0	2	.000	3	3	2	0	0	18	26	22	17	0	1	8	10	1.889	8.50	34	6.07	.336	1	.143	-11	0	-1.2
1905	Phi-N	1	1	.500	2	2	2	1	0	17	12	6	3	0	0	8	12	1.176	1.59	183	2.16	.203	1	.167	2	1	0.2
1906	Phi-N	1	3	.250	6	3	2	0	0	28	28	16	12	0	3	18	14	1.643	3.86	68	4.40	.255	0	.000	-4	0	-0.5
Total	**4**	**2**	**7**	**.222**	**15**	**9**	**7**	**1**	**0**	**86**	**100**	**65**	**46**	**2**	**4**	**50**	**43**	**1.744**	**4.81**	**62**	**5.25**	**.290**	**3**	**.100**	**-18**	**1**	**-2.0**

• KANTLEHNER, Erv

Erving Leslie "Peanuts" Kantlehner b: 7/31/1892, San Jose, CA d: 2/3/1990, Santa Barbara, CA BL/TL, 6', 190 lbs. Deb: 4/17/1914

YEAR	TM-L	W	L	PCT	G	GS	CG	SH	SV	IP	H	R	ER	HR	HB	BB	SO	RAT	ERA	ERA+	CERA	OAV	BH	AVG	PR+	WS	TPW
1914	Pit-N	3	2	.600	21	5	3	2	0	67	51	33	23	0	3	39	26	1.343	3.09	86	2.79	.218	1	.067	-4	3	-0.4
1915	Pit-N	5	12	.294	29	18	10	1	3	163	135	60	41	1	4	58	64	1.184	2.26	120	2.41	.230	15	.288	9	11	1.3

YEAR TM-L	W	L	PCT	G	GS	CG	SH	SV	IP	H	R	ER	HR	HB	BB	SO	RAT	ERA	ERA+	CERA	OAV	BH	AVG	PR+	WS	TPW
1916 Pit-N	5	15	.250	34	21	7	2	2	165	151	72	58	1	4	57	49	1.261	3.16	85	2.77	.249	8	.174	-5	6	-0.6
Phi-N	0	0	....	3	0	0	0	0	4	7	4	4	0	0	3	2	2.500	9.00	29	10.39	.500	0	....	-3	0	-0.3
Yr.	5	15	.250	37	21	7	2	2	169	158	76	62	1	4	60	51	1.290	3.30	81	2.95	.255	8	.174	-8	6	-0.9
Total 3	13	29	.310	87	44	20	5	5	399	344	169	126	2	11	157	141	1.256	2.84	95	2.70	.239	24	.212	-3	20	0.0

• KARCHNER, Matt Matthew Dean Karchner b: 6/28/1967, Berwick, PA BR/TR, 6'4", 245 lbs. Deb: 7/18/1995

YEAR TM-L	W	L	PCT	G	GS	CG	SH	SV	IP	H	R	ER	HR	HB	BB	SO	RAT	ERA	ERA+	CERA	OAV	BH	AVG	PR+	WS	TPW
1995 Chi-A	4	2	.667	31	0	0	0	0	32	33	8	6	2	1	12	24	1.406	1.69	264	3.96	.275	0	....	10	4	1.0
1996 Chi-A	7	4	.636	50	0	0	0	1	59^{1}	61	42	38	10	2	41	46	1.719	5.76	82	5.80	.266	0	....	-6	2	-0.6
1997 Chi-A	3	1	.750	52	0	0	0	15	52^{2}	50	18	17	4	0	26	30	1.443	2.91	151	3.96	.258	0	....	9	8	0.9
1998 Chi-A	2	4	.333	32	0	0	0	11	36^{2}	33	21	21	2	5	19	30	1.418	5.15	88	3.78	.243	0	....	-3	3	-0.2
* Chi-N	3	1	.750	29	0	0	0	0	28	30	18	16	6	2	14	22	1.571	5.14	86	5.71	.263	0	....	-2	1	-0.2
1999 Chi-N	1	0	1.000	16	0	0	0	0	18	16	5	5	3	2	9	9	1.389	2.50	181	4.73	.235	0	....	4	2	0.4
2000 Chi-N	1	1	.500	13	0	0	0	0	14^{2}	19	11	10	3	0	11	5	2.045	6.14	74	7.96	.311	0	....	-3	0	-0.2
Total 6	21	13	.618	223	0	0	0	27	241^{1}	242	123	113	30	12	132	166	1.550	4.21	108	4.89	.262	0	....	11	20	1.1

• KARDOW, Paul Paul Otto "Tex" Kardow b: 9/19/1915, Humble, TX d: 4/27/1968, San Antonio, TX BR/TR, 6'6", 210 lbs. Deb: 7/1/1936

YEAR TM-L	W	L	PCT	G	GS	CG	SH	SV	IP	H	R	ER	HR	HB	BB	SO	RAT	ERA	ERA+	CERA	OAV	BH	AVG	PR+	WS	TPW
1936 Cle-A	0	0	....	2	0	0	0	0	2	1	1	1	0	0	2	0	1.500	4.50	112	2.54	.167	0	....	0	0	0.0

• KARGER, Ed Edwin "Loose" Karger b: 5/6/1883, San Angelo, TX d: 9/9/1957, Delta, CO BR/TL, 5'11", 185 lbs. Deb: 4/15/1906 U

YEAR TM-L	W	L	PCT	G	GS	CG	SH	SV	IP	H	R	ER	HR	HB	BB	SO	RAT	ERA	ERA+	CERA	OAV	BH	AVG	PR+	WS	TPW
1906 Pit-N	2	3	.400	6	2	0	0	0	28	21	11	6	0	2	9	8	1.071	1.93	138	2.03	.204	1	.091	2	2	0.2
StL-N	5	16	.238	25	20	17	0	1	191^{2}	193	85	58	0	7	43	73	1.231	2.72	96	3.03	.271	17	.233	-0	10	0.4
Yr.	7	19	.269	31	22	17	0	1	219^{2}	214	96	64	0	9	52	81	1.211	2.62	100	2.90	.263	18	.214	2	12	0.6
1907 StL-N	15	19	.441	39	32	29	6	1	314	257	102	71	2	10	65	137	1.025	2.04	123	1.98	.223	20	.179	18	21	2.3
1908 StL-N	4	9	.308	22	15	9	1	0	141^{1}	148	77	48	1	2	50	34	1.401	3.06	77	3.39	.260	13	.241	-8	4	-0.6
1909 Cin-N	1	3	.250	9	5	1	0	0	34^{1}	26	22	17	0	2	30	8	1.631	4.46	58	3.87	.217	3	.273	-7	1	-0.6
Bos-A	5	2	.714	12	6	3	0	0	68	71	29	24	0	3	22	17	1.368	3.18	78	3.50	.273	3	.125	-6	3	-0.7
1910 Bos-A	11	7	.611	27	25	16	1	1	183^{1}	162	75	65	5	5	53	81	1.173	3.19	80	2.56	.230	20	.294	-12	11	-0.6
1911 Bos-A	5	8	.385	25	18	6	1	0	131	134	70	49	4	4	42	57	1.344	3.37	97	3.60	.272	11	.234	-2	7	0.1
Total 6	48	67	.417	165	123	81	9	3	1091^{2}	1012	471	338	12	35	314	415	1.215	2.79	93	2.79	.246	88	.220	-16	59	0.4

• KARL, Andy Anton Andrew Karl b: 4/8/1914, Mount Vernon, NY d: 4/8/1989, La Jolla, CA BR/TR, 6'1.5", 175 lbs. Deb: 4/24/1943

YEAR TM-L	W	L	PCT	G	GS	CG	SH	SV	IP	H	R	ER	HR	HB	BB	SO	RAT	ERA	ERA+	CERA	OAV	BH	AVG	PR+	WS	TPW
1943 Bos-A	1	1	.500	11	0	0	0	1	26	31	11	10	0	0	13	6	1.692	3.46	96	4.75	.310	2	.286	-1	2	0.0
Phi-N	1	2	.333	9	2	0	0	0	26^{2}	44	22	21	0	0	11	4	2.063	7.09	48	7.09	.383	2	.250	-11	0	-1.1
1944 Phi-N	3	2	.600	38	0	0	0	2	89	76	32	23	1	1	21	26	1.090	2.33	155	2.20	.238	3	.200	13	9	1.4
1945 Phi-N	8	8	.500	**67**	2	1	0	**15**	180^{2}	175	80	60	7	3	50	51	1.245	2.99	128	2.99	.253	7	.143	22	12	2.0
1946 Phi-N	3	7	.300	39	0	0	0	5	65^{1}	84	37	36	6	1	22	15	1.622	4.96	69	5.47	.321	1	.100	-11	1	-1.2
1947 Bos-N	2	3	.400	27	0	0	0	3	35	41	18	15	2	0	13	5	1.543	3.86	101	4.81	.318	1	.167	1	2	0.0
Total 5	18	23	.439	191	4	1	0	26	422^{2}	451	200	165	16	5	130	107	1.375	3.51	103	3.72	.279	16	.168	13	26	1.2

• KARL, Scott Randall Scott Karl b: 8/9/1971, Fontana, CA BL/TL, 6'2", 195 lbs. Deb: 5/4/1995

YEAR TM-L	W	L	PCT	G	GS	CG	SH	SV	IP	H	R	ER	HR	HB	BB	SO	RAT	ERA	ERA+	CERA	OAV	BH	AVG	PR+	WS	TPW
1995 Mil-A	6	7	.462	25	18	1	0	0	124	141	65	57	10	3	50	59	1.540	4.14	120	4.79	.288	0	....	9	8	0.9
1996 Mil-A	13	9	.591	32	32	3	1	0	207^{1}	220	124	112	29	11	72	121	1.408	4.86	107	4.72	.271	0	....	4	11	0.3
1997 Mil-A	10	13	.435	32	32	1	0	0	193^{1}	212	103	96	23	4	67	119	1.443	4.47	103	4.66	.279	0	.000	-3	10	-0.3
1998 Mil-N	10	11	.476	33	33	0	0	0	192^{1}	219	104	94	21	4	66	102	1.482	4.40	97	4.78	.290	4	.071	-5	8	-0.7
1999 Mil-N	11	11	.500	33	33	0	0	0	197^{2}	246	121	105	21	8	69	74	1.594	4.78	95	5.54	.312	11	.183	-3	9	0.0
2000 Col-N	2	3	.400	17	9	0	0	0	65^{2}	95	56	56	14	3	33	29	1.949	7.68	75	8.38	.343	4	.286	-14	1	-1.3
Ana-A	2	2	.500	6	4	0	0	0	21^{2}	31	21	16	2	0	12	9	1.985	6.65	76	7.30	.337	0	....	-4	0	-0.4
Total 6	54	56	.491	178	161	5	1	0	1002	1164	594	536	120	33	369	513	1.530	4.81	100	5.18	.293	19	.142	-16	47	-1.5

• KARNS, Bill William Arthur Karns b: 12/28/1875, Richmond, IA d: 11/15/1941, Seattle, WA BL/TL Deb: 8/14/1901

YEAR TM-L	W	L	PCT	G	GS	CG	SH	SV	IP	H	R	ER	HR	HB	BB	SO	RAT	ERA	ERA+	CERA	OAV	BH	AVG	PR+	WS	TPW
1901 Bal-A	1	0	1.000	3	1	1	0	0	17	30	18	12	0	0	9	5	2.294	6.35	61	8.33	.380	1	.143	-4	0	-0.4

• KARNUTH, Jason Jason Andre Karnuth b: 5/15/1976, La Grange, IL BR/TR, 6'2", 190 lbs. Deb: 4/20/2001

YEAR TM-L	W	L	PCT	G	GS	CG	SH	SV	IP	H	R	ER	HR	HB	BB	SO	RAT	ERA	ERA+	CERA	OAV	BH	AVG	PR+	WS	TPW
2001 StL-N	0	0	....	4	0	0	0	0	5	6	1	1	1	1	4	1	2.000	1.80	237	9.29	.316	0	....	1	1	0.1

• KARP, Ryan Ryan Jason Karp b: 4/5/1970, Los Angeles, CA BL/TL, 6'4", 220 lbs. Deb: 6/23/1995

YEAR TM-L	W	L	PCT	G	GS	CG	SH	SV	IP	H	R	ER	HR	HB	BB	SO	RAT	ERA	ERA+	CERA	OAV	BH	AVG	PR+	WS	TPW
1995 Phi-N	0	0	....	1	0	0	0	0	2	1	1	1	0	0	3	2	2.000	4.50	94	4.47	.143	0	....	-0	0	0.0
1997 Phi-N	1	1	.500	15	1	0	0	0	15	12	12	9	2	2	9	18	1.400	5.40	79	4.48	.218	0	....	-2	0	-0.2
Total 2	1	1	.500	16	1	0	0	0	17	13	13	10	2	2	12	20	1.471	5.29	80	4.48	.210	0	....	-2	0	-0.2

• KARPEL, Herb Herbert "Lefty" Karpel b: 12/27/1917, Brooklyn, NY d: 1/24/1995, San Diego, CA BL/TL, 5'9.5", 180 lbs. Deb: 4/19/1946

YEAR TM-L	W	L	PCT	G	GS	CG	SH	SV	IP	H	R	ER	HR	HB	BB	SO	RAT	ERA	ERA+	CERA	OAV	BH	AVG	PR+	WS	TPW
1946 NY-A	0	0	....	2	0	0	0	0	1^{2}	4	2	2	0	0	0	0	2.400	10.80	32	11.50	.500	0	....	-1	0	-0.1

• KARR, Benn Benjamin Joyce "Baldy" Karr b: 11/28/1893, Mount Pleasant, MS d: 12/8/1968, Memphis, TN BL/TR, 6', 175 lbs. Deb: 4/20/1920

YEAR TM-L	W	L	PCT	G	GS	CG	SH	SV	IP	H	R	ER	HR	HB	BB	SO	RAT	ERA	ERA+	CERA	OAV	BH	AVG	PR+	WS	TPW
1920 Bos-A	3	8	.273	26	2	0	0	1	91^{2}	109	55	49	3	1	24	21	1.451	4.81	76	4.19	.304	21	.280	-13	4	-0.7
1921 Bos-A	8	7	.533	26	7	5	0	0	117^{2}	123	53	48	8	1	38	37	1.368	3.67	115	3.80	.283	16	.258	5	10	0.5
1922 Bos-A	5	12	.294	41	13	7	0	1	183^{1}	212	115	91	10	5	45	41	1.402	4.47	92	4.12	.302	21	.214	-5	7	-0.5
1925 Cle-A	11	12	.478	32	24	12	1	0	197^{2}	248	127	105	8	6	80	41	1.659	4.78	92	5.15	.317	24	.261	-7	10	-0.3
1926 Cle-A	5	6	.455	30	7	4	0	1	113^{1}	137	72	63	9	6	41	23	1.571	5.00	81	4.83	.291	10	.222	-14	3	-1.3
1927 Cle-A	3	3	.500	22	5	1	0	2	76^{2}	92	49	43	5	1	32	17	1.617	5.05	83	5.06	.315	4	.200	-7	3	-0.6
Total 6	35	48	.422	177	58	29	1	5	780^{1}	921	471	399	43	20	260	180	1.513	4.60	90	4.54	.303	96	.245	-42	37	-2.8

• KARSAY, Steve Stefan Andrew Karsay b: 3/24/1972, Flushing, NY BR/TR, 6'3", 210 lbs. Deb: 8/17/1993

YEAR TM-L	W	L	PCT	G	GS	CG	SH	SV	IP	H	R	ER	HR	HB	BB	SO	RAT	ERA	ERA+	CERA	OAV	BH	AVG	PR+	WS	TPW
1993 Oak-A	3	3	.500	8	8	0	0	0	49	49	23	22	4	2	16	33	1.327	4.04	101	3.78	.258	0	....	0	3	0.0
1994 Oak-A	1	1	.500	4	4	1	0	0	28	26	8	8	1	1	8	15	1.214	2.57	172	3.01	.252	0	....	5	3	0.5
1997 Oak-A	3	12	.200	24	24	0	0	0	132^{2}	166	92	85	20	9	47	92	1.606	5.77	78	5.97	.304	0	....	-15	3	-1.5
1998 Cle-A	0	2	.000	11	1	0	0	0	24^{1}	31	16	16	3	2	6	13	1.521	5.92	81	5.40	.310	0	....	-3	0	-0.3
1999* Cle-A	10	2	.833	50	3	0	0	1	78^{2}	71	29	26	6	2	30	68	1.284	2.97	169	3.45	.247	0	....	18	9	1.7
2000 Cle-A	5	9	.357	72	0	0	0	20	76^{2}	79	33	32	5	3	25	66	1.357	3.76	132	3.79	.266	0	.000	11	11	1.0
2001 Cle-A	0	1	.000	31	0	0	0	1	43^{1}	29	6	6	1	0	8	44	.854	1.25	363	1.33	.188	0	....	17	6	1.6
* Atl-N	3	4	.429	43	0	0	0	7	44^{2}	44	21	17	4	1	17	39	1.366	3.43	129	3.68	.265	0	.000	5	5	0.4
2002* NY-A	6	4	.600	78	0	0	0	12	88^{1}	87	33	32	7	2	30	65	1.325	3.26	134	3.42	.258	0	.000	13	11	1.3
Total 8	31	38	.449	321	40	1	0	41	565^{2}	582	261	244	51	22	187	435	1.359	3.88	117	4.03	.267	0	.000	51	51	4.8

• KASHIWADA, Takashi Takashi Kashiwada b: 5/14/1971, Tokyo, Japan BL/TL, 5'11", 165 lbs. Deb: 5/1/1997

YEAR TM-L	W	L	PCT	G	GS	CG	SH	SV	IP	H	R	ER	HR	HB	BB	SO	RAT	ERA	ERA+	CERA	OAV	BH	AVG	PR+	WS	TPW
1997 NY-N	3	1	.750	35	0	0	0	0	31^{1}	35	15	15	4	3	18	19	1.691	4.31	94	6.17	.289	0	.000	-2	2	-0.2

• KATOLL, Jack John "Big Jack,Katy" Katoll b: 6/24/1872, Germany d: 6/18/1955, Hartland, IL BR/TR, 5'11", 195 lbs. Deb: 9/9/1898

YEAR TM-L	W	L	PCT	G	GS	CG	SH	SV	IP	H	R	ER	HR	HB	BB	SO	RAT	ERA	ERA+	CERA	OAV	BH	AVG	PR+	WS	TPW
1898 Chi-N	0	1	.000	2	1	1	0	0	11	8	4	1	0	0	1	3	.818	0.82	437	1.27	.202	0	.000	3	1	0.2
1899 Chi-N	1	1	.500	2	2	2	0	0	18	17	15	12	0	1	4	1	1.167	6.00	62	2.61	.250	0	.000	-5	0	-0.5
1901 Chi-A	11	10	.524	27	25	19	0	0	208	231	126	65	3	11	53	59	1.365	2.81	124	3.65	.278	10	.125	15	12	1.0
1902 Chi-A	0	0	....	1	0	0	0	0	1	1	0	0	0	0	0	2	1.000	0.00	....	2.02	.261	0	.000	0	0	0.0
Bal-A	5	10	.333	15	13	13	0	0	123	175	106	55	5	2	32	25	1.683	4.02	94	5.51	.334	10	.175	3	3	0.2
Yr.	5	10	.333	16	13	13	0	0	124	176	106	55	5	2	32	27	1.677	3.99	94	5.49	.334	10	.172	3	3	0.2
Total 4	17	22	.436	47	41	35	0	0	361	432	251	133	8	14	90	90	1.446	3.32	109	4.16	.295	20	.134	17	16	1.0

• KATZ, Bob Robert Clyde Katz b: 1/30/1911, Lancaster, PA d: 12/14/1962, St. Joseph, MI BR/TR, 5'11.5", 190 lbs. Deb: 5/12/1944

YEAR TM-L	W	L	PCT	G	GS	CG	SH	SV	IP	H	R	ER	HR	HB	BB	SO	RAT	ERA	ERA+	CERA	OAV	BH	AVG	PR+	WS	TPW
1944 Cin-N	0	1	.000	6	2	0	0	0	18^{1}	17	9	8	0	0	7	4	1.309	3.93	89	2.95	.254	0	.000	-1	1	-0.2

• KAUFMAN, Curt Curt Gerrard Kaufman b: 7/19/1957, Omaha, NE BR/TR, 6'2", 175 lbs. Deb: 9/10/1982

YEAR TM-L	W	L	PCT	G	GS	CG	SH	SV	IP	H	R	ER	HR	HB	BB	SO	RAT	ERA	ERA+	CERA	OAV	BH	AVG	PR+	WS	TPW
1982 NY-A	1	0	1.000	7	0	0	0	0	8^{2}	9	5	5	2	0	6	1	1.731	5.19	77	6.35	.265	0	....	-1	0	-0.1

YEAR	TM-L	W	L	PCT	G	GS	CG	SH	SV	IP	H	R	ER	HR	HB	BB	SO	RAT	ERA	ERA+	CERA	OAV	BH	AVG	PR+	WS	TPW
1983	NY-A	0	0	....	4	0	0	0	0	8^2	10	3	3	0	0	4	8	1.615	3.12	125	4.44	.303	0	....	1	1	0.1
1984	Cal-A	2	3	.400	29	1	0	0	1	69	68	37	35	13	0	20	41	1.275	4.57	87	4.03	.254	0	....	-5	3	-0.5
Total	3	3	3	.500	40	1	0	0	1	86^1	87	45	43	15	0	30	50	1.355	4.48	88	4.30	.260	0	....	-5	4	-0.5

• KAUFMANN, Tony Anthony Charles Kaufmann b: 12/16/1900, Chicago, IL d: 6/4/1982, Elgin, IL BR/TR, 5'11", 165 lbs. Deb: 9/23/1921 C ♦

YEAR	TM-L	W	L	PCT	G	GS	CG	SH	SV	IP	H	R	ER	HR	HB	BB	SO	RAT	ERA	ERA+	CERA	OAV	BH	AVG	PR+	WS	TPW
1921	Chi-N	1	0	1.000	2	1	1	0	1	13	12	6	6	0	0	3	6	1.154	4.15	92	2.29	.240	2	.400	-1	2	0.0
1922	Chi-N	7	13	.350	37	14	4	1	3	153	161	81	69	15	5	57	45	1.425	4.06	103	4.28	.270	9	.200	1	10	0.2
1923	Chi-N	14	10	.583	33	24	18	2	3	206^1	209	97	71	14	11	67	72	1.338	3.10	129	3.77	.260	16	.216	16	18	1.8
1924	Chi-N	16	11	.593	34	26	16	3	0	208^1	218	104	93	21	4	66	79	1.363	4.02	97	4.04	.270	24	.316	-6	16	0.0
1925	Chi-N	13	13	.500	31	23	14	2	2	196	221	107	98	9	7	77	49	1.520	4.50	96	4.49	.290	15	.192	-7	12	-0.6
1926	Chi-N	9	7	.563	26	22	14	1	2	169^2	169	71	57	6	6	44	52	1.255	3.02	127	3.15	.260	15	.250	12	14	1.4
1927	Chi-N	3	3	.500	9	6	3	0	0	53^1	75	44	38	8	4	19	21	1.763	6.41	60	6.88	.330	5	.313	-16	1	-1.3
	Phi-N	0	3	.000	5	5	1	0	0	18^2	37	25	22	2	0	8	4	2.411	10.61	39	10.29	.420	1	.143	-13	0	-1.3
	StL-N	0	0	....	1	0	0	0	0	0^1	4	3	3	0	0	1	0	15.00	81.00	5	132.90	1.000	0	....	-3	0	-0.3
	Yr.	3	6	.333	15	11	4	0	0	72^1	116	72	63	10	4	28	25	1.991	7.84	50	8.34	.363	6	.261	-32	1	-2.9
1928	StL-N	0	0	....	4	1	0	0	0	4^2	8	5	5	1	1	4	2	2.571	9.64	41	12.70	.440	0	....	-3	0	-0.3
1930	StL-N	0	1	.000	2	1	0	0	0	10^1	15	9	9	2	0	4	2	1.839	7.84	64	7.56	.350	1	.333	-3	0	-0.3
1931	StL-N	1	1	.500	15	1	0	0	1	49	65	34	33	3	1	17	13	1.673	6.06	65	5.38	.310	2	.111	-12	0	-1.3
1935	StL-N	0	0	....	3	0	0	0	0	3^2	4	1	1	0	0	1	0	1.364	2.45	167	3.23	.286	0	....	1	0	0.1
Total	11	64	62	.508	202	124	71	9	12	1086^1	1198	587	505	81	39	368	345	1.442	4.18	97	4.36	.280	91	.220	-34	73	-1.7

• KAYE, Justin Justin Malcolm Kaye b: 6/9/1976, Fort Lauderdale, FL BR/TR, 6'4", 195 lbs. Deb: 5/9/2002

YEAR	TM-L	W	L	PCT	G	GS	CG	SH	SV	IP	H	R	ER	HR	HB	BB	SO	RAT	ERA	ERA+	CERA	OAV	BH	AVG	PR+	WS	TPW
2002	Sea-A	0	0	....	3	0	0	0	0	3	6	4	4	0	0	1	3	2.333	12.00	35	9.61	.429	0	....	-3	0	-0.2

• KEAGLE, Greg Gregory Charles Keagle b: 6/28/1971, Corning, NY BR/TR, 6'1", 185 lbs. Deb: 4/1/1996

YEAR	TM-L	W	L	PCT	G	GS	CG	SH	SV	IP	H	R	ER	HR	HB	BB	SO	RAT	ERA	ERA+	CERA	OAV	BH	AVG	PR+	WS	TPW
1996	Det-A	3	6	.333	26	6	0	0	0	87^2	104	76	72	13	9	68	70	1.962	7.39	68	7.48	.298	0	....	-21	1	-1.9
1997	Det-A	3	5	.375	11	10	0	0	0	45^1	58	33	33	9	5	18	33	1.676	6.55	70	6.93	.309	0	.000	-10	0	-1.0
1998	Det-A	0	5	.000	9	7	0	0	0	38^2	46	26	24	5	4	20	25	1.707	5.59	84	6.41	.295	0	....	-4	1	-0.4
Total	3	6	16	.273	46	23	0	0	0	171^2	208	135	129	27	18	106	128	1.829	6.76	72	7.09	.300	0	.000	-36	2	-3.3

• KEALEY, Steve Steven William Kealey b: 5/13/1947, Torrance, CA BR/TR, 6', 185 lbs. Deb: 9/9/1968

YEAR	TM-L	W	L	PCT	G	GS	CG	SH	SV	IP	H	R	ER	HR	HB	BB	SO	RAT	ERA	ERA+	CERA	OAV	BH	AVG	PR+	WS	TPW
1968	Cal-A	0	1	.000	6	0	0	0	0	10	10	3	3	0	0	5	4	1.500	2.70	108	3.38	.256	0	....	0	1	0.0
1969	Cal-A	2	0	1.000	15	3	1	1	0	36^2	48	18	16	4	1	13	17	1.664	3.93	89	5.96	.322	0	.000	-2	2	-0.4
1970	Cal-A	1	0	1.000	17	0	0	0	1	21^2	19	11	10	2	0	6	14	1.154	4.15	87	2.99	.260	1	.250	-2	1	-0.2
1971	Chi-A	2	2	.500	54	1	0	0	6	77^1	69	40	33	10	0	26	50	1.228	3.84	93	3.24	.239	2	.200	-1	4	0.0
1972	Chi-A	3	2	.600	40	0	0	0	4	57^1	50	21	21	4	0	12	37	1.081	3.30	95	2.45	.234	0	.000	0	5	0.0
1973	Chi-A	0	0	....	7	0	0	0	0	11^1	23	22	19	2	0	7	4	2.647	15.09	26	11.88	.418	0	....	-14	0	-1.4
Total	6	8	5	.615	139	4	1	1	11	214^1	219	115	102	22	1	69	126	1.344	4.28	82	3.93	.267	3	.115	-19	13	-2.0

• KEAS, Ed Edward James Keas b: 2/2/1863, Dubuque, IA d: 1/12/1940, Dubuque, IA Deb: 8/25/1888

YEAR	TM-L	W	L	PCT	G	GS	CG	SH	SV	IP	H	R	ER	HR	HB	BB	SO	RAT	ERA	ERA+	CERA	OAV	BH	AVG	PR+	WS	TPW
1888	Cle-a	3	3	.500	6	6	6	0	0	51	53	28	13	1	1	12	18	1.275	2.29	135	....	.258	2	.087	5	2	0.3

• KEATING, Bob Robert M. Keating b: 9/22/1862, Springfield, MA d: 1/19/1922, Springfield, MA BL/TL, 6'4", 190 lbs. Deb: 8/27/1887

YEAR	TM-L	W	L	PCT	G	GS	CG	SH	SV	IP	H	R	ER	HR	HB	BB	SO	RAT	ERA	ERA+	CERA	OAV	BH	AVG	PR+	WS	TPW
1887	Bal-a	0	1	.000	1	1	1	0	0	9	22	16	11	0	0	6	0	2.444	11.00	37	....	.450	1	.250	-7	0	-0.5

• KEATING, Ray Raymond Herbert Keating b: 7/21/1891, Bridgeport, CT d: 12/28/1963, Sacramento, CA BR/TR, 5'11", 185 lbs. Deb: 9/12/1912

YEAR	TM-L	W	L	PCT	G	GS	CG	SH	SV	IP	H	R	ER	HR	HB	BB	SO	RAT	ERA	ERA+	CERA	OAV	BH	AVG	PR+	WS	TPW
1912	NY-A	0	3	.000	6	5	3	0	0	35^2	36	27	23	0	1	18	21	1.514	5.80	62	3.85	.265	6	.375	-7	1	-0.5
1913	NY-A	6	12	.333	28	21	9	2	0	151^1	147	77	54	3	2	51	83	1.308	3.21	93	3.14	.253	3	.070	-4	6	-0.7
1914	NY-A	8	11	.421	34	25	14	0	0	210	198	94	69	1	5	67	109	1.262	2.96	93	2.93	.253	12	.169	-7	9	-0.8
1915	NY-A	3	6	.333	11	10	8	1	0	79^1	66	41	32	3	3	45	37	1.399	3.63	81	3.41	.228	4	.154	-7	3	-0.8
1916	NY-A	5	6	.455	14	12	6	0	0	91	91	42	31	4	2	37	35	1.407	3.07	94	3.92	.272	7	.241	-3	4	-0.2
1918	NY-A	2	2	.500	15	6	1	0	0	48^1	39	27	21	0	2	30	16	1.428	3.91	72	3.30	.238	3	.188	-7	1	-0.8
1919	Bos-N	7	11	.389	22	13	9	1	0	136	129	61	45	2	2	45	48	1.279	2.98	96	3.01	.261	7	.152	-2	6	-0.3
Total	7	31	51	.378	130	92	50	4	0	751^2	706	369	275	13	17	293	349	1.329	3.29	88	3.22	.254	42	.170	-37	30	-4.1

• KECK, Cactus Frank Joseph Keck b: 1/13/1899, St. Louis, MO d: 2/6/1981, St. Louis, MO BR/TR, 5'11", 170 lbs. Deb: 5/26/1922

YEAR	TM-L	W	L	PCT	G	GS	CG	SH	SV	IP	H	R	ER	HR	HB	BB	SO	RAT	ERA	ERA+	CERA	OAV	BH	AVG	PR+	WS	TPW
1922	Cin-N	7	6	.538	27	15	5	1	1	131	138	71	49	4	5	29	27	1.275	3.37	118	3.31	.276	7	.159	6	8	0.4
1923	Cin-N	3	6	.333	35	6	1	0	2	87	84	49	36	5	3	32	16	1.333	3.72	104	3.47	.254	1	.059	1	4	0.0
Total	2	10	12	.455	62	21	6	1	3	218	222	120	85	9	8	61	43	1.298	3.51	112	3.37	.267	8	.131	7	12	0.4

• KEEFE, Bobby Robert Francis Keefe b: 6/16/1882, Folsom, CA d: 12/6/1964, Sacramento, CA BR/TR, 5'11", 155 lbs. Deb: 4/15/1907

YEAR	TM-L	W	L	PCT	G	GS	CG	SH	SV	IP	H	R	ER	HR	HB	BB	SO	RAT	ERA	ERA+	CERA	OAV	BH	AVG	PR+	WS	TPW
1907	NY-A	3	5	.375	19	3	0	0	3	57^2	60	18	16	1	1	20	20	1.387	2.50	112	3.51	.271	1	.053	3	5	0.1
1911	Cin-N	12	13	.480	39	26	15	0	3	234^1	196	88	70	7	3	76	105	1.161	2.69	123	2.53	.229	6	.086	16	15	1.4
1912	Cin-N	1	3	.250	17	6	0	0	2	68^2	78	52	40	0	4	33	29	1.617	5.24	64	4.48	.289	3	.167	-14	0	-1.4
Total	3	16	21	.432	75	35	15	0	8	360^2	334	158	126	8	8	129	154	1.284	3.14	103	3.06	.248	10	.093	6	20	0.2

• KEEFE, Dave David Edwin Keefe b: 1/9/1897, Williston, VT d: 2/4/1978, Kansas City, MO BL/TR, 5'9", 165 lbs. Deb: 4/21/1917 C

YEAR	TM-L	W	L	PCT	G	GS	CG	SH	SV	IP	H	R	ER	HR	HB	BB	SO	RAT	ERA	ERA+	CERA	OAV	BH	AVG	PR+	WS	TPW
1917	Phi-A	1	0	1.000	3	0	0	0	0	5	5	4	1	0	0	4	1	1.800	1.80	153	4.10	.278	0	.000	1	0	0.1
1919	Phi-A	0	1	.000	1	1	1	0	0	9	8	4	4	0	0	3	5	1.222	4.00	86	2.61	.242	0	.000	-0	0	-0.1
1920	Phi-A	6	7	.462	31	13	7	1	0	130^1	129	60	43	2	6	30	41	1.220	2.97	135	2.96	.262	10	.250	18	10	1.7
1921	Phi-A	2	9	.182	44	12	4	0	1	173	214	126	90	19	5	64	68	1.607	4.68	95	5.42	.311	10	.175	-1	6	-0.4
1922	Cle-A	0	0	....	18	1	0	0	0	36^1	47	30	25	2	0	12	11	1.624	6.19	65	5.24	.333	2	.333	-8	0	-0.7
Total	5	9	17	.346	97	27	12	1	1	353^2	403	224	163	23	11	113	126	1.459	4.15	102	4.40	.294	22	.206	9	16	0.6

• KEEFE, George George Washington Keefe b: 1/7/1867, Washington, DC d: 8/24/1935, Washington, DC BL/TL, 5'9", 168 lbs. Deb: 7/30/1886

YEAR	TM-L	W	L	PCT	G	GS	CG	SH	SV	IP	H	R	ER	HR	HB	BB	SO	RAT	ERA	ERA+	CERA	OAV	BH	AVG	PR+	WS	TPW
1886	Was-N	0	3	.000	4	4	4	0	0	31^1	28	22	18	0	....	15	5	1.372	5.17	63	....	.230	0	.000	-7	1	-0.8
1887	Was-N	0	1	.000	1	1	1	0	0	8	20	20	8	1	2	4	0	2.500	9.00	45	....	.459	0	.000	-4	0	-0.4
1888	Was-N	6	7	.462	13	13	13	1	0	114	87	55	36	2	4	43	52	1.140	2.84	98	....	.204	9	.214	-0	8	0.2
1889	Was-N	8	18	.308	30	27	24	0	0	230	266	182	131	6	4	143	90	**1.778**	5.13	77	....	.280	16	.163	-26	6	-2.3
1890	Buf-P	6	16	.273	25	22	22	0	0	196	280	229	142	11	0	138	55	**2.133**	6.52	63	....	.322	16	.203	-50	2	-3.8
1891	Was-a	0	3	.000	5	4	4	0	1	37	44	42	11	0	0	17	11	1.649	2.68	140	....	.286	2	.143	6	1	0.6
Total	6	20	48	.294	78	71	68	1	1	616^1	725	550	346	20	10	360	213	1.754	5.05	75	....	.283	43	.172	-81	18	-6.6

• KEEFE, John John Thomas Keefe b: 7/16/1867, Fitchburg, MA d: 8/10/1937, Fitchburg, MA TL Deb: 4/28/1890

YEAR	TM-L	W	L	PCT	G	GS	CG	SH	SV	IP	H	R	ER	HR	HB	BB	SO	RAT	ERA	ERA+	CERA	OAV	BH	AVG	PR+	WS	TPW
1890	Syr-a	17	24	.415	43	41	36	2	0	352^1	355	234	169	9	17	148	120	1.428	4.32	82	....	.254	30	.191	-24	12	-2.5

• KEEFE, Tim Timothy John "Smiling Tim,Sir Timothy" Keefe
b: 1/1/1857, Cambridge, MA d: 4/23/1933, Cambridge, MA BR/TR, 5'10.5", 185 lbs. Deb: 8/6/1880 U HOF: 1964

YEAR	TM-L	W	L	PCT	G	GS	CG	SH	SV	IP	H	R	ER	HR	HB	BB	SO	RAT	ERA	ERA+	CERA	OAV	BH	AVG	PR+	WS	TPW
1880	Tro-N	6	6	.500	12	12	12	0	0	105	68	27	10	0	....	16	39	.800	**0.86**	**295**	....	**.175**	10	.233	19	11	1.9
1881	Tro-N	18	27	.400	45	45	45	4	0	403	434	243	145	4	....	83	103	1.283	3.24	91	....	.263	35	.230	-32	23	-2.6
1882	Tro-N	17	26	.395	43	42	41	1	0	376	367	221	104	4	....	78	111	1.184	2.49	113	....	.241	43	.228	15	24	2.3
1883	NY-a	41	27	.603	**68**	**68**	**68**	5	0	**619**	488	244	166	6	....	108	**359**	.963	2.41	138	....	**.203**	57	.220	**58**	**70**	**5.6**
1884*	NY-a	37	17	.685	58	58	56	4	0	483	380	196	121	5	15	71	334	.934	2.25	138	....	.205	50	.238	28	47	3.8
1885	NY-N	32	13	.711	46	46	45	7	0	400	300	154	70	6	....	102	227	1.005	**1.58**	**169**	....	**.199**	27	.163	29	42	2.7
1886	NY-N	**42**	20	.677	**64**	**64**	**62**	2	0	**535**	479	250	152	9	....	102	297	1.086	2.56	124	....	.230	35	.171	37	38	3.4
1887	NY-N	35	19	.648	56	56	54	2	0	476^2	536	260	165	11	11	108	189	1.124	3.12	120	....	**.276**	62	.294	24	39	2.7
1888*	NY-N	**35**	12	.745	51	51	48	**8**	0	434^1	317	140	84	5	12	90	**335**	.937	**1.74**	**156**	....	**.197**	23	.127	35	35	2.8
1889*	NY-N	28	13	.683	47	45	39	3	1	364	319	212	134	9	18	151	225	1.291	3.31	119	....	**.228**	23	.154	23	27	1.7
1890	NY-P	17	11	.607	30	30	23	1	0	229	225	137	86	6	8	89	89	1.371	3.38	134	....	.246	10	.109	27	19	1.8

YEAR	TM-L	W	L	PCT	G	GS	CG	SH	SV	IP	H	R	ER	HR	HB	BB	SO	RAT	ERA	ERA+	CERA	OAV	BH	AVG	PR+	WS	TPW
1891	NY-N	2	5	.286	8	7	4	0	0	55	70	57	32	1	1	27	30	1.764	5.24	61	....	.299	2	.095	-13	0	-1.3
	Phi-N	3	6	.333	11	10	9	0	1	78^1	82	55	34	2	6	30	34	1.430	3.91	87	....	.259	5	.172	-5	4	-0.4
	Yr.	5	11	.313	19	17	13	0	1	133^1	152	112	66	3	7	57	64	1.568	4.46	74	....	.276	7	.140	-18	4	-1.7
1892	Phi-N	19	16	.543	39	38	31	2	0	313^1	279	142	82	4	13	98	136	1.203	2.36	138	2.63	.229	10	.085	26	24	1.9
1893	Phi-N	10	7	.588	22	22	17	0	0	178	202	131	87	3	12	80	56	1.584	4.40	104	4.68	.277	18	.228	1	10	0.1
Total	**14**	**342**	**225**	**.603**	**600**	**594**	**554**	**39**	**2**	**5049^2**	**4546**	**2469**	**1472**	**75**	**96**	**1233**	**2564**	**1.123**	**2.62**	**126**	**0.33**	**.230**	**410**	**.195**	**271**	**413**	**26.6**

• KEEGAN, Bob — Robert Charles "Smiley" Keegan b: 8/4/1920, Rochester, NY d: 6/20/2001, Rochester, NY BR/TR, 6'2.5", 207 lbs. Deb: 5/24/1953

YEAR	TM-L	W	L	PCT	G	GS	CG	SH	SV	IP	H	R	ER	HR	HB	BB	SO	RAT	ERA	ERA+	CERA	OAV	BH	AVG	PR+	WS	TPW
1953	Chi-A	7	5	.583	22	11	4	2	1	98^2	80	34	30	4	2	33	32	1.145	2.74	147	2.49	.223	9	.321	14	10	1.5
1954	Chi-A★	16	9	.640	31	27	14	2	2	209^2	211	84	72	16	1	82	61	1.397	3.09	121	3.88	.266	9	.120	13	14	1.1
1955	Chi-A	2	5	.286	18	11	1	0	0	58^2	83	39	38	4	1	28	29	1.892	5.83	68	6.61	.336	6	.333	-13	0	-1.2
1956	Chi-A	5	7	.417	20	16	4	0	0	105^1	119	56	46	15	2	35	32	1.462	3.93	104	4.89	.286	4	.125	1	5	0.0
1957	Chi-A	10	8	.556	30	20	6	2	2	142^2	131	62	56	22	2	37	36	1.178	3.53	106	3.49	.243	4	.103	0	8	-0.1
1958	Chi-A	0	2	.000	14	2	0	0	0	29^2	44	25	20	9	0	18	8	2.090	6.07	60	9.68	.358	0	.000	-8	0	-0.9
Total	**6**	**40**	**36**	**.526**	**135**	**87**	**29**	**6**	**5**	**644^2**	**668**	**300**	**262**	**70**	**8**	**233**	**198**	**1.398**	**3.66**	**105**	**4.26**	**.270**	**32**	**.163**	**7**	**37**	**0.5**

• KEEGAN, Ed — Edward Charles Keegan b: 7/8/1939, Camden, NJ BR/TR, 6'3", 165 lbs. Deb: 8/24/1959

YEAR	TM-L	W	L	PCT	G	GS	CG	SH	SV	IP	H	R	ER	HR	HB	BB	SO	RAT	ERA	ERA+	CERA	OAV	BH	AVG	PR+	WS	TPW
1959	Phi-N	0	3	.000	3	3	0	0	0	9	19	18	18	2	1	13	3	3.556	18.00	23	18.43	.432	0	.000	-14	0	-1.4
1961	KC-A	0	0	....	6	0	0	0	1	6	6	5	3	0	0	5	3	1.833	4.50	92	5.04	.261	0	....	-0	0	0.0
1962	Phi-N	0	0	....	4	0	0	0	0	8	6	2	2	1	1	5	5	1.375	2.25	172	4.41	.214	0	....	1	1	0.1
Total	**3**	**0**	**3**	**.000**	**13**	**3**	**0**	**0**	**1**	**23**	**31**	**25**	**23**	**3**	**2**	**23**	**11**	**2.348**	**9.00**	**45**	**10.06**	**.326**	**0**	**.000**	**-13**	**1**	**-1.3**

• KEELEY, Burt — Burton Elwood "Speed" Keeley b: 11/2/1879, Wilmington, IL d: 5/3/1952, Ely, MN BR/TR, 5'9", 170 lbs. Deb: 4/18/1908

YEAR	TM-L	W	L	PCT	G	GS	CG	SH	SV	IP	H	R	ER	HR	HB	BB	SO	RAT	ERA	ERA+	CERA	OAV	BH	AVG	PR+	WS	TPW
1908	Was-A	6	11	.353	28	15	12	1	1	169^2	173	87	56	3	4	48	68	**1.303**	2.97	77	3.17	.259	5	.102	-13	3	-1.8
1909	Was-A	0	0	....	2	0	0	0	0	7	12	13	9	0	1	1	0	1.857	11.57	21	6.82	.364	1	.500	-7	0	-0.8
Total	**2**	**6**	**11**	**.353**	**30**	**15**	**12**	**1**	**1**	**176^2**	**185**	**100**	**65**	**3**	**5**	**49**	**68**	**1.325**	**3.31**	**69**	**3.32**	**.264**	**6**	**.118**	**-21**	**3**	**-2.6**

• KEEN, Vic — Howard Victor Keen b: 3/16/1899, Bel Air, MD d: 12/10/1976, Salisbury, MD BR/TR, 5'9", 165 lbs. Deb: 8/13/1918

YEAR	TM-L	W	L	PCT	G	GS	CG	SH	SV	IP	H	R	ER	HR	HB	BB	SO	RAT	ERA	ERA+	CERA	OAV	BH	AVG	PR+	WS	TPW
1918	Phi-A	0	1	.000	1	1	0	0	0	8	9	3	3	1	0	1	1	1.250	3.38	87	4.15	.300	0	.000	-1	0	-0.1
1921	Chi-N	0	3	.000	5	4	1	0	0	25	29	17	13	0	1	9	9	1.520	4.68	82	4.41	.319	0	.000	-2	0	-0.3
1922	Chi-N	1	2	.333	7	2	2	0	1	34^2	36	20	15	4	1	10	11	1.327	3.89	108	4.02	.275	4	.333	1	2	0.2
1923	Chi-N	12	8	.600	35	17	10	0	1	177	169	70	59	8	5	57	46	1.277	3.00	133	3.22	.255	8	.151	15	15	1.2
1924	Chi-N	15	14	.517	40	28	15	0	3	234^2	242	112	99	17	4	80	75	1.372	3.80	103	3.86	.272	12	.156	-1	15	-0.5
1925	Chi-N	2	6	.250	30	8	1	0	1	83^1	125	61	58	8	0	41	19	1.992	6.26	69	7.55	.359	6	.240	-19	1	-1.8
1926★	StL-N	10	9	.526	26	21	12	1	0	152	179	89	77	15	1	42	29	1.454	4.56	86	4.57	.295	3	.057	-12	5	-1.8
1927	StL-N	2	1	.667	21	0	0	0	0	33^2	39	21	18	3	2	8	12	1.396	4.81	82	4.23	.293	1	.250	-4	1	-0.4
Total	**8**	**42**	**44**	**.488**	**165**	**81**	**41**	**1**	**6**	**748^1**	**828**	**393**	**342**	**56**	**14**	**248**	**202**	**1.438**	**4.11**	**97**	**4.31**	**.286**	**34**	**.148**	**-23**	**39**	**-3.4**

• KEENAN, Jimmie — James William "Sparkplug" Keenan b: 5/25/1899, Avon, NY d: 6/5/1980, Seminole, FL BL/TL, 5'7", 155 lbs. Deb: 9/9/1920

YEAR	TM-L	W	L	PCT	G	GS	CG	SH	SV	IP	H	R	ER	HR	HB	BB	SO	RAT	ERA	ERA+	CERA	OAV	BH	AVG	PR+	WS	TPW
1920	Phi-N	0	0	....	1	0	0	0	0	3	3	1	1	0	0	1	2	1.333	3.00	114	3.27	.333	0	.000	0	0	0.0
1921	Phi-N	1	2	.333	15	2	0	0	0	32^1	48	31	24	3	1	15	7	1.948	6.68	63	7.37	.364	0	.000	-8	0	-0.9
Total	**2**	**1**	**2**	**.333**	**16**	**2**	**0**	**0**	**0**	**35^1**	**51**	**32**	**25**	**3**	**1**	**16**	**9**	**1.896**	**6.37**	**66**	**7.02**	**.362**	**0**	**.000**	**-8**	**0**	**-0.9**

• KEENAN, Kid — Harry Leon Keenan b: 1875, Louisville, KY d: 6/11/1903, Covington, KY TR, 5'2" Deb: 8/11/1891

YEAR	TM-L	W	L	PCT	G	GS	CG	SH	SV	IP	H	R	ER	HR	HB	BB	SO	RAT	ERA	ERA+	CERA	OAV	BH	AVG	PR+	WS	TPW
1891	Cin-a	0	1	.000	1	1	1	0	0	8	6	9	0	0	0	4	5	1.250	0.00	....	....	.202	2	.500	4	1	0.4

• KEENER, Harry — Joshua Harry "Beans" Keener b: 9/1869, Easton, PA d: 3/25/1912, Easton, PA TR Deb: 6/27/1896

YEAR	TM-L	W	L	PCT	G	GS	CG	SH	SV	IP	H	R	ER	HR	HB	BB	SO	RAT	ERA	ERA+	CERA	OAV	BH	AVG	PR+	WS	TPW
1896	Phi-N	3	11	.214	16	13	11	0	0	113^1	144	102	74	5	0	39	28	1.615	5.88	73	4.90	.307	16	.314	-18	4	-1.4

• KEENER, Jeff — Jeffrey Bruce Keener b: 1/14/1959, Pana, IL BL/TR, 6', 170 lbs. Deb: 6/8/1982

YEAR	TM-L	W	L	PCT	G	GS	CG	SH	SV	IP	H	R	ER	HR	HB	BB	SO	RAT	ERA	ERA+	CERA	OAV	BH	AVG	PR+	WS	TPW
1982	StL-N	1	1	.500	19	0	0	0	0	22^1	19	8	4	1	0	19	25	1.701	1.61	225	4.16	.235	0	....	4	2	0.5
1983	StL-N	0	0	....	4	0	0	0	0	4^1	6	4	4	0	1	1	4	1.615	8.31	44	5.63	.333	0	....	-2	0	-0.2
Total	**2**	**1**	**1**	**.500**	**23**	**0**	**0**	**0**	**0**	**26^2**	**25**	**12**	**8**	**1**	**1**	**20**	**29**	**1.688**	**2.70**	**134**	**4.40**	**.253**	**0**	**....**	**2**	**2**	**0.2**

• KEENER, Joe — Joseph Donald Keener b: 4/21/1953, San Pedro, CA BR/TR, 6'4", 200 lbs. Deb: 9/18/1976

YEAR	TM-L	W	L	PCT	G	GS	CG	SH	SV	IP	H	R	ER	HR	HB	BB	SO	RAT	ERA	ERA+	CERA	OAV	BH	AVG	PR+	WS	TPW
1976	Mon-N	0	1	.000	2	2	0	0	0	4^1	7	7	5	0	1	8	1	3.462	10.38	36	15.27	.389	0	.000	-3	0	-0.4

• KEETON, Rickey — Rickey Keeton b: 3/18/1957, Cincinnati, OH BR/TR, 6'2", 190 lbs. Deb: 5/27/1980

YEAR	TM-L	W	L	PCT	G	GS	CG	SH	SV	IP	H	R	ER	HR	HB	BB	SO	RAT	ERA	ERA+	CERA	OAV	BH	AVG	PR+	WS	TPW
1980	Mil-A	2	2	.500	5	5	0	0	0	28^1	35	15	15	4	0	9	8	1.553	4.76	81	5.37	.307	0	....	-3	1	-0.3
1981	Mil-A	1	0	1.000	17	0	0	0	0	35^1	47	21	20	4	0	11	9	1.642	5.09	67	5.63	.329	0	....	-7	0	-0.7
Total	**2**	**3**	**2**	**.600**	**22**	**5**	**0**	**0**	**0**	**63^2**	**82**	**36**	**35**	**8**	**0**	**20**	**17**	**1.602**	**4.95**	**73**	**5.51**	**.319**	**0**	**....**	**-10**	**1**	**-1.0**

• KEFFER, Frank — Charles Franklin Keffer b: 7/1861, Bradford, PA Deb: 4/19/1890

YEAR	TM-L	W	L	PCT	G	GS	CG	SH	SV	IP	H	R	ER	HR	HB	BB	SO	RAT	ERA	ERA+	CERA	OAV	BH	AVG	PR+	WS	TPW
1890	Syr-a	1	1	.500	2	1	1	0	0	16	15	13	10	0	0	9	4	1.500	5.63	63	....	.241	1	.143	-3	0	-0.3

• KEHN, Chet — Chester Lawrence Kehn b: 10/30/1921, San Diego, CA d: 4/5/1984, San Diego, CA BR/TR, 5'11", 168 lbs. Deb: 4/30/1942

YEAR	TM-L	W	L	PCT	G	GS	CG	SH	SV	IP	H	R	ER	HR	HB	BB	SO	RAT	ERA	ERA+	CERA	OAV	BH	AVG	PR+	WS	TPW
1942	Bro-N	0	0	....	3	1	0	0	0	7^2	8	6	6	2	0	4	3	1.565	7.04	46	5.95	.267	2	1.000	-3	1	-0.2

• KEIFER, Katsy — Sherman Carl Keifer b: 9/3/1891, California, PA d: 2/19/1927, Outwood, KY BB/TL Deb: 10/8/1914

YEAR	TM-L	W	L	PCT	G	GS	CG	SH	SV	IP	H	R	ER	HR	HB	BB	SO	RAT	ERA	ERA+	CERA	OAV	BH	AVG	PR+	WS	TPW
1914	Ind-F	1	0	1.000	1	1	1	0	0	9	6	2	2	0	0	2	2	.889	2.00	173	1.28	.194	1	.333	1	1	0.2

• KEISLER, Randy — Randy Dean Keisler b: 2/24/1976, Richardson, TX BL/TL, 6'3", 190 lbs. Deb: 9/10/2000

YEAR	TM-L	W	L	PCT	G	GS	CG	SH	SV	IP	H	R	ER	HR	HB	BB	SO	RAT	ERA	ERA+	CERA	OAV	BH	AVG	PR+	WS	TPW
2000	NY-A	1	0	1.000	4	1	0	0	0	10^2	16	14	14	1	0	8	6	2.250	11.81	41	9.10	.364	0	....	-8	0	-0.7
2001	NY-A	1	2	.333	10	10	0	0	0	50^2	52	36	35	12	0	34	36	1.697	6.22	72	6.33	.259	0	.000	-9	0	-0.9
2003	SD-N	0	1	.000	2	2	0	0	0	6	7	9	8	3	1	7	5	2.333	12.00	33	12.82	.292	0	.000	-5	0	-0.5
Total	**3**	**2**	**3**	**.400**	**16**	**13**	**0**	**0**	**0**	**67^1**	**75**	**59**	**57**	**16**	**1**	**49**	**47**	**1.842**	**7.62**	**59**	**7.35**	**.279**	**0**	**.000**	**-22**	**0**	**-2.1**

• KEKICH, Mike — Michael Dennis Kekich b: 4/2/1945, San Diego, CA BR/TL, 6'1", 200 lbs. Deb: 6/9/1965

YEAR	TM-L	W	L	PCT	G	GS	CG	SH	SV	IP	H	R	ER	HR	HB	BB	SO	RAT	ERA	ERA+	CERA	OAV	BH	AVG	PR+	WS	TPW
1965	LA-N	0	1	.000	5	1	0	0	0	10^1	10	12	11	2	0	13	9	2.226	9.58	34	8.61	.263	0	.000	-7	0	-0.8
1968	LA-N	2	10	.167	25	20	1	1	0	115	116	54	50	9	1	46	84	1.409	3.91	71	4.04	.267	3	.081	-16	0	-2.0
1969	NY-A	4	6	.400	28	13	1	0	1	105	91	58	53	11	2	49	66	1.333	4.54	77	3.65	.236	3	.111	-13	2	-1.5
1970	NY-A	6	3	.667	26	14	1	0	0	98^2	103	59	53	12	1	55	63	1.601	4.83	73	5.10	.267	3	.094	-15	1	-1.6
1971	NY-A	10	9	.526	37	24	3	0	0	170^1	167	89	77	13	4	82	93	1.462	4.07	79	4.09	.257	8	.154	-15	5	-1.6
1972	NY-A	10	13	.435	29	28	2	0	0	175^1	172	77	72	13	4	76	78	1.414	3.70	80	4.04	.263	8	.136	-15	4	-1.8
1973	NY-A	1	1	.500	5	4	0	0	0	14^2	20	15	15	1	2	14	4	2.318	9.20	40	9.51	.351	0	....	-9	0	-0.9
	Cle-A	1	4	.200	16	6	0	0	0	50	73	47	39	6	0	35	26	2.160	7.02	56	8.55	.349	0	....	-17	0	-1.7
	Yr.	2	5	.286	21	10	0	0	0	64^2	93	62	54	7	2	49	30	2.196	7.52	51	8.77	.350	0	....	-26	0	-2.7
1975	Tex-A	0	0	....	23	0	0	0	2	31^1	33	16	13	2	0	21	19	1.723	3.73	101	5.16	.282	0	....	0	2	0.0
1977	Sea-A	5	4	.556	41	2	0	0	3	90	90	58	56	11	3	51	55	1.567	5.60	73	5.04	.265	0	....	-16	3	-1.6
Total	**9**	**39**	**51**	**.433**	**235**	**112**	**8**	**1**	**6**	**860^2**	**875**	**485**	**439**	**80**	**17**	**442**	**497**	**1.530**	**4.59**	**73**	**4.68**	**.268**	**25**	**.120**	**-123**	**17**	**-13.7**

• KELB, George — George Francis "Pugger,Lefty" Kelb b: 7/17/1870, Toledo, OH d: 10/20/1936, Toledo, OH BL/TL Deb: 4/17/1898

YEAR	TM-L	W	L	PCT	G	GS	CG	SH	SV	IP	H	R	ER	HR	HB	BB	SO	RAT	ERA	ERA+	CERA	OAV	BH	AVG	PR+	WS	TPW
1898	Cle-N	0	1	.000	3	1	1	0	0	16^1	23	17	8	0	4	1	8	1.469	4.41	82	5.21	.330	1	.200	-2	0	-0.2

• KELLEHER, Hal — Harold Joseph Kelleher b: 6/24/1914, Philadelphia, PA d: 8/27/1989, Cape May Court House, NJ BR/TR, 6', 165 lbs. Deb: 9/17/1935

YEAR	TM-L	W	L	PCT	G	GS	CG	SH	SV	IP	H	R	ER	HR	HB	BB	SO	RAT	ERA	ERA+	CERA	OAV	BH	AVG	PR+	WS	TPW
1935	Phi-N	2	0	1.000	3	3	2	1	0	25	26	7	5	0	1	12	12	1.520	1.80	252	3.78	.260	3	.375	8	4	0.9
1936	Phi-N	0	5	.000	14	4	1	0	0	44	60	38	26	2	3	29	13	2.023	5.32	85	6.99	.331	2	.167	-2	0	-0.3
1937	Phi-N	2	4	.333	27	2	1	0	0	58^1	72	51	43	3	7	31	20	1.766	6.63	65	5.92	.308	3	.176	-14	0	-1.4
1938	Phi-N	0	0	....	6	0	0	0	0	7^1	16	15	15	0	0	9	4	3.409	18.41	22	14.21	.432	1	.500	-12	0	-1.1
Total	**4**	**4**	**9**	**.308**	**50**	**9**	**4**	**1**	**0**	**134^2**	**174**	**111**	**89**	**5**	**11**	**81**	**49**	**1.894**	**5.95**	**73**	**6.33**	**.315**	**9**	**.231**	**-20**	**4**	**-1.9**

YEAR	TM-L	W	L	PCT	G	GS	CG	SH	SV	IP	H	R	ER	HR	HB	BB	SO	RAT	ERA	ERA+	CERA	OAV	BH	AVG	PR+	WS	TPW
• KELLER, Kris	Kristopher Shane Keller b: 3/1/1978, Williamsport, PA BR/TR, 6'2", 225 lbs. Deb: 5/24/2002																										
2002	Det-A	0	0	....	1	0	0	0	0	1	2	3	3	1	0	3	1	5.000	27.00	16	35.20	.400	0	....	-3	0	-0.2
• KELLER, Ron	Ronald Lee Keller b: 6/3/1943, Indianapolis, IN BR/TR, 6'2", 200 lbs. Deb: 7/9/1966																										
1966	Min-A	0	0	....	2	0	0	0	0	5^1	7	4	3	1	0	1	1	1.500	5.06	71	5.53	.318	0	.000	-1	0	-0.1
1968	Min-A	0	1	.000	7	1	0	0	0	16	18	6	5	2	1	4	11	1.375	2.81	110	4.78	.305	0	.000	1	1	0.1
Total	**2**	**0**	**1**	**.000**	**9**	**1**	**0**	**0**	**0**	**21^1**	**25**	**10**	**8**	**3**	**1**	**5**	**12**	**1.406**	**3.38**	**97**	**4.97**	**.309**	**0**	**.000**	**-0**	**1**	**0.0**
• KELLETT, Al	Alfred Henry Kellett b: 10/30/1901, Red Bank, NJ d: 7/14/1960, New York, NY BR/TR, 6'3", 200 lbs. Deb: 6/29/1923																										
1923	Phi-A	0	1	.000	5	0	0	0	0	10	11	9	7	0	0	8	1	1.900	6.30	65	5.05	.282	1	.333	-2	0	-0.2
1924	Bos-A	0	0	....	1	0	0	0	0	0	0	0	0	0	0	2	0	....	....	....	∞	.000	0	....	0	0	0.0
Total	**2**	**0**	**1**	**.000**	**6**	**0**	**0**	**0**	**0**	**10**	**11**	**9**	**7**	**0**	**0**	**10**	**1**	**2.100**	**6.30**	**65**	**5.05**	**.282**	**1**	**.333**	**-2**	**0**	**-0.2**
• KELLEY, Dick	Richard Anthony Kelley b: 1/8/1940, Brighton, MA d: 12/11/1991, Northridge, CA BR/TL, 5'11.5", 175 lbs. Deb: 4/15/1964																										
1964	Mil-N	0	0	....	2	0	0	0	0	2	2	4	4	0	0	3	2	2.500	18.00	20	7.45	.250	0	....	-3	0	-0.3
1965	Mil-N	1	1	.500	21	4	0	0	0	45	37	15	15	5	0	20	31	1.267	3.00	117	3.34	.226	0	.000	2	3	0.2
1966	Atl-N	7	5	.583	20	13	2	2	0	81	75	36	29	6	3	21	50	1.185	3.22	113	3.10	.247	1	.036	4	4	0.1
1967	Atl-N	2	9	.182	39	9	1	1	2	98	88	48	41	8	1	42	75	1.327	3.77	88	3.45	.247	4	.250	-5	4	-0.5
1968	Atl-N	2	4	.333	31	11	1	1	1	98	86	36	30	4	1	45	73	1.337	2.76	109	3.21	.238	1	.043	2	5	0.2
1969	SD-N	4	8	.333	27	23	1	1	0	136	113	60	54	11	5	61	96	1.279	3.57	99	3.28	.230	5	.106	1	8	-0.1
1971	SD-N	2	3	.400	48	1	0	0	2	59^2	52	26	23	5	4	23	42	1.257	3.47	95	3.29	.232	1	.333	-1	3	0.0
Total	**7**	**18**	**30**	**.375**	**188**	**61**	**5**	**5**	**5**	**519^2**	**453**	**225**	**196**	**39**	**14**	**215**	**369**	**1.285**	**3.39**	**100**	**3.29**	**.237**	**12**	**.096**	**-0**	**27**	**-0.5**
• KELLEY, Harry	Harry Leroy Kelley b: 2/13/1906, Parkin, AR d: 3/23/1958, Parkin, AR BR/TR, 5'9.5", 170 lbs. Deb: 4/16/1925																										
1925	Was-A	1	1	.500	6	1	0	0	0	16	30	23	16	0	0	12	7	2.625	9.00	47	9.85	.405	0	.000	-9	0	-0.9
1926	Was-A	0	0	....	7	1	0	0	0	10	17	10	9	0	1	8	6	2.500	8.10	48	10.11	.405	0	.000	-5	0	-0.5
1936	Phi-A	15	12	.556	35	27	20	1	3	235^1	250	112	101	21	2	75	82	1.381	3.86	132	4.02	.275	18	.198	32	20	2.7
1937	Phi-A	13	21	.382	41	29	14	0	0	205	267	154	122	16	3	79	68	1.688	5.36	88	5.42	.306	16	.225	-15	6	-1.2
1938	Phi-A	0	2	.000	4	3	0	0	0	8	17	16	15	0	0	10	3	3.375	16.88	29	14.16	.436	0	.000	-10	0	-1.0
	Was-A	9	8	.529	38	14	7	2	1	148^1	162	90	74	12	1	46	44	1.402	4.49	100	4.04	.276	12	.250	0	8	0.1
	Yr.	9	10	.474	42	17	7	2	1	156^1	179	106	89	12	1	56	47	1.503	5.12	89	4.56	.286	12	.240	-10	8	-0.9
1939	Was-A	4	3	.571	15	3	2	0	1	53^2	69	32	28	2	3	14	20	1.547	4.70	93	4.83	.314	4	.267	-3	3	-0.2
Total	**6**	**42**	**47**	**.472**	**146**	**78**	**43**	**3**	**5**	**676^1**	**812**	**437**	**365**	**51**	**10**	**244**	**230**	**1.561**	**4.86**	**97**	**4.86**	**.296**	**50**	**.216**	**-9**	**37**	**-0.9**
• KELLEY, Tom	Thomas Henry Kelley b: 1/5/1944, Manchester, CT BR/TR, 6', 191 lbs. Deb: 5/5/1964																										
1964	Cle-A	0	0	....	6	0	0	0	0	9^2	9	9	6	1	1	9	7	1.862	5.59	64	5.70	.237	0	....	-2	0	-0.2
1965	Cle-A	2	1	.667	4	4	1	0	0	30	19	8	8	3	0	13	31	1.067	2.40	145	2.43	.186	2	.222	4	3	0.4
1966	Cle-A	4	8	.333	31	7	1	0	0	95^1	97	55	46	14	0	42	64	1.458	4.34	79	4.65	.264	4	.143	-8	1	-1.0
1967	Cle-A	0	0	....	1	0	0	0	0	1	0	0	0	0	0	2	0	2.000	0.00	....	4.48	.000	0	....	0	0	0.0
1971	Atl-N	9	5	.643	28	20	5	0	0	143	140	56	47	8	1	69	68	1.462	2.96	125	4.01	.262	2	.047	13	12	1.0
1972	Atl-N	5	7	.417	27	14	2	1	0	116^1	122	65	59	12	0	65	59	1.607	4.56	83	5.02	.272	3	.088	-8	4	-1.0
1973	Atl-N	0	1	.000	7	0	0	0	0	12^2	13	5	4	0	0	7	5	1.579	2.84	138	3.77	.289	0	.000	2	1	0.1
Total	**7**	**20**	**22**	**.476**	**104**	**45**	**9**	**1**	**0**	**408**	**400**	**198**	**170**	**38**	**2**	**207**	**234**	**1.488**	**3.75**	**97**	**4.36**	**.260**	**11**	**.095**	**0**	**21**	**-0.6**
• KELLNER, Alex	Alexander Raymond Kellner b: 8/26/1924, Tucson, AZ d: 5/3/1996, Tucson, AZ BR/TL, 6', 200 lbs. Deb: 4/29/1948																										
1948	Phi-A	0	0	....	13	1	0	0	0	23	21	20	20	0	2	16	14	1.609	7.83	55	4.00	.239	0	.000	-9	0	-1.0
1949	Phi-A★	20	12	.625	38	27	19	0	1	245	243	120	102	18	2	129	94	1.518	3.75	110	4.29	.261	20	.217	4	17	0.5
1950	Phi-A	8	20	.286	36	29	15	0	2	225^1	253	157	137	28	2	112	85	1.620	5.47	83	5.25	.282	16	.200	-22	6	-2.1
1951	Phi-A	11	14	.440	33	29	11	1	2	209^2	218	118	104	20	4	93	94	1.483	4.46	96	4.47	.272	18	.228	-8	10	-0.9
1952	Phi-A	12	14	.462	34	33	14	2	0	231^1	223	124	112	21	4	86	105	1.336	4.36	91	3.66	.252	17	.207	-7	11	-0.6
1953	Phi-A	11	12	.478	25	25	14	2	0	201^2	210	98	88	8	4	51	81	1.294	3.93	109	3.34	.269	15	.217	9	15	1.0
1954	Phi-A	6	17	.261	27	27	8	1	0	173^2	204	118	104	16	6	88	69	**1.681**	5.39	72	5.51	.301	10	.182	-26	3	-2.7
1955	KC-A	11	8	.579	30	24	6	3	0	162^2	164	81	76	18	5	60	75	1.377	4.20	99	4.16	.265	12	.214	0	10	0.2
1956	KC-A	7	4	.636	20	17	5	0	0	91^2	103	49	44	15	2	33	44	1.484	4.32	100	5.20	.289	6	.200	-1	5	-0.1
1957	KC-A	6	5	.545	28	21	3	0	0	132^1	141	65	63	18	2	41	72	1.372	4.27	93	4.44	.278	11	.234	-4	7	0.0
1958	KC-A	0	2	.000	7	6	0	0	0	33^2	40	24	22	5	0	8	22	1.426	5.88	66	5.23	.315	1	.091	-7	0	-0.8
	Cin-N	7	3	.700	18	7	4	0	0	82	74	24	21	8	3	20	42	1.146	2.30	180	3.12	.243	10	.357	16	10	1.9
1959	StL-N	2	1	.667	12	4	0	0	0	37	31	17	13	9	1	10	19	1.108	3.16	134	3.53	.220	2	.222	5	3	0.5
Total	**12**	**101**	**112**	**.474**	**321**	**250**	**99**	**9**	**5**	**1849^1**	**1925**	**1015**	**906**	**184**	**37**	**747**	**816**	**1.445**	**4.41**	**94**	**4.35**	**.270**	**138**	**.215**	**-50**	**97**	**-3.9**
• KELLNER, Walt	Walter Joseph Kellner b: 4/26/1929, Tucson, AZ BR/TR, 6', 200 lbs. Deb: 9/6/1952																										
1952	Phi-A	0	0	....	1	0	0	0	0	4	4	3	3	0	0	3	2	1.750	6.75	59	4.32	.250	0	.000	-1	0	-0.1
1953	Phi-A	0	0	....	2	0	0	0	0	3	1	2	2	0	1	4	4	1.667	6.00	71	3.93	.111	0	....	-1	0	-0.1
Total	**2**	**0**	**0**	**....**	**3**	**0**	**0**	**0**	**0**	**7**	**5**	**5**	**5**	**0**	**1**	**7**	**6**	**1.714**	**6.43**	**63**	**4.16**	**.200**	**0**	**.000**	**-2**	**0**	**-0.2**
• KELLOGG, Al	Albert Clement Kellogg b: 9/9/1886, Providence, RI d: 7/21/1953, Portland, OR TL, 6'3", 208 lbs. Deb: 9/25/1908																										
1908	Phi-A	0	2	.000	3	3	2	0	0	17	20	19	11	1	1	9	8	1.706	5.82	44	5.45	.294	1	.125	-6	0	-0.7
• KELLUM, Win	Winford Ansley Kellum b: 4/11/1876, Waterford, Canada d: 8/10/1951, Big Rapids, MI BB/TL, 5'10", 190 lbs. Deb: 4/26/1901 U																										
1901	Bos-A	2	3	.400	6	6	5	0	0	48	61	42	34	3	3	7	8	1.417	6.38	55	4.52	.306	3	.167	-17	0	-1.6
1904	Cin-N	15	10	.600	31	24	22	1	2	224^2	206	98	65	1	10	46	70	1.122	2.60	112	2.41	.244	13	.159	2	17	0.4
1905	StL-N	3	3	.500	11	7	5	1	0	74	70	30	24	1	1	10	19	1.081	2.92	102	2.29	.255	5	.200	3	4	0.4
Total	**3**	**20**	**16**	**.556**	**48**	**37**	**32**	**2**	**2**	**346^2**	**337**	**170**	**123**	**5**	**14**	**63**	**97**	**1.154**	**3.19**	**96**	**2.68**	**.256**	**21**	**.168**	**-12**	**21**	**-0.8**
• KELLY, Bob	Robert Edward Kelly b: 10/4/1927, Cleveland, OH BR/TR, 6', 180 lbs. Deb: 5/4/1951																										
1951	Chi-N	7	4	.636	35	11	4	0	0	123^2	130	70	64	8	1	55	48	1.496	4.66	88	4.29	.275	5	.161	-7	6	-0.7
1952	Chi-N	4	9	.308	31	15	3	2	0	125^1	114	62	50	7	3	46	50	1.277	3.59	107	3.05	.236	8	.216	4	6	0.4
1953	Chi-N	0	1	.000	14	0	0	0	0	17	27	19	18	2	1	9	6	2.118	9.53	47	8.83	.375	0	.000	-9	0	-0.9
	Cin-N	1	2	.333	28	5	0	0	2	66^1	71	36	32	7	0	26	29	1.462	4.34	100	4.46	.276	2	.118	-1	3	-0.2
	Yr.	1	3	.250	42	5	0	0	2	83^1	98	55	50	9	1	35	35	1.596	5.40	81	5.35	.298	2	.111	-10	3	-1.1
1958	Cin-N	0	0	....	2	1	0	0	0	2	3	1	1	0	0	3	1	3.000	4.50	92	10.41	.500	0	....	-0	0	0.0
	Cle-A	0	2	.000	13	3	0	0	0	27^2	29	18	16	4	1	13	12	1.518	5.20	70	5.32	.282	1	.250	-5	0	-0.5
Total	**4**	**12**	**18**	**.400**	**123**	**35**	**7**	**2**	**2**	**362**	**374**	**206**	**181**	**28**	**6**	**152**	**146**	**1.453**	**4.50**	**90**	**4.22**	**.268**	**16**	**.178**	**-18**	**15**	**-1.9**
• KELLY, Bryan	Bryan Keith Kelly b: 2/24/1959, Silver Spring, MD BR/TR, 6'2", 195 lbs. Deb: 9/2/1986																										
1986	Det-A	1	2	.333	6	4	0	0	0	20	21	11	10	4	0	10	18	1.550	4.50	92	5.51	.269	0	....	-1	1	-0.1
1987	Det-A	0	1	.000	5	0	0	0	0	10^2	12	6	6	2	0	7	10	1.781	5.06	83	5.84	.286	0	....	-1	0	-0.1
Total	**2**	**1**	**3**	**.250**	**11**	**4**	**0**	**0**	**0**	**30^2**	**33**	**17**	**16**	**6**	**0**	**17**	**28**	**1.630**	**4.70**	**89**	**5.62**	**.275**	**0**	**....**	**-2**	**1**	**-0.2**
• KELLY, Ed	Edward Leo Kelly b: 12/10/1888, Pawtucket, RI d: 11/4/1928, Red Lodge, MT BR/TR, 5'11.5", 173 lbs. Deb: 4/14/1914																										
1914	Bos-A	0	0	....	3	0	0	0	0	2^1	1	1	0	0	0	1	4	.857	0.00	....	0.84	.100	0	.000	1	0	0.1
• KELLY, Herb	Herbert Barrett "Moke" Kelly b: 6/4/1892, Mobile, AL d: 5/18/1973, Torrance, CA BL/TL, 5'9", 160 lbs. Deb: 9/25/1914																										
1914	Pit-N	0	2	.000	5	2	2	0	0	25^2	24	11	7	1	0	7	6	1.208	2.45	108	2.81	.253	2	.222	0	2	0.1
1915	Pit-N	1	1	.500	5	1	0	0	0	11	10	9	5	0	1	4	6	1.273	4.09	67	2.90	.250	1	.500	-2	0	-0.1
Total	**2**	**1**	**3**	**.250**	**10**	**3**	**2**	**0**	**0**	**36^2**	**34**	**20**	**12**	**1**	**1**	**11**	**12**	**1.227**	**2.95**	**91**	**2.84**	**.252**	**3**	**.273**	**-1**	**2**	**0.0**
• KELLY, King	Michael Joseph Kelly b: 12/31/1857, Troy, NY d: 11/8/1894, Boston, MA BR/TR, 5'10", 170 lbs. Deb: 5/1/1878 M/U HOF: 1945 ♦																										
1880	Chi-N	0	0	....	1	0	0	0	0	3	3	2	0	0	....	1	1	1.333	0.00	....	....	.247	100	.291	1	16	1.3
1883	Chi-N	0	0	....	1	0	0	0	0	1	1	0	0	0	....	0	0	1.000	0.00	....	....	.245	109	.255	0	13	0.6
1884	Chi-N	0	1	.000	2	0	0	0	0	5^1	12	11	5	2	....	2	1	2.625	8.44	37	....	.424	160	.354	-3	21	4.2

YEAR	TM-L	W	L	PCT	G	GS	CG	SH	SV	IP	H	R	ER	HR	HB	BB	SO	RAT	ERA	ERA+	CERA	OAV	BH	AVG	PR+	WS	TPW
1887	Bos-N	1	0	1.000	3	0	0	0	0	13	31	16	5	1	0	14	0	2.385	3.46	113	....	.447	211	.391	0	23	2.3
1890	Bos-P	1	0	1.000	1	0	0	0	0	2	1	1	1	0	0	2	2	1.500	4.50	98	....	.142	111	.326	-0	16	1.1
1891	Cin-a	0	1	.000	3	0	0	0	0	15^{1}	21	15	9	2	1	7	0	1.826	5.28	78	....	.315	84	.297	-2	13	2.2
1892*	Bos-N	0	0	....	1	0	0	0	0	6	8	4	1	0	3	4	0	2.000	1.50	234	8.01	.308	53	.189	1	6	-0.9
Total	**7**	**2**	**2**	**.500**	**12**	**0**	**0**	**0**	**0**	**45^{2}**	**77**	**49**	**21**	**5**	**4**	**30**	**4**	**2.036**	**4.14**	**91**	**1.05**	**.361**	**1868**	**.314**	**-3**	**108**	**10.8**
• KELLY, Mike	Michael J. Kelly b: 11/9/1902, St. Louis, MO d: 2001, BR/TR, 6'1", 178 lbs. Deb: 9/3/1926 C																										
1926	Phi-N	0	0	....	4	0	0	0	0	6^{2}	9	7	7	0	1	4	2	1.950	9.45	44	6.56	.346	0	.000	-4	0	-0.4
• KELLY, Ren	Reynolds Joseph Kelly b: 11/18/1899, San Francisco, CA d: 8/24/1963, Millbrae, CA BR/TR, 6', 183 lbs. Deb: 9/18/1923																										
1923	Phi-A	0	0	....	1	0	0	0	0	7	7	3	2	0	0	4	1	1.571	2.57	160	3.61	.259	0	.000	1	1	0.1
• KELSO, Bill	William Eugene Kelso b: 2/19/1940, Kansas City, MO BR/TR, 6'4", 215 lbs. Deb: 7/31/1964																										
1964	LA-A	2	0	1.000	10	1	1	1	0	23^{2}	19	6	6	3	1	9	21	1.183	2.28	144	3.32	.218	0	.000	2	2	0.2
1966	Cal-A	1	1	.500	5	0	0	0	0	11^{1}	11	3	3	1	1	6	11	1.500	2.38	141	4.41	.244	0	.000	1	1	0.1
1967	Cal-A	5	3	.625	69	1	0	0	11	112	85	41	37	6	4	63	91	1.321	2.97	106	3.11	.219	2	.105	1	9	0.0
1968	Cin-N	4	1	.800	35	0	0	0	1	54	56	26	24	6	3	15	39	1.315	4.00	79	3.91	.277	0	.000	-5	2	-0.6
Total	**4**	**12**	**5**	**.706**	**119**	**2**	**1**	**1**	**12**	**201**	**171**	**76**	**70**	**16**	**9**	**93**	**162**	**1.313**	**3.13**	**101**	**3.42**	**.237**	**2**	**.059**	**-0**	**14**	**-0.3**
• KEMMERER, Russ	Russell Paul "Rusty,Dutch,Kimmersak" Kemmerer b: 11/1/1931, Pittsburgh, PA BR/TR, 6'2", 200 lbs. Deb: 6/27/1954																										
1954	Bos-A	5	3	.625	19	9	2	1	0	75^{1}	71	35	32	4	2	41	37	1.487	3.82	108	3.99	.257	3	.143	3	4	0.3
1955	Bos-A	1	1	.500	7	2	0	0	0	17^{1}	18	14	14	3	0	15	13	1.904	7.27	59	6.81	.269	0	.000	-6	0	-0.6
1957	Bos-A	0	0	....	1	0	0	0	0	4	5	2	2	0	0	2	1	1.750	4.50	89	4.53	.333	0	.000	-0	0	0.0
	Was-A	7	11	.389	39	26	6	0	0	172^{1}	214	110	95	20	2	71	81	1.654	4.96	79	5.75	.309	3	.067	-16	4	-1.8
	Yr.	7	11	.389	40	26	6	0	0	176^{1}	219	112	97	20	2	73	82	**1.656**	4.95	79	5.72	.310	3	.065	-16	4	-1.8
1958	Was-A	6	15	.286	40	30	6	0	0	224^{1}	234	122	115	25	4	74	111	1.373	4.61	83	4.14	.270	11	.159	-14	6	-1.7
1959	Was-A	8	17	.320	37	28	8	0	0	206	221	116	103	20	4	71	89	1.417	4.50	87	4.30	.276	8	.133	-6	7	-0.7
1960	Was-A	0	2	.000	3	3	0	0	0	17^{1}	18	15	15	2	1	10	10	1.615	7.79	51	5.38	.269	0	.000	-7	0	-0.7
	Chi-A	6	3	.667	36	7	2	1	2	120^{2}	111	45	40	5	1	45	76	1.293	2.98	127	3.13	.248	0	.000	9	9	0.6
	Yr.	6	5	.545	39	10	2	1	2	138	129	60	55	7	2	55	86	1.333	3.59	107	3.41	.250	0	.000	2	9	-0.1
1961	Chi-A	3	3	.500	47	2	0	0	2	96^{2}	102	53	47	10	0	26	35	1.324	4.38	89	3.93	.278	3	.200	-4	5	-0.3
1962	Chi-A	2	1	.667	20	0	0	0	0	28	30	14	12	3	0	11	17	1.464	3.86	101	4.34	.270	1	.500	0	2	0.1
	Hou-N	5	3	.625	36	2	0	0	3	68	72	34	31	10	3	15	23	1.279	4.10	91	4.25	.272	3	.333	-2	5	0.0
1963	Hou-N	0	0	....	17	0	0	0	1	36^{2}	48	28	23	1	0	8	12	1.527	5.65	56	4.51	.320	2	.286	-9	0	-1.0
Total	**9**	**43**	**59**	**.422**	**302**	**109**	**24**	**2**	**8**	**1066^{2}**	**1144**	**588**	**529**	**103**	**17**	**389**	**505**	**1.437**	**4.46**	**86**	**4.38**	**.277**	**34**	**.128**	**-52**	**42**	**-5.8**
• KEMNER, Dutch	Herman John Kemner b: 3/4/1899, Quincy, IL d: 1/16/1988, Quincy, IL BR/TR, 5'10.5", 175 lbs. Deb: 4/19/1929																										
1929	Cin-N	0	0	....	9	0	0	0	1	15^{1}	19	13	13	0	0	8	10	1.761	7.63	60	5.03	.328	1	.250	-5	0	-0.5
• KENNA, Ed	Edward Benninghaus "The Pitching Poet" Kenna b: 10/17/1877, Charleston, WV d: 3/22/1912, Grant, FL TR, 6', 180 lbs. Deb: 5/5/1902																										
1902	Phi-A	1	1	.500	2	1	1	0	0	17	19	15	10	1	1	11	5	1.765	5.29	69	5.47	.283	1	.125	-3	0	-0.3
• KENNEDY, Bill	William Gorman Kennedy b: 12/22/1918, Alexandria, VA d: 8/20/1995, Alexandria, VA BL/TL, 6'1", 175 lbs. Deb: 5/1/1942																										
1942	Was-A	0	1	.000	8	2	1	0	2	18	21	18	16	1	0	10	4	1.722	8.00	46	5.16	.296	0	.000	-8	0	-0.9
1946	Was-A	1	2	.333	21	2	0	0	3	39	40	29	26	1	0	29	18	1.769	6.00	56	4.77	.270	1	.125	-11	0	-1.2
1947	Was-A	0	0	....	2	0	0	0	0	6^{2}	10	8	6	1	0	5	1	2.250	8.10	46	8.96	.370	0	.000	-3	0	-0.4
Total	**3**	**1**	**3**	**.250**	**31**	**4**	**1**	**0**	**5**	**63^{2}**	**71**	**55**	**48**	**3**	**0**	**44**	**23**	**1.806**	**6.79**	**51**	**5.32**	**.289**	**1**	**.071**	**-22**	**0**	**-2.4**
• KENNEDY, Bill	William Aulton "Lefty" Kennedy b: 3/14/1921, Carnesville, GA d: 4/9/1983, Seattle, WA BL/TL, 6'2", 195 lbs. Deb: 4/26/1948																										
1948	Cle-A	1	0	1.000	6	3	0	0	0	11^{1}	16	14	14	0	0	13	12	2.559	11.12	37	8.37	.333	2	.667	-9	0	-0.8
	StL-A	7	8	.467	26	20	3	0	0	132	132	82	69	10	5	104	77	1.788	4.70	97	5.33	.259	11	.250	0	7	0.1
	Yr.	8	8	.500	32	23	3	0	0	143^{1}	148	96	83	10	5	117	89	1.849	5.21	86	5.57	.265	13	.277	-9	7	-0.7
1949	StL-A	4	11	.267	48	16	2	0	1	153^{2}	172	97	80	12	3	73	69	1.594	4.69	97	4.81	.285	6	.150	3	6	0.1
1950	StL-A	0	0	....	1	0	0	0	0	2	1	1	0	0	0	2	1	1.500	0.00	....	2.54	.143	0	....	1	0	0.1
1951	StL-A	1	5	.167	19	5	1	0	0	56	76	37	36	4	1	37	29	2.018	5.79	76	7.03	.332	2	.125	-7	1	-0.9
1952	Chi-A	2	2	.500	**47**	1	0	0	5	70^{2}	54	27	22	4	1	38	46	1.302	2.80	130	3.01	.213	3	.231	6	6	0.6
1953	Bos-A	0	0	....	16	0	0	0	2	24^{1}	24	13	10	2	1	17	14	1.685	3.70	114	4.83	.255	1	.500	1	2	0.2
1956	Cin-N	0	0	....	1	0	0	0	0	2	6	4	4	1	0	0	0	3.000	18.00	22	21.89	.667	0	....	-3	0	-0.3
1957	Cin-N	0	2	.000	8	0	0	0	3	12^{2}	16	9	9	1	1	5	8	1.658	6.39	64	5.46	.314	0	.000	-3	0	-0.3
Total	**8**	**15**	**28**	**.349**	**172**	**45**	**6**	**0**	**11**	**464^{2}**	**497**	**284**	**244**	**34**	**12**	**289**	**256**	**1.692**	**4.73**	**92**	**5.12**	**.275**	**25**	**.208**	**-12**	**22**	**-1.2**
• KENNEDY, Brickyard	William Park Kennedy b: 10/7/1867, Bellaire, OH d: 9/23/1915, Bellaire, OH BR/TR, 5'11", 160 lbs. Deb: 4/26/1892																										
1892	Bro-N	13	8	.619	26	21	18	0	1	191	189	115	82	3	4	95	108	1.487	3.86	82	3.73	.248	14	.165	-15	10	-1.5
1893	Bro-N	25	20	.556	46	44	40	2	1	382^{2}	376	238	158	15	7	168	107	1.422	3.72	119	3.66	.249	39	.248	34	29	3.0
1894	Bro-N	24	20	.545	48	41	34	0	2	360^{2}	445	291	197	15	11	149	107	1.647	4.92	100	5.04	.300	49	.304	5	24	0.8
1895	Bro-N	19	12	.613	40	34	27	2	1	288^{2}	334	199	159	14	7	93	41	1.479	4.96	89	4.29	.285	39	.307	-22	19	-1.4
1896	Bro-N	17	20	.459	42	38	28	1	1	305^{2}	334	211	150	12	12	130	76	1.518	4.42	93	4.29	.276	23	.189	-8	13	-1.3
1897	Bro-N	18	20	.474	44	40	36	2	1	343^{1}	370	206	149	6	8	149	81	1.512	3.91	105	4.01	.273	40	.272	11	25	1.3
1898	Bro-N	16	22	.421	40	39	38	0	0	339^{1}	360	183	127	12	5	123	73	1.423	3.37	106	3.78	.270	34	.252	12	20	1.4
1899	Bro-N	22	9	.710	40	33	27	2	2	277^{1}	297	133	86	11	3	86	55	1.381	2.79	140	3.67	.274	27	.248	29	28	3.0
1900	Bro-N	20	13	.606	42	35	26	2	0	292	316	160	127	5	8	111	75	1.462	3.91	98	3.86	.275	37	.301	-6	23	0.1
1901	Bro-N	3	5	.375	14	8	6	0	0	85^{1}	80	40	29	1	1	24	28	1.219	3.06	109	2.70	.247	6	.167	2	5	0.1
1902	NY-N	1	4	.200	6	6	4	1	0	38^{2}	44	25	17	0	0	16	9	1.552	3.96	71	4.06	.286	4	.267	-5	1	-0.4
1903*	Pit-N	9	6	.600	18	15	10	1	0	125^{1}	130	62	48	0	5	57	39	1.492	3.45	94	3.97	.277	21	.362	-8	11	0.0
Total	**12**	**187**	**159**	**.540**	**406**	**354**	**294**	**13**	**9**	**3030**	**3275**	**1863**	**1329**	**94**	**71**	**1201**	**799**	**1.477**	**3.95**	**102**	**4.02**	**.273**	**333**	**.261**	**30**	**208**	**5.1**
• KENNEDY, Joe	Joseph Darley Kennedy b: 5/24/1979, La Mesa, CA BR/TL, 6'4", 225 lbs. Deb: 6/6/2001																										
2001	TB-A	7	8	.467	20	20	0	0	0	117^{2}	122	63	58	16	3	34	78	1.326	4.44	101	4.23	.269	1	.250	0	6	0.0
2002	TB-A	8	11	.421	30	30	5	1	0	196^{2}	204	114	99	23	16	55	109	1.317	4.53	99	4.29	.269	3	.429	-5	9	-0.3
2003	TB-A	3	12	.200	32	22	1	1	1	133^{2}	167	101	91	19	11	47	77	1.601	6.13	74	5.92	.303	0	....	-27	0	-2.6
Total	**3**	**18**	**31**	**.367**	**82**	**72**	**6**	**2**	**1**	**448**	**493**	**278**	**248**	**58**	**30**	**136**	**264**	**1.404**	**4.98**	**90**	**4.76**	**.279**	**4**	**.364**	**-31**	**15**	**-2.9**
• KENNEDY, Monte	Monty Calvin Kennedy b: 5/11/1922, Amelia, VA d: 3/1/1997, Midlothian, VA BR/TL, 6'2", 185 lbs. Deb: 4/18/1946																										
1946	NY-N	9	10	.474	38	27	10	1	1	186^{2}	153	80	71	14	4	116	71	1.441	3.42	101	3.68	.224	15	.234	3	10	0.5
1947	NY-N	9	12	.429	34	24	9	0	0	148^{1}	158	90	80	8	4	88	60	1.658	4.85	84	4.79	.272	8	.167	-14	5	-1.4
1948	NY-N	3	9	.250	25	16	7	1	0	114^{1}	118	64	51	10	3	57	63	1.531	4.01	98	4.52	.264	4	.129	-1	4	-0.1
1949	NY-N	12	14	.462	38	32	14	4	1	223^{1}	208	105	85	13	3	100	95	1.379	3.43	116	3.49	.242	12	.145	14	13	1.3
1950	NY-N	5	4	.556	36	17	5	0	2	114^{1}	120	65	60	14	3	53	41	1.513	4.72	87	4.70	.269	2	.056	-11	4	-1.4
1951*	NY-N	1	2	.333	29	5	1	0	0	68	68	25	17	0	0	31	22	1.456	2.25	174	3.59	.270	3	.200	12	6	1.3
1952	NY-N	3	4	.429	31	6	2	1	0	83^{1}	73	37	28	6	2	31	48	1.248	3.02	122	3.05	.230	2	.091	7	5	0.5
1953	NY-N	0	0	....	18	0	0	0	0	22^{2}	30	18	18	2	1	19	11	2.162	7.15	60	7.85	.337	0	.000	-7	0	-0.7
Total	**8**	**42**	**55**	**.433**	**249**	**127**	**48**	**7**	**4**	**961**	**928**	**484**	**410**	**67**	**20**	**495**	**411**	**1.481**	**3.84**	**101**	**4.06**	**.253**	**46**	**.153**	**3**	**47**	**0.0**
• KENNEDY, Ted	Theodore A. Kennedy b: 2/7/1865, Henry, IL d: 10/28/1907, St. Louis, MO BL/TR, 5'8" Deb: 6/12/1885																										
1885	Chi-N	7	2	.778	9	9	8	0	0	78^{2}	91	54	30	5	....	28	36	1.513	3.43	88	....	.277	3	.083	-6	4	-0.9
1886	Phi-a	5	15	.250	20	19	19	0	0	172^{2}	196	143	87	4	8	65	68	1.512	4.53	77	....	.273	3	.044	-16	5	-2.1
	Lou-a	0	4	.000	4	4	4	0	0	32	53	43	19	1	1	16	14	2.156	5.34	68	....	.354	1	.077	-7	0	-0.7
	Yr.	5	19	.208	24	23	23	0	0	204^{2}	249	186	106	5	9	81	82	**1.612**	4.66	75	....	.287	4	.049	-22	5	-2.8
Total	**2**	**12**	**21**	**.364**	**33**	**32**	**31**	**0**	**0**	**283^{1}**	**340**	**240**	**136**	**10**	**9**	**109**	**118**	**1.585**	**4.32**	**79**	**....**	**.284**	**7**	**.060**	**-28**	**9**	**-3.7**

YEAR	TM-L	W	L	PCT	G	GS	CG	SH	SV	IP	H	R	ER	HR	HB	BB	SO	RAT	ERA	ERA+	CERA	OAV	BH	AVG	PR+	WS	TPW
• KENNEDY, Vern	Lloyd Vernon Kennedy b: 3/20/1907, Kansas City, MO d: 1/28/1993, Mendon, MO BL/TR, 6', 175 lbs. Deb: 9/18/1934																										
1934	Chi-A	0	2	.000	3	3	1	0	0	19^1	21	8	8	1	0	9	7	1.552	3.72	127	4.71	.300	2	.286	3	2	0.3
1935	Chi-A	11	11	.500	31	25	16	2	1	211^2	211	110	92	17	4	95	65	1.446	3.91	118	4.12	.262	18	.247	15	16	1.4
1936	Chi-A★	21	9	.700	35	34	20	1	0	274^1	282	167	141	13	3	147	99	1.564	4.63	112	4.32	.268	32	.283	14	20	1.7
1937	Chi-A	14	13	.519	32	30	15	1	0	221	238	150	125	16	3	124	114	1.638	5.09	90	4.83	.273	20	.230	-17	10	-1.4
1938	Det-A★	12	9	.571	33	26	11	0	2	190^1	215	123	107	13	1	113	53	1.723	5.06	99	5.22	.287	23	.291	-3	13	0.0
1939	Det-A	0	3	.000	4	4	1	0	0	21	25	15	15	4	1	9	9	1.619	6.43	76	6.14	.301	2	.286	-4	0	-0.3
	StL-A	9	17	.346	33	27	12	1	0	191^2	229	130	122	18	1	115	55	1.795	5.73	85	5.79	.297	10	.149	-14	6	-1.5
	Yr.	9	20	.310	37	31	13	1	0	212^2	254	145	137	22	2	124	64	1.777	5.80	84	5.82	.297	12	.162	-17	6	-1.8
1940	StL-A	12	17	.414	34	32	18	0	0	222^1	263	149	138	18	3	122	70	1.732	5.59	82	5.55	.298	25	.298	-23	11	-1.5
1941	StL-A	2	4	.333	6	6	2	0	0	45	44	27	22	5	0	27	6	1.578	4.40	98	4.76	.259	6	.400	0	3	0.2
	Was-A	1	7	.125	17	7	2	0	0	66^1	77	49	42	5	2	39	22	1.749	5.70	71	5.58	.297	3	.143	-11	0	-1.2
	Yr.	3	11	.214	23	13	4	0	0	111^1	121	76	64	10	2	66	28	1.680	5.17	80	5.25	.282	9	.250	-11	3	-0.9
1942	Cle-A	4	8	.333	28	12	4	0	1	108	99	57	49	1	1	50	37	1.380	4.08	84	3.15	.244	6	.200	-9	4	-0.9
1943	Cle-A	10	7	.588	28	17	8	1	0	146^2	130	47	40	4	2	59	63	1.289	2.45	127	3.02	.242	12	.231	7	10	0.9
1944	Cle-A	2	5	.286	12	10	2	0	0	59	66	36	33	0	0	37	17	1.746	5.03	66	4.69	.289	2	.087	-12	0	-1.5
	Phi-N	1	5	.167	12	7	3	0	0	55^1	60	31	26	3	0	20	23	1.446	4.23	85	3.91	.269	6	.286	-4	2	-0.3
1945	Phi-N	0	3	.000	12	3	0	0	0	36	43	29	22	2	0	14	13	1.583	5.50	70	4.68	.297	2	.182	-6	0	-0.6
	Cin-N	5	12	.294	24	20	11	1	1	157^2	170	74	70	10	3	69	38	1.516	4.00	94	4.39	.280	12	.226	-4	8	-0.2
	Yr.	5	15	.250	36	23	11	1	1	193^2	213	103	92	12	3	83	51	1.528	4.28	88	4.45	.283	14	.219	-10	8	-0.8
Total	12	104	132	.441	344	263	126	7	5	2025^2	2173	1202	1052	130	24	1049	691	1.591	4.67	94	4.64	.277	181	.244	-67	105	-4.6
• KENNEY, Art	Arthur Joseph Kenney b: 4/29/1916, Milford, MA BL/TL, 6', 175 lbs. Deb: 7/1/1938																										
1938	Bos-N	0	0	....	2	0	0	0	0	2^1	3	4	4	0	0	8	2	4.714	15.43	22	16.30	.300	0	....	-3	0	-0.3
• KENT, Ed	Edward C. Kent b: 1859, New York, NY BR/TR, 5'6.5", 152 lbs. Deb: 8/14/1884																										
1884	Tol-a	0	1	.000	1	1	1	0	0	9	14	11	6	0	1	3	4	1.889	6.00	57	....	.337	0	.000	-3	0	-0.3
• KENT, Maury	Maurice Allen Kent b: 9/17/1885, Marshalltown, IA d: 4/19/1966, Iowa City, IA BR/TR, 6', 168 lbs. Deb: 4/15/1912																										
1912	Bro-N	5	5	.500	20	9	2	1	0	93	107	74	50	3	1	46	24	1.645	4.84	69	4.68	.296	8	.229	-14	1	-1.3
1913	Bro-N	0	0	....	3	0	0	0	0	7^1	5	2	2	0	0	3	1	1.091	2.45	134	1.81	.192	0	.000	1	1	0.0
Total	2	5	5	.500	23	9	2	1	0	100^1	112	76	52	3	1	49	25	1.605	4.66	71	4.47	.289	8	.211	-14	2	-1.3
• KENT, Steve	Steven Patrick Kent b: 10/3/1978, Frankfurt, Germany BB/TL, 5'11", 170 lbs. Deb: 4/4/2002																										
2002	TB-A	0	2	.000	34	0	0	0	1	57^1	67	41	36	6	3	38	41	1.831	5.65	79	6.45	.294	0	....	-9	1	-0.8
• KEOUGH, Matt	Matthew Lon Keough b: 7/3/1955, Pomona, CA BR/TR, 6'3", 190 lbs. Deb: 9/3/1977																										
1977	Oak-A	1	3	.250	7	6	0	0	0	42^2	39	25	23	4	1	22	23	1.430	4.85	83	4.17	.247	0	....	-3	1	-0.3
1978	Oak-A★	8	15	.348	32	32	6	0	0	197^1	178	90	71	9	4	85	108	1.333	3.24	112	3.36	.241	0	....	12	12	1.3
1979	Oak-A	2	17	.105	30	28	7	1	0	176^2	220	115	99	18	7	78	95	**1.687**	5.04	80	5.97	.315	0	....	-15	3	-1.4
1980	Oak-A	16	13	.552	34	32	20	2	0	250	218	94	81	24	5	94	121	1.248	2.92	129	3.34	.236	0	....	21	18	2.1
1981*	Oak-A	10	6	.625	19	19	10	2	0	140^1	125	56	53	11	0	45	60	1.211	3.40	102	3.05	.239	0	....	-0	9	0.0
1982	Oak-A	11	18	.379	34	34	10	2	0	209^1	233	144	133	38	5	101	75	1.596	5.72	68	5.79	.284	0	....	-43	2	-4.3
1983	Oak-A	2	3	.400	14	4	0	0	0	44	50	29	27	7	0	31	28	1.841	5.52	70	6.52	.284	0	....	-9	1	-0.8
	NY-A	3	4	.429	12	12	0	0	0	55^2	59	42	32	12	2	20	26	1.419	5.17	75	5.16	.266	0	....	-8	0	-0.8
	Yr.	5	7	.417	26	16	0	0	0	99^2	109	71	59	19	2	51	54	1.605	5.33	73	5.76	.274	0	....	-16	1	-1.6
1985	StL-N	0	1	.000	4	1	0	0	0	10	10	5	5	0	1	4	10	1.400	4.50	78	3.65	.278	0	.000	-1	0	-0.2
1986	Chi-N	2	2	.500	19	2	0	0	0	29	36	17	16	4	1	12	19	1.655	4.97	81	6.06	.316	2	.400	-2	1	-0.2
	Hou-N	3	2	.600	10	5	0	0	0	35	22	14	12	5	1	18	25	1.143	3.09	117	2.85	.180	4	.364	2	3	0.3
	Yr.	5	4	.556	29	7	0	0	0	64	58	31	28	9	2	30	44	1.375	3.94	97	4.31	.246	6	.375	-1	4	0.2
Total	9	58	84	.408	215	175	53	7	0	1190	1190	631	552	132	27	510	590	1.429	4.17	92	4.42	.262	6	.333	-46	50	-4.3
• KEPSHIRE, Kurt	Kurt David Kepshire b: 7/3/1959, Bridgeport, CT BL/TR, 6'1", 180 lbs. Deb: 7/4/1984																										
1984	StL-N	6	5	.545	17	16	2	2	0	109	100	47	40	7	0	44	71	1.321	3.30	105	3.41	.249	2	.056	0	6	-0.2
1985	StL-N	10	9	.526	32	29	0	0	0	153^1	155	89	81	16	0	71	67	1.474	4.75	74	4.39	.264	6	.118	-24	2	-2.6
1986	StL-N	0	1	.000	2	1	0	0	0	8	8	4	4	2	0	4	6	1.500	4.50	81	5.64	.258	0	.000	-1	0	-0.1
Total	3	16	15	.516	51	46	2	2	0	270^1	263	140	125	25	0	119	144	1.413	4.16	84	4.03	.258	8	.091	-25	8	-2.9
• KERFELD, Charlie	Charles Patrick Kerfeld b: 9/28/1963, Knob Noster, MO BR/TR, 6'6", 225 lbs. Deb: 7/27/1985																										
1985	Hou-N	4	2	.667	11	6	0	0	0	44^1	44	22	20	2	0	25	30	1.556	4.06	85	4.30	.268	0	.000	-3	2	-0.5
1986*	Hou-N	11	2	.846	61	0	0	0	7	93^2	71	32	28	5	2	42	77	1.206	2.69	134	2.68	.213	1	.111	9	12	1.0
1987	Hou-N	0	2	.000	21	0	0	0	0	29^2	34	22	22	3	1	21	17	1.854	6.67	59	6.45	.309	0	.000	-9	0	-0.9
1990	Hou-N	0	2	.000	5	0	0	0	0	3^1	9	6	6	0	0	6	4	4.500	16.20	23	20.26	.529	0	....	-5	0	-0.5
	Atl-N	3	1	.750	25	0	0	0	2	30^2	31	22	19	2	0	23	27	1.761	5.58	72	5.06	.270	0	....	-5	1	-0.5
	Yr.	3	3	.500	30	0	0	0	2	34	40	28	25	2	0	29	31	2.029	6.62	60	6.55	.303	0	....	-9	1	-0.9
Total	4	18	9	.667	123	6	0	0	9	201^2	189	104	95	12	3	117	155	1.517	4.24	88	4.24	.256	1	.038	-12	15	-1.4
• KERIAZAKOS, Gus	Constantine Nicholas Keriazakos b: 7/28/1931, West Orange, NJ d: 5/4/1996, Hilton Head, SC BR/TR, 6'3", 187 lbs. Deb: 10/1/1950																										
1950	Chi-A	0	1	.000	1	1	0	0	0	2^1	7	5	5	0	0	5	1	5.143	19.29	23	24.27	.500	1	1.000	-4	0	-0.3
1954	Was-A	2	3	.400	22	3	2	0	0	59^2	59	29	25	4	0	30	33	1.492	3.77	94	4.03	.262	1	.067	-0	2	-0.1
1955	KC-A	0	1	.000	5	1	0	0	0	11^2	15	16	16	4	0	7	8	1.886	12.34	34	9.01	.333	0	.000	-11	0	-1.1
Total	3	2	5	.286	28	5	2	0	0	73^2	81	50	46	8	0	42	42	1.670	5.62	68	5.46	.285	2	.105	-15	2	-1.6
• KERKSIECK, Bill	Wayman William Kerksieck b: 12/6/1913, Ulm, AR d: 3/11/1970, Stuttgart, AR BR/TR, 6'1", 183 lbs. Deb: 6/21/1939																										
1939	Phi-N	0	2	.000	23	2	1	0	0	62^2	81	52	50	13	0	32	13	1.803	7.18	55	7.13	.328	1	.083	-23	0	-2.3
• KERN, Jim	James Lester Kern b: 3/15/1949, Gladwin, MI BR/TR, 6'5", 205 lbs. Deb: 9/6/1974																										
1974	Cle-A	0	1	.000	4	3	1	0	0	15^1	16	9	8	1	0	14	11	1.957	4.70	77	5.83	.262	0	....	-2	0	-0.2
1975	Cle-A	1	2	.333	13	7	0	0	0	71^2	60	31	30	5	5	45	55	1.465	3.77	100	4.13	.233	0	....	-0	4	0.0
1976	Cle-A	10	7	.588	50	2	0	0	15	117^2	91	38	31	2	5	50	111	1.198	2.37	147	2.54	.222	0	....	14	14	1.5
1977	Cle-A★	8	10	.444	60	0	0	0	18	92	85	39	35	3	6	47	91	1.435	3.42	115	3.82	.260	0	....	5	10	0.5
1978	Cle-A★	10	10	.500	58	0	0	0	13	99^1	77	36	34	4	3	58	95	1.359	3.08	121	3.16	.224	0	.000	8	10	0.8
1979	Tex-A★	13	5	.722	71	0	0	0	29	143	99	35	25	5	2	62	136	1.126	1.57	263	2.20	.199	0	....	39	25	3.8
1980	Tex-A	3	11	.214	38	1	0	0	2	63^1	65	38	34	4	2	45	40	1.737	4.83	81	5.00	.279	0	....	-6	2	-0.6
1981	Tex-A	1	2	.333	23	0	0	0	6	30	21	10	9	0	1	22	20	1.433	2.70	128	2.93	.204	0	....	2	3	0.2
1982	Cin-N	3	5	.375	50	0	0	0	2	76	61	27	24	3	2	48	43	1.434	2.84	130	3.19	.222	0	.000	7	6	0.7
	Chi-A	2	1	.667	13	1	0	0	3	28	20	16	16	3	0	12	23	1.143	5.14	78	2.78	.204	0	....	-3	2	-0.3
1983	Chi-A	0	0	....	1	0	0	0	0	0^2	1	1	0	0	0	0	0	1.500	0.00	....	4.47	.333	0	....	0	0	0.0
1984	Phi-N	0	1	.000	8	0	0	0	0	13^1	20	16	15	3	0	10	8	2.250	10.13	36	9.48	.339	0	.000	-9	0	-1.0
	Mil-A	1	0	1.000	6	0	0	0	0	4^2	6	0	0	0	0	3	4	1.929	0.00	....	5.77	.300	0	....	2	1	0.2
1985	Mil-A	0	1	.000	5	0	0	0	0	11	14	8	8	1	0	5	3	1.727	6.55	64	5.76	.318	0	....	-3	0	-0.3
1986	Cle-A	1	1	.500	16	0	0	0	0	27^1	34	28	24	1	3	23	11	2.085	7.90	52	7.09	.298	0	....	-11	0	-1.1
Total	13	53	57	.482	416	14	1	0	88	793^1	670	332	293	35	29	444	651	1.404	3.32	115	3.53	.235	0	.000	43	77	4.3
• KERR, Dickie	Richard Henry Kerr b: 7/3/1893, St. Louis, MO d: 5/4/1963, Houston, TX BL/TL, 5'7", 155 lbs. Deb: 4/25/1919																										
1919*	Chi-A	13	7	.650	39	17	10	1	0	212^1	208	78	68	2	2	64	79	1.281	2.88	110	3.03	.259	17	.250	2	16	0.7
1920	Chi-A	21	9	.700	45	27	19	3	**5**	253^2	266	116	95	7	4	72	72	1.332	3.37	112	3.51	.278	14	.156	8	20	0.4
1921	Chi-A	19	17	.528	44	37	25	3	1	308^2	357	182	162	12	11	96	80	1.468	4.72	90	4.20	.295	25	.238	-18	19	-1.2
1925	Chi-A	0	1	.000	12	2	0	0	0	36^2	45	23	21	3	1	18	4	1.718	5.15	81	5.60	.304	4	.333	-4	1	-0.3
Total	4	53	34	.609	140	83	54	7	6	811^1	876	399	346	24	18	250	235	1.388	3.84	100	3.74	.281	60	.218	-12	56	-0.3

YEAR TM-L	W	L	PCT	G	GS	CG	SH	SV	IP	H	R	ER	HR	HB	BB	SO	RAT	ERA	ERA+	CERA	OAV	BH	AVG	PR+	WS	TPW
• KERRIGAN, Joe	Joseph Thomas Kerrigan b: 11/30/1954, Philadelphia, PA BR/TR, 6'5", 205 lbs. Deb: 7/9/1976 M/C																									
1976 Mon-N	2	6	.250	38	0	0	0	1	56^{2}	63	27	24	3	2	23	22	1.518	3.81	97	4.53	.289	0	.000	-0	3	-0.1
1977 Mon-N	3	5	.375	66	0	0	0	11	89^{1}	80	37	32	4	3	33	43	1.265	3.22	118	3.07	.241	0	.000	5	9	0.4
1978 Bal-A	3	1	.750	26	2	0	0	3	71^{2}	75	44	38	10	2	36	41	1.549	4.77	73	5.08	.273	0	....	-11	1	-1.1
1980 Bal-A	0	0	....	1	0	0	0	0	2^{1}	3	1	1	0	0	0	1	1.286	3.86	102	2.96	.273	0	....	-0	0	0.0
Total 4	8	12	.400	131	2	0	0	15	220	221	109	95	17	7	92	107	1.423	3.89	94	4.10	.264	0	.000	-6	13	-0.8
• KERSHNER, Jason	Jason Ashley Kershner b: 12/19/1976, Scottsdale, AZ BL/TL, 6'2", 165 lbs. Deb: 7/25/2002																									
2002 SD-N	0	1	.000	15	0	0	0	0	18^{2}	15	14	12	2	2	10	11	1.339	5.79	65	4.00	.217	0	....	-4	0	-0.4
Tor-A	0	0	....	10	0	0	0	1	5^{1}	5	2	1	1	0	4	7	1.688	1.69	273	5.11	.227	0	....	2	1	0.2
2003 Tor-A	3	3	.500	40	0	0	0	0	54	43	21	19	5	2	15	32	1.074	3.17	145	2.56	.217	0	....	10	5	0.9
Total 2	3	4	.429	65	0	0	0	1	78	63	37	32	8	4	29	50	1.179	3.69	115	3.08	.218	0	....	7	6	0.7
• KESTER, Rick	Richard Lee Kester b: 7/7/1946, Iola, KS BR/TR, 6', 190 lbs. Deb: 8/18/1968																									
1968 Atl-N	0	0	....	5	0	0	0	0	6^{1}	8	4	4	0	0	3	9	1.737	5.68	53	5.16	.308	0	....	-2	0	-0.2
1969 Atl-N	0	0	....	1	0	0	0	0	2	5	3	3	1	0	0	2	2.500	13.50	27	15.86	.455	0	....	-2	0	-0.2
1970 Atl-N	0	0	....	15	0	0	0	0	32^{1}	36	24	20	3	0	19	20	1.701	5.57	77	5.42	.283	0	.000	-4	0	-0.5
Total 3	0	0	....	21	0	0	0	0	40^{2}	49	31	27	4	0	22	31	1.746	5.98	66	5.89	.299	0	.000	-8	0	-0.9
• KETCHUM, Gus	Augustus Franklin Ketchum b: 3/21/1897, Royce City, TX d: 9/6/1980, Oklahoma City, OK BR/TR, 5'9.5", 170 lbs. Deb: 8/7/1922																									
1922 Phi-A	0	1	.000	6	0	0	0	0	16	19	12	10	2	1	8	4	1.688	5.63	75	5.91	.302	0	.000	-2	0	-0.3
• KEUPPER, Henry	Henry J. Keupper b: 6/24/1887, Staunton, IL d: 8/14/1960, Marion, IL BL/TL, 6'1", 185 lbs. Deb: 4/19/1914																									
1914 StL-F	8	20	.286	42	25	12	1	0	213	256	132	101	3	4	49	70	1.432	4.27	81	3.90	.291	17	.250	-15	7	-1.3
• KEY, Jimmy	James Edward Key b: 4/22/1961, Huntsville, AL BR/TL, 6'1", 190 lbs. Deb: 4/6/1984																									
1984 Tor-A	4	5	.444	63	0	0	0	10	62	70	37	32	8	1	32	44	1.645	4.65	88	5.30	.286	0	....	-4	3	-0.4
1985* Tor-A★	14	6	.700	35	32	3	0	0	212^{2}	188	77	71	22	2	50	85	1.119	3.00	140	2.91	.237	0	....	25	19	2.5
1986 Tor-A	14	11	.560	36	35	4	2	0	232	222	98	92	24	3	74	141	1.276	3.57	118	3.66	.256	0	....	17	15	1.7
1987 Tor-A	17	8	.680	36	36	8	1	0	261	210	93	80	24	2	66	161	1.057	**2.76**	**163**	**2.48**	**.221**	0	....	47	23	4.4
1988 Tor-A	12	5	.706	21	21	2	2	0	131^{1}	127	55	48	13	5	30	65	1.195	3.29	119	3.31	.250	0	....	9	10	0.9
1989* Tor-A	13	14	.481	33	33	5	1	0	216	226	99	93	18	3	27	118	1.171	3.88	93	3.20	.270	0	....	-7	10	-0.7
1990 Tor-A	13	7	.650	27	27	0	0	0	154^{2}	169	79	73	20	1	22	88	1.235	4.25	96	3.82	.281	0	....	-2	8	-0.2
1991* Tor-A★	16	12	.571	33	33	2	2	0	209^{1}	207	84	71	12	3	44	125	1.199	3.05	138	2.99	.254	0	....	28	17	2.8
1992* Tor-A	13	13	.500	33	33	4	2	0	216^{2}	205	88	85	24	4	59	117	1.218	3.53	116	3.43	.248	0	....	14	14	1.4
1993 NY-A★	18	6	.750	34	34	4	2	0	236^{2}	219	84	79	26	1	43	173	1.107	3.00	138	2.94	.246	0	....	30	21	2.9
1994 NY-A★	**17**	4	.810	25	**25**	1	0	0	168	177	68	61	10	3	52	97	1.363	3.27	140	3.87	.273	0	....	21	15	2.0
1995 NY-A	1	2	.333	5	5	0	0	0	30^{1}	40	20	19	3	0	6	14	1.516	5.64	82	5.02	.323	0	....	-4	1	-0.3
1996* NY-A	12	11	.522	30	30	0	0	0	169^{1}	171	93	88	21	2	58	116	1.352	4.68	106	4.17	.266	0	....	8	10	0.7
1997* Bal-A	16	10	.615	34	34	1	1	0	212^{1}	210	90	81	24	5	82	141	1.375	3.43	128	4.20	.261	0	.000	22	17	2.1
1998 Bal-A	6	3	.667	25	11	0	0	0	79^{1}	77	39	37	5	3	23	53	1.261	4.20	108	3.47	.258	0	....	4	5	0.4
Total 15	186	117	.614	470	389	34	13	10	2591^{2}	2518	1104	1010	254	38	668	1538	1.229	3.51	121	3.44	.255	0	.000	208	188	20.1
• KEYSER, Brian	Brian Lee Keyser b: 10/31/1966, Castro Valley, CA BR/TR, 6'1", 180 lbs. Deb: 6/2/1995																									
1995 Chi-A	5	6	.455	23	10	0	0	0	92^{1}	114	53	51	10	2	27	48	1.527	4.97	90	5.22	.306	0	....	-4	3	-0.4
1996 Chi-A	1	2	.333	28	0	0	0	1	59^{2}	78	35	33	3	0	28	19	1.777	4.98	95	5.58	.328	0	....	-1	2	-0.1
Total 2	6	8	.429	51	10	0	0	1	152	192	88	84	13	2	55	67	1.625	4.97	92	5.36	.314	0	....	-5	5	-0.5
• KIDA, Masao	Masao Kida b: 9/12/1968, Tokyo, Japan BR/TR, 6'2", 210 lbs. Deb: 4/5/1999																									
1999 Det-A	1	0	1.000	49	0	0	0	1	64^{2}	73	48	45	6	4	30	50	1.593	6.26	79	5.23	.289	0	....	-10	2	-0.9
2000 Det-A	0	0	....	2	0	0	0	0	2^{2}	5	3	3	1	0	0	0	1.875	10.13	48	9.86	.385	0	....	-2	0	-0.1
2003 LA-N	0	1	.000	3	2	0	0	0	12	15	5	4	0	0	3	8	1.500	3.00	134	4.14	.300	1	.250	1	1	0.1
Total 3	1	1	.500	54	2	0	0	1	79^{1}	93	56	52	7	4	33	58	1.588	5.90	82	5.22	.294	1	.250	-10	3	-0.9
• KIECKER, Dana	Dana Ervin Kiecker b: 2/25/1961, Sleepy Eye, MN BR/TR, 6'3", 180 lbs. Deb: 4/12/1990																									
1990* Bos-A	8	9	.471	32	25	0	0	0	152	145	74	67	7	9	54	93	1.309	3.97	103	3.54	.253	0	....	5	9	0.5
1991 Bos-A	2	3	.400	18	5	0	0	0	40^{1}	56	34	33	6	2	23	21	1.959	7.36	58	7.73	.344	0	....	-14	0	-1.4
Total 2	10	12	.455	50	30	0	0	0	192^{1}	201	108	100	13	11	77	114	1.445	4.68	89	4.42	.273	0	....	-9	9	-0.9
• KIEFER, Joe	Joseph William "Harlem Joe,Smoke" Kiefer b: 7/19/1899, West Leyden, NY d: 7/5/1975, Utica, NY BR/TR, 5'11", 190 lbs. Deb: 10/1/1920																									
1920 Chi-A	0	1	.000	2	1	0	0	0	4^{2}	7	8	8	0	1	5	1	2.571	15.43	24	9.35	.333	0	.000	-6	0	-0.6
1925 Bos-A	0	2	.000	2	2	0	0	0	15	20	12	10	0	1	9	4	1.933	6.00	76	5.94	.351	0	.000	-2	0	-0.3
1926 Bos-A	0	2	.000	11	1	0	0	0	30	29	19	16	2	2	16	4	1.500	4.80	85	4.26	.266	1	.143	-2	1	-0.2
Total 3	0	5	.000	15	4	0	0	0	49^{2}	56	39	34	2	4	30	9	1.732	6.16	67	5.25	.299	1	.077	-10	1	-1.1
• KIEFER, Mark	Mark Andrew Kiefer b: 11/13/1968, Orange, CA BR/TR, 6'4", 175 lbs. Deb: 9/20/1993																									
1993 Mil-A	0	0	....	6	0	0	0	1	9^{1}	3	0	0	0	1	5	7	.857	0.00	....	1.18	.097	0	....	4	2	0.4
1994 Mil-A	1	0	1.000	7	0	0	0	0	10^{2}	15	12	10	4	0	8	8	2.156	8.44	60	11.01	.357	0	....	-4	0	-0.4
1995 Mil-A	4	1	.800	24	0	0	0	0	49^{2}	37	20	19	6	0	27	41	1.289	3.44	145	3.32	.203	0	....	8	5	0.7
1996 Mil-A	0	0	....	7	0	0	0	0	10	15	9	9	1	0	5	5	2.000	8.10	64	7.48	.366	0	....	-3	0	-0.3
Total 4	5	1	.833	44	0	0	0	1	79^{2}	70	41	38	11	1	45	61	1.444	4.29	117	4.62	.236	0	....	4	7	0.4
• KIELY, John	John Francis Kiely b: 10/4/1964, Boston, MA BR/TR, 6'3", 210 lbs. Deb: 7/26/1991																									
1991 Det-A	0	1	.000	7	0	0	0	0	6^{2}	13	11	11	0	1	9	1	3.300	14.85	28	13.49	.448	0	....	-8	0	-0.8
1992 Det-A	4	2	.667	39	0	0	0	0	55	44	14	13	2	0	28	18	1.309	2.13	186	2.91	.224	0	....	12	5	1.2
1993 Det-A	0	2	.000	8	0	0	0	0	11^{2}	13	11	10	2	1	13	5	2.229	7.71	56	8.07	.295	0	....	-4	0	-0.4
Total 3	4	5	.444	54	0	0	0	0	73^{1}	70	36	34	4	2	50	24	1.636	4.17	99	4.69	.260	0	....	-1	5	0.0
• KIELY, Leo	Leo Patrick "Kiki" Kiely b: 11/30/1929, Hoboken, NJ d: 1/18/1984, Montclair, NJ BL/TL, 6'2", 180 lbs. Deb: 6/27/1951																									
1951 Bos-A	7	7	.500	17	16	4	0	0	113^{1}	106	48	42	9	2	39	46	1.279	3.34	134	3.38	.251	5	.143	14	9	1.3
1954 Bos-A	5	8	.385	28	19	4	1	0	131	153	74	51	12	1	58	59	1.611	3.50	117	5.08	.295	9	.180	10	6	1.1
1955 Bos-A	3	3	.500	33	4	0	0	6	90	91	31	28	5	0	37	36	1.422	2.80	153	3.83	.269	5	.192	16	9	1.6
1956 Bos-A	2	2	.500	23	0	0	0	3	31^{1}	47	25	18	1	2	14	9	1.947	5.17	89	6.57	.362	1	.167	-2	1	-0.2
1958 Bos-A	5	2	.714	47	0	0	0	12	81	77	31	27	3	2	18	26	1.173	3.00	134	2.78	.254	0	.000	10	10	0.9
1959 Bos-A	3	3	.500	41	0	0	0	7	55^{2}	67	26	26	8	1	18	30	1.527	4.20	97	5.21	.299	0	.000	-1	4	-0.2
1960 KC-A	1	2	.333	20	0	0	0	1	20^{2}	21	4	4	1	1	5	6	1.258	1.74	229	3.44	.266	0	.000	5	3	0.6
Total 7	26	27	.491	209	39	8	1	29	523	562	239	196	39	9	189	212	1.436	3.37	125	4.18	.279	20	.144	53	42	5.1
• KIESCHNICK, Brooks	Michael Brooks Kieschnick b: 6/6/1972, Robstown, TX BL/TR, 6'4", 225 lbs. Deb: 4/3/1996 ♦																									
2003 Mil-N	1	1	.500	42	0	0	0	0	53	66	32	31	5	6	13	39	1.491	5.26	81	5.07	.299	21	.300	-5	3	0.4
• KILE, Darryl	Darryl Andrew Kile b: 12/2/1968, Garden Grove, CA d: 6/22/2002, Chicago, IL BR/TR, 6'5", 185 lbs. Deb: 4/8/1991																									
1991 Hou-N	7	11	.389	37	22	0	0	0	153^{2}	144	81	63	16	6	84	100	1.484	3.69	95	4.37	.246	0	.000	-4	5	-0.7
1992 Hou-N	5	10	.333	22	22	2	0	0	125^{1}	124	61	55	8	4	63	90	1.492	3.95	85	4.23	.261	5	.156	-8	3	-0.8
1993 Hou-N★	15	8	.652	32	26	4	2	0	171^{2}	152	73	67	12	15	69	141	1.287	3.51	110	3.59	.239	5	.094	5	11	0.5
1994 Hou-N	9	6	.600	24	24	0	0	0	147^{2}	153	84	75	13	9	82	105	1.591	4.57	87	5.04	.275	7	.149	-11	5	-1.0
1995 Hou-N	4	12	.250	25	21	0	0	0	127	114	81	70	5	12	73	113	1.472	4.96	78	4.04	.240	4	.111	-13	1	-1.3
1996 Hou-N	12	11	.522	35	33	4	0	0	219	233	113	102	16	16	97	219	1.507	4.19	92	4.66	.276	10	.137	-4	10	-0.4
1997* Hou-N★	19	7	.731	34	34	6	4	0	255^{2}	208	87	73	19	10	94	205	1.181	2.57	156	2.93	.225	11	.124	38	21	3.7
1998 Col-N	13	17	.433	36	**35**	4	1	0	230^{1}	257	141	133	28	7	96	158	1.533	5.20	100	5.11	.287	18	.254	-1	13	0.2
1999 Col-N	8	13	.381	32	32	1	0	0	190^{2}	225	150	140	33	6	109	116	**1.752**	6.61	88	6.55	.298	7	.135	-16	6	-1.6

YEAR	TM-L	W	L	PCT	G	GS	CG	SH	SV	IP	H	R	ER	HR	HB	BB	SO	RAT	ERA	ERA+	CERA	OAV	BH	AVG	PR+	WS	TPW
2000*	StL-N★	20	9	.690	34	34	5	1	0	232^1	215	109	101	33	13	58	192	1.175	3.91	118	3.59	.247	9	.123	15	17	1.5
2001*	StL-N	16	11	.593	34	34	2	1	0	227^1	228	83	78	22	11	65	179	1.289	3.09	138	3.84	.265	9	.127	25	18	2.5
2002	StL-N	5	4	.556	14	14	0	0	0	84^2	82	36	35	9	8	28	50	1.299	3.72	106	4.03	.257	2	.091	1	4	0.0
Total	12	133	119	.528	359	331	28	9	0	2165^1	2135	1099	992	214	117	918	1668	1.410	4.12	104	4.30	.260	87	.132	27	114	2.6

• KILGUS, Paul Paul Nelson Kilgus b: 2/2/1962, Bowling Green, KY BL/TL, 6'1", 185 lbs. Deb: 6/7/1987

YEAR	TM-L	W	L	PCT	G	GS	CG	SH	SV	IP	H	R	ER	HR	HB	BB	SO	RAT	ERA	ERA+	CERA	OAV	BH	AVG	PR+	WS	TPW
1987	Tex-A	2	7	.222	25	12	0	0	0	89^1	95	45	41	14	2	31	42	1.410	4.13	108	4.72	.271	0	....	4	5	0.4
1988	Tex-A	12	15	.444	32	32	5	3	0	203^1	190	105	94	18	10	71	88	1.284	4.16	98	3.58	.243	0	....	-3	10	-0.3
1989*	Chi-N	6	10	.375	35	23	0	0	2	145^2	164	90	71	9	5	49	61	1.462	4.39	86	4.31	.283	3	.073	-10	3	-1.3
1990	Tor-A	0	0	....	11	0	0	0	0	16^1	19	11	11	2	1	7	7	1.592	6.06	67	5.48	.306	0	....	-4	0	-0.4
1991	Bal-A	0	2	.000	38	0	0	0	1	62	60	38	35	8	3	24	32	1.355	5.08	78	4.20	.256	0	....	-8	1	-0.8
1993	StL-N	1	0	1.000	22	1	0	0	1	28^2	18	2	2	1	1	8	21	.907	0.63	631	1.58	.180	1	.200	11	5	1.1
Total	6	21	34	.382	163	68	5	3	4	545^1	546	291	254	52	22	190	251	1.350	4.19	96	3.98	.259	4	.087	-9	24	-1.3

• KILKENNY, Mike Michael David Kilkenny b: 4/11/1945, Bradford, Canada BR/TL, 6'3.5", 175 lbs. Deb: 4/11/1969

YEAR	TM-L	W	L	PCT	G	GS	CG	SH	SV	IP	H	R	ER	HR	HB	BB	SO	RAT	ERA	ERA+	CERA	OAV	BH	AVG	PR+	WS	TPW
1969	Det-A	8	6	.571	39	15	6	4	2	128^1	99	54	48	13	4	63	97	1.262	3.37	111	3.28	.211	2	.054	5	9	0.2
1970	Det-A	7	6	.538	36	21	3	0	0	129	141	77	74	10	2	70	105	1.636	5.16	72	5.06	.279	3	.077	-17	3	-2.0
1971	Det-A	4	5	.444	30	11	2	0	1	86^1	83	52	48	8	2	44	47	1.471	5.00	72	4.18	.247	2	.083	-14	1	-1.6
1972	Det-A	0	0	....	1	0	0	0	0	1	1	1	1	1	0	0	0	1.000	9.00	35	7.45	.250	0	....	-1	0	-0.1
	Oak-A	0	0	....	1	0	0	0	0	1	0	0	0	0	0	0	0	.000	0.00	....	0.00	.000	0	....	0	0	0.0
	SD-N	0	0	....	5	0	0	0	0	4^1	7	4	4	1	0	3	5	2.308	8.31	40	10.22	.350	0	....	-2	0	-0.3
	Cle-A	4	1	.800	22	7	1	0	1	58	51	23	22	5	0	39	44	1.552	3.41	94	4.30	.237	1	.071	-2	4	-0.3
	Yr.	4	1	.800	24	7	1	0	1	60	52	24	23	6	0	39	44	1.517	3.45	93	4.28	.237	1	.071	-2	4	-0.4
1973	Cle-A	0	0	....	5	0	0	0	0	2	5	5	5	1	1	5	3	5.000	22.50	17	32.60	.455	0	....	-4	0	-0.4
Total	5	23	18	.561	139	54	12	4	4	410	387	216	202	39	9	224	301	1.490	4.43	82	4.39	.248	8	.070	-34	17	-4.5

• KILLEEN, Evans Evans Henry Killeen b: 2/27/1936, Brooklyn, NY BR/TR, 6', 190 lbs. Deb: 9/7/1959

YEAR	TM-L	W	L	PCT	G	GS	CG	SH	SV	IP	H	R	ER	HR	HB	BB	SO	RAT	ERA	ERA+	CERA	OAV	BH	AVG	PR+	WS	TPW
1959	KC-A	0	0	....	4	0	0	0	0	5^2	4	3	3	0	0	4	1	1.412	4.76	84	3.15	.211	0	....	-0	0	0.0

• KILLEEN, Henry Henry Killeen b: 5/1872, Troy, NY d: 10/16/1916, Waterbury, CT, 5'9", 150 lbs. Deb: 9/11/1891

YEAR	TM-L	W	L	PCT	G	GS	CG	SH	SV	IP	H	R	ER	HR	HB	BB	SO	RAT	ERA	ERA+	CERA	OAV	BH	AVG	PR+	WS	TPW
1891	Cle-N	0	1	.000	1	1	1	0	0	8^2	11	8	6	1	0	8	3	2.192	6.23	55	....	.298	0	.000	-3	0	-0.2

• KILLEN, Frank Frank Bissell "Lefty" Killen b: 11/30/1870, Pittsburgh, PA d: 12/3/1939, Pittsburgh, PA BL/TL, 6'1", 200 lbs. Deb: 8/27/1891 U

YEAR	TM-L	W	L	PCT	G	GS	CG	SH	SV	IP	H	R	ER	HR	HB	BB	SO	RAT	ERA	ERA+	CERA	OAV	BH	AVG	PR+	WS	TPW
1891	Mil-a	7	4	.636	11	11	11	2	0	96^2	73	42	18	1	3	51	38	1.283	1.68	262	....	.203	8	.229	30	11	2.7
1892	Was-N	29	26	.527	60	52	46	2	0	459^2	448	286	169	15	20	182	147	1.371	3.31	98	3.51	.245	37	.199	-2	28	0.9
1893	Pit-N	**36**	14	.720	55	48	38	2	0	415	401	235	168	12	15	140	99	1.304	3.64	125	3.22	.246	47	.275	30	**42**	3.7
1894	Pit-N	14	11	.560	28	28	20	1	0	204	261	148	102	3	5	86	62	1.701	4.50	116	5.09	.308	21	.263	17	15	1.3
1895	Pit-N	5	5	.500	13	11	6	0	0	95	113	77	58	2	1	57	25	1.789	5.49	82	5.22	.291	13	.342	-11	6	-0.5
1896	Pit-N	**30**	18	.625	**52**	**50**	**44**	**5**	0	**432^1**	476	244	164	7	14	119	134	1.376	3.41	123	3.61	.278	40	.231	36	32	3.9
1897	Pit-N	17	23	.425	42	41	**38**	1	0	337^1	417	246	167	4	8	76	99	1.461	4.46	93	4.11	.301	32	.248	-4	22	0.1
1898	Pit-N	10	11	.476	23	23	17	0	0	177^2	201	106	74	3	11	41	48	1.362	3.75	95	3.73	.283	17	.262	-4	11	-0.2
	Was-N	6	9	.400	17	16	15	0	0	128^1	149	80	51	4	2	29	43	1.387	3.58	102	3.82	.288	15	.273	4	7	0.7
	Yr.	16	20	.444	40	39	32	0	0	306	350	186	125	7	13	70	91	1.373	3.68	98	3.77	.285	32	.267	-0	18	0.6
1899	Was-N	0	2	.000	2	2	1	0	0	12	18	11	8	0	1	4	3	1.833	6.00	65	6.18	.346	1	.200	-2	0	-0.2
	Bos-N	7	5	.583	12	12	11	0	0	99^1	108	65	47	3	3	26	23	1.349	4.26	98	3.59	.277	7	.171	-5	5	-0.6
	Yr.	7	7	.500	14	14	12	0	0	111^1	126	76	55	3	4	30	26	1.401	4.45	93	3.87	.285	8	.174	-7	5	-0.9
1900	Chi-N	3	3	.500	6	6	6	0	0	54	65	31	28	1	2	11	4	1.407	4.67	77	3.95	.297	3	.150	-5	2	-0.6
Total	10	164	131	.556	321	300	253	13	0	2511^1	2730	1571	1054	55	85	822	725	1.414	3.78	107	3.68	.272	241	.241	84	181	11.3

• KILLIAN, Ed Edwin Henry "Twilight Ed" Killian b: 11/12/1876, Racine, WI d: 7/18/1928, Detroit, MI BL/TL, 5'11", 170 lbs. Deb: 8/25/1903

YEAR	TM-L	W	L	PCT	G	GS	CG	SH	SV	IP	H	R	ER	HR	HB	BB	SO	RAT	ERA	ERA+	CERA	OAV	BH	AVG	PR+	WS	TPW
1903	Cle-A	3	4	.429	9	8	7	3	0	61^2	61	24	17	1	4	13	18	1.200	2.48	115	3.01	.258	5	.179	2	4	0.1
1904	Det-A	15	20	.429	40	34	32	4	1	331^2	293	118	90	0	17	93	124	1.164	2.44	104	2.48	.238	18	.143	-0	18	-0.3
1905	Det-A	23	14	.622	39	37	33	**8**	0	313^1	263	108	79	0	13	102	110	1.165	2.27	120	2.38	.230	32	.271	12	29	2.1
1906	Det-A	10	6	.625	21	16	14	0	2	149^2	165	71	57	0	5	54	47	1.463	3.43	81	3.80	.283	9	.170	-11	9	-1.3
1907*	Det-A	25	13	.658	42	34	29	3	1	314	286	103	62	2	11	91	96	1.201	1.78	146	2.62	.245	39	.320	30	29	**4.5**
1908*	Det-A	12	9	.571	27	23	15	0	1	180^2	170	78	60	3	8	53	47	1.234	2.99	81	2.98	.252	10	.137	-8	8	-1.3
1909	Det-A	11	9	.550	25	19	14	3	1	173^1	150	45	33	1	6	49	54	1.148	1.71	147	2.46	.236	10	.161	15	15	1.6
1910	Det-A	4	3	.571	11	9	5	1	0	74	75	38	25	2	6	27	20	1.378	3.04	86	3.82	.268	4	.148	-3	3	-0.5
Total	8	103	78	.569	214	180	149	22	6	1598^1	1463	585	423	9	70	482	516	1.217	2.38	109	2.75	.246	127	.209	36	115	5.0

• KILLILAY, Jack John William Killilay b: 5/24/1887, Leavenworth, KS d: 10/21/1968, Tulsa, OK BR/TR, 5'11", 165 lbs. Deb: 5/13/1911

YEAR	TM-L	W	L	PCT	G	GS	CG	SH	SV	IP	H	R	ER	HR	HB	BB	SO	RAT	ERA	ERA+	CERA	OAV	BH	AVG	PR+	WS	TPW
1911	Bos-A	4	2	.667	14	7	1	0	0	61	65	26	24	0	10	36	28	1.656	3.54	92	5.37	.302	1	.042	-2	4	-0.4

• KILROY, Matt Matthew Aloysius "Matches" Kilroy b: 6/21/1866, Philadelphia, PA d: 3/2/1940, Philadelphia, PA BL/TL, 5'9", 175 lbs. Deb: 4/17/1886 U

YEAR	TM-L	W	L	PCT	G	GS	CG	SH	SV	IP	H	R	ER	HR	HB	BB	SO	RAT	ERA	ERA+	CERA	OAV	BH	AVG	PR+	WS	TPW
1886	Bal-a	29	34	.460	**68**	**68**	**66**	5	0	583	476	350	218	10	19	182	**513**	1.129	3.37	101	....	.213	38	.174	17	32	1.2
1887	Bal-a	**46**	19	.708	**69**	**69**	**66**	**6**	0	**589^1**	742	326	201	9	20	157	217	1.259	3.07	133	....	.297	90	.333	**82**	51	**7.4**
1888	Bal-a	17	21	.447	40	40	35	2	0	321	347	224	144	5	0	79	135	1.327	4.04	74	....	.266	26	.179	-32	13	-2.9
1889	Bal-a	29	25	.537	59	56	**55**	5	0	480^2	476	283	152	8	0	142	217	1.286	2.85	133	....	.251	57	.274	**61**	44	**6.4**
1890	Bos-P	9	15	.375	30	27	18	0	0	217^2	268	161	103	14	9	87	48	1.631	4.26	103	....	.290	20	.215	1	15	0.0
1891	Cin-a	1	4	.200	7	6	4	0	0	45^1	51	42	15	1	0	19	6	1.544	2.98	138	....	.275	3	.150	6	2	0.4
1892	Was-N	1	1	.500	4	3	2	0	0	26^1	20	11	7	0	0	15	1	1.329	2.39	136	2.61	.202	2	.200	3	2	0.2
1893	Lou-N	3	2	.600	5	5	5	1	0	35	57	41	35	2	0	23	4	2.286	9.00	49	8.50	.355	7	.438	-17	1	-1.2
1894	Lou-N	0	5	.000	8	7	3	0	0	37	46	34	16	2	0	20	11	1.784	3.89	131	5.56	.302	2	.118	5	1	0.2
1898	Chi-N	6	7	.462	13	11	10	0	0	100^1	119	67	48	2	11	30	18	1.485	4.31	83	4.46	.293	22	.229	-9	5	-0.8
Total	10	141	133	.515	303	292	264	19	0	2435^2	2602	1539	939	53	59	754	1170	1.313	3.47	106	0.42	.264	267	.244	116	166	11.2

• KILROY, Mike Michael Joseph Kilroy b: 11/4/1872, Philadelphia, PA d: 10/2/1960, Philadelphia, PA BR/TR, 5'11", 180 lbs. Deb: 9/1/1888

YEAR	TM-L	W	L	PCT	G	GS	CG	SH	SV	IP	H	R	ER	HR	HB	BB	SO	RAT	ERA	ERA+	CERA	OAV	BH	AVG	PR+	WS	TPW
1888	Bal-a	0	1	.000	1	1	1	0	0	9	12	9	8	1	0	5	1	1.889	8.00	37	....	.309	0	.000	-5	0	-0.5
1891	Phi-N	0	2	.000	3	1	0	0	0	10	15	14	11	1	2	4	3	1.900	9.90	34	....	.334	2	.400	-7	0	-0.6
Total	2	0	3	.000	4	2	1	0	0	19	27	23	19	2	2	9	4	1.895	9.00	36	....	.323	2	.222	-12	0	-1.1

• KIM, Byung-Hyun Byung-Hyun Kim b: 1/21/1979, Kwangju, South Korea BR/TR, 5'11", 177 lbs. Deb: 5/29/1999

YEAR	TM-L	W	L	PCT	G	GS	CG	SH	SV	IP	H	R	ER	HR	HB	BB	SO	RAT	ERA	ERA+	CERA	OAV	BH	AVG	PR+	WS	TPW
1999	Ari-N	1	2	.333	25	0	0	0	1	27^1	20	15	14	2	5	20	31	1.463	4.61	99	4.35	.211	0	.000	-0	2	0.0
2000	Ari-N	6	6	.500	61	1	0	0	14	70^2	52	39	35	9	9	46	111	1.387	4.46	105	4.04	.200	0	.000	2	8	0.2
2001*	Ari-N	5	6	.455	78	0	0	0	19	98	58	32	32	10	8	44	113	1.041	2.94	156	2.45	.173	1	.167	16	16	1.6
2002*	Ari-N★	8	3	.727	72	0	0	0	36	84	64	20	19	5	6	26	92	1.071	2.04	218	2.45	.208	1	.500	23	20	2.4
2003	Ari-N	1	5	.167	7	7	0	0	0	43	34	17	17	6	4	15	33	1.140	3.56	131	3.32	.214	2	.154	6	3	0.6
	*Bos-A	8	5	.615	49	5	0	0	16	79^1	70	38	28	6	8	18	69	1.109	3.18	144	2.87	.230	2	.286	14	11	1.4
Total	5	29	27	.518	292	13	0	0	86	402^1	298	161	145	38	40	169	449	1.161	3.24	142	3.03	.204	6	.188	61	60	6.0

• KIM, Sun-Woo Sun Woo Kim b: 9/4/1977, Inchon, South Korea BR/TR, 6'2", 180 lbs. Deb: 6/15/2001

YEAR	TM-L	W	L	PCT	G	GS	CG	SH	SV	IP	H	R	ER	HR	HB	BB	SO	RAT	ERA	ERA+	CERA	OAV	BH	AVG	PR+	WS	TPW
2001	Bos-A	0	2	.000	20	2	0	0	0	41^2	54	27	27	1	4	21	27	1.800	5.83	77	5.72	.312	0	....	-5	1	-0.5
2002	Bos-A	2	0	1.000	15	2	0	0	0	29	34	24	24	5	1	7	18	1.414	7.45	60	5.01	.288	0	....	-10	0	-1.0
	Mon-N	1	0	1.000	4	3	0	0	0	20^1	18	2	2	0	1	7	11	1.230	0.89	481	2.82	.250	2	.250	8	3	0.8
2003	Mon-N	0	1	.000	4	3	0	0	0	14	24	13	13	6	4	8	5	2.286	8.36	60	14.93	.407	0	.000	-5	0	-0.5
Total	3	3	3	.500	43	10	0	0	0	105	130	66	66	12	10	43	61	1.648	5.66	81	6.19	.308	2	.182	-13	4	-1.2

• KIMBALL, Newt Newell W. Kimball b: 3/27/1915, Logan, UT d: 3/22/2001, Las Vegas, NV BR/TR, 6'2.5", 190 lbs. Deb: 5/7/1937

YEAR	TM-L	W	L	PCT	G	GS	CG	SH	SV	IP	H	R	ER	HR	HB	BB	SO	RAT	ERA	ERA+	CERA	OAV	BH	AVG	PR+	WS	TPW
1937	Chi-N	0	0	....	2	0	0	0	0	5	12	8	6	1	0	1	0	2.600	10.80	37	13.08	.444	0	.000	-4	0	-0.4
1938	Chi-N	0	0	....	1	0	0	0	0	1	3	1	1	0	0	0	1	3.000	9.00	42	14.52	.500	0	....	-1	0	-0.1

YEAR	TM-L	W	L	PCT	G	GS	CG	SH	SV	IP	H	R	ER	HR	HB	BB	SO	RAT	ERA	ERA+	CERA	OAV	BH	AVG	PR+	WS	TPW
1940	Bro-N	3	1	.750	21	0	0	0	1	33^2	29	15	12	2	0	15	21	1.307	3.21	125	3.12	.238	0	.000	3	3	0.2
	StL-N	1	0	1.000	2	1	1	0	0	14	11	5	4	1	0	6	6	1.214	2.57	155	2.70	.208	2	.333	2	2	0.3
	Yr.	4	1	.800	23	1	1	0	1	47^2	40	20	16	3	0	21	27	1.280	3.02	132	2.99	.229	2	.182	6	5	0.6
1941	Bro-N	3	1	.750	15	5	1	0	1	52	43	22	21	0	0	29	17	1.385	3.63	101	2.86	.225	3	.214	-1	3	0.0
1942	Bro-N	2	0	1.000	14	1	0	0	0	29^1	27	13	12	0	1	19	8	1.568	3.68	88	4.05	.265	1	.200	-2	1	-0.2
1943	Bro-N	1	1	.500	5	0	0	0	1	11	9	2	2	0	0	5	2	1.273	1.64	205	2.47	.214	0	.000	2	1	0.2
	Phi-N	1	6	.143	34	6	2	0	2	89^2	85	47	41	4	1	42	33	1.416	4.12	82	3.53	.253	3	.188	-6	2	-0.5
	Yr.	2	7	.222	39	6	2	0	3	100^2	94	49	43	4	1	47	35	1.401	3.84	88	3.41	.249	3	.158	-4	3	-0.3
Total	6	11	9	.550	94	13	4	0	5	235^2	219	113	99	8	2	117	88	1.426	3.78	94	3.54	.249	9	.180	-5	12	-0.5
• KIMBER, Sam		Samuel Jackson Kimber b: 10/29/1852, Philadelphia, PA d: 11/7/1925, Philadelphia, PA BR/TR, 5'10.5", 165 lbs. Deb: 5/1/1884																									
1884	Bro-a	18	20	.474	41	41	41	4	0	361^1	364	240	153	6	15	72	122	1.207	3.81	87	....	.248	21	.148	-13	16	-1.6
1885	Pro-N	0	1	.000	1	1	1	0	0	8	15	13	10	1	....	5	4	2.500	11.25	24	....	.383	0	.000	-8	0	-0.8
Total	2	18	21	.462	42	42	42	4	0	369^1	379	253	163	7	15	77	126	1.235	3.97	82	....	.251	21	.145	-21	16	-2.3
• KIMBERLIN, Harry		Harry Lydle "Murphy,Mule Trader" Kimberlin b: 3/13/1909, Sullivan, MO d: 12/31/1999, Poplar Bluff, MO BR/TR, 6'3", 175 lbs. Deb: 7/11/1936																									
1936	StL-A	0	0	....	13	0	0	0	0	20	24	13	12	3	0	16	4	2.000	5.40	100	7.11	.296	0	.000	0	1	0.0
1937	StL-A	0	2	.000	3	2	1	0	0	15^1	16	13	4	2	0	9	5	1.630	2.35	206	4.95	.254	1	.200	4	1	0.4
1938	StL-A	0	0	....	1	1	1	0	0	8	8	3	3	1	0	3	1	1.375	3.38	147	4.39	.286	0	.000	1	1	0.1
1939	StL-A	1	2	.333	17	3	0	0	0	41	59	35	25	6	2	19	11	1.902	5.49	89	7.20	.326	3	.333	-2	1	-0.1
Total	4	1	4	.200	34	6	2	0	0	84^1	107	64	44	12	2	47	21	1.826	4.70	106	6.50	.303	4	.250	4	4	0.4
• KIME, Hal		Harold Lee "Lefty" Kime b: 3/15/1899, West Salem, OH d: 5/16/1939, Columbus, OH BL/TL, 5'9", 160 lbs. Deb: 6/19/1920																									
1920	StL-N	0	0	....	4	0	0	0	0	7	9	4	2	0	1	2	1	1.571	2.57	119	5.34	.333	0	.000	0	0	0.0
• KIMSEY, Chad		Clyde Elias Kimsey b: 8/6/1906, Copperhill, TN d: 12/3/1942, Pryor, OK BL/TR, 6'2", 200 lbs. Deb: 4/21/1929																									
1929	StL-A	3	6	.333	24	3	1	0	1	64^1	83	42	36	2	0	19	13	1.585	5.04	88	5.12	.340	8	.267	-5	3	-0.2
1930	StL-A	6	10	.375	42	4	1	0	1	113^1	139	87	80	8	2	45	32	1.624	6.35	77	5.21	.312	24	.343	-20	6	-1.1
1931	StL-A	4	6	.400	42	1	0	0	7	94^1	121	60	46	1	2	27	27	1.569	4.39	106	4.54	.312	10	.270	2	8	0.7
1932	StL-A	4	2	.667	33	0	0	0	3	78^1	85	45	35	3	0	33	13	1.506	4.02	121	4.09	.281	6	.333	7	7	0.8
	Chi-A	1	1	.500	7	0	0	0	2	11	8	4	3	0	1	5	6	1.182	2.45	176	2.44	.211	0	.000	2	1	0.2
	Yr.	5	3	.625	40	0	0	0	5	89^1	93	49	38	3	1	38	19	1.466	3.83	125	3.89	.273	6	.300	9	8	1.0
1933	Chi-A	4	1	.800	28	2	0	0	0	96	124	67	59	7	4	36	19	1.667	5.53	77	5.54	.318	5	.152	-13	2	-1.4
1936	Det-A	2	3	.400	22	0	0	0	3	52	58	36	28	2	1	29	11	1.673	4.85	102	4.81	.284	5	.313	1	4	0.3
Total	6	24	29	.453	198	10	2	0	17	509^1	618	341	287	23	10	194	121	1.594	5.07	91	4.86	.307	58	.282	-25	31	-0.8
• KINDER, Ellis		Ellis Raymond "Old Folks" Kinder b: 7/26/1914, Atkins, AR d: 10/16/1968, Jackson, TN BR/TR, 6', 195 lbs. Deb: 4/30/1946																									
1946	StL-A	3	3	.500	33	7	1	0	1	86^2	78	35	32	8	0	36	59	1.315	3.32	112	3.44	.241	1	.053	4	6	0.3
1947	StL-A	8	15	.348	34	26	10	2	1	194^1	201	105	97	11	0	82	110	1.456	4.49	86	3.93	.264	8	.129	-11	8	-1.5
1948	Bos-A	10	7	.588	28	22	10	1	0	178	183	84	74	10	2	63	53	1.382	3.74	117	3.71	.266	6	.097	12	12	0.8
1949	Bos-A	23	6	.793	43	30	19	**6**	4	252	251	103	94	21	2	99	138	1.389	3.36	130	3.84	.260	12	.130	24	22	1.9
1950	Bos-A	14	12	.538	48	23	11	1	9	207	212	105	98	23	1	78	95	1.401	4.26	115	4.07	.263	13	.183	15	17	1.3
1951	Bos-A	11	2	.846	**63**	2	1	0	**14**	127	108	42	36	8	0	46	84	1.213	2.55	175	2.80	.230	4	.118	27	18	2.4
1952	Bos-A	5	6	.455	23	10	4	0	4	97^2	85	33	28	11	1	28	50	1.157	2.58	153	3.00	.234	0	.000	14	9	1.0
1953	Bos-A	10	6	.625	**69**	0	0	0	**27**	107	84	30	22	8	2	38	39	1.140	1.85	227	2.57	.215	11	.379	27	23	3.0
1954	Bos-A	8	8	.500	48	2	0	0	15	107	106	47	43	7	0	36	67	1.327	3.62	114	3.43	.260	5	.185	7	10	0.8
1955	Bos-A	5	5	.500	43	0	0	0	18	66^2	57	22	21	4	1	15	31	1.080	2.84	151	2.31	.229	3	.250	11	13	1.2
1956	StL-N	2	0	1.000	22	0	0	0	6	25^2	23	11	10	3	0	9	4	1.247	3.51	108	3.22	.245	0	.000	1	3	0.1
	Chi-A	3	1	.750	29	0	0	0	3	29^2	33	10	9	2	0	8	19	1.382	2.73	150	3.86	.277	0	.000	4	4	0.4
1957	Chi-A	0	0	....	1	0	0	0	0	1	0	0	0	0	0	1	0	1.000	0.00	....	0.00	.000	0	....	0	0	0.0
Total	12	102	71	.590	484	122	56	10	102	1479^2	1421	627	564	116	9	539	749	1.325	3.43	124	3.50	.252	63	.142	137	145	11.6
• KING, Clyde		Clyde Edward King b: 5/23/1924, Goldsboro, NC BB/TR, 6'1", 175 lbs. Deb: 6/21/1944 M/C																									
1944	Bro-N	2	1	.667	14	3	1	0	0	43^2	42	18	15	1	1	12	14	1.237	3.09	115	2.96	.256	2	.200	4	2	0.4
1945	Bro-N	5	5	.500	42	2	0	0	3	112^1	131	64	51	8	0	48	29	1.593	4.09	92	4.82	.295	4	.125	-4	4	-0.5
1947	Bro-N	6	5	.545	29	9	2	0	0	87^2	85	34	27	11	0	29	31	1.300	2.77	149	3.74	.252	3	.115	11	7	1.0
1948	Bro-N	0	1	.000	9	0	0	0	0	12^1	14	11	11	3	1	6	5	1.622	8.03	50	6.63	.286	0	.000	-6	0	-0.6
1951	Bro-N	14	7	.667	48	3	1	0	6	121^1	118	64	56	15	3	50	33	1.385	4.15	94	4.25	.263	4	.138	-6	8	-0.6
1952	Bro-N	2	0	1.000	23	0	0	0	0	42^2	56	25	24	5	1	12	17	1.594	5.06	72	5.61	.318	0	.000	-7	1	-0.8
1953	Cin-N	3	6	.333	35	4	0	0	2	76	78	47	44	15	2	32	21	1.447	5.21	84	5.13	.271	0	.000	-9	3	-0.9
Total	7	32	25	.561	200	21	4	0	11	496	524	263	228	58	8	189	150	1.438	4.14	95	4.49	.275	13	.114	-16	25	-2.0
• KING, Curtis		Curtis Albert King b: 10/25/1970, Norristown, PA BR/TR, 6'5", 205 lbs. Deb: 8/1/1997																									
1997	StL-N	4	2	.667	30	0	0	0	0	29^1	38	14	9	0	1	11	13	1.670	2.76	150	4.99	.325	0	.000	4	3	0.4
1998	StL-N	2	0	1.000	36	0	0	0	2	51	50	20	20	5	3	20	28	1.373	3.53	119	4.49	.262	0	.000	4	4	0.3
1999	StL-N	0	0	....	2	0	0	0	0	1	3	2	2	0	0	0	1	3.000	18.00	25	14.52	.500	0	....	-1	0	-0.1
Total	3	6	2	.750	68	0	0	0	2	81^1	91	36	31	5	4	31	42	1.500	3.43	123	4.54	.290	0	.000	7	7	0.6
• KING, Eric		Eric Steven King b: 4/10/1964, Oxnard, CA BR/TR, 6'2", 215 lbs. Deb: 5/15/1986																									
1986	Det-A	11	4	.733	33	16	3	1	3	138^1	108	54	54	11	8	63	79	1.236	3.51	117	3.17	.216	0	....	8	11	0.8
1987*	Det-A	6	9	.400	55	4	0	0	9	116	111	67	63	15	4	60	89	1.474	4.89	86	4.49	.251	0	....	-9	6	-0.9
1988	Det-A	4	1	.800	23	5	0	0	3	68^2	60	28	26	5	5	34	45	1.369	3.41	112	3.72	.233	0	....	3	5	0.3
1989	Chi-A	9	10	.474	25	25	1	1	0	159^1	144	69	60	13	4	64	72	1.305	3.39	112	3.58	.244	0	....	7	9	0.7
1990	Chi-A	12	4	.750	25	25	2	2	0	151	135	59	55	10	6	40	70	1.159	3.28	116	2.92	.237	0	....	6	12	0.6
1991	Cle-A	6	11	.353	25	24	2	1	0	150^2	166	83	77	7	3	44	59	1.394	4.60	90	3.83	.279	0	....	-5	5	-0.5
1992	Det-A	4	6	.400	17	14	0	0	1	79^1	90	47	46	12	1	28	45	1.487	5.22	76	5.09	.285	0	....	-10	2	-1.1
Total	7	52	45	.536	203	113	8	5	16	863^1	814	407	381	73	31	333	459	1.329	3.97	101	3.72	.249	0	....	-1	50	-0.1
• KING, Kevin		Kevin Ray King b: 2/11/1969, Atwater, CA BL/TL, 6'4", 170 lbs. Deb: 9/2/1993																									
1993	Sea-A	0	1	.000	13	0	0	0	0	11^2	9	8	8	3	1	4	8	1.114	6.17	71	3.76	.231	0	....	-2	0	-0.2
1994	Sea-A	0	2	.000	19	0	0	0	0	15^1	21	13	12	0	1	17	6	2.478	7.04	69	8.44	.333	0	....	-3	0	-0.3
1995	Sea-A	0	0	....	2	0	0	0	0	3^2	7	5	5	0	1	1	3	2.182	12.27	39	9.31	.412	0	....	-3	0	-0.3
Total	3	0	3	.000	34	0	0	0	0	30^2	37	26	25	3	3	22	17	1.924	7.34	64	6.77	.311	0	....	-9	0	-0.8
• KING, Nellie		Nelson Joseph King b: 3/15/1928, Shenandoah, PA BR/TR, 6'6", 185 lbs. Deb: 4/15/1954																									
1954	Pit-N	0	0	....	4	0	0	0	0	7	10	5	4	0	0	1	3	1.571	5.14	82	4.75	.400	0	....	-1	0	-0.1
1955	Pit-N	1	3	.250	17	4	0	0	0	54^1	60	24	18	2	2	14	21	1.362	2.98	138	3.74	.286	0	.000	7	4	0.5
1956	Pit-N	4	1	.800	38	0	0	0	5	60	54	24	21	8	1	19	25	1.217	3.15	120	3.42	.241	0	.000	5	6	0.4
1957	Pit-N	2	1	.667	36	0	0	0	1	52	69	27	26	7	2	16	23	1.635	4.50	84	6.07	.337	0	.000	-5	2	-0.5
Total	4	7	5	.583	95	4	0	0	6	173^1	193	80	69	17	5	50	72	1.402	3.58	108	4.37	.291	0	.000	7	12	0.3
• KING, Ray		Raymond Keith King b: 1/15/1974, Chicago, IL BL/TL, 6'1", 230 lbs. Deb: 5/21/1999																									
1999	Chi-N	0	0	....	10	0	0	0	0	10^2	11	8	7	2	1	10	5	1.969	5.91	77	8.10	.289	0	.000	-2	0	-0.2
2000	Mil-N	3	2	.600	36	0	0	0	0	28^2	18	7	4	1	0	10	19	.977	1.26	362	1.64	.180	0	....	10	4	0.9
2001	Mil-N	0	4	.000	82	0	0	0	1	55	49	22	22	5	1	25	49	1.345	3.60	119	3.51	.241	0	.000	4	5	0.4
2002	Mil-N	3	2	.600	76	0	0	0	0	65	61	24	22	5	3	24	50	1.308	3.05	134	3.55	.255	0	....	8	5	0.8
2003*	Atl-N	3	4	.429	80	0	0	0	0	59	46	30	23	3	1	27	43	1.237	3.51	120	2.79	.213	0	....	5	4	0.5
Total	5	9	12	.429	284	0	0	0	1	218^1	185	91	78	16	6	96	166	1.287	3.22	132	3.31	.232	0	.000	25	18	2.4

• KING, Silver Charles Frederick King b: 1/11/1868, St. Louis, MO d: 5/21/1938, St. Louis, MO BR/TR, 6', 170 lbs. Deb: 9/28/1886

YEAR	TM-L	W	L	PCT	G	GS	CG	SH	SV	IP	H	R	ER	HR	HB	BB	SO	RAT	ERA	ERA+	CERA	OAV	BH	AVG	PR+	WS	TPW
1886	KC-N	1	3	.250	5	5	5	0	0	39	43	35	21	1	....	9	23	1.333	4.85	77	....	.269	1	.045	-4	1	-0.6
1887*	StL-a	32	12	.727	46	44	43	2	1	390	510	231	164	4	17	109	128	1.308	3.78	120	....	.305	70	.285	24	37	1.0
1888*	StL-a	**45**	20	.692	**66**	**65**	**64**	**6**	0	**584^2**	435	203	107	6	30	76	258	.874	**1.65**	**198**	....	.200	43	.208	**89**	**71**	**9.2**
1889	StL-a	34	16	.680	55	52	46	2	1	458	462	257	160	15	12	125	188	1.282	3.14	134	....	.254	43	.228	44	44	3.9
1890	Chi-P	30	22	.577	56	**56**	48	**4**	0	461	420	233	138	5	15	163	185	1.265	**2.69**	**161**	....	**.232**	31	.168	**83**	**44**	**6.2**
1891	Pit-N	14	29	.326	48	44	40	3	1	384^1	382	243	133	7	18	144	160	1.369	3.11	105	....	.250	25	.169	10	20	0.9
1892	NY-N	23	24	.489	52	47	46	1	0	410	392	250	151	15	21	171	170	1.373	3.31	97	3.54	.242	34	.209	1	24	0.7
1893	NY-N	3	4	.429	7	7	4	0	0	49	69	58	47	4	2	26	13	1.939	8.63	54	6.94	.323	3	.176	-22	0	-1.7
	Cin-N	5	6	.455	17	15	8	1	1	105	119	69	57	2	7	56	30	1.667	4.89	98	4.84	.277	6	.162	-3	7	-0.2
	Yr.	8	10	.444	24	22	12	1	1	154	188	127	104	6	9	82	43	1.753	6.08	78	5.51	.292	9	.167	-25	7	-2.0
1896	Was-N	10	7	.588	22	16	12	0	1	145^1	179	106	66	3	4	43	35	1.528	4.09	108	4.42	.301	16	.276	8	8	1.0
1897	Was-N	6	9	.400	23	19	12	0	1	154	196	118	82	7	11	45	32	1.565	4.79	90	5.00	.307	11	.193	-10	7	-0.8
Total	**10**	**203**	**152**	**.572**	**397**	**370**	**328**	**19**	**6**	**3180^1**	**3207**	**1803**	**1126**	**69**	**137**	**967**	**1222**	**1.278**	**3.19**	**123**	**1.17**	**.253**	**283**	**.213**	**220**	**263**	**19.4**

• KINGMAN, Brian Brian Paul Kingman b: 7/27/1954, Los Angeles, CA BR/TR, 6'2", 200 lbs. Deb: 6/28/1979

YEAR	TM-L	W	L	PCT	G	GS	CG	SH	SV	IP	H	R	ER	HR	HB	BB	SO	RAT	ERA	ERA+	CERA	OAV	BH	AVG	PR+	WS	TPW
1979	Oak-A	8	7	.533	18	17	5	1	0	112^2	113	59	54	10	3	33	58	1.296	4.31	94	3.65	.258	0	....	-0	7	0.0
1980	Oak-A	8	20	.286	32	30	10	1	0	211^1	209	105	90	21	4	82	116	1.377	3.83	98	3.99	.256	0	....	-4	8	-0.4
1981*	Oak-A	3	6	.333	18	15	3	1	0	100^1	112	48	44	10	4	32	52	1.435	3.95	88	4.58	.286	0	....	-6	3	-0.7
1982	Oak-A	4	12	.250	23	20	3	0	1	122^2	131	64	61	11	7	57	46	1.533	4.48	87	4.90	.279	0	....	-8	4	-0.8
1983	SF-N	0	0	....	3	0	0	0	0	4^2	10	6	4	0	0	1	1	2.357	7.71	46	9.39	.417	0	....	-2	0	-0.2
Total	**5**	**23**	**45**	**.338**	**94**	**82**	**21**	**3**	**1**	**551^2**	**575**	**282**	**253**	**52**	**18**	**205**	**273**	**1.414**	**4.13**	**92**	**4.28**	**.269**	**0**	**....**	**-20**	**22**	**-2.1**

• KINNEY, Dennis Dennis Paul Kinney b: 2/26/1952, Toledo, OH BL/TL, 6'1", 190 lbs. Deb: 4/9/1978

YEAR	TM-L	W	L	PCT	G	GS	CG	SH	SV	IP	H	R	ER	HR	HB	BB	SO	RAT	ERA	ERA+	CERA	OAV	BH	AVG	PR+	WS	TPW
1978	Cle-A	0	2	.000	18	0	0	0	5	38^2	37	21	19	3	1	14	19	1.319	4.42	84	3.61	.259	0	....	-3	2	-0.3
	SD-N	0	1	.000	7	0	0	0	0	7	6	5	5	3	0	4	2	1.429	6.43	52	6.19	.222	0	.000	-2	0	-0.3
1979	SD-N	0	0	....	13	0	0	0	0	18	17	8	7	2	1	8	11	1.389	3.50	101	3.98	.250	0	.000	-0	1	0.0
1980	SD-N	4	6	.400	50	0	0	0	1	82^2	79	45	39	3	1	37	40	1.403	4.25	81	3.29	.252	1	.083	-9	2	-1.0
1981	Det-A	0	0	....	6	0	0	0	0	3^2	5	4	4	0	0	4	3	2.455	9.82	38	7.46	.313	0	....	-3	0	-0.3
1982	Oak-A	0	0	....	3	0	0	0	0	4^1	9	4	4	1	0	4	0	3.000	8.31	47	16.02	.474	0	....	-2	0	-0.2
Total	**5**	**4**	**9**	**.308**	**97**	**0**	**0**	**0**	**6**	**154^1**	**153**	**87**	**78**	**12**	**3**	**71**	**75**	**1.451**	**4.55**	**78**	**4.04**	**.261**	**1**	**.071**	**-18**	**5**	**-2.0**

• KINNEY, Matt Matthew John Kinney b: 12/16/1976, Bangor, ME BR/TR, 6'5", 220 lbs. Deb: 8/18/2000

YEAR	TM-L	W	L	PCT	G	GS	CG	SH	SV	IP	H	R	ER	HR	HB	BB	SO	RAT	ERA	ERA+	CERA	OAV	BH	AVG	PR+	WS	TPW
2000	Min-A	2	2	.500	8	8	0	0	0	42^1	41	26	24	7	0	25	24	1.559	5.10	101	5.20	.261	0	....	1	2	0.1
2002	Min-A	2	7	.222	14	12	0	0	0	66	78	39	34	13	1	33	45	1.682	4.64	97	6.35	.295	0	.000	-1	2	-0.1
2003	Mil-N	10	13	.435	33	31	1	0	0	190^2	201	121	110	27	6	80	152	1.474	5.19	82	4.82	.272	2	.036	-16	5	-2.0
Total	**3**	**14**	**22**	**.389**	**55**	**51**	**1**	**0**	**0**	**299**	**320**	**186**	**168**	**47**	**7**	**138**	**221**	**1.532**	**5.06**	**87**	**5.21**	**.276**	**2**	**.035**	**-17**	**9**	**-2.0**

• KINNEY, Walt Walter William Kinney b: 9/9/1893, Denison, TX d: 7/1/1971, Escondido, CA BL/TL, 6'2", 186 lbs. Deb: 7/26/1918

YEAR	TM-L	W	L	PCT	G	GS	CG	SH	SV	IP	H	R	ER	HR	HB	BB	SO	RAT	ERA	ERA+	CERA	OAV	BH	AVG	PR+	WS	TPW
1918	Bos-A	0	0	....	5	0	0	0	0	15	5	3	3	0	2	8	4	.867	1.80	149	1.22	.106	0	.000	1	1	0.0
1919	Phi-A	9	15	.375	43	21	13	0	2	202^2	199	110	82	7	8	91	97	1.431	3.64	94	3.86	.262	25	.284	4	10	1.2
1920	Phi-A	2	4	.333	10	8	5	1	0	61	59	38	21	3	1	28	19	1.426	3.10	130	3.87	.261	9	.346	7	4	0.9
1923	Phi-A	0	1	.000	5	1	0	0	0	12	11	13	10	0	0	9	9	1.667	7.50	55	3.65	.229	1	.167	-4	0	-0.4
Total	**4**	**11**	**20**	**.355**	**63**	**30**	**18**	**1**	**2**	**290^2**	**274**	**164**	**116**	**10**	**11**	**136**	**129**	**1.411**	**3.59**	**99**	**3.72**	**.254**	**35**	**.280**	**8**	**15**	**1.8**

• KINNUNEN, Mike Michael John Kinnunen b: 4/1/1958, Seattle, WA BL/TL, 6'1", 185 lbs. Deb: 6/12/1980

YEAR	TM-L	W	L	PCT	G	GS	CG	SH	SV	IP	H	R	ER	HR	HB	BB	SO	RAT	ERA	ERA+	CERA	OAV	BH	AVG	PR+	WS	TPW
1980	Min-A	0	0	....	21	0	0	0	0	24^2	29	18	14	1	1	9	8	1.541	5.11	85	4.51	.290	0	....	-2	0	-0.2
1986	Bal-A	0	0	....	9	0	0	0	0	7	8	6	5	1	0	5	1	1.857	6.43	64	7.08	.308	0	....	-2	0	-0.2
1987	Bal-A	0	0	....	18	0	0	0	0	20	27	14	11	3	0	16	14	2.150	4.95	89	8.59	.338	0	....	-1	0	-0.1
Total	**3**	**0**	**0**	**....**	**48**	**0**	**0**	**0**	**0**	**51^2**	**64**	**38**	**30**	**5**	**1**	**30**	**23**	**1.819**	**5.23**	**83**	**6.44**	**.311**	**0**	**....**	**-5**	**0**	**-0.5**

• KINSELLA, Ed Edward William "Rube" Kinsella b: 1/15/1882, Lexington, IL d: 1/17/1976, Bloomington, IL BR/TR, 6'1.5", 175 lbs. Deb: 9/16/1905

YEAR	TM-L	W	L	PCT	G	GS	CG	SH	SV	IP	H	R	ER	HR	HB	BB	SO	RAT	ERA	ERA+	CERA	OAV	BH	AVG	PR+	WS	TPW
1905	Pit-N	0	1	.000	3	2	2	0	0	17	19	6	5	0	1	3	11	1.294	2.65	113	3.52	.292	0	.000	0	1	0.0
1910	StL-A	1	3	.250	10	5	2	0	0	50	62	30	21	0	2	16	10	1.560	3.78	65	4.75	.321	3	.250	-7	1	-0.5
Total	**2**	**1**	**4**	**.200**	**13**	**7**	**4**	**0**	**0**	**67**	**81**	**36**	**26**	**0**	**3**	**19**	**21**	**1.493**	**3.49**	**73**	**4.44**	**.314**	**3**	**.200**	**-7**	**2**	**-0.5**

• KINZER, Matt Matthew Roy Kinzer b: 6/17/1963, Indianapolis, IN BR/TR, 6'2", 210 lbs. Deb: 5/18/1989

YEAR	TM-L	W	L	PCT	G	GS	CG	SH	SV	IP	H	R	ER	HR	HB	BB	SO	RAT	ERA	ERA+	CERA	OAV	BH	AVG	PR+	WS	TPW
1989	StL-N	0	2	.000	8	1	0	0	0	13^1	25	20	19	3	0	4	8	2.175	12.83	28	10.07	.403	0	.000	-14	0	-1.5
1990	Det-A	0	0	....	1	0	0	0	0	1^2	3	3	3	0	0	3	1	3.600	16.20	24	14.26	.375	0	....	-2	0	-0.2
Total	**2**	**0**	**2**	**.000**	**9**	**1**	**0**	**0**	**0**	**15**	**28**	**23**	**22**	**3**	**0**	**7**	**9**	**2.333**	**13.20**	**28**	**10.53**	**.400**	**0**	**.000**	**-16**	**0**	**-1.7**

• KINZY, Harry Harry Hersel "Slim" Kinzy b: 7/19/1910, Hallsville, TX d: 6/22/2003, Fort Worth, TX BR/TR, 6'4", 185 lbs. Deb: 6/8/1934

YEAR	TM-L	W	L	PCT	G	GS	CG	SH	SV	IP	H	R	ER	HR	HB	BB	SO	RAT	ERA	ERA+	CERA	OAV	BH	AVG	PR+	WS	TPW
1934	Chi-A	0	1	.000	13	2	1	0	0	34^1	38	23	19	1	4	31	12	2.010	4.98	95	6.41	.290	3	.300	0	1	0.1

• KIPP, Fred Fred Leo Kipp b: 10/1/1931, Piqua, KS BL/TL, 6'4", 200 lbs. Deb: 9/10/1957

YEAR	TM-L	W	L	PCT	G	GS	CG	SH	SV	IP	H	R	ER	HR	HB	BB	SO	RAT	ERA	ERA+	CERA	OAV	BH	AVG	PR+	WS	TPW
1957	Bro-N	0	0	....	1	0	0	0	0	4	6	4	4	2	0	0	3	1.500	9.00	46	8.13	.333	0	.000	-2	0	-0.2
1958	LA-N	6	6	.500	40	9	0	0	0	102^1	107	60	57	16	1	45	58	1.485	5.01	82	4.92	.273	9	.250	-11	4	-0.9
1959	LA-N	0	0	....	2	0	0	0	0	2^2	2	0	0	0	0	3	1	1.875	0.00	....	3.79	.222	0	....	1	0	0.1
1960	NY-A	0	1	.000	4	0	0	0	0	4^1	4	3	3	0	0	0	2	.923	6.23	57	1.64	.250	0	....	-1	0	-0.1
Total	**4**	**6**	**7**	**.462**	**47**	**9**	**0**	**0**	**0**	**113^1**	**119**	**67**	**64**	**18**	**1**	**48**	**64**	**1.474**	**5.08**	**80**	**4.88**	**.274**	**9**	**.243**	**-13**	**4**	**-1.2**

• KIPPER, Bob Robert Wayne Kipper b: 7/8/1964, Aurora, IL BR/TL, 6'2", 200 lbs. Deb: 4/12/1985

YEAR	TM-L	W	L	PCT	G	GS	CG	SH	SV	IP	H	R	ER	HR	HB	BB	SO	RAT	ERA	ERA+	CERA	OAV	BH	AVG	PR+	WS	TPW
1985	Cal-A	0	1	.000	2	1	0	0	0	3^1	7	8	8	1	0	3	0	3.000	21.60	19	15.56	.467	0	....	-7	0	-0.7
	Pit-N	1	2	.333	5	4	0	0	0	24^2	21	16	14	4	0	7	13	1.135	5.11	70	3.09	.221	2	.250	-4	0	-0.4
1986	Pit-N	6	8	.429	20	19	0	0	0	114	123	60	51	17	2	34	81	1.377	4.03	95	4.44	.271	1	.030	-2	4	-0.5
1987	Pit-N	5	9	.357	24	20	1	1	0	110^2	117	74	73	25	2	52	83	1.527	5.94	69	5.64	.271	8	.242	-24	1	-2.3
1988	Pit-N	2	6	.250	50	0	0	0	0	65	54	33	27	7	2	26	39	1.231	3.74	91	3.30	.234	0	.000	-3	2	-0.3
1989	Pit-N	3	4	.429	52	0	0	0	4	83	55	29	27	5	0	33	58	1.060	2.93	115	1.98	.188	1	.111	4	6	0.4
1990	Pit-N	5	2	.714	41	1	0	0	3	62^2	44	24	21	7	3	26	35	1.117	3.02	120	2.74	.195	1	.143	3	6	0.3
1991*	Pit-N	2	2	.500	52	0	0	0	4	60	66	34	31	7	0	22	38	1.467	4.65	77	4.51	.276	0	.000	-8	2	-0.8
1992	Min-A	3	3	.500	25	0	0	0	0	38^2	40	23	19	8	3	14	22	1.397	4.42	92	5.13	.268	0	....	-2	1	-0.2
Total	**8**	**27**	**37**	**.422**	**271**	**45**	**1**	**1**	**11**	**562**	**527**	**301**	**271**	**81**	**12**	**217**	**369**	**1.324**	**4.34**	**87**	**4.05**	**.247**	**13**	**.137**	**-42**	**22**	**-4.4**

• KIPPER, Thornton Thornton John Kipper b: 9/27/1928, Bagley, WI BR/TR, 6'3", 190 lbs. Deb: 6/7/1953

YEAR	TM-L	W	L	PCT	G	GS	CG	SH	SV	IP	H	R	ER	HR	HB	BB	SO	RAT	ERA	ERA+	CERA	OAV	BH	AVG	PR+	WS	TPW
1953	Phi-N	3	3	.500	20	3	0	0	0	45^2	59	26	24	8	0	12	15	1.555	4.73	89	5.75	.319	1	.091	-3	2	-0.3
1954	Phi-N	0	0	....	11	0	0	0	1	13^2	22	13	12	0	1	12	5	2.488	7.90	51	9.28	.379	0	.000	-6	0	-0.6
1955	Phi-N	0	1	.000	24	0	0	0	0	39^2	47	23	22	4	1	22	15	1.739	4.99	80	5.80	.301	1	.333	-5	1	-0.5
Total	**3**	**3**	**4**	**.429**	**55**	**3**	**0**	**0**	**1**	**99**	**128**	**62**	**58**	**12**	**2**	**46**	**35**	**1.758**	**5.27**	**77**	**6.26**	**.321**	**2**	**.125**	**-14**	**3**	**-1.4**

• KIRBY, Clay Clayton Laws Kirby b: 6/25/1948, Washington, DC d: 10/11/1991, Arlington, VA BR/TR, 6'3", 185 lbs. Deb: 4/11/1969

YEAR	TM-L	W	L	PCT	G	GS	CG	SH	SV	IP	H	R	ER	HR	HB	BB	SO	RAT	ERA	ERA+	CERA	OAV	BH	AVG	PR+	WS	TPW
1969	SD-N	7	20	.259	35	35	2	0	0	215^2	204	108	91	18	6	100	113	1.410	3.80	93	3.94	.252	4	.061	-4	10	-0.6
1970	SD-N	10	16	.385	36	34	6	1	0	214^2	198	118	108	29	9	120	154	1.481	4.53	88	4.66	.248	11	.149	-13	6	-1.3
1971	SD-N	15	13	.536	38	36	13	2	0	267^1	213	99	84	20	3	103	231	1.182	2.83	116	2.72	.216	8	.093	16	17	1.4
1972	SD-N	12	14	.462	34	34	9	2	0	238^2	197	87	83	21	2	116	175	1.311	3.13	105	3.36	.226	5	.068	8	14	0.4
1973	SD-N	8	18	.308	34	3[illegible]	4	2	0	191^2	214	122	102	30	1	66	129	1.461	4.79	72	4.87	.282	5	.093	-27	2	-3.1
1974	Cin-N	12	9	.571	36	35	7	1	0	230^2	210	97	84	15	2	91	160	1.305	3.28	106	3.32	.242	7	.095	1	12	-0.2
1975	Cin-N	10	6	.625	26	19	1	0	0	110^2	113	63	58	13	5	54	48	1.509	4.72	76	4.75	.263	6	.188	-17	3	-1.7
1976	Mon-N	1	8	.111	22	15	0	0	0	78^2	81	61	50	10	2	63	51	1.831	5.72	65	6.25	.273	1	.056	-17	0	-1.9
Total	**8**	**75**	**104**	**.419**	**261**	**239**	**42**	**8**	**0**	**1548**	**1430**	**755**	**660**	**156**	**30**	**713**	**1061**	**1.384**	**3.84**	**92**	**3.94**	**.246**	**47**	**.098**	**-53**	**64**	**-7.0**

YEAR	TM-L	W	L	PCT	G	GS	CG	SH	SV	IP	H	R	ER	HR	HB	BB	SO	RAT	ERA	ERA+	CERA	OAV	BH	AVG	PR+	WS	TPW
• KIRBY, John	John F. Kirby b: 1/13/1865, St. Louis, MO d: 10/6/1931, St. Louis, MO TR, 5'8", 172 lbs. Deb: 8/1/1884 U																										
1884	KC-U	0	1	.000	2	2	1	0	0	11	13	10	5	0	....	2	1	1.364	4.09	68	....	.275	1	.143	-2	0	-0.2
1885	StL-N	5	8	.385	14	14	14	0	0	129^1	118	66	51	0	....	44	46	1.253	3.55	77	....	.232	3	.060	-16	6	-2.0
1886	StL-N	11	26	.297	41	41	38	1	0	325	329	222	119	9	....	134	129	1.425	3.30	97	....	.253	15	.110	-12	11	-1.9
1887	Ind-N	1	6	.143	8	8	5	0	0	62	113	64	42	3	2	43	7	1.823	6.10	67	....	.382	4	.138	-14	1	-1.4
	Cle-a	0	5	.000	5	5	5	0	0	41	90	53	41	1	2	28	6	2.195	9.00	48	....	.424	3	.167	-20	0	-1.7
1888	KC-a	1	4	.200	5	5	5	0	0	43	48	36	20	0	1	7	11	1.279	4.19	82	....	.272	1	.063	-4	1	-0.5
Total	**5**	**18**	**50**	**.265**	**75**	**75**	**68**	**1**	**0**	**611^1**	**711**	**451**	**278**	**13**	**5**	**258**	**200**	**1.469**	**4.09**	**82**	**....**	**.280**	**27**	**.105**	**-67**	**19**	**-7.6**
• KIRCHER, Mike	Michael Andrew Kircher b: 9/30/1897, Rochester, NY d: 6/26/1972, Rochester, NY BB/TR, 6', 180 lbs. Deb: 8/8/1919																										
1919	Phi-A	0	0	....	2	0	0	0	0	8	15	8	7	0	0	3	2	2.250	7.88	43	9.13	.429	0	.000	-4	0	-0.4
1920	StL-N	2	1	.667	9	3	1	0	0	36^2	50	23	22	0	2	5	5	1.500	5.40	57	4.58	.333	3	.273	-10	0	-1.0
1921	StL-N	0	1	.000	3	0	0	0	0	3^1	4	3	3	0	1	1	2	1.500	8.10	45	5.29	.364	0	....	-2	0	-0.2
Total	**3**	**2**	**2**	**.500**	**14**	**3**	**1**	**0**	**0**	**48**	**69**	**34**	**32**	**0**	**3**	**9**	**9**	**1.625**	**6.00**	**53**	**5.39**	**.352**	**3**	**.214**	**-15**	**0**	**-1.6**
• KIRK, Bill	William Partlemore Kirk b: 7/19/1935, Coatesville, PA BL/TL, 6', 165 lbs. Deb: 9/23/1961																										
1961	KC-A	0	0	....	1	1	0	0	0	3	6	4	4	2	0	1	3	2.333	12.00	34	14.45	.375	0	....	-3	0	-0.3
• KIRKWOOD, Don	Donald Paul Kirkwood b: 9/24/1949, Pontiac, MI BR/TR, 6'3", 188 lbs. Deb: 9/13/1974																										
1974	Cal-A	0	0	....	3	0	0	0	0	7^1	12	8	7	0	0	6	4	2.455	8.59	40	9.19	.375	0	....	-4	0	-0.4
1975	Cal-A	6	5	.545	44	2	0	0	7	84	85	38	29	6	0	28	49	1.345	3.11	114	3.66	.270	0	....	4	7	0.4
1976	Cal-A	6	12	.333	28	26	4	0	0	157^2	167	91	81	12	1	57	78	1.421	4.62	72	4.07	.278	0	....	-22	2	-2.3
1977	Cal-A	1	0	1.000	13	0	0	0	1	17^2	20	12	10	3	0	9	10	1.642	5.09	77	5.70	.290	0	....	-2	0	-0.2
	Chi-A	1	1	.500	16	0	0	0	0	40	49	27	23	3	1	10	24	1.475	5.18	79	4.62	.310	0	....	-4	1	-0.4
	Yr.	2	1	.667	29	0	0	0	1	57^2	69	39	33	6	1	19	34	1.526	5.15	78	4.95	.304	0	....	-6	1	-0.6
1978	Tor-A	4	5	.444	16	9	3	0	0	68	76	36	32	6	0	25	29	1.485	4.24	93	4.59	.289	0	....	-2	3	-0.2
Total	**5**	**18**	**23**	**.439**	**120**	**37**	**7**	**0**	**8**	**374^2**	**409**	**212**	**182**	**30**	**2**	**135**	**194**	**1.452**	**4.37**	**82**	**4.31**	**.284**	**0**	**....**	**-29**	**13**	**-3.1**
• KIRSCH, Harry	Harry Louis "Casey" Kirsch b: 10/17/1887, Pittsburgh, PA d: 12/25/1925, Philadelphia, PA BR/TR, 5'11", 170 lbs. Deb: 4/16/1910																										
1910	Cle-A	0	0	....	2	0	0	0	0	3	5	2	2	0	0	1	5	2.000	6.00	43	7.23	.385	0	....	-1	0	-0.1
• KISER, Garland	Garland Routhard Kiser b: 7/8/1968, Charlotte, NC BL/TL, 6'3", 190 lbs. Deb: 9/9/1991																										
1991	Cle-A	0	0	....	7	0	0	0	0	4^2	7	5	5	0	1	4	3	2.357	9.64	43	9.27	.368	0	....	-3	0	-0.3
• KISINGER, Rube	Charles Samuel Kisinger b: 12/13/1876, Adrian, MI d: 7/17/1941, Huron, OH BR/TR, 6', 190 lbs. Deb: 9/10/1902																										
1902	Det-A	2	3	.400	5	5	5	0	0	43^1	48	20	15	0	3	14	7	1.431	3.12	117	3.85	.281	3	.158	2	3	0.1
1903	Det-A	7	9	.438	16	14	13	2	0	118^2	118	58	39	0	2	27	33	1.222	2.96	98	2.70	.259	6	.128	-0	5	-0.3
Total	**2**	**9**	**12**	**.429**	**21**	**19**	**18**	**2**	**0**	**162**	**166**	**78**	**54**	**0**	**5**	**41**	**40**	**1.278**	**3.00**	**103**	**3.01**	**.265**	**9**	**.136**	**2**	**8**	**-0.2**
• KISON, Bruce	Bruce Eugene Kison b: 2/18/1950, Pasco, WA BR/TR, 6'4", 178 lbs. Deb: 7/4/1971 C																										
1971★	Pit-N	6	5	.545	18	13	2	1	0	95^1	93	40	36	6	6	36	60	1.353	3.40	100	3.82	.259	2	.065	-1	4	-0.3
1972★	Pit-N	9	7	.563	32	18	6	1	3	152	123	61	55	11	9	69	102	1.263	3.26	102	3.28	.220	10	.189	-1	8	0.1
1973	Pit-N	3	0	1.000	7	7	0	0	0	43^2	36	17	15	4	1	24	26	1.374	3.09	114	3.77	.232	1	.083	2	3	0.2
1974★	Pit-N	9	8	.529	40	16	1	0	2	129	123	64	50	8	11	57	71	1.395	3.49	99	3.88	.247	4	.108	-1	6	-0.2
1975★	Pit-N	12	11	.522	33	29	6	0	0	192	160	89	69	10	4	92	89	1.313	3.23	109	3.13	.227	7	.119	6	9	0.5
1976	Pit-N	14	9	.609	31	29	6	1	1	193	180	83	66	10	3	52	98	1.202	3.08	113	2.92	.247	12	.203	8	13	1.2
1977	Pit-N	9	10	.474	33	32	3	1	0	193	209	113	105	25	6	55	122	1.368	4.90	81	4.37	.278	18	.261	-22	6	-1.9
1978	Pit-N	6	6	.500	28	11	0	0	0	96	81	40	34	3	5	39	62	1.250	3.19	116	2.97	.229	4	.138	7	6	0.8
1979★	Pit-N	13	7	.650	33	25	3	1	0	172^1	157	70	61	13	4	45	105	1.172	3.19	122	2.98	.246	8	.145	11	12	1.2
1980	Cal-A	3	6	.333	13	13	2	1	0	73^1	73	46	40	5	3	32	28	1.432	4.91	80	4.07	.264	0	....	-8	2	-0.8
1981	Cal-A	1	1	.500	11	4	0	0	0	44	40	18	17	8	0	14	19	1.227	3.48	105	3.83	.241	0	....	1	2	0.1
1982★	Cal-A	10	5	.667	33	16	3	1	1	142	120	54	50	15	5	44	86	1.155	3.17	128	3.06	.226	0	....	12	12	1.2
1983	Cal-A	11	5	.688	26	17	4	1	2	126^2	128	59	57	13	4	43	83	1.350	4.05	99	4.02	.264	0	....	-0	9	0.0
1984	Cal-A	4	5	.444	20	7	0	0	2	65^1	72	42	39	10	6	28	66	1.531	5.37	74	5.51	.280	0	....	-10	1	-1.0
1985	Bos-A	5	3	.625	22	9	0	0	1	92	98	43	42	9	1	32	56	1.413	4.11	104	4.20	.274	0	....	3	5	0.3
Total	**15**	**115**	**88**	**.567**	**380**	**246**	**36**	**8**	**12**	**1809^2**	**1693**	**839**	**736**	**150**	**68**	**662**	**1073**	**1.301**	**3.66**	**102**	**3.59**	**.248**	**66**	**.163**	**6**	**98**	**1.5**
• KISSINGER, Bill	William Francis "Shang,Shaney" Kissinger b: 8/15/1871, Dayton, KY d: 4/20/1929, Cincinnati, OH BR/TR, 5'11", 185 lbs. Deb: 5/30/1895																										
1895	Bal-N	1	0	1.000	2	2	1	0	0	11^1	18	11	5	0	0	2	3	1.765	3.97	120	5.79	.354	1	.200	0	1	0.0
	StL-N	4	12	.250	24	14	9	0	0	140^2	222	145	105	8	8	51	31	1.941	6.72	72	7.19	.353	24	.247	-26	3	-2.5
	Yr.	5	12	.294	26	16	10	0	0	152	240	156	110	8	8	53	34	1.928	6.51	74	7.09	.353	25	.245	-25	4	-2.5
1896	StL-N	2	9	.182	20	12	11	0	1	136	209	136	98	5	8	55	22	**1.941**	6.49	67	6.92	.349	22	.301	-29	2	-2.4
1897	StL-N	0	4	.000	7	4	2	0	0	31^1	51	50	40	2	8	15	5	2.106	11.49	38	8.88	.362	13	.333	-23	1	-1.9
Total	**3**	**7**	**25**	**.219**	**53**	**32**	**23**	**0**	**1**	**319^1**	**500**	**342**	**248**	**15**	**24**	**123**	**61**	**1.951**	**6.99**	**65**	**7.19**	**.352**	**60**	**.280**	**-77**	**7**	**-6.8**
• KITSON, Frank	Frank R. Kitson b: 9/11/1869, Hopkins, MI d: 4/14/1930, Allegan, MI BL/TR, 5'11", 165 lbs. Deb: 5/19/1898 U																										
1898	Bal-N	8	5	.615	17	13	13	1	0	119^1	123	71	43	0	8	35	32	1.324	3.24	110	3.31	.265	27	.314	1	9	0.5
1899	Bal-N	22	16	.579	40	37	34	2	0	326^2	327	144	101	6	12	65	75	1.200	2.78	142	2.88	.261	27	.201	41	31	3.6
1900★	Bro-N	15	13	.536	40	30	21	2	**4**	253^1	283	152	118	12	9	56	55	1.338	4.19	91	3.75	.282	32	.294	-13	19	-0.7
1901	Bro-N	19	11	.633	38	32	26	5	2	280^2	312	135	93	9	10	67	127	1.350	2.98	112	3.67	.280	35	.263	10	21	1.5
1902	Bro-N	19	13	.594	32	31	29	3	0	268^2	256	105	82	4	7	52	109	1.146	2.75	100	2.57	.251	32	.276	0	20	0.9
1903	Det-A	15	16	.484	31	28	28	2	0	257^2	277	112	74	8	6	38	102	1.223	2.58	113	3.03	.274	21	.181	10	14	0.7
1904	Det-A	9	13	.409	26	24	19	0	1	199^2	211	100	68	7	7	38	69	1.247	3.07	83	3.20	.272	15	.208	-14	7	-1.4
1905	Det-A	12	14	.462	33	27	21	3	1	225^2	230	120	87	3	11	57	78	1.272	3.47	79	3.15	.266	16	.184	-21	8	-2.4
1906	Was-A	6	14	.300	30	21	15	1	0	197	196	97	80	2	6	57	59	1.284	3.65	72	3.06	.262	22	.244	-19	8	-1.1
1907	Was-A	0	3	.000	5	3	2	0	0	32	41	20	14	1	2	9	11	1.563	3.94	61	5.07	.314	1	.100	-4	0	-0.5
	NY-A	4	0	1.000	12	4	3	0	0	61	75	31	21	0	4	17	14	1.508	3.10	90	4.36	.305	7	.280	-1	3	0.0
	Yr.	4	3	.571	17	7	5	0	0	93	116	51	35	1	6	26	25	1.527	3.39	78	4.60	.308	8	.229	-5	3	-0.6
Total	**10**	**129**	**118**	**.522**	**304**	**250**	**211**	**19**	**8**	**2221^2**	**2331**	**1087**	**781**	**52**	**82**	**491**	**731**	**1.270**	**3.16**	**97**	**3.22**	**.270**	**235**	**.240**	**-10**	**140**	**1.0**
• KLAERNER, Hugo	Hugo Emil "Dutch" Klaerner b: 10/15/1908, Fredericksburg, TX d: 1/3/1982, Fredericksburg, TX BR/TR, 5'11", 190 lbs. Deb: 9/10/1934																										
1934	Chi-A	0	2	.000	3	3	1	0	0	17^1	24	21	21	4	0	16	9	2.308	10.90	43	9.41	.329	2	.333	-11	0	-1.0
• KLAGES, Fred	Frederick Albert Anthony Klages b: 10/31/1943, Ambridge, PA BR/TR, 6'2", 185 lbs. Deb: 9/11/1966																										
1966	Chi-A	1	0	1.000	3	3	0	0	0	15^2	9	4	3	0	0	7	6	1.021	1.72	184	1.55	.167	3	.500	2	2	0.4
1967	Chi-A	4	4	.500	11	9	0	0	0	44^2	43	19	19	6	1	16	17	1.321	3.83	81	4.07	.256	0	.000	-4	1	-0.6
Total	**2**	**5**	**4**	**.556**	**14**	**12**	**0**	**0**	**0**	**60^1**	**52**	**23**	**22**	**6**	**1**	**23**	**23**	**1.243**	**3.28**	**95**	**3.42**	**.234**	**3**	**.167**	**-1**	**3**	**-0.2**
• KLAWITTER, Al	Albert C. "Dutch" Klawitter b: 4/12/1888, Wilkes-Barre, PA d: 5/2/1950, Milwaukee, WI BR/TR, 5'11.5", 187 lbs. Deb: 9/20/1909																										
1909	NY-N	1	1	.500	6	3	2	0	1	27	24	11	6	1	0	13	6	1.370	2.00	127	3.41	.247	3	.333	2	3	0.4
1910	NY-N	0	0	....	1	0	0	0	0	1	2	1	1	0	0	2	0	4.000	9.00	33	15.81	.400	0	....	-1	0	-0.1
1913	Det-A	1	2	.333	8	3	1	0	0	32	39	25	21	0	0	15	10	1.688	5.91	49	4.82	.305	0	.000	-10	0	-1.2
Total	**3**	**2**	**3**	**.400**	**15**	**6**	**3**	**0**	**1**	**60**	**65**	**37**	**28**	**1**	**0**	**30**	**16**	**1.583**	**4.20**	**67**	**4.37**	**.283**	**3**	**.150**	**-8**	**3**	**-0.9**
• KLAWITTER, Tom	Thomas Carl Klawitter b: 6/24/1958, La Crosse, WI BR/TL, 6'2", 190 lbs. Deb: 4/14/1985																										
1985	Min-A	0	0	....	7	2	0	0	0	9^1	7	7	7	2	0	13	5	2.143	6.75	65	8.00	.226	0	....	-2	0	-0.2
• KLEINE, Hal	Harold John Kleine b: 6/8/1923, St. Louis, MO d: 12/10/1957, St. Louis, MO BL/TL, 6'2", 193 lbs. Deb: 4/26/1944																										
1944	Cle-A	1	2	.333	11	6	1	0	0	40^2	38	29	26	0	0	36	13	1.820	5.75	57	4.60	.248	2	.143	-12	0	-1.3

YEAR	TM-L	W	L	PCT	G	GS	CG	SH	SV	IP	H	R	ER	HR	HB	BB	SO	RAT	ERA	ERA+	CERA	OAV	BH	AVG	PR+	WS	TPW
1945	Cle-A	0	0	....	3	0	0	0	0	7	8	4	3	0	0	7	5	2.143	3.86	84	6.20	.286	1	.333	-0	0	0.0
Total	2	1	2	.333	14	6	1	0	0	47^{2}	46	33	29	0	0	43	18	1.867	5.48	60	4.83	.254	3	.176	-12	0	-1.3
• KLEINHANS, Ted	Theodore Otto Kleinhans b: 4/8/1899, Deer Park, WI d: 7/24/1985, Redington Beach, FL BR/TL, 6', 170 lbs. Deb: 4/20/1934																										
1934	Phi-N	0	0	....	5	0	0	0	0	6	11	8	6	1	0	3	2	2.333	9.00	52	9.72	.379	0	.000	-3	0	-0.3
	Cin-N	2	6	.250	24	9	0	0	0	80	107	63	51	2	1	38	23	1.813	5.74	71	5.59	.321	3	.130	-13	0	-1.4
	Yr.	2	6	.250	29	9	0	0	0	86	118	71	57	3	1	41	25	1.849	5.97	69	5.87	.326	3	.125	-16	0	-1.7
1936	NY-A	1	1	.500	19	0	0	0	1	29^{1}	36	25	19	0	0	23	10	2.011	5.83	80	5.82	.300	1	.167	-4	0	-0.4
1937	Cin-N	1	2	.333	7	3	1	0	0	27^{1}	29	13	7	1	1	12	13	1.500	2.30	162	4.13	.271	2	.250	4	2	0.5
1938	Cin-N	0	0	....	1	0	0	0	0	1	2	1	1	0	0	0	0	2.000	9.00	40	7.48	.400	0	....	-1	0	-0.1
Total	4	4	9	.308	56	12	1	0	1	143^{2}	185	110	84	4	2	76	48	1.817	5.26	80	5.54	.311	6	.158	-16	2	-1.6
• KLEINKE, Nub	Norbert George Kleinke b: 5/19/1911, Fond du Lac, WI d: 3/16/1950, CA BR/TR, 6'1", 170 lbs. Deb: 4/25/1935																										
1935	StL-N	0	0	....	4	2	0	0	0	12^{2}	19	8	7	1	0	3	5	1.737	4.97	82	6.32	.358	0	.000	-1	0	-0.2
1937	StL-N	1	1	.500	5	2	1	0	0	20^{2}	25	14	11	0	0	7	9	1.548	4.79	83	4.45	.321	0	.000	-2	0	-0.3
Total	2	1	1	.500	9	4	1	0	0	33^{1}	44	22	18	1	0	10	14	1.620	4.86	83	5.16	.336	0	.000	-3	0	-0.4
• KLEPFER, Ed	Edward Lloyd "Big Ed" Klepfer b: 3/17/1888, Summerville, PA d: 8/9/1950, Tulsa, OK BR/TR, 6', 185 lbs. Deb: 7/4/1911																										
1911	NY-A	0	0	....	2	0	0	0	0	4	5	3	3	0	0	2	4	1.750	6.75	53	4.12	.250	0	.000	-1	0	-0.1
1913	NY-A	0	1	.000	8	1	0	0	0	24^{2}	38	22	21	2	2	12	10	2.027	7.66	39	8.27	.373	1	.167	-13	0	-1.3
1915	Chi-A	1	0	1.000	3	2	1	0	0	12^{2}	11	4	4	0	0	5	3	1.263	2.84	105	2.65	.234	0	.000	0	1	0.0
	Cle-A	1	6	.143	8	7	2	0	0	43	47	25	10	0	0	11	13	1.349	2.09	145	3.40	.283	2	.167	5	2	0.5
	Yr.	2	6	.250	11	9	3	0	0	55^{2}	58	29	14	0	0	16	16	1.329	2.26	134	3.23	.272	2	.133	5	3	0.5
1916	Cle-A	6	6	.500	31	13	4	1	2	143	136	52	40	0	4	46	62	1.273	2.52	119	3.05	.262	1	.025	7	9	0.4
1917	Cle-A	14	4	.778	41	27	9	0	1	213	208	84	56	0	0	55	66	1.235	2.37	120	2.85	.264	2	.032	5	16	-0.1
1919	Cle-A	0	0	....	5	0	0	0	0	7^{1}	12	14	6	1	0	6	7	2.455	7.36	45	10.31	.375	0	.000	-3	0	-0.4
Total	6	22	17	.564	98	50	16	1	3	447^{2}	457	204	140	3	6	137	165	1.327	2.81	105	3.39	.273	6	.048	0	28	-1.0
• KLIEMAN, Ed	Edward Frederick "Specs,Babe" Klieman b: 3/21/1918, Norwood, OH d: 11/15/1979, Homosassa, FL BR/TR, 6'1", 190 lbs. Deb: 9/24/1943																										
1943	Cle-A	0	1	.000	1	1	1	0	0	9	8	1	1	0	0	5	2	1.444	1.00	311	3.76	.286	0	.000	2	1	0.2
1944	Cle-A	11	13	.458	47	19	5	1	5	178^{1}	185	73	67	4	7	70	44	1.430	3.38	98	3.82	.274	6	.105	-4	11	-0.7
1945	Cle-A	5	8	.385	38	12	4	1	4	126^{1}	123	60	54	3	4	49	33	1.361	3.85	84	3.39	.261	8	.200	-7	5	-0.7
1946	Cle-A	0	0	....	9	0	0	0	0	15	18	13	11	0	0	10	2	1.867	6.60	50	5.24	.290	0	.000	-5	0	-0.6
1947	Cle-A	5	4	.556	**58**	0	0	0	**17**	92	78	32	31	5	2	39	21	1.272	3.03	115	3.04	.231	2	.105	3	9	0.2
1948*	Cle-A	3	2	.600	44	0	0	0	4	79^{2}	62	26	23	3	2	46	18	1.356	2.60	156	3.18	.229	2	.143	11	7	1.1
1949	Was-A	0	0	....	2	0	0	0	0	3	8	6	6	0	0	3	1	3.667	18.00	24	16.54	.500	1	1.000	-4	0	-0.4
	Chi-A	2	0	1.000	18	0	0	0	3	33	33	15	11	2	0	15	9	1.455	3.00	139	3.91	.273	2	.250	4	4	0.4
	Yr.	2	0	1.000	20	0	0	0	3	36	41	21	17	2	0	18	10	1.639	4.25	99	4.97	.299	3	.333	-0	4	0.0
1950	Phi-A	0	0	....	5	0	0	0	0	5^{2}	10	6	6	0	2	2	0	2.118	9.53	48	8.52	.357	0	.000	-3	0	-0.3
Total	8	26	28	.481	222	32	10	2	33	542	525	232	210	17	17	239	130	1.410	3.49	99	3.66	.261	21	.146	-4	37	-0.8
• KLIMKOWSKI, Ron	Ronald Bernard Klimkowski b: 3/1/1944, Jersey City, NJ BR/TR, 6'2", 190 lbs. Deb: 9/15/1969																										
1969	NY-A	0	0	....	3	1	0	0	0	14	6	1	1	0	0	5	3	.786	0.64	541	0.91	.130	0	.000	4	2	0.4
1970	NY-A	6	7	.462	45	3	1	1	1	98^{1}	80	36	29	7	3	33	40	1.149	2.65	132	2.70	.223	1	.053	9	7	0.8
1971	Oak-A	2	2	.500	26	0	0	0	2	45^{1}	37	19	17	3	1	23	25	1.324	3.38	99	3.02	.220	2	.400	-1	3	0.0
1972	NY-A	0	3	.000	16	2	0	0	1	31^{1}	32	15	14	3	1	15	11	1.500	4.02	73	4.28	.271	0	.000	-4	0	-0.5
Total	4	8	12	.400	90	6	1	1	4	189	155	71	61	13	5	76	79	1.222	2.90	114	2.91	.224	3	.091	9	12	0.7
• KLINE, Bob	Robert George "Junior" Kline b: 12/9/1909, Enterprise, OH d: 3/16/1987, Westerville, OH BR/TR, 6'3", 200 lbs. Deb: 9/17/1930																										
1930	Bos-A	0	0	....	1	0	0	0	0	1	1	0	0	0	0	0	0	1.000	0.00	....	1.95	.333	0	....	1	0	0.0
1931	Bos-A	5	5	.500	28	10	3	0	0	98	110	54	48	3	3	35	25	1.480	4.41	98	4.31	.298	9	.333	-1	7	0.2
1932	Bos-A	11	13	.458	47	19	4	1	2	172	203	117	101	10	1	76	31	1.622	5.28	85	4.82	.294	7	.130	-12	7	-1.4
1933	Bos-A	7	8	.467	46	8	1	0	4	127	127	70	64	5	6	67	16	1.528	4.54	97	4.17	.265	6	.176	-2	7	-0.3
1934	Phi-A	6	2	.750	20	0	0	0	1	39^{2}	50	34	28	6	0	13	14	1.588	6.35	69	5.60	.314	3	.333	-9	1	-0.8
	Was-A	1	0	1.000	6	0	0	0	0	4	10	8	7	0	1	4	1	3.500	15.75	27	16.37	.500	0	....	-5	0	-0.5
	Yr.	7	2	.778	26	0	0	0	1	43^{2}	60	42	35	6	1	17	15	1.763	7.21	61	6.58	.335	3	.333	-14	1	-1.2
Total	5	30	28	.517	148	37	8	1	7	441^{2}	501	283	248	24	11	195	87	1.576	5.05	87	4.69	.291	25	.202	-29	22	-2.7
• KLINE, Bobby	John Robert Kline b: 1/27/1929, St. Petersburg, FL BR/TR, 6', 179 lbs. Deb: 4/11/1955 ♦																										
1955	Was-A	0	0	....	1	0	0	0	0	1	4	3	3	1	0	1	0	5.000	27.00	14	41.46	.667	31	.221	-3	2	-0.7
• KLINE, Ron	Ronald Lee Kline b: 3/9/1932, Callery, PA d: 6/22/2002, Callery, PA BR/TR, 6'3", 205 lbs. Deb: 4/21/1952																										
1952	Pit-N	0	7	.000	27	11	0	0	0	78^{2}	74	55	48	3	6	66	27	1.780	5.49	73	5.08	.253	0	.000	-13	0	-1.5
1955	Pit-N	6	13	.316	36	19	2	1	2	136^{2}	161	78	63	13	5	53	48	1.566	4.15	99	5.13	.298	5	.132	1	6	-0.2
1956	Pit-N	14	18	.438	44	39	9	2	2	264	263	110	99	26	5	81	125	1.303	3.38	112	3.77	.263	10	.127	13	17	1.1
1957	Pit-N	9	16	.360	40	31	11	2	0	205	214	107	92	27	1	61	88	1.341	4.04	94	4.12	.268	4	.061	-8	7	-1.4
1958	Pit-N	13	16	.448	32	32	11	2	0	237^{1}	220	96	93	25	0	92	109	1.315	3.53	110	3.65	.252	2	.027	4	14	-0.2
1959	Pit-N	11	13	.458	33	29	7	0	0	186	186	95	88	23	2	70	91	1.376	4.26	91	4.13	.263	8	.136	-10	8	-1.1
1960	StL-N	4	9	.308	34	17	1	0	1	117^{2}	133	86	79	21	0	43	54	1.496	6.04	68	5.13	.284	5	.143	-25	0	-2.7
1961	LA-A	3	6	.333	26	12	0	0	1	104^{2}	119	62	57	16	1	44	70	1.557	4.90	92	5.35	.288	3	.097	-3	4	-0.5
	Det-A	5	3	.625	10	8	3	1	0	56^{1}	53	25	17	3	0	17	27	1.243	2.72	151	3.00	.245	3	.167	9	5	0.9
	Yr.	8	9	.471	36	20	3	1	1	161	172	87	74	19	1	61	97	1.447	4.14	107	4.53	.273	6	.122	5	9	0.3
1962	Det-A	3	6	.333	36	4	0	0	2	77^{1}	88	40	37	9	2	28	47	1.500	4.31	95	4.88	.284	2	.125	-1	4	-0.2
1963	Was-A	3	8	.273	62	1	0	0	17	93^{2}	85	36	29	3	3	30	49	1.228	2.79	133	2.90	.249	1	.091	10	10	1.0
1964	Was-A	10	7	.588	61	0	0	0	14	81^{1}	81	29	21	4	2	21	40	1.254	2.32	159	3.06	.262	1	.167	12	12	1.3
1965	Was-A	7	6	.538	74	0	0	0	**29**	99^{1}	106	36	29	7	2	32	52	1.389	2.63	132	3.73	.275	0	.000	10	14	1.0
1966	Was-A	6	4	.600	63	0	0	0	23	90^{1}	79	32	24	12	0	17	46	1.063	2.39	145	2.76	.237	1	.167	10	13	1.1
1967	Min-A	7	1	.875	54	0	0	0	5	71^{2}	71	33	30	10	1	15	36	1.200	3.77	92	3.48	.261	0	.000	-1	5	-0.2
1968	Pit-N	12	5	.706	56	0	0	0	7	112^{2}	94	26	21	3	2	31	48	1.109	1.68	174	2.26	.234	0	.000	14	13	1.5
1969	Pit-N	1	3	.250	20	0	0	0	3	31	37	23	20	3	1	5	15	1.355	5.81	60	4.18	.296	0	.000	-8	0	-0.9
	SF-N	0	2	.000	7	0	0	0	0	11	16	6	5	1	0	6	7	2.000	4.09	86	7.05	.364	0	....	-1	0	-0.1
	Yr.	1	5	.167	27	0	0	0	3	42	53	29	25	4	1	11	22	1.524	5.36	65	4.93	.314	0	.000	-8	0	-0.9
	Bos-A	0	1	.000	16	0	0	0	1	17	24	11	9	4	0	17	7	2.412	4.76	80	9.92	.329	0	....	-1	0	-0.2
1970	Atl-N	0	0	....	5	0	0	0	1	6^{1}	9	5	5	4	0	2	3	1.737	7.11	60	10.35	.321	0	....	-2	0	-0.2
Total	17	114	144	.442	736	203	44	8	108	2078	2113	991	866	217	33	731	989	1.369	3.75	103	4.03	.266	45	.092	10	132	-1.5
• KLINE, Steve	Steven Jack Kline b: 10/6/1947, Wenatchee, WA BR/TR, 6'3", 205 lbs. Deb: 7/10/1970																										
1970	NY-A	6	6	.500	16	15	5	0	0	100^{1}	99	42	38	8	0	24	49	1.226	3.41	103	3.17	.254	5	.179	1	5	0.3
1971	NY-A	12	13	.480	31	30	15	1	0	222^{1}	206	87	73	21	0	37	81	1.093	2.96	109	2.74	.244	9	.136	8	13	0.8
1972	NY-A	16	9	.640	32	32	11	4	0	236^{1}	210	79	63	11	10	44	58	1.075	2.40	123	2.47	.237	7	.092	14	14	1.3
1973	NY-A	4	7	.364	14	13	2	1	0	74	76	39	33	5	1	31	19	1.446	4.01	91	4.09	.270	0	....	-4	3	-0.4
1974	NY-A	2	2	.500	4	4	0	0	0	26	26	12	10	3	1	5	6	1.192	3.46	101	3.59	.263	0	....	-0	2	0.0
	Cle-A	3	8	.273	16	11	1	0	0	71	70	44	40	9	4	31	17	1.423	5.07	71	4.65	.266	0	....	-12	1	-1.2
	Yr.	5	10	.333	20	15	1	0	0	97	96	56	50	12	5	36	23	1.361	4.64	77	4.37	.265	0	....	-12	3	-1.3
1977	Atl-N	0	0	....	16	0	0	0	1	20^{1}	21	15	15	4	0	12	10	1.623	6.64	67	5.45	.259	0	....	-4	0	-0.4
Total	6	43	45	.489	129	105	34	6	1	750^{1}	708	318	272	61	16	184	240	1.189	3.26	103	3.13	.249	21	.124	3	38	0.3
• KLINE, Steve	Steven James Kline b: 8/22/1972, Sunbury, PA BB/TL, 6'2", 200 lbs. Deb: 4/2/1997																										
1997	Cle-A	3	1	.750	20	1	0	0	0	26^{1}	42	19	17	6	1	13	17	2.089	5.81	81	9.58	.365	0	....	-3	1	-0.3
	Mon-N	1	3	.250	26	0	0	0	0	26^{1}	31	18	18	4	1	10	20	1.557	6.15	68	5.39	.304	0	.000	-6	0	-0.6

YEAR TM-L	W	L	PCT	G	GS	CG	SH	SV	IP	H	R	ER	HR	HB	BB	SO	RAT	ERA	ERA+	CERA	OAV	BH	AVG	PR+	WS	TPW
1998 Mon-N	3	6	.333	78	0	0	0	1	71^2	62	25	22	4	3	41	76	1.437	2.76	152	3.60	.228	0	.000	13	6	1.2
1999 Mon-N	7	4	.636	**82**	0	0	0	0	69^2	56	32	29	8	3	33	69	1.278	3.75	120	3.40	.218	0	.000	7	7	0.7
2000 Mon-N	1	5	.167	**83**	0	0	0	14	82^1	88	36	32	8	3	27	64	1.397	3.50	137	4.37	.278	0	.000	13	9	1.2
2001* StL-N	3	3	.500	**89**	0	0	0	9	75	53	16	15	3	4	29	54	1.093	1.80	237	2.20	.203	1	.500	19	12	1.9
2002* StL-N	2	1	.667	66	0	0	0	6	58^1	54	23	22	3	1	21	41	1.286	3.39	116	3.28	.251	0	.000	3	6	0.3
2003 StL-N	5	5	.500	78	0	0	0	3	63^2	56	29	27	5	3	30	31	1.351	3.82	106	3.59	.237	1	.500	2	5	0.2
Total 7	25	28	.472	522	1	0	0	33	473^1	442	198	182	41	19	204	372	1.365	3.46	125	3.87	.249	2	.154	47	46	4.5

• KLING, Bill William Kling b: 1/14/1867, Kansas City, MO d: 8/26/1934, Kansas City, MO BL/TR, 6', 190 lbs. Deb: 8/13/1891 U

YEAR TM-L	W	L	PCT	G	GS	CG	SH	SV	IP	H	R	ER	HR	HB	BB	SO	RAT	ERA	ERA+	CERA	OAV	BH	AVG	PR+	WS	TPW
1891 Phi-N	4	2	.667	12	7	4	0	0	75	91	61	36	2	0	32	26	1.640	4.32	79	....	.289	6	.194	-8	3	-0.6
1892 Bal-N	0	2	.000	2	2	0	0	0	11	17	16	14	1	0	7	7	2.182	11.45	30	8.19	.340	1	.250	-9	0	-0.8
1895 Lou-N	0	0	....	1	0	0	0	0	1	0	0	0	0	0	1	0	1.000	0.00	....	0.82	.000	0	.000	1	0	0.0
Total 3	4	4	.500	15	9	4	0	0	87	108	77	50	3	0	40	33	1.701	5.17	66	1.04	.296	7	.194	-17	3	-1.3

• KLINGENBECK, Scott Scott Edward Klingenbeck b: 2/3/1971, Cincinnati, OH BR/TR, 6'2", 205 lbs. Deb: 6/2/1994

YEAR TM-L	W	L	PCT	G	GS	CG	SH	SV	IP	H	R	ER	HR	HB	BB	SO	RAT	ERA	ERA+	CERA	OAV	BH	AVG	PR+	WS	TPW
1994 Bal-A	1	0	1.000	1	1	0	0	0	7	6	4	3	1	1	4	5	1.429	3.86	130	4.63	.240	0	....	1	1	0.1
1995 Bal-A	2	2	.500	6	5	0	0	0	31^1	32	17	17	6	0	18	15	1.596	4.88	97	5.78	.269	0	....	-1	2	-0.1
Min-A	0	2	.000	18	4	0	0	0	48^1	69	48	46	16	4	24	27	1.924	8.57	56	9.53	.338	0	....	-20	0	-1.9
Yr.	2	4	.333	24	9	0	0	0	79^2	101	65	63	22	4	42	42	1.795	7.12	67	8.06	.313	0	....	-21	2	-2.0
1996 Min-A	1	1	.500	10	3	0	0	0	28^2	42	28	25	5	1	10	15	1.814	7.85	65	7.37	.339	0	....	-9	0	-0.8
1998 Cin-N	1	3	.250	4	4	0	0	0	22^2	26	17	15	6	1	7	13	1.456	5.96	72	5.82	.286	0	.000	-4	0	-0.5
Total 4	5	8	.385	39	17	0	0	0	138	175	114	106	34	7	63	75	1.725	6.91	69	7.37	.311	0	.000	-34	3	-3.2

• KLINGER, Bob Robert Harold Klinger b: 6/4/1908, Allenton, MO d: 8/19/1977, Villa Ridge, MO BR/TR, 6', 180 lbs. Deb: 4/19/1938

YEAR TM-L	W	L	PCT	G	GS	CG	SH	SV	IP	H	R	ER	HR	HB	BB	SO	RAT	ERA	ERA+	CERA	OAV	BH	AVG	PR+	WS	TPW
1938 Pit-N	12	5	.706	28	21	10	1	1	159^1	152	63	53	7	6	42	58	1.218	2.99	127	3.03	.253	10	.167	11	12	1.0
1939 Pit-N	14	17	.452	37	33	10	2	0	225	251	120	109	11	3	81	64	1.476	4.36	88	4.14	.284	17	.202	-8	10	-0.8
1940 Pit-N	8	13	.381	39	22	3	0	3	142	196	102	85	5	5	53	48	1.754	5.39	71	5.73	.329	6	.143	-21	1	-2.3
1941 Pit-N	9	4	.692	35	9	3	0	4	116^2	127	58	51	5	1	30	36	1.346	3.93	92	3.56	.276	8	.250	-3	8	-0.1
1942 Pit-N	8	11	.421	37	19	8	1	1	152^2	151	69	55	6	3	45	58	1.284	3.24	104	3.12	.252	8	.200	4	9	0.6
1943 Pit-N	11	8	.579	33	25	14	3	0	195	185	77	59	6	0	58	65	1.246	2.72	128	2.89	.252	16	.246	16	13	2.1
1946* Bos-A	3	2	.600	28	1	0	0	**9**	57	49	16	15	1	1	25	16	1.298	2.37	155	2.93	.238	5	.313	8	8	0.9
1947 Bos-A	1	1	.500	28	0	0	0	5	42	42	20	18	5	1	24	12	1.571	3.86	101	4.69	.253	1	.111	0	3	-0.1
Total 8	66	61	.520	265	130	48	7	23	1089^2	1153	525	445	46	20	358	357	1.387	3.68	100	3.72	.271	71	.204	8	64	1.4

• KLINK, Joe Joseph Charles Klink b: 2/3/1962, Johnstown, PA BL/TL, 5'11", 175 lbs. Deb: 4/9/1987

YEAR TM-L	W	L	PCT	G	GS	CG	SH	SV	IP	H	R	ER	HR	HB	BB	SO	RAT	ERA	ERA+	CERA	OAV	BH	AVG	PR+	WS	TPW
1987 Min-A	0	1	.000	12	0	0	0	0	23	37	18	17	4	0	11	17	2.087	6.65	69	8.71	.359	0	....	-5	0	-0.5
1990* Oak-A	0	0	....	40	0	0	0	1	39^2	34	9	9	1	0	18	19	1.311	2.04	182	3.05	.233	0	....	6	4	0.7
1991 Oak-A	10	3	.769	62	0	0	0	2	62	60	30	30	4	5	21	34	1.306	4.35	88	3.60	.259	0	....	-4	5	-0.4
1993 Fla-N	0	2	.000	59	0	0	0	0	37^2	37	22	21	0	0	24	22	1.619	5.02	86	4.00	.266	0	.000	-2	1	-0.2
1996 Sea-A	0	0	....	3	0	0	0	0	2^1	3	1	1	1	0	1	2	1.714	3.86	128	8.35	.300	0	....	0	0	0.0
Total 5	10	6	.625	176	0	0	0	3	164^2	171	80	78	10	5	75	94	1.494	4.26	96	4.34	.271	0	.000	-4	10	-0.4

• KLIPPSTEIN, Johnny John Calvin Klippstein b: 10/17/1927, Washington, DC d: 10/10/2003, Elgin, IL BR/TR, 6'1", 185 lbs. Deb: 5/3/1950

YEAR TM-L	W	L	PCT	G	GS	CG	SH	SV	IP	H	R	ER	HR	HB	BB	SO	RAT	ERA	ERA+	CERA	OAV	BH	AVG	PR+	WS	TPW
1950 Chi-N	2	9	.182	33	11	3	0	1	104^2	112	69	61	9	4	64	51	1.682	5.25	80	5.22	.279	11	.333	-9	3	-0.5
1951 Chi-N	6	6	.500	35	11	1	1	2	123^2	125	71	59	10	6	53	56	1.439	4.29	95	4.15	.263	4	.108	-2	6	-0.3
1952 Chi-N	9	14	.391	41	25	7	2	3	202^2	208	110	100	17	6	89	110	1.465	4.44	87	4.29	.265	11	.175	-13	7	-1.2
1953 Chi-N	10	11	.476	48	19	5	0	6	167^2	169	115	90	15	8	107	113	1.646	4.83	92	4.93	.258	9	.155	-2	8	-0.3
1954 Chi-N	4	11	.267	36	21	4	0	1	148	155	104	87	13	4	96	69	1.696	5.29	79	5.09	.272	6	.133	-16	2	-1.8
1955 Cin-N	9	10	.474	39	14	3	2	0	138	120	66	52	13	4	60	68	1.304	3.39	125	3.50	.233	2	.065	13	9	1.1
1956 Cin-N	12	11	.522	37	29	11	0	1	211	219	103	96	26	10	82	86	1.427	4.09	97	4.54	.275	7	.099	-0	11	-0.4
1957 Cin-N	8	11	.421	46	18	3	1	3	146	146	84	82	17	3	68	99	1.466	5.05	81	4.45	.261	3	.073	-16	6	-1.9
1958 Cin-N	3	2	.600	12	4	0	0	1	33	37	20	18	5	1	14	22	1.545	4.91	84	5.36	.285	1	.125	-3	1	-0.3
LA-N	3	5	.375	45	0	0	0	9	90	81	40	38	12	2	44	73	1.389	3.80	108	4.14	.248	1	.050	3	7	0.1
Yr.	6	7	.462	57	4	0	0	10	123	118	60	56	17	3	58	95	1.431	4.10	100	4.47	.259	2	.071	-0	8	-0.3
1959* LA-N	4	0	1.000	28	0	0	0	2	45^2	48	31	30	8	2	33	30	1.774	5.91	71	6.32	.276	1	.143	-9	1	-0.9
1960 Cle-A	5	5	.500	49	0	0	0	**14**	74^1	53	30	24	8	1	35	46	1.184	2.91	129	2.90	.205	2	.143	7	9	0.7
1961 Was-A	2	2	.500	42	1	0	0	0	71^2	83	59	54	13	4	43	41	1.758	6.78	58	6.74	.297	1	.143	-23	0	-2.3
1962 Cin-N	7	6	.538	40	7	0	0	4	108^2	113	66	54	13	4	64	67	1.629	4.47	90	5.35	.278	3	.125	-6	5	-0.6
1963 Phi-N	5	6	.455	49	1	0	0	8	112	80	28	24	3	3	46	86	1.125	1.93	168	2.18	.204	1	.038	14	12	1.3
1964 Phi-N	2	1	.667	11	0	0	0	1	22^1	22	10	10	6	2	8	13	1.343	4.03	86	5.27	.250	0	.000	-2	1	-0.2
Min-A	0	4	.000	33	0	0	0	2	45^2	44	12	10	4	1	20	39	1.401	1.97	182	3.78	.260	0	.000	9	4	0.9
1965* Min-A	9	3	.750	56	0	0	0	5	76^1	59	22	19	8	3	31	59	1.179	2.24	159	3.01	.217	0	.000	10	8	1.0
1966 Min-A	1	1	.500	26	0	0	0	3	39^2	35	15	15	2	2	20	26	1.387	3.40	106	3.59	.238	0	.000	1	3	0.1
1967 Det-A	0	0	....	5	0	0	0	0	6^2	6	4	4	1	0	1	4	1.050	5.40	60	2.97	.250	0	....	-2	0	-0.2
Total 18	101	118	.461	711	161	37	6	66	1967^2	1915	1059	927	203	70	978	1158	1.470	4.24	95	4.39	.258	63	.125	-45	103	-5.7

• KLOBEDANZ, Fred Frederick Augustus "Duke" Klobedanz b: 6/13/1871, Waterbury, CT d: 4/12/1940, Waterbury, CT BL/TL, 5'11", 190 lbs. Deb: 8/20/1896

YEAR TM-L	W	L	PCT	G	GS	CG	SH	SV	IP	H	R	ER	HR	HB	BB	SO	RAT	ERA	ERA+	CERA	OAV	BH	AVG	PR+	WS	TPW
1896 Bos-N	6	4	.600	10	9	9	0	0	80^2	69	41	27	5	0	31	26	1.240	3.01	151	2.92	.230	13	.317	12	8	1.2
1897* Bos-N	26	7	.788	38	37	30	2	0	309^1	344	198	158	13	23	125	92	1.516	4.60	97	4.47	.279	48	.324	-12	25	-0.1
1898 Bos-N	19	10	.655	35	33	25	0	0	270^2	281	168	117	13	12	99	51	1.404	3.89	95	3.86	.266	27	.213	-13	15	-1.5
1899 Bos-N	1	4	.200	5	5	4	0	0	33^1	39	22	18	2	2	9	8	1.440	4.86	85	4.39	.292	2	.182	-4	2	-0.2
1902 Bos-N	1	0	1.000	1	1	1	0	0	8	9	1	1	0	1	2	4	1.375	1.13	251	3.52	.284	1	.500	1	1	0.3
Total 5	53	25	.679	89	85	69	2	0	702	742	430	321	33	38	266	181	1.436	4.12	100	4.04	.270	91	.277	-16	51	-0.4

• KLOPP, Stan Stanley Harold "Betz" Klopp b: 12/22/1910, Womelsdorf, PA d: 3/11/1980, Robesonia, PA BR/TR, 6'1.5", 180 lbs. Deb: 4/29/1944

YEAR TM-L	W	L	PCT	G	GS	CG	SH	SV	IP	H	R	ER	HR	HB	BB	SO	RAT	ERA	ERA+	CERA	OAV	BH	AVG	PR+	WS	TPW
1944 Bos-N	1	2	.333	24	0	0	0	0	46^1	47	36	22	1	0	33	17	1.727	4.27	89	4.62	.272	2	.286	-2	0	-0.2

• KNACKERT, Brent Brent Bradley Knackert b: 8/1/1969, Los Angeles, CA BR/TR, 6'3", 185 lbs. Deb: 4/10/1990

YEAR TM-L	W	L	PCT	G	GS	CG	SH	SV	IP	H	R	ER	HR	HB	BB	SO	RAT	ERA	ERA+	CERA	OAV	BH	AVG	PR+	WS	TPW
1990 Sea-A	1	1	.500	24	2	0	0	0	37^1	50	28	27	5	2	21	28	1.902	6.51	61	6.99	.313	0	....	-11	0	-1.1
1996 Bos-A	0	1	.000	8	0	0	0	0	10	16	12	10	1	0	7	5	2.300	9.00	56	8.69	.356	0	....	-4	0	-0.4
Total 2	1	2	.333	32	2	0	0	0	47^1	66	40	37	6	2	28	33	1.986	7.04	60	7.35	.322	0	....	-15	0	-1.4

• KNAPP, Chris Robert Christian Knapp b: 9/16/1953, Cherry Point, NC BR/TR, 6'5", 195 lbs. Deb: 9/4/1975

YEAR TM-L	W	L	PCT	G	GS	CG	SH	SV	IP	H	R	ER	HR	HB	BB	SO	RAT	ERA	ERA+	CERA	OAV	BH	AVG	PR+	WS	TPW
1975 Chi-A	0	0	....	2	0	0	0	0	2	2	1	1	0	0	4	3	3.000	4.50	86	9.51	.250	0	....	-0	0	0.0
1976 Chi-A	3	1	.750	11	6	1	0	0	52^1	54	31	28	5	1	32	41	1.643	4.82	74	5.25	.273	0	....	-7	1	-0.7
1977 Chi-A	12	7	.632	27	26	4	0	0	146^1	166	90	78	16	7	61	103	1.551	4.80	85	5.12	.283	0	....	-7	6	-0.7
1978 Cal-A	14	8	.636	30	29	6	0	0	188^1	178	94	88	25	2	67	126	1.301	4.21	86	3.81	.250	0	....	-11	9	-1.2
1979* Cal-A	5	5	.500	20	18	3	0	0	98	109	73	60	8	2	35	36	1.469	5.51	74	4.36	.275	0	....	-15	1	-1.5
1980 Cal-A	2	11	.154	32	20	1	0	1	117^1	133	83	80	18	8	51	46	1.568	6.14	64	5.63	.289	0	....	-28	0	-2.8
Total 6	36	32	.529	122	99	15	0	1	604^1	642	372	335	72	20	250	355	1.476	4.99	77	4.71	.272	0	....	-69	17	-6.9

• KNAUSS, Frank Frank H. Knauss b: 1868, Cleveland, OH BL/TL, 5'10", 170 lbs. Deb: 6/25/1890

YEAR TM-L	W	L	PCT	G	GS	CG	SH	SV	IP	H	R	ER	HR	HB	BB	SO	RAT	ERA	ERA+	CERA	OAV	BH	AVG	PR+	WS	TPW
1890 Col-a	17	12	.586	37	34	28	3	2	275^2	206	131	86	3	21	106	148	1.132	2.81	128	....	**.202**	24	.226	13	22	1.7
1891 Cle-N	0	3	.000	3	3	1	0	0	15	23	29	12	2	4	8	6	2.067	7.20	48	....	.339	1	.167	-6	0	-0.6
1892 Cin-N	0	0	....	1	0	0	0	0	8	13	9	3	0	0	5	2	2.250	3.38	97	7.79	.352	1	.333	-0	0	0.0
1894 Cle-N	0	1	.000	2	2	1	0	0	11	7	9	7	0	3	14	2	1.909	5.73	95	5.06	.181	0	.000	-0	1	-0.1
1895 NY-N	0	0	....	1	1	0	0	0	3^2	9	7	7	0	0	2	1	3.000	17.18	27	13.29	.459	0	.000	-5	0	-0.4
Total 5	17	16	.515	44	40	30	3	2	313^1	258	185	115	5	28	135	159	1.254	3.30	112	0.53	.218	26	.217	1	23	0.6

YEAR	TM-L	W	L	PCT	G	GS	CG	SH	SV	IP	H	R	ER	HR	HB	BB	SO	RAT	ERA	ERA+	CERA	OAV	BH	AVG	PR+	WS	TPW
• KNEISCH, Rudy	Rudolph Frank Kneisch b: 4/10/1899, Baltimore, MD d: 4/6/1965, Baltimore, MD BR/TL, 5'10.5", 175 lbs. Deb: 9/21/1926																										
1926	Det-A	0	1	.000	2	2	1	0	0	17	18	7	5	2	2	6	4	1.412	2.65	153	4.72	.273	0	.000	3	1	0.2
• KNELL, Phil	Philip H. Knell b: 3/12/1865, Mill Valley, CA d: 6/5/1944, Santa Monica, CA BR/TL, 5'7.5", 154 lbs. Deb: 7/6/1888 U																										
1888	Pit-N	1	2	.333	3	3	3	0	0	26^{1}	20	19	11	1	5	18	15	1.443	3.76	70	....	.203	1	.091	-3	0	-0.4
1890	Phi-P	22	11	.667	35	31	30	2	0	286^{2}	287	199	122	10	28	166	99	1.580	3.83	112	....	.250	29	.220	14	21	1.1
1891	Col-a	28	27	.509	58	52	47	**5**	0	462	363	228	150	4	54	226	228	1.275	2.92	118	....	**.209**	34	.158	14	32	0.3
1892	Was-N	9	13	.409	22	21	17	1	0	170	156	114	69	4	11	76	74	1.365	3.65	89	3.39	.234	8	.118	-7	7	-1.1
	Phi-N	5	5	.500	11	9	7	0	0	80	87	47	36	0	11	35	43	1.525	4.05	80	4.34	.266	3	.088	-8	4	-1.0
	Yr.	14	18	.438	33	30	24	1	0	250	243	161	105	4	22	111	117	1.416	3.78	86	3.69	.245	11	.108	-16	11	-2.1
1894	Pit-N	0	0	....	1	0	0	0	0	7	11	9	9	0	1	6	0	2.429	11.57	45	8.94	.353	0	.000	-5	0	-0.4
	Lou-N	7	21	.250	32	28	25	0	0	247	330	237	146	9	14	104	67	1.757	5.32	96	5.73	.317	31	.274	-6	8	-0.4
	Yr.	7	21	.250	33	28	25	0	0	254	341	246	155	9	15	110	67	1.776	5.49	93	5.82	.318	31	.267	-11	8	-0.8
1895	Lou-N	0	6	.000	10	6	3	0	0	56^{2}	75	66	41	3	6	21	19	1.694	6.51	71	5.79	.314	6	.231	-9	1	-0.7
	Cle-N	7	5	.583	20	13	9	0	0	116^{2}	149	100	70	7	2	53	30	1.731	5.40	92	5.55	.306	11	.200	-5	5	-0.7
	Yr.	7	11	.389	30	19	12	0	0	173^{1}	224	166	111	10	8	74	49	1.719	5.76	84	5.63	.309	17	.210	-15	6	-1.4
Total	6	79	90	.467	192	163	141	8	0	1452^{1}	1478	1019	654	38	132	705	575	1.503	4.05	100	2.32	.256	123	.187	-16	78	-3.3
• KNEPPER, Bob	Robert Wesley Knepper b: 5/25/1954, Akron, OH BL/TL, 6'3", 200 lbs. Deb: 9/10/1976																										
1976	SF-N	1	2	.333	4	4	0	0	0	25	26	9	9	0	0	7	11	1.320	3.24	112	3.14	.277	1	.111	1	2	0.1
1977	SF-N	11	9	.550	27	27	6	2	0	166	151	73	62	14	3	72	100	1.343	3.36	116	3.65	.242	10	.182	12	12	1.4
1978	SF-N	17	11	.607	36	35	16	**6**	0	260	218	85	76	10	4	85	147	1.165	2.63	131	2.56	.229	5	.063	24	22	2.2
1979	SF-N	9	12	.429	34	34	6	2	0	207^{1}	241	117	107	30	3	77	123	1.534	4.64	75	5.20	.289	12	.182	-24	5	-2.2
1980	SF-N	9	16	.360	35	33	8	1	0	215^{1}	242	114	98	15	8	61	103	1.407	4.10	86	4.13	.281	10	.152	-9	6	-1.0
1981*	Hou-N★	9	5	.643	22	22	6	5	0	156^{2}	128	41	38	5	4	38	75	1.060	2.18	151	2.26	.226	7	.149	19	13	2.1
1982	Hou-N	5	15	.250	33	29	4	0	1	180	193	100	89	14	3	60	108	1.406	4.45	75	4.14	.278	3	.058	-24	2	-2.8
1983	Hou-N	6	13	.316	35	29	4	3	0	203	202	93	72	12	4	71	125	1.345	3.19	107	3.62	.261	12	.182	2	8	0.5
1984	Hou-N	15	10	.600	35	34	11	3	0	233^{2}	223	93	83	26	1	55	140	1.190	3.20	104	3.28	.251	13	.171	0	13	0.4
1985	Hou-N	15	13	.536	37	37	4	0	0	241	253	119	95	21	3	54	131	1.274	3.55	98	3.58	.271	11	.141	-5	9	-0.5
1986*	Hou-N	17	12	.586	40	38	8	**5**	0	258	232	100	90	19	4	62	143	1.140	3.14	115	2.75	.242	9	.099	12	17	1.0
1987	Hou-N	8	17	.320	33	31	1	0	0	177^{2}	226	118	104	26	4	54	76	**1.576**	5.27	74	5.74	.313	5	.098	-26	0	-2.7
1988	Hou-N★	14	5	.737	27	27	3	2	0	175	156	70	61	13	2	67	103	1.274	3.14	106	3.32	.243	6	.125	4	10	0.4
1989	Hou-N	4	10	.286	22	20	0	0	0	113	135	78	74	12	2	60	45	1.726	5.89	57	5.85	.303	7	.226	-31	1	-2.7
	SF-N	3	2	.600	13	6	1	1	0	52	55	20	20	4	1	15	19	1.346	3.46	97	3.74	.270	1	.083	-2	3	-0.1
	Yr.	7	12	.368	35	26	1	1	0	165	190	98	94	16	3	75	64	**1.606**	5.13	66	5.19	.292	8	.186	-32	4	-2.9
1990	SF-N	3	3	.500	12	7	0	0	0	44^{1}	56	28	28	7	1	19	24	1.692	5.68	64	6.21	.311	3	.231	-10	1	-1.0
Total	15	146	155	.485	445	413	78	30	1	2708	2737	1258	1106	228	47	857	1473	1.327	3.68	95	3.77	.264	115	.137	-55	124	-4.9
• KNEPPER, Charlie	Charles Knepper b: 2/18/1871, Anderson, IN d: 2/6/1946, Muncie, IN BR/TR, 6'4", 190 lbs. Deb: 5/26/1899																										
1899	Cle-N	4	22	.154	27	26	26	0	0	219^{2}	307	190	141	11	15	77	43	1.748	5.78	64	5.99	.330	12	.135	-40	6	-4.1
• KNERR, Lou	Wallace Luther Knerr b: 8/21/1921, Denver, PA d: 3/27/1980, Reading, PA BR/TR, 6'1", 210 lbs. Deb: 4/17/1945																										
1945	Phi-A	5	11	.313	27	17	5	0	0	130	142	77	61	6	1	74	41	1.662	4.22	81	4.71	.283	9	.191	-11	2	-1.3
1946	Phi-A	3	16	.158	30	22	6	0	0	148^{1}	171	95	89	13	1	67	58	1.604	5.40	66	4.93	.288	9	.180	-30	0	-3.1
1947	Was-A	0	0	....	6	0	0	0	0	9	17	13	11	1	0	8	5	2.778	11.00	34	11.34	.405	1	1.000	-7	0	-0.7
Total	3	8	27	.229	63	39	11	0	0	287^{1}	330	185	161	20	2	149	104	1.667	5.04	70	5.03	.290	19	.194	-48	2	-5.1
• KNETZER, Elmer	Elmer Ellsworth "Baron" Knetzer b: 7/22/1885, Carrick, PA d: 10/3/1975, Pittsburgh, PA BR/TR, 5'10", 180 lbs. Deb: 9/11/1909																										
1909	Bro-N	1	3	.250	5	4	3	0	0	35^{2}	33	22	12	2	0	22	7	1.542	3.03	85	4.17	.252	0	.000	-1	1	-0.3
1910	Bro-N	7	5	.583	20	15	10	3	0	132^{2}	122	63	47	1	1	60	56	1.372	3.19	95	3.30	.255	2	.053	-4	6	-0.6
1911	Bro-N	11	12	.478	35	20	11	3	0	204	202	101	79	1	1	93	66	1.446	3.49	95	3.76	.277	6	.097	-3	11	-0.6
1912	Bro-N	7	9	.438	33	16	4	1	0	140^{1}	135	86	71	6	4	70	61	1.461	4.55	73	3.81	.254	5	.135	-17	4	-1.8
1914	Pit-F	20	12	.625	37	30	20	3	1	272	257	123	87	9	2	88	146	1.268	2.88	107	3.10	.254	9	.099	7	18	0.0
1915	Pit-F	18	14	.563	41	33	22	3	3	279	256	105	80	5	1	89	120	1.237	2.58	120	2.86	.251	12	.132	17	20	1.3
1916	Bos-N	0	2	.000	2	0	0	0	0	5	11	9	4	0	0	2	2	2.600	7.20	34	12.35	.524	0	....	-3	0	-0.3
	Cin-N	5	12	.294	36	16	12	0	1	171^{1}	161	76	55	6	3	48	70	1.220	2.89	90	2.86	.252	8	.154	-7	6	-1.0
	Yr.	5	14	.263	38	16	12	0	1	176^{1}	172	85	59	6	3	50	72	1.259	3.01	86	3.13	.261	8	.154	-10	6	-1.2
1917	Cin-N	0	0	....	11	0	0	0	1	27^{1}	29	18	9	0	2	12	7	1.500	2.96	88	3.76	.282	0	.000	-1	0	-0.2
Total	8	69	69	.500	220	134	82	13	6	1267^{1}	1206	603	444	30	14	484	535	1.334	3.15	97	3.30	.259	42	.109	-12	66	-3.5
• KNIGHT, Brandon	Brandon Michael Knight b: 10/1/1975, Oxnard, CA BL/TR, 6', 170 lbs. Deb: 6/5/2001																										
2001	NY-A	0	0	....	4	0	0	0	0	10^{2}	18	12	12	5	0	3	7	1.969	10.13	44	11.03	.367	0	....	-6	0	-0.6
2002	NY-A	0	0	....	7	0	0	0	0	8^{2}	11	12	11	2	0	5	7	1.846	11.42	38	7.53	.306	0	....	-7	0	-0.6
Total	2	0	0	....	11	0	0	0	0	19^{1}	29	24	23	7	0	8	14	1.914	10.71	41	9.46	.341	0	....	-13	0	-1.2
• KNIGHT, George	George Henry Knight b: 11/24/1855, Lakeville, CT d: 10/4/1912, Lakeville, CT Deb: 9/28/1875 U																										
1875	NH-n	1	0	1.000	1	1	1	0	0	9	12	6	3	0	....	0	12	1.333	3.00	115	....	.293	0	.000	1	....	0.0
• KNIGHT, Jack	Elmer Russell Knight b: 1/12/1895, Pittsboro, MS d: 7/30/1976, San Antonio, TX BL/TR, 6', 175 lbs. Deb: 9/20/1922																										
1922	StL-N	0	0	....	1	1	0	0	0	4	9	4	4	0	0	3	1	3.000	9.00	43	12.91	.474	1	.500	-2	0	-0.2
1925	Phi-N	7	6	.538	33	11	4	0	3	105^{1}	161	100	80	14	1	36	19	1.870	6.84	70	7.17	.354	9	.205	-20	2	-1.9
1926	Phi-N	3	12	.200	35	15	5	0	2	142^{2}	206	122	105	14	0	48	29	1.780	6.62	63	6.33	.347	12	.214	-35	0	-3.4
1927	Bos-N	0	0	....	3	0	0	0	0	3	6	5	5	0	0	2	0	2.667	15.00	25	10.92	.429	0	....	-4	0	-0.4
Total	4	10	18	.357	72	27	9	0	5	255	382	231	194	28	1	89	49	1.847	6.85	64	6.83	.353	22	.216	-61	2	-5.8
• KNIGHT, Joe	Joseph William "Quiet Joe" Knight b: 9/28/1859, Port Stanley, Canada d: 10/16/1938, Lynhurst, Canada BL/TL, 5'11", 185 lbs. Deb: 5/16/1884 ♦																										
1884	Phi-N	2	4	.333	6	6	6	0	0	51	66	53	31	2	....	21	8	1.706	5.47	55	....	.297	6	.250	-12	1	-1.0
• KNIGHT, Lon	Alonzo P. Knight b: 6/16/1853, Philadelphia, PA d: 4/23/1932, Philadelphia, PA BR/TR, 5'11.5", 165 lbs. Deb: 9/4/1875 M/U ♦																										
1875	Ath-n	6	5	.545	13	13	12	0	0	107	114	....	27	0	....	12	10	1.178	2.27	108	....	.248	6	.128	-2	....	-0.5
1876	Phi-N	10	22	.313	34	32	27	0	0	282	383	288	82	0	....	34	12	1.479	2.62	93	....	.295	60	.248	13	5	0.4
1884	Phi-a	0	1	.000	2	1	1	0	0	14	24	19	14	0	1	4	2	2.000	9.00	38	....	.359	131	.271	-9	13	0.1
1885	Phi-a	0	0	....	1	0	0	0	0	5	4	1	1	0	0	2	1	1.200	1.80	191	....	.210	25	.210	1	2	-0.1
	Pro-N	0	0	....	1	0	0	0	0	4	4	4	3	1	....	4	1	2.000	6.75	39	....	.248	13	.160	-2	1	-0.3
Total	3	10	23	.303	38	33	28	0	0	305	415	312	100	1	1	44	16	1.505	2.95	86	....	.297	549	.245	3	21	0.0
• KNOLLS, Hub	Oscar Edward Knolls b: 12/18/1883, Valparaiso, IN d: 7/1/1946, Chicago, IL TR, 6'2", 190 lbs. Deb: 5/1/1906																										
1906	Bro-N	0	0	....	2	0	0	0	0	6^{2}	13	5	3	0	0	2	3	2.250	4.05	62	8.14	.382	1	1.000	-1	1	0.0
• KNOTT, Eric	Eric James Knott b: 9/23/1974, Harvey, IL BL/TL, 6', 188 lbs. Deb: 9/1/2001																										
2001	Ari-N	0	1	.000	3	1	0	0	0	4^{2}	8	9	1	0	2	0	4	1.714	1.93	237	7.20	.348	0	.000	1	0	0.1
2003	Mon-N	1	2	.333	13	1	0	0	0	19^{1}	23	12	11	2	0	6	17	1.500	5.12	99	4.77	.295	0	.000	-0	1	-0.1
Total	2	1	3	.250	16	2	0	0	0	24	31	21	12	2	2	6	21	1.542	4.50	111	5.24	.307	0	.000	1	1	0.1
• KNOTT, Jack	John Henry Knott b: 3/2/1907, Dallas, TX d: 10/13/1981, Brownwood, TX BR/TR, 6'2.5", 200 lbs. Deb: 4/13/1933																										
1933	StL-A	1	8	.111	20	9	0	0	0	82^{2}	88	51	46	11	2	33	19	1.464	5.01	93	4.59	.269	7	.304	-5	3	-0.4
1934	StL-A	10	3	.769	45	10	2	0	4	138	149	86	76	17	1	67	56	1.565	4.96	101	4.97	.278	4	.133	-1	9	-0.2
1935	StL-A	11	8	.579	48	19	7	2	**7**	187^{2}	219	119	96	8	1	78	45	1.583	4.60	104	4.48	.287	7	.115	5	14	0.0
1936	StL-A	9	17	.346	47	23	9	0	6	192^{2}	272	174	156	15	4	93	60	**1.894**	7.29	74	6.61	.330	4	.070	-37	4	-3.7
1937	StL-A	8	18	.308	38	22	8	0	2	191^{1}	220	117	104	25	5	91	74	1.625	4.89	99	5.49	.291	8	.140	0	11	-0.3

YEAR	TM-L	W	L	PCT	G	GS	CG	SH	SV	IP	H	R	ER	HR	HB	BB	SO	RAT	ERA	ERA+	CERA	OAV	BH	AVG	PR+	WS	TPW
1938	StL-A	1	2	.333	7	4	0	0	0	30	35	19	16	3	0	15	8	1.667	4.80	104	5.26	.285	1	.100	1	2	0.0
	Chi-A	5	10	.333	20	18	9	0	0	131	135	70	59	8	0	54	35	1.443	4.05	121	3.93	.271	5	.125	12	7	0.9
	Yr.	6	12	.333	27	22	9	0	0	161	170	89	75	11	0	69	43	1.484	4.19	117	4.18	.273	6	.120	13	9	0.9
1939	Chi-A	11	6	.647	25	23	8	0	0	149^2	157	71	69	13	1	41	56	1.323	4.15	114	3.68	.269	8	.151	8	12	0.5
1940	Chi-A	11	9	.550	25	23	4	2	0	158	166	88	80	12	2	52	44	1.380	4.56	97	3.83	.265	5	.088	-6	8	-0.9
1941	Phi-A	13	11	.542	27	26	11	0	0	194^1	212	108	95	20	2	81	54	1.508	4.40	95	4.62	.279	5	.077	-6	9	-0.9
1942	Phi-A	2	10	.167	20	14	4	0	0	95^1	127	84	59	7	1	36	31	1.710	5.57	68	5.43	.310	4	.138	-17	0	-1.8
1946	Phi-A	0	1	.000	3	1	0	0	0	6^1	7	4	4	1	1	1	2	1.263	5.68	62	4.56	.280	0	....	-1	0	-0.2
Total	**11**	**82**	**103**	**.443**	**325**	**192**	**62**	**4**	**19**	**1557**	**1787**	**991**	**860**	**140**	**20**	**642**	**484**	**1.560**	**4.97**	**95**	**4.82**	**.287**	**58**	**.120**	**-47**	**79**	**-6.9**

• KNOTTS, Gary Gary Everett Knotts b: 2/12/1977, Decatur, AL BR/TR, 6'4", 235 lbs. Deb: 7/28/2001

YEAR	TM-L	W	L	PCT	G	GS	CG	SH	SV	IP	H	R	ER	HR	HB	BB	SO	RAT	ERA	ERA+	CERA	OAV	BH	AVG	PR+	WS	TPW
2001	Fla-N	0	1	.000	2	1	0	0	0	6	7	4	4	1	2	1	9	1.333	6.00	70	5.84	.280	1	.500	-1	0	-0.1
2002	Fla-N	3	1	.750	28	0	0	0	0	30^2	21	15	15	6	1	16	21	1.207	4.40	89	3.62	.193	0	.000	-2	2	-0.2
2003	Det-A	3	8	.273	20	18	0	0	0	95^1	111	70	64	14	4	47	51	1.657	6.04	71	5.90	.288	0	.000	-18	1	-1.8
Total	**3**	**6**	**10**	**.375**	**50**	**19**	**0**	**0**	**0**	**132**	**139**	**89**	**83**	**21**	**7**	**64**	**81**	**1.538**	**5.66**	**75**	**5.37**	**.267**	**1**	**.250**	**-21**	**3**	**-2.0**

• KNOUFF, Ed Edward "Fred" Knouff b: 6/1868, Philadelphia, PA d: 9/14/1900, Philadelphia, PA BR/TR, 210 lbs. Deb: 7/1/1885

YEAR	TM-L	W	L	PCT	G	GS	CG	SH	SV	IP	H	R	ER	HR	HB	BB	SO	RAT	ERA	ERA+	CERA	OAV	BH	AVG	PR+	WS	TPW
1885	Phi-a	7	6	.538	14	13	12	0	0	106	103	76	43	0	9	44	43	1.387	3.65	94	....	.244	9	.188	-2	5	-0.3
1886	Bal-a	0	1	.000	1	1	1	0	0	9	2	5	2	0	3	5	8	.778	2.00	171	....	.068	0	.000	2	1	0.1
1887	Bal-a	2	6	.250	9	9	6	0	0	63	120	79	53	0	13	41	27	1.905	7.57	54	....	.390	10	.313	-23	1	-1.8
	StL-a	4	2	.667	6	6	6	1	0	50	76	34	25	0	3	36	18	1.520	4.50	101	....	.338	11	.193	-1	4	-0.6
	Yr.	6	8	.429	15	15	12	1	0	113	196	113	78	0	16	77	45	1.735	6.21	68	....	.368	21	.236	-24	5	-2.4
1888	StL-a	5	4	.556	9	9	9	0	0	81	66	45	24	0	8	37	25	1.272	2.67	122	....	.215	3	.097	3	6	0.1
	Cle-a	0	1	.000	2	2	1	0	0	9	8	2	1	0	1	3	2	1.222	1.00	309	....	.230	1	.167	2	1	0.2
	Yr.	5	5	.500	11	11	10	0	0	90	74	47	25	0	9	40	27	1.267	2.50	130	....	.216	4	.108	5	7	0.4
1889	Phi-a	2	0	1.000	3	3	2	0	0	25	37	17	11	2	1	9	5	1.840	3.96	95	....	.333	3	.250	-1	2	-0.1
Total	**5**	**20**	**20**	**.500**	**44**	**43**	**37**	**1**	**0**	**343**	**412**	**258**	**159**	**2**	**38**	**175**	**128**	**1.487**	**4.17**	**90**	**....**	**.287**	**37**	**.196**	**-20**	**20**	**-2.3**

• KNOWLES, Darold Darold Duane Knowles b: 12/9/1941, Brunswick, MO BL/TL, 6', 190 lbs. Deb: 4/18/1965 C

YEAR	TM-L	W	L	PCT	G	GS	CG	SH	SV	IP	H	R	ER	HR	HB	BB	SO	RAT	ERA	ERA+	CERA	OAV	BH	AVG	PR+	WS	TPW
1965	Bal-A	0	1	.000	5	1	0	0	0	14^2	14	15	15	2	3	10	12	1.636	9.20	38	5.85	.250	0	.000	-10	0	-1.1
1966	Phi-N	6	5	.545	69	0	0	0	13	100^1	98	38	34	4	7	46	88	1.435	3.05	118	3.85	.260	4	.250	6	10	0.7
1967	Was-A	6	8	.429	61	1	0	0	14	113^1	91	37	34	5	4	52	85	1.262	2.70	117	2.92	.228	1	.063	6	12	0.5
1968	Was-A	1	1	.500	32	0	0	0	4	41^1	38	11	10	0	1	12	37	1.210	2.18	134	2.52	.241	1	.250	4	3	0.5
1969	Was-A★	9	2	.818	53	0	0	0	13	84^1	73	25	21	8	4	31	59	1.233	2.24	155	3.34	.236	1	.077	11	11	1.2
1970	Was-A	2	14	.125	71	0	0	0	27	119^1	100	36	27	4	4	58	71	1.324	2.04	175	2.97	.231	1	.050	18	15	1.8
1971	Was-A	2	2	.500	12	0	0	0	2	15^1	17	6	6	2	0	6	16	1.500	3.52	94	4.58	.266	0	.000	-0	1	-0.1
	*Oak-A	5	2	.714	43	0	0	0	7	52^2	40	22	21	3	3	16	40	1.063	3.59	93	2.38	.221	1	.125	-2	5	-0.3
	Yr.	7	4	.636	55	0	0	0	9	68	57	28	27	5	3	22	56	1.162	3.57	93	2.88	.233	1	.100	-3	6	-0.4
1972	Oak-A	5	1	.833	54	0	0	0	11	65^2	49	12	10	1	0	37	36	1.310	1.37	207	2.72	.212	3	.250	10	9	1.2
1973*	Oak-A	6	8	.429	52	5	1	1	9	99	87	44	34	7	3	49	46	1.374	3.09	115	3.68	.246	0	....	2	6	0.2
1974	Oak-A	3	3	.500	45	1	0	0	3	53^1	61	29	25	6	2	35	18	1.800	4.22	79	6.18	.296	0	....	-6	1	-0.6
1975	Chi-N	6	9	.400	58	0	0	0	15	88^1	107	61	57	3	3	36	63	1.619	5.81	66	4.65	.298	1	.067	-16	3	-1.8
1976	Chi-N	5	7	.417	58	0	0	0	9	71^2	61	30	23	6	2	22	39	1.158	2.89	134	2.97	.242	1	.143	9	9	1.0
1977	Tex-A	5	2	.714	42	0	0	0	4	50^1	50	22	18	3	2	23	14	1.450	3.22	127	4.16	.272	0	....	4	5	0.4
1978	Mon-N	3	3	.500	60	0	0	0	6	72	63	20	19	5	0	30	34	1.292	2.38	148	3.30	.250	1	.167	7	7	0.7
1979	StL-N	2	5	.286	48	0	0	0	6	48^2	54	27	22	5	0	17	22	1.459	4.07	92	4.23	.277	0	.000	-3	3	-0.3
1980	StL-N	0	1	.000	2	0	0	0	0	1^2	3	2	2	1	0	0	1	1.800	10.80	34	11.17	.375	0	....	-1	0	-0.1
Total	**16**	**66**	**74**	**.471**	**765**	**8**	**1**	**1**	**143**	**1092**	**1006**	**437**	**378**	**65**	**38**	**480**	**681**	**1.361**	**3.12**	**113**	**3.58**	**.250**	**15**	**.120**	**38**	**100**	**4.0**

• KNOWLSON, Tom Thomas Herbert "Doc" Knowlson b: 4/23/1895, Ridgway, PA d: 4/11/1943, Miami Shores, FL BB/TR, 5'11", 178 lbs. Deb: 7/3/1915

YEAR	TM-L	W	L	PCT	G	GS	CG	SH	SV	IP	H	R	ER	HR	HB	BB	SO	RAT	ERA	ERA+	CERA	OAV	BH	AVG	PR+	WS	TPW
1915	Phi-A	4	6	.400	18	9	8	0	0	100^2	99	53	39	1	6	60	24	1.579	3.49	84	4.42	.273	3	.083	-5	2	-0.9

• KNOWLTON, Bill William Young Knowlton b: 8/18/1892, Philadelphia, PA d: 2/25/1944, Philadelphia, PA BR/TR Deb: 9/3/1920

YEAR	TM-L	W	L	PCT	G	GS	CG	SH	SV	IP	H	R	ER	HR	HB	BB	SO	RAT	ERA	ERA+	CERA	OAV	BH	AVG	PR+	WS	TPW
1920	Phi-A	0	1	.000	1	1	0	0	0	5^2	9	9	3	0	3	3	5	2.118	4.76	84	9.05	.346	0	.000	-0	0	-0.1

• KNUDSEN, Kurt Kurt David Knudsen b: 2/20/1967, Arlington Heights, IL BR/TR, 6'2", 200 lbs. Deb: 5/16/1992

YEAR	TM-L	W	L	PCT	G	GS	CG	SH	SV	IP	H	R	ER	HR	HB	BB	SO	RAT	ERA	ERA+	CERA	OAV	BH	AVG	PR+	WS	TPW
1992	Det-A	2	3	.400	48	1	0	0	5	70^2	70	39	36	9	1	41	51	1.571	4.58	86	4.85	.264	0	....	-4	3	-0.4
1993	Det-A	3	2	.600	30	0	0	0	2	37^2	41	22	20	9	4	16	29	1.513	4.78	90	6.08	.281	0	....	-2	2	-0.2
1994	Det-A	1	0	1.000	4	0	0	0	0	5^1	7	8	8	2	0	11	1	3.375	13.50	36	15.79	.304	0	....	-5	0	-0.5
Total	**3**	**6**	**5**	**.545**	**82**	**1**	**0**	**0**	**7**	**113^2**	**118**	**69**	**64**	**20**	**5**	**68**	**81**	**1.636**	**5.07**	**82**	**5.77**	**.272**	**0**	**....**	**-11**	**5**	**-1.1**

• KNUDSON, Mark Mark Richard Knudson b: 10/28/1960, Denver, CO BR/TR, 6'5", 215 lbs. Deb: 7/8/1985

YEAR	TM-L	W	L	PCT	G	GS	CG	SH	SV	IP	H	R	ER	HR	HB	BB	SO	RAT	ERA	ERA+	CERA	OAV	BH	AVG	PR+	WS	TPW
1985	Hou-N	0	2	.000	2	2	0	0	0	11	21	11	11	0	0	3	4	2.182	9.00	38	8.75	.429	0	.000	-7	0	-0.7
1986	Hou-N	1	5	.167	9	7	0	0	0	42^2	48	23	20	5	1	15	20	1.477	4.22	85	4.53	.279	0	.000	-3	1	-0.4
	Mil-A	0	1	.000	4	1	0	0	0	17^2	22	15	15	7	0	5	9	1.528	7.64	57	6.81	.286	0	....	-6	0	-0.6
1987	Mil-A	4	4	.500	15	8	1	0	0	62	88	46	37	7	0	14	26	1.645	5.37	85	5.75	.331	0	....	-5	2	-0.5
1988	Mil-A	0	0	....	5	0	0	0	0	16	17	3	2	1	0	2	7	1.188	1.13	354	3.27	.279	0	....	5	2	0.5
1989	Mil-A	8	5	.615	40	7	1	0	0	123^2	110	50	46	15	3	29	47	1.124	3.35	115	3.09	.237	0	....	6	8	0.6
1990	Mil-A	10	9	.526	30	27	4	2	0	168^1	187	84	77	14	3	40	56	1.349	4.12	94	4.00	.282	0	....	-3	7	-0.3
1991	Mil-A	1	3	.250	12	7	0	0	0	35	54	33	31	8	1	15	23	1.971	7.97	50	8.63	.355	0	....	-16	0	-1.6
1993	Col-N	0	0	....	4	0	0	0	0	5^2	16	14	14	4	0	5	3	3.706	22.24	21	25.48	.471	0	.000	-11	0	-1.1
Total	**8**	**24**	**29**	**.453**	**121**	**59**	**6**	**2**	**0**	**482**	**563**	**279**	**253**	**61**	**8**	**128**	**195**	**1.434**	**4.72**	**84**	**4.81**	**.290**	**0**	**.000**	**-39**	**20**	**-4.0**

• KOBEL, Kevin Kevin Richard Kobel b: 10/2/1953, Buffalo, NY BR/TL, 6', 195 lbs. Deb: 9/8/1973

YEAR	TM-L	W	L	PCT	G	GS	CG	SH	SV	IP	H	R	ER	HR	HB	BB	SO	RAT	ERA	ERA+	CERA	OAV	BH	AVG	PR+	WS	TPW
1973	Mil-A	0	1	.000	2	1	0	0	0	8^1	9	8	8	2	0	8	4	2.040	8.64	44	8.14	.273	0	....	-4	0	-0.5
1974	Mil-A	6	14	.300	34	24	3	2	0	169^1	166	84	75	16	2	54	74	1.299	3.99	91	3.67	.258	0	....	-8	6	-0.8
1976	Mil-A	0	1	.000	3	0	0	0	0	4	6	5	5	3	1	3	1	2.250	11.25	31	15.51	.375	0	....	-3	0	-0.4
1978	NY-N	5	6	.455	32	11	1	0	0	108^1	95	42	35	9	2	30	51	1.154	2.91	120	2.81	.239	4	.160	6	7	0.7
1979	NY-N	6	8	.429	30	27	1	1	0	161^2	169	74	63	14	3	46	67	1.330	3.51	104	3.85	.274	9	.196	1	8	0.1
1980	NY-N	1	4	.200	14	1	0	0	0	24^1	36	21	19	5	0	11	8	1.932	7.03	51	8.12	.353	0	.000	-9	0	-1.0
Total	**6**	**18**	**34**	**.346**	**115**	**64**	**5**	**3**	**0**	**476**	**481**	**234**	**205**	**49**	**8**	**152**	**205**	**1.330**	**3.88**	**93**	**3.94**	**.266**	**13**	**.178**	**-19**	**21**	**-1.9**

• KOCH, Alan Alan Goodman Koch b: 3/25/1938, Decatur, AL BR/TR, 6'4", 195 lbs. Deb: 7/26/1963

YEAR	TM-L	W	L	PCT	G	GS	CG	SH	SV	IP	H	R	ER	HR	HB	BB	SO	RAT	ERA	ERA+	CERA	OAV	BH	AVG	PR+	WS	TPW
1963	Det-A	1	1	.500	7	1	0	0	0	10	21	12	12	3	1	9	5	3.000	10.80	35	17.25	.467	2	.667	-8	0	-0.7
1964	Det-A	0	0	....	3	0	0	0	0	4	6	3	3	1	0	3	1	2.250	6.75	54	10.98	.375	0	....	-1	0	-0.1
	Was-A	3	10	.231	32	14	1	0	0	114	110	64	62	18	3	43	67	1.342	4.89	76	4.24	.253	8	.250	-16	2	-1.4
	Yr.	3	10	.231	35	14	1	0	0	118	116	67	65	19	3	46	68	1.373	4.96	75	4.47	.258	8	.250	-17	2	-1.6
Total	**2**	**4**	**11**	**.267**	**42**	**15**	**1**	**0**	**0**	**128**	**137**	**79**	**77**	**22**	**4**	**55**	**73**	**1.500**	**5.41**	**68**	**5.47**	**.277**	**10**	**.286**	**-25**	**2**	**-2.3**

• KOCH, Billy William Christopher Koch b: 12/14/1974, Rockville Centre, NY BR/TR, 6'3", 205 lbs. Deb: 5/5/1999

YEAR	TM-L	W	L	PCT	G	GS	CG	SH	SV	IP	H	R	ER	HR	HB	BB	SO	RAT	ERA	ERA+	CERA	OAV	BH	AVG	PR+	WS	TPW
1999	Tor-A	0	5	.000	56	0	0	0	31	63^2	55	26	24	5	3	30	57	1.335	3.39	145	3.53	.235	0	.000	11	10	1.0
2000	Tor-A	9	3	.750	68	0	0	0	33	78^2	78	28	23	6	2	18	60	1.220	2.63	193	3.25	.258	0	.000	21	16	1.9
2001	Tor-A	2	5	.286	69	0	0	0	36	69^1	69	39	37	7	6	33	55	1.471	4.80	96	4.54	.265	0	....	-2	8	-0.2
2002*	Oak-A	11	4	.733	**84**	0	0	0	44	93^2	73	38	34	7	4	46	93	1.270	3.27	135	3.10	.214	0	....	12	19	1.2
2003	Chi-A	5	5	.500	55	0	0	0	11	53	59	36	34	10	1	28	42	1.642	5.77	77	5.93	.281	0	....	-8	2	-0.8
Total	**5**	**27**	**22**	**.551**	**332**	**0**	**0**	**0**	**155**	**358^1**	**334**	**167**	**152**	**35**	**16**	**155**	**307**	**1.365**	**3.82**	**121**	**3.91**	**.248**	**0**	**.000**	**34**	**55**	**3.1**

• KOECHER, Dick Richard Finlay Koecher b: 3/30/1926, Philadelphia, PA BL/TL, 6'5", 196 lbs. Deb: 9/29/1946

YEAR	TM-L	W	L	PCT	G	GS	CG	SH	SV	IP	H	R	ER	HR	HB	BB	SO	RAT	ERA	ERA+	CERA	OAV	BH	AVG	PR+	WS	TPW
1946	Phi-N	0	1	.000	1	1	0	0	0	2^2	7	3	3	0	0	1	2	3.000	10.13	34	13.44	.467	0	.000	-2	0	-0.2
1947	Phi-N	0	2	.000	3	2	1	0	0	17	20	12	9	1	1	10	4	1.765	4.76	84	5.67	.299	0	.000	-2	0	-0.2

YEAR	TM-L	W	L	PCT	G	GS	CG	SH	SV	IP	H	R	ER	HR	HB	BB	SO	RAT	ERA	ERA+	CERA	OAV	BH	AVG	PR+	WS	TPW
1948	Phi-N	0	1	.000	3	0	0	0	0	6	4	2	2	0	0	3	2	1.167	3.00	131	2.39	.235	0	....	1	0	0.1
Total 3		0	4	.000	7	3	1	0	0	25^{2}	31	17	14	1	1	14	8	1.753	4.91	79	5.71	.313	0	.000	-3	0	-0.4
• KOENIG, Mark	Mark Anthony Koenig b: 7/19/1904, San Francisco, CA d: 4/22/1993, Willows, CA BB/TR, 6', 180 lbs. Deb: 9/8/1925 ♦																										
1930	Det-A	0	1	.000	2	1	0	0	0	9	11	10	10	0	1	8	6	2.111	10.00	48	6.97	.314	64	.240	-5	4	-1.8
1931	Det-A	0	0	....	3	0	0	0	0	7	7	5	5	0	0	11	3	2.571	6.43	71	7.83	.280	92	.253	-1	4	-2.8
Total 2		0	1	.000	5	1	0	0	0	16	18	15	15	0	1	19	9	2.313	8.44	56	7.34	.300	1190	.279	-7	8	-4.6
• KOENIGSMARK, Will	Willis Thomas Koenigsmark b: 2/27/1896, Waterloo, IL d: 7/1/1972, Waterloo, IL BR/TR, 6'4", 180 lbs. Deb: 9/10/1919																										
1919	StL-N	0	0	....	1	0	0	0	0	0	2	2	2	0	0	1	0	....	∞	....	∞	1.000	0	....	-2	0	-0.2
• KOESTNER, Elmer	Elmer Joseph "Bob" Koestner b: 11/30/1885, Piper City, IL d: 10/27/1959, Fairbury, IL BR/TR, 6'1.5", 175 lbs. Deb: 4/23/1910																										
1910	Cle-A	5	10	.333	27	13	8	1	2	145	145	76	49	0	6	63	44	1.434	3.04	85	3.88	.282	15	.313	-8	6	-0.6
1914	Chi-N	0	0	....	4	0	0	0	0	6^{1}	6	5	2	0	0	4	6	1.579	2.84	98	3.51	.261	0	.000	0	0	0.0
	Cin-N	0	0	....	5	1	0	0	0	18^{1}	18	15	9	0	0	9	6	1.473	4.42	66	3.38	.265	2	.400	-3	0	-0.2
	Yr.	0	0	....	9	1	0	0	0	24^{2}	24	20	11	0	0	13	12	1.500	4.01	72	3.42	.264	2	.333	-3	0	-0.2
Total 2		5	10	.333	36	14	8	1	2	169^{2}	169	96	60	0	6	76	56	1.444	3.18	83	3.81	.279	17	.315	-11	6	-0.9
• KOHLMAN, Joe	Joseph James "Blackie" Kohlman b: 1/28/1913, Philadelphia, PA d: 3/16/1974, Philadelphia, PA BR/TR, 6', 160 lbs. Deb: 9/26/1937																										
1937	Was-A	1	0	1.000	2	2	1	0	0	13	15	7	6	0	0	3	3	1.385	4.15	107	3.49	.283	1	.200	0	1	0.0
1938	Was-A	0	0	....	7	0	0	0	0	14^{1}	12	10	10	1	0	11	5	1.605	6.28	72	4.35	.240	0	.000	-3	0	-0.3
Total 2		1	0	1.000	9	2	1	0	0	27^{1}	27	17	16	1	0	14	8	1.500	5.27	85	3.94	.262	1	.125	-3	1	-0.3
• KOHLMEIER, Ryan	Ryan Lyle Kohlmeier b: 6/25/1977, Salina, KS BR/TR, 6'2", 223 lbs. Deb: 7/29/2000																										
2000	Bal-A	0	1	.000	25	0	0	0	13	26^{1}	30	9	7	1	0	15	17	1.709	2.39	197	4.98	.291	0	....	7	4	0.6
2001	Bal-A	1	2	.333	34	1	0	0	6	40^{2}	48	33	33	13	2	19	29	1.648	7.30	59	7.24	.291	0	....	-14	0	-1.3
Total 2		1	3	.250	59	1	0	0	19	67	78	42	40	14	2	34	46	1.672	5.37	81	6.35	.291	0	....	-7	4	-0.7
• KOLB, Brandon	Brandon Charles Kolb b: 11/20/1973, Oakland, CA BR/TR, 6'1", 190 lbs. Deb: 5/12/2000																										
2000	SD-N	0	1	.000	11	0	0	0	0	14	16	8	7	0	0	11	12	1.929	4.50	96	5.61	.296	0	.000	-0	0	-0.1
2001	Mil-N	0	0	....	10	0	0	0	0	9^{2}	16	16	14	6	0	8	8	2.483	13.03	33	15.04	.372	0	.000	-9	0	-0.9
Total 2		0	1	.000	21	0	0	0	0	23^{2}	32	24	21	6	0	19	20	2.155	7.99	54	9.46	.330	0	.000	-10	0	-1.0
• KOLB, Danny	Daniel Lee Kolb b: 3/29/1975, Sterling, IL BR/TR, 6'4", 215 lbs. Deb: 6/4/1999																										
1999	Tex-A	2	1	.667	16	0	0	0	0	31	33	18	16	2	1	15	15	1.548	4.65	109	4.63	.268	0	....	2	2	0.2
2000	Tex-A	0	0	....	1	0	0	0	0	0^{2}	5	5	5	0	0	2	0	10.50	67.50	7	69.84	.833	0	....	-5	0	-0.4
2001	Tex-A	0	0	....	17	0	0	0	0	15^{1}	15	8	8	2	0	10	15	1.630	4.70	99	5.03	.259	0	....	0	1	0.0
2002	Tex-A	3	6	.333	34	0	0	0	1	32	27	17	15	1	1	22	20	1.531	4.22	112	3.74	.227	0	....	2	2	0.2
2003	Mil-N	1	2	.333	37	0	0	0	21	41^{1}	34	10	9	2	1	19	39	1.282	1.96	217	2.96	.221	0	....	11	9	1.1
Total 5		6	9	.400	105	0	0	0	22	120^{1}	114	58	53	7	3	68	89	1.512	3.96	120	4.23	.248	0	....	11	14	1.1
• KOLB, Eddie	Edward William Kolb b: 7/20/1880, Cincinnati, OH BR/TR Deb: 10/15/1899																										
1899	Cle-N	0	1	.000	1	1	1	0	0	8	18	19	9	0	1	5	1	2.875	10.13	36	12.68	.442	1	.250	-5	0	-0.5
• KOLP, Ray	Raymond Carl "Jockey" Kolp b: 10/1/1894, New Berlin, OH d: 7/29/1967, New Orleans, LA BR/TR, 5'10.5", 187 lbs. Deb: 4/16/1921																										
1921	StL-A	8	7	.533	37	18	5	1	0	166^{2}	208	111	92	12	0	51	43	1.554	4.97	90	4.82	.314	7	.127	-8	6	-1.3
1922	StL-A	14	4	.778	32	18	9	1	0	169^{2}	199	89	74	10	5	36	54	1.385	3.93	105	4.03	.292	17	.298	-0	11	0.4
1923	StL-A	5	12	.294	34	17	11	1	1	171^{1}	178	91	74	11	6	54	44	1.354	3.89	107	3.76	.273	6	.111	3	9	0.0
1924	StL-A	5	7	.417	25	12	5	1	0	96^{2}	131	65	61	4	4	25	29	1.614	5.68	79	5.22	.329	6	.200	-13	3	-1.3
1927	Cin-N	3	3	.500	24	5	2	1	3	82^{1}	86	38	28	5	1	29	28	1.397	3.06	124	3.85	.278	6	.200	7	6	0.7
1928	Cin-N	13	10	.565	44	24	12	1	3	209	219	87	74	9	4	55	61	1.311	3.19	124	3.48	.280	15	.214	17	18	1.9
1929	Cin-N	8	10	.444	30	16	4	1	0	145^{1}	151	75	65	8	1	39	27	1.307	4.03	113	3.46	.278	8	.163	8	9	0.6
1930	Cin-N	7	12	.368	37	19	5	2	3	168^{1}	180	86	79	10	0	34	40	1.271	4.22	114	3.35	.278	12	.245	12	14	1.2
1931	Cin-N	4	9	.308	30	10	2	0	1	107	144	66	59	8	4	39	24	1.710	4.96	75	5.90	.332	4	.125	-16	2	-1.7
1932	Cin-N	6	10	.375	32	19	7	2	1	159^{2}	176	80	69	13	3	27	42	1.271	3.89	99	3.66	.280	9	.184	-0	8	-0.2
1933	Cin-N	6	9	.400	30	14	4	0	3	150^{1}	168	73	59	7	1	23	28	1.271	3.53	96	3.49	.290	7	.156	-1	8	-0.1
1934	Cin-N	0	2	.000	28	2	0	0	3	61^{2}	78	36	31	1	2	12	19	1.459	4.52	90	4.22	.312	1	.083	-1	3	-0.3
Total 12		79	95	.454	383	174	66	11	18	1688	1918	897	765	98	31	424	439	1.387	4.08	101	4.00	.292	98	.184	8	97	0.0
• KOLSTAD, Hal	Harold Everette Kolstad b: 6/1/1935, Rice Lake, WI BR/TR, 5'9", 190 lbs. Deb: 4/22/1962																										
1962	Bos-A	0	2	.000	27	2	0	0	2	61^{1}	65	44	37	11	2	35	36	1.630	5.43	76	5.79	.269	1	.056	-9	0	-1.1
1963	Bos-A	0	2	.000	7	0	0	0	0	11	16	16	16	4	2	6	6	2.000	13.09	29	10.91	.340	0	.000	-11	0	-1.2
Total 2		0	4	.000	34	2	0	0	2	72^{1}	81	60	53	15	4	41	42	1.687	6.59	61	6.57	.280	1	.053	-20	0	-2.3
• KOMIYAMA, Satoru	Satoru Komiyama b: 9/15/1965, Chiba, Japan BR/TR, 6', 195 lbs. Deb: 4/4/2002																										
2002	NY-N	0	3	.000	25	0	0	0	0	43^{1}	53	29	27	7	3	12	33	1.500	5.61	71	5.44	.301	0	.000	-8	0	-0.7
• KONIECZNY, Doug	Douglas James Konieczny b: 9/27/1951, Detroit, MI BR/TR, 6'4", 220 lbs. Deb: 9/11/1973																										
1973	Hou-N	0	1	.000	2	2	0	0	0	13	12	8	8	0	0	4	6	1.231	5.54	66	2.98	.279	0	.000	-3	0	-0.3
1974	Hou-N	0	3	.000	6	3	0	0	0	16	18	15	14	0	2	12	8	1.875	7.88	44	5.84	.290	0	.000	-8	0	-0.9
1975	Hou-N	6	13	.316	32	29	4	1	0	171	184	93	85	15	1	87	89	1.585	4.47	75	4.90	.280	8	.160	-22	3	-2.3
1977	Hou-N	1	1	.500	4	4	0	0	0	21	26	15	14	1	1	8	7	1.619	6.00	59	5.09	.302	1	.143	-6	0	-0.6
Total 4		7	18	.280	44	38	4	1	0	221	240	131	121	16	4	111	110	1.588	4.93	69	4.88	.283	9	.138	-39	3	-4.1
• KONIKOWSKI, Alex	Alexander James "Whitey" Konikowski b: 6/8/1928, Throop, PA d: 9/28/1997, Seymour, CT BR/TR, 6'1", 187 lbs. Deb: 6/16/1948																										
1948	NY-N	2	3	.400	22	1	0	0	1	33^{1}	46	34	28	7	0	17	9	1.890	7.56	52	7.90	.346	0	.000	-13	0	-1.3
1951*	NY-N	0	0	....	3	0	0	0	0	4	2	0	0	0	0	0	5	.500	0.00	....	0.58	.154	0	....	2	1	0.2
1954	NY-N	0	0	....	10	0	0	0	0	12	10	10	10	1	0	12	6	1.833	7.50	54	5.13	.244	0	.000	-5	0	-0.5
Total 3		2	3	.400	35	1	0	0	1	49^{1}	58	44	38	8	0	29	20	1.764	6.93	57	6.63	.310	0	.000	-16	1	-1.6
• KONSTANTY, Jim	Casimir James Konstanty b: 3/2/1917, Strykersville, NY d: 6/11/1976, Oneonta, NY BR/TR, 6'1.5", 202 lbs. Deb: 6/18/1944																										
1944	Cin-N	6	4	.600	20	12	5	1	0	112^{2}	113	46	35	11	1	33	19	1.296	2.80	125	3.69	.266	10	.294	6	9	0.8
1946	Bos-N	0	1	.000	10	1	0	0	0	15^{1}	17	9	9	2	0	7	9	1.565	5.28	65	5.16	.283	0	.000	-3	0	-0.3
1948	Phi-N	1	0	1.000	6	0	0	0	2	9^{2}	7	1	1	0	0	2	7	.931	0.93	423	1.67	.233	0	.000	3	2	0.3
1949	Phi-N	9	5	.643	53	0	0	0	7	97	98	38	35	9	1	29	43	1.309	3.25	121	3.92	.280	3	.176	6	11	0.6
1950*	Phi-N★	16	7	.696	**74**	0	0	0	**22**	152	108	51	45	11	0	50	56	1.039	2.66	152	2.14	.205	4	.108	23	23	2.0
1951	Phi-N	4	11	.267	58	1	0	0	9	115^{2}	127	58	52	9	0	31	27	1.366	4.05	95	3.88	.282	3	.158	-2	6	-0.3
1952	Phi-N	5	3	.625	42	2	2	1	6	80	87	44	35	9	0	21	16	1.350	3.94	93	4.03	.274	1	.071	-4	4	-0.4
1953	Phi-N	14	10	.583	48	19	7	0	5	170^{2}	198	90	84	18	3	42	45	1.406	4.43	95	4.44	.290	11	.220	-4	11	-0.4
1954	Phi-N	2	3	.400	33	1	0	0	3	50^{1}	62	27	21	7	0	12	11	1.470	3.75	108	5.11	.316	0	.000	1	3	0.0
	NY-A	1	1	.500	9	0	0	0	2	18^{1}	11	2	2	0	0	6	3	.927	0.98	350	1.35	.183	0	.000	5	3	0.4
1955	NY-A	7	2	.778	45	0	0	0	11	73^{2}	68	28	19	5	0	24	19	1.249	2.32	161	3.11	.247	1	.125	9	9	0.8
1956	NY-A	0	0	....	8	0	0	0	2	11	15	6	6	3	0	6	6	1.909	4.91	79	8.34	.319	0	.000	-2	0	-0.2
	StL-N	1	1	.500	27	0	0	0	5	39^{1}	46	20	20	4	0	6	7	1.322	4.58	83	4.00	.301	0	....	-3	2	-0.3
Total 11		66	48	.579	433	36	14	2	74	945^{2}	957	420	364	88	5	269	268	1.296	3.46	112	3.71	.268	33	.163	35	83	3.0
• KONUSZEWSKI, Dennis	Dennis John Konuszewski b: 2/4/1971, Bridgeport, MI BR/TR, 6'3", 210 lbs. Deb: 8/4/1995																										
1995	Pit-N	0	0	....	1	0	0	0	0	0^{1}	3	2	2	0	0	1	0	12.00	54.00	8	83.91	1.000	0	....	-2	0	-0.2
• KOOB, Ernie	Ernest Gerald Koob b: 9/11/1892, Keeler, MI d: 11/12/1941, Lemay, MO BL/TL, 5'10", 160 lbs. Deb: 6/23/1915																										
1915	StL-A	4	5	.444	28	13	6	0	1	133^{2}	119	50	35	2	10	50	37	1.264	2.36	121	3.24	.254	5	.135	6	8	0.5

YEAR	TM-L	W	L	PCT	G	GS	CG	SH	SV	IP	H	R	ER	HR	HB	BB	SO	RAT	ERA	ERA+	CERA	OAV	BH	AVG	PR+	WS	TPW
1916	StL-A	11	8	.579	33	20	10	2	2	166^{2}	153	54	47	1	6	56	26	1.254	2.54	108	2.95	.252	0	.000	-0	11	-0.1
1917	StL-A	6	14	.300	39	18	3	1	1	133^{2}	139	81	58	1	6	57	47	1.466	3.91	66	4.00	.280	4	.114	-19	2	-2.2
1919	StL-A	2	4	.333	25	4	0	0	0	66	77	37	34	3	2	23	11	1.515	4.64	71	4.57	.296	0	.000	-10	1	-1.3
Total	4	23	31	.426	125	55	19	3	4	500	488	222	174	7	24	186	121	1.348	3.13	90	3.52	.266	9	.070	-24	22	-3.1

• KOONCE, Cal

Calvin Lee Koonce b: 11/18/1940, Fayetteville, NC d: 10/28/1993, Winston-Salem, NC BR/TR, 6'1", 185 lbs. Deb: 4/14/1962

YEAR	TM-L	W	L	PCT	G	GS	CG	SH	SV	IP	H	R	ER	HR	HB	BB	SO	RAT	ERA	ERA+	CERA	OAV	BH	AVG	PR+	WS	TPW
1962	Chi-N	10	10	.500	35	30	3	1	0	190^{2}	200	93	84	17	7	86	84	1.500	3.97	105	4.61	.271	6	.094	4	12	0.0
1963	Chi-N	2	6	.250	21	13	0	0	0	72^{2}	75	43	37	9	2	32	44	1.472	4.58	77	4.69	.273	2	.105	-10	0	-1.1
1964	Chi-N	3	0	1.000	6	2	0	0	0	31	30	8	7	1	0	7	17	1.194	2.03	182	2.74	.254	0	.000	6	4	0.5
1965	Chi-N	7	9	.438	38	23	3	1	0	173	181	83	71	17	6	52	88	1.347	3.69	100	4.02	.271	5	.102	2	8	0.2
1966	Chi-N	5	5	.500	45	5	0	0	2	108^{2}	113	57	46	13	1	35	65	1.362	3.81	97	3.97	.268	3	.130	-0	5	0.0
1967	Chi-N	2	2	.500	34	0	0	0	2	51	52	27	26	2	1	21	28	1.431	4.59	77	3.73	.268	0	.000	-6	1	-0.8
	NY-N	3	3	.500	11	6	2	1	0	45	45	16	14	2	0	7	24	1.156	2.80	121	2.77	.259	2	.154	3	3	0.3
	Yr.	5	5	.500	45	6	2	1	2	96	97	43	40	4	1	28	52	1.302	3.75	93	3.28	.264	2	.100	-4	4	-0.5
1968	NY-N	6	4	.600	55	2	0	0	11	97	80	27	26	4	1	32	50	1.155	2.41	125	2.48	.235	0	.000	6	11	0.5
1969	NY-N	6	3	.667	40	0	0	0	7	83	85	53	46	8	3	42	48	1.530	4.99	73	4.63	.269	4	.235	-14	2	-1.5
1970	NY-N	0	2	.000	13	0	0	0	0	22	25	9	8	2	1	14	10	1.773	3.27	123	5.79	.301	0	.000	1	1	0.1
	Bos-A	3	4	.429	23	8	1	0	2	76^{1}	64	32	30	7	3	29	37	1.218	3.54	112	3.23	.231	2	.095	5	5	0.5
1971	Bos-A	0	1	.000	13	1	0	0	0	21	22	16	13	3	0	11	9	1.571	5.57	66	5.36	.278	0	.000	-4	0	-0.4
Total	10	47	49	.490	334	90	9	3	24	971^{1}	972	464	408	85	25	368	504	1.380	3.78	98	3.97	.264	24	.100	-9	52	-1.5

• KOOSMAN, Jerry

Jerome Martin Koosman b: 12/23/1942, Appleton, MN BR/TL, 6'2", 208 lbs. Deb: 4/14/1967

YEAR	TM-L	W	L	PCT	G	GS	CG	SH	SV	IP	H	R	ER	HR	HB	BB	SO	RAT	ERA	ERA+	CERA	OAV	BH	AVG	PR+	WS	TPW
1967	NY-N	0	2	.000	9	3	0	0	0	22^{1}	22	17	15	3	0	19	11	1.836	6.04	56	5.78	.259	0	.000	-7	0	-0.7
1968	NY-N★	19	12	.613	35	34	17	7	0	263^{2}	221	72	61	16	8	69	178	1.100	2.08	145	2.57	.228	7	.077	25	23	2.5
1969*	NY-N★	17	9	.654	32	32	16	6	0	241	187	66	61	14	4	68	180	1.058	2.28	160	2.24	.216	4	.048	31	25	2.5
1970	NY-N	12	7	.632	30	29	5	1	0	212	189	87	74	22	2	71	118	1.226	3.14	128	3.19	.237	6	.086	17	14	1.5
1971	NY-N	6	11	.353	26	24	4	0	0	165^{2}	160	66	56	12	1	51	96	1.274	3.04	112	3.34	.256	8	.160	5	9	0.6
1972	NY-N	11	12	.478	34	24	4	1	1	163	155	81	75	14	6	52	147	1.270	4.14	81	3.45	.250	4	.085	-13	5	-1.7
1973*	NY-N	14	15	.483	35	35	12	3	0	263	234	93	83	18	4	76	156	1.179	2.84	127	2.92	.242	8	.103	21	18	1.8
1974	NY-N	15	11	.577	35	35	13	0	0	265	258	113	99	16	7	85	188	1.294	3.36	106	3.43	.257	16	.186	5	17	0.8
1975	NY-N	14	13	.519	36	34	11	4	2	239^{2}	234	106	91	19	4	98	173	1.385	3.42	101	3.92	.261	14	.179	-2	13	-0.1
1976	NY-N	21	10	.677	34	32	17	3	0	247^{1}	205	81	74	19	1	66	200	1.096	2.69	122	2.52	.226	17	.215	15	20	1.9
1977	NY-N	8	20	.286	32	32	6	1	0	226^{2}	195	102	88	17	4	81	192	1.218	3.49	107	3.02	.232	8	.111	6	11	0.3
1978	NY-N	3	15	.167	38	32	3	0	2	235^{1}	221	110	98	17	8	84	160	1.296	3.75	93	3.49	.255	6	.086	-9	8	-1.3
1979	Min-A	20	13	.606	37	36	10	2	0	263^{2}	268	108	99	19	3	83	157	1.331	3.38	130	3.74	.268	0	....	30	23	2.9
1980	Min-A	16	13	.552	38	34	8	0	2	243^{1}	252	119	109	24	5	69	149	1.319	4.03	108	3.91	.272	0	....	8	16	0.8
1981	Min-A	3	9	.250	19	13	2	1	5	94^{1}	98	49	44	8	0	34	55	1.399	4.20	94	3.93	.272	0	....	-2	5	-0.2
	Chi-A	1	4	.200	8	3	1	0	0	27	27	10	10	2	0	7	21	1.259	3.33	107	3.35	.260	0	....	0	1	0.0
	Yr.	4	13	.235	27	16	3	1	5	121^{1}	125	59	54	10	0	41	76	1.368	4.01	97	3.80	.269	0	....	-1	6	-0.1
1982	Chi-A	11	7	.611	42	19	3	1	3	173^{1}	194	81	74	9	2	38	88	1.338	3.84	105	3.78	.287	0	....	5	10	0.5
1983*	Chi-A	11	7	.611	37	24	2	1	2	169^{2}	176	96	90	19	6	53	90	1.350	4.77	88	4.13	.266	0	....	-12	7	-1.2
1984	Phi-N	14	15	.483	36	34	3	1	0	224	232	95	81	8	3	60	137	1.304	3.25	112	3.32	.267	8	.108	13	12	1.0
1985	Phi-N	6	4	.600	19	18	3	1	0	99^{1}	107	56	51	14	3	34	60	1.419	4.62	80	4.65	.276	3	.088	-9	3	-1.1
Total	19	222	209	.515	612	527	140	33	17	3839^{1}	3635	1608	1433	290	71	1198	2556	1.259	3.36	110	3.34	.252	109	.119	127	240	10.9

• KOPLITZ, Howie

Howard Dean Koplitz b: 5/4/1938, Oshkosh, WI BR/TR, 5'10.5", 195 lbs. Deb: 9/8/1961

YEAR	TM-L	W	L	PCT	G	GS	CG	SH	SV	IP	H	R	ER	HR	HB	BB	SO	RAT	ERA	ERA+	CERA	OAV	BH	AVG	PR+	WS	TPW
1961	Det-A	2	0	1.000	4	1	1	0	0	12	16	6	3	0	0	8	9	2.000	2.25	182	6.09	.327	0	.000	2	1	0.2
1962	Det-A	3	0	1.000	10	6	1	0	0	37^{2}	54	24	22	5	0	10	10	1.699	5.26	77	6.34	.342	3	.231	-5	1	-0.4
1964	Was-A	0	0	....	6	1	0	0	0	17	20	9	9	3	0	13	9	1.941	4.76	78	7.19	.290	0	.000	-2	0	-0.2
1965	Was-A	4	7	.364	33	11	0	0	1	106^{2}	97	51	48	11	3	48	59	1.359	4.05	86	3.89	.249	3	.100	-6	4	-0.8
1966	Was-A	0	0	....	1	0	0	0	0	2	0	0	0	0	0	1	0	.500	0.00	....	0.28	.000	0	....	1	0	0.1
Total	5	9	7	.563	54	19	2	0	1	175^{1}	187	90	82	19	3	80	87	1.523	4.21	87	4.85	.281	6	.118	-10	6	-1.1

• KOPLOVE, Mike

Michael Paul Koplove b: 8/30/1976, Philadelphia, PA BR/TR, 6', 160 lbs. Deb: 9/6/2001

YEAR	TM-L	W	L	PCT	G	GS	CG	SH	SV	IP	H	R	ER	HR	HB	BB	SO	RAT	ERA	ERA+	CERA	OAV	BH	AVG	PR+	WS	TPW
2001	Ari-N	0	1	.000	9	0	0	0	0	10	8	7	4	1	2	9	14	1.700	3.60	127	5.25	.211	0	.000	1	0	0.1
2002*	Ari-N	6	1	.857	55	0	0	0	0	61^{2}	47	24	23	2	0	23	46	1.135	3.36	132	2.23	.213	0	.000	8	7	0.8
2003	Ari-N	3	0	1.000	31	0	0	0	0	37^{2}	31	11	9	3	5	10	27	1.088	2.15	217	2.93	.225	0	....	11	5	1.1
Total	3	9	2	.818	95	0	0	0	0	109^{1}	86	42	36	6	7	42	87	1.171	2.96	152	2.75	.217	0	.000	20	12	1.9

• KORINCE, George

George Eugene "Moose" Korince b: 1/10/1946, Ottawa, Canada BR/TR, 6'3", 210 lbs. Deb: 9/10/1966

YEAR	TM-L	W	L	PCT	G	GS	CG	SH	SV	IP	H	R	ER	HR	HB	BB	SO	RAT	ERA	ERA+	CERA	OAV	BH	AVG	PR+	WS	TPW
1966	Det-A	0	0	....	2	0	0	0	0	3	1	0	0	0	1	3	2	1.333	0.00	....	2.80	.091	0	....	1	0	0.1
1967	Det-A	1	0	1.000	9	0	0	0	0	14	10	8	8	1	0	11	11	1.500	5.14	63	3.49	.204	0	.000	-3	0	-0.3
Total	2	1	0	1.000	11	0	0	0	0	17	11	8	8	1	1	14	13	1.471	4.24	77	3.37	.183	0	.000	-2	0	-0.2

• KORWAN, Jim

James "Long Jim" Korwan b: 3/4/1874, Brooklyn, NY d: 7/24/1899, Brooklyn, NY BR/TR, 6'1", 181 lbs. Deb: 4/24/1894

YEAR	TM-L	W	L	PCT	G	GS	CG	SH	SV	IP	H	R	ER	HR	HB	BB	SO	RAT	ERA	ERA+	CERA	OAV	BH	AVG	PR+	WS	TPW
1894	Bro-N	0	0	....	1	0	0	0	0	5	9	14	8	1	0	5	2	2.800	14.40	34	12.69	.385	0	.000	-5	0	-0.4
1897	Chi-N	1	2	.333	5	4	3	0	0	34	47	36	22	1	1	28	12	2.206	5.82	76	7.41	.325	0	.000	-5	0	-0.6
Total	2	1	2	.333	6	4	3	0	0	39	56	50	30	2	1	33	14	2.282	6.92	66	8.08	.334	0	.000	-10	0	-1.0

• KOSKI, Bill

William John "T-Bone" Koski b: 2/6/1932, Madera, CA BR/TR, 6'4", 185 lbs. Deb: 4/28/1951

YEAR	TM-L	W	L	PCT	G	GS	CG	SH	SV	IP	H	R	ER	HR	HB	BB	SO	RAT	ERA	ERA+	CERA	OAV	BH	AVG	PR+	WS	TPW
1951	Pit-N	0	1	.000	13	1	0	0	0	27	26	23	20	2	0	28	6	2.000	6.67	63	5.93	.257	0	.000	-7	0	-0.7

• KOSLO, Dave

George Bernard Koslo b: 3/31/1920, Menasha, WI d: 12/1/1975, Menasha, WI BL/TL, 5'11", 180 lbs. Deb: 9/12/1941

YEAR	TM-L	W	L	PCT	G	GS	CG	SH	SV	IP	H	R	ER	HR	HB	BB	SO	RAT	ERA	ERA+	CERA	OAV	BH	AVG	PR+	WS	TPW
1941	NY-N	1	2	.333	4	3	2	0	0	23^{2}	17	6	5	0	0	10	12	1.141	1.90	194	2.03	.202	1	.111	5	2	0.4
1942	NY-N	3	6	.333	19	11	3	1	0	78	79	49	44	7	1	32	42	1.423	5.08	66	3.99	.261	3	.120	-16	0	-1.7
1946	NY-N	14	19	.424	40	**35**	17	3	1	265^{1}	251	119	107	15	5	101	121	1.327	3.63	95	3.36	.249	11	.125	-2	12	-0.6
1947	NY-N	15	10	.600	39	31	10	3	0	217^{1}	223	118	106	23	3	82	86	1.403	4.39	93	4.04	.259	10	.128	-9	11	-1.0
1948	NY-N	8	10	.444	35	18	5	3	3	149	168	69	64	7	1	62	58	1.544	3.87	102	4.44	.290	5	.114	2	8	0.0
1949	NY-N	11	14	.440	38	23	15	0	4	212	193	72	59	13	0	43	64	1.113	**2.50**	**159**	2.57	.239	10	.145	**35**	19	**3.6**
1950	NY-N	13	15	.464	40	22	7	1	3	186^{2}	190	89	81	18	5	68	56	1.382	3.91	105	4.09	.268	8	.123	-2	12	-0.2
1951*	NY-N	10	9	.526	39	16	5	2	3	149^{2}	153	68	55	18	2	45	54	1.323	3.31	118	3.87	.258	5	.100	10	11	0.8
1952	NY-N	10	7	.588	41	17	8	2	5	166^{1}	154	66	59	10	2	47	67	1.208	3.19	116	2.93	.242	2	.037	10	12	0.6
1953	NY-N	6	12	.333	37	12	2	0	2	111^{2}	135	70	59	8	1	36	36	1.531	4.76	90	4.69	.296	1	.033	-6	4	-0.9
1954	Bal-A	0	1	.000	3	1	0	0	0	14^{1}	20	7	5	1	0	3	3	1.605	3.14	114	5.45	.333	0	.000	1	1	0.0
	Mil-N	1	1	.500	12	0	0	0	1	17^{1}	13	6	6	0	0	9	7	1.269	3.12	120	2.46	.228	0	.000	1	2	0.1
1955	Mil-N	0	1	.000	1	0	0	0	0	0	1	1	1	1	0	0	0	....	∞	....	∞	1.000	0	....	-1	0	-0.1
Total	12	92	107	.462	348	189	74	15	22	1591^{1}	1597	740	651	121	20	538	606	1.342	3.68	105	3.65	.260	56	.109	28	94	1.2

• KOSTAL, Joe

Joseph William Kostal b: 3/17/1876, Chicago, IL d: 10/10/1933, Guelph, Canada BR/TR, 5'6", 130 lbs. Deb: 7/14/1896

YEAR	TM-L	W	L	PCT	G	GS	CG	SH	SV	IP	H	R	ER	HR	HB	BB	SO	RAT	ERA	ERA+	CERA	OAV	BH	AVG	PR+	WS	TPW
1896	Lou-N	0	0	....	2	0	0	0	0	2	4	4	0	0	0	0	0	2.000	0.00	....	7.69	.411	0	....	1	0	0.1

• KOUFAX, Sandy

Sanford Koufax b: 12/30/1935, Brooklyn, NY BR/TL, 6'2", 210 lbs. Deb: 6/24/1955 HOF: 1972

YEAR	TM-L	W	L	PCT	G	GS	CG	SH	SV	IP	H	R	ER	HR	HB	BB	SO	RAT	ERA	ERA+	CERA	OAV	BH	AVG	PR+	WS	TPW
1955	Bro-N	2	2	.500	12	5	2	2	0	41^{2}	33	15	14	2	1	28	30	1.464	3.02	134	3.64	.216	0	.000	5	3	0.3
1956	Bro-N	2	4	.333	16	10	0	0	0	58^{2}	66	37	32	10	0	29	30	1.619	4.91	81	5.83	.286	2	.118	-7	1	-0.8
1957	Bro-N	5	4	.556	34	13	2	0	0	104^{1}	83	49	45	14	2	51	122	1.284	3.88	107	3.56	.216	0	.000	3	6	0.0
1958	LA-N	11	11	.500	40	26	5	0	1	158^{2}	132	89	79	19	1	105	131	1.494	4.48	91	4.16	**.220**	6	.122	-7	7	-0.9
1959*	LA-N	8	6	.571	35	23	6	1	2	153^{1}	136	74	69	23	0	92	173	1.487	4.05	104	4.51	.235	6	.111	3	9	0.1
1960	LA-N	8	13	.381	37	26	7	2	1	175	133	83	76	20	1	100	197	1.331	3.91	102	3.45	**.207**	7	.123	-0	9	-0.2
1961	LA-N★	18	13	.581	42	35	15	2	1	255^{2}	212	117	100	27	3	96	**269**	1.205	3.52	123	3.08	**.222**	5	.065	22	20	1.7
1962	LA-N★	14	7	.667	28	26	11	2	1	184^{1}	134	61	52	13	2	57	216	1.036	**2.54**	143	**2.13**	**.197**	6	.087	22	15	1.9

YEAR TM-L	W	L	PCT	G	GS	CG	SH	SV	IP	H	R	ER	HR	HB	BB	SO	RAT	ERA	ERA+	CERA	OAV	BH	AVG	PR+	WS	TPW
1963* LA-N★	**25**	5	.833	40	40	20	**11**	0	311	214	68	65	18	3	58	**306**	.875	**1.88**	161	**1.55**	**.189**	7	.064	**42**	**32**	4.1
1964 LA-N★	19	5	.792	29	28	15	**7**	1	223	154	49	43	13	0	53	223	.928	**1.74**	**187**	**1.66**	**.191**	7	.095	38	24	3.8
1965* LA-N★	**26**	8	.765	43	41	**27**	8	2	**335^2**	216	90	76	26	5	71	**382**	.855	**2.04**	160	**1.56**	**.179**	20	.177	41	**33**	4.8
1966* LA-N★	**27**	9	.750	41	**41**	**27**	**5**	0	**323**	241	74	62	19	0	77	**317**	.985	**1.73**	**191**	1.92	.205	9	.076	**56**	**35**	5.2
Total 12	165	87	.655	397	314	137	40	9	2324^1	1754	806	713	204	18	817	2396	1.106	2.76	135	2.58	.205	75	.097	216	194	20.0

• KOUKALIK, Joe

Joseph Koukalik b: 3/3/1880, Chicago, IL d: 12/27/1945, Chicago, IL BR/TR, 5'8", 160 lbs. Deb: 9/1/1904

YEAR TM-L	W	L	PCT	G	GS	CG	SH	SV	IP	H	R	ER	HR	HB	BB	SO	RAT	ERA	ERA+	CERA	OAV	BH	AVG	PR+	WS	TPW
1904 Bro-N	0	1	.000	1	1	1	0	0	8	10	3	1	0	0	4	1	1.750	1.13	243	5.49	.333	0	.000	1	0	0.1

• KOUPAL, Lou

Louis Laddie Koupal b: 12/19/1898, Tabor, SD d: 12/8/1961, San Gabriel, CA BR/TR, 5'11", 175 lbs. Deb: 4/17/1925

YEAR TM-L	W	L	PCT	G	GS	CG	SH	SV	IP	H	R	ER	HR	HB	BB	SO	RAT	ERA	ERA+	CERA	OAV	BH	AVG	PR+	WS	TPW
1925 Pit-N	0	0	....	6	0	0	0	0	9	14	10	9	1	0	7	0	2.333	9.00	50	9.43	.378	0	.000	-5	0	-0.5
1926 Pit-N	0	2	.000	6	2	1	0	0	19^2	22	9	7	0	1	8	7	1.525	3.20	123	4.14	.289	1	.250	1	1	0.2
1928 Bro-N	1	0	1.000	17	1	1	0	1	37^1	43	22	10	0	1	15	10	1.554	2.41	165	4.24	.303	1	.111	7	2	0.6
1929 Bro-N	0	1	.000	18	3	0	0	4	40^1	49	36	24	3	0	25	17	1.835	5.36	86	5.80	.308	1	.071	-2	1	-0.4
Phi-N	5	5	.500	15	11	3	0	2	86^2	106	56	46	5	2	29	18	1.558	4.78	108	4.73	.305	4	.125	6	5	0.3
Yr.	5	6	.455	33	14	3	0	6	127	155	92	70	8	2	54	35	1.646	4.96	100	5.07	.306	5	.109	3	6	0.0
1930 Phi-N	0	4	.000	13	4	1	0	0	36^2	52	35	35	4	1	17	11	1.882	8.59	64	6.94	.344	1	.083	-12	0	-1.2
1937 StL-A	4	9	.308	26	13	6	0	0	105^2	150	87	77	10	0	55	24	1.940	6.56	74	6.98	.339	3	.094	-19	1	-2.0
Total 6	10	21	.323	101	34	12	0	7	335^1	436	255	208	23	5	156	87	1.765	5.58	87	5.85	.322	11	.106	-25	10	-2.9

• KOWALIK, Fabian

Fabian Lorenz Kowalik b: 4/22/1908, Falls City, TX d: 8/14/1954, Karnes City, TX BR/TR, 5'11", 185 lbs. Deb: 9/4/1932

YEAR TM-L	W	L	PCT	G	GS	CG	SH	SV	IP	H	R	ER	HR	HB	BB	SO	RAT	ERA	ERA+	CERA	OAV	BH	AVG	PR+	WS	TPW
1932 Chi-A	0	1	.000	2	1	0	0	0	10^1	16	11	8	2	1	4	2	1.935	6.97	62	8.28	.340	5	.385	-3	1	-0.2
1935* Chi-N	2	2	.500	20	2	1	0	1	55	60	31	27	2	0	19	20	1.436	4.42	89	3.82	.280	3	.200	-5	2	-0.5
1936 Chi-N	0	2	.000	6	0	0	0	1	16	24	12	12	1	0	7	1	1.938	6.75	59	7.01	.358	0	.000	-5	0	-0.6
Phi-N	1	5	.167	22	8	2	0	0	77	100	57	46	5	2	31	19	1.701	5.38	84	5.38	.308	13	.228	-5	1	-0.6
Bos-N	0	1	.000	1	1	1	0	0	9	18	8	8	0	0	2	0	2.222	8.00	48	8.40	.419	2	.400	-4	0	-0.4
Yr.	1	8	.111	29	9	3	0	1	102	142	77	66	6	2	40	20	1.784	5.82	74	5.91	.326	15	.224	-14	1	-1.5
Total 3	3	11	.214	51	12	4	0	2	167^1	218	119	101	10	3	63	42	1.679	5.43	78	5.37	.313	23	.242	-22	4	-2.2

• KOZLOWSKI, Ben

Benjamin Anthony Kozlowski b: 8/16/1980, St. Petersburg, FL BL/TL, 6'6", 220 lbs. Deb: 9/19/2002

YEAR TM-L	W	L	PCT	G	GS	CG	SH	SV	IP	H	R	ER	HR	HB	BB	SO	RAT	ERA	ERA+	CERA	OAV	BH	AVG	PR+	WS	TPW
2002 Tex-A	0	0	....	2	2	0	0	0	10	11	7	7	3	1	11	6	2.200	6.30	75	10.34	.289	0	....	-2	0	-0.2

• KRAEMER, Joe

Joseph Wayne Kraemer b: 9/10/1964, Olympia, WA BL/TL, 6'2", 185 lbs. Deb: 8/22/1989

YEAR TM-L	W	L	PCT	G	GS	CG	SH	SV	IP	H	R	ER	HR	HB	BB	SO	RAT	ERA	ERA+	CERA	OAV	BH	AVG	PR+	WS	TPW
1989 Chi-N	0	1	.000	1	1	0	0	0	3^2	7	6	2	0	0	2	5	2.455	4.91	77	8.25	.368	0	.000	-0	0	-0.1
1990 Chi-N	0	0	....	18	0	0	0	0	25	31	25	20	2	2	14	16	1.800	7.20	57	6.17	.310	0	....	-8	0	-0.8
Total 2	0	1	.000	19	1	0	0	0	28^2	38	31	22	2	2	16	21	1.884	6.91	59	6.44	.319	0	.000	-8	0	-0.9

• KRAKAUSKAS, Joe

Joseph Victor Lawrence Krakauskas b: 3/28/1915, Montreal, Canada d: 7/8/1960, Hamilton, Canada BL/TL, 6'1", 203 lbs. Deb: 9/9/1937

YEAR TM-L	W	L	PCT	G	GS	CG	SH	SV	IP	H	R	ER	HR	HB	BB	SO	RAT	ERA	ERA+	CERA	OAV	BH	AVG	PR+	WS	TPW
1937 Was-A	4	1	.800	5	4	3	0	0	40	33	14	12	0	0	22	18	1.375	2.70	164	2.92	.226	2	.125	7	4	0.6
1938 Was-A	7	5	.583	29	10	5	1	0	121^1	99	61	42	4	3	88	104	1.541	3.12	145	3.62	.220	6	.182	19	10	1.8
1939 Was-A	11	17	.393	39	29	12	0	1	217^1	230	125	111	13	1	114	110	1.583	4.60	95	4.52	.276	16	.208	-8	11	-0.5
1940 Was-A	1	6	.143	32	10	2	0	2	109	137	90	78	7	0	73	68	1.927	6.44	65	6.18	.309	8	.250	-26	0	-2.4
1941 Cle-A	1	2	.333	12	5	0	0	0	41^2	39	25	19	3	0	29	25	1.632	4.10	96	4.47	.245	1	.077	-1	1	-0.2
1942 Cle-A	0	0	....	3	0	0	0	0	7	7	3	3	1	0	4	2	1.571	3.86	89	4.82	.259	0	.000	-0	0	-0.1
1946 Cle-A	2	5	.286	29	5	0	0	1	47^1	60	31	29	2	0	25	20	1.796	5.51	60	5.57	.314	0	.000	-11	0	-1.3
Total 7	26	36	.419	149	63	22	1	4	583^2	605	349	294	30	4	355	347	1.645	4.53	92	4.62	.269	33	.180	-21	26	-2.1

• KRALICK, Jack

John Francis Kralick b: 6/1/1935, Youngstown, OH BL/TL, 6'2", 180 lbs. Deb: 4/15/1959

YEAR TM-L	W	L	PCT	G	GS	CG	SH	SV	IP	H	R	ER	HR	HB	BB	SO	RAT	ERA	ERA+	CERA	OAV	BH	AVG	PR+	WS	TPW
1959 Was-A	0	0	....	6	0	0	0	0	12^1	13	9	9	5	0	6	7	1.541	6.57	60	7.31	.289	0	.000	-3	0	-0.4
1960 Was-A	8	6	.571	35	18	7	2	1	151	139	54	51	12	4	45	71	1.219	3.04	130	3.19	.245	5	.122	17	12	1.7
1961 Min-A	13	11	.542	33	33	11	2	0	242	257	101	97	21	3	64	137	1.326	3.61	118	3.86	.274	13	.151	22	17	2.0
1962 Min-A	12	11	.522	39	37	7	1	0	242^2	239	121	104	30	3	61	139	1.236	3.86	106	3.61	.258	18	.202	5	13	0.8
1963 Min-A	1	4	.200	5	5	1	1	0	25^2	28	16	11	2	1	8	13	1.403	3.86	95	4.26	.280	1	.167	-1	1	0.1
Cle-A	13	9	.591	28	27	10	3	0	197^1	187	70	64	19	0	41	116	1.155	2.92	124	3.03	.249	11	.183	17	16	1.9
Yr.	14	13	.519	33	32	11	4	0	223	215	86	75	21	1	49	129	1.184	3.03	120	3.17	.253	12	.182	16	17	1.9
1964 Cle-A★	12	7	.632	30	29	8	3	0	190^2	196	79	68	17	9	51	119	1.295	3.21	112	3.77	.267	10	.156	13	12	1.3
1965 Cle-A	5	11	.313	30	16	1	0	0	86	106	58	47	9	2	21	34	1.477	4.92	71	4.73	.298	3	.143	-14	0	-1.5
1966 Cle-A	3	4	.429	27	4	0	0	0	68^1	69	30	29	9	1	20	31	1.302	3.82	90	3.82	.268	1	.077	-2	3	-0.3
1967 Cle-A	0	2	.000	2	0	0	0	0	2	4	3	2	0	0	1	1	2.500	9.00	36	10.75	.444	0	....	-1	0	-0.1
Total 9	67	65	.508	235	169	45	12	1	1218	1238	541	482	124	23	318	668	1.278	3.56	108	3.69	.264	62	.162	54	74	5.5

• KRALY, Steve

Steve Charles "Lefty" Kraly b: 4/18/1929, Whiting, IN BL/TL, 5'10", 152 lbs. Deb: 8/9/1953

YEAR TM-L	W	L	PCT	G	GS	CG	SH	SV	IP	H	R	ER	HR	HB	BB	SO	RAT	ERA	ERA+	CERA	OAV	BH	AVG	PR+	WS	TPW
1953 NY-A	0	2	.000	5	3	0	0	1	25	19	10	9	2	2	16	8	1.400	3.24	114	3.60	.209	0	.000	1	1	0.0

• KRAMER, Jack

John Henry Kramer b: 1/5/1918, New Orleans, LA d: 5/18/1995, Metairie, LA BR/TR, 6'2", 190 lbs. Deb: 4/25/1939

YEAR TM-L	W	L	PCT	G	GS	CG	SH	SV	IP	H	R	ER	HR	HB	BB	SO	RAT	ERA	ERA+	CERA	OAV	BH	AVG	PR+	WS	TPW
1939 StL-A	9	16	.360	40	31	10	2	0	211^2	269	150	137	18	3	127	68	**1.871**	5.83	83	6.34	.318	9	.136	-17	6	-1.7
1940 StL-A	3	7	.300	16	9	1	0	0	64^2	86	48	45	4	0	26	12	1.732	6.26	73	5.73	.327	1	.050	-12	1	-1.2
1941 StL-A	4	3	.571	29	3	0	0	2	59^1	69	48	34	5	0	40	20	1.837	5.16	83	5.74	.289	0	.000	-5	2	-0.4
1943 StL-A	0	0	....	3	0	0	0	0	9	11	8	8	0	1	8	4	2.111	8.00	42	6.64	.297	1	.500	-5	0	-0.4
1944* StL-A	17	13	.567	33	31	18	1	0	257	233	94	71	3	1	75	124	1.198	2.49	145	2.55	.241	14	.165	36	22	4.0
1945 StL-A★	10	15	.400	29	25	15	3	2	193	190	85	72	13	0	73	99	1.363	3.36	105	3.53	.254	9	.148	4	12	0.5
1946 StL-A★	13	11	.542	31	28	13	3	0	194^2	190	84	69	6	0	68	69	1.325	3.19	117	3.22	.257	8	.136	12	13	1.2
1947 StL-A★	11	16	.407	33	28	9	1	1	199^1	206	123	110	16	2	89	77	1.480	4.97	78	4.27	.270	7	.113	-22	5	-2.4
1948 Bos-A	18	5	.783	29	29	14	2	0	205	233	104	99	12	0	64	72	1.449	4.35	101	4.12	.284	11	.151	-0	14	-0.1
1949 Bos-A	6	8	.429	21	18	7	2	1	111^2	126	70	64	8	1	49	24	1.567	5.16	84	4.70	.286	9	.257	-12	5	-0.8
1950 NY-N	3	6	.333	35	9	1	0	1	86^2	91	46	34	6	2	39	27	1.500	3.53	116	4.21	.268	2	.100	3	5	0.4
1951 NY-N	0	0	....	4	1	0	0	0	4^2	11	8	8	0	0	3	2	3.000	15.43	25	13.68	.524	0	....	-6	0	-0.6
NY-A	1	3	.250	19	3	0	0	0	40^2	46	27	21	1	0	21	15	1.648	4.65	82	4.42	.280	1	.100	-4	0	-0.5
Total 12	95	103	.480	322	215	88	14	7	1637^1	1761	895	772	92	10	682	613	1.492	4.24	97	4.22	.276	72	.144	-27	85	-2.1

• KRAMER, Randy

Randall John Kramer b: 9/20/1960, Palo Alto, CA BR/TR, 6'2", 170 lbs. Deb: 9/11/1988

YEAR TM-L	W	L	PCT	G	GS	CG	SH	SV	IP	H	R	ER	HR	HB	BB	SO	RAT	ERA	ERA+	CERA	OAV	BH	AVG	PR+	WS	TPW
1988 Pit-N	1	2	.333	5	1	0	0	0	10	12	6	6	1	1	1	7	1.300	5.40	63	4.53	.316	0	.000	-2	0	-0.3
1989 Pit-N	5	9	.357	35	15	1	1	2	111^1	90	53	49	10	7	61	52	1.356	3.96	85	3.70	.224	5	.152	-8	3	-0.8
1990 Pit-N	0	1	.000	12	2	0	0	0	25^2	27	15	14	3	2	9	15	1.403	4.91	74	4.37	.273	0	.000	-4	0	-0.5
Chi-N	0	2	.000	10	2	0	0	0	20^1	20	10	9	3	1	12	12	1.574	3.98	102	4.95	.253	0	.000	1	1	0.1
Yr.	0	3	.000	22	4	0	0	0	46	47	25	23	6	3	21	27	1.478	4.50	84	4.62	.264	0	.000	-3	1	-0.4
1992 Sea-A	0	1	.000	4	4	0	0	0	16^1	30	14	14	2	1	7	6	2.265	7.71	51	10.13	.400	0	....	-7	0	-0.7
Total 4	6	15	.286	66	24	1	1	2	183^2	179	98	92	19	12	90	92	1.465	4.51	79	4.55	.259	5	.122	-20	4	-2.2

• KRAMER, Tom

Thomas Joseph Kramer b: 1/9/1968, Cincinnati, OH BB/TR, 6', 185 lbs. Deb: 9/12/1991

YEAR TM-L	W	L	PCT	G	GS	CG	SH	SV	IP	H	R	ER	HR	HB	BB	SO	RAT	ERA	ERA+	CERA	OAV	BH	AVG	PR+	WS	TPW
1991 Cle-A	0	0	....	4	0	0	0	0	4^2	10	9	9	1	0	6	4	3.429	17.36	24	16.90	.476	0	....	-7	0	-0.7
1993 Cle-A	7	3	.700	39	16	1	0	0	121	126	60	54	19	2	59	71	1.529	4.02	108	5.09	.269	0	....	4	6	0.4
Total 2	7	3	.700	43	16	1	0	0	125^2	136	69	63	20	2	65	75	1.599	4.51	95	5.53	.278	0	....	-3	6	-0.3

• KRAPP, Gene

Eugene Hamlet "Rubber Arm" Krapp b: 5/12/1887, Rochester, NY d: 4/13/1923, Detroit, MI BR/TR, 5'7", 165 lbs. Deb: 4/14/1911

YEAR TM-L	W	L	PCT	G	GS	CG	SH	SV	IP	H	R	ER	HR	HB	BB	SO	RAT	ERA	ERA+	CERA	OAV	BH	AVG	PR+	WS	TPW
1911 Cle-A	13	9	.591	35	26	14	1	1	222	188	115	84	1	13	138	132	1.468	3.41	100	3.62	.232	17	.230	-3	16	0.1
1912 Cle-A	2	5	.286	9	7	4	0	0	58^2	57	39	30	0	4	42	22	1.688	4.60	75	4.74	.273	7	.318	-9	2	-0.8
1914 Buf-F	16	14	.533	36	29	18	1	0	252^2	198	83	70	4	12	115	106	1.239	2.49	134	2.59	.210	11	.143	20	21	2.0
1915 Buf-F	9	19	.321	38	30	14	1	0	231	188	106	90	6	4	123	93	1.346	3.51	87	3.14	.230	9	.129	-11	10	-1.3
Total 4	40	47	.460	118	92	50	3	1	764^1	631	343	274	11	33	418	353	1.372	3.23	101	3.22	.227	44	.181	-3	49	0.0

• KRAUS, Jack John William "Tex,Texas Jack" Kraus b: 4/26/1918, San Antonio, TX d: 1/2/1976, San Antonio, TX BR/TL, 6'4", 190 lbs. Deb: 4/25/1943

YEAR	TM-L	W	L	PCT	G	GS	CG	SH	SV	IP	H	R	ER	HR	HB	BB	SO	RAT	ERA	ERA+	CERA	OAV	BH	AVG	PR+	WS	TPW
1943	Phi-N	9	15	.375	34	25	10	1	2	199^{2}	197	83	70	7	0	78	48	1.377	3.16	107	3.38	.259	4	.067	7	10	0.3
1945	Phi-N	4	9	.308	19	13	0	0	0	81^{2}	96	55	49	3	4	40	28	1.665	5.40	71	4.98	.293	3	.120	-12	1	-1.3
1946	NY-N	2	1	.667	17	1	0	0	0	25	25	17	17	4	1	15	7	1.600	6.12	56	5.30	.260	0	.000	-7	0	-0.8
Total	3	15	25	.375	70	39	10	1	2	306^{1}	318	155	136	14	5	133	83	1.472	4.00	88	3.96	.268	7	.080	-12	11	-1.8

• KRAUSE, Harry Harry William "Hal" Krause b: 7/12/1887, San Francisco, CA d: 10/23/1940, San Francisco, CA BB/TL, 5'10", 165 lbs. Deb: 4/20/1908

YEAR	TM-L	W	L	PCT	G	GS	CG	SH	SV	IP	H	R	ER	HR	HB	BB	SO	RAT	ERA	ERA+	CERA	OAV	BH	AVG	PR+	WS	TPW
1908	Phi-A	1	1	.500	4	2	2	0	0	21	20	11	6	0	3	4	10	1.143	2.57	99	2.81	.247	0	.000	0	1	-0.1
1909	Phi-A	18	8	.692	32	21	16	7	0	213	151	49	33	2	13	49	139	.939	**1.39**	**172**	1.72	.204	12	.156	22	20	2.3
1910	Phi-A	6	6	.500	16	11	9	2	0	112^{1}	99	46	36	4	8	42	60	1.255	2.88	82	3.36	.254	8	.211	-9	5	-0.9
1911	Phi-A	11	8	.579	27	19	12	1	2	169	155	65	57	2	9	47	85	1.195	3.04	104	2.92	.251	15	.254	1	12	0.3
1912	Phi-A	0	2	.000	4	2	0	0	0	5^{1}	10	8	8	0	1	2	3	2.250	13.50	23	10.07	.435	1	.250	-6	0	-0.6
	Cle-A	0	1	.000	2	2	0	0	0	4^{2}	11	6	6	0	0	2	1	2.786	11.57	30	13.27	.500	0	....	-4	0	-0.4
	Yr.	0	3	.000	6	4	0	0	0	10	21	14	14	0	1	4	4	2.500	12.60	26	11.56	.467	1	.250	-11	0	-1.1
Total	5	36	26	.581	85	57	39	10	2	525^{1}	446	185	146	8	34	146	298	1.127	2.50	109	2.69	.238	36	.195	4	38	0.6

• KRAUSSE, Lew Lewis Bernard Krausse, Sr. b: 6/8/1912, Media, PA d: 9/6/1988, Sarasota, FL BR/TR, 6'.5", 167 lbs. Deb: 6/11/1931

YEAR	TM-L	W	L	PCT	G	GS	CG	SH	SV	IP	H	R	ER	HR	HB	BB	SO	RAT	ERA	ERA+	CERA	OAV	BH	AVG	PR+	WS	TPW
1931	Phi-A	1	0	1.000	3	1	1	0	0	11	6	6	5	2	0	6	1	1.091	4.09	110	2.52	.150	0	.000	0	1	0.0
1932	Phi-A	4	1	.800	20	3	2	1	0	57	64	31	29	3	0	24	16	1.544	4.58	99	4.34	.281	2	.133	-1	4	-0.1
Total	2	5	1	.833	23	4	3	1	0	68	70	37	34	5	0	30	17	1.471	4.50	100	4.04	.261	2	.118	-0	5	0.0

• KRAUSSE, Lew Lewis Bernard Krausse, Jr. b: 4/25/1943, Media, PA BR/TR, 6', 186 lbs. Deb: 6/16/1961

YEAR	TM-L	W	L	PCT	G	GS	CG	SH	SV	IP	H	R	ER	HR	HB	BB	SO	RAT	ERA	ERA+	CERA	OAV	BH	AVG	PR+	WS	TPW
1961	KC-A	2	5	.286	12	8	2	1	0	55^{2}	49	33	30	3	1	46	32	1.707	4.85	85	4.82	.243	2	.118	-4	2	-0.5
1964	KC-A	0	2	.000	5	4	0	0	0	14^{2}	22	14	12	1	2	9	9	2.114	7.36	52	8.05	.349	0	.000	-6	0	-0.6
1965	KC-A	2	4	.333	7	5	0	0	0	25	29	14	14	1	0	8	22	1.480	5.04	69	4.20	.284	0	.000	-4	0	-0.5
1966	KC-A	14	9	.609	36	22	4	1	3	177^{2}	144	69	59	8	6	63	87	1.165	2.99	114	2.60	.222	8	.154	7	12	0.8
1967	KC-A	7	17	.292	48	19	0	0	6	160	140	85	76	17	4	67	96	1.294	4.28	74	3.52	.236	6	.146	-19	4	-2.0
1968	Oak-A	10	11	.476	36	25	2	0	4	185	147	68	64	16	3	62	105	1.130	3.11	90	2.63	.217	9	.161	-6	10	-0.4
1969	Oak-A	7	7	.500	43	16	4	2	7	140	134	75	69	23	5	48	85	1.300	4.44	78	4.16	.256	8	.167	-16	5	-1.2
1970	Mil-A	13	18	.419	37	35	8	1	0	216	235	130	114	33	4	67	130	1.398	4.75	80	4.50	.275	9	.138	-18	5	-1.9
1971	Mil-A	8	12	.400	43	22	1	0	0	180^{1}	164	67	59	23	5	62	92	1.253	2.94	118	3.56	.239	1	.023	9	11	0.6
1972	Bos-A	1	3	.250	24	7	0	0	1	60^{2}	74	48	43	9	3	28	35	1.681	6.38	50	6.16	.308	2	.125	-20	0	-2.3
1973	StL-N	0	0	....	1	0	0	0	0	2	2	0	0	0	0	1	1	1.500	0.00	....	3.63	.250	0	....	1	0	0.1
1974	Atl-N	4	3	.571	29	4	0	0	0	66^{2}	65	32	31	3	2	32	27	1.455	4.19	90	3.85	.258	2	.333	-4	4	-0.2
Total	12	68	91	.428	321	167	21	5	21	1283^{2}	1205	635	571	137	35	493	721	1.323	4.00	85	3.77	.248	47	.133	-81	53	-8.1

• KRAVEC, Ken Kenneth Peter Kravec b: 7/29/1951, Cleveland, OH BL/TL, 6'2", 185 lbs. Deb: 9/4/1975

YEAR	TM-L	W	L	PCT	G	GS	CG	SH	SV	IP	H	R	ER	HR	HB	BB	SO	RAT	ERA	ERA+	CERA	OAV	BH	AVG	PR+	WS	TPW
1975	Chi-A	0	1	.000	2	1	0	0	0	4^{1}	1	3	3	0	0	8	1	2.077	6.23	62	4.20	.071	0	....	-1	0	-0.1
1976	Chi-A	1	5	.167	9	8	1	0	0	49^{2}	49	28	27	3	1	32	38	1.631	4.89	73	4.74	.257	0	....	-7	1	-0.7
1977	Chi-A	11	8	.579	26	25	6	1	0	166^{2}	161	87	76	12	6	57	125	1.308	4.10	100	3.56	.250	0	....	5	9	0.5
1978	Chi-A	11	16	.407	30	30	7	2	0	203	188	104	92	22	10	95	154	1.394	4.08	93	4.14	.245	0	....	-4	9	-0.5
1979	Chi-A	15	13	.536	36	35	10	3	1	250	208	115	104	20	14	111	132	1.276	3.74	113	3.46	.233	0	....	13	16	1.3
1980	Chi-A	3	6	.333	20	15	0	0	0	81^{2}	100	71	63	13	5	44	37	1.763	6.94	58	6.49	.298	0	....	-26	0	-2.6
1981	Chi-N	1	6	.143	24	12	0	0	0	78^{1}	80	48	44	5	4	39	50	1.519	5.06	73	4.29	.268	0	.000	-10	0	-1.2
1982	Chi-N	1	1	.500	13	2	0	0	0	25	27	20	17	3	0	18	20	1.800	6.12	61	5.56	.267	0	.000	-6	0	-0.7
Total	8	43	56	.434	160	128	24	6	1	858^{2}	814	476	426	78	40	404	557	1.418	4.47	89	4.14	.251	0	.000	-37	35	-4.0

• KRAWCZYK, Ray Raymond Allen Krawczyk b: 10/9/1959, Sewickley, PA BR/TR, 6'1", 186 lbs. Deb: 6/29/1984

YEAR	TM-L	W	L	PCT	G	GS	CG	SH	SV	IP	H	R	ER	HR	HB	BB	SO	RAT	ERA	ERA+	CERA	OAV	BH	AVG	PR+	WS	TPW
1984	Pit-N	0	0	....	4	0	0	0	0	5^{1}	7	2	2	0	0	4	3	2.063	3.38	107	6.08	.350	0	....	0	0	0.0
1985	Pit-N	0	2	.000	8	0	0	0	0	8^{1}	20	13	13	1	1	6	9	3.120	14.04	25	14.89	.455	0	....	-10	0	-1.0
1986	Pit-N	0	1	.000	12	0	0	0	0	12^{1}	17	13	10	3	0	10	7	2.189	7.30	53	9.11	.321	0	....	-5	0	-0.5
1988	Cal-A	0	1	.000	14	1	0	0	1	24^{1}	29	13	13	2	2	8	17	1.521	4.81	80	5.09	.299	0	....	-3	1	-0.3
1989	Mil-A	0	0	....	1	0	0	0	0	2	4	3	3	0	0	1	6	2.500	13.50	28	9.72	.400	0	....	-2	0	-0.2
Total	5	0	4	.000	39	1	0	0	1	52^{1}	77	44	41	6	3	29	42	2.025	7.05	53	7.88	.344	0	....	-19	1	-2.0

• KREEGER, Frank Frank Kreeger d: 7/14/1899, Shelby County, IL Deb: 7/28/1884

YEAR	TM-L	W	L	PCT	G	GS	CG	SH	SV	IP	H	R	ER	HR	HB	BB	SO	RAT	ERA	ERA+	CERA	OAV	BH	AVG	PR+	WS	TPW
1884	KC-U	0	1	.000	1	1	0	0	0	7	9	8	0	0	....	5	3	2.000	0.00	....	....	.293	0	.000	2	0	0.1

• KREMER, Ray Remy Peter "Wiz" Kremer b: 3/23/1893, Oakland, CA d: 2/8/1965, Pinole, CA BR/TR, 6'1", 190 lbs. Deb: 4/18/1924

YEAR	TM-L	W	L	PCT	G	GS	CG	SH	SV	IP	H	R	ER	HR	HB	BB	SO	RAT	ERA	ERA+	CERA	OAV	BH	AVG	PR+	WS	TPW
1924	Pit-N	18	10	.643	**41**	30	17	**4**	1	259^{1}	262	102	92	7	4	51	64	1.207	3.19	120	2.91	.265	13	.151	8	21	0.5
1925*	Pit-N	17	8	.680	40	27	14	0	2	214^{2}	232	106	88	19	9	47	62	1.300	3.69	121	3.83	.278	14	.197	13	16	1.3
1926	Pit-N	**20**	6	.769	37	26	18	3	5	231^{1}	221	79	67	9	4	51	74	1.176	**2.61**	**151**	2.76	.252	21	.253	30	**25**	3.2
1927*	Pit-N	19	8	.704	35	28	18	3	2	226	205	73	62	9	0	53	63	1.142	**2.47**	**166**	2.50	.244	14	.169	**40**	22	3.8
1928	Pit-N	15	13	.536	34	31	17	1	0	219	253	124	113	15	4	68	61	1.466	4.64	87	4.34	.297	14	.179	-15	10	-1.4
1929	Pit-N	18	10	.643	34	27	14	0	0	221^{2}	226	114	105	21	1	60	66	1.290	4.26	112	3.61	.271	11	.128	9	15	0.6
1930	Pit-N	**20**	12	.625	39	**38**	18	1	0	**276**	366	181	154	29	1	63	58	1.554	5.02	99	5.25	.322	16	.157	-1	15	-0.5
1931	Pit-N	11	15	.423	30	30	15	1	0	230	246	110	85	6	5	65	58	1.352	3.33	116	3.45	.271	17	.227	9	15	1.3
1932	Pit-N	4	3	.571	11	10	3	1	0	56^{2}	61	35	27	5	1	16	6	1.359	4.29	89	3.91	.270	2	.105	-3	2	-0.5
1933	Pit-N	1	0	1.000	7	0	0	0	0	20	36	26	23	2	0	9	4	2.250	10.35	32	9.05	.387	0	.000	-16	0	-1.7
Total	10	143	85	.627	308	247	134	14	10	1954^{2}	2108	950	816	122	29	483	516	1.326	3.76	113	3.67	.278	122	.178	75	141	6.6

• KREMMEL, Jim James Louis Kremmel b: 2/28/1948, Belleville, IL BL/TL, 6', 175 lbs. Deb: 7/4/1973

YEAR	TM-L	W	L	PCT	G	GS	CG	SH	SV	IP	H	R	ER	HR	HB	BB	SO	RAT	ERA	ERA+	CERA	OAV	BH	AVG	PR+	WS	TPW
1973	Tex-A	0	2	.000	4	2	0	0	0	9	15	10	9	1	2	6	6	2.333	9.00	41	10.07	.366	0	....	-5	0	-0.5
1974	Chi-N	0	2	.000	23	2	0	0	0	31	37	21	18	3	1	18	22	1.774	5.23	73	6.00	.303	0	.000	-3	0	-0.4
Total	2	0	4	.000	27	4	0	0	0	40	52	31	27	4	3	24	28	1.900	6.08	62	6.92	.319	0	.000	-8	0	-0.9

• KRETLOW, Lou Louis Henry "Lena" Kretlow b: 6/27/1921, Apache, OK BR/TR, 6'2", 185 lbs. Deb: 9/26/1946

YEAR	TM-L	W	L	PCT	G	GS	CG	SH	SV	IP	H	R	ER	HR	HB	BB	SO	RAT	ERA	ERA+	CERA	OAV	BH	AVG	PR+	WS	TPW
1946	Det-A	1	0	1.000	1	1	1	0	0	9	7	3	3	2	0	2	4	1.000	3.00	122	2.85	.206	2	.500	1	1	0.2
1948	Det-A	2	1	.667	5	2	1	0	0	23^{1}	21	14	12	1	0	11	9	1.371	4.63	94	3.24	.233	4	.500	-0	2	0.1
1949	Det-A	3	2	.600	25	10	1	0	0	76	85	58	52	5	1	69	40	2.026	6.16	68	6.44	.290	0	.000	-16	0	-1.9
1950	StL-A	0	2	.000	9	2	0	0	0	14^{1}	25	19	19	2	2	18	10	3.000	11.93	41	13.67	.403	0	.000	-11	0	-1.0
	Chi-A	0	0	....	11	1	0	0	0	21^{1}	17	13	9	1	0	27	14	2.063	3.80	118	5.50	.221	0	.000	1	1	0.0
	Yr.	0	2	.000	20	3	0	0	0	35^{2}	42	32	28	3	2	45	24	2.439	7.07	68	8.78	.302	0	.000	-9	1	-1.0
1951	Chi-A	6	9	.400	26	18	7	1	0	137	129	77	64	7	3	74	89	1.482	4.20	96	3.89	.250	4	.083	-5	4	-1.0
1952	Chi-A	4	4	.500	19	11	4	2	1	79	52	31	26	5	1	56	63	1.367	2.96	123	2.95	.186	1	.050	5	5	0.5
1953	Chi-A	0	0	....	9	3	0	0	0	20^{2}	12	11	8	2	1	30	15	2.032	3.48	115	5.50	.171	0	.000	1	1	0.1
	StL-A	1	5	.167	22	11	0	0	0	81	93	56	46	5	0	52	37	1.790	5.11	82	5.41	.286	5	.200	-8	2	-0.8
	Yr.	1	5	.167	31	14	0	0	0	101^{2}	105	67	54	7	1	82	52	1.839	4.78	87	5.43	.266	5	.172	-7	3	-0.7
1954	Bal-A	6	11	.353	32	20	5	0	0	166^{2}	169	83	81	12	1	82	82	1.506	4.37	82	4.24	.269	8	.157	-13	6	-1.4
1955	Bal-A	0	4	.000	15	5	0	0	0	38^{1}	50	39	35	3	1	27	26	2.009	8.22	46	6.96	.316	1	.091	-18	0	-1.9
1956	KC-A	4	9	.308	25	20	3	0	0	118^{2}	121	75	70	17	0	74	61	1.643	5.31	82	5.33	.262	2	.061	-14	3	-1.6
Total	10	27	47	.365	199	104	22	3	1	785^{1}	781	479	425	62	10	522	450	1.659	4.87	82	4.87	.261	27	.114	-77	25	-8.8

• KREUGER, Rick Richard Allen Kreuger b: 11/3/1948, Grand Rapids, MI BR/TL, 6'2", 185 lbs. Deb: 9/6/1975

YEAR	TM-L	W	L	PCT	G	GS	CG	SH	SV	IP	H	R	ER	HR	HB	BB	SO	RAT	ERA	ERA+	CERA	OAV	BH	AVG	PR+	WS	TPW
1975	Bos-A	0	0	....	2	0	0	0	0	4	3	2	2	0	0	1	1	1.000	4.50	90	1.65	.200	0	....	-0	0	0.0
1976	Bos-A	2	1	.667	8	4	1	0	0	31	31	14	14	3	0	16	12	1.516	4.06	96	4.62	.272	0	....	-0	2	0.0
1977	Bos-A	0	1	.000	1	0	0	0	0	0	2	2	0	0	0	0	0	....	....	....	∞	1.000	0	....	0	0	0.0
1978	Cle-A	0	0	....	6	0	0	0	0	9^{1}	6	4	4	1	0	3	7	.964	3.86	97	1.91	.194	0	....	-0	0	0.0
Total	4	2	2	.500	17	4	1	0	0	44^{1}	42	22	20	4	0	20	20	1.398	4.06	96	3.79	.259	0	....	-0	2	0.0

YEAR	TM-L	W	L	PCT	G	GS	CG	SH	SV	IP	H	R	ER	HR	HB	BB	SO	RAT	ERA	ERA+	CERA	OAV	BH	AVG	PR+	WS	TPW
• KREUTZER, Frank	Franklin James Kreutzer b: 2/7/1939, Buffalo, NY BR/TL, 6'1", 190 lbs. Deb: 9/20/1962																										
1962	Chi-A	0	0	....	1	0	0	0	0	1^1	0	0	0	0	0	1	1	.750	0.00	....	0.57	.000	0	....	1	0	0.1
1963	Chi-A	1	0	1.000	1	1	0	0	0	5	3	1	1	1	0	1	0	.800	1.80	195	2.13	.188	0	.000	1	1	0.1
1964	Chi-A	3	1	.750	17	2	0	0	1	40^1	37	15	15	1	0	18	32	1.364	3.35	103	3.08	.239	1	.125	-1	3	-0.1
	Was-A	2	6	.250	13	9	0	0	0	45^1	48	26	24	6	1	23	27	1.566	4.76	78	5.11	.267	0	.000	-6	1	-0.7
	Yr.	5	7	.417	30	11	0	0	1	85^2	85	41	39	7	1	41	59	1.471	4.10	88	4.15	.254	1	.053	-6	4	-0.8
1965	Was-A	2	6	.250	33	14	2	1	0	85^1	73	48	41	7	2	54	65	1.488	4.32	80	4.09	.232	1	.045	-7	2	-0.9
1966	Was-A	0	5	.000	9	6	0	0	0	31^1	30	24	21	9	1	10	24	1.277	6.03	57	4.65	.236	2	.250	-9	0	-1.0
1969	Was-A	0	0	....	4	0	0	0	0	2	3	1	1	0	0	2	2	2.500	4.50	77	8.58	.333	0	....	-0	0	0.0
Total	**6**	**8**	**18**	**.308**	**78**	**32**	**2**	**1**	**1**	**210^2**	**194**	**115**	**103**	**24**	**4**	**109**	**151**	**1.438**	**4.40**	**80**	**4.17**	**.242**	**4**	**.078**	**-22**	**7**	**-2.5**
• KRIEGER, Kurt	Kurt Ferdinand "Dutch" Krieger b: 9/16/1926, Traisen, Austria d: 8/16/1970, St. Louis, MO BR/TR, 6'3", 212 lbs. Deb: 4/21/1949																										
1949	StL-N	0	0	....	1	0	0	0	0	1	0	0	0	0	0	1	0	1.000	0.00	....	0.80	.000	0	....	0	0	0.0
1951	StL-N	0	0	....	2	0	0	0	0	4	6	7	7	1	0	5	3	2.750	15.75	25	11.84	.353	0	....	-5	0	-0.5
Total	**2**	**0**	**0**	**....**	**3**	**0**	**0**	**0**	**0**	**5**	**6**	**7**	**7**	**1**	**0**	**6**	**3**	**2.400**	**12.60**	**31**	**9.63**	**.353**	**0**	**....**	**-5**	**0**	**-0.5**
• KRIST, Howie	Howard Wilbur "Spud" Krist b: 2/28/1916, West Henrietta, NY d: 4/23/1989, Buffalo, NY BL/TR, 6'1", 175 lbs. Deb: 9/12/1937																										
1937	StL-N	3	1	.750	6	4	1	0	0	27^2	34	13	13	0	0	10	6	1.590	4.23	94	4.41	.304	0	.000	-1	2	-0.2
1938	StL-N	0	0	....	2	0	0	0	0	1^1	1	0	0	0	0	0	1	.750	0.00	....	1.16	.250	0	....	1	0	0.1
1941	StL-N	10	0	1.000	37	8	2	0	2	114	107	57	51	10	1	35	36	1.246	4.03	94	3.26	.246	9	.237	-5	8	-0.4
1942	StL-N	13	3	.813	34	8	3	0	1	118^1	103	34	33	2	2	43	47	1.234	2.51	136	2.67	.233	6	.143	10	12	1.0
1943*	StL-N	11	5	.688	34	17	9	2	3	164^1	141	57	53	5	4	62	57	1.235	2.90	116	2.78	.233	10	.167	4	14	0.3
1946	StL-N	0	2	.000	15	0	0	0	0	18^2	22	15	14	3	1	8	3	1.607	6.75	51	5.88	.306	0	....	-7	0	-0.8
Total	**6**	**37**	**11**	**.771**	**128**	**37**	**15**	**2**	**6**	**444^1**	**408**	**176**	**164**	**20**	**8**	**158**	**150**	**1.274**	**3.32**	**107**	**3.10**	**.244**	**25**	**.168**	**3**	**36**	**0.0**
• KRIVDA, Rick	Rick Michael Krivda b: 1/19/1970, McKeesport, PA BR/TL, 6'1", 180 lbs. Deb: 7/7/1995																										
1995	Bal-A	2	7	.222	13	13	1	0	0	75^1	76	40	38	9	4	25	53	1.341	4.54	105	4.26	.266	0	....	1	4	0.1
1996	Bal-A	3	5	.375	22	11	0	0	0	81^2	89	48	45	14	1	39	54	1.567	4.96	99	5.57	.283	0	....	-0	4	0.0
1997	Bal-A	4	2	.667	10	10	0	0	0	50	67	36	35	7	0	18	29	1.700	6.30	70	6.34	.328	0	....	-11	1	-1.0
1998	Cle-A	2	0	1.000	11	1	0	0	0	25	24	10	9	2	0	16	10	1.600	3.24	147	4.59	.250	0	....	4	2	0.4
	Cin-N	0	2	.000	16	1	0	0	0	26^1	41	34	33	7	3	19	19	2.278	11.28	38	11.09	.366	0	.000	-20	0	-2.1
Total	**4**	**11**	**16**	**.407**	**72**	**36**	**1**	**0**	**0**	**258^1**	**297**	**168**	**160**	**39**	**8**	**117**	**165**	**1.603**	**5.57**	**83**	**5.81**	**.293**	**0**	**.000**	**-26**	**11**	**-2.6**
• KROCK, Gus	August H. Krock b: 5/9/1866, Milwaukee, WI d: 3/22/1905, Pasadena, CA BR/TL, 6', 196 lbs. Deb: 4/24/1888																										
1888	Chi-N	25	14	.641	39	39	39	4	0	339^2	295	143	92	20	9	45	161	1.001	2.44	123	....	.225	22	.164	13	26	1.1
1889	Chi-N	3	3	.500	7	7	5	0	0	60^2	86	43	33	10	2	14	16	1.648	4.90	85	....	.323	4	.167	-5	2	-0.6
	Ind-N	2	2	.500	4	4	3	0	0	32	48	38	26	2	0	14	10	1.938	7.31	57	....	.336	5	.357	-12	1	-0.9
	Was-N	2	4	.333	6	6	6	0	0	48	65	50	28	1	1	22	17	1.813	5.25	75	....	.313	2	.087	-6	0	-0.7
	Yr.	7	9	.438	17	17	14	0	0	140^2	199	131	87	13	3	50	43	1.770	5.57	74	....	.323	11	.180	-23	3	-2.2
1890	Buf-P	0	3	.000	4	3	3	0	0	25	43	37	17	1	0	15	5	2.320	6.12	67	....	.364	1	.083	-5	0	-0.5
Total	**3**	**32**	**26**	**.552**	**60**	**59**	**56**	**4**	**0**	**505^1**	**537**	**311**	**196**	**34**	**12**	**110**	**209**	**1.280**	**3.49**	**100**	**....**	**.263**	**34**	**.164**	**-15**	**29**	**-1.5**
• KROH, Rube	Floyd Myron Kroh b: 8/25/1886, Friendship, NY d: 3/17/1944, New Orleans, LA BL/TL, 6'2", 186 lbs. Deb: 9/30/1906																										
1906	Bos-A	1	0	1.000	1	1	1	1	0	9	2	0	0	0	0	4	5	.667	0.00	....	0.58	.074	0	.000	3	1	0.3
1907	Bos-A	1	4	.200	7	5	1	0	0	34^1	33	13	10	0	2	8	8	1.194	2.62	98	2.79	.255	3	.273	-2	2	-0.2
1908	Chi-N	0	0	....	2	1	0	0	0	12	9	3	2	0	0	4	11	1.083	1.50	156	1.82	.200	0	.000	1	1	0.1
1909	Chi-N	9	4	.692	17	13	10	2	0	120^1	97	26	22	2	1	30	51	1.055	1.65	154	2.08	.224	6	.150	11	11	1.2
1910	Chi-N	3	1	.750	6	4	1	0	0	34^1	33	19	17	1	2	15	16	1.398	4.46	65	3.66	.254	3	.250	-6	1	-0.7
1912	Bos-N	0	0	....	3	1	0	0	0	6^1	8	4	2	0	0	6	1	2.211	2.84	125	7.81	.364	1	.500	1	0	0.1
Total	**6**	**14**	**9**	**.609**	**36**	**25**	**13**	**3**	**0**	**216^1**	**182**	**65**	**53**	**3**	**5**	**67**	**92**	**1.151**	**2.20**	**121**	**2.54**	**.231**	**13**	**.181**	**7**	**16**	**0.8**
• KROLL, Gary	Gary Melvin Kroll b: 7/8/1941, Culver City, CA BR/TR, 6'6", 220 lbs. Deb: 7/26/1964																										
1964	Phi-N	0	0	....	2	0	0	0	0	3	3	1	1	0	0	2	2	1.667	3.00	116	4.23	.250	0	....	0	0	0.0
	NY-N	0	1	.000	8	2	0	0	0	21^2	19	11	10	1	1	15	24	1.569	4.15	86	4.33	.241	1	.333	-2	1	-0.1
	Yr.	0	1	.000	10	2	0	0	0	24^2	22	12	11	1	1	17	26	1.581	4.01	89	4.32	.242	1	.333	-1	1	-0.1
1965	NY-N	6	6	.500	32	11	1	0	1	87	83	48	43	12	6	41	62	1.425	4.45	79	4.54	.249	3	.115	-9	3	-1.0
1966	Hou-N	0	0	....	10	0	0	0	0	23^2	26	10	10	2	0	11	22	1.563	3.80	90	4.66	.280	0	.000	-1	1	-0.1
1969	Cle-A	0	0	....	19	0	0	0	0	24	16	14	11	3	0	22	28	1.583	4.13	91	4.35	.188	0	....	-1	1	-0.1
Total	**4**	**6**	**7**	**.462**	**71**	**13**	**1**	**0**	**1**	**159^1**	**147**	**84**	**75**	**18**	**7**	**91**	**138**	**1.494**	**4.24**	**84**	**4.50**	**.244**	**4**	**.125**	**-12**	**6**	**-1.3**
• KROON, Marc	Marc Jason Kroon b: 4/2/1973, Bronx, NY BB/TR, 6'2", 195 lbs. Deb: 7/7/1995																										
1995	SD-N	0	1	.000	2	0	0	0	0	1^2	1	2	2	0	0	2	2	1.800	10.80	37	4.62	.200	0	....	-1	0	-0.1
1997	SD-N	0	1	.000	12	0	0	0	0	11^1	14	9	9	2	1	5	12	1.676	7.15	54	6.21	.280	0	....	-4	0	-0.4
1998	SD-N	0	0	....	2	0	0	0	0	2^1	0	0	0	0	0	1	2	.429	0.00	....	0.20	.000	0	....	1	0	0.1
	Cin-N	0	0	....	4	0	0	0	0	5^1	7	8	8	0	1	8	4	2.813	13.50	32	11.01	.333	0	....	-5	0	-0.5
	Yr.	0	0	....	6	0	0	0	0	7^2	7	8	8	0	1	9	6	2.087	9.39	46	7.72	.333	0	....	-4	0	-0.4
Total	**3**	**0**	**2**	**.000**	**20**	**0**	**0**	**0**	**0**	**20^2**	**22**	**19**	**19**	**2**	**2**	**16**	**20**	**1.839**	**8.27**	**49**	**6.64**	**.289**	**0**	**....**	**-10**	**0**	**-1.0**
• KRUEGER, Bill	William Culp Krueger b: 4/24/1958, Waukegan, IL BL/TL, 6'5", 210 lbs. Deb: 4/10/1983																										
1983	Oak-A	7	6	.538	17	16	2	0	0	109^2	104	54	44	7	2	53	58	1.432	3.61	107	3.95	.252	0	....	2	6	0.2
1984	Oak-A	10	10	.500	26	24	1	0	0	142	156	95	75	9	2	85	61	1.697	4.75	79	5.24	.285	0	....	-16	3	-1.6
1985	Oak-A	9	10	.474	32	23	2	0	0	151^1	165	95	76	13	2	69	56	1.546	4.52	85	4.76	.276	0	....	-10	4	-1.0
1986	Oak-A	1	2	.333	11	3	0	0	1	34^1	40	25	23	4	0	13	10	1.544	6.03	64	5.20	.301	0	....	-8	0	-0.8
1987	Oak-A	0	3	.000	9	0	0	0	0	5^2	9	7	6	0	0	8	2	3.000	9.53	43	9.96	.360	0	....	-3	0	-0.3
	LA-N	0	0	....	2	0	0	0	0	2^1	3	2	0	0	0	1	2	1.714	0.00	....	4.08	.250	0	....	1	0	0.1
1988	LA-N	0	0	....	1	1	0	0	0	2^1	4	3	3	0	1	2	1	2.571	11.57	29	10.22	.364	0	....	-2	0	-0.2
1989	Mil-A	3	2	.600	34	5	0	0	3	93^2	96	43	40	9	0	33	72	1.377	3.84	100	3.93	.264	0	....	-0	5	0.0
1990	Mil-A	6	8	.429	30	17	0	0	0	129	137	70	57	10	3	54	64	1.481	3.98	97	4.37	.276	0	....	-0	5	0.0
1991	Sea-A	11	8	.579	35	25	1	0	0	175	194	82	70	15	4	60	91	1.451	3.60	114	4.51	.289	0	....	7	10	0.7
1992	Min-A	10	6	.625	27	27	2	2	0	161^1	166	82	77	18	3	46	86	1.314	4.30	94	3.92	.263	0	....	-6	8	-0.6
	Mon-N	0	2	.000	9	2	0	0	0	17^1	23	13	13	0	1	7	13	1.731	6.75	51	5.44	.315	0	.000	-6	0	-0.7
1993	Det-A	6	4	.600	32	7	0	0	0	82	90	43	31	6	4	30	60	1.463	3.40	126	4.46	.285	0	....	8	5	0.8
1994	Det-A	0	2	.000	16	2	0	0	0	19^2	26	24	21	3	1	17	17	2.186	9.61	50	8.32	.321	0	....	-10	0	-0.9
	SD-N	3	2	.600	8	7	1	0	0	41	42	24	22	5	1	7	30	1.195	4.83	85	3.46	.259	6	.500	-2	2	0.0
1995	SD-N	0	0	....	6	0	0	0	0	7^2	13	6	6	1	0	4	6	2.217	7.04	57	8.51	.371	0	....	-3	0	-0.3
	Sea-A	2	1	.667	6	5	0	0	0	20	37	17	13	4	0	4	10	2.050	5.85	81	9.58	.407	0	....	-2	1	-0.2
Total	**13**	**68**	**66**	**.507**	**301**	**164**	**9**	**2**	**4**	**1194^1**	**1305**	**685**	**577**	**104**	**24**	**493**	**639**	**1.505**	**4.35**	**91**	**4.64**	**.280**	**6**	**.400**	**-51**	**49**	**-4.8**
• KRUGER, Abe	Abraham Kruger b: 2/14/1885, Morris Run, PA d: 7/4/1962, Elmira, NY BR/TR, 6'2", 190 lbs. Deb: 10/6/1908																										
1908	Bro-N	0	1	.000	2	1	0	0	0	6^1	5	5	3	0	3	3	2	1.263	4.26	55	4.32	.238	0	.000	-1	0	-0.2
• KRUKOW, Mike	Michael Edward Krukow b: 1/21/1952, Long Beach, CA BR/TR, 6'5", 205 lbs. Deb: 9/6/1976																										
1976	Chi-N	0	0	....	2	0	0	0	0	4^1	6	4	4	0	0	2	1	1.846	8.31	46	5.94	.333	0	.000	-2	0	-0.2
1977	Chi-N	8	14	.364	34	33	1	1	0	172	195	96	84	16	3	61	106	1.488	4.40	100	4.53	.281	11	.200	3	8	0.3
1978	Chi-N	9	3	.750	27	20	3	1	0	138	125	62	60	11	5	53	81	1.290	3.91	103	3.47	.243	11	.244	3	11	0.6
1979	Chi-N	9	9	.500	28	28	0	0	0	164^2	172	84	77	13	3	81	119	**1.536**	4.21	98	4.56	.275	16	.314	1	10	0.6
1980	Chi-N	10	15	.400	34	34	3	0	0	205	200	117	100	13	8	80	130	1.366	4.39	89	3.75	.258	16	.246	-8	7	-0.6
1981	Chi-N	9	9	.500	25	**25**	2	1	0	144^1	146	68	59	11	2	55	101	1.393	3.68	100	3.89	.264	9	.180	4	8	0.4
1982	Phi-N	13	11	.542	33	33	7	2	0	208	211	87	72	8	3	82	138	1.409	3.12	118	3.70	.268	13	.181	13	15	1.3
1983	SF-N	11	11	.500	31	31	2	1	0	184^1	189	95	81	17	3	76	136	1.438	3.95	89	4.13	.261	16	.254	-7	8	-0.3

YEAR TM-L	W	L	PCT	G	GS	CG	SH	SV	IP	H	R	ER	HR	HB	BB	SO	RAT	ERA	ERA+	CERA	OAV	BH	AVG	PR+	WS	TPW
1984 SF-N	11	12	.478	35	33	3	1	1	199^1	234	117	101	22	5	78	141	**1.565**	4.56	77	5.13	.290	10	.139	-18	4	-2.1
1985 SF-N	8	11	.421	28	28	6	1	0	194^2	176	80	73	19	3	49	150	1.156	3.38	102	2.93	.238	12	.218	4	11	0.9
1986 SF-N★	20	9	.690	34	34	10	2	0	245	204	90	83	24	4	55	178	1.057	3.05	115	2.55	.223	12	.146	9	16	1.0
1987★SF-N	5	6	.455	30	28	3	0	0	163	182	98	87	24	2	46	104	1.399	4.80	80	4.63	.288	9	.167	-20	3	-1.9
1988 SF-N	7	4	.636	20	20	1	0	0	124^2	111	51	49	13	5	31	75	1.139	3.54	92	3.02	.236	3	.073	-4	6	-0.5
1989 SF-N	4	3	.571	8	8	0	0	0	43	37	20	19	5	1	18	18	1.279	3.98	85	3.58	.236	1	.063	-4	2	-0.5
Total 14	124	117	.515	369	355	41	10	1	2190^1	2188	1069	949	196	47	767	1478	1.349	3.90	96	3.83	.260	139	.193	-27	109	-0.9
• KRUMM, Al — Albert Krumm b: 1/13/1865, Pittsburgh, PA d: 6/15/1937, San Diego, CA TR Deb: 5/17/1889																										
1889 Pit-N	0	1	.000	1	1	1	0	0	9	8	11	10	0	0	10	4	2.000	10.00	38	....	.230	0	.000	-6	0	-0.6
• KUBENKA, Jeff — Jeffrey Scot Kubenka b: 8/24/1974, Weimar, TX BR/TL, 6'2", 191 lbs. Deb: 9/6/1998																										
1998 LA-N	1	0	1.000	6	0	0	0	0	9^1	4	1	1	0	0	8	10	1.286	0.96	411	2.03	.138	0	....	3	2	0.3
1999 LA-N	0	1	.000	6	0	0	0	0	7^2	13	12	10	1	0	4	2	2.217	11.74	36	8.56	.371	1	1.000	-6	0	-0.5
Total 2	1	1	.500	12	0	0	0	0	17	17	13	11	1	0	12	12	1.706	5.82	73	4.98	.266	1	1.000	-3	2	-0.2
• KUBINSKI, Tim — Timothy Mark Kubinski b: 1/20/1972, Pullman, WA BL/TL, 6'4", 205 lbs. Deb: 7/16/1997																										
1997 Oak-A	0	0	....	11	0	0	0	0	12^2	12	9	8	2	1	6	10	1.421	5.68	79	4.66	.255	0	....	-1	0	-0.1
1999 Oak-A	0	0	....	14	0	0	0	0	12^1	14	8	8	3	1	5	7	1.541	5.84	79	6.04	.280	0	....	-2	0	-0.1
Total 2	0	0	....	25	0	0	0	0	25	26	17	16	5	2	11	17	1.480	5.76	79	5.34	.268	0	....	-3	0	-0.3
• KUCAB, Johnny — John Albert Kucab b: 12/17/1919, Olyphant, PA d: 5/26/1977, Youngstown, OH BR/TR, 6'2", 185 lbs. Deb: 9/14/1950																										
1950 Phi-A	1	1	.500	4	2	2	0	0	26	29	10	10	4	0	8	8	1.423	3.46	131	4.70	.282	1	.111	3	2	0.3
1951 Phi-A	4	3	.571	30	1	0	0	4	74^2	76	37	35	9	1	23	23	1.326	4.22	101	3.97	.265	0	.000	-1	5	-0.2
1952 Phi-A	0	1	.000	25	0	0	0	2	51^1	64	37	30	5	1	20	17	1.636	5.26	75	5.48	.312	2	.200	-7	0	-0.7
Total 3	5	5	.500	59	3	2	0	6	152	169	84	75	18	2	51	48	1.447	4.44	94	4.60	.284	3	.086	-4	7	-0.7
• KUCEK, Jack — John Andrew Charles Kucek b: 6/8/1953, Warren, OH BR/TR, 6'2", 200 lbs. Deb: 8/8/1974																										
1974 Chi-A	1	4	.200	9	7	0	0	0	37^2	48	25	22	3	1	21	25	1.832	5.26	71	6.44	.320	0	....	-6	0	-0.6
1975 Chi-A	0	0	....	2	0	0	0	0	3^2	9	2	2	0	0	4	2	3.545	4.91	79	17.27	.500	0	....	-0	0	0.0
1976 Chi-A	0	0	....	2	0	0	0	0	4^2	9	5	5	2	0	4	2	2.786	9.64	37	16.01	.429	0	....	-3	0	-0.3
1977 Chi-A	0	1	.000	8	3	0	0	0	34^2	35	20	14	4	2	10	25	1.298	3.63	112	4.02	.267	0	....	3	1	0.3
1978 Chi-A	2	3	.400	10	5	3	0	1	52	42	23	19	5	0	27	30	1.327	3.29	116	3.36	.220	0	....	3	3	0.4
1979 Chi-A	0	0	....	1	0	0	0	0	0^2	0	4	0	0	0	3	0	4.500	0.00	....	10.78	.000	0	....	0	0	0.0
Phi-N	1	0	1.000	4	0	0	0	0	4^1	6	4	4	2	0	1	2	1.615	8.31	46	7.86	.333	0	....	-2	0	-0.2
1980 Tor-A	3	8	.273	23	12	0	0	1	68	83	56	51	9	1	41	35	1.824	6.75	64	6.45	.300	0	....	-19	0	-1.9
Total 7	7	16	.304	59	27	3	0	2	205^2	232	139	117	25	4	111	121	1.668	5.12	78	5.71	.288	0	....	-24	4	-2.5
• KUCKS, Johnny — John Charles Kucks b: 7/27/1933, Hoboken, NJ BR/TR, 6'3", 184 lbs. Deb: 4/17/1955																										
1955★NY-A	8	7	.533	29	13	3	1	0	126^2	122	54	48	8	2	44	49	1.311	3.41	110	3.40	.252	2	.050	-1	7	-0.5
1956★NY-A★	18	9	.667	34	31	12	3	0	224^1	223	113	96	19	10	72	67	1.315	3.85	101	3.85	.261	11	.143	-5	11	-0.6
1957★NY-A	8	10	.444	37	23	4	1	2	179^1	169	82	71	13	8	59	78	1.271	3.56	101	3.45	.251	6	.109	-2	7	-0.4
1958★NY-A	8	8	.500	34	15	4	1	4	126	132	67	55	14	6	39	46	1.357	3.93	90	4.22	.269	5	.125	-8	4	-0.9
1959 NY-A	0	1	.000	9	1	0	0	0	16^2	21	16	16	5	0	9	9	1.800	8.64	42	8.12	.323	0	.000	-9	0	-1.0
KC-A	8	11	.421	33	23	6	1	1	151^1	163	76	65	10	12	42	51	1.355	3.87	104	4.15	.278	4	.085	3	8	0.0
Yr.	8	12	.400	42	24	6	1	1	168	184	92	81	15	12	51	60	1.399	4.34	91	4.54	.282	4	.082	-6	8	-0.9
1960 KC-A	4	10	.286	31	17	1	0	0	114	140	85	76	22	1	43	38	1.605	6.00	66	5.99	.306	4	.133	-24	0	-2.5
Total 6	54	56	.491	207	123	30	7	7	938^1	970	493	427	91	39	308	338	1.362	4.10	93	4.15	.269	32	.110	-45	37	-5.8
• KUCZYNSKI, Bert — Bernard Carl Kuczynski b: 1/8/1920, Philadelphia, PA d: 1/19/1997, Allentown, PA BR/TR, 6', 195 lbs. Deb: 6/2/1943																										
1943 Phi-A	0	1	.000	6	1	0	0	0	24^2	36	15	11	2	2	9	8	1.824	4.01	85	6.69	.336	0	.000	-1	0	-0.1
• KUHAULUA, Fred — Fred Mahele Kuhaulua b: 2/23/1953, Honolulu, HI BL/TL, 5'11", 175 lbs. Deb: 8/2/1977																										
1977 Cal-A	0	0	....	3	1	0	0	0	6^1	15	11	11	1	0	7	3	3.474	15.63	25	17.51	.455	0	....	-8	0	-0.8
1981 SD-N	1	0	1.000	5	4	0	0	0	29^1	28	10	8	1	0	9	16	1.261	2.45	133	3.08	.257	1	.111	3	2	0.2
Total 2	1	0	1.000	8	5	0	0	0	35^2	43	21	19	2	0	16	19	1.654	4.79	75	5.65	.303	1	.111	-6	2	-0.6
• KUHN, Bub — Bernard Daniel Kuhn b: 10/12/1899, Vicksburg, MI d: 11/20/1956, Detroit, MI BL/TR, 6'1.5", 182 lbs. Deb: 9/1/1924																										
1924 Cle-A	0	1	.000	1	0	0	0	0	1	4	3	3	1	0	0	0	4.000	27.00	16	34.98	.667	0	....	-3	0	-0.2
• KULL, John — John A. Kull b: 6/24/1882, Shenandoah, PA d: 3/30/1936, Schuykill Haven, PA BL/TL, 6'2", 190 lbs. Deb: 10/2/1909																										
1909 Phi-A	1	0	1.000	1	0	0	0	0	3	3	1	1	0	1	5	4	2.667	3.00	80	8.74	.250	1	1.000	-0	1	0.0
• KUME, Mike — John Michael Kume b: 5/19/1926, Premier, WV BR/TR, 6'1", 195 lbs. Deb: 8/26/1955																										
1955 KC-A	0	2	.000	6	4	0	0	0	23^2	35	23	21	1	3	15	7	2.113	7.99	52	8.04	.354	1	.125	-10	0	-1.0
• KUNKEL, Bill — William Gustave James Kunkel b: 7/7/1936, Hoboken, NJ d: 5/4/1985, Red Bank, NJ BR/TR, 6'1", 187 lbs. Deb: 4/15/1961 U																										
1961 KC-A	3	4	.429	58	2	0	0	4	88^2	103	58	51	11	0	32	46	1.523	5.18	80	4.93	.289	1	.125	-10	3	-1.0
1962 KC-A	0	0	....	9	0	0	0	0	7^2	8	7	3	3	0	4	6	1.565	3.52	118	6.68	.258	0	....	1	0	0.1
1963 NY-A	3	2	.600	22	0	0	0	0	46^1	42	15	14	3	0	13	31	1.187	2.72	129	2.79	.239	2	.333	3	4	0.4
Total 3	6	6	.500	89	2	0	0	4	142^2	153	80	68	17	0	49	83	1.416	4.29	93	4.33	.272	3	.214	-6	7	-0.5
• KUNZ, Earl — Earl Dewey "Pinches" Kunz b: 12/25/1899, Sacramento, CA d: 4/14/1963, Sacramento, CA BR/TR, 5'10", 170 lbs. Deb: 4/19/1923																										
1923 Pit-N	1	2	.333	21	2	1	0	1	45^2	48	33	28	2	0	24	12	1.577	5.52	72	4.37	.293	1	.083	-8	0	-0.9
• KUROSAKI, Ryan — Ryan Yoshitomo Kurosaki b: 7/3/1952, Honolulu, HI BR/TR, 5'10", 160 lbs. Deb: 5/20/1975																										
1975 StL-N	0	0	....	7	0	0	0	0	13	15	11	11	3	0	7	6	1.692	7.62	49	6.29	.283	0	.000	-5	0	-0.6
• KURTZ, Hal — Harold James "Bud" Kurtz b: 8/20/1943, Washington, DC BR/TR, 6'3", 205 lbs. Deb: 4/18/1968																										
1968 Cle-A	1	0	1.000	28	0	0	0	1	38	37	24	22	2	5	15	16	1.368	5.21	57	3.76	.255	0	.000	-10	0	-1.2
• KUSEL, Ed — Edward D. Kusel b: 2/15/1886, Cleveland, OH d: 10/20/1948, Cleveland, OH TR, 6', 165 lbs. Deb: 9/18/1909																										
1909 StL-A	0	3	.000	3	3	3	0	0	24	43	32	19	1	0	1	2	1.833	7.13	34	5.08	.384	3	.300	-13	0	-1.4
• KUSH, Emil — Emil Benedict Kush b: 11/4/1916, Chicago, IL d: 11/26/1969, River Grove, IL BR/TR, 5'11", 185 lbs. Deb: 9/21/1941																										
1941 Chi-N	0	0	....	2	0	0	0	0	4	2	1	1	0	0	0	2	.500	2.25	156	0.54	.143	0	.000	1	0	0.1
1942 Chi-N	0	0	....	1	0	0	0	0	2	1	0	0	0	0	1	1	1.000	0.00	....	1.34	.167	0	.000	1	0	0.1
1946 Chi-N	9	2	.818	40	6	1	1	2	129^2	120	47	44	4	3	43	50	1.257	3.05	109	3.00	.253	8	.211	6	10	0.7
1947 Chi-N	8	3	.727	47	1	1	0	5	91	80	38	34	8	3	53	44	1.462	3.36	117	4.14	.247	5	.250	6	10	0.7
1948 Chi-N	1	4	.200	34	1	0	0	3	72	70	39	35	5	2	37	31	1.486	4.38	89	3.99	.253	2	.154	-3	3	-0.3
1949 Chi-N	3	3	.500	26	0	0	0	2	47^2	51	21	20	7	2	24	22	1.573	3.78	107	5.45	.283	3	.333	2	4	0.4
Total 6	21	12	.636	150	8	2	1	12	346^1	324	146	134	24	10	158	150	1.392	3.48	107	3.80	.254	18	.220	13	27	1.6
• KUTYNA, Marty — Marion John Kutyna b: 11/14/1932, Philadelphia, PA BR/TR, 6', 190 lbs. Deb: 9/19/1959																										
1959 KC-A	0	0	....	4	0	0	0	1	7^1	7	0	0	0	0	1	1	1.091	0.00	....	2.18	.250	0	....	3	1	0.3
1960 KC-A	3	2	.600	51	0	0	0	4	61^2	64	33	27	7	0	32	20	1.557	3.94	101	4.76	.274	1	.200	1	4	0.1
1961 Was-A	6	8	.429	50	6	0	0	3	143	147	79	63	12	2	48	64	1.364	3.97	99	3.90	.271	7	.206	-1	7	-0.1
1962 Was-A	5	6	.455	54	0	0	0	0	78	83	42	35	9	0	27	25	1.410	4.04	100	4.19	.275	1	.125	0	4	0.0
Total 4	14	16	.467	159	6	0	0	8	290	301	154	125	28	2	108	110	1.410	3.88	102	4.12	.272	9	.191	4	16	0.4
• KUTZLER, Jerry — Jerry Scott Kutzler b: 3/25/1965, Waukegan, IL BL/TR, 6'1", 175 lbs. Deb: 4/28/1990																										
1990 Chi-A	2	1	.667	7	7	0	0	0	31^1	38	23	21	2	0	14	21	1.660	6.03	63	5.22	.304	0	....	-8	0	-0.8

• KUZAVA, Bob

Robert Leroy "Sarge" Kuzava b: 5/28/1923, Wyandotte, MI BB/TL, 6'2", 204 lbs. Deb: 9/21/1946

YEAR TM-L	W	L	PCT	G	GS	CG	SH	SV	IP	H	R	ER	HR	HB	BB	SO	RAT	ERA	ERA+	CERA	OAV	BH	AVG	PR+	WS	TPW
1946 Cle-A	1	0	1.000	2	2	0	0	0	12	9	7	4	0	1	11	4	1.667	3.00	110	3.58	.191	1	.200	0	1	0.0
1947 Cle-A	1	1	.500	4	4	1	1	0	21^2	22	10	10	1	1	9	9	1.431	4.15	84	3.93	.265	1	.111	-2	1	-0.3
1949 Chi-A	10	6	.625	29	18	9	1	0	156^2	139	76	70	6	1	91	83	1.468	4.02	104	3.58	.240	2	.036	2	9	-0.4
1950 Chi-A	1	3	.250	10	7	1	0	0	44^1	43	28	28	5	0	27	21	1.579	5.68	79	4.74	.257	1	.083	-7	1	-0.7
Was-A	8	7	.533	22	22	8	1	0	155	156	80	68	8	1	75	84	1.490	3.95	114	4.00	.263	5	.100	10	10	0.7
Yr.	9	10	.474	32	29	9	1	0	199^1	199	108	96	13	1	102	105	1.510	4.33	104	4.16	.261	6	.097	3	11	0.1
1951 Was-A	3	3	.500	8	8	3	0	0	52^1	57	34	32	5	2	28	22	1.624	5.50	74	5.15	.284	3	.176	-8	1	-0.7
*NY-A	8	4	.667	23	8	4	1	5	82^1	76	27	22	5	1	27	50	1.251	2.40	159	3.08	.241	3	.136	12	9	1.2
Yr.	11	7	.611	31	16	7	1	5	134^2	133	61	54	10	3	55	72	1.396	3.61	110	3.88	.258	6	.154	4	10	0.4
1952* NY-A	8	8	.500	28	12	6	1	3	133	115	53	51	7	1	63	67	1.338	3.45	96	3.29	.240	4	.093	-6	7	-0.8
1953* NY-A	6	5	.545	33	6	2	2	4	92^1	92	35	34	9	0	34	48	1.365	3.31	111	3.92	.264	1	.048	1	6	0.0
1954 NY-A	1	3	.250	20	3	0	0	1	39^2	46	30	24	3	0	18	22	1.613	5.45	63	4.99	.297	0	.000	-10	0	-1.1
Bal-A	1	3	.250	4	4	0	0	0	23^2	30	11	11	0	0	11	15	1.732	4.18	86	5.08	.323	0	.000	-1	1	-0.2
Yr.	2	6	.250	24	7	0	0	1	63^1	76	41	35	3	0	29	37	1.658	4.97	70	5.02	.306	0	.000	-11	1	-1.3
1955 Bal-A	0	1	.000	6	1	0	0	0	12^1	10	7	5	0	0	4	5	1.135	3.65	104	2.01	.222	0	.000	0	0	0.0
Phi-N	1	0	1.000	17	4	0	0	0	32^1	47	26	26	5	0	12	13	1.825	7.24	55	7.00	.333	1	.143	-12	0	-1.2
1957 Pit-N	0	0	....	4	0	0	0	0	2	3	2	2	0	0	3	1	3.000	9.00	42	10.76	.333	0	....	-1	0	-0.1
StL-N	0	0	....	3	0	0	0	0	2^1	4	1	1	0	0	2	2	2.571	3.86	103	9.39	.364	0	....	0	0	0.0
Yr.	0	0	....	7	0	0	0	0	4^1	7	3	3	0	0	5	3	2.769	6.23	62	10.02	.350	0	....	-1	0	-0.1
Total 10	49	44	.527	213	99	34	7	13	862	849	427	388	54	8	415	446	1.466	4.05	97	4.01	.260	22	.086	-21	46	-3.6

• LABINE, Clem

Clement Walter Labine b: 8/6/1926, Lincoln, RI BR/TR, 6', 180 lbs. Deb: 4/18/1950

YEAR TM-L	W	L	PCT	G	GS	CG	SH	SV	IP	H	R	ER	HR	HB	BB	SO	RAT	ERA	ERA+	CERA	OAV	BH	AVG	PR+	WS	TPW
1950 Bro-N	0	0	....	1	0	0	0	0	2	2	1	1	0	0	1	0	1.500	4.50	91	4.01	.286	0	....	-0	0	0.0
1951 Bro-N	5	1	.833	14	6	5	2	0	65^1	52	17	16	4	0	20	39	1.102	2.20	178	2.41	.223	3	.143	11	7	1.0
1952 Bro-N	8	4	.667	25	9	0	0	0	77	76	44	44	3	1	47	43	1.597	5.14	71	4.30	.259	1	.045	-14	2	-1.6
1953* Bro-N	11	6	.647	37	7	0	0	7	110^1	92	39	34	9	0	30	44	1.106	2.77	154	2.56	.225	2	.071	17	13	1.5
1954 Bro-N	7	6	.538	47	2	0	0	5	108^1	101	60	50	7	1	56	43	1.449	4.15	98	3.73	.247	1	.033	-1	7	-0.3
1955* Bro-N	13	5	.722	**60**	8	1	0	11	144^1	121	61	52	12	0	55	67	1.219	3.24	125	3.02	.229	3	.097	12	15	1.3
1956* Bro-N★	10	6	.625	62	3	1	0	**19**	115^2	111	48	43	11	3	39	75	1.297	3.35	119	3.55	.253	2	.087	6	13	0.5
1957 Bro-N★	5	7	.417	58	0	0	0	**17**	104^2	104	50	40	8	1	27	67	1.252	3.44	121	3.22	.259	2	.100	9	11	0.7
1958 LA-N	6	6	.500	52	2	0	0	14	104	112	55	48	8	1	33	43	1.394	4.15	99	4.01	.283	1	.056	-1	9	-0.2
1959* LA-N	5	10	.333	56	0	0	0	9	84^2	91	39	37	11	1	25	37	1.370	3.93	107	4.22	.282	0	.000	3	7	0.1
1960 LA-N	0	1	.000	13	0	0	0	1	17	26	12	11	1	0	8	15	2.000	5.82	68	7.06	.356	1	.500	-4	0	-0.3
Det-A	0	3	.000	14	0	0	0	2	19^1	19	12	11	2	0	12	6	1.603	5.12	81	4.34	.257	0	.000	-2	0	-0.2
*Pit-N	3	0	1.000	15	0	0	0	3	30^1	29	5	5	0	1	11	21	1.319	1.48	253	2.97	.254	0	.000	7	5	0.7
Yr.	3	1	.750	28	0	0	0	4	47^1	55	17	16	1	1	19	36	1.563	3.04	128	4.44	.294	1	.167	3	5	0.4
1961 Pit-N	4	1	.800	56	1	0	0	8	92^2	102	43	38	4	2	31	49	1.435	3.69	108	3.96	.284	1	.100	3	7	0.2
1962 NY-N	0	0	....	3	0	0	0	0	4	5	6	5	1	0	1	2	1.500	11.25	37	5.54	.278	0	....	-3	0	-0.3
Total 13	77	56	.579	513	38	7	2	96	1079^2	1043	492	435	81	11	396	551	1.333	3.63	111	3.54	.256	17	.075	42	96	3.1

• LACEY, Bob

Robert Joseph Lacey b: 8/25/1953, Fredericksburg, VA BR/TL, 6'5", 210 lbs. Deb: 5/13/1977

YEAR TM-L	W	L	PCT	G	GS	CG	SH	SV	IP	H	R	ER	HR	HB	BB	SO	RAT	ERA	ERA+	CERA	OAV	BH	AVG	PR+	WS	TPW
1977 Oak-A	6	8	.429	64	0	0	0	7	121^2	100	46	41	13	0	43	69	1.175	3.03	133	2.91	.234	0	....	15	10	1.5
1978 Oak-A	8	9	.471	**74**	0	0	0	5	119^2	126	52	40	10	1	35	60	1.345	3.01	121	3.66	.271	0	....	11	10	1.1
1979 Oak-A	1	5	.167	42	0	0	0	4	47^2	66	34	31	7	1	24	33	1.888	5.85	69	6.94	.327	0	....	-8	0	-0.8
1980 Oak-A	3	2	.600	47	1	1	1	6	79^2	68	29	26	7	1	21	45	1.117	2.94	128	2.68	.234	0	....	7	7	0.7
1981 Cle-A	0	0	....	14	0	0	0	0	21^1	36	20	18	5	0	3	11	1.828	7.59	48	8.08	.371	0	....	-9	0	-0.9
Tex-A	0	0	....	1	0	0	0	0	1	1	1	1	1	0	0	0	1.000	9.00	39	7.45	.250	0	....	-1	0	-0.1
Yr.	0	0	....	15	0	0	0	0	22^1	37	21	19	6	0	3	11	1.791	7.66	47	8.05	.366	0	....	-9	0	-1.0
1983 Cal-A	1	2	.333	8	0	0	0	0	8^2	12	5	5	1	0	0	7	1.385	5.19	77	5.08	.343	0	....	-1	0	-0.1
1984 SF-N	1	3	.250	34	1	0	0	0	51	55	26	22	5	0	13	26	1.333	3.88	90	3.81	.276	2	.333	-1	2	0.0
Total 7	20	29	.408	284	2	1	1	22	450^2	464	213	184	49	3	139	251	1.338	3.67	103	3.89	.270	2	.333	12	29	1.3

• LACHEMANN, Marcel

Marcel Ernest Lachemann b: 6/13/1941, Los Angeles, CA BR/TR, 6', 185 lbs. Deb: 6/4/1969 M/C

YEAR TM-L	W	L	PCT	G	GS	CG	SH	SV	IP	H	R	ER	HR	HB	BB	SO	RAT	ERA	ERA+	CERA	OAV	BH	AVG	PR+	WS	TPW
1969 Oak-A	4	1	.800	28	0	0	0	2	43^1	43	24	19	1	2	19	16	1.431	3.95	87	3.76	.261	0	.000	-2	2	-0.3
1970 Oak-A	3	3	.500	41	0	0	0	3	58^1	58	20	18	6	2	18	39	1.303	2.78	127	3.76	.266	0	.000	4	5	0.4
1971 Oak-A	0	0	....	1	0	0	0	0	0^1	2	2	2	0	0	1	0	9.000	54.00	6	56.02	1.000	0	....	-2	0	-0.2
Total 3	7	4	.636	70	0	0	0	5	102	103	46	39	7	4	38	55	1.382	3.44	101	3.93	.268	0	.000	0	7	-0.1

• LACHOWICZ, Al

Allen Robert Lachowicz b: 9/6/1960, Pittsburgh, PA BR/TR, 6'3", 198 lbs. Deb: 9/13/1983

YEAR TM-L	W	L	PCT	G	GS	CG	SH	SV	IP	H	R	ER	HR	HB	BB	SO	RAT	ERA	ERA+	CERA	OAV	BH	AVG	PR+	WS	TPW
1983 Tex-A	0	1	.000	2	1	0	0	0	8	9	2	2	0	0	2	8	1.375	2.25	178	3.51	.281	0	....	2	1	0.2

• LACKEY,

William D. Lackey b: 12/8/1870, St. Albans, WV d: 5/15/1941, Columbus, OH Deb: 10/2/1890

YEAR TM-L	W	L	PCT	G	GS	CG	SH	SV	IP	H	R	ER	HR	HB	BB	SO	RAT	ERA	ERA+	CERA	OAV	BH	AVG	PR+	WS	TPW
1890 Phi-a	0	0	....	1	0	0	0	0	2	1	4	2	0	0	3	1	2.000	9.00	42	....	.145	0	.000	-1	0	-0.1

• LACKEY, John

John Derran Lackey b: 10/23/1978, Abilene, TX BR/TR, 6'6", 205 lbs. Deb: 6/24/2002

YEAR TM-L	W	L	PCT	G	GS	CG	SH	SV	IP	H	R	ER	HR	HB	BB	SO	RAT	ERA	ERA+	CERA	OAV	BH	AVG	PR+	WS	TPW
2002* Ana-A	9	4	.692	18	18	1	0	0	108^1	113	52	44	10	4	33	69	1.348	3.66	121	4.03	.267	0	....	6	7	0.6
2003 Ana-A	10	16	.385	33	33	2	**2**	0	204	223	117	105	31	10	66	151	1.417	4.63	93	4.88	.278	0	.000	-10	7	-1.0
Total 2	19	20	.487	51	51	3	2	0	312^1	336	169	149	41	14	99	220	1.393	4.29	101	4.59	.274	0	.000	-4	14	-0.4

• LACORTE, Frank

Frank Joseph LaCorte b: 10/13/1951, San Jose, CA BR/TR, 6'1", 180 lbs. Deb: 9/8/1975

YEAR TM-L	W	L	PCT	G	GS	CG	SH	SV	IP	H	R	ER	HR	HB	BB	SO	RAT	ERA	ERA+	CERA	OAV	BH	AVG	PR+	WS	TPW
1975 Atl-N	0	3	.000	3	2	0	0	0	13^2	13	10	8	1	0	6	10	1.390	5.27	72	3.75	.245	0	.000	-2	0	-0.3
1976 Atl-N	3	12	.200	19	17	1	0	0	105^1	97	58	55	6	6	53	79	1.424	4.70	81	3.88	.249	3	.091	-8	3	-1.1
1977 Atl-N	1	8	.111	14	7	0	0	0	37	67	51	48	10	2	29	28	2.595	11.68	38	12.94	.394	2	.200	-29	0	-2.9
1978 Atl-N	0	1	.000	2	2	0	0	0	14^2	9	6	6	0	0	4	7	.886	3.68	110	1.25	.180	0	.000	1	1	0.0
1979 Atl-N	0	0	....	6	0	0	0	0	8^1	9	7	7	2	0	5	6	1.680	7.56	54	6.28	.273	0	.000	-3	0	-0.3
Hou-N	1	2	.333	12	3	0	0	0	27	21	16	15	3	0	10	24	1.148	5.00	70	2.69	.208	0	.000	-4	0	-0.5
Yr.	1	2	.333	18	3	0	0	0	35^1	30	23	22	5	0	15	30	1.274	5.60	65	3.53	.224	0	.000	-7	0	-0.8
1980* Hou-N	8	5	.615	55	0	0	0	11	83	61	29	26	4	0	43	66	1.253	2.82	117	2.71	.210	1	.167	4	9	0.5
1981* Hou-N	4	2	.667	37	0	0	0	5	42	41	18	17	1	0	21	40	1.476	3.64	90	3.65	.258	1	.333	-2	3	-0.2
1982 Hou-N	1	5	.167	55	0	0	0	7	76^1	71	44	38	5	0	46	51	1.533	4.48	74	4.02	.247	0	.000	-11	2	-1.2
1983 Hou-N	4	4	.500	37	0	0	0	3	53^1	35	32	30	8	2	28	48	1.181	5.06	67	3.12	.190	1	.200	-11	1	-1.1
1984 Cal-A	1	2	.333	13	1	0	0	0	29^1	33	26	23	9	0	13	13	1.568	7.06	56	6.32	.282	0	....	-10	0	-1.0
Total 10	23	44	.343	253	32	1	0	26	490	457	297	273	49	10	258	372	1.459	5.01	74	4.32	.249	8	.104	-74	19	-8.0

• LACOSS, Mike

Michael James LaCoss b: 5/30/1956, Glendale, CA BR/TR, 6'5", 190 lbs. Deb: 7/18/1978

YEAR TM-L	W	L	PCT	G	GS	CG	SH	SV	IP	H	R	ER	HR	HB	BB	SO	RAT	ERA	ERA+	CERA	OAV	BH	AVG	PR+	WS	TPW
1978 Cin-N	4	8	.333	16	15	2	1	0	96	104	56	48	5	1	46	31	1.563	4.50	79	4.48	.288	2	.067	-9	2	-1.1
1979* Cin-N★	14	8	.636	35	32	6	1	0	205^2	202	92	80	13	2	79	73	1.366	3.50	107	3.70	.263	9	.129	5	12	0.4
1980 Cin-N	10	12	.455	34	29	4	2	0	169^1	207	101	87	9	1	68	59	1.624	4.62	77	4.97	.303	5	.091	-18	3	-2.1
1981 Cin-N	4	7	.364	20	13	1	1	1	78	102	55	53	7	1	30	22	1.692	6.12	58	5.78	.325	0	.000	-23	0	-2.7
1982 Hou-N	6	6	.500	41	8	0	0	0	115	107	41	37	3	4	54	51	1.400	2.90	115	3.57	.252	6	.250	4	9	0.6
1983 Hou-N	5	7	.417	38	17	2	0	1	138	142	81	68	10	2	56	53	1.435	4.43	77	4.07	.273	3	.086	-18	1	-2.1
1984 Hou-N	7	5	.583	39	18	2	1	3	132	132	64	59	3	0	55	86	1.417	4.02	83	3.56	.261	4	.129	-12	5	-1.3
1985 KC-A	1	1	.500	21	0	0	0	1	40^2	49	25	23	2	0	29	26	1.918	5.09	82	5.92	.304	0	....	-4	1	-0.4
1986 SF-N	10	13	.435	37	31	4	1	0	204^1	179	99	81	14	6	70	86	1.219	3.57	99	3.07	.240	14	.230	-4	9	0.1
1987* SF-N	13	10	.565	39	26	2	1	0	171	184	78	70	16	2	63	79	1.444	3.68	104	4.38	.283	3	.060	1	10	-0.2
1988 SF-N	7	7	.500	19	19	1	1	0	114^1	99	55	46	5	1	47	70	1.277	3.62	90	3.03	.234	8	.242	-5	5	-0.2
1989* SF-N	10	10	.500	45	18	1	0	6	150^1	143	62	53	3	7	65	78	1.384	3.17	106	3.52	.255	3	.073	-0	8	-0.1
1990 SF-N	6	4	.600	13	12	1	0	0	77^2	75	37	34	5	0	39	39	1.468	3.94	92	4.01	.259	1	.043	-3	4	-0.5

YEAR	TM-L	W	L	PCT	G	GS	CG	SH	SV	IP	H	R	ER	HR	HB	BB	SO	RAT	ERA	ERA+	CERA	OAV	BH	AVG	PR+	WS	TPW
1991	SF-N	1	5	.167	18	5	0	0	0	47^1	61	39	38	4	2	24	30	1.796	7.23	50	6.24	.314	2	.222	-20	0	-2.0
Total	14	98	103	.488	415	243	26	9	12	1739^2	1786	885	777	99	29	725	783	1.443	4.02	88	4.04	.270	60	.125	-105	69	-11.6

• LACY, Kerry Kerry Ardeen Lacy b: 8/7/1972, Chattanooga, TN BR/TR, 6'2", 195 lbs. Deb: 8/16/1996

YEAR	TM-L	W	L	PCT	G	GS	CG	SH	SV	IP	H	R	ER	HR	HB	BB	SO	RAT	ERA	ERA+	CERA	OAV	BH	AVG	PR+	WS	TPW
1996	Bos-A	2	0	1.000	11	0	0	0	0	10^2	15	5	4	2	1	8	9	2.156	3.38	150	9.45	.333	0	....	2	1	0.2
1997	Bos-A	1	1	.500	33	0	0	0	3	45^2	60	34	31	7	0	22	18	1.796	6.11	76	6.52	.314	0	....	-7	1	-0.7
Total	2	3	1	.750	44	0	0	0	3	56^1	75	39	35	9	1	30	27	1.864	5.59	84	7.07	.318	0	....	-5	2	-0.5

• LADD, Pete Peter Linwood Ladd b: 7/17/1956, Portland, ME BR/TR, 6'3", 240 lbs. Deb: 8/17/1979

YEAR	TM-L	W	L	PCT	G	GS	CG	SH	SV	IP	H	R	ER	HR	HB	BB	SO	RAT	ERA	ERA+	CERA	OAV	BH	AVG	PR+	WS	TPW
1979	Hou-N	1	1	.500	10	0	0	0	0	12^1	8	5	4	1	2	8	6	1.297	2.92	120	3.42	.178	0	.000	1	1	0.1
1982*	Mil-A	1	3	.250	16	0	0	0	3	18	16	8	8	5	0	6	12	1.222	4.00	95	4.10	.239	0	....	-1	1	-0.1
1983	Mil-A	3	4	.429	44	0	0	0	25	49^1	30	17	14	3	1	16	41	.932	2.55	146	1.63	.172	0	....	7	10	0.7
1984	Mil-A	4	9	.308	54	1	0	0	3	91	94	58	53	16	1	38	75	1.451	5.24	73	4.83	.266	0	....	-13	1	-1.3
1985	Mil-A	0	0	....	29	0	0	0	2	45^2	58	26	23	5	2	10	22	1.489	4.53	92	5.16	.315	0	....	-2	2	-0.2
1986	Sea-A	8	6	.571	52	0	0	0	6	70^2	69	33	30	10	3	18	53	1.231	3.82	111	3.79	.258	0	....	3	7	0.3
Total	6	17	23	.425	205	1	0	0	39	287	275	147	132	40	9	96	209	1.293	4.14	96	3.97	.252	0	.000	-5	22	-0.5

• LADE, Doyle Doyle Marion "Porky" Lade b: 2/17/1921, Fairbury, NE d: 5/18/2000, Lincoln, NE BR/TR, 5'10", 183 lbs. Deb: 9/18/1946

YEAR	TM-L	W	L	PCT	G	GS	CG	SH	SV	IP	H	R	ER	HR	HB	BB	SO	RAT	ERA	ERA+	CERA	OAV	BH	AVG	PR+	WS	TPW
1946	Chi-N	0	2	.000	3	2	0	0	0	15^1	15	8	7	0	1	3	8	1.174	4.11	81	2.55	.238	1	.200	-1	0	-0.1
1947	Chi-N	11	10	.524	34	25	7	1	0	187^1	202	105	82	15	1	79	62	1.500	3.94	100	4.37	.276	13	.217	1	11	0.3
1948	Chi-N	5	6	.455	19	12	6	0	0	87^1	99	44	39	4	1	31	29	1.489	4.02	97	4.18	.283	5	.156	-0	4	-0.1
1949	Chi-N	4	5	.444	36	13	5	1	1	129^2	141	73	72	14	2	58	43	1.535	5.00	81	4.73	.274	7	.219	-11	5	-1.0
1950	Chi-N	5	6	.455	34	12	2	0	2	117^2	126	68	62	14	2	50	36	1.496	4.74	89	4.71	.275	10	.286	-4	6	-0.1
Total	5	25	29	.463	126	64	20	2	3	537^1	583	298	262	47	7	221	178	1.496	4.39	91	4.45	.275	36	.220	-16	26	-1.0

• LAFFERTY, Flip Frank Bernard Lafferty b: 5/4/1854, Scranton, PA d: 2/8/1910, Wilmington, DE TR Deb: 9/15/1876 ♦

YEAR	TM-L	W	L	PCT	G	GS	CG	SH	SV	IP	H	R	ER	HR	HB	BB	SO	RAT	ERA	ERA+	CERA	OAV	BH	AVG	PR+	WS	TPW
1876	Phi-N	0	1	.000	1	1	1	0	0	9	5	3	0	0	....	0	0	.556	0.00	....	....	.151	0	.000	3	0	0.2

• LAFITTE, Ed Edward Francis "Doc" Lafitte b: 4/7/1886, New Orleans, LA d: 4/12/1971, Jenkintown, PA BR/TR, 6'2", 188 lbs. Deb: 4/16/1909

YEAR	TM-L	W	L	PCT	G	GS	CG	SH	SV	IP	H	R	ER	HR	HB	BB	SO	RAT	ERA	ERA+	CERA	OAV	BH	AVG	PR+	WS	TPW
1909	Det-A	0	1	.000	3	1	1	0	1	14	22	14	6	2	1	2	11	1.714	3.86	65	6.85	.344	1	.250	-2	0	-0.2
1911	Det-A	11	8	.579	29	20	15	0	1	172^1	205	113	75	2	5	52	63	**1.491**	3.92	88	4.30	.302	11	.157	-7	9	-1.0
1912	Det-A	0	0	....	1	0	0	0	0	1^2	2	4	3	0	0	2	0	2.400	16.20	20	8.04	.333	0	....	-2	0	-0.2
1914	Bro-F	18	15	.545	42	33	23	0	2	290^2	260	110	85	7	16	127	137	1.331	2.63	123	3.37	.248	26	.257	23	23	2.8
1915	Bro-F	6	9	.400	17	16	7	0	0	117^2	126	66	52	6	1	57	34	1.555	3.98	75	4.36	.288	14	.264	-14	4	-1.3
	Buf-F	2	2	.500	14	5	1	1	1	50^1	53	25	19	1	2	22	17	1.514	3.40	90	3.96	.286	2	.118	-2	2	-0.3
	Yr.	8	11	.421	31	21	8	1	1	168	179	91	71	7	3	79	51	**1.536**	3.80	79	4.24	.287	16	.229	-16	6	-1.5
Total	5	37	35	.514	106	75	47	1	5	646^2	668	332	240	18	25	262	262	1.438	3.34	96	3.93	.276	54	.220	-4	38	-0.1

• LAGGER, Ed Edwin Joseph Lagger b: 7/14/1912, Joliet, IL d: 11/10/1981, Joliet, IL BR/TR, 6'3", 200 lbs. Deb: 6/15/1934

YEAR	TM-L	W	L	PCT	G	GS	CG	SH	SV	IP	H	R	ER	HR	HB	BB	SO	RAT	ERA	ERA+	CERA	OAV	BH	AVG	PR+	WS	TPW
1934	Phi-A	0	0	....	8	0	0	0	0	18	27	23	22	1	1	14	2	2.278	11.00	40	8.22	.342	0	.000	-13	0	-1.3

• LAGROW, Lerrin Lerrin Harris LaGrow b: 7/8/1948, Phoenix, AZ BR/TR, 6'5", 220 lbs. Deb: 7/28/1970

YEAR	TM-L	W	L	PCT	G	GS	CG	SH	SV	IP	H	R	ER	HR	HB	BB	SO	RAT	ERA	ERA+	CERA	OAV	BH	AVG	PR+	WS	TPW
1970	Det-A	0	1	.000	10	0	0	0	0	12^1	16	11	10	2	0	6	7	1.784	7.30	51	6.55	.308	0	.000	-5	0	-0.5
1972*	Det-A	0	1	.000	16	0	0	0	2	27^1	22	4	4	0	0	6	9	1.024	1.32	239	1.77	.222	0	....	5	4	0.6
1973	Det-A	1	5	.167	21	3	0	0	3	54	54	26	26	8	1	23	33	1.426	4.33	94	4.56	.263	0	....	-1	3	-0.1
1974	Det-A	8	19	.296	37	34	11	0	0	216^1	245	132	112	21	3	80	85	1.502	4.66	82	4.72	.287	0	....	-19	6	-2.0
1975	Det-A	7	14	.333	32	26	7	2	0	164^1	183	105	80	15	2	66	75	1.515	4.38	92	4.60	.280	0	....	-3	6	-0.3
1976	StL-N	0	1	.000	8	2	1	0	0	24^1	21	4	4	0	1	7	10	1.151	1.48	239	2.35	.241	0	.000	5	3	0.5
1977	Chi-A	7	3	.700	66	0	0	0	25	98^2	81	32	27	10	1	35	63	1.176	2.46	166	3.00	.230	0	....	21	16	2.1
1978	Chi-A	6	5	.545	52	0	0	0	16	88	85	47	43	9	3	38	41	1.398	4.40	86	4.26	.260	0	....	-5	7	-0.5
1979	Chi-A	0	3	.000	11	2	0	0	1	17^2	27	21	18	2	1	16	9	2.434	9.17	46	9.82	.346	0	....	-10	0	-0.9
	LA-N	5	1	.833	31	0	0	0	4	37	38	16	14	2	0	18	22	1.514	3.41	107	4.20	.270	1	.333	1	4	0.2
1980	Phi-N	0	2	.000	25	0	0	0	3	39	42	22	18	5	0	17	21	1.513	4.15	91	4.75	.276	1	.250	-2	1	-0.2
Total	10	34	55	.382	309	67	19	2	54	779	814	420	356	74	12	312	375	1.445	4.11	94	4.36	.271	2	.154	-12	50	-1.2

• LAHTI, Jeff Jeffrey Allen Lahti b: 10/8/1956, Oregon City, OR BR/TR, 6', 180 lbs. Deb: 6/27/1982

YEAR	TM-L	W	L	PCT	G	GS	CG	SH	SV	IP	H	R	ER	HR	HB	BB	SO	RAT	ERA	ERA+	CERA	OAV	BH	AVG	PR+	WS	TPW
1982*	StL-N	5	4	.556	33	1	0	0	0	56^2	53	27	24	3	2	21	22	1.306	3.81	95	3.13	.245	1	.077	-3	3	-0.4
1983	StL-N	3	3	.500	53	0	0	0	0	74	64	31	26	2	1	29	26	1.257	3.16	114	2.68	.240	0	.000	4	5	0.3
1984	StL-N	4	2	.667	63	0	0	0	1	84^2	69	36	35	6	2	34	45	1.217	3.72	93	2.77	.225	1	.167	-4	5	-0.4
1985*	StL-N	5	2	.714	52	0	0	0	19	68^1	63	15	14	3	0	26	41	1.302	1.84	192	3.08	.251	0	.000	11	11	1.1
1986	StL-N	0	0	....	4	0	0	0	0	2^1	3	0	0	0	0	1	3	1.714	0.00	....	5.47	.333	0	....	1	0	0.1
Total	5	17	11	.607	205	1	0	0	20	286	252	109	99	14	5	111	137	1.269	3.12	114	2.91	.240	2	.053	10	24	0.7

• LAKE, Eddie Edward Erving "Sparky" Lake b: 3/18/1916, Antioch, CA d: 6/7/1995, Castro Valley, CA BR/TR, 5'7", 160 lbs. Deb: 9/26/1939 ♦

YEAR	TM-L	W	L	PCT	G	GS	CG	SH	SV	IP	H	R	ER	HR	HB	BB	SO	RAT	ERA	ERA+	CERA	OAV	BH	AVG	PR+	WS	TPW
1944	Bos-A	0	0	....	6	0	0	0	0	19^1	20	13	9	2	3	11	7	1.603	4.19	81	5.60	.278	26	.206	-2	3	-0.1

• LAKE, Joe Joseph Henry Lake b: 1/6/1881, Brooklyn, NY d: 6/30/1950, Brooklyn, NY BR/TR, 6', 185 lbs. Deb: 4/21/1908

YEAR	TM-L	W	L	PCT	G	GS	CG	SH	SV	IP	H	R	ER	HR	HB	BB	SO	RAT	ERA	ERA+	CERA	OAV	BH	AVG	PR+	WS	TPW
1908	NY-A	9	22	.290	38	27	19	2	0	269^1	252	157	95	6	6	77	118	1.222	3.17	78	2.78	.242	21	.188	-14	5	-1.5
1909	NY-A	14	11	.560	31	26	17	3	1	215^1	180	81	45	2	5	59	117	1.110	1.88	134	2.23	.225	14	.173	21	13	2.5
1910	StL-A	11	17	.393	35	29	24	1	2	261^1	243	116	64	2	1	77	141	1.224	2.20	112	2.72	.248	21	.231	9	10	1.3
1911	StL-A	10	15	.400	30	25	14	2	0	215^1	245	115	79	3	4	40	69	1.324	3.30	102	3.43	.282	21	.263	-0	10	0.2
1912	StL-A	1	7	.125	11	6	4	0	0	57	70	41	28	0	1	16	28	1.509	4.42	75	4.38	.314	3	.150	-8	0	-0.9
	Det-A	9	11	.450	26	14	11	0	1	162^2	190	94	56	3	3	39	86	1.408	3.10	106	3.94	.296	9	.145	4	7	0.1
	Yr.	10	18	.357	37	20	15	0	1	219^2	260	135	84	3	4	55	114	1.434	3.44	96	4.05	.301	12	.146	-3	7	-0.8
1913	Det-A	8	7	.533	28	12	6	0	1	137	149	67	50	3	0	24	35	1.263	3.28	89	3.20	.278	12	.267	-2	7	0.3
Total	6	62	90	.408	199	139	95	8	5	1318	1329	671	417	19	20	332	594	1.260	2.85	99	3.04	.261	101	.206	12	52	2.1

• LAMABE, Jack John Alexander Lamabe b: 10/3/1936, Farmingdale, NY BR/TR, 6'1", 198 lbs. Deb: 4/17/1962

YEAR	TM-L	W	L	PCT	G	GS	CG	SH	SV	IP	H	R	ER	HR	HB	BB	SO	RAT	ERA	ERA+	CERA	OAV	BH	AVG	PR+	WS	TPW
1962	Pit-N	3	1	.750	46	0	0	0	2	78	70	35	25	4	0	40	56	1.410	2.88	136	3.38	.238	0	.000	8	6	0.7
1963	Bos-A	7	4	.636	65	2	0	0	6	151^1	139	63	53	8	4	46	93	1.222	3.15	120	2.95	.247	3	.094	11	12	1.1
1964	Bos-A	9	13	.409	39	25	3	0	1	177^1	235	123	116	25	2	57	109	**1.647**	5.89	65	5.95	.318	6	.115	-36	0	-3.9
1965	Bos-A	0	3	.000	14	0	0	0	0	25^1	34	24	23	5	3	14	17	1.895	8.17	46	8.14	.340	0	.000	-12	0	-1.3
	Hou-N	0	2	.000	3	2	0	0	0	12^2	17	9	6	3	0	3	6	1.579	4.26	79	6.28	.315	1	.250	-1	0	-0.1
1966	Chi-A	7	9	.438	34	17	3	2	0	121^1	116	55	53	9	1	35	67	1.245	3.93	81	3.26	.251	2	.057	-11	3	-1.4
1967	Chi-A	1	0	1.000	3	0	0	0	0	5	7	2	1	0	0	1	3	1.600	1.80	172	4.34	.318	0	....	1	1	0.1
	NY-N	0	3	.000	16	2	0	0	1	31^2	24	15	14	4	0	8	23	1.011	3.98	85	2.30	.200	0	.000	-2	1	-0.3
	*StL-N	3	4	.429	23	1	1	1	4	47^2	43	16	15	2	0	10	30	1.112	2.83	115	2.43	.244	2	.200	2	4	0.2
	Yr.	3	7	.300	39	3	1	1	5	79^1	67	31	29	6	0	18	53	1.071	3.29	101	2.38	.226	2	.133	-0	5	0.0
1968	Chi-N	3	2	.600	42	0	0	0	1	61^1	68	33	29	7	1	24	30	1.500	4.26	74	4.61	.289	1	.200	-7	2	-0.8
Total	7	33	41	.446	285	49	7	3	15	711^2	753	375	335	67	11	238	434	1.393	4.24	85	4.13	.272	15	.096	-47	29	-5.6

• LAMACCHIA, Al Alfred Anthony LaMacchia b: 7/22/1921, St. Louis, MO BR/TR, 5'10.5", 190 lbs. Deb: 9/27/1943

YEAR	TM-L	W	L	PCT	G	GS	CG	SH	SV	IP	H	R	ER	HR	HB	BB	SO	RAT	ERA	ERA+	CERA	OAV	BH	AVG	PR+	WS	TPW
1943	StL-A	0	1	.000	1	1	0	0	0	4	9	6	5	0	0	2	2	2.750	11.25	30	11.28	.450	0	.000	-3	0	-0.4
1945	StL-A	2	0	1.000	5	0	0	0	0	9	6	2	2	0	0	3	2	1.000	2.00	176	1.61	.207	0	.000	2	1	0.2
1946	StL-A	0	0	....	8	0	0	0	0	15	17	10	10	2	0	7	3	1.600	6.00	62	5.04	.279	0	.000	-4	0	-0.4
	Was-A	0	1	.000	2	0	0	0	0	2^2	6	5	5	1	0	2	0	3.000	16.88	20	17.61	.462	0	....	-4	0	-0.4
	Yr.	0	1	.000	10	0	0	0	0	17^2	23	15	15	3	0	9	3	1.811	7.64	47	6.93	.311	0	.000	-8	0	-0.8
Total	3	2	2	.500	16	1	0	0	0	30^2	38	23	22	3	0	14	7	1.696	6.46	55	5.94	.309	0	.000	-10	1	-1.1

• LAMANNA, Frank Frank "Hank" LaManna b: 8/22/1919, Waterton, PA d: 9/1/1980, Syracuse, NY BR/TR, 6'2.5", 195 lbs. Deb: 4/16/1940

YEAR	TM-L	W	L	PCT	G	GS	CG	SH	SV	IP	H	R	ER	HR	HB	BB	SO	RAT	ERA	ERA+	CERA	OAV	BH	AVG	PR+	WS	TPW
1940	Bos-N	1	0	1.000	5	1	1	0	0	13^1	13	8	7	1	0	8	3	1.575	4.73	79	4.60	.271	1	.200	-2	0	-0.2

YEAR TM-L	W	L	PCT	G	GS	CG	SH	SV	IP	H	R	ER	HR	HB	BB	SO	RAT	ERA	ERA+	CERA	OAV	BH	AVG	PR+	WS	TPW
1941 Bos-N	5	4	.556	35	4	0	0	1	72^2	77	52	43	5	1	56	23	1.830	5.33	67	5.52	.285	9	.281	-15	1	-1.4
1942 Bos-N	0	1	.000	5	0	0	0	0	6^2	5	4	4	1	0	3	2	1.200	5.40	62	3.22	.208	0	.000	-1	0	-0.2
Total 3	6	5	.545	45	5	1	0	1	92^2	95	64	54	7	1	67	28	1.748	5.24	68	5.22	.278	10	.256	-18	1	-1.7
• LAMANSKE, Frank	Frank James "Lefty" Lamanske b: 9/30/1906, Oglesby, IL d: 8/4/1971, Olney, IL BL/TL, 5'11", 170 lbs. Deb: 4/27/1935																									
1935 Bro-N	0	0	....	2	0	0	0	0	3^2	5	3	3	0	0	1	1	1.636	7.36	54	4.69	.313	0	.000	-1	0	-0.2
• LAMASTER, Wayne	Noble Wayne LaMaster b: 2/13/1907, Speed, IN d: 8/4/1989, New Albany, IN BL/TL, 5'8", 170 lbs. Deb: 4/19/1937																									
1937 Phi-N	15	19	.441	50	30	10	1	4	220^1	255	139	130	24	2	82	135	1.530	5.31	81	4.89	.290	15	.190	-20	10	-2.2
1938 Phi-N	4	7	.364	18	12	1	1	0	63^2	80	58	55	8	3	31	35	1.743	7.77	51	6.11	.301	9	.409	-25	1	-2.1
Bro-N	0	1	.000	3	0	0	0	0	11^1	17	6	6	0	0	3	3	1.765	4.76	82	5.56	.340	1	.167	-1	0	-0.1
Yr.	4	8	.333	21	12	1	1	0	75	97	64	61	8	3	34	38	1.747	7.32	55	6.03	.307	10	.357	-26	1	-2.2
Total 2	19	27	.413	71	42	11	2	4	295^1	352	203	191	32	5	116	173	1.585	5.82	72	5.18	.295	25	.234	-46	11	-4.4
• LAMB, John	John Andrew Lamb b: 7/20/1946, Sharon, CT BR/TR, 6'3", 180 lbs. Deb: 8/12/1970																									
1970 Pit-N	0	1	.000	23	0	0	0	3	32^1	23	10	10	2	2	13	24	1.113	2.78	140	2.64	.209	0	.000	3	3	0.3
1971 Pit-N	0	0	....	2	0	0	0	0	4^1	3	0	0	0	0	1	1	.923	0.00	....	1.35	.188	0	.000	2	1	0.2
1973 Pit-N	0	1	.000	22	0	0	0	2	29^2	37	24	20	3	0	10	11	1.584	6.07	58	5.03	.308	0	.000	-8	0	-0.9
Total 3	0	2	.000	47	0	0	0	5	66^1	63	34	30	5	2	24	36	1.312	4.07	89	3.63	.256	0	.000	-4	4	-0.5
• LAMB, Ray	Raymond Richard Lamb b: 12/23/1944, Glendale, CA BR/TR, 6'1", 175 lbs. Deb: 8/1/1969																									
1969 LA-N	0	1	.000	10	0	0	0	1	15	12	3	3	2	0	7	11	1.267	1.80	185	3.66	.235	0	.000	2	2	0.2
1970 LA-N	6	1	.857	35	0	0	0	0	57	59	27	24	4	4	27	32	1.509	3.79	101	4.44	.277	0	.000	-1	4	-0.1
1971 Cle-A	6	12	.333	43	21	3	1	1	158^1	147	67	59	11	1	69	91	1.364	3.35	114	3.55	.247	4	.093	7	10	0.6
1972 Cle-A	5	6	.455	34	9	0	0	0	107^2	101	42	37	5	1	29	64	1.207	3.09	104	2.85	.248	0	.000	0	6	-0.1
1973 Cle-A	3	3	.500	32	1	0	0	2	86	98	44	44	7	2	42	60	1.628	4.60	85	5.13	.291	0	....	-6	4	-0.6
Total 5	20	23	.465	154	31	3	1	4	424	417	183	167	29	8	174	258	1.394	3.54	104	3.82	.260	4	.058	3	26	0.0
• LAMBERT, Clayton	Clayton Patrick Lambert b: 3/26/1917, Summit, IL d: 4/3/1981, Ogden, UT BR/TR, 6'2", 185 lbs. Deb: 4/22/1946																									
1946 Cin-N	2	2	.500	23	4	2	0	1	52^2	48	27	25	3	1	20	20	1.291	4.27	78	3.35	.251	2	.154	-7	2	-0.8
1947 Cin-N	0	0	....	3	0	0	0	0	5^2	12	10	10	3	0	6	1	3.176	15.88	26	19.87	.444	0	.000	-7	0	-0.7
Total 2	2	2	.500	26	4	2	0	1	58^1	60	37	35	6	1	26	21	1.474	5.40	65	4.95	.275	2	.143	-14	2	-1.5
• LAMBERT, Gene	Eugene Marion Lambert b: 4/26/1921, Crenshaw, MS d: 2/10/2000, Germantown, TN BR/TR, 5'11", 175 lbs. Deb: 9/14/1941																									
1941 Phi-N	0	1	.000	2	1	0	0	0	9	11	2	2	0	0	2	3	1.444	2.00	185	3.74	.297	0	.000	2	1	0.2
1942 Phi-N	0	0	....	1	0	0	0	0	1	3	1	1	0	0	0	1	3.000	9.00	37	14.52	.500	0	....	-1	0	-0.1
Total 2	0	1	.000	3	1	0	0	0	10	14	3	3	0	0	2	4	1.600	2.70	132	4.82	.326	0	.000	1	1	0.1
• LAMBETH, Otis	Otis Samuel Lambeth b: 5/13/1890, Berlin, KS d: 6/5/1976, Moran, KS BR/TR, 6', 175 lbs. Deb: 7/16/1916																									
1916 Cle-A	4	4	.500	15	9	3	0	1	74	69	33	24	1	3	38	28	1.446	2.92	103	3.70	.256	3	.111	1	4	-0.1
1917 Cle-A	7	6	.538	26	10	2	0	2	97^1	97	48	34	2	11	30	27	1.305	3.14	90	3.65	.274	6	.188	-6	5	-0.7
1918 Cle-A	0	0	....	2	0	0	0	0	7	10	5	5	0	0	6	3	2.286	6.43	47	8.18	.370	1	1.000	-3	0	-0.2
Total 3	11	10	.524	43	19	5	0	3	178^1	176	86	63	3	14	74	58	1.402	3.18	91	3.85	.271	10	.167	-8	9	-1.0
• LAMLINE, Fred	Frederick Arthur "Dutch" Lamline b: 8/14/1887, Port Huron, MI d: 9/20/1970, Port Huron, MI BR/TR, 5'11", 171 lbs. Deb: 9/18/1912																									
1912 Chi-A	0	0	....	1	0	0	0	0	2	7	7	7	0	0	2	1	4.500	31.50	10	24.81	.583	0	....	-6	0	-0.6
1915 StL-N	0	0	....	4	0	0	0	0	19	21	4	3	0	2	3	11	1.263	1.42	196	3.37	.300	1	.125	3	0	0.3
Total 2	0	0	....	5	0	0	0	0	21	28	11	10	0	2	5	12	1.571	4.29	72	5.41	.341	1	.125	-3	0	-0.3
• LAMP, Dennis	Dennis Patrick Lamp b: 9/23/1952, Los Angeles, CA BR/TR, 6'4", 210 lbs. Deb: 8/21/1977																									
1977 Chi-N	0	2	.000	11	3	0	0	0	30	43	21	21	3	2	8	12	1.700	6.30	70	6.25	.344	3	.375	-6	0	-0.5
1978 Chi-N	7	15	.318	37	36	6	3	0	223^2	221	96	82	16	4	56	73	1.238	3.30	122	3.28	.258	15	.205	20	15	2.2
1979 Chi-N	11	10	.524	38	32	6	1	0	200^1	223	96	78	14	5	46	86	1.343	3.50	117	3.92	.287	9	.155	17	12	1.7
1980 Chi-N	10	14	.417	41	37	2	1	0	202^2	259	123	117	16	1	82	83	**1.683**	5.20	75	5.56	.317	6	.098	-26	3	-3.0
1981 Chi-A	7	6	.538	27	10	3	0	0	127	103	41	34	4	1	43	71	1.150	2.41	148	2.46	.222	0	....	15	10	1.6
1982 Chi-A	11	8	.579	44	27	3	2	5	189^2	206	96	84	9	6	59	78	1.397	3.99	101	3.95	.279	0	....	3	10	0.3
1983* Chi-A	7	7	.500	49	5	1	0	15	116^1	123	52	48	6	4	29	44	1.307	3.71	113	3.60	.275	0	....	6	11	0.6
1984 Tor-A	8	8	.500	56	4	0	0	9	85	97	53	43	9	1	38	45	1.588	4.55	90	4.96	.285	0	....	-5	5	-0.5
1985* Tor-A	11	0	1.000	53	1	0	0	2	105^2	96	42	39	7	0	27	68	1.164	3.32	127	2.83	.247	0	....	9	10	0.9
1986 Tor-A	2	6	.250	40	2	0	0	2	73	93	50	41	5	0	23	30	1.589	5.05	83	4.90	.309	0	....	-7	2	-0.7
1987 Oak-A	1	3	.250	36	5	0	0	0	56^2	76	38	32	5	1	22	36	1.729	5.08	81	5.94	.326	0	....	-5	1	-0.5
1988 Bos-A	7	6	.538	46	0	0	0	0	82^2	92	39	32	3	2	19	49	1.343	3.48	118	3.66	.284	0	....	7	6	0.7
1989 Bos-A	4	2	.667	42	0	0	0	2	112^1	96	37	29	4	0	27	61	1.095	2.32	176	2.29	.235	0	....	23	10	2.4
1990* Bos-A	3	5	.375	47	1	0	0	0	105^2	114	61	55	10	3	30	49	1.363	4.68	87	4.02	.279	0	....	-5	4	-0.5
1991 Bos-A	6	3	.667	51	0	0	0	0	92	100	54	48	8	3	31	57	1.424	4.70	92	4.20	.275	0	....	-4	4	-0.4
1992 Pit-N	1	1	.500	21	0	0	0	0	28	33	16	16	3	2	9	15	1.500	5.14	67	4.88	.292	0	.000	-6	0	-0.6
Total 16	96	96	.500	639	163	21	7	35	1830^2	1975	915	799	122	35	549	857	1.379	3.93	103	3.95	.278	33	.164	36	103	3.5
• LAMPE, Henry	Henry Joseph Lampe b: 9/19/1872, Boston, MA d: 9/16/1936, Dorchester, MA BR/TL, 5'11.5", 175 lbs. Deb: 5/14/1894																									
1894 Bos-N	0	1	.000	2	1	0	0	0	5^1	17	19	7	5	0	7	1	4.500	11.81	50	35.30	.526	0	.000	-4	0	-0.3
1895 Phi-N	0	2	.000	7	3	2	0	0	44	68	54	37	3	1	33	18	2.295	7.57	63	8.53	.348	2	.125	-13	0	-1.2
Total 2	0	3	.000	9	4	2	0	0	49^1	85	73	44	8	1	40	19	2.534	8.03	61	11.43	.373	2	.111	-17	0	-1.4
• LANAHAN, Dick	Richard Anthony Lanahan b: 9/27/1911, Washington, DC d: 3/12/1975, Rochester, MN BL/TL, 6', 186 lbs. Deb: 9/15/1935																									
1935 Was-A	0	3	.000	3	3	0	0	0	20^2	27	13	13	2	2	17	10	2.129	5.66	76	7.77	.314	1	.167	-3	0	-0.3
1937 Was-A	0	1	.000	6	2	0	0	0	11^1	16	16	16	2	1	13	2	2.559	12.71	35	10.22	.320	0	.000	-11	0	-0.9
1940 Pit-N	6	8	.429	40	8	4	0	2	108	121	63	51	8	1	42	45	1.509	4.25	90	4.42	.279	4	.118	-2	4	-0.4
1941 Pit-N	0	1	.000	7	0	0	0	0	12	13	9	7	1	2	3	5	1.333	5.25	69	4.46	.283	0	.000	-2	0	-0.2
Total 4	6	13	.316	56	13	4	0	2	152	177	101	87	13	6	75	62	1.658	5.15	77	5.31	.288	5	.119	-18	4	-1.9
• LANCASTER, Les	Lester Wayne Lancaster b: 4/21/1962, Dallas, TX BR/TR, 6'2", 200 lbs. Deb: 4/7/1987																									
1987 Chi-N	8	3	.727	27	18	0	0	0	132^1	138	76	72	14	1	51	78	1.428	4.90	87	4.24	.268	4	.082	-6	6	-0.8
1988 Chi-N	4	6	.400	44	3	1	0	5	85^2	89	42	36	4	1	34	36	1.436	3.78	95	3.82	.273	1	.050	0	5	-0.1
1989* Chi-N	4	2	.667	42	0	0	0	8	72^2	60	12	11	2	0	15	56	1.032	1.36	276	2.01	.226	2	.182	20	13	2.1
1990 Chi-N	9	5	.643	55	6	1	1	6	109	121	57	56	11	1	40	65	1.477	4.62	88	4.48	.283	1	.050	-4	7	-0.4
1991 Chi-N	9	7	.563	64	11	1	0	3	156	150	68	61	13	4	49	102	1.276	3.52	110	3.48	.256	5	.179	9	11	1.0
1992 Det-A	3	4	.429	41	1	0	0	0	86^2	101	66	61	11	3	51	35	1.754	6.33	62	5.94	.294	0	....	-22	0	-2.2
1993 StL-N	4	1	.800	50	0	0	0	0	61^1	56	24	20	5	1	21	36	1.255	2.93	135	3.16	.242	0	.000	7	5	0.7
Total 7	41	28	.594	323	39	3	1	22	703^2	715	345	317	60	11	261	408	1.387	4.05	98	3.94	.265	13	.098	4	47	0.1
• LANCE, Gary	Gary Dean Lance b: 9/21/1948, Greenville, SC BB/TR, 6'3", 195 lbs. Deb: 9/28/1977																									
1977 KC-A	0	1	.000	1	0	0	0	0	2	2	1	1	0	0	2	0	2.000	4.50	90	5.48	.286	0	....	-0	0	0.0
• LANDIS, Bill	William Henry Landis b: 10/8/1942, Hanford, CA BL/TL, 6'2", 178 lbs. Deb: 9/28/1963																									
1963 KC-A	0	0	....	1	0	0	0	0	1^2	0	0	0	0	0	1	3	.600	0.00	....	0.38	.000	0	....	1	0	0.1
1967 Bos-A	1	0	1.000	18	1	0	0	0	25^2	24	16	15	6	0	11	23	1.364	5.26	66	4.57	.253	0	.000	-5	0	-0.6
1968 Bos-A	3	3	.500	38	1	0	0	3	60	48	22	21	4	2	30	59	1.300	3.15	100	3.24	.223	0	.000	0	4	0.0
1969 Bos-A	5	5	.500	45	5	0	0	1	82^1	82	53	48	7	3	49	50	1.591	5.25	73	4.84	.269	0	.000	-11	2	-1.2
Total 4	9	8	.529	102	7	0	0	4	169^2	154	91	84	17	5	91	135	1.444	4.46	80	4.19	.250	0	.000	-15	6	-1.7

YEAR TM-L	W	L	PCT	G	GS	CG	SH	SV	IP	H	R	ER	HR	HB	BB	SO	RAT	ERA	ERA+	CERA	OAV	BH	AVG	PR+	WS	TPW
• LANDIS, Doc	Samuel H. Landis b: 8/16/1854, Philadelphia, PA BR, 5'11", 172 lbs. Deb: 5/2/1882																									
1882 Phi-a	1	1	.500	2	2	2	0	0	17	16	12	6	1	....	1	13	1.000	3.18	94	....	.232	2	.167	-1	1	-0.2
Bal-a	11	28	.282	42	42	35	0	0	343	416	259	126	7	....	46	62	1.347	3.31	83	....	.278	29	.166	-15	10	-2.0
Yr.	12	29	.293	44	44	37	0	0	360	432	271	132	8	....	47	75	1.331	3.30	84	....	.276	31	.166	-15	11	-2.2
• LANDRETH, Larry	Larry Robert Landreth b: 3/11/1955, Stratford, Canada BR/TR, 6'1", 175 lbs. Deb: 9/16/1976																									
1976 Mon-N	1	2	.333	3	3	0	0	0	11	13	8	5	1	0	10	7	2.091	4.09	91	7.45	.310	0	.000	-0	0	-0.1
1977 Mon-N	0	2	.000	4	1	0	0	0	9^{1}	16	11	10	0	0	8	5	2.571	9.64	39	9.33	.381	0	.000	-6	0	-0.6
Total 2	1	4	.200	7	4	0	0	0	20^{1}	29	19	15	1	0	18	12	2.311	6.64	57	8.31	.345	0	.000	-7	0	-0.7
• LANDRUM, Bill	Thomas William Landrum b: 8/17/1957, Columbia, SC BR/TR, 6'2", 200 lbs. Deb: 8/31/1986																									
1986 Cin-N	0	0	....	10	0	0	0	0	13^{1}	23	11	10	0	0	4	14	2.025	6.75	57	7.27	.390	0	.000	-4	0	-0.5
1987 Cin-N	3	2	.600	44	2	0	0	2	65	68	35	34	3	0	34	42	1.569	4.71	90	4.50	.292	1	.200	-4	3	-0.4
1988 Chi-N	1	0	1.000	7	0	0	0	0	12^{1}	19	8	8	1	0	3	6	1.784	5.84	62	6.84	.365	0	.000	-3	0	-0.3
1989 Pit-N	2	3	.400	56	0	0	0	26	81	60	18	15	2	0	28	51	1.086	1.67	201	1.94	.205	0	.000	15	14	1.6
1990★ Pit-N	7	3	.700	54	0	0	0	13	71^{2}	69	22	17	4	0	21	39	1.256	2.13	169	3.15	.262	1	.111	11	10	1.1
1991★ Pit-N	4	4	.500	61	0	0	0	17	76^{1}	76	32	27	4	0	19	45	1.245	3.18	112	3.01	.252	0	.000	3	8	0.2
1992 Mon-N	1	1	.500	18	0	0	0	0	20	27	16	16	3	2	9	7	1.800	7.20	48	7.09	.325	0	....	-8	0	-0.9
1993 Cin-N	0	2	.000	18	0	0	0	0	21^{2}	18	9	9	1	0	6	14	1.108	3.74	108	2.38	.231	0	....	1	1	0.1
Total 8	18	15	.545	268	2	0	0	58	361^{1}	360	151	136	18	2	124	218	1.339	3.39	110	3.54	.265	2	.080	11	36	1.0
• LANDRUM, Joe	Joseph Butler Landrum b: 12/13/1928, Columbia, SC BR/TR, 5'11", 180 lbs. Deb: 7/13/1950																									
1950 Bro-N	0	0	....	7	0	0	0	1	6^{2}	12	8	6	2	1	1	5	1.950	8.10	51	10.13	.414	0	....	-3	0	-0.3
1952 Bro-N	1	3	.250	9	5	2	0	0	38	46	24	22	3	1	10	17	1.474	5.21	70	4.64	.301	1	.125	-7	0	-0.8
Total 2	1	3	.250	16	5	2	0	1	44^{2}	58	32	28	5	2	11	22	1.545	5.64	66	5.46	.319	1	.125	-10	0	-1.1
• LANE, Jerry	Gerald Hal Lane b: 2/7/1926, Ashland, NY d: 7/24/1988, Chattanooga, TN BR/TR, 6'.5", 205 lbs. Deb: 7/7/1953																									
1953 Was-A	1	4	.200	20	2	0	0	0	56^{2}	64	33	31	3	1	16	26	1.412	4.92	79	3.97	.288	1	.111	-7	1	-0.7
1954 Cin-N	1	0	1.000	3	0	0	0	0	10^{2}	9	2	2	0	0	3	2	1.125	1.69	248	2.27	.237	0	.000	3	1	0.3
1955 Cin-N	0	2	.000	8	0	0	0	1	11	11	6	6	2	0	6	5	1.545	4.91	86	5.18	.289	0	....	-1	0	-0.1
Total 3	2	6	.250	31	2	0	0	1	78^{1}	84	41	39	5	1	25	33	1.391	4.48	88	3.91	.282	1	.077	-5	2	-0.5
• LANFORD, Sam	Lewis Grover Lanford b: 1/8/1886, Woodruff, SC d: 9/14/1970, Woodruff, SC BR/TR, 5'7", 155 lbs. Deb: 8/19/1907																									
1907 Was-A	0	1	.000	2	1	0	0	0	7	10	10	4	0	3	5	2	2.143	5.14	47	8.80	.338	1	.333	-2	0	-0.2
• LANFRANCONI, Walt	Walter Oswald Lanfranconi b: 11/9/1916, Barre, VT d: 8/18/1986, Barre, VT BR/TR, 5'7.5", 155 lbs. Deb: 9/12/1941																									
1941 Chi-N	0	1	.000	2	1	0	0	0	6	7	3	2	0	0	2	1	1.500	3.00	117	3.82	.280	0	.000	1	0	0.0
1947 Bos-N	4	4	.500	36	4	1	0	1	64	65	23	21	2	0	27	18	1.438	2.95	132	3.75	.272	0	.000	7	6	0.6
Total 2	4	5	.444	38	5	1	0	1	70	72	26	23	2	0	29	19	1.443	2.96	130	3.76	.273	0	.000	8	6	0.6
• LANG, Chip	Robert David Lang b: 8/21/1952, Pittsburgh, PA BR/TR, 6'4", 205 lbs. Deb: 9/8/1975																									
1975 Mon-N	0	0	....	1	1	0	0	0	1^{2}	2	2	2	0	0	3	2	3.000	10.80	35	11.18	.333	0	....	-1	0	-0.1
1976 Mon-N	1	3	.250	29	2	0	0	0	62^{1}	56	32	29	3	3	34	30	1.444	4.19	89	3.81	.242	1	.167	-3	2	-0.3
Total 2	1	3	.250	30	3	0	0	0	64	58	34	31	3	3	37	32	1.484	4.36	85	4.00	.245	1	.167	-4	2	-0.5
• LANG, Marty	Martin John Lang b: 9/27/1905, Hooper, NE d: 1/13/1968, Lakewood, CO BR/TL, 5'11", 160 lbs. Deb: 7/4/1930																									
1930 Pit-N	0	0	....	2	0	0	0	0	1^{2}	9	10	10	2	0	3	2	7.200	54.00	9	65.71	.692	0	....	-9	0	-0.8
• LANGE, Dick	Richard Otto Lange b: 9/1/1948, Harbor Beach, MI BR/TR, 5'10", 185 lbs. Deb: 9/9/1972																									
1972 Cal-A	0	0	....	2	1	0	0	0	7^{2}	7	4	4	0	0	2	8	1.174	4.70	62	2.39	.233	0	.000	-2	0	-0.2
1973 Cal-A	2	1	.667	17	4	1	0	0	52^{2}	61	30	26	9	1	21	27	1.557	4.44	80	5.48	.292	0	....	-5	1	-0.5
1974 Cal-A	3	8	.273	21	18	1	0	0	113^{2}	111	63	48	10	4	47	57	1.390	3.80	90	3.94	.248	0	....	-4	2	-0.4
1975 Cal-A	4	6	.400	30	8	1	0	1	102	119	70	59	12	1	53	45	1.686	5.21	68	5.66	.292	0	....	-18	0	-1.9
Total 4	9	15	.375	70	31	3	0	1	276	298	167	137	31	6	123	137	1.525	4.47	78	4.83	.272	0	.000	-28	3	-3.0
• LANGE, Erv	Erwin Henry Lange b: 8/12/1887, Forest Park, IL d: 4/24/1971, Maywood, IL BR/TR, 5'10", 170 lbs. Deb: 4/19/1914																									
1914 Chi-F	12	11	.522	36	22	10	2	2	190	162	69	47	3	3	55	87	1.142	2.23	132	2.32	.224	9	.176	10	14	1.3
• LANGE, Frank	Frank Herman "Seagan,Bill" Lange b: 10/28/1883, Columbus, WI d: 12/26/1945, Madison, WI BR/TR, 5'11", 180 lbs. Deb: 5/16/1910																									
1910 Chi-A	9	4	.692	23	15	6	1	0	130^{2}	93	48	24	2	9	54	98	1.125	1.65	145	2.31	.204	13	.255	11	11	1.6
1911 Chi-A	8	8	.500	29	22	8	1	0	161^{2}	151	77	58	3	3	77	104	1.410	3.23	100	3.48	.251	22	.289	0	11	0.8
1912 Chi-A	10	10	.500	31	20	11	2	3	165^{1}	165	85	60	4	4	68	96	1.409	3.27	99	3.68	.270	14	.215	2	10	0.4
1913 Chi-A	1	3	.250	12	3	0	0	0	40^{2}	46	24	22	0	1	20	20	1.623	4.87	60	4.58	.295	3	.167	-9	0	-0.9
Total 4	28	25	.528	95	60	25	4	3	498^{1}	455	234	164	9	17	219	318	1.353	2.96	102	3.33	.249	52	.248	5	32	2.0
• LANGFORD, Rick	James Rick Langford b: 3/20/1952, Farmville, VA BR/TR, 6', 180 lbs. Deb: 6/13/1976 C																									
1976 Pit-N	0	1	.000	12	1	0	0	0	23	27	17	16	2	0	14	17	1.783	6.26	56	5.99	.307	1	.200	-7	0	-0.7
1977 Oak-A	8	19	.296	37	31	6	1	0	208^{1}	223	107	93	18	2	73	141	1.421	4.02	100	4.20	.273	0	....	3	9	0.3
1978 Oak-A	7	13	.350	37	24	4	2	0	175^{2}	169	77	67	15	3	56	92	1.281	3.43	106	3.45	.253	0	....	7	11	0.7
1979 Oak-A	12	16	.429	34	29	14	1	0	218^{2}	233	114	104	22	4	57	101	1.326	4.28	94	3.91	.273	0	....	1	12	0.1
1980 Oak-A	19	12	.613	35	33	**28**	2	0	**290**	276	119	105	29	1	64	102	1.172	3.26	116	3.18	.255	0	....	13	19	1.3
1981★ Oak-A	12	10	.545	24	24	**18**	2	0	195^{1}	190	81	65	14	3	58	84	1.270	2.99	116	3.37	.255	0	....	8	12	0.9
1982 Oak-A	11	16	.407	32	31	15	2	0	237^{1}	265	121	111	33	2	49	79	1.323	4.21	93	4.26	.281	0	.000	-8	10	-0.9
1983 Oak-A	0	4	.000	7	7	0	0	0	20	43	28	27	4	2	10	2	2.650	12.15	32	13.57	.448	0	....	-19	0	-1.9
1984 Oak-A	0	0	....	3	2	0	0	0	8^{2}	15	8	8	2	0	2	2	1.962	8.31	45	8.78	.366	0	....	-4	0	-0.4
1985 Oak-A	3	5	.375	23	3	0	0	0	59	60	24	23	8	0	15	21	1.271	3.51	110	3.79	.261	0	....	3	3	0.3
1986 Oak-A	1	10	.091	16	11	0	0	0	55	69	49	45	13	1	18	30	1.582	7.36	53	6.29	.300	0	....	-21	0	-2.1
Total 11	73	106	.408	260	196	85	10	0	1491	1570	745	664	160	18	416	671	1.332	4.01	95	4.01	.271	1	.167	-25	76	-2.5
• LANGSTON, Mark	Mark Edward Langston b: 8/20/1960, San Diego, CA BR/TL, 6'2", 190 lbs. Deb: 4/7/1984																									
1984 Sea-A	17	10	.630	35	33	5	2	0	225	188	99	85	16	8	118	**204**	1.360	3.40	117	3.56	.230	0	....	20	19	2.0
1985 Sea-A	7	14	.333	24	24	2	0	0	126^{2}	122	85	77	22	2	91	72	1.682	5.47	77	5.82	.255	0	....	-17	2	-1.7
1986 Sea-A	12	14	.462	37	36	9	0	0	239^{1}	234	142	129	30	4	123	**245**	1.492	4.85	87	4.64	.255	0	....	-16	11	-1.5
1987 Sea-A★	19	13	.594	35	35	14	3	0	272	242	132	116	30	5	114	**262**	1.309	3.84	123	3.69	.238	0	....	25	21	2.4
1988 Sea-A	15	11	.577	35	35	9	3	0	261^{1}	222	108	97	32	3	110	235	1.270	3.34	125	3.60	.233	0	....	25	19	2.5
1989 Sea-A	4	5	.444	10	10	2	1	0	73^{1}	60	30	29	3	4	19	60	1.077	3.56	113	2.43	.221	0	....	4	5	0.4
Mon-N	12	9	.571	24	24	6	4	0	176^{2}	138	57	47	13	0	93	175	1.308	2.39	147	3.17	.218	11	.172	23	15	2.5
1990 Cal-A	10	17	.370	33	33	5	1	0	223	215	120	109	13	5	104	195	1.430	4.40	87	4.02	.259	0	....	-14	8	-1.4
1991 Cal-A★	19	8	.704	34	34	7	0	0	246^{1}	190	89	82	30	2	96	183	1.161	3.00	137	3.03	.215	0	....	27	20	2.7
1992 Cal-A★	13	14	.481	32	32	9	2	0	229	206	103	93	14	6	74	174	1.223	3.66	109	3.12	.242	0	.000	7	15	0.7
1993 Cal-A★	16	11	.593	35	35	7	0	0	256^{1}	220	100	91	22	1	85	196	1.190	3.20	141	3.02	.234	0	....	34	20	3.3
1994 Cal-A	7	8	.467	18	18	2	1	0	119^{1}	121	67	62	19	0	54	109	1.466	4.68	104	4.83	.268	0	....	2	8	0.2
1995 Cal-A	15	7	.682	31	31	2	1	0	200^{1}	212	109	103	21	3	64	142	1.378	4.63	101	4.18	.272	0	....	-0	11	0.0
1996 Cal-A	6	5	.545	18	18	2	0	0	123^{1}	116	68	66	18	2	45	83	1.305	4.82	102	4.03	.247	0	....	1	7	0.1
1997 Ana-A	2	4	.333	9	9	0	0	0	47^{2}	61	34	31	8	0	29	30	1.888	5.85	79	7.21	.316	0	....	-7	1	-0.6
1998★ SD-N	4	6	.400	22	16	0	0	0	81^{1}	107	55	53	11	1	41	56	1.820	5.86	67	6.79	.325	2	.083	-18	0	-1.8
1999 Cle-A	1	2	.333	25	5	0	0	0	61^{2}	69	40	36	9	0	29	43	1.589	5.25	96	5.28	.288	1	.500	-1	2	-0.1
Total 16	179	158	.531	457	428	81	18	0	2962^{2}	2723	1438	1306	311	46	1289	2464	1.354	3.97	108	3.91	.246	14	.152	95	184	9.6
• LANIER, Max	Hubert Max Lanier b: 8/18/1915, Denton, NC BR/TL, 5'11", 187 lbs. Deb: 4/20/1938																									
1938 StL-N	0	3	.000	18	3	1	0	0	45	57	30	21	1	2	28	14	1.889	4.20	94	5.94	.317	1	.100	-1	1	-0.2

YEAR	TM-L	W	L	PCT	G	GS	CG	SH	SV	IP	H	R	ER	HR	HB	BB	SO	RAT	ERA	ERA+	CERA	OAV	BH	AVG	PR+	WS	TPW
1939	StL-N	2	1	.667	7	6	2	0	0	37^2	29	11	10	0	1	13	14	1.115	2.39	172	2.13	.220	4	.286	7	4	0.8
1940	StL-N	9	6	.600	35	11	4	2	3	105	113	50	39	1	1	38	49	1.438	3.34	119	3.63	.276	6	.200	9	8	0.9
1941	StL-N	10	8	.556	35	18	8	2	3	153	126	59	48	4	1	59	93	1.209	2.82	133	2.56	.225	10	.192	13	14	1.3
1942*	StL-N	13	8	.619	34	20	8	2	2	161	137	55	53	4	2	60	93	1.224	2.96	116	2.70	.234	12	.255	6	13	0.9
1943*	StL-N★	15	7	.682	32	25	14	2	3	213^1	195	62	45	3	2	75	123	1.266	1.90	**177**	2.84	.246	12	.164	**29**	23	2.9
1944*	StL-N★	17	12	.586	33	30	16	5	0	224^1	192	82	66	5	3	71	141	1.172	2.65	133	2.52	.234	14	.182	17	17	1.6
1945	StL-N	2	2	.500	4	3	3	0	0	26	22	10	5	0	0	8	16	1.154	1.73	216	2.17	.222	2	.182	5	2	0.5
1946	StL-N	6	0	1.000	6	6	6	2	0	56	45	13	12	1	1	19	36	1.143	1.93	179	2.38	.228	5	.200	9	7	0.9
1949	StL-N	5	4	.556	15	15	4	1	0	92	92	42	39	5	0	35	37	1.380	3.82	109	3.57	.261	2	.074	3	6	0.2
1950	StL-N	11	9	.550	27	27	10	2	0	181^1	173	70	63	13	1	68	89	1.329	3.13	137	3.46	.249	11	.162	25	16	2.3
1951	StL-N	11	9	.550	31	23	9	2	1	160	149	60	58	14	1	50	59	1.244	3.26	122	3.27	.248	8	.151	10	13	0.8
1952	NY-N	7	12	.368	37	16	6	1	5	137	124	64	60	11	3	65	47	1.380	3.94	94	3.71	.244	11	.268	-3	8	-0.1
1953	NY-N	0	0	....	3	0	0	0	0	5^1	8	4	4	1	0	3	2	2.063	6.75	64	8.58	.381	0	.000	-1	0	-0.2
	StL-A	0	1	.000	10	1	0	0	0	22^1	28	18	18	2	0	19	8	2.104	7.25	58	7.29	.322	1	.167	-7	0	-0.8
Total	14	108	82	.568	327	204	91	21	17	1619^1	1490	630	541	65	18	611	821	1.297	3.01	126	3.16	.247	99	.185	120	132	12.0

• LANKFORD, Frank Frank Greenfield Lankford b: 3/26/1971, Atlanta, GA BR/TR, 6'2" Deb: 3/31/1998

YEAR	TM-L	W	L	PCT	G	GS	CG	SH	SV	IP	H	R	ER	HR	HB	BB	SO	RAT	ERA	ERA+	CERA	OAV	BH	AVG	PR+	WS	TPW
1998	LA-N	0	2	.000	12	0	0	0	1	19^2	23	13	13	2	2	7	7	1.525	5.95	67	5.30	.288	0	.000	-4	0	-0.4

• LANNING, Johnny John Young "Tobacco Chewin' Johnny" Lanning b: 9/6/1910, Asheville, NC d: 11/8/1989, Asheville, NC BR/TR, 6'1", 185 lbs. Deb: 4/17/1936

YEAR	TM-L	W	L	PCT	G	GS	CG	SH	SV	IP	H	R	ER	HR	HB	BB	SO	RAT	ERA	ERA+	CERA	OAV	BH	AVG	PR+	WS	TPW
1936	Bos-N	7	11	.389	28	20	3	1	0	153	154	75	62	9	0	55	33	1.366	3.65	105	3.61	.263	7	.135	2	8	0.0
1937	Bos-N	5	7	.417	32	11	4	1	2	116^2	107	59	51	10	1	40	37	1.260	3.93	91	3.18	.236	4	.121	-7	5	-0.8
1938	Bos-N	8	7	.533	32	18	4	1	0	138	146	74	57	5	1	52	39	1.435	3.72	92	3.73	.267	9	.188	-5	5	-0.6
1939	Bos-N	5	6	.455	37	6	3	0	4	129	120	53	49	6	2	53	45	1.341	3.42	108	3.33	.252	6	.143	2	8	0.0
1940	Pit-N	8	4	.667	38	7	2	0	2	115^2	119	59	52	8	0	39	42	1.366	4.05	94	3.74	.268	7	.200	0	6	0.1
1941	Pit-N	11	11	.500	34	23	9	0	1	175^2	175	72	61	6	0	47	41	1.264	3.13	116	3.00	.256	6	.107	11	12	1.0
1942	Pit-N	6	8	.429	34	8	2	1	1	119^1	125	52	44	7	1	26	31	1.265	3.32	102	3.35	.274	4	.138	2	7	0.2
1943	Pit-N	4	1	.800	12	2	0	0	2	27	23	10	7	0	0	9	11	1.185	2.33	149	2.24	.223	1	.167	3	3	0.3
1945	Pit-N	0	0	....	1	0	0	0	0	2	8	8	8	1	0	0	0	4.000	36.00	11	28.70	.571	0	....	-7	0	-0.7
1946	Pit-N	4	5	.444	27	9	3	0	1	91	97	36	31	3	1	31	16	1.407	3.07	115	3.61	.269	3	.143	6	7	0.6
1947	Bos-N	0	0	....	3	0	0	0	0	3^2	4	5	4	0	0	6	0	2.727	9.82	40	9.42	.400	0	....	-2	0	-0.2
Total	11	58	60	.492	278	104	30	4	13	1071	1078	503	426	55	6	358	295	1.341	3.58	101	3.46	.261	47	.146	5	61	-0.1

• LANNING, Red Lester Alfred Lanning b: 5/13/1895, Harvard, IL d: 6/13/1962, Bristol, CT BL/TL, 5'9", 165 lbs. Deb: 6/20/1916 ♦

YEAR	TM-L	W	L	PCT	G	GS	CG	SH	SV	IP	H	R	ER	HR	HB	BB	SO	RAT	ERA	ERA+	CERA	OAV	BH	AVG	PR+	WS	TPW
1916	Phi-A	0	3	.000	6	3	1	0	0	24^1	38	27	22	1	2	17	9	2.260	8.14	35	8.61	.362	6	.182	-14	1	-1.6

• LANNING, Tom Thomas Newton Lanning b: 4/22/1907, Biltmore, NC d: 11/4/1967, Marietta, GA BL/TL, 6'1", 165 lbs. Deb: 9/14/1938

YEAR	TM-L	W	L	PCT	G	GS	CG	SH	SV	IP	H	R	ER	HR	HB	BB	SO	RAT	ERA	ERA+	CERA	OAV	BH	AVG	PR+	WS	TPW
1938	Phi-N	0	1	.000	3	1	0	0	0	7	9	7	5	0	0	2	2	1.571	6.43	62	4.16	.300	1	1.000	-2	0	-0.1

• LANSING, Gene Eugene Hewitt "Jigger" Lansing b: 1/11/1898, Albany, NY d: 1/18/1945, Rensselaer, NY BR/TR, 6'1", 185 lbs. Deb: 4/27/1922

YEAR	TM-L	W	L	PCT	G	GS	CG	SH	SV	IP	H	R	ER	HR	HB	BB	SO	RAT	ERA	ERA+	CERA	OAV	BH	AVG	PR+	WS	TPW
1922	Bos-N	0	1	.000	15	1	0	0	0	40^2	46	28	27	1	0	22	14	1.672	5.98	67	4.73	.301	0	.000	-8	0	-0.9

• LAPALME, Paul Paul Edmore "Lefty" LaPalme b: 12/14/1923, Springfield, MA BL/TL, 5'10", 184 lbs. Deb: 5/28/1951

YEAR	TM-L	W	L	PCT	G	GS	CG	SH	SV	IP	H	R	ER	HR	HB	BB	SO	RAT	ERA	ERA+	CERA	OAV	BH	AVG	PR+	WS	TPW
1951	Pit-N	1	5	.167	22	8	1	1	0	54^1	79	48	38	6	1	31	24	2.025	6.29	67	7.42	.333	1	.100	-12	0	-1.2
1952	Pit-N	1	2	.333	31	2	0	0	0	59^2	56	33	26	6	1	37	25	1.559	3.92	102	4.54	.253	1	.100	1	2	0.1
1953	Pit-N	8	16	.333	35	24	7	1	2	176^1	191	107	90	20	0	64	86	1.446	4.59	97	4.34	.272	5	.085	-1	9	-0.6
1954	Pit-N	4	10	.286	33	15	2	0	0	120^2	147	79	74	15	0	54	57	1.666	5.52	76	5.59	.302	5	.143	-15	3	-1.5
1955	StL-N	4	3	.571	56	0	0	0	3	91^2	76	36	28	10	1	34	39	1.200	2.75	148	3.01	.228	4	.211	14	9	1.5
1956	StL-N	0	0	....	1	0	0	0	0	0^2	4	6	6	0	0	2	0	9.000	81.00	5	56.02	.667	0	....	-6	0	-0.6
	Cin-N	2	4	.333	11	2	0	0	0	27	26	14	14	7	0	4	4	1.111	4.67	85	3.84	.257	2	.500	-2	2	-0.1
	Yr.	2	4	.333	12	2	0	0	0	27^2	30	20	20	7	0	6	4	1.301	6.51	60	5.10	.280	2	.500	-7	2	-0.7
	Chi-A	3	1	.750	29	0	0	0	2	45^2	31	14	12	2	0	27	23	1.270	2.36	173	2.61	.195	0	.000	9	5	0.7
1957	Chi-A	1	4	.200	35	0	0	0	7	40^1	35	16	15	5	1	19	19	1.339	3.35	112	3.94	.235	2	.500	1	4	0.2
Total	7	24	45	.348	253	51	10	2	14	616^1	645	353	303	71	4	272	277	1.488	4.42	95	4.56	.269	20	.136	-11	34	-1.5

• LAPIHUSKA, Andy Andrew "Apples" Lapihuska b: 11/1/1922, Delmont, NJ d: 2/17/1996, Millville, NJ BL/TR, 5'10.5", 175 lbs. Deb: 9/12/1942

YEAR	TM-L	W	L	PCT	G	GS	CG	SH	SV	IP	H	R	ER	HR	HB	BB	SO	RAT	ERA	ERA+	CERA	OAV	BH	AVG	PR+	WS	TPW
1942	Phi-N	0	2	.000	3	2	0	0	0	20^2	17	13	12	0	2	13	8	1.452	5.23	63	3.31	.221	2	.286	-4	0	-0.4
1943	Phi-N	0	0	....	1	0	0	0	0	2^1	5	6	6	1	0	3	0	3.429	23.14	15	18.89	.417	0	.000	-5	0	-0.6
Total	2	0	2	.000	4	2	0	0	0	23	22	19	18	1	2	16	8	1.652	7.04	47	4.89	.247	2	.222	-9	0	-1.0

• LAPOINT, Dave David Jeffrey LaPoint b: 7/29/1959, Glens Falls, NY BL/TL, 6'3", 215 lbs. Deb: 9/10/1980

YEAR	TM-L	W	L	PCT	G	GS	CG	SH	SV	IP	H	R	ER	HR	HB	BB	SO	RAT	ERA	ERA+	CERA	OAV	BH	AVG	PR+	WS	TPW
1980	Mil-A	1	0	1.000	5	3	0	0	1	15	17	14	10	2	0	13	5	2.000	6.00	64	6.78	.293	0	....	-4	0	-0.4
1981	StL-N	1	0	1.000	3	2	0	0	0	10^2	12	5	5	1	1	2	4	1.313	4.22	84	4.37	.293	0	.000	-1	1	-0.2
1982*	StL-N	9	3	.750	42	21	0	0	0	152^2	170	63	58	8	3	52	81	1.454	3.42	106	4.21	.290	2	.053	-0	9	-0.3
1983	StL-N	12	9	.571	37	29	1	0	0	191^1	191	92	84	12	4	84	113	1.437	3.95	92	3.98	.267	9	.153	-6	9	-0.5
1984	StL-N	12	10	.545	33	33	2	1	0	193	205	94	85	9	1	77	130	1.461	3.96	88	4.07	.278	4	.068	-13	7	-1.8
1985	SF-N	7	17	.292	31	31	2	1	0	206^2	215	99	82	18	0	74	122	1.398	3.57	96	4.02	.269	10	.167	-0	8	0.2
1986	Det-A	3	6	.333	16	8	0	0	0	67^2	85	49	43	11	0	32	36	1.729	5.72	72	6.28	.307	0	....	-13	0	-1.3
	SD-N	1	4	.200	24	4	0	0	0	61^1	67	37	29	8	1	24	41	1.484	4.26	86	4.67	.276	0	.000	-4	1	-0.5
1987	StL-N	1	1	.500	6	2	0	0	0	16	26	12	12	4	0	5	8	1.938	6.75	62	8.63	.351	0	.000	-5	0	-0.5
	Chi-A	6	3	.667	14	12	2	1	0	82^2	69	29	27	7	1	31	43	1.210	2.94	156	3.05	.224	0	....	13	8	1.2
1988	Chi-A	10	11	.476	25	25	1	1	0	161^1	151	69	61	10	2	47	79	1.227	3.40	117	3.07	.245	0	....	8	10	0.8
	Pit-N	4	2	.667	8	8	1	0	0	52	54	18	16	4	0	10	19	1.231	2.77	123	3.28	.271	1	.063	3	4	0.3
1989	NY-A	6	9	.400	20	20	0	0	0	113^2	146	73	71	12	2	45	51	1.680	5.62	69	5.75	.310	0	....	-22	2	-2.3
1990	NY-A	7	10	.412	28	27	2	0	0	157^2	180	84	72	11	1	57	67	1.503	4.11	97	4.50	.292	0	....	-3	7	-0.3
1991	Phi-N	0	1	.000	2	2	0	0	0	5	10	10	9	0	1	6	3	3.200	16.20	23	13.87	.435	0	.000	-7	0	-0.7
Total	12	80	86	.482	294	227	11	4	1	1486^2	1598	748	664	117	17	559	802	1.451	4.02	93	4.28	.277	26	.104	-54	66	-6.3

• LARA, Yovanny Yovanny B. Lara b: 9/20/1975, San Cristobal, Dominican Republic BR/TR, 6'4", 180 lbs. Deb: 6/28/2000

YEAR	TM-L	W	L	PCT	G	GS	CG	SH	SV	IP	H	R	ER	HR	HB	BB	SO	RAT	ERA	ERA+	CERA	OAV	BH	AVG	PR+	WS	TPW
2000	Mon-N	0	0	....	6	0	0	0	0	5^2	5	4	4	0	0	8	3	2.294	6.35	75	6.61	.250	0	....	-1	0	-0.1

• LARKIN, Andy Andrew Dane Larkin b: 6/27/1974, Chelan, WA BR/TR, 6'4", 180 lbs. Deb: 9/29/1996

YEAR	TM-L	W	L	PCT	G	GS	CG	SH	SV	IP	H	R	ER	HR	HB	BB	SO	RAT	ERA	ERA+	CERA	OAV	BH	AVG	PR+	WS	TPW
1996	Fla-N	0	0	....	1	1	0	0	0	5	3	1	1	0	1	4	2	1.400	1.80	226	3.47	.176	0	.000	1	0	0.1
1998	Fla-N	3	8	.273	17	14	0	0	0	74^2	101	87	80	12	4	55	43	2.089	9.64	42	8.41	.329	4	.138	-46	0	-4.6
2000	Cin-N	0	0	....	3	0	0	0	0	6^2	6	4	4	1	0	5	7	1.650	5.40	87	5.35	.240	0	.000	-1	0	-0.1
	KC-A	0	3	.000	18	0	0	0	1	19^1	29	20	19	5	0	11	17	2.069	8.84	58	8.97	.349	0	....	-8	0	-0.8
Total	3	3	11	.214	39	15	0	0	1	105^2	139	112	104	18	5	75	69	2.025	8.86	48	8.09	.322	4	.125	-53	0	-5.3

• LARKIN, Pat Patrick Clibborn Larkin b: 6/14/1960, Arcadia, CA BL/TL, 6', 180 lbs. Deb: 7/16/1983

YEAR	TM-L	W	L	PCT	G	GS	CG	SH	SV	IP	H	R	ER	HR	HB	BB	SO	RAT	ERA	ERA+	CERA	OAV	BH	AVG	PR+	WS	TPW
1983	SF-N	0	0	....	5	0	0	0	0	10^1	13	6	5	1	2	3	6	1.548	4.35	81	5.71	.317	0	.000	-1	0	-0.1

• LARKIN, Steve Stephen Patrick Larkin b: 12/9/1910, Cincinnati, OH d: 5/2/1969, Norristown, PA BR/TR, 6'1", 195 lbs. Deb: 5/6/1934

YEAR	TM-L	W	L	PCT	G	GS	CG	SH	SV	IP	H	R	ER	HR	HB	BB	SO	RAT	ERA	ERA+	CERA	OAV	BH	AVG	PR+	WS	TPW
1934	Det-A	0	0	....	2	1	0	0	0	6	8	7	1	0	0	5	8	2.167	1.50	293	6.33	.296	1	.333	2	0	0.2

• LARKIN, Terry Frank S. Larkin b: 1856, Brooklyn, NY d: 9/16/1894, Brooklyn, NY BR/TR Deb: 5/20/1876 ♦

YEAR	TM-L	W	L	PCT	G	GS	CG	SH	SV	IP	H	R	ER	HR	HB	BB	SO	RAT	ERA	ERA+	CERA	OAV	BH	AVG	PR+	WS	TPW
1876	NY-N	0	1	.000	1	1	1	0	0	9	9	7	3	0	....	0	0	1.000	3.00	71	....	.243	0	.000	-0	0	-0.1
1877	Har-N	29	25	.537	56	56	55	4	0	501	510	285	119	2	....	53	96	1.124	2.14	114	....	.249	52	.228	6	31	1.1
1878	Chi-N	29	26	.527	56	56	56	1	0	506	511	288	126	4	....	31	163	1.071	2.24	108	....	.249	65	.288	-1	34	1.4
1879	Chi-N	31	23	.574	58	58	57	4	0	513^1	514	277	139	5	....	30	142	1.060	2.44	105	....	.244	50	.219	-13	39	-1.0
1880	Tro-N	0	5	.000	5	5	3	0	0	38	83	65	37	1	....	10	5	2.447	8.76	29	....	.418	3	.150	-27	0	-2.6
Total	5	89	80	.527	176	176	172	9	0	1567^1	1627	922	424	12	....	124	406	1.117	2.43	102	....	.253	198	.234	-35	104	-1.3

• LAROCHE, Dave David Eugene LaRoche b: 5/14/1948, Colorado Springs, CO BL/TL, 6'2", 200 lbs. Deb: 5/11/1970 C

YEAR TM-L	W	L	PCT	G	GS	CG	SH	SV	IP	H	R	ER	HR	HB	BB	SO	RAT	ERA	ERA+	CERA	OAV	BH	AVG	PR+	WS	TPW
1970 Cal-A	4	1	.800	38	0	0	0	4	49^2	41	20	19	6	4	21	44	1.248	3.44	105	3.47	.224	2	.250	-0	4	0.1
1971 Cal-A	5	1	.833	56	0	0	0	9	72	55	21	20	3	1	27	63	1.139	2.50	129	2.21	.212	1	.091	5	10	0.5
1972 Min-A	5	7	.417	62	0	0	0	10	95^1	72	33	30	9	6	39	79	1.164	2.83	113	2.91	.209	1	.091	3	8	0.4
1973 Chi-N	4	1	.800	45	0	0	0	4	54^1	55	37	35	7	1	29	34	1.546	5.80	68	4.89	.274	2	.500	-10	2	-0.9
1974 Chi-N	5	6	.455	49	4	0	0	5	92	103	54	49	9	3	47	49	1.630	4.79	80	5.15	.286	9	.333	-5	5	-0.3
1975 Cle-A	5	3	.625	61	0	0	0	17	82^1	61	26	20	5	2	57	94	1.433	2.19	173	3.42	.210	0	....	14	11	1.4
1976 Cle-A★	1	4	.200	61	0	0	0	21	96^1	57	25	24	2	1	49	104	1.100	2.24	156	1.76	.175	0	....	13	14	1.4
1977 Cle-A	2	2	.500	13	0	0	0	4	18^2	15	13	11	3	0	7	18	1.179	5.30	74	3.32	.234	0	....	-3	1	-0.3
Cal-A★	6	5	.545	46	0	0	0	13	81^1	64	31	28	8	2	37	61	1.242	3.10	126	3.06	.218	0	....	8	9	0.8
Yr.	8	7	.533	59	0	0	0	17	100	79	44	39	11	2	44	79	1.230	3.51	112	3.11	.221	0	....	5	10	0.5
1978 Cal-A	10	9	.526	59	0	0	0	25	95^2	73	35	30	7	2	48	70	1.265	2.82	128	2.90	.215	0	....	9	14	0.9
1979* Cal-A	7	11	.389	53	1	0	0	10	85^2	107	54	53	13	2	32	59	1.623	5.57	73	5.87	.314	0	....	-14	2	-1.4
1980 Cal-A	3	5	.375	52	9	1	0	4	128	122	62	58	14	3	39	89	1.258	4.08	96	3.62	.256	0	....	-2	7	-0.2
1981* NY-A	4	1	.800	26	1	0	0	0	47	38	16	13	3	1	16	24	1.149	2.49	144	2.66	.229	0	....	5	4	0.6
1982 NY-A	4	2	.667	25	0	0	0	0	50	54	19	19	4	1	11	31	1.300	3.42	116	3.68	.273	0	....	3	4	0.3
1983 NY-A	0	0	....	1	0	0	0	0	1	2	2	2	1	0	0	0	2.000	18.00	22	16.28	.400	0	....	-2	0	-0.2
Total 14	65	58	.528	647	15	1	0	126	1049^1	919	448	411	94	29	459	819	1.313	3.53	106	3.51	.239	15	.246	25	95	3.2

• LAROSE, John Henry John LaRose b: 10/25/1951, Pawtucket, RI BL/TL, 6'1", 185 lbs. Deb: 9/20/1978

YEAR TM-L	W	L	PCT	G	GS	CG	SH	SV	IP	H	R	ER	HR	HB	BB	SO	RAT	ERA	ERA+	CERA	OAV	BH	AVG	PR+	WS	TPW
1978 Bos-A	0	0	....	1	0	0	0	0	2	3	5	5	1	0	3	0	3.000	22.50	18	16.41	.375	0	....	-4	0	-0.4

• LARSEN, Don Don James Larsen b: 8/7/1929, Michigan City, IN BR/TR, 6'4", 227 lbs. Deb: 4/18/1953

YEAR TM-L	W	L	PCT	G	GS	CG	SH	SV	IP	H	R	ER	HR	HB	BB	SO	RAT	ERA	ERA+	CERA	OAV	BH	AVG	PR+	WS	TPW
1953 StL-A	7	12	.368	38	22	7	2	2	192^2	201	99	89	11	4	64	96	1.375	4.16	101	3.75	.267	23	.284	2	14	0.9
1954 Bal-A	3	21	.125	29	28	12	1	0	201^2	213	106	98	18	1	89	80	1.498	4.37	82	4.36	.274	22	.250	-16	6	-0.8
1955* NY-A	9	2	.818	19	13	5	1	2	97	81	38	33	8	2	51	44	1.361	3.06	122	3.60	.229	6	.146	3	8	0.5
1956* NY-A	11	5	.688	38	20	6	1	1	179^2	133	72	65	19	7	96	107	1.275	3.26	119	3.38	.204	19	.241	8	14	1.3
1957* NY-A	10	4	.714	27	20	4	1	0	139^2	113	68	58	12	0	87	81	1.432	3.74	96	3.79	.220	14	.250	-4	7	0.0
1958* NY-A	9	6	.600	19	19	5	3	0	114^1	100	43	39	4	4	52	55	1.329	3.07	115	3.22	.233	15	.306	4	10	1.2
1959 NY-A	6	7	.462	25	18	3	1	3	124^2	122	65	60	14	2	76	69	1.588	4.33	84	4.93	.260	12	.255	-10	5	-0.6
1960 KC-A	1	10	.091	22	15	0	0	0	83^2	97	55	50	11	0	42	43	1.661	5.38	74	5.65	.293	6	.207	-12	0	-1.2
1961 KC-A	1	0	1.000	8	1	0	0	0	15	21	9	7	2	1	11	13	2.133	4.20	98	8.70	.344	6	.300	0	1	0.2
Chi-A	7	2	.778	25	3	0	0	2	74^1	64	36	34	5	1	29	53	1.251	4.12	95	3.03	.231	8	.320	-1	6	0.1
Yr.	8	2	.800	33	4	0	0	2	89^1	85	45	41	7	2	40	66	1.399	4.13	96	3.98	.251	14	.311	-1	7	0.3
1962* SF-N	5	4	.556	49	0	0	0	11	86^1	83	44	42	9	2	47	58	1.506	4.38	87	4.45	.256	5	.200	-6	6	-0.5
1963 SF-N	7	7	.500	46	0	0	0	3	62	46	23	21	8	0	30	44	1.226	3.05	105	2.93	.203	2	.182	2	5	0.3
1964 SF-N	0	1	.000	6	0	0	0	0	10^1	10	5	5	0	0	6	6	1.548	4.35	82	3.67	.256	0	.000	-1	0	-0.1
Hou-N	4	8	.333	30	10	2	1	1	103^1	92	36	26	4	1	20	58	1.084	2.26	151	2.27	.233	3	.097	15	9	1.6
Yr.	4	9	.308	36	10	2	1	1	113^2	102	41	31	4	1	26	64	1.126	2.45	140	2.40	.235	3	.094	14	9	1.5
1965 Hou-N	0	0	....	1	1	0	0	0	5^1	8	3	3	0	0	3	1	2.063	5.06	66	6.35	.348	0	.000	-1	0	-0.1
Bal-A	1	2	.333	27	1	0	0	1	54	53	22	16	4	1	20	40	1.352	2.67	130	3.64	.255	3	.273	4	4	0.5
1967 Chi-N	0	0	....	3	0	0	0	0	4	5	4	4	1	0	2	1	1.750	9.00	39	7.44	.333	0	....	-2	0	-0.3
Total 14	81	91	.471	412	171	44	11	26	1548	1442	728	650	130	26	725	849	1.400	3.78	99	3.87	.247	144	.242	-15	95	3.1

• LARSON, Dan Daniel James Larson b: 7/4/1954, Los Angeles, CA BR/TR, 6', 180 lbs. Deb: 7/18/1976

YEAR TM-L	W	L	PCT	G	GS	CG	SH	SV	IP	H	R	ER	HR	HB	BB	SO	RAT	ERA	ERA+	CERA	OAV	BH	AVG	PR+	WS	TPW
1976 Hou-N	5	8	.385	13	13	5	0	0	92^1	81	40	31	3	1	28	42	1.181	3.02	106	2.65	.236	9	.290	2	5	0.5
1977 Hou-N	1	7	.125	32	10	1	0	1	97^2	108	72	63	13	2	45	44	1.567	5.81	61	5.17	.280	6	.214	-24	0	-2.4
1978 Phi-N	0	0	....	1	0	0	0	0	1	1	1	1	1	0	1	2	2.000	9.00	40	14.27	.250	0	....	-1	0	-0.1
1979 Phi-N	1	1	.500	3	3	0	0	0	19	17	9	9	1	1	9	9	1.368	4.26	90	3.71	.250	0	.000	-1	1	-0.2
1980 Phi-N	0	5	.000	12	7	0	0	0	45^2	46	24	16	4	0	24	17	1.533	3.15	120	4.33	.271	2	.154	3	2	0.4
1981 Phi-N	3	0	1.000	5	4	1	0	0	28	27	13	13	4	0	15	15	1.500	4.18	87	4.73	.260	1	.111	-2	2	-0.2
1982 Chi-N	0	4	.000	12	6	0	0	0	39^2	51	30	25	4	2	18	22	1.739	5.67	66	6.30	.327	3	.273	-8	0	-0.8
Total 7	10	25	.286	78	43	7	0	1	323^1	331	189	158	30	6	140	151	1.457	4.40	81	4.37	.269	21	.216	-31	10	-2.7

• LARY, Al Alfred Allen Lary b: 9/26/1928, Northport, AL d: 7/10/2001, Northport, AL BR/TR, 6'3", 185 lbs. Deb: 9/6/1954

YEAR TM-L	W	L	PCT	G	GS	CG	SH	SV	IP	H	R	ER	HR	HB	BB	SO	RAT	ERA	ERA+	CERA	OAV	BH	AVG	PR+	WS	TPW
1954 Chi-N	0	0	....	1	1	0	0	0	6	3	2	2	0	0	7	4	1.667	3.00	140	3.15	.150	1	.500	1	1	0.1
1962 Chi-N	0	1	.000	15	3	0	0	0	34	42	27	27	5	0	15	18	1.676	7.15	58	6.01	.311	1	.167	-11	0	-1.1
Total 2	0	1	.000	16	4	0	0	0	40	45	29	29	5	0	22	22	1.675	6.53	64	5.58	.290	2	.250	-11	1	-1.0

• LARY, Frank Frank Strong "Mule,Taters,The Yankee Killer" Lary b: 4/10/1930, Northport, AL BR/TR, 5'11", 180 lbs. Deb: 9/14/1954

YEAR TM-L	W	L	PCT	G	GS	CG	SH	SV	IP	H	R	ER	HR	HB	BB	SO	RAT	ERA	ERA+	CERA	OAV	BH	AVG	PR+	WS	TPW
1954 Det-A	0	0	....	3	0	0	0	0	3^2	4	1	1	0	0	3	5	1.909	2.45	150	5.40	.286	0	....	0	0	0.1
1955 Det-A	14	15	.483	36	31	16	2	1	235	232	100	81	10	6	89	98	1.366	3.10	124	3.65	.262	16	.195	20	15	2.1
1956 Det-A	**21**	13	.618	41	**38**	20	3	1	**294**	289	116	103	20	12	116	165	1.378	3.15	131	3.88	.257	19	.184	32	22	3.1
1957 Det-A	11	16	.407	40	35	12	2	3	237^2	250	111	105	23	12	72	107	1.355	3.98	97	4.16	.276	9	.123	-5	12	-0.8
1958 Det-A	16	15	.516	39	34	**19**	3	1	**260**^{1}	249	91	84	20	12	68	131	1.218	2.90	139	3.31	.251	15	.170	30	21	3.0
1959 Det-A	17	10	.630	32	32	11	3	0	223	225	109	88	23	11	46	137	1.215	3.55	114	3.56	.261	10	.125	12	15	1.1
1960 Det-A★	15	15	.500	38	**36**	**15**	2	1	**274**^{1}	262	125	107	25	19	62	149	1.181	3.51	117	3.34	.249	17	.183	20	19	2.4
1961 Det-A★	23	9	.719	36	36	**22**	4	0	275^1	252	117	99	24	6	66	146	1.155	3.24	127	3.00	.243	25	.231	26	**22**	2.9
1962 Det-A	2	6	.250	17	14	2	1	0	80	98	59	51	17	4	21	41	1.488	5.74	71	5.71	.297	4	.167	-14	0	-1.4
1963 Det-A	4	9	.308	16	14	6	0	0	107^1	90	40	39	15	5	26	46	1.081	3.27	114	3.06	.226	8	.229	6	7	0.7
1964 Det-A	0	2	.000	6	4	0	0	0	18	24	15	14	3	3	10	6	1.889	7.00	52	7.84	.316	0	.000	-7	0	-0.8
NY-N	2	3	.400	13	8	3	1	1	57^1	62	33	29	7	4	14	27	1.326	4.55	78	4.37	.279	2	.118	-7	1	-0.6
Mil-N	1	0	1.000	5	2	0	0	0	12^1	15	7	6	4	0	0	4	1.216	4.38	80	5.13	.306	0	.000	-1	0	-0.2
Yr.	3	3	.500	18	10	3	1	1	69^2	77	40	35	11	4	14	31	1.306	4.52	79	4.50	.284	2	.100	-8	1	-0.8
1965 NY-N	1	3	.250	14	7	0	0	1	57^1	48	24	19	2	1	16	23	1.116	2.98	118	2.46	.233	4	.211	4	5	0.4
Chi-A	1	0	1.000	14	1	0	0	2	26^2	23	12	12	4	2	7	14	1.125	4.05	79	3.27	.230	1	.500	-3	2	-0.3
Total 12	128	116	.525	350	292	126	21	11	2162^1	2123	960	838	197	97	616	1099	1.267	3.49	113	3.64	.257	130	.177	113	141	11.7

• LASHER, Fred Frederick Walter Lasher b: 8/19/1941, Poughkeepsie, NY BR/TR, 6'3", 210 lbs. Deb: 4/12/1963

YEAR TM-L	W	L	PCT	G	GS	CG	SH	SV	IP	H	R	ER	HR	HB	BB	SO	RAT	ERA	ERA+	CERA	OAV	BH	AVG	PR+	WS	TPW
1963 Min-A	0	0	....	11	0	0	0	0	11^1	12	10	6	1	0	11	10	2.029	4.76	77	6.19	.286	0	.000	-1	0	-0.2
1967 Det-A	2	1	.667	17	0	0	0	9	30	25	14	13	1	1	11	28	1.200	3.90	84	2.66	.221	1	.111	-2	3	-0.3
1968* Det-A	5	1	.833	34	0	0	0	5	48^2	37	19	18	5	0	22	32	1.212	3.33	90	2.82	.215	1	.111	-2	4	-0.3
1969 Det-A	2	1	.667	32	0	0	0	0	44	34	16	15	5	2	22	26	1.273	3.07	122	3.57	.224	0	.000	3	3	0.3
1970 Det-A	1	3	.250	12	0	0	0	3	9	10	6	5	0	1	12	8	2.444	5.00	74	7.67	.278	0	.000	-1	0	-0.1
Cle-A	1	7	.125	43	1	0	0	5	57^2	57	34	26	6	3	30	44	1.509	4.06	98	4.68	.264	0	.000	-1	3	-0.2
Yr.	2	10	.167	55	1	0	0	8	66^2	67	40	31	6	4	42	52	1.635	4.19	94	5.08	.266	0	.000	-2	3	-0.3
1971 Cal-A	0	0	....	2	0	0	0	0	1^1	4	4	4	0	0	2	0	4.500	27.00	12	24.59	.667	0	....	-4	0	-0.4
Total 6	11	13	.458	151	1	0	0	22	202	179	103	87	18	7	110	148	1.431	3.88	91	4.04	.243	2	.063	-8	13	-1.1

• LASKEY, Bill William Alan Laskey b: 12/20/1957, Toledo, OH BR/TR, 6'5", 190 lbs. Deb: 4/23/1982

YEAR TM-L	W	L	PCT	G	GS	CG	SH	SV	IP	H	R	ER	HR	HB	BB	SO	RAT	ERA	ERA+	CERA	OAV	BH	AVG	PR+	WS	TPW
1982 SF-N	13	12	.520	32	31	7	1	0	189^1	186	74	66	14	2	43	88	1.210	3.14	115	3.18	.261	8	.129	13	12	1.2
1983 SF-N	13	10	.565	25	25	1	0	0	148^1	151	75	69	18	3	45	81	1.321	4.19	84	4.01	.266	5	.106	-10	6	-1.0
1984 SF-N	9	14	.391	35	34	2	0	0	207^2	222	112	100	20	6	50	71	1.310	4.33	81	3.87	.273	4	.063	-14	5	-1.8
1985 SF-N	5	11	.313	19	19	0	0	0	114	110	55	45	10	0	39	42	1.307	3.55	97	3.54	.255	4	.133	0	5	0.1
Mon-N	0	5	.000	11	7	0	0	0	34^1	55	36	36	9	2	14	18	2.010	9.44	36	9.43	.362	1	.143	-23	0	-2.5
Yr.	5	16	.238	30	26	0	0	0	148^1	165	91	81	19	2	53	60	1.470	4.91	69	4.91	.283	5	.135	-23	5	-2.4
1986 SF-N	1	1	.500	20	0	0	0	1	27^1	28	14	13	5	0	13	8	1.500	4.28	82	5.23	.275	0	.000	-3	1	-0.3
1988 Cle-A	1	0	1.000	17	0	0	0	1	24^1	32	16	14	0	0	6	17	1.562	5.18	79	4.44	.320	0	....	-2	1	-0.2
Total 6	42	53	.442	159	116	10	1	2	745^1	784	382	343	76	13	210	325	1.334	4.14	85	4.00	.272	22	.105	-38	30	-4.6

YEAR	TM-L	W	L	PCT	G	GS	CG	SH	SV	IP	H	R	ER	HR	HB	BB	SO	RAT	ERA	ERA+	CERA	OAV	BH	AVG	PR+	WS	TPW
• LASLEY, Bill					Willard Almond Lasley b: 7/13/1902, Gallipolis, OH d: 8/21/1990, Seattle, WA BB/TR, 6', 175 lbs. Deb: 9/19/1924																						
1924	StL-A	0	0	....	2	0	0	0	0	4	7	3	3	0	0	2	0	2.250	6.75	67	7.90	.412	0	.000	-1	0	-0.1
• LASORDA, Tom					Thomas Charles Lasorda b: 9/22/1927, Norristown, PA BL/TL, 5'10", 175 lbs. Deb: 8/5/1954 M/C HOF: 1997																						
1954	Bro-N	0	0	....	4	0	0	0	0	9	8	5	5	2	0	5	5	1.444	5.00	82	4.84	.242	0	.000	-1	0	-0.1
1955	Bro-N	0	0	....	4	1	0	0	0	4	5	6	6	1	1	6	4	2.750	13.50	30	12.88	.313	0	....	-4	0	-0.4
1956	KC-A	0	4	.000	18	5	0	0	1	45^1	40	38	31	6	3	45	28	1.875	6.15	70	6.15	.240	1	.077	-10	0	-1.1
Total	**3**	**0**	**4**	**.000**	**26**	**6**	**0**	**0**	**1**	58^1	**53**	**49**	**42**	**9**	**4**	**56**	**37**	**1.869**	**6.48**	**66**	**6.41**	**.245**	**1**	**.071**	**-15**	**0**	**-1.6**
• LATHAM, Bill					William Carol Latham b: 8/29/1960, Birmingham, AL BL/TL, 6'2", 190 lbs. Deb: 4/15/1985																						
1985	NY-N	1	3	.250	7	3	0	0	0	22^2	21	10	10	1	0	7	10	1.235	3.97	87	2.94	.250	1	.333	-1	1	-0.1
1986	Min-A	0	1	.000	7	2	0	0	0	16	24	14	13	1	1	6	8	1.875	7.31	59	6.95	.358	0	....	-5	0	-0.5
Total	**2**	**1**	**4**	**.200**	**14**	**5**	**0**	**0**	**0**	38^2	**45**	**24**	**23**	**2**	**1**	**13**	**18**	**1.500**	**5.35**	**73**	**4.60**	**.298**	**1**	**.333**	**-6**	**1**	**-0.6**
• LATHROP, Bill					William George Lathrop b: 8/12/1891, Hanover, WI d: 11/20/1958, Janesville, WI BR/TR, 6'2.5", 184 lbs. Deb: 7/29/1913																						
1913	Chi-A	0	1	.000	6	0	0	0	0	17	16	11	8	0	1	12	9	1.647	4.24	69	4.43	.262	0	.000	-3	0	-0.3
1914	Chi-A	1	2	.333	19	1	0	0	0	47^2	41	20	14	0	2	19	7	1.259	2.64	101	2.86	.241	0	.000	0	2	-0.1
Total	**2**	**1**	**3**	**.250**	**25**	**1**	**0**	**0**	**0**	64^2	**57**	**31**	**22**	**0**	**3**	**31**	**16**	**1.361**	**3.06**	**90**	**3.27**	**.247**	**0**	**.000**	**-2**	**2**	**-0.4**
• LATMAN, Barry					Arnold Barry Latman b: 5/21/1936, Los Angeles, CA BR/TR, 6'3", 210 lbs. Deb: 9/10/1957																						
1957	Chi-A	1	2	.333	7	2	0	0	1	12^1	12	11	11	2	1	13	9	2.027	8.03	47	7.70	.267	0	.000	-6	0	-0.6
1958	Chi-A	3	0	1.000	13	3	1	1	0	47^2	27	7	4	1	1	17	28	.923	0.76	481	1.45	.162	1	.083	15	7	1.5
1959	Chi-A	8	5	.615	37	21	5	2	0	156	138	71	65	15	4	72	97	1.346	3.75	100	3.68	.235	6	.128	-3	8	-0.4
1960	Cle-A	7	7	.500	31	20	4	0	0	147^1	146	78	66	19	6	72	94	1.480	4.03	93	4.70	.258	9	.220	-5	6	-0.4
1961	Cle-A★	13	5	.722	45	18	4	2	5	176^2	163	84	79	23	5	54	108	1.228	4.02	98	3.59	.244	4	.073	-2	11	-0.5
1962	Cle-A	8	13	.381	45	21	7	1	5	179^1	179	96	83	23	5	72	117	1.400	4.17	93	4.32	.261	10	.189	-7	9	-0.5
1963	Cle-A	7	12	.368	38	21	4	2	2	149^1	146	90	82	23	6	52	133	1.326	4.94	73	4.25	.257	8	.182	-21	2	-2.0
1964	LA-A	6	10	.375	40	18	2	1	2	138	128	72	59	15	7	52	81	1.304	3.85	85	3.75	.244	5	.125	-10	3	-1.1
1965	Cal-A	1	1	.500	18	0	0	0	0	31^2	30	12	10	3	0	16	18	1.453	2.84	120	4.03	.254	0	.000	2	2	0.2
1966	Hou-N	2	7	.222	31	9	1	1	1	103	88	42	31	5	7	35	74	1.194	2.71	126	2.95	.233	4	.154	9	6	1.0
1967	Hou-N	3	6	.333	39	1	0	0	0	77^2	73	42	39	13	6	34	70	1.378	4.52	73	4.65	.252	1	.091	-9	1	-1.0
Total	**11**	**59**	**68**	**.465**	**344**	**134**	**28**	**10**	**16**	**1219**	**1130**	**605**	**529**	**142**	**48**	**489**	**829**	**1.328**	**3.91**	**93**	**3.93**	**.246**	**48**	**.145**	**-37**	**55**	**-3.9**
• LATTIMORE, Bill					William Hershel "Slothful Bill" Lattimore b: 5/25/1884, Roxton, TX d: 10/30/1919, Colorado Springs, CO BL/TL, 5'9", 165 lbs. Deb: 4/17/1908																						
1908	Cle-A	1	2	.333	4	4	1	1	0	24	24	16	12	0	0	7	5	1.292	4.50	53	2.81	.247	4	.444	-6	1	-0.5
• LAUZERIQUE, George					George Albert Lauzerique b: 7/22/1947, Havana, Cuba BR/TR, 6'1", 180 lbs. Deb: 9/17/1967																						
1967	KC-A	0	2	.000	3	2	0	0	0	16	11	4	4	2	1	6	10	1.063	2.25	142	2.68	.193	0	.000	2	1	0.2
1968	Oak-A	0	0	....	1	0	0	0	0	1	0	0	0	0	0	1	0	1.000	0.00	....	0.95	.000	0	....	0	0	0.0
1969	Oak-A	3	4	.429	19	8	1	0	0	61^1	58	32	32	14	2	27	39	1.386	4.70	73	5.03	.250	2	.100	-9	1	-1.0
1970	Mil-A	1	2	.333	11	4	1	0	0	35	41	27	27	7	1	14	24	1.571	6.94	55	5.89	.295	2	.200	-12	0	-1.1
Total	**4**	**4**	**8**	**.333**	**34**	**14**	**2**	**0**	**0**	113^1	**110**	**63**	**63**	**23**	**4**	**48**	**73**	**1.394**	**5.00**	**71**	**4.93**	**.257**	**4**	**.121**	**-18**	**2**	**-1.9**
• LAVELLE, Gary					Gary Robert Lavelle b: 1/3/1949, Scranton, PA BB/TL, 6'2", 200 lbs. Deb: 9/10/1974																						
1974	SF-N	0	3	.000	10	0	0	0	0	16^2	14	7	4	1	0	10	12	1.440	2.16	176	3.34	.222	0	.000	3	1	0.3
1975	SF-N	6	3	.667	65	0	0	0	8	82^1	80	30	27	3	3	48	51	1.555	2.95	129	4.03	.260	1	.111	8	9	0.8
1976	SF-N	10	6	.625	65	0	0	0	12	110^1	102	37	33	6	2	52	71	1.396	2.69	135	3.52	.246	1	.077	13	14	1.3
1977	SF-N★	7	7	.500	73	0	0	0	20	118^1	106	35	27	4	0	37	93	1.208	2.05	190	2.55	.239	0	.000	26	18	2.5
1978	SF-N	13	10	.565	67	0	0	0	14	97^2	96	41	36	3	2	44	63	1.433	3.32	104	3.58	.263	1	.067	2	10	0.0
1979	SF-N	7	9	.438	70	0	0	0	20	96^2	86	31	27	5	2	42	80	1.324	2.51	139	3.14	.247	1	.250	12	11	1.2
1980	SF-N	6	8	.429	62	0	0	0	9	100	106	43	38	4	0	36	66	1.420	3.42	103	3.63	.275	0	.000	3	7	0.2
1981	SF-N	2	6	.250	34	3	0	0	4	65^2	58	33	28	3	2	23	45	1.234	3.84	89	2.99	.244	3	.273	-2	3	-0.2
1982	SF-N	10	7	.588	68	0	0	0	8	104^2	97	35	31	6	1	29	76	1.204	2.67	135	2.80	.247	2	.154	13	11	1.3
1983	SF-N★	7	4	.636	56	0	0	0	20	87	73	33	25	4	0	19	68	1.057	2.59	137	2.10	.229	0	.000	10	13	0.9
1984	SF-N	5	4	.556	77	0	0	0	12	101	92	34	31	5	1	42	71	1.327	2.76	127	3.15	.246	0	.000	11	8	1.1
1985*	Tor-A	5	7	.417	69	0	0	0	8	72^2	54	30	25	5	0	36	50	1.239	3.10	136	2.80	.214	0	....	8	8	0.8
1987	Tor-A	2	3	.400	23	0	0	0	1	27^2	36	20	17	2	0	19	17	1.988	5.53	81	6.38	.313	0	....	-4	1	-0.3
	Oak-A	0	0	....	6	0	0	0	0	4^1	4	4	4	0	0	3	6	1.615	8.31	50	4.14	.267	0	....	-2	0	-0.2
	Yr.	2	3	.400	29	0	0	0	1	32	40	24	21	2	0	22	23	1.938	5.91	75	6.07	.308	0	....	-6	1	-0.5
Total	**13**	**80**	**77**	**.510**	**745**	**3**	**0**	**0**	**136**	**1085**	**1004**	**413**	**353**	**51**	**13**	**440**	**769**	**1.331**	**2.93**	**125**	**3.21**	**.249**	**9**	**.081**	**100**	**114**	**9.7**
• LAVENDER, Jimmy					James Sanford Lavender b: 3/25/1884, Barnesville, GA d: 1/12/1960, Cartersville, GA BR/TR, 5'11", 165 lbs. Deb: 4/23/1912																						
1912	Chi-N	16	13	.552	42	31	15	3	3	251^2	240	116	85	8	10	89	109	1.307	3.04	109	3.28	.257	13	.149	2	18	-0.1
1913	Chi-N	10	14	.417	40	20	10	0	2	204	206	111	83	6	13	98	91	1.490	3.66	87	4.06	.267	8	.118	-12	7	-1.7
1914	Chi-N	11	11	.500	37	28	11	2	0	214^1	191	106	73	11	11	87	87	1.297	3.07	91	3.27	.247	11	.175	-3	10	0.0
1915	Chi-N	10	16	.385	41	24	13	1	4	220	178	77	63	5	10	67	117	1.114	2.58	108	2.36	.228	9	.134	8	15	0.7
1916	Chi-N	10	14	.417	36	25	9	4	2	188	163	76	59	3	9	62	91	1.197	2.82	103	2.69	.240	8	.151	4	12	0.3
1917	Phi-N	6	8	.429	28	14	7	0	1	129^1	119	61	51	5	3	44	52	1.260	3.55	79	3.05	.250	5	.139	-11	4	-1.4
Total	**6**	**63**	**76**	**.453**	**224**	**142**	**65**	**10**	**12**	1207^1	**1097**	**547**	**414**	**38**	**56**	**447**	**547**	**1.279**	**3.09**	**96**	**3.12**	**.248**	**54**	**.144**	**-13**	**66**	**-2.3**
• LAW, Ron					Ronald David Law b: 3/14/1946, Hamilton, Canada BR/TR, 6'2", 165 lbs. Deb: 6/29/1969																						
1969	Cle-A	3	4	.429	35	1	0	0	1	52^1	68	34	29	2	2	34	29	1.949	4.99	76	6.35	.325	1	.143	-7	0	-0.7
• LAW, Vance					Vance Aaron Law b: 10/1/1956, Boise, ID BR/TR, 6'2", 190 lbs. Deb: 6/1/1980 ♦																						
1986	Mon-N	0	0	....	3	0	0	0	0	4	3	2	1	0	0	2	0	1.250	2.25	164	2.58	.214	81	.225	1	8	0.4
1987	Mon-N	0	0	....	3	0	0	0	0	3^1	5	2	2	0	0	0	2	1.500	5.40	78	4.47	.333	119	.273	-0	16	0.8
1991	Oak-A	0	0	....	1	0	0	0	0	0^2	1	0	0	0	0	1	0	3.000	0.00	....	10.76	.333	28	.209	0	3	-0.9
Total	**3**	**0**	**0**	**....**	**7**	**0**	**0**	**0**	**0**	**8**	**9**	**4**	**3**	**0**	**0**	**3**	**2**	**1.500**	**3.38**	**119**	**4.05**	**.281**	**972**	**.256**	**1**	**27**	**0.4**
• LAW, Vern					Vernon Sanders "Deacon,Preacher" Law b: 3/12/1930, Meridan, ID BR/TR, 6'2", 195 lbs. Deb: 6/11/1950 C																						
1950	Pit-N	7	9	.438	27	17	5	1	0	128	137	83	70	11	4	49	57	1.453	4.92	89	4.31	.272	3	.073	-7	4	-0.9
1951	Pit-N	6	9	.400	28	14	2	1	2	114	109	66	57	9	6	51	41	1.404	4.50	94	3.93	.253	11	.344	-2	7	0.4
1954	Pit-N	9	13	.409	39	18	7	0	3	161^2	201	109	99	20	3	56	57	**1.590**	5.51	76	5.43	.311	12	.231	-20	5	-1.5
1955	Pit-N	10	10	.500	43	24	8	1	1	200^2	221	98	85	19	1	61	82	1.405	3.81	108	4.20	.280	16	.254	9	14	1.2
1956	Pit-N	8	16	.333	39	32	6	0	2	195^2	218	110	94	24	6	49	60	1.365	4.32	87	4.27	.281	10	.175	-11	6	-0.9
1957	Pit-N	10	8	.556	31	25	9	3	1	172^2	172	72	55	18	2	32	55	1.181	2.87	132	3.20	.256	12	.190	16	12	1.7
1958	Pit-N	14	12	.538	35	29	6	1	3	202^1	235	103	89	16	1	39	56	1.354	3.96	98	4.04	.297	12	.194	-6	11	0.0
1959	Pit-N	18	9	.667	34	33	20	2	1	266	245	91	88	25	2	53	110	1.120	2.98	130	2.82	.243	16	.167	24	**24**	2.5
1960*	Pit-N★	20	9	.690	35	35	**18**	3	0	271^2	266	104	93	25	4	40	120	1.126	3.08	122	3.00	.257	17	.181	16	20	1.9
1961	Pit-N	3	4	.429	11	10	1	0	0	59^1	72	33	31	10	1	18	20	1.517	4.70	85	5.53	.305	5	.263	-5	2	-0.3
1962	Pit-N	10	7	.588	23	20	7	2	0	139^1	156	67	61	21	1	27	78	1.313	3.94	100	4.21	.276	14	.311	-1	10	0.4
1963	Pit-N	4	5	.444	18	12	1	1	0	76^2	91	45	42	11	0	13	31	1.357	4.93	67	4.54	.296	5	.217	-14	0	-1.5
1964	Pit-N	12	13	.480	35	29	7	5	0	192	203	85	77	18	1	32	93	1.224	3.61	97	3.42	.270	19	.311	0	12	0.9
1965	Pit-N	17	9	.654	29	28	13	4	0	217^1	182	66	52	17	3	35	101	.998	2.15	163	2.29	.229	20	.244	28	21	3.4
1966	Pit-N	12	8	.600	31	28	8	4	0	177^2	203	85	80	19	4	24	88	1.278	4.05	88	4.02	.292	16	.242	-13	8	-0.9
1967	Pit-N	2	6	.250	25	10	1	0	0	97	122	57	45	5	1	18	43	1.443	4.18	81	4.16	.308	3	.111	-10	1	-1.1
Total	**16**	**162**	**147**	**.524**	**483**	**364**	**119**	**28**	**13**	**2672**	**2833**	**1274**	**1118**	**268**	**40**	**597**	**1092**	**1.284**	**3.77**	**102**	**3.75**	**.272**	**191**	**.216**	**4**	**157**	**5.2**
• LAWRENCE, Bob					Robert Andrew "Larry" Lawrence b: 12/14/1899, Brooklyn, NY d: 11/6/1983, Jamaica, NY BR/TR, 5'11", 180 lbs. Deb: 7/19/1924																						
1924	Chi-A	0	0	....	1	0	0	0	0	1	1	1	1	0	0	1	1	2.000	9.00	46	5.17	.250	0	....	-1	0	-0.1

YEAR TM-L	W	L	PCT	G	GS	CG	SH	SV	IP	H	R	ER	HR	HB	BB	SO	RAT	ERA	ERA+	CERA	OAV	BH	AVG	PR+	WS	TPW
• LAWRENCE, Brian	Brian Michael Lawrence b: 5/14/1976, Fort Collins, CO BR/TR, 6', 195 lbs. Deb: 4/15/2001																									
2001 SD-N	5	5	.500	27	15	1	0	0	114^{2}	107	53	44	10	5	34	84	1.230	3.45	116	3.30	.244	3	.115	9	6	0.8
2002 SD-N	12	12	.500	35	31	2	2	0	210	230	97	86	16	11	52	149	1.343	3.69	102	4.05	.281	6	.095	4	8	0.3
2003 SD-N	10	15	.400	33	33	1	0	0	210^{2}	206	106	98	27	11	57	116	1.248	4.19	94	3.81	.258	15	.224	-5	8	0.0
Total 3	**27**	**32**	**.458**	**95**	**79**	**4**	**2**	**0**	**535^{1}**	**543**	**256**	**228**	**53**	**27**	**143**	**349**	**1.281**	**3.83**	**101**	**3.79**	**.264**	**24**	**.154**	**8**	**22**	**1.1**
• LAWRENCE, Brooks	Brooks Ulysses "Bull" Lawrence b: 1/30/1925, Springfield, OH d: 4/27/2000, Springfield, OH BR/TR, 6', 205 lbs. Deb: 6/24/1954																									
1954 StL-N	15	6	.714	35	18	8	0	1	158^{2}	141	71	66	17	8	72	72	1.342	3.74	110	3.85	.243	10	.189	7	11	0.8
1955 StL-N	3	8	.273	46	10	2	1	1	96	102	73	70	11	7	58	52	1.667	6.56	62	5.58	.278	2	.095	-26	0	-2.7
1956 Cin-N★	19	10	.655	49	30	11	1	0	218^{2}	210	109	97	26	2	71	96	1.285	3.99	100	3.74	.256	11	.157	2	14	0.2
1957 Cin-N	16	13	.552	49	32	12	1	4	250^{1}	234	111	98	26	8	76	121	1.238	3.52	117	3.48	.247	14	.171	16	21	1.6
1958 Cin-N	8	13	.381	46	23	6	2	5	181	194	89	83	12	4	55	74	1.376	4.13	100	3.92	.275	6	.113	-0	10	-0.2
1959 Cin-N	7	12	.368	43	14	3	0	10	128^{1}	144	74	68	17	4	45	64	1.473	4.77	85	4.83	.281	6	.150	-10	5	-1.1
1960 Cin-N	1	0	1.000	7	0	0	0	1	7^{2}	9	12	9	1	0	8	2	2.217	10.57	36	8.06	.310	0	....	-6	0	-0.6
Total 7	**69**	**62**	**.527**	**275**	**127**	**42**	**5**	**22**	**1040^{2}**	**1034**	**539**	**491**	**110**	**33**	**385**	**481**	**1.364**	**4.25**	**96**	**4.06**	**.261**	**49**	**.154**	**-17**	**61**	**-2.1**
• LAWRENCE, Sean	Sean Christopher Lawrence b: 9/2/1970, Oak Park, IL BL/TL, 6'4" Deb: 8/25/1998																									
1998 Pit-N	2	1	.667	7	3	0	0	0	19^{2}	25	16	16	4	0	10	12	1.780	7.32	59	6.98	.313	0	.000	-7	0	-0.7
• LAWSON, Al	Alfred William Lawson b: 3/24/1869, London, England d: 11/29/1954, San Antonio, TX BR/TR, 5'11", 161 lbs. Deb: 5/13/1890																									
1890 Bos-N	0	1	.000	1	1	1	0	0	9	12	7	4	0	0	4	1	1.778	4.00	93	....	.311	0	.000	-0	0	0.0
Pit-N	0	2	.000	2	2	1	0	0	10	15	20	10	0	0	10	2	2.500	9.00	37	....	.337	0	.000	-6	0	-0.6
Yr.	0	3	.000	3	3	2	0	0	19	27	27	14	0	0	14	3	2.158	6.63	51	....	.325	0	.000	-6	0	-0.6
• LAWSON, Bob	Robert Baker Lawson b: 8/23/1875, Lynchburg, VA d: 10/28/1952, Durham, NC BR/TR, 5'10", 170 lbs. Deb: 5/7/1901																									
1901 Bos-N	2	2	.500	6	4	4	0	0	46	45	28	17	0	3	28	12	1.587	3.33	109	4.07	.255	4	.148	1	3	-0.2
1902 Bal-A	0	2	.000	3	2	1	0	0	13	21	11	7	0	2	3	5	1.846	4.85	78	6.78	.363	1	.167	-1	0	-0.1
Total 2	**2**	**4**	**.333**	**9**	**6**	**5**	**0**	**0**	**59**	**66**	**39**	**24**	**0**	**5**	**31**	**17**	**1.644**	**3.66**	**100**	**4.67**	**.281**	**5**	**.152**	**-0**	**3**	**-0.3**
• LAWSON, Roxie	Alfred Voyle Lawson b: 4/13/1906, Donnellson, IA d: 4/9/1977, Stockport, IA BR/TR, 6', 170 lbs. Deb: 8/3/1930																									
1930 Cle-A	1	2	.333	7	4	2	0	0	33^{2}	46	27	23	1	0	23	10	2.050	6.15	78	6.47	.324	1	.091	-4	1	-0.5
1931 Cle-A	0	2	.000	17	3	0	0	0	55^{2}	72	50	47	5	0	36	20	1.940	7.60	61	6.38	.304	2	.143	-17	0	-1.6
1933 Det-A	0	1	.000	4	2	0	0	0	16	17	16	13	2	0	17	6	2.125	7.31	59	7.08	.270	0	.000	-5	0	-0.6
1935 Det-A	3	1	.750	7	4	4	2	2	40	34	11	7	3	0	24	16	1.450	1.58	265	3.74	.233	4	.308	11	5	1.1
1936 Det-A	8	6	.571	41	8	3	0	3	128	139	87	78	13	4	71	34	1.641	5.48	90	5.24	.281	10	.222	-6	7	-0.5
1937 Det-A	18	7	.720	37	29	15	0	1	217^{1}	236	141	127	17	1	115	68	1.615	5.26	89	4.72	.271	21	.259	-11	13	-0.8
1938 Det-A	8	9	.471	27	16	5	0	1	127	154	85	77	13	0	82	39	1.858	5.46	92	6.09	.299	2	.044	-7	6	-1.1
1939 Det-A	1	1	.500	2	1	0	0	0	11^{1}	7	7	6	1	0	7	4	1.235	4.76	103	2.46	.167	0	.000	0	1	0.0
StL-A	3	7	.300	36	14	5	0	0	150^{2}	181	93	89	10	2	83	43	1.752	5.32	91	5.56	.307	8	.186	-4	6	-0.4
Yr.	4	8	.333	38	15	5	0	0	162	188	100	95	11	2	90	47	1.716	5.28	92	5.34	.297	8	.170	-4	7	-0.5
1940 StL-A	5	3	.625	30	2	0	0	4	72	77	45	41	5	0	54	18	1.819	5.13	89	5.46	.278	1	.045	-4	4	-0.6
Total 9	**47**	**39**	**.547**	**208**	**83**	**34**	**2**	**11**	**851^{2}**	**963**	**562**	**508**	**70**	**7**	**512**	**258**	**1.732**	**5.37**	**89**	**5.36**	**.285**	**49**	**.173**	**-48**	**43**	**-5.0**
• LAWSON, Steve	Steven George Lawson b: 12/28/1950, Oakland, CA BR/TL, 6'1", 175 lbs. Deb: 8/3/1972																									
1972 Tex-A	0	0	....	13	0	0	0	1	16	13	6	5	1	0	10	13	1.438	2.81	107	3.55	.213	1	1.000	1	1	0.1
• LAXTON, Bill	William Harry Laxton b: 1/5/1948, Camden, NJ BL/TL, 6'1", 190 lbs. Deb: 9/15/1970																									
1970 Phi-N	0	0	....	2	0	0	0	0	2	2	3	3	2	1	2	2	2.000	13.50	30	17.44	.250	0	....	-2	0	-0.2
1971 SD-N	0	2	.000	18	0	0	0	0	27^{2}	32	25	21	4	1	26	23	2.096	6.83	48	8.06	.305	0	....	-11	0	-1.1
1974 SD-N	0	1	.000	30	1	0	0	0	44^{2}	37	22	20	5	3	38	40	1.679	4.03	88	4.83	.226	1	.200	-1	2	-0.1
1976 Det-A	0	5	.000	26	3	0	0	2	94^{2}	77	49	43	13	6	51	74	1.352	4.09	91	4.07	.221	0	....	-3	4	-0.3
1977 Sea-A	3	2	.600	43	0	0	0	3	72^{2}	62	44	40	10	4	39	49	1.390	4.95	83	4.17	.233	0	....	-8	3	-0.8
Cle-A	0	0	....	2	0	0	0	0	1^{2}	2	1	1	0	0	2	1	2.400	5.40	73	7.49	.286	0	....	-0	0	0.0
Yr.	3	2	.600	45	0	0	0	3	74^{1}	64	45	41	10	4	41	50	1.413	4.96	83	4.25	.234	0	....	-8	3	-0.8
Total 5	**3**	**10**	**.231**	**121**	**4**	**0**	**0**	**5**	**243^{1}**	**212**	**144**	**128**	**34**	**15**	**158**	**189**	**1.521**	**4.73**	**79**	**4.83**	**.236**	**1**	**.200**	**-25**	**9**	**-2.6**
• LAXTON, Brett	Brett William Laxton b: 10/5/1973, Stratford, NJ BL/TR, 6'2", 210 lbs. Deb: 6/21/1999																									
1999 Oak-A	0	1	.000	3	2	0	0	0	9^{2}	12	12	8	1	2	7	9	1.966	7.45	62	7.39	.316	0	....	-3	0	-0.3
2000 KC-A	0	1	.000	6	1	0	0	0	16^{2}	23	15	15	0	2	10	14	1.980	8.10	63	7.06	.348	0	....	-6	0	-0.5
Total 2	**0**	**2**	**.000**	**9**	**3**	**0**	**0**	**0**	**26^{1}**	**35**	**27**	**23**	**1**	**4**	**17**	**23**	**1.975**	**7.86**	**63**	**7.18**	**.337**	**0**	**....**	**-9**	**0**	**-0.8**
• LAYANA, Tim	Timothy Joseph Layana b: 3/2/1964, Inglewood, CA d: 6/26/1999, Bakersfield, CA BR/TR, 6'2", 195 lbs. Deb: 4/9/1990																									
1990 Cin-N	5	3	.625	55	0	0	0	2	80	71	33	31	7	2	44	53	1.438	3.49	113	4.01	.244	0	.000	3	6	0.2
1991 Cin-N	0	2	.000	22	0	0	0	0	20^{2}	23	18	16	1	0	11	14	1.645	6.97	55	4.78	.277	0	.000	-7	0	-0.8
1993 SF-N	0	0	....	1	0	0	0	0	2	7	5	5	1	0	1	1	4.000	22.50	17	24.07	.538	0	....	-4	0	-0.4
Total 3	**5**	**5**	**.500**	**78**	**0**	**0**	**0**	**2**	**102^{2}**	**101**	**56**	**52**	**9**	**2**	**56**	**68**	**1.529**	**4.56**	**85**	**4.55**	**.261**	**0**	**.000**	**-9**	**6**	**-1.0**
• LAZAR, Danny	John Daniel Lazar b: 11/14/1943, East Chicago, IN BL/TL, 6'1", 190 lbs. Deb: 6/21/1968																									
1968 Chi-A	0	1	.000	8	1	0	0	0	13^{1}	14	6	6	1	0	4	11	1.350	4.05	75	3.77	.269	0	.000	-1	0	-0.2
1969 Chi-A	0	0	....	9	3	0	0	0	20^{2}	21	15	15	5	1	11	9	1.548	6.53	59	5.96	.280	0	.000	-6	0	-0.7
Total 2	**0**	**1**	**.000**	**17**	**4**	**0**	**0**	**0**	**34**	**35**	**21**	**21**	**6**	**1**	**15**	**20**	**1.471**	**5.56**	**64**	**5.10**	**.276**	**0**	**.000**	**-7**	**0**	**-0.8**
• LAZORKO, Jack	Jack Thomas Lazorko b: 3/30/1956, Hoboken, NJ BR/TR, 5'11", 200 lbs. Deb: 6/4/1984																									
1984 Mil-A	0	1	.000	15	1	0	0	1	39^{2}	37	19	19	7	1	22	24	1.487	4.31	89	4.90	.245	0	....	-2	1	-0.2
1985 Sea-A	0	0	....	15	0	0	0	1	20^{1}	23	10	8	1	3	8	7	1.525	3.54	119	4.96	.291	0	....	2	1	0.2
1986 Det-A	0	0	....	3	0	0	0	0	6^{2}	8	3	3	0	0	4	3	1.800	4.05	102	4.99	.296	0	....	-0	0	0.0
1987 Cal-A	5	6	.455	26	11	2	0	0	117^{2}	108	68	60	20	2	44	55	1.292	4.59	94	4.09	.248	0	....	-4	5	-0.4
1988 Cal-A	0	1	.000	10	3	0	0	0	37^{2}	37	15	14	5	1	16	19	1.407	3.35	115	4.37	.255	0	....	2	2	0.2
Total 5	**5**	**8**	**.385**	**69**	**15**	**2**	**0**	**2**	**222**	**213**	**115**	**104**	**33**	**7**	**94**	**108**	**1.383**	**4.22**	**98**	**4.39**	**.254**	**0**	**....**	**-2**	**9**	**-0.2**
• LEA, Charlie	Charles William Lea b: 12/25/1956, Orleans, France BR/TR, 6'4", 197 lbs. Deb: 6/12/1980																									
1980 Mon-N	7	5	.583	21	19	0	0	0	104	103	51	43	5	2	55	56	1.519	3.72	96	4.18	.262	3	.081	-1	4	-0.3
1981 Mon-N	5	4	.556	16	11	2	2	0	64^{1}	63	34	33	4	1	26	31	1.383	4.62	76	3.93	.268	2	.133	-8	2	-0.9
1982 Mon-N	12	10	.545	27	27	4	2	0	177^{2}	145	70	64	16	0	56	115	1.131	3.24	112	2.67	.222	8	.123	7	11	0.7
1983 Mon-N	16	11	.593	33	33	8	4	0	222	195	87	77	15	1	84	137	1.257	3.12	115	3.15	.238	8	.114	8	15	0.7
1984 Mon-N★	15	10	.600	30	30	8	0	0	224^{1}	198	82	72	19	3	68	123	1.186	2.89	119	3.03	.239	8	.111	11	15	0.8
1987 Mon-N	0	1	.000	1	1	0	0	0	1	4	4	4	1	0	2	1	6.000	36.00	12	47.63	.571	0	....	-4	0	-0.4
1988 Min-A	7	7	.500	24	23	0	0	0	130	156	79	70	19	5	50	72	1.585	4.85	84	5.69	.301	0	....	-11	4	-1.2
Total 7	**62**	**48**	**.564**	**152**	**144**	**22**	**8**	**0**	**923^{1}**	**864**	**407**	**363**	**79**	**12**	**341**	**535**	**1.305**	**3.54**	**103**	**3.61**	**.250**	**29**	**.112**	**2**	**51**	**-0.6**
• LEACH, Terry	Terry Hester Leach b: 3/13/1954, Selma, AL BR/TR, 6', 215 lbs. Deb: 8/12/1981																									
1981 NY-N	1	1	.500	21	1	0	0	0	35^{1}	26	11	10	2	0	12	16	1.075	2.55	137	2.23	.205	0	.000	4	3	0.5
1982 NY-N	2	1	.667	21	1	1	1	3	45^{1}	46	22	21	2	0	18	30	1.412	4.17	87	3.60	.271	1	.125	-2	3	-0.3
1985 NY-N	3	4	.429	22	4	1	1	1	55^{2}	48	19	18	3	1	14	30	1.114	2.91	119	2.49	.235	2	.167	4	4	0.4
1986 NY-N	0	0	....	6	0	0	0	0	6^{2}	6	3	2	0	0	3	4	1.350	2.70	131	2.83	.222	0	....	1	0	0.1
1987 NY-N	11	1	.917	44	12	1	1	0	131^{1}	132	54	47	14	1	29	61	1.226	3.22	117	3.45	.262	2	.061	10	10	0.8
1988★ NY-N	7	2	.778	52	0	0	0	3	92	95	32	26	5	3	24	51	1.293	2.54	127	3.43	.268	2	.143	7	7	0.8
1989 NY-N	0	0	....	10	0	0	0	0	21^{1}	19	11	10	1	1	4	2	1.078	4.22	77	2.59	.244	0	.000	-2	0	-0.3
KC-A	5	6	.455	30	3	0	0	0	73^{2}	78	46	34	4	1	36	34	1.548	4.15	93	4.26	.278	0	....	-1	2	-0.1
1990 Min-A	2	5	.286	55	0	0	0	2	81^{2}	84	31	29	2	1	21	46	1.286	3.20	130	3.02	.268	0	....	9	7	0.9

YEAR TM-L	W	L	PCT	G	GS	CG	SH	SV	IP	H	R	ER	HR	HB	BB	SO	RAT	ERA	ERA+	CERA	OAV	BH	AVG	PR+	WS	TPW
1991* Min-A	1	2	.333	50	0	0	0	0	67^{1}	82	28	27	3	0	14	32	1.426	3.61	118	4.01	.299	0	....	4	4	0.4
1992 Chi-A	6	5	.545	51	0	0	0	0	73^{2}	57	17	16	2	4	20	22	1.045	1.95	197	2.12	.215	0	....	16	8	1.6
1993 Chi-A	0	0	....	14	0	0	0	1	16	15	5	5	0	1	2	3	1.063	2.81	149	2.27	.250	0	....	2	2	0.2
Total 11	38	27	.585	376	21	3	3	10	700	688	279	245	38	13	197	331	1.264	3.15	119	3.21	.259	7	.097	50	50	5.0

• LEAL, Luis Luis Enrique (Alvarado) Leal b: 3/21/1957, Barquisimeto, Venezuela BR/TR, 6'3", 205 lbs. Deb: 5/25/1980

YEAR TM-L	W	L	PCT	G	GS	CG	SH	SV	IP	H	R	ER	HR	HB	BB	SO	RAT	ERA	ERA+	CERA	OAV	BH	AVG	PR+	WS	TPW
1980 Tor-A	3	4	.429	13	10	1	0	0	59^{2}	72	35	30	6	1	31	26	1.726	4.53	95	5.94	.314	0	....	-2	2	-0.2
1981 Tor-A	7	13	.350	29	19	3	0	1	129^{2}	127	63	53	8	5	44	71	1.319	3.68	107	3.48	.254	0	....	5	7	0.5
1982 Tor-A	12	15	.444	38	38	10	0	0	249^{2}	250	113	109	24	3	79	111	1.318	3.93	114	3.77	.262	0	....	17	17	1.7
1983 Tor-A	13	12	.520	35	35	7	1	0	217^{1}	216	113	104	23	6	65	116	1.293	4.31	100	3.77	.257	0	....	-1	12	-0.1
1984 Tor-A	13	8	.619	35	35	6	2	0	222^{1}	221	106	96	27	4	77	134	1.340	3.89	105	4.01	.258	0	....	4	14	0.4
1985 Tor-A	3	6	.333	15	14	0	0	0	67^{1}	82	46	43	13	3	24	33	1.574	5.75	73	6.02	.303	0	....	-13	0	-1.2
Total 6	51	58	.468	165	151	27	3	1	946	968	476	435	101	22	320	491	1.362	4.14	102	4.09	.265	0	....	11	52	1.1

• LEAR, King Charles Bernard Lear b: 1/23/1891, Greencastle, PA d: 10/31/1976, Waynesboro, PA BR/TR, 6', 175 lbs. Deb: 5/2/1914

YEAR TM-L	W	L	PCT	G	GS	CG	SH	SV	IP	H	R	ER	HR	HB	BB	SO	RAT	ERA	ERA+	CERA	OAV	BH	AVG	PR+	WS	TPW
1914 Cin-N	1	2	.333	17	4	3	1	1	55^{2}	55	23	19	3	2	19	20	1.329	3.07	95	3.57	.271	3	.188	-1	3	0.0
1915 Cin-N	6	10	.375	40	15	9	0	0	167^{2}	169	73	56	7	6	45	46	1.276	3.01	95	3.33	.270	8	.170	-6	7	-0.8
Total 2	7	12	.368	57	19	12	1	1	223^{1}	224	96	75	10	8	64	66	1.290	3.02	95	3.39	.270	11	.175	-7	10	-0.8

• LEARY, Frank Francis Patrick Leary b: 2/26/1881, Wayland, MA d: 10/4/1907, Natick, MA TR, 5'10" Deb: 4/30/1907

YEAR TM-L	W	L	PCT	G	GS	CG	SH	SV	IP	H	R	ER	HR	HB	BB	SO	RAT	ERA	ERA+	CERA	OAV	BH	AVG	PR+	WS	TPW
1907 Cin-N	0	1	.000	2	1	0	0	0	8	7	2	1	0	0	6	4	1.625	1.13	230	4.32	.269	0	.000	1	1	0.1

• LEARY, Jack John J. Leary b: 1858, New Haven, CT TL, 5'11", 186 lbs. Deb: 8/21/1880 ♦

YEAR TM-L	W	L	PCT	G	GS	CG	SH	SV	IP	H	R	ER	HR	HB	BB	SO	RAT	ERA	ERA+	CERA	OAV	BH	AVG	PR+	WS	TPW
1880 Bos-N	0	1	.000	1	1	0	0	0	3	8	5	5	0	....	0	1	2.667	15.00	15	....	.467	0	.000	-4	0	-0.4
1881 Det-N	0	2	.000	2	2	1	0	0	13	13	6	6	0	....	2	2	1.154	4.15	70	....	.249	3	.273	-2	1	-0.1
1882 Pit-a	1	0	1.000	3	2	1	0	0	18^{2}	28	22	13	0	....	3	5	1.661	6.27	42	....	.326	75	.292	-7	7	-0.9
Bal-a	2	1	.667	3	3	3	0	0	26	29	22	4	1	....	8	2	1.423	1.38	199	....	.264	4	.222	4	1	0.4
Yr.	3	1	.750	6	5	4	0	0	44^{2}	57	44	17	1	....	11	7	1.522	3.43	77	....	.291	79	.287	-3	8	-0.5
1884 Alt-U	0	3	.000	3	3	2	0	0	24	31	30	14	0	....	2	7	1.375	5.25	63	....	.294	3	.091	-3	0	-0.9
CP-U	0	2	.000	2	1	1	0	0	10	14	14	6	0	....	5	6	1.900	5.40	53	....	.311	7	.175	-3	0	-0.6
Yr.	0	5	.000	5	4	3	0	0	34	45	44	20	0	....	7	13	1.529	5.29	60	....	.299	10	.137	-6	0	-1.4
Total 4	3	9	.250	14	12	8	0	0	94^{2}	123	99	48	1	....	20	23	1.511	4.56	62	....	.296	125	.232	-15	9	-2.3

• LEARY, Tim Timothy James Leary b: 3/21/1958, Santa Monica, CA BR/TR, 6'3", 205 lbs. Deb: 4/12/1981

YEAR TM-L	W	L	PCT	G	GS	CG	SH	SV	IP	H	R	ER	HR	HB	BB	SO	RAT	ERA	ERA+	CERA	OAV	BH	AVG	PR+	WS	TPW
1981 NY-N	0	0	....	1	1	0	0	0	2	0	0	0	0	0	1	3	.500	0.00	....	0.27	.000	0	.000	1	0	0.1
1983 NY-N	1	1	.500	2	2	1	0	0	10^{2}	15	10	4	0	0	4	9	1.781	3.38	107	5.19	.319	1	.333	0	0	0.0
1984 NY-N	3	3	.500	20	7	0	0	0	53^{2}	61	28	24	2	2	18	29	1.472	4.02	88	4.17	.285	3	.300	-3	3	-0.1
1985 Mil-A	1	4	.200	5	5	0	0	0	33^{1}	40	18	15	5	1	8	29	1.440	4.05	103	5.05	.296	0	....	0	1	0.0
1986 Mil-A	12	12	.500	33	30	3	2	0	188^{1}	216	97	88	20	7	53	110	1.428	4.21	103	4.63	.289	0	....	4	11	0.4
1987 LA-N	3	11	.214	39	12	0	0	1	107^{2}	121	62	57	15	2	36	61	1.458	4.76	83	4.83	.285	7	.304	-9	3	-0.7
1988* LA-N	17	11	.607	35	34	9	6	0	228^{2}	201	87	74	13	6	56	180	1.124	2.91	114	2.65	.234	18	.269	13	17	1.9
1989 LA-N	6	7	.462	19	17	2	0	0	117^{1}	107	45	44	9	2	37	59	1.227	3.38	101	3.15	.247	2	.061	-0	5	-0.3
Cin-N	2	7	.222	14	14	0	0	0	89^{2}	98	39	37	8	3	31	64	1.439	3.71	97	4.28	.278	5	.192	-0	4	0.2
Yr.	8	14	.364	33	31	2	0	0	207	205	84	81	17	5	68	123	1.319	3.52	99	3.64	.261	7	.119	-1	9	-0.1
1990 NY-A	9	19	.321	31	31	6	1	0	208	202	105	95	18	7	78	138	1.346	4.11	97	3.90	.257	0	....	-3	10	-0.3
1991 NY-A	4	10	.286	28	18	1	0	0	120^{2}	150	89	87	20	4	57	83	1.715	6.49	64	6.58	.312	0	....	-31	0	-3.1
1992 NY-A	5	6	.455	18	15	2	0	0	97	84	62	60	9	4	57	34	1.454	5.57	70	4.28	.245	0	....	-18	1	-1.8
Sea-A	3	4	.429	8	8	1	0	0	44	47	27	24	3	5	30	12	1.750	4.91	81	5.65	.280	0	....	-4	1	-0.5
Yr.	8	10	.444	26	23	3	0	0	141	131	89	84	12	9	87	46	1.546	5.36	73	4.71	.256	0	....	-23	2	-2.3
1993 Sea-A	11	9	.550	33	27	0	0	0	169^{1}	202	104	95	21	8	58	68	1.535	5.05	87	5.38	.300	0	....	-13	6	-1.3
1994 Tex-A	1	1	.500	6	3	0	0	0	21	26	19	19	4	1	11	9	1.762	8.14	59	6.67	.306	0	....	-7	0	-0.7
Total 13	78	105	.426	292	224	25	9	1	1491^{1}	1570	792	723	147	52	535	888	1.411	4.36	90	4.37	.273	36	.221	-71	62	-6.1

• LECLAIR, George George Lewis "Frenchy" LeClair b: 10/18/1886, Milton, VT d: 10/10/1918, Farnham, Canada BR/TR, 5'9", 170 lbs. Deb: 6/5/1914

YEAR TM-L	W	L	PCT	G	GS	CG	SH	SV	IP	H	R	ER	HR	HB	BB	SO	RAT	ERA	ERA+	CERA	OAV	BH	AVG	PR+	WS	TPW
1914 Pit-F	5	2	.714	22	7	5	1	0	103^{1}	99	52	46	0	1	25	49	1.200	4.01	77	2.75	.262	5	.147	-10	4	-1.2
1915 Pit-F	1	2	.333	14	3	1	0	1	45^{2}	43	20	17	1	0	13	10	1.226	3.35	93	2.76	.253	2	.154	-1	2	-0.2
Buf-F	0	0	....	1	0	0	0	0	3	4	2	2	0	0	1	2	1.667	6.00	51	4.87	.333	0	....	-1	0	-0.1
Bal-F	1	8	.111	18	9	6	1	1	84	76	43	23	2	0	22	30	1.167	2.46	137	2.52	.246	2	.083	10	4	0.9
Yr.	2	10	.167	33	12	7	1	2	132^{2}	123	65	42	3	0	36	42	1.198	2.85	114	2.66	.251	4	.108	8	6	0.6
Total 2	7	12	.368	55	19	12	2	2	236	222	117	88	3	1	61	91	1.199	3.36	94	2.70	.256	9	.127	-3	10	-0.6

• LEDBETTER, Razor Ralph Overton Ledbetter b: 12/8/1894, Rutherford College, NC d: 2/1/1969, West Palm Beach, FL BR/TR, 6'3", 190 lbs. Deb: 4/16/1915

YEAR TM-L	W	L	PCT	G	GS	CG	SH	SV	IP	H	R	ER	HR	HB	BB	SO	RAT	ERA	ERA+	CERA	OAV	BH	AVG	PR+	WS	TPW
1915 Det-A	0	0	....	1	0	0	0	0	1	1	0	0	0	0	0	0	1.000	0.00	....	2.02	.333	0	....	0	0	0.0

• LEDEZMA, Wilfredo Wilfredo J. Ledezma b: 1/21/1981, Guarico, Venezuela BL/TL, 6'3", 150 lbs. Deb: 4/2/2003

YEAR TM-L	W	L	PCT	G	GS	CG	SH	SV	IP	H	R	ER	HR	HB	BB	SO	RAT	ERA	ERA+	CERA	OAV	BH	AVG	PR+	WS	TPW
2003 Det-A	3	7	.300	34	8	0	0	0	84	99	55	54	12	3	35	49	1.595	5.79	75	5.67	.297	0	....	-14	2	-1.3

• LEE, Bill William Crutcher "Big Bill" Lee b: 10/21/1909, Plaquemine, LA d: 6/15/1977, Plaquemine, LA BR/TR, 6'3", 195 lbs. Deb: 4/29/1934

YEAR TM-L	W	L	PCT	G	GS	CG	SH	SV	IP	H	R	ER	HR	HB	BB	SO	RAT	ERA	ERA+	CERA	OAV	BH	AVG	PR+	WS	TPW
1934 Chi-N	13	14	.481	35	29	16	4	1	214^{1}	218	91	81	9	2	74	104	1.362	3.40	114	3.53	.263	10	.132	10	16	0.7
1935* Chi-N	20	6	.769	39	32	18	3	1	252	241	106	83	11	5	84	100	1.290	2.96	133	3.21	.251	24	.235	18	21	1.9
1936 Chi-N	18	11	.621	43	33	20	**4**	1	258^{2}	238	106	95	14	3	93	102	1.280	3.31	120	3.16	.246	12	.138	14	20	1.1
1937 Chi-N	14	15	.483	42	**34**	17	2	3	272^{1}	289	122	107	14	0	73	108	1.329	3.54	112	3.53	.273	15	.172	12	18	1.1
1938* Chi-N★	**22**	9	.710	44	**37**	19	**9**	2	291	281	95	86	18	2	74	121	1.220	**2.66**	**144**	3.08	.254	20	.198	**36**	**28**	**3.7**
1939 Chi-N★	19	15	.559	37	**36**	20	1	0	282^{1}	295	125	108	18	1	85	105	1.346	3.44	114	3.63	.272	13	.126	23	20	1.9
1940 Chi-N	9	17	.346	37	30	9	1	0	211^{1}	246	129	118	12	2	70	70	1.495	5.03	75	4.38	.294	10	.132	-29	3	-3.2
1941 Chi-N	8	14	.364	28	22	12	0	1	167^{1}	179	87	70	6	2	43	62	1.327	3.76	93	3.37	.270	11	.186	-0	7	0.1
1942 Chi-N	13	13	.500	32	30	18	1	0	219^{2}	221	99	94	4	1	67	75	1.311	3.85	83	3.08	.258	11	.159	-12	10	-1.2
1943 Chi-N	3	7	.300	13	12	4	0	0	78^{1}	83	37	31	4	0	27	18	1.404	3.56	94	3.78	.273	7	.269	-1	3	0.1
Phi-N	1	5	.167	13	7	2	0	3	60^{2}	70	35	31	4	1	21	17	1.500	4.60	73	4.59	.298	1	.059	-8	1	-1.0
Yr.	4	12	.250	26	19	6	0	3	139	153	72	62	8	1	48	35	1.446	4.01	84	4.13	.284	8	.186	-8	4	-0.9
1944 Phi-N	10	11	.476	31	28	11	3	1	208^{1}	199	88	73	9	3	57	50	1.229	3.15	115	2.94	.248	14	.194	11	15	1.1
1945 Phi-N	3	6	.333	13	13	2	0	0	77^{1}	107	52	40	0	0	30	13	1.772	4.66	82	5.16	.318	4	.167	-5	2	-0.6
Bos-N	6	3	.667	16	13	6	1	0	106^{1}	112	43	33	6	0	36	12	1.392	2.79	137	3.84	.279	4	.129	12	9	1.2
Yr.	9	9	.500	29	26	8	1	0	183^{2}	219	95	73	6	0	66	25	1.552	3.58	107	4.39	.297	8	.145	7	11	0.6
1946 Bos-N	10	9	.526	25	21	8	0	0	140	148	73	65	7	1	45	32	1.379	4.18	82	3.67	.273	8	.170	-11	4	-1.2
1947 Chi-N	0	2	.000	14	2	0	0	0	24	26	16	12	2	1	14	9	1.667	4.50	88	4.88	.268	1	.333	-1	0	-0.1
Total 14	169	157	.518	462	379	182	29	13	2864	2953	1304	1127	138	24	893	998	1.343	3.54	105	3.51	.266	165	.168	69	177	5.6

• LEE, Bill William Francis "Spaceman" Lee b: 12/28/1946, Burbank, CA BL/TL, 6'3", 210 lbs. Deb: 6/25/1969

YEAR TM-L	W	L	PCT	G	GS	CG	SH	SV	IP	H	R	ER	HR	HB	BB	SO	RAT	ERA	ERA+	CERA	OAV	BH	AVG	PR+	WS	TPW
1969 Bos-A	1	3	.250	20	1	0	0	0	52	56	27	26	9	2	28	45	1.615	4.50	85	5.94	.281	0	.000	-3	2	-0.4
1970 Bos-A	2	2	.500	11	5	0	0	1	37	48	20	19	3	0	14	19	1.676	4.62	86	5.60	.320	0	.000	-2	1	-0.3
1971 Bos-A	9	2	.818	47	3	0	0	2	102	102	35	31	7	1	46	74	1.451	2.74	135	3.91	.256	5	.217	12	10	1.4
1972 Bos-A	7	4	.636	47	0	0	0	5	84^{1}	75	31	30	5	1	32	43	1.269	3.20	100	3.10	.248	3	.188	2	7	0.4
1973 Bos-A★	17	11	.607	38	33	18	1	1	284^{2}	275	100	87	20	5	76	120	1.233	2.75	146	3.28	.257	0	....	38	24	3.9
1974 Bos-A	17	15	.531	38	37	16	1	0	282^{1}	320	123	110	25	4	67	95	1.371	3.51	110	4.24	.290	0	....	13	19	1.4
1975* Bos-A	17	9	.654	41	34	17	4	0	260	274	123	114	20	3	69	78	1.319	3.95	103	3.76	.273	0	....	4	18	0.4
1976 Bos-A	5	7	.417	24	14	1	0	3	96	124	68	60	13	3	28	29	1.583	5.63	69	5.62	.307	0	....	-17	0	-1.8
1977 Bos-A	9	5	.643	27	16	4	0	1	128	155	67	63	14	0	29	31	1.438	4.43	101	4.75	.306	0	....	3	8	0.3
1978 Bos-A	10	10	.500	28	24	8	1	0	177	198	89	68	20	2	59	44	1.452	3.46	119	4.64	.285	0	....	12	11	1.2
1979 Mon-N	16	10	.615	33	33	6	3	0	222	230	91	75	20	1	46	59	1.243	3.04	120	3.46	.265	16	.216	14	16	1.6

YEAR	TM-L	W	L	PCT	G	GS	CG	SH	SV	IP	H	R	ER	HR	HB	BB	SO	RAT	ERA	ERA+	CERA	OAV	BH	AVG	PR+	WS	TPW
1980	Mon-N	4	6	.400	24	18	2	0	0	118	156	71	65	13	3	22	34	1.508	4.96	72	5.24	.319	9	.220	-18	1	-1.8
1981*	Mon-N	5	6	.455	31	7	0	0	6	88^2	90	33	29	6	2	14	34	1.173	2.94	119	3.07	.265	8	.364	5	8	0.9
1982	Mon-N	0	0	....	7	0	0	0	0	12^1	19	7	6	1	0	1	8	1.622	4.38	83	5.75	.352	0	....	-1	0	-0.1
Total	**14**	**119**	**90**	**.569**	**416**	**225**	**72**	**10**	**19**	**1944^1**	**2122**	**885**	**783**	**176**	**27**	**531**	**713**	**1.364**	**3.62**	**107**	**4.11**	**.280**	**41**	**.208**	**62**	**125**	**6.9**

• LEE, Bob Robert Dean "Moose,Horse" Lee b: 11/26/1937, Ottumwa, IA BR/TR, 6'3", 230 lbs. Deb: 4/15/1964

YEAR	TM-L	W	L	PCT	G	GS	CG	SH	SV	IP	H	R	ER	HR	HB	BB	SO	RAT	ERA	ERA+	CERA	OAV	BH	AVG	PR+	WS	TPW
1964	LA-A	6	5	.545	64	5	0	0	19	137	87	31	23	6	1	58	111	1.058	1.51	217	1.91	.182	0	.000	26	20	2.5
1965	Cal-A★	9	7	.563	69	0	0	0	23	131^1	95	35	28	11	1	42	89	1.043	1.92	177	2.18	.205	3	.143	21	20	2.3
1966	Cal-A	5	4	.556	61	0	0	0	16	101^2	90	39	31	8	1	31	46	1.190	2.74	122	2.95	.237	0	.000	6	11	0.6
1967	LA-N	0	0	....	4	0	0	0	0	6^2	6	8	4	2	1	3	2	1.350	5.40	57	5.27	.222	0	....	-2	0	-0.2
	Cin-N	3	3	.500	27	1	0	0	2	50^2	51	26	25	0	0	25	33	1.500	4.44	84	3.43	.262	3	.375	-4	2	-0.3
	Yr.	3	3	.500	31	1	0	0	2	57^1	57	34	29	2	1	28	35	1.483	4.55	80	3.64	.257	3	.375	-5	2	-0.5
1968	Cin-N	2	4	.333	44	1	0	0	3	65^1	73	38	37	4	1	37	34	1.684	5.10	62	5.02	.302	1	.200	-14	0	-1.6
Total	**5**	**25**	**23**	**.521**	**269**	**7**	**0**	**0**	**63**	**492^2**	**402**	**177**	**148**	**31**	**5**	**196**	**315**	**1.214**	**2.70**	**124**	**2.81**	**.225**	**7**	**.104**	**34**	**53**	**3.4**

• LEE, Cliff Clifton Phifer Lee b: 8/30/1978, Benton, AR BL/TL, 6'3", 190 lbs. Deb: 9/15/2002

YEAR	TM-L	W	L	PCT	G	GS	CG	SH	SV	IP	H	R	ER	HR	HB	BB	SO	RAT	ERA	ERA+	CERA	OAV	BH	AVG	PR+	WS	TPW
2002	Cle-A	0	1	.000	2	2	0	0	0	10^1	6	2	2	0	0	8	6	1.355	1.74	252	2.38	.171	0	....	3	1	0.3
2003	Cle-A	3	3	.500	9	9	0	0	0	52^1	41	28	21	7	2	20	44	1.166	3.61	122	3.29	.220	0	....	4	3	0.3
Total	**2**	**3**	**4**	**.429**	**11**	**11**	**0**	**0**	**0**	**62^2**	**47**	**30**	**23**	**7**	**2**	**28**	**50**	**1.197**	**3.30**	**134**	**3.14**	**.213**	**0**	**....**	**7**	**4**	**0.6**

• LEE, Corey Corey Wayne Lee b: 12/26/1974, Raleigh, NC BL/TL, 6'2", 185 lbs. Deb: 8/24/1999

YEAR	TM-L	W	L	PCT	G	GS	CG	SH	SV	IP	H	R	ER	HR	HB	BB	SO	RAT	ERA	ERA+	CERA	OAV	BH	AVG	PR+	WS	TPW
1999	Tex-A	0	1	.000	1	0	0	0	0	1	2	3	3	1	0	1	0	3.000	27.00	19	23.01	.400	0	....	-2	0	-0.2

• LEE, David David Emmer Lee b: 3/12/1973, Pittsburgh, PA BR/TR, 6'1", 202 lbs. Deb: 5/22/1999

YEAR	TM-L	W	L	PCT	G	GS	CG	SH	SV	IP	H	R	ER	HR	HB	BB	SO	RAT	ERA	ERA+	CERA	OAV	BH	AVG	PR+	WS	TPW
1999	Col-N	3	2	.600	36	0	0	0	0	49	43	21	20	4	4	29	38	1.469	3.67	158	4.43	.247	1	.200	12	5	1.1
2000	Col-N	0	0	....	7	0	0	0	1	5^2	10	9	7	3	1	6	6	2.824	11.12	52	16.73	.357	0	....	-3	0	-0.3
2001	SD-N	1	0	1.000	41	0	0	0	0	48^2	52	20	20	6	6	27	42	1.623	3.70	108	5.86	.278	0	.000	2	3	0.2
2003	Cle-A	1	0	1.000	8	0	0	0	0	7^2	4	4	4	1	0	6	7	1.304	4.70	94	2.79	.143	0	....	-0	0	0.0
Total	**4**	**5**	**2**	**.714**	**92**	**0**	**0**	**0**	**1**	**111**	**109**	**54**	**51**	**14**	**11**	**68**	**93**	**1.595**	**4.14**	**117**	**5.57**	**.261**	**1**	**.167**	**10**	**8**	**1.0**

• LEE, Don Donald Edward Lee b: 2/26/1934, Globe, AZ BR/TR, 6'4", 210 lbs. Deb: 4/23/1957

YEAR	TM-L	W	L	PCT	G	GS	CG	SH	SV	IP	H	R	ER	HR	HB	BB	SO	RAT	ERA	ERA+	CERA	OAV	BH	AVG	PR+	WS	TPW
1957	Det-A	1	3	.250	11	6	0	0	0	38^2	48	22	20	6	1	18	19	1.707	4.66	83	6.31	.308	2	.167	-4	1	-0.4
1958	Det-A	0	0	....	1	0	0	0	0	2	1	2	2	1	1	1	0	1.000	9.00	45	6.46	.143	0	....	-1	0	-0.1
1960	Was-A	8	7	.533	44	20	1	0	3	165	160	72	63	16	3	64	88	1.358	3.44	115	3.94	.258	5	.116	12	11	1.2
1961	Min-A	3	6	.333	37	10	4	0	3	115	93	49	45	12	4	35	65	1.113	3.52	120	2.86	.221	2	.067	12	8	0.9
1962	Min-A	3	3	.500	9	9	1	0	0	52	51	27	26	8	7	24	28	1.442	4.50	91	5.18	.256	4	.211	-3	2	-0.2
	LA-A	8	8	.500	27	22	4	2	2	153^1	153	64	53	12	3	39	74	1.252	3.11	124	3.38	.256	9	.184	14	11	1.4
	Yr.	11	11	.500	36	31	5	2	2	205^1	204	91	79	20	10	63	102	1.300	3.46	113	3.84	.256	13	.191	11	13	1.1
1963	LA-A	8	11	.421	40	22	3	2	1	154	148	74	63	12	9	51	89	1.292	3.68	93	3.60	.251	7	.156	-4	5	-0.5
1964	LA-A	5	4	.556	33	8	0	0	2	89^1	99	39	27	6	1	25	73	1.388	2.72	121	3.96	.279	6	.261	5	6	0.7
1965	Cal-A	0	1	.000	10	0	0	0	0	14	21	11	10	4	1	5	12	1.857	6.43	53	8.49	.350	1	.333	-5	0	-0.4
	Hou-N	0	0	....	7	0	0	0	0	8	8	3	3	0	1	3	3	1.375	3.38	99	3.88	.267	0	.000	0	0	0.0
1966	Hou-N	2	0	1.000	9	0	0	0	0	18	17	5	5	1	0	4	9	1.167	2.50	137	2.72	.250	1	1.000	2	2	0.3
	Chi-N	2	1	.667	16	0	0	0	0	19	28	19	15	3	0	12	7	2.105	7.11	52	8.27	.346	0	....	-7	0	-0.7
	Yr.	4	1	.800	25	0	0	0	0	37	45	24	20	4	0	16	16	1.649	4.86	74	5.57	.302	1	1.000	-5	2	-0.5
Total	**9**	**40**	**44**	**.476**	**244**	**97**	**13**	**4**	**11**	**828^1**	**827**	**387**	**332**	**81**	**31**	**281**	**467**	**1.338**	**3.61**	**104**	**3.97**	**.260**	**37**	**.164**	**21**	**46**	**2.0**

• LEE, Mark Mark Linden Lee b: 6/14/1953, Inglewood, CA BR/TR, 6'4", 225 lbs. Deb: 4/23/1978

YEAR	TM-L	W	L	PCT	G	GS	CG	SH	SV	IP	H	R	ER	HR	HB	BB	SO	RAT	ERA	ERA+	CERA	OAV	BH	AVG	PR+	WS	TPW
1978	SD-N	5	1	.833	56	0	0	0	2	85	74	34	31	2	2	36	31	1.294	3.28	101	2.81	.240	0	.000	0	5	0.0
1979	SD-N	2	4	.333	46	1	0	0	5	65	88	34	31	3	2	25	25	1.738	4.29	82	5.66	.332	2	.333	-6	2	-0.6
1980	Pit-N	0	1	.000	4	0	0	0	0	5^2	5	3	3	0	0	3	2	1.412	4.76	76	2.99	.227	0	....	-1	0	0.0
1981	Pit-N	0	2	.000	12	0	0	0	2	19^2	17	6	6	1	0	5	5	1.119	2.75	131	2.31	.233	1	.500	2	2	0.2
Total	**4**	**7**	**8**	**.467**	**118**	**1**	**0**	**0**	**9**	**175^1**	**184**	**77**	**71**	**6**	**4**	**69**	**63**	**1.443**	**3.64**	**95**	**3.82**	**.275**	**3**	**.231**	**-5**	**9**	**-0.4**

• LEE, Mark Mark Owen Lee b: 7/20/1964, Williston, ND BL/TL, 6'3", 198 lbs. Deb: 9/8/1988

YEAR	TM-L	W	L	PCT	G	GS	CG	SH	SV	IP	H	R	ER	HR	HB	BB	SO	RAT	ERA	ERA+	CERA	OAV	BH	AVG	PR+	WS	TPW
1988	KC-A	0	0	....	4	0	0	0	0	5	6	2	2	0	0	1	0	1.400	3.60	111	3.80	.300	0	....	0	0	0.0
1990	Mil-A	1	0	1.000	11	0	0	0	0	21^1	20	5	5	1	0	4	14	1.125	2.11	183	2.66	.256	0	....	4	2	0.4
1991	Mil-A	2	5	.286	62	0	0	0	1	67^2	72	33	29	10	1	31	43	1.522	3.86	103	5.09	.283	0	....	1	3	0.1
1995	Bal-A	2	0	1.000	39	0	0	0	1	33^1	31	18	18	5	1	18	27	1.470	4.86	98	4.53	.246	0	....	-1	2	-0.1
Total	**4**	**5**	**5**	**.500**	**116**	**0**	**0**	**0**	**2**	**127^1**	**129**	**58**	**54**	**16**	**2**	**54**	**84**	**1.437**	**3.82**	**110**	**4.49**	**.270**	**0**	**....**	**5**	**7**	**0.5**

• LEE, Mike Michael Randall Lee b: 5/19/1941, Bell, CA BL/TL, 6'5", 220 lbs. Deb: 5/6/1960

YEAR	TM-L	W	L	PCT	G	GS	CG	SH	SV	IP	H	R	ER	HR	HB	BB	SO	RAT	ERA	ERA+	CERA	OAV	BH	AVG	PR+	WS	TPW
1960	Cle-A	0	0	....	7	0	0	0	0	9	6	2	2	1	1	11	6	1.889	2.00	187	6.24	.207	0	....	2	1	0.2
1963	LA-A	1	1	.500	6	4	0	0	0	26	30	11	11	3	1	14	11	1.692	3.81	90	6.05	.300	0	.000	-1	1	-0.2
Total	**2**	**1**	**1**	**.500**	**13**	**4**	**0**	**0**	**0**	**35**	**36**	**13**	**13**	**4**	**2**	**25**	**17**	**1.743**	**3.34**	**104**	**6.10**	**.279**	**0**	**.000**	**1**	**2**	**0.0**

• LEE, Roy Roy Edwin Lee b: 9/28/1917, Elmira, NY d: 11/11/1985, St. Louis, MO BL/TL, 5'11.5", 175 lbs. Deb: 9/23/1945

YEAR	TM-L	W	L	PCT	G	GS	CG	SH	SV	IP	H	R	ER	HR	HB	BB	SO	RAT	ERA	ERA+	CERA	OAV	BH	AVG	PR+	WS	TPW
1945	NY-N	0	2	.000	3	1	0	0	0	7	8	9	9	3	0	3	0	1.571	11.57	34	7.02	.267	0	.000	-6	0	-0.6

• LEE, Sang-Hoon Sang-Hoon Lee b: 3/11/1971, Seoul, South Korea BL/TL, 6'1", 190 lbs. Deb: 6/29/2000

YEAR	TM-L	W	L	PCT	G	GS	CG	SH	SV	IP	H	R	ER	HR	HB	BB	SO	RAT	ERA	ERA+	CERA	OAV	BH	AVG	PR+	WS	TPW
2000	Bos-A	0	0	....	9	0	0	0	0	11^2	11	4	4	2	1	5	6	1.371	3.09	163	4.94	.262	0	....	3	1	0.2

• LEE, Thornton Thornton Starr "Lefty" Lee b: 9/13/1906, Sonoma, CA d: 6/9/1997, Tucson, AZ BL/TL, 6'3", 205 lbs. Deb: 9/19/1933

YEAR	TM-L	W	L	PCT	G	GS	CG	SH	SV	IP	H	R	ER	HR	HB	BB	SO	RAT	ERA	ERA+	CERA	OAV	BH	AVG	PR+	WS	TPW
1933	Cle-A	1	1	.500	3	2	2	0	0	17^1	13	9	8	1	0	11	7	1.385	4.15	107	3.13	.203	3	.375	1	2	0.2
1934	Cle-A	1	1	.500	24	6	0	0	0	85^2	105	57	48	8	3	44	41	1.739	5.04	90	5.79	.308	2	.095	-4	3	-0.5
1935	Cle-A	7	10	.412	32	20	8	1	1	180^2	179	90	81	6	4	71	81	1.384	4.04	112	3.48	.259	12	.197	12	12	1.0
1936	Cle-A	3	5	.375	43	8	2	0	3	127	138	86	69	2	2	67	49	1.614	4.89	103	4.26	.271	5	.122	3	7	0.1
1937	Chi-A	12	10	.545	30	25	13	2	0	204^2	209	91	80	17	1	60	80	1.314	3.52	131	3.56	.260	15	.211	20	18	1.9
1938	Chi-A	13	12	.520	33	30	18	1	1	245^1	252	123	95	12	3	94	77	1.410	3.49	140	3.69	.263	25	.258	**39**	19	**4.0**
1939	Chi-A	15	11	.577	33	29	15	2	3	235	260	121	110	14	3	70	81	1.404	4.21	112	3.99	.285	15	.165	11	18	0.8
1940	Chi-A	12	13	.480	28	27	24	1	0	228	223	100	88	13	2	56	87	1.224	3.47	127	3.05	.254	23	.274	19	19	2.2
1941	Chi-A★	22	11	.667	35	34	**30**	3	1	300^1	258	98	79	18	4	92	130	1.165	**2.37**	**173**	**2.71**	.232	29	.254	**54**	**32**	**5.7**
1942	Chi-A	2	6	.250	11	8	6	1	0	76	82	38	28	4	2	31	25	1.487	3.32	109	4.21	.278	6	.200	2	4	0.2
1943	Chi-A	5	9	.357	19	19	7	1	0	127	129	66	59	8	4	50	35	1.409	4.18	80	3.90	.266	3	.071	-13	2	-1.8
1944	Chi-A	3	9	.250	15	14	6	0	0	113^1	105	51	38	3	1	25	39	1.147	3.02	114	2.53	.246	4	.095	5	6	0.2
1945	Chi-A★	15	12	.556	29	28	19	1	0	228^1	208	81	62	6	10	76	108	1.244	2.44	136	2.95	.245	14	.179	25	18	2.6
1946	Chi-A	2	4	.333	7	7	2	0	0	43^1	39	24	17	1	1	23	23	1.431	3.53	97	3.46	.244	4	.267	-1	2	0.0
1947	Chi-A	3	7	.300	21	11	2	1	1	86^2	86	50	43	5	2	56	57	1.638	4.47	82	4.60	.261	6	.207	-8	2	-0.8
1948	NY-N	1	3	.250	11	4	1	0	0	32^2	41	20	16	3	1	12	17	1.622	4.41	89	5.32	.304	1	.091	-2	1	-0.2
Total	**16**	**117**	**124**	**.485**	**374**	**272**	**155**	**14**	**10**	**2331^1**	**2327**	**1105**	**921**	**121**	**43**	**838**	**937**	**1.358**	**3.56**	**118**	**3.56**	**.260**	**167**	**.200**	**164**	**165**	**15.5**

• LEE, Tom Thomas Frank Lee b: 6/8/1862, Milwaukee, WI d: 3/4/1886, Milwaukee, WI Deb: 6/14/1884 U

YEAR	TM-L	W	L	PCT	G	GS	CG	SH	SV	IP	H	R	ER	HR	HB	BB	SO	RAT	ERA	ERA+	CERA	OAV	BH	AVG	PR+	WS	TPW
1884	Chi-N	1	4	.200	5	5	5	0	0	45^1	55	43	19	12	....	15	14	1.544	3.77	83	....	.284	3	.125	-5	1	-0.6
	Bal-U	5	8	.385	15	14	12	0	0	122	121	88	46	1	....	29	81	1.230	3.39	98	....	.242	23	.280	-2	9	0.0

• LEE, Watty Wyatt Arnold Lee b: 8/12/1879, Lynch Station, VA d: 3/6/1936, Washington, DC BL/TL, 5'10.5", 171 lbs. Deb: 4/30/1901 ♦

YEAR	TM-L	W	L	PCT	G	GS	CG	SH	SV	IP	H	R	ER	HR	HB	BB	SO	RAT	ERA	ERA+	CERA	OAV	BH	AVG	PR+	WS	TPW
1901	Was-A	16	16	.500	36	33	25	2	0	262	328	184	128	14	11	45	63	1.424	4.40	83	4.38	.303	33	.256	-21	14	-1.5
1902	Was-A	5	6	.455	13	10	10	0	0	98	118	66	55	5	8	20	24	1.408	5.05	73	4.36	.298	100	.256	-13	11	-2.0
1903	Was-A	8	12	.400	22	20	15	2	0	166^2	169	86	57	5	7	40	70	1.254	3.08	102	3.15	.262	48	.208	3	13	-0.3

YEAR TM-L	W	L	PCT	G	GS	CG	SH	SV	IP	H	R	ER	HR	HB	BB	SO	RAT	ERA	ERA+	CERA	OAV	BH	AVG	PR+	WS	TPW
1904 Pit-N	1	2	.333	5	3	1	0	0	22^2	34	25	22	0	3	9	5	1.897	8.74	31	6.50	.337	4	.333	-15	1	-1.5
Total 4	30	36	.455	76	66	51	4	0	549^1	649	361	262	24	29	114	162	1.389	4.29	80	4.09	.292	185	.242	-46	39	-5.3
• LEEVER, Sam	Samuel "Deacon,The Goshen Schoolmaster" Leever b: 12/23/1871, Goshen, OH d: 5/19/1953, Goshen, OH BR/TR, 5'10.5", 175 lbs. Deb: 5/26/1898 U																									
1898 Pit-N	1	0	1.000	5	3	2	0	0	33	26	10	9	0	1	5	15	.939	2.45	145	1.63	.216	3	.250	4	4	0.4
1899 Pit-N	21	23	.477	**51**	39	35	4	**3**	**379**	353	191	134	7	11	122	121	1.253	3.18	120	2.90	.247	33	.226	25	27	2.6
1900* Pit-N	15	13	.536	30	29	25	3	0	232^2	236	101	70	2	8	48	84	1.221	2.71	134	2.89	.263	18	.205	23	20	2.1
1901 Pit-N	14	5	.737	21	20	18	2	0	176	182	82	56	2	7	39	82	1.256	2.86	114	3.08	.265	13	.183	6	11	0.5
1902 Pit-N	15	7	.682	28	26	23	4	2	222	203	73	59	2	8	31	86	1.054	2.39	114	2.21	.244	16	.178	3	17	0.2
1903* Pit-N	25	7	.781	36	34	30	**7**	1	284^1	255	98	65	2	5	60	90	1.108	**2.06**	**157**	2.26	.238	19	.165	26	28	2.1
1904 Pit-N	18	11	.621	34	32	26	1	0	253^1	224	85	61	2	5	54	63	1.097	2.17	126	2.28	.237	26	.263	14	22	2.2
1905 Pit-N	20	5	.800	33	29	20	3	1	229^2	199	94	69	3	12	54	81	1.102	2.70	111	2.36	.231	9	.102	3	19	0.0
1906 Pit-N	22	7	.759	36	31	25	6	0	260^1	232	84	67	3	7	48	76	1.076	2.32	115	2.31	.243	20	.211	9	21	1.2
1907 Pit-N	14	9	.609	31	24	17	5	0	216^2	182	70	40	3	8	46	65	1.052	1.66	146	2.17	.229	11	.151	22	17	2.4
1908 Pit-N	15	7	.682	38	20	14	4	2	192^2	179	60	45	1	6	41	28	1.142	2.10	109	2.53	.249	9	.148	4	13	0.5
1909 Pit-N	8	1	.889	19	4	2	0	2	70	74	30	22	0	4	14	23	1.257	2.83	91	3.21	.276	4	.167	-3	5	-0.3
1910 Pit-N	6	5	.545	26	8	4	0	2	111	104	45	34	2	6	25	33	1.162	2.76	114	2.88	.259	2	.065	4	8	0.1
Total 13	194	100	.660	388	299	241	39	13	2660^2	2449	1023	731	29	88	587	847	1.141	2.47	122	2.53	.245	183	.184	139	212	14.1
• LEFEBVRE, Bill	Wilfred Henry "Lefty" Lefebvre b: 11/11/1915, Natick, RI BL/TL, 5'11.5", 180 lbs. Deb: 6/10/1938																									
1938 Bos-A	0	0	....	1	0	0	0	0	4	8	6	6	2	1	0	0	2.000	13.50	37	13.23	.400	1	1.000	-4	1	-0.2
1939 Bos-A	1	1	.500	5	3	0	0	0	26^1	35	17	17	2	0	14	8	1.861	5.81	81	6.39	.333	3	.300	-3	2	-0.2
1943 Was-A	2	0	1.000	6	3	1	0	0	32^1	33	18	16	3	0	16	10	1.515	4.45	72	4.49	.268	4	.286	-4	1	-0.3
1944 Was-A	2	4	.333	24	4	2	0	3	69^2	86	48	35	3	1	21	18	1.536	4.52	72	4.56	.305	16	.258	-9	2	-0.3
Total 4	5	5	.500	36	10	3	0	3	132^1	162	89	74	10	2	51	36	1.610	5.03	72	5.17	.306	24	.276	-20	6	-1.0
• LEFFERTS, Craig	Craig Lindsay Lefferts b: 9/29/1957, Munich, West Germany BL/TL, 6'1", 210 lbs. Deb: 4/7/1983																									
1983 Chi-N	3	4	.429	56	5	0	0	1	89	80	35	31	13	2	29	60	1.225	3.13	121	3.62	.243	2	.111	8	6	0.8
1984* SD-N	3	4	.429	62	0	0	0	10	105^2	88	29	25	4	1	24	56	1.060	2.13	168	2.22	.229	5	.294	15	12	1.7
1985 SD-N	7	6	.538	60	0	0	0	2	83^1	75	34	31	7	0	30	48	1.260	3.35	105	3.23	.244	1	.250	0	6	0.0
1986 SD-N	9	8	.529	**83**	0	0	0	4	107^2	98	41	37	7	1	44	72	1.319	3.09	118	3.34	.253	1	.125	7	9	0.8
1987 SD-N	2	2	.500	33	0	0	0	2	51^1	56	29	25	9	2	15	39	1.383	4.38	90	4.63	.272	1	.333	-3	2	-0.3
*SF-N	3	3	.500	44	0	0	0	4	47^1	36	18	17	4	0	18	18	1.141	3.23	119	2.49	.216	1	.250	3	5	0.3
Yr.	5	5	.500	77	0	0	0	6	98^2	92	47	42	13	2	33	57	1.267	3.83	102	3.60	.247	2	.286	-0	7	0.0
1988 SF-N	3	8	.273	64	0	0	0	11	92^1	74	33	30	7	1	23	58	1.051	2.92	112	2.35	.225	0	.000	3	8	0.3
1989* SF-N	2	4	.333	70	0	0	0	20	107	93	38	32	11	1	22	71	1.075	2.69	125	2.64	.233	0	.000	6	11	0.5
1990 SD-N	7	5	.583	56	0	0	0	23	78^2	68	26	22	10	1	22	60	1.144	2.52	152	2.97	.228	1	.250	11	13	1.2
1991 SD-N	1	6	.143	54	0	0	0	23	69	74	35	30	5	1	14	48	1.275	3.91	97	3.51	.285	0	.000	-1	7	-0.2
1992 SD-N	13	9	.591	27	27	0	0	0	163^1	180	76	67	16	0	35	81	1.316	3.69	97	3.92	.285	4	.077	-2	9	-0.5
Bal-A	1	3	.250	5	5	1	0	0	33	34	19	15	3	0	6	23	1.212	4.09	98	3.34	.268	0	....	-0	1	0.0
1993 Tex-A	3	9	.250	52	8	0	0	0	83^1	102	57	56	17	1	28	58	1.560	6.05	69	5.89	.304	0	....	-16	0	-1.6
1994 Cal-A	1	1	.500	30	0	0	0	1	34^2	50	20	18	7	0	12	27	1.788	4.67	104	7.39	.350	0	....	1	2	0.1
Total 12	58	72	.446	696	45	1	0	101	1145^2	1108	490	436	120	11	322	719	1.248	3.43	109	3.50	.257	16	.121	31	91	3.1
• LEFTWICH, Phil	Philip Dale Leftwich b: 5/19/1969, Lynchburg, VA BR/TR, 6'5", 205 lbs. Deb: 7/29/1993																									
1993 Cal-A	4	6	.400	12	12	1	0	0	80^2	81	35	34	5	3	27	31	1.339	3.79	119	3.73	.262	0	....	5	5	0.5
1994 Cal-A	5	10	.333	20	20	1	0	0	114	127	75	72	16	3	42	67	1.482	5.68	86	5.02	.283	0	....	-11	5	-1.0
1996 Cal-A	0	1	.000	2	2	0	0	0	7^1	12	9	6	1	0	3	4	2.045	7.36	67	8.66	.375	0	....	-2	0	-0.2
Total 3	9	17	.346	34	34	2	0	0	202	220	119	112	22	6	72	102	1.446	4.99	95	4.64	.279	0	....	-7	10	-0.6
• LEHENY, Regis	Regis Francis Leheny b: 1/5/1908, Pittsburgh, PA d: 11/2/1976, Pittsburgh, PA BL/TL, 6'.5", 180 lbs. Deb: 5/21/1932																									
1932 Bos-A	0	0	....	2	0	0	0	0	2^2	5	5	5	0	0	3	1	3.000	16.88	27	11.27	.417	0	.000	-4	0	-0.3
• LEHEW, Jim	James Anthony Lehew b: 8/19/1937, Baltimore, MD BR/TR, 6', 185 lbs. Deb: 9/13/1961																									
1961 Bal-A	0	0	....	2	0	0	0	0	2	1	0	0	0	0	0	0	.500	0.00	....	0.54	.167	0	....	1	0	0.1
1962 Bal-A	0	0	....	6	0	0	0	0	9^2	10	3	2	0	0	3	2	1.345	1.86	202	3.43	.303	0	.000	2	1	0.2
Total 2	0	0	....	8	0	0	0	0	11^2	11	3	2	0	0	3	2	1.200	1.54	244	2.93	.282	0	.000	3	1	0.3
• LEHMAN, Ken	Kenneth Karl Lehman b: 6/10/1928, Seattle, WA BL/TL, 6', 186 lbs. Deb: 9/5/1952																									
1952* Bro-N	1	2	.333	4	3	0	0	0	15^1	19	11	9	1	0	6	7	1.630	5.28	69	5.00	.297	0	.000	-3	0	-0.3
1956 Bro-N	2	3	.400	25	4	0	0	0	49^1	65	35	31	11	0	23	29	1.784	5.66	70	7.17	.325	3	.300	-10	0	-1.0
1957 Bro-N	0	0	....	3	0	0	0	0	7	7	0	0	0	0	1	3	1.143	0.00	....	2.52	.259	1	.500	3	1	0.4
Bal-A	8	3	.727	30	3	1	0	6	68	57	21	21	1	0	22	32	1.162	2.78	129	2.38	.232	4	.200	5	9	0.7
1958 Bal-A	2	1	.667	31	1	1	0	0	62	64	26	24	5	2	18	36	1.323	3.48	103	3.74	.276	1	.071	1	4	0.0
1961 Phi-N	1	1	.500	41	2	0	0	1	63^1	61	32	30	6	1	25	27	1.358	4.26	95	3.71	.260	0	.000	-2	3	-0.3
Total 5	14	10	.583	134	13	2	0	7	265	273	125	115	24	3	95	134	1.389	3.91	98	4.06	.272	9	.161	-6	17	-0.6
• LEHR, Norm	Norman Carl Michael "King" Lehr b: 5/28/1901, Rochester, NY d: 7/17/1968, Livonia, NY BR/TR, 6', 168 lbs. Deb: 5/20/1926																									
1926 Cle-A	0	0	....	4	0	0	0	0	14^2	11	5	5	0	0	4	4	1.023	3.07	132	1.69	.216	0	.000	1	1	0.1
• LEIBRANDT, Charlie	Charles Louis Leibrandt b: 10/4/1956, Chicago, IL BR/TL, 6'3", 200 lbs. Deb: 9/17/1979																									
1979* Cin-N	0	0	....	3	0	0	0	0	4^1	2	2	0	0	0	2	1	.923	0.00	....	1.31	.154	0	....	2	0	0.2
1980 Cin-N	10	9	.526	36	27	5	2	0	173^2	200	84	82	15	2	54	62	1.463	4.25	84	4.53	.292	11	.196	-11	7	-1.0
1981 Cin-N	1	1	.500	7	4	1	1	0	30	28	12	12	0	0	15	9	1.433	3.60	99	3.33	.262	0	.000	-0	2	-0.1
1982 Cin-N	5	7	.417	36	11	0	0	2	107^2	130	68	61	4	2	48	34	1.653	5.10	73	4.97	.308	2	.080	-17	1	-2.0
1984* KC-A	11	7	.611	23	23	0	0	0	143^2	158	65	58	11	3	38	53	1.364	3.63	111	3.96	.277	0	....	5	9	0.5
1985* KC-A	17	9	.654	33	33	8	3	0	237^2	223	86	71	17	2	68	108	1.224	2.69	155	3.14	.248	0	....	42	**24**	4.1
1986 KC-A	14	11	.560	35	34	8	1	0	231^1	238	112	105	18	4	63	108	1.301	4.09	104	3.67	.268	0	....	7	14	0.7
1987 KC-A	16	11	.593	35	35	8	3	0	240^1	235	104	91	23	1	74	151	1.286	3.41	134	3.55	.253	0	....	34	20	3.2
1988 KC-A	13	12	.520	35	35	7	2	0	243	244	98	86	20	4	62	125	1.259	3.19	125	3.53	.264	0	....	26	17	2.6
1989 KC-A	5	11	.313	33	27	3	1	0	161	196	98	92	13	2	54	73	1.553	5.14	75	4.98	.304	0	....	-21	2	-2.1
1990 Atl-N	9	11	.450	24	24	5	2	0	162^1	164	72	57	9	4	35	76	1.226	3.16	128	3.17	.261	9	.180	20	11	2.1
1991* Atl-N	15	13	.536	36	36	1	1	0	229^2	212	105	89	18	4	56	128	1.167	3.49	111	2.95	.245	3	.043	10	13	0.7
1992* Atl-N	15	7	.682	32	31	5	2	0	193	191	78	72	9	5	42	104	1.207	3.36	109	3.04	.258	7	.121	6	12	0.5
1993 Tex-A	9	10	.474	26	26	1	0	0	150^1	169	84	76	15	4	45	89	1.424	4.55	91	4.41	.284	0	....	-4	6	-0.4
Total 14	140	119	.541	394	346	52	18	2	2308	2390	1068	952	172	37	656	1121	1.320	3.71	107	3.70	.268	32	.120	98	138	9.1
• LEIFIELD, Lefty	Albert Peter Leifield b: 9/5/1883, Trenton, IL d: 10/10/1970, Alexandria, VA BL/TL, 6'1", 165 lbs. Deb: 9/3/1905 C																									
1905 Pit-N	5	2	.714	8	7	6	1	0	56	52	23	18	0	4	14	10	1.179	2.89	103	2.73	.248	7	.350	-0	6	0.3
1906 Pit-N	18	13	.581	37	31	24	8	1	255^2	214	90	53	3	14	68	111	1.103	1.87	143	2.39	.231	11	.125	21	19	2.1
1907 Pit-N	20	16	.556	40	33	24	6	1	286	270	107	74	1	12	100	112	1.294	2.33	104	3.12	.256	15	.147	8	18	0.9
1908 Pit-N	15	14	.517	34	26	18	5	2	218^2	168	69	51	1	12	86	87	1.162	2.10	109	2.35	.212	17	.227	5	15	0.9
1909* Pit-N	19	8	.704	32	27	13	3	0	201^2	172	76	53	4	6	54	43	1.121	2.37	109	2.38	.229	14	.192	2	16	0.4
1910 Pit-N	15	13	.536	40	30	13	3	2	218^1	197	84	64	6	10	67	64	1.209	2.64	119	3.02	.253	11	.183	11	17	1.2
1911 Pit-N	16	16	.500	42	37	26	2	1	318	301	114	93	7	16	82	111	1.204	2.63	130	3.04	.260	24	.235	22	24	2.9
1912 Pit-N	1	2	.333	6	1	1	1	0	23^2	29	15	11	0	2	10	8	1.648	4.18	78	4.74	.302	1	.143	-3	0	-0.2
Chi-N	7	2	.778	13	9	4	1	0	70^2	68	26	19	0	3	21	23	1.259	2.42	137	2.90	.258	3	.115	5	7	0.4
Yr.	8	4	.667	19	10	5	2	0	94^1	97	41	30	0	5	31	31	1.357	2.86	115	3.36	.270	4	.121	3	7	0.2
1913 Chi-N	0	1	.000	6	1	0	0	0	21^1	28	14	13	0	0	5	4	1.547	5.48	58	4.48	.329	0	.000	-6	0	-0.7
1918 StL-A	2	6	.250	15	6	3	1	0	67	61	23	19	1	2	19	22	1.194	2.55	107	2.78	.252	1	.053	1	4	-0.1

YEAR TM-L	W	L	PCT	G	GS	CG	SH	SV	IP	H	R	ER	HR	HB	BB	SO	RAT	ERA	ERA+	CERA	OAV	BH	AVG	PR+	WS	TPW
1919 StL-A	6	4	.600	19	9	6	2	0	92	96	40	30	4	4	25	18	1.315	2.93	113	3.59	.270	3	.100	3	6	0.1
1920 StL-A	0	0	....	4	0	0	0	0	9	17	12	7	0	0	3	3	2.222	7.00	56	8.51	.405	0	.000	-3	0	-0.3
Total 12	124	97	.561	296	217	138	33	7	1838	1673	693	505	27	85	554	616	1.212	2.47	115	2.87	.248	107	.175	66	132	7.8
• LEIPER, Dave	David Paul Leiper b: 6/18/1962, Whittier, CA BL/TL, 6'1", 160 lbs. Deb: 9/2/1984																									
1984 Oak-A	1	0	1.000	8	0	0	0	0	7	12	7	7	2	0	5	3	2.429	9.00	42	11.26	.353	0	....	-4	0	-0.4
1986 Oak-A	2	2	.500	33	0	0	0	1	31^2	28	17	17	3	2	18	15	1.453	4.83	80	4.21	.252	0	....	-3	1	-0.3
1987 Oak-A	2	1	.667	45	0	0	0	1	52^1	49	28	22	6	1	18	33	1.280	3.78	109	3.62	.246	0	....	3	4	0.2
SD-N	1	0	1.000	12	0	0	0	1	16	16	8	8	2	0	5	10	1.313	4.50	88	3.95	.267	0	....	-1	1	-0.1
1988 SD-N	3	0	1.000	35	0	0	0	1	54	45	19	13	1	0	14	33	1.093	2.17	157	2.06	.231	1	.500	7	5	0.7
1989 SD-N	0	1	.000	22	0	0	0	0	28^2	40	19	16	2	2	20	7	2.093	5.02	70	7.56	.333	0	.000	-5	0	-0.6
1994 Oak-A	0	0	....	26	0	0	0	1	18^2	13	4	4	0	1	6	14	1.018	1.93	229	1.74	.206	0	....	5	2	0.5
1995 Oak-A	1	1	.500	24	0	0	0	0	22^2	23	10	9	3	1	13	10	1.588	3.57	124	5.19	.258	0	....	2	1	0.2
Mon-N	0	2	.000	26	0	0	0	2	22	16	8	7	2	0	6	12	1.000	2.86	150	2.11	.200	0	.000	4	3	0.4
1996 Phi-N	2	0	1.000	26	0	0	0	0	21	31	16	15	4	0	7	10	1.810	6.43	67	7.36	.348	0	....	-5	0	-0.5
Mon-N	0	1	.000	7	0	0	0	0	4	9	5	5	0	0	2	3	2.750	11.25	38	11.46	.474	0	....	-3	0	-0.3
Yr.	2	1	.667	33	0	0	0	0	25	40	21	20	4	0	9	13	1.960	7.20	60	8.02	.370	0	....	-8	0	-0.8
Total 8	12	8	.600	264	0	0	0	7	278	282	141	123	25	7	114	150	1.424	3.98	99	4.28	.266	1	.250	-2	17	-0.2
• LEIPER, Jack	John Henry Thomas Leiper b: 12/23/1867, Chester, PA d: 8/23/1960, West Goshen, PA BL/TL, 5'11" Deb: 9/4/1891																									
1891 Col-a	2	2	.500	6	5	4	0	0	45	41	43	27	3	4	39	19	1.778	5.40	64	....	.235	3	.143	-11	0	-1.1
• LEISTER, John	John William Leister b: 1/3/1961, San Antonio, TX BR/TR, 6'2", 200 lbs. Deb: 5/28/1987																									
1987 Bos-A	0	2	.000	8	6	0	0	0	30^1	49	31	31	9	0	12	16	2.011	9.20	49	9.71	.368	0	....	-16	0	-1.5
1990 Bos-A	0	0	....	2	1	0	0	0	5^2	7	5	3	0	0	4	3	1.941	4.76	85	5.50	.304	0	....	-0	0	0.0
Total 2	0	2	.000	10	7	0	0	0	36	56	36	34	9	0	16	19	2.000	8.50	53	9.05	.359	0	....	-16	0	-1.5
• LEITER, Al	Alois Terry Leiter b: 10/23/1965, Toms River, NJ BL/TL, 6'2", 215 lbs. Deb: 9/15/1987																									
1987 NY-A	2	2	.500	4	4	0	0	0	22^2	24	16	16	2	0	15	28	1.721	6.35	69	5.41	.273	0	....	-5	0	-0.5
1988 NY-A	4	4	.500	14	14	0	0	0	57^1	49	27	25	7	5	33	60	1.430	3.92	100	4.51	.231	0	....	1	3	0.1
1989 NY-A	1	2	.333	4	4	0	0	0	26^2	23	20	18	1	2	21	22	1.650	6.08	64	4.62	.235	0	....	-7	0	-0.7
Tor-A	0	0	....	1	1	0	0	0	6^2	9	3	3	1	0	2	4	1.650	4.05	89	5.96	.310	0	....	-0	0	0.0
Yr.	1	2	.333	5	5	0	0	0	33^1	32	23	21	2	2	23	26	1.650	5.67	68	4.89	.252	0	....	-7	0	-0.7
1990 Tor-A	0	0	....	4	0	0	0	0	6^1	1	0	0	0	0	2	5	.474	0.00	....	0.33	.050	0	....	3	1	0.3
1991 Tor-A	0	0	....	3	0	0	0	0	1^2	3	5	5	0	0	5	1	4.800	27.00	16	19.88	.429	0	....	-4	0	-0.4
1992 Tor-A	0	0	....	1	0	0	0	0	1	1	1	1	0	0	2	0	3.000	9.00	45	8.07	.200	0	....	-1	0	-0.1
1993* Tor-A	9	6	.600	34	12	1	1	2	105	93	52	48	8	4	56	66	1.419	4.11	105	3.94	.240	0	....	3	8	0.3
1994 Tor-A	6	7	.462	20	20	1	0	0	111^2	125	68	63	6	2	65	100	1.701	5.08	95	5.14	.285	0	....	-2	5	-0.2
1995 Tor-A	11	11	.500	28	28	2	1	0	183	162	80	74	15	6	108	153	1.475	3.64	129	4.18	.238	0	....	21	14	2.0
1996 Fla-N★	16	12	.571	33	33	2	1	0	215^1	153	74	70	14	11	119	200	1.263	2.93	139	3.09	**.202**	7	.100	24	19	2.1
1997* Fla-N	11	9	.550	27	27	0	0	0	151^1	133	78	73	13	12	91	132	1.480	4.34	93	4.39	.241	5	.104	-6	7	-0.7
1998 NY-N	17	6	.739	28	28	4	2	0	193	151	55	53	8	11	71	174	1.150	2.47	167	2.65	.216	6	.105	35	21	3.5
1999* NY-N	13	12	.520	32	32	1	1	0	213	209	107	100	19	9	93	162	1.418	4.23	104	4.17	.262	6	.105	2	11	0.0
2000* NY-N★	16	8	.667	31	31	2	1	0	208	176	84	74	19	11	76	200	1.212	3.20	138	3.23	.228	3	.052	29	17	2.4
2001 NY-N	11	11	.500	29	29	0	0	0	187^1	178	81	69	18	4	46	142	1.196	3.31	125	3.26	.252	4	.065	16	14	1.3
2002 NY-N	13	13	.500	33	33	2	2	0	204^1	194	99	79	23	8	69	172	1.287	3.48	114	3.75	.250	8	.151	13	11	1.4
2003 NY-N	15	9	.625	30	30	1	1	0	180^2	176	83	80	15	9	94	139	1.494	3.99	104	4.40	.260	1	.019	4	10	0.0
Total 17	145	112	.564	356	326	16	10	2	2075	1860	933	851	169	94	968	1760	1.363	3.69	115	3.81	.241	40	.087	127	141	10.8
• LEITER, Mark	Mark Edward Leiter b: 4/13/1963, Joliet, IL BR/TR, 6'3", 210 lbs. Deb: 7/24/1990																									
1990 NY-A	1	1	.500	8	3	0	0	0	26^1	33	20	20	5	2	9	21	1.595	6.84	58	6.42	.314	0	....	-8	0	-0.9
1991 Det-A	9	7	.563	38	15	1	0	1	134^2	125	66	63	16	6	50	103	1.300	4.21	99	3.79	.245	0	....	-1	7	-0.1
1992 Det-A	8	5	.615	35	14	1	0	0	112	116	57	52	9	3	43	75	1.420	4.18	95	4.22	.277	0	....	-2	5	-0.2
1993 Det-A	6	6	.500	27	13	1	0	0	106^2	111	61	56	17	3	44	70	1.453	4.73	91	4.79	.267	0	....	-5	4	-0.5
1994 Cal-A	4	7	.364	40	7	0	0	2	95^1	99	56	50	13	9	35	71	1.406	4.72	103	4.64	.265	0	....	1	6	0.1
1995 SF-N	10	12	.455	30	29	7	1	0	195^2	185	91	83	19	17	55	129	1.227	3.82	107	3.65	.254	6	.098	4	10	0.2
1996 SF-N	4	10	.286	23	22	1	0	0	135^1	151	93	78	25	9	50	118	1.485	5.19	79	5.45	.283	6	.143	-17	2	-1.8
Mon-N	4	2	.667	12	12	1	0	0	69^2	68	35	34	12	7	19	46	1.249	4.39	98	4.24	.254	2	.080	-0	4	-0.1
Yr.	8	12	.400	35	34	2	0	0	205	219	128	112	37	16	69	164	1.405	4.92	85	5.03	.273	8	.119	-18	6	-1.9
1997 Phi-N	10	17	.370	31	31	3	0	0	182^2	216	132	115	25	9	64	148	1.533	5.67	75	5.28	.292	6	.118	-28	2	-2.9
1998 Phi-N	7	5	.583	69	0	0	0	23	88^2	67	36	35	8	8	47	84	1.286	3.55	122	3.45	.216	0	.000	7	14	0.7
1999 Sea-A	0	0	....	2	0	0	0	0	1^1	2	1	1	0	0	0	1	1.500	6.75	74	4.47	.333	0	....	-0	0	0.0
2001 Mil-N	2	1	.667	20	3	0	0	0	36	32	16	15	6	2	8	26	1.111	3.75	114	3.31	.232	1	.143	2	2	0.2
Total 11	65	73	.471	335	149	15	1	26	1184^1	1205	664	602	155	75	424	892	1.375	4.57	92	4.43	.265	21	.112	-47	56	-5.2
• LEITH, Bill	William "Shady Bill" Leith b: 5/31/1873, Matteawan, NY d: 7/16/1940, Beacon, NY TL, 6'1" Deb: 9/25/1899																									
1899 Was-N	0	0	....	1	0	0	0	0	2	4	5	4	0	1	2	1	3.000	18.00	22	14.08	.413	0	.000	-3	0	-0.3
• LEITNER, Doc	George Aloysius Leitner b: 9/14/1865, Piermont, NY d: 5/18/1937, New York, NY BR/TR, 5'11.5", 185 lbs. Deb: 8/10/1887																									
1887 Ind-N	2	6	.250	8	8	8	0	0	65	110	66	41	6	0	41	27	1.692	5.68	72	....	.364	4	.148	-12	1	-1.2
• LEITNER, Dummy	George Michael Leitner b: 6/19/1871, Parkton, MD d: 2/20/1960, Baltimore, MD BL/TR, 5'7", 120 lbs. Deb: 6/29/1901																									
1901 Phi-A	0	0	....	1	0	0	0	0	2	1	0	0	0	0	1	1	1.000	0.00	....	1.38	.148	0	.000	1	0	0.1
NY-N	0	2	.000	2	2	2	0	0	18	27	9	9	0	1	4	3	1.722	4.50	73	5.79	.344	1	.143	-2	0	-0.2
1902 Cle-A	0	0	....	1	1	0	0	0	8	11	4	4	0	0	1	0	1.500	4.50	76	4.35	.327	1	.250	-1	0	-0.1
Chi-A	0	0	....	1	0	0	0	0	4	9	7	6	0	2	2	0	2.750	13.50	25	13.78	.443	0	.000	-5	0	-0.4
Yr.	0	0	....	2	1	0	0	0	12	20	11	10	0	2	3	0	1.917	7.50	45	7.49	.370	1	.143	-6	0	-0.5
Total 2	0	2	.000	5	3	2	0	0	32	48	20	19	0	3	8	4	1.750	5.34	63	6.15	.345	2	.133	-7	0	-0.7
• LELIVELT, Bill	William John Lelivelt b: 10/21/1884, Chicago, IL d: 2/14/1968, Chicago, IL BR/TR, 6', 168 lbs. Deb: 7/19/1909																									
1909 Det-A	0	1	.000	4	2	1	0	1	20	27	12	10	0	0	2	4	1.450	4.50	56	4.22	.325	2	.333	-4	0	-0.4
1910 Det-A	0	1	.000	1	1	1	0	0	9	6	4	1	0	0	3	2	1.000	1.00	263	1.73	.207	1	.500	2	1	0.3
Total 2	0	2	.000	5	3	2	0	1	29	33	16	11	0	0	5	6	1.310	3.41	74	3.44	.294	3	.375	-3	1	-0.1
• LEMANCZYK, Dave	David Lawrence Lemanczyk b: 8/17/1950, Syracuse, NY BR/TR, 6'4", 235 lbs. Deb: 4/15/1973																									
1973 Det-A	0	0	....	1	0	0	0	0	2^1	4	3	3	0	0	0	0	1.714	11.57	35	5.71	.364	0	....	-2	0	-0.2
1974 Det-A	2	1	.667	22	3	0	0	0	78^2	79	43	35	12	2	44	52	1.564	4.00	95	5.13	.261	0	....	-1	4	-0.1
1975 Det-A	2	7	.222	26	6	4	0	0	109	120	62	54	8	3	46	67	1.523	4.46	90	4.55	.281	0	....	-3	4	-0.3
1976 Det-A	4	6	.400	20	10	1	0	0	81^1	86	47	46	7	0	34	51	1.475	5.09	73	4.38	.271	0	....	-12	2	-1.2
1977 Tor-A	13	16	.448	34	34	11	0	0	252	278	143	119	20	4	87	105	1.448	4.25	99	4.35	.282	0	....	5	13	0.5
1978 Tor-A	4	14	.222	29	20	3	0	0	136^2	170	97	95	16	3	65	62	1.720	6.26	63	6.18	.313	0	....	-35	0	-3.6
1979 Tor-A★	8	10	.444	22	20	11	3	0	143	137	65	59	12	6	45	63	1.273	3.71	117	3.60	.258	0	....	9	10	0.9
1980 Tor-A	2	5	.286	10	8	0	0	0	43^1	57	29	26	4	0	15	10	1.662	5.40	80	5.72	.322	0	....	-6	1	-0.6
Cal-A	2	4	.333	21	2	0	0	0	66^2	81	40	32	8	2	27	19	1.620	4.32	91	5.57	.301	0	....	-3	2	-0.3
Yr.	4	9	.308	31	10	0	0	0	110	138	69	58	12	2	42	29	1.636	4.75	86	5.63	.309	0	....	-8	3	-0.8
Total 8	37	63	.370	185	103	30	3	0	913	1012	529	469	87	20	363	429	1.506	4.62	87	4.76	.284	0	....	-47	36	-4.9
• LEMASTER, Denny	Denver Clayton Lemaster b: 2/25/1939, Corona, CA BR/TL, 6'1", 185 lbs. Deb: 7/15/1962																									
1962 Mil-N	3	4	.429	17	12	4	1	0	86^2	75	36	29	11	3	32	69	1.235	3.01	126	3.61	.238	4	.121	7	6	0.6
1963 Mil-N	11	14	.440	46	31	10	1	1	237	199	87	80	30	1	85	190	1.198	3.04	106	3.17	.227	14	.189	1	14	0.4
1964 Mil-N	17	11	.607	39	35	9	3	1	221	216	112	102	27	4	75	185	1.317	4.15	85	3.87	.252	9	.134	-16	8	-1.6

YEAR	TM-L	W	L	PCT	G	GS	CG	SH	SV	IP	H	R	ER	HR	HB	BB	SO	RAT	ERA	ERA+	CERA	OAV	BH	AVG	PR+	WS	TPW
1965	Mil-N	7	13	.350	32	23	4	1	0	146^1	140	75	72	12	3	58	111	1.353	4.43	79	3.71	.251	4	.089	-16	4	-1.8
1966	Atl-N	11	8	.579	27	27	10	3	0	171	170	78	71	25	1	41	139	1.234	3.74	97	3.71	.258	7	.119	-2	8	-0.3
1967	Atl-N★	9	9	.500	31	31	8	2	0	215^1	184	86	80	20	3	72	148	1.189	3.34	99	3.00	.229	7	.104	-2	12	-0.4
1968	Hou-N	10	15	.400	33	32	7	2	0	224	231	79	70	11	4	72	146	1.353	2.81	105	3.55	.263	2	.031	8	13	0.5
1969	Hou-N	13	17	.433	38	37	11	1	1	244^2	232	97	86	20	1	72	173	1.243	3.16	112	3.19	.246	15	.170	13	15	1.7
1970	Hou-N	7	12	.368	39	21	3	0	3	162	169	88	82	22	2	65	103	1.444	4.56	85	4.53	.268	8	.178	-12	6	-1.0
1971	Hou-N	0	2	.000	42	0	0	0	2	60	59	23	23	4	1	22	28	1.350	3.45	97	3.58	.262	1	.167	-1	3	-0.1
1972	Mon-N	2	0	1.000	13	0	0	0	0	19^2	28	17	17	2	1	6	13	1.729	7.78	46	6.25	.329	1	.333	-9	0	-0.9
Total	11	90	105	.462	357	249	66	14	8	1787^2	1703	778	712	184	24	600	1305	1.288	3.58	96	3.57	.249	72	.130	-28	89	-2.9

• LEMAY, Dick Richard Paul LeMay b: 8/28/1938, Cincinnati, OH BL/TL, 6'3", 190 lbs. Deb: 6/13/1961

YEAR	TM-L	W	L	PCT	G	GS	CG	SH	SV	IP	H	R	ER	HR	HB	BB	SO	RAT	ERA	ERA+	CERA	OAV	BH	AVG	PR+	WS	TPW
1961	SF-N	3	6	.333	27	5	1	0	3	83^1	65	35	33	11	4	36	54	1.212	3.56	107	3.28	.217	2	.077	3	5	0.1
1962	SF-N	0	1	.000	9	0	0	0	1	9^1	9	8	8	2	0	9	5	1.929	7.71	49	6.93	.265	0	....	-4	0	-0.4
1963	Chi-N	0	1	.000	9	1	0	0	0	15^1	26	9	9	1	0	4	10	1.957	5.28	66	7.20	.394	0	.000	-3	0	-0.4
Total	3	3	8	.273	45	6	1	0	4	108	100	52	50	14	4	49	69	1.380	4.17	90	4.15	.250	2	.071	-4	5	-0.6

• LEMON, Bob Robert Granville Lemon b: 9/22/1920, San Bernardino, CA d: 1/11/2000, Long Beach, CA BL/TR, 6', 185 lbs. Deb: 9/9/1941 M/C HOF: 1976 ♦

YEAR	TM-L	W	L	PCT	G	GS	CG	SH	SV	IP	H	R	ER	HR	HB	BB	SO	RAT	ERA	ERA+	CERA	OAV	BH	AVG	PR+	WS	TPW
1946	Cle-A	4	5	.444	32	5	1	0	1	94	77	40	26	1	0	68	39	1.543	2.49	133	3.51	.229	16	.180	9	6	0.7
1947	Cle-A	11	5	.688	37	15	6	1	3	167^1	150	68	64	7	4	97	65	1.476	3.44	101	3.77	.242	18	.321	-2	13	0.8
1948*	Cle-A★	20	14	.588	43	37	**20**	**10**	2	**293^2**	231	104	92	12	3	129	147	1.226	2.82	144	**2.65**	.216	34	.286	34	26	4.5
1949	Cle-A★	22	10	.688	37	33	22	2	1	279^2	211	101	93	19	6	137	138	1.244	2.99	133	2.88	.211	29	.269	28	**31**	4.2
1950	Cle-A★	**23**	11	.676	44	**37**	**22**	3	3	**288**	281	144	123	28	2	146	**170**	1.483	3.84	113	4.28	.257	37	.272	14	**25**	2.8
1951	Cle-A★	17	14	.548	42	**34**	17	1	2	263^1	244	119	103	19	2	124	132	1.397	3.52	108	3.65	.244	21	.206	8	19	1.2
1952	Cle-A★	22	11	.667	42	**36**	**28**	5	4	**309^2**	236	104	86	15	6	105	131	1.101	2.50	134	**2.28**	**.208**	28	.226	32	25	3.9
1953	Cle-A★	21	15	.583	41	36	23	5	1	**286^2**	283	119	107	16	11	110	98	1.371	3.36	112	3.74	.262	26	.232	12	22	2.0
1954*	Cle-A★	**23**	7	.767	36	33	**21**	2	0	258^1	228	95	78	12	4	92	110	1.239	2.72	135	2.89	.238	21	.214	24	**24**	**3.0**
1955	Cle-A	**18**	10	.643	35	31	5	0	2	211^1	218	103	91	17	5	74	100	1.382	3.88	103	4.00	.266	19	.244	2	15	0.8
1956	Cle-A	20	14	.588	39	35	**21**	2	3	255^1	230	103	86	23	6	89	94	1.249	3.03	139	3.34	.239	18	.194	34	23	3.8
1957	Cle-A	6	11	.353	21	17	2	0	0	117^1	129	70	60	9	7	64	45	1.645	4.60	81	5.19	.287	3	.065	-10	3	-1.4
1958	Cle-A	0	1	.000	11	1	0	0	0	25^1	41	15	15	3	1	16	8	2.250	5.33	68	9.34	.376	3	.231	-5	0	-0.5
Total	13	207	128	.618	460	350	188	31	22	2850	2559	1185	1024	181	57	1251	1277	1.337	3.23	119	3.44	.241	274	.232	180	232	26.0

• LEMONDS, Dave David Lee Lemonds b: 7/5/1948, Charlotte, NC BL/TL, 6'1.5", 180 lbs. Deb: 6/30/1969

YEAR	TM-L	W	L	PCT	G	GS	CG	SH	SV	IP	H	R	ER	HR	HB	BB	SO	RAT	ERA	ERA+	CERA	OAV	BH	AVG	PR+	WS	TPW
1969	Chi-N	0	1	.000	2	1	0	0	0	4^2	5	2	2	0	0	5	0	2.143	3.86	104	7.14	.313	0	.000	0	0	0.0
1972	Chi-A	4	7	.364	31	18	0	0	0	94^2	87	39	31	6	1	38	69	1.320	2.95	106	3.39	.247	3	.120	4	5	0.4
Total	2	4	8	.333	33	19	0	0	0	99^1	92	41	33	6	1	43	69	1.359	2.99	106	3.57	.250	3	.115	4	5	0.4

• LEMONGELLO, Mark Mark Lemongello b: 7/21/1955, Jersey City, NJ BR/TR, 6'1", 180 lbs. Deb: 9/14/1976

YEAR	TM-L	W	L	PCT	G	GS	CG	SH	SV	IP	H	R	ER	HR	HB	BB	SO	RAT	ERA	ERA+	CERA	OAV	BH	AVG	PR+	WS	TPW
1976	Hou-N	3	1	.750	4	4	1	0	0	29	26	12	9	2	0	7	9	1.138	2.79	114	2.52	.236	0	.000	1	2	0.1
1977	Hou-N	9	14	.391	34	30	5	0	0	214^2	237	88	83	20	3	52	83	1.346	3.48	102	4.04	.281	6	.087	3	10	-0.1
1978	Hou-N	9	14	.391	33	30	9	1	1	210^1	204	100	92	20	9	66	77	1.284	3.94	84	3.66	.259	11	.172	-10	7	-1.0
1979	Tor-A	1	9	.100	18	10	2	0	0	83	97	64	58	14	3	34	40	1.578	6.29	69	5.69	.299	0	....	-18	0	-1.8
Total	4	22	38	.367	89	74	17	1	1	537	564	264	242	56	15	159	209	1.346	4.06	89	4.07	.273	17	.121	-25	19	-2.8

• LENNON, Ed Edward Francis Lennon b: 8/17/1897, Philadelphia, PA d: 9/13/1947, Philadelphia, PA BR/TR, 5'11", 170 lbs. Deb: 6/30/1928

YEAR	TM-L	W	L	PCT	G	GS	CG	SH	SV	IP	H	R	ER	HR	HB	BB	SO	RAT	ERA	ERA+	CERA	OAV	BH	AVG	PR+	WS	TPW
1928	Phi-N	0	0	....	5	0	0	0	0	12^1	19	14	12	0	0	10	6	2.351	8.76	49	7.90	.373	0	.000	-6	0	-0.6

• LEON, Danilo Danilo Enrique (Lineco) Leon b: 4/3/1967, La Concepcion, Venezuela BR/TR, 6'1", 170 lbs. Deb: 6/6/1992

YEAR	TM-L	W	L	PCT	G	GS	CG	SH	SV	IP	H	R	ER	HR	HB	BB	SO	RAT	ERA	ERA+	CERA	OAV	BH	AVG	PR+	WS	TPW
1992	Tex-A	1	1	.500	15	0	0	0	0	18^1	18	14	12	5	3	10	15	1.527	5.89	64	6.61	.254	0	....	-4	0	-0.4

• LEON, Izzy Isidoro (Becerra) Leon b: 1/4/1911, Cruces, Cuba d: 7/25/2002, Miami, FL BR/TR, 5'10", 160 lbs. Deb: 6/21/1945

YEAR	TM-L	W	L	PCT	G	GS	CG	SH	SV	IP	H	R	ER	HR	HB	BB	SO	RAT	ERA	ERA+	CERA	OAV	BH	AVG	PR+	WS	TPW
1945	Phi-N	0	4	.000	14	4	0	0	0	38^2	49	25	23	3	0	19	11	1.759	5.35	72	5.73	.312	1	.111	-6	0	-0.6

• LEON, Max Maximino (Molino) Leon b: 2/4/1950, Pozo Hondo, Mexico BR/TR, 5'10", 170 lbs. Deb: 7/18/1973

YEAR	TM-L	W	L	PCT	G	GS	CG	SH	SV	IP	H	R	ER	HR	HB	BB	SO	RAT	ERA	ERA+	CERA	OAV	BH	AVG	PR+	WS	TPW
1973	Atl-N	2	2	.500	12	1	1	0	0	27	30	18	16	6	3	9	18	1.444	5.33	74	5.62	.278	2	.286	-4	1	-0.4
1974	Atl-N	4	7	.364	34	2	1	1	3	75	68	22	22	5	1	14	38	1.093	2.64	143	2.61	.242	2	.133	8	7	0.8
1975	Atl-N	2	1	.667	50	1	0	0	6	85	90	52	39	5	7	33	53	1.447	4.13	91	4.16	.274	3	.333	-1	4	0.0
1976	Atl-N	2	4	.333	30	0	0	0	3	36	32	15	11	2	2	15	16	1.306	2.75	138	3.25	.234	0	.000	5	4	0.5
1977	Atl-N	4	4	.500	31	9	0	0	1	81^2	89	42	36	9	9	25	44	1.396	3.97	112	4.70	.280	6	.316	7	6	0.8
1978	Atl-N	0	0	....	5	0	0	0	0	5^2	6	4	4	1	1	4	1	1.765	6.35	64	6.64	.273	0	....	-1	0	-0.1
Total	6	14	18	.438	162	13	2	1	13	310^1	315	153	128	28	23	100	170	1.337	3.71	107	3.99	.264	13	.250	13	22	1.5

• LEONARD, Dennis Dennis Patrick Leonard b: 5/18/1951, Brooklyn, NY BR/TR, 6'1", 190 lbs. Deb: 9/4/1974

YEAR	TM-L	W	L	PCT	G	GS	CG	SH	SV	IP	H	R	ER	HR	HB	BB	SO	RAT	ERA	ERA+	CERA	OAV	BH	AVG	PR+	WS	TPW
1974	KC-A	0	4	.000	5	4	0	0	0	22	28	15	13	0	3	12	8	1.818	5.32	72	6.09	.329	0	....	-3	0	-0.4
1975	KC-A	15	7	.682	32	30	8	0	0	212^1	212	98	89	18	9	90	146	1.422	3.77	102	4.25	.263	0	....	5	14	0.5
1976*	KC-A	17	10	.630	35	34	16	2	0	259	247	113	101	16	11	70	150	1.224	3.51	100	3.24	.255	0	....	-1	14	-0.1
1977*	KC-A	**20**	12	.625	38	37	21	5	1	292^2	246	117	99	18	8	79	244	1.110	3.04	133	2.61	.227	0	....	30	24	3.0
1978*	KC-A	21	17	.553	40	**40**	20	4	0	294^2	283	125	109	27	9	78	183	1.225	3.33	115	3.40	.254	0	....	14	19	1.4
1979	KC-A	14	12	.538	32	32	12	**5**	0	236	226	117	107	33	2	56	126	1.195	4.08	104	3.52	.253	0	....	3	14	0.2
1980*	KC-A	20	11	.645	38	**38**	9	3	0	280^1	271	127	118	30	1	80	155	1.252	3.79	107	3.48	.253	0	....	9	18	0.9
1981*	KC-A	13	11	.542	26	**26**	9	2	0	**201^2**	202	79	67	15	3	41	107	1.205	2.99	121	3.17	.258	0	....	15	14	1.5
1982	KC-A	10	6	.625	21	21	2	0	0	130^2	145	82	74	20	2	46	58	1.462	5.10	80	4.86	.279	0	....	-15	4	-1.5
1983	KC-A	6	3	.667	10	10	1	0	0	63	69	29	26	3	0	19	31	1.397	3.71	110	3.84	.277	0	....	3	4	0.3
1985	KC-A	0	0	....	2	0	0	0	0	2	1	0	0	0	0	0	1	.500	0.00	....	0.54	.143	0	....	1	0	0.1
1986	KC-A	8	13	.381	33	30	5	2	0	192^2	207	106	95	22	4	51	114	1.339	4.44	96	4.10	.275	0	....	-2	8	-0.2
Total	12	144	106	.576	312	302	103	23	1	2187	2137	1008	898	202	52	622	1323	1.262	3.70	107	3.54	.257	0	....	58	133	5.9

• LEONARD, Dutch Hubert Benjamin Leonard b: 4/16/1892, Birmingham, OH d: 7/11/1952, Fresno, CA BL/TL, 5'10.5", 185 lbs. Deb: 4/12/1913 C

YEAR	TM-L	W	L	PCT	G	GS	CG	SH	SV	IP	H	R	ER	HR	HB	BB	SO	RAT	ERA	ERA+	CERA	OAV	BH	AVG	PR+	WS	TPW
1913	Bos-A	14	17	.452	42	28	14	3	1	259^1	245	108	69	0	4	94	144	1.307	2.39	123	3.01	.253	15	.181	20	17	2.3
1914	Bos-A	19	5	.792	36	25	17	7	3	224^2	139	34	24	3	8	60	176	.886	**0.96**	**279**	**1.43**	**.180**	10	.147	39	29	4.2
1915*	Bos-A	15	7	.682	32	21	10	2	0	183^1	130	57	48	3	14	67	116	1.075	2.36	118	2.25	**.208**	14	.264	7	18	1.3
1916*	Bos-A	18	12	.600	48	34	17	6	6	274	244	87	72	6	8	66	144	1.131	2.36	117	2.62	.247	17	.200	16	22	1.9
1917	Bos-A	16	17	.485	37	36	26	4	1	294^1	257	88	71	4	5	72	144	1.118	2.17	119	2.35	.236	9	.087	12	22	0.6
1918	Bos-A	8	6	.571	16	16	12	3	0	125^2	119	51	38	0	2	53	47	1.369	2.72	98	3.10	.254	8	.186	-1	7	-0.1
1919	Det-A	14	13	.519	29	28	18	4	0	217^1	212	89	67	7	7	65	102	1.275	2.77	115	3.17	.254	11	.155	14	14	1.1
1920	Det-A	10	17	.370	28	27	10	3	0	191^1	192	107	92	8	8	63	76	1.333	4.33	86	3.68	.271	12	.211	-9	9	-0.7
1921	Det-A	11	13	.458	36	32	16	1	1	245	273	125	102	15	10	63	120	1.371	3.75	114	3.96	.286	14	.171	20	13	1.5
1924	Det-A	3	2	.600	9	7	3	0	1	51^1	68	32	26	1	1	18	26	1.675	4.56	90	5.24	.327	4	.211	-3	2	-0.3
1925	Det-A	11	4	.733	18	18	9	0	0	125^2	143	73	63	7	1	43	65	1.480	4.51	95	4.21	.289	10	.200	-3	7	-0.4
Total	11	139	113	.552	331	272	152	33	13	2192	2022	851	672	54	68	664	1160	1.225	2.76	117	2.95	.249	124	.173	111	160	11.5

• LEONARD, Dutch Emil John Leonard b: 3/25/1909, Auburn, IL d: 4/17/1983, Springfield, IL BR/TR, 6', 175 lbs. Deb: 8/31/1933

YEAR	TM-L	W	L	PCT	G	GS	CG	SH	SV	IP	H	R	ER	HR	HB	BB	SO	RAT	ERA	ERA+	CERA	OAV	BH	AVG	PR+	WS	TPW
1933	Bro-N	2	3	.400	10	3	2	0	0	40	42	17	13	0	0	10	6	1.300	2.93	110	2.93	.261	0	.000	2	2	0.1
1934	Bro-N	14	11	.560	44	21	11	2	5	183^2	210	90	67	12	4	33	58	1.323	3.28	119	3.83	.286	12	.179	14	12	1.3
1935	Bro-N	2	9	.182	43	11	4	0	**8**	137^2	152	67	60	11	1	29	41	1.315	3.92	101	3.77	.280	1	.026	-1	7	-0.5
1936	Bro-N	0	0	....	16	0	0	0	1	32	34	18	13	2	0	5	8	1.219	3.66	113	3.01	.262	2	.400	2	2	0.3
1938	Was-A	12	15	.444	33	31	15	3	0	223^1	221	109	85	11	7	53	68	1.227	3.43	132	**3.08**	.256	19	.232	27	17	2.7
1939	Was-A	20	8	.714	34	34	21	2	0	269^1	273	124	106	16	5	59	88	1.233	3.54	123	3.16	.262	21	.221	22	21	2.0
1940	Was-A★	14	19	.424	35	35	23	2	0	289	328	136	112	19	2	78	124	1.405	3.49	120	4.04	.286	16	.158	26	20	2.0
1941	Was-A	18	13	.581	34	33	19	4	0	256	271	117	98	6	3	54	91	1.270	3.45	117	3.14	.270	9	.102	20	19	1.4
1942	Was-A	2	2	.500	6	5	1	1	0	35	28	16	16	1	0	5	15	.943	4.11	89	1.66	.214	1	.100	-0	1	-0.1

YEAR TM-L	W	L	PCT	G	GS	CG	SH	SV	IP	H	R	ER	HR	HB	BB	SO	RAT	ERA	ERA+	CERA	OAV	BH	AVG	PR+	WS	TPW
1943 Was-A★	11	13	.458	31	31	15	2	1	219^2	218	96	80	9	4	46	51	1.202	3.28	98	2.92	.257	7	.104	-2	10	-0.6
1944 Was-A★	14	14	.500	32	31	17	3	0	229^1	222	97	78	8	3	37	62	1.129	3.06	106	2.59	.252	18	.228	8	13	1.0
1945 Was-A★	17	7	.708	31	29	12	4	1	216	208	72	51	5	2	35	96	1.125	2.13	146	2.46	.248	18	.231	25	19	2.7
1946 Was-A	10	10	.500	26	23	7	2	0	161^2	182	85	64	9	4	36	62	1.348	3.56	94	3.78	.281	9	.170	-1	7	-0.2
1947 Phi-N	17	12	.586	32	29	19	3	0	235	224	86	70	14	2	57	103	1.196	2.68	150	3.03	.258	14	.175	33	23	3.2
1948 Phi-N	12	17	.414	34	31	16	1	0	225^2	226	85	63	9	4	54	92	1.241	2.51	157	3.16	.265	12	.145	36	19	3.4
1949 Chi-N	7	16	.304	33	28	10	1	0	180	198	94	83	4	7	43	83	1.339	4.15	97	3.45	.272	12	.203	1	9	0.2
1950 Chi-N	5	1	.833	35	1	0	0	6	74	70	41	31	7	2	27	28	1.311	3.77	111	3.57	.248	1	.063	5	7	0.4
1951 Chi-N★	10	6	.625	41	1	0	0	3	81^2	69	30	24	3	2	28	30	1.188	2.64	155	2.63	.234	0	.000	14	10	1.1
1952 Chi-N	2	2	.500	45	0	0	0	11	66^2	56	18	16	3	3	24	37	1.200	2.16	178	2.73	.235	2	.200	13	10	1.3
1953 Chi-N	2	3	.400	45	0	0	0	8	62^2	72	34	32	9	1	24	27	1.532	4.60	97	5.21	.289	3	.300	1	5	0.1
Total 20	**191**	**181**	**.513**	**640**	**377**	**192**	**30**	**44**	**3218^1**	**3304**	**1432**	**1162**	**158**	**56**	**737**	**1170**	**1.256**	**3.25**	**119**	**3.24**	**.265**	**177**	**.168**	**245**	**233**	**21.9**

• LEONARD, Elmer Elmer Ellsworth "Tiny" Leonard b: 11/12/1888, Napa, CA d: 5/27/1981, Napa, CA BR/TR, 6'3.5", 210 lbs. Deb: 6/22/1911

YEAR TM-L	W	L	PCT	G	GS	CG	SH	SV	IP	H	R	ER	HR	HB	BB	SO	RAT	ERA	ERA+	CERA	OAV	BH	AVG	PR+	WS	TPW
1911 Phi-A	2	2	.500	5	1	1	0	0	19	26	11	6	0	2	10	10	1.895	2.84	111	6.31	.329	2	.286	1	1	0.1

• LEONHARD, Dave David Paul Leonhard b: 1/22/1941, Arlington, VA BR/TR, 5'11", 165 lbs. Deb: 9/21/1967

YEAR TM-L	W	L	PCT	G	GS	CG	SH	SV	IP	H	R	ER	HR	HB	BB	SO	RAT	ERA	ERA+	CERA	OAV	BH	AVG	PR+	WS	TPW
1967 Bal-A	0	0	....	3	2	0	0	1	14^1	11	5	5	1	1	6	9	1.186	3.14	100	2.84	.200	0	.000	-0	1	-0.1
1968 Bal-A	7	7	.500	28	18	5	2	1	126^1	95	46	44	10	2	57	61	1.203	3.13	93	2.94	.216	4	.129	-5	6	-0.7
1969* Bal-A	7	4	.636	37	3	1	1	1	94	78	28	26	8	0	38	37	1.234	2.49	143	3.01	.228	2	.095	8	8	0.8
1970 Bal-A	0	0	....	23	0	0	0	1	28^1	32	18	16	5	0	18	14	1.765	5.08	72	6.22	.294	0	.000	-5	0	-0.5
1971* Bal-A	2	3	.400	12	6	1	1	1	54	51	18	17	5	1	19	18	1.296	2.83	118	3.65	.252	5	.278	2	4	0.4
1972 Bal-A	0	0	....	14	0	0	0	0	20	20	10	10	3	0	12	7	1.600	4.50	68	5.14	.260	1	1.000	-4	0	-0.3
Total 6	**16**	**14**	**.533**	**117**	**29**	**7**	**4**	**5**	**337**	**287**	**125**	**118**	**32**	**4**	**150**	**146**	**1.297**	**3.15**	**102**	**3.48**	**.234**	**12**	**.156**	**-4**	**19**	**-0.4**

• LEOPOLD, Rudy Rudolph Matas Leopold b: 7/27/1905, Grand Cane, LA d: 9/3/1965, Baton Rouge, LA BL/TL, 6', 160 lbs. Deb: 7/4/1928

YEAR TM-L	W	L	PCT	G	GS	CG	SH	SV	IP	H	R	ER	HR	HB	BB	SO	RAT	ERA	ERA+	CERA	OAV	BH	AVG	PR+	WS	TPW
1928 Chi-A	0	0	....	2	0	0	0	0	2^1	3	3	1	0	0	0	0	1.286	3.86	105	2.67	.273	0	.000	0	0	0.0

• LERCH, Randy Randy Louis Lerch b: 10/9/1954, Sacramento, CA BL/TL, 6'5", 190 lbs. Deb: 9/14/1975

YEAR TM-L	W	L	PCT	G	GS	CG	SH	SV	IP	H	R	ER	HR	HB	BB	SO	RAT	ERA	ERA+	CERA	OAV	BH	AVG	PR+	WS	TPW
1975 Phi-N	0	0	....	3	0	0	0	0	7	6	5	5	1	0	1	8	1.000	6.43	58	2.67	.231	0	....	-2	0	-0.2
1976 Phi-N	0	0	....	1	0	0	0	1	3	3	1	1	0	0	0	0	1.000	3.00	118	1.95	.250	1	1.000	0	1	0.1
1977 Phi-N	10	6	.625	32	28	3	0	0	168^2	207	102	95	20	1	75	81	**1.672**	5.07	79	5.81	.312	9	.167	-23	4	-2.3
1978* Phi-N	11	8	.579	33	28	5	0	0	184	183	89	81	15	1	70	96	1.375	3.96	90	3.86	.263	15	.250	-12	10	-0.5
1979 Phi-N	10	13	.435	37	35	6	1	0	214	228	98	89	20	3	60	92	1.346	3.74	102	4.02	.281	11	.153	-1	12	0.0
1980 Phi-N	4	14	.222	30	22	2	0	0	150	178	98	86	15	0	55	57	1.553	5.16	73	4.99	.302	12	.267	-23	1	-2.0
1981* Mil-A	7	9	.438	23	18	1	0	0	110^2	134	63	53	8	0	43	53	1.599	4.31	79	5.03	.303	0	....	-12	3	-1.3
1982 Mil-A	8	7	.533	21	20	1	1	0	108^2	123	68	60	12	3	51	33	1.601	4.97	76	5.28	.286	0	....	-16	2	-1.6
Mon-N	2	0	1.000	6	4	0	0	0	23^2	26	11	9	0	0	8	4	1.437	3.42	106	3.62	.289	2	.250	0	1	0.1
1983 Mon-N	1	3	.250	19	5	0	0	0	38^2	45	29	29	6	1	18	24	1.629	6.75	53	5.74	.292	2	.222	-14	0	-1.4
SF-N	1	0	1.000	7	0	0	0	0	10^2	9	4	4	1	0	8	6	1.594	3.38	105	4.35	.231	0	....	0	1	0.0
Yr.	2	3	.400	26	5	0	0	0	49^1	54	33	33	7	1	26	30	1.622	6.02	59	5.44	.280	2	.222	-14	1	-1.4
1984 SF-N	5	3	.625	37	4	0	0	2	72^1	80	36	34	3	1	36	48	1.604	4.23	83	4.61	.287	2	.133	-4	3	-0.4
1986 Phi-N	1	1	.500	4	0	0	0	0	8	10	8	7	0	0	7	5	2.125	7.88	49	6.06	.286	1	.333	-4	0	-0.3
Total 11	**60**	**64**	**.484**	**253**	**164**	**18**	**2**	**3**	**1099^1**	**1232**	**612**	**553**	**101**	**10**	**432**	**507**	**1.514**	**4.53**	**82**	**4.72**	**.289**	**55**	**.206**	**-109**	**38**	**-9.8**

• LEROY, John John Michael Leroy b: 4/19/1975, Bellevue, WA d: 6/26/2001, Sioux City, IA BR/TR, 6'3", 175 lbs. Deb: 9/26/1997

YEAR TM-L	W	L	PCT	G	GS	CG	SH	SV	IP	H	R	ER	HR	HB	BB	SO	RAT	ERA	ERA+	CERA	OAV	BH	AVG	PR+	WS	TPW
1997 Atl-N	1	0	1.000	1	0	0	0	0	2	1	0	0	0	0	3	3	2.000	0.00	....	3.47	.143	0	....	1	0	0.1

• LEROY, Louis Louis Paul "Chief" Leroy b: 2/18/1879, Omro, WI d: 10/10/1944, Shawano, WI BR/TR, 5'10", 180 lbs. Deb: 9/22/1905

YEAR TM-L	W	L	PCT	G	GS	CG	SH	SV	IP	H	R	ER	HR	HB	BB	SO	RAT	ERA	ERA+	CERA	OAV	BH	AVG	PR+	WS	TPW
1905 NY-A	1	1	.500	3	3	2	0	0	24	26	14	10	2	1	1	8	1.125	3.75	78	3.03	.278	1	.125	-2	1	-0.2
1906 NY-A	2	0	1.000	11	2	1	0	1	44^2	33	19	11	0	2	12	28	1.007	2.22	134	1.77	.209	2	.143	4	4	0.4
1910 Bos-A	0	0	....	1	0	0	0	0	4	7	9	5	1	0	2	3	2.250	11.25	23	10.79	.389	0	.000	-4	0	-0.4
Total 3	**3**	**1**	**.750**	**15**	**5**	**3**	**0**	**1**	**72^2**	**66**	**42**	**26**	**3**	**3**	**15**	**39**	**1.115**	**3.22**	**89**	**2.69**	**.245**	**3**	**.130**	**-2**	**5**	**-0.3**

• LERSCH, Barry Barry Lee Lersch b: 9/7/1944, Denver, CO BB/TR, 6', 180 lbs. Deb: 4/8/1969

YEAR TM-L	W	L	PCT	G	GS	CG	SH	SV	IP	H	R	ER	HR	HB	BB	SO	RAT	ERA	ERA+	CERA	OAV	BH	AVG	PR+	WS	TPW
1969 Phi-N	0	3	.000	10	0	0	0	2	17^2	20	14	14	6	1	10	13	1.698	7.13	50	7.44	.286	0	.000	-7	0	-0.8
1970 Phi-N	6	3	.667	42	11	3	0	3	138	119	52	50	17	1	47	92	1.203	3.26	122	3.21	.232	2	.065	13	13	1.1
1971 Phi-N	5	14	.263	38	30	3	0	0	214^1	203	97	90	28	3	50	113	1.180	3.78	93	3.42	.252	10	.169	-9	10	-0.7
1972 Phi-N	4	6	.400	36	8	3	1	0	100^2	86	37	34	8	3	33	48	1.182	3.04	118	2.90	.231	0	.000	5	7	0.3
1973 Phi-N	3	6	.333	42	4	0	0	1	98^1	105	49	48	10	2	27	51	1.342	4.39	86	4.01	.279	3	.176	-8	4	-0.8
1974 StL-N	0	0	....	1	0	0	0	0	1^1	3	6	6	1	0	5	0	6.000	40.50	9	38.11	.429	0	....	-5	0	-0.6
Total 6	**18**	**32**	**.360**	**169**	**53**	**9**	**1**	**6**	**570^1**	**536**	**255**	**242**	**70**	**10**	**172**	**317**	**1.241**	**3.82**	**96**	**3.58**	**.250**	**15**	**.113**	**-11**	**34**	**-1.5**

• LESHNOCK, Don Donald Lee Leshnock b: 11/25/1946, Youngstown, OH BR/TL, 6'3", 195 lbs. Deb: 6/7/1972

YEAR TM-L	W	L	PCT	G	GS	CG	SH	SV	IP	H	R	ER	HR	HB	BB	SO	RAT	ERA	ERA+	CERA	OAV	BH	AVG	PR+	WS	TPW
1972 Det-A	0	0	....	1	0	0	0	0	1	2	0	0	0	0	0	2	2.000	0.00	....	7.48	.400	0	....	0	0	0.0

• LESKANIC, Curt Curtis John Leskanic b: 4/2/1968, Homestead, PA BR/TR, 6', 180 lbs. Deb: 6/27/1993

YEAR TM-L	W	L	PCT	G	GS	CG	SH	SV	IP	H	R	ER	HR	HB	BB	SO	RAT	ERA	ERA+	CERA	OAV	BH	AVG	PR+	WS	TPW
1993 Col-N	1	5	.167	18	8	0	0	0	57	59	40	34	7	2	27	30	1.509	5.37	89	4.71	.266	2	.154	-2	2	-0.2
1994 Col-N	1	1	.500	8	3	0	0	0	22^1	27	14	14	2	0	10	17	1.657	5.64	88	5.62	.314	1	.167	-1	1	-0.1
1995* Col-N	6	3	.667	**76**	0	0	0	10	98	83	38	37	7	0	33	107	1.184	3.40	159	2.79	.226	1	.143	25	14	2.4
1996 Col-N	7	5	.583	70	0	0	0	6	73^2	82	51	51	12	2	38	76	1.629	6.23	84	5.81	.285	1	.333	-7	5	-0.6
1997 Col-N	4	0	1.000	55	0	0	0	2	58^1	59	36	36	8	0	24	53	1.423	5.55	93	4.55	.271	0	.000	-2	4	-0.2
1998 Col-N	6	4	.600	66	0	0	0	2	75^2	75	37	37	9	1	40	55	1.520	4.40	118	4.74	.258	0	.000	6	7	0.6
1999 Col-N	6	2	.750	63	0	0	0	0	85	87	54	48	7	5	49	77	1.600	5.08	114	5.00	.272	2	.500	7	8	0.8
2000 Mil-N	9	3	.750	73	0	0	0	12	77^1	58	23	22	7	3	51	75	1.409	2.56	178	3.72	.212	0	.000	16	12	1.5
2001 Mil-N	2	6	.250	70	0	0	0	17	69^1	63	30	28	11	2	31	64	1.356	3.63	118	4.18	.241	0	.000	5	7	0.5
2003 Mil-N	4	0	1.000	26	0	0	0	0	26^2	22	8	8	1	1	18	28	1.500	2.70	157	3.93	.227	0	....	5	4	0.5
KC-A	1	0	1.000	27	0	0	0	2	26	16	7	5	1	0	11	22	1.038	1.73	298	1.84	.180	0	....	10	5	1.0
Total 10	**47**	**29**	**.618**	**552**	**11**	**0**	**0**	**51**	**669^1**	**631**	**338**	**320**	**72**	**16**	**332**	**604**	**1.439**	**4.30**	**118**	**4.30**	**.251**	**7**	**.179**	**62**	**69**	**6.1**

• LESLEY, Brad Bradley Jay Lesley b: 9/11/1958, Turlock, CA BR/TR, 6'6", 230 lbs. Deb: 7/31/1982

YEAR TM-L	W	L	PCT	G	GS	CG	SH	SV	IP	H	R	ER	HR	HB	BB	SO	RAT	ERA	ERA+	CERA	OAV	BH	AVG	PR+	WS	TPW
1982 Cin-N	0	2	.000	28	0	0	0	4	38^1	27	13	11	1	0	13	29	1.043	2.58	143	1.78	.197	0	.000	5	4	0.5
1983 Cin-N	0	0	....	5	0	0	0	0	8^1	9	2	2	1	0	0	5	1.080	2.16	176	3.24	.290	0	....	2	1	0.2
1984 Cin-N	0	1	.000	16	0	0	0	2	19^1	17	11	11	3	0	14	7	1.603	5.12	74	5.01	.246	1	.500	-3	0	-0.2
1985 Mil-A	1	0	1.000	5	0	0	0	0	6^1	8	7	7	2	0	2	5	1.579	9.95	42	6.76	.296	0	....	-4	0	-0.4
Total 4	**1**	**3**	**.250**	**54**	**0**	**0**	**0**	**6**	**72^1**	**61**	**33**	**31**	**7**	**0**	**29**	**46**	**1.244**	**3.86**	**99**	**3.25**	**.231**	**1**	**.333**	**-1**	**5**	**0.0**

• LEVERENZ, Walt Walter Fred "Tiny" Leverenz b: 7/21/1888, Chicago, IL d: 3/19/1973, Atascadero, CA BL/TL, 5'10", 175 lbs. Deb: 4/18/1913

YEAR TM-L	W	L	PCT	G	GS	CG	SH	SV	IP	H	R	ER	HR	HB	BB	SO	RAT	ERA	ERA+	CERA	OAV	BH	AVG	PR+	WS	TPW
1913 StL-A	6	17	.261	30	27	13	2	1	202^2	159	80	58	3	12	89	87	1.224	2.58	114	2.78	.222	12	.176	5	11	0.4
1914 StL-A	1	12	.077	27	16	5	0	0	111^1	107	67	47	5	4	63	41	1.527	3.80	71	4.30	.264	6	.182	-12	0	-1.4
1915 StL-A	1	2	.333	5	1	0	0	0	9	11	9	8	0	1	8	3	2.111	8.00	36	7.33	.333	0	.000	-5	0	-0.6
Total 3	**8**	**31**	**.205**	**62**	**44**	**18**	**2**	**1**	**323**	**277**	**156**	**113**	**8**	**17**	**160**	**131**	**1.353**	**3.15**	**90**	**3.43**	**.240**	**18**	**.176**	**-13**	**11**	**-1.6**

• LEVERETT, Dixie Gorham Vance Leverett b: 3/29/1894, Georgetown, TX d: 2/20/1957, Beaverton, OR BR/TR, 5'11", 190 lbs. Deb: 5/6/1922

YEAR TM-L	W	L	PCT	G	GS	CG	SH	SV	IP	H	R	ER	HR	HB	BB	SO	RAT	ERA	ERA+	CERA	OAV	BH	AVG	PR+	WS	TPW
1922 Chi-A	13	10	.565	33	27	16	4	2	223^2	224	95	83	11	3	79	60	1.355	3.34	122	3.48	.264	21	.253	15	18	1.8
1923 Chi-A	10	13	.435	38	24	9	0	3	192^2	212	108	87	6	6	64	64	1.433	4.06	97	3.69	.280	16	.267	-2	11	0.3
1924 Chi-A	2	3	.400	21	11	4	0	0	99	123	72	64	2	3	41	29	1.657	5.82	71	4.86	.314	6	.188	-18	1	-1.8
1926 Chi-A	1	1	.500	6	3	1	0	0	24	31	18	16	1	0	7	12	1.583	6.00	64	4.72	.316	1	.143	-6	0	-0.6
1929 Bos-N	3	7	.300	24	12	3	0	1	97^2	135	81	69	5	5	30	28	1.689	6.36	74	5.65	.339	6	.188	-18	1	-1.6
Total 5	**29**	**34**	**.460**	**122**	**77**	**33**	**4**	**6**	**637**	**725**	**374**	**319**	**25**	**17**	**221**	**193**	**1.485**	**4.51**	**92**	**4.14**	**.291**	**50**	**.234**	**-28**	**31**	**-2.0**

YEAR	TM-L	W	L	PCT	G	GS	CG	SH	SV	IP	H	R	ER	HR	HB	BB	SO	RAT	ERA	ERA+	CERA	OAV	BH	AVG	PR+	WS	TPW
• LEVERETTE, Hod	Horace Wilbur "Levy" Leverette b: 2/4/1889, Shreveport, LA d: 4/10/1958, St. Petersburg, FL BR/TR, 6', 180 lbs. Deb: 4/22/1920																										
1920	StL-A	0	2	.000	3	2	0	0	0	10^1	9	6	6	1	0	12	0	2.032	5.23	75	6.37	.250	0	.000	-2	0	-0.2
• LEVINE, Alan	Alan Brian Levine b: 5/22/1968, Park Ridge, IL BL/TR, 6'3", 180 lbs. Deb: 6/22/1996																										
1996	Chi-A	0	1	.000	16	0	0	0	0	18^1	22	14	11	1	1	7	12	1.582	5.40	88	4.80	.289	0	....	-1	0	-0.1
1997	Chi-A	2	2	.500	25	0	0	0	0	27^1	35	22	21	4	2	16	22	1.866	6.91	63	7.10	.313	0	....	-7	0	-0.7
1998	Tex-A	0	1	.000	30	0	0	0	0	58	68	30	29	6	0	16	19	1.448	4.50	107	4.58	.294	0	....	3	3	0.3
1999	Ana-A	1	1	.500	50	1	0	0	0	85	76	40	32	13	3	29	37	1.235	3.39	143	3.81	.247	0	....	13	7	1.2
2000	Ana-A	3	4	.429	51	5	0	0	2	95^1	98	44	41	10	2	49	42	1.542	3.87	131	4.71	.266	0	....	10	7	1.0
2001	Ana-A	8	10	.444	64	1	0	0	2	75^2	71	25	20	7	2	28	40	1.308	2.38	192	3.66	.257	0	....	18	10	1.7
2002	Ana-A	4	4	.500	52	0	0	0	5	63^2	61	35	30	8	2	34	40	1.492	4.24	104	4.53	.253	0	....	-1	4	-0.1
2003	TB-A	3	5	.375	36	0	0	0	0	49^2	45	23	16	7	2	18	25	1.268	2.90	156	3.89	.243	0	....	8	4	0.8
	KC-A	0	1	.000	18	0	0	0	1	21^1	22	6	6	2	1	11	5	1.547	2.53	204	4.82	.268	0	....	6	3	0.6
	Yr.	3	6	.333	54	0	0	0	1	71	67	29	22	9	3	29	30	1.352	2.79	168	4.17	.251	0	....	14	7	1.3
Total	**8**	**21**	**29**	**.420**	**342**	**7**	**0**	**0**	**10**	**494^1**	**498**	**239**	**206**	**58**	**15**	**208**	**242**	**1.428**	**3.75**	**126**	**4.41**	**.265**	**0**	**....**	**49**	**38**	**4.6**
• LEVRAULT, Allen	Allen Harry Levrault b: 8/15/1977, Fall River, MA BR/TR, 6'3", 230 lbs. Deb: 6/13/2000																										
2000	Mil-N	0	1	.000	5	1	0	0	0	12	10	7	6	0	0	7	9	1.417	4.50	101	3.21	.238	0	.000	-0	0	0.0
2001	Mil-N	6	10	.375	32	20	1	0	0	130^2	146	93	88	27	7	59	80	1.569	6.06	71	5.89	.281	2	.061	-26	1	-2.8
2003	Fla-N	1	0	1.000	19	0	0	0	0	28	38	12	12	3	1	15	21	1.893	3.86	106	6.96	.333	0	.000	1	2	0.0
Total	**3**	**7**	**11**	**.389**	**56**	**21**	**1**	**0**	**0**	**170^2**	**194**	**112**	**106**	**30**	**8**	**81**	**110**	**1.611**	**5.59**	**77**	**5.88**	**.287**	**2**	**.053**	**-26**	**3**	**-2.8**
• LEVSEN, Dutch	Emil Henry Levsen b: 4/29/1898, Wyoming, IA d: 3/12/1972, St. Louis Park, MN BR/TR, 6', 180 lbs. Deb: 9/28/1923																										
1923	Cle-A	0	0	....	3	0	0	0	0	4^1	4	0	0	0	0	0	1	.923	0.00	....	1.76	.267	0	.000	2	1	0.2
1924	Cle-A	1	1	.500	4	1	1	0	0	16^1	22	8	8	0	0	4	3	1.592	4.41	97	4.71	.333	0	.000	-0	1	-0.1
1925	Cle-A	1	2	.333	4	3	2	0	0	24^1	30	16	15	1	1	16	9	1.890	5.55	80	6.15	.313	2	.250	-3	1	-0.2
1926	Cle-A	16	13	.552	33	31	18	2	0	237^1	235	110	90	11	8	85	53	1.348	3.41	119	3.51	.261	17	.205	12	17	1.1
1927	Cle-A	3	7	.300	25	13	2	1	0	80^1	96	54	49	1	2	37	15	1.656	5.49	76	4.75	.303	5	.200	-11	2	-1.2
1928	Cle-A	0	3	.000	11	3	0	0	0	41^1	39	30	25	4	2	31	7	1.694	5.44	76	4.77	.258	0	.000	-6	0	-0.8
Total	**6**	**21**	**26**	**.447**	**80**	**51**	**23**	**3**	**0**	**404**	**426**	**218**	**187**	**17**	**13**	**173**	**88**	**1.483**	**4.17**	**99**	**4.07**	**.276**	**24**	**.178**	**-6**	**22**	**-1.0**
• LEWALLYN, Dennis	Dennis Dale Lewallyn b: 8/11/1953, Pensacola, FL BR/TR, 6'4", 200 lbs. Deb: 9/21/1975																										
1975	LA-N	0	0	....	2	0	0	0	0	3	1	0	0	0	0	0	0	.333	0.00	....	0.25	.100	0	....	1	1	0.1
1976	LA-N	1	1	.500	4	2	0	0	0	16^2	12	5	4	1	0	6	4	1.080	2.16	156	2.23	.207	0	.000	2	2	0.1
1977	LA-N	3	1	.750	5	1	0	0	1	17	22	8	8	1	0	4	8	1.529	4.24	90	4.64	.306	0	.000	-1	1	-0.2
1978	LA-N	0	0	....	1	0	0	0	0	2	2	0	0	0	0	0	0	1.000	0.00	....	1.95	.250	0	....	1	0	0.1
1979	LA-N	0	1	.000	7	0	0	0	0	12^1	19	8	7	0	1	5	1	1.946	5.11	71	6.29	.358	1	.500	-2	0	-0.2
1980	Tex-A	0	0	....	4	0	0	0	0	5^2	7	5	5	0	0	4	1	1.941	7.94	49	5.59	.304	0	....	-2	0	-0.2
1981	Cle-A	0	0	....	7	0	0	0	0	13^1	16	8	8	1	0	2	11	1.350	5.40	67	4.01	.296	0	....	-2	0	-0.2
1982	Cle-A	0	1	.000	4	0	0	0	0	10^1	13	8	8	3	0	1	3	1.355	6.97	58	5.51	.310	0	....	-3	0	-0.3
Total	**8**	**4**	**4**	**.500**	**34**	**3**	**0**	**0**	**1**	**80^1**	**92**	**42**	**40**	**6**	**1**	**22**	**28**	**1.419**	**4.48**	**84**	**4.24**	**.288**	**1**	**.077**	**-7**	**4**	**-0.8**
• LEWANDOWSKI, Dan	Daniel William Lewandowski b: 1/6/1928, Buffalo, NY d: 7/19/1996, Hamilton, Canada BR/TR, 6', 180 lbs. Deb: 9/22/1951																										
1951	StL-N	0	1	.000	2	0	0	0	0	1	3	1	1	0	0	1	1	4.000	9.00	44	16.66	.500	0	....	-1	0	-0.1
• LEWIS, Bert	William Burton Lewis b: 10/3/1895, Tonawanda, NY d: 3/24/1950, Tonawanda, NY BR/TR, 6'2", 176 lbs. Deb: 4/19/1924																										
1924	Phi-N	0	0	....	12	0	0	0	0	18	23	12	12	1	1	7	3	1.667	6.00	74	5.40	.315	0	.000	-3	0	-0.3
• LEWIS, Colby	Colby Preston Lewis b: 8/2/1979, Bakersfield, CA BR/TR, 6'4", 215 lbs. Deb: 4/1/2002																										
2002	Tex-A	1	3	.250	15	4	0	0	0	34^1	42	26	24	4	2	26	28	1.981	6.29	75	7.22	.304	0	....	-6	0	-0.5
2003	Tex-A	10	9	.526	26	26	0	0	0	127	163	104	103	23	5	70	88	1.835	7.30	68	7.38	.317	0	.000	-31	1	-3.0
Total	**2**	**11**	**12**	**.478**	**41**	**30**	**0**	**0**	**0**	**161^1**	**205**	**130**	**127**	**27**	**7**	**96**	**116**	**1.866**	**7.08**	**69**	**7.35**	**.314**	**0**	**.000**	**-37**	**1**	**-3.6**
• LEWIS, Jim	James Martin Lewis b: 10/12/1955, Miami, FL BR/TR, 6'3", 190 lbs. Deb: 9/12/1979																										
1979	Sea-A	0	0	....	2	0	0	0	0	2^1	10	7	4	1	0	1	0	4.714	15.43	28	34.81	.625	0	....	-3	0	-0.3
1982	NY-A	0	0	....	1	0	0	0	0	0^2	3	7	4	0	0	3	0	9.000	54.00	7	44.72	.500	0	....	-4	0	-0.4
1983	Min-A	0	0	....	6	0	0	0	0	18	24	13	13	5	1	7	8	1.722	6.50	65	7.93	.324	0	....	-5	0	-0.5
1985	Sea-A	0	1	.000	2	1	0	0	0	4^2	8	4	4	1	2	1	1	1.929	7.71	55	11.48	.421	0	....	-2	0	-0.2
Total	**4**	**0**	**1**	**.000**	**11**	**1**	**0**	**0**	**0**	**25^2**	**45**	**31**	**25**	**7**	**3**	**12**	**9**	**2.221**	**8.77**	**48**	**11.97**	**.391**	**0**	**....**	**-13**	**0**	**-1.3**
• LEWIS, Jim	James Steven Lewis b: 7/20/1964, Jackson, MI BR/TR, 6'2", 200 lbs. Deb: 8/9/1991																										
1991	SD-N	0	0	....	12	0	0	0	0	13	14	7	6	2	0	11	10	1.923	4.15	91	6.35	.275	0	.000	-1	0	-0.1
• LEWIS, Richie	Richie Todd Lewis b: 1/25/1966, Muncie, IN BR/TR, 5'10", 175 lbs. Deb: 7/31/1992																										
1992	Bal-A	1	1	.500	2	2	0	0	0	6^2	13	8	8	1	0	7	4	3.000	10.80	37	13.54	.406	0	....	-5	0	-0.5
1993	Fla-N	6	3	.667	57	0	0	0	0	77^1	68	37	28	7	1	43	65	1.435	3.26	132	3.81	.239	1	.500	11	6	1.1
1994	Fla-N	1	4	.200	45	0	0	0	0	54	62	44	34	7	1	38	45	1.852	5.67	77	6.09	.284	0	.000	-8	0	-0.9
1995	Fla-N	0	1	.000	21	1	0	0	0	36	30	15	15	9	1	15	32	1.250	3.75	112	4.10	.224	0	.000	2	2	0.2
1996	Det-A	4	6	.400	72	0	0	0	2	90^1	78	45	42	9	4	65	78	1.583	4.18	121	4.51	.238	0	.000	11	5	0.9
1997	Oak-A	2	0	1.000	14	0	0	0	0	18^2	24	21	20	7	1	15	12	2.089	9.64	47	10.29	.316	0	....	-10	0	-1.0
	Cin-N	0	0	....	4	0	0	0	0	5^2	4	5	4	3	0	3	4	1.235	6.35	68	5.43	.200	1	1.000	-1	0	-0.1
1998	Bal-A	0	0	....	2	1	0	0	0	4^2	8	8	8	2	0	5	4	2.786	15.43	30	16.11	.421	0	....	-6	0	-0.5
Total	**7**	**14**	**15**	**.483**	**217**	**4**	**0**	**0**	**2**	**293^1**	**287**	**183**	**159**	**45**	**8**	**191**	**244**	**1.630**	**4.88**	**92**	**5.34**	**.258**	**2**	**.200**	**-8**	**13**	**-0.7**
• LEWIS, Scott	Scott Allen Lewis b: 12/5/1965, Grants Pass, OR BR/TR, 6'3", 178 lbs. Deb: 9/25/1990																										
1990	Cal-A	1	1	.500	2	2	1	0	0	16^1	10	4	4	2	0	2	9	.735	2.20	173	1.42	.172	0	....	3	2	0.3
1991	Cal-A	3	5	.375	16	11	0	0	0	60^1	81	43	42	9	2	21	37	1.691	6.27	65	6.36	.316	0	....	-15	0	-1.5
1992	Cal-A	4	0	1.000	21	2	0	0	0	38^1	36	18	17	3	2	14	18	1.304	3.99	100	3.71	.255	0	....	-0	3	0.0
1993	Cal-A	1	2	.333	15	4	0	0	0	32	37	16	15	3	2	12	10	1.531	4.22	107	5.09	.311	0	....	1	2	0.1
1994	Cal-A	0	1	.000	20	0	0	0	0	31	46	23	21	5	2	10	10	1.806	6.10	80	7.59	.359	0	....	-4	1	-0.4
Total	**5**	**9**	**9**	**.500**	**74**	**19**	**1**	**0**	**0**	**178**	**210**	**104**	**99**	**22**	**8**	**59**	**84**	**1.511**	**5.01**	**85**	**5.32**	**.299**	**0**	**....**	**-16**	**8**	**-1.6**
• LEWIS, Ted	Edward Morgan "Parson" Lewis b: 12/25/1872, Machynlleth, Wales d: 5/24/1936, Durham, NH BR/TR, 5'10.5", 158 lbs. Deb: 7/6/1896																										
1896	Bos-N	1	4	.200	6	5	4	0	0	41^2	37	32	15	2	0	27	12	1.536	3.24	140	3.87	.237	2	.111	5	2	0.3
1897*	Bos-N	21	12	.636	38	34	30	2	1	290	316	177	124	11	10	125	65	1.521	3.85	116	4.26	.275	28	.248	13	22	1.0
1898	Bos-N	26	8	.765	41	33	29	1	2	313^1	267	131	101	9	9	109	72	1.200	2.90	127	2.66	.229	37	.282	19	31	2.2
1899	Bos-N	17	11	.607	29	25	23	2	0	234^2	245	119	91	10	8	73	60	1.355	3.49	119	3.63	.269	25	.260	9	20	0.9
1900	Bos-N	13	12	.520	30	22	19	1	0	209	215	122	96	11	4	86	66	1.440	4.13	100	3.92	.265	10	.137	-5	13	-0.7
1901	Bos-A	16	17	.485	39	34	31	1	1	316^1	299	172	124	14	8	91	103	1.233	3.53	100	3.02	.247	21	.174	-13	18	-1.4
Total	**6**	**94**	**64**	**.595**	**183**	**153**	**136**	**7**	**4**	**1405**	**1379**	**753**	**551**	**57**	**39**	**511**	**378**	**1.345**	**3.53**	**112**	**3.46**	**.255**	**123**	**.223**	**27**	**106**	**2.2**
• LEY, Terry	Terrence Richard Ley b: 2/21/1947, Portland, OR BL/TL, 6', 190 lbs. Deb: 8/20/1971																										
1971	NY-A	0	0	....	6	0	0	0	0	9	9	9	5	1	2	9	7	2.000	5.00	65	6.60	.257	0	....	-2	0	-0.2
• LIDDLE, Don	Donald Eugene Liddle b: 5/25/1925, Mount Carmel, IL d: 6/5/2000, Mount Carmel, IL BL/TL, 5'10", 165 lbs. Deb: 4/17/1953																										
1953	Mil-N	7	6	.538	31	15	4	0	2	128^2	119	54	44	6	2	55	63	1.352	3.08	127	3.40	.248	3	.088	11	9	0.9
1954*	NY-N	9	4	.692	28	19	4	3	0	126^2	100	48	43	5	3	55	44	1.224	3.06	132	2.70	.223	7	.189	12	11	1.4
1955	NY-N	10	4	.714	33	13	4	0	1	106^1	97	54	50	18	4	61	56	1.486	4.23	95	4.87	.246	5	.185	-2	7	-0.1

YEAR	TM-L	W	L	PCT	G	GS	CG	SH	SV	IP	H	R	ER	HR	HB	BB	SO	RAT	ERA	ERA+	CERA	OAV	BH	AVG	PR+	WS	TPW
1956	NY-N	1	2	.333	11	5	1	0	1	41^1	45	22	18	5	1	14	21	1.427	3.92	96	4.35	.278	2	.167	-0	2	0.0
	StL-N	1	2	.333	14	2	0	0	0	24^2	36	25	23	8	0	18	14	2.189	8.39	45	10.27	.353	0	.000	-13	0	-1.3
	Yr.	2	4	.333	25	7	1	0	1	66	81	47	41	13	1	32	35	1.712	5.59	68	6.56	.307	2	.143	-13	2	-1.4
Total	4	28	18	.609	117	54	13	3	4	427^2	397	203	178	42	10	203	198	1.403	3.75	105	4.05	.250	17	.152	8	29	0.8

• LIDGE, Brad Bradley Thomas Lidge b: 12/23/1976, Sacramento, CA BR/TR, 6'5", 200 lbs. Deb: 4/26/2002

YEAR	TM-L	W	L	PCT	G	GS	CG	SH	SV	IP	H	R	ER	HR	HB	BB	SO	RAT	ERA	ERA+	CERA	OAV	BH	AVG	PR+	WS	TPW
2002	Hou-N	1	0	1.000	6	1	0	0	0	8^2	12	6	6	0	2	9	12	2.423	6.23	68	8.90	.333	2	1.000	-2	1	-0.1
2003	Hou-N	6	3	.667	78	0	0	0	1	85	60	36	34	6	5	42	97	1.200	3.60	123	2.82	.202	0	.000	6	8	0.5
Total	2	7	3	.700	84	1	0	0	1	93^2	72	42	40	6	7	51	109	1.313	3.84	115	3.38	.216	2	.333	4	9	0.5

• LIDLE, Cory Cory Fulton Lidle b: 3/22/1972, Hollywood, CA BR/TR, 5'11", 175 lbs. Deb: 5/8/1997

YEAR	TM-L	W	L	PCT	G	GS	CG	SH	SV	IP	H	R	ER	HR	HB	BB	SO	RAT	ERA	ERA+	CERA	OAV	BH	AVG	PR+	WS	TPW
1997	NY-N	7	2	.778	54	2	0	0	2	81^2	86	38	32	7	3	20	54	1.298	3.53	115	3.75	.274	0	.000	3	6	0.3
1999	TB-A	1	0	1.000	5	1	0	0	0	5	8	4	4	0	0	2	4	2.000	7.20	69	6.98	.364	0	....	-1	0	-0.1
2000	TB-A	4	6	.400	31	11	0	0	0	96^2	114	61	54	13	3	29	62	1.479	5.03	98	5.06	.294	0	.000	-2	4	-0.2
2001*	Oak-A	13	6	.684	29	29	1	0	0	188	170	84	75	23	10	47	118	1.154	3.59	123	3.35	.242	0	.000	17	13	1.6
2002*	Oak-A	8	10	.444	31	30	2	2	0	192	191	90	83	17	6	39	111	1.198	3.89	113	3.31	.258	0	.000	12	13	1.1
2003	Tor-A	12	15	.444	31	31	2	0	0	192^2	216	133	123	24	5	60	112	1.433	5.75	80	4.67	.282	2	.333	-21	6	-2.0
Total	6	45	39	.536	181	104	5	2	2	756	785	410	371	84	27	197	461	1.299	4.42	102	3.96	.268	2	.125	7	42	0.7

• LIEBER, Dutch Charles Edwin Lieber b: 2/1/1910, Alameda, CA d: 12/31/1961, Sawtelle, CA BR/TR, 6'.5", 180 lbs. Deb: 4/18/1935

YEAR	TM-L	W	L	PCT	G	GS	CG	SH	SV	IP	H	R	ER	HR	HB	BB	SO	RAT	ERA	ERA+	CERA	OAV	BH	AVG	PR+	WS	TPW
1935	Phi-A	1	1	.500	18	1	0	0	2	46^2	45	18	16	1	1	19	14	1.371	3.09	147	3.44	.263	2	.143	8	4	0.7
1936	Phi-A	0	1	.000	3	0	0	0	0	11^2	17	11	10	0	0	6	1	1.971	7.71	66	6.62	.362	0	.000	-3	0	-0.3
Total	2	1	2	.333	21	1	0	0	2	58^1	62	29	26	1	1	25	15	1.491	4.01	118	4.07	.284	2	.118	5	4	0.3

• LIEBER, Jon Jonathan Ray Lieber b: 4/2/1970, Council Bluffs, IA BL/TR, 6'3", 220 lbs. Deb: 5/15/1994

YEAR	TM-L	W	L	PCT	G	GS	CG	SH	SV	IP	H	R	ER	HR	HB	BB	SO	RAT	ERA	ERA+	CERA	OAV	BH	AVG	PR+	WS	TPW
1994	Pit-N	6	7	.462	17	17	1	0	0	108^2	116	62	45	12	1	25	71	1.298	3.73	116	3.83	.271	4	.103	6	6	0.5
1995	Pit-N	4	7	.364	21	12	0	0	0	72^2	103	56	51	7	4	14	45	1.610	6.32	68	5.96	.346	1	.048	-15	0	-1.7
1996	Pit-N	9	5	.643	51	15	0	0	1	142	156	70	63	19	3	28	94	1.296	3.99	109	4.12	.279	7	.194	8	9	0.9
1997	Pit-N	11	14	.440	33	32	1	0	0	188^1	193	102	94	23	1	51	160	1.296	4.49	96	3.78	.263	7	.121	-2	9	-0.3
1998	Pit-N	8	14	.364	29	28	2	0	1	171	182	93	78	23	3	40	138	1.298	4.11	105	4.00	.269	8	.167	3	8	0.3
1999	Chi-N	10	11	.476	31	31	3	1	0	203^1	226	107	92	28	1	46	186	1.338	4.07	111	4.19	.279	7	.121	13	13	1.1
2000	Chi-N	12	11	.522	35	**35**	6	1	0	**251**	248	130	123	36	10	54	192	1.203	4.41	103	3.70	.256	18	.220	5	12	0.7
2001	Chi-N★	20	6	.769	34	34	5	1	0	232^1	226	104	98	25	7	41	148	1.149	3.80	109	3.19	.255	12	.158	13	16	1.3
2002	Chi-N	6	8	.429	21	21	3	0	0	141	153	64	58	15	1	12	87	1.170	3.70	108	3.33	.277	7	.163	6	7	0.6
Total	9	86	83	.509	272	225	21	3	2	1510^1	1603	788	702	188	31	311	1121	1.267	4.18	103	3.85	.271	71	.154	35	80	3.5

• LIEBHARDT, Glenn Glenn John Liebhardt b: 3/10/1883, Milton, IN d: 7/13/1956, Cleveland, OH BR/TR, 5'10", 175 lbs. Deb: 10/2/1906

YEAR	TM-L	W	L	PCT	G	GS	CG	SH	SV	IP	H	R	ER	HR	HB	BB	SO	RAT	ERA	ERA+	CERA	OAV	BH	AVG	PR+	WS	TPW
1906	Cle-A	2	0	1.000	2	2	2	0	0	18	13	4	3	0	0	1	9	.778	1.50	175	1.19	.205	0	.000	2	2	0.1
1907	Cle-A	18	14	.563	38	34	27	4	1	280^1	254	100	64	1	10	85	110	1.209	2.05	122	2.64	.244	14	.161	9	19	0.8
1908	Cle-A	15	16	.484	38	26	19	3	0	262	222	93	64	2	3	81	146	1.156	2.20	108	2.43	.235	14	.175	3	17	0.4
1909	Cle-A	1	5	.167	12	4	1	0	1	52^1	54	28	17	0	1	16	15	1.338	2.92	87	3.86	.314	0	.000	-3	1	-0.5
Total	4	36	35	.507	90	66	49	7	2	612^2	543	225	148	3	14	183	280	1.185	2.17	113	2.61	.245	28	.147	11	39	0.8

• LIEBHARDT, Glenn Glenn Ignatius "Sandy" Liebhardt b: 7/31/1910, Cleveland, OH d: 3/14/1992, Winston-Salem, NC BR/TR, 5'10.5", 170 lbs. Deb: 4/22/1930

YEAR	TM-L	W	L	PCT	G	GS	CG	SH	SV	IP	H	R	ER	HR	HB	BB	SO	RAT	ERA	ERA+	CERA	OAV	BH	AVG	PR+	WS	TPW
1930	Phi-A	0	1	.000	5	0	0	0	0	9	14	12	11	2	0	8	2	2.444	11.00	42	10.59	.359	0	.000	-6	0	-0.6
1936	StL-A	0	0	....	24	0	0	0	0	55^1	98	58	54	4	2	27	20	2.259	8.78	61	8.88	.375	0	.000	-20	0	-1.9
1938	StL-A	0	0	....	2	0	0	0	0	3	4	2	2	1	0	0	1	1.333	6.00	83	5.82	.308	0	....	-0	0	0.0
Total	3	0	1	.000	31	0	0	0	0	67^1	116	72	67	7	2	35	23	2.243	8.96	58	8.97	.371	0	.000	-27	0	-2.5

• LIGTENBERG, Kerry Kerry Dale Ligtenberg b: 5/11/1971, Rapid City, SD BR/TR, 6'2", 185 lbs. Deb: 8/12/1997

YEAR	TM-L	W	L	PCT	G	GS	CG	SH	SV	IP	H	R	ER	HR	HB	BB	SO	RAT	ERA	ERA+	CERA	OAV	BH	AVG	PR+	WS	TPW
1997*	Atl-N	1	0	1.000	15	0	0	0	1	15	12	5	5	4	0	4	19	1.067	3.00	140	3.26	.211	0	....	2	2	0.2
1998*	Atl-N	3	2	.600	75	0	0	0	30	73	51	24	22	6	0	24	79	1.027	2.71	153	2.13	.193	0	....	11	15	1.1
2000*	Atl-N	2	3	.400	59	0	0	0	12	52^1	43	21	21	7	0	24	51	1.280	3.61	127	3.46	.226	0	....	6	8	0.6
2001*	Atl-N	3	3	.500	53	0	0	0	1	59^2	50	22	20	4	0	30	56	1.341	3.02	146	3.14	.226	0	....	9	5	0.9
2002*	Atl-N	3	4	.429	52	0	0	0	0	66^2	52	23	22	6	0	33	51	1.275	2.97	138	3.10	.213	0	....	7	6	0.7
2003	Bal-A	4	2	.667	68	0	0	0	1	59^1	60	23	22	9	2	14	47	1.247	3.34	132	3.93	.263	0	....	7	6	0.7
Total	6	16	14	.533	322	0	0	0	45	326	268	118	112	36	2	129	303	1.218	3.09	139	3.11	.223	0	....	42	42	4.1

• LILLARD, Gene Robert Eugene Lillard b: 11/12/1913, Santa Barbara, CA d: 4/12/1991, Goleta, CA BR/TR, 5'10.5", 178 lbs. Deb: 5/8/1936 ♦

YEAR	TM-L	W	L	PCT	G	GS	CG	SH	SV	IP	H	R	ER	HR	HB	BB	SO	RAT	ERA	ERA+	CERA	OAV	BH	AVG	PR+	WS	TPW
1939	Chi-N	3	5	.375	20	7	2	0	0	55	68	48	40	2	3	36	31	1.891	6.55	60	6.03	.309	1	.100	-14	0	-1.3
1940	StL-N	0	1	.000	2	1	0	0	0	4^2	8	7	7	1	1	4	2	2.571	13.50	30	12.21	.364	0	....	-5	0	-0.5
Total	2	3	6	.333	22	8	2	0	0	59^2	76	55	47	3	4	40	33	1.944	7.09	56	6.51	.314	8	.182	-19	0	-1.8

• LILLIE, Jim James J. "Grasshopper" Lillie b: 7/27/1861, New Haven, CT d: 11/9/1890, Kansas City, MO Deb: 5/17/1883 ♦

YEAR	TM-L	W	L	PCT	G	GS	CG	SH	SV	IP	H	R	ER	HR	HB	BB	SO	RAT	ERA	ERA+	CERA	OAV	BH	AVG	PR+	WS	TPW
1883	Buf-N	0	1	.000	3	0	0	0	0	12	16	12	4	0	....	2	4	1.500	3.00	106	....	.302	47	.234	0	3	-1.3
1884	Buf-N	0	1	.000	2	1	0	0	0	13	22	24	9	0	....	5	4	2.077	6.23	51	....	.356	105	.223	-4	6	-1.4
1886	KC-N	0	0	....	1	0	0	0	0	6	8	5	3	0	....	1	0	1.500	4.50	83	....	.308	73	.175	-0	2	-3.2
Total	3	0	2	.000	6	1	0	0	0	31	46	41	16	0	....	8	8	1.742	4.65	70	....	.327	332	.219	-4	11	-5.8

• LILLIQUIST, Derek Derek Jansen Lilliquist b: 2/20/1966, Winter Park, FL BL/TL, 6', 214 lbs. Deb: 4/13/1989

YEAR	TM-L	W	L	PCT	G	GS	CG	SH	SV	IP	H	R	ER	HR	HB	BB	SO	RAT	ERA	ERA+	CERA	OAV	BH	AVG	PR+	WS	TPW
1989	Atl-N	8	10	.444	32	30	0	0	0	165^2	202	87	73	16	2	34	79	1.425	3.97	92	4.52	.301	12	.190	-4	6	-0.4
1990	Atl-N	2	8	.200	12	11	0	0	0	61^2	75	45	43	10	1	19	34	1.524	6.28	64	5.26	.301	8	.348	-14	1	-1.0
	SD-N	3	3	.500	16	7	1	1	0	60^1	61	29	29	6	2	23	29	1.392	4.33	88	4.23	.266	3	.150	-4	2	-0.4
	Yr.	5	11	.313	28	18	1	1	0	122	136	74	72	16	3	42	63	1.459	5.31	74	4.75	.285	11	.256	-18	3	-1.4
1991	SD-N	0	2	.000	6	2	0	0	0	14^1	25	14	14	3	0	4	7	2.023	8.79	43	9.05	.379	0	.000	-8	0	-0.9
1992	Cle-A	5	3	.625	71	0	0	0	6	61^2	39	13	12	5	2	18	47	.924	1.75	223	1.73	.186	0	....	15	10	1.5
1993	Cle-A	4	4	.500	56	2	0	0	10	64	64	20	16	5	1	19	40	1.297	2.25	192	3.45	.263	0	....	15	8	1.4
1994	Cle-A	1	3	.250	36	0	0	0	1	29^1	34	17	16	6	1	8	15	1.432	4.91	96	5.37	.304	0	....	-1	2	-0.1
1995	Bos-A	2	1	.667	28	0	0	0	0	23	27	17	16	7	0	9	9	1.565	6.26	78	6.44	.303	0	....	-4	1	-0.3
1996	Cin-N	0	0	....	5	0	0	0	0	3^2	5	3	3	1	0	0	1	1.364	7.36	56	6.01	.357	0	....	-1	0	-0.1
Total	8	25	34	.424	262	52	1	1	17	483^2	532	245	222	59	9	134	261	1.377	4.13	96	4.37	.283	23	.213	-5	30	-0.2

• LILLY, Ted Theodore Roosevelt Lilly b: 1/4/1976, Lomita, CA BL/TL, 6'1", 185 lbs. Deb: 5/14/1999

YEAR	TM-L	W	L	PCT	G	GS	CG	SH	SV	IP	H	R	ER	HR	HB	BB	SO	RAT	ERA	ERA+	CERA	OAV	BH	AVG	PR+	WS	TPW
1999	Mon-N	0	1	.000	9	3	0	0	0	23^2	30	20	20	7	3	9	28	1.648	7.61	59	7.76	.309	1	.200	-8	0	-0.7
2000	NY-A	0	0	....	7	0	0	0	0	8	8	6	5	1	0	5	11	1.625	5.63	86	4.76	.235	0	....	-1	0	-0.1
2001	NY-A	5	6	.455	26	21	0	0	0	120^2	126	81	72	20	7	51	112	1.467	5.37	84	5.10	.267	0	.000	-9	3	-0.9
2002	NY-A	3	6	.333	16	11	2	1	0	76^2	57	31	29	10	5	24	59	1.057	3.40	128	2.74	.202	0	.000	10	5	1.0
	* Oak-A	2	1	.667	6	5	0	0	0	23^1	23	12	12	5	1	7	18	1.286	4.63	95	4.56	.253	0	....	-0	1	0.0
	Yr.	5	7	.417	22	16	2	1	0	100	80	43	41	15	6	31	77	1.110	3.69	118	3.16	.214	0	.000	10	6	0.9
2003*	Oak-A	12	10	.545	32	31	0	0	0	178^1	179	92	86	24	5	58	147	1.329	4.34	104	4.06	.255	0	.000	3	10	0.3
Total	5	22	24	.478	96	71	2	1	0	430^2	423	242	224	67	21	154	375	1.340	4.68	96	4.36	.252	1	.071	-4	19	-0.5

• LIMA, Jose Jose Desiderio Rodriguez Lima b: 9/30/1972, Santiago, Dominican Republic BR/TR, 6'2", 170 lbs. Deb: 4/20/1994

YEAR	TM-L	W	L	PCT	G	GS	CG	SH	SV	IP	H	R	ER	HR	HB	BB	SO	RAT	ERA	ERA+	CERA	OAV	BH	AVG	PR+	WS	TPW
1994	Det-A	0	1	.000	3	1	0	0	0	6^2	11	10	10	2	0	3	7	2.100	13.50	36	9.61	.355	0	....	-6	0	-0.6
1995	Det-A	3	9	.250	15	15	0	0	0	73^2	85	52	50	10	4	18	37	1.398	6.11	78	4.73	.288	0	....	-10	2	-0.9
1996	Det-A	5	6	.455	39	4	0	0	3	72^2	87	48	46	13	5	22	59	1.500	5.70	89	5.53	.296	0	....	-4	3	-0.3
1997*	Hou-N	1	6	.143	52	1	0	0	2	75	79	45	44	9	5	16	63	1.267	5.28	76	3.96	.271	0	.000	-12	1	-1.2
1998	Hou-N	16	8	.667	33	33	3	1	0	233^1	229	100	96	34	7	32	169	1.119	3.70	110	3.36	.256	11	.139	8	14	0.7
1999*	Hou-N★	21	10	.677	35	**35**	3	0	0	246^1	256	108	98	30	2	44	187	1.218	3.58	123	3.58	.265	6	.080	21	18	1.6
2000	Hou-N	7	16	.304	33	33	0	0	0	196^1	251	152	145	48	2	68	124	1.625	6.65	73	6.59	.313	10	.167	-36	2	-3.4

YEAR	TM-L	W	L	PCT	G	GS	CG	SH	SV	IP	H	R	ER	HR	HB	BB	SO	RAT	ERA	ERA+	CERA	OAV	BH	AVG	PR+	WS	TPW
2001	Hou-N	1	2	.333	14	9	0	0	0	53	77	48	43	12	5	16	41	1.755	7.30	63	7.90	.350	0	.000	-16	0	-1.7
	Det-A	5	10	.333	18	18	2	0	0	112^{2}	120	66	59	23	4	22	43	1.260	4.71	92	4.49	.274	0	.000	-3	4	-0.3
2002	Det-A	4	6	.400	20	12	0	0	0	68^{1}	86	60	59	12	2	21	33	1.566	7.77	55	5.97	.314	0	....	-26	0	-2.5
2003	KC-A	8	3	.727	14	14	0	0	0	73^{1}	80	40	40	7	5	26	32	1.445	4.91	105	4.69	.280	1	.500	2	5	0.2
Total	10	71	77	.480	276	175	8	1	5	1211^{1}	1361	729	690	200	41	288	795	1.361	5.13	88	4.74	.284	28	.119	-81	49	-8.4

• LINCOLN, Ezra Ezra Perry Lincoln b: 11/17/1868, Raynham, MA d: 5/7/1951, Taunton, MA BL/TL, 5'11", 160 lbs. Deb: 5/2/1890

YEAR	TM-L	W	L	PCT	G	GS	CG	SH	SV	IP	H	R	ER	HR	HB	BB	SO	RAT	ERA	ERA+	CERA	OAV	BH	AVG	PR+	WS	TPW
1890	Cle-N	3	11	.214	15	15	13	0	0	118	157	102	58	1	0	53	22	1.780	4.42	81	....	.310	8	.157	-11	2	-1.3
	Syr-a	0	3	.000	3	3	2	0	0	20	33	27	23	1	0	4	6	1.850	10.35	34	....	.358	0	.000	-15	0	-1.4

• LINCOLN, Mike Michael George Lincoln b: 4/10/1975, Carmichael, CA BR/TR, 6'2", 210 lbs. Deb: 4/7/1999

YEAR	TM-L	W	L	PCT	G	GS	CG	SH	SV	IP	H	R	ER	HR	HB	BB	SO	RAT	ERA	ERA+	CERA	OAV	BH	AVG	PR+	WS	TPW
1999	Min-A	3	10	.231	18	15	0	0	0	76^{1}	102	59	58	11	1	26	27	1.677	6.84	74	6.16	.321	0	.000	-15	1	-1.4
2000	Min-A	0	3	.000	8	4	0	0	0	20^{2}	36	25	25	10	2	13	15	2.371	10.89	47	14.32	.383	0	....	-13	0	-1.2
2001	Pit-N	2	1	.667	31	0	0	0	0	40^{1}	34	16	12	3	4	11	24	1.116	2.68	168	2.94	.225	1	.250	8	4	0.8
2002	Pit-N	2	4	.333	55	0	0	0	0	72^{1}	80	28	25	7	0	27	50	1.479	3.11	134	4.49	.290	0	.000	8	6	0.7
2003	Pit-N	3	4	.429	36	0	0	0	5	36^{1}	38	22	21	5	1	13	28	1.404	5.20	84	4.70	.277	0	....	-3	2	-0.3
Total	5	10	22	.313	148	19	0	0	5	246	290	150	141	36	8	90	144	1.545	5.16	92	5.61	.297	1	.100	-14	13	-1.3

• LINDAMAN, Vive Vivan Alexander Lindaman b: 10/28/1877, Charles City, IA d: 2/13/1927, Charles City, IA BR/TR, 6'1", 200 lbs. Deb: 4/14/1906 U

YEAR	TM-L	W	L	PCT	G	GS	CG	SH	SV	IP	H	R	ER	HR	HB	BB	SO	RAT	ERA	ERA+	CERA	OAV	BH	AVG	PR+	WS	TPW
1906	Bos-N	12	23	.343	39	36	32	2	0	307^{1}	303	132	83	4	11	90	115	1.279	2.43	110	3.20	.264	14	.132	11	20	1.2
1907	Bos-N	11	15	.423	34	28	24	2	1	260	252	130	105	10	15	108	90	1.385	3.63	70	3.84	.265	11	.122	-34	6	-4.0
1908	Bos-N	12	16	.429	43	30	21	2	1	270^{2}	246	112	71	7	10	70	68	1.167	2.36	101	2.79	.249	15	.176	-5	13	-0.5
1909	Bos-N	1	6	.143	15	6	6	1	0	66	75	44	34	1	1	28	13	1.561	4.64	61	4.50	.299	6	.273	-13	0	-1.4
Total	4	36	60	.375	131	100	83	7	2	904	876	418	293	22	37	296	286	1.296	2.92	88	3.36	.262	46	.152	-41	39	-4.8

• LINDBLAD, Paul Paul Aaron Lindblad b: 8/9/1941, Chanute, KS BL/TL, 6'1", 195 lbs. Deb: 9/15/1965

YEAR	TM-L	W	L	PCT	G	GS	CG	SH	SV	IP	H	R	ER	HR	HB	BB	SO	RAT	ERA	ERA+	CERA	OAV	BH	AVG	PR+	WS	TPW
1965	KC-A	0	1	.000	4	0	0	0	0	7^{1}	12	9	9	3	1	0	12	1.636	11.05	32	9.15	.353	0	.000	-6	0	-0.7
1966	KC-A	5	10	.333	38	14	0	0	1	121	138	63	56	14	3	37	69	1.446	4.17	82	4.66	.292	5	.147	-11	2	-1.2
1967	KC-A	5	8	.385	46	10	1	1	6	115^{2}	106	59	46	15	6	35	83	1.219	3.58	89	3.50	.241	7	.206	-5	5	-0.4
1968	Oak-A	4	3	.571	47	1	0	0	2	56^{1}	51	19	15	6	0	14	42	1.154	2.40	117	2.85	.237	3	.375	3	4	0.4
1969	Oak-A	9	6	.600	60	0	0	0	9	78^{1}	72	37	36	8	2	33	64	1.340	4.14	83	3.61	.240	4	.333	-6	6	-0.5
1970	Oak-A	8	2	.800	62	0	0	0	3	63^{1}	52	23	19	7	0	28	42	1.263	2.70	131	3.16	.222	0	.000	5	6	0.5
1971	Oak-A	1	0	1.000	8	0	0	0	0	16	18	7	7	1	1	2	4	1.250	3.94	85	3.74	.295	1	.333	-1	1	-0.1
	Was-A	6	4	.600	43	0	0	0	8	83^{2}	58	25	24	6	2	29	50	1.040	2.58	128	2.14	.196	3	.158	6	9	0.7
	Yr.	7	4	.636	51	0	0	0	8	99^{2}	76	32	31	7	3	31	54	1.074	2.80	118	2.40	.213	4	.182	5	10	0.6
1972	Tex-A	5	8	.385	**66**	0	0	0	9	99^{2}	95	31	29	7	0	29	51	1.244	2.62	115	3.16	.257	3	.200	6	7	0.7
1973*	Oak-A	1	5	.167	36	3	0	0	2	78	89	38	32	8	3	28	33	1.500	3.69	96	4.93	.292	0	....	-3	2	-0.3
1974	Oak-A	4	4	.500	45	2	0	0	6	100^{2}	85	30	23	4	2	30	46	1.142	2.06	161	2.40	.231	0	....	13	10	1.3
1975*	Oak-A	9	1	.900	68	0	0	0	7	122^{1}	105	44	37	6	0	43	58	1.210	2.72	133	2.72	.237	0	.000	12	11	1.2
1976	Oak-A	6	5	.545	65	0	0	0	5	114^{2}	111	50	39	5	3	24	37	1.177	3.06	110	2.79	.253	0	....	6	8	0.6
1977	Tex-A	4	5	.444	42	1	0	0	4	98^{2}	103	50	46	16	1	29	46	1.338	4.20	97	4.38	.270	0	....	-2	5	-0.2
1978	Tex-A	1	1	.500	18	0	0	0	2	39^{2}	41	16	16	2	2	15	25	1.412	3.63	103	3.80	.279	0	....	1	3	0.1
	*NY-A	0	0	....	7	1	0	0	0	18^{1}	21	9	9	4	0	8	9	1.582	4.42	82	5.83	.284	0	....	-2	0	-0.2
	Yr.	1	1	.500	25	1	0	0	2	58	62	25	25	6	2	23	34	1.466	3.88	95	4.44	.281	0	....	-1	3	-0.1
Total	14	68	63	.519	655	32	1	1	64	1213^{2}	1157	510	443	112	26	384	671	1.270	3.29	104	3.46	.253	26	.195	14	79	2.0

• LINDE, Lyman Lyman Gilbert Linde b: 9/30/1920, Rolling Prairie, WI d: 10/26/1995, Beaver Dam, WI BR/TR, 5'11", 185 lbs. Deb: 9/11/1947

YEAR	TM-L	W	L	PCT	G	GS	CG	SH	SV	IP	H	R	ER	HR	HB	BB	SO	RAT	ERA	ERA+	CERA	OAV	BH	AVG	PR+	WS	TPW
1947	Cle-A	0	0	....	1	0	0	0	0	0^{2}	3	2	2	0	0	1	0	6.000	27.00	13	33.87	.600	0	....	-2	0	-0.2
1948	Cle-A	0	0	....	3	0	0	0	0	10	9	6	6	1	0	4	0	1.300	5.40	75	3.55	.243	0	.000	-2	0	-0.2
Total	2	0	0	....	4	0	0	0	0	10^{2}	12	8	8	1	0	5	0	1.594	6.75	58	5.44	.286	0	.000	-3	0	-0.4

• LINDELL, Johnny John Harlan Lindell b: 8/30/1916, Greeley, CO d: 8/27/1985, Newport Beach, CA BR/TR, 6'4.5", 217 lbs. Deb: 4/18/1941 ♦

YEAR	TM-L	W	L	PCT	G	GS	CG	SH	SV	IP	H	R	ER	HR	HB	BB	SO	RAT	ERA	ERA+	CERA	OAV	BH	AVG	PR+	WS	TPW
1942	NY-A	2	1	.667	23	2	0	0	1	52^{2}	52	25	22	3	1	22	28	1.405	3.76	91	3.68	.254	6	.250	-4	3	-0.3
1953	Pit-N	5	16	.238	27	23	13	1	0	175^{2}	173	106	92	17	6	116	102	1.645	4.71	95	4.98	.262	26	.286	-4	12	1.0
	Phi-N	1	1	.500	5	3	2	0	0	23^{1}	22	16	11	0	0	23	16	1.929	4.24	99	4.94	.259	7	.389	-0	2	0.3
	Yr.	6	17	.261	32	26	15	1	0	199	195	122	103	17	6	139	118	**1.678**	4.66	95	4.98	.261	33	.303	-4	14	1.3
Total	2	8	18	.308	55	28	15	1	1	251^{2}	247	147	125	20	7	161	146	1.621	4.47	95	4.71	.260	762	.273	-8	17	1.0

• LINDEMANN, Ernie Ernest Lindemann b: 6/10/1883, New York, NY d: 12/27/1951, Brooklyn, NY BR/TR Deb: 6/28/1907

YEAR	TM-L	W	L	PCT	G	GS	CG	SH	SV	IP	H	R	ER	HR	HB	BB	SO	RAT	ERA	ERA+	CERA	OAV	BH	AVG	PR+	WS	TPW
1907	Bos-N	0	0	....	1	1	0	0	0	6^{1}	6	5	4	0	0	4	3	1.579	5.68	45	4.33	.286	1	.500	-2	0	-0.2

• LINDQUIST, Carl Carl Emil Lindquist b: 5/9/1919, Morris Run, PA d: 9/3/2001, Blossburg, PA BR/TR, 6'2", 185 lbs. Deb: 9/27/1943

YEAR	TM-L	W	L	PCT	G	GS	CG	SH	SV	IP	H	R	ER	HR	HB	BB	SO	RAT	ERA	ERA+	CERA	OAV	BH	AVG	PR+	WS	TPW
1943	Bos-N	0	2	.000	2	2	0	0	0	13	17	10	9	3	0	4	1	1.615	6.23	55	6.51	.315	0	.000	-4	0	-0.5
1944	Bos-N	0	0	....	5	0	0	0	0	8^{2}	8	5	3	1	0	2	4	1.154	3.12	123	2.72	.222	0	.000	1	0	0.1
Total	2	0	2	.000	7	2	0	0	0	21^{2}	25	15	12	4	0	6	5	1.431	4.98	70	5.00	.278	0	.000	-4	0	-0.5

• LINDSEY, Jim James Kendrick Lindsey b: 1/24/1896, Greensburg, LA d: 10/25/1963, Jackson, LA BR/TR, 6'1", 175 lbs. Deb: 5/1/1922

YEAR	TM-L	W	L	PCT	G	GS	CG	SH	SV	IP	H	R	ER	HR	HB	BB	SO	RAT	ERA	ERA+	CERA	OAV	BH	AVG	PR+	WS	TPW
1922	Cle-A	4	5	.444	29	5	0	0	1	83^{2}	105	60	56	4	3	24	29	1.542	6.02	66	4.78	.324	4	.167	-17	1	-1.7
1924	Cle-A	0	0	....	3	0	0	0	0	3	8	7	7	0	0	3	0	3.667	21.00	20	15.72	.500	0	.000	-6	0	-0.6
1929	StL-N	1	1	.500	2	2	1	0	0	16^{1}	20	11	10	1	1	2	8	1.347	5.51	85	4.05	.290	1	.200	-1	1	-0.1
1930*	StL-N	7	5	.583	39	6	3	0	5	105^{2}	131	59	52	6	4	46	50	1.675	4.43	113	5.26	.312	8	.286	6	8	0.6
1931*	StL-N	6	4	.600	35	2	1	1	7	74^{2}	77	32	23	2	0	45	32	1.634	2.77	142	4.34	.270	1	.111	9	8	0.9
1932	StL-N	3	3	.500	33	5	0	0	3	89^{1}	96	53	49	6	2	38	31	1.500	4.94	80	4.36	.279	3	.143	-9	3	-1.0
1933	StL-N	0	0	....	1	0	0	0	0	2	2	1	1	0	0	1	1	1.500	4.50	77	4.01	.286	0	....	-0	0	0.0
1934	Cin-N	0	0	....	4	0	0	0	0	4	4	3	2	0	1	2	2	1.500	4.50	91	4.08	.286	0	....	-0	0	0.0
	StL-N	0	1	.000	11	0	0	0	1	14	21	13	10	2	0	3	7	1.714	6.43	66	6.19	.328	0	.000	-4	0	-0.4
	Yr.	0	1	.000	15	0	0	0	1	18	25	16	12	2	1	5	9	1.667	6.00	70	5.72	.321	0	.000	-4	0	-0.4
1937	Bro-N	0	1	.000	20	0	0	0	2	38^{1}	43	22	15	4	1	12	15	1.435	3.52	115	4.57	.295	1	.167	3	2	0.3
Total	9	21	20	.512	177	20	5	1	19	431	507	261	225	25	12	176	175	1.585	4.70	90	4.80	.300	18	.186	-18	23	-2.1

• LINDSTROM, Axel Axel Olaf Lindstrom b: 8/26/1895, Gustavsberg, Sweden d: 6/24/1940, Asheville, NC BR/TR, 5'10", 180 lbs. Deb: 10/3/1916

YEAR	TM-L	W	L	PCT	G	GS	CG	SH	SV	IP	H	R	ER	HR	HB	BB	SO	RAT	ERA	ERA+	CERA	OAV	BH	AVG	PR+	WS	TPW
1916	Phi-A	0	0	....	1	0	0	0	1	4	2	2	2	0	1	0	1	.500	4.50	63	0.94	.182	1	.500	-1	0	0.0

• LINEBRINK, Scott Scott Cameron Linebrink b: 8/4/1976, Austin, TX BR/TR, 6'3", 185 lbs. Deb: 4/15/2000

YEAR	TM-L	W	L	PCT	G	GS	CG	SH	SV	IP	H	R	ER	HR	HB	BB	SO	RAT	ERA	ERA+	CERA	OAV	BH	AVG	PR+	WS	TPW
2000	SF-N	0	0	....	3	0	0	0	0	2^{1}	7	3	3	1	0	2	0	3.857	11.57	37	24.13	.500	0	....	-2	0	-0.2
	Hou-N	0	0	....	8	0	0	0	0	9^{2}	11	5	5	3	3	6	6	1.759	4.66	104	9.21	.289	1	1.000	0	1	0.1
	Yr.	0	0	....	11	0	0	0	0	12	18	8	8	4	3	8	6	2.167	6.00	77	12.11	.346	1	1.000	-2	1	-0.1
2001	Hou-N	0	0	....	9	0	0	0	0	10^{1}	6	4	3	0	2	6	9	1.161	2.61	175	2.54	.176	0	....	2	1	0.2
2002	Hou-N	0	0	....	22	0	0	0	0	24^{1}	31	21	19	2	1	13	24	1.808	7.03	61	5.70	.298	0	....	-7	0	-0.7
2003	Hou-N	1	1	.500	9	6	0	0	0	31^{2}	38	15	15	4	3	14	17	1.642	4.26	104	6.27	.317	0	.000	-0	1	-0.1
	SD-N	2	1	.667	43	0	0	0	0	60^{2}	55	22	19	5	3	22	51	1.269	2.82	140	3.41	.244	2	.500	8	4	0.9
	Yr.	3	2	.600	52	6	0	0	0	92^{1}	93	37	34	9	6	36	68	1.397	3.31	125	4.39	.270	2	.167	8	5	0.8
Total	4	3	2	.600	94	6	0	0	0	139	148	70	64	15	12	63	107	1.518	4.14	102	5.15	.277	3	.231	1	7	0.2

• LINES, Dick Richard George Lines b: 8/17/1938, Montreal, Canada BR/TL, 6'1", 175 lbs. Deb: 4/16/1966

YEAR	TM-L	W	L	PCT	G	GS	CG	SH	SV	IP	H	R	ER	HR	HB	BB	SO	RAT	ERA	ERA+	CERA	OAV	BH	AVG	PR+	WS	TPW
1966	Was-A	5	2	.714	53	0	0	0	2	83	63	23	21	4	1	24	49	1.048	2.28	152	2.08	.213	0	.000	10	8	1.0
1967	Was-A	2	5	.286	54	0	0	0	4	85^{2}	83	43	32	6	0	24	54	1.249	3.36	94	3.01	.245	1	.111	-2	4	-0.2
Total	2	7	7	.500	107	0	0	0	6	168^{2}	146	66	53	10	1	48	103	1.150	2.83	116	2.55	.230	1	.053	8	12	0.8

YEAR	TM-L	W	L	PCT	G	GS	CG	SH	SV	IP	H	R	ER	HR	HB	BB	SO	RAT	ERA	ERA+	CERA	OAV	BH	AVG	PR+	WS	TPW
• LINK, Fred	Frederick Theodore "Laddie" Link b: 3/11/1886, Columbus, OH d: 5/22/1939, Houston, TX BL/TL, 6', 170 lbs. Deb: 4/15/1910																										
1910	Cle-A	5	6	.455	22	13	6	1	1	127^2	121	53	45	0	7	50	55	1.339	3.17	81	3.48	.259	7	.167	-9	6	-1.1
	StL-A	0	1	.000	3	3	0	0	0	17	24	10	8	0	1	13	5	2.176	4.24	58	8.07	.375	1	.167	-3	0	-0.4
	Yr.	5	7	.417	25	16	6	1	1	144^2	145	63	53	0	8	63	60	1.438	3.30	78	4.02	.273	8	.167	-12	6	-1.5
• LINKE, Ed	Edward Karl "Babe" Linke b: 11/9/1911, Chicago, IL d: 6/21/1988, Chicago, IL BR/TR, 5'11", 180 lbs. Deb: 4/27/1933																										
1933	Was-A	1	0	1.000	3	2	0	0	0	16	15	10	9	0	0	11	6	1.625	5.06	83	3.90	.250	1	.167	-2	1	-0.2
1934	Was-A	2	2	.500	7	4	2	0	0	34^2	38	20	16	1	0	9	9	1.356	4.15	104	3.47	.277	2	.182	1	2	0.1
1935	Was-A	11	7	.611	40	22	10	1	3	178	211	111	99	6	1	80	51	1.635	5.01	86	4.72	.296	20	.294	-13	8	-0.6
1936	Was-A	1	5	.167	13	6	1	0	0	52	73	46	41	4	0	14	11	1.673	7.10	67	5.59	.330	6	.400	-14	1	-0.8
1937	Was-A	6	1	.857	36	7	0	0	3	128^2	158	89	80	11	4	59	61	1.687	5.60	79	5.54	.304	10	.217	-19	4	-1.6
1938	StL-A	1	7	.125	21	2	0	0	0	39^2	60	37	35	6	0	33	18	2.345	7.94	63	9.41	.357	2	.200	-13	0	-1.1
Total	6	22	22	.500	120	43	13	1	6	449	555	313	280	28	5	206	156	1.695	5.61	80	5.34	.305	41	.263	-60	16	-4.3
• LINT, Royce	Royce James Lint b: 1/1/1921, Birmingham, AL BL/TL, 6'1", 165 lbs. Deb: 4/13/1954																										
1954	StL-N	2	3	.400	30	4	1	1	0	70^1	75	46	38	9	0	30	36	1.493	4.86	85	4.59	.273	1	.100	-5	2	-0.4
• LINTON, Doug	Douglas Warren Linton b: 2/9/1965, Santa Ana, CA BR/TR, 6'1", 190 lbs. Deb: 8/3/1992																										
1992	Tor-A	1	3	.250	8	3	0	0	0	24	31	23	23	5	0	17	16	2.000	8.63	47	8.19	.323	0	....	-12	0	-1.2
1993	Tor-A	0	1	.000	4	1	0	0	0	11	11	8	8	0	1	9	4	1.818	6.55	66	5.03	.256	0	....	-3	0	-0.3
	Cal-A	2	0	1.000	19	0	0	0	0	25^2	35	22	22	8	0	14	19	1.909	7.71	58	8.65	.324	0	....	-9	0	-0.9
	Yr.	2	1	.667	23	1	0	0	0	36^2	46	30	30	8	1	23	23	1.882	7.36	60	7.56	.305	0	....	-12	0	-1.2
1994	NY-N	6	2	.750	32	3	0	0	0	50^1	74	27	25	4	0	20	29	1.868	4.47	93	6.55	.341	0	.000	-2	3	-0.2
1995	KC-A	0	1	.000	7	2	0	0	0	22^1	22	21	18	4	2	10	13	1.433	7.25	66	5.10	.256	0	....	-6	0	-0.6
1996	KC-A	7	9	.438	21	18	0	0	0	104	111	65	58	13	8	26	87	1.317	5.02	100	4.28	.271	0	....	-0	5	0.0
1999	Bal-A	1	4	.200	14	8	0	0	0	59	69	41	39	14	2	25	31	1.593	5.95	79	6.42	.296	0	....	-9	1	-0.9
2003	Tor-A	0	0	....	7	0	0	0	0	9	7	3	3	2	0	4	7	1.222	3.00	153	4.14	.226	0	....	2	1	0.2
Total	7	17	20	.459	112	35	0	0	0	305^1	360	210	196	50	13	125	206	1.588	5.78	80	5.82	.294	0	.000	-40	10	-4.0
• LINZY, Frank	Frank Alfred Linzy b: 9/15/1940, Fort Gibson, OK BR/TR, 6'1", 190 lbs. Deb: 8/14/1963																										
1963	SF-N	0	0	....	8	1	0	0	0	16^2	22	9	9	0	1	10	14	1.920	4.86	66	6.29	.324	0	.000	-3	0	-0.3
1965	SF-N	9	3	.750	57	0	0	0	21	81^2	76	19	13	2	3	23	35	1.212	1.43	251	2.80	.250	4	.222	21	16	2.3
1966	SF-N	7	11	.389	51	0	0	0	16	100^1	107	40	33	4	2	34	57	1.405	2.96	124	3.67	.273	3	.150	8	10	0.8
1967	SF-N	7	7	.500	57	0	0	0	17	95^2	67	21	16	4	0	34	38	1.056	1.51	218	1.96	.203	0	.000	19	15	1.9
1968	SF-N	9	8	.529	57	0	0	0	12	94^2	76	30	22	1	1	27	36	1.088	2.09	141	1.87	.218	0	.000	10	11	1.0
1969	SF-N	14	9	.609	58	0	0	0	11	116^1	129	57	47	5	3	38	62	1.436	3.64	96	3.80	.283	8	.267	-1	10	0.2
1970	SF-N	2	1	.667	20	0	0	0	1	25^2	33	20	20	2	1	11	16	1.714	7.01	57	5.67	.327	0	.000	-8	0	-0.9
	StL-N	3	5	.375	47	0	0	0	2	61^1	66	26	25	3	0	23	19	1.451	3.67	112	3.83	.282	0	.000	4	4	0.3
	Yr.	5	6	.455	67	0	0	0	3	87	99	46	45	5	1	34	35	1.529	4.66	87	4.37	.296	0	.000	-4	4	-0.5
1971	StL-N	4	3	.571	50	0	0	0	6	59^1	49	18	14	2	0	27	24	1.281	2.12	169	2.60	.226	2	.500	11	8	1.3
1972	Mil-A	2	2	.500	47	0	0	0	12	77^1	70	30	26	4	2	27	24	1.254	3.03	100	2.91	.248	1	.111	0	6	0.0
1973	Mil-A	2	6	.250	42	1	0	0	13	63	68	34	25	7	1	21	21	1.413	3.57	105	4.35	.282	0	....	2	4	0.2
1974	Phi-N	3	2	.600	22	0	0	0	0	24^2	27	11	9	1	0	7	12	1.378	3.28	115	3.77	.284	0	....	1	2	0.1
Total	11	62	57	.521	516	2	0	0	111	816^2	790	315	259	35	14	282	358	1.313	2.85	123	3.23	.257	18	.149	63	86	6.8
• LIPETRI, Angelo	Michael Angelo Lipetri b: 7/6/1929, Brooklyn, NY BR/TR, 6'1.5", 180 lbs. Deb: 4/25/1956																										
1956	Phi-N	0	0	....	6	0	0	0	0	11	7	5	4	2	1	3	8	.909	3.27	114	2.43	.175	0	.000	1	1	0.1
1958	Phi-N	0	0	....	4	0	0	0	0	4	6	5	5	1	1	0	1	1.500	11.25	35	7.93	.353	0	....	-3	0	-0.3
Total	2	0	0	....	10	0	0	0	0	15	13	10	9	3	2	3	9	1.067	5.40	71	3.90	.228	0	.000	-2	1	-0.3
• LIPP, Tom	Thomas Charles Lipp b: 6/4/1870, Baltimore, MD d: 5/30/1932, Baltimore, MD, 5'11.5", 170 lbs. Deb: 9/18/1897																										
1897	Phi-N	0	1	.000	1	1	0	0	0	3	8	5	5	0	0	2	1	3.333	15.00	28	15.45	.482	1	1.000	-4	0	-0.3
• LIRA, Felipe	Antonio Felipe Lira b: 4/26/1972, Santa Teresa, Venezuela BR/TR, 6', 170 lbs. Deb: 4/27/1995																										
1995	Det-A	9	13	.409	37	22	0	0	1	146^1	151	74	70	17	8	56	89	1.415	4.31	110	4.48	.271	0	....	9	10	0.9
1996	Det-A	6	14	.300	32	32	3	2	0	194^2	204	123	113	30	10	66	113	1.387	5.22	97	4.66	.269	0	....	1	6	0.1
1997	Det-A	5	7	.417	20	15	1	1	0	92	101	61	59	15	2	45	64	1.587	5.77	79	5.53	.277	0	....	-13	2	-1.3
	Sea-A	0	4	.000	8	3	0	0	0	18^2	31	21	19	3	4	10	9	2.196	9.16	49	10.14	.365	0	....	-9	0	-0.9
	Yr.	5	11	.313	28	18	1	1	0	110^2	132	82	78	18	6	55	73	1.690	6.34	72	6.31	.294	0	....	-23	2	-2.2
1998	Sea-A	1	0	1.000	7	0	0	0	0	15^2	22	10	8	5	0	5	16	1.723	4.60	101	7.63	.319	0	....	0	1	0.0
1999	Det-A	0	0	....	2	0	0	0	0	3^1	7	5	4	2	0	2	3	2.700	10.80	46	16.24	.389	0	....	-2	0	-0.2
2000	Mon-N	5	8	.385	53	7	0	0	0	101^2	129	71	61	11	4	36	51	1.623	5.40	89	5.51	.310	4	.211	-6	3	-0.4
2001	Mon-N	0	0	....	4	0	0	0	0	5	11	7	7	1	0	2	3	2.600	12.60	35	12.69	.440	0	....	-4	0	-0.4
Total	7	26	46	.361	163	79	4	3	1	577^1	656	372	341	84	28	222	348	1.521	5.32	90	5.30	.286	4	.211	-25	22	-2.2
• LISENBEE, Hod	Horace Milton Lisenbee b: 9/23/1898, Clarksville, TN d: 11/14/1987, Clarksville, TN BR/TR, 5'11", 170 lbs. Deb: 4/23/1927																										
1927	Was-A	18	9	.667	39	34	17	**4**	0	242	221	114	96	6	3	78	105	1.236	3.57	114	2.75	.245	11	.133	11	16	0.6
1928	Was-A	2	6	.250	16	9	3	0	0	77	102	58	52	4	5	32	13	1.740	6.08	66	5.73	.326	4	.174	-19	0	-1.8
1929	Bos-A	0	0	....	5	0	0	0	0	8^2	10	5	5	1	0	4	2	1.615	5.19	82	5.08	.294	0	.000	-1	0	-0.1
1930	Bos-A	10	17	.370	37	31	15	0	0	237^1	254	130	116	20	5	86	47	1.433	4.40	105	4.22	.280	20	.267	3	15	0.4
1931	Bos-A	5	12	.294	41	17	6	0	0	164^2	190	108	95	13	3	49	42	1.451	5.19	83	4.26	.281	12	.226	-16	6	-1.4
1932	Bos-A	0	4	.000	19	6	3	0	0	73^1	87	55	46	9	1	25	13	1.527	5.65	80	5.03	.296	1	.048	-8	1	-0.9
1936	Phi-A	1	7	.125	19	7	4	0	0	85^2	115	69	59	9	0	24	17	1.623	6.20	82	5.55	.322	3	.120	-11	2	-1.0
1945	Cin-N	1	3	.250	31	3	0	0	1	80^1	97	56	49	12	2	16	14	1.407	5.49	68	4.82	.294	0	.000	-15	0	-1.8
Total	8	37	58	.389	207	107	48	4	1	969	1076	595	518	74	19	314	253	1.434	4.81	90	4.22	.282	51	.169	-56	40	-6.2
• LISKA, Ad	Adolph James Liska b: 7/10/1906, Dwight, NE d: 11/30/1998, Portland, OR BR/TR, 5'11.5", 160 lbs. Deb: 4/17/1929																										
1929	Was-A	3	9	.250	24	10	4	0	0	94^1	87	53	50	1	3	42	33	1.367	4.77	89	3.20	.249	5	.172	-7	4	-0.7
1930	Was-A	9	7	.563	32	16	7	1	1	150^2	140	69	55	6	5	71	40	1.400	3.29	140	3.56	.250	5	.096	17	12	1.2
1931	Was-A	0	1	.000	2	1	0	0	0	4	9	3	3	0	0	1	2	2.500	6.75	64	10.72	.450	0	.000	-1	0	-0.1
1932	Phi-N	2	0	1.000	8	0	0	0	1	26^2	22	5	5	0	1	10	6	1.200	1.69	261	2.51	.239	0	.000	8	4	0.7
1933	Phi-N	3	1	.750	45	1	0	0	1	75^2	96	46	38	5	0	26	23	1.612	4.52	84	5.00	.310	1	.071	-6	3	-0.8
Total	5	17	18	.486	111	28	11	1	3	351^1	354	176	151	12	9	150	104	1.435	3.87	110	3.78	.266	11	.107	11	23	0.3
• LITTELL, Mark	Mark Alan Littell b: 1/17/1953, Cape Girardeau, MO BL/TR, 6'3", 210 lbs. Deb: 6/14/1973																										
1973	KC-A	1	3	.250	8	7	1	0	0	38	44	25	24	5	0	23	16	1.763	5.68	72	5.97	.288	0	....	-6	1	-0.6
1975	KC-A	1	2	.333	7	3	1	0	0	24^1	19	11	10	1	0	15	19	1.397	3.70	104	3.39	.229	0	....	1	1	0.1
1976*	KC-A	8	4	.667	60	1	0	0	16	104	68	26	24	1	0	60	92	1.231	2.08	168	2.28	.188	0	.000	16	14	1.7
1977*	KC-A	8	4	.667	48	5	0	0	12	104^2	73	49	42	6	1	55	106	1.223	3.61	112	2.61	.198	0	.000	4	10	0.4
1978	StL-N	4	8	.333	72	2	0	0	11	106^1	80	38	33	8	4	59	130	1.307	2.79	126	3.10	.213	0	.000	8	9	0.8
1979	StL-N	9	4	.692	63	0	0	0	13	82^1	60	22	20	2	0	39	67	1.202	2.19	172	2.32	.203	0	.000	13	14	1.2
1980	StL-N	0	2	.000	14	0	0	0	2	10^2	14	11	11	2	0	7	7	1.969	9.28	40	7.39	.318	0	.000	-7	0	-0.7
1981	StL-N	1	3	.250	28	1	0	0	2	41	36	21	20	2	0	31	22	1.634	4.39	81	4.07	.237	2	.250	-4	1	-0.5
1982	StL-N	0	1	.000	16	0	0	0	0	20^2	22	14	12	1	0	15	7	1.790	5.23	69	4.80	.272	0	.000	-4	0	-0.5
Total	9	32	31	.508	316	19	2	0	56	532	416	217	196	28	5	304	466	1.353	3.32	113	3.17	.217	2	.059	20	50	1.9
• LITTLE, Jeff	Donald Jeffrey Little b: 12/25/1954, Fremont, OH BR/TL, 6'6", 220 lbs. Deb: 9/6/1980																										
1980	StL-N	1	1	.500	7	2	0	0	0	18^2	18	9	8	0	0	9	17	1.446	3.86	96	3.48	.250	1	.167	-1	1	-0.1
1982	Min-A	2	0	1.000	33	0	0	0	0	36^1	33	20	17	6	0	27	26	1.651	4.21	101	5.29	.244	0	....	-0	2	0.0
Total	2	3	1	.750	40	2	0	0	0	55	51	29	25	6	0	36	43	1.582	4.09	99	4.68	.246	1	.167	-1	3	-0.1

• LITTLEFIELD, Dick Richard Bernard Littlefield b: 3/18/1926, Detroit, MI d: 11/20/1997, Detroit, MI BL/TL, 6', 180 lbs. Deb: 7/7/1950

YEAR	TM-L	W	L	PCT	G	GS	CG	SH	SV	IP	H	R	ER	HR	HB	BB	SO	RAT	ERA	ERA+	CERA	OAV	BH	AVG	PR+	WS	TPW
1950	Bos-A	2	2	.500	15	2	0	0	1	23^1	27	25	24	6	1	24	13	2.186	9.26	53	9.16	.297	0	.000	-11	0	-1.1
1951	Chi-A	1	1	.500	4	2	0	0	0	9^2	9	12	9	1	0	17	7	2.690	8.38	48	8.66	.243	0	.000	-5	0	-0.4
1952	Det-A	0	3	.000	28	1	0	0	1	47^2	46	24	23	4	0	25	32	1.490	4.34	88	4.06	.257	1	.143	-2	2	-0.2
	StL-A	2	3	.400	7	5	3	0	0	46^1	35	18	14	4	0	17	34	1.122	2.72	144	2.47	.205	1	.063	6	3	0.4
	Yr.	2	6	.250	35	6	3	0	1	94	81	42	37	8	0	42	66	1.309	3.54	108	3.27	.231	2	.087	4	5	0.2
1953	StL-A	7	12	.368	36	22	2	0	0	152^1	153	93	86	17	4	84	104	1.556	5.08	83	4.76	.264	8	.190	-14	5	-1.5
1954	Bal-A	0	0	....	3	0	0	0	0	6	8	7	7	0	1	6	5	2.333	10.50	34	8.34	.333	0	.000	-5	0	-0.5
	Pit-N	10	11	.476	23	21	7	1	0	155	140	78	62	10	2	85	92	1.452	3.60	116	3.71	.239	8	.163	14	11	1.4
1955	Pit-N	5	12	.294	35	17	4	1	0	130	148	91	74	15	2	68	70	1.662	5.12	80	5.41	.290	6	.176	-13	2	-1.3
1956	Pit-N	0	0	....	6	2	0	0	0	12^2	14	8	6	2	0	6	10	1.579	4.26	88	5.61	.286	0	.000	-1	0	-0.1
	StL-N	0	2	.000	3	2	0	0	0	9^2	9	9	8	2	0	4	5	1.345	7.45	51	4.12	.237	0	.000	-4	0	-0.4
	NY-N	4	4	.500	31	7	0	0	2	97	78	45	44	16	0	39	65	1.206	4.08	93	3.42	.231	2	.083	-3	6	-0.4
	Yr.	4	6	.400	40	11	0	0	2	119^1	101	62	58	20	0	49	80	1.257	4.37	86	3.71	.238	2	.071	-7	6	-1.0
1957	Chi-N	2	3	.400	48	2	0	0	4	65^2	76	46	39	12	1	37	51	1.721	5.35	72	6.24	.295	2	.182	-10	0	-1.0
1958	Mil-N	0	1	.000	4	0	0	0	1	6^1	7	5	3	2	1	1	7	1.263	4.26	83	5.99	.280	0	....	-1	0	-0.1
Total	**9**	**33**	**54**	**.379**	**243**	**83**	**16**	**2**	**9**	**761^2**	**750**	**461**	**399**	**91**	**12**	**413**	**495**	**1.527**	**4.71**	**86**	**4.66**	**.260**	**28**	**.145**	**-48**	**29**	**-5.2**

• LITTLEFIELD, John John Andrew Littlefield b: 1/5/1954, Covina, CA BR/TR, 6'2", 200 lbs. Deb: 6/8/1980

YEAR	TM-L	W	L	PCT	G	GS	CG	SH	SV	IP	H	R	ER	HR	HB	BB	SO	RAT	ERA	ERA+	CERA	OAV	BH	AVG	PR+	WS	TPW
1980	StL-N	5	5	.500	52	0	0	0	9	66	71	31	23	2	1	20	22	1.379	3.14	118	3.51	.282	0	.000	3	5	0.2
1981	SD-N	2	3	.400	42	0	0	0	2	64	53	28	26	5	1	28	21	1.266	3.66	89	3.22	.235	0	.000	-3	3	-0.3
Total	**2**	**7**	**8**	**.467**	**94**	**0**	**0**	**0**	**11**	**130**	**124**	**59**	**49**	**7**	**2**	**48**	**43**	**1.323**	**3.39**	**102**	**3.37**	**.259**	**0**	**.000**	**0**	**8**	**-0.1**

• LITTLEJOHN, Carlisle Charles Carlisle Littlejohn b: 10/6/1901, Irene, TX d: 10/27/1977, Kansas City, MO BR/TR, 5'10", 175 lbs. Deb: 5/11/1927

YEAR	TM-L	W	L	PCT	G	GS	CG	SH	SV	IP	H	R	ER	HR	HB	BB	SO	RAT	ERA	ERA+	CERA	OAV	BH	AVG	PR+	WS	TPW
1927	StL-N	3	1	.750	14	2	1	0	0	42	47	21	21	4	0	14	16	1.452	4.50	88	4.50	.292	5	.417	-3	3	-0.2
1928	StL-N	2	1	.667	12	2	1	0	0	32	36	16	13	2	0	14	6	1.563	3.66	109	4.49	.286	0	.000	1	2	-0.1
Total	**2**	**5**	**2**	**.714**	**26**	**4**	**2**	**0**	**0**	**74**	**83**	**37**	**34**	**6**	**0**	**28**	**22**	**1.500**	**4.14**	**96**	**4.50**	**.289**	**5**	**.217**	**-2**	**5**	**-0.2**

• LIVELY, Buddy Everett Adrian "Red" Lively b: 2/14/1925, Birmingham, AL BR/TR, 6'.5", 200 lbs. Deb: 4/17/1947

YEAR	TM-L	W	L	PCT	G	GS	CG	SH	SV	IP	H	R	ER	HR	HB	BB	SO	RAT	ERA	ERA+	CERA	OAV	BH	AVG	PR+	WS	TPW
1947	Cin-N	4	7	.364	38	17	3	1	0	123	126	75	64	16	0	63	52	1.537	4.68	88	4.69	.265	6	.188	-6	4	-0.5
1948	Cin-N	0	0	....	10	0	0	0	0	22^2	13	7	6	0	1	11	12	1.059	2.38	164	1.64	.165	0	.000	4	2	0.4
1949	Cin-N	4	6	.400	31	10	3	1	1	103^1	91	47	45	11	0	53	30	1.394	3.92	107	3.92	.245	4	.154	3	6	0.3
Total	**3**	**8**	**13**	**.381**	**79**	**27**	**6**	**2**	**1**	**249**	**230**	**129**	**115**	**27**	**1**	**127**	**94**	**1.434**	**4.16**	**99**	**4.09**	**.248**	**10**	**.167**	**1**	**12**	**0.3**

• LIVELY, Jack Henry Everett Lively b: 5/29/1885, Joppa, AL d: 12/5/1967, Arab, AL BR/TR, 5'9", 185 lbs. Deb: 4/16/1911

YEAR	TM-L	W	L	PCT	G	GS	CG	SH	SV	IP	H	R	ER	HR	HB	BB	SO	RAT	ERA	ERA+	CERA	OAV	BH	AVG	PR+	WS	TPW
1911	Det-A	7	5	.583	18	14	10	0	0	113^2	143	73	58	1	7	34	45	1.557	4.59	75	4.75	.313	11	.256	-13	6	-1.0

• LIVENGOOD, Wes Wesley Amos Livengood b: 7/18/1910, Salisbury, NC d: 9/2/1996, Winston-Salem, NC BR/TR, 6'2", 172 lbs. Deb: 5/30/1939

YEAR	TM-L	W	L	PCT	G	GS	CG	SH	SV	IP	H	R	ER	HR	HB	BB	SO	RAT	ERA	ERA+	CERA	OAV	BH	AVG	PR+	WS	TPW
1939	Cin-N	0	0	....	5	0	0	0	0	5^2	9	6	6	3	0	3	4	2.118	9.53	40	12.24	.360	0	....	-4	0	-0.4

• LIVINGSTONE, Jake Jacob M. Livingstone b: 1/1/1880, St. Petersburg, Russia d: 3/22/1949, Wassaic, NY Deb: 9/6/1901

YEAR	TM-L	W	L	PCT	G	GS	CG	SH	SV	IP	H	R	ER	HR	HB	BB	SO	RAT	ERA	ERA+	CERA	OAV	BH	AVG	PR+	WS	TPW
1901	NY-N	0	0	....	2	0	0	0	0	12	26	13	12	0	3	7	6	2.750	9.00	37	12.44	.431	1	.167	-7	0	-0.7

• LLEWELLYN, Clem Clement Manly "Lew" Llewellyn b: 8/1/1895, Dobson, NC d: 11/26/1969, Concord, NC BL/TR, 6'2", 195 lbs. Deb: 6/18/1922

YEAR	TM-L	W	L	PCT	G	GS	CG	SH	SV	IP	H	R	ER	HR	HB	BB	SO	RAT	ERA	ERA+	CERA	OAV	BH	AVG	PR+	WS	TPW
1922	NY-A	0	0	....	1	0	0	0	0	1	1	0	0	0	0	0	0	1.000	0.00	....	1.95	.250	0	....	0	0	0.0

• LLOYD, Graeme Graeme John Lloyd b: 4/9/1967, Victoria, Australia BL/TL, 6'8", 234 lbs. Deb: 4/11/1993

YEAR	TM-L	W	L	PCT	G	GS	CG	SH	SV	IP	H	R	ER	HR	HB	BB	SO	RAT	ERA	ERA+	CERA	OAV	BH	AVG	PR+	WS	TPW
1993	Mil-A	3	4	.429	55	0	0	0	0	63^2	64	24	20	5	3	13	31	1.209	2.83	150	3.26	.256	0	....	11	5	1.0
1994	Mil-A	2	3	.400	43	0	0	0	3	47	49	28	27	4	3	15	31	1.362	5.17	97	3.94	.269	0	....	-2	3	-0.2
1995	Mil-A	0	5	.000	33	0	0	0	4	32	28	16	16	4	0	8	13	1.125	4.50	111	2.98	.246	0	....	1	3	0.1
1996	Mil-A	2	4	.333	52	0	0	0	0	51	49	19	16	3	1	17	24	1.294	2.82	184	3.28	.254	0	....	12	6	1.1
	★NY-A	0	2	.000	13	0	0	0	0	5^2	12	11	11	1	0	5	6	3.000	17.47	28	13.39	.429	0	....	-8	0	-0.7
	Yr.	2	6	.250	65	0	0	0	0	56^2	61	30	27	4	1	22	30	1.465	4.29	119	4.29	.276	0	....	5	6	0.4
1997★	NY-A	1	1	.500	46	0	0	0	1	49	55	24	18	6	1	20	26	1.531	3.31	135	4.84	.293	0	....	7	3	0.6
1998★	NY-A	3	0	1.000	50	0	0	0	0	37^2	26	10	7	3	2	6	20	.850	1.67	262	1.67	.191	0	....	11	5	1.0
1999	Tor-A	5	3	.625	74	0	0	0	3	72	68	36	29	11	4	23	47	1.264	3.63	136	4.00	.250	0	....	10	7	0.9
2001	Mon-N	9	5	.643	84	0	0	0	1	70^1	74	38	34	6	6	21	44	1.351	4.35	103	4.19	.272	0	.000	2	6	0.2
2002	Mon-N	2	3	.400	41	0	0	0	5	30^2	41	21	20	5	1	8	17	1.598	5.87	73	5.97	.325	0	.000	-5	1	-0.6
	Fla-N	2	2	.500	25	0	0	0	0	26^1	26	13	13	1	1	11	20	1.405	4.44	89	3.69	.263	0	....	-2	1	-0.2
	Yr.	4	5	.444	66	0	0	0	5	57	67	34	33	6	2	19	37	1.509	5.21	79	4.91	.298	0	.000	-7	2	-0.7
2003	NY-N	1	2	.333	36	0	0	0	0	35^1	39	16	13	2	0	7	17	1.302	3.31	125	3.47	.281	0	....	4	2	0.3
	KC-A	0	2	.000	16	0	0	0	0	12^1	29	18	15	0	1	7	8	2.919	10.95	47	12.89	.453	0	....	-8	0	-0.8
Total	**10**	**30**	**36**	**.455**	**568**	**0**	**0**	**0**	**17**	**533**	**560**	**274**	**239**	**51**	**23**	**161**	**304**	**1.353**	**4.04**	**114**	**4.08**	**.271**	**0**	**.000**	**33**	**42**	**3.0**

• LOAIZA, Esteban Esteban Antonio (Veyna) Loaiza b: 12/31/1971, Tijuana, Mexico BR/TR, 6'4", 190 lbs. Deb: 4/29/1995

YEAR	TM-L	W	L	PCT	G	GS	CG	SH	SV	IP	H	R	ER	HR	HB	BB	SO	RAT	ERA	ERA+	CERA	OAV	BH	AVG	PR+	WS	TPW
1995	Pit-N	8	9	.471	32	**31**	1	0	0	172^2	205	115	99	21	5	55	85	1.506	5.16	83	5.10	.300	10	.192	-15	5	-1.3
1996	Pit-N	2	3	.400	10	10	1	1	0	52^2	65	32	29	11	2	19	32	1.595	4.96	88	6.30	.308	2	.118	-3	2	-0.3
1997	Pit-N	11	11	.500	33	32	1	0	0	196^1	214	99	90	17	12	56	122	1.375	4.13	104	4.20	.279	10	.167	5	11	0.5
1998	Pit-N	6	5	.545	21	14	0	0	0	91^2	96	50	46	13	3	30	53	1.375	4.52	95	4.48	.275	7	.241	-3	4	-0.2
	Tex-A	3	6	.333	14	14	1	0	0	79^1	103	57	52	15	2	22	55	1.576	5.90	82	6.04	.316	0	....	-8	2	-0.8
1999★	Tex-A	9	5	.643	30	15	0	0	0	120^1	128	65	61	10	0	40	77	1.396	4.56	111	4.03	.275	0	....	9	8	0.8
2000	Tex-A	5	6	.455	20	17	0	0	1	107^1	133	67	64	21	3	31	75	1.528	5.37	93	5.81	.302	0	.000	-2	5	-0.2
	Tor-A	5	7	.417	14	14	1	1	0	92	95	45	37	8	10	26	62	1.315	3.62	140	4.22	.270	0	....	15	7	1.4
	Yr.	10	13	.435	34	31	1	1	1	199^1	228	112	101	29	13	57	137	1.430	4.56	110	5.08	.288	0	.000	13	12	1.1
2001	Tor-A	11	11	.500	36	30	1	1	0	190	239	113	106	27	9	40	110	1.468	5.02	91	5.30	.307	0	.000	-10	8	-1.0
2002	Tor-A	9	10	.474	25	25	3	1	0	151^1	192	102	96	18	4	38	87	1.520	5.71	81	5.26	.309	1	.167	-17	4	-1.7
2003	Chi-A★	21	9	.700	34	34	1	0	0	226^1	196	75	73	17	10	56	**207**	1.113	2.90	154	2.79	.233	1	.200	37	**23**	3.5
Total	**9**	**90**	**82**	**.523**	**269**	**236**	**10**	**4**	**1**	**1480**	**1666**	**820**	**753**	**178**	**60**	**413**	**965**	**1.405**	**4.58**	**100**	**4.63**	**.286**	**31**	**.178**	**7**	**79**	**0.7**

• LOCKE, Bobby Lawrence Donald Locke b: 3/3/1934, Rowes Run, PA BR/TR, 5'11", 185 lbs. Deb: 6/18/1959

YEAR	TM-L	W	L	PCT	G	GS	CG	SH	SV	IP	H	R	ER	HR	HB	BB	SO	RAT	ERA	ERA+	CERA	OAV	BH	AVG	PR+	WS	TPW
1959	Cle-A	3	2	.600	24	7	0	0	2	77^2	66	33	27	6	3	41	40	1.378	3.13	118	3.66	.233	8	.333	4	6	0.8
1960	Cle-A	3	5	.375	32	11	2	2	2	123	121	51	46	10	2	37	53	1.285	3.37	111	3.48	.255	9	.237	5	8	0.8
1961	Cle-A	4	4	.500	37	4	0	0	2	95^1	112	50	48	12	2	40	37	1.594	4.53	87	5.45	.300	4	.211	-6	4	-0.6
1962	StL-N	0	0	....	1	0	0	0	0	2	1	0	0	0	0	2	1	1.500	0.00	....	2.80	.143	0	....	1	0	0.1
	Phi-N	1	0	1.000	5	0	0	0	0	15^2	16	12	10	4	0	10	9	1.660	5.74	67	6.34	.262	2	.286	-3	0	-0.3
	Yr.	1	0	1.000	6	0	0	0	0	17^2	17	12	10	4	0	12	10	1.642	5.09	76	5.94	.250	2	.286	-2	0	-0.2
1963	Phi-N	0	0	....	9	0	0	0	0	10^2	10	7	7	0	0	5	7	1.406	5.91	55	3.13	.244	0	.000	-3	0	-0.4
1964	Phi-N	0	0	....	8	0	0	0	0	19^1	21	6	6	2	0	6	11	1.397	2.79	124	3.99	.276	0	.000	1	1	0.1
1965	Cin-N	0	1	.000	11	0	0	0	0	17^1	20	15	11	2	0	8	8	1.615	5.71	66	4.90	.299	0	.000	-4	0	-0.4
1967	Cal-A	3	0	1.000	9	1	0	0	2	19^1	14	6	5	1	1	3	7	.879	2.33	135	1.74	.203	2	.667	2	3	0.3
1968	Cal-A	2	3	.400	29	0	0	0	2	36^1	51	29	26	3	1	13	21	1.761	6.44	45	6.04	.331	0	.000	-15	0	-1.7
Total	**9**	**16**	**15**	**.516**	**165**	**23**	**2**	**2**	**10**	**416^2**	**432**	**209**	**186**	**40**	**9**	**165**	**194**	**1.433**	**4.02**	**89**	**4.28**	**.269**	**25**	**.255**	**-19**	**22**	**-1.3**

• LOCKE, Chuck Charles Edward Locke b: 5/5/1932, Malden, MO BR/TR, 5'11", 185 lbs. Deb: 9/16/1955

YEAR	TM-L	W	L	PCT	G	GS	CG	SH	SV	IP	H	R	ER	HR	HB	BB	SO	RAT	ERA	ERA+	CERA	OAV	BH	AVG	PR+	WS	TPW
1955	Bal-A	0	0	....	2	0	0	0	0	3	0	0	0	0	0	1	1	.333	0.00	....	0.11	.000	0	....	1	0	0.1

• LOCKE, Ron Ronald Thomas Locke b: 4/4/1942, Wakefield, RI BR/TL, 5'11", 168 lbs. Deb: 4/23/1964

YEAR	TM-L	W	L	PCT	G	GS	CG	SH	SV	IP	H	R	ER	HR	HB	BB	SO	RAT	ERA	ERA+	CERA	OAV	BH	AVG	PR+	WS	TPW
1964	NY-N	1	2	.333	25	3	0	0	0	41^1	46	23	16	3	1	22	17	1.645	3.48	103	5.16	.289	0	.000	0	1	0.0

• LOCKER, Bob Robert Awtry Locker b: 3/15/1938, George, IA BB/TR, 6'3", 200 lbs. Deb: 4/14/1965

YEAR	TM-L	W	L	PCT	G	GS	CG	SH	SV	IP	H	R	ER	HR	HB	BB	SO	RAT	ERA	ERA+	CERA	OAV	BH	AVG	PR+	WS	TPW
1965	Chi-A	5	2	.714	51	0	0	0	2	91^1	71	36	32	6	2	30	69	1.106	3.15	101	2.36	.216	0	.000	-1	5	-0.2

YEAR	TM-L	W	L	PCT	G	GS	CG	SH	SV	IP	H	R	ER	HR	HB	BB	SO	RAT	ERA	ERA+	CERA	OAV	BH	AVG	PR+	WS	TPW
1966	Chi-A	9	8	.529	56	0	0	0	12	95	73	32	26	2	5	23	70	1.011	2.46	129	1.80	.206	4	.250	7	12	0.9
1967	Chi-A	7	5	.583	**77**	0	0	0	20	124^{2}	102	34	29	5	10	23	80	1.003	2.09	148	2.19	.222	0	.000	14	16	1.4
1968	Chi-A	5	4	.556	70	0	0	0	10	90^{1}	78	27	23	4	1	27	62	1.162	2.29	132	2.43	.234	0	.000	8	9	0.8
1969	Chi-A	2	3	.400	17	0	0	0	4	22	26	18	16	6	0	6	15	1.455	6.55	59	5.78	.292	0	.000	-6	0	-0.7
	Sea-A	3	3	.500	51	0	0	0	6	78^{1}	69	29	19	3	3	26	46	1.213	2.18	166	2.73	.234	1	.083	15	7	1.5
	Yr.	5	6	.455	68	0	0	0	10	100^{1}	95	47	35	9	3	32	61	1.266	3.14	119	3.40	.247	1	.077	9	7	0.8
1970	Mil-A	0	1	.000	28	0	0	0	3	31^{2}	37	18	12	1	5	10	19	1.484	3.41	111	4.97	.306	0	.000	2	1	0.2
	Oak-A	3	3	.500	38	0	0	0	4	56^{1}	49	21	18	1	1	19	33	1.207	2.88	123	2.56	.232	1	.167	4	5	0.4
	Yr.	3	4	.429	66	0	0	0	7	88	86	39	30	2	6	29	52	1.307	3.07	118	3.42	.259	1	.143	6	6	0.6
1971*	Oak-A	7	2	.778	47	0	0	0	6	72^{1}	68	28	23	2	1	19	46	1.203	2.86	116	2.62	.249	0	.000	2	7	0.2
1972*	Oak-A	6	1	.857	56	0	0	0	10	78	69	25	23	1	2	16	47	1.090	2.65	107	2.19	.235	0	.000	1	7	0.1
1973	Chi-N	10	6	.625	63	0	0	0	18	106^{1}	96	40	30	6	4	42	76	1.298	2.54	155	3.23	.244	1	.067	19	17	1.9
1975	Chi-N	0	1	.000	22	0	0	0	0	32^{2}	38	21	18	3	2	16	14	1.653	4.96	77	5.56	.306	0	....	-3	1	-0.3
Total	10	57	39	.594	576	0	0	0	95	879	776	329	269	40	36	257	577	1.175	2.75	122	2.74	.237	7	.074	61	87	6.2

• LOCKWOOD, Milo Milo Hathaway Lockwood b: 4/7/1858, Solon, OH d: 10/9/1897, Economy, PA, 5'10", 160 lbs. Deb: 4/17/1884 ♦

YEAR	TM-L	W	L	PCT	G	GS	CG	SH	SV	IP	H	R	ER	HR	HB	BB	SO	RAT	ERA	ERA+	CERA	OAV	BH	AVG	PR+	WS	TPW
1884	Was-U	1	9	.100	11	10	6	0	0	67^{2}	99	95	56	4	....	15	48	1.685	7.45	40	....	.320	14	.209	-32	1	-2.8

• LOCKWOOD, Skip Claude Edward Lockwood b: 8/17/1946, Roslindale, MA BR/TR, 6'1", 190 lbs. Deb: 4/23/1965 ♦

YEAR	TM-L	W	L	PCT	G	GS	CG	SH	SV	IP	H	R	ER	HR	HB	BB	SO	RAT	ERA	ERA+	CERA	OAV	BH	AVG	PR+	WS	TPW
1969	Sea-A	0	1	.000	6	3	0	0	0	23	24	9	9	3	0	6	10	1.304	3.52	103	4.07	.279	0	.000	1	1	0.0
1970	Mil-A	5	12	.294	27	26	3	1	0	173^{2}	173	91	83	22	6	79	93	1.451	4.30	88	4.65	.266	12	.226	-6	6	-0.4
1971	Mil-A	10	15	.400	33	32	5	1	0	208	191	93	77	13	5	91	115	1.356	3.33	104	3.58	.246	5	.081	1	9	0.0
1972	Mil-A	8	15	.348	29	27	5	3	0	170	148	75	68	11	4	71	106	1.288	3.60	84	3.21	.232	7	.132	-11	5	-1.3
1973	Mil-A	5	12	.294	37	15	3	0	0	154^{2}	164	75	67	10	6	59	87	1.442	3.90	96	4.27	.280	0	....	-2	6	-0.2
1974	Cal-A	2	5	.286	37	2	0	0	1	81^{1}	81	42	39	8	5	32	39	1.389	4.32	80	4.17	.264	0	....	-7	2	-0.8
1975	NY-N	1	3	.250	24	0	0	0	2	48^{1}	28	9	8	3	1	25	61	1.097	1.49	232	2.05	.174	1	.167	10	5	1.0
1976	NY-N	10	7	.588	56	0	0	0	19	94^{1}	62	31	28	6	2	34	108	1.018	2.67	123	1.92	.186	6	.333	6	15	0.9
1977	NY-N	4	8	.333	63	0	0	0	20	104	87	40	39	5	4	31	84	1.135	3.38	111	2.48	.227	3	.200	4	13	0.4
1978	NY-N	7	13	.350	57	0	0	0	15	90^{2}	78	36	36	10	0	31	73	1.202	3.57	97	3.12	.236	2	.182	-2	8	0.0
1979	NY-N	2	5	.286	27	0	0	0	9	42^{1}	33	7	7	3	0	14	42	1.110	1.49	244	2.44	.224	0	.000	10	7	1.0
1980	Bos-A	3	1	.750	24	1	0	0	2	45^{2}	61	31	27	4	0	17	11	1.708	5.32	79	5.69	.321	0	....	-6	2	-0.6
Total	12	57	97	.370	420	106	16	5	68	1236	1130	539	488	98	33	490	829	1.311	3.55	99	3.54	.246	40	.154	-1	79	0.0

• LOES, Billy William Loes b: 12/13/1929, Long Island City, NY BR/TR, 6'1", 170 lbs. Deb: 5/18/1950

YEAR	TM-L	W	L	PCT	G	GS	CG	SH	SV	IP	H	R	ER	HR	HB	BB	SO	RAT	ERA	ERA+	CERA	OAV	BH	AVG	PR+	WS	TPW
1950	Bro-N	0	0	....	10	0	0	0	0	12^{2}	16	11	11	5	0	5	2	1.658	7.82	52	8.09	.314	0	.000	-6	0	-0.5
1952*	Bro-N	13	8	.619	39	21	8	4	1	187^{1}	154	62	56	12	3	71	115	1.201	2.69	135	2.80	.224	5	.093	18	16	1.6
1953*	Bro-N	14	8	.636	32	25	9	1	0	162^{2}	165	92	82	21	3	53	75	1.340	4.54	94	4.08	.261	7	.125	-7	8	-0.9
1954	Bro-N	13	5	.722	28	21	6	0	0	147^{2}	154	73	68	14	1	60	97	1.449	4.14	99	4.21	.269	6	.118	-1	9	-0.4
1955*	Bro-N	10	4	.714	22	19	6	0	0	128	116	59	51	16	2	46	85	1.266	3.59	113	3.61	.240	4	.091	6	8	0.3
1956	Bro-N	0	1	.000	1	1	0	0	0	1^{1}	5	6	6	1	0	1	2	4.500	40.50	10	34.22	.556	0	....	-5	0	-0.6
	Bal-A	2	7	.222	21	6	1	0	3	56^{2}	65	33	30	4	2	23	22	1.553	4.76	82	4.79	.291	3	.176	-5	2	-0.5
1957	Bal-A★	12	7	.632	31	18	8	3	4	155^{1}	142	59	56	8	4	37	86	1.152	3.24	111	2.79	.245	4	.080	3	11	0.0
1958	Bal-A	3	9	.250	32	10	1	0	5	114	106	51	46	10	8	44	44	1.316	3.63	99	3.77	.252	2	.067	0	6	-0.3
1959	Bal-A	4	7	.364	37	0	0	0	14	64^{1}	58	31	29	5	3	25	34	1.290	4.06	93	3.42	.239	1	.125	-2	6	-0.3
1960	SF-N	3	2	.600	37	0	0	0	5	45^{2}	40	26	25	9	4	17	28	1.248	4.93	71	4.33	.247	1	.250	-7	1	-0.7
1961	SF-N	6	5	.545	26	18	3	1	0	114^{2}	114	62	54	13	5	39	55	1.334	4.24	90	4.00	.258	5	.156	-5	4	-0.5
Total	11	80	63	.559	316	139	42	9	32	1190^{1}	1135	565	514	118	35	421	645	1.307	3.89	99	3.72	.252	38	.110	-11	71	-2.8

• LOEWER, Carlton Carlton Ernest Loewer b: 9/24/1973, Lafayette, LA BR/TR, 6'6", 211 lbs. Deb: 6/14/1998

YEAR	TM-L	W	L	PCT	G	GS	CG	SH	SV	IP	H	R	ER	HR	HB	BB	SO	RAT	ERA	ERA+	CERA	OAV	BH	AVG	PR+	WS	TPW
1998	Phi-N	7	8	.467	21	21	1	0	0	122^{2}	154	86	83	18	3	39	58	1.573	6.09	71	5.70	.312	3	.086	-24	1	-2.5
1999	Phi-N	2	6	.250	20	13	2	1	0	89^{2}	100	54	51	9	0	26	48	1.405	5.12	92	4.31	.287	5	.227	-5	3	-0.4
2001	SD-N	0	2	.000	2	2	0	0	0	4^{1}	13	12	12	2	0	3	1	3.692	24.92	16	23.60	.520	0	....	-10	0	-1.0
2003	SD-N	1	2	.333	5	5	0	0	0	21^{2}	35	17	16	3	1	8	11	1.985	6.65	59	8.30	.368	0	.000	-6	0	-0.7
Total	4	10	18	.357	48	41	3	1	0	238^{1}	302	169	162	32	4	76	118	1.586	6.12	72	5.74	.314	8	.129	-46	4	-4.6

• LOFTUS, Frank Francis Patrick Loftus b: 3/10/1898, Scranton, PA d: 10/27/1980, Belchertown, MA BR/TR, 5'9", 190 lbs. Deb: 9/26/1926

YEAR	TM-L	W	L	PCT	G	GS	CG	SH	SV	IP	H	R	ER	HR	HB	BB	SO	RAT	ERA	ERA+	CERA	OAV	BH	AVG	PR+	WS	TPW
1926	Was-A	0	0	....	1	0	0	0	0	1	3	2	1	0	0	2	0	5.000	9.00	43	27.09	.600	0	....	-1	0	-0.1

• LOGAN, Bob Robert Dean "Lefty" Logan b: 2/10/1910, Thompson, NE d: 5/20/1978, Indianapolis, IN BR/TL, 5'10", 170 lbs. Deb: 4/18/1935

YEAR	TM-L	W	L	PCT	G	GS	CG	SH	SV	IP	H	R	ER	HR	HB	BB	SO	RAT	ERA	ERA+	CERA	OAV	BH	AVG	PR+	WS	TPW
1935	Bro-N	0	1	.000	2	0	0	0	0	2^{2}	2	1	1	0	0	1	1	1.125	3.38	118	1.73	.182	0	....	0	0	0.0
1937	Det-A	0	0	....	1	0	0	0	0	0^{2}	1	0	0	0	0	1	1	3.000	0.00	....	10.19	.333	0	....	0	0	0.0
	Chi-N	0	0	....	4	0	0	0	1	6^{1}	6	1	1	0	0	4	2	1.579	1.42	280	3.81	.261	0	.000	2	1	0.2
1938	Chi-N	0	2	.000	14	0	0	0	2	22^{2}	18	9	7	0	1	17	10	1.544	2.78	137	3.54	.222	0	.000	2	2	0.2
1941	Cin-N	0	1	.000	2	0	0	0	0	3^{1}	5	5	3	0	0	5	0	3.000	8.10	44	10.19	.333	0	....	-2	0	-0.1
1945	Bos-N	7	11	.389	34	25	5	1	1	187	213	84	66	9	1	53	53	1.422	3.18	121	3.94	.283	13	.213	13	13	1.4
Total	5	7	15	.318	57	25	5	1	4	222^{2}	245	100	78	9	2	81	67	1.464	3.15	121	3.98	.277	13	.200	16	16	1.7

• LOHRMAN, Bill William Leroy Lohrman b: 5/22/1913, Brooklyn, NY d: 9/13/1999, Poughkeepsie, NY BR/TR, 6'1", 185 lbs. Deb: 6/19/1934

YEAR	TM-L	W	L	PCT	G	GS	CG	SH	SV	IP	H	R	ER	HR	HB	BB	SO	RAT	ERA	ERA+	CERA	OAV	BH	AVG	PR+	WS	TPW
1934	Phi-N	0	1	.000	4	0	0	0	1	6	5	5	3	0	0	1	2	1.000	4.50	105	1.71	.217	1	.500	0	0	0.0
1937	NY-N	1	0	1.000	2	1	1	0	1	10	5	1	1	0	0	2	3	.700	0.90	432	0.88	.152	0	.000	3	2	0.3
1938	NY-N	9	6	.600	31	14	3	0	0	152	152	72	56	9	2	33	52	1.217	3.32	113	3.05	.253	4	.082	7	10	0.4
1939	NY-N	12	13	.480	38	24	9	1	1	185^{2}	200	91	84	15	3	45	70	1.320	4.07	96	3.86	.282	14	.233	-3	12	0.1
1940	NY-N	10	15	.400	31	27	11	4	1	195	200	98	82	19	3	43	73	1.246	3.78	103	3.53	.264	8	.123	3	10	0.0
1941	NY-N	9	10	.474	33	20	6	2	3	159	184	87	71	7	0	40	61	1.409	4.02	92	3.87	.286	11	.229	-7	9	-0.3
1942	StL-N	1	1	.500	5	0	0	0	0	12^{2}	11	3	2	0	0	2	6	1.026	1.42	241	1.89	.244	2	.667	3	2	0.4
	NY-N	13	4	.765	26	19	12	2	0	158	143	52	45	11	2	33	41	1.114	2.56	131	2.65	.240	7	.121	12	13	1.1
	Yr.	14	5	.737	31	19	12	2	0	170^{2}	154	55	47	11	2	35	47	1.107	2.48	136	2.59	.240	9	.148	15	15	1.4
1943	NY-N	5	6	.455	17	12	3	0	1	80^{1}	110	51	46	7	2	25	16	1.680	5.15	67	5.78	.324	1	.037	-14	1	-1.8
	Bro-N	0	2	.000	6	2	2	0	0	27^{2}	29	14	11	2	1	10	5	1.410	3.58	94	4.01	.274	1	.143	-0	1	0.0
	Yr.	5	8	.385	23	14	5	0	1	108	139	65	57	9	3	35	21	1.611	4.75	72	5.33	.312	2	.059	-15	2	-1.8
1944	Bro-N	0	0	....	3	0	0	0	0	2^{2}	4	0	0	0	0	4	1	3.000	0.00	....	13.77	.500	0	....	1	0	0.1
	Cin-N	0	1	.000	2	1	0	0	0	1^{2}	5	5	5	0	0	2	0	4.200	27.00	13	20.02	.500	0	....	-4	0	-0.5
	Yr.	0	1	.000	5	1	0	0	0	4^{1}	9	5	5	0	0	6	1	3.462	10.38	34	16.17	.500	0	....	-3	0	-0.3
Total	9	60	59	.504	198	120	47	9	8	990^{2}	1048	479	406	70	13	240	330	1.300	3.69	100	3.62	.271	49	.153	1	60	-0.2

• LOHSE, Kyle Kyle Matthew Lohse b: 10/4/1978, Chico, CA BR/TR, 6'2", 190 lbs. Deb: 6/22/2001

YEAR	TM-L	W	L	PCT	G	GS	CG	SH	SV	IP	H	R	ER	HR	HB	BB	SO	RAT	ERA	ERA+	CERA	OAV	BH	AVG	PR+	WS	TPW
2001	Min-A	4	7	.364	19	16	0	0	0	90^{1}	102	60	57	16	8	29	64	1.450	5.68	81	5.43	.284	2	.400	-10	3	-0.9
2002*	Min-A	13	8	.619	32	31	1	1	0	180^{2}	181	92	85	26	9	70	124	1.389	4.23	106	4.55	.259	1	.250	5	11	0.5
2003*	Min-A	14	11	.560	33	33	2	1	0	201	211	107	103	28	5	45	130	1.274	4.61	98	4.00	.268	1	.333	2	11	0.3
Total	3	31	26	.544	84	80	3	2	0	472	494	259	245	70	22	144	318	1.352	4.67	97	4.48	.268	4	.333	-3	25	-0.1

• LOISELLE, Rich Richard Frank Loiselle b: 1/12/1972, Neenah, WI BR/TR, 6'5", 225 lbs. Deb: 9/7/1996

YEAR	TM-L	W	L	PCT	G	GS	CG	SH	SV	IP	H	R	ER	HR	HB	BB	SO	RAT	ERA	ERA+	CERA	OAV	BH	AVG	PR+	WS	TPW
1996	Pit-N	1	0	1.000	5	3	0	0	0	20^{2}	22	8	7	3	0	8	9	1.452	3.05	143	4.64	.268	2	.250	3	2	0.4
1997	Pit-N	1	5	.167	72	0	0	0	29	72^{2}	76	29	25	7	1	24	66	1.376	3.10	139	4.02	.269	0	.000	10	11	1.0
1998	Pit-N	2	7	.222	54	0	0	0	19	55	56	26	21	2	2	36	48	1.673	3.44	125	4.43	.262	0	....	5	6	0.5
1999	Pit-N	3	2	.600	13	0	0	0	0	15^{1}	16	9	9	2	2	9	14	1.630	5.28	86	5.82	.281	0	....	-1	1	-0.1
2000	Pit-N	2	3	.400	40	0	0	0	0	42^{1}	43	27	24	5	3	30	32	1.724	5.10	90	5.48	.262	0	....	-2	2	-0.2
2001	Pit-N	0	1	.000	18	0	0	0	1	18	28	24	23	3	4	17	9	2.500	11.50	39	11.11	.359	0	....	-14	0	-1.4
Total	6	9	18	.333	202	3	0	0	49	224	241	123	109	22	12	124	178	1.629	4.38	101	5.15	.274	2	.222	2	22	0.2

YEAR	TM-L	W	L	PCT	G	GS	CG	SH	SV	IP	H	R	ER	HR	HB	BB	SO	RAT	ERA	ERA+	CERA	OAV	BH	AVG	PR+	WS	TPW
• LOLICH, Mickey	Michael Stephen Lolich b: 9/12/1940, Portland, OR BB/TL, 6'1", 210 lbs. Deb: 5/12/1963																										
1963	Det-A	5	9	.357	33	18	4	0	0	144^{1}	145	64	57	13	5	56	103	1.393	3.55	105	4.15	.265	2	.056	3	7	0.3
1964	Det-A	18	9	.667	44	33	12	6	2	232	196	88	84	26	5	64	192	1.121	3.26	112	2.92	.225	7	.109	10	18	1.1
1965	Det-A	15	9	.625	43	37	7	3	3	243^{2}	216	103	93	23	12	72	226	1.182	3.44	101	3.19	.236	5	.058	3	15	-0.3
1966	Det-A	14	14	.500	40	33	5	1	3	203^{2}	204	119	108	24	6	83	173	**1.409**	4.77	73	4.25	.257	9	.141	-30	4	-3.1
1967	Det-A	14	13	.519	31	30	11	**6**	0	204	165	71	69	14	7	56	174	1.083	3.04	107	2.54	.221	12	.197	3	13	0.6
1968*	Det-A	17	9	.654	39	32	8	4	1	220	178	84	78	23	11	65	197	1.105	3.19	94	2.83	.219	8	.114	-5	12	-0.6
1969	Det-A★	19	11	.633	37	36	15	1	1	280^{2}	214	111	98	22	14	122	271	1.197	3.14	119	2.92	.210	8	.088	17	20	1.6
1970	Det-A	14	19	.424	40	39	13	3	0	272^{2}	272	125	115	27	5	109	230	1.397	3.80	98	4.10	.260	11	.134	6	17	0.7
1971	Det-A★	**25**	14	.641	45	**45**	**29**	4	0	**376**	336	133	122	36	7	92	**308**	1.138	2.92	123	2.94	.237	15	.130	28	29	3.2
1972*	Det-A★	22	14	.611	41	41	23	4	0	327^{1}	282	100	91	29	11	74	250	1.088	2.50	126	2.73	.234	6	.067	20	26	2.3
1973	Det-A	16	15	.516	42	42	17	3	0	308^{2}	315	143	131	35	5	79	214	1.276	3.82	107	3.79	.266	0	....	11	19	1.2
1974	Det-A	16	21	.432	41	41	27	3	0	308	310	155	142	38	3	78	202	1.260	4.15	92	3.77	.268	0	....	-10	17	-1.1
1975	Det-A	12	18	.400	32	32	19	1	0	240^{2}	260	119	101	19	0	64	139	1.346	3.78	106	3.85	.279	0	....	11	15	1.1
1976	NY-N	8	13	.381	31	30	5	2	0	192^{2}	184	83	69	14	0	52	120	1.225	3.22	102	3.15	.252	7	.130	0	8	0.1
1978	SD-N	2	1	.667	20	2	0	0	1	34^{2}	30	6	6	0	1	11	13	1.183	1.56	213	2.44	.240	0	.000	7	4	0.7
1979	SD-N	0	2	.000	27	5	0	0	0	49^{1}	59	33	26	4	0	22	20	1.642	4.74	74	5.16	.304	0	.000	-7	0	-0.8
Total	16	217	191	.532	586	496	195	41	11	3638^{1}	3366	1537	1390	347	92	1099	2832	1.227	3.44	104	3.35	.246	90	.110	67	224	6.9
• LOLLAR, Tim	William Timothy Lollar b: 3/17/1956, Poplar Bluff, MO BL/TL, 6'3", 200 lbs. Deb: 6/28/1980																										
1980	NY-A	1	0	1.000	14	1	0	0	2	32^{1}	33	14	12	3	0	20	13	1.639	3.34	117	5.00	.280	0	....	2	2	0.2
1981	SD-N	2	8	.200	24	11	0	0	1	76^{2}	87	56	52	4	3	51	38	1.800	6.10	53	5.52	.293	3	.167	-24	0	-2.5
1982	SD-N	16	9	.640	34	34	4	2	0	232^{2}	192	82	81	20	4	87	150	1.199	3.13	109	2.99	.224	21	.247	5	17	1.5
1983	SD-N	7	12	.368	30	30	1	0	0	175^{2}	170	98	90	22	4	85	135	1.452	4.61	76	4.57	.258	14	.241	-25	5	-2.0
1984*	SD-N	11	13	.458	31	31	3	2	0	195^{2}	168	89	85	18	1	105	131	1.395	3.91	91	3.81	.234	15	.221	-12	10	-0.5
1985	Chi-A	3	5	.375	18	13	0	0	0	83	83	48	43	10	1	58	61	1.699	4.66	93	5.53	.266	0	....	-4	3	-0.4
	Bos-A	5	5	.500	16	10	1	0	1	67	57	37	34	9	1	40	44	1.448	4.57	94	4.35	.230	0	.000	-1	3	-0.1
	Yr.	8	10	.444	34	23	1	0	1	150	140	85	77	19	2	98	105	1.587	4.62	93	5.01	.250	0	.000	-5	6	-0.5
1986	Bos-A	2	0	1.000	32	1	0	0	0	43	51	35	33	7	3	34	28	1.977	6.91	60	7.57	.304	1	1.000	-13	0	-1.2
Total	7	47	52	.475	199	131	9	4	4	906	841	459	430	93	17	480	600	1.458	4.27	85	4.31	.249	54	.234	-70	40	-4.9
• LOMBARDI, Vic	Victor Alvin Lombardi b: 9/20/1922, Reedley, CA d: 12/3/1997, Fresno, CA BL/TL, 5'7", 158 lbs. Deb: 4/18/1945																										
1945	Bro-N	10	11	.476	38	24	9	0	4	203^{2}	195	106	75	11	5	86	64	1.380	3.31	113	3.58	.252	13	.183	11	12	1.0
1946	Bro-N	13	10	.565	41	25	13	2	3	193	170	76	62	10	2	84	60	1.316	2.89	117	3.11	.235	14	.230	9	14	1.1
1947*	Bro-N	12	11	.522	33	20	7	3	3	174^{2}	156	73	58	12	2	65	72	1.265	2.99	138	3.17	.241	16	.242	19	15	2.0
1948	Pit-N	10	9	.526	38	17	9	0	4	163	156	72	67	9	2	67	54	1.368	3.70	110	3.57	.255	10	.208	6	13	0.7
1949	Pit-N	5	5	.500	34	12	4	0	1	134	149	74	68	14	3	68	64	1.619	4.57	92	5.22	.286	17	.347	-5	9	0.1
1950	Pit-N	0	5	.000	39	2	0	0	1	76^{1}	93	61	56	14	2	48	26	1.847	6.60	66	7.10	.310	4	.250	-18	0	-1.7
Total	6	50	51	.495	223	100	42	5	16	944^{2}	919	462	386	70	16	418	340	1.415	3.68	107	3.92	.257	74	.238	21	63	3.2
• LOMBARDO, Lou	Louis Lombardo b: 11/18/1928, Carlstadt, NJ d: 6/11/2001, Rock Hill, SC BL/TL, 6'2", 210 lbs. Deb: 9/22/1948																										
1948	NY-N	0	0	....	2	0	0	0	0	5^{1}	5	4	4	1	1	5	0	1.875	6.75	58	6.92	.250	0	.000	-2	0	-0.2
• LOMON, Kevin	Kevin Dale Lomon b: 11/20/1971, Fort Smith, AR BR/TR, 6'1", 195 lbs. Deb: 4/27/1995																										
1995	NY-N	0	1	.000	6	0	0	0	0	9^{1}	17	8	7	0	0	5	6	2.357	6.75	60	9.02	.405	0	....	-3	0	-0.3
1996	Atl-N	0	0	....	6	0	0	0	0	7^{1}	7	4	4	0	1	3	1	1.364	4.91	90	3.82	.259	0	....	-0	0	0.0
Total	2	0	1	.000	12	0	0	0	0	16^{2}	24	12	11	0	1	8	7	1.920	5.94	70	6.73	.348	0	....	-3	0	-0.3
• LONBORG, Jim	James Reynold Lonborg b: 4/16/1942, Santa Maria, CA BR/TR, 6'5", 210 lbs. Deb: 4/23/1965																										
1965	Bos-A	9	17	.346	32	31	7	1	0	185^{1}	193	112	92	20	3	65	113	1.392	4.47	83	4.13	.262	8	.136	-12	5	-1.2
1966	Bos-A	10	10	.500	45	23	3	1	2	181^{2}	173	86	78	18	7	55	131	1.255	3.86	98	3.51	.249	5	.093	-0	9	-0.2
1967*	Bos-A★	**22**	9	.710	39	**39**	15	2	0	273^{1}	228	102	96	23	19	83	**246**	1.138	3.16	110	2.95	.225	14	.141	11	19	1.1
1968	Bos-A	6	10	.375	23	17	4	1	0	113^{1}	89	57	54	11	11	59	73	1.306	4.29	74	3.66	.216	11	.282	-14	4	-1.2
1969	Bos-A	7	11	.389	29	23	4	0	0	143^{2}	148	78	72	15	7	65	100	1.483	4.51	84	4.72	.270	4	.098	-8	5	-0.9
1970	Bos-A	4	1	.800	9	4	0	0	0	34	33	12	12	3	0	9	21	1.235	3.18	125	3.41	.260	4	.444	4	4	0.6
1971	Bos-A	10	7	.588	27	26	5	1	0	167^{2}	167	86	77	15	14	67	100	1.396	4.13	89	4.24	.259	9	.170	-6	7	-0.6
1972	Mil-A	14	12	.538	33	30	11	2	1	223	197	75	70	17	11	76	143	1.224	2.83	107	3.19	.238	10	.145	5	14	0.5
1973	Phi-N	13	16	.448	38	30	6	0	0	199^{1}	218	124	108	25	9	80	106	1.495	4.88	78	4.92	.279	8	.136	-26	5	-2.7
1974	Phi-N	17	13	.567	39	39	16	3	0	283	280	113	101	22	6	70	121	1.237	3.21	118	3.35	.261	9	.096	12	21	0.9
1975	Phi-N	8	6	.571	27	26	6	2	0	159^{1}	161	84	73	12	5	45	72	1.293	4.12	90	3.51	.257	1	.023	-11	6	-1.5
1976*	Phi-N	18	10	.643	33	32	8	1	1	222	210	85	76	18	5	50	118	1.171	3.08	115	3.04	.249	11	.164	8	15	1.0
1977*	Phi-N	11	4	.733	25	25	4	1	0	157^{2}	157	77	72	15	5	50	76	1.313	4.11	97	3.80	.261	5	.104	-5	7	-0.7
1978	Phi-N	8	10	.444	22	22	1	0	0	113^{2}	132	69	66	16	2	45	48	1.557	5.23	68	5.40	.293	6	.176	-23	1	-2.4
1979	Phi-N	0	1	.000	4	1	0	0	0	7^{1}	14	10	9	3	1	4	7	2.455	11.05	35	14.09	.389	0	.000	-6	0	-0.6
Total	15	157	137	.534	425	368	90	15	4	2464^{1}	2400	1170	1056	233	105	823	1475	1.308	3.86	94	3.78	.255	105	.136	-71	122	-7.8
• LONG, Bill	William Douglas Long b: 2/29/1960, Cincinnati, OH BR/TR, 6', 185 lbs. Deb: 7/21/1985																										
1985	Chi-A	0	1	.000	4	3	0	0	0	14	25	17	16	4	0	5	13	2.143	10.29	42	10.14	.391	0	....	-9	0	-0.9
1987	Chi-A	8	8	.500	29	23	5	2	1	169	179	85	82	20	3	28	72	1.225	4.37	105	3.69	.272	0	....	-1	10	-0.1
1988	Chi-A	8	11	.421	47	18	3	0	2	174	187	89	78	21	4	43	77	1.322	4.03	98	4.14	.280	0	....	-4	8	-0.4
1989	Chi-A	5	5	.500	30	8	0	0	1	98^{2}	101	49	43	8	4	37	51	1.399	3.92	97	4.10	.265	0	....	-1	4	-0.1
1990	Chi-A	0	1	.000	4	0	0	0	0	5^{2}	6	5	4	2	0	2	2	1.412	6.35	60	5.65	.261	0	....	-2	0	-0.2
	Chi-N	6	1	.857	42	0	0	0	5	55^{2}	66	29	27	8	1	21	32	1.563	4.37	93	5.47	.301	0	.000	-0	4	0.0
1991	Mon-N	0	0	....	3	0	0	0	0	1^{2}	4	2	2	0	0	4	0	4.800	10.80	33	23.59	.500	0	....	-1	0	-0.1
Total	6	27	27	.500	159	52	8	2	9	518^{2}	568	276	252	63	12	140	247	1.365	4.37	95	4.37	.281	0	.000	-19	26	-1.9
• LONG, Bob	Robert Earl Long b: 11/11/1954, Jasper, TN BR/TR, 6'3", 178 lbs. Deb: 9/2/1981																										
1981	Pit-N	1	2	.333	5	3	0	0	0	19^{2}	23	14	13	2	0	10	8	1.678	5.95	60	5.51	.299	0	.000	-5	0	-0.6
1985	Sea-A	0	0	....	28	0	0	0	0	38^{1}	30	17	16	7	2	17	29	1.226	3.76	112	3.75	.210	0	....	2	2	0.2
Total	2	1	2	.333	33	3	0	0	0	58	53	31	29	9	2	27	37	1.379	4.50	87	4.35	.241	0	.000	-3	2	-0.4
• LONG, Joey	Joey J. Long b: 7/15/1970, Sidney, OH BR/TL, 6'2", 220 lbs. Deb: 4/25/1997																										
1997	SD-N	0	0	....	10	0	0	0	0	11	17	11	10	1	1	8	8	2.273	8.18	47	8.63	.340	0	....	-5	0	-0.5
• LONG, Lep	Lester Long b: 7/12/1888, Summit, NJ d: 10/21/1958, Birmingham, AL BR/TR, 5'10", 153 lbs. Deb: 6/29/1911																										
1911	Phi-A	0	0	....	4	0	0	0	0	8	15	6	4	0	0	5	4	2.500	4.50	70	9.69	.405	0	.000	-1	0	-0.2
• LONG, Red	Nelson Long b: 9/28/1876, Burlington, Canada d: 8/11/1929, Hamilton, Canada BR/TR, 6'1", 190 lbs. Deb: 9/11/1902																										
1902	Bos-N	0	0	....	1	1	1	0	0	8	4	2	1	0	1	3	5	.875	1.13	251	1.30	.150	0	.000	1	1	0.1
• LONG, Tom	Thomas Francis "Little Hawk" Long b: 4/22/1898, Memphis, TN d: 9/16/1973, Louisville, KY BL/TL, 5'9", 154 lbs. Deb: 4/26/1924																										
1924	Bro-N	0	0	....	1	0	0	0	0	2	2	2	2	0	0	2	0	2.000	9.00	42	5.81	.333	0	....	-1	0	-0.1
• LOONEY, Brian	Brian James Looney b: 9/26/1969, New Haven, CT BL/TL, 5'10", 180 lbs. Deb: 9/26/1993																										
1993	Mon-N	0	0	....	3	1	0	0	0	6	8	2	2	0	0	2	7	1.667	3.00	139	4.83	.308	0	.000	1	0	0.1
1994	Mon-N	0	0	....	1	0	0	0	0	2	4	5	5	1	1	0	2	2.000	22.50	19	14.72	.400	0	....	-4	0	-0.4
1995	Bos-A	0	1	.000	3	1	0	0	0	4^{2}	12	9	9	1	0	4	2	3.429	17.36	28	18.09	.545	0	....	-6	0	-0.6
Total	3	0	1	.000	7	2	0	0	0	12^{2}	24	16	16	2	1	6	11	2.368	11.37	40	11.28	.414	0	.000	-10	0	-0.9
• LOOPER, Aaron	Aaron Joseph Looper b: 9/7/1976, Ada, OK BR/TR, 6'2", 185 lbs. Deb: 8/2/2003																										
2003	Sea-A	0	0	....	6	0	0	0	0	7	7	4	4	1	1	2	6	1.286	5.14	84	4.73	.269	0	....	-1	0	-0.1

YEAR TM-L	W	L	PCT	G	GS	CG	SH	SV	IP	H	R	ER	HR	HB	BB	SO	RAT	ERA	ERA+	CERA	OAV	BH	AVG	PR+	WS	TPW
• LOOPER, Braden	Braden LaVern Looper b: 10/28/1974, Weatherford, OK BR/TR, 6'4", 225 lbs. Deb: 3/31/1998																									
1998 StL-N	0	1	.000	4	0	0	0	0	3^1	5	4	2	1	0	1	4	1.800	5.40	78	8.14	.357	0	....	-0	0	0.0
1999 Fla-N	3	3	.500	72	0	0	0	0	83	96	43	35	7	1	31	50	1.530	3.80	115	4.67	.293	0	....	5	5	0.5
2000 Fla-N	5	1	.833	73	0	0	0	2	67^1	71	41	33	3	5	36	29	1.589	4.41	100	4.55	.268	0	.000	1	5	0.0
2001 Fla-N	3	3	.500	71	0	0	0	3	71	63	28	28	8	2	30	52	1.310	3.55	119	3.77	.242	0	.000	5	7	0.4
2002 Fla-N	2	5	.286	78	0	0	0	13	86	73	31	30	8	1	28	55	1.174	3.14	125	2.98	.230	0	.000	7	11	0.7
2003* Fla-N	6	4	.600	74	0	0	0	28	80^2	82	34	33	4	1	29	56	1.376	3.68	111	3.67	.264	1	1.000	3	11	0.4
Total 6	19	17	.528	372	0	0	0	46	391^1	390	181	161	31	10	155	246	1.393	3.70	114	3.94	.261	1	.167	21	39	2.0
• LOOS, Pete	Ivan Loos b: 3/23/1878, Philadelphia, PA d: 2/23/1956, Darby, PA TR Deb: 5/2/1901																									
1901 Phi-A	0	1	.000	1	1	0	0	0	1	2	5	3	0	0	4	0	6.000	27.00	14	24.88	.410	0	....	-3	0	-0.2
• LOPAT, Ed	Edmund Walter Lopat b: 6/21/1918, New York, NY d: 6/15/1992, Darien, CT BL/TL, 5'10", 185 lbs. Deb: 4/30/1944 M/C																									
1944 Chi-A	11	10	.524	27	25	13	1	0	210	217	96	76	12	2	59	75	1.314	3.26	105	3.43	.265	25	.309	4	16	1.1
1945 Chi-A	10	13	.435	26	24	17	1	1	199^1	226	101	91	8	6	56	74	1.415	4.11	81	3.92	.285	24	.293	-15	9	-1.0
1946 Chi-A	13	13	.500	29	29	20	2	0	231	216	80	70	18	1	48	89	1.143	2.73	125	2.85	.248	22	.253	15	19	2.3
1947 Chi-A	16	13	.552	31	31	22	3	0	252^2	241	88	79	17	2	73	109	1.243	2.81	130	3.16	.253	19	.198	24	21	2.5
1948 NY-A	17	11	.607	33	31	13	3	0	226^2	246	106	92	16	2	66	83	1.376	3.65	112	3.94	.284	14	.173	8	14	0.6
1949* NY-A	15	10	.600	31	30	14	4	1	215^1	222	93	78	19	5	69	70	1.351	3.26	124	3.93	.269	20	.263	14	17	2.0
1950* NY-A	18	8	.692	35	32	15	3	1	236^1	244	110	91	19	4	65	72	1.307	3.47	124	3.64	.266	19	.232	19	20	2.4
1951* NY-A★	21	9	.700	31	31	20	4	0	234^2	209	86	76	12	3	71	93	1.193	2.91	131	2.79	.239	15	.179	21	19	2.1
1952* NY-A	10	5	.667	20	19	10	2	0	149^1	127	47	42	11	4	53	56	1.205	2.53	131	3.01	.234	9	.173	8	12	0.9
1953* NY-A	16	4	.800	25	24	9	3	0	178^1	169	58	48	13	4	32	50	1.127	**2.42**	**152**	2.85	.250	12	.190	20	16	2.1
1954 NY-A	12	4	.750	26	23	7	0	0	170	189	74	67	14	6	33	54	1.306	3.55	97	3.90	.288	1	.018	-6	8	-1.2
1955 NY-A	4	8	.333	16	12	3	1	0	86^2	101	45	36	12	1	16	24	1.350	3.74	100	4.49	.294	4	.138	-4	3	-0.5
Bal-A	3	4	.429	10	7	1	0	0	49	57	24	23	8	3	9	10	1.347	4.22	90	4.80	.294	3	.176	-2	2	-0.1
Yr.	7	12	.368	26	19	4	1	0	135^2	158	69	59	20	4	25	34	1.349	3.91	96	4.60	.294	7	.152	-5	5	-0.6
Total 12	166	112	.597	340	318	164	27	3	2439^1	2464	1008	869	179	43	650	859	1.277	3.21	115	3.47	.264	187	.211	107	176	13.2
• LOPATKA, Art	Arthur Joseph Lopatka b: 5/28/1919, Chicago, IL BB/TL, 5'10", 170 lbs. Deb: 9/12/1945																									
1945 StL-N	1	0	1.000	4	1	1	0	0	11^2	7	4	2	0	1	3	5	.857	1.54	242	1.29	.159	1	.250	3	1	0.3
1946 Phi-N	0	1	.000	4	1	0	0	0	5^1	13	11	10	1	0	4	4	3.188	16.88	20	15.84	.448	0	....	-8	0	-0.8
Total 2	1	1	.500	8	2	1	0	0	17	20	15	12	1	1	7	9	1.588	6.35	55	5.85	.274	1	.250	-5	1	-0.6
• LOPEZ, Albie	Albert Anthony Lopez b: 8/18/1971, Mesa, AZ BR/TR, 6'1", 205 lbs. Deb: 7/6/1993																									
1993 Cle-A	3	1	.750	9	9	0	0	0	49^2	49	34	33	7	1	32	25	1.631	5.98	72	5.45	.262	0	....	-9	1	-0.9
1994 Cle-A	1	2	.333	4	4	1	1	0	17	20	11	8	3	1	6	18	1.529	4.24	111	5.76	.290	0	....	1	1	0.1
1995 Cle-A	0	0	....	6	2	0	0	0	23	17	8	8	4	1	7	22	1.043	3.13	150	2.91	.205	0	....	4	2	0.4
1996 Cle-A	5	4	.556	13	10	0	0	0	62	80	47	44	14	2	22	45	1.645	6.39	77	6.74	.311	0	....	-10	2	-0.9
1997 Cle-A	3	7	.300	37	6	0	0	0	76^2	101	61	59	11	4	40	63	1.839	6.93	68	6.89	.321	0	.000	-18	0	-1.8
1998 TB-A	7	4	.636	54	0	0	0	1	79^2	73	31	23	7	3	32	62	1.318	2.60	185	3.66	.249	0	.000	16	9	1.5
1999 TB-A	3	2	.600	51	0	0	0	1	64	66	40	33	8	1	24	37	1.406	4.64	107	4.27	.263	0	....	3	4	0.2
2000 TB-A	11	13	.458	45	24	4	1	2	185^1	199	95	85	24	1	70	96	1.451	4.13	120	4.68	.277	0	.000	14	13	1.2
2001 TB-A	5	12	.294	20	20	1	1	0	124^2	152	87	74	16	4	51	67	1.628	5.34	84	5.74	.302	0	.000	-12	3	-1.2
* Ari-N	4	7	.364	13	13	2	2	0	81	74	36	36	10	0	24	69	1.210	4.00	114	3.39	.247	1	.042	4	5	0.3
2002 Atl-N	1	4	.200	30	4	0	0	0	55^2	66	29	27	1	0	18	39	1.509	4.37	94	4.19	.300	1	.111	-3	2	-0.3
2003 KC-A	4	2	.667	15	0	0	0	0	22^2	41	32	32	7	0	17	15	2.559	12.71	41	12.68	.383	0	....	-19	0	-1.8
Total 11	47	58	.448	297	92	8	5	4	841^1	938	511	462	112	18	343	558	1.523	4.94	95	5.14	.284	2	.043	-30	42	-3.2
• LOPEZ, Aquilino	Aquilino Lopez b: 4/21/1975, Villa Altagracia, Dominican Republic BR/TR, 6'3", 165 lbs. Deb: 4/2/2003																									
2003 Tor-A	1	3	.250	72	0	0	0	14	73^2	58	31	28	5	5	34	64	1.249	3.42	134	3.04	.212	0	....	11	10	1.1
• LOPEZ, Aurelio	Aurelio Alejandro (Rios) Lopez b: 9/21/1948, Tecamachalco, Mexico d: 9/22/1992, Matehuala, Mexico BR/TR, 6', 220 lbs. Deb: 9/1/1974																									
1974 KC-A	0	0	....	8	1	0	0	0	16	21	12	10	0	0	10	5	1.938	5.63	68	6.11	.344	0	....	-3	0	-0.3
1978 StL-N	4	2	.667	25	4	0	0	0	65	52	35	31	4	1	32	46	1.292	4.29	82	3.03	.218	3	.214	-6	2	-0.6
1979 Det-A	10	5	.667	61	0	0	0	21	127	95	37	34	12	3	51	106	1.150	2.41	180	2.78	.210	0	....	26	19	2.5
1980 Det-A	13	6	.684	67	1	0	0	21	124	125	56	52	15	3	45	97	1.371	3.77	109	4.15	.263	0	....	6	13	0.6
1981 Det-A	5	2	.714	29	3	0	0	3	81^2	70	34	33	8	2	31	53	1.237	3.64	104	3.31	.233	0	....	-1	6	-0.1
1982 Det-A	3	1	.750	19	0	0	0	3	41	41	27	24	8	0	19	26	1.463	5.27	77	4.96	.268	0	....	-6	1	-0.6
1983 Det-A★	9	8	.529	57	0	0	0	18	115^1	87	36	36	12	1	49	90	1.179	2.81	139	2.84	.210	0	....	13	14	1.3
1984* Det-A	10	1	.909	71	0	0	0	14	137^2	109	51	45	16	2	52	94	1.169	2.94	133	3.02	.221	0	....	14	13	1.4
1985 Det-A	3	7	.300	51	0	0	0	5	86^1	82	50	46	15	1	41	53	1.425	4.80	85	4.44	.250	0	....	-7	3	-0.7
1986* Hou-N	3	3	.500	45	0	0	0	7	78	64	32	30	6	0	25	44	1.141	3.46	104	2.63	.221	0	.000	1	6	0.0
1987 Hou-N	2	1	.667	26	0	0	0	1	38	39	22	19	6	2	12	21	1.342	4.50	87	4.50	.273	0	.000	-2	2	-0.2
Total 11	62	36	.633	459	9	0	0	93	910	785	392	360	102	15	367	635	1.266	3.56	110	3.45	.234	3	.125	34	79	3.2
• LOPEZ, Javier	Javier Alfonso Lopez b: 7/11/1977, San Juan, Puerto Rico BL/TL, 6'4", 200 lbs. Deb: 4/1/2003																									
2003 Col-N	4	1	.800	75	0	0	0	1	58^1	58	25	24	5	4	12	40	1.200	3.70	133	3.44	.258	1	.200	9	6	0.9
• LOPEZ, Marcelino	Marcelino Pons Lopez b: 9/23/1943, Havana, Cuba BR/TL, 6'3", 210 lbs. Deb: 4/14/1963																									
1963 Phi-N	1	0	1.000	4	2	0	0	0	6	8	5	4	0	0	7	2	2.500	6.00	54	8.09	.333	0	.000	-2	0	-0.2
1965 Cal-A	14	13	.519	35	32	8	1	1	215^1	185	79	70	12	4	82	122	1.240	2.93	116	2.97	.230	14	.203	10	15	1.5
1966 Cal-A	7	14	.333	37	32	6	2	1	199	188	95	87	20	9	68	132	1.286	3.93	85	3.72	.251	11	.190	-15	7	-1.4
1967 Cal-A	0	2	.000	4	3	0	0	0	9	11	10	9	1	0	9	6	2.222	9.00	35	8.04	.324	1	.500	-6	0	-0.6
Bal-A	1	0	1.000	4	4	0	0	0	17^2	15	5	5	1	0	10	15	1.415	2.55	124	3.60	.227	0	.000	1	1	0.1
Yr.	1	2	.333	8	7	0	0	0	26^2	26	15	14	2	0	19	21	1.688	4.73	67	5.09	.260	1	.143	-5	1	-0.5
1969* Bal-A	5	3	.625	27	4	0	0	0	69^1	65	34	34	3	2	34	57	1.428	4.41	81	3.73	.252	3	.214	-9	3	-0.8
1970* Bal-A	1	1	.500	25	3	0	0	0	60^2	47	19	14	2	0	37	49	1.385	2.08	176	3.09	.217	1	.077	9	5	1.0
1971 Mil-A	2	7	.222	31	11	0	0	0	67^2	64	48	35	5	0	60	42	1.833	4.66	75	5.35	.251	1	.059	-10	0	-1.2
1972 Cle-A	0	0	....	4	2	0	0	0	8^1	8	5	5	0	0	10	1	2.160	5.40	60	6.50	.276	0	.000	-2	0	-0.3
Total 8	31	40	.437	171	93	14	3	2	653	591	300	263	44	15	317	426	1.391	3.62	94	3.72	.243	31	.171	-23	31	-2.0
• LOPEZ, Ramon	Jose Ramon (Hevia) Lopez b: 5/26/1933, Las Villas, Cuba d: 9/4/1982, Miami, FL BR/TR, 6', 175 lbs. Deb: 8/21/1966																									
1966 Cal-A	0	1	.000	4	1	0	0	0	7	4	5	4	1	0	4	2	1.143	5.14	65	2.58	.154	0	....	-1	0	-0.2
• LOPEZ, Rodrigo	Rodrigo (Munoz) Lopez b: 12/14/1975, Tlalnepantla, Mexico BR/TR, 6'1", 180 lbs. Deb: 4/29/2000																									
2000 SD-N	0	3	.000	6	6	0	0	0	24^2	40	24	24	5	0	13	17	2.149	8.76	49	9.78	.377	1	.111	-12	0	-1.2
2002 Bal-A	15	9	.625	33	28	1	0	0	196^2	172	83	78	23	5	62	136	1.190	3.57	120	3.27	.234	0	.000	13	15	1.2
2003 Bal-A	7	10	.412	26	26	3	1	0	147	188	101	95	24	10	43	103	1.571	5.82	76	6.00	.313	0	.000	-23	3	-2.2
Total 3	22	22	.500	65	60	4	1	0	368^1	400	208	197	52	15	118	256	1.406	4.81	90	4.80	.277	1	.071	-22	18	-2.2
• LORENZEN, Lefty	Adolph Andreas Lorenzen b: 1/12/1893, Davenport, IA d: 3/5/1963, Davenport, IA BL/TL, 5'10", 164 lbs. Deb: 9/12/1913																									
1913 Det-A	0	0	....	1	0	0	0	0	2	4	4	4	0	0	3	0	3.500	18.00	16	20.06	.667	1	.500	-3	0	-0.3
• LORRAINE, Andrew	Andrew Jason Lorraine b: 8/11/1972, Los Angeles, CA BL/TL, 6'3", 195 lbs. Deb: 7/17/1994																									
1994 Cal-A	0	2	.000	4	3	0	0	0	18^2	30	23	22	7	0	11	10	2.196	10.61	46	11.13	.366	0	....	-12	0	-1.1
1995 Chi-A	0	0	....	5	0	0	0	0	8	3	3	3	0	1	2	5	.625	3.38	132	0.85	.111	0	....	1	1	0.1
1997 Oak-A	3	1	.750	12	6	0	0	0	29^2	45	22	21	2	1	15	18	2.022	6.37	71	7.57	.354	0	....	-5	1	-0.5
1998 Sea-A	0	0	....	4	0	0	0	0	3^2	3	1	1	0	0	4	0	1.909	2.45	189	5.44	.250	0	....	1	0	0.1
1999 Chi-N	2	5	.286	11	11	2	1	0	61^2	71	42	38	9	0	22	40	1.508	5.55	82	5.03	.293	2	.133	-6	2	-0.6

YEAR	TM-L	W	L	PCT	G	GS	CG	SH	SV	IP	H	R	ER	HR	HB	BB	SO	RAT	ERA	ERA+	CERA	OAV	BH	AVG	PR+	WS	TPW
2000	Chi-N	1	2	.333	8	5	0	0	0	32	36	25	23	5	0	18	25	1.688	6.47	70	5.80	.286	1	.125	-7	0	-0.6
	Cle-A	0	0	....	10	0	0	0	0	9^1	8	4	4	1	0	5	5	1.393	3.86	129	3.78	.222	0	....	1	1	0.1
2002	Mil-N	0	1	.000	5	1	0	0	0	12	22	18	15	7	0	6	10	2.333	11.25	36	13.99	.379	0	.000	-10	0	-1.0
Total	**7**	**6**	**11**	**.353**	**59**	**26**	**2**	**1**	**0**	**175**	**218**	**138**	**127**	**31**	**2**	**83**	**113**	**1.720**	**6.53**	**69**	**6.61**	**.307**	**3**	**.125**	**-37**	**5**	**-3.5**

• LOTZ, Joe Joseph Peter "Smokey" Lotz b: 1/2/1891, Remsen, IA d: 1/1/1971, Castro Valley, CA BR/TR, 5'8.5", 175 lbs. Deb: 7/15/1916

YEAR	TM-L	W	L	PCT	G	GS	CG	SH	SV	IP	H	R	ER	HR	HB	BB	SO	RAT	ERA	ERA+	CERA	OAV	BH	AVG	PR+	WS	TPW
1916	StL-N	0	3	.000	12	3	1	0	0	40	31	20	19	1	1	17	18	1.200	4.28	62	2.56	.225	4	.333	-7	1	-0.7

• LOUDELL, Art Arthur Loudell b: 4/10/1882, Latham, MO d: 2/19/1961, Kansas City, MO BR/TR, 5'11", 173 lbs. Deb: 8/13/1910

YEAR	TM-L	W	L	PCT	G	GS	CG	SH	SV	IP	H	R	ER	HR	HB	BB	SO	RAT	ERA	ERA+	CERA	OAV	BH	AVG	PR+	WS	TPW
1910	Det-A	1	1	.500	5	2	1	0	0	21^1	23	13	8	0	0	14	12	1.734	3.38	78	4.75	.284	1	.143	-2	0	-0.2

• LOUGHLIN, Larry Larry John Loughlin b: 8/16/1941, Tacoma, WA d: 1/26/1999, Denver, CO BL/TL, 6'1", 190 lbs. Deb: 5/27/1967

YEAR	TM-L	W	L	PCT	G	GS	CG	SH	SV	IP	H	R	ER	HR	HB	BB	SO	RAT	ERA	ERA+	CERA	OAV	BH	AVG	PR+	WS	TPW
1967	Phi-N	0	0	....	3	0	0	0	0	5^1	9	9	9	1	0	4	5	2.438	15.19	22	10.55	.375	1	1.000	-7	0	-0.7

• LOUN, Don Donald Nelson Loun b: 11/9/1940, Frederick, MD BR/TL, 6'2", 185 lbs. Deb: 9/23/1964

YEAR	TM-L	W	L	PCT	G	GS	CG	SH	SV	IP	H	R	ER	HR	HB	BB	SO	RAT	ERA	ERA+	CERA	OAV	BH	AVG	PR+	WS	TPW
1964	Was-A	1	1	.500	2	2	1	1	0	13	13	4	3	0	0	3	3	1.231	2.08	178	2.70	.250	0	.000	2	1	0.2

• LOUX, Shane Shane A. Loux b: 8/13/1979, Rapid City, SD BR/TR, 6'2", 205 lbs. Deb: 9/10/2002

YEAR	TM-L	W	L	PCT	G	GS	CG	SH	SV	IP	H	R	ER	HR	HB	BB	SO	RAT	ERA	ERA+	CERA	OAV	BH	AVG	PR+	WS	TPW
2002	Det-A	0	3	.000	3	3	0	0	0	14	19	16	14	4	1	3	7	1.571	9.00	48	7.12	.317	0	....	-7	0	-0.7
2003	Det-A	1	1	.500	11	4	0	0	0	30^1	37	24	24	4	4	12	8	1.615	7.12	61	6.12	.303	0	....	-10	0	-0.9
Total	**2**	**1**	**4**	**.200**	**14**	**7**	**0**	**0**	**0**	**44^1**	**56**	**40**	**38**	**8**	**5**	**15**	**15**	**1.602**	**7.71**	**56**	**6.44**	**.308**	**0**	**....**	**-17**	**0**	**-1.6**

• LOVE, Slim Edward Haughton Love b: 8/1/1890, Love, MS d: 11/30/1942, Memphis, TN BL/TL, 6'7", 195 lbs. Deb: 9/8/1913

YEAR	TM-L	W	L	PCT	G	GS	CG	SH	SV	IP	H	R	ER	HR	HB	BB	SO	RAT	ERA	ERA+	CERA	OAV	BH	AVG	PR+	WS	TPW
1913	Was-A	1	0	1.000	5	1	0	0	1	16^2	14	5	3	0	0	6	5	1.200	1.62	182	2.38	.226	1	.200	2	2	0.3
1916	NY-A	2	0	1.000	20	1	0	0	0	47^2	46	29	26	2	0	23	21	1.448	4.91	59	4.02	.274	0	.000	-11	0	-1.4
1917	NY-A	6	5	.545	33	9	2	0	1	130^1	115	50	34	0	1	57	82	1.320	2.35	114	3.05	.251	6	.167	4	9	0.4
1918	NY-A	13	12	.520	38	29	13	1	1	228^2	207	92	78	3	10	116	95	1.413	3.07	92	3.50	.253	17	.230	-13	11	-1.2
1919	Det-A	6	4	.600	22	8	4	0	1	89^2	92	40	30	3	6	40	46	1.472	3.01	106	4.25	.275	6	.222	3	6	0.4
1920	Det-A	0	0	....	1	0	0	0	0	4^1	6	4	4	0	0	4	2	2.308	8.31	45	8.37	.375	0	....	-2	0	-0.2
Total	**6**	**28**	**21**	**.571**	**119**	**48**	**19**	**1**	**4**	**517^1**	**480**	**220**	**175**	**8**	**17**	**246**	**251**	**1.403**	**3.04**	**95**	**3.57**	**.259**	**30**	**.192**	**-17**	**28**	**-1.9**

• LOVELACE, Vance Vance Odell Lovelace b: 8/9/1963, Tampa, FL BL/TL, 6'5", 205 lbs. Deb: 9/10/1988

YEAR	TM-L	W	L	PCT	G	GS	CG	SH	SV	IP	H	R	ER	HR	HB	BB	SO	RAT	ERA	ERA+	CERA	OAV	BH	AVG	PR+	WS	TPW
1988	Cal-A	0	0	....	3	0	0	0	0	1^1	2	2	2	1	0	3	0	3.750	13.50	29	26.26	.400	0	....	-1	0	-0.1
1989	Cal-A	0	0	....	1	0	0	0	0	1	0	0	0	0	0	1	1	1.000	0.00	....	0.00	.000	0	....	0	0	0.0
1990	Sea-A	0	0	....	5	0	0	0	0	2^1	3	1	1	0	1	6	1	3.857	3.86	103	15.94	.300	0	....	0	0	0.0
Total	**3**	**0**	**0**	**....**	**9**	**0**	**0**	**0**	**0**	**4^2**	**5**	**3**	**3**	**1**	**1**	**10**	**2**	**3.214**	**5.79**	**67**	**15.47**	**.333**	**0**	**....**	**-1**	**0**	**-0.1**

• LOVENGUTH, Lynn Lynn Richard Lovenguth b: 11/29/1922, Camden, NJ d: 9/29/2000, Beaverton, OR BL/TR, 5'10.5", 170 lbs. Deb: 4/18/1955

YEAR	TM-L	W	L	PCT	G	GS	CG	SH	SV	IP	H	R	ER	HR	HB	BB	SO	RAT	ERA	ERA+	CERA	OAV	BH	AVG	PR+	WS	TPW
1955	Phi-N	0	1	.000	14	0	0	0	0	18	17	9	9	1	2	10	14	1.500	4.50	88	4.42	.258	0	.000	-1	1	-0.2
1957	StL-N	0	1	.000	2	1	0	0	0	9	6	3	2	0	0	6	6	1.333	2.00	198	2.54	.182	0	.000	2	1	0.2
Total	**2**	**0**	**2**	**.000**	**16**	**1**	**0**	**0**	**0**	**27**	**23**	**12**	**11**	**1**	**2**	**16**	**20**	**1.444**	**3.67**	**108**	**3.79**	**.232**	**0**	**.000**	**1**	**2**	**0.0**

• LOVETT, John John Lovett b: 5/6/1877, Monday, OH d: 12/5/1937, Murray City, OH Deb: 5/22/1903

YEAR	TM-L	W	L	PCT	G	GS	CG	SH	SV	IP	H	R	ER	HR	HB	BB	SO	RAT	ERA	ERA+	CERA	OAV	BH	AVG	PR+	WS	TPW
1903	StL-N	0	0	....	3	1	0	0	0	5	6	5	7	0	1	5	3	2.200	12.60	60	7.38	.300	1	.333	-1	0	-0.1

• LOVETT, Tom Thomas Joseph Lovett b: 12/7/1863, Providence, RI d: 3/19/1928, Providence, RI BR, 5'8", 162 lbs. Deb: 6/4/1885

YEAR	TM-L	W	L	PCT	G	GS	CG	SH	SV	IP	H	R	ER	HR	HB	BB	SO	RAT	ERA	ERA+	CERA	OAV	BH	AVG	PR+	WS	TPW
1885	Phi-a	7	8	.467	16	16	15	1	0	138^2	130	96	57	3	5	38	56	1.212	3.70	93	....	.238	13	.224	-3	6	-0.3
1889*	Bro-a	17	10	.630	29	28	23	1	0	229	234	132	110	3	0	65	92	1.306	4.32	86	....	.257	19	.190	-16	15	-1.4
1890*	Bro-N	30	11	.732	44	41	39	4	0	372	327	195	115	14	0	141	124	1.258	2.78	123	....	.229	33	.201	26	29	2.2
1891	Bro-N	23	19	.548	44	43	39	3	0	365^2	361	229	150	14	0	129	129	1.340	3.69	89	....	.248	25	.163	-7	19	-1.0
1893	Bro-N	3	5	.375	14	8	6	0	1	96	134	92	70	2	0	35	15	1.760	6.56	67	5.53	.321	9	.180	-22	1	-2.1
1894	Bos-N	8	6	.571	15	13	10	0	0	104	155	96	69	12	0	36	23	1.837	5.97	99	6.84	.341	7	.143	-4	6	-0.7
Total	**6**	**88**	**59**	**.599**	**162**	**149**	**132**	**9**	**1**	**1305^1**	**1341**	**840**	**571**	**48**	**5**	**444**	**439**	**1.367**	**3.94**	**95**	**0.95**	**.257**	**106**	**.185**	**-26**	**76**	**-3.1**

• LOVRICH, Pete Peter Lovrich b: 10/16/1942, Blue Island, IL BR/TR, 6'4", 200 lbs. Deb: 4/26/1963

YEAR	TM-L	W	L	PCT	G	GS	CG	SH	SV	IP	H	R	ER	HR	HB	BB	SO	RAT	ERA	ERA+	CERA	OAV	BH	AVG	PR+	WS	TPW
1963	KC-A	1	1	.500	20	1	0	0	0	20^2	25	23	18	5	1	10	16	1.694	7.84	49	6.68	.291	0	....	-9	0	-0.9

• LOWDERMILK, Grover Grover Cleveland "Slim" Lowdermilk b: 1/15/1885, Sandborn, IN d: 3/31/1968, Odin, IL BR/TR, 6'4", 190 lbs. Deb: 7/3/1909

YEAR	TM-L	W	L	PCT	G	GS	CG	SH	SV	IP	H	R	ER	HR	HB	BB	SO	RAT	ERA	ERA+	CERA	OAV	BH	AVG	PR+	WS	TPW
1909	StL-N	0	2	.000	7	3	1	0	0	29	28	24	20	0	3	30	14	2.000	6.21	41	6.33	.292	1	.100	-11	0	-1.3
1911	StL-N	0	1	.000	11	2	1	1	0	33^1	37	30	27	1	2	33	15	2.100	7.29	46	6.87	.301	1	.111	-15	0	-1.5
1912	Chi-N	0	1	.000	2	1	1	0	0	13	17	18	14	1	0	14	8	2.385	9.69	34	7.81	.304	0	.000	-10	0	-1.0
1915	StL-A	9	17	.346	38	29	14	1	0	222^1	183	110	77	1	16	133	130	1.421	3.12	92	3.45	.234	9	.125	-9	8	-1.2
	Det-A	4	1	.800	7	5	0	0	0	28	17	16	13	0	1	24	18	1.464	4.18	72	3.00	.185	1	.125	-3	1	-0.4
	Yr.	13	18	.419	45	34	14	1	0	250^1	200	126	90	1	17	157	148	1.426	3.24	89	3.40	.229	10	.125	-12	9	-1.6
1916	Det-A	0	0	....	1	0	0	0	0	0^1	0	0	0	0	0	3	0	9.000	0.00	....	28.30	.000	0	....	0	0	0.0
	Cle-A	1	5	.167	10	9	2	0	0	51^1	52	33	18	0	3	45	28	1.890	3.16	95	5.45	.277	3	.167	-1	1	-0.1
	Yr.	1	5	.167	11	9	2	0	0	51^2	52	33	18	0	3	48	28	1.935	3.14	96	5.60	.277	3	.167	-1	1	-0.1
1917	StL-A	2	1	.667	3	2	2	1	0	19	16	5	3	0	0	4	9	1.053	1.42	183	1.72	.225	0	.000	3	1	0.2
1918	StL-A	2	6	.250	13	11	4	0	0	80	74	44	28	1	3	38	25	1.400	3.15	87	3.41	.255	7	.250	-4	2	-0.3
1919	StL-A	0	0	....	7	0	0	0	0	12	6	2	1	0	5	4	6	.833	0.75	442	2.31	.176	0	.000	3	2	0.3
	*Chi-A	5	5	.500	20	11	5	0	0	96^2	95	44	30	0	4	43	43	1.428	2.79	114	3.66	.268	3	.088	2	5	-0.1
	Yr.	5	5	.500	27	11	5	0	0	108^2	101	46	31	0	9	47	49	1.362	2.57	124	3.51	.260	3	.086	5	7	0.2
1920	Chi-A	0	0	....	3	0	0	0	0	5^1	9	4	4	0	0	5	0	2.625	6.75	56	10.31	.409	0	....	-2	0	-0.2
Total	**9**	**23**	**39**	**.371**	**122**	**73**	**30**	**3**	**0**	**590^1**	**534**	**330**	**235**	**4**	**37**	**376**	**296**	**1.542**	**3.58**	**82**	**4.06**	**.253**	**25**	**.131**	**-46**	**20**	**-5.6**

• LOWDERMILK, Lou Louis Bailey Lowdermilk b: 2/23/1887, Sandborn, IN d: 12/27/1975, Centralia, IL BR/TL, 6'1", 180 lbs. Deb: 4/20/1911

YEAR	TM-L	W	L	PCT	G	GS	CG	SH	SV	IP	H	R	ER	HR	HB	BB	SO	RAT	ERA	ERA+	CERA	OAV	BH	AVG	PR+	WS	TPW
1911	StL-N	3	4	.429	16	3	3	0	0	65	72	39	25	0	5	29	20	1.554	3.46	97	4.67	.304	2	.111	-1	2	-0.2
1912	StL-N	1	1	.500	4	1	1	0	1	15	14	8	5	0	0	9	2	1.533	3.00	114	3.42	.246	1	.250	1	1	0.1
Total	**2**	**4**	**5**	**.444**	**20**	**4**	**4**	**0**	**1**	**80**	**86**	**47**	**30**	**0**	**5**	**38**	**22**	**1.550**	**3.38**	**100**	**4.44**	**.293**	**3**	**.136**	**-0**	**3**	**-0.1**

• LOWE, Derek Derek Christopher Lowe b: 6/1/1973, Dearborn, MI BR/TR, 6'6", 170 lbs. Deb: 4/26/1997

YEAR	TM-L	W	L	PCT	G	GS	CG	SH	SV	IP	H	R	ER	HR	HB	BB	SO	RAT	ERA	ERA+	CERA	OAV	BH	AVG	PR+	WS	TPW
1997	Sea-A	2	4	.333	12	9	0	0	0	53	59	43	41	11	2	20	39	1.491	6.96	65	5.55	.282	0	.000	-14	0	-1.3
	Bos-A	0	2	.000	8	0	0	0	0	16	15	6	6	0	2	3	13	1.125	3.38	137	2.78	.268	0	.000	2	1	0.2
	Yr.	2	6	.250	20	9	0	0	0	69	74	49	47	11	4	23	52	1.406	6.13	74	4.91	.279	0	.000	-12	1	-1.1
1998*	Bos-A	3	9	.250	63	10	0	0	4	123	126	65	55	5	4	42	77	1.366	4.02	117	3.64	.267	0	.000	8	7	0.8
1999*	Bos-A	6	3	.667	74	0	0	0	15	109^1	84	35	32	7	4	25	80	.997	2.63	188	2.14	.208	0	....	28	19	2.6
2000	Bos-A★	4	4	.500	74	0	0	0	**42**	91^1	90	27	26	6	2	22	79	1.226	2.56	197	3.17	.257	0	.000	25	19	2.3
2001	Bos-A	5	10	.333	67	3	0	0	24	91^2	103	39	36	7	5	29	82	1.440	3.53	127	4.31	.283	0	.000	11	11	1.1
2002	Bos-A★	21	8	.724	32	32	1	1	0	219^2	166	65	63	12	12	48	127	.974	2.58	174	2.13	.211	1	.333	43	22	4.2
2003*	Bos-A	17	7	.708	33	33	1	0	0	203^1	216	113	101	17	11	72	110	1.416	4.47	102	4.32	.272	0	.000	6	12	0.5
Total	**7**	**58**	**47**	**.552**	**363**	**87**	**2**	**1**	**85**	**907^1**	**859**	**393**	**360**	**65**	**42**	**261**	**607**	**1.234**	**3.57**	**129**	**3.36**	**.250**	**1**	**.063**	**111**	**91**	**10.4**

• LOWE, George George Wesley "Doc" Lowe b: 4/25/1895, Ridgefield Park, NJ d: 9/3/1981, Somers Point, NJ BR/TR, 6'2", 180 lbs. Deb: 7/28/1920

YEAR	TM-L	W	L	PCT	G	GS	CG	SH	SV	IP	H	R	ER	HR	HB	BB	SO	RAT	ERA	ERA+	CERA	OAV	BH	AVG	PR+	WS	TPW
1920	Cin-N	0	0	....	1	0	0	0	0	2	1	0	0	0	0	1	0	1.000	0.00	....	1.54	.167	0	....	1	0	0.1

• LOWE, Sean Jonathan Sean Lowe b: 3/29/1971, Dallas, TX BR/TR, 6'2", 205 lbs. Deb: 8/29/1997

YEAR	TM-L	W	L	PCT	G	GS	CG	SH	SV	IP	H	R	ER	HR	HB	BB	SO	RAT	ERA	ERA+	CERA	OAV	BH	AVG	PR+	WS	TPW
1997	StL-N	0	2	.000	6	4	0	0	0	17^1	27	21	18	2	1	10	8	2.135	9.35	44	8.57	.360	1	.333	-10	0	-1.0
1998	StL-N	0	3	.000	4	1	0	0	0	5^1	11	9	9	1	0	5	2	3.000	15.19	28	14.71	.440	0	.000	-6	0	-0.7
1999	Chi-A	4	1	.800	64	0	0	0	0	95^2	90	39	39	10	4	46	62	1.422	3.67	133	4.38	.262	0	....	13	8	1.2
2000	Chi-A	4	1	.800	50	5	0	0	0	70^2	78	47	43	10	6	39	53	1.656	5.48	91	5.95	.284	0	....	-5	3	-0.5
2001	Chi-A	9	4	.692	45	11	0	0	3	127	123	55	51	12	7	32	71	1.220	3.61	127	3.51	.256	1	.333	13	10	1.3

YEAR TM-L	W	L	PCT	G	GS	CG	SH	SV	IP	H	R	ER	HR	HB	BB	SO	RAT	ERA	ERA+	CERA	OAV	BH	AVG	PR+	WS	TPW
2002 Pit-N	4	2	.667	43	1	0	0	0	69	85	45	41	8	7	34	57	1.725	5.35	78	6.20	.307	1	.077	-9	2	-1.0
Col-N	1	1	.500	8	0	0	0	0	10^1	16	13	10	1	0	7	7	2.226	8.71	55	8.60	.348	0	.000	-4	0	-0.5
Yr.	5	3	.625	51	1	0	0	0	79^1	101	58	51	9	7	41	64	1.790	5.79	74	6.51	.313	1	.071	-14	2	-1.5
2003 KC-A	1	1	.500	28	0	0	0	0	44^2	55	32	31	7	2	21	28	1.701	6.25	83	6.14	.301	0	....	-5	1	-0.5
Total 7	23	15	.605	248	22	0	0	3	440	485	261	242	51	27	194	288	1.543	4.95	94	5.23	.284	3	.136	-14	24	-1.5
• LOWN, Turk	Omar Joseph Lown b: 5/30/1924, Brooklyn, NY BR/TR, 6', 185 lbs. Deb: 4/24/1951																									
1951 Chi-N	4	9	.308	31	18	3	1	0	127	125	80	77	14	1	90	39	1.693	5.46	75	5.13	.260	8	.205	-18	2	-1.7
1952 Chi-N	4	11	.267	33	19	5	0	0	156^2	154	87	76	13	3	93	73	**1.577**	4.37	88	4.53	.257	7	.140	-9	4	-0.9
1953 Chi-N	8	7	.533	49	12	2	0	3	148^1	166	93	85	20	2	84	76	1.685	5.16	86	5.61	.282	6	.125	-7	7	-0.9
1954 Chi-N	0	2	.000	15	0	0	0	0	22	23	18	15	1	0	15	16	1.727	6.14	68	4.61	.261	0	....	-4	0	-0.4
1956 Chi-N	9	8	.529	61	0	0	0	13	110^2	95	49	44	10	1	78	74	1.563	3.58	105	4.30	.240	5	.217	0	10	0.3
1957 Chi-N	5	7	.417	**67**	0	0	0	12	93	74	45	39	10	0	51	51	1.344	3.77	103	3.55	.221	2	.200	2	8	0.3
1958 Chi-N	0	0	....	4	0	0	0	0	4	2	2	2	0	0	3	4	1.250	4.50	87	2.19	.154	0	....	-0	0	0.0
Cin-N	0	2	.000	11	0	0	0	0	11^2	12	8	7	2	0	12	9	2.057	5.40	77	7.20	.273	0	.000	-2	0	-0.2
Yr.	0	2	.000	15	0	0	0	0	15^2	14	10	9	2	0	15	13	1.851	5.17	79	5.92	.246	0	.000	-2	0	-0.2
Chi-A	3	3	.500	27	0	0	0	8	40^2	49	22	18	1	0	28	40	1.893	3.98	91	5.61	.308	3	.333	-2	2	-0.2
1959* Chi-A	9	2	.818	60	0	0	0	**15**	93^1	73	32	30	12	2	42	63	1.232	2.89	130	3.28	.215	3	.250	7	13	0.8
1960 Chi-A	2	3	.400	45	0	0	0	5	67^1	60	31	29	6	0	34	39	1.396	3.88	97	3.63	.239	1	.200	-2	4	-0.1
1961 Chi-A	7	5	.583	59	0	0	0	11	101	87	37	31	13	0	35	50	1.208	2.76	142	3.28	.238	0	.000	14	12	1.2
1962 Chi-A	4	2	.667	42	0	0	0	6	56^1	58	21	19	3	1	25	40	1.473	3.04	129	3.96	.269	0	.000	6	6	0.5
Total 11	55	61	.474	504	49	10	1	73	1032	978	525	472	105	10	590	574	1.519	4.12	97	4.39	.252	35	.164	-15	68	-1.3
• LOWRY, Noah	Noah Ryan Lowry b: 10/10/1980, Ventura, CA BL/TL, 6'2", 190 lbs. Deb: 9/5/2003																									
2003 SF-N	0	0	....	4	0	0	0	0	6^1	1	0	0	0	1	2	5	.474	0.00	....	0.50	.048	1	.500	3	1	0.3
• LOWRY, Sam	Samuel Joseph Lowry b: 3/25/1920, Philadelphia, PA d: 12/1/1992, Philadelphia, PA BR/TR, 5'11", 170 lbs. Deb: 9/19/1942																									
1942 Phi-A	0	0	....	1	0	0	0	0	3	3	2	2	0	0	1	0	1.333	6.00	63	2.97	.250	0	.000	-1	0	-0.1
1943 Phi-A	0	0	....	5	0	0	0	0	18	18	10	10	1	0	9	3	1.500	5.00	68	4.02	.269	1	.167	-3	0	-0.3
Total 2	0	0	....	6	0	0	0	0	21	21	12	12	1	0	10	3	1.476	5.14	67	3.87	.266	1	.143	-3	0	-0.4
• LOYND, Mike	Michael Wallace Loynd b: 3/26/1964, St. Louis, MO BR/TR, 6'4", 210 lbs. Deb: 7/24/1986																									
1986 Tex-A	2	2	.500	9	8	0	0	1	42	49	30	25	4	2	19	33	1.619	5.36	80	5.32	.290	0	....	-5	1	-0.5
1987 Tex-A	1	5	.167	26	8	0	0	1	69^1	82	53	47	14	1	38	48	1.731	6.10	73	6.51	.287	0	....	-12	1	-1.1
Total 2	3	7	.300	35	16	0	0	2	111^1	131	83	72	18	3	57	81	1.689	5.82	76	6.06	.288	0	....	-17	2	-1.6
• LUBY, Pat	John Perkins Luby b: 1/1869, Charleston, SC d: 4/24/1899, Charleston, SC TR, 6', 185 lbs. Deb: 6/16/1890																									
1890 Chi-N	20	9	.690	34	31	26	0	1	267^2	226	129	95	6	0	95	85	1.199	3.19	114	....	.222	31	.267	7	27	1.4
1891 Chi-N	8	11	.421	30	24	18	0	1	206	221	148	109	11	0	94	52	1.529	4.76	70	....	.264	24	.245	-37	12	-2.6
1892 Chi-N	11	16	.407	31	27	24	1	0	252^1	248	157	86	10	0	103	66	1.391	3.07	108	3.50	.247	31	.190	10	14	0.6
1895 Lou-N	1	5	.167	11	6	5	0	0	71^1	115	90	54	5	0	19	12	1.879	6.81	68	6.90	.358	15	.283	-14	2	-0.8
Total 4	40	41	.494	106	88	73	1	2	797^1	810	524	344	32	0	311	215	1.406	3.88	92	1.72	.255	101	.235	-34	55	-1.4
• LUCAS, Gary	Gary Paul Lucas b: 11/8/1954, Riverside, CA BL/TL, 6'5", 200 lbs. Deb: 4/16/1980																									
1980 SD-N	5	8	.385	46	18	0	0	3	150	138	59	54	8	1	43	85	1.207	3.24	106	2.83	.250	6	.171	1	9	0.1
1981 SD-N	7	7	.500	**57**	0	0	0	13	90	78	26	20	1	3	36	53	1.267	2.00	163	2.71	.247	1	.100	12	11	1.3
1982 SD-N	1	10	.091	65	0	0	0	16	97^1	89	42	35	5	1	29	64	1.212	3.24	106	2.81	.245	0	.000	1	7	0.0
1983 SD-N	5	8	.385	62	0	0	0	17	91	85	38	29	9	0	34	60	1.308	2.87	122	3.35	.245	0	.000	5	9	0.4
1984 Mon-N	0	3	.000	55	0	0	0	8	53	54	20	16	4	0	20	42	1.396	2.72	126	3.82	.267	0	.000	4	4	0.3
1985 Mon-N	6	2	.750	49	0	0	0	1	67^2	63	29	24	6	0	24	31	1.286	3.19	106	3.27	.251	0	.000	1	4	0.0
1986* Cal-A	4	1	.800	27	0	0	0	2	45^2	45	19	16	1	0	6	31	1.117	3.15	130	2.49	.253	0	....	4	4	0.4
1987 Cal-A	1	5	.167	48	0	0	0	3	74^1	66	41	30	7	2	35	44	1.359	3.63	118	3.68	.241	0	....	5	4	0.5
Total 8	29	44	.397	409	18	0	0	63	669	618	274	224	41	7	227	410	1.263	3.01	118	3.07	.249	7	.088	33	52	3.0
• LUCAS, Ray	Ray Wesley "Luke" Lucas b: 10/2/1908, Springfield, OH d: 10/9/1969, Harrison, MI BR/TR, 6'2", 175 lbs. Deb: 9/28/1929																									
1929 NY-N	0	0	....	3	0	0	0	1	8	3	0	0	0	0	3	1	.750	0.00	....	0.81	.111	1	.500	4	2	0.4
1930 NY-N	0	0	....	6	0	0	0	0	10^1	9	8	8	2	1	10	1	1.839	6.97	68	6.61	.265	0	.000	-3	0	-0.2
1931 NY-N	0	0	....	1	0	0	0	0	2	1	1	1	1	0	1	0	1.000	4.50	82	3.98	.143	0	....	-0	0	0.0
1933 Bro-N	0	0	....	2	0	0	0	0	5	6	4	4	0	1	4	0	2.000	7.20	45	6.63	.316	0	....	-2	0	-0.2
1934 Bro-N	1	1	.500	10	2	0	0	0	30^2	39	24	23	2	3	14	3	1.728	6.75	58	5.94	.328	2	.333	-10	0	-0.8
Total 5	1	1	.500	22	2	0	0	1	56	58	37	36	5	5	32	5	1.607	5.79	68	5.32	.282	3	.333	-10	2	-0.9
• LUCAS, Red	Charles Fred "The Nashville Narcissus" Lucas b: 4/28/1902, Columbia, TN d: 7/9/1986, Nashville, TN BL/TR, 5'9.5", 170 lbs. Deb: 4/19/1923 ♦																									
1923 NY-N	0	0	....	3	0	0	0	1	5^1	9	5	0	0	0	4	3	2.438	0.00	....	8.18	.346	0	.000	2	0	0.2
1924 Bos-N	1	4	.200	27	4	1	0	0	83^2	112	60	48	5	6	18	30	1.554	5.16	74	5.27	.332	11	.333	-12	2	-1.0
1926 Cin-N	8	5	.615	39	11	7	1	2	154	161	68	63	6	2	30	34	1.240	3.68	100	3.14	.277	23	.303	-0	12	0.8
1927 Cin-N	18	11	.621	37	23	19	4	2	239^2	231	96	90	6	0	39	51	1.127	3.38	112	**2.47**	.256	47	.313	12	23	2.2
1928 Cin-N	13	9	.591	27	19	13	**4**	1	167^1	164	73	63	9	0	42	35	1.231	3.39	117	3.04	.258	23	.315	10	15	1.6
1929 Cin-N	19	12	.613	32	32	**28**	2	0	270	267	119	108	14	1	58	72	1.204	3.60	127	**2.92**	**.257**	41	.293	27	**26**	3.5
1930 Cin-N	14	16	.467	33	28	18	1	1	210^2	270	135	126	15	1	44	53	1.491	5.38	90	4.66	.315	38	.336	-12	14	0.3
1931 Cin-N	14	13	.519	29	29	**24**	3	0	238	261	110	95	10	0	39	56	1.261	3.59	104	3.29	.280	43	.281	2	17	1.3
1932 Cin-N	13	17	.433	31	31	**28**	0	0	269^1	261	110	88	10	1	35	63	1.099	2.94	131	**2.44**	.249	43	.287	28	23	4.2
1933 Cin-N	10	16	.385	29	29	21	3	0	219^2	248	106	83	13	2	18	40	1.211	3.40	100	3.31	.289	35	.287	2	15	1.6
1934 Pit-N	10	9	.526	29	22	12	1	0	172^2	198	89	84	14	2	40	44	1.378	4.38	94	4.05	.283	23	.219	-3	9	-0.1
1935 Pit-N	8	6	.571	20	19	8	2	0	125^2	136	60	48	10	2	23	29	1.265	3.44	119	3.51	.272	21	.318	10	11	1.7
1936 Pit-N	15	4	.789	27	22	12	0	0	175^2	178	70	62	7	3	26	53	1.161	3.18	128	2.78	.257	26	.241	18	15	2.2
1937 Pit-N	8	10	.444	20	20	9	1	0	126^1	150	69	60	12	1	23	20	1.369	4.27	90	4.14	.290	22	.268	-6	7	-0.1
1938 Pit-N	6	3	.667	13	13	4	0	0	84	90	33	33	5	1	16	19	1.262	3.54	107	3.49	.283	5	.109	1	5	-0.1
Total 15	157	135	.538	396	302	204	22	7	2542	2736	1203	1051	136	22	455	602	1.255	3.72	107	3.33	.275	404	.281	79	194	18.3
• LUCEY, Joe	Joseph Earl "Scotch" Lucey b: 3/27/1897, Holyoke, MA d: 7/30/1980, Holyoke, MA BR/TR, 6', 168 lbs. Deb: 7/6/1920 ♦																									
1925 Bos-A	0	1	.000	7	2	0	0	0	11	18	20	11	0	0	14	2	2.909	9.00	50	10.05	.360	2	.133	-5	0	-0.9
• LUCID, Con	Cornelius Cecil Lucid b: 2/24/1874, Dublin, Ireland d: 6/25/1931, Houston, TX, 5'7", 170 lbs. Deb: 5/1/1893																									
1893 Lou-N	0	1	.000	2	1	0	0	0	6	10	14	10	0	1	10	0	3.333	15.00	29	13.02	.361	1	.333	-7	0	-0.6
1894 Bro-N	5	3	.625	10	9	7	0	0	71^1	87	68	52	6	9	44	15	1.836	6.56	75	6.45	.298	7	.212	-12	3	-1.1
1895 Bro-N	10	7	.588	21	19	12	2	0	137	164	113	84	4	7	72	24	1.723	5.52	80	5.21	.292	13	.245	-19	7	-1.3
Phi-N	6	3	.667	10	10	7	1	0	69^2	80	56	46	3	9	35	19	1.651	5.94	80	5.24	.284	10	.345	-9	4	-0.4
Yr.	16	10	.615	31	29	19	3	0	206^2	244	169	130	7	16	107	43	1.698	5.66	80	5.22	.290	23	.280	-28	11	-1.7
1896 Phi-N	1	4	.200	5	5	5	0	0	42	75	43	39	2	2	17	3	2.190	8.36	51	8.61	.384	2	.125	-18	0	-1.7
1897 StL-N	1	5	.167	6	6	5	0	0	49	66	46	20	0	0	26	4	1.878	3.67	120	5.68	.320	3	.176	6	1	0.5
Total 5	23	23	.500	54	50	36	3	0	375	482	340	251	15	28	204	65	1.829	6.02	76	6.02	.308	36	.238	-59	15	-4.6
• LUCIER, Lou	Louis Joseph Lucier b: 3/23/1918, Northbridge, MA BR/TR, 5'8", 160 lbs. Deb: 4/23/1943																									
1943 Bos-A	3	4	.429	16	9	3	0	0	74	94	35	32	1	2	33	23	1.716	3.89	85	5.30	.322	4	.200	-5	3	-0.6
1944 Bos-A	0	0	....	3	0	0	0	0	5^1	7	3	3	0	0	7	2	2.625	5.06	67	7.93	.292	0	.000	-1	0	-0.1
Phi-N	0	0	....	1	0	0	0	0	2	3	3	3	0	0	2	1	2.500	13.50	27	8.24	.333	0	....	-2	0	-0.2
1945 Phi-N	0	1	.000	13	0	0	0	1	20^1	14	9	5	1	0	5	5	.934	2.21	173	1.61	.194	1	.250	4	1	0.4
Total 3	3	5	.375	33	9	3	0	1	101^2	118	50	43	2	2	47	31	1.623	3.81	89	4.76	.297	5	.200	-4	4	-0.5

YEAR	TM-L	W	L	PCT	G	GS	CG	SH	SV	IP	H	R	ER	HR	HB	BB	SO	RAT	ERA	ERA+	CERA	OAV	BH	AVG	PR+	WS	TPW
• LUDOLPH, Willie	William Francis "Wee Willie" Ludolph b: 1/21/1900, San Francisco, CA d: 4/8/1952, Oakland, CA BR/TR, 6'1.5", 170 lbs. Deb: 5/28/1924																										
1924	Det-A	0	0	....	3	0	0	0	0	5^{2}	5	3	3	0	1	2	1	1.235	4.76	86	3.31	.250	0	.000	-0	0	-0.1
• LUDWICK, Eric	Eric David Ludwick b: 12/14/1971, Whiteman AFB, MO BR/TR, 6'5", 210 lbs. Deb: 9/1/1996																										
1996	StL-N	0	1	.000	6	1	0	0	0	10	11	11	10	4	1	3	12	1.400	9.00	47	6.73	.275	0	.000	-6	0	-0.6
1997	StL-N	0	1	.000	5	0	0	0	0	6^{2}	12	7	7	1	0	6	7	2.700	9.45	44	12.40	.400	0	....	-4	0	-0.4
	Oak-A	1	4	.200	6	5	0	0	0	24	32	24	22	7	1	16	14	2.000	8.25	55	9.23	.330	0	.000	-9	0	-0.9
1998	Fla-N	1	4	.200	13	6	0	0	0	32^{2}	46	31	27	7	0	17	27	1.929	7.44	55	7.89	.333	0	.000	-12	0	-1.3
1999	Tor-A	0	0	....	1	0	0	0	0	1	3	3	3	0	0	2	0	5.000	27.00	18	24.59	.500	0	....	-2	0	-0.2
Total	4	2	10	.167	31	12	0	0	0	74^{1}	104	76	69	19	2	44	60	1.991	8.35	51	8.80	.334	0	.000	-33	0	-3.4
• LUEBBER, Steve	Stephen Lee Luebber b: 7/9/1949, Clinton, MO BR/TR, 6'3", 195 lbs. Deb: 6/27/1971																										
1971	Min-A	2	5	.286	18	12	0	0	1	68	73	42	38	7	4	37	35	1.618	5.03	71	5.31	.278	1	.053	-10	0	-1.2
1972	Min-A	0	0	....	2	0	0	0	0	2^{1}	3	0	0	0	0	2	1	2.143	0.00	....	5.73	.333	0	....	1	0	0.1
1976	Min-A	4	5	.444	38	12	2	1	2	119^{1}	109	57	53	9	1	62	45	1.433	4.00	90	3.97	.248	0	....	-5	5	-0.6
1979	Tor-A	0	0	....	1	0	0	0	0	0	2	1	1	0	0	1	0	....	∞	....	∞	1.000	0	....	-1	0	-0.1
1981	Bal-A	0	0	....	7	0	0	0	0	16^{2}	26	14	14	3	1	4	12	1.800	7.56	48	7.83	.366	0	....	-7	0	-0.8
Total	5	6	10	.375	66	24	2	1	3	206^{1}	213	114	106	19	6	106	93	1.546	4.62	78	4.74	.271	1	.053	-23	5	-2.6
• LUEBBERS, Larry	Larry Christopher Luebbers b: 10/11/1969, Cincinnati, OH BR/TR, 6'6", 190 lbs. Deb: 7/3/1993																										
1993	Cin-N	2	5	.286	14	14	0	0	0	77^{1}	74	49	39	7	1	38	38	1.448	4.54	89	4.19	.261	6	.250	-4	2	-0.2
1999	StL-N	3	3	.500	8	8	1	0	0	45^{2}	46	27	26	8	3	16	16	1.358	5.12	89	4.69	.261	2	.125	-3	2	-0.3
2000	Cin-N	0	2	.000	14	1	0	0	1	20^{1}	27	15	14	1	0	12	9	1.918	6.20	76	6.46	.333	0	....	-4	0	-0.3
Total	3	5	10	.333	36	23	1	0	1	143^{1}	147	91	79	16	4	66	63	1.486	4.96	87	4.67	.272	8	.200	-10	4	-0.9
• LUEBKE, Dick	Richard Raymond Luebke b: 4/8/1935, Chicago, IL d: 12/4/1974, San Diego, CA BR/TL, 6'4", 200 lbs. Deb: 8/11/1962																										
1962	Bal-A	0	1	.000	10	0	0	0	0	13^{1}	12	4	4	0	0	6	7	1.350	2.70	139	3.08	.250	0	....	1	1	0.1
• LUECKEN, Rick	Richard Fred Luecken b: 11/15/1960, McAllen, TX BR/TR, 6'6", 210 lbs. Deb: 6/6/1989																										
1989	KC-A	2	1	.667	19	0	0	0	1	23^{2}	23	9	9	3	0	13	16	1.521	3.42	112	4.45	.258	0	....	2	2	0.2
1990	Atl-N	1	4	.200	36	0	0	0	1	53	73	36	34	5	3	30	35	1.943	5.77	70	7.09	.336	1	.333	-9	0	-0.9
	Tor-A	0	0	....	1	0	0	0	0	1	2	1	1	1	0	1	0	3.000	9.00	45	27.72	.500	0	....	-1	0	-0.1
Total	2	3	5	.375	56	0	0	0	2	77^{2}	98	46	44	9	3	44	51	1.828	5.10	78	6.55	.316	1	.333	-8	2	-0.8
• LUFF, Henry	Henry T. Luff b: 9/14/1856, Philadelphia, PA d: 10/11/1916, Philadelphia, PA, 5'11", 175 lbs. Deb: 4/21/1875 ♦																										
1875	NH-n	1	6	.143	10	7	5	0	0	69^{2}	98	91	25	2	....	3	5	1.450	3.23	48	....	.304	45	.271	-16	....	-1.2
• LUGO, Urbano	Rafael Urbano (Colina) Lugo b: 8/12/1962, Punto Fijo, Venezuela BR/TR, 6', 190 lbs. Deb: 4/28/1985																										
1985	Cal-A	3	4	.429	20	10	1	0	0	83	86	36	34	10	4	29	42	1.386	3.69	111	4.53	.274	0	....	1	5	0.1
1986	Cal-A	1	1	.500	6	3	0	0	0	21^{1}	21	9	9	4	0	6	9	1.266	3.80	108	4.29	.266	0	....	0	1	0.0
1987	Cal-A	0	2	.000	7	5	0	0	0	28	42	34	29	8	0	18	24	2.143	9.32	46	9.76	.339	0	....	-16	0	-1.5
1988	Cal-A	0	0	....	1	0	0	0	0	2	2	2	2	1	0	1	1	1.500	9.00	43	7.30	.250	0	....	-1	0	-0.1
1989	Mon-N	0	0	....	3	0	0	0	0	4	4	3	3	1	0	0	3	1.000	6.75	52	3.33	.250	0	....	-1	0	-0.2
1990	Det-A	2	0	1.000	13	1	0	0	0	24^{1}	30	19	19	9	3	13	12	1.767	7.03	56	8.81	.313	0	....	-9	0	-0.9
Total	6	6	7	.462	50	19	1	0	0	162^{2}	185	103	96	33	7	67	91	1.549	5.31	77	6.04	.290	0	....	-25	6	-2.5
• LUHRSEN, Wild Bill	William Ferdinand Luhrsen b: 4/14/1884, Buckley, IL d: 8/15/1973, Little Rock, AR BR/TR, 5'9", 165 lbs. Deb: 8/23/1913																										
1913	Pit-N	3	1	.750	5	3	2	0	0	29	25	10	8	3	2	16	11	1.414	2.48	121	4.31	.248	0	.000	2	2	0.1
• LUKASIEWICZ, Mark	Mark Francis Lukasiewicz b: 3/8/1973, Jersey City, NJ BL/TL, 6'5", 240 lbs. Deb: 5/11/2001																										
2001	Ana-A	0	2	.000	24	0	0	0	0	22^{1}	21	17	15	6	2	9	25	1.343	6.04	75	5.12	.247	0	....	-4	0	-0.4
2002	Ana-A	2	0	1.000	17	0	0	0	0	14	17	6	6	0	0	9	15	1.857	3.86	115	5.43	.298	0	....	0	1	0.0
Total	2	2	2	.500	41	0	0	0	0	36^{1}	38	23	21	6	2	18	40	1.541	5.20	87	5.24	.268	0	....	-3	1	-0.3
• LUKENS, Al	Albert P. Lukens b: 1872, Vineland, NJ TR, 5'9", 168 lbs. Deb: 6/23/1894																										
1894	Phi-N	0	1	.000	3	2	1	0	0	15	26	22	17	0	3	10	0	2.400	10.20	50	9.50	.376	0	.000	-8	0	-0.8
• LUMENTI, Ralph	Raphael Anthony Lumenti b: 12/21/1936, Milford, MA BL/TL, 6'3", 185 lbs. Deb: 9/7/1957																										
1957	Was-A	0	1	.000	3	2	0	0	0	9^{1}	9	7	7	1	1	5	8	1.500	6.75	58	4.90	.250	0	.000	-3	0	-0.3
1958	Was-A	1	2	.333	8	4	0	0	0	21	21	20	20	2	1	36	20	2.714	8.57	44	9.86	.266	2	.250	-11	0	-1.1
1959	Was-A	0	0	....	2	0	0	0	0	3	2	0	0	0	0	1	2	1.000	0.00	....	1.73	.200	0	....	1	0	0.1
Total	3	1	3	.250	13	6	0	0	0	33^{1}	32	27	27	3	2	42	30	2.220	7.29	53	7.74	.256	2	.200	-12	0	-1.2
• LUNA, Memo	Guillermo Romero Luna b: 6/25/1930, Tacubaya, Mexico BL/TL, 6', 168 lbs. Deb: 4/20/1954																										
1954	StL-N	0	1	.000	1	1	0	0	0	0^{2}	2	2	2	0	0	2	0	6.000	27.00	15	28.10	.667	0	....	-2	0	-0.2
• LUNDBOM, Jack	John Frederick Lundbom b: 3/10/1877, Manistee, MI d: 10/31/1949, Manistee, MI BR/TR, 6'2", 187 lbs. Deb: 5/9/1902																										
1902	Cle-A	1	1	.500	8	3	1	0	0	34	48	35	25	1	1	16	7	1.882	6.62	52	6.22	.333	4	.267	-12	0	-1.1
• LUNDGREN, Carl	Carl Leonard Lundgren b: 2/16/1880, Marengo, IL d: 8/21/1934, Marengo, IL BR/TR, 5'11", 175 lbs. Deb: 6/19/1902 U																										
1902	Chi-N	9	9	.500	18	18	17	1	0	160	158	59	35	2	6	45	68	1.269	1.97	137	3.04	.258	7	.106	12	10	0.7
1903	Chi-N	11	9	.550	27	20	16	0	**3**	193	191	103	63	1	6	60	67	1.301	2.94	106	3.16	.262	7	.115	1	11	0.0
1904	Chi-N	17	9	.654	31	27	25	2	1	242	203	97	70	2	4	77	106	1.157	2.60	102	2.35	.226	20	.222	-3	19	0.1
1905	Chi-N	13	5	.722	23	19	16	3	0	169^{1}	132	58	42	3	9	53	69	1.093	2.23	133	2.31	.220	11	.180	8	15	0.9
1906	Chi-N	17	6	.739	27	24	21	5	2	207^{2}	160	63	51	3	8	89	103	1.199	2.21	119	2.59	.221	12	.179	5	19	0.8
1907	Chi-N	18	7	.720	28	25	21	7	0	207	130	42	27	0	2	92	84	1.072	1.17	212	1.77	**.185**	7	.106	25	25	2.5
1908	Chi-N	6	9	.400	23	15	9	1	0	138^{2}	149	72	65	5	0	56	38	1.478	4.22	55	4.15	.284	7	.149	-30	0	-3.7
1909	Chi-N	0	1	.000	2	1	0	0	0	4^{1}	6	2	2	0	0	4	0	2.308	4.15	61	7.95	.353	1	.500	-1	0	-0.1
Total	8	91	55	.623	179	149	125	19	6	1322	1129	496	355	16	35	476	535	1.214	2.42	111	2.70	.235	72	.157	17	99	1.3
• LUNDGREN, Del	Ebin Delmar Lundgren b: 9/21/1899, Lindsborg, KS d: 10/19/1984, Lindsborg, KS BR/TR, 5'8", 160 lbs. Deb: 4/27/1924																										
1924	Pit-N	0	1	.000	8	1	0	0	0	16^{2}	25	13	12	0	1	3	4	1.680	6.48	59	5.75	.403	0	.000	-6	0	-0.6
1926	Bos-A	0	2	.000	18	2	0	0	0	31	35	28	26	2	3	28	11	2.032	7.55	54	7.14	.307	0	.000	-11	0	-1.1
1927	Bos-A	5	12	.294	30	17	5	2	0	136^{1}	160	100	95	7	4	87	39	1.812	6.27	67	5.63	.302	7	.159	-30	1	-3.0
Total	3	5	15	.250	56	20	5	2	0	184	220	141	133	9	8	118	54	1.837	6.51	64	5.90	.312	7	.137	-47	1	-4.7
• LUNDQUIST, David	David Bruce Lundquist b: 6/4/1973, Beverly, MA BR/TR, 6'2", 200 lbs. Deb: 4/6/1999																										
1999	Chi-A	1	1	.500	17	0	0	0	0	22	28	21	21	3	1	12	18	1.818	8.59	57	6.70	.315	0	....	-9	0	-0.8
2001	SD-N	0	1	.000	17	0	0	0	0	19^{2}	20	13	13	1	1	7	19	1.373	5.95	67	3.72	.260	0	....	-4	0	-0.4
2002	SD-N	0	0	....	3	0	0	0	0	2^{2}	8	5	5	0	1	5	0	4.875	16.88	22	27.23	.615	0	....	-4	0	-0.4
Total	3	1	2	.333	37	0	0	0	0	44^{1}	56	39	39	4	3	24	37	1.805	7.92	55	6.61	.313	0	....	-17	0	-1.6
• LUQUE, Dolf	Adolfo Domingo De Guzman "The Pride Of Havana" Luque b: 8/4/1890, Havana, Cuba d: 7/3/1957, Havana, Cuba BR/TR, 5'7", 160 lbs. Deb: 5/20/1914 C																										
1914	Bos-N	0	1	.000	2	1	1	0	0	8^{2}	5	5	4	0	0	4	1	1.038	4.15	66	1.50	.167	0	.000	-2	0	-0.2
1915	Bos-N	0	0	....	2	1	0	0	0	5	6	3	2	0	0	4	3	2.000	3.60	74	5.63	.286	0	.000	-1	0	-0.1
1918	Cin-N	6	3	.667	12	10	9	1	0	83	84	44	35	1	1	32	26	1.398	3.80	70	3.51	.277	9	.321	-11	4	-0.7
1919*	Cin-N	10	3	.769	30	9	6	2	3	106	89	35	31	2	2	36	40	1.179	2.63	105	2.52	.237	4	.125	-0	9	-0.1
1920	Cin-N	13	9	.591	37	23	10	1	1	207^{2}	168	65	58	5	4	60	72	1.098	2.51	121	2.25	**.225**	17	.266	12	16	1.7
1921	Cin-N	17	19	.472	41	36	25	**3**	3	304	318	132	114	13	1	64	102	1.257	3.38	106	3.20	.273	30	.270	11	23	1.6
1922	Cin-N	13	23	.361	39	33	18	0	0	261	266	123	96	7	1	72	79	1.295	3.31	120	3.17	.268	18	.209	14	18	1.4

YEAR TM-L	W	L	PCT	G	GS	CG	SH	SV	IP	H	R	ER	HR	HB	BB	SO	RAT	ERA	ERA+	CERA	OAV	BH	AVG	PR+	WS	TPW
1923 Cin-N	**27**	8	.771	41	37	28	**6**	2	322	279	90	69	2	5	88	151	1.140	**1.93**	**200**	**2.32**	**.235**	21	.202	**69**	**39**	**6.7**
1924 Cin-N	10	15	.400	31	28	13	2	0	219^1	229	99	77	5	2	53	86	1.286	3.16	119	3.15	.271	13	.178	15	14	1.4
1925 Cin-N	16	18	.471	36	36	22	**4**	0	291	263	109	85	7	2	78	140	1.172	**2.63**	**156**	**2.53**	**.239**	26	.255	**43**	27	**4.5**
1926 Cin-N	13	16	.448	34	31	16	1	0	233^2	231	123	89	7	2	77	83	1.318	3.43	108	3.20	.260	27	.346	6	14	1.4
1927 Cin-N	13	12	.520	29	27	17	2	0	230^2	225	103	82	10	0	56	76	1.218	3.20	118	2.93	.260	18	.217	16	16	1.8
1928 Cin-N	11	10	.524	33	29	11	1	1	234^1	254	112	93	12	2	84	72	1.442	3.57	111	4.02	.284	8	.119	9	15	0.8
1929 Cin-N	5	16	.238	32	22	8	1	0	176	213	103	88	7	2	56	43	1.528	4.50	101	4.52	.310	15	.278	0	9	0.4
1930 Bro-N	14	8	.636	31	24	16	2	2	199	221	107	95	18	0	58	62	1.402	4.30	114	4.17	.287	18	.240	9	15	0.9
1931 Bro-N	7	6	.538	19	15	5	0	0	102^2	122	59	52	6	1	27	25	1.451	4.56	84	4.31	.297	4	.133	-7	4	-0.7
1932 NY-N	6	7	.462	38	5	1	0	5	110	128	53	49	4	0	32	32	1.455	4.01	93	3.99	.290	1	.040	-2	6	-0.4
1933* NY-N	8	2	.800	35	0	0	0	4	80^1	75	27	24	4	0	19	23	1.170	2.69	119	2.74	.251	5	.263	3	8	0.4
1934 NY-N	4	3	.571	26	0	0	0	7	42^1	54	20	18	3	1	17	12	1.677	3.83	101	5.42	.316	2	.286	-0	3	0.0
1935 NY-N	1	0	1.000	2	0	0	0	0	3^2	1	0	0	0	0	1	2	.545	0.00	....	0.42	.091	1	1.000	2	1	0.2
Total 20	194	179	.520	550	367	206	26	28	3220^1	3231	1412	1161	113	26	918	1130	1.288	3.24	116	3.22	.265	237	.227	185	241	21.1

• LUSH, Johnny

John Charles Lush b: 10/8/1885, Williamsport, PA d: 11/18/1946, Beverly Hills, CA BL/TL, 5'9.5", 165 lbs. Deb: 4/22/1904 ♦

YEAR TM-L	W	L	PCT	G	GS	CG	SH	SV	IP	H	R	ER	HR	HB	BB	SO	RAT	ERA	ERA+	CERA	OAV	BH	AVG	PR+	WS	TPW
1904 Phi-N	0	6	.000	7	6	3	0	0	42^2	52	40	17	0	7	27	27	1.852	3.59	74	5.95	.301	102	.276	-4	12	-0.7
1905 Phi-N	2	0	1.000	2	2	1	0	0	17	12	4	3	0	1	8	8	1.176	1.59	183	2.21	.194	5	.313	2	2	0.2
1906 Phi-N	18	15	.545	37	35	24	5	0	281	254	128	74	2	16	119	151	1.327	2.37	110	3.07	.236	56	.264	11	19	1.9
1907 Phi-N	3	5	.375	8	8	5	2	0	57^1	48	22	19	0	3	21	20	1.203	2.98	81	2.57	.227	8	.200	-5	3	-0.7
StL-N	7	10	.412	20	19	15	3	0	144	132	63	40	2	8	42	71	1.208	2.50	100	2.86	.246	23	.280	1	10	0.8
Yr.	10	15	.400	28	27	20	5	0	201^1	180	85	59	2	11	63	91	1.207	2.64	94	2.77	.241	31	.254	-4	13	0.1
1908 StL-N	11	18	.379	38	32	23	3	1	250^2	221	102	59	6	11	57	93	1.109	2.12	110	2.42	.231	15	.169	12	13	1.6
1909 StL-N	11	18	.379	34	28	21	2	0	221^1	215	96	77	1	10	69	66	1.283	3.13	81	3.13	.260	22	.239	-10	7	-0.5
1910 StL-N	14	13	.519	36	25	13	1	1	225^1	235	116	80	6	7	70	54	1.354	3.20	93	3.65	.276	21	.226	1	10	0.6
Total 7	66	85	.437	182	155	105	16	2	1239^1	1169	571	369	17	63	413	490	1.276	2.68	97	3.09	.249	252	.254	9	76	3.2

• LYLE, Jim

James Charles Lyle b: 7/24/1900, Lake, MS d: 10/10/1977, Williamsport, PA BR/TR, 6'1", 180 lbs. Deb: 10/2/1925

YEAR TM-L	W	L	PCT	G	GS	CG	SH	SV	IP	H	R	ER	HR	HB	BB	SO	RAT	ERA	ERA+	CERA	OAV	BH	AVG	PR+	WS	TPW
1925 Was-A	0	0	....	1	0	0	0	0	3	5	2	2	0	0	1	3	2.000	6.00	70	6.26	.333	0	....	-1	0	-0.1

• LYLE, Sparky

Albert Walter Lyle b: 7/22/1944, Du Bois, PA BL/TL, 6'1", 192 lbs. Deb: 7/4/1967

YEAR TM-L	W	L	PCT	G	GS	CG	SH	SV	IP	H	R	ER	HR	HB	BB	SO	RAT	ERA	ERA+	CERA	OAV	BH	AVG	PR+	WS	TPW
1967 Bos-A	1	2	.333	27	0	0	0	5	43^1	33	13	11	3	2	14	42	1.085	2.28	153	2.53	.213	2	.250	6	5	0.7
1968 Bos-A	6	1	.857	49	0	0	0	11	65^2	67	25	20	6	0	14	52	1.234	2.74	115	3.34	.261	1	.125	3	7	0.4
1969 Bos-A	8	3	.727	71	0	0	0	17	102^2	91	33	29	8	1	48	93	1.354	2.54	150	3.53	.240	2	.118	17	14	1.7
1970 Bos-A	1	7	.125	63	0	0	0	20	67^1	62	37	29	5	1	34	51	1.426	3.88	102	3.73	.244	0	.000	2	6	0.1
1971 Bos-A	6	4	.600	50	0	0	0	16	52^1	41	16	16	5	0	23	37	1.223	2.75	134	3.11	.228	3	1.000	6	10	0.8
1972 NY-A	9	5	.643	59	0	0	0	**35**	107^2	84	25	23	3	0	29	75	1.050	1.92	153	1.95	.216	4	.190	12	18	1.5
1973 NY-A★	5	9	.357	51	0	0	0	27	82^1	66	30	23	4	0	18	63	1.020	2.51	146	2.01	.216	0	....	10	14	1.0
1974 NY-A	9	3	.750	66	0	0	0	15	114	93	30	21	6	1	43	89	1.193	1.66	210	2.65	.226	0	.000	21	16	2.2
1975 NY-A	5	7	.417	49	0	0	0	6	89^1	94	34	31	1	2	36	65	1.455	3.12	117	3.77	.275	0	....	3	7	0.3
1976* NY-A★	7	8	.467	64	0	0	0	**23**	103^2	82	33	26	5	0	42	61	1.196	2.26	151	2.60	.225	0	....	10	14	1.0
1977* NY-A★	13	5	.722	**72**	0	0	0	26	137	131	41	33	7	2	33	68	1.197	2.17	182	2.98	.257	0	....	25	20	2.4
1978* NY-A	9	3	.750	59	0	0	0	9	111^2	116	46	43	6	4	33	33	1.334	3.47	104	3.65	.278	0	....	1	9	0.1
1979 Tex-A	5	8	.385	67	0	0	0	13	95	78	37	33	9	0	28	48	1.116	3.13	133	2.62	.226	0	....	10	10	1.0
1980 Tex-A	3	2	.600	49	0	0	0	8	80^2	97	47	42	9	0	28	43	1.550	4.69	83	5.08	.306	0	....	-6	3	-0.6
Phi-N	0	0	....	10	0	0	0	2	14	11	5	3	0	0	6	6	1.214	1.93	196	2.23	.220	0	....	3	2	0.3
1981* Phi-N	9	6	.600	48	0	0	0	2	75	85	40	37	4	1	33	29	1.573	4.44	82	4.55	.301	2	.400	-7	4	-0.7
1982 Phi-N	3	3	.500	34	0	0	0	2	36^2	50	23	21	3	0	12	12	1.691	5.15	71	5.66	.327	1	.500	-6	1	-0.6
Chi-A	0	0	....	11	0	0	0	1	12	11	4	4	0	0	7	6	1.500	3.00	134	3.82	.262	0	....	1	1	0.2
Total 16	99	76	.566	899	0	0	0	238	1390^1	1292	519	445	84	14	481	873	1.275	2.88	127	3.23	.251	15	.192	109	161	11.7

• LYNCH, Adrian

Adrian Ryan Lynch b: 2/9/1897, Laurens, IA d: 3/16/1934, Davenport, IA BB/TR, 6'1.5", 185 lbs. Deb: 8/4/1920

YEAR TM-L	W	L	PCT	G	GS	CG	SH	SV	IP	H	R	ER	HR	HB	BB	SO	RAT	ERA	ERA+	CERA	OAV	BH	AVG	PR+	WS	TPW
1920 StL-A	2	0	1.000	5	3	1	0	0	22^1	23	15	13	1	1	17	8	1.791	5.24	75	5.00	.277	2	.222	-3	1	-0.3

• LYNCH, Ed

Edward Francis Lynch b: 2/25/1956, Brooklyn, NY BR/TR, 6'6", 230 lbs. Deb: 8/31/1980

YEAR TM-L	W	L	PCT	G	GS	CG	SH	SV	IP	H	R	ER	HR	HB	BB	SO	RAT	ERA	ERA+	CERA	OAV	BH	AVG	PR+	WS	TPW
1980 NY-N	1	1	.500	5	4	0	0	0	19^1	24	12	11	0	1	5	9	1.500	5.12	69	4.34	.304	2	.333	-3	0	-0.3
1981 NY-N	4	5	.444	17	13	0	0	0	80^1	79	32	26	6	1	21	27	1.245	2.91	120	3.28	.254	3	.143	6	5	0.8
1982 NY-N	4	8	.333	43	12	0	0	2	139^1	145	57	55	6	1	40	51	1.328	3.55	102	3.49	.273	0	.000	3	8	-0.1
1983 NY-N	10	10	.500	30	27	1	0	0	174^2	208	94	83	17	3	41	44	1.426	4.28	85	4.52	.302	8	.154	-15	5	-1.6
1984 NY-N	9	8	.529	40	13	0	0	2	124	169	77	62	14	4	24	62	1.556	4.50	79	5.53	.324	6	.222	-13	3	-1.3
1985 NY-N	10	8	.556	31	29	6	1	0	191	188	76	73	19	1	27	65	1.126	3.44	100	3.00	.256	4	.077	1	10	-0.1
1986 NY-N	0	0	....	1	0	0	0	0	1^2	2	0	0	0	0	0	1	1.200	0.00	....	2.89	.286	0	....	1	0	0.1
Chi-N	7	5	.583	23	13	1	1	0	99^2	105	48	42	10	1	23	57	1.284	3.79	107	3.76	.279	1	.033	4	6	0.3
Yr.	7	5	.583	24	13	1	1	0	101^1	107	48	42	10	1	23	58	1.283	3.73	108	3.75	.279	1	.033	5	6	0.3
1987 Chi-N	2	9	.182	58	8	0	0	4	110^1	130	74	66	17	2	48	80	1.613	5.38	79	5.66	.295	3	.188	-11	2	-1.1
Total 8	47	54	.465	248	119	8	2	8	940^1	1050	470	418	89	14	229	396	1.360	4.00	92	4.13	.284	27	.114	-27	39	-3.4

• LYNCH, Jack

John H. Lynch b: 2/5/1857, New York, NY d: 4/20/1923, Bronx, NY BR/TR, 5'8", 185 lbs. Deb: 5/2/1881 U

YEAR TM-L	W	L	PCT	G	GS	CG	SH	SV	IP	H	R	ER	HR	HB	BB	SO	RAT	ERA	ERA+	CERA	OAV	BH	AVG	PR+	WS	TPW
1881 Buf-N	10	9	.526	20	19	17	0	0	165^2	203	112	66	2	....	29	32	1.400	3.59	77	....	.289	13	.167	-9	8	-1.2
1883 NY-a	13	15	.464	29	29	29	1	0	255	263	161	116	6	....	25	119	1.129	4.09	82	....	.250	20	.187	-24	15	-2.3
1884 NY-a	37	15	.712	55	53	53	5	0	496	420	225	147	10	10	42	292	.931	2.67	117	....	.217	30	.152	6	36	0.0
1885 NY-a	23	21	.523	44	43	43	1	0	379	410	243	152	17	3	42	177	1.193	3.61	82	....	.264	30	.196	-26	12	-2.0
1886 NY-a	20	30	.400	51	50	50	1	0	432^2	485	307	190	10	12	116	193	1.389	3.95	86	....	.271	27	.160	-32	22	-3.2
1887 NY-a	7	14	.333	21	21	21	0	0	187	281	158	106	8	4	36	45	1.503	5.10	83	....	.335	21	.233	-12	5	-1.3
1890 Bro-a	0	1	.000	1	1	1	0	0	9	22	18	12	1	0	5	1	3.000	12.00	32	....	.452	3	.750	-8	1	-0.5
Total 7	110	105	.512	221	216	214	8	0	1924^1	2084	1224	789	54	29	295	859	1.218	3.69	89	....	.263	144	.180	-105	99	-10.5

• LYNCH, Mike

Michael Joseph Lynch b: 6/28/1880, Holyoke, MA d: 4/2/1927, Garrison, NY BR/TR, 6'2", 170 lbs. Deb: 6/21/1904

YEAR TM-L	W	L	PCT	G	GS	CG	SH	SV	IP	H	R	ER	HR	HB	BB	SO	RAT	ERA	ERA+	CERA	OAV	BH	AVG	PR+	WS	TPW
1904 Pit-N	15	11	.577	27	24	24	1	0	222^2	200	90	67	1	15	91	95	1.307	2.71	101	3.12	.243	20	.230	-1	15	0.3
1905 Pit-N	17	8	.680	33	22	13	0	2	206^1	191	102	87	3	5	107	106	1.444	3.79	79	3.63	.254	11	.136	-22	11	-2.4
1906 Pit-N	6	5	.545	18	12	7	0	0	119	101	48	32	2	8	31	48	1.109	2.42	110	2.48	.232	8	.205	3	7	0.3
1907 Pit-N	2	2	.500	7	4	2	0	0	36	37	21	9	0	1	22	9	1.639	2.25	108	4.53	.282	3	.250	1	2	0.2
NY-N	3	6	.333	12	10	7	0	1	72	68	35	27	3	0	30	34	1.361	3.38	73	3.38	.249	8	.296	-5	3	-0.3
Yr.	5	8	.385	19	14	9	0	1	108	105	56	36	3	1	52	43	1.454	3.00	82	3.77	.260	11	.282	-4	5	-0.1
Total 4	43	32	.573	97	72	53	1	3	656	597	296	222	9	29	281	292	1.338	3.05	91	3.27	.247	50	.203	-24	38	-1.9

• LYNCH, Tom

Thomas S. Lynch b: 1863, Peru, IL d: 5/13/1903, Peru, IL BL, 5'11", 175 lbs. Deb: 8/5/1884

YEAR TM-L	W	L	PCT	G	GS	CG	SH	SV	IP	H	R	ER	HR	HB	BB	SO	RAT	ERA	ERA+	CERA	OAV	BH	AVG	PR+	WS	TPW
1884 Chi-N	0	0	....	1	1	0	0	0	7	7	4	2	1	....	3	2	1.429	2.57	122	....	.246	0	.000	0	0	-0.1

• LYNN, Red

Japhet Monroe Lynn b: 12/27/1913, Kenney, TX d: 10/27/1977, Bellville, TX BR/TR, 6', 162 lbs. Deb: 4/25/1939

YEAR TM-L	W	L	PCT	G	GS	CG	SH	SV	IP	H	R	ER	HR	HB	BB	SO	RAT	ERA	ERA+	CERA	OAV	BH	AVG	PR+	WS	TPW
1939 Det-A	0	1	.000	4	0	0	0	0	8^1	11	8	8	2	1	3	3	1.680	8.64	57	7.16	.324	0	.000	-3	0	-0.4
NY-N	1	0	1.000	26	0	0	0	1	49^2	44	21	17	3	2	21	22	1.309	3.08	127	3.26	.240	0	.000	5	4	0.4
1940 NY-N	4	3	.571	33	0	0	0	3	42^1	40	21	18	3	1	24	25	1.512	3.83	101	4.11	.247	0	.000	0	3	0.0
1944 Chi-N	5	4	.556	22	7	4	1	1	84^1	80	41	38	4	1	37	35	1.387	4.06	87	3.55	.251	6	.207	-4	4	-0.4
Total 3	10	8	.556	85	7	4	1	5	184^2	175	91	81	12	5	85	85	1.408	3.95	96	3.76	.251	6	.146	-2	11	-0.3

• LYON, Brandon

Brandon James Lyon b: 8/10/1979, Salt Lake City, UT BR/TR, 6'1", 170 lbs. Deb: 8/4/2001

YEAR TM-L	W	L	PCT	G	GS	CG	SH	SV	IP	H	R	ER	HR	HB	BB	SO	RAT	ERA	ERA+	CERA	OAV	BH	AVG	PR+	WS	TPW
2001 Tor-A	5	4	.556	11	11	0	0	0	63	63	31	30	6	1	15	35	1.238	4.29	107	3.50	.266	0	....	2	4	0.2
2002 Tor-A	1	4	.200	15	10	0	0	0	62	78	47	45	14	2	19	30	1.565	6.53	71	6.24	.308	0	....	-13	0	-1.2

YEAR	TM-L	W	L	PCT	G	GS	CG	SH	SV	IP	H	R	ER	HR	HB	BB	SO	RAT	ERA	ERA+	CERA	OAV	BH	AVG	PR+	WS	TPW
2003	Bos-A	4	6	.400	49	0	0	0	9	59	73	33	27	6	2	19	50	1.559	4.12	111	4.96	.296	0	....	4	5	0.4
Total	3	10	14	.417	75	21	0	0	9	184	214	111	102	26	5	53	115	1.451	4.99	92	4.89	.290	0	....	-7	9	-0.7
• LYONS, Al	Albert Harold Lyons b: 7/18/1918, St. Joseph, MO d: 12/20/1965, Inglewood, CA BR/TR, 6'2", 195 lbs. Deb: 4/19/1944																										
1944	NY-A	0	0	....	11	0	0	0	0	39^2	43	22	20	2	2	24	14	1.689	4.54	77	5.15	.291	9	.346	-5	2	-0.3
1946	NY-A	0	1	.000	2	1	0	0	0	8^1	11	5	5	0	1	6	4	2.040	5.40	64	6.67	.314	0	.000	-2	0	-0.3
1947	NY-A	1	0	1.000	6	0	0	0	0	11	18	11	11	2	0	9	7	2.455	9.00	39	10.40	.367	4	.667	-7	1	-0.5
	Pit-N	1	2	.333	13	0	0	0	0	28^1	36	24	23	4	1	12	16	1.694	7.31	58	6.01	.300	2	.200	-10	0	-0.8
1948	Bos-N	1	0	1.000	7	0	0	0	0	12^2	17	11	11	1	0	8	5	1.974	7.82	49	6.44	.309	2	.167	-6	0	-0.6
Total	4	3	3	.500	39	1	0	0	0	100	125	73	70	9	4	59	46	1.840	6.30	60	6.26	.307	17	.293	-29	3	-2.5
• LYONS, Curt	Curt Russell Lyons b: 10/17/1974, Greencastle, IN BR/TR, 6'5", 230 lbs. Deb: 9/19/1996																										
1996	Cin-N	2	0	1.000	3	3	0	0	0	16	17	8	8	1	1	7	14	1.500	4.50	92	4.65	.274	0	.000	-1	1	-0.1
• LYONS, George	George Tony "Smooth" Lyons b: 1/25/1891, Bible Grove, IL d: 8/12/1981, Nevada, MO BR/TR, 5'11", 180 lbs. Deb: 9/6/1920																										
1920	StL-N	2	1	.667	7	2	1	0	0	23^1	21	8	8	2	1	9	5	1.286	3.09	99	3.69	.262	1	.143	-0	2	0.0
1924	StL-A	3	2	.600	26	6	2	0	0	77^2	97	52	45	2	5	45	25	1.828	5.21	87	5.94	.323	5	.250	-7	3	-0.6
Total	2	5	3	.625	33	8	3	0	0	101	118	60	53	4	6	54	30	1.703	4.72	89	5.42	.310	6	.222	-7	5	-0.7
• LYONS, Hersh	Herschel Englebert Lyons b: 7/23/1915, Fresno, CA BR/TR, 5'11", 195 lbs. Deb: 4/17/1941																										
1941	StL-N	0	0	....	1	0	0	0	0	1^1	1	0	0	0	0	3	1	3.000	0.00	....	8.02	.200	0	....	1	0	0.1
• LYONS, Ted	Theodore Amar "Sunday Teddy" Lyons b: 12/28/1900, Lake Charles, LA d: 7/25/1986, Sulphur, LA BB/TR, 5'11", 200 lbs. Deb: 7/2/1923 M/C HOF: 1955																										
1923	Chi-A	2	1	.667	9	1	0	0	0	22^2	30	21	16	2	1	15	6	1.985	6.35	62	6.87	.323	1	.200	-6	0	-0.6
1924	Chi-A	12	11	.522	41	22	12	0	3	216^1	279	143	117	10	2	72	52	1.622	4.87	85	5.01	.322	17	.221	-17	8	-1.6
1925	Chi-A	**21**	11	.656	43	32	19	**5**	3	262^2	274	111	95	7	2	83	45	1.359	3.26	128	3.47	.278	18	.186	26	23	2.1
1926	Chi-A	18	16	.529	39	31	24	3	2	283^2	268	108	95	6	1	106	51	1.318	3.01	128	3.03	.252	22	.212	24	24	2.3
1927	Chi-A	**22**	14	.611	39	34	**30**	2	2	**307^2**	291	125	97	7	0	67	71	1.164	2.84	143	2.54	.251	28	.255	36	**30**	**4.0**
1928	Chi-A	15	14	.517	39	27	21	0	6	240	276	133	106	11	2	68	60	1.433	3.98	102	3.81	.295	23	.253	1	15	0.2
1929	Chi-A	14	20	.412	37	31	21	1	2	259^1	276	136	118	11	2	76	57	1.357	4.10	104	3.59	.278	20	.220	1	16	0.3
1930	Chi-A	22	15	.595	42	36	**29**	1	1	**297^2**	331	160	125	12	2	57	69	1.303	3.78	122	3.44	.285	38	.311	36	26	4.0
1931	Chi-A	4	6	.400	22	12	7	0	0	101	117	50	45	6	0	33	16	1.485	4.01	106	4.39	.296	5	.152	5	6	0.3
1932	Chi-A	10	15	.400	33	26	19	1	2	230^2	243	104	84	10	3	71	58	1.361	3.28	132	3.62	.272	19	.260	29	14	3.2
1933	Chi-A	10	21	.323	36	27	14	2	1	228	260	142	111	10	0	74	74	1.465	4.38	97	3.98	.280	26	.286	-1	12	0.4
1934	Chi-A	11	13	.458	30	24	21	0	1	205^1	249	138	111	15	2	66	53	1.534	4.87	97	4.64	.293	20	.206	3	10	0.4
1935	Chi-A	15	8	.652	23	22	19	3	0	190^2	194	79	64	15	3	56	54	1.311	3.02	153	3.58	.262	18	.220	32	20	3.0
1936	Chi-A	10	13	.435	26	24	15	1	0	182	227	115	104	21	3	45	48	1.495	5.14	101	4.98	.305	11	.157	-1	9	-0.3
1937	Chi-A	12	7	.632	22	22	11	0	0	169^1	182	86	78	21	1	45	45	1.341	4.15	111	4.18	.278	12	.211	5	13	0.6
1938	Chi-A	9	11	.450	23	23	17	1	0	194^2	238	93	80	13	0	52	54	1.490	3.70	132	4.45	.299	14	.194	26	14	2.3
1939	Chi-A★	14	6	.700	21	21	16	0	0	172^2	162	71	53	7	1	26	65	1.089	2.76	171	**2.40**	.247	18	.295	36	20	3.7
1940	Chi-A	12	8	.600	22	22	17	**4**	0	186^1	188	85	67	17	0	37	72	1.208	3.24	137	3.15	.252	18	.240	20	15	2.1
1941	Chi-A	12	10	.545	22	22	19	2	0	187^1	199	87	77	9	4	37	63	1.260	3.70	111	3.27	.269	20	.270	6	13	0.9
1942	Chi-A	14	6	.700	20	20	20	1	0	180^1	167	52	42	11	2	26	50	1.070	**2.10**	**172**	2.50	.245	16	.239	29	21	**3.3**
1946	Chi-A	1	4	.200	5	5	5	0	0	42^2	38	17	11	2	0	9	10	1.102	2.32	147	2.38	.235	0	.000	5	3	0.3
Total	21	260	230	.531	594	484	356	27	23	4161	4489	2056	1696	223	31	1121	1073	1.348	3.67	118	3.64	.276	364	.233	294	312	30.9
• LYONS, Toby	Thomas A. Lyons b: 3/27/1869, Cambridge, MA d: 8/29/1920, Boston, MA Deb: 4/18/1890 U																										
1890	Syr-a	0	2	.000	3	3	2	0	0	22^1	40	36	26	1	1	21	6	2.731	10.48	34	....	.377	4	.333	-17	0	-1.4
• LYSANDER, Rick	Richard Eugene Lysander b: 2/21/1953, Huntington Park, CA BR/TR, 6'2", 190 lbs. Deb: 4/12/1980																										
1980	Oak-A	0	0	....	5	0	0	0	0	13^2	24	13	12	3	0	4	5	2.049	7.90	48	9.45	.381	0	....	-6	0	-0.6
1983	Min-A	5	12	.294	61	4	1	1	3	125	132	63	47	8	2	43	58	1.400	3.38	125	3.79	.275	0	....	10	8	1.0
1984	Min-A	4	3	.571	36	0	0	0	5	56^2	62	23	22	2	0	27	22	1.571	3.49	120	4.23	.283	0	....	3	5	0.3
1985	Min-A	0	2	.000	35	1	0	0	3	61	72	43	41	3	0	22	26	1.541	6.05	73	4.68	.305	0	....	-11	1	-1.1
Total	4	9	17	.346	137	5	1	1	11	256^1	290	142	122	16	2	96	111	1.506	4.28	99	4.40	.291	0	....	-4	14	-0.4
• LYSTON, John	John Michael Lyston b: 5/28/1867, Baltimore, MD d: 10/29/1909, Baltimore, MD BR/TR, 5'111" Deb: 8/29/1891 U																										
1891	Col-a	0	1	.000	1	1	1	0	0	6	10	8	7	0	1	6	1	2.667	10.50	33	....	.359	0	.000	-5	0	-0.4
1894	Cle-N	0	0	....	1	1	0	0	0	3^2	5	6	4	1	0	4	0	2.455	9.82	56	10.69	.322	0	.000	-2	0	-0.2
Total	2	0	1	.000	2	2	1	0	0	9^2	15	14	11	1	1	10	1	2.586	10.24	39	4.05	.346	0	.000	-7	0	-0.6
• MAAS, Duke	Duane Fredrick Maas b: 1/31/1929, Utica, MI d: 12/7/1976, Mount Clemens, MI BR/TR, 5'10", 170 lbs. Deb: 4/21/1955																										
1955	Det-A	5	6	.455	18	16	5	2	0	86^2	91	52	47	7	2	50	42	1.627	4.88	79	4.96	.271	5	.167	-10	2	-1.0
1956	Det-A	0	7	.000	26	7	0	0	0	63^1	81	51	46	9	6	32	34	1.784	6.54	63	6.69	.313	3	.188	-17	0	-1.7
1957	Det-A	10	14	.417	45	26	8	2	6	219^1	210	92	80	23	4	65	116	1.254	3.28	117	3.47	.252	6	.085	12	15	0.9
1958	KC-A	4	5	.444	10	7	3	1	1	55^1	49	25	24	3	1	13	19	1.120	3.90	100	2.70	.241	3	.176	0	4	0.1
	*NY-A	7	3	.700	22	13	2	1	0	101^1	93	51	43	9	2	36	50	1.273	3.82	93	3.44	.242	3	.088	-5	4	-0.7
	Yr.	11	8	.579	32	20	5	2	1	156^2	142	76	67	12	3	49	69	1.219	3.85	95	3.18	.242	6	.118	-5	8	-0.7
1959	NY-A	14	8	.636	38	21	3	1	4	138	149	82	68	14	2	53	67	1.464	4.43	82	4.56	.278	5	.125	-12	5	-1.4
1960	*NY-A	5	1	.833	35	1	0	0	4	70^1	70	44	32	6	1	35	28	1.493	4.09	87	4.29	.265	0	.000	-6	3	-0.7
1961	NY-A	0	0	....	1	0	0	0	0	0^1	2	2	2	0	0	0	0	6.000	54.00	7	39.65	1.000	0	....	-2	0	-0.2
Total	7	45	44	.506	195	91	21	7	15	734^2	745	399	342	71	18	284	356	1.401	4.19	90	4.16	.264	25	.117	-39	33	-4.7
• MABE, Bob	Robert Lee Mabe b: 10/8/1929, Danville, VA BR/TR, 5'11", 165 lbs. Deb: 4/18/1958																										
1958	StL-N	3	9	.250	31	13	4	0	0	111^2	113	66	56	11	4	41	74	1.379	4.51	92	4.01	.260	1	.042	-5	4	-0.7
1959	Cin-N	4	2	.667	18	1	0	0	3	29^2	29	28	18	6	0	19	8	1.618	5.46	74	5.59	.254	0	.000	-5	0	-0.6
1960	Bal-A	0	0	....	2	0	0	0	0	0^2	4	6	2	0	0	1	0	7.500	27.00	14	41.86	.571	0	....	-2	0	-0.2
Total	3	7	11	.389	51	14	4	0	3	142	146	100	76	17	4	61	82	1.458	4.82	85	4.52	.263	1	.032	-11	4	-1.4
• MACARTHUR, Mac	Malcolm M. MacArthur b: 1/19/1862, Glasgow, Scotland d: 10/18/1932, Detroit, MI TR, 5'9.5", 164 lbs. Deb: 5/2/1884																										
1884	Ind-a	1	5	.167	6	6	6	0	0	52	57	49	29	1	2	21	19	1.500	5.02	65	....	.264	2	.095	-8	1	-0.8
• MACCORMACK, Frank	Frank Louis MacCormack b: 9/21/1954, Jersey City, NJ BR/TR, 6'4", 210 lbs. Deb: 6/14/1976																										
1976	Det-A	0	5	.000	9	8	0	0	0	32^2	35	24	21	1	1	34	14	2.112	5.79	64	7.00	.294	0	.000	-7	0	-0.8
1977	Sea-A	0	0	....	3	3	0	0	0	7	4	3	3	0	3	12	4	2.286	3.86	107	7.71	.174	0	....	0	0	0.0
Total	2	0	5	.000	12	11	0	0	0	39^2	39	27	24	1	4	46	18	2.143	5.45	69	7.12	.275	0	.000	-7	0	-0.8
• MACDONALD, Bill	William Paul MacDonald b: 3/28/1929, Alameda, CA d: 5/4/1991, Shasta Lake, CA BR/TR, 5'10", 170 lbs. Deb: 5/6/1950																										
1950	Pit-N	8	10	.444	32	20	6	2	1	153	138	88	73	17	1	88	60	1.477	4.29	102	4.23	.243	6	.122	2	7	0.1
1953	Pit-N	0	1	.000	4	1	0	0	0	7^1	12	10	10	0	1	8	4	2.727	12.27	36	11.12	.400	0	....	-6	0	-0.6
Total	2	8	11	.421	36	21	6	2	1	160^1	150	98	83	17	2	96	64	1.534	4.66	94	4.54	.251	6	.122	-4	7	-0.5
• MACDONALD, Bob	Robert Joseph MacDonald b: 4/27/1965, East Orange, NJ BL/TL, 6'3", 208 lbs. Deb: 8/14/1990																										
1990	Tor-A	0	0	....	4	0	0	0	0	2^1	0	0	0	0	0	2	0	.857	0.00	....	0.81	.000	0	....	1	0	0.1
1991	*Tor-A	3	3	.500	45	0	0	0	0	53^2	51	19	17	5	0	25	24	1.416	2.85	148	3.91	.252	0	....	8	5	0.8
1992	Tor-A	1	0	1.000	27	0	0	0	0	47^1	50	24	23	4	1	16	26	1.394	4.37	93	4.03	.270	0	....	-1	2	-0.1
1993	Det-A	3	3	.500	68	0	0	0	3	65^2	67	42	39	8	1	33	39	1.523	5.35	80	4.67	.268	0	....	-8	3	-0.7
1995	NY-A	1	1	.500	33	0	0	0	0	46^1	50	25	25	7	1	22	41	1.554	4.86	95	5.46	.282	0	....	-2	2	-0.1

YEAR	TM-L	W	L	PCT	G	GS	CG	SH	SV	IP	H	R	ER	HR	HB	BB	SO	RAT	ERA	ERA+	CERA	OAV	BH	AVG	PR+	WS	TPW
1996	NY-N	0	2	.000	20	0	0	0	0	19	16	10	9	2	0	9	12	1.316	4.26	94	3.61	.235	0	....	-1	1	-0.1
Total	**6**	**8**	**9**	**.471**	**197**	**0**	**0**	**0**	**3**	**234^1**	**234**	**120**	**113**	**26**	**3**	**107**	**142**	**1.455**	**4.34**	**99**	**4.40**	**.265**	**0**	**....**	**-2**	**13**	**-0.2**

• MACDOUGAL, Mike Robert Meiklejohn MacDougal b: 3/5/1977, Las Vegas, NV BR/TR, 6'4", 195 lbs. Deb: 9/22/2001

YEAR	TM-L	W	L	PCT	G	GS	CG	SH	SV	IP	H	R	ER	HR	HB	BB	SO	RAT	ERA	ERA+	CERA	OAV	BH	AVG	PR+	WS	TPW
2001	KC-A	1	1	.500	3	3	0	0	0	15^1	18	10	8	2	1	4	7	1.435	4.70	104	5.04	.290	0	....	-0	1	0.0
2002	KC-A	0	1	.000	6	0	0	0	0	9	5	5	5	0	0	7	10	1.333	5.00	100	2.26	.161	0	....	0	0	0.0
2003	KC-A★	3	5	.375	68	0	0	0	27	64	64	36	29	4	8	32	57	1.500	4.08	127	4.76	.267	0	....	8	9	0.7
Total	**3**	**4**	**7**	**.364**	**77**	**3**	**0**	**0**	**27**	**88^1**	**87**	**51**	**42**	**6**	**9**	**43**	**74**	**1.472**	**4.28**	**119**	**4.55**	**.261**	**0**	**....**	**8**	**10**	**0.7**

• MACE, Jimmy Harry F. Mace b: 1870, Washington, DC, 5'11", 185 lbs. Deb: 5/5/1891

YEAR	TM-L	W	L	PCT	G	GS	CG	SH	SV	IP	H	R	ER	HR	HB	BB	SO	RAT	ERA	ERA+	CERA	OAV	BH	AVG	PR+	WS	TPW
1891	Was-a	0	1	.000	3	1	1	0	0	16	18	14	13	0	1	8	3	1.625	7.31	51	....	.275	0	.000	-5	0	-0.5

• MACFAYDEN, Danny Daniel Knowles "Deacon Danny" MacFayden b: 6/10/1905, North Truro, MA d: 8/26/1972, Brunswick, ME BR/TR, 5'11", 170 lbs. Deb: 8/25/1926

YEAR	TM-L	W	L	PCT	G	GS	CG	SH	SV	IP	H	R	ER	HR	HB	BB	SO	RAT	ERA	ERA+	CERA	OAV	BH	AVG	PR+	WS	TPW
1926	Bos-A	0	1	.000	3	1	1	0	0	13	10	7	7	0	0	7	1	1.308	4.85	84	2.60	.217	1	.333	-1	0	-0.1
1927	Bos-A	5	8	.385	34	16	6	1	2	160^1	176	88	76	9	6	59	42	1.466	4.27	99	4.32	.294	13	.283	1	11	0.5
1928	Bos-A	9	15	.375	33	28	9	0	0	195	215	123	103	12	7	78	61	1.503	4.75	86	4.21	.289	9	.143	-15	7	-1.6
1929	Bos-A	10	18	.357	32	27	14	**4**	0	221	225	108	89	8	5	81	61	1.385	3.62	118	3.65	.271	13	.176	17	15	1.3
1930	Bos-A	11	14	.440	36	33	18	1	2	269^1	293	141	126	9	6	93	76	1.433	4.21	109	3.88	.281	13	.141	9	17	0.4
1931	Bos-A	16	12	.571	35	32	17	2	0	230^2	263	121	103	4	7	79	74	1.483	4.02	107	3.97	.281	10	.123	8	17	0.3
1932	Bos-A	1	10	.091	12	11	6	0	0	77^2	91	55	44	3	1	33	29	1.597	5.10	88	4.53	.289	3	.120	-4	2	-0.5
	NY-A	7	5	.583	17	15	9	0	1	121^1	137	69	53	11	2	37	33	1.434	3.93	104	4.31	.281	5	.102	2	6	-0.1
	Yr.	8	15	.348	29	26	15	0	1	199	228	124	97	14	3	70	62	1.497	4.39	97	4.40	.284	8	.108	-2	8	-0.6
1933	NY-A	3	2	.600	25	6	2	0	0	90^1	120	62	59	8	2	37	28	1.738	5.88	66	5.90	.319	1	.029	-19	1	-2.2
1934	NY-A	4	3	.571	22	11	4	0	0	96	110	57	48	5	2	31	41	1.469	4.50	90	4.23	.288	4	.103	-6	3	-0.8
1935	Cin-N	1	2	.333	7	4	1	0	0	36	39	22	19	1	0	13	13	1.444	4.75	84	3.84	.281	1	.091	-3	1	-0.4
	Bos-N	5	13	.278	28	20	7	1	0	151^2	200	96	86	8	5	34	46	1.543	5.10	74	4.85	.314	8	.157	-17	3	-1.8
	Yr.	6	15	.286	35	24	8	1	0	187^2	239	118	105	9	5	47	59	1.524	5.04	76	4.65	.308	9	.145	-20	4	-2.1
1936	Bos-N	17	13	.567	37	31	21	2	0	266^2	268	97	85	5	5	66	86	1.253	2.87	134	2.99	.259	8	.096	26	22	2.1
1937	Bos-N	14	14	.500	32	32	16	2	0	246	250	96	80	5	2	60	70	1.260	2.93	122	3.05	.268	13	.157	12	17	1.0
1938	Bos-N	14	9	.609	29	29	19	5	0	219^2	208	82	72	6	5	64	58	1.238	2.95	116	2.88	.247	9	.117	11	16	0.6
1939	Bos-N	8	14	.364	33	28	8	0	2	191^2	221	100	83	11	4	59	46	1.461	3.90	95	4.23	.291	12	.179	-7	7	-0.8
1940	Pit-N	5	4	.556	35	8	0	0	2	91^1	112	47	36	5	4	27	24	1.522	3.55	107	4.68	.302	5	.179	5	5	0.5
1941	Was-A	0	1	.000	5	0	0	0	0	7	12	9	8	1	0	5	3	2.429	10.29	39	10.20	.375	0	....	-5	0	-0.5
1943	Bos-N	2	1	.667	10	1	0	0	0	21^1	31	14	14	1	1	9	5	1.875	5.91	58	6.67	.344	1	.250	-6	0	-0.7
Total	**17**	**132**	**159**	**.454**	**465**	**333**	**158**	**18**	**9**	**2706**	**2981**	**1394**	**1191**	**112**	**64**	**872**	**797**	**1.424**	**3.96**	**101**	**3.93**	**.281**	**129**	**.142**	**9**	**150**	**-2.4**

• MACHADO, Julio Julio Segundo (Rondon) Machado b: 12/1/1965, Zulia, Venezuela BR/TR, 5'9", 165 lbs. Deb: 9/7/1989

YEAR	TM-L	W	L	PCT	G	GS	CG	SH	SV	IP	H	R	ER	HR	HB	BB	SO	RAT	ERA	ERA+	CERA	OAV	BH	AVG	PR+	WS	TPW
1989	NY-N	0	1	.000	10	0	0	0	0	11	9	4	4	0	0	3	14	1.091	3.27	100	2.00	.214	0	....	0	1	0.0
1990	NY-N	4	1	.800	27	0	0	0	0	34^1	32	13	12	4	2	17	27	1.427	3.15	119	4.21	.248	0	....	3	3	0.3
	Mil-A	0	0	....	10	0	0	0	3	13	9	1	1	0	0	8	12	1.308	0.69	559	2.26	.191	0	....	5	2	0.5
1991	Mil-A	3	3	.500	54	0	0	0	3	88^2	65	36	34	12	3	55	98	1.353	3.45	115	3.94	.211	0	....	5	6	0.5
Total	**3**	**7**	**5**	**.583**	**101**	**0**	**0**	**0**	**6**	**147**	**115**	**54**	**51**	**16**	**5**	**83**	**151**	**1.347**	**3.12**	**123**	**3.71**	**.219**	**0**	**....**	**13**	**12**	**1.3**

• MACHEMEHL, Chuck Charles Walter Machemehl b: 4/20/1946, Brenham, TX BR/TR, 6'4", 200 lbs. Deb: 4/6/1971

YEAR	TM-L	W	L	PCT	G	GS	CG	SH	SV	IP	H	R	ER	HR	HB	BB	SO	RAT	ERA	ERA+	CERA	OAV	BH	AVG	PR+	WS	TPW
1971	Cle-A	0	2	.000	14	0	0	0	3	18^1	16	16	13	2	0	15	9	1.691	6.38	60	4.78	.246	1	.500	-5	0	-0.5

• MACK, Bill William Francis Mack b: 2/12/1885, Elmira, NY d: 9/30/1971, Elmira, NY BL/TL, 6'1", 155 lbs. Deb: 7/14/1908

YEAR	TM-L	W	L	PCT	G	GS	CG	SH	SV	IP	H	R	ER	HR	HB	BB	SO	RAT	ERA	ERA+	CERA	OAV	BH	AVG	PR+	WS	TPW
1908	Chi-N	0	0	....	2	0	0	0	0	6	5	3	2	1	1	1	2	1.000	3.00	78	3.93	.263	2	.667	-1	1	0.1

• MACK, Frank Frank George "Stubby" Mack b: 2/2/1900, Oklahoma City, OK d: 7/2/1971, Clearwater, FL BR/TR, 6'1.5", 180 lbs. Deb: 8/16/1922

YEAR	TM-L	W	L	PCT	G	GS	CG	SH	SV	IP	H	R	ER	HR	HB	BB	SO	RAT	ERA	ERA+	CERA	OAV	BH	AVG	PR+	WS	TPW
1922	Chi-A	2	2	.500	8	4	1	1	0	34^1	36	16	14	2	0	16	11	1.515	3.67	111	4.26	.281	3	.250	1	2	0.2
1923	Chi-A	0	1	.000	11	0	0	0	0	23^1	23	13	11	0	0	11	6	1.457	4.24	93	3.54	.284	0	.000	-1	1	-0.2
1925	Chi-A	0	0	....	8	0	0	0	0	13^1	24	14	14	1	0	13	6	2.775	9.45	44	12.08	.444	1	.333	-8	0	-0.7
Total	**3**	**2**	**3**	**.400**	**27**	**4**	**1**	**1**	**0**	**71**	**83**	**43**	**39**	**3**	**0**	**40**	**23**	**1.732**	**4.94**	**82**	**5.49**	**.315**	**4**	**.190**	**-7**	**3**	**-0.7**

• MACK, Tony Tony Lynn Mack b: 4/30/1961, Lexington, KY BR/TR, 5'10", 177 lbs. Deb: 7/27/1985

YEAR	TM-L	W	L	PCT	G	GS	CG	SH	SV	IP	H	R	ER	HR	HB	BB	SO	RAT	ERA	ERA+	CERA	OAV	BH	AVG	PR+	WS	TPW
1985	Cal-A	0	1	.000	1	1	0	0	0	2^1	8	4	4	0	0	0	0	3.429	15.43	27	19.13	.571	0	....	-3	0	-0.3

• MACKENZIE, Ken Kenneth Purvis Mackenzie b: 3/10/1934, Gore Bay, Canada BR/TL, 6', 185 lbs. Deb: 5/2/1960

YEAR	TM-L	W	L	PCT	G	GS	CG	SH	SV	IP	H	R	ER	HR	HB	BB	SO	RAT	ERA	ERA+	CERA	OAV	BH	AVG	PR+	WS	TPW
1960	Mil-N	0	1	.000	9	0	0	0	0	8^1	9	7	6	2	0	3	9	1.440	6.48	53	4.87	.281	0	.000	-3	0	-0.3
1961	Mil-N	0	1	.000	5	0	0	0	0	7	8	5	4	1	1	2	5	1.429	5.14	73	5.40	.296	0	.000	-1	0	-0.1
1962	NY-N	5	4	.556	42	1	0	0	1	80	87	47	44	10	3	34	51	1.513	4.95	84	4.97	.280	1	.083	-5	3	-0.6
1963	NY-N	3	1	.750	34	0	0	0	3	58	63	35	32	11	2	12	41	1.293	4.97	70	4.37	.267	0	.000	-9	2	-1.1
	StL-N	0	0	....	8	0	0	0	0	9	9	6	4	1	0	3	7	1.333	4.00	89	3.63	.250	0	....	-0	0	-0.1
	Yr.	3	1	.750	42	0	0	0	3	67	72	41	36	12	2	15	48	1.299	4.84	72	4.27	.265	0	.000	-9	2	-1.1
1964	SF-N	0	0	....	10	0	0	0	1	9	9	7	5	1	0	3	3	1.333	5.00	71	3.59	.265	0	....	-2	0	-0.2
1965	Hou-N	0	3	.000	21	0	0	0	0	37	46	22	16	7	0	6	26	1.405	3.89	86	5.08	.299	3	.273	-2	1	-0.1
Total	**6**	**8**	**10**	**.444**	**129**	**1**	**0**	**0**	**5**	**208^1**	**231**	**129**	**111**	**33**	**6**	**63**	**142**	**1.411**	**4.80**	**78**	**4.71**	**.278**	**4**	**.111**	**-22**	**6**	**-2.4**

• MACKINSON, John John Joseph Mackinson b: 10/29/1923, Orange, NJ d: 10/17/1989, Reseda, CA BR/TR, 5'10.5", 160 lbs. Deb: 4/16/1953

YEAR	TM-L	W	L	PCT	G	GS	CG	SH	SV	IP	H	R	ER	HR	HB	BB	SO	RAT	ERA	ERA+	CERA	OAV	BH	AVG	PR+	WS	TPW
1953	Phi-A	0	0	....	1	0	0	0	0	1^1	1	0	0	0	0	2	0	2.250	0.00	....	5.42	.200	0	....	1	0	0.1
1955	StL-N	0	1	.000	8	1	0	0	0	20^2	24	18	18	3	1	10	8	1.645	7.84	52	5.53	.296	0	.000	-8	0	-0.9
Total	**2**	**0**	**1**	**.000**	**9**	**1**	**0**	**0**	**0**	**22**	**25**	**18**	**18**	**3**	**1**	**12**	**8**	**1.682**	**7.36**	**55**	**5.53**	**.291**	**0**	**.000**	**-8**	**0**	**-0.8**

• MACLEOD, Billy William Daniel Macleod b: 5/13/1942, Gloucester, MA BL/TL, 6'2", 190 lbs. Deb: 9/13/1962

YEAR	TM-L	W	L	PCT	G	GS	CG	SH	SV	IP	H	R	ER	HR	HB	BB	SO	RAT	ERA	ERA+	CERA	OAV	BH	AVG	PR+	WS	TPW
1962	Bos-A	0	1	.000	2	0	0	0	0	1^2	4	1	1	0	0	1	2	3.000	5.40	76	13.02	.444	0	....	-0	0	0.0

• MACON, Max Max Cullen Macon b: 10/14/1915, Pensacola, FL d: 8/5/1989, Jupiter, FL BL/TL, 6'3", 175 lbs. Deb: 4/21/1938 ♦

YEAR	TM-L	W	L	PCT	G	GS	CG	SH	SV	IP	H	R	ER	HR	HB	BB	SO	RAT	ERA	ERA+	CERA	OAV	BH	AVG	PR+	WS	TPW
1938	StL-N	4	11	.267	38	12	5	1	2	129^1	133	83	59	9	4	61	39	1.500	4.11	96	4.27	.268	11	.306	-2	5	0.0
1940	Bro-N	1	0	1.000	2	0	0	0	0	2	5	5	5	2	0	0	1	2.500	22.50	18	20.86	.455	1	1.000	-4	0	-0.4
1942	Bro-N	5	3	.625	14	8	4	1	1	84	67	22	18	3	2	33	27	1.190	1.93	169	2.54	.220	12	.279	11	9	1.6
1943	Bro-N	7	5	.583	25	9	0	0	0	77	91	54	51	4	4	32	21	1.597	5.96	56	4.84	.291	9	.164	-21	0	-2.6
1944	Bos-N	0	0	....	1	0	0	0	0	3	10	7	7	2	0	1	1	3.667	21.00	18	26.72	.556	100	.273	-6	6	-2.3
1947	Bos-N	0	0	....	1	0	0	0	0	2	1	0	0	0	0	1	1	1.000	0.00	....	1.54	.167	0	.000	1	0	0.1
Total	**6**	**17**	**19**	**.472**	**81**	**29**	**9**	**2**	**3**	**297^1**	**307**	**171**	**140**	**20**	**10**	**128**	**90**	**1.463**	**4.24**	**85**	**4.25**	**.267**	**133**	**.265**	**-20**	**20**	**-3.6**

• MACPHERSON, Harry Harry William Macpherson b: 7/10/1926, North Andover, MA BR/TR, 5'10", 150 lbs. Deb: 8/14/1944

YEAR	TM-L	W	L	PCT	G	GS	CG	SH	SV	IP	H	R	ER	HR	HB	BB	SO	RAT	ERA	ERA+	CERA	OAV	BH	AVG	PR+	WS	TPW
1944	Bos-N	0	0	....	1	0	0	0	0	1	0	0	0	0	0	1	1	1.000	0.00	....	0.80	.000	0	....	0	0	0.0

• MACRAE, Scott Scott Patrick MacRae b: 8/13/1974, Dearborn, MI BR/TR, 6'3", 205 lbs. Deb: 7/24/2001

YEAR	TM-L	W	L	PCT	G	GS	CG	SH	SV	IP	H	R	ER	HR	HB	BB	SO	RAT	ERA	ERA+	CERA	OAV	BH	AVG	PR+	WS	TPW
2001	Cin-N	0	1	.000	24	0	0	0	0	31^1	33	15	14	0	2	8	18	1.309	4.02	113	3.30	.266	0	.000	2	2	0.2

• MACWHORTER, Keith Keith Macwhorter b: 12/30/1955, Worcester, MA BR/TR, 6'4", 190 lbs. Deb: 5/10/1980

YEAR	TM-L	W	L	PCT	G	GS	CG	SH	SV	IP	H	R	ER	HR	HB	BB	SO	RAT	ERA	ERA+	CERA	OAV	BH	AVG	PR+	WS	TPW
1980	Bos-A	0	3	.000	14	2	0	0	0	42^1	46	27	26	3	2	18	21	1.512	5.53	76	4.51	.280	0	....	-6	1	-0.6

• MADDEN, Kid Michael Joseph Madden b: 10/2/1867, Portland, ME d: 3/16/1896, Portland, ME BL/TL, 5'7.5", 130 lbs. Deb: 5/6/1887 U

YEAR	TM-L	W	L	PCT	G	GS	CG	SH	SV	IP	H	R	ER	HR	HB	BB	SO	RAT	ERA	ERA+	CERA	OAV	BH	AVG	PR+	WS	TPW
1887	Bos-N	21	14	.600	37	37	36	3	0	321	439	203	135	20	20	122	81	1.368	3.79	104	....	.317	44	.306	-1	21	0.3
1888	Bos-N	7	11	.389	20	18	17	1	0	165	142	76	54	6	15	24	53	1.006	2.95	98	....	.224	11	.164	-3	10	-0.4
1889	Bos-N	10	10	.500	22	19	18	1	1	178	194	131	87	7	16	71	64	1.489	4.40	95	....	.269	25	.291	-3	10	0.0
1890	Bos-P	3	2	.600	10	7	5	1	0	62	85	55	33	2	6	25	24	1.774	4.79	92	....	.313	7	.184	-3	3	-0.4

YEAR TM-L	W	L	PCT	G	GS	CG	SH	SV	IP	H	R	ER	HR	HB	BB	SO	RAT	ERA	ERA+	CERA	OAV	BH	AVG	PR+	WS	TPW
1891 Bos-a	0	1	.000	1	1	1	0	0	8	10	12	6	2	0	6	6	2.000	6.75	52	....	.296	2	.667	-3	0	-0.2
Bal-a	13	12	.520	32	27	20	1	1	224	239	168	102	4	0	88	56	1.460	4.10	91	....	.264	29	.271	-6	13	-0.1
Yr.	13	13	.500	33	28	21	1	1	232	249	180	108	6	0	94	62	1.478	4.19	89	....	.265	31	.282	-9	13	-0.3
Total 5	54	50	.519	122	109	97	7	2	958	1109	645	417	41	57	336	284	1.381	3.92	96	....	.281	118	.265	-20	57	-0.8
• MADDEN, Len	Leonard Joseph "Lefty" Madden b: 7/2/1890, Toledo, OH d: 9/9/1949, Toledo, OH BL/TL, 6'2", 165 lbs. Deb: 8/31/1912																									
1912 Chi-N	0	1	.000	6	2	0	0	0	12^1	16	10	4	1	1	9	5	2.027	2.92	114	6.76	.302	1	.250	0	0	0.0
• MADDEN, Mike	Michael Anthony Madden b: 1/13/1957, Denver, CO BL/TL, 6'1", 190 lbs. Deb: 4/5/1983																									
1983 Hou-N	9	5	.643	28	13	0	0	0	94^2	76	37	33	4	1	45	44	1.278	3.14	108	3.00	.231	1	.045	1	6	0.0
1984 Hou-N	2	3	.400	17	7	0	0	0	40^2	46	27	25	1	0	35	29	1.992	5.53	60	6.10	.297	2	.333	-11	0	-1.0
1985 Hou-N	0	0	....	13	0	0	0	0	19	29	15	9	1	0	11	16	2.105	4.26	81	7.88	.363	0	....	-2	0	-0.2
1986 Hou-N	1	2	.333	13	6	0	0	0	39^2	47	20	18	3	0	22	30	1.739	4.08	88	5.40	.297	0	.000	-2	1	-0.3
Total 4	12	10	.545	71	26	0	0	0	194	198	99	85	9	1	113	119	1.603	3.94	87	4.62	.274	3	.081	-13	7	-1.5
• MADDEN, Morris	Morris De Wayne Madden b: 8/31/1960, Laurens, SC BL/TL, 6', 155 lbs. Deb: 6/11/1987																									
1987 Det-A	0	0	....	2	0	0	0	0	1^2	4	3	3	0	0	3	0	4.200	16.20	26	17.04	.444	0	....	-2	0	-0.2
1988 Pit-N	0	0	....	5	0	0	0	0	5^2	5	0	0	0	0	7	3	2.118	0.00	....	6.26	.294	0	....	2	1	0.2
1989 Pit-N	2	2	.500	9	3	0	0	0	14	17	14	11	0	0	13	6	2.143	7.07	47	7.00	.327	0	.000	-6	0	-0.6
Total 3	2	2	.500	16	3	0	0	0	21^1	26	17	14	0	0	23	9	2.297	5.91	59	7.59	.333	0	.000	-6	1	-0.6
• MADDOX, Nick	Nicholas Maddox b: 11/9/1886, Govans, MD d: 11/27/1954, Pittsburgh, PA BL/TR, 6', 175 lbs. Deb: 9/13/1907																									
1907 Pit-N	5	1	.833	6	6	6	1	0	54	32	8	5	0	4	13	38	.833	0.83	291	1.36	.178	5	.250	10	7	1.4
1908 Pit-N	23	8	.742	36	32	22	4	1	260^2	209	89	66	5	11	90	70	1.147	2.28	100	2.46	.223	25	.266	0	20	1.0
1909* Pit-N	13	8	.619	31	27	17	4	0	203^1	173	72	50	2	15	39	56	1.043	2.21	116	2.25	.232	15	.224	5	16	1.0
1910 Pit-N	2	3	.400	20	7	2	0	0	87^1	73	40	33	0	5	28	29	1.156	3.40	92	2.66	.246	6	.214	-3	5	-0.2
Total 4	43	20	.683	93	72	47	9	1	605^1	487	209	154	7	35	170	193	1.085	2.29	110	2.32	.226	51	.244	13	48	3.2
• MADDUX, Greg	Gregory Alan "Mad Dog" Maddux b: 4/14/1966, San Angelo, TX BR/TR, 6', 170 lbs. Deb: 9/3/1986																									
1986 Chi-N	2	4	.333	6	5	1	0	0	31	44	20	19	3	1	11	20	1.774	5.52	73	6.45	.336	4	.333	-5	1	-0.4
1987 Chi-N	6	14	.300	30	27	1	1	0	155^2	181	111	97	17	4	74	101	1.638	5.61	76	5.42	.294	5	.119	-19	1	-2.1
1988 Chi-N★	18	8	.692	34	34	9	3	0	249	230	97	88	13	9	81	140	1.249	3.18	113	3.09	.244	19	.198	17	20	2.1
1989* Chi-N	19	12	.613	35	35	7	1	0	238^1	222	90	78	13	6	82	135	1.276	2.95	128	3.20	.249	17	.210	22	20	2.6
1990 Chi-N	15	15	.500	35	35	8	2	0	237	242	116	91	11	4	71	144	1.321	3.46	118	3.41	.265	12	.145	23	15	2.2
1991 Chi-N	15	11	.577	37	37	7	2	0	263	232	113	98	18	6	66	198	1.133	3.35	116	2.73	.237	18	.205	20	17	2.4
1992 Chi-N★	20	11	.645	35	35	9	4	0	268	201	68	65	7	14	70	199	1.011	2.18	165	2.01	.210	15	.170	42	27	4.7
1993* Atl-N	20	10	.667	36	36	8	1	0	267	228	85	70	14	6	52	197	1.049	2.36	170	2.32	.232	15	.165	47	25	4.6
1994 Atl-N★	16	6	.727	25	25	10	3	0	202	150	44	35	4	6	31	156	.896	1.56	272	1.59	.207	14	.222	62	26	6.3
1995* Atl-N★	19	2	.905	28	28	10	3	0	209^2	147	39	38	8	4	23	181	.811	1.63	261	1.41	.197	11	.153	64	30	6.2
1996* Atl-N★	15	11	.577	35	35	5	1	0	245	225	85	74	11	3	28	172	1.033	2.72	162	2.22	.241	10	.147	49	23	4.8
1997* Atl-N★	19	4	.826	33	33	5	2	0	232^2	200	58	57	9	6	20	177	.946	2.20	191	1.95	.236	7	.104	50	26	4.9
1998* Atl-N★	18	9	.667	34	34	9	5	0	251	201	75	62	13	7	45	204	.980	2.22	187	2.01	.220	18	.240	51	25	5.4
1999* Atl-N	19	9	.679	33	33	4	0	0	219^1	258	103	87	16	4	37	136	1.345	3.57	126	3.95	.294	11	.172	25	17	2.6
2000* Atl-N★	19	9	.679	35	35	6	3	0	249^1	225	91	83	19	10	42	190	1.071	3.00	153	2.60	.238	15	.188	45	24	4.4
2001* Atl-N	17	11	.607	34	34	3	3	0	233	220	86	79	20	7	27	173	1.060	3.05	144	2.70	.253	12	.188	34	20	3.4
2002* Atl-N	16	6	.727	34	34	0	0	0	199^1	194	67	58	14	4	45	118	1.199	2.62	156	3.11	.257	11	.186	29	19	3.0
2003* Atl-N	16	11	.593	36	36	1	0	0	218^1	225	112	96	24	8	33	124	1.182	3.96	107	3.44	.268	10	.147	7	11	0.6
Total 18	289	163	.639	575	571	103	34	0	3968^2	3625	1460	1275	234	109	838	2765	1.125	2.89	142	2.75	.244	224	.178	564	347	57.8
• MADDUX, Mike	Michael Ausley Maddux b: 8/27/1961, Dayton, OH BL/TR, 6'2", 190 lbs. Deb: 6/3/1986 C																									
1986 Phi-N	3	7	.300	16	16	0	0	0	78	88	56	47	6	3	34	44	1.564	5.42	71	4.84	.286	1	.045	-13	0	-1.5
1987 Phi-N	2	0	1.000	7	2	0	0	0	17	17	5	5	0	0	5	15	1.294	2.65	160	2.96	.254	0	.000	3	2	0.2
1988 Phi-N	4	3	.571	25	11	0	0	0	88^2	91	41	37	6	5	34	59	1.410	3.76	95	4.16	.275	3	.130	-1	4	-0.1
1989 Phi-N	1	3	.250	16	4	2	1	1	43^2	52	29	25	3	2	14	26	1.511	5.15	69	4.77	.304	0	.000	-8	0	-0.9
1990 LA-N	0	1	.000	11	2	0	0	0	20^2	24	15	15	3	1	4	11	1.355	6.53	56	4.74	.293	0	.000	-7	0	-0.7
1991 SD-N	7	2	.778	64	1	0	0	5	98^2	78	30	27	4	1	27	57	1.064	2.46	154	2.20	.221	1	.077	14	11	1.5
1992 SD-N	2	2	.500	50	1	0	0	5	79^2	71	25	21	2	0	24	60	1.192	2.37	151	2.54	.236	1	.111	11	9	1.2
1993 NY-N	3	8	.273	58	0	0	0	5	75	67	34	30	3	4	27	57	1.253	3.60	111	2.95	.243	0	.000	3	6	0.3
1994 NY-N	2	1	.667	27	0	0	0	2	44	45	25	25	7	0	13	32	1.318	5.11	82	4.06	.263	0	.000	-5	2	-0.5
1995 Pit-N	1	0	1.000	8	0	0	0	0	9	14	9	9	0	0	3	4	1.889	9.00	48	6.22	.359	0	....	-5	0	-0.5
* Bos-A	4	1	.800	36	4	0	0	1	89^2	86	40	36	5	2	15	65	1.126	3.61	135	2.71	.247	0	....	12	8	1.1
1996 Bos-A	3	2	.600	23	7	0	0	0	64^1	76	37	32	12	5	27	32	1.601	4.48	113	6.15	.295	0	....	6	4	0.5
1997 Sea-A	1	0	1.000	6	0	0	0	0	10^2	20	12	12	1	1	8	7	2.625	10.13	44	11.34	.400	0	....	-7	0	-0.6
1998 Mon-N	3	4	.429	51	0	0	0	1	55^2	50	24	23	3	1	15	33	1.168	3.72	113	2.79	.243	0	.000	4	4	0.4
1999 Mon-N	0	0	....	4	0	0	0	0	5	9	5	5	1	1	3	4	2.400	9.00	50	12.70	.409	0	....	-2	0	-0.2
LA-N	1	1	.500	49	0	0	0	0	54^2	54	21	20	5	4	19	41	1.335	3.29	130	4.01	.261	0	....	6	4	0.6
Yr.	1	1	.500	53	0	0	0	0	59^2	63	26	25	6	5	22	45	1.425	3.77	115	4.74	.275	0	....	4	4	0.4
2000 Hou-N	2	2	.500	21	0	0	0	0	27^1	31	20	19	6	2	12	17	1.573	6.26	78	6.05	.282	0	.000	-4	1	-0.4
Total 15	39	37	.513	472	48	2	1	20	861^2	873	428	388	67	32	284	564	1.343	4.05	101	3.88	.265	6	.065	9	55	0.4
• MADIGAN, Tony	William J. "Tice" Madigan b: 7/1868, Washington, DC d: 12/4/1954, Washington, DC TR, 5'5.5", 126 lbs. Deb: 7/10/1886																									
1886 Was-N	1	13	.071	14	13	13	0	0	114^2	154	110	65	3	....	44	29	1.727	5.10	64	....	.310	4	.083	-23	1	-2.5
• MADISON, Dave	David Pledger Madison b: 2/1/1921, Brooksville, MS d: 12/8/1985, Macon, MS BR/TR, 6'3", 190 lbs. Deb: 9/26/1950																									
1950 NY-A	0	0	....	1	0	0	0	0	3	3	2	2	1	0	1	1	1.333	6.00	72	5.71	.273	0	....	-1	0	0.0
1952 StL-A	4	2	.667	31	4	0	0	0	78	78	46	38	7	4	48	35	1.615	4.38	89	4.86	.264	2	.118	-5	3	-0.6
Det-A	1	1	.500	10	1	0	0	0	15	16	14	13	1	1	10	7	1.733	7.80	49	5.71	.291	0	.000	-6	0	-0.7
Yr.	5	3	.625	41	5	0	0	0	93	94	60	51	8	5	58	42	1.634	4.94	79	4.99	.268	2	.105	-11	3	-1.2
1953 Det-A	3	4	.429	32	1	0	0	0	62	76	55	47	7	3	44	27	1.935	6.82	60	6.67	.303	1	.091	-17	0	-1.8
Total 3	8	7	.533	74	6	0	0	0	158	173	117	100	16	8	103	70	1.747	5.70	70	5.67	.282	3	.100	-29	3	-3.1
• MADRID, Alex	Alexander Madrid b: 4/18/1963, Springerville, AZ BR/TR, 6'3", 200 lbs. Deb: 7/20/1987																									
1987 Mil-A	0	0	....	3	0	0	0	0	5^1	11	9	9	1	0	1	1	2.250	15.19	30	10.50	.440	0	....	-6	0	-0.6
1988 Phi-N	1	1	.500	5	2	1	0	0	16^1	15	5	5	0	0	6	2	1.286	2.76	129	2.58	.246	0	.000	2	1	0.1
1989 Phi-N	1	2	.333	6	3	0	0	0	24^2	32	16	15	3	1	14	13	1.865	5.47	65	6.59	.314	0	.000	-5	0	-0.6
Total 3	2	3	.400	14	5	1	0	0	46^1	58	30	29	4	1	21	16	1.705	5.63	68	5.63	.309	0	.000	-10	1	-1.0
• MADSON, Ryan	Ryan Michael Madson b: 8/28/1980, Long Beach, CA BL/TR, 6'6", 180 lbs. Deb: 9/27/2003																									
2003 Phi-N	0	0	....	1	0	0	0	0	2	0	0	0	0	0	0	0	.000	0.00	....	0.00	.000	0	....	1	0	0.1
• MADURO, Calvin	Calvin Gregory Maduro b: 9/5/1974, Santa Cruz, Aruba BR/TR, 6', 175 lbs. Deb: 9/8/1996																									
1996 Phi-N	0	1	.000	4	2	0	0	0	15^1	13	6	6	1	2	3	11	1.043	3.52	123	2.81	.232	0	.000	1	1	0.1
1997 Phi-N	3	7	.300	15	13	0	0	0	71	83	59	57	12	3	41	31	1.746	7.23	59	6.44	.294	1	.050	-23	0	-2.4
2000 Bal-A	0	0	....	15	2	0	0	0	23^1	29	25	25	8	2	16	18	1.929	9.64	49	9.30	.315	0	....	-13	0	-1.2
2001 Bal-A	5	6	.455	22	12	0	0	0	93^2	83	44	44	10	4	36	51	1.270	4.23	101	3.71	.240	0	....	-0	5	0.0
2002 Bal-A	2	5	.286	12	10	0	0	0	56^2	64	37	35	12	1	22	29	1.518	5.56	77	5.62	.279	0	....	-9	1	-0.8
Total 5	10	19	.345	68	39	0	0	0	260	272	171	167	43	12	118	140	1.500	5.78	75	5.32	.271	1	.042	-44	7	-4.4
• MAESTRI, Hector	Hector Anibal (Garcia) Maestri b: 4/19/1935, Havana, Cuba BR/TR, 5'10", 158 lbs. Deb: 9/24/1960																									
1960 Was-A	0	0	....	1	0	0	0	0	2	1	0	0	0	0	1	1	1.000	0.00	....	1.62	.167	0	....	1	0	0.1

YEAR TM-L	W	L	PCT	G	GS	CG	SH	SV	IP	H	R	ER	HR	HB	BB	SO	RAT	ERA	ERA+	CERA	OAV	BH	AVG	PR+	WS	TPW
1961 Was-A	0	1	.000	1	1	0	0	0	6	6	3	1	1	0	2	2	1.333	1.50	261	4.18	.250	0	.000	2	0	0.1
Total 2	0	1	.000	2	1	0	0	0	8	7	3	1	1	0	3	3	1.250	1.13	348	3.54	.233	0	.000	3	0	0.2
• MAGEE, Bill	William J. Magee b: 1875, Canada BR/TR, 5'10", 154 lbs. Deb: 5/18/1897																									
1897 Lou-N	4	12	.250	23	17	13	1	0	156^1	187	137	93	6	10	101	44	1.842	5.35	79	5.73	.294	13	.210	-18	4	-1.7
1898 Lou-N	16	15	.516	38	33	29	3	0	295^1	294	163	133	8	19	129	55	1.432	4.05	88	3.80	.258	14	.126	-14	16	-2.1
1899 Lou-N	3	7	.300	12	10	6	1	0	71	91	58	41	1	9	28	13	1.676	5.20	74	5.33	.311	3	.111	-9	1	-1.0
Phi-N	3	5	.375	9	9	7	0	0	70	82	50	44	0	7	32	4	1.629	5.66	65	4.66	.292	5	.161	-16	1	-1.6
Was-N	1	4	.200	8	7	4	0	0	42	54	45	40	3	7	28	11	1.952	8.57	46	7.24	.312	5	.333	-20	0	-1.7
Yr.	7	16	.304	29	26	17	1	0	183	227	153	125	4	23	88	28	1.721	6.15	62	5.51	.304	13	.178	-46	2	-4.4
1901 StL-N	0	0	....	1	1	0	0	0	8	8	4	4	0	0	4	3	1.500	4.50	71	3.62	.259	2	.500	-1	1	0.0
NY-N	0	4	.000	6	5	4	0	0	42^1	56	36	28	4	4	11	14	1.583	5.95	56	5.50	.316	2	.143	-11	0	-1.2
Yr.	0	4	.000	7	6	4	0	0	50^1	64	40	32	4	4	15	17	1.570	5.72	57	5.20	.307	4	.222	-13	1	-1.2
1902 NY-N	0	0	....	2	1	0	0	0	5	5	2	2	0	0	1	2	1.200	3.60	78	2.56	.260	0	.000	-0	0	-0.1
Phi-N	2	4	.333	8	6	6	0	0	53^2	61	28	22	1	3	18	15	1.472	3.69	76	4.34	.286	4	.211	-4	3	-0.4
Yr.	2	4	.333	10	7	6	0	0	58^2	66	30	24	1	3	19	17	1.449	3.68	76	4.19	.284	4	.200	-4	3	-0.5
Total 5	29	51	.363	107	89	69	5	0	743^2	838	523	407	23	59	352	161	1.600	4.93	75	4.75	.283	48	.169	-95	26	-9.8
• MAGLIE, Sal	Salvatore Anthony "The Barber" Maglie b: 4/26/1917, Niagara Falls, NY d: 12/28/1992, Niagara Falls, NY BR/TR, 6'2", 180 lbs. Deb: 8/9/1945 C																									
1945 NY-N	5	4	.556	13	10	7	3	0	84^1	72	22	22	2	2	22	32	1.115	2.35	166	2.35	.231	5	.167	15	9	1.4
1950 NY-N	18	4	.818	47	16	12	**5**	1	206	169	71	62	14	10	86	96	1.238	**2.71**	**151**	3.08	.226	8	.121	25	21	2.3
1951★ NY-N★	**23**	6	.793	42	37	22	3	4	298	254	110	97	27	6	86	146	1.141	2.93	**134**	2.84	**.230**	17	.152	**32**	**28**	2.9
1952 NY-N★	18	8	.692	35	31	12	5	1	216	199	80	70	16	6	75	112	1.269	2.92	127	3.31	.244	5	.072	19	17	1.7
1953 NY-N	8	9	.471	27	24	9	3	0	145^1	158	79	67	19	1	47	80	1.411	4.15	103	4.50	.278	13	.271	2	7	0.4
1954★ NY-N	14	6	.700	34	32	9	1	2	218^1	222	83	79	21	3	70	117	1.337	3.26	124	3.80	.262	8	.127	16	18	1.4
1955 NY-N	9	5	.643	23	21	6	0	0	129^2	142	67	54	18	3	48	71	1.465	3.75	107	4.83	.278	5	.125	4	8	0.2
Cle-A	0	2	.000	10	2	0	0	2	25^2	26	14	11	0	1	7	11	1.286	3.86	103	3.01	.252	0	.000	0	1	0.0
1956 Cle-A	0	0	....	2	0	0	0	0	5	6	2	2	1	0	2	2	1.600	3.60	117	6.16	.300	0	....	0	0	0.0
*Bro-N	13	5	.722	28	26	9	3	0	191	154	65	61	21	5	52	108	1.079	2.87	**138**	2.78	.222	9	.129	19	16	1.7
1957 Bro-N	6	6	.500	19	17	4	1	1	101^1	94	42	33	12	4	26	50	1.184	2.93	142	3.38	.245	1	.034	14	8	1.1
NY-A	2	0	1.000	6	3	1	1	3	26	22	6	5	1	1	7	9	1.115	1.73	207	2.53	.227	2	.250	5	3	0.5
1958 NY-A	1	1	.500	7	3	0	0	0	23^1	27	12	12	3	0	9	7	1.543	4.63	76	5.13	.300	1	.143	-3	1	-0.3
StL-N	2	6	.250	10	10	2	0	0	53	46	31	28	14	2	25	21	1.340	4.75	87	4.81	.232	2	.125	-4	2	-0.4
Total 10	119	62	.657	303	232	93	25	14	1723	1591	684	603	169	44	562	862	1.250	3.15	127	3.44	.245	76	.135	146	139	13.0
• MAGNANTE, Mike	Michael Anthony Magnante b: 6/17/1965, Glendale, CA BL/TL, 6'1", 190 lbs. Deb: 4/22/1991																									
1991 KC-A	0	1	.000	38	0	0	0	0	55	55	19	15	3	0	23	42	1.418	2.45	168	3.76	.262	0	....	12	4	1.2
1992 KC-A	4	9	.308	44	12	0	0	0	89^1	115	53	49	5	2	35	31	1.679	4.94	82	5.47	.325	0	....	-7	2	-0.8
1993 KC-A	1	2	.333	7	6	0	0	0	35^1	37	16	16	3	1	11	16	1.358	4.08	112	4.16	.282	0	....	2	2	0.2
1994 KC-A	2	3	.400	36	1	0	0	0	47	55	27	24	5	0	16	21	1.511	4.60	109	4.73	.289	0	....	2	3	0.2
1995 KC-A	1	1	.500	28	0	0	0	0	44^2	45	23	21	6	2	16	28	1.366	4.23	113	4.41	.268	0	....	2	3	0.2
1996 KC-A	2	2	.500	38	0	0	0	0	54	58	38	34	5	4	24	32	1.519	5.67	89	4.99	.282	0	....	-4	2	-0.4
1997★ Hou-N	3	1	.750	40	0	0	0	1	47^2	39	16	12	2	0	11	43	1.049	2.27	177	2.08	.223	0	.000	9	5	0.8
1998 Hou-N	4	7	.364	48	0	0	0	2	51^2	56	28	28	2	4	26	39	1.587	4.88	83	4.62	.276	2	1.000	-5	2	-0.4
1999 Ana-A	5	2	.714	53	0	0	0	0	69^1	68	30	26	2	3	29	44	1.399	3.38	143	3.63	.262	0	....	11	7	1.0
2000★ Oak-A	1	1	.500	55	0	0	0	0	39^2	50	22	19	3	2	19	17	1.739	4.31	110	5.49	.309	0	.000	2	2	0.2
2001★ Oak-A	3	1	.750	65	0	0	0	0	55^1	50	23	17	7	1	13	23	1.139	2.77	160	3.13	.244	0	....	10	5	1.0
2002 Oak-A	0	2	.000	32	0	0	0	0	28^2	38	22	19	2	1	11	11	1.709	5.97	74	5.71	.317	0	....	-5	0	-0.5
Total 12	26	32	.448	484	19	0	0	3	617^2	666	317	280	45	20	234	347	1.457	4.08	110	4.33	.279	2	.333	28	37	2.8
• MAGNUSON, Jim	James Robert Magnuson b: 8/18/1946, Marinette, WI d: 5/30/1991, Green Bay, WI BR/TL, 6'2", 190 lbs. Deb: 6/28/1970																									
1970 Chi-A	1	5	.167	13	6	0	0	0	44^2	45	28	24	7	1	16	20	1.366	4.84	81	4.46	.263	0	.000	-4	1	-0.5
1971 Chi-A	1	1	.500	15	4	0	0	0	30	30	18	15	0	2	16	11	1.533	4.50	80	4.23	.265	0	.000	-3	1	-0.3
1973 NY-A	0	1	.000	8	0	0	0	0	27^1	38	17	13	2	0	9	9	1.720	4.28	86	5.91	.342	0	....	-2	0	-0.2
Total 3	2	7	.222	36	10	0	0	0	102	113	63	52	9	3	41	40	1.510	4.59	82	4.78	.286	0	.000	-9	2	-1.1
• MAGRANE, Joe	Joseph David Magrane b: 7/2/1964, Des Moines, IA BR/TL, 6'6", 230 lbs. Deb: 4/25/1987																									
1987★ StL-N	9	7	.563	27	26	4	2	0	170^1	157	75	67	9	10	60	101	1.274	3.54	117	3.31	.245	7	.135	10	11	1.2
1988 StL-N	5	9	.357	24	24	4	3	0	165^1	133	57	40	6	2	51	100	1.113	**2.18**	**160**	2.29	.217	8	.167	22	13	2.6
1989 StL-N	18	9	.667	34	33	9	3	0	234^2	219	81	76	5	6	72	127	1.240	2.91	124	2.92	.251	11	.138	16	18	1.8
1990 StL-N	10	17	.370	31	31	3	2	0	203^1	204	86	81	10	8	59	100	1.293	3.59	106	3.45	.264	7	.127	6	12	0.6
1992 StL-N	1	2	.333	5	5	0	0	0	31^1	34	15	14	2	2	15	20	1.564	4.02	84	4.81	.279	2	.200	-3	1	-0.2
1993 StL-N	8	10	.444	22	20	0	0	0	116	127	68	64	15	5	37	38	1.414	4.97	80	4.70	.286	4	.114	-13	3	-1.4
Cal-A	3	2	.600	8	8	0	0	0	48	48	27	21	4	0	21	24	1.438	3.94	114	4.09	.265	0	....	2	3	0.2
1994 Cal-A	2	6	.250	20	11	1	0	0	74	89	63	60	18	6	51	33	1.892	7.30	67	8.16	.300	0	....	-20	0	-1.9
1996 Chi-A	1	5	.167	19	8	0	0	0	53^2	70	45	41	10	3	25	21	1.770	6.88	69	7.12	.318	0	....	-12	0	-1.1
Total 8	57	67	.460	190	166	21	10	0	1096^2	1081	517	464	79	42	391	564	1.342	3.81	105	3.84	.260	39	.139	9	61	1.8
• MAGRINI, Pete	Peter Alexander Magrini b: 6/8/1942, San Francisco, CA BR/TR, 6', 195 lbs. Deb: 4/13/1966																									
1966 Bos-A	0	1	.000	3	1	0	0	0	7^1	8	9	8	0	1	8	3	2.182	9.82	39	7.32	.308	0	.000	-5	0	-0.6
• MAHAFFEY, Art	Arthur Mahaffey b: 6/4/1938, Cincinnati, OH BR/TR, 6'1", 200 lbs. Deb: 7/30/1960																									
1960 Phi-N	7	3	.700	14	12	5	1	0	93^1	78	29	24	9	1	34	56	1.200	2.31	168	3.10	.229	3	.100	16	10	1.4
1961 Phi-N★	11	19	.367	36	32	12	3	0	219^1	205	110	100	27	7	70	158	1.254	4.10	99	3.67	.249	8	.127	-4	11	-0.6
1962 Phi-N★	19	14	.576	41	39	20	2	0	274	253	131	120	36	12	81	177	1.219	3.94	98	3.64	.246	13	.141	-4	17	-0.3
1963 Phi-N	7	10	.412	26	22	6	1	0	149	143	73	66	18	5	48	97	1.282	3.99	81	3.82	.255	10	.200	-15	4	-1.4
1964 Phi-N	12	9	.571	34	29	2	2	0	157^1	161	84	79	17	6	82	80	1.544	4.52	77	4.91	.269	6	.120	-19	4	-2.0
1965 Phi-N	2	5	.286	22	9	1	0	0	71	82	53	49	11	7	32	52	1.606	6.21	56	5.93	.294	2	.095	-22	0	-2.4
1966 StL-N	1	4	.200	12	5	0	0	1	35	37	27	25	7	1	21	19	1.657	6.43	56	5.98	.276	0	.000	-11	0	-1.3
Total 7	59	64	.480	185	148	46	9	1	999	959	507	463	125	39	368	639	1.328	4.17	88	4.06	.255	42	.134	-60	46	-6.5
• MAHAFFEY, Lou	Louis Wood Mahaffey b: 1/3/1874, Madison, WI d: 10/26/1949, Torrance, CA BR/TR, 5'9", 170 lbs. Deb: 4/26/1898																									
1898 Lou-N	0	1	.000	1	1	1	0	0	9	10	9	3	0	0	5	1	1.667	3.00	119	4.52	.279	0	.000	1	0	0.0
• MAHAFFEY, Roy	Lee Roy "Popeye" Mahaffey b: 2/9/1903, Belton, SC d: 7/23/1969, Anderson, SC BR/TR, 6', 180 lbs. Deb: 8/31/1926																									
1926 Pit-N	0	0	....	4	0	0	0	0	4^2	5	4	0	0	1	1	3	1.286	0.00	....	3.85	.294	0	.000	2	0	0.2
1927 Pit-N	1	0	1.000	2	1	0	0	0	9^1	9	8	8	0	3	9	4	1.929	7.71	53	6.53	.300	2	.400	-4	0	-0.3
1930 Phi-A	9	5	.643	33	17	6	0	0	152^2	186	108	85	16	4	53	38	1.566	5.01	93	5.07	.298	7	.119	-6	6	-1.0
1931★ Phi-A	15	4	.789	30	20	8	0	2	162^1	161	87	76	9	3	82	59	1.497	4.21	107	4.41	.258	12	.190	1	13	0.1
1932 Phi-A	13	13	.500	37	28	13	0	0	222^2	245	136	126	27	5	96	106	1.531	5.09	89	4.84	.274	15	.172	-15	10	-1.5
1933 Phi-A	13	10	.565	33	23	9	0	0	179^1	198	114	103	5	4	74	66	1.517	5.17	83	4.05	.275	14	.215	-12	7	-1.2
1934 Phi-A	6	7	.462	37	14	3	0	2	129	142	88	77	10	1	55	37	1.527	5.37	82	4.46	.276	13	.271	-15	5	-1.2
1935 Phi-A	8	4	.667	27	17	5	0	0	136	153	66	59	11	5	42	39	1.434	3.90	116	4.34	.283	9	.176	12	9	0.9
1936 StL-A	2	6	.250	21	9	1	0	1	60	82	62	54	6	1	40	13	2.033	8.10	66	7.07	.315	1	.063	-17	0	-1.6
Total 9	67	49	.578	224	129	45	0	5	1056	1181	673	588	84	27	452	365	1.546	5.01	91	4.70	.280	73	.184	-55	50	-5.7
• MAHAY, Ron	Ronald Matthew Mahay b: 6/28/1971, Crestwood, IL BL/TL, 6'2", 185 lbs. Deb: 5/21/1995 ♦																									
1997 Bos-A	3	0	1.000	28	0	0	0	0	25	19	7	7	3	0	11	22	1.200	2.52	184	3.01	.204	0	....	6	3	0.6
1998 Bos-A	1	1	.500	29	0	0	0	1	26	26	16	10	2	2	15	14	1.577	3.46	136	4.76	.263	0	....	3	2	0.3
1999 Oak-A	2	0	1.000	6	1	0	0	1	19^1	8	4	4	2	0	3	15	.569	1.86	249	0.88	.123	0	....	6	3	0.6

YEAR	TM-L	W	L	PCT	G	GS	CG	SH	SV	IP	H	R	ER	HR	HB	BB	SO	RAT	ERA	ERA+	CERA	OAV	BH	AVG	PR+	WS	TPW
2000	Oak-A	0	1	.000	5	2	0	0	0	16	26	18	16	4	0	9	5	2.188	9.00	53	9.97	.366	0	....	-7	0	-0.7
	Fla-N	1	0	1.000	18	0	0	0	0	25^1	31	17	17	6	0	16	27	1.855	6.04	73	7.67	.310	2	.500	-4	1	-0.3
2001	Chi-N	0	0	....	17	0	0	0	0	20^2	14	6	6	4	0	15	24	1.403	2.61	159	4.32	.197	0	.000	4	2	0.4
2002	Chi-N	2	0	1.000	11	0	0	0	0	14^2	13	14	14	6	0	8	14	1.432	8.59	47	6.11	.228	0	....	-7	0	-0.7
2003	Tex-A	3	3	.500	35	0	0	0	0	45^1	33	19	16	3	0	20	38	1.169	3.18	156	2.31	.195	0	....	10	4	0.9
Total	7	12	5	.706	149	3	0	0	2	192^1	170	101	90	30	2	97	159	1.388	4.21	108	4.44	.234	6	.231	10	15	1.0

• MAHLER, Mickey Michael James Mahler b: 7/30/1952, Montgomery, AL BB/TL, 6'3", 189 lbs. Deb: 9/13/1977

YEAR	TM-L	W	L	PCT	G	GS	CG	SH	SV	IP	H	R	ER	HR	HB	BB	SO	RAT	ERA	ERA+	CERA	OAV	BH	AVG	PR+	WS	TPW
1977	Atl-N	1	2	.333	5	5	0	0	0	23	31	19	16	4	1	9	14	1.739	6.26	71	6.80	.326	3	.500	-4	1	-0.2
1978	Atl-N	4	11	.267	34	21	1	0	0	134^2	130	82	70	16	7	66	92	1.455	4.68	86	4.48	.255	4	.098	-7	3	-1.0
1979	Atl-N	5	11	.313	26	18	1	0	0	100	123	72	65	11	3	47	71	1.700	5.85	69	5.68	.304	3	.111	-17	0	-1.8
1980	Pit-N	0	0	....	2	0	0	0	0	1	4	7	7	1	0	3	1	7.000	63.00	6	53.56	.571	0	....	-7	0	-0.7
1981	Cal-A	0	0	....	6	0	0	0	0	6^1	1	0	0	0	0	2	5	.474	0.00	....	0.36	.056	0	....	3	1	0.3
1982	Cal-A	2	0	1.000	6	0	0	0	0	8	9	1	1	0	0	6	5	1.875	1.13	360	5.30	.300	0	....	2	1	0.2
1985	Mon-N	1	4	.200	9	7	1	1	1	48^1	40	22	19	3	1	24	32	1.324	3.54	96	3.34	.229	3	.188	-1	2	0.0
	Det-A	1	2	.333	3	2	0	0	0	20^2	19	8	4	2	0	4	14	1.113	1.74	234	2.69	.241	0	....	5	2	0.5
1986	Tex-A	0	2	.000	29	5	0	0	3	63	71	31	29	3	3	29	28	1.587	4.14	104	4.91	.295	0	....	1	3	0.1
	Tor-A	0	0	....	2	0	0	0	0	1	1	0	0	0	1	0	0	1.000	0.00	....	4.47	.200	0	....	0	0	0.0
	Yr.	0	2	.000	31	5	0	0	3	64	72	31	29	3	4	29	28	1.578	4.08	105	4.91	.293	0	....	2	3	0.2
Total	8	14	32	.304	122	58	3	1	4	406	429	242	211	40	16	190	262	1.525	4.68	86	4.82	.274	13	.144	-24	13	-2.6

• MAHLER, Rick Richard Keith Mahler b: 8/5/1953, Austin, TX BR/TR, 6'1", 202 lbs. Deb: 4/20/1979

YEAR	TM-L	W	L	PCT	G	GS	CG	SH	SV	IP	H	R	ER	HR	HB	BB	SO	RAT	ERA	ERA+	CERA	OAV	BH	AVG	PR+	WS	TPW
1979	Atl-N	0	0	....	15	0	0	0	0	22	28	16	15	4	0	11	12	1.773	6.14	66	6.72	.311	1	.500	-4	0	-0.4
1980	Atl-N	0	0	....	2	0	0	0	0	3^2	2	1	1	0	0	0	1	.545	2.45	152	0.63	.154	0	....	1	0	0.1
1981	Atl-N	8	6	.571	34	14	1	0	2	112^1	109	41	35	5	1	43	54	1.353	2.80	128	3.44	.258	4	.148	10	9	1.0
1982*	Atl-N	9	10	.474	39	33	5	2	0	205^1	213	105	96	18	1	62	105	1.339	4.21	89	3.88	.272	11	.190	-11	8	-1.0
1983	Atl-N	0	0	....	10	0	0	0	0	14^1	16	8	8	0	0	9	7	1.744	5.02	77	4.76	.296	0	.000	-2	0	-0.2
1984	Atl-N	13	10	.565	38	29	9	1	0	222	209	86	77	13	3	62	106	1.221	3.12	123	3.04	.251	21	.296	19	18	2.6
1985	Atl-N	17	15	.531	39	**39**	6	1	0	266^2	272	116	103	24	2	79	107	1.316	3.48	111	3.77	.268	14	.156	13	17	1.3
1986	Atl-N	14	18	.438	39	**39**	7	1	0	237^2	283	139	129	25	3	95	137	**1.590**	4.88	81	5.27	.301	16	.193	-21	7	-2.0
1987	Atl-N	8	13	.381	39	28	3	1	0	197	212	118	109	24	2	85	95	1.508	4.98	87	4.91	.283	11	.169	-13	7	-1.2
1988	Atl-N	9	16	.360	39	34	5	0	0	249	279	125	102	17	8	42	131	1.289	3.69	100	3.67	.282	9	.125	3	10	0.2
1989	Cin-N	9	13	.409	40	31	5	2	0	220^2	242	113	94	15	10	51	102	1.328	3.83	94	3.83	.282	11	.177	-3	9	-0.2
1990*	Cin-N	7	6	.538	35	16	2	1	4	134^2	134	67	64	16	3	39	68	1.285	4.28	92	3.82	.261	4	.114	-7	6	-0.8
1991	Mon-N	1	3	.250	10	6	0	0	0	37^1	37	17	15	2	0	15	17	1.393	3.62	100	3.77	.268	1	.111	-0	1	-0.1
	Atl-N	1	1	.500	13	2	0	0	0	28^2	33	20	18	2	2	13	10	1.605	5.65	69	5.06	.282	1	.200	-6	0	-0.5
	Yr.	2	4	.333	23	8	0	0	0	66	70	37	33	4	2	28	27	1.485	4.50	84	4.33	.275	2	.143	-6	1	-0.6
Total	13	96	111	.464	392	271	43	9	6	1951^1	2069	972	866	165	35	606	952	1.371	3.99	96	4.03	.275	104	.179	-23	92	-1.3

• MAHOMES, Pat Patrick Lavon Mahomes b: 8/9/1970, Bryan, TX BR/TR, 6'1", 210 lbs. Deb: 4/12/1992

YEAR	TM-L	W	L	PCT	G	GS	CG	SH	SV	IP	H	R	ER	HR	HB	BB	SO	RAT	ERA	ERA+	CERA	OAV	BH	AVG	PR+	WS	TPW
1992	Min-A	3	4	.429	14	13	0	0	0	69^2	73	41	39	5	0	37	44	1.579	5.04	80	4.83	.279	0	....	-8	2	-0.8
1993	Min-A	1	5	.167	12	5	0	0	0	37^1	47	34	32	8	1	16	23	1.688	7.71	56	6.71	.309	0	....	-14	0	-1.3
1994	Min-A	9	5	.643	21	21	0	0	0	120	121	68	63	22	1	62	53	1.525	4.73	103	5.41	.269	0	....	4	8	0.4
1995	Min-A	4	10	.286	47	7	0	0	3	94^2	100	74	67	22	2	47	67	1.553	6.37	75	5.88	.271	0	....	-17	2	-1.6
1996	Min-A	1	4	.200	20	5	0	0	0	45	63	38	36	10	0	27	30	2.000	7.20	71	8.43	.330	0	....	-11	0	-1.0
	Bos-A	2	0	1.000	11	0	0	0	2	12^1	9	8	8	3	0	6	6	1.216	5.84	87	3.89	.209	0	....	-1	1	-0.1
	Yr.	3	4	.429	31	5	0	0	2	57^1	72	46	44	13	0	33	36	1.831	6.91	74	7.46	.308	0	....	-12	1	-1.1
1997	Bos-A	1	0	1.000	10	0	0	0	0	10	15	10	9	2	2	10	5	2.500	8.10	57	11.95	.366	0	....	-4	0	-0.4
1999*	NY-N	8	0	1.000	39	0	0	0	0	63^2	44	26	26	7	2	37	51	1.272	3.68	119	3.22	.197	5	.313	5	7	0.6
2000	NY-N	5	3	.625	53	5	0	0	0	94	96	63	57	15	2	66	76	1.723	5.46	81	5.87	.263	4	.235	-10	2	-0.9
2001	Tex-A	7	6	.538	56	4	0	0	0	107^1	115	71	68	17	0	55	61	1.584	5.70	82	5.31	.280	1	1.000	-11	3	-1.1
2002	Chi-N	1	1	.500	16	2	0	0	0	32^2	36	15	14	3	1	17	23	1.622	3.86	104	5.10	.286	0	.000	1	2	0.0
2003	Pit-N	0	1	.000	9	1	0	0	0	22^1	19	13	12	2	0	12	13	1.388	4.84	91	3.60	.241	1	.250	-1	1	-0.1
Total	11	42	39	.519	308	63	0	0	5	709	738	461	431	116	11	392	452	1.594	5.47	84	5.52	.272	11	.256	-67	28	-6.1

• MAHON, Al Alfred Gwinn "Lefty" Mahon b: 9/23/1909, Albion, NE d: 12/26/1977, New Haven, CT BL/TL, 5'11", 160 lbs. Deb: 4/22/1930

YEAR	TM-L	W	L	PCT	G	GS	CG	SH	SV	IP	H	R	ER	HR	HB	BB	SO	RAT	ERA	ERA+	CERA	OAV	BH	AVG	PR+	WS	TPW
1930	Phi-A	0	0	....	3	0	0	0	0	4^1	11	11	11	0	0	7	0	4.154	22.85	20	19.57	.579	0	.000	-9	0	-0.8

• MAHONEY, Bob Robert Paul Mahoney b: 6/20/1928, Leroy, MN d: 8/27/2000, Lincoln, NE BR/TR, 6'1", 185 lbs. Deb: 5/3/1951

YEAR	TM-L	W	L	PCT	G	GS	CG	SH	SV	IP	H	R	ER	HR	HB	BB	SO	RAT	ERA	ERA+	CERA	OAV	BH	AVG	PR+	WS	TPW
1951	Chi-A	0	0	....	3	0	0	0	0	6^2	5	4	4	1	0	5	3	1.500	5.40	75	4.28	.208	0	....	-1	0	-0.1
	StL-A	2	5	.286	30	4	0	0	0	81	86	47	40	7	0	41	30	1.568	4.44	99	4.64	.274	4	.222	1	4	0.1
	Yr.	2	5	.286	33	4	0	0	0	87^2	91	51	44	8	0	46	33	1.563	4.52	96	4.61	.269	4	.222	0	4	0.0
1952	StL-A	0	0	....	3	0	0	0	0	3	8	6	6	0	0	4	1	4.000	18.00	22	18.02	.500	0	....	-5	0	-0.5
Total	2	2	5	.286	36	4	0	0	0	90^2	99	57	50	8	0	50	34	1.643	4.96	87	5.06	.280	4	.222	-4	4	-0.5

• MAHONEY, Chris Christopher John Mahoney b: 6/11/1885, Milton, MA d: 7/15/1954, Visalia, CA BR/TR, 5'9", 160 lbs. Deb: 7/12/1910

YEAR	TM-L	W	L	PCT	G	GS	CG	SH	SV	IP	H	R	ER	HR	HB	BB	SO	RAT	ERA	ERA+	CERA	OAV	BH	AVG	PR+	WS	TPW
1910	Bos-A	0	1	.000	2	1	0	0	1	11	16	11	4	1	0	5	6	1.909	3.27	78	6.66	.327	1	.143	-1	0	-0.2

• MAILS, Duster John Walter "Walter,The Great" Mails b: 10/1/1894, San Quentin, CA d: 7/5/1974, San Francisco, CA BL/TL, 6', 195 lbs. Deb: 9/28/1915

YEAR	TM-L	W	L	PCT	G	GS	CG	SH	SV	IP	H	R	ER	HR	HB	BB	SO	RAT	ERA	ERA+	CERA	OAV	BH	AVG	PR+	WS	TPW
1915	Bro-N	0	1	.000	2	0	0	0	0	5	6	5	2	2	0	5	3	2.200	3.60	77	10.96	.333	0	.000	-0	0	-0.1
1916	Bro-N	0	1	.000	11	0	0	0	0	17^1	15	9	7	1	0	9	13	1.385	3.63	74	3.45	.242	1	.250	-2	0	-0.2
1920*	Cle-A	7	0	1.000	9	8	6	2	0	63^1	54	18	13	1	0	18	25	1.137	1.85	205	2.32	.230	4	.200	12	8	1.2
1921	Cle-A	14	8	.636	34	24	10	2	2	194^1	210	103	85	4	2	89	87	1.539	3.94	108	4.10	.283	6	.094	7	12	0.3
1922	Cle-A	4	7	.364	26	13	4	1	0	104	122	69	61	8	4	40	54	1.558	5.28	76	4.76	.291	5	.161	-12	3	-1.2
1925	StL-N	7	7	.500	21	16	9	0	0	131	145	78	67	11	7	58	49	1.550	4.60	94	4.79	.279	6	.133	-5	6	-0.7
1926	StL-N	0	1	.000	1	0	0	0	0	1	2	1	0	0	0	1	1	3.000	0.00	....	8.58	.400	0	....	0	0	0.0
Total	7	32	25	.561	104	61	29	5	2	516	554	283	235	27	13	220	232	1.500	4.10	100	4.24	.277	22	.133	0	29	-0.7

• MAIN, Alex Miles Grant Main b: 5/13/1884, Montrose, MI d: 12/29/1965, Royal Oak, MI BL/TR, 6'5", 195 lbs. Deb: 4/18/1914

YEAR	TM-L	W	L	PCT	G	GS	CG	SH	SV	IP	H	R	ER	HR	HB	BB	SO	RAT	ERA	ERA+	CERA	OAV	BH	AVG	PR+	WS	TPW
1914	Det-A	6	6	.500	32	12	5	1	3	138^1	131	51	41	2	3	59	55	1.373	2.67	105	3.43	.259	4	.100	4	8	0.2
1915	KC-F	13	14	.481	35	28	18	2	3	230	181	88	65	4	5	75	91	1.113	2.54	115	2.26	.222	15	.197	11	17	1.3
1918	Phi-N	2	2	.500	8	4	1	1	0	35	30	20	18	1	5	16	14	1.314	4.63	65	3.40	.240	1	.091	-6	1	-0.8
Total	3	21	22	.488	75	44	24	4	6	403^1	342	159	124	7	13	150	160	1.220	2.77	105	2.76	.236	20	.157	8	26	0.7

• MAIN, Woody Forrest Harry Main b: 2/12/1922, Delano, CA d: 6/27/1992, Whittier, CA BR/TR, 6'3.5", 195 lbs. Deb: 4/21/1948

YEAR	TM-L	W	L	PCT	G	GS	CG	SH	SV	IP	H	R	ER	HR	HB	BB	SO	RAT	ERA	ERA+	CERA	OAV	BH	AVG	PR+	WS	TPW
1948	Pit-N	1	1	.500	17	0	0	0	0	27	35	27	25	4	0	19	12	2.000	8.33	49	7.46	.324	0	.000	-13	0	-1.3
1950	Pit-N	1	0	1.000	12	0	0	0	1	20^1	21	12	11	2	1	11	12	1.574	4.87	90	4.67	.256	2	.400	-1	1	0.0
1952	Pit-N	2	12	.143	48	11	2	0	2	153^1	149	78	76	14	0	52	79	1.311	4.46	89	3.52	.253	2	.054	-7	6	-1.0
1953	Pit-N	0	0	....	2	0	0	0	0	4	5	5	5	1	0	2	4	1.750	11.25	40	6.88	.294	0	....	-3	0	-0.3
Total	4	4	13	.235	79	11	2	0	3	204^2	210	122	117	21	1	84	107	1.436	5.14	79	4.22	.264	4	.091	-24	7	-2.7

• MAINS, Jim James Royal Mains b: 6/12/1922, Bridgton, ME d: 3/17/1969, Bridgton, ME BR/TR, 6'2", 190 lbs. Deb: 8/22/1943

YEAR	TM-L	W	L	PCT	G	GS	CG	SH	SV	IP	H	R	ER	HR	HB	BB	SO	RAT	ERA	ERA+	CERA	OAV	BH	AVG	PR+	WS	TPW
1943	Phi-A	0	1	.000	1	1	1	0	0	8	9	5	5	0	0	3	4	1.500	5.63	60	3.74	.281	0	.000	-2	0	-0.2

• MAINS, Willard Willard Eben "Grasshopper" Mains b: 7/7/1868, North Windham, ME d: 5/23/1923, Bridgton, ME TR, 6'2", 190 lbs. Deb: 8/3/1888

YEAR	TM-L	W	L	PCT	G	GS	CG	SH	SV	IP	H	R	ER	HR	HB	BB	SO	RAT	ERA	ERA+	CERA	OAV	BH	AVG	PR+	WS	TPW
1888	Chi-N	1	1	.500	2	2	1	0	0	11	8	10	6	0	1	6	5	1.273	4.91	61	....	.196	1	.143	-3	0	-0.3
1891	Cin-a	12	12	.500	30	23	19	0	0	204	196	127	61	3	12	107	76	1.485	2.69	153	....	.244	22	.244	32	17	2.9
	Mil-a	0	2	.000	2	2	1	0	0	10	14	19	12	1	0	10	2	2.400	10.80	41	....	.320	3	.600	-7	0	-0.5
	Yr.	12	14	.462	32	25	20	0	0	214	210	146	73	4	12	117	78	1.528	3.07	135	....	.248	25	.263	25	17	2.4

YEAR TM-L	W	L	PCT	G	GS	CG	SH	SV	IP	H	R	ER	HR	HB	BB	SO	RAT	ERA	ERA+	CERA	OAV	BH	AVG	PR+	WS	TPW
1896 Bos-N	3	2	.600	8	5	3	0	1	42^2	43	35	26	1	2	31	13	1.734	5.48	83	4.77	.260	6	.273	-6	2	-0.5
Total 3	**16**	**17**	**.485**	**42**	**32**	**24**	**0**	**1**	**267^2**	**261**	**191**	**105**	**5**	**15**	**154**	**96**	**1.550**	**3.53**	**118**	**0.76**	**.248**	**32**	**.258**	**17**	**19**	**1.6**

• MAIRENA, Oswaldo — Oswaldo Antonio Mairena b: 7/30/1975, Chinandega, Nicaragua BL/TL, 5'11", 165 lbs. Deb: 9/5/2000

YEAR TM-L	W	L	PCT	G	GS	CG	SH	SV	IP	H	R	ER	HR	HB	BB	SO	RAT	ERA	ERA+	CERA	OAV	BH	AVG	PR+	WS	TPW
2000 Chi-N	0	0	....	2	0	0	0	0	2	7	4	4	1	0	2	0	4.500	18.00	25	32.37	.583	0	....	-3	0	-0.3
2002 Fla-N	2	3	.400	31	0	0	0	0	33^2	38	21	20	7	0	12	21	1.485	5.35	74	5.42	.288	0	....	-5	1	-0.5
Total 2	**2**	**3**	**.400**	**33**	**0**	**0**	**0**	**0**	**35^2**	**45**	**25**	**24**	**8**	**0**	**14**	**21**	**1.654**	**6.06**	**66**	**6.94**	**.313**	**0**	**....**	**-8**	**1**	**-0.8**

• MAKOSKY, Frank — Frank Makosky b: 1/20/1910, Boonton, NJ d: 1/10/1987, Stroudsburg, PA BR/TR, 6'1", 185 lbs. Deb: 4/30/1937

YEAR TM-L	W	L	PCT	G	GS	CG	SH	SV	IP	H	R	ER	HR	HB	BB	SO	RAT	ERA	ERA+	CERA	OAV	BH	AVG	PR+	WS	TPW
1937 NY-A	5	2	.714	26	1	1	0	3	58	64	42	32	6	0	24	27	1.517	4.97	90	4.47	.277	5	.313	-4	3	-0.3

• MAKOWSKI, Tom — Thomas Anthony Makowski b: 12/22/1950, Buffalo, NY BR/TL, 5'11", 185 lbs. Deb: 5/1/1975

YEAR TM-L	W	L	PCT	G	GS	CG	SH	SV	IP	H	R	ER	HR	HB	BB	SO	RAT	ERA	ERA+	CERA	OAV	BH	AVG	PR+	WS	TPW
1975 Det-A	0	0	....	3	0	0	0	0	9^1	10	11	5	2	0	9	3	2.036	4.82	83	7.49	.278	0	....	-1	0	-0.1

• MALARKEY, Bill — William John Malarkey b: 11/26/1878, Port Byron, IL d: 12/12/1956, Phoenix, AZ BR/TR, 5'10", 185 lbs. Deb: 4/16/1908

YEAR TM-L	W	L	PCT	G	GS	CG	SH	SV	IP	H	R	ER	HR	HB	BB	SO	RAT	ERA	ERA+	CERA	OAV	BH	AVG	PR+	WS	TPW
1908 NY-N	0	2	.000	15	0	0	0	2	35	31	16	10	1	1	10	12	1.171	2.57	93	2.73	.242	0	.000	-0	1	-0.1

• MALARKEY, John — John S. "Liz" Malarkey b: 5/4/1872, Springfield, OH d: 10/29/1949, Cincinnati, OH TR, 5'11", 155 lbs. Deb: 9/21/1894

YEAR TM-L	W	L	PCT	G	GS	CG	SH	SV	IP	H	R	ER	HR	HB	BB	SO	RAT	ERA	ERA+	CERA	OAV	BH	AVG	PR+	WS	TPW
1894 Was-N	2	1	.667	3	3	3	0	0	26	42	22	12	1	0	5	3	1.808	4.15	127	6.35	.360	1	.071	4	1	0.1
1895 Was-N	0	8	.000	22	8	5	0	2	100^2	135	113	67	3	8	60	32	1.937	5.99	80	6.46	.317	5	.135	-12	2	-1.3
1896 Was-N	0	1	.000	1	1	0	0	0	7	9	7	1	1	0	3	0	1.714	1.29	342	6.12	.310	1	.500	3	1	0.3
1899 Chi-N	0	1	.000	1	1	1	0	0	9	19	13	13	0	1	5	7	2.667	13.00	29	11.31	.426	1	.200	-9	0	-0.8
1902 Bos-N	8	10	.444	21	19	17	1	1	170^1	158	82	49	0	0	58	39	1.268	2.59	109	2.73	.246	13	.210	3	9	0.5
1903 Bos-N	11	16	.407	32	27	25	2	0	253	266	150	87	5	11	96	98	1.431	3.09	103	3.85	.272	14	.161	-2	13	-0.1
Total 6	**21**	**37**	**.362**	**80**	**59**	**51**	**3**	**3**	**566**	**629**	**387**	**229**	**10**	**20**	**227**	**179**	**1.512**	**3.64**	**97**	**4.24**	**.281**	**35**	**.169**	**-13**	**26**	**-1.3**

• MALASKA, Mark — Dennis Mark Malaska b: 1/17/1978, Youngstown, OH BL/TL, 6'3", 191 lbs. Deb: 7/17/2003

YEAR TM-L	W	L	PCT	G	GS	CG	SH	SV	IP	H	R	ER	HR	HB	BB	SO	RAT	ERA	ERA+	CERA	OAV	BH	AVG	PR+	WS	TPW
2003 TB-A	2	1	.667	22	0	0	0	0	16	13	7	5	0	1	12	17	1.563	2.81	161	3.64	.232	0	....	3	2	0.3

• MALDONADO, Carlos — Carlos Cesar (Delgado) Maldonado b: 10/18/1966, Chepo, Panama BB/TR, 6'2", 210 lbs. Deb: 9/16/1990

YEAR TM-L	W	L	PCT	G	GS	CG	SH	SV	IP	H	R	ER	HR	HB	BB	SO	RAT	ERA	ERA+	CERA	OAV	BH	AVG	PR+	WS	TPW
1990 KC-A	0	0	....	4	0	0	0	0	6	9	6	6	0	0	4	9	2.167	9.00	43	7.17	.346	0	....	-3	0	-0.3
1991 KC-A	0	0	....	5	0	0	0	0	7^2	11	9	7	0	0	9	1	2.609	8.22	50	8.59	.333	0	....	-3	0	-0.3
1993 Mil-A	2	2	.500	29	0	0	0	1	37^1	40	20	19	2	0	17	18	1.527	4.58	93	4.07	.282	0	....	-1	2	-0.1
Total 3	**2**	**2**	**.500**	**38**	**0**	**0**	**0**	**1**	**51**	**60**	**35**	**32**	**2**	**0**	**30**	**28**	**1.765**	**5.65**	**73**	**5.12**	**.299**	**0**	**....**	**-8**	**2**	**-0.8**

• MALIS, Cy — Cyrus Sol Malis b: 2/26/1907, Philadelphia, PA d: 1/12/1971, North Hollywood, CA BR/TR, 5'11", 175 lbs. Deb: 8/17/1934

YEAR TM-L	W	L	PCT	G	GS	CG	SH	SV	IP	H	R	ER	HR	HB	BB	SO	RAT	ERA	ERA+	CERA	OAV	BH	AVG	PR+	WS	TPW
1934 Phi-N	0	0	....	1	0	0	0	0	3^2	4	2	2	0	0	2	1	1.636	4.91	96	4.13	.267	0	....	-0	0	0.0

• MALLETTE, Brian — Brian Drew Mallette b: 1/19/1975, Dublin, GA BR/TR, 6', 185 lbs. Deb: 4/12/2002

YEAR TM-L	W	L	PCT	G	GS	CG	SH	SV	IP	H	R	ER	HR	HB	BB	SO	RAT	ERA	ERA+	CERA	OAV	BH	AVG	PR+	WS	TPW
2002 Mil-N	0	0	....	5	0	0	0	0	5	7	6	6	3	1	3	5	2.000	10.80	38	12.26	.350	0	....	-4	0	-0.4

• MALLETTE, Mal — Malcolm Francis Mallette b: 1/30/1922, Syracuse, NY BL/TL, 6'2", 200 lbs. Deb: 9/25/1950

YEAR TM-L	W	L	PCT	G	GS	CG	SH	SV	IP	H	R	ER	HR	HB	BB	SO	RAT	ERA	ERA+	CERA	OAV	BH	AVG	PR+	WS	TPW
1950 Bro-N	0	0	....	2	0	0	0	0	1^1	2	0	0	0	0	1	2	2.250	0.00	....	7.28	.333	0	....	1	0	0.1

• MALLICOAT, Rob — Robbin Dale Mallicoat b: 11/16/1964, St. Helens, OR BL/TL, 6'3", 180 lbs. Deb: 9/11/1987

YEAR TM-L	W	L	PCT	G	GS	CG	SH	SV	IP	H	R	ER	HR	HB	BB	SO	RAT	ERA	ERA+	CERA	OAV	BH	AVG	PR+	WS	TPW
1987 Hou-N	0	0	....	4	1	0	0	0	6^2	8	5	5	0	0	6	4	2.100	6.75	58	6.94	.320	0	....	-2	0	-0.2
1991 Hou-N	0	2	.000	24	0	0	0	1	23^1	22	10	10	2	2	13	18	1.500	3.86	91	4.61	.259	0	.000	-1	1	-0.1
1992 Hou-N	0	0	....	23	0	0	0	0	23^2	26	19	19	2	5	19	20	1.901	7.23	46	6.77	.283	0	.000	-10	0	-1.1
Total 3	**0**	**2**	**.000**	**51**	**1**	**0**	**0**	**1**	**53^2**	**56**	**34**	**34**	**4**	**7**	**38**	**42**	**1.752**	**5.70**	**61**	**5.85**	**.277**	**0**	**.000**	**-13**	**1**	**-1.4**

• MALLOY, Alex — Archibald Alexander "Lick" Malloy b: 10/31/1886, Laurinburg, NC d: 3/1/1961, Ferris, TX BR/TR, 6'2", 180 lbs. Deb: 9/10/1910

YEAR TM-L	W	L	PCT	G	GS	CG	SH	SV	IP	H	R	ER	HR	HB	BB	SO	RAT	ERA	ERA+	CERA	OAV	BH	AVG	PR+	WS	TPW
1910 StL-A	0	6	.000	7	6	4	0	0	52^2	47	26	15	0	2	17	27	1.215	2.56	96	2.93	.261	1	.063	-0	1	-0.2

• MALLOY, Bob — Robert William Malloy b: 11/24/1964, Arlington, VA BR/TR, 6'5", 200 lbs. Deb: 5/26/1987

YEAR TM-L	W	L	PCT	G	GS	CG	SH	SV	IP	H	R	ER	HR	HB	BB	SO	RAT	ERA	ERA+	CERA	OAV	BH	AVG	PR+	WS	TPW
1987 Tex-A	0	0	....	2	2	0	0	0	11	13	11	8	6	0	3	8	1.455	6.55	68	7.36	.271	0	....	-2	0	-0.2
1990 Mon-N	0	0	....	1	0	0	0	0	2	1	0	0	0	0	1	1	1.000	0.00	....	1.41	.143	0	....	1	0	0.1
Total 2	**0**	**0**	**....**	**3**	**2**	**0**	**0**	**0**	**13**	**14**	**11**	**8**	**6**	**0**	**4**	**9**	**1.385**	**5.54**	**81**	**6.45**	**.255**	**0**	**....**	**-2**	**0**	**-0.1**

• MALLOY, Bob — Robert Paul Malloy b: 5/28/1918, Canonsburg, PA BR/TR, 5'11", 185 lbs. Deb: 5/4/1943

YEAR TM-L	W	L	PCT	G	GS	CG	SH	SV	IP	H	R	ER	HR	HB	BB	SO	RAT	ERA	ERA+	CERA	OAV	BH	AVG	PR+	WS	TPW
1943 Cin-N	0	0	....	6	0	0	0	0	10	14	8	7	1	0	8	4	2.200	6.30	53	7.98	.778	2	.667	-4	0	-0.3
1944 Cin-N	1	1	.500	9	0	0	0	0	23^1	22	10	8	0	0	11	4	1.414	3.09	113	3.43	.265	0	.000	0	1	0.0
1946 Cin-N	2	5	.286	27	3	1	0	2	72	71	29	22	2	2	26	24	1.347	2.75	122	3.38	.265	5	.278	3	5	0.4
1947 Cin-N	0	0	....	1	0	0	0	0	1	3	2	2	1	0	0	1	3.000	18.00	23	30.73	.600	0	....	-2	0	-0.2
1949 StL-A	1	1	.500	5	0	0	0	0	9^2	6	3	3	0	0	7	2	1.345	2.79	162	2.55	.200	0	.000	2	1	0.2
Total 5	**4**	**7**	**.364**	**48**	**3**	**1**	**0**	**2**	**116**	**116**	**52**	**42**	**4**	**2**	**52**	**35**	**1.448**	**3.26**	**106**	**3.96**	**.287**	**7**	**.226**	**0**	**7**	**0.1**

• MALLOY, Herm — Herman "Tug" Malloy b: 6/1/1885, Massillon, OH d: 5/9/1942, Louisville, OH BR/TR, 6' Deb: 10/6/1907

YEAR TM-L	W	L	PCT	G	GS	CG	SH	SV	IP	H	R	ER	HR	HB	BB	SO	RAT	ERA	ERA+	CERA	OAV	BH	AVG	PR+	WS	TPW
1907 Det-A	0	1	.000	1	1	1	0	0	8	13	10	5	1	0	5	6	2.250	5.63	46	8.76	.367	1	.250	-3	0	-0.3
1908 Det-A	0	2	.000	3	2	2	0	0	17	20	11	7	1	2	4	8	1.412	3.71	65	4.32	.278	3	.333	-2	0	-0.2
Total 2	**0**	**3**	**.000**	**4**	**3**	**3**	**0**	**0**	**25**	**33**	**21**	**12**	**2**	**2**	**9**	**14**	**1.680**	**4.32**	**58**	**5.74**	**.307**	**4**	**.308**	**-5**	**0**	**-0.4**

• MALONE, Chuck — Charles Ray Malone b: 7/8/1965, Harrisburg, AR BR/TR, 6'7", 250 lbs. Deb: 9/6/1990

YEAR TM-L	W	L	PCT	G	GS	CG	SH	SV	IP	H	R	ER	HR	HB	BB	SO	RAT	ERA	ERA+	CERA	OAV	BH	AVG	PR+	WS	TPW
1990 Phi-N	1	0	1.000	7	0	0	0	0	7^1	3	4	3	1	0	11	7	1.909	3.68	104	5.48	.130	0	....	0	1	0.0

• MALONE, Martin — Martin Malone Deb: 6/20/1872

YEAR TM-L	W	L	PCT	G	GS	CG	SH	SV	IP	H	R	ER	HR	HB	BB	SO	RAT	ERA	ERA+	CERA	OAV	BH	AVG	PR+	WS	TPW
1872 Eck-n	0	3	.000	3	3	3	0	0	27	85	86	31	1	....	0	0	3.148	10.33	12	....	.515	5	.313	-73	....	-5.0

• MALONE, Pat — Perce Leigh Malone b: 9/25/1902, Altoona, PA d: 5/13/1943, Altoona, PA BL/TR, 6', 200 lbs. Deb: 4/12/1928

YEAR TM-L	W	L	PCT	G	GS	CG	SH	SV	IP	H	R	ER	HR	HB	BB	SO	RAT	ERA	ERA+	CERA	OAV	BH	AVG	PR+	WS	TPW
1928 Chi-N	18	13	.581	42	25	16	2	2	250^2	218	99	79	15	6	99	155	1.265	2.84	135	3.09	.236	18	.189	19	23	2.0
1929* Chi-N	**22**	10	.688	40	30	19	**5**	2	267	283	120	106	12	6	102	**166**	1.442	3.57	129	3.98	.276	22	.210	26	23	2.5
1930 Chi-N	**20**	9	.690	45	35	**22**	1	4	271^2	290	145	119	14	6	96	142	1.421	3.94	124	3.85	.271	26	.248	30	24	3.0
1931 Chi-N	16	9	.640	36	30	12	2	0	228^1	229	115	99	9	4	88	112	1.388	3.90	99	3.55	.258	17	.215	1	13	0.3
1932* Chi-N	15	17	.469	37	32	17	2	0	237	222	111	89	13	6	78	120	1.266	3.38	111	3.15	.244	14	.179	6	16	0.6
1933 Chi-N	10	14	.417	31	26	13	2	0	186^1	186	91	81	10	5	59	72	1.315	3.91	84	3.42	.258	10	.159	-17	5	-2.1
1934 Chi-N	14	7	.667	34	21	8	1	0	191	200	85	75	14	3	55	111	1.335	3.53	110	3.70	.270	11	.172	6	14	0.4
1935 NY-A	3	5	.375	29	2	0	0	3	56^1	53	45	34	7	1	33	25	1.527	5.43	75	4.50	.252	0	.000	-10	0	-1.1
1936* NY-A	12	4	.750	35	9	5	0	**9**	134^2	144	60	57	4	4	60	72	1.515	3.81	122	4.07	.273	10	.196	12	13	1.0
1937 NY-A	4	4	.500	28	9	3	0	6	92	109	65	56	5	4	35	49	1.565	5.48	81	4.70	.291	1	.030	-12	3	-1.6
Total 10	**134**	**92**	**.593**	**357**	**219**	**115**	**15**	**26**	**1915**	**1934**	**936**	**795**	**103**	**45**	**705**	**1024**	**1.378**	**3.74**	**109**	**3.66**	**.262**	**129**	**.188**	**61**	**134**	**4.9**

• MALONEY, Charlie — Charles Michael Maloney b: 5/22/1886, Cambridge, MA d: 1/17/1967, Arlington, MA BR/TR, 5'8", 155 lbs. Deb: 8/10/1908

YEAR TM-L	W	L	PCT	G	GS	CG	SH	SV	IP	H	R	ER	HR	HB	BB	SO	RAT	ERA	ERA+	CERA	OAV	BH	AVG	PR+	WS	TPW
1908 Bos-N	0	0	....	1	0	0	0	0	2	3	1	1	0	0	1	0	2.000	4.50	53	8.05	.429	0	....	-1	0	-0.1

• MALONEY, Jim — James William Maloney b: 6/2/1940, Fresno, CA BL/TR, 6'2", 207 lbs. Deb: 7/27/1960

YEAR TM-L	W	L	PCT	G	GS	CG	SH	SV	IP	H	R	ER	HR	HB	BB	SO	RAT	ERA	ERA+	CERA	OAV	BH	AVG	PR+	WS	TPW
1960 Cin-N	2	6	.250	11	10	2	1	0	63^2	61	35	33	5	2	37	48	1.539	4.66	82	4.52	.255	2	.111	-6	1	-0.7
1961* Cin-N	6	7	.462	27	11	1	0	2	94^2	86	54	46	16	1	59	57	1.532	4.37	93	4.89	.242	11	.379	-3	6	0.1
1962 Cin-N	9	7	.563	22	17	3	0	1	115^1	90	52	45	11	2	66	105	1.353	3.51	115	3.52	.214	8	.186	6	8	0.6
1963 Cin-N	23	7	.767	33	33	13	6	0	250^1	183	84	77	17	6	88	265	1.083	2.77	121	2.38	.202	15	.169	16	22	1.8
1964 Cin-N	15	10	.600	31	31	11	2	0	216	175	72	65	16	1	83	214	1.194	2.71	133	2.84	.222	11	.151	19	18	2.2
1965 Cin-N★	20	9	.690	33	33	14	5	0	255^1	189	77	72	13	5	110	244	1.171	2.54	148	2.56	.206	20	.225	34	23	4.3
1966 Cin-N	16	8	.667	32	32	10	**5**	0	224^2	174	75	70	18	10	90	216	1.175	2.80	139	2.89	.214	18	.222	30	21	3.5
1967 Cin-N	15	11	.577	30	29	6	3	0	196^1	181	76	71	8	3	72	153	1.289	3.25	115	3.16	.247	11	.159	12	13	1.3
1968 Cin-N	16	10	.615	33	32	8	5	0	207	183	100	83	17	2	80	181	1.271	3.61	88	3.29	.239	18	.243	-9	10	-0.3

YEAR TM-L	W	L	PCT	G	GS	CG	SH	SV	IP	H	R	ER	HR	HB	BB	SO	RAT	ERA	ERA+	CERA	OAV	BH	AVG	PR+	WS	TPW
1969 Cin-N	12	5	.706	30	27	6	3	0	178^{2}	135	64	55	11	1	86	102	1.237	2.77	136	2.80	.208	11	.200	20	15	2.7
1970 Cin-N	0	1	.000	7	3	0	0	1	16^{2}	26	22	21	3	2	15	7	2.460	11.34	37	11.02	.366	0	.000	-13	0	-1.4
1971 Cal-A	0	3	.000	13	4	0	0	0	30^{1}	35	18	17	3	1	24	13	1.945	5.04	64	6.62	.294	1	.200	-6	0	-0.7
Total 12	134	84	.615	302	262	74	30	4	1849	1518	729	655	138	36	810	1605	1.259	3.19	115	3.17	.224	126	.201	99	137	13.4
• MALONEY, Sean	Sean Patrick Maloney b: 5/25/1971, South Kingstown, RI BR/TR, 6'7", 210 lbs. Deb: 4/28/1997																									
1997 Mil-A	0	0	....	3	0	0	0	0	7	7	4	4	1	2	2	5	1.286	5.14	90	5.54	.304	0	....	-1	0	-0.1
1998 LA-N	0	1	.000	11	0	0	0	0	12^{2}	13	7	7	2	2	5	11	1.421	4.97	80	5.26	.265	0	.000	-1	0	-0.1
Total 2	0	1	.000	14	0	0	0	0	19^{2}	20	11	11	3	4	7	16	1.373	5.03	83	5.36	.278	0	.000	-2	0	-0.2
• MALOY, Paul	Paul Augustus "Biff" Maloy b: 6/4/1892, Bascom, OH d: 3/18/1976, Sandusky, OH BR/TR, 5'11", 185 lbs. Deb: 7/11/1913																									
1913 Bos-A	0	0	....	2	0	0	0	0	2	2	2	2	0	2	1	0	1.500	9.00	33	8.59	.286	0	....	-1	0	-0.1
• MALTZBERGER, Gordon	Gordon Ralph "Maltzy" Maltzberger b: 9/4/1912, Utopia, TX d: 12/11/1974, Rialto, CA BR/TR, 6', 170 lbs. Deb: 4/27/1943 C																									
1943 Chi-A	7	4	.636	37	0	0	0	**14**	98^{2}	86	29	27	8	2	24	48	1.115	2.46	136	2.74	.236	3	.120	9	13	1.0
1944 Chi-A	10	5	.667	46	0	0	0	**12**	91^{1}	81	31	30	2	1	19	49	1.095	2.96	116	2.25	.235	3	.136	5	13	0.4
1946 Chi-A	2	0	1.000	19	0	0	0	2	39^{2}	30	7	7	3	1	6	17	.908	1.59	215	1.85	.205	0	.000	8	5	0.8
1947 Chi-A	1	4	.200	33	0	0	0	5	63^{2}	61	26	24	4	1	25	22	1.351	3.39	108	3.54	.257	1	.143	2	5	0.3
Total 4	20	13	.606	135	0	0	0	33	293^{1}	258	93	88	17	5	74	136	1.132	2.70	128	2.64	.236	7	.117	23	36	2.5
• MAMAUX, Al	Albert Leon Mamaux b: 5/30/1894, Pittsburgh, PA d: 12/31/1962, Santa Monica, CA BR/TR, 6'.5", 168 lbs. Deb: 9/23/1913																									
1913 Pit-N	0	0	....	1	0	0	0	0	3	2	1	1	0	0	2	2	1.333	3.00	100	2.17	.167	0	.000	0	0	0.0
1914 Pit-N	5	2	.714	13	6	4	2	0	63	41	19	12	1	2	24	30	1.032	1.71	154	1.78	.186	5	.250	6	6	0.8
1915 Pit-N	21	8	.724	38	30	17	8	0	251^{2}	182	70	57	3	9	96	152	1.105	2.04	134	2.11	.208	15	.163	20	21	1.9
1916 Pit-N	21	15	.583	45	37	26	1	2	310	264	123	87	3	9	136	163	1.290	2.53	106	2.85	.239	21	.191	12	19	1.5
1917 Pit-N	2	11	.154	16	13	5	0	0	85^{2}	92	59	50	1	3	50	22	1.658	5.25	54	4.48	.278	7	.226	-22	0	-2.5
1918 Bro-N	0	1	.000	2	1	0	0	0	8	14	6	6	0	0	2	2	2.000	6.75	41	7.73	.438	0	.000	-4	0	-0.4
1919 Bro-N	10	12	.455	30	22	16	2	0	199^{1}	174	89	59	2	4	66	80	1.204	2.66	111	2.61	.245	11	.175	11	11	1.3
1920* Bro-N	12	8	.600	41	17	9	2	4	190^{2}	172	70	57	2	4	63	101	1.233	2.69	119	2.82	.255	10	.167	13	16	1.4
1921 Bro-N	3	3	.500	12	1	0	0	1	43	36	17	15	1	1	13	21	1.140	3.14	124	2.42	.240	2	.182	4	4	0.4
1922 Bro-N	1	4	.200	37	7	1	0	3	87^{2}	97	46	36	7	2	33	35	1.483	3.70	110	4.47	.290	4	.235	4	6	0.7
1923 Bro-N	0	2	.000	5	1	0	0	0	13	20	13	12	0	0	6	5	2.000	8.31	47	6.87	.385	1	.500	-6	0	-0.6
1924 NY-A	1	1	.500	14	2	0	0	0	38	44	28	24	2	1	20	12	1.684	5.68	73	5.04	.308	1	.077	-7	0	-0.8
Total 12	76	67	.531	254	137	78	15	10	1293	1138	541	416	22	35	511	625	1.275	2.90	105	2.95	.245	77	.182	32	83	3.7
• MANDERS, Hal	Harold Carl Manders b: 6/14/1917, Waukee, IA BR/TR, 6', 187 lbs. Deb: 8/12/1941																									
1941 Det-A	1	0	1.000	8	0	0	0	0	15^{1}	13	5	4	0	1	8	7	1.370	2.35	194	3.17	.236	0	.000	4	2	0.4
1942 Det-A	2	0	1.000	18	0	0	0	0	33	39	19	15	4	1	15	14	1.636	4.09	97	5.70	.307	1	.250	-0	2	0.0
1946 Det-A	0	0	....	2	0	0	0	0	6	8	7	7	1	1	2	3	1.667	10.50	35	7.57	.364	1	.500	-4	0	-0.4
Chi-N	0	1	.000	2	1	0	0	0	6	11	6	6	1	1	3	4	2.333	9.00	37	11.91	.423	0	.000	-4	0	-0.4
Total 3	3	1	.750	30	1	0	0	0	60^{1}	71	37	32	6	4	28	28	1.641	4.77	80	5.86	.309	2	.167	-4	4	-0.5
• MANGUM, Leo	Leo Allan "Blackie" Mangum b: 5/24/1896, Durham, NC d: 7/9/1974, Lima, OH BR/TR, 6'1", 187 lbs. Deb: 7/11/1924																									
1924 Chi-A	1	4	.200	13	7	1	0	0	47	69	43	37	3	1	25	12	2.000	7.09	58	7.26	.359	1	.071	-15	0	-1.5
1925 Chi-A	1	0	1.000	7	0	0	0	0	15	25	15	13	0	0	6	6	2.067	7.80	53	7.18	.373	2	.500	-6	0	-0.5
1928 NY-N	0	0	....	1	1	0	0	0	3	6	5	5	0	0	5	1	3.667	15.00	26	14.42	.500	1	1.000	-4	0	-0.3
1932 Bos-N	0	0	....	7	0	0	0	0	10^{1}	17	8	6	1	0	0	3	1.645	5.23	72	5.32	.333	0	.000	-2	0	-0.2
1933 Bos-N	4	3	.571	25	5	2	1	0	84	93	33	31	2	0	11	28	1.238	3.32	92	3.05	.280	2	.091	-2	5	-0.4
1934 Bos-N	5	3	.625	29	3	1	0	1	94^{1}	127	67	60	9	0	23	28	1.590	5.72	67	5.22	.315	9	.281	-20	1	-1.8
1935 Bos-N	0	0	....	3	0	0	0	0	4^{2}	6	3	2	0	0	2	0	1.714	3.86	98	4.81	.300	0	....	0	0	0.0
Total 7	11	10	.524	85	16	4	1	1	258^{1}	343	174	154	15	1	72	78	1.606	5.37	69	5.10	.318	15	.200	-48	6	-4.6
• MANN, Jim	James Joseph Mann b: 11/17/1974, Brockton, MA BR/TR, 6'3", 225 lbs. Deb: 5/29/2000																									
2000 NY-N	0	0	....	2	0	0	0	0	2^{2}	6	3	3	1	0	1	0	2.625	10.13	44	14.73	.429	0	....	-2	0	-0.2
2001 Hou-N	0	0	....	4	0	0	0	0	5^{1}	3	2	2	0	2	4	5	1.313	3.38	135	3.87	.176	0	....	1	0	0.1
2002 Hou-N	0	1	.000	17	0	0	0	0	22	19	10	10	3	5	7	19	1.182	4.09	104	4.12	.235	0	.000	1	1	0.1
2003 Pit-N	0	0	....	2	0	0	0	0	1^{2}	5	4	2	1	0	1	1	3.600	10.80	41	22.63	.455	0	....	-1	0	-0.1
Total 4	0	1	.000	25	0	0	0	0	31^{2}	33	19	17	5	7	13	25	1.453	4.83	90	5.95	.268	0	.000	-2	1	-0.2
• MANNING, David	David Anthony Manning b: 8/14/1972, Buffalo, NY BR/TR, 6'3", 210 lbs. Deb: 8/2/2003																									
2003 Mil-N	0	2	.000	2	2	0	0	0	6^{2}	11	13	12	1	0	8	2	2.850	16.20	26	12.41	.393	0	.000	-9	0	-0.9
• MANNING, Ernie	Ernest Devon "Ed" Manning b: 10/9/1890, Florala, AL d: 4/28/1973, Pensacola, FL BL/TR, 6', 175 lbs. Deb: 5/3/1914																									
1914 StL-A	0	0	....	4	0	0	0	0	10	11	6	4	0	0	3	3	1.400	3.60	75	3.76	.297	0	.000	-1	0	-0.2
• MANNING, Jack	John E. Manning b: 12/20/1853, Braintree, MA d: 8/15/1929, Boston, MA BR/TR, 5'8.5", 158 lbs. Deb: 4/23/1873 M ♦																									
1874 Bal-n	4	16	.200	22	20	17	0	0	176^{2}	222	....	41	2	....	10	12	1.313	2.09	88	....	.275	61	.351	-6	....	-0.6
1875 Bos-n	15	2	.882	27	18	8	1	7	144	152	....	38	1	....	14	34	1.153	2.38	111	....	.247	94	.270	-2	....	0.3
1876 Bos-N	18	5	.783	34	20	13	0	**5**	197^{1}	213	139	47	1	....	32	24	1.242	2.14	105	....	.248	76	.258	3	19	0.0
1877 Cin-N	0	4	.000	10	4	2	0	1	44	83	65	34	1	....	7	6	2.045	6.95	38	....	.380	80	.317	-19	8	-1.2
1878 Bos-N	1	0	1.000	3	1	1	0	0	11^{1}	24	19	18	1	....	5	2	2.559	14.29	17	....	.411	63	.254	-15	7	-3.2
Total 2 n	19	18	.514	49	38	25	1	7	320^{2}	374	....	79	3	....	24	46	1.241	2.22	97	....	.263	199	.290	-8	....	-0.3
Total 3	19	9	.679	47	25	16	0	6	252^{2}	320	223	99	3	....	44	32	1.441	3.53	68	....	.281	725	.256	-31	34	-4.4
• MANNING, Jim	James Benjamin Manning b: 7/21/1943, L'Anse, MI BR/TR, 6'1", 185 lbs. Deb: 4/15/1962																									
1962 Min-A	0	0	....	5	1	0	0	0	7	14	10	4	0	1	1	3	2.143	5.14	79	8.28	.389	0	.000	-1	0	-0.1
• MANNING, Rube	Walter S. Manning b: 4/29/1883, Chambersburg, PA d: 4/23/1930, Williamsport, PA BR/TR, 6', 180 lbs. Deb: 9/25/1907																									
1907 NY-A	0	1	.000	1	1	1	0	0	9	8	3	3	0	1	3	3	1.222	3.00	93	3.05	.241	0	.000	-0	0	-0.1
1908 NY-A	13	16	.448	41	26	19	2	1	245	228	114	80	4	18	86	113	1.282	2.94	84	3.29	.256	17	.187	-6	7	-0.6
1909 NY-A	7	11	.389	26	21	11	2	1	173	167	76	61	2	9	48	71	1.243	3.17	80	3.14	.265	11	.183	-8	6	-0.9
1910 NY-A	2	4	.333	16	9	4	0	0	75	80	43	31	4	4	25	25	1.400	3.72	71	4.17	.283	5	.192	-7	2	-0.7
Total 4	22	32	.407	84	57	35	4	2	502	483	236	175	10	32	162	212	1.285	3.14	81	3.37	.263	33	.183	-21	15	-2.3
• MANON, Julio	Julio Alberto Manon b: 6/10/1973, Guerra Distrito, Dominican Republic BR/TR, 6', 200 lbs. Deb: 6/5/2003																									
2003 Mon-N	1	2	.333	23	0	0	0	1	28^{1}	26	13	13	3	1	17	15	1.518	4.13	122	4.57	.252	0	.000	3	3	0.3
• MANON, Ramon	Ramon (Reyes) Manon b: 1/20/1968, Santo Domingo, Dominican Republic BR/TR, 6', 150 lbs. Deb: 4/19/1990																									
1990 Tex-A	0	0	....	1	0	0	0	0	2	3	3	3	0	0	3	0	3.000	13.50	29	9.50	.333	0	....	-2	0	-0.2
• MANSELL, Tom	Thomas E. "Brick" Mansell b: 1/1/1855, Auburn, NY d: 10/6/1934, Auburn, NY BL/TR, 5'8", 160 lbs. Deb: 5/1/1879 ♦																									
1883 Det-N	0	0	....	1	0	0	0	0	6^{2}	21	18	14	2	....	5	3	3.900	18.90	16	....	.506	29	.221	-12	1	-1.8
• MANSKE, Lou	Louis Hugo Manske b: 7/4/1884, Milwaukee, WI d: 4/27/1963, Milwaukee, WI BL/TL, 6' Deb: 8/31/1906																									
1906 Pit-N	0	0	....	2	1	0	0	0	8	12	6	5	0	0	5	6	2.125	5.63	47	7.82	.387	0	.000	-3	0	-0.4
• MANTEI, Matt	Matthew Bruce Mantei b: 7/7/1973, Tampa, FL BR/TR, 6'1", 180 lbs. Deb: 6/18/1995																									
1995 Fla-N	0	1	.000	12	0	0	0	0	13^{1}	12	8	7	1	0	13	15	1.875	4.73	89	5.54	.245	0	....	-1	0	-0.1
1996 Fla-N	1	0	1.000	14	0	0	0	0	18^{1}	13	13	13	2	1	21	25	1.855	6.38	64	5.46	.197	0	.000	-5	0	-0.5
1998 Fla-N	3	4	.429	42	0	0	0	9	54^{2}	38	19	18	1	7	23	63	1.116	2.96	138	2.44	.203	1	.333	7	5	0.7

YEAR	TM-L	W	L	PCT	G	GS	CG	SH	SV	IP	H	R	ER	HR	HB	BB	SO	RAT	ERA	ERA+	CERA	OAV	BH	AVG	PR+	WS	TPW
1999	Fla-N	1	2	.333	35	0	0	0	10	36^1	24	11	11	4	2	25	50	1.349	2.72	160	3.55	.186	0	.000	7	6	0.6
	*Ari-N	0	1	.000	30	0	0	0	22	29	20	10	9	1	3	19	49	1.345	2.79	164	3.25	.192	0	....	6	6	0.5
	Yr.	1	3	.250	65	0	0	0	32	65^1	44	21	20	5	5	44	99	1.347	2.76	161	3.42	.189	0	.000	12	12	1.1
2000	Ari-N	1	1	.500	47	0	0	0	17	45^1	31	24	23	4	2	35	53	1.456	4.57	103	3.80	.193	0	....	1	6	0.1
2001	Ari-N	0	0	....	8	0	0	0	2	7	6	2	2	2	0	4	12	1.429	2.57	178	5.18	.222	0	....	1	1	0.1
2002*	Ari-N	2	2	.500	31	0	0	0	0	26^2	28	15	14	3	1	12	26	1.500	4.73	94	4.64	.257	0	....	-1	1	-0.1
2003	Ari-N	5	4	.556	50	0	0	0	29	55	37	17	16	6	2	18	68	1.000	2.62	178	2.26	.191	0	....	13	13	1.3
Total	8	13	15	.464	269	0	0	0	89	285^2	209	119	113	24	18	170	361	1.327	3.56	124	3.46	.204	1	.200	29	38	2.8

• MANUEL, Barry
Barry Paul Manuel b: 8/12/1965, Mamou, LA BR/TR, 5'11", 180 lbs. Deb: 9/6/1991

YEAR	TM-L	W	L	PCT	G	GS	CG	SH	SV	IP	H	R	ER	HR	HB	BB	SO	RAT	ERA	ERA+	CERA	OAV	BH	AVG	PR+	WS	TPW
1991	Tex-A	1	0	1.000	8	0	0	0	0	16	7	2	2	0	0	6	5	.813	1.13	358	1.06	.143	0	....	5	2	0.5
1992	Tex-A	1	0	1.000	3	0	0	0	0	5^2	6	3	3	2	1	1	9	1.235	4.76	80	5.90	.261	0	....	-1	0	-0.1
1996	Mon-N	4	1	.800	53	0	0	0	0	86	70	34	31	10	7	26	62	1.116	3.24	133	3.00	.219	0	.000	11	7	1.0
1997	NY-N	0	1	.000	19	0	0	0	0	25^2	35	18	15	6	1	13	21	1.870	5.26	77	7.97	.324	0	.000	-4	0	-0.4
1998	Ari-N	1	0	1.000	13	0	0	0	0	15^2	17	14	13	5	1	14	12	1.979	7.47	56	8.26	.266	0	....	-6	0	-0.6
Total	5	7	2	.778	96	0	0	0	0	149	135	71	64	23	10	60	109	1.309	3.87	109	4.31	.240	0	.000	6	9	0.5

• MANUEL, Moxie
Mark Garfield Manuel b: 10/16/1881, Metropolis, IL d: 4/26/1924, Memphis, TN BR/TR, 5'11", 170 lbs. Deb: 9/25/1905

YEAR	TM-L	W	L	PCT	G	GS	CG	SH	SV	IP	H	R	ER	HR	HB	BB	SO	RAT	ERA	ERA+	CERA	OAV	BH	AVG	PR+	WS	TPW
1905	Was-A	0	0	....	3	1	1	0	0	10	9	9	6	0	1	3	3	1.200	5.40	49	2.78	.243	1	.250	-3	0	-0.4
1908	Chi-A	3	4	.429	18	6	3	0	1	60^1	52	25	22	0	2	25	25	1.276	3.28	70	3.01	.251	1	.063	-6	2	-0.8
Total	2	3	4	.429	21	7	4	0	1	70^1	61	34	28	0	3	28	28	1.265	3.58	66	2.98	.250	2	.100	-9	2	-1.2

• MANVILLE, Dick
Richard Wesley Manville b: 12/25/1926, Des Moines, IA BR/TR, 6'4", 192 lbs. Deb: 4/30/1950

YEAR	TM-L	W	L	PCT	G	GS	CG	SH	SV	IP	H	R	ER	HR	HB	BB	SO	RAT	ERA	ERA+	CERA	OAV	BH	AVG	PR+	WS	TPW
1950	Bos-N	0	0	....	1	0	0	0	0	2	0	0	0	0	0	3	2	1.500	0.00	....	1.44	.000	0	....	1	0	0.1
1952	Chi-N	0	0	....	11	0	0	0	0	17	25	17	15	2	0	12	6	2.176	7.94	48	8.53	.362	1	.500	-8	0	-0.8
Total	2	0	0	....	12	0	0	0	0	19	25	17	15	2	0	15	8	2.105	7.11	54	7.78	.362	1	.500	-7	0	-0.7

• MANZANILLO, Josias
Josias (Adams) Manzanillo b: 10/16/1967, San Pedro de Macoris, Dominican Republic BR/TR, 6', 190 lbs. Deb: 10/5/1991

YEAR	TM-L	W	L	PCT	G	GS	CG	SH	SV	IP	H	R	ER	HR	HB	BB	SO	RAT	ERA	ERA+	CERA	OAV	BH	AVG	PR+	WS	TPW
1991	Bos-A	0	0	....	1	0	0	0	0	1	2	2	2	0	0	3	1	5.000	18.00	24	21.46	.400	0	....	-2	0	-0.2
1993	Mil-A	1	1	.500	10	1	0	0	1	17	22	20	18	1	2	10	10	1.882	9.53	45	6.15	.314	0	....	-10	0	-1.0
	NY-N	0	0	....	6	0	0	0	0	12	8	7	4	1	0	9	11	1.417	3.00	134	3.32	.186	0	.000	1	1	0.1
1994	NY-N	3	2	.600	37	0	0	0	2	47^1	34	15	14	4	3	13	48	.993	2.66	157	2.28	.200	0	.000	8	6	0.7
1995	NY-N	1	2	.333	12	0	0	0	0	16	18	15	14	3	0	6	14	1.500	7.88	51	4.93	.273	0	....	-7	0	-0.7
	NY-A	0	0	....	11	0	0	0	0	17^1	19	4	4	1	2	9	11	1.615	2.08	222	4.96	.279	0	....	5	2	0.4
1997	Sea-A	0	1	.000	16	0	0	0	0	18^1	19	13	11	3	0	17	18	1.964	5.40	83	6.97	.275	0	.000	-2	0	-0.2
1999	NY-N	0	0	....	12	0	0	0	0	18^2	19	12	12	5	2	4	25	1.232	5.79	76	4.90	.264	1	1.000	-3	1	-0.2
2000	Pit-N	2	2	.500	43	0	0	0	0	58^2	50	23	22	6	0	32	39	1.398	3.38	136	3.85	.240	0	.000	9	5	0.8
2001	Pit-N	3	2	.600	71	0	0	0	2	79^2	60	32	30	4	5	26	80	1.079	3.39	132	2.33	.211	0	.000	10	8	1.0
2002	Pit-N	0	0	....	13	0	0	0	0	13	20	11	11	5	1	5	4	1.923	7.62	55	10.63	.364	0	....	-5	0	-0.5
2003	Cin-N	0	2	.000	9	0	0	0	0	10^2	21	20	15	7	0	4	12	2.344	12.66	34	14.74	.389	0	....	-10	0	-1.0
Total	10	10	12	.455	241	1	0	0	5	309^2	292	174	157	40	15	138	273	1.389	4.56	95	4.41	.251	1	.091	-5	23	-0.6

• MANZANILLO, Ravelo
Ravelo (Adams) Manzanillo b: 10/17/1963, San Pedro de Macoris, Dominican Republic BL/TL, 6', 210 lbs. Deb: 9/25/1988

YEAR	TM-L	W	L	PCT	G	GS	CG	SH	SV	IP	H	R	ER	HR	HB	BB	SO	RAT	ERA	ERA+	CERA	OAV	BH	AVG	PR+	WS	TPW
1988	Chi-A	0	1	.000	2	2	0	0	0	9^1	7	6	6	1	1	12	10	2.036	5.79	69	6.79	.212	0	....	-2	0	-0.2
1994	Pit-N	4	2	.667	46	0	0	0	1	50	45	30	23	4	3	42	39	1.740	4.14	104	5.10	.245	2	.667	1	4	0.2
1995	Pit-N	0	0	....	5	0	0	0	0	3^2	3	3	2	0	1	2	1	1.364	4.91	88	4.07	.231	0	.000	-0	0	0.0
Total	3	4	3	.571	53	2	0	0	1	63	55	39	31	5	5	56	50	1.762	4.43	96	5.29	.239	2	.500	-2	4	-0.1

• MAPEL, Rolla
Rolla Hamilton "Lefty" Mapel b: 3/9/1890, Lee's Summit, MO d: 4/6/1966, San Diego, CA BL/TL, 5'11.5", 165 lbs. Deb: 8/31/1919

YEAR	TM-L	W	L	PCT	G	GS	CG	SH	SV	IP	H	R	ER	HR	HB	BB	SO	RAT	ERA	ERA+	CERA	OAV	BH	AVG	PR+	WS	TPW
1919	StL-A	0	3	.000	4	3	2	0	0	20	17	12	10	0	3	17	2	1.700	4.50	74	5.02	.262	1	.167	-3	0	-0.3

• MARAK, Paul
Paul Patrick Marak b: 8/2/1965, Lakenheath, England BR/TR, 6'2", 175 lbs. Deb: 9/1/1990

YEAR	TM-L	W	L	PCT	G	GS	CG	SH	SV	IP	H	R	ER	HR	HB	BB	SO	RAT	ERA	ERA+	CERA	OAV	BH	AVG	PR+	WS	TPW
1990	Atl-N	1	2	.333	7	7	1	1	0	39	39	16	16	2	3	19	15	1.487	3.69	109	4.28	.267	1	.091	2	2	0.2

• MARANDA, Georges
Georges Henri Maranda b: 1/15/1932, Levis, Canada d: 7/14/2000, Levis, Canada BR/TR, 6'2", 195 lbs. Deb: 4/26/1960

YEAR	TM-L	W	L	PCT	G	GS	CG	SH	SV	IP	H	R	ER	HR	HB	BB	SO	RAT	ERA	ERA+	CERA	OAV	BH	AVG	PR+	WS	TPW
1960	SF-N	1	4	.200	17	4	0	0	0	50^2	50	32	26	6	0	30	28	1.579	4.62	75	4.59	.254	2	.167	-6	0	-0.6
1962	Min-A	1	3	.250	32	4	0	0	0	72^2	69	43	36	10	4	35	36	1.431	4.46	92	4.56	.252	4	.250	-3	2	-0.2
Total	2	2	7	.222	49	8	0	0	0	123^1	119	75	62	16	4	65	64	1.492	4.52	84	4.57	.253	6	.214	-9	2	-0.8

• MARBERRY, Firpo
Frederick Marberry b: 11/30/1898, Streetman, TX d: 6/30/1976, Mexia, TX BR/TR, 6'1", 190 lbs. Deb: 8/11/1923 U

YEAR	TM-L	W	L	PCT	G	GS	CG	SH	SV	IP	H	R	ER	HR	HB	BB	SO	RAT	ERA	ERA+	CERA	OAV	BH	AVG	PR+	WS	TPW
1923	Was-A	4	0	1.000	11	4	2	0	0	44^2	42	16	14	1	3	17	18	1.321	2.82	134	3.31	.258	2	.143	3	4	0.2
1924*	Was-A	11	12	.478	**50**	14	6	0	**15**	195^1	190	88	67	3	9	70	68	1.331	3.09	131	3.24	.262	8	.136	16	17	1.1
1925*	Was-A	9	5	.643	**55**	0	0	0	**15**	93^1	84	50	36	4	4	45	53	1.382	3.47	122	3.51	.246	5	.263	5	11	0.6
1926	Was-A	12	7	.632	**64**	5	3	0	**22**	138	120	55	46	4	3	66	43	1.348	3.00	129	3.14	.243	6	.176	13	16	1.2
1927	Was-A	10	7	.588	56	10	2	0	9	155^1	177	92	80	4	3	68	74	1.577	4.64	88	4.43	.296	5	.122	-12	8	-1.4
1928	Was-A	13	13	.500	**48**	11	7	1	3	161^1	160	79	69	4	3	42	76	1.252	3.85	104	3.00	.268	5	.109	0	11	-0.3
1929	Was-A	19	12	.613	**49**	26	16	0	**11**	250^1	233	100	85	6	6	69	121	1.206	3.06	139	**2.78**	.252	19	.235	30	26	2.9
1930	Was-A	15	5	.750	33	22	9	2	1	185	190	92	84	15	0	53	56	1.314	4.09	112	3.63	.270	24	.329	4	16	0.8
1931	Was-A	16	4	.800	45	25	11	1	7	219	211	92	84	13	3	63	88	1.251	3.45	124	3.17	.252	19	.232	18	20	1.8
1932	Was-A	8	4	.667	**54**	15	8	1	**13**	197^2	202	98	88	13	2	72	66	1.386	4.01	108	3.79	.268	11	.167	2	16	0.0
1933	Det-A	16	11	.593	37	32	15	1	2	238^1	232	98	87	13	1	61	84	1.229	3.29	131	3.03	.254	11	.122	25	20	1.9
1934*	Det-A	15	5	.750	38	19	6	1	3	155^2	174	92	79	12	0	48	64	1.426	4.57	96	4.07	.276	12	.218	-4	10	-0.2
1935	Det-A	0	1	.000	5	2	1	0	0	19	22	11	9	2	0	9	7	1.632	4.26	98	5.01	.289	1	.200	-0	1	0.0
1936	NY-N	0	0	....	1	0	0	0	0	0^1	1	1	0	0	0	0	0	3.000	0.00	....	9.49	.500	0	.000	0	0	0.0
	Was-A	0	2	.000	5	1	0	0	0	14	11	7	6	2	1	3	4	1.000	3.86	124	2.61	.208	0	.000	1	1	0.1
Total	14	148	88	.627	551	186	86	7	101	2067^1	2049	971	834	96	38	686	822	1.323	3.63	116	3.39	.262	128	.192	102	177	8.7

• MARBET, Walt
Walter William Marbet b: 9/13/1890, Plymouth County, IA d: 9/24/1956, Hohenwald, TN BR/TR, 6'1", 175 lbs. Deb: 6/17/1913

YEAR	TM-L	W	L	PCT	G	GS	CG	SH	SV	IP	H	R	ER	HR	HB	BB	SO	RAT	ERA	ERA+	CERA	OAV	BH	AVG	PR+	WS	TPW
1913	StL-N	0	1	.000	3	1	0	0	0	3^1	9	7	6	0	0	4	1	3.900	16.20	20	18.51	.500	0	....	-5	0	-0.5

• MARCHILDON, Phil
Philip Joseph "Babe" Marchildon b: 10/25/1913, Penetanguishene, Canada d: 1/10/1997, Toronto, Canada BR/TR, 5'10.5", 175 lbs. Deb: 9/22/1940

YEAR	TM-L	W	L	PCT	G	GS	CG	SH	SV	IP	H	R	ER	HR	HB	BB	SO	RAT	ERA	ERA+	CERA	OAV	BH	AVG	PR+	WS	TPW
1940	Phi-A	0	2	.000	2	2	1	0	0	10	12	9	8	1	0	8	4	2.000	7.20	62	6.37	.286	0	.000	-3	0	-0.3
1941	Phi-A	10	15	.400	30	27	14	1	0	204^1	188	94	81	15	3	118	74	1.498	3.57	118	4.05	.245	11	.167	13	13	1.3
1942	Phi-A	17	14	.548	38	31	18	1	1	244	215	126	114	14	4	140	110	1.455	4.20	90	3.64	.235	20	.238	-6	13	-0.4
1945	Phi-A	0	1	.000	3	2	0	0	0	9	5	5	4	0	0	11	2	1.778	4.00	86	3.66	.179	1	.500	-1	0	0.0
1946	Phi-A	13	16	.448	36	29	16	1	1	226^2	197	104	88	14	4	114	95	1.372	3.49	102	3.47	.237	5	.067	3	12	-0.3
1947	Phi-A	19	9	.679	35	35	21	2	0	276^2	228	110	99	15	7	141	128	1.334	3.22	119	3.21	.224	15	.153	11	21	1.0
1948	Phi-A	9	15	.375	33	30	12	1	0	226^1	214	133	114	19	4	131	66	1.524	4.53	95	4.26	.251	5	.069	-8	9	-1.3
1949	Phi-A	0	3	.000	7	6	0	0	0	16	24	23	21	3	1	19	2	2.688	11.81	35	11.57	.358	1	.167	-14	0	-1.4
1950	Bos-A	0	0	....	1	0	0	0	0	1^1	1	1	1	0	0	2	0	2.250	6.75	73	5.42	.200	0	....	-0	0	0.0
Total	9	68	75	.476	185	162	82	6	2	1214^1	1084	605	530	81	23	684	481	1.456	3.93	100	3.82	.240	58	.143	-5	68	-1.4

• MARCUM, Johnny
John Alfred "Footsie" Marcum b: 9/9/1909, Campbellsburg, KY d: 9/10/1984, Louisville, KY BL/TR, 5'11", 197 lbs. Deb: 9/7/1933

YEAR	TM-L	W	L	PCT	G	GS	CG	SH	SV	IP	H	R	ER	HR	HB	BB	SO	RAT	ERA	ERA+	CERA	OAV	BH	AVG	PR+	WS	TPW
1933	Phi-A	3	2	.600	5	5	4	2	0	37	28	12	8	0	0	20	14	1.297	1.95	220	2.40	.200	2	.167	11	4	1.0
1934	Phi-A	14	11	.560	37	31	17	2	0	232	257	131	116	13	4	88	92	1.487	4.50	97	4.21	.280	30	.268	-5	15	0.0
1935	Phi-A	17	12	.586	39	27	19	2	3	242^2	256	125	110	9	2	83	99	1.397	4.08	111	3.59	.268	37	.311	16	19	2.4
1936	Bos-A	8	13	.381	31	23	9	1	1	174	194	100	93	14	0	52	57	1.414	4.81	111	4.12	.281	18	.205	9	11	0.9
1937	Bos-A	13	11	.542	37	23	9	1	3	183^2	230	104	99	17	2	47	59	1.508	4.85	98	4.88	.306	23	.267	2	14	0.6
1938	Bos-A	5	6	.455	15	11	7	0	0	92^1	113	49	42	11	0	25	25	1.495	4.09	121	4.88	.298	5	.135	8	7	0.6

YEAR TM-L	W	L	PCT	G	GS	CG	SH	SV	IP	H	R	ER	HR	HB	BB	SO	RAT	ERA	ERA+	CERA	OAV	BH	AVG	PR+	WS	TPW
1939 StL-A	2	5	.286	12	6	2	0	0	47^2	66	43	41	12	1	10	14	1.594	7.74	63	6.79	.332	10	.455	-14	1	-1.0
Chi-A	3	3	.500	19	6	2	0	0	90	125	66	60	15	0	19	32	1.600	6.00	79	5.87	.326	16	.281	-14	3	-1.0
Yr.	5	8	.385	31	12	4	0	0	137^2	191	109	101	27	1	29	46	1.598	6.60	72	6.19	.328	26	.329	-28	4	-2.0
Total 7	65	63	.508	195	132	69	8	7	1099^1	1269	630	569	91	9	344	392	1.467	4.66	101	4.41	.287	141	.265	12	74	3.6
• MARENTETTE, Leo	Leo John Marentette b: 2/18/1941, Detroit, MI BR/TR, 6'2", 200 lbs. Deb: 9/26/1965																									
1965 Det-A	0	0	....	2	0	0	0	0	3	1	0	0	0	0	1	3	.667	0.00	....	0.75	.111	0	....	1	0	0.1
1969 Mon-N	0	0	....	3	0	0	0	0	5^1	9	4	4	1	0	1	4	1.875	6.75	54	7.87	.391	0	.000	-2	0	-0.2
Total 2	0	0	....	5	0	0	0	0	8^1	10	4	4	1	0	2	7	1.440	4.32	85	5.31	.313	0	.000	-1	0	-0.1
• MARGONERI, Joe	Joseph Emanuel Margoneri b: 1/13/1930, Somerset, PA BL/TL, 6', 185 lbs. Deb: 4/25/1956																									
1956 NY-N	6	6	.500	23	13	2	0	0	91^2	88	45	40	12	0	49	49	1.495	3.93	96	4.53	.254	3	.103	-1	5	-0.2
1957 NY-N	1	1	.500	13	2	1	0	0	34^1	44	23	20	1	1	21	18	1.893	5.24	75	6.02	.314	0	.000	-5	0	-0.6
Total 2	7	7	.500	36	15	3	0	0	126	132	68	60	13	1	70	67	1.603	4.29	89	4.94	.271	3	.081	-6	5	-0.8
• MARICHAL, Juan	Juan Antonio (Sanchez) "Manito" Marichal b: 10/20/1937, Laguna Verde, Dominican Republic BR/TR, 6', 185 lbs. Deb: 7/19/1960 HOF: 1983																									
1960 SF-N	6	2	.750	11	11	6	1	0	81^1	59	29	24	5	0	28	58	1.070	2.66	131	2.18	.200	4	.129	8	6	0.8
1961 SF-N	13	10	.565	29	27	9	3	0	185	183	88	80	24	2	48	124	1.249	3.89	98	3.69	.257	7	.119	-0	10	-0.3
1962★ SF-N★	18	11	.621	37	36	18	3	1	262^2	233	112	98	34	3	90	153	1.230	3.36	113	3.42	.234	21	.236	13	19	1.7
1963 SF-N★	**25**	8	.758	41	40	18	5	0	**321^1**	259	102	86	27	2	61	248	.996	2.41	133	2.19	.216	20	.179	34	26	3.9
1964 SF-N★	21	8	.724	33	33	**22**	4	0	269	241	89	74	18	1	52	206	1.089	2.48	144	2.50	.236	14	.144	30	25	3.1
1965 SF-N★	22	13	.629	39	37	24	**10**	1	295^1	224	78	70	27	4	46	240	.914	2.13	**169**	1.92	.205	17	.173	**52**	30	**5.6**
1966 SF-N★	25	6	.806	37	36	25	4	0	307^1	228	88	76	32	5	36	222	.859	2.23	165	**1.80**	**.202**	28	.250	49	33	**5.8**
1967 SF-N★	14	10	.583	26	26	18	2	0	202^1	195	79	62	20	1	42	166	1.171	2.76	119	3.05	.249	14	.177	12	14	1.5
1968 SF-N★	**26**	9	.743	38	38	**30**	5	0	**326**	295	106	88	21	6	46	218	1.046	2.43	121	2.41	.238	20	.163	21	24	2.6
1969 SF-N★	21	11	.656	37	36	27	**8**	0	299^2	244	90	70	15	6	54	205	.994	**2.10**	**167**	**2.07**	.222	15	.138	49	29	5.0
1970 SF-N	12	10	.545	34	33	14	1	0	242^2	269	128	111	28	1	48	123	1.306	4.12	97	3.94	.277	5	.059	1	11	-0.5
1971★ SF-N★	18	11	.621	37	37	18	4	0	279	244	113	91	27	3	56	159	1.075	2.94	116	2.64	.233	14	.133	16	18	1.7
1972 SF-N	6	16	.273	25	24	6	0	0	165	176	82	68	15	3	46	72	1.345	3.71	94	3.95	.277	10	.196	-4	5	-0.3
1973 SF-N	11	15	.423	34	32	9	2	0	207^1	231	104	88	22	1	37	87	1.293	3.82	100	3.77	.277	13	.188	2	10	0.4
1974 Bos-A	5	1	.833	11	9	0	0	0	57^1	61	32	31	3	2	14	21	1.308	4.87	79	3.59	.270	0	....	-6	3	-0.6
1975 LA-N	0	1	.000	2	2	0	0	0	6	11	9	9	2	0	5	1	2.667	13.50	25	13.14	.407	0	.000	-7	0	-0.7
Total 16	243	142	.631	471	457	244	52	2	3507^1	3153	1329	1126	320	40	709	2303	1.101	2.89	122	2.76	.237	202	.165	271	263	29.6
• MARION, Dan	Donald G. "Rube" Marion b: 7/31/1890, Cleveland, OH d: 1/18/1933, Milwaukee, WI BR/TR, 6'1", 187 lbs. Deb: 4/23/1914																									
1914 Bro-F	3	2	.600	17	9	4	0	0	89^1	97	52	39	1	6	38	41	1.511	3.93	82	4.25	.281	7	.194	-6	3	-0.7
1915 Bro-F	12	9	.571	35	25	15	2	0	208^1	193	92	74	1	3	64	46	1.234	3.20	93	2.76	.248	13	.176	-6	10	-0.7
Total 2	15	11	.577	52	34	19	2	0	297^2	290	144	113	2	9	102	87	1.317	3.42	90	3.21	.258	20	.182	-12	13	-1.5
• MARKELL, Duke	Harry Duquesne Markell b: 8/17/1923, Paris, France d: 6/14/1984, Fort Lauderdale, FL BR/TR, 6'1.5", 209 lbs. Deb: 9/6/1951																									
1951 StL-A	1	1	.500	5	2	1	0	0	21^1	25	16	15	3	0	20	10	2.109	6.33	69	7.61	.298	1	.167	-4	0	-0.4
• MARKLE, Cliff	Clifford Monroe Markle b: 5/3/1894, Dravosburg, PA d: 5/24/1974, Temple City, CA BR/TR, 5'9", 163 lbs. Deb: 9/18/1915																									
1915 NY-A	2	0	1.000	3	2	2	0	0	23	15	3	1	1	0	6	12	.913	0.39	749	1.56	.185	0	.000	6	3	0.7
1916 NY-A	4	3	.571	11	7	3	1	0	45^2	41	26	23	0	4	31	14	1.577	4.53	64	4.23	.256	0	.000	-9	1	-1.1
1921 Cin-N	2	6	.250	10	6	5	0	0	67	75	36	28	0	0	20	23	1.418	3.76	95	3.59	.291	3	.125	-0	3	-0.2
1922 Cin-N	4	5	.444	25	3	2	1	0	75^2	75	41	32	3	0	33	34	1.427	3.81	105	3.62	.268	3	.150	-0	4	0.0
1924 NY-A	0	3	.000	7	3	0	0	0	23^1	29	26	23	5	0	20	7	2.100	8.87	47	8.11	.333	0	.000	-12	0	-1.3
Total 5	12	17	.414	56	21	12	2	0	234^2	235	132	107	9	4	110	90	1.470	4.10	88	3.98	.271	6	.087	-16	11	-2.0
• MARLOWE, Dick	Richard Burton Marlowe b: 6/27/1929, Hickory, NC d: 12/30/1968, Toledo, OH BR/TR, 6'2", 170 lbs. Deb: 9/19/1951																									
1951 Det-A	0	1	.000	2	1	0	0	0	1^2	5	6	6	0	0	2	1	4.200	32.40	13	20.02	.500	0	....	-5	0	-0.5
1952 Det-A	0	2	.000	4	1	0	0	0	11	21	10	9	1	0	3	3	2.182	7.36	52	9.56	.420	0	.000	-4	0	-0.5
1953 Det-A	6	7	.462	42	11	2	0	0	119^2	152	74	70	13	2	42	52	1.621	5.26	77	5.56	.319	7	.219	-12	3	-1.3
1954 Det-A	5	4	.556	38	2	0	0	2	84	76	45	39	11	0	40	39	1.381	4.18	88	3.92	.244	3	.167	-5	4	-0.5
1955 Det-A	1	0	1.000	4	1	1	0	1	15	12	4	3	1	0	4	9	1.067	1.80	213	2.29	.218	0	.000	3	2	0.3
1956 Det-A	1	1	.500	7	1	0	0	0	11	12	8	7	1	0	9	4	1.909	5.73	72	6.21	.279	0	.000	-2	0	-0.2
Chi-A	0	0	....	1	0	0	0	0	1	2	1	1	1	0	1	0	3.000	9.00	46	27.72	.500	0	....	-1	0	-0.1
Yr.	1	1	.500	8	1	0	0	0	12	14	9	8	2	0	10	4	2.000	6.00	69	8.00	.298	0	.000	-3	0	-0.3
Total 6	13	15	.464	98	17	3	0	3	243^1	280	148	135	28	2	101	108	1.566	4.99	79	5.19	.295	10	.175	-26	9	-2.7
• MARONE, Lou	Louis Stephen Marone b: 12/3/1945, San Diego, CA BR/TL, 5'11", 185 lbs. Deb: 5/30/1969																									
1969 Pit-N	1	1	.500	29	0	0	0	0	35^1	24	10	10	2	2	13	25	1.047	2.55	137	2.21	.195	0	....	4	3	0.4
1970 Pit-N	0	0	....	1	0	0	0	0	2^1	2	1	1	1	0	0	0	.857	3.86	101	3.45	.222	0	....	-0	0	0.0
Total 2	1	1	.500	30	0	0	0	0	37^2	26	11	11	3	2	13	25	1.035	2.63	134	2.28	.197	0	....	4	3	0.4
• MAROTH, Mike	Michael Warren Maroth b: 8/17/1977, Orlando, FL BL/TL, 6', 180 lbs. Deb: 6/8/2002																									
2002 Det-A	6	10	.375	21	21	0	0	0	128^2	136	68	64	7	2	36	58	1.337	4.48	96	3.73	.276	1	.167	-2	6	-0.2
2003 Det-A	9	21	.300	33	33	1	0	0	193^1	231	131	123	34	8	50	87	1.453	5.73	75	5.36	.299	1	.500	-31	4	-2.9
Total 2	15	31	.326	54	54	1	0	0	322	367	199	187	41	10	86	145	1.407	5.23	82	4.71	.290	2	.250	-32	10	-3.0
• MARQUARD, Rube	Richard William Marquard b: 10/9/1886, Cleveland, OH d: 6/1/1980, Baltimore, MD BB/TL, 6'3", 180 lbs. Deb: 9/25/1908 HOF: 1971																									
1908 NY-N	0	1	.000	1	1	0	0	0	5	6	5	2	0	1	2	2	1.600	3.60	67	5.42	.316	0	.000	-1	0	-0.1
1909 NY-N	5	13	.278	29	21	8	0	1	173	155	81	50	2	9	73	109	1.318	2.60	98	3.22	.248	8	.148	1	7	-0.1
1910 NY-N	4	4	.500	13	8	2	0	0	70^2	65	35	35	2	4	40	52	1.486	4.46	66	3.99	.254	3	.111	-11	2	-1.3
1911★ NY-N	24	7	.774	45	33	22	5	3	277^2	221	98	77	9	4	106	**237**	1.178	2.50	134	2.48	**.219**	17	.163	31	26	3.0
1912★ NY-N	**26**	11	.703	43	38	22	1	1	294^2	286	112	84	9	3	80	175	1.242	2.57	132	2.93	.255	21	.219	26	26	2.7
1913★ NY-N	23	10	.697	42	33	20	4	3	288	248	100	80	10	3	49	151	1.031	2.50	125	2.17	.237	23	.219	18	26	2.1
1914 NY-N	12	22	.353	39	33	15	4	2	268	261	117	91	9	2	47	92	1.149	3.06	87	2.67	.262	15	.179	-12	11	-1.4
1915 NY-N	9	8	.529	27	21	10	2	2	169	178	85	70	8	1	33	79	1.249	3.73	69	3.22	.272	6	.109	-20	4	-2.5
Bro-N	2	2	.500	6	3	0	0	1	24^2	29	17	17	0	0	5	13	1.378	6.20	45	3.29	.276	1	.125	-10	0	-1.1
Yr.	11	10	.524	33	24	10	2	3	193^2	207	102	87	8	1	38	92	1.265	4.04	64	3.23	.273	7	.111	-30	4	-3.7
1916★ Bro-N	13	6	.684	36	21	15	2	5	205	169	54	36	2	0	38	107	1.010	1.58	169	1.87	.229	9	.143	21	20	2.3
1917 Bro-N	19	12	.613	37	29	14	2	0	232^2	200	84	66	5	0	60	117	1.117	2.55	109	2.26	.232	15	.200	4	17	0.5
1918 Bro-N	9	18	.333	34	29	19	4	0	239	231	97	70	7	1	59	89	1.213	2.64	106	2.83	.260	13	.171	4	14	0.3
1919 Bro-N	3	3	.500	8	7	3	0	0	59	54	17	15	1	0	10	29	1.085	2.29	130	2.21	.244	6	.261	6	5	0.7
1920★ Bro-N	10	7	.588	28	26	10	1	0	189^2	181	83	68	5	1	35	89	1.139	3.23	99	2.50	.251	10	.169	2	11	0.1
1921 Cin-N	17	14	.548	39	36	18	2	0	265^2	291	123	100	8	7	50	88	1.284	3.39	106	3.37	.285	19	.200	9	17	0.8
1922 Bos-N	11	15	.423	39	25	7	0	1	198	255	131	112	12	0	66	57	1.621	5.09	78	5.14	.322	14	.222	-22	7	-2.1
1923 Bos-N	11	14	.440	38	29	11	3	0	239	265	127	99	10	2	65	78	1.381	3.73	107	3.78	.288	12	.140	9	12	0.3
1924 Bos-N	1	2	.333	6	6	1	0	0	36	33	17	12	3	1	13	10	1.278	3.00	127	3.42	.254	3	.273	4	3	0.4
1925 Bos-N	2	8	.200	26	8	0	0	0	72	105	60	46	5	0	27	19	1.833	5.75	70	6.21	.341	3	.136	-15	0	-1.5
Total 18	201	177	.532	536	407	197	30	19	3306^2	3233	1443	1130	107	39	858	1593	1.237	3.08	103	3.01	.260	198	.179	45	208	2.9
• MARQUEZ, Isidro	Isidro (Espinoza) Marquez b: 5/14/1965, Navojoa, Mexico BR/TR, 6'3", 190 lbs. Deb: 4/26/1995																									
1995 Chi-A	0	1	.000	7	0	0	0	0	6^2	9	5	5	3	0	2	8	1.650	6.75	66	8.30	.321	0	....	-2	0	-0.2
• MARQUIS, Jason	Jason Scott Marquis b: 8/21/1978, Manhasset, NY BL/TR, 6'1", 185 lbs. Deb: 6/6/2000																									
2000 Atl-N	1	0	1.000	15	0	0	0	0	23^1	23	16	13	4	1	12	17	1.500	5.01	91	5.13	.261	0	.000	-1	1	-0.1
2001★ Atl-N	5	6	.455	38	16	0	0	0	129^1	113	62	50	14	4	59	98	1.330	3.48	127	3.70	.234	1	.032	13	8	1.0

YEAR	TM-L	W	L	PCT	G	GS	CG	SH	SV	IP	H	R	ER	HR	HB	BB	SO	RAT	ERA	ERA+	CERA	OAV	BH	AVG	PR+	WS	TPW
2002	Atl-N	8	9	.471	22	22	0	0	0	114^1	127	66	64	19	3	49	84	1.539	5.04	81	5.43	.283	5	.132	-14	3	-1.4
2003	Atl-N	0	0	....	21	2	0	0	1	40^2	43	27	25	3	2	18	19	1.500	5.53	76	4.45	.270	1	.500	-6	1	-0.5
Total	**4**	**14**	**15**	**.483**	**96**	**40**	**0**	**0**	**1**	**307^2**	**306**	**171**	**152**	**40**	**10**	**138**	**218**	**1.443**	**4.45**	**96**	**4.55**	**.260**	**7**	**.096**	**-8**	**13**	**-1.0**

• MARQUIS, Jim James Milburn Marquis b: 11/18/1900, Yoakum, TX d: 8/5/1992, Jackson, CA BR/TR, 5'11", 174 lbs. Deb: 8/8/1925

YEAR	TM-L	W	L	PCT	G	GS	CG	SH	SV	IP	H	R	ER	HR	HB	BB	SO	RAT	ERA	ERA+	CERA	OAV	BH	AVG	PR+	WS	TPW
1925	NY-A	0	0	....	2	0	0	0	0	7^1	12	8	8	1	0	6	0	2.455	9.82	43	10.31	.414	0	.000	-5	0	-0.5

• MARRERO, Connie Conrado Eugenio (Ramos) Marrero b: 5/1/1911, Las Villas, Cuba BR/TR, 5'5", 158 lbs. Deb: 4/21/1950

YEAR	TM-L	W	L	PCT	G	GS	CG	SH	SV	IP	H	R	ER	HR	HB	BB	SO	RAT	ERA	ERA+	CERA	OAV	BH	AVG	PR+	WS	TPW
1950	Was-A	6	10	.375	27	19	8	1	1	152	159	84	76	17	4	55	63	1.408	4.50	100	4.26	.269	6	.122	0	8	-0.1
1951	Was-A★	11	9	.550	25	25	16	2	0	187	198	87	81	8	3	71	66	1.439	3.90	105	3.85	.268	10	.164	6	11	0.5
1952	Was-A	11	8	.579	22	22	16	2	0	184^1	175	68	59	9	4	53	77	1.237	2.88	123	3.03	.249	5	.079	15	14	1.1
1953	Was-A	8	7	.533	22	20	10	2	2	145^2	130	56	49	14	5	48	65	1.222	3.03	129	3.28	.241	6	.125	13	10	1.1
1954	Was-A	3	6	.333	22	8	1	0	0	66^1	74	37	35	12	0	22	26	1.447	4.75	75	5.00	.287	0	.000	-8	1	-0.9
Total	**5**	**39**	**40**	**.494**	**118**	**94**	**51**	**7**	**3**	**735^1**	**736**	**332**	**300**	**60**	**16**	**249**	**297**	**1.340**	**3.67**	**108**	**3.72**	**.260**	**27**	**.114**	**27**	**44**	**1.6**

• MARROW, Buck Charles Kennon Marrow b: 8/29/1909, Tarboro, NC d: 11/21/1982, Newport News, VA BR/TR, 6'4", 200 lbs. Deb: 7/3/1932

YEAR	TM-L	W	L	PCT	G	GS	CG	SH	SV	IP	H	R	ER	HR	HB	BB	SO	RAT	ERA	ERA+	CERA	OAV	BH	AVG	PR+	WS	TPW
1932	Det-A	2	5	.286	18	7	2	0	1	63^2	70	40	34	6	6	29	31	1.555	4.81	98	5.08	.278	3	.158	-2	3	-0.2
1937	Bro-N	1	2	.333	6	3	1	0	0	16^1	19	13	12	2	0	9	2	1.714	6.61	61	5.61	.284	0	.000	-4	0	-0.5
1938	Bro-N	0	1	.000	15	0	0	0	0	19^2	23	10	10	1	3	11	6	1.729	4.58	85	5.57	.291	0	.000	-1	1	-0.1
Total	**3**	**3**	**8**	**.273**	**39**	**10**	**3**	**0**	**1**	**99^2**	**112**	**63**	**56**	**9**	**9**	**49**	**39**	**1.615**	**5.06**	**87**	**5.27**	**.282**	**3**	**.120**	**-7**	**4**	**-0.8**

• MARS, Ed Edward M. Mars b: 12/4/1866, Chicago, IL d: 12/9/1941, Chicago, IL, 5'9", 166 lbs. Deb: 8/12/1890

YEAR	TM-L	W	L	PCT	G	GS	CG	SH	SV	IP	H	R	ER	HR	HB	BB	SO	RAT	ERA	ERA+	CERA	OAV	BH	AVG	PR+	WS	TPW
1890	Syr-a	9	5	.643	16	14	14	0	0	121^1	132	80	63	2	5	49	59	1.492	4.67	75	....	.269	14	.275	-13	6	-0.8

• MARSHALL, Cuddles Clarence Westly Marshall b: 4/28/1925, Bellingham, WA BR/TR, 6'3", 200 lbs. Deb: 4/24/1946

YEAR	TM-L	W	L	PCT	G	GS	CG	SH	SV	IP	H	R	ER	HR	HB	BB	SO	RAT	ERA	ERA+	CERA	OAV	BH	AVG	PR+	WS	TPW
1946	NY-A	3	4	.429	23	11	1	0	0	81	96	49	48	4	0	56	32	1.877	5.33	65	5.92	.308	4	.143	-19	0	-2.1
1948	NY-A	0	0	....	1	0	0	0	0	1	0	0	0	0	0	3	0	3.000	0.00	....	5.85	.000	0	....	0	0	0.0
1949	NY-A	3	0	1.000	21	2	0	0	3	49^1	48	31	28	3	2	48	13	1.946	5.11	79	5.80	.259	1	.111	-7	1	-0.7
1950	StL-A	1	3	.250	28	2	0	0	1	53^2	72	52	47	1	1	51	24	2.292	7.88	63	7.43	.321	4	.333	-16	0	-1.4
Total	**4**	**7**	**7**	**.500**	**73**	**15**	**1**	**0**	**4**	**185**	**216**	**132**	**123**	**8**	**3**	**158**	**69**	**2.022**	**5.98**	**68**	**6.33**	**.300**	**9**	**.184**	**-42**	**1**	**-4.2**

• MARSHALL, Mike Michael Grant Marshall b: 1/15/1943, Adrian, MI BR/TR, 5'10", 180 lbs. Deb: 5/31/1967

YEAR	TM-L	W	L	PCT	G	GS	CG	SH	SV	IP	H	R	ER	HR	HB	BB	SO	RAT	ERA	ERA+	CERA	OAV	BH	AVG	PR+	WS	TPW
1967	Det-A	1	3	.250	37	0	0	0	10	59	51	15	13	6	2	20	41	1.203	1.98	165	3.25	.233	2	.222	8	7	0.9
1969	Sea-A	3	10	.231	20	14	3	1	0	87^2	99	54	50	8	2	35	47	1.529	5.13	71	4.73	.281	7	.259	-12	2	-0.9
1970	Hou-N	0	1	.000	4	0	0	0	0	5^1	8	5	5	0	1	4	5	2.250	8.44	46	8.98	.400	0	....	-3	0	-0.3
	Mon-N	3	7	.300	24	5	0	0	3	64^2	56	34	25	4	0	29	38	1.314	3.48	118	3.07	.225	1	.091	4	4	0.4
	Yr.	3	8	.273	28	5	0	0	3	70	64	39	30	4	1	33	43	1.386	3.86	105	3.52	.238	1	.091	1	4	0.2
1971	Mon-N	5	8	.385	66	0	0	0	23	111^1	100	56	53	9	4	50	85	1.347	4.28	82	3.57	.247	3	.188	-9	9	-0.9
1972	Mon-N	14	8	.636	**65**	0	0	0	18	116	82	26	23	3	2	47	95	1.112	1.78	199	2.12	.202	3	.136	23	22	2.5
1973	Mon-N	14	11	.560	**92**	0	0	0	**31**	179	163	62	53	10	4	75	124	1.330	2.66	143	3.42	.252	8	.242	23	23	2.5
1974*	LA-N★	15	12	.556	**106**	0	0	0	**21**	208^1	191	66	56	9	1	56	143	1.186	2.42	140	2.77	.247	8	.235	24	21	2.6
1975	LA-N★	9	14	.391	57	0	0	0	13	109^1	98	46	40	8	4	39	64	1.253	3.29	103	3.17	.242	1	.067	0	8	-0.1
1976	LA-N	4	3	.571	30	0	0	0	8	62^2	64	33	31	2	1	25	39	1.420	4.45	76	3.69	.270	0	.000	-9	4	-0.9
	Atl-N	2	1	.667	24	0	0	0	6	36^2	35	15	13	4	1	14	17	1.336	3.19	119	3.92	.259	1	.167	3	4	0.4
	Yr.	6	4	.600	54	0	0	0	14	99^1	99	48	44	6	2	39	56	1.389	3.99	88	3.78	.266	1	.091	-5	8	-0.5
1977	Atl-N	1	0	1.000	4	0	0	0	0	6	12	6	6	1	0	2	6	2.333	9.00	49	10.57	.400	1	1.000	-3	0	-0.2
	Tex-A	2	2	.500	12	4	0	0	1	35^2	42	19	16	0	2	13	18	1.542	4.04	101	4.46	.304	0	....	-0	2	0.0
1978	Min-A	10	12	.455	54	0	0	0	21	99	80	31	27	3	1	37	56	1.182	2.45	156	2.56	.225	0	....	15	14	1.5
1979	Min-A	10	15	.400	**90**	1	0	0	**32**	142^2	132	47	42	8	4	48	81	1.262	2.65	165	3.30	.254	0	....	28	23	2.7
1980	Min-A	1	3	.250	18	0	0	0	1	32^1	42	23	22	2	2	12	13	1.670	6.12	71	5.58	.323	0	....	-7	0	-0.6
1981	NY-N	3	2	.600	20	0	0	0	0	31	26	10	9	2	0	8	8	1.097	2.61	133	2.38	.224	0	....	3	3	0.4
Total	**14**	**97**	**112**	**.464**	**723**	**24**	**3**	**1**	**188**	**1386^2**	**1281**	**548**	**484**	**79**	**31**	**514**	**880**	**1.294**	**3.14**	**118**	**3.32**	**.249**	**35**	**.196**	**89**	**146**	**9.9**

• MARSHALL, Rube Roy De Verne "Cy" Marshall b: 1/19/1890, Salineville, OH d: 6/11/1980, Dover, OH BR/TR, 5'11", 170 lbs. Deb: 9/28/1912

YEAR	TM-L	W	L	PCT	G	GS	CG	SH	SV	IP	H	R	ER	HR	HB	BB	SO	RAT	ERA	ERA+	CERA	OAV	BH	AVG	PR+	WS	TPW
1912	Phi-N	0	1	.000	2	1	0	0	0	3	12	11	7	0	0	1	2	4.333	21.00	17	22.97	.632	0	....	-6	0	-0.6
1913	Phi-N	0	1	.000	14	1	0	0	1	45^1	54	29	23	2	1	22	18	1.676	4.57	73	5.03	.297	1	.091	-6	1	-0.7
1914	Phi-N	6	7	.462	27	17	7	0	1	134^1	144	77	56	2	5	50	49	1.444	3.75	78	3.77	.279	6	.140	-8	4	-1.1
1915	Buf-F	2	1	.667	21	4	2	0	0	59^1	62	34	26	1	2	33	21	1.601	3.94	78	4.52	.281	5	.294	-6	3	-0.5
Total	**4**	**8**	**10**	**.444**	**64**	**23**	**9**	**0**	**2**	**242**	**272**	**151**	**112**	**5**	**8**	**106**	**90**	**1.562**	**4.17**	**74**	**4.43**	**.290**	**12**	**.169**	**-26**	**8**	**-2.8**

• MARTE, Damaso Damaso (Sabinon) Marte b: 2/14/1975, Santo Domingo, Dominican Republic BL/TL, 6', 170 lbs. Deb: 6/30/1999

YEAR	TM-L	W	L	PCT	G	GS	CG	SH	SV	IP	H	R	ER	HR	HB	BB	SO	RAT	ERA	ERA+	CERA	OAV	BH	AVG	PR+	WS	TPW
1999	Sea-A	0	1	.000	5	0	0	0	0	8^2	16	9	9	3	0	6	3	2.538	9.35	53	13.32	.390	0	....	-4	0	-0.4
2001	Pit-N	0	1	.000	23	0	0	0	0	36^1	34	21	19	5	3	12	39	1.266	4.71	95	3.93	.250	0	.000	-1	1	-0.1
2002	Chi-A	1	1	.500	68	0	0	0	10	60^1	44	19	19	5	4	18	72	1.028	2.83	161	2.42	.204	0	.000	11	8	1.1
2003	Chi-A	4	2	.667	71	0	0	0	11	79^2	50	16	14	3	3	34	87	1.054	1.58	283	1.96	.185	0	....	25	15	2.4
Total	**4**	**5**	**5**	**.500**	**167**	**0**	**0**	**0**	**21**	**185**	**144**	**65**	**61**	**16**	**10**	**70**	**201**	**1.157**	**2.97**	**154**	**3.03**	**.217**	**0**	**.000**	**31**	**24**	**2.9**

• MARTIN, Barney Barnes Robertson Martin b: 3/3/1923, Columbia, SC d: 10/30/1997, Columbia, SC BR/TR, 5'11", 170 lbs. Deb: 4/22/1953

YEAR	TM-L	W	L	PCT	G	GS	CG	SH	SV	IP	H	R	ER	HR	HB	BB	SO	RAT	ERA	ERA+	CERA	OAV	BH	AVG	PR+	WS	TPW
1953	Cin-N	0	0	....	1	0	0	0	0	2	3	2	2	0	0	1	1	2.000	9.00	48	6.33	.333	0	....	-1	0	-0.1

• MARTIN, Doc Harold Winthrop Martin b: 9/23/1887, Roxbury, MA d: 4/14/1935, Milton, MA BR/TR, 5'11", 165 lbs. Deb: 10/7/1908

YEAR	TM-L	W	L	PCT	G	GS	CG	SH	SV	IP	H	R	ER	HR	HB	BB	SO	RAT	ERA	ERA+	CERA	OAV	BH	AVG	PR+	WS	TPW
1908	Phi-A	0	1	.000	1	1	0	0	0	2	2	4	3	0	1	3	2	2.500	13.50	19	9.59	.286	0	.000	-2	0	-0.3
1911	Phi-A	1	1	.500	11	3	1	0	0	38	40	26	19	1	5	17	21	1.500	4.50	70	4.44	.272	3	.214	-6	1	-0.6
1912	Phi-A	0	0	....	2	0	0	0	0	4^1	5	5	5	0	1	5	4	2.308	10.38	30	8.62	.333	0	.000	-4	0	-0.4
Total	**3**	**1**	**2**	**.333**	**14**	**4**	**1**	**0**	**0**	**44^1**	**47**	**35**	**27**	**1**	**7**	**25**	**27**	**1.624**	**5.48**	**56**	**5.08**	**.278**	**3**	**.167**	**-12**	**1**	**-1.2**

• MARTIN, Fred Fred Turner Martin b: 6/27/1915, Williams, OK d: 6/11/1979, Chicago, IL BR/TR, 6'1", 185 lbs. Deb: 4/21/1946 C

YEAR	TM-L	W	L	PCT	G	GS	CG	SH	SV	IP	H	R	ER	HR	HB	BB	SO	RAT	ERA	ERA+	CERA	OAV	BH	AVG	PR+	WS	TPW
1946	StL-N	2	1	.667	6	3	2	0	0	28^2	29	13	13	0	0	8	19	1.291	4.08	85	2.86	.254	3	.273	-2	2	-0.2
1949	StL-N	6	0	1.000	21	5	3	0	0	70	65	24	19	3	0	20	30	1.214	2.44	170	2.79	.243	6	.300	13	8	1.4
1950	StL-N	4	2	.667	30	2	0	0	0	63^1	87	43	36	4	1	30	19	1.847	5.12	84	6.29	.331	4	.267	-5	2	-0.4
Total	**3**	**12**	**3**	**.800**	**57**	**10**	**5**	**0**	**0**	**162**	**181**	**80**	**68**	**7**	**1**	**58**	**68**	**1.475**	**3.78**	**108**	**4.17**	**.281**	**13**	**.283**	**5**	**12**	**0.7**

• MARTIN, John John Robert Martin b: 4/11/1956, Wyandotte, MI BB/TL, 6', 190 lbs. Deb: 8/27/1980

YEAR	TM-L	W	L	PCT	G	GS	CG	SH	SV	IP	H	R	ER	HR	HB	BB	SO	RAT	ERA	ERA+	CERA	OAV	BH	AVG	PR+	WS	TPW
1980	StL-N	2	3	.400	9	5	1	0	0	42	39	20	20	1	0	9	23	1.143	4.29	86	2.51	.247	3	.273	-3	2	-0.3
1981	StL-N	8	5	.615	17	15	4	0	0	102^2	85	43	39	10	2	26	36	1.081	3.42	104	2.73	.228	7	.212	-0	6	0.2
1982	StL-N	4	5	.444	24	7	0	0	0	66	56	33	31	6	0	30	21	1.303	4.23	86	3.36	.230	1	.091	-6	2	-0.7
1983	StL-N	3	1	.750	26	5	0	0	0	66^1	60	31	26	6	2	26	29	1.296	3.53	103	3.44	.242	4	.222	1	4	0.2
	Det-A	0	0	....	15	0	0	0	1	13^1	15	11	11	2	0	4	11	1.425	7.43	53	4.78	.294	0	....	-5	0	-0.5
Total	**4**	**17**	**14**	**.548**	**91**	**32**	**5**	**0**	**1**	**290^1**	**255**	**138**	**127**	**25**	**4**	**95**	**120**	**1.206**	**3.94**	**92**	**3.10**	**.238**	**15**	**.205**	**-14**	**14**	**-1.1**

• MARTIN, Morrie Morris Webster "Lefty" Martin b: 9/3/1922, Dixon, MO BL/TL, 6', 180 lbs. Deb: 4/25/1949

YEAR	TM-L	W	L	PCT	G	GS	CG	SH	SV	IP	H	R	ER	HR	HB	BB	SO	RAT	ERA	ERA+	CERA	OAV	BH	AVG	PR+	WS	TPW
1949	Bro-N	1	3	.250	10	4	0	0	0	30^2	39	25	24	5	2	15	15	1.761	7.04	58	6.78	.320	2	.200	-11	0	-1.1
1951	Phi-A	11	4	.733	35	13	3	1	0	138	139	70	58	13	5	63	35	1.464	3.78	113	4.30	.259	11	.220	5	9	0.5
1952	Phi-A	0	2	.000	5	5	0	0	0	25^1	32	19	18	1	2	15	13	1.855	6.39	62	5.99	.302	1	.111	-6	0	-0.7
1953	Phi-A	10	12	.455	58	11	2	0	7	156^1	158	85	77	12	8	59	64	1.388	4.43	97	3.97	.262	4	.095	-2	10	-0.6
1954	Phi-A	2	4	.333	13	6	2	0	0	52^2	57	32	32	9	2	19	24	1.443	5.47	71	4.93	.278	4	.235	-8	1	-0.8
	Chi-A	5	4	.556	35	2	1	0	5	70	52	18	16	5	1	24	31	1.086	2.06	181	2.35	.210	2	.133	12	8	1.2
	Yr.	7	8	.467	48	8	3	0	5	122^2	109	50	48	14	3	43	55	1.239	3.52	109	3.46	.241	6	.188	4	9	0.4
1955	Chi-A	2	3	.400	37	0	0	0	2	52	50	27	21	4	2	20	22	1.346	3.63	109	3.73	.259	3	.300	1	3	0.1

YEAR TM-L	W	L	PCT	G	GS	CG	SH	SV	IP	H	R	ER	HR	HB	BB	SO	RAT	ERA	ERA+	CERA	OAV	BH	AVG	PR+	WS	TPW
1956 Chi-A	1	0	1.000	10	0	0	0	0	18^1	21	10	10	1	0	7	9	1.527	4.91	84	4.56	.292	1	.200	-2	1	-0.2
Bal-A	1	1	.500	9	0	0	0	0	5	10	6	6	1	1	2	3	2.400	10.80	36	11.78	.400	0	....	-4	0	-0.4
Yr.	2	1	.667	19	0	0	0	0	23^1	31	16	16	2	1	9	12	1.714	6.17	65	6.11	.320	1	.200	-6	1	-0.5
1957 StL-N	0	0	....	4	1	0	0	0	10^2	5	3	3	0	1	4	7	.844	2.53	157	1.29	.143	0	.000	2	1	0.1
1958 StL-N	3	1	.750	17	0	0	0	0	24^2	19	13	13	3	2	12	16	1.257	4.74	87	3.65	.211	0	.000	-2	2	-0.2
Cle-A	2	0	1.000	14	0	0	0	1	18^2	20	7	5	0	0	8	5	1.500	2.41	151	3.97	.294	0	....	2	2	0.3
1959 Chi-N	0	0	....	3	0	0	0	0	2^1	5	5	5	2	1	1	1	2.571	19.29	20	21.79	.455	0	....	-4	0	-0.4
Total 10	38	34	.528	250	42	8	1	15	604^2	607	320	288	56	27	249	245	1.416	4.29	96	4.24	.262	28	.170	-16	37	-2.1

• MARTIN, Pat — Patrick Francis Martin b: 4/13/1894, Brooklyn, NY d: 2/4/1949, Brooklyn, NY BL/TL, 5'11.5", 170 lbs. Deb: 9/20/1919

YEAR TM-L	W	L	PCT	G	GS	CG	SH	SV	IP	H	R	ER	HR	HB	BB	SO	RAT	ERA	ERA+	CERA	OAV	BH	AVG	PR+	WS	TPW
1919 Phi-A	0	2	.000	2	2	1	0	0	11	11	8	5	0	0	8	6	1.727	4.09	84	4.34	.256	0	.000	-0	0	-0.1
1920 Phi-A	1	4	.200	8	5	2	0	0	32^1	48	36	22	2	4	25	14	2.258	6.12	66	9.06	.364	4	.400	-7	0	-0.6
Total 2	1	6	.143	10	7	3	0	0	43^1	59	44	27	2	4	33	20	2.123	5.61	69	7.86	.337	4	.308	-7	0	-0.6

• MARTIN, Paul — Paul Charles Martin b: 3/10/1932, Brownstown, PA BR/TR, 6'6", 235 lbs. Deb: 7/2/1955

YEAR TM-L	W	L	PCT	G	GS	CG	SH	SV	IP	H	R	ER	HR	HB	BB	SO	RAT	ERA	ERA+	CERA	OAV	BH	AVG	PR+	WS	TPW
1955 Pit-N	0	1	.000	7	1	0	0	0	7	13	12	11	0	1	17	3	4.286	14.14	29	19.45	.464	0	....	-8	0	-0.8

• MARTIN, Phonney — Alphonse Case Martin b: 8/4/1845, New York, NY d: 5/24/1933, Hollis, NY, 5'7", 148 lbs. Deb: 4/26/1872 U ♦

YEAR TM-L	W	L	PCT	G	GS	CG	SH	SV	IP	H	R	ER	HR	HB	BB	SO	RAT	ERA	ERA+	CERA	OAV	BH	AVG	PR+	WS	TPW
1872 Tro-n	1	2	.333	8	3	0	0	0	37^1	70	59	20	0	....	2	1	1.929	4.82	64	....	.354	36	.308	-10	....	-0.7
Eck-n	2	7	.222	10	9	9	0	0	85	144	106	40	1	....	4	2	1.741	4.24	78	....	.331	12	.154	-1	....	-0.3
Yr.	3	9	.250	18	12	9	0	0	122^1	214	165	60	1	....	6	3	1.798	4.41	73	....	.338	48	.246	-11	....	-1.0
1873 Mut-n	0	1	.000	6	1	1	0	0	34	50	37	13	0	....	7	1	1.676	3.44	92	....	.304	31	.221	-0	....	-1.0
Total 2 n	3	10	.231	24	13	10	0	0	156^1	264	202	73	1	....	13	4	1.772	4.20	77	....	.331	79	.236	-11	....	-2.0

• MARTIN, Ray — Raymond Joseph Martin b: 3/13/1925, Norwood, MA BR/TR, 6'2", 177 lbs. Deb: 8/15/1943

YEAR TM-L	W	L	PCT	G	GS	CG	SH	SV	IP	H	R	ER	HR	HB	BB	SO	RAT	ERA	ERA+	CERA	OAV	BH	AVG	PR+	WS	TPW
1943 Bos-N	0	0	....	2	0	0	0	0	3^1	3	3	3	0	0	1	1	1.200	8.10	42	2.39	.231	0	.000	-2	0	-0.2
1947 Bos-N	1	0	1.000	1	1	1	0	0	9	7	1	1	0	0	4	2	1.222	1.00	390	2.33	.212	0	.000	3	1	0.3
1948 Bos-N	0	0	....	2	0	0	0	0	2^1	0	0	0	0	0	1	0	.429	0.00	....	0.17	.000	0	....	1	0	0.1
Total 3	1	0	1.000	5	1	1	0	0	14^2	10	4	4	0	0	6	3	1.091	2.45	143	2.00	.217	0	.000	2	1	0.2

• MARTIN, Renie — Donald Renie Martin b: 8/30/1955, Dover, DE BR/TR, 6'4", 190 lbs. Deb: 5/9/1979

YEAR TM-L	W	L	PCT	G	GS	CG	SH	SV	IP	H	R	ER	HR	HB	BB	SO	RAT	ERA	ERA+	CERA	OAV	BH	AVG	PR+	WS	TPW
1979 KC-A	0	3	.000	25	0	0	0	5	34^2	32	20	20	1	1	14	25	1.327	5.19	82	3.12	.248	0	....	-4	2	-0.4
1980* KC-A	10	10	.500	32	20	2	0	2	137^1	133	84	67	18	1	70	68	1.478	4.39	92	4.60	.255	0	....	-5	5	-0.5
1981* KC-A	4	5	.444	29	0	0	0	4	61^2	55	25	19	2	0	29	25	1.362	2.77	130	3.09	.244	0	....	6	5	0.6
1982 SF-N	7	10	.412	29	25	1	0	0	141^1	148	91	73	14	0	64	63	1.500	4.65	77	4.46	.274	13	.265	-14	2	-1.1
1983 SF-N	2	4	.333	37	6	0	0	1	94^1	95	50	44	11	3	51	43	1.548	4.20	84	4.87	.268	9	.346	-6	4	-0.2
1984 SF-N	1	1	.500	12	0	0	0	0	23^1	29	13	10	2	0	16	8	1.929	3.86	91	6.61	.305	3	.500	-0	1	0.1
Phi-N	0	2	.000	9	0	0	0	0	15^2	17	12	8	2	0	12	5	1.851	4.60	79	5.57	.274	0	.000	-1	0	-0.2
Yr.	1	3	.250	21	0	0	0	0	39	46	25	18	4	0	28	13	1.897	4.15	86	6.19	.293	3	.375	-2	1	-0.1
Total 6	24	35	.407	173	51	3	0	12	508^1	509	295	241	50	5	256	237	1.505	4.27	88	4.45	.264	25	.301	-25	19	-1.6

• MARTIN, Speed — Elwood Good Martin b: 9/15/1893, Wawawai, WA d: 6/14/1983, Lemon Grove, CA BR/TR, 6', 165 lbs. Deb: 7/5/1917

YEAR TM-L	W	L	PCT	G	GS	CG	SH	SV	IP	H	R	ER	HR	HB	BB	SO	RAT	ERA	ERA+	CERA	OAV	BH	AVG	PR+	WS	TPW
1917 StL-A	0	2	.000	9	2	0	0	0	15^2	20	13	10	0	0	5	5	1.596	5.74	45	4.99	.339	0	.000	-5	0	-0.6
1918 Chi-N	5	2	.714	9	5	4	1	1	53^2	47	19	11	0	1	14	16	1.137	1.84	151	2.27	.246	3	.188	7	5	0.7
1919 Chi-N	8	8	.500	35	14	7	2	2	163^2	158	58	45	2	4	52	54	1.283	2.47	116	3.04	.259	8	.182	9	11	0.9
1920 Chi-N	4	15	.211	35	13	6	0	2	136	165	96	73	2	1	50	44	1.581	4.83	66	4.38	.305	7	.159	-23	0	-2.5
1921 Chi-N	11	15	.423	37	28	13	1	1	217^1	245	115	105	12	2	68	86	1.440	4.35	88	4.18	.298	17	.233	-13	12	-1.1
1922 Chi-N	1	0	1.000	1	1	0	0	0	6	10	5	5	0	0	2	2	2.000	7.50	56	7.23	.385	0	.000	-2	0	-0.2
Total 6	29	42	.408	126	63	30	4	6	592^1	645	306	249	16	8	191	207	1.411	3.78	88	3.79	.287	35	.194	-28	28	-2.8

• MARTIN, Tom — Thomas Edgar Martin b: 5/21/1970, Charleston, SC BL/TL, 6'1", 185 lbs. Deb: 4/2/1997

YEAR TM-L	W	L	PCT	G	GS	CG	SH	SV	IP	H	R	ER	HR	HB	BB	SO	RAT	ERA	ERA+	CERA	OAV	BH	AVG	PR+	WS	TPW
1997* Hou-N	5	3	.625	55	0	0	0	2	56	52	13	13	2	1	23	36	1.339	2.09	191	3.34	.254	0	.000	11	7	1.1
1998 Cle-A	1	1	.500	14	0	0	0	0	14^2	29	21	21	3	0	12	9	2.795	12.89	37	13.19	.408	0	....	-13	0	-1.2
1999 Cle-A	0	1	.000	6	0	0	0	0	9^1	13	9	9	2	0	3	8	1.714	8.68	58	6.64	.325	0	....	-4	0	-0.3
2000 Cle-A	1	0	1.000	31	0	0	0	0	33^1	32	16	15	3	1	15	21	1.410	4.05	123	4.05	.254	0	....	4	2	0.3
2001 NY-N	1	0	1.000	14	0	0	0	0	17	23	22	19	4	1	10	12	1.941	10.06	41	8.02	.319	0	.000	-11	0	-1.1
2002 TB-A	0	0	....	2	0	0	0	0	1^2	5	3	3	0	0	1	1	3.600	16.20	28	17.54	.500	0	....	-2	0	-0.2
2003 LA-N	1	2	.333	80	0	0	0	0	51	36	21	20	6	2	24	51	1.176	3.53	114	2.94	.198	0	.000	2	5	0.2
Total 7	9	7	.563	202	0	0	0	2	183	190	105	100	20	5	88	138	1.519	4.92	90	4.88	.269	0	.000	-14	14	-1.3

• MARTINA, Joe — Joseph John "Oyster Joe" Martina b: 7/8/1889, New Orleans, LA d: 3/22/1962, New Orleans, LA BR/TR, 6', 183 lbs. Deb: 4/19/1924

YEAR TM-L	W	L	PCT	G	GS	CG	SH	SV	IP	H	R	ER	HR	HB	BB	SO	RAT	ERA	ERA+	CERA	OAV	BH	AVG	PR+	WS	TPW
1924* Was-A	6	8	.429	24	14	8	0	0	125^1	129	69	65	7	6	56	57	1.476	4.67	86	4.09	.271	14	.326	-12	6	-0.9

• MARTINEZ, Alfredo — Alfredo Martinez b: 3/15/1957, Los Angeles, CA BR/TR, 6'3", 185 lbs. Deb: 4/20/1980

YEAR TM-L	W	L	PCT	G	GS	CG	SH	SV	IP	H	R	ER	HR	HB	BB	SO	RAT	ERA	ERA+	CERA	OAV	BH	AVG	PR+	WS	TPW
1980 Cal-A	7	9	.438	30	23	4	1	0	149^1	150	81	75	14	1	59	57	1.400	4.52	87	4.01	.259	0	....	-9	6	-0.9
1981 Cal-A	0	0	....	2	0	0	0	0	6	5	2	2	1	0	3	4	1.333	3.00	122	4.10	.227	0	....	0	0	0.0
Total 2	7	9	.438	32	23	4	1	0	155^1	155	83	77	15	1	62	61	1.397	4.46	88	4.01	.257	0	....	-9	6	-0.9

• MARTINEZ, Dennis — Jose Dennis (Emilia) "El Presidente" Martinez b: 5/14/1955, Granada, Nicaragua BR/TR, 6'1", 185 lbs. Deb: 9/14/1976

YEAR TM-L	W	L	PCT	G	GS	CG	SH	SV	IP	H	R	ER	HR	HB	BB	SO	RAT	ERA	ERA+	CERA	OAV	BH	AVG	PR+	WS	TPW
1976 Bal-A	1	2	.333	4	2	1	0	0	27^2	23	8	8	1	0	8	18	1.120	2.60	126	2.54	.237	0	....	2	2	0.2
1977 Bal-A	14	7	.667	42	13	5	0	4	166^2	157	86	76	10	8	64	107	1.326	4.10	92	3.58	.253	0	....	-10	10	-1.0
1978 Bal-A	16	11	.593	40	38	15	2	0	276^1	257	121	108	20	3	93	142	1.267	3.52	99	3.35	.250	0	....	-4	16	-0.5
1979* Bal-A	15	16	.484	40	**39**	**18**	3	0	**292^1**	279	129	119	28	1	78	132	1.221	3.66	109	3.31	.253	0	....	6	18	0.6
1980 Bal-A	6	4	.600	25	12	2	0	1	99^2	103	44	44	12	2	44	42	1.475	3.97	99	4.68	.272	0	....	-2	6	-0.2
1981 Bal-A	**14**	5	.737	25	24	9	2	0	179	173	84	66	10	2	62	88	1.313	3.32	109	3.44	.254	0	....	7	12	0.7
1982 Bal-A	16	12	.571	40	39	10	2	0	252	262	123	118	30	7	87	111	1.385	4.21	96	4.30	.267	0	....	-5	14	-0.5
1983 Bal-A	7	16	.304	32	25	4	0	0	153	209	108	94	21	2	45	71	1.660	5.53	71	6.25	.330	0	....	-26	0	-2.6
1984 Bal-A	6	9	.400	34	20	2	0	0	141^2	145	81	79	26	5	37	77	1.285	5.02	77	4.36	.263	0	....	-21	3	-2.1
1985 Bal-A	13	11	.542	33	31	3	1	0	180	203	110	103	29	9	63	68	1.478	5.15	78	5.30	.288	0	....	-21	5	-2.0
1986 Bal-A	0	0	....	4	0	0	0	0	6^2	11	5	5	0	0	2	2	1.950	6.75	61	6.57	.367	0	....	-2	0	-0.2
Mon-N	3	6	.333	19	15	1	1	0	98	103	52	50	11	3	28	63	1.337	4.59	80	4.09	.274	3	.100	-10	2	-1.1
1987 Mon-N	11	4	.733	22	22	2	1	0	144^2	133	59	53	9	6	40	84	1.196	3.30	127	3.07	.244	3	.065	17	11	1.4
1988 Mon-N	15	13	.536	34	34	9	2	0	235^1	215	94	71	21	6	55	120	1.147	2.72	132	2.97	.239	15	.192	20	15	2.3
1989 Mon-N	16	7	.696	34	33	5	2	0	232	227	88	82	21	7	49	142	1.190	3.18	111	3.30	.257	9	.125	10	16	1.0
1990 Mon-N★	10	11	.476	32	32	7	2	0	226	191	80	74	16	6	49	156	1.062	2.95	124	2.44	.228	7	.103	17	15	1.6
1991 Mon-N★	14	11	.560	31	31	**9**	**5**	0	222	187	70	59	9	4	62	123	1.122	**2.39**	151	2.46	.226	11	.153	28	18	2.9
1992 Mon-N★	16	11	.593	32	32	6	0	0	226^1	172	75	62	12	9	60	147	1.025	2.47	140	2.19	.211	14	.189	25	17	2.8
1993 Mon-N	15	9	.625	35	34	2	0	1	224^2	211	110	96	27	11	64	138	1.224	3.85	108	3.56	.246	11	.159	8	12	0.8
1994 Cle-A	11	6	.647	24	24	7	3	0	176^2	166	75	69	14	7	44	92	1.189	3.52	134	3.18	.247	0	....	24	14	2.2
1995* Cle-A★	12	5	.706	28	28	3	2	0	187	174	71	64	17	12	46	99	1.176	3.08	152	3.31	.247	0	....	34	16	3.2
1996 Cle-A	9	6	.600	20	20	1	1	0	112	122	63	56	12	2	37	48	1.420	4.50	109	4.43	.278	0	....	5	7	0.5
1997 Sea-A	1	5	.167	9	9	0	0	0	49	65	46	42	8	7	29	17	1.918	7.71	58	8.11	.327	0	....	-17	0	-1.6
1998* Atl-N	4	6	.400	53	5	1	1	2	91	109	53	45	8	3	19	62	1.407	4.45	94	4.37	.295	1	.091	-4	4	-0.4
Total 23	245	193	.559	692	562	122	30	8	3999^2	3897	1835	1643	372	122	1165	2149	1.266	3.70	106	3.62	.256	74	.142	79	233	7.9

• MARTINEZ, Javier — Javier Antonio Martinez b: 2/5/1977, Bayamon, Puerto Rico BR/TR, 6'2" Deb: 4/2/1998

YEAR TM-L	W	L	PCT	G	GS	CG	SH	SV	IP	H	R	ER	HR	HB	BB	SO	RAT	ERA	ERA+	CERA	OAV	BH	AVG	PR+	WS	TPW
1998 Pit-N	0	1	.000	37	0	0	0	0	41	39	32	22	5	4	34	42	1.780	4.83	89	5.94	.248	0	.000	-3	0	-0.3

• MARTINEZ, Jose — Jose Miguel (Martinez) Martinez b: 4/1/1971, Guayubin, Dominican Republic BR/TR, 6'2", 180 lbs. Deb: 5/10/1994

YEAR TM-L	W	L	PCT	G	GS	CG	SH	SV	IP	H	R	ER	HR	HB	BB	SO	RAT	ERA	ERA+	CERA	OAV	BH	AVG	PR+	WS	TPW
1994 SD-N	0	2	.000	4	1	0	0	0	12	18	9	9	2	0	5	7	1.917	6.75	61	7.96	.375	0	.000	-3	0	-0.3

YEAR TM-L	W	L	PCT	G	GS	CG	SH	SV	IP	H	R	ER	HR	HB	BB	SO	RAT	ERA	ERA+	CERA	OAV	BH	AVG	PR+	WS	TPW
• MARTINEZ, Luis	Luis Martinez b: 1/20/1980, Santo Domingo, Dominican Republic BL/TL, 6'6", 200 lbs. Deb: 9/3/2003																									
2003 Mil-N	0	3	.000	4	4	0	0	0	16^{1}	25	18	18	3	0	15	10	2.449	9.92	43	10.34	.373	0	.000	-10	0	-1.0
• MARTINEZ, Pedro	Pedro Jaime Martinez b: 10/25/1971, Manoguayabo, Dominican Republic BR/TR, 5'11", 170 lbs. Deb: 9/24/1992																									
1992 LA-N	0	1	.000	2	1	0	0	0	8	6	2	2	0	0	1	8	.875	2.25	153	1.38	.200	0	.000	1	1	0.1
1993 LA-N	10	5	.667	65	2	0	0	2	107	76	34	31	5	4	57	119	1.243	2.61	146	2.79	.201	0	.000	15	12	1.4
1994 Mon-N	11	5	.688	24	23	1	1	1	144^{2}	115	58	55	11	11	45	142	1.106	3.42	123	2.81	.220	4	.091	13	11	1.2
1995 Mon-N	14	10	.583	30	30	2	2	0	194^{2}	158	79	76	21	11	66	174	1.151	3.51	122	3.19	.227	7	.111	19	14	1.6
1996 Mon-N★	13	10	.565	33	33	4	1	0	216^{2}	189	100	89	19	3	70	222	1.195	3.70	117	3.02	.232	6	.094	16	14	1.4
1997 Mon-N★	17	8	.680	31	31	**13**	4	0	241^{1}	158	65	51	16	9	67	305	.932	**1.90**	**221**	**1.79**	**.184**	8	.116	**61**	**26**	**6.0**
1998* Bos-A★	19	7	.731	33	33	3	2	0	233^{2}	188	82	75	26	8	67	251	1.091	2.89	163	2.78	.217	0	.000	45	21	4.2
1999* Bos-A★	**23**	4	.852	31	29	5	1	0	213^{1}	160	56	49	9	9	37	**313**	.923	**2.07**	**240**	**1.79**	**.205**	0	.000	**69**	**27**	**6.3**
2000 Bos-A★	18	6	.750	29	29	7	**4**	0	217	128	44	42	17	14	32	**284**	.737	**1.74**	**289**	**1.39**	**.167**	0	....	**79**	**29**	**7.3**
2001 Bos-A	7	3	.700	18	18	1	0	0	116^{2}	84	33	31	5	6	25	163	.934	2.39	187	1.84	.199	0	....	29	12	2.8
2002 Bos-A★	20	4	.833	30	30	2	0	0	199^{1}	144	62	50	13	15	40	**239**	.923	**2.26**	**199**	**1.98**	**.198**	0	.000	46	21	**4.4**
2003* Bos-A	14	4	.778	29	29	3	0	0	186^{2}	147	52	46	7	9	47	206	1.039	**2.22**	**206**	**2.22**	**.215**	0	.000	**52**	20	**5.0**
Total 12	166	67	.712	355	288	41	15	3	2079	1553	667	597	149	99	554	2426	1.013	2.58	172	2.30	.206	25	.095	447	208	41.7
• MARTINEZ, Pedro	Pedro (Aquino) Martinez b: 11/29/1968, Villa Mella, Dominican Republic BL/TL, 6'2", 185 lbs. Deb: 6/29/1993																									
1993 SD-N	3	1	.750	32	0	0	0	0	37	23	11	10	4	1	13	32	.973	2.43	170	2.04	.172	0	.000	7	4	0.7
1994 SD-N	3	2	.600	48	1	0	0	3	68^{1}	52	31	22	4	1	49	52	1.478	2.90	142	3.40	.210	0	.000	11	6	1.0
1995 Hou-N	0	0	....	25	0	0	0	0	20^{2}	29	18	17	3	2	16	17	2.177	7.40	52	8.69	.330	0	....	-8	0	-0.7
1996 NY-N	0	0	....	5	0	0	0	0	7	8	7	5	1	0	7	6	2.143	6.43	63	6.44	.296	0	....	-2	0	-0.2
Cin-N	0	0	....	4	0	0	0	0	3	5	2	2	1	0	1	3	2.000	6.00	69	9.75	.357	0	....	-1	0	-0.1
Yr.	0	0	....	9	0	0	0	0	10	13	9	7	2	0	8	9	2.100	6.30	64	7.43	.317	0	....	-3	0	-0.3
1997 Cin-N	1	1	.500	8	0	0	0	0	6^{2}	8	9	7	1	1	7	4	2.250	9.45	46	8.70	.286	0	....	-4	0	-0.4
Total 5	7	4	.636	122	1	0	0	3	142^{2}	125	78	63	14	5	93	114	1.528	3.97	102	4.34	.232	0	.000	4	10	0.3
• MARTINEZ, Ramon	Ramon Jaime Martinez b: 3/22/1968, Santo Domingo, Dominican Republic BR/TR, 6'4", 173 lbs. Deb: 8/13/1988																									
1988 LA-N	1	3	.250	9	6	0	0	0	35^{2}	27	17	15	0	0	22	23	1.374	3.79	88	2.87	.216	0	.000	-1	1	-0.2
1989 LA-N	6	4	.600	15	15	2	2	0	98^{2}	79	39	35	11	5	41	89	1.216	3.19	107	3.34	.219	6	.162	2	5	0.2
1990 LA-N★	20	6	.769	33	33	**12**	3	0	234^{1}	191	89	76	22	4	67	223	1.101	2.92	125	2.66	.220	10	.125	18	17	1.7
1991 LA-N	17	13	.567	33	33	6	4	0	220^{1}	190	89	80	18	7	69	150	1.175	3.27	110	2.96	.229	9	.117	8	14	0.7
1992 LA-N	8	11	.421	25	25	1	1	0	150^{2}	141	82	67	11	5	69	101	1.394	4.00	86	3.78	.245	6	.120	-6	3	-0.8
1993 LA-N	10	12	.455	32	32	4	3	0	211^{2}	202	88	81	15	4	104	127	1.446	3.44	111	4.00	.255	9	.129	9	13	0.7
1994 LA-N	12	7	.632	24	24	4	**3**	0	170	160	83	75	18	6	56	119	1.271	3.97	99	3.64	.249	18	.273	-0	10	0.4
1995* LA-N	17	7	.708	30	30	4	2	0	206^{1}	176	95	84	19	5	81	138	1.246	3.66	104	3.28	.231	11	.172	3	13	0.4
1996* LA-N	15	6	.714	28	27	2	2	0	168^{2}	153	76	64	12	8	86	133	1.417	3.42	113	3.94	.245	7	.119	10	12	0.8
1997 LA-N	10	5	.667	22	22	1	0	0	133^{2}	123	64	54	14	6	68	120	1.429	3.64	106	4.22	.243	8	.190	5	8	0.5
1998 LA-N	7	3	.700	15	15	1	0	0	101^{2}	76	41	32	8	3	41	91	1.151	2.83	140	2.71	.206	6	.176	13	8	1.4
1999* Bos-A	2	1	.667	4	4	0	0	0	20^{2}	14	8	7	2	2	8	15	1.065	3.05	163	2.69	.192	0	....	4	2	0.4
2000 Bos-A	10	8	.556	27	27	0	0	0	127^{2}	143	94	87	16	9	67	89	1.645	6.13	82	5.71	.283	1	.200	-16	4	-1.4
2001 Pit-N	0	2	.000	4	4	0	0	0	15^{2}	16	15	15	4	2	16	9	2.043	8.62	52	9.01	.276	0	.000	-7	0	-0.7
Total 14	135	88	.605	301	297	37	20	0	1895^{2}	1691	880	772	170	66	795	1427	1.311	3.67	105	3.61	.239	91	.153	42	110	3.9
• MARTINEZ, Rogelio	Rogelio (Ulloa) "Limonar" Martinez b: 11/5/1918, Cidra, Cuba BR/TR, 6', 180 lbs. Deb: 7/13/1950																									
1950 Was-A	0	1	.000	2	1	0	0	0	1^{1}	4	4	4	0	0	2	0	4.500	27.00	17	21.38	.500	0	....	-3	0	-0.3
• MARTINEZ, Silvio	Silvio Ramon (Cabrera) Martinez b: 8/19/1955, Santiago, Dominican Republic BR/TR, 5'10", 170 lbs. Deb: 4/9/1977																									
1977 Chi-A	0	1	.000	10	0	0	0	1	21	28	14	13	4	0	12	10	1.905	5.57	73	7.52	.337	0	....	-3	0	-0.3
1978 StL-N	9	8	.529	22	22	5	2	0	138^{1}	114	65	56	11	2	71	45	1.337	3.64	97	3.41	.228	8	.170	-3	6	-0.3
1979 StL-N	15	8	.652	32	29	7	2	0	206^{2}	204	92	75	14	0	67	102	1.311	3.27	115	3.50	.259	8	.129	7	14	0.5
1980 StL-N	5	10	.333	25	20	2	0	0	119^{2}	127	75	64	8	2	48	39	1.462	4.81	77	4.20	.273	3	.086	-17	1	-1.9
1981 StL-N	2	5	.286	18	16	0	0	0	97	95	48	43	4	1	39	34	1.381	3.99	89	3.58	.260	7	.200	-6	3	-0.6
Total 5	31	32	.492	107	87	14	4	1	582^{2}	568	294	251	41	5	237	230	1.382	3.88	95	3.78	.258	26	.145	-22	24	-2.6
• MARTINEZ, Tippy	Felix Anthony Martinez b: 3/31/1950, La Junta, CO BL/TL, 5'10" Deb: 8/9/1974																									
1974 NY-A	0	0	....	10	0	0	0	0	12^{2}	14	7	6	0	1	9	10	1.816	4.26	82	5.16	.286	0	....	-1	0	-0.1
1975 NY-A	1	2	.333	23	2	0	0	8	37	27	15	11	2	1	32	20	1.595	2.68	136	3.97	.208	0	....	3	4	0.3
1976 NY-A	2	0	1.000	11	0	0	0	2	28	18	6	6	1	0	14	14	1.143	1.93	177	2.33	.191	0	....	4	3	0.4
Bal-A	3	1	.750	28	0	0	0	8	41^{2}	32	13	12	0	1	28	31	1.440	2.59	126	3.14	.222	0	....	3	5	0.3
Yr.	5	1	.833	39	0	0	0	10	69^{2}	50	19	18	1	1	42	45	1.321	2.33	143	2.82	.210	0	....	6	8	0.7
1977 Bal-A	5	1	.833	41	0	0	0	9	50	47	17	15	2	0	27	29	1.480	2.70	140	3.97	.266	0	....	5	7	0.5
1978 Bal-A	3	3	.500	42	0	0	0	5	69	77	41	37	4	1	40	57	1.696	4.83	72	5.13	.281	0	....	-11	1	-1.1
1979* Bal-A	10	3	.769	39	0	0	0	3	78	59	29	25	0	1	31	61	1.154	2.88	139	2.13	.210	0	....	8	9	0.8
1980 Bal-A	4	4	.500	53	0	0	0	10	80^{2}	69	30	27	5	1	34	68	1.277	3.01	131	3.18	.240	0	....	7	8	0.7
1981 Bal-A	3	3	.500	37	0	0	0	11	59	48	21	19	4	0	32	50	1.356	2.90	125	3.28	.231	0	....	5	7	0.5
1982 Bal-A	8	8	.500	76	0	0	0	16	95	81	39	36	6	1	37	78	1.242	3.41	118	3.02	.240	0	....	6	12	0.6
1983* Bal-A★	9	3	.750	65	0	0	0	21	103^{1}	76	30	27	10	0	37	81	1.094	2.35	168	2.55	.211	0	....	19	17	1.9
1984 Bal-A	4	9	.308	55	0	0	0	17	89^{2}	88	42	39	9	0	51	72	1.550	3.91	99	4.35	.260	0	....	-2	7	-0.2
1985 Bal-A	3	3	.500	49	0	0	0	4	70	70	48	42	8	0	37	47	1.529	5.40	75	4.47	.261	0	....	-10	2	-1.0
1986 Bal-A	0	2	.000	14	0	0	0	1	16	18	10	10	1	0	12	11	1.875	5.63	73	5.99	.295	0	....	-3	0	-0.3
1988 Min-A	0	0	....	3	0	0	0	0	4	8	9	8	1	1	4	3	3.000	18.00	23	16.72	.471	0	....	-6	0	-0.6
Total 14	55	42	.567	546	2	0	0	115	834	732	357	320	53	8	425	632	1.387	3.45	111	3.59	.242	0	....	26	82	2.6
• MARTINEZ, Willie	William Jose Martinez b: 1/4/1978, Barquisimeto, Venezuela BR/TR, 6'2", 180 lbs. Deb: 6/14/2000																									
2000 Cle-A	0	0	....	1	0	0	0	0	3	1	1	1	0	0	1	1	.667	3.00	166	0.69	.111	0	....	1	0	0.1
• MARTINI, Wedo	Guido Joe "Southern" Martini b: 7/1/1913, Birmingham, AL d: 10/28/1970, Philadelphia, PA BR/TR, 5'10", 165 lbs. Deb: 7/28/1935																									
1935 Phi-A	0	2	.000	3	2	0	0	0	6^{1}	8	13	12	0	0	11	1	3.000	17.05	27	10.06	.333	0	.000	-9	0	-0.8
• MARTZ, Randy	Randy Carl Martz b: 5/28/1956, Harrisburg, PA BL/TR, 6'4", 210 lbs. Deb: 9/6/1980																									
1980 Chi-N	1	2	.333	6	6	0	0	0	30^{1}	28	14	7	1	0	11	5	1.286	2.08	189	2.94	.241	1	.111	7	2	0.6
1981 Chi-N	5	7	.417	33	14	1	0	6	107^{2}	103	49	44	6	1	49	32	1.412	3.68	100	3.77	.256	6	.214	3	7	0.4
1982 Chi-N	11	10	.524	28	24	1	0	1	147^{2}	157	80	69	17	3	36	40	1.307	4.21	89	3.93	.272	6	.143	-6	6	-0.5
1983 Chi-A	0	0	....	1	1	0	0	0	5	4	2	2	0	0	4	1	1.600	3.60	116	3.64	.211	0	....	0	0	0.0
Total 4	17	19	.472	68	45	2	0	7	290^{2}	292	145	122	24	4	100	78	1.349	3.78	99	3.76	.262	13	.165	3	15	0.6
• MASAOKA, Onan	Onan Kainoa Satoshi Masaoka b: 10/27/1977, Hilo, HI BR/TL, 6', 188 lbs. Deb: 4/5/1999																									
1999 LA-N	2	4	.333	54	0	0	0	1	66^{2}	55	33	32	8	2	47	61	1.530	4.32	99	4.44	.222	0	.000	0	4	0.0
2000 LA-N	1	1	.500	29	0	0	0	0	27	23	12	12	2	1	15	27	1.407	4.00	108	3.81	.230	0	....	1	2	0.1
Total 2	3	5	.375	83	0	0	0	1	93^{2}	78	45	44	10	3	62	88	1.495	4.23	102	4.25	.224	0	.000	1	6	0.1
• MASON, Del	Adelbert William Mason b: 10/29/1883, Newfane, NY d: 12/31/1962, Winter Park, FL BR/TR, 6', 160 lbs. Deb: 4/23/1904																									
1904 Was-A	0	3	.000	5	3	2	0	0	33	45	30	22	1	2	13	16	1.758	6.00	44	5.45	.325	0	.000	-11	0	-1.5
1906 Cin-N	0	1	.000	2	1	1	0	0	12	10	6	6	1	1	6	4	1.333	4.50	61	4.03	.250	0	.000	-2	0	-0.3
1907 Cin-N	5	12	.294	25	17	13	1	0	146	144	68	51	2	6	55	45	1.363	3.14	82	3.68	.277	8	.182	-11	3	-1.2
Total 3	5	16	.238	32	21	16	1	0	191	199	104	79	4	9	74	65	1.429	3.72	70	4.01	.285	8	.125	-24	3	-3.1

• MASON, Ernie Ernest Mason b: New Orleans, LA d: 7/30/1904, Covington, LA, 6', 150 lbs. Deb: 7/17/1894

YEAR	TM-L	W	L	PCT	G	GS	CG	SH	SV	IP	H	R	ER	HR	HB	BB	SO	RAT	ERA	ERA+	CERA	OAV	BH	AVG	PR+	WS	TPW
1894	StL-N	0	3	.000	4	2	2	0	0	22^2	34	29	18	1	0	10	3	1.941	7.15	76	6.67	.343	3	.250	-4	0	-0.4

• MASON, Hank Henry Mason b: 6/19/1931, Marshall, MO BR/TR, 6', 185 lbs. Deb: 9/12/1958

YEAR	TM-L	W	L	PCT	G	GS	CG	SH	SV	IP	H	R	ER	HR	HB	BB	SO	RAT	ERA	ERA+	CERA	OAV	BH	AVG	PR+	WS	TPW
1958	Phi-N	0	0	....	1	0	0	0	0	5	7	7	6	0	1	2	3	1.800	10.80	37	6.56	.368	0	.000	-4	0	-0.4
1960	Phi-N	0	0	....	3	0	0	0	0	5^2	9	6	6	1	0	5	3	2.471	9.53	41	10.01	.375	0	.000	-4	0	-0.4
Total	2	0	0	....	4	0	0	0	0	10^2	16	13	12	1	1	7	6	2.156	10.13	39	8.39	.372	0	.000	-7	0	-0.8

• MASON, Mike Michael Paul Mason b: 11/21/1958, Fairbault, MN BL/TL, 6'2", 205 lbs. Deb: 9/13/1982

YEAR	TM-L	W	L	PCT	G	GS	CG	SH	SV	IP	H	R	ER	HR	HB	BB	SO	RAT	ERA	ERA+	CERA	OAV	BH	AVG	PR+	WS	TPW
1982	Tex-A	1	2	.333	4	4	0	0	0	23	21	13	13	3	0	9	8	1.304	5.09	76	3.75	.244	0	....	-3	1	-0.3
1983	Tex-A	0	2	.000	5	0	0	0	0	10^2	10	7	7	0	1	6	9	1.500	5.91	68	3.77	.244	0	....	-2	0	-0.2
1984	Tex-A	9	13	.409	36	24	4	0	0	184^1	159	78	74	18	2	51	113	1.139	3.61	115	2.88	.233	0	....	13	11	1.3
1985	Tex-A	8	15	.348	38	30	1	1	0	179	212	113	96	22	3	73	92	**1.592**	4.83	88	5.43	.299	0	....	-9	7	-0.9
1986	Tex-A	7	3	.700	27	22	2	1	0	135	135	71	65	11	0	56	85	1.415	4.33	99	3.94	.257	0	....	-0	7	0.0
1987	Tex-A	0	2	.000	8	6	0	0	0	29	37	20	18	6	4	22	21	2.034	5.59	80	9.00	.322	0	....	-3	0	-0.3
	Chi-N	4	1	.800	17	4	0	0	0	38	43	25	24	4	1	23	28	1.737	5.68	75	5.97	.303	2	.222	-5	2	-0.5
1988	Min-A	0	1	.000	5	0	0	0	0	6^2	8	8	8	1	0	9	7	2.550	10.80	38	9.62	.286	0	....	-5	0	-0.5
Total	7	29	39	.426	140	90	7	2	0	605^2	625	335	305	65	11	249	363	1.443	4.53	93	4.48	.268	2	.222	-15	28	-1.4

• MASON, Roger Roger Le Roy Mason b: 9/18/1958, Bellaire, MI BR/TR, 6'6", 220 lbs. Deb: 9/4/1984

YEAR	TM-L	W	L	PCT	G	GS	CG	SH	SV	IP	H	R	ER	HR	HB	BB	SO	RAT	ERA	ERA+	CERA	OAV	BH	AVG	PR+	WS	TPW
1984	Det-A	1	1	.500	5	2	0	0	1	22	23	11	11	1	0	10	15	1.500	4.50	87	4.13	.271	0	....	-2	1	-0.2
1985	SF-N	1	3	.250	5	5	1	1	0	29^2	28	13	7	1	0	11	26	1.315	2.12	162	3.07	.243	1	.091	5	2	0.5
1986	SF-N	3	4	.429	11	11	1	0	0	60	56	35	32	5	3	30	43	1.433	4.80	73	4.11	.250	1	.048	-9	1	-1.2
1987	SF-N	1	1	.500	5	5	0	0	0	26	30	15	13	4	0	10	18	1.538	4.50	85	5.59	.303	1	.125	-2	1	-0.2
1989	Hou-N	0	0	....	2	0	0	0	0	1^1	2	3	3	0	0	2	3	3.000	20.25	17	10.76	.333	0	....	-2	0	-0.3
1991*	Pit-N	3	2	.600	24	0	0	0	3	29^2	21	11	10	2	1	6	21	.910	3.03	118	1.80	.200	0	....	2	3	0.2
1992*	Pit-N	5	7	.417	65	0	0	0	8	88	80	41	40	11	4	33	56	1.284	4.09	84	3.68	.246	0	.000	-7	5	-0.8
1993	SD-N	0	7	.000	34	0	0	0	0	50	43	20	18	1	2	18	39	1.220	3.24	128	2.70	.242	0	.000	5	3	0.5
	*Phi-N	5	5	.500	34	0	0	0	0	49^2	47	28	27	9	0	16	32	1.268	4.89	81	3.95	.246	1	.333	-5	2	-0.4
	Yr.	5	12	.294	68	0	0	0	0	99^2	90	48	45	10	2	34	71	1.244	4.06	99	3.32	.244	1	.167	0	5	0.0
1994	Phi-N	1	1	.500	6	0	0	0	0	8^2	11	6	5	2	0	5	7	1.846	5.19	83	7.31	.306	0	....	-1	0	-0.1
	NY-N	2	4	.333	41	0	0	0	1	51^1	44	23	20	6	2	20	26	1.247	3.51	119	3.42	.232	0	....	4	4	0.4
	Yr.	3	5	.375	47	0	0	0	1	60	55	29	25	8	2	25	33	1.333	3.75	112	3.98	.243	0	....	3	4	0.3
Total	9	22	35	.386	232	23	2	1	13	416^1	385	206	186	42	12	161	286	1.311	4.02	93	3.69	.248	4	.071	-13	22	-1.6

• MASTERS, Walt Walter Thomas Masters b: 3/28/1907, Pen Argyl, PA d: 7/10/1992, Ottawa, Canada BR/TR, 5'10.5", 180 lbs. Deb: 7/9/1931

YEAR	TM-L	W	L	PCT	G	GS	CG	SH	SV	IP	H	R	ER	HR	HB	BB	SO	RAT	ERA	ERA+	CERA	OAV	BH	AVG	PR+	WS	TPW
1931	Was-A	0	0	....	3	0	0	0	1	9	7	2	2	0	0	4	1	1.222	2.00	215	2.41	.226	0	.000	2	1	0.2
1937	Phi-N	0	0	....	1	0	0	0	0	1	5	4	4	0	0	1	0	6.000	36.00	12	40.34	.714	0	....	-4	0	-0.3
1939	Phi-A	0	0	....	4	0	0	0	0	11	15	9	8	0	0	8	2	2.091	6.55	72	6.11	.306	0	.000	-2	0	-0.2
Total	3	0	0	....	8	0	0	0	1	21	27	15	14	0	0	13	3	1.905	6.00	75	6.15	.310	0	.000	-3	1	-0.4

• MASTERSON, Paul Paul Nicholas "Lefty" Masterson b: 10/16/1915, Chicago, IL d: 11/27/1997, Chicago, IL BL/TL, 5'11", 165 lbs. Deb: 9/15/1940

YEAR	TM-L	W	L	PCT	G	GS	CG	SH	SV	IP	H	R	ER	HR	HB	BB	SO	RAT	ERA	ERA+	CERA	OAV	BH	AVG	PR+	WS	TPW
1940	Phi-N	0	0	....	2	0	0	0	0	5	5	4	4	0	0	2	3	1.400	7.20	54	3.36	.263	0	.000	-2	0	-0.2
1941	Phi-N	1	0	1.000	2	1	1	0	0	11^1	11	6	6	0	0	6	8	1.500	4.76	78	3.53	.250	0	.000	-1	1	-0.2
1942	Phi-N	0	0	....	4	0	0	0	0	8^1	10	6	6	1	0	5	3	1.800	6.48	51	6.08	.303	0	....	-3	0	-0.3
Total	3	1	0	1.000	8	1	1	0	0	24^2	26	16	16	1	0	13	14	1.581	5.84	61	4.36	.271	0	.000	-6	1	-0.7

• MASTERSON, Walt Walter Edward Masterson b: 6/22/1920, Philadelphia, PA BR/TR, 6'2", 189 lbs. Deb: 5/8/1939

YEAR	TM-L	W	L	PCT	G	GS	CG	SH	SV	IP	H	R	ER	HR	HB	BB	SO	RAT	ERA	ERA+	CERA	OAV	BH	AVG	PR+	WS	TPW
1939	Was-A	2	2	.500	24	5	1	0	0	58^1	66	44	36	2	2	48	12	1.954	5.55	78	5.82	.293	2	.154	-8	1	-0.8
1940	Was-A	3	13	.188	31	19	3	0	2	130^1	128	92	71	6	3	88	68	1.657	4.90	85	4.49	.257	7	.184	-9	3	-0.8
1941	Was-A	4	3	.571	34	6	1	0	3	78^1	101	56	52	3	1	53	40	1.966	5.97	68	6.35	.321	2	.105	-16	1	-1.7
1942	Was-A	5	9	.357	25	15	8	4	2	142^2	138	75	53	6	2	54	63	1.346	3.34	109	3.31	.251	7	.156	11	5	1.1
1945	Was-A	1	2	.333	4	2	1	1	0	25	21	8	3	1	0	10	14	1.240	1.08	287	2.73	.228	1	.111	6	2	0.5
1946	Was-A	5	6	.455	29	9	2	0	1	91^1	105	70	61	8	3	67	61	1.883	6.01	56	6.18	.295	2	.080	-25	0	-2.8
1947	Was-A★	12	16	.429	35	31	14	4	1	253	215	98	88	11	2	97	135	1.233	3.13	119	2.83	.234	11	.133	21	21	1.9
1948	Was-A★	8	15	.348	33	27	9	2	2	188	171	88	80	12	4	122	72	1.559	3.83	113	4.25	.247	11	.193	14	13	1.3
1949	Was-A	3	2	.600	10	7	3	0	0	53	42	22	19	4	3	21	17	1.189	3.23	132	2.92	.216	1	.056	8	4	0.6
	Bos-A	3	4	.429	18	5	1	0	4	55	58	30	26	2	0	35	19	1.691	4.25	102	4.82	.283	2	.118	-0	3	-0.1
	Yr.	6	6	.500	28	12	4	0	4	108	100	52	45	6	3	56	36	1.444	3.75	115	3.89	.251	3	.086	8	7	0.6
1950	Bos-A	8	6	.571	33	15	6	0	1	129^1	145	91	81	15	1	82	60	1.755	5.64	87	5.78	.287	6	.136	-10	5	-1.2
1951	Bos-A	3	0	1.000	30	1	0	0	2	59^1	53	24	22	1	0	32	39	1.433	3.34	134	3.16	.228	2	.182	7	6	0.7
1952	Bos-A	1	1	.500	5	1	0	0	0	9^1	18	12	12	1	0	11	3	3.107	11.57	34	13.07	.400	0	.000	-8	0	-0.9
	Was-A	9	8	.529	24	21	11	0	2	160^2	153	71	66	11	3	72	89	1.400	3.70	96	3.79	.253	6	.120	-1	9	-0.3
	Yr.	10	9	.526	29	22	11	0	2	170	171	83	78	12	3	83	92	1.494	4.13	87	4.29	.263	6	.115	-9	9	-1.2
1953	Was-A	10	12	.455	29	20	10	4	0	166^1	145	79	67	16	3	62	95	1.244	3.63	107	3.22	.232	7	.137	4	8	0.3
1956	Det-A	1	1	.500	35	0	0	0	0	49^2	54	28	23	2	1	32	28	1.732	4.17	99	5.11	.289	1	.250	-0	2	0.0
Total	14	78	100	.438	399	184	70	15	20	1649^2	1613	888	760	101	28	886	815	1.515	4.15	96	4.19	.258	68	.140	-8	83	-2.0

• MATARAZZO, Len Leonard Matarazzo b: 9/12/1928, New Castle, PA BR/TR, 6'4", 195 lbs. Deb: 9/6/1952

YEAR	TM-L	W	L	PCT	G	GS	CG	SH	SV	IP	H	R	ER	HR	HB	BB	SO	RAT	ERA	ERA+	CERA	OAV	BH	AVG	PR+	WS	TPW
1952	Phi-A	0	0	....	1	0	0	0	0	1	1	0	0	0	0	1	0	2.000	0.00	....	5.17	.250	0	....	0	0	0.0

• MATEO, Julio Julio Cesar Mateo b: 8/22/1978, Bani, Dominican Republic BR/TR, 6', 177 lbs. Deb: 5/7/2002

YEAR	TM-L	W	L	PCT	G	GS	CG	SH	SV	IP	H	R	ER	HR	HB	BB	SO	RAT	ERA	ERA+	CERA	OAV	BH	AVG	PR+	WS	TPW
2002	Sea-A	0	0	....	12	0	0	0	0	21	20	10	10	2	1	12	15	1.524	4.29	99	4.63	.247	0	....	0	1	0.0
2003	Sea-A	4	0	1.000	50	0	0	0	1	85^2	69	32	30	14	5	13	71	.957	3.15	137	2.71	.220	0	....	9	7	0.8
Total	2	4	0	1.000	62	0	0	0	1	106^2	89	42	40	16	6	25	86	1.069	3.38	127	3.09	.225	0	....	9	8	0.8

• MATHEWS, Bobby Robert T. Mathews b: 11/21/1851, Baltimore, MD d: 4/17/1898, Baltimore, MD BR/TR, 5'5.5", 140 lbs. Deb: 5/4/1871 U ♦

YEAR	TM-L	W	L	PCT	G	GS	CG	SH	SV	IP	H	R	ER	HR	HB	BB	SO	RAT	ERA	ERA+	CERA	OAV	BH	AVG	PR+	WS	TPW
1871	Kek-n	6	11	.353	19	19	19	**1**	0	169	261	243	97	5	....	21	17	1.669	5.17	88	....	.310	24	.270	4	....	0.2
1872	Bal-n	25	18	.581	49	47	39	0	0	406	480	356	144	3	....	52	**55**	1.310	3.19	119	....	.257	50	.224	30	....	1.3
1873	Mut-n	29	23	.558	52	52	47	2	0	443	489	348	126	5	....	62	**75**	1.244	2.56	124	....	.247	43	.193	41	....	2.6
1874	Mut-n	42	22	.656	65	65	62	**4**	0	578	652	371	122	3	....	39	**101**	1.196	1.90	133	....	.254	72	.242	46	....	3.6
1875	Mut-n	29	38	.433	70	**70**	**69**	2	0	**626^2**	711	421	172	4	....	20	75	1.166	2.47	107	....	.260	48	.182	13	....	0.3
1876	NY-N	21	34	.382	56	56	55	2	0	516	693	395	164	8	....	24	37	1.390	2.86	75	....	.298	40	.181	-6	18	-1.1
1877	Cin-N	3	12	.200	15	15	13	0	0	129^1	208	132	58	0	....	17	9	**1.740**	4.04	66	....	.343	10	.169	-13	1	-1.5
1879	Pro-N	12	6	.667	27	25	15	1	**1**	189	194	85	48	4	....	26	90	1.164	2.29	103	....	.249	35	.202	-0	14	-0.7
1881	Pro-N	4	8	.333	14	14	10	1	0	102^1	121	81	36	2	....	21	28	1.388	3.17	84	....	.282	11	.193	-3	3	-0.4
	Bos-N	1	0	1.000	5	1	1	0	2	23	22	11	6	0	....	11	5	1.435	2.35	113	....	.241	12	.169	1	2	-0.8
	Yr.	5	8	.385	19	15	11	1	**2**	125^1	143	92	42	2	....	32	33	1.396	3.02	88	....	.275	23	.180	-2	5	-1.2
1882	Bos-N	19	15	.559	34	32	31	0	0	285	278	151	91	5	....	22	153	1.053	2.87	99	....	.241	38	.225	4	21	-0.3
1883	Phi-a	30	13	.698	44	44	41	1	0	381	396	224	104	11	....	31	203	1.121	2.46	141	....	.251	31	.186	54	30	4.2
1884	Phi-a	30	18	.625	49	49	48	3	0	430^2	401	238	159	10	12	49	286	1.045	3.32	102	....	.234	34	.185	3	31	-0.1
1885	Phi-a	30	17	.638	48	48	46	2	0	422^1	394	229	114	3	20	57	286	1.068	2.43	141	....	.237	30	.168	50	26	4.0
1886	Phi-a	13	9	.591	24	24	22	0	0	197^2	226	148	87	3	13	53	93	1.411	3.96	88	....	.274	21	.239	-6	11	-0.5
1887	Phi-a	3	4	.429	7	7	7	0	0	58	100	64	43	4	3	25	9	1.724	6.67	64	....	.366	9	.310	-16	1	-1.3
Total	5 n	131	112	.539	255	253	236	9	0	2222^2	2593	1739	661	20	....	194	323	1.254	2.68	116	....	.260	237	.216	135	....	8.1
Total	10	166	136	.550	323	315	289	10	3	2734^1	3033	1758	910	50	48	336	1199	1.223	3.00	97	....	.265	271	.194	69	158	1.4

• MATHEWS, Greg Gregory Inman Mathews b: 5/17/1962, Harbor City, CA BR/TL, 6'2", 180 lbs. Deb: 6/3/1986

YEAR	TM-L	W	L	PCT	G	GS	CG	SH	SV	IP	H	R	ER	HR	HB	BB	SO	RAT	ERA	ERA+	CERA	OAV	BH	AVG	PR+	WS	TPW
1986	StL-N	11	8	.579	23	22	1	0	0	145^1	139	61	59	15	2	44	67	1.259	3.65	100	3.63	.259	2	.047	-5	8	-0.8
1987*	StL-N	11	11	.500	32	32	2	1	0	197^2	184	87	82	17	0	71	108	1.290	3.73	111	3.45	.249	13	.191	8	12	0.9

YEAR	TM-L	W	L	PCT	G	GS	CG	SH	SV	IP	H	R	ER	HR	HB	BB	SO	RAT	ERA	ERA+	CERA	OAV	BH	AVG	PR+	WS	TPW
1988	StL-N	4	6	.400	13	13	1	0	0	68	61	34	32	4	2	33	31	1.382	4.24	82	3.65	.247	4	.174	-6	2	-0.6
1990	StL-N	0	5	.000	11	10	0	0	0	50^{2}	53	34	30	2	2	30	18	1.638	5.33	72	4.81	.277	3	.214	-8	0	-0.7
1992	Phi-N	2	3	.400	14	7	0	0	0	52^{1}	54	31	30	7	1	24	27	1.490	5.16	68	4.82	.270	0	.000	-9	0	-1.1
Total	5	28	33	.459	93	84	4	1	0	514	491	247	233	45	7	202	251	1.348	4.08	93	3.80	.256	22	.136	-22	22	-2.4

• MATHEWS, T.J. Timothy Jay Mathews b: 1/9/1970, Belleville, IL BR/TR, 6'2", 200 lbs. Deb: 7/28/1995

YEAR	TM-L	W	L	PCT	G	GS	CG	SH	SV	IP	H	R	ER	HR	HB	BB	SO	RAT	ERA	ERA+	CERA	OAV	BH	AVG	PR+	WS	TPW
1995	StL-N	1	1	.500	23	0	0	0	2	29^{2}	21	7	5	1	0	11	28	1.079	1.52	276	1.99	.200	0	.000	8	5	0.8
1996*	StL-N	2	6	.250	67	0	0	0	6	83^{2}	62	32	28	8	2	32	80	1.124	3.01	139	2.60	.203	0	.000	9	8	0.8
1997	StL-N	4	4	.500	40	0	0	0	0	46	41	14	11	4	1	18	46	1.283	2.15	193	3.29	.238	0	.000	10	5	1.0
	Oak-A	6	2	.750	24	0	0	0	3	28^{2}	34	18	14	5	1	12	24	1.605	4.40	102	5.80	.293	0	....	1	3	0.1
1998	Oak-A	7	4	.636	66	0	0	0	1	72^{2}	71	44	37	6	4	29	53	1.376	4.58	100	3.91	.258	0	....	1	5	0.1
1999	Oak-A	9	5	.643	50	0	0	0	3	59	46	28	25	9	2	20	42	1.119	3.81	122	3.02	.215	0	....	6	7	0.5
2000	Oak-A	2	3	.400	50	0	0	0	0	59^{2}	73	40	40	10	2	25	42	1.642	6.03	79	5.98	.303	0	....	-8	2	-0.7
2001	Oak-A	0	1	.000	20	0	0	0	1	23	28	14	13	2	0	11	19	1.696	5.09	87	5.18	.295	0	....	-2	1	-0.2
	StL-N	1	0	1.000	10	0	0	0	0	14^{2}	11	6	5	2	0	1	10	.818	3.07	139	1.77	.204	0	.000	2	1	0.1
2002	Hou-N	0	0	....	12	0	0	0	0	18^{1}	19	7	7	2	0	5	13	1.309	3.44	124	3.66	.271	0	.000	2	1	0.2
Total	8	32	26	.552	362	0	0	0	16	435^{1}	406	210	185	49	12	164	357	1.309	3.82	117	3.73	.246	0	.000	29	38	2.8

• MATHEWS, Terry Terry Alan Mathews b: 10/5/1964, Alexandria, LA BL/TR, 6'2", 225 lbs. Deb: 6/21/1991

YEAR	TM-L	W	L	PCT	G	GS	CG	SH	SV	IP	H	R	ER	HR	HB	BB	SO	RAT	ERA	ERA+	CERA	OAV	BH	AVG	PR+	WS	TPW
1991	Tex-A	4	0	1.000	34	2	0	0	1	57^{1}	54	24	23	5	1	18	51	1.256	3.61	112	3.40	.251	0	....	4	4	0.4
1992	Tex-A	2	4	.333	40	0	0	0	0	42^{1}	48	29	28	4	1	31	26	1.866	5.95	64	6.25	.294	0	....	-9	0	-1.0
1994	Fla-N	2	1	.667	24	2	0	0	0	43	45	16	16	4	1	9	21	1.256	3.35	131	3.63	.268	3	.500	4	4	0.6
1995	Fla-N	4	4	.500	57	0	0	0	3	82^{2}	70	32	31	9	1	27	72	1.173	3.38	125	3.09	.235	6	.462	8	7	1.0
1996	Fla-N	2	4	.333	57	0	0	0	4	55	59	33	30	7	1	27	49	1.564	4.91	83	4.97	.273	0	.000	-6	2	-0.6
	*Bal-A	2	2	.500	14	0	0	0	0	18^{2}	20	7	7	3	0	7	13	1.446	3.38	146	4.97	.282	0	....	3	2	0.3
1997*	Bal-A	4	4	.500	57	0	0	0	1	63^{1}	63	35	31	8	0	36	39	1.563	4.41	100	4.82	.267	0	....	-0	4	0.0
1998	Bal-A	0	1	.000	17	0	0	0	0	20^{1}	26	15	14	6	0	8	10	1.672	6.20	73	7.22	.342	0	....	-4	0	-0.3
1999	KC-A	2	1	.667	24	1	0	0	1	39	44	21	19	4	2	17	19	1.564	4.38	114	5.17	.289	0	.000	2	3	0.2
Total	8	22	21	.512	324	5	0	0	10	421^{2}	429	212	199	50	7	180	300	1.444	4.25	100	4.48	.269	9	.375	1	26	0.4

• MATHEWSON, Christy Christopher "Big Six,Matty" Mathewson
b: 8/12/1878, Factoryville, PA d: 10/7/1925, Saranac Lake, NY BR/TR, 6'1.5", 195 lbs. Deb: 7/17/1900 M/C/U HOF: 1936

YEAR	TM-L	W	L	PCT	G	GS	CG	SH	SV	IP	H	R	ER	HR	HB	BB	SO	RAT	ERA	ERA+	CERA	OAV	BH	AVG	PR+	WS	TPW
1900	NY-N	0	3	.000	6	1	1	0	0	33^{2}	37	32	19	1	4	20	15	1.693	5.08	71	5.13	.279	2	.182	-6	0	-0.5
1901	NY-N	20	17	.541	40	38	36	5	0	336	288	131	90	3	13	97	221	1.146	2.41	137	2.38	.230	28	.215	**42**	21	**4.1**
1902	NY-N	14	17	.452	35	33	30	**8**	0	284^{2}	246	118	65	3	10	77	164	1.135	2.06	136	2.43	.233	26	.205	26	22	2.9
1903	NY-N	30	13	.698	45	42	37	3	2	366^{1}	321	136	92	4	10	100	**267**	1.149	2.26	148	2.37	.231	28	.226	36	37	3.8
1904	NY-N	33	12	.733	48	**46**	33	4	1	367^{2}	306	120	83	7	4	78	**212**	1.044	2.03	134	2.04	.226	30	.226	21	34	2.8
1905*	NY-N	**31**	9	.775	43	37	32	**8**	2	338^{2}	252	85	48	4	1	64	**206**	.933	**1.28**	**229**	**1.54**	.205	30	.236	**64**	**39**	**7.6**
1906	NY-N	22	12	.647	38	35	22	6	1	266^{2}	262	100	88	3	3	77	128	1.271	2.97	88	2.93	.259	24	.264	-12	20	-0.5
1907	NY-N	**24**	12	.667	41	36	31	**8**	2	315	250	88	70	5	2	53	**178**	.962	2.00	124	**1.67**	.212	20	.187	27	29	**3.4**
1908	NY-N	**37**	11	.771	**56**	**44**	**34**	**11**	**5**	**390^{2}**	285	86	62	5	3	42	**259**	.837	**1.43**	**168**	1.34	.200	20	.155	**46**	**39**	**5.6**
1909	NY-N	25	6	.806	37	33	26	8	2	275^{1}	192	57	35	2	0	36	149	.828	**1.14**	**223**	**1.29**	.200	25	.263	**46**	34	**5.8**
1910	NY-N	**27**	9	.750	38	35	**27**	2	0	318^{1}	292	100	67	5	3	60	184	1.106	1.89	156	2.35	.248	25	.234	**42**	**30**	**5.2**
1911*	NY-N	26	13	.667	45	37	29	5	3	307	303	102	68	5	1	38	141	1.111	**1.99**	**168**	2.43	.259	22	.196	**51**	32	**5.1**
1912*	NY-N	23	12	.657	43	34	27	0	4	310	311	107	73	5	2	34	134	1.113	2.12	159	2.44	.260	29	.264	**43**	**31**	**4.7**
1913*	NY-N	25	11	.694	40	35	25	4	2	306	291	94	70	8	0	21	93	1.020	**2.06**	**151**	2.16	.252	19	.184	**35**	**30**	3.6
1914	NY-N	24	13	.649	41	35	29	5	2	312	314	133	104	16	2	23	80	1.080	3.00	88	2.58	.263	23	.219	-12	19	-0.7
1915	NY-N	8	14	.364	27	24	11	1	0	186	199	97	74	9	1	20	57	1.177	3.58	71	2.96	.277	8	.157	-19	5	-1.9
1916	NY-N	3	4	.429	12	6	4	1	2	65^{2}	59	27	17	3	0	7	16	1.005	2.33	104	2.15	.243	0	.000	-0	3	-0.1
	Cin-N	1	0	1.000	1	1	1	0	0	9	15	8	8	1	0	1	3	1.778	8.00	32	6.76	.366	3	.600	-5	1	-0.5
	Yr.	4	4	.500	13	7	5	1	2	74^{2}	74	35	25	4	0	8	19	1.098	3.01	82	2.70	.261	3	.136	-6	4	-0.6
Total	17	373	188	.665	636	552	435	79	28	4788^{2}	4223	1621	1133	89	59	848	2507	1.059	2.13	134	2.18	.236	362	.215	424	426	50.3

• MATHEWSON, Henry Henry Mathewson b: 12/24/1886, Factoryville, PA d: 7/1/1917, Factoryville, PA BR/TR, 6'3", 175 lbs. Deb: 9/28/1906

YEAR	TM-L	W	L	PCT	G	GS	CG	SH	SV	IP	H	R	ER	HR	HB	BB	SO	RAT	ERA	ERA+	CERA	OAV	BH	AVG	PR+	WS	TPW
1906	NY-N	0	1	.000	2	1	1	0	1	10	7	7	6	0	1	14	2	2.100	5.40	48	5.24	.194	0	.000	-3	0	-0.4
1907	NY-N	0	0	....	1	0	0	0	1	1	1	0	0	0	0	0	0	1.000	0.00	....	1.95	.250	0	....	0	0	0.0
Total	2	0	1	.000	3	1	1	0	2	11	8	7	6	0	1	14	2	2.000	4.91	53	4.94	.200	0	.000	-3	0	-0.3

• MATHIAS, Carl Carl Lynwood "Stubby" Mathias b: 6/13/1936, Bechtelsville, PA BB/TL, 5'11", 195 lbs. Deb: 7/31/1960

YEAR	TM-L	W	L	PCT	G	GS	CG	SH	SV	IP	H	R	ER	HR	HB	BB	SO	RAT	ERA	ERA+	CERA	OAV	BH	AVG	PR+	WS	TPW
1960	Cle-A	0	1	.000	7	0	0	0	0	15^{1}	14	7	6	2	0	8	13	1.435	3.52	106	4.19	.233	0	.000	0	1	0.0
1961	Was-A	0	1	.000	4	3	0	0	0	13^{2}	22	19	17	3	1	4	7	1.902	11.20	35	8.51	.361	1	.200	-11	0	-1.1
Total	2	0	2	.000	11	3	0	0	0	29	36	26	23	5	1	12	20	1.655	7.14	54	6.23	.298	1	.167	-11	1	-1.1

• MATHIS, Ron Ronald Vance Mathis b: 9/25/1958, Kansas City, MO BR/TR, 6', 175 lbs. Deb: 4/13/1985

YEAR	TM-L	W	L	PCT	G	GS	CG	SH	SV	IP	H	R	ER	HR	HB	BB	SO	RAT	ERA	ERA+	CERA	OAV	BH	AVG	PR+	WS	TPW
1985	Hou-N	3	5	.375	23	8	0	0	1	70	83	54	47	7	1	27	34	1.571	6.04	57	5.03	.293	1	.071	-21	0	-2.2
1987	Hou-N	0	1	.000	8	0	0	0	0	12	10	8	7	2	0	11	8	1.750	5.25	75	5.80	.233	0	.000	-2	0	-0.2
Total	2	3	6	.333	31	8	0	0	1	82	93	62	54	9	1	38	42	1.598	5.93	59	5.14	.285	1	.063	-22	0	-2.4

• MATLACK, Jon Jonathan Trumpbour Matlack b: 1/19/1950, West Chester, PA BL/TL, 6'3", 205 lbs. Deb: 7/11/1971 C

YEAR	TM-L	W	L	PCT	G	GS	CG	SH	SV	IP	H	R	ER	HR	HB	BB	SO	RAT	ERA	ERA+	CERA	OAV	BH	AVG	PR+	WS	TPW
1971	NY-N	0	3	.000	7	6	0	0	0	37	31	18	17	2	0	15	24	1.243	4.14	82	2.94	.228	3	.273	-3	1	-0.3
1972	NY-N	15	10	.600	34	32	8	4	0	244	215	79	63	14	2	71	169	1.172	2.32	145	2.70	.234	10	.128	30	22	3.3
1973*	NY-N	14	16	.467	34	34	14	3	0	242	210	93	86	16	2	99	205	1.277	3.20	113	3.13	.236	9	.138	10	16	1.2
1974	NY-N★	13	15	.464	34	34	14	**7**	0	265^{1}	221	82	71	8	5	76	195	1.119	2.41	148	**2.35**	.226	8	.101	33	24	3.1
1975	NY-N★	16	12	.571	33	32	8	3	0	228^{2}	224	105	86	15	1	58	154	1.233	3.38	102	3.14	.254	7	.100	-1	12	-0.1
1976	NY-N★	17	10	.630	35	35	16	**6**	0	262	236	94	86	18	3	57	153	1.118	2.95	111	2.70	.242	17	.193	8	18	1.3
1977	NY-N	7	15	.318	26	26	5	3	0	169	175	86	79	19	2	43	123	1.290	4.21	89	3.83	.273	3	.060	-9	6	-1.1
1978	Tex-A	15	13	.536	35	33	18	2	1	270	252	93	68	14	4	51	157	1.122	2.27	165	2.65	.245	0	....	45	25	4.7
1979	Tex-A	5	4	.556	13	13	2	0	0	85	98	43	39	9	1	15	35	1.329	4.13	100	4.20	.293	0	....	-1	4	-0.1
1980	Tex-A	10	10	.500	35	34	8	1	1	234^{2}	265	111	96	17	0	48	142	1.334	3.68	106	3.87	.287	0	....	9	13	0.9
1981	Tex-A	4	7	.364	17	16	1	1	0	104^{1}	101	59	48	8	1	41	43	1.361	4.14	84	3.73	.258	0	....	-10	2	-1.0
1982	Tex-A	7	7	.500	33	14	1	0	1	147^{2}	158	64	58	14	2	37	78	1.321	3.53	110	3.89	.275	0	....	7	11	0.7
1983	Tex-A	2	4	.333	25	9	2	0	0	73^{1}	90	43	38	7	3	27	38	1.595	4.66	86	5.41	.307	0	....	-5	2	-0.5
Total	13	125	126	.498	361	318	97	30	3	2363	2276	970	835	161	26	638	1516	1.233	3.18	114	3.20	.254	57	.129	113	156	12.0

• MATTERN, Al Alonzo Albert Mattern b: 6/16/1883, West Rush, NY d: 11/6/1958, West Rush, NY BL/TR, 5'10", 165 lbs. Deb: 9/16/1908

YEAR	TM-L	W	L	PCT	G	GS	CG	SH	SV	IP	H	R	ER	HR	HB	BB	SO	RAT	ERA	ERA+	CERA	OAV	BH	AVG	PR+	WS	TPW
1908	Bos-N	1	2	.333	5	3	1	1	0	30^{1}	30	10	7	0	0	6	8	1.187	2.08	115	2.70	.265	1	.125	0	2	0.0
1909	Bos-N	15	21	.417	47	32	24	2	3	316^{1}	322	142	100	4	3	108	98	1.359	2.85	99	3.40	.268	17	.168	-2	17	-0.2
1910	Bos-N	16	19	.457	**51**	37	17	**6**	1	305	288	145	101	5	6	121	94	1.341	2.98	111	3.31	.257	16	.163	6	20	0.3
1911	Bos-N	4	15	.211	33	21	11	0	0	186^{1}	228	129	103	13	1	63	51	1.562	4.97	77	5.20	.320	11	.175	-20	3	-2.2
1912	Bos-N	0	1	.000	2	1	0	0	0	6^{1}	10	9	5	0	0	1	3	1.737	7.11	50	4.64	.313	0	.000	-2	0	-0.3
Total	5	36	58	.383	138	94	53	9	4	844^{1}	878	435	316	22	10	299	254	1.394	3.37	96	3.75	.276	45	.165	-18	42	-2.4

• MATTES, Troy Troy Walter Mattes b: 8/26/1975, Champaign, IL BR/TR, 6'7", 230 lbs. Deb: 6/19/2001

YEAR	TM-L	W	L	PCT	G	GS	CG	SH	SV	IP	H	R	ER	HR	HB	BB	SO	RAT	ERA	ERA+	CERA	OAV	BH	AVG	PR+	WS	TPW
2001	Mon-N	3	3	.500	8	8	0	0	0	45	51	33	30	9	4	21	26	1.600	6.00	74	6.18	.285	7	.467	-7	1	-0.4

• MATTESON, C.V. Clifford Virgil Matteson b: 11/24/1861, Seville, OH d: 12/18/1931, Seville, OH Deb: 6/13/1884 ♦

YEAR	TM-L	W	L	PCT	G	GS	CG	SH	SV	IP	H	R	ER	HR	HB	BB	SO	RAT	ERA	ERA+	CERA	OAV	BH	AVG	PR+	WS	TPW
1884	StL-U	1	0	1.000	1	1	0	0	0	6	9	11	6	1	....	3	3	2.000	9.00	33	....	.325	0	.000	-4	0	-0.5

• MATTESON, Eddie Henry Edson "Matty" Matteson b: 9/7/1884, Guy's Mills, PA d: 9/1/1943, Westfield, NY BR/TR, 5'10.5", 160 lbs. Deb: 5/30/1914

YEAR	TM-L	W	L	PCT	G	GS	CG	SH	SV	IP	H	R	ER	HR	HB	BB	SO	RAT	ERA	ERA+	CERA	OAV	BH	AVG	PR+	WS	TPW
1914	Phi-N	3	2	.600	15	3	2	0	0	58	58	29	20	1	1	23	28	1.397	3.10	95	3.56	.278	4	.182	1	3	0.0

YEAR	TM-L	W	L	PCT	G	GS	CG	SH	SV	IP	H	R	ER	HR	HB	BB	SO	RAT	ERA	ERA+	CERA	OAV	BH	AVG	PR+	WS	TPW
1918	Was-A	5	3	.625	14	6	2	0	0	67^{2}	57	20	13	2	1	15	17	1.064	1.73	157	2.32	.238	2	.105	5	6	0.4
Total	2	8	5	.615	29	9	4	0	0	125^{2}	115	49	33	3	2	38	45	1.218	2.36	120	2.89	.257	6	.146	6	9	0.5
• MATTHEWS, Joe		John Joseph "Lefty" Matthews b: 9/29/1898, Baltimore, MD d: 2/8/1968, Hagerstown, MD BB/TL, 6', 170 lbs. Deb: 9/18/1922																									
1922	Bos-N	0	1	.000	3	1	0	0	0	10	5	6	4	1	1	6	0	1.100	3.60	111	2.23	.143	0	.000	1	0	0.0
• MATTHEWS, Mike		Michael Scott Matthews b: 10/24/1973, Fredericksburg, VA BL/TL, 6'2", 175 lbs. Deb: 5/31/2000																									
2000	StL-N	0	0	....	14	0	0	0	0	9^{1}	15	12	12	2	1	10	8	2.679	11.57	40	11.83	.349	0	....	-7	0	-0.7
2001*	StL-N	3	4	.429	51	10	0	0	1	89	74	32	32	11	4	33	72	1.202	3.24	132	3.34	.227	2	.118	8	7	0.8
2002	StL-N	2	1	.667	43	0	0	0	0	41^{2}	40	21	18	5	2	22	32	1.488	3.89	102	4.64	.260	1	.167	-0	2	0.0
	Mil-N	0	0	....	4	0	0	0	0	4	3	2	2	0	0	7	2	2.500	4.50	91	6.63	.214	0	....	-0	0	0.0
	Yr.	2	1	.667	47	0	0	0	0	45^{2}	43	23	20	5	2	29	34	1.577	3.94	101	4.81	.256	1	.167	-1	2	-0.1
2003	SD-N	6	4	.600	77	0	0	0	0	64^{2}	65	34	32	4	4	29	44	1.454	4.45	88	4.20	.271	0	.000	-3	7	-0.4
Total	4	11	9	.550	189	10	0	0	1	208^{2}	197	101	96	22	11	101	158	1.428	4.14	100	4.31	.254	3	.120	-3	16	-0.3
• MATTHEWS, William		William Calvin Matthews b: 1/12/1878, Mahanoy City, PA d: 1/23/1946, Mount Carbon, PA TR Deb: 8/28/1909																									
1909	Bos-A	0	0	....	5	1	0	0	0	16^{2}	16	8	6	1	0	10	6	1.560	3.24	77	4.54	.271	0	.000	-2	1	-0.3
• MATTHEWSON, Dale		Dale Wesley Matthewson b: 5/15/1923, Catasauqua, PA d: 2/20/1984, Blairsville, GA BR/TR, 5'11.5", 145 lbs. Deb: 7/3/1943																									
1943	Phi-N	0	3	.000	11	1	0	0	0	26	26	14	14	1	0	8	8	1.308	4.85	70	3.29	.271	0	.000	-4	0	-0.5
1944	Phi-N	0	0	....	17	0	0	0	0	32	27	14	14	1	0	16	8	1.344	3.94	92	3.07	.237	1	.333	-1	2	-0.1
Total	2	0	3	.000	28	1	0	0	0	58	53	28	28	2	0	24	16	1.328	4.34	80	3.17	.252	1	.200	-5	2	-0.5
• MATTIMORE, Mike		Michael Joseph Mattimore b: 1859, Renovo, PA d: 4/28/1931, Butte, MT BL/TL, 5'8.5", 160 lbs. Deb: 5/3/1887 U ♦																									
1887	NY-N	3	3	.500	7	7	6	1	0	57^{1}	75	39	15	2	4	28	12	1.308	2.35	159	....	.307	8	.250	8	4	0.6
1888	Phi-a	15	10	.600	26	24	24	4	0	221	221	146	83	6	13	65	80	1.294	3.38	88	....	.251	38	.268	-11	15	-0.1
1889	Phi-a	2	1	.667	5	1	1	0	1	31	43	27	20	0	1	13	6	1.806	5.81	65	....	.319	17	.233	-8	3	-0.8
	KC-a	0	0	....	1	0	0	0	0	3	3	3	1	1	0	2	1	1.667	3.00	139	....	.252	12	.160	0	0	-0.9
	Yr.	2	1	.667	6	1	1	0	1	34	46	30	21	1	1	15	7	1.794	5.56	68	....	.314	29	.196	-8	3	-1.7
1890	Bro-a	6	13	.316	19	19	19	0	0	178^{1}	201	149	90	3	13	76	33	1.553	4.54	86	....	.276	17	.132	-12	4	-2.0
Total	4	26	27	.491	58	51	50	5	1	490^{2}	543	364	209	12	31	184	132	1.425	3.83	90	....	.272	92	.204	-22	26	-3.1
• MATTINGLY, Earl		Laurence Earl Mattingly b: 11/4/1904, New Port, MD d: 9/8/1993, Brookeville, MD BR/TR, 5'10.5", 164 lbs. Deb: 4/15/1931																									
1931	Bro-N	0	1	.000	8	0	0	0	0	14^{1}	15	4	4	0	2	10	6	1.744	2.51	152	5.04	.268	0	.000	2	1	0.2
• MATULA, Rick		Richard Carlton Matula b: 11/22/1953, Wharton, TX BR/TR, 6', 190 lbs. Deb: 4/8/1979																									
1979	Atl-N	8	10	.444	28	28	1	0	0	171^{1}	193	90	79	14	3	64	67	1.500	4.15	98	4.55	.286	5	.094	3	8	0.0
1980	Atl-N	11	13	.458	33	30	3	1	0	176^{2}	195	100	90	17	0	60	62	1.443	4.58	82	4.35	.286	6	.105	-16	5	-2.0
1981	Atl-N	0	0	....	5	0	0	0	0	7	8	5	5	1	0	2	0	1.429	6.43	56	4.80	.286	0	.000	-2	0	-0.2
Total	3	19	23	.452	66	58	4	1	0	355	396	195	174	32	3	126	129	1.470	4.41	88	4.46	.286	11	.099	-16	13	-2.2
• MATUZAK, Harry		Harry George "Matty" Matuzak b: 1/27/1910, Omer, MI d: 11/16/1978, Fairhope, AL BR/TR, 5'11.5", 185 lbs. Deb: 4/19/1934																									
1934	Phi-A	0	3	.000	11	0	0	0	0	24	28	16	13	2	1	10	9	1.583	4.88	90	4.89	.292	1	.167	-2	1	-0.1
1936	Phi-A	0	1	.000	6	1	0	0	0	15	21	14	12	0	0	4	8	1.667	7.20	71	4.80	.318	0	.000	-4	0	-0.4
Total	2	0	4	.000	17	1	0	0	0	39	49	30	25	2	1	14	17	1.615	5.77	81	4.86	.302	1	.111	-5	1	-0.5
• MAUCK, Hal		Alfred Maris Mauck b: 3/6/1869, Princeton, IN d: 4/27/1921, Princeton, IN BR/TR, 5'11", 185 lbs. Deb: 4/29/1893																									
1893	Chi-N	8	10	.444	23	18	12	1	0	143	168	112	70	2	9	60	23	1.594	4.41	105	4.62	.284	9	.148	4	8	-0.1
• MAUL, Al		Albert Joseph "Smiling Al" Maul b: 10/9/1865, Philadelphia, PA d: 5/3/1958, Philadelphia, PA BR/TR, 6', 175 lbs. Deb: 6/20/1884 ♦																									
1884	Phi-U	0	1	.000	1	1	1	0	0	8	10	7	4	0	....	1	7	1.375	4.50	64	....	.287	0	.000	-1	0	-0.2
1887	Phi-N	4	2	.667	7	5	4	0	0	50^{1}	87	50	31	2	2	15	18	1.728	5.54	76	....	.369	32	.451	-6	4	-0.2
1888	Pit-N	0	2	.000	3	1	1	0	0	17	26	20	12	0	0	5	12	1.824	6.35	42	....	.339	54	.208	-7	5	-1.5
1889	Pit-N	1	4	.200	6	4	4	0	0	42	64	53	46	3	1	28	11	2.190	9.86	38	....	.339	71	.276	-29	9	-1.1
1890	Pit-P	16	12	.571	30	28	26	2	0	246^{2}	258	189	104	13	12	104	81	1.468	3.79	103	....	.258	42	.259	10	18	1.3
1891	Pit-N	1	2	.333	8	3	3	0	1	39	44	22	10	0	3	16	13	1.538	2.31	142	....	.274	28	.188	4	4	-0.4
1893	Was-N	12	21	.364	37	33	29	1	0	297	355	254	175	17	18	144	72	1.680	5.30	87	5.32	.288	34	.254	-15	11	-0.3
1894	Was-N	11	15	.423	28	26	21	0	0	201^{2}	272	200	135	12	10	73	34	1.711	6.02	87	5.75	.319	30	.242	-12	8	-0.8
1895	Was-N	10	5	.667	16	16	14	0	0	135^{2}	136	67	37	5	3	37	34	1.275	**2.45**	**195**	3.20	.257	18	.250	38	10	3.1
1896	Was-N	5	2	.714	8	8	7	0	0	62	75	50	25	0	4	20	18	1.532	3.63	121	4.36	.297	8	.286	7	3	0.7
1897	Was-N	0	1	.000	1	1	0	0	0	2	4	2	2	0	0	1	0	2.500	9.00	48	9.81	.411	0	.000	-1	0	-0.1
	Bal-N	0	0	....	2	2	0	0	0	7^{2}	9	8	6	0	4	8	2	2.217	7.04	59	8.49	.291	1	.333	-3	0	-0.2
	Yr.	0	1	.000	3	3	0	0	0	9^{2}	13	10	8	0	4	9	2	2.276	7.45	56	8.76	.319	1	.250	-4	0	-0.3
1898	Bal-N	20	7	.741	28	28	26	1	0	239^{2}	207	74	56	3	4	49	31	1.068	2.10	170	2.14	.232	19	.204	33	24	3.4
1899	Bro-N	2	0	1.000	4	4	2	0	0	26	35	19	13	1	2	6	2	1.577	4.50	87	5.16	.322	3	.273	-2	1	-0.2
1900	Phi-N	2	3	.400	5	4	3	0	0	38	53	31	26	2	2	3	6	1.474	6.16	59	4.88	.329	3	.200	-11	1	-1.0
1901	NY-N	0	3	.000	3	3	2	0	0	19	39	27	24	1	2	8	5	2.474	11.37	29	10.84	.417	3	.375	-17	0	-1.6
Total	15	84	80	.512	187	167	143	4	1	1431^{2}	1674	1073	706	59	67	518	346	1.521	4.44	95	3.19	.286	346	.249	-12	98	1.2
• MAUN, Ernie		Ernest Gerald Maun b: 2/3/1901, Clearwater, KS d: 1/1/1987, Corpus Christi, TX BR/TR, 6', 165 lbs. Deb: 5/16/1924																									
1924	NY-N	1	1	.500	22	0	0	0	1	35	46	24	23	2	1	10	5	1.600	5.91	62	5.18	.326	2	.667	-9	0	-0.8
1926	Phi-N	1	4	.200	14	5	0	0	0	37^{2}	57	36	27	4	1	18	9	1.991	6.45	64	7.32	.339	3	.250	-8	0	-0.8
Total	2	2	5	.286	36	5	0	0	1	72^{2}	103	60	50	6	2	28	14	1.803	6.19	63	6.29	.333	5	.333	-17	0	-1.6
• MAUNEY, Dick		Richard Mauney b: 1/26/1920, Concord, NC d: 2/6/1970, Albemarle, NC BR/TR, 5'11.5", 164 lbs. Deb: 6/13/1945																									
1945	Phi-N	6	10	.375	20	16	6	2	1	122^{2}	127	54	42	7	2	27	35	1.255	3.08	124	3.32	.268	6	.146	13	6	1.3
1946	Phi-N	6	4	.600	24	7	3	1	2	90	98	36	27	4	3	18	31	1.289	2.70	127	3.51	.279	4	.167	8	7	0.8
1947	Phi-N	0	0	....	9	1	0	0	1	16^{1}	15	8	7	1	1	7	6	1.347	3.86	104	4.14	.288	0	.000	0	1	0.0
Total	3	12	14	.462	53	24	9	3	4	229	240	98	76	12	6	52	72	1.275	2.99	124	3.45	.274	10	.149	21	14	2.1
• MAUPIN, Harry		Harry Carr Maupin b: 7/11/1872, Wellsville, MO d: 8/25/1952, Parsons, KS TR, 5'7", 150 lbs. Deb: 10/5/1898																									
1898	StL-N	0	2	.000	2	2	2	0	0	18	22	11	11	0	3	3	3	1.389	5.50	69	4.24	.299	3	.429	-3	1	-0.2
1899	Cle-N	0	3	.000	5	3	2	0	0	25	55	36	35	0	1	7	3	2.480	12.60	29	10.44	.436	0	.000	-24	0	-2.3
Total	2	0	5	.000	7	5	4	0	0	43	77	47	46	0	4	10	6	2.023	9.63	38	7.84	.386	3	.176	-26	1	-2.5
• MAURER, Dave		David Charles Maurer b: 2/23/1975, Minneapolis, MN BR/TL, 6'2", 205 lbs. Deb: 7/22/2000																									
2000	SD-N	1	0	1.000	14	0	0	0	0	14^{2}	15	8	6	2	2	5	13	1.364	3.68	117	4.71	.263	0	....	1	1	0.1
2001	SD-N	0	0	....	3	0	0	0	0	5	8	6	6	1	0	4	4	2.400	10.80	37	10.33	.348	0	.000	-4	0	-0.4
2002	Cle-A	0	1	.000	2	0	0	0	0	1^{1}	3	2	2	1	0	0	0	2.250	13.50	33	16.20	.429	0	....	-1	0	-0.1
Total	3	1	1	.500	19	0	0	0	0	21	26	16	14	4	2	9	17	1.667	6.00	70	6.78	.299	0	.000	-4	1	-0.4
• MAURIELLO, Ralph		Ralph "Tami" Mauriello b: 8/25/1934, Brooklyn, NY BR/TR, 6'3", 195 lbs. Deb: 9/13/1958																									
1958	LA-N	1	1	.500	3	2	0	0	0	11^{2}	10	6	6	1	0	8	11	1.543	4.63	89	4.37	.238	0	.000	-1	1	-0.1
• MAUSER, Tim		Timothy Edward Mauser b: 10/4/1966, Fort Worth, TX BR/TR, 6', 185 lbs. Deb: 7/7/1991																									
1991	Phi-N	0	0	....	3	0	0	0	0	10^{2}	18	10	9	3	0	3	6	1.969	7.59	48	9.17	.367	0	.000	-5	0	-0.5
1993	Phi-N	0	0	....	8	0	0	0	0	16^{1}	15	9	9	1	1	7	14	1.347	4.96	80	3.67	.238	0	.000	-2	0	-0.2
	SD-N	0	1	.000	28	0	0	0	0	37^{2}	36	19	15	5	0	17	32	1.407	3.58	115	4.01	.248	0	.000	2	2	0.2
	Yr.	0	1	.000	36	0	0	0	0	54	51	28	24	6	1	24	46	1.389	4.00	102	3.90	.245	0	.000	1	2	0.0
1994	SD-N	2	4	.333	35	0	0	0	2	49	50	21	19	3	1	19	32	1.408	3.49	118	3.87	.269	1	.250	5	4	0.5

YEAR TM-L	W	L	PCT	G	GS	CG	SH	SV	IP	H	R	ER	HR	HB	BB	SO	RAT	ERA	ERA+	CERA	OAV	BH	AVG	PR+	WS	TPW
1995 SD-N	0	1	.000	5	0	0	0	0	5^{2}	4	6	6	0	0	9	9	2.294	9.53	42	5.98	.190	0	.000	-4	0	-0.4
Total 4	2	6	.250	79	0	0	0	2	119^{1}	123	65	58	12	2	55	93	1.492	4.37	92	4.46	.265	1	.071	-3	6	-0.3
• MAXCY, Brian	David Brian Maxcy b: 5/4/1971, Amory, MS BR/TR, 6'1", 170 lbs. Deb: 5/27/1995																									
1995 Det-A	4	5	.444	41	0	0	0	0	52^{1}	61	48	40	6	2	31	20	1.758	6.88	69	5.81	.293	0	....	-12	0	-1.1
1996 Det-A	0	0	....	2	0	0	0	0	3^{1}	8	5	5	2	0	2	1	3.000	13.50	37	20.67	.471	0	....	-3	0	-0.3
Total 2	4	5	.444	43	0	0	0	0	55^{2}	69	53	45	8	2	33	21	1.832	7.28	66	6.70	.307	0	....	-15	0	-1.4
• MAXIE, Larry	Larry Hans Maxie b: 10/10/1940, Upland, CA BR/TR, 6'4", 220 lbs. Deb: 8/30/1969																									
1969 Atl-N	0	0	....	2	0	0	0	0	3	1	1	1	0	1	1	1	.667	3.00	120	0.94	.111	0	....	0	0	0.0
• MAXWELL, Bert	James Albert Maxwell b: 10/17/1886, Texarkana, AR d: 12/10/1961, Brady, TX BB/TR, 6', 180 lbs. Deb: 9/12/1906 U																									
1906 Pit-N	0	1	.000	1	1	0	0	0	8	8	6	5	0	0	2	1	1.250	5.63	47	3.15	.286	0	.000	-3	0	-0.3
1908 Phi-A	0	0	....	4	0	0	0	0	13	23	21	16	0	2	9	7	2.462	11.08	23	8.89	.348	0	.000	-12	0	-1.4
1911 NY-N	1	2	.333	4	3	3	0	0	31	37	15	10	0	2	7	8	1.419	2.90	115	4.20	.311	1	.111	2	2	0.2
1914 Bro-F	3	4	.429	12	8	6	1	1	71^{1}	76	31	26	0	1	24	19	1.402	3.28	99	3.55	.276	2	.087	0	4	-0.1
Total 4	4	7	.364	21	12	9	1	1	123^{1}	144	73	57	0	5	42	35	1.508	4.16	72	4.25	.295	3	.075	-12	6	-1.7
• MAY, Buckshot	William Herbert May b: 12/13/1899, Bakersfield, CA d: 3/15/1984, Bakersfield, CA BR/TR, 6'2", 169 lbs. Deb: 5/9/1924																									
1924 Pit-N	0	0	....	1	0	0	0	0	1	2	0	0	0	0	0	1	2.000	0.00	....	9.49	.500	0	....	0	0	0.0
• MAY, Darrell	Darrell Kevin May b: 6/13/1972, San Bernardino, CA BL/TL, 6'2", 170 lbs. Deb: 9/10/1995																									
1995 Atl-N	0	0	....	2	0	0	0	0	4	10	5	5	0	0	0	1	2.500	11.25	38	11.41	.500	0	....	-3	0	-0.3
1996 Pit-N	0	1	.000	5	2	0	0	0	8^{2}	15	10	9	5	1	4	5	2.192	9.35	47	13.48	.357	1	.333	-5	0	-0.4
Cal-A	0	0	....	5	0	0	0	0	2^{2}	3	3	3	1	0	2	1	1.875	10.13	48	8.41	.333	0	....	-2	0	-0.1
1997 Ana-A	2	1	.667	29	2	0	0	0	51^{2}	56	31	30	6	0	25	42	1.568	5.23	88	4.87	.277	0	.000	-4	2	-0.4
2002 KC-A	4	10	.286	30	21	2	1	0	131^{1}	144	83	78	28	1	50	95	1.477	5.35	94	5.35	.277	0	.000	-4	5	-0.4
2003 KC-A	10	8	.556	35	32	2	1	0	210	197	98	88	31	2	53	115	1.190	3.77	137	3.50	.246	0	.000	33	17	3.1
Total 5	16	20	.444	106	57	4	2	0	408^{1}	425	230	213	71	4	134	259	1.369	4.69	106	4.59	.266	1	.077	15	24	1.4
• MAY, Jakie	Frank Spruiell May b: 11/25/1895, Youngsville, NC d: 6/3/1970, Wendell, NC BR/TL, 5'8", 178 lbs. Deb: 6/26/1917																									
1917 StL-N	0	0	....	15	1	0	0	0	29^{1}	29	13	11	0	3	11	18	1.364	3.38	80	3.88	.302	0	.000	-3	1	-0.4
1918 StL-N	5	6	.455	29	15	6	0	0	152^{2}	149	83	65	2	13	69	61	1.428	3.83	71	3.71	.264	3	.067	-20	2	-2.3
1919 StL-N	3	12	.200	28	19	8	1	0	125^{2}	99	64	45	1	14	87	58	1.480	3.22	87	3.61	.230	6	.162	-8	3	-1.0
1920 StL-N	1	4	.200	16	5	3	0	0	70^{2}	65	38	24	0	7	37	33	1.443	3.06	100	3.53	.251	5	.227	-0	3	0.1
1921 StL-N	1	3	.250	5	5	1	0	0	21	29	14	11	0	0	12	5	1.952	4.71	77	6.20	.333	2	.333	-2	1	-0.2
1924 Cin-N	3	3	.500	38	3	2	0	**6**	99	104	39	33	2	6	29	59	1.343	3.00	126	3.57	.276	3	.111	8	8	0.7
1925 Cin-N	8	9	.471	36	12	7	1	2	137^{1}	146	74	59	3	7	45	74	1.391	3.87	106	3.68	.272	8	.186	1	8	0.1
1926 Cin-N	13	9	.591	45	15	9	1	3	167^{2}	175	66	60	4	7	44	103	1.306	3.22	115	3.40	.276	7	.146	8	12	0.7
1927 Cin-N	15	12	.556	44	28	17	2	1	235^{2}	242	110	92	4	14	70	121	1.324	3.51	108	3.41	.274	14	.184	8	15	0.8
1928 Cin-N	3	5	.375	21	11	1	1	1	79^{1}	99	44	39	1	1	35	39	1.689	4.42	89	4.95	.315	8	.296	-4	3	-0.3
1929 Cin-N	10	14	.417	41	24	10	0	3	199	219	111	102	7	5	75	92	1.477	4.61	99	4.07	.285	13	.203	-2	12	-0.3
1930 Cin-N	3	11	.214	26	18	5	1	0	112^{1}	147	83	72	6	6	41	44	1.674	5.77	84	5.46	.320	5	.128	-11	2	-1.1
1931 Chi-N	5	5	.500	31	4	1	0	2	79	81	35	34	2	3	43	38	1.570	3.87	100	4.29	.275	5	.227	1	5	0.1
1932* Chi-N	2	2	.500	35	0	0	0	1	53^{2}	61	34	26	3	2	19	20	1.491	4.36	86	4.22	.281	1	.125	-4	2	-0.5
Total 14	72	95	.431	410	160	70	7	19	1562^{1}	1645	808	673	35	88	617	765	1.448	3.88	96	3.92	.278	80	.171	-28	77	-3.4
• MAY, Rudy	Rudolph May b: 7/18/1944, Coffeyville, KS BL/TL, 6'2", 207 lbs. Deb: 4/18/1965																									
1965 Cal-A	4	9	.308	30	19	2	1	0	124	111	59	54	7	4	78	76	1.524	3.92	87	4.23	.245	6	.200	-8	4	-0.5
1969 Cal-A	10	13	.435	43	25	4	0	2	180^{1}	142	81	69	20	3	66	133	1.153	3.44	101	2.99	.220	4	.082	-2	10	-0.4
1970 Cal-A	7	13	.350	38	34	2	2	0	208^{2}	190	102	93	20	3	81	164	1.299	4.01	90	3.55	.245	6	.087	-14	5	-1.8
1971 Cal-A	11	12	.478	32	31	7	2	0	208^{1}	160	74	70	12	2	87	156	1.186	3.02	107	2.65	.213	10	.147	2	13	0.3
1972 Cal-A	12	11	.522	35	30	10	3	1	205^{1}	162	79	67	15	0	82	169	1.188	2.94	99	2.72	.215	7	.113	-2	11	-0.4
1973 Cal-A	7	17	.292	34	28	10	4	0	185	177	101	90	20	3	80	134	1.389	4.38	81	4.01	.254	0	....	-15	5	-1.5
1974 Cal-A	0	1	.000	18	3	0	0	2	27	29	24	21	2	1	10	12	1.444	7.00	49	4.19	.274	0	....	-10	0	-1.1
NY-A	8	4	.667	17	15	8	2	0	114^{1}	75	36	29	5	4	48	90	1.076	2.28	153	2.16	.188	0	....	13	10	1.4
Yr.	8	5	.615	35	18	8	2	2	141^{1}	104	60	50	7	5	58	102	1.146	3.18	109	2.55	.206	0	....	3	10	0.3
1975 NY-A	14	12	.538	32	31	13	1	0	212	179	87	72	9	2	99	145	1.311	3.06	119	3.13	.231	0	....	8	15	0.8
1976 NY-A	4	3	.571	11	11	2	1	0	68	49	32	27	5	1	28	38	1.132	3.57	96	2.58	.206	0	....	-3	3	-0.4
Bal-A	11	7	.611	24	21	5	1	0	152^{1}	156	73	64	11	0	42	71	1.300	3.78	86	3.53	.267	0	....	-10	7	-1.1
Yr.	15	10	.600	35	32	7	2	0	220^{1}	205	105	91	16	1	70	109	1.248	3.72	89	3.24	.249	0	....	-14	10	-1.5
1977 Bal-A	18	14	.563	37	37	11	4	0	251^{2}	243	114	101	25	5	78	105	1.275	3.61	105	3.65	.255	0	....	-2	16	-0.2
1978 Mon-N	8	10	.444	27	23	4	1	0	144	141	73	62	15	6	42	87	1.271	3.88	91	3.69	.255	6	.143	-10	4	-1.0
1979 Mon-N	10	3	.769	33	7	2	1	0	93^{2}	88	30	24	4	4	31	67	1.270	2.31	159	3.21	.255	3	.143	14	9	1.4
1980* NY-A	15	5	.750	41	17	3	1	3	175^{1}	144	56	48	14	0	39	133	1.044	**2.46**	**159**	2.38	.224	0	....	29	17	2.9
1981* NY-A	6	11	.353	27	22	4	0	1	147^{2}	137	71	68	10	2	41	79	1.205	4.14	86	3.06	.246	0	....	-10	4	-1.1
1982 NY-A	6	6	.500	41	6	0	0	3	106	109	43	34	4	1	14	85	1.160	2.89	138	2.74	.267	0	....	14	8	1.4
1983 NY-A	1	5	.167	15	0	0	0	0	18^{1}	22	15	14	1	1	12	16	1.855	6.87	57	5.88	.293	0	....	-6	0	-0.6
Total 16	152	156	.494	535	360	87	24	12	2622	2314	1150	1007	199	42	958	1760	1.248	3.46	101	3.21	.238	42	.123	-14	141	-2.0
• MAY, Scott	Scott Francis May b: 11/11/1961, West Bend, WI BR/TR, 6'1", 185 lbs. Deb: 9/2/1988																									
1988 Tex-A	0	0	....	3	1	0	0	0	7^{1}	8	7	7	3	0	4	4	1.636	8.59	47	7.45	.296	0	....	-4	0	-0.4
1991 Chi-N	0	0	....	2	0	0	0	0	2	6	4	4	0	0	1	1	3.500	18.00	22	18.50	.545	0	....	-3	0	-0.3
Total 2	0	0	....	5	1	0	0	0	9^{1}	14	11	11	3	0	5	5	2.036	10.61	38	9.82	.368	0	....	-7	0	-0.7
• MAYER, Ed	Edwin David Mayer b: 11/30/1931, San Francisco, CA BL/TL, 6'2", 185 lbs. Deb: 9/15/1957																									
1957 Chi-N	0	0	....	3	1	0	0	0	7^{2}	8	5	5	2	1	2	3	1.304	5.87	66	5.33	.258	1	.500	-2	0	-0.1
1958 Chi-N	2	2	.500	19	0	0	0	1	23^{2}	15	12	10	0	3	16	14	1.310	3.80	103	2.91	.190	1	.200	1	2	0.0
Total 2	2	2	.500	22	1	0	0	1	31^{1}	23	17	15	2	4	18	17	1.309	4.31	91	3.50	.209	2	.286	-1	2	-0.1
• MAYER, Erskine	Erskine John Mayer b: 1/16/1889, Atlanta, GA d: 3/10/1957, Los Angeles, CA BR/TR, 6', 168 lbs. Deb: 9/4/1912																									
1912 Phi-N	0	1	.000	7	1	0	0	0	21^{1}	27	15	15	1	1	7	5	1.594	6.33	57	5.10	.318	0	.000	-6	0	-0.7
1913 Phi-N	9	9	.500	39	19	7	2	1	170^{2}	172	77	59	6	9	46	51	1.277	3.11	107	3.39	.272	6	.120	4	11	0.3
1914 Phi-N	21	19	.525	48	38	24	4	2	321	308	135	92	8	13	91	116	1.243	2.58	114	2.99	.256	21	.194	23	21	2.7
1915* Phi-N	21	15	.583	43	33	20	2	2	274^{2}	240	94	72	9	14	59	114	1.089	2.36	116	2.49	.243	21	.239	11	24	1.8
1916 Phi-N	7	7	.500	28	16	7	2	0	140	148	58	49	7	4	33	62	1.293	3.15	84	3.54	.281	5	.132	-8	6	-1.0
1917 Phi-N	11	6	.647	28	18	11	1	0	160	160	62	49	6	4	33	64	1.206	2.76	102	3.04	.268	10	.196	-0	11	0.0
1918 Phi-N	7	4	.636	13	13	7	0	0	104	108	46	36	2	4	26	16	1.288	3.12	96	3.30	.276	8	.216	-1	7	0.0
Pit-N	9	3	.750	15	14	11	1	0	123^{1}	122	40	31	1	4	27	25	1.208	2.26	127	2.81	.268	7	.167	4	10	0.7
Yr.	16	7	.696	28	27	18	1	0	227^{1}	230	86	67	3	8	53	41	1.245	2.65	111	3.04	.272	15	.190	3	17	0.7
1919 Pit-N	5	3	.625	18	10	6	0	1	88^{1}	100	50	44	2	2	12	20	1.268	4.48	67	3.06	.267	6	.207	-14	2	-1.5
* Chi-A	1	3	.250	6	2	0	0	0	23^{2}	30	23	22	1	0	11	9	1.732	8.37	38	5.50	.316	0	.000	-14	0	-1.6
Total 8	91	70	.565	245	164	93	12	6	1427	1415	600	469	43	55	345	482	1.233	2.96	99	3.09	.265	84	.185	-1	92	0.7
• MAYS, Al	Albert C. Mays b: 5/17/1865, Canal Dover, OH d: 5/17/1905, Parkersburg, WV BR Deb: 5/10/1885 U																									
1885 Lou-a	6	11	.353	17	17	17	0	0	150	129	102	46	3	8	43	61	1.147	2.76	117	....	.222	13	.213	8	9	0.8
1886 NY-a	11	27	.289	41	40	39	1	0	350	330	231	132	7	14	140	163	1.343	3.39	100	....	.238	16	.119	-4	19	-1.1
1887 NY-a	17	34	.333	52	52	50	0	0	441^{1}	687	359	232	11	20	136	124	1.557	4.73	90	....	.343	55	.238	-10	14	-0.9
1888 Bro-a	9	9	.500	18	18	17	1	0	160^{2}	150	81	50	1	11	32	67	1.133	2.80	106	....	.238	5	.079	3	12	-0.1
1889 Col-a	10	7	.588	21	19	13	1	0	140	167	119	75	4	4	56	52	1.593	4.82	75	....	.287	7	.130	-19	5	-1.7

YEAR TM-L	W	L	PCT	G	GS	CG	SH	SV	IP	H	R	ER	HR	HB	BB	SO	RAT	ERA	ERA+	CERA	OAV	BH	AVG	PR+	WS	TPW
1890 Col-a	0	1	.000	1	1	1	0	0	9	14	13	8	0	1	8	2	2.444	8.00	45	....	.345	0	.000	-5	0	-0.4
Total 6	53	89	.373	150	147	137	3	0	1251	1477	905	543	26	58	415	469	1.404	3.91	94	....	.283	96	.176	-27	59	-3.5
• MAYS, Carl	Carl William "Sub" Mays b: 11/12/1891, Liberty, KY d: 4/4/1971, El Cajon, CA BL/TR, 5'11.5", 195 lbs. Deb: 4/15/1915																									
1915 Bos-A	6	5	.545	38	6	2	0	**7**	131^{2}	119	54	38	0	5	21	65	1.063	2.60	107	2.24	.244	9	.237	2	11	0.3
1916* Bos-A	18	13	.581	44	24	14	2	3	245	208	79	65	3	9	74	76	1.151	2.39	116	2.51	.234	18	.234	13	22	2.3
1917 Bos-A	22	9	.710	35	33	27	2	0	289	230	81	56	1	14	74	91	1.052	1.74	148	2.08	.221	27	.252	25	30	3.5
1918* Bos-A	21	13	.618	35	33	**30**	**8**	0	293^{1}	230	94	72	2	11	81	114	1.060	2.21	121	2.04	.221	30	.288	14	25	2.6
1919 Bos-A	5	11	.313	21	16	14	2	2	146	131	53	40	3	5	40	53	1.171	2.47	122	2.74	.247	8	.151	7	9	0.5
NY-A	9	3	.750	13	13	12	1	0	120	96	38	22	2	5	37	54	1.108	1.65	193	2.25	.216	14	.311	17	14	2.0
Yr.	14	14	.500	34	29	26	3	2	266	227	91	62	5	10	77	107	1.143	2.10	147	2.52	.233	22	.224	24	23	2.6
1920 NY-A	26	11	.703	45	37	26	**6**	2	312	310	127	106	13	7	84	92	1.263	3.06	125	3.19	.263	26	.239	26	27	2.7
1921* NY-A	**27**	9	.750	**49**	38	30	1	**7**	**336^{2}**	332	145	114	11	9	76	70	1.212	3.05	139	2.93	.257	49	.343	40	35	4.8
1922* NY-A	13	14	.481	34	29	21	1	2	240	257	111	96	12	7	50	41	1.279	3.60	111	3.53	.285	23	.250	9	17	0.9
1923 NY-A	5	2	.714	23	7	2	0	0	81^{1}	119	59	56	8	4	32	16	1.857	6.20	64	7.03	.357	4	.148	-21	1	-2.0
1924 Cin-N	20	9	.690	37	27	15	2	0	226	238	97	79	3	4	36	63	1.212	3.15	120	2.88	.270	24	.289	15	20	2.2
1925 Cin-N	3	5	.375	12	5	3	0	2	51^{2}	60	22	19	0	2	13	10	1.413	3.31	124	3.75	.294	4	.250	4	5	0.4
1926 Cin-N	19	12	.613	39	33	**24**	3	1	281	286	112	98	3	4	53	58	1.206	3.14	118	2.80	.269	22	.224	17	20	1.9
1927 Cin-N	3	7	.300	14	9	6	0	0	82	89	39	32	1	1	10	17	1.207	3.51	108	2.87	.276	13	.406	3	6	0.8
1928 Cin-N	4	1	.800	14	6	4	1	1	62^{2}	67	33	27	3	0	22	10	1.420	3.88	102	3.84	.275	8	.296	0	5	0.2
1929 NY-N	7	2	.778	37	8	1	0	4	123	140	67	59	8	2	31	32	1.390	4.32	106	3.95	.287	12	.353	2	9	0.6
Total 15	208	126	.623	490	324	231	29	31	3021^{1}	2912	1211	979	73	89	734	862	1.207	2.92	120	2.90	.257	291	.268	172	256	23.8
• MAYS, Joe	Joseph Emerson Mays b: 12/10/1975, Flint, MI BB/TR, 6'1", 185 lbs. Deb: 4/7/1999																									
1999 Min-A	6	11	.353	49	20	2	1	0	171	179	92	83	24	2	67	115	1.439	4.37	116	4.62	.270	0	.000	14	10	1.4
2000 Min-A	7	15	.318	31	28	2	1	0	160^{1}	193	105	99	20	2	67	102	1.622	5.56	93	5.59	.299	2	.400	-5	6	-0.3
2001 Min-A★	17	13	.567	34	34	4	2	0	233^{2}	205	87	82	25	5	64	123	1.151	3.16	**145**	3.05	.235	0	.000	39	**22**	3.7
2002* Min-A	4	8	.333	17	17	1	1	0	95^{1}	113	60	57	14	2	25	38	1.448	5.38	83	4.99	.292	0	....	-9	2	-0.9
2003 Min-A	8	8	.500	31	21	0	0	0	130	159	92	91	21	4	39	50	1.523	6.30	72	5.55	.302	1	.333	-23	2	-2.1
Total 5	42	55	.433	162	120	9	5	0	790^{1}	849	436	412	104	15	262	428	1.406	4.69	102	4.55	.274	3	.250	16	42	1.7
• MAYSEY, Matt	Matthew Samuel Maysey b: 1/8/1967, Hamilton, Canada BR/TR, 6'4", 225 lbs. Deb: 7/8/1992																									
1992 Mon-N	0	0	....	2	0	0	0	0	2^{1}	4	1	1	1	1	0	1	1.714	3.86	90	11.45	.364	0	....	-0	0	0.0
1993 Mil-A	1	2	.333	23	0	0	0	1	22	28	14	14	4	1	13	10	1.864	5.73	74	7.35	.322	1	1.000	-3	1	-0.3
Total 2	1	2	.333	25	0	0	0	1	24^{1}	32	15	15	5	2	13	11	1.849	5.55	75	7.74	.327	1	1.000	-4	1	-0.3
• MCADAMS, Jack	George D. McAdams b: 12/17/1886, Benton, AR d: 5/21/1937, San Francisco, CA BR/TR, 6'1.5", 170 lbs. Deb: 7/22/1911																									
1911 StL-N	0	0	....	6	0	0	0	0	9^{2}	7	5	4	0	2	5	4	1.241	3.72	90	3.26	.226	0	.000	-0	0	-0.1
• MCAFEE, Bill	William Fort McAfee b: 9/7/1907, Smithville, GA d: 7/8/1958, Culpepper, VA BR/TR, 6'2", 186 lbs. Deb: 5/12/1930																									
1930 Chi-N	0	0	....	2	0	0	0	0	1	3	5	0	0	0	2	0	5.000	0.00	....	18.79	.375	0	....	1	0	0.0
1931 Bos-N	0	1	.000	18	1	0	0	0	29^{2}	39	22	21	2	0	10	9	1.652	6.37	59	5.57	.333	0	.000	-8	0	-0.9
1932 Was-A	6	1	.857	8	5	2	0	0	41^{1}	47	22	18	3	0	22	10	1.669	3.92	110	5.03	.287	2	.111	1	3	-0.1
1933 Was-A	3	2	.600	27	1	0	0	5	53	64	40	39	3	1	21	14	1.604	6.62	63	4.76	.296	4	.267	-16	1	-1.3
1934 StL-A	1	0	1.000	28	0	0	0	0	61^{2}	84	48	40	4	3	26	11	1.784	5.84	86	6.16	.332	3	.188	-7	2	-0.6
Total 5	10	4	.714	83	7	2	0	5	186^{2}	237	137	118	12	4	81	44	1.704	5.69	77	5.49	.313	9	.173	-29	6	-2.8
• MCALLISTER, Sport	Lewis William McAllister b: 7/23/1874, Austin, MS d: 7/17/1962, Wyandotte, MI BB/TR, 5'11", 180 lbs. Deb: 8/7/1896 U ♦																									
1896 Cle-N	0	0	....	1	0	0	0	0	4	9	3	3	0	0	2	0	2.750	6.75	67	11.58	.440	6	.222	-1	0	-0.5
1897 Cle-N	1	2	.333	4	3	3	0	0	28	29	20	14	3	0	9	10	1.357	4.50	100	3.96	.265	30	.219	-2	2	-1.3
1898 Cle-N	3	4	.429	9	7	6	0	0	65^{1}	73	43	33	2	3	23	9	1.469	4.55	79	4.12	.281	13	.228	-7	3	-0.6
1899 Cle-N	0	1	.000	3	1	1	0	0	16	29	22	17	0	4	10	2	2.438	9.56	38	10.08	.390	99	.237	-10	1	-3.8
Total 4	4	7	.364	17	11	10	0	0	113^{1}	140	88	67	5	7	44	21	1.624	5.32	72	5.19	.301	358	.247	-20	6	-6.3
• MCANALLY, Ernie	Ernest Lee McAnally b: 8/15/1946, Pittsburg, TX BR/TR, 6'1", 190 lbs. Deb: 4/11/1971																									
1971 Mon-N	11	12	.478	31	25	8	2	0	177^{2}	150	85	77	9	8	87	98	1.334	3.90	90	3.38	.228	7	.117	-7	8	-0.9
1972 Mon-N	6	15	.286	29	27	4	2	0	170	165	79	72	13	4	71	102	1.388	3.81	93	3.89	.259	6	.113	-4	7	-0.6
1973 Mon-N	7	9	.438	27	24	4	0	0	147	158	84	66	13	3	54	72	1.442	4.04	94	4.27	.274	9	.184	-4	5	-0.5
1974 Mon-N	6	13	.316	25	21	5	2	0	128^{2}	126	73	64	10	4	56	79	1.415	4.48	86	3.99	.256	5	.119	-9	3	-1.1
Total 4	30	49	.380	112	97	21	6	0	623^{1}	599	321	279	45	19	268	351	1.391	4.03	91	3.86	.253	27	.132	-23	23	-3.1
• MCANDREW, Jamie	James Brian McAndrew b: 9/2/1967, Williamsport, PA BR/TR, 6'2", 190 lbs. Deb: 7/17/1995																									
1995 Mil-A	2	3	.400	10	4	0	0	0	36^{1}	37	21	19	2	1	12	19	1.349	4.71	106	3.68	.266	0	....	0	2	0.0
1997 Mil-A	1	1	.500	5	4	0	0	0	19^{1}	24	19	18	1	2	23	8	2.431	8.38	55	8.93	.304	0	....	-9	0	-0.8
Total 2	3	4	.429	15	8	0	0	0	55^{2}	61	40	37	3	3	35	27	1.725	5.98	80	5.50	.280	0	....	-8	2	-0.8
• MCANDREW, Jim	James Clement McAndrew b: 1/11/1944, Lost Nation, IA BR/TR, 6'2", 185 lbs. Deb: 7/21/1968																									
1968 NY-N	4	7	.364	12	12	2	1	0	79	66	20	20	5	4	17	46	1.051	2.28	133	2.45	.230	1	.045	6	6	0.5
1969 NY-N	6	7	.462	27	21	4	2	0	135	112	57	52	12	2	44	90	1.156	3.47	105	2.81	.225	5	.135	-1	7	-0.1
1970 NY-N	10	14	.417	32	27	9	3	2	184^{1}	166	77	73	18	2	38	111	1.107	3.56	113	2.79	.239	8	.148	6	12	0.7
1971 NY-N	2	5	.286	24	10	0	0	0	90^{1}	78	50	44	10	1	32	42	1.218	4.38	78	3.12	.227	1	.043	-11	0	-1.3
1972 NY-N	11	8	.579	28	23	4	0	1	160^{2}	133	54	50	12	5	38	81	1.064	2.80	120	2.49	.225	2	.047	11	13	0.9
1973 NY-N	3	8	.273	23	12	0	0	1	80^{1}	109	60	48	9	3	31	38	1.743	5.38	67	6.26	.330	2	.133	-16	0	-1.5
1974 SD-N	1	4	.200	15	5	1	0	0	41^{2}	48	30	26	7	0	13	16	1.464	5.62	63	4.83	.284	1	.143	-8	0	-0.9
Total 7	37	53	.411	161	110	20	6	4	771^{1}	712	348	313	73	17	213	424	1.199	3.65	98	3.21	.245	20	.100	-13	38	-1.6
• MCARTHUR, Dixie	Oland Alexander McArthur b: 2/1/1892, Vernon, AL d: 5/31/1986, West Point, MS BR/TR, 6'1", 185 lbs. Deb: 7/10/1914																									
1914 Pit-N	0	0	....	1	0	0	0	0	1	1	0	0	0	0	0	1	1.000	0.00	....	1.95	.250	0	....	0	0	0.0
• MCAVOY, Tom	Thomas John McAvoy b: 8/12/1936, Brooklyn, NY BL/TL, 6'3", 200 lbs. Deb: 9/27/1959																									
1959 Was-A	0	0	....	1	0	0	0	0	2^{2}	1	0	0	0	0	2	0	1.125	0.00	....	1.70	.125	0	.000	1	0	0.1
• MCAVOY, Wickey	James Eugene McAvoy b: 10/22/1894, Rochester, NY d: 7/6/1973, Rochester, NY BR/TR, 5'11", 172 lbs. Deb: 9/29/1913 ♦																									
1918 Phi-A	0	0	....	1	0	0	0	0	0^{2}	1	1	1	1	0	0	0	1.500	13.50	22	15.46	.500	66	.244	-1	6	0.6
• MCBEAN, Al	Alvin O'Neal McBean b: 5/15/1938, Charlotte Amalie, V.I. BR/TR, 5'11.5", 180 lbs. Deb: 7/2/1961																									
1961 Pit-N	3	2	.600	27	2	0	0	0	74^{1}	72	35	31	4	4	42	49	1.534	3.75	106	4.34	.263	4	.267	2	5	0.3
1962 Pit-N	15	10	.600	33	29	6	2	0	189^{2}	212	93	78	11	7	65	119	1.460	3.70	106	4.40	.285	14	.209	3	12	0.5
1963 Pit-N	13	3	.813	55	7	2	1	11	122^{1}	100	42	35	5	2	39	74	1.136	2.57	128	2.39	.222	6	.194	9	14	1.1
1964 Pit-N	8	3	.727	58	0	0	0	22	89^{2}	76	23	19	4	4	17	41	1.037	1.91	184	2.24	.234	1	.083	17	16	1.7
1965 Pit-N	6	6	.500	62	1	0	0	18	114	111	33	29	5	3	42	54	1.342	2.29	153	3.40	.260	6	.222	13	14	1.5
1966 Pit-N	4	3	.571	47	0	0	0	3	86^{2}	95	38	31	9	2	24	54	1.373	3.22	111	4.18	.280	1	.100	2	5	0.1
1967 Pit-N	7	4	.636	51	8	5	0	4	131	118	41	37	6	1	43	54	1.229	2.54	132	2.96	.248	6	.207	10	11	1.4
1968 Pit-N	9	12	.429	36	28	9	2	0	198^{1}	204	88	79	10	5	63	100	1.346	3.58	82	3.67	.269	13	.194	-17	5	-1.7
1969 SD-N	0	1	.000	1	1	0	0	0	7	10	4	4	1	0	2	1	1.714	5.14	69	6.77	.345	1	.500	-1	0	-0.1
LA-N	2	6	.250	31	0	0	0	4	48^{1}	46	22	21	6	2	21	26	1.386	3.91	85	4.18	.258	0	.000	-4	2	-0.4
Yr.	2	7	.222	32	1	0	0	4	55^{1}	56	26	25	7	2	23	27	1.428	4.07	83	4.50	.271	1	.200	-5	2	-0.5

YEAR TM-L	W	L	PCT	G	GS	CG	SH	SV	IP	H	R	ER	HR	HB	BB	SO	RAT	ERA	ERA+	CERA	OAV	BH	AVG	PR+	WS	TPW
1970 LA-N	0	0	....	1	0	0	0	0	1	1	0	0	0	0	0	0	1.000	0.00	....	2.02	.333	0	....	0	0	0.0
Pit-N	0	0	....	7	0	0	0	1	10	13	11	9	2	0	7	3	2.000	8.10	48	8.19	.317	0	.000	-5	0	-0.5
Yr.	0	0	....	8	0	0	0	1	11	14	11	9	2	0	7	3	1.909	7.36	53	7.63	.318	0	.000	-5	0	-0.5
Total 10	67	50	.573	409	76	22	5	63	1072^1	1058	430	373	63	30	365	575	1.327	3.13	110	3.59	.262	52	.197	30	84	4.0
• MCBEE, Pryor	Pryor Edward "Lefty" McBee b: 6/20/1901, Blanco, OK d: 4/19/1963, Roseville, CA BR/TL, 6'1", 190 lbs. Deb: 5/22/1926																									
1926 Chi-A	0	0	....	1	0	0	0	0	1^1	1	2	1	0	0	3	1	3.000	6.75	57	8.02	.250	0	....	-0	0	0.0
• MCBRIDE, Dick	James Dickson McBride b: 1845, Philadelphia, PA d: 10/10/1916, Philadelphia, PA TR, 5'9", 150 lbs. Deb: 5/20/1871 M																									
1871 Ath-n	18	5	.783	25	25	25	0	0	222	285	....	113	3	....	40	15	1.464	4.58	88	....	.272	31	.235	-17	....	-1.3
1872 Ath-n	30	14	.682	47	47	47	1	0	419^1	513	....	133	3	....	26	44	1.285	2.85	121	....	.263	74	.287	15	....	1.4
1873 Ath-n	24	19	.558	46	46	38	**3**	0	382^2	453	....	141	3	....	47	25	1.307	3.32	103	....	.260	71	.281	-7	....	-0.4
1874 Ath-n	33	22	.600	55	55	55	0	0	487	514	....	89	6	....	32	37	1.121	**1.64**	124	....	**.241**	57	.217	23	....	1.3
1875 Ath-n	44	14	.759	60	60	59	6	0	538	602	....	139	4	....	24	27	1.164	2.33	134	....	.258	73	.270	19	....	2.0
1876 Bos-N	0	4	.000	4	4	3	0	0	33	53	35	10	1	....	5	2	1.758	2.73	83	....	.329	3	.188	-2	0	-0.2
Total 5 n	149	74	.668	233	233	224	10	0	2049	2367	....	615	19	....	169	148	1.238	2.70	116	....	.257	306	.260	33	....	2.9
• MCBRIDE, Ken	Kenneth Faye McBride b: 8/12/1935, Huntsville, AL BR/TR, 6'1", 195 lbs. Deb: 8/4/1959 C																									
1959 Chi-A	0	1	.000	11	2	0	0	1	22^2	20	11	8	1	0	17	12	1.632	3.18	118	4.24	.230	1	.167	1	1	0.1
1960 Chi-A	0	1	.000	5	0	0	0	0	4^2	6	2	2	0	1	3	4	1.929	3.86	98	6.63	.333	0	....	-0	0	0.0
1961 LA-A★	12	15	.444	38	36	11	1	1	241^2	229	114	98	28	7	102	180	1.370	3.65	124	4.08	.252	7	.084	26	17	2.1
1962 LA-A★	11	5	.688	24	23	6	4	0	149^1	136	66	58	9	9	70	83	1.379	3.50	110	3.82	.249	9	.164	7	10	0.7
1963 LA-A★	13	12	.520	36	36	11	2	0	251	198	101	91	22	14	82	147	1.116	3.26	105	2.83	.218	15	.172	5	13	0.7
1964 LA-A	4	13	.235	29	21	0	0	1	116^1	104	77	68	14	16	75	66	1.539	5.26	62	5.14	.239	6	.214	-26	0	-2.5
1965 Cal-A	0	3	.000	8	4	0	0	0	22	24	17	15	1	2	14	11	1.727	6.14	55	5.34	.270	0	.000	-7	0	-0.7
Total 7	40	50	.444	151	122	28	7	3	807^2	717	388	340	75	49	363	503	1.337	3.79	98	3.85	.240	38	.144	6	41	0.4
• MCBRIDE, Pete	Peter William McBride b: 7/9/1875, Adams, MA d: 7/3/1944, North Adams, MA BR/TR, 5'10", 170 lbs. Deb: 9/20/1898																									
1898 Cle-N	0	1	.000	1	1	1	0	0	7	9	6	5	0	1	4	6	1.857	6.43	56	6.00	.310	2	1.000	-2	1	-0.1
1899 StL-N	2	4	.333	11	6	4	0	0	64	65	46	29	4	4	40	26	1.641	4.08	98	4.83	.263	5	.185	-1	3	-0.1
Total 2	2	5	.286	12	7	5	0	0	71	74	52	34	4	5	44	32	1.662	4.31	91	4.95	.268	7	.241	-4	4	-0.2
• MCCABE, Dick	Richard James McCabe b: 2/21/1896, Mamaroneck, NY d: 4/11/1950, Buffalo, NY BR/TR, 5'10.5", 159 lbs. Deb: 5/30/1918																									
1918 Bos-A	0	1	.000	3	1	0	0	0	9^2	13	4	3	0	0	2	3	1.552	2.79	96	4.84	.351	0	.000	-0	0	-0.1
1922 Chi-A	1	0	1.000	3	0	0	0	0	3^1	4	2	2	0	0	0	1	1.200	5.40	75	3.15	.308	0	....	-1	0	-0.1
Total 2	1	1	.500	6	1	0	0	0	13	17	6	5	0	0	2	4	1.462	3.46	90	4.41	.340	0	.000	-1	0	-0.1
• MCCABE, Ralph	Ralph Herbert "Mack" McCabe b: 10/21/1918, Napanee, Canada d: 5/3/1974, Windsor, Canada BR/TR, 6'4", 195 lbs. Deb: 9/18/1946																									
1946 Cle-A	0	1	.000	1	1	0	0	0	4	5	5	5	3	1	2	3	1.750	11.25	29	13.02	.313	0	.000	-4	0	-0.4
• MCCABE, Tim	Timothy J. McCabe b: 10/19/1894, Ironton, MO d: 4/12/1977, Ironton, MO BR/TR, 6', 190 lbs. Deb: 8/16/1915																									
1915 StL-A	3	1	.750	7	4	4	1	0	41^2	25	11	6	1	1	9	17	.816	1.30	221	1.32	.177	1	.067	7	4	0.6
1916 StL-A	2	0	1.000	13	0	0	0	0	25^2	29	20	9	0	2	7	7	1.403	3.16	87	3.80	.282	0	.000	-2	0	-0.2
1917 StL-A	0	0	....	1	0	0	0	0	2^1	4	6	6	1	0	4	2	3.429	23.14	11	18.86	.400	0	....	-5	0	-0.6
1918 StL-A	0	0	....	1	0	0	0	0	1^1	2	2	2	0	0	1	0	2.250	13.50	20	6.30	.333	0	....	-2	0	-0.2
Total 4	5	1	.833	22	4	4	1	0	71	60	39	23	2	3	21	26	1.141	2.92	94	2.89	.231	1	.053	-2	4	-0.3
• MCCAHAN, Bill	William Glenn McCahan b: 6/7/1921, Philadelphia, PA d: 7/3/1986, Fort Worth, TX BR/TR, 5'11", 200 lbs. Deb: 9/15/1946																									
1946 Phi-A	1	1	.500	4	2	2	1	0	18	16	2	2	0	0	9	6	1.389	1.00	355	3.04	.246	2	.400	5	3	0.6
1947 Phi-A	10	5	.667	29	19	10	1	0	165^1	160	73	61	7	0	62	47	1.343	3.32	115	3.31	.252	9	.164	5	11	0.4
1948 Phi-A	4	7	.364	17	15	5	0	0	86^2	98	58	55	8	0	65	20	1.881	5.71	75	5.93	.284	8	.258	-14	2	-1.3
1949 Phi-A	1	1	.500	7	4	0	0	0	20^2	23	9	6	0	0	9	3	1.548	2.61	157	4.03	.291	1	.200	3	2	0.3
Total 4	16	14	.533	57	40	17	2	0	290^2	297	142	124	15	0	145	76	1.521	3.84	105	4.13	.264	20	.208	-1	18	0.0
• MCCALL, Dutch	Robert Leonard McCall b: 12/27/1920, Columbia, TN d: 1/7/1996, Little Rock, AR BL/TL, 6'1", 184 lbs. Deb: 4/27/1948																									
1948 Chi-N	4	13	.235	30	20	5	0	0	151^1	158	93	81	14	1	85	89	1.606	4.82	81	4.78	.268	9	.170	-14	3	-1.3
• MCCALL, Larry	Larry Stephen McCall b: 9/8/1952, Asheville, NC BL/TR, 6'2", 195 lbs. Deb: 9/10/1977																									
1977 NY-A	0	1	.000	2	0	0	0	0	6	12	7	5	1	0	1	0	2.167	7.50	53	9.13	.375	0	....	-2	0	-0.2
1978 NY-A	1	1	.500	5	1	0	0	0	16	20	10	10	2	1	6	7	1.625	5.63	64	6.10	.323	0	....	-4	0	-0.4
1979 Tex-A	1	0	1.000	2	1	0	0	0	8^1	7	2	2	0	0	3	3	1.200	2.16	192	2.37	.226	0	....	2	1	0.2
Total 3	2	2	.500	9	2	0	0	0	30^1	39	19	17	3	1	10	10	1.615	5.04	75	5.68	.312	0	....	-4	1	-0.5
• MCCALL, Windy	John William McCall b: 7/18/1925, San Francisco, CA BL/TL, 6', 180 lbs. Deb: 4/25/1948																									
1948 Bos-A	0	1	.000	1	1	0	0	0	1^1	6	3	3	1	0	1	0	5.250	20.25	22	40.76	.600	0	....	-2	0	-0.2
1949 Bos-A	0	0	....	5	0	0	0	0	9^1	13	12	12	2	0	10	8	2.464	11.57	38	10.37	.333	2	.667	-8	0	-0.7
1950 Pit-N	0	0	....	2	0	0	0	0	6^2	12	7	7	2	0	4	5	2.400	9.45	46	11.90	.387	0	.000	-4	0	-0.4
1954 NY-N	2	5	.286	33	4	0	0	2	61	50	26	22	5	3	29	38	1.295	3.25	124	3.26	.219	0	.000	5	4	0.3
1955 NY-N	6	5	.545	42	6	4	0	3	95	86	45	39	8	6	37	50	1.295	3.69	109	3.61	.244	2	.118	4	7	0.3
1956 NY-N	3	4	.429	46	4	0	0	7	77^1	74	36	31	7	1	20	41	1.216	3.61	105	3.18	.252	3	.200	2	6	0.2
1957 NY-N	0	0	....	5	0	0	0	0	3	8	5	5	1	1	2	2	3.333	15.00	26	22.12	.533	0	....	-4	0	-0.4
Total 7	11	15	.423	134	15	4	0	12	253^2	249	134	119	26	11	103	144	1.388	4.22	95	4.27	.257	7	.146	-7	17	-0.8
• MCCAMENT, Randy	Larry Randall McCament b: 7/29/1962, Albuquerque, NM BR/TR, 6'3", 195 lbs. Deb: 6/28/1989																									
1989 SF-N	1	1	.500	25	0	0	0	0	36^2	32	22	16	4	1	23	12	1.500	3.93	86	4.44	.241	1	.333	-3	0	-0.3
1990 SF-N	0	0	....	3	0	0	0	0	6	8	2	2	0	0	5	5	2.167	3.00	121	7.07	.333	0	.000	0	0	0.0
Total 2	1	1	.500	28	0	0	0	0	42^2	40	24	18	4	1	28	17	1.594	3.80	90	4.81	.255	1	.250	-3	0	-0.3
• MCCANN, Gene	Henry Eugene "Mike" McCann b: 6/13/1876, Baltimore, MD d: 4/26/1943, New York, NY TR, 5'10" Deb: 4/19/1901																									
1901 Bro-N	2	3	.400	6	5	3	0	0	34	34	25	13	1	4	16	9	1.471	3.44	97	4.13	.259	0	.000	-1	1	-0.1
1902 Bro-N	1	2	.333	3	3	3	0	0	30	32	18	8	0	0	12	9	1.467	2.40	115	3.65	.273	1	.083	1	1	0.0
Total 2	3	5	.375	9	8	6	0	0	64	66	43	21	1	4	28	18	1.469	2.95	105	3.90	.265	1	.045	1	2	-0.1
• MCCARTHY, Arch	Archibald Joseph McCarthy b: 1/21/1881, Ypsilanti, MI TR, 6', 160 lbs. Deb: 8/14/1902																									
1902 Det-A	2	7	.222	10	8	8	0	0	72	90	57	49	2	4	31	10	1.681	6.13	59	5.18	.306	2	.071	-21	0	-2.2
• MCCARTHY, Bill	William Thomas McCarthy b: 4/11/1882, Ashland, MA d: 5/29/1939, Boston, MA BR/TR, 5'11", 180 lbs. Deb: 4/21/1906																									
1906 Bos-N	0	0	....	1	0	0	0	0	2	2	6	2	0	0	3	0	2.500	9.00	30	5.32	.182	0	.000	-1	0	-0.2
• MCCARTHY, Greg	Gregory O'Neil McCarthy b: 10/30/1968, Norwalk, CT BL/TL, 6'2", 195 lbs. Deb: 8/28/1996																									
1996 Sea-A	0	0	....	10	0	0	0	0	9^2	8	2	2	0	4	4	7	1.241	1.86	266	3.88	.229	0	....	3	1	0.3
1997 Sea-A	1	1	.500	37	0	0	0	0	29^2	26	21	18	4	1	16	34	1.416	5.46	82	4.29	.230	0	....	-3	1	-0.3
1998 Sea-A	1	2	.333	29	0	0	0	0	23^1	18	13	13	6	3	17	25	1.500	5.01	92	5.64	.214	0	....	-1	1	-0.1
Total 3	2	3	.400	76	0	0	0	0	62^2	52	36	33	10	8	37	66	1.420	4.74	97	4.73	.224	0	....	-0	3	0.0
• MCCARTHY, Tom	Thomas Patrick McCarthy b: 5/22/1884, Fort Wayne, IN d: 3/28/1933, Mishawaka, IN TR, 5'7", 170 lbs. Deb: 5/10/1908																									
1908 Cin-N	0	1	.000	1	1	0	0	0	3^2	6	5	4	0	0	3	3	2.455	9.82	23	7.25	.300	0	.000	-3	0	-0.4
Pit-N	0	0	....	2	1	0	0	0	6	3	1	0	0	0	6	1	1.500	0.00	....	3.08	.176	0	.000	2	1	0.1
Bos-N	7	3	.700	14	11	7	2	0	94	77	24	17	0	1	28	27	1.117	1.63	147	2.01	.235	6	.171	6	8	0.7
Yr.	7	4	.636	17	13	7	2	0	103^2	86	30	21	0	1	37	31	1.186	1.82	130	2.26	.236	6	.146	4	9	0.5

YEAR TM-L	W	L	PCT	G	GS	CG	SH	SV	IP	H	R	ER	HR	HB	BB	SO	RAT	ERA	ERA+	CERA	OAV	BH	AVG	PR+	WS	TPW
1909 Bos-N	0	5	.000	8	7	3	0	0	46^{1}	47	28	18	3	2	28	11	1.619	3.50	80	4.90	.272	2	.125	-4	1	-0.4
Total 2	7	9	.438	25	20	10	2	0	150	133	58	39	3	3	65	42	1.320	2.34	109	3.07	.247	8	.140	1	10	0.0
• MCCARTHY, Tom	Thomas Michael McCarthy b: 6/18/1961, Lundstahl, West Germany BR/TR, 6', 180 lbs. Deb: 7/5/1985																									
1985 Bos-A	0	0	....	3	0	0	0	0	5	7	6	6	1	0	4	2	2.200	10.80	40	9.34	.350	0	....	-4	0	-0.3
1988 Chi-A	2	0	1.000	6	0	0	0	1	13	9	2	2	0	2	2	5	.846	1.38	287	1.63	.191	0	....	4	2	0.4
1989 Chi-A	1	2	.333	31	0	0	0	0	66^{2}	72	32	26	8	2	20	27	1.380	3.51	108	4.44	.280	0	....	2	3	0.2
Total 3	3	2	.600	40	0	0	0	1	84^{2}	88	40	34	9	4	26	34	1.346	3.61	108	4.30	.272	0	....	2	5	0.2
• MCCARTHY, Tommy	Thomas Francis Michael McCarthy b: 7/24/1863, Boston, MA d: 8/5/1922, Boston, MA BR/TR, 5'7", 170 lbs. Deb: 7/10/1884 M/U HOF: 1946 ♦																									
1884 Bos-U	0	7	.000	7	6	5	0	0	56	73	53	30	2	....	14	18	1.554	4.82	62	....	.295	45	.215	-12	4	-1.9
1886 Phi-N	0	0	....	1	0	0	0	0	1	0	0	0	0	....	1	1	1.000	0.00	....	....	.000	5	.185	0	1	-0.1
1888* StL-a	0	1	.000	2	1	0	0	0	5^{1}	5	5	2	1	0	2	1	1.313	3.38	96	....	.239	140	.274	-0	19	1.8
1889 StL-a	0	0	....	1	0	0	0	0	5	4	4	4	0	0	6	1	2.000	7.20	59	....	.213	176	.291	-2	19	-0.4
1891 StL-a	0	0	....	1	0	0	0	0	1	2	2	1	0	0	0	0	2.000	9.00	47	....	.402	176	.309	-1	22	0.4
1894 Bos-N	0	0	....	1	0	0	0	0	2	1	1	1	0	0	3	0	2.000	4.50	131	4.13	.148	188	.349	0	19	0.1
Total 6	0	8	.000	13	7	5	0	0	70^{1}	85	65	38	3	0	26	21	1.578	4.86	65	0.12	.285	1495	.292	-14	84	0.0
• MCCARTY, John	John A. McCarty b: St. Louis, MO TR Deb: 4/18/1889 U																									
1889 KC-a	8	6	.571	15	14	13	0	0	119^{2}	147	108	52	4	6	61	36	1.738	3.91	107	....	.293	18	.228	7	6	0.5
• MCCASKILL, Kirk	Kirk Edward McCaskill b: 4/9/1961, Kapuskasing, Canada BR/TR, 6'1", 196 lbs. Deb: 5/1/1985																									
1985 Cal-A	12	12	.500	30	29	6	1	0	189^{2}	189	105	99	23	4	64	102	1.334	4.70	88	4.05	.258	0	....	-18	7	-1.8
1986* Cal-A	17	10	.630	34	33	10	2	0	246^{1}	207	98	92	19	5	92	202	1.214	3.36	122	3.07	.229	0	....	16	18	1.5
1987 Cal-A	4	6	.400	14	13	1	1	0	74^{2}	84	52	47	14	2	34	56	1.580	5.67	76	5.86	.286	0	....	-11	1	-1.1
1988 Cal-A	8	6	.571	23	23	4	2	0	146^{1}	155	78	70	9	1	61	98	1.476	4.31	90	4.24	.274	0	....	-7	6	-0.7
1989 Cal-A	15	10	.600	32	32	6	4	0	212	202	73	69	16	3	59	107	1.231	2.93	130	3.32	.254	0	....	17	18	1.8
1990 Cal-A	12	11	.522	29	29	2	1	0	174^{1}	161	77	63	9	2	72	78	1.337	3.25	117	3.43	.244	0	....	11	12	1.1
1991 Cal-A	10	19	.345	30	30	1	0	0	177^{2}	193	93	84	19	3	66	71	1.458	4.26	96	4.67	.283	0	....	-6	7	-0.6
1992 Chi-A	12	13	.480	34	34	0	0	0	209	193	116	97	11	6	95	109	1.378	4.18	92	3.56	.242	0	....	-7	8	-0.7
1993* Chi-A	4	8	.333	30	14	0	0	2	113^{2}	144	71	66	12	1	36	65	1.584	5.23	80	5.36	.313	0	....	-13	3	-1.3
1994 Chi-A	1	4	.200	40	0	0	0	3	52^{2}	51	22	20	6	0	22	37	1.386	3.42	136	3.91	.252	0	....	7	4	0.7
1995 Chi-A	6	4	.600	55	1	0	0	2	81	97	50	44	10	5	33	50	1.605	4.89	91	5.68	.302	0	....	-3	3	-0.3
1996 Chi-A	5	5	.500	29	4	0	0	0	51^{2}	72	41	40	6	2	31	28	1.994	6.97	68	7.55	.344	0	....	-12	0	-1.1
Total 12	106	108	.495	380	242	30	11	7	1729	1748	876	791	154	34	665	1003	1.396	4.12	99	4.12	.264	0	....	-27	87	-2.5
• MCCATTY, Steve	Steven Earl McCatty b: 3/20/1954, Detroit, MI BR/TR, 6'3", 205 lbs. Deb: 9/17/1977																									
1977 Oak-A	0	0	....	4	2	0	0	0	14^{1}	16	9	8	1	1	7	9	1.605	5.02	80	5.10	.276	0	....	-1	0	-0.1
1978 Oak-A	0	0	....	9	0	0	0	0	20	26	14	10	1	0	9	10	1.750	4.50	81	5.22	.306	0	....	-2	0	-0.2
1979 Oak-A	11	12	.478	31	23	8	0	0	185^{2}	207	106	87	17	10	80	87	1.546	4.22	96	4.90	.284	0	....	2	10	0.2
1980 Oak-A	14	14	.500	33	31	11	1	0	221^{2}	202	104	95	27	8	99	114	1.358	3.86	98	4.02	.240	0	....	-4	11	-0.4
1981* Oak-A	**14**	7	.667	22	22	16	**4**	0	185^{2}	140	50	48	12	2	61	91	1.083	**2.33**	150	2.37	**.211**	0	....	**22**	**18**	**2.3**
1982 Oak-A	6	3	.667	21	20	2	0	0	128^{2}	124	62	57	16	4	70	66	1.508	3.99	98	4.76	.255	0	....	-1	7	-0.1
1983 Oak-A	6	9	.400	38	24	3	2	5	167	156	79	74	16	1	82	65	1.425	3.99	97	4.02	.247	0	....	-4	8	-0.4
1984 Oak-A	8	14	.364	33	30	4	0	0	179^{2}	206	101	95	24	1	71	63	1.542	4.76	79	5.22	.290	0	....	-21	4	-2.1
1985 Oak-A	4	4	.500	30	9	1	0	0	85^{2}	95	56	53	10	4	41	36	1.588	5.57	69	5.33	.286	0	....	-16	1	-1.5
Total 9	63	63	.500	221	161	45	7	5	1188^{1}	1172	581	527	124	31	520	541	1.424	3.99	96	4.29	.258	0	....	-26	59	-2.5
• MCCAULEY, Al	Allen A. McCauley b: 3/4/1863, Indianapolis, IN d: 8/24/1917, Indianapolis, IN BL/TL, 6', 180 lbs. Deb: 6/21/1884 U ♦																									
1884 Ind-a	2	7	.222	10	9	9	0	0	76	87	74	43	2	0	25	34	1.474	5.09	64	....	.273	10	.189	-12	3	-0.9
• MCCLAIN, Joe	Joseph Fred McClain b: 5/5/1933, Johnson City, TN BR/TR, 6', 183 lbs. Deb: 4/14/1961																									
1961 Was-A	8	18	.308	33	29	7	2	1	212	221	105	91	22	4	48	76	1.269	3.86	101	3.67	.270	14	.206	1	10	0.2
1962 Was-A	0	4	.000	10	4	0	0	0	24	33	25	25	8	2	11	6	1.833	9.38	43	8.75	.327	1	.143	-14	0	-1.5
Total 2	8	22	.267	43	33	7	2	1	236	254	130	116	30	6	59	82	1.326	4.42	89	4.18	.276	15	.200	-13	10	-1.2
• MCCLELLAN, Paul	Paul William McClellan b: 2/3/1966, San Mateo, CA BR/TR, 6'2", 180 lbs. Deb: 9/2/1990																									
1990 SF-N	0	1	.000	4	1	0	0	0	7^{2}	14	10	10	3	1	6	2	2.609	11.74	31	14.50	.389	1	.500	-7	0	-0.7
1991 SF-N	3	6	.333	13	12	1	0	0	71	68	41	36	12	1	25	44	1.310	4.56	78	4.18	.252	3	.143	-8	1	-0.9
Total 2	3	7	.300	17	13	1	0	0	78^{2}	82	51	46	15	2	31	46	1.436	5.26	68	5.18	.268	4	.174	-15	1	-1.6
• MCCLOSKEY, Jim	James Ellwood "Irish" McCloskey b: 5/26/1910, Danville, PA d: 8/18/1971, Jersey City, NJ BL/TL, 5'9.5", 180 lbs. Deb: 4/21/1936																									
1936 Bos-N	0	0	....	4	1	0	0	0	8	14	10	10	1	1	3	2	2.125	11.25	34	9.07	.378	0	.000	-7	0	-0.7
• MCCLOSKEY, John	James John McCloskey b: 8/20/1882, Wyoming, PA d: 6/5/1919, Wilkes-Barre, PA Deb: 5/3/1906																									
1906 Phi-N	3	2	.600	9	4	3	0	0	41	46	21	13	2	1	9	6	1.341	2.85	91	3.75	.280	3	.200	-1	2	-0.1
1907 Phi-N	0	0	....	3	0	0	0	0	9	15	9	7	0	1	6	3	2.333	7.00	35	9.71	.417	0	.000	-5	0	-0.6
Total 2	3	2	.600	12	4	3	0	0	50	61	30	20	2	2	15	9	1.520	3.60	70	4.82	.305	3	.158	-5	2	-0.6
• MCCLUNG, Seth	Michael Seth McClung b: 2/7/1981, Lewisburg, WV BL/TR, 6'6", 235 lbs. Deb: 3/31/2003																									
2003 TB-A	4	1	.800	12	5	0	0	0	38^{2}	33	23	23	6	3	25	25	1.500	5.35	85	5.11	.241	0	....	-4	2	-0.4
• MCCLURE, Bob	Robert Craig McClure b: 4/29/1952, Oakland, CA BR/TL, 5'11", 170 lbs. Deb: 8/13/1975 C																									
1975 KC-A	1	0	1.000	12	0	0	0	1	15^{1}	4	0	0	0	0	14	15	1.174	0.00	....	1.34	.077	0	....	7	3	0.7
1976 KC-A	0	0	....	8	0	0	0	0	4	3	4	4	0	0	8	3	2.750	9.00	39	8.25	.214	0	....	-2	0	-0.3
1977 Mil-A	2	1	.667	68	0	0	0	6	71^{1}	64	25	20	2	1	34	57	1.374	2.52	161	3.29	.249	0	....	12	8	1.2
1978 Mil-A	2	6	.250	44	0	0	0	9	65	53	30	27	8	6	30	47	1.277	3.74	101	3.65	.223	0	....	-0	5	0.0
1979 Mil-A	5	2	.714	36	0	0	0	5	51	53	29	22	6	3	24	37	1.510	3.88	107	4.93	.269	0	....	2	4	0.2
1980 Mil-A	5	8	.385	52	5	2	1	10	90^{2}	83	34	31	6	2	37	47	1.324	3.08	126	3.42	.241	0	....	7	8	0.7
1981* Mil-A	0	0	....	4	0	0	0	0	7^{2}	7	3	3	1	0	4	6	1.435	3.52	97	3.98	.233	0	....	-0	0	0.0
1982* Mil-A	12	7	.632	34	26	5	0	0	172^{2}	160	90	81	21	4	74	99	1.355	4.22	90	4.03	.248	0	....	-11	7	-1.1
1983 Mil-A	9	9	.500	24	23	4	0	0	142	152	75	71	11	5	68	68	1.549	4.50	83	4.85	.277	0	....	-12	5	-1.2
1984 Mil-A	4	8	.333	39	18	1	0	1	139^{2}	154	76	68	9	2	52	68	1.475	4.38	88	4.27	.282	0	....	-7	4	-0.7
1985 Mil-A	4	1	.800	38	1	0	0	3	85^{2}	91	43	41	10	3	30	57	1.412	4.31	97	4.49	.274	0	....	-1	5	-0.1
1986 Mil-A	2	1	.667	13	0	0	0	0	16^{1}	18	7	7	2	0	10	11	1.714	3.86	112	5.62	.286	0	....	1	1	0.1
Mon-N	2	5	.286	52	0	0	0	6	62^{2}	53	22	21	2	1	23	42	1.213	3.02	122	2.73	.232	1	.250	5	6	0.5
1987 Mon-N	6	1	.857	52	0	0	0	5	52^{1}	47	30	20	8	0	20	33	1.280	3.44	122	3.67	.241	0	.000	5	5	0.5
1988 Mon-N	1	3	.250	19	0	0	0	2	19	23	13	13	3	1	6	12	1.526	6.16	58	5.47	.307	0	.000	-6	0	-0.6
NY-N	1	0	1.000	14	0	0	0	1	11	12	5	5	1	1	2	7	1.273	4.09	79	4.12	.279	0	....	-1	1	-0.1
Yr.	2	3	.400	33	0	0	0	3	30	35	18	18	4	2	8	19	1.433	5.40	65	4.98	.297	0	.000	-7	1	-0.7
1989 Cal-A	6	1	.857	48	0	0	0	3	52^{1}	39	14	9	2	1	15	36	1.032	1.55	246	2.06	.212	0	....	12	8	1.3
1990 Cal-A	2	0	1.000	11	0	0	0	0	7	7	6	5	0	0	3	6	1.429	6.43	59	3.51	.269	0	....	-2	0	-0.2
1991 Cal-A	0	0	....	13	0	0	0	0	9^{2}	13	11	10	3	1	5	5	1.862	9.31	44	8.73	.317	0	....	-6	0	-0.6
StL-N	1	1	.500	32	0	0	0	0	23	24	8	8	1	1	8	15	1.391	3.13	119	3.81	.282	1	1.000	1	2	0.2
1992 StL-N	2	2	.500	71	0	0	0	0	54	52	21	19	6	2	25	24	1.426	3.17	107	4.31	.261	0	....	1	3	0.1
1993 Fla-N	1	1	.500	14	0	0	0	0	6^{1}	13	5	5	2	0	5	6	2.842	7.11	61	15.22	.419	0	....	-2	0	-0.2
Total 19	68	57	.544	698	73	12	1	52	1158^{2}	1125	551	490	104	34	497	701	1.400	3.81	101	4.07	.257	2	.222	2	75	0.2
• MCCLUSKEY, Harry	Harry Robert McCluskey b: 3/29/1892, Clay Center, OH d: 6/7/1962, Toledo, OH BL/TL, 5'11.5", 173 lbs. Deb: 7/29/1915																									
1915 Cin-N	0	0	....	3	0	0	0	0	5	4	3	3	0	0	0	2	.800	5.40	53	1.05	.182	0	.000	-2	0	-0.2

YEAR TM-L	W	L	PCT	G	GS	CG	SH	SV	IP	H	R	ER	HR	HB	BB	SO	RAT	ERA	ERA+	CERA	OAV	BH	AVG	PR+	WS	TPW
• MCCOLL, Alex	Alexander Boyd "Red" McColl b: 3/29/1894, Eagleville, OH d: 2/6/1991, Kingsville, OH BB/TR, 6'1", 178 lbs. Deb: 8/27/1933																									
1933* Was-A	1	0	1.000	4	1	1	0	0	17	13	5	5	0	0	7	5	1.176	2.65	158	2.18	.210	2	.333	3	2	0.3
1934 Was-A	3	4	.429	42	2	1	0	1	112	129	56	48	6	1	36	29	1.473	3.86	112	4.22	.291	3	.097	6	7	0.4
Total 2	4	4	.500	46	3	2	0	1	129	142	61	53	6	1	43	34	1.434	3.70	116	3.95	.281	5	.135	9	9	0.7
• MCCONNAUGHEY, Ralph	Ralph James McConnaughey b: 8/5/1889, Vandergrift, PA d: 6/4/1966, Detroit, MI BR/TR, 5'8.5", 166 lbs. Deb: 7/8/1914																									
1914 Ind-F	0	2	.000	7	2	1	0	0	26	23	15	14	3	1	16	7	1.500	4.85	72	4.39	.245	1	.125	-4	0	-0.5
• MCCONNELL, George	George Neely "Slats" McConnell b: 9/16/1877, Shelbyville, TN d: 5/10/1964, Chattanooga, TN BR/TR, 6'3", 190 lbs. Deb: 4/13/1909 ♦																									
1909 NY-A	0	1	.000	2	1	0	0	0	4	3	2	1	0	0	3	4	1.500	2.25	112	3.47	.231	9	.209	0	0	-0.1
1912 NY-A	8	12	.400	23	20	19	0	0	176^2	172	96	54	3	4	52	91	1.268	2.75	131	3.11	.269	27	.297	27	12	3.1
1913 NY-A	4	15	.211	35	20	8	0	3	180	162	90	64	2	7	60	72	1.233	3.20	93	2.86	.245	12	.179	-4	7	-0.6
1914 Chi-N	0	1	.000	1	1	0	0	0	7	3	1	1	0	0	3	3	.857	1.29	216	1.02	.125	0	.000	1	1	0.1
1915 Chi-F	**25**	10	.714	44	35	23	4	1	303	262	103	74	8	8	89	151	1.158	2.20	127	2.55	.232	31	.248	20	25	2.8
1916 Chi-N	4	12	.250	28	21	8	1	0	171^1	137	66	49	8	5	35	82	1.004	2.57	113	2.05	.223	9	.158	9	10	0.8
Total 6	41	51	.446	133	98	58	5	4	842	739	358	243	21	24	242	403	1.165	2.60	116	2.62	.240	88	.229	53	55	6.2
• MCCOOL, Billy	William John McCool b: 7/14/1944, Batesville, IN BR/TL, 6'2", 203 lbs. Deb: 4/24/1964																									
1964 Cin-N	6	5	.545	40	3	0	0	7	89^1	66	27	24	3	1	29	87	1.063	2.42	149	2.01	.206	0	.000	11	10	1.0
1965 Cin-N	9	10	.474	62	2	0	0	21	105^1	93	53	50	9	4	47	120	1.329	4.27	88	3.56	.237	1	.037	-6	8	-0.8
1966 Cin-N★	8	8	.500	57	0	0	0	18	105^1	76	32	29	5	3	41	104	1.111	2.48	157	2.29	.205	3	.167	18	16	1.9
1967 Cin-N	3	7	.300	31	11	0	0	2	97^1	92	45	37	8	5	56	83	1.521	3.42	110	4.32	.246	2	.077	4	4	0.3
1968 Cin-N	3	4	.429	30	4	0	0	2	50^2	59	35	28	4	0	41	30	1.974	4.97	64	6.34	.294	1	.125	-10	0	-1.2
1969 SD-N	3	5	.375	54	0	0	0	7	58^2	59	32	28	2	6	42	35	1.722	4.30	82	4.98	.266	0	.000	-4	3	-0.5
1970 StL-N	0	3	.000	18	0	0	0	1	21^2	20	15	15	0	0	16	12	1.662	6.23	66	4.17	.250	0	.000	-5	0	-0.5
Total 7	32	42	.432	292	20	0	0	58	528^1	465	239	211	31	19	272	471	1.395	3.59	102	3.64	.237	7	.069	8	41	0.2
• MCCORMICK, Harry	Patrick Henry McCormick b: 10/25/1855, Syracuse, NY d: 8/8/1889, Syracuse, NY BR/TR, 5'9", 155 lbs. Deb: 5/1/1879																									
1879 Syr-N	18	33	.353	54	54	49	5	0	457^1	517	291	152	3	....	31	96	1.198	2.99	79	....	.267	51	.222	-9	19	-1.0
1881 Wor-N	1	8	.111	9	9	9	1	0	78^1	89	50	31	1	....	15	7	1.328	3.56	85	....	.274	6	.133	-3	3	-0.6
1882 Cin-a	14	11	.560	25	25	24	3	0	219^2	177	87	37	4	....	42	33	.997	1.52	174	....	.206	12	.129	24	20	1.6
1883 Cin-a	8	6	.571	15	15	14	1	0	128^2	139	70	41	1	....	27	21	1.290	2.87	113	....	.258	17	.309	1	10	0.4
Total 4	41	58	.414	103	103	96	10	0	884	922	498	261	9	....	115	157	1.173	2.66	97	....	.252	86	.203	12	52	0.4
• MCCORMICK, Jim	James McCormick b: 11/3/1856, Glasgow, Scotland d: 3/10/1918, Paterson, NJ BR/TR, 5'10.5", 215 lbs. Deb: 5/20/1878 M/U																									
1878 Ind-N	5	8	.385	14	14	12	1	0	117	128	47	22	0	....	15	36	1.222	1.69	120	....	.265	8	.143	5	6	0.3
1879 Cle-N	20	40	.333	62	60	59	3	0	546^1	582	308	147	4	....	74	197	1.201	2.42	103	....	.256	62	.220	**24**	33	1.8
1880 Cle-N	**45**	28	.616	**74**	**74**	**72**	7	0	**657^2**	585	274	135	2	....	75	260	1.004	1.85	127	....	.226	71	.246	25	**54**	2.5
1881 Cle-N	26	30	.464	59	58	**57**	2	0	526	484	267	143	4	....	84	178	1.080	2.45	107	....	**.234**	79	.256	6	34	1.3
1882 Cle-N	**36**	30	.545	**68**	**67**	**65**	4	0	**595^2**	550	274	157	14	....	103	200	1.096	2.37	117	....	.231	57	.218	4	42	-0.1
1883 Cle-N	28	12	.700	43	41	36	1	1	342	316	151	70	1	....	65	145	1.114	**1.84**	**171**	....	.231	37	.236	37	40	3.1
1884 Cle-N	19	22	.463	42	41	39	3	0	359	357	206	114	17	....	75	182	1.203	2.86	110	....	.245	50	.263	9	26	1.1
Cin-U	21	3	.875	24	24	24	**7**	0	210	151	57	36	3	....	14	161	.786	**1.54**	**207**	....	**.188**	27	.245	**39**	27	3.3
1885 Pro-N	1	3	.250	4	4	4	0	0	37	34	26	10	1	....	20	8	1.459	2.43	109	....	.233	3	.214	1	2	0.1
* Chi-N	20	4	.833	24	24	24	3	0	215	187	103	58	8	....	40	88	1.056	2.43	125	....	.223	23	.223	8	19	0.8
Yr.	21	7	.750	28	28	28	3	0	252	221	129	68	9	....	60	96	1.115	2.43	122	....	.225	26	.222	9	21	0.9
1886* Chi-N	31	11	.738	42	42	38	2	0	347^2	341	165	109	18	....	100	172	1.268	2.82	128	....	.247	41	.236	17	33	1.8
1887 Pit-N	13	23	.361	36	36	36	0	0	322^1	461	217	154	12	12	84	77	1.430	4.30	90	....	.326	35	.254	-12	18	-1.0
Total 10	265	214	.553	492	485	466	33	1	4275^2	4176	2095	1155	84	12	749	1704	1.132	2.43	119	....	.243	493	.237	162	334	15.0
• MCCORMICK, Mike	Michael Francis McCormick b: 9/29/1938, Pasadena, CA BL/TL, 6'2", 195 lbs. Deb: 9/3/1956																									
1956 NY-N	0	1	.000	3	2	0	0	0	6^2	7	7	7	1	0	10	4	2.550	9.45	40	9.55	.269	0	.000	-4	0	-0.4
1957 NY-N	3	1	.750	24	5	1	0	0	74^2	79	37	34	7	3	32	50	1.487	4.10	96	4.74	.280	6	.273	-1	4	0.0
1958 SF-N	11	8	.579	42	28	8	2	1	178^1	192	103	91	20	3	60	82	1.413	4.59	83	4.36	.276	12	.222	-14	7	-1.3
1959 SF-N	12	16	.429	47	31	7	3	4	225^2	213	117	100	24	1	86	151	1.325	3.99	96	3.60	.248	7	.106	-4	9	-0.6
1960 SF-N★	15	12	.556	40	34	15	4	3	253	228	87	76	15	1	65	154	1.158	**2.70**	129	2.70	.241	16	.182	24	18	2.6
1961 SF-N★	13	16	.448	40	35	13	3	0	250	235	99	89	33	2	75	163	1.240	3.20	119	3.62	.249	15	.188	19	17	1.9
1962 SF-N	5	5	.500	28	15	1	0	0	98^2	112	64	59	18	1	45	42	1.591	5.38	71	5.69	.286	3	.107	-17	1	-1.7
1963 Bal-A	6	8	.429	25	21	2	0	0	136	132	70	65	18	0	66	75	1.456	4.30	82	4.45	.256	8	.174	-12	3	-1.2
1964 Bal-A	0	2	.000	4	2	0	0	0	17^1	21	10	10	1	0	8	13	1.673	5.19	69	5.09	.288	1	.167	-4	0	-0.4
1965 Was-A	8	8	.500	44	21	3	1	1	158	158	64	59	17	0	36	88	1.228	3.36	103	3.43	.260	3	.073	3	10	0.3
1966 Was-A	11	14	.440	41	32	8	3	0	216	193	98	83	23	2	51	101	1.130	3.46	100	2.88	.236	14	.212	-2	11	0.2
1967 SF-N	**22**	10	.688	40	35	14	5	0	262^1	220	88	83	25	5	81	150	1.147	2.85	115	2.81	.226	10	.119	12	20	1.3
1968 SF-N	12	14	.462	38	28	9	2	1	198^1	196	92	79	17	2	49	121	1.235	3.58	82	3.21	.254	6	.103	-13	6	-1.3
1969 SF-N	11	9	.550	32	28	9	0	0	196^2	175	81	73	20	1	77	76	1.281	3.34	105	3.42	.237	9	.136	5	12	0.6
1970 SF-N	3	4	.429	23	11	1	0	2	78^1	80	58	54	15	3	36	37	1.481	6.20	64	5.05	.262	4	.160	-18	0	-1.8
NY-A	2	0	1.000	9	4	0	0	0	20^2	26	15	14	2	0	13	12	1.887	6.10	58	6.28	.295	1	.200	-6	0	-0.6
1971 KC-A	0	0	....	4	1	0	0	0	9^2	14	10	10	0	0	5	2	1.966	9.31	37	6.53	.350	0	.000	-6	0	-0.7
Total 16	134	128	.511	484	333	91	23	12	2380^1	2281	1100	986	256	24	795	1321	1.292	3.73	95	3.63	.251	115	.156	-36	118	-3.1
• MCCORRY, Bill	William Charles McCorry b: 7/9/1887, Saranac Lake, NY d: 3/22/1973, Augusta, GA BL/TR, 5'9", 157 lbs. Deb: 9/17/1909																									
1909 StL-A	0	2	.000	2	2	2	0	0	15	29	21	15	1	0	6	10	2.333	9.00	27	9.46	.397	0	.000	-11	0	-1.3
• MCCRABB, Les	Lester William "Buster" McCrabb b: 11/4/1914, Wakefield, PA BR/TR, 5'11", 175 lbs. Deb: 9/7/1939 C																									
1939 Phi-A	1	2	.333	5	4	2	0	0	35^2	42	20	16	4	1	10	11	1.458	4.04	117	4.61	.290	0	.000	4	2	0.2
1940 Phi-A	0	0	....	4	0	0	0	0	11^2	19	13	9	2	1	2	4	1.800	6.94	64	7.50	.365	1	.250	-3	0	-0.3
1941 Phi-A	9	13	.409	26	23	11	1	2	157^1	188	105	96	16	3	49	40	1.506	5.49	76	4.76	.294	8	.143	-24	4	-2.5
1942 Phi-A	0	0	....	1	0	0	0	0	4	14	14	14	2	1	2	0	4.000	31.50	12	28.39	.560	0	.000	-12	0	-1.3
1950 Phi-A	0	0	....	2	0	0	0	0	1^1	7	4	4	0	0	0	2	5.250	27.00	17	30.23	.583	0	....	-3	0	-0.3
Total 5	10	15	.400	38	27	13	1	2	210	270	156	139	24	6	63	57	1.586	5.96	71	5.50	.309	9	.122	-39	6	-4.3
• MCCREERY, Ed	Esley Porterfield "Big Ed" McCreery b: 12/24/1889, Cripple Creek, CO d: 10/19/1960, Sacramento, CA BR/TR, 6', 190 lbs. Deb: 8/16/1914																									
1914 Det-A	1	0	1.000	3	1	0	0	0	4	6	5	5	0	0	3	4	2.250	11.25	25	6.92	.316	0	.000	-4	0	-0.4
• MCCREERY, Tom	Thomas Livingston McCreery b: 10/19/1874, Beaver, PA d: 7/3/1941, Beaver, PA BB/TR, 5'11", 180 lbs. Deb: 6/8/1895 ♦																									
1895 Lou-N	3	1	.750	8	4	3	1	1	48^2	51	40	29	0	5	38	14	1.829	5.36	86	5.19	.266	35	.324	-2	4	-0.4
1896 Lou-N	0	1	.000	1	1	0	0	0	1	4	10	4	1	0	5	0	9.000	36.00	12	63.73	.583	155	.351	-3	16	2.3
1900 Pit-N	0	0	....	1	0	0	0	0	3	3	4	4	2	0	1	0	1.333	12.00	30	7.69	.260	29	.220	-3	2	-0.6
Total 3	3	2	.600	10	5	3	1	1	52^2	58	54	37	3	5	44	14	1.937	6.32	71	6.44	.276	857	.289	-8	22	1.3
• MCCULLERS, Lance	Lance Graye McCullers b: 3/8/1964, Tampa, FL BB/TR, 6'1", 218 lbs. Deb: 8/12/1985																									
1985 SD-N	0	2	.000	21	0	0	0	5	35	23	15	9	3	1	16	27	1.114	2.31	153	2.40	.195	0	.000	4	3	0.4
1986 SD-N	10	10	.500	70	7	0	0	5	136	103	46	42	12	4	58	92	1.184	2.78	131	2.90	.216	2	.091	13	12	1.5
1987 SD-N	8	10	.444	78	0	0	0	16	123^1	115	60	51	11	2	59	126	1.411	3.72	106	3.80	.244	1	.071	2	10	0.2
1988 SD-N	3	6	.333	60	0	0	0	10	97^2	70	29	27	8	0	55	81	1.280	2.49	136	2.89	.205	2	.250	8	10	1.0
1989 NY-A	4	3	.571	52	1	0	0	3	84^2	83	46	43	9	3	37	82	1.417	4.57	85	4.17	.255	0	....	-7	4	-0.7
1990 NY-A	1	0	1.000	11	0	0	0	0	15	14	8	6	2	0	6	11	1.333	3.60	110	3.64	.241	0	....	1	1	0.1
Det-A	1	0	1.000	9	1	0	0	0	29^2	18	11	9	2	0	13	20	1.045	2.73	145	1.90	.170	0	....	3	2	0.3
Yr.	2	0	1.000	20	1	0	0	0	44^2	32	19	15	4	0	19	31	1.142	3.02	131	2.49	.195	0	....	4	3	0.4

YEAR	TM-L	W	L	PCT	G	GS	CG	SH	SV	IP	H	R	ER	HR	HB	BB	SO	RAT	ERA	ERA+	CERA	OAV	BH	AVG	PR+	WS	TPW
1992	Tex-A	1	0	1.000	5	0	0	0	0	5	1	4	3	0	0	8	3	1.800	5.40	70	3.38	.067	0	....	-1	0	-0.1
Total	7	28	31	.475	306	9	0	0	39	526^1	427	219	190	47	10	252	442	1.290	3.25	116	3.25	.223	5	.104	24	42	2.6
• MCCULLOUGH, Charlie	Charles F. McCullough b: 1867, Dublin, Ireland TR, 6'1", 185 lbs. Deb: 4/23/1890																										
1890	Bro-a	4	21	.160	26	25	24	0	0	215^2	247	174	110	5	16	102	61	1.618	4.59	85	....	.279	2	.023	-15	4	-2.4
	Syr-a	1	2	.333	3	3	3	0	0	26	29	25	21	1	0	14	8	1.654	7.27	48	....	.274	1	.111	-10	0	-0.9
	Yr.	5	23	.179	29	28	27	0	0	241^2	276	199	131	6	16	116	69	1.622	4.88	78	....	.279	3	.032	-26	4	-3.3
• MCCULLOUGH, Paul	Paul Willard McCullough b: 7/28/1898, New Castle, PA d: 11/7/1970, New Castle, PA BR/TR, 5'9.5", 190 lbs. Deb: 7/2/1929																										
1929	Was-A	0	0	....	3	0	0	0	0	7^1	7	7	7	1	0	2	3	1.227	8.59	49	3.57	.250	0	.000	-4	0	-0.4
• MCCULLOUGH, Phil	Pinson Lamar McCullough b: 7/22/1917, Stockbridge, GA d: 1/16/2003, Decatur, GA BR/TR, 6'4", 204 lbs. Deb: 4/22/1942																										
1942	Was-A	0	0	....	1	0	0	0	0	3	5	4	2	0	0	2	2	2.333	6.00	61	7.51	.333	0	.000	-1	0	-0.1
• MCCURRY, Jeff	Jeffrey Dee McCurry b: 1/21/1970, Tokyo, Japan BR/TR, 6'7", 210 lbs. Deb: 5/6/1995																										
1995	Pit-N	1	4	.200	55	0	0	0	1	61	82	38	34	9	5	30	27	1.836	5.02	86	7.46	.337	0	.000	-4	2	-0.4
1996	Det-A	0	0	....	2	0	0	0	0	3^1	9	9	9	3	0	2	0	3.300	24.30	21	25.61	.474	0	....	-7	0	-0.6
1997	Col-N	1	4	.200	33	0	0	0	0	40^2	43	22	20	7	0	20	19	1.549	4.43	117	5.39	.277	0	.000	4	3	0.4
1998	Pit-N	1	3	.250	16	0	0	0	0	19^1	24	14	14	4	1	9	11	1.707	6.52	66	7.11	.324	0	....	-5	0	-0.5
1999	Hou-N	0	1	.000	5	0	0	0	0	4	11	8	7	1	0	2	3	3.250	15.75	28	17.98	.478	0	....	-5	0	-0.5
Total	5	3	12	.200	111	0	0	0	1	128^1	169	91	84	24	6	63	60	1.808	5.89	78	7.55	.329	0	.000	-17	5	-1.7
• MCDANIEL, Lindy	Lyndall Dale McDaniel b: 12/13/1935, Hollis, OK BR/TR, 6'3", 195 lbs. Deb: 9/2/1955																										
1955	StL-N	0	0	....	4	2	0	0	0	19	22	10	10	4	0	7	7	1.526	4.74	86	5.61	.293	1	.200	-1	1	-0.1
1956	StL-N	7	6	.538	39	7	1	0	0	116^1	121	60	44	7	0	42	59	1.401	3.40	111	3.78	.273	7	.219	5	6	0.7
1957	StL-N	15	9	.625	30	26	10	1	0	191	196	87	74	13	3	53	75	1.304	3.49	114	3.57	.266	19	.257	10	14	1.5
1958	StL-N	5	7	.417	26	17	2	1	0	108^2	139	76	70	17	2	31	47	1.564	5.80	71	5.64	.305	2	.067	-20	1	-2.3
1959	StL-N	14	12	.538	62	7	1	0	**15**	132	144	61	56	11	1	41	86	1.402	3.82	111	4.11	.283	1	.034	7	14	0.6
1960	StL-N★	12	4	.750	65	2	1	0	**26**	116^1	85	28	27	8	1	24	105	.937	2.09	196	1.85	.207	6	.231	26	25	2.8
1961	StL-N	10	6	.625	55	0	0	0	9	94^1	117	57	51	11	2	31	65	1.569	4.87	90	5.17	.305	4	.235	-5	6	-0.5
1962	StL-N	3	10	.231	55	2	0	0	14	107	96	53	49	12	1	29	79	1.168	4.12	104	3.00	.239	2	.095	1	8	0.0
1963	Chi-N	13	7	.650	57	0	0	0	**22**	88	82	32	28	9	0	27	75	1.239	2.86	123	3.30	.251	2	.091	5	14	0.5
1964	Chi-N	1	7	.125	63	0	0	0	15	95	104	43	41	4	1	23	71	1.337	3.88	95	3.51	.276	2	.125	-1	8	-0.1
1965	Chi-N	5	6	.455	71	0	0	0	2	128^2	115	45	37	12	0	47	92	1.259	2.59	142	3.08	.241	0	.000	17	11	1.7
1966	SF-N	10	5	.667	64	0	0	0	6	121^2	103	48	36	5	0	35	93	1.134	2.66	138	2.36	.228	2	.091	14	11	1.3
1967	SF-N	2	6	.250	41	3	0	0	3	72^2	69	34	30	5	2	24	48	1.280	3.72	88	3.18	.248	1	.091	-4	3	-0.4
1968	SF-N	0	0	....	12	0	0	0	0	19^1	30	16	16	2	0	5	9	1.810	7.45	40	6.90	.357	0	.000	-10	0	-1.1
	NY-A	4	1	.800	24	0	0	0	10	51^1	30	10	10	5	1	12	43	.818	1.75	165	1.49	.166	0	.000	7	9	0.7
1969	NY-A	5	6	.455	51	0	0	0	5	83^2	84	37	33	4	0	23	60	1.279	3.55	98	3.10	.261	0	.000	-1	6	-0.2
1970	NY-A	9	5	.643	62	0	0	0	29	111^2	88	29	25	7	0	23	81	.994	2.01	174	2.01	.217	4	.167	18	19	1.9
1971	NY-A	5	10	.333	44	0	0	0	4	69^2	82	41	39	12	0	24	39	1.522	5.04	64	5.23	.296	1	.111	-14	0	-1.5
1972	NY-A	3	1	.750	37	0	0	0	0	68	54	23	17	4	0	25	47	1.162	2.25	131	2.49	.217	2	.286	5	5	0.7
1973	NY-A	12	6	.667	47	3	1	0	10	160^1	148	54	51	11	1	49	93	1.229	2.86	128	3.07	.250	0	.000	13	15	1.2
1974	KC-A	1	4	.200	38	5	2	0	1	106^2	109	50	41	6	0	24	47	1.247	3.46	110	3.16	.265	0	....	6	6	0.6
1975	KC-A	5	1	.833	40	0	0	0	1	78	81	40	36	3	0	24	40	1.346	4.15	93	3.39	.273	0	....	-2	4	-0.2
Total	21	141	119	.542	987	74	18	2	172	2139^1	2099	934	821	172	15	623	1361	1.272	3.45	109	3.40	.258	56	.148	78	186	7.8
• MCDANIEL, Von	Max Von McDaniel b: 4/18/1939, Hollis, OK d: 8/20/1995, Lawton, OK BR/TR, 6'2.5", 180 lbs. Deb: 6/13/1957																										
1957	StL-N	7	5	.583	17	13	4	2	0	86^2	71	37	31	7	1	31	45	1.177	3.22	123	2.82	.225	0	.000	7	6	0.4
1958	StL-N	0	0	....	2	1	0	0	0	2	5	3	3	0	0	5	0	5.000	13.50	31	23.02	.500	0	....	-2	0	-0.2
Total	2	7	5	.583	19	14	4	2	0	88^2	76	40	34	7	1	36	45	1.263	3.45	115	3.28	.233	0	.000	5	6	0.2
• MCDERMOTT, Joe	Joseph McDermott Deb: 5/4/1871 ♦																										
1872	Eck-n	0	7	.000	7	7	7	0	0	63	143	144	57	3	....	12	1	**2.460**	8.14	42	....	.399	9	.281	-27	....	-1.7
• MCDERMOTT, Mickey	Maurice Joseph "Maury" McDermott b: 4/29/1929, Poughkeepsie, NY d: 8/7/2003, Phoenix, AZ BL/TL, 6'2", 170 lbs. Deb: 4/24/1948 C																										
1948	Bos-A	0	0	....	7	0	0	0	0	23^1	16	18	16	2	1	35	17	2.186	6.17	71	6.45	.208	3	.375	-5	1	-0.4
1949	Bos-A	5	4	.556	12	12	6	2	0	80	63	37	36	5	3	52	50	1.438	4.05	108	3.57	.220	7	.212	1	6	0.2
1950	Bos-A	7	3	.700	38	15	4	0	5	130	119	80	75	8	2	124	96	1.869	5.19	94	5.35	.249	16	.364	-4	10	0.3
1951	Bos-A	8	8	.500	34	19	9	1	3	172	141	72	64	9	5	92	127	1.355	3.35	133	3.29	.226	18	.273	21	16	2.3
1952	Bos-A	10	9	.526	30	21	7	2	0	162	139	70	67	14	3	92	117	1.426	3.72	106	3.84	.234	14	.226	3	12	0.6
1953	Bos-A	18	10	.643	32	30	8	4	0	206^1	169	82	69	9	2	109	92	1.347	3.01	140	3.11	.224	28	.301	26	22	3.3
1954	Was-A	7	15	.318	30	26	11	1	1	196^1	172	95	75	8	3	110	95	1.436	3.44	103	3.51	.239	19	.200	6	9	0.9
1955	Was-A	10	10	.500	31	20	8	1	1	156	140	75	65	9	9	100	78	1.538	3.75	102	4.33	.243	25	.263	6	10	1.3
1956★	NY-A	2	6	.250	23	9	1	0	0	87	85	46	41	10	0	47	38	1.517	4.24	91	4.58	.261	11	.212	-6	3	-0.3
1957	KC-A	1	4	.200	29	4	0	0	0	69	68	47	42	9	0	50	29	1.710	5.48	72	5.52	.266	12	.245	-11	2	-0.5
1958	Det-A	0	0	....	2	0	0	0	0	2	6	4	2	0	0	2	0	4.000	9.00	45	19.55	.500	1	.333	-1	0	-0.1
1961	StL-N	1	0	1.000	19	0	0	0	4	27	29	17	11	3	0	15	15	1.630	3.67	120	4.95	.271	1	.071	2	2	0.1
	KC-A	0	0	....	4	0	0	0	0	5^2	14	12	9	0	0	10	3	4.235	14.29	29	19.18	.452	1	.200	-6	0	-0.6
Total	12	69	69	.500	291	156	54	11	14	1316^2	1161	655	572	86	28	838	757	1.518	3.91	105	4.09	.240	156	.252	32	93	7.2
• MCDERMOTT, Mike	Michael H. McDermott b: 5/6/1864, Fall River, MA d: 5/7/1947, Fall River, MA TR, 5'10", 152 lbs. Deb: 9/2/1889																										
1889	Lou-a	1	8	.111	9	9	9	0	0	84^1	108	65	39	4	2	34	22	1.684	4.16	92	....	.302	6	.182	-2	2	-0.2
• MCDERMOTT, Mike	Michael Joseph McDermott b: 9/7/1862, St. Louis, MO d: 6/30/1943, St. Louis, MO TR, 5'8", 145 lbs. Deb: 4/20/1895																										
1895	Lou-N	4	19	.174	33	26	18	0	0	207^1	258	203	138	8	0	103	42	1.741	5.99	77	5.27	.301	13	.159	-22	4	-1.9
1896	Lou-N	2	7	.222	12	10	4	1	0	65	87	77	53	4	0	44	12	2.015	7.34	59	6.74	.318	8	.296	-20	0	-1.6
1897	Cle-N	4	5	.444	9	7	4	0	0	62	75	44	31	2	3	25	12	1.613	4.50	100	4.85	.297	8	.320	-3	4	-0.2
	StL-N	1	2	.333	4	4	1	0	0	21^1	23	23	22	2	2	19	3	1.969	9.28	47	6.59	.273	2	.222	-11	0	-0.9
	Yr.	5	7	.417	13	11	5	0	0	83^1	98	67	53	4	5	44	15	1.704	5.72	78	5.30	.291	10	.294	-14	4	-1.1
Total	3	11	33	.250	58	47	27	1	0	355^2	443	347	244	16	5	191	69	1.783	6.17	73	5.54	.302	31	.217	-57	8	-4.6
• MCDEVITT, Danny	Daniel Eugene McDevitt b: 11/18/1932, New York, NY BL/TL, 5'10", 175 lbs. Deb: 6/17/1957																										
1957	Bro-N	7	4	.636	22	17	5	2	0	119	105	55	43	5	6	72	90	1.487	3.25	128	3.98	.238	6	.154	12	8	1.2
1958	LA-N	2	6	.250	13	10	2	0	0	48^1	71	43	40	6	0	31	26	2.110	7.45	55	8.28	.355	2	.133	-18	0	-1.9
1959	LA-N	10	8	.556	39	22	6	2	4	145	149	83	64	16	14	51	106	1.379	3.97	106	4.36	.263	5	.109	4	8	0.2
1960	LA-N	0	4	.000	24	7	0	0	0	53	51	26	25	7	6	42	30	1.755	4.25	93	6.17	.260	2	.200	-2	2	-0.2
1961	NY-A	1	2	.333	8	2	0	0	1	13	18	11	11	2	1	8	8	2.000	7.62	49	8.64	.353	0	.000	-6	0	-0.6
	Min-A	1	0	1.000	16	1	0	0	0	26^2	20	11	7	1	4	19	15	1.463	2.36	180	3.92	.213	0	.000	6	2	0.6
	Yr.	2	2	.500	24	3	0	0	1	39^2	38	22	18	3	5	27	23	1.639	4.08	96	5.47	.262	0	.000	0	2	0.0
1962	KC-A	0	3	.000	33	1	0	0	2	51	47	37	33	5	1	41	28	1.725	5.82	71	5.26	.250	2	.222	-9	0	-0.9
Total	6	21	27	.438	155	60	13	4	7	456	461	266	223	42	32	264	303	1.590	4.40	94	5.09	.265	17	.138	-13	20	-1.6
• MCDILL, Allen	Allen Gabriel McDill b: 8/23/1971, Greenville, MS BL/TL, 6', 155 lbs. Deb: 5/15/1997																										
1997	KC-A	0	0	....	3	0	0	0	0	4	3	6	6	1	1	8	2	2.750	13.50	35	11.63	.214	0	....	-4	0	-0.4
1998	KC-A	0	0	....	7	0	0	0	0	6	9	7	7	3	0	2	3	1.833	10.50	46	9.97	.333	0	....	-4	0	-0.4
2000	Det-A	0	0	....	13	0	0	0	0	10	13	9	8	2	1	1	7	1.400	7.20	67	5.88	.317	0	....	-3	0	-0.2
2001	Bos-A	0	0	....	15	0	0	0	0	14^2	13	9	9	2	1	7	16	1.364	5.52	81	4.14	.236	0	....	-1	0	-0.1
Total	4	0	0	....	38	0	0	0	0	34^2	38	31	30	8	3	18	28	1.615	7.79	60	6.51	.277	0	....	-12	0	-1.1

• MCDONALD, Ben Larry Benard McDonald b: 11/24/1967, Baton Rouge, LA BR/TR, 6'7", 213 lbs. Deb: 9/6/1989

YEAR	TM-L	W	L	PCT	G	GS	CG	SH	SV	IP	H	R	ER	HR	HB	BB	SO	RAT	ERA	ERA+	CERA	OAV	BH	AVG	PR+	WS	TPW
1989	Bal-A	1	0	1.000	6	0	0	0	0	7^1	8	7	7	2	0	4	3	1.636	8.59	44	6.61	.286	0	....	-4	0	-0.4
1990	Bal-A	8	5	.615	21	15	3	2	0	118^2	88	36	32	9	0	35	65	1.037	2.43	156	2.20	.205	0	....	17	10	1.7
1991	Bal-A	6	8	.429	21	21	1	0	0	126^1	126	71	68	16	1	43	85	1.338	4.84	81	4.07	.261	0	....	-13	4	-1.3
1992	Bal-A	13	13	.500	35	35	4	2	0	227	213	113	107	32	9	74	158	1.264	4.24	95	3.85	.247	0	....	-7	11	-0.7
1993	Bal-A	13	14	.481	34	34	7	1	0	220^1	185	92	83	17	5	86	171	1.230	3.39	132	3.10	.228	0	....	23	17	2.3
1994	Bal-A	14	7	.667	24	24	5	1	0	157^1	151	75	71	14	2	54	94	1.303	4.06	123	3.65	.255	0	....	14	12	1.3
1995	Bal-A	3	6	.333	14	13	1	0	0	80	67	40	37	10	3	38	62	1.313	4.16	114	3.72	.224	0	....	4	5	0.4
1996	Mil-A	12	10	.545	35	35	2	0	0	221^1	228	104	96	25	6	67	146	1.333	3.90	133	4.03	.264	0	....	27	16	2.5
1997	Mil-A	8	7	.533	21	21	1	0	0	133	120	68	60	13	5	36	110	1.173	4.06	114	3.15	.237	0	.000	4	8	0.4
Total	9	78	70	.527	211	198	24	6	0	1291^1	1186	606	561	138	31	437	894	1.257	3.91	114	3.53	.243	0	.000	66	83	6.2

• MCDONALD, Hank Henry Monroe McDonald b: 1/16/1911, Santa Monica, CA d: 10/17/1982, Hemet, CA BR/TR, 6'3", 200 lbs. Deb: 4/16/1931

YEAR	TM-L	W	L	PCT	G	GS	CG	SH	SV	IP	H	R	ER	HR	HB	BB	SO	RAT	ERA	ERA+	CERA	OAV	BH	AVG	PR+	WS	TPW
1931	Phi-A	2	4	.333	19	10	1	1	0	70^1	62	43	29	3	1	41	23	1.464	3.71	121	3.65	.239	2	.095	4	4	0.3
1933	Phi-A	1	1	.500	4	1	0	0	0	12^1	14	12	7	0	0	4	1	1.459	5.11	84	3.41	.264	0	.000	-1	0	-0.1
	StL-A	0	4	.000	25	5	0	0	0	58^1	83	59	56	6	3	34	22	2.006	8.64	54	7.31	.332	2	.143	-27	0	-2.6
	Yr.	1	5	.167	29	6	0	0	0	70^2	97	71	63	6	3	38	23	1.910	8.02	57	6.63	.320	2	.111	-28	0	-2.7
Total	2	3	9	.250	48	16	1	1	0	141	159	114	92	9	4	79	46	1.688	5.87	78	5.14	.283	4	.103	-24	4	-2.4

• MCDONALD, Jim Jimmie Le Roy "Hot Rod" McDonald b: 5/17/1927, Grants Pass, OR BR/TR, 5'10.5", 185 lbs. Deb: 7/27/1950

YEAR	TM-L	W	L	PCT	G	GS	CG	SH	SV	IP	H	R	ER	HR	HB	BB	SO	RAT	ERA	ERA+	CERA	OAV	BH	AVG	PR+	WS	TPW
1950	Bos-A	1	0	1.000	9	0	0	0	0	19	23	9	8	1	1	10	5	1.737	3.79	129	5.76	.329	1	.333	2	2	0.3
1951	StL-A	4	7	.364	16	11	5	0	1	84	84	48	38	5	2	46	28	1.548	4.07	108	4.30	.260	6	.207	5	5	0.5
1952	NY-A	3	4	.429	26	5	1	0	0	69^1	71	31	27	1	2	40	20	1.601	3.50	95	4.22	.268	6	.316	-4	4	0.0
1953★	NY-A	9	7	.563	27	18	6	2	0	129^2	128	64	55	4	1	39	43	1.288	3.82	97	3.16	.260	4	.098	-5	5	-0.8
1954	NY-A	4	1	.800	16	10	3	1	0	71	54	28	25	3	1	45	20	1.394	3.17	108	3.20	.213	4	.211	0	5	0.2
1955	Bal-A	3	5	.375	21	8	0	0	0	51^2	76	48	41	5	0	30	20	2.052	7.14	53	7.71	.345	2	.182	-18	0	-1.8
1956	Chi-A	0	2	.000	8	3	0	0	0	18^2	29	18	18	2	1	7	10	1.929	8.68	47	7.91	.377	0	.000	-10	0	-1.0
1957	Chi-A	0	1	.000	10	0	0	0	0	22^1	18	8	5	2	0	10	12	1.254	2.01	185	3.12	.234	0	.000	4	2	0.4
1958	Chi-A	0	0	....	3	0	0	0	0	2^1	6	8	5	1	0	4	0	4.286	19.29	19	23.84	.429	0	....	-4	0	-0.4
Total	9	24	27	.471	136	55	15	3	1	468	489	262	222	24	8	231	158	1.538	4.27	89	4.42	.273	23	.180	-29	23	-2.6

• MCDONALD, John John Joseph McDonald b: 1/27/1883, Throop, PA d: 4/9/1950, Roselle, NJ BR/TR, 6'1", 170 lbs. Deb: 9/3/1907

YEAR	TM-L	W	L	PCT	G	GS	CG	SH	SV	IP	H	R	ER	HR	HB	BB	SO	RAT	ERA	ERA+	CERA	OAV	BH	AVG	PR+	WS	TPW
1907	Was-A	0	0	....	1	0	0	0	0	6	12	11	6	0	0	2	3	2.333	9.00	27	8.31	.416	1	.333	-4	0	-0.4

• MCDOOLAN, McDoolan Deb: 4/14/1873

YEAR	TM-L	W	L	PCT	G	GS	CG	SH	SV	IP	H	R	ER	HR	HB	BB	SO	RAT	ERA	ERA+	CERA	OAV	BH	AVG	PR+	WS	TPW
1873	Mar-n	0	1	.000	1	1	1	0	0	9	18	....	3	0	....	0	0	2.000	3.00	108	....	.373	0	.000	2	....	0.1

• MCDOUGAL, Dewey James H. McDougal b: 9/19/1871, Aledo, IL d: 4/28/1935, Galesburg, IL TR, 5'10", 170 lbs. Deb: 4/24/1895

YEAR	TM-L	W	L	PCT	G	GS	CG	SH	SV	IP	H	R	ER	HR	HB	BB	SO	RAT	ERA	ERA+	CERA	OAV	BH	AVG	PR+	WS	TPW
1895	StL-N	3	10	.231	18	14	10	0	0	114^2	187	146	106	11	10	46	23	2.032	8.32	58	8.18	.360	6	.146	-41	0	-3.5
1896	StL-N	0	1	.000	3	1	0	0	0	10	13	11	9	2	1	4	0	1.700	8.10	54	6.98	.312	0	.000	-4	0	-0.4
Total	2	3	11	.214	21	15	10	0	0	124^2	200	157	115	13	11	50	23	2.005	8.30	58	8.09	.357	6	.136	-45	0	-3.9

• MCDOUGAL, Sandy John Auchanbolt McDougal b: 5/21/1874, Buffalo, NY d: 10/2/1910, Buffalo, NY BR/TR, 5'10", 155 lbs. Deb: 6/12/1895

YEAR	TM-L	W	L	PCT	G	GS	CG	SH	SV	IP	H	R	ER	HR	HB	BB	SO	RAT	ERA	ERA+	CERA	OAV	BH	AVG	PR+	WS	TPW
1895	Bro-N	0	0	....	1	0	0	0	1	3	3	4	4	0	0	5	2	2.667	12.00	37	7.73	.257	0	.000	-3	0	-0.2
1905	StL-N	1	4	.200	5	5	5	0	0	44^2	50	24	17	0	0	12	10	1.388	3.43	87	3.76	.301	2	.133	-1	1	-0.1
Total	2	1	4	.200	6	5	5	0	1	47^2	53	28	21	0	0	17	12	1.469	3.97	80	4.01	.298	2	.125	-3	1	-0.4

• MCDOWELL, Jack Jack Burns McDowell b: 1/16/1966, Van Nuys, CA BR/TR, 6'5", 180 lbs. Deb: 9/15/1987

YEAR	TM-L	W	L	PCT	G	GS	CG	SH	SV	IP	H	R	ER	HR	HB	BB	SO	RAT	ERA	ERA+	CERA	OAV	BH	AVG	PR+	WS	TPW
1987	Chi-A	3	0	1.000	4	4	0	0	0	28	16	6	6	1	2	6	15	.786	1.93	238	1.39	.168	0	....	7	3	0.7
1988	Chi-A	5	10	.333	26	26	1	0	0	158^2	147	85	70	12	7	68	84	1.355	3.97	100	3.71	.245	0	....	-2	6	-0.2
1990	Chi-A	14	9	.609	33	33	4	0	0	205	189	93	87	20	7	77	165	1.298	3.82	100	3.69	.244	0	....	-4	12	-0.4
1991	Chi-A★	17	10	.630	35	**35**	**15**	3	0	253^2	212	97	96	19	4	82	191	1.159	3.41	117	2.84	.228	0	....	9	18	0.9
1992	Chi-A★	20	10	.667	34	34	**13**	1	0	260^2	247	95	92	21	7	75	178	1.235	3.18	122	3.31	.251	0	....	20	20	2.0
1993★	Chi-A★	**22**	10	.688	34	34	10	**4**	0	256^2	261	104	96	20	3	69	158	1.286	3.37	124	3.57	.266	0	....	23	21	2.2
1994	Chi-A	10	9	.526	25	**25**	6	2	0	181	186	82	75	12	5	42	127	1.260	3.73	125	3.46	.266	0	....	19	12	1.8
1995★	NY-A	15	10	.600	30	30	**8**	2	0	217^2	211	106	95	25	5	78	157	1.328	3.93	118	3.93	.254	0	....	15	15	1.4
1996★	Cle-A	13	9	.591	30	30	5	1	0	192	214	119	109	22	4	67	141	1.464	5.11	96	4.67	.282	0	....	-4	10	-0.4
1997	Cle-A	3	3	.500	8	6	0	0	0	40^2	44	25	23	6	1	18	38	1.525	5.09	92	5.13	.282	0	....	-1	2	-0.1
1998	Ana-A	5	3	.625	14	14	0	0	0	76	96	45	43	11	1	19	45	1.513	5.09	92	5.39	.311	0	....	-3	3	-0.3
1999	Ana-A	0	4	.000	4	4	0	0	0	19	31	17	17	4	2	5	12	1.895	8.05	60	8.79	.369	0	....	-7	0	-0.6
Total	12	127	87	.593	277	275	62	13	0	1889	1854	874	809	173	48	606	1311	1.302	3.85	111	3.73	.257	0	....	72	122	7.0

• MCDOWELL, Roger Roger Alan McDowell b: 12/21/1960, Cincinnati, OH BR/TR, 6'1", 182 lbs. Deb: 4/11/1985

YEAR	TM-L	W	L	PCT	G	GS	CG	SH	SV	IP	H	R	ER	HR	HB	BB	SO	RAT	ERA	ERA+	CERA	OAV	BH	AVG	PR+	WS	TPW
1985	NY-N	6	5	.545	62	2	0	0	17	127^1	108	43	40	9	1	37	70	1.139	2.83	122	2.63	.230	3	.158	10	13	1.1
1986★	NY-N	14	9	.609	75	0	0	0	22	128	107	48	43	4	3	42	65	1.164	3.02	117	2.53	.228	5	.278	7	16	0.8
1987	NY-N	7	5	.583	56	0	0	0	25	88^2	95	41	41	7	2	28	32	1.387	4.16	91	3.99	.276	3	.231	-3	9	-0.2
1988★	NY-N	5	5	.500	62	0	0	0	16	89	80	31	26	1	3	31	46	1.247	2.63	122	2.70	.238	3	.333	6	10	0.8
1989	NY-N	1	5	.167	25	0	0	0	4	35^1	34	21	13	1	2	16	15	1.415	3.31	99	3.59	.254	1	.500	0	1	0.1
	Phi-N	3	3	.500	44	0	0	0	19	56^2	45	15	7	2	1	22	32	1.182	1.11	319	2.49	.220	0	.000	16	10	1.7
	Yr.	4	8	.333	69	0	0	0	23	92	79	36	20	3	3	38	47	1.272	1.96	172	2.91	.233	1	.333	16	11	1.7
1990	Phi-N	6	8	.429	72	0	0	0	22	86^1	92	41	37	2	2	35	39	1.471	3.86	99	3.89	.286	0	.000	-1	9	-0.2
1991	Phi-N	3	6	.333	38	0	0	0	3	59	61	28	21	1	2	32	28	1.576	3.20	114	3.87	.266	0	.000	3	4	0.3
	LA-N	6	3	.667	33	0	0	0	7	42^1	39	12	12	3	0	16	22	1.299	2.55	141	3.16	.257	0	....	5	6	0.5
	Yr.	9	9	.500	71	0	0	0	10	101^1	100	40	33	4	2	48	50	1.461	2.93	124	3.58	.262	0	.000	8	10	0.8
1992	LA-N	6	10	.375	65	0	0	0	14	83^2	103	46	38	3	1	42	50	1.733	4.09	84	5.00	.306	0	.000	-4	3	-0.4
1993	LA-N	5	3	.625	54	0	0	0	2	68	76	32	17	2	2	30	27	1.559	2.25	169	4.30	.288	1	.500	12	6	1.2
1994	LA-N	0	3	.000	32	0	0	0	0	41^1	50	25	24	3	1	22	29	1.742	5.23	75	5.43	.303	0	.000	-6	0	-0.6
1995	Tex-A	7	4	.636	64	0	0	0	4	85	86	39	38	5	6	34	49	1.412	4.02	120	4.11	.277	0	....	8	9	0.7
1996	Bal-A	1	1	.500	41	0	0	0	4	59^1	69	32	28	7	2	23	20	1.551	4.25	116	5.30	.296	0	....	4	4	0.4
Total	12	70	70	.500	723	2	0	0	159	1050	1045	454	385	50	28	410	524	1.386	3.30	114	3.64	.263	16	.222	57	100	6.3

• MCDOWELL, Sam Samuel Edward Thomas "Sudden Sam" McDowell b: 9/21/1942, Pittsburgh, PA BL/TL, 6'5", 218 lbs. Deb: 9/15/1961

YEAR	TM-L	W	L	PCT	G	GS	CG	SH	SV	IP	H	R	ER	HR	HB	BB	SO	RAT	ERA	ERA+	CERA	OAV	BH	AVG	PR+	WS	TPW
1961	Cle-A	0	0	....	1	1	0	0	0	6^1	3	0	0	0	0	5	5	1.263	0.00	....	2.03	.136	0	.000	3	1	0.2
1962	Cle-A	3	7	.300	25	13	0	0	1	87^2	81	64	59	9	4	70	70	1.722	6.06	64	5.39	.243	4	.154	-22	0	-2.3
1963	Cle-A	3	5	.375	14	12	3	1	0	65	63	37	35	6	0	44	63	1.646	4.85	75	5.00	.256	4	.211	-8	1	-0.8
1964	Cle-A	11	6	.647	31	24	6	2	1	173^1	148	60	52	8	3	100	177	1.431	2.70	133	3.54	.229	8	.143	21	14	2.3
1965	Cle-A★	17	11	.607	42	35	14	3	4	273	178	80	66	9	6	132	**325**	1.136	**2.18**	**160**	2.19	**.185**	12	.126	**40**	**25**	**4.0**
1966	Cle-A★	9	8	.529	35	28	8	**5**	3	194^1	130	66	62	12	6	102	**225**	1.194	2.87	120	2.63	**.188**	12	.200	15	17	1.8
1967	Cle-A	13	15	.464	37	37	10	1	0	236^1	201	112	101	21	7	123	236	1.371	3.85	85	3.75	.233	15	.183	-13	8	-1.3
1968	Cle-A★	15	14	.517	38	37	11	3	0	269	181	78	54	13	10	110	**283**	1.082	1.81	164	2.16	.189	13	.153	32	23	3.6
1969	Cle-A★	18	14	.563	39	38	18	4	1	285	222	111	93	13	7	102	**279**	1.137	2.94	128	2.45	.213	16	.174	28	20	2.8
1970	Cle-A★	20	12	.625	39	39	19	1	0	**305**	236	108	99	25	7	131	**304**	1.203	2.92	135	2.92	.213	13	.124	**34**	**30**	**3.2**
1971	Cle-A★	13	17	.433	35	31	8	2	1	214^2	160	89	81	22	3	153	192	1.458	3.40	113	3.83	.207	13	.178	9	15	0.9
1972	SF-N	10	8	.556	28	25	4	0	0	164^1	155	86	79	12	6	86	122	1.467	4.33	81	4.16	.253	7	.119	-15	4	-1.8
1973	SF-N	1	2	.333	18	3	0	0	3	40	45	23	20	4	0	29	35	1.850	4.50	85	6.12	.285	2	.167	-3	1	-0.3
	NY-A	5	8	.385	16	15	2	1	0	95^2	73	47	42	4	0	64	75	1.432	3.95	93	3.34	.212	0	....	-4	4	-0.4
1974	NY-A	1	6	.143	13	7	0	0	0	48	42	27	25	6	0	41	33	1.729	4.69	74	5.23	.236	0	....	-7	0	-0.8
1975	Pit-N	2	1	.667	14	1	0	0	0	34^2	30	11	11	0	0	20	29	1.442	2.86	124	3.19	.242	0	.000	3	3	0.2
Total	15	141	134	.513	425	346	103	23	14	2492^1	1948	999	879	164	59	1312	2453	1.308	3.17	113	3.22	.215	119	.154	112	166	11.3

• MCELROY, Chuck — Charles Dwayne McElroy b: 10/1/1967, Port Arthur, TX BL/TL, 6', 195 lbs. Deb: 9/4/1989

YEAR	TM-L	W	L	PCT	G	GS	CG	SH	SV	IP	H	R	ER	HR	HB	BB	SO	RAT	ERA	ERA+	CERA	OAV	BH	AVG	PR+	WS	TPW
1989	Phi-N	0	0	....	11	0	0	0	0	10^{1}	12	2	2	1	0	4	8	1.548	1.74	204	4.75	.286	0	....	2	1	0.2
1990	Phi-N	0	1	.000	16	0	0	0	0	14	24	13	12	0	0	10	16	2.429	7.71	50	8.44	.369	0	....	-6	0	-0.6
1991	Chi-N	6	2	.750	71	0	0	0	3	101^{1}	73	33	22	7	0	57	92	1.283	1.95	199	2.93	.210	3	.300	23	12	2.5
1992	Chi-N	4	7	.364	72	0	0	0	6	83^{2}	73	40	33	5	0	51	83	1.482	3.55	101	3.66	.237	4	.667	0	6	0.3
1993	Chi-N	2	2	.500	49	0	0	0	0	47^{1}	51	30	24	4	1	25	31	1.606	4.56	87	4.81	.280	0	.000	-4	2	-0.4
1994	Cin-N	1	2	.333	52	0	0	0	5	57^{2}	52	15	15	3	0	15	38	1.162	2.34	177	2.74	.244	1	.167	11	7	1.1
1995	Cin-N	3	4	.429	44	0	0	0	0	40^{1}	46	29	27	5	1	15	27	1.512	6.02	68	4.95	.291	0	.000	-9	0	-1.0
1996	Cin-N	2	0	1.000	12	0	0	0	0	12^{1}	13	10	9	2	0	10	13	1.865	6.57	63	6.39	.265	0	.000	-3	0	-0.4
	Cal-A	5	1	.833	40	0	0	0	0	36^{2}	32	12	12	2	2	13	32	1.227	2.95	166	3.10	.239	0	....	8	4	0.7
1997	Ana-A	0	0	....	13	0	0	0	0	15^{2}	17	7	6	2	0	3	18	1.277	3.45	134	3.89	.270	0	....	2	1	0.2
	Chi-A	1	3	.250	48	0	0	0	1	59^{1}	56	29	26	3	2	19	44	1.264	3.94	111	3.17	.247	0	....	4	4	0.4
	Yr.	1	3	.250	61	0	0	0	1	75	73	36	32	5	2	22	62	1.267	3.84	115	3.32	.252	0	....	6	5	0.5
1998	Col-N	6	4	.600	78	0	0	0	2	68^{1}	68	23	22	3	0	24	61	1.346	2.90	179	3.61	.268	1	.200	17	10	1.7
1999	Col-N	3	1	.750	41	0	0	0	0	40^{2}	48	29	28	9	0	28	37	1.869	6.20	94	7.29	.296	0	.000	-2	3	-0.2
	NY-N	0	0	....	15	0	0	0	0	13^{1}	12	5	5	0	1	8	7	1.500	3.38	130	3.74	.250	0	....	1	1	0.1
	Yr.	3	1	.750	56	0	0	0	0	54	60	34	33	9	1	36	44	1.778	5.50	101	6.41	.286	0	.000	-0	4	0.0
2000	Bal-A	3	0	1.000	43	2	0	0	0	63^{1}	60	36	33	6	2	34	50	1.484	4.69	101	4.31	.247	0	....	0	4	0.0
2001	Bal-A	1	2	.333	18	5	0	0	0	45^{1}	49	29	27	8	2	28	22	1.699	5.36	80	6.06	.269	0	....	-6	1	-0.6
	SD-N	1	1	.500	31	0	0	0	0	29^{2}	38	24	17	6	0	18	25	1.888	5.16	78	7.10	.306	0	.000	-3	0	-0.4
Total	**13**	**38**	**30**	**.559**	**654**	**7**	**0**	**0**	**17**	**739^{1}**	**724**	**366**	**320**	**66**	**11**	**362**	**604**	**1.469**	**3.90**	**110**	**4.26**	**.258**	**9**	**.214**	**36**	**56**	**3.8**

• MCELROY, Jim — James D. McElroy b: 11/5/1862, Napa County, CA d: 2/24/1889, Needles, CA, 5'10", 170 lbs. Deb: 5/26/1884

YEAR	TM-L	W	L	PCT	G	GS	CG	SH	SV	IP	H	R	ER	HR	HB	BB	SO	RAT	ERA	ERA+	CERA	OAV	BH	AVG	PR+	WS	TPW
1884	Phi-N	1	12	.077	13	13	13	0	0	111	115	112	60	1	....	54	45	1.523	4.86	61	....	.253	7	.146	-18	1	-1.9
	Wil-U	0	1	.000	1	1	0	0	0	5	10	6	6	0	....	0	3	2.000	10.80	31	....	.391	0	.000	-4	0	-0.4

• MCENANEY, Will — William Henry McEnaney b: 2/14/1952, Springfield, OH BL/TL, 6', 180 lbs. Deb: 7/3/1974

YEAR	TM-L	W	L	PCT	G	GS	CG	SH	SV	IP	H	R	ER	HR	HB	BB	SO	RAT	ERA	ERA+	CERA	OAV	BH	AVG	PR+	WS	TPW
1974	Cin-N	2	1	.667	24	0	0	0	2	27	24	16	13	4	0	9	13	1.222	4.33	80	3.58	.250	0	....	-3	1	-0.3
1975*	Cin-N	5	2	.714	70	0	0	0	15	91	92	29	25	6	2	23	48	1.264	2.47	145	3.32	.264	0	.000	8	10	0.7
1976*	Cin-N	2	6	.250	55	0	0	0	7	72^{1}	97	44	39	3	1	23	28	1.659	4.85	72	5.07	.323	1	.167	-11	1	-1.2
1977	Mon-N	3	5	.375	69	0	0	0	3	86^{2}	92	39	38	6	2	22	38	1.315	3.95	96	3.60	.271	0	.000	-2	5	-0.2
1978	Pit-N	0	0	....	6	0	0	0	0	8^{2}	15	11	10	3	1	2	6	1.962	10.38	36	10.91	.395	0	....	-6	0	-0.7
1979	StL-N	0	3	.000	45	0	0	0	2	64	60	26	21	3	2	16	15	1.188	2.95	127	2.72	.251	0	.000	4	5	0.4
Total	**6**	**12**	**17**	**.414**	**269**	**0**	**0**	**0**	**29**	**349^{2}**	**380**	**165**	**146**	**25**	**8**	**95**	**148**	**1.358**	**3.76**	**97**	**3.85**	**.279**	**1**	**.032**	**-10**	**22**	**-1.3**

• MCEVOY, Lou — Louis Anthony McEvoy b: 5/30/1902, Williamsburg, KS d: 12/17/1953, Webster Groves, MO BR/TR, 6'2.5", 203 lbs. Deb: 4/28/1930

YEAR	TM-L	W	L	PCT	G	GS	CG	SH	SV	IP	H	R	ER	HR	HB	BB	SO	RAT	ERA	ERA+	CERA	OAV	BH	AVG	PR+	WS	TPW
1930	NY-A	1	3	.250	28	1	0	0	3	52^{1}	64	51	39	4	2	29	14	1.777	6.71	64	5.36	.288	2	.125	-13	0	-1.3
1931	NY-A	0	0	....	6	0	0	0	1	12^{1}	19	17	17	1	1	12	3	2.514	12.41	32	9.84	.358	0	.000	-12	0	-1.1
Total	**2**	**1**	**3**	**.250**	**34**	**1**	**0**	**0**	**4**	**64^{2}**	**83**	**68**	**56**	**5**	**3**	**41**	**17**	**1.918**	**7.79**	**54**	**6.21**	**.301**	**2**	**.100**	**-25**	**0**	**-2.5**

• MCFADDEN, Barney — Bernard Joseph McFadden b: 3/20/1877, Eckley, PA d: 4/28/1924, Mauch Chuck, PA BR/TR, 6'1", 195 lbs. Deb: 4/24/1901

YEAR	TM-L	W	L	PCT	G	GS	CG	SH	SV	IP	H	R	ER	HR	HB	BB	SO	RAT	ERA	ERA+	CERA	OAV	BH	AVG	PR+	WS	TPW
1901	Cin-N	3	4	.429	8	5	4	0	0	46	54	39	31	2	6	40	11	2.043	6.07	53	6.78	.291	3	.150	-14	0	-1.4
1902	Phi-N	0	1	.000	1	1	1	0	0	9	14	13	8	0	0	7	3	2.333	8.00	35	7.57	.354	0	.000	-5	0	-0.6
Total	**2**	**3**	**5**	**.375**	**9**	**6**	**5**	**0**	**0**	**55**	**68**	**52**	**39**	**2**	**6**	**47**	**14**	**2.091**	**6.38**	**49**	**6.91**	**.302**	**3**	**.130**	**-19**	**0**	**-2.0**

• MCFARLAN, Dan — Anderson Daniel McFarlan b: 11/26/1874, Gainesville, TX d: 9/24/1924, Louisville, KY Deb: 9/2/1895

YEAR	TM-L	W	L	PCT	G	GS	CG	SH	SV	IP	H	R	ER	HR	HB	BB	SO	RAT	ERA	ERA+	CERA	OAV	BH	AVG	PR+	WS	TPW
1895	Lou-N	0	7	.000	7	7	6	0	0	46	80	56	34	4	0	15	10	2.065	6.65	70	8.13	.375	5	.238	-8	0	-0.7
1899	Bro-N	0	0	....	1	0	0	0	0	6	6	1	1	1	0	3	0	1.500	1.50	261	4.86	.260	0	.000	1	1	0.1
	Was-N	8	18	.308	32	28	22	1	0	211^{2}	268	166	112	5	11	64	41	1.569	4.76	82	4.75	.308	16	.186	-12	5	-1.0
	Yr.	8	18	.308	33	28	22	1	0	217^{2}	274	167	113	6	11	67	41	1.567	4.67	84	4.75	.307	16	.182	-10	6	-0.9
Total	**2**	**8**	**25**	**.242**	**40**	**35**	**28**	**1**	**0**	**263^{2}**	**354**	**223**	**147**	**10**	**11**	**82**	**51**	**1.654**	**5.02**	**81**	**5.34**	**.320**	**21**	**.193**	**-19**	**6**	**-1.7**

• MCFARLAND, Chappie — Charles A. McFarland b: 3/13/1875, White Hall, IL d: 12/14/1924, Houston, TX TR, 6'1" Deb: 9/15/1902

YEAR	TM-L	W	L	PCT	G	GS	CG	SH	SV	IP	H	R	ER	HR	HB	BB	SO	RAT	ERA	ERA+	CERA	OAV	BH	AVG	PR+	WS	TPW
1902	StL-N	0	1	.000	2	1	1	0	0	11	11	7	7	1	0	3	3	1.273	5.73	48	3.55	.260	0	.000	-3	0	-0.4
1903	StL-N	9	19	.321	28	26	25	1	0	229	253	133	78	2	6	48	76	1.314	3.07	106	3.44	.284	8	.108	1	11	-0.3
1904	StL-N	14	18	.438	32	31	28	1	0	269^{1}	266	149	96	7	4	56	111	1.196	3.21	84	2.64	.248	13	.131	-10	9	-1.3
1905	StL-N	8	18	.308	31	28	22	3	1	250^{1}	281	145	106	3	6	65	85	1.382	3.81	78	3.68	.284	14	.165	-15	7	-1.4
1906	StL-N	2	1	.667	6	4	2	0	1	37^{1}	33	18	8	1	0	8	16	1.098	1.93	136	2.12	.219	2	.133	3	2	0.3
	Pit-N	1	3	.250	6	5	2	1	0	35^{1}	39	14	10	0	2	7	11	1.302	2.55	105	3.62	.298	5	.385	0	2	0.2
	Bro-N	0	1	.000	1	1	1	0	0	9	10	8	8	1	0	5	5	1.667	8.00	31	5.44	.286	0	.000	-5	0	-0.6
	Yr.	3	5	.375	13	10	5	1	1	81^{2}	82	40	26	2	2	20	32	1.249	2.87	91	3.13	.259	7	.226	-2	4	-0.2
Total	**5**	**34**	**61**	**.358**	**106**	**96**	**81**	**6**	**2**	**841^{1}**	**893**	**474**	**313**	**15**	**18**	**192**	**307**	**1.290**	**3.35**	**87**	**3.23**	**.270**	**42**	**.143**	**-30**	**31**	**-3.6**

• MCFARLAND, Monte — Lamont Amos McFarland b: 11/7/1872, White Hall, IL d: 11/15/1913, Peoria, IL BR, 5'10" Deb: 9/14/1895

YEAR	TM-L	W	L	PCT	G	GS	CG	SH	SV	IP	H	R	ER	HR	HB	BB	SO	RAT	ERA	ERA+	CERA	OAV	BH	AVG	PR+	WS	TPW
1895	Chi-N	2	0	1.000	2	2	2	0	0	14	21	11	8	0	0	5	5	1.857	5.14	99	5.95	.341	1	.143	-0	1	-0.1
1896	Chi-N	0	4	.000	4	3	2	0	0	25	32	25	20	0	2	21	3	2.120	7.20	63	6.73	.309	0	.000	-8	0	-0.9
Total	**2**	**2**	**4**	**.333**	**6**	**5**	**4**	**0**	**0**	**39**	**53**	**36**	**28**	**0**	**2**	**26**	**8**	**2.026**	**6.46**	**72**	**6.45**	**.321**	**1**	**.053**	**-8**	**1**	**-0.9**

• MCFETRIDGE, Jack — John Reed McFetridge b: 8/25/1869, Philadelphia, PA d: 1/10/1917, Philadelphia, PA, 6', 175 lbs. Deb: 6/7/1890

YEAR	TM-L	W	L	PCT	G	GS	CG	SH	SV	IP	H	R	ER	HR	HB	BB	SO	RAT	ERA	ERA+	CERA	OAV	BH	AVG	PR+	WS	TPW
1890	Phi-N	1	0	1.000	1	1	1	0	0	9	5	1	1	0	0	2	4	.778	1.00	364	....	.158	3	.750	3	2	0.3
1903	Phi-N	1	11	.083	14	13	11	0	0	103	120	71	56	2	3	49	31	1.641	4.89	67	4.86	.299	6	.176	-20	1	-1.9
Total	**2**	**2**	**11**	**.154**	**15**	**14**	**12**	**0**	**0**	**112**	**125**	**72**	**57**	**2**	**3**	**51**	**35**	**1.571**	**4.58**	**71**	**4.47**	**.289**	**9**	**.237**	**-18**	**3**	**-1.5**

• MCGAFFIGAN, Andy — Andrew Joseph McGaffigan b: 10/25/1956, West Palm Beach, FL BR/TR, 6'3", 195 lbs. Deb: 9/22/1981

YEAR	TM-L	W	L	PCT	G	GS	CG	SH	SV	IP	H	R	ER	HR	HB	BB	SO	RAT	ERA	ERA+	CERA	OAV	BH	AVG	PR+	WS	TPW
1981	NY-A	0	0	....	2	0	0	0	0	7	5	3	2	1	0	3	2	1.143	2.57	139	2.66	.200	0	....	1	0	0.1
1982	SF-N	1	0	1.000	4	0	0	0	0	8	5	1	0	0	1	1	4	.750	0.00	....	1.32	.179	0	.000	3	1	0.3
1983	SF-N	3	9	.250	43	16	0	0	2	134^{1}	131	67	64	17	1	39	93	1.266	4.29	82	3.68	.255	2	.067	-10	4	-1.2
1984	Mon-N	3	4	.429	21	3	0	0	1	46	37	14	13	2	0	15	39	1.130	2.54	135	2.40	.220	0	.000	4	4	0.3
	Cin-N	0	2	.000	9	3	0	0	0	23	23	14	14	2	0	8	18	1.348	5.48	69	3.78	.261	0	.000	-4	0	-0.5
	Yr.	3	6	.333	30	6	0	0	1	69	60	28	27	4	0	23	57	1.203	3.52	102	2.86	.234	0	.000	-0	4	-0.1
1985	Cin-N	3	3	.500	15	15	2	0	0	94^{1}	88	40	39	4	2	30	83	1.251	3.72	102	3.05	.247	1	.034	-0	5	-0.2
1986	Mon-N	10	5	.667	48	14	1	1	2	142^{2}	114	49	42	9	2	55	104	1.185	2.65	139	2.71	.223	2	.061	16	13	1.5
1987	Mon-N	5	2	.714	69	0	0	0	12	120^{1}	105	38	32	5	3	42	100	1.222	2.39	176	2.82	.235	0	.000	26	16	2.5
1988	Mon-N	6	0	1.000	63	0	0	0	4	91^{1}	81	31	28	4	2	37	71	1.292	2.76	130	3.00	.233	0	.000	7	9	0.8
1989	Mon-N	3	5	.375	57	0	0	0	2	75	85	40	39	3	3	30	40	1.533	4.68	75	4.48	.293	1	1.000	-9	2	-0.9
1990	SF-N	0	0	....	4	0	0	0	0	4^{2}	10	9	9	2	0	4	4	3.000	17.36	21	17.74	.455	0	....	-7	0	-0.7
	KC-A	4	3	.571	24	11	0	0	1	78^{2}	75	40	27	6	2	28	49	1.309	3.09	124	3.54	.248	0	....	9	4	0.9
1991	KC-A	0	0	....	4	0	0	0	0	8	14	5	4	0	0	2	3	2.000	4.50	92	7.17	.389	0	....	-0	0	0.0
Total	**11**	**38**	**33**	**.535**	**363**	**62**	**3**	**1**	**24**	**833^{1}**	**773**	**351**	**313**	**55**	**16**	**294**	**610**	**1.280**	**3.38**	**109**	**3.32**	**.247**	**6**	**.048**	**35**	**58**	**2.7**

• MCGEACHEY, Jack — John Charles McGeachey b: 5/13/1864, Clinton, MA d: 4/5/1930, Cambridge, MA BR/TR, 5'8", 165 lbs. Deb: 6/17/1886 ♦

YEAR	TM-L	W	L	PCT	G	GS	CG	SH	SV	IP	H	R	ER	HR	HB	BB	SO	RAT	ERA	ERA+	CERA	OAV	BH	AVG	PR+	WS	TPW
1887	Ind-N	0	1	.000	1	0	0	0	0	6^{1}	17	17	8	2	0	4	3	2.684	11.37	36	....	.476	114	.278	-5	6	-1.7
1888	Ind-N	0	0	....	1	0	0	0	0	5	5	5	4	1	0	3	0	1.600	7.20	41	....	.251	99	.219	-2	5	-2.7
1889	Ind-N	0	0	....	3	0	0	0	0	4^{2}	7	9	6	2	0	6	3	2.786	11.57	36	....	.336	142	.267	-4	7	-1.9
Total	**3**	**0**	**1**	**.000**	**5**	**0**	**0**	**0**	**0**	**16**	**29**	**31**	**18**	**5**	**0**	**13**	**6**	**2.375**	**10.13**	**38**	**....**	**.379**	**609**	**.247**	**-11**	**18**	**-6.3**

• MCGEE, Bill — William Henry "Fiddler Bill" McGee b: 11/16/1909, Batchtown, IL d: 2/11/1987, St. Louis, MO BR/TR, 6'1", 215 lbs. Deb: 9/29/1935

YEAR	TM-L	W	L	PCT	G	GS	CG	SH	SV	IP	H	R	ER	HR	HB	BB	SO	RAT	ERA	ERA+	CERA	OAV	BH	AVG	PR+	WS	TPW
1935	StL-N	1	0	1.000	1	1	1	0	0	9	3	1	1	0	0	1	2	.444	1.00	410	0.38	.103	1	.333	3	1	0.3
1936	StL-N	1	1	.500	7	2	0	0	0	16	23	14	14	3	0	4	8	1.688	7.88	50	7.02	.359	1	.250	-7	0	-0.7
1937	StL-N	1	0	1.000	4	1	1	0	0	14	13	4	4	1	1	4	9	1.214	2.57	155	3.37	.255	1	.200	2	1	0.2

YEAR	TM-L	W	L	PCT	G	GS	CG	SH	SV	IP	H	R	ER	HR	HB	BB	SO	RAT	ERA	ERA+	CERA	OAV	BH	AVG	PR+	WS	TPW
1938	StL-N	7	12	.368	47	25	10	1	5	216	216	101	77	4	1	78	104	1.361	3.21	123	3.25	.257	14	.209	19	15	2.0
1939	StL-N	12	5	.706	43	17	5	4	0	156	155	68	66	14	0	59	56	1.372	3.81	108	3.82	.260	8	.145	4	10	0.1
1940	StL-N	16	10	.615	38	31	11	3	0	218	222	108	92	13	2	96	78	1.459	3.80	105	3.95	.263	13	.178	8	13	0.8
1941	StL-N	0	1	.000	4	3	0	0	0	14	17	9	8	1	1	13	2	2.143	5.14	73	7.32	.298	0	.000	-2	0	-0.3
	NY-N	2	9	.182	22	14	1	0	0	106	117	68	58	9	0	54	41	1.613	4.92	75	4.89	.285	5	.161	-15	1	-1.7
	Yr.	2	10	.167	26	17	1	0	0	120	134	77	66	10	1	67	43	1.675	4.95	75	5.17	.286	5	.143	-17	1	-2.0
1942	NY-N	6	3	.667	31	8	2	1	1	104	95	50	34	8	1	46	40	1.356	2.94	114	3.51	.244	3	.103	4	6	0.2
Total	**8**	**46**	**41**	**.529**	**197**	**102**	**31**	**9**	**6**	**853**	**861**	**423**	**354**	**53**	**6**	**355**	**340**	**1.426**	**3.74**	**104**	**3.88**	**.263**	**46**	**.170**	**15**	**47**	**0.9**

• MCGEEHAN, Conny Cornelius Bernard McGeehan b: 8/25/1882, Drifton, PA d: 7/4/1907, Hazleton, PA TR Deb: 7/15/1903

YEAR	TM-L	W	L	PCT	G	GS	CG	SH	SV	IP	H	R	ER	HR	HB	BB	SO	RAT	ERA	ERA+	CERA	OAV	BH	AVG	PR+	WS	TPW
1903	Phi-A	1	0	1.000	3	0	0	0	0	10	9	5	5	0	1	1	4	1.000	4.50	68	2.10	.240	0	.000	-2	0	-0.3

• MCGEHEE, Kevin George Kevin McGehee b: 1/18/1969, Alexandria, LA BR/TR, 6', 190 lbs. Deb: 8/23/1993

YEAR	TM-L	W	L	PCT	G	GS	CG	SH	SV	IP	H	R	ER	HR	HB	BB	SO	RAT	ERA	ERA+	CERA	OAV	BH	AVG	PR+	WS	TPW
1993	Bal-A	0	0	....	5	0	0	0	0	16^{2}	18	11	11	5	2	7	7	1.500	5.94	75	6.49	.281	0	....	-3	0	-0.3

• MCGEHEE, Pat Patrick Henry McGehee b: 7/2/1888, Meadville, MS d: 12/30/1946, Paducah, KY BL/TR, 6'2.5", 180 lbs. Deb: 8/23/1912

YEAR	TM-L	W	L	PCT	G	GS	CG	SH	SV	IP	H	R	ER	HR	HB	BB	SO	RAT	ERA	ERA+	CERA	OAV	BH	AVG	PR+	WS	TPW
1912	Det-A	0	0	....	1	1	0	0	0	0	1	0	0	0	0	1	0	....	....	....	∞	1.000	0	....	0	0	0.0

• MCGILBERRY, Randy Randall Kent McGilberry b: 10/29/1953, Mobile, AL BB/TR, 6'1", 195 lbs. Deb: 9/6/1977

YEAR	TM-L	W	L	PCT	G	GS	CG	SH	SV	IP	H	R	ER	HR	HB	BB	SO	RAT	ERA	ERA+	CERA	OAV	BH	AVG	PR+	WS	TPW
1977	KC-A	0	1	.000	3	0	0	0	0	7	7	4	4	1	0	1	1	1.143	5.14	78	3.72	.280	0	....	-1	0	-0.1
1978	KC-A	0	1	.000	18	0	0	0	0	25^{2}	27	16	12	2	0	18	12	1.753	4.21	91	5.30	.276	0	....	-1	0	-0.1
Total	**2**	**0**	**2**	**.000**	**21**	**0**	**0**	**0**	**0**	**32^{2}**	**34**	**20**	**16**	**3**	**0**	**19**	**13**	**1.622**	**4.41**	**88**	**4.96**	**.276**	**0**	**....**	**-2**	**0**	**-0.2**

• MCGILL, Bill William Jacob "Parson" McGill b: 6/29/1880, Galva, KS d: 8/7/1959, Alva, OK BR/TR, 6'2", 185 lbs. Deb: 9/16/1907

YEAR	TM-L	W	L	PCT	G	GS	CG	SH	SV	IP	H	R	ER	HR	HB	BB	SO	RAT	ERA	ERA+	CERA	OAV	BH	AVG	PR+	WS	TPW
1907	StL-A	1	0	1.000	2	2	1	0	0	18^{1}	22	8	7	0	0	2	8	1.309	3.44	73	3.50	.300	0	.000	-2	1	-0.4

• MCGILL, Willie William Vaness "Kid" McGill b: 11/10/1873, Atlanta, GA d: 8/29/1944, Indianapolis, IN TL, 5'6.5", 170 lbs. Deb: 5/8/1890

YEAR	TM-L	W	L	PCT	G	GS	CG	SH	SV	IP	H	R	ER	HR	HB	BB	SO	RAT	ERA	ERA+	CERA	OAV	BH	AVG	PR+	WS	TPW
1890	Cle-P	11	9	.550	24	20	19	0	0	183^{2}	222	146	84	5	12	96	82	1.731	4.12	97	....	.286	10	.147	-3	8	0.0
1891	Cin-a	2	5	.286	8	8	6	0	0	65	69	56	36	1	3	37	19	1.631	4.98	83	....	.263	2	.100	-6	3	-0.5
	StL-a	18	9	.667	33	29	20	1	1	233^{1}	207	140	81	10	12	126	146	1.427	3.12	135	....	.230	14	.161	25	22	2.4
	Yr.	20	14	.588	41	37	26	1	1	298^{1}	276	196	117	11	15	163	165	1.472	3.53	118	....	.237	16	.150	19	25	1.9
1892	Cin-N	1	1	.500	3	3	1	0	0	17	18	14	10	0	0	5	7	1.353	5.29	62	3.23	.261	2	.286	-4	1	-0.4
1893	Chi-N	17	18	.486	39	34	26	1	0	302^{2}	311	206	155	6	14	181	91	1.626	4.61	100	4.40	.258	29	.234	2	20	0.4
1894	Chi-N	7	19	.269	27	23	22	0	0	208	272	195	135	2	10	117	58	1.870	5.84	96	5.83	.313	20	.244	-1	11	0.0
1895	Phi-N	10	8	.556	20	20	13	0	0	146	177	122	90	2	4	81	70	1.767	5.55	86	5.19	.295	14	.222	-12	7	-1.0
1896	Phi-N	5	4	.556	12	11	7	0	0	79^{2}	87	62	47	0	4	53	29	1.757	5.31	81	4.85	.276	6	.207	-8	4	-0.7
Total	**7**	**71**	**73**	**.493**	**166**	**148**	**114**	**2**	**1**	**1235^{1}**	**1363**	**941**	**638**	**26**	**59**	**696**	**502**	**1.667**	**4.65**	**98**	**3.03**	**.273**	**97**	**.202**	**-8**	**76**	**0.2**

• MCGILLEN, John John Joseph McGillen b: 8/6/1917, Eddystone, PA d: 8/11/1987, Upland, PA BL/TL, 6'1", 175 lbs. Deb: 4/20/1944

YEAR	TM-L	W	L	PCT	G	GS	CG	SH	SV	IP	H	R	ER	HR	HB	BB	SO	RAT	ERA	ERA+	CERA	OAV	BH	AVG	PR+	WS	TPW
1944	Phi-A	0	0	....	2	0	0	0	0	1	1	2	2	0	0	2	0	3.000	18.00	19	10.60	.333	0	....	-2	0	-0.2

• MCGINLEY, Jim James William McGinley b: 10/2/1878, Groveland, MA d: 9/20/1961, Haverhill, MA BR/TR, 5'9.5", 165 lbs. Deb: 9/22/1904

YEAR	TM-L	W	L	PCT	G	GS	CG	SH	SV	IP	H	R	ER	HR	HB	BB	SO	RAT	ERA	ERA+	CERA	OAV	BH	AVG	PR+	WS	TPW
1904	StL-N	2	1	.667	3	3	3	0	0	27	28	8	6	0	3	6	6	1.259	2.00	134	3.29	.267	1	.091	3	2	0.2
1905	StL-N	0	1	.000	1	1	0	0	0	3	5	6	5	1	0	2	0	2.333	15.00	20	10.53	.333	1	1.000	-4	0	-0.4
Total	**2**	**2**	**2**	**.500**	**4**	**4**	**3**	**0**	**0**	**30**	**33**	**14**	**11**	**1**	**3**	**8**	**6**	**1.367**	**3.30**	**85**	**4.01**	**.275**	**2**	**.167**	**-1**	**2**	**-0.2**

• MCGINN, Dan Daniel Michael McGinn b: 11/29/1943, Omaha, NE BL/TL, 6', 190 lbs. Deb: 9/3/1968

YEAR	TM-L	W	L	PCT	G	GS	CG	SH	SV	IP	H	R	ER	HR	HB	BB	SO	RAT	ERA	ERA+	CERA	OAV	BH	AVG	PR+	WS	TPW
1968	Cin-N	0	1	.000	14	0	0	0	0	12	13	7	7	1	1	11	16	2.000	5.25	60	6.49	.271	0	.000	-3	0	-0.3
1969	Mon-N	7	10	.412	74	1	0	0	6	132^{1}	123	67	58	8	5	65	112	1.421	3.94	93	3.79	.245	5	.172	-3	7	-0.3
1970	Mon-N	7	10	.412	52	19	3	2	0	130^{2}	154	88	79	13	7	78	83	1.776	5.44	76	6.11	.296	4	.114	-20	2	-2.2
1971	Mon-N	1	4	.200	28	6	1	0	0	71	74	51	47	7	1	42	40	1.634	5.96	59	5.11	.274	4	.235	-19	0	-2.0
1972	Chi-N	0	5	.000	42	2	0	0	4	62^{2}	78	46	41	5	4	29	42	1.707	5.89	65	5.58	.301	2	.250	-14	0	-1.5
Total	**5**	**15**	**30**	**.333**	**210**	**28**	**4**	**2**	**10**	**408^{2}**	**442**	**259**	**232**	**34**	**18**	**225**	**293**	**1.632**	**5.11**	**74**	**5.12**	**.276**	**15**	**.165**	**-60**	**9**	**-6.3**

• MCGINNIS, Gus August McGinnis b: 8/1870, Barnesville, OH d: 4/20/1904, Barnesville, OH TL, 5'11", 168 lbs. Deb: 4/27/1893

YEAR	TM-L	W	L	PCT	G	GS	CG	SH	SV	IP	H	R	ER	HR	HB	BB	SO	RAT	ERA	ERA+	CERA	OAV	BH	AVG	PR+	WS	TPW
1893	Chi-N	2	5	.286	13	5	3	0	0	67^{1}	85	67	40	2	3	31	13	1.723	5.35	87	5.33	.299	6	.240	-5	3	-0.3
	Phi-N	1	3	.250	5	4	4	1	0	37^{1}	39	20	18	0	2	17	12	1.500	4.34	105	3.88	.261	3	.200	0	2	0.0
	Yr.	3	8	.273	18	9	7	1	0	104^{2}	124	87	58	2	5	48	25	1.643	4.99	92	4.81	.286	9	.225	-5	5	-0.3

• MCGINNIS, Jumbo George Washington McGinnis b: 2/22/1864, St. Louis, MO d: 5/18/1934, St. Louis, MO, 5'10", 197 lbs. Deb: 5/2/1882 U

YEAR	TM-L	W	L	PCT	G	GS	CG	SH	SV	IP	H	R	ER	HR	HB	BB	SO	RAT	ERA	ERA+	CERA	OAV	BH	AVG	PR+	WS	TPW
1882	StL-a	25	18	.581	45	45	43	3	0	388^{1}	391	241	112	2	....	53	134	1.143	2.60	108	....	.245	44	.217	16	26	1.6
1883	StL-a	28	16	.636	45	45	41	**6**	0	382^{2}	325	174	99	3	....	69	128	1.030	2.33	149	....	.215	36	.200	23	42	1.5
1884	StL-a	24	16	.600	40	40	39	5	0	354^{1}	331	196	112	4	12	35	141	1.033	2.84	114	....	.234	34	.233	7	28	0.9
1885	StL-a	6	6	.500	13	13	12	3	0	112	98	65	42	1	6	19	41	1.045	3.38	97	....	.225	11	.220	-5	7	-0.4
1886	StL-a	5	5	.500	10	10	10	1	0	87^{2}	107	75	37	2	7	27	30	1.529	3.80	90	....	.288	7	.189	-4	4	-0.4
	Bal-a	11	13	.458	26	25	24	0	0	209^{1}	235	141	81	6	14	48	70	1.352	3.48	98	....	.271	16	.188	3	11	0.2
	Yr.	16	18	.471	36	35	34	1	0	297	342	216	118	8	21	75	100	1.404	3.58	96	....	.276	23	.189	-1	15	-0.2
1887	Cin-a	3	5	.375	8	8	8	0	0	69^{1}	128	66	42	3	8	43	18	1.846	5.45	80	....	.382	7	.219	-12	3	-0.9
Total	**6**	**102**	**79**	**.564**	**187**	**186**	**177**	**18**	**0**	**1603^{2}**	**1615**	**958**	**525**	**21**	**47**	**294**	**562**	**1.164**	**2.95**	**111**	**....**	**.247**	**155**	**.211**	**29**	**121**	**2.5**

• MCGINNITY, Joe Joseph Jerome "Iron Man" McGinnity
b: 3/19/1871, Rock Island, IL d: 11/14/1929, Brooklyn, NY BR/TR, 5'11", 206 lbs. Deb: 4/18/1899 C/U HOF: 1946

YEAR	TM-L	W	L	PCT	G	GS	CG	SH	SV	IP	H	R	ER	HR	HB	BB	SO	RAT	ERA	ERA+	CERA	OAV	BH	AVG	PR+	WS	TPW
1899	Bal-N	**28**	16	.636	48	41	38	4	2	366^{1}	358	164	109	3	28	93	74	1.231	2.68	148	2.92	.256	28	.193	51	35	4.1
1900*	Bro-N	**28**	8	.778	44	37	32	1	0	**343**	350	179	112	5	41	113	93	1.350	2.94	130	3.64	.264	28	.193	30	**30**	2.3
1901	Bal-A	26	20	.565	**48**	**43**	**39**	1	1	**382**	412	219	151	7	21	96	75	1.330	3.56	109	3.38	.272	31	.209	25	27	1.9
1902	Bal-A	13	10	.565	25	23	19	0	0	198^{2}	219	102	76	3	8	46	39	1.334	3.44	109	3.43	.280	25	.287	18	11	2.1
	NY-N	8	8	.500	19	16	16	1	0	153	122	52	35	1	9	32	67	1.007	2.06	136	1.87	.219	8	.121	14	12	0.8
1903	NY-N	**31**	20	.608	**55**	**48**	**44**	3	2	**434**	391	162	117	4	19	109	171	1.152	2.43	138	2.45	.236	34	.206	35	**40**	3.2
1904	NY-N	**35**	8	.814	**51**	44	38	**9**	**5**	**408**	307	103	73	8	13	86	144	.963	**1.61**	**169**	1.71	.206	25	.176	**42**	**42**	**4.3**
1905*	NY-N	21	15	.583	**46**	38	26	2	3	320^{1}	289	131	102	6	14	71	125	1.124	2.87	102	2.45	.240	28	.233	4	22	1.0
1906	NY-N	**27**	12	.692	**45**	37	32	3	2	339^{2}	316	127	85	1	7	71	105	1.139	2.25	115	2.34	.246	15	.130	12	24	1.0
1907	NY-N	18	18	.500	**47**	34	23	3	**4**	310^{1}	320	126	109	6	15	58	120	1.218	3.16	78	2.97	.266	18	.175	-13	16	-1.5
1908	NY-N	11	7	.611	37	20	7	5	**5**	186	192	73	47	8	7	37	55	1.231	2.27	105	3.16	.267	11	.180	5	10	0.5
Total	**10**	**246**	**142**	**.634**	**465**	**381**	**314**	**32**	**24**	**3441^{1}**	**3276**	**1438**	**1016**	**52**	**182**	**812**	**1068**	**1.188**	**2.66**	**119**	**2.74**	**.249**	**251**	**.194**	**223**	**269**	**19.8**

• MCGLINCHY, Kevin Kevin Michael McGlinchy b: 6/28/1977, Malden, MA BR/TR, 6'5", 220 lbs. Deb: 4/5/1999

YEAR	TM-L	W	L	PCT	G	GS	CG	SH	SV	IP	H	R	ER	HR	HB	BB	SO	RAT	ERA	ERA+	CERA	OAV	BH	AVG	PR+	WS	TPW
1999*	Atl-N	7	3	.700	64	0	0	0	0	70^{1}	66	25	22	6	1	30	67	1.365	2.82	160	3.68	.255	0	.000	14	8	1.3
2000	Atl-N	0	0	....	10	0	0	0	0	8^{1}	11	4	2	1	0	6	9	2.040	2.16	212	7.10	.314	0	....	2	1	0.2
Total	**2**	**7**	**3**	**.700**	**74**	**0**	**0**	**0**	**0**	**78^{2}**	**77**	**29**	**24**	**7**	**1**	**36**	**76**	**1.436**	**2.75**	**164**	**4.04**	**.262**	**0**	**.000**	**16**	**9**	**1.5**

• MCGLOTHEN, Lynn Lynn Everett McGlothen b: 3/27/1950, Monroe, LA d: 8/14/1984, Dubach, LA BL/TR, 6'2", 195 lbs. Deb: 6/25/1972

YEAR	TM-L	W	L	PCT	G	GS	CG	SH	SV	IP	H	R	ER	HR	HB	BB	SO	RAT	ERA	ERA+	CERA	OAV	BH	AVG	PR+	WS	TPW
1972	Bos-A	8	7	.533	22	22	4	1	0	145	135	66	55	9	7	59	112	1.338	3.41	94	3.65	.247	10	.189	-0	7	0.1
1973	Bos-A	1	2	.333	6	3	0	0	0	23	39	23	21	6	1	8	16	2.043	8.22	49	9.86	.386	0	....	-11	0	-1.1
1974	StL-N★	16	12	.571	31	31	8	3	0	237^{1}	212	80	71	12	2	89	142	1.268	2.69	133	3.04	.241	15	.181	20	21	2.0
1975	StL-N	15	13	.536	35	34	9	2	0	239	231	110	104	21	4	97	146	1.372	3.92	96	3.81	.254	7	.088	2	12	-0.4
1976	StL-N	13	15	.464	33	32	10	4	0	205	209	96	89	10	4	68	106	1.351	3.91	91	3.63	.268	15	.211	-9	10	-0.8
1977	SF-N	2	9	.182	21	15	2	0	0	80	94	62	50	9	1	52	42	1.825	5.63	70	6.29	.299	2	.105	-14	0	-1.5
1978	SF-N	0	0	....	5	1	0	0	0	12^{2}	15	9	7	0	0	4	9	1.500	4.97	69	4.02	.313	0	.000	-2	0	-0.3
	Chi-N	5	3	.625	49	1	0	0	0	80	77	33	27	7	0	39	60	1.450	3.04	133	4.09	.257	3	.231	9	7	1.1
	Yr.	5	3	.625	54	2	0	0	0	92^{2}	92	42	34	7	0	43	69	1.457	3.30	118	4.08	.264	3	.188	7	7	0.8
1979	Chi-N	13	14	.481	42	29	6	1	2	212	236	103	97	27	3	55	147	1.373	4.12	100	4.37	.283	16	.225	3	12	0.5

YEAR	TM-L	W	L	PCT	G	GS	CG	SH	SV	IP	H	R	ER	HR	HB	BB	SO	RAT	ERA	ERA+	CERA	OAV	BH	AVG	PR+	WS	TPW
1980	Chi-N	12	14	.462	39	27	2	2	0	182^1	211	105	97	24	1	64	119	1.508	4.79	82	4.98	.293	10	.196	-15	6	-1.4
1981	Chi-N	1	4	.200	20	6	0	0	0	54^2	71	32	29	1	1	28	26	1.811	4.77	77	5.50	.317	1	.083	-5	1	-0.6
	Chi-A	0	0	....	11	0	0	0	0	21^2	14	10	10	0	1	7	12	.969	4.15	86	1.52	.189	0	....	-2	1	-0.2
1982	NY-A	0	0	....	4	0	0	0	0	5	9	6	6	1	0	2	2	2.200	10.80	37	9.81	.375	0	....	-4	0	-0.4
Total	**11**	**86**	**93**	**.480**	**318**	**201**	**41**	**13**	**2**	**1497^2**	**1553**	**735**	**663**	**127**	**25**	**572**	**939**	**1.419**	**3.98**	**94**	**4.16**	**.270**	**79**	**.173**	**-29**	**77**	**-2.9**

• MCGLOTHIN, Pat

Ezra Mac McGlothin b: 10/20/1920, Coalfield, TN BL/TR, 6'3.5", 180 lbs. Deb: 4/25/1949

YEAR	TM-L	W	L	PCT	G	GS	CG	SH	SV	IP	H	R	ER	HR	HB	BB	SO	RAT	ERA	ERA+	CERA	OAV	BH	AVG	PR+	WS	TPW
1949	Bro-N	1	1	.500	7	0	0	0	0	15^2	13	8	8	2	0	5	11	1.149	4.60	89	3.02	.224	0	.000	-1	1	-0.2
1950	Bro-N	0	0	....	1	0	0	0	0	2	5	3	3	0	0	1	2	3.000	13.50	30	13.07	.455	0	....	-2	0	-0.2
Total	**2**	**1**	**1**	**.500**	**8**	**0**	**0**	**0**	**0**	**17^2**	**18**	**11**	**11**	**2**	**0**	**6**	**13**	**1.358**	**5.60**	**73**	**4.15**	**.261**	**0**	**.000**	**-3**	**1**	**-0.4**

• MCGLOTHLIN, Jim

James Milton "Red" McGlothlin b: 10/6/1943, Los Angeles, CA d: 12/23/1975, Union, KY BR/TR, 6'1", 185 lbs. Deb: 9/20/1965

YEAR	TM-L	W	L	PCT	G	GS	CG	SH	SV	IP	H	R	ER	HR	HB	BB	SO	RAT	ERA	ERA+	CERA	OAV	BH	AVG	PR+	WS	TPW
1965	Cal-A	0	3	.000	3	3	1	0	0	18	18	9	7	1	0	7	9	1.389	3.50	97	3.70	.261	0	.000	-0	0	-0.1
1966	Cal-A	3	1	.750	19	11	0	0	0	67^2	79	37	34	9	1	19	41	1.448	4.52	74	4.88	.292	1	.059	-9	1	-1.0
1967	Cal-A★	12	8	.600	32	29	9	**6**	0	197^1	163	74	65	13	4	56	137	1.110	2.96	106	2.59	.226	8	.140	2	12	0.2
1968	Cal-A	10	15	.400	40	32	8	0	3	208^1	187	87	82	19	8	60	135	1.186	3.54	82	3.21	.244	7	.111	-17	8	-2.1
1969	Cal-A	8	16	.333	37	35	4	1	0	201	188	86	71	19	5	58	96	1.224	3.18	110	3.40	.249	7	.121	4	10	0.3
1970*	Cin-N	14	10	.583	35	34	5	3	0	210^2	192	91	84	19	3	86	97	1.320	3.59	116	3.56	.245	8	.121	13	15	1.4
1971	Cin-N	8	12	.400	30	26	6	0	0	170^2	151	65	61	15	4	47	93	1.160	3.22	101	3.05	.243	7	.137	-3	9	-0.3
1972*	Cin-N	9	8	.529	31	21	3	1	0	145	165	71	63	15	0	49	69	1.476	3.91	82	4.57	.287	8	.174	-14	4	-1.2
1973	Cin-N	3	3	.500	24	9	0	0	0	63^1	91	52	47	13	0	23	18	1.800	6.68	51	7.38	.340	2	.125	-24	0	-2.5
	Chi-A	0	1	.000	5	1	0	0	0	18^1	13	8	8	2	0	13	14	1.418	3.93	101	3.81	.203	0	....	0	1	0.0
Total	**9**	**67**	**77**	**.465**	**256**	**201**	**36**	**11**	**3**	**1300^1**	**1247**	**580**	**522**	**125**	**25**	**418**	**709**	**1.280**	**3.61**	**93**	**3.64**	**.255**	**48**	**.126**	**-50**	**60**	**-5.3**

• MCGLYNN, Stoney

Ulysses Simpson Grant McGlynn b: 5/26/1872, Lancaster, PA d: 8/26/1941, Manitowoc, WI BR/TR, 5'11", 185 lbs. Deb: 9/20/1906

YEAR	TM-L	W	L	PCT	G	GS	CG	SH	SV	IP	H	R	ER	HR	HB	BB	SO	RAT	ERA	ERA+	CERA	OAV	BH	AVG	PR+	WS	TPW
1906	StL-N	2	2	.500	6	6	6	0	0	48	43	16	13	0	1	15	25	1.208	2.44	107	2.70	.249	1	.059	1	3	0.0
1907	StL-N	14	25	.359	45	**39**	**33**	3	1	**352^1**	329	159	114	6	4	112	109	1.252	2.91	86	2.93	.251	25	.200	-15	14	-1.3
1908	StL-N	1	6	.143	16	6	4	0	1	75^2	76	40	29	0	2	17	23	1.229	3.45	68	2.80	.256	2	.077	-8	1	-0.9
Total	**3**	**17**	**33**	**.340**	**67**	**51**	**43**	**3**	**2**	**476**	**448**	**215**	**156**	**6**	**7**	**144**	**157**	**1.244**	**2.95**	**84**	**2.88**	**.252**	**28**	**.167**	**-21**	**18**	**-2.2**

• MCGOWAN, Mickey

Tullis Earl McGowan b: 11/26/1921, Dothan, AL BL/TL, 6'2", 200 lbs. Deb: 4/22/1948

YEAR	TM-L	W	L	PCT	G	GS	CG	SH	SV	IP	H	R	ER	HR	HB	BB	SO	RAT	ERA	ERA+	CERA	OAV	BH	AVG	PR+	WS	TPW
1948	NY-N	0	0	....	3	0	0	0	0	3^2	3	3	3	1	0	4	2	1.909	7.36	53	6.78	.231	0	.000	-1	0	-0.2

• MCGRANER, Howard

Howard "Muck" McGraner b: 9/11/1889, Hamley Run, OH d: 10/22/1952, Zaleski, OH BL/TL, 5'7", 155 lbs. Deb: 9/12/1912

YEAR	TM-L	W	L	PCT	G	GS	CG	SH	SV	IP	H	R	ER	HR	HB	BB	SO	RAT	ERA	ERA+	CERA	OAV	BH	AVG	PR+	WS	TPW
1912	Cin-N	1	0	1.000	4	0	0	0	0	19	22	17	15	2	1	7	5	1.526	7.11	47	5.00	.293	2	.250	-8	0	-0.7

• MCGRAW, Bob

Robert Emmett McGraw b: 4/10/1895, La Veta, CO d: 6/2/1978, Seal Beach, CA BR/TR, 6'2", 160 lbs. Deb: 9/25/1917

YEAR	TM-L	W	L	PCT	G	GS	CG	SH	SV	IP	H	R	ER	HR	HB	BB	SO	RAT	ERA	ERA+	CERA	OAV	BH	AVG	PR+	WS	TPW
1917	NY-A	0	1	.000	2	2	1	0	0	11	9	5	1	0	0	3	3	1.091	0.82	328	2.41	.257	0	.000	2	1	0.2
1918	NY-A	0	1	.000	1	1	0	0	0	0	0	4	0	0	0	4	0	....	....	....	∞	.000	0	....	0	0	0.0
1919	NY-A	1	0	1.000	6	0	0	0	0	16^1	11	6	6	1	1	10	3	1.286	3.31	96	3.34	.216	0	.000	-1	1	-0.1
	Bos-A	0	2	.000	10	1	0	0	0	26^2	33	23	20	0	3	17	6	1.875	6.75	45	6.65	.347	1	.100	-11	0	-1.3
	Yr.	1	2	.333	16	1	0	0	0	43	44	29	26	1	4	27	9	1.651	5.44	56	5.39	.301	1	.077	-12	1	-1.4
1920	NY-A	0	0	....	15	0	0	0	0	27	24	18	14	1	1	20	11	1.630	4.67	82	4.22	.240	0	.000	-3	0	-0.4
1925	Bro-N	0	2	.000	2	2	2	0	0	19^2	14	9	7	0	0	13	3	1.373	3.20	130	2.81	.222	1	.167	3	1	0.3
1926	Bro-N	9	13	.409	33	21	10	0	1	174^1	197	104	89	12	2	67	49	1.514	4.59	83	4.43	.292	8	.145	-12	7	-1.3
1927	Bro-N	0	1	.000	1	1	0	0	0	4	5	5	4	1	0	2	2	1.750	9.00	44	6.88	.313	0	.000	-2	0	-0.2
	StL-N	4	5	.444	18	12	4	1	0	94	121	65	53	3	0	30	37	1.606	5.07	78	4.81	.323	6	.182	-13	2	-1.2
	Yr.	4	6	.400	19	13	4	1	0	98	126	70	57	4	0	32	39	1.612	5.23	75	4.89	.323	6	.176	-16	2	-1.5
1928	Phi-N	7	8	.467	39	3	0	0	1	132	150	86	68	7	1	56	28	1.561	4.64	92	4.81	.326	4	.111	-3	6	-0.5
1929	Phi-N	5	5	.500	41	4	0	0	4	86^1	113	68	55	6	2	43	22	1.807	5.73	90	5.91	.324	4	.200	-4	4	-0.3
Total	**9**	**26**	**38**	**.406**	**168**	**47**	**17**	**1**	**6**	**591^1**	**677**	**393**	**317**	**31**	**10**	**265**	**164**	**1.593**	**4.82**	**84**	**4.78**	**.305**	**24**	**.138**	**-44**	**22**	**-4.9**

• MCGRAW, John

John McGraw b: 12/8/1890, Intercourse, PA d: 4/27/1967, Torrance, CA BR/TR, 5'9", 160 lbs. Deb: 7/29/1914

YEAR	TM-L	W	L	PCT	G	GS	CG	SH	SV	IP	H	R	ER	HR	HB	BB	SO	RAT	ERA	ERA+	CERA	OAV	BH	AVG	PR+	WS	TPW
1914	Bro-F	0	0	....	1	0	0	0	0	2	0	0	0	0	1	0	2	.000	0.00	....	0.23	.000	0	....	1	0	0.1

• MCGRAW, Tom

Thomas Virgil McGraw b: 12/8/1967, Portland, OR BL/TL, 6'2", 195 lbs. Deb: 5/7/1997

YEAR	TM-L	W	L	PCT	G	GS	CG	SH	SV	IP	H	R	ER	HR	HB	BB	SO	RAT	ERA	ERA+	CERA	OAV	BH	AVG	PR+	WS	TPW
1997	StL-N	0	0	....	2	0	0	0	0	1^2	2	0	0	0	0	1	0	1.800	0.00	....	5.10	.333	0	....	1	0	0.1

• MCGRAW, Tug

Frank Edwin McGraw b: 8/30/1944, Martinez, CA d: 1/5/2004, Nashville, TN BR/TL, 6', 185 lbs. Deb: 4/18/1965

YEAR	TM-L	W	L	PCT	G	GS	CG	SH	SV	IP	H	R	ER	HR	HB	BB	SO	RAT	ERA	ERA+	CERA	OAV	BH	AVG	PR+	WS	TPW
1965	NY-N	2	7	.222	37	9	2	0	1	97^2	88	47	36	8	3	48	57	1.392	3.32	106	3.91	.249	3	.130	3	5	0.2
1966	NY-N	2	9	.182	15	12	1	0	0	62^1	72	38	37	11	0	25	34	1.556	5.34	68	5.54	.294	4	.235	-12	0	-1.2
1967	NY-N	0	3	.000	4	4	0	0	0	17^1	13	16	15	3	0	13	18	1.500	7.79	43	4.29	.206	1	.250	-9	0	-0.9
1969*	NY-N	9	3	.750	42	4	1	0	12	100^1	89	31	25	6	0	47	92	1.355	2.24	163	3.37	.243	4	.167	13	14	1.4
1970	NY-N	4	6	.400	57	0	0	0	10	90^2	77	40	33	6	1	49	81	1.390	3.28	123	3.21	.231	4	.308	6	9	0.7
1971	NY-N	11	4	.733	51	1	0	0	8	111	73	22	21	4	3	41	109	1.027	1.70	200	1.80	.189	4	.222	20	17	2.3
1972	NY-N★	8	6	.571	54	0	0	0	27	106	71	26	20	3	3	40	92	1.047	1.70	198	1.86	.197	2	.100	20	22	2.1
1973*	NY-N	5	6	.455	60	2	0	0	25	118^2	106	53	51	11	3	55	81	1.357	3.87	93	3.71	.243	4	.167	-4	10	-0.4
1974	NY-N	6	11	.353	41	4	1	1	3	88^2	96	43	41	12	0	32	54	1.444	4.16	86	4.47	.279	1	.071	-6	4	-0.7
1975	Phi-N★	9	6	.600	56	0	0	0	14	102^2	84	38	34	6	3	36	55	1.169	2.98	125	2.71	.226	2	.154	6	12	0.6
1976*	Phi-N	7	6	.538	58	0	0	0	11	97^1	81	34	27	4	0	42	76	1.264	2.50	142	2.73	.226	1	.143	10	10	1.1
1977*	Phi-N	7	3	.700	45	0	0	0	9	79	62	25	23	6	1	24	58	1.089	2.62	153	2.47	.221	4	.400	11	10	1.3
1978*	Phi-N	8	7	.533	55	1	0	0	9	89^2	82	39	32	6	0	23	63	1.171	3.21	111	2.78	.245	0	.000	2	8	0.1
1979	Phi-N	4	3	.571	65	1	0	0	16	83^2	83	56	48	9	2	29	57	1.339	5.16	74	3.84	.259	1	.167	-13	5	-1.4
1980*	Phi-N	5	4	.556	57	0	0	0	20	92^1	62	16	15	3	2	23	75	.921	1.46	259	1.53	.194	2	.250	24	18	2.6
1981*	Phi-N	2	4	.333	34	0	0	0	10	44	35	13	13	2	0	14	26	1.114	2.66	136	2.26	.219	0	.000	4	6	0.5
1982	Phi-N	3	3	.500	34	0	0	0	5	39^2	50	19	19	3	1	12	25	1.563	4.31	85	4.74	.305	0	.000	-3	3	-0.3
1983	Phi-N	2	1	.667	34	1	0	0	0	55^2	58	24	22	4	0	19	30	1.383	3.56	100	3.82	.271	1	.333	1	3	0.1
1984	Phi-N	2	0	1.000	25	0	0	0	0	38	36	17	16	1	0	10	26	1.211	3.79	96	2.57	.245	1	.333	-0	2	0.0
Total	**19**	**96**	**92**	**.511**	**824**	**39**	**5**	**1**	**180**	**1514^2**	**1318**	**597**	**528**	**108**	**22**	**582**	**1109**	**1.254**	**3.14**	**116**	**3.11**	**.237**	**39**	**.182**	**72**	**158**	**8.2**

• MCGREGOR, Scott

Scott Houston McGregor b: 1/18/1954, Inglewood, CA BB/TL, 6'1", 190 lbs. Deb: 9/19/1976

YEAR	TM-L	W	L	PCT	G	GS	CG	SH	SV	IP	H	R	ER	HR	HB	BB	SO	RAT	ERA	ERA+	CERA	OAV	BH	AVG	PR+	WS	TPW
1976	Bal-A	0	1	.000	3	2	0	0	0	14^2	17	7	6	0	0	5	6	1.500	3.68	89	4.11	.293	0	....	-1	0	-0.1
1977	Bal-A	3	5	.375	29	5	1	0	4	114	119	57	56	8	7	30	55	1.307	4.42	86	3.85	.275	0	....	-11	5	-1.1
1978	Bal-A	15	13	.536	35	32	13	4	1	233	217	98	86	19	1	47	94	1.133	3.32	105	2.87	.248	0	....	1	15	0.1
1979*	Bal-A	13	6	.684	27	23	7	2	0	174^2	165	70	65	19	2	23	81	1.076	3.35	120	**2.83**	.248	0	....	10	14	1.0
1980	Bal-A	20	8	.714	36	36	12	4	0	252	254	101	93	16	2	58	119	1.238	3.32	119	3.28	.265	0	....	12	18	1.2
1981	Bal-A★	13	5	.722	24	22	8	3	0	160	167	63	58	13	0	40	82	1.294	3.26	111	3.61	.273	0	....	7	12	0.8
1982	Bal-A	14	12	.538	37	37	7	1	0	226^1	238	126	116	31	1	52	84	1.281	4.61	87	3.89	.267	0	....	-15	9	-1.5
1983*	Bal-A	18	7	.720	36	36	12	2	0	260	271	101	92	24	1	45	86	1.215	3.18	124	3.39	.269	0	....	23	21	2.3
1984	Bal-A	15	12	.556	30	30	10	3	0	196^1	216	93	86	18	5	54	67	1.375	3.94	98	4.20	.280	0	....	-5	11	-0.5
1985	Bal-A	14	14	.500	35	34	8	1	0	204	226	118	109	34	1	65	86	1.426	4.81	84	4.85	.283	0	....	-16	7	-1.6
1986	Bal-A	11	15	.423	34	33	4	2	0	203	216	110	102	35	3	57	95	1.345	4.52	91	4.52	.270	0	....	-7	9	-0.7
1987	Bal-A	2	7	.222	26	15	1	1	0	85^1	112	69	63	15	3	35	39	1.723	6.64	66	6.79	.326	0	....	-21	0	-2.0
1988	Bal-A	0	3	.000	4	4	0	0	0	17^1	27	18	17	3	0	7	10	1.962	8.83	44	8.35	.370	0	....	-10	0	-1.0
Total	**13**	**138**	**108**	**.561**	**356**	**309**	**83**	**23**	**5**	**2140^2**	**2245**	**1031**	**949**	**235**	**26**	**518**	**904**	**1.291**	**3.99**	**98**	**3.87**	**.271**	**0**	**....**	**-33**	**121**	**-3.1**

• MCGREW, Slim

Walter Howard McGrew b: 8/5/1899, Yoakum, TX d: 8/21/1967, Houston, TX BR/TR, 6'7.5", 235 lbs. Deb: 4/18/1922

YEAR	TM-L	W	L	PCT	G	GS	CG	SH	SV	IP	H	R	ER	HR	HB	BB	SO	RAT	ERA	ERA+	CERA	OAV	BH	AVG	PR+	WS	TPW
1922	Was-A	0	0	....	1	0	0	0	0	1^2	4	6	2	0	0	2	1	3.600	10.80	36	14.07	.500	0	.000	-1	0	-0.1
1923	Was-A	0	0	....	3	0	0	0	0	5	11	9	7	0	0	3	1	2.800	12.60	30	11.78	.440	0	.000	-5	0	-0.5

YEAR TM-L	W	L	PCT	G	GS	CG	SH	SV	IP	H	R	ER	HR	HB	BB	SO	RAT	ERA	ERA+	CERA	OAV	BH	AVG	PR+	WS	TPW
1924 Was-A	0	1	.000	6	2	0	0	0	23^1	25	15	13	1	0	12	8	1.586	5.01	80	4.34	.281	0	.000	-3	0	-0.4
Total 3	0	1	.000	10	2	0	0	0	30	40	30	22	1	0	17	10	1.900	6.60	60	6.12	.328	0	.000	-10	0	-1.1

• MCGUIRE,

McGuire TL Deb: 6/16/1894

YEAR TM-L	W	L	PCT	G	GS	CG	SH	SV	IP	H	R	ER	HR	HB	BB	SO	RAT	ERA	ERA+	CERA	OAV	BH	AVG	PR+	WS	TPW
1894 Cin-N	0	0	....	1	0	0	0	0	6	15	9	7	0	0	5	1	3.333	10.50	53	14.93	.465	1	.250	-3	0	-0.3

• MCGUIRE, Tom

Thomas Patrick "Elmer" McGuire b: 2/1/1892, Chicago, IL d: 12/7/1959, Phoenix, AZ BR/TR, 6', 175 lbs. Deb: 4/18/1914

YEAR TM-L	W	L	PCT	G	GS	CG	SH	SV	IP	H	R	ER	HR	HB	BB	SO	RAT	ERA	ERA+	CERA	OAV	BH	AVG	PR+	WS	TPW
1914 Chi-F	5	6	.455	24	12	7	0	0	131^1	143	76	54	7	4	57	37	1.523	3.70	80	4.60	.288	19	.271	-14	4	-0.9
1919 Chi-A	0	0	....	1	0	0	0	0	3	5	4	3	0	0	3	0	2.667	9.00	35	12.38	.500	0	.000	-2	0	-0.2
Total 2	5	6	.455	25	12	7	0	0	134^1	148	80	57	7	4	60	37	1.548	3.82	78	4.77	.292	19	.268	-16	4	-1.1

• MCGUNNIGLE, Bill

William Henry "Gunner" McGunnigle b: 1/1/1855, Boston, MA d: 3/9/1899, Brockton, MA BR/TR, 5'9", 155 lbs. Deb: 5/2/1879 M/U ♦

YEAR TM-L	W	L	PCT	G	GS	CG	SH	SV	IP	H	R	ER	HR	HB	BB	SO	RAT	ERA	ERA+	CERA	OAV	BH	AVG	PR+	WS	TPW
1879 Buf-N	9	5	.643	14	13	13	2	0	120	113	66	35	0	....	16	62	1.075	2.63	100	....	**.233**	30	.175	-3	12	-1.2
1880 Buf-N	2	3	.400	5	5	4	1	0	37	43	19	14	0	....	8	3	1.378	3.41	72	....	.276	4	.182	-2	1	-0.4
Total 2	11	8	.579	19	18	17	3	0	157	156	85	49	0	....	24	65	1.146	2.81	91	....	.243	35	.173	-5	13	-1.6

• MCHALE, Marty

Martin Joseph McHale b: 10/30/1886, Stoneham, MA d: 5/7/1979, Hempstead, NY BR/TR, 5'11.5", 174 lbs. Deb: 9/28/1910

YEAR TM-L	W	L	PCT	G	GS	CG	SH	SV	IP	H	R	ER	HR	HB	BB	SO	RAT	ERA	ERA+	CERA	OAV	BH	AVG	PR+	WS	TPW
1910 Bos-A	0	2	.000	2	2	1	0	0	13^2	15	8	7	0	1	6	14	1.537	4.61	55	3.92	.259	0	.000	-3	0	-0.4
1911 Bos-A	0	0	....	4	1	0	0	0	9^1	19	12	10	1	1	3	3	2.357	9.64	34	12.33	.475	0	.000	-7	0	-0.7
1913 NY-A	2	4	.333	7	6	4	1	0	48^2	49	21	16	1	1	10	11	1.212	2.96	101	2.99	.266	0	.000	0	2	-0.1
1914 NY-A	7	16	.304	31	23	12	0	1	191	195	82	63	3	4	33	75	1.194	2.97	93	2.91	.268	12	.200	-7	9	-0.5
1915 NY-A	3	6	.333	13	11	6	0	0	78^1	86	45	37	1	0	19	25	1.340	4.25	69	3.37	.277	3	.143	-13	2	-1.3
1916 Bos-A	0	1	.000	2	1	0	0	0	6	7	7	2	0	1	4	1	1.833	3.00	92	5.56	.280	0	....	-0	0	0.0
Cle-A	0	0	....	5	0	0	0	0	11^1	10	7	7	1	0	6	2	1.412	5.56	54	4.30	.270	0	.000	-3	0	-0.4
Yr.	0	1	.000	7	1	0	0	0	17^1	17	14	9	1	1	10	3	1.558	4.67	63	4.74	.274	0	.000	-3	0	-0.4
Total 6	12	29	.293	64	44	23	1	1	358^1	381	182	142	7	8	81	131	1.289	3.57	80	3.39	.276	15	.140	-32	13	-3.4

• MCILREE, Vance

Vance Elmer McIlree b: 10/14/1897, Riverside, IA d: 5/6/1959, Kansas City, MO BR/TR, 6', 160 lbs. Deb: 9/13/1921

YEAR TM-L	W	L	PCT	G	GS	CG	SH	SV	IP	H	R	ER	HR	HB	BB	SO	RAT	ERA	ERA+	CERA	OAV	BH	AVG	PR+	WS	TPW
1921 Was-A	0	0	....	1	0	0	0	0	1	1	1	1	0	0	0	0	1.000	9.00	46	1.51	.200	0	....	-1	0	-0.1

• MCILWAIN, Stover

Stover William "Smokey" McIlwain b: 9/22/1939, Savannah, GA d: 1/15/1966, Buffalo, NY BR/TR, 6'4", 195 lbs. Deb: 9/25/1957

YEAR TM-L	W	L	PCT	G	GS	CG	SH	SV	IP	H	R	ER	HR	HB	BB	SO	RAT	ERA	ERA+	CERA	OAV	BH	AVG	PR+	WS	TPW
1957 Chi-A	0	0	....	1	0	0	0	0	1	2	0	0	0	0	1	0	3.000	0.00	....	14.53	.500	0	....	0	0	0.0
1958 Chi-A	0	0	....	1	1	0	0	0	4	4	1	1	1	0	0	4	1.000	2.25	162	3.33	.250	0	.000	1	0	0.0
Total 2	0	0	....	2	1	0	0	0	5	6	1	1	1	0	1	4	1.400	1.80	202	5.57	.300	0	.000	1	0	0.1

• MCINTIRE, Harry

John Reid McIntire b: 1/11/1879, Dayton, OH d: 1/9/1949, Daytona Beach, FL BR/TR, 5'11", 180 lbs. Deb: 4/14/1905

YEAR TM-L	W	L	PCT	G	GS	CG	SH	SV	IP	H	R	ER	HR	HB	BB	SO	RAT	ERA	ERA+	CERA	OAV	BH	AVG	PR+	WS	TPW
1905 Bro-N	8	25	.242	40	35	29	1	1	308^2	340	188	127	6	20	101	135	1.429	3.70	78	3.93	.285	34	.246	-20	10	-1.4
1906 Bro-N	13	21	.382	39	31	25	4	3	276	254	123	91	2	14	89	121	1.243	2.97	85	2.92	.247	18	.175	-11	10	-1.2
1907 Bro-N	7	15	.318	28	22	19	3	0	199^2	178	82	53	6	7	79	49	1.287	2.39	98	3.21	.248	15	.217	1	11	0.7
1908 Bro-N	11	20	.355	40	35	26	4	2	288	259	106	86	5	20	90	108	1.212	2.69	87	3.02	.252	20	.200	-13	14	-1.3
1909 Bro-N	7	17	.292	32	26	20	2	1	228	200	114	92	5	21	91	84	1.276	3.63	71	3.29	.246	13	.171	-24	6	-2.6
1910* Chi-N	13	9	.591	28	19	10	2	0	176	152	70	60	5	10	50	65	1.148	3.07	94	2.73	.240	17	.258	-6	13	-0.2
1911 Chi-N	11	7	.611	25	17	9	1	0	149	147	81	68	5	4	33	56	1.208	4.11	80	2.97	.257	14	.264	-16	7	-1.2
1912 Chi-N	1	2	.333	4	3	2	0	0	23^2	22	11	10	0	0	6	8	1.183	3.80	87	2.51	.256	3	.300	-2	2	-0.1
1913 Cin-N	0	1	.000	1	0	0	0	0	1	3	3	3	0	0	0	0	3.000	27.00	12	17.53	.600	0	....	-3	0	-0.3
Total 9	71	117	.378	237	188	140	17	7	1650	1555	778	590	34	96	539	626	1.269	3.22	83	3.20	.256	134	.218	-95	73	-7.5

• MCINTOSH, Joe

Joseph Anthony McIntosh b: 8/4/1951, Billings, MT BB/TR, 6'2", 185 lbs. Deb: 4/5/1974

YEAR TM-L	W	L	PCT	G	GS	CG	SH	SV	IP	H	R	ER	HR	HB	BB	SO	RAT	ERA	ERA+	CERA	OAV	BH	AVG	PR+	WS	TPW
1974 SD-N	0	4	.000	10	5	0	0	0	37^1	36	19	15	3	1	17	22	1.420	3.62	98	3.92	.250	0	.000	1	1	0.0
1975 SD-N	8	15	.348	37	28	4	1	0	183	195	88	75	14	2	60	71	1.393	3.69	94	3.95	.273	9	.188	-2	9	0.0
Total 2	8	19	.296	47	33	4	1	0	220^1	231	107	90	17	3	77	93	1.398	3.68	95	3.95	.270	9	.155	-1	10	-0.1

• MCINTYRE, Frank

Frank W. McIntyre b: 7/12/1859, Walled Lake, MI d: 7/8/1887, Detroit, MI Deb: 5/16/1883

YEAR TM-L	W	L	PCT	G	GS	CG	SH	SV	IP	H	R	ER	HR	HB	BB	SO	RAT	ERA	ERA+	CERA	OAV	BH	AVG	PR+	WS	TPW
1883 Det-N	1	0	1.000	1	1	1	0	0	11	11	10	1	0	....	1	0	1.091	0.82	380	....	.245	0	.000	3	1	0.2
Col-a	1	1	.500	2	2	2	0	0	19	20	19	11	0	....	7	6	1.421	5.21	59	....	.253	0	.000	-5	0	-0.4

• MCJAMES, Doc

James McCutchen McJames b: 8/27/1873, Williamsburg, SC d: 9/23/1901, Charleston, SC TR Deb: 9/24/1895

YEAR TM-L	W	L	PCT	G	GS	CG	SH	SV	IP	H	R	ER	HR	HB	BB	SO	RAT	ERA	ERA+	CERA	OAV	BH	AVG	PR+	WS	TPW
1895 Was-N	1	1	.500	2	2	2	0	0	17	17	11	3	0	0	16	9	1.941	1.59	302	5.11	.257	1	.143	6	1	0.4
1896 Was-N	12	20	.375	37	33	29	0	1	280^1	310	208	133	2	6	135	103	1.587	4.27	103	4.25	.278	18	.162	10	11	0.1
1897 Was-N	15	23	.395	44	39	33	**3**	2	323^2	361	212	130	7	21	137	**156**	1.539	3.61	120	4.36	.280	21	.169	21	19	1.2
1898 Bal-N	27	15	.643	45	42	40	2	0	374	327	148	98	5	12	113	178	1.176	2.36	151	2.54	.234	27	.181	41	30	3.4
1899 Bro-N	19	15	.559	37	34	27	1	1	275^1	295	166	107	4	10	122	105	1.515	3.50	112	4.03	.274	19	.170	8	19	0.3
1901 Bro-N	5	6	.455	13	12	6	0	0	91	104	71	48	1	7	40	42	1.582	4.75	71	4.53	.285	1	.029	-15	1	-1.8
Total 6	79	80	.497	178	162	137	6	4	1361^1	1414	816	519	19	56	563	593	1.452	3.43	116	3.79	.266	87	.162	71	81	3.7

• MCKAIN, Archie

Archie Richard "Happy" McKain b: 5/12/1911, Delphos, KS d: 5/21/1985, Salina, KS BB/TL, 5'10", 175 lbs. Deb: 4/25/1937

YEAR TM-L	W	L	PCT	G	GS	CG	SH	SV	IP	H	R	ER	HR	HB	BB	SO	RAT	ERA	ERA+	CERA	OAV	BH	AVG	PR+	WS	TPW
1937 Bos-A	8	8	.500	36	18	3	0	2	137	152	84	71	7	0	64	66	1.577	4.66	102	4.33	.273	13	.265	4	9	0.6
1938 Bos-A	5	4	.556	37	5	1	0	6	99^2	119	60	50	6	2	44	27	1.635	4.52	109	5.01	.297	2	.065	4	7	0.1
1939 Det-A	5	6	.455	32	11	4	1	4	129^2	120	66	53	6	0	54	49	1.342	3.68	133	3.24	.247	9	.220	17	12	2.0
1940* Det-A	5	0	1.000	27	0	0	0	3	51	48	18	16	2	0	25	24	1.431	2.82	168	3.49	.247	1	.143	12	7	1.1
1941 Det-A	2	1	.667	15	0	0	0	0	43	58	24	24	3	0	11	14	1.605	5.02	90	5.23	.330	0	.000	-1	2	-0.2
StL-A	0	1	.000	8	0	0	0	1	10	16	9	9	2	1	4	2	2.000	8.10	53	9.13	.364	0	.000	-4	0	-0.4
Yr.	2	2	.500	23	0	0	0	1	53	74	33	33	5	1	15	16	1.679	5.60	80	5.96	.336	0	.000	-5	2	-0.6
1943 StL-A	1	1	.500	10	0	0	0	0	16	16	9	7	0	0	6	6	1.375	3.94	84	3.00	.242	0	.000	-1	1	-0.1
Total 6	26	21	.553	165	34	8	1	16	486^1	529	270	230	26	3	208	188	1.515	4.26	111	4.23	.275	25	.176	31	38	3.1

• MCKAIN, Hal

Harold Le Roy McKain b: 7/10/1906, Logan, IA d: 1/24/1970, Sacramento, CA BL/TR, 5'11", 185 lbs. Deb: 9/22/1927

YEAR TM-L	W	L	PCT	G	GS	CG	SH	SV	IP	H	R	ER	HR	HB	BB	SO	RAT	ERA	ERA+	CERA	OAV	BH	AVG	PR+	WS	TPW
1927 Cle-A	0	1	.000	2	1	0	0	0	11	18	6	5	0	0	4	5	2.000	4.09	103	7.21	.391	0	.000	0	0	0.0
1929 Chi-A	6	9	.400	34	10	4	1	1	158	158	84	64	10	10	85	33	1.538	3.65	117	4.50	.275	10	.227	9	11	1.1
1930 Chi-A	6	4	.600	32	5	0	0	5	89	108	67	55	0	3	42	52	1.685	5.56	83	4.72	.299	13	.419	-7	6	0.0
1931 Chi-A	6	9	.400	27	8	3	0	0	112	134	82	71	10	3	57	39	1.705	5.71	75	5.49	.295	5	.119	-16	2	-1.5
1932 Chi-A	0	0	....	8	0	0	0	0	11^1	17	15	14	1	0	5	7	1.941	11.12	39	6.74	.340	0	.000	-8	0	-0.8
Total 5	18	23	.439	103	24	7	1	6	381^1	435	254	209	21	16	193	136	1.647	4.93	88	4.99	.293	28	.230	-22	19	-1.3

• MCKAY, Reeve

Reeve Stewart "Rip" McKay b: 11/16/1881, Morgan, TX d: 1/18/1946, Dallas, TX TR, 6'1.5", 168 lbs. Deb: 10/2/1915

YEAR TM-L	W	L	PCT	G	GS	CG	SH	SV	IP	H	R	ER	HR	HB	BB	SO	RAT	ERA	ERA+	CERA	OAV	BH	AVG	PR+	WS	TPW
1915 StL-A	0	0	....	1	0	0	0	0	1	1	1	1	0	0	0	0	1.000	9.00	32	2.02	.500	0	....	-1	0	-0.1

• MCKEE, Jim

James Marion McKee b: 2/1/1947, Columbus, OH d: 9/14/2002, Pickaway County, OH BR/TR, 6'7", 215 lbs. Deb: 9/15/1972

YEAR TM-L	W	L	PCT	G	GS	CG	SH	SV	IP	H	R	ER	HR	HB	BB	SO	RAT	ERA	ERA+	CERA	OAV	BH	AVG	PR+	WS	TPW
1972 Pit-N	1	0	1.000	2	0	0	0	0	5	2	0	0	0	0	1	4	.600	0.00	....	0.63	.125	0	....	2	1	0.2
1973 Pit-N	0	1	.000	15	1	0	0	0	27	31	21	17	2	1	17	13	1.778	5.67	62	5.67	.287	0	.000	-6	0	-0.7
Total 2	1	1	.500	17	1	0	0	0	32	33	21	17	2	1	18	17	1.594	4.78	74	4.88	.266	0	.000	-5	1	-0.5

• MCKEE, Rogers

Rogers Hornsby McKee b: 9/16/1926, Shelby, NC BL/TL, 6'1", 160 lbs. Deb: 8/18/1943

YEAR TM-L	W	L	PCT	G	GS	CG	SH	SV	IP	H	R	ER	HR	HB	BB	SO	RAT	ERA	ERA+	CERA	OAV	BH	AVG	PR+	WS	TPW
1943 Phi-N	1	0	1.000	4	1	1	0	0	13^1	12	9	9	0	0	5	1	1.275	6.08	55	2.51	.226	1	.200	-4	0	-0.4
1944 Phi-N	0	0	....	1	0	0	0	0	2	2	1	1	1	0	1	0	1.500	4.50	80	7.17	.250	0	....	-0	0	0.0
Total 2	1	0	1.000	5	1	1	0	0	15^1	14	10	10	1	0	6	1	1.304	5.87	58	3.12	.230	1	.200	-4	0	-0.4

• MCKEITHAN, Tim

Emmett James McKeithan b: 11/2/1906, Lawndale, NC d: 8/20/1969, Forest City, NC BR/TR, 6'2", 182 lbs. Deb: 7/21/1932

YEAR TM-L	W	L	PCT	G	GS	CG	SH	SV	IP	H	R	ER	HR	HB	BB	SO	RAT	ERA	ERA+	CERA	OAV	BH	AVG	PR+	WS	TPW
1932 Phi-A	0	1	.000	4	2	0	0	0	12^2	18	11	10	0	0	5	0	1.816	7.11	64	5.67	.340	0	.000	-4	0	-0.3
1933 Phi-A	1	0	1.000	3	1	0	0	0	9	10	4	4	0	0	4	3	1.556	4.00	107	3.90	.278	1	.333	1	1	0.1

YEAR	TM-L	W	L	PCT	G	GS	CG	SH	SV	IP	H	R	ER	HR	HB	BB	SO	RAT	ERA	ERA+	CERA	OAV	BH	AVG	PR+	WS	TPW
1934	Phi-A	0	0	....	3	0	0	0	0	4	7	7	7	2	0	5	0	3.000	15.75	28	17.14	.389	0	.000	-5	0	-0.5
Total	3	1	1	.500	10	3	0	0	0	25^2	35	22	21	2	0	14	3	1.909	7.36	60	6.84	.327	1	.143	-8	1	-0.7
• MCKENNA, Kit	James William McKenna b: 2/10/1873, Lynchburg, VA d: 3/31/1941, Lynchburg, VA TR, 5'9" Deb: 7/7/1898																										
1898	Bro-N	2	6	.250	14	9	7	0	0	100^2	118	75	63	4	17	57	27	1.738	5.63	64	5.74	.290	9	.225	-22	1	-2.0
1899	Bal-N	2	3	.400	8	4	4	0	1	45	66	38	23	1	3	19	7	1.889	4.60	86	6.45	.340	1	.059	-3	1	-0.4
Total	2	4	9	.308	22	13	11	0	1	145^2	184	113	86	5	20	76	34	1.785	5.31	69	5.96	.307	10	.175	-25	2	-2.4
• MCKENRY, Limb	Frank Gordon "Big Pete" McKenry b: 8/13/1888, Piney Flats, TN d: 11/1/1956, Fresno, CA BR/TR, 6'4", 205 lbs. Deb: 8/27/1915																										
1915	Cin-N	5	5	.500	21	11	5	0	0	110^1	94	43	36	2	3	39	37	1.205	2.94	97	2.62	.238	5	.152	-3	6	-0.3
1916	Cin-N	1	1	.500	6	1	0	0	0	14^2	14	8	7	0	2	8	2	1.500	4.30	60	3.99	.259	2	.400	-3	1	-0.1
Total	2	6	6	.500	27	12	5	0	0	125	108	51	43	2	5	47	39	1.240	3.10	91	2.78	.241	7	.184	-6	7	-0.4
• MCKEON, Joel	Joel Jacob McKeon b: 2/25/1963, Covington, KY BL/TL, 6', 185 lbs. Deb: 5/6/1986																										
1986	Chi-A	3	1	.750	30	0	0	0	1	33	18	10	9	2	0	17	18	1.061	2.45	176	1.91	.165	0	....	6	4	0.6
1987	Chi-A	1	2	.333	13	0	0	0	0	21	27	22	22	8	0	15	14	2.000	9.43	49	9.69	.318	0	....	-12	0	-1.1
Total	2	4	3	.571	43	0	0	0	1	54	45	32	31	10	0	32	32	1.426	5.17	87	4.94	.232	0	....	-6	4	-0.5
• MCKEON, Larry	Lawrence G. McKeon b: 3/25/1866, New York, NY d: 7/18/1915, Indianapolis, IN, 5'10", 168 lbs. Deb: 5/1/1884																										
1884	Ind-a	18	41	.305	61	60	59	2	0	512	488	350	199	20	18	94	308	1.137	3.50	94	....	.238	53	.212	12	17	0.8
1885	Cin-a	20	13	.606	33	33	32	2	0	290	273	143	92	5	13	50	117	1.114	2.86	114	....	.238	20	.165	10	22	0.5
1886	Cin-a	8	8	.500	19	19	16	0	0	156	174	118	88	6	3	54	46	1.462	5.08	69	....	.270	19	.253	-28	6	-2.4
	KC-N	0	2	.000	3	3	3	0	0	21	44	32	25	0	....	8	3	2.476	10.71	35	....	.412	0	.000	-16	0	-1.5
Total	3	46	64	.418	116	115	110	4	0	979	979	643	404	31	34	206	474	1.210	3.71	90	....	.248	92	.202	-22	45	-2.6
• MCKNIGHT, Tony	Tony Mark McKnight b: 6/29/1977, Texarkana, AR BL/TR, 6'5", 205 lbs. Deb: 8/10/2000																										
2000	Hou-N	4	1	.800	6	6	1	0	0	35	35	19	15	4	2	9	23	1.257	3.86	126	3.61	.245	0	.000	4	3	0.3
2001	Hou-N	1	0	1.000	3	3	0	0	0	18	21	8	8	4	2	3	10	1.333	4.00	114	5.29	.288	0	.000	1	1	0.0
	Pit-N	2	6	.250	12	12	0	0	0	69^1	88	44	40	15	3	21	36	1.572	5.19	86	6.16	.307	0	.000	-5	2	-0.6
	Yr.	3	6	.333	15	15	0	0	0	87^1	109	52	48	19	5	24	46	1.523	4.95	91	5.98	.303	0	.000	-4	3	-0.6
Total	2	7	7	.500	21	21	1	0	0	122^1	144	71	63	23	7	33	69	1.447	4.63	99	5.31	.286	0	.000	0	6	-0.3
• MCLAIN, Denny	Dennis Dale McLain b: 3/29/1944, Chicago, IL BR/TR, 6'1", 185 lbs. Deb: 9/21/1963																										
1963	Det-A	2	1	.667	3	3	2	0	0	21	20	12	10	2	0	16	22	1.714	4.29	87	5.26	.253	1	.200	-1	1	0.0
1964	Det-A	4	5	.444	19	16	3	0	0	100	84	48	45	16	1	37	70	1.210	4.05	90	3.51	.225	5	.135	-5	4	-0.6
1965	Det-A	16	6	.727	33	29	13	4	1	220^1	174	73	64	25	2	62	192	1.071	2.61	133	2.65	.216	4	.054	22	20	2.0
1966	Det-A★	20	14	.588	38	38	14	4	0	264^1	205	120	115	42	3	104	192	1.169	3.92	89	3.27	.214	17	.183	-13	13	-1.3
1967	Det-A	17	16	.515	37	37	10	3	0	235	209	110	99	35	3	73	161	1.200	3.79	86	3.46	.237	10	.118	-16	8	-2.1
1968*	Det-A★	**31**	6	.838	41	**41**	**28**	6	0	**336**	241	86	73	31	6	63	280	.905	1.96	154	1.91	.200	18	.162	**38**	**33**	**4.4**
1969	Det-A★	**24**	9	.727	42	**41**	23	**9**	0	**325**	288	105	101	25	4	67	181	1.092	2.80	133	2.63	.237	17	.160	**32**	**29**	**3.3**
1970	Det-A	3	5	.375	14	14	1	0	0	91^1	100	51	47	19	3	28	52	1.401	4.63	80	5.07	.273	2	.065	-6	3	-0.9
1971	Was-A	10	22	.313	33	32	9	3	0	216^2	233	115	103	31	3	72	103	1.410	4.28	77	4.57	.281	6	.103	-24	4	-2.7
1972	Oak-A	1	2	.333	5	5	0	0	0	22^1	32	17	15	4	0	8	8	1.791	6.04	47	6.90	.323	0	.000	-8	0	-1.0
	Atl-N	3	5	.375	15	8	2	0	1	54	60	41	39	12	1	18	21	1.444	6.50	58	5.38	.279	2	.167	-15	0	-1.6
Total	10	131	91	.590	280	264	105	29	2	1886	1646	778	711	242	26	548	1282	1.163	3.39	101	3.24	.234	82	.133	3	115	-0.5
• MCLAUGHLIN, Barney	Bernard McLaughlin b: 1857, Ireland d: 2/13/1921, Lowell, MA BR/TR, 5'8" Deb: 8/9/1882 ♦																										
1884	KC-U	1	3	.250	7	4	4	0	0	48^2	62	44	29	2	....	15	14	1.582	5.36	52	....	.291	37	.228	-14	4	-1.0
• MCLAUGHLIN, Bo	Michael Duane McLaughlin b: 10/23/1953, Oakland, CA BR/TR, 6'5", 210 lbs. Deb: 7/20/1976																										
1976	Hou-N	4	5	.444	17	11	4	2	1	79	71	31	25	6	2	17	32	1.114	2.85	112	2.83	.244	0	.000	3	4	0.2
1977	Hou-N	4	7	.364	46	6	0	0	5	84^2	81	44	40	6	6	34	59	1.358	4.25	84	3.89	.260	0	.000	-6	3	-0.7
1978	Hou-N	0	1	.000	12	1	0	0	2	23^1	30	17	13	2	2	16	10	1.971	5.01	66	7.00	.313	0	.000	-4	0	-0.5
1979	Hou-N	1	2	.333	12	0	0	0	0	16^1	22	15	10	2	0	4	12	1.592	5.51	64	5.42	.314	0	.000	-4	0	-0.4
	Atl-N	1	1	.500	37	1	0	0	0	49^2	63	33	27	2	2	16	45	1.591	4.89	83	4.67	.303	0	.000	-3	1	-0.4
	Yr.	2	3	.400	49	1	0	0	0	66	85	48	37	4	2	20	57	1.591	5.05	77	4.86	.306	0	.000	-7	1	-0.8
1981	Oak-A	0	0	....	11	0	0	0	1	11^2	17	15	15	1	1	9	3	2.229	11.57	30	8.67	.333	0	....	-11	0	-1.1
1982	Oak-A	0	4	.000	21	2	1	0	0	48^1	51	31	26	3	1	27	27	1.614	4.84	81	4.68	.267	0	....	-5	1	-0.5
Total	6	10	20	.333	156	21	5	2	9	313	335	186	156	22	14	123	188	1.463	4.49	80	4.36	.275	0	.000	-30	9	-3.4
• MCLAUGHLIN, Byron	Byron Scott McLaughlin b: 9/29/1955, Van Nuys, CA BR/TR, 6'1", 185 lbs. Deb: 9/18/1977																										
1977	Sea-A	0	0	....	1	0	0	0	0	1^1	5	4	4	1	0	0	1	3.750	27.00	15	33.31	.625	0	....	-3	0	-0.3
1978	Sea-A	4	8	.333	20	17	4	0	0	107	97	58	52	15	6	39	87	1.271	4.37	87	3.89	.238	0	....	-6	4	-0.6
1979	Sea-A	7	7	.500	47	7	1	0	14	123^2	114	58	58	13	2	60	74	1.407	4.22	103	4.02	.251	0	....	2	11	0.2
1980	Sea-A	3	6	.333	45	4	0	0	2	90^2	124	74	69	15	2	50	41	1.919	6.85	60	7.26	.331	0	....	-27	0	-2.7
1983	Cal-A	2	4	.333	16	7	0	0	0	55^2	63	32	32	3	2	22	45	1.527	5.17	78	4.47	.286	0	....	-7	2	-0.7
Total	5	16	25	.390	129	35	5	0	16	378^1	403	226	215	47	12	171	248	1.517	5.11	80	4.93	.275	0	....	-41	17	-4.1
• MCLAUGHLIN, Jim	James Thomas McLaughlin b: 11/18/1860, Cleveland, OH d: 11/16/1895, Cleveland, OH BL/TL, 157 lbs. Deb: 5/30/1884																										
1884	Bal-a	1	2	.333	3	2	2	0	0	22	27	22	9	2	0	11	8	1.727	3.68	94	....	.287	5	.227	-0	1	0.1
• MCLAUGHLIN, Joey	Joey Richard McLaughlin b: 7/11/1956, Tulsa, OK BR/TR, 6'2", 205 lbs. Deb: 6/11/1977																										
1977	Atl-N	0	0	....	3	2	0	0	0	6	10	10	10	3	0	3	0	2.167	15.00	30	12.13	.385	0	.000	-7	0	-0.7
1979	Atl-N	5	3	.625	37	0	0	0	5	69	54	23	19	3	1	34	40	1.275	2.48	163	2.90	.224	2	.182	14	8	1.5
1980	Tor-A	6	9	.400	55	10	0	0	4	135^2	159	79	68	16	4	53	70	1.563	4.51	95	5.23	.302	0	....	-5	6	-0.5
1981	Tor-A	1	5	.167	40	0	0	0	10	60	55	24	19	2	0	21	38	1.267	2.85	138	2.96	.249	0	....	8	7	0.8
1982	Tor-A	8	6	.571	44	0	0	0	8	70	54	27	25	7	1	30	49	1.200	3.21	139	2.95	.212	0	....	10	10	1.0
1983	Tor-A	7	4	.636	50	0	0	0	9	64^2	63	33	32	11	0	37	47	1.546	4.45	97	5.01	.259	0	....	-1	5	-0.1
1984	Tor-A	0	0	....	6	0	0	0	0	10^2	12	6	3	0	0	7	3	1.781	2.53	162	4.81	.286	0	....	2	1	0.2
	Tex-A	2	1	.667	15	0	0	0	0	32^2	33	17	16	4	0	13	21	1.408	4.41	94	4.20	.260	0	....	-1	1	-0.1
	Yr.	2	1	.667	21	0	0	0	0	43^1	45	23	19	4	0	20	24	1.500	3.95	105	4.35	.266	0	....	1	2	0.1
Total	7	29	28	.509	250	12	0	0	36	448^2	440	219	192	46	6	198	268	1.422	3.85	110	4.19	.262	2	.167	21	38	2.2
• MCLAUGHLIN, Jud	Justin Theodore McLaughlin b: 3/24/1912, Brighton, MA d: 9/27/1964, Cambridge, MA BL/TL, 5'11", 155 lbs. Deb: 6/23/1931																										
1931	Bos-A	0	0	....	9	0	0	0	0	12	23	16	16	1	0	8	3	2.583	12.00	36	10.52	.397	0	....	-10	0	-1.0
1932	Bos-A	0	0	....	1	0	0	0	0	3	5	5	5	0	0	4	0	3.000	15.00	30	11.33	.385	0	.000	-3	0	-0.3
1933	Bos-A	0	0	....	6	0	0	0	0	8^2	14	7	6	1	0	5	1	2.192	6.23	70	8.61	.359	0	....	-2	0	-0.2
Total	3	0	0	....	16	0	0	0	0	23^2	42	28	27	2	0	17	4	2.493	10.27	42	9.92	.382	0	.000	-15	0	-1.5
• MCLAUGHLIN, Pat	Patrick Elmer McLaughlin b: 8/17/1910, Taylor, TX d: 11/1/1999, Houston, TX BR/TR, 6'2", 175 lbs. Deb: 4/25/1937																										
1937	Det-A	0	2	.000	10	3	0	0	0	32^2	39	23	23	3	0	16	8	1.684	6.34	74	5.35	.291	1	.100	-6	1	-0.6
1940	Phi-A	0	0	....	1	0	0	0	0	1^2	4	3	3	1	0	1	0	3.000	16.20	27	19.38	.444	0	....	-2	0	-0.2
1945	Det-A	0	0	....	1	0	0	0	0	1	2	2	1	0	0	0	0	2.000	9.00	39	7.48	.400	0	....	-1	0	-0.1
Total	3	0	2	.000	12	3	0	0	0	35^1	45	28	27	4	0	17	8	1.755	6.88	67	6.07	.304	1	.100	-8	1	-0.8
• MCLAUGHLIN, Warren	Warren A. McLaughlin b: 1/22/1876, North Plainfield, NJ d: 10/22/1923, Plainfield, NJ TL Deb: 7/7/1900																										
1900	Phi-N	0	0	....	1	0	0	0	0	6	4	4	3	0	0	6	1	1.667	4.50	80	3.46	.190	1	.500	-1	1	0.0
1902	Pit-N	3	0	1.000	3	3	3	0	0	26	27	13	8	0	1	9	13	1.385	2.77	99	3.40	.268	4	.364	-1	2	0.0
1903	Phi-N	0	3	.000	3	2	2	0	0	23	38	24	18	0	1	11	3	2.130	7.04	46	7.78	.376	2	.200	-10	0	-1.0
Total	3	3	3	.500	7	5	5	0	0	55	69	41	29	0	2	26	17	1.727	4.75	66	5.23	.309	7	.304	-11	3	-0.9

• MCLEAN, Al

Albert Eldon "Elrod" McLean b: 9/20/1912, Chicago, IL d: 9/29/1990, Asheboro, NC BR/TR, 6', 175 lbs. Deb: 7/16/1935

YEAR TM-L	W	L	PCT	G	GS	CG	SH	SV	IP	H	R	ER	HR	HB	BB	SO	RAT	ERA	ERA+	CERA	OAV	BH	AVG	PR+	WS	TPW
1935 Was-A	0	0	....	4	0	0	0	0	8^{2}	12	8	7	0	0	5	3	1.962	7.27	59	6.07	.324	0	.000	-3	0	-0.3

• MCLELAND, Wayne

Wayne Gaffney "Nubbin" McLeland b: 8/29/1924, Milton, IA BR/TR, 6', 180 lbs. Deb: 4/20/1951

YEAR TM-L	W	L	PCT	G	GS	CG	SH	SV	IP	H	R	ER	HR	HB	BB	SO	RAT	ERA	ERA+	CERA	OAV	BH	AVG	PR+	WS	TPW
1951 Det-A	0	1	.000	6	1	0	0	0	11	20	10	10	1	1	4	0	2.182	8.18	51	9.54	.400	0	.000	-5	0	-0.5
1952 Det-A	0	0	....	4	0	0	0	0	2^{2}	4	3	3	0	0	6	0	3.750	10.13	38	13.16	.444	0	....	-2	0	-0.2
Total 2	**0**	**1**	**.000**	**10**	**1**	**0**	**0**	**0**	13^{2}	**24**	**13**	**13**	**1**	**1**	**10**	**0**	**2.488**	**8.56**	**48**	**10.25**	**.407**	**0**	**.000**	**-7**	**0**	**-0.7**

• MCLISH, Cal

Calvin Coolidge Julius Caesar Tuskahoma "Bus,Buster" McLish b: 12/1/1925, Anadarko, OK BB/TR, 6', 200 lbs. Deb: 5/13/1944 C

YEAR TM-L	W	L	PCT	G	GS	CG	SH	SV	IP	H	R	ER	HR	HB	BB	SO	RAT	ERA	ERA+	CERA	OAV	BH	AVG	PR+	WS	TPW
1944 Bro-N	3	10	.231	23	13	3	0	0	84	110	81	73	10	1	48	24	1.881	7.82	45	6.67	.321	7	.219	-37	0	-3.8
1946 Bro-N	0	0	....	1	0	0	0	0	0	1	2	0	0	0	0	0		....	....	∞	1.000	0	....	0	0	0.0
1947 Pit-N	0	0	....	1	0	0	0	0	1	2	2	2	0	1	0	0	2.000	18.00	23	11.63	.400	0	....	-2	0	-0.1
1948 Pit-N	0	0	....	2	1	0	0	0	5	8	5	5	0	0	2	1	2.000	9.00	45	7.53	.400	0	.000	-3	0	-0.3
1949 Chi-N	1	1	.500	8	2	0	0	0	23	31	21	15	5	0	12	6	1.870	5.87	69	7.70	.341	3	.333	-4	0	-0.3
1951 Chi-N	4	10	.286	30	17	5	1	0	145^{2}	159	76	72	16	3	52	46	1.449	4.45	92	4.55	.283	5	.119	-4	6	-0.5
1956 Cle-A	2	4	.333	37	2	0	0	1	61^{2}	67	36	34	5	0	32	27	1.605	4.96	85	4.79	.282	1	.111	-5	2	-0.3
1957 Cle-A	9	7	.563	42	7	2	0	1	144^{1}	118	55	44	11	2	67	88	1.282	2.74	136	3.07	.220	8	.186	18	13	2.1
1958 Cle-A	16	8	.667	39	30	13	0	1	225^{2}	214	92	75	25	1	70	97	1.258	2.99	122	3.52	.251	6	.094	15	15	1.5
1959 Cle-A★	19	8	.704	35	32	13	0	1	235^{1}	253	110	95	26	5	72	113	1.381	3.63	101	4.21	.270	14	.189	-0	14	0.1
1960 Cin-N	4	14	.222	37	21	2	1	0	151^{1}	170	85	70	16	7	48	56	1.441	4.16	92	4.59	.287	2	.049	-6	4	-1.0
1961 Chi-A	10	13	.435	31	27	4	0	1	162^{1}	178	87	79	21	1	47	80	1.386	4.38	89	4.38	.280	9	.167	-7	7	-0.8
1962 Phi-N	11	5	.688	32	24	5	1	1	154^{2}	184	84	73	15	2	45	71	1.481	4.25	91	4.67	.293	4	.078	-8	8	-0.9
1963 Phi-N	13	11	.542	32	32	10	2	0	209^{2}	184	85	76	14	4	56	98	1.145	3.26	99	2.80	.239	14	.203	-4	12	0.0
1964 Phi-N	0	1	.000	2	1	0	0	0	5^{1}	6	3	2	0	0	1	6	1.313	3.38	103	2.74	.261	0	.000	0	0	0.0
Total 15	**92**	**92**	**.500**	**352**	**209**	**57**	**5**	**6**	**1609**	**1685**	**824**	**715**	**164**	**27**	**552**	**713**	**1.390**	**4.00**	**93**	**4.17**	**.270**	**73**	**.149**	**-47**	**81**	**-4.3**

• MCMACKIN, Sam

Samuel McMackin b: 1872, Cleveland, OH d: 2/11/1903, Columbus, OH BR/TL Deb: 9/4/1902

YEAR TM-L	W	L	PCT	G	GS	CG	SH	SV	IP	H	R	ER	HR	HB	BB	SO	RAT	ERA	ERA+	CERA	OAV	BH	AVG	PR+	WS	TPW
1902 Chi-A	0	0	....	1	0	0	0	0	3	1	1	0	0	0	0	2	.333	0.00	....	0.26	.105	0	.000	1	0	0.1
Det-A	0	1	.000	1	1	1	0	0	8^{1}	9	5	3	0	1	4	2	1.560	3.24	112	4.52	.276	2	.500	0	1	0.1
Yr.	0	1	.000	2	1	1	0	0	11^{1}	10	6	3	0	1	4	4	1.235	2.38	153	3.39	.238	2	.400	1	1	0.2

• MCMAHAN, Jack

Jack Wally McMahan b: 7/25/1932, Hot Springs, AR BR/TL, 6', 175 lbs. Deb: 4/18/1956

YEAR TM-L	W	L	PCT	G	GS	CG	SH	SV	IP	H	R	ER	HR	HB	BB	SO	RAT	ERA	ERA+	CERA	OAV	BH	AVG	PR+	WS	TPW
1956 Pit-N	0	0	....	11	0	0	0	0	13^{1}	18	9	9	1	0	9	9	2.025	6.08	62	7.30	.340	0	.000	-3	0	-0.4
KC-A	0	5	.000	23	9	0	0	0	61^{2}	69	40	33	7	2	31	13	1.622	4.82	90	5.45	.290	0	.000	-4	1	-0.6

• MCMAHON, Doc

Henry John McMahon b: 12/19/1886, Woburn, MA d: 12/11/1929, Woburn, MA TR Deb: 10/6/1908

YEAR TM-L	W	L	PCT	G	GS	CG	SH	SV	IP	H	R	ER	HR	HB	BB	SO	RAT	ERA	ERA+	CERA	OAV	BH	AVG	PR+	WS	TPW
1908 Bos-A	1	0	1.000	1	1	1	0	0	9	14	3	3	0	0	0	3	1.556	3.00	82	4.91	.350	2	.400	-1	1	0.0

• MCMAHON, Don

Donald John McMahon b: 1/4/1930, Brooklyn, NY d: 7/22/1987, Los Angeles, CA BR/TR, 6'2", 222 lbs. Deb: 6/30/1957 C

YEAR TM-L	W	L	PCT	G	GS	CG	SH	SV	IP	H	R	ER	HR	HB	BB	SO	RAT	ERA	ERA+	CERA	OAV	BH	AVG	PR+	WS	TPW
1957★ Mil-N	2	3	.400	32	0	0	0	9	46^{2}	33	13	8	0	0	29	46	1.329	1.54	227	2.48	.196	2	.250	9	7	1.1
1958★ Mil-N★	7	2	.778	38	0	0	0	8	58^{2}	50	25	24	4	2	29	37	1.347	3.68	96	3.43	.235	1	.111	-2	6	-0.2
1959 Mil-N	5	3	.625	60	0	0	0	**15**	80^{2}	81	26	23	5	1	37	55	1.463	2.57	138	3.92	.259	2	.222	9	10	1.0
1960 Mil-N	3	6	.333	48	0	0	0	10	63^{2}	66	48	42	9	2	32	50	1.539	5.94	58	4.96	.263	0	.000	-17	0	-1.9
1961 Mil-N	6	4	.600	53	0	0	0	8	92	84	35	29	4	2	51	55	1.467	2.84	132	3.77	.249	3	.188	9	9	0.9
1962 Mil-N	0	1	.000	2	0	0	0	0	3	3	2	2	1	0	0	3	1.000	6.00	63	3.79	.250	0	....	-1	0	-0.1
Hou-N	5	5	.500	51	0	0	0	8	76^{2}	53	14	13	4	1	33	69	1.122	1.53	245	2.36	.201	1	.083	20	12	1.9
Yr.	5	6	.455	53	0	0	0	8	79^{2}	56	16	15	5	1	33	72	1.117	1.69	221	2.41	.203	1	.083	19	12	1.9
1963 Hou-N	1	5	.167	49	2	0	0	5	80	83	38	36	10	0	26	51	1.363	4.05	78	4.09	.270	1	.083	-6	3	-0.6
1964 Cle-A	6	4	.600	70	0	0	0	16	101	67	31	27	7	2	52	92	1.178	2.41	150	2.52	.189	2	.143	16	14	1.6
1965 Cle-A	3	3	.500	58	0	0	0	11	85	79	36	31	8	1	37	60	1.365	3.28	106	3.73	.248	2	.222	2	6	0.2
1966 Cle-A	1	1	.500	12	0	0	0	1	12^{1}	8	4	4	1	0	6	5	1.135	2.92	118	2.45	.190	0	.000	1	1	0.1
Bos-A	8	7	.533	49	0	0	0	9	78	65	29	23	7	3	38	57	1.321	2.65	143	3.40	.232	1	.091	10	9	1.1
Yr.	9	8	.529	61	0	0	0	10	90^{1}	73	33	27	8	3	44	62	1.295	2.69	139	3.27	.227	1	.077	11	10	1.2
1967 Bos-A	1	2	.333	11	0	0	0	2	17^{2}	14	8	7	3	0	13	10	1.528	3.57	98	4.71	.215	0	.000	-0	1	0.0
Chi-A	5	0	1.000	52	0	0	0	3	91^{2}	54	21	17	5	6	27	74	.884	1.67	186	1.61	.173	2	.182	14	10	1.6
Yr.	6	2	.750	63	0	0	0	5	109^{1}	68	29	24	8	6	40	84	.988	1.98	162	2.11	.180	2	.154	14	11	1.6
1968 Chi-A	2	1	.667	25	0	0	0	0	46	31	10	10	2	3	20	32	1.109	1.96	155	2.17	.190	1	.333	6	4	0.7
★Det-A	3	1	.750	20	0	0	0	1	35^{2}	22	8	8	2	0	10	33	.897	2.02	149	1.55	.180	0	.000	4	4	0.4
Yr.	5	2	.714	45	0	0	0	1	81^{2}	53	18	18	4	3	30	65	1.016	1.98	152	1.90	.186	1	.143	9	8	1.1
1969 Det-A	3	5	.375	34	0	0	0	11	37	25	17	16	2	1	18	38	1.162	3.89	96	2.44	.192	0	.000	-1	5	-0.2
SF-N	3	1	.750	13	0	0	0	2	23^{2}	13	9	8	1	0	9	21	.930	3.04	115	1.50	.157	1	.333	1	3	0.2
1970 SF-N	9	5	.643	61	0	0	0	19	94^{1}	70	32	31	9	2	45	74	1.219	2.96	134	2.78	.202	2	.143	13	14	1.3
1971★ SF-N	10	6	.625	61	0	0	0	4	82	73	40	37	9	7	37	71	1.341	4.06	84	3.94	.242	0	.000	-6	5	-0.7
1972 SF-N	3	3	.500	44	0	0	0	5	63	46	26	26	8	1	21	45	1.063	3.71	94	2.57	.206	1	.250	-2	4	-0.2
1973 SF-N	4	0	1.000	22	0	0	0	6	30^{1}	21	5	5	1	0	7	20	.923	1.48	257	1.47	.189	1	1.000	8	7	0.9
1974 SF-N	0	0	....	9	0	0	0	0	11^{2}	13	5	4	2	0	2	5	1.286	3.09	123	4.19	.283	0	....	1	1	0.1
Total 18	**90**	**68**	**.570**	**874**	**2**	**0**	**0**	**153**	1310^{2}	**1054**	**482**	**431**	**104**	**34**	**579**	**1003**	**1.246**	**2.96**	**118**	**3.08**	**.221**	**23**	**.137**	**91**	**135**	**9.3**

• MCMAHON, Sadie

John Joseph McMahon b: 9/19/1867, Wilmington, DE d: 2/20/1954, Wilmington, DE BR/TR, 5'9.5", 165 lbs. Deb: 7/5/1889 U

YEAR TM-L	W	L	PCT	G	GS	CG	SH	SV	IP	H	R	ER	HR	HB	BB	SO	RAT	ERA	ERA+	CERA	OAV	BH	AVG	PR+	WS	TPW
1889 Phi-a	14	12	.538	28	27	27	2	0	242	230	160	95	5	14	102	117	1.372	3.53	107	....	.243	16	.154	-2	14	-0.7
1890 Phi-a	29	18	.617	48	46	44	0	1	410	414	238	152	5	20	133	225	1.334	3.34	115	....	.254	40	.229	46	25	4.4
Bal-a	7	3	.700	12	11	11	1	0	99	84	49	33	1	6	33	66	1.182	3.00	142	....	.223	4	.103	14	8	0.9
Yr.	**36**	21	.632	**60**	**57**	**55**	1	1	**509**	498	287	185	6	26	166	**291**	1.305	3.27	119	....	.249	44	.206	60	33	5.3
1891 Bal-a	**35**	24	.593	61	**58**	**53**	**5**	1	**503**	493	259	157	13	17	149	219	1.276	2.81	133	....	.248	43	.205	60	39	4.9
1892 Bal-N	19	25	.432	48	46	44	2	1	397	430	260	143	9	9	145	118	1.448	3.24	106	3.84	.266	25	.141	26	11	1.6
1893 Bal-N	23	18	.561	43	40	35	0	1	346^{1}	378	232	168	6	9	156	79	1.542	4.37	109	4.15	.270	36	.243	21	26	1.5
1894 Bal-N	25	8	.758	35	33	26	0	0	275^{2}	317	175	129	7	9	111	60	1.553	4.21	129	4.40	.286	36	.286	30	24	2.3
1895★ Bal-N	10	4	.714	15	15	15	**4**	0	122^{1}	110	54	40	1	4	32	37	1.161	2.94	162	2.50	.237	16	.314	17	15	1.5
1896 Bal-N	11	9	.550	22	22	19	0	0	175^{2}	195	109	68	4	3	55	33	1.423	3.48	123	3.79	.279	9	.123	12	11	0.4
1897 Bro-N	0	6	.000	9	7	5	0	0	63	75	56	41	1	3	29	13	1.651	5.86	70	4.81	.293	5	.200	-12	1	-1.1
Total 9	**173**	**127**	**.577**	**321**	**305**	**279**	**14**	**4**	**2634**	**2726**	**1592**	**1026**	**52**	**94**	**945**	**967**	**1.394**	**3.51**	**117**	**2.07**	**.260**	**230**	**.204**	**212**	**174**	**15.9**

• MCMAKIN, John

John Weaver "Spartenburg John" McMakin b: 3/6/1878, Spartanburg, SC d: 9/25/1956, Lyman, SC BR/TL, 5'11", 165 lbs. Deb: 4/19/1902

YEAR TM-L	W	L	PCT	G	GS	CG	SH	SV	IP	H	R	ER	HR	HB	BB	SO	RAT	ERA	ERA+	CERA	OAV	BH	AVG	PR+	WS	TPW
1902 Bro-N	2	2	.500	4	4	4	0	0	32	34	18	11	0	2	11	6	1.406	3.09	89	3.52	.272	2	.182	-1	1	-0.1

• MCMANUS, Joe

Joab Logan McManus b: 9/7/1887, Palmyra, IL d: 12/23/1955, Beckley, WV BR/TR, 6'1", 180 lbs. Deb: 4/12/1913

YEAR TM-L	W	L	PCT	G	GS	CG	SH	SV	IP	H	R	ER	HR	HB	BB	SO	RAT	ERA	ERA+	CERA	OAV	BH	AVG	PR+	WS	TPW
1913 Cin-N	0	0	....	1	0	0	0	0	2	3	4	4	0	0	4	1	3.500	18.00	18	13.22	.375	0	....	-3	0	-0.3

• MCMANUS, Patrick

Patrick A. McManus b: 1859, Ireland d: 5/19/1917, Orange County, NY Deb: 5/22/1879

YEAR TM-L	W	L	PCT	G	GS	CG	SH	SV	IP	H	R	ER	HR	HB	BB	SO	RAT	ERA	ERA+	CERA	OAV	BH	AVG	PR+	WS	TPW
1879 Tro-N	0	2	.000	2	2	2	0	0	21	24	21	7	1	....	1	6	1.190	3.00	83	....	.269	1	.125	-1	0	-0.1

• MCMICHAEL, Greg

Gregory Winston McMichael b: 12/1/1966, Knoxville, TN BR/TR, 6'3", 215 lbs. Deb: 4/12/1993

YEAR TM-L	W	L	PCT	G	GS	CG	SH	SV	IP	H	R	ER	HR	HB	BB	SO	RAT	ERA	ERA+	CERA	OAV	BH	AVG	PR+	WS	TPW
1993★ Atl-N	2	3	.400	74	0	0	0	19	91^{2}	68	22	21	3	0	29	89	1.058	2.06	195	1.98	.206	0	.000	19	17	1.9
1994 Atl-N	4	6	.400	51	0	0	0	21	58^{2}	66	29	25	1	0	19	47	1.449	3.84	111	3.64	.280	0	.000	3	8	0.3
1995★ Atl-N	7	2	.778	67	0	0	0	2	80^{2}	64	27	25	8	0	32	74	1.190	2.79	153	2.74	.213	0	.000	14	11	1.4
1996★ Atl-N	5	3	.625	73	0	0	0	2	86^{2}	84	37	31	4	1	27	78	1.281	3.22	137	3.11	.253	0	....	13	9	1.2
1997 NY-N	7	10	.412	73	0	0	0	7	87^{2}	73	34	29	8	2	27	81	1.141	2.98	136	2.80	.233	2	.667	9	10	0.9
1998 NY-N	1	2	.333	22	0	0	0	0	22^{1}	23	12	10	1	1	14	22	1.657	4.03	107	4.53	1.000	0	.000	1	0	0.1
LA-N	0	1	.000	12	0	0	0	1	14^{1}	17	8	7	1	1	6	11	1.605	4.40	90	4.84	.309	0	....	-1	1	-0.1
NY-N	4	1	.800	30	0	0	0	1	31	41	19	14	7	2	15	22	1.806	4.06	102	7.31	.318	0	....	0	3	0.0
Yr.	5	4	.556	64	0	0	0	2	67^{2}	81	39	31	9	4	35	55	1.714	4.12	101	5.87	.391	0	.000	0	4	0.0

YEAR	TM-L	W	L	PCT	G	GS	CG	SH	SV	IP	H	R	ER	HR	HB	BB	SO	RAT	ERA	ERA+	CERA	OAV	BH	AVG	PR+	WS	TPW
1999	NY-N	1	1	.500	19	0	0	0	0	18^2	20	10	10	3	0	8	18	1.500	4.82	91	4.66	.270	0	....	-1	1	-0.1
	Oak-A	0	0	....	17	0	0	0	0	15	15	9	9	3	2	12	3	1.800	5.40	86	7.21	.283	0	....	-1	0	-0.1
2000	Atl-N	0	0	....	15	0	0	0	0	16^1	12	8	8	3	0	4	14	.980	4.41	104	2.68	.214	0	....	0	1	0.0
Total	8	31	29	.517	453	0	0	0	53	523	483	215	189	42	9	193	459	1.293	3.25	130	3.38	.254	2	.133	56	61	5.5

• MCMULLEN, George George McMullen b: CA Deb: 7/2/1887

YEAR	TM-L	W	L	PCT	G	GS	CG	SH	SV	IP	H	R	ER	HR	HB	BB	SO	RAT	ERA	ERA+	CERA	OAV	BH	AVG	PR+	WS	TPW
1887	NY-a	2	1	.667	3	3	2	0	0	21	44	44	18	2	0	19	2	2.095	7.71	55	....	.413	1	.083	-7	0	-0.8

• MCMULLIN, John John F. "Lefty" McMullin b: 1849, Philadelphia, PA d: 4/11/1881, Philadelphia, PA BR/TL, 5'9", 160 lbs. Deb: 5/9/1871 ♦

YEAR	TM-L	W	L	PCT	G	GS	CG	SH	SV	IP	H	R	ER	HR	HB	BB	SO	RAT	ERA	ERA+	CERA	OAV	BH	AVG	PR+	WS	TPW
1871	Tro-n	12	15	.444	29	29	28	0	0	249	430	362	153	4	....	75	12	**2.028**	5.53	76	....	.335	38	.279	-38	....	-2.3
1872	Mut-n	1	0	1.000	3	1	1	0	0	15	18	15	6	0	....	2	1	1.333	3.60	96	....	.260	61	.257	-1	....	0.4
1873	Ath-n	1	0	1.000	1	1	1	0	0	8	10	5	2	0	....	1	2	1.375	2.25	152	....	.271	62	.273	1	....	-0.6
1875	Phi-n	0	0	....	4	0	0	0	0	11^1	32	23	10	0	....	1	22	2.912	7.94	35	....	.467	57	.257	-6	....	-0.7
Total	4 n	14	15	.483	37	31	30	0	0	283^1	490	405	171	4	....	79	37	2.008	5.43	75	....	.336	308	.285	-44	....	-3.2

• MCMURTRY, Craig Joe Craig McMurtry b: 11/5/1959, Temple, TX BR/TR, 6'5", 195 lbs. Deb: 4/10/1983

YEAR	TM-L	W	L	PCT	G	GS	CG	SH	SV	IP	H	R	ER	HR	HB	BB	SO	RAT	ERA	ERA+	CERA	OAV	BH	AVG	PR+	WS	TPW
1983	Atl-N	15	9	.625	36	35	6	3	0	224^2	204	86	77	13	1	88	105	1.300	3.08	126	3.28	.243	6	.086	17	16	1.5
1984	Atl-N	9	17	.346	37	30	0	0	0	183^1	184	100	88	16	1	102	99	1.560	4.32	89	4.65	.268	6	.115	-8	6	-1.0
1985	Atl-N	0	3	.000	17	6	0	0	1	45	56	36	33	6	1	27	28	1.844	6.60	58	6.49	.306	1	.071	-13	0	-1.5
1986	Atl-N	1	6	.143	37	5	0	0	0	79^2	82	46	42	7	2	43	50	1.569	4.74	84	4.72	.265	2	.125	-6	2	-0.6
1988	Tex-A	3	3	.500	32	0	0	0	3	60	37	16	15	5	1	24	35	1.017	2.25	181	2.01	.180	0	....	12	7	1.2
1989	Tex-A	0	0	....	19	0	0	0	0	23	29	21	19	3	2	13	14	1.826	7.43	53	6.82	.312	0	....	-9	0	-0.9
1990	Tex-A	0	3	.000	23	3	0	0	0	41^2	43	25	20	4	1	30	14	1.752	4.32	91	5.83	.281	0	....	-2	1	-0.2
1995	Hou-N	0	1	.000	11	0	0	0	0	10^1	15	11	9	0	1	9	4	2.323	7.84	49	7.91	.357	0	.000	-4	0	-0.4
Total	8	28	42	.400	212	79	6	3	4	667^2	650	341	303	54	10	336	349	1.477	4.08	95	4.29	.259	15	.098	-13	32	-1.9

• MCNABB, Edgar Edgar J. "Texas" McNabb b: 10/24/1865, Coshocton, OH d: 2/28/1894, Pittsburgh, PA BR/TR, 5'11.5", 170 lbs. Deb: 5/12/1893

YEAR	TM-L	W	L	PCT	G	GS	CG	SH	SV	IP	H	R	ER	HR	HB	BB	SO	RAT	ERA	ERA+	CERA	OAV	BH	AVG	PR+	WS	TPW
1893	Bal-N	8	7	.533	21	14	12	0	0	142	167	109	65	5	8	53	18	1.549	4.12	115	4.60	.285	13	.194	13	10	0.9

• MCNALLY, Dave David Arthur McNally b: 10/31/1942, Billings, MT d: 12/2/2002, Billings, MT BR/TL, 5'11", 190 lbs. Deb: 9/26/1962

YEAR	TM-L	W	L	PCT	G	GS	CG	SH	SV	IP	H	R	ER	HR	HB	BB	SO	RAT	ERA	ERA+	CERA	OAV	BH	AVG	PR+	WS	TPW
1962	Bal-A	1	0	1.000	1	1	1	1	0	9	2	0	0	0	0	3	4	.556	0.00	....	0.47	.071	0	.000	4	2	0.3
1963	Bal-A	7	8	.467	29	20	2	0	1	125^2	133	67	64	9	5	55	78	1.496	4.58	77	4.49	.276	2	.053	-15	2	-1.8
1964	Bal-A	9	11	.450	30	23	5	3	0	159^1	157	72	65	15	9	51	88	1.305	3.67	97	3.93	.260	7	.137	-6	8	-0.6
1965	Bal-A	11	6	.647	35	29	6	2	0	198^2	163	69	63	15	6	73	116	1.188	2.85	122	2.89	.222	6	.092	10	14	0.8
1966*	Bal-A	13	6	.684	34	33	5	1	0	213	212	91	75	22	4	64	158	1.296	3.17	105	3.73	.256	15	.195	3	12	0.6
1967	Bal-A	7	7	.500	24	22	3	1	0	119	134	65	60	13	2	39	70	1.454	4.54	69	4.77	.295	6	.158	-20	1	-2.3
1968	Bal-A	22	10	.688	35	35	18	5	0	273	175	67	59	24	10	55	202	.842	1.95	150	1.66	.182	11	.128	25	26	3.2
1969*	Bal-A★	20	7	.741	41	40	11	4	0	268^2	232	103	96	21	5	84	166	1.176	3.22	111	2.95	.234	8	.085	0	17	-0.2
1970*	Bal-A★	**24**	9	.727	40	**40**	16	1	0	296	277	114	106	29	7	78	185	1.199	3.22	113	3.29	.250	14	.133	7	22	1.2
1971*	Bal-A	21	5	.808	30	30	11	1	0	224^1	188	75	72	24	5	58	91	1.097	2.89	116	2.83	.229	12	.162	9	19	1.2
1972	Bal-A★	13	17	.433	36	36	12	6	0	241	220	85	79	15	2	68	120	1.195	2.95	104	2.90	.247	12	.152	-2	12	-0.1
1973*	Bal-A	17	17	.500	38	38	17	4	0	266	247	100	95	16	5	81	87	1.233	3.21	116	3.18	.251	0	....	4	18	0.4
1974*	Bal-A	16	10	.615	39	37	13	4	1	259	260	112	103	19	8	81	111	1.317	3.58	96	3.77	.270	0	....	-7	14	-0.7
1975	Mon-N	3	6	.333	12	12	0	0	0	77^1	88	50	45	8	4	36	36	1.603	5.24	73	5.18	.280	4	.190	-12	1	-1.1
Total	14	184	119	.607	424	396	120	33	2	2730	2488	1070	982	230	72	826	1512	1.214	3.24	106	3.26	.245	97	.133	-0	168	1.1

• MCNAMARA, Tim Timothy Augustine McNamara b: 11/20/1898, Millville, MA d: 11/5/1994, North Smithfield, RI BR/TR, 5'11", 170 lbs. Deb: 6/27/1922

YEAR	TM-L	W	L	PCT	G	GS	CG	SH	SV	IP	H	R	ER	HR	HB	BB	SO	RAT	ERA	ERA+	CERA	OAV	BH	AVG	PR+	WS	TPW
1922	Bos-N	3	4	.429	24	5	4	2	0	70^2	55	26	19	2	1	26	16	1.146	2.42	165	2.39	.225	2	.118	13	7	1.2
1923	Bos-N	3	13	.188	32	16	3	0	0	139^1	185	95	76	8	5	29	32	1.536	4.91	81	4.92	.320	7	.179	-13	3	-1.1
1924	Bos-N	8	12	.400	35	21	6	2	0	179	242	119	103	9	3	31	35	1.525	5.18	74	4.84	.334	6	.140	-25	4	-2.6
1925	Bos-N	0	0	....	1	0	0	0	0	0^2	6	6	6	0	0	2	1	12.00	81.00	5	91.26	.857	0	....	-6	0	-0.5
1926	NY-N	0	0	....	6	0	0	0	0	6	7	6	6	0	0	4	4	1.833	9.00	42	4.97	.304	0	....	-4	0	-0.4
Total	5	14	29	.326	98	42	13	4	0	395^2	495	252	210	19	9	92	88	1.484	4.78	82	4.58	.314	15	.152	-34	14	-3.4

• MCNAUGHTON, Gordon Gordon Joseph McNaughton b: 7/31/1910, Chicago, IL d: 8/6/1942, Chicago, IL BR/TR, 6'1", 190 lbs. Deb: 8/13/1932

YEAR	TM-L	W	L	PCT	G	GS	CG	SH	SV	IP	H	R	ER	HR	HB	BB	SO	RAT	ERA	ERA+	CERA	OAV	BH	AVG	PR+	WS	TPW
1932	Bos-A	0	1	.000	6	2	0	0	0	21	21	15	15	1	3	22	6	2.048	6.43	70	6.47	.259	2	.250	-4	0	-0.4

• MCNEAL, Harry John Harley McNeal b: 8/11/1877, Iberia, OH d: 1/11/1945, Cleveland, OH BR/TR, 6'3", 175 lbs. Deb: 8/5/1901

YEAR	TM-L	W	L	PCT	G	GS	CG	SH	SV	IP	H	R	ER	HR	HB	BB	SO	RAT	ERA	ERA+	CERA	OAV	BH	AVG	PR+	WS	TPW
1901	Cle-A	5	5	.500	12	10	9	0	0	85^1	120	68	42	4	8	30	15	1.758	4.43	80	6.12	.328	6	.162	-8	3	-0.9

• MCNICHOL, Brian Brian David McNichol b: 5/20/1974, Fairfax, VA BL/TL, 6'6", 225 lbs. Deb: 9/7/1999

YEAR	TM-L	W	L	PCT	G	GS	CG	SH	SV	IP	H	R	ER	HR	HB	BB	SO	RAT	ERA	ERA+	CERA	OAV	BH	AVG	PR+	WS	TPW
1999	Chi-N	0	2	.000	4	2	0	0	0	10^2	15	8	8	4	1	7	12	2.063	6.75	67	10.58	.333	0	.000	-3	0	-0.3

• MCNICHOL, Ed Edwin Briggs McNichol b: 1/10/1879, Martins Ferry, OH d: 11/1/1952, Salineville, OH BR/TR, 5'5", 170 lbs. Deb: 7/9/1904

YEAR	TM-L	W	L	PCT	G	GS	CG	SH	SV	IP	H	R	ER	HR	HB	BB	SO	RAT	ERA	ERA+	CERA	OAV	BH	AVG	PR+	WS	TPW
1904	Bos-N	2	12	.143	17	15	12	1	0	122	120	70	58	3	5	74	39	1.590	4.28	64	4.33	.262	4	.093	-17	2	-2.2

• MCPARTLIN, Frank Frank McPartlin b: 2/16/1872, Hoosick Falls, NY d: 11/13/1943, New York, NY TR, 6', 180 lbs. Deb: 8/22/1899

YEAR	TM-L	W	L	PCT	G	GS	CG	SH	SV	IP	H	R	ER	HR	HB	BB	SO	RAT	ERA	ERA+	CERA	OAV	BH	AVG	PR+	WS	TPW
1899	NY-N	0	0	....	1	0	0	0	0	4	4	4	2	0	2	3	2	1.750	4.50	83	6.21	.260	0	.000	-0	0	0.0

• MCPHERSON, John John Jacob McPherson b: 3/9/1869, Easton, PA d: 9/30/1941, Easton, PA TR Deb: 7/12/1901

YEAR	TM-L	W	L	PCT	G	GS	CG	SH	SV	IP	H	R	ER	HR	HB	BB	SO	RAT	ERA	ERA+	CERA	OAV	BH	AVG	PR+	WS	TPW
1901	Phi-A	0	1	.000	1	1	0	0	0	4	7	5	5	0	1	4	0	2.750	11.25	33	11.20	.378	0	.000	-3	0	-0.3
1904	Phi-N	1	12	.077	15	12	11	1	0	128	130	82	52	1	6	46	32	1.375	3.66	73	3.49	.264	3	.064	-12	1	-1.7
Total	2	1	13	.071	16	13	11	1	0	132	137	87	57	1	7	50	32	1.417	3.89	70	3.72	.268	3	.063	-15	1	-2.0

• MCQUAID, Herb Herbert George McQuaid b: 3/29/1899, San Francisco, CA d: 4/4/1966, Richmond, CA BR/TR, 6'2", 185 lbs. Deb: 6/22/1923

YEAR	TM-L	W	L	PCT	G	GS	CG	SH	SV	IP	H	R	ER	HR	HB	BB	SO	RAT	ERA	ERA+	CERA	OAV	BH	AVG	PR+	WS	TPW
1923	Cin-N	1	0	1.000	12	1	0	0	0	34^1	31	11	9	0	3	10	9	1.194	2.36	164	2.71	.238	0	.000	6	3	0.4
1926	NY-A	1	0	1.000	17	1	0	0	0	38^1	48	34	26	5	2	13	6	1.591	6.10	63	5.61	.329	0	.000	-9	0	-1.0
Total	2	2	0	1.000	29	2	0	0	0	72^2	79	45	35	5	5	23	15	1.404	4.33	89	4.24	.286	0	.000	-3	3	-0.5

• MCQUEEN, Mike Michael Robert McQueen b: 8/30/1950, Oklahoma City, OK BL/TL, 6', 190 lbs. Deb: 10/2/1969

YEAR	TM-L	W	L	PCT	G	GS	CG	SH	SV	IP	H	R	ER	HR	HB	BB	SO	RAT	ERA	ERA+	CERA	OAV	BH	AVG	PR+	WS	TPW
1969	Atl-N	0	0	....	1	1	0	0	0	3	2	1	1	0	0	3	3	1.667	3.00	120	3.63	.182	0	....	0	0	0.0
1970	Atl-N	1	5	.167	22	8	1	0	1	66	67	48	41	10	1	31	54	1.485	5.59	77	4.82	.266	6	.300	-8	1	-0.6
1971	Atl-N	4	1	.800	17	3	0	0	1	56	47	24	22	7	2	23	38	1.250	3.54	105	3.45	.228	4	.211	1	5	0.2
1972	Atl-N	0	5	.000	23	7	1	0	1	78^1	79	45	40	11	1	44	40	1.570	4.60	82	4.97	.260	2	.087	-6	1	-0.8
1974	Cin-N	0	0	....	10	0	0	0	0	15	17	10	9	4	0	11	5	1.867	5.40	65	7.70	.288	1	1.000	-3	0	-0.3
Total	5	5	11	.313	73	19	2	0	3	218^1	212	128	113	32	4	112	140	1.484	4.66	84	4.71	.255	13	.206	-16	7	-1.5

• MCQUILLAN, George George Watt McQuillan b: 5/1/1885, Brooklyn, NY d: 5/30/1940, Columbus, OH BR/TR, 5'11.5", 175 lbs. Deb: 5/8/1907

YEAR	TM-L	W	L	PCT	G	GS	CG	SH	SV	IP	H	R	ER	HR	HB	BB	SO	RAT	ERA	ERA+	CERA	OAV	BH	AVG	PR+	WS	TPW
1907	Phi-N	4	0	1.000	6	5	5	3	0	41	21	3	3	0	1	11	28	.780	0.66	367	1.09	.158	4	.364	7	8	1.2
1908	Phi-N	23	17	.575	48	42	32	7	2	359^2	263	88	61	1	6	91	114	.984	1.53	157	1.64	.207	18	.151	31	33	3.6
1909	Phi-N	13	16	.448	41	28	16	4	2	247^2	202	87	59	5	1	54	96	1.034	2.14	121	2.04	.226	9	.118	8	18	0.6
1910	Phi-N	9	6	.600	24	17	13	3	1	152^1	109	42	27	2	3	50	71	1.044	**1.60**	195	1.92	.204	7	.149	25	13	2.5
1911	Cin-N	2	6	.250	19	5	2	0	0	77	92	60	40	2	4	31	28	1.597	4.68	71	4.96	.308	2	.091	-12	0	-1.3
1913	Pit-N	8	6	.571	25	16	7	0	1	141^2	144	60	54	1	1	35	59	1.264	3.43	88	2.99	.273	4	.103	-5	7	-0.7
1914	Pit-N	13	17	.433	45	28	15	0	4	259^1	248	100	86	8	8	60	96	1.188	2.98	89	2.87	.261	5	.068	-11	14	-1.6
1915	Pit-N	8	10	.444	30	20	9	0	1	149	160	64	47	1	2	39	56	1.336	2.84	96	3.34	.284	4	.091	-1	7	-0.4
	Phi-N	4	3	.571	9	8	5	0	0	63^2	60	31	15	1	1	11	13	1.115	2.12	129	2.35	.247	1	.043	4	4	0.3
	Yr.	12	13	.480	39	28	14	0	1	212^2	220	95	62	2	3	50	69	1.270	2.62	104	3.04	.273	5	.075	3	11	-0.2
1916	Phi-N	1	7	.125	21	3	1	0	2	62	58	33	19	2	3	15	22	1.177	2.76	96	2.76	.251	1	.091	-1	1	-0.1
1918	Cle-A	0	1	.000	5	1	0	0	1	23	25	10	6	0	0	4	7	1.261	2.35	128	3.00	.284	0	.000	2	1	0.2
Total	10	85	89	.489	273	173	105	17	14	1576^1	1382	578	417	23	30	401	590	1.131	2.38	115	2.46	.241	55	.117	49	106	4.2

• MCQUILLAN, Hugh

Hugh A. "Handsome Hugh" McQuillan b: 9/15/1897, New York, NY d: 8/26/1947, New York, NY BR/TR, 6', 170 lbs. Deb: 7/26/1918

YEAR	TM-L	W	L	PCT	G	GS	CG	SH	SV	IP	H	R	ER	HR	HB	BB	SO	RAT	ERA	ERA+	CERA	OAV	BH	AVG	PR+	WS	TPW
1918	Bos-N	1	0	1.000	1	1	1	0	0	9	7	3	3	0	0	5	1	1.333	3.00	90	2.58	.219	1	.250	-0	1	0.0
1919	Bos-N	2	3	.400	16	7	2	0	1	60	66	34	23	3	1	14	13	1.333	3.45	83	3.64	.288	4	.222	-4	2	-0.4
1920	Bos-N	11	15	.423	38	27	17	1	5	225^{2}	230	110	89	3	2	70	53	1.329	3.55	86	3.22	.273	19	.257	-15	13	-1.0
1921	Bos-N	13	17	.433	45	31	13	2	5	250	284	137	111	9	2	90	94	1.496	4.00	91	4.17	.291	18	.205	-11	11	-1.0
1922	Bos-N	5	10	.333	28	17	7	0	0	136	154	70	64	3	1	56	33	1.544	4.24	94	4.27	.299	7	.167	-2	7	-0.3
	*NY-N	6	5	.545	15	13	5	0	1	94^{1}	111	48	40	7	0	34	24	1.537	3.82	105	4.71	.301	7	.189	-1	6	-0.2
	Yr.	11	15	.423	43	30	12	0	1	230^{1}	265	118	104	10	1	90	57	1.541	4.06	98	4.45	.300	14	.177	-3	13	-0.5
1923*	NY-N	15	14	.517	38	32	15	5	0	229^{2}	224	96	87	12	5	66	75	1.263	3.41	112	3.21	.259	14	.171	7	17	0.5
1924*	NY-N	14	8	.636	27	23	14	1	3	184	179	68	55	8	2	43	49	1.207	2.69	136	2.94	.259	14	.209	19	14	1.8
1925	NY-N	2	3	.400	14	11	2	0	1	70	95	49	47	9	1	23	23	1.686	6.04	67	6.35	.343	3	.143	-15	1	-1.5
1926	NY-N	11	10	.524	33	22	12	1	0	167	171	72	69	7	1	42	47	1.275	3.72	101	3.26	.271	7	.132	-2	11	-0.4
1927	NY-N	5	4	.556	11	9	5	0	0	58	73	32	29	4	1	22	17	1.638	4.50	86	5.21	.309	4	.211	-4	3	-0.3
	Bos-N	3	5	.375	13	11	2	0	0	78	109	65	48	2	2	24	17	1.705	5.54	67	5.26	.332	5	.227	-14	0	-1.4
	Yr.	8	9	.471	24	20	7	0	0	136	182	97	77	6	3	46	34	1.676	5.10	74	5.24	.322	9	.220	-18	3	-1.7
Total 10		88	94	.484	279	204	95	10	16	1561^{2}	1703	784	665	67	18	489	446	1.404	3.83	95	3.85	.284	103	.195	-42	86	-4.2

• MCRAE, Norm

Norman McRae b: 9/26/1947, Elizabeth, NJ d: 7/25/2003, Garland, TX BR/TR, 6'1", 195 lbs. Deb: 9/13/1969

YEAR	TM-L	W	L	PCT	G	GS	CG	SH	SV	IP	H	R	ER	HR	HB	BB	SO	RAT	ERA	ERA+	CERA	OAV	BH	AVG	PR+	WS	TPW
1969	Det-A	0	0	....	3	0	0	0	0	3	2	2	2	0	0	1	3	1.000	6.00	62	1.57	.200	0	....	-1	0	-0.1
1970	Det-A	0	0	....	19	0	0	0	0	31^{1}	26	13	10	1	1	25	16	1.628	2.87	130	4.25	.226	0	.000	4	2	0.4
Total 2		0	0	....	22	0	0	0	0	34^{1}	28	15	12	1	1	26	19	1.573	3.15	118	4.02	.224	0	.000	3	2	0.3

• MCTIGUE, Bill

William Patrick "Rebel" McTigue b: 1/3/1891, Nashville, TN d: 5/8/1920, Nashville, TN BL/TL, 6'1.5", 175 lbs. Deb: 5/2/1911

YEAR	TM-L	W	L	PCT	G	GS	CG	SH	SV	IP	H	R	ER	HR	HB	BB	SO	RAT	ERA	ERA+	CERA	OAV	BH	AVG	PR+	WS	TPW
1911	Bos-N	0	5	.000	14	8	0	0	0	37	37	32	29	3	2	49	23	2.324	7.05	54	7.96	.280	1	.083	-13	0	-1.3
1912	Bos-N	2	0	1.000	10	1	1	0	0	34^{2}	39	26	21	0	0	18	17	1.644	5.45	65	4.42	.289	1	.077	-7	1	-0.8
1916	Det-A	0	0	....	3	0	0	0	0	5^{1}	5	6	3	0	0	5	1	1.875	5.06	57	5.28	.278	0	.000	-1	0	-0.1
Total 3		2	5	.286	27	9	1	0	0	77	81	64	53	3	2	72	41	1.987	6.19	59	6.18	.284	2	.077	-21	1	-2.3

• MCVEY, Cal

Calvin Alexander McVey b: 8/30/1850, Montrose, IA d: 8/20/1926, San Francisco, CA BR/TR, 5'9", 170 lbs. Deb: 5/5/1871 M ♦

YEAR	TM-L	W	L	PCT	G	GS	CG	SH	SV	IP	H	R	ER	HR	HB	BB	SO	RAT	ERA	ERA+	CERA	OAV	BH	AVG	PR+	WS	TPW
1875	Bos-n	1	0	1.000	3	2	0	0	1	11	15	....	6	0	....	1	13	1.455	4.91	72	....	.297	138	.355	-2	....	3.4
1876	Chi-N	5	2	.714	11	6	5	0	2	59^{1}	57	22	10	0	....	2	9	.994	1.52	161	....	.234	107	.345	3	16	0.8
1877	Chi-N	4	8	.333	17	10	6	0	**2**	92	129	87	46	2	....	11	20	1.522	4.50	66	....	.313	98	.368	-15	14	-0.4
1879	Cin-N	0	2	.000	3	1	1	0	0	14	34	23	13	1	....	2	7	2.571	8.36	28	....	.439	105	.297	-9	13	-0.8
Total 3		9	12	.429	31	17	12	0	4	165^{1}	220	132	69	3	....	15	36	1.421	3.76	73	....	.300	393	.327	-21	43	-0.4

• MCWEENY, Doug

Douglas Lawrence "Buzz" McWeeny b: 8/17/1896, Chicago, IL d: 1/1/1953, Melrose Park, IL BR/TR, 6'2", 190 lbs. Deb: 4/24/1921

YEAR	TM-L	W	L	PCT	G	GS	CG	SH	SV	IP	H	R	ER	HR	HB	BB	SO	RAT	ERA	ERA+	CERA	OAV	BH	AVG	PR+	WS	TPW
1921	Chi-A	3	6	.333	27	8	3	0	2	97^{2}	127	76	66	7	0	45	46	1.761	6.08	70	5.86	.325	1	.032	-20	1	-2.2
1922	Chi-A	0	1	.000	4	1	0	0	0	10^{2}	13	8	7	0	0	7	5	1.875	5.91	69	5.23	.325	0	.000	-2	0	-0.2
1924	Chi-A	1	3	.250	13	5	2	0	0	43^{1}	47	25	22	2	2	17	18	1.477	4.57	90	4.41	.294	0	.000	-2	2	-0.2
1926	Bro-N	11	13	.458	42	24	10	1	1	216^{1}	213	97	73	6	8	84	96	1.373	3.04	126	3.43	.258	7	.109	23	17	1.8
1927	Bro-N	4	8	.333	34	22	6	0	1	164^{1}	167	80	65	13	8	70	73	1.442	3.56	111	4.17	.266	2	.043	7	9	0.3
1928	Bro-N	14	14	.500	42	32	12	**4**	1	244	218	108	86	11	5	114	79	1.361	3.17	125	3.23	.235	14	.173	23	17	2.2
1929	Bro-N	4	10	.286	36	22	4	0	1	146	167	119	99	17	3	93	59	1.781	6.10	76	5.84	.288	5	.104	-21	2	-2.1
1930	Cin-N	0	2	.000	8	2	0	0	0	25^{2}	28	23	21	0	0	20	10	1.870	7.36	66	5.07	.283	1	.143	-7	0	-0.6
Total 8		37	57	.394	206	116	37	5	6	948	980	536	439	56	26	450	386	1.508	4.17	100	4.24	.268	30	.104	1	48	-1.0

• MCWILLIAMS, Larry

Larry Dean McWilliams b: 2/10/1954, Wichita, KS BL/TL, 6'5", 180 lbs. Deb: 7/17/1978

YEAR	TM-L	W	L	PCT	G	GS	CG	SH	SV	IP	H	R	ER	HR	HB	BB	SO	RAT	ERA	ERA+	CERA	OAV	BH	AVG	PR+	WS	TPW
1978	Atl-N	9	3	.750	15	15	3	1	0	99^{1}	84	38	31	11	2	35	42	1.198	2.81	144	3.10	.224	2	.063	15	10	1.4
1979	Atl-N	3	2	.600	13	13	1	0	0	66^{1}	69	41	41	4	4	22	32	1.372	5.56	73	3.94	.272	5	.208	-9	2	-0.9
1980	Atl-N	9	14	.391	30	30	4	1	0	163^{2}	188	97	90	27	7	39	77	1.387	4.95	76	4.85	.285	8	.157	-22	3	-2.3
1981	Atl-N	2	1	.667	6	5	2	1	0	37^{2}	31	13	13	2	0	8	23	1.035	3.11	115	2.23	.230	1	.100	2	3	0.2
1982	Atl-N	2	3	.400	27	2	0	0	0	37^{2}	52	30	26	3	2	20	24	1.912	6.21	60	6.60	.327	1	.167	-10	0	-1.1
	Pit-N	6	5	.545	19	18	2	2	1	121^{2}	106	49	42	9	4	24	94	1.068	3.11	119	2.57	.232	6	.188	9	8	0.9
	Yr.	8	8	.500	46	20	2	2	1	159^{1}	158	79	68	12	6	44	118	1.268	3.84	97	3.52	.256	7	.184	-2	8	-0.2
1983	Pit-N	15	8	.652	35	35	8	4	0	238	205	99	86	19	3	87	199	1.227	3.25	114	3.02	.230	9	.114	13	15	1.1
1984	Pit-N	12	11	.522	34	32	7	2	1	227^{1}	226	86	74	18	2	78	149	1.337	2.93	123	3.71	.263	9	.122	14	14	1.1
1985	Pit-N	7	9	.438	30	19	2	0	0	126^{1}	139	70	66	9	7	62	52	1.591	4.70	76	4.91	.283	5	.125	-14	3	-1.5
1986	Pit-N	3	11	.214	49	15	0	0	0	122^{1}	129	75	70	16	7	49	80	1.455	5.15	74	4.73	.268	4	.138	-18	1	-1.8
1987	Atl-N	0	1	.000	9	2	0	0	0	20^{1}	25	15	13	2	2	7	13	1.574	5.75	75	5.35	.301	1	.200	-3	0	-0.3
1988	StL-N	6	9	.400	42	17	2	1	1	136	130	64	59	10	4	45	70	1.287	3.90	89	3.38	.253	6	.162	-8	6	-0.7
1989	Phi-N	2	11	.154	40	16	2	1	0	120^{2}	123	67	55	3	4	49	54	1.425	4.10	86	3.70	.265	3	.111	-7	2	-0.8
	KC-A	2	2	.500	8	5	1	0	0	32^{2}	31	15	15	2	3	8	24	1.194	4.13	93	3.28	.254	0	....	-1	2	-0.1
1990	KC-A	0	0	....	13	0	0	0	0	8^{1}	10	9	9	2	1	9	7	2.280	9.72	39	10.04	.313	0	....	-5	0	-0.5
Total 13		78	90	.464	370	224	34	13	3	1558^{1}	1548	768	690	137	52	542	940	1.341	3.99	93	3.83	.259	60	.135	-43	69	-5.3

• MEACHAM, Rusty

Russell Loren Meacham b: 1/27/1968, Stuart, FL BR/TR, 6'3", 175 lbs. Deb: 6/29/1991

YEAR	TM-L	W	L	PCT	G	GS	CG	SH	SV	IP	H	R	ER	HR	HB	BB	SO	RAT	ERA	ERA+	CERA	OAV	BH	AVG	PR+	WS	TPW
1991	Det-A	2	1	.667	10	4	0	0	0	27^{2}	35	17	16	4	0	11	14	1.663	5.20	80	5.97	.315	0	....	-3	1	-0.3
1992	KC-A	10	4	.714	64	0	0	0	2	101^{2}	88	39	31	5	1	21	64	1.072	2.74	148	2.28	.233	0	....	16	11	1.7
1993	KC-A	2	2	.500	15	0	0	0	0	21	31	15	13	2	3	5	13	1.714	5.57	82	6.42	.326	0	....	-2	1	-0.2
1994	KC-A	3	3	.500	36	0	0	0	4	50^{2}	51	23	21	7	2	12	36	1.243	3.73	134	3.85	.263	0	....	7	6	0.7
1995	KC-A	4	3	.571	49	0	0	0	2	59^{2}	72	36	33	6	1	19	30	1.525	4.98	96	4.92	.304	0	....	-2	4	-0.2
1996	Sea-A	1	1	.500	15	5	0	0	1	42^{1}	57	28	27	9	4	13	25	1.654	5.74	86	7.19	.328	0	....	-4	1	-0.4
2000	Hou-N	0	0	....	5	0	0	0	0	4^{2}	8	6	6	3	0	2	3	2.143	11.57	42	14.02	.381	0	....	-3	0	-0.3
2001	TB-A	1	3	.250	24	0	0	0	0	35^{1}	39	24	22	3	2	10	13	1.387	5.60	80	4.18	.277	0	....	-5	1	-0.4
Total 8		23	17	.575	218	9	0	0	9	343	381	188	169	39	13	93	198	1.382	4.43	103	4.48	.282	0	....	4	25	0.5

• MEADOR, Johnny

John Davis Meador b: 12/4/1892, Madison, NC d: 4/11/1970, Winston-Salem, NC BR/TR, 5'10.5", 165 lbs. Deb: 4/24/1920

YEAR	TM-L	W	L	PCT	G	GS	CG	SH	SV	IP	H	R	ER	HR	HB	BB	SO	RAT	ERA	ERA+	CERA	OAV	BH	AVG	PR+	WS	TPW
1920	Pit-N	0	2	.000	12	2	0	0	0	36^{1}	48	18	17	1	0	7	5	1.514	4.21	76	4.73	.340	1	.167	-4	1	-0.4

• MEADOWS, Brian

Matthew Brian Meadows b: 11/21/1975, Montgomery, AL BR/TR, 6'4", 220 lbs. Deb: 4/4/1998

YEAR	TM-L	W	L	PCT	G	GS	CG	SH	SV	IP	H	R	ER	HR	HB	BB	SO	RAT	ERA	ERA+	CERA	OAV	BH	AVG	PR+	WS	TPW
1998	Fla-N	11	13	.458	31	31	1	0	0	174^{1}	222	106	101	20	3	46	88	1.537	5.21	79	5.29	.315	7	.130	-21	4	-2.1
1999	Fla-N	11	15	.423	31	31	0	0	0	178^{1}	214	117	111	31	5	57	72	1.520	5.60	78	5.51	.302	7	.140	-24	4	-2.3
2000	SD-N	7	8	.467	22	22	0	0	0	124^{2}	150	80	74	24	8	50	53	1.604	5.34	81	6.23	.301	6	.150	-16	2	-1.6
	KC-A	6	2	.750	11	10	2	0	0	71^{2}	84	39	38	8	0	14	26	1.367	4.77	107	4.35	.293	0	....	1	5	0.1
2001	KC-A	1	6	.143	10	10	0	0	0	50^{1}	73	41	39	12	1	12	21	1.689	6.97	70	7.47	.351	0	....	-13	0	-1.2
2002	Pit-N	1	6	.143	11	11	0	0	0	62^{2}	62	29	27	7	1	14	31	1.213	3.88	108	3.29	.256	0	.000	2	3	0.0
2003	Pit-N	2	1	.667	34	7	0	0	1	76^{1}	91	45	40	8	1	11	38	1.336	4.72	93	4.12	.290	1	.071	-3	3	-0.3
Total 6		39	51	.433	150	122	3	0	1	738^{1}	896	457	430	110	19	204	329	1.490	5.24	83	5.27	.302	21	.119	-73	21	-7.5

• MEADOWS, Lee

Henry Lee "Specs" Meadows b: 7/12/1894, Oxford, NC d: 1/29/1963, Daytona Beach, FL BL/TR, 6', 190 lbs. Deb: 4/19/1915

YEAR	TM-L	W	L	PCT	G	GS	CG	SH	SV	IP	H	R	ER	HR	HB	BB	SO	RAT	ERA	ERA+	CERA	OAV	BH	AVG	PR+	WS	TPW
1915	StL-N	13	11	.542	39	26	14	1	0	244	232	112	81	5	5	88	104	1.311	2.99	93	3.16	.259	8	.096	-3	10	-0.7
1916	StL-N	12	23	.343	**51**	36	11	1	2	289	261	117	83	3	14	119	120	1.315	2.58	102	3.09	.247	15	.158	2	14	0.2
1917	StL-N	15	9	.625	43	37	18	4	2	265^{2}	253	99	91	5	4	90	100	1.291	3.08	87	3.12	.262	9	.101	-15	16	-2.3
1918	StL-N	8	14	.364	30	23	12	0	1	165^{1}	176	91	66	1	10	56	49	1.403	3.59	75	3.69	.280	7	.127	-17	3	-2.1
1919	StL-N	4	10	.286	22	12	3	1	0	92	100	44	31	3	2	30	28	1.413	3.03	92	3.90	.292	3	.103	-4	3	-0.6
	Phi-N	8	10	.444	18	17	15	3	0	158^{1}	128	55	41	2	7	49	88	1.118	2.33	138	2.33	.229	6	.118	16	9	1.5
	Yr.	12	20	.375	40	29	18	4	0	250^{1}	228	99	72	5	9	79	116	1.226	2.59	117	2.90	.253	9	.113	13	12	0.9
1920	Phi-N	16	14	.533	35	33	19	3	0	247	249	104	78	5	8	90	95	1.372	2.84	120	3.52	.270	14	.171	16	19	1.4
1921	Phi-N	11	16	.407	28	27	15	2	0	194^{1}	226	118	93	10	4	62	52	1.482	4.31	98	4.21	.288	13	.210	2	11	0.4
1922	Phi-N	12	18	.400	33	33	19	2	0	237	264	127	106	8	11	71	62	1.414	4.03	116	3.96	.288	27	.314	18	17	2.1

YEAR	TM-L	W	L	PCT	G	GS	CG	SH	SV	IP	H	R	ER	HR	HB	BB	SO	RAT	ERA	ERA+	CERA	OAV	BH	AVG	PR+	WS	TPW
1923	Phi-N	1	3	.250	8	5	0	0	1	19^2	40	32	29	0	0	15	10	2.797	13.27	35	11.40	.430	4	.400	-18	1	-1.6
	Pit-N	16	10	.615	31	25	17	1	0	227	250	97	76	3	1	44	66	1.295	3.01	133	3.26	.284	22	.250	21	20	2.3
	Yr.	17	13	.567	39	30	17	1	1	246^2	290	129	105	3	1	59	76	1.415	3.83	108	3.90	.298	26	.265	3	21	0.7
1924	Pit-N	13	12	.520	36	30	15	3	0	229^1	240	99	83	7	4	51	61	1.269	3.26	118	3.28	.278	16	.195	6	17	0.4
1925*	Pit-N	19	10	.655	35	31	20	1	1	255^1	272	128	104	11	8	67	87	1.328	3.67	122	3.54	.273	17	.175	17	18	1.5
1926	Pit-N	**20**	9	.690	36	31	15	1	0	226^2	254	125	100	10	4	52	54	1.350	3.97	99	3.70	.287	20	.227	-5	13	-0.5
1927*	Pit-N	19	10	.655	40	**38**	**25**	2	0	299^1	315	131	113	11	8	66	84	1.273	3.40	121	3.27	.273	18	.157	22	20	1.7
1928	Pit-N	1	1	.500	4	2	1	0	0	10	18	11	9	0	0	5	3	2.300	8.10	50	8.06	.383	2	.500	-5	0	-0.4
1929	Pit-N	0	0	....	1	0	0	0	0	0^2	2	1	1	0	0	1	0	4.500	13.50	35	21.38	.500	0	.000	-1	0	-0.1
Total	**15**	**188**	**180**	**.511**	**490**	**406**	**219**	**25**	**7**	**3160^2**	**3280**	**1491**	**1185**	**84**	**90**	**956**	**1063**	**1.340**	**3.37**	**105**	**3.48**	**.273**	**201**	**.180**	**53**	**191**	**3.1**

• MEADOWS, Rufus Rufus Rivers Meadows b: 8/25/1907, Chase City, VA d: 5/10/1970, Wichita, KS BL/TL, 5'11", 175 lbs. Deb: 4/23/1926

YEAR	TM-L	W	L	PCT	G	GS	CG	SH	SV	IP	H	R	ER	HR	HB	BB	SO	RAT	ERA	ERA+	CERA	OAV	BH	AVG	PR+	WS	TPW
1926	Cin-N	0	0	....	1	0	0	0	0	0^1	0	0	0	0	0	0	0	.000	0.00	....	0.00	.000	0	.000	0	0	0.0

• MEADS, Dave David Donald Meads b: 1/7/1964, Montclair, NJ BL/TL, 6'.5", 175 lbs. Deb: 4/13/1987

YEAR	TM-L	W	L	PCT	G	GS	CG	SH	SV	IP	H	R	ER	HR	HB	BB	SO	RAT	ERA	ERA+	CERA	OAV	BH	AVG	PR+	WS	TPW
1987	Hou-N	5	3	.625	45	0	0	0	0	48^2	60	31	30	8	1	16	32	1.562	5.55	71	5.91	.321	1	.333	-9	1	-0.8
1988	Hou-N	3	1	.750	22	2	0	0	0	39^2	37	20	14	4	0	14	27	1.286	3.18	105	3.43	.240	1	.250	1	2	0.2
Total	**2**	**8**	**4**	**.667**	**67**	**2**	**0**	**0**	**0**	**88^1**	**97**	**51**	**44**	**12**	**1**	**30**	**59**	**1.438**	**4.48**	**83**	**4.80**	**.284**	**2**	**.286**	**-8**	**3**	**-0.6**

• MEAKIM, George George Clinton Meakim b: 7/11/1865, Brooklyn, NY d: 2/17/1923, Queens, NY BR/TR, 5'7.5", 154 lbs. Deb: 5/2/1890

YEAR	TM-L	W	L	PCT	G	GS	CG	SH	SV	IP	H	R	ER	HR	HB	BB	SO	RAT	ERA	ERA+	CERA	OAV	BH	AVG	PR+	WS	TPW
1890*	Lou-a	12	7	.632	28	21	16	3	1	192	173	100	62	4	8	63	123	1.229	2.91	132	....	.233	11	.153	19	17	1.6
1891	Phi-a	1	4	.200	6	6	4	0	0	35	51	45	27	1	0	22	13	2.086	6.94	55	....	.329	3	.200	-12	0	-1.0
1892	Chi-N	0	1	.000	1	1	1	0	0	9	18	14	11	0	0	2	0	2.222	11.00	30	8.63	.400	2	.400	-8	0	-0.7
	Cin-N	1	1	.500	3	3	1	0	0	13^2	19	18	13	1	0	9	4	2.049	8.56	38	7.10	.317	0	.000	-8	0	-0.8
	Yr.	1	2	.333	4	4	2	0	0	22^2	37	32	24	1	0	11	4	2.118	9.53	35	7.71	.353	2	.200	-16	0	-1.5
1895	Lou-N	1	0	1.000	1	1	1	0	0	7	7	2	2	0	0	4	2	1.571	2.57	180	3.85	.257	1	.333	2	1	0.2
Total	**4**	**15**	**13**	**.536**	**39**	**32**	**23**	**3**	**1**	**256^2**	**268**	**179**	**115**	**6**	**8**	**100**	**142**	**1.434**	**4.03**	**92**	**0.79**	**.261**	**17**	**.170**	**-7**	**18**	**-0.7**

• MEARS, Chris Christopher Peter Mears b: 1/20/1978, Ottawa, Canada BR/TR, 6'4", 190 lbs. Deb: 6/29/2003

YEAR	TM-L	W	L	PCT	G	GS	CG	SH	SV	IP	H	R	ER	HR	HB	BB	SO	RAT	ERA	ERA+	CERA	OAV	BH	AVG	PR+	WS	TPW
2003	Det-A	1	3	.250	29	3	0	0	5	41^1	50	28	25	5	3	11	21	1.476	5.44	79	5.38	.307	0	....	-5	1	-0.5

• MECHE, Gil Gilbert Allen Meche b: 9/8/1978, Lafayette, LA BR/TR, 6'3", 200 lbs. Deb: 7/6/1999

YEAR	TM-L	W	L	PCT	G	GS	CG	SH	SV	IP	H	R	ER	HR	HB	BB	SO	RAT	ERA	ERA+	CERA	OAV	BH	AVG	PR+	WS	TPW
1999	Sea-A	8	4	.667	16	15	0	0	0	85^2	73	48	45	9	2	57	47	1.518	4.73	105	4.47	.237	0	....	3	6	0.3
2000	Sea-A	4	4	.500	15	15	1	1	0	85^2	75	37	36	7	1	40	60	1.342	3.78	120	3.60	.240	0	....	6	6	0.6
2003	Sea-A	15	13	.536	32	32	1	0	0	186^1	187	97	95	30	3	63	130	1.342	4.59	94	4.39	.263	1	.200	-11	9	-1.0
Total	**3**	**27**	**21**	**.563**	**63**	**62**	**2**	**1**	**0**	**357^2**	**335**	**182**	**176**	**46**	**6**	**160**	**237**	**1.384**	**4.43**	**102**	**4.22**	**.252**	**1**	**.200**	**-1**	**21**	**-0.2**

• MECIR, Jim James Jason Mecir b: 5/16/1970, Bayside, NY BB/TR, 6'1", 195 lbs. Deb: 9/4/1995

YEAR	TM-L	W	L	PCT	G	GS	CG	SH	SV	IP	H	R	ER	HR	HB	BB	SO	RAT	ERA	ERA+	CERA	OAV	BH	AVG	PR+	WS	TPW
1995	Sea-A	0	0	....	2	0	0	0	0	4^2	5	1	0	0	0	2	3	1.500	0.00	....	3.75	.263	0	....	3	1	0.2
1996	NY-A	1	1	.500	26	0	0	0	0	40^1	42	24	23	6	0	23	38	1.612	5.13	96	5.10	.275	0	....	-0	2	0.0
1997	NY-A	0	4	.000	25	0	0	0	0	33^2	36	23	22	5	2	10	25	1.366	5.88	76	4.73	.279	0	....	-5	0	-0.5
1998	TB-A	7	2	.778	68	0	0	0	0	84	68	30	29	6	3	33	77	1.202	3.11	154	2.95	.225	0	.000	12	9	1.2
1999	TB-A	0	1	.000	17	0	0	0	0	20^2	15	7	6	0	1	14	15	1.403	2.61	190	3.05	.203	0	....	5	2	0.5
2000	TB-A	7	2	.778	38	0	0	0	1	49^2	35	17	17	2	1	22	33	1.148	3.08	160	2.44	.201	0	....	10	7	0.9
	*Oak-A	3	1	.750	25	0	0	0	4	35^1	35	14	11	2	1	14	37	1.387	2.80	169	3.71	.255	0	....	8	5	0.7
	Yr.	10	3	.769	63	0	0	0	5	85	70	31	28	4	2	36	70	1.247	2.96	164	2.97	.225	0	....	18	12	1.6
2001*	Oak-A	2	8	.200	54	0	0	0	3	63	54	25	24	4	1	26	61	1.270	3.43	129	3.00	.231	0	....	7	6	0.6
2002*	Oak-A	6	4	.600	61	0	0	0	1	67^2	68	36	32	5	4	29	53	1.433	4.26	103	4.05	.259	0	....	1	6	0.1
2003*	Oak-A	2	3	.400	41	0	0	0	1	37	40	25	23	4	1	16	25	1.514	5.59	81	4.77	.280	0	....	-4	1	-0.4
Total	**9**	**28**	**26**	**.519**	**357**	**0**	**0**	**0**	**10**	**436**	**398**	**202**	**187**	**34**	**14**	**189**	**367**	**1.346**	**3.86**	**120**	**3.64**	**.244**	**0**	**.000**	**37**	**39**	**3.4**

• MEDICH, Doc George Francis Medich b: 12/9/1948, Aliquippa, PA BR/TR, 6'5", 227 lbs. Deb: 9/5/1972

YEAR	TM-L	W	L	PCT	G	GS	CG	SH	SV	IP	H	R	ER	HR	HB	BB	SO	RAT	ERA	ERA+	CERA	OAV	BH	AVG	PR+	WS	TPW
1972	NY-A	0	0	....	1	1	0	0	0	0	2	2	0	0	0	2	0	....	....	....	∞	1.000	0	....	0	0	0.0
1973	NY-A	14	9	.609	34	32	11	3	0	235	217	84	77	20	3	74	145	1.238	2.95	124	3.20	.241	0	....	16	18	1.7
1974	NY-A	19	15	.559	38	38	17	4	0	279^2	275	122	112	24	8	91	154	1.309	3.60	97	3.72	.259	0	....	-9	16	-0.9
1975	NY-A	16	16	.500	38	37	15	2	0	272^1	271	115	106	25	1	72	132	1.259	3.50	104	3.52	.264	0	....	-4	16	-0.4
1976	Pit-N	8	11	.421	29	26	3	0	0	179	193	80	70	10	2	48	86	1.346	3.52	99	3.67	.281	5	.096	-1	8	-0.3
1977	Oak-A	10	6	.625	26	25	1	0	0	147^2	155	89	77	19	3	49	74	1.381	4.69	86	4.26	.265	0	....	-9	5	-0.9
	Sea-A	2	0	1.000	3	3	1	0	0	22^1	26	9	9	1	2	4	3	1.343	3.63	113	4.02	.286	0	....	1	2	0.1
	Yr.	12	6	.667	29	28	2	0	0	170	181	98	86	20	5	53	77	1.376	4.55	89	4.23	.268	0	....	-8	7	-0.8
	NY-N	0	1	.000	1	1	0	0	0	7	6	3	3	0	0	1	3	1.000	3.86	97	2.05	.261	0	.000	-0	0	0.0
1978	Tex-A	9	8	.529	28	22	6	2	2	171	166	78	71	10	3	52	71	1.275	3.74	100	3.33	.255	0	....	1	10	0.1
1979	Tex-A	10	7	.588	29	19	4	1	0	149	156	78	69	9	4	49	58	1.376	4.17	99	3.82	.269	0	....	-2	8	-0.2
1980	Tex-A	14	11	.560	34	32	6	0	0	204^1	230	104	89	13	3	56	91	1.400	3.92	99	4.10	.285	0	....	2	11	0.2
1981	Tex-A	10	6	.625	20	20	4	**4**	0	143^1	136	51	49	8	2	33	65	1.179	3.08	113	2.90	.252	0	....	4	10	0.4
1982	Tex-A	7	11	.389	21	21	2	0	0	122^2	146	73	69	8	3	61	37	1.688	5.06	76	5.41	.307	0	....	-15	4	-1.5
	*Mil-A	5	4	.556	10	10	1	0	0	63	57	37	35	4	1	32	36	1.413	5.00	76	3.77	.242	0	....	-9	2	-0.9
	Yr.	12	15	.444	31	31	3	0	0	185^2	203	110	104	12	4	93	73	1.594	5.04	76	4.85	.286	0	....	-25	6	-2.5
Total	**11**	**124**	**105**	**.541**	**312**	**287**	**71**	**16**	**2**	**1996^1**	**2036**	**925**	**836**	**151**	**35**	**624**	**955**	**1.332**	**3.77**	**99**	**3.72**	**.266**	**5**	**.093**	**-26**	**110**	**-2.8**

• MEDINA, Rafael Rafael Eduardo Medina b: 2/15/1975, Panama City, Panama BR/TR, 6'3", 240 lbs. Deb: 4/2/1998

YEAR	TM-L	W	L	PCT	G	GS	CG	SH	SV	IP	H	R	ER	HR	HB	BB	SO	RAT	ERA	ERA+	CERA	OAV	BH	AVG	PR+	WS	TPW
1998	Fla-N	2	6	.250	12	12	0	0	0	67^1	76	50	45	8	3	52	49	1.901	6.01	68	6.59	.289	1	.053	-14	0	-1.5
1999	Fla-N	1	1	.500	20	0	0	0	0	23^1	20	15	15	3	1	20	16	1.714	5.79	75	5.23	.227	0	....	-4	0	-0.3
Total	**2**	**3**	**7**	**.300**	**32**	**12**	**0**	**0**	**0**	**90^2**	**96**	**65**	**60**	**11**	**4**	**72**	**65**	**1.853**	**5.96**	**70**	**6.24**	**.274**	**1**	**.053**	**-18**	**0**	**-1.9**

• MEDLINGER, Irv Irving John Medlinger b: 6/18/1927, Chicago, IL d: 9/3/1975, Wheeling, IL BL/TL, 5'11", 185 lbs. Deb: 4/20/1949

YEAR	TM-L	W	L	PCT	G	GS	CG	SH	SV	IP	H	R	ER	HR	HB	BB	SO	RAT	ERA	ERA+	CERA	OAV	BH	AVG	PR+	WS	TPW
1949	StL-A	0	0	....	3	0	0	0	0	4	11	13	12	1	0	3	4	3.500	27.00	17	19.01	.478	0	....	-10	0	-1.0
1951	StL-A	0	0	....	6	0	0	0	0	9^2	10	10	9	1	0	12	5	2.276	8.38	52	7.35	.270	0	....	-4	0	-0.4
Total	**2**	**0**	**0**	**....**	**9**	**0**	**0**	**0**	**0**	**13^2**	**21**	**23**	**21**	**2**	**0**	**15**	**9**	**2.634**	**13.83**	**32**	**10.76**	**.350**	**0**	**....**	**-14**	**0**	**-1.4**

• MEDVIN, Scott Scott Howard Medvin b: 9/16/1961, North Olmsted, OH BR/TR, 6'1", 195 lbs. Deb: 5/11/1988

YEAR	TM-L	W	L	PCT	G	GS	CG	SH	SV	IP	H	R	ER	HR	HB	BB	SO	RAT	ERA	ERA+	CERA	OAV	BH	AVG	PR+	WS	TPW
1988	Pit-N	3	0	1.000	17	0	0	0	0	27^2	23	16	15	1	1	9	16	1.157	4.88	70	2.57	.230	0	.000	-5	1	-0.5
1989	Pit-N	0	1	.000	6	0	0	0	0	6^1	6	5	4	0	0	5	4	1.737	5.68	59	3.81	.240	0	....	-2	0	-0.2
1990	Sea-A	0	1	.000	5	0	0	0	0	4^1	7	4	3	0	1	2	1	2.077	6.23	63	8.41	.368	0	....	-1	0	-0.1
Total	**3**	**3**	**2**	**.600**	**28**	**0**	**0**	**0**	**0**	**38^1**	**36**	**25**	**22**	**1**	**2**	**16**	**21**	**1.357**	**5.17**	**67**	**3.43**	**.250**	**0**	**.000**	**-7**	**1**	**-0.8**

• MEEGAN, Pete Peter James "Steady Pete" Meegan b: 11/13/1863, San Francisco, CA d: 3/15/1905, San Francisco, CA Deb: 8/12/1884

YEAR	TM-L	W	L	PCT	G	GS	CG	SH	SV	IP	H	R	ER	HR	HB	BB	SO	RAT	ERA	ERA+	CERA	OAV	BH	AVG	PR+	WS	TPW
1884	Ric-a	7	12	.368	22	22	22	1	0	179	177	130	86	7	14	29	106	1.151	4.32	76	....	.244	12	.160	-19	5	-1.9
1885	Pit-a	7	8	.467	18	16	14	1	0	146	146	90	55	1	10	38	58	1.260	3.39	95	....	.249	13	.194	-4	10	-0.2
Total	**2**	**14**	**20**	**.412**	**40**	**38**	**36**	**2**	**0**	**325**	**323**	**220**	**141**	**8**	**24**	**67**	**164**	**1.200**	**3.90**	**84**	**....**	**.247**	**25**	**.176**	**-23**	**15**	**-2.1**

• MEEHAN, Bill William Thomas Meehan b: 9/4/1889, Osceola Mills, PA d: 10/8/1982, Douglas, WY BR/TR, 5'9", 155 lbs. Deb: 9/17/1915

YEAR	TM-L	W	L	PCT	G	GS	CG	SH	SV	IP	H	R	ER	HR	HB	BB	SO	RAT	ERA	ERA+	CERA	OAV	BH	AVG	PR+	WS	TPW
1915	Phi-A	0	1	.000	1	1	0	0	0	4	7	5	5	0	0	3	4	2.500	11.25	26	9.34	.389	1	1.000	-4	0	-0.3

• MEEKER, Roy Charles Roy Meeker b: 9/15/1900, Lead Mine, MO d: 3/25/1929, Orlando, FL BL/TL, 5'9", 175 lbs. Deb: 9/22/1923

YEAR	TM-L	W	L	PCT	G	GS	CG	SH	SV	IP	H	R	ER	HR	HB	BB	SO	RAT	ERA	ERA+	CERA	OAV	BH	AVG	PR+	WS	TPW
1923	Phi-A	3	0	1.000	5	2	2	0	0	25	24	10	10	0	0	13	12	1.480	3.60	114	3.40	.253	1	.111	2	2	0.1
1924	Phi-A	5	12	.294	30	14	5	1	0	146	166	86	76	7	5	81	37	1.692	4.68	91	5.02	.288	11	.229	-5	7	-0.5
1926	Cin-N	0	2	.000	7	1	1	0	0	21	24	18	15	1	0	9	5	1.571	6.43	57	4.83	.324	0	.000	-6	0	-0.7
Total	**3**	**8**	**14**	**.364**	**42**	**17**	**8**	**1**	**0**	**192**	**214**	**114**	**101**	**8**	**5**	**103**	**54**	**1.651**	**4.73**	**88**	**4.78**	**.287**	**12**	**.190**	**-9**	**9**	**-1.1**

YEAR TM-L	W	L	PCT	G	GS	CG	SH	SV	IP	H	R	ER	HR	HB	BB	SO	RAT	ERA	ERA+	CERA	OAV	BH	AVG	PR+	WS	TPW
• MEEKIN, Jouett	George Jouett Meekin b: 2/21/1867, New Albany, IN d: 12/14/1944, New Albany, IN BR/TR, 6'1", 180 lbs. Deb: 6/13/1891 U																									
1891 Lou-a	10	16	.385	29	26	25	2	0	221^{1}	223	154	109	2	6	106	141	1.486	4.43	82	....	.253	21	.216	-21	12	-1.4
1892 Lou-N	7	10	.412	19	18	17	0	0	156^{1}	168	108	70	3	4	78	67	1.574	4.03	76	4.24	.264	5	.078	-18	5	-2.1
Was-N	3	10	.231	14	14	13	1	0	112	112	91	43	2	6	48	58	1.429	3.46	94	3.68	.250	6	.133	-2	4	-0.2
Yr.	10	20	.333	33	32	30	1	0	268^{1}	280	199	113	5	10	126	125	1.513	3.79	83	4.01	.258	11	.101	-20	9	-2.3
1893 Was-N	10	15	.400	31	28	24	1	0	245	289	201	135	6	7	140	91	1.751	4.96	93	5.15	.285	29	.257	-3	7	0.0
1894* NY-N	33	9	.786	52	48	40	1	2	409	404	240	168	13	11	176	137	1.418	3.70	142	3.59	.256	48	.282	66	48	5.6
1895 NY-N	16	11	.593	29	29	24	1	0	225^{2}	296	170	133	10	9	73	76	1.635	5.30	87	5.21	.312	28	.292	-18	14	-1.1
1896 NY-N	26	14	.650	42	41	34	0	0	334^{1}	378	205	142	8	15	127	110	1.510	3.82	110	4.24	.283	43	.299	12	27	2.1
1897 NY-N	20	11	.645	37	34	30	2	0	303^{2}	328	176	127	9	8	99	83	1.406	3.76	110	3.75	.274	41	.299	13	23	1.6
1898 NY-N	16	18	.471	38	37	34	1	0	320	329	185	134	9	12	108	82	1.366	3.77	92	3.54	.264	27	.209	-11	15	-0.9
1899 NY-N	5	11	.313	18	18	16	0	0	148^{1}	169	103	72	4	8	70	30	1.611	4.37	86	4.67	.286	12	.207	-12	6	-0.9
Bos-N	7	6	.538	13	13	12	0	0	108	111	52	34	0	2	23	23	1.241	2.83	147	2.87	.266	7	.171	12	10	1.0
Yr.	12	17	.414	31	31	28	0	0	256^{1}	280	155	106	4	10	93	53	1.455	3.72	104	3.91	.278	19	.192	0	16	0.0
1900 Pit-N	0	2	.000	2	2	1	0	0	13	20	21	10	1	1	8	3	2.154	6.92	52	8.24	.351	0	.000	-5	0	-0.5
Total 10	153	133	.535	324	308	270	9	2	2596^{2}	2827	1706	1177	67	89	1056	901	1.495	4.08	100	3.77	.273	267	.243	14	171	3.0
• MEELER, Phil	Charles Phillip Meeler b: 7/3/1948, South Boston, VA BR/TR, 6'5", 215 lbs. Deb: 5/10/1972																									
1972 Det-A	0	1	.000	7	0	0	0	0	8^{1}	10	6	4	0	0	7	5	2.040	4.32	73	5.79	.303	0	.000	-1	0	-0.2
• MEERS, Russ	Russell Harlan "Babe" Meers b: 11/28/1918, Tilton, IL d: 11/16/1994, Lancaster, PA BL/TL, 5'10", 170 lbs. Deb: 9/28/1941																									
1941 Chi-N	0	1	.000	1	1	0	0	0	8	5	2	1	0	1	0	5	.625	1.13	312	1.02	.172	0	.000	2	1	0.2
1946 Chi-N	1	2	.333	7	2	0	0	0	11^{1}	10	6	4	0	0	10	2	1.765	3.18	105	4.21	.238	1	1.000	0	1	0.1
1947 Chi-N	2	0	1.000	35	1	0	0	0	64^{1}	61	34	32	5	2	38	28	1.539	4.48	88	4.49	.263	2	.143	-4	3	-0.4
Total 3	3	3	.500	43	4	0	0	0	83^{2}	76	42	37	5	3	48	35	1.482	3.98	97	4.12	.251	3	.176	-1	5	-0.1
• MEINE, Heinie	Henry William "The Count Of Luxemburg" Meine b: 5/1/1896, St. Louis, MO d: 3/18/1968, St. Louis, MO BR/TR, 5'11", 180 lbs. Deb: 8/16/1922																									
1922 StL-A	0	0	....	1	0	0	0	0	4	5	3	2	1	0	2	0	1.750	4.50	92	7.30	.313	0	.000	-0	0	0.0
1929 Pit-N	7	6	.538	22	13	7	1	1	108	120	62	54	4	7	34	19	1.426	4.50	106	4.12	.291	4	.103	1	6	-0.1
1930 Pit-N	6	8	.429	20	16	4	0	1	117^{1}	168	89	80	6	5	44	18	1.807	6.14	81	6.25	.346	5	.122	-15	3	-1.6
1931 Pit-N	**19**	13	.594	36	**35**	22	3	0	**284**	278	121	94	8	7	87	58	1.285	2.98	129	3.11	.254	14	.146	23	22	2.0
1932 Pit-N	12	9	.571	28	25	13	1	1	172^{1}	193	92	74	6	3	45	32	1.381	3.86	99	3.66	.278	10	.164	-2	9	-0.4
1933 Pit-N	15	8	.652	32	29	12	2	0	207^{1}	227	99	84	10	2	50	50	1.336	3.65	91	3.57	.278	13	.173	-9	9	-1.1
1934 Pit-N	7	6	.538	26	14	2	0	0	106^{1}	134	60	51	12	1	25	22	1.495	4.32	95	4.93	.306	3	.107	-1	5	-0.2
Total 7	66	50	.569	165	132	60	7	3	999^{1}	1125	526	439	47	25	287	199	1.413	3.95	101	3.99	.284	49	.144	-4	54	-1.4
• MEINKE, Frank	Frank Louis Meinke b: 10/18/1863, Chicago, IL d: 11/8/1931, Chicago, IL BR, 5'10.5", 172 lbs. Deb: 5/1/1884 ♦																									
1884 Det-N	8	23	.258	35	31	31	1	0	289	341	217	102	10	....	63	124	1.398	3.18	91	....	.278	56	.164	1	11	-1.3
1885 Det-N	0	1	.000	1	1	0	0	0	5	13	12	2	0	....	4	0	3.400	3.60	79	....	.462	0	.000	-0	0	-0.1
Total 2	8	24	.250	36	32	31	1	0	294	354	229	104	10	....	67	124	1.432	3.18	91	....	.282	56	.163	1	11	-1.4
• MELENDEZ, Jose	Jose Luis (Garcia) Melendez b: 9/2/1965, Naguabo, Puerto Rico BR/TR, 6'2", 175 lbs. Deb: 9/11/1990																									
1990 Sea-A	0	0	....	3	0	0	0	0	5^{1}	8	8	7	2	1	3	7	2.063	11.81	33	11.06	.333	0	....	-5	0	-0.5
1991 SD-N	8	5	.615	31	9	0	0	3	93^{2}	77	35	34	11	1	24	60	1.078	3.27	116	2.66	.221	2	.100	5	8	0.5
1992 SD-N	6	7	.462	56	3	0	0	0	89^{1}	82	32	29	9	3	20	82	1.142	2.92	122	3.01	.249	0	.000	7	8	0.7
1993 Bos-A	2	1	.667	9	0	0	0	0	16	10	4	4	2	0	5	14	.938	2.25	205	1.74	.179	0	....	4	2	0.4
1994 Bos-A	0	1	.000	10	0	0	0	0	16^{1}	20	11	11	3	2	8	9	1.714	6.06	83	6.87	.323	0	....	-2	0	-0.2
Total 5	16	14	.533	109	12	0	0	3	220^{2}	197	90	85	27	7	60	172	1.165	3.47	112	3.25	.241	2	.080	9	18	0.9
• MELTER, Steve	Stephen Blazius Melter b: 1/2/1886, Cherokee, IA d: 1/28/1962, Mishawaka, IN BR/TR, 6'2", 180 lbs. Deb: 6/27/1909																									
1909 StL-N	0	1	.000	23	1	0	0	3	64^{1}	79	49	25	1	2	20	24	1.539	3.50	72	4.79	.322	2	.133	-5	1	-0.6
• MELTON, Cliff	Clifford George "Mickey Mouse,Mountain Music" Melton b: 1/3/1912, Brevard, NC d: 7/28/1986, Baltimore, MD BL/TL, 6'5.5", 203 lbs. Deb: 4/25/1937																									
1937* NY-N	20	9	.690	46	27	14	2	**7**	248	216	90	72	9	6	55	142	1.093	2.61	149	**2.37**	.233	10	.122	**30**	25	2.5
1938 NY-N	14	14	.500	36	31	10	1	0	243	266	126	105	19	1	61	101	1.346	3.89	97	3.79	.276	14	.175	-4	12	-0.5
1939 NY-N	12	15	.444	41	23	9	2	5	207^{1}	214	94	82	7	4	65	95	1.346	3.56	110	3.45	.269	12	.182	8	15	0.7
1940 NY-N	10	11	.476	37	21	4	1	2	166^{2}	185	103	91	9	3	68	91	1.518	4.91	79	4.36	.285	12	.222	-18	5	-1.7
1941 NY-N	8	11	.421	42	22	9	3	1	194^{1}	181	83	65	14	2	61	100	1.245	3.01	123	3.12	.246	7	.115	14	14	1.1
1942 NY-N★	11	5	.688	23	17	12	2	1	143^{2}	122	51	42	9	2	33	61	1.079	2.63	128	2.43	.229	11	.234	10	12	1.3
1943 NY-N	9	13	.409	34	28	6	2	0	186^{1}	184	85	66	7	3	69	55	1.358	3.19	108	3.38	.257	8	.148	8	10	0.9
1944 NY-N	2	2	.500	13	10	1	0	0	64^{1}	78	40	29	5	1	19	15	1.508	4.06	90	4.57	.294	3	.120	-3	2	-0.5
Total 8	86	80	.518	272	179	65	13	16	1453^{2}	1446	672	552	79	22	431	660	1.291	3.42	109	3.32	.259	77	.164	45	95	3.7
• MELTON, Rube	Reuben Franklin Melton b: 2/27/1917, Cramerton, NC d: 9/11/1971, Greer, SC BR/TR, 6'5", 205 lbs. Deb: 4/17/1941																									
1941 Phi-N	1	5	.167	25	5	2	0	0	83^{2}	81	48	44	7	0	47	57	1.530	4.73	78	4.29	.258	2	.105	-9	2	-1.1
1942 Phi-N	9	20	.310	42	29	10	1	4	209^{1}	180	95	86	7	3	114	107	1.404	3.70	89	3.31	.234	8	.123	-9	13	-1.1
1943 Bro-N	5	8	.385	30	17	4	2	0	119^{1}	106	62	52	3	5	79	63	1.550	3.92	86	3.93	.243	4	.105	-6	3	-0.9
1944 Bro-N	9	13	.409	37	23	6	1	0	187^{1}	178	92	72	1	2	96	91	1.463	3.46	103	3.44	.254	7	.123	8	7	0.6
1946 Bro-N	6	3	.667	24	12	3	2	1	99^{2}	72	27	22	3	3	52	44	1.244	1.99	170	2.61	.206	3	.107	14	9	1.4
1947 Bro-N	0	1	.000	4	1	0	0	0	4^{2}	7	7	7	1	0	7	1	3.000	13.50	31	13.03	.350	1	1.000	-5	0	-0.4
Total 6	30	50	.375	162	87	25	6	5	704	624	331	283	22	13	395	363	1.447	3.62	96	3.53	.241	25	.120	-6	34	-1.5
• MENDOZA, Mike	Michael Joseph Mendoza b: 11/26/1955, Inglewood, CA BR/TR, 6'5", 215 lbs. Deb: 9/7/1979																									
1979 Hou-N	0	0	....	1	0	0	0	0	1	0	0	0	0	0	0	0	.000	0.00	....	0.00	.000	0	....	0	0	0.0
• MENDOZA, Ramiro	Ramiro Mendoza b: 6/15/1972, Los Santos, Panama BR/TR, 6'2", 154 lbs. Deb: 5/25/1996																									
1996 NY-A	4	5	.444	12	11	0	0	0	53	80	43	40	5	4	10	34	1.698	6.79	73	6.42	.343	0	....	-10	1	-0.9
1997* NY-A	8	6	.571	39	15	0	0	2	133^{2}	157	67	63	15	5	28	82	1.384	4.24	105	4.52	.292	0	....	4	7	0.4
1998* NY-A	10	2	.833	41	14	1	1	1	130^{1}	131	50	47	9	9	30	56	1.235	3.25	135	3.44	.264	0	....	14	12	1.3
1999* NY-A	9	9	.500	53	6	0	0	3	123^{2}	141	68	59	13	3	27	80	1.358	4.29	110	4.19	.284	0	....	7	8	0.6
2000 NY-A	7	4	.636	14	9	1	1	0	65^{2}	66	32	31	9	4	20	30	1.310	4.25	114	4.21	.260	0	....	5	5	0.5
2001* NY-A	8	4	.667	56	2	0	0	6	100^{2}	89	44	42	9	2	23	70	1.113	3.75	120	2.84	.241	0	.000	10	10	1.0
2002* NY-A	8	4	.667	62	0	0	0	4	91^{2}	102	43	35	8	2	16	61	1.287	3.44	127	3.70	.275	0	.000	12	8	1.2
2003 Bos-A	3	5	.375	37	5	0	0	0	66^{2}	98	51	50	10	5	20	36	1.770	6.75	68	7.22	.349	0	....	-15	0	-1.4
Total 8	57	39	.594	314	62	2	2	16	765^{1}	864	398	367	78	34	174	449	1.356	4.32	106	4.30	.284	0	.000	29	51	2.7
• MENEFEE, Jock	John Menefee b: 1/15/1868, Rowlesburg, WV d: 3/11/1953, Belle Vernon, PA BR/TR, 6', 165 lbs. Deb: 8/17/1892 U ♦																									
1892 Pit-N	0	0	....	1	0	0	0	0	4	10	6	5	0	0	2	0	3.000	11.25	29	13.42	.455	0	.000	-4	0	-0.4
1893 Lou-N	8	7	.533	15	15	14	1	0	129^{1}	150	95	61	3	3	40	30	1.469	4.24	103	4.07	.282	20	.274	4	10	0.7
1894 Lou-N	8	17	.320	28	24	20	1	0	211^{2}	258	153	101	3	9	50	43	1.455	4.29	119	4.14	.298	13	.165	19	10	1.1
Pit-N	5	8	.385	13	13	13	0	0	111^{2}	159	95	67	4	2	39	33	1.773	5.40	97	5.83	.331	12	.255	-2	6	-0.1
Yr.	13	25	.342	41	37	33	1	0	323^{1}	417	248	168	7	11	89	76	1.565	4.68	110	4.72	.310	25	.198	17	16	1.0
1895 Pit-N	0	1	.000	2	1	0	0	0	1^{2}	2	8	3	0	1	7	0	5.400	16.20	28	21.72	.293	0	....	-2	0	-0.2
1898 NY-N	0	1	.000	1	1	1	0	0	9^{1}	11	8	5	0	2	2	3	1.393	4.82	72	4.33	.291	0	.000	-1	0	-0.2
1900 Chi-N	9	4	.692	16	13	11	0	0	117	140	74	50	1	10	35	30	1.496	3.85	94	4.35	.296	5	.109	-1	6	-0.4
1901 Chi-N	8	12	.400	21	20	19	0	0	182^{1}	201	102	77	4	6	34	55	1.289	3.80	85	3.36	.278	39	.257	-10	11	-0.8
1902 Chi-N	12	10	.545	22	21	20	4	0	197^{1}	201	81	53	1	6	26	60	1.150	2.42	112	2.64	.264	50	.231	6	14	0.0
1903 Chi-N	8	10	.444	20	17	13	1	0	147	157	85	49	3	6	38	39	1.327	3.00	104	3.51	.275	13	.203	-0	7	0.0
Total 9	58	70	.453	139	125	111	7	0	1111^{1}	1289	707	471	19	45	273	293	1.406	3.81	100	3.91	.288	152	.222	9	64	-0.2

YEAR TM-L	W	L	PCT	G	GS	CG	SH	SV	IP	H	R	ER	HR	HB	BB	SO	RAT	ERA	ERA+	CERA	OAV	BH	AVG	PR+	WS	TPW
• MENENDEZ, Tony	Antonio Gustavo (Remon) Menendez b: 2/20/1965, Havana, Cuba BR/TR, 6'2", 190 lbs. Deb: 6/22/1992																									
1992 Cin-N	1	0	1.000	3	0	0	0	0	4^{2}	1	1	1	1	0	0	5	.214	1.93	186	0.34	.067	0	....	1	1	0.1
1993 Pit-N	2	0	1.000	14	0	0	0	0	21	20	8	7	4	1	4	13	1.143	3.00	135	3.84	.256	0	.000	2	2	0.2
1994 SF-N	0	1	.000	6	0	0	0	0	3^{1}	8	8	8	2	0	2	2	3.000	21.60	19	20.67	.471	0	....	-7	0	-0.7
Total 3	3	1	.750	23	0	0	0	0	29	29	17	16	7	1	6	20	1.207	4.97	80	5.21	.264	0	.000	-4	3	-0.3
• MENHART, Paul	Paul Gerard Menhart b: 3/25/1969, St. Louis, MO BR/TR, 6'2", 190 lbs. Deb: 4/27/1995																									
1995 Tor-A	1	4	.200	21	9	1	0	0	78^{2}	72	49	43	9	6	47	50	1.513	4.92	96	4.75	.248	0	....	-2	3	-0.2
1996 Sea-A	2	2	.500	11	6	0	0	0	42	55	36	34	9	2	25	18	1.905	7.29	68	8.27	.327	0	....	-11	0	-1.0
1997 SD-N	2	3	.400	9	8	0	0	0	44	42	23	23	6	0	13	22	1.250	4.70	82	3.74	.256	0	.000	-4	1	-0.5
Total 3	5	9	.357	41	23	1	0	0	164^{2}	169	108	100	24	8	85	90	1.543	5.47	83	5.38	.272	0	.000	-17	4	-1.7
• MEOLA, Mike	Emile Michael Meola b: 10/19/1905, New York, NY d: 9/1/1976, Fairlawn, NJ BR/TR, 5'11", 175 lbs. Deb: 4/24/1933																									
1933 Bos-A	0	0	....	3	0	0	0	0	2^{1}	5	6	6	0	0	2	1	3.000	23.14	19	12.04	.417	0	....	-5	0	-0.5
1936 StL-A	0	1	.000	9	0	0	0	0	19^{1}	29	20	20	0	1	13	6	2.172	9.31	58	7.67	.358	1	.500	-8	0	-0.7
Bos-A	0	2	.000	6	3	1	0	1	21^{1}	29	17	13	0	1	10	8	1.828	5.48	97	5.49	.326	1	.143	-0	1	-0.1
Yr.	0	3	.000	15	3	1	0	1	40^{2}	58	37	33	0	2	23	14	1.992	7.30	73	6.52	.341	2	.222	-9	1	-0.7
Total 2	0	3	.000	18	3	1	0	1	43	63	43	39	0	2	25	15	2.047	8.16	63	6.82	.346	2	.222	-13	1	-1.2
• MERCADO, Hector	Hector Luis Mercado b: 4/29/1974, Catano, Puerto Rico BL/TL, 6'3", 235 lbs. Deb: 4/4/2000																									
2000 Cin-N	0	0	....	12	0	0	0	0	14	12	7	7	2	0	8	13	1.429	4.50	104	4.32	.240	0	.000	0	1	0.0
2001 Cin-N	3	2	.600	56	0	0	0	0	53	55	27	24	6	0	30	59	1.604	4.08	112	4.99	.266	0	.000	4	3	0.3
2002 Phi-N	2	2	.500	31	3	0	0	0	39	32	21	20	2	3	25	40	1.462	4.62	84	3.86	.224	1	.250	-3	1	-0.3
2003 Phi-N	0	0	....	13	0	0	0	1	18^{2}	18	12	12	5	1	12	15	1.607	5.79	69	6.32	.254	0	.000	-4	0	-0.4
Total 4	5	4	.556	112	3	0	0	1	124^{2}	117	67	63	15	4	75	127	1.540	4.55	93	4.76	.248	1	.111	-3	5	-0.4
• MERCEDES, Jose	Jose Miguel (Santana) Mercedes b: 3/5/1971, El Seibo, Dominican Republic BR/TR, 6'1", 180 lbs. Deb: 5/31/1994																									
1994 Mil-A	2	0	1.000	19	0	0	0	0	31	22	9	8	4	2	16	11	1.226	2.32	217	3.69	.216	0	....	8	4	0.8
1995 Mil-A	0	1	.000	5	0	0	0	0	7^{1}	12	9	8	1	0	8	6	2.727	9.82	51	11.32	.375	0	....	-4	0	-0.4
1996 Mil-A	0	2	.000	11	0	0	0	0	16^{2}	20	18	17	6	0	5	6	1.500	9.18	57	6.70	.294	0	....	-8	0	-0.7
1997 Mil-A	7	10	.412	29	23	2	1	0	159	146	76	67	24	5	53	80	1.252	3.79	122	3.92	.248	0	.000	10	10	0.9
1998 Mil-N	2	2	.500	7	5	0	0	0	32	42	25	24	5	1	9	11	1.594	6.75	63	5.87	.316	1	.091	-9	0	-0.9
2000 Bal-A	14	7	.667	36	20	1	0	0	145^{2}	150	71	65	15	3	64	70	1.469	4.02	117	4.52	.270	0	.000	12	11	1.1
2001 Bal-A	8	17	.320	33	31	2	0	0	184	219	125	119	20	10	63	123	1.533	5.82	74	5.18	.294	0	.000	-33	2	-3.2
2003 Mon-N	0	0	....	5	0	0	0	0	7^{1}	6	3	0	0	0	5	3	1.500	0.00	....	3.58	.231	0	....	4	1	0.4
Total 8	33	39	.458	145	79	5	1	0	583	617	336	308	75	21	223	310	1.441	4.75	95	4.73	.274	1	.053	-20	28	-2.1
• MERCER, Jack	Harry Vernon Mercer b: 3/10/1889, Zanesville, OH d: 6/25/1945, Dayton, OH Deb: 8/2/1910																									
1910 Pit-N	0	0	....	1	0	0	0	0	1	0	0	0	0	0	2	1	2.000	0.00	....	3.72	.000	0	....	0	0	0.0
• MERCER, Mark	Mark Kenneth Mercer b: 5/22/1954, Fort Bragg, NC BL/TL, 6'5", 220 lbs. Deb: 9/1/1981																									
1981 Tex-A	0	1	.000	7	0	0	0	2	7^{2}	7	4	4	1	0	7	8	1.826	4.70	74	5.91	.241	0	....	-1	0	-0.1
• MERCER, Win	George Barclay Mercer b: 6/20/1874, Chester, WV d: 1/12/1903, San Francisco, CA BR/TR, 5'7", 140 lbs. Deb: 4/21/1894 U ♦																									
1894 Was-N	17	23	.425	50	39	30	0	3	339^{1}	445	285	144	9	14	126	72	1.683	3.82	138	5.25	.313	48	.291	62	19	5.0
1895 Was-N	13	23	.361	44	38	32	0	2	313^{1}	432	281	154	17	18	96	85	1.685	4.42	108	5.70	.323	51	.254	18	13	1.0
1896 Was-N	25	18	.581	46	45	38	2	0	366^{1}	456	266	168	10	20	117	94	1.564	4.13	107	4.73	.303	38	.244	19	18	1.7
1897 Was-N	21	20	.512	**47**	**43**	35	**3**	**3**	342	403	219	120	5	28	104	91	1.482	3.16	137	4.30	.291	44	.317	40	27	4.2
1898 Was-N	12	18	.400	33	30	24	0	0	233^{2}	309	181	125	3	18	71	52	**1.626**	4.81	76	5.09	.316	80	.321	-25	13	-1.5
1899 Was-N	7	14	.333	23	21	21	0	0	186	234	128	95	2	6	53	28	1.543	4.60	85	4.47	.307	112	.299	-7	15	-1.3
1900 NY-N	13	17	.433	33	29	26	1	0	242^{2}	303	138	104	5	20	58	39	1.488	3.86	94	4.51	.305	73	.294	-7	20	-0.5
1901 Was-A	9	13	.409	24	22	19	1	1	179^{2}	217	126	91	8	10	50	31	1.486	4.56	80	4.51	.295	42	.300	-17	13	-0.9
1902 Det-A	15	18	.455	35	33	28	4	1	281^{2}	282	129	95	5	10	80	40	1.285	3.04	120	3.15	.261	18	.180	15	19	1.3
Total 9	132	164	.446	335	300	253	11	10	2484^{2}	3081	1753	1096	64	144	755	532	1.544	3.97	105	4.66	.302	506	.285	97	157	8.9
• MERCKER, Kent	Kent Franklin Mercker b: 2/1/1968, Indianapolis, IN BL/TL, 6'1", 195 lbs. Deb: 9/22/1989																									
1989 Atl-N	0	0	....	2	1	0	0	0	4^{1}	8	6	6	0	0	6	4	3.231	12.46	29	13.19	.400	0	.000	-4	0	-0.5
1990 Atl-N	4	7	.364	36	0	0	0	7	48^{1}	43	22	17	6	2	24	39	1.386	3.17	127	4.04	.236	0	.000	6	5	0.6
1991* Atl-N	5	3	.625	50	4	0	0	6	73^{1}	56	23	21	5	1	35	62	1.241	2.58	151	2.88	.211	1	.100	11	9	1.1
1992* Atl-N	3	2	.600	53	0	0	0	6	68^{1}	51	27	26	4	3	35	49	1.259	3.42	107	2.99	.207	0	.000	2	6	0.1
1993* Atl-N	3	1	.750	43	6	0	0	0	66	52	24	21	2	2	36	59	1.333	2.86	140	3.02	.212	0	.000	8	6	0.6
1994 Atl-N	9	4	.692	20	17	2	1	0	112^{1}	90	46	43	16	0	45	111	1.202	3.45	123	3.27	.220	2	.054	11	9	0.9
1995* Atl-N	7	8	.467	29	26	0	0	0	143	140	73	66	16	3	61	102	1.406	4.15	103	4.19	.258	5	.104	3	7	0.2
1996 Bal-A	3	6	.333	14	12	0	0	0	58	73	56	50	12	3	35	22	1.862	7.76	64	7.45	.307	0	....	-18	0	-1.7
Cle-A	1	0	1.000	10	0	0	0	0	11^{2}	10	4	4	1	0	3	7	1.114	3.09	159	2.65	.244	0	....	2	1	0.2
Yr.	4	6	.400	24	12	0	0	0	69^{2}	83	60	54	13	3	38	29	1.737	6.98	71	6.64	.297	0	....	-16	1	-1.4
1997 Cin-N	8	11	.421	28	25	0	0	0	144^{2}	135	65	63	16	2	62	75	1.362	3.92	110	3.91	.250	7	.156	6	9	0.7
1998 StL-N	11	11	.500	30	29	0	0	0	161^{2}	199	99	91	11	3	53	72	1.559	5.07	83	4.96	.310	8	.148	-15	5	-1.4
1999 StL-N	6	5	.545	25	18	0	0	0	103^{2}	125	73	59	16	2	51	64	1.698	5.12	89	6.15	.303	5	.179	-6	4	-0.5
* Bos-A	2	0	1.000	5	5	0	0	0	25^{2}	23	12	10	0	1	13	17	1.403	3.51	142	3.29	.235	0	....	4	2	0.4
2000 Ana-A	1	3	.250	21	7	0	0	0	48^{1}	57	35	35	12	2	29	30	1.779	6.52	78	7.35	.300	0	....	-9	1	-0.8
2002 Col-N	3	1	.750	58	0	0	0	0	44	55	33	30	12	2	22	37	1.750	6.14	78	7.45	.299	0	.000	-6	1	-0.6
2003 Cin-N	0	2	.000	49	0	0	0	0	38^{1}	31	13	10	5	0	25	41	1.461	2.35	182	4.09	.225	0	....	8	4	0.8
* Atl-N	0	0	....	18	0	0	0	1	17	15	3	2	1	0	7	7	1.294	1.06	398	2.95	.231	0	.000	6	2	0.6
Yr.	0	2	.000	67	0	0	0	1	55^{1}	46	16	12	6	0	32	48	1.410	1.95	218	3.74	.227	0	.000	14	6	1.4
Total 14	66	64	.508	491	150	2	1	20	1168^{2}	1163	614	554	135	26	542	798	1.459	4.27	102	4.51	.261	28	.114	9	71	0.7
• MERENA, Spike	John Joseph Merena b: 11/18/1909, Paterson, NJ d: 3/9/1977, Bridgeport, CT BL/TL, 6', 185 lbs. Deb: 9/16/1934																									
1934 Bos-A	1	2	.333	4	3	2	1	0	24^{2}	20	8	8	2	1	16	7	1.459	2.92	165	3.85	.222	1	.143	5	2	0.5
• MERIDITH, Ron	Ronald Knox Meridith b: 11/26/1956, San Pedro, CA BL/TL, 6', 175 lbs. Deb: 9/16/1984																									
1984 Chi-N	0	0	....	3	0	0	0	0	5^{1}	6	5	2	1	0	2	4	1.500	3.38	116	4.68	.273	0	....	0	0	0.0
1985 Chi-N	3	2	.600	32	0	0	0	1	46^{1}	53	24	23	3	1	24	23	1.662	4.47	89	5.03	.301	1	.250	-2	3	-0.2
1986 Tex-A	1	0	1.000	5	0	0	0	0	3	2	1	1	0	0	1	2	1.000	3.00	143	1.51	.286	0	....	0	0	0.0
1987 Tex-A	1	0	1.000	11	0	0	0	0	20^{2}	25	18	14	7	0	12	17	1.790	6.10	73	7.94	.298	0	....	-3	0	-0.3
Total 4	5	2	.714	51	0	0	0	1	75^{1}	86	48	40	11	1	39	46	1.659	4.78	87	5.67	.298	1	.250	-5	3	-0.4
• MERRIMAN, Brett	Brett Alan Merriman b: 7/15/1966, Jacksonville, IL BR/TR, 6'2", 180 lbs. Deb: 4/8/1993																									
1993 Min-A	1	1	.500	19	0	0	0	0	27	36	29	29	3	3	23	14	2.185	9.67	45	8.78	.343	0	....	-16	0	-1.5
1994 Min-A	0	1	.000	15	0	0	0	0	17	18	13	12	0	4	14	10	1.882	6.35	77	6.05	.269	0	....	-3	0	-0.2
Total 2	1	2	.333	34	0	0	0	0	44	54	42	41	3	7	37	24	2.068	8.39	54	7.72	.314	0	....	-18	0	-1.8
• MERRITT, Jim	James Joseph Merritt b: 12/9/1943, Altadena, CA BL/TL, 6'3", 180 lbs. Deb: 8/2/1965																									
1965* Min-A	5	4	.556	16	9	1	0	2	76^{2}	68	29	27	11	0	20	61	1.148	3.17	112	3.21	.239	3	.136	2	5	0.3
1966 Min-A	7	14	.333	31	18	5	1	3	144	112	57	54	17	0	33	124	1.007	3.38	106	2.36	.212	4	.103	4	9	0.4
1967 Min-A	13	7	.650	37	28	11	4	0	227^{2}	196	72	64	21	7	30	161	.993	2.53	137	2.35	.230	10	.135	27	19	3.0
1968 Min-A	12	16	.429	38	34	11	1	1	238^{1}	207	102	86	21	7	52	181	1.087	3.25	95	2.71	.232	10	.141	-1	11	0.0
1969 Cin-N	17	9	.654	42	36	8	1	0	251	269	127	122	33	5	61	144	1.315	4.37	86	4.07	.273	11	.143	-17	10	-1.8
1970* Cin-N★	20	12	.625	35	35	12	1	0	234	248	114	106	21	1	53	136	1.286	4.08	102	3.59	.270	14	.169	2	15	0.4
1971 Cin-N	1	11	.083	28	11	0	0	0	107	115	55	52	14	3	31	38	1.364	4.37	74	4.31	.279	4	.138	-16	0	-1.7

YEAR TM-L	W	L	PCT	G	GS	CG	SH	SV	IP	H	R	ER	HR	HB	BB	SO	RAT	ERA	ERA+	CERA	OAV	BH	AVG	PR+	WS	TPW
1972 Cin-N	1	0	1.000	4	1	0	0	0	8	13	4	4	1	0	2	4	1.875	4.50	71	7.22	.361	0	.000	-1	0	-0.2
1973 Tex-A	5	13	.278	35	19	8	1	1	160	191	79	72	18	1	34	65	1.406	4.05	92	4.48	.296	0	....	-2	6	-0.2
1974 Tex-A	0	0	....	26	1	0	0	0	32^2	46	17	15	3	0	6	18	1.592	4.13	86	5.30	.329	0	....	-2	1	-0.2
1975 Tex-A	0	0	....	5	0	0	0	0	3^2	3	1	0	0	1	0	0	.818	0.00	....	2.00	.214	0	....	2	0	0.2
Total 11	81	86	.485	297	192	56	9	7	1483	1468	657	602	160	25	322	932	1.207	3.65	98	3.40	.257	56	.141	-2	76	0.2
• MERRITT, Lloyd	Lloyd Wesley Merritt b: 4/8/1933, St. Louis, MO BR/TR, 6', 189 lbs. Deb: 4/22/1957																									
1957 StL-N	1	2	.333	44	0	0	0	7	65^1	60	29	24	7	4	28	35	1.347	3.31	120	3.93	.251	0	.000	5	5	0.5
• MERTZ, Jim	James Verlin Mertz b: 8/10/1916, Lima, OH d: 2/4/2003, Waycross, GA BR/TR, 5'10.5", 170 lbs. Deb: 5/1/1943																									
1943 Was-A	5	7	.417	33	10	2	0	3	116^2	109	65	60	7	0	58	53	1.431	4.63	69	3.74	.251	7	.184	-18	2	-1.9
• MESA, Jose	Jose Ramon Nova "Joe Table" Mesa b: 5/22/1966, Pueblo Viejo, Dominican Republic BR/TR, 6'3", 225 lbs. Deb: 9/10/1987																									
1987 Bal-A	1	3	.250	6	5	0	0	0	31^1	38	23	21	7	0	15	17	1.691	6.03	73	6.67	.297	0	....	-6	0	-0.5
1990 Bal-A	3	2	.600	7	7	0	0	0	46^2	37	20	20	2	1	27	24	1.371	3.86	98	3.21	.218	0	....	-1	3	-0.1
1991 Bal-A	6	11	.353	23	23	2	1	0	123^2	151	86	82	11	3	62	64	1.722	5.97	66	5.85	.307	0	....	-28	0	-2.8
1992 Bal-A	3	8	.273	13	12	0	0	0	67^2	77	41	39	9	2	27	22	1.537	5.19	78	5.25	.287	0	....	-9	1	-0.9
Cle-A	4	4	.500	15	15	1	1	0	93	92	45	43	5	2	43	40	1.452	4.16	94	4.09	.262	0	....	-2	4	-0.2
Yr.	7	12	.368	28	27	1	1	0	160^2	169	86	82	14	4	70	62	1.488	4.59	86	4.58	.273	0	....	-11	5	-1.1
1993 Cle-A	10	12	.455	34	33	3	0	0	208^2	232	122	114	21	7	62	118	1.409	4.92	88	4.48	.286	0	....	-14	6	-1.4
1994 Cle-A	7	5	.583	51	0	0	0	2	73	71	33	31	3	3	26	63	1.329	3.82	123	3.31	.254	0	....	7	7	0.7
1995* Cle-A★	3	0	1.000	62	0	0	0	**46**	64	49	9	8	3	0	17	58	1.031	1.13	417	2.06	.216	0	....	26	17	2.4
1996* Cle-A★	2	7	.222	69	0	0	0	39	72^1	69	32	30	6	3	28	64	1.341	3.73	131	3.81	.257	0	....	10	12	0.9
1997* Cle-A	4	4	.500	66	0	0	0	16	82^1	83	28	22	7	3	28	69	1.348	2.40	195	3.83	.259	0	....	22	11	2.1
1998 Cle-A	3	4	.429	44	0	0	0	1	54	61	36	31	7	4	20	35	1.500	5.17	92	5.07	.282	0	....	-2	2	-0.2
SF-N	5	3	.625	32	0	0	0	0	30^2	30	14	12	1	0	18	28	1.565	3.52	113	3.99	.256	0	....	2	3	0.2
1999 Sea-A	3	6	.333	68	0	0	0	33	68^2	84	42	38	11	4	40	42	1.806	4.98	100	6.83	.305	0	....	0	5	0.0
2000* Sea-A	4	6	.400	66	0	0	0	1	80^2	89	48	48	11	5	41	84	1.612	5.36	85	5.60	.280	0	....	-8	3	-0.7
2001 Phi-N	3	3	.500	71	0	0	0	42	69^1	65	26	18	4	2	20	59	1.226	2.34	182	3.07	.246	0	....	14	14	1.4
2002 Phi-N	4	6	.400	74	0	0	0	45	75^2	65	26	25	5	4	39	64	1.374	2.97	131	3.51	.231	0	....	7	13	0.7
2003 Phi-N	5	7	.417	61	0	0	0	24	58	71	44	42	7	1	31	45	1.759	6.52	61	6.07	.296	0	....	-16	1	-1.6
Total 15	70	91	.435	762	95	6	2	249	1299^2	1364	675	624	120	44	544	896	1.468	4.32	99	4.51	.271	0	....	1	102	-0.2
• MESSENGER, Bud	Andrew Warren Messenger b: 2/1/1898, Grand Blanc, MI d: 11/4/1971, Lansing, MI BR/TR, 6', 175 lbs. Deb: 7/31/1924																									
1924 Cle-A	2	0	1.000	5	2	1	0	0	25	28	13	12	4	0	14	4	1.680	4.32	99	5.77	.283	1	.125	0	1	0.0
• MESSERSMITH, Andy	John Alexander Messersmith b: 8/6/1945, Toms River, NJ BR/TR, 6'1", 200 lbs. Deb: 7/4/1968																									
1968 Cal-A	4	2	.667	28	5	2	1	4	81^1	44	21	20	3	1	35	74	.971	2.21	131	1.54	.157	2	.100	5	7	0.5
1969 Cal-A	16	11	.593	40	33	10	2	2	250	169	81	70	17	5	100	211	1.076	2.52	138	2.23	**.190**	12	.156	23	22	2.6
1970 Cal-A	11	10	.524	37	26	6	1	5	194^2	144	75	65	21	6	78	162	1.140	3.01	120	2.83	**.205**	11	.157	8	14	0.9
1971 Cal-A★	20	13	.606	38	38	14	4	0	276^2	224	112	92	16	7	121	179	1.247	2.99	108	2.94	.218	16	.172	4	19	0.8
1972 Cal-A	8	11	.421	25	21	10	3	2	169^2	125	56	53	5	2	68	142	1.138	2.81	103	2.24	.207	10	.189	0	12	0.3
1973 LA-N	14	10	.583	33	33	10	3	0	249^2	196	90	75	24	6	77	177	1.093	2.70	127	2.63	.214	15	.169	17	18	1.9
1974* LA-N★	**20**	6	.769	39	39	13	3	0	292^1	227	93	84	24	3	94	221	1.098	2.59	131	2.54	.212	23	.240	28	25	3.9
1975 LA-N★	19	14	.576	42	**40**	**19**	**7**	1	**321^2**	244	92	82	22	5	96	213	1.057	2.29	148	2.33	**.213**	17	.157	36	**28**	3.9
1976 Atl-N★	11	11	.500	29	28	12	3	1	207^1	166	83	70	14	2	74	135	1.158	3.04	125	2.68	.219	12	.179	22	17	2.4
1977 Atl-N	5	4	.556	16	16	1	1	0	102^1	101	54	50	12	2	39	69	1.368	4.40	101	3.97	.256	4	.118	4	6	0.4
1978 NY-A	0	3	.000	6	5	0	0	0	22^1	24	21	14	7	1	15	16	1.746	5.64	64	7.48	.267	0	....	-5	0	-0.5
1979 LA-N	2	4	.333	11	11	1	0	0	62^1	55	34	34	9	0	34	26	1.428	4.91	74	4.34	.244	2	.091	-8	1	-0.9
Total 12	130	99	.568	344	295	98	27	15	2230^1	1719	812	709	174	40	831	1625	1.143	2.86	121	2.68	.212	124	.170	136	169	16.3
• METCALF, Tom	Thomas John Metcalf b: 7/16/1940, Amherst, WI BR/TR, 6'2.5", 174 lbs. Deb: 8/4/1963																									
1963 NY-A	1	0	1.000	8	0	0	0	0	13	12	4	4	1	0	3	3	1.154	2.77	127	2.89	.250	0	....	1	1	0.1
• METIVIER, Dewey	George Dewey Metivier b: 5/6/1898, Cambridge, MA d: 3/2/1947, Cambridge, MA BL/TR, 5'11", 175 lbs. Deb: 9/15/1922																									
1922 Cle-A	2	0	1.000	2	2	2	0	0	18	18	9	9	1	1	3	1	1.167	4.50	89	3.18	.265	1	.167	-1	1	0.0
1923 Cle-A	4	2	.667	26	5	1	0	1	73^1	111	66	53	1	6	38	9	2.032	6.50	61	7.01	.368	3	.150	-20	0	-2.0
1924 Cle-A	1	5	.167	26	6	1	0	3	76^1	110	50	45	3	0	34	14	1.886	5.31	81	6.36	.358	3	.125	-8	2	-0.9
Total 3	7	7	.500	54	13	4	0	4	167^2	239	125	107	5	7	75	24	1.873	5.74	71	6.30	.353	7	.140	-28	3	-2.9
• METZGER, Butch	Clarence Edward Metzger b: 5/23/1952, Lafayette, IN BR/TR, 6'1", 185 lbs. Deb: 9/8/1974																									
1974 SF-N	1	0	1.000	10	0	0	0	0	12^2	11	5	5	0	0	12	5	1.816	3.55	107	3.55	.239	0	....	0	1	0.0
1975 SD-N	1	0	1.000	4	0	0	0	0	4^2	6	4	4	1	0	4	6	2.143	7.71	45	8.14	.316	0	....	-2	0	-0.2
1976 SD-N	11	4	.733	77	0	0	0	16	123^1	119	44	40	5	3	52	89	1.386	2.92	112	3.48	.258	0	.000	5	12	0.5
1977 SD-N	0	0	....	17	1	0	0	0	22^2	27	16	14	5	1	12	6	1.721	5.56	64	6.61	.307	0	.000	-5	0	-0.5
StL-N	4	2	.667	58	0	0	0	7	92^2	78	36	32	8	1	38	48	1.252	3.11	124	3.16	.228	0	.000	6	8	0.5
Yr.	4	2	.667	75	1	0	0	7	115^1	105	52	46	13	2	50	54	1.344	3.59	104	3.84	.244	0	.000	1	8	0.0
1978 NY-N	1	3	.250	25	0	0	0	0	37^1	48	28	27	4	1	22	21	1.875	6.51	54	6.32	.324	0	....	-13	0	-1.4
Total 5	18	9	.667	191	1	0	0	23	293^1	289	133	122	23	6	140	175	1.463	3.74	94	4.06	.262	0	.000	-9	21	-1.0
• MEYER, Bob	Robert Bernard Meyer b: 8/4/1939, Toledo, OH BR/TL, 6'2", 185 lbs. Deb: 4/20/1964																									
1964 NY-A	0	3	.000	7	1	0	0	0	18^1	16	12	10	1	0	12	12	1.527	4.91	74	3.97	.235	0	.000	-3	0	-0.3
LA-A	1	1	.500	6	5	0	0	0	18	25	10	10	2	1	13	13	2.111	5.00	66	8.35	.333	0	.000	-4	0	-0.4
KC-A	1	4	.200	9	7	2	0	0	42	37	23	18	2	0	33	30	1.667	3.86	99	4.60	.248	0	.000	1	1	-0.1
Yr.	2	8	.200	22	13	2	0	0	78^1	78	45	38	5	1	58	55	1.736	4.37	83	5.31	.267	0	.000	-6	1	-0.8
1969 Sea-A	0	3	.000	6	5	1	0	0	32^2	30	14	12	4	2	10	17	1.224	3.31	110	3.73	.252	1	.091	2	1	0.2
1970 Mil-A	0	1	.000	10	0	0	0	0	18^1	24	13	13	2	0	12	20	1.964	6.38	59	7.15	.329	1	.333	-5	0	-0.5
Total 3	2	12	.143	38	18	3	0	0	129^1	132	72	63	11	3	80	92	1.639	4.38	83	5.17	.273	2	.057	-9	2	-1.2
• MEYER, Brian	Brian Scott Meyer b: 1/29/1963, Camden, NJ BR/TR, 6'1", 190 lbs. Deb: 9/3/1988																									
1988 Hou-N	0	0	....	8	0	0	0	0	12^1	9	2	2	2	0	4	10	1.054	1.46	228	2.98	.225	0	....	3	1	0.3
1989 Hou-N	0	1	.000	12	0	0	0	1	18	16	13	9	0	1	13	13	1.611	4.50	75	3.84	.239	0	....	-2	0	-0.2
1990 Hou-N	0	4	.000	14	0	0	0	1	20^1	16	7	5	3	0	6	6	1.082	2.21	168	2.75	.211	0	.000	3	2	0.3
Total 3	0	5	.000	34	0	0	0	2	50^2	41	22	16	5	1	23	29	1.263	2.84	122	3.19	.224	0	.000	4	3	0.4
• MEYER, Jack	John Robert Meyer b: 3/23/1932, Philadelphia, PA d: 3/6/1967, Philadelphia, PA BR/TR, 6'1", 175 lbs. Deb: 4/16/1955																									
1955 Phi-N	6	11	.353	50	5	0	0	**16**	110^1	75	50	42	14	3	66	97	1.278	3.43	116	3.27	.190	2	.100	5	11	0.5
1956 Phi-N	7	11	.389	41	7	2	0	2	96	86	49	47	8	4	51	66	1.427	4.41	84	3.87	.242	4	.200	-5	4	-0.4
1957 Phi-N	0	2	.000	19	2	0	0	0	37^2	44	30	24	6	1	28	34	1.912	5.73	66	7.09	.297	1	.167	-8	0	-0.8
1958 Phi-N	3	6	.333	37	5	1	0	2	90^1	77	38	36	8	1	33	87	1.218	3.59	110	3.07	.232	5	.278	5	6	0.6
1959 Phi-N	5	3	.625	47	1	1	0	1	93^2	76	43	35	9	1	53	71	1.377	3.36	122	3.63	.222	1	.071	8	7	0.7
1960 Phi-N	3	1	.750	7	4	0	0	0	25	25	13	12	2	0	11	18	1.440	4.32	90	4.07	.272	1	.125	-1	2	-0.1
1961 Phi-N	0	0	....	1	0	0	0	0	2	2	2	2	1	0	2	2	2.000	9.00	45	11.03	.286	0	....	-1	0	-0.1
Total 7	24	34	.414	202	24	4	0	21	455	385	225	198	48	10	244	375	1.382	3.92	100	3.83	.230	14	.163	3	30	0.4
• MEYER, Russ	Russell Charles "Rowdy,The Mad Monk" Meyer b: 10/25/1923, Peru, IL d: 11/16/1997, Oglesby, IL BB/TR, 6'1", 185 lbs. Deb: 9/13/1946 C																									
1946 Chi-N	0	0	....	4	1	0	0	1	17	21	7	6	2	0	10	10	1.824	3.18	105	6.40	.309	1	.200	1	1	0.1
1947 Chi-N	3	2	.600	23	2	1	0	0	45	43	17	17	4	1	14	22	1.267	3.40	116	3.51	.257	3	.250	3	5	0.3
1948 Chi-N	10	10	.500	29	26	8	3	0	164^2	157	75	67	8	1	77	89	1.421	3.66	107	3.68	.254	6	.107	6	10	0.3
1949 Phi-N	17	8	.680	37	28	14	2	1	213	199	84	73	14	1	70	78	1.263	3.08	128	3.22	.250	10	.143	18	20	1.6
1950* Phi-N	9	11	.450	32	25	3	0	1	159^2	193	108	94	21	2	67	74	1.628	5.30	76	5.67	.304	7	.140	-22	2	-2.3

YR	TM-L	W	L	PCT	G	GS	CG	SH	SV	IP	H	R	ER	HR	HB	BB	SO	RAT	ERA	ERA+	CERA	OAV	BH	AVG	PR+	WS	TPW
	Bal-A	14	12	.538	37	**36**	3	2	0	243	233	105	101	21	2	88	113	1.321	3.74	101	3.65	.254	0	....	-0	14	0.0
	Bal-A	5	8	.385	27	24	1	1	0	135^1	143	73	67	18	0	61	60	1.507	4.46	85	4.85	.273	0	....	-11	4	-1.1
	Bal-A	10	9	.526	31	26	3	1	0	184	175	86	82	17	1	53	108	1.239	4.01	98	3.36	.253	0	....	-2	9	-0.2
	Bal-A	6	8	.429	23	20	0	0	1	115^2	140	78	75	16	2	44	51	1.591	5.84	69	5.51	.296	0	....	-24	0	-2.4
	Cle-A	1	1	.500	5	2	0	0	0	16	19	8	6	3	0	11	7	1.875	3.38	128	7.36	.302	0	....	2	1	0.2
	KC-A	0	5	.000	10	10	0	0	0	55^2	68	43	38	6	1	20	17	1.581	6.14	81	5.14	.298	0	....	-7	1	-0.7
	Sea-A	1	4	.200	7	4	0	0	0	21	30	20	16	3	0	15	13	2.143	6.86	72	8.09	.330	0	....	-5	0	-0.4
l	**8**	**39**	**47**	**.453**	**143**	**125**	**8**	**5**	**1**	**795^2**	**817**	**415**	**387**	**85**	**6**	**301**	**387**	**1.405**	**4.38**	**92**	**4.27**	**.266**	**0**	**....**	**-39**	**33**	**-3.8**
ILCHIN, Mike	Michael Wayne Milchin b: 2/28/1968, Knoxville, TN BL/TL, 6'3", 190 lbs. Deb: 5/14/1996																										
	Min-A	2	1	.667	26	0	0	0	0	21^2	31	21	20	6	0	12	19	1.985	8.31	62	8.87	.341	0	....	-8	0	-0.7
	Bal-A	1	0	1.000	13	0	0	0	0	11	13	7	7	0	0	5	10	1.636	5.73	86	4.48	.325	0	....	-1	0	-0.1
	Yr.	3	1	.750	39	0	0	0	0	32^2	44	28	27	6	0	17	29	1.867	7.44	68	7.39	.336	0	....	-9	0	-0.8
ILES, Carl	Carl Thomas Miles b: 3/22/1918, Trenton, MO BB/TL, 5'11", 178 lbs. Deb: 6/8/1940																										
	Phi-A	0	0	....	2	0	0	0	0	8	9	12	12	2	0	8	6	2.125	13.50	33	8.18	.281	3	.750	-8	0	-0.6
ILES, Jim	James Charlie Miles b: 8/8/1943, Grenada, MS BR/TR, 6'2", 210 lbs. Deb: 9/7/1968																										
	Was-A	0	0	....	3	0	0	0	0	4^1	8	6	6	0	0	2	5	2.308	12.46	23	8.52	.421	0	....	-5	0	-0.5
	Was-A	0	1	.000	10	1	0	0	0	20^1	19	15	14	2	4	15	15	1.672	6.20	56	5.71	.257	1	.333	-6	0	-0.6
l	**2**	**0**	**1**	**.000**	**13**	**1**	**0**	**0**	**0**	**24^2**	**27**	**21**	**20**	**2**	**4**	**17**	**20**	**1.784**	**7.30**	**45**	**6.21**	**.290**	**1**	**.333**	**-11**	**0**	**-1.2**
ILITELLO, Sam	Sam Salvatore Militello b: 11/26/1969, Tampa, FL BR/TR, 6'3", 200 lbs. Deb: 8/9/1992																										
2	NY-A	3	3	.500	9	9	0	0	0	60	43	24	23	6	2	32	42	1.250	3.45	114	3.12	.195	0	....	3	3	0.3
3	NY-A	1	1	.500	3	2	0	0	0	9^1	10	8	7	1	2	7	5	1.821	6.75	61	6.65	.270	0	....	-3	0	-0.3
l	**2**	**4**	**4**	**.500**	**12**	**11**	**0**	**0**	**0**	**69^1**	**53**	**32**	**30**	**7**	**4**	**39**	**47**	**1.327**	**3.89**	**102**	**3.59**	**.205**	**0**	**....**	**0**	**3**	**0.0**
ILJUS, Johnny	John Kenneth "Jovo,Big Serb" Miljus b: 6/30/1895, Pittsburgh, PA d: 2/11/1976, Fort Harrison, MT BR/TR, 6'1", 178 lbs. Deb: 10/2/1915																										
5	Pit-F	0	0	....	1	0	0	0	0	1	1	0	0	0	0	0	0	1.000	0.00	....	2.02	.250	0	....	0	0	0.0
7	Bro-N	0	1	.000	4	1	1	0	0	15	14	3	1	0	3	8	9	1.467	0.60	465	3.91	.250	0	.000	3	2	0.3
0	Bro-N	1	0	1.000	9	0	0	0	0	23^1	24	10	8	2	0	4	9	1.200	3.09	104	3.10	.267	2	.333	1	2	0.2
	Bro-N	6	3	.667	28	9	3	0	1	93^2	115	49	44	1	2	27	37	1.516	4.23	92	4.35	.312	5	.167	-3	5	-0.5
7*	Pit-N	8	3	.727	19	6	3	2	0	75^2	62	21	16	0	0	17	24	1.044	1.90	216	1.89	.228	5	.179	18	8	1.7
3	Pit-N	5	7	.417	21	10	3	0	1	69^2	90	48	41	2	3	33	26	1.766	5.30	77	5.41	.313	8	.308	-10	2	-0.8
	Cle-A	1	4	.200	11	4	1	0	1	50^2	46	25	15	1	0	20	19	1.303	2.66	155	2.67	.243	3	.200	9	4	0.8
9	Cle-A	8	8	.500	34	15	4	0	2	128^1	174	93	74	10	3	64	42	1.855	5.19	86	6.32	.331	11	.256	-10	5	-0.8
l	**7**	**29**	**26**	**.527**	**127**	**45**	**15**	**2**	**5**	**457^1**	**526**	**249**	**199**	**16**	**11**	**173**	**166**	**1.528**	**3.92**	**105**	**4.39**	**.293**	**34**	**.222**	**9**	**28**	**0.9**
ILLER, Bert	Herbert A. Miller b: 10/26/1875, Riley, MI d: 6/14/1937, Flint, MI Deb: 7/15/1897																										
7	Lou-N	0	1	.000	4	1	1	0	0	17	32	23	15	0	0	3	3	2.059	7.94	54	7.65	.396	1	.167	-7	0	-0.6
ILLER, Bill	William Paul "Lefty,Hooks" Miller b: 7/26/1927, Minersville, PA d: 7/1/2003, Lititz, PA BL/TL, 6', 175 lbs. Deb: 4/20/1952																										
2	NY-A	4	6	.400	21	13	5	2	0	88	78	43	34	5	2	49	45	1.443	3.48	95	3.73	.241	6	.214	-4	4	-0.4
3	NY-A	2	1	.667	13	3	0	0	1	34	46	19	18	3	1	19	17	1.912	4.76	77	6.75	.324	2	.200	-5	1	-0.5
4	NY-A	0	1	.000	2	1	0	0	0	5^2	9	4	4	0	0	1	6	1.765	6.35	54	5.87	.375	0	.000	-2	0	-0.2
5	Bal-A	0	1	.000	5	1	0	0	0	4	3	6	6	0	0	10	4	3.250	13.50	28	9.26	.200	1	1.000	-4	0	-0.4
l	**4**	**6**	**9**	**.400**	**41**	**18**	**5**	**2**	**1**	**131^2**	**136**	**72**	**62**	**8**	**3**	**79**	**72**	**1.633**	**4.24**	**82**	**4.77**	**.270**	**9**	**.225**	**-16**	**5**	**-1.5**
ILLER, Bill	William Francis "Wild Bill" Miller b: 4/12/1910, Hannibal, MO d: 2/26/1982, Hannibal, MO BR/TR, 6', 180 lbs. Deb: 10/2/1937																										
7	StL-A	0	1	.000	1	1	0	0	0	4	7	6	6	1	1	4	1	2.750	13.50	36	13.66	.389	0	.000	-4	0	-0.4
ILLER, Bob	Robert John Miller b: 6/16/1926, Detroit, MI BR/TR, 6'3", 190 lbs. Deb: 9/16/1949																										
9	Phi-N	0	0	....	3	0	0	0	0	2^2	2	0	0	0	0	2	0	1.500	0.00	....	3.02	.200	0	....	1	1	0.1
0*	Phi-N	11	6	.647	35	22	7	2	1	174	190	78	69	9	5	57	44	1.420	3.57	113	3.99	.277	11	.180	9	12	0.8
1	Phi-N	2	1	.667	17	3	0	0	0	34^1	47	33	26	2	1	18	10	1.893	6.82	56	6.45	.331	3	.429	-11	0	-1.0
2	Phi-N	0	1	.000	3	1	0	0	0	9	13	6	6	2	0	1	2	1.556	6.00	61	6.76	.351	0	.000	-2	0	-0.3
3	Phi-N	8	9	.471	35	20	8	3	2	157^1	169	76	70	14	2	42	63	1.341	4.00	105	3.83	.271	10	.182	4	10	0.2
4	Phi-N	7	9	.438	30	16	5	0	0	150	176	84	76	14	3	39	42	1.433	4.56	89	4.49	.300	8	.160	-9	5	-0.9
5	Phi-N	8	4	.667	40	0	0	0	1	89^2	80	26	24	6	1	28	28	1.204	2.41	165	2.89	.242	5	.278	14	10	1.5
6	Phi-N	3	6	.333	49	6	3	1	5	122^1	115	55	44	14	3	34	53	1.218	3.24	115	3.30	.248	2	.091	9	7	0.8
7	Phi-N	2	5	.286	32	1	0	0	6	60^1	61	18	18	4	1	17	12	1.293	2.69	142	3.39	.265	2	.250	8	8	1.0
8	Phi-N	1	1	.500	17	0	0	0	0	22^1	36	30	29	7	0	9	9	2.015	11.69	34	9.27	.360	0	.000	-19	0	-1.9
l	**10**	**42**	**42**	**.500**	**261**	**69**	**23**	**6**	**15**	**822**	**889**	**406**	**362**	**72**	**16**	**247**	**263**	**1.382**	**3.96**	**101**	**4.06**	**.277**	**41**	**.184**	**3**	**53**	**0.4**
ILLER, Bob	Robert W. Miller b: 1862, d: 5/23/1931, Newark, NJ Deb: 8/30/1890																										
0	Roc-a	3	7	.300	13	12	11	0	1	92^1	89	58	44	2	3	26	20	1.245	4.29	83	....	.246	6	.150	-8	4	-0.9
1	Was-a	2	5	.286	7	7	3	0	0	42	53	51	20	3	6	24	13	1.833	4.29	87	....	.298	2	.111	-0	0	-0.2
l	**2**	**5**	**12**	**.294**	**20**	**19**	**14**	**0**	**1**	**134^1**	**142**	**109**	**64**	**5**	**9**	**50**	**33**	**1.429**	**4.29**	**84**	**....**	**.263**	**8**	**.138**	**-8**	**4**	**-1.0**
ILLER, Bob	Robert Gerald Miller b: 7/15/1935, Berwyn, IL BR/TL, 6'1", 185 lbs. Deb: 6/25/1953																										
3	Det-A	1	2	.333	13	1	0	0	0	36^1	43	25	24	2	1	21	9	1.761	5.94	68	5.41	.289	1	.125	-6	0	-0.7
4	Det-A	1	1	.500	32	1	0	0	1	69^2	62	25	19	1	0	26	27	1.263	2.45	150	2.77	.244	2	.133	9	6	0.9
5	Det-A	2	1	.667	7	3	1	0	0	25^1	26	12	7	4	0	12	11	1.500	2.49	154	4.86	.263	2	.222	4	2	0.4
6	Det-A	0	2	.000	11	3	0	0	0	31^2	37	23	20	5	0	22	16	1.863	5.68	72	6.88	.308	1	.143	-5	0	-0.5
2	Cin-N	0	0	....	6	0	0	0	0	5^1	14	13	13	1	2	3	4	3.188	21.94	18	19.73	.538	0	.000	-11	0	-1.1
	NY-N	2	2	.500	17	0	0	0	1	20^1	24	16	16	2	1	8	8	1.574	7.08	59	5.54	.312	0	.000	-6	3	-0.6
	Yr.	2	2	.500	23	0	0	0	1	25^2	38	29	29	3	3	11	12	1.909	10.17	40	8.49	.369	0	.000	-17	3	-1.7
al	**5**	**6**	**8**	**.429**	**86**	**8**	**1**	**0**	**2**	**188^2**	**206**	**114**	**99**	**15**	**4**	**92**	**75**	**1.580**	**4.72**	**85**	**5.02**	**.284**	**6**	**.146**	**-16**	**11**	**-1.6**
ILLER, Bob	Robert Lane Miller b: 2/18/1939, St. Louis, MO d: 8/6/1993, Rancho Bernardo, CA BR/TR, 6'1", 182 lbs. Deb: 6/26/1957 C																										
7	StL-N	0	0	....	5	0	0	0	0	9	13	9	7	2	0	5	7	2.000	7.00	57	8.13	.325	0	....	-3	0	-0.3
9	StL-N	4	3	.571	11	10	3	0	0	70^2	66	31	26	2	1	21	43	1.231	3.31	128	2.86	.248	5	.208	8	6	0.8
0	StL-N	4	3	.571	15	7	0	0	0	52^2	53	21	20	2	1	17	33	1.329	3.42	120	3.38	.262	2	.143	4	4	0.4
1	StL-N	1	3	.250	34	5	0	0	3	74^1	82	41	35	6	0	46	39	1.722	4.24	104	5.40	.290	5	.357	1	5	0.3
2	NY-N	1	12	.077	33	21	1	0	0	143^2	146	98	78	20	6	62	91	1.448	4.89	86	4.61	.259	5	.122	-9	0	-0.9
3	LA-N	10	8	.556	42	23	2	0	1	187	171	71	60	7	3	65	125	1.262	2.89	105	2.99	.244	4	.070	4	11	0.2
4	LA-N	7	7	.500	**74**	2	0	0	9	137^2	115	49	40	1	2	63	94	1.293	2.62	124	2.64	.226	3	.158	10	12	1.1
5*	LA-N	6	7	.462	61	1	0	0	9	103	82	37	34	9	3	26	77	1.049	2.97	110	2.44	.225	0	.000	2	8	0.1
6*	LA-N	4	2	.667	46	0	0	0	5	84^1	70	31	26	5	1	29	58	1.174	2.77	119	2.64	.230	1	.077	5	7	0.4
7	LA-N	2	9	.182	52	4	0	0	0	85^2	88	46	41	9	3	27	32	1.342	4.31	72	3.95	.273	1	.125	-11	0	-1.2
8	Min-A	0	3	.000	45	0	0	0	2	72^1	65	26	22	1	5	24	41	1.230	2.74	113	2.81	.239	1	.143	4	4	0.4
9*	Min-A	5	5	.500	48	11	1	0	3	119^1	118	42	40	9	0	32	57	1.257	3.02	121	3.35	.264	0	.000	7	8	0.4
0	Cle-A	2	2	.500	15	2	0	0	1	28	35	14	13	1	0	15	15	1.786	4.18	95	5.34	.310	1	.200	-1	2	0.0
	Chi-A	4	6	.400	15	12	0	0	0	70	88	42	39	11	4	33	36	1.729	5.01	78	6.57	.315	4	.174	-8	2	-0.7
	Yr.	6	8	.429	30	14	0	0	1	98	123	56	52	12	4	48	51	1.745	4.78	82	6.22	.314	5	.179	-8	4	-0.8
	Chi-N	0	0	....	7	1	0	0	2	9	6	5	5	3	0	6	4	1.333	5.00	90	4.62	.194	0	....	-1	1	-0.1
1	Chi-N	0	0	....	2	0	0	0	0	7	10	4	4	0	0	1	2	1.571	5.14	76	4.97	.357	0	.000	-1	0	-0.1
	SD-N	7	3	.700	38	0	0	0	7	63^2	53	12	10	0	1	26	36	1.241	1.41	233	2.46	.227	0	.000	14	10	1.3
*	Pit-N	1	2	.333	16	0	0	0	3	28	20	8	4	1	0	13	13	1.179	1.29	265	2.19	.200	0	.000	6	3	0.7
	Yr.	8	5	.615	56	0	0	0	10	98^2	83	24	18	1	1	40	51	1.247	1.64	210	2.56	.230	0	.000	19	13	2.0
2*	Pit-N	5	2	.714	36	0	0	0	3	54^1	54	19	16	3	1	24	18	1.436	2.65	125	3.73	.263	0	.000	3	4	0.3

YEAR	TM-L	W	L	PCT	G	GS	CG	SH	SV	IP	H	R	ER	HR	HB	BB	SO	RAT	ERA	ERA+	CERA	OAV	BH	AVG	PR+
1951	Phi-N	8	9	.471	28	24	7	2	0	168	172	69	65	13	2	55	65	1.351	3.48	110	3.72	.263	5	.104	7
1952	Phi-N	13	14	.481	37	32	14	1	1	232^1	235	99	81	10	2	65	92	1.291	3.14	116	3.24	.260	7	.089	10
1953*	Bro-N	15	5	.750	34	32	10	2	0	191^1	201	109	97	25	1	63	106	1.380	4.56	93	4.25	.269	11	.147	-9
1954	Bro-N	11	6	.647	36	28	6	2	0	180^1	193	89	80	17	2	49	70	1.342	3.99	102	3.91	.275	2	.043	2
1955*	Bro-N	6	2	.750	18	11	2	1	0	73	86	46	44	8	0	31	26	1.603	5.42	75	5.16	.300	1	.037	-11
1956	Chi-N	1	6	.143	20	9	0	0	0	57	71	41	40	11	2	26	28	1.702	6.32	60	6.52	.313	1	.083	-17
	Cin-N	0	0	....	1	0	0	0	0	1	1	0	0	0	0	0	1	1.000	0.00	....	1.95	.250	0	....	0
	Yr.	1	6	.143	21	9	0	0	0	58	72	41	40	11	2	26	29	1.690	6.21	61	6.44	.312	1	.083	-17
1957	Bos-A	0	0	....	2	1	0	0	0	5	10	5	3	0	0	3	1	2.600	5.40	74	10.18	.417	1	1.000	-1
1959	KC-A	1	0	1.000	18	0	0	0	1	24	24	12	12	3	1	11	10	1.458	4.50	89	4.59	.261	0	.000	-1
Total	**13**	**94**	**73**	**.563**	**319**	**219**	**65**	**13**	**5**	**1531^1**	**1606**	**761**	**679**	**136**	**15**	**541**	**672**	**1.402**	**3.99**	**99**	**4.09**	**.271**	**55**	**.114**	**-16**
• MIADICH, Bart		John Barton Miadich b: 2/3/1976, Torrance, CA BR/TR, 6'4", 205 lbs. Deb: 9/2/2001																							
2001	Ana-A	0	0	....	11	0	0	0	0	10	6	5	5	2	0	8	11	1.400	4.50	101	4.38	.182	0	....	0
2003	Ana-A	0	0	....	1	0	0	0	0	2	5	4	4	0	1	1	3	3.000	18.00	24	17.04	.500	0	....	-3
Total	**2**	**0**	**0**	**....**	**12**	**0**	**0**	**0**	**0**	**12**	**11**	**9**	**9**	**2**	**1**	**9**	**14**	**1.667**	**6.75**	**66**	**6.49**	**.256**	**0**	**....**	**-3**
• MICELI, Dan		Daniel Miceli b: 9/9/1970, Newark, NJ BR/TR, 6'1", 207 lbs. Deb: 9/9/1993																							
1993	Pit-N	0	0	....	9	0	0	0	0	5^1	6	3	3	0	0	3	4	1.688	5.06	80	4.53	.273	0	....	-1
1994	Pit-N	2	1	.667	28	0	0	0	2	27^1	28	19	18	5	2	11	27	1.427	5.93	73	4.98	.267	0	.000	-5
1995	Pit-N	4	4	.500	58	0	0	0	21	58	61	30	30	7	4	28	56	1.534	4.66	92	4.93	.270	0	.000	-2
1996	Pit-N	2	10	.167	44	9	0	0	1	85^2	99	65	55	15	3	45	66	1.681	5.78	76	6.09	.291	0	.000	-12
1997	Det-A	3	2	.600	71	0	0	0	3	82^2	77	49	46	13	1	38	79	1.391	5.01	92	4.30	.248	0	....	-5
1998*	SD-N	10	5	.667	67	0	0	0	2	72^2	64	28	26	6	1	27	70	1.252	3.22	122	3.20	.238	1	1.000	5
1999	SD-N	4	5	.444	66	0	0	0	2	68^2	67	39	34	7	2	36	59	1.500	4.46	94	4.57	.266	0	.000	-2
2000	Fla-N	6	4	.600	45	0	0	0	0	48^2	45	23	23	4	1	18	40	1.295	4.25	104	3.42	.242	0	....	[illegible]
2001	Fla-N	0	5	.000	29	0	0	0	0	24^2	29	21	19	5	0	11	31	1.622	6.93	61	5.80	.287	0	....	[illegible]
	Col-N	2	0	1.000	22	0	0	0	1	20^1	18	8	5	2	0	5	17	1.131	2.21	241	2.77	.231	0	....	[illegible]
	Yr.	2	5	.286	51	0	0	0	1	45	47	29	24	7	0	16	48	1.400	4.80	92	4.43	.263	0	....	[illegible]
2002	Tex-A	0	2	.000	9	0	0	0	0	8^1	13	8	8	1	0	3	5	1.920	8.64	55	7.11	.333	0	....	[illegible]
2003	Col-N	0	2	.000	14	0	0	0	0	20^2	24	13	13	7	1	9	18	1.597	5.66	87	7.07	.286	0	....	[illegible]
	Cle-A	1	1	.500	13	0	0	0	0	15	9	4	2	1	0	6	19	1.000	1.20	368	1.70	.164	0	....	
	NY-A	0	0	....	7	0	0	0	1	4^2	4	3	3	2	0	3	1	1.500	5.79	75	6.21	.211	0	....	[illegible]
	Yr.	1	1	.500	20	0	0	0	1	19^2	13	7	5	3	0	9	20	1.119	2.29	192	2.77	.176	0	....	
	Hou-N	1	1	.500	23	0	0	0	0	30	22	7	7	3	1	7	20	.967	2.10	211	2.22	.208	0	.000	
	Yr.	1	3	.250	37	0	0	0	0	50^2	46	20	20	10	2	16	38	1.224	3.55	133	4.20	.242	0	.000	
Total	**11**	**35**	**42**	**.455**	**505**	**9**	**0**	**0**	**33**	**572^2**	**566**	**320**	**292**	**78**	**16**	**250**	**512**	**1.425**	**4.59**	**95**	**4.47**	**.258**	**1**	**.050**	**-1**
• MICHAELS, John		John Joseph Michaels b: 7/10/1907, Bridgeport, CT d: 11/18/1996, Sebring, FL BL/TL, 5'10.5", 154 lbs. Deb: 4/16/1932																							
1932	Bos-A	1	6	.143	28	8	2	0	0	80^2	101	59	46	4	3	27	16	1.587	5.13	88	4.85	.304	3	.143	
• MICHAELSON, John		John August "Mike" Michaelson b: 8/12/1893, Taivalkoski, Finland d: 4/16/1968, Woodruff, WI BR/TR, 5'9", 165 lbs. Deb: 8/28/1921																							
1921	Chi-A	0	0	....	2	0	0	0	0	2^2	4	3	3	0	0	1	1	1.875	10.13	42	7.02	.400	0	....	
• MICHALAK, Chris		Christian Matthew Michalak b: 1/4/1971, Joliet, IL BL/TL, 6'2", 195 lbs. Deb: 8/22/1998																							
1998	Ari-N	0	0	....	5	0	0	0	0	5^1	9	7	7	1	0	4	5	2.438	11.81	36	10.59	.375	0	....	
2001	Tor-A	6	7	.462	24	18	0	0	0	115	133	66	59	14	12	49	57	1.583	4.62	99	5.73	.296	1	.333	
	Tex-A	2	2	.500	11	0	0	0	1	21^2	24	8	8	5	1	6	10	1.385	3.32	140	5.39	.279	0	....	
	Yr.	8	9	.471	35	18	0	0	1	136^2	157	74	67	19	13	55	67	1.551	4.41	104	5.67	.293	1	.333	
2002	Tex-A	0	2	.000	13	0	0	0	0	14^1	20	7	7	1	1	10	5	2.093	4.40	107	7.62	.339	0	....	
Total	**3**	**8**	**11**	**.421**	**53**	**18**	**0**	**0**	**1**	**156^1**	**186**	**88**	**81**	**21**	**14**	**69**	**77**	**1.631**	**4.66**	**98**	**6.02**	**.301**	**1**	**.333**	
• MICKENS, Glenn		Glenn Roger Mickens b: 7/26/1930, Wilmar, CA BR/TR, 6', 175 lbs. Deb: 7/19/1953																							
1953	Bro-N	0	1	.000	4	2	0	0	0	6^1	11	9	8	2	0	4	5	2.368	11.37	37	11.76	.393	0	.000	
• MIDDLEBROOK, Jason		Jason Douglas Middlebrook b: 6/26/1975, Jackson, MI BR/TR, 6'3", 215 lbs. Deb: 9/17/2001																							
2001	SD-N	2	1	.667	4	3	0	0	0	19^1	18	11	11	6	1	10	10	1.448	5.12	78	5.85	.247	1	.143	
2002	SD-N	1	3	.250	12	2	0	0	0	35^1	31	20	20	1	1	15	28	1.302	5.09	74	3.05	.244	2	.333	
	NY-N	1	0	1.000	3	3	0	0	0	16	13	7	7	1	0	7	14	1.250	3.94	101	2.95	.220	0	.000	
	Yr.	2	3	.400	15	5	0	0	0	51^1	44	27	27	2	1	22	42	1.286	4.73	81	3.02	.237	2	.182	
2003	NY-N	0	0	....	5	0	0	0	0	7	13	8	8	0	0	4	3	2.429	10.29	40	9.62	.433	0	....	
Total	**3**	**4**	**4**	**.500**	**24**	**8**	**0**	**0**	**0**	**77^2**	**75**	**46**	**46**	**8**	**2**	**36**	**55**	**1.429**	**5.33**	**73**	**4.32**	**.260**	**3**	**.167**	
• MIDDLETON, Jim		James Blaine "Rifle Jim" Middleton b: 5/28/1889, Argos, IN d: 1/12/1974, Argos, IN BR/TR, 5'11.5", 165 lbs. Deb: 4/18/1917																							
1917	NY-N	1	1	.500	13	0	0	0	1	36	35	18	11	1	1	8	9	1.194	2.75	93	2.71	.255	0	.000	
1921	Det-A	6	11	.353	38	10	2	0	**7**	121^2	149	83	68	5	2	44	31	1.586	5.03	85	4.64	.302	5	.147	
Total	**2**	**7**	**12**	**.368**	**51**	**10**	**2**	**0**	**8**	**157^2**	**184**	**101**	**79**	**6**	**3**	**52**	**40**	**1.497**	**4.51**	**86**	**4.20**	**.292**	**5**	**.119**	
• MIDDLETON, John		John Wayne "Lefty" Middleton b: 4/11/1900, Mount Calm, TX d: 11/3/1986, Amarillo, TX BL/TL, 6'1", 185 lbs. Deb: 9/6/1922																							
1922	Cle-A	0	1	.000	2	1	0	0	0	7^1	8	7	6	1	0	6	2	1.909	7.36	54	6.42	.286	1	.333	
• MIDKIFF, Dick		Richard James Midkiff b: 9/28/1914, Gonzales, TX d: 10/30/1956, Temple, TX BR/TR, 6'2", 185 lbs. Deb: 4/24/1938																							
1938	Bos-A	1	1	.500	13	2	0	0	0	35^1	43	30	20	5	0	21	10	1.811	5.09	97	6.21	.305	2	.200	
• MIELKE, Gary		Gary Roger Mielke b: 1/28/1963, St. James, MN BR/TR, 6'3", 185 lbs. Deb: 8/19/1987																							
1987	Tex-A	0	0	....	3	0	0	0	0	3	3	2	2	2	0	1	3	1.333	6.00	75	6.98	.250	0	....	
1989	Tex-A	1	0	1.000	43	0	0	0	1	49^2	52	18	18	4	2	25	26	1.550	3.26	122	4.80	.280	0	....	
1990	Tex-A	0	3	.000	33	0	0	0	0	41	42	17	17	4	2	15	13	1.390	3.73	105	4.16	.271	0	....	
Total	**3**	**1**	**3**	**.250**	**79**	**0**	**0**	**0**	**1**	**93^2**	**97**	**37**	**37**	**10**	**4**	**41**	**42**	**1.473**	**3.56**	**112**	**4.59**	**.275**	**0**	**....**	
• MIKKELSEN, Pete		Peter James Mikkelsen b: 10/25/1939, Staten Island, NY BR/TR, 6'2", 220 lbs. Deb: 4/17/1964																							
1964*	NY-A	7	4	.636	50	0	0	0	12	86	79	35	34	3	4	41	63	1.395	3.56	102	3.56	.247	1	.063	
1965	NY-A	4	9	.308	41	3	0	0	1	82^1	78	40	30	10	3	36	69	1.385	3.28	104	4.04	.249	1	.100	
1966	Pit-N	9	8	.529	71	0	0	0	14	126	106	45	43	8	5	51	76	1.246	3.07	116	3.13	.234	3	.150	
1967	Pit-N	1	2	.333	32	0	0	0	2	56^1	50	29	27	7	3	19	30	1.225	4.31	78	3.43	.237	0	.000	
	Chi-N	0	0	....	7	0	0	0	0	7	9	6	5	1	1	5	0	2.000	6.43	55	7.93	.333	0	....	
	Yr.	1	2	.333	39	0	0	0	2	63^1	59	35	32	8	4	24	30	1.311	4.55	75	3.92	.248	0	.000	
1968	Chi-N	0	0	....	3	0	0	0	0	4^2	7	4	4	3	0	1	5	1.714	7.71	41	10.46	.350	1	1.000	
	StL-N	0	0	....	5	0	0	0	0	16	10	5	2	0	0	7	8	1.063	1.13	257	1.48	.179	0	.000	
	Yr.	0	0	....	8	0	0	0	0	20^2	17	9	6	3	0	8	13	1.210	2.61	117	3.51	.224	1	.250	
1969	LA-N	7	5	.583	48	0	0	0	4	81^1	57	34	25	9	4	30	51	1.070	2.77	120	2.44	.193	1	.167	
1970	LA-N	4	2	.667	33	0	0	0	6	62	48	20	19	5	4	20	47	1.097	2.76	139	2.60	.211	2	.333	
1971	LA-N	8	5	.615	41	0	0	0	5	74	67	38	30	10	1	17	46	1.135	3.65	89	3.10	.242	2	.200	
1972	LA-N	5	5	.500	33	0	0	0	5	57^2	65	32	26	3	5	23	41	1.526	4.06	82	4.55	.283	0	.000	
Total	**9**	**45**	**40**	**.529**	**364**	**3**	**0**	**0**	**49**	**653^1**	**576**	**288**	**245**	**59**	**30**	**250**	**436**	**1.264**	**3.38**	**102**	**3.38**	**.237**	**11**	**.133**	
• MIKLOS, Hank		John Joseph Miklos b: 11/27/1910, Chicago, IL d: 3/29/2000, Adrian, MI BL/TL, 5'11", 175 lbs. Deb: 4/23/1944																							
1944	Chi-N	0	0	....	2	0	0	0	0	7	9	6	6	1	0	3	0	1.714	7.71	46	6.37	.333	0	.000	
• MILACKI, Bob		Robert Milacki b: 7/28/1964, Trenton, NJ BR/TR, 6'4", 234 lbs. Deb: 9/18/1988																							
1988	Bal-A	2	0	1.000	3	3	1	1	0	25	9	2	2	1	0	9	18	.720	0.72	542	0.94	.110	0	....	

YEAR	TM-L	W	L	PCT	G	GS	CG	SH	SV	IP	H	R	ER	HR	HB	BB	SO	RAT	ERA	ERA+	CERA	OAV	BH	AVG	PR+	WS	TPW
1973	SD-N	0	0	....	18	0	0	0	0	30^{2}	29	18	14	4	0	12	15	1.337	4.11	84	3.81	.244	0	.000	-2	1	-0.2
	Det-A	4	2	.667	22	0	0	0	1	42	34	16	16	3	0	22	23	1.333	3.43	119	3.34	.230	0	....	3	4	0.3
	NY-N	0	0	....	1	0	0	0	0	1	0	0	0	0	0	0	1	.000	0.00	....	0.00	.000	0	....	0	0	0.0
	Yr.	0	0	....	19	0	0	0	0	31^{2}	29	18	14	4	0	12	16	1.295	3.98	87	3.69	.244	0	.000	-2	1	-0.2
1974	NY-N	2	2	.500	58	0	0	0	2	78	89	39	31	2	1	39	35	1.641	3.58	100	4.48	.296	1	.111	-0	4	-0.1
Total	**17**	**69**	**81**	**.460**	**694**	**99**	**7**	**0**	**51**	**1551^{1}**	**1487**	**679**	**581**	**101**	**32**	**608**	**895**	**1.350**	**3.37**	**106**	**3.59**	**.255**	**33**	**.110**	**38**	**96**	**3.2**
• MILLER, Cyclone		Joseph H. Miller b: 9/24/1859, Springfield, MA d: 10/13/1916, New London, CT TL, 5'9.5", 165 lbs. Deb: 7/11/1884 U																									
1884	CP-U	1	0	1.000	1	1	1	0	0	9	4	2	1	0	....	0	13	.444	1.00	288	....	.125	1	.250	2	1	0.2
	Pro-N	3	2	.600	6	5	2	0	0	34^{2}	36	24	8	0	....	11	12	1.356	2.08	136	....	.253	1	.043	2	2	-0.1
	Phi-N	0	1	.000	1	1	1	0	0	9	17	19	10	5	....	6	1	2.556	10.00	30	....	.382	0	.000	-7	0	-0.7
	Yr.	3	3	.500	7	6	3	0	0	43^{2}	53	43	18	5	....	17	13	1.603	3.71	78	....	.284	1	.037	-5	2	-0.8
1886	Phi-a	10	8	.556	19	19	19	1	0	169^{2}	158	109	56	6	4	59	99	1.279	2.97	118	....	.236	9	.136	14	11	1.1
Total	**2**	**14**	**11**	**.560**	**27**	**26**	**23**	**1**	**0**	**222^{1}**	**215**	**154**	**75**	**11**	**4**	**76**	**125**	**1.309**	**3.04**	**110**	**....**	**.242**	**11**	**.113**	**11**	**14**	**0.5**
• MILLER, Dyar		Dyar K. Miller b: 5/29/1946, Batesville, IN BR/TR, 6'1", 195 lbs. Deb: 6/9/1975 C																									
1975	Bal-A	6	3	.667	30	0	0	0	8	46^{1}	32	14	14	3	0	16	33	1.036	2.72	129	1.96	.199	0	....	3	7	0.3
1976	Bal-A	2	4	.333	49	0	0	0	7	88^{2}	79	31	29	5	1	36	37	1.297	2.94	111	3.21	.246	0	....	2	7	0.2
1977	Bal-A	2	2	.500	12	0	0	0	1	22^{1}	25	14	14	6	0	10	9	1.567	5.64	67	6.16	.278	0	....	-5	0	-0.5
	Cal-A	4	4	.500	41	0	0	0	4	92^{1}	81	35	31	10	0	30	49	1.202	3.02	129	3.13	.242	0	....	10	7	1.0
	Yr.	6	6	.500	53	0	0	0	5	114^{2}	106	49	45	16	0	40	58	1.273	3.53	110	3.72	.249	0	....	5	7	0.5
1978	Cal-A	6	2	.750	41	0	0	0	1	84^{2}	85	29	25	3	5	41	34	1.488	2.66	136	4.14	.264	0	....	10	7	1.0
1979	Cal-A	1	0	1.000	14	1	0	0	0	35^{1}	44	14	13	2	2	13	16	1.613	3.31	123	5.42	.319	0	....	3	2	0.3
	Tor-A	0	0	....	10	0	0	0	0	15^{1}	27	18	18	3	0	5	7	2.087	10.57	41	9.53	.391	0	....	-11	0	-1.0
	Yr.	1	0	1.000	24	1	0	0	0	50^{2}	71	32	31	5	2	18	23	1.757	5.51	77	6.66	.343	0	....	-8	2	-0.7
1980	NY-N	1	2	.333	31	0	0	0	1	42	37	9	9	1	0	11	28	1.143	1.93	184	2.36	.242	0	.000	7	4	0.8
1981	NY-N	1	0	1.000	23	0	0	0	0	38^{1}	49	20	14	2	1	15	22	1.670	3.29	106	5.36	.327	1	.333	1	2	0.2
Total	**7**	**23**	**17**	**.575**	**251**	**1**	**0**	**0**	**22**	**465^{1}**	**459**	**184**	**167**	**35**	**9**	**177**	**235**	**1.367**	**3.23**	**114**	**3.86**	**.264**	**1**	**.250**	**20**	**36**	**2.2**
• MILLER, Elmer		Elmer Joseph "Lefty" Miller b: 4/17/1903, Detroit, MI d: 1/8/1987, Corona, CA BL/TL, 5'11", 189 lbs. Deb: 6/21/1929																									
1929	Phi-N	0	1	.000	8	2	0	0	0	11^{1}	12	18	14	1	3	21	5	2.912	11.12	47	10.89	.279	9	.237	-7	0	-0.7
• MILLER, Frank		Frank Lee "Bullet" Miller b: 5/13/1886, Allegan, MI d: 2/19/1974, Allegan, MI BR/TR, 6', 188 lbs. Deb: 7/12/1913																									
1913	Chi-A	0	1	.000	1	1	0	0	0	1^{2}	4	5	5	0	0	3	2	4.200	27.00	11	21.71	.571	0	....	-4	0	-0.5
1916	Pit-N	7	10	.412	30	20	10	2	1	173	135	55	44	4	7	49	88	1.064	2.29	117	2.19	.226	7	.137	11	11	1.2
1917	Pit-N	10	19	.345	38	28	14	5	1	224	216	98	78	1	5	60	92	1.232	3.13	90	2.66	.251	9	.118	-6	8	-1.1
1918	Pit-N	11	8	.579	23	23	14	2	0	170^{1}	152	60	45	1	7	37	47	1.110	2.38	121	2.39	.250	6	.105	4	11	0.1
1919	Pit-N	13	12	.520	32	26	16	3	0	201^{2}	170	79	68	6	5	34	59	1.012	3.03	99	2.06	.234	7	.106	1	12	-0.4
1922	Bos-N	11	13	.458	31	23	14	2	1	200	213	100	78	7	2	60	65	1.365	3.51	114	3.58	.279	8	.118	13	13	0.8
1923	Bos-N	0	3	.000	8	6	0	0	1	39^{1}	54	26	20	2	3	11	6	1.653	4.58	87	5.65	.335	1	.143	-2	1	-0.2
Total	**7**	**52**	**66**	**.441**	**163**	**127**	**68**	**14**	**4**	**1010**	**944**	**423**	**338**	**21**	**29**	**254**	**359**	**1.186**	**3.01**	**103**	**2.74**	**.253**	**38**	**.117**	**17**	**56**	**-0.2**
• MILLER, Fred		Frederick Holman "Speedy" Miller b: 6/28/1886, Fairfield, IN d: 5/2/1953, Brookville, IN BL/TL, 6'2", 190 lbs. Deb: 7/8/1910																									
1910	Bro-N	1	1	.500	6	2	0	0	0	21	25	19	11	1	3	13	2	1.810	4.71	64	6.39	.309	2	.250	-4	0	-0.4
• MILLER, Jake		Walter Miller b: 2/28/1898, Wagram, OH d: 8/20/1975, Venice, FL BL/TL, 6'2", 170 lbs. Deb: 9/11/1924																									
1924	Cle-A	0	1	.000	2	2	1	0	0	12	13	6	4	0	0	5	4	1.500	3.00	142	3.59	.265	0	.000	2	1	0.1
1925	Cle-A	10	13	.435	32	22	13	0	2	190^{1}	207	85	70	4	7	62	51	1.413	3.31	133	3.72	.279	13	.183	24	15	1.9
1926	Cle-A	7	4	.636	18	11	5	3	1	82^{2}	99	34	30	1	2	18	24	1.415	3.27	124	3.92	.307	2	.083	5	7	0.3
1927	Cle-A	10	8	.556	34	23	11	0	0	185^{1}	189	80	66	4	6	48	53	1.279	3.21	131	3.19	.271	8	.138	21	15	1.7
1928	Cle-A	8	9	.471	25	24	8	0	0	158	203	89	78	6	5	43	37	1.557	4.44	93	4.91	.332	7	.135	-4	7	-0.9
1929	Cle-A	14	12	.538	29	29	14	2	0	206	227	98	82	7	7	60	58	1.393	3.58	124	3.78	.279	15	.200	21	17	1.8
1930	Cle-A	4	4	.500	24	9	1	0	0	88^{1}	147	89	70	6	4	38	31	2.094	7.13	68	7.93	.373	10	.303	-21	0	-1.8
1931	Cle-A	2	1	.667	10	5	1	1	0	41^{1}	45	26	20	2	0	19	17	1.548	4.35	106	4.25	.273	1	.077	2	2	0.1
1933	Chi-A	5	6	.455	26	14	4	2	0	105^{2}	130	75	66	3	6	47	30	1.675	5.62	75	5.00	.297	7	.189	-15	2	-1.5
Total	**9**	**60**	**58**	**.508**	**200**	**139**	**58**	**8**	**3**	**1069^{2}**	**1260**	**582**	**486**	**33**	**37**	**340**	**305**	**1.496**	**4.09**	**106**	**4.32**	**.298**	**63**	**.171**	**36**	**66**	**1.6**
• MILLER, John		John Ernest Miller b: 5/30/1941, Baltimore, MD BR/TR, 6'2", 210 lbs. Deb: 9/22/1962																									
1962	Bal-A	1	1	.500	2	1	0	0	0	10	2	1	1	0	0	5	4	.700	0.90	417	0.66	.065	0	.000	3	1	0.3
1963	Bal-A	1	1	.500	3	2	0	0	0	17	12	6	6	0	0	14	16	1.529	3.18	111	3.24	.194	0	.000	1	1	0.0
1965	Bal-A	6	4	.600	16	16	1	0	0	93^{1}	75	38	33	4	1	58	71	1.425	3.18	109	3.49	.223	3	.100	2	5	0.1
1966	Bal-A	4	8	.333	23	16	0	0	0	100^{2}	92	59	53	15	0	58	81	1.490	4.74	70	4.58	.241	4	.118	-16	0	-1.9
1967	Bal-A	0	0	....	2	0	0	0	0	6	7	5	5	1	2	3	6	1.667	7.50	42	7.84	.304	0	....	-3	0	-0.3
Total	**5**	**12**	**14**	**.462**	**46**	**35**	**1**	**0**	**0**	**227**	**188**	**109**	**98**	**20**	**3**	**138**	**178**	**1.436**	**3.89**	**87**	**3.94**	**.225**	**7**	**.096**	**-14**	**7**	**-1.8**
• MILLER, Justin		Justin Mark Miller b: 8/27/1977, Torrance, CA BR/TR, 6'2", 195 lbs. Deb: 4/12/2002																									
2002	Tor-A	9	5	.643	25	18	0	0	0	102^{1}	103	70	63	12	11	66	68	1.651	5.54	83	5.73	.268	0	.000	-10	3	-1.0
• MILLER, Kurt		Kurt Everett Miller b: 8/24/1972, Tucson, AZ BR/TR, 6'5", 205 lbs. Deb: 6/11/1994																									
1994	Fla-N	1	3	.250	4	4	0	0	0	20	26	18	18	3	2	7	11	1.650	8.10	54	6.53	.317	1	.167	-9	0	-0.8
1996	Fla-N	1	3	.250	26	5	0	0	0	46^{1}	57	41	35	5	2	33	30	1.942	6.80	60	6.77	.313	3	.375	-15	0	-1.4
1997	Fla-N	0	1	.000	7	0	0	0	0	7^{1}	12	8	8	2	1	7	7	2.591	9.82	41	13.07	.364	0	....	-5	0	-0.5
1998	Chi-N	0	0	....	3	0	0	0	0	4	3	0	0	0	0	0	6	.750	0.00	....	1.13	.200	0	....	2	1	0.2
1999	Chi-N	0	0	....	4	0	0	0	0	3	6	6	6	1	0	3	1	3.000	18.00	25	16.63	.462	0	....	-4	0	-0.4
Total	**5**	**2**	**7**	**.222**	**44**	**9**	**0**	**0**	**0**	**80^{2}**	**104**	**73**	**67**	**11**	**5**	**50**	**55**	**1.909**	**7.48**	**56**	**7.37**	**.320**	**4**	**.286**	**-30**	**1**	**-2.9**
• MILLER, Larry		Larry Don Miller b: 6/19/1937, Topeka, KS BL/TL, 6', 195 lbs. Deb: 6/21/1964																									
1964	LA-N	4	8	.333	16	14	1	0	0	79^{2}	87	44	37	1	2	28	50	1.444	4.18	77	3.68	.275	7	.269	-8	1	-0.7
1965	NY-N	1	4	.200	28	5	0	0	0	57^{1}	66	32	32	6	1	25	36	1.587	5.02	70	5.16	.289	2	.182	-9	1	-1.0
1966	NY-N	0	2	.000	4	1	0	0	0	8^{1}	9	7	7	3	0	4	7	1.560	7.56	48	6.89	.273	1	.500	-4	0	-0.3
Total	**3**	**5**	**14**	**.263**	**48**	**20**	**1**	**0**	**0**	**145^{1}**	**162**	**83**	**76**	**10**	**3**	**57**	**93**	**1.507**	**4.71**	**72**	**4.45**	**.281**	**10**	**.256**	**-21**	**2**	**-2.0**
• MILLER, Matt		Matthew Lincoln Miller b: 8/2/1974, Lubbock, TX BL/TL, 6'3", 175 lbs. Deb: 5/8/2001																									
2001	Det-A	0	0	....	13	0	0	0	0	9^{2}	16	8	8	0	1	4	6	2.069	7.45	58	7.86	.372	0	....	-3	0	-0.3
2002	Det-A	0	0	....	2	0	0	0	0	0^{2}	4	2	1	1	0	1	1	7.500	13.50	32	62.48	.571	0	....	-1	0	-0.1
Total	**2**	**0**	**0**	**....**	**15**	**0**	**0**	**0**	**0**	**10^{1}**	**20**	**10**	**9**	**1**	**1**	**5**	**7**	**2.419**	**7.84**	**55**	**11.38**	**.400**	**0**	**....**	**-4**	**0**	**-0.4**
• MILLER, Matt		Matt Jacob Miller b: 11/23/1971, Greenwood, MS BR/TR, 6'3", 215 lbs. Deb: 6/27/2003																									
2003	Col-N	0	0	....	4	0	0	0	0	4^{1}	5	1	1	0	0	2	5	1.615	2.08	236	4.86	.313	0	....	1	1	0.1
• MILLER, Ox		John Anthony Miller b: 5/4/1915, Gause, TX BR/TR, 6'1", 190 lbs. Deb: 8/7/1943																									
1943	Was-A	0	0	....	3	0	0	0	0	6	10	7	7	1	0	5	1	2.500	10.50	30	10.34	.370	0	.000	-5	0	-0.5
	StL-A	0	0	....	2	0	0	0	0	6	7	8	8	2	2	3	3	1.667	12.00	28	8.80	.304	0	.000	-6	0	-0.6
	Yr.	0	0	....	5	0	0	0	0	12	17	15	15	3	2	8	4	2.083	11.25	29	9.57	.340	0	.000	-11	0	-1.2
1945	StL-A	2	1	.667	4	3	3	0	0	28^{1}	23	5	5	2	0	5	4	.988	1.59	221	2.08	.219	2	.182	6	4	0.6
1946	StL-A	1	3	.250	11	3	0	0	1	35^{1}	52	28	27	5	0	15	12	1.896	6.88	54	7.17	.338	2	.286	-12	0	-1.2
1947	Chi-N	1	2	.333	4	4	1	0	0	16	31	18	18	2	0	5	7	2.250	10.13	39	9.66	.397	3	.429	-11	1	-0.9
Total	**4**	**4**	**6**	**.400**	**24**	**10**	**4**	**0**	**1**	**91^{2}**	**123**	**66**	**65**	**12**	**2**	**33**	**27**	**1.702**	**6.38**	**57**	**6.34**	**.318**	**7**	**.259**	**-28**	**5**	**-2.6**
• MILLER, Paul		Paul Robert Miller b: 4/27/1965, Burlington, WI BR/TR, 6'5", 215 lbs. Deb: 7/30/1991																									
1991	Pit-N	0	0	....	1	1	0	0	0	5	4	3	3	0	0	3	2	1.400	5.40	66	3.13	.222	0	.000	-1	0	-0.1

YEAR TM-L	W	L	PCT	G	GS	CG	SH	SV	IP	H	R	ER	HR	HB	BB	SO	RAT	ERA	ERA+	CERA	OAV	BH	AVG	PR+	WS	TPW
1992 Pit-N	1	0	1.000	6	0	0	0	0	11^{1}	11	3	3	0	0	1	5	1.059	2.38	144	2.10	.256	0	.000	1	1	0.1
1993 Pit-N	0	0	....	3	2	0	0	0	10	15	6	6	2	0	2	2	1.700	5.40	75	6.85	.349	0	.000	-2	0	-0.2
Total 3	**1**	**0**	**1.000**	**10**	**3**	**0**	**0**	**0**	**26^{1}**	**30**	**12**	**12**	**2**	**0**	**6**	**9**	**1.367**	**4.10**	**92**	**4.10**	**.288**	**0**	**.000**	**-1**	**1**	**-0.2**
• MILLER, Ralph	Ralph Darwin Miller b: 3/15/1873, Cincinnati, OH d: 5/8/1973, Cincinnati, OH BR/TR, 5'11", 170 lbs. Deb: 5/4/1898																									
1898 Bro-N	4	14	.222	23	21	16	0	0	151^{2}	161	119	90	4	13	86	43	1.629	5.34	67	4.68	.270	12	.194	-28	2	-2.7
1899 Bal-N	1	3	.250	6	4	3	0	0	37	44	28	18	0	4	14	3	1.568	4.38	90	4.60	.295	2	.182	-2	2	0.0
Total 2	**5**	**17**	**.227**	**29**	**25**	**19**	**0**	**0**	**188^{2}**	**205**	**147**	**108**	**4**	**17**	**100**	**46**	**1.617**	**5.15**	**71**	**4.66**	**.275**	**14**	**.192**	**-30**	**4**	**-2.7**
• MILLER, Ralph	Ralph Henry "Moose,Lefty" Miller b: 1/14/1899, Vinton, IA d: 2/18/1967, White Bear Lake, MN BR/TL, 6'1.5", 190 lbs. Deb: 9/16/1921																									
1921 Was-A	0	0	....	1	0	0	0	0	1	0	0	0	0	0	0	0	.000	0.00	....	0.00	.000	0	....	0	0	0.0
• MILLER, Randy	Randall Scott Miller b: 3/18/1953, Oxnard, CA BR/TR, 6'1", 180 lbs. Deb: 9/7/1977																									
1977 Bal-A	0	0	....	1	0	0	0	0	0^{2}	4	3	3	0	0	0	0	6.000	40.50	9	39.65	.800	0	....	-3	0	-0.3
1978 Mon-N	0	1	.000	5	0	0	0	0	7	11	9	8	1	0	3	6	2.000	10.29	34	7.36	.393	0	.000	-5	0	-0.6
Total 2	**0**	**1**	**.000**	**6**	**0**	**0**	**0**	**0**	**7^{2}**	**15**	**12**	**11**	**1**	**0**	**3**	**6**	**2.348**	**12.91**	**28**	**10.17**	**.455**	**0**	**.000**	**-8**	**0**	**-0.9**
• MILLER, Red	Leo Alphonso Miller b: 2/11/1897, Philadelphia, PA d: 10/20/1973, Orlando, FL BR/TR, 5'11", 195 lbs. Deb: 7/13/1923																									
1923 Phi-N	0	0	....	1	0	0	0	0	1^{2}	6	6	6	0	0	1	0	4.200	32.40	14	22.05	.545	0	.000	-5	0	-0.5
• MILLER, Roger	Roger Wesley Miller b: 8/1/1954, Connellsville, PA d: 4/26/1993, Mill Run, PA BR/TR, 6'3", 200 lbs. Deb: 9/8/1974																									
1974 Mil-A	0	0	....	2	0	0	0	0	2^{1}	3	3	3	1	1	0	2	1.286	11.57	31	8.35	.300	0	....	-2	0	-0.2
• MILLER, Ronnie	Ronald Arthur Miller b: 8/28/1918, Mason City, IA d: 1/6/1998, Ferguson, MO BB/TR, 5'11", 167 lbs. Deb: 9/10/1941																									
1941 Was-A	0	0	....	1	0	0	0	0	2	2	1	1	0	0	1	0	1.500	4.50	90	4.66	.333	0	....	-0	0	0.0
• MILLER, Roscoe	Roscoe Clyde "Roxy,Rubberlegs" Miller b: 12/2/1876, Greenville, IN d: 4/18/1913, Croydon, IN BR/TR, 6'2", 190 lbs. Deb: 4/25/1901																									
1901 Det-A	23	13	.639	38	36	35	3	1	332	339	168	109	1	13	98	79	1.316	2.95	130	3.19	.262	27	.208	29	30	2.7
1902 Det-A	6	12	.333	20	18	15	1	1	148^{2}	158	85	61	3	9	57	39	1.446	3.69	99	3.91	.273	11	.183	-3	7	-0.4
NY-N	1	8	.111	10	9	7	0	0	72^{2}	77	40	37	1	5	11	15	1.211	4.58	61	3.09	.272	1	.048	-14	1	-1.7
1903 NY-N	2	5	.286	15	8	6	0	**3**	85	101	53	39	1	1	24	30	1.471	4.13	81	4.16	.302	5	.161	-9	4	-1.0
1904 Pit-N	7	7	.500	19	17	11	2	0	134^{1}	133	67	50	4	4	39	35	1.280	3.35	82	3.18	.256	2	.043	-10	5	-1.4
Total 4	**39**	**45**	**.464**	**102**	**88**	**74**	**6**	**5**	**772^{2}**	**808**	**413**	**296**	**10**	**32**	**229**	**198**	**1.342**	**3.45**	**97**	**3.43**	**.268**	**46**	**.160**	**-7**	**47**	**-1.8**
• MILLER, Russ	Russell Lewis Miller b: 3/25/1900, Etna, OH d: 4/30/1962, Bucyrus, OH BR/TR, 5'11", 165 lbs. Deb: 9/24/1927																									
1927 Phi-N	1	1	.500	2	2	1	0	0	15^{1}	21	9	9	2	1	3	4	1.565	5.28	78	5.78	.339	1	.333	-2	1	-0.2
1928 Phi-N	0	12	.000	33	12	1	0	1	108	137	79	65	14	0	34	19	1.583	5.42	79	5.42	.315	4	.148	-12	2	-1.3
Total 2	**1**	**13**	**.071**	**35**	**14**	**2**	**0**	**1**	**123^{1}**	**158**	**88**	**74**	**16**	**1**	**37**	**23**	**1.581**	**5.40**	**79**	**5.46**	**.318**	**5**	**.167**	**-14**	**3**	**-1.4**
• MILLER, Stu	Stuart Leonard Miller b: 12/26/1927, Northampton, MA BR/TR, 5'11.5", 165 lbs. Deb: 8/12/1952																									
1952 StL-N	6	3	.667	12	11	6	2	0	88	63	25	20	3	2	26	64	1.011	2.05	181	1.85	.197	3	.120	16	9	1.5
1953 StL-N	7	8	.467	40	18	8	2	4	137^{2}	161	86	85	19	2	47	79	1.511	5.56	77	5.07	.293	8	.186	-18	4	-1.7
1954 StL-N	2	3	.400	19	4	0	0	2	46^{2}	55	36	30	5	3	29	22	1.800	5.79	71	6.25	.307	4	.308	-8	1	-0.7
1956 StL-N	0	1	.000	3	0	0	0	1	7^{1}	12	6	4	3	0	5	5	2.318	4.91	77	12.71	.387	0	.000	-1	0	-0.1
Phi-N	5	8	.385	24	15	2	0	0	106^{2}	109	65	53	16	4	51	55	1.500	4.47	83	4.79	.263	4	.160	-7	3	-0.4
Yr.	5	9	.357	27	15	2	0	1	114	121	71	57	19	4	56	60	1.553	4.50	83	5.30	.271	4	.154	-7	3	-0.5
1957 NY-N	7	9	.438	38	13	0	0	1	124	110	53	50	15	3	45	60	1.250	3.63	108	3.52	.242	2	.057	5	8	0.1
1958 SF-N	6	9	.400	41	20	4	1	0	182	160	60	50	16	2	49	119	1.148	**2.47**	**154**	**2.87**	.233	6	.120	29	15	2.9
1959 SF-N	8	7	.533	59	9	2	0	8	167^{2}	164	66	53	15	5	57	95	1.318	2.84	134	3.63	.260	2	.044	19	13	1.6
1960 SF-N	7	6	.538	47	3	2	0	2	101^{2}	100	49	44	9	3	31	65	1.289	3.90	89	3.51	.256	5	.200	-4	4	-0.3
1961 SF-N★	14	5	.737	63	0	0	0	**17**	122	95	41	36	4	1	37	89	1.082	2.66	143	2.08	.215	4	.200	17	18	1.8
1962* SF-N	5	8	.385	59	0	0	0	19	107	107	55	49	8	2	42	78	1.393	4.12	92	3.84	.268	2	.125	-4	8	-0.4
1963 Bal-A	5	8	.385	**71**	0	0	0	**27**	112^{1}	93	36	28	5	3	53	114	1.300	2.24	157	2.99	.232	5	.313	16	16	1.9
1964 Bal-A	7	7	.500	66	0	0	0	23	97	77	37	33	7	3	34	87	1.144	3.06	117	2.56	.222	1	.111	3	13	0.3
1965 Bal-A	14	7	.667	67	0	0	0	24	119^{1}	87	26	25	5	1	32	104	.997	1.89	184	1.84	.207	1	.063	19	22	2.0
1966 Bal-A	9	4	.692	51	0	0	0	18	92	65	24	23	5	4	22	67	.946	2.25	148	1.82	.201	2	.105	11	14	1.0
1967 Bal-A	3	10	.231	42	0	0	0	8	81^{1}	63	28	23	5	1	36	60	1.217	2.55	124	2.60	.220	0	.000	4	6	0.3
1968 Atl-N	0	0	....	2	0	0	0	0	1^{1}	1	4	4	0	0	4	1	3.750	27.00	11	10.23	.500	0	....	-4	0	-0.4
Total 16	**105**	**103**	**.505**	**704**	**93**	**24**	**5**	**154**	**1694**	**1522**	**697**	**610**	**140**	**39**	**600**	**1164**	**1.253**	**3.24**	**116**	**3.27**	**.242**	**49**	**.133**	**93**	**154**	**9.3**
• MILLER, Travis	Travis Eugene Miller b: 11/2/1972, Dayton, OH BR/TL, 6'3", 205 lbs. Deb: 8/25/1996																									
1996 Min-A	1	2	.333	7	7	0	0	0	26^{1}	45	29	27	7	0	9	15	2.051	9.23	55	10.05	.388	0	....	-12	0	-1.1
1997 Min-A	1	5	.167	13	7	0	0	0	48^{1}	64	49	41	8	1	23	26	1.800	7.63	61	6.90	.320	0	....	-16	0	-1.5
1998 Min-A	0	2	.000	14	0	0	0	0	23^{1}	25	10	10	0	0	11	23	1.543	3.86	124	3.92	.272	0	....	3	1	0.3
1999 Min-A	2	2	.500	52	0	0	0	0	49^{2}	55	18	15	3	0	16	40	1.430	2.72	187	4.01	.284	0	....	13	5	1.2
2000 Min-A	2	3	.400	67	0	0	0	1	67	83	35	29	4	1	32	62	1.716	3.90	132	5.35	.297	0	....	10	5	1.0
2001 Min-A	1	4	.200	45	0	0	0	0	48^{2}	54	30	26	5	1	20	30	1.521	4.81	96	4.82	.283	0	....	-1	2	-0.1
2002 Min-A	0	0	....	5	0	0	0	0	4	5	2	2	0	0	2	3	1.750	4.50	100	4.07	.294	0	....	-0	0	0.0
Total 7	**7**	**18**	**.280**	**203**	**14**	**0**	**0**	**1**	**267^{1}**	**331**	**173**	**150**	**27**	**3**	**113**	**199**	**1.661**	**5.05**	**96**	**5.60**	**.304**	**0**	**....**	**-3**	**13**	**-0.3**
• MILLER, Trever	Trever Douglas Miller b: 5/29/1973, Louisville, KY BR/TL, 6'3", 175 lbs. Deb: 9/4/1996																									
1996 Det-A	0	4	.000	5	4	0	0	0	16^{2}	28	17	17	3	2	9	8	2.220	9.18	55	10.15	.384	0	....	-7	0	-0.7
1998* Hou-N	2	0	1.000	37	1	0	0	1	53^{1}	57	21	18	4	1	20	30	1.444	3.04	134	4.18	.266	1	.333	6	4	0.6
1999* Hou-N	3	2	.600	47	0	0	0	1	49^{2}	58	29	28	6	5	29	37	1.752	5.07	87	6.48	.299	0	.000	-4	2	-0.4
2000 Phi-N	0	0	....	14	0	0	0	0	14	19	16	13	3	1	9	10	2.000	8.36	56	8.14	.317	0	....	-6	0	-0.5
LA-N	0	0	....	2	0	0	0	0	2^{1}	8	6	6	0	1	3	1	4.714	23.14	19	28.18	.571	0	....	-5	0	-0.5
Yr.	0	0	....	16	0	0	0	0	16^{1}	27	22	19	3	2	12	11	2.388	10.47	43	11.00	.365	0	....	-11	0	-1.0
2003 Tor-A	2	2	.500	**79**	0	0	0	4	52^{2}	46	30	27	7	5	28	44	1.405	4.61	100	4.38	.231	0	....	1	4	0.1
Total 5	**7**	**8**	**.467**	**184**	**5**	**0**	**0**	**6**	**188^{2}**	**216**	**119**	**109**	**23**	**15**	**98**	**130**	**1.664**	**5.20**	**87**	**5.96**	**.286**	**1**	**.167**	**-15**	**10**	**-1.4**
• MILLER, Wade	Wade T. Miller b: 9/13/1976, Reading, PA BR/TR, 6'2", 185 lbs. Deb: 7/7/1999																									
1999 Hou-N	0	1	.000	5	1	0	0	0	10^{1}	17	11	11	4	0	5	8	2.129	9.58	46	11.07	.362	0	.000	-6	0	-0.6
2000 Hou-N	6	6	.500	16	16	2	0	0	105	104	66	60	14	3	42	89	1.390	5.14	94	4.37	.257	4	.100	-2	4	-0.3
2001* Hou-N	16	8	.667	32	32	1	0	0	212	183	91	80	31	4	76	183	1.222	3.40	134	3.57	.234	11	.167	27	17	2.6
2002 Hou-N	15	4	.789	26	26	1	1	0	164^{2}	151	63	60	14	6	62	144	1.294	3.28	130	3.54	.249	11	.177	19	14	2.0
2003 Hou-N	14	13	.519	33	33	1	0	0	187^{1}	168	96	86	17	10	77	161	1.308	4.13	107	3.70	.242	10	.159	2	9	0.2
Total 5	**51**	**32**	**.614**	**112**	**108**	**5**	**1**	**0**	**679^{1}**	**623**	**327**	**297**	**80**	**23**	**262**	**585**	**1.303**	**3.93**	**115**	**3.84**	**.246**	**36**	**.155**	**41**	**44**	**3.9**
• MILLER, Walt	Walter W. Miller b: 10/19/1884, Spiceland, IN d: 3/1/1956, Marion, IN BR/TR, 5'11.5", 180 lbs. Deb: 9/20/1911																									
1911 Bro-N	0	1	.000	3	2	0	0	0	11	16	14	8	0	1	6	0	2.000	6.55	51	7.11	.356	0	.000	-4	0	-0.4
• MILLER, Whitey	Kenneth Albert Miller b: 5/2/1915, St. Louis, MO d: 4/3/1991, St. Louis, MO BR/TR, 6'1", 195 lbs. Deb: 9/15/1944																									
1944 NY-N	0	1	.000	4	0	0	0	0	5	1	2	0	0	0	4	2	1.000	0.00	....	0.97	.059	0	.000	2	1	0.2
• MILLIGAN, Billy	William Joseph Milligan b: 8/19/1878, Buffalo, NY d: 10/14/1928, Buffalo, NY BR/TL, 5'7" Deb: 4/30/1901																									
1901 Phi-A	0	3	.000	6	3	2	0	0	33	43	24	16	1	2	14	5	1.727	4.36	86	5.51	.311	5	.333	-2	2	0.0
1904 NY-N	0	1	.000	5	1	1	0	2	25	36	22	15	2	1	4	6	1.600	5.40	50	5.23	.310	1	.111	-8	0	-0.8
Total 2	**0**	**4**	**.000**	**11**	**4**	**3**	**0**	**2**	**58**	**79**	**46**	**31**	**3**	**3**	**18**	**11**	**1.672**	**4.81**	**66**	**5.39**	**.311**	**6**	**.250**	**-10**	**2**	**-0.8**
• MILLIGAN, John	John Alexander Milligan b: 1/22/1904, Schuylerville, NY d: 5/15/1972, Fort Pierce, FL BR/TL, 5'10", 172 lbs. Deb: 8/11/1928																									
1928 Phi-N	2	5	.286	13	7	3	0	0	68	69	39	33	2	1	32	22	1.485	4.37	98	3.94	.274	1	.050	0	3	-0.2

YEAR TM-L	W	L	PCT	G	GS	CG	SH	SV	IP	H	R	ER	HR	HB	BB	SO	RAT	ERA	ERA+	CERA	OAV	BH	AVG	PR+	WS	TPW
1929 Phi-N	0	1	.000	8	3	0	0	0	9^2	29	19	18	0	2	10	2	4.034	16.76	31	20.82	.527	1	.333	-12	0	-1.1
1930 Phi-N	1	2	.333	9	2	1	0	0	28^1	26	16	10	0	2	21	7	1.659	3.18	172	4.26	.255	1	.111	8	2	0.6
1931 Phi-N	0	0	....	3	0	0	0	0	8	11	5	3	0	1	4	6	1.875	3.38	126	6.21	.324	0	.000	1	0	0.1
1934 Was-A	0	0	....	2	0	0	0	0	2^2	6	3	3	0	0	0	1	2.250	10.13	43	10.75	.500	0	....	-2	0	-0.2
Total 5	**3**	**8**	**.273**	**35**	**12**	**4**	**0**	**0**	116^2	**141**	**82**	**67**	**2**	**6**	**67**	**38**	**1.783**	**5.17**	**90**	**5.73**	**.310**	**3**	**.088**	**-5**	**5**	**-0.8**
• MILLIKEN, Bob	Robert Fogle "Bobo" Milliken b: 8/25/1926, Majorsville, WV BR/TR, 6', 195 lbs. Deb: 4/22/1953 C																									
1953* Bro-N	8	4	.667	37	10	3	0	2	117^2	94	52	44	13	0	42	65	1.156	3.37	127	2.80	.214	4	.118	10	9	0.8
1954 Bro-N	5	2	.714	24	3	0	0	2	62^2	58	31	28	12	2	18	25	1.213	4.02	102	3.89	.246	3	.176	0	5	0.0
Total 2	**13**	**6**	**.684**	**61**	**13**	**3**	**0**	**4**	180^1	**152**	**83**	**72**	**25**	**2**	**60**	**90**	**1.176**	**3.59**	**117**	**3.18**	**.225**	**7**	**.137**	**10**	**14**	**0.8**
• MILLS, Alan	Alan Bernard Mills b: 10/18/1966, Lakeland, FL BR/TR, 6'1", 192 lbs. Deb: 4/14/1990																									
1990 NY-A	1	5	.167	36	0	0	0	0	41^2	48	21	19	4	1	33	24	1.944	4.10	97	6.44	.298	0	....	-1	2	-0.1
1991 NY-A	1	1	.500	6	2	0	0	0	16^1	16	9	8	1	0	8	11	1.469	4.41	94	3.99	.254	0	....	-0	1	0.0
1992 Bal-A	10	4	.714	35	3	0	0	2	103^1	78	33	30	5	1	54	60	1.277	2.61	154	2.81	.215	0	....	16	11	1.6
1993 Bal-A	5	4	.556	45	0	0	0	4	100^1	80	39	36	14	4	51	68	1.306	3.23	138	3.80	.225	0	....	12	9	1.2
1994 Bal-A	3	3	.500	47	0	0	0	2	45^1	43	26	26	7	2	24	44	1.478	5.16	97	4.85	.251	0	....	-1	3	-0.1
1995 Bal-A	3	0	1.000	21	0	0	0	0	23	30	20	19	4	2	18	16	2.087	7.43	64	8.10	.309	0	....	-7	0	-0.7
1996* Bal-A	3	2	.600	49	0	0	0	3	54^2	40	26	26	10	1	35	50	1.372	4.28	115	4.17	.208	0	....	4	5	0.4
1997* Bal-A	2	3	.400	39	0	0	0	0	38^2	41	23	21	5	1	33	32	1.914	4.89	90	6.39	.268	0	....	-2	1	-0.2
1998 Bal-A	3	4	.429	72	0	0	0	2	77	55	32	32	8	1	50	57	1.364	3.74	122	3.42	.203	0	....	8	7	0.7
1999 LA-N	3	4	.429	68	0	0	0	0	72^1	70	33	30	10	4	43	49	1.562	3.73	115	5.17	.261	0	.000	5	5	0.4
2000 LA-N	2	1	.667	18	0	0	0	1	25^2	31	12	12	3	1	16	18	1.831	4.21	103	6.72	.304	0	.000	0	2	0.0
Bal-A	2	0	1.000	23	0	0	0	1	23^2	25	17	17	6	1	19	18	1.859	6.46	73	7.36	.263	0	....	-5	1	-0.4
2001 Bal-A	1	1	.500	15	0	0	0	0	14	20	15	15	6	2	11	9	2.214	9.64	44	11.82	.333	0	....	-8	0	-0.8
Total 12	**39**	**32**	**.549**	**474**	**5**	**0**	**0**	**15**	**636**	**577**	**306**	**291**	**83**	**21**	**395**	**456**	**1.528**	**4.12**	**108**	**4.77**	**.245**	**0**	**.000**	**20**	**47**	**2.0**
• MILLS, Art	Arthur Grant Mills b: 3/2/1903, Utica, NY d: 7/23/1975, Utica, NY BR/TR, 5'10", 155 lbs. Deb: 4/16/1927 C																									
1927 Bos-N	0	1	.000	15	1	0	0	0	37^2	41	19	16	1	3	18	7	1.566	3.82	97	4.42	.287	0	.000	0	2	-0.1
1928 Bos-N	0	0	....	4	0	0	0	0	7^2	17	11	11	3	2	8	0	3.261	12.91	30	19.95	.472	0	.000	-7	0	-0.7
Total 2	**0**	**1**	**.000**	**19**	**1**	**0**	**0**	**0**	45^1	**58**	**30**	**27**	**4**	**5**	**26**	**7**	**1.853**	**5.36**	**71**	**7.05**	**.324**	**0**	**.000**	**-7**	**2**	**-0.8**
• MILLS, Dick	Richard Alan Mills b: 1/29/1945, Boston, MA BR/TR, 6'3", 195 lbs. Deb: 9/7/1970																									
1970 Bos-A	0	0	....	2	0	0	0	0	3^2	6	4	1	0	1	3	3	2.455	2.45	161	9.42	.353	0	....	1	0	0.1
• MILLS, Lefty	Howard Robinson Mills b: 5/12/1910, Dedham, MA d: 9/23/1982, Riverside, CA BL/TL, 6'1", 187 lbs. Deb: 6/10/1934																									
1934 StL-A	0	0	....	4	0	0	0	0	8^2	10	4	4	0	0	11	2	2.423	4.15	120	7.57	.303	1	.333	1	1	0.1
1937 StL-A	1	1	.500	2	2	1	0	0	12^2	16	13	9	1	0	10	10	2.053	6.39	75	6.46	.286	0	.000	-2	0	-0.3
1938 StL-A	10	12	.455	30	27	15	1	0	210^1	216	139	124	16	8	116	134	1.578	5.31	94	4.57	.262	6	.091	-8	11	-0.9
1939 StL-A	4	11	.267	34	14	4	0	2	144^1	147	114	105	16	8	113	103	1.801	6.55	74	5.71	.264	11	.234	-23	3	-2.0
1940 StL-A	0	6	.000	26	5	1	0	0	59	64	55	51	7	3	52	18	1.966	7.78	59	6.60	.275	2	.154	-21	0	-2.0
Total 5	**15**	**30**	**.333**	**96**	**48**	**21**	**1**	**2**	**435**	**453**	**325**	**293**	**40**	**19**	**302**	**267**	**1.736**	**6.06**	**80**	**5.34**	**.266**	**20**	**.149**	**-53**	**15**	**-5.1**
• MILLS, Willie	William Grant "Wee Willie" Mills b: 8/15/1877, Scheneves, NY d: 7/5/1914, Norwood, NY BR/TR, 5'7", 150 lbs. Deb: 7/13/1901																									
1901 NY-N	0	2	.000	2	2	2	0	0	16	21	15	15	2	1	4	3	1.563	8.44	39	5.68	.314	1	.167	-9	0	-0.8
• MILLWOOD, Kevin	Kevin Austin Millwood b: 12/24/1974, Gastonia, NC BR/TR, 6'4", 205 lbs. Deb: 7/14/1997																									
1997 Atl-N	5	3	.625	12	8	0	0	0	51^1	55	26	23	1	2	21	42	1.481	4.03	104	4.03	.281	0	.000	1	3	0.0
1998 Atl-N	17	8	.680	31	29	3	1	0	174^1	175	86	79	18	3	56	163	1.325	4.08	102	3.81	.258	4	.080	-0	10	-0.1
1999* Atl-N★	18	7	.720	33	33	2	0	0	228	168	80	68	24	4	59	205	.996	2.68	167	**2.26**	**.202**	12	.154	48	22	4.5
2000* Atl-N	10	13	.435	36	**35**	0	0	0	212^2	213	115	110	26	3	62	168	1.293	4.66	98	3.83	.258	7	.119	-0	10	-0.2
2001* Atl-N	7	7	.500	21	21	0	0	0	121	121	66	58	20	1	40	84	1.331	4.31	102	4.20	.260	4	.093	1	5	-0.1
2002* Atl-N	18	8	.692	35	34	1	1	0	217	186	83	78	16	8	65	178	1.157	3.24	126	2.85	.230	14	.200	17	19	2.0
2003 Phi-N	14	12	.538	35	35	5	**3**	0	222	210	103	99	19	4	68	169	1.252	4.01	99	3.35	.250	4	.059	-0	12	-0.3
Total 7	**89**	**58**	**.605**	**203**	**195**	**11**	**5**	**0**	1226^1	**1128**	**559**	**515**	**124**	**25**	**371**	**1009**	**1.222**	**3.78**	**113**	**3.32**	**.243**	**45**	**.118**	**65**	**81**	**5.7**
• MILNAR, Al	Albert Joseph "Happy" Milnar b: 12/26/1913, Cleveland, OH BL/TL, 6'2", 195 lbs. Deb: 4/30/1936																									
1936 Cle-A	1	2	.333	4	3	1	0	0	22	26	20	18	0	0	18	9	2.000	7.36	68	5.54	.286	3	.300	-6	0	-0.5
1938 Cle-A	3	1	.750	23	5	2	0	1	68^1	90	48	38	5	0	26	29	1.698	5.00	93	5.57	.320	4	.154	-3	3	-0.3
1939 Cle-A	14	12	.538	37	26	12	2	3	209	212	96	88	11	0	99	76	1.488	3.79	116	3.96	.264	20	.253	14	18	1.6
1940 Cle-A★	18	10	.643	37	33	15	**4**	3	242^1	242	120	88	14	1	99	99	1.407	3.27	129	3.70	.257	17	.181	20	17	1.7
1941 Cle-A	12	19	.387	35	30	9	1	0	229^1	236	128	111	9	1	116	82	1.535	4.36	91	4.08	.266	14	.171	-12	10	-0.9
1942 Cle-A	6	8	.429	28	19	8	2	0	157	146	82	72	3	4	85	35	1.471	4.13	84	3.62	.251	12	.171	-14	5	-1.3
1943 Cle-A	1	3	.250	16	6	0	0	0	39	51	38	35	0	1	35	12	2.205	8.08	38	7.10	.329	4	.211	-22	0	-2.4
StL-A	1	2	.333	3	2	1	0	0	14^2	23	11	9	0	0	9	7	2.182	5.52	60	7.18	.354	2	.333	-3	0	-0.3
Yr.	2	5	.286	19	8	1	0	0	53^2	74	49	44	0	1	44	19	2.199	7.38	43	7.13	.336	6	.240	-26	0	-2.7
1946 StL-A	1	1	.500	4	2	1	1	0	14^2	15	4	4	1	0	6	1	1.432	2.45	152	4.10	.278	3	.750	2	2	0.4
Phi-N	0	0	....	1	1	0	0	0	0	2	4	0	0	0	2	0		....	....	∞	1.000	0	....	0	0	0.0
Total 8	**57**	**58**	**.496**	**188**	**127**	**49**	**10**	**7**	996^1	**1043**	**551**	**463**	**43**	**7**	**495**	**350**	**1.544**	**4.18**	**95**	**4.19**	**.270**	**79**	**.203**	**-24**	**55**	**-1.9**
• MILSTEAD, George	George Earl "Cowboy" Milstead b: 6/26/1903, Cleburne, TX d: 8/9/1977, Cleburne, TX BL/TL, 5'10", 144 lbs. Deb: 6/27/1924																									
1924 Chi-N	1	1	.500	13	2	1	0	0	29^2	41	25	20	3	1	13	6	1.820	6.07	64	6.46	.328	1	.167	-8	0	-0.7
1925 Chi-N	1	1	.500	5	3	1	0	0	21	26	12	7	0	0	8	7	1.619	3.00	144	4.64	.310	0	.000	3	1	0.1
1926 Chi-N	1	5	.167	18	4	0	0	2	55^1	63	30	22	0	1	24	14	1.572	3.58	107	4.32	.309	1	.053	1	2	-0.2
Total 3	**3**	**7**	**.300**	**36**	**9**	**2**	**0**	**2**	**106**	**130**	**67**	**49**	**3**	**2**	**45**	**27**	**1.651**	**4.16**	**94**	**4.99**	**.315**	**2**	**.063**	**-4**	**3**	**-0.8**
• MILTON, Eric	Eric Robert Milton b: 8/4/1975, State College, PA BL/TL, 6'3", 220 lbs. Deb: 4/5/1998																									
1998 Min-A	8	14	.364	32	32	1	0	0	172^1	195	113	108	25	2	70	107	1.538	5.64	85	5.21	.282	4	.444	-14	6	-1.2
1999 Min-A	7	11	.389	34	34	4	2	0	206^1	190	111	103	28	3	63	163	1.226	4.49	113	3.56	.243	0	.000	14	12	1.3
2000 Min-A	13	10	.565	33	33	0	0	0	200	205	123	108	35	7	44	160	1.245	4.86	106	4.09	.260	0	.000	10	11	0.9
2001 Min-A★	15	7	.682	35	34	2	1	0	220^2	222	109	106	35	5	61	157	1.282	4.32	106	4.05	.257	0	.000	8	15	0.7
2002* Min-A	13	9	.591	29	29	2	1	0	171	173	96	92	24	3	30	121	1.187	4.84	93	3.59	.258	2	.400	-7	9	-0.6
2003* Min-A	1	0	1.000	3	3	0	0	0	17	15	5	5	2	0	1	7	.941	2.65	172	2.29	.234	0	....	4	2	0.4
Total 6	**57**	**51**	**.528**	**166**	**165**	**9**	**4**	**0**	987^1	**1000**	**557**	**522**	**149**	**20**	**269**	**715**	**1.285**	**4.76**	**101**	**4.05**	**.259**	**6**	**.300**	**15**	**55**	**1.6**
• MILTON, Larry	Samuel Lawrence "Tug" Milton b: 5/4/1879, Owensboro, KY d: 5/16/1942, Tulsa, OK TR Deb: 5/7/1903																									
1903 StL-N	0	0	....	1	0	0	0	0	4	3	1	1	0	0	1	0	1.000	2.25	145	1.61	.200	1	.500	0	0	0.1
• MIMBS, Mike	Michael Randall Mimbs b: 2/13/1969, Macon, GA BL/TL, 6'2", 180 lbs. Deb: 5/6/1995																									
1995 Phi-N	9	7	.563	35	19	2	1	1	136^2	127	70	63	10	6	75	93	1.478	4.15	102	4.22	.250	5	.143	0	8	-0.1
1996 Phi-N	3	9	.250	21	17	0	0	0	99^1	116	66	61	13	2	41	56	1.581	5.53	78	5.38	.294	4	.121	-14	1	-1.5
1997 Phi-N	0	3	.000	17	1	0	0	0	28^2	31	27	24	6	3	27	29	2.023	7.53	56	8.03	.272	0	.000	-10	0	-1.0
Total 3	**12**	**19**	**.387**	**73**	**37**	**2**	**1**	**1**	264^2	**274**	**163**	**148**	**29**	**11**	**143**	**178**	**1.576**	**5.03**	**85**	**5.07**	**.270**	**9**	**.129**	**-24**	**9**	**-2.6**
• MINAHAN, Cotton	Edmund Joseph Minahan b: 12/10/1882, Springfield, OH d: 5/20/1958, East Orange, NJ BR/TR, 6', 190 lbs. Deb: 4/21/1907																									
1907 Cin-N	0	2	.000	2	2	1	0	0	14	12	8	2	0	1	13	4	1.786	1.29	201	5.03	.261	0	.000	2	0	0.1
• MINARCIN, Rudy	Rudy Anthony "Buster" Minarcin b: 3/25/1930, North Vandergrift, PA BR/TR, 6', 195 lbs. Deb: 4/11/1955																									
1955 Cin-N	5	9	.357	41	12	3	1	1	115^2	116	73	63	17	3	51	45	1.444	4.90	86	4.60	.261	5	.179	-9	3	-0.9
1956 Bos-A	1	0	1.000	3	1	0	0	0	9^2	9	4	3	2	1	8	5	1.759	2.79	166	6.88	.250	1	.500	2	1	0.2

YEAR TM-L	W	L	PCT	G	GS	CG	SH	SV	IP	H	R	ER	HR	HB	BB	SO	RAT	ERA	ERA+	CERA	OAV	BH	AVG	PR+	WS	TPW
1957 Bos-A	0	0	....	26	0	0	0	2	44^{2}	44	30	22	5	1	30	20	1.657	4.43	90	5.08	.267	0	.000	-2	1	-0.1
Total 3	6	9	.400	70	13	3	1	3	170	169	107	88	24	5	89	70	1.518	4.66	90	4.86	.262	6	.188	-8	5	-0.8

• MINCHEY, Nate Nathan Derek Minchey b: 8/31/1969, Austin, TX BR/TR, 6'8", 225 lbs. Deb: 9/12/1993

YEAR TM-L	W	L	PCT	G	GS	CG	SH	SV	IP	H	R	ER	HR	HB	BB	SO	RAT	ERA	ERA+	CERA	OAV	BH	AVG	PR+	WS	TPW
1993 Bos-A	1	2	.333	5	5	1	0	0	33	35	16	13	5	0	8	18	1.303	3.55	130	3.99	.265	0	....	4	2	0.4
1994 Bos-A	2	3	.400	6	5	0	0	0	23	44	26	22	1	0	14	15	2.522	8.61	58	10.38	.427	0	....	-9	0	-0.9
1996 Bos-A	0	2	.000	2	2	0	0	0	6	16	11	10	1	0	5	4	3.500	15.00	34	19.67	.533	0	....	-6	0	-0.6
1997 Col-N	0	0	....	2	0	0	0	0	2	5	3	3	0	0	1	1	3.000	13.50	38	13.27	.556	0	....	-2	0	-0.2
Total 4	3	7	.300	15	12	1	0	0	64	100	56	48	7	0	28	38	2.000	6.75	73	8.04	.365	0	....	-14	2	-1.3

• MINER, Ray Raymond Theadore "Lefty" Miner b: 4/4/1897, Glens Falls, NY d: 9/15/1963, Glenridge, NY BR/TL, 5'11", 160 lbs. Deb: 9/15/1921

YEAR TM-L	W	L	PCT	G	GS	CG	SH	SV	IP	H	R	ER	HR	HB	BB	SO	RAT	ERA	ERA+	CERA	OAV	BH	AVG	PR+	WS	TPW
1921 Phi-A	0	0	....	1	0	0	0	0	1	2	4	4	0	0	3	0	5.000	36.00	12	20.02	.400	0	....	-3	0	-0.3

• MINETTO, Craig Craig Stephen Minetto b: 4/25/1954, Stockton, CA BL/TL, 6', 185 lbs. Deb: 7/4/1978

YEAR TM-L	W	L	PCT	G	GS	CG	SH	SV	IP	H	R	ER	HR	HB	BB	SO	RAT	ERA	ERA+	CERA	OAV	BH	AVG	PR+	WS	TPW
1978 Oak-A	0	0	....	4	1	0	0	0	12	13	10	5	1	2	7	3	1.667	3.75	97	5.92	.283	0	....	0	0	0.0
1979 Oak-A	1	5	.167	36	13	0	0	0	118^{1}	131	85	73	16	3	58	64	1.597	5.55	73	5.34	.282	0	....	-16	1	-1.6
1980 Oak-A	0	2	.000	7	1	0	0	1	8	11	7	7	2	0	3	5	1.750	7.88	48	7.02	.324	0	....	-4	0	-0.4
1981 Oak-A	0	0	....	8	0	0	0	0	6^{2}	7	2	2	0	1	4	4	1.650	2.70	129	4.99	.280	0	....	0	1	0.1
Total 4	1	7	.125	55	15	0	0	1	145	162	104	87	19	6	72	76	1.614	5.40	74	5.47	.284	0	....	-20	2	-1.9

• MINGORI, Steve Steven Bernard Mingori b: 2/29/1944, Kansas City, MO BL/TL, 5'10", 170 lbs. Deb: 8/5/1970

YEAR TM-L	W	L	PCT	G	GS	CG	SH	SV	IP	H	R	ER	HR	HB	BB	SO	RAT	ERA	ERA+	CERA	OAV	BH	AVG	PR+	WS	TPW
1970 Cle-A	1	0	1.000	21	0	0	0	1	20^{1}	17	8	6	2	1	12	16	1.426	2.66	149	3.62	.227	0	.000	3	2	0.3
1971 Cle-A	1	2	.333	54	0	0	0	4	56^{2}	31	10	9	2	1	24	45	.971	1.43	267	1.51	.166	1	.500	15	9	1.6
1972 Cle-A	0	6	.000	41	0	0	0	10	57	67	28	25	4	2	36	47	1.807	3.95	81	5.64	.293	1	.125	-5	0	-0.7
1973 Cle-A	0	0	....	5	0	0	0	0	11^{2}	10	8	8	3	0	10	4	1.714	6.17	63	6.29	.233	0	....	-3	0	-0.3
KC-A	3	3	.500	19	1	0	0	1	56^{1}	59	21	19	6	3	23	46	1.456	3.04	135	4.46	.267	0	....	7	5	0.8
Yr.	3	3	.500	24	1	0	0	1	68	69	29	27	9	3	33	50	1.500	3.57	113	4.78	.261	0	....	5	5	0.5
1974 KC-A	2	3	.400	36	0	0	0	2	67^{1}	53	31	21	4	2	23	43	1.129	2.81	136	2.41	.212	0	....	9	5	0.9
1975 KC-A	0	3	.000	36	0	0	0	2	50^{1}	42	21	14	2	1	20	25	1.232	2.50	154	2.70	.226	0	.000	8	4	0.8
1976* KC-A	5	5	.500	55	0	0	0	10	85^{1}	73	23	22	3	3	25	38	1.148	2.32	151	2.57	.238	0	....	11	10	1.2
1977* KC-A	2	4	.333	43	0	0	0	4	64	59	26	22	4	1	19	19	1.219	3.09	130	3.03	.254	0	....	6	5	0.6
1978* KC-A	1	4	.200	45	0	0	0	7	69	64	25	21	5	3	16	28	1.159	2.74	140	2.89	.242	0	....	8	6	0.8
1979 KC-A	3	3	.500	30	1	0	0	1	46^{2}	69	36	30	10	1	17	18	1.843	5.79	74	7.75	.348	0	....	-8	1	-0.8
Total 10	18	33	.353	385	2	0	0	42	584^{2}	544	237	197	45	18	225	329	1.315	3.03	126	3.55	.248	2	.167	50	47	5.2

• MINNER, Paul Paul Edison "Lefty" Minner b: 7/30/1923, New Wilmington, PA BL/TL, 6'5", 210 lbs. Deb: 9/12/1946

YEAR TM-L	W	L	PCT	G	GS	CG	SH	SV	IP	H	R	ER	HR	HB	BB	SO	RAT	ERA	ERA+	CERA	OAV	BH	AVG	PR+	WS	TPW
1946 Bro-N	0	1	.000	3	0	0	0	0	4	6	4	3	1	0	3	3	2.250	6.75	50	9.17	.333	0	....	-2	0	-0.2
1948 Bro-N	4	3	.571	28	2	0	0	1	62^{2}	61	23	17	5	0	26	23	1.388	2.44	164	3.75	.257	4	.190	9	6	1.1
1949* Bro-N	3	1	.750	27	1	0	0	2	47^{1}	49	22	20	7	1	18	17	1.415	3.80	108	4.59	.272	3	.214	1	3	0.1
1950 Chi-N	8	13	.381	39	24	9	1	4	190^{1}	217	105	87	18	1	72	99	1.518	4.11	102	4.69	.287	14	.215	7	11	0.9
1951 Chi-N	6	17	.261	33	28	14	3	1	201^{2}	219	97	85	20	0	64	68	1.403	3.79	108	4.19	.277	18	.254	9	13	1.4
1952 Chi-N	14	9	.609	28	27	12	2	0	180^{2}	180	84	75	13	1	54	61	1.295	3.74	103	3.42	.258	15	.234	3	13	0.9
1953 Chi-N	12	15	.444	31	27	9	2	1	201	227	109	94	15	3	40	64	1.328	4.21	106	3.81	.283	15	.221	11	14	1.3
1954 Chi-N	11	11	.500	32	29	12	0	1	218	236	107	96	19	1	50	79	1.312	3.96	106	3.78	.280	13	.171	8	12	1.1
1955 Chi-N	9	9	.500	22	22	7	1	0	157^{2}	173	67	61	15	1	47	53	1.395	3.48	117	4.13	.283	13	.232	10	14	1.2
1956 Chi-N	2	5	.286	10	9	1	0	0	47	60	38	36	9	2	19	14	1.681	6.89	55	6.70	.324	3	.250	-17	0	-1.6
Total 10	69	84	.451	253	169	64	9	10	1310^{1}	1428	656	574	122	10	393	481	1.390	3.94	104	4.12	.279	98	.219	39	86	6.2

• MINNICK, Don Donald Athey Minnick b: 4/14/1931, Lynchburg, VA BR/TR, 6'3", 195 lbs. Deb: 9/23/1957

YEAR TM-L	W	L	PCT	G	GS	CG	SH	SV	IP	H	R	ER	HR	HB	BB	SO	RAT	ERA	ERA+	CERA	OAV	BH	AVG	PR+	WS	TPW
1957 Was-A	0	1	.000	2	1	0	0	0	9^{1}	14	8	5	1	0	2	7	1.714	4.82	81	6.17	.341	0	.000	-1	0	-0.1

• MINOR, Blas Blas Minor b: 3/20/1966, Merced, CA BR/TR, 6'3", 203 lbs. Deb: 7/28/1992

YEAR TM-L	W	L	PCT	G	GS	CG	SH	SV	IP	H	R	ER	HR	HB	BB	SO	RAT	ERA	ERA+	CERA	OAV	BH	AVG	PR+	WS	TPW
1992 Pit-N	0	0	....	1	0	0	0	0	2	3	2	1	0	0	0	0	1.500	4.50	76	4.47	.333	0	....	-0	0	0.0
1993 Pit-N	8	6	.571	65	0	0	0	2	94^{1}	94	43	43	8	4	26	84	1.272	4.10	99	3.59	.263	2	.200	-1	8	-0.1
1994 Pit-N	0	1	.000	17	0	0	0	1	19	27	17	17	4	1	9	17	1.895	8.05	54	8.09	.351	0	....	-8	0	-0.8
1995 NY-N	4	2	.667	35	0	0	0	1	46^{2}	44	21	19	6	1	13	43	1.221	3.66	110	3.58	.253	0	.000	2	3	0.2
1996 NY-N	0	0	....	17	0	0	0	0	25^{2}	23	11	10	4	0	6	20	1.130	3.51	115	3.13	.237	0	.000	1	1	0.1
Sea-A	0	1	.000	11	0	0	0	0	25^{1}	27	14	14	6	0	11	14	1.500	4.97	100	5.75	.276	0	....	-0	1	0.0
1997 Hou-N	1	0	1.000	11	0	0	0	1	12	13	7	6	1	1	5	6	1.500	4.50	89	4.71	.277	0	....	-1	1	-0.1
Total 6	13	10	.565	157	0	0	0	5	225	231	115	110	29	7	70	184	1.338	4.40	95	4.23	.269	2	.154	-8	14	-0.7

• MINSHALL, Jim James Edward Minshall b: 7/4/1947, Covington, KY BR/TR, 6'6", 215 lbs. Deb: 9/14/1974

YEAR TM-L	W	L	PCT	G	GS	CG	SH	SV	IP	H	R	ER	HR	HB	BB	SO	RAT	ERA	ERA+	CERA	OAV	BH	AVG	PR+	WS	TPW
1974 Pit-N	0	1	.000	5	0	0	0	0	4^{1}	1	1	0	0	0	2	3	.692	0.00	....	0.52	.083	0	....	2	0	0.2
1975 Pit-N	0	0	....	1	0	0	0	0	1	0	0	0	0	0	2	2	2.000	0.00	....	3.47	.000	0	....	0	0	0.0
Total 2	0	1	.000	6	0	0	0	0	5^{1}	1	1	0	0	0	4	5	.938	0.00	....	1.08	.083	0	....	2	0	0.2

• MINTON, Greg Gregory Brian Minton b: 7/29/1951, Lubbock, TX BB/TR, 6'2", 190 lbs. Deb: 9/7/1975

YEAR TM-L	W	L	PCT	G	GS	CG	SH	SV	IP	H	R	ER	HR	HB	BB	SO	RAT	ERA	ERA+	CERA	OAV	BH	AVG	PR+	WS	TPW
1975 SF-N	1	1	.500	4	2	0	0	0	17	19	14	13	1	1	11	6	1.765	6.88	55	5.40	.288	0	.000	-6	0	-0.7
1976 SF-N	0	3	.000	10	2	0	0	0	25^{2}	32	18	14	0	1	12	7	1.714	4.91	74	5.17	.317	1	.200	-3	0	-0.3
1977 SF-N	1	1	.500	2	2	0	0	0	14	14	8	7	0	0	4	5	1.286	4.50	87	3.07	.264	1	.333	-1	1	0.0
1978 SF-N	0	1	.000	11	0	0	0	0	15^{2}	22	14	14	3	1	8	6	1.915	8.04	43	7.97	.338	0	.000	-8	0	-0.9
1979 SF-N	4	3	.571	46	0	0	0	4	79^{2}	59	25	16	0	2	27	33	1.079	1.81	193	1.92	.215	0	.000	16	8	1.6
1980 SF-N	4	6	.400	68	0	0	0	19	91^{1}	81	28	25	0	0	34	42	1.259	2.46	144	2.63	.243	1	.125	13	13	1.3
1981 SF-N	4	5	.444	55	0	0	0	21	84^{1}	84	28	27	0	0	36	29	1.423	2.88	119	3.35	.267	0	.000	6	10	0.5
1982 SF-N★	10	4	.714	78	0	0	0	30	123	108	29	25	5	2	42	58	1.220	1.83	197	2.76	.244	3	.176	26	21	2.8
1983 SF-N	7	11	.389	73	0	0	0	22	106^{2}	117	51	42	6	0	47	38	1.538	3.54	100	4.22	.283	6	.545	1	10	0.5
1984 SF-N	4	9	.308	74	1	0	0	19	124^{1}	130	60	52	6	0	57	48	1.504	3.76	93	3.84	.267	1	.048	-0	6	-0.2
1985 SF-N	5	4	.556	68	0	0	0	4	96^{2}	98	42	38	6	0	54	37	1.572	3.54	97	4.26	.272	0	.000	0	6	0.0
1986 SF-N	4	4	.500	48	0	0	0	5	68^{2}	63	35	30	4	1	34	34	1.413	3.93	90	3.40	.251	2	.400	-4	4	-0.3
1987 SF-N	1	0	1.000	15	0	0	0	1	23^{1}	30	9	9	2	1	10	9	1.714	3.47	111	5.90	.323	0	.000	1	2	0.0
Cal-A	5	4	.556	41	0	0	0	10	76	71	28	26	4	1	29	35	1.316	3.08	140	3.40	.257	0	....	10	9	1.0
1988 Cal-A	4	5	.444	44	0	0	0	7	79	67	37	25	1	3	34	46	1.278	2.85	135	2.75	.233	0	....	9	7	0.9
1989 Cal-A	4	3	.571	62	0	0	0	8	90	76	22	22	4	2	37	42	1.256	2.20	173	2.96	.230	0	....	15	12	1.5
1990 Cal-A	1	1	.500	11	0	0	0	0	15^{1}	11	4	4	1	1	7	4	1.174	2.35	162	2.85	.212	0	....	3	2	0.3
Total 16	59	65	.476	710	7	0	0	150	1130^{2}	1082	452	389	43	16	483	479	1.384	3.10	117	3.45	.257	15	.146	77	111	8.1

• MINTZ, Steve Stephen Wayne Mintz b: 11/24/1968, Wilmington, NC BL/TR, 5'11", 190 lbs. Deb: 5/18/1995

YEAR TM-L	W	L	PCT	G	GS	CG	SH	SV	IP	H	R	ER	HR	HB	BB	SO	RAT	ERA	ERA+	CERA	OAV	BH	AVG	PR+	WS	TPW
1995 SF-N	1	2	.333	14	0	0	0	0	19^{1}	26	16	16	4	2	12	7	1.966	7.45	55	8.16	.329	0	.000	-7	0	-0.8
1999 Ana-A	0	0	....	3	0	0	0	0	5	8	2	2	1	0	2	2	2.000	3.60	135	9.22	.381	0	....	1	0	0.1
Total 2	1	2	.333	17	0	0	0	0	24^{1}	34	18	18	5	2	14	9	1.973	6.66	62	8.38	.340	0	.000	-7	0	-0.7

• MINUTELLI, Gino Gino Michael Minutelli b: 5/23/1964, Wilmington, DE BL/TL, 6', 180 lbs. Deb: 9/18/1990

YEAR TM-L	W	L	PCT	G	GS	CG	SH	SV	IP	H	R	ER	HR	HB	BB	SO	RAT	ERA	ERA+	CERA	OAV	BH	AVG	PR+	WS	TPW
1990 Cin-N	0	0	....	2	0	0	0	0	1	0	1	1	0	1	2	0	2.000	9.00	44	7.00	.000	0	....	-1	0	-0.1
1991 Cin-N	0	2	.000	16	3	0	0	0	25^{1}	30	17	17	5	0	18	21	1.895	6.04	63	7.04	.288	0	.000	-6	0	-0.7
1993 SF-N	0	1	.000	9	0	0	0	0	14^{1}	7	9	6	2	0	15	10	1.535	3.77	104	4.00	.152	0	.000	-0	0	-0.1
Total 3	0	3	.000	27	3	0	0	0	40^{2}	37	27	24	7	1	35	31	1.770	5.31	72	5.96	.247	0	.000	-7	0	-0.8

• MIRABELLA, Paul Paul Thomas Mirabella b: 3/20/1954, Belleville, NJ BL/TL, 6'1", 196 lbs. Deb: 7/28/1978

YEAR TM-L	W	L	PCT	G	GS	CG	SH	SV	IP	H	R	ER	HR	HB	BB	SO	RAT	ERA	ERA+	CERA	OAV	BH	AVG	PR+	WS	TPW
1978 Tex-A	3	2	.600	10	4	0	0	1	28	30	18	18	2	0	17	23	1.679	5.79	65	5.23	.286	0	....	-6	0	-0.6
1979 NY-A	0	4	.000	10	1	0	0	0	14^{1}	16	15	14	3	1	10	4	1.814	8.79	46	6.79	.276	0	....	-8	0	-0.8

YEAR	TM-L	W	L	PCT	G	GS	CG	SH	SV	IP	H	R	ER	HR	HB	BB	SO	RAT	ERA	ERA+	CERA	OAV	BH	AVG	PR+	WS	TPW
1980	Tor-A	5	12	.294	33	22	3	1	0	130^{2}	151	73	63	11	3	66	53	1.661	4.34	99	5.35	.294	0	....	-2	5	-0.2
1981	Tor-A	0	0	....	8	1	0	0	0	14^{2}	20	16	12	2	1	7	9	1.841	7.36	54	6.90	.313	0	....	-5	0	-0.6
1982	Tex-A	1	1	.500	40	0	0	0	3	50^{2}	46	28	27	4	2	22	29	1.342	4.80	81	3.55	.241	0	....	-5	2	-0.5
1983	Bal-A	0	0	....	3	2	0	0	0	9^{2}	9	6	6	1	0	7	4	1.655	5.59	71	4.87	.243	0	....	-2	0	-0.2
1984	Sea-A	2	5	.286	52	1	0	0	3	68	74	39	33	6	1	32	41	1.559	4.37	91	4.69	.282	0	....	-1	3	-0.1
1985	Sea-A	0	0	....	10	0	0	0	0	13^{2}	9	4	2	0	2	4	8	.951	1.32	320	1.67	.188	0	....	4	1	0.4
1986	Sea-A	0	0	....	8	0	0	0	0	6^{1}	13	7	6	1	0	3	6	2.526	8.53	50	11.91	.419	0	....	-3	0	-0.3
1987	Mil-A	2	1	.667	29	0	0	0	2	29^{1}	30	20	16	0	0	16	14	1.568	4.91	93	3.77	.268	0	....	-1	2	-0.1
1988	Mil-A	2	2	.500	38	0	0	0	4	60	44	12	11	3	0	21	33	1.083	1.65	241	2.09	.204	0	....	15	8	1.5
1989	Mil-A	0	0	....	13	0	0	0	0	15^{1}	18	14	13	1	1	7	6	1.630	7.63	50	4.67	.290	0	....	-7	0	-0.7
1990	Mil-A	4	2	.667	44	2	0	0	0	59	66	32	26	9	2	27	28	1.576	3.97	98	5.46	.281	0	....	0	3	0.0
Total	**13**	**19**	**29**	**.396**	**298**	**33**	**3**	**1**	**13**	**499^{2}**	**526**	**284**	**247**	**43**	**13**	**239**	**258**	**1.531**	**4.45**	**91**	**4.64**	**.272**	**0**	**....**	**-20**	**24**	**-2.0**

• MIRANDA, Angel Angel Luis (Andujar) Miranda b: 11/9/1969, Arecibo, Puerto Rico BL/TL, 6'1", 195 lbs. Deb: 6/5/1993

YEAR	TM-L	W	L	PCT	G	GS	CG	SH	SV	IP	H	R	ER	HR	HB	BB	SO	RAT	ERA	ERA+	CERA	OAV	BH	AVG	PR+	WS	TPW
1993	Mil-A	4	5	.444	22	17	2	0	0	120	100	53	44	12	2	52	88	1.267	3.30	129	3.33	.226	0	....	13	8	1.3
1994	Mil-A	2	5	.286	8	8	1	0	0	46	39	28	27	8	0	27	24	1.435	5.28	95	4.59	.234	0	....	-3	2	-0.2
1995	Mil-A	4	5	.444	30	10	0	0	1	74	83	47	43	8	0	49	45	1.784	5.23	95	6.00	.291	0	....	-3	3	-0.3
1996	Mil-A	7	6	.538	46	12	0	0	1	109^{1}	116	68	60	12	2	69	78	1.692	4.94	105	5.45	.277	0	....	1	6	0.1
1997	Mil-A	0	0	....	10	0	0	0	0	14	17	6	6	1	3	9	8	1.857	3.86	120	6.85	.309	0	....	1	1	0.1
Total	**5**	**17**	**21**	**.447**	**116**	**47**	**3**	**0**	**2**	**363^{1}**	**355**	**202**	**180**	**41**	**7**	**206**	**243**	**1.544**	**4.46**	**109**	**4.81**	**.260**	**0**	**....**	**9**	**20**	**0.9**

• MISURACA, Mike Michael William Misuraca b: 8/21/1968, Long Beach, CA BR/TR, 6', 190 lbs. Deb: 7/27/1997

YEAR	TM-L	W	L	PCT	G	GS	CG	SH	SV	IP	H	R	ER	HR	HB	BB	SO	RAT	ERA	ERA+	CERA	OAV	BH	AVG	PR+	WS	TPW
1997	Mil-A	0	0	....	5	0	0	0	0	10^{1}	15	13	13	5	0	7	10	2.129	11.32	41	11.35	.333	0	....	-8	0	-0.8

• MITCHELL, Bobby Robert McKasha Mitchell b: 2/6/1856, Cincinnati, OH d: 5/1/1933, Springfield, OH BL/TL, 5'5", 135 lbs. Deb: 9/6/1877

YEAR	TM-L	W	L	PCT	G	GS	CG	SH	SV	IP	H	R	ER	HR	HB	BB	SO	RAT	ERA	ERA+	CERA	OAV	BH	AVG	PR+	WS	TPW
1877	Cin-N	6	5	.545	12	12	11	1	0	100	123	69	39	0	....	11	41	1.340	3.51	75	....	.286	10	.204	-4	2	-0.4
1878	Cin-N	7	2	.778	9	9	9	1	0	80	69	32	19	1	....	18	51	1.088	2.14	99	....	**.221**	12	.245	-1	7	0.0
1879	Cle-N	7	15	.318	23	22	20	0	0	194^{2}	236	153	71	0	....	42	90	1.428	3.28	76	....	.281	16	.147	-10	6	-1.8
1882	StL-a	0	1	.000	1	1	0	0	0	7	12	13	6	0	....	2	2	2.000	7.71	36	....	.356	0	.000	-4	0	-0.4
Total	**4**	**20**	**23**	**.465**	**45**	**44**	**40**	**2**	**0**	**381^{2}**	**440**	**267**	**135**	**1**	**....**	**73**	**184**	**1.344**	**3.18**	**78**	**....**	**.272**	**38**	**.180**	**-19**	**15**	**-2.6**

• MITCHELL, Charlie Charles Ross Mitchell b: 6/24/1962, Dickson, TN BR/TR, 6'3", 170 lbs. Deb: 8/9/1984

YEAR	TM-L	W	L	PCT	G	GS	CG	SH	SV	IP	H	R	ER	HR	HB	BB	SO	RAT	ERA	ERA+	CERA	OAV	BH	AVG	PR+	WS	TPW
1984	Bos-A	0	0	....	10	0	0	0	0	16^{1}	14	7	5	1	2	6	7	1.224	2.76	151	3.01	.226	0	....	3	1	0.3
1985	Bos-A	0	0	....	2	0	0	0	0	1^{2}	5	3	3	1	0	0	2	3.000	16.20	26	21.12	.500	0	....	-2	0	-0.2
Total	**2**	**0**	**0**	**....**	**12**	**0**	**0**	**0**	**0**	**18**	**19**	**10**	**8**	**2**	**2**	**6**	**9**	**1.389**	**4.00**	**105**	**4.68**	**.264**	**0**	**....**	**1**	**1**	**0.1**

• MITCHELL, Clarence Clarence Elmer Mitchell b: 2/22/1891, Franklin, NE d: 11/6/1963, Grand Island, NE BL/TL, 5'11.5", 190 lbs. Deb: 6/2/1911 C ♦

YEAR	TM-L	W	L	PCT	G	GS	CG	SH	SV	IP	H	R	ER	HR	HB	BB	SO	RAT	ERA	ERA+	CERA	OAV	BH	AVG	PR+	WS	TPW
1911	Det-A	1	0	1.000	5	1	0	0	0	14^{1}	20	13	13	1	0	7	4	1.884	8.16	42	6.89	.350	2	.500	-7	0	-0.6
1916	Cin-N	11	10	.524	29	24	17	1	0	194^{2}	211	87	68	4	10	45	52	1.315	3.14	82	3.52	.280	28	.239	-14	9	-1.5
1917	Cin-N	9	15	.375	32	20	10	2	1	159^{1}	166	73	57	4	2	34	37	1.255	3.22	81	3.06	.260	25	.278	-10	7	-0.8
1918	Bro-N	0	1	.000	1	1	0	0	0	0^{1}	4	4	4	0	0	0	0	12.00	108.00	3	120.07	1.000	6	.250	-4	0	-0.6
1919	Bro-N	7	5	.583	23	11	9	0	0	108^{2}	123	49	37	0	0	23	43	1.344	3.06	97	3.42	.290	18	.367	1	8	0.8
1920*	Bro-N	5	2	.714	19	7	3	1	1	78^{2}	85	35	27	1	0	23	18	1.373	3.09	104	3.51	.280	25	.234	2	6	0.1
1921	Bro-N	11	9	.550	37	18	13	**3**	2	190	206	91	61	7	5	46	39	1.326	2.89	134	3.53	.280	24	.264	22	17	2.5
1922	Bro-N	0	3	.000	5	3	0	0	0	12^{2}	28	24	20	0	1	7	1	2.763	14.21	29	11.73	.460	45	.290	-14	6	-1.2
1923	Phi-N	9	10	.474	29	19	8	1	0	139^{1}	170	93	73	8	4	46	41	1.550	4.72	97	4.72	.290	21	.269	2	8	0.6
1924	Phi-N	6	13	.316	30	26	9	1	1	165	223	113	103	10	6	58	36	1.703	5.62	79	5.57	.320	26	.255	-18	5	-1.7
1925	Phi-N	10	17	.370	32	26	12	1	1	199^{1}	245	130	117	23	5	51	46	1.485	5.28	90	4.93	.300	18	.196	-3	10	-0.5
1926	Phi-N	9	14	.391	28	25	12	0	1	178^{2}	232	111	91	7	4	55	52	1.606	4.58	90	4.98	.310	19	.244	-3	9	-0.2
1927	Phi-N	6	3	.667	13	12	8	1	0	94^{2}	99	44	43	7	2	28	17	1.342	4.09	101	3.78	.270	10	.238	2	7	0.4
1928	Phi-N	0	0	....	3	0	0	0	0	5^{2}	13	6	6	0	0	2	0	2.647	9.53	45	12.60	.540	1	.250	-3	0	-0.3
	* StL-N	8	9	.471	19	18	9	1	0	150	149	59	55	8	3	38	31	1.247	3.30	121	3.20	.260	7	.125	11	10	0.7
	Yr.	8	9	.471	22	18	9	1	0	155^{2}	162	65	61	8	3	40	31	1.298	3.53	114	3.54	.271	8	.133	7	10	0.4
1929	StL-N	8	11	.421	25	22	16	0	0	173	221	89	82	13	5	60	39	1.624	4.27	109	5.40	.320	18	.273	8	12	1.1
1930	StL-N	1	0	1.000	1	1	0	0	0	3	5	2	2	0	0	2	1	2.333	6.00	84	8.02	.350	1	.500	-0	0	0.0
	NY-N	10	3	.769	24	16	5	0	0	129	151	68	57	10	1	36	40	1.450	3.98	119	4.40	.290	12	.255	10	10	0.9
	Yr.	11	3	.786	25	17	5	0	0	132	156	70	59	10	1	38	41	1.470	4.02	118	4.48	.292	13	.265	9	10	0.9
1931	NY-N	13	11	.542	27	25	13	0	0	190^{1}	221	103	86	12	3	52	39	1.434	4.07	91	4.14	.280	16	.219	-10	8	-0.8
1932	NY-N	1	3	.250	8	3	1	0	2	30^{1}	41	21	14	1	1	11	7	1.714	4.15	89	5.46	.320	2	.200	-1	1	-0.1
Total	**18**	**125**	**139**	**.473**	**390**	**278**	**145**	**12**	**9**	**2217**	**2613**	**1215**	**1016**	**116**	**52**	**624**	**543**	**1.460**	**4.12**	**94**	**4.34**	**.293**	**324**	**.252**	**-30**	**133**	**-1.3**

• MITCHELL, Craig Craig Seton Mitchell b: 4/14/1954, Santa Rosa, CA BR/TR, 6'3", 180 lbs. Deb: 9/25/1975

YEAR	TM-L	W	L	PCT	G	GS	CG	SH	SV	IP	H	R	ER	HR	HB	BB	SO	RAT	ERA	ERA+	CERA	OAV	BH	AVG	PR+	WS	TPW
1975	Oak-A	0	1	.000	1	1	0	0	0	3^{2}	6	5	5	0	0	2	2	2.182	12.27	30	7.97	.375	0	....	-4	0	-0.4
1976	Oak-A	0	0	....	1	0	0	0	0	3^{1}	3	1	1	0	0	0	1	.900	2.70	124	1.57	.231	0	....	0	0	0.0
1977	Oak-A	0	1	.000	3	1	0	0	0	5^{2}	9	6	5	1	0	2	1	1.941	7.94	51	7.64	.346	0	....	-2	0	-0.2
Total	**3**	**0**	**2**	**.000**	**5**	**2**	**0**	**0**	**0**	**12^{2}**	**18**	**12**	**11**	**1**	**0**	**4**	**3**	**1.737**	**7.82**	**48**	**6.14**	**.327**	**0**	**....**	**-6**	**0**	**-0.6**

• MITCHELL, Fred Frederick Francis Mitchell b: 6/5/1878, Cambridge, MA d: 10/13/1970, Newton, MA BR/TR, 5'9.5", 185 lbs. Deb: 4/27/1901 M/C ♦

YEAR	TM-L	W	L	PCT	G	GS	CG	SH	SV	IP	H	R	ER	HR	HB	BB	SO	RAT	ERA	ERA+	CERA	OAV	BH	AVG	PR+	WS	TPW
1901	Bos-A	6	6	.500	17	13	10	0	0	108^{2}	115	67	46	2	11	51	34	1.528	3.81	92	4.31	.268	7	.159	-8	5	-1.0
1902	Bos-A	0	1	.000	1	0	0	0	0	4	8	5	5	1	0	5	2	3.250	11.25	32	15.94	.414	0	.000	-4	0	-0.3
	Phi-A	5	8	.385	18	14	9	0	1	107^{2}	120	71	43	4	8	59	22	1.663	3.59	102	4.96	.282	9	.188	1	5	0.0
	Yr.	5	9	.357	19	14	9	0	1	111^{2}	128	76	48	5	8	64	24	1.719	3.87	94	5.35	.288	9	.184	-2	5	-0.3
1903	Phi-N	11	16	.407	28	28	24	1	0	227	250	155	113	4	19	102	69	1.551	4.48	73	4.53	.284	19	.200	-34	5	-3.4
1904	Phi-N	4	7	.364	13	13	11	0	0	108^{2}	133	62	41	3	7	25	29	1.454	3.40	79	4.45	.306	17	.207	-7	3	-0.8
	Bro-N	2	5	.286	8	8	8	1	0	66	73	37	28	0	3	23	16	1.455	3.82	72	4.02	.291	7	.292	-8	2	-0.5
	Yr.	6	12	.333	21	21	19	1	0	174^{2}	206	99	69	3	10	48	45	1.454	3.56	76	4.28	.301	24	.226	-14	5	-1.3
1905	Bro-N	3	7	.300	12	10	9	0	0	96^{1}	107	73	51	2	5	38	44	1.505	4.76	60	4.28	.285	15	.190	-18	1	-2.5
Total	**5**	**31**	**50**	**.383**	**97**	**86**	**71**	**2**	**1**	**718^{1}**	**806**	**470**	**327**	**16**	**53**	**303**	**216**	**1.544**	**4.10**	**77**	**4.53**	**.286**	**120**	**.210**	**-76**	**21**	**-8.5**

• MITCHELL, John John Kyle Mitchell b: 8/11/1965, Dickson, TN BR/TR, 6'2", 195 lbs. Deb: 9/8/1986

YEAR	TM-L	W	L	PCT	G	GS	CG	SH	SV	IP	H	R	ER	HR	HB	BB	SO	RAT	ERA	ERA+	CERA	OAV	BH	AVG	PR+	WS	TPW
1986	NY-N	0	1	.000	4	1	0	0	0	10	10	4	4	1	0	4	2	1.400	3.60	98	4.43	.278	0	.000	-0	0	0.0
1987	NY-N	3	6	.333	20	19	1	0	0	111^{2}	124	64	51	6	2	36	57	1.433	4.11	92	4.02	.279	4	.114	-3	3	-0.4
1988	NY-N	0	0	....	1	0	0	0	0	1	2	0	0	0	0	1	1	3.000	0.00	....	14.53	.500	0	.000	0	0	0.0
1989	NY-N	0	1	.000	2	0	0	0	0	3	3	7	2	0	0	4	4	2.333	6.00	54	5.65	.231	0	....	-1	0	-0.1
1990	Bal-A	6	6	.500	24	17	0	0	0	114^{1}	133	63	59	7	3	48	43	1.583	4.64	82	4.92	.300	0	....	-12	3	-1.2
Total	**5**	**9**	**14**	**.391**	**51**	**37**	**1**	**0**	**0**	**240**	**272**	**138**	**116**	**14**	**5**	**93**	**107**	**1.521**	**4.35**	**87**	**4.53**	**.289**	**4**	**.105**	**-15**	**6**	**-1.7**

• MITCHELL, Larry Larry Paul Mitchell b: 10/16/1971, Flint, MI BR/TR, 6'1", 200 lbs. Deb: 8/11/1996

YEAR	TM-L	W	L	PCT	G	GS	CG	SH	SV	IP	H	R	ER	HR	HB	BB	SO	RAT	ERA	ERA+	CERA	OAV	BH	AVG	PR+	WS	TPW
1996	Phi-N	0	0	....	7	0	0	0	0	12	14	6	6	1	0	5	7	1.583	4.50	96	5.12	.311	0	.000	-0	1	-0.1

• MITCHELL, Monroe Monroe Barr Mitchell b: 9/11/1901, Starkville, MS d: 9/4/1976, Valdosta, GA BR/TL, 6'1.5", 170 lbs. Deb: 7/11/1923

YEAR	TM-L	W	L	PCT	G	GS	CG	SH	SV	IP	H	R	ER	HR	HB	BB	SO	RAT	ERA	ERA+	CERA	OAV	BH	AVG	PR+	WS	TPW
1923	Was-A	2	4	.333	10	6	3	1	2	41^{2}	57	35	30	0	1	22	8	1.896	6.48	58	5.98	.350	3	.250	-14	0	-1.3

• MITCHELL, Paul Paul Michael Mitchell b: 8/19/1949, Worcester, MA BR/TR, 6'1", 195 lbs. Deb: 7/1/1975

YEAR	TM-L	W	L	PCT	G	GS	CG	SH	SV	IP	H	R	ER	HR	HB	BB	SO	RAT	ERA	ERA+	CERA	OAV	BH	AVG	PR+	WS	TPW
1975	Bal-A	3	0	1.000	11	4	1	0	0	57	41	23	23	8	0	19	31	1.053	3.63	97	2.56	.204	0	....	-3	3	-0.3
1976	Oak-A	9	7	.563	26	26	4	1	0	142	169	74	67	15	1	30	67	1.401	4.25	79	4.44	.294	0	....	-12	4	-1.2
1977	Oak-A	0	3	.000	5	3	0	0	0	13^{2}	21	16	16	3	0	7	5	2.049	10.54	38	8.45	.339	0	....	-10	0	-1.0
	Sea-A	3	3	.500	9	9	0	0	0	39^{2}	50	26	22	7	1	16	20	1.664	4.99	82	6.24	.311	0	....	-5	1	-0.5
	Yr.	3	6	.333	14	12	0	0	0	53^{1}	71	42	38	10	1	23	25	1.763	6.41	64	6.81	.318	0	....	-14	1	-1.4
1978	Sea-A	8	14	.364	29	29	4	2	0	168	173	86	78	21	2	79	75	1.500	4.18	91	4.80	.270	0	....	-6	8	-0.6

YEAR	TM-L	W	L	PCT	G	GS	CG	SH	SV	IP	H	R	ER	HR	HB	BB	SO	RAT	ERA	ERA+	CERA	OAV	BH	AVG	PR+	WS	TPW
1979	Sea-A	1	4	.200	10	6	1	0	0	36^2	46	26	18	4	0	15	18	1.664	4.42	99	5.71	.309	0	....	-0	1	0.0
	Mil-A	3	3	.500	18	8	0	0	0	75	81	50	48	11	3	10	32	1.213	5.76	72	3.95	.276	0	....	-13	1	-1.3
	Yr.	4	7	.364	28	14	1	0	0	111^2	127	76	66	15	3	25	50	1.361	5.32	79	4.53	.287	0	....	-13	2	-1.3
1980	Mil-A	5	5	.500	17	11	1	1	1	89^1	92	40	35	7	1	15	29	1.198	3.53	110	3.20	.267	0	....	2	5	0.2
Total	6	32	39	.451	125	96	11	4	1	621^1	673	341	307	76	8	191	277	1.391	4.45	85	4.41	.278	0	....	-45	23	-4.6

• MITCHELL, Roy Albert Roy Mitchell b: 4/19/1885, Belton, TX d: 9/8/1959, Temple, TX BR/TR, 5'9.5", 170 lbs. Deb: 9/10/1910

YEAR	TM-L	W	L	PCT	G	GS	CG	SH	SV	IP	H	R	ER	HR	HB	BB	SO	RAT	ERA	ERA+	CERA	OAV	BH	AVG	PR+	WS	TPW
1910	StL-A	4	2	.667	6	6	6	0	0	52	43	24	15	0	2	12	23	1.058	2.60	95	2.28	.244	4	.211	-0	2	0.0
1911	StL-A	4	8	.333	28	12	8	1	0	133^1	134	79	57	4	6	45	40	1.343	3.85	88	3.67	.273	11	.224	-8	5	-0.6
1912	StL-A	3	4	.429	13	7	5	0	0	62	81	36	32	2	4	17	22	1.581	4.65	72	5.17	.323	6	.316	-10	3	-0.6
1913	StL-A	13	16	.448	33	27	21	4	1	245^1	265	111	82	6	5	47	59	1.272	3.01	97	3.31	.280	13	.148	-6	12	-0.7
1914	StL-A	4	5	.444	28	9	4	0	**4**	103^1	134	77	50	1	6	38	38	1.665	4.35	62	5.23	.320	7	.206	-18	0	-1.9
1918	Chi-A	0	1	.000	2	2	0	0	0	12	18	14	10	1	0	4	3	1.833	7.50	36	6.28	.346	0	.000	-6	0	-0.7
	Cin-N	4	0	1.000	5	3	3	2	0	36^1	27	3	3	0	0	5	9	.881	0.74	359	1.41	.208	3	.214	7	4	0.9
1919	Cin-N	0	1	.000	7	1	0	0	0	31	32	16	8	0	0	9	10	1.323	2.32	119	3.10	.276	0	.000	1	1	-0.1
Total	7	32	37	.464	122	67	47	7	5	675^1	734	360	257	14	23	177	204	1.349	3.42	86	3.71	.284	44	.187	-40	27	-3.8

• MITCHELL, Willie William Mitchell b: 12/1/1889, Pleasant Grove, MS d: 11/23/1973, Sardis, MS BR/TL, 6', 176 lbs. Deb: 9/22/1909

YEAR	TM-L	W	L	PCT	G	GS	CG	SH	SV	IP	H	R	ER	HR	HB	BB	SO	RAT	ERA	ERA+	CERA	OAV	BH	AVG	PR+	WS	TPW
1909	Cle-A	1	2	.333	3	3	3	0	0	23	18	6	4	0	4	10	8	1.217	1.57	163	3.00	.225	2	.286	2	2	0.3
1910	Cle-A	12	8	.600	35	18	11	1	0	183^2	155	77	53	2	15	55	102	1.143	2.60	99	2.65	.236	10	.159	-1	11	-0.4
1911	Cle-A	7	14	.333	30	22	9	0	0	177^1	190	102	74	1	13	60	78	1.410	3.76	91	3.93	.284	7	.109	-9	7	-1.4
1912	Cle-A	5	8	.385	29	15	8	0	1	163^2	149	88	51	0	7	56	94	1.253	2.80	122	2.78	.240	6	.113	8	9	0.5
1913	Cle-A	14	8	.636	35	22	14	4	0	217	153	62	46	1	8	88	141	1.111	1.91	159	1.80	.199	10	.143	24	20	2.3
1914	Cle-A	11	17	.393	39	32	16	3	1	257	228	127	91	3	7	124	179	1.370	3.19	90	3.19	.238	7	.086	-5	9	-0.9
1915	Cle-A	11	14	.440	36	30	12	1	1	236	210	103	74	1	2	84	149	1.246	2.82	108	2.71	.241	10	.127	7	14	0.3
1916	Cle-A	2	5	.286	12	6	1	0	1	43^2	55	35	25	1	0	19	24	1.695	5.15	58	5.08	.309	0	.000	-11	0	-1.3
	Det-A	7	5	.583	23	17	7	2	0	127^2	119	53	47	1	5	48	60	1.308	3.31	86	3.16	.253	9	.250	-4	7	-0.2
	Yr.	9	10	.474	35	23	8	2	1	171^1	174	88	72	2	5	67	84	1.407	3.78	77	3.65	.268	9	.191	-14	7	-1.5
1917	Det-A	12	8	.600	30	22	12	5	0	185^1	172	66	45	2	13	46	80	1.176	2.19	121	2.82	.250	7	.119	13	11	1.0
1918	Det-A	0	1	.000	1	1	0	0	0	4	3	4	4	0	0	5	2	2.000	9.00	30	4.59	.200	0	.000	-3	0	-0.3
1919	Det-A	1	2	.333	3	2	0	0	0	13^2	12	8	8	2	1	10	4	1.610	5.27	61	5.58	.255	1	.200	-3	0	-0.3
Total	11	83	92	.474	276	190	93	16	4	1632	1464	731	522	14	75	605	921	1.268	2.88	103	2.94	.243	69	.130	19	90	-0.5

• MITRE, Sergio Sergio Armando Mitre b: 2/16/1981, Los Angeles, CA BR/TR, 6'4", 210 lbs. Deb: 7/22/2003

YEAR	TM-L	W	L	PCT	G	GS	CG	SH	SV	IP	H	R	ER	HR	HB	BB	SO	RAT	ERA	ERA+	CERA	OAV	BH	AVG	PR+	WS	TPW
2003	Chi-N	0	1	.000	3	2	0	0	0	8^2	15	8	8	1	0	4	3	2.192	8.31	51	9.02	.395	1	.500	-4	0	-0.4

• MIZELL, Vinegar Bend Wilmer David Mizell b: 8/13/1930, Leakesville, MS d: 2/21/1999, Kerrville, TX BR/TL, 6'3.5", 205 lbs. Deb: 4/22/1952

YEAR	TM-L	W	L	PCT	G	GS	CG	SH	SV	IP	H	R	ER	HR	HB	BB	SO	RAT	ERA	ERA+	CERA	OAV	BH	AVG	PR+	WS	TPW
1952	StL-N	10	8	.556	30	30	7	2	0	190	171	89	77	12	1	103	146	1.442	3.65	102	3.65	.237	3	.044	1	9	-0.4
1953	StL-N	13	11	.542	33	33	10	1	0	224^1	193	93	87	12	4	114	173	1.368	3.49	122	3.27	.227	7	.084	22	17	1.7
1956	StL-N	14	14	.500	33	33	11	3	0	208^2	172	93	84	20	7	92	153	1.265	3.62	104	3.34	.222	8	.107	4	11	0.1
1957	StL-N	8	10	.444	33	21	7	2	0	149^1	136	69	62	18	1	51	87	1.252	3.74	106	3.47	.241	4	.089	4	8	0.2
1958	StL-N	10	14	.417	30	29	8	2	0	189^2	178	81	72	17	2	91	80	1.418	3.42	121	3.95	.252	7	.115	15	14	1.2
1959	StL-N★	13	10	.565	31	30	8	1	0	201^1	196	104	94	21	8	89	108	1.416	4.20	101	4.16	.252	14	.187	3	12	0.3
1960	StL-N	1	3	.250	9	9	0	0	0	55^1	64	31	28	7	0	28	42	1.663	4.55	90	5.50	.291	2	.111	-3	2	-0.3
	*Pit-N	13	5	.722	23	23	8	3	0	155^2	141	59	54	7	3	46	71	1.201	3.12	120	2.90	.247	7	.137	8	11	0.8
	Yr.	14	8	.636	32	32	8	3	0	211	205	90	82	14	3	74	113	1.322	3.50	110	3.58	.259	9	.130	6	13	0.5
1961	Pit-N	7	10	.412	25	17	2	1	0	100	120	61	56	16	0	31	37	1.510	5.04	79	5.22	.299	3	.130	-12	3	-1.3
1962	Pit-N	1	1	.500	4	3	0	0	0	16^1	15	10	9	3	1	10	6	1.531	4.96	79	5.46	.254	0	.000	-2	0	-0.2
	NY-N	0	2	.000	17	2	0	0	0	38	48	35	31	10	1	25	15	1.921	7.34	57	8.36	.324	2	.250	-13	0	-1.2
	Yr.	1	3	.250	21	5	0	0	0	54^1	63	45	40	13	2	35	21	1.804	6.63	62	7.49	.304	2	.143	-15	0	-1.5
Total	9	90	88	.506	268	230	61	15	0	1528^2	1434	725	654	143	28	680	918	1.383	3.85	104	3.87	.247	57	.111	28	87	0.9

• MLICKI, Dave David John Mlicki b: 6/8/1968, Cleveland, OH BR/TR, 6'4", 190 lbs. Deb: 9/12/1992

YEAR	TM-L	W	L	PCT	G	GS	CG	SH	SV	IP	H	R	ER	HR	HB	BB	SO	RAT	ERA	ERA+	CERA	OAV	BH	AVG	PR+	WS	TPW
1992	Cle-A	0	2	.000	4	4	0	0	0	21^2	23	14	12	3	1	16	16	1.800	4.98	78	6.44	.280	0	....	-2	0	-0.2
1993	Cle-A	0	0	....	3	3	0	0	0	13^1	11	6	5	2	2	6	7	1.275	3.38	128	4.23	.220	0	....	1	1	0.1
1995	NY-N	9	7	.563	29	25	0	0	0	160^2	160	82	76	23	4	54	123	1.332	4.26	95	4.11	.256	2	.051	-4	7	-0.5
1996	NY-N	6	7	.462	51	2	0	0	1	90	95	46	33	9	6	33	83	1.422	3.30	122	4.40	.277	1	.100	6	6	0.6
1997	NY-N	8	12	.400	32	32	1	1	0	193^2	194	89	86	21	5	76	157	1.394	4.00	101	4.16	.259	9	.188	-3	10	-0.1
1998	NY-N	1	4	.200	10	10	1	0	0	57	68	38	36	8	5	25	39	1.632	5.68	73	5.89	.297	3	.188	-10	0	-0.9
	LA-N	7	3	.700	20	20	2	1	0	124^1	120	64	56	15	2	38	78	1.271	4.05	98	3.69	.253	2	.059	-1	6	-0.3
	Yr.	8	7	.533	30	30	3	1	0	181^1	188	102	92	23	7	63	117	1.384	4.57	88	4.38	.267	5	.100	-11	6	-1.2
1999	LA-N	0	1	.000	2	0	0	0	0	7^1	10	4	4	1	0	2	1	1.636	4.91	87	6.01	.323	1	1.000	-0	0	0.0
	Det-A	14	12	.538	31	31	2	0	0	191^2	209	108	98	24	12	70	119	1.456	4.60	107	4.86	.276	0	.000	7	12	0.7
2000	Det-A	6	11	.353	24	21	0	0	0	119^1	143	79	74	17	3	44	57	1.567	5.58	86	5.39	.291	0	.000	-10	4	-0.9
2001	Det-A	4	8	.333	15	15	0	0	0	81	118	69	66	19	6	41	48	1.963	7.33	59	8.98	.348	0	.000	-26	0	-2.5
	*Hou-N	7	3	.700	19	14	0	0	0	86^2	85	53	49	18	9	33	49	1.362	5.09	90	5.04	.260	3	.115	-5	4	-0.6
2002	Hou-N	4	10	.286	22	16	0	0	0	86	101	57	51	11	3	34	57	1.570	5.34	80	5.26	.290	5	.185	-10	1	-0.9
Total	10	66	80	.452	262	193	6	2	1	1232^2	1337	709	646	171	58	472	834	1.468	4.72	92	4.94	.276	26	.125	-56	51	-5.5

• MMAHAT, Kevin Kevin Paul Mmahat b: 11/9/1964, Memphis, TN BL/TL, 6'5", 220 lbs. Deb: 9/9/1989

YEAR	TM-L	W	L	PCT	G	GS	CG	SH	SV	IP	H	R	ER	HR	HB	BB	SO	RAT	ERA	ERA+	CERA	OAV	BH	AVG	PR+	WS	TPW
1989	NY-A	0	2	.000	4	2	0	0	0	7^2	13	12	11	2	1	8	3	2.739	12.91	30	13.79	.406	0	....	-8	0	-0.8

• MODAK, Mike Michael Modak b: 5/18/1922, Campbell, OH d: 12/12/1995, Lakeland, FL BR/TR, 5'10.5", 195 lbs. Deb: 7/4/1945

YEAR	TM-L	W	L	PCT	G	GS	CG	SH	SV	IP	H	R	ER	HR	HB	BB	SO	RAT	ERA	ERA+	CERA	OAV	BH	AVG	PR+	WS	TPW
1945	Cin-N	1	2	.333	20	3	1	1	1	42^1	52	27	27	0	0	23	7	1.772	5.74	65	5.08	.308	1	.100	-9	0	-1.0

• MOEHLER, Brian Brian Merritt Moehler b: 12/3/1971, Rockingham, NC BR/TR, 6'3", 195 lbs. Deb: 9/22/1996

YEAR	TM-L	W	L	PCT	G	GS	CG	SH	SV	IP	H	R	ER	HR	HB	BB	SO	RAT	ERA	ERA+	CERA	OAV	BH	AVG	PR+	WS	TPW
1996	Det-A	0	1	.000	2	2	0	0	0	10^1	11	10	5	1	0	8	2	1.839	4.35	116	5.49	.262	0	....	1	0	0.1
1997	Det-A	11	12	.478	31	31	2	1	0	175^1	198	97	91	22	5	61	97	1.477	4.67	98	4.92	.285	0	.000	-4	9	-0.4
1998	Det-A	14	13	.519	33	33	4	3	0	221^1	220	103	96	30	2	56	123	1.247	3.90	121	3.79	.259	0	.000	17	17	1.5
1999	Det-A	10	16	.385	32	32	2	2	0	196^1	229	116	110	22	7	59	106	1.467	5.04	98	4.85	.294	0	.000	-2	10	-0.2
2000	Det-A	12	9	.571	29	29	2	0	0	178	222	99	89	20	2	40	103	1.472	4.50	107	4.95	.305	0	.000	7	10	0.6
2001	Det-A	0	0	....	1	1	0	0	0	8	6	3	3	0	0	1	2	.875	3.38	129	1.43	.207	0	....	1	1	0.1
2002	Det-A	1	1	.500	3	3	0	0	0	19^2	17	5	5	3	0	2	13	.966	2.29	188	2.54	.233	0	....	5	2	0.4
	Cin-N	2	4	.333	10	9	0	0	0	43^1	61	34	29	8	1	11	18	1.662	6.02	70	6.56	.330	0	.000	-9	0	-1.0
2003	Hou-N	0	0	....	3	3	0	0	0	13^2	22	12	12	4	0	6	5	2.049	7.90	56	9.97	.379	0	.000	-6	0	-0.6
Total	8	50	56	.472	144	143	10	6	0	866	986	479	440	110	17	244	469	1.420	4.57	103	4.70	.287	0	.000	10	49	0.6

• MOELLER, Dennis Dennis Michael Moeller b: 9/15/1967, Tarzana, CA BR/TL, 6'2", 195 lbs. Deb: 7/28/1992

YEAR	TM-L	W	L	PCT	G	GS	CG	SH	SV	IP	H	R	ER	HR	HB	BB	SO	RAT	ERA	ERA+	CERA	OAV	BH	AVG	PR+	WS	TPW
1992	KC-A	0	3	.000	5	4	0	0	0	18	24	17	14	5	0	11	6	1.944	7.00	58	8.10	.333	0	....	-6	0	-0.6
1993	Pit-N	1	0	1.000	10	0	0	0	0	16^1	26	20	18	2	1	7	13	2.020	9.92	41	8.09	.356	0	....	-11	0	-1.1
Total	2	1	3	.250	15	4	0	0	0	34^1	50	37	32	7	1	18	19	1.981	8.39	48	8.10	.345	0	....	-16	0	-1.7

• MOELLER, Joe Joseph Douglas Moeller b: 2/15/1943, Blue Island, IL BR/TR, 6'5", 208 lbs. Deb: 4/12/1962

YEAR	TM-L	W	L	PCT	G	GS	CG	SH	SV	IP	H	R	ER	HR	HB	BB	SO	RAT	ERA	ERA+	CERA	OAV	BH	AVG	PR+	WS	TPW
1962	LA-N	6	5	.545	19	15	1	0	1	85^2	87	55	50	10	0	58	46	1.693	5.25	69	5.45	.266	7	.212	-15	1	-1.5
1964	LA-N	7	13	.350	27	24	1	0	0	145^1	153	89	68	14	4	31	97	1.266	4.21	77	3.59	.265	3	.067	-15	0	-1.9
1966★	LA-N	2	4	.333	29	8	0	0	0	78^2	73	31	22	4	3	14	31	1.106	2.52	131	2.48	.244	2	.167	7	5	0.7
1967	LA-N	0	0	....	6	0	0	0	0	5	9	5	5	1	0	3	2	2.400	9.00	34	10.33	.409	0	....	-3	0	-0.3
1968	LA-N	1	1	.500	3	3	0	0	0	16	17	10	9	1	1	2	11	1.188	5.06	55	3.32	.270	0	.000	-4	0	-0.6
1969	LA-N	1	0	1.000	23	4	0	0	1	51^1	54	23	19	4	0	13	25	1.305	3.33	100	3.71	.278	2	.200	-1	2	0.0
1970	LA-N	7	9	.438	31	19	2	1	4	135^1	131	63	59	16	1	43	63	1.286	3.92	98	3.64	.248	6	.154	-4	6	-0.4

YEAR	TM-L	W	L	PCT	G	GS	CG	SH	SV	IP	H	R	ER	HR	HB	BB	SO	RAT	ERA	ERA+	CERA	OAV	BH	AVG	PR+	WS	TPW
1971	LA-N	2	4	.333	28	1	0	0	1	66^1	72	32	28	5	0	12	32	1.266	3.80	85	3.44	.279	0	.000	-4	2	-0.5
Total	**8**	**26**	**36**	**.419**	**166**	**74**	**4**	**1**	**7**	**583^2**	**596**	**308**	**260**	**55**	**9**	**176**	**307**	**1.323**	**4.01**	**85**	**3.77**	**.263**	**20**	**.129**	**-41**	**16**	**-4.5**
• MOELLER, Ron	Ronald Ralph "The Kid" Moeller b: 10/13/1938, Cincinnati, OH BL/TL, 6', 180 lbs. Deb: 9/8/1956																										
1956	Bal-A	0	1	.000	4	1	0	0	0	8^2	10	5	4	0	0	3	2	1.500	4.15	94	3.89	.286	0	.000	-0	0	0.0
1958	Bal-A	0	0	....	4	0	0	0	0	4^1	6	2	2	0	0	3	3	2.077	4.15	87	6.90	.333	0	....	-0	0	0.0
1961	LA-A	4	8	.333	33	18	1	1	0	112^2	122	80	73	15	2	83	87	1.820	5.83	77	6.28	.275	6	.207	-15	3	-1.3
1963	LA-A	0	0	....	3	0	0	0	0	2^2	5	2	2	1	0	1	2	2.250	6.75	51	11.86	.385	0	....	-1	0	-0.1
	Was-A	2	0	1.000	8	3	0	0	0	24^1	31	17	17	4	1	10	10	1.685	6.29	59	6.58	.316	2	.222	-7	0	-0.7
	Yr.	2	0	1.000	11	3	0	0	0	27	36	19	19	5	1	11	12	1.741	6.33	58	7.10	.324	2	.222	-8	0	-0.8
Total	**4**	**6**	**9**	**.400**	**52**	**22**	**1**	**1**	**0**	**152^2**	**174**	**106**	**98**	**20**	**3**	**100**	**104**	**1.795**	**5.78**	**74**	**6.31**	**.287**	**8**	**.205**	**-24**	**3**	**-2.2**
• MOFFETT, Sam	Samuel R. Moffett b: 3/14/1857, Wheeling, WV d: 5/5/1907, Butte, MT BR/TR, 6', 175 lbs. Deb: 5/15/1884 ♦																										
1884	Cle-N	3	19	.136	24	22	21	0	0	197^2	236	165	85	9	....	58	84	1.487	3.87	81	....	.281	47	.184	-17	7	-2.4
1887	Ind-N	1	5	.167	6	6	6	0	0	50	70	45	21	1	4	23	3	1.400	3.78	109	....	.322	6	.143	1	1	-0.3
1888	Ind-N	2	5	.286	7	7	6	1	0	56	62	40	29	3	2	17	7	1.411	4.66	63	....	.271	4	.114	-10	1	-1.1
Total	**3**	**6**	**29**	**.171**	**37**	**35**	**33**	**1**	**0**	**303^2**	**368**	**250**	**135**	**13**	**6**	**98**	**94**	**1.459**	**4.00**	**80**	**....**	**.286**	**57**	**.171**	**-26**	**9**	**-3.9**
• MOFFITT, Randy	Randall James Moffitt b: 10/13/1948, Long Beach, CA BR/TR, 6'3", 190 lbs. Deb: 6/11/1972																										
1972	SF-N	1	5	.167	40	0	0	0	4	70^2	72	31	29	5	2	30	37	1.443	3.69	94	4.06	.266	0	.000	-2	3	-0.3
1973	SF-N	4	4	.500	60	0	0	0	14	100^1	86	30	27	9	1	31	65	1.166	2.42	158	2.82	.225	1	.059	17	12	1.6
1974	SF-N	5	7	.417	61	1	0	0	15	102	99	52	51	9	2	29	49	1.255	4.50	84	3.37	.256	5	.313	-8	9	-0.6
1975	SF-N	4	5	.444	55	0	0	0	11	74	73	35	32	6	3	32	39	1.419	3.89	98	3.96	.257	3	.214	-1	6	0.0
1976	SF-N	6	6	.500	58	0	0	0	14	103	92	36	26	6	1	35	50	1.233	2.27	160	2.83	.238	2	.143	17	14	1.8
1977	SF-N	4	9	.308	64	0	0	0	11	87^2	91	41	35	4	3	39	68	1.483	3.59	109	3.93	.273	0	.000	4	7	0.4
1978	SF-N	8	4	.667	70	0	0	0	12	81^2	79	35	30	5	3	33	52	1.371	3.31	104	3.49	.258	1	.143	1	8	0.2
1979	SF-N	2	5	.286	28	0	0	0	2	35	53	33	30	5	2	14	16	1.914	7.71	45	7.48	.356	0	.000	-16	0	-1.7
1980	SF-N	1	1	.500	13	0	0	0	0	16^2	18	10	9	2	1	4	10	1.320	4.86	73	4.24	.281	0	.000	-2	0	-0.2
1981	SF-N	0	0	....	10	0	0	0	0	11^1	15	10	10	2	0	2	11	1.500	7.94	43	5.32	.313	0	....	-6	0	-0.6
1982	Hou-N	2	4	.333	30	0	0	0	3	41^2	36	15	14	3	5	13	20	1.176	3.02	110	3.09	.228	0	.000	1	4	0.1
1983	Tor-A	6	2	.750	45	0	0	0	10	57^1	52	27	24	5	1	24	38	1.326	3.77	114	3.40	.243	0	....	3	7	0.3
Total	**12**	**43**	**52**	**.453**	**534**	**1**	**0**	**0**	**96**	**781^1**	**766**	**355**	**317**	**61**	**24**	**286**	**455**	**1.346**	**3.65**	**101**	**3.64**	**.257**	**12**	**.140**	**10**	**70**	**0.9**
• MOFORD, Herb	Herbert Moford b: 8/6/1928, Brooksville, KY BR/TR, 6'1", 175 lbs. Deb: 4/12/1955																										
1955	StL-N	1	1	.500	14	1	0	0	2	24	29	23	21	5	1	15	8	1.833	7.88	52	6.99	.299	0	.000	-10	0	-1.0
1958	Det-A	4	9	.308	25	11	6	0	1	109^2	83	45	44	10	9	42	58	1.140	3.61	112	2.93	.214	1	.027	4	6	0.0
1959	Bos-A	0	2	.000	4	2	0	0	0	8^2	10	11	11	3	0	6	7	1.846	11.42	36	8.30	.286	0	.000	-7	0	-0.7
1962	NY-N	0	1	.000	7	0	0	0	0	15	21	15	12	3	0	1	5	1.467	7.20	58	5.44	.318	1	.250	-5	0	-0.5
Total	**4**	**5**	**13**	**.278**	**50**	**14**	**6**	**0**	**3**	**157^1**	**143**	**94**	**88**	**21**	**10**	**64**	**78**	**1.316**	**5.03**	**81**	**4.09**	**.244**	**2**	**.045**	**-18**	**6**	**-2.2**
• MOGRIDGE, George	George Anthony Mogridge b: 2/18/1889, Rochester, NY d: 3/4/1962, Rochester, NY BL/TL, 6'2", 165 lbs. Deb: 8/17/1911																										
1911	Chi-A	0	2	.000	4	1	0	0	0	12^2	12	10	7	1	0	1	5	1.026	4.97	65	2.58	.255	2	.400	-2	0	-0.2
1912	Chi-A	3	4	.429	17	8	2	0	3	64^2	69	32	29	2	1	15	31	1.299	4.04	80	3.26	.264	2	.125	-5	3	-0.5
1915	NY-A	2	3	.400	6	5	3	1	0	41	33	11	8	0	3	11	11	1.073	1.76	167	2.16	.219	1	.083	5	4	0.5
1916	NY-A	6	12	.333	30	21	10	2	0	194^2	174	71	50	3	7	45	66	1.125	2.31	125	2.63	.252	14	.212	10	12	1.2
1917	NY-A	9	11	.450	29	25	15	1	0	196^1	185	82	65	5	9	39	46	1.141	2.98	90	2.78	.255	11	.159	-7	10	-0.9
1918	NY-A	16	13	.552	**45**	19	13	1	**7**	239^1	232	78	58	6	8	43	62	1.149	2.18	129	2.77	.263	15	.190	10	17	1.1
1919	NY-A	10	9	.526	35	18	13	3	0	169	159	68	52	6	7	46	58	1.213	2.77	115	2.85	.250	6	.125	3	12	0.2
1920	NY-A	5	9	.357	26	15	7	0	1	125^1	146	83	60	4	3	36	35	1.452	4.31	89	4.06	.287	7	.167	-7	4	-0.8
1921	Was-A	18	14	.563	38	36	21	4	0	288	301	119	96	12	7	66	101	1.274	3.00	137	3.28	.269	15	.153	31	26	2.4
1922	Was-A	18	13	.581	34	32	18	3	0	251^2	300	120	100	12	11	72	61	1.478	3.58	108	4.03	.304	21	.244	1	17	0.5
1923	Was-A	13	13	.500	33	30	17	3	1	211	228	90	73	10	3	56	62	1.346	3.11	121	3.68	.285	17	.227	8	14	0.9
1924*	Was-A	16	11	.593	30	30	13	2	0	213	217	97	89	2	7	61	48	1.305	3.76	107	3.14	.270	13	.176	1	14	-0.1
1925	Was-A	3	4	.429	10	8	3	0	0	53	58	23	20	2	4	18	12	1.434	3.40	124	4.23	.291	2	.105	3	3	0.1
	StL-A	1	1	.500	2	2	1	0	0	15^1	17	10	10	2	1	5	8	1.435	5.87	80	4.75	.279	0	.000	-2	1	-0.2
	Yr.	4	5	.444	12	10	4	0	0	68^1	75	33	30	4	5	23	20	1.434	3.95	111	4.35	.288	2	.087	1	4	-0.1
1926	Bos-N	6	10	.375	39	10	2	0	3	142	173	82	71	6	3	36	46	1.472	4.50	79	4.35	.311	8	.174	-13	4	-1.5
1927	Bos-N	6	4	.600	20	1	0	0	5	48^2	48	23	20	4	2	15	26	1.295	3.70	100	3.51	.257	3	.200	1	5	0.1
Total	**15**	**132**	**133**	**.498**	**398**	**261**	**138**	**20**	**20**	**2265^2**	**2352**	**999**	**808**	**77**	**76**	**565**	**678**	**1.287**	**3.21**	**109**	**3.33**	**.273**	**137**	**.182**	**36**	**146**	**2.8**
• MOHART, George	George Benjamin Mohart b: 3/6/1892, Buffalo, NY d: 10/2/1970, Silver Creek, NY BR/TR, 5'9", 165 lbs. Deb: 4/15/1920																										
1920	Bro-N	0	1	.000	13	1	0	0	0	35^2	33	17	7	0	3	7	13	1.121	1.77	181	2.55	.250	1	.125	6	2	0.7
1921	Bro-N	0	0	....	2	0	0	0	0	7	8	5	3	0	1	1	1	1.286	3.86	101	3.54	.296	1	.500	0	0	0.0
Total	**2**	**0**	**1**	**.000**	**15**	**1**	**0**	**0**	**0**	**42^2**	**41**	**22**	**10**	**0**	**4**	**8**	**14**	**1.148**	**2.11**	**160**	**2.72**	**.258**	**2**	**.200**	**6**	**2**	**0.7**
• MOHLER, Mike	Michael Ross Mohler b: 7/26/1968, Dayton, OH BR/TL, 6'2", 195 lbs. Deb: 4/7/1993																										
1993	Oak-A	1	6	.143	42	9	0	0	0	64^1	57	45	40	10	2	44	42	1.570	5.60	73	4.99	.241	0	....	-11	0	-1.0
1994	Oak-A	0	1	.000	1	1	0	0	0	2^1	2	3	2	1	0	2	4	1.714	7.71	57	5.83	.167	0	....	-1	0	-0.1
1995	Oak-A	1	1	.500	28	0	0	0	1	23^2	16	8	8	0	0	18	15	1.437	3.04	146	2.98	.198	0	....	4	2	0.4
1996	Oak-A	6	3	.667	72	0	0	0	7	81	79	36	33	9	1	41	64	1.481	3.67	134	4.42	.263	0	....	10	9	0.9
1997	Oak-A	1	10	.091	62	10	0	0	1	101^2	116	65	58	11	7	54	66	1.672	5.13	88	5.75	.301	0	....	-5	3	-0.5
1998	Oak-A	3	3	.500	57	0	0	0	0	61	70	38	35	6	4	26	42	1.574	5.16	88	5.19	.289	0	....	-3	2	-0.3
1999	StL-N	1	1	.500	48	0	0	0	1	49^1	47	26	24	3	1	23	31	1.419	4.38	104	3.87	.254	0	.000	1	3	0.1
2000	StL-N	1	1	.500	22	0	0	0	0	19	26	20	19	1	2	15	8	2.158	9.00	51	7.85	.321	1	1.000	-9	0	-0.9
	Cle-A	0	1	.000	2	0	0	0	0	1	1	1	1	1	0	0	2	1.000	9.00	55	7.45	.250	0	....	-0	0	0.0
2001	Ari-N	0	0	....	13	0	0	0	0	13^2	14	11	11	3	0	9	7	1.683	7.24	63	6.39	.286	0	....	-4	0	-0.4
Total	**9**	**14**	**27**	**.341**	**347**	**20**	**0**	**0**	**10**	**417**	**428**	**253**	**231**	**45**	**17**	**232**	**281**	**1.583**	**4.99**	**90**	**5.03**	**.272**	**1**	**.250**	**-19**	**19**	**-1.8**
• MOHORCIC, Dale	Dale Robert Mohorcic b: 1/25/1956, Cleveland, OH BR/TR, 6'3", 220 lbs. Deb: 5/31/1986																										
1986	Tex-A	2	4	.333	58	0	0	0	7	79	86	25	22	5	1	15	29	1.278	2.51	172	3.51	.279	0	....	16	8	1.6
1987	Tex-A	7	6	.538	74	0	0	0	16	99^1	88	34	33	11	2	19	48	1.077	2.99	150	2.82	.244	0	....	17	13	1.7
1988	Tex-A	2	6	.250	43	0	0	0	5	52	62	35	28	6	5	20	25	1.577	4.85	84	5.41	.295	0	....	-5	1	-0.5
	NY-A	2	2	.500	13	0	0	0	1	22^2	21	7	7	1	3	9	19	1.324	2.78	142	3.49	.239	0	....	3	2	0.3
	Yr.	4	8	.333	56	0	0	0	6	74^2	83	42	35	7	8	29	44	1.500	4.22	96	4.82	.279	0	....	-2	3	-0.2
1989	NY-A	2	1	.667	32	0	0	0	2	57^2	65	41	32	8	6	18	24	1.439	4.99	77	5.12	.286	0	....	-7	1	-0.7
1990	Mon-N	1	2	.333	34	0	0	0	2	53	56	21	19	6	4	18	29	1.396	3.23	113	4.59	.286	1	.125	2	3	0.2
Total	**5**	**16**	**21**	**.432**	**254**	**0**	**0**	**0**	**33**	**363^2**	**378**	**163**	**141**	**37**	**21**	**99**	**174**	**1.312**	**3.49**	**117**	**4.01**	**.272**	**1**	**.125**	**27**	**28**	**2.5**
• MOISAN, Bill	William Joseph Moisan b: 7/30/1925, Bradford, MA BL/TR, 6'1", 170 lbs. Deb: 9/17/1953																										
1953	Chi-N	0	0	....	3	0	0	0	0	5	5	3	3	0	1	2	1	1.400	5.40	82	4.03	.278	0	....	-0	0	0.0
• MOLESWORTH, Carlton	Carlton Molesworth b: 2/15/1876, Frederick, MD d: 7/25/1961, Frederick, MD BL/TL, 5'7.5", 200 lbs. Deb: 9/14/1895																										
1895	Was-N	0	2	.000	4	3	1	0	0	16	33	34	26	1	4	15	7	3.000	14.63	33	13.94	.416	1	.143	-17	0	-1.5
• MOLINA, Gabe	Cruz Gabriel Molina b: 5/3/1975, Denver, CO BR/TR, 5'11", 220 lbs. Deb: 5/1/1999																										
1999	Bal-A	1	2	.333	20	0	0	0	0	23	22	19	17	4	0	16	14	1.652	6.65	70	5.67	.256	0	....	-5	0	-0.5
2000	Bal-A	0	0	....	9	0	0	0	0	13	25	14	13	2	0	9	8	2.615	9.00	52	11.48	.397	0	....	-6	0	-0.6
	Atl-N	0	0	....	2	0	0	0	0	2	3	4	2	1	1	1	1	2.000	9.00	51	13.58	.375	0	....	-1	0	-0.1
2002	StL-N	1	0	1.000	12	0	0	0	0	11^1	6	2	2	1	0	6	4	1.059	1.59	249	2.21	.162	0	....	3	2	0.3

YEAR TM-L	W	L	PCT	G	GS	CG	SH	SV	IP	H	R	ER	HR	HB	BB	SO	RAT	ERA	ERA+	CERA	OAV	BH	AVG	PR+	WS	TPW
2003 StL-N	0	0	....	3	0	0	0	0	2^2	5	4	4	1	0	1	1	2.250	13.50	30	11.86	.385	0	....	-3	0	-0.3
Total 4	2	2	.500	46	0	0	0	0	52	61	43	38	9	1	33	28	1.808	6.58	69	6.99	.295	0	....	-13	2	-1.2
• MOLONEY, Richie	Richard Henry Moloney b: 6/7/1950, Brookline, MA BR/TR, 6'3", 185 lbs. Deb: 9/20/1970																									
1970 Chi-A	0	0	....	1	0	0	0	0	1	2	0	0	0	0	0	1	2.000	0.00	....	7.48	.400	0	....	0	0	0.0
• MOLYNEAUX, Vince	Vincent Leo Molyneaux b: 8/17/1888, Lewiston, NY d: 5/4/1950, Stamford, CT BR/TR, 6', 180 lbs. Deb: 7/5/1917																									
1917 StL-A	0	0	....	7	0	0	0	0	22	18	15	12	0	0	20	4	1.727	4.91	53	4.23	.237	0	.000	-6	0	-0.7
1918 Bos-A	1	0	1.000	6	0	0	0	0	10^2	3	4	4	0	0	8	1	1.031	3.38	79	1.16	.086	0	.000	-1	1	-0.1
Total 2	1	0	1.000	13	0	0	0	0	32^2	21	19	16	0	0	28	5	1.500	4.41	59	3.23	.189	0	.000	-7	1	-0.8
• MONAHAN, Rinty	Edward Francis Monahan b: 4/28/1928, Brooklyn, NY BR/TR, 6'1.5", 195 lbs. Deb: 8/9/1953																									
1953 Phi-A	0	0	....	4	0	0	0	0	10^2	11	5	5	0	0	7	2	1.688	4.22	102	4.48	.275	0	.000	0	1	0.0
• MONBOUQUETTE, Bill	William Charles Monbouquette b: 8/11/1936, Medford, MA BR/TR, 5'11", 195 lbs. Deb: 7/18/1958 C																									
1958 Bos-A	3	4	.429	10	8	3	0	0	54^1	52	25	20	4	0	20	30	1.325	3.31	121	3.41	.251	3	.176	5	3	0.5
1959 Bos-A	7	7	.500	34	17	4	0	0	151^2	165	86	70	15	3	33	87	1.305	4.15	98	3.99	.285	3	.065	-2	6	-0.6
1960 Bos-A★	14	11	.560	35	30	12	3	0	215	217	91	87	18	2	68	134	1.326	3.64	111	3.68	.263	6	.092	15	16	1.3
1961 Bos-A	14	14	.500	32	32	12	1	0	236^1	233	106	89	24	0	100	161	1.409	3.39	123	4.05	.254	9	.130	21	17	2.1
1962 Bos-A★	15	13	.536	35	35	11	4	0	235^1	227	100	87	22	3	65	153	1.241	3.33	124	3.39	.251	7	.096	20	17	1.7
1963 Bos-A★	20	10	.667	37	36	13	1	0	266^2	258	119	113	31	0	42	174	1.125	3.81	99	3.01	.250	10	.114	1	16	-0.3
1964 Bos-A	13	14	.481	36	35	7	5	1	234	258	114	105	34	1	40	120	1.274	4.04	95	4.01	.277	6	.083	1	11	-0.1
1965 Bos-A	10	18	.357	35	35	10	2	0	228^2	239	114	94	32	1	40	110	1.220	3.70	101	3.68	.269	4	.059	5	10	0.2
1966 Det-A	7	8	.467	30	14	2	1	0	102^2	120	60	54	14	3	22	61	1.383	4.73	74	4.59	.293	4	.154	-15	2	-1.6
1967 Det-A	0	0	....	2	0	0	0	0	2	1	0	0	0	0	0	2	.500	0.00	....	0.54	.143	0	....	1	0	0.1
NY-A	6	5	.545	33	10	2	1	1	133^1	122	39	35	6	4	17	53	1.043	2.36	132	2.35	.246	5	.156	13	12	1.4
Yr.	6	5	.545	35	10	2	1	1	135^1	123	39	35	6	4	17	55	1.034	2.33	134	2.33	.245	5	.156	14	12	1.5
1968 NY-A	5	7	.417	17	11	2	0	0	89^1	92	47	44	7	3	13	32	1.175	4.43	65	3.20	.264	3	.115	-14	0	-1.6
SF-N	0	1	.000	7	0	0	0	1	12^1	11	9	5	4	0	2	5	1.054	3.65	81	3.84	.239	0	....	-1	0	-0.1
Total 11	114	112	.504	343	263	78	18	3	1961^2	1995	910	803	211	20	462	1122	1.253	3.68	103	3.59	.263	60	.103	49	110	3.0
• MONGE, Sid	Isidro Pedroza Monge b: 4/11/1951, Agua Prieta, Mexico BB/TL, 6'2", 195 lbs. Deb: 9/12/1975																									
1975 Cal-A	0	2	.000	4	2	2	0	0	23^2	22	12	11	3	1	10	17	1.352	4.18	85	4.08	.242	0	....	-2	1	-0.2
1976 Cal-A	6	7	.462	32	13	2	0	0	117^2	108	50	44	10	1	49	53	1.334	3.37	99	3.71	.248	0	....	0	6	0.0
1977 Cal-A	0	1	.000	4	0	0	0	1	12^1	14	6	4	2	0	6	4	1.622	2.92	134	5.66	.304	0	....	1	1	0.1
Cle-A	1	2	.333	33	0	0	0	3	39	47	31	27	6	0	27	25	1.897	6.23	63	6.79	.309	0	....	-10	0	-1.0
Yr.	1	3	.250	37	0	0	0	4	51^1	61	37	31	8	0	33	29	1.831	5.44	72	6.52	.308	0	....	-9	1	-0.8
1978 Cle-A	4	3	.571	48	2	0	0	6	84^2	71	36	26	4	0	51	54	1.441	2.76	135	3.40	.225	0	....	10	7	1.0
1979 Cle-A★	12	10	.545	76	0	0	0	19	131	96	37	35	9	1	64	108	1.221	2.40	177	2.73	.209	0	....	30	21	2.9
1980 Cle-A	3	5	.375	67	0	0	0	14	94^1	80	39	37	12	3	40	61	1.272	3.53	115	3.52	.227	0	....	6	10	0.6
1981 Cle-A	3	5	.375	31	0	0	0	4	58	58	31	28	9	0	21	41	1.362	4.34	83	4.33	.266	0	....	-3	3	-0.3
1982 Phi-N	7	1	.875	47	0	0	0	2	72	70	35	30	8	2	22	43	1.278	3.75	98	3.66	.256	1	.111	-1	5	-0.1
1983 Phi-N	3	0	1.000	14	0	0	0	0	11^2	20	10	9	4	0	6	7	2.229	6.94	51	10.92	.377	0	.000	-4	0	-0.5
SD-N	7	3	.700	47	0	0	0	7	68^2	65	24	24	4	1	31	32	1.398	3.15	111	3.65	.257	1	.100	1	7	0.1
Yr.	10	3	.769	61	0	0	0	7	80^1	85	34	33	8	1	37	39	1.519	3.70	95	4.70	.278	1	.091	-3	7	-0.3
1984 SD-N	2	1	.667	13	0	0	0	0	15	17	10	8	3	0	17	7	2.267	4.80	74	8.37	.293	0	.000	-2	0	-0.3
Det-A	1	0	1.000	19	0	0	0	0	36	40	21	17	5	2	12	19	1.444	4.25	92	4.94	.282	0	....	-2	1	-0.2
Total 10	49	40	.551	435	17	4	0	56	764	708	342	300	79	11	356	471	1.393	3.53	106	3.98	.248	2	.095	26	62	2.4
• MONROE, Ed	Edward Oliver "Peck" Monroe b: 2/22/1895, Louisville, KY d: 4/29/1969, Louisville, KY BR/TR, 6'5", 187 lbs. Deb: 5/29/1917																									
1917 NY-A	1	0	1.000	9	1	1	0	1	28^2	35	15	11	1	2	6	12	1.430	3.45	78	4.38	.310	2	.167	-3	1	-0.3
1918 NY-A	0	0	....	1	0	0	0	0	2	1	2	1	0	0	2	1	1.500	4.50	63	2.54	.143	0	....	-0	0	0.0
Total 2	1	0	1.000	10	1	1	0	1	30^2	36	17	12	1	2	8	13	1.435	3.52	76	4.26	.300	2	.167	-3	1	-0.4
• MONROE, Larry	Lawrence James Monroe b: 6/20/1956, Detroit, MI BR/TR, 6'4", 200 lbs. Deb: 8/23/1976																									
1976 Chi-A	0	1	.000	8	2	0	0	0	21^2	23	11	10	0	0	13	9	1.662	4.15	86	4.58	.284	0	....	-1	1	-0.1
• MONROE, Zach	Zachary Charles Monroe b: 7/8/1931, Peoria, IL BR/TR, 6', 198 lbs. Deb: 6/27/1958																									
1958★ NY-A	4	2	.667	21	6	1	0	1	58	57	29	21	8	0	27	18	1.448	3.26	108	4.54	.263	2	.118	1	3	0.0
1959 NY-A	0	0	....	3	0	0	0	0	3^1	3	2	2	2	0	2	1	1.500	5.40	68	7.86	.231	0	....	-1	0	-0.1
Total 2	4	2	.667	24	6	1	0	1	61^1	60	31	23	10	0	29	19	1.451	3.38	105	4.72	.261	2	.118	-0	3	-0.1
• MONTAGUE, John	John Evans Montague b: 9/12/1947, Newport News, VA BR/TR, 6'2", 213 lbs. Deb: 9/9/1973																									
1973 Mon-N	0	0	....	4	0	0	0	0	7^2	8	3	3	0	1	2	7	1.304	3.52	108	3.27	.286	0	.000	0	1	0.0
1974 Mon-N	3	4	.429	46	1	0	0	3	82^2	73	37	29	5	4	38	43	1.343	3.16	121	3.51	.241	1	.100	7	6	0.7
1975 Mon-N	0	1	.000	12	0	0	0	2	17^2	23	11	11	4	2	6	9	1.642	5.60	68	7.12	.324	0	.000	-4	0	-0.4
Phi-N	0	0	....	3	0	0	0	0	5	8	5	5	1	0	4	1	2.400	9.00	41	10.72	.400	0	....	-3	0	-0.3
Yr.	0	1	.000	15	0	0	0	2	22^2	31	16	16	5	2	10	10	1.809	6.35	60	7.91	.341	0	.000	-7	0	-0.7
1977 Sea-A	8	12	.400	47	15	2	0	4	182^1	193	95	87	20	4	75	98	1.470	4.29	96	4.60	.272	0	....	-7	10	-0.7
1978 Sea-A	1	3	.250	19	0	0	0	2	43^2	52	31	30	2	0	24	14	1.740	6.18	62	5.31	.308	0	....	-11	0	-1.2
1979 Sea-A	6	4	.600	41	1	0	0	1	116^1	125	73	72	14	2	47	60	1.479	5.57	78	4.58	.284	0	....	-15	4	-1.5
★Cal-A	2	0	1.000	14	0	0	0	6	17^2	16	12	10	3	0	9	6	1.415	5.09	80	4.58	.242	0	....	-2	1	-0.2
Yr.	8	4	.667	55	1	0	0	7	134	141	85	82	17	2	56	66	1.470	5.51	78	4.58	.279	0	....	-17	5	-1.7
1980 Cal-A	4	2	.667	37	0	0	0	3	73^2	97	47	42	8	1	21	22	1.602	5.13	77	5.59	.324	0	....	-10	2	-1.0
Total 7	24	26	.480	223	17	2	0	21	546^2	595	314	289	57	14	226	260	1.502	4.76	85	4.74	.283	1	.083	-45	24	-4.5
• MONTALVO, Rafael	Rafael Edgardo (Torres) Montalvo b: 3/31/1964, Rio Piedras, Puerto Rico BR/TR, 6', 185 lbs. Deb: 4/13/1986																									
1986 Hou-N	0	0	....	1	0	0	0	0	1	1	1	1	0	0	2	0	3.000	9.00	40	9.51	.250	0	....	-1	0	-0.1
• MONTEAGUDO, Aurelio	Aurelio Faustino (Cintra) Monteagudo b: 11/19/1943, Caibarien, Cuba d: 11/10/1990, Saltillo, Mexico BR/TR, 5'11", 185 lbs. Deb: 9/1/1963																									
1963 KC-A	0	0	....	4	0	0	0	0	7	4	2	2	0	0	3	3	1.000	2.57	150	1.48	.182	0	....	1	1	0.1
1964 KC-A	0	4	.000	11	6	0	0	0	31^1	40	32	31	11	1	10	14	1.596	8.90	43	7.69	.317	2	.286	-17	0	-1.7
1965 KC-A	0	0	....	4	0	0	0	0	7	5	4	3	1	0	4	5	1.286	3.86	90	3.06	.185	0	....	-0	0	0.0
1966 KC-A	0	0	....	6	0	0	0	0	12^2	12	4	4	0	0	7	3	1.500	2.84	119	3.77	.261	0	....	1	1	0.1
Hou-N	0	0	....	10	0	0	0	1	15^1	14	8	8	1	0	11	7	1.630	4.70	73	4.33	.241	0	.000	-2	1	-0.2
1967 Chi-A	0	1	.000	1	1	0	0	0	1^1	4	3	3	1	0	2	0	4.500	20.25	15	31.96	.500	0	....	-3	0	-0.3
1970 KC-A	1	1	.500	21	0	0	0	0	27^1	20	11	9	2	1	9	18	1.061	2.96	126	2.36	.200	0	.000	2	2	0.2
1973 Cal-A	2	1	.667	15	0	0	0	3	30	23	18	14	2	4	16	8	1.300	4.20	84	3.45	.215	0	....	-2	2	-0.2
Total 7	3	7	.300	72	7	0	0	4	132	122	82	74	18	6	62	58	1.394	5.05	72	4.53	.247	2	.200	-20	7	-2.0
• MONTEAGUDO, Rene	Rene (Miranda) Monteagudo b: 3/12/1916, Havana, Cuba d: 9/14/1973, Hialeah, FL BL/TL, 5'7", 165 lbs. Deb: 9/6/1938 ♦																									
1938 Was-A	1	1	.500	5	3	2	0	0	22	26	15	14	3	0	15	13	1.864	5.73	79	6.32	.286	3	.500	-3	1	-0.2
1940 Was-A	2	6	.250	27	8	3	0	2	100^2	128	70	68	7	3	52	64	1.788	6.08	69	5.95	.316	6	.182	-20	1	-1.9
1945 Phi-N	0	0	....	14	0	0	0	0	45^2	67	42	38	1	2	28	16	2.080	7.49	51	6.98	.347	58	.301	-17	5	-1.4
Total 3	3	7	.300	46	11	5	0	2	168^1	221	127	120	11	5	95	93	1.877	6.42	64	6.28	.321	78	.289	-40	7	-3.5
• MONTEFUSCO, John	John Joseph "The Count" Montefusco b: 5/25/1950, Long Branch, NJ BR/TR, 6'1", 180 lbs. Deb: 9/3/1974																									
1974 SF-N	3	2	.600	7	5	1	1	0	39^1	41	22	21	3	0	19	34	1.525	4.81	79	4.33	.256	4	.286	-4	2	-0.2
1975 SF-N	15	9	.625	35	34	10	4	0	243^2	210	85	78	11	8	86	215	1.215	2.88	132	2.83	.233	7	.088	25	20	2.4
1976 SF-N★	16	14	.533	37	36	11	**6**	0	253^1	224	90	80	11	4	74	172	1.176	2.84	128	2.69	.238	8	.103	**26**	**21**	2.5
1977 SF-N	7	12	.368	26	25	4	0	0	157^1	170	82	61	10	3	46	110	1.373	3.49	112	3.77	.273	6	.122	10	8	0.9

YEAR	TM-L	W	L	PCT	G	GS	CG	SH	SV	IP	H	R	ER	HR	HB	BB	SO	RAT	ERA	ERA+	CERA	OAV	BH	AVG	PR+	WS	TPW
1978	SF-N	11	9	.550	36	36	3	0	0	238^{2}	233	110	101	25	4	68	177	1.261	3.81	90	3.55	.255	4	.057	-9	9	-1.3
1979	SF-N	3	8	.273	22	22	0	0	0	137	145	64	60	15	2	51	76	1.431	3.94	89	4.43	.279	7	.167	-5	5	-0.4
1980	SF-N	4	8	.333	22	17	1	0	0	113^{1}	120	61	55	15	2	39	85	1.403	4.37	81	4.33	.265	1	.033	-8	2	-1.1
1981	Atl-N	2	3	.400	26	9	0	0	1	77^{1}	75	32	30	9	0	27	34	1.319	3.49	103	3.84	.260	1	.067	1	4	0.0
1982	SD-N	10	11	.476	32	32	1	0	0	184^{1}	177	93	82	17	3	41	83	1.183	4.00	86	3.12	.251	5	.086	-13	5	-1.6
1983	SD-N	9	4	.692	31	10	1	0	4	95^{1}	94	38	35	6	1	32	52	1.322	3.30	106	3.50	.265	1	.053	0	8	0.0
	NY-A	5	0	1.000	6	6	0	0	0	38	39	14	14	3	1	10	15	1.289	3.32	117	3.74	.271	0	....	3	4	0.3
1984	NY-A	5	3	.625	11	11	0	0	0	55^{1}	55	26	22	5	1	13	23	1.229	3.58	106	3.29	.253	0	....	2	3	0.2
1985	NY-A	0	0	....	3	1	0	0	0	7	12	8	8	3	0	2	2	2.000	10.29	39	11.01	.387	0	....	-5	0	-0.5
1986	NY-A	0	0	....	4	0	0	0	0	12^{1}	9	3	3	2	0	5	3	1.135	2.19	187	3.06	.200	0	....	3	1	0.2
Total	**13**	**90**	**83**	**.520**	**298**	**244**	**32**	**11**	**5**	**1652^{1}**	**1604**	**728**	**650**	**135**	**29**	**513**	**1081**	**1.281**	**3.54**	**102**	**3.46**	**.255**	**44**	**.097**	**23**	**92**	**1.3**

• MONTEJO, Manny Manuel (Bofill) Montejo b: 10/16/1935, Caibarien, Cuba BR/TR, 5'11", 150 lbs. Deb: 7/25/1961

YEAR	TM-L	W	L	PCT	G	GS	CG	SH	SV	IP	H	R	ER	HR	HB	BB	SO	RAT	ERA	ERA+	CERA	OAV	BH	AVG	PR+	WS	TPW
1961	Det-A	0	0	....	12	0	0	0	0	16^{1}	13	7	7	2	2	6	15	1.163	3.86	106	3.41	.217	0	....	0	1	0.0

• MONTELEONE, Rich Richard Monteleone b: 3/22/1963, Tampa, FL BR/TR, 6'2", 234 lbs. Deb: 4/15/1987 C

YEAR	TM-L	W	L	PCT	G	GS	CG	SH	SV	IP	H	R	ER	HR	HB	BB	SO	RAT	ERA	ERA+	CERA	OAV	BH	AVG	PR+	WS	TPW
1987	Sea-A	0	0	....	3	0	0	0	0	7	10	5	5	2	1	4	2	2.000	6.43	73	10.14	.345	0	....	-1	0	-0.1
1988	Cal-A	0	0	....	3	0	0	0	0	4^{1}	4	0	0	0	1	1	3	1.154	0.00	....	2.57	.222	0	....	2	1	0.2
1989	Cal-A	2	2	.500	24	0	0	0	0	39^{2}	39	15	14	3	1	13	27	1.311	3.18	120	3.55	.255	0	....	2	3	0.2
1990	NY-A	0	1	.000	5	0	0	0	0	7^{1}	8	5	5	0	0	2	8	1.364	6.14	65	3.42	.276	0	....	-2	0	-0.2
1991	NY-A	3	1	.750	26	0	0	0	0	47	42	27	19	5	0	19	34	1.298	3.64	114	3.40	.236	0	....	3	3	0.3
1992	NY-A	7	3	.700	47	0	0	0	0	92^{2}	82	35	34	7	0	27	62	1.176	3.30	119	2.84	.235	0	....	6	7	0.6
1993	NY-A	7	4	.636	42	0	0	0	0	85^{2}	85	52	47	14	0	35	50	1.401	4.94	84	4.33	.262	0	....	-7	3	-0.7
1994	SF-N	4	3	.571	39	0	0	0	0	45^{1}	43	18	16	6	0	13	16	1.235	3.18	126	3.49	.253	0	.000	2	4	0.2
1995	Cal-A	1	0	1.000	9	0	0	0	0	9	8	2	2	1	0	3	5	1.222	2.00	235	3.43	.267	0	....	3	1	0.2
1996	Cal-A	0	3	.000	12	0	0	0	0	15^{1}	23	11	10	5	1	2	5	1.630	5.87	83	8.20	.348	0	....	-2	0	-0.2
Total	**10**	**24**	**17**	**.585**	**210**	**0**	**0**	**0**	**0**	**353^{1}**	**344**	**170**	**152**	**43**	**4**	**119**	**212**	**1.310**	**3.87**	**106**	**3.84**	**.255**	**0**	**.000**	**6**	**22**	**0.6**

• MONTGOMERY, Jeff Jeffrey Thomas Montgomery b: 1/7/1962, Wellston, OH BR/TR, 5'11", 180 lbs. Deb: 8/1/1987

YEAR	TM-L	W	L	PCT	G	GS	CG	SH	SV	IP	H	R	ER	HR	HB	BB	SO	RAT	ERA	ERA+	CERA	OAV	BH	AVG	PR+	WS	TPW
1987	Cin-N	2	2	.500	14	1	0	0	0	19^{1}	25	15	14	2	0	9	13	1.759	6.52	65	6.07	.313	0	.000	-5	0	-0.5
1988	KC-A	7	2	.778	45	0	0	0	1	62^{2}	54	25	24	6	2	30	47	1.340	3.45	116	3.65	.231	0	....	5	6	0.5
1989	KC-A	7	3	.700	63	0	0	0	18	92	66	16	14	3	2	25	94	.989	1.37	281	1.79	.198	0	....	27	19	2.7
1990	KC-A	6	5	.545	73	0	0	0	24	94^{1}	81	36	25	6	5	34	94	1.219	2.39	161	2.95	.227	0	....	18	12	1.8
1991	KC-A	4	4	.500	67	0	0	0	33	90	83	32	29	6	2	28	77	1.233	2.90	142	3.14	.246	0	....	15	15	1.5
1992	KC-A★	1	6	.143	65	0	0	0	39	82^{2}	61	23	20	5	3	27	69	1.065	2.18	186	2.30	.205	0	....	18	16	1.9
1993	KC-A★	7	5	.583	69	0	0	0	**45**	87^{1}	65	22	22	3	2	23	66	1.008	2.27	202	1.89	.206	0	....	22	22	2.1
1994	KC-A	2	3	.400	42	0	0	0	27	44^{2}	48	21	20	5	1	15	50	1.410	4.03	124	4.40	.276	0	....	5	7	0.4
1995	KC-A	2	3	.400	54	0	0	0	31	65^{2}	60	27	25	7	2	25	49	1.294	3.43	140	3.65	.252	0	....	9	11	0.8
1996	KC-A★	4	6	.400	48	0	0	0	24	63^{1}	59	31	30	14	3	19	45	1.232	4.26	118	4.32	.251	0	....	5	9	0.5
1997	KC-A	1	4	.200	55	0	0	0	14	59^{1}	53	24	23	9	0	18	48	1.197	3.49	135	3.33	.240	0	....	7	8	0.7
1998	KC-A	2	5	.286	56	0	0	0	36	56	58	35	31	8	2	22	54	1.429	4.98	97	4.60	.264	0	....	-0	8	0.0
1999	KC-A	1	4	.200	49	0	0	0	12	51^{1}	72	40	39	7	2	21	27	1.812	6.84	73	7.08	.343	0	....	-12	1	-1.1
Total	**13**	**46**	**52**	**.469**	**700**	**1**	**0**	**0**	**304**	**868^{2}**	**785**	**347**	**316**	**81**	**26**	**296**	**733**	**1.244**	**3.27**	**137**	**3.40**	**.241**	**0**	**.000**	**114**	**134**	**11.4**

• MONTGOMERY, Monty Monty Bryson Montgomery b: 9/1/1946, Albemarle, NC BR/TR, 6'3", 200 lbs. Deb: 9/14/1971

YEAR	TM-L	W	L	PCT	G	GS	CG	SH	SV	IP	H	R	ER	HR	HB	BB	SO	RAT	ERA	ERA+	CERA	OAV	BH	AVG	PR+	WS	TPW
1971	KC-A	3	0	1.000	3	2	0	0	0	21^{1}	16	5	5	0	0	3	12	.891	2.11	163	1.43	.205	0	.000	3	3	0.3
1972	KC-A	3	3	.500	9	8	1	1	0	56^{1}	55	21	19	2	0	17	24	1.278	3.04	100	3.18	.263	3	.176	1	3	0.1
Total	**2**	**6**	**3**	**.667**	**12**	**10**	**1**	**1**	**0**	**77^{2}**	**71**	**26**	**24**	**2**	**0**	**20**	**36**	**1.172**	**2.78**	**112**	**2.70**	**.247**	**3**	**.125**	**4**	**6**	**0.4**

• MONTGOMERY, Steve Steven Lewis Montgomery b: 12/25/1970, Westminster, CA BR/TR, 6'4", 210 lbs. Deb: 4/3/1996

YEAR	TM-L	W	L	PCT	G	GS	CG	SH	SV	IP	H	R	ER	HR	HB	BB	SO	RAT	ERA	ERA+	CERA	OAV	BH	AVG	PR+	WS	TPW
1996	Oak-A	1	0	1.000	8	0	0	0	0	13^{2}	18	14	14	5	0	13	8	2.268	9.22	53	10.50	.310	0	....	-7	0	-0.6
1997	Oak-A	0	1	.000	4	0	0	0	0	6^{1}	10	7	7	2	0	8	1	2.842	9.95	45	13.63	.385	0	....	-4	0	-0.4
1999	Phi-N	1	5	.167	53	0	0	0	3	64^{2}	54	25	24	10	0	31	55	1.314	3.34	141	3.87	.229	1	1.000	9	6	0.9
2000	SD-N	0	2	.000	7	0	0	0	0	5^{2}	6	6	5	3	0	4	3	1.765	7.94	54	9.01	.273	0	....	-2	0	-0.2
Total	**4**	**2**	**8**	**.200**	**72**	**0**	**0**	**0**	**3**	**90^{1}**	**88**	**52**	**50**	**20**	**0**	**56**	**67**	**1.594**	**4.98**	**94**	**5.88**	**.257**	**1**	**1.000**	**-4**	**6**	**-0.3**

• MONZANT, Ramon Ramon Segundo (Espino) Monzant b: 1/4/1933, Maracaibo, Venezuela BR/TR, 6', 165 lbs. Deb: 7/2/1954

YEAR	TM-L	W	L	PCT	G	GS	CG	SH	SV	IP	H	R	ER	HR	HB	BB	SO	RAT	ERA	ERA+	CERA	OAV	BH	AVG	PR+	WS	TPW
1954	NY-N	0	0	....	6	1	0	0	0	7^{2}	8	5	4	0	0	11	5	2.478	4.70	86	7.14	.276	0	.000	-1	0	-0.1
1955	NY-N	4	8	.333	28	12	3	0	0	94^{2}	98	47	42	11	3	43	54	1.489	3.99	101	4.76	.278	3	.125	0	5	0.0
1956	NY-N	1	0	1.000	4	1	1	0	0	13	8	7	6	4	0	7	11	1.154	4.15	91	3.79	.170	0	.000	-0	1	-0.1
1957	NY-N	3	2	.600	24	2	0	0	0	49^{2}	55	27	22	6	2	16	37	1.430	3.99	99	4.66	.286	3	.300	-0	3	0.0
1958	SF-N	8	11	.421	43	16	4	1	1	150^{2}	160	89	79	20	6	57	93	1.440	4.72	81	4.66	.273	8	.163	-14	4	-1.5
1960	SF-N	0	0	....	1	0	0	0	0	1	1	1	1	1	0	0	1	1.000	9.00	39	7.45	.250	0	....	-1	0	-0.1
Total	**6**	**16**	**21**	**.432**	**106**	**32**	**8**	**1**	**1**	**316^{2}**	**330**	**176**	**154**	**42**	**11**	**134**	**201**	**1.465**	**4.38**	**89**	**4.73**	**.273**	**14**	**.157**	**-15**	**13**	**-1.8**

• MOODY, Eric Eric Lane Moody b: 1/6/1971, Greenville, SC BR/TR, 6'6", 185 lbs. Deb: 8/3/1997

YEAR	TM-L	W	L	PCT	G	GS	CG	SH	SV	IP	H	R	ER	HR	HB	BB	SO	RAT	ERA	ERA+	CERA	OAV	BH	AVG	PR+	WS	TPW
1997	Tex-A	0	1	.000	10	1	0	0	0	19	26	10	9	4	0	2	12	1.474	4.26	112	5.90	.329	0	....	1	1	0.1

• MOON, Leo Leo "Lefty" Moon b: 6/22/1899, Bellemont, NC d: 8/25/1970, New Orleans, LA BR/TL, 5'11", 165 lbs. Deb: 7/9/1932

YEAR	TM-L	W	L	PCT	G	GS	CG	SH	SV	IP	H	R	ER	HR	HB	BB	SO	RAT	ERA	ERA+	CERA	OAV	BH	AVG	PR+	WS	TPW
1932	Cle-A	0	0	....	1	0	0	0	0	5^{2}	11	8	7	0	0	7	1	3.176	11.12	43	11.84	.379	1	.500	-4	0	-0.3

• MOONEY, Jim Jim Irving Mooney b: 9/4/1906, Mooresburg, TN d: 4/27/1979, Johnson City, TN BR/TL, 5'11", 168 lbs. Deb: 8/14/1931

YEAR	TM-L	W	L	PCT	G	GS	CG	SH	SV	IP	H	R	ER	HR	HB	BB	SO	RAT	ERA	ERA+	CERA	OAV	BH	AVG	PR+	WS	TPW
1931	NY-N	7	1	.875	10	8	6	2	0	71^{2}	71	19	16	1	1	16	38	1.214	2.01	184	2.84	.262	4	.160	13	7	1.2
1932	NY-N	6	10	.375	29	18	4	1	0	124^{2}	154	79	70	18	0	42	37	1.572	5.05	74	5.35	.299	5	.122	-16	2	-1.8
1933	StL-N	2	5	.286	21	8	2	0	1	77^{1}	87	36	32	1	0	26	14	1.461	3.72	93	3.92	.296	1	.050	-2	3	-0.4
1934★	StL-N	2	4	.333	32	7	1	0	1	82^{1}	114	59	50	3	4	49	27	1.980	5.47	77	6.63	.326	1	.053	-12	1	-1.4
Total	**4**	**17**	**20**	**.459**	**92**	**41**	**13**	**3**	**2**	**356**	**426**	**193**	**168**	**23**	**5**	**133**	**116**	**1.570**	**4.25**	**89**	**4.83**	**.298**	**11**	**.105**	**-18**	**13**	**-2.5**

• MOONEYHAM, Bill William Craig Mooneyham b: 8/16/1960, Livermore, CA BR/TR, 6', 175 lbs. Deb: 4/19/1986

YEAR	TM-L	W	L	PCT	G	GS	CG	SH	SV	IP	H	R	ER	HR	HB	BB	SO	RAT	ERA	ERA+	CERA	OAV	BH	AVG	PR+	WS	TPW
1986	Oak-A	4	5	.444	45	6	0	0	2	99^{2}	103	53	50	4	3	67	75	1.706	4.52	86	4.98	.270	0	....	-7	4	-0.7

• MOORE, Balor Balor Lilbon Moore b: 1/25/1951, Smithville, TX BL/TL, 6'2", 184 lbs. Deb: 5/21/1970

YEAR	TM-L	W	L	PCT	G	GS	CG	SH	SV	IP	H	R	ER	HR	HB	BB	SO	RAT	ERA	ERA+	CERA	OAV	BH	AVG	PR+	WS	TPW
1970	Mon-N	0	2	.000	6	2	0	0	0	9^{2}	14	9	8	0	0	8	6	2.276	7.45	55	8.02	.368	1	.333	-4	0	-0.3
1972	Mon-N	9	9	.500	22	22	6	3	0	147^{2}	122	61	57	15	5	59	161	1.226	3.47	102	3.25	.226	8	.145	2	9	0.2
1973	Mon-N	7	16	.304	35	32	3	1	0	176^{1}	151	98	88	18	3	109	151	1.474	4.49	85	4.19	.233	3	.057	-14	4	-1.7
1974	Mon-N	0	2	.000	8	2	0	0	0	13^{2}	13	8	6	1	0	15	16	2.049	3.95	97	6.32	.245	0	.000	-0	0	0.0
1977	Cal-A	0	2	.000	7	3	0	0	0	22^{2}	28	19	10	7	3	10	14	1.676	3.97	98	7.45	.298	0	....	0	0	0.0
1978	Tor-A	6	9	.400	37	18	2	0	0	144^{1}	165	85	79	16	7	54	75	1.517	4.93	80	5.14	.294	0	....	-15	4	-1.6
1979	Tor-A	5	7	.417	34	16	5	0	0	139^{1}	135	85	75	17	8	79	51	1.536	4.84	90	5.02	.262	0	....	-9	6	-0.8
1980	Tor-A	1	1	.500	31	3	0	0	1	64^{2}	76	43	38	6	4	31	22	1.655	5.29	81	5.70	.309	0	....	-8	1	-0.8
Total	**8**	**28**	**48**	**.368**	**180**	**98**	**16**	**4**	**1**	**718^{1}**	**704**	**408**	**361**	**80**	**30**	**365**	**496**	**1.488**	**4.52**	**87**	**4.68**	**.261**	**12**	**.106**	**-47**	**24**	**-5.1**

• MOORE, Barry Robert Barry Moore b: 4/3/1943, Statesville, NC BL/TL, 6'1", 190 lbs. Deb: 5/29/1965

YEAR	TM-L	W	L	PCT	G	GS	CG	SH	SV	IP	H	R	ER	HR	HB	BB	SO	RAT	ERA	ERA+	CERA	OAV	BH	AVG	PR+	WS	TPW
1965	Was-A	0	0	....	1	0	0	0	0	1	1	1	0	0	0	1	0	2.000	0.00	....	5.48	.333	0	....	0	0	0.0
1966	Was-A	3	3	.500	12	11	1	0	0	62^{1}	55	26	26	3	1	39	28	1.508	3.75	92	4.00	.240	2	.105	-3	3	-0.4
1967	Was-A	7	11	.389	27	26	3	1	0	143^{2}	127	67	60	15	3	71	74	1.378	3.76	84	3.87	.240	6	.130	-10	5	-1.1
1968	Was-A	4	6	.400	32	18	0	0	3	117^{2}	116	55	44	8	2	42	56	1.343	3.37	87	3.64	.261	3	.097	-5	3	-0.7
1969	Was-A	9	8	.529	31	25	4	0	0	134	123	70	64	12	2	67	51	1.418	4.30	81	3.98	.246	9	.209	-13	4	-1.2

YEAR TM-L	W	L	PCT	G	GS	CG	SH	SV	IP	H	R	ER	HR	HB	BB	SO	RAT	ERA	ERA+	CERA	OAV	BH	AVG	PR+	WS	TPW
1970 Cle-A	3	5	.375	13	12	0	0	0	70^1	70	34	33	8	1	46	35	1.649	4.22	94	5.20	.262	2	.095	-2	4	-0.4
Chi-A	0	4	.000	24	7	0	0	0	70^2	85	56	50	12	8	34	34	1.684	6.37	61	6.64	.302	5	.263	-18	0	-1.8
Yr.	3	9	.250	37	19	0	0	0	141	155	90	83	20	9	80	69	1.667	5.30	74	5.92	.283	7	.175	-20	4	-2.2
Total 6	**26**	**37**	**.413**	**140**	**99**	**8**	**1**	**3**	**599^2**	**577**	**309**	**277**	**58**	**17**	**300**	**278**	**1.462**	**4.16**	**82**	**4.35**	**.256**	**27**	**.151**	**-50**	**19**	**-5.5**

• MOORE, Bill William Christopher Moore b: 9/3/1902, Corning, NY d: 1/24/1984, Corning, NY BR/TR, 6'3", 195 lbs. Deb: 4/15/1925

YEAR TM-L	W	L	PCT	G	GS	CG	SH	SV	IP	H	R	ER	HR	HB	BB	SO	RAT	ERA	ERA+	CERA	OAV	BH	AVG	PR+	WS	TPW
1925 Det-A	0	0	....	1	0	0	0	0	0	0	0	0	0	3	0	....	....	....	....	∞	.000	0	....	0	0	0.0

• MOORE, Bobby Robert Devell Moore b: 11/8/1958, Jena, LA BR/TR, 6'4", 200 lbs. Deb: 9/11/1985

YEAR TM-L	W	L	PCT	G	GS	CG	SH	SV	IP	H	R	ER	HR	HB	BB	SO	RAT	ERA	ERA+	CERA	OAV	BH	AVG	PR+	WS	TPW
1985 SF-N	0	0	....	11	0	0	0	0	16^2	18	6	6	1	0	10	10	1.680	3.24	106	4.68	.269	0	.000	1	1	0.0

• MOORE, Brad Bradley Alan Moore b: 6/21/1964, Loveland, CO BR/TR, 6'1", 185 lbs. Deb: 6/14/1988

YEAR TM-L	W	L	PCT	G	GS	CG	SH	SV	IP	H	R	ER	HR	HB	BB	SO	RAT	ERA	ERA+	CERA	OAV	BH	AVG	PR+	WS	TPW
1988 Phi-N	0	0	....	5	0	0	0	0	5^2	4	0	0	0	0	4	2	1.412	0.00	....	3.16	.267	0	....	2	1	0.2
1990 Phi-N	0	0	....	3	0	0	0	0	2^2	4	1	1	0	0	2	1	2.250	3.38	113	7.27	.400	0	....	0	0	0.0
Total 2	**0**	**0**	**....**	**8**	**0**	**0**	**0**	**0**	**8^1**	**8**	**1**	**1**	**0**	**0**	**6**	**3**	**1.680**	**1.08**	**354**	**4.48**	**.320**	**0**	**....**	**2**	**1**	**0.3**

• MOORE, Carlos Carlos Whitman Moore b: 8/13/1906, Clinton, TN d: 7/2/1958, New Orleans, LA BR/TR, 6'1.5", 180 lbs. Deb: 5/4/1930

YEAR TM-L	W	L	PCT	G	GS	CG	SH	SV	IP	H	R	ER	HR	HB	BB	SO	RAT	ERA	ERA+	CERA	OAV	BH	AVG	PR+	WS	TPW
1930 Was-A	0	0	....	4	0	0	0	0	11^2	9	3	3	0	0	4	2	1.114	2.31	198	1.99	.225	0	.000	3	1	0.2

• MOORE, Cy William Austin Moore b: 2/7/1905, Elberton, GA d: 3/28/1972, Augusta, GA BR/TR, 6'1", 178 lbs. Deb: 6/7/1929

YEAR TM-L	W	L	PCT	G	GS	CG	SH	SV	IP	H	R	ER	HR	HB	BB	SO	RAT	ERA	ERA+	CERA	OAV	BH	AVG	PR+	WS	TPW
1929 Bro-N	3	3	.500	32	3	0	0	2	68	87	45	42	3	0	31	17	1.735	5.56	83	5.31	.320	3	.188	-5	3	-0.5
1930 Bro-N	0	0	....	1	0	0	0	0	0	2	1	0	0	0	0	0	....	....	....	∞	1.000	0	....	0	0	0.0
1931 Bro-N	1	2	.333	23	1	1	0	0	61^2	62	31	26	5	4	13	35	1.216	3.79	100	3.46	.260	2	.154	1	3	0.0
1932 Bro-N	0	3	.000	20	2	0	0	0	48^2	56	32	26	3	1	17	21	1.500	4.81	79	4.43	.290	3	.214	-5	1	-0.5
1933 Phi-N	8	9	.471	36	18	9	3	1	161^1	177	74	67	7	3	42	53	1.357	3.74	102	3.68	.270	3	.063	2	11	-0.3
1934 Phi-N	4	9	.308	35	15	3	0	0	126^2	163	98	91	11	2	65	55	1.800	6.47	73	6.00	.309	6	.143	-26	1	-2.8
Total 6	**16**	**26**	**.381**	**147**	**39**	**13**	**3**	**3**	**466^1**	**547**	**281**	**252**	**29**	**10**	**168**	**181**	**1.533**	**4.86**	**87**	**4.60**	**.290**	**17**	**.128**	**-35**	**19**	**-4.1**

• MOORE, Donnie Donnie Ray Moore b: 2/13/1954, Lubbock, TX d: 7/18/1989, Anaheim, CA BL/TR, 6', 185 lbs. Deb: 9/14/1975

YEAR TM-L	W	L	PCT	G	GS	CG	SH	SV	IP	H	R	ER	HR	HB	BB	SO	RAT	ERA	ERA+	CERA	OAV	BH	AVG	PR+	WS	TPW
1975 Chi-N	0	0	....	4	1	0	0	0	8^2	12	4	4	1	0	4	8	1.846	4.15	92	6.60	.316	0	.000	-0	0	0.0
1977 Chi-N	4	2	.667	27	1	0	0	0	48^2	51	27	22	1	0	18	34	1.418	4.07	108	3.48	.285	3	.300	3	4	0.4
1978 Chi-N	9	7	.563	71	1	0	0	4	102^2	117	55	47	7	2	31	50	1.442	4.12	98	4.12	.287	4	.267	-0	8	0.1
1979 Chi-N	1	4	.200	39	1	0	0	1	73	95	46	42	8	2	25	43	1.644	5.18	79	5.68	.321	2	.154	-8	1	-0.8
1980 StL-N	1	1	.500	11	0	0	0	0	21^2	25	15	15	1	1	5	10	1.385	6.23	59	4.03	.298	3	.750	-6	0	-0.5
1981 Mil-A	0	0	....	3	0	0	0	0	4	4	3	3	0	0	4	2	2.000	6.75	51	5.79	.286	0	....	-2	0	-0.2
1982* Atl-N	3	1	.750	16	0	0	0	1	27^2	32	13	13	1	2	7	17	1.410	4.23	88	4.02	.294	0	.000	-2	2	-0.2
1983 Atl-N	2	3	.400	43	0	0	0	6	68^2	72	30	28	6	0	10	41	1.194	3.67	106	3.30	.279	4	.500	1	5	0.2
1984 Atl-N	4	5	.444	47	0	0	0	16	64^1	63	27	21	3	1	18	47	1.259	2.94	131	3.04	.258	0	.000	7	9	0.7
1985 Cal-A★	8	8	.500	65	0	0	0	31	103	91	28	22	9	0	21	72	1.087	1.92	214	2.58	.237	0	....	22	20	2.2
1986* Cal-A	4	5	.444	49	0	0	0	21	72^2	60	28	24	10	0	22	53	1.128	2.97	138	2.94	.228	0	....	8	11	0.8
1987 Cal-A	2	2	.500	14	0	0	0	5	26^2	28	12	8	2	0	13	17	1.538	2.70	159	4.24	.259	0	....	5	3	0.4
1988 Cal-A	5	2	.714	27	0	0	0	4	33	48	20	18	4	0	8	22	1.697	4.91	79	6.24	.343	0	....	-4	2	-0.4
Total 13	**43**	**40**	**.518**	**416**	**4**	**0**	**0**	**89**	**654^2**	**698**	**308**	**267**	**53**	**8**	**186**	**416**	**1.350**	**3.67**	**109**	**3.83**	**.276**	**16**	**.281**	**24**	**65**	**2.8**

• MOORE, Earl Earl Alonzo "Crossfire,Big Ebbie" Moore b: 7/29/1879, Pickerington, OH d: 11/28/1961, Columbus, OH BR/TR, 6', 195 lbs. Deb: 4/25/1901 U

YEAR TM-L	W	L	PCT	G	GS	CG	SH	SV	IP	H	R	ER	HR	HB	BB	SO	RAT	ERA	ERA+	CERA	OAV	BH	AVG	PR+	WS	TPW
1901 Cle-A	16	14	.533	31	30	28	4	0	251^1	234	129	81	4	8	107	99	1.357	2.90	122	3.20	.244	16	.162	19	16	1.3
1902 Cle-A	17	17	.500	36	34	29	4	1	293	304	158	96	8	7	101	84	1.382	2.95	117	3.57	.268	24	.212	15	17	1.4
1903 Cle-A	20	9	.690	29	27	27	3	0	247^2	196	88	48	0	5	62	148	1.042	**1.74**	**164**	1.83	**.217**	8	.092	28	19	2.4
1904 Cle-A	12	11	.522	26	24	22	1	0	227^2	186	83	57	2	10	61	139	1.085	2.25	113	2.13	.224	12	.140	6	13	0.5
1905 Cle-A	15	15	.500	31	30	28	3	0	269	232	111	79	6	18	92	131	1.204	2.64	99	2.77	.235	10	.104	-0	15	-0.5
1906 Cle-A	1	1	.500	5	4	2	0	0	29^2	27	15	13	1	2	18	8	1.517	3.94	66	3.97	.246	0	.000	-5	0	-0.7
1907 Cle-A	1	1	.500	3	2	1	0	0	19^1	18	14	10	0	1	8	7	1.345	4.66	54	3.05	.249	0	.000	-5	0	-0.6
NY-A	2	6	.250	12	9	3	0	1	64	72	49	28	1	4	30	28	1.594	3.94	71	4.26	.286	6	.273	-7	1	-0.7
Yr.	3	7	.300	15	11	4	0	1	83^1	90	63	38	1	5	38	35	1.536	4.10	66	3.98	.278	6	.207	-12	1	-1.3
1908 Phi-N	2	1	.667	3	3	3	1	0	26	20	4	0	0	2	8	16	1.077	0.00	....	2.20	.217	2	.222	7	4	0.8
1909 Phi-N	18	12	.600	38	34	24	4	0	299^2	238	93	70	7	9	108	173	1.155	2.10	123	2.32	.210	9	.094	11	24	0.9
1910 Phi-N	22	15	.595	46	35	18	**6**	0	283	228	98	81	5	10	121	**185**	1.233	2.58	121	2.77	.228	20	.230	15	21	1.8
1911 Phi-N	15	19	.441	42	36	21	5	1	308^1	265	123	90	11	12	164	174	1.391	2.63	131	3.53	.240	11	.109	27	24	2.2
1912 Phi-N	9	14	.391	31	24	10	1	0	182^1	186	101	67	3	7	77	79	1.442	3.31	109	3.81	.275	6	.107	6	9	0.2
1913 Phi-N	1	3	.250	12	5	0	0	1	52	50	37	29	3	1	40	24	1.731	5.02	66	4.73	.254	0	.000	-10	0	-1.2
Chi-N	1	1	.500	7	2	0	0	0	28^1	34	19	14	3	0	12	12	1.624	4.45	71	5.31	.321	1	.125	-4	0	-0.5
Yr.	2	4	.333	19	7	0	0	1	80^1	84	56	43	6	1	52	36	1.693	4.82	68	4.94	.277	1	.042	-14	0	-1.7
1914 Buf-F	11	15	.423	36	27	14	2	2	194^2	184	109	93	3	10	99	96	1.454	4.30	78	3.87	.263	9	.161	-24	6	-2.6
Total 14	**163**	**154**	**.514**	**388**	**326**	**230**	**34**	**6**	**2776**	**2474**	**1231**	**856**	**57**	**106**	**1108**	**1403**	**1.290**	**2.78**	**111**	**3.04**	**.241**	**134**	**.141**	**79**	**169**	**4.6**

• MOORE, Euel Euel Walton "Chief" Moore b: 5/27/1908, Reagan, OK d: 2/12/1989, Tishomingo, OK BR/TR, 6'2", 185 lbs. Deb: 7/8/1934

YEAR TM-L	W	L	PCT	G	GS	CG	SH	SV	IP	H	R	ER	HR	HB	BB	SO	RAT	ERA	ERA+	CERA	OAV	BH	AVG	PR+	WS	TPW
1934 Phi-N	5	7	.417	20	16	3	0	1	122^1	145	60	55	9	0	41	38	1.520	4.05	117	4.45	.288	5	.109	7	7	0.4
1935 Phi-N	1	6	.143	15	8	1	0	1	40^1	63	40	35	5	2	20	15	2.058	7.81	58	8.09	.354	6	.400	-14	0	-1.2
NY-N	1	0	1.000	6	0	0	0	0	8	9	5	5	0	0	4	3	1.625	5.63	69	4.16	.281	0	.000	-2	0	-0.2
Yr.	2	6	.250	21	8	1	0	1	48^1	72	45	40	5	2	24	18	1.986	7.45	60	7.44	.343	6	.353	-16	0	-1.4
1936 Phi-N	2	3	.400	20	5	1	0	1	54^1	76	50	42	4	1	12	19	1.620	6.96	65	5.18	.311	4	.222	-13	0	-1.3
Total 3	**9**	**16**	**.360**	**61**	**29**	**5**	**0**	**3**	**225**	**293**	**155**	**137**	**18**	**3**	**77**	**75**	**1.644**	**5.48**	**84**	**5.27**	**.306**	**15**	**.185**	**-21**	**7**	**-2.3**

• MOORE, Frank Frank J. Moore b: 9/12/1877, Dover, OH d: 5/20/1964, Portsmouth, OH BB/TR, 6'4", 200 lbs. Deb: 6/14/1905

YEAR TM-L	W	L	PCT	G	GS	CG	SH	SV	IP	H	R	ER	HR	HB	BB	SO	RAT	ERA	ERA+	CERA	OAV	BH	AVG	PR+	WS	TPW
1905 Pit-N	0	0	....	1	0	0	0	0	3	2	0	0	0	0	0	1	.667	0.00	....	1.01	.200	0	.000	1	1	0.1

• MOORE, Gene Eugene "Blue Goose" Moore, Sr. b: 11/9/1885, Lancaster, TX d: 8/31/1938, Dallas, TX BL/TL, 6'2", 185 lbs. Deb: 9/28/1909

YEAR TM-L	W	L	PCT	G	GS	CG	SH	SV	IP	H	R	ER	HR	HB	BB	SO	RAT	ERA	ERA+	CERA	OAV	BH	AVG	PR+	WS	TPW
1909 Pit-N	0	0	....	1	0	0	0	0	2	4	4	4	0	0	3	2	3.500	18.00	14	12.70	.364	0	.000	-3	0	-0.4
1910 Pit-N	2	1	.667	4	1	0	0	0	17^1	19	7	6	1	0	7	9	1.500	3.12	101	3.58	.268	0	.000	-0	1	-0.1
1912 Cin-N	0	1	.000	5	2	0	0	1	14^2	17	11	8	0	2	11	6	1.909	4.91	68	6.06	.304	0	.000	-2	0	-0.3
Total 3	**2**	**2**	**.500**	**10**	**3**	**0**	**0**	**1**	**34**	**40**	**22**	**18**	**1**	**2**	**21**	**17**	**1.794**	**4.76**	**64**	**5.19**	**.290**	**0**	**.000**	**-6**	**1**	**-0.8**

• MOORE, Jim James Stanford Moore b: 12/14/1903, Prescott, AR d: 5/19/1973, Seattle, WA BR/TR, 6', 165 lbs. Deb: 9/21/1928

YEAR TM-L	W	L	PCT	G	GS	CG	SH	SV	IP	H	R	ER	HR	HB	BB	SO	RAT	ERA	ERA+	CERA	OAV	BH	AVG	PR+	WS	TPW
1928 Cle-A	0	1	.000	1	1	1	0	0	9	5	2	2	0	0	5	1	1.111	2.00	207	1.66	.161	0	.000	2	1	0.2
1929 Cle-A	0	0	....	2	0	0	0	0	5^2	6	6	6	1	0	4	0	1.765	9.53	47	5.70	.273	0	.000	-3	0	-0.3
1930 Chi-A	2	1	.667	9	5	2	0	1	40	42	18	16	0	0	12	11	1.350	3.60	128	3.05	.268	3	.231	6	4	0.5
1931 Chi-A	0	2	.000	33	4	0	0	0	83^2	93	52	46	3	1	27	15	1.434	4.95	86	3.86	.282	1	.063	-5	3	-0.6
1932 Chi-A	0	0	....	1	0	0	0	0	1	1	0	0	0	0	1	2	2.000	0.00	....	5.17	.250	0	.000	0	0	0.0
Total 5	**2**	**4**	**.333**	**46**	**10**	**3**	**0**	**1**	**139^1**	**147**	**78**	**70**	**4**	**1**	**49**	**29**	**1.407**	**4.52**	**96**	**3.57**	**.270**	**4**	**.114**	**0**	**8**	**-0.2**

• MOORE, Marcus Marcus Braymont Moore b: 11/2/1970, Oakland, CA BB/TR, 6'5", 195 lbs. Deb: 7/9/1993

YEAR TM-L	W	L	PCT	G	GS	CG	SH	SV	IP	H	R	ER	HR	HB	BB	SO	RAT	ERA	ERA+	CERA	OAV	BH	AVG	PR+	WS	TPW
1993 Col-N	3	1	.750	27	0	0	0	0	26^1	30	25	20	4	1	20	13	1.899	6.84	70	6.94	.291	0	.000	-5	1	-0.5
1994 Col-N	1	1	.500	29	0	0	0	0	33^2	33	26	23	4	5	21	33	1.604	6.15	81	5.44	.252	0	.000	-3	1	-0.3
1996 Cin-N	3	3	.500	23	0	0	0	2	26^1	26	21	17	3	2	22	27	1.823	5.81	72	5.96	.263	1	.333	-5	1	-0.4
Total 3	**7**	**5**	**.583**	**79**	**0**	**0**	**0**	**2**	**86^1**	**89**	**72**	**60**	**11**	**8**	**63**	**73**	**1.761**	**6.25**	**74**	**6.05**	**.267**	**1**	**.200**	**-14**	**3**	**-1.3**

• MOORE, Mike Michael Wayne Moore b: 11/26/1959, Carnegie, OK BR/TR, 6'4", 205 lbs. Deb: 4/11/1982

YEAR TM-L	W	L	PCT	G	GS	CG	SH	SV	IP	H	R	ER	HR	HB	BB	SO	RAT	ERA	ERA+	CERA	OAV	BH	AVG	PR+	WS	TPW
1982 Sea-A	7	14	.333	28	27	1	1	0	144^1	159	91	86	21	2	79	73	1.649	5.36	79	5.74	.285	0	....	-18	3	-1.8
1983 Sea-A	6	8	.429	22	21	3	2	0	128	130	75	67	10	3	60	108	1.484	4.71	90	4.39	.267	0	....	-6	5	-0.6
1984 Sea-A	7	17	.292	34	33	6	0	0	212	236	127	117	16	5	85	158	1.514	4.97	80	4.57	.282	0	....	-18	7	-1.9
1985 Sea-A	17	10	.630	35	34	14	2	0	247	230	100	95	18	4	70	155	1.215	3.46	122	3.16	.247	0	....	22	19	2.1

YEAR	TM-L	W	L	PCT	G	GS	CG	SH	SV	IP	H	R	ER	HR	HB	BB	SO	RAT	ERA	ERA+	CERA	OAV	BH	AVG	PR+	WS	TPW
1986	Sea-A	11	13	.458	38	**37**	11	1	1	266	279	141	127	28	12	94	146	1.402	4.30	99	4.40	.273	0	....	-1	15	-0.1
1987	Sea-A	9	19	.321	33	33	12	0	0	231	268	145	121	29	0	84	115	1.524	4.71	100	5.03	.292	0	.000	-1	10	-0.1
1988	Sea-A	9	15	.375	37	32	9	3	1	228^{2}	196	104	96	24	3	63	182	1.133	3.78	110	2.94	.232	0	....	10	13	1.1
1989*	Oak-A★	19	11	.633	35	35	6	3	0	241^{2}	193	82	70	14	2	83	172	1.142	2.61	141	2.59	.219	0	....	25	19	2.6
1990*	Oak-A	13	15	.464	33	33	3	0	0	199^{1}	204	113	103	14	3	84	73	1.445	4.65	80	4.16	.267	0	....	-25	4	-2.6
1991	Oak-A	17	8	.680	33	33	3	1	0	210	176	75	69	11	5	105	153	1.338	2.96	130	3.37	.229	0	....	21	16	2.1
1992*	Oak-A	17	12	.586	36	**36**	2	0	0	223	229	113	102	20	8	103	117	1.489	4.12	91	4.53	.268	0	....	-11	9	-1.1
1993	Det-A	13	9	.591	36	**36**	4	3	0	213^{2}	227	135	124	35	3	89	89	1.479	5.22	82	4.93	.271	0	....	-22	7	-2.1
1994	Det-A	11	10	.524	25	**25**	4	0	0	154^{1}	152	97	93	27	3	89	62	1.562	5.42	89	5.37	.263	0	....	-8	6	-0.7
1995	Det-A	5	15	.250	25	25	1	0	0	132^{2}	179	118	111	24	2	68	64	1.862	7.53	63	7.35	.323	0	....	-39	0	-3.7
Total	14	161	176	.478	450	440	79	16	2	2831^{2}	2858	1516	1381	291	55	1156	1667	1.418	4.39	95	4.30	.264	0	.000	-71	133	-6.8

• MOORE, Ray Raymond Leroy "Farmer,Old Blue" Moore b: 6/1/1926, Meadows, MD d: 3/2/1995, Clinton, MD BR/TR, 6', 205 lbs. Deb: 8/1/1952

YEAR	TM-L	W	L	PCT	G	GS	CG	SH	SV	IP	H	R	ER	HR	HB	BB	SO	RAT	ERA	ERA+	CERA	OAV	BH	AVG	PR+	WS	TPW
1952	Bro-N	1	2	.333	14	2	0	0	0	28^{1}	29	17	15	3	2	26	11	1.941	4.76	76	6.45	.274	0	.000	-4	0	-0.4
1953	Bro-N	0	1	.000	1	1	1	0	0	8	6	3	3	1	0	4	4	1.250	3.38	126	3.09	.214	0	.000	1	0	0.0
1955	Bal-A	10	10	.500	46	14	3	1	6	151^{2}	128	75	66	14	4	80	80	1.371	3.92	97	3.72	.229	6	.136	0	8	-0.1
1956	Bal-A	12	7	.632	32	27	9	1	0	185	161	90	86	12	1	99	105	1.405	4.18	94	3.68	.238	19	.271	-4	15	0.2
1957	Bal-A	11	13	.458	34	32	7	1	0	227^{1}	196	99	94	17	2	112	117	1.355	3.72	97	3.54	.236	18	.214	-7	12	-0.4
1958	Chi-A	9	7	.563	32	20	4	2	2	136^{2}	107	63	58	10	0	70	73	1.295	3.82	95	3.16	.220	9	.205	-5	8	-0.3
1959*	Chi-A	3	6	.333	29	8	0	0	0	89^{2}	86	46	41	10	1	46	49	1.472	4.12	91	4.42	.261	2	.087	-5	3	-0.7
1960	Chi-A	1	1	.500	14	0	0	0	0	20^{2}	19	13	13	5	0	11	3	1.452	5.66	67	5.25	.253	0	.000	-5	0	-0.5
	Was-A	3	2	.600	37	0	0	0	13	65^{2}	49	24	21	5	1	27	29	1.157	2.88	137	2.66	.213	1	.071	9	9	0.8
	Yr.	4	3	.571	51	0	0	0	13	86^{1}	68	37	34	10	1	38	32	1.228	3.54	109	3.28	.223	1	.063	4	9	0.3
1961	Min-A	4	4	.500	46	0	0	0	14	56^{1}	49	23	23	8	1	38	45	1.544	3.67	115	4.65	.233	0	.000	5	6	0.5
1962	Min-A	8	3	.727	49	0	0	0	9	64^{2}	55	35	34	8	2	30	58	1.314	4.73	86	3.65	.231	0	.000	-5	6	-0.6
1963	Min-A	1	3	.250	31	1	0	0	2	38^{2}	50	34	30	8	1	17	38	1.733	6.98	52	6.78	.309	1	.333	-14	0	-1.5
Total	11	63	59	.516	365	105	24	5	46	1072^{2}	935	522	484	101	15	560	612	1.394	4.06	93	3.85	.238	56	.187	-34	67	-3.0

• MOORE, Roy Roy Daniel Moore b: 10/26/1898, Austin, TX d: 4/5/1951, Seattle, WA BB/TL, 6', 185 lbs. Deb: 4/15/1920

YEAR	TM-L	W	L	PCT	G	GS	CG	SH	SV	IP	H	R	ER	HR	HB	BB	SO	RAT	ERA	ERA+	CERA	OAV	BH	AVG	PR+	WS	TPW
1920	Phi-A	1	13	.071	24	14	5	0	0	132^{2}	161	89	69	6	3	64	45	1.696	4.68	86	5.48	.314	10	.200	-7	3	-0.8
1921	Phi-A	10	10	.500	29	26	12	0	0	191^{2}	206	110	96	4	4	122	64	**1.711**	4.51	99	4.67	.280	19	.257	2	12	0.6
1922	Phi-A	0	3	.000	15	6	0	0	0	50^{2}	65	43	43	1	3	32	29	1.914	7.64	56	6.09	.319	5	.263	-19	0	-1.7
	Det-A	0	0	....	9	0	0	0	2	19^{2}	29	14	13	0	5	10	9	1.983	5.95	65	7.64	.367	3	.429	-4	0	-0.3
	Yr.	0	3	.000	24	6	0	0	2	70^{1}	94	57	56	1	8	42	38	1.934	7.17	58	6.52	.332	8	.308	-23	0	-2.0
1923	Det-A	0	0	....	3	0	0	0	1	12	15	4	4	0	0	11	7	2.167	3.00	129	6.24	.288	0	.000	1	1	0.0
Total	4	11	26	.297	80	46	17	0	3	406^{2}	476	260	225	11	15	239	154	1.758	4.98	85	5.30	.301	37	.239	-26	16	-2.2

• MOORE, Tommy Tommy Joe Moore b: 7/7/1948, Lynwood, CA BR/TR, 5'11", 175 lbs. Deb: 9/15/1972

YEAR	TM-L	W	L	PCT	G	GS	CG	SH	SV	IP	H	R	ER	HR	HB	BB	SO	RAT	ERA	ERA+	CERA	OAV	BH	AVG	PR+	WS	TPW
1972	NY-N	0	0	....	3	1	0	0	0	12^{1}	12	4	4	1	0	1	5	1.054	2.92	115	2.75	.273	1	.333	1	1	0.1
1973	NY-N	0	1	.000	3	1	0	0	0	3^{1}	6	5	4	1	0	3	1	2.700	10.80	33	14.05	.400	0	....	-3	0	-0.3
1975	StL-N	0	0	....	10	0	0	0	0	18^{2}	15	10	8	2	0	12	6	1.446	3.86	97	3.65	.203	1	.500	0	1	0.1
	Tex-A	0	2	.000	12	0	0	0	0	21	31	21	19	1	1	12	15	2.048	8.14	46	7.15	.352	0	....	-10	0	-1.0
1977	Sea-A	2	1	.667	14	1	0	0	0	33	36	22	18	1	3	21	13	1.727	4.91	84	5.24	.281	0	....	-3	1	-0.3
Total	4	2	4	.333	42	3	0	0	0	88^{1}	100	62	53	6	4	49	40	1.687	5.40	71	5.34	.287	2	.400	-15	3	-1.5

• MOORE, Trey Warren Neal Moore b: 10/2/1972, Houston, TX BL/TL, 6'1", 190 lbs. Deb: 4/5/1998

YEAR	TM-L	W	L	PCT	G	GS	CG	SH	SV	IP	H	R	ER	HR	HB	BB	SO	RAT	ERA	ERA+	CERA	OAV	BH	AVG	PR+	WS	TPW
1998	Mon-N	2	5	.286	13	11	0	0	0	61	78	37	34	5	1	17	35	1.557	5.02	84	4.95	.306	4	.235	-5	2	-0.3
2000	Mon-N	1	5	.167	8	8	0	0	0	35^{1}	55	31	26	7	4	21	24	2.151	6.62	72	9.97	.364	1	.125	-7	0	-0.7
2001	Atl-N	0	0	....	2	0	0	0	0	4	7	5	5	0	0	2	1	2.250	11.25	39	8.06	.368	1	1.000	-3	0	-0.2
Total	3	3	10	.231	23	19	0	0	0	100^{1}	140	73	65	12	5	40	60	1.794	5.83	76	6.84	.329	6	.231	-15	2	-1.2

• MOORE, Whitey Lloyd Albert Moore b: 6/10/1912, Tuscarawas, OH d: 12/10/1987, Uhrichsville, OH BR/TR, 6'1", 195 lbs. Deb: 9/27/1936

YEAR	TM-L	W	L	PCT	G	GS	CG	SH	SV	IP	H	R	ER	HR	HB	BB	SO	RAT	ERA	ERA+	CERA	OAV	BH	AVG	PR+	WS	TPW
1936	Cin-N	1	0	1.000	1	0	0	0	0	5	3	3	3	0	0	3	4	1.200	5.40	71	1.90	.167	0	.000	-1	0	-0.1
1937	Cin-N	0	3	.000	13	6	0	0	0	38^{2}	32	22	21	1	4	39	27	1.836	4.89	76	5.09	.239	0	.000	-5	0	-0.6
1938	Cin-N	6	4	.600	19	11	3	1	0	90^{1}	66	41	35	4	3	42	38	1.196	3.49	104	2.55	.205	2	.077	0	5	-0.2
1939*	Cin-N	13	12	.520	42	24	9	2	3	187^{2}	177	88	72	10	6	95	81	1.449	3.45	111	3.84	.254	6	.098	3	12	-0.1
1940*	Cin-N	8	8	.500	25	15	5	1	1	116^{2}	100	48	47	8	7	56	60	1.337	3.63	104	3.48	.231	5	.128	-2	7	-0.4
1941	Cin-N	2	1	.667	23	4	1	0	0	61^{2}	62	35	30	2	3	45	17	1.735	4.38	82	4.63	.246	3	.167	-5	2	-0.6
1942	Cin-N	0	0	....	1	0	0	0	0	1	0	0	0	0	0	1	0	1.000	0.00	....	0.80	.000	0	....	0	0	0.0
	StL-N	0	1	.000	9	0	0	0	0	12^{1}	10	6	6	0	1	11	1	1.703	4.38	78	4.11	.217	0	.000	-1	0	-0.2
	Yr.	0	1	.000	10	0	0	0	0	13^{1}	10	6	6	0	1	12	1	1.650	4.05	85	3.86	.217	0	.000	-1	0	-0.1
Total	7	30	29	.508	133	60	18	4	4	513^{1}	450	243	214	25	24	292	228	1.445	3.75	99	3.70	.237	16	.103	-11	26	-2.1

• MOORE, Wilcy William Wilcy "Cy" Moore b: 5/20/1897, Bonita, TX d: 3/29/1963, Hollis, OK BR/TR, 6', 195 lbs. Deb: 4/14/1927

YEAR	TM-L	W	L	PCT	G	GS	CG	SH	SV	IP	H	R	ER	HR	HB	BB	SO	RAT	ERA	ERA+	CERA	OAV	BH	AVG	PR+	WS	TPW
1927*	NY-A	19	7	.731	50	12	6	1	**13**	213	185	68	54	3	1	59	75	1.146	**2.28**	**169**	**2.33**	**.234**	6	.080	**37**	24	2.8
1928	NY-A	4	4	.500	35	2	0	0	2	60^{1}	71	44	28	4	0	31	18	1.691	4.18	90	4.52	.286	2	.143	-2	2	-0.3
1929	NY-A	6	4	.600	41	0	0	0	8	61	64	36	28	4	0	19	21	1.361	4.13	93	3.68	.268	1	.067	-3	5	-0.4
1931	Bos-A	11	13	.458	53	15	8	1	**10**	185^{1}	195	88	80	7	1	55	37	1.349	3.88	111	3.43	.269	9	.161	9	18	0.6
1932	Bos-A	4	10	.286	37	2	0	0	4	84^{1}	98	59	49	5	1	42	28	1.660	5.23	86	4.80	.284	1	.045	-5	3	-0.7
	*NY-A	2	0	1.000	10	1	0	0	4	25	27	8	7	1	0	6	8	1.320	2.52	162	3.38	.273	0	.000	4	4	0.3
	Yr.	6	10	.375	47	3	0	0	8	109^{1}	125	67	56	6	1	48	36	1.582	4.61	96	4.47	.282	1	.033	-1	7	-0.4
1933	NY-A	5	6	.455	35	0	0	0	8	62	92	53	38	1	0	20	17	1.806	5.52	70	5.70	.333	2	.133	-10	1	-1.1
Total	6	51	44	.537	261	32	14	2	49	691	732	356	284	25	3	232	204	1.395	3.70	110	3.58	.269	21	.102	30	57	1.2

• MOORHEAD, Bob Charles Robert Moorhead b: 1/23/1938, Chambersburg, PA d: 12/3/1986, Lemoyne, PA BR/TR, 6'1", 208 lbs. Deb: 4/11/1962

YEAR	TM-L	W	L	PCT	G	GS	CG	SH	SV	IP	H	R	ER	HR	HB	BB	SO	RAT	ERA	ERA+	CERA	OAV	BH	AVG	PR+	WS	TPW
1962	NY-N	0	2	.000	38	7	0	0	0	105^{1}	118	69	53	13	4	42	63	1.519	4.53	92	5.11	.289	1	.045	-2	3	-0.2
1965	NY-N	0	1	.000	9	0	0	0	0	14^{1}	16	7	7	0	0	5	5	1.465	4.40	80	3.70	.271	0	....	-1	1	-0.1
Total	2	0	3	.000	47	7	0	0	0	119^{2}	134	76	60	13	4	47	68	1.513	4.51	91	4.94	.287	1	.045	-3	4	-0.4

• MOOSE, Bob Robert Ralph Moose b: 10/9/1947, Export, PA d: 10/9/1976, Martins Ferry, OH BR/TR, 6', 200 lbs. Deb: 9/19/1967

YEAR	TM-L	W	L	PCT	G	GS	CG	SH	SV	IP	H	R	ER	HR	HB	BB	SO	RAT	ERA	ERA+	CERA	OAV	BH	AVG	PR+	WS	TPW
1967	Pit-N	1	0	1.000	2	2	1	0	0	14^{2}	14	6	6	1	1	4	7	1.227	3.68	91	3.57	.259	2	.333	-1	1	0.0
1968	Pit-N	8	12	.400	38	22	3	3	3	171^{1}	136	61	52	5	3	41	126	1.033	2.73	107	1.99	.218	5	.093	1	9	-0.1
1969	Pit-N	14	3	.824	44	19	6	1	4	170	149	64	55	9	5	62	165	1.241	2.91	120	3.02	.231	4	.075	12	14	1.1
1970*	Pit-N	11	10	.524	28	27	9	2	0	189^{2}	186	88	84	14	3	64	119	1.318	3.99	97	3.68	.262	12	.182	-7	10	-0.4
1971*	Pit-N	11	7	.611	30	18	3	1	1	140	169	73	64	12	2	35	68	1.457	4.11	83	4.44	.301	4	.103	-12	4	-1.4
1972*	Pit-N	13	10	.565	31	30	6	3	1	226	213	84	73	11	4	47	144	1.150	2.91	114	2.71	.248	12	.169	7	14	1.0
1973	Pit-N	12	13	.480	33	29	6	3	0	201^{1}	219	86	79	11	4	70	111	1.435	3.53	100	4.06	.280	9	.134	-0	8	-0.1
1974	Pit-N	1	5	.167	7	6	0	0	0	35^{2}	59	30	30	4	2	7	15	1.850	7.57	45	7.46	.386	2	.182	-17	0	-1.7
1975	Pit-N	2	2	.500	23	5	1	0	0	67^{2}	63	30	28	4	2	25	34	1.300	3.72	95	3.34	.246	3	.167	-1	3	-0.1
1976	Pit-N	3	9	.250	53	2	0	0	10	88	100	44	36	4	3	32	38	1.500	3.68	95	4.38	.294	3	.250	-2	5	0.0
Total	10	76	71	.517	289	160	35	13	19	1304^{1}	1308	566	507	75	30	387	827	1.300	3.50	99	3.48	.262	56	.141	-20	68	-1.7

• MOOTY, Jake Jake T. Mooty b: 4/13/1912, Bennett, TX d: 4/20/1970, Fort Worth, TX BR/TR, 5'10.5", 170 lbs. Deb: 9/9/1936

YEAR	TM-L	W	L	PCT	G	GS	CG	SH	SV	IP	H	R	ER	HR	HB	BB	SO	RAT	ERA	ERA+	CERA	OAV	BH	AVG	PR+	WS	TPW
1936	Cin-N	0	0	....	8	0	0	0	1	13^{2}	10	6	6	0	0	4	11	1.024	3.95	97	1.71	.204	0	.000	-0	1	0.0
1937	Cin-N	0	3	.000	14	2	0	0	1	39	54	39	36	2	0	22	11	1.949	8.31	45	6.39	.327	0	.000	-20	0	-2.1
1940	Chi-N	6	6	.500	20	12	6	0	1	114	101	45	37	11	1	49	42	1.316	2.92	128	3.48	.238	10	.263	11	9	1.2
1941	Chi-N	8	9	.471	33	14	7	1	4	153^{1}	143	69	57	9	2	56	45	1.298	3.35	105	3.28	.251	10	.200	7	9	0.8
1942	Chi-N	2	5	.286	19	10	1	0	1	84^{1}	89	48	44	11	0	44	28	1.577	4.70	68	4.88	.266	6	.214	-12	1	-1.3
1943	Chi-N	0	0	....	2	0	0	0	0	1	2	0	0	0	0	1	1	3.000	0.00	....	11.63	.400	0	....	0	0	0.0

YEAR TM-L	W	L	PCT	G	GS	CG	SH	SV	IP	H	R	ER	HR	HB	BB	SO	RAT	ERA	ERA+	CERA	OAV	BH	AVG	PR+	WS	TPW
1944 Det-A	0	0	....	15	0	0	0	0	28^{1}	35	20	14	0	1	18	7	1.871	4.45	80	5.46	.310	1	.143	-3	0	-0.3
Total 7	**16**	**23**	**.410**	**111**	**38**	**14**	**1**	**8**	**433^{2}**	**434**	**227**	**194**	**33**	**4**	**194**	**145**	**1.448**	**4.03**	**88**	**4.04**	**.261**	**27**	**.205**	**-17**	**20**	**-1.7**
• MORAGA, David	David Michael Moraga b: 7/8/1975, Torrance, CA BL/TL, 6', 185 lbs. Deb: 6/11/2000																									
2000 Mon-N	0	0	....	3	0	0	0	0	1^{2}	6	7	7	0	0	2	2	4.800	37.80	13	23.58	.600	0	....	-6	0	-0.6
Col-N	0	0	....	1	0	0	0	0	1	4	5	5	1	1	0	0	4.000	45.00	13	41.46	.667	0	....	-4	0	-0.4
Yr.	0	0	....	4	0	0	0	0	2^{2}	10	12	12	1	1	2	2	4.500	40.50	13	30.28	.625	0	....	-10	0	-1.0
• MORAN, Bill	Carl William "Bugs" Moran b: 9/26/1950, Portsmouth, VA BR/TR, 6'4", 210 lbs. Deb: 4/12/1974																									
1974 Chi-A	1	3	.250	15	5	0	0	0	46^{1}	57	27	24	5	6	23	17	1.727	4.66	80	6.32	.302	0	....	-4	1	-0.5
• MORAN, Harry	Harry Edwin Moran b: 4/2/1889, Slater, WV d: 11/28/1962, Beckley, WV BL/TL, 6'1", 165 lbs. Deb: 6/23/1912																									
1912 Det-A	0	1	.000	5	2	1	0	0	14^{2}	19	14	8	1	2	12	3	2.114	4.91	67	8.21	.339	1	.200	-3	0	-0.3
1914 Buf-F	10	7	.588	34	16	7	2	2	154	159	87	73	7	11	53	73	1.377	4.27	78	4.02	.276	10	.196	-18	6	-1.8
1915 New-F	13	9	.591	34	23	13	2	0	205^{2}	193	80	58	2	18	66	87	1.259	2.54	112	3.28	.262	11	.180	6	14	0.8
Total 3	**23**	**17**	**.575**	**73**	**41**	**21**	**4**	**2**	**374^{1}**	**371**	**181**	**139**	**10**	**31**	**131**	**163**	**1.341**	**3.34**	**93**	**3.78**	**.271**	**22**	**.188**	**-15**	**20**	**-1.3**
• MORAN, Hiker	Albert Thomas Moran b: 1/1/1912, Rochester, NY d: 1/7/1998, Saratoga Springs, NY BR/TR, 6'4.5", 185 lbs. Deb: 9/29/1938																									
1938 Bos-N	0	0	....	1	0	0	0	0	3	1	0	0	0	0	1	0	.667	0.00	....	0.72	.111	0	.000	1	1	0.1
1939 Bos-N	1	1	.500	6	2	1	0	0	20	21	10	10	3	0	11	4	1.600	4.50	82	5.20	.276	1	.200	-2	1	-0.1
Total 2	**1**	**1**	**.500**	**7**	**2**	**1**	**0**	**0**	**23**	**22**	**10**	**10**	**3**	**0**	**12**	**4**	**1.478**	**3.91**	**94**	**4.62**	**.259**	**1**	**.167**	**-1**	**2**	**0.0**
• MORAN, Sam	Samuel Moran b: 9/16/1870, Rochester, NY d: 8/27/1897, Rochester, NY TL, 160 lbs. Deb: 8/28/1895																									
1895 Pit-N	2	4	.333	10	6	6	0	0	62^{2}	78	63	52	2	3	51	19	2.059	7.47	60	6.59	.301	4	.154	-21	0	-1.7
• MORE, Forrest	Forrest T. More b: 9/30/1883, Hayden, IN d: 8/17/1968, Columbus, IN BR/TR, 6', 180 lbs. Deb: 4/15/1909																									
1909 StL-N	1	5	.167	15	2	1	0	0	50	48	33	28	0	3	20	17	1.360	5.04	50	3.39	.258	2	.154	-13	0	-1.3
Bos-N	1	5	.167	10	4	3	0	0	48^{2}	47	47	24	0	4	20	10	1.377	4.44	63	3.68	.270	1	.067	-9	0	-1.1
Yr.	2	10	.167	25	6	4	0	0	98^{2}	95	80	52	0	7	40	27	1.368	4.74	56	3.53	.264	3	.107	-22	0	-2.5
• MOREHEAD, Dave	David Michael "Moe" Morehead b: 9/5/1942, San Diego, CA BR/TR, 6'1", 185 lbs. Deb: 4/13/1963																									
1963 Bos-A	10	13	.435	29	29	6	1	0	174^{2}	137	82	74	20	0	99	136	1.351	3.81	99	3.58	.211	6	.105	0	9	-0.3
1964 Bos-A	8	15	.348	32	30	3	1	0	166^{2}	156	101	92	14	4	112	139	1.608	4.97	78	4.67	.248	5	.093	-17	3	-2.0
1965 Bos-A	10	18	.357	34	33	5	2	0	192^{2}	157	103	87	18	3	113	163	1.401	4.06	92	3.72	.217	8	.131	-4	7	-0.3
1966 Bos-A	1	2	.333	12	5	0	0	0	28	31	17	17	7	0	7	20	1.357	5.46	70	5.01	.274	3	.500	-5	1	-0.4
1967* Bos-A	5	4	.556	10	9	1	1	0	47^{2}	48	24	23	0	2	22	40	1.469	4.34	80	3.82	.264	1	.083	-4	2	-0.5
1968 Bos-A	1	4	.200	11	9	3	1	0	55	52	17	15	3	2	20	28	1.309	2.45	129	3.48	.249	2	.125	5	4	0.5
1969 KC-A	2	3	.400	21	2	0	0	0	33	28	22	21	7	0	28	32	1.697	5.73	64	5.99	.239	0	.000	-7	0	-0.7
1970 KC-A	3	5	.375	28	17	1	0	1	121^{2}	121	64	49	9	1	62	69	1.504	3.62	103	4.28	.261	6	.167	0	5	0.0
Total 8	**40**	**64**	**.385**	**177**	**134**	**19**	**6**	**1**	**819^{1}**	**730**	**430**	**378**	**78**	**12**	**463**	**627**	**1.456**	**4.15**	**90**	**4.09**	**.237**	**31**	**.127**	**-32**	**31**	**-3.7**
• MOREHEAD, Seth	Seth Marvin "Moe" Morehead b: 8/15/1934, Houston, TX BL/TL, 6'.5", 195 lbs. Deb: 4/27/1957																									
1957 Phi-N	1	1	.500	34	1	1	0	1	58^{2}	57	27	24	1	2	20	36	1.313	3.68	103	3.09	.254	0	.000	1	4	0.0
1958 Phi-N	1	6	.143	27	11	0	0	0	92^{1}	121	67	60	8	1	26	54	1.592	5.85	68	5.27	.319	4	.182	-18	0	-1.8
1959 Phi-N	0	2	.000	3	3	0	0	0	10	15	11	11	3	1	3	8	1.800	9.90	41	8.63	.333	0	.000	-6	0	-0.7
Chi-N	0	1	.000	11	2	0	0	0	18^{2}	25	13	10	1	0	8	9	1.768	4.82	82	5.54	.313	1	.500	-2	0	-0.1
Yr.	0	3	.000	14	5	0	0	0	28^{2}	40	24	21	4	1	11	17	1.779	6.59	61	6.62	.320	1	.200	-8	0	-0.8
1960 Chi-N	2	9	.182	45	7	2	0	4	123^{1}	123	61	54	17	2	46	64	1.370	3.94	96	4.20	.258	4	.138	-2	5	-0.3
1961 Mil-N	1	0	1.000	12	0	0	0	0	15^{1}	16	11	11	4	1	7	13	1.500	6.46	58	5.90	.271	0	....	-5	0	-0.5
Total 5	**5**	**19**	**.208**	**132**	**24**	**3**	**0**	**5**	**318^{1}**	**357**	**190**	**170**	**34**	**7**	**110**	**184**	**1.467**	**4.81**	**81**	**4.60**	**.282**	**9**	**.145**	**-32**	**9**	**-3.3**
• MOREL, Ramon	Ramon Rafael Morel b: 8/15/1974, Villa Gonzalez, Dominican Republic BR/TR, 6'2", 175 lbs. Deb: 7/6/1995																									
1995 Pit-N	0	1	.000	5	0	0	0	0	6^{1}	6	2	2	0	0	2	3	1.263	2.84	151	3.03	.300	0	....	1	1	0.1
1996 Pit-N	2	1	.667	29	0	0	0	0	42	57	27	25	4	1	19	22	1.810	5.36	81	6.26	.324	0	.000	-4	1	-0.4
1997 Pit-N	0	0	....	5	0	0	0	0	7^{2}	11	4	4	2	0	4	4	1.957	4.70	91	8.66	.344	0	....	-0	0	0.0
Chi-N	0	0	....	3	0	0	0	0	3^{2}	3	2	2	1	0	3	3	1.636	4.91	88	5.91	.214	0	....	-0	0	0.0
Yr.	0	0	....	8	0	0	0	0	11^{1}	14	6	6	3	0	7	7	1.853	4.76	90	7.77	.304	0	....	-1	0	-0.1
Total 3	**2**	**2**	**.500**	**42**	**0**	**0**	**0**	**0**	**59^{2}**	**77**	**35**	**33**	**7**	**1**	**28**	**32**	**1.760**	**4.98**	**87**	**6.20**	**.318**	**0**	**.000**	**-3**	**2**	**-0.4**
• MOREN, Lew	Lewis Howard "Hicks" Moren b: 8/4/1883, Pittsburgh, PA d: 11/2/1966, Pittsburgh, PA BR/TR, 5'11", 150 lbs. Deb: 9/21/1903																									
1903 Pit-N	0	1	.000	1	1	1	0	0	6	9	7	6	0	1	2	2	1.833	9.00	36	6.56	.346	0	.000	-4	0	-0.4
1904 Pit-N	0	0	....	1	0	0	0	0	4	7	6	4	1	1	4	0	2.750	9.00	30	14.95	.412	0	.000	-3	0	-0.3
1907 Phi-N	11	18	.379	37	31	21	3	1	255	202	106	72	3	9	101	98	1.188	2.54	95	2.57	.226	6	.081	-8	13	-1.2
1908 Phi-N	8	9	.471	28	16	9	4	0	154	146	68	50	1	2	49	72	1.266	2.92	82	2.99	.258	12	.245	-10	6	-1.0
1909 Phi-N	16	15	.516	40	31	19	2	1	257^{2}	226	103	76	6	4	93	110	1.238	2.65	97	2.82	.239	10	.111	-6	16	-0.9
1910 Phi-N	13	14	.481	34	26	12	1	1	205^{1}	207	104	81	6	9	82	74	1.407	3.55	88	3.83	.269	11	.149	-12	8	-1.3
Total 6	**48**	**57**	**.457**	**141**	**105**	**62**	**10**	**3**	**882**	**797**	**394**	**289**	**17**	**26**	**331**	**356**	**1.279**	**2.95**	**90**	**3.10**	**.248**	**39**	**.134**	**-43**	**43**	**-5.1**
• MORENO, Angel	Angel (Veneroso) Moreno b: 6/6/1955, La Mendosa, Mexico BL/TL, 5'9", 165 lbs. Deb: 8/15/1981																									
1981 Cal-A	1	3	.250	8	4	1	0	0	31^{1}	27	10	10	2	0	14	12	1.309	2.87	127	3.30	.233	0	....	3	2	0.3
1982 Cal-A	3	7	.300	13	8	2	0	1	49^{1}	55	31	26	7	1	23	22	1.581	4.74	85	5.52	.288	0	....	-5	1	-0.5
Total 2	**4**	**10**	**.286**	**21**	**12**	**3**	**0**	**1**	**80^{2}**	**82**	**41**	**36**	**9**	**1**	**37**	**34**	**1.475**	**4.02**	**98**	**4.66**	**.267**	**0**	**....**	**-2**	**3**	**-0.2**
• MORENO, Juan	Juan Carlos (Vegas) Moreno b: 2/28/1975, Maiquetia, Venezuela BL/TL, 6'1", 205 lbs. Deb: 5/17/2001																									
2001 Tex-A	3	3	.500	45	0	0	0	0	41^{1}	22	21	18	6	0	28	36	1.210	3.92	119	2.83	.153	0	....	4	3	0.4
2002 SD-N	0	0	....	4	0	0	0	0	6	6	6	5	1	0	10	3	2.667	7.50	50	9.45	.261	0	....	-2	0	-0.2
Total 2	**3**	**3**	**.500**	**49**	**0**	**0**	**0**	**0**	**47^{1}**	**28**	**27**	**23**	**7**	**0**	**38**	**39**	**1.394**	**4.37**	**101**	**3.67**	**.168**	**0**	**....**	**1**	**3**	**0.1**
• MORENO, Julio	Julio (Gonzalez) "Jiqui" Moreno b: 1/28/1922, Guines, Cuba d: 1/2/1987, Miami, FL BR/TR, 5'8", 165 lbs. Deb: 9/8/1950																									
1950 Was-A	1	1	.500	4	3	1	0	0	21^{1}	22	13	11	1	1	12	7	1.594	4.64	97	4.60	.268	1	.125	-0	1	-0.1
1951 Was-A	5	11	.313	31	18	5	0	2	132^{2}	132	82	72	18	1	80	37	1.598	4.88	84	4.99	.256	7	.175	-10	3	-1.1
1952 Was-A	9	9	.500	26	22	7	0	0	147^{1}	154	75	65	10	5	52	62	1.398	3.97	89	3.99	.270	6	.122	-6	6	-0.8
1953 Was-A	3	1	.750	12	2	1	0	0	35^{1}	41	11	11	2	0	13	13	1.528	2.80	139	4.45	.291	0	.000	4	3	0.3
Total 4	**18**	**22**	**.450**	**73**	**45**	**14**	**0**	**2**	**336^{2}**	**349**	**181**	**159**	**31**	**7**	**157**	**119**	**1.503**	**4.25**	**91**	**4.47**	**.267**	**14**	**.132**	**-12**	**13**	**-1.7**
• MORENO, Orber	Orber (Aquiles) Moreno b: 4/27/1977, Caracas, Venezuela BR/TR, 6'2", 200 lbs. Deb: 5/25/1999																									
1999 KC-A	0	0	....	7	0	0	0	0	8	4	5	5	1	0	6	7	1.250	5.63	89	2.84	.143	0	....	-1	0	-0.1
2003 NY-N	0	0	....	7	0	0	0	0	8	10	7	7	1	0	3	5	1.625	7.88	53	5.65	.313	0	.000	-3	0	-0.3
Total 2	**0**	**0**	**....**	**14**	**0**	**0**	**0**	**0**	**16**	**14**	**12**	**12**	**2**	**0**	**9**	**12**	**1.438**	**6.75**	**66**	**4.25**	**.233**	**0**	**.000**	**-4**	**0**	**-0.4**
• MORET, Roger	Rogelio (Torres) Moret b: 9/16/1949, Guayama, Puerto Rico BB/TL, 6'4", 175 lbs. Deb: 9/13/1970																									
1970 Bos-A	1	0	1.000	3	1	0	0	0	8^{1}	7	3	3	0	0	4	2	1.320	3.24	122	2.85	.226	0	.000	1	1	0.1
1971 Bos-A	4	3	.571	13	7	4	1	0	71	50	24	23	5	2	40	47	1.268	2.92	127	3.02	.205	2	.087	7	6	0.7
1972 Bos-A	0	0	....	3	0	0	0	0	5	5	3	2	0	0	6	4	2.200	3.60	89	6.52	.263	0	.000	-0	0	0.0
1973 Bos-A	13	2	.867	30	15	5	2	3	156^{1}	138	60	55	19	3	67	90	1.311	3.17	127	3.78	.238	0	....	14	14	1.4
1974 Bos-A	9	10	.474	31	21	10	1	2	173^{1}	158	79	72	15	2	79	111	1.367	3.74	103	3.71	.243	0	....	4	11	0.4
1975* Bos-A	14	3	.824	36	16	4	1	1	145	132	60	58	8	2	76	80	1.434	3.60	113	3.77	.248	0	....	8	13	0.8
1976 Atl-N	3	5	.375	27	12	1	0	1	77^{1}	84	44	43	7	1	27	30	1.435	5.00	76	4.32	.280	3	.130	-9	2	-1.0
1977 Tex-A	3	3	.500	18	8	0	0	4	72^{1}	59	41	30	6	0	38	39	1.341	3.73	109	3.30	.220	0	....	2	4	0.2
1978 Tex-A	0	1	.000	7	2	0	0	1	14^{2}	23	8	8	1	1	2	5	1.705	4.91	76	6.76	.390	0	....	-2	0	-0.2
Total 9	**47**	**27**	**.635**	**168**	**82**	**24**	**5**	**12**	**723^{1}**	**656**	**322**	**294**	**61**	**11**	**339**	**408**	**1.376**	**3.66**	**107**	**3.76**	**.245**	**5**	**.100**	**24**	**51**	**2.3**

YEAR	TM-L	W	L	PCT	G	GS	CG	SH	SV	IP	H	R	ER	HR	HB	BB	SO	RAT	ERA	ERA+	CERA	OAV	BH	AVG	PR+	WS	TPW
• MOREY, Dave					David Beale Morey b: 2/25/1889, Malden, MA d: 1/4/1986, Oak Bluffs, MA BL/TR, 6', 185 lbs. Deb: 7/4/1913																						
1913	Phi-A	0	0	....	2	0	0	0	0	4	2	2	2	0	1	2	1	1.000	4.50	61	2.38	.182	0	.000	-1	0	-0.1
• MORGAN, Cy					Cyril Arlon Morgan b: 11/11/1895, Lakeville, MA d: 9/11/1946, Lakeville, MA BR/TR, 6', 170 lbs. Deb: 6/8/1921																						
1921	Bos-N	1	1	.500	17	0	0	0	1	30^1	37	24	22	0	1	17	8	1.780	6.53	56	5.25	.314	0	.000	-10	0	-1.1
1922	Bos-N	0	0	....	2	0	0	0	0	1^1	8	8	4	0	0	2	0	7.500	27.00	15	47.10	.667	0	....	-3	0	-0.3
Total	2	1	1	.500	19	0	0	0	1	31^2	45	32	26	0	1	19	8	2.021	7.39	50	7.02	.347	0	.000	-13	0	-1.4
• MORGAN, Cy					Harry Richard Morgan b: 11/10/1878, Pomeroy, OH d: 6/28/1962, Wheeling, WV BR/TR, 6', 175 lbs. Deb: 9/18/1903																						
1903	StL-A	0	2	.000	2	1	1	0	0	13	12	12	6	0	2	6	6	1.385	4.15	70	3.34	.245	1	.250	-2	0	-0.2
1904	StL-A	0	2	.000	8	3	2	0	0	51	51	23	21	3	2	10	24	1.196	3.71	67	3.08	.261	1	.056	-6	1	-0.9
1905	StL-A	2	5	.286	13	8	5	1	0	77^1	82	59	31	1	9	37	44	1.539	3.61	70	4.36	.274	8	.258	-8	0	-0.7
1907	StL-A	2	5	.286	10	6	4	0	0	55	77	43	37	3	2	17	14	1.709	6.05	41	5.67	.333	2	.100	-22	0	-2.5
	Bos-A	6	6	.500	16	13	9	2	0	114^1	77	35	25	1	3	34	50	.971	1.97	131	1.62	.194	2	.057	3	8	-0.1
	Yr.	8	11	.421	26	19	13	2	0	169^1	154	78	62	4	5	51	64	1.211	3.30	77	2.93	.245	4	.073	-19	8	-2.7
1908	Bos-A	14	13	.519	30	26	17	2	1	205	166	78	56	7	10	90	99	1.249	2.46	100	2.94	.226	8	.127	-4	10	-0.8
1909	Bos-A	2	6	.250	12	10	5	0	1	64^2	52	19	17	0	6	31	30	1.284	2.37	105	3.13	.240	1	.050	-0	4	-0.2
	Phi-A	16	11	.593	28	26	21	5	0	228^2	152	56	42	3	16	71	81	.975	1.65	145	1.77	.191	8	.108	17	18	1.6
	Yr.	18	17	.514	40	36	26	5	1	293^1	204	75	59	3	22	102	111	1.043	1.81	134	2.07	**.201**	9	.096	17	22	1.4
1910	Phi-A	18	12	.600	36	34	23	3	0	290^2	214	92	50	0	18	117	134	1.139	1.55	153	2.35	.216	14	.141	21	20	1.9
1911	Phi-A	15	7	.682	38	30	15	2	1	249^2	217	109	75	0	21	113	136	1.322	2.70	116	3.21	.243	15	.160	11	15	0.5
1912	Phi-A	3	8	.273	16	14	5	0	0	93^2	75	56	39	0	5	51	47	1.345	3.75	83	3.02	.226	1	.033	-8	2	-1.2
1913	Cin-N	0	1	.000	1	1	0	0	0	2^1	5	4	4	0	1	1	2	2.571	15.43	21	14.14	.500	0	.000	-3	0	-0.3
Total	10	78	78	.500	210	172	107	15	3	1445^1	1180	586	403	18	95	578	667	1.216	2.51	105	2.80	.229	61	.125	-3	78	-3.0
• MORGAN, Mike					Michael Thomas Morgan b: 10/8/1959, Tulare, CA BR/TR, 6'3", 215 lbs. Deb: 6/11/1978																						
1978	Oak-A	0	3	.000	3	3	1	0	0	12^1	19	12	10	1	0	8	0	2.189	7.30	50	8.68	.373	0	....	-5	0	-0.5
1979	Oak-A	2	10	.167	13	13	2	0	0	77^1	102	57	51	7	3	50	17	1.966	5.94	68	7.32	.332	0	....	-14	0	-1.4
1982	NY-A	7	11	.389	30	23	2	0	0	150^1	167	77	73	15	2	67	71	1.557	4.37	91	4.98	.285	0	....	-5	6	-0.5
1983	Tor-A	0	3	.000	16	4	0	0	0	45^1	48	26	26	6	0	21	22	1.522	5.16	83	4.98	.273	0	....	-4	1	-0.4
1985	Sea-A	1	1	.500	2	2	0	0	0	6	11	8	8	2	0	5	2	2.667	12.00	35	13.97	.393	0	....	-5	0	-0.5
1986	Sea-A	11	17	.393	37	33	9	1	1	216^1	243	122	109	24	4	86	116	1.521	4.53	94	4.96	.286	0	....	-6	11	-0.6
1987	Sea-A	12	17	.414	34	31	8	2	0	207	245	117	107	25	5	53	85	1.440	4.65	101	4.80	.296	0	....	0	11	0.0
1988	Bal-A	1	6	.143	22	10	2	0	1	71^1	70	45	43	6	1	23	29	1.304	5.43	72	3.63	.255	0	....	-13	1	-1.3
1989	LA-N	8	11	.421	40	19	0	0	0	152^2	130	51	43	6	2	33	72	1.068	2.53	135	2.26	.234	3	.083	14	10	1.3
1990	LA-N	11	15	.423	33	33	6	**4**	0	211	216	100	88	19	5	60	106	1.308	3.75	98	3.76	.266	8	.113	-3	9	-0.6
1991	LA-N★	14	10	.583	34	33	5	1	1	236^1	197	85	73	12	3	61	140	1.092	2.78	129	2.37	.226	7	.092	21	17	1.8
1992	Chi-N	16	8	.667	34	34	6	1	0	240	203	80	68	14	3	79	123	1.175	2.55	141	2.77	.234	8	.108	27	19	2.7
1993	Chi-N	10	15	.400	32	32	1	1	0	207^2	206	100	93	15	7	74	111	1.348	4.03	99	3.77	.262	4	.061	-3	11	-0.7
1994	Chi-N	2	10	.167	15	15	1	0	0	80^2	111	65	60	12	4	35	57	1.810	6.69	62	7.10	.338	3	.125	-23	0	-2.3
1995	Chi-N	2	1	.667	4	4	0	0	0	24^2	19	8	6	2	1	9	15	1.135	2.19	188	2.74	.216	1	.143	5	2	0.5
	StL-N	5	6	.455	17	17	1	0	0	106^2	114	48	46	10	5	25	46	1.303	3.88	108	4.00	.283	1	.032	2	6	0.0
	Yr.	7	7	.500	21	21	1	0	0	131^1	133	56	52	12	6	34	61	1.272	3.56	117	3.76	.271	2	.053	7	8	0.5
1996	StL-N	4	8	.333	18	18	0	0	0	103	118	63	60	14	0	40	55	1.534	5.24	80	5.19	.294	2	.061	-14	2	-1.7
	Cin-N	2	3	.400	5	5	0	0	0	27^1	28	9	7	2	1	7	19	1.280	2.30	180	3.63	.267	0	.000	5	2	0.4
	Yr.	6	11	.353	23	23	0	0	0	130^1	146	72	67	16	1	47	74	1.481	4.63	91	4.87	.289	2	.050	-9	4	-1.2
1997	Cin-N	9	12	.429	31	30	1	0	0	162	165	91	86	13	8	49	103	1.321	4.78	90	3.83	.266	4	.091	-9	6	-1.0
1998	Min-A	4	2	.667	18	17	0	0	0	98	108	41	38	13	7	24	50	1.347	3.49	137	4.68	.286	1	.500	15	8	1.5
	*Chi-N	0	1	.000	5	5	0	0	0	22^2	30	21	18	8	1	15	10	1.985	7.15	62	9.46	.323	4	.667	-7	1	-0.5
1999	Tex-A	13	10	.565	34	25	1	0	0	140	184	108	97	25	7	48	61	1.657	6.24	81	6.64	.323	1	.250	-16	4	-1.5
2000	Ari-N	5	5	.500	60	4	0	0	5	101^2	123	55	55	10	1	40	56	1.603	4.87	97	5.34	.311	7	.438	-1	7	0.1
2001*	Ari-N	1	0	1.000	31	1	0	0	0	38	45	20	18	2	0	17	24	1.632	4.26	107	4.90	.306	0	....	1	2	0.1
2002	Ari-N	1	1	.500	29	0	0	0	0	34	41	22	20	7	3	9	13	1.471	5.29	84	5.65	.289	0	....	-3	1	-0.3
Total	22	141	186	.431	597	411	46	10	8	2772^1	2943	1431	1303	270	73	938	1403	1.400	4.23	98	4.35	.276	54	.109	-42	137	-5.3
• MORGAN, Pidgey					Daniel Morgan b: 5/1853, MO d: 1/31/1910, St. Louis, MO Deb: 5/4/1875 ♦																						
1875	RS-n	1	3	.250	7	4	4	1	0	42	38	....	16	0	....	1	8	.929	3.43	71	....	.219	18	.261	-2	....	-0.2
• MORGAN, Tom					Tom Stephen "Plowboy" Morgan b: 5/20/1930, El Monte, CA d: 1/13/1987, Anaheim, CA BR/TR, 6'1", 195 lbs. Deb: 4/20/1951 C																						
1951*	NY-A	9	3	.750	27	16	4	2	2	124^2	119	56	51	11	3	36	57	1.243	3.68	104	3.38	.253	12	.273	0	9	0.2
1952	NY-A	5	4	.556	16	12	2	1	2	93^2	86	34	32	8	4	33	35	1.270	3.07	108	3.56	.252	6	.182	-1	6	0.0
1954	NY-A	11	5	.688	32	17	7	4	1	143	149	58	53	8	5	40	34	1.322	3.34	103	3.65	.274	7	.143	-2	8	-0.2
1955*	NY-A	7	3	.700	40	1	0	0	10	72	72	29	26	3	5	24	17	1.333	3.25	115	3.62	.267	4	.222	1	7	0.1
1956*	NY-A	6	7	.462	41	0	0	0	11	71^1	74	41	33	2	3	27	20	1.416	4.16	93	3.85	.284	2	.154	-4	5	-0.4
1957	KC-A	9	7	.563	46	13	5	0	7	143^2	160	76	74	19	3	61	32	1.538	4.64	85	5.24	.299	3	.091	-10	6	-1.3
1958	Det-A	2	5	.286	39	1	0	0	1	62^2	70	28	22	7	1	4	32	1.181	3.16	128	3.57	.286	2	.200	5	4	0.5
1959	Det-A	1	4	.200	46	1	0	0	9	92^2	94	48	41	11	6	18	39	1.209	3.98	102	3.70	.265	9	.391	1	8	0.5
1960	Det-A	3	2	.600	22	0	0	0	1	29	33	17	15	6	0	10	12	1.483	4.66	89	5.38	.295	0	....	-2	1	-0.2
	Was-A	1	3	.250	14	0	0	0	0	24	36	15	10	6	1	5	11	1.708	3.75	105	7.32	.343	0	.000	1	1	0.0
	Yr.	4	5	.444	36	0	0	0	1	53	69	32	25	12	1	15	23	1.585	4.25	95	6.26	.318	0	.000	-1	2	-0.1
1961	LA-A	8	2	.800	59	0	0	0	10	91^2	74	31	24	7	5	17	39	.993	2.36	191	2.31	.224	1	.083	23	14	2.2
1962	LA-A	5	2	.714	48	0	0	0	9	58^2	53	23	19	6	1	19	29	1.227	2.91	132	3.22	.247	0	.000	7	7	0.6
1963	LA-A	0	0	....	13	0	0	0	1	16^1	20	11	10	1	3	6	7	1.592	5.51	62	5.59	.313	0	.000	-4	0	-0.4
Total	12	67	47	.588	443	61	18	7	64	1023^1	1040	467	410	95	40	300	364	1.309	3.61	106	3.86	.270	46	.186	16	76	1.7
• MORLAN, John					John Glen Morlan b: 11/22/1947, Columbus, OH BR/TR, 6', 178 lbs. Deb: 7/20/1973																						
1973	Pit-N	2	2	.500	10	7	1	0	0	41	42	18	18	4	0	23	23	1.585	3.95	89	4.79	.276	2	.182	-2	2	-0.1
1974	Pit-N	0	3	.000	39	0	0	0	0	65	54	37	31	2	3	48	38	1.569	4.29	80	3.89	.227	0	.000	-6	1	-0.7
Total	2	2	5	.286	49	7	1	0	0	106	96	55	49	6	3	71	61	1.575	4.16	83	4.24	.246	2	.111	-8	3	-0.9
• MORMAN, Alvin					Alvin Morman b: 1/6/1969, Rockingham, NC BL/TL, 6'3", 210 lbs. Deb: 4/2/1996																						
1996	Hou-N	4	1	.800	53	0	0	0	0	42	43	24	23	8	0	24	31	1.595	4.93	79	5.25	.261	0	....	-4	2	-0.4
1997*	Cle-A	0	0	....	34	0	0	0	2	18^1	19	13	12	2	1	14	13	1.800	5.89	80	5.81	.268	0	.000	-2	0	-0.2
1998	Cle-A	0	1	.000	31	0	0	0	0	22	25	13	13	1	0	11	16	1.636	5.32	90	4.96	.298	0	....	-1	1	-0.1
	SF-N	0	1	.000	9	0	0	0	0	7	8	4	4	4	0	3	7	1.571	5.14	77	8.45	.276	0	....	-1	0	-0.1
1999	KC-A	2	4	.333	49	0	0	0	1	53^1	66	27	24	6	4	23	31	1.669	4.05	124	6.04	.307	0	....	5	3	0.4
Total	4	6	7	.462	176	0	0	0	3	142^2	161	81	76	21	5	75	98	1.654	4.79	93	5.73	.285	0	.000	-4	6	-0.4
• MOROGIELLO, Dan					Daniel Joseph Morogiello b: 3/26/1955, Brooklyn, NY BL/TL, 6'1", 200 lbs. Deb: 5/20/1983																						
1983	Bal-A	0	1	.000	22	0	0	0	1	37^2	39	10	10	1	1	10	15	1.301	2.39	165	3.21	.265	0	....	7	4	0.7
• MORONEY, Jim					James Francis Moroney b: 12/4/1883, Boston, MA d: 2/26/1929, Philadelphia, PA BL/TL, 6'1", 175 lbs. Deb: 4/24/1906																						
1906	Bos-N	0	3	.000	3	3	3	0	0	27	28	20	16	1	6	12	11	1.481	5.33	50	4.58	.259	1	.100	-8	0	-0.9
1910	Phi-N	1	2	.333	12	2	1	0	0	42	43	20	10	1	4	11	13	1.286	2.14	145	3.89	.295	0	.000	4	2	0.3
1912	Chi-N	1	1	.500	10	3	1	0	1	23^2	25	13	12	0	4	17	5	1.775	4.56	73	5.69	.316	3	.500	-4	2	-0.3
Total	3	2	6	.250	25	8	5	0	2	92^2	96	53	38	2	14	40	29	1.468	3.69	80	4.55	.288	4	.154	-7	4	-0.9
• MORRELL, Bill					Willard Blackmer Morrell b: 4/9/1893, Hyde Park, MA d: 8/5/1975, Birmingham, AL BR/TR, 6', 172 lbs. Deb: 4/20/1926																						
1926	Was-A	3	3	.500	26	2	1	0	1	69^2	83	48	41	5	2	29	16	1.608	5.30	73	5.16	.311	4	.235	-11	2	-1.0
1930	NY-N	0	0	....	2	0	0	0	0	8	6	1	1	0	0	1	3	.875	1.13	421	1.46	.214	0	.000	3	1	0.2

YEAR TM-L	W	L	PCT	G	GS	CG	SH	SV	IP	H	R	ER	HR	HB	BB	SO	RAT	ERA	ERA+	CERA	OAV	BH	AVG	PR+	WS	TPW
1931 NY-N	5	3	.625	20	7	2	0	1	66	83	34	32	4	0	27	16	1.667	4.36	85	5.19	.306	2	.111	-6	3	-0.6
Total 3	8	6	.571	48	9	3	0	2	143^{2}	172	83	74	9	2	57	35	1.594	4.64	82	4.97	.304	6	.162	-14	6	-1.4

• MORRILL, John

John Francis "Honest John" Morrill b: 2/19/1855, Boston, MA d: 4/2/1932, Brookline, MA BR/TR, 5'10.5", 155 lbs. Deb: 4/24/1876 M/U ♦

YEAR TM-L	W	L	PCT	G	GS	CG	SH	SV	IP	H	R	ER	HR	HB	BB	SO	RAT	ERA	ERA+	CERA	OAV	BH	AVG	PR+	WS	TPW
1880 Bos-N	0	0	....	3	0	0	0	0	10^{2}	9	3	1	0	....	1	0	.938	0.84	269	....	.217	81	.237	2	10	0.1
1881 Bos-N	0	1	.000	3	0	0	0	1	5^{2}	9	8	4	0	....	1	0	1.765	6.35	42	....	.345	90	.289	-2	11	1.2
1882 Bos-N	0	0	....	1	0	0	0	0	2	3	0	0	0	....	0	2	1.500	0.00	....	....	.328	101	.289	1	12	0.9
1883 Bos-N	1	0	1.000	2	1	1	0	0	13	15	11	4	0	....	4	5	1.462	2.77	112	....	.273	129	.319	1	20	2.1
1884 Bos-N	0	1	.000	7	1	1	0	**2**	23	34	23	19	0	....	6	13	1.739	7.43	39	....	.326	114	.260	-12	14	-0.7
1886 Bos-N	0	0	....	1	0	0	0	0	4	5	1	0	0	....	0	2	1.250	0.00	....	....	.295	106	.247	1	17	1.8
1889 Was-N	0	0	....	1	0	0	0	0	0^{1}	0	0	0	0	0	0	0	.000	0.00	....	....	.000	27	.185	0	2	-0.8
Total 7	1	2	.333	18	2	2	0	3	58^{2}	75	46	28	0	0	12	22	1.483	4.30	66	....	.296	1312	.265	-9	86	4.5

• MORRIS, Danny

Danny Walker Morris b: 6/11/1946, Greenville, KY BR/TR, 6'1", 200 lbs. Deb: 9/10/1968

YEAR TM-L	W	L	PCT	G	GS	CG	SH	SV	IP	H	R	ER	HR	HB	BB	SO	RAT	ERA	ERA+	CERA	OAV	BH	AVG	PR+	WS	TPW
1968 Min-A	0	1	.000	3	2	0	0	0	10^{2}	11	5	2	0	0	4	6	1.406	1.69	183	3.44	.262	0	.000	2	0	0.2
1969 Min-A	0	1	.000	3	1	0	0	0	5^{1}	5	4	3	1	0	4	1	1.688	5.06	72	5.11	.238	0	....	-1	0	-0.1
Total 2	0	2	.000	6	3	0	0	0	16	16	9	5	1	0	8	7	1.500	2.81	121	3.99	.254	0	.000	1	0	0.1

• MORRIS, Ed

Edward "Cannonball" Morris b: 9/29/1862, Brooklyn, NY d: 4/12/1937, Pittsburgh, PA BB/TL, 5'7", 165 lbs. Deb: 5/1/1884

YEAR TM-L	W	L	PCT	G	GS	CG	SH	SV	IP	H	R	ER	HR	HB	BB	SO	RAT	ERA	ERA+	CERA	OAV	BH	AVG	PR+	WS	TPW
1884 Col-a	34	13	.723	52	52	47	3	0	429^{2}	335	159	104	3	13	51	302	.898	2.18	139	....	**.203**	37	.186	29	44	2.9
1885 Pit-a	39	24	.619	**63**	**63**	**63**	**7**	0	**581**	459	245	152	5	14	101	**298**	.964	2.35	137	....	**.208**	44	.186	51	**56**	4.3
1886 Pit-a	**41**	20	.672	64	63	63	**12**	**1**	555^{1}	455	244	151	5	7	118	326	1.032	2.45	138	....	.213	38	.167	52	44	4.0
1887 Pit-N	14	22	.389	38	38	37	1	0	317^{2}	446	225	152	13	8	71	91	1.404	4.31	90	....	.322	30	.229	-12	16	-1.3
1888 Pit-N	29	23	.558	**55**	**55**	**54**	5	0	480	470	216	123	7	8	74	135	1.133	2.31	115	....	.247	19	.101	21	34	1.1
1889 Pit-N	6	13	.316	21	21	18	0	0	170	196	107	78	4	6	48	40	1.435	4.13	91	....	.280	7	.097	-7	7	-1.1
1890 Pit-P	8	7	.533	18	15	15	1	0	144^{1}	178	116	78	5	3	35	25	1.476	4.86	80	....	.291	9	.143	-11	7	-1.2
Total 7	171	122	.584	311	307	297	29	1	2678	2539	1312	838	42	59	498	1217	1.108	2.82	118	....	.240	184	.165	123	208	8.8

• MORRIS, Ed

Walter Edward "Big Ed" Morris b: 12/7/1899, Foshee, AL d: 3/3/1932, Century, FL BR/TR, 6'2", 185 lbs. Deb: 8/5/1922

YEAR TM-L	W	L	PCT	G	GS	CG	SH	SV	IP	H	R	ER	HR	HB	BB	SO	RAT	ERA	ERA+	CERA	OAV	BH	AVG	PR+	WS	TPW
1922 Chi-N	0	0	....	5	0	0	0	0	12	22	17	11	1	0	6	5	2.333	8.25	51	9.09	.386	1	.250	-5	0	-0.5
1928 Bos-A	19	15	.559	47	29	20	0	5	257^{2}	255	118	101	7	5	80	104	1.300	3.53	116	3.07	.264	14	.154	15	21	1.2
1929 Bos-A	14	14	.500	33	26	17	2	1	208^{1}	227	118	103	7	2	95	73	1.546	4.45	96	4.21	.282	16	.232	-3	13	-0.1
1930 Bos-A	4	9	.308	18	9	3	0	0	65^{1}	67	42	30	1	0	38	28	1.607	4.13	111	3.93	.260	6	.316	3	4	0.4
1931 Bos-A	5	7	.417	37	14	3	0	0	130^{2}	131	80	69	4	5	74	46	1.569	4.75	91	4.15	.260	6	.158	-6	6	-0.7
Total 5	42	45	.483	140	78	43	2	6	674	702	375	314	20	12	293	256	1.476	4.19	101	3.82	.271	43	.195	3	44	0.3

• MORRIS, Jack

John Scott Morris b: 5/16/1955, St. Paul, MN BR/TR, 6'3", 200 lbs. Deb: 7/26/1977

YEAR TM-L	W	L	PCT	G	GS	CG	SH	SV	IP	H	R	ER	HR	HB	BB	SO	RAT	ERA	ERA+	CERA	OAV	BH	AVG	PR+	WS	TPW
1977 Det-A	1	1	.500	7	6	1	0	0	45^{2}	38	20	19	4	0	23	28	1.336	3.74	114	3.58	.235	0	....	3	3	0.3
1978 Det-A	3	5	.375	28	7	0	0	0	106	107	57	51	8	3	49	48	1.472	4.33	89	4.20	.268	0	....	-7	4	-0.7
1979 Det-A	17	7	.708	27	27	9	1	0	197^{2}	179	76	72	19	4	59	113	1.204	3.28	132	3.26	.244	0	....	21	17	2.0
1980 Det-A	16	15	.516	36	36	11	2	0	250	252	125	116	20	4	87	112	1.356	4.18	98	3.79	.263	0	....	1	14	0.1
1981 Det-A★	**14**	7	.667	25	25	15	1	0	198	153	69	67	14	2	78	97	1.167	3.05	124	2.67	.218	0	....	12	16	1.2
1982 Det-A	17	16	.515	37	37	17	3	0	266^{1}	247	131	120	37	0	96	135	1.288	4.06	100	3.80	.247	0	....	-6	14	-0.6
1983 Det-A	20	13	.606	37	37	20	1	0	**293^{2}**	257	117	109	30	3	83	**232**	1.158	3.34	117	2.98	.233	0	....	15	20	1.5
1984* Det-A★	19	11	.633	35	35	9	1	0	240^{1}	221	108	96	20	2	87	148	1.282	3.60	109	3.35	.241	0	....	7	14	0.7
1985 Det-A★	16	11	.593	35	35	13	4	0	257	212	102	95	21	5	110	191	1.253	3.33	122	3.15	.225	0	....	21	19	2.1
1986 Det-A	21	8	.724	35	35	15	**6**	0	267	229	105	97	40	0	82	223	1.165	3.27	126	3.24	.229	0	....	22	20	2.2
1987* Det-A★	18	11	.621	34	34	13	0	0	266	227	111	100	39	1	93	208	1.203	3.38	125	3.36	.228	0	.000	23	21	2.2
1988 Det-A	15	13	.536	34	34	10	2	0	235	225	115	103	20	4	83	168	1.311	3.94	97	3.57	.251	0	....	-5	12	-0.5
1989 Det-A	6	14	.300	24	24	10	0	0	170^{1}	189	102	92	23	2	59	115	1.456	4.86	79	4.77	.283	0	....	-18	4	-1.8
1990 Det-A	15	18	.455	36	**36**	**11**	3	0	249^{2}	231	144	125	26	6	97	162	1.314	4.51	88	3.61	.242	0	....	-21	8	-2.1
1991* Min-A★	18	12	.600	35	**35**	10	2	0	246^{2}	226	107	94	18	5	92	163	1.289	3.43	124	3.41	.245	0	....	20	18	2.0
1992* Tor-A	**21**	6	.778	34	34	6	1	0	240^{2}	222	114	108	18	10	80	132	1.255	4.04	101	3.40	.246	0	....	2	15	0.2
1993 Tor-A	7	12	.368	27	27	4	1	0	152^{2}	189	116	105	18	3	65	103	1.664	6.19	70	5.74	.302	0	....	-31	1	-3.0
1994 Cle-A	10	6	.625	23	23	1	0	0	141^{1}	163	96	88	14	4	67	100	1.627	5.60	84	5.41	.292	0	....	-14	5	-1.3
Total 18	254	186	.577	549	527	175	28	0	3824	3567	1815	1657	389	58	1390	2478	1.296	3.90	104	3.62	.247	0	.000	46	225	4.5

• MORRIS, Jim

James Samuel Morris b: 1/19/1964, Brownwood, TX BL/TL, 6'3", 215 lbs. Deb: 9/18/1999

YEAR TM-L	W	L	PCT	G	GS	CG	SH	SV	IP	H	R	ER	HR	HB	BB	SO	RAT	ERA	ERA+	CERA	OAV	BH	AVG	PR+	WS	TPW
1999 TB-A	0	0	....	5	0	0	0	0	4^{2}	3	3	3	1	1	2	3	1.071	5.79	86	3.56	.167	0	....	-0	0	0.0
2000 TB-A	0	0	....	16	0	0	0	0	10^{1}	10	9	5	1	0	7	10	1.645	4.35	113	4.68	.250	0	....	1	0	0.0
Total 2	0	0	....	21	0	0	0	0	15	13	12	8	2	1	9	13	1.467	4.80	103	4.33	.224	0	....	0	0	0.0

• MORRIS, John

John Wallace Morris b: 8/23/1941, Lewes, DE BR/TL, 6'2", 198 lbs. Deb: 7/19/1966

YEAR TM-L	W	L	PCT	G	GS	CG	SH	SV	IP	H	R	ER	HR	HB	BB	SO	RAT	ERA	ERA+	CERA	OAV	BH	AVG	PR+	WS	TPW
1966 Phi-N	1	1	.500	13	0	0	0	0	13^{2}	15	8	8	2	1	3	8	1.317	5.27	68	4.47	.278	0	....	-3	0	-0.3
1968 Bal-A	2	0	1.000	19	0	0	0	0	31^{2}	19	11	9	4	4	17	22	1.137	2.56	114	3.00	.173	0	.000	1	2	0.0
1969 Sea-A	0	0	....	6	0	0	0	0	12^{2}	16	10	9	2	0	8	8	1.895	6.39	57	6.78	.308	1	1.000	-4	0	-0.3
1970 Mil-A	4	3	.571	20	9	2	0	0	73^{1}	70	33	32	4	2	22	40	1.255	3.93	96	3.24	.253	3	.176	0	4	0.1
1971 Mil-A	2	2	.500	43	1	0	0	1	67^{2}	69	34	28	4	1	27	42	1.419	3.72	93	3.70	.270	1	.200	-3	3	-0.3
1972 SF-N	0	0	....	7	0	0	0	0	6^{1}	9	6	3	2	0	2	5	1.737	4.26	82	7.54	.310	0	....	-1	0	-0.1
1973 SF-N	1	0	1.000	7	0	0	0	0	6^{1}	12	8	6	0	0	3	3	2.368	8.53	45	9.49	.429	0	.000	-3	0	-0.4
1974 SF-N	1	1	.500	17	0	0	0	1	20^{2}	17	7	7	1	0	4	9	1.016	3.05	125	1.99	.215	1	1.000	2	2	0.2
Total 8	11	7	.611	132	10	2	0	2	232^{1}	227	117	102	19	8	86	137	1.347	3.95	90	3.78	.256	6	.194	-9	11	-0.9

• MORRIS, Matt

Matthew Christian Morris b: 8/9/1974, Middletown, NY BR/TR, 6'5", 210 lbs. Deb: 4/4/1997

YEAR TM-L	W	L	PCT	G	GS	CG	SH	SV	IP	H	R	ER	HR	HB	BB	SO	RAT	ERA	ERA+	CERA	OAV	BH	AVG	PR+	WS	TPW
1997 StL-N	12	9	.571	33	33	3	0	0	217	208	88	77	12	7	69	149	1.276	3.19	130	3.41	.258	15	.205	23	16	2.5
1998 StL-N	7	5	.583	17	17	2	1	0	113^{2}	101	37	32	8	3	42	79	1.258	2.53	166	3.25	.243	2	.069	21	10	2.1
2000* StL-N	3	3	.500	31	0	0	0	4	53	53	22	21	3	2	17	34	1.321	3.57	129	3.58	.261	1	.333	6	6	0.5
2001* StL-N★	**22**	8	.733	34	34	2	1	0	216^{1}	218	86	76	13	13	54	185	1.257	3.16	135	3.50	.265	10	.139	22	17	2.0
2002* StL-N★	17	9	.654	32	32	1	1	0	210^{1}	210	86	80	16	6	64	171	1.303	3.42	115	3.63	.261	12	.169	9	13	1.0
2003 StL-N	11	8	.579	27	27	5	**3**	0	172^{1}	164	76	72	20	4	39	120	1.178	3.76	108	3.37	.252	10	.192	6	10	0.8
Total 6	72	42	.632	174	143	13	6	4	982^{2}	954	395	358	72	35	285	738	1.261	3.28	126	3.46	.257	50	.167	86	72	9.0

• MORRISETTE, Bill

William Lee Morrisette b: 1/17/1893, Baltimore, MD d: 3/25/1966, Virginia Beach, VA BR/TR, 6', 176 lbs. Deb: 9/19/1915

YEAR TM-L	W	L	PCT	G	GS	CG	SH	SV	IP	H	R	ER	HR	HB	BB	SO	RAT	ERA	ERA+	CERA	OAV	BH	AVG	PR+	WS	TPW
1915 Phi-A	2	0	1.000	4	1	1	0	0	20	15	6	3	0	0	5	11	1.000	1.35	216	1.57	.195	2	.286	4	1	0.4
1916 Phi-A	0	0	....	1	0	0	0	0	4	6	3	3	0	0	5	2	2.750	6.75	42	11.26	.429	0	.000	-2	0	-0.2
1920 Det-A	1	1	.500	8	3	1	0	0	27	25	21	13	0	3	19	15	1.630	4.33	86	4.21	.245	0	.000	-1	1	-0.3
Total 3	3	1	.750	13	4	2	0	0	51	46	30	19	0	3	29	28	1.471	3.35	102	3.73	.238	2	.125	1	2	0.0

• MORRISON, Guy

Walter Guy Morrison b: 8/29/1895, Hinton, WV d: 8/14/1934, Grand Rapids, MI BR/TR, 5'11", 185 lbs. Deb: 8/31/1927

YEAR TM-L	W	L	PCT	G	GS	CG	SH	SV	IP	H	R	ER	HR	HB	BB	SO	RAT	ERA	ERA+	CERA	OAV	BH	AVG	PR+	WS	TPW
1927 Bos-N	1	2	.333	11	3	1	0	0	34^{1}	40	22	17	1	0	15	6	1.602	4.46	83	4.39	.296	1	.125	-2	1	-0.1
1928 Bos-N	0	0	....	1	0	0	0	0	3	4	4	4	1	0	3	0	2.333	12.00	33	10.38	.308	0	....	-3	0	-0.3
Total 2	1	2	.333	12	3	1	0	0	37^{1}	44	26	21	2	0	18	6	1.661	5.06	74	4.87	.297	1	.125	-5	1	-0.4

• MORRISON, Hank

Stephen Henry Morrison b: 5/22/1866, Olneyville, RI d: 9/30/1927, Attleboro, MA BR/TR, 5'10", 180 lbs. Deb: 5/28/1887

YEAR TM-L	W	L	PCT	G	GS	CG	SH	SV	IP	H	R	ER	HR	HB	BB	SO	RAT	ERA	ERA+	CERA	OAV	BH	AVG	PR+	WS	TPW
1887 Ind-N	3	4	.429	7	7	5	0	0	57	106	73	48	2	1	27	13	1.860	7.58	54	....	.387	5	.179	-22	0	-2.1

• MORRISON, Johnny

John Dewey "Jughandle Johnny" Morrison b: 10/22/1895, Pellville, KY d: 3/20/1966, Louisville, KY BR/TR, 5'11", 188 lbs. Deb: 9/28/1920

YEAR TM-L	W	L	PCT	G	GS	CG	SH	SV	IP	H	R	ER	HR	HB	BB	SO	RAT	ERA	ERA+	CERA	OAV	BH	AVG	PR+	WS	TPW
1920 Pit-N	1	0	1.000	2	1	1	1	0	7	4	0	0	0	0	1	3	.714	0.00	....	0.95	.167	0	.000	3	1	0.2
1921 Pit-N	9	7	.563	21	17	11	**3**	0	144	131	49	46	3	1	33	52	1.139	2.88	133	2.56	.258	5	.119	15	13	1.3
1922 Pit-N	17	11	.607	45	33	20	**5**	1	286^{1}	315	130	109	10	6	87	104	1.404	3.43	119	3.82	.286	20	.198	25	21	2.1

YEAR TM-L	W	L	PCT	G	GS	CG	SH	SV	IP	H	R	ER	HR	HB	BB	SO	RAT	ERA	ERA+	CERA	OAV	BH	AVG	PR+	WS	TPW
1923 Pit-N	25	13	.658	42	37	27	2	2	301^2	287	136	117	6	5	110	114	1.316	3.49	115	3.12	.253	21	.183	12	23	0.8
1924 Pit-N	11	16	.407	**41**	25	10	0	2	237^2	213	114	99	7	4	73	85	1.203	3.75	102	2.70	.245	13	.169	-7	14	-0.9
1925* Pit-N	17	14	.548	**44**	26	10	0	**4**	211	245	113	91	12	7	60	60	1.445	3.88	115	4.23	.291	13	.178	9	13	0.6
1926 Pit-N	6	8	.429	26	13	6	2	2	122^1	119	52	46	2	2	44	39	1.332	3.38	116	3.22	.267	3	.077	5	8	0.2
1927 Pit-N	3	2	.600	21	2	1	0	3	53^2	63	27	25	2	0	21	21	1.565	4.19	98	4.53	.304	2	.154	-1	3	-0.1
1929 Bro-N	13	7	.650	39	10	4	0	**8**	136^2	150	87	68	11	3	61	57	1.544	4.48	103	4.58	.279	7	.163	5	11	0.3
1930 Bro-N	1	2	.333	16	0	0	0	1	34^2	47	29	21	4	0	16	11	1.817	5.45	90	6.63	.346	0	.000	-3	1	-0.3
Total 10	103	80	.563	297	164	90	13	23	1535	1574	737	622	57	28	506	546	1.355	3.65	113	3.54	.271	84	.164	63	108	4.2

• MORRISON, Mike — Michael Morrison b: 2/6/1867, Erie, PA d: 6/16/1955, Erie, PA BR/TR, 5'8.5", 156 lbs. Deb: 4/19/1887

YEAR TM-L	W	L	PCT	G	GS	CG	SH	SV	IP	H	R	ER	HR	HB	BB	SO	RAT	ERA	ERA+	CERA	OAV	BH	AVG	PR+	WS	TPW
1887 Cle-a	12	25	.324	40	40	35	0	0	316^2	590	341	173	13	22	205	158	**1.863**	4.92	88	....	.385	38	.250	-9	7	-0.9
1888 Cle-a	1	3	.250	4	4	4	0	0	35	40	35	21	3	1	19	14	1.686	5.40	57	....	.277	4	.235	-9	0	-0.8
1890 Syr-a	6	9	.400	17	14	13	1	0	127	131	112	83	4	13	81	69	1.669	5.88	60	....	.259	29	.242	-31	4	-2.7
Bal-a	1	2	.333	4	4	3	0	0	26	15	20	11	0	2	20	13	1.346	3.81	112	....	.163	1	.111	1	1	0.1
Yr.	7	11	.389	21	18	16	1	0	153	146	132	94	4	15	101	82	1.614	5.53	65	....	.244	30	.233	-30	5	-2.6
Total 3	20	39	.339	65	62	55	1	0	504^2	776	508	288	20	38	325	254	1.775	5.14	77	....	.341	72	.242	-47	12	-4.3

• MORRISON, Phil — Philip Melvin Morrison b: 10/18/1894, Rockport, IN d: 1/18/1955, Lexington, KY BB/TR, 6'2", 190 lbs. Deb: 9/30/1921

YEAR TM-L	W	L	PCT	G	GS	CG	SH	SV	IP	H	R	ER	HR	HB	BB	SO	RAT	ERA	ERA+	CERA	OAV	BH	AVG	PR+	WS	TPW
1921 Pit-N	0	0	....	1	0	0	0	0	0^2	1	0	0	0	0	0	1	1.500	0.00	....	4.47	.333	0	....	0	0	0.0

• MORRISSEY, Frank — Michael Joseph "Deacon" Morrissey b: 5/3/1876, Baltimore, MD d: 2/22/1939, Baltimore, MD TR, 5'4", 140 lbs. Deb: 7/13/1901

YEAR TM-L	W	L	PCT	G	GS	CG	SH	SV	IP	H	R	ER	HR	HB	BB	SO	RAT	ERA	ERA+	CERA	OAV	BH	AVG	PR+	WS	TPW
1901 Bos-A	0	0	....	1	0	0	0	0	4^1	5	1	1	0	2	2	1	1.615	2.08	170	5.96	.286	0	.000	1	1	0.0
1902 Chi-N	1	3	.250	5	5	5	0	0	40	40	16	10	0	2	8	13	1.200	2.25	120	2.79	.260	2	.091	2	2	-0.1
Total 2	1	3	.250	6	5	5	0	0	44^1	45	17	11	0	4	10	14	1.241	2.23	123	3.10	.263	2	.080	2	3	-0.1

• MORTON, Carl — Carl Wendle Morton b: 1/18/1944, Kansas City, MO d: 4/12/1983, Tulsa, OK BR/TR, 6', 200 lbs. Deb: 4/11/1969

YEAR TM-L	W	L	PCT	G	GS	CG	SH	SV	IP	H	R	ER	HR	HB	BB	SO	RAT	ERA	ERA+	CERA	OAV	BH	AVG	PR+	WS	TPW
1969 Mon-N	0	3	.000	8	5	0	0	0	29^1	29	15	15	2	2	18	16	1.602	4.60	80	4.61	.264	0	.000	-3	1	-0.3
1970 Mon-N	18	11	.621	43	37	10	4	0	284^2	281	123	114	27	4	125	154	1.426	3.60	114	4.15	.262	15	.161	14	21	1.6
1971 Mon-N	10	18	.357	36	35	9	0	1	213^2	252	129	114	22	4	83	84	1.568	4.80	73	5.05	.295	14	.182	-30	4	-3.0
1972 Mon-N	7	13	.350	27	27	3	1	0	172	170	84	75	16	3	53	51	1.297	3.92	90	3.65	.258	7	.135	-6	7	-0.6
1973 Atl-N	15	10	.600	38	37	10	4	0	256^1	254	114	97	18	4	70	112	1.264	3.41	115	3.36	.259	17	.181	17	18	2.2
1974 Atl-N	16	12	.571	38	38	7	1	0	274^2	293	110	96	10	2	89	113	1.391	3.15	120	3.68	.277	10	.112	15	17	1.2
1975 Atl-N	17	16	.515	39	39	11	2	0	277^2	302	122	108	19	3	82	78	1.383	3.50	108	3.94	.278	15	.160	15	17	1.5
1976 Atl-N	4	9	.308	26	24	1	1	0	140^1	172	79	65	6	5	45	42	1.546	4.17	91	4.70	.306	8	.178	-3	6	-0.2
Total 8	87	92	.486	255	242	51	13	1	1648^2	1753	776	684	120	27	565	650	1.406	3.73	101	4.03	.275	86	.156	20	91	2.5

• MORTON, Guy — Guy "Alabama Blossom" Morton, Sr. b: 6/1/1893, Vernon, AL d: 10/18/1934, Sheffield, AL BR/TR, 6'1", 175 lbs. Deb: 6/20/1914

YEAR TM-L	W	L	PCT	G	GS	CG	SH	SV	IP	H	R	ER	HR	HB	BB	SO	RAT	ERA	ERA+	CERA	OAV	BH	AVG	PR+	WS	TPW
1914 Cle-A	1	13	.071	25	13	5	0	1	128	116	62	43	1	3	55	80	1.336	3.02	95	3.27	.257	1	.029	-0	4	-0.4
1915 Cle-A	16	15	.516	34	27	15	6	1	240	189	75	57	5	2	60	134	1.038	2.14	142	2.00	.216	12	.146	26	21	2.2
1916 Cle-A	12	6	.667	27	18	9	0	0	149^2	139	63	48	1	3	42	88	1.209	2.89	104	2.69	.246	12	.211	2	9	0.1
1917 Cle-A	10	10	.500	35	18	6	1	2	161	158	74	49	3	2	59	62	1.348	2.74	103	3.40	.266	4	.085	-3	9	-0.8
1918 Cle-A	14	8	.636	30	28	13	1	0	214^2	189	87	63	1	3	77	123	1.239	2.64	113	2.62	.240	12	.156	13	14	1.3
1919 Cle-A	9	9	.500	26	20	9	3	0	147^1	128	65	46	3	0	47	64	1.188	2.81	119	2.53	.233	9	.161	9	9	0.7
1920 Cle-A	8	6	.571	29	17	6	1	1	137	140	80	68	2	1	57	72	1.438	4.47	85	3.65	.270	10	.217	-13	6	-1.4
1921 Cle-A	8	3	.727	30	7	3	2	0	107^2	98	45	33	1	2	32	45	1.207	2.76	154	2.59	.244	6	.171	18	9	1.5
1922 Cle-A	14	9	.609	38	23	13	3	0	202^2	218	117	90	7	4	85	102	1.495	4.00	100	4.03	.277	13	.191	5	12	0.3
1923 Cle-A	6	6	.500	33	14	3	2	1	129^1	133	67	61	3	2	56	54	1.461	4.24	93	3.78	.276	7	.159	-3	6	-0.5
1924 Cle-A	0	1	.000	10	0	0	0	0	12^1	12	12	9	0	0	13	6	2.027	6.57	65	5.20	.250	0	.000	-3	0	-0.3
Total 11	98	86	.533	317	185	82	19	6	1629^2	1520	747	567	27	22	583	830	1.290	3.13	108	3.03	.251	86	.157	51	99	2.8

• MORTON, Kevin — Kevin Joseph Morton b: 8/3/1968, Norwalk, CT BR/TL, 6'2", 185 lbs. Deb: 7/5/1991

YEAR TM-L	W	L	PCT	G	GS	CG	SH	SV	IP	H	R	ER	HR	HB	BB	SO	RAT	ERA	ERA+	CERA	OAV	BH	AVG	PR+	WS	TPW
1991 Bos-A	6	5	.545	16	15	1	0	0	86^1	93	49	44	9	1	40	45	1.541	4.59	94	4.88	.284	0	....	-3	4	-0.3

• MORTON, Sparrow — William P. Morton TL Deb: 7/15/1884

YEAR TM-L	W	L	PCT	G	GS	CG	SH	SV	IP	H	R	ER	HR	HB	BB	SO	RAT	ERA	ERA+	CERA	OAV	BH	AVG	PR+	WS	TPW
1884 Phi-N	0	2	.000	2	2	2	0	0	17	16	20	10	0	....	11	5	1.588	5.29	56	....	.235	3	.375	-4	0	-0.2

• MOSELEY, Earl — Earl Victor "Vic" Moseley b: 9/7/1884, Middleburg, OH d: 7/1/1963, Alliance, OH BR/TR, 5'9.5", 168 lbs. Deb: 6/17/1913

YEAR TM-L	W	L	PCT	G	GS	CG	SH	SV	IP	H	R	ER	HR	HB	BB	SO	RAT	ERA	ERA+	CERA	OAV	BH	AVG	PR+	WS	TPW
1913 Bos-A	8	5	.615	24	15	7	3	0	120^2	105	56	42	1	0	49	62	1.276	3.13	94	3.13	.245	3	.081	-0	6	-0.3
1914 Ind-F	19	18	.514	43	38	29	4	1	316^2	303	149	122	5	4	123	205	1.345	3.47	100	3.30	.258	12	.110	-3	17	-1.0
1915 New-F	15	15	.500	38	32	22	5	1	268	222	87	57	2	2	99	142	1.198	**1.91**	148	2.49	.229	13	.148	27	21	2.6
1916 Cin-N	7	10	.412	31	15	7	0	1	150^1	145	75	65	5	0	69	60	1.424	3.89	67	3.50	.257	4	.087	-23	3	-2.9
Total 4	49	48	.505	136	100	65	12	3	855^2	775	367	286	13	6	340	469	1.303	3.01	100	3.06	.247	32	.114	-0	47	-1.6

• MOSER, Walter — Walter Frederick Moser b: 2/27/1881, Concord, NC d: 12/10/1946, Philadelphia, PA BR/TR, 5'9", 170 lbs. Deb: 9/3/1906

YEAR TM-L	W	L	PCT	G	GS	CG	SH	SV	IP	H	R	ER	HR	HB	BB	SO	RAT	ERA	ERA+	CERA	OAV	BH	AVG	PR+	WS	TPW
1906 Phi-N	0	4	.000	6	4	4	0	0	42^2	49	35	17	0	1	15	17	1.500	3.59	73	4.14	.295	0	.000	-4	0	-0.7
1911 Bos-A	0	1	.000	6	3	1	0	0	24^2	37	28	11	0	1	11	11	1.946	4.01	81	6.88	.366	0	.000	-2	0	-0.3
StL-A	0	2	.000	2	2	0	0	0	3^1	11	12	8	0	0	4	2	4.500	21.60	16	20.72	.478	1	1.000	-7	0	-0.6
Yr.	0	3	.000	8	5	1	0	0	28	48	40	19	0	1	15	13	2.250	6.11	54	8.53	.387	1	.125	-9	0	-0.9
Total 2	0	7	.000	14	9	5	0	0	70^2	97	75	36	0	2	30	30	1.797	4.58	64	5.88	.334	1	.045	-13	0	-1.6

• MOSES, John — John William Moses b: 8/9/1957, Los Angeles, CA BB/TL, 5'10", 170 lbs. Deb: 8/23/1982 C ♦

YEAR TM-L	W	L	PCT	G	GS	CG	SH	SV	IP	H	R	ER	HR	HB	BB	SO	RAT	ERA	ERA+	CERA	OAV	BH	AVG	PR+	WS	TPW
1989 Min-A	0	0	....	1	0	0	0	0	1	0	0	0	0	0	1	0	1.000	0.00	....	0.97	.000	68	.281	0	8	-0.6
1990 Min-A	0	0	....	2	0	0	0	0	2	5	3	3	0	0	2	0	3.500	13.50	31	15.69	.455	38	.221	-2	1	-1.5
Total 2	0	0	....	3	0	0	0	0	3	5	3	3	0	0	3	0	2.667	9.00	46	10.78	.455	438	.254	-2	9	-2.0

• MOSKAU, Paul — Paul Richard Moskau b: 12/20/1953, St. Joseph, MO BR/TR, 6'2", 210 lbs. Deb: 6/21/1977

YEAR TM-L	W	L	PCT	G	GS	CG	SH	SV	IP	H	R	ER	HR	HB	BB	SO	RAT	ERA	ERA+	CERA	OAV	BH	AVG	PR+	WS	TPW
1977 Cin-N	6	6	.500	20	19	2	2	0	108	116	51	48	10	1	40	71	1.444	4.00	98	4.35	.278	7	.184	-2	6	0.0
1978 Cin-N	6	4	.600	26	25	2	1	1	145	139	65	64	17	3	57	88	1.352	3.97	89	4.04	.255	10	.204	-4	8	-0.1
1979 Cin-N	5	4	.556	21	15	1	0	0	106^1	107	53	46	9	0	51	58	1.486	3.89	96	4.23	.263	3	.081	-2	4	-0.4
1980 Cin-N	9	7	.563	33	19	2	1	2	152^2	147	69	68	13	1	41	94	1.231	4.01	89	3.30	.257	7	.159	-6	8	-0.6
1981 Cin-N	2	1	.667	27	1	0	0	2	54^2	54	31	30	4	1	32	32	1.573	4.94	72	4.43	.258	0	.000	-9	1	-1.0
1982 Pit-N	1	3	.250	13	5	0	0	0	35	43	21	17	7	0	8	15	1.457	4.37	85	5.45	.303	1	.091	-2	1	-0.3
1983 Chi-N	3	2	.600	8	8	0	0	0	32	44	25	24	7	0	14	16	1.813	6.75	56	7.49	.331	2	.182	-10	0	-1.0
Total 7	32	27	.542	148	92	7	4	5	633^2	650	315	297	67	6	243	374	1.409	4.22	87	4.23	.268	30	.153	-35	28	-3.5

• MOSOLF, Jim — James Frederick Mosolf b: 8/21/1905, Puyallup, WA d: 12/28/1979, Dallas, OR BL/TR, 5'10", 186 lbs. Deb: 9/9/1929 ♦

YEAR TM-L	W	L	PCT	G	GS	CG	SH	SV	IP	H	R	ER	HR	HB	BB	SO	RAT	ERA	ERA+	CERA	OAV	BH	AVG	PR+	WS	TPW
1930 Pit-N	0	0	....	1	0	0	0	0	0^1	1	1	1	0	0	0	1	3.000	27.00	18	14.52	.500	17	.333	-1	1	-0.2

• MOSS, Damian — Damian Joseph Moss b: 11/24/1976, Darlinghurst, Australia BR/TL, 6', 187 lbs. Deb: 4/26/2001

YEAR TM-L	W	L	PCT	G	GS	CG	SH	SV	IP	H	R	ER	HR	HB	BB	SO	RAT	ERA	ERA+	CERA	OAV	BH	AVG	PR+	WS	TPW
2001 Atl-N	0	0	....	5	1	0	0	0	9	3	3	3	1	0	9	8	1.333	3.00	147	2.61	.097	0	.000	1	1	0.2
2002* Atl-N	12	6	.667	33	29	0	0	0	179	140	80	68	20	6	89	111	1.279	3.42	120	3.51	.221	5	.100	10	12	0.9
2003 SF-N	9	7	.563	21	20	0	0	0	115	121	62	60	12	5	63	57	1.600	4.70	87	5.18	.273	7	.241	-10	5	-0.9
Bal-A	1	5	.167	10	9	0	0	0	50^2	63	40	35	12	6	29	22	1.816	6.22	71	7.87	.307	0	....	-10	0	-1.0
Total 3	22	18	.550	69	59	0	0	0	353^2	327	185	166	45	17	190	198	1.462	4.22	99	4.65	.249	12	.150	-8	18	-0.8

• MOSS, Mal — Charles Malcolm Moss b: 4/18/1905, Sullivan, IN d: 2/6/1983, Savannah, GA BR/TL, 6', 175 lbs. Deb: 4/29/1930

YEAR TM-L	W	L	PCT	G	GS	CG	SH	SV	IP	H	R	ER	HR	HB	BB	SO	RAT	ERA	ERA+	CERA	OAV	BH	AVG	PR+	WS	TPW
1930 Chi-N	0	0	....	12	1	0	0	1	18^2	18	13	13	0	0	14	4	1.714	6.27	78	4.18	.254	3	.273	-3	1	-0.2

• MOSS, Ray — Raymond Earl Moss b: 12/5/1901, Chattanooga, TN d: 8/9/1998, Chattanooga, TN BR/TR, 6'1", 185 lbs. Deb: 4/17/1926

YEAR TM-L	W	L	PCT	G	GS	CG	SH	SV	IP	H	R	ER	HR	HB	BB	SO	RAT	ERA	ERA+	CERA	OAV	BH	AVG	PR+	WS	TPW
1926 Bro-N	0	0	....	1	0	0	0	0	1	3	1	1	0	0	0	0	3.000	9.00	42	14.52	.600	0	.000	-1	0	-0.1
1927 Bro-N	1	0	1.000	1	1	0	0	0	8^1	11	3	3	0	0	1	1	1.440	3.24	122	4.17	.333	1	.333	1	1	0.1

YEAR	TM-L	W	L	PCT	G	GS	CG	SH	SV	IP	H	R	ER	HR	HB	BB	SO	RAT	ERA	ERA+	CERA	OAV	BH	AVG	PR+	WS	TPW
1928	Bro-N	0	3	.000	22	5	1	1	1	60^{1}	62	43	33	5	0	35	5	1.608	4.92	81	4.74	.279	8	.320	-6	1	-0.4
1929	Bro-N	11	6	.647	39	20	7	2	0	182	214	115	102	9	7	81	59	1.621	5.04	91	4.89	.296	5	.076	-4	9	-0.9
1930	Bro-N	9	6	.600	36	11	5	0	1	118^{1}	127	78	67	13	4	55	30	1.538	5.10	96	4.74	.270	6	.154	-5	6	-0.6
1931	Bro-N	0	0	....	1	0	0	0	0	1	1	0	0	0	0	1	0	2.000	0.00	....	5.17	.333	0	....	0	0	0.0
	Bos-N	1	3	.250	12	5	0	0	0	45	56	32	23	2	0	16	14	1.600	4.60	82	4.71	.306	2	.133	-4	0	-0.4
	Yr.	1	3	.250	13	5	0	0	0	46	57	32	23	2	0	17	14	1.609	4.50	84	4.72	.306	2	.133	-3	0	-0.4
Total	6	22	18	.550	112	42	13	3	2	416	474	272	229	29	11	189	109	1.594	4.95	90	4.81	.289	22	.148	-19	17	-2.2

• MOSSI, Don

Donald Louis "The Sphinx,Ears" Mossi b: 1/11/1929, St. Helena, CA BL/TL, 6'1", 195 lbs. Deb: 4/17/1954

YEAR	TM-L	W	L	PCT	G	GS	CG	SH	SV	IP	H	R	ER	HR	HB	BB	SO	RAT	ERA	ERA+	CERA	OAV	BH	AVG	PR+	WS	TPW
1954*	Cle-A	6	1	.857	40	5	2	0	7	93	56	22	20	5	1	39	55	1.022	1.94	190	1.81	.176	3	.158	17	13	1.7
1955	Cle-A	4	3	.571	57	1	0	0	9	81^{2}	81	28	22	4	1	18	69	1.212	2.42	164	2.93	.253	1	.111	14	10	1.4
1956	Cle-A	6	5	.545	48	3	0	0	11	87^{2}	79	38	35	6	1	33	59	1.278	3.59	117	3.16	.240	3	.150	6	9	0.6
1957	Cle-A★	11	10	.524	36	22	6	1	2	159	165	82	73	16	2	57	97	1.396	4.13	90	4.08	.265	12	.218	-5	9	-0.4
1958	Cle-A	7	8	.467	43	5	0	0	3	101^{2}	106	49	44	6	4	30	55	1.338	3.90	94	3.62	.269	3	.115	-3	5	-0.5
1959	Det-A	17	9	.654	34	30	15	3	0	228	210	92	85	20	3	49	125	1.136	3.36	121	2.93	.243	13	.169	18	18	1.8
1960	Det-A	9	8	.529	23	22	9	2	0	158^{1}	158	68	61	17	1	32	69	1.200	3.47	119	3.29	.258	5	.116	12	11	1.2
1961	Det-A	15	7	.682	35	34	12	1	1	240^{1}	237	97	79	29	0	47	137	1.182	2.96	139	3.35	.258	13	.165	**30**	20	**3.1**
1962	Det-A	11	13	.458	35	27	8	1	1	180^{1}	195	92	84	24	1	36	121	1.281	4.19	97	3.88	.270	9	.164	-1	10	0.1
1963	Det-A	7	7	.500	24	16	3	0	2	122^{2}	110	58	51	20	4	17	68	1.035	3.74	100	3.00	.236	8	.205	-0	8	0.2
1964	Chi-A	3	1	.750	34	0	0	0	7	40	37	16	13	9	1	7	36	1.100	2.93	118	3.58	.240	1	.167	1	4	0.1
1965	KC-A	5	8	.385	51	0	0	0	7	55^{1}	59	30	23	0	0	20	41	1.428	3.74	93	3.36	.278	0	.000	-1	3	-0.2
Total	12	101	80	.558	460	165	55	8	50	1548	1493	672	590	156	19	385	932	1.213	3.43	114	3.29	.252	71	.163	88	120	9.3

• MOSSOR, Earl

Earl Dalton Mossor b: 7/21/1925, Forbus, TN d: 12/29/1988, Batavia, OH BL/TR, 6'1", 175 lbs. Deb: 4/30/1951

YEAR	TM-L	W	L	PCT	G	GS	CG	SH	SV	IP	H	R	ER	HR	HB	BB	SO	RAT	ERA	ERA+	CERA	OAV	BH	AVG	PR+	WS	TPW
1951	Bro-N	0	0	....	3	0	0	0	0	1^{2}	2	6	6	1	0	7	1	5.400	32.40	12	29.36	.333	1	1.000	-5	0	-0.5

• MOTA, Danny

Daniel Avila Mota b: 10/9/1975, Seybol, Dominican Republic BR/TR, 6', 180 lbs. Deb: 9/15/2000

YEAR	TM-L	W	L	PCT	G	GS	CG	SH	SV	IP	H	R	ER	HR	HB	BB	SO	RAT	ERA	ERA+	CERA	OAV	BH	AVG	PR+	WS	TPW
2000	Min-A	0	0	....	4	0	0	0	0	5^{1}	10	5	5	1	0	1	3	2.063	8.44	61	8.84	.370	0	....	-2	0	-0.2

• MOTA, Guillermo

Guillermo Mota b: 7/25/1973, San Pedro de Macoris, Dominican Republic BR/TR, 6'6", 205 lbs. Deb: 5/2/1999

YEAR	TM-L	W	L	PCT	G	GS	CG	SH	SV	IP	H	R	ER	HR	HB	BB	SO	RAT	ERA	ERA+	CERA	OAV	BH	AVG	PR+	WS	TPW
1999	Mon-N	2	4	.333	51	0	0	0	0	55^{1}	54	24	18	5	2	25	27	1.428	2.93	153	4.10	.257	1	1.000	11	5	1.1
2000	Mon-N	1	1	.500	29	0	0	0	0	30	27	21	20	3	2	12	24	1.300	6.00	80	3.86	.245	0	.000	-4	1	-0.4
2001	Mon-N	1	3	.250	53	0	0	0	0	49^{2}	51	30	29	9	1	18	31	1.389	5.26	85	4.77	.271	1	.333	-3	2	-0.3
2002	LA-N	1	3	.250	43	0	0	0	0	60^{2}	45	30	28	4	2	27	49	1.187	4.15	92	2.57	.202	1	.250	-3	2	-0.2
2003	LA-N	6	3	.667	76	0	0	0	1	105	78	23	23	7	1	26	99	.990	1.97	204	2.01	.206	2	.222	22	14	2.3
Total	5	11	14	.440	252	0	0	0	1	300^{2}	255	128	118	28	8	108	230	1.207	3.53	120	3.15	.230	5	.278	23	24	2.5

• MOULDER, Glen

Glen Hubert Moulder b: 9/28/1917, Cleveland, OK d: 11/27/1994, Decatur, GA BR/TR, 6', 180 lbs. Deb: 4/28/1946

YEAR	TM-L	W	L	PCT	G	GS	CG	SH	SV	IP	H	R	ER	HR	HB	BB	SO	RAT	ERA	ERA+	CERA	OAV	BH	AVG	PR+	WS	TPW
1946	Bro-N	0	0	....	1	0	0	0	0	2	2	1	1	1	0	1	1	1.500	4.50	75	8.13	.286	0	....	-0	0	0.0
1947	StL-A	4	2	.667	32	2	0	0	2	73	78	37	31	4	0	43	23	1.658	3.82	102	4.76	.283	4	.235	1	5	0.1
1948	Chi-A	3	6	.333	33	9	0	0	2	85^{2}	108	67	61	8	1	54	26	1.891	6.41	66	6.42	.316	6	.300	-21	0	-1.9
Total	3	7	8	.467	66	11	0	0	4	160^{2}	188	105	93	13	1	98	50	1.780	5.21	79	5.69	.301	10	.270	-20	5	-1.8

• MOUNCE, Tony

Anthony David Mounce b: 2/8/1975, Sacramento, CA BL/TL, 6'2", 170 lbs. Deb: 6/13/2003

YEAR	TM-L	W	L	PCT	G	GS	CG	SH	SV	IP	H	R	ER	HR	HB	BB	SO	RAT	ERA	ERA+	CERA	OAV	BH	AVG	PR+	WS	TPW
2003	Tex-A	1	5	.167	11	11	0	0	0	50^{2}	65	42	40	9	5	25	30	1.776	7.11	70	7.34	.317	0	.000	-11	0	-1.1

• MOUNTAIN, Frank

Frank Henry Mountain b: 5/17/1860, Fort Edward, NY d: 11/19/1939, Schenectady, NY BR/TR, 5'11", 185 lbs. Deb: 7/19/1880 U ♦

YEAR	TM-L	W	L	PCT	G	GS	CG	SH	SV	IP	H	R	ER	HR	HB	BB	SO	RAT	ERA	ERA+	CERA	OAV	BH	AVG	PR+	WS	TPW
1880	Tro-N	1	1	.500	2	2	2	0	0	17	23	17	10	0	....	6	2	1.706	5.29	48	....	.308	2	.222	-5	0	-0.5
1881	Det-N	3	4	.429	7	7	7	0	0	60	80	63	35	2	....	18	13	1.633	5.25	56	....	.307	4	.160	-16	0	-1.5
1882	Wor-N	0	5	.000	5	5	5	0	0	42	47	30	14	0	....	11	5	1.381	3.00	103	....	.267	1	.063	2	0	-0.1
	Phi-a	2	6	.250	8	8	8	0	0	69	72	49	30	1	....	11	15	1.203	3.91	76	....	.251	12	.333	-8	5	-0.5
	Wor-N	2	11	.154	13	13	11	0	0	102	138	93	45	4	....	24	24	1.588	3.97	78	....	.306	19	.271	-5	3	-0.3
	Yr.	2	16	.111	18	18	16	0	0	144	185	123	59	4	....	35	29	1.528	3.69	84	....	.295	20	.233	-3	3	-0.4
1883	Col-a	26	33	.441	59	59	57	4	0	503	546	345	201	8	....	123	159	1.330	3.60	85	....	.259	60	.217	-31	18	-1.9
1884	Col-a	23	17	.575	42	41	40	5	**1**	360^{2}	289	163	98	7	11	78	156	1.018	2.45	124	....	.208	50	.238	14	36	2.4
1885	Pit-a	1	4	.200	5	5	5	0	0	46	56	31	22	1	2	24	7	1.739	4.30	75	....	.288	2	.100	-6	2	-0.6
1886	Pit-a	0	2	.000	2	2	2	0	0	16	22	21	14	0	5	14	2	2.250	7.88	43	....	.313	8	.145	-8	1	-1.0
Total	7	58	83	.411	143	142	137	9	1	1215^{2}	1273	812	469	23	18	309	383	1.301	3.47	88	....	.254	158	.220	-63	65	-4.1

• MOUNTJOY, Bill

William Henry "Medicine Bill" Mountjoy b: 12/11/1858, London, Canada d: 5/19/1894, London, Canada BL/TR, 5'6", 150 lbs. Deb: 9/29/1883

YEAR	TM-L	W	L	PCT	G	GS	CG	SH	SV	IP	H	R	ER	HR	HB	BB	SO	RAT	ERA	ERA+	CERA	OAV	BH	AVG	PR+	WS	TPW
1883	Cin-a	0	1	.000	1	1	1	0	0	8	9	4	2	0	....	2	3	1.375	2.25	144	....	.266	0	.000	1	0	0.0
1884	Cin-a	19	12	.613	33	33	32	3	0	289	274	148	94	5	16	43	96	1.097	2.93	114	....	.237	18	.151	8	21	0.5
1885	Cin-a	10	7	.588	17	17	17	1	0	153^{2}	149	89	54	5	7	52	50	1.308	3.16	103	....	.244	10	.167	0	11	0.1
	Bal-a	2	4	.333	6	6	6	1	0	53	72	47	32	1	4	13	15	1.604	5.43	60	....	.311	1	.056	-12	2	-1.0
	Yr.	12	11	.522	23	23	23	2	0	206^{2}	221	136	86	6	11	65	65	1.384	3.75	87	....	.262	11	.141	-12	13	-1.0
Total	3	31	24	.564	57	57	56	5	0	503^{2}	504	288	182	11	27	110	164	1.219	3.25	101	....	.248	29	.145	-3	34	-0.5

• MOYER, Ed

Charles Edward Moyer b: 8/15/1885, Andover, OH d: 11/18/1962, Jacksonville, FL Deb: 7/20/1910

YEAR	TM-L	W	L	PCT	G	GS	CG	SH	SV	IP	H	R	ER	HR	HB	BB	SO	RAT	ERA	ERA+	CERA	OAV	BH	AVG	PR+	WS	TPW
1910	Was-A	0	3	.000	6	3	2	0	0	25	22	15	9	1	3	13	3	1.400	3.24	77	4.04	.253	1	.125	-3	0	-0.3

• MOYER, Jamie

Jamie Moyer b: 11/18/1962, Sellersville, PA BL/TL, 6', 170 lbs. Deb: 6/16/1986

YEAR	TM-L	W	L	PCT	G	GS	CG	SH	SV	IP	H	R	ER	HR	HB	BB	SO	RAT	ERA	ERA+	CERA	OAV	BH	AVG	PR+	WS	TPW
1986	Chi-N	7	4	.636	16	16	1	1	0	87^{1}	107	52	49	10	3	42	45	1.706	5.05	80	6.13	.311	2	.091	-8	3	-0.9
1987	Chi-N	12	15	.444	35	33	1	0	0	201	210	127	114	28	5	97	147	1.527	5.10	84	4.96	.271	14	.230	-14	7	-1.0
1988	Chi-N	9	15	.375	34	30	3	1	0	202	212	84	78	20	4	55	121	1.322	3.48	104	3.89	.272	5	.083	7	12	0.6
1989	Tex-A	4	9	.308	15	15	1	0	0	76	84	51	41	10	2	33	44	1.539	4.86	82	5.20	.283	0	....	-7	1	-0.7
1990	Tex-A	2	6	.250	33	10	1	0	0	102^{1}	115	59	53	6	4	39	58	1.505	4.66	84	4.57	.290	0	....	-9	3	-0.9
1991	StL-N	0	5	.000	8	7	0	0	0	31^{1}	38	21	20	5	1	16	20	1.723	5.74	65	6.58	.319	0	.000	-7	0	-0.8
1993	Bal-A	12	9	.571	25	25	3	1	0	152	154	63	58	11	6	38	90	1.263	3.43	130	3.58	.265	0	....	15	13	1.5
1994	Bal-A	5	7	.417	23	23	0	0	0	149	158	81	79	23	2	38	87	1.315	4.77	105	4.24	.271	0	....	2	8	0.2
1995	Bal-A	8	6	.571	27	18	0	0	0	115^{2}	117	70	67	18	3	30	65	1.271	5.21	91	4.11	.265	0	....	-7	5	-0.7
1996	Bos-A	7	1	.875	23	10	0	0	0	90	111	50	45	14	1	27	50	1.533	4.50	113	5.37	.300	0	....	8	6	0.7
	Sea-A	6	2	.750	11	11	0	0	0	70^{2}	66	36	26	9	1	19	29	1.203	3.31	150	3.31	.243	0	....	13	5	1.2
	Yr.	13	3	.813	34	21	0	0	0	160^{2}	177	86	71	23	2	46	79	1.388	3.98	127	4.46	.276	0	....	20	11	1.9
1997*	Sea-A	17	5	.773	30	30	2	0	0	188^{2}	187	82	81	21	7	43	113	1.219	3.86	116	3.56	.256	1	.333	15	14	1.5
1998	Sea-A	15	9	.625	34	34	4	3	0	234^{1}	234	99	92	23	10	42	158	1.178	3.53	131	3.34	.256	0	.000	32	18	3.0
1999	Sea-A	14	8	.636	32	32	4	0	0	228	235	108	98	23	9	48	137	1.241	3.87	129	3.71	.267	1	.500	29	18	2.7
2000	Sea-A	13	10	.565	26	26	0	0	0	154	173	103	94	22	3	53	98	1.468	5.49	83	4.91	.281	0	.000	-18	5	-1.6
2001*	Sea-A	20	6	.769	33	33	1	0	0	209^{2}	187	84	80	24	10	44	119	1.102	3.43	121	3.03	.239	0	.000	11	15	1.0
2002	Sea-A	13	8	.619	34	34	4	2	0	230^{2}	198	89	85	28	9	50	147	1.075	3.32	127	2.89	.230	1	.200	25	16	2.4
2003	Sea-A★	21	7	.750	33	33	1	0	0	215	199	83	78	19	8	66	129	1.233	3.27	132	3.37	.246	2	.400	19	18	1.9
Total	17	185	132	.584	472	420	26	8	0	2737^{2}	2785	1342	1238	314	88	780	1657	1.302	4.07	108	3.96	.264	26	.152	106	167	10.1

• MROZINSKI, Ron

Ronald Frank Mrozinski b: 9/16/1930, White Haven, PA BR/TL, 5'11", 160 lbs. Deb: 6/20/1954

YEAR	TM-L	W	L	PCT	G	GS	CG	SH	SV	IP	H	R	ER	HR	HB	BB	SO	RAT	ERA	ERA+	CERA	OAV	BH	AVG	PR+	WS	TPW
1954	Phi-N	1	1	.500	15	4	1	0	0	48	49	26	24	10	0	25	26	1.542	4.50	90	5.34	.261	1	.083	-3	2	-0.4
1955	Phi-N	0	2	.000	22	1	0	0	1	34^{1}	38	26	25	2	4	19	18	1.660	6.55	61	5.50	.299	0	.000	-10	0	-1.1
Total	2	1	3	.250	37	5	1	0	1	82^{1}	87	52	49	12	4	44	44	1.591	5.36	75	5.41	.276	1	.063	-13	2	-1.4

• MUDROCK, Phil

Philip Ray Mudrock b: 1/12/1937, Louisville, CO BR/TR, 6'1", 190 lbs. Deb: 4/19/1963

YEAR	TM-L	W	L	PCT	G	GS	CG	SH	SV	IP	H	R	ER	HR	HB	BB	SO	RAT	ERA	ERA+	CERA	OAV	BH	AVG	PR+	WS	TPW
1963	Chi-N	0	0	....	1	0	0	0	0	1	2	1	1	0	0	0	0	2.000	9.00	39	7.48	.400	0	....	-1	0	-0.1

• MUELLER, Gordie Joseph Gordon Mueller b: 12/10/1922, Baltimore, MD BR/TR, 6'4", 200 lbs. Deb: 4/19/1950

YEAR	TM-L	W	L	PCT	G	GS	CG	SH	SV	IP	H	R	ER	HR	HB	BB	SO	RAT	ERA	ERA+	CERA	OAV	BH	AVG	PR+	WS	TPW
1950	Bos-A	0	0	....	8	0	0	0	0	7	11	8	8	1	0	13	1	3.429	10.29	48	13.77	.344	0	.000	-4	0	-0.4

• MUELLER, Les Leslie Clyde Mueller b: 3/4/1919, Belleville, IL BR/TR, 6'3", 190 lbs. Deb: 8/15/1941

YEAR	TM-L	W	L	PCT	G	GS	CG	SH	SV	IP	H	R	ER	HR	HB	BB	SO	RAT	ERA	ERA+	CERA	OAV	BH	AVG	PR+	WS	TPW
1941	Det-A	0	0	....	4	0	0	0	0	13	9	9	7	1	0	10	8	1.462	4.85	94	3.42	.205	0	.000	-0	0	0.0
1945*	Det-A	6	8	.429	26	18	6	2	1	134^{2}	117	63	55	8	2	58	42	1.300	3.68	96	3.15	.234	8	.182	-3	7	-0.3
Total	2	6	8	.429	30	18	6	2	1	147^{2}	126	72	62	9	2	68	50	1.314	3.78	95	3.17	.231	8	.170	-3	7	-0.3

• MUELLER, Willie Willard Lawrence Mueller b: 8/30/1956, West Bend, WI BR/TR, 6'4", 220 lbs. Deb: 8/12/1978

YEAR	TM-L	W	L	PCT	G	GS	CG	SH	SV	IP	H	R	ER	HR	HB	BB	SO	RAT	ERA	ERA+	CERA	OAV	BH	AVG	PR+	WS	TPW
1978	Mil-A	1	0	1.000	5	0	0	0	0	12^{2}	16	11	9	1	0	6	6	1.737	6.39	59	5.51	.291	0	....	-4	0	-0.4
1981	Mil-A	0	0	....	1	0	0	0	0	2	4	1	1	0	0	0	1	2.000	4.50	76	7.48	.400	0	....	-0	0	0.0
Total	2	1	0	1.000	6	0	0	0	0	14^{2}	20	12	10	1	0	6	7	1.773	6.14	61	5.78	.308	0	....	-4	0	-0.4

• MUFFETT, Billy Billy Arnold "Muff" Muffett b: 9/21/1930, Hammond, IN BR/TR, 6'1", 198 lbs. Deb: 8/3/1957 C

YEAR	TM-L	W	L	PCT	G	GS	CG	SH	SV	IP	H	R	ER	HR	HB	BB	SO	RAT	ERA	ERA+	CERA	OAV	BH	AVG	PR+	WS	TPW
1957	StL-N	3	2	.600	23	0	0	0	8	44	35	11	11	1	0	13	21	1.091	2.25	176	2.07	.222	0	.000	8	7	0.8
1958	StL-N	4	6	.400	35	6	1	0	5	84	107	52	46	11	5	42	41	1.774	4.93	84	6.43	.316	4	.200	-8	3	-0.7
1959	SF-N	0	0	....	5	0	0	0	0	6^{2}	11	6	4	2	0	3	3	2.100	5.40	71	10.59	.407	0	....	-1	0	-0.1
1960	Bos-A	6	4	.600	23	14	4	1	0	125	116	53	45	6	5	36	75	1.216	3.24	125	2.98	.242	11	.268	14	11	1.7
1961	Bos-A	3	11	.214	38	11	2	0	2	112^{2}	130	87	71	18	2	36	47	1.473	5.67	74	5.04	.291	5	.217	-19	1	-1.6
1962	Bos-A	0	0	....	1	1	0	0	0	4	8	4	4	0	0	2	1	2.500	9.00	46	10.75	.471	0	.000	-2	0	-0.2
Total	6	16	23	.410	125	32	7	1	15	376^{1}	407	213	181	38	12	132	188	1.432	4.33	95	4.48	.277	20	.217	-6	22	-0.2

• MUICH, Joe Ignatius Andrew Muich b: 11/23/1903, St. Louis, MO d: 7/2/1993, St. Louis, MO BR/TR, 6'2", 175 lbs. Deb: 9/4/1924

YEAR	TM-L	W	L	PCT	G	GS	CG	SH	SV	IP	H	R	ER	HR	HB	BB	SO	RAT	ERA	ERA+	CERA	OAV	BH	AVG	PR+	WS	TPW
1924	Bos-N	0	0	....	3	0	0	0	0	9	19	12	11	1	0	5	1	2.667	11.00	35	11.94	.432	0	.000	-7	0	-0.8

• MUIR, Joe Joseph Allen Muir b: 11/26/1922, Oriole, MD d: 6/25/1980, Baltimore, MD BL/TL, 6'1", 172 lbs. Deb: 4/21/1951

YEAR	TM-L	W	L	PCT	G	GS	CG	SH	SV	IP	H	R	ER	HR	HB	BB	SO	RAT	ERA	ERA+	CERA	OAV	BH	AVG	PR+	WS	TPW
1951	Pit-N	0	2	.000	9	1	0	0	0	16^{1}	11	6	5	2	0	7	5	1.102	2.76	153	2.34	.180	0	.000	3	1	0.3
1952	Pit-N	2	3	.400	12	5	1	0	0	35^{2}	42	28	25	3	0	18	17	1.682	6.31	63	5.24	.288	1	.111	-9	0	-0.9
Total	2	2	5	.286	21	6	1	0	0	52	53	34	30	5	0	25	22	1.500	5.19	78	4.33	.256	1	.100	-6	1	-0.7

• MULCAHY, Hugh Hugh Noyes "Losing Pitcher" Mulcahy b: 9/9/1913, Brighton, MA d: 10/19/2001, Aliquippa, PA BR/TR, 6'2", 190 lbs. Deb: 7/24/1935 C

YEAR	TM-L	W	L	PCT	G	GS	CG	SH	SV	IP	H	R	ER	HR	HB	BB	SO	RAT	ERA	ERA+	CERA	OAV	BH	AVG	PR+	WS	TPW
1935	Phi-N	1	5	.167	18	5	0	0	1	52^{2}	62	35	28	2	5	25	11	1.652	4.78	95	5.09	.295	0	.000	-1	2	-0.3
1936	Phi-N	1	1	.500	3	2	2	0	0	22^{2}	20	8	8	0	2	12	2	1.412	3.18	143	3.35	.238	2	.250	4	2	0.4
1937	Phi-N	8	18	.308	**56**	25	9	1	3	215^{2}	256	147	123	17	7	97	54	**1.637**	5.13	84	5.22	.296	11	.151	-16	7	-1.8
1938	Phi-N	10	20	.333	46	34	15	0	1	267^{1}	294	162	137	14	6	120	90	1.549	4.61	87	4.41	.278	16	.170	-10	9	-1.2
1939	Phi-N	9	16	.360	38	31	14	1	4	225^{2}	246	144	125	19	11	93	59	1.502	4.99	79	4.58	.282	12	.158	-26	7	-2.8
1940	Phi-N★	13	22	.371	36	36	21	3	0	280	283	141	112	12	3	91	82	1.336	3.60	108	3.42	.261	19	.202	9	19	1.0
1945	Phi-N	1	3	.250	5	4	1	0	0	28^{1}	33	17	12	1	0	9	2	1.482	3.81	100	4.09	.295	0	.000	1	1	0.0
1946	Phi-N	2	4	.333	16	5	1	0	0	62^{2}	69	34	31	3	5	33	12	1.628	4.45	77	4.98	.295	3	.188	-7	2	-0.6
1947	Pit-N	0	0	....	2	1	0	0	0	6^{2}	8	7	3	1	0	7	2	2.250	4.05	104	9.04	.333	1	.333	0	0	0.0
Total	9	45	89	.336	220	143	63	5	9	1161^{2}	1271	695	579	69	39	487	314	1.513	4.49	90	4.42	.280	64	.165	-45	49	-5.2

• MULDER, Mark Mark Alan Mulder b: 8/5/1977, South Holland, IL BL/TL, 6'6", 200 lbs. Deb: 4/18/2000

YEAR	TM-L	W	L	PCT	G	GS	CG	SH	SV	IP	H	R	ER	HR	HB	BB	SO	RAT	ERA	ERA+	CERA	OAV	BH	AVG	PR+	WS	TPW
2000	Oak-A	9	10	.474	27	27	0	0	0	154	191	106	93	22	4	69	88	1.688	5.44	87	6.14	.308	0	.000	-10	5	-0.9
2001*	Oak-A	**21**	8	.724	34	34	6	**4**	0	229^{1}	214	92	88	16	5	51	153	1.156	3.45	128	2.95	.249	1	.200	24	18	2.3
2002*	Oak-A	19	7	.731	30	30	2	1	0	207^{1}	182	88	80	21	11	55	159	1.143	3.47	127	3.06	.232	0	.000	23	18	2.1
2003	Oak-A★	15	9	.625	26	26	**9**	**2**	0	186^{2}	180	66	65	15	2	40	128	1.179	3.13	144	3.17	.259	0	.000	29	17	2.7
Total	4	64	34	.653	117	117	17	7	0	777^{1}	767	352	326	74	22	215	528	1.263	3.77	120	3.66	.259	1	.056	65	58	6.2

• MULHOLLAND, Terry Terence John Mulholland b: 3/9/1963, Uniontown, PA BR/TL, 6'3", 206 lbs. Deb: 6/8/1986

YEAR	TM-L	W	L	PCT	G	GS	CG	SH	SV	IP	H	R	ER	HR	HB	BB	SO	RAT	ERA	ERA+	CERA	OAV	BH	AVG	PR+	WS	TPW
1986	SF-N	1	7	.125	15	10	0	0	0	54^{2}	51	33	30	3	1	35	27	1.573	4.94	71	4.31	.251	1	.053	-9	0	-1.1
1988	SF-N	2	1	.667	9	6	2	1	0	46	50	20	19	3	1	7	18	1.239	3.72	88	3.46	.281	0	.000	-2	2	-0.3
1989	SF-N	0	0	....	5	1	0	0	0	11	15	5	5	0	0	4	6	1.727	4.09	82	5.23	.319	0	.000	-1	0	-0.1
	Phi-N	4	7	.364	20	17	2	1	0	104^{1}	122	61	58	8	4	32	60	1.476	5.00	71	4.58	.292	2	.059	-16	1	-2.0
	Yr.	4	7	.364	25	18	2	1	0	115^{1}	137	66	63	8	4	36	66	1.500	4.92	72	4.64	.295	2	.056	-17	1	-2.1
1990	Phi-N	9	10	.474	33	26	6	1	0	180^{2}	172	78	67	15	2	42	75	1.185	3.34	114	3.04	.252	6	.097	7	11	0.5
1991	Phi-N	16	13	.552	34	34	8	3	0	232	231	100	93	15	3	49	142	1.207	3.61	102	3.15	.260	7	.088	3	14	-0.1
1992	Phi-N	13	11	.542	32	32	**12**	2	0	229	227	101	97	14	3	46	125	1.192	3.81	91	3.07	.261	8	.096	-7	9	-1.0
1993*	Phi-N★	12	9	.571	29	28	7	2	0	191	177	80	69	20	3	40	116	1.136	3.25	122	2.99	.241	4	.065	17	13	1.2
1994	NY-A	6	7	.462	24	19	2	0	0	120^{2}	150	94	87	24	3	37	72	1.550	6.49	70	5.92	.303	0	....	-28	1	-2.6
1995	SF-N	5	13	.278	29	24	2	0	0	149	190	112	96	25	4	38	65	1.530	5.80	70	5.67	.313	5	.102	-30	0	-3.0
1996	Phi-N	8	7	.533	21	21	3	0	0	133^{1}	157	74	69	17	3	21	52	1.335	4.66	93	4.36	.293	8	.178	-6	5	-0.5
	Sea-A	5	4	.556	12	12	0	0	0	69^{1}	75	38	36	5	2	28	34	1.486	4.67	106	4.49	.286	0	....	2	4	0.2
1997	Chi-N	6	12	.333	25	25	1	0	0	157	162	79	71	20	9	45	74	1.318	4.07	106	4.24	.271	8	.163	4	8	0.4
	SF-N	0	1	.000	15	2	0	0	0	29^{2}	28	21	17	4	2	6	25	1.146	5.16	78	3.34	.248	1	.167	-4	0	-0.3
	Yr.	6	13	.316	40	27	1	0	0	186^{2}	190	100	88	24	11	51	99	1.291	4.24	100	4.10	.267	9	.164	1	8	0.1
1998*	Chi-N	6	5	.545	70	6	0	0	3	112	100	49	36	7	4	39	72	1.241	2.89	152	3.04	.235	5	.294	21	12	2.3
1999	Chi-N	6	6	.500	26	16	0	0	0	110	137	71	63	16	1	32	44	1.536	5.15	88	5.42	.309	3	.094	-6	5	-0.8
	*Atl-N	4	2	.667	16	8	0	0	1	60^{1}	64	24	20	5	0	13	39	1.276	2.98	151	3.55	.274	2	.125	11	6	1.0
	Yr.	10	8	.556	42	24	0	0	1	170^{1}	201	95	83	21	1	45	83	1.444	4.39	103	4.76	.297	5	.104	4	11	0.2
2000*	Atl-N	9	9	.500	54	20	1	0	1	156^{2}	198	96	89	24	4	41	78	1.526	5.11	90	5.43	.308	9	.250	-8	7	-0.6
2001	Pit-N	0	0	....	22	1	0	0	0	36^{1}	38	15	15	5	1	10	17	1.321	3.72	121	4.32	.277	0	.000	3	3	0.3
	LA-N	1	1	.500	19	3	0	0	0	29^{1}	40	20	19	7	1	7	25	1.602	5.83	69	6.67	.315	0	.000	-6	0	-0.6
	Yr.	1	1	.500	41	4	0	0	0	65^{2}	78	35	34	12	2	17	42	1.447	4.66	90	5.37	.295	0	.000	-3	3	-0.3
2002	LA-N	0	0	....	21	0	0	0	0	32	45	29	26	10	2	7	17	1.625	7.31	52	7.68	.331	0	.000	-13	0	-1.3
	Cle-A	3	2	.600	16	3	0	0	0	47	56	27	24	5	4	14	21	1.489	4.60	96	5.05	.301	0	....	-1	3	0.0
2003	Cle-A	3	4	.429	45	3	0	0	0	99	117	60	54	17	6	37	42	1.556	4.91	90	5.75	.295	0	.000	-7	3	-0.7
Total	17	119	131	.476	592	317	46	10	5	2390^{1}	2602	1287	1160	269	63	630	1246	1.352	4.37	93	4.23	.278	69	.112	-77	107	-9.2

• MULLANE, Tony Anthony John "Count,The Apollo Of The Box" Mullane
b: 1/30/1859, Cork, Ireland d: 4/25/1944, Chicago, IL BB/TR, 5'10.5", 165 lbs. Deb: 8/27/1881 U ♦

YEAR	TM-L	W	L	PCT	G	GS	CG	SH	SV	IP	H	R	ER	HR	HB	BB	SO	RAT	ERA	ERA+	CERA	OAV	BH	AVG	PR+	WS	TPW
1881	Det-N	1	4	.200	5	5	5	0	0	44	55	42	24	2	....	17	7	1.636	4.91	59	....	.293	5	.263	-10	0	-0.9
1882	Lou-a	30	24	.556	**55**	**55**	51	5	0	460^{1}	418	212	96	4	....	78	**170**	1.077	1.88	132	....	.226	78	.257	27	36	3.6
1883	StL-a	35	15	.700	53	49	49	3	**1**	460^{2}	372	222	112	3	....	74	191	.968	2.19	**159**	....	.207	69	.225	35	55	3.0
1884	Tol-a	36	26	.581	67	65	64	**7**	0	567	481	276	159	5	32	89	325	1.005	2.52	135	....	.217	97	.276	51	58	6.4
1886	Cin-a	33	27	.550	63	56	55	1	0	529^{2}	501	315	218	11	18	166	250	1.259	3.70	95	....	.238	73	.225	-15	34	-1.6
1887	Cin-a	31	17	.646	48	48	47	**6**	0	416^{1}	535	234	150	11	32	121	97	1.285	3.24	134	....	.301	60	.279	33	46	2.9
1888	Cin-a	26	16	.619	44	42	41	4	**1**	380^{1}	341	194	120	9	29	75	186	1.094	2.84	112	....	.231	44	.251	4	33	0.9
1889	Cin-a	11	9	.550	33	24	17	0	**5**	220	218	133	73	4	13	89	112	1.395	2.99	131	....	.251	58	.296	20	24	2.5
1890	Cin-N	12	10	.545	25	21	21	0	1	209	175	101	52	7	8	96	91	1.297	2.24	158	....	.221	79	.276	27	28	3.3
1891	Cin-N	23	26	.469	51	47	42	1	0	426^{1}	390	250	153	15	18	187	124	1.353	3.23	104	....	.234	31	.148	4	24	-0.3
1892	Cin-N	21	13	.618	37	34	30	3	1	295	222	131	85	12	12	127	109	1.183	2.59	126	2.55	**.201**	20	.169	16	26	1.4
1893	Cin-N	6	6	.500	15	13	11	0	1	122^{1}	130	84	60	4	9	65	24	1.594	4.41	108	4.57	.264	15	.288	3	10	0.5
	Bal-N	12	16	.429	34	26	23	0	1	244^{2}	277	177	121	4	7	124	71	1.639	4.45	106	4.58	.277	26	.228	13	17	0.8
	Yr.	18	22	.450	49	39	34	0	**2**	367	407	261	181	8	16	189	95	1.624	4.44	107	4.58	.273	41	.247	16	27	1.3
1894	Bal-N	6	9	.400	21	15	9	0	4	122^{2}	155	117	86	4	7	90	43	1.997	6.31	86	6.44	.305	21	.396	-15	7	-0.7
	Cle-N	1	2	.333	4	4	3	0	0	33	46	35	28	3	0	10	3	1.697	7.64	71	5.85	.326	1	.077	-8	1	-0.7
	Yr.	7	11	.389	25	19	12	0	**4**	155^{2}	201	152	114	7	7	100	46	1.934	6.59	83	6.32	.310	22	.333	-23	8	-1.4
Total	13	284	220	.563	555	504	468	30	15	4531^{1}	4316	2523	1537	98	185	1408	1803	1.237	3.05	119	0.75	.240	677	.247	186	399	20.9

YEAR TM-L	W	L	PCT	G	GS	CG	SH	SV	IP	H	R	ER	HR	HB	BB	SO	RAT	ERA	ERA+	CERA	OAV	BH	AVG	PR+	WS	TPW
• MULLEN, Scott	Kenneth Scott Mullen b: 1/17/1975, San Benito, TX BR/TL, 6'2", 190 lbs. Deb: 8/31/2000																									
2000 KC-A	0	0	....	11	0	0	0	0	10^1	10	5	5	2	0	3	7	1.258	4.35	118	4.00	.244	0	....	1	1	0.1
2001 KC-A	0	0	....	17	0	0	0	0	10	13	6	5	0	0	9	3	2.200	4.50	109	6.89	.310	0	....	0	0	0.0
2002 KC-A	4	5	.444	44	0	0	0	0	40	40	16	14	5	2	13	21	1.325	3.15	159	4.08	.267	0	....	8	4	0.8
2003 KC-A	0	0	....	2	0	0	0	0	4^1	11	8	8	2	0	5	3	3.692	16.62	31	22.33	.458	0	....	-6	0	-0.5
LA-N	0	0	....	1	1	0	0	0	3	2	3	3	0	1	5	1	2.333	9.00	45	7.34	.200	0	.000	-2	0	-0.2
Total 4	**4**	**5**	**.444**	**75**	**1**	**0**	**0**	**0**	**67^2**	**76**	**38**	**35**	**9**	**3**	**35**	**35**	**1.640**	**4.66**	**106**	**5.80**	**.285**	**0**	**.000**	**2**	**5**	**0.2**
• MULLIGAN, Dick	Richard Charles Mulligan b: 3/18/1918, Swoyersville, PA d: 12/15/1992, Victoria, TX BL/TL, 6', 167 lbs. Deb: 9/24/1941																									
1941 Was-A	0	1	.000	1	1	1	0	0	9	11	5	5	0	0	2	2	1.444	5.00	81	3.85	.306	0	.000	-1	0	-0.1
1946 Phi-N	2	2	.500	19	5	1	0	1	54^2	61	32	29	0	4	27	16	1.610	4.77	72	4.50	.289	0	.000	-8	1	-0.9
Bos-N	1	0	1.000	4	0	0	0	0	15^1	6	4	4	1	0	9	4	.978	2.35	146	1.53	.122	0	.000	2	1	0.2
Yr.	3	2	.600	23	5	1	0	1	70	67	36	33	1	4	36	20	1.471	4.24	81	3.85	.258	0	.000	-6	2	-0.7
1947 Bos-N	0	0	....	1	0	0	0	0	2	4	2	2	0	0	1	1	2.500	9.00	43	9.55	.400	0	....	-1	0	-0.1
Total 3	**3**	**3**	**.500**	**25**	**6**	**2**	**0**	**1**	**81**	**82**	**43**	**40**	**1**	**4**	**39**	**23**	**1.494**	**4.44**	**79**	**3.99**	**.268**	**0**	**.000**	**-8**	**2**	**-0.9**
• MULLIGAN, Joe	Joseph Ignatius "Big Joe" Mulligan b: 7/31/1913, Weymouth, MA d: 6/5/1986, West Roxbury, MA BR/TR, 6'4", 210 lbs. Deb: 6/28/1934																									
1934 Bos-A	1	0	1.000	14	2	1	0	0	44^2	46	21	18	1	2	27	13	1.634	3.63	132	4.60	.279	0	.000	6	3	0.4
• MULLIN, George	George Joseph "Wabash George" Mullin b: 7/4/1880, Toledo, OH d: 1/7/1944, Wabash, IN BR/TR, 5'11", 188 lbs. Deb: 5/4/1902																									
1902 Det-A	13	16	.448	35	30	25	0	0	260	282	155	106	4	7	95	78	1.450	3.67	99	3.75	.277	39	.325	-4	16	0.6
1903 Det-A	19	15	.559	41	36	31	6	**2**	320^2	284	128	80	4	8	106	170	1.216	2.25	130	2.65	.237	35	.278	24	23	3.5
1904 Det-A	17	23	.425	45	44	42	7	0	382^1	345	154	102	1	10	131	161	1.245	2.40	106	2.70	.242	45	.290	2	25	1.7
1905 Det-A	21	21	.500	44	**41**	**35**	1	0	**347^2**	303	149	97	4	8	138	168	1.268	2.51	109	2.73	.237	35	.259	4	26	1.3
1906 Det-A	21	18	.538	40	40	35	2	0	330	315	139	102	3	15	108	123	1.282	2.78	99	2.98	.255	32	.225	-1	26	0.3
1907* Det-A	20	20	.500	46	42	35	5	3	357^1	346	153	103	1	15	106	146	1.265	2.59	100	2.96	.257	34	.217	1	21	0.7
1908* Det-A	17	13	.567	39	30	26	1	0	290^2	301	142	100	1	7	71	121	1.280	3.10	78	3.02	.271	32	.256	-17	14	-1.1
1909* Det-A	**29**	8	.784	40	35	29	3	1	303^2	258	96	75	1	8	78	124	1.106	2.22	113	2.18	.234	27	.214	10	28	1.8
1910 Det-A	21	12	.636	38	32	27	5	0	289	260	125	92	7	14	102	98	1.253	2.87	92	3.04	.254	33	.256	-7	19	-0.1
1911 Det-A	18	10	.643	30	29	25	2	0	234^1	245	99	80	7	12	61	87	1.306	3.07	112	3.43	.276	28	.286	13	23	2.0
1912 Det-A	12	17	.414	30	29	22	2	0	226	214	112	89	3	9	92	88	1.354	3.54	93	3.25	.255	25	.278	-5	14	0.4
1913 Det-A	1	6	.143	7	7	4	0	0	52^1	53	28	16	1	2	18	16	1.357	2.75	106	3.36	.268	7	.350	2	3	0.6
Was-A	3	5	.375	11	9	3	0	0	57^1	69	34	32	1	5	25	14	1.640	5.02	59	4.57	.283	4	.190	-14	0	-1.5
Yr.	4	11	.267	18	16	7	0	0	109^2	122	62	48	2	7	43	30	1.505	3.94	75	3.99	.276	11	.268	-12	3	-0.9
1914 Ind-F	14	10	.583	36	20	11	1	2	203	202	100	61	4	10	91	74	1.443	2.70	128	3.66	.261	24	.312	15	17	2.5
1915 New-F	2	2	.500	5	4	3	0	0	32^1	41	22	21	0	0	16	14	1.763	5.85	49	5.16	.318	1	.100	-11	0	-1.2
Total 14	**228**	**196**	**.538**	**487**	**428**	**353**	**35**	**8**	**3686^2**	**3518**	**1636**	**1156**	**42**	**130**	**1238**	**1482**	**1.290**	**2.82**	**101**	**3.03**	**.255**	**401**	**.262**	**11**	**255**	**11.6**
• MULLINS, Greg	Gregory Eugene Mullins b: 12/13/1971, Palatka, FL BL/TL, 5'10" Deb: 9/18/1998																									
1998 Mil-N	0	0	....	2	0	0	0	0	1	1	0	0	0	1	0	1	1.000	0.00	....	5.48	.250	0	....	0	0	0.0
• MULRENAN, Dominic	Dominic Joseph Mulrenan b: 12/18/1893, Woburn, MA d: 7/27/1964, Melrose, MA BR/TR, 5'11", 170 lbs. Deb: 4/24/1921																									
1921 Chi-A	2	8	.200	12	10	3	0	0	56	84	52	45	2	2	36	10	2.143	7.23	59	7.65	.359	3	.150	-19	0	-1.9
• MULRONEY, Frank	Francis Joseph Mulroney b: 4/8/1903, Mallard, IA d: 11/11/1985, Aberdeen, WA BR/TR, 6', 170 lbs. Deb: 4/15/1930																									
1930 Bos-A	0	1	.000	2	0	0	0	0	3	3	2	1	0	0	0	2	1.000	3.00	153	1.95	.273	0	....	1	0	0.0
• MUNCRIEF, Bob	Robert Cleveland Muncrief b: 1/28/1916, Madill, OK d: 2/6/1996, Duncanville, TX BR/TR, 6'2", 190 lbs. Deb: 9/30/1937																									
1937 StL-A	0	0	....	1	1	0	0	0	2	3	2	1	1	0	2	0	2.500	4.50	107	12.08	.300	0	....	0	0	0.0
1939 StL-A	0	0	....	2	0	0	0	0	3	7	5	5	1	0	3	1	3.333	15.00	32	18.92	.500	0	....	-3	0	-0.3
1941 StL-A	13	9	.591	36	24	12	2	1	214^1	221	95	87	18	5	53	67	1.278	3.65	118	3.59	.266	18	.237	18	18	2.0
1942 StL-A	6	8	.429	24	18	7	1	0	134^1	149	61	58	11	0	31	39	1.340	3.89	95	3.83	.280	5	.111	-1	7	-0.3
1943 StL-A	13	12	.520	35	27	12	3	1	205	211	80	64	13	2	48	80	1.263	2.81	118	3.34	.264	10	.152	15	13	1.4
1944* StL-A★	13	8	.619	33	27	12	3	1	219^1	216	83	75	11	3	50	88	1.213	3.08	117	3.02	.258	18	.231	17	17	1.9
1945 StL-A	13	4	.765	27	15	10	0	1	145^2	132	51	44	8	2	44	54	1.208	2.72	129	2.86	.239	3	.067	13	14	1.0
1946 StL-A	3	12	.200	29	14	4	1	0	115^1	149	75	64	6	0	31	49	1.561	4.99	75	4.79	.314	1	.031	-16	0	-2.0
1947 StL-A	8	14	.364	31	23	7	0	0	176^1	210	108	96	14	2	51	74	1.480	4.90	79	4.56	.299	6	.105	-18	4	-2.2
1948* Cle-A	5	4	.556	21	9	1	1	0	72^1	76	37	32	8	0	31	24	1.479	3.98	102	4.57	.279	2	.111	-1	3	-0.2
1949 Pit-N	1	5	.167	13	4	1	0	3	35^2	44	27	25	8	0	13	11	1.598	6.31	67	6.21	.310	1	.143	-8	0	-0.8
Chi-N	5	6	.455	34	3	1	0	2	75	80	42	38	9	1	31	36	1.480	4.56	88	4.59	.276	4	.286	-3	5	-0.1
Yr.	6	11	.353	47	7	2	0	5	110^2	124	69	63	17	1	44	47	1.518	5.12	80	5.12	.287	5	.238	-11	5	-1.0
1951 NY-A	0	0	....	2	0	0	0	0	3	5	3	3	0	0	4	2	3.000	9.00	43	11.33	.417	0	....	-2	0	-0.2
Total 12	**80**	**82**	**.494**	**288**	**165**	**67**	**11**	**9**	**1401^1**	**1503**	**669**	**592**	**108**	**15**	**392**	**525**	**1.352**	**3.80**	**100**	**3.86**	**.275**	**68**	**.155**	**11**	**81**	**0.2**
• MUNGER, Red	George David Munger b: 10/4/1918, Houston, TX d: 7/23/1996, Houston, TX BR/TR, 6'2", 200 lbs. Deb: 5/1/1943																									
1943 StL-N	9	5	.643	32	9	5	0	2	93^1	101	47	41	2	0	42	45	1.532	3.95	85	4.05	.281	6	.214	-8	5	-0.8
1944 StL-N★	11	3	.786	21	12	7	2	2	121	92	23	18	2	2	41	55	1.099	1.34	263	2.12	.212	5	.114	27	15	2.4
1946* StL-N	2	2	.500	10	7	2	0	1	48^2	47	19	18	0	0	12	28	1.212	3.33	104	2.63	.255	4	.250	-0	4	0.1
1947 StL-N★	16	5	.762	40	31	13	6	3	224^1	218	94	84	12	2	76	123	1.311	3.37	123	3.37	.255	15	.185	19	18	1.9
1948 StL-N	10	11	.476	39	25	7	2	0	166	179	91	83	13	1	74	72	1.524	4.50	91	4.43	.272	8	.160	-7	7	-0.7
1949 StL-N★	15	8	.652	35	28	12	2	2	188^1	179	86	81	13	2	87	82	1.412	3.87	108	3.81	.255	17	.258	5	15	0.9
1950 StL-N	7	8	.467	32	20	5	1	0	154^2	158	73	67	15	3	70	61	1.474	3.90	110	4.32	.262	7	.137	8	10	0.6
1951 StL-N	4	6	.400	23	11	3	0	0	94^2	106	58	56	13	0	46	44	1.606	5.32	74	5.29	.286	5	.172	-16	2	-1.6
1952 StL-N	0	1	.000	1	1	0	0	0	4^1	7	6	6	2	1	1	1	1.846	12.46	30	11.59	.389	0	.000	-4	0	-0.5
Pit-N	0	3	.000	5	4	0	0	0	26^1	30	21	21	5	0	10	8	1.519	7.18	56	5.29	.283	0	.000	-9	0	-1.0
Yr.	0	4	.000	6	5	0	0	0	30^2	37	27	27	7	1	11	9	1.565	7.92	50	6.18	.298	0	.000	-13	0	-1.5
1956 Pit-N	3	4	.429	35	13	0	0	2	107	126	56	48	8	0	41	45	1.561	4.04	93	4.76	.299	3	.107	-2	4	-0.3
Total 10	**77**	**56**	**.579**	**273**	**161**	**54**	**13**	**12**	**1228^2**	**1243**	**574**	**523**	**85**	**11**	**500**	**564**	**1.419**	**3.83**	**103**	**3.94**	**.264**	**70**	**.174**	**12**	**80**	**1.1**
• MUNGO, Van	Van Lingle Mungo b: 6/8/1911, Pageland, SC d: 2/12/1985, Pageland, SC BR/TR, 6'2", 185 lbs. Deb: 9/7/1931 C																									
1931 Bro-N	3	1	.750	5	4	2	1	0	31	27	9	8	0	1	13	12	1.290	2.32	164	2.92	.241	3	.250	5	4	0.6
1932 Bro-N	13	11	.542	39	33	11	1	2	223^1	224	120	110	9	6	115	107	1.518	4.43	86	4.07	.260	16	.203	-16	11	-1.5
1933 Bro-N	16	15	.516	41	28	18	3	0	248	223	89	75	7	0	84	110	1.238	2.72	118	2.70	.236	15	.179	20	17	2.1
1934 Bro-N★	18	16	.529	45	**38**	22	3	3	**315^1**	300	137	118	15	3	104	184	1.281	3.37	116	3.13	.249	30	.248	21	22	2.4
1935 Bro-N	16	10	.615	37	26	18	**4**	2	214^1	205	100	87	13	2	90	143	1.376	3.65	109	3.57	.252	26	.289	5	15	1.0
1936 Bro-N★	18	19	.486	45	**37**	22	2	3	311^2	275	137	116	8	3	118	**238**	1.261	3.35	123	2.79	**.234**	22	.179	31	24	2.6
1937 Bro-N★	9	11	.450	25	21	14	0	3	161	136	65	52	3	3	56	122	1.193	2.91	139	2.51	**.229**	16	.250	24	16	2.6
1938 Bro-N	4	11	.267	24	18	6	2	0	133^1	133	78	58	11	2	72	72	1.538	3.92	100	4.41	.259	9	.191	1	5	0.2
1939 Bro-N	4	5	.444	14	10	1	0	0	77^1	70	36	28	7	3	33	34	1.332	3.26	123	3.58	.239	10	.345	7	7	1.0
1940 Bro-N	1	0	1.000	7	0	0	0	1	22	24	6	6	1	0	10	9	1.545	2.45	163	4.37	.282	0	.000	4	2	0.3
1941 Bro-N	0	0	....	2	0	0	0	0	2	1	1	1	0	0	2	0	1.500	4.50	81	2.54	.143	0	....	-0	0	0.0
1942 NY-N	1	2	.333	9	5	0	0	0	36^1	38	32	24	4	0	21	27	1.624	5.94	56	5.05	.273	3	.214	-11	0	-1.2
1943 NY-N	3	7	.300	45	13	2	2	2	154^1	140	68	67	7	6	79	83	1.419	3.91	88	3.57	.243	7	.159	-6	7	-0.8
1945 NY-N★	14	7	.667	26	26	7	2	0	183	161	77	65	4	4	71	101	1.268	3.20	122	2.83	.238	17	.233	14	17	1.8
Total 14	**120**	**115**	**.511**	**364**	**259**	**123**	**20**	**16**	**2113**	**1957**	**955**	**815**	**89**	**33**	**868**	**1242**	**1.337**	**3.47**	**110**	**3.27**	**.245**	**174**	**.221**	**100**	**147**	**11.3**
• MUNIZ, Manny	Manuel (Rodriguez) Muniz b: 12/31/1947, Caguas, Puerto Rico BR/TR, 5'11", 190 lbs. Deb: 9/3/1971																									
1971 Phi-N	0	1	.000	5	0	0	0	0	10^1	9	8	8	2	0	8	6	1.645	6.97	51	5.26	.225	0	.000	-4	0	-0.4

YEAR	TM-L	W	L	PCT	G	GS	CG	SH	SV	IP	H	R	ER	HR	HB	BB	SO	RAT	ERA	ERA+	CERA	OAV	BH	AVG	PR+	WS	TPW
• MUNNINGHOFF, Scott	Scott Andrew Munninghoff b: 12/5/1958, Cincinnati, OH BR/TR, 6', 175 lbs. Deb: 4/13/1980																										
1980	Phi-N	0	0	....	4	0	0	0	0	6	8	3	3	0	0	5	2	2.167	4.50	84	6.82	.320	1	1.000	-0	0	0.1
• MUNNS, Les	Leslie Ernest "Nemo,Big Ed" Munns b: 12/1/1908, Fort Bragg, CA d: 2/28/1997, Cedar Rapids, IA BR/TR, 6'5", 212 lbs. Deb: 4/22/1934																										
1934	Bro-N	3	7	.300	33	9	4	0	0	99^1	106	67	52	7	0	60	41	1.671	4.71	83	5.00	.280	7	.241	-8	3	-0.6
1935	Bro-N	1	3	.250	21	5	0	0	1	58^1	74	47	36	5	4	33	13	1.834	5.55	72	6.49	.319	3	.188	-11	0	-1.1
1936	StL-N	0	3	.000	7	1	0	0	1	24	23	18	8	2	0	12	4	1.458	3.00	131	3.81	.240	1	.111	3	1	0.2
Total	**3**	**4**	**13**	**.235**	**61**	**15**	**4**	**0**	**2**	**181^2**	**203**	**132**	**96**	**14**	**4**	**105**	**58**	**1.695**	**4.76**	**83**	**5.32**	**.287**	**11**	**.204**	**-17**	**4**	**-1.6**
• MUNOZ, Bobby	Roberto (Sbert) Munoz b: 3/3/1968, Rio Piedras, Puerto Rico BR/TR, 6'7", 252 lbs. Deb: 5/29/1993																										
1993	NY-A	3	3	.500	38	0	0	0	0	45^2	48	27	27	1	0	26	33	1.620	5.32	78	4.19	.270	0	....	-6	2	-0.6
1994	Phi-N	7	5	.583	21	14	1	0	1	104^1	101	40	31	8	1	35	59	1.304	2.67	161	3.47	.252	7	.206	20	9	2.1
1995	Phi-N	0	2	.000	3	3	0	0	0	15^2	15	13	10	2	3	9	6	1.532	5.74	74	5.72	.268	0	.000	-3	0	-0.3
1996	Phi-N	0	3	.000	6	6	0	0	0	25^1	42	28	22	5	1	7	8	1.934	7.82	55	8.55	.375	1	.143	-10	0	-1.0
1997	Phi-N	1	5	.167	8	7	0	0	0	33^1	47	35	33	4	2	15	20	1.860	8.91	48	7.08	.338	3	.300	-17	0	-1.6
1998	Bal-A	0	0	....	9	1	0	0	0	12	18	13	13	4	1	6	6	2.000	9.75	47	10.37	.383	0	....	-7	0	-0.6
2001	Mon-N	0	4	.000	15	7	0	0	0	42	53	25	24	6	2	21	21	1.762	5.14	87	6.71	.321	0	.000	-2	1	-0.3
Total	**7**	**11**	**22**	**.333**	**100**	**38**	**1**	**0**	**1**	**278^1**	**324**	**181**	**160**	**30**	**10**	**119**	**153**	**1.592**	**5.17**	**83**	**5.40**	**.295**	**11**	**.164**	**-26**	**12**	**-2.4**
• MUNOZ, Mike	Michael Anthony Munoz b: 7/12/1965, Baldwin Park, CA BL/TL, 6'2", 200 lbs. Deb: 9/6/1989																										
1989	LA-N	0	0	....	3	0	0	0	0	2^2	5	5	5	1	0	2	3	2.625	16.88	20	14.88	.417	0	....	-4	0	-0.4
1990	LA-N	0	1	.000	8	0	0	0	0	5^2	6	2	2	0	0	3	2	1.588	3.18	115	4.43	.300	0	.000	0	0	0.0
1991	Det-A	0	0	....	6	0	0	0	0	9^1	14	10	10	0	0	5	3	2.036	9.64	43	6.78	.350	0	....	-6	0	-0.6
1992	Det-A	1	2	.333	65	0	0	0	2	48	44	16	16	3	0	25	23	1.438	3.00	132	3.57	.246	0	....	6	4	0.6
1993	Det-A	0	1	.000	8	0	0	0	0	3	4	2	2	1	0	6	1	3.333	6.00	71	14.77	.308	0	....	-1	0	-0.1
	Col-N	2	1	.667	21	0	0	0	0	18	21	12	9	1	0	9	16	1.667	4.50	106	4.79	.309	0	....	1	1	0.1
1994	Col-N	4	2	.667	57	0	0	0	1	45^2	37	22	19	3	0	31	32	1.489	3.74	133	3.68	.223	0	....	8	5	0.8
1995*	Col-N	2	4	.333	64	0	0	0	2	43^2	54	38	36	9	1	27	37	1.855	7.42	73	7.40	.307	1	.500	-9	1	-0.7
1996	Col-N	2	2	.500	54	0	0	0	0	44^2	55	33	33	4	1	16	45	1.590	6.65	79	5.13	.302	0	.000	-6	2	-0.6
1997	Col-N	3	3	.500	64	0	0	0	2	45^2	52	25	23	4	0	13	26	1.423	4.53	114	4.45	.294	0	.000	4	5	0.4
1998	Col-N	2	2	.500	40	0	0	0	3	41^1	53	32	26	2	1	16	24	1.669	5.66	91	5.29	.312	0	.000	-2	2	-0.3
1999	Tex-A	2	1	.667	56	0	0	0	1	52^2	52	24	23	5	1	18	27	1.329	3.93	129	3.82	.263	0	....	7	5	0.7
2000	Tex-A	0	1	.000	7	0	0	0	0	4	11	6	6	1	0	3	1	3.500	13.50	37	19.41	.524	0	....	-4	0	-0.3
Total	**12**	**18**	**20**	**.474**	**453**	**0**	**0**	**0**	**11**	**364^1**	**408**	**227**	**210**	**34**	**4**	**174**	**240**	**1.597**	**5.19**	**95**	**5.08**	**.287**	**1**	**.143**	**-5**	**25**	**-0.5**
• MUNOZ, Oscar	Juan Oscar Munoz b: 9/25/1969, Hialeah, FL BR/TR, 6'3", 222 lbs. Deb: 8/6/1995																										
1995	Min-A	2	1	.667	10	3	0	0	0	35^1	40	28	22	6	1	17	25	1.613	5.60	85	5.69	.276	0	....	-3	1	-0.3
• MUNRO, Peter	Peter Daniel Munro b: 6/14/1975, Flushing, NY BR/TR, 6'2", 210 lbs. Deb: 4/6/1999																										
1999	Tor-A	0	2	.000	31	2	0	0	0	55^1	70	38	37	6	2	23	38	1.681	6.02	82	6.04	.318	0	....	-7	1	-0.6
2000	Tor-A	1	1	.500	9	3	0	0	0	25^2	38	22	17	1	3	16	16	2.104	5.96	85	8.18	.355	0	.000	-3	0	-0.2
2002	Hou-N	5	5	.500	19	14	0	0	0	80^2	89	37	32	5	3	23	45	1.388	3.57	119	4.04	.283	3	.136	7	5	0.6
2003	Hou-N	3	4	.429	40	2	0	0	0	54	63	30	28	7	5	26	27	1.648	4.67	95	5.97	.294	0	.000	-3	2	-0.2
Total	**4**	**9**	**12**	**.429**	**99**	**21**	**0**	**0**	**0**	**215^2**	**260**	**127**	**114**	**19**	**13**	**88**	**126**	**1.614**	**4.76**	**97**	**5.53**	**.304**	**3**	**.125**	**-5**	**8**	**-0.5**
• MURA, Steve	Stephen Andrew Mura b: 2/12/1955, New Orleans, LA BR/TR, 6'2", 190 lbs. Deb: 9/5/1978																										
1978	SD-N	0	2	.000	5	2	0	0	0	7^2	15	10	10	1	0	5	5	2.609	11.74	28	12.35	.441	0	.000	-7	0	-0.8
1979	SD-N	4	4	.500	38	5	0	0	2	73	57	30	25	6	1	37	59	1.288	3.08	114	3.17	.217	0	.000	3	5	0.2
1980	SD-N	8	7	.533	37	23	3	1	2	168^2	149	74	69	9	3	86	109	1.393	3.68	93	3.61	.246	7	.137	-7	8	-0.8
1981	SD-N	5	14	.263	23	22	2	0	0	138^2	156	72	66	10	0	50	70	1.486	4.28	76	4.36	.285	6	.136	-16	2	-1.8
1982	StL-N	12	11	.522	35	30	7	1	0	184^1	196	89	83	16	0	80	84	1.497	4.05	89	4.53	.278	3	.057	-13	7	-1.8
1983	Chi-A	0	0	....	6	0	0	0	0	12^1	13	11	6	1	0	6	4	1.541	4.38	96	4.38	.260	0	....	-0	0	0.0
1985	Oak-A	1	1	.500	23	1	0	0	1	48	41	25	22	3	0	25	29	1.375	4.13	93	3.28	.225	0	....	-1	2	-0.1
Total	**7**	**30**	**39**	**.435**	**167**	**83**	**12**	**2**	**5**	**632^2**	**627**	**311**	**281**	**46**	**4**	**289**	**360**	**1.448**	**4.00**	**87**	**4.09**	**.263**	**16**	**.101**	**-42**	**24**	**-5.0**
• MURAKAMI, Masanori	Masanori Murakami b: 5/6/1944, Otsuki, Japan BL/TL, 6', 180 lbs. Deb: 9/1/1964																										
1964	SF-N	1	0	1.000	9	0	0	0	1	15	8	3	3	1	0	1	15	.600	1.80	198	0.91	.163	0	.000	3	2	0.3
1965	SF-N	4	1	.800	45	1	0	0	8	74^1	57	31	31	9	3	22	85	1.063	3.75	96	2.60	.205	2	.154	-0	7	0.0
Total	**2**	**5**	**1**	**.833**	**54**	**1**	**0**	**0**	**9**	**89^1**	**65**	**34**	**34**	**10**	**3**	**23**	**100**	**.985**	**3.43**	**105**	**2.32**	**.199**	**2**	**.125**	**3**	**9**	**0.2**
• MURCHISON, Tim	Thomas Malcolm Murchison b: 10/8/1896, Liberty, NC d: 10/20/1962, Liberty, NC BR/TL, 6', 185 lbs. Deb: 6/21/1917																										
1917	StL-N	0	0	....	1	0	0	0	0	1	0	0	0	0	0	2	2	2.000	0.00	....	2.86	.000	0	....	0	0	0.0
1920	Cle-A	0	0	....	2	0	0	0	0	5	3	1	0	0	0	4	0	1.400	0.00	....	2.92	.200	0	.000	2	1	0.2
Total	**2**	**0**	**0**	**....**	**3**	**0**	**0**	**0**	**0**	**6**	**3**	**1**	**0**	**0**	**0**	**6**	**2**	**1.500**	**0.00**	**....**	**2.91**	**.200**	**0**	**.000**	**2**	**1**	**0.2**
• MURFF, Red	John Robert Murff b: 4/1/1921, Burlington, TX BR/TR, 6'3", 195 lbs. Deb: 4/21/1956																										
1956	Mil-N	0	0	....	14	1	0	0	1	24^1	25	14	12	3	0	7	18	1.315	4.44	78	3.94	.272	1	.200	-3	0	-0.3
1957	Mil-N	2	2	.500	12	1	0	0	2	26	31	14	14	3	0	11	13	1.615	4.85	72	5.45	.301	0	.000	-4	1	-0.5
Total	**2**	**2**	**2**	**.500**	**26**	**2**	**0**	**0**	**3**	**50^1**	**56**	**28**	**26**	**6**	**0**	**18**	**31**	**1.470**	**4.65**	**75**	**4.72**	**.287**	**1**	**.091**	**-7**	**1**	**-0.8**
• MURPHY, Bob	Robert J. Murphy b: 12/26/1866, Dutchess County, NY, 6', 173 lbs. Deb: 5/27/1890																										
1890	NY-N	1	0	1.000	3	2	1	0	0	18	23	17	11	0	0	10	8	1.833	5.50	63	....	.302	1	.111	-4	0	-0.4
	Bro-a	3	9	.250	12	12	10	0	0	96	121	95	61	6	0	46	26	1.740	5.72	68	....	.299	9	.180	-19	1	-1.8
• MURPHY, Con	Cornelius B. "Monk,Razzle Dazzle" Murphy b: 10/15/1863, Worcester, MA d: 8/1/1914, Worcester, MA TR, 5'9", 130 lbs. Deb: 9/11/1884																										
1884	Phi-N	0	3	.000	3	3	3	0	0	26	37	34	19	1	....	6	10	1.654	6.58	45	....	.317	0	.000	-9	0	-0.9
1890	Bro-P	4	10	.286	20	14	11	0	2	139	168	134	74	2	6	82	29	1.799	4.79	93	....	.286	15	.217	-7	7	-0.7
Total	**2**	**4**	**13**	**.235**	**23**	**17**	**14**	**0**	**2**	**165**	**205**	**168**	**93**	**3**	**6**	**88**	**39**	**1.776**	**5.07**	**80**	**....**	**.292**	**15**	**.190**	**-16**	**7**	**-1.6**
• MURPHY, Dan	Daniel Lee Murphy b: 9/18/1964, Artesia, CA BR/TR, 6'2", 195 lbs. Deb: 8/10/1989 C																										
1989	SD-N	0	0	....	7	0	0	0	0	6^1	6	6	4	1	0	4	1	1.579	5.68	61	4.57	.231	0	....	-2	0	-0.2
• MURPHY, Danny	Daniel Francis Murphy b: 8/23/1942, Beverly, MA BL/TR, 5'11", 185 lbs. Deb: 6/18/1960 ♦																										
1969	Chi-A	2	1	.667	17	0	0	0	4	31^1	28	8	7	2	2	10	16	1.213	2.01	192	3.35	.252	0	.000	7	5	0.8
1970	Chi-A	2	3	.400	51	0	0	0	5	80^2	82	55	51	11	4	49	42	1.624	5.69	69	5.34	.273	2	.333	-15	2	-1.3
Total	**2**	**4**	**4**	**.500**	**68**	**0**	**0**	**0**	**9**	**112**	**110**	**63**	**58**	**13**	**6**	**59**	**58**	**1.509**	**4.66**	**84**	**4.78**	**.268**	**23**	**.177**	**-8**	**7**	**-0.5**
• MURPHY, Ed	Edward J. Murphy b: 1/22/1877, Auburn, NY d: 1/29/1935, Weedsport, NY TR, 6'1", 186 lbs. Deb: 4/23/1898																										
1898	Phi-N	1	2	.333	7	3	2	0	0	30	41	23	17	3	1	10	8	1.700	5.10	67	6.01	.323	5	.357	-5	1	-0.4
1901	StL-N	10	9	.526	23	21	16	0	0	165	201	105	77	5	1	32	42	1.412	4.20	76	3.97	.298	16	.250	-23	6	-1.9
1902	StL-N	10	6	.625	23	17	12	1	1	164	187	86	55	7	2	31	37	1.329	3.02	91	3.64	.286	16	.262	-2	7	-0.1
1903	StL-N	4	8	.333	15	12	9	0	0	106	108	62	39	2	6	38	16	1.377	3.31	98	3.58	.262	13	.203	-3	5	-0.6
Total	**4**	**25**	**25**	**.500**	**68**	**53**	**39**	**1**	**1**	**465**	**537**	**276**	**188**	**17**	**10**	**111**	**103**	**1.394**	**3.64**	**84**	**3.90**	**.288**	**50**	**.246**	**-33**	**19**	**-3.0**
• MURPHY, Joe	Joseph Akin Murphy b: 9/7/1866, St. Louis, MO d: 3/28/1951, Coral Gables, FL, 5'11", 160 lbs. Deb: 4/28/1886 U																										
1886	Cin-a	2	3	.400	5	5	5	0	0	46	50	34	25	0	1	21	11	1.543	4.89	72	....	.265	0	.000	-7	1	-0.9
	StL-N	0	4	.000	4	4	3	0	0	33	45	41	30	3	....	16	11	1.848	8.18	39	....	.313	3	.214	-19	0	-1.7
	StL-a	1	0	1.000	1	1	1	0	0	7	5	4	3	0	0	3	3	1.143	3.86	89	....	.191	0	.000	-0	1	-0.1
	Yr.	3	3	.500	6	6	6	0	0	53	55	38	28	0	1	24	14	1.491	4.75	74	....	.256	0	.000	-8	2	-1.0

YEAR TM-L	W	L	PCT	G	GS	CG	SH	SV	IP	H	R	ER	HR	HB	BB	SO	RAT	ERA	ERA+	CERA	OAV	BH	AVG	PR+	WS	TPW
1887 StL-a	1	0	1.000	1	1	1	0	0	9	17	8	5	0	1	4	5	1.889	5.00	91	....	.326	1	.167	-1	1	-0.1
Total 2	4	7	.364	11	11	10	0	0	95	117	87	63	3	2	44	30	1.653	5.97	57	....	.285	4	.098	-28	3	-2.8

• MURPHY, John

John Henry Murphy, 5'11", 165 lbs. Deb: 4/17/1884 ♦

YEAR TM-L	W	L	PCT	G	GS	CG	SH	SV	IP	H	R	ER	HR	HB	BB	SO	RAT	ERA	ERA+	CERA	OAV	BH	AVG	PR+	WS	TPW
1884 Wil-U	0	6	.000	7	6	5	0	0	48	52	36	16	3	....	2	27	1.125	3.00	111	....	.258	2	.065	3	1	-0.2
Alt-U	5	6	.455	14	10	10	0	0	111^{2}	141	90	48	3	....	9	46	1.343	3.87	86	....	.289	14	.149	3	5	-0.5
Yr.	5	12	.294	21	16	15	0	0	159^{2}	193	126	64	6	....	11	73	1.278	3.61	92	....	.280	16	.128	6	6	-0.7

• MURPHY, Johnny

John Joseph "Fireman,Grandma,Fordham Johnny" Murphy b: 7/14/1908, New York, NY d: 1/14/1970, New York, NY BR/TR, 6'2", 190 lbs. Deb: 5/19/1932

YEAR TM-L	W	L	PCT	G	GS	CG	SH	SV	IP	H	R	ER	HR	HB	BB	SO	RAT	ERA	ERA+	CERA	OAV	BH	AVG	PR+	WS	TPW
1932 NY-A	0	0	....	2	0	0	0	0	3^{1}	7	6	6	0	0	3	2	3.000	16.20	25	12.58	.438	1	1.000	-4	0	-0.4
1934 NY-A	14	10	.583	40	20	10	0	4	207^{2}	193	79	72	11	0	76	70	1.295	3.12	130	3.22	.250	7	.099	19	18	1.4
1935 NY-A	10	5	.667	40	8	4	0	5	117	110	67	53	7	0	55	28	1.410	4.08	99	3.57	.243	5	.156	-2	8	0.0
1936* NY-A	9	3	.750	27	5	2	0	5	88	90	38	33	5	1	36	34	1.432	3.38	138	3.87	.262	13	.361	12	10	1.4
1937* NY-A★	13	4	.765	39	4	0	0	10	110	121	59	51	7	1	50	36	1.555	4.17	107	4.44	.277	8	.229	2	10	0.3
1938* NY-A★	8	2	.800	32	2	1	0	**11**	91^{1}	90	47	43	5	1	41	43	1.434	4.24	107	3.78	.256	2	.063	2	9	0.0
1939* NY-A★	3	6	.333	38	0	0	0	**19**	61^{1}	57	33	30	2	0	28	30	1.386	4.40	99	3.37	.252	2	.182	-3	7	-0.2
1940 NY-A	8	4	.667	35	1	0	0	9	63^{1}	58	27	26	5	0	15	23	1.153	3.69	109	2.86	.247	1	.077	2	8	0.2
1941* NY-A	8	3	.727	35	0	0	0	**15**	77^{1}	68	20	17	1	0	40	29	1.397	1.98	199	3.12	.237	1	.056	14	12	1.2
1942 NY-A	4	10	.286	31	0	0	0	**11**	58	66	27	22	2	2	23	24	1.534	3.41	101	4.35	.293	2	.154	-2	4	-0.2
1943* NY-A	12	4	.750	37	0	0	0	8	68	44	22	19	2	0	30	31	1.088	2.51	128	1.87	.183	1	.053	4	9	0.2
1946 NY-A	4	2	.667	27	0	0	0	7	45	40	22	17	4	0	19	19	1.311	3.40	102	3.34	.240	0	.000	-1	4	-0.2
1947 Bos-A	0	0	....	32	0	0	0	3	54^{2}	41	17	17	1	0	28	9	1.262	2.80	139	2.47	.206	3	.273	7	5	0.8
Total 13	93	53	.637	415	40	17	0	107	1045	985	464	406	52	5	444	378	1.367	3.50	117	3.44	.249	46	.154	48	104	4.4

• MURPHY, Rob

Robert Albert Murphy b: 5/26/1960, Miami, FL BL/TL, 6'2", 215 lbs. Deb: 9/13/1985

YEAR TM-L	W	L	PCT	G	GS	CG	SH	SV	IP	H	R	ER	HR	HB	BB	SO	RAT	ERA	ERA+	CERA	OAV	BH	AVG	PR+	WS	TPW
1985 Cin-N	0	0	....	2	0	0	0	0	3	2	2	2	1	0	2	1	1.333	6.00	63	5.24	.200	0	....	-1	0	-0.1
1986 Cin-N	6	0	1.000	34	0	0	0	1	50^{1}	26	4	4	0	0	21	36	.934	0.72	541	1.28	.155	0	.000	18	9	1.8
1987 Cin-N	8	5	.615	87	0	0	0	3	100^{2}	91	37	34	7	0	32	99	1.222	3.04	140	2.99	.239	1	.200	13	11	1.3
1988 Cin-N	0	6	.000	**76**	0	0	0	3	84^{2}	69	31	29	3	1	38	74	1.264	3.08	116	2.81	.229	0	....	3	6	0.3
1989 Bos-A	5	7	.417	74	0	0	0	9	105	97	38	32	7	1	41	107	1.314	2.74	149	3.37	.251	0	....	17	10	1.7
1990* Bos-A	0	6	.000	68	0	0	0	7	57	85	46	40	10	1	32	54	2.053	6.32	64	8.34	.348	0	....	-13	0	-1.3
1991 Sea-A	0	1	.000	57	0	0	0	4	48	47	17	16	4	1	19	34	1.375	3.00	137	3.68	.250	0	....	5	4	0.5
1992 Hou-N	3	1	.750	59	0	0	0	0	55^{2}	56	28	25	2	0	21	42	1.383	4.04	83	3.40	.260	0	.000	-4	2	-0.4
1993 StL-N	5	7	.417	73	0	0	0	1	64^{2}	73	37	35	8	1	20	41	1.438	4.87	81	4.57	.290	1	.500	-7	3	-0.6
1994 StL-N	4	3	.571	50	0	0	0	2	40^{1}	35	18	17	7	0	13	25	1.190	3.79	110	3.46	.230	0	....	2	4	0.2
NY-A	0	0	....	3	0	0	0	0	1^{2}	3	3	3	2	0	0	0	1.800	16.20	28	16.12	.375	0	....	-2	0	-0.2
1995 LA-N	0	1	.000	6	0	0	0	0	5	6	7	7	2	0	3	2	1.800	12.60	30	8.79	.300	1	1.000	-5	0	-0.4
Fla-N	1	1	.500	8	0	0	0	0	7^{1}	8	9	8	1	0	5	5	1.773	9.82	43	5.65	.286	0	....	-5	0	-0.5
Yr.	1	2	.333	14	0	0	0	0	12^{1}	14	16	15	3	0	8	7	1.784	10.95	37	6.92	.292	1	1.000	-9	0	-0.9
Total 11	32	38	.457	597	0	0	0	30	623^{1}	598	277	252	54	5	247	520	1.356	3.64	108	3.79	.254	3	.250	21	49	2.3

• MURPHY, Tom

Thomas Andrew Murphy b: 12/30/1945, Cleveland, OH BR/TR, 6'3", 185 lbs. Deb: 6/13/1968

YEAR TM-L	W	L	PCT	G	GS	CG	SH	SV	IP	H	R	ER	HR	HB	BB	SO	RAT	ERA	ERA+	CERA	OAV	BH	AVG	PR+	WS	TPW
1968 Cal-A	5	6	.455	15	15	3	0	0	99^{1}	67	30	24	5	5	28	56	.956	2.17	134	1.89	.191	0	.000	7	7	0.5
1969 Cal-A	10	16	.385	36	35	4	0	0	215^{2}	213	110	101	12	21	69	100	1.308	4.21	83	3.80	.260	10	.141	-21	6	-2.2
1970 Cal-A	16	13	.552	39	38	5	2	0	227	223	114	107	32	7	81	99	1.339	4.24	85	4.24	.261	14	.184	-22	8	-2.0
1971 Cal-A	6	17	.261	37	36	7	0	0	243^{1}	228	108	102	24	9	82	89	1.274	3.77	86	3.67	.256	13	.173	-17	8	-1.8
1972 Cal-A	0	0	....	6	0	0	0	0	10	13	6	6	0	0	8	2	2.100	5.40	54	6.70	.342	0	.000	-3	0	-0.3
KC-A	4	4	.500	18	9	1	1	1	70^{1}	77	26	24	3	6	16	34	1.322	3.07	99	4.02	.287	0	.000	1	4	-0.1
Yr.	4	4	.500	24	9	1	1	1	80^{1}	90	32	30	3	6	24	36	1.419	3.36	89	4.36	.294	0	.000	-2	4	-0.4
1973 StL-N	3	7	.300	19	13	2	0	0	88^{2}	89	38	37	5	3	22	42	1.252	3.76	97	3.40	.269	4	.174	-1	3	-0.1
1974 Mil-A	10	10	.500	70	0	0	0	20	123	97	27	26	6	2	51	47	1.203	1.90	190	2.59	.224	1	.500	23	19	2.4
1975 Mil-A	1	9	.100	52	0	0	0	20	72^{1}	85	43	37	5	5	27	32	1.548	4.60	83	4.88	.295	0	....	-6	3	-0.6
1976 Mil-A	0	1	.000	15	0	0	0	1	18^{1}	25	18	15	2	2	9	7	1.855	7.36	47	6.45	.313	0	....	-8	0	-0.8
Bos-A	4	5	.444	37	0	0	0	8	81	91	43	31	5	2	25	32	1.432	3.44	113	4.03	.290	0	....	5	6	0.5
Yr.	4	6	.400	52	0	0	0	9	99^{1}	116	61	46	7	4	34	39	1.510	4.17	90	4.47	.294	0	....	-3	6	-0.3
1977 Bos-A	0	1	.000	16	0	0	0	0	30^{2}	44	25	23	6	0	12	13	1.826	6.75	67	7.55	.338	0	....	-7	0	-0.7
Tor-A	2	1	.667	19	1	0	0	2	52	63	22	21	6	1	18	26	1.558	3.63	115	5.21	.304	0	....	5	4	0.4
Yr.	2	2	.500	35	1	0	0	2	82^{2}	107	47	44	12	1	30	39	1.657	4.79	91	6.08	.318	0	....	-3	4	-0.3
1978 Tor-A	6	9	.400	50	0	0	0	7	94	87	43	41	11	0	37	36	1.319	3.93	100	3.61	.256	0	....	1	7	0.1
1979 Tor-A	1	2	.333	10	0	0	0	0	18^{1}	23	11	11	1	0	8	6	1.691	5.40	80	5.49	.311	0	....	-2	1	-0.2
Total 12	68	101	.402	439	147	22	3	59	1444	1425	664	606	123	63	493	621	1.328	3.78	94	3.86	.263	42	.145	-47	76	-4.9

• MURPHY, Walter

Walter Joseph Murphy b: 9/27/1907, New York, NY d: 3/23/1976, Houston, TX BR/TR, 6'1.5", 180 lbs. Deb: 4/19/1931

YEAR TM-L	W	L	PCT	G	GS	CG	SH	SV	IP	H	R	ER	HR	HB	BB	SO	RAT	ERA	ERA+	CERA	OAV	BH	AVG	PR+	WS	TPW
1931 Bos-A	0	0	....	2	0	0	0	0	2	4	2	2	0	0	1	0	2.500	9.00	48	10.56	.444	0	....	-1	0	-0.1

• MURRAY, Amby

Ambrose Joseph Murray b: 6/14/1913, Fall River, MA d: 2/6/1997, Port Salerno, FL BL/TL, 5'7", 150 lbs. Deb: 7/5/1936

YEAR TM-L	W	L	PCT	G	GS	CG	SH	SV	IP	H	R	ER	HR	HB	BB	SO	RAT	ERA	ERA+	CERA	OAV	BH	AVG	PR+	WS	TPW
1936 Bos-N	0	0	....	4	1	0	0	0	11	15	5	5	1	0	3	2	1.636	4.09	94	5.40	.319	1	.250	-0	0	0.0

• MURRAY, Dale

Dale Albert Murray b: 2/2/1950, Cuero, TX BR/TR, 6'4", 205 lbs. Deb: 7/7/1974

YEAR TM-L	W	L	PCT	G	GS	CG	SH	SV	IP	H	R	ER	HR	HB	BB	SO	RAT	ERA	ERA+	CERA	OAV	BH	AVG	PR+	WS	TPW
1974 Mon-N	1	1	.500	32	0	0	0	10	69^{2}	46	12	8	1	0	23	31	.990	1.03	371	1.62	.187	0	.000	22	12	2.2
1975 Mon-N	15	8	.652	63	0	0	0	9	111^{1}	134	59	49	0	3	39	43	1.554	3.96	96	4.22	.305	3	.214	-2	10	-0.1
1976 Mon-N	4	9	.308	**81**	0	0	0	13	113^{1}	117	47	41	1	0	37	35	1.359	3.26	114	3.20	.277	0	.000	6	10	0.5
1977 Cin-N	7	2	.778	61	1	0	0	4	102	125	60	56	13	2	46	42	1.676	4.94	79	5.95	.314	2	.167	-12	3	-1.3
1978 Cin-N	1	1	.500	15	0	0	0	2	32^{2}	34	20	15	1	1	17	25	1.561	4.13	86	4.14	.272	0	.000	-2	1	-0.2
NY-N	8	5	.615	53	0	0	0	5	86^{1}	85	39	35	4	2	36	37	1.402	3.65	95	3.41	.266	0	.000	-2	6	-0.3
Yr.	9	6	.600	68	0	0	0	7	119	119	59	50	5	3	53	62	1.445	3.78	93	3.61	.268	0	.000	-4	7	-0.5
1979 NY-N	4	8	.333	58	0	0	0	4	97	105	58	52	6	0	52	37	1.619	4.82	75	4.65	.287	0	.000	-14	2	-1.5
Mon-N	1	2	.333	9	0	0	0	1	13^{1}	14	4	4	1	0	3	4	1.275	2.70	136	3.48	.292	0	.000	1	1	0.1
Yr.	5	10	.333	67	0	0	0	5	110^{1}	119	62	56	7	0	55	41	1.577	4.57	80	4.51	.287	0	.000	-12	3	-1.3
1980 Mon-N	0	1	.000	16	0	0	0	0	29^{1}	39	23	20	3	0	12	16	1.739	6.14	58	5.89	.315	0	.000	-8	0	-0.9
1981 Tor-A	1	0	1.000	11	0	0	0	0	15^{1}	12	2	2	0	0	5	12	1.109	1.17	336	2.05	.211	0	....	5	2	0.5
1982 Tor-A	8	7	.533	56	0	0	0	11	111	115	48	39	3	3	32	60	1.324	3.16	142	3.39	.268	0	....	17	13	1.7
1983 NY-A	2	4	.333	40	0	0	0	1	94^{1}	113	56	47	5	1	22	45	1.431	4.48	87	4.10	.297	0	....	-6	3	-0.6
1984 NY-A	1	2	.333	19	0	0	0	0	23^{2}	30	15	13	2	2	5	13	1.479	4.94	77	5.06	.306	0	....	-3	0	-0.3
1985 NY-A	0	0	....	3	0	0	0	0	2	4	3	3	0	0	0	0	2.000	13.50	30	7.48	.400	0	....	-2	0	-0.2
Tex-A	0	0	....	1	0	0	0	0	1	3	2	2	0	0	0	0	3.000	18.00	24	17.53	.750	0	....	-2	0	-0.1
Yr.	0	0	....	4	0	0	0	0	3	7	5	5	0	0	0	0	2.333	15.00	27	10.83	.500	0	....	-4	0	-0.4
Total 12	53	50	.515	518	1	0	0	60	902^{1}	976	448	386	40	14	329	400	1.446	3.85	99	3.99	.282	5	.077	-1	63	-0.4

• MURRAY, Dan

Daniel Saffle Murray b: 11/21/1973, Los Alamitos, CA BR/TR, 6'1", 195 lbs. Deb: 8/9/1999

YEAR TM-L	W	L	PCT	G	GS	CG	SH	SV	IP	H	R	ER	HR	HB	BB	SO	RAT	ERA	ERA+	CERA	OAV	BH	AVG	PR+	WS	TPW
1999 NY-N	0	0	....	1	0	0	0	0	2	4	3	3	0	0	2	1	3.000	13.50	32	12.01	.444	0	....	-2	0	-0.2
KC-A	0	0	....	4	0	0	0	0	8^{1}	9	8	6	4	1	4	8	1.560	6.48	77	8.21	.265	0	....	-2	0	-0.1
2000 KC-A	0	0	....	10	0	0	0	0	19^{1}	20	10	10	7	1	10	16	1.552	4.66	110	7.09	.278	0	....	1	1	0.1
Total 2	0	0	....	15	0	0	0	0	29^{2}	33	21	19	11	2	16	25	1.652	5.76	86	7.74	.287	0	....	-3	1	-0.3

• MURRAY, George

George King "Smiler" Murray b: 9/23/1898, Charlotte, NC d: 10/18/1955, Memphis, TN BR/TR, 6'2", 200 lbs. Deb: 5/8/1922

YEAR TM-L	W	L	PCT	G	GS	CG	SH	SV	IP	H	R	ER	HR	HB	BB	SO	RAT	ERA	ERA+	CERA	OAV	BH	AVG	PR+	WS	TPW
1922 NY-A	3	2	.600	22	2	0	0	0	56^{2}	53	27	25	0	1	26	14	1.394	3.97	101	3.24	.255	5	.278	-0	4	0.1
1923 Bos-A	7	11	.389	39	18	5	0	0	177^{2}	190	111	97	9	7	87	40	1.559	4.91	84	4.57	.291	9	.164	-15	6	-1.7
1924 Bos-A	2	9	.182	28	7	0	0	0	80^{1}	97	68	60	6	7	32	27	1.606	6.72	65	4.96	.307	4	.182	-20	0	-1.9
1926 Was-A	6	3	.667	12	12	5	0	0	81^{1}	89	56	51	1	6	37	28	1.549	5.64	68	4.27	.287	5	.139	-16	1	-1.8

YEAR	TM-L	W	L	PCT	G	GS	CG	SH	SV	IP	H	R	ER	HR	HB	BB	SO	RAT	ERA	ERA+	CERA	OAV	BH	AVG	PR+	WS	TPW
1927	Was-A	1	1	.500	7	3	0	0	0	18	18	18	14	1	2	15	5	1.833	7.00	58	5.46	.265	1	.167	-6	0	-0.6
1933	Chi-A	0	0	....	2	0	0	0	0	2^1	3	2	2	0	0	2	0	2.143	7.71	55	6.98	.375	0	....	-1	0	-0.1
Total	6	19	26	.422	110	42	10	0	0	416^1	450	282	249	17	23	199	114	1.559	5.38	76	4.46	.288	24	.175	-59	11	-6.0
• MURRAY, Heath	Heath Robertson Murray b: 4/19/1973, Troy, OH BL/TL, 6'4", 205 lbs. Deb: 5/24/1997																										
1997	SD-N	1	2	.333	17	3	0	0	0	33^1	50	25	25	3	4	21	16	2.130	6.75	57	8.88	.376	0	.000	-10	0	-1.1
1999	SD-N	0	4	.000	22	8	0	0	0	50	60	33	32	7	1	26	25	1.720	5.76	73	5.93	.297	2	.154	-9	0	-0.8
2001	Det-A	1	7	.125	40	4	0	0	0	63^1	82	48	46	11	3	40	42	1.926	6.54	66	7.69	.322	0	....	-14	0	-1.4
2002	Cle-A	0	2	.000	9	0	0	0	0	12	12	10	10	3	2	7	11	1.583	7.50	59	6.82	.267	0	....	-4	0	-0.4
Total	4	2	15	.118	88	15	0	0	0	158^2	204	116	113	24	10	94	94	1.878	6.41	65	7.32	.321	2	.105	-38	0	-3.7
• MURRAY, Jim	James Francis "Big Jim" Murray b: 12/31/1900, Scranton, PA d: 7/15/1973, Queens, NY BB/TL, 6'2", 210 lbs. Deb: 7/3/1922																										
1922	Bro-N	0	0	....	4	0	0	0	1	6	8	3	3	0	0	3	3	1.833	4.50	90	5.55	.320	1	.500	-0	0	0.0
• MURRAY, Joe	Joseph Ambrose Murray b: 11/11/1920, Wilkes-Barre, PA d: 10/19/2001, San Clemente, CA BL/TL, 6', 165 lbs. Deb: 8/17/1950																										
1950	Phi-A	0	3	.000	8	2	0	0	0	30	34	20	19	1	0	21	8	1.833	5.70	80	5.25	.283	0	.000	-4	0	-0.5
• MURRAY, Matt	Matthew Michael Murray b: 9/26/1970, Boston, MA BL/TR, 6'6", 240 lbs. Deb: 8/12/1995																										
1995	Atl-N	0	2	.000	4	1	0	0	0	10^2	10	8	8	3	1	5	3	1.406	6.75	63	5.86	.256	1	.500	-3	0	-0.2
	Bos-A	0	1	.000	2	1	0	0	0	3^1	11	10	7	1	0	3	1	4.200	18.90	26	25.29	.524	0	....	-5	0	-0.5
• MURRAY, Pat	Patrick Joseph Murray b: 7/18/1897, Scottsville, NY d: 11/5/1983, Rochester, NY BR/TL, 6', 175 lbs. Deb: 7/1/1919																										
1919	Phi-N	0	2	.000	8	2	1	0	0	34^1	50	28	24	0	4	12	11	1.806	6.29	51	6.13	.347	0	.000	-12	0	-1.4
• MUSGRAVES, Dennis	Dennis Eugene Musgraves b: 12/25/1943, Indianapolis, IN BR/TR, 6'4", 188 lbs. Deb: 7/9/1965																										
1965	NY-N	0	0	....	5	1	0	0	0	16	11	2	1	0	2	7	11	1.125	0.56	627	2.44	.200	0	.000	5	3	0.5
• MUSSELMAN, Jeff	Jeffrey Joseph Musselman b: 6/21/1963, Doylestown, PA BL/TL, 6', 180 lbs. Deb: 9/2/1986																										
1986	Tor-A	0	0	....	6	0	0	0	0	5^1	8	7	6	1	0	5	4	2.438	10.13	42	9.74	.333	0	....	-3	0	-0.3
1987	Tor-A	12	5	.706	68	1	0	0	3	89	75	43	41	7	3	54	54	1.449	4.15	108	3.86	.237	0	....	2	8	0.2
1988	Tor-A	8	5	.615	15	15	0	0	0	85	80	34	30	4	3	30	39	1.294	3.18	124	3.38	.252	0	....	7	6	0.7
1989	Tor-A	0	1	.000	5	3	0	0	0	11	19	15	13	2	0	9	3	2.545	10.64	34	11.74	.404	0	....	-9	0	-0.9
	NY-N	3	2	.600	20	0	0	0	0	26^1	27	11	9	1	0	14	11	1.557	3.08	106	4.00	.267	0	....	1	2	0.1
1990	NY-N	0	2	.000	28	0	0	0	0	32	40	22	20	3	1	11	14	1.594	5.63	67	5.35	.310	0	.000	-6	0	-0.7
Total	5	23	15	.605	142	19	0	0	3	248^2	249	132	119	18	7	123	125	1.496	4.31	92	4.38	.266	0	.000	-9	16	-0.9
• MUSSELMAN, Ron	Ralph Ronald Musselman b: 11/11/1954, Wilmington, NC BR/TR, 6'2", 185 lbs. Deb: 8/18/1982																										
1982	Sea-A	1	0	1.000	12	0	0	0	0	15^2	18	7	6	2	1	6	9	1.532	3.45	123	5.34	.300	0	....	1	1	0.1
1984	Tor-A	0	2	.000	11	0	0	0	1	21^1	18	7	5	2	0	10	9	1.313	2.11	194	3.18	.225	0	....	5	2	0.5
1985	Tor-A	3	0	1.000	25	4	0	0	0	52^1	59	28	26	2	0	24	29	1.586	4.47	94	4.47	.284	0	....	-2	3	-0.2
Total	3	4	2	.667	48	4	0	0	1	89^1	95	42	37	6	1	40	47	1.511	3.73	113	4.31	.273	0	....	4	6	0.4
• MUSSER, Paul	Paul Musser b: 6/24/1889, Millheim, PA d: 7/7/1973, State College, PA BR/TR, 6', 175 lbs. Deb: 6/6/1912																										
1912	Was-A	0	0	....	7	2	0	0	2	20^2	16	7	6	0	2	16	10	1.548	2.61	128	3.84	.225	0	.000	1	2	0.0
1919	Bos-A	0	2	.000	5	4	1	0	0	19^2	26	16	9	0	0	8	14	1.729	4.12	73	5.52	.342	0	.000	-3	0	-0.4
Total	2	0	2	.000	12	6	1	0	2	40^1	42	23	15	0	2	24	24	1.636	3.35	94	4.66	.285	0	.000	-2	2	-0.4
• MUSSILL, Barney	Bernard James Mussill b: 10/1/1919, Bower Hill, PA BR/TL, 6'1", 200 lbs. Deb: 4/20/1944																										
1944	Phi-N	0	1	.000	16	0	0	0	0	19^1	20	16	13	1	0	13	5	1.707	6.05	60	4.61	.267	0	.000	-5	0	-0.5
• MUSSINA, Mike	Michael Cole "Moose" Mussina b: 12/8/1968, Williamsport, PA BL/TR, 6'2", 185 lbs. Deb: 8/4/1991																										
1991	Bal-A	4	5	.444	12	12	2	0	0	87^2	77	31	28	7	1	21	52	1.118	2.87	137	2.80	.239	0	....	10	6	1.0
1992	Bal-A★	18	5	.783	32	32	8	4	0	241	212	70	68	16	2	48	130	1.079	2.54	158	2.54	.239	0	....	38	24	3.9
1993	Bal-A★	14	6	.700	25	25	3	2	0	167^2	163	84	83	20	3	44	117	1.235	4.46	100	3.61	.256	0	....	-2	11	-0.2
1994	Bal-A★	16	5	.762	24	24	3	0	0	176^1	163	63	60	19	1	42	99	1.163	3.06	163	3.16	.248	0	....	36	18	3.3
1995	Bal-A	**19**	9	.679	32	32	7	**4**	0	221^2	187	86	81	24	1	50	158	1.069	3.29	144	2.66	.226	0	....	33	20	3.1
1996*	Bal-A	19	11	.633	36	**36**	4	1	0	243^1	264	137	130	31	3	69	204	1.368	4.81	103	4.36	.275	0	....	3	13	0.3
1997*	Bal-A★	15	8	.652	33	33	4	1	0	224^2	197	87	80	27	3	54	218	1.117	3.20	137	3.00	.234	1	.250	29	19	2.8
1998	Bal-A	13	10	.565	29	29	4	2	0	206^1	189	85	80	22	4	41	175	1.115	3.49	131	2.96	.242	0	.000	26	15	2.5
1999	Bal-A★	18	7	.720	31	31	4	0	0	203^1	207	88	79	16	1	52	172	1.274	3.50	134	3.54	.268	3	.273	23	17	2.2
2000	Bal-A	11	15	.423	34	34	6	1	0	**237^2**	236	105	100	28	3	46	210	1.187	3.79	125	3.37	.255	0	.000	26	18	2.3
2001*	NY-A	17	11	.607	34	34	4	3	0	228^2	202	87	80	20	4	42	214	1.067	3.15	143	2.65	.237	1	.143	**39**	20	**3.7**
2002*	NY-A	18	10	.643	33	33	2	2	0	215^2	208	103	97	27	5	48	182	1.187	4.05	108	3.46	.253	3	.600	14	15	1.5
2003*	NY-A	17	8	.680	31	31	2	1	0	214^2	192	86	81	21	3	40	195	1.081	3.40	129	2.75	.238	0	.000	28	18	2.7
Total	13	199	110	.644	386	386	53	21	0	2668^2	2497	1112	1047	278	34	597	2126	1.159	3.53	129	3.15	.247	8	.216	303	214	29.0
• MUSTAIKIS, Alex	Alexander Dominick Mustaikis b: 3/26/1909, Chelsea, MA d: 1/17/1970, Scranton, PA BR/TR, 6'3", 180 lbs. Deb: 7/7/1940																										
1940	Bos-A	0	1	.000	6	1	0	0	0	15	15	18	15	1	0	15	6	2.000	9.00	50	5.67	.254	2	.333	-7	0	-0.6
• MUTIS, Jeff	Jeffrey Thomas Mutis b: 12/20/1966, Allentown, PA BL/TL, 6'2", 185 lbs. Deb: 6/15/1991																										
1991	Cle-A	0	3	.000	3	3	0	0	0	12^1	23	16	16	1	0	7	6	2.432	11.68	36	9.58	.397	0	....	-10	0	-1.0
1992	Cle-A	0	2	.000	3	2	0	0	0	11^1	24	14	12	4	0	6	8	2.647	9.53	41	14.31	.429	0	....	-7	0	-0.7
1993	Cle-A	3	6	.333	17	13	1	1	0	81	93	56	52	14	7	33	29	1.556	5.78	75	5.91	.289	0	....	-13	1	-1.3
1994	Fla-N	1	0	1.000	35	0	0	0	0	38^1	51	25	23	6	1	15	30	1.722	5.40	81	6.45	.331	0	.000	-5	1	-0.5
Total	4	4	11	.267	58	18	1	1	0	143	191	111	103	25	8	61	73	1.762	6.48	66	7.04	.324	0	.000	-35	2	-3.5
• MYERS, Brett	Brett Allen Myers b: 8/17/1980, Jacksonville, FL BR/TR, 6'4", 215 lbs. Deb: 7/24/2002																										
2002	Phi-N	4	5	.444	12	12	1	0	0	72	73	38	34	11	6	29	34	1.417	4.25	92	5.04	.277	3	.130	-3	3	-0.4
2003	Phi-N	14	9	.609	32	32	1	1	0	193	205	99	95	20	9	76	143	1.456	4.43	90	4.56	.272	9	.145	-9	9	-0.9
Total	2	18	14	.563	44	44	2	1	0	265	278	137	129	31	15	105	177	1.445	4.38	91	4.69	.273	12	.141	-12	12	-1.3
• MYERS, Elmer	Elmer Glenn Myers b: 3/2/1894, York Springs, PA d: 7/29/1976, Collingswood, NJ BR/TR, 6'2", 185 lbs. Deb: 10/6/1915																										
1915	Phi-A	1	0	1.000	1	1	1	1	0	9	2	0	0	0	0	5	12	.778	0.00	....	0.76	.074	0	.000	3	0	0.2
1916	Phi-A	14	23	.378	44	35	31	2	1	315	280	169	128	7	14	168	182	1.422	3.66	78	3.63	.248	27	.214	-21	5	-2.0
1917	Phi-A	9	16	.360	38	23	13	2	3	201^2	221	122	99	2	5	79	88	**1.488**	4.42	62	3.88	.283	18	.247	-34	3	-3.6
1918	Phi-A	4	8	.333	18	15	5	1	1	95^1	101	66	49	4	4	42	17	1.500	4.63	63	4.26	.283	5	.143	-21	0	-2.6
1919	Cle-A	8	7	.533	23	15	6	1	1	134^2	134	68	56	3	10	43	38	1.314	3.74	89	3.51	.264	11	.239	-5	7	-0.3
1920	Cle-A	2	4	.333	16	7	2	0	1	71^2	93	52	38	1	4	23	16	1.619	4.77	79	5.03	.316	6	.240	-9	1	-0.9
	Bos-A	9	1	.900	12	10	9	1	0	97	90	30	23	1	2	24	34	1.175	2.13	171	2.53	.249	12	.316	15	12	1.8
	Yr.	11	5	.688	28	17	11	1	1	168^2	183	82	61	2	6	47	50	1.364	3.25	115	3.59	.279	18	.286	6	13	0.9
1921	Bos-A	8	12	.400	30	20	11	0	0	172	217	107	93	11	10	53	40	1.570	4.87	87	5.07	.315	14	.215	-16	6	-1.7
1922	Bos-A	0	1	.000	3	1	0	0	0	5^2	10	11	11	1	2	3	1	2.294	17.47	23	11.34	.370	0	.000	-8	0	-0.8
Total	8	55	72	.433	185	127	78	8	7	1102	1148	625	497	30	51	440	428	1.441	4.06	79	3.95	.275	93	.226	-98	34	-9.9
• MYERS, Henry	Henry C. Myers b: 5/1858, Philadelphia, PA d: 4/18/1895, Philadelphia, PA BR/TR, 5'9", 159 lbs. Deb: 8/20/1881 M ♦																										
1882	Bal-a	0	2	.000	6	2	1	0	0	26	30	28	19	2	....	4	7	1.308	6.58	42	....	.271	53	.180	-11	2	-2.9
• MYERS, Jimmy	James Xavier Myers b: 4/28/1969, Oklahoma City, OK BR/TR, 6'1", 190 lbs. Deb: 4/6/1996																										
1996	Bal-A	0	0	....	11	0	0	0	0	14	18	13	11	4	0	3	6	1.500	7.07	70	5.98	.305	0	....	-3	0	-0.3
• MYERS, Joseph	Joseph William Myers b: 3/18/1882, Wilmington, DE d: 2/11/1956, Delaware City, DE BR/TR, 5'10.5", 205 lbs. Deb: 10/7/1905																										
1905	Phi-A	0	0	....	1	1	1	0	0	5	3	3	2	0	1	3	5	1.200	3.60	74	2.59	.176	0	.000	-0	0	-0.1

YEAR TM-L	W	L	PCT	G	GS	CG	SH	SV	IP	H	R	ER	HR	HB	BB	SO	RAT	ERA	ERA+	CERA	OAV	BH	AVG	PR+	WS	TPW
• MYERS, Mike				Michael Stanley Myers b: 6/26/1969, Cook County, IL BL/TL, 6'3", 200 lbs. Deb: 4/25/1995																						
1995 Fla-N	0	0	....	2	0	0	0	0	2	1	0	0	0	0	3	0	2.000	0.00	....	5.03	.167	0	....	1	0	0.1
Det-A	1	0	1.000	11	0	0	0	0	6^1	10	7	7	1	2	4	4	2.211	9.95	48	11.13	.385	0	....	-4	0	-0.3
1996 Det-A	1	5	.167	**83**	0	0	0	6	64^2	70	41	36	6	4	34	69	1.608	5.01	101	4.97	.272	0	....	2	3	0.2
1997 Det-A	0	4	.000	**88**	0	0	0	2	53^2	58	36	34	12	2	25	50	1.547	5.70	80	5.70	.274	0	....	-7	1	-0.7
1998 Mil-N	2	2	.500	70	0	0	0	1	50	44	19	15	5	6	22	40	1.320	2.70	158	4.14	.249	0	....	8	6	0.8
1999 Mil-N	2	1	.667	71	0	0	0	0	41^1	46	24	24	7	3	13	35	1.427	5.23	87	5.24	.291	0	.000	-3	2	-0.3
2000 Col-N	0	1	.000	78	0	0	0	1	45^1	24	10	10	2	2	24	41	1.059	1.99	292	1.94	.160	0	....	19	7	1.8
2001 Col-N	2	3	.400	73	0	0	0	0	40	32	17	16	2	1	24	36	1.400	3.60	148	3.29	.225	0	....	7	4	0.7
2002* Ari-N	4	3	.571	69	0	0	0	4	37	39	18	18	2	8	17	31	1.514	4.38	101	5.13	.275	0	....	1	3	0.1
2003 Ari-N	0	1	.000	64	0	0	0	0	36^1	38	23	23	4	5	21	21	1.624	5.70	82	5.54	.262	0	....	-4	1	-0.4
Total 9	12	20	.375	609	0	0	0	14	376^2	362	195	183	41	33	187	327	1.458	4.37	109	4.62	.256	0	.000	21	27	2.0
• MYERS, Randy				Randall Kirk Myers b: 9/19/1962, Vancouver, WA BL/TL, 6'1", 215 lbs. Deb: 10/6/1985																						
1985 NY-N	0	0	....	1	0	0	0	0	2	0	0	0	0	0	1	2	.500	0.00	....	0.27	.000	0	....	1	0	0.1
1986 NY-N	0	0	....	10	0	0	0	0	10^2	11	5	5	1	1	9	13	1.875	4.22	84	6.05	.256	0	....	-1	0	-0.1
1987 NY-N	3	6	.333	54	0	0	0	6	75	61	36	33	6	0	30	92	1.213	3.96	95	2.81	.225	2	.286	-1	6	0.0
1988* NY-N	7	3	.700	55	0	0	0	26	68	45	15	13	5	2	17	69	.912	1.72	187	1.78	.190	1	.250	11	14	1.3
1989 NY-N	7	4	.636	65	0	0	0	24	84^1	62	23	22	4	0	40	88	1.209	2.35	139	2.53	.206	0	.000	9	13	0.9
1990* Cin-N★	4	6	.400	66	0	0	0	31	86^2	59	24	20	6	3	38	98	1.119	2.08	190	2.35	.193	1	.250	16	17	1.7
1991 Cin-N	6	13	.316	58	12	1	0	6	132	116	61	52	8	1	80	108	1.485	3.55	107	3.92	.242	5	.172	4	8	0.5
1992 SD-N	3	6	.333	66	0	0	0	38	79^2	84	38	38	7	1	34	66	1.481	4.29	83	4.42	.279	1	.143	-6	7	-0.7
1993 Chi-N	2	4	.333	73	0	0	0	**53**	75^1	65	26	26	7	1	26	86	1.208	3.11	128	3.08	.230	1	.500	7	15	0.8
1994 Chi-N★	1	5	.167	38	0	0	0	21	40^1	40	18	17	3	0	16	32	1.388	3.79	110	3.78	.260	0	.000	1	5	0.1
1995 Chi-N★	1	2	.333	57	0	0	0	**38**	55^2	49	25	24	7	0	28	59	1.383	3.88	106	3.95	.237	0	....	1	8	0.1
1996* Bal-A	4	4	.500	62	0	0	0	31	58^2	60	24	23	7	1	29	74	1.517	3.53	140	4.64	.265	0	....	9	9	0.8
1997* Bal-A★	2	3	.400	61	0	0	0	**45**	59^2	47	12	10	2	0	22	56	1.156	1.51	292	2.40	.217	0	....	19	15	1.8
1998 Tor-A	3	4	.429	41	0	0	0	28	42^1	44	21	21	4	2	19	32	1.488	4.46	105	4.42	.265	0	.000	1	6	0.1
*SD-N	1	3	.250	21	0	0	0	0	14^1	15	10	10	2	0	7	9	1.535	6.28	63	4.84	.273	0	....	-4	0	-0.4
Total 14	44	63	.411	728	12	1	0	347	884^2	758	338	314	69	12	396	884	1.304	3.19	122	3.35	.233	11	.183	68	123	7.0
• MYERS, Rodney				Rodney Luther Myers b: 6/26/1969, Rockford, IL BR/TR, 6'1", 200 lbs. Deb: 4/3/1996																						
1996 Chi-N	2	1	.667	45	0	0	0	0	67^1	61	38	35	6	3	38	50	1.470	4.68	93	4.20	.243	0	.000	-3	3	-0.4
1997 Chi-N	0	0	....	5	1	0	0	0	9	12	6	6	1	1	7	6	2.111	6.00	72	8.42	.333	0	....	-2	0	-0.2
1998 Chi-N	0	0	....	12	0	0	0	0	18	26	14	14	3	0	6	15	1.778	7.00	63	7.19	.342	0	.000	-5	0	-0.5
1999 Chi-N	3	1	.750	46	0	0	0	0	63^2	71	34	31	10	1	25	41	1.508	4.38	103	5.22	.289	3	.429	2	5	0.3
2000 SD-N	0	0	....	3	0	0	0	0	2	2	1	1	0	0	0	3	1.000	4.50	96	1.95	.250	0	....	-0	0	0.0
2001 SD-N	1	2	.333	37	0	0	0	1	47^1	53	31	28	6	4	20	29	1.542	5.32	75	5.50	.291	0	.000	-6	1	-0.6
2002 SD-N	1	1	.500	14	0	0	0	0	21^1	29	20	14	1	3	10	11	1.828	5.91	64	6.83	.333	0	.000	-5	0	-0.5
2003 LA-N	0	0	....	4	0	0	0	0	9	10	7	6	1	1	4	5	1.556	6.00	67	5.30	.270	0	.000	-2	0	-0.2
Total 8	7	5	.583	166	1	0	0	1	237^2	264	151	135	28	13	110	160	1.574	5.11	83	5.38	.286	3	.167	-21	9	-2.1
• MYETTE, Aaron				Aaron Kenneth Myette b: 9/26/1977, New Westminster, Canada BR/TR, 6'4", 195 lbs. Deb: 9/7/1999																						
1999 Chi-A	0	2	.000	4	3	0	0	0	15^2	17	11	11	2	2	14	11	1.979	6.32	77	7.09	.266	0	....	-2	0	-0.2
2000 Chi-A	0	0	....	2	0	0	0	0	2^2	0	0	0	0	0	4	1	1.500	0.00	....	1.96	.000	0	....	1	0	0.1
2001 Tex-A	4	5	.444	19	15	0	0	0	80^2	94	65	64	12	11	37	67	1.624	7.14	65	6.23	.293	0	....	-22	0	-2.1
2002 Tex-A	2	5	.286	15	12	0	0	0	48^1	64	57	54	11	6	41	48	2.172	10.06	47	9.79	.325	0	....	-28	0	-2.7
2003 Cle-A	0	0	....	2	0	0	0	0	2^2	7	7	7	1	1	2	1	3.375	23.63	19	21.83	.467	0	....	-6	0	-0.6
Total 5	6	12	.333	42	30	0	0	0	150	182	140	136	26	20	98	128	1.867	8.16	57	7.67	.305	0	....	-56	0	-5.4
• MYRICK, Bob				Robert Howard Myrick b: 10/1/1952, Hattiesburg, MS BR/TL, 6'1", 195 lbs. Deb: 5/28/1976																						
1976 NY-N	1	1	.500	21	1	0	0	0	27^2	34	13	10	2	0	13	11	1.699	3.25	101	5.46	.306	0	.000	-0	1	0.0
1977 NY-N	2	2	.500	44	4	0	0	2	87^1	86	39	35	5	1	33	49	1.363	3.61	104	3.64	.265	2	.182	1	5	0.1
1978 NY-N	0	3	.000	17	0	0	0	0	24^2	18	10	9	3	0	13	13	1.257	3.28	106	3.17	.207	0	.000	0	1	0.0
Total 3	3	6	.333	82	5	0	0	2	139^2	138	62	54	10	1	59	73	1.411	3.48	104	3.91	.264	2	.125	1	7	0.1
• NABHOLZ, Chris				Christopher William Nabholz b: 1/5/1967, Harrisburg, PA BL/TL, 6'5", 212 lbs. Deb: 6/11/1990																						
1990 Mon-N	6	2	.750	11	11	1	1	0	70	43	23	22	6	2	32	53	1.071	2.83	129	2.29	.176	0	.000	6	6	0.5
1991 Mon-N	8	7	.533	24	24	1	0	0	153^2	134	66	62	5	2	57	99	1.243	3.63	100	2.89	.237	6	.115	-2	7	-0.3
1992 Mon-N	11	12	.478	32	32	1	1	0	195	176	80	72	11	5	74	130	1.282	3.32	104	3.30	.244	8	.123	3	10	0.3
1993 Mon-N	9	8	.529	26	21	1	0	0	116^2	100	57	53	9	8	63	74	1.397	4.09	102	3.91	.236	5	.128	1	6	0.0
1994 Cle-A	0	1	.000	6	4	0	0	0	11	23	16	14	1	1	9	5	2.909	11.45	41	13.24	.418	0	....	-8	0	-0.8
Bos-A	3	4	.429	8	8	0	0	0	42	44	32	31	5	2	29	23	1.738	6.64	76	6.12	.282	0	....	-8	1	-0.7
Yr.	3	5	.375	14	12	0	0	0	53	67	48	45	6	3	38	28	1.981	7.64	64	7.60	.318	0	....	-16	1	-1.5
1995 Chi-N	0	1	.000	34	0	0	0	0	23^1	22	15	14	4	0	14	21	1.543	5.40	76	4.85	.253	0	.000	-4	1	-0.4
Total 6	37	35	.514	141	100	4	2	0	611^2	542	289	268	41	20	278	405	1.341	3.94	98	3.63	.240	19	.107	-11	31	-1.4
• NABORS, Jack				Herman John Nabors b: 11/19/1887, Montevallo, AL d: 11/20/1923, Wilton, AL BR/TR, 6'3", 185 lbs. Deb: 8/9/1915																						
1915 Phi-A	0	5	.000	10	7	2	0	0	54	58	46	33	1	5	35	18	1.722	5.50	53	5.54	.304	2	.125	-15	0	-1.7
1916 Phi-A	1	20	.048	40	30	11	0	1	212^2	206	110	82	2	3	95	74	1.415	3.47	82	3.60	.266	7	.101	-10	3	-1.6
1917 Phi-A	0	0	....	2	0	0	0	0	3	2	1	1	0	0	1	2	1.000	3.00	92	1.66	.200	0	....	-0	0	0.0
Total 3	1	25	.038	52	37	13	0	1	269^2	266	157	116	3	8	131	94	1.472	3.87	74	3.96	.273	9	.106	-25	3	-3.3
• NAGLE, Judge				Walter Harold "Lucky" Nagle b: 3/10/1880, Santa Rosa, CA d: 5/26/1971, Santa Rosa, CA BR/TR, 6', 176 lbs. Deb: 4/26/1911																						
1911 Pit-N	4	2	.667	8	3	1	0	1	27^1	33	16	11	3	1	6	11	1.427	3.62	94	5.18	.324	1	.143	-1	1	-0.1
Bos-A	1	1	.500	5	1	0	0	0	27	27	12	10	2	0	6	12	1.222	3.33	98	3.26	.262	1	.100	-0	2	-0.1
• NAGY, Charles				Charles Harrison Nagy b: 5/5/1967, Bridgeport, CT BL/TR, 6'3", 200 lbs. Deb: 6/29/1990																						
1990 Cle-A	2	4	.333	9	8	0	0	0	45^2	58	31	30	7	1	21	26	1.730	5.91	66	6.54	.315	0	....	-9	0	-1.0
1991 Cle-A	10	15	.400	33	33	6	1	0	211^1	228	103	97	15	6	66	109	1.391	4.13	101	4.02	.275	0	....	4	10	0.4
1992 Cle-A★	17	10	.630	33	33	10	3	0	252	245	91	83	11	6	57	169	1.198	2.96	132	2.99	.260	0	....	28	20	2.9
1993 Cle-A	2	6	.250	9	9	1	0	0	48^2	66	38	34	6	2	13	30	1.623	6.29	69	5.90	.322	0	....	-11	0	-1.0
1994 Cle-A	10	8	.556	23	23	3	0	0	169^1	175	76	65	15	5	48	108	1.317	3.45	136	3.86	.265	0	....	24	13	2.2
1995* Cle-A	16	6	.727	29	29	2	1	0	178	194	95	90	20	6	61	139	1.433	4.55	103	4.63	.278	0	....	3	11	0.3
1996* Cle-A★	17	5	.773	32	32	5	0	0	222	217	89	84	21	3	61	167	1.252	3.41	144	3.50	.255	0	....	37	21	3.4
1997* Cle-A	15	11	.577	34	34	1	1	0	227	253	115	108	27	7	77	149	1.454	4.28	110	4.74	.282	1	.200	12	13	1.2
1998* Cle-A	15	10	.600	33	33	2	0	0	210^1	250	139	122	34	9	66	120	1.502	5.22	91	5.39	.297	0	.000	-10	9	-1.0
1999* Cle-A★	17	11	.607	33	32	1	0	0	202	238	120	111	26	6	59	126	1.470	4.95	102	4.97	.293	0	.000	3	11	0.2
2000 Cle-A	2	7	.222	11	11	0	0	0	57	71	53	52	15	2	21	41	1.614	8.21	60	6.54	.300	0	....	-20	0	-1.8
2001 Cle-A	5	6	.455	15	13	0	0	0	70^1	102	53	50	10	0	20	29	1.735	6.40	71	6.60	.342	1	1.000	-13	1	-1.2
2002 Cle-A	1	4	.200	19	7	0	0	0	48^2	76	51	48	10	2	13	22	1.829	8.88	49	8.01	.360	0	....	-24	0	-2.3
2003 SD-N	0	2	.000	5	0	0	0	0	12^1	15	7	6	0	0	3	7	1.459	4.38	90	4.10	.313	0	.000	-1	0	-0.1
Total 14	129	105	.551	318	297	31	6	0	1954^2	2188	1061	980	217	51	586	1242	1.419	4.51	101	4.57	.284	2	.105	25	109	2.2
• NAGY, Mike				Michael Timothy Nagy b: 3/25/1948, New York, NY BR/TR, 6'3", 200 lbs. Deb: 4/21/1969																						
1969 Bos-A	12	2	.857	33	28	7	1	0	196^2	183	84	68	10	11	106	84	**1.469**	3.11	122	4.06	.245	5	.077	19	14	1.8
1970 Bos-A	6	5	.545	23	20	4	0	0	128^2	138	71	64	16	2	64	56	1.570	4.48	88	5.13	.275	11	.250	-5	5	-0.3
1971 Bos-A	1	3	.250	12	7	0	0	0	38	46	29	28	4	0	20	9	1.737	6.63	56	6.04	.315	1	.083	-12	0	-1.3
1972 Bos-A	0	0	....	1	0	0	0	0	2	3	2	2	0	1	0	2	1.500	9.00	36	6.48	.375	0	....	-1	0	-0.1
1973 StL-N	0	2	.000	9	7	0	0	0	40^2	44	21	19	4	1	15	14	1.451	4.20	87	4.48	.282	1	.091	-3	0	-0.3

YEAR	TM-L	W	L	PCT	G	GS	CG	SH	SV	IP	H	R	ER	HR	HB	BB	SO	RAT	ERA	ERA+	CERA	OAV	BH	AVG	PR+	WS	TPW
1974	Hou-N	1	1	.500	9	0	0	0	0	12^2	17	13	12	3	1	5	5	1.737	8.53	41	7.26	.309	0	.000	-7	0	-0.8
Total	**6**	**20**	**13**	**.606**	**87**	**62**	**11**	**1**	**0**	418^2	**431**	**220**	**193**	**37**	**16**	**210**	**170**	**1.531**	**4.15**	**91**	**4.72**	**.267**	**18**	**.135**	**-8**	**19**	**-1.1**
• NAGY, Steve	Stephen Nagy b: 5/28/1919, Franklin, NJ BL/TL, 5'9", 170 lbs. Deb: 4/20/1947																										
1947	Pit-N	1	3	.250	6	1	0	0	0	14	18	10	9	1	0	9	4	1.929	5.79	73	6.29	.310	1	.250	-2	0	-0.2
1950	Was-A	2	5	.286	9	9	2	0	0	53^1	69	50	39	5	0	29	17	1.838	6.58	68	6.05	.307	5	.227	-12	0	-1.0
Total	**2**	**3**	**8**	**.273**	**15**	**10**	**2**	**0**	**0**	67^1	**87**	**60**	**48**	**6**	**0**	**38**	**21**	**1.856**	**6.42**	**69**	**6.10**	**.307**	**6**	**.231**	**-15**	**0**	**-1.2**
• NAHEM, Sam	Samuel Ralph "Subway Sam" Nahem b: 10/19/1915, New York, NY BR/TR, 6'1.5", 190 lbs. Deb: 10/2/1938																										
1938	Bro-N	1	0	1.000	1	1	1	0	0	9	6	3	3	0	0	4	2	1.111	3.00	130	1.90	.194	2	.400	1	1	0.1
1941	StL-N	5	2	.714	26	8	2	0	1	81^2	76	35	27	2	2	38	31	1.396	2.98	127	3.31	.243	4	.174	6	6	0.5
1942	Phi-N	1	3	.250	35	2	0	0	0	74^2	72	48	41	2	2	40	38	1.500	4.94	67	3.78	.254	2	.100	-14	0	-1.6
1948	Phi-N	3	3	.500	28	1	0	0	0	59	68	52	46	4	3	45	30	1.915	7.02	56	6.08	.288	2	.154	-20	0	-2.0
Total	**4**	**10**	**8**	**.556**	**90**	**12**	**3**	**0**	**1**	224^1	**222**	**138**	**117**	**8**	**7**	**127**	**101**	**1.556**	**4.69**	**78**	**4.14**	**.257**	**10**	**.164**	**-27**	**7**	**-2.9**
• NAKAMURA, Mike	Micheal Yoshihide Nakamura b: 9/6/1976, Nara, Japan BR/TR, 5'10", 178 lbs. Deb: 6/7/2003																										
2003	Min-A	0	0	....	12	0	0	0	1	12^2	20	11	11	4	1	2	14	1.737	7.82	58	8.35	.339	0	....	-4	0	-0.4
• NAKTENIS, Pete	Peter Ernest Naktenis b: 6/12/1914, Aberdeen, WA BL/TL, 6'1", 185 lbs. Deb: 6/13/1936																										
1936	Phi-A	0	1	.000	7	1	0	0	0	18^2	24	26	26	2	2	27	18	2.732	12.54	41	10.61	.324	1	.200	-15	0	-1.4
1939	Cin-N	0	0	....	3	0	0	0	0	4	2	1	1	0	2	0	1	.500	2.25	170	1.43	.154	0	....	1	0	0.1
Total	**2**	**0**	**1**	**.000**	**10**	**1**	**0**	**0**	**0**	22^2	**26**	**27**	**27**	**2**	**4**	**27**	**19**	**2.338**	**10.72**	**47**	**8.99**	**.299**	**1**	**.200**	**-15**	**0**	**-1.3**
• NANCE, Shane	Joseph Shane Nance b: 9/7/1977, Houston, TX BL/TL, 5'8", 180 lbs. Deb: 8/24/2002																										
2002	Mil-N	0	0	....	4	0	0	0	0	6^1	4	3	3	1	0	4	5	1.263	4.26	96	3.29	.174	1	.333	-0	1	0.0
2003	Mil-N	0	2	.000	26	0	0	0	0	24^1	34	16	13	5	1	10	25	1.808	4.81	88	7.31	.327	0	....	-1	1	-0.1
Total	**2**	**0**	**2**	**.000**	**30**	**0**	**0**	**0**	**0**	30^2	**38**	**19**	**16**	**6**	**1**	**14**	**30**	**1.696**	**4.70**	**90**	**6.48**	**.299**	**1**	**.333**	**-1**	**2**	**-0.1**
• NAPIER, Buddy	Skelton Le Roy Napier b: 12/18/1889, Byromville, GA d: 3/29/1968, Hutchins, TX BR/TR, 5'11", 165 lbs. Deb: 8/14/1912																										
1912	StL-A	1	2	.333	7	2	0	0	0	25^1	33	21	14	0	3	5	10	1.500	4.97	67	4.73	.317	0	.000	-5	0	-0.6
1918	Chi-N	0	0	....	1	0	0	0	0	6^2	10	4	4	0	0	4	2	2.100	5.40	52	7.16	.357	1	.333	-2	0	-0.2
1920	Cin-N	4	2	.667	9	5	5	1	0	49	47	12	7	0	1	7	17	1.102	1.29	236	2.34	.254	3	.214	9	5	1.1
1921	Cin-N	0	2	.000	22	6	1	0	1	56^2	72	38	35	2	0	13	14	1.500	5.56	64	4.50	.329	2	.143	-12	1	-1.0
Total	**4**	**5**	**6**	**.455**	**39**	**13**	**6**	**1**	**1**	137^2	**162**	**75**	**60**	**2**	**4**	**29**	**43**	**1.387**	**3.92**	**86**	**3.90**	**.302**	**6**	**.158**	**-9**	**6**	**-0.7**
• NARANJO, Cholly	Lazaro Ramon Gonzalo "Gonzalo" Naranjo b: 11/25/1934, Havana, Cuba BL/TR, 5'11.5", 165 lbs. Deb: 7/8/1956																										
1956	Pit-N	1	2	.333	17	3	0	0	0	34^1	37	22	17	7	1	17	26	1.573	4.46	85	5.76	.282	1	.143	-2	1	-0.2
• NARLESKI, Ray	Raymond Edmond Narleski b: 11/25/1928, Camden, NJ BR/TR, 6'1", 175 lbs. Deb: 4/17/1954																										
1954*	Cle-A	3	3	.500	42	2	1	0	13	89	59	25	22	8	2	44	52	1.157	2.22	165	2.59	.189	0	.000	13	12	1.2
1955	Cle-A	9	1	.900	**60**	1	1	0	**19**	111^2	91	47	46	11	0	52	94	1.281	3.71	108	3.26	.220	7	.292	3	14	0.4
1956	Cle-A★	3	2	.600	32	0	0	0	4	59^1	36	11	10	5	1	19	42	.927	1.52	277	1.75	.170	2	.250	18	9	1.8
1957	Cle-A	11	5	.688	46	15	7	1	16	154^1	136	65	53	15	4	70	93	1.335	3.09	120	3.63	.235	4	.093	13	15	1.1
1958	Cle-A★	13	10	.565	44	24	7	0	1	183^1	179	87	83	21	3	91	102	**1.473**	4.07	90	4.40	.255	11	.204	-10	9	-0.9
1959	Det-A	4	12	.250	42	10	1	0	5	104^1	105	83	67	21	1	59	71	1.572	5.78	70	5.30	.254	2	.095	-20	0	-2.1
Total	**6**	**43**	**33**	**.566**	**266**	**52**	**17**	**1**	**58**	**702**	**606**	**318**	**281**	**81**	**11**	**335**	**454**	**1.340**	**3.60**	**106**	**3.73**	**.230**	**26**	**.157**	**17**	**59**	**1.4**
• NARUM, Buster	Leslie Ferdinand Narum b: 11/16/1940, Philadelphia, PA BR/TR, 6'1", 200 lbs. Deb: 4/14/1963																										
1963	Bal-A	0	0	....	7	0	0	0	0	9	8	3	3	0	0	5	5	1.444	3.00	118	3.07	.242	1	1.000	1	1	0.2
1964	Was-A	9	15	.375	38	32	7	2	0	199	195	104	95	31	5	73	121	1.347	4.30	86	4.33	.259	4	.061	-14	6	-1.9
1965	Was-A	4	12	.250	46	24	2	0	0	173^2	176	98	86	16	7	91	86	**1.537**	4.46	78	4.60	.267	2	.043	-18	3	-2.1
1966	Was-A	0	0	....	3	0	0	0	0	3^1	11	9	8	2	0	4	0	4.500	21.60	16	30.89	.579	0	....	-7	0	-0.7
1967	Was-A	1	0	1.000	2	2	0	0	0	11^2	8	4	4	1	0	4	8	1.029	3.09	102	2.24	.195	0	.000	0	1	-0.1
Total	**5**	**14**	**27**	**.341**	**96**	**58**	**9**	**2**	**0**	396^2	**398**	**218**	**196**	**50**	**12**	**177**	**220**	**1.450**	**4.45**	**80**	**4.59**	**.264**	**7**	**.059**	**-38**	**11**	**-4.6**
• NASH, Jim	James Edwin Nash b: 2/9/1945, Hawthorne, NV BR/TR, 6'5", 230 lbs. Deb: 7/3/1966																										
1966	KC-A	12	1	.923	18	17	5	0	1	127	95	32	29	6	0	47	98	1.118	2.06	165	2.28	.204	5	.102	18	12	1.8
1967	KC-A	12	17	.414	37	34	8	2	0	222^1	200	103	93	21	4	87	186	1.291	3.76	85	3.52	.242	7	.100	-14	7	-1.8
1968	Oak-A	13	13	.500	34	33	12	6	0	228^2	185	63	58	18	3	55	169	1.050	2.28	123	2.34	.219	5	.068	13	16	1.3
1969	Oak-A	8	8	.500	26	19	3	1	0	115^1	112	53	47	17	2	30	75	1.231	3.67	94	3.66	.247	4	.111	-3	5	-0.4
1970	Atl-N	13	9	.591	34	33	6	2	0	212^1	211	105	96	22	5	90	153	1.418	4.07	105	4.13	.257	7	.088	10	13	0.8
1971	Atl-N	9	7	.563	32	19	2	0	2	133	166	81	73	17	0	50	65	1.624	4.94	75	5.66	.314	7	.149	-17	3	-2.0
1972	Atl-N	1	1	.500	11	4	0	0	1	31^1	35	20	19	2	0	25	10	1.915	5.46	69	6.36	.307	2	.222	-5	0	-0.6
	Phi-N	0	8	.000	9	8	0	0	0	37^1	46	33	26	5	3	17	15	1.688	6.27	57	6.03	.311	1	.100	-12	0	-1.3
	Yr.	1	9	.100	20	12	0	0	1	68^2	81	53	45	7	3	42	25	1.791	5.90	62	6.18	.309	3	.158	-17	0	-1.8
Total	**7**	**68**	**64**	**.515**	**201**	**167**	**36**	**11**	**4**	1107^1	**1050**	**490**	**441**	**108**	**17**	**401**	**771**	**1.310**	**3.58**	**97**	**3.69**	**.250**	**38**	**.101**	**-10**	**56**	**-2.2**
• NASTU, Philip	Philip "Phil" Nastu b: 3/8/1955, Bridgeport, CT BL/TL, 6'2", 180 lbs. Deb: 9/15/1978																										
1978	SF-N	0	1	.000	3	1	0	0	0	8	8	5	5	1	0	2	5	1.250	5.63	61	3.70	.258	0	.000	-2	0	-0.2
1979	SF-N	3	4	.429	25	14	1	0	0	100	105	51	48	14	2	41	47	1.460	4.32	81	4.73	.272	1	.042	-8	3	-0.9
1980	SF-N	0	0	....	6	0	0	0	0	6	10	9	4	1	0	5	1	2.500	6.00	59	10.25	.357	0	....	-2	0	-0.2
Total	**3**	**3**	**5**	**.375**	**34**	**15**	**1**	**0**	**0**	**114**	**123**	**65**	**57**	**16**	**2**	**48**	**53**	**1.500**	**4.50**	**78**	**4.95**	**.276**	**1**	**.040**	**-11**	**3**	**-1.3**
• NATHAN, Joe	Joseph Michael Nathan b: 11/22/1974, Houston, TX BR/TR, 6'4", 195 lbs. Deb: 4/21/1999																										
1999	SF-N	7	4	.636	19	14	0	0	1	90^1	84	45	42	17	1	46	54	1.439	4.18	100	4.78	.243	5	.179	0	5	0.1
2000	SF-N	5	2	.714	20	15	0	0	0	93^1	89	63	54	12	4	63	61	1.629	5.21	81	5.23	.255	5	.156	-10	2	-0.7
2002	SF-N	0	0	....	4	0	0	0	0	3^2	1	0	0	0	0	0	2	.273	0.00	....	0.17	.083	0	....	2	1	0.2
2003*	SF-N	12	4	.750	78	0	0	0	0	79	51	26	26	7	3	33	83	1.063	2.96	138	2.34	.186	0	.000	8	11	0.8
Total	**4**	**24**	**10**	**.706**	**121**	**29**	**0**	**0**	**1**	266^1	**225**	**134**	**122**	**36**	**8**	**142**	**200**	**1.378**	**4.12**	**102**	**4.15**	**.229**	**10**	**.164**	**-0**	**19**	**0.3**
• NATION, Joey	Joseph Paul Nation b: 9/28/1978, Oklahoma City, OK BL/TL, 6'2", 205 lbs. Deb: 9/23/2000																										
2000	Chi-N	0	2	.000	2	2	0	0	0	11^2	12	9	9	2	2	8	8	1.714	6.94	65	6.81	.279	2	.500	-3	0	-0.2
• NAULTY, Dan	Daniel Donovan Naulty b: 1/6/1970, Los Angeles, CA BR/TR, 6'6", 210 lbs. Deb: 4/2/1996																										
1996	Min-A	3	2	.600	49	0	0	0	4	57	43	26	24	5	0	35	56	1.368	3.79	135	3.37	.207	0	....	8	6	0.7
1997	Min-A	1	1	.500	29	0	0	0	1	30^2	29	20	20	8	0	10	23	1.272	5.87	79	4.58	.254	0	....	-4	1	-0.4
1998	Min-A	0	2	.000	19	0	0	0	0	23^2	25	16	13	3	0	10	15	1.479	4.94	96	4.60	.269	0	....	-0	1	0.0
1999	NY-A	1	0	1.000	33	0	0	0	0	49^1	40	24	24	8	4	22	25	1.257	4.38	108	4.04	.225	0	....	2	3	0.2
Total	**4**	**5**	**5**	**.500**	**130**	**0**	**0**	**0**	**5**	160^2	**137**	**86**	**81**	**24**	**4**	**77**	**119**	**1.332**	**4.54**	**106**	**3.99**	**.231**	**0**	**....**	**6**	**11**	**0.5**
• NAVARRO, Jaime	Jaime (Cintron) Navarro b: 3/27/1967, Bayamon, Puerto Rico BR/TR, 6'4", 210 lbs. Deb: 6/20/1989																										
1989	Mil-A	7	8	.467	19	17	1	0	0	109^2	119	47	38	6	1	32	56	1.377	3.12	123	3.80	.277	0	....	8	7	0.8
1990	Mil-A	8	7	.533	32	22	3	0	1	149^1	176	83	74	11	4	41	75	1.453	4.46	87	4.47	.293	0	....	-8	5	-0.8
1991	Mil-A	15	12	.556	34	34	10	2	0	234	237	117	102	18	6	73	114	1.325	3.92	101	3.70	.261	0	....	1	12	0.1
1992	Mil-A	17	11	.607	34	34	5	3	0	246	224	98	91	14	6	64	100	1.171	3.33	115	2.88	.246	0	....	9	15	0.9
1993	Mil-A	11	12	.478	35	34	5	1	0	214^1	254	135	127	21	11	73	114	1.526	5.33	80	5.08	.300	0	....	-24	6	-2.4
1994	Mil-A	4	9	.308	29	10	0	0	0	89^2	115	71	66	10	4	35	65	1.673	6.62	76	5.93	.314	0	....	-19	1	-1.7
1995	Chi-N	14	6	.700	29	29	1	1	0	200^1	194	79	73	19	3	56	128	1.248	3.28	125	3.41	.251	12	.185	17	15	1.8
1996	Chi-N	15	12	.556	35	35	4	1	0	236^2	244	116	103	25	10	72	158	1.335	3.92	111	4.08	.269	10	.130	8	13	0.6
1997	Chi-A	9	14	.391	33	33	2	0	0	209^2	267	155	135	22	3	73	142	**1.622**	5.79	76	5.46	.309	0	.000	-30	3	-2.8
1998	Chi-A	8	16	.333	37	27	1	0	1	172^2	223	135	122	30	7	77	71	**1.737**	6.36	72	6.80	.315	0	.000	-35	1	-3.3

YEAR TM-L	W	L	PCT	G	GS	CG	SH	SV	IP	H	R	ER	HR	HB	BB	SO	RAT	ERA	ERA+	CERA	OAV	BH	AVG	PR+	WS	TPW
1999 Chi-A	8	13	.381	32	27	0	0	0	159^2	206	126	108	29	11	71	74	1.735	6.09	80	6.96	.313	0	.000	-20	2	-1.9
2000 Mil-N	0	5	.000	5	5	0	0	0	18^2	34	31	26	6	0	18	7	2.786	12.54	36	14.01	.410	0	.000	-17	0	-1.6
Cle-A	0	1	.000	7	2	0	0	0	14^2	20	13	13	3	1	5	9	1.705	7.98	62	7.08	.328	0	....	-5	0	-0.4
Total 12	116	126	.479	361	309	32	8	2	2055^1	2313	1206	1078	214	67	690	1113	1.461	4.72	91	4.73	.285	22	.145	-115	80	-10.8
• NAVARRO, Julio	Julio (Ventura) "Whiplash" Navarro b: 1/9/1936, Vieques, Puerto Rico BR/TR, 6', 190 lbs. Deb: 9/3/1962																									
1962 LA-A	1	1	.500	9	0	0	0	0	15^1	20	9	8	2	0	4	11	1.565	4.70	82	5.23	.317	1	.500	-1	1	-0.1
1963 LA-A	4	5	.444	57	0	0	0	12	90^1	75	36	29	7	2	32	53	1.185	2.89	119	2.82	.228	3	.200	6	8	0.7
1964 LA-A	0	0	....	5	0	0	0	1	9^1	5	2	2	0	2	5	8	1.071	1.93	170	2.41	.167	0	.000	1	1	0.1
Det-A	2	1	.667	26	0	0	0	2	41	40	19	18	9	2	16	36	1.366	3.95	93	4.77	.250	0	.000	-1	2	-0.2
Yr.	2	1	.667	31	0	0	0	3	50^1	45	21	20	9	4	21	44	1.311	3.58	101	4.33	.237	0	.000	-0	3	-0.1
1965 Det-A	0	2	.000	15	1	0	0	1	30	25	16	14	5	0	12	22	1.233	4.20	83	3.62	.238	0	.000	-2	1	-0.3
1966 Det-A	0	0	....	1	0	0	0	0	0	2	3	3	2	1	0	0	....	∞	....	∞	1.000	0	....	-3	0	-0.3
1970 Atl-N	0	0	....	17	0	0	0	1	26^1	24	12	12	7	1	1	21	.949	4.10	105	3.25	.233	1	.167	1	2	0.1
Total 6	7	9	.438	130	1	0	0	17	212^1	191	97	86	32	8	70	151	1.229	3.65	103	3.52	.241	5	.147	0	15	0.0
• NAYLOR, Earl	Earl Eugene Naylor b: 5/19/1919, Kansas City, MO d: 1/16/1990, Winter Haven, FL BR/TR, 6', 190 lbs. Deb: 4/15/1942 ♦																									
1942 Phi-N	0	5	.000	20	4	1	0	0	60^1	68	43	41	5	0	29	19	1.608	6.12	54	4.86	.286	33	.196	-19	0	-3.2
• NAYLOR, Rollie	Roleine Cecil Naylor b: 2/4/1892, Krum, TX d: 6/18/1966, Fort Worth, TX BR/TR, 6'1.5", 180 lbs. Deb: 9/14/1917																									
1917 Phi-A	2	2	.500	5	5	3	0	0	33	30	10	6	1	1	11	11	1.242	1.64	168	2.97	.265	1	.091	5	2	0.4
1919 Phi-A	5	18	.217	31	23	17	0	0	204^2	210	109	76	2	4	64	68	1.339	3.34	102	3.50	.280	12	.169	11	7	0.9
1920 Phi-A	10	23	.303	42	36	20	0	0	251^1	306	147	97	7	6	86	90	1.560	3.47	116	4.78	.312	14	.163	20	12	1.4
1921 Phi-A	3	13	.188	32	19	6	0	0	169^1	214	106	91	10	3	55	39	1.589	4.84	92	4.95	.315	6	.115	-4	6	-0.7
1922 Phi-A	10	15	.400	35	26	11	0	0	171^1	212	115	90	7	3	51	37	1.535	4.73	90	4.49	.309	11	.200	-8	7	-0.6
1923 Phi-A	12	7	.632	26	20	9	2	0	143	149	68	55	5	0	59	27	1.455	3.46	119	3.78	.273	11	.244	14	12	1.5
1924 Phi-A	0	5	.000	10	7	1	0	0	38^1	53	29	27	2	0	20	10	1.904	6.34	68	6.01	.333	3	.375	-8	0	-0.7
Total 7	42	83	.336	181	136	67	2	0	1011	1174	584	442	34	17	346	282	1.503	3.93	102	4.35	.300	58	.177	29	46	2.1
• NAYMICK, Mike	Michael John Naymick b: 9/6/1917, Berlin, PA BR/TR, 6'8", 225 lbs. Deb: 9/24/1939																									
1939 Cle-A	0	1	.000	2	1	1	0	0	4^2	3	1	1	0	0	5	3	1.714	1.93	228	3.46	.188	0	.000	1	0	0.1
1940 Cle-A	1	2	.333	13	4	0	0	0	30	36	17	17	1	3	17	15	1.767	5.10	83	5.48	.290	1	.167	-4	1	-0.3
1943 Cle-A	4	4	.500	29	4	0	0	2	62^2	32	23	16	3	3	47	41	1.261	2.30	135	2.43	.160	3	.188	4	4	0.4
1944 Cle-A	0	0	....	7	0	0	0	0	13	16	15	14	1	0	10	4	2.000	9.69	34	6.28	.314	0	.000	-9	0	-1.0
StL-N	0	0	....	1	0	0	0	0	2	2	1	1	0	0	1	1	1.500	4.50	78	4.01	.333	0	....	-0	0	0.0
Total 4	5	7	.417	52	9	1	0	2	112^1	89	57	49	5	6	80	64	1.504	3.93	90	3.76	.224	4	.154	-8	5	-0.9
• NEAGLE, Denny	Dennis Edward Neagle b: 9/13/1968, Gambrills, MD BL/TL, 6'4", 217 lbs. Deb: 7/27/1991																									
1991 Min-A	0	1	.000	7	3	0	0	0	20	28	9	9	3	0	7	14	1.750	4.05	105	6.53	.329	0	....	0	1	0.0
1992* Pit-N	4	6	.400	55	6	0	0	2	86^1	81	46	43	9	2	43	77	1.436	4.48	77	4.04	.247	0	.000	-11	2	-1.3
1993 Pit-N	3	5	.375	50	7	0	0	1	81^1	82	49	48	10	3	37	73	1.463	5.31	76	4.57	.258	0	.000	-12	2	-1.4
1994 Pit-N	9	10	.474	24	24	2	0	0	137	135	80	78	18	3	49	122	1.343	5.12	84	4.09	.259	8	.190	-13	6	-1.2
1995 Pit-N★	13	8	.619	31	**31**	5	1	0	**209^2**	221	91	80	20	3	45	150	1.269	3.43	125	3.67	.273	9	.122	23	16	2.2
1996 Pit-N	14	6	.700	27	27	1	0	0	182^2	186	67	62	21	3	34	131	1.204	3.05	143	3.55	.267	10	.182	29	16	2.8
*Atl-N	2	3	.400	6	6	1	0	0	38^2	40	26	24	5	0	14	18	1.397	5.59	79	4.37	.268	2	.143	-5	1	-0.5
Yr.	16	9	.640	33	33	2	0	0	221^1	226	93	86	26	3	48	149	1.238	3.50	125	3.69	.267	12	.174	24	17	2.4
1997* Atl-N★	**20**	5	.800	34	34	4	4	0	233^1	204	87	77	18	6	49	172	1.084	2.97	142	2.60	.233	11	.153	31	21	3.1
1998* Atl-N	16	11	.593	32	31	5	2	0	210^1	196	91	83	25	6	60	165	1.217	3.55	117	3.55	.250	11	.175	12	14	1.3
1999 Cin-N	9	5	.643	20	19	0	0	0	111^2	95	54	53	23	4	40	76	1.209	4.27	109	3.88	.229	6	.162	1	7	0.1
2000 Cin-N	8	2	.800	18	18	0	0	0	117^2	111	48	46	15	3	50	88	1.368	3.52	134	4.12	.247	7	.189	14	10	1.4
*NY-A	7	7	.500	16	15	1	0	0	91^1	99	61	59	16	2	31	58	1.423	5.81	83	4.89	.278	0	....	-8	3	-0.8
2001 Col-N	9	8	.529	30	30	0	0	0	170^2	192	107	102	29	7	60	139	1.477	5.38	99	5.21	.284	11	.196	-2	8	0.1
2002 Col-N	8	11	.421	35	28	1	0	0	164^1	170	101	96	26	10	63	111	1.418	5.26	91	4.80	.266	12	.267	-7	8	-0.5
2003 Col-N	2	4	.333	7	7	0	0	0	35^1	47	31	31	12	1	12	21	1.670	7.90	62	7.90	.320	0	.000	-11	0	-1.2
Total 13	124	92	.574	392	286	20	7	3	1890^1	1887	948	891	250	53	594	1415	1.312	4.24	105	4.06	.260	87	.164	41	115	4.3
• NEAGLE, Jack	John Henry Neagle b: 1/2/1858, Syracuse, NY d: 9/20/1904, Syracuse, NY BR/TR, 5'6", 155 lbs. Deb: 7/8/1879 ♦																									
1879 Cin-N	0	1	.000	2	2	1	0	0	13	13	12	5	0	....	5	4	1.385	3.46	67	....	.244	2	.167	-2	0	-0.3
1883 Phi-N	1	7	.125	8	7	6	0	0	61^1	88	77	47	0	....	21	13	1.777	6.90	45	....	.318	12	.164	-21	0	-2.5
Bal-a	1	4	.200	6	5	4	0	0	46	48	48	25	1	....	20	9	1.478	4.89	71	....	.252	10	.286	-5	2	-0.3
Pit-a	3	12	.200	16	16	12	0	0	114	156	123	74	9	....	25	41	1.588	5.84	55	....	.306	19	.188	-31	1	-3.2
Yr.	4	16	.200	22	21	16	0	0	160	204	171	99	10	....	45	50	1.556	5.57	59	....	.291	29	.213	-36	3	-3.5
1884 Pit-a	11	26	.297	38	38	37	2	0	326	354	219	135	6	18	70	85	1.301	3.73	90	....	.262	22	.149	-3	14	-1.0
Total 3	16	50	.242	70	68	60	2	0	560^1	659	479	286	16	18	141	152	1.428	4.59	71	....	.277	65	.176	-62	17	-7.3
• NEAL, Blaine	Blaine Neal b: 4/6/1978, Marlton, NJ BL/TR, 6'5", 205 lbs. Deb: 9/3/2001																									
2001 Fla-N	0	0	....	4	0	0	0	0	5^1	7	4	4	0	0	5	3	2.250	6.75	62	7.12	.304	0	....	-2	0	-0.1
2002 Fla-N	3	0	1.000	32	0	0	0	0	33	32	12	10	1	0	14	33	1.394	2.73	144	3.35	.248	0	....	4	3	0.4
2003 Fla-N	0	0	....	18	0	0	0	0	21	38	20	19	2	1	9	10	2.238	8.14	50	9.42	.413	0	....	-10	0	-0.9
Total 3	3	0	1.000	54	0	0	0	0	59^1	77	36	33	3	1	28	46	1.770	5.01	81	5.84	.316	0	....	-7	3	-0.7
• NEALE, Joe	Joseph Hunt Neale b: 5/7/1866, Wadsworth, OH d: 12/30/1913, Akron, OH BR/TR, 5'8", 153 lbs. Deb: 6/21/1886 ♦																									
1886 Lou-a	0	1	.000	1	1	0	0	0	7	11	12	6	0	1	7	0	2.571	7.71	47	....	.342	0	.000	-3	0	-0.4
1887 Lou-a	1	4	.200	5	4	4	0	0	41^1	75	50	32	4	2	15	11	1.815	6.97	63	....	.378	4	.182	-13	0	-1.2
1890 StL-a	5	3	.625	10	9	8	0	0	69	53	37	26	4	4	15	23	.986	3.39	127	....	.206	2	.067	7	6	0.3
1891 StL-a	6	4	.600	15	11	9	1	1	110^1	109	73	52	4	7	36	24	1.314	4.24	99	....	.249	6	.118	-2	7	-0.4
Total 4	12	12	.500	31	25	21	1	1	227^2	248	172	116	12	14	73	58	1.344	4.59	92	....	.268	12	.111	-11	13	-1.7
• NECCIAI, Ron	Ronald Andrew Necciai b: 6/18/1932, Gallatin, PA BR/TR, 6'5", 185 lbs. Deb: 8/10/1952																									
1952 Pit-N	1	6	.143	12	9	0	0	0	54^2	63	45	43	5	1	32	31	1.738	7.08	56	5.70	.296	1	.059	-18	0	-2.0
• NEGRAY, Ron	Ronald Alvin Negray b: 2/26/1930, Akron, OH BR/TR, 6'1", 185 lbs. Deb: 9/14/1952																									
1952 Bro-N	0	0	....	4	1	0	0	0	13	15	5	5	0	0	5	5	1.538	3.46	105	4.17	.294	0	.000	0	1	0.0
1955 Phi-N	4	3	.571	19	10	2	0	0	71^2	71	31	28	13	0	21	30	1.284	3.52	113	4.11	.257	0	.000	3	5	-0.1
1956 Phi-N	2	3	.400	39	4	0	0	3	66^2	72	36	31	6	1	24	44	1.440	4.19	89	4.14	.280	3	.429	-2	3	-0.1
1958 LA-N	0	0	....	4	0	0	0	0	11^1	12	9	9	4	0	7	2	1.676	7.15	57	7.46	.279	0	.000	-4	0	-0.4
Total 4	6	6	.500	66	15	2	0	3	162^2	170	81	73	23	1	57	81	1.395	4.04	95	4.36	.271	3	.086	-3	9	-0.6
• NEHER, Jim	James Gilmore Neher b: 2/5/1889, Rochester, NY d: 11/11/1951, Buffalo, NY BR/TR, 5'11", 185 lbs. Deb: 9/10/1912																									
1912 Cle-A	0	0	....	1	0	0	0	0	1	0	0	0	0	0	0	0	.000	0.00	....	0.00	.000	0	....	0	0	0.0
• NEHF, Art	Arthur Neukom Nehf b: 7/31/1892, Terre Haute, IN d: 12/18/1960, Phoenix, AZ BL/TL, 5'9.5", 176 lbs. Deb: 8/13/1915																									
1915 Bos-N	5	4	.556	12	10	6	4	0	78^1	60	29	22	0	3	21	39	1.034	2.53	106	1.87	.214	4	.143	0	5	-0.1
1916 Bos-N	7	5	.583	22	13	6	1	0	121	110	40	27	1	3	20	36	1.074	2.01	122	2.22	.244	5	.125	6	7	0.6
1917 Bos-N	17	8	.680	38	23	16	5	0	233^1	197	78	56	4	4	39	101	1.011	2.16	118	1.98	.231	12	.171	13	19	2.0
1918 Bos-N	15	15	.500	32	31	**28**	2	0	284^1	274	107	85	2	6	76	96	1.231	2.69	100	2.82	.259	16	.168	6	15	0.9
1919 Bos-N	8	9	.471	22	19	13	1	0	168^2	151	66	58	6	6	40	53	1.132	3.09	92	2.57	.242	13	.206	-5	9	-0.3
NY-N	9	2	.818	13	12	9	2	0	102	70	23	17	2	2	19	24	.873	1.50	187	1.46	.196	8	.229	13	11	1.8
Yr.	17	11	.607	35	31	22	3	0	270^2	221	89	75	8	8	59	77	1.034	2.49	114	2.15	.225	21	.214	9	20	1.6
1920 NY-N	21	12	.636	40	33	22	4	0	280^2	273	113	96	8	1	45	79	1.133	3.08	97	2.58	.260	26	.268	-7	19	-0.2
1921* NY-N	20	10	.667	41	34	18	2	1	260^2	266	116	105	18	2	55	67	1.231	3.63	101	3.29	.271	18	.202	-6	17	-0.6

YEAR TM-L	W	L	PCT	G	GS	CG	SH	SV	IP	H	R	ER	HR	HB	BB	SO	RAT	ERA	ERA+	CERA	OAV	BH	AVG	PR+	WS	TPW
1922* NY-N	19	13	.594	37	35	20	2	1	268^{1}	286	122	98	15	4	64	60	1.304	3.29	122	3.54	.276	25	.255	13	21	1.5
1923* NY-N	13	10	.565	34	27	7	1	2	196	219	112	98	14	2	49	50	1.367	4.50	85	3.91	.281	12	.190	-17	9	-1.6
1924* NY-N	14	4	.778	30	20	11	0	2	171^{2}	167	75	69	14	2	42	72	1.217	3.62	101	3.20	.254	13	.228	0	12	0.6
1925 NY-N	11	9	.550	29	20	8	1	1	155	193	86	65	7	1	50	63	1.568	3.77	107	4.77	.308	11	.216	5	12	0.5
1926 NY-N	0	0	....	2	0	0	0	0	1^{2}	2	2	2	0	0	1	0	1.800	10.80	35	4.93	.286	0	.000	-1	0	-0.1
Cin-N	0	1	.000	7	0	0	0	0	17	25	10	7	0	1	5	4	1.765	3.71	100	5.92	.379	1	.200	-0	0	0.0
Yr.	0	1	.000	9	0	0	0	0	18^{2}	27	12	9	0	1	6	4	1.768	4.34	85	5.83	.370	1	.167	-1	0	-0.2
1927 Cin-N	3	5	.375	21	5	1	0	4	45^{1}	59	33	28	2	0	14	21	1.610	5.56	68	4.97	.319	1	.077	-9	0	-1.0
Chi-N	1	1	.500	8	2	2	1	1	26^{1}	25	5	4	0	0	9	12	1.291	1.37	282	2.84	.260	3	.429	7	4	0.8
Yr.	4	6	.400	29	7	3	1	5	71^{2}	84	38	32	2	0	23	33	1.493	4.02	94	4.19	.299	4	.200	-2	4	-0.2
1928 Chi-N	13	7	.650	31	21	10	2	0	176^{2}	190	62	52	3	1	52	40	1.370	2.65	145	3.45	.281	11	.190	17	18	1.9
1929* Chi-N	8	5	.615	32	15	4	0	1	120^{2}	148	85	75	11	2	39	27	1.550	5.59	82	5.08	.310	13	.289	-15	5	-1.0
Total 15	184	120	.605	451	320	181	28	13	2707^{2}	2715	1164	964	107	40	640	844	1.239	3.20	105	3.13	.265	192	.210	21	183	5.8

• NEIBAUER, Gary Gary Wayne Neibauer b: 10/29/1944, Billings, MT BR/TR, 6'3", 200 lbs. Deb: 4/12/1969

YEAR TM-L	W	L	PCT	G	GS	CG	SH	SV	IP	H	R	ER	HR	HB	BB	SO	RAT	ERA	ERA+	CERA	OAV	BH	AVG	PR+	WS	TPW
1969* Atl-N	1	2	.333	29	0	0	0	0	57^{2}	42	28	25	9	1	31	42	1.266	3.90	92	3.48	.204	0	.000	-2	2	-0.3
1970 Atl-N	0	3	.000	7	0	0	0	0	12^{2}	11	7	7	0	0	8	9	1.500	4.97	86	3.35	.239	0	.000	-1	0	-0.1
1971 Atl-N	1	0	1.000	6	1	0	0	1	21	14	5	5	3	1	9	6	1.095	2.14	173	2.79	.187	0	.000	4	3	0.3
1972 Atl-N	0	0	....	8	0	0	0	0	17^{1}	27	15	14	6	1	6	8	1.904	7.27	52	9.81	.360	0	.000	-6	0	-0.7
Phi-N	0	2	.000	9	2	0	0	0	18^{2}	17	12	11	1	1	14	7	1.661	5.30	68	4.73	.239	1	.250	-4	0	-0.4
Yr.	0	2	.000	17	2	0	0	0	36	44	27	25	7	2	20	15	1.778	6.25	59	7.17	.301	1	.125	-10	0	-1.1
1973 Atl-N	2	1	.667	16	1	0	0	0	21^{1}	24	19	17	3	2	19	9	2.016	7.17	55	7.48	.282	1	.250	-7	0	-0.7
Total 5	4	8	.333	75	4	0	0	1	148^{2}	135	86	79	22	6	87	81	1.493	4.78	79	4.84	.242	2	.069	-16	5	-1.8

• NEIDLINGER, Jim James Llewellyn Neidlinger b: 9/24/1964, Vallejo, CA BB/TR, 6'4", 180 lbs. Deb: 8/1/1990

YEAR TM-L	W	L	PCT	G	GS	CG	SH	SV	IP	H	R	ER	HR	HB	BB	SO	RAT	ERA	ERA+	CERA	OAV	BH	AVG	PR+	WS	TPW
1990 LA-N	5	3	.625	12	12	0	0	0	74	67	30	27	4	1	15	46	1.108	3.28	111	2.56	.241	3	.120	3	5	0.3

• NEIGER, Al Alvin Edward Neiger b: 3/26/1939, Wilmington, DE BL/TL, 6', 195 lbs. Deb: 7/30/1960

YEAR TM-L	W	L	PCT	G	GS	CG	SH	SV	IP	H	R	ER	HR	HB	BB	SO	RAT	ERA	ERA+	CERA	OAV	BH	AVG	PR+	WS	TPW
1960 Phi-N	0	0	....	6	0	0	0	0	12^{2}	16	8	8	2	2	4	3	1.579	5.68	68	6.21	.340	1	.500	-3	0	-0.2

• NEKOLA, Bots Francis Joseph Nekola b: 12/10/1906, New York, NY d: 3/11/1987, Rockville Centre, NY BL/TL, 5'11.5", 175 lbs. Deb: 7/19/1929

YEAR TM-L	W	L	PCT	G	GS	CG	SH	SV	IP	H	R	ER	HR	HB	BB	SO	RAT	ERA	ERA+	CERA	OAV	BH	AVG	PR+	WS	TPW
1929 NY-A	0	0	....	9	1	0	0	0	18^{2}	21	10	9	0	0	15	2	1.929	4.34	89	5.47	.296	2	.500	-1	1	0.0
1933 Det-A	0	0	....	2	0	0	0	0	1^{1}	4	4	4	1	0	1	0	3.750	27.00	16	27.14	.500	0	....	-3	0	-0.3
Total 2	0	0	....	11	1	0	0	0	20	25	14	13	1	0	16	2	2.050	5.85	68	6.92	.317	2	.500	-5	1	-0.3

• NELSON, Andy Andrew A. “Peaches” Nelson b: 11/30/1884, St. Paul, MN TL Deb: 5/26/1908

YEAR TM-L	W	L	PCT	G	GS	CG	SH	SV	IP	H	R	ER	HR	HB	BB	SO	RAT	ERA	ERA+	CERA	OAV	BH	AVG	PR+	WS	TPW
1908 Chi-A	0	0	....	2	1	0	0	0	9	11	4	2	0	1	4	1	1.667	2.00	116	5.78	.282	0	.000	0	0	0.1

• NELSON, Bill William F. Nelson b: 9/28/1863, Terre Haute, IN d: 6/23/1941, Terre Haute, IN TR Deb: 9/3/1884

YEAR TM-L	W	L	PCT	G	GS	CG	SH	SV	IP	H	R	ER	HR	HB	BB	SO	RAT	ERA	ERA+	CERA	OAV	BH	AVG	PR+	WS	TPW
1884 Pit-a	1	2	.333	3	3	3	0	0	26	26	21	13	1	4	8	6	1.308	4.50	75	....	.247	2	.167	-2	1	-0.3

• NELSON, Emmett George Emmett “Ramrod” Nelson b: 2/26/1905, Viborg, SD d: 8/25/1967, Sioux Falls, SD BR/TR, 6'3", 180 lbs. Deb: 6/24/1935

YEAR TM-L	W	L	PCT	G	GS	CG	SH	SV	IP	H	R	ER	HR	HB	BB	SO	RAT	ERA	ERA+	CERA	OAV	BH	AVG	PR+	WS	TPW
1935 Cin-N	4	4	.500	19	7	3	1	1	60^{1}	70	31	29	2	2	23	14	1.541	4.33	92	4.46	.295	2	.133	-2	3	-0.3
1936 Cin-N	1	0	1.000	6	1	0	0	0	17	24	8	6	1	1	4	3	1.647	3.18	120	5.66	.333	1	.167	1	1	0.1
Total 2	5	4	.556	25	8	3	1	1	77^{1}	94	39	35	3	3	27	17	1.565	4.07	97	4.73	.304	3	.143	-0	4	-0.1

• NELSON, Gene Wayland Eugene Nelson b: 12/3/1960, Tampa, FL BR/TR, 6', 174 lbs. Deb: 5/4/1981

YEAR TM-L	W	L	PCT	G	GS	CG	SH	SV	IP	H	R	ER	HR	HB	BB	SO	RAT	ERA	ERA+	CERA	OAV	BH	AVG	PR+	WS	TPW
1981 NY-A	3	1	.750	8	7	0	0	0	39^{1}	40	24	21	5	1	23	16	1.602	4.81	74	5.15	.261	0	....	-6	1	-0.6
1982 Sea-A	6	9	.400	22	19	2	1	0	122^{2}	133	70	63	16	2	60	71	1.573	4.62	92	5.26	.279	0	....	-5	5	-0.5
1983 Sea-A	0	3	.000	10	5	1	0	0	32	38	29	28	6	1	21	11	1.844	7.88	54	6.97	.295	0	....	-13	0	-1.3
1984 Chi-A	3	5	.375	20	9	2	0	1	74^{2}	72	38	37	9	1	17	36	1.192	4.46	93	3.45	.254	0	....	-3	4	-0.3
1985 Chi-A	10	10	.500	46	18	1	0	2	145^{2}	144	74	69	23	7	67	101	1.449	4.26	101	4.81	.258	0	.000	0	8	0.0
1986 Chi-A	6	6	.500	54	1	0	0	6	114^{2}	118	52	49	7	3	41	70	1.387	3.85	112	3.89	.271	0	....	3	9	0.3
1987 Oak-A	6	5	.545	54	6	0	0	3	123^{2}	120	58	54	12	5	35	94	1.253	3.93	105	3.52	.249	0	....	4	8	0.4
1988* Oak-A	9	6	.600	54	1	0	0	3	111^{2}	93	42	38	9	3	38	67	1.173	3.06	123	2.91	.228	0	....	7	9	0.8
1989* Oak-A	3	5	.375	50	0	0	0	3	80	60	33	29	5	2	30	70	1.125	3.26	113	2.39	.203	0	....	2	6	0.3
1990* Oak-A	3	3	.500	51	0	0	0	5	74^{2}	55	14	13	5	3	17	38	.964	1.57	237	2.06	.208	0	....	16	10	1.6
1991 Oak-A	1	5	.167	44	0	0	0	0	48^{2}	60	38	37	12	3	23	23	1.705	6.84	56	7.10	.306	0	....	-16	0	-1.6
1992 Oak-A	3	1	.750	28	2	0	0	0	51^{2}	68	37	37	5	0	22	23	1.742	6.45	58	5.98	.335	0	....	-16	0	-1.6
1993 Cal-A	0	5	.000	46	0	0	0	4	52^{2}	50	25	18	3	2	23	31	1.386	3.08	147	3.60	.251	0	....	8	4	0.8
Tex-A	0	0	....	6	0	0	0	1	8	10	3	3	0	0	1	4	1.375	3.38	123	3.51	.303	0	....	1	1	0.1
Yr.	0	5	.000	52	0	0	0	5	60^{2}	60	28	21	3	2	24	35	1.385	3.12	143	3.59	.259	0	....	9	5	0.8
Total 13	53	64	.453	493	68	6	1	28	1080	1061	537	496	117	33	418	655	1.369	4.13	98	4.12	.258	0	.000	-16	65	-1.7

• NELSON, Jeff Jeffrey Allan Nelson b: 11/17/1966, Baltimore, MD BR/TR, 6'8", 235 lbs. Deb: 4/16/1992

YEAR TM-L	W	L	PCT	G	GS	CG	SH	SV	IP	H	R	ER	HR	HB	BB	SO	RAT	ERA	ERA+	CERA	OAV	BH	AVG	PR+	WS	TPW
1992 Sea-A	1	7	.125	66	0	0	0	6	81	71	34	31	7	6	44	46	1.420	3.44	115	3.93	.245	0	....	5	5	0.5
1993 Sea-A	5	3	.625	71	0	0	0	1	60	57	30	29	5	8	34	61	1.517	4.35	101	4.62	.258	0	....	0	4	0.0
1994 Sea-A	0	0	....	28	0	0	0	0	42^{1}	35	18	13	3	8	20	44	1.299	2.76	177	3.77	.226	0	....	10	3	1.0
1995* Sea-A	7	3	.700	62	0	0	0	2	78^{2}	58	21	19	4	6	27	96	1.081	2.17	218	2.39	.209	0	....	24	10	2.3
1996* NY-A	4	4	.500	73	0	0	0	2	74^{1}	75	38	36	6	2	36	91	1.493	4.36	113	4.41	.262	0	....	6	6	0.6
1997* NY-A	3	7	.300	77	0	0	0	2	78^{2}	53	32	25	7	4	37	81	1.144	2.86	156	2.48	.191	0	....	15	8	1.4
1998* NY-A	5	3	.625	45	0	0	0	3	40^{1}	44	18	17	1	8	22	35	1.636	3.79	116	5.13	.278	0	.000	2	4	0.2
1999* NY-A	2	1	.667	39	0	0	0	1	30^{1}	27	14	14	2	3	22	35	1.615	4.15	114	4.76	.245	0	....	2	2	0.2
2000* NY-A	8	4	.667	73	0	0	0	0	69^{2}	44	24	19	2	2	45	71	1.278	2.45	197	2.61	.183	0	.000	20	9	1.8
2001* Sea-A★	4	3	.571	69	0	0	0	4	65^{1}	30	21	20	3	6	44	88	1.133	2.76	151	2.20	.136	0	....	8	8	0.8
2002 Sea-A	3	2	.600	41	0	0	0	2	45^{2}	36	20	20	4	3	27	55	1.380	3.94	107	3.70	.221	0	....	2	4	0.2
2003 Sea-A	3	2	.600	46	0	0	0	7	37^{2}	34	16	14	3	2	14	47	1.274	3.35	129	3.48	.248	0	....	3	4	0.3
* NY-A	1	0	1.000	24	0	0	0	1	17^{2}	17	9	9	1	2	10	21	1.528	4.58	95	4.37	.246	0	....	-0	2	0.0
Yr.	4	2	.667	70	0	0	0	8	55^{1}	51	25	23	4	4	24	68	1.355	3.74	116	3.76	.248	0	....	3	6	0.3
Total 12	46	39	.541	714	0	0	0	31	721^{2}	581	295	266	48	60	382	771	1.334	3.32	135	3.49	.223	0	.000	98	69	9.1

• NELSON, Jim James Lorin Nelson b: 7/4/1947, Birmingham, AL BR/TR, 6', 180 lbs. Deb: 5/30/1970

YEAR TM-L	W	L	PCT	G	GS	CG	SH	SV	IP	H	R	ER	HR	HB	BB	SO	RAT	ERA	ERA+	CERA	OAV	BH	AVG	PR+	WS	TPW
1970 Pit-N	4	2	.667	15	10	1	1	0	68^{1}	64	32	26	5	3	38	42	1.493	3.42	113	4.26	.255	4	.200	2	4	0.2
1971 Pit-N	2	2	.500	17	2	0	0	0	34^{2}	27	9	9	0	5	26	11	1.529	2.34	146	3.90	.225	3	.500	4	4	0.6
Total 2	6	4	.600	32	12	1	1	0	103	91	41	35	5	8	64	53	1.505	3.06	123	4.14	.245	7	.269	6	8	0.8

• NELSON, Joe Joseph George Nelson b: 10/25/1974, Alameda, CA BR/TR, 6'2", 185 lbs. Deb: 6/13/2001

YEAR TM-L	W	L	PCT	G	GS	CG	SH	SV	IP	H	R	ER	HR	HB	BB	SO	RAT	ERA	ERA+	CERA	OAV	BH	AVG	PR+	WS	TPW
2001 Atl-N	0	0	....	2	0	0	0	0	2	7	9	8	1	1	2	0	4.500	36.00	12	33.03	.583	0	....	-7	0	-0.7

• NELSON, Luke Luther Martin Nelson b: 12/4/1893, Cable, IL d: 11/14/1985, Moline, IL BR/TR, 6', 180 lbs. Deb: 5/25/1919

YEAR TM-L	W	L	PCT	G	GS	CG	SH	SV	IP	H	R	ER	HR	HB	BB	SO	RAT	ERA	ERA+	CERA	OAV	BH	AVG	PR+	WS	TPW
1919 NY-A	3	0	1.000	9	1	0	0	0	24^{1}	22	9	8	1	1	11	11	1.356	2.96	108	3.47	.244	1	.143	-0	2	0.0

• NELSON, Lynn Lynn Bernard “Line Drive” Nelson b: 2/24/1905, Sheldon, ND d: 2/15/1955, Kansas City, MO BL/TR, 5'10.5", 170 lbs. Deb: 4/18/1930

YEAR TM-L	W	L	PCT	G	GS	CG	SH	SV	IP	H	R	ER	HR	HB	BB	SO	RAT	ERA	ERA+	CERA	OAV	BH	AVG	PR+	WS	TPW
1930 Chi-N	3	2	.600	37	3	0	0	0	81^{1}	97	52	46	10	6	28	29	1.537	5.09	96	5.35	.300	4	.222	-1	4	-0.1
1933 Chi-N	5	5	.500	24	3	3	0	1	75^{2}	65	34	27	2	0	30	20	1.256	3.21	102	2.65	.232	5	.238	-1	5	0.0
1934 Chi-N	0	1	.000	2	1	0	0	0	1	4	4	4	1	0	1	0	5.000	36.00	11	46.92	.667	0	....	-4	0	-0.3
1937 Phi-A	4	9	.308	30	4	1	0	2	116	140	78	76	12	2	51	49	1.647	5.90	80	5.39	.300	40	.354	-15	7	-0.1
1938 Phi-A	10	11	.476	32	23	13	0	2	191	215	142	120	29	5	79	75	1.539	5.65	85	5.12	.277	31	.277	-12	8	-0.7
1939 Phi-A	10	13	.435	35	24	12	2	1	197^{2}	233	117	105	27	3	64	75	1.503	4.78	98	5.02	.292	15	.188	5	10	0.3
1940 Det-A	1	1	.500	6	2	0	0	0	14	23	19	17	5	0	9	7	2.286	10.93	44	11.33	.371	8	.348	-9	1	-0.7
Total 7	33	42	.440	166	60	29	2	6	676^{2}	777	446	395	86	16	262	255	1.535	5.25	88	5.08	.286	103	.281	-39	35	-1.6

YEAR	TM-L	W	L	PCT	G	GS	CG	SH	SV	IP	H	R	ER	HR	HB	BB	SO	RAT	ERA	ERA+	CERA	OAV	BH	AVG	PR+	WS	TPW
• NELSON, Mel	Melvin Frederick Nelson b: 5/30/1936, San Diego, CA BR/TL, 6', 185 lbs. Deb: 9/27/1960																										
1960	StL-N	0	1	.000	2	1	0	0	0	8	7	3	3	1	0	2	7	1.125	3.38	121	2.76	.226	1	.500	1	1	0.1
1963	LA-A	2	3	.400	36	3	0	0	1	52^2	55	34	31	7	2	32	41	1.652	5.30	65	5.21	.263	1	.091	-11	0	-1.2
1965	Min-A	0	4	.000	28	3	0	0	3	54^2	57	29	25	7	2	23	31	1.463	4.12	86	4.53	.261	1	.111	-4	1	-0.5
1967	Min-A	0	0	....	1	0	0	0	0	0^1	3	2	2	1	0	0	0	9.000	54.00	6	116.77	.750	0	....	-2	0	-0.2
1968*	StL-N	2	1	.667	18	4	1	0	1	52^2	49	20	17	3	0	9	16	1.101	2.91	100	2.50	.254	2	.167	-0	3	0.0
1969	StL-N	0	1	.000	8	0	0	0	0	5^1	13	7	7	0	0	3	3	3.000	11.81	30	14.02	.520	0	....	-5	0	-0.5
Total	**6**	**4**	**10**	**.286**	**93**	**11**	**1**	**0**	**5**	**173^2**	**184**	**95**	**85**	**19**	**4**	**69**	**98**	**1.457**	**4.40**	**77**	**4.54**	**.271**	**5**	**.147**	**-22**	**5**	**-2.3**
• NELSON, Red	Albert Francis Nelson b: 5/19/1886, Cleveland, OH d: 10/26/1956, St. Petersburg, FL BR/TR, 5'11", 190 lbs. Deb: 9/9/1910																										
1910	StL-A	5	1	.833	7	6	6	1	0	60	57	26	17	0	4	14	30	1.183	2.55	97	2.88	.261	6	.261	-0	3	0.2
1911	StL-A	3	9	.250	16	13	6	0	0	81	103	68	47	1	7	44	24	1.815	5.22	65	6.01	.324	3	.111	-17	0	-1.9
1912	StL-A	0	2	.000	8	3	0	0	1	18	21	14	14	0	0	13	9	1.889	7.00	48	5.82	.318	1	.333	-8	0	-0.7
	Phi-N	2	0	1.000	4	2	1	0	0	19^1	25	10	8	2	2	6	2	1.603	3.72	97	5.62	.305	1	.100	-0	1	-0.1
1913	Phi-N	0	0	....	2	0	0	0	0	8^1	9	2	2	0	0	4	3	1.560	2.16	154	4.23	.290	1	.333	1	1	0.1
	Cin-N	0	0	....	2	0	0	0	0	1^2	6	7	7	1	1	4	0	6.000	37.80	9	42.21	.667	0	....	-6	0	-0.7
	Yr.	0	0	....	4	0	0	0	0	10	15	9	9	1	1	8	3	2.300	8.10	40	10.56	.375	1	.333	-5	1	-0.5
Total	**4**	**10**	**12**	**.455**	**39**	**24**	**13**	**1**	**1**	**188^1**	**221**	**127**	**95**	**4**	**14**	**85**	**68**	**1.625**	**4.54**	**70**	**5.20**	**.305**	**12**	**.182**	**-31**	**5**	**-3.0**
• NELSON, Roger	Roger Eugene "Spider" Nelson b: 6/7/1944, Altadena, CA BR/TR, 6'3", 205 lbs. Deb: 9/9/1967																										
1967	Chi-A	0	1	.000	5	0	0	0	0	7	4	1	1	1	2	0	4	.571	1.29	241	2.02	.182	0	....	1	1	0.2
1968	Bal-A	4	3	.571	19	6	0	0	1	71	49	21	19	3	1	26	70	1.056	2.41	121	2.01	.192	1	.063	3	5	0.3
1969	KC-A	7	13	.350	29	29	8	1	0	193^1	170	78	71	12	6	65	82	1.216	3.31	112	3.09	.243	8	.138	11	12	1.0
1970	KC-A	0	2	.000	4	2	0	0	0	9	18	10	10	3	1	0	3	2.000	10.00	37	11.26	.419	0	....	-6	0	-0.6
1971	KC-A	0	1	.000	13	1	0	0	0	34	35	20	20	1	0	5	29	1.176	5.29	65	2.82	.269	2	.333	-7	0	-0.6
1972	KC-A	11	6	.647	34	19	10	6	2	173^1	120	41	40	13	1	31	120	.871	2.08	146	**1.66**	.196	5	.093	21	16	2.1
1973*	Cin-N	3	2	.600	14	8	1	0	0	54^2	49	25	21	4	3	24	17	1.335	3.46	98	3.67	.246	2	.111	-1	2	-0.3
1974	Cin-N	4	4	.500	14	12	1	0	1	85^1	67	36	32	7	1	35	42	1.195	3.38	103	2.87	.213	5	.179	-1	5	0.0
1976	KC-A	0	0	....	3	0	0	0	0	8^2	4	2	2	0	2	4	4	.923	2.08	168	1.57	.138	0	....	1	1	0.1
Total	**9**	**29**	**32**	**.475**	**135**	**77**	**20**	**7**	**4**	**636^1**	**516**	**234**	**216**	**44**	**17**	**190**	**371**	**1.109**	**3.06**	**111**	**2.67**	**.224**	**23**	**.128**	**21**	**42**	**2.1**
• NEN, Robb	Robert Allen Nen b: 11/28/1969, San Pedro, CA BR/TR, 6'4", 200 lbs. Deb: 4/10/1993																										
1993	Tex-A	1	1	.500	9	3	0	0	0	22^2	28	17	16	1	0	26	12	2.382	6.35	65	8.60	.326	0	....	-5	0	-0.5
	Fla-N	1	0	1.000	15	1	0	0	0	33^1	35	28	26	5	0	20	27	1.650	7.02	61	5.28	.255	0	.000	-9	0	-1.0
1994	Fla-N	5	5	.500	44	0	0	0	15	58	46	20	19	6	0	17	60	1.086	2.95	148	2.63	.222	0	.000	8	11	0.8
1995	Fla-N	0	7	.000	62	0	0	0	23	65^2	62	26	24	6	1	23	68	1.294	3.29	128	3.48	.244	0	....	7	8	0.7
1996	Fla-N	5	1	.833	75	0	0	0	35	83	67	21	18	2	1	21	92	1.060	1.95	209	2.07	.225	0	.000	18	19	1.8
1997*	Fla-N	9	3	.750	73	0	0	0	35	74	72	35	32	7	0	40	81	1.514	3.89	104	4.20	.250	0	....	1	11	0.1
1998	SF-N★	7	7	.500	78	0	0	0	40	88^2	59	21	15	4	1	25	110	.947	1.52	261	1.58	.180	0	.000	24	19	2.4
1999	SF-N★	3	8	.273	72	0	0	0	37	72^1	79	36	32	8	0	27	77	1.465	3.98	106	4.44	.275	0	....	2	8	0.2
2000*	SF-N	4	3	.571	68	0	0	0	41	66	37	15	11	4	2	19	92	.848	1.50	282	1.44	.162	0	....	20	15	1.9
2001	SF-N	4	5	.444	79	0	0	0	**45**	77^2	58	28	26	6	1	22	93	1.030	3.01	132	2.12	.203	0	.000	8	14	0.8
2002*	SF-N★	6	2	.750	68	0	0	0	43	73^2	64	19	18	2	1	20	81	1.140	2.20	176	2.33	.232	1	.500	13	15	1.3
Total	**10**	**45**	**42**	**.517**	**643**	**4**	**0**	**0**	**314**	**715**	**607**	**266**	**237**	**51**	**7**	**260**	**793**	**1.213**	**2.98**	**138**	**2.97**	**.227**	**1**	**.067**	**87**	**120**	**8.3**
• NEU, Mike	Michael David Neu b: 3/9/1978, Napa, CA BB/TR, 5'10", 175 lbs. Deb: 4/9/2003																										
2003	Oak-A	0	0	....	32	0	0	0	1	42	43	18	17	2	2	26	20	1.643	3.64	124	4.73	.261	0	....	4	3	0.4
• NEUBAUER, Hal	Harold Charles Neubauer b: 5/13/1902, Hoboken, NJ d: 9/9/1949, Barrington, RI BR/TR, 6'.5", 185 lbs. Deb: 6/12/1925																										
1925	Bos-A	1	0	1.000	7	0	0	0	0	10^1	17	18	14	2	0	11	4	2.710	12.19	37	11.27	.378	0	....	-8	0	-0.8
• NEUER, Tex	John S. Neuer b: 6/8/1877, Fremont, OH d: 1/14/1966, Northumberland, PA TL Deb: 8/28/1907																										
1907	NY-A	4	2	.667	7	6	6	3	0	54	40	21	13	1	0	19	22	1.093	2.17	129	1.95	.209	2	.095	5	4	0.3
• NEUGEBAUER, Nick	Nickolas Donald Neugebauer b: 7/15/1980, Riverside, CA BR/TR, 6'3", 225 lbs. Deb: 8/19/2001																										
2001	Mil-N	1	1	.500	2	2	0	0	0	6	6	5	5	1	0	6	11	2.000	7.50	57	6.94	.250	0	.000	-2	0	-0.2
2002	Mil-N	1	7	.125	12	12	0	0	0	55^1	56	33	29	10	0	44	47	1.807	4.72	87	6.32	.264	2	.105	-4	1	-0.4
Total	**2**	**2**	**8**	**.200**	**14**	**14**	**0**	**0**	**0**	**61^1**	**62**	**38**	**34**	**11**	**0**	**50**	**58**	**1.826**	**4.99**	**83**	**6.38**	**.263**	**2**	**.091**	**-6**	**1**	**-0.7**
• NEUMEIER, Dan	Daniel George Neumeier b: 3/9/1948, Shawano, WI BR/TR, 6'5", 205 lbs. Deb: 9/8/1972																										
1972	Chi-A	0	0	....	3	0	0	0	0	3	2	3	3	0	0	3	0	1.667	9.00	35	3.96	.200	0	.000	-2	0	-0.2
• NEVEL, Ernie	Ernie Wyre Nevel b: 8/17/1919, Charleston, MO d: 7/10/1988, Springfield, MO BR/TR, 5'11", 200 lbs. Deb: 9/26/1950																										
1950	NY-A	0	1	.000	3	1	0	0	0	6^1	10	7	7	0	0	6	3	2.526	9.95	43	8.55	.345	0	.000	-4	0	-0.4
1951	NY-A	0	0	....	1	0	0	0	1	4	1	0	0	0	0	1	1	.500	0.00	....	0.41	.083	0	.000	2	1	0.1
1953	Cin-N	0	0	....	10	0	0	0	0	10^1	16	7	7	0	0	1	5	1.645	6.10	71	5.61	.390	0	....	-2	0	-0.2
Total	**3**	**0**	**1**	**.000**	**14**	**1**	**0**	**0**	**1**	**20^2**	**27**	**14**	**14**	**0**	**0**	**8**	**9**	**1.694**	**6.10**	**71**	**5.51**	**.329**	**0**	**.000**	**-5**	**1**	**-0.5**
• NEVERS, Ernie	Ernest Alonzo Nevers b: 6/11/1902, Willow River, MN d: 5/3/1976, San Rafael, CA BR/TR, 6', 205 lbs. Deb: 4/26/1926																										
1926	StL-A	2	4	.333	11	7	4	0	0	74^2	82	41	37	4	1	24	16	1.420	4.46	96	3.92	.290	5	.185	-2	4	-0.3
1927	StL-A	3	8	.273	27	5	2	0	2	94^2	105	61	52	8	2	35	22	1.479	4.94	88	4.69	.311	7	.219	-7	4	-0.7
1928	StL-A	1	0	1.000	6	0	0	0	0	9	9	4	3	1	0	2	1	1.222	3.00	140	3.55	.281	0	.000	1	1	0.1
Total	**3**	**6**	**12**	**.333**	**44**	**12**	**6**	**0**	**2**	**178^1**	**196**	**106**	**92**	**13**	**3**	**61**	**39**	**1.441**	**4.64**	**93**	**4.31**	**.300**	**12**	**.200**	**-8**	**9**	**-0.9**
• NEWCOMBE, Don	Donald "Newk" Newcombe b: 6/14/1926, Madison, NJ BL/TR, 6'4", 225 lbs. Deb: 5/20/1949																										
1949*	Bro-N★	17	8	.680	38	31	19	**5**	1	244^1	223	89	86	17	3	73	149	1.211	3.17	129	3.02	.243	22	.229	21	21	2.4
1950	Bro-N★	19	11	.633	40	35	20	4	3	267^1	258	120	110	22	2	75	130	1.246	3.70	111	3.32	.254	24	.247	6	22	1.2
1951	Bro-N★	20	9	.690	40	36	18	3	0	272	235	115	99	19	6	91	**164**	1.199	3.28	120	2.91	.230	23	.223	14	21	1.8
1954	Bro-N	9	8	.529	29	25	6	0	0	144^1	158	81	73	24	5	49	82	1.434	4.55	90	4.83	.274	15	.319	-8	8	-0.3
1955*	Bro-N★	20	5	.800	34	31	17	1	0	233^2	222	103	83	35	1	38	143	1.113	3.20	127	3.22	.249	42	.359	21	25	**4.1**
1956*	Bro-N	**27**	7	.794	38	36	18	5	0	268	219	101	91	33	3	46	139	.989	3.06	130	**2.42**	**.221**	26	.234	22	**27**	**3.1**
1957	Bro-N	11	12	.478	28	28	12	4	0	198^2	199	86	77	28	1	33	90	1.168	3.49	119	3.42	.258	17	.230	15	15	2.0
1958	LA-N	0	6	.000	11	8	1	0	0	34^1	53	37	30	11	0	8	16	1.777	7.86	52	8.27	.346	5	.417	-14	1	-1.3
	Cin-N	7	7	.500	20	18	7	0	1	133^1	159	61	57	20	1	28	53	1.403	3.85	108	4.78	.298	21	.350	4	11	1.2
	Yr.	7	13	.350	31	26	8	0	1	167^2	212	98	87	31	1	36	69	1.479	4.67	88	5.50	.309	26	.361	-11	12	0.0
1959	Cin-N	13	8	.619	30	29	17	2	1	222	216	87	78	25	5	27	100	1.095	3.16	128	3.00	.253	32	.305	22	21	**3.7**
1960	Cin-N	4	6	.400	16	15	1	0	0	82^2	99	48	42	12	3	14	36	1.367	4.57	84	4.77	.304	5	.139	-7	2	-0.7
	Cle-A	2	3	.400	20	2	0	0	1	54	61	28	26	6	0	8	27	1.278	4.33	86	3.94	.289	6	.300	-4	2	-0.2
Total	**10**	**149**	**90**	**.623**	**344**	**294**	**136**	**24**	**7**	**2154^2**	**2102**	**956**	**852**	**252**	**30**	**490**	**1129**	**1.203**	**3.56**	**113**	**3.43**	**.254**	**238**	**.271**	**91**	**176**	**17.0**
• NEWELL, Tom	Thomas Dean Newell b: 5/17/1963, Monrovia, CA BR/TR, 6'1", 185 lbs. Deb: 9/9/1987																										
1987	Phi-N	0	0	....	2	0	0	0	0	1	4	4	4	1	0	3	1	7.000	36.00	12	50.03	.571	0	....	-4	0	-0.4
• NEWHAUSER, Don	Donald Louis Newhauser b: 11/7/1947, Miami, FL BR/TR, 6'4", 200 lbs. Deb: 6/15/1972																										
1972	Bos-A	4	2	.667	31	0	0	0	4	37	30	11	10	2	2	25	27	1.486	2.43	132	3.73	.226	0	.000	4	4	0.4
1973	Bos-A	0	0	....	9	0	0	0	1	12	9	2	0	0	1	13	8	1.833	0.00	....	4.34	.205	0	....	5	2	0.5
1974	Bos-A	0	1	.000	2	0	0	0	0	3^2	5	4	4	0	0	4	2	2.455	9.82	39	7.46	.357	0	....	-2	0	-0.3
Total	**3**	**4**	**3**	**.571**	**42**	**0**	**0**	**0**	**5**	**52^2**	**44**	**17**	**14**	**2**	**3**	**42**	**37**	**1.633**	**2.39**	**141**	**4.13**	**.230**	**0**	**.000**	**7**	**6**	**0.7**
• NEWHOUSER, Hal	Harold "Prince Hal" Newhouser b: 5/20/1921, Detroit, MI d: 11/10/1998, Detroit, MI BL/TL, 6'2", 192 lbs. Deb: 9/29/1939 HOF: 1992																										
1939	Det-A	0	1	.000	1	1	1	0	0	5	3	3	3	0	0	4	4	1.400	5.40	91	2.45	.188	0	.000	-0	0	0.0

YEAR	TM-L	W	L	PCT	G	GS	CG	SH	SV	IP	H	R	ER	HR	HB	BB	SO	RAT	ERA	ERA+	CERA	OAV	BH	AVG	PR+	WS	TPW
1940	Det-A	9	9	.500	28	20	7	0	0	133^1	149	81	72	12	2	76	89	1.688	4.86	98	5.26	.282	8	.200	1	7	0.0
1941	Det-A	9	11	.450	33	27	5	1	0	173	166	109	92	6	1	137	106	**1.751**	4.79	95	4.63	.249	9	.150	0	8	-0.1
1942	Det-A★	8	14	.364	38	23	11	1	5	183^2	137	73	50	4	2	114	103	1.367	2.45	161	2.86	**.207**	8	.154	**33**	17	3.3
1943	Det-A★	8	17	.320	37	25	10	1	1	195^2	163	88	66	3	0	111	144	1.400	3.04	116	3.03	.224	12	.185	11	10	1.2
1944	Det-A★	**29**	9	.763	47	34	25	6	2	312^1	264	94	77	6	1	102	**187**	1.172	2.22	161	2.42	.230	29	.242	48	35	5.4
1945*	Det-A★	**25**	9	.735	40	**36**	**29**	**8**	2	**313^1**	239	73	63	5	0	110	**212**	1.114	**1.81**	**194**	2.07	**.211**	28	.257	**58**	**38**	**6.6**
1946	Det-A★	**26**	9	.743	37	34	29	6	1	292^2	215	77	63	10	1	98	275	1.069	**1.94**	**189**	**2.00**	**.201**	13	.126	**60**	**33**	**6.2**
1947	Det-A★	17	17	.500	40	36	**24**	3	2	285	268	105	91	9	2	110	176	1.326	2.87	131	3.14	.249	19	.198	**35**	**24**	**3.9**
1948	Det-A★	**21**	12	.636	39	35	19	2	1	272^1	249	109	91	10	1	99	143	1.278	3.01	145	2.96	.242	19	.207	**47**	**27**	**4.7**
1949	Det-A	18	11	.621	38	35	22	3	1	292	277	118	109	19	0	111	144	1.329	3.36	124	3.42	.251	18	.198	29	25	2.9
1950	Det-A	15	13	.536	35	30	15	1	3	213^2	232	110	103	23	4	81	87	1.465	4.34	108	4.55	.279	13	.176	7	15	0.5
1951	Det-A	6	6	.500	15	14	7	1	0	96^1	98	47	42	9	3	19	37	1.215	3.92	106	3.49	.268	9	.310	4	7	0.6
1952	Det-A	9	9	.500	25	19	8	0	0	154	148	72	64	13	0	47	57	1.266	3.74	102	3.33	.254	10	.217	4	10	0.8
1953	Det-A	0	1	.000	7	4	0	0	1	21^2	31	22	17	4	2	8	6	1.800	7.06	58	7.65	.348	4	.500	-7	1	-0.5
1954*	Cle-A	7	2	.778	26	1	0	0	7	46^2	34	16	13	3	0	18	25	1.114	2.51	146	2.33	.209	2	.154	5	7	0.5
1955	Cle-A	0	0	....	2	0	0	0	0	2^1	1	0	0	0	0	4	1	2.143	0.00	....	3.94	.125	0	....	1	0	0.1
Total	**17**	**207**	**150**	**.580**	**488**	**374**	**212**	**33**	**26**	**2993**	**2674**	**1197**	**1016**	**136**	**19**	**1249**	**1796**	**1.311**	**3.06**	**132**	**3.15**	**.239**	**201**	**.201**	**336**	**264**	**36.0**

• NEWKIRK, Floyd Floyd Elmo "Three Finger" Newkirk b: 7/16/1908, Norris City, IL d: 4/15/1976, Clayton, MO BR/TR, 5'11", 178 lbs. Deb: 8/21/1934

YEAR	TM-L	W	L	PCT	G	GS	CG	SH	SV	IP	H	R	ER	HR	HB	BB	SO	RAT	ERA	ERA+	CERA	OAV	BH	AVG	PR+	WS	TPW
1934	NY-A	0	0	....	1	0	0	0	0	1	1	0	0	0	0	1	0	2.000	0.00	....	5.17	.333	0	....	0	0	0.0

• NEWKIRK, Joel Joel Inez "Sailor" Newkirk b: 6/1/1896, Kyana, IN d: 1/22/1966, Eldorado, IL BR/TR, 6', 180 lbs. Deb: 8/20/1919

YEAR	TM-L	W	L	PCT	G	GS	CG	SH	SV	IP	H	R	ER	HR	HB	BB	SO	RAT	ERA	ERA+	CERA	OAV	BH	AVG	PR+	WS	TPW
1919	Chi-N	0	0	....	1	0	0	0	0	2	2	3	3	0	1	3	1	2.500	13.50	21	9.59	.286	0	.000	-2	0	-0.3
1920	Chi-N	0	1	.000	2	1	0	0	0	6^2	8	6	4	1	0	6	2	2.100	5.40	59	8.11	.333	0	.000	-2	0	-0.2
Total	**2**	**0**	**1**	**.000**	**3**	**1**	**0**	**0**	**0**	**8^2**	**10**	**9**	**7**	**1**	**1**	**9**	**3**	**2.192**	**7.27**	**42**	**8.45**	**.322**	**0**	**.000**	**-4**	**0**	**-0.5**

• NEWLIN, Maury Maurice Milton Newlin b: 6/22/1914, Bloomingdale, IN d: 8/14/1978, Houston, TX BR/TR, 6', 176 lbs. Deb: 9/20/1940

YEAR	TM-L	W	L	PCT	G	GS	CG	SH	SV	IP	H	R	ER	HR	HB	BB	SO	RAT	ERA	ERA+	CERA	OAV	BH	AVG	PR+	WS	TPW
1940	StL-A	1	0	1.000	1	1	0	0	0	6	4	4	4	1	0	2	3	1.000	6.00	76	2.52	.190	1	.500	-1	0	-0.1
1941	StL-A	0	2	.000	14	0	0	0	1	27^2	43	24	20	4	0	12	10	1.988	6.51	66	7.86	.361	0	.000	-6	0	-0.7
Total	**2**	**1**	**2**	**.333**	**15**	**1**	**0**	**0**	**1**	**33^2**	**47**	**28**	**24**	**5**	**0**	**14**	**13**	**1.812**	**6.42**	**68**	**6.90**	**.336**	**1**	**.125**	**-7**	**0**	**-0.8**

• NEWMAN, Alan Alan Spencer Newman b: 10/2/1969, La Habra, CA BL/TL, 6'6", 240 lbs. Deb: 5/14/1999

YEAR	TM-L	W	L	PCT	G	GS	CG	SH	SV	IP	H	R	ER	HR	HB	BB	SO	RAT	ERA	ERA+	CERA	OAV	BH	AVG	PR+	WS	TPW
1999	TB-A	2	2	.500	18	0	0	0	0	15^2	22	12	12	2	1	9	20	1.979	6.89	72	7.92	.333	0	....	-3	0	-0.3
2000	Cle-A	0	0	....	1	0	0	0	0	1^1	6	3	3	1	0	1	0	5.250	20.25	25	45.29	.667	0	....	-2	0	-0.2
Total	**2**	**2**	**2**	**.500**	**19**	**0**	**0**	**0**	**0**	**17**	**28**	**15**	**15**	**3**	**1**	**10**	**20**	**2.235**	**7.94**	**63**	**10.85**	**.373**	**0**	**....**	**-6**	**0**	**-0.5**

• NEWMAN, Fred Frederick William Newman b: 2/21/1942, Boston, MA d: 6/24/1987, Framingham, MA BR/TR, 6'3", 190 lbs. Deb: 9/16/1962

YEAR	TM-L	W	L	PCT	G	GS	CG	SH	SV	IP	H	R	ER	HR	HB	BB	SO	RAT	ERA	ERA+	CERA	OAV	BH	AVG	PR+	WS	TPW
1962	LA-A	0	1	.000	4	1	0	0	0	6^1	11	7	7	0	0	3	4	2.211	9.95	39	8.04	.393	0	.000	-4	0	-0.4
1963	LA-A	1	5	.167	12	8	0	0	0	44	56	27	26	6	2	15	16	1.614	5.32	64	5.96	.316	4	.250	-9	0	-0.9
1964	LA-A	13	10	.565	32	28	7	2	0	190	177	68	58	9	7	39	83	1.137	2.75	120	2.71	.246	11	.180	10	14	1.3
1965	Cal-A	14	16	.467	36	36	10	2	0	260^2	225	94	85	15	1	64	109	1.109	2.93	116	2.50	.234	7	.095	12	16	1.3
1966	Cal-A	4	7	.364	21	19	1	0	0	102^2	112	54	54	7	6	31	42	1.393	4.73	71	4.32	.289	6	.200	-17	2	-1.7
1967	Cal-A	1	0	1.000	3	1	0	0	0	6^1	8	5	1	1	1	2	0	1.579	1.42	221	6.48	.320	0	.000	1	0	0.1
Total	**6**	**33**	**39**	**.458**	**108**	**93**	**18**	**4**	**0**	**610**	**589**	**255**	**231**	**38**	**17**	**154**	**254**	**1.218**	**3.41**	**99**	**3.22**	**.256**	**28**	**.153**	**-6**	**32**	**-0.3**

• NEWMAN, Ray Raymond Francis Newman b: 6/20/1945, Evansville, IN BL/TL, 6'5", 205 lbs. Deb: 5/16/1971

YEAR	TM-L	W	L	PCT	G	GS	CG	SH	SV	IP	H	R	ER	HR	HB	BB	SO	RAT	ERA	ERA+	CERA	OAV	BH	AVG	PR+	WS	TPW
1971	Chi-N	1	2	.333	30	0	0	0	2	38^1	30	15	15	4	0	17	35	1.226	3.52	112	3.17	.219	0	.000	2	3	0.2
1972	Mil-A	0	0	....	4	0	0	0	1	7	4	0	0	0	0	2	1	.857	0.00	....	1.29	.182	1	1.000	2	2	0.3
1973	Mil-A	2	1	.667	11	0	0	0	1	18^1	19	6	6	2	0	5	10	1.309	2.95	128	3.61	.260	0	....	2	2	0.2
Total	**3**	**3**	**3**	**.500**	**45**	**0**	**0**	**0**	**4**	**63^2**	**53**	**21**	**21**	**6**	**0**	**24**	**46**	**1.209**	**2.97**	**131**	**3.09**	**.228**	**1**	**.143**	**7**	**7**	**0.7**

• NEWSOM, Bobo Louis Norman "Buck" Newsom b: 8/11/1907, Hartsville, SC d: 12/7/1962, Orlando, FL BR/TR, 6'3", 220 lbs. Deb: 9/11/1929

YEAR	TM-L	W	L	PCT	G	GS	CG	SH	SV	IP	H	R	ER	HR	HB	BB	SO	RAT	ERA	ERA+	CERA	OAV	BH	AVG	PR+	WS	TPW
1929	Bro-N	0	3	.000	3	2	0	0	0	9^1	15	12	11	0	0	5	6	2.143	10.61	43	7.29	.375	0	.000	-6	0	-0.6
1930	Bro-N	0	0	....	2	0	0	0	0	3	2	2	0	0	0	2	1	1.333	0.00	....	2.17	.167	0	....	2	0	0.1
1932	Chi-N	0	0	....	1	0	0	0	0	1	1	0	0	0	0	0	0	1.000	0.00	....	2.02	.333	0	....	0	0	0.0
1934	StL-A	16	20	.444	47	32	15	2	5	262^1	259	138	117	15	1	149	135	1.555	4.01	124	4.25	.261	17	.183	25	21	2.1
1935	StL-A	0	6	.000	7	6	1	0	1	42^2	54	29	23	2	0	13	22	1.570	4.85	99	4.67	.303	1	.091	-0	2	-0.1
	Was-A	11	12	.478	28	23	17	2	2	198^1	222	108	98	9	4	84	65	1.543	4.45	97	4.47	.288	22	.301	-2	10	0.2
	Yr.	11	18	.379	35	29	18	2	3	241	276	137	121	11	4	97	87	1.548	4.52	98	4.51	.291	23	.274	-2	12	0.1
1936	Was-A	17	15	.531	43	**38**	24	4	2	285^2	294	160	137	13	3	146	156	1.540	4.32	111	4.22	.268	23	.213	11	19	0.9
1937	Was-A	3	4	.429	11	10	3	0	0	67^2	76	49	44	4	3	48	39	1.833	5.85	76	5.70	.287	3	.120	-12	1	-1.1
	Bos-A	13	10	.565	30	27	14	1	0	207^2	193	114	103	14	3	119	127	1.502	4.46	106	3.98	.243	19	.253	11	15	1.2
	Yr.	16	14	.533	41	**37**	17	1	0	275^1	269	163	147	18	6	167	166	1.584	4.81	97	4.40	.254	22	.220	-1	16	0.1
1938	StL-A★	20	16	.556	44	**40**	**31**	0	1	**329^2**	334	205	186	30	5	192	226	1.596	5.08	98	4.75	.265	31	.250	-4	21	-0.1
1939	StL-A	3	1	.750	6	6	3	0	0	45^2	50	26	24	5	1	22	28	1.577	4.73	103	4.83	.266	4	.222	2	3	0.2
	Det-A★	17	10	.630	35	31	21	3	2	246	222	100	92	14	2	104	164	1.325	3.37	145	3.24	.238	18	.186	41	23	3.5
	Yr.	20	11	.645	41	**37**	**24**	3	2	291^2	272	126	116	19	3	126	192	1.365	3.58	136	3.49	.243	22	.191	43	26	3.6
1940*	Det-A★	21	5	.808	36	34	20	3	0	264	235	110	83	19	3	100	164	1.269	2.83	**168**	3.18	.238	23	.215	**61**	26	**5.7**
1941	Det-A	12	20	.375	43	36	12	2	2	250^1	265	140	128	15	3	118	175	1.530	4.60	99	4.23	.264	9	.102	6	14	0.0
1942	Was-A	11	17	.393	30	29	15	2	0	213^2	236	135	117	5	3	92	**113**	1.535	4.93	74	4.12	.280	12	.160	-21	4	-2.4
	Bro-N	2	2	.500	6	5	2	1	0	32	28	13	12	1	1	14	21	1.313	3.38	97	3.10	.235	0	.000	-1	2	-0.2
1943	Bro-N	9	4	.692	22	12	6	1	1	125	113	51	42	4	2	57	75	1.360	3.02	111	3.29	.244	11	.250	6	8	0.8
	StL-A	1	6	.143	10	9	0	0	0	52^1	69	45	43	7	1	35	37	1.987	7.39	45	7.26	.318	5	.333	-23	0	-2.4
	Was-A	3	3	.500	6	6	2	0	0	40	38	22	17	1	2	21	11	1.475	3.83	84	3.72	.247	2	.133	-3	1	-0.4
	Yr.	4	9	.308	16	15	2	0	0	92^1	107	67	60	8	3	56	48	1.765	5.85	56	5.73	.288	7	.233	-26	1	-2.8
1944	Phi-A★	13	15	.464	37	33	18	2	1	265	243	100	83	11	4	82	142	1.226	2.82	124	2.90	.244	10	.114	20	20	1.6
1945	Phi-A	8	20	.286	36	34	16	3	0	257^1	255	111	94	12	3	103	127	1.391	3.29	104	3.56	.260	14	.163	5	12	0.1
1946	Phi-A	3	5	.375	10	9	3	1	0	58^2	61	27	22	2	5	30	32	1.551	3.38	105	4.38	.266	2	.105	1	3	0.1
	Was-A	11	8	.579	24	22	14	2	1	178	163	63	55	5	2	60	82	1.253	2.78	120	2.86	.242	10	.161	15	13	1.3
	Yr.	14	13	.519	34	31	17	3	1	236^2	224	90	77	7	7	90	114	1.327	2.93	116	3.24	.248	12	.148	16	16	1.4
1947	Was-A	4	6	.400	14	13	1	0	0	83^2	99	44	38	2	1	37	40	1.625	4.09	91	4.60	.296	7	.241	-2	4	-0.1
	*NY-A	7	5	.583	17	15	6	2	0	115^2	109	38	36	8	2	30	42	1.202	2.80	126	3.05	.250	4	.095	9	8	0.5
	Yr.	11	11	.500	31	28	7	2	0	199^1	208	82	74	10	3	67	82	1.380	3.34	109	3.71	.270	11	.155	7	12	0.4
1948	NY-N	0	4	.000	11	4	0	0	0	25^2	35	16	12	1	0	13	9	1.870	4.21	94	5.97	.330	3	.429	-1	1	0.0
1952	Was-A	1	1	.500	10	0	0	0	2	12^2	16	7	7	2	0	9	5	1.974	4.97	71	7.06	.302	0	.000	-2	0	-0.2
	Phi-A	3	3	.500	14	5	1	0	1	47^2	38	19	19	2	2	23	22	1.280	3.59	110	2.94	.220	2	.133	3	4	0.2
	Yr.	4	4	.500	24	5	1	0	3	60^1	54	26	26	4	2	32	27	1.425	3.88	99	3.81	.239	2	.118	1	4	0.0
1953	Phi-A	2	1	.667	17	2	1	0	0	38^2	44	24	21	3	5	24	16	1.759	4.89	88	5.82	.282	1	.167	-2	2	-0.3
Total	**20**	**211**	**222**	**.487**	**600**	**483**	**246**	**31**	**21**	**3759^1**	**3769**	**1908**	**1664**	**206**	**61**	**1732**	**2082**	**1.463**	**3.98**	**106**	**3.96**	**.261**	**253**	**.189**	**140**	**237**	**10.6**

• NEWSOME, Dick Heber Hampton Newsome b: 12/13/1909, Ahoskie, NC d: 12/15/1965, Ahoskie, NC BR/TR, 6', 185 lbs. Deb: 4/25/1941

YEAR	TM-L	W	L	PCT	G	GS	CG	SH	SV	IP	H	R	ER	HR	HB	BB	SO	RAT	ERA	ERA+	CERA	OAV	BH	AVG	PR+	WS	TPW
1941	Bos-A	19	10	.655	36	29	17	2	0	213^2	235	115	98	13	7	79	58	1.470	4.13	101	4.24	.277	19	.244	3	14	0.6
1942	Bos-A	8	10	.444	24	23	11	0	0	158	174	98	88	11	0	67	40	1.525	5.01	74	4.40	.278	13	.236	-26	3	-2.5
1943	Bos-A	8	13	.381	25	22	8	2	0	154^1	166	83	77	8	5	68	40	**1.516**	4.49	74	4.29	.274	7	.146	-21	3	-2.4
Total	**3**	**35**	**33**	**.515**	**85**	**74**	**36**	**4**	**0**	**526**	**575**	**296**	**263**	**32**	**12**	**214**	**138**	**1.500**	**4.50**	**83**	**4.30**	**.276**	**39**	**.215**	**-44**	**20**	**-4.3**

• NEWTON, Doc Eustace James Newton b: 10/26/1877, Indianapolis, IN d: 5/14/1931, Memphis, TN BL/TL, 6', 185 lbs. Deb: 4/27/1900 U

YEAR	TM-L	W	L	PCT	G	GS	CG	SH	SV	IP	H	R	ER	HR	HB	BB	SO	RAT	ERA	ERA+	CERA	OAV	BH	AVG	PR+	WS	TPW
1900	Cin-N	9	15	.375	35	27	22	1	0	234^2	255	146	108	4	12	100	88	1.513	4.14	88	4.13	.276	17	.198	-13	10	-1.2

YEAR	TM-L	W	L	PCT	G	GS	CG	SH	SV	IP	H	R	ER	HR	HB	BB	SO	RAT	ERA	ERA+	CERA	OAV	BH	AVG	PR+	WS	TPW
1901	Cin-N	4	13	.235	20	18	17	0	0	168^{1}	190	117	77	6	14	59	65	1.479	4.12	78	4.35	.283	9	.130	-13	4	-1.7
	Bro-N	6	5	.545	13	12	9	0	0	105	110	42	33	1	7	30	45	1.333	2.83	118	3.44	.268	9	.220	5	8	0.6
	Yr.	10	18	.357	33	30	26	0	0	273^{1}	300	159	110	7	21	89	110	1.423	3.62	89	4.00	.277	18	.164	-8	12	-1.1
1902	Bro-N	15	14	.517	31	28	26	4	2	264^{1}	208	95	71	2	11	87	107	1.116	2.42	114	2.20	**.217**	19	.174	10	18	0.9
1905	NY-A	2	2	.500	11	7	2	0	0	59^{2}	61	23	14	1	2	24	15	1.425	2.11	139	3.64	.267	3	.136	6	4	0.6
1906	NY-A	7	5	.583	21	15	6	2	0	125	118	53	44	3	7	33	52	1.208	3.17	94	2.90	.252	9	.220	-2	9	-0.2
1907	NY-A	7	10	.412	19	15	10	0	0	133	132	66	47	0	7	31	70	1.226	3.18	88	2.37	.262	4	.108	-4	6	-0.5
1908	NY-A	4	5	.444	23	13	6	1	1	88^{1}	78	52	29	0	7	41	49	1.347	2.95	84	3.25	.242	4	.160	-2	2	-0.3
1909	NY-A	0	3	.000	4	4	1	0	0	22^{1}	27	17	7	0	3	11	11	1.701	2.82	89	5.29	.300	1	.167	-0	0	0.0
Total	8	54	72	.429	177	139	99	8	3	1200^{2}	1179	611	430	17	70	416	502	1.328	3.22	95	3.28	.258	75	.172	-13	61	-1.9
• NICHOLS, Chet	Chester Raymond "Nick" Nichols, Sr. b: 7/3/1897, Woonsocket, RI d: 7/11/1982, Pawtucket, RI BR/TR, 5'11", 160 lbs. Deb: 7/30/1926																										
1926	Pit-N	0	0	....	3	0	0	0	0	7^{2}	13	11	7	0	0	5	2	2.348	8.22	48	7.74	.342	1	.333	-4	0	-0.4
1927	Pit-N	0	3	.000	8	0	0	0	0	27^{2}	34	19	18	1	1	17	9	1.843	5.86	70	5.72	.309	1	.111	-6	0	-0.6
1928	NY-N	0	0	....	3	0	0	0	0	2^{2}	11	13	7	0	1	3	1	5.250	23.63	17	29.36	.611	0	....	-6	0	-0.6
1930	Phi-N	1	2	.333	16	5	1	0	0	59^{2}	76	51	45	8	2	16	15	1.542	6.79	80	5.31	.306	6	.300	-7	2	-0.6
1931	Phi-N	0	1	.000	3	0	0	0	0	5^{2}	10	6	6	0	0	1	1	1.941	9.53	45	7.26	.435	0	.000	-3	0	-0.4
1932	Phi-N	0	2	.000	11	0	0	0	1	19^{1}	23	16	15	2	0	14	5	1.914	6.98	63	6.33	.299	0	.000	-6	0	-0.6
Total	6	1	8	.111	44	5	1	0	1	122^{2}	167	116	98	11	4	56	33	1.818	7.19	65	6.33	.325	8	.211	-31	2	-3.1
• NICHOLS, Chet	Chester Raymond Nichols, Jr. b: 2/22/1931, Pawtucket, RI d: 3/27/1995, Lincoln, RI BB/TL, 6'1.5", 195 lbs. Deb: 4/19/1951																										
1951	Bos-N	11	8	.579	33	19	12	3	2	156	142	61	50	4	1	69	71	1.353	**2.88**	127	3.16	.246	7	.137	15	12	1.3
1954	Mil-N	9	11	.450	35	20	5	1	1	122^{1}	132	68	60	5	4	65	55	1.610	4.41	84	4.66	.286	3	.086	-11	3	-1.4
1955	Mil-N	9	8	.529	34	21	6	0	1	144	139	79	64	20	1	67	44	1.431	4.00	94	4.38	.253	8	.154	-4	5	-0.6
1956	Mil-N	0	1	.000	2	0	0	0	0	4	9	3	3	1	0	3	2	3.000	6.75	51	17.82	.563	0	.000	-1	0	-0.2
1960	Bos-A	0	2	.000	6	1	0	0	0	12^{2}	12	6	6	0	0	4	11	1.263	4.26	95	2.67	.240	0	.000	0	0	0.0
1961	Bos-A	3	2	.600	26	2	0	0	3	51^{2}	40	12	12	3	0	26	20	1.277	2.09	199	2.97	.221	1	.111	12	7	1.2
1962	Bos-A	1	1	.500	29	1	0	0	3	57	61	25	19	3	0	22	33	1.456	3.00	138	4.01	.276	0	.000	7	4	0.6
1963	Bos-A	1	3	.250	21	7	0	0	0	52^{2}	61	30	28	8	0	24	27	1.614	4.78	79	5.66	.298	3	.231	-6	1	-0.6
1964	Cin-N	0	0	....	3	0	0	0	0	3	4	2	2	1	0	0	3	1.333	6.00	60	5.82	.308	0	....	-1	0	-0.1
Total	9	34	36	.486	189	71	23	4	10	603^{1}	600	286	244	45	6	280	266	1.459	3.64	104	4.14	.264	22	.127	12	32	0.3
• NICHOLS, Dolan	Dolan Levon "Nick" Nichols b: 2/28/1930, Tishomingo, MS d: 11/20/1989, Tupelo, MS BR/TR, 6', 195 lbs. Deb: 4/15/1958																										
1958	Chi-N	0	4	.000	24	0	0	0	1	41^{1}	46	27	23	1	1	16	9	1.500	5.01	78	4.21	.295	0	.000	-5	0	-0.5
• NICHOLS, Kid	Charles Augustus Nichols b: 9/14/1869, Madison, WI d: 4/11/1953, Kansas City, MO BB/TR, 5'10.5", 175 lbs. Deb: 4/23/1890 M/U HOF: 1949																										
1890	Bos-N	27	19	.587	48	47	47	**7**	0	424	374	175	105	8	12	112	222	1.146	2.23	168	....	.230	43	.247	**74**	43	**6.7**
1891	Bos-N	30	17	.638	52	48	45	5	**3**	425^{1}	413	219	113	15	17	103	240	1.213	2.39	**153**	....	.245	36	.197	**60**	39	**5.2**
1892*	Bos-N	35	16	.686	53	51	49	5	0	453	404	211	143	15	10	121	192	1.159	2.84	124	2.56	.229	39	.198	20	48	1.8
1893	Bos-N	34	14	.708	52	44	43	1	1	425	426	222	166	15	15	118	94	1.280	3.52	140	3.28	.253	39	.220	62	40	4.9
1894	Bos-N	32	13	.711	50	46	40	**3**	0	407	488	308	215	23	9	121	113	1.496	4.75	124	4.36	.294	50	.294	40	37	3.3
1895	Bos-N	26	16	.619	48	43	43	1	**3**	389^{2}	429	220	144	15	5	90	147	1.332	3.33	150	3.54	.275	37	.236	69	34	5.4
1896	Bos-N	**30**	14	.682	49	43	37	3	1	372^{1}	387	211	117	14	7	101	102	1.311	2.83	160	3.30	.266	28	.190	**61**	33	4.9
1897*	Bos-N	**31**	11	.738	46	40	37	2	**3**	**368**	362	152	108	9	5	68	127	1.168	2.64	**169**	**2.68**	.255	39	.265	**66**	**41**	**6.0**
1898	Bos-N	**31**	12	.721	**50**	42	40	5	**4**	388	316	136	92	7	14	85	138	1.034	2.13	173	**1.99**	**.221**	38	.241	56	**44**	**5.5**
1899	Bos-N	21	19	.525	42	37	37	4	1	343^{1}	326	155	114	11	6	82	108	1.188	2.99	139	2.79	.251	26	.191	32	31	2.5
1900	Bos-N	13	16	.448	29	27	25	**4**	0	231^{1}	215	116	79	11	11	72	53	1.241	3.07	134	3.13	.246	18	.200	22	18	1.9
1901	Bos-N	19	16	.543	38	34	33	4	0	321	306	146	115	8	10	90	143	1.234	3.22	112	2.89	.250	46	.282	9	32	2.0
1904	StL-N	21	13	.618	36	35	35	3	1	317	268	97	71	3	5	50	134	1.003	2.02	133	1.83	.222	17	.156	30	27	3.2
1905	StL-N	1	5	.167	7	7	5	0	0	51^{2}	64	47	31	1	0	18	16	1.587	5.40	55	4.35	.296	5	.227	-12	0	-1.3
	Phi-N	10	6	.625	17	16	15	1	0	138^{2}	129	47	35	1	4	28	50	1.132	2.27	128	2.46	.250	10	.189	8	11	0.8
	Yr.	11	11	.500	24	23	20	1	0	190^{1}	193	94	66	2	4	46	66	1.256	3.12	94	2.98	.264	15	.200	-4	11	-0.4
1906	Phi-N	0	1	.000	4	2	1	0	0	11	17	16	12	0	2	13	1	2.727	9.82	27	10.83	.386	0	.000	-9	0	-1.0
Total	15	361	208	.634	621	562	532	48	17	5066^{1}	4924	2478	1660	156	132	1272	1880	1.223	2.95	139	2.48	.251	471	.226	588	478	51.7
• NICHOLS, Rod	Rodney Lea Nichols b: 12/29/1964, Burlington, IA BR/TR, 6'2", 200 lbs. Deb: 7/30/1988																										
1988	Cle-A	1	7	.125	11	10	3	0	0	69^{1}	73	41	39	5	2	23	31	1.385	5.06	81	4.03	.272	0	....	-6	1	-0.6
1989	Cle-A	4	6	.400	15	11	0	0	0	71^{2}	81	42	35	9	2	24	42	1.465	4.40	90	4.86	.285	0	....	-3	2	-0.3
1990	Cle-A	0	3	.000	4	2	0	0	0	16	24	14	14	5	2	6	3	1.875	7.88	50	9.35	.343	0	....	-7	0	-0.7
1991	Cle-A	2	11	.154	31	16	3	1	1	137^{1}	145	63	54	6	6	30	76	1.274	3.54	117	3.44	.273	0	....	12	7	1.2
1992	Cle-A	4	3	.571	30	9	0	0	0	105^{1}	114	58	53	13	2	31	56	1.377	4.53	86	4.32	.273	0	....	-7	4	-0.7
1993	LA-N	0	1	.000	4	0	0	0	0	6^{1}	9	5	4	1	0	2	3	1.737	5.68	67	6.42	.360	0	....	-1	0	-0.1
1995	Atl-N	0	0	....	5	0	0	0	0	6^{2}	14	11	4	3	0	5	3	2.850	5.40	79	16.45	.424	0	....	-1	0	-0.1
Total	7	11	31	.262	100	48	6	1	1	412^{2}	460	234	203	42	14	121	214	1.408	4.43	91	4.50	.282	0	....	-13	14	-1.3
• NICHOLS, Tricky	Frederick C. Nichols b: 7/26/1850, Bridgeport, CT d: 8/22/1897, Bridgeport, CT BR/TR, 5'7.5", 150 lbs. Deb: 4/21/1875																										
1875	NH-n	4	29	.121	34	33	30	0	0	288	319	....	76	2	....	10	10	1.142	2.38	76	....	.256	23	.193	-9	....	-0.8
1876	Bos-N	1	0	1.000	1	1	1	0	0	9	7	5	1	0	....	0	0	.778	1.00	225	....	.200	0	.000	1	1	0.0
1877	StL-N	18	23	.439	42	39	35	1	0	350	376	195	101	2	....	53	80	1.226	2.60	100	....	.259	31	.167	1	24	-1.0
1878	Pro-N	4	7	.364	11	10	10	0	0	98	157	98	46	0	....	8	21	**1.684**	4.22	52	....	.345	9	.184	-23	1	-2.2
1880	Wor-N	0	2	.000	2	2	2	0	0	17^{2}	29	16	8	0	....	4	4	1.868	4.08	64	....	.350	0	.000	-3	0	-0.4
1882	Bal-a	1	12	.077	16	13	12	0	0	118^{1}	155	113	66	2	....	17	21	1.454	5.02	55	....	.297	15	.158	-28	1	-3.0
Total	5	24	44	.353	72	65	60	1	0	593	724	427	222	4	....	82	126	1.359	3.37	75	....	.284	55	.161	-52	27	-6.6
• NICHOLSON, Frank	Frank Collins Nicholson b: 8/29/1889, Berlin, PA d: 11/10/1972, Jersey Shore, PA BR/TR, 6'2", 175 lbs. Deb: 9/6/1912																										
1912	Phi-N	0	0	....	2	0	0	0	0	4	8	3	3	1	0	2	1	2.500	6.75	54	14.04	.471	0	....	-1	0	-0.1
• NICHTING, Chris	Christopher Thomas Nichting b: 5/13/1966, Cincinnati, OH BR/TR, 6'1", 205 lbs. Deb: 5/15/1995																										
1995	Tex-A	0	0	....	13	0	0	0	0	24^{1}	36	19	19	1	1	13	6	2.014	7.03	69	7.01	.343	0	....	-6	0	-0.6
2000	Cle-A	0	0	....	7	0	0	0	0	9	13	7	7	0	2	5	7	2.000	7.00	71	7.21	.342	0	....	-2	0	-0.2
2001	Cin-N	0	3	.000	36	0	0	0	1	36^{1}	46	24	18	6	0	8	33	1.486	4.46	102	5.22	.307	0	.000	1	1	0.1
	Col-N	0	0	....	7	0	0	0	0	6	9	3	3	2	0	0	7	1.500	4.50	119	6.91	.346	0	....	1	0	0.1
	Yr.	0	3	.000	43	0	0	0	1	42^{1}	55	27	21	8	0	8	40	1.488	4.46	104	5.46	.313	0	.000	1	1	0.1
2002	Col-N	1	1	.500	29	0	0	0	0	36^{1}	40	18	18	7	1	5	25	1.239	4.46	107	4.36	.280	1	.333	2	2	0.2
Total	4	1	4	.200	92	0	0	0	1	112	144	71	65	16	4	31	78	1.563	5.22	91	5.58	.312	1	.250	-5	3	-0.4
• NICKLE, Doug	Douglas Alan Nickle b: 10/2/1974, Sonoma, CA BR/TR, 6'4", 210 lbs. Deb: 9/18/2000																										
2000	Phi-N	0	0	....	4	0	0	0	0	2^{2}	5	4	4	0	1	2	0	2.625	13.50	35	12.52	.417	0	....	-3	0	-0.2
2001	Phi-N	0	0	....	2	0	0	0	0	2	1	0	0	0	0	0	1	.500	0.00	....	0.54	.143	0	....	1	0	0.1
2002	Phi-N	0	0	....	4	0	0	0	0	4^{1}	6	3	3	2	0	4	2	2.308	6.23	63	11.93	.316	0	.000	-1	0	-0.1
	SD-N	1	0	1.000	10	0	0	0	0	11^{2}	20	13	11	1	1	9	7	2.486	8.49	44	9.93	.357	0	....	-6	0	-0.6
	Yr.	1	0	1.000	14	0	0	0	0	16	26	16	14	3	1	13	9	2.438	7.88	48	10.47	.347	0	.000	-7	0	-0.7
Total	3	1	0	1.000	20	0	0	0	0	20^{2}	32	20	18	3	2	15	10	2.274	7.84	50	9.78	.340	0	.000	-9	0	-0.9
• NICOL, George	George Edward Nicol b: 10/17/1870, Barry, IL d: 8/4/1924, Milwaukee, WI TL, 5'7", 155 lbs. Deb: 9/23/1890 ♦																										
1890	StL-a	2	1	.667	3	3	2	0	0	17	11	13	9	1	2	19	16	1.765	4.76	90	....	.179	2	.286	-1	1	0.0
1891	Chi-N	0	1	.000	3	2	0	0	0	11	14	20	6	0	1	10	12	2.182	4.91	68	....	.299	2	.333	-2	0	-0.1

YEAR TM-L	W	L	PCT	G	GS	CG	SH	SV	IP	H	R	ER	HR	HB	BB	SO	RAT	ERA	ERA+	CERA	OAV	BH	AVG	PR+	WS	TPW
1894 Pit-N	3	4	.429	9	5	3	0	0	46^1	58	38	32	2	5	39	13	2.094	6.22	84	7.08	.303	9	.450	-5	3	-0.2
Lou-N	0	1	.000	2	2	2	0	0	17^1	35	35	15	4	1	16	4	2.942	7.79	65	14.60	.412	38	.352	-5	2	-0.6
Yr.	3	5	.375	11	7	5	0	0	63^2	93	73	47	6	6	55	17	2.325	6.64	78	9.13	.337	47	.367	-10	5	-0.8
Total 3	5	7	.417	17	12	7	0	0	91^2	118	106	62	7	9	84	45	2.204	6.09	79	6.34	.307	51	.362	-13	6	-0.8
• NIED, David	David Glen Nied b: 12/22/1968, Dallas, TX BR/TR, 6'2", 188 lbs. Deb: 9/1/1992																									
1992 Atl-N	3	0	1.000	6	2	0	0	0	23	10	3	3	0	0	5	19	.652	1.17	311	0.74	.130	2	.286	6	3	0.7
1993 Col-N	5	9	.357	16	16	1	0	0	87	99	53	50	8	1	42	46	1.621	5.17	92	5.11	.296	4	.174	-1	5	-0.1
1994 Col-N	9	7	.563	22	22	2	1	0	122	137	70	65	15	4	47	74	1.508	4.80	104	4.99	.287	4	.100	6	7	0.4
1995 Col-N	0	0	....	2	0	0	0	0	4^1	11	10	10	2	0	3	3	3.231	20.77	26	19.74	.458	0	....	-7	0	-0.7
1996 Col-N	0	2	.000	6	1	0	0	0	5^1	5	8	8	1	0	8	4	2.438	13.50	39	8.90	.250	0	.000	-5	0	-0.5
Total 5	17	18	.486	52	41	3	1	0	241^2	262	144	136	26	5	105	146	1.519	5.06	97	4.98	.281	10	.141	-1	15	-0.1
• NIEDENFUER, Tom	Thomas Edward Niedenfuer b: 8/13/1959, St. Louis Park, MN BR/TR, 6'5", 225 lbs. Deb: 8/15/1981																									
1981* LA-N	3	1	.750	17	0	0	0	2	26	25	11	11	1	1	6	12	1.192	3.81	87	2.87	.258	0	....	-1	2	-0.1
1982 LA-N	3	4	.429	55	0	0	0	9	69^2	71	22	21	3	2	25	60	1.378	2.71	128	3.56	.269	0	.000	6	7	0.7
1983* LA-N	8	3	.727	66	0	0	0	11	94^2	55	22	20	6	1	29	66	.887	1.90	189	1.44	.170	0	.000	20	15	2.0
1984 LA-N	2	5	.286	33	0	0	0	11	47^1	39	14	13	3	2	23	45	1.310	2.47	143	3.09	.227	0	.000	6	7	0.6
1985* LA-N	7	9	.438	64	0	0	0	19	106^1	86	32	32	6	1	24	102	1.034	2.71	128	2.20	.223	1	.111	9	13	0.9
1986 LA-N	6	6	.500	60	0	0	0	11	80	86	35	33	11	1	29	55	1.438	3.71	93	4.41	.280	2	.500	-1	7	0.0
1987 LA-N	1	0	1.000	15	0	0	0	1	16^1	13	5	5	1	1	9	10	1.347	2.76	144	3.42	.220	0	....	2	2	0.2
Bal-A	3	5	.375	45	0	0	0	13	52^1	55	32	29	11	1	22	37	1.471	4.99	88	5.17	.266	0	....	-3	4	-0.3
1988 Bal-A	3	4	.429	52	0	0	0	18	59	59	23	23	8	2	19	40	1.322	3.51	111	4.07	.259	0	....	2	7	0.2
1989 Sea-A	0	3	.000	25	0	0	0	0	36^1	46	29	27	7	1	15	15	1.679	6.69	60	6.14	.309	0	....	-11	0	-1.1
1990 StL-N	0	6	.000	52	0	0	0	2	65	66	26	25	3	0	25	32	1.400	3.46	110	3.60	.269	0	.000	3	5	0.3
Total 10	36	46	.439	484	0	0	0	97	653	601	251	239	60	13	226	474	1.266	3.29	113	3.39	.247	3	.115	32	69	3.3
• NIEHAUS, Dick	Richard J. Niehaus b: 10/24/1892, Covington, KY d: 3/12/1957, Atlanta, GA BL/TL, 5'11", 165 lbs. Deb: 9/9/1913																									
1913 StL-N	0	2	.000	3	3	2	0	0	24	20	17	11	1	0	13	4	1.375	4.13	78	3.12	.241	2	.286	-2	1	-0.2
1914 StL-N	1	0	1.000	8	1	1	0	0	17^1	18	11	6	1	0	8	6	1.500	3.12	90	4.12	.269	1	.250	-1	1	0.0
1915 StL-N	2	1	.667	15	2	0	0	0	45^1	48	35	20	2	1	22	21	1.544	3.97	70	4.28	.281	1	.071	-5	0	-0.7
1920 Cle-A	1	2	.333	19	3	0	0	2	40	42	21	16	0	1	16	12	1.450	3.60	105	3.66	.269	4	.444	0	3	0.2
Total 4	4	5	.444	45	9	3	0	2	126^2	128	84	53	4	2	59	43	1.476	3.77	83	3.84	.268	8	.235	-9	5	-0.7
• NIEKRO, Joe	Joseph Franklin Niekro b: 11/7/1944, Martins Ferry, OH BR/TR, 6'1", 190 lbs. Deb: 4/16/1967																									
1967 Chi-N	10	7	.588	36	22	7	2	0	169^2	171	68	63	15	2	32	77	1.196	3.34	106	3.18	.257	9	.196	2	10	0.4
1968 Chi-N	14	10	.583	34	29	2	1	2	177	204	93	85	18	3	59	65	**1.486**	4.32	73	4.75	.294	6	.100	-23	5	-2.8
1969 Chi-N	0	1	.000	4	3	0	0	0	19^1	24	9	8	3	0	6	7	1.552	3.72	108	5.53	.304	1	.200	1	1	0.1
SD-N	8	17	.320	37	31	8	3	0	202	213	91	83	15	0	45	55	1.277	3.70	96	3.46	.273	6	.118	-1	12	-0.1
Yr.	8	18	.308	41	34	8	3	0	221^1	237	100	91	18	0	51	62	1.301	3.70	97	3.64	.276	7	.125	-0	13	0.0
1970 Det-A	12	13	.480	38	34	6	2	0	213	221	107	96	28	3	72	101	1.376	4.06	92	4.30	.266	13	.197	-1	12	0.2
1971 Det-A	6	7	.462	31	15	0	0	1	122^1	136	62	61	13	2	49	43	1.512	4.49	80	4.80	.283	4	.133	-12	3	-1.3
1972 Det-A	3	2	.600	18	7	1	0	1	47	62	20	20	3	1	8	24	1.489	3.83	82	4.98	.330	3	.250	-4	2	-0.4
1973 Atl-N	2	4	.333	20	0	0	0	3	24	23	11	11	2	0	11	12	1.417	4.13	95	4.10	.277	1	.333	-0	2	0.0
1974 Atl-N	3	2	.600	27	2	0	0	0	43	36	19	17	5	2	18	31	1.256	3.56	106	3.56	.237	0	.000	0	3	0.0
1975 Hou-N	6	4	.600	40	4	1	1	4	88	79	32	30	3	2	39	54	1.341	3.07	110	3.22	.240	3	.214	2	7	0.3
1976 Hou-N	4	8	.333	36	13	0	0	0	118	107	60	44	8	1	56	77	1.381	3.36	95	3.58	.238	5	.185	-2	4	0.0
1977 Hou-N	13	8	.619	44	14	9	2	5	180^2	155	66	61	14	1	64	101	1.212	3.04	117	3.04	.237	7	.140	11	14	1.0
1978 Hou-N	14	14	.500	35	29	10	1	0	202^2	190	97	87	13	9	73	97	1.298	3.86	86	3.50	.248	9	.138	-8	8	-1.0
1979 Hou-N★	**21**	11	.656	38	38	11	**5**	0	263^2	221	102	88	17	7	107	119	1.244	3.00	117	3.11	.228	10	.120	16	19	1.4
1980* Hou-N	20	12	.625	37	36	11	2	0	256	268	119	101	12	4	79	127	1.355	3.55	93	3.64	.270	22	.275	-8	14	0.0
1981* Hou-N	9	9	.500	24	24	5	2	0	166	150	60	52	8	0	47	77	1.187	2.82	117	2.78	.243	9	.176	8	9	0.9
1982 Hou-N	17	12	.586	35	35	16	5	0	270	224	79	74	12	5	64	130	1.067	2.47	134	**2.35**	.229	8	.090	23	**25**	2.0
1983 Hou-N	15	14	.517	38	**38**	9	1	0	263^2	238	115	102	15	3	101	152	1.286	3.48	98	3.19	.241	8	.094	-6	11	-1.0
1984 Hou-N	16	12	.571	38	**38**	6	1	0	248^1	223	104	84	16	4	89	127	1.256	3.04	109	3.21	.241	11	.133	4	13	0.3
1985 Hou-N	9	12	.429	32	32	4	1	0	213	197	100	88	21	5	99	117	1.390	3.72	93	3.93	.247	17	.250	-8	8	-0.5
NY-A	2	1	.667	3	3	0	0	0	12^1	14	8	8	3	0	8	4	1.784	5.84	69	7.04	.280	0	....	-3	0	-0.3
1986 NY-A	9	10	.474	25	25	0	0	0	125^2	139	84	68	15	1	63	59	1.607	4.87	84	5.20	.275	0	....	-12	4	-1.2
1987 NY-A	3	4	.429	8	8	1	0	0	50^2	40	25	20	4	4	19	30	1.164	3.55	123	3.01	.215	0	....	4	3	0.4
* Min-A	4	9	.308	19	18	0	0	0	96^1	115	76	67	11	6	45	54	1.661	6.26	74	5.86	.296	0	....	-18	0	-1.7
Yr.	7	13	.350	27	26	1	0	0	147	155	101	87	15	10	64	84	1.490	5.33	86	4.88	.270	0	....	-13	3	-1.3
1988 Min-A	1	1	.500	5	2	0	0	0	11^2	16	13	13	2	0	9	7	2.143	10.03	41	8.53	.320	0	....	-8	0	-0.8
Total 22	221	204	.520	702	500	107	29	16	3584	3466	1620	1431	276	65	1262	1747	1.319	3.59	98	3.63	.255	152	.156	-43	189	-4.1
• NIEKRO, Phil	Philip Henry Niekro b: 4/1/1939, Blaine, OH BR/TR, 6'1", 180 lbs. Deb: 4/15/1964 HOF: 1997																									
1964 Mil-N	0	0	....	10	0	0	0	0	15	15	10	8	1	1	7	8	1.467	4.80	73	4.39	.273	0	....	-2	0	-0.2
1965 Mil-N	2	3	.400	41	1	0	0	6	74^2	73	32	24	5	3	26	49	1.326	2.89	122	3.55	.258	1	.100	5	5	0.5
1966 Atl-N	4	3	.571	28	0	0	0	2	50^1	48	32	23	4	2	23	17	1.411	4.11	88	3.79	.249	0	.000	-3	2	-0.4
1967 Atl-N	11	9	.550	46	20	10	1	9	207	164	64	43	9	7	55	129	1.058	**1.87**	**178**	2.27	.218	7	.123	32	21	3.4
1968 Atl-N	14	12	.538	37	34	15	5	2	257	228	83	74	16	5	45	140	1.062	2.59	116	2.50	.239	8	.104	10	18	1.1
1969* Atl-N★	23	13	.639	40	35	21	4	1	284^1	235	93	81	21	5	57	193	1.027	2.56	141	2.27	.221	20	.211	34	28	3.9
1970 Atl-N	12	18	.400	34	32	10	3	0	229^2	222	124	109	40	6	68	168	1.263	4.27	100	4.01	.248	12	.152	6	11	0.5
1971 Atl-N	15	14	.517	42	36	18	4	2	268^2	248	112	89	27	3	70	173	1.184	2.98	125	3.16	.245	14	.152	23	22	2.3
1972 Atl-N	16	12	.571	38	36	17	1	0	282^1	254	112	96	22	5	53	164	1.087	3.06	124	2.62	.236	18	.194	27	22	3.1
1973 Atl-N	13	10	.565	42	30	9	1	4	245	214	103	90	21	5	89	131	1.237	3.31	119	3.21	.234	10	.122	19	17	1.9
1974 Atl-N	**20**	13	.606	41	39	**18**	6	1	**302**^{1}	249	91	80	19	6	88	195	1.115	2.38	159	2.59	.225	20	.192	**42**	**28**	**4.4**
1975 Atl-N★	15	15	.500	39	37	13	1	0	275^2	285	115	98	29	11	72	144	1.295	3.20	118	3.93	.269	17	.172	24	19	2.5
1976 Atl-N	17	11	.607	38	37	10	2	0	270^2	249	116	99	18	8	101	173	1.293	3.29	115	3.34	.242	18	.191	22	**21**	2.4
1977 Atl-N	16	20	.444	44	**43**	**20**	2	0	**330**^{1}	315	166	148	26	8	164	**262**	1.450	4.03	110	4.13	.255	19	.174	25	20	2.3
1978 Atl-N★	19	18	.514	44	**42**	**22**	4	1	**334**^{1}	295	129	107	16	13	102	248	1.187	2.88	140	2.86	.235	27	.225	**48**	**30**	**5.5**
1979 Atl-N	**21**	20	.512	44	**44**	**23**	1	0	**342**	311	160	129	41	11	113	208	1.240	3.39	119	3.53	.241	24	.195	**35**	**24**	**3.8**
1980 Atl-N	15	18	.455	40	**38**	11	3	1	275	256	119	111	30	3	85	176	1.240	3.63	103	3.47	.249	12	.133	4	17	0.2
1981 Atl-N	7	7	.500	22	22	3	3	0	139^1	120	56	48	6	1	56	62	1.263	3.10	116	2.99	.233	4	.077	8	8	0.4
1982* Atl-N★	17	4	.810	35	35	4	2	0	234^1	225	106	94	23	3	73	144	1.272	3.61	103	3.61	.255	17	.195	2	14	0.5
1983 Atl-N	11	10	.524	34	33	2	0	0	201^2	212	94	89	18	2	105	128	**1.572**	3.97	98	4.87	.276	12	.185	-4	9	-0.4
1984 NY-A★	16	8	.667	32	31	5	1	0	215^2	219	85	74	15	3	76	136	1.368	3.09	123	3.86	.267	0	....	18	15	1.8
1985 NY-A	16	12	.571	33	33	7	1	0	220	203	110	100	29	2	120	149	1.468	4.09	98	4.53	.245	0	....	-5	10	-0.5
1986 Cle-A	11	11	.500	34	32	5	0	0	210^1	241	126	101	24	6	95	81	1.597	4.32	96	5.35	.287	0	....	-3	9	-0.3
1987 Cle-A	7	11	.389	22	22	2	0	0	123^2	142	83	81	18	4	53	57	1.577	5.89	77	5.48	.286	0	....	-17	4	-1.6
Tor-A	0	2	.000	3	3	0	0	0	12	15	11	11	4	0	7	7	1.833	8.25	54	8.41	.306	0	....	-5	0	-0.5
Yr.	7	13	.350	25	25	2	0	0	135^2	157	94	92	22	4	60	64	1.600	6.10	74	5.74	.288	0	....	-22	4	-2.1
Atl-N	0	0	....	1	1	0	0	0	3	6	5	5	0	0	6	0	4.000	15.00	29	17.55	.429	0	.000	-4	0	-0.4
Total 24	318	274	.537	864	716	245	45	29	5404^1	5044	2337	2012	482	123	1809	3342	1.268	3.35	116	3.49	.247	260	.169	343	374	36.2
• NIELSEN, Jerry	Gerald Arthur Nielsen b: 8/5/1966, Sacramento, CA BL/TL, 6'3", 185 lbs. Deb: 7/12/1992																									
1992 NY-A	1	0	1.000	20	0	0	0	0	19^2	17	10	10	1	0	18	12	1.780	4.58	86	4.85	.243	0	....	-1	1	-0.2
1993 Cal-A	0	0	....	10	0	0	0	0	12^1	18	13	11	1	1	4	8	1.784	8.03	56	6.30	.340	0	....	-5	0	-0.5
Total 2	1	0	1.000	30	0	0	0	0	32	35	23	21	2	1	22	20	1.781	5.91	71	5.41	.285	0	....	-6	1	-0.6

YEAR	TM-L	W	L	PCT	G	GS	CG	SH	SV	IP	H	R	ER	HR	HB	BB	SO	RAT	ERA	ERA+	CERA	OAV	BH	AVG	PR+	WS	TPW
• NIELSEN, Scott					Jeffrey Scott Nielsen b: 12/18/1958, Salt Lake City, UT BR/TR, 6'1", 190 lbs. Deb: 7/7/1986																						
1986	NY-A	4	4	.500	10	9	2	2	0	56	66	29	25	12	2	12	20	1.393	4.02	102	5.51	.299	0	....	0	3	0.0
1987	Chi-A	3	5	.375	19	7	1	1	2	66^1	83	48	46	9	1	25	23	1.628	6.24	73	5.81	.307	0	....	-14	1	-1.3
1988	NY-A	1	2	.333	7	2	0	0	0	19^2	27	16	15	5	0	13	4	2.034	6.86	57	8.89	.333	0	....	-6	0	-0.6
1989	NY-A	1	0	1.000	2	0	0	0	0	0^2	2	1	1	0	0	1	0	4.500	13.50	29	18.30	.500	0	....	-1	0	-0.1
Total	4	9	11	.450	38	18	3	3	2	142^2	178	94	87	26	3	51	47	1.605	5.49	78	6.17	.309	0	....	-21	4	-2.0
• NIEMANN, Randy					Randal Harold Niemann b: 11/15/1955, Scotia, CA BL/TL, 6'4", 200 lbs. Deb: 5/20/1979 C																						
1979	Hou-N	3	2	.600	26	7	3	2	1	67	68	32	28	1	1	22	24	1.343	3.76	93	3.26	.272	2	.133	-2	3	-0.2
1980	Hou-N	0	1	.000	22	1	0	0	1	33	40	21	20	2	0	12	18	1.576	5.45	60	4.82	.299	2	.333	-8	0	-0.8
1982	Pit-N	1	1	.500	20	0	0	0	1	35^1	34	22	20	1	2	17	26	1.443	5.09	73	3.64	.254	2	1.000	-5	1	-0.5
1983	Pit-N	0	1	.000	8	1	0	0	0	13^2	20	14	14	2	1	7	8	1.976	9.22	40	8.14	.357	0	.000	-8	0	-0.9
1984	Chi-A	0	0	....	5	0	0	0	0	5^1	5	1	1	0	0	5	5	1.875	1.69	246	4.94	.263	0	....	1	1	0.1
1985	NY-N	0	0	....	4	0	0	0	0	4^2	5	0	0	0	0	0	2	1.071	0.00	....	2.43	.278	0	....	2	1	0.2
1986	NY-N	2	3	.400	31	1	0	0	0	35^2	44	17	15	2	0	12	18	1.570	3.79	93	4.77	.308	2	.333	-1	2	0.0
1987	Min-A	1	0	1.000	6	0	0	0	0	5^1	3	5	5	0	2	7	1	1.875	8.44	55	5.51	.158	0	....	-2	0	-0.2
Total	8	7	8	.467	122	10	3	2	3	200	219	112	103	8	6	82	102	1.505	4.64	77	4.27	.283	8	.267	-23	8	-2.2
• NIEMES, Jack					Jacob Leland Niemes b: 10/19/1919, Cincinnati, OH d: 3/4/1966, Hamilton, OH BR/TL, 6'1", 180 lbs. Deb: 5/30/1943																						
1943	Cin-N	0	0	....	3	0	0	0	0	3	5	3	2	0	0	2	1	2.333	6.00	55	8.59	.385	0	....	-1	0	-0.1
• NIESON, Chuck					Charles Bassett Nieson b: 9/24/1942, Hanford, CA BR/TR, 6'2", 185 lbs. Deb: 9/18/1964																						
1964	Min-A	0	0	....	2	0	0	0	0	2	1	1	1	1	0	1	5	1.000	4.50	80	4.08	.143	0	....	-0	0	0.0
• NIEVES, Juan					Juan Manuel (Cruz) Nieves b: 1/5/1965, Santurce, Puerto Rico BL/TL, 6'3", 175 lbs. Deb: 4/10/1986																						
1986	Mil-A	11	12	.478	35	33	4	3	0	184^2	224	124	101	17	1	77	116	**1.630**	4.92	88	5.36	.299	0	....	-11	6	-1.1
1987	Mil-A	14	8	.636	34	33	3	1	0	195^2	199	112	106	24	2	100	163	**1.528**	4.88	94	4.79	.264	0	....	-5	10	-0.5
1988	Mil-A	7	5	.583	25	15	1	1	1	110^1	84	53	50	13	1	50	73	1.215	4.08	98	3.09	.208	0	....	-2	6	-0.2
Total	3	32	25	.561	94	81	8	5	1	490^2	507	289	257	54	4	227	352	1.496	4.71	92	4.62	.266	0	....	-18	22	-1.8
• NIGGELING, Johnny					John Arnold Niggeling b: 7/10/1903, Remsen, IA d: 9/16/1963, Le Mars, IA BR/TR, 6', 170 lbs. Deb: 4/30/1938																						
1938	Bos-N	1	0	1.000	2	0	0	0	0	2	4	2	2	0	0	1	1	2.500	9.00	38	9.55	.400	0	....	-1	0	-0.1
1939	Cin-N	2	1	.667	10	5	2	1	0	40^1	51	28	26	2	2	13	20	1.587	5.80	66	4.93	.309	2	.154	-10	0	-1.0
1940	StL-A	7	11	.389	28	20	10	0	0	153^2	148	88	76	9	5	69	82	1.412	4.45	103	3.76	.250	9	.176	3	9	0.2
1941	StL-A	7	9	.438	24	20	13	1	0	168^1	168	83	71	17	1	63	68	1.372	3.80	113	3.83	.255	10	.167	12	11	1.0
1942	StL-A	15	11	.577	28	27	16	3	0	206^1	173	76	61	10	11	93	107	1.289	2.66	139	3.09	.226	10	.139	26	17	2.5
1943	StL-A	6	8	.429	20	20	7	0	0	150^1	122	61	53	7	6	57	73	1.191	3.17	105	2.67	.220	3	.061	5	8	0.0
	Was-A	4	2	.667	6	6	5	3	0	51	27	6	5	0	0	17	24	.863	0.88	363	1.14	.153	5	.278	13	7	1.5
	Yr.	10	10	.500	26	26	12	3	0	201^1	149	67	58	7	6	74	97	1.108	2.59	128	2.28	.204	8	.119	18	15	1.6
1944	Was-A	10	8	.556	24	24	14	2	0	206	164	65	53	5	4	88	121	1.223	2.32	141	2.59	.221	9	.130	24	15	2.3
1945	Was-A	7	12	.368	26	25	8	2	0	176^2	161	80	62	7	3	73	90	1.325	3.16	98	3.17	.240	7	.119	-0	7	-0.4
1946	Was-A	3	2	.600	8	6	3	0	0	38	39	22	17	1	1	21	10	1.579	4.03	83	4.15	.265	2	.182	-2	1	-0.2
	Bos-N	2	5	.286	8	8	3	0	0	58	54	23	21	2	1	21	24	1.293	3.26	105	3.05	.243	2	.111	2	3	0.0
Total	9	64	69	.481	184	161	81	12	0	1250^2	1111	534	447	60	34	516	620	1.301	3.22	114	3.17	.236	59	.140	71	78	5.9
• NIPPER, Al					Albert Samuel Nipper b: 4/2/1959, San Diego, CA BR/TR, 6', 194 lbs. Deb: 9/6/1983 C																						
1983	Bos-A	1	1	.500	3	2	1	0	0	16	17	4	4	0	1	7	5	1.500	2.25	193	4.37	.293	0	....	4	2	0.4
1984	Bos-A	11	6	.647	29	24	6	0	0	182^2	183	86	79	18	7	52	84	1.286	3.89	107	3.75	.257	0	....	12	12	1.2
1985	Bos-A	9	12	.429	25	25	5	0	0	162	157	83	73	14	9	82	85	1.475	4.06	106	4.44	.256	0	....	7	8	0.7
1986*	Bos-A	10	12	.455	26	26	3	0	0	159	186	108	95	24	4	47	79	1.465	5.38	77	5.05	.290	0	....	-20	3	-2.0
1987	Bos-A	11	12	.478	30	30	6	0	0	174	196	115	105	30	7	62	89	1.483	5.43	84	5.27	.284	0	....	-16	6	-1.5
1988	Chi-N	2	4	.333	22	12	0	0	1	80	72	37	27	9	3	34	27	1.325	3.04	119	3.83	.238	2	.087	7	5	0.6
1990	Cle-A	2	3	.400	9	5	0	0	0	24	35	19	18	2	2	19	12	2.250	6.75	58	8.80	.354	0	....	-7	0	-0.7
Total	7	46	50	.479	144	124	21	0	1	797^2	846	452	401	97	33	303	381	1.440	4.52	93	4.65	.271	2	.087	-14	36	-1.3
• NIPPERT, Merlin					Merlin Lee Nippert b: 9/1/1938, Mangum, OK BR/TR, 6'1", 175 lbs. Deb: 9/12/1962																						
1962	Bos-A	0	0	....	4	0	0	0	0	6	4	3	3	1	0	4	3	1.333	4.50	92	3.26	.200	0	....	-0	0	0.0
• NISCHWITZ, Ron					Ronald Lee Nischwitz b: 7/1/1937, Dayton, OH BB/TL, 6'3", 205 lbs. Deb: 9/4/1961																						
1961	Det-A	0	1	.000	6	1	0	0	0	11^1	13	12	7	2	0	8	8	1.853	5.56	74	6.39	.295	0	.000	-2	0	-0.2
1962	Det-A	4	5	.444	48	0	0	0	4	64^2	73	30	28	5	1	26	28	1.531	3.90	104	4.64	.285	5	.417	2	5	0.4
1963	Cle-A	0	2	.000	14	0	0	0	1	16^2	17	13	12	3	0	8	10	1.500	6.48	56	4.78	.262	0	.000	-5	0	-0.6
1965	Det-A	1	0	1.000	20	0	0	0	1	22^2	21	10	7	2	0	6	12	1.191	2.78	125	3.15	.259	0	.000	2	2	0.2
Total	4	5	8	.385	88	1	0	0	6	115^1	124	65	54	12	1	48	58	1.491	4.21	92	4.54	.278	5	.278	-3	7	-0.2
• NITCHOLAS, Otho					Otho James Nitcholas b: 9/13/1908, McKinney, TX d: 9/11/1986, McKinney, TX BR/TR, 6', 190 lbs. Deb: 4/18/1945																						
1945	Bro-N	1	0	1.000	7	0	0	0	0	18^2	19	14	11	4	0	1	4	1.071	5.30	71	3.33	.257	1	.250	-3	0	-0.3
• NITKOWSKI, C.J.					Christopher John Nitkowski b: 3/9/1973, Suffern, NY BL/TL, 6'2", 185 lbs. Deb: 6/3/1995																						
1995	Cin-N	1	3	.250	9	7	0	0	0	32^1	41	25	22	4	2	15	18	1.732	6.12	67	6.20	.306	2	.200	-8	0	-0.8
	Det-A	1	4	.200	11	11	0	0	0	39^1	53	32	31	7	3	20	13	1.856	7.09	67	7.76	.335	0	....	-10	0	-0.9
1996	Det-A	2	3	.400	11	8	0	0	0	45^2	62	44	41	7	7	38	36	2.190	8.08	63	9.44	.332	0	....	-14	0	-1.3
1998	Hou-N	3	3	.500	43	0	0	0	3	59^2	49	27	25	4	6	23	44	1.207	3.77	108	3.19	.228	0	.000	2	4	0.1
1999	Det-A	4	5	.444	68	7	0	0	0	81^2	63	44	39	11	3	45	66	1.322	4.30	115	3.73	.213	0	.000	6	6	0.5
2000	Det-A	4	9	.308	67	11	0	0	0	109^2	124	79	64	13	4	49	81	1.578	5.25	92	5.23	.286	0	....	-5	3	-0.4
2001	Det-A	0	3	.000	56	0	0	0	0	45^1	51	30	28	7	5	31	38	1.809	5.56	78	6.53	.283	0	....	-5	1	-0.5
	NY-N	1	0	1.000	5	0	0	0	0	5^2	3	0	0	0	0	3	4	1.059	0.00	....	1.52	.167	0	....	3	1	0.3
2002	Tex-A	0	1	.000	12	0	0	0	0	13^2	11	4	4	0	0	13	14	1.756	2.63	179	4.35	.224	0	....	3	1	0.3
2003	Tex-A	0	0	....	6	0	0	0	0	9^2	17	8	8	0	0	8	5	2.586	7.45	67	9.69	.415	0	....	-3	0	-0.2
Total	8	16	31	.340	288	44	0	0	3	442^2	474	293	262	53	30	245	319	1.624	5.33	87	5.57	.277	2	.133	-31	16	-3.0
• NIXON, Willard					Willard Lee Nixon b: 6/17/1928, Taylorsville, GA d: 12/10/2000, Rome, GA BL/TR, 6'2", 195 lbs. Deb: 7/7/1950																						
1950	Bos-A	8	6	.571	22	15	2	0	2	101^1	126	75	68	8	2	58	57	1.816	6.04	81	5.99	.310	5	.139	-12	3	-1.3
1951	Bos-A	7	4	.636	33	14	2	1	1	125	136	79	68	12	7	56	70	1.536	4.90	91	4.93	.285	13	.289	-6	7	-0.3
1952	Bos-A	5	4	.556	23	13	5	0	0	103^2	115	64	56	12	4	61	50	1.698	4.86	81	5.74	.290	11	.208	-11	3	-1.0
1953	Bos-A	4	8	.333	23	15	5	1	0	116^2	114	57	51	6	1	59	57	1.483	3.93	107	3.88	.254	8	.190	3	7	0.3
1954	Bos-A	11	12	.478	31	30	8	2	0	199^2	182	102	90	16	9	87	102	1.347	4.06	101	3.69	.248	18	.265	3	11	0.9
1955	Bos-A	12	10	.545	31	31	7	3	0	208	207	102	94	10	3	85	95	1.404	4.07	105	3.73	.259	18	.261	7	14	1.3
1956	Bos-A	9	8	.529	23	22	9	1	0	145^1	142	79	68	9	8	57	74	1.369	4.21	110	3.83	.255	11	.204	7	9	0.6
1957	Bos-A	12	13	.480	29	29	11	1	0	191	207	86	78	10	7	56	96	1.377	3.68	109	3.99	.280	22	.293	10	15	1.5
1958	Bos-A	1	7	.125	10	8	2	0	0	43^1	48	30	29	7	0	11	15	1.362	6.02	67	4.48	.281	5	.294	-9	0	-0.8
Total	9	69	72	.489	225	177	51	9	3	1234	1277	674	602	90	41	530	616	1.464	4.39	97	4.29	.270	111	.242	-9	69	1.2
• NOLAN, Gary					Gary Lynn Nolan b: 5/27/1948, Herlong, CA BR/TR, 6'2.5", 197 lbs. Deb: 4/15/1967																						
1967	Cin-N	14	8	.636	33	32	8	5	0	226^2	193	73	65	18	5	62	206	1.125	2.58	145	2.69	.228	7	.104	31	19	3.2
1968	Cin-N	9	4	.692	23	22	4	2	0	150	105	48	40	10	3	49	111	1.027	2.40	132	2.14	.196	6	.130	14	11	1.8
1969	Cin-N	8	8	.500	16	15	2	1	0	108^2	102	45	43	11	0	40	83	1.307	3.56	106	3.57	.247	8	.229	2	7	0.6
1970*	Cin-N	18	7	.720	37	37	4	2	0	250^2	226	102	91	25	1	96	181	1.285	3.27	128	3.44	.240	13	.159	25	19	2.5
1971	Cin-N	12	15	.444	35	35	9	0	0	244^2	208	91	86	12	2	59	146	1.091	3.16	103	2.33	.227	11	.147	-3	13	-0.5
1972*	Cin-N★	15	5	.750	25	25	6	2	0	176	147	48	39	13	1	30	90	1.006	1.99	161	2.22	.227	7	.117	20	15	2.1
1973	Cin-N	0	1	.000	2	2	0	0	0	10^1	6	4	4	1	0	7	3	1.258	3.48	98	2.66	.167	0	.000	-0	0	0.0

YEAR TM-L	W	L	PCT	G	GS	CG	SH	SV	IP	H	R	ER	HR	HB	BB	SO	RAT	ERA	ERA+	CERA	OAV	BH	AVG	PR+	WS	TPW
1975* Cin-N	15	9	.625	32	32	5	1	0	210^2	202	75	74	18	1	29	74	1.097	3.16	114	2.74	.251	12	.176	4	15	0.6
1976* Cin-N	15	9	.625	34	34	7	1	0	239^1	232	96	92	28	1	27	113	1.082	3.46	101	2.94	.254	8	.101	-1	12	-0.5
1977 Cin-N	4	1	.800	8	8	0	0	0	39^1	53	22	21	5	0	12	28	1.653	4.81	82	5.89	.321	1	.067	-4	2	-0.5
Cal-A	0	3	.000	5	5	0	0	0	18^1	31	19	18	5	0	2	4	1.800	8.84	44	8.17	.365	0	....	-10	0	-1.0
Total 10	110	70	.611	250	247	45	14	0	1674^2	1505	623	573	146	14	413	1039	1.145	3.08	116	2.88	.239	73	.138	77	113	8.3

• NOLAN, The Only Edward Sylvester Nolan b: 11/7/1857, Paterson, NJ d: 5/18/1913, Paterson, NJ BL/TR, 5'8", 171 lbs. Deb: 5/1/1878 U

YEAR TM-L	W	L	PCT	G	GS	CG	SH	SV	IP	H	R	ER	HR	HB	BB	SO	RAT	ERA	ERA+	CERA	OAV	BH	AVG	PR+	WS	TPW
1878 Ind-N	13	22	.371	38	38	37	1	0	347	357	208	99	1	....	56	125	1.190	2.57	79	....	.253	37	.243	-19	15	-1.2
1881 Cle-N	8	14	.364	22	21	20	0	0	180	183	111	61	3	....	38	54	1.228	3.05	86	....	.252	41	.244	-10	9	-1.4
1883 Pit-a	0	7	.000	7	7	6	0	0	55	81	44	26	0	....	10	23	1.655	4.25	75	....	.322	8	.308	-5	2	-0.3
1884 Wil-U	1	4	.200	5	5	5	0	0	40	44	28	13	1	....	7	52	1.275	2.93	114	....	.261	9	.273	3	2	0.4
1885 Phi-N	1	5	.167	7	7	6	0	0	54	55	43	25	1	....	24	20	1.463	4.17	67	....	.252	2	.077	-9	1	-0.9
Total 5	23	52	.307	79	78	74	1	0	676	720	434	224	6	....	135	274	1.265	2.98	81	....	.259	97	.240	-40	29	-3.5

• NOLD, Dick Richard Louis Nold b: 5/4/1943, San Francisco, CA BR/TR, 6'2", 190 lbs. Deb: 8/19/1967

YEAR TM-L	W	L	PCT	G	GS	CG	SH	SV	IP	H	R	ER	HR	HB	BB	SO	RAT	ERA	ERA+	CERA	OAV	BH	AVG	PR+	WS	TPW
1967 Was-A	0	2	.000	7	3	0	0	0	20^1	19	13	11	1	0	13	10	1.574	4.87	65	4.20	.241	0	.000	-4	0	-0.4

• NOLES, Dickie Dickie Ray Noles b: 11/19/1956, Charlotte, NC BR/TR, 6'2", 190 lbs. Deb: 7/5/1979

YEAR TM-L	W	L	PCT	G	GS	CG	SH	SV	IP	H	R	ER	HR	HB	BB	SO	RAT	ERA	ERA+	CERA	OAV	BH	AVG	PR+	WS	TPW
1979 Phi-N	3	4	.429	14	14	0	0	0	90	80	40	38	6	2	38	42	1.311	3.80	101	3.43	.246	3	.100	-1	5	-0.2
1980* Phi-N	1	4	.200	48	3	0	0	6	81	80	42	35	5	1	42	57	1.506	3.89	97	3.89	.254	4	.308	-1	4	0.0
1981* Phi-N	2	2	.500	13	8	0	0	0	58^1	57	30	27	2	3	23	34	1.371	4.17	87	3.66	.260	2	.105	-4	2	-0.5
1982 Chi-N	10	13	.435	31	30	2	2	0	171	180	99	84	11	5	61	85	1.409	4.42	84	4.03	.274	6	.107	-11	5	-1.4
1983 Chi-N	5	10	.333	24	18	1	1	0	116^1	133	69	61	9	1	37	59	1.461	4.72	80	4.41	.287	9	.237	-10	3	-0.9
1984 Chi-N	2	2	.500	21	1	0	0	0	50^2	60	29	29	4	1	16	14	1.500	5.15	76	4.87	.305	0	.000	-6	1	-0.8
Tex-A	2	3	.400	18	6	0	0	0	57^2	60	38	33	6	5	30	39	1.561	5.15	81	5.13	.262	0	....	-6	1	-0.6
1985 Tex-A	4	8	.333	28	13	0	0	1	110^1	129	67	62	11	6	33	59	1.468	5.06	84	4.84	.289	0	....	-8	4	-0.8
1986 Cle-A	3	2	.600	32	0	0	0	0	54^2	56	33	31	9	5	30	32	1.573	5.10	81	5.52	.269	0	....	-5	2	-0.5
1987 Chi-N	4	2	.667	41	1	0	0	2	64^1	59	31	25	1	5	27	33	1.337	3.50	122	3.27	.239	0	.000	7	6	0.6
Det-A	0	0	....	4	0	0	0	2	2	2	1	1	0	0	1	0	1.500	4.50	94	3.63	.250	0	....	-0	0	0.0
1988 Bal-A	0	2	.000	2	2	0	0	0	3^1	11	10	9	2	1	0	1	3.300	24.30	16	24.42	.500	0	....	-8	0	-0.8
1990 Phi-N	0	1	.000	1	0	0	0	0	0^1	2	1	1	0	0	0	0	6.000	27.00	14	39.65	.667	0	....	-1	0	-0.1
Total 11	36	53	.404	277	96	3	3	11	860	909	490	436	66	35	338	455	1.450	4.56	86	4.34	.272	24	.136	-55	33	-6.0

• NOLTE, Eric Eric Carl Nolte b: 4/28/1964, Canoga Park, CA BL/TL, 6'3", 205 lbs. Deb: 8/1/1987

YEAR TM-L	W	L	PCT	G	GS	CG	SH	SV	IP	H	R	ER	HR	HB	BB	SO	RAT	ERA	ERA+	CERA	OAV	BH	AVG	PR+	WS	TPW
1987 SD-N	2	6	.250	12	12	1	0	0	67^1	57	28	24	6	2	36	44	1.381	3.21	123	3.71	.226	2	.095	5	4	0.4
1988 SD-N	0	0	....	2	0	0	0	0	3	3	2	2	1	0	2	1	1.667	6.00	57	6.85	.273	0	....	-1	0	-0.1
1989 SD-N	0	0	....	3	1	0	0	0	9	15	12	11	1	0	7	8	2.444	11.00	32	9.57	.375	0	.000	-8	0	-0.8
1991 SD-N	3	2	.600	6	6	0	0	0	22	37	27	27	6	0	10	15	2.136	11.05	34	10.11	.378	1	.111	-18	0	-1.9
Tex-A	0	0	....	3	0	0	0	0	2^2	3	1	1	0	0	3	1	2.250	3.38	119	6.72	.273	0	....	0	0	0.0
Total 4	5	8	.385	26	19	1	0	0	104	115	70	65	14	2	58	69	1.663	5.63	67	5.74	.279	3	.094	-21	4	-2.4

• NOMO, Hideo Hideo "The Tornado" Nomo b: 8/31/1968, Osaka, Japan BR/TR, 6'2", 210 lbs. Deb: 5/2/1995

YEAR TM-L	W	L	PCT	G	GS	CG	SH	SV	IP	H	R	ER	HR	HB	BB	SO	RAT	ERA	ERA+	CERA	OAV	BH	AVG	PR+	WS	TPW
1995* LA-N★	13	6	.684	28	28	4	**3**	0	191^1	124	63	54	14	5	78	**236**	1.056	2.54	149	2.16	**.182**	6	.091	26	17	2.2
1996* LA-N	16	11	.593	33	33	3	2	0	228^1	180	93	81	23	2	85	234	1.161	3.19	121	2.86	.218	10	.133	19	16	1.8
1997 LA-N	14	12	.538	33	33	1	0	0	207^1	193	104	98	23	9	92	233	1.375	4.25	91	4.06	.243	11	.159	-7	9	-0.5
1998 LA-N	2	7	.222	12	12	2	0	0	67^2	57	39	38	8	3	38	73	1.404	5.05	79	4.13	.228	1	.050	-8	1	-0.9
NY-N	4	5	.444	17	16	1	0	0	89^2	73	49	48	11	1	56	94	1.439	4.82	86	4.07	.224	8	.267	-7	3	-0.5
Yr.	6	12	.333	29	28	3	0	0	157^1	130	88	86	19	4	94	167	1.424	4.92	83	4.10	.226	9	.180	-15	4	-1.4
1999 Mil-N	12	8	.600	28	28	0	0	0	176^1	173	96	89	27	3	78	161	1.423	4.54	100	4.57	.256	12	.214	2	10	0.4
2000 Det-A	8	12	.400	32	31	1	0	0	190	191	102	100	31	3	89	181	1.474	4.74	102	4.95	.263	0	.000	3	10	0.2
2001 Bos-A	13	10	.565	33	33	2	2	0	198	171	105	99	26	3	96	**220**	1.348	4.50	100	3.90	.231	1	.200	3	11	0.3
2002 LA-N	16	6	.727	34	34	0	0	0	220^1	189	92	83	26	2	101	193	1.316	3.39	113	3.68	.236	4	.063	9	13	0.8
2003 LA-N	16	13	.552	33	33	2	2	0	218^1	175	82	75	24	1	98	177	1.250	3.09	130	3.30	.223	9	.138	19	17	1.9
Total 9	114	90	.559	283	281	16	9	0	1787^1	1526	825	765	213	32	811	1802	1.308	3.85	108	3.69	.231	62	.136	59	107	5.6

• NOMURA, Takahito Takahito Nomura b: 1/10/1969, Kouchi, Japan BL/TL, 5'7", 175 lbs. Deb: 4/3/2002

YEAR TM-L	W	L	PCT	G	GS	CG	SH	SV	IP	H	R	ER	HR	HB	BB	SO	RAT	ERA	ERA+	CERA	OAV	BH	AVG	PR+	WS	TPW
2002 Mil-N	0	0	....	21	0	0	0	0	13^2	11	14	13	2	2	18	9	2.122	8.56	48	6.95	.224	0	....	-7	0	-0.7

• NOPS, Jerry Jeremiah H. Nops b: 6/23/1875, Toledo, OH d: 3/26/1937, Camden, NJ BL/TL, 5'8.5", 168 lbs. Deb: 9/7/1896

YEAR TM-L	W	L	PCT	G	GS	CG	SH	SV	IP	H	R	ER	HR	HB	BB	SO	RAT	ERA	ERA+	CERA	OAV	BH	AVG	PR+	WS	TPW
1896 Phi-N	1	0	1.000	1	1	1	0	0	7	11	5	4	0	0	1	1	1.714	5.14	84	5.23	.354	0	.000	-1	0	-0.1
Bal-N	2	1	.667	3	3	3	0	0	22	29	15	15	0	0	2	8	1.409	6.14	70	3.75	.315	1	.111	-5	1	-0.5
Yr.	3	1	.750	4	4	4	0	0	29	40	20	19	0	0	3	9	1.483	5.90	73	4.11	.325	1	.077	-6	1	-0.6
1897* Bal-N	20	6	.769	30	25	23	1	0	220^2	235	107	69	5	9	52	69	1.301	2.81	148	3.36	.271	18	.196	30	18	2.3
1898 Bal-N	16	9	.640	33	29	23	2	0	235	241	130	93	5	16	78	91	1.357	3.56	100	3.57	.264	20	.220	-6	14	-0.4
1899 Bal-N	17	11	.607	33	33	26	2	0	259	296	156	116	1	11	71	60	1.417	4.03	98	3.78	.287	29	.276	-3	17	-0.1
1900 Bro-N	4	4	.500	9	8	6	1	0	68	79	45	29	1	2	18	22	1.426	3.84	100	3.88	.290	4	.160	-1	4	-0.1
1901 Bal-A	12	10	.545	27	23	17	1	1	176^2	192	123	80	5	13	59	43	1.421	4.08	95	3.97	.274	13	.220	2	10	0.2
Total 6	72	41	.637	136	122	99	7	1	988^1	1083	581	406	17	51	281	294	1.380	3.70	105	3.69	.277	85	.221	16	64	1.2

• NORIEGA, John John Alan Noriega b: 12/20/1943, Ogden, UT BR/TR, 6'4", 185 lbs. Deb: 5/1/1969

YEAR TM-L	W	L	PCT	G	GS	CG	SH	SV	IP	H	R	ER	HR	HB	BB	SO	RAT	ERA	ERA+	CERA	OAV	BH	AVG	PR+	WS	TPW
1969 Cin-N	0	0	....	5	0	0	0	0	7^2	12	6	5	1	0	3	4	1.957	5.87	64	8.01	.400	0	....	-2	0	-0.2
1970 Cin-N	0	0	....	8	0	0	0	0	18	25	17	16	0	2	10	6	1.944	8.00	52	6.45	.333	1	.250	-8	0	-0.8
Total 2	0	0	....	13	0	0	0	0	25^2	37	23	21	1	2	13	10	1.948	7.36	55	6.91	.352	1	.250	-10	0	-0.9

• NORMAN, Fred Fredie Hubert Norman b: 8/20/1942, San Antonio, TX BB/TL, 5'8", 160 lbs. Deb: 9/21/1962

YEAR TM-L	W	L	PCT	G	GS	CG	SH	SV	IP	H	R	ER	HR	HB	BB	SO	RAT	ERA	ERA+	CERA	OAV	BH	AVG	PR+	WS	TPW
1962 KC-A	0	0	....	2	0	0	0	0	4	4	1	1	0	0	1	2	1.250	2.25	185	2.77	.250	0	....	1	1	0.1
1963 KC-A	0	1	.000	2	2	0	0	0	6^1	9	9	8	1	0	7	6	2.526	11.37	34	10.10	.346	0	.000	-5	0	-0.6
1964 Chi-N	0	4	.000	8	5	0	0	0	31^2	34	25	23	9	1	21	20	1.737	6.54	57	7.12	.279	1	.091	-10	0	-1.1
1966 Chi-N	0	0	....	2	0	0	0	0	4	5	2	2	0	0	2	6	1.750	4.50	82	4.82	.313	0	....	-0	0	0.0
1967 Chi-N	0	0	....	1	0	0	0	0	1	0	0	0	0	0	0	3	.000	0.00	....	0.00	.000	0	....	0	0	0.0
1970 LA-N	2	0	1.000	30	0	0	0	1	62	65	40	36	8	2	33	47	1.581	5.23	73	5.16	.273	1	.143	-11	1	-1.0
StL-N	0	0	....	1	0	0	0	0	1	1	0	0	0	0	0	0	1.000	0.00	....	1.95	.333	0	....	0	0	0.0
Yr.	2	0	1.000	31	0	0	0	1	63	66	40	36	8	2	33	47	1.571	5.14	75	5.11	.274	1	.143	-10	1	-1.0
1971 StL-N	0	0	....	4	0	0	0	0	3^2	7	5	5	1	0	7	4	3.818	12.27	29	19.75	.438	0	....	-3	0	-0.4
SD-N	3	12	.200	20	18	5	0	0	127^1	114	48	47	7	2	56	77	1.335	3.32	99	3.31	.240	9	.237	1	7	0.3
Yr.	3	12	.200	24	18	5	0	0	131	121	53	52	8	2	63	81	1.405	3.57	93	3.77	.246	9	.237	-3	7	0.0
1972 SD-N	9	11	.450	42	28	10	6	2	211^2	195	88	81	18	2	88	167	1.337	3.44	95	3.53	.244	8	.125	-0	11	0.1
1973 SD-N	1	7	.125	12	11	1	0	0	74	72	35	35	9	1	29	49	1.365	4.26	81	4.12	.262	3	.136	-6	2	-0.7
*Cin-N	12	6	.667	24	24	7	3	0	166^1	136	67	61	18	1	72	112	1.251	3.30	103	3.21	.224	3	.052	-2	10	-0.6
Yr.	13	13	.500	36	35	8	3	0	240^1	208	102	96	27	2	101	161	1.286	3.60	95	3.49	.236	6	.075	-8	12	-1.3
1974 Cin-N	13	12	.520	35	26	8	2	0	186^1	170	69	65	15	2	68	141	1.277	3.14	111	3.26	.241	8	.131	4	12	0.1
1975* Cin-N	12	4	.750	34	26	2	0	0	188	163	85	78	23	0	84	119	1.314	3.73	96	3.64	.235	7	.117	-9	9	-1.1
1976* Cin-N	12	7	.632	33	24	8	3	0	180^1	153	71	62	10	3	70	126	1.237	3.09	113	2.97	.231	7	.140	7	11	0.6
1977 Cin-N	14	13	.519	35	34	8	1	0	221^1	200	97	83	28	3	98	160	1.346	3.38	116	3.89	.241	8	.110	12	13	1.0
1978 Cin-N	11	9	.550	36	31	0	0	1	177^1	173	86	73	19	3	82	111	1.438	3.70	96	4.22	.255	7	.140	-0	9	-0.1
1979* Cin-N	11	13	.458	34	31	5	0	0	195^1	193	86	79	14	0	57	95	1.280	3.64	102	3.38	.258	9	.153	2	11	0.2
1980 Mon-N	4	4	.500	48	8	2	0	4	98	96	50	45	8	3	40	58	1.388	4.13	86	3.89	.259	1	.050	-6	4	-0.8
Total 16	104	103	.502	403	268	56	15	8	1939^2	1790	864	784	188	23	815	1303	1.343	3.64	98	3.71	.246	72	.125	-25	101	-3.8

• NORRIS, Mike Michael Kelvin Norris b: 3/19/1955, San Francisco, CA BR/TR, 6'2", 175 lbs. Deb: 4/10/1975

YEAR	TM-L	W	L	PCT	G	GS	CG	SH	SV	IP	H	R	ER	HR	HB	BB	SO	RAT	ERA	ERA+	CERA	OAV	BH	AVG	PR+	WS	TPW
1975	Oak-A	1	0	1.000	4	3	1	1	0	16^2	6	2	0	0	0	8	5	.840	0.00	....	0.98	.107	0	....	7	2	0.7
1976	Oak-A	4	5	.444	24	19	1	1	0	96	91	53	51	10	2	56	44	1.531	4.78	70	4.55	.250	0	....	-14	1	-1.4
1977	Oak-A	2	7	.222	16	12	1	1	0	77^1	77	45	41	14	4	31	35	1.397	4.77	84	4.86	.260	0	.000	-5	2	-0.5
1978	Oak-A	0	5	.000	14	5	1	0	0	49	46	35	30	2	3	35	36	1.653	5.51	66	4.60	.247	0	....	-9	0	-1.0
1979	Oak-A	5	8	.385	29	18	3	0	0	146^1	146	87	78	11	9	94	96	1.640	4.80	84	4.99	.265	0	....	-8	5	-0.8
1980	Oak-A	22	9	.710	33	33	24	1	0	284^1	215	88	80	18	6	83	180	1.048	2.53	149	**2.26**	**.209**	0	....	**36**	**25**	**3.6**
1981*	Oak-A★	12	9	.571	23	23	12	2	0	172^2	145	77	72	17	10	63	78	1.205	3.75	93	3.29	.228	0	....	-7	9	-0.8
1982	Oak-A	7	11	.389	28	28	7	1	0	166^1	154	103	88	25	6	84	83	1.431	4.76	82	4.52	.242	0	....	-16	4	-1.6
1983	Oak-A	4	5	.444	16	16	2	0	0	88^2	68	42	37	11	3	36	63	1.173	3.76	103	3.15	.213	0	....	0	4	0.0
1990	Oak-A	1	0	1.000	14	0	0	0	0	27	24	10	9	0	2	9	16	1.222	3.00	124	2.84	.242	0	....	2	2	0.2
Total	**10**	**58**	**59**	**.496**	**201**	**157**	**52**	**7**	**0**	**1124^1**	**972**	**542**	**486**	**108**	**45**	**499**	**636**	**1.308**	**3.89**	**97**	**3.65**	**.233**	**0**	**.000**	**-15**	**54**	**-1.6**

• NORTH, Lou Louis Alexander North b: 6/15/1891, Elgin, IL d: 5/15/1974, Shelton, CT BR/TR, 5'11", 175 lbs. Deb: 8/22/1913

YEAR	TM-L	W	L	PCT	G	GS	CG	SH	SV	IP	H	R	ER	HR	HB	BB	SO	RAT	ERA	ERA+	CERA	OAV	BH	AVG	PR+	WS	TPW
1913	Det-A	0	1	.000	1	1	0	0	0	6	10	11	10	1	0	9	3	3.167	15.00	19	13.22	.357	0	.000	-8	0	-0.9
1917	StL-N	0	0	....	5	0	0	0	0	11^1	14	5	5	1	0	4	4	1.588	3.97	68	5.65	.350	0	.000	-2	0	-0.2
1920	StL-N	3	2	.600	24	6	3	0	1	88	90	42	32	3	2	32	37	1.386	3.27	94	3.70	.278	7	.226	-2	4	-0.2
1921	StL-N	4	4	.500	40	0	0	0	**7**	86^1	81	39	34	5	1	32	28	1.309	3.54	103	3.37	.256	3	.158	1	6	0.0
1922	StL-N	10	3	.769	**53**	11	4	0	4	149^2	164	90	74	4	6	64	84	1.523	4.45	87	4.24	.283	11	.234	-6	10	-0.4
1923	StL-N	3	4	.429	34	3	0	0	1	71^2	90	50	41	8	3	31	24	1.688	5.15	76	5.85	.308	4	.182	-9	1	-1.0
1924	StL-N	0	0	....	6	0	0	0	0	14^2	15	12	11	1	0	9	8	1.636	6.75	56	4.84	.273	1	.250	-5	0	-0.5
	Bos-N	1	2	.333	9	4	1	0	0	35^1	45	25	21	1	0	19	11	1.811	5.35	71	5.61	.321	1	.111	-6	0	-0.6
	Yr.	1	2	.333	15	4	1	0	0	50	60	37	32	2	0	28	19	1.760	5.76	66	5.39	.307	2	.154	-11	0	-1.1
Total	**7**	**21**	**16**	**.568**	**172**	**25**	**8**	**0**	**13**	**463**	**509**	**274**	**228**	**24**	**12**	**200**	**199**	**1.531**	**4.43**	**81**	**4.50**	**.287**	**27**	**.197**	**-37**	**21**	**-3.8**

• NORTHROP, Jake George Howard "Jerky" Northrop b: 3/5/1888, Monroeton, PA d: 11/16/1945, Monroeton, PA BL/TR, 5'11", 170 lbs. Deb: 7/29/1918

YEAR	TM-L	W	L	PCT	G	GS	CG	SH	SV	IP	H	R	ER	HR	HB	BB	SO	RAT	ERA	ERA+	CERA	OAV	BH	AVG	PR+	WS	TPW
1918	Bos-N	5	1	.833	7	4	4	1	0	40	26	9	6	0	0	3	4	.725	1.35	199	0.99	.183	2	.154	7	4	0.7
1919	Bos-N	1	5	.167	11	3	2	0	0	37^1	43	22	19	2	1	10	9	1.420	4.58	62	4.29	.301	4	.500	-7	1	-0.5
Total	**2**	**6**	**6**	**.500**	**18**	**7**	**6**	**1**	**0**	**77^1**	**69**	**31**	**25**	**2**	**1**	**13**	**13**	**1.060**	**2.91**	**97**	**2.59**	**.242**	**6**	**.286**	**-0**	**5**	**0.2**

• NORTON, Effie Elisha Strong "Leiter" Norton b: 8/17/1873, Conneaut, OH d: 3/5/1950, Aspinwall, PA BR/TR, 5'10.5" Deb: 8/8/1896

YEAR	TM-L	W	L	PCT	G	GS	CG	SH	SV	IP	H	R	ER	HR	HB	BB	SO	RAT	ERA	ERA+	CERA	OAV	BH	AVG	PR+	WS	TPW
1896	Was-N	3	1	.750	8	5	2	0	0	44	49	25	15	2	6	14	13	1.432	3.07	143	4.42	.280	4	.211	7	3	0.6
1897	Was-N	2	1	.667	4	2	1	0	0	17	31	18	13	0	0	11	3	2.471	6.88	63	9.21	.389	5	.278	-5	1	-0.4
Total	**2**	**5**	**2**	**.714**	**12**	**7**	**3**	**0**	**0**	**61**	**80**	**43**	**28**	**2**	**6**	**25**	**16**	**1.721**	**4.13**	**106**	**5.75**	**.314**	**9**	**.243**	**2**	**4**	**0.2**

• NORTON, Phil Phillip Douglas Norton b: 2/1/1976, Texarkana, TX BR/TL, 6'1", 190 lbs. Deb: 8/3/2000

YEAR	TM-L	W	L	PCT	G	GS	CG	SH	SV	IP	H	R	ER	HR	HB	BB	SO	RAT	ERA	ERA+	CERA	OAV	BH	AVG	PR+	WS	TPW
2000	Chi-N	0	1	.000	2	2	0	0	0	8^2	14	10	9	5	0	7	6	2.423	9.35	49	14.18	.350	2	.667	-5	0	-0.4
2003	Chi-N	0	0	....	4	0	0	0	0	3^1	2	2	2	0	0	3	0	1.500	5.40	78	3.21	.182	0	....	-0	0	0.0
	Cin-N	0	0	....	17	0	0	0	0	14^2	7	4	4	0	0	6	7	.886	2.45	174	1.24	.149	0	.000	3	2	0.3
	Yr.	0	0	....	21	0	0	0	0	18	9	6	6	0	0	9	7	1.000	3.00	141	1.60	.155	0	.000	3	2	0.2
Total	**2**	**0**	**1**	**.000**	**23**	**2**	**0**	**0**	**0**	**26^2**	**23**	**16**	**15**	**5**	**0**	**16**	**13**	**1.463**	**5.06**	**87**	**5.69**	**.235**	**2**	**.500**	**-2**	**2**	**-0.1**

• NORTON, Tom Thomas John Norton b: 4/26/1950, Elyria, OH BR/TR, 6'1", 200 lbs. Deb: 4/18/1972

YEAR	TM-L	W	L	PCT	G	GS	CG	SH	SV	IP	H	R	ER	HR	HB	BB	SO	RAT	ERA	ERA+	CERA	OAV	BH	AVG	PR+	WS	TPW
1972	Min-A	0	1	.000	21	0	0	0	0	32^1	31	14	10	1	1	14	22	1.392	2.78	115	3.63	.252	0	....	1	1	0.1

• NOSEK, Randy Randall William Nosek b: 1/8/1967, Omaha, NE BR/TR, 6'4", 215 lbs. Deb: 5/27/1989

YEAR	TM-L	W	L	PCT	G	GS	CG	SH	SV	IP	H	R	ER	HR	HB	BB	SO	RAT	ERA	ERA+	CERA	OAV	BH	AVG	PR+	WS	TPW
1989	Det-A	0	2	.000	2	2	0	0	0	5^1	7	8	8	2	0	10	4	3.188	13.50	28	16.38	.333	0	....	-6	0	-0.6
1990	Det-A	1	1	.500	3	2	0	0	0	7	7	7	6	1	0	9	3	2.286	7.71	51	8.10	.280	0	....	-3	0	-0.3
Total	**2**	**1**	**3**	**.250**	**5**	**4**	**0**	**0**	**0**	**12^1**	**14**	**15**	**14**	**3**	**0**	**19**	**7**	**2.676**	**10.22**	**38**	**11.68**	**.304**	**0**	**....**	**-9**	**0**	**-0.9**

• NOTTEBART, Don Donald Edward Nottebart b: 1/23/1936, West Newton, MA BR/TR, 6'1", 190 lbs. Deb: 7/1/1960

YEAR	TM-L	W	L	PCT	G	GS	CG	SH	SV	IP	H	R	ER	HR	HB	BB	SO	RAT	ERA	ERA+	CERA	OAV	BH	AVG	PR+	WS	TPW
1960	Mil-N	1	0	1.000	5	1	0	0	1	15^1	14	10	7	0	0	15	8	1.891	4.11	83	4.51	.233	0	.000	-1	0	-0.2
1961	Mil-N	6	7	.462	38	11	2	0	3	126^1	117	61	57	11	2	48	66	1.306	4.06	92	3.56	.251	7	.184	-4	6	-0.4
1962	Mil-N	2	2	.500	39	0	0	0	2	64	64	30	23	4	4	20	36	1.313	3.23	117	3.58	.258	2	.333	4	5	0.5
1963	Hou-N	11	8	.579	31	27	9	2	0	193	170	80	68	10	1	39	118	1.083	3.17	100	2.39	.234	11	.167	4	12	0.4
1964	Hou-N	6	11	.353	28	24	2	0	0	157	165	76	68	12	1	37	90	1.287	3.90	88	3.58	.275	3	.064	-6	5	-0.9
1965	Hou-N	4	15	.211	29	25	3	0	0	158	166	99	82	14	5	55	77	1.399	4.67	72	4.09	.273	5	.104	-20	0	-2.2
1966	Cin-N	5	4	.556	59	1	0	0	11	111^1	97	45	38	11	2	43	69	1.257	3.07	127	3.31	.235	4	.167	12	11	1.2
1967	Cin-N	0	3	.000	47	0	0	0	4	79^1	75	25	17	4	2	19	48	1.185	1.93	194	2.92	.253	0	.000	17	8	1.8
1969	NY-A	0	0	....	4	0	0	0	0	6	6	3	3	1	1	0	5	1.000	4.50	77	3.69	.261	0	....	-1	0	-0.1
	Chi-N	1	1	.500	16	0	0	0	0	18	28	14	14	2	0	7	8	1.944	7.00	58	7.32	.350	0	.000	-6	0	-0.6
Total	**9**	**36**	**51**	**.414**	**296**	**89**	**16**	**2**	**21**	**928^1**	**902**	**443**	**377**	**69**	**18**	**283**	**525**	**1.276**	**3.65**	**96**	**3.42**	**.256**	**32**	**.134**	**-3**	**47**	**-0.5**

• NOURSE, Chet Chester Linwood Nourse b: 8/7/1887, Ipswich, MA d: 4/20/1958, Clearwater, FL BR/TR, 6'3", 185 lbs. Deb: 7/27/1909

YEAR	TM-L	W	L	PCT	G	GS	CG	SH	SV	IP	H	R	ER	HR	HB	BB	SO	RAT	ERA	ERA+	CERA	OAV	BH	AVG	PR+	WS	TPW
1909	Bos-A	0	0	....	3	0	0	0	0	5	5	5	4	0	0	5	3	2.000	7.20	35	5.41	.263	0	.000	-3	0	-0.3

• NOVOA, Rafael Rafael Angel Novoa b: 10/26/1967, New York, NY BL/TL, 6', 180 lbs. Deb: 7/31/1990

YEAR	TM-L	W	L	PCT	G	GS	CG	SH	SV	IP	H	R	ER	HR	HB	BB	SO	RAT	ERA	ERA+	CERA	OAV	BH	AVG	PR+	WS	TPW
1990	SF-N	0	1	.000	7	2	0	0	1	18^2	21	14	14	3	0	13	14	1.821	6.75	54	6.43	.284	1	.200	-7	0	-0.6
1993	Mil-A	0	3	.000	15	7	2	0	0	56	58	32	28	7	4	22	17	1.429	4.50	94	4.61	.267	0	....	-1	2	-0.1
Total	**2**	**0**	**4**	**.000**	**22**	**9**	**2**	**0**	**1**	**74^2**	**79**	**46**	**42**	**10**	**4**	**35**	**31**	**1.527**	**5.06**	**80**	**5.06**	**.271**	**1**	**.200**	**-8**	**2**	**-0.7**

• NOYES, Win Winfield Charles Noyes b: 6/16/1889, Pleasanton, NE d: 4/8/1969, Cashmere, WA BR/TR, 6', 180 lbs. Deb: 5/19/1913

YEAR	TM-L	W	L	PCT	G	GS	CG	SH	SV	IP	H	R	ER	HR	HB	BB	SO	RAT	ERA	ERA+	CERA	OAV	BH	AVG	PR+	WS	TPW
1913	Bos-N	0	0	....	11	0	0	0	0	20^2	22	18	11	1	4	6	5	1.355	4.79	68	4.53	.289	1	.250	-3	0	-0.3
1917	Phi-A	10	10	.500	27	22	11	1	1	171	156	74	56	5	4	77	64	1.363	2.95	93	3.40	.258	6	.115	-1	6	-0.3
1919	Phi-A	1	5	.167	10	6	3	0	0	49	66	34	31	1	1	15	20	1.653	5.69	60	5.31	.332	2	.125	-10	0	-1.2
	Chi-A	0	0	....	1	1	0	0	0	6	10	5	5	0	0	0	4	1.667	7.50	42	5.88	.385	1	.500	-3	0	-0.3
	Yr.	1	5	.167	11	7	3	0	0	55	76	39	36	1	1	15	24	1.655	5.89	57	5.37	.338	3	.167	-13	0	-1.5
Total	**3**	**11**	**15**	**.423**	**49**	**29**	**14**	**1**	**1**	**246^2**	**254**	**131**	**103**	**7**	**9**	**98**	**93**	**1.427**	**3.76**	**80**	**3.94**	**.280**	**10**	**.135**	**-18**	**6**	**-2.1**

• NUNEZ, Edwin Edwin (Martinez) Nunez b: 5/27/1963, Humacao, Puerto Rico BR/TR, 6'5", 237 lbs. Deb: 4/7/1982

YEAR	TM-L	W	L	PCT	G	GS	CG	SH	SV	IP	H	R	ER	HR	HB	BB	SO	RAT	ERA	ERA+	CERA	OAV	BH	AVG	PR+	WS	TPW
1982	Sea-A	1	2	.333	8	5	0	0	0	35^1	36	18	18	7	0	16	27	1.472	4.58	92	5.18	.269	0	....	-1	2	-0.1
1983	Sea-A	0	4	.000	14	5	0	0	0	37	40	21	18	3	3	22	35	1.676	4.38	97	5.53	.278	0	....	-0	1	0.0
1984	Sea-A	2	2	.500	37	0	0	0	7	67^2	55	26	24	8	3	21	57	1.123	3.19	125	2.94	.218	0	....	7	8	0.8
1985	Sea-A	7	3	.700	70	0	0	0	16	90^1	79	36	31	13	0	34	58	1.251	3.09	136	3.50	.234	0	....	12	12	1.2
1986	Sea-A	1	2	.333	14	1	0	0	0	21^2	25	15	14	5	0	5	17	1.385	5.82	73	5.12	.284	0	....	-4	0	-0.4
1987	Sea-A	3	4	.429	48	0	0	0	12	47^1	45	20	20	7	1	18	34	1.331	3.80	124	4.13	.262	0	....	5	7	0.4
1988	Sea-A	1	4	.200	14	3	0	0	0	29^1	45	33	26	4	2	14	19	2.011	7.98	52	8.13	.366	0	....	-12	0	-1.2
	NY-N	1	0	1.000	10	0	0	0	0	14	21	7	7	1	0	3	8	1.714	4.50	72	5.99	.339	0	....	-2	0	-0.2
1989	Det-A	3	4	.429	27	0	0	0	1	54	49	33	25	6	0	36	41	1.574	4.17	92	4.34	.254	0	....	-2	2	-0.2
1990	Det-A	3	1	.750	42	0	0	0	6	80^1	65	26	20	4	2	37	66	1.270	2.24	177	2.87	.218	0	....	14	8	1.4
1991	Mil-A	2	1	.667	23	0	0	0	8	25^1	28	20	17	6	0	13	24	1.618	6.04	66	5.82	.277	0	....	-6	0	-0.6
1992	Mil-A	1	1	.500	10	0	0	0	0	13^2	12	5	4	1	0	6	10	1.317	2.63	146	3.37	.231	0	....	2	1	0.2
	Tex-A	0	2	.000	39	0	0	0	3	45^2	51	29	28	5	2	16	39	1.467	5.52	69	4.70	.279	0	....	-8	1	-0.8
	Yr.	1	3	.250	49	0	0	0	3	59^1	63	34	32	6	2	22	49	1.433	4.85	78	4.39	.268	0	....	-6	2	-0.7
1993	Oak-A	3	6	.333	56	0	0	0	1	75^2	89	36	32	2	6	29	58	1.559	3.81	107	4.75	.298	0	....	3	4	0.3
1994	Oak-A	0	0	....	15	0	0	0	0	15	26	20	20	2	0	10	15	2.400	12.00	37	10.11	.382	0	....	-13	0	-1.2
Total	**13**	**28**	**36**	**.438**	**427**	**14**	**0**	**0**	**54**	**652^1**	**666**	**345**	**304**	**74**	**19**	**280**	**508**	**1.450**	**4.19**	**97**	**4.47**	**.266**	**0**	**....**	**-7**	**46**	**-0.6**

• NUNEZ, Jose Jose (Jimenez) Nunez b: 1/13/1964, Jarabacoa, Dominican Republic BR/TR, 6'3", 175 lbs. Deb: 4/9/1987

YEAR	TM-L	W	L	PCT	G	GS	CG	SH	SV	IP	H	R	ER	HR	HB	BB	SO	RAT	ERA	ERA+	CERA	OAV	BH	AVG	PR+	WS	TPW
1987	Tor-A	5	2	.714	37	9	0	0	0	97	91	57	54	12	0	58	99	1.536	5.01	90	4.59	.256	0	....	-7	4	-0.7

YEAR	TM-L	W	L	PCT	G	GS	CG	SH	SV	IP	H	R	ER	HR	HB	BB	SO	RAT	ERA	ERA+	CERA	OAV	BH	AVG	PR+	WS	TPW
1988	Tor-A	0	1	.000	13	2	0	0	0	29^1	28	11	10	3	1	17	18	1.534	3.07	128	4.66	.259	0	....	3	2	0.3
1989	Tor-A	0	0	....	6	1	0	0	0	10^2	8	3	3	0	0	2	14	.938	2.53	143	1.52	.200	0	....	1	1	0.1
1990	Chi-N	4	7	.364	21	10	0	0	0	60^2	61	47	44	5	0	34	40	1.566	6.53	62	4.44	.270	0	.000	-15	0	-1.6
Total 4		9	10	.474	77	22	0	0	0	197^2	188	118	111	20	1	111	171	1.513	5.05	84	4.39	.258	0	.000	-18	7	-1.9
• NUNEZ, Jose Antonio	Jose Antonio Nunez b: 3/14/1979, Monte Cristi, Dominican Republic BL/TL, 6'2", 165 lbs. Deb: 4/3/2001																										
2001	LA-N	0	1	.000	6	0	0	0	0	7^1	14	15	11	4	0	5	11	2.591	13.50	30	15.10	.389	0	....	-8	0	-0.7
	SD-N	4	1	.800	56	0	0	0	0	51^2	48	20	19	3	4	20	49	1.316	3.31	121	3.53	.245	0	.000	5	4	0.4
	Yr.	4	2	.667	62	0	0	0	0	59	62	35	30	7	4	25	60	1.475	4.58	87	4.97	.267	0	.000	-3	4	-0.3
2002	SD-N	0	0	....	1	0	0	0	0	1	0	0	0	0	0	1	0	1.000	0.00	....	0.95	.000	0	....	0	0	0.0
Total 2		4	2	.667	63	0	0	0	0	60	62	35	30	7	4	26	60	1.467	4.50	89	4.90	.267	0	.000	-2	4	-0.3
• NUNEZ, Vladimir	Vladimir (Zarabaza) Nunez b: 3/15/1975, Havana, Cuba BR/TR, 6'5", 224 lbs. Deb: 9/11/1998																										
1998	Ari-N	0	0	....	4	0	0	0	0	5^1	7	6	6	0	0	2	2	1.688	10.13	42	4.87	.318	0	....	-4	0	-0.3
1999	Ari-N	3	2	.600	27	0	0	0	1	34	29	15	11	2	1	20	28	1.441	2.91	157	3.63	.242	0	.000	6	3	0.5
	Fla-N	4	8	.333	17	12	0	0	0	74^2	66	48	38	9	3	34	58	1.339	4.58	95	3.98	.243	4	.160	-2	2	-0.2
	Yr.	7	10	.412	44	12	0	0	1	108^2	95	63	49	11	4	54	86	1.371	4.06	108	3.87	.242	4	.143	4	5	0.3
2000	Fla-N	0	6	.000	17	12	0	0	0	68^1	88	63	60	12	2	34	45	1.785	7.90	56	6.88	.319	2	.118	-26	0	-2.4
2001	Fla-N	4	5	.444	52	3	0	0	0	92	79	33	28	9	5	30	64	1.185	2.74	154	3.17	.234	1	.111	15	8	1.4
2002	Fla-N	6	5	.545	77	0	0	0	20	97^2	80	38	37	8	0	37	73	1.198	3.41	115	2.88	.224	1	.200	5	14	0.5
2003	Fla-N	0	3	.000	14	0	0	0	0	10^2	21	21	19	7	0	7	10	2.625	16.03	26	16.12	.396	0	....	-14	0	-1.4
Total 6		17	29	.370	208	27	0	0	21	382^2	370	224	199	47	11	164	280	1.395	4.68	91	4.34	.257	8	.136	-19	27	-1.9
• NUNN, Howie	Howard Ralph Nunn b: 10/18/1935, Westfield, NC BR/TR, 6', 173 lbs. Deb: 4/11/1959																										
1959	StL-N	2	2	.500	16	0	0	0	0	21^1	23	18	18	3	0	15	20	1.781	7.59	56	5.82	.291	0	.000	-8	0	-0.8
1961	Cin-N	2	1	.667	24	0	0	0	0	37^2	35	17	15	0	1	24	26	1.566	3.58	113	3.73	.252	2	.250	2	3	0.2
1962	Cin-N	0	0	....	6	0	0	0	0	9^2	15	6	6	0	0	3	4	1.862	5.59	72	6.10	.375	0	.000	-2	0	-0.2
Total 3		4	3	.571	46	0	0	0	0	68^2	73	41	39	3	1	42	50	1.675	5.11	81	4.71	.283	2	.200	-7	3	-0.8
• NUXHALL, Joe	Joseph Henry Nuxhall b: 7/30/1928, Hamilton, OH BL/TL, 6'3", 219 lbs. Deb: 6/10/1944																										
1944	Cin-N	0	0	....	1	0	0	0	0	0^2	2	5	5	0	0	5	0	10.50	67.50	5	47.83	.500	0	....	-5	0	-0.5
1952	Cin-N	1	4	.200	37	5	2	0	1	92^1	83	33	33	4	3	42	52	1.354	3.22	117	3.42	.246	2	.087	5	6	0.4
1953	Cin-N	9	11	.450	30	17	5	1	2	141^2	136	77	68	13	8	69	52	1.447	4.32	101	4.19	.252	16	.327	-2	11	0.5
1954	Cin-N	12	5	.706	35	14	5	1	0	166^2	188	77	72	11	6	59	85	1.482	3.89	108	4.47	.292	9	.173	4	13	0.8
1955	Cin-N★	17	12	.586	50	33	14	**5**	3	257	240	108	99	25	5	78	98	1.237	3.47	122	3.41	.249	17	.198	22	20	2.5
1956	Cin-N★	13	11	.542	44	32	10	2	3	200^2	196	96	83	18	6	87	120	1.410	3.72	107	4.11	.257	11	.186	8	14	1.1
1957	Cin-N	10	10	.500	39	28	6	2	1	174^1	192	104	92	24	7	53	99	1.405	4.75	87	4.61	.275	14	.237	-13	8	-1.0
1958	Cin-N	12	11	.522	36	26	5	0	0	175^2	169	78	74	15	1	63	111	1.321	3.79	109	3.64	.257	13	.210	6	12	0.6
1959	Cin-N	9	9	.500	28	21	6	1	1	131^2	155	76	62	10	1	35	75	1.443	4.24	96	4.38	.292	11	.250	-3	6	0.0
1960	Cin-N	1	8	.111	38	6	0	0	0	112	130	58	55	8	4	27	72	1.402	4.42	86	4.24	.297	2	.077	-8	3	-0.9
1961	KC-A	5	8	.385	37	13	1	0	1	128	135	81	76	12	3	65	81	1.563	5.34	77	4.78	.268	19	.292	-16	6	-0.8
1962	LA-A	0	0	....	5	0	0	0	0	5^1	7	6	6	0	1	5	2	2.250	10.13	38	7.90	.304	0	....	-4	0	-0.4
	Cin-N	5	0	1.000	12	9	1	0	1	66	59	20	18	4	1	25	57	1.273	2.45	164	3.21	.240	7	.269	11	8	1.4
1963	Cin-N	15	8	.652	35	29	14	2	2	217^1	194	73	63	14	6	39	169	1.072	2.61	128	2.54	.237	12	.158	18	19	1.9
1964	Cin-N	9	8	.529	32	22	7	4	2	154^2	146	73	70	19	6	51	111	1.274	4.07	89	3.81	.250	7	.130	-10	7	-1.1
1965	Cin-N	11	4	.733	32	16	5	1	2	148^2	142	57	57	18	3	31	117	1.164	3.45	109	3.35	.252	8	.178	5	10	0.6
1966	Cin-N	6	8	.429	35	16	2	1	0	130	136	71	65	14	9	42	71	1.369	4.50	87	4.28	.270	4	.100	-7	4	-1.0
Total 16		135	117	.536	526	287	83	20	19	2302^2	2310	1093	998	209	70	776	1372	1.340	3.90	102	3.88	.262	152	.198	11	147	4.1
• NYE, Rich	Richard Raymond Nye b: 8/4/1944, Oakland, CA BL/TL, 6'4", 185 lbs. Deb: 9/16/1966																										
1966	Chi-N	0	2	.000	3	2	0	0	0	17	16	4	4	1	0	7	9	1.353	2.12	174	3.40	.254	1	.250	3	1	0.3
1967	Chi-N	13	10	.565	35	30	7	0	0	205	179	82	73	15	2	52	119	1.127	3.20	111	2.68	.234	16	.213	5	13	0.9
1968	Chi-N	7	12	.368	27	20	6	1	1	132^2	145	65	56	16	1	34	74	1.349	3.80	83	4.12	.276	8	.182	-9	4	-1.1
1969	Chi-N	3	5	.375	34	5	1	0	3	68^2	72	43	39	13	1	21	39	1.354	5.11	79	4.56	.271	1	.063	-8	1	-1.0
1970	StL-N	0	0	....	6	0	0	0	0	8	13	5	4	2	0	6	5	2.375	4.50	91	10.48	.371	1	.500	-0	1	0.0
	Mon-N	3	2	.600	8	6	2	0	0	46^1	47	23	21	3	0	20	21	1.446	4.08	101	3.89	.260	3	.176	-0	3	-0.1
	Yr.	3	2	.600	14	6	2	0	0	54^1	60	28	25	5	0	26	26	1.583	4.14	99	4.86	.278	4	.211	-0	4	0.0
Total 5		26	31	.456	113	63	16	1	4	477^2	472	222	197	50	4	140	267	1.281	3.71	96	3.62	.257	30	.190	-9	23	-0.8
• NYE, Ryan	Ryan Craig Nye b: 6/24/1973, Biloxi, MS BR/TR, 6'2", 195 lbs. Deb: 6/7/1997																										
1997	Phi-N	0	2	.000	4	2	0	0	0	12	20	11	11	2	2	9	7	2.417	8.25	52	11.38	.392	0	.000	-5	0	-0.5
1998	Phi-N	0	0	....	1	0	0	0	0	1	3	3	3	1	0	0	3	3.000	27.00	16	25.51	.500	0	....	-3	0	-0.2
Total 2		0	2	.000	5	2	0	0	0	13	23	14	14	3	2	9	10	2.462	9.69	44	12.47	.404	0	.000	-8	0	-0.8
• NYMAN, Jerry	Gerald Smith Nyman b: 11/23/1942, Logan, UT BL/TL, 5'10", 165 lbs. Deb: 8/24/1968																										
1968	Chi-A	2	1	.667	8	7	1	1	0	40^1	38	13	9	1	0	16	27	1.339	2.01	151	3.11	.247	2	.154	5	3	0.5
1969	Chi-A	4	4	.500	20	10	2	1	0	64^2	58	40	38	7	0	39	40	1.500	5.29	73	4.38	.244	1	.050	-9	1	-1.1
1970	SD-N	0	2	.000	2	2	0	0	0	5^1	8	9	9	1	0	2	2	1.875	15.19	26	7.55	.364	0	....	-7	0	-0.6
Total 3		6	7	.462	30	19	3	2	0	110^1	104	62	56	9	0	57	69	1.459	4.57	81	4.07	.251	3	.091	-11	4	-1.2
• OANA, Prince	Henry Kawaihoa Oana b: 1/22/1908, Waipahu, HI d: 6/19/1976, Austin, TX BR/TR, 6'2", 193 lbs. Deb: 4/22/1934 ♦																										
1943	Det-A	3	2	.600	10	0	0	0	0	34	34	21	17	4	2	19	15	1.559	4.50	78	4.86	.262	10	.385	-4	2	0.1
1945	Det-A	0	0	....	3	1	0	0	1	11^1	3	2	2	0	0	7	3	.882	1.59	221	0.95	.086	1	.200	2	2	0.2
Total 2		3	2	.600	13	1	0	0	1	45^1	37	23	19	4	2	26	18	1.390	3.77	93	3.88	.224	16	.308	-1	4	0.3
• OBERBECK, Henry	Henry A. Oberbeck b: 5/17/1858, St. Louis, MO d: 8/26/1921, St. Louis, MO Deb: 5/7/1883 U ♦																										
1884	Bal-U	0	0	....	2	1	0	0	0	6	9	3	2	0	....	2	1	1.833	3.00	111	....	.325	23	.184	0	1	-0.6
	KC-U	0	5	.000	6	4	3	0	0	29^2	47	35	19	0	....	3	6	1.685	5.76	48	....	.338	17	.189	-10	1	-0.6
	Yr.	0	5	.000	8	5	3	0	0	35^2	56	38	21	0	....	5	7	1.710	5.30	54	....	.336	40	.186	-10	2	-1.2
• OBERLANDER, Doc	Hartman Louis Oberlander b: 5/12/1864, Waukegan, IL d: 11/14/1922, Pryor, MT TL, 5'10.5", 165 lbs. Deb: 5/16/1888																										
1888	Cle-a	1	2	.333	3	3	3	0	0	25^2	27	33	15	2	1	18	23	1.753	5.26	59	....	.261	3	.214	-6	0	-0.5
• OBERLIN, Frank	Frank Rufus "Flossie" Oberlin b: 3/29/1876, Elsie, MI d: 1/6/1952, Ashley, IN BR/TR, 6'1", 165 lbs. Deb: 9/20/1906																										
1906	Bos-A	1	3	.250	4	4	4	0	0	34	38	20	12	0	2	13	13	1.500	3.18	86	3.93	.286	2	.154	-1	1	-0.1
1907	Bos-A	1	5	.167	12	4	2	0	0	46	48	31	22	2	2	24	18	1.565	4.30	60	4.42	.271	2	.154	-11	0	-1.2
	Was-A	2	6	.250	11	8	3	0	0	48^2	57	38	25	0	2	12	18	1.418	4.62	52	3.71	.295	1	.056	-10	0	-1.4
	Yr.	3	11	.214	23	12	5	0	0	94^2	105	69	47	2	4	36	36	1.489	4.47	56	4.06	.284	3	.097	-21	0	-2.6
1909	Was-A	1	4	.200	9	4	1	0	0	41	41	22	17	1	6	16	13	1.390	3.73	65	4.05	.266	2	.143	-6	1	-0.7
1910	Was-A	0	6	.000	8	6	6	0	0	57^1	52	32	19	0	2	23	18	1.308	2.98	83	3.15	.259	1	.053	-4	1	-0.7
Total 4		5	24	.172	44	26	16	0	0	227	236	143	95	3	14	88	80	1.427	3.77	67	3.81	.275	8	.104	-32	3	-4.0
• OBERMUELLER, Wes	Wesley Mitchell Obermueller b: 12/22/1976, Cedar Rapids, IA BR/TR, 6'2", 195 lbs. Deb: 9/20/2002																										
2002	KC-A	0	2	.000	2	2	0	0	0	7^2	14	10	10	3	0	2	5	2.087	11.74	43	11.04	.378	0	....	-6	0	-0.5
2003	Mil-N	2	5	.286	12	11	0	0	0	65^2	81	40	37	10	6	25	34	1.614	5.07	84	6.08	.301	3	.130	-5	2	-0.5
Total 2		2	7	.222	14	13	0	0	0	73^1	95	50	47	13	6	27	39	1.664	5.77	76	6.60	.310	3	.130	-10	2	-1.1
• O'BRIEN, Billy	William Smith O'Brien b: 3/14/1860, Albany, NY d: 5/26/1911, Kansas City, MO BR/TR, 6', 185 lbs. Deb: 9/27/1884 ♦																										
1884	StP-U	1	0	1.000	2	0	0	0	0	10	8	5	2	0	....	3	7	1.100	1.80	169	....	.205	7	.233	1	2	0.2

YEAR TM-L	W	L	PCT	G	GS	CG	SH	SV	IP	H	R	ER	HR	HB	BB	SO	RAT	ERA	ERA+	CERA	OAV	BH	AVG	PR+	WS	TPW
• O'BRIEN, Bob	Robert Allen O'Brien b: 4/23/1949, Pittsburgh, PA BL/TL, 5'10", 170 lbs. Deb: 4/11/1971																									
1971 LA-N	2	2	.500	14	4	1	1	0	42	42	18	14	4	1	13	15	1.310	3.00	108	3.78	.263	1	.111	1	2	0.1
• O'BRIEN, Buck	Thomas Joseph O'Brien b: 5/9/1882, Brockton, MA d: 7/25/1959, Boston, MA BR/TR, 5'10", 188 lbs. Deb: 9/9/1911																									
1911 Bos-A	5	1	.833	6	5	5	2	0	47^2	30	9	2	0	1	21	31	1.070	0.38	866	1.72	.180	2	.125	15	6	1.4
1912* Bos-A	20	13	.606	37	34	25	2	0	275^2	237	107	79	3	10	90	115	1.186	2.58	133	2.64	.237	13	.138	26	23	2.2
1913 Bos-A	4	9	.308	15	12	6	0	0	90^1	103	42	37	0	0	35	54	1.528	3.69	80	4.29	.305	5	.167	-6	3	-0.6
Chi-A	0	2	.000	6	3	0	0	0	18^1	21	14	8	0	0	13	4	1.855	3.93	74	5.70	.318	0	.000	-2	0	-0.3
Yr.	4	11	.267	21	15	6	0	0	108^2	124	56	45	0	0	48	58	1.583	3.73	79	4.53	.307	5	.152	-8	3	-0.9
Total 3	29	25	.537	64	54	36	4	0	432	391	172	126	3	11	159	204	1.273	2.63	123	3.01	.249	20	.140	34	32	2.7
• O'BRIEN, Dan	Daniel Jogues O'Brien b: 4/22/1954, St. Petersburg, FL BR/TR, 6'4", 215 lbs. Deb: 9/4/1978																									
1978 StL-N	0	2	.000	7	2	0	0	0	18	22	12	9	1	2	8	12	1.667	4.50	78	5.30	.301	0	.000	-2	0	-0.3
1979 StL-N	1	1	.500	6	0	0	0	0	11	21	10	10	0	0	3	5	2.182	8.18	46	8.41	.420	0	.000	-6	0	-0.6
Total 2	1	3	.250	13	2	0	0	0	29	43	22	19	1	2	11	17	1.862	5.90	62	6.48	.350	0	.000	-8	0	-0.9
• O'BRIEN, Darby	John F. O'Brien b: 4/15/1867, Troy, NY d: 3/11/1892, West Troy, NY BR/TR, 5'10", 165 lbs. Deb: 6/23/1888 U																									
1888 Cle-a	11	19	.367	30	30	30	1	0	259	245	162	95	5	12	99	135	1.328	3.30	94	....	.241	20	.183	-5	9	-0.7
1889 Cle-N	22	17	.564	41	41	39	1	0	346^2	345	216	160	9	24	167	122	1.477	4.15	97	....	.251	35	.250	-16	23	-0.9
1890 Cle-P	8	16	.333	25	25	22	0	0	206^1	229	171	78	9	19	93	54	1.561	3.40	117	....	.269	15	.156	13	9	0.6
1891 Bos-a	18	13	.581	40	30	22	0	**2**	268^2	300	197	109	13	20	127	87	1.589	3.65	96	....	.273	30	.234	-11	14	-0.9
Total 4	59	65	.476	136	126	113	2	2	1080^2	1119	746	442	36	75	486	398	1.485	3.68	99	....	.258	100	.211	-19	55	-1.8
• O'BRIEN, Darby	William D. O'Brien b: 9/1/1863, Peoria, IL d: 6/15/1893, Peoria, IL BR/TR, 6'1", 186 lbs. Deb: 4/16/1887 U ♦																									
1887 NY-a	0	0	....	1	0	0	0	0	1	2	0	0	0	0	1	0	2.000	0.00	....	....	.401	197	.351	1	18	1.8
• O'BRIEN, Johnny	John Thomas O'Brien b: 12/11/1930, South Amboy, NJ BR/TR, 5'9", 170 lbs. Deb: 4/19/1953 ♦																									
1956 Pit-N	1	0	1.000	8	0	0	0	0	19	8	6	6	2	2	9	9	.895	2.84	133	1.90	.133	18	.173	2	1	-0.9
1957 Pit-N	0	3	.000	16	1	0	0	0	40	46	32	27	7	1	24	19	1.750	6.08	62	6.35	.293	11	.314	-11	1	-1.0
1958 StL-N	0	0	....	1	0	0	0	0	2	7	5	5	0	0	2	2	4.500	22.50	18	23.57	.538	0	.000	-4	0	-0.7
Total 3	1	3	.250	25	1	0	0	0	61	61	43	38	9	3	35	30	1.574	5.61	68	5.53	.265	204	.250	-13	2	-2.7
• OCKEY, Walter	Walter Andrew "Footie" Ockey b: 1/4/1920, New York, NY d: 12/4/1971, Staten Island, NY BR/TR, 6', 175 lbs. Deb: 5/3/1944																									
1944 NY-N	0	0	....	2	0	0	0	0	2^2	2	1	1	1	0	2	1	1.500	3.38	109	5.77	.200	0	....	0	0	0.0
• O'CONNOR, Andy	Andrew James O'Connor b: 9/14/1884, Roxbury, MA d: 9/26/1980, Norwood, MA BR/TR, 6', 160 lbs. Deb: 10/6/1908																									
1908 NY-A	0	1	.000	1	1	1	0	0	8	15	11	9	0	3	7	5	2.750	10.13	24	12.88	.429	0	.000	-7	0	-0.8
• O'CONNOR, Brian	Brian Michael O'Connor b: 1/4/1977, Cincinnati, OH BL/TL, 6'2", 170 lbs. Deb: 5/13/2000																									
2000 Pit-N	0	0	....	6	1	0	0	0	12^1	12	11	7	2	1	11	7	1.865	5.11	90	6.50	.250	1	.500	-1	0	0.0
• O'CONNOR, Frank	Frank Henry O'Connor b: 9/15/1870, Keeseville, NY d: 12/26/1913, Brattleboro, VT BL/TL, 6', 185 lbs. Deb: 8/3/1893																									
1893 Phi-N	0	0	....	3	1	0	0	1	4	2	5	5	0	0	9	0	2.750	11.25	41	6.62	.145	2	1.000	-3	0	-0.1
• O'CONNOR, Jack	Jack William O'Connor b: 6/2/1958, Twenty-Nine Palms, CA BL/TL, 6'3", 215 lbs. Deb: 4/9/1981																									
1981 Min-A	3	2	.600	28	0	0	0	0	35^1	46	27	23	3	2	30	16	2.151	5.86	67	7.85	.336	0	....	-7	0	-0.8
1982 Min-A	8	9	.471	23	19	6	1	0	126	122	63	60	13	2	57	56	1.421	4.29	99	4.18	.256	0	....	-2	6	-0.2
1983 Min-A	2	3	.400	27	8	0	0	0	83	107	59	54	13	0	36	56	1.723	5.86	72	6.36	.315	0	....	-16	1	-1.6
1984 Min-A	0	0	....	2	0	0	0	0	4^2	1	1	1	1	0	4	0	1.071	1.93	218	2.38	.067	0	....	1	0	0.1
1985 Mon-N	0	2	.000	20	1	0	0	0	23^2	21	14	13	1	0	13	16	1.437	4.94	69	3.01	.239	0	....	-4	0	-0.4
1987 Bal-A	1	1	.500	29	0	0	0	2	46	46	23	22	5	0	23	33	1.500	4.30	102	4.40	.263	0	....	1	3	0.0
Total 6	14	17	.452	129	28	6	1	2	318^2	343	187	173	36	4	163	177	1.588	4.89	85	5.07	.278	0	....	-28	10	-2.8
• O'DAY, Hank	Henry Francis O'Day b: 7/8/1862, Chicago, IL d: 7/2/1935, Chicago, IL TR, 6', 180 lbs. Deb: 5/2/1884 M/U																									
1884 Tol-a	9	28	.243	41	40	35	2	**1**	326^2	335	241	136	6	18	66	163	1.228	3.75	91	....	.251	51	.211	-15	16	-1.5
1885 Pit-a	5	7	.417	12	12	10	0	0	103	110	77	42	4	7	16	36	1.223	3.67	88	....	.262	12	.245	-6	6	-0.5
1886 Was-N	2	2	.500	6	6	6	0	0	49	41	17	9	1	....	17	47	1.184	1.65	197	....	.219	1	.053	9	3	0.6
1887 Was-N	8	20	.286	30	30	29	0	0	254^2	364	197	118	15	9	109	86	1.429	4.17	97	....	.326	30	.244	1	12	-0.2
1888 Was-N	16	29	.356	46	46	46	3	0	403	359	208	139	19	16	117	186	1.181	3.10	90	....	.230	23	.139	-12	20	-1.7
1889 Was-N	2	10	.167	13	13	11	0	0	108	117	88	52	7	6	57	23	1.611	4.33	91	....	.267	8	.182	-3	3	-0.3
*NY-N	9	1	.900	10	10	8	0	0	78	83	51	37	2	7	35	28	1.513	4.27	92	....	.264	3	.097	-3	5	-0.4
Yr.	11	11	.500	23	23	19	0	0	186	200	139	89	9	13	92	51	1.570	4.31	92	....	.266	11	.147	-6	8	-0.6
1890 NY-P	22	13	.629	43	35	32	1	**3**	329	355	249	154	11	18	161	94	1.568	4.21	108	....	.264	34	.227	8	23	0.5
Total 7	73	110	.399	201	192	177	6	4	1651^1	1764	1128	687	65	81	578	663	1.352	3.74	96	....	.263	162	.197	-22	88	-3.5
• O'DELL, Billy	William Oliver O'Dell b: 2/10/1933, Whitmire, SC BB/TL, 5'11", 170 lbs. Deb: 6/20/1954																									
1954 Bal-A	1	1	.500	7	2	1	0	0	16^1	15	7	5	0	0	5	6	1.224	2.76	130	2.59	.242	0	.000	2	1	0.1
1956 Bal-A	0	0	....	4	1	0	0	0	8	6	1	1	0	0	6	6	1.500	1.13	349	3.21	.222	0	.000	3	1	0.2
1957 Bal-A	4	10	.286	35	15	2	1	4	140^1	107	48	42	12	5	39	97	1.040	2.69	133	2.42	.212	5	.147	12	11	1.1
1958 Bal-A★	14	11	.560	41	25	12	3	8	221^1	201	83	73	13	4	51	137	1.139	2.97	121	2.67	.241	8	.111	16	20	1.6
1959 Bal-A★	10	12	.455	38	24	6	2	1	199^1	163	74	65	18	1	67	88	1.154	2.93	129	2.73	.220	5	.083	17	15	1.4
1960 SF-N	8	13	.381	43	24	6	1	2	202^2	198	80	72	16	2	72	145	1.332	3.20	109	3.55	.252	6	.107	8	11	0.9
1961 SF-N	7	5	.583	46	14	4	1	2	130^1	132	63	52	10	1	33	110	1.266	3.59	106	3.32	.260	4	.103	4	7	0.2
1962* SF-N	19	14	.576	43	39	20	2	0	280^2	282	126	110	18	7	66	195	1.240	3.53	108	3.30	.258	12	.133	9	17	0.7
1963 SF-N	14	10	.583	36	33	10	3	1	222^1	218	90	78	14	7	70	116	1.295	3.16	101	3.38	.253	16	.205	5	13	0.9
1964 SF-N	8	7	.533	36	8	1	0	2	85	82	55	51	10	4	35	54	1.376	5.40	66	4.08	.252	0	.000	-18	1	-2.1
1965 Mil-N	10	6	.625	62	1	0	0	18	111^1	87	35	27	10	2	30	78	1.051	2.18	161	2.34	.215	4	.174	16	16	1.7
1966 Atl-N	2	3	.400	24	0	0	0	6	41^1	44	14	11	3	2	18	20	1.500	2.40	152	4.55	.272	2	.250	6	4	0.6
Pit-N	3	2	.600	37	2	0	0	4	71^1	74	24	22	3	4	23	47	1.360	2.78	129	3.82	.275	1	.063	5	6	0.4
Yr.	5	5	.500	61	2	0	0	10	112^2	118	38	33	6	6	41	67	1.411	2.64	136	4.09	.274	3	.125	11	10	1.0
1967 Pit-N	5	6	.455	27	11	1	0	0	86^2	88	58	56	10	3	41	34	1.488	5.82	58	4.60	.265	3	.115	-25	0	-2.7
Total 13	105	100	.512	479	199	63	13	48	1817	1697	758	665	137	42	556	1133	1.240	3.29	108	3.21	.246	66	.125	60	123	5.1
• ODENWALD, Ted	Theodore Joseph "Lefty" Odenwald b: 1/4/1902, Hudson, WI d: 10/23/1965, Shakopee, MN BR/TL, 5'10", 147 lbs. Deb: 4/13/1921																									
1921 Cle-A	1	0	1.000	10	0	0	0	0	17^1	16	5	3	0	1	6	4	1.269	1.56	273	3.01	.262	0	.000	5	2	0.4
1922 Cle-A	0	0	....	1	0	0	0	0	1^1	6	6	6	0	0	2	2	6.000	40.50	10	33.87	.600	0	....	-5	0	-0.5
Total 2	1	0	1.000	11	0	0	0	0	18^2	22	11	9	0	1	8	6	1.607	4.34	94	5.21	.310	0	.000	-0	2	-0.1
• ODOM, Blue Moon	Johnny Lee Odom b: 5/29/1945, Macon, GA BR/TR, 6', 185 lbs. Deb: 9/5/1964																									
1964 KC-A	1	2	.333	5	5	1	1	0	17	29	21	19	5	0	11	10	2.353	10.06	38	11.25	.363	0	.000	-12	0	-1.2
1965 KC-A	0	0	....	1	0	0	0	0	1	2	1	1	0	0	2	0	4.000	9.00	39	16.69	.400	0	....	-1	0	-0.1
1966 KC-A	5	5	.500	14	14	4	2	0	90^1	70	31	25	1	2	53	47	1.362	2.49	136	2.99	.215	3	.097	9	6	0.9
1967 KC-A	3	8	.273	29	17	0	0	0	103^2	94	67	58	9	3	68	67	1.563	5.04	63	4.43	.243	8	.286	-21	0	-2.1
1968 Oak-A★	16	10	.615	32	31	9	4	0	231^1	179	74	63	9	7	98	143	1.197	2.45	115	2.65	.216	17	.218	9	17	1.7
1969 Oak-A★	15	6	.714	32	32	10	3	0	231^1	179	87	75	15	6	112	150	1.258	2.92	118	3.03	.215	21	.266	13	18	2.5
1970 Oak-A	9	8	.529	29	29	4	1	0	156^1	128	77	66	14	8	100	88	1.458	3.80	93	4.12	.227	13	.241	-6	8	0.0
1971 Oak-A	10	12	.455	25	25	3	1	0	140^2	147	78	67	13	0	71	69	1.550	4.29	78	4.57	.271	8	.160	-17	2	-1.7
1972* Oak-A	15	6	.714	31	30	4	2	0	194^1	164	62	54	10	3	87	86	1.292	2.50	114	3.20	.234	8	.121	5	12	0.6
1973* Oak-A	5	12	.294	30	24	3	0	0	150^1	153	86	75	14	2	67	83	1.463	4.49	79	4.33	.263	0	.000	-20	2	-2.1
1974* Oak-A	1	5	.167	34	5	1	0	1	87^1	85	39	37	4	3	52	52	1.569	3.81	87	4.47	.267	0	....	-6	3	-0.6

YEAR	TM-L	W	L	PCT	G	GS	CG	SH	SV	IP	H	R	ER	HR	HB	BB	SO	RAT	ERA	ERA+	CERA	OAV	BH	AVG	PR+	WS	TPW
1975	Oak-A	0	2	.000	7	2	0	0	0	11	19	15	15	1	1	11	4	2.727	12.27	30	12.26	.422	0	....	-11	0	-1.1
	Cle-A	1	0	1.000	3	1	1	1	0	10^1	4	3	3	1	0	8	10	1.161	2.61	145	2.27	.118	0	....	1	1	0.1
	Yr.	1	2	.333	10	3	1	1	0	21^1	23	18	18	2	1	19	14	1.969	7.59	48	7.42	.291	0	....	-9	1	-1.0
	Atl-N	1	7	.125	15	10	0	0	0	56	78	46	44	5	0	28	30	1.893	7.07	53	6.89	.342	1	.077	-19	0	-2.1
1976	Chi-A	2	2	.500	8	4	0	0	0	28	31	21	18	2	1	20	18	1.821	5.79	62	5.88	.282	0	....	-7	0	-0.7
Total	13	84	85	.497	295	229	40	15	1	1509	1362	708	620	103	36	788	857	1.425	3.70	90	3.92	.244	79	.195	-82	69	-5.9

• ODOM, Dave

David Everett "Blimp,Porky" Odom b: 6/5/1918, Dinuba, CA d: 11/19/1987, Myrtle Beach, SC BR/TR, 6'1", 220 lbs. Deb: 5/31/1943

YEAR	TM-L	W	L	PCT	G	GS	CG	SH	SV	IP	H	R	ER	HR	HB	BB	SO	RAT	ERA	ERA+	CERA	OAV	BH	AVG	PR+	WS	TPW
1943	Bos-N	0	3	.000	22	3	1	0	2	54^2	54	32	32	3	4	30	17	1.537	5.27	65	4.54	.269	0	.000	-12	0	-1.4

• O'DONNELL, George

George Dana O'Donnell b: 5/27/1929, Winchester, IL BR/TR, 6'3", 175 lbs. Deb: 4/18/1954

YEAR	TM-L	W	L	PCT	G	GS	CG	SH	SV	IP	H	R	ER	HR	HB	BB	SO	RAT	ERA	ERA+	CERA	OAV	BH	AVG	PR+	WS	TPW
1954	Pit-N	3	9	.250	21	10	3	0	1	87^1	105	50	44	4	2	21	8	1.443	4.53	92	4.32	.315	2	.087	-1	4	-0.2

• O'DONOGHUE, John

John Eugene O'Donoghue b: 10/7/1939, Kansas City, MO BR/TL, 6'4", 210 lbs. Deb: 9/29/1963

YEAR	TM-L	W	L	PCT	G	GS	CG	SH	SV	IP	H	R	ER	HR	HB	BB	SO	RAT	ERA	ERA+	CERA	OAV	BH	AVG	PR+	WS	TPW
1963	KC-A	0	1	.000	1	1	0	0	0	6	6	2	1	0	0	2	1	1.333	1.50	256	3.52	.286	0	.000	2	1	0.1
1964	KC-A	10	14	.417	39	32	2	1	0	173^2	202	104	95	24	3	65	79	1.537	4.92	78	5.12	.286	13	.236	-18	5	-1.7
1965	KC-A★	9	18	.333	34	30	4	1	0	177^2	183	92	78	15	1	66	82	1.402	3.95	88	3.98	.267	12	.218	-8	6	-0.6
1966	Cle-A	6	8	.429	32	13	2	0	0	108	109	50	46	13	2	23	49	1.222	3.83	90	3.59	.264	5	.152	-3	5	-0.4
1967	Cle-A	8	9	.471	33	17	5	2	2	130^2	120	52	47	10	2	33	81	1.171	3.24	101	2.99	.247	4	.100	2	7	0.2
1968	Bal-A	0	0	....	16	0	0	0	2	22	34	15	15	2	0	7	11	1.864	6.14	48	6.93	.374	0	.000	-8	0	-1.0
1969	Sea-A	2	2	.500	55	0	0	0	6	70	58	28	23	5	3	37	48	1.357	2.96	123	3.53	.230	1	.077	7	5	0.7
1970	Mil-A	2	0	1.000	25	0	0	0	0	23^1	29	15	13	4	0	9	13	1.629	5.01	76	5.71	.299	0	.000	-3	1	-0.3
	Mon-N	2	3	.400	9	3	0	0	0	22^1	20	14	13	2	2	11	6	1.388	5.24	78	4.24	.263	0	.000	-3	1	-0.3
1971	Mon-N	0	0	....	13	0	0	0	0	17^1	19	10	9	3	0	7	7	1.500	4.67	75	4.96	.271	0	....	-2	0	-0.2
Total	9	39	55	.415	257	96	13	4	10	751	780	382	340	78	13	260	377	1.385	4.07	87	4.14	.269	35	.170	-35	31	-3.4

• O'DONOGHUE, John

John Preston O'Donoghue b: 5/26/1969, Wilmington, DE BL/TL, 6'6", 198 lbs. Deb: 6/27/1993

YEAR	TM-L	W	L	PCT	G	GS	CG	SH	SV	IP	H	R	ER	HR	HB	BB	SO	RAT	ERA	ERA+	CERA	OAV	BH	AVG	PR+	WS	TPW
1993	Bal-A	0	1	.000	11	1	0	0	0	19^2	22	12	10	4	1	10	16	1.627	4.58	98	6.14	.278	0	....	-1	1	0.0

• O'DOUL, Lefty

Francis Joseph O'Doul b: 3/4/1897, San Francisco, CA d: 12/7/1969, San Francisco, CA BL/TL, 6', 180 lbs. Deb: 4/29/1919 ♦

YEAR	TM-L	W	L	PCT	G	GS	CG	SH	SV	IP	H	R	ER	HR	HB	BB	SO	RAT	ERA	ERA+	CERA	OAV	BH	AVG	PR+	WS	TPW
1919	NY-A	0	0	....	3	0	0	0	0	5	7	6	2	0	0	4	2	2.200	3.60	89	6.57	.304	4	.250	-0	0	-0.1
1920	NY-A	0	0	....	2	0	0	0	0	3^2	4	2	2	0	1	2	2	1.636	4.91	78	5.40	.286	2	.167	-0	0	-0.1
1922	NY-A	0	0	....	6	0	0	0	0	16	24	13	6	0	0	12	5	2.250	3.38	118	7.67	.353	3	.333	1	0	0.2
1923	Bos-A	1	1	.500	23	1	0	0	0	53	69	50	32	2	4	31	10	1.887	5.43	76	6.46	.337	5	.143	-8	0	-1.0
Total	4	1	1	.500	34	1	0	0	0	77^2	104	71	42	2	5	49	19	1.970	4.87	83	6.67	.336	1140	.349	-7	0	-1.0

• OELKERS, Bryan

Bryan Alois Oelkers b: 3/11/1961, Zaragoza, Spain BL/TL, 6'3", 192 lbs. Deb: 4/9/1983

YEAR	TM-L	W	L	PCT	G	GS	CG	SH	SV	IP	H	R	ER	HR	HB	BB	SO	RAT	ERA	ERA+	CERA	OAV	BH	AVG	PR+	WS	TPW
1983	Min-A	0	5	.000	10	8	0	0	0	34^1	56	34	33	7	0	17	13	2.126	8.65	49	9.66	.376	0	....	-17	0	-1.7
1986	Cle-A	3	3	.500	35	4	0	0	1	69	70	38	36	13	6	40	33	1.594	4.70	88	5.84	.262	0	....	-4	3	-0.4
Total	2	3	8	.273	45	12	0	0	1	103^1	126	72	69	20	6	57	46	1.771	6.01	70	7.11	.303	0	....	-21	3	-2.1

• OESCHGER, Joe

Joseph Carl Oeschger b: 5/24/1892, Chicago, IL d: 7/28/1986, Rohnert Park, CA BR/TR, 6', 190 lbs. Deb: 4/21/1914

YEAR	TM-L	W	L	PCT	G	GS	CG	SH	SV	IP	H	R	ER	HR	HB	BB	SO	RAT	ERA	ERA+	CERA	OAV	BH	AVG	PR+	WS	TPW
1914	Phi-N	4	8	.333	32	10	5	0	1	124	129	74	52	5	10	54	47	1.476	3.77	78	4.23	.279	3	.075	-8	3	-1.2
1915	Phi-N	1	0	1.000	6	1	1	0	0	23^2	21	13	9	1	0	9	8	1.268	3.42	80	2.92	.247	0	.000	-2	1	-0.3
1916	Phi-N	1	0	1.000	14	0	0	0	0	30^1	18	8	8	2	1	14	17	1.055	2.37	111	2.08	.184	0	.000	1	2	0.0
1917	Phi-N	15	14	.517	42	30	18	5	1	262	241	108	80	7	6	72	123	1.195	2.75	102	2.77	.249	10	.114	0	15	-0.4
1918	Phi-N	6	18	.250	30	23	13	2	**3**	184	159	87	62	3	7	83	60	1.315	3.03	99	3.00	.238	5	.083	-0	8	-0.5
1919	Phi-N	0	1	.000	5	4	2	0	0	38	52	29	25	1	2	16	5	1.789	5.92	54	5.91	.340	0	.000	-11	0	-1.5
	NY-N	0	1	.000	5	1	0	0	0	8	12	4	4	0	0	2	3	1.750	4.50	62	6.29	.400	0	.000	-2	0	-0.2
	Bos-N	4	2	.667	7	7	4	1	0	56^2	63	19	16	0	1	21	16	1.482	2.54	112	4.02	.300	2	.091	2	4	0.1
	Yr.	4	4	.500	17	12	6	1	0	102^2	127	52	45	1	3	39	24	1.617	3.94	77	4.90	.323	2	.053	-11	4	-1.6
1920	Bos-N	15	13	.536	38	30	20	5	0	299	294	124	115	10	8	99	80	1.314	3.46	88	3.34	.265	18	.178	-17	16	-2.1
1921	Bos-N	20	14	.588	46	36	19	**3**	0	299	303	128	117	11	15	97	68	1.338	3.52	104	3.63	.274	28	.255	2	20	0.4
1922	Bos-N	6	21	.222	46	23	10	1	1	195^2	234	137	110	8	8	81	51	1.610	5.06	79	4.83	.303	12	.190	-21	4	-2.0
1923	Bos-N	5	15	.250	44	19	6	1	2	166^1	227	117	105	4	5	54	33	1.689	5.68	70	5.39	.330	12	.231	-30	2	-2.8
1924	NY-N	2	0	1.000	10	2	0	0	0	29	35	17	10	1	0	14	10	1.690	3.10	118	4.79	.287	3	.429	2	2	0.2
	Phi-N	2	7	.222	19	8	0	0	0	65^1	88	44	32	6	3	16	8	1.592	4.41	101	5.60	.333	5	.250	2	3	0.1
	Yr.	4	7	.364	29	10	0	0	0	94^1	123	61	42	7	3	30	18	1.622	4.01	106	5.35	.318	8	.296	4	5	0.4
1925	Bro-N	1	2	.333	21	3	1	0	0	37	60	38	25	2	1	19	6	2.135	6.08	69	8.05	.382	1	.125	-7	0	-0.7
Total	12	82	116	.414	365	197	99	18	8	1818	1936	947	770	61	67	651	535	1.423	3.81	89	3.94	.281	99	.165	-88	80	-10.7

• OGDEN, Curly

Warren Harvey Ogden b: 1/24/1901, Ogden, PA d: 8/6/1964, Upland, PA BR/TR, 6'1.5", 180 lbs. Deb: 7/18/1922

YEAR	TM-L	W	L	PCT	G	GS	CG	SH	SV	IP	H	R	ER	HR	HB	BB	SO	RAT	ERA	ERA+	CERA	OAV	BH	AVG	PR+	WS	TPW
1922	Phi-A	1	4	.200	15	6	4	0	0	72^1	59	29	25	4	5	33	20	1.272	3.11	136	3.25	.237	7	.241	10	6	0.9
1923	Phi-A	1	2	.333	18	2	0	0	0	46^1	63	39	29	2	3	32	14	2.050	5.63	73	6.88	.330	5	.294	-7	0	-0.6
1924	Phi-A	0	3	.000	5	1	0	0	0	12^2	14	5	5	1	1	7	4	1.658	3.55	121	5.14	.275	0	.000	1	0	0.1
	*Was-A	9	5	.643	16	16	9	3	0	108	83	40	33	3	2	51	23	1.241	2.75	147	2.57	.221	13	.277	13	12	1.4
	Yr.	9	8	.529	21	17	9	3	0	120^2	97	45	38	4	3	58	27	1.285	2.83	143	2.84	.227	13	.260	14	12	1.4
1925	Was-A	3	1	.750	17	4	2	1	0	42	45	24	21	1	2	18	6	1.500	4.50	94	4.23	.288	3	.250	-2	2	-0.2
1926	Was-A	4	4	.500	22	9	4	0	0	96^1	114	55	46	2	5	45	21	1.651	4.30	90	4.80	.305	5	.185	-5	4	-0.6
Total	5	18	19	.486	93	38	19	4	0	377^2	378	192	159	13	18	186	88	1.493	3.79	107	4.07	.271	33	.244	9	24	1.0

• OGDEN, Jack

John Mahlon Ogden b: 11/5/1897, Ogden, PA d: 11/9/1977, Philadelphia, PA BR/TR, 6', 190 lbs. Deb: 6/22/1918

YEAR	TM-L	W	L	PCT	G	GS	CG	SH	SV	IP	H	R	ER	HR	HB	BB	SO	RAT	ERA	ERA+	CERA	OAV	BH	AVG	PR+	WS	TPW
1918	NY-N	0	0	....	5	0	0	0	0	8^2	8	4	3	0	2	3	1	1.269	3.12	84	3.80	.296	0	.000	-1	0	-0.1
1928	StL-A	15	16	.484	38	31	18	1	2	242^2	257	121	112	23	1	80	67	1.389	4.15	101	3.83	.274	17	.200	1	16	0.1
1929	StL-A	4	8	.333	34	14	7	0	0	131^1	154	83	72	8	0	44	32	1.508	4.93	90	4.48	.301	11	.244	-9	5	-0.8
1931	Cin-N	4	8	.333	22	9	3	1	1	89	79	42	29	3	0	32	24	1.247	2.93	127	2.76	.242	4	.148	7	5	0.6
1932	Cin-N	2	2	.500	24	3	1	0	0	57	72	40	33	5	0	22	20	1.649	5.21	74	5.35	.310	2	.167	-8	1	-0.8
Total	5	25	34	.424	123	57	29	2	3	528^2	570	290	249	39	3	181	144	1.421	4.24	97	3.98	.280	34	.200	-9	27	-1.0

• OGEA, Chad

Chad Wayne Ogea b: 11/9/1970, Lake Charles, LA BR/TR, 6'2", 200 lbs. Deb: 5/3/1994

YEAR	TM-L	W	L	PCT	G	GS	CG	SH	SV	IP	H	R	ER	HR	HB	BB	SO	RAT	ERA	ERA+	CERA	OAV	BH	AVG	PR+	WS	TPW
1994	Cle-A	0	1	.000	4	1	0	0	0	16^1	21	11	11	2	1	10	11	1.898	6.06	78	6.80	.304	0	....	-2	0	-0.2
1995*	Cle-A	8	3	.727	20	14	1	0	0	106^1	95	38	36	11	1	29	57	1.166	3.05	154	3.03	.233	0	....	20	10	1.9
1996*	Cle-A	10	6	.625	29	21	1	1	0	146^2	151	82	78	22	5	42	101	1.316	4.79	102	4.28	.266	0	....	2	9	0.2
1997*	Cle-A	8	9	.471	21	21	1	0	0	126^1	139	79	70	13	5	47	80	1.472	4.99	94	4.71	.283	0	.000	-3	5	-0.3
1998*	Cle-A	5	4	.556	19	9	0	0	0	69	74	44	43	9	7	25	43	1.435	5.61	85	4.93	.273	0	....	-6	3	-0.6
1999	Phi-N	6	12	.333	36	28	0	0	0	168	192	110	105	36	4	61	77	1.506	5.63	84	5.68	.288	4	.091	-19	4	-2.0
Total	6	37	35	.514	129	94	3	1	0	632^2	672	364	343	93	23	214	369	1.400	4.88	97	4.66	.272	4	.087	-9	31	-1.0

• OGRODOWSKI, Joe

Joseph Anthony Ogrodowski b: 11/20/1906, Hoytville, PA d: 6/24/1959, Elmira, NY BR/TR, 5'11", 165 lbs. Deb: 4/27/1925

YEAR	TM-L	W	L	PCT	G	GS	CG	SH	SV	IP	H	R	ER	HR	HB	BB	SO	RAT	ERA	ERA+	CERA	OAV	BH	AVG	PR+	WS	TPW
1925	Bos-N	0	0	....	1	0	0	0	0	1	6	8	6	0	0	3	0	9.000	54.00	7	50.08	.600	0	....	-6	0	-0.5

• OHKA, Tomokazu

Tomokazu Ohka b: 3/18/1976, Kyoto, Japan BR/TR, 6'1", 180 lbs. Deb: 7/19/1999

YEAR	TM-L	W	L	PCT	G	GS	CG	SH	SV	IP	H	R	ER	HR	HB	BB	SO	RAT	ERA	ERA+	CERA	OAV	BH	AVG	PR+	WS	TPW
1999	Bos-A	1	2	.333	8	2	0	0	0	13	21	12	9	2	0	6	8	2.077	6.23	80	8.56	.362	0	....	-2	0	-0.2
2000	Bos-A	3	6	.333	13	12	0	0	0	69^1	70	25	24	7	2	26	40	1.385	3.12	162	4.19	.263	0	....	15	6	1.4
2001	Bos-A	2	5	.286	12	11	0	0	0	52^1	69	40	36	7	2	19	37	1.682	6.19	72	6.24	.317	0	.000	-9	1	-0.9
	Mon-N	1	4	.200	10	10	0	0	0	54^2	65	30	29	8	1	10	31	1.372	4.77	93	4.83	.302	3	.200	-1	2	-0.1
2002	Mon-N	13	8	.619	32	31	2	0	0	192^2	194	83	68	19	7	45	118	1.240	3.18	134	3.55	.264	7	.127	23	14	2.3
2003	Mon-N	10	12	.455	34	34	2	0	0	199	233	106	92	24	9	45	118	1.397	4.16	121	4.59	.292	10	.182	20	13	2.0
Total	5	30	37	.448	109	100	4	0	0	581	652	296	258	67	21	151	352	1.382	4.00	117	4.46	.285	20	.156	47	35	4.5

YEAR TM-L	W	L	PCT	G	GS	CG	SH	SV	IP	H	R	ER	HR	HB	BB	SO	RAT	ERA	ERA+	CERA	OAV	BH	AVG	PR+	WS	TPW
• OHL, Joe				Joseph Earl Ohl b: 1/10/1888, Jobstown, NJ d: 12/18/1951, Camden, NJ BL/TL, 6'1" Deb: 7/29/1909																						
1909 Was-A	0	0	....	4	0	0	0	0	8^2	7	4	2	0	1	1	2	.923	2.08	117	1.62	.194	0	.000	0	0	0.0
• OHMAN, Will				William McDaniel Ohman b: 8/13/1977, Frankfurt, West Germany BL/TL, 6'2", 195 lbs. Deb: 9/19/2000																						
2000 Chi-N	1	0	1.000	6	0	0	0	0	3^1	4	3	3	0	0	4	2	2.400	8.10	56	7.25	.308	0	....	-1	0	-0.1
2001 Chi-N	0	1	.000	11	0	0	0	0	11^2	14	10	10	2	0	6	12	1.714	7.71	54	6.26	.292	0	.000	-4	0	-0.5
Total 2	1	1	.500	17	0	0	0	0	15	18	13	13	2	0	10	14	1.867	7.80	54	6.48	.295	0	.000	-6	0	-0.6
• OHME, Kevin				Kevin Arthur Ohme b: 4/13/1971, Palm Beach, FL BL/TL, 6'1", 180 lbs. Deb: 4/14/2003																						
2003 StL-N	0	0	....	2	0	0	0	0	4^1	3	0	0	0	0	1	2	.923	0.00	....	1.23	.200	1	1.000	2	1	0.2
• OJALA, Kirt				Kirt Stanley Ojala b: 12/24/1968, Kalamazoo, MI BL/TL, 6'2", 200 lbs. Deb: 8/18/1997																						
1997 Fla-N	1	2	.333	7	5	0	0	0	28^2	28	10	10	4	0	18	19	1.605	3.14	129	5.12	.252	0	.000	3	2	0.2
1998 Fla-N	2	7	.222	41	13	1	0	0	125	128	71	59	14	4	59	75	1.496	4.25	96	4.66	.267	4	.154	-1	3	-0.1
1999 Fla-N	0	1	.000	8	1	0	0	0	10^2	21	17	17	1	0	6	5	2.531	14.34	30	11.34	.438	0	....	-12	0	-1.1
Total 3	3	10	.231	56	19	1	0	0	164^1	177	98	86	19	4	83	99	1.582	4.71	88	5.17	.277	4	.121	-10	5	-1.0
• OJEDA, Bob				Robert Michael Ojeda b: 12/17/1957, Los Angeles, CA BL/TL, 6'1", 190 lbs. Deb: 7/13/1980																						
1980 Bos-A	1	1	.500	7	7	0	0	0	26	39	20	20	2	0	14	12	2.038	6.92	61	7.82	.361	0	....	-8	0	-0.8
1981 Bos-A	6	2	.750	10	10	2	0	0	66^1	50	25	23	6	2	25	28	1.131	3.12	124	2.75	.212	0	....	7	5	0.7
1982 Bos-A	4	6	.400	22	14	0	0	0	78^1	95	53	49	13	1	29	52	1.583	5.63	76	5.75	.296	0	....	-10	2	-1.0
1983 Bos-A	12	7	.632	29	28	5	0	0	173^2	173	85	78	15	3	73	94	1.417	4.04	108	4.13	.265	0	....	7	11	0.7
1984 Bos-A	12	12	.500	33	32	8	**5**	0	216^2	211	106	96	17	2	96	137	1.417	3.99	104	4.02	.259	0	....	12	14	1.2
1985 Bos-A	9	11	.450	39	22	5	0	1	157^2	166	74	70	11	2	48	102	1.357	4.00	107	3.76	.273	0	....	8	9	0.8
1986★ NY-N	18	5	.783	32	30	7	2	0	217^1	185	72	62	15	2	52	148	1.090	2.57	138	2.53	.230	8	.113	23	18	2.1
1987 NY-N	3	5	.375	10	7	0	0	0	46^1	45	23	20	5	0	10	21	1.187	3.88	97	3.20	.253	1	.071	-0	2	0.0
1988 NY-N	10	13	.435	29	29	5	5	0	190^1	158	74	61	6	4	33	133	1.004	2.88	112	2.02	.225	10	.164	7	9	0.8
1989 NY-N	13	11	.542	31	31	5	2	0	192	179	83	74	16	2	78	95	1.339	3.47	94	3.58	.245	7	.106	-3	8	-0.5
1990 NY-N	7	6	.538	38	12	0	0	0	118	123	53	48	10	2	40	62	1.381	3.66	102	4.05	.272	4	.133	3	6	0.2
1991 LA-N	12	9	.571	31	31	2	1	0	189^1	181	78	67	15	3	70	120	1.326	3.18	113	3.57	.257	9	.161	8	12	1.0
1992 LA-N	6	9	.400	29	29	2	1	0	166^1	169	80	67	8	1	81	94	**1.503**	3.63	95	4.08	.268	5	.102	1	6	0.0
1993 Cle-A	2	1	.667	9	7	0	0	0	43	48	22	21	5	0	21	27	1.605	4.40	98	5.22	.289	0	....	-0	2	0.0
1994 NY-A	0	0	....	2	2	0	0	0	3	11	8	8	1	0	6	3	5.667	24.00	19	36.34	.611	0	....	-7	0	-0.6
Total 15	115	98	.540	351	291	41	16	1	1884^1	1833	856	764	145	24	676	1128	1.332	3.65	104	3.69	.257	44	.127	47	104	4.5
• OKRIE, Frank				Frank Anthony "Lefty" Okrie b: 10/28/1896, Detroit, MI d: 10/16/1959, Detroit, MI BL/TL, 5'11", 175 lbs. Deb: 4/20/1920																						
1920 Det-A	1	2	.333	21	1	1	0	0	41	44	29	24	2	5	18	9	1.512	5.27	71	4.99	.295	1	.200	-6	1	-0.6
• OLDHAM, Red				John Cyrus Oldham b: 7/15/1893, Zion, MD d: 1/28/1961, Costa Mesa, CA BB/TL, 6', 176 lbs. Deb: 8/19/1914																						
1914 Det-A	2	4	.333	9	7	3	0	0	45^1	42	22	17	1	3	8	23	1.103	3.38	83	2.56	.243	4	.267	-2	2	-0.1
1915 Det-A	3	0	1.000	17	2	1	0	4	57^2	52	22	18	1	4	17	17	1.197	2.81	108	2.86	.243	2	.143	3	5	0.3
1920 Det-A	8	13	.381	39	22	10	1	1	215^1	248	132	92	5	6	91	62	1.574	3.85	97	4.64	.302	12	.174	1	9	0.0
1921 Det-A	11	14	.440	40	28	12	1	1	229^1	258	129	108	11	6	81	67	1.478	4.24	101	4.21	.288	19	.224	6	11	0.8
1922 Det-A	10	13	.435	43	28	9	0	3	212	256	130	110	14	11	59	72	1.486	4.67	83	4.65	.305	19	.260	-14	9	-1.0
1925★ Pit-N	3	2	.600	11	4	3	0	1	53	66	27	23	2	2	18	10	1.585	3.91	114	4.96	.313	6	.333	2	4	0.4
1926 Pit-N	2	2	.500	17	2	0	0	2	41^2	56	27	26	1	1	18	16	1.776	5.62	70	5.92	.359	2	.222	-8	1	-0.8
Total 7	39	48	.448	176	93	38	2	12	854^1	978	489	394	35	33	292	267	1.487	4.15	93	4.38	.295	64	.226	-13	41	-0.4
• OLIN, Steve				Steven Robert Olin b: 10/4/1965, Portland, OR d: 3/22/1993, Little Lake Nellie, FL BR/TR, 6'3", 185 lbs. Deb: 7/29/1989																						
1989 Cle-A	1	4	.200	25	0	0	0	1	36	35	16	15	1	0	14	24	1.361	3.75	106	3.33	.255	0	....	1	2	0.1
1990 Cle-A	4	4	.500	50	1	0	0	1	92^1	96	41	35	3	6	26	64	1.321	3.41	115	3.60	.270	0	....	7	6	0.7
1991 Cle-A	3	6	.333	48	0	0	0	17	56^1	61	26	21	2	1	23	38	1.491	3.36	124	3.94	.274	0	....	6	6	0.6
1992 Cle-A	8	5	.615	72	0	0	0	29	88^1	80	25	23	8	4	27	47	1.211	2.34	167	3.30	.248	0	....	16	14	1.6
Total 4	16	19	.457	195	1	0	0	48	273	272	108	94	14	11	90	173	1.326	3.10	128	3.54	.262	0	....	30	28	3.0
• OLIVARES, Omar				Omar (Palqu) Olivares b: 7/6/1967, Mayaguez, Puerto Rico BR/TR, 6'1", 193 lbs. Deb: 8/18/1990																						
1990 StL-N	1	1	.500	9	6	0	0	0	49^1	45	17	16	2	2	17	20	1.257	2.92	131	3.26	.249	3	.176	5	4	0.6
1991 StL-N	11	7	.611	28	24	0	0	1	167^1	148	72	69	13	5	61	91	1.249	3.71	100	3.35	.243	12	.226	-2	10	0.1
1992 StL-N	9	9	.500	32	30	1	0	0	197	189	84	84	20	4	63	124	1.279	3.84	88	3.65	.257	16	.235	-12	9	-0.9
1993 StL-N	5	3	.625	58	9	0	0	1	118^2	134	60	55	10	9	54	63	1.584	4.17	95	5.16	.288	7	.269	-3	6	-0.1
1994 StL-N	3	4	.429	14	12	1	0	1	73^2	84	53	47	10	4	37	26	1.643	5.74	72	5.92	.294	6	.214	-13	1	-1.1
1995 Col-N	1	3	.250	11	6	0	0	0	31^2	44	28	26	4	2	21	15	2.053	7.39	73	8.49	.349	1	.143	-6	0	-0.6
Phi-N	0	1	.000	5	0	0	0	0	10	11	6	6	1	1	2	7	1.300	5.40	78	4.14	.282	1	.500	-1	0	0.0
Yr.	1	4	.200	16	6	0	0	0	41^2	55	34	32	5	3	23	22	1.872	6.91	74	7.45	.333	2	.222	-8	0	-0.6
1996 Det-A	7	11	.389	25	25	4	0	0	160	169	90	87	16	9	75	81	1.525	4.89	103	4.92	.275	0	....	6	7	0.6
1997 Det-A	5	6	.455	19	19	3	2	0	115	110	68	60	8	9	53	74	1.417	4.70	98	4.17	.253	2	.667	-3	6	-0.1
Sea-A	1	4	.200	13	12	0	0	0	62^1	81	41	38	10	4	28	29	1.749	5.49	82	6.77	.315	1	.500	-6	2	-0.6
Yr.	6	10	.375	32	31	3	2	0	177^1	191	109	98	18	13	81	103	1.534	4.97	92	5.09	.276	3	.600	-9	8	-0.7
1998 Ana-A	9	9	.500	37	26	1	0	0	183	189	92	82	19	5	91	112	1.530	4.03	116	4.85	.270	0	.000	15	11	1.4
1999 Ana-A	8	9	.471	20	20	3	0	0	131	135	62	59	11	6	49	49	1.405	4.05	119	4.32	.273	2	.333	10	10	1.0
Oak-A	7	2	.778	12	12	1	0	0	74^2	82	43	36	8	3	32	36	1.527	4.34	107	5.08	.283	0	....	3	5	0.3
Yr.	15	11	.577	32	32	4	0	0	205^2	217	105	95	19	9	81	85	1.449	4.16	115	4.59	.276	2	.333	13	15	1.3
2000 Oak-A	4	8	.333	21	16	1	0	0	108	134	86	81	10	7	60	57	1.796	6.75	70	6.42	.309	1	1.000	-23	1	-2.0
2001 Pit-N	6	9	.400	45	12	1	0	1	110	123	87	80	17	10	42	69	1.500	6.55	69	5.34	.283	6	.222	-25	1	-2.2
Total 12	77	86	.472	349	229	16	2	4	1591^2	1678	889	826	159	80	685	853	1.485	4.67	93	4.78	.275	58	.240	-54	73	-3.6
• OLIVER, Darren				Darren Christopher Oliver b: 10/6/1970, Kansas City, MO BR/TL, 6', 200 lbs. Deb: 9/1/1993																						
1993 Tex-A	0	0	....	2	0	0	0	0	3^1	2	1	1	1	0	1	4	.900	2.70	154	2.15	.154	0	....	1	0	0.1
1994 Tex-A	4	0	1.000	43	0	0	0	2	50	40	24	19	4	6	35	50	1.500	3.42	141	4.29	.223	0	....	9	5	0.8
1995 Tex-A	4	2	.667	17	7	0	0	0	49	47	25	23	3	1	32	39	1.612	4.22	114	4.59	.257	0	....	3	4	0.3
1996★ Tex-A	14	6	.700	30	30	1	1	0	173^2	190	97	90	20	10	76	112	1.532	4.66	112	5.10	.279	0	....	11	12	1.0
1997 Tex-A	13	12	.520	32	32	3	1	0	201^1	213	111	94	29	11	82	104	1.465	4.20	114	4.98	.271	1	.500	16	12	1.6
1998 Tex-A	6	7	.462	19	19	2	0	0	103^1	140	84	75	11	10	43	58	1.771	6.53	74	6.68	.325	1	.167	-18	2	-1.7
StL-N	4	4	.500	10	10	0	0	0	57	64	31	27	7	0	23	29	1.526	4.26	98	4.85	.283	2	.087	-0	2	-0.1
1999 StL-N	9	9	.500	30	30	2	1	0	196^1	197	96	93	16	11	74	119	1.380	4.26	107	4.11	.265	20	.274	7	13	1.2
2000 Tex-A	2	9	.182	21	21	0	0	0	108	151	95	89	16	4	42	49	1.787	7.42	67	7.04	.339	0	.000	-27	0	-2.5
2001 Tex-A	11	11	.500	28	28	1	0	0	154	189	109	103	23	6	65	104	1.649	6.02	77	6.14	.305	2	.333	-22	3	-2.0
2002 Bos-A	4	5	.444	14	9	1	1	0	58	70	30	30	7	6	27	32	1.672	4.66	97	6.49	.317	0	.000	-2	3	-0.2
2003 Col-N	13	11	.542	33	32	1	0	0	180^1	201	108	101	21	8	61	88	1.453	5.04	97	4.80	.284	17	.254	1	10	0.5
Total 11	84	76	.525	279	218	11	4	2	1334^1	1504	811	745	158	73	561	788	1.548	5.02	96	5.29	.287	43	.239	-21	66	-1.0
• OLIVERAS, Francisco				Francisco Javier (Noa) Oliveras b: 1/31/1963, Santurce, Puerto Rico BR/TR, 5'10", 170 lbs. Deb: 5/3/1989																						
1989 Min-A	3	4	.429	12	8	1	0	0	55^2	64	28	28	8	1	15	24	1.419	4.53	91	4.85	.288	0	....	-2	3	-0.2
1990 SF-N	2	2	.500	33	2	0	0	2	55^1	47	22	17	5	2	21	41	1.229	2.77	132	3.10	.230	0	.000	5	4	0.5
1991 SF-N	6	6	.500	55	1	0	0	3	79^1	69	36	34	12	1	22	48	1.147	3.86	93	3.31	.242	2	.200	-3	5	-0.3
1992 SF-N	0	3	.000	16	7	0	0	0	44^2	41	19	18	11	1	10	17	1.142	3.63	91	3.99	.250	1	.143	-3	1	-0.2
Total 4	11	15	.423	116	18	1	0	5	235	221	105	97	36	5	68	130	1.230	3.71	99	3.75	.253	3	.136	-3	13	-0.3

• OLIVO, Chi-Chi
Federico Emilio (Maldonado) Olivo
b: 3/18/1928, Guayubin, Dominican Republic d: 2/3/1977, Guayubin, Dominican Republic BR/TR, 6'2", 215 lbs. Deb: 6/5/1961

YEAR	TM-L	W	L	PCT	G	GS	CG	SH	SV	IP	H	R	ER	HR	HB	BB	SO	RAT	ERA	ERA+	CERA	OAV	BH	AVG	PR+	WS	TPW
1961	Mil-N	0	0	....	3	0	0	0	0	2	3	4	4	1	0	5	1	4.000	18.00	21	23.54	.500	0	....	-3	0	-0.3
1964	Mil-N	2	1	.667	38	0	0	0	5	60	55	25	25	7	0	21	45	1.267	3.75	94	3.41	.247	1	.250	-2	4	-0.2
1965	Mil-N	0	1	.000	8	0	0	0	0	13	12	2	2	1	0	5	11	1.308	1.38	254	3.26	.267	0	....	3	1	0.3
1966	Atl-N	5	4	.556	47	0	0	0	7	66	59	34	31	4	1	19	41	1.182	4.23	86	2.73	.240	1	.111	-4	4	-0.5
Total	**4**	**7**	**6**	**.538**	**96**	**0**	**0**	**0**	**12**	**141**	**129**	**65**	**62**	**13**	**1**	**50**	**98**	**1.270**	**3.96**	**91**	**3.37**	**.248**	**2**	**.154**	**-6**	**9**	**-0.7**

• OLIVO, Diomedes
Diomedes Antonio (Maldonado) Olivo
b: 1/22/1919, Guayubin, Dominican Republic d: 2/15/1977, Santo Domingo, Dominican Republic BL/TL, 6'1", 195 lbs. Deb: 9/5/1960

YEAR	TM-L	W	L	PCT	G	GS	CG	SH	SV	IP	H	R	ER	HR	HB	BB	SO	RAT	ERA	ERA+	CERA	OAV	BH	AVG	PR+	WS	TPW
1960	Pit-N	0	0	....	4	0	0	0	0	9^{2}	8	3	3	1	0	5	10	1.345	2.79	134	3.36	.216	0	.000	1	1	0.1
1962	Pit-N	5	1	.833	62	1	0	0	7	84^{1}	88	30	26	5	0	25	66	1.340	2.77	142	3.52	.277	3	.188	10	9	1.1
1963	StL-N	0	5	.000	19	0	0	0	0	13^{1}	16	9	8	1	1	9	9	1.875	5.40	66	6.18	.296	0	....	-3	0	-0.3
Total	**3**	**5**	**6**	**.455**	**85**	**1**	**0**	**0**	**7**	107^{1}	**112**	**42**	**37**	**7**	**1**	**39**	**85**	**1.407**	**3.10**	**123**	**3.84**	**.274**	**3**	**.176**	**8**	**10**	**0.8**

• OLLOM, Jim
James Donald Ollom b: 7/8/1945, Snohomish, WA BR/TL, 6'4", 210 lbs. Deb: 9/3/1966

YEAR	TM-L	W	L	PCT	G	GS	CG	SH	SV	IP	H	R	ER	HR	HB	BB	SO	RAT	ERA	ERA+	CERA	OAV	BH	AVG	PR+	WS	TPW
1966	Min-A	0	0	....	3	1	0	0	0	10	6	4	4	1	1	1	11	.700	3.60	100	1.46	.167	0	.000	0	1	0.0
1967	Min-A	0	1	.000	21	2	0	0	0	35	33	24	21	4	4	11	17	1.257	5.40	64	3.95	.258	1	.200	-7	0	-0.8
Total	**2**	**0**	**1**	**.000**	**24**	**3**	**0**	**0**	**0**	**45**	**39**	**28**	**25**	**5**	**5**	**12**	**28**	**1.133**	**5.00**	**70**	**3.40**	**.238**	**1**	**.143**	**-7**	**1**	**-0.8**

• OLMSTEAD, Fred
Frederic William Olmstead b: 7/3/1881, Grand Rapids, MI d: 10/22/1936, Muskogee, OK BR/TR, 5'11", 170 lbs. Deb: 7/2/1908

YEAR	TM-L	W	L	PCT	G	GS	CG	SH	SV	IP	H	R	ER	HR	HB	BB	SO	RAT	ERA	ERA+	CERA	OAV	BH	AVG	PR+	WS	TPW
1908	Chi-A	0	0	....	1	0	0	0	0	2	6	3	3	0	0	1	1	3.500	13.50	17	19.99	.600	0	.000	-2	0	-0.2
1909	Chi-A	3	2	.600	8	6	5	0	0	54^{2}	52	17	11	1	1	12	21	1.171	1.81	129	2.99	.277	2	.095	3	4	0.2
1910	Chi-A	10	12	.455	32	20	14	4	0	184^{1}	174	64	40	1	4	50	68	1.215	1.95	123	2.87	.260	10	.154	10	11	0.9
1911	Chi-A	6	6	.500	25	11	7	1	2	117^{2}	146	78	55	3	6	30	45	1.496	4.21	77	4.58	.309	7	.189	-13	3	-1.2
Total	**4**	**19**	**20**	**.487**	**66**	**37**	**26**	**5**	**2**	358^{2}	**378**	**162**	**109**	**5**	**11**	**93**	**135**	**1.313**	**2.74**	**100**	**3.54**	**.282**	**19**	**.153**	**-2**	**18**	**-0.3**

• OLMSTED, Al
Alan Ray Olmsted b: 3/18/1957, St. Louis, MO BR/TL, 6'2", 195 lbs. Deb: 9/12/1980

YEAR	TM-L	W	L	PCT	G	GS	CG	SH	SV	IP	H	R	ER	HR	HB	BB	SO	RAT	ERA	ERA+	CERA	OAV	BH	AVG	PR+	WS	TPW
1980	StL-N	1	1	.500	5	5	0	0	0	34^{2}	32	13	11	2	1	14	14	1.327	2.86	129	3.46	.244	2	.182	3	2	0.3

• OLMSTED, Hank
Henry Theodore Olmsted b: 1/12/1879, Sac Bay, MI d: 1/6/1969, Bradenton, FL BR/TR, 5'8.5", 147 lbs. Deb: 7/15/1905

YEAR	TM-L	W	L	PCT	G	GS	CG	SH	SV	IP	H	R	ER	HR	HB	BB	SO	RAT	ERA	ERA+	CERA	OAV	BH	AVG	PR+	WS	TPW
1905	Bos-A	1	2	.333	3	3	3	0	0	25	18	10	9	0	0	12	6	1.200	3.24	83	2.17	.204	1	.125	-1	1	-0.2

• OLSEN, Kevin
Kevin Gary Olsen b: 7/26/1976, Covina, CA BR/TR, 6'2", 200 lbs. Deb: 9/7/2001

YEAR	TM-L	W	L	PCT	G	GS	CG	SH	SV	IP	H	R	ER	HR	HB	BB	SO	RAT	ERA	ERA+	CERA	OAV	BH	AVG	PR+	WS	TPW
2001	Fla-N	0	0	....	4	2	0	0	0	15	11	2	2	0	0	2	13	.867	1.20	351	1.34	.204	0	.000	5	2	0.4
2002	Fla-N	0	5	.000	17	8	0	0	0	55^{2}	57	31	28	5	1	31	38	1.581	4.53	87	4.81	.270	1	.083	-4	1	-0.5
2003	Fla-N	0	0	....	7	0	0	0	0	12	25	18	17	2	0	4	12	2.417	12.75	32	11.54	.431	0	....	-12	0	-1.1
Total	**3**	**0**	**5**	**.000**	**28**	**10**	**0**	**0**	**0**	82^{2}	**93**	**51**	**47**	**7**	**1**	**37**	**63**	**1.573**	**5.12**	**78**	**5.16**	**.288**	**1**	**.067**	**-11**	**3**	**-1.2**

• OLSEN, Ole
Arthur Ole Olsen b: 9/12/1894, South Norwalk, CT d: 9/12/1980, Norwalk, CT BR/TR, 5'10", 163 lbs. Deb: 4/12/1922

YEAR	TM-L	W	L	PCT	G	GS	CG	SH	SV	IP	H	R	ER	HR	HB	BB	SO	RAT	ERA	ERA+	CERA	OAV	BH	AVG	PR+	WS	TPW
1922	Det-A	7	6	.538	37	15	5	0	3	137	147	84	69	8	14	40	52	1.365	4.53	85	4.07	.281	7	.179	-7	5	-0.8
1923	Det-A	1	1	.500	17	2	1	0	0	41^{1}	42	30	29	1	5	17	12	1.427	6.31	61	4.07	.290	1	.125	-11	0	-1.1
Total	**2**	**8**	**7**	**.533**	**54**	**17**	**6**	**0**	**3**	178^{1}	**189**	**114**	**98**	**9**	**19**	**57**	**64**	**1.379**	**4.95**	**78**	**4.07**	**.283**	**8**	**.170**	**-18**	**5**	**-2.0**

• OLSEN, Vern
Vern Jarl Olsen b: 3/16/1918, Hillsboro, OR d: 7/13/1989, Maywood, IL BR/TL, 6'.5", 175 lbs. Deb: 9/8/1939

YEAR	TM-L	W	L	PCT	G	GS	CG	SH	SV	IP	H	R	ER	HR	HB	BB	SO	RAT	ERA	ERA+	CERA	OAV	BH	AVG	PR+	WS	TPW
1939	Chi-N	1	0	1.000	4	0	0	0	0	7^{2}	2	0	0	0	0	7	3	1.174	0.00	....	1.47	.087	0	.000	4	2	0.4
1940	Chi-N	13	9	.591	34	20	9	4	0	172^{2}	172	64	57	5	2	62	71	1.355	2.97	126	3.37	.260	15	.263	16	15	1.9
1941	Chi-N	10	8	.556	37	23	10	2	1	185^{2}	202	84	65	7	1	59	73	1.406	3.15	111	3.71	.276	15	.238	12	12	1.6
1942	Chi-N	6	9	.400	32	17	4	1	1	140^{1}	161	75	70	6	1	55	46	1.539	4.49	71	4.31	.283	9	.188	-17	4	-1.7
1946	Chi-N	0	0	....	5	0	0	0	0	9^{2}	10	3	3	0	0	9	8	1.966	2.79	119	5.65	.294	0	....	1	1	0.1
Total	**5**	**30**	**26**	**.536**	**112**	**60**	**23**	**7**	**2**	**516**	**547**	**226**	**195**	**18**	**4**	**192**	**201**	**1.432**	**3.40**	**101**	**3.76**	**.271**	**39**	**.231**	**15**	**34**	**2.3**

• OLSON, Gregg
Greggory William Olson b: 10/11/1966, Scribner, NE BR/TR, 6'4", 206 lbs. Deb: 9/2/1988

YEAR	TM-L	W	L	PCT	G	GS	CG	SH	SV	IP	H	R	ER	HR	HB	BB	SO	RAT	ERA	ERA+	CERA	OAV	BH	AVG	PR+	WS	TPW
1988	Bal-A	1	1	.500	10	0	0	0	0	11	10	4	4	1	0	10	9	1.818	3.27	119	5.42	.244	0	....	1	1	0.1
1989	Bal-A	5	2	.714	64	0	0	0	27	85	57	17	16	1	1	46	90	1.212	1.69	224	2.13	.188	0	....	19	18	2.0
1990	Bal-A★	6	5	.545	64	0	0	0	37	74^{1}	57	20	20	3	3	31	74	1.184	2.42	157	2.63	.213	0	....	11	14	1.1
1991	Bal-A	4	6	.400	72	0	0	0	31	73^{2}	74	28	26	1	1	29	72	1.398	3.18	124	3.39	.261	0	....	6	10	0.6
1992	Bal-A	1	5	.167	60	0	0	0	36	61^{1}	46	14	14	3	0	24	58	1.141	2.05	196	2.48	.211	0	....	13	13	1.3
1993	Bal-A	0	2	.000	50	0	0	0	29	45	37	9	8	1	0	18	44	1.222	1.60	279	2.49	.223	0	.000	14	10	1.3
1994	Atl-N	0	2	.000	16	0	0	0	1	14^{2}	19	15	15	1	1	13	10	2.182	9.20	46	7.28	.317	0	.000	-8	0	-0.8
1995	Cle-A	0	0	....	3	0	0	0	0	2^{2}	5	4	4	1	0	2	0	2.625	13.50	35	14.88	.417	0	....	-3	0	-0.2
	KC-A	3	3	.500	20	0	0	0	3	30^{1}	23	11	11	3	0	17	21	1.319	3.26	147	3.31	.215	0	....	5	4	0.4
	Yr.	3	3	.500	23	0	0	0	3	33	28	15	15	4	0	19	21	1.424	4.09	116	4.25	.235	0	....	2	4	0.2
1996	Det-A	3	0	1.000	43	0	0	0	8	43	43	25	24	6	1	28	29	1.651	5.02	101	5.34	.259	0	....	1	3	0.1
	Hou-N	1	0	1.000	9	0	0	0	0	9^{1}	12	5	5	1	0	7	8	2.036	4.82	80	6.71	.308	0	....	-1	1	-0.1
1997	Min-A	0	0	....	11	0	0	0	0	8^{1}	19	17	17	0	0	11	6	3.600	18.36	25	15.24	.432	0	....	-13	0	-1.2
	KC-A	4	3	.571	34	0	0	0	1	41^{2}	39	18	14	3	1	17	28	1.344	3.02	156	3.71	.260	0	....	7	4	0.7
	Yr.	4	3	.571	45	0	0	0	1	50	58	35	31	3	1	28	34	1.720	5.58	84	5.63	.299	0	....	-5	4	-0.5
1998	Ari-N	3	4	.429	64	0	0	0	30	68^{2}	56	25	23	4	1	25	55	1.180	3.01	140	2.74	.223	1	.500	9	12	1.0
1999*	Ari-N	9	4	.692	61	0	0	0	14	60^{2}	54	28	25	9	2	25	45	1.302	3.71	123	3.94	.238	0	....	6	9	0.6
2000	LA-N	0	1	.000	13	0	0	0	0	17^{2}	21	11	10	4	1	7	15	1.585	5.09	85	6.32	.296	0	....	-1	0	-0.1
2001	LA-N	0	1	.000	28	0	0	0	0	24^{2}	26	24	22	4	0	20	24	1.865	8.03	50	6.36	.268	0	....	-11	0	-1.1
Total	**14**	**40**	**39**	**.506**	**622**	**0**	**0**	**0**	**217**	**672**	**598**	**275**	**258**	**46**	**12**	**330**	**588**	**1.381**	**3.46**	**124**	**3.67**	**.239**	**1**	**.250**	**55**	**99**	**5.7**

• OLSON, Ted
Theodore Otto Olson b: 8/27/1912, Quincy, MA d: 12/9/1980, Weymouth, MA BR/TR, 6'2.5", 185 lbs. Deb: 6/21/1936

YEAR	TM-L	W	L	PCT	G	GS	CG	SH	SV	IP	H	R	ER	HR	HB	BB	SO	RAT	ERA	ERA+	CERA	OAV	BH	AVG	PR+	WS	TPW
1936	Bos-A	1	1	.500	5	3	1	0	0	18^{1}	24	16	15	3	0	8	5	1.745	7.36	72	6.45	.324	1	.143	-4	0	-0.4
1937	Bos-A	0	0	....	11	0	0	0	0	32^{1}	42	28	26	4	0	15	11	1.763	7.24	66	6.10	.318	3	.300	-8	0	-0.7
1938	Bos-A	0	0	....	2	0	0	0	0	7	9	5	5	0	0	2	2	1.571	6.43	77	4.46	.310	0	.000	-1	0	-0.1
Total	**3**	**1**	**1**	**.500**	**18**	**3**	**1**	**0**	**0**	57^{2}	**75**	**49**	**46**	**7**	**0**	**25**	**18**	**1.734**	**7.18**	**69**	**6.01**	**.319**	**4**	**.222**	**-14**	**0**	**-1.2**

• OLWINE, Ed
Edward R. Olwine b: 5/28/1958, Greenville, OH BL/TL, 6'2", 165 lbs. Deb: 6/2/1986

YEAR	TM-L	W	L	PCT	G	GS	CG	SH	SV	IP	H	R	ER	HR	HB	BB	SO	RAT	ERA	ERA+	CERA	OAV	BH	AVG	PR+	WS	TPW
1986	Atl-N	0	0	....	37	0	0	0	1	47^{2}	35	20	18	5	1	17	37	1.091	3.40	117	2.48	.207	1	.333	4	4	0.4
1987	Atl-N	0	1	.000	27	0	0	0	1	23^{1}	25	16	13	4	1	8	12	1.414	5.01	87	4.76	.269	0	....	-2	1	-0.2
1988	Atl-N	0	0	....	16	0	0	0	1	18^{2}	22	15	14	4	1	4	5	1.393	6.75	54	5.25	.286	0	....	-6	0	-0.7
Total	**3**	**0**	**1**	**.000**	**80**	**0**	**0**	**0**	**3**	89^{2}	**82**	**51**	**45**	**13**	**3**	**29**	**54**	**1.238**	**4.52**	**88**	**3.65**	**.242**	**1**	**.333**	**-4**	**5**	**-0.4**

• O'NEAL, Randy
Randall Jeffrey O'Neal b: 8/30/1960, Ashland, KY BR/TR, 6'2", 195 lbs. Deb: 9/12/1984

YEAR	TM-L	W	L	PCT	G	GS	CG	SH	SV	IP	H	R	ER	HR	HB	BB	SO	RAT	ERA	ERA+	CERA	OAV	BH	AVG	PR+	WS	TPW
1984	Det-A	2	1	.667	4	3	0	0	0	18^{2}	16	7	7	0	0	6	12	1.179	3.38	116	2.33	.222	0	....	1	1	0.1
1985	Det-A	5	5	.500	28	12	1	0	1	94^{1}	82	42	34	8	2	36	52	1.251	3.24	126	3.30	.240	0	....	9	7	0.8
1986	Det-A	3	7	.300	37	11	1	0	2	122^{2}	121	69	59	13	3	44	68	1.345	4.33	95	3.88	.260	0	....	-4	4	-0.4
1987	Atl-N	4	2	.667	16	10	0	0	0	61	79	41	38	12	2	24	33	1.689	5.61	77	6.68	.316	2	.105	-8	2	-0.9
	StL-N	0	0	....	1	1	0	0	0	5	2	1	1	0	0	2	4	.800	1.80	231	0.86	.111	1	1.000	1	1	0.2
	Yr.	4	2	.667	17	11	0	0	0	66	81	42	39	12	2	26	37	1.621	5.32	82	6.24	.302	3	.150	-7	3	-0.7
1988	StL-N	2	3	.400	10	8	0	0	0	53	57	29	27	7	2	10	20	1.264	4.58	76	4.03	.274	0	.000	-7	1	-1.0
1989	Phi-N	0	1	.000	20	1	0	0	0	39	46	28	27	5	0	9	29	1.410	6.23	57	4.57	.301	0	.000	-11	0	-1.3
1990	SF-N	1	0	1.000	26	0	0	0	0	47	58	23	20	3	0	18	30	1.617	3.83	95	5.03	.314	1	.167	-1	2	-0.1
Total	**7**	**17**	**19**	**.472**	**142**	**46**	**2**	**0**	**3**	440^{2}	**461**	**240**	**213**	**48**	**9**	**149**	**248**	**1.384**	**4.35**	**90**	**4.25**	**.272**	**4**	**.080**	**-21**	**18**	**-2.5**

• O'NEAL, Skinny
Oran Herbert O'Neal b: 5/2/1899, Gatewood, MO d: 6/2/1981, Springfield, MO BR/TR, 5'11", 160 lbs. Deb: 4/18/1925

YEAR	TM-L	W	L	PCT	G	GS	CG	SH	SV	IP	H	R	ER	HR	HB	BB	SO	RAT	ERA	ERA+	CERA	OAV	BH	AVG	PR+	WS	TPW
1925	Phi-N	0	0	....	11	1	0	0	0	20^{1}	35	23	21	2	0	12	6	2.311	9.30	51	9.57	.407	1	.167	-9	0	-0.9

YEAR	TM-L	W	L	PCT	G	GS	CG	SH	SV	IP	H	R	ER	HR	HB	BB	SO	RAT	ERA	ERA+	CERA	OAV	BH	AVG	PR+	WS	TPW
1927	Phi-N	0	0	....	2	0	0	0	0	5	9	5	5	0	0	2	2	2.200	9.00	46	8.15	.409	0	.000	-3	0	-0.3
Total	2	0	0	....	13	1	0	0	0	25^1	44	28	26	2	0	14	8	2.289	9.24	50	9.29	.407	1	.143	-12	0	-1.2
• O'NEIL, Ed	Edward J. O'Neil b: 3/11/1859, Fall River, MA d: 9/30/1892, Fall River, MA TR, 5'11", 180 lbs. Deb: 6/20/1890																										
1890	Tol-a	0	2	.000	2	2	2	0	0	16	27	18	14	0	0	13	2	2.500	7.88	50	....	.363	0	.000	-7	0	-0.8
	Phi-a	0	6	.000	6	6	6	0	0	52	84	77	56	0	7	32	17	2.231	9.69	39	....	.353	5	.161	-31	0	-3.0
	Yr.	0	8	.000	8	8	8	0	0	68	111	95	70	0	7	45	19	2.294	9.26	42	....	.356	5	.125	-38	0	-3.8
• O'NEILL, Emmett	Robert Emmett "Pinky" O'Neill b: 1/13/1918, San Mateo, CA d: 10/11/1993, Sparks, NV BR/TR, 6'3", 180 lbs. Deb: 8/3/1943																										
1943	Bos-A	1	4	.200	11	5	1	0	0	57^2	56	31	29	3	1	46	20	1.769	4.53	73	4.89	.256	3	.188	-8	1	-0.8
1944	Bos-A	6	11	.353	28	22	8	1	0	151^2	154	88	78	6	2	89	68	1.602	4.63	73	4.36	.265	10	.182	-21	3	-2.2
1945	Bos-A	8	11	.421	24	22	10	1	0	141^2	134	87	81	5	5	117	55	1.772	5.15	66	4.92	.258	9	.180	-29	2	-2.8
1946	Chi-N	0	0	....	1	0	0	0	0	1	0	0	0	0	0	3	1	3.000	0.00	....	5.85	.000	0	....	0	0	0.0
	Chi-A	0	0	....	2	0	0	0	0	3^2	4	2	0	0	0	5	0	2.455	0.00	....	7.84	.333	0	.000	1	0	0.1
Total	4	15	26	.366	66	49	19	2	0	355^2	348	208	188	14	8	260	144	1.709	4.76	71	4.70	.261	22	.180	-56	6	-5.7
• O'NEILL, Harry	Joseph Henry O'Neill b: 11/20/1892, Lindsay, Canada d: 9/5/1969, Ridgetown, Canada BR/TR, 6', 180 lbs. Deb: 9/15/1922																										
1922	Phi-A	0	0	....	1	0	0	0	0	3	2	1	1	0	1	1	0	1.000	3.00	141	2.62	.200	0	.000	0	0	0.0
1923	Phi-A	0	0	....	3	0	0	0	0	2	1	0	0	0	0	3	2	2.000	0.00	....	4.52	.167	0	....	1	0	0.1
Total	2	0	0	....	4	0	0	0	0	5	3	1	1	0	1	4	2	1.400	1.80	236	3.38	.188	0	.000	1	0	0.1
• O'NEILL, J.	J. O'Neill b: Brooklyn, NY Deb: 8/20/1875																										
1875	Atl-n	0	4	.000	5	4	3	0	0	34	56	....	19	2	....	0	14	1.647	5.03	48	....	.338	2	.077	-7	....	-0.8
• O'NEILL, Mike	Michael Joyce O'Neill b: 9/7/1877, Maam, Ireland d: 8/12/1959, Scranton, PA BR/TR, 5'11", 185 lbs. Deb: 9/20/1901 U ♦																										
1901	StL-N	2	2	.500	5	4	4	1	0	41	29	12	6	2	5	10	16	.951	1.32	241	2.07	.198	6	.400	8	5	1.0
1902	StL-N	16	15	.516	36	32	29	2	2	288^1	297	136	93	3	12	66	105	1.259	2.90	94	3.08	.266	43	.319	0	18	1.4
1903	StL-N	4	13	.235	19	17	12	0	0	145	184	124	61	2	6	43	39	1.566	3.79	86	4.61	.304	25	.227	-11	4	-0.9
1904	StL-N	10	14	.417	25	24	23	1	0	220	229	86	51	1	3	50	68	1.268	2.09	129	2.96	.262	21	.231	19	17	2.7
Total	4	32	44	.421	85	77	68	4	2	694^1	739	358	211	8	26	169	228	1.308	2.73	105	3.30	.270	97	.255	15	44	4.1
• O'NEILL, Tip	James Edward O'Neill b: 5/25/1858, Woodstock, Canada d: 12/31/1915, Montreal, Canada BR/TR, 6'1.5", 167 lbs. Deb: 5/5/1883 ♦																										
1883	NY-N	5	12	.294	19	19	15	0	0	148	182	129	67	5	....	64	55	1.662	4.07	76	....	.286	15	.197	-17	5	-1.7
1884	StL-a	11	4	.733	17	14	14	0	0	141	125	95	42	3	4	51	36	1.248	2.68	121	....	.225	82	.276	5	21	1.0
Total	2	16	16	.500	36	33	29	0	0	289	307	224	109	8	4	115	91	1.460	3.39	93	....	.257	1435	.334	-11	26	-0.7
• ONTIVEROS, Steve	Steven Ontiveros b: 3/5/1961, Tularosa, NM BR/TR, 6', 190 lbs. Deb: 6/14/1985																										
1985	Oak-A	1	3	.250	39	0	0	0	8	74^2	45	17	16	4	2	19	36	.857	1.93	200	1.48	.174	0	....	17	9	1.6
1986	Oak-A	2	2	.500	46	0	0	0	10	72^2	72	40	38	10	1	25	54	1.335	4.71	82	4.13	.265	0	....	-7	4	-0.7
1987	Oak-A	10	8	.556	35	22	2	1	1	150^2	141	78	67	19	4	50	97	1.268	4.00	103	3.64	.242	0	....	4	8	0.3
1988	Oak-A	3	4	.429	10	10	0	0	0	54^2	57	32	28	4	0	21	30	1.427	4.61	82	3.95	.265	0	....	-6	1	-0.6
1989	Phi-N	2	1	.667	6	5	0	0	0	30^2	34	15	13	2	0	15	12	1.598	3.82	93	4.88	.288	1	.083	-1	1	-0.1
1990	Phi-N	0	0	....	5	0	0	0	0	10	9	3	3	1	0	3	6	1.200	2.70	142	3.00	.225	0	....	1	1	0.1
1993	Sea-A	0	2	.000	14	0	0	0	0	18	18	3	2	0	0	6	13	1.333	1.00	440	3.16	.277	0	....	7	2	0.7
1994	Oak-A	6	4	.600	27	13	2	0	0	115^1	93	39	34	7	6	26	56	1.032	**2.65**	167	**2.35**	.217	0	....	21	10	2.0
1995	Oak-A★	9	6	.600	22	22	2	1	0	129^2	144	75	63	12	4	38	77	1.404	4.37	102	4.38	.283	0	....	1	6	0.1
2000	Bos-A	1	1	.500	3	1	0	0	0	5^1	9	6	6	1	0	4	1	2.438	10.13	50	10.99	.375	0	....	-3	0	-0.3
Total	10	34	31	.523	207	73	6	2	19	661^2	622	308	270	60	17	207	382	1.253	3.67	112	3.49	.248	1	.083	35	42	3.3
• OQUIST, Mike	Michael Lee Oquist b: 5/30/1968, La Junta, CO BR/TR, 6'2", 170 lbs. Deb: 8/14/1993																										
1993	Bal-A	0	0	....	5	0	0	0	0	11^2	12	5	5	0	0	4	8	1.371	3.86	116	3.16	.261	0	....	1	1	0.1
1994	Bal-A	3	3	.500	15	9	0	0	0	58^1	75	41	40	7	6	30	39	1.800	6.17	81	6.76	.319	0	....	-8	1	-0.8
1995	Bal-A	2	1	.667	27	0	0	0	0	54	51	27	25	6	2	41	27	1.704	4.17	114	5.22	.246	0	....	3	3	0.3
1996	SD-N	0	0	....	8	0	0	0	0	7^2	6	2	2	0	0	4	4	1.304	2.35	168	2.50	.231	0	....	1	1	0.1
1997	Oak-A	4	6	.400	19	17	1	0	0	107^2	111	62	60	15	6	43	72	1.430	5.02	90	4.71	.266	1	.250	-4	5	-0.3
1998	Oak-A	7	11	.389	31	29	0	0	0	175	210	125	121	27	5	57	112	1.526	6.22	73	5.47	.298	0	.000	-30	2	-2.9
1999	Oak-A	9	10	.474	28	24	0	0	0	140^2	158	86	84	18	2	64	89	1.578	5.37	86	5.24	.283	0	.000	-11	6	-1.0
Total	7	25	31	.446	133	79	1	0	0	555	623	348	337	73	21	243	351	1.560	5.46	85	5.28	.284	1	.143	-48	19	-4.5
• O'RILEY, Don	Donald Lee O'Riley b: 3/12/1945, Topeka, KS d: 5/2/1997, Kansas City, MO BR/TR, 6'3", 205 lbs. Deb: 6/20/1969																										
1969	KC-A	1	1	.500	18	0	0	0	1	23^1	32	23	18	0	0	15	10	2.014	6.94	53	5.89	.311	0	.000	-8	0	-0.9
1970	KC-A	0	0	....	9	2	0	0	0	23^1	26	15	14	5	1	9	13	1.500	5.40	69	5.58	.277	0	.000	-5	0	-0.5
Total	2	1	1	.500	27	2	0	0	1	46^2	58	38	32	5	1	24	23	1.757	6.17	60	5.73	.294	0	.000	-13	0	-1.4
• OROPESA, Eddie	Edilberto Oropesa b: 11/23/1971, Colon, Cuba BL/TL, 6'3", 215 lbs. Deb: 4/2/2001																										
2001	Phi-N	1	0	1.000	30	0	0	0	0	19	16	10	10	1	0	17	15	1.737	4.74	90	4.20	.232	0	....	-1	1	-0.1
2002	Ari-N	2	0	1.000	32	0	0	0	0	25^1	39	30	29	6	2	15	18	2.132	10.30	43	9.65	.348	0	....	-16	0	-1.6
2003	Ari-N	3	3	.500	47	0	0	0	0	38^2	38	27	25	3	2	27	39	1.681	5.82	80	5.06	.257	0	....	-5	1	-0.5
Total	3	6	3	.667	109	0	0	0	0	83	93	67	64	10	4	59	72	1.831	6.94	65	6.26	.283	0	....	-22	2	-2.2
• OROSCO, Jesse	Jesse Russell Orosco b: 4/21/1957, Santa Barbara, CA BR/TL, 6'2", 185 lbs. Deb: 4/5/1979																										
1979	NY-N	1	2	.333	18	2	0	0	0	35	33	20	19	4	2	22	22	1.571	4.89	74	5.16	.260	0	.000	-5	0	-0.6
1981	NY-N	0	1	.000	8	0	0	0	1	17^1	13	4	3	2	0	6	18	1.096	1.56	224	2.53	.213	0	.000	4	2	0.4
1982	NY-N	4	10	.286	54	2	0	0	4	109^1	92	37	33	7	2	40	89	1.207	2.72	134	2.92	.230	2	.143	12	9	1.3
1983	NY-N★	13	7	.650	62	0	0	0	17	110	76	27	18	3	1	38	84	1.036	1.47	246	1.84	.197	4	.333	25	20	2.8
1984	NY-N★	10	6	.625	60	0	0	0	31	87	58	29	25	7	2	34	85	1.057	2.59	137	2.14	.185	1	.250	9	17	1.1
1985	NY-N	8	6	.571	54	0	0	0	17	79	66	26	24	6	0	34	68	1.266	2.73	126	3.00	.224	3	.429	7	10	0.8
1986*	NY-N	8	6	.571	58	0	0	0	21	81	64	23	21	6	3	35	62	1.222	2.33	152	2.99	.217	0	.000	11	13	1.1
1987	NY-N	3	9	.250	58	0	0	0	16	77	78	41	38	5	2	31	78	1.416	4.44	85	3.81	.266	0	.000	-5	5	-0.6
1988*	LA-N	3	2	.600	55	0	0	0	9	53	41	18	16	4	2	30	43	1.340	2.72	123	3.33	.215	0	.000	4	6	0.4
1989	Cle-A	3	4	.429	69	0	0	0	3	78	54	20	18	7	2	26	79	1.026	2.08	191	2.20	.198	0	....	17	10	1.7
1990	Cle-A	5	4	.556	55	0	0	0	2	64^2	58	35	28	9	0	38	55	1.485	3.90	101	4.25	.239	0	....	1	3	0.1
1991	Cle-A	2	0	1.000	47	0	0	0	0	45^2	52	20	19	4	1	15	36	1.467	3.74	111	4.24	.286	0	....	3	3	0.3
1992	Mil-A	3	1	.750	59	0	0	0	1	39	33	15	14	5	1	13	40	1.179	3.23	119	3.31	.232	0	....	2	3	0.2
1993	Mil-A	3	5	.375	57	0	0	0	8	56^2	47	25	20	2	3	17	67	1.129	3.18	134	2.50	.224	0	.000	7	7	0.7
1994	Mil-A	3	1	.750	40	0	0	0	0	39	32	26	22	4	2	26	36	1.487	5.08	99	4.22	.222	0	....	-1	2	-0.1
1995	Bal-A	2	4	.333	**65**	0	0	0	3	49^2	28	19	18	4	1	27	58	1.107	3.26	146	2.12	.169	0	....	8	6	0.7
1996*	Bal-A	3	1	.750	66	0	0	0	0	55^2	42	22	21	5	2	28	52	1.257	3.40	145	3.07	.207	0	....	9	6	0.9
1997*	Bal-A	6	3	.667	71	0	0	0	0	50^1	29	13	13	6	0	30	46	1.172	2.32	189	2.73	.169	0	....	11	7	1.1
1998	Bal-A	4	1	.800	69	0	0	0	7	56^2	46	20	20	6	1	28	50	1.306	3.18	143	3.45	.221	0	....	9	7	0.9
1999	Bal-A	0	2	.000	65	0	0	0	1	32	28	21	19	5	2	20	35	1.500	5.34	88	4.73	.239	0	....	-3	1	-0.3
2000	StL-N	0	0	....	6	0	0	0	0	2^1	3	3	1	1	2	3	4	2.571	3.86	119	13.85	.273	0	....	0	0	0.0
2001	LA-N	0	1	.000	35	0	0	0	0	16	17	7	7	3	0	7	21	1.500	3.94	102	5.25	.279	0	....	0	1	0.0
2002	LA-N	1	2	.333	56	0	0	0	1	27	24	10	9	4	0	12	22	1.333	3.00	127	3.75	.229	0	....	2	2	0.3
2003	SD-N	1	1	.500	42	0	0	0	2	25	33	22	21	4	2	10	22	1.720	7.56	52	6.76	.317	0	....	-10	0	-1.0
	NY-A	0	0	....	15	0	0	0	0	4^1	4	6	5	0	0	6	4	2.308	10.38	42	4.76	.250	0	....	-3	0	-0.3
	Min-A	1	1	.500	8	0	0	0	0	4^1	4	3	3	0	1	5	3	2.077	6.23	73	6.21	.235	0	....	-1	0	-0.1
	Yr.	1	1	.500	23	0	0	0	0	8^2	8	9	8	0	1	11	7	2.192	8.31	53	5.49	.242	0	....	-4	0	-0.3
Total	24	87	80	.521	1252	4	0	0	144	1295	1055	512	455	113	34	581	1179	1.263	3.16	125	3.20	.223	10	.169	114	140	11.8

YEAR	TM-L	W	L	PCT	G	GS	CG	SH	SV	IP	H	R	ER	HR	HB	BB	SO	RAT	ERA	ERA+	CERA	OAV	BH	AVG	PR+	WS	TPW
• O'ROURKE,					O'Rourke Deb: 7/9/1872																						
1872	Eck-n	0	1	.000	1	1	1	0	0	9	16	15	8	0	....	2	0	2.000	8.00	58	....	.342	0	.000	-2	....	-0.2
• O'ROURKE, Jim					James Henry "Orator Jim" O'Rourke b: 9/1/1850, Bridgeport, CT d: 1/8/1919, Bridgeport, CT BR/TR, 5'8", 185 lbs. Deb: 4/26/1872 M/U HOF: 1945 ♦																						
1883	Buf-N	0	0	....	2	0	0	0	1	7	10	9	5	0	....	1	1	1.571	6.43	49	....	.317	143	.328	-2	17	1.0
1884	Buf-N	0	1	.000	4	0	0	0	1	12^2	7	5	4	0	....	1	3	.632	2.84	111	....	.153	162	.347	1	25	2.3
Total	**2**	**0**	**1**	**.000**	**6**	**0**	**0**	**0**	**2**	19^2	**17**	**14**	**9**	**0**	**....**	**2**	**4**	**.966**	**4.12**	**77**	**....**	**.220**	**2340**	**.313**	**-2**	**42**	**3.3**
• O'ROURKE, Mike					Michael J. O'Rourke Deb: 9/1/1890																						
1890	Bal-a	1	2	.333	5	5	5	0	0	41	45	19	18	0	3	10	8	1.341	3.95	108	....	.271	3	.115	1	3	0.0
• ORRELL, Joe					Forrest Gordon Orrell b: 3/6/1917, National City, CA d: 1/12/1993, Chula Vista, CA BR/TR, 6'4", 210 lbs. Deb: 8/12/1943																						
1943	Det-A	0	0	....	10	0	0	0	1	19^1	18	9	8	0	2	11	2	1.500	3.72	94	3.95	.257	1	.250	-0	1	0.0
1944	Det-A	2	1	.667	10	2	0	0	0	22^1	26	13	6	0	1	11	10	1.657	2.42	148	4.56	.286	1	.250	3	2	0.3
1945	Det-A	2	3	.400	12	5	1	0	0	48	46	18	16	1	2	24	14	1.458	3.00	117	3.76	.260	2	.133	3	3	0.2
Total	**3**	**4**	**4**	**.500**	**32**	**7**	**1**	**0**	**1**	89^2	**90**	**40**	**30**	**1**	**5**	**46**	**26**	**1.517**	**3.01**	**117**	**4.00**	**.266**	**4**	**.174**	**5**	**6**	**0.5**
• ORTEGA, Phil					Filomeno Coronada "Kemo" Ortega b: 10/7/1939, Gilbert, AZ BR/TR, 6'2", 175 lbs. Deb: 9/10/1960																						
1960	LA-N	0	0	....	3	1	0	0	0	6^1	12	12	12	1	0	5	4	2.684	17.05	23	11.61	.400	0	.000	-9	0	-1.0
1961	LA-N	0	2	.000	4	2	1	0	0	13	10	9	8	6	0	2	15	.923	5.54	78	3.92	.208	1	.250	-2	0	-0.2
1962	LA-N	0	2	.000	24	3	0	0	1	53^2	60	43	41	8	3	39	30	1.845	6.88	53	6.55	.276	0	.000	-19	0	-2.0
1963	LA-N	0	0	....	1	0	0	0	0	1	2	2	2	1	0	0	1	2.000	18.00	17	16.28	.400	0	....	-2	0	-0.2
1964	LA-N	7	9	.438	34	25	4	3	1	157^1	149	74	70	22	6	56	107	1.303	4.00	81	3.98	.249	6	.136	-13	4	-1.4
1965	Was-A	12	15	.444	35	29	4	2	0	179^2	176	107	102	33	5	97	88	1.519	5.11	68	5.30	.262	11	.208	-31	4	-2.9
1966	Was-A	12	12	.500	33	31	5	1	0	197^1	158	91	86	29	5	53	121	1.069	3.92	88	2.88	.218	3	.056	-12	8	-1.5
1967	Was-A	10	10	.500	34	34	5	2	0	219^2	189	77	74	16	6	57	122	1.120	3.03	104	2.72	.231	4	.061	3	14	0.0
1968	Was-A	5	12	.294	31	16	1	1	0	115^2	115	70	64	12	5	62	57	1.530	4.98	59	4.65	.263	4	.167	-25	0	-2.7
1969	Cal-A	0	0	....	5	0	0	0	0	8	13	13	9	3	0	7	4	2.500	10.13	34	11.77	.333	0	....	-6	0	-0.6
Total	**10**	**46**	**62**	**.426**	**204**	**141**	**20**	**9**	**2**	951^2	**884**	**498**	**468**	**131**	**30**	**378**	**549**	**1.326**	**4.43**	**75**	**4.07**	**.246**	**29**	**.115**	**-117**	**30**	**-12.5**
• ORTH, Al					Albert Lewis "Smiling Al,The Curveless Wonder" Orth b: 9/5/1872, Tipton, IN d: 10/8/1948, Lynchburg, VA BL/TR, 6', 200 lbs. Deb: 8/15/1895 U ♦																						
1895	Phi-N	8	1	.889	11	10	9	0	1	88	103	50	38	0	2	22	25	1.420	3.89	123	3.75	.288	16	.356	9	9	1.0
1896	Phi-N	15	10	.600	25	23	19	0	0	196	244	128	96	10	3	46	23	1.480	4.41	98	4.46	.303	21	.256	0	14	0.2
1897	Phi-N	14	19	.424	36	34	29	2	0	282^1	349	194	145	12	6	82	64	1.527	4.62	91	4.57	.301	50	.329	-7	16	0.2
1898	Phi-N	15	13	.536	32	28	25	1	0	250	290	131	84	2	8	53	52	1.372	3.02	113	3.65	.288	36	.293	13	18	2.1
1899	Phi-N	14	3	.824	21	15	13	3	1	144^2	149	67	40	0	3	19	35	1.161	**2.49**	148	2.63	.266	13	.210	17	14	1.6
1900	Phi-N	14	14	.500	33	30	24	2	1	262	302	145	110	4	13	60	68	1.382	3.78	96	3.78	.288	40	.310	-3	18	0.3
1901	Phi-N	20	12	.625	35	33	30	**6**	1	281^2	250	101	71	3	8	32	92	1.001	2.27	150	**2.00**	.237	36	.281	35	29	4.0
1902	Was-A	19	18	.514	38	37	36	1	0	324	367	181	143	18	9	40	76	1.256	3.97	93	3.41	.286	38	.217	-4	19	-0.5
1903	Was-A	10	22	.313	36	32	30	2	**2**	279^2	326	174	135	8	7	62	88	1.387	4.34	72	3.77	.290	49	.302	-35	15	-2.5
1904	Was-A	3	4	.429	10	7	7	0	0	73^2	88	49	39	2	3	15	23	1.398	4.76	56	3.92	.297	22	.216	-15	1	-2.5
	NY-A	11	6	.647	20	18	11	2	0	137^2	122	47	41	0	3	19	47	1.024	2.68	101	2.01	.239	19	.297	-3	14	0.0
	Yr.	14	10	.583	30	25	18	2	0	211^1	210	96	80	2	6	34	70	1.155	3.41	79	2.67	.260	41	.247	-18	15	-2.5
1905	NY-A	18	16	.529	40	37	26	6	0	305^1	273	122	97	8	7	61	121	1.094	2.86	102	2.37	.241	24	.183	6	18	0.6
1906	NY-A	**27**	17	.614	45	39	**36**	3	0	$\mathbf{338^2}$	317	115	88	2	1	66	133	1.131	2.34	127	2.26	.251	37	.274	26	**36**	**3.7**
1907	NY-A	14	21	.400	36	33	21	2	0	248^2	244	134	72	2	6	53	78	1.194	2.61	107	2.68	.259	34	.324	9	16	1.9
1908	NY-A	2	13	.133	21	17	8	1	0	139^1	134	62	53	4	4	30	22	1.177	3.42	72	2.84	.255	20	.290	-11	5	-0.7
1909	NY-A	0	0	....	1	1	0	0	0	3	6	4	4	0	0	1	1	2.333	12.00	21	9.49	.429	9	.265	-3	1	-0.4
Total	**15**	**204**	**189**	**.519**	**440**	**394**	**324**	**31**	**6**	3354^2	**3564**	**1704**	**1256**	**75**	**83**	**661**	**948**	**1.259**	**3.37**	**99**	**3.17**	**.272**	**464**	**.273**	**34**	**243**	**9.2**
• ORTIZ, Baby					Oliverio (Nunez) Ortiz b: 12/5/1919, Camaguey, Cuba d: 3/27/1984, Central Senado, Cuba BR/TR, 6', 190 lbs. Deb: 9/23/1944																						
1944	Was-A	0	2	.000	2	2	1	0	0	13	13	11	9	0	0	6	4	1.462	6.23	52	3.38	.255	1	.167	-4	0	-0.5
• ORTIZ, Ramon					Ramon Diogenes (Ortiz) Ortiz b: 3/23/1973, Cotui, Dominican Republic BR/TR, 6', 170 lbs. Deb: 8/19/1999																						
1999	Ana-A	2	3	.400	9	9	0	0	0	48^1	50	35	35	7	2	25	44	1.552	6.52	74	5.23	.265	0	....	-9	1	-0.9
2000	Ana-A	8	6	.571	18	18	2	0	0	111^1	96	69	63	18	2	55	73	1.356	5.09	100	4.24	.236	0	....	-3	6	-0.3
2001	Ana-A	13	11	.542	32	32	2	0	0	208^2	223	114	101	25	12	76	135	1.433	4.36	105	4.65	.274	0	.000	4	12	0.3
2002*	Ana-A	15	9	.625	32	32	4	1	0	217^1	188	97	91	40	5	68	162	1.178	3.77	118	3.64	.230	0	.000	9	14	0.8
2003	Ana-A	16	13	.552	32	32	1	0	0	180	209	121	104	28	12	63	94	1.511	5.20	83	5.44	.287	0	.000	-20	5	-2.0
Total	**5**	**54**	**42**	**.563**	**123**	**123**	**9**	**1**	**0**	765^2	**766**	**436**	**394**	**118**	**33**	**287**	**508**	**1.375**	**4.63**	**98**	**4.53**	**.259**	**0**	**.000**	**-20**	**38**	**-2.1**
• ORTIZ, Russ					Russell Reid Ortiz b: 6/5/1974, Van Nuys, CA BR/TR, 6'1", 210 lbs. Deb: 4/2/1998																						
1998	SF-N	4	4	.500	22	13	0	0	0	88^1	90	51	49	11	4	46	75	1.540	4.99	80	5.05	.269	7	.280	-10	3	-0.7
1999	SF-N	18	9	.667	33	33	3	0	0	207^2	189	109	88	24	6	125	164	1.512	3.81	110	4.56	.244	14	.197	9	12	1.1
2000*	SF-N	14	12	.538	33	32	0	0	0	195^2	192	117	109	28	7	112	167	1.554	5.01	84	5.17	.261	12	.197	-17	7	-1.3
2001	SF-N	17	9	.654	33	33	1	1	0	218^2	187	90	80	13	0	91	169	1.271	3.29	121	3.08	.232	13	.194	16	15	2.0
2002*	SF-N	14	10	.583	33	33	2	0	0	214^1	191	89	86	15	4	94	137	1.330	3.61	107	3.46	.241	17	.246	4	13	1.2
2003*	Atl-N★	**21**	7	.750	34	34	1	1	0	212^1	177	101	90	17	4	102	149	1.314	3.81	111	3.32	.223	18	.257	10	16	1.7
Total	**6**	**88**	**51**	**.633**	**188**	**178**	**7**	**2**	**0**	**1137**	**1026**	**557**	**502**	**108**	**25**	**570**	**861**	**1.404**	**3.97**	**103**	**3.98**	**.242**	**81**	**.223**	**12**	**66**	**4.1**
• ORWOLL, Ossie					Oswald Christian Orwoll b: 11/17/1900, Portland, OR d: 5/8/1967, Decorah, IA BL/TL, 6', 174 lbs. Deb: 4/13/1928 ♦																						
1928	Phi-A	6	5	.545	27	8	3	0	2	106	110	59	54	7	2	50	53	1.509	4.58	87	4.17	.274	52	.306	-6	10	-0.4
1929	Phi-A	0	2	.000	12	0	0	0	1	30	32	23	16	6	0	6	12	1.267	4.80	88	4.30	.278	13	.255	-2	1	-0.4
Total	**2**	**6**	**7**	**.462**	**39**	**8**	**3**	**0**	**3**	**136**	**142**	**82**	**70**	**13**	**2**	**56**	**65**	**1.456**	**4.63**	**88**	**4.20**	**.275**	**65**	**.294**	**-8**	**11**	**-0.8**
• OSBORN, Bob					John Bode Osborn b: 4/17/1903, San Diego, TX d: 4/19/1960, Paris, TX BR/TR, 6'1" Deb: 9/16/1925																						
1925	Chi-N	0	0	....	1	0	0	0	0	2	6	2	0	0	0	0	0	3.000	0.00	....	15.89	.600	0	....	1	0	0.1
1926	Chi-N	6	5	.545	31	15	6	0	1	136^1	157	64	55	3	0	58	43	1.577	3.63	106	4.36	.301	6	.146	0	7	-0.2
1927	Chi-N	5	5	.500	24	12	2	0	0	107^2	125	54	50	2	1	48	45	1.607	4.18	92	4.47	.294	8	.205	-6	5	-0.6
1929	Chi-N	0	0	....	3	1	0	0	0	9	8	3	3	0	0	2	1	1.111	3.00	154	2.19	.242	1	.250	1	1	0.1
1930	Chi-N	10	6	.625	35	13	3	0	1	126^2	147	74	70	9	1	53	42	1.579	4.97	98	4.81	.300	4	.095	-1	8	-0.5
1931	Pit-N	6	1	.857	27	2	0	0	0	64^2	85	43	36	3	1	20	9	1.624	5.01	77	5.05	.316	3	.167	-9	2	-1.0
Total	**6**	**27**	**17**	**.614**	**121**	**43**	**11**	**0**	**2**	446^1	**528**	**240**	**214**	**17**	**3**	**181**	**140**	**1.588**	**4.32**	**96**	**4.63**	**.302**	**22**	**.153**	**-13**	**23**	**-2.1**
• OSBORN, Ozzie					Danny Leon Osborn b: 6/19/1946, Springfield, MO BR/TR, 6'2", 195 lbs. Deb: 4/26/1975																						
1975	Chi-A	3	0	1.000	24	0	0	0	0	58	57	29	29	2	2	37	38	1.621	4.50	86	4.63	.265	0	....	-3	3	-0.3
• OSBORNE, Donovan					Donovan Alan Osborne b: 6/21/1969, Roseville, CA BB/TL, 6'2", 210 lbs. Deb: 4/9/1992																						
1992	StL-N	11	9	.550	34	29	0	0	0	179	193	91	75	14	2	38	104	1.291	3.77	90	3.65	.275	7	.121	-10	6	-1.2
1993	StL-N	10	7	.588	26	26	1	0	0	155^2	153	73	65	18	7	47	83	1.285	3.76	105	3.86	.257	10	.204	3	9	0.5
1995	StL-N	4	6	.400	19	19	0	0	0	113^1	112	58	48	17	2	34	82	1.288	3.81	110	4.01	.260	5	.161	3	6	0.5
1996*	StL-N	13	9	.591	30	30	2	1	0	198^2	191	87	78	22	1	57	134	1.248	3.53	119	3.51	.254	13	.220	10	14	1.3
1997	StL-N	3	7	.300	14	14	0	0	0	80^1	84	46	44	10	1	23	51	1.332	4.93	84	4.13	.274	5	.208	-7	2	-0.6
1998	StL-N	5	4	.556	14	14	1	1	0	83^2	84	42	38	11	1	22	60	1.267	4.09	103	3.70	.256	1	.040	1	4	0.0
1999	StL-N	1	3	.250	6	6	0	0	0	29^1	34	18	18	4	2	10	21	1.500	5.52	83	5.35	.298	1	.100	-3	1	-0.3
2002	Chi-N	0	1	.000	11	0	0	0	0	16	19	11	11	1	0	10	13	1.813	6.19	65	5.40	.297	0	.000	-4	0	-0.4
Total	**8**	**47**	**46**	**.505**	**154**	**138**	**4**	**2**	**0**	**856**	**870**	**426**	**377**	**97**	**16**	**241**	**548**	**1.298**	**3.96**	**100**	**3.85**	**.264**	**42**	**.162**	**-6**	**42**	**-0.2**

YEAR TM-L	W	L	PCT	G	GS	CG	SH	SV	IP	H	R	ER	HR	HB	BB	SO	RAT	ERA	ERA+	CERA	OAV	BH	AVG	PR+	WS	TPW
• OSBORNE, Fred	Frederick W. Osborne b: 5/1865, TL Deb: 7/14/1890 ♦																									
1890 Pit-N	0	5	.000	8	5	5	0	0	58	82	87	54	6	7	45	14	2.190	8.38	39	....	.324	40	.238	-30	1	-2.9
• OSBORNE, Tiny	Earnest Preston Osborne b: 4/9/1893, Porterdale, GA d: 1/5/1969, Atlanta, GA BL/TR, 6'4.5" Deb: 4/15/1922																									
1922 Chi-N	9	5	.643	41	14	7	1	3	184	183	113	92	7	12	95	81	1.511	4.50	93	4.19	.271	9	.134	-8	8	-1.1
1923 Chi-N	8	15	.348	37	25	8	1	1	179^2	174	117	91	14	2	89	69	1.464	4.56	88	3.99	.255	12	.200	-16	6	-1.6
1924 Chi-N	0	0	....	2	0	0	0	1	3	3	1	1	0	0	2	2	1.667	3.00	130	4.40	.300	0	....	0	0	0.0
Bro-N	6	5	.545	21	13	6	0	0	104^1	123	67	59	1	4	54	52	1.696	5.09	74	4.85	.298	9	.250	-13	3	-1.2
Yr.	6	5	.545	23	13	6	0	1	107^1	126	68	60	1	4	56	54	1.696	5.03	75	4.84	.298	9	.250	-13	3	-1.2
1925 Bro-N	8	15	.348	41	22	10	0	1	175	210	111	96	9	4	75	59	1.629	4.94	85	4.97	.304	14	.246	-9	7	-0.7
Total 4	**31**	**40**	**.437**	**142**	**74**	**31**	**2**	**6**	**646**	**693**	**409**	**339**	**31**	**22**	**315**	**263**	**1.560**	**4.72**	**86**	**4.45**	**.280**	**44**	**.200**	**-45**	**24**	**-4.6**
• OSBORNE, Wayne	Wayne Harold Osborne b: 10/11/1912, Watsonville, CA d: 3/13/1987, Vancouver, WA BL/TR, 6'2.5" Deb: 4/18/1935																									
1935 Pit-N	0	0	....	2	0	0	0	0	1^1	1	1	1	0	0	0	1	.750	6.75	61	1.13	.250	0	....	-0	0	0.0
1936 Bos-N	1	1	.500	5	3	0	0	0	20	31	13	13	1	0	9	8	2.000	5.85	66	7.03	.352	2	.250	-5	0	-0.4
Total 2	**1**	**1**	**.500**	**7**	**3**	**0**	**0**	**0**	**21^1**	**32**	**14**	**14**	**1**	**0**	**9**	**9**	**1.922**	**5.91**	**65**	**6.66**	**.348**	**2**	**.250**	**-5**	**0**	**-0.5**
• OSBURN, Pat	Larry Patrick Osburn b: 5/4/1949, Murray, KY BL/TL, 6'4", 195 lbs. Deb: 4/13/1974																									
1974 Cin-N	0	0	....	6	0	0	0	0	9	11	9	8	2	0	4	4	1.667	8.00	44	6.37	.297	0	.000	-5	0	-0.5
1975 Mil-A	0	1	.000	6	1	0	0	0	11^2	19	9	7	2	2	9	1	2.400	5.40	71	11.68	.404	0	....	-2	0	-0.2
Total 2	**0**	**1**	**.000**	**12**	**1**	**0**	**0**	**0**	**20^2**	**30**	**18**	**15**	**4**	**2**	**13**	**5**	**2.081**	**6.53**	**56**	**9.37**	**.357**	**0**	**.000**	**-7**	**0**	**-0.7**
• OSGOOD, Charlie	Charles Benjamin Osgood b: 11/23/1926, Somerville, MA BR/TR, 5'10", 180 lbs. Deb: 6/18/1944																									
1944 Bro-N	0	0	....	1	0	0	0	0	3	2	1	1	0	1	3	0	1.667	3.00	118	5.16	.222	0	....	0	0	0.0
• OSINSKI, Dan	Daniel Osinski b: 11/17/1933, Chicago, IL BR/TR, 6'1.5", 195 lbs. Deb: 4/11/1962																									
1962 KC-A	0	0	....	4	0	0	0	0	4^2	8	9	9	1	0	8	4	3.429	17.36	24	15.75	.381	0	....	-7	0	-0.7
LA-A	6	4	.600	33	0	0	0	4	54^1	45	22	17	3	0	30	44	1.380	2.82	137	3.24	.223	0	.000	7	5	0.6
Yr.	6	4	.600	37	0	0	0	4	59	53	31	26	4	0	38	48	1.542	3.97	100	4.23	.238	0	.000	-0	5	-0.1
1963 LA-A	8	8	.500	47	16	4	1	0	159^1	145	66	58	15	2	80	100	1.412	3.28	105	3.90	.242	5	.111	3	8	0.1
1964 LA-A	3	3	.500	47	4	1	1	2	93	87	47	36	8	2	39	88	1.355	3.48	94	3.61	.244	1	.056	-3	3	-0.4
1965 Mil-N	0	3	.000	61	0	0	0	6	83	81	28	26	4	1	40	54	1.458	2.82	125	3.78	.261	1	.167	6	6	0.6
1966 Bos-A	4	3	.571	44	1	0	0	2	67^1	68	33	27	8	1	28	44	1.426	3.61	105	4.37	.274	2	.333	2	4	0.2
1967* Bos-A	3	1	.750	34	0	0	0	2	63^2	61	19	18	5	0	14	38	1.178	2.54	137	2.88	.243	3	.333	7	6	0.9
1969 Chi-A	5	5	.500	51	0	0	0	2	60^2	56	28	24	3	0	23	27	1.302	3.56	108	3.14	.251	0	.000	3	5	0.3
1970 Hou-N	0	1	.000	3	0	0	0	0	3^2	5	4	4	0	0	2	1	1.909	9.82	39	5.31	.357	0	....	-2	0	-0.2
Total 8	**29**	**28**	**.509**	**324**	**21**	**5**	**2**	**18**	**589^2**	**556**	**256**	**219**	**47**	**6**	**264**	**400**	**1.391**	**3.34**	**107**	**3.75**	**.250**	**12**	**.122**	**16**	**37**	**1.4**
• OSTEEN, Claude	Claude Wilson Osteen b: 8/9/1939, Caney Springs, TN BL/TL, 5'11", 173 lbs. Deb: 7/6/1957 C																									
1957 Cin-N	0	0	....	3	0	0	0	0	4	4	1	1	0	0	3	3	1.750	2.25	183	4.54	.250	0	.000	1	0	0.1
1959 Cin-N	0	0	....	2	0	0	0	0	7^2	11	10	6	1	0	9	3	2.609	7.04	58	9.69	.333	0	.000	-3	0	-0.3
1960 Cin-N	0	1	.000	20	3	0	0	0	48^1	53	29	27	5	1	30	15	1.717	5.03	76	5.68	.293	1	.083	-7	1	-0.8
1961 Cin-N	0	0	....	1	0	0	0	0	0^1	0	0	0	0	0	0	0	.000	0.00	....	0.00	.000	0	....	0	0	0.0
Was-A	1	1	.500	3	3	0	0	0	18^1	14	11	10	3	1	9	14	1.255	4.91	80	3.87	.219	1	.143	-2	1	-0.2
1962 Was-A	8	13	.381	28	22	7	2	1	150^1	140	62	61	12	4	47	59	1.244	3.65	111	3.29	.246	10	.208	7	10	0.8
1963 Was-A	9	14	.391	40	29	8	2	0	212^1	222	101	79	23	1	60	109	1.328	3.35	111	3.92	.270	12	.171	9	11	1.0
1964 Was-A	15	13	.536	37	36	13	0	0	257	256	107	95	20	3	64	133	1.245	3.33	111	3.33	.259	14	.156	10	17	1.2
1965* LA-N	15	15	.500	40	40	9	1	0	287	253	95	89	19	3	78	162	1.153	2.79	117	2.74	.236	12	.121	11	18	1.0
1966* LA-N	17	14	.548	39	38	8	3	0	240^1	238	92	76	6	2	65	137	1.261	2.85	116	2.97	.261	16	.211	11	17	1.7
1967 LA-N★	17	17	.500	39	39	14	5	0	288^1	298	116	103	19	2	52	152	1.214	3.22	96	3.18	.270	18	.178	-0	16	0.5
1968 LA-N	12	18	.400	39	36	5	3	0	253^2	267	109	87	14	5	54	119	1.265	3.09	90	3.39	.275	15	.179	-11	8	-1.0
1969 LA-N	20	15	.571	41	41	16	7	0	321	293	103	95	17	6	74	183	1.143	2.66	125	2.75	.245	24	.216	21	26	2.7
1970 LA-N★	16	14	.533	37	37	11	4	0	258^2	280	121	110	24	4	52	114	1.284	3.83	100	3.76	.276	19	.204	-5	13	0.0
1971 LA-N	14	11	.560	38	38	11	4	0	259	262	108	101	25	3	63	109	1.255	3.51	92	3.59	.266	16	.186	-9	12	-0.7
1972 LA-N	20	11	.645	33	33	14	4	0	252	232	82	74	16	4	69	100	1.194	2.64	126	2.99	.245	24	.273	19	22	3.0
1973 LA-N★	16	11	.593	33	33	12	3	0	236^2	227	97	87	20	2	61	86	1.217	3.31	104	3.30	.258	12	.154	0	14	0.0
1974 Hou-N	9	9	.500	23	21	7	2	0	138^1	158	67	57	8	2	47	45	1.482	3.71	93	4.43	.292	13	.283	-6	8	-0.2
StL-N	0	2	.000	8	2	0	0	0	22^2	26	14	11	1	0	11	6	1.632	4.37	82	4.36	.286	0	.000	-2	0	-0.3
Yr.	9	11	.450	31	23	7	2	0	161	184	81	68	9	2	58	51	1.503	3.80	92	4.42	.291	13	.245	-8	8	-0.6
1975 Chi-A	7	16	.304	37	37	5	0	0	204^1	237	110	99	16	2	92	63	**1.610**	4.36	89	5.08	.294	0	....	-8	7	-0.8
Total 18	**196**	**195**	**.501**	**541**	**488**	**140**	**40**	**1**	**3460^1**	**3471**	**1435**	**1268**	**249**	**45**	**940**	**1612**	**1.275**	**3.30**	**104**	**3.46**	**.263**	**207**	**.188**	**36**	**201**	**7.5**
• OSTEEN, Darrell	Milton Darrell Osteen b: 2/14/1943, Oklahoma City, OK BR/TR, 6'1", 170 lbs. Deb: 9/2/1965																									
1965 Cin-N	0	0	....	3	0	0	0	0	3	2	0	0	0	0	4	1	2.000	0.00	....	5.19	.200	0	....	1	1	0.1
1966 Cin-N	0	2	.000	13	0	0	0	1	15	26	21	20	3	0	9	17	2.333	12.00	32	10.15	.371	1	.500	-13	0	-1.4
1967 Cin-N	0	2	.000	10	0	0	0	2	14^1	10	10	10	1	3	13	13	1.605	6.28	60	4.72	.196	0	.000	-4	0	-0.4
1970 Oak-A	1	0	1.000	3	1	0	0	0	5^2	9	4	4	0	0	3	3	2.118	6.35	56	7.15	.346	0	.000	-2	0	-0.2
Total 4	**1**	**4**	**.200**	**29**	**1**	**0**	**0**	**3**	**38**	**47**	**35**	**34**	**4**	**3**	**29**	**34**	**2.000**	**8.05**	**47**	**7.26**	**.299**	**1**	**.200**	**-18**	**1**	**-1.9**
• OSTENDORF, Fred	Frederick K. Ostendorf b: 8/5/1890, Baltimore, MD d: 3/2/1965, Kecoughtan, VA BL/TL, 6'.5", 169 lbs. Deb: 7/16/1914																									
1914 Ind-F	0	0	....	1	0	0	0	0	2	5	5	5	0	1	2	0	3.500	22.50	15	17.93	.500	0	.000	-4	0	-0.5
• OSTER, Bill	William Charles Oster b: 1/2/1933, New York, NY BL/TL, 6'3", 198 lbs. Deb: 8/23/1954																									
1954 Phi-A	0	1	.000	8	1	0	0	0	15^2	19	15	11	2	0	12	5	1.979	6.32	62	6.99	.311	1	.333	-4	0	-0.4
• OSTERMUELLER, Fritz	Frederick Raymond Ostermueller b: 9/15/1907, Quincy, IL d: 12/17/1957, Quincy, IL BL/TL, 5'11", 175 lbs. Deb: 4/21/1934																									
1934 Bos-A	10	13	.435	33	23	10	0	3	198^2	200	93	77	7	1	99	75	1.505	3.49	138	3.88	.262	13	.167	31	17	2.7
1935 Bos-A	7	8	.467	22	19	10	0	1	137^2	135	67	60	0	3	78	41	1.547	3.92	121	3.78	.257	14	.286	12	11	1.3
1936 Bos-A	10	16	.385	43	23	7	1	2	180^2	210	115	98	8	3	84	90	1.627	4.88	109	4.73	.288	15	.234	8	11	0.7
1937 Bos-A	3	7	.300	25	7	2	0	1	86^2	101	64	48	2	1	44	29	1.673	4.98	95	4.69	.286	11	.333	-0	4	0.2
1938 Bos-A	13	5	.722	31	18	10	1	2	176^2	199	98	90	15	3	58	46	1.455	4.58	108	4.24	.275	16	.216	5	13	0.6
1939 Bos-A	11	7	.611	34	20	8	0	4	159^1	173	86	75	6	2	58	61	1.450	4.24	111	3.88	.277	9	.161	9	13	0.7
1940 Bos-A	5	9	.357	31	16	5	0	0	143^2	166	86	79	7	0	70	80	1.643	4.95	91	4.71	.284	17	.315	-6	8	-0.2
1941 StL-A	0	3	.000	15	2	0	0	0	46	45	26	23	3	0	23	20	1.478	4.50	96	4.00	.257	3	.214	-0	2	0.0
1942 StL-A	3	1	.750	10	4	2	0	0	43^2	46	22	18	4	0	17	21	1.443	3.71	100	4.15	.266	3	.188	0	2	0.0
1943 StL-A	0	2	.000	11	3	0	0	0	28^2	36	16	16	1	0	13	4	1.709	5.02	66	5.35	.321	2	.286	-5	0	-0.5
Bro-N	1	1	.500	7	1	0	0	0	27^1	21	11	10	0	0	12	15	1.207	3.29	102	2.27	1.000	0	.000	1	1	-0.1
1944 Bro-N	2	1	.667	10	4	3	0	1	41^2	46	17	15	3	0	12	17	1.392	3.24	110	3.73	.267	2	.154	3	2	0.3
Pit-N	11	7	.611	28	24	14	1	1	204^2	201	79	62	7	1	65	80	1.300	2.73	136	3.17	.260	20	.250	24	17	2.7
Yr.	13	8	.619	38	28	17	1	2	246^1	247	96	77	10	1	77	97	1.315	2.81	131	3.27	.261	22	.237	27	19	3.0
1945 Pit-N	5	4	.556	14	11	4	1	0	80^2	74	45	41	6	2	37	29	1.376	4.57	86	3.50	.236	9	.321	-5	4	-0.2
1946 Pit-N	13	10	.565	27	25	16	2	0	193^1	193	70	61	5	3	56	57	1.288	2.84	124	3.14	.263	21	.328	17	19	2.6
1947 Pit-N	12	10	.545	26	24	12	3	0	183	181	94	78	18	1	68	66	1.361	3.84	110	3.79	.254	12	.188	9	10	0.9
1948 Pit-N	8	11	.421	23	22	10	2	0	134^1	143	73	66	13	1	41	43	1.370	4.42	92	3.83	.262	8	.182	-6	6	-0.6
Total 15	**114**	**115**	**.498**	**390**	**246**	**113**	**11**	**15**	**2066^2**	**2170**	**1062**	**917**	**105**	**21**	**835**	**774**	**1.454**	**3.99**	**109**	**3.91**	**.270**	**175**	**.234**	**97**	**140**	**11.1**
• OSTING, Jimmy	James Michael Osting b: 4/7/1977, Louisville, KY BR/TL, 6'5", 190 lbs. Deb: 5/2/2001																									
2001 SD-N	0	0	....	3	0	0	0	0	2	1	0	0	0	0	2	3	1.500	0.00	....	1.96	.143	0	....	1	0	0.1
2002 Mil-N	0	2	.000	3	3	0	0	0	12	18	11	10	3	0	10	7	2.333	7.50	55	10.28	.340	0	.000	-5	0	-0.5
Total 2	**0**	**2**	**.000**	**6**	**3**	**0**	**0**	**0**	**14**	**19**	**11**	**10**	**3**	**0**	**12**	**10**	**2.214**	**6.43**	**64**	**9.09**	**.317**	**0**	**.000**	**-4**	**0**	**-0.4**

YEAR	TM-L	W	L	PCT	G	GS	CG	SH	SV	IP	H	R	ER	HR	HB	BB	SO	RAT	ERA	ERA+	CERA	OAV	BH	AVG	PR+	WS	TPW
• OSTROWSKI, Joe	Joseph Paul "Professor,Specs" Ostrowski b: 11/15/1916, West Wyoming, PA d: 1/3/2003, Wilkes-Barre, PA BL/TL, 6', 180 lbs. Deb: 7/18/1948																										
1948	StL-A	4	6	.400	26	9	3	0	3	78^1	108	54	52	6	0	17	20	1.596	5.97	76	5.37	.333	4	.222	-11	3	-1.0
1949	StL-A	8	8	.500	40	13	4	0	2	141	185	94	75	16	0	27	34	1.504	4.79	95	4.96	.307	7	.189	1	7	0.3
1950	StL-A	2	4	.333	9	7	2	0	0	57^1	57	22	16	2	0	7	15	1.116	2.51	197	2.49	.251	4	.222	17	7	1.8
	NY-A	1	1	.500	21	4	1	0	3	43^2	50	26	25	11	0	15	15	1.489	5.15	83	5.95	.294	1	.111	-5	2	-0.5
	Yr.	3	5	.375	30	11	3	0	3	101	107	48	41	13	0	22	30	1.277	3.65	124	3.98	.270	5	.185	13	9	1.3
1951*	NY-A	6	4	.600	34	3	2	0	5	95^1	103	44	37	4	1	18	30	1.269	3.49	110	3.33	.279	3	.107	2	6	0.0
1952	NY-A	2	2	.500	20	1	0	0	2	40	56	31	25	5	1	14	17	1.750	5.63	59	6.33	.327	0	.000	-12	0	-1.3
Total	5	23	25	.479	150	37	12	0	15	455^2	559	271	230	44	2	98	131	1.442	4.54	93	4.59	.300	19	.161	-7	25	-0.6
• OSUNA, Al	Alfonso Osuna b: 8/10/1965, Inglewood, CA BR/TL, 6'3", 200 lbs. Deb: 9/2/1990																										
1990	Hou-N	2	0	1.000	12	0	0	0	0	11^1	10	6	6	1	3	6	6	1.412	4.76	78	5.13	.270	0	....	-1	1	-0.1
1991	Hou-N	7	6	.538	71	0	0	0	12	81^2	59	39	31	5	3	46	68	1.286	3.42	103	2.90	.201	0	.000	1	8	0.0
1992	Hou-N	6	3	.667	66	0	0	0	0	61^2	52	29	29	8	1	38	37	1.459	4.23	79	4.19	.236	0	....	-6	3	-0.6
1993	Hou-N	1	1	.500	44	0	0	0	2	25^1	17	10	9	3	1	13	21	1.184	3.20	121	2.84	.200	0	....	2	3	0.2
1994	LA-N	2	0	1.000	15	0	0	0	0	8^2	13	6	6	0	0	4	7	1.962	6.23	63	6.32	.333	0	....	-2	0	-0.2
1996	SD-N	0	0	....	10	0	0	0	0	4	5	1	1	0	1	2	4	1.750	2.25	176	5.47	.313	0	.000	1	0	0.1
Total	6	18	10	.643	218	0	0	0	14	192^2	156	91	82	17	9	109	143	1.375	3.83	92	3.65	.226	0	.000	-6	15	-0.7
• OSUNA, Antonio	Antonio Pedro Osuna b: 4/12/1973, Sinaloa, Mexico BR/TR, 5'11", 160 lbs. Deb: 4/25/1995																										
1995*	LA-N	2	4	.333	39	0	0	0	0	44^2	39	22	22	5	1	20	46	1.321	4.43	86	3.76	.241	0	.000	-3	2	-0.3
1996*	LA-N	9	6	.600	73	0	0	0	4	84	65	33	28	6	2	32	85	1.155	3.00	129	2.53	.220	0	.000	9	10	0.9
1997	LA-N	3	4	.429	48	0	0	0	0	61^2	46	15	15	6	1	19	68	1.054	2.19	176	2.43	.209	1	.500	12	7	1.2
1998	LA-N	7	1	.875	54	0	0	0	6	64^2	50	26	22	8	2	32	72	1.268	3.06	130	3.50	.214	0	.000	7	8	0.6
1999	LA-N	0	0	....	5	0	0	0	0	4^2	4	5	4	0	1	3	5	1.500	7.71	56	4.14	.222	0	....	-2	0	-0.2
2000	LA-N	3	6	.333	46	0	0	0	0	67^1	57	30	28	7	2	35	70	1.366	3.74	116	3.74	.229	0	.000	5	4	0.4
2001	Chi-A	0	0	....	4	0	0	0	0	4^1	8	10	10	3	1	2	6	2.308	20.77	22	16.71	.421	0	....	-8	0	-0.7
2002	Chi-A	8	2	.800	59	0	0	0	11	67^2	64	32	29	1	4	28	66	1.360	3.86	118	3.31	.250	0	....	5	8	0.4
2003	NY-A	2	5	.286	48	0	0	0	0	50^2	58	22	21	3	2	20	47	1.539	3.73	117	4.51	.282	0	....	5	4	0.5
Total	9	34	28	.548	376	0	0	0	21	449^2	391	195	179	39	16	191	465	1.294	3.58	116	3.45	.236	1	.111	29	43	2.8
• OSWALT, Roy	Roy Edward Oswalt b: 8/29/1977, Kosciusko, MS BR/TR, 6', 170 lbs. Deb: 5/6/2001																										
2001	Hou-N	14	3	.824	28	20	3	1	0	141^2	126	48	43	13	6	24	144	1.059	2.73	167	2.68	.235	9	.191	28	15	2.8
2002	Hou-N	19	9	.679	35	34	0	0	0	233	215	86	78	17	5	62	208	1.189	3.01	141	3.05	.247	10	.130	34	20	3.4
2003	Hou-N	10	5	.667	21	21	0	0	0	127^1	116	48	42	15	5	29	108	1.139	2.97	149	3.26	.246	7	.179	18	10	1.8
Total	3	43	17	.717	84	75	3	1	0	502	457	182	163	45	16	115	460	1.139	2.92	150	3.00	.243	26	.160	81	45	8.0
• OTEY, Bill	William Tilford "Steamboat Bill" Otey b: 12/16/1886, Dayton, OH d: 4/23/1931, Dayton, OH BL/TL, 6'2", 181 lbs. Deb: 9/27/1907																										
1907	Pit-N	0	1	.000	3	2	1	0	0	16^1	23	11	8	1	1	4	5	1.653	4.41	55	5.55	.319	1	.250	-3	0	-0.4
1910	Was-A	0	1	.000	9	1	1	0	0	34^2	40	17	13	1	1	6	12	1.327	3.38	74	3.84	.301	5	.385	-4	1	-0.2
1911	Was-A	1	3	.250	12	2	0	0	0	49^2	68	44	35	2	3	15	16	1.671	6.34	52	5.71	.333	1	.059	-17	0	-1.8
Total	3	1	5	.167	24	5	2	0	0	100^2	131	72	56	4	5	25	33	1.550	5.01	58	5.04	.320	7	.206	-25	1	-2.5
• OTIS, Harry	Harry George "Cannonball" Otis b: 10/5/1886, West New York, NJ d: 1/29/1976, Teaneck, NJ BR/TL, 6', 180 lbs. Deb: 9/5/1909																										
1909	Cle-A	2	2	.500	5	3	0	0	0	26^1	26	11	4	0	3	18	6	1.671	1.37	187	4.99	.283	1	.111	3	2	0.3
• O'TOOLE, Dennis	Dennis Joseph O'Toole b: 3/13/1949, Chicago, IL BR/TR, 6'3", 195 lbs. Deb: 9/8/1969																										
1969	Chi-A	0	0	....	2	0	0	0	0	4	5	3	3	0	0	2	4	1.750	6.75	57	5.31	.333	0	....	-1	0	-0.1
1970	Chi-A	0	0	....	3	0	0	0	0	3^1	5	1	1	0	0	2	3	2.100	2.70	144	6.89	.357	0	....	0	0	0.1
1971	Chi-A	0	0	....	1	0	0	0	0	2	0	0	0	0	0	1	2	.500	0.00	....	0.27	.000	0	....	1	0	0.1
1972	Chi-A	0	0	....	3	0	0	0	0	5	10	3	3	0	0	2	5	2.400	5.40	58	9.65	.417	0	....	-1	0	-0.1
1973	Chi-A	0	0	....	6	0	0	0	0	16	23	11	10	3	0	3	8	1.625	5.63	70	6.30	.329	0	....	-3	0	-0.3
Total	5	0	0	....	15	0	0	0	0	30^1	43	18	17	3	0	10	22	1.747	5.04	75	6.39	.350	0	....	-4	0	-0.4
• O'TOOLE, Jim	James Jerome O'Toole b: 1/10/1937, Chicago, IL BB/TL, 6', 198 lbs. Deb: 9/26/1958																										
1958	Cin-N	0	1	.000	1	1	0	0	0	7	4	2	1	0	0	5	4	1.286	1.29	322	2.15	.154	0	.000	2	1	0.2
1959	Cin-N	5	8	.385	28	19	3	1	0	129^1	144	78	74	14	4	73	68	1.678	5.15	79	5.60	.287	5	.135	-16	3	-1.6
1960	Cin-N	12	12	.500	34	31	7	2	1	196^1	198	94	83	14	4	66	124	1.345	3.80	100	3.75	.263	7	.106	-0	10	-0.3
1961*	Cin-N	19	9	.679	39	35	11	3	2	252^2	229	101	87	16	3	93	178	1.274	3.10	131	3.20	.240	16	.172	**28**	22	2.6
1962	Cin-N	16	13	.552	36	34	11	3	0	251^2	222	115	98	20	5	87	170	1.228	3.50	115	3.18	.238	10	.110	13	16	0.8
1963	Cin-N★	17	14	.548	33	32	12	5	0	234^1	208	85	75	13	3	57	146	1.131	2.88	116	2.62	.239	11	.149	12	17	1.2
1964	Cin-N	17	7	.708	30	30	9	3	0	220	194	71	65	8	0	51	145	1.114	2.66	136	2.38	.235	7	.100	20	19	2.1
1965	Cin-N	3	10	.231	29	22	2	0	1	127^2	154	98	84	14	3	47	71	1.574	5.92	63	5.14	.294	4	.089	-31	0	-3.4
1966	Cin-N	5	7	.417	25	24	2	0	0	142	139	65	56	16	3	49	96	1.324	3.55	110	3.84	.254	6	.128	7	8	0.6
1967	Chi-A	4	3	.571	15	10	1	1	0	54^1	53	21	17	4	1	18	37	1.307	2.82	110	3.46	.251	1	.077	2	3	0.1
Total	10	98	84	.538	270	238	58	18	4	1615^1	1545	730	640	119	26	546	1039	1.294	3.57	106	3.47	.251	67	.125	37	99	2.3
• O'TOOLE, Marty	Martin James O'Toole b: 11/27/1888, William Penn, PA d: 2/18/1949, Aberdeen, WA BR/TR, 5'11", 175 lbs. Deb: 9/21/1908																										
1908	Cin-N	1	0	1.000	3	2	1	0	0	15	15	8	4	0	0	7	5	1.467	2.40	95	3.71	.273	1	.200	0	1	0.0
1911	Pit-N	3	2	.600	5	5	3	0	0	38	28	17	10	1	0	20	34	1.263	2.37	144	2.72	.215	5	.357	4	3	0.5
1912	Pit-N	15	17	.469	37	36	17	**6**	0	275^1	237	110	83	4	2	159	150	1.438	2.71	120	3.34	.241	22	.222	14	20	1.5
1913	Pit-N	6	8	.429	26	16	7	0	1	144^2	148	69	53	3	3	55	58	1.403	3.30	91	3.56	.271	7	.132	-3	6	-0.6
1914	Pit-N	1	8	.111	19	9	1	0	1	92^1	92	56	48	3	0	47	36	1.505	4.68	57	3.89	.270	5	.167	-21	0	-2.2
	NY-N	1	1	.500	10	5	2	0	0	34	34	17	16	0	0	12	13	1.353	4.24	63	3.13	.262	3	.300	-6	1	-0.6
	Yr.	2	9	.182	29	14	3	0	1	126^1	126	73	64	3	0	59	49	1.464	4.56	58	3.69	.268	8	.200	-27	1	-2.8
Total	5	27	36	.429	100	73	31	6	2	599^1	554	277	214	11	5	300	296	1.425	3.21	92	3.44	.254	43	.204	-13	31	-1.4
• OTTEN, Jim	James Edward Otten b: 7/1/1951, Lewiston, MT BR/TR, 6'2", 195 lbs. Deb: 7/31/1974																										
1974	Chi-A	0	1	.000	5	1	0	0	0	16^1	22	11	10	0	1	12	11	2.082	5.51	68	6.76	.324	0	....	-3	0	-0.3
1975	Chi-A	0	0	....	2	0	0	0	0	5^1	4	5	4	1	0	7	3	2.063	6.75	57	7.17	.235	0	....	-2	0	-0.2
1976	Chi-A	0	0	....	2	0	0	0	0	6	9	6	3	0	0	2	3	1.833	4.50	79	5.80	.333	0	....	-1	0	-0.1
1980	StL-N	0	5	.000	31	4	0	0	0	55^1	71	38	34	3	2	26	38	1.753	5.53	67	5.65	.323	1	.200	-12	0	-1.3
1981	StL-N	1	0	1.000	24	0	0	0	0	35^2	44	23	21	3	0	20	20	1.794	5.30	67	5.99	.319	0	.000	-7	0	-0.8
Total	5	1	6	.143	64	5	0	0	0	118^2	150	83	72	7	3	67	75	1.829	5.46	67	5.98	.319	1	.143	-25	0	-2.7
• OTTO, Dave	David Alan Otto b: 11/12/1964, Chicago, IL BL/TL, 6'7", 210 lbs. Deb: 9/8/1987																										
1987	Oak-A	0	0	....	3	0	0	0	0	6	7	6	6	1	0	1	3	1.333	9.00	46	4.85	.304	0	....	-3	0	-0.3
1988	Oak-A	0	0	....	3	2	0	0	0	10	9	2	2	0	0	6	7	1.500	1.80	210	3.65	.243	0	....	2	1	0.2
1989	Oak-A	0	0	....	1	1	0	0	0	6^2	6	2	2	0	0	2	4	1.200	2.70	136	2.69	.261	0	....	1	0	0.1
1990	Oak-A	0	0	....	2	0	0	0	0	2^1	3	3	2	0	0	3	2	2.571	7.71	48	8.40	.300	0	....	-1	0	-0.1
1991	Cle-A	2	8	.200	18	14	1	0	0	100	108	52	47	7	4	27	47	1.350	4.23	98	3.91	.283	0	....	1	3	0.1
1992	Cle-A	5	9	.357	18	16	0	0	0	80^1	110	64	63	12	1	33	32	1.780	7.06	55	6.95	.333	0	....	-28	0	-2.8
1993	Pit-N	3	4	.429	28	8	0	0	0	68	85	40	38	9	3	28	30	1.662	5.03	80	6.15	.317	4	.222	-8	3	-0.7
1994	Chi-N	0	1	.000	36	0	0	0	0	45	49	20	19	4	1	22	19	1.578	3.80	109	4.85	.283	0	.000	1	2	0.1
Total	8	10	22	.313	109	41	1	0	0	318^1	377	189	179	33	9	122	144	1.568	5.06	80	5.30	.303	4	.200	-35	9	-3.4
• OVERALL, Orval	Orval Overall b: 2/2/1881, Farmersville, CA d: 7/14/1947, Fresno, CA BB/TR, 6'2", 214 lbs. Deb: 4/16/1905 U																										
1905	Cin-N	18	23	.439	42	39	32	2	0	318	290	146	101	4	14	147	173	1.374	2.86	115	3.43	.252	17	.145	9	17	0.9

YEAR	TM-L	W	L	PCT	G	GS	CG	SH	SV	IP	H	R	ER	HR	HB	BB	SO	RAT	ERA	ERA+	CERA	OAV	BH	AVG	PR+	WS	TPW
1906	Cin-N	4	5	.444	13	10	6	0	0	82^1	77	52	39	1	4	46	33	1.494	4.26	64	3.71	.253	6	.194	-15	1	-1.6
	*Chi-N	12	3	.800	18	14	13	2	1	144	116	43	30	1	4	51	94	1.160	1.88	140	2.25	.217	9	.170	9	13	0.9
	Yr.	16	8	.667	31	24	19	2	1	226^1	193	95	69	2	8	97	127	1.281	2.74	98	2.78	.230	15	.179	-6	14	-0.7
1907*	Chi-N	23	7	.767	36	30	26	**8**	3	268^1	201	62	50	3	11	69	141	1.006	1.68	148	1.87	.208	20	.213	18	**32**	2.4
1908*	Chi-N	15	11	.577	37	27	16	4	4	225	165	74	48	3	2	78	167	1.080	1.92	122	2.01	.208	9	.129	8	17	0.9
1909	Chi-N	20	11	.645	38	32	23	**9**	3	285	204	66	45	1	8	80	**205**	.996	1.42	178	1.69	**.198**	22	.229	33	30	4.5
1910*	Chi-N	12	6	.667	23	21	11	4	1	144^2	106	44	43	2	1	54	92	1.106	2.68	107	2.13	.212	5	.122	2	12	0.1
1913	Chi-N	4	5	.444	11	9	6	1	0	68	73	33	25	1	1	26	30	1.456	3.31	96	3.77	.284	6	.250	-1	4	0.0
Total	7	108	71	.603	218	182	133	30	12	1535^1	1232	520	381	16	45	551	935	1.161	2.23	124	2.42	.223	94	.179	63	126	8.0

• OVERMIRE, Stubby Frank W. Overmire b: 5/16/1919, Moline, MI d: 3/3/1977, Lakeland, FL BR/TL, 5'7", 170 lbs. Deb: 4/25/1943 C

YEAR	TM-L	W	L	PCT	G	GS	CG	SH	SV	IP	H	R	ER	HR	HB	BB	SO	RAT	ERA	ERA+	CERA	OAV	BH	AVG	PR+	WS	TPW
1943	Det-A	7	6	.538	29	18	8	3	1	147	135	56	52	5	1	38	48	1.177	3.18	111	2.64	.243	7	.167	6	9	0.7
1944	Det-A	11	11	.500	32	28	11	3	1	199^2	214	84	68	2	2	41	57	1.277	3.07	117	3.06	.271	11	.175	12	14	1.3
1945*	Det-A	9	9	.500	31	22	9	0	4	162^1	189	81	70	6	3	42	36	1.423	3.88	91	4.01	.294	10	.189	-7	8	-0.7
1946	Det-A	5	7	.417	24	13	3	0	1	97^1	106	54	50	6	0	29	34	1.387	4.62	79	3.78	.274	5	.152	-9	3	-1.0
1947	Det-A	11	5	.688	28	17	7	3	0	140^2	142	62	59	9	1	44	33	1.322	3.77	100	3.47	.259	7	.149	3	9	0.2
1948	Det-A	3	4	.429	37	4	0	0	3	66^1	89	48	44	5	0	31	14	1.809	5.97	73	6.01	.326	1	.071	-10	1	-1.1
1949	Det-A	1	3	.250	14	1	0	0	0	17^1	29	21	19	2	1	9	3	2.192	9.87	42	9.00	.377	1	.333	-11	0	-1.0
1950	StL-A	9	12	.429	31	19	8	2	0	161	200	89	75	11	1	45	39	1.522	4.19	118	4.62	.298	8	.167	19	12	1.9
1951	StL-A	1	6	.143	8	7	3	0	0	53^1	61	26	21	5	0	21	13	1.538	3.54	124	4.67	.281	1	.071	6	3	0.6
	NY-A	1	1	.500	15	4	1	0	0	44^2	50	27	23	2	2	18	14	1.522	4.63	83	4.44	.287	1	.143	-5	1	-0.4
	Yr.	2	7	.222	23	11	4	0	0	98	111	53	44	7	2	39	27	1.531	4.04	101	4.57	.284	2	.095	2	4	0.1
1952	StL-A	0	3	.000	17	4	0	0	0	41	44	21	17	3	0	7	10	1.244	3.73	105	3.33	.270	2	.182	1	1	0.1
Total	10	58	67	.464	266	137	50	11	10	1130^2	1259	569	498	56	11	325	301	1.401	3.96	98	3.88	.280	54	.161	4	61	0.4

• OVERY, Mike Harry Michael Overy b: 1/27/1951, Clinton, IL BR/TR, 6'2", 190 lbs. Deb: 8/14/1976

YEAR	TM-L	W	L	PCT	G	GS	CG	SH	SV	IP	H	R	ER	HR	HB	BB	SO	RAT	ERA	ERA+	CERA	OAV	BH	AVG	PR+	WS	TPW
1976	Cal-A	0	2	.000	5	0	0	0	0	7^1	6	5	5	1	1	3	8	1.227	6.14	54	3.59	.214	0	....	-2	0	-0.2

• OVITZ, Ernie Ernest Gayhart Ovitz b: 10/7/1885, Mineral Point, WI d: 9/11/1980, Green Bay, WI BR/TR, 5'8.5", 156 lbs. Deb: 6/22/1911

YEAR	TM-L	W	L	PCT	G	GS	CG	SH	SV	IP	H	R	ER	HR	HB	BB	SO	RAT	ERA	ERA+	CERA	OAV	BH	AVG	PR+	WS	TPW
1911	Chi-N	0	0	....	1	0	0	0	0	2	3	2	1	0	0	3	0	3.000	4.50	73	11.16	.375	0	....	-0	0	0.0

• OWCHINKO, Bob Robert Dennis Owchinko b: 1/1/1955, Detroit, MI BL/TL, 6'2", 195 lbs. Deb: 9/25/1976

YEAR	TM-L	W	L	PCT	G	GS	CG	SH	SV	IP	H	R	ER	HR	HB	BB	SO	RAT	ERA	ERA+	CERA	OAV	BH	AVG	PR+	WS	TPW
1976	SD-N	0	2	.000	2	2	0	0	0	4^1	11	8	8	0	0	3	4	3.231	16.62	20	13.88	.478	0	.000	-6	0	-0.7
1977	SD-N	9	12	.429	30	28	3	2	0	170	191	93	84	20	0	67	101	1.518	4.45	79	4.90	.287	4	.082	-16	4	-1.9
1978	SD-N	10	13	.435	36	33	4	1	0	202^1	198	87	80	14	1	78	94	1.364	3.56	93	3.68	.263	11	.175	-6	9	-0.5
1979	SD-N	6	12	.333	42	20	2	0	0	149^1	144	73	62	16	2	55	66	1.333	3.74	94	3.83	.259	4	.121	-5	6	-0.5
1980	Cle-A	2	9	.182	29	14	1	1	0	114^1	138	71	67	13	2	47	66	1.618	5.27	77	5.49	.301	0	....	-15	2	-1.5
1981*	Oak-A	4	3	.571	29	0	0	0	2	39^1	34	15	14	2	1	19	26	1.347	3.20	109	3.43	.245	0	....	1	3	0.1
1982	Oak-A	2	4	.333	54	0	0	0	3	102	111	60	59	11	0	52	67	1.598	5.21	75	4.94	.275	0	....	-15	2	-1.5
1983	Pit-N	0	0	....	1	0	0	0	0	0	2	1	1	1	0	0	0	....	∞	....	∞	1.000	0	....	-1	0	-0.1
1984	Cin-N	3	5	.375	49	4	0	0	2	94	91	47	43	10	0	39	60	1.383	4.12	92	3.93	.253	2	.167	-3	5	-0.2
1986	Mon-N	1	0	1.000	3	3	0	0	0	15	17	6	6	1	0	3	6	1.333	3.60	102	3.91	.288	1	.200	0	1	0.1
Total	10	37	60	.381	275	104	10	4	7	890^2	937	461	424	88	6	363	490	1.460	4.28	85	4.38	.274	22	.135	-65	32	-6.7

• OWEN, Frank Frank Malcolm "Yip" Owen b: 12/23/1879, Ypsilanti, MI d: 11/24/1942, Dearborn, MI BB/TR, 5'11", 160 lbs. Deb: 4/26/1901

YEAR	TM-L	W	L	PCT	G	GS	CG	SH	SV	IP	H	R	ER	HR	HB	BB	SO	RAT	ERA	ERA+	CERA	OAV	BH	AVG	PR+	WS	TPW
1901	Det-A	1	3	.250	8	5	3	0	0	56	70	43	27	1	4	30	17	1.786	4.34	89	5.54	.302	1	.050	-4	2	-0.6
1903	Chi-A	8	12	.400	26	20	15	1	1	167^1	167	85	65	1	7	44	66	1.261	3.50	80	2.91	.259	7	.123	-10	6	-1.2
1904	Chi-A	21	15	.583	37	36	34	4	1	315	243	95	68	2	11	61	103	.965	1.94	126	1.70	.214	23	.215	11	26	1.8
1905	Chi-A	21	13	.618	42	38	32	3	0	334	276	110	78	6	9	56	125	.994	2.10	117	1.92	.227	18	.145	4	22	0.0
1906*	Chi-A	22	13	.629	42	36	27	7	0	293	289	114	76	4	4	54	66	1.171	2.33	109	2.65	.261	14	.136	3	18	0.2
1907	Chi-A	2	3	.400	11	4	2	0	0	47	43	22	13	1	0	13	15	1.191	2.49	96	2.54	.246	4	.250	-0	2	0.0
1908	Chi-A	6	7	.462	25	14	5	1	0	140	142	79	53	2	3	37	48	1.279	3.41	68	3.08	.260	9	.180	-15	1	-1.7
1909	Chi-A	1	1	.500	3	2	1	0	0	16	19	8	8	0	1	3	3	1.375	4.50	52	3.59	.279	1	.167	-4	0	-0.5
Total	8	82	67	.550	194	155	119	16	2	1368^1	1249	556	388	17	39	298	443	1.131	2.55	101	2.45	.244	77	.159	-15	77	-1.9

• OWENS, Jim James Philip "Bear" Owens b: 1/16/1934, Gifford, PA BR/TR, 5'11", 190 lbs. Deb: 4/19/1955 C

YEAR	TM-L	W	L	PCT	G	GS	CG	SH	SV	IP	H	R	ER	HR	HB	BB	SO	RAT	ERA	ERA+	CERA	OAV	BH	AVG	PR+	WS	TPW
1955	Phi-N	0	2	.000	3	2	0	0	0	8^2	13	8	8	2	0	7	6	2.308	8.31	48	10.71	.382	0	.000	-4	0	-0.4
1956	Phi-N	0	4	.000	10	5	0	0	0	29^2	35	26	24	3	2	22	22	1.921	7.28	51	6.97	.313	1	.167	-11	0	-1.1
1958	Phi-N	1	0	1.000	1	1	0	0	0	7	4	4	2	1	0	5	3	1.286	2.57	154	3.06	.154	0	.000	1	1	0.1
1959	Phi-N	12	12	.500	31	30	11	1	1	221^1	203	97	79	14	4	73	135	1.247	3.21	128	3.11	.244	9	.120	23	16	2.2
1960	Phi-N	4	14	.222	31	22	6	0	0	150	182	95	84	21	1	64	83	1.640	5.04	77	5.64	.299	3	.068	-20	1	-2.3
1961	Phi-N	5	10	.333	20	17	3	0	0	106^2	119	62	53	8	0	32	38	1.416	4.47	91	4.15	.287	2	.074	-6	4	-0.8
1962	Phi-N	2	4	.333	23	12	1	0	0	69^2	90	53	49	12	0	33	21	1.766	6.33	61	6.75	.318	2	.143	-20	0	-2.0
1963	Cin-N	0	2	.000	19	3	0	0	4	42^1	42	28	25	6	0	24	29	1.559	5.31	63	4.84	.259	1	.125	-9	0	-1.0
1964	Hou-N	8	7	.533	48	11	0	0	6	118	115	48	43	7	0	32	88	1.246	3.28	104	3.11	.262	3	.103	3	9	0.3
1965	Hou-N	6	5	.545	50	0	0	0	8	71^1	64	28	26	4	0	29	53	1.304	3.28	102	3.01	.238	1	.125	2	7	0.2
1966	Hou-N	4	7	.364	40	0	0	0	2	50	53	29	26	5	1	17	32	1.400	4.68	73	3.97	.273	0	.000	-6	1	-0.7
1967	Hou-N	0	1	.000	10	0	0	0	0	10^2	12	5	5	1	0	2	6	1.313	4.22	78	3.95	.308	0	....	-1	0	-0.1
Total	12	42	68	.382	286	103	21	1	21	885^1	932	483	424	84	8	340	516	1.437	4.31	87	4.29	.273	22	.101	-49	39	-5.7

• OWNBEY, Rick Richard Wayne Ownbey b: 10/20/1957, Corona, CA BR/TR, 6'3", 185 lbs. Deb: 8/17/1982

YEAR	TM-L	W	L	PCT	G	GS	CG	SH	SV	IP	H	R	ER	HR	HB	BB	SO	RAT	ERA	ERA+	CERA	OAV	BH	AVG	PR+	WS	TPW
1982	NY-N	1	2	.333	8	8	2	0	0	50^1	44	23	21	3	0	43	28	1.728	3.75	97	4.80	.242	3	.200	-0	2	0.1
1983	NY-N	1	3	.250	10	4	0	0	0	34^2	31	19	18	4	1	21	19	1.500	4.67	78	4.57	.240	1	.111	-4	1	-0.5
1984	StL-N	0	3	.000	4	4	0	0	0	19	23	13	10	1	0	8	11	1.632	4.74	73	4.88	.303	0	.000	-3	0	-0.4
1986	StL-N	1	3	.250	17	3	0	0	0	42^2	47	20	18	4	2	19	25	1.547	3.80	96	5.18	.294	0	.000	-2	2	-0.3
Total	4	3	11	.214	39	19	2	0	0	146^2	145	75	67	12	3	91	83	1.609	4.11	88	4.87	.265	4	.114	-10	5	-1.1

• OZMER, Doc Horace Robert Ozmer b: 5/25/1901, Atlanta, GA d: 12/28/1970, Atlanta, GA BR/TR, 5'10.5", 185 lbs. Deb: 5/11/1923

YEAR	TM-L	W	L	PCT	G	GS	CG	SH	SV	IP	H	R	ER	HR	HB	BB	SO	RAT	ERA	ERA+	CERA	OAV	BH	AVG	PR+	WS	TPW
1923	Phi-A	0	0	....	1	0	0	0	0	2	1	1	1	0	0	1	1	1.000	4.50	91	1.34	.167	0	....	-0	0	0.0

• PABOR, Charlie Charles Henry Pabor b: 9/24/1846, Brooklyn, NY d: 4/23/1913, New Haven, CT BL/TL, 5'8", 155 lbs. Deb: 5/4/1871 M/U ♦

YEAR	TM-L	W	L	PCT	G	GS	CG	SH	SV	IP	H	R	ER	HR	HB	BB	SO	RAT	ERA	ERA+	CERA	OAV	BH	AVG	PR+	WS	TPW
1871	Cle-n	0	2	.000	7	1	1	0	0	29^1	50	53	22	4	....	6	0	1.909	6.75	61	....	.332	42	.296	-6	....	-0.7
1872	Cle-n	1	1	.500	2	2	2	0	0	18	20	15	8	0	....	3	0	1.278	4.00	121	....	.245	19	.207	2	....	-0.4
1875	Atl-n	0	1	.000	1	1	0	0	0	4	11	12	4	0	....	1	0	3.000	9.00	26	....	.460	36	.235	-3	....	-0.1
Total	3 n	1	4	.200	10	4	3	0	0	51^1	81	80	34	4	....	10	0	1.773	5.96	65	....	.316	204	.285	-7	....	-1.3

• PACELLA, John John Lewis Pacella b: 9/15/1956, Brooklyn, NY BR/TR, 6'3", 195 lbs. Deb: 9/15/1977

YEAR	TM-L	W	L	PCT	G	GS	CG	SH	SV	IP	H	R	ER	HR	HB	BB	SO	RAT	ERA	ERA+	CERA	OAV	BH	AVG	PR+	WS	TPW
1977	NY-N	0	0	....	3	0	0	0	0	4	2	2	0	0	0	2	1	1.000	0.00	....	1.33	.133	0	....	2	0	0.2
1979	NY-N	0	2	.000	4	3	0	0	0	16^1	16	8	8	0	0	4	12	1.224	4.41	83	2.65	.246	0	.000	-2	0	-0.2
1980	NY-N	3	4	.429	32	15	0	0	0	84	89	51	48	5	2	59	68	1.762	5.14	69	5.43	.280	2	.100	-15	0	-1.7
1982	NY-A	0	1	.000	3	1	0	0	0	10	13	8	8	0	1	9	2	2.200	7.20	55	7.38	.342	0	....	-4	0	-0.4
	Min-A	1	2	.333	21	1	0	0	2	51^2	61	48	42	14	0	37	20	1.897	7.32	58	8.05	.299	0	....	-18	0	-1.8
	Yr.	1	3	.250	24	2	0	0	2	61^2	74	56	50	14	1	46	22	1.946	7.30	57	7.94	.306	0	....	-22	0	-2.2
1984	Bal-A	0	1	.000	6	1	0	0	0	14^2	15	13	11	2	0	9	8	1.636	6.75	57	5.27	.268	0	....	-5	0	-0.5
1986	Det-A	0	0	....	5	0	0	0	1	11	10	5	5	0	0	13	5	2.091	4.09	101	6.04	.294	0	....	-0	1	0.0
Total	6	4	10	.286	74	21	0	0	3	191^2	206	135	122	21	3	133	116	1.769	5.73	67	5.94	.282	2	.083	-42	1	-4.4

• PACHECO, Alex Alexander Melchor (Lara) Pacheco b: 7/19/1973, Caracas, Venezuela BR/TR, 6'3", 200 lbs. Deb: 4/17/1996

YEAR	TM-L	W	L	PCT	G	GS	CG	SH	SV	IP	H	R	ER	HR	HB	BB	SO	RAT	ERA	ERA+	CERA	OAV	BH	AVG	PR+	WS	TPW
1996	Mon-N	0	0	....	5	0	0	0	0	5^2	8	7	7	2	0	1	7	1.588	11.12	39	7.35	.320	0	....	-4	0	-0.4

• PACILLO, Pat Patrick Michael Pacillo b: 7/23/1963, Jersey City, NJ BR/TR, 6'2", 205 lbs. Deb: 5/23/1987

YEAR	TM-L	W	L	PCT	G	GS	CG	SH	SV	IP	H	R	ER	HR	HB	BB	SO	RAT	ERA	ERA+	CERA	OAV	BH	AVG	PR+	WS	TPW
1987	Cin-N	3	3	.500	12	7	0	0	0	39^2	41	30	27	7	1	19	23	1.513	6.13	69	5.27	.270	1	.091	-8	0	-0.8
1988	Cin-N	1	0	1.000	6	0	0	0	0	10^2	14	7	6	2	0	4	11	1.688	5.06	71	6.50	.318	0	.000	-2	0	-0.2
Total	2	4	3	.571	18	7	0	0	0	50^1	55	37	33	9	1	23	34	1.550	5.90	70	5.53	.281	1	.083	-10	0	-1.1

• PACKARD, Gene Eugene Milo Packard b: 7/13/1887, Colorado Springs, CO d: 5/19/1959, Riverside, CA BL/TL, 5'10", 155 lbs. Deb: 9/27/1912

YEAR	TM-L	W	L	PCT	G	GS	CG	SH	SV	IP	H	R	ER	HR	HB	BB	SO	RAT	ERA	ERA+	CERA	OAV	BH	AVG	PR+	WS	TPW
1912	Cin-N	1	0	1.000	1	1	1	0	0	9	7	3	3	0	0	4	2	1.222	3.00	112	2.25	.206	1	.250	0	1	0.1
1913	Cin-N	7	11	.389	39	21	9	2	0	190^2	208	97	63	2	8	64	73	1.427	2.97	109	3.78	.286	11	.180	5	9	0.5
1914	KC-F	20	14	.588	42	34	24	4	5	302	282	127	97	5	3	88	154	1.225	2.89	106	2.78	.246	28	.241	5	21	0.9
1915	KC-F	20	12	.625	42	31	21	5	2	281^2	250	111	84	3	9	74	108	1.150	2.68	109	2.55	.242	22	.232	9	22	1.3
1916	Chi-N	10	6	.625	37	16	5	2	5	155^1	154	60	48	4	3	38	36	1.236	2.78	104	2.87	.256	7	.130	4	12	0.3
1917	Chi-N	0	0	....	2	0	0	0	0	1^2	3	2	2	1	0	0	1	1.800	10.80	27	11.17	.375	0	....	-1	0	-0.2
	StL-N	9	6	.600	34	11	6	0	2	153^1	138	48	42	4	3	25	44	1.063	2.47	109	2.28	.246	15	.288	2	15	0.6
	Yr.	9	6	.600	36	11	6	0	2	155	141	50	44	5	3	25	45	1.071	2.55	105	2.38	.248	15	.288	1	15	0.5
1918	StL-N	12	12	.500	30	23	10	1	2	182^1	184	84	71	6	5	33	46	1.190	3.50	77	2.95	.266	12	.174	-17	7	-2.0
1919	Phi-N	6	8	.429	21	16	10	1	1	134^1	167	70	62	3	4	30	24	1.467	4.15	77	4.41	.321	7	.137	-13	4	-1.6
Total	8	85	69	.552	248	153	86	15	17	1410^1	1393	602	472	28	35	356	488	1.240	3.01	99	3.01	.262	103	.205	-6	91	-0.1

• PACTWA, Joe Joseph Martin Pactwa b: 6/2/1948, Hammond, IN BL/TL, 5'11", 185 lbs. Deb: 9/15/1975

YEAR	TM-L	W	L	PCT	G	GS	CG	SH	SV	IP	H	R	ER	HR	HB	BB	SO	RAT	ERA	ERA+	CERA	OAV	BH	AVG	PR+	WS	TPW
1975	Cal-A	1	0	1.000	4	3	0	0	0	16^1	23	7	7	0	0	10	3	2.020	3.86	92	6.64	.343	0	....	-1	1	-0.1

• PADILLA, Vicente Vicente de la Cruz Padilla b: 9/27/1977, Chinandega, Nicaragua BR/TR, 6'2", 200 lbs. Deb: 6/29/1999

YEAR	TM-L	W	L	PCT	G	GS	CG	SH	SV	IP	H	R	ER	HR	HB	BB	SO	RAT	ERA	ERA+	CERA	OAV	BH	AVG	PR+	WS	TPW
1999	Ari-N	0	1	.000	5	0	0	0	0	2^2	7	5	5	1	0	3	0	3.750	16.88	27	20.65	.467	0	....	-4	0	-0.3
2000	Ari-N	2	1	.667	27	0	0	0	0	35	32	10	9	0	0	10	30	1.200	2.31	203	2.48	.242	1	1.000	9	5	0.9
	Phi-N	2	6	.250	28	0	0	0	2	30^1	40	23	18	3	1	18	21	1.912	5.34	87	6.52	.328	0	....	-2	1	-0.2
	Yr.	4	7	.364	55	0	0	0	2	65^1	72	33	27	3	1	28	51	1.531	3.72	126	4.35	.283	1	1.000	7	6	0.7
2001	Phi-N	3	1	.750	23	0	0	0	0	34	36	18	16	1	0	12	29	1.412	4.24	100	3.80	.273	1	.333	-0	3	0.1
2002	Phi-N★	14	11	.560	32	32	1	1	0	206	198	83	75	16	15	53	128	1.218	3.28	119	3.42	.254	3	.052	13	14	0.9
2003	Phi-N	14	12	.538	32	32	1	1	0	208^2	196	94	84	22	16	62	133	1.236	3.62	110	3.68	.251	4	.060	9	13	0.6
Total	5	35	32	.522	147	64	2	2	2	516^2	509	233	207	43	32	158	341	1.291	3.61	113	3.76	.259	9	.070	25	36	1.9

• PAGAN, Dave David Percy Pagan b: 9/15/1949, Nipawin, Canada BR/TR, 6'2", 175 lbs. Deb: 7/1/1973

YEAR	TM-L	W	L	PCT	G	GS	CG	SH	SV	IP	H	R	ER	HR	HB	BB	SO	RAT	ERA	ERA+	CERA	OAV	BH	AVG	PR+	WS	TPW
1973	NY-A	0	0	....	4	1	0	0	0	12^2	16	4	4	1	0	1	9	1.342	2.84	129	4.38	.320	0	....	1	1	0.1
1974	NY-A	1	3	.250	16	6	1	0	0	49^1	49	29	28	1	0	28	39	1.561	5.11	68	4.22	.265	0	....	-10	0	-1.0
1975	NY-A	0	0	....	13	0	0	0	1	31	30	16	14	2	2	13	18	1.387	4.06	90	3.70	.256	0	....	-2	1	-0.2
1976	NY-A	1	1	.500	7	2	1	0	0	23^2	18	7	6	0	0	4	13	.930	2.28	150	1.61	.222	0	....	2	2	0.2
	Bal-A	1	4	.200	20	5	0	0	1	46^2	54	33	31	2	1	23	34	1.650	5.98	55	4.95	.298	0	....	-15	0	-1.5
	Yr.	2	5	.286	27	7	1	0	1	70^1	72	40	37	2	1	27	47	1.408	4.73	70	3.83	.275	0	....	-12	2	-1.3
1977	Sea-A	1	1	.500	24	4	1	1	2	66	86	52	45	3	2	26	30	1.697	6.14	67	5.55	.323	0	....	-16	0	-1.6
	Pit-N	0	0	....	1	0	0	0	0	3	1	0	0	0	0	0	4	.333	0.00	....	0.25	.100	0	....	1	0	0.1
Total	5	4	9	.308	85	18	3	1	4	232^1	254	141	128	9	5	95	147	1.502	4.96	73	4.37	.285	0	....	-38	4	-3.9

• PAGE, Joe Joseph Francis "Fireman" Page b: 10/28/1917, Cherry Valley, PA d: 4/21/1980, Latrobe, PA BL/TL, 6'3", 205 lbs. Deb: 4/19/1944

YEAR	TM-L	W	L	PCT	G	GS	CG	SH	SV	IP	H	R	ER	HR	HB	BB	SO	RAT	ERA	ERA+	CERA	OAV	BH	AVG	PR+	WS	TPW
1944	NY-A★	5	7	.417	19	16	4	0	0	102^2	100	65	52	3	3	52	63	1.481	4.56	76	3.79	.258	5	.156	-14	1	-1.5
1945	NY-A	6	3	.667	20	9	4	0	0	102	95	43	32	1	0	46	50	1.382	2.82	122	3.14	.246	9	.250	5	7	0.6
1946	NY-A	9	8	.529	31	17	6	1	3	136	126	66	54	7	4	72	77	1.456	3.57	97	3.85	.252	7	.163	-6	7	-0.6
1947*	NY-A★	14	8	.636	56	2	0	0	**17**	141^1	105	41	39	5	1	72	116	1.252	2.48	142	2.63	.208	10	.217	16	17	1.7
1948	NY-A★	7	8	.467	**55**	1	0	0	16	107^2	116	59	51	6	1	66	77	1.690	4.26	96	4.79	.275	7	.292	-4	8	0.0
1949*	NY-A	13	8	.619	**60**	0	0	0	**27**	135^1	103	44	39	8	5	75	99	1.315	2.59	156	3.12	.215	7	.175	19	19	1.7
1950	NY-A	3	7	.300	37	0	0	0	13	55^1	66	34	31	8	0	31	33	1.753	5.04	85	6.02	.295	2	.250	-5	3	-0.4
1954	Pit-N	0	0	....	7	0	0	0	0	9^2	16	17	12	4	1	7	4	2.379	11.17	38	12.45	.364	0	....	-7	0	-0.7
Total	8	57	49	.538	285	45	14	1	76	790	727	369	310	42	15	421	519	1.453	3.53	106	3.79	.247	47	.205	3	62	0.7

• PAGE, Phil Philippe Rausac Page b: 8/23/1905, Springfield, MA d: 7/27/1958, Springfield, MA BR/TL, 6'2", 175 lbs. Deb: 9/18/1928 C

YEAR	TM-L	W	L	PCT	G	GS	CG	SH	SV	IP	H	R	ER	HR	HB	BB	SO	RAT	ERA	ERA+	CERA	OAV	BH	AVG	PR+	WS	TPW
1928	Det-A	2	0	1.000	3	2	2	0	0	22	21	9	6	1	0	10	3	1.409	2.45	167	3.62	.256	2	.222	4	2	0.4
1929	Det-A	0	2	.000	10	4	1	0	0	25^1	29	24	23	1	1	19	6	1.895	8.17	52	5.57	.296	1	.125	-10	0	-1.0
1930	Det-A	0	1	.000	12	0	0	0	0	12	23	16	13	1	0	9	2	2.667	9.75	49	11.59	.434	0	....	-7	0	-0.6
1934	Bro-N	1	0	1.000	6	0	0	0	0	10	13	7	6	1	0	6	4	1.900	5.40	72	6.81	.342	0	.000	-2	0	-0.2
Total	4	3	3	.500	31	6	3	0	0	69^1	86	56	48	4	1	44	15	1.875	6.23	70	6.17	.317	3	.167	-14	2	-1.4

• PAGE, Sam Samuel Walter Page b: 2/11/1916, Woodruff, SC d: 5/29/2002, Greenville, SC BL/TR, 6', 172 lbs. Deb: 9/11/1939

YEAR	TM-L	W	L	PCT	G	GS	CG	SH	SV	IP	H	R	ER	HR	HB	BB	SO	RAT	ERA	ERA+	CERA	OAV	BH	AVG	PR+	WS	TPW
1939	Phi-A	0	3	.000	4	3	1	0	0	22	34	27	17	1	0	15	11	2.227	6.95	68	7.73	.343	3	.429	-5	0	-0.3

• PAGE, Vance Vance Linwood Page b: 9/15/1905, Elm City, NC d: 7/14/1951, Wilson, NC BR/TR, 6', 180 lbs. Deb: 8/6/1938

YEAR	TM-L	W	L	PCT	G	GS	CG	SH	SV	IP	H	R	ER	HR	HB	BB	SO	RAT	ERA	ERA+	CERA	OAV	BH	AVG	PR+	WS	TPW
1938*	Chi-N	5	4	.556	13	9	3	0	1	68	90	33	29	4	0	13	18	1.515	3.84	100	4.82	.323	4	.154	-1	4	-0.2
1939	Chi-N	7	7	.500	27	17	8	1	1	139^1	169	77	60	8	1	37	43	1.478	3.88	102	4.32	.298	12	.255	5	8	0.7
1940	Chi-N	1	3	.250	30	1	0	0	2	59	65	38	29	1	0	26	22	1.542	4.42	85	3.80	.271	4	.308	-4	2	-0.3
1941	Chi-N	2	2	.500	25	3	1	0	1	48^1	48	24	23	2	2	30	17	1.614	4.28	82	4.36	.254	2	.286	-3	2	-0.2
Total	4	15	16	.484	95	30	12	1	5	314^2	372	172	141	15	3	106	100	1.519	4.03	94	4.34	.292	22	.237	-3	16	0.1

• PAIGE, Pat George Lynn "Piggy" Paige b: 5/5/1882, Paw Paw, MI d: 6/8/1939, Berlin, WI BL/TR, 5'10", 175 lbs. Deb: 5/20/1911

YEAR	TM-L	W	L	PCT	G	GS	CG	SH	SV	IP	H	R	ER	HR	HB	BB	SO	RAT	ERA	ERA+	CERA	OAV	BH	AVG	PR+	WS	TPW
1911	Cle-A	1	0	1.000	2	1	1	0	0	16	21	12	8	0	0	7	6	1.750	4.50	76	5.55	.339	1	.143	-2	0	-0.2

• PAIGE, Satchel Leroy Robert Paige b: 7/7/1906, Mobile, AL d: 6/8/1982, Kansas City, MO BR/TR, 6'3.5", 180 lbs. Deb: 7/9/1948 C HOF: 1971

YEAR	TM-L	W	L	PCT	G	GS	CG	SH	SV	IP	H	R	ER	HR	HB	BB	SO	RAT	ERA	ERA+	CERA	OAV	BH	AVG	PR+	WS	TPW
1948*	Cle-A	6	1	.857	21	7	3	2	1	72^2	61	21	20	2	1	22	43	1.142	2.48	164	2.37	.226	2	.087	11	7	0.8
1949	Cle-A	4	7	.364	31	5	1	0	5	83	70	29	28	4	1	33	54	1.241	3.04	131	2.81	.230	1	.063	8	8	0.7
1951	StL-A	3	4	.429	23	3	0	0	5	62	67	39	33	6	1	29	48	1.548	4.79	92	4.69	.276	2	.125	-1	3	-0.3
1952	StL-A★	12	10	.545	46	6	3	2	10	138	116	51	47	5	3	57	91	1.254	3.07	128	2.80	.226	5	.128	12	13	1.1
1953	StL-A★	3	9	.250	57	4	0	0	11	117^1	114	51	46	12	1	39	51	1.304	3.53	119	3.68	.257	2	.069	10	11	0.6
1965	KC-A	0	0	....	1	1	0	0	0	3	1	0	0	0	0	0	1	.333	0.00	....	0.25	.100	0	.000	1	0	0.1
Total	6	28	31	.475	179	26	7	4	32	476	429	191	174	29	7	180	288	1.279	3.29	125	3.18	.240	12	.097	41	42	3.0

• PAINE, Phil Phillips Steere "Flip" Paine b: 6/8/1930, Chepachet, RI d: 2/19/1978, Lebanon, PA BR/TR, 6'2", 181 lbs. Deb: 7/14/1951

YEAR	TM-L	W	L	PCT	G	GS	CG	SH	SV	IP	H	R	ER	HR	HB	BB	SO	RAT	ERA	ERA+	CERA	OAV	BH	AVG	PR+	WS	TPW
1951	Bos-N	2	0	1.000	21	0	0	0	0	35^1	36	15	12	2	4	20	17	1.585	3.06	120	4.90	.271	0	.000	3	3	0.2
1954	Mil-N	1	0	1.000	11	0	0	0	0	14	14	9	6	1	1	12	11	1.857	3.86	97	6.02	.292	0	....	-0	1	0.0
1955	Mil-N	2	0	1.000	15	0	0	0	0	25^1	20	8	7	2	0	14	26	1.342	2.49	151	3.14	.225	1	.333	4	2	0.4
1956	Mil-N	0	0	....	1	0	0	0	0	0	3	2	0	0	0	0	0	....	....	....	∞	1.000	0	....	0	0	0.0
1957	Mil-N	0	0	....	1	0	0	0	0	2	1	0	0	0	0	3	2	2.000	0.00	....	4.47	.143	0	....	1	0	0.1
1958	StL-N	5	1	.833	46	0	0	0	1	73^1	70	33	29	7	5	31	45	1.377	3.56	116	4.13	.256	2	.286	5	7	0.5
Total	6	10	1	.909	95	0	0	0	1	150	144	67	54	12	10	80	101	1.493	3.24	121	4.33	.260	3	.214	11	13	1.1

• PAINTER, Lance Lance Telford Painter b: 7/21/1967, Bedford, England BL/TL, 6'1", 195 lbs. Deb: 5/19/1993

YEAR	TM-L	W	L	PCT	G	GS	CG	SH	SV	IP	H	R	ER	HR	HB	BB	SO	RAT	ERA	ERA+	CERA	OAV	BH	AVG	PR+	WS	TPW
1993	Col-N	2	2	.500	10	6	1	0	0	39	52	26	26	5	0	9	16	1.564	6.00	79	5.83	.333	3	.300	-4	2	-0.3
1994	Col-N	4	6	.400	15	14	0	0	0	73^2	91	51	50	9	1	26	41	1.588	6.11	81	5.35	.302	3	.143	-7	2	-0.7
1995*	Col-N	3	0	1.000	33	1	0	0	1	45^1	55	23	22	9	2	10	36	1.434	4.37	123	5.50	.296	1	.111	6	4	0.6
1996	Col-N	4	2	.667	34	1	0	0	0	50^2	56	37	33	12	3	25	48	1.599	5.86	89	6.19	.280	2	.133	-2	3	-0.3
1997	StL-N	1	1	.500	14	0	0	0	0	17	13	9	9	1	0	8	11	1.235	4.76	87	2.71	.213	0	.000	-1	1	-0.1
1998	StL-N	4	0	1.000	65	0	0	0	1	47^1	42	24	21	5	4	28	39	1.479	3.99	105	4.56	.249	1	1.000	1	4	0.2
1999	StL-N	4	5	.444	56	4	0	0	1	63^1	63	37	34	6	2	25	56	1.389	4.83	95	4.12	.265	0	.000	-2	4	-0.2
2000	Tor-A	2	0	1.000	42	2	0	0	0	66^2	69	37	35	9	2	22	53	1.365	4.73	107	4.37	.271	0	....	3	4	0.2

YEAR	TM-L	W	L	PCT	G	GS	CG	SH	SV	IP	H	R	ER	HR	HB	BB	SO	RAT	ERA	ERA+	CERA	OAV	BH	AVG	PR+	WS	TPW
2001	Tor-A	0	1	.000	10	0	0	0	0	18^1	27	17	16	4	1	11	14	2.073	7.85	58	9.25	.342	0	....	-7	0	-0.6
	Mil-N	1	0	1.000	13	0	0	0	0	10^2	11	5	5	3	0	7	6	1.688	4.22	102	6.53	.268	0	....	0	1	0.0
2003	StL-N	0	1	.000	22	0	0	0	0	18	17	12	11	3	0	7	11	1.333	5.50	74	4.07	.246	0	.000	-3	0	-0.3
Total	10	25	18	.581	314	28	1	0	3	450	496	278	262	66	15	178	331	1.498	5.24	91	5.14	.283	10	.154	-16	25	-1.6
• PALACIOS, Vicente					Vicente (Diaz) Palacios b: 7/19/1963, Veracruz, Mexico BR/TR, 6'3", 195 lbs. Deb: 9/4/1987																						
1987	Pit-N	2	1	.667	6	4	0	0	0	29^1	27	14	14	1	1	9	13	1.227	4.30	96	3.00	.250	1	.111	-1	2	-0.1
1988	Pit-N	1	2	.333	7	3	0	0	0	24^1	28	18	18	3	0	15	15	1.767	6.66	51	5.98	.295	0	.000	-9	0	-1.0
1990	Pit-N	0	0	....	7	0	0	0	3	15	4	0	0	0	0	2	8	.400	0.00	....	0.30	.083	0	.000	6	4	0.6
1991	Pit-N	6	3	.667	36	7	1	1	3	81^2	69	34	34	12	1	38	64	1.310	3.75	95	3.80	.228	1	.071	-2	5	-0.3
1992	Pit-N	3	2	.600	20	8	0	0	0	53	56	25	25	1	0	27	33	1.566	4.25	81	4.27	.280	1	.071	-5	2	-0.6
1994	StL-N	3	8	.273	31	17	1	1	1	117^2	104	60	58	16	3	43	95	1.249	4.44	94	3.70	.245	0	.000	-4	5	-0.8
1995	StL-N	2	3	.400	20	5	0	0	0	40^1	48	29	26	7	2	19	34	1.661	5.80	72	6.29	.300	1	.167	-8	0	-0.8
2000	SD-N	0	1	.000	7	0	0	0	0	10^2	12	10	8	4	0	5	8	1.594	6.75	64	7.37	.308	0	....	-3	0	-0.3
Total	8	17	20	.459	134	44	2	2	7	372	348	190	183	44	7	158	270	1.360	4.43	87	4.15	.253	4	.045	-26	18	-3.3
• PALAGYI, Mike					Michael Raymond Palagyi b: 7/4/1917, Conneaut, OH BR/TR, 6'2", 185 lbs. Deb: 8/18/1939																						
1939	Was-A	0	0	....	1	0	0	0	0	0	0	3	3	0	1	3	0	....	∞	....	∞	1.000	0	....	-3	0	-0.3
• PALICA, Erv					Ervin Martin Palica b: 2/9/1928, Lomita, CA d: 5/29/1982, Huntington Beach, CA BR/TR, 6'1.5", 180 lbs. Deb: 4/21/1945																						
1947	Bro-N	0	1	.000	3	0	0	0	0	3	2	1	1	0	1	2	1	1.333	3.00	138	3.10	.182	0	....	0	0	0.0
1948	Bro-N	6	6	.500	41	10	3	0	3	125^1	111	63	62	13	3	58	74	1.348	4.45	90	3.74	.239	5	.128	-9	6	-0.9
1949*	Bro-N	8	9	.471	49	1	0	0	6	97	93	43	39	6	1	49	44	1.464	3.62	113	4.01	.261	3	.158	3	8	0.4
1950	Bro-N	13	8	.619	43	19	10	2	1	201^1	176	89	80	13	2	98	131	1.361	3.58	115	3.44	.237	15	.221	7	16	0.9
1951	Bro-N	2	6	.250	19	8	0	0	0	53	55	28	28	10	0	20	15	1.415	4.75	83	4.68	.259	2	.154	-6	2	-0.6
1953	Bro-N	0	0	....	4	0	0	0	0	6	10	8	8	1	0	8	3	3.000	12.00	36	12.87	.370	1	1.000	-5	0	-0.5
1954	Bro-N	3	3	.500	25	3	0	0	0	67^2	77	45	40	9	1	31	25	1.596	5.32	77	5.18	.285	4	.250	-9	2	-0.8
1955	Bal-A	5	11	.313	33	25	5	1	0	169^2	165	91	78	10	2	83	68	1.462	4.14	92	3.99	.260	13	.236	-4	6	-0.1
1956	Bal-A	4	11	.267	29	14	2	0	0	116^1	117	64	58	10	1	50	62	1.436	4.49	87	4.06	.264	5	.156	-7	4	-0.8
Total	9	41	55	.427	246	80	20	3	10	839^1	806	432	394	72	11	399	423	1.436	4.22	94	4.03	.255	48	.198	-29	44	-2.4
• PALL, Donn					Donn Steven Pall b: 1/11/1962, Chicago, IL BR/TR, 6'2", 183 lbs. Deb: 8/1/1988																						
1988	Chi-A	0	2	.000	17	0	0	0	0	28^2	39	11	11	1	0	8	16	1.640	3.45	115	5.11	.328	0	....	1	2	0.1
1989	Chi-A	4	5	.444	53	0	0	0	6	87	90	35	32	9	8	19	58	1.253	3.31	115	3.89	.270	0	....	5	6	0.5
1990	Chi-A	3	5	.375	56	0	0	0	2	76	63	33	28	7	4	24	39	1.145	3.32	115	2.91	.232	0	....	3	6	0.3
1991	Chi-A	7	2	.778	51	0	0	0	0	71	59	22	19	7	3	20	40	1.113	2.41	165	2.91	.231	0	....	10	8	1.0
1992	Chi-A	5	2	.714	39	0	0	0	1	73	79	43	40	9	2	27	27	1.452	4.93	78	4.47	.272	0	....	-9	2	-0.9
1993	Chi-A	2	3	.400	39	0	0	0	1	58^2	62	25	21	5	2	11	29	1.244	3.22	130	3.43	.268	0	....	6	5	0.6
	Phi-N	1	0	1.000	8	0	0	0	0	17^2	15	7	5	1	0	3	11	1.019	2.55	156	2.21	.231	0	....	3	2	0.3
1994	NY-A	1	2	.333	26	0	0	0	0	35	43	18	14	3	1	9	21	1.486	3.60	127	4.73	.295	0	....	3	2	0.3
	Chi-N	0	0	....	2	0	0	0	0	4	8	2	2	1	0	1	2	2.250	4.50	92	12.16	.444	0	....	-0	0	0.0
1996	Fla-N	1	1	.500	12	0	0	0	0	18^2	16	15	12	3	0	9	9	1.339	5.79	70	3.91	.232	0	.000	-4	0	-0.4
1997	Fla-N	0	0	....	2	0	0	0	0	2^1	3	1	1	1	0	1	0	1.714	3.86	105	8.35	.300	0	.000	0	0	0.0
1998	Fla-N	0	1	.000	23	0	0	0	0	33^1	42	19	19	5	1	7	26	1.470	5.13	80	5.42	.326	0	.000	-4	1	-0.4
Total	10	24	23	.511	328	0	0	0	10	505^1	519	231	204	52	21	139	278	1.302	3.63	109	3.89	.268	0	.000	15	34	1.4
• PALM, Mike					Richard Paul Palm b: 2/13/1925, Boston, MA BR/TR, 6'3.5", 190 lbs. Deb: 7/11/1948																						
1948	Bos-A	0	0	....	3	0	0	0	0	3	6	2	2	0	0	5	1	3.667	6.00	73	14.42	.400	0	.000	-1	0	-0.1
• PALMER, Billy					Billy Palmer b: St. Louis, MO Deb: 5/28/1885																						
1885	StL-N	0	4	.000	4	4	4	0	0	34	46	33	13	2	....	20	9	1.941	3.44	80	....	.309	1	.091	-4	0	-0.3
• PALMER, David					David William Palmer b: 8/19/1957, Glens Falls, NY BR/TR, 6'1", 205 lbs. Deb: 9/9/1978																						
1978	Mon-N	0	1	.000	5	1	0	0	0	9^2	9	4	3	1	0	2	7	1.138	2.79	126	3.02	.243	0	.000	0	0	0.0
1979	Mon-N	10	2	.833	36	11	2	1	2	122^2	110	41	36	10	2	30	72	1.141	2.64	139	2.79	.237	1	.032	13	11	1.1
1980	Mon-N	8	6	.571	24	19	3	1	0	129^2	124	53	43	11	2	30	73	1.188	2.98	120	3.18	.255	9	.200	9	8	1.1
1982	Mon-N	6	4	.600	13	13	1	0	0	73^2	60	34	26	3	2	36	46	1.303	3.18	115	3.07	.224	1	.042	3	4	0.1
1984	Mon-N	7	3	.700	20	19	1	1	0	105^1	101	45	45	5	0	44	66	1.377	3.84	89	3.55	.256	5	.152	-6	5	-0.6
1985	Mon-N	7	10	.412	24	23	0	0	0	135^2	128	60	56	5	3	67	106	1.437	3.71	91	3.72	.250	4	.111	-6	5	-0.8
1986	Atl-N	11	10	.524	35	35	2	0	0	209^2	181	98	85	17	5	102	170	1.350	3.65	109	3.60	.234	12	.182	10	13	1.2
1987	Atl-N	8	11	.421	28	28	0	0	0	152^1	169	94	83	17	7	64	111	1.530	4.90	89	4.97	.281	6	.125	-9	5	-0.9
1988	Phi-N	7	9	.438	22	22	1	1	0	129	129	67	64	8	0	48	85	1.372	4.47	80	3.65	.261	10	.256	-11	5	-0.7
1989	Det-A	0	3	.000	5	5	0	0	0	17^1	25	19	15	1	0	11	12	2.077	7.79	49	7.47	.342	0	....	-7	0	-0.8
Total	10	64	59	.520	212	176	10	4	2	1085	1036	515	456	78	21	434	748	1.355	3.78	99	3.69	.252	48	.149	-3	56	-0.1
• PALMER, Jim					James Alvin "Cakes" Palmer b: 10/15/1945, New York, NY BR/TR, 6'3", 196 lbs. Deb: 4/17/1965 HOF: 1990																						
1965	Bal-A	5	4	.556	27	6	0	0	1	92	75	49	38	6	2	56	75	1.424	3.72	93	3.74	.229	5	.192	-4	4	-0.3
1966*	Bal-A	15	10	.600	30	30	6	0	0	208^1	176	83	80	21	0	91	147	1.282	3.46	96	3.41	.231	7	.096	-4	11	-0.6
1967	Bal-A	3	1	.750	9	9	2	1	0	49	34	18	16	6	0	20	23	1.102	2.94	107	2.70	.199	1	.077	0	3	0.0
1969*	Bal-A	16	4	.800	26	23	11	6	0	181	131	48	47	11	1	64	123	1.077	2.34	152	2.26	.200	13	.203	18	18	2.1
1970*	Bal-A★	20	10	.667	39	39	17	**5**	0	**305**	263	98	92	21	1	100	199	1.190	2.71	134	2.85	.231	17	.150	25	25	2.4
1971*	Bal-A★	20	9	.690	37	37	20	3	0	282	231	94	84	19	4	106	184	1.195	2.68	125	2.83	.221	20	.196	18	22	2.1
1972	Bal-A★	21	10	.677	36	36	18	3	0	274^1	219	73	63	21	1	70	184	1.053	2.07	149	2.35	.217	22	.224	24	25	3.2
1973*	Bal-A	22	9	.710	38	37	19	6	1	296^1	225	86	79	16	3	113	158	1.141	**2.40**	156	**2.51**	.211	0	....	31	28	3.2
1974*	Bal-A	7	12	.368	26	26	5	2	0	178^2	176	78	65	12	3	69	84	1.371	3.27	105	3.72	.257	0	....	1	9	0.1
1975	Bal-A★	**23**	11	.676	39	38	25	**10**	1	323	253	87	75	20	2	80	193	1.031	**2.09**	**168**	2.20	.216	0	....	**41**	**31**	**4.2**
1976	Bal-A	**22**	13	.629	40	**40**	23	6	0	**315**	255	101	88	20	8	84	159	1.076	2.51	130	2.46	.224	0	....	23	**27**	2.5
1977	Bal-A★	**20**	11	.645	39	**39**	**22**	3	0	**319**	263	106	103	24	3	99	193	1.135	2.91	130	2.76	.229	0	....	23	**29**	2.2
1978	Bal-A★	21	12	.636	38	38	19	6	0	**296**	246	94	81	19	1	97	138	1.159	2.46	142	2.72	.227	0	....	30	27	3.1
1979*	Bal-A	10	6	.625	23	22	7	0	0	155^2	144	66	57	12	0	43	67	1.201	3.30	122	3.06	.246	0	....	10	12	1.0
1980	Bal-A	16	10	.615	34	33	4	0	0	224	238	108	99	26	3	74	109	1.393	3.98	99	4.36	.275	0	....	-5	12	-0.5
1981	Bal-A	7	8	.467	22	22	5	0	0	127^1	117	60	53	14	2	46	35	1.280	3.75	97	3.63	.247	0	....	-1	6	-0.1
1982	Bal-A	15	5	.750	36	32	8	2	1	227	195	85	79	22	4	63	103	1.137	3.13	129	**2.92**	.231	0	....	22	20	2.2
1983*	Bal-A	5	4	.556	14	11	0	0	0	76^2	86	42	36	11	0	19	34	1.370	4.23	93	4.43	.283	0	....	-2	3	-0.2
1984	Bal-A	0	3	.000	5	3	0	0	0	17^2	22	19	18	2	0	17	4	2.208	9.17	42	8.02	.319	0	....	-11	0	-1.1
Total	19	268	152	.638	558	521	211	53	4	3948	3349	1395	1253	303	38	1311	2212	1.180	2.86	125	2.93	.230	85	.174	239	312	25.5
• PALMER, Lowell					Lowell Raymond Palmer b: 8/18/1947, Sacramento, CA BR/TR, 6'1", 190 lbs. Deb: 6/21/1969																						
1969	Phi-N	2	8	.200	26	9	1	1	0	90	91	54	52	12	6	47	68	1.533	5.20	68	4.98	.264	3	.136	-17	1	-1.7
1970	Phi-N	1	2	.333	38	5	0	0	0	102	98	66	62	15	5	55	85	1.500	5.47	73	4.93	.255	4	.148	-16	1	-1.5
1971	Phi-N	0	0	....	3	1	0	0	0	15	13	11	10	3	4	13	6	1.733	6.00	59	7.17	.236	1	.200	-4	0	-0.5
1972	StL-N	0	3	.000	16	2	0	0	0	34^2	30	16	15	2	1	26	25	1.615	3.89	87	4.50	.244	0	.000	-2	1	-0.3
	Cle-A	0	0	....	1	0	0	0	0	2	2	1	1	0	0	2	3	2.000	4.50	71	4.93	.222	0	....	-0	0	0.0
1974	SD-N	2	5	.286	22	8	1	0	0	73	68	48	46	9	7	59	52	1.740	5.67	63	5.78	.256	2	.087	-15	0	-1.7
Total	5	5	18	.217	106	25	2	1	0	316^2	302	196	186	41	23	202	239	1.592	5.29	69	5.20	.255	10	.122	-54	3	-5.6
• PALMERO, Emilio					Emilio Antonio "Pal" Palmero b: 6/13/1895, Guanabacoa, Cuba d: 7/15/1970, Toledo, OH BL/TL, 5'11", 157 lbs. Deb: 9/21/1915																						
1915	NY-N	0	2	.000	3	2	1	0	0	11^2	10	4	4	0	3	9	8	1.629	3.09	83	4.55	.233	1	.250	-1	0	-0.1
1916	NY-N	0	3	.000	4	2	0	0	0	15^2	17	14	14	2	1	8	8	1.596	8.04	30	5.36	.288	0	.000	-10	0	-1.1
1921	StL-A	4	7	.364	24	9	4	0	0	90	109	63	50	1	6	49	26	1.756	5.00	90	5.39	.319	8	.216	-5	4	-0.4

YEAR TM-L	W	L	PCT	G	GS	CG	SH	SV	IP	H	R	ER	HR	HB	BB	SO	RAT	ERA	ERA+	CERA	OAV	BH	AVG	PR+	WS	TPW
1926 Was-A	2	2	.500	7	3	0	0	0	17	22	15	9	1	1	15	6	2.176	4.76	81	7.63	.344	1	.333	-2	0	-0.2
1928 Bos-N	0	1	.000	3	1	0	0	0	6^2	14	8	4	0	0	2	0	2.400	5.40	72	9.98	.452	0	.000	-1	0	-0.1
Total 5	6	15	.286	41	17	5	0	0	141	172	104	81	4	11	83	48	1.809	5.17	72	5.81	.319	10	.208	-18	4	-1.8

• PALMQUIST, Ed — Edwin Lee Palmquist b: 6/10/1933, Los Angeles, CA BR/TR, 6'3", 195 lbs. Deb: 6/10/1960

YEAR TM-L	W	L	PCT	G	GS	CG	SH	SV	IP	H	R	ER	HR	HB	BB	SO	RAT	ERA	ERA+	CERA	OAV	BH	AVG	PR+	WS	TPW
1960 LA-N	0	1	.000	22	0	0	0	0	39	34	16	11	6	1	16	23	1.282	2.54	156	3.75	.243	0	.000	6	3	0.5
1961 LA-N	0	1	.000	5	0	0	0	1	8^2	10	8	6	0	2	7	5	1.962	6.23	70	6.88	.333	0	....	-2	0	-0.2
Min-A	1	1	.500	9	2	0	0	0	21	33	23	22	7	3	13	13	2.190	9.43	45	11.13	.359	0	.000	-12	0	-1.2
Total 2	1	3	.250	36	2	0	0	1	68^2	77	47	39	13	6	36	41	1.646	5.11	82	6.40	.294	0	.000	-8	3	-0.9

• PANIAGUA, Jose — Jose Luis (Sanchez) Paniagua b: 8/20/1973, San Jose de Ocoa, Dominican Republic BR/TR, 6'2", 185 lbs. Deb: 4/4/1996

YEAR TM-L	W	L	PCT	G	GS	CG	SH	SV	IP	H	R	ER	HR	HB	BB	SO	RAT	ERA	ERA+	CERA	OAV	BH	AVG	PR+	WS	TPW
1996 Mon-N	2	4	.333	13	11	0	0	0	51	55	24	20	7	3	23	27	1.529	3.53	123	5.41	.282	0	.000	5	3	0.4
1997 Mon-N	1	2	.333	9	3	0	0	0	18	29	24	24	2	4	16	8	2.500	12.00	35	11.18	.372	0	.000	-16	0	-1.6
1998 Sea-A	2	0	1.000	18	0	0	0	1	22	15	5	5	3	3	5	16	.909	2.05	226	2.68	.200	0	....	7	3	0.6
1999 Sea-A	6	11	.353	59	0	0	0	3	77^2	75	37	35	5	7	52	74	1.635	4.06	123	5.06	.264	0	....	8	7	0.8
2000★ Sea-A	3	0	1.000	69	0	0	0	5	80^1	68	31	31	6	7	38	71	1.320	3.47	131	3.64	.234	0	....	9	8	0.8
2001★ Sea-A	4	3	.571	60	0	0	0	3	66	59	35	32	7	4	38	46	1.470	4.36	95	4.34	.233	0	.000	-3	4	-0.3
2002 Det-A	0	1	.000	41	0	0	0	1	41^2	50	30	27	10	3	15	34	1.560	5.83	74	6.35	.294	0	....	-7	0	-0.7
2003 Chi-A	0	0	....	1	0	0	0	0	0^1	3	4	4	0	0	1	0	12.00	108.00	4	83.91	.750	0	....	-4	0	-0.4
Total 8	18	21	.462	270	14	0	0	13	357	354	190	178	40	31	188	276	1.518	4.49	99	5.04	.262	0	.000	-1	25	-0.4

• PANTHER, Jim — James Edward Panther b: 3/1/1945, Burlington, IA BR/TR, 6'1", 190 lbs. Deb: 4/5/1971

YEAR TM-L	W	L	PCT	G	GS	CG	SH	SV	IP	H	R	ER	HR	HB	BB	SO	RAT	ERA	ERA+	CERA	OAV	BH	AVG	PR+	WS	TPW
1971 Oak-A	0	1	.000	4	0	0	0	0	5^2	10	9	7	1	0	5	4	2.647	11.12	30	10.48	.385	0	.000	-5	0	-0.6
1972 Tex-A	5	9	.357	58	4	0	0	0	93^2	101	55	43	8	5	46	44	1.569	4.13	73	4.85	.277	1	.125	-10	1	-1.1
1973 Atl-N	2	3	.400	23	0	0	0	0	30^2	45	26	26	3	0	9	8	1.761	7.63	52	6.52	.363	0	....	-12	0	-1.3
Total 3	7	13	.350	85	4	0	0	0	130	156	90	76	12	5	60	56	1.662	5.26	63	5.49	.303	1	.111	-27	1	-2.9

• PAPA, John — John Paul Papa b: 12/5/1940, Bridgeport, CT BR/TR, 5'11", 190 lbs. Deb: 4/11/1961

YEAR TM-L	W	L	PCT	G	GS	CG	SH	SV	IP	H	R	ER	HR	HB	BB	SO	RAT	ERA	ERA+	CERA	OAV	BH	AVG	PR+	WS	TPW
1961 Bal-A	0	0	....	2	0	0	0	0	1	2	2	2	1	0	3	3	5.000	18.00	22	35.20	.400	0	....	-2	0	-0.2
1962 Bal-A	0	0	....	1	0	0	0	0	1	3	3	3	0	0	1	0	4.000	27.00	14	19.55	.600	0	....	-3	0	-0.3
Total 2	0	0	....	3	0	0	0	0	2	5	5	5	1	0	4	3	4.500	22.50	17	27.38	.500	0	....	-4	0	-0.4

• PAPAI, Al — Alfred Thomas Papai b: 5/7/1917, Divernon, IL d: 9/7/1995, Springfield, IL BR/TR, 6'3", 185 lbs. Deb: 4/24/1948

YEAR TM-L	W	L	PCT	G	GS	CG	SH	SV	IP	H	R	ER	HR	HB	BB	SO	RAT	ERA	ERA+	CERA	OAV	BH	AVG	PR+	WS	TPW
1948 StL-N	0	1	.000	10	0	0	0	0	16	14	10	9	3	0	7	8	1.313	5.06	81	4.08	.241	0	.000	-2	0	-0.2
1949 StL-A	4	11	.267	42	15	6	0	2	142^1	175	103	80	8	1	81	31	1.799	5.06	90	5.54	.298	3	.079	-4	4	-0.5
1950 Bos-A	4	2	.667	16	3	2	0	2	50^2	61	41	38	5	0	28	19	1.757	6.75	73	5.66	.293	3	.176	-10	1	-1.0
StL-N	1	0	1.000	13	0	0	0	0	19	21	12	11	0	0	14	7	1.842	5.21	82	5.18	.300	0	.000	-2	1	-0.2
1955 Chi-A	0	0	....	7	0	0	0	0	11^2	10	5	5	1	0	8	5	1.543	3.86	102	3.97	.244	0	.000	-0	1	0.0
Total 4	9	14	.391	88	18	8	0	4	239^2	281	171	143	17	1	138	70	1.748	5.37	85	5.36	.291	6	.097	-17	7	-1.9

• PAPE, Larry — Laurence Albert Pape b: 7/21/1883, Norwood, OH d: 7/21/1918, Swissvale, PA BR/TR, 5'11", 175 lbs. Deb: 7/6/1909

YEAR TM-L	W	L	PCT	G	GS	CG	SH	SV	IP	H	R	ER	HR	HB	BB	SO	RAT	ERA	ERA+	CERA	OAV	BH	AVG	PR+	WS	TPW
1909 Bos-A	2	0	1.000	11	3	2	1	2	57^1	46	17	13	0	5	12	18	1.012	2.04	122	2.02	....	3	.143	2	5	0.2
1911 Bos-A	10	8	.556	27	19	10	1	0	176^1	167	68	48	3	4	63	49	1.304	2.45	133	3.30	.264	13	.203	16	13	1.4
1912 Bos-A	1	1	.500	13	2	1	0	1	48^2	74	36	27	0	2	16	17	1.849	4.99	68	6.49	.366	4	.235	-8	1	-0.8
Total 3	13	9	.591	51	24	13	2	3	282^1	287	121	88	3	11	91	84	1.339	2.81	113	3.59	.344	20	.196	9	19	0.8

• PAPISH, Frank — Frank Richard "Pap" Papish b: 10/21/1917, Pueblo, CO d: 8/30/1965, Pueblo, CO BR/TL, 6'2", 192 lbs. Deb: 5/8/1945

YEAR TM-L	W	L	PCT	G	GS	CG	SH	SV	IP	H	R	ER	HR	HB	BB	SO	RAT	ERA	ERA+	CERA	OAV	BH	AVG	PR+	WS	TPW
1945 Chi-A	4	4	.500	19	5	3	0	1	84^1	75	36	35	3	0	40	45	1.364	3.74	89	3.19	.241	6	.231	-3	5	-0.2
1946 Chi-A	7	5	.583	31	15	6	2	0	138	122	52	42	7	1	63	66	1.341	2.74	125	3.33	.243	8	.186	9	10	0.9
1947 Chi-A	12	12	.500	38	26	6	1	3	199	185	82	72	6	2	98	79	1.422	3.26	112	3.42	.245	5	.086	9	14	0.4
1948 Chi-A	2	8	.200	32	14	2	0	4	95^1	97	65	53	7	3	75	41	1.804	5.00	85	5.37	.265	5	.185	-9	3	-0.9
1949 Cle-A	1	0	1.000	25	3	1	0	1	62	54	24	22	2	0	39	23	1.500	3.19	125	3.61	.240	1	.125	5	5	0.5
1950 Pit-N	0	0	....	4	1	0	0	0	2^1	8	7	7	1	0	4	1	5.143	27.00	16	31.79	.533	0	....	-6	0	-0.6
Total 6	26	29	.473	149	64	18	3	9	581	541	266	231	26	6	319	255	1.480	3.58	104	3.82	.249	25	.154	5	37	0.2

• PAPPALAU, John — John Joseph Pappalau b: 4/3/1875, Albany, NY d: 5/12/1944, Albany, NY BR/TR, 6', 175 lbs. Deb: 6/9/1897

YEAR TM-L	W	L	PCT	G	GS	CG	SH	SV	IP	H	R	ER	HR	HB	BB	SO	RAT	ERA	ERA+	CERA	OAV	BH	AVG	PR+	WS	TPW
1897 Cle-N	0	1	.000	2	1	1	0	0	12	22	16	14	0	2	6	3	2.333	10.50	43	9.36	.390	0	.000	-9	0	-0.8

• PAPPAS, Milt — Milton Stephen "Gimpy" Pappas b: 5/11/1939, Detroit, MI BR/TR, 6'3", 190 lbs. Deb: 8/10/1957

YEAR TM-L	W	L	PCT	G	GS	CG	SH	SV	IP	H	R	ER	HR	HB	BB	SO	RAT	ERA	ERA+	CERA	OAV	BH	AVG	PR+	WS	TPW
1957 Bal-A	0	0	....	4	0	0	0	0	9	6	1	1	0	0	3	3	1.000	1.00	359	1.66	.200	0	.000	2	1	0.2
1958 Bal-A	10	10	.500	31	21	3	0	0	135^1	135	67	61	8	2	48	72	1.352	4.06	89	3.68	.262	6	.143	-6	6	-0.8
1959 Bal-A	15	9	.625	33	27	15	4	3	209^1	175	82	76	8	4	75	120	1.194	3.27	116	2.73	.226	11	.139	10	17	0.7
1960 Bal-A	15	11	.577	30	27	11	3	0	205^2	184	81	77	15	6	83	126	1.298	3.37	113	3.45	.243	3	.043	6	14	0.1
1961 Bal-A	13	9	.591	26	23	11	4	1	177^2	134	67	60	16	7	78	89	1.193	3.04	129	2.96	.208	9	.136	15	15	1.5
1962 Bal-A★	12	10	.545	35	32	9	1	0	205^1	200	105	92	31	2	75	130	1.339	4.03	93	4.17	.257	6	.087	-8	8	-0.8
1963 Bal-A	16	9	.640	34	32	11	4	0	216^2	186	80	73	21	5	69	120	1.177	3.03	116	3.05	.233	9	.127	12	15	1.2
1964 Bal-A	16	7	.696	37	36	13	7	0	251^2	225	89	83	21	7	48	157	1.085	2.97	120	2.71	.239	12	.129	10	18	0.9
1965 Bal-A★	13	9	.591	34	34	9	3	0	221^1	192	81	64	22	3	52	127	1.102	2.60	133	2.79	.233	5	.071	18	15	1.5
1966 Cin-N	12	11	.522	33	32	6	2	0	209^2	224	106	100	23	3	39	133	1.254	4.29	91	3.71	.275	8	.107	-7	9	-0.9
1967 Cin-N	16	13	.552	34	32	5	3	0	217^2	218	88	81	19	5	38	129	1.176	3.35	112	3.20	.259	7	.097	11	14	1.0
1968 Cin-N	2	5	.286	15	11	0	0	0	62^2	70	41	39	9	2	10	43	1.277	5.60	56	4.06	.275	1	.063	-17	0	-2.0
Atl-N	10	8	.556	22	19	3	1	0	121^1	111	36	32	8	3	22	75	1.096	2.37	126	2.65	.246	6	.162	8	11	1.1
Yr.	12	13	.480	37	30	3	1	0	184	181	77	71	17	5	32	118	1.158	3.47	89	3.13	.256	7	.132	-9	11	-0.9
1969★ Atl-N	6	10	.375	26	24	1	0	0	144	149	66	58	14	4	44	72	1.340	3.63	100	3.89	.267	7	.156	0	8	0.3
1970 Atl-N	2	2	.500	11	3	1	0	0	35^2	44	25	24	6	2	7	25	1.430	6.06	71	5.15	.293	0	.000	-6	0	-0.7
Chi-N	10	8	.556	21	20	6	2	0	144^2	135	53	43	14	0	36	80	1.182	2.68	168	3.04	.248	12	.240	29	15	3.3
Yr.	12	10	.545	32	23	7	2	0	180^1	179	78	67	20	2	43	105	1.231	3.34	132	3.45	.258	12	.200	23	15	2.6
1971 Chi-N	17	14	.548	35	35	14	**5**	0	261^1	279	109	102	25	5	62	99	1.305	3.51	112	3.85	.274	14	.154	17	20	1.8
1972 Chi-N	17	7	.708	29	28	10	3	0	195	187	72	60	18	8	29	80	1.108	2.77	138	2.99	.251	13	.191	23	17	2.6
1973 Chi-N	7	12	.368	30	29	1	1	0	162	192	82	77	20	4	40	48	1.432	4.28	92	4.78	.299	3	.063	-2	7	-0.5
Total 17	209	164	.560	520	465	129	43	4	3186	3046	1331	1203	298	72	858	1728	1.225	3.40	110	3.37	.252	132	.123	116	210	10.6

• PARK, Chan Ho — Chan Ho Park b: 6/30/1973, Kongju, South Korea BR/TR, 6'2", 185 lbs. Deb: 4/8/1994

YEAR TM-L	W	L	PCT	G	GS	CG	SH	SV	IP	H	R	ER	HR	HB	BB	SO	RAT	ERA	ERA+	CERA	OAV	BH	AVG	PR+	WS	TPW
1994 LA-N	0	0	....	2	0	0	0	0	4	5	5	5	1	1	5	6	2.500	11.25	35	11.69	.294	0	....	-3	0	-0.3
1995 LA-N	0	0	....	2	1	0	0	0	4	2	2	2	1	0	2	7	1.000	4.50	84	2.70	.143	0	.000	-0	0	0.0
1996 LA-N	5	5	.500	48	10	0	0	0	108^2	82	48	44	7	4	71	119	1.408	3.64	106	3.50	.209	1	.053	4	7	0.2
1997 LA-N	14	8	.636	32	29	2	0	0	192	149	80	72	24	8	70	166	1.141	3.38	114	3.04	.213	9	.176	13	13	1.5
1998 LA-N	15	9	.625	34	34	2	0	0	220^2	199	101	91	16	11	97	191	1.341	3.71	107	3.69	.244	14	.194	7	13	0.9
1999 LA-N	13	11	.542	33	33	0	0	0	194^1	208	120	113	31	14	100	174	1.585	5.23	82	5.68	.276	9	.153	-19	6	-1.8
2000 LA-N	18	10	.643	34	34	3	1	0	226	173	92	82	21	12	124	217	1.314	3.27	133	3.51	.214	15	.214	28	18	3.1
2001 LA-N★	15	11	.577	36	**35**	2	1	0	234	183	98	91	23	20	91	218	1.171	3.50	114	3.15	.216	10	.145	14	16	1.5
2002 Tex-A	9	8	.529	25	25	0	0	0	145^2	154	95	93	20	17	78	121	1.593	5.75	82	5.75	.273	0	.000	-15	5	-1.5
2003 Tex-A	1	3	.250	7	7	0	0	0	29^2	34	26	25	5	6	25	16	1.989	7.58	65	8.56	.306	0	....	-8	0	-0.8
Total 10	90	65	.581	253	208	9	2	0	1359	1189	667	618	149	93	663	1235	1.363	4.09	102	4.09	.237	58	.168	19	78	2.9

• PARK, Jim — James Park b: 11/10/1892, Richmond, KY d: 12/17/1970, Lexington, KY BR/TR, 6'2", 175 lbs. Deb: 9/7/1915

YEAR TM-L	W	L	PCT	G	GS	CG	SH	SV	IP	H	R	ER	HR	HB	BB	SO	RAT	ERA	ERA+	CERA	OAV	BH	AVG	PR+	WS	TPW
1915 StL-A	2	0	1.000	3	3	1	0	0	22^2	18	8	3	1	0	9	5	1.191	1.19	240	2.53	.214	4	.400	4	3	0.6
1916 StL-A	1	4	.200	26	6	1	0	0	79	69	28	23	2	1	25	26	1.190	2.62	105	2.74	.244	2	.100	-1	4	-0.3
1917 StL-A	1	1	.500	13	0	0	0	0	20^1	27	20	15	1	0	12	9	1.918	6.64	39	6.55	.333	0	.000	-9	0	-1.0
Total 3	4	5	.444	42	9	2	0	0	122	114	56	41	4	1	46	40	1.311	3.02	89	3.34	.254	6	.188	-6	7	-0.7

YEAR TM-L	W	L	PCT	G	GS	CG	SH	SV	IP	H	R	ER	HR	HB	BB	SO	RAT	ERA	ERA+	CERA	OAV	BH	AVG	PR+	WS	TPW
• PARKER, Christian	Christian Michael Parker b: 7/3/1975, Albuquerque, NM BR/TR, 6'1", 200 lbs. Deb: 4/6/2001																									
2001 NY-A	0	1	.000	1	1	0	0	0	3	8	7	7	2	0	1	1	3.000	21.00	21	21.01	.471	0	....	-5	0	-0.5
• PARKER, Clay	James Clayton Parker b: 12/19/1962, Columbia, LA BR/TR, 6'1", 185 lbs. Deb: 9/14/1987																									
1987 Sea-A	0	0	....	3	1	0	0	0	7^{2}	15	10	9	2	1	4	8	2.478	10.57	45	12.78	.405	0	....	-5	0	-0.5
1989 NY-A	4	5	.444	22	17	2	0	0	120	123	53	49	12	2	31	53	1.283	3.68	105	3.67	.264	0	....	2	7	0.2
1990 NY-A	1	1	.500	5	2	0	0	0	22	19	11	11	5	0	7	20	1.182	4.50	88	3.74	.229	0	....	-1	1	-0.1
Det-A	2	2	.500	24	1	0	0	0	51	45	18	18	6	1	25	20	1.373	3.18	125	3.87	.242	0	....	3	3	0.3
Yr.	3	3	.500	29	3	0	0	0	73	64	29	29	11	1	32	40	1.315	3.58	111	3.83	.238	0	....	2	4	0.2
1992 Sea-A	0	2	.000	8	6	0	0	0	33^{1}	47	28	28	6	2	11	20	1.740	7.56	53	7.27	.338	0	....	-13	0	-1.3
Total 4	7	10	.412	62	27	2	0	0	234	249	120	115	31	6	78	121	1.397	4.42	90	4.53	.273	0	....	-14	11	-1.4
• PARKER, Doc	Harley Park Parker b: 6/14/1872, Theresa, NY d: 3/3/1941, Chicago, IL BR/TR, 6'2", 200 lbs. Deb: 7/11/1893 U																									
1893 Chi-N	0	0	....	1	0	0	0	1	2	5	3	3	0	0	1	0	3.000	13.50	34	13.42	.458	0	.000	-2	0	-0.2
1895 Chi-N	4	2	.667	7	6	5	1	0	51^{1}	65	30	21	1	0	9	9	1.442	3.68	138	4.07	.304	7	.318	8	5	0.7
1896 Chi-N	1	5	.167	9	7	7	0	0	73	100	71	50	3	0	27	15	1.740	6.16	73	5.56	.323	10	.278	-14	2	-1.2
1901 Cin-N	0	1	.000	1	1	1	0	0	8	26	21	14	1	0	2	0	3.500	15.75	20	19.47	.532	0	.000	-11	0	-1.1
Total 4	5	8	.385	18	14	13	1	1	134^{1}	196	125	88	5	0	39	24	1.749	5.90	74	5.94	.336	17	.274	-19	7	-1.7
• PARKER, Harry	Harry William Parker b: 9/14/1947, Highland, IL BR/TR, 6'3", 190 lbs. Deb: 8/8/1970																									
1970 StL-N	1	1	.500	7	4	0	0	0	22^{1}	24	13	8	0	0	15	9	1.746	3.22	128	4.71	.276	2	.250	3	1	0.3
1971 StL-N	0	0	....	4	0	0	0	0	5	6	4	4	2	0	2	2	1.600	7.20	50	7.40	.286	0	....	-2	0	-0.2
1973* NY-N	8	4	.667	38	9	0	0	5	96^{2}	79	40	36	7	3	36	63	1.190	3.35	108	2.80	.217	4	.174	2	7	0.2
1974 NY-N	4	12	.250	40	16	1	0	4	131	145	64	57	10	3	46	58	1.458	3.92	91	4.33	.281	0	.000	-6	5	-1.0
1975 NY-N	2	3	.400	18	1	0	0	2	34^{2}	37	17	17	2	0	19	22	1.615	4.41	78	4.38	.272	0	.000	-4	2	-0.3
StL-N	0	1	.000	14	0	0	0	1	18^{2}	21	13	13	3	0	10	13	1.661	6.27	60	5.50	.288	0	.000	-5	0	-0.5
Yr.	2	4	.333	32	1	0	0	3	53^{1}	58	30	30	5	0	29	35	1.631	5.06	71	4.77	.278	0	.000	-9	2	-0.8
1976 Cle-A	0	0	....	3	0	0	0	0	7	3	0	0	0	0	0	5	.429	0.00	....	0.44	.136	0	....	3	1	0.3
Total 6	15	21	.417	124	30	1	0	12	315^{1}	315	151	135	24	6	128	172	1.405	3.85	94	3.93	.258	6	.086	-9	16	-1.2
• PARKER, Jay	Jay Parker b: 7/8/1874, Theresa, NY d: 6/8/1935, Hartford, MI BR/TR, 5'11", 185 lbs. Deb: 9/27/1899																									
1899 Pit-N	0	0	....	1	1	0	0	0	0	0	2	0	0	1	2	0	....	....	....	∞	-1.000	0	....	0	0	0.0
• PARKER, Roy	Roy William Parker b: 2/29/1896, Union, MO d: 5/17/1954, Tulsa, OK BR/TR, 6'3", 200 lbs. Deb: 9/10/1919																									
1919 StL-N	0	0	....	2	0	0	0	0	2	6	7	7	0	1	1	0	3.500	31.50	9	13.21	.333	0	....	-6	0	-0.7
• PARKS, Bill	William Robert Parks b: 6/4/1849, Easton, PA d: 10/10/1911, Easton, PA BR/TR, 5'8", 150 lbs. Deb: 4/26/1875 M ♦																									
1875 Was-n	4	8	.333	14	11	9	0	0	106^{2}	144	120	39	3	....	5	3	1.397	3.29	65	....	.295	20	.180	-6	....	-0.8
Phi-n	0	0	....	2	0	0	0	0	5^{1}	13	11	5	0	....	1	0	2.625	8.44	37	....	.431	1	.167	-3	....	-0.3
Yr.	4	8	.333	16	11	9	0	0	112	157	131	44	3	....	6	3	1.455	3.54	63	....	.303	21	.179	-9	....	-1.1
• PARKS, Slicker	Vernon Henry Parks b: 11/10/1895, Dallas, MI d: 2/21/1978, Royal Oak, MI BR/TR, 5'10", 158 lbs. Deb: 7/11/1921																									
1921 Det-A	3	2	.600	10	1	0	0	0	25^{1}	33	17	16	2	1	16	10	1.934	5.68	75	6.46	.306	1	.111	-3	1	-0.4
• PARMELEE, Roy	Le Roy Earl "Bud,Tarzan" Parmelee b: 4/25/1907, Lambertville, MI d: 8/31/1981, Monroe, MI BR/TR, 6'1", 190 lbs. Deb: 9/28/1929																									
1929 NY-N	1	0	1.000	2	1	0	0	0	7	13	7	7	1	1	3	1	2.286	9.00	51	11.57	.481	1	.500	-4	0	-0.3
1930 NY-N	0	1	.000	11	1	0	0	0	21	18	26	22	3	0	26	19	2.095	9.43	50	6.52	.228	1	.250	-11	0	-0.9
1931 NY-N	2	2	.500	13	5	4	0	0	58^{2}	47	25	24	1	3	33	30	1.364	3.68	100	3.12	.223	4	.200	-1	3	-0.1
1932 NY-N	0	3	.000	8	3	0	0	0	25^{1}	25	18	11	0	2	14	23	1.539	3.91	95	3.79	.250	2	.400	-0	1	0.1
1933 NY-N	13	8	.619	32	32	14	3	0	218^{1}	191	94	77	9	14	77	132	1.227	3.17	101	2.94	.232	19	.235	-3	12	0.1
1934 NY-N	10	6	.625	22	20	7	2	0	152^{2}	134	59	58	6	6	60	83	1.271	3.42	113	3.04	**.238**	11	.200	6	11	0.7
1935 NY-N	14	10	.583	34	31	13	0	0	226	214	117	106	20	9	97	79	1.376	4.22	91	3.83	.249	18	.209	-10	12	-0.7
1936 StL-N	11	11	.500	37	28	9	0	2	221	226	125	112	13	10	107	79	1.507	4.56	86	4.33	.270	15	.197	-15	10	-1.5
1937 Chi-N	7	8	.467	33	18	8	0	0	145^{2}	165	93	83	13	7	79	55	1.675	5.13	78	5.37	.286	9	.173	-19	3	-1.9
1939 Phi-A	1	6	.143	14	5	0	0	1	44^{2}	42	41	32	2	3	35	13	1.724	6.45	73	4.56	.235	2	.133	-7	0	-0.7
Total 10	59	55	.518	206	144	55	5	3	1120^{1}	1075	605	532	68	55	531	514	1.434	4.27	90	3.94	.253	82	.207	-64	52	-5.3
• PARNELL, Mel	Melvin Lloyd "Dusty" Parnell b: 6/13/1922, New Orleans, LA BL/TL, 6', 180 lbs. Deb: 4/20/1947																									
1947 Bos-A	2	3	.400	15	5	1	0	0	50^{2}	60	41	36	1	1	27	23	1.717	6.39	61	5.02	.296	1	.056	-14	0	-1.7
1948 Bos-A	15	8	.652	35	27	16	1	0	212	205	87	74	7	4	90	77	1.392	3.14	140	3.47	.252	13	.163	28	18	2.3
1949 Bos-A★	**25**	7	.781	39	33	**27**	4	2	**295^{1}**	258	102	91	8	5	134	122	1.327	2.77	157	3.09	.237	29	.254	**47**	**31**	**4.7**
1950 Bos-A	18	10	.643	40	31	21	2	3	249	244	116	100	17	7	106	93	1.406	3.61	136	3.87	.259	19	.194	37	22	3.3
1951 Bos-A★	18	11	.621	36	29	11	3	2	221	229	99	80	11	0	77	77	1.385	3.26	137	3.72	.272	25	.309	**29**	22	**3.3**
1952 Bos-A	12	12	.500	33	29	15	3	2	214	207	94	86	13	5	89	107	1.383	3.62	109	3.67	.255	8	.095	6	13	0.3
1953 Bos-A	21	8	.724	38	34	12	5	0	241	217	98	82	15	4	116	136	1.382	3.06	137	3.52	.239	21	.223	29	23	3.1
1954 Bos-A	3	7	.300	19	15	4	1	0	92^{1}	104	45	38	7	1	35	38	1.505	3.70	111	4.46	.287	3	.088	5	4	0.4
1955 Bos-A	2	3	.400	13	9	0	0	1	46	62	44	40	12	1	25	18	1.891	7.83	55	7.98	.318	6	.316	-18	0	-1.6
1956 Bos-A	7	6	.538	21	20	6	1	0	131^{1}	129	71	55	13	0	59	41	1.431	3.77	123	4.16	.256	7	.152	13	8	1.1
Total 10	123	75	.621	289	232	113	20	10	1752^{2}	1715	797	682	104	28	758	732	1.411	3.50	124	3.79	.257	132	.198	163	141	15.2
• PARNHAM, Rube	James Arthur Parnham b: 2/1/1894, Heidelberg, PA d: 11/25/1963, McKeesport, PA BR/TR, 6'3", 185 lbs. Deb: 9/20/1916																									
1916 Phi-A	2	1	.667	4	3	2	0	0	24^{2}	27	14	11	0	0	13	8	1.622	4.01	71	4.59	.300	3	.273	-3	1	-0.2
1917 Phi-A	0	1	.000	2	2	0	0	0	11	12	6	5	1	0	9	4	1.909	4.09	67	6.35	.316	0	.000	-1	0	-0.2
Total 2	2	2	.500	6	5	2	0	0	35^{2}	39	20	16	1	0	22	12	1.710	4.04	70	5.13	.305	3	.214	-4	1	-0.4
• PARONTO, Chad	Chad Michael Paronto b: 7/28/1975, Woodsville, NH BR/TR, 6'5", 250 lbs. Deb: 4/18/2001																									
2001 Bal-A	1	3	.250	24	0	0	0	0	27	33	24	15	5	1	11	16	1.630	5.00	86	5.98	.289	0	....	-2	0	-0.2
2002 Cle-A	0	2	.000	29	0	0	0	0	35^{2}	34	19	16	3	2	11	23	1.262	4.04	109	3.45	.248	0	....	2	2	0.2
2003 Cle-A	0	2	.000	6	0	0	0	0	6^{2}	7	8	7	1	0	3	6	1.500	9.45	47	5.00	.292	0	....	-4	0	-0.4
Total 3	1	7	.125	59	0	0	0	0	69^{1}	74	51	38	9	3	25	45	1.428	4.93	88	4.58	.269	0	....	-4	2	-0.4
• PARQUE, Jim	Jim Vo Parque b: 2/8/1975, Norwalk, CA BL/TL, 5'11", 170 lbs. Deb: 5/26/1998																									
1998 Chi-A	7	5	.583	21	21	0	0	0	113	135	72	64	14	6	49	77	1.628	5.10	89	5.88	.299	0	.000	-7	4	-0.7
1999 Chi-A	9	15	.375	31	30	1	0	0	173^{2}	210	111	99	23	10	79	111	1.664	5.13	95	5.98	.299	2	.400	-4	7	-0.3
2000* Chi-A	13	6	.684	33	32	0	0	0	187	208	105	89	21	11	71	111	1.492	4.28	116	4.99	.283	0	.000	12	11	1.0
2001 Chi-A	0	3	.000	5	5	1	0	0	28	36	26	25	7	2	10	15	1.643	8.04	57	6.86	.308	0	....	-11	0	-1.0
2002 Chi-A	1	4	.200	8	4	0	0	0	25^{1}	34	29	28	11	1	16	13	1.974	9.95	46	10.13	.318	0	....	-15	0	-1.5
2003 TB-A	1	1	.500	5	5	0	0	0	17^{1}	27	23	23	2	1	16	8	2.481	11.94	38	10.16	.351	0	....	-15	0	-1.4
Total 6	31	34	.477	103	97	2	0	0	544^{1}	650	366	328	78	31	241	335	1.637	5.42	88	5.99	.297	2	.200	-40	22	-3.9
• PARRA, Jose	Jose Miguel Parra b: 11/28/1972, Jacagua, Dominican Republic BR/TR, 5'11", 160 lbs. Deb: 5/7/1995																									
1995 LA-N	0	0	....	8	0	0	0	0	10^{1}	10	8	5	2	1	6	7	1.548	4.35	87	5.56	.256	0	....	-1	0	-0.1
Min-A	1	5	.167	12	12	0	0	0	61^{2}	83	59	52	11	2	22	29	1.703	7.59	63	6.55	.313	0	....	-19	0	-1.8
1996 Min-A	5	5	.500	27	5	0	0	0	70	88	48	47	15	3	27	50	1.643	6.04	85	6.63	.308	0	....	-8	2	-0.7
2000 Pit-N	0	1	.000	6	2	0	0	0	11^{2}	17	9	9	3	1	7	9	2.057	6.94	66	9.86	.354	0	....	-3	0	-0.2
2002 Ari-N	0	1	.000	16	0	0	0	0	14	13	5	5	0	1	11	8	1.714	3.21	138	4.57	.255	0	....	2	1	0.2
Total 4	6	12	.333	69	19	0	0	0	167^{2}	211	129	118	31	8	73	103	1.694	6.33	76	6.59	.306	0	....	-29	3	-2.6
• PARRETT, Jeff	Jeffrey Dale Parrett b: 8/26/1961, Indianapolis, IN BR/TR, 6'4", 193 lbs. Deb: 4/11/1986																									
1986 Mon-N	0	1	.000	12	0	0	0	0	20^{1}	19	11	11	3	0	13	21	1.574	4.87	76	5.02	.247	1	.500	-3	0	-0.2
1987 Mon-N	7	6	.538	45	0	0	0	6	62	53	33	29	8	0	30	56	1.339	4.21	100	3.65	.229	0	.000	1	5	0.0

YEAR	TM-L	W	L	PCT	G	GS	CG	SH	SV	IP	H	R	ER	HR	HB	BB	SO	RAT	ERA	ERA+	CERA	OAV	BH	AVG	PR+	WS	TPW
1988	Mon-N	12	4	.750	61	0	0	0	6	91^{2}	66	29	27	8	1	45	62	1.211	2.65	136	2.84	.214	0	....	8	10	0.9
1989	Phi-N	12	6	.667	72	0	0	0	6	105^{2}	90	43	35	6	0	44	98	1.268	2.98	119	2.85	.232	0	.000	7	10	0.7
1990	Phi-N	4	9	.308	47	5	0	0	1	81^{2}	92	51	47	10	1	36	69	1.567	5.18	74	5.18	.293	0	.000	-13	1	-1.5
	Atl-N	1	1	.500	20	0	0	0	1	27	27	11	9	1	1	19	17	1.704	3.00	134	4.83	.281	1	1.000	4	3	0.4
	Yr.	5	10	.333	67	5	0	0	2	108^{2}	119	62	56	11	2	55	86	1.601	4.64	83	5.10	.290	1	.091	-10	4	-1.1
1991	Atl-N	1	2	.333	18	0	0	0	1	21^{1}	31	18	15	2	0	12	14	2.016	6.33	61	6.95	.326	0	....	-6	0	-0.6
1992*	Oak-A	9	1	.900	66	0	0	0	0	98^{1}	81	35	33	7	2	42	78	1.251	3.02	124	3.08	.226	0	....	7	9	0.7
1993	Col-N	3	3	.500	40	6	0	0	1	73^{2}	78	47	44	6	2	45	66	1.670	5.38	89	4.95	.274	1	.091	-3	4	-0.3
1995	StL-N	4	7	.364	59	0	0	0	0	76^{2}	71	33	31	8	1	28	71	1.291	3.64	115	3.46	.243	1	.500	4	5	0.4
1996	StL-N	2	2	.500	33	0	0	0	0	42^{1}	40	20	20	2	1	20	42	1.417	4.25	99	3.64	.245	0	.000	-1	2	-0.1
	Phi-N	1	1	.500	18	0	0	0	0	24	24	5	5	0	0	11	22	1.458	1.88	230	3.54	.270	0	....	6	3	0.6
	Yr.	3	3	.500	51	0	0	0	0	66^{1}	64	25	25	2	1	31	64	1.432	3.39	124	3.60	.254	0	.000	5	5	0.5
Total	10	56	43	.566	491	11	0	0	22	724^{2}	672	336	306	61	9	345	616	1.403	3.80	105	3.81	.249	4	.105	11	52	1.1
• PARRIS, Steve	Steven Michael Parris b: 12/17/1967, Joliet, IL BR/TR, 6', 190 lbs. Deb: 6/21/1995																										
1995	Pit-N	6	6	.500	15	15	1	1	0	82	89	49	49	12	7	33	61	1.488	5.38	80	5.36	.283	7	.250	-9	4	-0.7
1996	Pit-N	0	3	.000	8	4	0	0	0	26^{1}	35	22	21	4	1	11	27	1.747	7.18	61	6.70	.321	1	.167	-8	0	-0.7
1998	Cin-N	6	5	.545	18	16	1	1	0	99	89	44	41	9	4	32	77	1.222	3.73	115	3.22	.236	4	.138	6	6	0.5
1999	Cin-N	11	4	.733	22	21	2	1	0	128^{2}	124	59	50	16	6	52	86	1.368	3.50	133	4.29	.260	6	.158	13	9	1.1
2000	Cin-N	12	17	.414	33	33	0	0	0	192^{2}	227	109	103	30	4	71	117	1.547	4.81	98	5.44	.294	7	.127	-5	9	-0.6
2001	Tor-A	4	6	.400	19	19	1	0	0	105^{2}	126	60	54	18	2	41	49	1.580	4.60	100	5.75	.299	0	.000	-1	5	-0.1
2002	Tor-A	5	5	.500	14	14	0	0	0	75^{1}	96	50	50	13	3	35	48	1.739	5.97	77	6.68	.314	0	.000	-11	2	-1.1
2003	TB-A	0	3	.000	10	7	0	0	0	43^{2}	60	32	30	12	0	13	14	1.672	6.18	73	7.23	.328	0	.000	-9	0	-0.9
Total	8	44	49	.473	139	129	5	3	0	753^{1}	846	425	398	114	27	288	479	1.505	4.75	96	5.26	.286	25	.154	-23	35	-2.5
• PARRISH, John	John Henry Parrish b: 11/26/1977, Lancaster, PA BL/TL, 5'11", 181 lbs. Deb: 7/24/2000																										
2000	Bal-A	2	4	.333	8	8	0	0	0	36^{1}	40	32	29	6	1	35	28	2.064	7.18	66	7.75	.288	0	....	-10	0	-0.9
2001	Bal-A	1	2	.333	16	1	0	0	0	22	22	17	15	5	3	17	20	1.773	6.14	70	7.06	.256	0	....	-5	0	-0.5
2003	Bal-A	0	1	.000	14	0	0	0	0	23^{2}	17	7	5	2	1	8	15	1.056	1.90	231	2.39	.205	0	....	7	2	0.6
Total	3	3	7	.300	38	9	0	0	0	82	79	56	49	13	5	60	63	1.695	5.38	84	6.02	.256	0	....	-8	2	-0.7
• PARROTT, Mike	Michael Everett Arch Parrott b: 12/6/1954, Oxnard, CA BR/TR, 6'4", 210 lbs. Deb: 9/5/1977																										
1977	Bal-A	0	0	....	3	0	0	0	0	4^{1}	4	1	1	0	0	2	2	1.385	2.08	183	3.31	.250	0	....	1	0	0.1
1978	Sea-A	1	5	.167	27	10	0	0	1	82^{1}	108	59	47	8	3	32	41	1.700	5.14	74	5.75	.316	0	....	-12	1	-1.2
1979	Sea-A	14	12	.538	38	30	13	2	0	229^{1}	231	104	96	17	6	86	127	1.382	3.77	116	3.90	.267	0	....	16	17	1.5
1980	Sea-A	1	16	.059	27	16	1	0	3	94	136	83	76	16	1	42	53	1.894	7.28	57	7.58	.348	0	....	-32	0	-3.2
1981	Sea-A	3	6	.333	24	12	0	0	1	85	102	51	48	3	1	28	43	1.529	5.08	76	4.46	.299	0	....	-10	2	-1.1
Total	5	19	39	.328	119	68	14	2	5	495	581	298	268	44	11	190	266	1.558	4.87	84	5.00	.297	0	....	-38	20	-3.9
• PARROTT, Tom	Thomas William "Tacky Tom" Parrott b: 4/10/1868, Portland, OR d: 1/1/1932, Dundee, OR BR/TR, 5'10.5", 170 lbs. Deb: 6/18/1893 ♦																										
1893	Chi-N	0	3	.000	4	3	2	0	0	27	35	30	20	1	0	17	7	1.926	6.67	69	6.07	.305	7	.259	-6	0	-0.5
	Cin-N	10	7	.588	22	17	11	1	0	154	174	95	70	1	9	70	33	1.584	4.09	117	4.41	.276	13	.191	9	12	0.5
	Yr.	10	10	.500	26	20	13	1	0	181	209	125	90	2	9	87	40	1.635	4.48	106	4.66	.281	20	.211	3	12	0.0
1894	Cin-N	17	19	.472	41	36	31	1	1	308^{2}	402	268	192	19	11	126	61	1.711	5.60	99	5.61	.312	74	.323	-3	22	0.4
1895	Cin-N	11	18	.379	41	31	23	0	**3**	263^{1}	382	228	160	8	5	76	57	1.739	5.47	91	5.72	.334	69	.343	-16	18	-0.4
1896	StL-N	1	1	.500	7	2	2	0	0	42	62	39	29	4	3	18	8	1.905	6.21	70	7.21	.340	138	.291	-8	10	-1.1
Total	4	39	48	.448	115	89	69	2	4	795	1055	660	471	33	28	307	166	1.713	5.33	96	5.51	.314	301	.301	-23	62	-1.1
• PARSON, Jiggs	William Edwin Parson b: 12/28/1885, Parker, SD d: 5/19/1967, Los Angeles, CA BR/TR, 6'2", 180 lbs. Deb: 5/16/1910																										
1910	Bos-N	0	2	.000	10	4	0	0	0	35^{1}	35	23	15	2	2	26	7	1.726	3.82	87	5.41	.278	1	.083	-3	1	-0.4
1911	Bos-N	0	1	.000	7	0	0	0	0	25	36	30	18	2	4	15	7	2.040	6.48	59	8.76	.375	2	.200	-7	0	-0.7
Total	2	0	3	.000	17	4	0	0	0	60^{1}	71	53	33	4	6	41	14	1.856	4.92	72	6.80	.320	3	.136	-9	1	-1.1
• PARSONS, Bill	William Raymond Parsons b: 8/17/1948, Riverside, CA BR/TR, 6'6", 195 lbs. Deb: 4/13/1971																										
1971	Mil-A	13	17	.433	36	35	12	4	0	244^{2}	219	95	87	19	4	93	139	1.275	3.20	108	3.30	.241	12	.167	5	15	0.9
1972	Mil-A	13	13	.500	33	30	10	2	0	214	194	102	93	27	3	68	111	1.224	3.91	77	3.41	.240	11	.164	-21	6	-2.3
1973	Mil-A	3	6	.333	20	17	0	0	0	59^{2}	59	50	45	6	0	67	30	2.112	6.79	55	6.89	.257	0	....	-20	0	-2.0
1974	Oak-A	0	0	....	4	0	0	0	0	2	1	0	0	0	0	3	2	2.000	0.00	....	4.47	.143	0	....	1	0	0.1
Total	4	29	36	.446	93	82	22	6	0	520^{1}	473	247	225	52	7	231	282	1.353	3.89	85	3.76	.242	23	.165	-35	21	-3.4
• PARSONS, Charlie	Charles James Parsons b: 7/18/1863, Cherry Flats, PA d: 3/24/1936, Mansfield, PA BL/TL, 5'10", 160 lbs. Deb: 5/29/1886																										
1886	Bos-N	0	2	.000	2	2	2	0	0	16	20	13	7	0	....	4	5	1.500	3.94	80	....	.295	3	.375	-1	1	0.0
1887	NY-a	1	1	.500	4	4	4	0	0	34	57	36	17	0	1	6	5	1.676	4.50	94	....	.360	4	.250	0	1	0.0
1890	Cle-N	0	1	.000	2	1	0	0	0	9	12	11	6	0	4	6	2	2.000	6.00	59	....	.311	3	.750	-2	0	-0.1
Total	3	1	4	.200	8	7	6	0	0	59	89	60	30	0	5	16	12	1.678	4.58	83	....	.336	10	.357	-3	2	-0.1
• PARSONS, Tom	Thomas Anthony Parsons b: 9/13/1939, Lakeville, CT BR/TR, 6'7", 210 lbs. Deb: 9/5/1963																										
1963	Pit-N	0	1	.000	1	1	0	0	0	4^{1}	7	6	4	1	0	2	2	2.077	8.31	40	9.11	.368	0	.000	-2	0	-0.3
1964	NY-N	1	2	.333	4	2	1	0	0	19^{1}	20	9	9	1	0	6	10	1.345	4.19	85	3.65	.274	0	.000	-1	1	-0.2
1965	NY-N	1	10	.091	35	11	1	1	1	90^{2}	108	53	47	17	0	17	58	1.379	4.67	76	4.85	.290	1	.056	-11	1	-1.3
Total	3	2	13	.133	40	14	2	1	1	114^{1}	135	68	60	19	0	25	70	1.399	4.72	74	4.81	.291	1	.037	-15	2	-1.8
• PARTENHEIMER, Stan	Stanwood Wendell "Party" Partenheimer b: 10/21/1922, Chicopee Falls, MA d: 1/28/1989, Wilson, NC BR/TL, 5'11", 175 lbs. Deb: 5/27/1944																										
1944	Bos-A	0	0	....	1	1	0	0	0	1	3	2	2	0	0	2	0	5.000	18.00	19	23.63	.500	0	.000	-2	0	-0.2
1945	StL-N	0	0	....	8	2	0	0	0	13^{1}	12	9	9	2	0	16	6	2.100	6.08	62	6.85	.250	0	.000	-4	0	-0.4
Total	2	0	0	....	9	3	0	0	0	14^{1}	15	11	11	2	0	18	6	2.302	6.91	53	8.02	.278	0	.000	-5	0	-0.6
• PASCHALL, Bill	William Herbert Paschall b: 4/22/1954, Norfolk, VA BR/TR, 6', 175 lbs. Deb: 9/20/1978																										
1978	KC-A	0	1	.000	2	0	0	0	1	8	6	3	3	0	1	0	5	.750	3.38	113	1.38	.207	0	....	0	1	0.0
1979	KC-A	0	1	.000	7	0	0	0	0	13^{2}	18	11	10	2	2	5	3	1.683	6.59	65	6.03	.300	0	....	-4	0	-0.4
1981	KC-A	0	0	....	2	0	0	0	0	2	2	1	1	0	0	0	1	1.000	4.50	80	2.31	.286	0	....	-0	0	0.0
Total	3	0	2	.000	11	0	0	0	1	23^{2}	26	15	14	2	3	5	9	1.310	5.32	77	4.15	.271	0	....	-4	1	-0.3
• PASCUAL, Camilo	Camilo Alberto (Lus) "Camile,Little Potato" Pascual b: 1/20/1934, Havana, Cuba BR/TR, 5'11", 185 lbs. Deb: 4/15/1954 C																										
1954	Was-A	4	7	.364	48	4	1	0	3	119^{1}	126	65	56	7	6	61	60	1.567	4.22	84	4.56	.276	4	.133	-7	4	-0.8
1955	Was-A	2	12	.143	43	16	1	0	3	129	158	94	88	5	6	70	82	1.767	6.14	62	5.59	.311	7	.219	-30	0	-2.9
1956	Was-A	6	18	.250	39	27	6	0	2	188^{2}	194	131	123	33	6	89	162	1.500	5.87	74	5.10	.261	8	.138	-27	4	-2.8
1957	Was-A	8	17	.320	29	26	8	2	0	175^{2}	168	85	80	11	3	76	113	1.389	4.10	95	3.75	.258	7	.140	0	7	-0.1
1958	Was-A	8	12	.400	31	27	6	2	0	177^{1}	166	66	62	14	3	60	146	1.274	3.15	121	3.41	.248	9	.158	18	13	1.7
1959	Was-A★	17	10	.630	32	30	**17**	**6**	0	238^{2}	202	80	70	10	3	69	185	1.135	2.64	148	2.45	.226	26	.302	**42**	**24**	**4.9**
1960	Was-A★	12	8	.600	26	22	8	3	2	151^{2}	139	65	51	11	2	53	143	1.266	3.03	130	3.26	.240	9	.176	18	13	2.1
1961	Min-A★	15	16	.484	35	33	15	**8**	0	252^{1}	205	114	97	26	3	100	**221**	1.209	3.46	123	3.08	.217	14	.165	27	17	2.7
1962	Min-A★	20	11	.645	34	33	**18**	**5**	0	257^{2}	236	100	95	25	2	59	**206**	1.145	3.32	123	2.95	.241	26	.268	21	**23**	2.9
1963	Min-A	21	9	.700	31	31	**18**	3	0	248^{1}	205	76	68	21	3	81	**202**	1.152	2.46	148	2.81	.224	23	.250	**33**	22	**4.1**
1964	Min-A★	15	12	.556	36	36	14	1	0	267^{1}	245	121	98	30	3	98	213	1.283	3.30	109	3.54	.241	17	.181	12	14	1.6
1965*	Min-A	9	3	.750	27	27	5	1	0	156	126	67	58	12	5	63	96	1.212	3.35	106	2.97	.217	12	.200	2	9	0.5
1966	Min-A	8	6	.571	21	19	2	0	0	103	113	63	56	9	2	30	56	1.388	4.89	73	4.15	.278	8	.216	-14	2	-1.4
1967	Was-A	12	10	.545	28	27	5	1	0	164^{2}	147	73	60	15	3	43	106	1.154	3.28	96	2.97	.237	9	.176	-3	10	-0.1
1968	Was-A	13	12	.520	31	31	8	4	0	201	181	72	60	11	4	59	111	1.194	2.69	109	2.89	.239	12	.185	7	9	0.9

YEAR	TM-L	W	L	PCT	G	GS	CG	SH	SV	IP	H	R	ER	HR	HB	BB	SO	RAT	ERA	ERA+	CERA	OAV	BH	AVG	PR+	WS	TPW
1969	Was-A	2	5	.286	14	13	0	0	0	55^1	49	42	42	12	5	38	34	1.572	6.83	51	5.93	.239	4	.235	-21	0	-2.2
	Cin-N	0	0	....	5	1	0	0	0	7^1	14	7	7	2	0	4	3	2.455	8.59	44	13.03	.424	0	....	-4	0	-0.4
1970	LA-N	0	0	....	10	0	0	0	0	14	12	4	4	2	1	5	8	1.214	2.57	149	3.58	.231	0	....	2	1	0.2
1971	Cle-A	2	2	.500	9	1	0	0	0	23^1	17	9	8	0	1	11	20	1.200	3.09	124	2.40	.205	3	.600	2	3	0.3
Total	**18**	**174**	**170**	**.506**	**529**	**404**	**132**	**36**	**10**	**2930^2**	**2703**	**1334**	**1183**	**256**	**61**	**1069**	**2167**	**1.287**	**3.63**	**103**	**3.49**	**.244**	**198**	**.205**	**79**	**175**	**11.2**

• PASCUAL, Carlos — Carlos Alberto (Lus) "Patato" Pascual b: 3/13/1931, Havana, Cuba BR/TR, 5'6", 165 lbs. Deb: 9/24/1950

YEAR	TM-L	W	L	PCT	G	GS	CG	SH	SV	IP	H	R	ER	HR	HB	BB	SO	RAT	ERA	ERA+	CERA	OAV	BH	AVG	PR+	WS	TPW
1950	Was-A	1	1	.500	2	2	2	0	0	17	12	5	4	0	1	8	3	1.176	2.12	212	2.21	.194	1	.250	5	2	0.4

• PASHNICK, Larry — Larry John Pashnick b: 4/25/1956, Lincoln Park, MI BR/TR, 6'3", 205 lbs. Deb: 4/10/1982

YEAR	TM-L	W	L	PCT	G	GS	CG	SH	SV	IP	H	R	ER	HR	HB	BB	SO	RAT	ERA	ERA+	CERA	OAV	BH	AVG	PR+	WS	TPW
1982	Det-A	4	4	.500	28	13	1	0	0	94^1	110	46	42	17	1	25	19	1.431	4.01	101	5.17	.297	0	....	-2	5	-0.2
1983	Det-A	1	3	.250	12	6	0	0	0	37^2	48	27	22	5	3	18	17	1.752	5.26	74	6.46	.308	0	....	-6	0	-0.6
1984	Min-A	2	1	.667	13	1	0	0	0	38^1	38	19	15	3	2	11	10	1.278	3.52	119	3.67	.260	0	....	2	3	0.2
Total	**3**	**7**	**8**	**.467**	**53**	**20**	**1**	**0**	**0**	**170^1**	**196**	**92**	**79**	**25**	**6**	**54**	**46**	**1.468**	**4.17**	**97**	**5.11**	**.292**	**0**	**....**	**-6**	**8**	**-0.6**

• PASSEAU, Claude — Claude William Passeau b: 4/9/1909, Waynesboro, MS d: 8/30/2003, Lucedale, MS BR/TR, 6'3", 198 lbs. Deb: 9/29/1935

YEAR	TM-L	W	L	PCT	G	GS	CG	SH	SV	IP	H	R	ER	HR	HB	BB	SO	RAT	ERA	ERA+	CERA	OAV	BH	AVG	PR+	WS	TPW
1935	Pit-N	0	1	.000	1	1	0	0	0	3	7	4	4	0	0	2	1	3.000	12.00	34	14.24	.500	0	.000	-3	0	-0.3
1936	Phi-N	11	15	.423	49	21	8	2	3	217^1	247	118	84	7	4	55	85	1.390	3.48	130	3.70	.280	22	.282	33	15	3.6
1937	Phi-N	14	18	.438	50	**34**	18	1	2	**292^1**	348	158	141	16	5	79	135	1.461	4.34	100	4.31	.296	21	.196	5	18	0.5
1938	Phi-N	11	18	.379	44	33	15	0	1	239	281	147	120	8	8	93	100	1.565	4.52	89	4.45	.287	13	.163	-6	8	-0.9
1939	Phi-N	2	4	.333	8	8	4	1	0	53^1	54	26	25	1	1	25	29	1.481	4.22	93	3.74	.263	4	.200	-2	2	-0.2
	Chi-N	13	9	.591	34	27	13	1	3	221	215	86	75	8	4	48	108	1.190	3.05	129	2.82	.254	12	.156	28	19	2.6
	Yr.	15	13	.536	42	35	17	2	3	274^1	269	112	100	9	5	73	**137**	1.247	3.28	120	3.00	.256	16	.165	26	21	2.4
1940	Chi-N	20	13	.606	46	31	20	4	5	280^2	259	97	78	8	4	59	124	1.133	2.50	150	**2.42**	.237	20	.204	**40**	28	**4.6**
1941	Chi-N★	14	14	.500	34	30	20	3	0	231	262	99	86	10	1	52	80	1.359	3.35	105	3.67	.281	19	.221	10	15	1.5
1942	Chi-N★	19	14	.576	35	34	24	3	0	278^1	284	116	83	13	3	74	89	1.286	2.68	119	3.26	.260	19	.181	21	19	2.3
1943	Chi-N★	15	12	.556	35	31	18	1	1	257	245	96	83	10	4	66	93	1.210	2.91	115	2.84	.249	19	.198	17	16	1.9
1944	Chi-N	15	9	.625	34	27	18	2	3	227	234	80	73	8	1	50	89	1.251	2.89	122	3.10	.266	13	.163	19	18	1.9
1945*	Chi-N★	17	9	.654	34	27	19	**5**	1	227	205	70	62	4	2	59	98	1.163	2.46	149	2.46	.238	17	.187	27	22	**2.8**
1946	Chi-N★	9	8	.529	21	21	10	2	0	129^1	118	53	45	5	1	42	47	1.237	3.13	106	2.81	.237	10	.204	5	9	0.8
1947	Chi-N	2	6	.250	19	6	1	1	2	63^1	97	54	44	7	1	24	26	1.911	6.25	63	7.14	.353	0	.000	-16	0	-1.8
Total	**13**	**162**	**150**	**.519**	**444**	**331**	**188**	**26**	**21**	**2719^2**	**2856**	**1204**	**1003**	**105**	**39**	**728**	**1104**	**1.318**	**3.32**	**114**	**3.40**	**.267**	**189**	**.192**	**177**	**189**	**19.5**

• PASTORE, Frank — Frank Enrico Pastore b: 8/21/1957, Alhambra, CA BR/TR, 6'2", 205 lbs. Deb: 4/4/1979

YEAR	TM-L	W	L	PCT	G	GS	CG	SH	SV	IP	H	R	ER	HR	HB	BB	SO	RAT	ERA	ERA+	CERA	OAV	BH	AVG	PR+	WS	TPW
1979*	Cin-N	6	7	.462	30	9	2	1	4	95^1	102	47	45	8	1	23	63	1.311	4.25	88	3.65	.271	4	.160	-6	5	-0.6
1980	Cin-N	13	7	.650	27	27	9	2	0	184^2	161	72	67	13	0	42	110	1.099	3.27	110	2.54	.233	10	.156	9	12	0.8
1981	Cin-N	4	9	.308	22	22	2	1	0	132	125	73	59	11	3	35	81	1.212	4.02	88	3.18	.247	5	.114	-8	3	-1.1
1982	Cin-N	8	13	.381	31	29	3	2	0	188^1	210	86	83	13	4	57	94	1.418	3.97	93	4.16	.286	10	.172	-7	8	-0.6
1983	Cin-N	9	12	.429	36	29	4	1	0	184^1	207	104	100	20	1	64	93	1.470	4.88	78	4.73	.290	11	.186	-22	5	-2.1
1984	Cin-N	3	8	.273	24	16	1	0	0	98^1	110	74	71	10	3	40	53	1.525	6.50	58	4.88	.285	2	.071	-29	0	-3.2
1985	Cin-N	2	1	.667	17	6	1	0	0	54	60	23	23	1	1	16	29	1.407	3.83	99	3.78	.287	2	.143	-1	3	-0.1
1986	Min-A	3	1	.750	33	1	0	0	2	49^1	54	28	22	4	0	24	18	1.581	4.01	107	4.56	.283	0	....	2	3	0.2
Total	**8**	**48**	**58**	**.453**	**220**	**139**	**22**	**7**	**6**	**986^1**	**1029**	**507**	**470**	**80**	**13**	**301**	**541**	**1.348**	**4.29**	**87**	**3.85**	**.270**	**44**	**.151**	**-61**	**39**	**-6.7**

• PASTORIUS, Jim — James W. "Sunny Jim" Pastorius b: 7/12/1881, Pittsburgh, PA d: 5/10/1941, Pittsburgh, PA BL/TL, 5'9", 165 lbs. Deb: 4/15/1906

YEAR	TM-L	W	L	PCT	G	GS	CG	SH	SV	IP	H	R	ER	HR	HB	BB	SO	RAT	ERA	ERA+	CERA	OAV	BH	AVG	PR+	WS	TPW
1906	Bro-N	10	14	.417	29	24	16	3	0	211^2	225	111	85	4	3	69	58	**1.389**	3.61	70	3.62	.274	10	.141	-24	4	-2.7
1907	Bro-N	16	12	.571	28	26	20	4	0	222	218	74	58	2	6	77	70	1.329	2.35	99	3.30	.264	15	.205	2	16	0.6
1908	Bro-N	4	20	.167	28	25	16	2	0	213^2	171	88	58	5	7	74	54	1.147	2.44	95	2.59	.216	8	.129	-4	8	-0.5
1909	Bro-N	1	9	.100	12	9	5	1	0	79^2	91	65	51	4	1	58	23	1.870	5.76	45	6.19	.313	2	.080	-27	0	-3.1
Total	**4**	**31**	**55**	**.360**	**97**	**84**	**57**	**10**	**0**	**727**	**705**	**338**	**252**	**15**	**17**	**278**	**205**	**1.352**	**3.12**	**78**	**3.50**	**.258**	**35**	**.152**	**-53**	**28**	**-5.7**

• PATE, Joe — Joseph William Pate b: 6/6/1892, Alice, TX d: 12/26/1948, Fort Worth, TX BL/TL, 5'10", 184 lbs. Deb: 4/15/1926

YEAR	TM-L	W	L	PCT	G	GS	CG	SH	SV	IP	H	R	ER	HR	HB	BB	SO	RAT	ERA	ERA+	CERA	OAV	BH	AVG	PR+	WS	TPW
1926	Phi-A	9	0	1.000	47	2	0	0	6	113	109	38	34	3	2	51	24	1.416	2.71	154	3.51	.262	4	.148	18	14	1.8
1927	Phi-A	0	3	.000	32	0	0	0	6	53^2	67	36	31	3	1	21	14	1.640	5.20	82	4.99	.318	3	.300	-5	2	-0.4
Total	**2**	**9**	**3**	**.750**	**79**	**2**	**0**	**0**	**12**	**166^2**	**176**	**74**	**65**	**6**	**3**	**72**	**38**	**1.488**	**3.51**	**120**	**3.99**	**.281**	**7**	**.189**	**13**	**16**	**1.4**

• PATRICK, Bronswell — Bronswell Dante Patrick b: 9/16/1970, Greenville, NC BR/TR, 6'1", 237 lbs. Deb: 5/18/1998

YEAR	TM-L	W	L	PCT	G	GS	CG	SH	SV	IP	H	R	ER	HR	HB	BB	SO	RAT	ERA	ERA+	CERA	OAV	BH	AVG	PR+	WS	TPW
1998	Mil-N	4	1	.800	32	3	0	0	0	78^2	83	43	41	9	0	29	49	1.424	4.69	91	4.44	.279	3	.200	-4	4	-0.3
1999	SF-N	1	0	1.000	6	0	0	0	1	5^1	9	7	6	1	0	3	6	2.250	10.13	41	9.69	.375	0	.000	-4	0	-0.3
Total	**2**	**5**	**1**	**.833**	**38**	**3**	**0**	**0**	**1**	**84**	**92**	**50**	**47**	**10**	**0**	**32**	**55**	**1.476**	**5.04**	**85**	**4.78**	**.286**	**3**	**.188**	**-8**	**4**	**-0.6**

• PATTEN, Case — Case Lyman "Pat" Patten b: 5/7/1876, Westport, NY d: 5/31/1935, Rochester, NY BB/TL, 6', 175 lbs. Deb: 5/4/1901 U

YEAR	TM-L	W	L	PCT	G	GS	CG	SH	SV	IP	H	R	ER	HR	HB	BB	SO	RAT	ERA	ERA+	CERA	OAV	BH	AVG	PR+	WS	TPW
1901	Was-A	18	10	.643	32	30	26	4	0	254^1	285	163	111	8	17	74	109	1.412	3.93	93	4.01	.280	13	.135	-7	14	-1.0
1902	Was-A	18	16	.529	36	34	33	1	1	299^2	331	186	135	11	11	89	92	1.402	4.05	91	3.72	.281	12	.096	-6	14	-1.6
1903	Was-A	11	22	.333	36	34	32	0	1	300	313	163	120	11	4	80	133	1.310	3.60	87	3.29	.268	14	.132	-12	15	-1.8
1904	Was-A	14	23	.378	45	39	37	2	**3**	357^2	367	162	122	2	20	79	150	1.247	3.07	87	3.03	.266	16	.127	-7	8	-1.3
1905	Was-A	14	22	.389	42	36	29	2	0	309^2	300	145	108	3	10	86	113	1.247	3.14	84	2.90	.256	16	.155	-26	13	-3.0
1906	Was-A	19	16	.543	38	32	28	7	0	282^2	253	106	68	2	6	79	96	1.175	2.17	122	2.49	.243	11	.117	19	11	1.7
1907	Was-A	12	16	.429	36	29	20	1	0	237^1	272	135	94	3	6	63	58	1.412	3.56	68	3.64	.290	11	.126	-22	4	-2.7
1908	Was-A	0	2	.000	4	3	1	0	0	18	25	14	7	0	0	6	6	1.722	3.50	65	5.33	.333	1	.200	-2	0	-0.3
	Bos-A	0	1	.000	1	1	0	0	0	3	8	5	5	0	0	1	0	3.000	15.00	16	15.32	.533	0	.000	-4	0	-0.5
	Yr.	0	3	.000	5	4	1	0	0	21	33	19	12	0	0	7	6	1.905	5.14	46	6.76	.366	1	.167	-7	0	-0.8
Total	**8**	**106**	**128**	**.453**	**270**	**238**	**206**	**17**	**5**	**2062^1**	**2154**	**1079**	**770**	**40**	**74**	**557**	**757**	**1.315**	**3.36**	**88**	**3.30**	**.270**	**94**	**.127**	**-67**	**79**	**-10.5**

• PATTERSON, Bob — Robert Chandler Patterson b: 5/16/1959, Jacksonville, FL BR/TL, 6'2", 192 lbs. Deb: 9/2/1985

YEAR	TM-L	W	L	PCT	G	GS	CG	SH	SV	IP	H	R	ER	HR	HB	BB	SO	RAT	ERA	ERA+	CERA	OAV	BH	AVG	PR+	WS	TPW
1985	SD-N	0	0	....	3	0	0	0	0	4	13	11	11	2	0	3	1	4.000	24.75	14	28.64	.565	0	....	-9	0	-1.0
1986	Pit-N	2	3	.400	11	5	0	0	0	36^1	49	20	20	0	0	5	20	1.486	4.95	77	4.19	.322	1	.125	-5	1	-0.5
1987	Pit-N	1	4	.200	15	7	0	0	0	43	49	34	32	5	1	22	27	1.651	6.70	61	5.26	.290	1	.083	-13	0	-1.4
1989	Pit-N	4	3	.571	12	3	0	0	1	26^2	23	13	12	3	0	8	20	1.163	4.05	83	2.93	.232	0	.000	-2	1	-0.2
1990*	Pit-N	8	5	.615	55	5	0	0	5	94^2	88	33	31	9	3	21	70	1.151	2.95	123	3.02	.249	1	.053	6	9	0.5
1991*	Pit-N	4	3	.571	54	1	0	0	2	65^2	67	32	30	7	0	15	57	1.249	4.11	87	3.59	.267	1	.250	-4	4	-0.4
1992*	Pit-N	6	3	.667	60	0	0	0	9	64^2	59	22	21	7	0	23	43	1.268	2.92	118	3.38	.246	2	.333	3	8	0.5
1993	Tex-A	2	4	.333	52	0	0	0	1	52^2	59	28	28	8	1	11	46	1.329	4.78	87	4.43	.282	0	....	-3	2	-0.3
1994	Cal-A	2	3	.400	47	0	0	0	1	42	35	21	19	6	2	15	30	1.190	4.07	120	3.51	.229	0	....	4	4	0.3
1995	Cal-A	5	2	.714	62	0	0	0	0	53^1	48	18	18	6	1	13	41	1.144	3.04	154	3.11	.246	0	....	9	6	0.9
1996	Chi-N	3	3	.500	79	0	0	0	8	54^2	46	19	19	6	1	22	53	1.244	3.13	139	3.14	.229	1	.333	7	7	0.7
1997	Chi-N	1	6	.143	76	0	0	0	0	59^1	47	23	22	9	0	10	58	.961	3.34	129	2.42	.222	0	.000	6	6	0.6
1998	Chi-N	1	1	.500	33	0	0	0	1	20^1	36	20	17	2	0	12	17	2.361	7.52	59	9.40	.391	0	....	-7	0	-0.7
Total	**13**	**39**	**40**	**.494**	**559**	**21**	**0**	**0**	**28**	**617^1**	**619**	**294**	**280**	**70**	**9**	**180**	**483**	**1.294**	**4.08**	**97**	**3.83**	**.263**	**7**	**.125**	**-8**	**48**	**-1.0**

• PATTERSON, Danny — Danny Shane Patterson b: 2/17/1971, San Gabriel, CA BR/TR, 6', 170 lbs. Deb: 7/26/1996

YEAR	TM-L	W	L	PCT	G	GS	CG	SH	SV	IP	H	R	ER	HR	HB	BB	SO	RAT	ERA	ERA+	CERA	OAV	BH	AVG	PR+	WS	TPW
1996*	Tex-A	0	0	....	7	0	0	0	0	8^2	10	4	0	0	0	3	5	1.500	0.00	....	3.81	.286	0	....	5	1	0.5
1997	Tex-A	10	6	.625	54	0	0	0	1	71	70	29	27	3	0	23	69	1.310	3.42	140	3.27	.263	0	....	12	8	1.1
1998	Tex-A	2	5	.286	56	0	0	0	2	60^2	64	31	30	11	2	19	33	1.368	4.45	108	4.79	.274	0	....	3	5	0.3
1999*	Tex-A	2	0	1.000	53	0	0	0	0	60^1	77	38	38	5	1	19	43	1.591	5.67	89	5.11	.304	0	.000	-3	3	-0.3
2000	Det-A	5	1	.833	58	0	0	0	0	56^2	69	26	25	4	2	14	29	1.465	3.97	121	4.68	.309	0	....	6	5	0.5
2001	Det-A	5	4	.556	60	0	0	0	1	64^2	64	24	22	4	4	12	27	1.175	3.06	142	3.21	.274	0	....	10	7	1.0
2002	Det-A	0	2	.000	6	0	0	0	0	3	5	5	5	0	1	2	1	2.333	15.00	29	9.70	.357	0	....	-4	0	-0.3
2003	Det-A	0	0	....	19	0	0	0	3	17^2	15	8	8	1	1	4	19	1.075	4.08	106	2.51	.227	0	....	0	2	0.0
Total	**8**	**24**	**18**	**.571**	**313**	**0**	**0**	**0**	**7**	**342^2**	**374**	**165**	**155**	**28**	**11**	**96**	**226**	**1.372**	**4.07**	**117**	**4.12**	**.282**	**0**	**.000**	**30**	**31**	**2.8**

YEAR TM-L	W	L	PCT	G	GS	CG	SH	SV	IP	H	R	ER	HR	HB	BB	SO	RAT	ERA	ERA+	CERA	OAV	BH	AVG	PR+	WS	TPW
• PATTERSON, Daryl	Daryl Alan Patterson b: 11/21/1943, Coalinga, CA BL/TR, 6'4", 195 lbs. Deb: 4/10/1968																									
1968* Det-A	2	3	.400	38	1	0	0	7	68	53	19	16	3	4	27	49	1.176	2.12	142	2.71	.213	0	.000	6	7	0.6
1969 Det-A	0	2	.000	18	0	0	0	0	22^{1}	15	8	7	2	0	19	12	1.522	2.82	132	3.85	.205	0	.000	2	1	0.2
1970 Det-A	7	1	.875	43	0	0	0	2	78	81	47	42	9	5	39	55	1.538	4.85	77	5.05	.269	0	.000	-7	4	-0.9
1971 Det-A	0	1	.000	12	0	0	0	0	9^{1}	14	7	5	1	1	6	5	2.143	4.82	74	8.49	.359	0	....	-1	0	-0.1
Oak-A	0	0	....	4	0	0	0	0	5^{2}	5	5	5	2	1	4	2	1.588	7.94	42	7.55	.238	0	.000	-3	0	-0.3
Yr.	0	1	.000	16	0	0	0	0	15	19	12	10	3	2	10	7	1.933	6.00	58	8.13	.317	0	.000	-4	0	-0.5
StL-N	0	1	.000	13	2	0	0	1	26^{2}	20	14	13	3	0	15	11	1.313	4.39	82	3.40	.211	0	.000	-2	1	-0.2
1974 Pit-N	2	1	.667	14	0	0	0	1	21	35	19	17	3	0	9	8	2.095	7.29	47	8.67	.376	0	.000	-9	0	-1.0
Total 5	11	9	.550	142	3	0	0	11	231	223	119	105	23	11	119	142	1.481	4.09	86	4.58	.256	0	.000	-14	13	-1.7
• PATTERSON, Dave	David Glenn Patterson b: 7/25/1956, Springfield, MO BR/TR, 6', 170 lbs. Deb: 6/9/1979																									
1979 LA-N	4	1	.800	36	0	0	0	6	53	62	35	31	5	0	22	34	1.585	5.26	69	4.86	.292	1	.143	-9	2	-1.0
• PATTERSON, Gil	Gilbert Thomas Patterson b: 9/5/1955, Philadelphia, PA BR/TR, 6'1", 185 lbs. Deb: 4/19/1977																									
1977 NY-A	1	2	.333	10	6	0	0	1	33^{1}	38	20	20	3	3	20	29	1.740	5.40	73	6.00	.290	0	....	-6	0	-0.6
• PATTERSON, Jeff	Jeffrey Simmons Patterson b: 10/1/1968, Anaheim, CA BR/TR, 6'2", 200 lbs. Deb: 4/30/1995																									
1995 NY-A	0	0	....	3	0	0	0	0	3^{1}	3	1	1	1	0	3	3	1.800	2.70	171	7.01	.231	0	....	1	0	0.1
• PATTERSON, John	John Hollis Patterson b: 1/30/1978, Orange, TX BR/TR, 6'6", 183 lbs. Deb: 7/20/2002																									
2002 Ari-N	2	0	1.000	7	5	0	0	0	30^{2}	27	11	11	7	1	7	31	1.109	3.23	137	3.76	.235	1	.100	4	3	0.4
2003 Ari-N	1	4	.200	16	8	0	0	1	55	61	39	37	7	2	30	43	1.655	6.05	77	5.50	.281	1	.077	-8	0	-0.9
Total 2	3	4	.429	23	13	0	0	1	85^{2}	88	50	48	14	3	37	74	1.459	5.04	91	4.88	.265	2	.087	-4	3	-0.4
• PATTERSON, Ken	Kenneth Brian Patterson b: 7/8/1964, Costa Mesa, CA BL/TL, 6'4", 210 lbs. Deb: 7/9/1988																									
1988 Chi-A	0	2	.000	9	2	0	0	1	20^{2}	25	11	11	2	0	7	8	1.548	4.79	83	5.00	.294	0	....	-2	1	-0.2
1989 Chi-A	6	1	.857	50	1	0	0	0	65^{2}	64	37	33	11	2	28	43	1.401	4.52	84	4.59	.257	0	....	-5	3	-0.5
1990 Chi-A	2	1	.667	43	0	0	0	2	66^{1}	58	27	25	6	2	34	40	1.387	3.39	113	3.90	.242	0	....	2	5	0.2
1991 Chi-A	3	0	1.000	43	0	0	0	1	63^{2}	48	22	20	5	1	35	32	1.304	2.83	140	3.27	.214	0	....	6	5	0.6
1992 Chi-N	2	3	.400	32	1	0	0	0	41^{2}	41	25	18	7	1	27	23	1.632	3.89	93	5.31	.268	0	.000	-1	1	-0.2
1993 Cal-A	1	1	.500	46	0	0	0	1	59	54	30	30	7	0	35	36	1.508	4.58	98	4.46	.249	0	....	-1	3	-0.1
1994 Cal-A	0	0	....	1	0	0	0	0	0^{2}	0	0	0	0	0	0	1	.000	0.00	....	0.00	.000	0	....	0	0	0.0
Total 7	14	8	.636	224	4	0	0	5	317^{2}	290	152	137	38	6	166	183	1.435	3.88	102	4.27	.248	0	.000	-2	18	-0.2
• PATTERSON, Reggie	Reginald Allen Patterson b: 11/7/1958, Birmingham, AL BR/TR, 6'4", 180 lbs. Deb: 8/13/1981																									
1981 Chi-A	0	1	.000	6	1	0	0	0	7^{1}	14	11	11	1	0	6	2	2.727	13.50	27	12.60	.412	0	....	-8	0	-0.9
1983 Chi-N	1	2	.333	5	2	0	0	0	18^{2}	17	12	10	3	2	6	10	1.232	4.82	79	4.20	.246	0	.000	-2	0	-0.3
1984 Chi-N	0	1	.000	3	1	0	0	0	6	10	7	7	1	0	2	5	2.000	10.50	37	8.28	.357	0	.000	-4	0	-0.5
1985 Chi-N	3	0	1.000	8	5	1	0	0	39	36	13	13	2	0	10	17	1.179	3.00	133	2.83	.250	1	.100	5	4	0.5
Total 4	4	4	.500	22	9	1	0	0	71	77	43	41	7	2	24	34	1.423	5.20	73	4.66	.280	1	.056	-10	4	-1.1
• PATTERSON, Roy	Roy Lewis "Pat,St. Croix,Boy Wonder" Patterson b: 12/17/1876, Stoddard, WI d: 4/14/1953, St. Croix Falls, WI BR/TR, 6', 185 lbs. Deb: 4/24/1901																									
1901 Chi-A	20	15	.571	41	35	30	4	0	312^{1}	345	164	117	11	11	62	127	1.303	3.37	103	3.51	.277	26	.222	3	20	0.3
1902 Chi-A	19	14	.576	34	30	26	2	0	268	262	111	91	5	3	67	61	1.228	3.06	111	2.84	.257	20	.190	5	19	0.3
1903 Chi-A	15	15	.500	34	30	26	2	1	293	275	119	88	5	11	69	89	1.174	2.70	104	2.67	.248	11	.105	9	17	0.3
1904 Chi-A	9	9	.500	22	17	14	4	0	165	148	52	42	1	7	24	64	1.042	2.29	107	2.06	.241	6	.103	-1	10	-0.5
1905 Chi-A	4	6	.400	13	9	7	0	0	88^{2}	73	34	18	0	0	16	29	1.004	1.83	135	1.77	.227	8	.267	4	6	0.6
1906 Chi-A	10	7	.588	21	18	12	3	1	142	119	46	33	1	4	17	45	.958	2.09	121	1.78	.231	3	.061	5	10	0.1
1907 Chi-A	4	6	.400	19	13	4	1	0	96	105	42	28	0	2	18	27	1.281	2.63	91	3.15	.281	3	.097	-2	4	-0.5
Total 7	81	72	.529	184	152	119	16	2	1365	1327	568	417	23	38	273	442	1.172	2.75	108	2.71	.255	77	.156	24	86	0.7
• PATTIN, Marty	Martin William Pattin b: 4/6/1943, Charleston, IL BR/TR, 5'11", 180 lbs. Deb: 5/14/1968 C																									
1968 Cal-A	4	4	.500	52	4	0	0	3	84	67	27	26	7	2	37	66	1.238	2.79	104	3.06	.221	1	.083	0	6	-0.1
1969 Sea-A	7	12	.368	34	27	2	1	0	158^{2}	166	104	99	29	2	71	126	1.494	5.62	65	5.16	.268	9	.155	-30	0	-3.3
1970 Mil-A	14	12	.538	37	29	11	0	0	233^{1}	204	91	88	20	6	71	161	1.179	3.39	112	3.01	.235	9	.129	15	15	1.4
1971 Mil-A★	14	14	.500	36	36	9	5	0	264^{2}	225	100	92	29	4	73	169	1.126	3.13	111	2.93	.235	7	.084	8	16	0.5
1972 Bos-A	17	13	.567	38	35	13	4	0	253	232	102	91	19	9	65	168	1.174	3.24	99	3.03	.243	12	.140	4	14	0.5
1973 Bos-A	15	15	.500	34	30	11	2	1	219^{1}	238	112	105	31	8	69	119	1.400	4.31	93	4.64	.277	0	....	-8	10	-0.9
1974 KC-A	3	7	.300	25	11	2	0	0	117^{1}	121	55	52	10	2	28	50	1.270	3.99	96	3.51	.264	0	....	-1	5	-0.1
1975 KC-A	10	10	.500	44	15	5	1	5	177	173	77	64	13	3	45	89	1.232	3.25	118	3.22	.253	0	....	14	13	1.4
1976* KC-A	8	14	.364	44	15	4	1	5	141	114	51	39	9	3	38	65	1.078	2.49	140	2.32	.216	0	....	16	11	1.7
1977* KC-A	10	3	.769	31	10	4	0	0	128^{1}	115	56	51	16	2	37	55	1.184	3.58	113	3.28	.242	0	....	5	9	0.5
1978* KC-A	3	3	.500	32	5	2	0	4	78^{2}	72	41	29	8	2	25	30	1.233	3.32	115	3.30	.248	0	....	4	4	0.4
1979 KC-A	5	2	.714	31	7	1	0	3	94^{1}	109	50	48	11	1	21	41	1.378	4.58	93	4.40	.293	0	....	-4	5	-0.4
1980* KC-A	4	0	1.000	37	0	0	0	4	89	97	39	36	7	1	23	40	1.348	3.64	111	3.81	.277	0	....	4	6	0.4
Total 13	114	109	.511	475	224	64	14	25	2038^{2}	1933	905	820	209	45	603	1179	1.244	3.62	102	3.47	.250	38	.123	27	114	2.2
• PATTISON, Jimmy	James Wells Pattison b: 12/18/1908, Bronx, NY d: 2/22/1991, Melbourne, FL BL/TL, 6', 185 lbs. Deb: 4/18/1929																									
1929 Bro-N	0	1	.000	6	0	0	0	0	11^{2}	9	6	6	1	0	4	5	1.114	4.63	100	2.72	.231	1	.500	0	1	0.1
• PATTON, Harry	Harry Claude Patton b: 6/29/1884, Gillespie, IL d: 6/9/1930, St. Louis, MO Deb: 8/22/1910																									
1910 StL-N	0	0	....	1	0	0	0	0	4	4	2	1	0	0	2	2	1.500	2.25	132	3.74	.267	0	....	0	0	0.0
• PAUL, Mike	Michael George Paul b: 4/18/1945, Detroit, MI BL/TL, 6', 183 lbs. Deb: 5/27/1968 C																									
1968 Cle-A	5	8	.385	36	7	0	0	3	91^{2}	72	42	40	11	5	35	87	1.167	3.93	75	3.08	.213	4	.167	-11	2	-1.2
1969 Cle-A	5	10	.333	47	12	0	0	2	117^{1}	104	48	47	12	2	54	98	1.347	3.61	104	3.65	.241	0	.000	3	6	0.0
1970 Cle-A	2	8	.200	30	15	1	0	0	88	91	51	47	13	0	45	70	1.545	4.81	82	5.10	.271	4	.154	-9	2	-1.0
1971 Cle-A	2	7	.222	17	12	1	0	0	62	78	42	41	8	5	14	33	1.484	5.95	64	5.45	.318	1	.053	-15	0	-1.7
1972 Tex-A	8	9	.471	49	20	2	1	1	161^{2}	149	50	39	4	2	52	108	1.243	2.17	139	2.79	.246	8	.167	18	11	2.2
1973 Tex-A	5	4	.556	36	10	1	0	2	87^{1}	104	55	48	9	5	36	49	1.603	4.95	75	5.40	.295	0	....	-10	2	-1.0
Chi-N	0	1	.000	11	1	0	0	0	18^{1}	17	7	7	2	0	9	6	1.418	3.44	115	4.11	.258	0	.000	1	1	0.1
1974 Chi-N	0	1	.000	2	0	0	0	0	1^{1}	4	4	4	1	0	1	1	3.750	27.00	14	25.36	.500	0	....	-3	0	-0.4
Total 7	27	48	.360	228	77	5	1	8	627^{2}	619	299	273	60	19	246	452	1.378	3.91	90	4.03	.260	17	.115	-25	24	-3.0
• PAULSEN, Gil	Guilford Paul Hans Paulsen b: 11/14/1902, Graettinger, IA d: 4/2/1994, Harlan, IA BR/TR, 6'2.5", 190 lbs. Deb: 10/3/1925																									
1925 StL-N	0	0	....	1	0	0	0	0	2	1	0	0	0	0	0	1	.500	0.00	....	0.47	.125	0	....	1	0	0.1
• PAVANO, Carl	Carl Anthony Pavano b: 1/8/1976, New Britain, CT BR/TR, 6'5", 230 lbs. Deb: 5/23/1998																									
1998 Mon-N	6	9	.400	24	23	0	0	0	134^{2}	130	70	63	18	8	43	83	1.285	4.21	100	3.97	.251	6	.158	2	6	0.1
1999 Mon-N	6	8	.429	19	18	1	1	0	104	117	66	65	8	4	35	70	1.462	5.63	80	4.51	.285	2	.061	-11	3	-1.3
2000 Mon-N	8	4	.667	15	15	0	0	0	97	89	40	33	8	8	34	64	1.268	3.06	157	3.67	.248	5	.143	19	8	1.8
2001 Mon-N	1	6	.143	8	8	0	0	0	42^{2}	59	33	30	7	2	16	36	1.758	6.33	71	6.99	.331	1	.077	-8	0	-0.9
2002 Mon-N	3	8	.273	15	14	0	0	0	74^{1}	98	55	52	14	7	31	51	1.735	6.30	68	7.07	.318	5	.208	-17	0	-1.6
Fla-N	3	2	.600	22	8	0	0	0	61^{2}	76	33	26	5	3	14	41	1.459	3.79	104	4.74	.306	3	.188	1	3	0.1
Yr.	6	10	.375	37	22	0	0	0	136	174	88	78	19	10	45	92	1.610	5.16	80	6.01	.313	8	.200	-16	3	-1.5
2003* Fla-N	12	13	.480	33	32	2	0	0	201	204	99	96	19	7	49	133	1.259	4.30	95	3.57	.265	6	.098	-6	9	-0.7
Total 6	39	50	.438	136	118	3	1	0	715^{1}	773	396	365	79	39	222	478	1.391	4.59	93	4.46	.277	28	.127	-20	29	-2.4
• PAVLAS, Dave	David Lee Pavlas b: 8/12/1962, Frankfurt, West Germany BR/TR, 6'7", 180 lbs. Deb: 8/21/1990																									
1990 Chi-N	2	0	1.000	13	0	0	0	0	21^{1}	23	7	5	2	0	6	12	1.359	2.11	193	3.76	.271	0	.000	5	2	0.6

YEAR	TM-L	W	L	PCT	G	GS	CG	SH	SV	IP	H	R	ER	HR	HB	BB	SO	RAT	ERA	ERA+	CERA	OAV	BH	AVG	PR+	WS	TPW
1991	Chi-N	0	0	....	1	0	0	0	0	1	3	2	2	1	0	0	0	3.000	18.00	22	30.73	.750	0	....	-2	0	-0.2
1995	NY-A	0	0	....	4	0	0	0	0	5^{2}	8	2	2	0	0	0	3	1.412	3.18	145	4.17	.333	0	....	1	0	0.1
1996	NY-A	0	0	....	16	0	0	0	1	23	23	7	6	0	1	7	18	1.304	2.35	211	3.07	.264	0	....	7	3	0.6
Total	4	2	0	1.000	34	0	0	0	1	51	57	18	15	3	1	13	33	1.373	2.65	167	4.02	.285	0	.000	12	5	1.1
• PAVLIK, Roger	Roger Allen Pavlik b: 10/4/1967, Houston, TX BB/TR, 6'3", 220 lbs. Deb: 5/2/1992																										
1992	Tex-A	4	4	.500	13	12	1	0	0	62	66	32	29	3	3	34	45	1.613	4.21	90	4.97	.280	0	....	-2	3	-0.2
1993	Tex-A	12	6	.667	26	26	2	0	0	166^{1}	151	67	63	18	5	80	131	1.389	3.41	122	4.08	.245	0	....	17	12	1.6
1994	Tex-A	2	5	.286	11	11	0	0	0	50^{1}	61	45	43	8	4	30	31	1.808	7.69	63	6.80	.300	0	....	-15	0	-1.4
1995	Tex-A	10	10	.500	31	31	2	1	0	191^{2}	174	96	93	19	4	90	149	1.377	4.37	110	3.91	.243	0	....	10	14	1.0
1996*	Tex-A★	15	8	.652	34	34	7	0	0	201	216	120	116	28	5	81	127	1.478	5.19	101	4.91	.276	0	....	1	12	0.1
1997	Tex-A	3	5	.375	11	11	0	0	0	57^{2}	59	29	28	7	1	31	35	1.561	4.37	110	5.01	.267	0	....	4	3	0.3
1998	Tex-A	1	1	.500	5	0	0	0	1	14	16	8	6	2	1	5	8	1.500	3.86	125	5.18	.286	0	....	2	1	0.2
Total	7	47	39	.547	131	125	12	1	1	743	743	397	378	85	23	351	526	1.472	4.58	103	4.61	.262	0	....	17	45	1.6
• PAWLOWSKI, John	John Pawlowski b: 9/6/1963, Johnson City, NY BR/TR, 6'2", 175 lbs. Deb: 9/19/1987																										
1987	Chi-A	0	0	....	2	0	0	0	0	3^{2}	7	2	2	0	0	3	2	2.727	4.91	93	11.10	.438	0	....	-0	0	0.0
1988	Chi-A	1	0	1.000	6	0	0	0	0	14	20	14	13	2	0	3	10	1.643	8.36	48	6.02	.328	0	....	-7	0	-0.7
Total	2	1	0	1.000	8	0	0	0	0	17^{2}	27	16	15	2	0	6	12	1.868	7.64	53	7.07	.351	0	....	-7	0	-0.7
• PAXTON, Mike	Michael De Wayne Paxton b: 9/3/1953, Memphis, TN BR/TR, 5'11", 190 lbs. Deb: 5/25/1977																										
1977	Bos-A	10	5	.667	29	12	2	1	0	108	134	53	46	7	3	25	58	1.472	3.83	117	4.68	.311	0	....	9	8	0.9
1978	Cle-A	12	11	.522	33	27	5	2	1	191	179	89	82	13	8	63	96	1.267	3.86	97	3.36	.247	0	....	-1	10	-0.1
1979	Cle-A	8	8	.500	33	24	3	0	0	159^{2}	210	118	105	14	2	52	70	1.641	5.92	72	5.50	.315	0	....	-26	2	-2.6
1980	Cle-A	0	0	....	4	0	0	0	0	7^{2}	13	11	11	4	0	6	6	2.478	12.91	32	14.55	.394	0	....	-7	0	-0.7
Total	4	30	24	.556	99	63	10	3	1	466^{1}	536	271	244	38	13	146	230	1.462	4.71	87	4.58	.289	0	....	-25	20	-2.5
• PAYNE, George	George Washington Payne b: 5/23/1890, Mount Vernon, KY d: 1/24/1959, Long Beach, CA BR/TR, 5'11", 172 lbs. Deb: 5/8/1920																										
1920	Chi-A	1	1	.500	12	0	0	0	0	29^{2}	39	24	18	2	0	9	7	1.618	5.46	69	5.17	.312	1	.125	-6	0	-0.6
• PAYNE, Harley	Harley Fenwick "Lady" Payne b: 1/9/1868, Windsor, OH d: 12/29/1935, Orwell, OH BB/TL, 6', 160 lbs. Deb: 4/18/1896																										
1896	Bro-N	14	16	.467	34	28	24	2	0	241^{2}	284	129	91	4	8	58	52	1.415	3.39	122	3.83	.291	21	.214	21	17	1.8
1897	Bro-N	14	17	.452	40	38	30	1	0	280	350	215	144	8	17	71	86	1.504	4.63	88	4.40	.304	26	.236	-13	14	-1.2
1898	Bro-N	1	0	1.000	1	1	1	0	0	9	11	8	4	0	0	3	2	1.556	4.00	89	4.24	.299	3	.750	-0	1	0.1
1899	Pit-N	1	3	.250	5	5	2	0	0	26^{1}	33	19	11	2	2	4	8	1.405	3.76	101	4.52	.306	1	.100	0	1	-0.1
Total	4	30	36	.455	80	72	57	3	0	557	678	371	250	14	27	136	148	1.461	4.04	101	4.16	.298	51	.230	7	33	0.6
• PAYNE, Mike	Michael Earl Payne b: 11/15/1961, Woonsocket, RI d: 8/4/2002, Dunnellon, FL BR/TR, 5'11", 165 lbs. Deb: 8/22/1984																										
1984	Atl-N	0	1	.000	3	1	0	0	0	5^{2}	7	4	4	0	0	3	3	1.765	6.35	61	5.47	.333	0	.000	-2	0	-0.2
• PAZIK, Mike	Michael Joseph Pazik b: 1/26/1950, Lynn, MA BL/TL, 6'2", 195 lbs. Deb: 5/11/1975 C																										
1975	Min-A	0	4	.000	5	3	0	0	0	19^{2}	28	20	18	5	0	10	8	1.932	8.24	47	8.33	.329	0	....	-9	0	-1.0
1976	Min-A	0	0	....	5	0	0	0	0	9	13	9	7	0	1	4	6	1.889	7.00	51	6.69	.342	0	....	-3	0	-0.4
1977	Min-A	1	0	1.000	3	3	0	0	0	18	18	5	5	1	0	6	6	1.333	2.50	159	3.48	.265	0	....	3	2	0.3
Total	3	1	4	.200	13	6	0	0	0	46^{2}	59	34	30	6	1	20	20	1.693	5.79	66	6.14	.309	0	....	-10	2	-1.0
• PEARCE, Frank	Franklin Johnson Pearce b: 3/30/1860, Jefferson County, KY d: 11/13/1926, Louisville, KY Deb: 10/4/1876																										
1876	Lou-N	0	0	....	1	0	0	0	0	4	5	4	2	0	....	1	1	1.500	4.50	60	....	.271	0	.000	-1	0	-0.1
• PEARCE, Frank	Franklin Thomas Pearce b: 8/31/1905, Middletown, KY d: 9/3/1950, Van Buren, KY BR/TR, 6', 170 lbs. Deb: 4/20/1933																										
1933	Phi-N	5	4	.556	20	7	3	1	0	82	78	41	33	5	0	29	18	1.305	3.62	105	3.25	.251	5	.192	2	5	0.2
1934	Phi-N	0	2	.000	7	1	0	0	0	20	25	16	16	4	0	5	4	1.500	7.20	66	5.59	.301	2	.667	-6	0	-0.5
1935	Phi-N	0	0	....	5	0	0	0	0	13	22	15	12	0	0	6	7	2.154	8.31	55	7.26	.361	2	.500	-5	0	-0.5
Total	3	5	6	.455	32	8	3	1	0	115	125	72	61	9	0	40	29	1.435	4.77	87	4.11	.275	9	.273	-9	5	-0.8
• PEARCE, George	George Thomas "Filbert" Pearce b: 1/10/1888, Shabbona Grove, IL d: 10/11/1935, Joliet, IL BL/TL, 5'10.5", 175 lbs. Deb: 4/16/1912																										
1912	Chi-N	0	0	....	3	2	0	0	0	14^{2}	15	13	9	0	0	12	9	1.841	5.52	60	5.08	.185	1	.167	-4	0	-0.4
1913	Chi-N	13	5	.722	25	21	14	3	0	164^{1}	137	60	42	4	3	59	73	1.193	2.30	138	2.60	....	4	.073	15	13	1.2
1914	Chi-N	9	12	.429	30	17	4	0	1	141	122	82	55	3	2	65	78	1.326	3.51	79	2.96	.239	4	.089	-9	4	-1.3
1915	Chi-N	13	9	.591	36	20	8	2	0	176	158	83	65	1	4	77	96	**1.335**	3.32	83	2.98	.244	11	.196	-8	9	-0.8
1916	Chi-N	0	0	....	4	1	0	0	0	4^{1}	6	5	1	0	0	1	0	1.615	2.08	140	3.98	.300	0	....	0	0	0.1
1917	StL-N	1	1	.500	5	0	0	0	0	10^{1}	7	7	4	0	1	3	4	.968	3.48	77	1.55	.184	0	.000	-1	0	-0.2
Total	6	36	27	.571	103	61	26	5	1	510^{2}	445	250	176	8	10	217	260	1.296	3.10	93	2.89	.343	20	.120	-7	26	-1.4
• PEARCE, Jim	James Madison Pearce b: 6/9/1925, Zebulon, NC BR/TR, 6'6", 180 lbs. Deb: 9/8/1949																										
1949	Was-A	0	1	.000	2	1	0	0	0	5^{1}	9	10	5	1	0	5	1	2.625	8.44	50	11.15	.375	0	.000	-2	0	-0.3
1950	Was-A	2	1	.667	20	3	1	0	0	56^{2}	58	40	38	2	1	37	18	1.676	6.04	74	4.62	.270	2	.154	-10	1	-1.0
1953	Was-A	0	1	.000	4	1	0	0	0	9^{1}	15	10	8	3	0	6	0	2.250	7.71	50	12.12	.405	0	.000	-4	0	-0.4
1954	Cin-N	1	0	1.000	2	1	1	0	0	11	7	1	0	0	1	5	3	1.091	0.00	....	2.08	.194	0	.000	5	2	0.5
1955	Cin-N	0	1	.000	2	1	0	0	0	3^{1}	8	5	4	0	0	0	0	2.400	10.80	39	10.16	.471	0	....	-2	0	-0.2
Total	5	3	4	.429	30	7	2	0	0	85^{2}	97	66	55	6	2	53	22	1.751	5.78	75	5.74	.295	2	.105	-13	3	-1.4
• PEARCE, Josh	Joshua Ray Pearce b: 8/20/1977, Yakima, WA BR/TR, 6'3", 215 lbs. Deb: 4/20/2002																										
2002	StL-N	0	0	....	3	3	0	0	0	13	20	13	11	1	1	8	1	2.154	7.62	52	8.51	.377	1	.250	-5	0	-0.5
2003	StL-N	0	0	....	7	0	0	0	0	9	11	3	3	0	1	2	4	1.444	3.00	135	4.45	.306	0	....	1	1	0.1
Total	2	0	0	....	10	3	0	0	0	22	31	16	14	1	2	10	5	1.864	5.73	69	6.85	.348	1	.250	-4	1	-0.4
• PEARS, Frank	Frank H. Pears b: 8/30/1866, Louisville, KY d: 11/29/1923, St. Louis, MO TR, 5'9", 145 lbs. Deb: 10/6/1889 U																										
1889	KC-a	0	2	.000	3	2	2	0	0	22	21	16	12	2	1	9	5	1.364	4.91	85	....	.244	1	.091	-1	1	-0.2
1893	StL-N	0	0	....	1	0	0	0	0	4	9	7	6	0	1	2	0	2.750	13.50	35	12.68	.432	0	.000	-4	0	-0.4
Total	2	0	2	.000	4	2	2	0	0	26	30	23	18	2	2	11	5	1.577	6.23	70	1.95	.280	1	.077	-5	1	-0.6
• PEARSON, Alex	Alexander Franklin Pearson b: 3/7/1877, Greensboro, PA d: 10/30/1966, Rochester, PA BR/TR, 5'10.5", 160 lbs. Deb: 8/1/1902																										
1902	StL-N	2	6	.250	11	10	8	0	0	82	90	47	36	0	3	22	24	1.366	3.95	69	3.47	.279	9	.265	-10	2	-0.9
1903	Cle-A	1	2	.333	4	3	2	0	0	30^{1}	34	15	12	1	1	3	12	1.220	3.56	80	3.08	.282	1	.083	-3	1	-0.4
Total	2	3	8	.273	15	13	10	0	0	112^{1}	124	62	48	1	4	25	36	1.326	3.85	72	3.37	.280	10	.217	-12	3	-1.3
• PEARSON, Ike	Isaac Overton Pearson b: 3/1/1917, Grenada, MS d: 3/17/1985, Sarasota, FL BR/TR, 6'1", 180 lbs. Deb: 6/6/1939																										
1939	Phi-N	2	13	.133	26	13	4	0	0	125	144	84	80	15	5	56	29	1.600	5.76	68	5.30	.296	2	.054	-25	1	-2.9
1940	Phi-N	3	14	.176	29	20	5	1	1	145^{1}	160	91	88	13	3	57	43	1.493	5.45	72	4.46	.275	9	.205	-25	2	-2.4
1941	Phi-N	4	14	.222	46	10	0	0	6	136	139	75	54	8	8	70	38	1.537	3.57	104	4.38	.266	5	.125	3	7	0.1
1942	Phi-N	1	6	.143	35	7	0	0	0	85^{1}	87	48	43	4	4	50	21	1.605	4.54	73	4.60	.271	1	.043	-12	2	-1.5
1946	Phi-N	1	0	1.000	5	2	1	1	0	14^{1}	16	8	6	1	1	8	6	1.674	3.77	91	5.03	.271	1	.200	-0	1	0.0
1948	Chi-A	2	3	.400	23	2	0	0	1	53	62	32	29	8	2	27	12	1.679	4.92	86	5.91	.292	2	.200	-4	2	-0.5
Total	6	13	50	.206	164	54	10	2	8	559	608	338	300	49	23	268	149	1.567	4.83	79	4.80	.279	20	.126	-64	15	-7.1
• PEARSON, Jason	Jason John Pearson b: 12/29/1975, Freeport, IL BL/TL, 6', 195 lbs. Deb: 6/4/2002																										
2002	SD-N	0	0	....	2	0	0	0	0	1^{2}	1	0	0	0	0	0	3	.600	0.00	....	0.75	.167	0	....	1	0	0.1
2003	StL-N	0	0	....	2	0	0	0	0	1	4	7	7	1	0	3	1	7.000	63.00	6	53.56	.571	0	....	-7	0	-0.6
Total	2	0	0	....	4	0	0	0	0	2^{2}	5	7	7	1	0	3	4	3.000	23.63	17	20.56	.385	0	....	-6	0	-0.6

• PEARSON, Monte Montgomery Marcellus "Hoot" Pearson b: 9/2/1908, Oakland, CA d: 1/27/1978, Fresno, CA BR/TR, 6', 175 lbs. Deb: 4/22/1932

YEAR TM-L	W	L	PCT	G	GS	CG	SH	SV	IP	H	R	ER	HR	HB	BB	SO	RAT	ERA	ERA+	CERA	OAV	BH	AVG	PR+	WS	TPW
1932 Cle-A	0	0	....	8	0	0	0	0	8	10	9	9	1	0	11	5	2.625	10.13	47	9.79	.323	0	....	-5	0	-0.4
1933 Cle-A	10	5	.667	19	16	10	0	0	135^1	111	45	35	5	0	55	54	1.227	**2.33**	191	2.63	.221	13	.260	32	16	3.1
1934 Cle-A	18	13	.581	39	33	19	0	2	254^2	257	144	128	16	1	130	140	1.520	4.52	101	4.13	.260	25	.272	2	17	0.7
1935 Cle-A	8	13	.381	30	24	10	1	0	181^2	199	117	99	9	0	103	90	1.662	4.90	92	4.72	.279	11	.177	-6	7	-0.5
1936* NY-A★	19	7	.731	33	31	15	1	1	223	191	99	92	13	3	135	118	1.462	3.71	125	3.71	**.233**	23	.253	22	20	2.4
1937* NY-A	9	3	.750	22	20	7	1	1	144^2	145	60	51	6	1	64	71	1.445	3.17	140	3.78	.261	11	.216	18	12	1.7
1938* NY-A	16	7	.696	28	27	17	1	0	202	198	107	89	12	0	113	98	1.540	3.97	114	4.19	.258	13	.171	11	15	1.0
1939* NY-A	12	5	.706	22	20	8	0	0	146^1	151	77	73	9	1	70	76	1.510	4.49	97	4.23	.272	17	.321	-8	9	-0.2
1940 NY-A★	7	5	.583	16	16	7	1	0	109^2	108	48	45	8	0	44	43	1.386	3.69	109	3.77	.262	4	.121	3	8	0.2
1941 Cin-N	1	3	.250	7	4	1	0	0	24^1	22	15	14	3	0	15	8	1.521	5.18	69	4.39	.242	0	.000	-4	0	-0.5
Total 10	100	61	.621	224	191	94	5	4	1429^2	1392	721	635	82	6	740	703	1.491	4.00	111	3.99	.256	117	.228	66	104	7.5

• PEARSON, Terry Terry Bobby Gene Pearson b: 11/10/1971, Tuscaloosa, AL BR/TR, 6', 200 lbs. Deb: 4/4/2002

YEAR TM-L	W	L	PCT	G	GS	CG	SH	SV	IP	H	R	ER	HR	HB	BB	SO	RAT	ERA	ERA+	CERA	OAV	BH	AVG	PR+	WS	TPW
2002 Det-A	0	0	....	4	0	0	0	0	6	8	7	7	2	0	2	4	1.667	10.50	41	7.43	.320	0	....	-4	0	-0.4

• PEASLEY, Marv Marvin Warren Peasley b: 7/16/1888, Jonesport, ME d: 12/27/1948, San Francisco, CA BL/TL, 6'1", 175 lbs. Deb: 9/27/1910

YEAR TM-L	W	L	PCT	G	GS	CG	SH	SV	IP	H	R	ER	HR	HB	BB	SO	RAT	ERA	ERA+	CERA	OAV	BH	AVG	PR+	WS	TPW
1910 Det-A	0	1	.000	2	1	0	0	0	10	13	14	9	0	1	11	4	2.400	8.10	32	7.56	.295	0	.000	-6	0	-0.7

• PEAVY, Jake Jacob Edward Peavy b: 5/31/1981, Mobile, AL BR/TR, 6'1", 180 lbs. Deb: 6/22/2002

YEAR TM-L	W	L	PCT	G	GS	CG	SH	SV	IP	H	R	ER	HR	HB	BB	SO	RAT	ERA	ERA+	CERA	OAV	BH	AVG	PR+	WS	TPW
2002 SD-N	6	7	.462	17	17	0	0	0	97^2	106	54	49	11	3	33	90	1.423	4.52	83	4.41	.274	7	.212	-7	3	-0.6
2003 SD-N	12	11	.522	32	32	0	0	0	194^2	173	94	89	33	6	82	156	1.310	4.11	96	4.13	.238	4	.073	-3	7	-0.5
Total 2	18	18	.500	49	49	0	0	0	292^1	279	148	138	44	9	115	246	1.348	4.25	91	4.22	.250	11	.125	-10	10	-1.1

• PECHINEY, George George Adolphe "Pisch" Pechiney b: 9/20/1861, Cincinnati, OH d: 7/14/1943, Cincinnati, OH BR/TR, 5'9", 184 lbs. Deb: 8/4/1885

YEAR TM-L	W	L	PCT	G	GS	CG	SH	SV	IP	H	R	ER	HR	HB	BB	SO	RAT	ERA	ERA+	CERA	OAV	BH	AVG	PR+	WS	TPW
1885 Cin-a	7	4	.636	11	11	11	1	0	98	95	45	22	1	6	30	49	1.276	2.02	161	....	.244	6	.150	12	8	1.0
1886 Cin-a	15	21	.417	40	40	35	2	0	330^1	355	230	152	4	14	133	110	1.477	4.14	85	....	.262	30	.208	-25	15	-2.3
1887 Cle-a	1	9	.100	10	10	10	0	0	86	162	124	68	8	3	44	24	1.884	7.12	61	....	.387	11	.289	-23	0	-1.9
Total 3	23	34	.404	61	61	56	3	0	514^1	612	399	242	13	23	207	183	1.507	4.23	87	....	.283	47	.212	-36	23	-3.2

• PEEK, Steve Stephen George Peek b: 7/30/1914, Springfield, MA d: 9/20/1991, Syracuse, NY BB/TR, 6'2", 195 lbs. Deb: 4/16/1941

YEAR TM-L	W	L	PCT	G	GS	CG	SH	SV	IP	H	R	ER	HR	HB	BB	SO	RAT	ERA	ERA+	CERA	OAV	BH	AVG	PR+	WS	TPW
1941 NY-A	4	2	.667	17	8	2	0	0	80	85	48	45	6	0	39	18	1.550	5.06	78	4.55	.276	1	.036	-13	2	-1.5

• PEERY, Red George Allan Peery b: 8/15/1906, Payson, UT d: 5/6/1985, Salt Lake City, UT BL/TL, 5'11", 160 lbs. Deb: 9/22/1927

YEAR TM-L	W	L	PCT	G	GS	CG	SH	SV	IP	H	R	ER	HR	HB	BB	SO	RAT	ERA	ERA+	CERA	OAV	BH	AVG	PR+	WS	TPW
1927 Pit-N	0	0	....	1	0	0	0	0	1	0	1	0	0	0	1	0	1.000	0.00	....	0.64	.000	0	....	0	0	0.0
1929 Bos-N	0	1	.000	9	1	0	0	0	44	53	28	25	1	0	9	3	1.409	5.11	91	3.91	.305	3	.214	-2	2	-0.1
Total 2	0	1	.000	10	1	0	0	0	45	53	29	25	1	0	10	3	1.400	5.00	94	3.84	.305	3	.214	-1	2	-0.1

• PELTY, Barney Barney Pelty b: 9/10/1880, Farmington, MO d: 5/24/1939, Farmington, MO BR/TR, 5'9", 175 lbs. Deb: 8/20/1903 U

YEAR TM-L	W	L	PCT	G	GS	CG	SH	SV	IP	H	R	ER	HR	HB	BB	SO	RAT	ERA	ERA+	CERA	OAV	BH	AVG	PR+	WS	TPW
1903 StL-A	3	3	.500	7	6	5	0	1	48^2	49	25	13	1	2	15	20	1.315	2.40	121	3.31	.261	3	.150	3	3	0.3
1904 StL-A	15	18	.455	39	35	31	2	0	301	270	121	95	7	20	77	126	1.153	2.84	87	2.65	.241	15	.127	-8	15	-1.6
1905 StL-A	14	14	.500	31	28	27	1	0	258^2	222	106	79	3	12	68	114	1.121	2.75	92	2.35	.234	15	.153	-2	11	-0.5
1906 StL-A	16	11	.593	34	30	25	4	2	260^2	189	77	46	1	18	59	92	.951	1.59	163	1.69	**.206**	15	.165	**28**	21	2.9
1907 StL-A	12	21	.364	36	31	29	5	1	273	234	101	78	1	18	64	85	1.092	2.57	98	2.32	.234	16	.168	-2	14	-0.4
1908 StL-A	7	4	.636	20	13	7	2	0	122	104	44	27	0	10	32	36	1.115	1.99	120	2.54	.241	5	.119	-0	8	-0.3
1909 StL-A	11	11	.500	27	23	17	5	0	199^1	158	63	51	2	5	53	88	1.059	2.30	105	2.09	.222	15	.165	2	12	0.0
1910 StL-A	5	11	.313	27	19	13	3	0	165^1	157	81	64	3	8	70	48	1.373	3.48	71	3.60	.263	5	.089	-18	4	-2.5
1911 StL-A	7	15	.318	28	22	18	1	0	197	197	87	65	4	4	69	59	1.350	2.97	113	3.44	.265	9	.138	7	10	0.3
1912 StL-A	1	5	.167	6	6	2	0	0	38^2	43	27	24	0	3	15	10	1.500	5.59	60	4.37	.297	0	.000	-10	0	-1.2
Was-A	1	4	.200	11	4	1	0	0	43^2	40	18	16	0	4	10	15	1.145	3.30	102	2.72	.250	2	.222	-1	3	-0.1
Yr.	2	9	.182	17	10	3	0	0	82^1	83	45	40	0	7	25	25	1.312	4.37	76	3.50	.272	2	.095	-11	3	-1.3
Total 10	92	117	.440	266	217	175	23	4	1908	1663	750	558	22	104	532	693	1.150	2.63	100	2.58	.239	100	.143	-1	101	-3.3

• PEMBER, Dave David Joseph Pember b: 5/24/1978, Cincinnati, OH BR/TR, 6'5", 225 lbs. Deb: 9/3/2002

YEAR TM-L	W	L	PCT	G	GS	CG	SH	SV	IP	H	R	ER	HR	HB	BB	SO	RAT	ERA	ERA+	CERA	OAV	BH	AVG	PR+	WS	TPW
2002 Mil-N	0	1	.000	4	1	0	0	0	8^2	7	6	5	1	0	6	5	1.500	5.19	79	4.04	.219	0	.000	-1	0	-0.1

• PENA, Alejandro Alejandro (Vasquez) Pena b: 6/25/1959, Cambiaso Puerta Plata, Dominican Republic BR/TR, 6'1", 205 lbs. Deb: 8/13/1981

YEAR TM-L	W	L	PCT	G	GS	CG	SH	SV	IP	H	R	ER	HR	HB	BB	SO	RAT	ERA	ERA+	CERA	OAV	BH	AVG	PR+	WS	TPW
1981* LA-N	1	1	.500	14	0	0	0	2	25^1	18	8	8	2	0	11	14	1.145	2.84	117	2.47	.194	0	.000	1	2	0.1
1982 LA-N	0	2	.000	29	0	0	0	0	35^2	37	24	19	2	1	21	20	1.626	4.79	72	4.52	.272	0	....	-5	0	-0.5
1983* LA-N	12	9	.571	34	26	4	3	1	177	152	67	54	7	1	51	120	1.147	2.75	131	2.45	.229	6	.100	20	13	1.9
1984 LA-N	12	6	.667	28	28	8	**4**	0	199^1	186	67	55	7	3	46	135	1.164	**2.48**	**142**	2.68	.246	8	.121	**25**	18	2.5
1985 LA-N	0	1	.000	2	1	0	0	0	4^1	7	5	4	1	0	3	2	2.308	8.31	42	9.72	.350	0	.000	-2	0	-0.3
1986 LA-N	1	2	.333	24	10	0	0	1	70	74	40	38	6	1	30	46	1.486	4.89	71	4.33	.270	3	.176	-10	1	-1.0
1987 LA-N	2	7	.222	37	7	0	0	11	87^1	82	41	34	9	2	37	76	1.363	3.50	113	3.83	.251	1	.077	5	6	0.4
1988* LA-N	6	7	.462	60	0	0	0	12	94^1	75	29	20	4	1	27	83	1.081	1.91	174	2.19	.218	0	.000	16	12	1.6
1989 LA-N	4	3	.571	53	0	0	0	5	76	62	20	18	6	2	18	75	1.053	2.13	160	2.39	.220	1	1.000	10	9	1.1
1990 NY-N	3	3	.500	52	0	0	0	5	76	71	31	27	4	1	22	76	1.224	3.20	117	2.89	.245	1	.167	6	6	0.6
1991 NY-N	6	1	.857	44	0	0	0	4	63	63	20	19	5	0	19	49	1.302	2.71	134	3.52	.267	0	....	8	8	0.8
*Atl-N	2	0	1.000	15	0	0	0	11	19^1	11	3	3	1	0	3	13	.724	1.40	278	1.15	.167	0	.000	5	5	0.6
Yr.	8	1	.889	59	0	0	0	15	82^1	74	23	22	6	0	22	62	1.166	2.40	153	2.97	.245	0	.000	13	13	1.4
1992 Atl-N	1	6	.143	41	0	0	0	15	42	40	19	19	7	0	13	34	1.262	4.07	90	3.79	.255	0	.000	-2	3	-0.2
1994 Pit-N	3	2	.600	22	0	0	0	7	28^2	22	16	16	4	1	10	27	1.116	5.02	86	2.90	.206	0	.000	-2	4	-0.3
1995 Bos-A	1	1	.500	17	0	0	0	0	24^1	33	23	20	5	0	12	25	1.849	7.40	66	7.22	.314	0	....	-7	0	-0.7
Fla-N	2	0	1.000	13	0	0	0	0	18	11	3	3	2	0	3	21	.778	1.50	281	1.41	.169	0	.000	5	3	0.5
*Atl-N	0	0	....	14	0	0	0	0	13	11	6	6	1	0	4	18	1.154	4.15	103	2.76	.224	0	....	0	1	0.0
Yr.	2	0	1.000	27	0	0	0	0	31	22	9	9	3	0	7	39	.935	2.61	163	1.98	.193	0	.000	6	4	0.5
1996 Fla-N	0	1	.000	4	0	0	0	0	4	4	5	2	2	0	1	5	1.250	4.50	91	5.64	.235	0	....	-0	0	0.0
Total 15	56	52	.519	503	72	12	7	74	1057^2	959	427	365	75	13	331	839	1.220	3.11	118	3.05	.240	20	.110	74	91	7.3

• PENA, Hipolito Hipolito (Concepcion) Pena b: 1/30/1964, Fantino, Dominican Republic BL/TL, 6'3", 165 lbs. Deb: 9/1/1986

YEAR TM-L	W	L	PCT	G	GS	CG	SH	SV	IP	H	R	ER	HR	HB	BB	SO	RAT	ERA	ERA+	CERA	OAV	BH	AVG	PR+	WS	TPW
1986 Pit-N	0	3	.000	10	1	0	0	1	8^1	7	10	8	3	1	3	6	1.200	8.64	44	4.70	.206	0	....	-4	0	-0.5
1987 Pit-N	0	3	.000	16	1	0	0	1	25^2	16	14	13	2	0	26	16	1.636	4.56	90	4.00	.184	1	.167	-2	1	-0.2
1988 NY-A	1	1	.500	16	0	0	0	0	14^1	10	8	5	1	0	9	10	1.326	3.14	125	2.92	.192	0	....	1	1	0.1
Total 3	1	7	.125	42	2	0	0	2	48^1	33	32	26	6	1	38	32	1.469	4.84	82	3.80	.191	1	.167	-5	2	-0.5

• PENA, Jesus Jesus Pena b: 3/8/1975, Santo Domingo, Dominican Republic BL/TL, 6', 170 lbs. Deb: 8/7/1999

YEAR TM-L	W	L	PCT	G	GS	CG	SH	SV	IP	H	R	ER	HR	HB	BB	SO	RAT	ERA	ERA+	CERA	OAV	BH	AVG	PR+	WS	TPW
1999 Chi-A	0	0	....	26	0	0	0	0	20^1	21	15	12	3	1	23	20	2.164	5.31	92	7.22	.259	0	....	-1	0	-0.1
2000 Chi-A	2	1	.667	20	0	0	0	1	23^1	25	18	14	6	1	16	19	1.757	5.40	92	7.18	.278	0	....	-1	1	-0.1
Bos-A	0	0	....	2	0	0	0	0	3	3	1	1	1	0	3	1	2.000	3.00	168	9.05	.273	0	....	1	0	0.1
Yr.	2	1	.667	22	0	0	0	1	26^1	28	19	15	7	1	19	20	1.785	5.13	97	7.40	.277	0	....	-1	1	-0.1
Total 2	2	1	.667	48	0	0	0	1	46^2	49	34	27	10	2	42	40	1.950	5.21	95	7.32	.269	0	....	-2	1	-0.1

• PENA, Jim James Patrick Pena b: 9/17/1964, Los Angeles, CA BL/TL, 6'1", 175 lbs. Deb: 7/7/1992

YEAR TM-L	W	L	PCT	G	GS	CG	SH	SV	IP	H	R	ER	HR	HB	BB	SO	RAT	ERA	ERA+	CERA	OAV	BH	AVG	PR+	WS	TPW
1992 SF-N	1	1	.500	25	2	0	0	0	44	49	19	17	4	1	20	32	1.568	3.48	95	4.60	.282	1	.200	-2	2	-0.2

• PENA, Jose Jose (Gutierrez) Pena b: 12/3/1942, Ciudad Juarez, Mexico BR/TR, 6'2", 190 lbs. Deb: 6/1/1969

YEAR TM-L	W	L	PCT	G	GS	CG	SH	SV	IP	H	R	ER	HR	HB	BB	SO	RAT	ERA	ERA+	CERA	OAV	BH	AVG	PR+	WS	TPW
1969 Cin-N	1	1	.500	6	0	0	0	0	5	10	10	10	0	0	5	3	3.000	18.00	21	11.51	.400	0	....	-8	0	-0.8
1970 LA-N	4	3	.571	29	0	0	0	4	57	51	32	28	8	3	29	31	1.404	4.42	87	4.22	.241	1	.125	-5	3	-0.4
1971 LA-N	2	0	1.000	21	0	0	0	1	43	32	18	17	7	1	18	44	1.163	3.56	91	3.26	.211	2	.667	-2	3	-0.1

YEAR	TM-L	W	L	PCT	G	GS	CG	SH	SV	IP	H	R	ER	HR	HB	BB	SO	RAT	ERA	ERA+	CERA	OAV	BH	AVG	PR+	WS	TPW
1972	LA-N	0	0	....	5	0	0	0	0	7^1	13	8	7	1	0	6	4	2.591	8.59	39	10.41	.371	0	....	-4	0	-0.5
Total	4	7	4	.636	61	0	0	0	5	112^1	106	68	62	16	4	58	82	1.460	4.97	72	4.58	.250	3	.273	-19	6	-1.8
• PENA, Juan	Juan Francisco Pena b: 6/27/1977, Santo Domingo, Dominican Republic BR/TR, 6'5", 215 lbs. Deb: 5/8/1999																										
1999	Bos-A	2	0	1.000	2	2	0	0	0	13	9	1	1	0	0	3	15	.923	0.69	717	1.49	.196	0	....	6	2	0.6
• PENA, Orlando	Orlando Gregorio (Quevara) Pena b: 11/17/1933, Victoria de las Tunas, Cuba BR/TR, 5'11", 154 lbs. Deb: 8/24/1958																										
1958	Cin-N	1	0	1.000	9	0	0	0	3	15	10	1	1	0	0	4	11	.933	0.60	691	1.35	.185	0	....	6	4	0.6
1959	Cin-N	5	9	.357	46	8	1	0	5	136	150	80	72	26	0	39	76	1.390	4.76	85	4.77	.280	3	.088	-11	5	-1.1
1960	Cin-N	0	1	.000	4	0	0	0	0	9^1	8	3	3	0	0	3	9	1.179	2.89	132	2.02	.222	0	.000	1	1	0.1
1962	KC-A	6	4	.600	13	12	6	1	0	89^2	71	31	30	9	1	27	56	1.093	3.01	138	2.58	.213	5	.161	12	8	1.2
1963	KC-A	12	20	.375	35	33	9	3	0	217	218	93	89	24	5	53	128	1.249	3.69	104	3.62	.260	9	.145	5	14	0.6
1964	KC-A	12	14	.462	40	32	5	0	0	219^1	231	126	108	40	8	73	184	1.386	4.43	86	4.80	.268	12	.160	-11	8	-1.1
1965	KC-A	0	6	.000	12	5	0	0	0	35^1	42	30	27	4	2	13	24	1.557	6.88	51	5.42	.302	1	.111	-13	0	-1.4
	Det-A	4	6	.400	30	0	0	0	4	57^1	54	18	16	5	1	20	55	1.291	2.51	138	3.45	.252	2	.250	6	6	0.8
	Yr.	4	12	.250	42	5	0	0	4	92^2	96	48	43	9	3	33	79	1.392	4.18	83	4.20	.272	3	.176	-7	6	-0.6
1966	Det-A	4	2	.667	54	0	0	0	7	108	105	47	37	16	5	35	79	1.296	3.08	113	3.96	.252	2	.111	4	7	0.4
1967	Det-A	0	1	.000	2	0	0	0	0	2	5	3	3	0	1	0	2	2.500	13.50	24	13.27	.500	0	....	-2	0	-0.3
	Cle-A	0	3	.000	48	1	0	0	8	88^1	67	34	33	8	1	22	72	1.008	3.36	97	2.15	.208	0	.000	-0	6	-0.1
	Yr.	0	4	.000	50	1	0	0	8	90^1	72	37	36	8	2	22	74	1.041	3.59	91	2.39	.217	0	.000	-2	6	-0.4
1970	Pit-N	2	1	.667	23	0	0	0	2	37^2	38	21	20	6	1	7	25	1.195	4.78	81	3.81	.268	0	.000	-5	2	-0.5
1971	Bal-A	0	1	.000	5	0	0	0	0	14^2	16	7	5	0	0	5	4	1.432	3.07	109	3.49	.281	0	.000	0	0	0.0
1973	Bal-A	1	1	.500	11	2	0	0	1	44^2	36	20	20	10	2	8	23	.985	4.03	93	3.09	.218	0	....	-3	2	-0.3
	StL-N	4	4	.500	42	0	0	0	6	62	60	17	15	3	0	14	38	1.194	2.18	167	2.76	.251	1	.143	10	6	1.0
1974	StL-N	5	2	.714	42	0	0	0	1	45	45	15	13	0	1	20	23	1.444	2.60	138	3.52	.269	1	.500	4	5	0.5
	Cal-A	0	0	....	4	0	0	0	3	8	6	0	0	0	0	1	5	.875	0.00	....	1.48	.214	0	....	3	2	0.3
1975	Cal-A	0	2	.000	7	0	0	0	0	12^2	13	3	3	0	0	8	4	1.658	2.13	166	4.44	.283	0	....	2	1	0.2
Total	14	56	77	.421	427	93	21	4	40	1202	1175	549	495	151	28	352	818	1.270	3.71	101	3.76	.255	36	.136	9	77	0.8
• PENA, Ramon	Ramon Arturo (Padilla) Pena b: 5/5/1962, Santiago, Dominican Republic BR/TR, 5'10", 155 lbs. Deb: 4/27/1989																										
1989	Det-A	0	0	....	8	0	0	0	0	18	26	13	12	0	2	8	12	1.889	6.00	64	6.18	.338	0	....	-4	0	-0.4
• PENCE, Rusty	Russell William Pence b: 3/11/1900, Marine, IL d: 8/11/1971, Hot Springs, AR BR/TR, 6', 185 lbs. Deb: 5/13/1921																										
1921	Chi-A	0	0	....	4	0	0	0	0	5^1	6	5	5	0	1	7	2	2.438	8.44	50	7.44	.286	0	.000	-3	0	-0.3
• PENNER, Ken	Kenneth William Penner b: 4/24/1896, Booneville, IN d: 5/28/1959, Sacramento, CA BL/TR, 5'11.5", 170 lbs. Deb: 9/11/1916																										
1916	Cle-A	1	0	1.000	4	2	0	0	0	12^2	14	6	6	0	0	4	5	1.421	4.26	70	3.93	.304	0	.000	-2	0	-0.2
1929	Chi-N	0	1	.000	5	0	0	0	0	12^2	14	11	4	1	0	6	3	1.579	2.84	162	4.57	.280	1	.250	2	0	0.2
Total	2	1	1	.500	9	2	0	0	0	25^1	28	17	10	1	0	10	8	1.500	3.55	98	4.25	.292	1	.167	0	0	0.0
• PENNINGTON, Brad	Brad Lee Pennington b: 4/14/1969, Salem, IN BL/TL, 6'5", 205 lbs. Deb: 4/17/1993																										
1993	Bal-A	3	2	.600	34	0	0	0	4	33	34	25	24	7	2	25	39	1.788	6.55	68	6.83	.266	0	....	-8	0	-0.8
1994	Bal-A	0	1	.000	8	0	0	0	0	6	9	8	8	2	0	8	7	2.833	12.00	42	13.59	.346	0	....	-5	0	-0.4
1995	Bal-A	0	1	.000	8	0	0	0	0	6^2	3	7	6	1	0	11	10	2.100	8.10	59	5.97	.136	0	....	-3	0	-0.2
	Cin-N	0	0	....	6	0	0	0	0	9^2	9	8	6	0	1	11	7	2.069	5.59	74	6.42	.273	0	.000	-2	0	-0.2
1996	Bos-A	0	2	.000	14	0	0	0	0	13	6	5	4	1	0	15	13	1.615	2.77	183	3.63	.140	0	....	4	1	0.3
	Cal-A	0	0	....	8	0	0	0	0	7^1	5	10	10	1	0	16	7	2.864	12.27	40	9.62	.185	0	....	-6	0	-0.5
	Yr.	0	2	.000	22	0	0	0	0	20^1	11	15	14	2	0	31	20	2.066	6.20	80	5.79	.157	0	....	-2	1	-0.2
1998	TB-A	0	0	....	1	0	0	0	0	0	1	1	1	0	0	3	0	....	∞	....	∞	1.000	0	....	-1	0	-0.1
Total	5	3	6	.333	79	0	0	0	4	75^2	67	64	59	12	3	89	83	2.062	7.02	67	6.96	.239	0	.000	-21	1	-2.0
• PENNINGTON, Kewpie	George Louis Pennington b: 9/24/1896, New York, NY d: 5/3/1953, Newark, NJ BR/TR, 5'8.5", 168 lbs. Deb: 4/14/1917																										
1917	StL-A	0	0	....	1	0	0	0	0	1	1	0	0	0	0	0	0	1.000	0.00	....	1.95	.250	0	....	0	0	0.0
• PENNOCK, Herb	Herbert Jefferis "The Knight Of Kennett Square" Pennock b: 2/10/1894, Kennett Square, PA d: 1/30/1948, New York, NY BB/TL, 6', 160 lbs. Deb: 5/14/1912 C HOF: 1948																										
1912	Phi-A	1	2	.333	17	2	1	0	2	50	48	31	25	1	3	30	38	1.560	4.50	69	4.28	.262	2	.133	-9	1	-0.9
1913	Phi-A	2	1	.667	14	3	1	0	0	33^1	30	24	19	4	0	22	17	1.560	5.13	54	4.21	.221	1	.111	-9	0	-1.0
1914*	Phi-A	11	4	.733	28	14	8	3	3	151^2	136	56	47	1	2	65	90	1.325	2.79	93	3.09	.248	12	.214	-4	10	-0.2
1915	Phi-A	3	6	.333	11	8	3	1	1	44	46	34	26	2	2	29	24	1.705	5.32	55	4.92	.266	5	.278	-11	1	-1.1
	Bos-A	0	0	....	5	1	0	0	0	14	23	16	15	0	0	10	7	2.357	9.64	29	8.80	.390	1	.167	-11	0	-1.1
	Yr.	3	6	.333	16	9	3	1	1	58	69	50	41	2	2	39	31	1.862	6.36	45	5.86	.298	6	.250	-22	1	-2.3
1916	Bos-A	0	2	.000	9	2	0	0	1	26^2	23	11	9	0	1	8	12	1.163	3.04	91	2.58	.245	1	.125	-0	1	-0.1
1917	Bos-A	5	5	.500	24	5	4	1	1	100^2	90	49	37	2	3	23	35	1.123	3.31	78	2.52	.243	4	.167	-9	4	-0.8
1919	Bos-A	16	8	.667	32	26	16	5	0	219	223	78	66	2	3	48	70	1.237	2.71	111	3.06	.274	13	.173	4	16	0.5
1920	Bos-A	16	13	.552	37	31	19	4	2	242^1	244	108	99	9	4	61	68	1.259	3.68	99	3.15	.264	20	.260	-4	19	0.0
1921	Bos-A	13	14	.481	32	31	15	1	0	222^2	268	121	100	7	2	59	91	1.469	4.04	104	4.19	.307	18	.212	-0	14	0.2
1922	Bos-A	10	17	.370	32	26	15	1	1	202	230	108	97	7	1	74	59	1.505	4.32	95	4.19	.297	9	.138	-2	11	-0.4
1923*	NY-A	19	6	.760	35	27	21	1	3	238^1	235	86	83	11	2	68	93	1.271	3.13	126	3.19	.261	16	.193	19	23	1.9
1924	NY-A	21	9	.700	40	34	25	4	3	286^1	302	104	90	13	1	64	101	1.278	2.83	147	3.22	.273	16	.158	**41**	27	3.6
1925	NY-A	16	17	.485	47	31	21	2	2	**277**	267	117	91	11	2	71	88	1.220	2.96	144	**2.92**	.254	20	.202	**41**	23	3.5
1926*	NY-A	23	11	.676	40	33	19	1	2	266^1	294	133	107	11	4	43	78	1.265	3.62	107	3.31	.282	18	.212	12	18	1.4
1927*	NY-A	19	8	.704	34	26	18	1	2	209^2	225	89	70	5	2	48	51	1.302	3.00	128	3.29	.283	15	.217	19	17	1.8
1928	NY-A	17	6	.739	28	24	18	**5**	3	211	215	71	60	2	0	40	53	1.209	2.56	147	2.74	.267	15	.203	31	20	2.9
1929	NY-A	9	11	.450	27	23	8	1	2	157^1	205	101	86	11	3	28	49	1.481	4.92	78	4.65	.318	9	.176	-20	5	-2.0
1930	NY-A	11	7	.611	25	19	11	1	0	156^1	194	95	75	8	0	20	46	1.369	4.32	99	3.92	.301	11	.183	1	7	-0.1
1931	NY-A	11	6	.647	25	25	12	1	0	189^1	247	96	90	7	1	30	65	1.463	4.28	93	4.36	.315	10	.152	-8	10	-0.7
1932*	NY-A	9	5	.643	22	21	9	1	0	146^2	191	94	75	8	0	38	54	1.561	4.60	89	4.75	.310	8	.151	-8	6	-0.8
1933	NY-A	7	4	.636	23	5	2	1	4	65	96	46	40	4	0	21	22	1.800	5.54	70	6.16	.342	5	.238	-11	2	-1.0
1934	Bos-A	2	0	1.000	30	2	1	0	1	62	68	31	21	2	0	16	16	1.355	3.05	158	3.51	.276	3	.214	13	5	1.2
Total	22	241	162	.598	617	419	247	35	33	3571^2	3900	1699	1428	128	36	916	1227	1.348	3.60	104	3.59	.281	232	.191	74	240	6.7
• PENNY, Brad	Bradley Wayne Penny b: 5/24/1978, Broken Arrow, OK BR/TR, 6'4", 200 lbs. Deb: 4/7/2000																										
2000	Fla-N	8	7	.533	23	22	0	0	0	119^2	120	70	64	13	5	60	80	1.504	4.81	92	4.70	.263	5	.111	-4	5	-0.6
2001	Fla-N	10	10	.500	31	31	1	1	0	205	183	92	84	15	7	54	154	1.156	3.69	114	2.96	.240	10	.161	11	12	1.1
2002	Fla-N	8	7	.533	24	24	1	1	0	129^1	148	76	67	18	1	50	93	1.531	4.66	84	5.08	.288	8	.167	-11	4	-1.1
2003*	Fla-N	14	10	.583	32	32	0	0	0	196^1	195	96	90	21	3	56	138	1.278	4.13	99	3.73	.264	9	.132	-2	10	-0.1
Total	4	40	34	.541	110	109	2	2	0	650^1	646	334	305	67	16	220	465	1.332	4.22	98	3.93	.261	32	.143	-6	31	-0.7
• PENSON, Paul	Paul Eugene Penson b: 7/12/1931, Kansas City, KS BR/TR, 6'1", 185 lbs. Deb: 4/21/1954																										
1954	Phi-N	1	1	.500	5	3	0	0	0	16	14	11	8	1	0	14	3	1.750	4.50	90	4.57	.237	0	.000	-1	0	-0.2
• PENTZ, Gene	Eugene David Pentz b: 6/21/1953, Johnstown, PA BR/TR, 6'1", 200 lbs. Deb: 7/29/1975																										
1975	Det-A	0	4	.000	13	0	0	0	0	25^1	27	14	9	0	0	20	21	1.855	3.20	126	4.98	.293	0	....	3	1	0.3
1976	Hou-N	3	3	.500	40	0	0	0	5	63^2	62	26	21	5	1	31	36	1.461	2.97	108	4.12	.259	1	.200	2	4	0.2
1977	Hou-N	5	2	.714	41	4	0	0	2	87	76	41	37	8	1	44	51	1.379	3.83	93	3.67	.236	0	.000	-2	4	-0.4
1978	Hou-N	0	0	....	10	0	0	0	0	15	12	13	10	1	1	13	8	1.667	6.00	55	4.14	.214	0	.000	-4	0	-0.5
Total	4	8	9	.471	104	4	0	0	7	191	177	94	77	14	3	108	116	1.492	3.63	95	4.03	.250	1	.053	-2	9	-0.4
• PEPPER, Bob	Robert Ernest Pepper b: 5/3/1895, Rosston, PA d: 4/8/1968, Ford Cliff, PA BR/TR, 6'2", 178 lbs. Deb: 7/23/1915																										
1915	Phi-A	0	0	....	1	0	0	0	0	5	6	5	1	0	1	4	0	2.000	1.80	162	7.25	.333	0	.000	1	0	0.0

YEAR TM-L	W	L	PCT	G	GS	CG	SH	SV	IP	H	R	ER	HR	HB	BB	SO	RAT	ERA	ERA+	CERA	OAV	BH	AVG	PR+	WS	TPW
• PEPPER, Laurin	Hugh McLaurin Pepper b: 1/18/1931, Vaughan, MS BR/TR, 5'11", 190 lbs. Deb: 7/4/1954																									
1954 Pit-N	1	5	.167	14	8	0	0	0	50^2	63	53	45	4	0	43	17	2.092	7.99	52	6.89	.315	4	.235	-20	0	-2.0
1955 Pit-N	0	1	.000	14	1	0	0	0	20	30	24	23	5	2	25	7	2.750	10.35	40	13.50	.370	0	.000	-14	0	-1.4
1956 Pit-N	1	1	.500	11	7	0	0	0	30	30	17	10	1	0	25	12	1.833	3.00	126	5.14	.256	0	.000	3	2	0.2
1957 Pit-N	0	1	.000	5	1	0	0	0	9	11	8	8	1	0	5	4	1.778	8.00	47	5.55	.297	0	....	-4	0	-0.4
Total 4	2	8	.200	44	17	0	0	0	109^2	134	102	86	11	2	98	40	2.116	7.06	58	7.51	.308	4	.160	-35	2	-3.5
• PEPPERS, Harrison	Harrison Peppers b: 9/1866, KY d: 11/5/1903, Webb City, MO BL Deb: 6/30/1894																									
1894 Lou-N	0	1	.000	2	1	0	0	0	8	10	7	6	0	0	4	0	1.750	6.75	75	5.00	.303	0	.000	-1	0	-0.2
• PERAZA, Luis	Luis (Rios) Peraza b: 6/17/1942, Rio Piedras, Puerto Rico BR/TR, 5'11", 185 lbs. Deb: 4/9/1969																									
1969 Phi-N	0	0	....	8	0	0	0	0	9	12	6	6	1	0	2	7	1.556	6.00	59	5.69	.364	0	.000	-2	0	-0.3
• PERAZA, Oswaldo	Oswald Jose Peraza b: 10/19/1962, Puerto Cabello, Venezuela BR/TR, 6'4", 172 lbs. Deb: 4/4/1988																									
1988 Bal-A	5	7	.417	19	15	1	0	0	86	98	62	53	10	2	37	61	1.570	5.55	70	5.09	.282	0	....	-16	1	-1.7
• PERCIVAL, Troy	Troy Eugene Percival b: 8/9/1969, Fontana, CA BR/TR, 6'3", 200 lbs. Deb: 4/26/1995																									
1995 Cal-A	3	2	.600	62	0	0	0	3	74	37	19	16	6	1	26	94	.851	1.95	241	1.44	.147	0	....	22	12	2.1
1996 Cal-A★	0	2	.000	62	0	0	0	36	74	38	20	19	8	2	31	100	.932	2.31	212	1.76	.149	0	.000	21	16	1.9
1997 Ana-A	5	5	.500	55	0	0	0	27	52	40	20	20	6	4	22	72	1.192	3.46	133	3.15	.205	0	....	6	10	0.6
1998 Ana-A★	2	7	.222	67	0	0	0	42	66^2	45	31	27	5	3	37	87	1.230	3.65	129	2.74	.186	0	....	8	12	0.8
1999 Ana-A★	4	6	.400	60	0	0	0	31	57	38	24	24	9	3	22	58	1.053	3.79	128	2.83	.186	0	....	6	11	0.6
2000 Ana-A	5	5	.500	54	0	0	0	32	50	42	27	25	7	2	30	49	1.440	4.50	113	4.24	.228	0	....	2	8	0.2
2001 Ana-A★	4	2	.667	57	0	0	0	39	57^2	39	19	17	3	2	18	71	.988	2.65	172	1.90	.187	0	....	12	14	1.1
2002* Ana-A	4	1	.800	58	0	0	0	40	56^1	38	12	12	5	0	25	68	1.118	1.92	231	2.45	.188	0	....	14	13	1.3
2003 Ana-A	0	5	.000	52	0	0	0	33	49^1	33	22	19	7	3	23	48	1.135	3.47	124	2.99	.184	0	....	4	8	0.4
Total 9	27	35	.435	527	0	0	0	283	537	350	194	179	56	20	234	647	1.088	3.00	157	2.52	.182	0	.000	96	104	9.0
• PERDUE, Hub	Herbert Rodney "The Gallatin Squash" Perdue b: 6/7/1882, Bethpage, TN d: 10/31/1968, Gallatin, TN BR/TR, 5'10.5", 192 lbs. Deb: 4/19/1911																									
1911 Bos-N	6	10	.375	24	19	9	0	1	137^1	180	100	76	10	4	41	40	1.609	4.98	77	5.46	.321	10	.208	-15	2	-1.6
1912 Bos-N	13	16	.448	37	30	20	1	3	249	295	135	105	11	2	54	101	1.402	3.80	94	4.02	.303	12	.138	-3	13	-0.8
1913 Bos-N	16	13	.552	38	32	16	3	1	212^1	201	107	77	7	4	39	91	1.130	3.26	100	2.53	.249	7	.104	4	9	-0.1
1914 Bos-N	2	5	.286	9	9	2	0	0	51	60	35	33	5	3	11	13	1.392	5.82	47	4.73	.311	1	.071	-19	0	-2.1
StL-N	8	8	.500	22	19	12	0	1	153^1	160	60	48	3	5	35	43	1.272	2.82	99	3.32	.290	8	.167	-1	9	-0.2
Yr.	10	13	.435	31	28	14	0	1	204^1	220	95	81	8	8	46	56	1.302	3.57	78	3.67	.295	9	.145	-21	9	-2.3
1915 StL-N	6	12	.333	31	13	5	1	1	115^1	141	66	54	7	2	19	29	1.387	4.21	66	4.18	.311	4	.111	-17	1	-2.0
Total 5	51	64	.443	161	122	64	5	7	918^1	1037	503	393	43	20	199	317	1.346	3.85	84	3.83	.293	42	.140	-52	34	-6.8
• PEREZ, Carlos	Carlos Gross Perez b: 4/14/1971, Nigua, Dominican Republic BL/TL, 6'3", 195 lbs. Deb: 4/27/1995																									
1995 Mon-N★	10	8	.556	28	23	2	1	0	141^1	142	61	58	18	5	28	106	1.203	3.69	116	3.58	.257	6	.133	11	10	1.2
1997 Mon-N	12	13	.480	33	32	8	**5**	0	206^2	206	109	89	21	4	48	110	1.229	3.88	108	3.50	.260	11	.172	7	11	0.9
1998 Mon-N	7	10	.412	23	23	3	0	0	163^1	177	79	68	12	3	33	82	1.286	3.75	112	3.62	.277	9	.191	11	8	1.2
LA-N	4	4	.500	11	11	4	2	0	77^2	67	30	28	9	0	30	46	1.249	3.24	122	3.42	.234	2	.083	6	5	0.6
Yr.	11	14	.440	34	34	7	2	0	241	244	109	96	21	3	63	128	1.274	3.59	115	3.55	.263	11	.155	17	13	1.8
1999 LA-N	2	10	.167	17	16	0	0	0	89^2	116	77	74	23	6	39	40	1.729	7.43	58	7.54	.317	8	.296	-31	1	-2.5
2000 LA-N	5	8	.385	30	22	0	0	0	144	192	95	89	25	8	33	64	1.563	5.56	78	6.21	.324	2	.047	-19	2	-2.1
Total 5	40	53	.430	142	127	17	8	0	822^2	900	451	406	108	26	211	448	1.350	4.44	95	4.44	.279	38	.152	-15	37	-0.7
• PEREZ, George	George Thomas Perez b: 12/29/1937, San Fernando, CA BR/TR, 6'2.5", 200 lbs. Deb: 4/17/1958																									
1958 Pit-N	0	1	.000	4	0	0	0	1	8^1	9	5	5	1	0	4	2	1.560	5.40	72	5.35	.300	0	.000	-2	0	-0.2
• PEREZ, Melido	Melido Turpen Gross Perez b: 2/15/1966, San Cristobal, Dominican Republic BR/TR, 6'4", 180 lbs. Deb: 9/4/1987																									
1987 KC-A	1	1	.500	3	3	0	0	0	10^1	18	12	9	2	0	5	5	2.226	7.84	58	9.94	.375	0	....	-4	0	-0.3
1988 Chi-A	12	10	.545	32	32	3	1	0	197	186	105	83	26	2	72	138	1.310	3.79	105	3.88	.248	0	....	1	10	0.1
1989 Chi-A	11	14	.440	31	31	2	0	0	183^1	187	106	102	23	3	90	141	1.511	5.01	76	4.79	.264	0	....	-25	4	-2.5
1990 Chi-A	13	14	.481	35	35	3	3	0	197	177	111	101	14	2	86	161	1.335	4.61	83	3.52	.241	0	....	-21	7	-2.2
1991 Chi-A	8	7	.533	49	8	0	0	1	135^2	111	49	47	15	1	52	128	1.201	3.12	127	3.18	.224	0	....	9	11	0.9
1992 NY-A	13	16	.448	33	33	10	1	0	247^2	212	94	79	16	5	93	218	1.231	2.87	136	3.09	.235	0	....	28	17	2.9
1993 NY-A	6	14	.300	25	25	0	0	0	163	173	103	94	22	1	64	148	1.454	5.19	80	4.58	.267	0	....	-19	3	-1.8
1994 NY-A	9	4	.692	22	22	1	0	0	151^1	134	74	69	16	3	58	109	1.269	4.10	111	3.48	.238	0	....	5	9	0.5
1995 NY-A	5	5	.500	13	12	1	0	0	69^1	70	46	43	10	1	31	44	1.457	5.58	83	4.64	.261	0	....	-8	2	-0.7
Total 9	78	85	.479	243	201	20	5	1	1354^2	1268	700	627	144	18	551	1092	1.343	4.17	97	3.86	.248	0	....	-33	63	-3.2
• PEREZ, Mike	Michael Irvin (Ortega) Perez b: 10/19/1964, Yauco, Puerto Rico BR/TR, 6', 187 lbs. Deb: 9/5/1990																									
1990 StL-N	1	0	1.000	13	0	0	0	1	13^2	12	6	6	0	0	3	5	1.098	3.95	97	2.15	.240	0	.000	-0	2	0.0
1991 StL-N	0	2	.000	14	0	0	0	0	17	19	11	11	1	1	7	7	1.529	5.82	64	4.59	.288	0	....	-4	0	-0.4
1992 StL-N	9	3	.750	77	0	0	0	0	93	70	23	19	4	1	32	46	1.097	1.84	184	2.12	.210	0	.000	15	11	1.5
1993 StL-N	7	2	.778	65	0	0	0	7	72^2	65	24	20	4	1	20	58	1.170	2.48	160	2.78	.243	0	.000	12	10	1.2
1994 StL-N	2	3	.400	36	0	0	0	12	31	52	32	30	5	3	10	20	2.000	8.71	48	8.82	.391	0	....	-16	0	-1.5
1995 Chi-N	2	6	.250	68	0	0	0	2	71^1	72	30	29	8	4	27	49	1.388	3.66	112	4.20	.268	0	.000	3	5	0.3
1996 Chi-N	1	0	1.000	24	0	0	0	0	27	29	14	14	2	3	13	22	1.556	4.67	93	4.84	.264	0	.000	-1	1	-0.1
1997 KC-A	2	0	1.000	16	0	0	0	0	20^1	15	8	8	2	1	8	17	1.131	3.54	133	2.98	.214	0	....	2	2	0.2
Total 8	24	16	.600	313	0	0	0	22	346	334	148	137	26	14	120	224	1.312	3.56	112	3.67	.257	0	.000	11	31	1.2
• PEREZ, Odalis	Odalis Amadol Perez b: 6/11/1978, Las Matas de Farfan, Dominican Republic BL/TL, 6', 150 lbs. Deb: 9/1/1998																									
1998* Atl-N	0	1	.000	10	0	0	0	0	10^2	10	5	5	1	0	4	5	1.313	4.22	99	3.60	.244	0	....	-0	1	0.0
1999 Atl-N	4	6	.400	18	17	0	0	0	93	100	65	62	12	1	53	82	1.645	6.00	75	5.42	.275	4	.133	-15	1	-1.5
2001 Atl-N	7	8	.467	24	16	0	0	0	95^1	108	55	52	7	1	39	71	1.542	4.91	90	4.79	.290	5	.192	-6	3	-0.5
2002 LA-N★	15	10	.600	32	32	4	2	0	222^1	182	76	74	21	4	38	155	.990	3.00	127	**2.31**	.226	10	.156	19	16	2.1
2003 LA-N	12	12	.500	30	30	0	0	0	185^1	191	98	93	28	3	46	141	1.279	4.52	89	4.07	.267	5	.096	-13	6	-1.6
Total 5	38	37	.507	114	95	4	2	0	606^2	591	299	286	69	9	180	454	1.271	4.24	97	3.74	.257	24	.140	-15	27	-1.5
• PEREZ, Oliver	Oliver (Martinez) Perez b: 8/15/1981, Culiacan, Mexico BL/TL, 6'3", 160 lbs. Deb: 6/16/2002																									
2002 SD-N	4	5	.444	16	15	0	0	0	90	71	37	35	13	5	48	94	1.322	3.50	108	3.93	.218	4	.133	4	4	0.3
2003 SD-N	4	7	.364	19	19	0	0	0	103^2	103	65	62	20	3	65	117	1.621	5.38	73	5.74	.258	7	.212	-16	1	-1.5
Pit-N	0	3	.000	5	5	0	0	0	23	26	15	15	2	1	12	24	1.652	5.87	75	5.29	.283	0	.000	-4	0	-0.4
Yr.	4	10	.286	24	24	0	0	0	126^2	129	80	77	22	4	77	141	1.626	5.47	73	5.66	.263	7	.179	-20	1	-1.9
Total 2	8	15	.348	40	39	0	0	0	216^2	200	117	112	35	9	125	235	1.500	4.65	85	4.94	.245	11	.159	-16	5	-1.7
• PEREZ, Pascual	Pascual Gross Perez b: 5/17/1957, San Cristobal, Dominican Republic BR/TR, 6'2", 163 lbs. Deb: 5/7/1980																									
1980 Pit-N	0	1	.000	2	2	0	0	0	12	15	6	5	0	2	2	7	1.417	3.75	97	4.75	.341	1	.250	-0	0	0.0
1981 Pit-N	2	7	.222	17	13	2	0	0	86^1	92	50	38	5	3	34	46	1.459	3.96	91	4.06	.273	3	.136	-3	1	-0.4
1982* Atl-N	4	4	.500	16	11	0	0	0	79^1	85	35	27	4	0	17	29	1.286	3.06	122	3.35	.276	3	.167	6	5	0.7
1983 Atl-N★	15	8	.652	33	33	7	1	0	215^1	213	88	82	20	4	51	144	1.226	3.43	113	3.41	.260	12	.160	9	14	0.8
1984 Atl-N	14	8	.636	30	30	4	1	0	211^2	208	96	88	26	3	51	145	1.224	3.74	103	3.61	.260	5	.076	4	12	0.3
1985 Atl-N	1	13	.071	22	22	0	0	0	95^1	115	72	65	10	1	57	57	1.804	6.14	63	5.92	.297	3	.120	-24	0	-2.5
1987 Mon-N	7	0	1.000	10	10	2	0	0	70^1	52	21	18	5	1	16	58	.967	2.30	182	2.00	.206	1	.042	16	8	1.4
1988 Mon-N	12	8	.600	27	27	4	2	0	188	133	59	51	15	7	44	131	.941	2.44	147	**1.94**	.196	2	.037	21	14	1.9
1989 Mon-N	9	13	.409	33	28	2	0	0	198^1	178	85	73	15	4	45	152	1.124	3.31	106	2.69	.237	11	.204	6	11	0.8
1990 NY-A	1	2	.333	3	3	0	0	0	14	8	3	2	0	0	3	12	.786	1.29	309	1.08	.163	0	....	4	2	0.4

YEAR	TM-L	W	L	PCT	G	GS	CG	SH	SV	IP	H	R	ER	HR	HB	BB	SO	RAT	ERA	ERA+	CERA	OAV	BH	AVG	PR+	WS	TPW
1991	NY-A	2	4	.333	14	14	0	0	0	73^{2}	68	26	26	7	0	24	41	1.249	3.18	130	3.42	.250	0	....	8	5	0.8
Total	11	67	68	.496	207	193	21	4	0	1244^{1}	1167	541	475	107	25	344	822	1.214	3.44	110	3.25	.249	41	.120	46	72	4.4
• PEREZ, Tomas	Tomas Orlando Perez b: 12/29/1973, Barquisimeto, Venezuela BB/TR, 5'11", 165 lbs. Deb: 5/3/1995 ♦																										
2002	Phi-N	0	0	....	1	0	0	0	0	0^{1}	0	0	0	0	0	0	0	.000	0.00	....	0.00	.000	53	.250	0	4	1.0
• PEREZ, Yorkis	Yorkis Miguel Vargas Perez b: 9/30/1967, Bajos de Haina, Dominican Republic BL/TL, 6', 180 lbs. Deb: 9/30/1991																										
1991	Chi-N	1	0	1.000	3	0	0	0	0	4^{1}	2	1	1	0	0	2	3	.923	2.08	187	1.31	.167	0	....	1	1	0.1
1994	Fla-N	3	0	1.000	44	0	0	0	0	40^{2}	33	18	16	4	1	14	41	1.156	3.54	124	2.83	.220	0	.000	3	5	0.3
1995	Fla-N	2	6	.250	69	0	0	0	1	46^{2}	35	29	27	6	2	28	47	1.350	5.21	81	3.62	.203	0	.000	-5	2	-0.5
1996	Fla-N	3	4	.429	64	0	0	0	0	47^{2}	51	28	28	2	1	31	47	1.720	5.29	77	4.91	.274	0	.000	-7	2	-0.7
1997	NY-N	0	1	.000	9	0	0	0	0	8^{2}	15	8	8	2	0	4	7	2.192	8.31	49	9.91	.375	0	.000	-4	0	-0.4
1998	Phi-N	0	2	.000	57	0	0	0	0	52	40	23	22	3	0	25	42	1.250	3.81	114	2.80	.209	0	.000	3	4	0.3
1999	Phi-N	3	1	.750	35	0	0	0	0	32	29	15	14	4	0	15	26	1.375	3.94	120	3.96	.244	0	.000	2	3	0.2
2000	Hou-N	2	1	.667	33	0	0	0	0	22^{2}	25	18	13	4	0	14	21	1.721	5.16	94	5.64	.266	0	.000	-0	1	0.0
2002	Bal-A	0	0	....	23	0	0	0	1	27^{1}	21	12	10	4	0	14	25	1.280	3.29	130	3.33	.198	0	....	3	2	0.3
Total	9	14	15	.483	337	0	0	0	2	282	251	152	139	29	4	147	259	1.411	4.44	97	3.90	.235	0	.000	-5	20	-0.6
• PERISHO, Matt	Matthew Alan Perisho b: 6/8/1975, Burlington, IA BL/TL, 6', 175 lbs. Deb: 5/27/1997																										
1997	Ana-A	0	2	.000	11	8	0	0	0	45	59	34	30	6	3	28	35	1.933	6.00	77	7.56	.324	0	.000	-7	0	-0.7
1998	Tex-A	0	2	.000	2	2	0	0	0	5	15	17	15	2	2	8	2	4.600	27.00	18	30.09	.500	0	....	-12	0	-1.2
1999	Tex-A	0	0	....	4	1	0	0	0	10^{1}	8	3	3	0	0	2	17	.968	2.61	194	1.55	.211	0	....	3	1	0.3
2000	Tex-A	2	7	.222	34	13	0	0	0	105	136	99	86	20	6	67	74	1.933	7.37	68	7.79	.316	0	.000	-26	0	-2.4
2001	Det-A	2	3	.400	30	4	0	0	0	39^{1}	54	29	25	5	4	14	19	1.729	5.72	76	6.71	.327	0	....	-5	1	-0.5
2002	Det-A	0	0	....	5	0	0	0	0	10^{1}	16	11	10	2	0	6	3	2.129	8.71	49	9.45	.372	0	....	-5	0	-0.5
Total	6	4	14	.222	86	28	0	0	0	215	288	193	169	35	15	125	150	1.921	7.07	67	7.84	.324	0	.000	-52	2	-4.9
• PERKINS, Cecil	Cecil Boyce Perkins b: 12/1/1940, Baltimore, MD BR/TR, 6', 175 lbs. Deb: 7/5/1967																										
1967	NY-A	0	1	.000	2	1	0	0	0	5	6	5	5	1	0	2	1	1.600	9.00	35	6.48	.316	0	.000	-3	0	-0.4
• PERKINS, Charlie	Charles Sullivan "Lefty" Perkins b: 9/9/1905, Ensley, AL d: 5/25/1988, Salem, OR BR/TL, 6'1", 175 lbs. Deb: 5/1/1930																										
1930	Phi-A	0	0	....	8	1	0	0	0	23^{2}	25	20	17	0	0	15	15	1.690	6.46	72	4.67	.313	1	.125	-5	0	-0.5
1934	Bro-N	0	3	.000	11	2	0	0	0	24^{1}	37	25	23	3	2	14	5	2.096	8.51	46	8.06	.336	2	.286	-12	0	-1.2
Total	2	0	3	.000	19	3	0	0	0	48	62	45	40	3	2	29	20	1.896	7.50	56	6.38	.327	3	.200	-17	0	-1.7
• PERKINS, Dan	Daniel Lee Perkins b: 3/15/1975, Miami, FL BR/TR, 6'2", 193 lbs. Deb: 4/7/1999																										
1999	Min-A	1	7	.125	29	12	0	0	0	86^{2}	117	69	63	14	5	43	44	1.846	6.54	78	7.40	.326	1	.500	-14	0	-1.2
• PERKOVICH, John	John Joseph "Perky" Perkovich b: 3/10/1924, Chicago, IL d: 9/16/2000, Little Rock, AR BR/TR, 5'11", 170 lbs. Deb: 5/6/1950																										
1950	Chi-A	0	0	....	1	0	0	0	0	5	7	4	4	3	0	1	3	1.600	7.20	62	9.22	.318	0	.000	-2	0	-0.2
• PERKOWSKI, Harry	Harry Walter Perkowski b: 9/6/1922, Dante, VA BL/TL, 6'2.5", 196 lbs. Deb: 9/13/1947																										
1947	Cin-N	0	0	....	3	1	0	0	0	7^{1}	12	3	3	1	0	3	2	2.045	3.68	111	8.52	.375	0	.000	0	1	0.1
1949	Cin-N	1	1	.500	5	3	2	0	0	23^{2}	21	14	12	2	0	14	3	1.479	4.56	92	3.88	.236	3	.333	-1	1	0.0
1950	Cin-N	0	0	....	22	0	0	0	0	34^{1}	36	21	20	6	1	23	19	1.718	5.24	81	6.00	.286	7	.318	-3	2	-0.2
1951	Cin-N	3	6	.333	35	7	1	0	1	102	96	42	32	2	1	46	56	1.392	2.82	144	3.34	.251	1	.040	15	8	1.2
1952	Cin-N	12	10	.545	33	24	11	1	0	194	197	91	82	9	3	89	86	1.474	3.80	99	3.94	.265	12	.160	-1	11	-0.1
1953	Cin-N	12	11	.522	33	25	7	2	2	193	204	107	97	26	1	62	70	1.378	4.52	96	4.31	.271	14	.203	-8	11	-0.6
1954	Cin-N	2	8	.200	28	12	3	1	0	95^{2}	100	71	65	16	1	62	32	1.693	6.11	69	5.84	.276	4	.160	-21	0	-2.1
1955	Chi-N	3	4	.429	25	4	0	0	2	47^{2}	53	32	28	3	0	25	28	1.636	5.29	77	4.80	.283	2	.154	-7	1	-0.7
Total	8	33	40	.452	184	76	24	4	5	697^{2}	719	381	339	65	7	324	296	1.495	4.37	94	4.42	.269	43	.180	-26	35	-2.5
• PERLMAN, Jon	Jonathan Samuel Perlman b: 12/13/1956, Dallas, TX BL/TR, 6'3", 185 lbs. Deb: 9/6/1985																										
1985	Chi-N	1	0	1.000	6	0	0	0	0	8^{2}	10	11	11	3	0	8	4	2.077	11.42	35	9.17	.313	0	.000	-7	0	-0.8
1987	SF-N	0	0	....	10	0	0	0	0	11^{1}	11	7	5	1	1	4	3	1.324	3.97	97	3.89	.256	0	....	-0	0	0.0
1988	Cle-A	0	2	.000	10	0	0	0	0	19^{2}	25	12	12	0	0	11	10	1.831	5.49	75	5.12	.309	0	....	-3	0	-0.3
Total	3	1	2	.333	26	0	0	0	0	39^{2}	46	30	28	4	1	23	17	1.739	6.35	63	5.65	.295	0	.000	-10	0	-1.1
• PERME, Len	Leonard John Perme b: 11/25/1917, Cleveland, OH BL/TL, 6', 170 lbs. Deb: 9/8/1942																										
1942	Chi-A	0	1	.000	4	1	1	0	0	13	5	2	2	0	1	4	4	.692	1.38	260	0.86	.119	1	.333	3	2	0.3
1946	Chi-A	0	0	....	4	0	0	0	0	4^{1}	6	4	4	0	0	7	2	3.000	8.31	41	9.85	.316	0	....	-2	0	-0.3
Total	2	0	1	.000	8	1	1	0	0	17^{1}	11	6	6	0	1	11	6	1.269	3.12	111	3.11	.180	1	.333	1	2	0.1
• PERNOLL, Hub	Henry Hubbard "Piano Legs" Pernoll b: 3/14/1888, Grants Pass, OR d: 2/18/1944, Grants Pass, OR BR/TL, 5'8", 175 lbs. Deb: 4/25/1910																										
1910	Det-A	4	3	.571	11	5	4	0	0	54^{2}	54	20	18	1	5	14	25	1.244	2.96	89	3.38	.270	1	.063	-2	3	-0.4
1912	Det-A	0	0	....	3	0	0	0	0	9	9	6	6	0	0	4	3	1.444	6.00	55	3.53	.265	0	.000	-3	0	-0.3
Total	2	4	3	.571	14	5	4	0	0	63^{2}	63	26	24	1	5	18	28	1.272	3.39	81	3.40	.269	1	.053	-5	3	-0.7
• PERRANOSKI, Ron	Ronald Peter Perranoski b: 4/1/1936, Paterson, NJ BL/TL, 6', 192 lbs. Deb: 4/14/1961 C																										
1961	LA-N	7	5	.583	53	1	0	0	6	91^{2}	82	31	27	5	4	41	56	1.342	2.65	164	3.41	.244	1	.083	17	11	1.6
1962	LA-N	6	6	.500	**70**	0	0	0	20	107^{1}	103	40	34	1	0	36	68	1.295	2.85	127	2.87	.255	1	.071	9	12	0.9
1963*	LA-N	16	3	.842	**69**	0	0	0	21	129	112	30	24	7	4	43	75	1.202	1.67	180	2.73	.231	3	.125	20	20	2.2
1964	LA-N	5	7	.417	72	0	0	0	14	125^{1}	128	62	43	5	1	46	79	1.388	3.09	105	3.37	.263	2	.105	2	7	0.2
1965*	LA-N	6	6	.500	59	0	0	0	17	104^{2}	85	28	26	2	3	40	53	1.194	2.24	146	2.50	.226	3	.158	10	13	1.2
1966*	LA-N	6	7	.462	55	0	0	0	7	82	82	32	29	4	1	31	50	1.378	3.18	104	3.44	.269	2	.250	1	7	0.2
1967	LA-N	6	7	.462	**70**	0	0	0	16	110	97	36	30	4	3	45	75	1.291	2.45	126	2.96	.240	1	.100	9	12	0.9
1968	Min-A	8	7	.533	66	0	0	0	6	87	86	36	30	5	0	38	65	1.425	3.10	100	3.47	.252	0	.000	1	6	0.1
1969*	Min-A	9	10	.474	75	0	0	0	**31**	119^{2}	85	32	28	4	1	52	62	1.145	2.11	173	2.13	.205	2	.083	19	20	1.9
1970*	Min-A	7	8	.467	67	0	0	0	**34**	111	108	38	30	7	1	42	55	1.351	2.43	153	3.54	.259	1	.042	15	15	1.4
1971	Min-A	1	4	.200	36	0	0	0	5	42^{2}	60	39	32	2	3	28	21	2.063	6.75	53	7.10	.337	0	.000	-14	0	-1.6
	Det-A	0	1	.000	11	0	0	0	2	18	16	9	5	2	1	3	8	1.056	2.50	144	2.83	.254	0	.000	2	1	0.2
	Yr.	1	5	.167	47	0	0	0	7	60^{2}	76	48	37	4	4	31	29	1.764	5.49	65	5.84	.315	0	.000	-12	1	-1.4
1972	Det-A	0	1	.000	17	0	0	0	0	18^{2}	23	16	16	2	1	8	10	1.661	7.71	41	5.80	.307	0	.000	-10	0	-1.1
	LA-N	2	0	1.000	9	0	0	0	0	16^{2}	19	8	5	0	0	8	5	1.620	2.70	123	4.50	.292	0	....	1	1	0.1
1973	Cal-A	0	2	.000	8	0	0	0	0	11	11	5	5	0	1	7	5	1.636	4.09	87	4.87	.282	0	....	-1	0	-0.1
Total	13	79	74	.516	737	1	0	0	179	1174^{2}	1097	442	364	50	24	468	687	1.332	2.79	122	3.24	.250	16	.096	83	125	8.1
• PERRIN, Bill	William Joseph "Lefty" Perrin b: 6/23/1910, New Orleans, LA d: 6/30/1974, New Orleans, LA BR/TL, 5'11", 172 lbs. Deb: 9/30/1934																										
1934	Cle-A	0	1	.000	1	1	0	0	0	5	13	9	8	0	1	2	3	3.000	14.40	32	14.75	.520	0	.000	-5	0	-0.5
• PERRING, George	George Wilson Perring b: 8/13/1884, Sharon, WI d: 8/20/1960, Beloit, WI BR/TR, 6', 190 lbs. Deb: 4/25/1908 ♦																										
1914	KC-F	0	0	....	1	0	0	0	0	0^{2}	2	1	1	0	0	1	0	4.500	13.50	23	21.94	1.000	138	.278	-1	17	1.6
• PERRITT, Pol	William Dayton Perritt b: 8/30/1892, Arcadia, LA d: 10/15/1947, Shreveport, LA BR/TR, 6'2", 168 lbs. Deb: 9/7/1912																										
1912	StL-N	1	1	.500	6	3	1	0	0	31	25	16	11	0	0	10	13	1.129	3.19	107	2.23	.243	2	.222	1	2	0.0
1913	StL-N	6	14	.300	36	21	8	0	0	175	205	123	102	9	8	64	64	**1.537**	5.25	61	4.69	.300	12	.203	-40	1	-4.2
1914	StL-N	16	13	.552	41	32	18	3	2	286	248	106	75	7	15	93	115	1.192	2.36	118	2.76	.245	13	.141	12	20	1.1
1915	NY-N	12	18	.400	35	30	16	4	0	220	226	95	65	6	12	59	91	1.295	2.66	96	3.32	.266	11	.162	-0	9	-0.1
1916	NY-N	18	11	.621	40	28	17	5	2	251	243	82	73	11	7	56	115	1.191	2.62	93	2.94	.257	7	.084	-9	15	-1.5
1917*	NY-N	17	7	.708	35	26	14	5	1	215	186	61	45	3	7	45	72	1.074	1.88	135	2.23	.237	11	.157	13	17	1.2
1918	NY-N	18	13	.581	35	31	19	6	0	233	212	82	71	5	1	38	60	1.073	2.74	96	2.24	.246	14	.175	-4	14	-0.6

YEAR TM-L	W	L	PCT	G	GS	CG	SH	SV	IP	H	R	ER	HR	HB	BB	SO	RAT	ERA	ERA+	CERA	OAV	BH	AVG	PR+	WS	TPW
1919 NY-N	1	1	.500	11	3	0	0	1	19	27	18	15	0	2	12	2	2.053	7.11	39	7.21	.386	0	.000	-9	0	-1.1
1920 NY-N	0	0	....	8	0	0	0	2	15	9	3	3	0	0	4	3	.867	1.80	166	1.21	.167	0	.000	2	2	0.1
1921 NY-N	2	0	1.000	5	1	0	0	0	11^2	17	9	5	0	0	2	5	1.629	3.86	95	4.66	.321	0	.000	-1	1	-0.1
Det-A	1	0	1.000	4	2	0	0	0	13	18	9	7	0	1	7	3	1.923	4.85	88	6.73	.383	2	.400	-1	1	0.0
Total 10	92	78	.541	256	177	93	23	8	1469^2	1416	604	472	41	53	390	543	1.229	2.89	95	3.02	.259	72	.151	-35	82	-5.2

• PERRY, Gaylord Gaylord Jackson Perry b: 9/15/1938, Williamston, NC BR/TR, 6'4", 215 lbs. Deb: 4/14/1962 HOF: 1991

YEAR TM-L	W	L	PCT	G	GS	CG	SH	SV	IP	H	R	ER	HR	HB	BB	SO	RAT	ERA	ERA+	CERA	OAV	BH	AVG	PR+	WS	TPW
1962 SF-N	3	1	.750	13	7	1	0	0	43	54	29	25	3	0	14	20	1.581	5.23	73	4.87	.310	3	.231	-7	1	-0.7
1963 SF-N	1	6	.143	31	4	0	0	2	76	84	41	34	10	2	29	52	1.487	4.03	79	4.71	.279	4	.222	-6	1	-0.5
1964 SF-N	12	11	.522	44	19	5	2	5	206^1	179	65	63	16	5	43	155	1.076	2.75	130	2.56	.232	3	.054	17	19	1.5
1965 SF-N	8	12	.400	47	26	6	0	1	195^2	194	105	91	21	6	70	170	1.349	4.19	86	3.86	.256	10	.156	-10	6	-1.1
1966 SF-N★	21	8	.724	36	35	13	3	0	255^2	242	92	85	15	5	40	201	1.103	2.99	123	2.67	.247	16	.186	19	21	2.0
1967 SF-N	15	17	.469	39	37	18	3	1	293	231	98	85	20	4	84	230	1.075	2.61	126	2.32	.214	13	.143	21	20	2.2
1968 SF-N	16	15	.516	39	38	19	3	1	291	240	93	79	10	4	59	173	1.027	2.44	120	2.04	.222	11	.113	18	19	1.8
1969 SF-N	19	14	.576	40	39	26	3	0	**325^1**	290	115	90	23	11	91	233	1.171	2.49	141	2.90	.237	14	.120	39	26	3.9
1970 SF-N★	**23**	13	.639	41	**41**	23	**5**	0	**328^2**	292	138	117	27	8	84	214	1.144	3.20	124	2.90	.237	14	.117	35	24	3.1
1971★SF-N	16	12	.571	37	37	14	2	0	280	255	116	86	20	5	67	158	1.150	2.76	123	2.84	.242	10	.102	21	17	1.9
1972 Cle-A★	**24**	16	.600	41	40	**29**	5	1	342^2	253	79	73	17	12	82	234	.978	1.92	168	1.93	.205	17	.155	**45**	**39**	**5.2**
1973 Cle-A	19	19	.500	41	41	**29**	7	0	344	315	143	129	34	5	115	238	1.250	3.38	116	3.45	.246	0	....	22	24	2.3
1974 Cle-A★	21	13	.618	37	37	28	4	0	322^1	230	98	90	25	6	99	216	1.021	2.51	**144**	**2.20**	.204	0	....	**38**	**30**	**4.0**
1975 Cle-A	6	9	.400	15	15	10	1	0	121^2	120	57	48	16	1	34	85	1.266	3.55	107	3.72	.256	0	....	2	6	0.3
Tex-A	12	8	.600	22	22	15	4	0	184	157	70	62	12	3	36	148	1.049	3.03	124	2.37	.227	0	....	15	15	1.6
Yr.	18	17	.514	37	37	25	5	0	305^2	277	127	110	28	4	70	233	1.135	3.24	116	2.91	.239	0	....	18	21	1.8
1976 Tex-A	15	14	.517	32	32	21	2	0	250^1	232	93	90	14	0	52	143	1.134	3.24	111	2.70	.247	0	....	8	17	0.9
1977 Tex-A	15	12	.556	34	34	13	4	0	238	239	108	89	21	5	56	177	1.239	3.37	121	3.47	.262	0	....	16	16	1.6
1978 SD-N	**21**	6	.778	37	37	5	2	0	260^2	241	96	79	9	2	66	154	1.178	2.73	122	2.72	.248	8	.092	17	18	1.4
1979 SD-N★	12	11	.522	32	32	10	0	0	232^2	225	90	79	12	4	67	140	1.255	3.06	115	3.18	.257	6	.085	10	16	0.8
1980 Tex-A	6	9	.400	24	24	6	2	0	155	159	74	59	12	7	46	107	1.323	3.43	114	3.85	.268	0	....	10	9	1.0
NY-A	4	4	.500	10	8	0	0	0	50^2	65	33	25	2	1	18	28	1.638	4.44	88	5.18	.320	0	....	-3	2	-0.3
Yr.	10	13	.435	34	32	6	2	0	205^2	224	107	84	14	8	64	135	1.400	3.68	106	4.18	.281	0	....	8	11	0.8
1981 Atl-N	8	9	.471	23	23	3	0	0	150^2	182	70	66	9	4	24	60	1.367	3.94	91	4.12	.304	12	.250	-6	7	-0.3
1982 Sea-A	10	12	.455	32	32	6	0	0	216^2	245	117	106	27	4	54	116	1.380	4.40	96	4.48	.287	0	....	-3	10	-0.3
1983 Sea-A	3	10	.231	16	16	2	0	0	102	116	60	56	18	3	23	42	1.363	4.94	86	4.78	.286	0	....	-8	3	-0.8
KC-A	4	4	.500	14	14	1	1	0	84^1	98	48	40	6	1	26	40	1.470	4.27	95	4.39	.292	0	....	-1	3	-0.1
Yr.	7	14	.333	30	30	3	1	0	186^1	214	108	96	24	4	49	82	1.411	4.64	90	4.60	.289	0	....	-9	6	-0.9
Total 22	314	265	.542	777	690	303	53	11	5350^1	4938	2128	1846	399	108	1379	3534	1.181	3.11	117	3.03	.245	141	.131	314	369	31.5

• PERRY, Jim James Evan Perry b: 10/30/1935, Williamston, NC BB/TR, 6'4", 200 lbs. Deb: 4/23/1959

YEAR TM-L	W	L	PCT	G	GS	CG	SH	SV	IP	H	R	ER	HR	HB	BB	SO	RAT	ERA	ERA+	CERA	OAV	BH	AVG	PR+	WS	TPW
1959 Cle-A	12	10	.545	44	13	8	2	4	153	122	54	45	10	2	55	79	1.157	2.65	139	2.67	.225	15	.300	16	15	2.0
1960 Cle-A	**18**	10	.643	41	**36**	10	**4**	1	261^1	257	118	105	35	4	91	120	1.332	3.62	103	4.10	.260	22	.242	3	16	0.5
1961 Cle-A★	10	17	.370	35	35	6	1	0	223^2	238	132	117	28	6	87	90	1.453	4.71	84	4.64	.273	12	.164	-19	6	-2.0
1962 Cle-A	12	12	.500	35	27	7	3	0	193^2	213	94	89	21	2	59	74	1.404	4.14	94	4.46	.285	11	.183	-7	10	-0.7
1963 Cle-A	0	0	....	5	0	0	0	0	10^1	12	6	6	0	0	2	7	1.355	5.23	69	3.29	.293	0	.000	-2	0	-0.2
Min-A	9	9	.500	35	25	5	1	1	168^1	167	77	70	17	2	57	65	1.331	3.74	97	3.77	.256	11	.216	-1	8	0.1
Yr.	9	9	.500	40	25	5	1	1	178^2	179	83	76	17	2	59	72	1.332	3.83	95	3.74	.258	11	.208	-3	8	-0.1
1964 Min-A	6	3	.667	42	1	0	0	2	65^1	61	26	25	7	1	23	55	1.286	3.44	104	3.49	.245	2	.154	2	5	0.2
1965★Min-A	12	7	.632	36	19	4	2	0	167^2	142	57	49	18	3	47	88	1.127	2.63	135	2.92	.232	9	.170	15	13	1.7
1966 Min-A	11	7	.611	33	25	8	1	0	184^1	149	61	52	17	5	53	122	1.096	2.54	142	2.68	.222	13	.220	23	17	2.9
1967 Min-A	8	7	.533	37	11	3	2	0	130^2	123	51	44	8	3	50	94	1.324	3.03	114	3.50	.255	8	.190	8	9	1.0
1968 Min-A	8	6	.571	32	18	3	2	1	139	113	37	35	8	5	26	69	1.000	2.27	136	2.16	.219	6	.143	15	13	1.9
1969★Min-A	20	6	.769	46	36	12	3	0	261^2	244	87	82	18	9	66	153	1.185	2.82	129	3.03	.247	16	.172	21	20	2.3
1970★Min-A★	**24**	12	.667	40	**40**	13	4	0	278^2	258	112	94	20	9	57	168	1.130	3.04	123	**2.82**	.243	24	.247	20	21	2.6
1971 Min-A★	17	17	.500	40	39	8	0	1	270	263	135	127	39	5	102	126	1.352	4.23	84	4.21	.259	17	.185	-16	10	-1.5
1972 Min-A	13	16	.448	35	35	5	2	0	217^2	191	93	81	14	8	60	85	1.153	3.35	96	2.81	.236	11	.155	-5	9	-0.6
1973 Det-A	14	13	.519	35	34	7	1	0	203	225	96	91	22	4	55	66	1.379	4.03	101	4.31	.282	0	....	3	12	0.3
1974 Cle-A	17	12	.586	36	36	8	3	0	252	242	94	83	11	5	64	71	1.214	2.96	122	2.96	.254	0	....	17	20	1.8
1975 Cle-A	1	6	.143	8	6	0	0	0	37^2	46	34	28	8	0	18	11	1.699	6.69	57	6.47	.309	0	....	-12	0	-1.3
Oak-A	3	4	.429	15	11	2	1	0	67^2	61	43	35	7	7	26	33	1.286	4.66	78	3.80	.237	0	....	-8	1	-0.8
Yr.	4	10	.286	23	17	2	1	0	105^1	107	77	63	15	7	44	44	1.434	5.38	69	4.75	.264	0	....	-20	1	-2.1
Total 17	215	174	.553	630	447	109	32	10	3285^2	3127	1407	1258	308	80	998	1576	1.255	3.45	106	3.49	.252	177	.199	72	205	10.2

• PERRY, Pat William Patrick Perry b: 2/4/1959, Taylorville, IL BL/TL, 6'1", 170 lbs. Deb: 9/12/1985

YEAR TM-L	W	L	PCT	G	GS	CG	SH	SV	IP	H	R	ER	HR	HB	BB	SO	RAT	ERA	ERA+	CERA	OAV	BH	AVG	PR+	WS	TPW
1985 StL-N	1	0	1.000	6	0	0	0	0	12^1	3	0	0	0	0	3	6	.486	0.00	....	0.35	.077	1	.500	5	2	0.5
1986 StL-N	2	3	.400	46	0	0	0	2	68^2	59	31	29	5	0	34	29	1.354	3.80	96	3.34	.239	0	.000	-4	4	-0.5
1987 StL-N	4	2	.667	45	0	0	0	1	65^2	54	34	32	7	2	21	33	1.142	4.39	95	2.92	.222	1	.143	-2	3	-0.2
Cin-N	1	0	1.000	12	0	0	0	1	15^1	6	0	0	0	1	4	6	.652	0.00	....	0.79	.122	0	....	7	3	0.7
Yr.	5	2	.714	57	0	0	0	2	81	60	34	32	7	3	25	39	1.049	3.56	117	2.51	.205	1	.143	5	6	0.5
1988 Cin-N	2	2	.500	12	0	0	0	0	20^2	21	17	13	4	0	9	11	1.452	5.66	63	4.50	.263	0	.000	-5	0	-0.6
Chi-N	2	2	.500	35	0	0	0	1	38	40	15	14	5	1	7	24	1.237	3.32	109	3.86	.270	1	1.000	2	4	0.4
Yr.	4	4	.500	47	0	0	0	1	58^2	61	32	27	9	1	16	35	1.313	4.14	87	4.08	.268	1	.333	-3	4	-0.2
1989 Chi-N	0	1	.000	19	0	0	0	1	35^2	23	8	7	2	0	16	20	1.093	1.77	213	2.08	.187	1	.167	8	4	0.8
1990 LA-N	0	0	....	7	0	0	0	0	6^2	9	7	6	0	1	5	2	2.100	8.10	45	6.67	.310	0	.000	-3	0	-0.4
Total 6	12	10	.545	182	0	0	0	6	263	215	112	101	23	5	99	131	1.194	3.46	109	3.02	.224	4	.148	8	20	0.8

• PERRY, Scott Herbert Scott Perry b: 4/17/1891, Denison, TX d: 10/27/1959, Kansas City, MO BR/TR, 6'1", 175 lbs. Deb: 5/13/1915

YEAR TM-L	W	L	PCT	G	GS	CG	SH	SV	IP	H	R	ER	HR	HB	BB	SO	RAT	ERA	ERA+	CERA	OAV	BH	AVG	PR+	WS	TPW
1915 StL-A	0	0	....	1	1	0	0	0	2	5	3	3	0	1	1	0	3.000	13.50	21	15.27	.455	0	....	-2	0	-0.3
1916 Chi-N	2	1	.667	4	3	2	1	0	28^1	30	9	8	0	0	3	10	1.165	2.54	114	2.65	.291	3	.273	2	3	0.2
1917 Cin-N	0	0	....	4	1	0	0	0	13^1	17	15	10	0	1	8	4	1.875	6.75	39	5.72	.321	0	.000	-6	0	-0.8
1918 Phi-A	20	19	.513	44	**36**	**30**	3	2	**332^1**	295	97	73	1	2	111	81	1.222	1.98	148	2.61	.247	15	.134	24	30	2.1
1919 Phi-A	4	17	.190	25	21	12	0	1	183^2	193	92	73	4	2	72	38	1.443	3.58	96	3.94	.282	8	.136	5	7	0.3
1920 Phi-A	11	25	.306	42	34	20	1	1	263^2	310	151	106	14	7	65	79	1.422	3.62	111	4.31	.300	13	.157	17	13	1.3
1921 Phi-A	3	6	.333	12	8	5	0	1	70	77	36	32	4	1	24	19	1.443	4.11	108	4.02	.288	1	.038	4	4	0.0
Total 7	40	68	.370	132	104	69	5	5	893^1	927	403	305	23	14	284	231	1.356	3.07	113	3.57	.277	40	.135	43	57	2.9

• PERRYMAN, Parson Emmett Key Perryman b: 10/24/1888, Everett Springs, GA d: 9/12/1966, Starke, FL BR/TR, 6'4.5", 193 lbs. Deb: 4/14/1915

YEAR TM-L	W	L	PCT	G	GS	CG	SH	SV	IP	H	R	ER	HR	HB	BB	SO	RAT	ERA	ERA+	CERA	OAV	BH	AVG	PR+	WS	TPW
1915 StL-A	2	4	.333	24	3	0	0	0	50^1	52	27	22	2	1	16	19	1.351	3.93	73	3.78	.281	0	.000	-7	1	-0.8

• PERSON, Robert Robert Alan Person b: 10/6/1969, Lowell, MA BR/TR, 6', 180 lbs. Deb: 9/18/1995

YEAR TM-L	W	L	PCT	G	GS	CG	SH	SV	IP	H	R	ER	HR	HB	BB	SO	RAT	ERA	ERA+	CERA	OAV	BH	AVG	PR+	WS	TPW
1995 NY-N	1	0	1.000	3	1	0	0	0	12	5	1	1	1	0	2	10	.583	0.75	540	0.82	.119	2	.667	4	2	0.5
1996 NY-N	4	5	.444	27	13	0	0	0	89^2	86	50	45	16	2	35	76	1.349	4.52	89	4.32	.247	3	.143	-6	3	-0.6
1997 Tor-A	5	10	.333	23	22	0	0	0	128^1	125	86	80	19	5	60	99	1.442	5.61	82	4.65	.255	0	.000	-17	2	-1.6
1998 Tor-A	3	1	.750	27	0	0	0	6	38^1	45	31	30	9	2	22	31	1.748	7.04	66	6.94	.294	0	....	-10	0	-1.0
1999 Tor-A	0	2	.000	11	0	0	0	2	11	9	12	12	1	4	15	12	2.182	9.82	50	8.06	.231	0	....	-6	0	-0.6
Phi-N	10	5	.667	31	22	0	0	0	137	130	72	65	23	2	70	127	1.460	4.27	110	4.78	.252	3	.073	5	8	0.2
2000 Phi-N	9	7	.563	28	28	1	1	0	173^1	144	73	70	13	6	95	164	1.379	3.63	128	3.70	.229	7	.132	19	13	1.8
2001 Phi-N	15	7	.682	33	33	3	1	0	208^1	179	103	97	34	8	80	183	1.243	4.19	101	3.84	.234	8	.119	-1	12	0.0
2002 Phi-N	4	5	.444	16	16	0	0	0	87^2	79	58	53	13	5	51	61	1.483	5.44	72	4.85	.241	2	.083	-16	1	-1.4
2003 Bos-A	0	0	....	7	0	0	0	1	11^2	11	10	10	0	1	8	10	1.629	7.71	59	4.30	.250	0	.000	-4	0	-0.4
Total 9	51	42	.548	206	135	4	2	9	897^1	813	496	463	129	35	438	773	1.394	4.64	95	4.37	.242	25	.117	-31	41	-3.0

• PERTICA, Bill William Andrew Pertica b: 8/17/1898, Santa Barbara, CA d: 12/28/1967, Los Angeles, CA BR/TR, 5'9", 165 lbs. Deb: 8/7/1918

YEAR	TM-L	W	L	PCT	G	GS	CG	SH	SV	IP	H	R	ER	HR	HB	BB	SO	RAT	ERA	ERA+	CERA	OAV	BH	AVG	PR+	WS	TPW
1918	Bos-A	0	0	....	1	0	0	0	0	3	3	1	1	0	0	0	1	1.000	3.00	89	2.18	.273	0	.000	-0	0	0.0
1921	StL-N	14	10	.583	38	31	15	2	2	208^1	212	104	78	9	10	70	67	1.354	3.37	108	3.62	.267	10	.143	6	11	0.3
1922	StL-N	8	8	.500	34	15	2	0	0	117^1	153	94	77	5	3	65	30	1.858	5.91	65	6.15	.333	6	.182	-24	2	-2.4
1923	StL-N	0	0	....	1	1	0	0	0	2^1	2	2	1	0	1	3	0	2.143	3.86	101	6.80	.250	0	.000	0	0	0.0
Total	**4**	**22**	**18**	**.550**	**74**	**47**	**17**	**2**	**2**	**331**	**370**	**201**	**157**	**14**	**14**	**138**	**98**	**1.535**	**4.27**	**88**	**4.53**	**.291**	**16**	**.152**	**-18**	**13**	**-2.1**

• PERZANOWSKI, Stan Stanley Perzanowski b: 8/25/1950, East Chicago, IN BB/TR, 6'2", 170 lbs. Deb: 6/20/1971

YEAR	TM-L	W	L	PCT	G	GS	CG	SH	SV	IP	H	R	ER	HR	HB	BB	SO	RAT	ERA	ERA+	CERA	OAV	BH	AVG	PR+	WS	TPW
1971	Chi-A	0	1	.000	5	0	0	0	1	6	14	10	8	1	0	3	5	2.833	12.00	30	12.70	.412	0	.000	-6	0	-0.6
1974	Chi-A	0	0	....	2	1	0	0	0	2^1	8	7	5	1	0	2	2	4.286	19.29	19	27.80	.533	0	....	-4	0	-0.4
1975	Tex-A	3	3	.500	12	8	1	0	0	66	59	25	22	1	5	25	26	1.273	3.00	125	3.16	.246	0	....	6	5	0.6
1976	Tex-A	0	0	....	5	0	0	0	0	11^2	20	15	13	3	2	4	6	2.057	10.03	36	10.67	.385	0	....	-8	0	-0.9
1978	Min-A	2	7	.222	13	7	1	0	1	56^2	59	37	33	1	4	26	31	1.500	5.24	73	4.22	.276	0	....	-9	0	-0.9
Total	**5**	**5**	**11**	**.313**	**37**	**16**	**2**	**0**	**2**	**142^2**	**160**	**94**	**81**	**7**	**11**	**60**	**70**	**1.542**	**5.11**	**73**	**5.00**	**.288**	**0**	**.000**	**-21**	**5**	**-2.3**

• PETEREK, Jeff Jeffrey Allen Peterek b: 9/22/1963, Michigan City, IN BR/TR, 6'2", 195 lbs. Deb: 8/14/1989

YEAR	TM-L	W	L	PCT	G	GS	CG	SH	SV	IP	H	R	ER	HR	HB	BB	SO	RAT	ERA	ERA+	CERA	OAV	BH	AVG	PR+	WS	TPW
1989	Mil-A	0	2	.000	7	4	0	0	0	31^1	31	14	14	3	0	14	16	1.436	4.02	95	4.09	.252	0	....	-1	1	-0.1

• PETERS, Chris Christopher Michael Peters b: 1/28/1972, Fort Thomas, KY BL/TL, 6'1", 170 lbs. Deb: 7/19/1996

YEAR	TM-L	W	L	PCT	G	GS	CG	SH	SV	IP	H	R	ER	HR	HB	BB	SO	RAT	ERA	ERA+	CERA	OAV	BH	AVG	PR+	WS	TPW
1996	Pit-N	2	4	.333	16	10	0	0	0	64	72	43	40	9	1	25	28	1.516	5.63	78	5.14	.287	4	.211	-8	1	-0.8
1997	Pit-N	2	2	.500	31	1	0	0	0	37^1	38	23	19	6	3	21	17	1.580	4.58	94	5.55	.277	1	.250	-1	2	-0.1
1998	Pit-N	8	10	.444	39	21	1	0	1	148	142	63	57	13	3	55	103	1.331	3.47	124	3.70	.252	9	.231	13	10	1.4
1999	Pit-N	5	4	.556	19	11	0	0	0	71	98	59	52	17	4	27	46	1.761	6.59	69	7.47	.322	6	.273	-16	1	-1.3
2000	Pit-N	0	1	.000	18	0	0	0	1	28^1	23	9	9	2	1	14	16	1.306	2.86	161	3.22	.221	1	.167	6	3	0.5
2001	Mon-N	2	4	.333	13	6	0	0	0	31	47	26	26	7	2	15	14	2.000	7.55	59	9.24	.367	1	.091	-10	0	-1.0
Total	**6**	**19**	**25**	**.432**	**136**	**49**	**1**	**0**	**2**	**379^2**	**420**	**223**	**203**	**54**	**14**	**157**	**224**	**1.520**	**4.81**	**92**	**5.24**	**.282**	**22**	**.218**	**-16**	**17**	**-1.2**

• PETERS, Gary Gary Charles Peters b: 4/21/1937, Grove City, PA BL/TL, 6'2", 200 lbs. Deb: 9/10/1959

YEAR	TM-L	W	L	PCT	G	GS	CG	SH	SV	IP	H	R	ER	HR	HB	BB	SO	RAT	ERA	ERA+	CERA	OAV	BH	AVG	PR+	WS	TPW
1959	Chi-A	0	0	....	2	0	0	0	0	1	2	0	0	0	0	2	1	4.000	0.00	....	16.69	.400	0	....	0	0	0.0
1960	Chi-A	0	0	....	2	0	0	0	0	3^1	4	1	1	0	0	1	4	1.500	2.70	140	3.97	.286	0	....	0	0	0.0
1961	Chi-A	0	0	....	3	0	0	0	1	10^1	10	2	2	0	0	2	6	1.161	1.74	225	2.57	.270	1	.333	3	1	0.3
1962	Chi-A	0	1	.000	5	0	0	0	0	6^1	8	5	4	0	1	1	4	1.421	5.68	69	4.37	.308	0	....	-1	0	-0.1
1963	Chi-A	19	8	.704	41	30	13	4	1	243	192	69	63	9	8	68	189	1.070	**2.33**	**150**	2.26	.216	21	.259	30	**25**	4.0
1964	Chi-A★	**20**	8	.714	37	36	11	3	0	273^2	217	89	76	20	7	104	205	1.173	2.50	138	2.80	.219	25	.208	22	22	3.1
1965	Chi-A	10	12	.455	33	30	1	0	0	176^1	181	76	71	19	4	63	95	1.384	3.62	88	4.11	.265	13	.181	-11	7	-0.9
1966	Chi-A	12	10	.545	30	27	11	4	0	204^2	156	54	45	11	3	45	129	.982	**1.98**	**160**	**1.96**	.212	19	.235	26	20	3.4
1967	Chi-A★	16	11	.593	38	36	11	3	0	260	187	81	66	15	11	91	215	1.069	2.28	136	2.25	**.199**	21	.212	23	21	**3.2**
1968	Chi-A	4	13	.235	31	25	6	1	1	162^2	146	79	68	7	7	60	110	1.266	3.76	80	3.13	.242	15	.208	-13	3	-0.7
1969	Chi-A	10	15	.400	36	32	7	3	0	218^2	238	118	110	21	5	78	140	1.445	4.53	85	4.51	.283	12	.169	-13	9	-1.1
1970	Bos-A	16	11	.593	34	34	10	4	0	221^2	221	114	100	20	7	83	155	1.371	4.06	98	3.98	.257	20	.244	2	13	0.9
1971	Bos-A	14	11	.560	34	32	9	1	1	214	241	111	104	25	6	70	100	1.453	4.37	84	4.78	.288	26	.271	-13	11	-0.6
1972	Bos-A	3	3	.500	33	4	0	0	1	85^1	91	48	41	10	3	38	67	1.512	4.32	74	4.76	.279	6	.200	-9	1	-0.9
Total	**14**	**124**	**103**	**.546**	**359**	**286**	**79**	**23**	**5**	**2081**	**1894**	**847**	**751**	**157**	**62**	**706**	**1420**	**1.249**	**3.25**	**107**	**3.32**	**.243**	**179**	**.222**	**46**	**133**	**10.8**

• PETERS, John John Paul Peters b: 4/8/1850, Louisiana, MO d: 1/4/1924, St. Louis, MO BR/TR, 5'7", 180 lbs. Deb: 5/23/1874 ♦

YEAR	TM-L	W	L	PCT	G	GS	CG	SH	SV	IP	H	R	ER	HR	HB	BB	SO	RAT	ERA	ERA+	CERA	OAV	BH	AVG	PR+	WS	TPW
1876	Chi-N	0	0	....	1	0	0	0	1	1	1	1	0	0	....	1	0	2.000	0.00	....	....	.195	111	.348	0	12	1.8

• PETERS, Ray Raymond James Peters b: 8/27/1946, Buffalo, NY BR/TR, 6'5.5", 210 lbs. Deb: 6/4/1970

YEAR	TM-L	W	L	PCT	G	GS	CG	SH	SV	IP	H	R	ER	HR	HB	BB	SO	RAT	ERA	ERA+	CERA	OAV	BH	AVG	PR+	WS	TPW
1970	Mil-A	0	2	.000	2	2	0	0	0	2	7	7	7	0	0	5	1	6.000	31.50	12	31.30	.583	0	....	-6	0	-0.6

• PETERS, Rube Oscar Casper Peters b: 3/15/1885, Grantfork, IL d: 2/7/1965, Pequannock, NJ BR/TR, 6'1", 195 lbs. Deb: 4/13/1912

YEAR	TM-L	W	L	PCT	G	GS	CG	SH	SV	IP	H	R	ER	HR	HB	BB	SO	RAT	ERA	ERA+	CERA	OAV	BH	AVG	PR+	WS	TPW
1912	Chi-A	5	6	.455	28	11	4	0	0	108^2	134	72	50	2	6	33	39	1.537	4.14	78	4.68	.309	6	.194	-9	2	-1.0
1914	Bro-F	2	2	.500	11	3	1	0	0	37^2	52	27	16	1	0	16	13	1.805	3.82	85	5.71	.335	1	.091	-2	1	-0.3
Total	**2**	**7**	**8**	**.467**	**39**	**14**	**5**	**0**	**0**	**146^1**	**186**	**99**	**66**	**3**	**6**	**49**	**52**	**1.606**	**4.06**	**79**	**4.95**	**.316**	**7**	**.167**	**-11**	**3**	**-1.2**

• PETERS, Steve Steven Bradley Peters b: 11/14/1962, Oklahoma City, OK BL/TL, 5'10", 170 lbs. Deb: 8/11/1987

YEAR	TM-L	W	L	PCT	G	GS	CG	SH	SV	IP	H	R	ER	HR	HB	BB	SO	RAT	ERA	ERA+	CERA	OAV	BH	AVG	PR+	WS	TPW
1987	StL-N	0	0	....	12	0	0	0	1	15	17	3	3	1	0	6	11	1.533	1.80	231	4.66	.298	0	.000	4	2	0.4
1988	StL-N	3	3	.500	44	0	0	0	0	45	57	34	32	8	0	22	30	1.756	6.40	54	6.24	.313	0	.000	-15	0	-1.6
Total	**2**	**3**	**3**	**.500**	**56**	**0**	**0**	**0**	**1**	**60**	**74**	**37**	**35**	**9**	**0**	**28**	**41**	**1.700**	**5.25**	**67**	**5.84**	**.310**	**0**	**.000**	**-11**	**2**	**-1.3**

• PETERSON, Adam Adam Charles Peterson b: 12/11/1965, Long Beach, CA BR/TR, 6'3", 190 lbs. Deb: 9/19/1987

YEAR	TM-L	W	L	PCT	G	GS	CG	SH	SV	IP	H	R	ER	HR	HB	BB	SO	RAT	ERA	ERA+	CERA	OAV	BH	AVG	PR+	WS	TPW
1987	Chi-A	0	0	....	1	1	0	0	0	4	8	6	6	1	0	3	1	2.750	13.50	34	14.13	.444	0	....	-4	0	-0.4
1988	Chi-A	0	1	.000	2	2	0	0	0	6	6	9	9	0	0	6	5	2.000	13.50	29	4.96	.240	0	....	-6	0	-0.7
1989	Chi-A	0	1	.000	3	2	0	0	0	5^1	13	9	9	1	0	2	3	2.813	15.19	25	14.21	.464	0	....	-7	0	-0.7
1990	Chi-A	2	5	.286	20	11	2	0	0	85	90	46	43	12	2	26	29	1.365	4.55	84	4.53	.278	0	....	-9	2	-0.9
1991	SD-N	3	4	.429	13	11	0	0	0	54^2	50	33	27	10	0	28	37	1.427	4.45	85	4.49	.242	0	.000	-4	1	-0.5
Total	**5**	**5**	**11**	**.313**	**39**	**27**	**2**	**0**	**0**	**155**	**167**	**103**	**94**	**24**	**2**	**65**	**75**	**1.497**	**5.46**	**71**	**5.12**	**.277**	**0**	**.000**	**-30**	**3**	**-3.1**

• PETERSON, Fritz Fritz Fred Peterson b: 2/8/1942, Chicago, IL BB/TL, 6', 200 lbs. Deb: 4/15/1966

YEAR	TM-L	W	L	PCT	G	GS	CG	SH	SV	IP	H	R	ER	HR	HB	BB	SO	RAT	ERA	ERA+	CERA	OAV	BH	AVG	PR+	WS	TPW
1966	NY-A	12	11	.522	34	32	11	2	0	215	196	89	79	15	3	40	96	1.098	3.31	100	2.58	.241	15	.224	1	12	0.5
1967	NY-A	8	14	.364	36	30	6	1	0	181^1	179	88	70	11	3	43	102	1.224	3.47	90	3.10	.256	7	.146	-5	6	-0.4
1968	NY-A	12	11	.522	36	27	6	2	0	212^1	187	72	62	13	4	29	115	1.017	2.63	110	2.28	.241	5	.079	9	13	0.8
1969	NY-A	17	16	.515	37	37	16	4	0	272	228	95	77	15	3	43	150	.996	2.55	137	2.08	.229	9	.113	27	23	2.8
1970	NY-A★	20	11	.645	39	37	8	2	0	260^1	247	102	84	24	3	40	127	1.102	2.90	121	2.83	.248	20	.222	17	19	2.3
1971	NY-A	15	13	.536	37	35	16	4	1	274	269	106	93	25	4	42	139	1.135	3.05	106	3.03	.258	7	.082	7	16	0.4
1972	NY-A	17	15	.531	35	35	12	3	0	250^1	270	98	90	17	5	44	100	1.254	3.24	91	3.49	.276	19	.232	-8	11	-0.6
1973	NY-A	8	15	.348	31	31	6	0	0	184^1	207	93	81	18	7	49	59	1.389	3.95	93	4.34	.286	0	....	-8	7	-0.8
1974	NY-A	0	0	....	3	1	0	0	0	7^2	13	4	4	1	0	2	5	1.957	4.70	74	7.56	.361	0	....	-1	0	-0.1
	Cle-A	9	14	.391	29	29	3	0	0	152^2	187	89	74	16	4	37	52	1.467	4.36	83	4.85	.305	0	....	-13	5	-1.4
	Yr.	9	14	.391	32	30	3	0	0	160^1	200	93	78	17	4	39	57	1.491	4.38	82	4.98	.308	0	....	-14	5	-1.5
1975	Cle-A	14	8	.636	25	25	6	2	0	146^1	154	73	64	15	6	40	47	1.326	3.94	96	4.13	.275	0	....	-3	8	-0.3
1976	Cle-A	0	3	.000	9	9	0	0	0	47	59	31	29	3	0	10	19	1.468	5.55	63	4.55	.309	0	....	-11	0	-1.2
	Tex-A	1	0	1.000	4	2	0	0	0	15	21	7	6	0	0	7	4	1.867	3.60	100	6.11	.344	0	....	-0	1	0.0
	Yr.	1	3	.250	13	11	0	0	0	62	80	38	35	3	0	17	23	1.565	5.08	69	4.92	.317	0	....	-11	1	-1.2
Total	**11**	**133**	**131**	**.504**	**355**	**330**	**90**	**20**	**1**	**2218^1**	**2217**	**947**	**813**	**173**	**42**	**426**	**1015**	**1.191**	**3.30**	**101**	**3.21**	**.261**	**82**	**.159**	**11**	**121**	**2.0**

• PETERSON, Jim James Niels Peterson b: 8/18/1908, Philadelphia, PA d: 8/8/1975, Palm Beach, FL BR/TR, 6'.5", 200 lbs. Deb: 7/9/1931

YEAR	TM-L	W	L	PCT	G	GS	CG	SH	SV	IP	H	R	ER	HR	HB	BB	SO	RAT	ERA	ERA+	CERA	OAV	BH	AVG	PR+	WS	TPW
1931	Phi-A	0	1	.000	6	1	1	0	0	13	18	10	9	0	0	4	7	1.692	6.23	72	5.03	.321	1	.500	-3	0	-0.2
1933	Phi-A	2	5	.286	32	5	0	0	0	90^2	114	64	50	6	0	36	18	1.654	4.96	86	5.05	.305	4	.148	-4	2	-0.5
1937	Bro-N	0	0	....	3	0	0	0	0	5^2	8	5	5	3	0	2	4	1.765	7.94	51	9.96	.333	0	....	-2	0	-0.2
Total	**3**	**2**	**6**	**.250**	**41**	**6**	**1**	**0**	**0**	**109^1**	**140**	**79**	**64**	**9**	**0**	**42**	**29**	**1.665**	**5.27**	**82**	**5.30**	**.308**	**5**	**.172**	**-9**	**2**	**-0.9**

• PETERSON, Kent Kent Franklin "Pete" Peterson b: 12/21/1925, Goshen, UT d: 4/27/1995, Highland, UT BR/TL, 5'10", 175 lbs. Deb: 7/15/1944

YEAR	TM-L	W	L	PCT	G	GS	CG	SH	SV	IP	H	R	ER	HR	HB	BB	SO	RAT	ERA	ERA+	CERA	OAV	BH	AVG	PR+	WS	TPW
1944	Cin-N	0	0	....	1	0	0	0	0	1	0	0	0	0	0	0	0	.000	0.00	....	0.00	.000	0	....	0	0	0.0
1947	Cin-N	6	13	.316	37	17	3	1	2	152^1	156	74	72	8	3	62	78	1.431	4.25	96	3.88	.265	3	.068	-1	8	-0.4
1948	Cin-N	2	15	.118	43	17	2	0	1	137	146	82	70	10	6	59	64	1.496	4.60	85	4.39	.271	5	.139	-8	4	-1.0
1949	Cin-N	4	5	.444	30	7	2	0	0	66^1	66	54	46	8	4	46	28	1.688	6.24	67	5.40	.261	1	.056	-15	0	-1.7
1950	Cin-N	0	3	.000	9	2	0	0	0	20	25	20	16	4	0	17	6	2.100	7.20	59	8.18	.305	1	.333	-6	0	-0.6
1951	Cin-N	1	1	.500	9	0	0	0	0	9^2	13	8	7	0	1	8	5	2.172	6.52	63	7.14	.317	0	.000	-3	0	-0.3
1952	Phi-N	0	0	....	3	0	0	0	2	7	2	0	0	0	0	2	7	.571	0.00	....	0.51	.091	0	.000	3	2	0.3

YEAR	TM-L	W	L	PCT	G	GS	CG	SH	SV	IP	H	R	ER	HR	HB	BB	SO	RAT	ERA	ERA+	CERA	OAV	BH	AVG	PR+	WS	TPW
1953	Phi-N	0	1	.000	15	0	0	0	0	27	26	20	20	3	1	21	20	1.741	6.67	63	5.29	.252	0	.000	-7	0	-0.8
Total	**8**	**13**	**38**	**.255**	**147**	**43**	**7**	**1**	**5**	**420^{1}**	**434**	**258**	**231**	**33**	**15**	**215**	**208**	**1.544**	**4.95**	**82**	**4.59**	**.267**	**10**	**.091**	**-37**	**14**	**-4.4**
• PETERSON, Kyle	Kyle Johnathan Peterson b: 4/9/1976, Elkhorn, NE BL/TR, 6'3", 215 lbs. Deb: 7/19/1999																										
1999	Mil-N	4	7	.364	17	12	0	0	0	77	87	46	39	3	4	25	34	1.455	4.56	99	4.20	.285	3	.136	1	3	0.0
2001	Mil-N	1	2	.333	3	2	0	0	0	14^{2}	19	10	9	3	0	4	12	1.568	5.52	78	5.60	.302	1	.200	-2	0	-0.2
Total	**2**	**5**	**9**	**.357**	**20**	**14**	**0**	**0**	**0**	**91^{2}**	**106**	**56**	**48**	**6**	**4**	**29**	**46**	**1.473**	**4.71**	**95**	**4.42**	**.288**	**4**	**.148**	**-1**	**3**	**-0.1**
• PETERSON, Sid	Sidney Herbert Peterson b: 1/31/1918, Havelock, ND d: 8/29/2001, Wichita Falls, TX BR/TR, 6'3", 220 lbs. Deb: 5/4/1943																										
1943	StL-A	2	0	1.000	3	0	0	0	0	10	15	3	3	0	1	3	0	1.800	2.70	123	6.09	.341	0	.000	1	1	0.1
• PETKOVSEK, Mark	Mark Joseph Petkovsek b: 11/18/1965, Beaumont, TX BR/TR, 6', 185 lbs. Deb: 6/8/1991																										
1991	Tex-A	0	1	.000	4	1	0	0	0	9^{1}	21	16	15	4	0	4	6	2.679	14.46	28	15.57	.438	0	....	-11	0	-1.1
1993	Pit-N	3	0	1.000	26	0	0	0	0	32^{1}	43	25	25	7	0	9	14	1.608	6.96	58	6.33	.328	0	....	-11	0	-1.1
1995	StL-N	6	6	.500	26	21	1	1	0	137^{1}	136	71	61	11	6	35	71	1.245	4.00	105	3.52	.262	3	.081	1	7	0.0
1996*	StL-N	11	2	.846	48	6	0	0	0	88^{2}	83	37	35	9	5	35	45	1.331	3.55	118	3.94	.251	3	.188	4	8	0.4
1997	StL-N	4	7	.364	55	2	0	0	2	96	109	61	54	14	6	31	51	1.458	5.06	82	5.21	.292	1	.091	-10	2	-1.0
1998	StL-N	7	4	.636	48	10	0	0	0	105^{2}	131	63	56	9	8	36	55	1.580	4.77	88	5.43	.312	7	.318	-6	5	-0.4
1999	Ana-A	10	4	.714	64	0	0	0	1	83	85	37	32	6	2	21	43	1.277	3.47	140	3.51	.269	0	....	12	9	1.1
2000	Ana-A	4	2	.667	64	1	0	0	2	81	86	39	38	8	3	23	31	1.346	4.22	120	4.07	.277	0	....	6	7	0.5
2001	Tex-A	1	2	.333	55	0	0	0	0	76^{2}	103	61	57	14	5	28	42	1.709	6.69	70	6.74	.323	0	.000	-17	0	-1.6
Total	**9**	**46**	**28**	**.622**	**390**	**41**	**1**	**1**	**5**	**710**	**797**	**410**	**373**	**82**	**35**	**222**	**358**	**1.435**	**4.73**	**92**	**4.78**	**.288**	**14**	**.161**	**-31**	**38**	**-3.1**
• PETRY, Dan	Daniel Joseph Petry b: 11/13/1958, Palo Alto, CA BR/TR, 6'4", 200 lbs. Deb: 7/8/1979																										
1979	Det-A	6	5	.545	15	15	2	0	0	98	90	46	43	11	4	33	43	1.255	3.95	110	3.67	.254	0	....	3	6	0.3
1980	Det-A	10	9	.526	27	25	4	3	0	164^{2}	156	82	72	9	1	83	88	1.451	3.94	104	3.75	.253	0	....	5	9	0.5
1981	Det-A	10	9	.526	23	22	7	2	0	141	115	53	47	10	1	57	79	1.220	3.00	126	2.91	.224	0	....	9	10	0.9
1982	Det-A	15	9	.625	35	35	8	1	0	246	220	98	88	15	4	100	132	1.301	3.22	126	3.32	.241	0	....	18	18	1.8
1983	Det-A	19	11	.633	38	**38**	9	2	0	266^{1}	256	126	116	37	6	99	122	1.333	3.92	100	4.16	.256	0	....	-4	14	-0.4
1984*	Det-A	18	8	.692	35	35	7	2	0	233^{1}	231	94	84	21	3	66	144	1.273	3.24	121	3.57	.259	0	....	16	16	1.6
1985	Det-A★	15	13	.536	34	34	8	0	0	238^{2}	190	98	89	24	3	81	109	1.135	3.36	121	2.80	.217	0	....	19	17	1.8
1986	Det-A	5	10	.333	20	20	2	0	0	116	122	78	60	15	5	53	56	1.509	4.66	89	4.91	.268	0	....	-8	2	-0.8
1987*	Det-A	9	7	.563	30	21	0	0	0	134^{2}	148	101	84	22	10	76	93	1.663	5.61	75	6.02	.279	0	....	-22	2	-2.1
1988	Cal-A	3	9	.250	22	22	4	1	0	139^{2}	139	70	68	18	6	59	64	1.418	4.38	88	4.51	.263	0	....	-8	5	-0.8
1989	Cal-A	3	2	.600	19	4	0	0	0	51	53	32	31	8	1	23	21	1.490	5.47	70	5.06	.275	0	....	-10	1	-1.0
1990	Det-A	10	9	.526	32	23	1	0	0	149^{2}	148	78	74	14	1	77	73	1.503	4.45	89	4.40	.263	0	....	-12	6	-1.2
1991	Det-A	2	3	.400	17	6	0	0	0	54^{2}	66	35	30	9	0	19	18	1.555	4.94	84	5.54	.300	0	....	-5	1	-0.5
	Atl-N	0	0	....	10	0	0	0	0	24^{1}	29	17	15	2	1	14	9	1.767	5.55	70	5.77	.296	1	.200	-4	0	-0.5
	Bos-A	0	0	....	13	0	0	0	1	22^{1}	21	17	11	3	1	12	12	1.478	4.43	97	4.61	.250	0	....	-0	1	0.0
	Yr.	2	3	.400	30	6	0	0	1	77	87	52	41	12	1	31	30	1.532	4.79	87	5.27	.286	0	....	-5	2	-0.5
Total	**13**	**125**	**104**	**.546**	**370**	**300**	**52**	**11**	**1**	**2080^{1}**	**1984**	**1025**	**912**	**218**	**47**	**852**	**1063**	**1.363**	**3.95**	**102**	**3.98**	**.253**	**1**	**.200**	**-3**	**108**	**-0.3**
• PETTIBONE, Jay	Harry Jonathan Pettibone b: 6/21/1957, Mount Clemens, MI BR/TR, 6'4", 182 lbs. Deb: 9/11/1983																										
1983	Min-A	0	4	.000	4	4	1	0	0	27	28	16	16	8	2	8	10	1.333	5.33	80	5.88	.280	0	....	-4	0	-0.4
• PETTIT, Bob	Robert Henry Pettit b: 7/19/1861, Williamstown, MA d: 11/1/1910, Derby, CT BL/TR, 5'9", 160 lbs. Deb: 9/3/1887 ♦																										
1887	Chi-N	0	0	....	1	0	0	0	**1**	1	5	8	0	0	0	2	0	5.000	0.00	....	....	.629	44	.301	0	2	-0.4
• PETTIT, Leon	Leon Arthur "Lefty" Pettit b: 6/23/1902, Waynesburg, PA d: 11/21/1974, Columbia, TN BL/TL, 5'10.5", 165 lbs. Deb: 4/18/1935																										
1935	Was-A	8	5	.615	41	7	1	0	3	109	129	65	60	6	4	58	45	1.716	4.95	87	5.36	.301	2	.080	-7	5	-0.6
1937	Phi-N	0	1	.000	3	1	0	0	0	4	6	5	5	1	0	4	0	2.500	11.25	38	11.27	.353	0	....	-3	0	-0.3
Total	**2**	**8**	**6**	**.571**	**44**	**8**	**1**	**0**	**3**	**113**	**135**	**70**	**65**	**7**	**4**	**62**	**45**	**1.743**	**5.18**	**84**	**5.57**	**.303**	**2**	**.080**	**-10**	**5**	**-0.9**
• PETTIT, Paul	George William Paul "Lefty" Pettit b: 11/29/1931, Los Angeles, CA BL/TL, 6'2", 195 lbs. Deb: 5/4/1951																										
1951	Pit-N	0	0	....	2	0	0	0	0	2^{2}	2	1	1	1	0	1	0	1.125	3.38	125	4.18	.200	0	.000	0	0	0.0
1953	Pit-N	1	2	.333	10	5	0	0	0	28	33	27	24	1	0	20	14	1.893	7.71	58	5.79	.297	2	.250	-10	0	-0.9
Total	**2**	**1**	**2**	**.333**	**12**	**5**	**0**	**0**	**0**	**30^{2}**	**35**	**28**	**25**	**2**	**0**	**21**	**14**	**1.826**	**7.34**	**61**	**5.65**	**.289**	**2**	**.222**	**-10**	**0**	**-0.9**
• PETTITTE, Andy	Andrew Eugene Pettitte b: 6/15/1972, Baton Rouge, LA BL/TL, 6'5", 235 lbs. Deb: 4/29/1995																										
1995*	NY-A	12	9	.571	31	26	3	0	0	175	183	86	81	15	1	63	114	1.406	4.17	111	4.13	.272	0	....	8	11	0.7
1996*	NY-A★	**21**	8	.724	35	34	2	0	0	221	229	105	95	23	3	72	162	1.362	3.87	128	4.14	.271	0	....	30	18	2.8
1997*	NY-A	18	7	.720	35	**35**	4	1	0	240^{1}	233	86	77	7	3	65	166	1.240	2.88	154	3.05	.256	0	....	44	20	4.2
1998*	NY-A	16	11	.593	33	32	5	0	0	216^{1}	226	110	102	20	6	87	146	1.447	4.24	103	4.46	.274	0	.000	-1	13	-0.1
1999*	NY-A	14	11	.560	31	31	0	0	0	191^{2}	216	105	100	20	3	89	121	1.591	4.70	101	5.22	.289	1	.200	2	10	0.2
2000*	NY-A	19	9	.679	32	32	3	1	0	204^{2}	219	111	99	17	4	80	125	1.461	4.35	111	4.32	.271	0	.000	15	14	1.3
2001*	NY-A★	15	10	.600	31	31	2	0	0	200^{2}	224	103	89	14	6	41	164	1.321	3.99	112	3.82	.281	0	.000	15	13	1.4
2002*	NY-A	13	5	.722	22	22	3	1	0	134^{2}	144	58	49	6	4	32	97	1.307	3.27	133	3.55	.272	1	.333	20	12	2.0
2003*	NY-A	21	8	.724	33	33	1	0	0	208^{1}	227	109	93	21	1	50	180	1.330	4.02	109	3.89	.272	1	.143	13	14	1.2
Total	**9**	**149**	**78**	**.656**	**283**	**276**	**23**	**3**	**0**	**1792^{2}**	**1901**	**873**	**785**	**143**	**31**	**579**	**1275**	**1.383**	**3.94**	**116**	**4.06**	**.273**	**3**	**.107**	**147**	**125**	**13.8**
• PETTY, Charlie	Charles E. Petty b: 1/28/1866, Nashville, TN TR Deb: 7/30/1889																										
1889	Cin-a	2	3	.400	5	5	5	0	0	44	44	29	27	3	6	20	10	1.455	5.52	71	....	.252	6	.300	-8	2	-0.6
1893	NY-N	5	2	.714	9	6	4	0	0	54	66	36	20	0	1	28	12	1.741	3.33	139	4.97	.292	7	.318	7	5	0.8
1894	Was-N	3	8	.273	16	12	8	0	0	103	156	114	64	4	9	32	14	1.825	5.59	94	6.54	.345	8	.195	-1	3	-0.2
	Cle-N	0	2	.000	4	3	2	0	0	27	42	37	26	4	3	14	4	2.074	8.67	63	8.77	.351	1	.083	-10	0	-0.9
	Yr.	3	10	.231	20	15	10	0	0	130	198	151	90	8	12	46	18	1.877	6.23	85	7.00	.346	9	.170	-11	3	-1.1
Total	**3**	**10**	**15**	**.400**	**34**	**26**	**19**	**0**	**0**	**228**	**308**	**216**	**137**	**11**	**19**	**94**	**40**	**1.763**	**5.41**	**90**	**5.17**	**.317**	**22**	**.232**	**-12**	**10**	**-0.9**
• PETTY, Jesse	Jesse Lee "The Silver Fox" Petty b: 11/23/1894, Orr, OK d: 10/23/1971, St. Paul, MN BR/TL, 6', 195 lbs. Deb: 4/14/1921																										
1921	Cle-A	0	0	....	4	0	0	0	0	9	10	2	2	0	0	0	0	1.111	2.00	213	2.63	.345	0	.000	2	1	0.2
1925	Bro-N	9	9	.500	28	21	7	0	0	153	188	97	83	15	2	47	39	1.536	4.88	86	4.96	.304	7	.140	-7	5	-0.9
1926	Bro-N	17	17	.500	38	33	23	1	1	275^{2}	246	118	87	9	3	79	101	1.179	2.84	135	2.56	**.240**	17	.175	35	24	3.2
1927	Bro-N	13	18	.419	42	33	19	2	1	271^{2}	263	108	90	13	4	53	101	1.163	2.98	133	2.73	.254	9	.099	29	21	2.2
1928	Bro-N	15	15	.500	40	31	15	2	1	234	264	119	105	18	5	56	74	1.368	4.04	98	4.02	.289	9	.111	-1	12	-0.6
1929	Pit-N	11	10	.524	36	25	12	1	0	184^{1}	197	100	76	12	0	42	58	1.297	3.71	129	3.45	.277	7	.104	19	12	1.2
1930	Pit-N	1	6	.143	10	7	0	0	1	41^{1}	67	43	38	8	2	13	16	1.935	8.27	60	8.32	.362	1	.083	-15	0	-1.5
	Chi-N	1	3	.250	9	3	0	0	0	39^{1}	51	18	13	2	0	6	18	1.449	2.97	164	4.35	.317	3	.231	9	3	0.7
	Yr.	2	9	.182	19	10	0	0	1	80^{2}	118	61	51	10	2	19	34	1.698	5.69	87	6.38	.341	4	.160	-7	3	-0.7
Total	**7**	**67**	**78**	**.462**	**207**	**153**	**76**	**6**	**4**	**1208^{1}**	**1286**	**605**	**494**	**77**	**16**	**296**	**407**	**1.309**	**3.68**	**113**	**3.58**	**.275**	**53**	**.128**	**71**	**78**	**4.5**
• PETTYJOHN, Adam	Adam Christopher Pettyjohn b: 6/11/1977, Phoenix, AZ BR/TL, 6'3", 190 lbs. Deb: 7/16/2001																										
2001	Det-A	1	6	.143	16	9	0	0	0	65	81	48	42	10	4	21	40	1.569	5.82	75	5.84	.309	0	.000	-10	0	-0.9
• PEZZULLO, Pretzel	John Pezzullo b: 12/10/1910, Bridgeport, CT d: 5/16/1990, Dallas, TX BL/TL, 5'11.5", 180 lbs. Deb: 4/18/1935																										
1935	Phi-N	3	5	.375	41	7	2	0	1	84^{1}	115	74	60	5	7	45	24	1.897	6.40	71	6.44	.321	6	.250	-16	1	-1.5
1936	Phi-N	0	0	....	1	0	0	0	0	2	1	1	1	0	0	6	0	3.500	4.50	101	9.85	.167	0	....	0	0	0.0
Total	**2**	**3**	**5**	**.375**	**42**	**7**	**2**	**0**	**1**	**86^{1}**	**116**	**75**	**61**	**5**	**7**	**51**	**24**	**1.934**	**6.36**	**71**	**6.52**	**.319**	**6**	**.250**	**-16**	**1**	**-1.5**
• PFANN, Bill	William F. Pfann b: 6/1863, Hamilton, Canada d: 6/3/1904, Hamilton, Canada, 6', 205 lbs. Deb: 6/16/1894																										
1894	Cin-N	0	1	.000	1	1	0	0	0	3	10	10	9	1	0	4	0	4.667	27.00	21	29.05	.537	0	.000	-7	0	-0.6

YEAR	TM-L	W	L	PCT	G	GS	CG	SH	SV	IP	H	R	ER	HR	HB	BB	SO	RAT	ERA	ERA+	CERA	OAV	BH	AVG	PR+	WS	TPW
• PFEFFER, Big Jeff	Francis Xavier Pfeffer b: 3/31/1882, Champaign, IL d: 12/19/1954, Kankakee, IL BR/TR, 6'1", 185 lbs. Deb: 4/15/1905																										
1905	Chi-N	4	4	.500	15	11	9	0	0	101	84	36	28	2	4	36	56	1.188	2.50	119	2.77	.240	8	.200	2	7	0.2
1906	Bos-N	13	22	.371	36	36	33	4	0	302^1	270	138	99	4	16	114	158	1.270	2.95	91	2.94	.246	31	.196	-6	18	-0.4
1907	Bos-N	6	8	.429	19	16	12	1	0	144	129	62	48	3	7	61	65	1.319	3.00	85	3.36	.253	15	.250	-8	6	-0.6
1908	Bos-N	0	0	....	4	0	0	0	0	10	18	16	14	1	0	8	3	2.600	12.60	19	10.65	.383	0	.000	-12	0	-1.4
1910	Chi-N	1	0	1.000	13	1	1	0	0	41^1	43	31	15	1	1	16	11	1.427	3.27	88	3.94	.281	3	.176	-2	0	-0.2
1911	Bos-N	7	5	.583	26	6	4	1	2	97	116	74	51	3	0	57	24	1.784	4.73	81	5.39	.301	9	.196	-8	2	-0.7
Total	6	31	39	.443	113	70	59	6	2	695^2	660	357	255	14	28	292	317	1.368	3.30	86	3.52	.260	66	.204	-35	33	-3.0
• PFEFFER, Fred	Nathaniel Frederick "Fritz,Dandelion" Pfeffer b: 3/17/1860, Louisville, KY d: 4/10/1932, Chicago, IL BR/TR, 5'10.5", 184 lbs. Deb: 5/1/1882 M/U ♦																										
1884	Chi-N	0	0	....	1	0	0	0	0	1	3	2	1	0	....	1	0	4.000	9.00	35	....	.495	135	.289	-1	19	4.5
1885*	Chi-N	2	1	.667	5	2	2	0	**2**	31^2	26	15	9	1	....	8	13	1.074	2.56	118	....	.213	113	.241	1	18	0.9
1892	Lou-N	0	0	....	1	0	0	0	0	5	4	3	1	0	0	5	0	1.800	1.80	170	4.18	.211	121	.257	1	20	1.7
1894	Lou-N	0	0	....	1	0	0	0	0	7	8	6	2	0	0	6	0	2.000	2.57	198	5.66	.284	128	.309	2	11	0.6
Total	4	2	1	.667	8	2	2	0	2	44^2	41	26	13	1	0	20	13	1.366	2.62	124	1.35	.234	1707	.259	3	68	7.7
• PFEFFER, Jeff	Edward Joseph Pfeffer b: 3/4/1888, Seymour, IL d: 8/15/1972, Chicago, IL BR/TR, 6'3", 210 lbs. Deb: 4/16/1911																										
1911	StL-A	0	0	....	2	0	0	0	0	10	11	11	8	0	0	4	4	1.500	7.20	47	4.11	.297	0	.000	-4	0	-0.5
1913	Bro-N	0	1	.000	5	2	1	0	0	24^1	28	16	9	0	4	13	13	1.685	3.33	99	5.18	.311	0	.000	-0	0	-0.1
1914	Bro-N	23	12	.657	43	34	27	3	4	315	264	99	69	9	7	91	135	1.127	1.97	145	2.40	.232	23	.198	30	26	3.2
1915	Bro-N	19	14	.576	40	34	26	6	3	291^2	243	93	68	8	17	76	84	1.094	2.10	132	2.39	.231	27	.255	20	26	2.7
1916*	Bro-N	25	11	.694	41	36	30	6	1	328^2	274	91	70	5	17	63	128	1.025	1.92	139	2.10	.230	34	.279	22	32	3.2
1917	Bro-N	11	15	.423	30	30	24	3	0	266	225	84	66	4	16	66	115	1.094	2.23	125	2.32	.234	13	.130	14	18	1.0
1918	Bro-N	1	0	1.000	1	1	1	1	0	9	2	0	0	0	0	3	1	.556	0.00	....	0.44	.071	1	.250	3	2	0.3
1919	Bro-N	17	13	.567	30	30	26	4	0	267	270	95	79	7	12	49	92	1.195	2.66	111	2.97	.267	20	.206	15	18	1.8
1920*	Bro-N	16	9	.640	30	28	20	2	0	215	225	81	72	5	5	45	80	1.256	3.01	106	3.12	.273	18	.243	7	16	0.9
1921	Bro-N	1	5	.167	6	5	2	0	0	31^2	36	19	16	0	1	9	8	1.421	4.55	85	3.79	.310	0	.000	-2	1	-0.4
	StL-N	9	3	.750	18	13	7	1	0	98^2	115	51	47	3	5	28	22	1.449	4.29	85	4.24	.305	4	.138	-7	5	-0.8
	Yr.	10	8	.556	24	18	9	1	0	130^1	151	70	63	3	6	37	30	1.442	4.35	85	4.13	.306	4	.100	-9	6	-1.1
1922	StL-N	19	12	.613	44	32	19	1	2	261^1	286	126	104	12	11	58	83	1.316	3.58	108	3.59	.279	24	.245	14	21	1.7
1923	StL-N	8	9	.471	26	18	7	1	0	152^1	171	80	68	8	9	40	32	1.385	4.02	97	4.00	.287	7	.127	-1	7	-0.4
1924	StL-N	4	5	.444	16	12	3	0	0	78	102	52	46	3	1	30	20	1.692	5.31	71	5.29	.318	3	.115	-13	1	-1.6
	Pit-N	5	3	.625	15	4	1	0	0	58^2	68	23	20	3	0	17	19	1.449	3.07	125	4.17	.293	6	.240	3	5	0.2
	Yr.	9	8	.529	31	16	4	0	0	136^2	170	75	66	6	1	47	39	1.588	4.35	87	4.81	.308	9	.176	-10	6	-1.3
Total	13	158	112	.585	347	279	194	28	10	2407^1	2320	921	742	67	105	592	836	1.210	2.77	116	2.97	.258	180	.206	99	178	11.2
• PFIESTER, Jack	John Albert "Jack The Giant Killer" Pfiester b: 5/24/1878, Cincinnati, OH d: 9/3/1953, Loveland, OH BR/TL, 5'11", 180 lbs. Deb: 9/8/1903																										
1903	Pit-N	0	3	.000	3	3	2	0	0	19	26	21	13	0	2	10	15	1.895	6.16	52	6.16	.321	0	.000	-7	0	-0.8
1904	Pit-N	1	1	.500	3	2	1	0	0	20	28	18	16	0	0	9	6	1.850	7.20	38	5.54	.318	2	.286	-10	1	-0.9
1906*	Chi-N	20	8	.714	31	29	20	4	0	250^2	173	63	42	3	13	63	153	.941	1.51	175	1.66	.194	4	.048	25	24	2.0
1907*	Chi-N	14	9	.609	30	22	13	3	0	195	143	61	25	1	5	48	90	.979	**1.15**	**216**	1.71	.207	6	.094	24	19	2.5
1908*	Chi-N	12	10	.545	33	29	18	3	0	252	204	80	56	1	11	70	117	1.087	2.00	117	2.19	.223	8	.101	7	16	0.4
1909	Chi-N	17	6	.739	29	25	13	5	0	196^2	179	67	53	1	5	49	73	1.159	2.43	104	2.48	.240	11	.169	1	14	0.2
1910*	Chi-N	6	3	.667	14	13	5	2	0	100^1	82	28	20	0	1	26	34	1.076	1.79	160	2.05	.225	3	.091	11	9	0.9
1911	Chi-N	1	4	.200	6	5	3	0	0	33^2	34	25	15	0	2	18	15	1.545	4.01	82	4.01	.262	2	.182	-3	0	-0.3
Total	8	71	44	.617	149	128	75	17	0	1067^1	869	363	240	6	39	293	503	1.089	2.02	128	2.21	.222	36	.103	48	83	3.9
• PFISTER, Dan	Daniel Albin Pfister b: 12/20/1936, Plainfield, NJ BR/TR, 6', 187 lbs. Deb: 9/9/1961																										
1961	KC-A	0	0	....	2	0	0	0	0	2^1	5	4	4	2	0	4	3	3.857	15.43	27	27.02	.417	0	....	-3	0	-0.3
1962	KC-A	4	14	.222	41	25	2	0	1	196^1	175	112	99	27	9	106	123	1.431	4.54	92	4.42	.238	12	.185	-7	8	-0.8
1963	KC-A	1	0	1.000	3	1	0	0	0	9^1	8	2	2	1	1	3	9	1.179	1.93	199	3.38	.229	0	.000	2	1	0.2
1964	KC-A	1	5	.167	19	3	0	0	0	41^1	50	32	30	10	6	29	21	1.911	6.53	58	8.43	.311	0	.000	-12	0	-1.3
Total	4	6	19	.240	65	29	2	0	1	249^1	238	150	135	40	16	142	156	1.524	4.87	84	5.26	.252	12	.162	-20	9	-2.2
• PFUND, Lee	Le Roy Herbert Pfund b: 10/18/1918, Oak Park, IL BR/TR, 6'1", 185 lbs. Deb: 4/21/1945																										
1945	Bro-N	3	2	.600	15	10	2	0	0	62^1	69	51	36	4	5	35	27	1.668	5.20	72	5.03	.274	4	.182	-10	0	-0.9
• PHEBUS, Bill	Raymond William Phebus b: 8/2/1909, Cherryvale, KS d: 10/11/1989, Bartow, FL BR/TR, 5'9", 170 lbs. Deb: 9/6/1936																										
1936	Was-A	0	0	....	2	1	0	0	0	7^1	4	6	2	1	1	4	4	1.091	2.45	195	2.00	.114	0	.000	2	0	0.2
1937	Was-A	3	2	.600	6	5	4	1	1	40^2	33	13	10	2	2	24	12	1.402	2.21	200	3.55	.232	0	.000	9	5	0.9
1938	Was-A	0	0	....	5	0	0	0	1	6^1	9	9	8	1	0	7	2	2.526	11.37	40	9.72	.346	0	.000	-5	0	-0.5
Total	3	3	2	.600	13	6	4	1	2	54^1	46	28	20	4	3	35	18	1.491	3.31	136	4.06	.227	0	.000	6	5	0.7
• PHELPS, Ray	Raymond Clifford Phelps b: 12/11/1903, Dunlap, TN d: 7/7/1971, Fort Pierce, FL BR/TR, 6'2", 200 lbs. Deb: 4/23/1930																										
1930	Bro-N	14	7	.667	36	24	11	2	0	179^2	198	98	82	21	3	52	64	1.391	4.11	120	4.30	.280	10	.147	12	13	0.8
1931	Bro-N	7	9	.438	28	26	3	1	0	149^1	184	88	83	3	4	44	50	1.527	5.00	76	4.46	.306	8	.157	-18	4	-1.9
1932	Bro-N	4	5	.444	20	9	4	1	0	79^1	101	58	52	5	3	27	21	1.613	5.90	65	5.30	.323	2	.087	-19	0	-1.9
1935	Chi-A	4	8	.333	27	17	4	0	1	125	126	77	67	10	3	55	38	1.448	4.82	96	4.09	.262	5	.122	-4	5	-0.7
1936	Chi-A	4	6	.400	15	4	2	0	0	68^2	91	54	46	9	2	42	17	1.937	6.03	86	7.28	.331	6	.231	-7	2	-0.6
Total	5	33	35	.485	126	80	24	4	1	602	700	375	330	48	15	220	190	1.528	4.93	89	4.77	.294	31	.148	-36	24	-4.3
• PHELPS, Tommy	Thomas Allen Phelps b: 3/4/1974, Seoul, South Korea BL/TL, 6'3", 192 lbs. Deb: 3/31/2003																										
2003	Fla-N	3	2	.600	27	7	0	0	0	63	70	32	28	3	2	23	43	1.476	4.00	102	4.31	.282	1	.091	0	3	0.0
• PHELPS, Travis	Travis Howard Phelps b: 7/25/1977, Neosho, MO BR/TR, 6'2", 170 lbs. Deb: 4/19/2001																										
2001	TB-A	2	2	.500	49	0	0	0	5	62	53	30	24	6	3	24	54	1.242	3.48	129	3.27	.226	0	....	7	6	0.6
2002	TB-A	1	2	.333	26	0	0	0	0	37^2	30	20	20	7	5	27	36	1.513	4.78	93	5.45	.222	0	....	-2	2	-0.2
Total	2	3	4	.429	75	0	0	0	5	99^2	83	50	44	13	8	51	90	1.344	3.97	113	4.09	.224	0	....	5	8	0.5
• PHILLIPPE, Deacon	Charles Louis Phillippe b: 5/23/1872, Rural Retreat, VA d: 3/30/1952, Avalon, PA BR/TR, 6'.5", 180 lbs. Deb: 4/21/1899 U																										
1899	Lou-N	21	17	.553	42	38	33	2	1	321	331	178	113	10	7	64	68	1.231	3.17	122	3.06	.266	26	.203	30	23	2.6
1900*	Pit-N	20	13	.606	38	33	29	1	0	279	274	127	88	7	7	42	75	1.133	2.84	128	2.63	.257	19	.181	23	23	1.9
1901	Pit-N	22	12	.647	37	32	30	1	2	296	274	115	73	7	10	38	103	1.054	2.22	147	2.25	.244	26	.230	31	25	3.4
1902	Pit-N	20	9	.690	31	30	29	5	0	272	265	90	62	1	4	26	122	1.070	2.05	133	2.21	.255	25	.221	14	23	1.7
1903*	Pit-N	25	9	.735	36	33	31	4	2	289^1	269	115	78	4	4	29	123	1.030	2.43	133	**2.10**	.241	26	.210	14	27	1.5
1904	Pit-N	10	10	.500	21	19	17	3	1	166^2	183	82	60	1	3	26	82	1.254	3.24	84	3.04	.272	8	.123	-11	7	-1.5
1905	Pit-N	20	13	.606	38	33	25	5	0	279	235	95	68	0	10	48	133	1.014	2.19	136	2.01	.233	9	.093	20	26	1.6
1906	Pit-N	15	10	.600	33	24	19	3	0	218^2	216	78	60	3	2	26	90	1.107	2.47	108	2.42	.252	20	.244	4	16	0.7
1907	Pit-N	14	11	.560	35	26	17	1	2	214	214	90	62	2	5	36	61	1.168	2.61	93	2.76	.264	12	.185	-1	13	0.1
1908	Pit-N	0	0	....	5	0	0	0	0	12	20	15	15	0	0	3	1	1.917	11.25	20	6.39	.357	1	.250	-12	0	-1.3
1909*	Pit-N	8	3	.727	22	13	7	1	0	131^2	121	41	34	2	4	14	38	1.025	2.32	110	2.29	.253	3	.071	2	10	-0.1
1910	Pit-N	14	2	.875	31	8	5	1	4	121^2	111	46	31	4	3	9	30	.986	2.29	137	2.10	.239	9	.220	11	13	1.2
1911	Pit-N	0	0	....	3	0	0	0	0	6	5	5	5	0	0	2	3	1.167	7.50	46	2.42	.238	1	1.000	-3	0	-0.2
Total	13	189	109	.634	372	289	242	27	12	2607	2518	1077	749	41	59	363	929	1.105	2.59	117	2.47	.253	185	.189	122	206	11.7
• PHILLIPS, Bill	William Corcoran "Whoa Bill,Silver Bill" Phillips b: 11/9/1868, Allenport, PA d: 10/25/1941, Charleroi, PA BR/TR, 5'11", 180 lbs. Deb: 8/11/1890 M																										
1890	Pit-N	1	9	.100	10	10	9	0	0	82	123	97	69	8	1	29	25	1.854	7.57	43	....	.337	11	.239	-35	1	-3.0
1895	Cin-N	6	7	.462	18	9	6	0	2	109	126	90	73	6	7	44	15	1.560	6.03	82	4.78	.285	15	.313	-13	6	-0.9
1899	Cin-N	17	9	.654	33	27	18	1	1	227^2	234	121	84	3	14	71	43	1.340	3.32	118	3.43	.266	12	.130	14	17	0.8
1900	Cin-N	9	11	.450	29	24	17	3	0	208^1	229	140	99	5	13	67	51	1.421	4.28	86	3.93	.279	13	.165	-15	7	-1.6

YEAR	TM-L	W	L	PCT	G	GS	CG	SH	SV	IP	H	R	ER	HR	HB	BB	SO	RAT	ERA	ERA+	CERA	OAV	BH	AVG	PR+	WS	TPW
1901	Cin-N	14	18	.438	37	36	29	1	0	281^{1}	364	196	145	7	12	67	109	1.532	4.64	69	4.65	.311	22	.202	-39	8	-3.7
1902	Cin-N	16	16	.500	33	33	30	0	0	269	267	121	75	3	9	55	85	1.197	2.51	119	2.79	.259	39	.342	9	20	2.0
1903	Cin-N	7	6	.538	16	13	11	1	0	118^{1}	134	74	44	0	7	30	46	1.386	3.35	106	3.64	.279	10	.175	3	6	0.2
Total	**7**	70	76	.479	176	152	120	6	3	1295^{2}	1477	839	589	32	63	363	374	1.420	4.09	86	3.56	.285	122	.224	-75	65	-6.2

• PHILLIPS, Buz Albert Abernathy Phillips b: 5/25/1904, Newton, NC d: 11/6/1964, Baltimore, MD BR/TR, 5'11.5", 185 lbs. Deb: 8/5/1930

YEAR	TM-L	W	L	PCT	G	GS	CG	SH	SV	IP	H	R	ER	HR	HB	BB	SO	RAT	ERA	ERA+	CERA	OAV	BH	AVG	PR+	WS	TPW
1930	Phi-N	0	0	....	14	1	0	0	0	43^{2}	68	44	39	6	1	18	9	1.969	8.04	68	7.71	.354	6	.462	-11	1	-0.8

• PHILLIPS, Ed Norman Edwin Phillips b: 9/20/1944, Ardmore, OK BR/TR, 6'1", 190 lbs. Deb: 4/9/1970

YEAR	TM-L	W	L	PCT	G	GS	CG	SH	SV	IP	H	R	ER	HR	HB	BB	SO	RAT	ERA	ERA+	CERA	OAV	BH	AVG	PR+	WS	TPW
1970	Bos-A	0	2	.000	18	0	0	0	0	23^{2}	29	14	14	4	2	10	23	1.648	5.32	74	6.48	.312	0	.000	-3	0	-0.4

• PHILLIPS, Jack John Stephen Phillips b: 5/24/1919, St. Louis, MO d: 6/16/1958, St. Louis, MO BR/TR, 6'1", 185 lbs. Deb: 7/13/1945

YEAR	TM-L	W	L	PCT	G	GS	CG	SH	SV	IP	H	R	ER	HR	HB	BB	SO	RAT	ERA	ERA+	CERA	OAV	BH	AVG	PR+	WS	TPW
1945	NY-N	0	0	....	1	0	0	0	0	4^{1}	5	5	5	1	1	4	0	2.077	10.38	38	9.26	.294	1	.500	-3	0	-0.3

• PHILLIPS, Jason Jason Charles Phillips b: 3/22/1974, Williamsport, PA BR/TR, 6'6", 225 lbs. Deb: 4/5/1999

YEAR	TM-L	W	L	PCT	G	GS	CG	SH	SV	IP	H	R	ER	HR	HB	BB	SO	RAT	ERA	ERA+	CERA	OAV	BH	AVG	PR+	WS	TPW
1999	Pit-N	0	0	....	6	0	0	0	0	7	11	9	9	2	0	6	7	2.429	11.57	39	11.24	.393	0	....	-5	0	-0.5
2002	Cle-A	1	3	.250	8	6	0	0	0	41^{2}	41	24	23	7	4	20	23	1.464	4.97	88	5.23	.259	0	....	-2	2	-0.2
2003	Cle-A	0	1	.000	3	0	0	0	0	5	9	5	5	1	0	2	2	2.200	9.00	49	10.22	.409	0	....	-3	0	-0.3
Total	**3**	1	4	.200	17	6	0	0	0	53^{2}	61	38	37	10	4	28	32	1.658	6.20	71	6.48	.293	0	....	-10	2	-1.0

• PHILLIPS, Red Clarence Lemuel Phillips b: 11/3/1908, Pauls Valley, OK d: 2/1/1988, Wichita, KS BR/TR, 6'3.5", 195 lbs. Deb: 7/24/1934

YEAR	TM-L	W	L	PCT	G	GS	CG	SH	SV	IP	H	R	ER	HR	HB	BB	SO	RAT	ERA	ERA+	CERA	OAV	BH	AVG	PR+	WS	TPW
1934	Det-A	2	0	1.000	7	1	1	0	1	23^{1}	31	17	16	1	0	16	3	2.014	6.17	71	6.54	.316	3	.250	-5	1	-0.4
1936	Det-A	2	4	.333	22	6	3	0	0	87^{1}	124	67	63	12	0	22	15	1.672	6.49	76	6.16	.332	10	.303	-14	2	-1.1
Total	**2**	4	4	.500	29	7	4	0	1	110^{2}	155	84	79	13	0	38	18	1.744	6.42	75	6.24	.329	13	.289	-19	3	-1.5

• PHILLIPS, Taylor William Taylor "T-Bone" Phillips b: 6/18/1933, Atlanta, GA BL/TL, 5'11", 185 lbs. Deb: 6/8/1956

YEAR	TM-L	W	L	PCT	G	GS	CG	SH	SV	IP	H	R	ER	HR	HB	BB	SO	RAT	ERA	ERA+	CERA	OAV	BH	AVG	PR+	WS	TPW
1956	Mil-N	5	3	.625	23	6	3	0	2	87^{2}	69	25	22	6	7	33	36	1.163	2.26	153	2.88	.223	0	.000	11	8	0.9
1957	Mil-N	3	2	.600	27	6	0	0	2	73	82	46	45	3	1	40	36	1.671	5.55	63	5.07	.300	2	.100	-18	0	-2.0
1958	Chi-N	7	10	.412	39	27	5	1	1	170^{1}	178	102	90	22	6	79	102	1.509	4.76	82	4.87	.266	3	.056	-14	4	-1.9
1959	Chi-N	0	2	.000	7	2	0	0	0	16^{2}	22	14	14	3	2	11	5	1.980	7.56	52	8.00	.319	0	.000	-7	0	-0.7
	Phi-N	1	4	.200	32	3	1	0	1	63	72	35	35	4	4	31	35	1.635	5.00	82	5.38	.303	1	.091	-6	2	-0.7
	Yr.	1	6	.143	39	5	1	0	1	79^{2}	94	49	49	7	6	42	40	1.707	5.54	73	5.93	.306	1	.067	-13	2	-1.4
1960	Phi-N	0	1	.000	10	1	0	0	0	14	21	13	13	2	1	4	6	1.786	8.36	46	7.21	.356	0	.000	-7	0	-0.7
1963	Chi-A	0	0	....	9	0	0	0	0	14	16	16	16	2	1	13	13	2.071	10.29	34	7.10	.302	0	.000	-11	0	-1.1
Total	**6**	16	22	.421	147	45	9	1	6	438^{2}	460	251	235	42	22	211	233	1.530	4.82	78	4.84	.275	6	.053	-52	14	-6.2

• PHILLIPS, Tom Thomas Gerald Phillips b: 4/5/1889, Phillipsburg, PA d: 4/12/1929, Phillipsburg, PA BR/TR, 6'2", 190 lbs. Deb: 9/13/1915

YEAR	TM-L	W	L	PCT	G	GS	CG	SH	SV	IP	H	R	ER	HR	HB	BB	SO	RAT	ERA	ERA+	CERA	OAV	BH	AVG	PR+	WS	TPW
1915	StL-A	1	3	.250	5	4	1	0	0	27^{1}	28	13	9	0	2	12	5	1.463	2.96	97	4.08	.283	1	.111	-1	1	-0.2
1919	Cle-A	3	2	.600	22	3	2	0	0	55	55	27	18	2	3	34	18	1.618	2.95	113	4.72	.272	4	.364	3	4	0.4
1921	Was-A	1	0	1.000	1	1	1	0	0	9	9	2	2	0	0	3	2	1.333	2.00	206	3.38	.290	0	.000	2	1	0.1
1922	Was-A	3	7	.300	17	7	2	1	0	70	72	43	38	2	4	22	19	1.343	4.89	79	3.56	.273	3	.150	-10	1	-1.0
Total	**4**	8	12	.400	45	15	6	1	0	161^{1}	164	85	67	4	9	71	44	1.457	3.74	95	4.03	.275	8	.186	-6	7	-0.7

• PHOEBUS, Tom Thomas Harold Phoebus b: 4/7/1942, Baltimore, MD BR/TR, 5'8", 185 lbs. Deb: 9/15/1966

YEAR	TM-L	W	L	PCT	G	GS	CG	SH	SV	IP	H	R	ER	HR	HB	BB	SO	RAT	ERA	ERA+	CERA	OAV	BH	AVG	PR+	WS	TPW
1966	Bal-A	2	1	.667	3	3	2	2	0	22	16	3	3	0	0	6	17	1.000	1.23	271	1.77	.213	1	.167	5	3	0.6
1967	Bal-A	14	9	.609	33	33	7	4	0	208	177	84	77	16	0	114	179	1.399	3.33	95	3.63	.227	11	.145	-8	9	-0.8
1968	Bal-A	15	15	.500	36	36	9	3	0	240^{2}	186	81	70	10	4	105	193	1.209	2.62	112	2.66	.212	15	.183	4	15	0.8
1969	Bal-A	14	7	.667	35	33	6	2	0	202	180	89	79	23	4	87	117	1.322	3.52	101	3.78	.241	15	.200	-7	11	-0.5
1970*	Bal-A	5	5	.500	27	21	3	0	0	135	106	58	46	11	6	62	72	1.244	3.07	119	3.17	.219	7	.163	6	7	0.5
1971	SD-N	3	11	.214	29	21	2	0	0	133^{1}	144	67	66	14	3	64	80	1.560	4.46	74	4.94	.280	6	.167	-16	2	-1.6
1972	SD-N	0	1	.000	1	1	0	0	0	5^{2}	3	5	5	2	0	6	8	1.588	7.94	41	5.82	.150	0	.000	-3	0	-0.3
	Chi-N	3	3	.500	37	1	0	0	6	83^{1}	76	40	35	9	2	45	59	1.452	3.78	101	4.25	.247	2	.133	0	5	0.0
	Yr.	3	4	.429	38	2	0	0	6	89	79	45	40	11	2	51	67	1.461	4.04	92	4.35	.241	2	.118	-3	5	-0.4
Total	**7**	56	52	.519	201	149	29	11	6	1030	888	427	381	85	19	489	725	1.337	3.33	100	3.57	.233	57	.170	-19	52	-1.4

• PHOENIX, Steve Steven Robert Phoenix b: 1/31/1968, Phoenix, AZ BR/TR, 6'2", 175 lbs. Deb: 7/30/1994

YEAR	TM-L	W	L	PCT	G	GS	CG	SH	SV	IP	H	R	ER	HR	HB	BB	SO	RAT	ERA	ERA+	CERA	OAV	BH	AVG	PR+	WS	TPW
1994	Oak-A	0	0	....	2	0	0	0	0	4^{1}	4	3	3	0	0	2	3	1.385	6.23	71	3.10	.235	0	....	-1	0	-0.1
1995	Oak-A	0	0	....	1	0	0	0	0	1^{2}	3	6	6	1	0	3	3	3.600	32.40	14	21.45	.429	0	....	-5	0	-0.5
Total	**2**	0	0	....	3	0	0	0	0	6	7	9	9	1	0	5	6	2.000	13.50	33	8.20	.292	0	....	-6	0	-0.6

• PHYLE, Bill William Joseph Phyle b: 6/25/1875, Duluth, MN d: 8/6/1953, Los Angeles, CA TR Deb: 9/17/1898 ♦

YEAR	TM-L	W	L	PCT	G	GS	CG	SH	SV	IP	H	R	ER	HR	HB	BB	SO	RAT	ERA	ERA+	CERA	OAV	BH	AVG	PR+	WS	TPW
1898	Chi-N	2	1	.667	3	3	3	2	0	23	24	15	2	0	2	6	4	1.304	0.78	457	3.33	.267	1	.111	7	2	0.6
1899	Chi-N	1	8	.111	10	9	9	0	1	83^{2}	92	58	39	2	4	29	10	1.446	4.20	89	3.96	.279	6	.176	-4	2	-0.6
1901	NY-N	7	10	.412	24	19	16	0	1	168^{2}	208	121	80	2	6	54	62	**1.553**	4.27	77	4.48	.301	12	.182	-14	3	-1.5
Total	**3**	10	19	.345	37	31	28	2	2	275^{1}	324	194	121	4	12	89	76	1.500	3.96	87	4.22	.292	32	.176	-11	7	-1.5

• PIATT, Doug Douglas William Piatt b: 9/26/1965, Beaver, PA BL/TR, 6'1", 185 lbs. Deb: 6/11/1991

YEAR	TM-L	W	L	PCT	G	GS	CG	SH	SV	IP	H	R	ER	HR	HB	BB	SO	RAT	ERA	ERA+	CERA	OAV	BH	AVG	PR+	WS	TPW
1991	Mon-N	0	0	....	21	0	0	0	0	34^{2}	29	11	10	3	0	17	29	1.327	2.60	139	3.50	.230	0	.000	4	3	0.4

• PIATT, Wiley Wiley Harold "Iron Man" Piatt b: 7/13/1874, Blue Creek, OH d: 9/20/1946, Cincinnati, OH BL/TL, 5'10", 175 lbs. Deb: 4/22/1898

YEAR	TM-L	W	L	PCT	G	GS	CG	SH	SV	IP	H	R	ER	HR	HB	BB	SO	RAT	ERA	ERA+	CERA	OAV	BH	AVG	PR+	WS	TPW
1898	Phi-N	24	14	.632	39	37	33	**6**	0	306	285	156	108	2	19	97	121	1.248	3.18	108	2.91	.245	32	.262	11	21	1.4
1899	Phi-N	23	15	.605	39	38	31	2	0	305	323	173	117	6	23	86	89	1.341	3.45	107	3.59	.272	33	.270	3	21	0.7
1900	Phi-N	9	10	.474	22	20	16	1	0	160^{2}	194	120	84	5	16	71	47	**1.649**	4.71	77	5.16	.298	17	.250	-19	6	-1.5
1901	Phi-A	5	12	.294	18	16	15	0	1	140	176	112	72	4	3	60	45	1.686	4.63	81	5.09	.304	13	.224	-14	5	-1.2
	Chi-A	4	2	.667	7	6	4	1	0	51^{2}	42	29	16	2	4	14	19	1.084	2.79	125	2.45	.220	2	.118	4	3	0.3
	Yr.	9	14	.391	25	22	19	1	1	191^{2}	218	141	88	6	7	74	64	1.523	4.13	90	4.38	.283	15	.200	-10	8	-0.9
1902	Chi-A	12	12	.500	32	30	22	2	0	246	263	129	96	3	7	66	96	1.337	3.51	96	3.38	.274	17	.200	-8	14	-0.5
1903	Bos-N	9	14	.391	25	23	18	0	0	181	198	107	64	5	4	61	100	1.431	3.18	100	3.92	.280	16	.225	-3	10	-0.1
Total	**6**	86	79	.521	182	170	139	12	1	1390^{1}	1481	826	557	27	76	455	517	1.392	3.61	97	3.73	.272	130	.239	-25	80	-1.0

• PICHARDO, Hipolito Hipolito Antonio (Balbina) Pichardo b: 8/22/1969, Esperanza, Dominican Republic BR/TR, 6'1", 185 lbs. Deb: 4/21/1992

YEAR	TM-L	W	L	PCT	G	GS	CG	SH	SV	IP	H	R	ER	HR	HB	BB	SO	RAT	ERA	ERA+	CERA	OAV	BH	AVG	PR+	WS	TPW
1992	KC-A	9	6	.600	31	24	1	1	0	143^{2}	148	71	63	9	3	49	59	1.371	3.95	103	3.84	.267	0	....	4	8	0.4
1993	KC-A	7	8	.467	30	25	2	0	0	165	183	85	74	10	6	53	70	1.430	4.04	113	4.22	.282	0	....	9	10	0.9
1994	KC-A	5	3	.625	45	0	0	0	3	67^{2}	82	42	37	4	7	24	36	1.567	4.92	102	5.19	.308	0	....	1	5	0.0
1995	KC-A	8	4	.667	44	0	0	0	1	64	66	34	31	4	4	30	43	1.500	4.36	110	4.27	.265	0	.000	2	5	0.2
1996	KC-A	3	5	.375	57	0	0	0	3	68	74	41	41	5	2	26	43	1.471	5.43	92	4.39	.284	0	....	-3	4	-0.3
1997	KC-A	3	5	.375	47	0	0	0	11	49	51	24	23	7	1	24	34	1.531	4.22	112	4.87	.271	0	....	2	5	0.2
1998	KC-A	7	8	.467	27	18	0	0	1	112^{1}	126	73	64	11	4	43	55	1.504	5.13	94	4.75	.280	0	.000	-2	6	-0.3
2000	Bos-A	6	3	.667	38	1	0	0	1	65	63	29	25	1	3	26	37	1.369	3.46	146	3.51	.260	0	.000	11	6	1.0
2001	Bos-A	2	1	.667	30	0	0	0	0	34^{2}	42	23	19	3	5	10	17	1.500	4.93	91	5.11	.300	0	....	-1	1	-0.1
2002	Hou-N	0	1	.000	1	0	0	0	0	0^{1}	3	3	3	0	0	2	0	15.00	81.00	5	87.43	.750	0	....	-3	0	-0.3
Total	**10**	50	44	.532	350	68	3	1	20	769^{2}	838	425	380	54	35	287	394	1.462	4.44	105	4.39	.279	0	.000	19	50	1.8

• PICHE, Ron Ronald Jacques Piche b: 5/22/1935, Verdun, Canada BR/TR, 5'11", 165 lbs. Deb: 5/30/1960 C

YEAR	TM-L	W	L	PCT	G	GS	CG	SH	SV	IP	H	R	ER	HR	HB	BB	SO	RAT	ERA	ERA+	CERA	OAV	BH	AVG	PR+	WS	TPW
1960	Mil-N	3	5	.375	37	0	0	0	9	48	48	26	19	3	3	23	38	1.479	3.56	96	4.10	.258	0	.000	-0	3	0.0
1961	Mil-N	2	2	.500	12	1	1	0	1	23^{1}	20	12	9	1	0	16	16	1.543	3.47	108	3.80	.238	0	.000	1	1	0.0
1962	Mil-N	3	2	.600	14	8	2	0	0	52	54	32	28	6	3	29	28	1.596	4.85	78	5.22	.273	1	.056	-6	1	-0.7
1963	Mil-N	1	1	.500	37	1	0	0	0	53	53	32	20	4	0	25	40	1.472	3.40	95	3.91	.256	0	.000	-2	1	-0.3
1965	Cal-A	0	3	.000	14	1	0	0	0	19^{2}	20	15	15	5	0	12	14	1.627	6.86	50	6.05	.267	0	.000	-8	0	-0.8
1966	StL-N	1	3	.250	20	0	0	0	2	25^{1}	21	13	12	4	1	18	21	1.539	4.26	84	4.41	.214	0	.000	-2	1	-0.3
Total	**6**	10	16	.385	134	11	3	0	12	221^{1}	216	130	103	23	7	123	157	1.532	4.19	84	4.49	.255	1	.024	-17	7	-2.1

YEAR TM-L	W	L	PCT	G	GS	CG	SH	SV	IP	H	R	ER	HR	HB	BB	SO	RAT	ERA	ERA+	CERA	OAV	BH	AVG	PR+	WS	TPW
• PICKETT, Charlie	Charles Albert Pickett b: 3/1/1883, Delaware, OH d: 5/20/1969, Springfield, OH BR/TR, 6'1", 175 lbs. Deb: 6/21/1910																									
1910 StL-N	0	0	....	2	0	0	0	0	6	7	2	1	0	0	2	2	1.500	1.50	198	3.82	.280	0	....	1	0	0.2
• PICKETT, Ricky	Cecil Lee Pickett b: 1/19/1970, Fort Worth, TX BL/TL, 6'1" Deb: 4/28/1998																									
1998 Ari-N	0	0	....	2	0	0	0	0	0^2	3	6	6	0	0	4	2	10.50	81.00	5	58.14	.600	0	....	-6	0	-0.6
• PICKFORD, Kevin	Kevin Patrick Pickford b: 3/12/1975, Fresno, CA BL/TL, 6'4", 200 lbs. Deb: 5/16/2002																									
2002 SD-N	0	2	.000	16	4	0	0	0	30	37	23	20	3	3	20	18	1.900	6.00	63	7.06	.314	0	.000	-7	0	-0.8
• PICKREL, Clarence	Clarence Douglas Pickrel b: 3/28/1911, Gretna, VA d: 11/4/1983, Rocky Mount, VA BR/TR, 6'1", 180 lbs. Deb: 4/22/1933																									
1933 Phi-N	1	0	1.000	9	0	0	0	0	13^2	20	7	6	0	1	3	6	1.683	3.95	96	5.72	.357	0	.000	-0	1	0.0
1934 Bos-N	0	0	....	10	1	0	0	0	16	24	9	9	0	0	7	9	1.938	5.06	76	6.09	.333	0	.000	-2	0	-0.2
Total 2	1	0	1.000	19	1	0	0	0	29^2	44	16	15	0	1	10	15	1.820	4.55	84	5.92	.344	0	.000	-2	1	-0.3
• PICO, Jeff	Jeffrey Mark Pico b: 2/12/1966, Antioch, CA BR/TR, 6'1", 190 lbs. Deb: 5/31/1988																									
1988 Chi-N	6	7	.462	29	13	3	2	1	112^2	108	57	52	6	0	37	57	1.287	4.15	87	3.19	.252	5	.147	-4	5	-0.5
1989 Chi-N	3	1	.750	53	5	0	0	2	90^2	99	43	38	8	0	31	38	1.434	3.77	100	4.09	.278	1	.100	0	5	0.0
1990 Chi-N	4	4	.500	31	8	0	0	2	92	120	53	49	7	1	37	37	1.707	4.79	85	5.56	.321	6	.273	-5	4	-0.3
Total 3	13	12	.520	113	26	3	2	5	295^1	327	153	139	21	1	105	132	1.463	4.24	90	4.20	.282	12	.182	-9	14	-0.8
• PICONE, Mario	Mario Peter "Babe" Picone b: 7/5/1926, Brooklyn, NY BR/TR, 5'11", 180 lbs. Deb: 9/27/1947																									
1947 NY-N	0	0	....	2	1	0	0	0	7	10	6	6	1	0	2	1	1.714	7.71	53	6.69	.345	1	.500	-3	0	-0.2
1952 NY-N	0	1	.000	2	1	0	0	0	9	11	8	7	2	0	5	3	1.778	7.00	53	7.07	.306	0	.000	-3	0	-0.4
1954 NY-N	0	0	....	5	0	0	0	0	13^2	13	8	8	1	0	11	6	1.756	5.27	77	5.28	.283	0	.000	-2	0	-0.2
Cin-N	0	1	.000	4	1	0	0	0	10^1	9	7	7	3	0	7	1	1.548	6.10	69	5.85	.243	0	.000	-2	0	-0.2
Yr.	0	1	.000	9	1	0	0	0	24	22	15	15	4	0	18	7	1.667	5.63	73	5.53	.265	0	.000	-4	0	-0.4
Total 3	0	2	.000	13	3	0	0	0	40	43	29	28	7	0	25	11	1.700	6.30	63	6.08	.291	1	.167	-10	0	-1.0
• PIECHOTA, Al	Aloysius Edward "Pie" Piechota b: 1/19/1914, Chicago, IL d: 6/13/1996, Chicago, IL BR/TR, 6', 195 lbs. Deb: 5/7/1940																									
1940 Bos-N	2	5	.286	21	8	2	0	0	61	68	45	39	6	0	41	18	1.787	5.75	65	5.57	.278	4	.200	-15	0	-1.4
1941 Bos-N	0	0	....	1	0	0	0	0	1	0	0	0	0	0	1	0	1.000	0.00	....	0.80	.000	0	....	0	0	0.0
Total 2	2	5	.286	22	8	2	0	0	62	68	45	39	6	0	42	18	1.774	5.66	66	5.49	.278	4	.200	-15	0	-1.4
• PIEH, Cy	Edwin John Pieh b: 9/29/1886, Waunakee, WI d: 9/12/1945, Jacksonville, FL BR/TR, 6'2", 190 lbs. Deb: 9/6/1913																									
1913 NY-A	1	0	1.000	4	0	0	0	0	10^1	10	8	5	0	0	7	6	1.645	4.35	69	4.01	.250	1	.250	-2	1	-0.1
1914 NY-A	3	4	.429	18	4	1	0	0	62^1	68	41	35	6	0	29	24	1.556	5.05	54	4.98	.289	2	.118	-17	0	-1.8
1915 NY-A	4	5	.444	21	8	3	2	0	94	78	40	30	2	5	39	46	1.245	2.87	102	2.94	.234	2	.067	-1	5	-0.4
Total 3	8	9	.471	43	12	4	2	0	166^2	156	89	70	8	5	75	76	1.386	3.78	75	3.77	.256	5	.098	-19	6	-2.4
• PIERCE, Billy	Walter William Pierce b: 4/2/1927, Detroit, MI BL/TL, 5'10", 160 lbs. Deb: 6/1/1945																									
1945 Det-A	0	0	....	5	0	0	0	0	10	6	2	2	1	1	10	10	1.600	1.80	195	4.33	.182	0	.000	2	1	0.2
1948 Det-A	3	0	1.000	22	5	0	0	0	55^1	47	40	39	5	1	51	36	1.771	6.34	69	5.02	.234	5	.294	-11	1	-0.9
1949 Chi-A	7	15	.318	32	26	8	0	0	171^2	145	89	74	11	0	112	95	1.497	3.88	108	3.73	.228	9	.176	5	9	0.4
1950 Chi-A	12	16	.429	33	29	15	1	1	219^1	189	112	97	11	2	137	118	1.486	3.98	113	3.62	.228	20	.260	8	16	1.1
1951 Chi-A	15	14	.517	37	28	18	1	2	240^1	237	93	81	14	1	73	113	1.290	3.03	133	3.30	.258	16	.203	23	19	2.2
1952 Chi-A	15	12	.556	33	32	14	4	1	255^1	214	76	73	12	3	79	144	1.148	2.57	142	2.52	.227	17	.187	28	23	2.9
1953 Chi-A★	18	12	.600	40	33	19	7	3	271^1	216	94	82	20	3	102	**186**	1.172	2.72	148	2.69	**.218**	11	.126	**38**	24	3.4
1954 Chi-A	9	10	.474	36	26	12	4	3	188^2	179	86	73	15	3	86	148	1.405	3.48	107	3.80	.249	11	.193	3	10	0.4
1955 Chi-A★	15	10	.600	33	26	16	6	1	205^2	162	50	45	16	3	64	157	1.099	**1.97**	**200**	**2.49**	.213	12	.171	42	**23**	**4.2**
1956 Chi-A★	20	9	.690	35	33	**21**	1	1	276^1	261	108	102	24	3	100	192	1.306	3.32	124	3.55	.249	16	.157	22	21	1.7
1957 Chi-A★	**20**	12	.625	37	34	**16**	4	2	257	228	98	93	18	1	71	171	1.163	3.26	115	2.74	.234	17	.172	9	18	0.7
1958 Chi-A★	17	11	.607	35	32	**19**	3	2	245	204	83	73	33	1	66	144	1.102	2.68	136	2.93	.227	17	.205	23	**22**	2.5
1959* Chi-A★	14	15	.483	34	33	12	2	0	224	217	98	90	26	3	62	114	1.246	3.62	104	3.57	.253	13	.191	-1	14	0.2
1960 Chi-A	14	7	.667	32	30	8	1	0	196^1	201	81	79	24	0	46	108	1.258	3.62	104	3.73	.266	12	.179	1	13	0.2
1961 Chi-A★	10	9	.526	39	28	5	1	3	180	190	85	76	17	1	54	106	1.356	3.80	103	3.98	.275	8	.143	3	11	0.1
1962* SF-N	16	6	.727	30	23	7	2	1	162^1	147	67	63	19	3	35	76	1.121	3.49	109	3.04	.239	12	.214	6	13	0.7
1963 SF-N	3	11	.214	38	13	3	1	8	99	106	49	47	12	1	20	52	1.273	4.27	75	3.81	.272	4	.129	-10	3	-1.1
1964 SF-N	3	0	1.000	34	1	0	0	4	49	40	14	12	6	0	10	29	1.020	2.20	162	2.47	.222	3	.333	7	7	0.8
Total 18	211	169	.555	585	432	193	38	32	3306^2	2989	1325	1201	234	30	1178	1999	1.260	3.27	119	3.26	.240	203	.184	198	248	19.7
• PIERCE, Ed	Edward John Pierce b: 10/6/1968, Arcadia, CA BL/TL, 6'1", 185 lbs. Deb: 9/6/1992																									
1992 KC-A	0	0	....	2	1	0	0	0	5^1	9	2	2	1	0	4	3	2.438	3.38	120	11.87	.429	0	....	0	0	0.0
• PIERCE, Jeff	Jeffrey Charles Pierce b: 6/7/1969, Poughkeepsie, NY BR/TR, 6'1", 190 lbs. Deb: 4/26/1995																									
1995 Bos-A	0	3	.000	12	0	0	0	0	15	16	12	11	0	0	14	12	2.000	6.60	74	5.31	.286	0	....	-3	0	-0.3
• PIERCE, Ray	Raymond Lester "Lefty" Pierce b: 6/6/1897, Emporia, KS d: 5/4/1963, Denver, CO BL/TL, 5'7", 156 lbs. Deb: 5/12/1924																									
1924 Chi-N	0	0	....	6	0	0	0	0	7^1	7	6	6	2	0	4	2	1.500	7.36	53	5.41	.269	0	....	-3	0	-0.3
1925 Phi-N	5	4	.556	23	8	4	0	0	90	134	67	55	7	1	24	18	1.756	5.50	87	6.37	.356	5	.179	-4	4	-0.3
1926 Phi-N	2	7	.222	37	7	1	0	0	84^2	128	71	53	3	1	35	18	1.925	5.63	74	6.42	.348	3	.125	-11	0	-1.3
Total 3	7	11	.389	66	15	5	0	0	182	269	144	114	12	2	63	38	1.824	5.64	78	6.35	.349	8	.154	-18	4	-1.9
• PIERCE, Tony	Tony Michael Pierce b: 1/29/1946, Brunswick, GA BR/TL, 6'1", 190 lbs. Deb: 4/14/1967																									
1967 KC-A	3	4	.429	49	6	0	0	7	97^2	79	42	33	6	5	30	61	1.116	3.04	105	2.57	.221	0	.000	1	6	-0.1
1968 Oak-A	1	2	.333	17	3	0	0	1	32^2	39	16	14	3	1	10	16	1.500	3.86	73	4.72	.295	0	.000	-4	0	-0.5
Total 2	4	6	.400	66	9	0	0	8	130^1	118	58	47	9	6	40	77	1.212	3.25	94	3.11	.241	0	.000	-2	6	-0.6
• PIERCY, Bill	William Benton "Wild Bill" Piercy b: 5/2/1896, El Monte, CA d: 8/28/1951, Long Beach, CA BR/TR, 6'1.5", 185 lbs. Deb: 10/3/1917																									
1917 NY-A	0	1	.000	1	1	1	0	0	9	9	3	3	0	0	2	4	1.222	3.00	89	2.71	.257	0	.000	-0	0	0.0
1921* NY-A	5	4	.556	14	10	5	1	0	81^2	82	40	27	4	7	28	35	1.347	2.98	142	3.74	.263	6	.214	10	7	1.0
1922 Bos-A	3	9	.250	29	12	7	1	0	121^1	140	77	63	2	6	62	24	1.665	4.67	88	4.79	.304	5	.147	-6	4	-0.7
1923 Bos-A	8	17	.320	30	24	11	0	0	187^1	193	105	71	5	14	73	51	1.420	3.41	120	3.88	.277	7	.132	15	11	1.2
1924 Bos-A	5	7	.417	23	18	3	0	0	121	156	87	80	4	10	66	20	1.835	5.95	73	6.07	.335	6	.154	-20	2	-2.1
1926 Chi-N	6	5	.545	19	5	1	0	0	90^1	96	52	45	1	6	37	31	1.472	4.48	86	3.93	.280	9	.257	-8	4	-0.7
Total 6	27	43	.386	116	70	28	2	0	610^2	676	364	289	16	43	268	165	1.546	4.26	97	4.47	.292	33	.173	-8	28	-1.3
• PIERETTI, Marino	Marino Paul "Chick" Pieretti b: 9/23/1920, Luccia, Italy d: 1/30/1981, San Francisco, CA BR/TR, 5'7", 158 lbs. Deb: 4/19/1945																									
1945 Was-A	14	13	.519	44	27	14	3	2	233^1	235	114	86	3	1	91	66	1.397	3.32	93	3.32	.257	18	.222	-4	10	-0.3
1946 Was-A	2	2	.500	30	2	1	0	0	62	70	48	41	9	2	40	20	1.774	5.95	56	6.15	.292	3	.214	-17	0	-1.7
1947 Was-A	2	4	.333	23	10	2	1	0	83^1	97	50	39	3	2	47	32	1.728	4.21	88	5.00	.287	6	.231	-3	2	-0.3
1948 Was-A	0	2	.000	8	1	0	0	0	11^2	18	14	14	1	0	7	6	2.143	10.80	40	8.35	.375	0	.000	-8	0	-0.8
Chi-A	8	10	.444	21	18	4	0	1	120	117	70	66	6	0	52	28	1.408	4.95	86	3.62	.262	7	.179	-10	6	-1.1
Yr.	8	12	.400	29	19	4	0	1	131^2	135	84	80	7	0	59	34	1.473	5.47	78	4.04	.273	7	.171	-19	6	-1.9
1949 Chi-A	4	6	.400	39	9	0	0	4	116	131	77	71	10	0	54	25	1.595	5.51	76	4.89	.289	9	.237	-18	3	-1.7
1950 Cle-A	0	1	.000	29	1	0	0	1	47^1	45	24	22	2	0	30	11	1.585	4.18	104	4.11	.253	2	.286	1	3	0.1
Total 6	30	38	.441	194	68	21	4	8	673^2	713	397	339	34	5	321	188	1.535	4.53	82	4.25	.272	45	.217	-60	24	-5.8
• PIEROTTI, Al	Albert Felix Pierotti b: 10/24/1895, Boston, MA d: 2/12/1964, Everett, MA BR/TR, 5'10.5", 195 lbs. Deb: 8/9/1920																									
1920 Bos-N	1	1	.500	6	2	2	0	0	25	23	9	8	2	0	9	12	1.280	2.88	106	3.38	.250	2	.250	0	2	0.0
1921 Bos-N	0	1	.000	2	0	0	0	0	1^2	3	4	4	0	0	3	1	3.600	21.60	17	12.33	.375	0	.000	-3	0	-0.3
Total 2	1	2	.333	8	2	2	0	0	26^2	26	13	12	2	0	12	13	1.425	4.05	80	3.94	.260	2	.222	-3	2	-0.3

YEAR TM-L	W	L	PCT	G	GS	CG	SH	SV	IP	H	R	ER	HR	HB	BB	SO	RAT	ERA	ERA+	CERA	OAV	BH	AVG	PR+	WS	TPW
• PIERRO, Bill	William Leonard "Wild Bill" Pierro b: 4/15/1926, Brooklyn, NY BR/TR, 6'1", 155 lbs. Deb: 7/17/1950																									
1950 Pit-N	0	2	.000	12	3	0	0	0	29	33	34	34	2	2	28	13	2.103	10.55	42	6.94	.289	2	.222	-20	0	-1.9
• PIERSOLL, Chris	Christopher Earl Piersoll b: 9/25/1977, Van Nuys, CA BR/TR, 6'4", 195 lbs. Deb: 8/31/2001																									
2001 Cin-N	0	0	....	11	0	0	0	0	11^1	12	4	3	0	1	6	7	1.588	2.38	191	4.47	.267	0	....	3	1	0.3
• PIERSON, William	William Morris Pierson b: 6/14/1899, Atlantic City, NJ d: 2/20/1959, Atlantic City, NJ BL/TL, 6'2", 180 lbs. Deb: 7/4/1918																									
1918 Phi-A	0	1	.000	8	1	0	0	0	21^2	20	10	8	0	2	20	6	1.846	3.32	88	5.59	.286	1	.250	-2	1	-0.2
1919 Phi-A	0	0	....	2	1	0	0	0	7^2	9	3	3	0	0	8	4	2.217	3.52	97	7.34	.333	1	.333	0	0	0.0
1924 Phi-A	0	0	....	1	0	0	0	0	2^2	3	1	1	0	0	3	0	2.250	3.38	127	6.88	.300	0	....	0	0	0.0
Total 3	0	1	.000	11	2	0	0	0	32	32	14	12	0	2	31	10	1.969	3.38	93	6.12	.299	2	.286	-1	1	-0.1
• PIKTUZIS, George	George Richard Piktuzis b: 1/3/1932, Chicago, IL d: 11/28/1993, Long Beach, CA BR/TL, 6'2", 200 lbs. Deb: 4/25/1956																									
1956 Chi-N	0	0	....	2	0	0	0	0	5	6	4	4	1	0	2	3	1.600	7.20	52	6.48	.333	0	....	-2	0	-0.2
• PILLETTE, Duane	Duane Xavier "Dee" Pillette b: 7/24/1922, Detroit, MI BR/TR, 6'3", 205 lbs. Deb: 7/19/1949																									
1949 NY-A	2	4	.333	12	3	2	0	0	37^1	43	20	18	6	0	19	9	1.661	4.34	93	5.90	.299	0	.000	-2	1	-0.3
1950 NY-A	0	0	....	4	0	0	0	0	7	9	3	1	0	0	3	4	1.714	1.29	334	4.97	.321	0	....	2	1	0.2
StL-A	3	5	.375	24	7	1	0	2	73^2	104	62	58	6	2	44	18	2.009	7.09	70	7.21	.337	3	.136	-15	1	-1.5
Yr.	3	5	.375	28	7	1	0	2	80^2	113	65	59	6	2	47	22	1.983	6.58	75	7.02	.335	3	.136	-13	2	-1.3
1951 StL-A	6	14	.300	35	24	6	1	0	191	205	113	106	14	5	115	65	**1.675**	4.99	88	5.07	.276	8	.136	-8	6	-1.1
1952 StL-A	10	13	.435	30	30	9	1	0	205^1	222	94	82	14	7	55	62	1.349	3.59	109	3.85	.274	12	.182	6	11	0.7
1953 StL-A	7	13	.350	31	25	5	1	0	166^2	181	90	83	16	2	62	58	1.458	4.48	94	4.38	.277	7	.132	-4	8	-0.5
1954 Bal-A	10	14	.417	25	25	11	1	0	179	158	79	62	9	1	67	66	1.257	3.12	115	2.90	.234	7	.132	11	12	1.0
1955 Bal-A	0	3	.000	7	5	0	0	0	20^2	31	16	15	0	0	14	13	2.177	6.53	58	7.26	.344	1	.167	-6	0	-0.6
1956 Phi-N	0	0	....	20	0	0	0	0	23^1	32	21	17	2	0	12	10	1.886	6.56	57	6.16	.330	0	.000	-7	0	-0.7
Total 8	38	66	.365	188	119	34	4	2	904	985	498	442	67	17	391	305	1.522	4.40	94	4.52	.277	38	.140	-24	40	-2.8
• PILLETTE, Herman	Herman Polycarp "Old Folks" Pillette b: 12/26/1895, St. Paul, OR d: 4/30/1960, Sacramento, CA BR/TR, 6'2", 190 lbs. Deb: 7/30/1917																									
1917 Cin-N	0	0	....	1	0	0	0	0	1	4	2	2	0	0	0	0	4.000	18.00	14	22.42	.571	0	....	-2	0	-0.2
1922 Det-A	19	12	.613	40	37	18	4	1	274^2	270	110	87	6	15	95	71	1.329	2.85	136	3.32	.258	17	.172	37	22	3.3
1923 Det-A	14	19	.424	47	36	14	0	1	250^1	280	138	107	7	6	83	64	1.450	3.85	100	3.97	.288	21	.247	3	15	0.6
1924 Det-A	1	1	.500	19	3	1	0	1	37^2	46	30	20	1	3	14	13	1.593	4.78	86	4.65	.297	4	.364	-3	1	-0.2
Total 4	34	32	.515	107	76	33	4	3	563^2	600	280	216	14	24	192	148	1.405	3.45	112	3.73	.275	42	.215	35	38	3.5
• PILLION, Squiz	Cecil Randolph Pillion b: 4/13/1894, Hartford, CT d: 9/30/1962, Pittsburgh, PA BL/TL, 6', 178 lbs. Deb: 8/20/1915																									
1915 Phi-A	0	0	....	2	0	0	0	0	5^1	10	5	4	0	1	2	0	2.250	6.75	43	9.31	.400	0	.000	-2	0	-0.3
• PINA, Horacio	Horacio (Garcia) Pina b: 3/12/1945, Coahuila, Mexico BR/TR, 6'2", 177 lbs. Deb: 8/14/1968																									
1968 Cle-A	1	1	.500	12	3	0	0	2	31^1	24	7	6	0	1	15	24	1.245	1.72	172	2.60	.218	0	.000	4	3	0.4
1969 Cle-A	4	2	.667	31	4	0	0	1	46^2	44	29	27	6	5	27	32	1.521	5.21	72	5.12	.256	3	.500	-7	1	-0.7
1970 Was-A	5	3	.625	61	0	0	0	6	71	66	25	22	4	3	35	41	1.423	2.79	127	3.69	.250	0	.000	5	7	0.5
1971 Was-A	1	1	.500	56	0	0	0	2	57^2	47	26	23	2	4	31	38	1.353	3.59	92	3.18	.227	0	.000	-2	3	-0.2
1972 Tex-A	2	7	.222	60	0	0	0	15	76	61	33	27	3	8	43	60	1.368	3.20	94	3.51	.228	1	.200	-0	5	0.0
1973* Oak-A	6	3	.667	47	0	0	0	8	88	58	31	27	8	8	34	41	1.045	2.76	128	2.51	.193	0	....	5	8	0.5
1974 Chi-N	3	4	.429	34	0	0	0	4	47^1	49	22	21	4	2	28	32	1.627	3.99	95	4.91	.268	1	.200	1	3	0.1
Cal-A	1	2	.333	11	0	0	0	0	11^2	9	3	3	1	0	3	6	1.029	2.31	148	2.07	.209	0	....	2	1	0.2
1978 Phi-N	0	0	....	2	0	0	0	0	2^1	0	0	0	0	0	0	4	.000	0.00	....	0.00	.000	0	.000	1	0	0.1
Total 8	23	23	.500	314	7	0	0	38	432	358	176	156	28	31	216	278	1.329	3.25	106	3.50	.232	5	.185	9	31	1.0
• PINEDA, Luis	Luis A. Pineda b: 10/17/1974, San Cristobal, Dominican Republic BR/TR, 6'1", 160 lbs. Deb: 8/4/2001																									
2001 Det-A	0	1	.000	16	0	0	0	0	18^1	16	10	10	2	0	14	13	1.636	4.91	88	4.73	.239	0	....	-1	1	-0.1
2002 Cin-N	1	3	.250	26	2	0	0	0	32^1	25	16	15	4	2	24	31	1.515	4.18	102	4.54	.221	0	.000	0	2	0.0
Total 2	1	4	.200	42	2	0	0	0	50^2	41	26	25	6	2	38	44	1.559	4.44	96	4.61	.228	0	.000	-1	3	-0.1
• PINEIRO, Joel	Joel Alberto Pineiro b: 9/25/1978, Rio Piedras, Puerto Rico BR/TR, 6'1", 180 lbs. Deb: 8/8/2000																									
2000 Sea-A	1	0	1.000	8	1	0	0	0	19^1	25	13	12	3	0	13	10	1.966	5.59	81	7.44	.316	0	....	-2	0	-0.2
2001* Sea-A	6	2	.750	17	11	0	0	0	75^1	50	24	17	2	3	21	56	.942	2.03	204	1.71	.191	0	....	16	7	1.5
2002 Sea-A	14	7	.667	37	28	2	1	0	194^1	189	75	70	24	7	54	136	1.250	3.24	130	3.77	.256	1	.143	23	14	2.2
2003 Sea-A	16	11	.593	32	32	3	**2**	0	211^2	192	94	89	19	6	76	151	1.266	3.78	114	3.43	.241	0	.000	7	13	0.6
Total 4	37	20	.649	94	72	5	3	0	500^2	456	206	188	48	16	164	353	1.238	3.38	127	3.46	.243	1	.091	43	34	4.1
• PINNANCE, Ed	Edward D. "Peanuts" Pinnance b: 10/22/1879, Walpole Island, Canada d: 12/12/1944, Walpole Island, Canada BL/TR, 6'1", 180 lbs. Deb: 9/14/1903																									
1903 Phi-A	0	0	....	2	1	0	0	1	7	5	2	2	0	0	2	2	1.000	2.57	119	1.70	.200	0	.000	0	1	0.0
• PINTO, Lerton	William Lerton Pinto b: 4/8/1899, Chillicothe, OH d: 5/13/1983, Oxnard, CA BL/TL, 6', 190 lbs. Deb: 5/23/1922																									
1922 Phi-N	0	1	.000	9	0	0	0	0	24^2	31	20	14	1	0	14	4	1.824	5.11	91	5.68	.320	1	.111	-1	1	-0.1
1924 Phi-N	0	0	....	3	0	0	0	0	4	7	4	4	1	0	0	1	1.750	9.00	50	10.21	.467	0	.000	-2	0	-0.2
Total 2	0	1	.000	12	0	0	0	0	28^2	38	24	18	2	0	14	5	1.814	5.65	82	6.31	.340	1	.100	-3	1	-0.4
• PIPGRAS, Ed	Edward John Pipgras b: 6/15/1904, Schleswig, IA d: 4/13/1964, Currie, MN BR/TR, 6'2.5", 175 lbs. Deb: 8/25/1932																									
1932 Bro-N	0	1	.000	5	1	0	0	0	10	16	11	6	2	0	6	5	2.200	5.40	71	9.19	.348	0	.000	-2	0	-0.2
• PIPGRAS, George	George William Pipgras b: 12/20/1899, Ida Grove, IA d: 10/19/1986, Gainesville, FL BR/TR, 6'1.5", 185 lbs. Deb: 6/9/1923 U																									
1923 NY-A	1	3	.250	8	2	2	0	0	33^1	34	22	22	2	1	25	12	1.770	5.94	66	5.29	.276	0	.000	-8	0	-0.9
1924 NY-A	0	1	.000	9	1	0	0	1	15^1	20	18	17	0	4	18	4	2.478	9.98	42	9.30	.351	1	.333	-10	0	-0.9
1927* NY-A	10	3	.769	29	21	9	1	0	166^1	148	81	76	2	1	77	81	1.353	4.11	94	3.04	.247	16	.239	-5	9	-0.4
1928* NY-A	**24**	13	.649	46	**38**	22	4	3	**300^2**	314	132	113	4	3	103	139	1.387	3.38	111	3.26	.272	18	.157	17	21	1.2
1929 NY-A	18	12	.600	39	33	13	3	0	225^1	229	132	106	16	5	95	125	1.438	4.23	91	4.00	.264	12	.143	-12	10	-1.5
1930 NY-A	15	15	.500	44	30	15	**3**	4	221	230	133	101	9	8	70	111	1.357	4.11	104	3.51	.263	12	.150	7	11	0.4
1931 NY-A	7	6	.538	36	14	6	1	3	137^2	134	73	58	8	2	58	59	1.395	3.79	105	3.58	.251	1	.024	2	7	-0.4
1932* NY-A	16	9	.640	32	27	14	2	0	219	235	120	102	15	6	87	111	1.470	4.19	97	4.16	.269	18	.220	-2	13	-0.2
1933 NY-A	2	2	.500	4	4	3	0	0	33	32	13	12	1	0	12	14	1.333	3.27	119	3.12	.252	1	.091	3	2	0.2
Bos-A	9	8	.529	22	17	9	2	1	128^1	140	65	58	5	2	45	56	1.442	4.07	108	3.91	.276	9	.196	5	8	0.4
Yr.	11	10	.524	26	21	12	2	1	161^1	172	78	70	6	2	57	70	1.419	3.90	110	3.75	.271	10	.175	7	10	0.6
1934 Bos-A	0	0	....	2	1	0	0	0	3^1	4	3	3	1	0	3	0	2.100	8.10	59	9.29	.308	0	.000	-1	0	-0.1
1935 Bos-A	0	1	.000	5	1	0	0	0	5	9	9	8	3	1	5	2	2.800	14.40	33	17.65	.391	0	....	-5	0	-0.5
Total 11	102	73	.583	276	189	93	16	12	1488^1	1529	801	676	66	33	598	714	1.429	4.09	98	3.77	.266	88	.163	-11	81	-2.6
• PIPPEN, Cotton	Henry Harold Pippen b: 4/2/1911, Cisco, TX d: 2/15/1981, Williams, CA BR/TR, 6'2", 180 lbs. Deb: 8/28/1936																									
1936 StL-N	0	2	.000	6	3	0	0	0	21	37	18	18	5	2	8	8	2.143	7.71	51	10.62	.402	1	.167	-9	0	-0.9
1939 Phi-A	4	11	.267	25	17	5	0	1	118^2	169	97	79	13	1	40	33	1.761	5.99	79	6.19	.329	3	.086	-13	2	-1.4
Det-A	0	1	.000	3	2	0	0	0	14	18	13	11	1	0	6	5	1.714	7.07	69	5.12	.310	2	.400	-3	0	-0.3
Yr.	4	12	.250	28	19	5	0	1	132^2	187	110	90	14	1	46	38	1.756	6.11	77	6.08	.327	5	.125	-17	2	-1.7
1940 Det-A	1	2	.333	4	3	0	0	0	21^1	29	16	16	3	1	10	9	1.828	6.75	70	6.88	.326	0	.000	-4	0	-0.5
Total 3	5	16	.238	38	25	5	0	1	175	253	144	124	22	4	64	55	1.811	6.38	72	6.72	.336	6	.111	-30	2	-3.1
• PIRTLE, Gerry	Gerald Eugene Pirtle b: 12/3/1947, Tulsa, OK BR/TR, 6'1", 185 lbs. Deb: 7/2/1978																									
1978 Mon-N	0	2	.000	19	0	0	0	0	25^2	33	24	17	5	2	23	14	2.182	5.96	59	8.50	.314	0	....	-8	0	-0.8

YEAR TM-L	W	L	PCT	G	GS	CG	SH	SV	IP	H	R	ER	HR	HB	BB	SO	RAT	ERA	ERA+	CERA	OAV	BH	AVG	PR+	WS	TPW
• PISCIOTTA, Marc	Marc George Pisciotta b: 8/7/1970, Edison, NJ BR/TR, 6'5", 240 lbs. Deb: 6/30/1997																									
1997 Chi-N	3	1	.750	24	0	0	0	0	28^1	20	10	10	1	1	16	21	1.271	3.18	136	2.83	.200	0	.000	4	4	0.3
1998 Chi-N	1	2	.333	43	0	0	0	0	44	44	21	20	4	2	32	31	1.727	4.09	108	5.35	.259	1	.333	2	2	0.3
1999 KC-A	0	2	.000	8	0	0	0	0	8^1	9	8	8	1	0	10	3	2.280	8.64	58	8.28	.281	0	....	-4	0	-0.3
Total 3	4	5	.444	75	0	0	0	0	80^2	73	39	38	6	3	58	55	1.624	4.24	106	4.77	.242	1	.250	2	6	0.3
• PITLOCK, Skip	Lee Patrick Thomas Pitlock b: 11/6/1947, Hillside, IL BL/TL, 6'2", 180 lbs. Deb: 6/12/1970																									
1970 SF-N	5	5	.500	18	15	1	0	0	87	92	48	45	13	4	48	56	1.609	4.66	85	5.58	.274	2	.080	-5	3	-0.5
1974 Chi-A	3	3	.500	40	5	0	0	1	105^2	103	58	52	7	7	55	68	1.495	4.43	84	4.34	.257	0	....	-7	3	-0.7
1975 Chi-A	0	0	....	1	0	0	0	0	0	1	0	0	0	0	0	0	....	....	....	∞	1.000	0	....	0	0	0.0
Total 3	8	8	.500	59	20	1	0	1	192^2	196	106	97	20	11	103	124	1.552	4.53	85	4.90	.266	2	.080	-12	6	-1.2
• PITTINGER, Togie	Charles Reno Pittinger b: 1/12/1872, Greencastle, PA d: 1/14/1909, Greencastle, PA BL/TR, 6'2", 175 lbs. Deb: 4/26/1900																									
1900 Bos-N	2	9	.182	18	13	8	0	0	114	135	97	65	7	8	54	27	1.658	5.13	80	5.28	.294	6	.130	-15	2	-1.8
1901 Bos-N	13	16	.448	34	33	27	1	0	281^1	288	135	94	7	8	76	129	1.294	3.01	120	3.18	.263	11	.110	15	21	0.7
1902 Bos-N	27	16	.628	46	40	36	7	0	389^1	360	139	109	4	16	128	174	1.253	2.52	112	2.95	.246	20	.136	10	24	0.2
1903 Bos-N	18	22	.450	44	39	35	3	1	351^2	396	205	136	12	17	143	140	1.533	3.48	92	4.62	.294	14	.109	-18	17	-2.5
1904 Bos-N	15	21	.417	38	38	35	5	0	335^1	298	149	99	1	14	144	146	1.318	2.66	103	3.06	.242	13	.107	13	19	0.4
1905 Phi-N	23	14	.622	**46**	37	29	4	2	337^1	311	155	116	3	16	104	136	1.230	3.09	94	2.88	.247	19	.156	-12	19	-1.5
1906 Phi-N	8	10	.444	20	16	9	2	0	129^2	128	62	49	2	12	50	43	1.373	3.40	77	3.55	.252	4	.091	-10	3	-1.3
1907 Phi-N	9	5	.643	16	12	8	1	0	102	101	43	34	3	5	35	37	1.333	3.00	81	3.49	.261	5	.139	-8	6	-1.0
Total 8	115	113	.504	262	228	187	23	3	2040^2	2017	985	702	39	96	734	832	1.348	3.10	98	3.47	.260	92	.124	-26	111	-6.7
• PITTSLEY, Jim	James Michael Pittsley b: 4/3/1974, Du Bois, PA BR/TR, 6'7", 215 lbs. Deb: 5/23/1995																									
1995 KC-A	0	0	....	1	1	0	0	0	3^1	7	5	5	3	0	1	0	2.400	13.50	35	19.40	.438	0	....	-3	0	-0.3
1997 KC-A	5	8	.385	21	21	0	0	0	112	120	72	68	15	6	54	52	1.554	5.46	86	5.32	.277	1	.500	-10	4	-0.9
1998 KC-A	1	1	.500	39	2	0	0	0	68^1	88	56	50	13	2	37	44	1.829	6.59	73	7.35	.322	0	.000	-13	0	-1.2
1999 KC-A	1	2	.333	5	5	0	0	0	23^1	33	22	18	2	1	15	7	2.057	6.94	72	7.77	.337	0	....	-6	0	-0.5
Mil-N	0	1	.000	15	0	0	0	0	18^2	20	12	10	3	1	10	13	1.607	4.82	94	5.74	.274	0	.000	-0	1	0.0
Total 4	7	12	.368	81	29	0	0	0	225^2	268	167	151	36	10	117	116	1.706	6.02	79	6.43	.300	1	.200	-32	5	-3.0
• PITULA, Stan	Stanley Pitula b: 3/23/1931, Hackensack, NJ d: 8/15/1965, Hackensack, NJ BR/TR, 5'10", 170 lbs. Deb: 4/24/1957																									
1957 Cle-A	2	2	.500	23	5	1	0	0	59^2	67	37	33	8	2	32	17	1.659	4.98	75	5.81	.296	3	.200	-8	1	-0.8
• PIZARRO, Juan	Juan Ramon (Cordova) Pizarro b: 2/7/1937, Santurce, Puerto Rico BL/TL, 5'11", 190 lbs. Deb: 5/4/1957																									
1957* Mil-N	5	6	.455	24	10	3	0	0	99^1	99	58	51	16	1	51	68	1.510	4.62	76	4.96	.261	9	.250	-14	2	-1.2
1958* Mil-N	6	4	.600	16	10	7	1	1	96^2	75	36	29	12	4	47	84	1.262	2.70	130	3.51	.212	8	.250	8	8	1.1
1959 Mil-N	6	2	.750	29	14	6	2	0	133^2	117	61	56	13	8	70	126	1.399	3.77	94	4.08	.237	5	.122	-3	6	-0.3
1960 Mil-N	6	7	.462	21	17	3	0	0	114^2	105	63	58	13	4	72	88	1.544	4.55	75	4.72	.244	11	.275	-13	3	-1.0
1961 Chi-A	14	7	.667	39	25	12	1	2	194^2	164	73	66	17	4	89	188	1.300	3.05	128	3.38	.226	17	.246	20	18	2.5
1962 Chi-A	12	14	.462	36	32	9	1	1	203^1	182	97	86	16	1	97	173	1.372	3.81	103	3.56	.236	11	.159	3	11	0.3
1963 Chi-A★	16	8	.667	32	28	10	3	1	214^2	177	69	57	14	3	63	163	1.118	2.39	147	2.57	.224	13	.178	25	19	2.9
1964 Chi-A★	19	9	.679	33	33	11	4	0	239	193	78	68	23	3	55	162	1.038	2.56	135	2.43	.219	19	.211	17	19	2.3
1965 Chi-A	6	3	.667	18	18	2	1	0	97	96	42	37	9	1	37	65	1.371	3.43	93	3.86	.254	8	.235	-4	5	-0.1
1966 Chi-A	8	6	.571	34	9	1	0	3	88^2	91	49	37	9	1	39	42	1.466	3.76	84	4.34	.269	4	.154	-6	3	-0.6
1967 Pit-N	8	10	.444	50	9	1	1	9	107	99	55	47	10	2	52	96	1.411	3.95	85	3.79	.245	7	.259	-8	5	-0.7
1968 Pit-N	1	1	.500	12	0	0	0	0	11	14	7	4	2	1	10	6	2.182	3.27	89	8.30	.311	0	.000	-1	0	-0.1
Bos-A	6	8	.429	19	12	6	0	2	107^2	97	46	43	15	0	44	84	1.310	3.59	88	3.79	.242	5	.161	-5	5	-0.4
1969 Bos-A	0	1	.000	6	0	0	0	2	9	14	7	6	2	0	6	4	2.222	6.00	63	9.82	.359	1	.333	-2	0	-0.2
Cle-A	3	3	.500	48	4	1	0	4	82^2	67	34	29	6	2	49	44	1.403	3.16	119	3.57	.229	3	.200	6	6	0.7
Oak-A	1	1	.500	3	0	0	0	1	7^2	3	2	2	1	0	3	4	.783	2.35	146	1.41	.125	1	.500	1	1	0.1
Yr.	4	5	.444	57	4	1	0	7	99^1	84	43	37	9	2	58	52	1.430	3.35	112	3.97	.236	5	.250	5	7	0.6
1970 Chi-N	0	0	....	12	0	0	0	1	15^2	16	9	8	2	1	9	14	1.596	4.60	98	5.24	.262	0	.000	-0	1	0.0
1971 Chi-N	7	6	.538	16	14	6	3	0	101^1	78	43	39	10	2	40	67	1.164	3.46	114	2.83	.209	6	.176	7	8	0.9
1972 Chi-N	4	5	.444	16	7	1	0	1	59^1	66	28	26	7	1	32	24	1.652	3.94	97	5.50	.293	3	.143	-1	3	-0.1
1973 Chi-N	0	1	.000	2	0	0	0	0	4	6	5	5	1	1	1	3	1.750	11.25	35	8.24	.353	0	.000	-3	0	-0.3
Hou-N	2	2	.500	15	1	0	0	0	23^1	28	17	17	1	1	11	10	1.671	6.56	55	4.93	.301	0	.000	-8	0	-0.8
Yr.	2	3	.400	17	1	0	0	0	27^1	34	22	22	2	2	12	13	1.683	7.24	51	5.41	.309	0	.000	-11	0	-1.1
1974* Pit-N	1	1	.500	7	2	0	0	0	24	20	11	5	2	0	11	7	1.292	1.88	184	3.01	.220	2	.333	4	2	0.5
Total 18	131	105	.555	488	245	79	17	28	2034^1	1807	890	776	201	41	888	1522	1.325	3.43	103	3.64	.237	133	.202	24	125	5.2
• PLADSON, Gordie	Gordon Cecil Pladson b: 7/31/1956, New Westminster, Canada BR/TR, 6'4", 210 lbs. Deb: 9/7/1979																									
1979 Hou-N	0	0	....	4	0	0	0	0	4	9	2	2	1	0	2	2	2.750	4.50	78	14.76	.450	0	....	-0	0	0.0
1980 Hou-N	0	4	.000	12	6	0	0	0	41^1	38	23	20	3	0	16	13	1.306	4.35	76	3.39	.244	0	.000	-5	0	-0.6
1981 Hou-N	0	0	....	2	0	0	0	0	4	9	4	4	0	0	3	3	3.000	9.00	37	12.64	.429	0	....	-3	0	-0.3
1982 Hou-N	0	0	....	2	0	0	0	0	1^1	10	8	8	0	0	2	0	9.000	54.00	6	61.66	.769	0	....	-8	0	-0.8
Total 4	0	4	.000	20	6	0	0	0	50^2	66	37	34	4	0	23	18	1.757	6.04	55	6.55	.314	0	.000	-15	0	-1.7
• PLANETA, Emil	Emil Joseph Planeta b: 1/31/1909, Higganum, CT d: 2/2/1963, Rocky Hill, CT BR/TR, 6', 190 lbs. Deb: 9/20/1931																									
1931 NY-N	0	0	....	2	0	0	0	0	5^1	7	7	6	0	0	4	0	2.063	10.13	36	5.88	.292	0	.000	-4	0	-0.4
• PLANK, Ed	Edward Arthur Plank b: 4/9/1952, Chicago, IL BR/TR, 6'1", 205 lbs. Deb: 9/6/1978																									
1978 SF-N	0	0	....	5	0	0	0	0	6^2	6	3	3	1	0	2	1	1.200	4.05	85	3.63	.273	0	....	-0	0	0.0
1979 SF-N	0	0	....	4	0	0	0	0	3^2	9	5	3	0	0	2	1	3.000	7.36	47	12.46	.450	0	....	-2	0	-0.2
Total 2	0	0	....	9	0	0	0	0	10^1	15	8	6	1	0	4	2	1.839	5.23	66	6.77	.357	0	....	-2	0	-0.2
• PLANK, Eddie	Edward Stewart "Gettysburg Eddie" Plank b: 8/31/1875, Gettysburg, PA d: 2/24/1926, Gettysburg, PA BL/TL, 5'11.5", 175 lbs. Deb: 5/13/1901 HOF: 1946																									
1901 Phi-A	17	13	.567	33	32	28	1	0	260^2	254	133	96	2	7	68	90	1.235	3.31	114	2.83	.253	18	.182	13	19	0.9
1902 Phi-A	20	15	.571	36	32	31	1	0	300	319	140	110	5	18	61	107	1.267	3.30	111	3.30	.273	35	.292	13	25	1.8
1903 Phi-A	23	16	.590	**43**	**40**	33	3	0	336	317	128	89	5	23	65	176	1.137	2.38	128	2.65	.249	25	.187	**28**	28	2.8
1904 Phi-A	26	17	.605	44	43	37	7	0	357^1	311	111	86	2	19	86	201	1.111	2.17	123	2.32	.235	31	.240	29	29	3.6
1905* Phi-A	24	12	.667	41	**41**	**35**	4	0	346^2	287	113	87	3	24	75	210	1.044	2.26	117	2.14	.228	29	.230	26	31	3.2
1906 Phi-A	19	6	.760	26	25	21	5	0	211^2	173	70	53	1	15	51	108	1.058	2.25	121	2.13	.226	17	.233	11	16	1.5
1907 Phi-A	24	16	.600	43	40	33	**8**	0	343^2	282	115	84	5	17	85	183	1.068	2.20	118	2.16	.226	26	.211	14	29	1.8
1908 Phi-A	14	16	.467	34	28	21	4	1	244^2	202	71	59	1	9	46	135	1.014	2.17	118	1.91	.224	16	.180	16	19	1.8
1909 Phi-A	19	10	.655	34	33	24	3	0	265^1	215	74	52	1	8	62	132	1.044	1.76	136	1.95	.224	21	.219	16	22	2.2
1910 Phi-A	16	10	.615	38	32	22	1	2	250^1	218	89	56	3	8	55	123	1.091	2.01	118	2.25	.237	11	.128	5	16	0.2
1911* Phi-A	23	8	.742	40	30	24	**6**	**4**	256^2	237	85	60	2	14	77	149	1.223	2.10	150	2.87	.255	18	.191	28	22	2.6
1912 Phi-A	26	6	.813	37	30	23	5	2	259^2	234	90	64	1	6	83	110	1.221	2.22	140	2.63	.245	24	.267	21	25	2.5
1913* Phi-A	18	10	.643	41	30	18	7	4	242^2	211	87	70	3	5	57	151	1.104	2.60	106	2.24	.234	8	.105	4	16	0.4
1914* Phi-A	15	7	.682	34	22	12	4	3	185^1	178	68	59	2	6	42	110	1.187	2.87	91	2.80	.266	9	.150	-6	11	-0.7
1915 StL-F	21	11	.656	42	31	23	6	3	268^1	212	75	62	1	3	54	147	.991	2.08	**149**	**1.74**	.218	24	.258	26	29	**3.4**
1916 StL-A	16	15	.516	37	26	17	3	3	235^2	203	78	61	2	6	67	88	1.146	2.33	118	2.39	.237	15	.185	5	17	0.6
1917 StL-A	5	6	.455	20	14	8	1	1	131	105	39	26	2	2	38	26	1.092	1.79	145	2.14	.225	4	.105	12	7	1.2
Total 17	326	194	.627	623	529	410	69	23	4495^2	3958	1566	1174	41	190	1072	2246	1.119	2.35	122	2.39	.239	331	.206	261	361	29.7
• PLANTENBERG, Erik	Erik John Plantenberg b: 10/30/1968, Renton, WA BB/TL, 6'1", 180 lbs. Deb: 7/31/1993																									
1993 Sea-A	0	0	....	20	0	0	0	1	9^2	11	7	7	0	1	12	3	2.379	6.52	68	7.45	.282	0	....	-2	0	-0.2
1994 Sea-A	0	0	....	6	0	0	0	0	7	4	0	0	0	1	7	1	1.571	0.00	....	3.89	.174	0	....	4	1	0.4

YEAR	TM-L	W	L	PCT	G	GS	CG	SH	SV	IP	H	R	ER	HR	HB	BB	SO	RAT	ERA	ERA+	CERA	OAV	BH	AVG	PR+	WS	TPW
1997	Phi-N	0	0	....	35	0	0	0	0	25^2	25	14	14	1	1	12	12	1.442	4.91	87	3.88	.255	0	....	-2	1	-0.2
Total	**3**	0	0	....	61	0	0	0	1	42^1	40	21	21	1	3	31	16	1.677	4.46	96	4.70	.250	0	....	-0	2	0.0

• PLEIS, Bill William Pleis b: 8/5/1937, St. Louis, MO BL/TL, 5'10", 175 lbs. Deb: 4/16/1961

YEAR	TM-L	W	L	PCT	G	GS	CG	SH	SV	IP	H	R	ER	HR	HB	BB	SO	RAT	ERA	ERA+	CERA	OAV	BH	AVG	PR+	WS	TPW
1961	Min-A	4	2	.667	37	0	0	0	2	56^1	59	35	31	4	4	34	32	1.651	4.95	86	4.90	.266	1	.111	-3	3	-0.4
1962	Min-A	2	5	.286	21	4	0	0	3	45	46	27	22	7	1	14	31	1.333	4.40	93	4.16	.264	4	.286	-2	2	-0.1
1963	Min-A	6	2	.750	36	4	1	0	0	68	67	37	33	10	0	16	37	1.221	4.37	83	3.60	.258	2	.125	-5	3	-0.5
1964	Min-A	4	1	.800	47	0	0	0	4	50^2	43	23	22	6	1	31	42	1.461	3.91	92	4.16	.232	1	.250	-1	3	-0.1
1965*	Min-A	4	4	.500	41	2	0	0	4	51^1	49	20	17	3	0	27	33	1.481	2.98	119	3.77	.250	0	.000	3	4	0.2
1966	Min-A	1	2	.333	8	0	0	0	0	9^1	5	6	2	1	0	4	9	.964	1.93	186	1.79	.152	0	....	2	1	0.2
Total	**6**	21	16	.568	190	10	1	0	13	280^2	269	148	127	31	6	126	184	1.407	4.07	94	4.02	.251	8	.160	-7	16	-0.7

• PLESAC, Dan Daniel Thomas Plesac b: 2/4/1962, Gary, IN BL/TL, 6'5", 215 lbs. Deb: 4/11/1986

YEAR	TM-L	W	L	PCT	G	GS	CG	SH	SV	IP	H	R	ER	HR	HB	BB	SO	RAT	ERA	ERA+	CERA	OAV	BH	AVG	PR+	WS	TPW
1986	Mil-A	10	7	.588	51	0	0	0	14	91	81	34	30	5	0	29	75	1.209	2.97	146	2.86	.240	0	....	14	13	1.4
1987	Mil-A★	5	6	.455	57	0	0	0	23	79^1	63	30	23	8	3	23	89	1.084	2.61	175	2.67	.213	0	....	18	14	1.7
1988	Mil-A★	1	2	.333	50	0	0	0	30	52^1	46	14	14	2	0	12	52	1.108	2.41	165	2.36	.234	0	....	9	10	0.9
1989	Mil-A★	3	4	.429	52	0	0	0	33	61^1	47	16	16	6	0	17	52	1.043	2.35	163	2.39	.213	0	....	10	11	1.0
1990	Mil-A	3	7	.300	66	0	0	0	24	69	67	36	34	5	3	31	65	1.420	4.43	87	3.97	.257	0	....	-4	6	-0.4
1991	Mil-A	2	7	.222	45	10	0	0	8	92^1	92	49	44	12	3	39	61	1.419	4.29	93	4.48	.263	0	....	-3	4	-0.3
1992	Mil-A	5	4	.556	44	4	0	0	1	79	64	28	26	5	3	35	54	1.253	2.96	130	3.04	.229	0	....	6	6	0.6
1993	Chi-N	2	1	.667	57	0	0	0	0	62^2	74	37	33	10	0	21	47	1.516	4.74	84	5.15	.298	0	.000	-6	3	-0.6
1994	Chi-N	2	3	.400	54	0	0	0	1	54^2	61	30	28	9	1	13	53	1.354	4.61	90	4.59	.279	0	.000	-3	2	-0.3
1995	Pit-N	4	4	.500	58	0	0	0	3	60^1	53	26	24	3	1	27	57	1.326	3.58	120	3.09	.237	1	.250	5	6	0.6
1996	Pit-N	6	5	.545	73	0	0	0	11	70^1	67	35	32	4	0	24	76	1.294	4.09	107	3.12	.247	0	.000	3	8	0.2
1997	Tor-A	2	4	.333	73	0	0	0	1	50^1	47	22	20	8	0	19	61	1.311	3.58	128	3.86	.244	0	....	5	5	0.5
1998	Tor-A	4	3	.571	78	0	0	0	4	50	41	23	21	4	1	16	55	1.140	3.78	123	2.76	.224	0	....	5	7	0.5
1999	Tor-A	0	3	.000	30	0	0	0	0	22^2	28	21	21	4	0	9	26	1.632	8.34	59	5.87	.308	0	....	-9	0	-0.8
*	Ari-N	2	1	.667	34	0	0	0	1	21^2	22	9	8	3	0	8	27	1.385	3.32	138	4.19	.259	0	.000	3	2	0.3
2000	Ari-N	5	1	.833	62	0	0	0	0	40	34	21	14	4	0	26	45	1.500	3.15	149	3.98	.228	0	....	7	4	0.7
2001	Tor-A	4	5	.444	62	0	0	0	1	45^1	34	18	18	4	1	24	68	1.279	3.57	128	3.07	.207	0	....	5	5	0.5
2002	Tor-A	1	2	.333	19	0	0	0	0	13^1	11	5	5	1	0	6	14	1.275	3.38	137	3.02	.216	0	....	2	1	0.2
	Phi-N	2	1	.667	41	0	0	0	1	23	16	12	12	5	0	12	27	1.217	4.70	83	3.45	.190	0	....	-2	2	-0.2
2003	Phi-N	2	1	.667	58	0	0	0	2	33^1	29	12	10	3	1	11	37	1.200	2.70	148	3.04	.228	0	....	5	4	0.5
Total	**18**	65	71	.478	1064	14	0	0	158	1072	977	478	433	105	17	402	1041	1.286	3.64	116	3.47	.242	1	.067	70	113	6.7

• PLITT, Norman Norman William Plitt b: 2/21/1893, York, PA d: 2/1/1954, New York, NY BR/TR, 5'11", 180 lbs. Deb: 4/26/1918

YEAR	TM-L	W	L	PCT	G	GS	CG	SH	SV	IP	H	R	ER	HR	HB	BB	SO	RAT	ERA	ERA+	CERA	OAV	BH	AVG	PR+	WS	TPW
1918	Bro-N	0	0	....	1	0	0	0	0	2	3	1	1	0	0	1	0	2.000	4.50	62	8.05	.429	1	1.000	-0	1	0.0
1927	Bro-N	2	6	.250	19	8	1	0	0	62^1	73	40	34	3	1	36	9	1.749	4.91	81	5.31	.303	4	.222	-7	1	-0.7
	NY-N	1	0	1.000	3	0	0	0	0	7^1	9	3	3	0	1	1	0	1.364	3.68	105	4.23	.310	0	.000	0	1	0.0
	Yr.	3	6	.333	22	8	1	0	0	69^2	82	43	37	3	2	37	9	1.708	4.78	83	5.20	.304	4	.211	-7	2	-0.7
Total	**2**	3	6	.333	23	8	1	0	0	71^2	85	44	38	3	2	38	9	1.716	4.77	82	5.28	.307	5	.250	-7	3	-0.7

• PLODINEC, Tim Timothy Alfred Plodinec b: 1/27/1947, Aliquippa, PA BR/TR, 6'4", 190 lbs. Deb: 6/2/1972

YEAR	TM-L	W	L	PCT	G	GS	CG	SH	SV	IP	H	R	ER	HR	HB	BB	SO	RAT	ERA	ERA+	CERA	OAV	BH	AVG	PR+	WS	TPW
1972	StL-N	0	0	....	1	0	0	0	0	0^1	3	1	1	0	0	0	0	9.000	27.00	13	67.29	.750	0	....	-1	0	-0.1

• PLUNK, Eric Eric Vaughn Plunk b: 9/3/1963, Wilmington, CA BR/TR, 6'5", 217 lbs. Deb: 5/12/1986

YEAR	TM-L	W	L	PCT	G	GS	CG	SH	SV	IP	H	R	ER	HR	HB	BB	SO	RAT	ERA	ERA+	CERA	OAV	BH	AVG	PR+	WS	TPW
1986	Oak-A	4	7	.364	26	15	0	0	0	120^1	91	75	71	14	5	102	98	1.604	5.31	73	4.81	.214	0	....	-19	2	-1.9
1987	Oak-A	4	6	.400	32	11	0	0	2	95	91	53	50	8	2	62	90	1.611	4.74	87	4.72	.253	0	....	-5	4	-0.5
1988*	Oak-A	7	2	.778	49	0	0	0	5	78	62	27	26	6	1	39	79	1.295	3.00	126	3.14	.217	0	....	6	7	0.6
1989	Oak-A	1	1	.500	23	0	0	0	1	28^2	17	7	7	1	1	12	24	1.012	2.20	167	1.83	.172	0	....	4	3	0.4
	NY-A	7	5	.583	27	7	0	0	0	75^2	65	36	31	9	0	52	61	1.546	3.69	105	4.58	.237	0	....	1	5	0.1
	Yr.	8	6	.571	50	7	0	0	1	104^1	82	43	38	10	1	64	85	1.399	3.28	117	3.82	.220	0	....	6	8	0.6
1990	NY-A	6	3	.667	47	0	0	0	0	72^2	58	27	22	6	2	43	67	1.390	2.72	146	3.65	.225	0	....	10	7	1.0
1991	NY-A	2	5	.286	43	8	0	0	0	111^2	128	69	59	18	1	62	103	1.701	4.76	87	5.99	.286	0	....	-7	3	-0.7
1992	Cle-A	9	6	.600	58	0	0	0	4	71^2	61	31	29	5	0	38	50	1.381	3.64	107	3.48	.229	0	....	3	6	0.3
1993	Cle-A	4	5	.444	70	0	0	0	15	71	61	29	22	5	0	30	77	1.282	2.79	155	3.02	.226	0	....	12	9	1.2
1994	Cle-A	7	2	.778	41	0	0	0	3	71	61	25	20	3	2	37	73	1.380	2.54	186	3.35	.231	0	....	17	9	1.6
1995*	Cle-A	6	2	.750	56	0	0	0	2	64	48	19	19	5	4	27	71	1.172	2.67	176	2.91	.211	0	....	15	8	1.4
1996*	Cle-A	3	2	.600	56	0	0	0	2	77^2	56	21	21	6	3	34	85	1.159	2.43	201	2.72	.203	0	....	21	11	2.0
1997*	Cle-A	4	5	.444	55	0	0	0	0	65^2	62	37	34	12	1	36	66	1.492	4.66	101	4.78	.245	0	.000	1	3	0.1
1998	Cle-A	3	1	.750	37	0	0	0	0	41	44	23	22	6	2	15	38	1.439	4.83	99	4.91	.282	0	....	-0	3	0.0
	Mil-N	1	2	.333	26	0	0	0	1	31^2	33	14	13	3	3	15	36	1.516	3.69	116	4.88	.270	0	.000	2	2	0.2
1999	Mil-N	4	4	.500	68	0	0	0	0	75^1	71	44	42	15	5	43	63	1.513	5.02	90	5.33	.251	0	....	-3	4	-0.3
Total	**14**	72	58	.554	714	41	0	0	35	1151	1009	537	488	122	32	647	1081	1.439	3.82	110	4.15	.236	0	.000	56	86	5.3

• PLYMPTON, Jeff Jeffrey Hunter Plympton b: 11/24/1965, Framingham, MA BR/TR, 6'2", 205 lbs. Deb: 6/15/1991

YEAR	TM-L	W	L	PCT	G	GS	CG	SH	SV	IP	H	R	ER	HR	HB	BB	SO	RAT	ERA	ERA+	CERA	OAV	BH	AVG	PR+	WS	TPW
1991	Bos-A	0	0	....	4	0	0	0	0	5^1	5	0	0	0	0	4	2	1.688	0.00	....	4.39	.263	0	....	3	1	0.3

• POAT, Ray Raymond Willis Poat b: 12/19/1917, Chicago, IL d: 4/29/1990, Oak Lawn, IL BR/TR, 6'2", 200 lbs. Deb: 4/15/1942

YEAR	TM-L	W	L	PCT	G	GS	CG	SH	SV	IP	H	R	ER	HR	HB	BB	SO	RAT	ERA	ERA+	CERA	OAV	BH	AVG	PR+	WS	TPW
1942	Cle-A	1	3	.250	4	4	1	1	0	18^1	24	11	11	1	1	9	8	1.800	5.40	64	5.68	.296	0	.000	-4	0	-0.5
1943	Cle-A	2	5	.286	17	4	1	0	0	45	44	22	22	3	0	20	31	1.422	4.40	71	3.79	.259	2	.154	-7	0	-0.9
1944	Cle-A	4	8	.333	36	6	1	0	1	80^2	82	50	46	9	0	37	40	1.475	5.13	64	4.40	.265	0	.000	-17	1	-2.1
1947	NY-N	4	3	.571	7	7	5	0	0	60	53	18	17	8	0	13	25	1.100	2.55	160	2.96	.238	4	.190	10	6	1.2
1948	NY-N	11	10	.524	39	24	7	3	0	157^2	162	95	76	21	3	67	57	1.452	4.34	91	4.48	.262	7	.125	-6	5	-0.8
1949	NY-N	0	0	....	2	0	0	0	0	2^1	8	6	5	0	0	1	0	3.857	19.29	21	21.22	.615	0	....	-4	0	-0.4
	Pit-N	0	1	.000	11	2	0	0	0	36	52	29	25	6	0	15	17	1.861	6.25	67	7.17	.335	1	.100	-8	0	-0.9
	Yr.	0	1	.000	13	2	0	0	0	38^1	60	35	30	6	0	16	17	1.983	7.04	59	8.03	.357	1	.100	-12	0	-1.3
Total	**6**	22	30	.423	116	47	15	4	1	400	425	231	202	48	4	162	178	1.468	4.55	81	4.55	.271	14	.115	-38	12	-4.2

• PODBIELAN, Bud Clarence Anthony Podbielan b: 3/6/1924, Curlew, WA d: 10/26/1982, Syracuse, NY BR/TR, 6'1.5", 170 lbs. Deb: 4/25/1949

YEAR	TM-L	W	L	PCT	G	GS	CG	SH	SV	IP	H	R	ER	HR	HB	BB	SO	RAT	ERA	ERA+	CERA	OAV	BH	AVG	PR+	WS	TPW
1949	Bro-N	0	1	.000	7	1	0	0	0	12^1	9	9	5	1	1	9	5	1.459	3.65	112	3.87	.205	0	.000	0	0	0.0
1950	Bro-N	5	4	.556	20	10	2	0	1	72^2	93	47	43	10	2	29	28	1.679	5.33	77	6.02	.307	3	.107	-12	2	-1.3
1951	Bro-N	2	2	.500	27	5	1	0	0	79^2	67	32	31	9	2	36	26	1.293	3.50	112	3.54	.233	7	.304	2	5	0.3
1952	Bro-N	0	0	....	3	0	0	0	0	2	4	5	4	1	0	3	1	3.500	18.00	20	19.64	.444	0	....	-3	0	-0.3
	Cin-N	4	5	.444	24	7	4	1	1	86^2	78	30	27	8	1	26	22	1.200	2.80	134	3.12	.245	4	.160	9	8	0.9
	Yr.	4	5	.444	27	7	4	1	1	88^2	82	35	31	9	1	29	23	1.252	3.15	119	3.49	.251	4	.160	6	8	0.6
1953	Cin-N	6	16	.273	36	24	8	1	1	186^1	214	112	98	21	8	67	74	1.508	4.73	92	5.00	.290	7	.125	-12	7	-1.4
1954	Cin-N	7	10	.412	27	24	4	0	0	131	157	92	78	20	2	58	42	1.641	5.36	78	5.76	.300	6	.143	-18	3	-1.9
1955	Cin-N	1	2	.333	17	2	0	0	0	42	36	16	15	4	1	11	26	1.119	3.21	132	2.85	.234	2	.400	5	3	0.6
1957	Cin-N	0	1	.000	5	3	1	0	0	16	18	11	11	4	0	4	13	1.375	6.19	66	5.37	.290	0	.000	-4	0	-0.4
1959	Cle-A	0	1	.000	6	0	0	0	0	12^1	17	8	8	1	0	2	5	1.541	5.84	63	5.34	.354	0	.000	-3	0	-0.3
Total	**9**	25	42	.373	172	76	20	2	3	641	693	362	320	79	17	245	242	1.463	4.49	92	4.74	.279	29	.154	-36	28	-3.8

• PODGAJNY, Johnny John Sigmund "Specs" Podgajny b: 6/10/1920, Chester, PA d: 3/2/1971, Chester, PA BR/TR, 6'2", 173 lbs. Deb: 9/15/1940

YEAR	TM-L	W	L	PCT	G	GS	CG	SH	SV	IP	H	R	ER	HR	HB	BB	SO	RAT	ERA	ERA+	CERA	OAV	BH	AVG	PR+	WS	TPW
1940	Phi-N	1	3	.250	4	4	3	0	0	35	33	14	11	0	1	1	12	.971	2.83	138	1.96	.250	2	.167	4	3	0.4
1941	Phi-N	9	12	.429	34	24	8	0	0	181^1	191	96	93	8	4	70	53	1.439	4.62	80	3.89	.270	8	.129	-17	7	-2.0
1942	Phi-N	6	14	.300	43	23	6	0	0	186^2	191	95	81	9	11	63	40	1.361	3.91	85	3.75	.268	11	.183	-12	8	-1.4
1943	Phi-N	4	4	.500	13	5	3	0	0	64	77	32	30	4	0	16	13	1.453	4.22	80	4.36	.310	5	.250	-5	2	-0.5
	Pit-N	0	4	.000	15	5	0	0	0	34^1	37	28	18	1	0	13	7	1.456	4.72	74	3.61	.266	1	.143	-5	0	-0.5
	Yr.	4	8	.333	28	10	3	0	0	98^1	114	60	48	5	0	29	20	1.454	4.39	78	4.10	.295	6	.222	-10	2	-1.0

YEAR TM-L	W	L	PCT	G	GS	CG	SH	SV	IP	H	R	ER	HR	HB	BB	SO	RAT	ERA	ERA+	CERA	OAV	BH	AVG	PR+	WS	TPW
1946 Cle-A	0	0	....	6	0	0	0	0	9	13	8	5	0	0	2	4	1.667	5.00	66	4.60	.302	0	....	-2	0	-0.2
Total 5	20	37	.351	115	61	20	0	0	510^{1}	542	273	238	22	16	165	129	1.385	4.20	83	3.76	.273	27	.168	-37	20	-4.2
• PODRES, Johnny	John Joseph Podres b: 9/30/1932, Witherbee, NY BL/TL, 5'11", 192 lbs. Deb: 4/17/1953 C																									
1953* Bro-N	9	4	.692	33	18	3	1	0	115	126	62	54	12	1	64	82	1.652	4.23	101	5.24	.282	11	.306	-1	7	0.1
1954 Bro-N	11	7	.611	29	21	6	2	0	151^{2}	147	77	72	13	1	53	79	1.319	4.27	96	3.56	.255	17	.283	-3	10	0.2
1955* Bro-N	9	10	.474	27	24	5	2	0	159^{1}	160	80	70	15	4	57	114	1.362	3.95	103	3.97	.259	11	.183	1	8	0.0
1957 Bro-N	12	9	.571	31	27	10	**6**	3	196	168	64	58	15	1	44	109	1.082	**2.66**	**156**	**2.55**	.230	15	.208	33	19	3.4
1958 LA-N★	13	15	.464	39	31	10	2	1	210^{1}	208	96	87	27	2	78	143	1.360	3.72	110	4.13	.261	9	.127	8	14	0.5
1959* LA-N	14	9	.609	34	29	6	2	0	195	192	93	89	23	3	74	145	1.364	4.11	103	4.11	.261	16	.246	2	14	0.6
1960 LA-N★	14	12	.538	34	33	8	1	0	227^{2}	217	88	78	25	1	71	159	1.265	3.08	129	3.51	.250	9	.136	20	18	2.0
1961 LA-N	18	5	.783	32	29	6	1	0	182^{2}	192	81	76	27	4	51	124	1.330	3.74	116	4.33	.271	16	.232	11	16	1.2
1962 LA-N★	15	13	.536	40	40	8	0	0	255	270	121	108	20	3	71	178	1.337	3.81	95	3.75	.272	14	.159	-5	12	-0.4
1963* LA-N	14	12	.538	37	34	10	5	1	198^{1}	196	91	78	16	3	64	134	1.311	3.54	85	3.51	.257	9	.141	-10	8	-1.0
1964 LA-N	0	2	.000	2	2	0	0	0	2^{2}	5	5	5	1	0	3	0	3.000	16.88	19	14.88	.417	0	....	-4	0	-0.4
1965 LA-N	7	6	.538	27	22	2	1	1	134	126	57	51	17	2	39	63	1.231	3.43	95	3.51	.247	8	.178	-4	6	-0.4
1966 LA-N	0	0	....	1	0	0	0	0	1^{2}	2	0	0	0	0	1	1	1.800	0.00	....	3.96	.400	0	....	1	0	0.1
Det-A	4	5	.444	36	13	2	1	4	107^{2}	106	48	41	12	1	34	53	1.300	3.43	102	3.69	.259	7	.233	0	6	0.3
1967 Det-A	3	1	.750	21	8	0	0	1	63^{1}	58	29	27	12	1	11	34	1.089	3.84	85	3.39	.244	2	.100	-5	2	-0.6
1969 SD-N	5	6	.455	17	9	1	0	0	64^{2}	66	34	31	7	1	28	17	1.454	4.31	82	4.29	.264	1	.063	-5	3	-0.6
Total 15	148	116	.561	440	340	77	24	11	2265	2239	1026	925	242	28	743	1435	1.317	3.68	104	3.79	.259	145	.190	39	143	4.9
• POETZ, Joe	Joseph Frank "Bull Montana" Poetz b: 6/22/1900, St. Louis, MO d: 2/7/1942, St. Louis, MO BR/TR, 5'10.5", 175 lbs. Deb: 9/14/1926																									
1926 NY-N	0	1	.000	2	1	0	0	0	8	5	3	3	2	1	8	0	1.625	3.38	111	5.89	.192	0	.000	0	0	0.0
• POFFENBERGER, Boots	Cletus Elwood Poffenberger b: 7/1/1915, Williamsport, MD d: 9/1/1999, Williamsport, MD BR/TR, 5'10", 178 lbs. Deb: 6/11/1937																									
1937 Det-A	10	5	.667	29	16	5	0	3	137^{1}	147	83	71	8	4	79	35	1.646	4.65	100	4.82	.277	11	.216	2	10	0.2
1938 Det-A	6	7	.462	25	15	8	1	1	125	147	74	67	8	2	66	28	1.704	4.82	104	5.32	.297	8	.182	2	8	0.0
1939 Bro-N	0	0	....	3	1	0	0	0	5	7	3	3	1	0	4	2	2.200	5.40	75	8.70	.318	0	.000	-1	0	-0.1
Total 3	16	12	.571	57	32	13	1	4	267^{1}	301	160	141	17	6	149	65	1.683	4.75	101	5.13	.287	19	.198	3	18	0.1
• POHOLSKY, Tom	Thomas George Poholsky b: 8/26/1929, Detroit, MI d: 1/6/2001, Kirkwood, MO BR/TR, 6'3", 205 lbs. Deb: 4/20/1950																									
1950 StL-N	0	0	....	5	1	0	0	0	14^{2}	16	6	6	2	0	3	2	1.295	3.68	117	4.14	.281	0	.000	1	1	0.1
1951 StL-N	7	13	.350	38	26	10	1	1	195	204	106	96	15	0	68	70	1.395	4.43	89	3.93	.271	14	.209	-13	7	-1.2
1954 StL-N	5	7	.417	25	13	4	0	0	106	101	43	36	11	4	20	55	1.142	3.06	135	3.13	.254	4	.148	13	7	1.2
1955 StL-N	9	11	.450	30	24	8	2	0	151	143	71	64	26	2	35	66	1.179	3.81	106	3.58	.244	8	.182	6	10	0.5
1956 StL-N	9	14	.391	33	29	7	2	0	203	210	100	81	27	5	44	95	1.251	3.59	105	3.83	.268	11	.159	5	9	0.4
1957 Chi-N	1	7	.125	28	11	1	0	0	84	117	55	46	9	2	22	28	1.655	4.93	78	5.84	.330	2	.105	-9	0	-0.9
Total 6	31	52	.373	159	104	30	5	1	753^{2}	791	381	329	90	13	192	316	1.304	3.93	100	3.94	.270	39	.171	3	34	0.0
• POINDEXTER, Jennings	Chester Jennings "Jinx" Poindexter b: 9/30/1910, Pauls Valley, OK d: 3/3/1983, Norman, OK BL/TL, 5'10", 165 lbs. Deb: 9/15/1936																									
1936 Bos-A	0	2	.000	3	3	0	0	0	10^{2}	13	11	8	0	0	16	2	2.719	6.75	79	8.46	.302	0	.000	-2	0	-0.2
1939 Phi-N	0	0	....	11	1	0	0	0	30^{1}	29	19	14	0	0	15	12	1.451	4.15	95	3.29	.250	2	.200	-1	1	-0.1
Total 2	0	2	.000	14	4	0	0	0	41	42	30	22	0	0	31	14	1.780	4.83	90	4.64	.264	2	.143	-2	1	-0.3
• POLCHOW, Lou	Louis William Polchow b: 3/14/1881, Mankato, MN d: 8/15/1912, Good Thunder, MN, 5'9" Deb: 9/14/1902																									
1902 Cle-A	0	1	.000	1	1	1	0	0	8	9	5	5	0	0	4	2	1.625	5.63	61	4.16	.284	0	.000	-2	0	-0.2
• POLE, Dick	Richard Henry Pole b: 10/13/1950, Trout Creek, MI BR/TR, 6'3", 210 lbs. Deb: 8/3/1973 C																									
1973 Bos-A	3	2	.600	12	7	0	0	0	54^{2}	70	35	34	4	0	18	24	1.610	5.60	72	5.41	.318	0	....	-10	1	-1.0
1974 Bos-A	1	1	.500	15	2	0	0	1	45	55	28	21	6	1	13	32	1.511	4.20	91	5.29	.304	0	....	-1	1	-0.1
1975* Bos-A	4	6	.400	18	11	2	1	0	89^{2}	102	46	44	11	2	32	42	1.494	4.42	92	4.90	.290	0	....	-3	5	-0.3
1976 Bos-A	6	5	.545	31	15	1	0	0	120^{2}	131	62	58	8	2	48	49	1.483	4.33	90	4.35	.279	0	.000	-4	5	-0.5
1977 Sea-A	7	12	.368	25	24	3	0	0	122^{1}	106	76	70	16	6	57	51	1.504	5.15	80	4.99	.270	0	....	-16	4	-1.6
1978 Sea-A	4	11	.267	21	18	2	0	0	98^{2}	122	82	71	16	3	41	41	1.652	6.48	59	6.10	.306	0	....	-29	0	-2.9
Total 6	25	37	.403	122	77	8	1	1	531	607	329	298	61	14	209	239	1.537	5.05	78	5.10	.290	0	.000	-64	16	-6.5
• POLITTE, Cliff	Clifford Anthony Politte b: 2/27/1974, Kirkwood, MO BR/TR, 5'11", 185 lbs. Deb: 4/2/1998																									
1998 StL-N	2	3	.400	8	8	0	0	0	37	45	32	26	6	1	18	22	1.703	6.32	66	6.28	.302	1	.071	-9	0	-0.9
1999 Phi-N	1	0	1.000	13	0	0	0	0	17^{2}	19	14	14	2	0	15	15	1.925	7.13	66	6.47	.275	0	....	-5	0	-0.5
2000 Phi-N	4	3	.571	12	8	0	0	0	59	55	24	24	8	0	27	50	1.390	3.66	127	4.20	.248	2	.133	6	5	0.6
2001 Phi-N	2	3	.400	23	0	0	0	0	26	24	8	7	2	1	8	23	1.231	2.42	175	3.11	.250	0	.000	5	3	0.5
2002 Phi-N	2	0	1.000	13	0	0	0	0	16^{1}	19	10	7	0	1	9	15	1.714	3.86	101	4.89	.288	0	.000	-0	1	0.0
Tor-A	1	3	.250	55	0	0	0	1	57^{1}	38	23	23	5	1	19	57	.994	3.61	128	2.06	.186	0	....	7	6	0.7
2003 Tor-A	1	5	.167	54	0	0	0	12	49^{1}	52	32	31	11	1	17	40	1.399	5.66	81	4.93	.268	0	....	-5	3	-0.5
Total 6	13	17	.433	178	16	0	0	13	262^{2}	252	143	132	34	5	113	222	1.390	4.52	99	4.25	.252	3	.094	-0	18	-0.1
• POLIVKA, Ken	Kenneth Lyle "Soup" Polivka b: 1/21/1921, Chicago, IL d: 7/23/1988, Aurora, IL BL/TL, 5'10.5", 175 lbs. Deb: 4/18/1947																									
1947 Cin-N	0	0	....	2	0	0	0	0	3	3	1	1	0	0	3	1	2.000	3.00	137	5.17	.250	0	....	0	0	0.0
• POLLET, Howie	Howard Joseph Pollet b: 6/26/1921, New Orleans, LA d: 8/8/1974, Houston, TX BL/TL, 6'1.5", 175 lbs. Deb: 8/20/1941 C																									
1941 StL-N	5	2	.714	9	8	6	2	0	70	55	18	15	1	1	27	37	1.171	1.93	195	2.23	.212	5	.179	13	8	1.3
1942* StL-N	7	5	.583	27	13	5	2	0	109^{1}	102	43	35	7	2	39	42	1.290	2.88	119	3.24	.242	7	.226	5	8	0.9
1943 StL-N★	8	4	.667	16	14	12	5	0	118^{1}	83	26	23	2	2	32	61	.972	**1.75**	192	1.66	.200	7	.163	18	14	1.8
1946* StL-N★	**21**	10	.677	40	32	22	4	5	**266**	228	84	62	12	5	86	107	1.180	**2.10**	**165**	2.70	.234	14	.161	36	**27**	3.8
1947 StL-N	9	11	.450	37	24	9	0	2	176^{1}	195	96	85	11	3	87	73	**1.599**	4.34	95	4.77	.286	15	.231	-4	8	-0.2
1948 StL-N	13	8	.619	36	26	11	0	0	186^{1}	216	102	94	10	2	67	80	1.519	4.54	90	4.41	.289	8	.118	-9	8	-1.1
1949 StL-N★	20	9	.690	39	28	17	**5**	1	230^{2}	228	80	71	9	2	59	108	1.244	2.77	150	3.01	.256	16	.195	35	**24**	3.6
1950 StL-N	14	13	.519	37	30	14	2	2	232^{1}	228	103	85	19	1	68	117	1.274	3.29	130	3.39	.256	12	.143	27	19	2.5
1951 StL-N	0	3	.000	6	2	0	0	1	12^{1}	10	10	6	1	0	8	10	1.459	4.38	91	3.52	.208	0	.000	-1	0	0.0
Pit-N	6	10	.375	21	21	4	1	0	128^{2}	149	81	72	24	1	51	47	1.554	5.04	84	5.62	.294	5	.139	-10	4	-1.0
Yr.	6	13	.316	27	23	4	1	1	141	159	91	78	25	1	59	57	1.546	4.98	84	5.44	.287	5	.135	-11	4	-1.0
1952 Pit-N	7	16	.304	31	30	9	1	0	214	217	111	98	22	3	71	90	1.346	4.12	97	3.92	.266	13	.191	-2	9	0.1
1953 Pit-N	1	1	.500	5	2	0	0	0	12^{2}	27	15	15	2	0	6	8	2.605	10.66	42	12.90	.482	1	.333	-9	0	-0.8
Chi-N	5	6	.455	25	17	2	0	1	111^{1}	120	62	51	6	1	44	45	1.473	4.12	108	4.02	.271	4	.129	7	7	0.6
Yr.	6	7	.462	30	19	2	0	1	124	147	77	66	8	1	50	53	1.589	4.79	93	4.93	.295	5	.147	-1	7	-0.2
1954 Chi-N	8	10	.444	20	20	4	2	0	128^{1}	131	60	51	4	0	54	58	1.442	3.58	117	3.64	.263	13	.277	10	8	1.3
1955 Chi-N	4	3	.571	24	7	1	1	5	61	62	41	38	11	0	27	27	1.459	5.61	73	4.83	.265	6	.400	-11	3	-0.8
1956 Chi-A	3	1	.750	11	4	0	0	0	26^{1}	27	15	12	2	0	11	14	1.443	4.10	100	3.94	.252	3	.375	-0	2	0.0
Pit-N	0	4	.000	19	0	0	0	3	23^{1}	18	10	8	3	0	8	10	1.114	3.09	122	2.72	.212	0	.000	2	2	0.2
Total 14	131	116	.530	403	278	116	25	20	2107^{1}	2096	957	821	146	23	745	934	1.348	3.51	115	3.66	.260	129	.185	110	151	12.2
• POLLEY, Dale	Ezra Dale Polley b: 8/9/1965, Georgetown, KY BR/TL, 6', 165 lbs. Deb: 6/23/1996																									
1996 NY-A	1	3	.250	32	0	0	0	0	21^{2}	23	20	19	5	3	11	14	1.569	7.89	63	6.18	.264	0	....	-7	0	-0.6
• POLLI, Lou	Louis Americo "Crip" Polli b: 7/9/1901, Baveno, Italy d: 12/19/2000, Berlin, VT BR/TR, 5'10.5", 165 lbs. Deb: 4/18/1932																									
1932 StL-A	0	0	....	5	0	0	0	0	6^{2}	13	8	4	0	0	3	5	2.400	5.40	90	9.28	.406	1	.500	-0	0	0.0
1944 NY-N	0	2	.000	19	0	0	0	3	35^{2}	42	25	18	3	0	20	6	1.738	4.54	81	5.45	.294	0	.000	-4	1	-0.5
Total 2	0	2	.000	24	0	0	0	3	42^{1}	55	33	22	3	0	23	11	1.843	4.68	82	6.05	.314	1	.125	-4	1	-0.5

YEAR	TM-L	W	L	PCT	G	GS	CG	SH	SV	IP	H	R	ER	HR	HB	BB	SO	RAT	ERA	ERA+	CERA	OAV	BH	AVG	PR+	WS	TPW
• POLONI, John					John Paul Poloni b: 2/28/1954, Dearborn, MI BL/TL, 6'5", 210 lbs. Deb: 9/16/1977																						
1977	Tex-A	1	0	1.000	2	1	0	0	0	7	8	5	5	1	0	1	5	1.286	6.43	63	4.20	.286	0	....	-2	0	-0.2
• POMORSKI, John					John Leon Pomorski b: 12/30/1905, Brooklyn, NY d: 12/6/1977, Brampton, Canada BR/TR, 6', 178 lbs. Deb: 4/17/1934																						
1934	Chi-A	0	0	....	3	0	0	0	0	1^{2}	1	2	1	0	0	2	0	1.800	5.40	88	3.16	.143	0	....	-0	0	0.0
• POND, Arlie					Erasmus Arlington Pond b: 1/19/1873, Saugus, MA d: 9/19/1930, Cebu, Philippines BR/TR, 5'10", 160 lbs. Deb: 7/4/1895																						
1895	Bal-N	0	1	.000	6	1	1	0	2	13^{2}	10	13	9	0	0	12	13	1.610	5.93	80	3.42	.202	2	.333	-3	1	-0.2
1896	Bal-N	16	8	.667	28	26	21	2	0	214^{1}	232	133	83	4	0	57	80	1.348	3.49	123	3.39	.274	19	.235	15	16	1.3
1897	Bal-N	18	9	.667	32	28	23	0	0	248	267	131	97	4	15	72	59	1.367	3.52	118	3.63	.273	22	.244	14	19	1.3
1898	Bal-N	1	1	.500	3	2	1	1	0	20	8	4	1	0	2	9	4	.850	0.45	794	1.18	.122	2	.286	6	3	0.7
Total	4	35	19	.648	69	57	46	3	2	496	517	281	190	8	17	150	156	1.345	3.45	123	3.42	.267	45	.245	33	39	3.1
• PONDER, Elmer					Charles Elmer Ponder b: 6/26/1893, Reed, OK d: 4/20/1974, Albuquerque, NM BR/TR, 6', 178 lbs. Deb: 9/18/1917																						
1917	Pit-N	1	1	.500	3	2	1	1	0	21^{1}	12	5	4	0	1	6	11	.844	1.69	168	1.26	.167	0	.000	3	2	0.2
1919	Pit-N	0	5	.000	9	5	0	0	0	47^{1}	55	26	21	0	3	6	6	1.289	3.99	76	3.36	.297	2	.133	-5	0	-0.6
1920	Pit-N	11	15	.423	33	23	13	2	0	196	182	76	57	3	2	40	62	1.133	2.62	123	2.39	.246	7	.119	14	14	1.0
1921	Pit-N	2	0	1.000	8	1	1	0	0	24^{2}	29	8	6	1	0	3	3	1.297	2.19	175	3.63	.305	0	.000	4	3	0.3
	Chi-N	3	6	.333	16	11	5	0	0	89^{1}	117	58	47	7	3	17	31	1.500	4.74	81	4.95	.321	4	.121	-9	2	-1.1
	Yr.	5	6	.455	24	12	6	0	0	114	146	66	53	8	3	20	34	1.456	4.18	91	4.66	.318	4	.093	-5	5	-0.9
Total	4	17	27	.386	69	42	20	3	0	378^{2}	395	173	135	11	9	72	113	1.233	3.21	105	3.13	.271	13	.105	7	21	-0.3
• PONSON, Sidney					Sidney Alton Ponson b: 11/2/1976, Noord, Aruba BR/TR, 6'1", 225 lbs. Deb: 4/19/1998																						
1998	Bal-A	8	9	.471	31	20	0	0	1	135	157	82	79	19	3	42	85	1.474	5.27	86	5.07	.293	2	.500	-9	5	-0.8
1999	Bal-A	12	12	.500	32	32	6	0	0	210	227	118	110	35	1	80	112	1.462	4.71	99	5.08	.282	0	.000	-5	10	-0.5
2000	Bal-A	9	13	.409	32	32	6	1	0	222	223	125	119	30	1	83	152	1.378	4.82	98	4.26	.258	0	.000	-2	11	-0.2
2001	Bal-A	5	10	.333	23	23	3	1	0	138^{1}	161	83	76	21	6	37	84	1.431	4.94	87	5.04	.289	0	.000	-12	4	-1.1
2002	Bal-A	7	9	.438	28	28	3	0	0	176	172	84	80	26	2	63	120	1.335	4.09	105	4.24	.258	1	.333	2	10	0.2
2003	Bal-A	14	6	.700	21	21	4	0	0	148	147	65	62	10	4	43	100	1.284	3.77	117	3.50	.258	0	.000	11	12	1.0
	*SF-N	3	6	.333	10	10	0	0	0	68	64	29	28	6	1	18	34	1.206	3.71	111	3.23	.255	2	.091	2	4	0.1
Total	6	58	65	.472	177	166	22	2	1	1097^{1}	1151	586	554	147	18	366	687	1.382	4.54	99	4.45	.271	5	.122	-14	56	-1.4
• POOLE, Ed					Edward I. Poole b: 9/7/1874, Canton, OH d: 3/11/1919, Malvern, OH BR/TR, 5'10", 175 lbs. Deb: 10/6/1900 ♦																						
1900	Pit-N	1	0	1.000	1	0	0	0	0	7	4	1	1	0	0	0	3	.571	1.29	282	0.71	.167	2	.500	2	2	0.3
1901	Pit-N	5	4	.556	12	10	8	1	0	80	78	45	32	3	6	30	26	1.350	3.60	91	3.58	.254	16	.205	-4	4	-0.7
1902	Pit-N	0	0	....	1	0	0	0	0	8	7	4	1	0	0	3	2	1.250	1.13	243	2.04	.236	1	.250	1	0	0.1
	Cin-N	12	4	.750	16	16	16	2	0	138	129	47	33	2	8	54	55	1.326	2.15	139	3.21	.248	7	.115	10	11	0.5
	Yr.	12	4	.750	17	16	16	2	0	146	136	51	34	2	8	57	57	1.322	2.10	142	3.14	.247	8	.123	11	11	0.7
1903	Cin-N	7	13	.350	25	21	18	1	0	184	188	105	67	4	12	77	73	1.440	3.28	108	3.97	.270	17	.243	6	10	0.6
1904	Bro-N	8	14	.364	25	23	19	1	1	178	178	86	67	4	8	74	67	1.416	3.39	81	3.86	.268	8	.129	-12	6	-1.6
Total	5	33	35	.485	80	70	61	5	1	595	584	288	201	13	34	238	226	1.382	3.04	102	3.64	.260	51	.183	3	33	-0.7
• POOLE, Jim					James Richard Poole b: 4/28/1966, Rochester, NY BL/TL, 6'2", 203 lbs. Deb: 6/15/1990																						
1990	LA-N	0	0	....	16	0	0	0	0	10^{2}	7	5	5	1	0	8	6	1.406	4.22	87	2.88	.184	0	....	-1	0	-0.1
1991	Tex-A	0	0	....	5	0	0	0	1	6	10	4	3	0	0	3	4	2.167	4.50	90	7.52	.370	0	....	-0	0	0.0
	Bal-A	3	2	.600	24	0	0	0	0	36	19	10	8	3	0	9	34	.778	2.00	197	1.26	.157	0	....	8	4	0.8
	Yr.	3	2	.600	29	0	0	0	1	42	29	14	11	3	0	12	38	.976	2.36	168	2.16	.196	0	....	7	4	0.7
1992	Bal-A	0	0	....	6	0	0	0	0	3^{1}	3	3	0	0	0	1	3	1.200	0.00	....	2.46	.231	0	....	1	0	0.1
1993	Bal-A	2	1	.667	55	0	0	0	2	50^{1}	30	18	12	2	0	21	29	1.013	2.15	208	1.64	.175	0	....	12	7	1.2
1994	Bal-A	1	0	1.000	38	0	0	0	0	20^{1}	32	15	15	4	0	11	18	2.115	6.64	75	9.06	.372	0	....	-4	0	-0.4
1995*	Cle-A	3	3	.500	42	0	0	0	0	50^{1}	40	22	21	7	2	17	41	1.132	3.75	125	3.15	.217	0	....	5	4	0.5
1996	Cle-A	4	0	1.000	32	0	0	0	0	26^{2}	29	15	9	3	0	14	19	1.613	3.04	161	4.88	.274	0	....	6	3	0.5
	SF-N	2	1	.667	35	0	0	0	0	23^{2}	15	7	7	2	1	13	19	1.183	2.66	154	2.60	.188	0	.000	4	3	0.3
1997	SF-N	3	1	.750	63	0	0	0	0	49^{1}	73	44	39	6	4	25	26	1.986	7.11	57	7.91	.353	0	....	-17	0	-1.6
1998	SF-N	1	3	.250	26	0	0	0	0	32^{1}	38	20	19	5	0	9	16	1.454	5.29	75	4.76	.302	1	.250	-5	0	-0.4
	*Cle-A	0	0	....	12	0	0	0	0	7	9	4	4	0	1	3	11	1.714	5.14	93	5.21	.300	0	....	-0	0	0.0
1999	Phi-N	1	1	.500	51	0	0	0	1	35^{1}	48	20	17	3	3	15	22	1.783	4.33	109	6.58	.327	0	.000	1	2	0.1
	Cle-A	1	0	1.000	3	0	0	0	0	1	2	2	2	0	0	3	0	5.000	18.00	28	21.00	.667	0	....	-1	0	-0.1
2000	Det-A	1	0	1.000	18	0	0	0	0	8^{2}	13	8	7	4	1	1	5	1.615	7.27	66	9.09	.361	0	....	-2	0	-0.2
	Mon-N	0	0	....	5	0	0	0	0	2	8	6	6	1	0	3	3	5.500	27.00	18	35.83	.571	0	....	-5	0	-0.5
Total	11	22	12	.647	431	0	0	0	4	363	376	203	174	41	12	156	256	1.466	4.31	101	4.77	.271	1	.125	2	23	0.2
• POORMAN, Tom					Thomas Iverson Poorman b: 10/14/1857, Lock Haven, PA d: 2/18/1905, Lock Haven, PA BL/TR, 5'7", 135 lbs. Deb: 5/5/1880 ♦																						
1880	Buf-N	1	8	.111	11	9	9	0	1	85	117	90	39	3	....	19	13	1.600	4.13	60	....	.311	11	.157	-12	0	-1.8
	Chi-N	2	0	1.000	2	1	0	0	0	15	12	5	4	0	....	8	0	1.333	2.40	101	....	.208	5	.200	-0	2	-0.2
	Yr.	3	8	.273	13	10	9	0	1	100	129	95	43	3	....	27	13	**1.560**	3.87	63	....	.298	16	.168	-12	2	-2.0
1884	Tol-a	0	1	.000	1	1	1	0	0	9	13	11	3	1	0	2	0	1.667	3.00	113	....	.321	89	.233	0	6	-0.8
1887	Phi-a	0	0	....	1	0	0	0	0	0^{2}	6	4	3	1	0	1	1	9.000	40.50	11	....	.751	190	.306	-3	13	-1.0
Total	3	3	9	.250	15	11	10	0	1	109^{2}	148	110	49	5	0	30	14	1.614	4.02	64	....	.307	533	.256	-14	21	-3.7
• POPP, Bill					William Peter Popp b: 6/7/1877, St. Louis, MO d: 9/5/1909, St. Louis, MO TR, 5'10.5", 170 lbs. Deb: 4/19/1902																						
1902	StL-N	2	6	.250	9	7	5	0	0	60^{1}	87	60	33	2	5	26	20	1.873	4.92	56	6.49	.337	1	.048	-14	0	-1.7
• PORRAY, Ed					Edmund Joseph Porray b: 12/5/1888, Atlantic Ocean d: 7/13/1954, Lackawaxen, PA BR/TR, 5'11", 170 lbs. Deb: 4/17/1914																						
1914	Buf-F	0	1	.000	3	3	0	0	0	10^{1}	18	9	5	2	0	7	0	2.419	4.35	77	10.73	.391	0	.000	-1	0	-0.2
• PORTER, Chuck					Charles William Porter b: 1/12/1955, Baltimore, MD BR/TR, 6'3", 188 lbs. Deb: 9/14/1981																						
1981	Mil-A	0	0	....	3	0	0	0	0	4^{1}	6	2	2	0	0	1	1	1.615	4.15	82	4.72	.316	0	....	-0	0	0.0
1982	Mil-A	0	0	....	3	0	0	0	0	3^{2}	3	2	2	0	0	1	3	1.091	4.91	77	2.39	.250	0	....	-1	0	-0.1
1983	Mil-A	7	9	.438	25	21	6	1	0	134	162	72	67	9	2	38	76	1.493	4.50	83	4.55	.298	0	....	-11	5	-1.1
1984	Mil-A	6	4	.600	17	12	1	0	0	81^{1}	92	37	35	8	0	12	48	1.279	3.87	99	3.78	.284	0	....	1	5	0.1
1985	Mil-A	0	0	....	6	1	0	0	0	13^{2}	15	8	3	1	0	2	8	1.244	1.98	211	3.36	.273	0	....	3	1	0.3
Total	5	13	13	.500	54	34	7	1	0	237	278	121	109	18	2	54	136	1.401	4.14	91	4.19	.291	0	....	-8	11	-0.8
• PORTER, Henry					Henry Porter b: 6/1858, Vergennes, VT d: 12/30/1906, Brockton, MA BR/TR, 142 lbs. Deb: 9/27/1884																						
1884	Mil-U	3	3	.500	6	6	6	1	0	51	32	25	17	1	....	9	71	.804	3.00	102	....	.168	11	.275	-6	6	-0.4
1885	Bro-a	33	21	.611	54	54	53	2	0	481^{2}	427	261	149	11	16	107	197	1.109	2.78	118	....	.228	40	.205	30	35	2.7
1886	Bro-a	27	19	.587	48	48	48	1	0	424	439	277	161	8	5	120	163	1.318	3.42	102	....	.255	33	.179	6	27	-0.2
1887	Bro-a	15	24	.385	40	40	38	1	0	339^{2}	512	264	159	7	7	96	74	1.507	4.21	102	....	.336	39	.250	3	18	0.1
1888	KC-a	18	37	.327	55	54	53	4	0	474	527	336	219	16	23	120	145	1.365	4.16	82	....	.272	28	.144	-39	22	-4.6
1889	KC-a	0	3	.000	4	4	3	0	0	23	52	46	32	0	1	14	9	2.870	12.52	33	....	.433	1	.100	-21	0	-1.8
Total	6	96	107	.473	207	206	201	9	0	1793^{1}	1989	1209	737	43	52	466	659	1.315	3.70	97	....	.270	152	.195	-27	108	-4.3
• PORTER, Ned					Ned Swindell Porter b: 7/6/1905, Apalachicola, FL d: 6/30/1968, Gainesville, FL BR/TR, 6', 173 lbs. Deb: 8/7/1926																						
1926	NY-N	0	0	....	2	0	0	0	0	2	2	1	1	1	0	0	1	1.000	4.50	83	4.70	.250	0	....	-0	0	0.0
1927	NY-N	0	0	....	1	0	0	0	0	2	3	1	0	0	0	1	0	2.000	0.00	....	6.33	.333	0	....	1	0	0.1
Total	2	0	0	....	3	0	0	0	0	4	5	2	1	1	0	1	1	1.500	2.25	167	5.51	.294	0	....	1	0	0.1
• PORTER, Odie					Odie Oscar Porter b: 5/24/1877, Borden, IN d: 5/2/1903, Borden, IN TL Deb: 6/16/1902																						
1902	Phi-A	0	1	.000	1	1	1	0	0	8	12	10	3	0	0	5	2	2.125	3.38	109	6.30	.346	0	.000	0	0	0.0

YEAR TM-L	W	L	PCT	G	GS	CG	SH	SV	IP	H	R	ER	HR	HB	BB	SO	RAT	ERA	ERA+	CERA	OAV	BH	AVG	PR+	WS	TPW
• PORTERFIELD, Bob	Erwin Coolidge Porterfield b: 8/10/1923, Newport, VA d: 4/28/1980, Charlotte, NC BR/TR, 6', 190 lbs. Deb: 8/8/1948																									
1948 NY-A	5	3	.625	16	12	2	1	0	78	85	42	39	5	0	34	30	1.526	4.50	91	4.29	.273	6	.250	-5	4	-0.4
1949 NY-A	2	5	.286	12	8	3	0	0	57^{2}	53	26	26	3	1	29	25	1.422	4.06	100	3.66	.251	1	.053	-1	3	-0.3
1950 NY-A	1	1	.500	10	2	0	0	1	19^{2}	28	19	19	2	0	8	9	1.831	8.69	49	6.67	.341	1	.333	-10	0	-0.9
1951 NY-A	0	0	....	2	0	0	0	0	3	5	6	5	0	0	3	2	2.667	15.00	26	9.95	.385	0	....	-4	0	-0.4
Was-A	9	8	.529	19	19	10	3	0	133^{1}	109	51	48	8	0	54	53	1.223	3.24	126	2.79	.224	6	.130	14	10	1.1
Yr.	9	8	.529	21	19	10	3	0	136^{1}	114	57	53	8	0	57	55	1.254	3.50	116	2.95	.228	6	.130	11	10	0.7
1952 Was-A	13	14	.481	31	29	15	3	0	231^{1}	222	80	70	7	4	85	80	1.327	2.72	130	3.26	.254	15	.190	23	20	2.4
1953 Was-A	**22**	10	.688	34	32	**24**	**9**	0	255	243	99	95	19	1	73	77	1.239	3.35	116	3.25	.257	25	.255	14	21	2.2
1954 Was-A★	13	15	.464	32	31	**21**	2	0	244	249	104	90	14	3	77	82	1.336	3.32	107	3.55	.266	9	.102	11	13	0.7
1955 Was-A	10	17	.370	30	27	8	2	0	178	197	103	88	14	2	54	74	1.410	4.45	86	4.14	.282	12	.190	-7	5	-0.7
1956 Bos-A	3	12	.200	25	18	4	1	0	126	127	82	72	21	1	64	53	1.516	5.14	90	5.04	.260	14	.326	-7	4	-0.4
1957 Bos-A	4	4	.500	28	9	3	1	1	102^{1}	107	54	46	8	1	30	28	1.339	4.05	99	3.77	.272	5	.172	1	6	0.1
1958 Bos-A	0	0	....	2	0	0	0	0	4	3	2	2	1	0	0	1	.750	4.50	89	2.05	.214	0	....	-0	0	0.0
Pit-N	4	6	.400	37	6	2	1	5	87^{2}	78	33	32	7	1	19	39	1.106	3.29	118	2.69	.241	1	.050	4	7	0.3
1959 Pit-N	0	0	....	6	0	0	0	0	5^{1}	6	2	1	1	0	2	1	1.500	1.69	229	4.48	.261	0	....	1	0	0.1
Chi-N	0	0	....	4	0	0	0	0	6^{1}	14	9	8	1	0	3	0	2.684	11.37	35	12.70	.424	0	.000	-5	0	-0.5
Pit-N	1	2	.333	30	0	0	0	1	36	45	20	19	2	0	17	18	1.722	4.75	81	5.43	.326	0	.000	-4	2	-0.4
Yr.	1	2	.333	40	0	0	0	1	47^{2}	65	31	28	4	0	22	19	1.825	5.29	74	6.29	.335	0	.000	-8	2	-0.8
Total 12	87	97	.473	318	193	92	23	8	1567^{2}	1571	732	660	113	14	552	572	1.354	3.79	103	3.72	.263	95	.184	24	95	3.0
• PORTO, Al	Alfred "Lefty" Porto b: 6/27/1926, Heilwood, PA BL/TL, 5'11", 176 lbs. Deb: 4/22/1948																									
1948 Phi-N	0	0	....	3	0	0	0	0	4	2	0	0	0	0	1	1	.750	0.00	....	0.91	.143	0	....	2	1	0.2
• PORTOCARRERO, Arnie	Arnold Mario Portocarrero b: 7/5/1931, New York, NY d: 6/21/1986, Kansas City, KS BR/TR, 6'3", 196 lbs. Deb: 4/18/1954																									
1954 Phi-A	9	18	.333	34	33	16	1	0	248	233	124	112	25	5	114	132	1.399	4.06	96	3.88	.249	8	.107	-1	12	-0.3
1955 KC-A	5	9	.357	24	20	4	1	0	111^{1}	109	66	59	12	4	67	34	1.581	4.77	87	4.86	.259	4	.108	-7	4	-0.8
1956 KC-A	0	1	.000	3	1	0	0	0	8	9	9	9	2	0	7	2	2.000	10.13	43	8.37	.300	0	.000	-5	0	-0.5
1957 KC-A	4	9	.308	33	17	1	0	0	114^{2}	103	55	50	10	3	34	42	1.195	3.92	101	3.13	.240	3	.107	1	5	0.0
1958 Bal-A	15	11	.577	32	27	10	3	2	204^{2}	173	81	74	17	3	57	90	1.124	3.25	111	2.75	.229	11	.164	9	16	0.9
1959 Bal-A	2	7	.222	27	14	1	0	0	90	107	73	68	10	2	32	23	1.544	6.80	56	5.07	.294	0	.000	-31	0	-3.4
1960 Bal-A	3	2	.600	13	5	1	0	0	40^{2}	44	23	20	6	0	9	15	1.303	4.43	86	4.19	.275	0	.000	-4	1	-0.5
Total 7	38	57	.400	166	117	33	5	2	817^{1}	778	431	392	82	17	320	338	1.343	4.32	90	3.82	.252	26	.108	-38	38	-4.6
• PORTUGAL, Mark	Mark Steven Portugal b: 10/30/1962, Los Angeles, CA BR/TR, 6', 190 lbs. Deb: 8/14/1985																									
1985 Min-A	1	3	.250	6	4	0	0	0	24^{1}	24	16	15	3	0	14	12	1.562	5.55	79	5.06	.270	0	....	-3	1	-0.3
1986 Min-A	6	10	.375	27	15	3	0	1	112^{2}	112	56	54	10	1	50	67	1.438	4.31	100	4.25	.265	0	....	1	7	0.1
1987 Min-A	1	3	.250	13	7	0	0	0	44	58	40	38	13	1	24	28	1.864	7.77	59	8.59	.326	0	....	-16	0	-1.5
1988 Min-A	3	3	.500	26	0	0	0	3	57^{2}	60	30	29	11	1	17	31	1.335	4.53	90	4.64	.274	0	....	-3	3	-0.3
1989 Hou-N	7	1	.875	20	15	2	1	0	108	91	34	33	7	2	37	86	1.185	2.75	123	2.90	.232	7	.206	8	9	1.2
1990 Hou-N	11	10	.524	32	32	1	0	0	196^{2}	187	90	79	21	4	67	136	1.292	3.62	103	3.67	.250	9	.136	1	9	0.0
1991 Hou-N	10	12	.455	32	27	1	0	1	168^{1}	163	91	84	19	2	59	120	1.319	4.49	78	3.82	.256	9	.196	-19	5	-1.7
1992 Hou-N	6	3	.667	18	16	1	1	0	101^{1}	76	32	30	7	1	41	62	1.155	2.66	126	2.64	.213	3	.107	8	6	0.8
1993 Hou-N	18	4	.818	33	33	1	1	0	208	194	75	64	10	4	77	131	1.303	2.77	140	3.31	.248	15	.231	24	19	2.7
1994 SF-N	10	8	.556	21	21	1	0	0	137^{1}	135	68	60	17	6	45	87	1.311	3.93	102	4.06	.260	17	.354	-4	9	0.3
1995 SF-N	5	5	.500	17	17	1	0	0	104	106	56	48	10	2	34	63	1.346	4.15	98	3.91	.262	3	.103	-2	4	-0.2
★Cin-N	6	5	.545	14	14	0	0	0	77^{2}	79	35	33	7	2	22	33	1.300	3.82	108	3.74	.262	5	.172	1	5	0.2
Yr.	11	10	.524	31	**31**	1	0	0	181^{2}	185	91	81	17	4	56	96	1.327	4.01	102	3.84	.262	8	.138	-1	9	0.0
1996 Cin-N	8	9	.471	27	26	1	1	0	156	146	77	69	20	2	42	93	1.205	3.98	104	3.44	.248	8	.167	2	8	0.2
1997 Phi-N	0	2	.000	3	3	0	0	0	13^{2}	17	8	7	0	0	5	2	1.610	4.61	92	4.70	.321	0	.000	-1	0	-0.1
1998 Phi-N	10	5	.667	26	26	3	0	0	166^{1}	186	88	82	26	4	32	104	1.311	4.44	98	4.39	.283	13	.260	-2	10	0.2
1999 Bos-A	7	12	.368	31	27	1	0	0	150^{1}	179	100	92	28	4	41	79	1.463	5.51	90	5.33	.292	0	.000	-9	5	-0.9
Total 15	109	95	.534	346	283	16	4	5	1826^{1}	1813	896	817	209	36	607	1134	1.325	4.03	100	3.98	.261	89	.198	-13	100	0.8
• PORZIO, Mike	Lawrence Michael Porzio b: 8/20/1972, Waterbury, CT BL/TL, 6'3", 190 lbs. Deb: 7/9/1999																									
1999 Col-N	0	0	....	16	0	0	0	0	14^{2}	21	14	14	5	0	10	10	2.114	8.59	68	9.91	.328	0	....	-4	0	-0.4
2002 Chi-A	2	2	.500	32	0	0	0	0	43	40	25	23	10	3	23	33	1.465	4.81	95	5.44	.248	0	....	-2	2	-0.2
2003 Chi-A	1	1	.500	3	3	0	0	0	14	18	10	10	2	2	1	9	1.357	6.43	70	5.25	.321	0	....	-3	0	-0.3
Total 3	3	3	.500	51	3	0	0	0	71^{2}	79	49	47	17	5	34	52	1.577	5.90	82	6.32	.281	0	....	-9	2	-0.9
• POSEDEL, Bill	William John "Sailor Bill,Barnacle Bill" Posedel b: 8/2/1906, San Francisco, CA d: 11/28/1989, Livermore, CA BR/TR, 5'11", 175 lbs. Deb: 4/23/1938 C																									
1938 Bro-N	8	9	.471	33	17	6	1	1	140	178	96	88	14	2	46	49	1.600	5.66	69	5.35	.311	10	.227	-26	2	-2.5
1939 Bos-N	15	13	.536	33	29	18	5	0	220^{2}	221	103	96	8	0	78	73	1.355	3.92	94	3.43	.268	8	.110	-9	10	-1.3
1940 Bos-N	12	17	.414	35	32	18	0	1	233	263	118	107	16	1	81	86	1.476	4.13	90	4.36	.288	14	.171	-16	11	-1.5
1941 Bos-N	4	4	.500	18	9	3	0	0	57^{1}	61	36	31	6	1	30	10	1.587	4.87	73	5.01	.279	8	.320	-9	2	-0.7
1946 Bos-N	2	0	1.000	19	0	0	0	4	28^{1}	34	24	22	4	0	13	9	1.659	6.99	49	5.78	.304	0	.000	-11	0	-1.2
Total 5	41	43	.488	138	87	45	6	6	679^{1}	757	377	344	48	4	248	227	1.479	4.56	82	4.37	.286	40	.176	-71	25	-7.2
• POSER, Bob	John Falk Poser b: 3/16/1910, Columbus, WI d: 5/21/2002, Columbus, WI BL/TR, 6', 173 lbs. Deb: 4/17/1932																									
1932 Chi-A	0	0	....	1	0	0	0	0	0^{2}	3	2	2	0	0	2	1	7.500	27.00	16	40.91	.600	0	.000	-2	0	-0.2
1935 StL-A	1	1	.500	4	1	0	0	0	13^{2}	26	15	14	0	0	4	1	2.195	9.22	52	8.30	.400	1	.250	-7	0	-0.6
Total 2	1	1	.500	5	1	0	0	0	14^{1}	29	17	16	0	0	6	2	2.442	10.05	47	9.82	.414	1	.143	-8	0	-0.8
• POSSEHL, Lou	Louis Thomas Possehl b: 4/12/1926, Chicago, IL d: 10/7/1997, Sarasota, FL BR/TR, 6'2", 180 lbs. Deb: 8/25/1946																									
1946 Phi-N	1	2	.333	4	4	0	0	0	13^{2}	19	9	9	0	1	10	4	2.122	5.93	58	7.12	.339	0	.000	-4	0	-0.4
1947 Phi-N	0	0	....	2	0	0	0	0	4^{1}	5	2	2	0	1	0	1	1.154	4.15	97	4.16	.385	0	....	-0	0	0.0
1948 Phi-N	1	1	.500	3	2	1	0	0	14^{2}	17	8	8	3	0	4	7	1.432	4.91	80	5.50	.304	1	.250	-2	1	-0.1
1951 Phi-N	0	1	.000	2	1	0	0	0	6	9	5	4	0	0	3	6	2.000	6.00	64	6.33	.333	0	.000	-1	0	-0.2
1952 Phi-N	0	1	.000	4	1	0	0	0	12^{2}	12	9	7	3	0	7	4	1.500	4.97	73	5.04	.235	0	.000	-2	0	-0.2
Total 5	2	5	.286	15	8	1	0	0	51^{1}	62	33	30	6	2	24	22	1.675	5.26	70	5.80	.305	1	.100	-9	1	-1.0
• POTE, Lou	Louis William Pote b: 8/21/1971, Evergreen Park, IL BR/TR, 6'3", 200 lbs. Deb: 8/11/1999																									
1999 Ana-A	1	1	.500	20	0	0	0	3	29^{1}	23	9	7	1	0	12	20	1.193	2.15	225	2.56	.219	0	....	9	5	0.8
2000 Ana-A	1	1	.500	32	1	0	0	1	50^{1}	52	23	19	4	0	17	44	1.371	3.40	149	3.87	.267	0	....	8	4	0.7
2001 Ana-A	2	0	1.000	44	1	0	0	2	86^{2}	88	41	40	11	3	32	66	1.385	4.15	110	4.21	.258	0	....	3	6	0.3
2002 Ana-A	0	2	.000	31	0	0	0	0	50^{1}	33	20	18	7	3	26	32	1.172	3.22	138	3.16	.194	0	....	5	3	0.5
Total 4	4	4	.500	127	2	0	0	6	216^{2}	196	93	84	23	6	87	162	1.306	3.49	134	3.66	.242	0	....	25	18	2.4
• POTT, Nellie	Nelson Adolph "Lefty" Pott b: 7/16/1899, Cincinnati, OH d: 12/3/1963, Cincinnati, OH BL/TL, 6', 185 lbs. Deb: 4/19/1922																									
1922 Cle-A	0	0	....	2	0	0	0	0	2	7	7	7	1	0	2	0	4.500	31.50	13	29.71	.583	0	....	-6	0	-0.6
• POTTER, Dykes	Maryland Dykes Potter b: 11/18/1910, Ashland, KY d: 2/27/2002, Greenup, KY BR/TR, 6', 185 lbs. Deb: 4/26/1938																									
1938 Bro-N	0	0	....	2	0	0	0	0	2	4	1	1	1	0	0	1	2.000	4.50	87	11.88	.400	0	....	-0	0	0.0
• POTTER, Nels	Nelson Thomas "Nellie" Potter b: 8/23/1911, Mount Morris, IL d: 9/30/1990, Mount Morris, IL BL/TR, 5'11", 180 lbs. Deb: 4/25/1936																									
1936 StL-N	0	0	....	1	0	0	0	0	1	0	0	0	0	0	0	0	.000	0.00	....	0.00	.000	0	....	0	0	0.0
1938 Phi-A	2	12	.143	35	9	4	0	5	111^{1}	139	95	80	15	2	49	43	1.689	6.47	75	5.86	.306	10	.256	-17	2	-1.5
1939 Phi-A	8	12	.400	41	25	9	0	2	196^{1}	258	163	144	26	5	88	60	1.762	6.60	71	6.35	.321	12	.179	-35	3	-3.3
1940 Phi-A	9	14	.391	31	25	13	0	0	200^{2}	213	115	99	18	1	71	73	1.415	4.44	100	4.05	.269	18	.254	3	10	0.5

YEAR	TM-L	W	L	PCT	G	GS	CG	SH	SV	IP	H	R	ER	HR	HB	BB	SO	RAT	ERA	ERA+	CERA	OAV	BH	AVG	PR+	WS	TPW
1941	Phi-A	1	1	.500	10	3	1	0	2	23^1	35	26	24	3	0	16	7	2.186	9.26	45	8.22	.337	1	.167	-13	0	-1.3
	Bos-A	2	0	1.000	10	0	0	0	0	20	21	10	10	0	0	16	6	1.850	4.50	93	5.06	.284	0	.000	-1	1	-0.1
	Yr.	3	1	.750	20	3	1	0	2	43^1	56	36	34	3	0	32	13	2.031	7.06	59	6.76	.315	1	.111	-14	1	-1.3
1943	StL-A	10	5	.667	33	13	8	0	1	168^1	146	56	52	11	3	54	80	1.188	2.78	120	2.85	.235	8	.145	13	13	1.2
1944*	StL-A	19	7	.731	32	29	16	3	0	232	211	79	73	6	1	70	91	1.211	2.83	127	2.69	.244	13	.159	24	20	2.3
1945	StL-A	15	11	.577	32	32	21	3	0	255^1	212	75	70	10	1	68	129	1.097	2.47	143	2.27	.226	28	.304	31	27	3.7
1946	StL-A	8	9	.471	23	19	10	0	0	145	152	72	60	9	3	59	72	1.455	3.72	100	4.02	.268	12	.231	1	8	0.3
1947	StL-A	4	10	.286	32	10	3	0	2	122^2	130	61	55	13	2	44	65	1.418	4.04	96	4.29	.277	9	.257	-1	8	0.2
1948	StL-A	1	1	.500	2	2	0	0	0	10^1	11	7	6	1	2	4	4	1.452	5.23	87	4.75	.262	2	.500	-1	1	0.0
	Phi-A	2	2	.500	8	0	0	0	1	18	17	8	8	1	0	5	13	1.222	4.00	107	2.93	.250	1	.250	0	2	0.1
	Yr.	3	3	.500	10	2	0	0	1	28^1	28	15	14	2	2	9	17	1.306	4.45	99	3.60	.255	3	.375	-0	3	0.1
	*Bos-N	5	2	.714	18	7	3	0	2	85	77	27	22	4	0	8	47	1.000	2.33	165	2.14	.245	11	.379	14	9	1.7
1949	Bos-N	6	11	.353	41	3	1	0	7	96^2	99	49	45	6	1	30	57	1.334	4.19	90	3.49	.265	3	.130	-4	6	-0.4
Total	**12**	**92**	**97**	**.487**	**349**	**177**	**89**	**6**	**22**	**1686**	**1721**	**843**	**748**	**123**	**21**	**582**	**747**	**1.366**	**3.99**	**102**	**3.81**	**.265**	**128**	**.228**	**14**	**110**	**3.7**

• POTTER, Squire Robert Potter b: 3/18/1902, Flatwoods, KY d: 1/27/1983, Ashland, KY BR/TR, 6'1", 185 lbs. Deb: 8/7/1923

YEAR	TM-L	W	L	PCT	G	GS	CG	SH	SV	IP	H	R	ER	HR	HB	BB	SO	RAT	ERA	ERA+	CERA	OAV	BH	AVG	PR+	WS	TPW
1923	Was-A	0	0	....	1	0	0	0	0	3	11	9	7	0	0	4	1	5.000	21.00	18	31.36	.688	0	....	-6	0	-0.6

• POTTS, Mike Michael Larry Potts b: 9/5/1970, Langdale, AL BL/TL, 5'9", 179 lbs. Deb: 4/6/1996

YEAR	TM-L	W	L	PCT	G	GS	CG	SH	SV	IP	H	R	ER	HR	HB	BB	SO	RAT	ERA	ERA+	CERA	OAV	BH	AVG	PR+	WS	TPW
1996	Mil-A	1	2	.333	24	0	0	0	1	45^1	58	39	36	7	0	30	21	1.941	7.15	73	7.29	.319	0	....	-11	0	-1.0

• POUNDS, Bill Jeared Wells Pounds b: 3/11/1878, Paterson, NJ d: 7/7/1936, Paterson, NJ BR/TR, 5'10.5", 178 lbs. Deb: 5/2/1903

YEAR	TM-L	W	L	PCT	G	GS	CG	SH	SV	IP	H	R	ER	HR	HB	BB	SO	RAT	ERA	ERA+	CERA	OAV	BH	AVG	PR+	WS	TPW
1903	Cle-A	0	0	....	1	0	0	0	0	5	8	7	6	0	0	0	2	1.600	10.80	26	4.59	.360	1	.500	-4	0	-0.4
	Bro-N	0	0	....	1	0	0	0	0	6	8	5	4	1	0	2	2	1.667	6.00	53	6.84	.348	2	.667	-1	0	0.0

• POWELL, Abner Charles Abner "Ab" Powell b: 12/15/1860, Shenandoah, PA d: 8/7/1953, New Orleans, LA BL/TR, 5'7", 160 lbs. Deb: 8/4/1884 ♦

YEAR	TM-L	W	L	PCT	G	GS	CG	SH	SV	IP	H	R	ER	HR	HB	BB	SO	RAT	ERA	ERA+	CERA	OAV	BH	AVG	PR+	WS	TPW
1884	Was-U	6	12	.333	18	17	14	1	0	134	135	107	51	3	....	19	78	1.149	3.43	87	....	.245	54	.283	-3	12	0.3
1886	Bal-a	2	5	.286	7	7	7	0	0	60	66	51	34	2	1	26	15	1.533	5.10	67	....	.267	7	.179	-10	1	-1.1
	Cin-a	0	1	.000	4	1	1	0	0	15^1	16	13	8	0	0	9	4	1.630	4.70	75	....	.257	17	.230	-2	2	-0.4
	Yr.	2	6	.250	11	8	8	0	0	75^1	82	64	42	2	1	35	19	1.553	5.02	68	....	.265	24	.212	-12	3	-1.5
Total	**2**	**8**	**18**	**.308**	**29**	**25**	**22**	**1**	**0**	**209^1**	**217**	**171**	**93**	**5**	**1**	**54**	**97**	**1.295**	**4.00**	**80**	**....**	**.252**	**78**	**.257**	**-14**	**15**	**-1.2**

• POWELL, Bill William Burris "Big Bill" Powell b: 5/8/1885, Taylor County, WV d: 9/28/1967, East Liverpool, OH BR/TR, 6'2.5", 182 lbs. Deb: 4/16/1909

YEAR	TM-L	W	L	PCT	G	GS	CG	SH	SV	IP	H	R	ER	HR	HB	BB	SO	RAT	ERA	ERA+	CERA	OAV	BH	AVG	PR+	WS	TPW
1909	Pit-N	0	1	.000	3	1	0	0	0	7^1	7	6	3	0	1	6	2	1.773	3.68	70	5.62	.290	1	.333	-1	0	-0.1
1910	Pit-N	4	6	.400	12	9	4	2	0	75	65	32	20	0	5	34	23	1.320	2.40	131	3.13	.240	6	.261	6	6	0.7
1912	Chi-N	0	0	....	1	0	0	0	0	2	2	2	2	0	0	1	0	1.500	9.00	37	3.50	.250	0	....	-1	0	-0.1
1913	Cin-N	0	1	.000	1	1	0	0	0	0^1	2	2	2	0	0	2	0	12.00	54.00	6	68.21	1.000	0	....	-2	0	-0.2
Total	**4**	**4**	**8**	**.333**	**17**	**11**	**4**	**2**	**0**	**84^2**	**76**	**42**	**27**	**0**	**6**	**43**	**25**	**1.406**	**2.87**	**107**	**3.61**	**.249**	**7**	**.269**	**1**	**6**	**0.3**

• POWELL, Brian William Brian Powell b: 10/10/1973, Bainbridge, GA BR/TR, 6'2", 205 lbs. Deb: 6/27/1998

YEAR	TM-L	W	L	PCT	G	GS	CG	SH	SV	IP	H	R	ER	HR	HB	BB	SO	RAT	ERA	ERA+	CERA	OAV	BH	AVG	PR+	WS	TPW
1998	Det-A	3	8	.273	18	16	0	0	0	83^2	101	67	59	17	2	36	46	1.637	6.35	74	6.25	.294	0	.000	-16	1	-1.6
2000	Hou-N	2	1	.667	9	5	0	0	0	31^1	34	21	20	8	1	13	14	1.500	5.74	84	5.88	.279	2	.222	-3	1	-0.2
2001	Hou-N	0	1	.000	1	1	0	0	0	3	5	6	6	1	0	3	3	2.667	18.00	25	13.15	.357	0	.000	-4	0	-0.4
2002	Det-A	1	5	.167	13	9	0	0	0	57^2	64	34	31	11	1	21	30	1.474	4.84	89	5.29	.278	0	....	-3	2	-0.3
2003	SF-N	0	1	.000	1	1	0	0	0	4^2	8	7	7	3	0	1	3	1.929	13.50	30	12.71	.381	0	.000	-5	0	-0.5
Total	**5**	**6**	**16**	**.273**	**42**	**32**	**0**	**0**	**0**	**180^1**	**212**	**135**	**123**	**40**	**4**	**74**	**96**	**1.586**	**6.14**	**75**	**6.16**	**.290**	**2**	**.154**	**-31**	**4**	**-3.0**

• POWELL, Dennis Dennis Clay Powell b: 8/13/1963, Moultrie, GA BR/TL, 6'3", 200 lbs. Deb: 7/7/1985

YEAR	TM-L	W	L	PCT	G	GS	CG	SH	SV	IP	H	R	ER	HR	HB	BB	SO	RAT	ERA	ERA+	CERA	OAV	BH	AVG	PR+	WS	TPW
1985	LA-N	1	1	.500	16	2	0	0	1	29^1	30	19	17	7	1	13	19	1.466	5.22	67	5.20	.263	0	.000	-6	0	-0.6
1986	LA-N	2	7	.222	27	6	0	0	0	65^1	65	32	31	5	1	25	31	1.378	4.27	81	3.84	.272	3	.214	-5	2	-0.3
1987	Sea-A	1	3	.250	16	3	0	0	0	34^1	32	13	12	3	0	15	17	1.369	3.15	150	3.75	.250	0	....	6	3	0.6
1988	Sea-A	1	3	.250	12	2	0	0	0	18^2	29	20	18	2	2	11	15	2.143	8.68	48	8.70	.363	0	....	-9	0	-0.9
1989	Sea-A	2	2	.500	43	1	0	0	2	45	49	25	25	6	2	21	27	1.556	5.00	81	5.33	.285	0	....	-5	2	-0.5
1990	Sea-A	0	0	....	2	0	0	0	0	3	5	3	3	0	1	2	0	2.333	9.00	44	9.70	.357	0	....	-2	0	-0.2
	Mil-A	0	4	.000	9	7	0	0	0	39^1	59	37	30	0	1	19	23	1.983	6.86	56	6.51	.341	0	....	-13	0	-1.3
	Yr.	0	4	.000	11	7	0	0	0	42^1	64	40	33	0	2	21	23	2.008	7.02	55	6.74	.342	0	....	-14	0	-1.5
1992	Sea-A	4	2	.667	49	0	0	0	0	57	49	30	29	5	3	29	35	1.368	4.58	87	3.85	.238	0	....	-4	3	-0.4
1993	Sea-A	0	0	....	33	2	0	0	0	47^2	42	22	22	7	1	24	32	1.385	4.15	106	4.38	.255	0	....	1	3	0.1
Total	**8**	**11**	**22**	**.333**	**207**	**23**	**0**	**0**	**3**	**339^2**	**360**	**201**	**187**	**35**	**12**	**159**	**199**	**1.528**	**4.95**	**79**	**4.85**	**.279**	**3**	**.176**	**-36**	**13**	**-3.6**

• POWELL, Grover Grover David Powell b: 10/10/1940, Sayre, PA d: 5/21/1985, Raleigh, NC BL/TL, 5'10", 175 lbs. Deb: 7/13/1963

YEAR	TM-L	W	L	PCT	G	GS	CG	SH	SV	IP	H	R	ER	HR	HB	BB	SO	RAT	ERA	ERA+	CERA	OAV	BH	AVG	PR+	WS	TPW
1963	NY-N	1	1	.500	20	4	1	1	0	49^2	37	23	15	2	1	32	39	1.389	2.72	128	3.20	.202	2	.200	5	3	0.6

• POWELL, Jack John Joseph "Red" Powell b: 7/9/1874, Bloomington, IL d: 10/17/1944, Chicago, IL BR/TR, 5'11", 195 lbs. Deb: 6/23/1897

YEAR	TM-L	W	L	PCT	G	GS	CG	SH	SV	IP	H	R	ER	HR	HB	BB	SO	RAT	ERA	ERA+	CERA	OAV	BH	AVG	PR+	WS	TPW
1897	Cle-N	15	10	.600	27	26	24	2	0	225	245	117	79	2	9	62	61	1.364	3.16	142	3.52	.275	20	.206	21	21	1.5
1898	Cle-N	23	15	.605	42	41	36	**6**	0	342	328	154	114	8	16	112	93	1.287	3.00	120	3.15	.251	18	.132	21	25	1.3
1899	StL-N	23	19	.548	48	**43**	**40**	2	0	373	433	197	146	15	15	85	87	1.389	3.52	113	3.97	.290	27	.201	16	29	1.4
1900	StL-N	17	16	.515	38	37	28	3	0	287^2	325	194	142	9	3	77	77	1.397	4.44	82	3.78	.284	31	.284	-21	14	-1.0
1901	StL-N	19	19	.500	**45**	37	33	2	**3**	338^1	351	168	133	14	12	50	133	1.185	3.54	90	2.85	.266	21	.176	-21	17	-2.0
1902	StL-A	22	17	.564	42	39	36	3	**2**	328^1	320	144	117	12	9	93	137	1.258	3.21	110	3.06	.256	26	.205	7	31	1.0
1903	StL-A	15	19	.441	38	34	33	4	**2**	306^1	294	131	99	11	5	58	169	1.149	2.91	100	2.62	.252	25	.208	-0	20	0.2
1904	NY-A	23	19	.548	47	45	38	3	0	390^1	340	154	106	15	10	92	202	1.107	2.44	111	2.45	.235	26	.178	3	29	0.1
1905	NY-A	8	13	.381	37	23	13	1	1	203	214	107	79	4	6	57	84	1.335	3.50	84	3.40	.273	12	.185	-10	6	-1.1
	StL-A	2	1	.667	3	3	3	0	0	28	22	6	5	0	1	5	12	.964	1.61	158	1.70	.219	1	.100	3	2	0.3
	Yr.	10	14	.417	40	26	16	1	1	231	236	113	84	4	7	62	96	1.290	3.27	89	3.20	.267	13	.173	-7	8	-0.8
1906	StL-A	13	14	.481	28	26	25	3	1	244	196	77	48	2	8	55	132	1.029	1.77	146	1.95	.223	21	.231	22	20	2.7
1907	StL-A	13	16	.448	32	31	27	4	1	255^2	229	104	76	4	5	62	96	1.138	2.68	94	2.37	.242	12	.132	-5	12	-0.9
1908	StL-A	16	13	.552	33	32	23	5	1	256	208	73	60	1	6	47	85	.996	2.11	113	1.94	.231	21	.236	-4	20	-0.1
1909	StL-A	12	16	.429	34	27	18	4	3	239	221	83	56	1	4	42	82	1.100	2.11	114	2.37	.250	14	.179	7	15	0.9
1910	StL-A	7	11	.389	21	18	8	3	0	129^1	121	45	33	0	1	28	52	1.152	2.30	108	2.47	.250	7	.163	3	5	0.2
1911	StL-A	8	19	.296	31	27	18	1	1	207^2	224	120	76	7	7	44	52	1.291	3.29	102	3.27	.262	12	.164	-0	8	-0.3
1912	StL-A	9	17	.346	32	27	19	0	0	235^1	248	117	81	5	3	52	67	1.275	3.10	108	3.28	.276	15	.183	3	13	0.4
Total	**16**	**245**	**254**	**.491**	**578**	**516**	**422**	**46**	**15**	**4389**	**4319**	**1991**	**1450**	**110**	**120**	**1021**	**1621**	**1.217**	**2.97**	**106**	**2.92**	**.258**	**309**	**.192**	**44**	**287**	**4.6**

• POWELL, Jack Reginald Bertrand Powell b: 8/17/1891, Holcomb, MO d: 3/12/1930, Memphis, TN TR, 6'2" Deb: 6/14/1913

YEAR	TM-L	W	L	PCT	G	GS	CG	SH	SV	IP	H	R	ER	HR	HB	BB	SO	RAT	ERA	ERA+	CERA	OAV	BH	AVG	PR+	WS	TPW
1913	StL-A	0	0	....	2	0	0	0	0	2	1	3	0	0	0	2	0	1.500	0.00	....	2.54	.143	0	....	1	0	0.1

• POWELL, Jay James Willard Powell b: 1/9/1972, Meridian, MS BR/TR, 6'4", 220 lbs. Deb: 9/10/1995

YEAR	TM-L	W	L	PCT	G	GS	CG	SH	SV	IP	H	R	ER	HR	HB	BB	SO	RAT	ERA	ERA+	CERA	OAV	BH	AVG	PR+	WS	TPW
1995	Fla-N	0	0	....	9	0	0	0	0	8^1	7	2	1	0	2	6	4	1.560	1.08	390	4.44	.241	0	....	3	1	0.3
1996	Fla-N	4	3	.571	67	0	0	0	2	71^1	71	41	36	5	4	36	52	1.500	4.54	90	4.39	.255	0	.000	-5	4	-0.5
1997*	Fla-N	7	2	.778	74	0	0	0	2	79^2	71	35	29	3	4	30	65	1.268	3.28	123	3.10	.242	2	.500	6	9	0.7
1998	Fla-N	4	4	.500	33	0	0	0	3	36^1	36	19	17	5	2	22	24	1.596	4.21	97	5.07	.263	0	....	-0	2	0.0
	*Hou-N	3	3	.500	29	0	0	0	4	34	22	9	9	1	1	15	38	1.088	2.38	170	1.96	.182	0	.000	6	5	0.6
	Yr.	7	7	.500	62	0	0	0	7	70^1	58	28	26	6	3	37	62	1.351	3.33	123	3.57	.225	0	.000	6	7	0.6
1999*	Hou-N	5	4	.556	67	0	0	0	4	75	82	38	36	3	3	40	77	1.627	4.32	102	4.75	.282	0	....	0	6	0.0
2000	Hou-N	1	1	.500	29	0	0	0	0	27	29	18	17	1	0	19	16	1.778	5.67	86	5.10	.271	0	.000	-2	1	-0.2
2001	Hou-N	2	2	.500	35	0	0	0	0	36^1	41	18	15	4	0	19	28	1.651	3.72	123	5.23	.275	0	.000	3	3	0.3
	Col-N	3	1	.750	39	0	0	0	7	38^2	34	18	12	5	2	12	26	1.190	2.79	191	3.45	.245	0	....	11	6	1.0
	Yr.	5	3	.625	74	0	0	0	7	75	75	36	27	9	2	31	54	1.413	3.24	151	4.31	.260	0	.000	14	9	1.4
2002	Tex-A	3	2	.600	51	0	0	0	0	49^2	50	28	19	5	1	24	35	1.490	3.44	137	4.28	.253	0	....	8	4	0.7

YEAR TM-L	W	L	PCT	G	GS	CG	SH	SV	IP	H	R	ER	HR	HB	BB	SO	RAT	ERA	ERA+	CERA	OAV	BH	AVG	PR+	WS	TPW
2003 Tex-A	3	0	1.000	51	0	0	0	0	58^{2}	75	58	51	7	2	34	40	1.858	7.82	63	6.72	.318	0	....	-18	0	-1.7
Total 9	35	22	.614	484	0	0	0	22	515	518	284	242	39	21	257	405	1.505	4.23	106	4.41	.262	2	.167	12	41	1.2
• POWELL, Jeremy	Jeremy Robert Powell b: 6/18/1976, Bellflower, CA BR/TR, 6'5", 230 lbs. Deb: 7/23/1998																									
1998 Mon-N	1	5	.167	7	6	0	0	0	25	27	25	22	5	4	11	14	1.520	7.92	53	6.29	.290	0	.000	-10	0	-1.0
1999 Mon-N	4	8	.333	17	17	0	0	0	97	113	60	51	14	8	44	44	1.619	4.73	95	6.03	.302	4	.133	-1	4	-0.1
2000 Mon-N	0	3	.000	11	4	0	0	0	26	35	27	23	6	0	9	19	1.692	7.96	60	6.84	.321	3	.600	-9	1	-0.7
Total 3	5	16	.238	35	27	0	0	0	148	175	112	96	25	12	64	77	1.615	5.84	77	6.21	.304	7	.171	-20	5	-1.8
• POWELL, Ross	Ross John Powell b: 1/24/1968, Grand Rapids, MI BL/TL, 6', 180 lbs. Deb: 9/5/1993																									
1993 Cin-N	0	3	.000	9	1	0	0	0	16^{1}	13	8	8	1	0	6	17	1.163	4.41	91	2.66	.224	0	.000	-1	1	-0.1
1994 Hou-N	0	0	....	12	0	0	0	0	7^{1}	6	1	1	0	1	5	5	1.500	1.23	322	4.07	.240	0	....	2	1	0.2
1995 Hou-N	0	0	....	15	0	0	0	0	9	16	12	11	1	0	11	8	3.000	11.00	35	11.34	.381	0	....	-7	0	-0.7
Pit-N	0	2	.000	12	3	0	0	0	20^{2}	20	14	12	5	2	10	12	1.452	5.23	82	5.62	.253	0	.000	-2	0	-0.2
Yr.	0	2	.000	27	3	0	0	0	29^{2}	36	26	23	6	2	21	20	1.921	6.98	59	7.36	.298	0	.000	-9	0	-0.9
Total 3	0	5	.000	48	4	0	0	0	53^{1}	55	35	32	7	3	32	42	1.631	5.40	75	5.47	.270	0	.000	-7	2	-0.8
• POWER, Ted	Ted Henry Power b: 1/31/1955, Guthrie, OK BR/TR, 6'4", 225 lbs. Deb: 9/9/1981																									
1981 LA-N	1	3	.250	5	2	0	0	0	14^{1}	16	6	5	0	1	7	7	1.605	3.14	106	4.29	.286	0	.000	0	1	0.0
1982 LA-N	1	1	.500	12	4	0	0	0	33^{2}	38	27	25	4	0	23	15	1.812	6.68	52	6.02	.288	0	.000	-12	0	-1.3
1983 Cin-N	5	6	.455	49	6	1	0	2	111	120	62	56	10	1	49	57	1.523	4.54	84	4.75	.286	0	.000	-9	4	-1.1
1984 Cin-N	9	7	.563	**78**	0	0	0	11	108^{2}	93	37	34	4	0	46	81	1.279	2.82	134	2.85	.237	0	.000	13	14	1.3
1985 Cin-N	8	6	.571	64	0	0	0	27	80	65	27	24	2	1	45	42	1.375	2.70	140	3.05	.227	0	....	9	14	1.0
1986 Cin-N	10	6	.625	56	10	0	0	1	129	115	59	53	13	1	52	95	1.295	3.70	105	3.46	.245	3	.125	3	9	0.4
1987 Cin-N	10	13	.435	34	34	2	1	0	204	213	115	102	28	3	71	133	1.392	4.50	94	4.35	.267	7	.119	-7	8	-0.7
1988 KC-A	5	6	.455	22	12	2	2	0	80^{1}	98	54	53	7	3	30	44	1.593	5.94	67	5.28	.305	0	....	-16	1	-1.6
Det-A	1	1	.500	4	2	0	0	0	18^{2}	23	13	12	1	0	8	13	1.661	5.79	66	4.91	.307	0	....	-4	0	-0.4
Yr.	6	7	.462	26	14	2	2	0	99	121	67	65	8	3	38	57	1.606	5.91	67	5.21	.306	0	....	-20	1	-2.1
1989 StL-N	7	7	.500	23	15	0	0	0	97	96	47	40	7	1	21	43	1.206	3.71	98	3.07	.255	3	.091	-2	4	-0.4
1990* Pit-N	1	3	.250	40	0	0	0	7	51^{2}	50	23	21	5	0	17	42	1.297	3.66	99	3.41	.255	1	.125	-1	4	-0.1
1991 Cin-N	5	3	.625	68	0	0	0	3	87	87	37	35	6	2	31	51	1.356	3.62	105	3.71	.265	0	.000	2	6	0.2
1992 Cle-A	3	3	.500	64	0	0	0	6	99^{1}	88	33	28	7	4	35	51	1.238	2.54	154	3.16	.248	0	....	16	10	1.6
1993 Cle-A	0	2	.000	20	0	0	0	0	20	30	17	16	2	0	8	11	1.900	7.20	60	6.41	.333	0	....	-6	0	-0.6
Sea-A	2	2	.500	25	0	0	0	13	25^{1}	27	11	11	1	0	9	16	1.421	3.91	113	3.96	.287	0	....	1	4	0.1
Yr.	2	4	.333	45	0	0	0	13	45^{1}	57	28	27	3	0	17	27	1.632	5.36	81	5.04	.310	0	....	-5	4	-0.5
Total 13	68	69	.496	564	85	5	3	70	1160	1159	568	515	97	17	452	701	1.389	4.00	97	3.91	.264	14	.089	-13	79	-1.6
• POWERS, Ike	John Lloyd Powers b: 3/13/1906, Hancock, MD d: 12/22/1968, Hancock, MD BR/TR, 6'.5", 188 lbs. Deb: 7/26/1927																									
1927 Phi-A	1	1	.500	11	1	0	0	0	26	26	16	13	1	0	7	3	1.269	4.50	95	3.05	.271	2	.400	-0	1	0.0
1928 Phi-A	1	0	1.000	9	0	0	0	2	12	8	6	6	1	1	10	4	1.500	4.50	89	4.08	.222	0	....	-1	1	-0.1
Total 2	2	1	.667	20	1	0	0	2	38	34	22	19	2	1	17	7	1.342	4.50	93	3.38	.258	2	.400	-1	2	0.0
• POWERS, Jim	James T. Powers b: 1868, New York, NY, 5'10", 150 lbs. Deb: 4/18/1890																									
1890 Bro-a	1	2	.333	4	2	2	0	0	30	38	29	19	1	1	16	3	1.800	5.70	68	....	.300	2	.154	-6	0	-0.5
• PRALL, Willie	Wilfred Anthony Prall b: 4/20/1950, Hackensack, NJ BL/TL, 6'3", 200 lbs. Deb: 9/3/1975																									
1975 Chi-N	0	2	.000	3	3	0	0	0	14^{2}	21	15	14	1	0	8	7	1.977	8.59	45	7.05	.339	0	.000	-7	0	-0.8
• PRATT, Al	Albert George "Uncle Al" Pratt b: 11/19/1847, Pittsburgh, PA d: 11/21/1937, Pittsburgh, PA TR, 5'7", 140 lbs. Deb: 5/4/1871 M/U																									
1871 Cle-n	10	17	.370	28	28	22	0	0	224^{2}	296	288	94	9	....	47	**34**	1.527	3.77	110	....	.277	34	.262	26	....	1.9
1872 Cle-n	2	9	.182	15	12	8	0	0	105^{2}	150	133	68	3	....	14	7	1.552	5.79	84	....	.293	18	.277	-4	....	-0.3
Total 2 n	12	26	.316	43	40	30	0	0	330^{1}	446	421	162	12	....	61	41	1.535	4.41	100	....	.283	52	.267	22	....	1.6
• PRATT, Andy	Andrew Elias Pratt b: 8/27/1979, Mesa, AZ BL/TL, 5'11", 160 lbs. Deb: 9/28/2002																									
2002 Atl-N	0	0	....	1	0	0	0	0	1^{1}	1	1	1	0	0	4	1	3.750	6.75	61	12.03	.200	0	....	-0	0	0.0
• PREGENZER, John	John Arthur Pregenzer b: 8/2/1935, Burlington, WI BR/TR, 6'5", 220 lbs. Deb: 4/20/1963																									
1963 SF-N	0	0	....	6	0	0	0	1	9^{1}	8	5	5	0	1	8	5	1.714	4.82	66	4.34	.242	0	....	-2	0	-0.2
1964 SF-N	2	0	1.000	13	0	0	0	0	18^{1}	21	15	10	1	1	11	8	1.745	4.91	73	5.27	.296	0	....	-3	0	-0.3
Total 2	2	0	1.000	19	0	0	0	1	27^{2}	29	20	15	1	2	19	13	1.735	4.88	70	4.96	.279	0	....	-4	0	-0.5
• PRENDERGAST, Jim	James Bartholomew Prendergast b: 8/23/1917, Brooklyn, NY d: 8/23/1994, Amherst, NY BL/TL, 6'1", 208 lbs. Deb: 4/25/1948																									
1948 Bos-N	1	1	.500	10	2	0	0	1	16^{2}	30	20	19	1	0	5	3	2.100	10.26	37	8.06	.380	0	.000	-12	0	-1.3
• PRENDERGAST, Mike	Michael Thomas Prendergast b: 12/15/1888, Arlington, IL d: 11/18/1967, Omaha, NE BR/TR, 5'9.5", 165 lbs. Deb: 4/26/1914																									
1914 Chi-F	5	9	.357	30	19	7	1	0	136	131	53	36	6	3	40	71	1.257	2.38	124	3.20	.255	4	.108	5	7	0.4
1915 Chi-F	14	12	.538	42	30	16	3	0	253^{2}	220	93	70	6	4	67	95	1.131	2.48	112	2.52	.240	6	.075	9	15	0.2
1916 Chi-N	6	11	.353	35	10	4	2	2	152	127	53	39	5	1	23	56	.987	2.31	126	1.92	.228	7	.152	12	11	1.2
1917 Chi-N	3	6	.333	35	8	1	0	1	99^{1}	112	42	37	6	0	21	43	1.339	3.35	86	3.83	.302	7	.250	-4	5	-0.3
1918 Phi-N	13	14	.481	33	30	20	0	1	252^{1}	257	102	81	6	1	46	41	1.201	2.89	104	2.85	.273	7	.082	3	15	-0.4
1919 Phi-N	0	1	.000	5	1	0	0	0	15	20	15	14	0	1	10	5	2.000	8.40	38	6.28	.351	1	.333	-9	0	-0.9
Total 6	41	53	.436	180	98	48	6	4	908^{1}	867	358	277	29	10	207	311	1.182	2.74	106	2.82	.258	32	.115	17	53	0.2
• PRENTISS, George	George Pepper Prentiss b: 6/10/1876, Wilmington, DE d: 9/8/1902, Wilmington, DE BB/TR, 5'11", 175 lbs. Deb: 9/23/1901																									
1901 Bos-A	1	0	1.000	2	1	1	0	0	10	7	4	2	0	0	6	0	1.300	1.80	196	2.42	.195	1	.333	2	1	0.2
1902 Bos-A	2	2	.500	7	4	3	0	0	41	55	31	24	0	0	10	9	1.585	5.27	68	4.59	.321	5	.313	-9	1	-0.8
Bal-A	0	1	.000	2	2	0	0	0	6^{2}	14	10	8	1	0	5	1	2.850	10.80	35	13.24	.426	0	.000	-5	0	-0.5
Yr.	2	3	.400	9	6	3	0	0	47^{2}	69	41	32	1	0	15	10	1.762	6.04	60	5.80	.338	5	.250	-14	1	-1.3
Total 2	3	3	.500	11	7	4	0	0	57^{2}	76	45	34	1	0	21	10	1.682	5.31	68	5.21	.317	6	.261	-12	2	-1.1
• PRESKO, Joe	Joseph Edward "Baby Joe,Little Joe" Presko b: 10/7/1928, Kansas City, MO BR/TR, 5'9.5", 170 lbs. Deb: 5/3/1951																									
1951 StL-N	7	4	.636	15	12	5	0	2	88^{2}	86	36	34	9	2	20	38	1.195	3.45	115	3.28	.251	6	.162	4	7	0.3
1952 StL-N	7	10	.412	28	18	5	1	0	146^{2}	140	74	66	15	1	57	63	1.343	4.05	92	3.69	.247	4	.093	-6	5	-0.8
1953 StL-N	6	13	.316	34	25	4	0	1	161^{2}	165	95	90	19	5	65	56	1.423	5.01	85	4.32	.261	13	.220	-11	6	-1.0
1954 StL-N	4	9	.308	37	6	1	1	0	71^{2}	97	56	55	14	5	41	36	1.926	6.91	60	7.97	.327	4	.250	-22	0	-2.1
1957 Det-A	1	1	.500	7	0	0	0	0	11	10	3	2	0	1	4	3	1.273	1.64	236	3.02	.278	0	.000	3	1	0.3
1958 Det-A	0	0	....	7	0	0	0	2	10^{2}	13	4	4	0	0	1	6	1.313	3.38	120	3.58	.317	0	....	1	1	0.1
Total 6	25	37	.403	128	61	15	2	5	490^{1}	511	268	251	57	14	188	202	1.426	4.61	87	4.43	.267	27	.173	-32	20	-3.3
• PRESSNELL, Tot	Forest Charles Pressnell b: 8/8/1906, Findlay, OH d: 1/6/2001, Findlay, OH BR/TR, 5'10.5", 175 lbs. Deb: 4/21/1938																									
1938 Bro-N	11	14	.440	43	19	6	1	3	192	209	86	76	11	8	56	57	1.380	3.56	109	3.89	.276	9	.143	9	12	0.8
1939 Bro-N	9	7	.563	31	18	10	2	2	156^{2}	171	76	70	8	1	33	43	1.302	4.02	100	3.43	.273	10	.196	1	10	0.0
1940 Bro-N	6	5	.545	24	4	1	1	2	68^{1}	58	31	28	4	2	17	21	1.098	3.69	108	2.41	.221	0	.000	3	5	0.0
1941 Chi-N	5	3	.625	29	1	0	0	1	70	69	26	24	2	4	23	27	1.314	3.09	114	3.33	.253	3	.200	5	6	0.6
1942 Chi-N	1	1	.500	27	0	0	0	4	39^{1}	40	28	24	5	5	5	9	1.144	5.49	58	3.64	.260	2	.667	-9	1	-0.8
Total 5	32	30	.516	154	42	17	4	12	526^{1}	547	247	222	30	20	134	157	1.294	3.80	100	3.47	.264	24	.161	8	34	0.5
• PRICE, Bill	William Price b: Philadelphia, PA Deb: 4/27/1890																									
1890 Phi-a	1	0	1.000	1	1	1	0	0	9	6	3	2	0	0	7	1	1.444	2.00	191	....	.184	1	.250	2	1	0.2

YEAR TM-L	W	L	PCT	G	GS	CG	SH	SV	IP	H	R	ER	HR	HB	BB	SO	RAT	ERA	ERA+	CERA	OAV	BH	AVG	PR+	WS	TPW
• PRICE, Joe	Joseph Walter Price b: 11/29/1956, Inglewood, CA BR/TL, 6'4", 220 lbs. Deb: 6/14/1980																									
1980 Cin-N	7	3	.700	24	13	2	0	0	111^1	95	45	44	10	1	37	44	1.186	3.56	101	3.08	.236	5	.128	2	7	0.0
1981 Cin-N	6	1	.857	41	0	0	0	4	53^2	42	19	15	3	0	18	41	1.118	2.52	141	2.38	.222	0	.000	6	7	0.6
1982 Cin-N	3	4	.429	59	1	0	0	3	72^2	73	26	23	7	4	32	71	1.445	2.85	130	4.29	.263	1	.333	6	6	0.7
1983 Cin-N	10	6	.625	21	21	5	0	0	144	118	46	46	12	0	46	83	1.139	2.88	132	2.72	.225	4	.098	15	14	1.4
1984 Cin-N	7	13	.350	30	30	3	1	0	171^2	176	91	80	19	2	61	129	1.381	4.19	90	4.05	.261	7	.146	-6	7	-0.7
1985 Cin-N	2	2	.500	26	8	0	0	1	64^2	59	35	28	10	0	23	52	1.268	3.90	97	3.58	.242	0	.000	-1	3	-0.3
1986 Cin-N	1	2	.333	25	2	0	0	0	41^2	49	30	25	5	0	22	30	1.704	5.40	72	5.62	.293	1	.143	-7	0	-0.7
1987* SF-N	2	2	.500	20	0	0	0	1	35	19	10	10	5	1	13	42	.914	2.57	150	1.93	.154	1	.167	4	3	0.4
1988 SF-N	1	6	.143	38	3	0	0	4	61^2	59	33	27	5	1	27	49	1.395	3.94	83	3.71	.249	0	.000	-5	1	-0.6
1989 SF-N	1	1	.500	7	1	0	0	0	14	16	9	9	3	0	4	10	1.429	5.79	58	5.18	.314	0	.000	-4	0	-0.4
Bos-A	2	5	.286	31	5	0	0	0	70^1	71	35	34	8	0	30	52	1.436	4.35	94	4.27	.262	0	....	-1	3	-0.1
1990 Bal-A	3	4	.429	50	0	0	0	0	65^1	62	29	26	8	0	24	54	1.316	3.58	106	3.83	.253	0	....	1	4	0.1
Total 11	45	49	.479	372	84	10	1	13	906	839	408	367	95	9	337	657	1.298	3.65	102	3.59	.246	19	.111	9	55	0.5
• PRIDDY, Bob	Robert Simpson Priddy b: 12/10/1939, Pittsburgh, PA BR/TR, 6'1", 200 lbs. Deb: 9/20/1962																									
1962 Pit-N	1	0	1.000	2	0	0	0	0	3	4	1	1	0	0	1	1	1.667	3.00	131	4.83	.308	0	....	0	0	0.0
1964 Pit-N	1	2	.333	19	0	0	0	1	34^1	35	16	15	2	1	15	23	1.456	3.93	89	4.20	.282	0	.000	-1	2	-0.1
1965 SF-N	1	0	1.000	8	0	0	0	0	10^1	6	2	2	1	0	2	7	.774	1.74	207	1.41	.176	0	.000	2	1	0.2
1966 SF-N	6	3	.667	38	3	0	0	1	91	88	45	40	8	3	28	51	1.275	3.96	93	3.59	.259	3	.176	-3	4	-0.3
1967 Was-A	3	7	.300	46	8	1	0	4	110	98	48	42	12	0	33	57	1.191	3.44	92	3.14	.240	4	.182	-4	6	-0.2
1968 Chi-A	3	11	.214	35	18	2	0	0	114	106	50	46	14	4	41	66	1.289	3.63	83	3.77	.244	1	.042	-7	2	-0.9
1969 Chi-A	0	0	....	4	0	0	0	0	8	10	5	4	2	0	2	5	1.500	4.50	86	5.88	.303	0	....	-0	0	0.0
Cal-A	0	1	.000	15	0	0	0	0	26^1	24	14	14	4	0	7	15	1.177	4.78	73	3.36	.242	0	.000	-4	0	-0.4
Yr.	0	1	.000	19	0	0	0	0	34^1	34	19	18	6	0	9	20	1.252	4.72	75	3.95	.258	0	.000	-5	0	-0.5
Atl-N	0	0	....	1	0	0	0	0	2	1	0	0	0	0	1	1	1.000	0.00	....	1.41	.143	0	....	1	0	0.1
1970 Atl-N	5	5	.500	41	0	0	0	8	73	75	46	44	9	3	24	32	1.356	5.42	79	4.25	.269	3	.200	-7	4	-0.7
1971 Atl-N	4	9	.308	40	0	0	0	4	64	71	36	30	8	1	44	36	1.797	4.22	88	6.05	.289	2	.182	-3	2	-0.3
Total 9	24	38	.387	249	29	3	0	18	536	518	263	238	60	12	198	294	1.336	4.00	88	3.94	.257	13	.137	-27	21	-2.7
• PRIEST, Eddie	Eddie Lee Priest b: 4/8/1974, Boaz, AL BR/TL, 6'1" Deb: 5/27/1998																									
1998 Cin-N	0	1	.000	2	2	0	0	0	6	12	8	7	2	0	1	1	2.167	10.50	41	12.11	.444	0	.000	-4	0	-0.4
• PRIETO, Ariel	Ariel Prieto b: 10/22/1969, Havana, Cuba BR/TR, 6'3", 225 lbs. Deb: 7/2/1995																									
1995 Oak-A	2	6	.250	14	9	1	0	0	58	57	35	32	4	5	32	37	1.534	4.97	89	4.73	.264	0	....	-3	2	-0.3
1996 Oak-A	6	7	.462	21	21	2	0	0	125^2	130	66	58	9	7	54	75	1.464	4.15	118	4.45	.273	0	....	9	8	0.8
1997 Oak-A	6	8	.429	22	22	0	0	0	125	155	84	70	16	5	70	90	1.800	5.04	89	6.55	.306	0	....	-5	4	-0.4
1998 Oak-A	0	1	.000	2	2	0	0	0	8^1	17	11	11	2	1	5	8	2.640	11.88	38	13.54	.415	0	....	-7	0	-0.6
2000 Oak-A	1	2	.333	8	6	0	0	0	31^2	42	21	18	3	1	13	19	1.737	5.12	93	6.12	.321	0	.000	-1	1	-0.1
2001 TB-A	0	0	....	3	0	0	0	0	3^2	6	1	1	0	1	2	2	2.182	2.45	183	9.19	.375	0	....	1	0	0.1
Total 6	15	24	.385	70	60	3	0	0	352^1	407	218	190	34	20	176	231	1.655	4.85	95	5.66	.294	0	.000	-6	15	-0.6
• PRIM, Ray	Raymond Lee "Pop" Prim b: 12/30/1906, Salitpa, AL d: 4/29/1995, Monte Rio, CA BR/TL, 6', 178 lbs. Deb: 9/24/1933																									
1933 Was-A	0	1	.000	2	1	0	0	0	14^1	13	6	5	0	0	2	6	1.047	3.14	133	1.91	.232	0	.000	1	1	0.1
1934 Was-A	0	2	.000	8	1	0	0	0	14^2	19	11	11	1	0	8	3	1.841	6.75	64	6.23	.339	0	.000	-4	0	-0.4
1935 Phi-N	3	4	.429	29	6	1	0	0	73^1	110	54	47	4	0	15	27	1.705	5.77	79	5.65	.340	2	.083	-9	2	-1.1
1943 Chi-N	4	3	.571	29	5	0	0	1	60	67	24	17	2	0	14	27	1.350	2.55	131	3.51	.282	2	.167	6	4	0.7
1945* Chi-N	13	8	.619	34	19	9	2	2	165^1	142	58	44	9	1	23	88	.998	**2.40**	**152**	**2.08**	**.228**	13	.255	21	17	2.3
1946 Chi-N	2	3	.400	14	2	0	0	1	23^1	28	17	15	5	0	10	10	1.629	5.79	57	5.99	.289	1	.200	-6	0	-0.6
Total 6	22	21	.512	116	34	10	2	4	351	379	170	139	21	1	72	161	1.285	3.56	109	3.50	.272	18	.180	9	24	1.0
• PRINCE, Don	Donald Mark Prince b: 4/5/1938, Clarkton, NC BR/TR, 6'4", 200 lbs. Deb: 9/21/1962																									
1962 Chi-N	0	0	....	1	0	0	0	0	1	0	0	0	0	1	1	0	1.000	0.00	....	4.48	.000	0		0	0	0.0
• PRINZ, Bret	Bret Randolph Prinz b: 6/15/1977, Chicago Heights, IL BR/TR, 6'3", 185 lbs. Deb: 4/22/2001																									
2001 Ari-N	4	1	.800	46	0	0	0	9	41	33	13	12	4	1	19	27	1.268	2.63	174	3.27	.220	0	....	8	7	0.8
2002 Ari-N	0	2	.000	20	0	0	0	0	13^1	23	14	14	1	1	10	10	2.475	9.45	47	10.34	.404	0	....	-7	0	-0.7
2003 Ari-N	0	0	....	1	0	0	0	0	1	1	0	0	0	0	1	1	2.000	0.00	....	3.46	.250	0	....	1	0	0.1
NY-A	0	0	....	2	0	0	0	0	2	6	4	4	1	0	3	2	4.500	18.00	24	27.15	.500	0	....	-3	0	-0.3
Total 3	4	3	.571	69	0	0	0	9	57^1	63	31	30	6	2	33	40	1.674	4.71	95	5.75	.283	0	....	-1	7	-0.2
• PRIOR, Mark	Mark William Prior b: 9/7/1980, San Diego, CA BR/TR, 6'5", 225 lbs. Deb: 5/22/2002																									
2002 Chi-N	6	6	.500	19	19	1	0	0	116^2	98	45	43	14	7	38	147	1.166	3.32	121	3.27	.226	6	.171	10	7	1.2
2003* Chi-N★	18	6	.750	30	30	3	1	0	211^1	183	67	57	15	9	50	245	1.103	2.43	173	2.69	.231	18	.250	42	22	4.6
Total 2	24	12	.667	49	49	4	1	0	328	281	112	100	29	16	88	392	1.125	2.74	150	2.90	.229	24	.224	52	29	5.8
• PROCTOR, Jim	James Arthur Proctor b: 9/9/1935, Brandywine, MD BR/TR, 6', 165 lbs. Deb: 9/14/1959																									
1959 Det-A	0	1	.000	2	1	0	0	0	2^2	8	5	5	0	0	3	0	4.125	16.88	24	20.18	.533	0	....	-4	0	-0.4
• PROCTOR, Red	Noah Richard Proctor b: 10/27/1900, Williamsburg, VA d: 12/17/1954, Richmond, VA BR/TR, 6'1", 165 lbs. Deb: 8/6/1923																									
1923 Chi-A	0	0	....	2	0	0	0	0	4	11	8	6	0	0	2	0	3.250	13.50	29	16.27	.550	0	....	-4	0	-0.4
• PROESER, George	George "Yatz" Proeser b: 5/30/1864, Cincinnati, OH d: 10/13/1941, New Burlington, OH BL/TL, 5'10", 190 lbs. Deb: 9/15/1888 ♦																									
1888 Cle-a	3	4	.429	7	7	7	1	0	59	53	39	25	4	7	30	20	1.407	3.81	81	....	.232	7	.304	-4	3	-0.2
• PROKOPEC, Luke	Kenneth Luke Prokopec b: 2/23/1978, Blackwood, Australia BL/TR, 5'11", 166 lbs. Deb: 9/4/2000																									
2000 LA-N	1	1	.500	5	3	0	0	0	21	19	10	7	2	2	9	12	1.333	3.00	144	4.15	.253	0	.000	3	1	0.2
2001 LA-N	8	7	.533	29	22	0	0	0	138^1	146	80	75	27	4	40	91	1.345	4.88	82	4.69	.268	7	.194	-13	4	-1.2
2002 Tor-A	2	9	.182	22	12	0	0	0	71^2	90	57	54	19	7	25	41	1.605	6.78	68	6.91	.302	0	....	-17	0	-1.6
Total 3	11	17	.393	56	37	0	0	0	231	255	147	136	48	13	74	144	1.424	5.30	80	5.33	.278	7	.171	-26	5	-2.5
• PROLY, Mike	Michael James Proly b: 12/15/1950, Jamaica, NY BR/TR, 6', 185 lbs. Deb: 4/10/1976																									
1976 StL-N	1	0	1.000	14	0	0	0	0	17	21	9	7	0	0	6	4	1.588	3.71	95	4.51	.328	0	....	-0	1	0.0
1978 Chi-A	5	2	.714	14	6	2	0	1	65^2	63	24	20	4	0	12	19	1.142	2.74	139	2.80	.250	0	....	8	6	0.9
1979 Chi-A	3	8	.273	38	6	0	0	9	88^1	89	43	38	6	1	40	32	1.460	3.87	110	4.00	.260	0	....	3	6	0.3
1980 Chi-A	5	10	.333	62	3	0	0	8	146^2	136	67	50	7	3	58	56	1.323	3.07	131	3.32	.253	0	....	17	12	1.7
1981 Phi-N	2	1	.667	35	2	0	0	2	63	66	29	27	6	1	19	19	1.349	3.86	94	3.98	.282	0	.000	-2	3	-0.3
1982 Chi-N	5	3	.625	44	1	0	0	1	82	77	22	21	5	2	22	24	1.207	2.30	162	3.09	.257	4	.286	14	9	1.6
1983 Chi-N	1	5	.167	60	0	0	0	1	83	79	35	33	5	1	38	31	1.410	3.58	106	3.63	.259	1	.091	3	4	0.3
Total 7	22	29	.431	267	18	2	0	22	545^2	531	229	196	33	8	195	185	1.330	3.23	120	3.49	.261	5	.156	43	41	4.4
• PROUGH, Bill	Herschel Clinton "Clint" Prough b: 11/28/1887, Markle, IN d: 12/29/1936, Richmond, IN BR/TR, 6'3", 185 lbs. Deb: 4/27/1912																									
1912 Cin-N	0	0	....	1	0	0	0	0	3	7	5	2	0	0	1	0	2.667	6.00	56	12.71	.538	0	.000	-1	0	-0.1
• PRUDHOMME, Augie	John Olgus Prudhomme b: 11/20/1902, Frierson, LA d: 10/4/1992, Shreveport, LA BR/TR, 6'2", 186 lbs. Deb: 4/19/1929																									
1929 Det-A	1	6	.143	34	6	2	0	1	94	119	78	65	7	2	53	26	1.830	6.22	69	6.00	.322	5	.238	-17	1	-1.5
• PRUETT, Hub	Hubert Shelby "Shucks" Pruett b: 9/1/1900, Malden, MO d: 1/28/1982, Ladue, MO BL/TL, 5'10.5", 165 lbs. Deb: 4/26/1922																									
1922 StL-A	7	7	.500	39	8	4	0	7	119^2	99	48	31	2	5	59	70	1.320	2.33	177	2.95	.235	5	.147	21	12	1.9
1923 StL-A	4	7	.364	32	8	3	0	2	104^1	109	57	50	3	3	64	59	1.658	4.31	97	4.60	.279	3	.130	-3	6	-0.3
1924 StL-A	3	4	.429	33	1	0	0	0	65	64	42	33	1	4	42	27	1.631	4.57	99	4.34	.270	3	.200	-1	3	-0.1

YEAR TM-L	W	L	PCT	G	GS	CG	SH	SV	IP	H	R	ER	HR	HB	BB	SO	RAT	ERA	ERA+	CERA	OAV	BH	AVG	PR+	WS	TPW
1927 Phi-N	7	17	.292	31	28	12	1	1	186	238	147	125	6	12	89	90	**1.758**	6.05	68	5.56	.314	13	.217	-36	2	-3.4
1928 Phi-N	2	4	.333	13	9	4	0	0	71^1	78	49	36	2	3	49	35	1.780	4.54	94	5.19	.291	5	.208	-1	3	-0.1
1930 NY-N	5	4	.556	45	8	1	0	3	135^2	152	83	72	11	4	63	49	1.585	4.78	99	4.90	.287	5	.135	-2	7	-0.3
1932 Bos-N	1	5	.167	18	7	4	0	0	63	76	42	36	3	6	30	27	1.683	5.14	73	5.41	.308	2	.105	-10	0	-1.0
Total 7	29	48	.377	211	69	28	1	13	745	816	468	383	28	37	396	357	1.627	4.63	92	4.73	.286	36	.170	-32	33	-3.4
• PRUIETT, Tex	Charles Le Roy Pruiett b: 4/10/1883, Osgood, IN d: 3/6/1953, Ventura, CA BL/TR, 5'8", 176 lbs. Deb: 4/26/1907																									
1907 Bos-A	3	11	.214	35	17	6	2	3	173^2	166	77	60	1	8	59	54	1.296	3.11	83	3.10	.254	8	.157	-18	6	-2.0
1908 Bos-A	1	7	.125	13	6	1	1	2	58^2	55	26	13	1	2	21	28	1.295	1.99	123	3.05	.257	1	.063	2	2	0.0
Total 2	4	18	.182	48	23	7	3	5	232^1	221	103	73	2	10	80	82	1.296	2.83	90	3.09	.255	9	.134	-16	8	-2.0
• PUCKETT, Troy	Troy Levi Puckett b: 12/10/1889, Winchester, IN d: 4/13/1971, Winchester, IN BL/TR, 6'2", 186 lbs. Deb: 10/4/1911																									
1911 Phi-N	0	0	....	1	0	0	0	0	2	4	3	3	0	1	2	1	3.000	13.50	25	14.91	.444	0	....	-2	0	-0.2
• PUENTE, Miguel	Migel Antonio (Aguilar) Puente b: 5/8/1948, San Luis Potosi, Mexico BR/TR, 6', 160 lbs. Deb: 5/3/1970																									
1970 SF-N	1	3	.250	6	4	1	0	0	18^2	25	18	17	5	0	11	14	1.929	8.20	48	7.98	.325	0	.000	-8	0	-0.9
• PUFFER, Brandon	Brandon Duane Puffer b: 10/5/1975, Downey, CA BR/TR, 6'3", 190 lbs. Deb: 4/17/2002																									
2002 Hou-N	3	3	.500	55	0	0	0	0	69	67	37	34	3	5	38	48	1.522	4.43	96	4.15	.258	0	.000	-1	3	-0.1
2003 Hou-N	0	0	....	13	0	0	0	0	21	24	13	12	2	1	16	10	1.905	5.14	86	6.46	.300	0	.000	-2	0	-0.2
Total 2	3	3	.500	68	0	0	0	0	90	91	50	46	5	6	54	58	1.611	4.60	93	4.69	.268	0	.000	-3	3	-0.4
• PUGH, Tim	Timothy Dean Pugh b: 1/26/1967, South Lake Tahoe, CA BR/TR, 6'6", 230 lbs. Deb: 9/1/1992																									
1992 Cin-N	4	2	.667	7	7	0	0	0	45^1	47	15	13	2	1	13	18	1.324	2.58	139	3.56	.276	1	.077	5	4	0.5
1993 Cin-N	10	15	.400	31	27	3	1	0	164^1	200	102	96	19	7	59	94	1.576	5.26	77	5.48	.303	12	.222	-21	4	-2.0
1994 Cin-N	3	3	.500	10	9	1	0	0	47^2	60	37	32	5	3	26	24	1.804	6.04	68	6.51	.314	5	.357	-10	1	-0.8
1995 Cin-N	6	5	.545	28	12	0	0	0	98^1	100	46	42	13	1	32	38	1.342	3.84	107	4.18	.266	4	.143	1	5	0.1
1996 Cin-N	1	0	1.000	9	0	0	0	0	15^1	20	18	18	3	1	11	9	2.022	10.57	39	7.93	.317	0	....	-11	0	-1.1
KC-A	0	1	.000	19	1	0	0	0	36^1	42	24	22	9	2	12	27	1.486	5.45	92	5.88	.282	0	....	-2	1	-0.2
Cin-N	0	1	.000	1	0	0	0	0	0^1	4	2	2	0	0	0	0	12.00	54.00	8	95.94	.800	0	....	-2	0	-0.2
Yr.	1	1	.500	10	0	0	0	0	15^2	24	20	20	3	1	11	9	2.234	11.49	36	9.81	.353	0	....	-13	0	-1.3
1997 Det-A	1	1	.500	2	2	0	0	0	9	6	5	5	0	0	5	4	1.222	5.00	92	2.26	.188	0	....	-1	0	0.0
Total 6	25	28	.472	107	58	4	1	0	416^2	479	249	230	51	15	158	214	1.529	4.97	83	5.21	.291	22	.202	-41	15	-3.6
• PULEO, Charlie	Charles Michael Puleo b: 2/7/1955, Glen Ridge, NJ BR/TR, 6'2", 200 lbs. Deb: 9/16/1981																									
1981 NY-N	0	0	....	4	1	0	0	0	13^1	8	1	0	0	0	8	8	1.200	0.00	....	1.95	.182	0	.000	5	2	0.5
1982 NY-N	9	9	.500	36	24	1	1	1	171	179	99	85	13	2	90	98	1.573	4.47	81	4.69	.275	6	.125	-14	4	-1.6
1983 Cin-N	6	12	.333	27	24	0	0	0	143^2	145	86	78	18	5	91	71	1.643	4.89	78	5.36	.269	5	.100	-17	2	-1.9
1984 Cin-N	1	2	.333	5	4	0	0	0	22	27	15	14	2	0	15	6	1.909	5.73	66	6.24	.297	1	.200	-5	0	-0.4
1986 Atl-N	1	2	.333	5	3	1	0	0	24^1	13	10	8	4	1	12	18	1.027	2.96	134	2.51	.160	2	.333	3	2	0.4
1987 Atl-N	6	8	.429	35	16	1	0	0	123^1	122	63	58	11	3	40	99	1.314	4.23	103	3.74	.262	5	.179	2	7	0.3
1988 Atl-N	5	5	.500	53	3	0	0	1	106^1	101	46	41	9	3	47	70	1.392	3.47	106	3.84	.251	3	.231	4	7	0.4
1989 Atl-N	1	1	.500	15	1	0	0	0	29	26	15	15	2	0	16	17	1.448	4.66	78	3.75	.245	0	.000	-3	1	-0.3
Total 8	29	39	.426	180	76	3	1	2	633	621	335	299	59	14	319	387	1.485	4.25	90	4.38	.261	22	.144	-24	25	-2.7
• PULIDO, Alfonso	Alfonso (Manzo) Pulido b: 1/23/1957, Veracruz, Mexico BL/TL, 5'11", 170 lbs. Deb: 9/5/1983																									
1983 Pit-N	0	0	....	1	1	0	0	0	2	4	3	2	2	0	1	1	2.500	9.00	41	19.72	.400	0	....	-1	0	-0.1
1984 Pit-N	0	0	....	1	0	0	0	0	2	3	2	2	0	0	1	2	2.000	9.00	40	6.48	.333	0	....	-1	0	-0.1
1986 NY-A	1	1	.500	10	3	0	0	1	30^2	38	17	16	8	0	9	13	1.533	4.70	87	6.29	.306	0	....	-2	1	-0.2
Total 3	1	1	.500	12	4	0	0	1	34^2	45	22	20	10	0	11	16	1.615	5.19	77	7.07	.315	0	....	-5	1	-0.5
• PULIDO, Carlos	Juan Carlos (Valera) Pulido b: 8/5/1971, Caracas, Venezuela BL/TL, 6', 195 lbs. Deb: 4/9/1994																									
1994 Min-A	3	7	.300	19	14	0	0	0	84^1	87	57	56	17	1	40	32	1.506	5.98	81	5.45	.273	0	....	-9	3	-0.8
2003 Min-A	0	1	.000	7	1	0	0	0	15^2	15	9	7	0	0	3	6	1.149	4.02	113	2.37	.254	0	....	1	1	0.1
Total 2	3	8	.273	26	15	0	0	0	100	102	66	63	17	1	43	38	1.450	5.67	85	4.97	.270	0	....	-8	4	-0.7
• PULSIPHER, Bill	William Thomas Pulsipher b: 10/9/1973, Fort Benning, GA BL/TL, 6'3", 210 lbs. Deb: 6/17/1995																									
1995 NY-N	5	7	.417	17	17	2	0	0	126^2	122	58	56	11	4	45	81	1.318	3.98	102	3.81	.255	4	.105	1	6	0.1
1998 NY-N	0	0	....	15	1	0	0	0	14^1	23	11	11	2	0	5	13	1.953	6.91	60	7.92	.371	0	.000	-4	0	-0.5
Mil-N	3	4	.429	11	10	0	0	0	58	63	30	30	6	1	26	38	1.534	4.66	92	4.90	.289	3	.158	-3	3	-0.3
Yr.	3	4	.429	26	11	0	0	0	72^1	86	41	41	8	1	31	51	1.618	5.10	83	5.50	.307	3	.150	-8	3	-0.8
1999 Mil-N	5	6	.455	19	16	0	0	0	87^1	100	65	58	19	2	36	42	1.557	5.98	76	5.81	.286	3	.143	-13	1	-1.3
2000 NY-N	0	2	.000	2	2	0	0	0	6^2	12	9	9	1	1	6	7	2.700	12.15	36	12.44	.387	0	.000	-6	0	-0.6
2001 Bos-A	0	0	....	23	0	0	0	0	22	25	15	13	3	2	14	16	1.773	5.32	84	6.71	.294	0	....	-2	1	-0.2
Chi-A	0	0	....	14	0	0	0	0	8	11	8	7	2	1	7	4	2.250	7.88	58	9.96	.314	0	....	-3	0	-0.3
Yr.	0	0	....	37	0	0	0	0	30	36	23	20	5	3	21	20	1.900	6.00	75	7.58	.300	0	....	-5	1	-0.4
Total 5	13	19	.406	101	46	2	0	0	323	356	196	184	44	11	139	201	1.533	5.13	84	5.26	.283	10	.123	-30	11	-3.0
• PUMPELLY, Spencer	Spencer Armstrong Pumpelly b: 4/11/1893, Owego, NY d: 12/5/1973, Sayre, PA TR, 5'11", 175 lbs. Deb: 7/11/1925																									
1925 Was-A	0	0	....	1	0	0	0	0	1	1	1	1	1	0	1	0	2.000	9.00	47	17.60	.333	0	....	-1	0	-0.1
• PURCELL, Blondie	William Aloysius Purcell b: 3/16/1854, Paterson, NJ d: 2/20/1912, Trenton, NJ BR/TR, 5'9.5", 159 lbs. Deb: 5/1/1879 M ♦																									
1879 Syr-N	4	15	.211	22	17	15	0	0	179^2	245	165	75	1	....	19	28	1.469	3.76	63	....	.305	72	.260	-19	9	-2.9
Cin-N	0	2	.000	2	2	2	0	0	18	27	15	8	0	....	2	3	1.611	4.00	58	....	.326	11	.220	-3	1	-0.6
Yr.	4	17	.190	24	19	17	0	0	197^2	272	180	83	1	....	21	31	**1.482**	3.78	63	....	.307	83	.254	-22	10	-3.4
1880 Cin-N	3	17	.150	25	21	21	0	0	196	235	149	70	1	....	32	47	1.362	3.21	77	....	.283	95	.292	-12	12	-0.7
1881 Buf-N	4	1	.800	9	5	5	0	0	61^2	62	37	19	2	....	9	15	1.151	2.77	100	....	.250	33	.292	2	8	0.0
1882 Buf-N	2	1	.667	6	3	2	0	0	31	44	30	17	2	....	4	9	1.548	4.94	59	....	.316	105	.276	-6	11	-1.1
1883 Phi-N	2	6	.250	11	9	7	0	0	80	110	71	39	0	....	12	30	1.525	4.39	70	....	.309	114	.268	-5	7	-0.3
1884 Phi-N	0	0	....	1	0	0	0	0	4	3	1	1	0	....	0	1	.750	2.25	133	....	.197	108	.252	1	13	-0.6
1885 Phi-a	0	1	.000	1	0	0	0	0	6	11	9	4	0	0	2	3	2.167	6.00	57	....	.379	90	.296	-2	9	0.2
1886 Bal-a	0	0	....	1	0	0	0	0	1	1	1	1	0	0	0	0	1.000	9.00	38	....	.249	19	.224	-1	3	-0.1
1887 Bal-a	0	0	....	1	0	0	0	0	4	12	8	7	0	1	4	2	3.000	15.75	26	....	.501	188	.307	-5	13	-1.4
Total 9	15	43	.259	79	57	52	0	0	581^1	750	486	241	6	1	84	138	1.428	3.73	70	....	.296	1263	.274	-50	86	-7.3
• PURDIN, John	John Nolan Purdin b: 7/16/1942, Lynx, OH BR/TR, 6'2", 185 lbs. Deb: 9/16/1964																									
1964 LA-N	2	0	1.000	3	2	1	1	0	16	6	1	1	1	0	6	8	.750	0.56	576	1.09	.115	1	.200	5	3	0.5
1965 LA-N	2	1	.667	11	2	0	0	0	22^2	26	19	17	8	0	13	16	1.721	6.75	48	7.36	.283	0	.000	-9	0	-1.0
1968 LA-N	2	3	.400	35	1	0	0	2	55^2	42	22	19	2	0	21	38	1.132	3.07	90	2.07	.206	3	.500	-2	3	-0.1
1969 LA-N	0	0	....	9	0	0	0	0	16^1	19	11	11	7	0	12	6	1.898	6.06	55	9.06	.292	0	.000	-5	0	-0.6
Total 4	6	4	.600	58	5	1	1	2	110^2	93	53	48	18	0	52	68	1.310	3.90	78	4.04	.225	4	.250	-12	6	-1.2
• PURKEY, Bob	Robert Thomas Purkey b: 7/14/1929, Pittsburgh, PA BR/TR, 6'2", 195 lbs. Deb: 4/14/1954																									
1954 Pit-N	3	8	.273	36	11	0	0	0	131^1	145	78	74	3	7	62	38	1.576	5.07	83	4.54	.293	2	.077	-10	4	-1.0
1955 Pit-N	2	7	.222	14	10	2	0	1	67^2	77	47	40	5	2	25	24	1.507	5.32	77	4.68	.287	6	.316	-8	2	-0.7
1956 Pit-N	0	0	....	2	0	0	0	0	4	2	1	1	1	0	0	1	.500	2.25	168	1.13	.143	0	....	1	0	0.1
1957 Pit-N	11	14	.440	48	21	6	1	2	179^2	194	84	77	10	7	38	51	1.291	3.86	98	3.55	.278	5	.111	-3	9	-0.4
1958 Cin-N★	17	11	.607	37	34	17	3	0	250	259	106	100	25	4	49	70	1.232	3.60	115	3.53	.268	9	.111	14	17	1.3
1959 Cin-N	13	18	.419	38	33	9	1	1	218	241	118	103	25	6	43	78	1.303	4.25	95	4.05	.279	11	.167	-5	11	-0.2
1960 Cin-N	17	11	.607	41	33	11	1	0	252^2	259	114	101	23	9	59	97	1.259	3.60	106	3.61	.265	11	.133	6	15	0.5
1961★ Cin-N★	16	12	.571	36	34	13	1	1	246^1	245	118	102	27	6	51	116	1.202	3.73	109	3.39	.255	8	.100	10	16	0.6

YEAR	TM-L	W	L	PCT	G	GS	CG	SH	SV	IP	H	R	ER	HR	HB	BB	SO	RAT	ERA	ERA+	CERA	OAV	BH	AVG	PR+	WS	TPW
1962	Cin-N★	23	5	.821	37	37	18	2	0	288^1	260	109	90	28	14	64	141	1.124	2.81	143	3.02	.240	11	.103	**37**	**26**	3.5
1963	Cin-N	6	10	.375	21	21	4	1	0	137	143	60	54	12	2	33	55	1.285	3.55	94	3.65	.272	4	.098	-3	6	-0.4
1964	Cin-N	11	9	.550	34	25	9	2	1	195^2	181	77	66	16	7	49	78	1.175	3.04	119	3.09	.246	3	.052	10	13	0.7
1965	StL-N	10	9	.526	32	17	3	1	2	124^1	148	83	80	20	7	33	39	1.456	5.79	66	5.25	.294	1	.029	-27	1	-3.2
1966	Pit-N	0	1	.000	10	0	0	0	1	19^2	16	3	3	0	0	4	5	1.017	1.37	260	1.89	.235	0	.000	4	2	0.4
Total	13	129	115	.529	386	276	92	13	9	2114^2	2170	998	891	195	71	510	793	1.267	3.79	103	3.66	.266	71	.110	24	122	1.2

• PURNER, Oscar Oscar E. Purner b: 12/9/1873, Washington, DC Deb: 9/2/1895

YEAR	TM-L	W	L	PCT	G	GS	CG	SH	SV	IP	H	R	ER	HR	HB	BB	SO	RAT	ERA	ERA+	CERA	OAV	BH	AVG	PR+	WS	TPW
1895	Was-N	0	0	....	1	0	0	0	0	2	4	2	2	1	0	3	0	3.500	9.00	53	20.16	.409	0	.000	-1	0	-0.1

• PUTTMANN, Ambrose Ambrose Nicholas "Putty,Brose" Puttmann b: 9/9/1880, Cincinnati, OH d: 6/21/1936, Jamaica, NY TL, 6'4", 185 lbs. Deb: 9/4/1903

YEAR	TM-L	W	L	PCT	G	GS	CG	SH	SV	IP	H	R	ER	HR	HB	BB	SO	RAT	ERA	ERA+	CERA	OAV	BH	AVG	PR+	WS	TPW
1903	NY-A	2	0	1.000	3	2	1	0	0	19	16	9	2	0	1	4	8	1.053	0.95	329	1.87	.228	1	.143	5	2	0.5
1904	NY-A	2	0	1.000	9	3	2	1	0	49^1	40	21	15	0	0	17	26	1.155	2.74	99	2.06	.223	5	.278	-1	4	0.0
1905	NY-A	2	7	.222	17	9	5	1	1	86^1	79	50	41	2	5	37	39	1.344	4.27	68	3.29	.246	10	.313	-12	2	-1.0
1906	StL-N	2	2	.500	4	4	0	0	0	18^2	23	13	11	2	2	9	12	1.714	5.30	49	6.19	.303	2	.333	-5	0	-0.5
Total	4	8	9	.471	33	18	8	2	1	173^1	158	93	69	4	8	67	85	1.298	3.58	79	3.10	.244	18	.286	-14	8	-1.0

• PUTZ, J.J. Joseph Jason Putz b: 2/22/1977, Trenton, MI BR/TR, 6'5", 220 lbs. Deb: 8/11/2003

YEAR	TM-L	W	L	PCT	G	GS	CG	SH	SV	IP	H	R	ER	HR	HB	BB	SO	RAT	ERA	ERA+	CERA	OAV	BH	AVG	PR+	WS	TPW
2003	Sea-A	0	0	....	3	0	0	0	0	3^2	4	2	2	0	0	3	3	1.909	4.91	88	5.31	.267	0	....	-0	0	0.0

• PYECHA, John John Nicholas Pyecha b: 11/25/1931, Aliquippa, PA BR/TR, 6'5", 200 lbs. Deb: 4/24/1954

YEAR	TM-L	W	L	PCT	G	GS	CG	SH	SV	IP	H	R	ER	HR	HB	BB	SO	RAT	ERA	ERA+	CERA	OAV	BH	AVG	PR+	WS	TPW
1954	Chi-N	0	1	.000	1	0	0	0	0	2^2	4	3	3	1	0	2	2	2.250	10.13	41	10.81	.333	0	.000	-2	0	-0.2

• PYLE, Ewald Herbert Ewald "Lefty" Pyle b: 8/27/1910, St. Louis, MO BL/TL, 6'.5", 175 lbs. Deb: 4/23/1939

YEAR	TM-L	W	L	PCT	G	GS	CG	SH	SV	IP	H	R	ER	HR	HB	BB	SO	RAT	ERA	ERA+	CERA	OAV	BH	AVG	PR+	WS	TPW
1939	StL-A	0	2	.000	6	1	0	0	0	8^1	17	15	12	3	0	11	5	3.360	12.96	38	16.78	.405	0	.000	-7	0	-0.7
1942	StL-A	0	0	....	2	0	0	0	0	5^1	6	4	4	0	0	4	1	1.875	6.75	55	5.25	.286	0	.000	-2	0	-0.2
1943	Was-A	4	8	.333	18	11	2	1	1	72^2	70	38	33	0	1	45	25	1.583	4.09	78	3.77	.254	2	.100	-7	2	-0.9
1944	NY-N	7	10	.412	31	21	3	0	0	164	152	89	79	12	6	68	79	1.341	4.34	84	3.51	.241	8	.157	-14	7	-1.4
1945	NY-N	0	0	....	6	1	0	0	0	6^1	16	12	12	0	0	4	2	3.158	17.05	23	13.85	.457	0	.000	-9	0	-1.0
	Bos-N	0	1	.000	4	2	0	0	0	13^2	16	15	11	1	0	18	10	2.488	7.24	53	8.29	.302	2	.333	-5	0	-0.5
	Yr.	0	1	.000	10	3	0	0	0	20	32	27	23	1	0	22	12	2.700	10.35	37	10.05	.364	2	.250	-14	0	-1.4
Total	5	11	21	.344	67	36	5	1	1	270^1	277	173	151	16	7	150	122	1.580	5.03	73	4.51	.262	12	.143	-44	9	-4.6

• PYLE, Harlan Harlan Albert "Firpo" Pyle b: 11/29/1905, Burchard, NE d: 1/13/1993, Beatrice, NE BR/TR, 6'2", 180 lbs. Deb: 9/21/1928

YEAR	TM-L	W	L	PCT	G	GS	CG	SH	SV	IP	H	R	ER	HR	HB	BB	SO	RAT	ERA	ERA+	CERA	OAV	BH	AVG	PR+	WS	TPW
1928	Cin-N	0	0	....	2	1	0	0	0	1^1	1	3	3	0	0	4	1	3.750	20.25	20	8.70	.143	0	.000	-2	0	-0.3

• PYLE, Shadow Harry Thomas Pyle b: 11/29/1861, Reading, PA d: 12/26/1908, Reading, PA TL, 5'8", 136 lbs. Deb: 10/15/1884

YEAR	TM-L	W	L	PCT	G	GS	CG	SH	SV	IP	H	R	ER	HR	HB	BB	SO	RAT	ERA	ERA+	CERA	OAV	BH	AVG	PR+	WS	TPW
1884	Phi-N	0	1	.000	1	1	1	0	0	9	9	8	4	0	....	6	4	1.667	4.00	75	....	.246	0	.000	-1	0	-0.1
1887	Chi-N	1	3	.250	4	4	3	0	0	26^2	53	27	14	1	2	21	5	1.988	4.73	94	....	.402	3	.188	-1	1	-0.1
Total	2	1	4	.200	5	5	4	0	0	35^2	62	35	18	1	2	27	9	1.907	4.54	88	....	.369	3	.150	-1	1	-0.3

• QUALTERS, Tom Thomas Francis "Money Bags" Qualters b: 4/1/1935, McKeesport, PA BR/TR, 6'.5", 190 lbs. Deb: 9/13/1953

YEAR	TM-L	W	L	PCT	G	GS	CG	SH	SV	IP	H	R	ER	HR	HB	BB	SO	RAT	ERA	ERA+	CERA	OAV	BH	AVG	PR+	WS	TPW
1953	Phi-N	0	0	....	1	0	0	0	0	0^1	4	6	6	1	1	1	0	15.00	162.00	3	181.36	.800	0	....	-6	0	-0.6
1957	Phi-N	0	0	....	6	0	0	0	0	7^1	12	6	6	0	0	4	6	2.182	7.36	52	7.90	.400	0	....	-3	0	-0.3
1958	Phi-N	0	0	....	1	0	0	0	0	2	2	1	1	0	0	1	0	1.500	4.50	88	3.21	.222	0	....	-0	0	0.0
	Chi-A	0	0	....	26	0	0	0	0	43	45	22	20	1	0	20	14	1.512	4.19	87	4.00	.281	0	.000	-3	1	-0.3
Total	3	0	0	....	34	0	0	0	0	52^2	63	35	33	2	1	26	20	1.690	5.64	67	5.64	.309	0	.000	-12	1	-1.1

• QUANTRILL, Paul Paul John Quantrill b: 11/3/1968, London, Canada BL/TR, 6'1", 185 lbs. Deb: 7/20/1992

YEAR	TM-L	W	L	PCT	G	GS	CG	SH	SV	IP	H	R	ER	HR	HB	BB	SO	RAT	ERA	ERA+	CERA	OAV	BH	AVG	PR+	WS	TPW
1992	Bos-A	2	3	.400	27	0	0	0	1	49^1	55	18	12	1	1	15	24	1.419	2.19	192	3.70	.288	0	....	11	5	1.1
1993	Bos-A	6	12	.333	49	14	1	1	1	138	151	73	60	13	2	44	66	1.413	3.91	118	4.16	.279	0	....	10	8	0.9
1994	Bos-A	1	1	.500	17	0	0	0	0	23	25	10	9	4	2	5	15	1.304	3.52	143	4.53	.278	0	....	4	2	0.3
	Phi-N	2	2	.500	18	1	0	0	1	30	39	21	20	3	3	10	13	1.633	6.00	72	5.97	.331	0	.000	-5	0	-0.6
1995	Phi-N	11	12	.478	33	29	0	0	0	179^1	212	102	93	20	6	44	103	1.428	4.67	91	4.67	.295	6	.105	-10	7	-1.2
1996	Tor-A	5	14	.263	38	20	0	0	0	134^1	172	90	81	27	2	51	86	1.660	5.43	92	6.52	.316	0	....	-9	4	-0.8
1997	Tor-A	6	7	.462	77	0	0	0	5	88	103	25	19	5	1	17	56	1.364	1.94	236	3.94	.297	0	.000	24	12	2.3
1998	Tor-A	3	4	.429	82	0	0	0	7	80	88	26	23	5	3	22	59	1.375	2.59	180	3.90	.285	0	....	18	11	1.7
1999	Tor-A	3	2	.600	41	0	0	0	0	48^2	53	19	18	5	4	17	28	1.438	3.33	148	4.77	.282	0	....	9	5	0.8
2000	Tor-A	2	5	.286	68	0	0	0	1	83^2	100	45	42	7	2	25	47	1.494	4.52	112	4.78	.298	0	....	5	6	0.5
2001	Tor-A★	11	2	.846	**80**	0	0	0	2	83	86	29	28	6	6	12	58	1.181	3.04	151	3.31	.274	0	....	14	11	1.3
2002	LA-N	5	4	.556	**86**	0	0	0	1	76^2	80	27	23	1	3	25	53	1.370	2.70	141	3.42	.267	1	.333	9	8	0.9
2003	LA-N	2	5	.286	**89**	0	0	0	1	77^1	61	18	15	2	3	15	44	.983	1.75	230	2.03	.227	0	.000	18	11	1.8
Total	12	59	73	.447	705	64	1	1	20	1091^1	1225	503	443	99	38	302	652	1.399	3.65	125	4.34	.287	7	.108	97	90	9.1

• QUARLES, Bill William H. Quarles b: 1869, Petersburg, VA d: 3/25/1897, Petersburg, VA, 6'3" Deb: 5/21/1891

YEAR	TM-L	W	L	PCT	G	GS	CG	SH	SV	IP	H	R	ER	HR	HB	BB	SO	RAT	ERA	ERA+	CERA	OAV	BH	AVG	PR+	WS	TPW
1891	Was-a	1	1	.500	3	2	2	0	0	22	32	27	20	1	2	12	10	2.000	8.18	46	....	.329	0	.000	-10	0	-1.0
1893	Bos-N	2	1	.667	3	3	3	0	0	27	31	20	14	2	2	5	6	1.333	4.67	106	4.12	.280	2	.222	0	2	0.0
Total	2	3	2	.600	6	5	5	0	0	49	63	47	34	3	4	17	16	1.633	6.24	67	2.27	.303	2	.100	-9	2	-0.9

• QUEEN, Mel Melvin Joseph Queen b: 3/4/1918, Maxwell, PA d: 4/4/1982, Fort Smith, AR BR/TR, 6'.5", 204 lbs. Deb: 4/18/1942

YEAR	TM-L	W	L	PCT	G	GS	CG	SH	SV	IP	H	R	ER	HR	HB	BB	SO	RAT	ERA	ERA+	CERA	OAV	BH	AVG	PR+	WS	TPW
1942	NY-A	1	0	1.000	4	0	0	0	0	5^2	6	0	0	0	2	3	0	1.588	0.00	....	5.78	.300	0	....	2	1	0.2
1944	NY-A	6	3	.667	10	10	4	1	0	81^2	68	32	30	7	1	34	30	1.249	3.31	105	3.07	.227	6	.194	0	6	0.0
1946	NY-A	1	1	.500	14	3	1	0	0	30^1	40	28	22	2	0	21	26	2.011	6.53	53	6.53	.315	1	.143	-11	0	-1.2
1947	NY-A	0	0	....	5	0	0	0	0	6^2	9	7	7	2	1	4	2	1.950	9.45	37	9.36	.321	0	.000	-4	0	-0.5
	Pit-N	3	7	.300	14	12	2	0	0	74	70	39	33	8	1	51	34	1.635	4.01	105	4.74	.244	2	.077	2	3	0.0
1948	Pit-N	4	4	.500	25	8	0	0	1	66^1	82	51	49	8	3	40	34	1.839	6.65	61	6.50	.308	1	.059	-19	0	-2.1
1950	Pit-N	5	14	.263	33	21	4	1	0	120^1	135	95	80	18	2	73	76	1.729	5.98	73	5.88	.284	2	.057	-21	0	-2.3
1951	Pit-N	7	9	.438	39	21	4	1	0	168^1	149	90	83	21	1	99	123	1.473	4.44	95	4.21	.233	5	.106	-2	7	-0.4
1952	Pit-N	0	2	.000	2	2	0	0	0	3^1	8	12	11	2	0	4	3	3.600	29.70	13	19.82	.381	0	....	-9	0	-1.0
Total	8	27	40	.403	146	77	15	3	1	556^2	567	354	315	68	11	329	328	1.610	5.09	80	5.04	.262	17	.104	-63	17	-7.3

• QUEEN, Mel Melvin Douglas Queen b: 3/26/1942, Johnson City, NY BL/TR, 6'1", 197 lbs. Deb: 4/13/1964 M/C ♦

YEAR	TM-L	W	L	PCT	G	GS	CG	SH	SV	IP	H	R	ER	HR	HB	BB	SO	RAT	ERA	ERA+	CERA	OAV	BH	AVG	PR+	WS	TPW
1966	Cin-N	0	0	....	7	0	0	0	1	7	11	5	5	0	0	6	9	2.429	6.43	61	8.68	.367	7	.127	-2	0	-1.1
1967	Cin-N	14	8	.636	31	24	6	2	0	195^2	155	69	60	17	6	52	154	1.058	2.76	136	2.47	.215	17	.210	23	17	2.8
1968	Cin-N	0	1	.000	5	4	0	0	0	18^1	25	15	12	7	0	6	20	1.691	5.89	54	7.90	.333	1	.125	-5	0	-0.6
1969	Cin-N	1	0	1.000	2	2	0	0	0	12	7	3	3	2	1	3	7	.833	2.25	167	2.06	.163	1	.167	2	1	0.2
1970	Cal-A	3	6	.333	34	3	0	0	9	60	58	28	28	5	5	28	44	1.433	4.20	86	4.18	.261	4	.250	-5	3	-0.5
1971	Cal-A	2	2	.500	44	0	0	0	4	65^2	49	17	13	3	8	29	53	1.188	1.78	181	2.84	.212	0	.000	10	7	1.0
1972	Cal-A	0	0	....	17	0	0	0	0	31	31	17	15	2	3	19	19	1.613	4.35	67	4.96	.265	0	.000	-5	0	-0.6
Total	7	20	17	.541	140	33	6	2	14	389^2	336	154	136	36	23	143	306	1.229	3.14	112	3.35	.233	49	.179	17	28	1.2

• QUEVEDO, Ruben Ruben Eduardo Quevedo b: 1/5/1979, Valencia, Venezuela BR/TR, 6'1", 245 lbs. Deb: 4/14/2000

YEAR	TM-L	W	L	PCT	G	GS	CG	SH	SV	IP	H	R	ER	HR	HB	BB	SO	RAT	ERA	ERA+	CERA	OAV	BH	AVG	PR+	WS	TPW
2000	Chi-N	3	10	.231	21	15	1	0	0	88	96	81	73	21	3	54	65	1.705	7.47	61	6.49	.271	4	.133	-28	0	-2.8
2001	Mil-N	4	5	.444	10	10	0	0	0	56^2	56	30	29	9	0	30	60	1.518	4.61	93	4.79	.257	4	.250	-2	3	-0.2
2002	Mil-N	6	11	.353	26	25	1	1	0	139	159	100	89	28	4	68	93	1.633	5.76	71	6.16	.288	4	.095	-25	0	-2.7
2003	Mil-N	1	4	.200	9	8	0	0	0	42^2	53	32	32	12	0	23	19	1.781	6.75	63	7.69	.314	3	.300	-11	0	-1.0
Total	4	14	30	.318	66	58	2	1	0	326^1	364	243	223	70	7	175	237	1.652	6.15	70	6.21	.281	15	.153	-67	3	-6.7

• QUICK, Eddie Edward Quick b: 12/1881, Baltimore, MD d: 6/19/1913, Rocky Ford, CO TR, 5'11" Deb: 9/28/1903

YEAR	TM-L	W	L	PCT	G	GS	CG	SH	SV	IP	H	R	ER	HR	HB	BB	SO	RAT	ERA	ERA+	CERA	OAV	BH	AVG	PR+	WS	TPW
1903	NY-A	0	0	....	1	1	0	0	0	2	5	5	2	0	0	1	0	3.000	9.00	35	12.03	.467	0	.000	-1	0	-0.1

YEAR	TM-L	W	L	PCT	G	GS	CG	SH	SV	IP	H	R	ER	HR	HB	BB	SO	RAT	ERA	ERA+	CERA	OAV	BH	AVG	PR+	WS	TPW
• QUINN, Frank	Frank William Quinn b: 11/27/1927, Springfield, MA d: 1/11/1993, Boynton Beach, FL BR/TR, 6'2", 180 lbs. Deb: 5/29/1949																										
1949	Bos-A	0	0	....	8	0	0	0	0	22	18	7	7	2	1	9	4	1.227	2.86	152	3.14	.222	1	.167	3	2	0.3
1950	Bos-A	0	0	....	1	0	0	0	0	2	2	2	2	0	0	1	0	1.500	9.00	54	3.50	.250	0	....	-1	0	-0.1
Total	2	0	0	....	9	0	0	0	0	24	20	9	9	2	1	10	4	1.250	3.38	132	3.17	.225	1	.167	2	2	0.2
• QUINN, Jack	John Picus Quinn b: 7/5/1883, Janesville, PA d: 4/17/1946, Pottsville, PA BR/TR, 6', 196 lbs. Deb: 4/15/1909																										
1909	NY-A	9	5	.643	23	11	8	0	1	118^2	110	45	26	1	4	24	36	1.129	1.97	128	2.57	.252	7	.156	10	7	1.2
1910	NY-A	18	12	.600	35	31	20	0	0	235^2	214	88	62	2	6	58	82	1.154	2.37	112	2.57	.247	19	.232	14	19	2.0
1911	NY-A	8	10	.444	40	16	7	0	2	174^2	203	111	73	2	4	41	71	1.397	3.76	95	3.88	.297	10	.164	0	9	0.0
1912	NY-A	5	7	.417	18	11	7	0	0	102^2	139	89	66	4	4	23	47	1.578	5.79	62	5.13	.325	8	.205	-19	0	-1.9
1913	Bos-N	4	3	.571	8	7	6	1	0	56^1	55	22	15	1	1	7	33	1.101	2.40	137	2.44	.261	4	.200	6	4	0.8
1914	Bal-F	26	14	.650	46	42	27	4	1	342^2	335	129	99	3	8	65	164	1.167	2.60	122	2.79	.266	33	.273	30	32	4.0
1915	Bal-F	9	22	.290	44	31	21	0	1	273^2	289	137	105	9	8	63	118	1.286	3.45	98	3.48	.278	29	.264	2	13	0.8
1918	Chi-A	5	1	.833	6	5	5	0	0	51	38	13	13	0	0	7	22	.882	2.29	119	1.43	.216	4	.222	3	5	0.5
1919	NY-A	15	14	.517	38	31	18	4	0	266	242	96	77	8	6	65	97	1.154	2.61	122	2.67	.244	19	.209	9	22	1.1
1920	NY-A	18	10	.643	41	32	17	2	3	253^1	271	110	90	8	2	48	101	1.259	3.20	119	2.85	.273	8	.091	17	19	1.2
1921*	NY-A	8	7	.533	33	13	6	0	0	119	158	61	50	2	5	32	44	1.597	3.78	112	4.85	.327	9	.220	5	8	0.5
1922	Bos-A	13	16	.448	40	32	16	4	0	256	263	119	99	9	3	59	67	1.258	3.48	118	3.05	.267	9	.099	22	19	1.6
1923	Bos-A	13	17	.433	42	28	16	1	7	243	302	125	105	6	6	53	71	1.461	3.89	106	4.27	.316	18	.225	7	18	0.7
1924	Bos-A	12	13	.480	44	25	13	2	7	228^2	241	109	83	10	12	52	64	1.281	3.27	134	3.40	.273	14	.179	31	18	2.6
1925	Bos-A	7	8	.467	19	15	8	0	0	105	140	68	51	3	3	26	24	1.581	4.37	104	4.77	.315	3	.094	5	5	0.3
	Phi-A	6	3	.667	18	14	4	0	0	99^2	119	56	43	3	3	16	19	1.355	3.88	120	3.74	.296	3	.097	9	6	0.6
	Yr.	13	11	.542	37	29	12	0	0	204^2	259	124	94	6	6	42	43	1.471	4.13	111	4.27	.306	6	.095	14	11	0.9
1926	Phi-A	10	11	.476	31	21	8	3	1	163^2	191	74	62	4	1	36	58	1.387	3.41	122	3.70	.296	8	.174	14	13	1.3
1927	Phi-A	15	10	.600	34	25	11	3	1	201^1	211	82	73	8	4	37	43	1.232	3.26	131	3.19	.278	6	.091	25	17	1.7
1928	Phi-A	18	7	.720	31	28	18	4	1	211^1	239	92	68	3	7	34	43	1.292	2.90	138	3.29	.286	13	.165	27	18	2.3
1929*	Phi-A	11	9	.550	35	18	7	0	2	161	182	87	71	8	1	39	41	1.373	3.97	107	3.81	.290	8	.133	4	10	0.0
1930*	Phi-A	9	7	.563	35	7	0	0	6	89^2	109	51	44	6	1	22	28	1.461	4.42	106	4.36	.302	9	.265	2	8	0.3
1931	Bro-N	5	4	.556	39	1	0	0	**15**	64^1	65	28	19	1	1	24	25	1.383	2.66	143	3.36	.266	3	.200	9	10	0.9
1932	Bro-N	3	7	.300	42	0	0	0	**8**	87^1	102	36	32	1	1	24	28	1.443	3.30	116	3.88	.296	4	.200	5	7	0.5
1933	Cin-N	0	1	.000	14	0	0	0	1	15^2	20	9	7	0	0	5	3	1.596	4.02	84	4.44	.323	0	.000	-1	0	-0.1
Total	23	247	218	.531	756	444	243	28	57	3920^1	4238	1837	1433	102	91	860	1329	1.300	3.29	114	3.39	.280	248	.184	237	287	22.9
• QUINN, Tad	Clarence Carr Quinn b: 9/21/1882, Torrington, CT d: 8/7/1946, Waterbury, CT TR, 6'1", 210 lbs. Deb: 9/27/1902																										
1902	Phi-A	0	1	.000	1	1	1	0	0	8	12	9	4	1	0	1	3	1.625	4.50	81	5.89	.346	0	.000	-1	0	-0.1
1903	Phi-A	0	0	....	2	0	0	0	0	9	11	6	5	0	0	5	1	1.778	5.00	61	4.77	.300	2	.667	-2	0	-0.1
Total	2	0	1	.000	3	1	1	0	0	17	23	15	9	1	0	6	4	1.706	4.76	69	5.30	.323	2	.333	-3	0	-0.2
• QUINN, Wimpy	Wellington Hunt Quinn b: 5/14/1918, Birmingham, AL d: 9/1/1954, Santa Monica, CA BR/TR, 6'2", 187 lbs. Deb: 6/8/1941																										
1941	Chi-N	0	0	....	3	0	0	0	0	5	3	4	4	0	0	3	2	1.200	7.20	49	1.78	.158	1	.500	-2	0	-0.2
• QUINTANA, Luis	Luis Joaquin (Santos) Quintana b: 12/25/1951, Vega Baja, Puerto Rico BL/TL, 6'2", 175 lbs. Deb: 7/9/1974																										
1974	Cal-A	2	1	.667	18	0	0	0	0	12^2	17	6	6	0	0	14	11	2.447	4.26	81	7.95	.327	0	....	-1	1	-0.1
1975	Cal-A	0	2	.000	4	0	0	0	0	7	13	6	5	2	0	6	5	2.714	6.43	55	13.35	.394	0	....	-2	0	-0.2
Total	2	2	3	.400	22	0	0	0	0	19^2	30	12	11	2	0	20	16	2.542	5.03	69	9.87	.353	0	....	-3	1	-0.3
• QUIRICO, Rafael	Rafael Octavio (Dottin) Quirico b: 9/7/1969, Santo Domingo, Dominican Republic BL/TL, 6'3", 170 lbs. Deb: 6/25/1996																										
1996	Phi-N	0	1	.000	1	1	0	0	0	1^2	4	7	7	1	0	5	1	5.400	37.80	11	33.15	.444	0	....	-6	0	-0.6
• QUIRK, Art	Arthur Lincoln Quirk b: 4/11/1938, Providence, RI BR/TL, 5'11", 170 lbs. Deb: 4/17/1962																										
1962	Bal-A	2	2	.500	7	5	0	0	0	27^1	36	20	18	3	0	18	18	1.976	5.93	63	7.03	.308	1	.143	-7	0	-0.7
1963	Was-A	1	0	1.000	7	3	0	0	0	21	23	13	10	3	0	8	12	1.476	4.29	87	4.72	.280	1	.250	-1	1	-0.1
Total	2	3	2	.600	14	8	0	0	0	48^1	59	33	28	6	0	26	30	1.759	5.21	72	6.02	.296	2	.182	-8	1	-0.8
• QUISENBERRY, Dan	Daniel Raymond Quisenberry b: 2/7/1953, Santa Monica, CA d: 9/30/1998, Leawood, KS BR/TR, 6'2", 180 lbs. Deb: 7/8/1979																										
1979	KC-A	3	2	.600	32	0	0	0	5	40	42	16	14	5	0	7	13	1.225	3.15	135	3.52	.278	0	....	5	4	0.4
1980*	KC-A	12	7	.632	**75**	0	0	0	**33**	128^1	129	47	44	5	1	27	37	1.216	3.09	131	2.85	.265	0	....	14	19	1.4
1981*	KC-A	1	4	.200	40	0	0	0	18	62^1	59	16	12	1	1	15	20	1.187	1.73	208	2.54	.258	0	....	13	10	1.4
1982	KC-A★	9	7	.563	72	0	0	0	**35**	136^2	126	43	39	12	0	12	46	1.010	2.57	159	2.46	.252	0	....	23	22	2.3
1983	KC-A★	5	3	.625	**69**	0	0	0	**45**	139	118	35	30	6	0	11	48	.928	1.94	210	1.80	.229	0	....	34	28	3.4
1984*	KC-A★	6	3	.667	72	0	0	0	**44**	129^1	121	39	38	10	0	12	41	1.028	2.64	152	2.44	.247	0	....	19	24	1.9
1985*	KC-A	8	9	.471	**84**	0	0	0	**37**	129	142	41	34	8	1	16	54	1.225	2.37	175	3.29	.280	0	....	27	23	2.7
1986	KC-A	3	7	.300	62	0	0	0	12	81^1	92	30	25	2	3	24	36	1.426	2.77	154	3.78	.291	0	....	14	10	1.4
1987	KC-A	4	1	.800	47	0	0	0	8	49	58	15	15	3	1	10	17	1.388	2.76	165	3.95	.287	0	....	10	7	1.0
1988	KC-A	0	1	.000	20	0	0	0	1	25^1	32	11	10	0	0	5	9	1.461	3.55	112	3.91	.305	0	....	2	2	0.2
	StL-N	2	0	1.000	33	0	0	0	0	38	54	26	26	4	0	6	19	1.579	6.16	56	5.61	.344	0	.000	-12	0	-1.2
1989	StL-N	3	1	.750	63	0	0	0	6	78^1	78	25	23	2	0	14	37	1.174	2.64	137	2.60	.261	1	.250	8	8	0.8
1990	SF-N	0	1	.000	5	0	0	0	0	6^2	13	12	10	1	0	3	2	2.400	13.50	27	9.67	.419	0	.000	-7	0	-0.8
Total	12	56	46	.549	674	0	0	0	244	1043^1	1064	356	320	59	7	162	379	1.175	2.76	144	2.95	.267	1	.167	150	157	14.9
• RABE, Charlie	Charles Henry Rabe b: 5/6/1932, Boyce, TX BL/TL, 6'1", 180 lbs. Deb: 9/21/1957																										
1957	Cin-N	0	1	.000	2	1	0	0	0	8^1	5	2	2	2	0	0	6	.600	2.16	190	1.41	.167	0	.000	2	1	0.2
1958	Cin-N	0	3	.000	9	1	0	0	0	18^2	25	10	9	3	0	9	10	1.821	4.34	96	7.03	.321	0	.000	-0	0	-0.1
Total	2	0	4	.000	11	2	0	0	0	27	30	12	11	5	0	9	16	1.444	3.67	113	5.30	.278	0	.000	1	1	0.1
• RACHUNOK, Steve	Stephen Stepanovich "The Mad Russian" Rachunok b: 12/5/1916, Rittman, OH d: 5/11/2002, Corona, CA BR/TR, 6'4.5", 205 lbs. Deb: 9/17/1940																										
1940	Bro-N	0	1	.000	2	1	1	0	0	10	9	5	5	0	0	5	10	1.400	4.50	89	3.08	.243	0	.000	-1	0	0.0
• RACZKA, Mike	Michael Raczka b: 11/16/1962, New Britain, CT BL/TL, 6'2", 200 lbs. Deb: 8/15/1992																										
1992	Oak-A	0	0	....	8	0	0	0	0	6^1	8	7	6	0	0	5	2	2.053	8.53	44	6.01	.308	0	....	-3	0	-0.3
• RADATZ, Dick	Richard Raymond "The Monster,Moose" Radatz b: 4/2/1937, Detroit, MI BR/TR, 6'6", 235 lbs. Deb: 4/10/1962																										
1962	Bos-A	9	6	.600	**62**	0	0	0	**24**	124^2	95	32	31	9	4	40	144	1.083	2.24	184	2.45	.211	3	.097	26	21	2.4
1963	Bos-A★	15	6	.714	66	0	0	0	25	132^1	94	31	29	9	5	51	162	1.096	1.97	192	2.29	.201	2	.069	27	24	2.7
1964	Bos-A★	16	9	.640	79	0	0	0	**29**	157	103	44	40	13	7	58	181	1.025	2.29	168	2.14	.186	6	.162	31	24	3.2
1965	Bos-A	9	11	.450	63	0	0	0	22	124^1	104	57	54	11	5	53	121	1.263	3.91	95	3.22	.227	5	.185	-0	11	0.1
1966	Bos-A	0	2	.000	16	0	0	0	4	19	24	10	10	3	0	11	19	1.842	4.74	80	6.50	.304	0	.000	-2	0	-0.2
	Cle-A	0	3	.000	39	0	0	0	10	56^2	49	33	29	6	3	34	49	1.465	4.61	75	4.12	.233	1	.111	-6	2	-0.7
	Yr.	0	5	.000	55	0	0	0	14	75^2	73	43	39	9	3	45	68	1.559	4.64	76	4.72	.253	1	.091	-8	2	-1.0
1967	Cle-A	0	0	....	3	0	0	0	0	3	5	2	2	1	0	2	1	2.333	6.00	54	11.45	.357	0	....	-1	0	-0.1
	Chi-N	1	0	1.000	20	0	0	0	5	23^1	12	21	17	4	5	24	18	1.543	6.56	54	4.90	.154	1	.250	-8	0	-0.9
1969	Det-A	2	2	.500	11	0	0	0	0	18^2	14	8	7	3	0	5	18	1.018	3.38	111	2.63	.212	0	.000	1	1	0.0
	Mon-N	0	4	.000	22	0	0	0	3	34^2	32	22	22	6	1	18	32	1.442	5.71	64	4.71	.244	1	.250	-8	1	-0.8
Total	7	52	43	.547	381	0	0	0	122	693^2	532	260	241	65	30	296	745	1.194	3.13	120	2.97	.212	19	.131	59	84	5.8
• RADBOURN, Charley	Charles Gardner "Old Hoss" Radbourn b: 12/11/1854, Rochester, NY d: 2/5/1897, Bloomington, IL BR/TR, 5'9", 168 lbs. Deb: 5/5/1880 HOF: 1939 ♦																										
1881	Pro-N	25	11	.694	41	36	34	3	0	325^1	309	162	88	1	....	64	117	1.147	2.43	109	....	.240	59	.219	18	24	0.8
1882	Pro-N	33	20	.623	54	51	50	**6**	0	466	422	213	110	6	....	51	**201**	1.015	2.12	132	....	.228	78	.239	**25**	**50**	2.2
1883	Pro-N	**48**	25	.658	**76**	68	66	4	1	632^1	563	275	144	7	....	56	315	.979	2.05	150	....	.224	108	.283	46	**60**	5.0
1884*	Pro-N	**59**	12	.831	**75**	**73**	**73**	11	1	**678^2**	528	216	104	18	....	98	**441**	.922	**1.38**	**205**	....	.203	83	.230	91	**89**	**8.5**
1885	Pro-N	28	21	.571	49	49	49	2	0	445^2	423	209	109	4	....	83	154	1.135	2.20	120	....	.239	58	.233	22	39	3.1

YEAR	TM-L	W	L	PCT	G	GS	CG	SH	SV	IP	H	R	ER	HR	HB	BB	SO	RAT	ERA	ERA+	CERA	OAV	BH	AVG	PR+	WS	TPW
1886	Bos-N	27	31	.466	58	58	57	3	0	509^1	521	300	170	18	....	111	218	1.241	3.00	105	....	.255	60	.237	21	32	2.6
1887	Bos-N	24	23	.511	50	50	48	1	0	425	638	305	215	20	14	133	87	1.501	4.55	86	....	.337	58	.301	-38	22	-2.9
1888	Bos-N	7	16	.304	24	24	24	1	0	207	187	110	66	8	8	45	64	1.121	2.87	100	....	.232	17	.215	-2	11	0.0
1889	Bos-N	20	11	.645	33	31	28	1	0	277	282	151	113	14	8	72	99	1.278	3.67	114	....	.255	23	.189	18	21	1.4
1890	Bos-P	27	12	.692	41	38	36	1	0	343	352	183	126	8	11	100	80	1.318	3.31	133	....	.254	39	.253	38	34	3.0
1891	Cin-N	11	13	.458	26	24	23	2	0	218	236	149	103	13	13	62	54	1.367	4.25	79	....	.266	17	.177	-23	9	-2.1
Total	11	309	195	.613	527	502	488	35	2	4527^1	4461	2273	1348	117	54	875	1830	1.149	2.68	121	....	.246	603	.241	216	391	21.6
• RADBOURN, George	George B. "Dandy,Dordy" Radbourn b: 4/8/1856, Bloomington, IL d: 1/1/1904, Bloomington, IL, 160 lbs. Deb: 5/30/1883																										
1883	Det-N	1	2	.333	3	3	2	0	0	22	38	28	16	1	....	7	2	2.045	6.55	47	....	.360	2	.167	-8	0	-0.8
• RADEBAUGH, Roy	Roy Radebaugh b: 2/22/1884, Champaign, IL d: 1/17/1945, Cedar Rapids, IA BR/TR, 5'7", 160 lbs. Deb: 9/22/1911																										
1911	StL-N	0	0	....	2	1	0	0	0	10	6	3	3	0	0	4	1	1.000	2.70	125	1.53	.176	0	.000	1	1	0.0
• RADER, Drew	Drew Leon "Lefty" Rader b: 5/14/1901, Elmira, NY d: 6/5/1975, Catskill, NY BR/TL, 6'2", 187 lbs. Deb: 7/18/1921																										
1921	Pit-N	0	0	....	1	0	0	0	0	2	2	0	0	0	0	0	0	1.000	0.00	....	2.31	.286	0	.000	1	0	0.1
• RADFORD, Paul	Paul Revere "Shorty" Radford b: 10/14/1861, Roxbury, MA d: 2/21/1945, Boston, MA BR/TR, 5'6", 148 lbs. Deb: 5/1/1883 ♦																										
1884*	Pro-N	0	2	.000	2	2	1	0	0	13	27	19	11	0	....	3	2	2.308	7.62	37	....	.404	70	.197	-7	7	-1.8
1885	Pro-N	0	2	.000	3	2	2	0	0	18^1	34	27	16	1	....	8	3	2.291	7.85	34	....	.380	90	.243	-11	13	-0.7
1887	NY-a	0	0	....	2	0	0	0	0	5	18	16	10	1	0	3	4	3.600	18.00	24	....	.547	235	.397	-7	18	0.0
1890	Cle-P	0	0	....	1	0	0	0	0	5	7	5	2	1	0	1	3	1.600	3.60	110	....	.317	136	.292	0	17	2.5
1891	Bos-a	0	0	....	1	0	0	0	0	1	0	0	0	0	0	0	0	.000	0.00	....	....	.000	118	.259	0	22	2.2
1893	Was-N	0	0	....	1	0	0	0	0	1	2	2	2	2	0	2	1	4.000	18.00	26	42.01	.404	106	.228	-1	10	-0.4
Total	6	0	4	.000	10	4	3	0	0	43^1	88	69	41	5	0	17	13	2.354	8.52	36	0.97	.407	1312	.258	-26	87	1.8
• RADINSKY, Scott	Scott David Radinsky b: 3/3/1968, Glendale, CA BL/TL, 6'3", 204 lbs. Deb: 4/9/1990																										
1990	Chi-A	6	1	.857	62	0	0	0	4	52^1	47	29	28	1	2	36	46	1.586	4.82	79	4.11	.241	0	....	-7	4	-0.7
1991	Chi-A	5	5	.500	67	0	0	0	8	71^1	53	18	16	4	1	23	49	1.065	2.02	197	2.17	.206	0	....	14	11	1.4
1992	Chi-A	3	7	.300	68	0	0	0	15	59^1	54	21	18	3	2	34	48	1.483	2.73	141	3.89	.243	0	....	7	7	0.8
1993*	Chi-A	8	2	.800	73	0	0	0	4	54^2	61	33	26	3	1	19	44	1.463	4.28	98	3.97	.268	0	....	-1	5	-0.1
1995	Chi-A	2	1	.667	46	0	0	0	1	38	46	23	23	7	0	17	14	1.658	5.45	82	6.05	.309	0	....	-4	1	-0.3
1996*	LA-N	5	1	.833	58	0	0	0	1	52^1	52	19	14	2	0	17	48	1.318	2.41	161	3.18	.264	0	.000	9	6	0.9
1997	LA-N	5	1	.833	75	0	0	0	3	62^1	54	22	20	4	1	21	44	1.203	2.89	134	2.83	.236	0	.000	7	8	0.7
1998	LA-N	6	6	.500	62	0	0	0	13	61^2	63	21	18	5	4	20	45	1.346	2.63	151	4.03	.272	0	....	9	8	0.9
1999	StL-N	2	1	.667	43	0	0	0	3	27^2	27	16	15	2	1	18	17	1.627	4.88	94	4.67	.270	0	....	-1	2	-0.1
2000	StL-N	0	0	....	1	0	0	0	0	0	0	0	0	0	0	1	0		....	....	∞	1.000	0	....	0	0	0.0
2001	Cle-A	0	0	....	2	0	0	0	0	2	4	6	6	2	0	3	3	3.500	27.00	17	26.18	.400	0	....	-5	0	-0.5
Total	11	42	25	.627	557	0	0	0	52	481^2	461	208	184	33	12	209	358	1.391	3.44	118	3.78	.253	0	.000	30	52	2.9
• RADKE, Brad	Brad William Radke b: 10/27/1972, Eau Claire, WI BR/TR, 6'2", 180 lbs. Deb: 4/29/1995																										
1995	Min-A	11	14	.440	29	28	2	1	0	181	195	112	107	32	4	47	75	1.337	5.32	90	4.58	.275	0	....	-11	7	-1.0
1996	Min-A	11	16	.407	35	35	3	0	0	232	231	125	115	40	4	57	148	1.241	4.46	115	3.97	.256	0	....	15	14	1.3
1997	Min-A	20	10	.667	35	**35**	4	1	0	239^2	238	114	103	28	3	48	174	1.193	3.87	120	3.41	.257	0	.000	21	16	2.0
1998	Min-A★	12	14	.462	32	32	5	1	0	213^2	238	109	102	23	9	43	146	1.315	4.30	111	4.18	.283	0	.000	15	14	1.4
1999	Min-A	12	14	.462	33	33	4	0	0	218^2	239	97	91	28	1	44	121	1.294	3.75	136	4.07	.280	0	.000	33	17	3.0
2000	Min-A	12	16	.429	34	34	4	1	0	226^2	261	119	112	27	5	51	141	1.376	4.45	116	4.44	.286	0	.000	21	15	1.9
2001	Min-A	15	11	.577	33	33	6	2	0	226	235	105	99	24	10	26	137	1.155	3.94	116	3.45	.271	2	.500	18	17	1.8
2002*	Min-A	9	5	.643	21	21	2	1	0	118^1	124	64	62	12	7	20	62	1.217	4.72	95	3.73	.272	0	....	-3	6	-0.3
2003*	Min-A	14	10	.583	33	33	3	1	0	212^1	242	111	106	32	5	28	120	1.272	4.49	101	4.24	.288	1	.200	5	13	0.5
Total	9	116	110	.513	285	284	33	8	0	1868^1	2003	956	897	246	48	364	1124	1.267	4.32	111	4.00	.274	3	.143	114	119	10.6
• RADLOSKY, Rob	Robert Vincent Radlosky b: 1/7/1974, West Palm Beach, FL BR/TR, 6'2", 204 lbs. Deb: 5/25/1999																										
1999	Min-A	0	1	.000	7	0	0	0	0	8^2	15	12	12	7	1	4	3	2.192	12.46	41	16.36	.375	0	....	-7	0	-0.7
• RAETHER, Hal	Harold Herman "Bud" Raether b: 10/10/1932, Lake Mills, WI BR/TR, 6'1", 185 lbs. Deb: 7/4/1954																										
1954	Phi-A	0	0	....	1	0	0	0	0	2	1	1	1	0	0	4	0	2.500	4.50	87	6.98	.200	0	....	-0	0	0.0
1957	KC-A	0	0	....	1	0	0	0	0	2	2	2	2	1	0	0	0	1.000	9.00	44	4.70	.250	0	....	-1	0	-0.1
Total	2	0	0	....	2	0	0	0	0	4	3	3	3	1	0	4	0	1.750	6.75	58	5.84	.231	0	....	-1	0	-0.1
• RAFFENSBERGER, Ken	Kenneth David Raffensberger b: 8/8/1917, York, PA d: 11/10/2002, York, PA BR/TL, 6'2", 185 lbs. Deb: 4/25/1939																										
1939	StL-N	0	0	....	1	0	0	0	0	1	2	0	0	0	0	0	1	2.000	0.00	....	7.48	.400	0	....	0	0	0.0
1940	Chi-N	7	9	.438	43	10	3	0	3	114^2	120	54	43	10	2	29	55	1.299	3.38	111	3.72	.271	5	.167	5	7	0.4
1941	Chi-N	0	1	.000	10	1	0	0	0	18	17	9	9	0	0	7	5	1.333	4.50	78	3.11	.262	0	.000	-1	0	-0.2
1943	Phi-N	0	1	.000	1	1	1	0	0	8	7	3	1	0	0	2	3	1.125	1.13	300	2.13	.241	0	.000	2	1	0.2
1944	Phi-N★	13	20	.394	37	31	18	3	0	258^2	257	101	88	9	2	45	136	1.168	3.06	118	2.65	.252	11	.138	16	18	1.3
1945	Phi-N	0	3	.000	5	4	1	0	0	24^1	28	19	12	3	0	14	6	1.726	4.44	86	5.50	.283	0	.000	-1	0	-0.2
1946	Phi-N	8	15	.348	39	23	14	2	**6**	196	203	89	79	10	1	39	73	1.235	3.63	95	3.12	.265	10	.167	-4	10	-0.4
1947	Phi-N	2	6	.250	10	7	3	1	0	41	50	30	25	4	1	8	16	1.415	5.49	73	4.58	.307	4	.267	-7	0	-0.6
	Cin-N	6	5	.545	19	15	7	0	1	106^2	132	54	49	11	0	29	38	1.509	4.13	99	4.85	.305	6	.162	1	6	0.0
	Yr.	8	11	.421	29	22	10	1	1	147^2	182	84	74	15	1	37	54	1.483	4.51	90	4.78	.305	10	.192	-6	6	-0.6
1948	Cin-N	11	12	.478	40	24	7	4	0	180^1	187	88	77	15	1	37	57	1.242	3.84	102	3.27	.259	7	.113	4	12	0.1
1949	Cin-N	18	17	.514	41	**38**	20	**5**	0	284	289	129	107	23	2	80	103	1.299	3.39	123	3.57	.264	16	.178	25	20	2.6
1950	Cin-N	14	19	.424	38	35	18	4	0	239	271	127	113	34	2	40	87	1.301	4.26	100	4.10	.279	11	.134	2	13	0.1
1951	Cin-N	16	17	.485	42	33	14	5	5	248^2	232	108	95	29	6	38	81	1.086	3.44	119	2.92	.246	10	.122	19	18	1.6
1952	Cin-N	17	13	.567	38	33	18	**6**	1	247	247	85	77	18	2	45	93	1.182	2.81	134	3.08	.261	8	.107	26	22	2.4
1953	Cin-N	7	14	.333	26	26	9	1	0	174	200	87	76	23	0	33	47	1.339	3.93	111	4.29	.289	8	.140	5	10	0.3
1954	Cin-N	0	2	.000	6	1	0	0	0	10^1	15	10	9	2	0	3	5	1.742	7.84	53	6.67	.333	1	.500	-4	0	-0.4
Total	15	119	154	.436	396	282	133	31	16	2151^2	2257	993	860	191	19	449	806	1.258	3.60	110	3.50	.267	97	.141	89	137	7.3
• RAFFO, Al	Albert Martin Raffo b: 11/27/1941, San Francisco, CA BR/TR, 6'5", 210 lbs. Deb: 4/29/1969																										
1969	Phi-N	1	3	.250	45	0	0	0	1	72^1	81	35	33	6	4	25	38	1.465	4.11	86	4.61	.286	1	.167	-5	3	-0.4
• RAGAN, Pat	Don Carlos Patrick Ragan b: 11/15/1888, Blanchard, IA d: 9/4/1956, Los Angeles, CA BR/TR, 5'10.5", 185 lbs. Deb: 4/21/1909 C																										
1909	Cin-N	0	1	.000	2	0	0	0	0	8	7	4	3	0	0	4	2	1.375	3.38	77	3.32	.259	1	.500	-1	0	0.0
	Chi-N	0	0	....	2	0	0	0	0	3^2	4	2	1	0	0	1	2	1.364	2.45	103	3.48	.286	0	.000	0	0	0.0
	Yr.	0	1	.000	4	0	0	0	0	11^2	11	6	4	0	0	5	4	1.371	3.09	83	3.37	.268	1	.250	-1	0	-0.1
1911	Bro-N	4	3	.571	22	7	5	1	1	93^2	81	32	22	0	2	31	39	1.196	2.11	157	2.72	.252	4	.138	13	9	1.2
1912	Bro-N	7	18	.280	36	25	12	1	1	208	211	101	84	7	4	65	101	1.327	3.63	92	3.35	.270	4	.060	-4	8	-1.1
1913	Bro-N	15	18	.455	44	32	14	0	0	264^2	284	145	111	10	4	64	109	1.315	3.77	87	3.46	.281	15	.165	-18	10	-2.0
1914	Bro-N	10	15	.400	38	26	14	1	3	208^1	214	104	69	5	3	85	106	1.435	2.98	96	3.68	.270	10	.133	-4	8	-0.7
1915	Bro-N	1	0	1.000	5	0	0	0	0	19^2	11	6	2	0	0	8	7	.966	0.92	303	1.36	.164	1	.167	4	2	0.4
	Bos-N	16	12	.571	33	26	13	3	0	227	208	71	62	2	7	59	81	1.176	2.46	109	2.65	.255	12	.150	3	16	0.2
	Yr.	17	12	.586	38	26	13	3	0	246^2	219	77	64	2	7	67	88	1.159	2.34	115	2.55	.248	13	.151	7	18	0.6
1916	Bos-N	9	9	.500	28	23	14	3	0	182	143	53	42	3	0	47	94	1.044	2.08	118	1.92	.218	13	.217	8	12	1.2
1917	Bos-N	6	9	.400	30	13	5	1	1	147^2	138	59	48	6	1	35	61	1.172	2.93	87	2.67	.250	6	.125	-5	6	-0.6
1918	Bos-N	8	17	.320	30	25	15	2	0	206^1	212	95	74	4	4	54	68	1.289	3.23	83	3.16	.270	13	.183	-8	6	-1.0
1919	Bos-N	0	2	.000	4	3	0	0	0	12^2	16	13	10	0	0	3	3	1.500	7.11	40	3.71	.281	1	.250	-6	0	-0.7
	NY-N	1	0	1.000	7	1	1	0	0	22^2	19	7	4	0	0	14	7	1.456	1.59	176	3.17	.247	3	.429	3	3	0.4
	Yr.	1	2	.333	11	4	1	0	0	35^1	35	20	14	0	0	17	10	1.472	3.57	80	3.36	.261	4	.364	-3	3	-0.2
	Chi-A	0	0	....	1	0	0	0	0	1	1	0	0	0	0	0	0	1.000	0.00	....	1.95	.250	0	....	0	0	0.0

YEAR	TM-L	W	L	PCT	G	GS	CG	SH	SV	IP	H	R	ER	HR	HB	BB	SO	RAT	ERA	ERA+	CERA	OAV	BH	AVG	PR+	WS	TPW
1923	Phi-N	0	0	....	1	0	0	0	0	3	6	2	2	1	0	0	0	2.000	6.00	77	10.41	.400	1	.500	-0	0	0.0
Total	11	77	104	.425	283	181	93	12	6	1608^1	1555	694	534	38	25	470	680	1.259	2.99	97	3.02	.260	84	.154	-15	80	-2.9

• RAGGIO, Brady Brady John Raggio b: 9/17/1972, Los Angeles, CA BR/TR, 6'4", 210 lbs. Deb: 4/15/1997

YEAR	TM-L	W	L	PCT	G	GS	CG	SH	SV	IP	H	R	ER	HR	HB	BB	SO	RAT	ERA	ERA+	CERA	OAV	BH	AVG	PR+	WS	TPW
1997	StL-N	1	2	.333	15	4	0	0	0	31^1	44	24	24	1	1	16	21	1.915	6.89	60	6.53	.336	0	.000	-10	0	-1.0
1998	StL-N	1	1	.500	4	1	0	0	0	7	22	12	12	1	1	3	3	3.571	15.43	27	22.18	.579	0	.000	-9	0	-0.9
2003	Ari-N	0	0	....	10	0	0	0	1	8^1	9	6	6	1	0	6	8	1.800	6.48	72	5.96	.290	0	....	-2	0	-0.2
Total	3	2	3	.400	29	5	0	0	1	46^2	75	42	42	3	2	25	32	2.143	8.10	52	8.78	.375	0	.000	-20	0	-2.0

• RAGLAND, Frank Frank Roland Ragland b: 5/26/1904, Water Valley, MS d: 7/28/1959, Paris, MS BR/TR, 6'1", 186 lbs. Deb: 4/17/1932

YEAR	TM-L	W	L	PCT	G	GS	CG	SH	SV	IP	H	R	ER	HR	HB	BB	SO	RAT	ERA	ERA+	CERA	OAV	BH	AVG	PR+	WS	TPW
1932	Was-A	1	0	1.000	12	1	0	0	0	37^2	54	33	31	5	3	21	11	1.991	7.41	58	7.99	.346	3	.273	-14	0	-1.2
1933	Phi-N	0	4	.000	11	5	0	0	0	38^1	51	32	29	1	1	10	4	1.591	6.81	56	4.82	.317	2	.200	-13	0	-1.3
Total	2	1	4	.200	23	6	0	0	0	76	105	65	60	6	4	31	15	1.789	7.11	57	6.39	.331	5	.238	-27	0	-2.6

• RAICH, Eric Eric James Raich b: 11/1/1951, Detroit, MI BR/TR, 6'4", 225 lbs. Deb: 5/24/1975

YEAR	TM-L	W	L	PCT	G	GS	CG	SH	SV	IP	H	R	ER	HR	HB	BB	SO	RAT	ERA	ERA+	CERA	OAV	BH	AVG	PR+	WS	TPW
1975	Cle-A	7	8	.467	18	17	2	0	0	92^2	118	61	57	12	1	31	34	1.608	5.54	68	5.61	.320	0	....	-19	1	-1.9
1976	Cle-A	0	0	....	1	0	0	0	0	2^2	7	5	5	1	0	0	1	2.625	16.88	21	15.60	.467	0	....	-4	0	-0.4
Total	2	7	8	.467	19	17	2	0	0	95^1	125	66	62	13	1	31	35	1.636	5.85	64	5.89	.326	0	....	-23	1	-2.3

• RAIN, Steve Steven Nicholas Rain b: 6/2/1975, Los Angeles, CA BR/TR, 6'6", 260 lbs. Deb: 7/17/1999

YEAR	TM-L	W	L	PCT	G	GS	CG	SH	SV	IP	H	R	ER	HR	HB	BB	SO	RAT	ERA	ERA+	CERA	OAV	BH	AVG	PR+	WS	TPW
1999	Chi-N	0	1	.000	16	0	0	0	0	14^2	28	17	15	1	1	7	12	2.386	9.20	49	10.12	.418	0	....	-7	0	-0.7
2000	Chi-N	3	4	.429	37	0	0	0	0	49^2	46	25	24	10	1	27	54	1.470	4.35	104	5.17	.250	0	.000	1	3	0.1
Total	2	3	5	.375	53	0	0	0	0	64^1	74	42	39	11	2	34	66	1.679	5.46	83	6.30	.295	0	.000	-6	3	-0.6

• RAINEY, Chuck Charles David Rainey b: 7/14/1954, San Diego, CA BR/TR, 5'11", 190 lbs. Deb: 4/8/1979

YEAR	TM-L	W	L	PCT	G	GS	CG	SH	SV	IP	H	R	ER	HR	HB	BB	SO	RAT	ERA	ERA+	CERA	OAV	BH	AVG	PR+	WS	TPW
1979	Bos-A	8	5	.615	20	16	4	1	1	103^2	97	47	44	7	3	41	41	1.331	3.82	115	3.63	.250	0	....	8	8	0.7
1980	Bos-A	8	3	.727	16	13	2	1	0	87	92	49	47	7	2	41	43	1.529	4.86	87	4.63	.273	0	....	-6	4	-0.6
1981	Bos-A	0	1	.000	11	2	0	0	0	40	39	21	12	2	0	13	20	1.300	2.70	143	3.21	.252	0	....	6	2	0.6
1982	Bos-A	7	5	.583	27	25	3	3	0	129	146	75	72	14	2	63	57	1.620	5.02	86	5.41	.294	0	....	-8	5	-0.8
1983	Chi-N	14	13	.519	34	34	1	1	0	191	219	109	95	17	3	74	84	1.534	4.48	85	4.91	.295	9	.161	-12	6	-1.1
1984	Chi-N	5	7	.417	17	16	0	0	0	88^1	102	55	42	4	2	38	45	1.585	4.28	91	4.72	.290	3	.097	-3	3	-0.4
	Oak-A	1	1	.500	16	0	0	0	1	30^2	43	27	23	2	0	17	10	1.957	6.75	55	6.55	.341	0	....	-10	0	-1.0
Total	6	43	35	.551	141	106	10	6	2	669^2	738	383	335	53	12	287	300	1.531	4.50	90	4.72	.284	12	.138	-25	28	-2.6

• RAJSICH, Dave David Christopher Rajsich b: 9/28/1951, Youngstown, OH BL/TL, 6'5", 175 lbs. Deb: 7/2/1978

YEAR	TM-L	W	L	PCT	G	GS	CG	SH	SV	IP	H	R	ER	HR	HB	BB	SO	RAT	ERA	ERA+	CERA	OAV	BH	AVG	PR+	WS	TPW
1978	NY-A	0	0	....	4	2	0	0	0	13^1	16	6	6	0	0	6	9	1.650	4.05	89	4.88	.320	0	....	-1	0	-0.1
1979	Tex-A	1	3	.250	27	3	0	0	0	53^2	56	25	21	7	0	18	32	1.379	3.52	118	4.30	.267	0	....	3	3	0.3
1980	Tex-A	2	1	.667	24	1	0	0	2	48^1	56	34	32	7	3	22	35	1.614	5.96	65	5.83	.295	0	....	-10	0	-1.0
Total	3	3	4	.429	55	6	0	0	2	115^1	128	65	59	14	3	46	76	1.509	4.60	86	5.01	.284	0	....	-8	3	-0.8

• RAKERS, Jason Jason Paul Rakers b: 6/29/1973, Pittsburgh, PA BR/TR, 6'2", 200 lbs. Deb: 5/6/1998

YEAR	TM-L	W	L	PCT	G	GS	CG	SH	SV	IP	H	R	ER	HR	HB	BB	SO	RAT	ERA	ERA+	CERA	OAV	BH	AVG	PR+	WS	TPW
1998	Cle-A	0	0	....	1	0	0	0	0	1	0	1	1	0	0	3	0	3.000	9.00	53	7.00	.000	0	....	-0	0	0.0
1999	Cle-A	0	0	....	1	0	0	0	0	2	2	1	1	1	0	1	0	1.500	4.50	112	7.30	.250	0	....	0	0	0.0
2000	KC-A	2	0	1.000	11	0	0	0	0	21^2	33	22	22	5	0	7	16	1.846	9.14	56	8.07	.351	0	....	-10	0	-0.9
Total	3	2	0	1.000	13	0	0	0	0	24^2	35	24	24	6	0	11	16	1.865	8.76	58	7.97	.343	0	....	-10	0	-1.0

• RAKOW, Ed Edward Charles "Rock" Rakow b: 5/30/1935, Pittsburgh, PA d: 8/26/2000, West Palm Beach, FL BB/TR, 5'11", 178 lbs. Deb: 4/22/1960

YEAR	TM-L	W	L	PCT	G	GS	CG	SH	SV	IP	H	R	ER	HR	HB	BB	SO	RAT	ERA	ERA+	CERA	OAV	BH	AVG	PR+	WS	TPW
1960	LA-N	0	1	.000	9	2	0	0	0	22	30	19	18	5	0	11	9	1.864	7.36	54	7.38	.323	2	.333	-9	0	-0.8
1961	KC-A	2	8	.200	45	11	1	0	1	124^2	131	80	66	14	8	49	81	1.444	4.76	86	4.61	.269	3	.103	-8	4	-0.9
1962	KC-A	14	17	.452	42	35	11	2	1	235^1	232	126	111	31	4	98	159	1.402	4.25	98	4.38	.260	8	.098	-1	12	-0.5
1963	KC-A	9	10	.474	34	26	7	1	0	174^1	173	85	76	18	5	61	104	1.342	3.92	98	3.99	.261	6	.105	-0	9	-0.2
1964	Det-A	8	9	.471	42	13	1	0	3	152^1	155	70	63	14	6	59	96	1.405	3.72	98	4.27	.266	0	.000	-2	8	-0.5
1965	Det-A	0	0	....	6	0	0	0	0	13^1	14	11	9	2	0	11	10	1.875	6.08	57	6.48	.280	0	.000	-4	0	-0.4
1967	Atl-N	3	2	.600	17	3	0	0	0	39^1	36	23	23	4	1	15	25	1.297	5.26	63	3.50	.240	0	.000	-9	0	-1.1
Total	7	36	47	.434	195	90	20	3	5	761^1	771	414	366	88	24	304	484	1.412	4.33	90	4.38	.264	19	.084	-31	33	-4.5

• RALEIGH, John John Austin Raleigh b: 4/21/1890, Elkhorn, WI d: 8/24/1955, Escondido, CA BR/TL, 5'9", 165 lbs. Deb: 8/4/1909

YEAR	TM-L	W	L	PCT	G	GS	CG	SH	SV	IP	H	R	ER	HR	HB	BB	SO	RAT	ERA	ERA+	CERA	OAV	BH	AVG	PR+	WS	TPW
1909	StL-N	1	10	.091	15	10	3	0	0	80^2	85	42	34	0	3	21	26	1.314	3.79	66	3.46	.285	2	.087	-9	1	-1.2
1910	StL-N	0	0	....	3	1	0	0	0	5	8	5	5	0	0	0	2	1.600	9.00	33	5.29	.364	0	.000	-3	0	-0.4
Total	2	1	10	.091	18	11	3	0	0	85^2	93	47	39	0	3	21	28	1.331	4.10	63	3.56	.290	2	.083	-13	1	-1.6

• RAMBERT, Pep Elmer Donald Rambert b: 8/1/1916, Cleveland, OH d: 11/16/1974, West Palm Beach, FL BR/TR, 6', 175 lbs. Deb: 9/23/1939

YEAR	TM-L	W	L	PCT	G	GS	CG	SH	SV	IP	H	R	ER	HR	HB	BB	SO	RAT	ERA	ERA+	CERA	OAV	BH	AVG	PR+	WS	TPW
1939	Pit-N	0	0	....	2	0	0	0	0	3^2	7	4	4	0	0	1	4	2.182	9.82	39	8.01	.389	0	....	-2	0	-0.2
1940	Pit-N	0	1	.000	3	1	0	0	0	8^1	12	8	7	0	3	4	0	1.920	7.56	50	7.24	.333	0	.000	-3	0	-0.3
Total	2	0	1	.000	5	1	0	0	0	12	19	12	11	0	3	5	4	2.000	8.25	46	7.48	.352	0	.000	-6	0	-0.6

• RAMBO, Pete Warren Dawson Rambo b: 11/1/1906, Thorofare, NJ d: 6/19/1991, Camden, NJ BR/TR, 5'9", 150 lbs. Deb: 9/16/1926

YEAR	TM-L	W	L	PCT	G	GS	CG	SH	SV	IP	H	R	ER	HR	HB	BB	SO	RAT	ERA	ERA+	CERA	OAV	BH	AVG	PR+	WS	TPW
1926	Phi-N	0	0	....	1	0	0	0	0	3^2	6	8	6	0	0	4	4	2.727	14.73	28	9.49	.353	1	1.000	-4	0	-0.4

• RAMIREZ, Allan Daniel Allan Ramirez b: 5/1/1957, Victoria, TX BR/TR, 5'10", 180 lbs. Deb: 6/8/1983

YEAR	TM-L	W	L	PCT	G	GS	CG	SH	SV	IP	H	R	ER	HR	HB	BB	SO	RAT	ERA	ERA+	CERA	OAV	BH	AVG	PR+	WS	TPW
1983	Bal-A	4	4	.500	11	10	1	0	0	57	46	22	22	6	0	30	20	1.333	3.47	114	3.68	.229	0	....	3	4	0.3

• RAMIREZ, Erasmo Erasmo Ramirez b: 4/29/1976, Santa Ana, CA BL/TL, 6', 180 lbs. Deb: 4/30/2003

YEAR	TM-L	W	L	PCT	G	GS	CG	SH	SV	IP	H	R	ER	HR	HB	BB	SO	RAT	ERA	ERA+	CERA	OAV	BH	AVG	PR+	WS	TPW
2003	Tex-A	3	1	.750	34	0	0	0	0	49	46	21	21	4	4	9	28	1.122	3.86	129	3.15	.251	0	....	7	4	0.6

• RAMIREZ, Hector Hector Bienvenido Ramirez b: 12/15/1971, El Seibo, Dominican Republic BR/TR, 6'3", 218 lbs. Deb: 8/28/1999

YEAR	TM-L	W	L	PCT	G	GS	CG	SH	SV	IP	H	R	ER	HR	HB	BB	SO	RAT	ERA	ERA+	CERA	OAV	BH	AVG	PR+	WS	TPW
1999	Mil-N	1	2	.333	15	0	0	0	0	21	19	8	8	1	0	11	9	1.429	3.43	132	3.63	.247	0	.000	3	2	0.2
2000	Mil-N	0	1	.000	6	0	0	0	0	9	11	10	10	1	0	5	4	1.778	10.00	46	5.96	.289	1	1.000	-6	0	-0.5
Total	2	1	3	.250	21	0	0	0	0	30	30	18	18	2	0	16	13	1.533	5.40	84	4.33	.261	1	.250	-3	2	-0.2

• RAMIREZ, Horacio Horacio Ramirez b: 11/24/1979, Carson, CA BL/TL, 6'1", 170 lbs. Deb: 4/2/2003

YEAR	TM-L	W	L	PCT	G	GS	CG	SH	SV	IP	H	R	ER	HR	HB	BB	SO	RAT	ERA	ERA+	CERA	OAV	BH	AVG	PR+	WS	TPW
2003	Atl-N	12	4	.750	29	29	1	0	0	182^1	181	91	81	21	6	72	100	1.388	4.00	105	4.21	.263	6	.098	5	9	0.2

• RAMIREZ, Roberto Roberto Sanchez Ramirez b: 8/17/1972, Veracruz, Mexico BL/TL, 6', 170 lbs. Deb: 6/12/1998

YEAR	TM-L	W	L	PCT	G	GS	CG	SH	SV	IP	H	R	ER	HR	HB	BB	SO	RAT	ERA	ERA+	CERA	OAV	BH	AVG	PR+	WS	TPW
1998	SD-N	1	0	1.000	21	0	0	0	0	14^2	12	13	10	4	0	12	17	1.636	6.14	64	5.61	.211	0	....	-4	0	-0.4
1999	Col-N	1	5	.167	32	4	0	0	1	40^1	68	42	37	8	0	22	32	2.231	8.26	70	9.69	.368	1	.143	-11	0	-1.0
Total	2	2	5	.286	53	4	0	0	1	55	80	55	47	12	0	34	49	2.073	7.69	69	8.60	.331	1	.143	-14	0	-1.4

• RAMOS, Edgar Edgar Jose (Malave) Ramos b: 3/6/1975, Cumana, Venezuela BR/TR, 6'4", 190 lbs. Deb: 5/21/1997

YEAR	TM-L	W	L	PCT	G	GS	CG	SH	SV	IP	H	R	ER	HR	HB	BB	SO	RAT	ERA	ERA+	CERA	OAV	BH	AVG	PR+	WS	TPW
1997	Phi-N	0	2	.000	4	2	0	0	0	14	15	9	8	3	1	6	4	1.500	5.14	83	6.04	.288	0	.000	-1	0	-0.2

• RAMOS, Mario Mario Martin Ramos b: 10/19/1977, Aurora, IL BL/TL, 5'11", 180 lbs. Deb: 6/19/2003

YEAR	TM-L	W	L	PCT	G	GS	CG	SH	SV	IP	H	R	ER	HR	HB	BB	SO	RAT	ERA	ERA+	CERA	OAV	BH	AVG	PR+	WS	TPW
2003	Tex-A	1	1	.500	3	3	0	0	0	13	11	9	9	3	2	13	8	1.846	6.23	80	7.20	.224	0	.000	-2	0	-0.2

• RAMOS, Pedro Pedro (Guerra) "Pete" Ramos b: 4/28/1935, Pinar del Rio, Cuba BB/TR, 6', 185 lbs. Deb: 4/11/1955

YEAR	TM-L	W	L	PCT	G	GS	CG	SH	SV	IP	H	R	ER	HR	HB	BB	SO	RAT	ERA	ERA+	CERA	OAV	BH	AVG	PR+	WS	TPW
1955	Was-A	5	11	.313	45	9	3	1	5	130	121	62	56	13	11	39	34	1.231	3.88	99	3.61	.253	3	.079	3	6	0.0
1956	Was-A	12	10	.545	37	18	4	0	0	152	178	95	89	23	3	76	54	1.671	5.27	82	6.03	.299	9	.205	-11	7	-1.1
1957	Was-A	12	16	.429	43	30	7	1	0	231	251	131	123	43	7	69	91	1.385	4.79	81	4.80	.271	13	.171	-17	7	-1.9
1958	Was-A	14	18	.438	43	**37**	10	4	3	259^1	277	133	122	38	5	77	132	1.365	4.23	90	4.40	.273	21	.239	-5	13	-0.4
1959	Was-A★	13	19	.406	37	35	11	0	0	233^2	233	127	108	30	9	52	95	1.220	4.16	94	3.67	.257	11	.147	2	10	0.2
1960	Was-A	11	18	.379	43	**36**	14	1	2	274	254	126	105	24	7	99	160	1.288	3.45	114	3.48	.245	10	.116	19	16	1.7
1961	Min-A	11	20	.355	42	34	9	3	2	264^1	265	134	116	39	4	79	174	1.301	3.95	107	4.02	.258	16	.172	14	15	1.6

YEAR	TM-L	W	L	PCT	G	GS	CG	SH	SV	IP	H	R	ER	HR	HB	BB	SO	RAT	ERA	ERA+	CERA	OAV	BH	AVG	PR+	WS	TPW
1962	Cle-A	10	12	.455	37	27	7	2	1	201^{1}	189	104	83	28	5	85	96	1.361	3.71	104	4.12	.246	10	.147	2	11	0.4
1963	Cle-A	9	8	.529	36	22	5	0	0	184^{2}	156	74	64	29	4	41	169	1.067	3.12	116	2.94	.226	6	.109	12	13	1.3
1964	Cle-A	7	10	.412	36	19	3	1	0	133	144	84	76	18	4	26	98	1.278	5.14	70	3.96	.273	7	.179	-20	2	-1.8
	NY-A	1	0	1.000	13	0	0	0	8	21^{2}	13	3	3	1	0	0	21	.600	1.25	291	0.93	.183	0	.000	6	6	0.5
	Yr.	8	10	.444	49	19	3	1	8	154^{2}	157	87	79	19	4	26	119	1.183	4.60	78	3.53	.263	7	.159	-14	8	-1.3
1965	NY-A	5	5	.500	65	0	0	0	19	92^{1}	80	34	30	7	1	27	68	1.159	2.92	116	2.74	.237	1	.083	6	11	0.5
1966	NY-A	3	9	.250	52	1	0	0	13	89^{2}	98	43	36	10	1	18	58	1.294	3.61	92	3.87	.283	2	.154	-3	5	-0.3
1967	Phi-N	0	0	....	6	0	0	0	0	8	14	8	8	1	2	8	1	2.750	9.00	38	13.01	.412	0	.000	-5	0	-0.5
1969	Pit-N	0	1	.000	5	0	0	0	0	6	8	4	4	2	0	0	4	1.333	6.00	58	5.82	.320	0	.000	-2	0	-0.2
	Cin-N	4	3	.571	38	0	0	0	2	66^{1}	73	41	38	8	5	24	40	1.462	5.16	73	4.59	.284	0	.000	-10	1	-1.1
	Yr.	4	4	.500	43	0	0	0	2	72^{1}	81	45	42	10	5	24	44	1.452	5.23	71	4.69	.287	0	.000	-12	1	-1.3
1970	Was-A	0	0	....	4	0	0	0	0	8^{1}	10	7	7	2	0	4	10	1.680	7.56	47	6.53	.294	0	.000	-4	0	-0.4
Total	15	117	160	.422	582	268	73	13	55	2355^{2}	2364	1210	1068	316	68	724	1305	1.311	4.08	95	4.05	.261	109	.155	-14	123	-1.6

• RAMSAY, Robert Robert Arthur Ramsay b: 12/3/1973, Vancouver, WA BL/TL, 6'5", 215 lbs. Deb: 8/27/1999

YEAR	TM-L	W	L	PCT	G	GS	CG	SH	SV	IP	H	R	ER	HR	HB	BB	SO	RAT	ERA	ERA+	CERA	OAV	BH	AVG	PR+	WS	TPW
1999	Sea-A	0	2	.000	6	3	0	0	0	18^{1}	23	13	13	3	0	9	11	1.745	6.38	78	6.71	.324	0	....	-3	0	-0.3
2000*	Sea-A	1	1	.500	37	1	0	0	0	50^{1}	43	22	19	3	1	40	32	1.649	3.40	134	4.44	.234	0	....	6	4	0.5
Total	2	1	3	.250	43	4	0	0	0	68^{2}	66	35	32	6	1	49	43	1.675	4.19	112	5.05	.259	0	....	3	4	0.3

• RAMSDELL, Willie James Willard "Willie the Knuck" Ramsdell b: 4/4/1916, Williamsburg, KS d: 10/8/1969, Wichita, KS BR/TR, 5'11", 180 lbs. Deb: 9/24/1947

YEAR	TM-L	W	L	PCT	G	GS	CG	SH	SV	IP	H	R	ER	HR	HB	BB	SO	RAT	ERA	ERA+	CERA	OAV	BH	AVG	PR+	WS	TPW
1947	Bro-N	1	1	.500	2	0	0	0	0	2^{2}	4	6	2	0	1	3	3	2.625	6.75	61	9.55	.333	1	1.000	-1	0	0.0
1948	Bro-N	4	4	.500	27	1	0	0	4	50^{1}	48	35	29	6	3	41	34	1.768	5.19	77	5.53	.251	1	.091	-8	1	-0.9
1950	Bro-N	1	2	.333	5	0	0	0	1	6^{1}	7	3	2	0	1	2	2	1.421	2.84	144	4.31	.292	0	.000	1	1	0.0
	Cin-N	7	12	.368	27	22	8	1	0	157^{1}	151	77	65	17	2	75	83	1.436	3.72	114	4.23	.255	10	.200	11	11	1.2
	Yr.	8	14	.364	32	22	8	1	1	163^{2}	158	80	67	17	3	77	85	1.436	3.68	115	4.23	.257	10	.189	12	12	1.2
1951	Cin-N	9	17	.346	31	31	10	1	0	196	204	103	88	18	8	70	88	1.398	4.04	101	4.11	.266	9	.155	2	8	0.1
1952	Chi-N	2	3	.400	19	4	0	0	0	67	41	22	18	5	5	24	30	.970	2.42	159	1.93	.173	1	.056	11	6	1.0
Total	5	24	39	.381	111	58	18	2	5	479^{2}	455	246	204	46	20	215	240	1.397	3.83	107	4.03	.250	22	.156	16	27	1.4

• RAMSEY, Toad Thomas A. Ramsey b: 8/8/1864, Indianapolis, IN d: 3/27/1906, Indianapolis, IN BR/TL Deb: 9/5/1885

YEAR	TM-L	W	L	PCT	G	GS	CG	SH	SV	IP	H	R	ER	HR	HB	BB	SO	RAT	ERA	ERA+	CERA	OAV	BH	AVG	PR+	WS	TPW
1885	Lou-a	3	6	.333	9	9	9	0	0	79	44	38	17	1	1	28	83	.911	1.94	166	....	.156	4	.129	11	6	0.8
1886	Lou-a	38	27	.585	67	67	**66**	3	0	**588^{2}**	447	297	160	3	12	207	499	1.111	2.45	148	....	**.201**	58	.241	68	47	5.9
1887	Lou-a	37	27	.578	65	64	61	0	0	561	711	358	214	9	16	167	**355**	1.267	3.43	128	....	.298	62	.254	49	46	3.3
1888	Lou-a	8	30	.211	40	40	37	1	0	342^{1}	362	278	130	10	11	86	228	1.309	3.42	90	....	.262	17	.120	-4	5	-0.9
1889	Lou-a	1	16	.059	18	18	15	0	0	140	175	152	87	7	2	71	60	1.757	5.59	69	....	.297	15	.263	-25	2	-2.1
	StL-a	3	1	.750	5	3	3	0	0	41	44	29	18	0	1	10	33	1.317	3.95	107	....	.266	5	.294	0	3	0.1
	Yr.	4	17	.190	23	21	18	0	0	181	219	181	105	7	3	81	93	1.657	5.22	75	....	.290	20	.270	-25	5	-2.0
1890	StL-a	24	17	.585	44	40	34	1	0	348^{2}	325	221	143	10	8	102	257	1.225	3.69	117	....	.240	33	.228	23	28	2.0
Total	6	114	124	.479	248	241	225	5	0	2100^{2}	2108	1373	769	40	51	671	1515	1.243	3.29	116	....	.251	194	.221	122	137	9.2

• RANDALL, Scott Scott Phillip Randall b: 10/29/1975, Fullerton, CA BR/TR, 6'3", 225 lbs. Deb: 8/26/2003

YEAR	TM-L	W	L	PCT	G	GS	CG	SH	SV	IP	H	R	ER	HR	HB	BB	SO	RAT	ERA	ERA+	CERA	OAV	BH	AVG	PR+	WS	TPW
2003	Cin-N	2	5	.286	15	2	0	0	0	27^{2}	34	20	20	1	2	11	25	1.627	6.51	66	4.98	.304	1	.250	-7	0	-0.7

• RANDOLPH, Stephen Stephen LeCharles Randolph b: 5/1/1974, Okinawa, Japan BL/TL, 6'3", 185 lbs. Deb: 3/31/2003

YEAR	TM-L	W	L	PCT	G	GS	CG	SH	SV	IP	H	R	ER	HR	HB	BB	SO	RAT	ERA	ERA+	CERA	OAV	BH	AVG	PR+	WS	TPW
2003	Ari-N	8	1	.889	50	0	0	0	0	60	50	28	27	7	2	43	50	1.550	4.05	115	4.51	.226	0	.000	5	6	0.4

• RANEY, Ribs Frank Robert Donald Raney b: 2/16/1923, Detroit, MI BR/TR, 6'4", 190 lbs. Deb: 9/18/1949

YEAR	TM-L	W	L	PCT	G	GS	CG	SH	SV	IP	H	R	ER	HR	HB	BB	SO	RAT	ERA	ERA+	CERA	OAV	BH	AVG	PR+	WS	TPW
1949	StL-A	1	2	.333	3	3	1	0	0	16^{1}	23	15	14	2	0	12	5	2.143	7.71	59	7.97	.333	0	.000	-5	0	-0.6
1950	StL-A	0	1	.000	1	0	0	0	0	2	2	2	1	0	0	2	2	2.000	4.50	110	5.17	.250	0	.000	0	0	0.0
Total	2	1	3	.250	4	3	1	0	0	18^{1}	25	17	15	2	0	14	7	2.127	7.36	62	7.67	.325	0	.000	-5	0	-0.6

• RAPP, Pat Patrick Leland Rapp b: 7/13/1967, Jennings, LA BR/TR, 6'3", 215 lbs. Deb: 7/10/1992

YEAR	TM-L	W	L	PCT	G	GS	CG	SH	SV	IP	H	R	ER	HR	HB	BB	SO	RAT	ERA	ERA+	CERA	OAV	BH	AVG	PR+	WS	TPW
1992	SF-N	0	2	.000	3	2	0	0	0	10	8	8	8	0	1	6	3	1.400	7.20	46	3.30	.235	0	.000	-5	0	-0.5
1993	Fla-N	4	6	.400	16	16	1	0	0	94	101	49	42	7	2	39	57	1.489	4.02	107	4.47	.281	6	.194	5	5	0.5
1994	Fla-N	7	8	.467	24	23	2	1	0	133^{1}	132	67	57	13	7	69	75	1.508	3.85	114	4.73	.266	5	.122	6	8	0.5
1995	Fla-N	14	7	.667	28	28	3	2	0	167^{1}	158	72	64	10	7	76	102	1.398	3.44	122	3.90	.253	6	.107	14	11	1.1
1996	Fla-N	8	16	.333	30	29	0	0	0	162^{1}	184	95	92	12	3	91	86	**1.694**	5.10	80	5.46	.301	7	.121	-21	3	-2.3
1997	Fla-N	4	6	.400	19	19	1	1	0	108^{2}	121	59	54	11	3	51	64	1.583	4.47	90	5.15	.286	5	.143	-6	4	-0.6
	SF-N	1	2	.333	8	6	0	0	0	33	37	24	22	5	2	21	28	1.758	6.00	67	6.44	.294	0	.000	-7	0	-0.8
	Yr.	5	8	.385	27	25	1	1	0	141^{2}	158	83	76	16	5	72	92	1.624	4.83	84	5.45	.288	5	.106	-13	4	-1.4
1998	KC-A	12	13	.480	32	32	1	1	0	188^{1}	208	117	111	24	10	107	132	1.673	5.30	91	5.84	.285	0	.000	-8	9	-0.8
1999*	Bos-A	6	7	.462	37	26	0	0	0	146^{1}	147	78	67	13	7	69	90	1.476	4.12	120	4.56	.263	0	.000	14	9	1.3
2000	Bal-A	9	12	.429	31	30	0	0	0	174	203	125	114	18	5	83	106	**1.644**	5.90	80	5.42	.289	0	.000	-22	4	-2.1
2001	Ana-A	5	12	.294	31	28	1	0	0	170	169	96	90	20	2	71	82	1.412	4.76	96	4.30	.261	0	.000	-5	7	-0.5
Total	10	70	91	.435	259	239	9	5	0	1387^{1}	1468	790	721	133	49	683	825	1.550	4.68	95	4.93	.276	29	.117	-35	60	-4.1

• RASCHI, Vic Victor John Angelo Raschi b: 3/28/1919, West Springfield, MA d: 10/14/1988, Groveland, NY BR/TR, 6'1", 205 lbs. Deb: 9/23/1946

YEAR	TM-L	W	L	PCT	G	GS	CG	SH	SV	IP	H	R	ER	HR	HB	BB	SO	RAT	ERA	ERA+	CERA	OAV	BH	AVG	PR+	WS	TPW
1946	NY-A	2	0	1.000	2	2	2	0	0	16	14	7	7	0	0	5	11	1.188	3.94	88	2.31	.230	1	.250	-1	1	-0.1
1947*	NY-A	7	2	.778	15	14	6	1	0	104^{2}	89	47	45	11	1	38	51	1.213	3.87	91	3.10	.226	10	.250	-5	6	-0.3
1948	NY-A★	19	8	.704	36	31	18	6	1	222^{2}	208	103	95	15	3	74	124	1.266	3.84	106	3.23	.247	19	.235	3	15	0.5
1949*	NY-A★	21	10	.677	38	**37**	21	3	0	274^{2}	247	120	102	16	6	138	124	1.402	3.34	121	3.58	.241	13	.157	15	19	1.5
1950*	NY-A★	21	8	.724	33	32	17	2	1	256^{2}	232	120	114	19	3	116	155	1.356	4.00	107	3.55	.243	17	.198	5	18	0.6
1951*	NY-A	21	10	.677	35	**34**	15	4	0	258^{1}	233	110	94	20	5	103	**164**	1.301	3.27	117	3.40	.242	15	.176	12	17	1.0
1952*	NY-A★	16	6	.727	31	31	13	4	0	223	174	78	69	12	6	91	127	1.188	2.78	119	2.67	.216	13	.188	6	17	0.8
1953*	NY-A	13	6	.684	28	26	7	4	1	181	150	74	67	11	1	55	76	1.133	3.33	111	**2.51**	.224	9	.143	2	11	0.0
1954	StL-N	8	9	.471	30	29	6	2	0	179	182	99	94	24	0	71	73	1.413	4.73	87	4.36	.268	9	.141	-11	6	-1.3
1955	StL-N	0	1	.000	1	1	0	0	0	1^{2}	5	4	4	0	0	1	1	3.600	21.60	19	15.89	.556	0	....	-3	0	-0.3
	KC-A	4	6	.400	20	18	1	0	0	101^{1}	132	66	61	10	1	35	38	1.648	5.42	77	5.52	.312	6	.182	-14	3	-1.4
Total	10	132	66	.667	269	255	106	26	3	1819	1666	828	752	138	26	727	944	1.316	3.72	105	3.45	.244	112	.184	10	113	0.9

• RASMUSSEN, Dennis Dennis Lee Rasmussen b: 4/18/1959, Los Angeles, CA BL/TL, 6'7", 230 lbs. Deb: 9/16/1983

YEAR	TM-L	W	L	PCT	G	GS	CG	SH	SV	IP	H	R	ER	HR	HB	BB	SO	RAT	ERA	ERA+	CERA	OAV	BH	AVG	PR+	WS	TPW
1983	SD-N	0	0	....	4	1	0	0	0	13^{2}	10	5	3	1	0	8	13	1.317	1.98	176	3.14	.200	0	.000	2	1	0.2
1984	NY-A	9	6	.600	24	24	1	0	0	147^{2}	127	79	75	16	4	60	110	1.266	4.57	83	3.54	.234	0	....	-12	5	-1.2
1985	NY-A	3	5	.375	22	16	2	0	0	101^{2}	97	56	45	10	1	42	63	1.367	3.98	101	3.96	.255	0	....	-1	4	-0.1
1986	NY-A	18	6	.750	31	31	3	1	0	202	160	91	87	28	2	74	131	1.158	3.88	105	3.16	.217	0	....	3	14	0.3
1987	NY-A	9	7	.563	26	25	2	0	0	146	145	78	77	31	4	55	89	1.370	4.75	92	4.86	.260	0	....	-7	8	-0.6
	Cin-N	4	1	.800	7	7	0	0	0	45^{1}	39	22	20	5	1	12	39	1.125	3.97	107	2.92	.229	1	.067	1	3	0.0
1988	Cin-N	2	6	.250	11	11	1	1	0	56^{1}	68	36	36	8	2	22	27	1.598	5.75	62	5.59	.300	5	.227	-15	0	-1.5
	SD-N	14	4	.778	20	20	6	0	0	148^{1}	131	48	42	9	2	36	85	1.126	2.55	133	2.69	.238	9	.188	12	13	1.5
	Yr.	16	10	.615	31	31	7	1	0	204^{2}	199	84	78	17	4	58	112	1.256	3.43	101	3.48	.256	14	.200	-3	13	0.1
1989	SD-N	10	10	.500	33	33	1	0	0	183^{2}	190	100	87	18	3	72	87	1.426	4.26	82	4.23	.270	11	.169	-18	5	-1.8
1990	SD-N	11	15	.423	32	32	3	1	0	187^{2}	217	110	94	28	3	62	86	1.487	4.51	85	5.09	.292	18	.290	-15	6	-1.0
1991	SD-N	6	13	.316	24	24	1	1	0	146^{2}	155	74	61	12	2	49	75	1.391	3.74	102	4.02	.271	6	.136	0	5	0.1
1992	Chi-N	0	0	....	3	1	0	0	0	5	7	6	6	2	1	2	0	1.800	10.80	33	9.81	.350	0	....	-4	0	-0.4
	KC-A	4	1	.800	5	5	1	1	0	37^{2}	25	7	6	0	0	6	12	.823	1.43	283	1.30	.197	0	....	11	5	1.2
1993	KC-A	1	2	.333	9	4	0	0	0	29	40	25	24	4	1	14	12	1.862	7.45	62	7.14	.328	0	....	-9	0	-0.9
1995	KC-A	0	1	.000	5	1	0	0	0	10	13	10	10	3	0	8	6	2.100	9.00	53	8.78	.302	0	....	-5	0	-0.5
Total	12	91	77	.542	256	235	21	5	0	1460^{2}	1424	747	673	175	26	522	835	1.332	4.15	93	4.02	.257	50	.193	-55	69	-4.7

YEAR	TM-L	W	L	PCT	G	GS	CG	SH	SV	IP	H	R	ER	HR	HB	BB	SO	RAT	ERA	ERA+	CERA	OAV	BH	AVG	PR+	WS	TPW
• RASMUSSEN, Eric	Eric Ralph Rasmussen b: 3/22/1952, Racine, WI BR/TR, 6'3", 205 lbs. Deb: 7/21/1975																										
1975	StL-N	5	5	.500	14	13	2	1	0	81	86	44	34	8	0	20	59	1.309	3.78	99	3.69	.264	4	.154	2	3	0.2
1976	StL-N	6	12	.333	43	17	2	1	0	150^1	139	67	59	10	2	54	76	1.284	3.53	100	3.28	.247	4	.105	-1	7	-0.2
1977	StL-N	11	17	.393	34	34	11	3	0	233	223	103	90	24	5	63	120	1.227	3.48	111	3.43	.254	10	.139	5	12	0.5
1978	StL-N	2	5	.286	10	10	2	1	0	60^1	61	32	28	4	0	20	32	1.343	4.18	84	3.61	.270	2	.111	-5	1	-0.6
	SD-N	12	10	.545	27	24	3	2	0	146^1	154	72	66	16	1	43	59	1.346	4.06	82	4.06	.277	7	.152	-12	5	-1.4
	Yr.	14	15	.483	37	34	5	3	0	206^2	215	104	94	20	1	63	91	1.345	4.09	83	3.93	.275	9	.141	-17	6	-2.0
1979	SD-N	6	9	.400	45	20	5	3	3	156^2	142	59	57	9	0	42	54	1.174	3.27	108	2.74	.244	2	.056	3	11	0.1
1980	SD-N	4	11	.267	40	14	0	0	1	111^1	130	60	54	9	3	33	50	1.464	4.37	79	4.50	.295	2	.095	-13	2	-1.5
1982	StL-N	1	2	.333	8	3	0	0	0	18^1	21	13	9	2	0	8	15	1.582	4.42	82	4.69	.288	0	.000	-2	0	-0.2
1983	StL-N	0	0	....	6	0	0	0	1	7^2	16	11	10	1	0	4	6	2.609	11.74	31	12.02	.444	0	....	-7	0	-0.7
	KC-A	3	6	.333	11	9	2	1	0	52^2	61	28	28	4	0	22	18	1.576	4.78	85	4.86	.289	0	....	-4	2	-0.4
Total	**8**	**50**	**77**	**.394**	**238**	**144**	**27**	**12**	**5**	**1017^2**	**1033**	**489**	**435**	**87**	**11**	**309**	**489**	**1.319**	**3.85**	**93**	**3.70**	**.266**	**31**	**.119**	**-34**	**43**	**-4.1**
• RASMUSSEN, Hans	Henry Florian Rasmussen b: 4/18/1895, Chicago, IL d: 1/1/1949, Chicago, IL BR/TR, 6'6", 220 lbs. Deb: 8/11/1915																										
1915	Chi-F	0	0	....	2	0	0	0	0	2	3	3	3	0	0	2	2	2.500	13.50	21	8.46	.600	0	.000	-2	0	-0.3
• RATH, Fred	Frederick Helsher Rath, Jr. b: 1/5/1973, Dallas, TX BR/TR, 6'3" Deb: 7/29/1998																										
1998	Col-N	0	0	....	2	0	0	0	0	5^1	6	1	1	0	0	2	2	1.500	1.69	307	4.03	.300	0	.000	2	1	0.2
• RATH, Fred	Frederick Helsher Rath, Sr. b: 9/1/1943, Little Rock, AR BR/TR, 6'3", 200 lbs. Deb: 9/10/1968																										
1968	Chi-A	0	0	....	5	0	0	0	0	11^1	8	5	2	0	1	3	3	.971	1.59	190	1.55	.182	0	....	2	1	0.2
1969	Chi-A	0	2	.000	3	2	0	0	0	11^2	11	10	10	4	0	8	4	1.629	7.71	50	6.76	.256	0	.000	-5	0	-0.5
Total	**2**	**0**	**2**	**.000**	**8**	**2**	**0**	**0**	**0**	**23**	**19**	**15**	**12**	**4**	**1**	**11**	**7**	**1.304**	**4.70**	**79**	**4.19**	**.218**	**0**	**.000**	**-3**	**1**	**-0.3**
• RATH, Gary	Alfred Gary Rath b: 1/10/1973, Gulfport, MS BL/TL, 6'2", 186 lbs. Deb: 6/2/1998																										
1998	LA-N	0	0	....	3	0	0	0	0	3^1	3	4	4	1	0	2	4	1.500	10.80	37	5.66	.250	0	....	-3	0	-0.2
1999	Min-A	0	1	.000	5	1	0	0	0	4^2	6	6	6	1	0	5	1	2.357	11.57	44	9.58	.300	0	....	-3	0	-0.3
Total	**2**	**0**	**1**	**.000**	**8**	**1**	**0**	**0**	**0**	**8**	**9**	**10**	**10**	**2**	**0**	**7**	**5**	**2.000**	**11.25**	**41**	**7.95**	**.281**	**0**	**....**	**-6**	**0**	**-0.6**
• RATLIFF, Jon	Jon Charles Ratliff b: 12/22/1971, Syracuse, NY BR/TR, 6'4", 195 lbs. Deb: 9/15/2000																										
2000	Oak-A	0	0	....	1	0	0	0	0	1	0	0	0	0	0	0	0	.000	0.00	....	0.00	.000	0	....	1	0	0.0
• RATZER, Steve	Steven Wayne Ratzer b: 9/9/1953, Paterson, NJ BR/TR, 6'1", 192 lbs. Deb: 10/5/1980																										
1980	Mon-N	0	0	....	1	1	0	0	0	4	9	5	5	0	0	2	0	2.750	11.25	32	12.01	.450	0	.000	-3	0	-0.4
1981	Mon-N	1	1	.500	12	0	0	0	0	17^1	23	14	12	2	0	7	4	1.731	6.23	56	5.89	.311	0	.000	-5	0	-0.6
Total	**2**	**1**	**1**	**.500**	**13**	**1**	**0**	**0**	**0**	**21^1**	**32**	**19**	**17**	**2**	**0**	**9**	**4**	**1.922**	**7.17**	**49**	**7.03**	**.340**	**0**	**.000**	**-9**	**0**	**-1.0**
• RAU, Doug	Douglas James Rau b: 12/15/1948, Columbus, TX BL/TL, 6'2", 175 lbs. Deb: 9/2/1972																										
1972	LA-N	2	2	.500	7	3	2	0	0	32^2	18	11	8	1	1	11	19	.888	2.20	151	1.34	.159	1	.143	4	3	0.5
1973	LA-N	4	2	.667	31	3	0	0	3	63^2	64	28	28	5	1	28	51	1.445	3.96	87	4.08	.259	1	.091	-4	3	-0.5
1974*	LA-N	13	11	.542	36	35	3	1	0	198^1	191	90	82	20	4	70	126	1.316	3.72	91	3.74	.251	9	.141	-6	8	-0.7
1975	LA-N	15	9	.625	38	38	8	2	0	257^2	227	96	89	18	3	61	151	1.118	3.11	109	2.67	.236	17	.195	6	16	0.8
1976	LA-N	16	12	.571	34	32	8	3	0	231	221	71	66	18	7	69	98	1.255	2.57	131	3.49	.258	9	.150	16	**21**	1.8
1977*	LA-N	14	8	.636	32	32	4	2	0	212^1	232	87	81	15	6	49	126	1.323	3.43	111	3.86	.282	10	.141	7	13	0.7
1978*	LA-N	15	9	.625	30	30	7	2	0	199	219	82	72	17	2	68	95	1.442	3.26	108	4.35	.284	9	.143	4	12	0.4
1979	LA-N	1	5	.167	11	11	1	1	0	56	73	37	33	3	4	22	28	1.696	5.30	69	5.77	.320	2	.143	-10	0	-0.9
1981	Cal-A	1	2	.333	3	3	0	0	0	10^1	14	10	10	2	0	4	3	1.742	8.71	42	7.37	.341	0	....	-6	0	-0.6
Total	**9**	**81**	**60**	**.574**	**222**	**187**	**33**	**11**	**3**	**1261**	**1259**	**512**	**469**	**99**	**28**	**382**	**697**	**1.301**	**3.35**	**105**	**3.67**	**.262**	**58**	**.154**	**12**	**76**	**1.4**
• RAUCH, Bob	Robert John Rauch b: 6/16/1949, Brookings, SD BR/TR, 6'4", 200 lbs. Deb: 6/29/1972																										
1972	NY-N	0	1	.000	19	0	0	0	1	27	27	16	15	3	0	21	23	1.778	5.00	67	5.55	.273	0	.000	-5	0	-0.5
• RAUCH, Jon	Jon Erich Rauch b: 9/27/1978, Louisville, KY BR/TR, 6'10", 230 lbs. Deb: 4/2/2002																										
2002	Chi-A	2	1	.667	8	6	0	0	0	28^2	28	26	21	7	2	14	19	1.465	6.59	69	5.41	.248	0	....	-7	0	-0.6
• RAUTZHAN, Lance	Clarence George Rautzhan b: 8/20/1952, Pottsville, PA BR/TL, 6'1", 195 lbs. Deb: 7/23/1977																										
1977*	LA-N	4	1	.800	25	0	0	0	2	20^2	25	10	10	0	0	7	13	1.548	4.35	88	4.34	.313	0	.000	-1	2	-0.2
1978*	LA-N	2	1	.667	43	0	0	0	4	61^1	61	22	20	1	1	19	25	1.304	2.93	119	3.13	.263	0	.000	4	5	0.3
1979	LA-N	0	2	.000	12	0	0	0	1	9^2	9	9	8	0	1	11	5	2.069	7.45	49	5.95	.273	0	....	-4	0	-0.4
	Mil-A	0	0	....	3	0	0	0	0	3	3	3	3	0	0	10	2	4.333	9.00	46	16.89	.300	0	....	-2	0	-0.2
Total	**3**	**6**	**4**	**.600**	**83**	**0**	**0**	**0**	**7**	**94^2**	**98**	**44**	**41**	**1**	**2**	**47**	**45**	**1.532**	**3.90**	**94**	**4.12**	**.276**	**0**	**.000**	**-3**	**7**	**-0.4**
• RAWLEY, Shane	Shane William Rawley b: 7/27/1955, Racine, WI BR/TL, 6', 180 lbs. Deb: 4/6/1978																										
1978	Sea-A	4	9	.308	52	2	0	0	4	111^1	114	57	51	7	5	51	66	1.482	4.12	92	4.39	.275	0	....	-3	6	-0.3
1979	Sea-A	5	9	.357	48	3	0	0	11	84^1	88	40	36	2	1	40	48	1.518	3.84	113	4.10	.278	0	....	5	8	0.5
1980	Sea-A	7	7	.500	59	0	0	0	13	113^2	103	44	42	3	3	63	68	1.460	3.33	124	3.60	.258	0	....	11	12	1.1
1981	Sea-A	4	6	.400	46	0	0	0	8	68^1	64	31	30	1	1	38	35	1.493	3.95	98	3.69	.257	0	....	0	5	0.0
1982	NY-A	11	10	.524	47	17	3	0	3	164	165	79	74	10	2	54	111	1.335	4.06	98	3.56	.267	0	....	-0	9	0.0
1983	NY-A	14	14	.500	34	33	13	2	1	238^1	246	111	100	19	3	79	124	1.364	3.78	103	3.94	.269	0	....	4	14	0.4
1984	NY-A	2	3	.400	11	10	0	0	0	42	46	33	29	0	0	27	24	1.738	6.21	61	4.69	.272	0	....	-11	0	-1.1
	Phi-N	10	6	.625	18	18	3	0	0	120^1	117	55	51	13	1	27	58	1.197	3.81	95	3.35	.257	5	.116	-1	6	-0.2
1985	Phi-N	13	8	.619	36	31	6	2	0	198^2	188	82	73	16	2	81	106	1.354	3.31	111	3.67	.249	8	.138	11	13	1.2
1986	Phi-N★	11	7	.611	23	23	7	1	0	157^2	166	67	62	13	1	50	73	1.370	3.54	109	3.92	.270	9	.173	6	10	0.7
1987	Phi-N	17	11	.607	36	**36**	4	1	0	229^2	250	118	112	23	5	86	123	1.463	4.39	97	4.52	.279	12	.152	-6	12	-0.6
1988	Phi-N	8	16	.333	32	32	4	1	0	198	220	111	92	27	4	78	87	**1.505**	4.18	85	5.00	.286	6	.105	-11	4	-1.3
1989	Min-A	5	12	.294	27	25	1	0	0	145	167	89	84	19	0	60	68	1.566	5.21	79	5.31	.293	0	....	-17	3	-1.7
Total	**12**	**111**	**118**	**.485**	**469**	**230**	**41**	**7**	**40**	**1871^1**	**1934**	**917**	**836**	**153**	**28**	**734**	**991**	**1.426**	**4.02**	**97**	**4.15**	**.271**	**40**	**.138**	**-12**	**102**	**-1.4**
• RAY, Carl	Carl Grady Ray b: 1/31/1889, Danbury, NC d: 4/2/1970, Lexington, NC BL/TL, 5'11", 170 lbs. Deb: 9/25/1915																										
1915	Phi-A	0	1	.000	2	1	0	0	0	7^1	11	7	4	0	4	6	6	2.318	4.91	59	9.65	.333	0	.000	-2	0	-0.2
1916	Phi-A	0	1	.000	3	1	0	0	0	9^1	9	8	5	0	1	14	5	2.464	4.82	59	7.39	.257	0	.000	-2	0	-0.3
Total	**2**	**0**	**2**	**.000**	**5**	**2**	**0**	**0**	**0**	**16^2**	**20**	**15**	**9**	**0**	**5**	**20**	**11**	**2.400**	**4.86**	**59**	**8.39**	**.294**	**0**	**.000**	**-3**	**0**	**-0.4**
• RAY, Farmer	Robert Henry Ray b: 9/17/1886, Fort Lyon, CO d: 3/11/1963, Electra, TX BL/TR, 5'11", 160 lbs. Deb: 6/13/1910																										
1910	StL-A	4	10	.286	21	16	11	0	0	140^2	146	77	56	3	7	49	35	1.386	3.58	69	3.92	.285	7	.175	-16	3	-1.8
• RAY, Jim	James Francis "Sting" Ray b: 12/1/1944, Rock Hill, SC BR/TR, 6'1", 195 lbs. Deb: 9/16/1965																										
1965	Hou-N	0	2	.000	3	2	0	0	0	7^2	11	9	9	1	0	6	7	2.217	10.57	32	8.94	.355	0	.000	-6	0	-0.7
1966	Hou-N	0	0	....	1	0	0	0	0	0	0	1	0	0	0	1	0	....	....	....	∞	1.000	0	....	0	0	0.0
1968	Hou-N	2	3	.400	41	2	1	0	1	80^2	65	26	24	5	1	25	71	1.116	2.68	110	2.33	.220	1	.067	4	5	0.4
1969	Hou-N	8	2	.800	40	13	0	0	0	115	105	55	50	11	2	48	115	1.330	3.91	90	3.65	.245	3	.115	-3	6	-0.4
1970	Hou-N	6	3	.667	52	2	0	0	5	105	97	39	38	13	0	49	67	1.390	3.26	119	4.14	.251	5	.185	7	9	0.7
1971	Hou-N	10	4	.714	47	1	0	0	3	97^2	72	27	23	3	2	31	46	1.055	2.12	159	2.06	.211	3	.167	13	11	1.4
1972	Hou-N	10	9	.526	54	0	0	0	8	90^1	77	50	43	10	3	44	50	1.339	4.28	78	3.63	.227	1	.063	-9	5	-1.1
1973	Hou-N	6	4	.600	42	0	0	0	6	69	65	37	34	5	3	38	25	1.493	4.43	82	4.11	.253	3	.231	-6	4	-0.6
1974	Det-A	1	3	.250	28	0	0	0	2	52^1	49	27	26	4	1	29	26	1.490	4.47	85	4.13	.254	0	....	-4	3	-0.4
Total	**9**	**43**	**30**	**.589**	**308**	**20**	**1**	**0**	**25**	**617^2**	**541**	**271**	**247**	**52**	**12**	**271**	**407**	**1.315**	**3.60**	**97**	**3.47**	**.238**	**16**	**.137**	**-4**	**43**	**-0.7**
• RAY, Ken	Kenneth Alan Ray b: 11/27/1974, Atlanta, GA BR/TR, 6'2", 200 lbs. Deb: 7/10/1999																										
1999	KC-A	1	0	1.000	13	0	0	0	0	11^1	23	12	11	2	1	6	0	2.559	8.74	57	13.86	.460	0	....	-5	0	-0.5

YEAR TM-L	W	L	PCT	G	GS	CG	SH	SV	IP	H	R	ER	HR	HB	BB	SO	RAT	ERA	ERA+	CERA	OAV	BH	AVG	PR+	WS	TPW
• RAYDON, Curt				Curtis Lowell Raydon b: 11/18/1933, Bloomington, IL BR/TR, 6'4", 190 lbs. Deb: 4/15/1958																						
1958 Pit-N	8	4	.667	31	20	2	1	1	134^1	118	64	54	18	5	61	85	1.333	3.62	107	3.97	.236	1	.026	1	7	-0.1
• RAYMOND, Bugs				Arthur Lawrence Raymond b: 2/24/1882, Chicago, IL d: 9/7/1912, Chicago, IL BR/TR, 5'10", 180 lbs. Deb: 9/23/1904																						
1904 Det-A	0	1	.000	5	2	1	0	0	14^2	14	9	5	0	2	6	7	1.364	3.07	83	3.61	.252	0	.000	-1	0	-0.2
1907 StL-N	2	4	.333	8	6	6	1	0	64^2	56	34	12	3	1	21	34	1.191	1.67	149	2.73	.230	2	.091	6	3	0.7
1908 StL-N	15	25	.375	48	37	23	5	2	324^1	236	116	73	2	14	95	145	1.021	2.03	116	1.90	.207	17	.189	19	19	2.4
1909 NY-N	18	12	.600	39	30	18	2	0	270	239	98	74	7	6	87	121	1.207	2.47	103	2.84	.245	13	.146	5	18	0.6
1910 NY-N	4	11	.267	19	11	6	0	0	99^1	106	63	42	2	8	40	55	1.470	3.81	78	4.22	.280	5	.156	-8	1	-0.9
1911 NY-N	6	4	.600	17	9	4	1	0	81^2	73	40	30	1	2	33	39	1.298	3.31	101	3.08	.248	5	.200	2	5	0.1
Total 6	**45**	**57**	**.441**	**136**	**95**	**58**	**9**	**2**	**854^2**	**724**	**360**	**236**	**15**	**33**	**282**	**401**	**1.177**	**2.49**	**105**	**2.67**	**.234**	**42**	**.160**	**23**	**46**	**2.8**
• RAYMOND, Claude				Jean Claude Marc "Frenchy" Raymond b: 5/7/1937, St. Jean, Canada BR/TR, 5'10", 175 lbs. Deb: 4/15/1959																						
1959 Chi-A	0	0	....	3	0	0	0	0	4	5	4	4	2	0	2	1	1.750	9.00	42	9.05	.333	0	....	-2	0	-0.2
1961 Mil-N	1	0	1.000	13	0	0	0	2	20^1	22	9	9	2	1	9	13	1.525	3.98	94	4.81	.275	0	.000	-1	1	-0.1
1962 Mil-N	5	5	.500	26	0	0	0	10	42^2	37	15	13	5	2	15	40	1.219	2.74	138	3.45	.236	0	.000	5	6	0.4
1963 Mil-N	4	6	.400	45	0	0	0	5	53^1	57	36	32	12	4	27	44	1.575	5.40	60	5.97	.268	2	.500	-14	1	-1.3
1964 Hou-N	5	5	.500	38	0	0	0	0	79^2	64	28	25	3	3	22	56	1.079	2.82	121	2.39	.229	1	.071	6	6	0.6
1965 Hou-N	7	4	.636	33	7	2	0	5	96^1	87	35	31	6	5	16	79	1.069	2.90	116	2.63	.244	3	.115	7	8	0.6
1966 Hou-N★	7	5	.583	62	0	0	0	16	92	85	39	32	10	4	25	73	1.196	3.13	109	3.26	.242	1	.111	4	10	0.4
1967 Hou-N	0	4	.000	21	0	0	0	5	31	31	12	11	5	2	7	17	1.226	3.19	104	3.84	.256	1	.200	1	2	0.2
Atl-N	4	1	.800	28	0	0	0	5	34^1	33	11	10	2	0	11	14	1.282	2.62	127	3.08	.260	0	.000	2	4	0.2
Yr.	4	5	.444	49	0	0	0	10	65^1	64	23	21	7	2	18	31	1.255	2.89	115	3.44	.258	1	.143	3	6	0.4
1968 Atl-N	3	5	.375	36	0	0	0	10	60^1	56	21	19	4	1	18	37	1.227	2.83	106	2.97	.256	1	.143	1	6	0.1
1969 Atl-N	2	2	.500	33	0	0	0	1	48	56	34	28	4	2	13	15	1.438	5.25	69	4.51	.298	2	.286	-9	0	-0.9
Mon-N	1	2	.333	15	0	0	0	1	22	21	12	10	2	2	8	11	1.318	4.09	90	3.70	.256	0	.000	-1	1	-0.1
Yr.	3	4	.429	48	0	0	0	2	70	77	46	38	6	4	21	26	1.400	4.89	74	4.26	.285	2	.182	-9	1	-1.0
1970 Mon-N	6	7	.462	59	0	0	0	23	83^1	76	48	41	13	2	27	68	1.236	4.43	93	3.57	.240	0	.000	-4	9	-0.4
1971 Mon-N	1	7	.125	37	0	0	0	0	53^2	81	34	28	5	0	25	29	1.975	4.70	75	7.45	.373	0	.000	-7	0	-0.7
Total 12	**46**	**53**	**.465**	**449**	**7**	**2**	**0**	**83**	**721**	**711**	**338**	**293**	**75**	**28**	**225**	**497**	**1.298**	**3.66**	**96**	**3.80**	**.261**	**11**	**.109**	**-11**	**54**	**-1.3**
• RAZIANO, Barry				Barry John Raziano b: 2/5/1947, New Orleans, LA BB/TR, 5'10", 175 lbs. Deb: 8/18/1973																						
1973 KC-A	0	0	....	2	0	0	0	0	5	6	3	3	1	1	1	0	1.400	5.40	76	5.79	.316	0	....	-1	0	-0.1
1974 Cal-A	1	2	.333	13	0	0	0	1	16^2	15	14	12	1	0	8	9	1.380	6.48	53	3.60	.246	0	....	-5	0	-0.6
Total 2	**1**	**2**	**.333**	**15**	**0**	**0**	**0**	**1**	**21^2**	**21**	**17**	**15**	**2**	**1**	**9**	**9**	**1.385**	**6.23**	**57**	**4.11**	**.263**	**0**	**....**	**-6**	**0**	**-0.6**
• REAGAN, Rip				Arthur Edgar Reagan b: 6/5/1878, Lincoln, IL d: 6/8/1953, Kansas City, MO BR/TR, 5'11", 170 lbs. Deb: 9/19/1903																						
1903 Cin-N	0	2	.000	3	2	2	0	0	18	40	30	12	0	1	7	7	2.611	6.00	59	11.56	.455	2	.250	-5	0	-0.4
• REAMES, Britt				William Britt Reames b: 8/19/1973, Seneca, SC BR/TR, 5'11", 175 lbs. Deb: 8/20/2000																						
2000* StL-N	2	1	.667	8	7	0	0	0	40^2	30	17	13	4	1	23	31	1.303	2.88	160	3.39	.207	2	.167	7	3	0.7
2001 Mon-N	4	8	.333	41	13	0	0	0	95	101	68	59	16	5	48	86	1.568	5.59	80	5.52	.273	2	.118	-10	2	-0.8
2002 Mon-N	1	4	.200	42	6	0	0	0	68	70	42	38	8	3	38	76	1.588	5.03	85	5.04	.266	1	.111	-6	1	-0.6
2003 Mon-N	0	0	....	2	0	0	0	0	1^1	4	4	4	0	0	2	1	4.500	27.00	19	22.07	.500	0	.000	-3	0	-0.3
Total 4	**7**	**13**	**.350**	**93**	**26**	**0**	**0**	**0**	**205**	**205**	**131**	**114**	**28**	**9**	**111**	**194**	**1.541**	**5.00**	**88**	**5.04**	**.261**	**5**	**.128**	**-12**	**6**	**-1.1**
• REARDON, Jeff				Jeffrey James Reardon b: 10/1/1955, Pittsfield, MA BR/TR, 6', 195 lbs. Deb: 8/25/1979																						
1979 NY-N	1	2	.333	18	0	0	0	2	20^2	12	7	4	2	0	9	10	1.016	1.74	209	1.88	.174	0	....	4	3	0.4
1980 NY-N	8	7	.533	61	0	0	0	6	110^1	96	36	32	10	0	47	101	1.296	2.61	136	3.11	.231	0	.000	11	11	1.1
1981 NY-N	1	0	1.000	18	0	0	0	2	28^2	27	11	11	2	1	12	28	1.360	3.45	101	3.50	.245	0	.000	0	2	0.0
* Mon-N	2	0	1.000	25	0	0	0	6	41^2	21	6	6	3	1	9	21	.720	1.30	270	1.18	.148	0	.000	10	7	1.0
Yr.	3	0	1.000	43	0	0	0	8	70^1	48	17	17	5	2	21	49	.981	2.18	160	2.12	.190	0	.000	10	9	1.1
1982 Mon-N	7	4	.636	75	0	0	0	26	109	87	28	25	6	2	36	86	1.128	2.06	176	2.48	.221	1	.100	19	18	1.9
1983 Mon-N	7	9	.438	66	0	0	0	21	92	87	34	31	7	1	44	78	1.424	3.03	118	3.75	.250	1	.125	4	10	0.4
1984 Mon-N	7	7	.500	68	0	0	0	23	87	70	31	28	5	3	37	79	1.230	2.90	118	2.85	.220	0	.000	4	12	0.3
1985 Mon-N★	2	8	.200	63	0	0	0	**41**	87^2	68	31	31	7	1	26	67	1.072	3.18	107	2.34	.209	2	.286	1	13	0.2
1986 Mon-N★	7	9	.438	62	0	0	0	35	89	83	42	39	12	1	26	67	1.225	3.94	93	3.55	.251	1	.125	-3	11	-0.3
1987* Min-A	8	8	.500	63	0	0	0	31	80^1	70	41	40	14	3	28	83	1.220	4.48	103	3.72	.232	0	....	1	12	0.1
1988 Min-A★	2	4	.333	63	0	0	0	42	73	68	21	20	6	2	15	56	1.137	2.47	165	2.91	.245	0	....	13	13	1.3
1989 Min-A	5	4	.556	65	0	0	0	31	73	68	33	33	8	3	12	46	1.096	4.07	102	2.96	.246	0	....	1	11	0.1
1990* Bos-A	5	3	.625	47	0	0	0	21	51^1	39	19	18	5	1	19	33	1.130	3.16	129	2.63	.206	0	....	6	10	0.6
1991 Bos-A★	1	4	.200	57	0	0	0	40	59^1	54	21	20	9	1	16	44	1.180	3.03	142	3.35	.236	0	....	8	10	0.8
1992 Bos-A	2	2	.500	46	0	0	0	27	42^1	53	20	20	6	1	7	32	1.417	4.25	99	4.99	.308	0	....	-0	5	0.0
* Atl-N	3	0	1.000	14	0	0	0	3	15^2	14	2	2	0	1	2	7	1.021	1.15	318	2.08	.241	0	....	4	4	0.5
1993 Cin-N	4	6	.400	58	0	0	0	8	61^2	66	34	28	4	5	10	35	1.232	4.09	98	3.51	.270	0	.000	0	5	0.0
1994 NY-A	1	0	1.000	11	0	0	0	2	9^2	17	9	9	3	0	3	4	2.069	8.38	55	10.30	.386	0	....	-4	0	-0.4
Total 16	**73**	**77**	**.487**	**880**	**0**	**0**	**0**	**367**	**1132^1**	**1000**	**426**	**397**	**109**	**27**	**358**	**877**	**1.199**	**3.16**	**122**	**3.12**	**.236**	**5**	**.088**	**81**	**157**	**8.2**
• REARDON, Jeremiah				Jeremiah J. Reardon b: 9/1868, St. Louis, MO d: 4/22/1907, St. Louis, MO Deb: 7/17/1886																						
1886 StL-N	0	1	.000	1	1	1	0	0	8	10	8	6	1	....	5	0	1.875	6.75	47	....	.295	1	.250	-3	0	-0.3
Cin-a	0	1	.000	1	1	0	0	0	2	5	4	4	0	0	4	0	4.500	18.00	20	....	.453	0	.000	-3	0	-0.3
• REBERGER, Frank				Frank Beall "Crane" Reberger b: 6/7/1944, Caldwell, ID BL/TR, 6'5", 200 lbs. Deb: 6/6/1968 C																						
1968 Chi-N	0	1	.000	3	1	0	0	0	6	9	4	3	1	0	2	3	1.833	4.50	70	7.46	.346	0	....	-1	0	-0.1
1969 SD-N	1	2	.333	67	0	0	0	6	87^2	83	38	35	6	2	41	65	1.414	3.59	98	3.82	.258	1	.200	1	7	0.1
1970 SF-N	7	8	.467	45	18	3	0	2	152	178	108	94	13	7	98	117	1.816	5.57	71	6.03	.293	11	.234	-24	2	-2.2
1971 SF-N	3	0	1.000	13	7	0	0	0	43^2	37	20	19	5	2	19	21	1.282	3.92	87	3.64	.228	3	.231	-2	2	-0.2
1972 SF-N	3	4	.429	20	11	2	0	0	99^1	97	49	44	10	5	37	52	1.349	3.99	87	4.02	.257	8	.229	-5	4	-0.4
Total 5	**14**	**15**	**.483**	**148**	**37**	**5**	**0**	**8**	**388^2**	**404**	**219**	**195**	**35**	**16**	**197**	**258**	**1.546**	**4.52**	**82**	**4.77**	**.270**	**23**	**.230**	**-32**	**15**	**-2.8**
• RECCIUS, John				John Reccius b: 10/29/1859, Louisville, KY d: 9/1/1930, Louisville, KY, 5'6.5" Deb: 5/2/1882 ♦																						
1882 Lou-a	4	6	.400	13	10	9	1	0	95	106	70	32	3	....	22	31	1.347	3.03	82	....	.264	63	.237	-7	10	0.0
1883 Lou-a	0	0	....	1	0	0	0	0	4	10	3	1	0	....	0	0	2.500	2.25	133	....	.446	9	.143	0	0	-0.5
Total 2	**4**	**6**	**.400**	**14**	**10**	**9**	**1**	**0**	**99**	**116**	**73**	**33**	**3**	**....**	**22**	**31**	**1.394**	**3.00**	**83**	**....**	**.274**	**72**	**.219**	**-6**	**10**	**-0.5**
• RECCIUS, Phil				Phillip Reccius b: 6/7/1862, Louisville, KY d: 2/15/1903, Louisville, KY, 5'9", 163 lbs. Deb: 9/25/1882 ♦																						
1884 Lou-a	6	7	.462	18	11	11	0	0	129^1	118	80	39	2	4	19	46	1.059	2.71	113	....	.230	63	.240	0	13	0.1
1885 Lou-a	0	4	.000	7	5	4	0	1	40	46	35	17	0	1	11	10	1.425	3.83	84	....	.277	97	.241	-3	8	-1.0
1886 Lou-a	0	1	.000	1	1	0	0	0	3	7	6	3	0	0	3	0	3.333	9.00	40	....	.436	4	.308	-2	1	0.1
1887 Cle-a	0	0	....	1	0	0	0	0	7	13	7	6	0	0	5	0	1.857	7.71	56	....	.384	71	.281	-2	3	-0.9
Total 4	**6**	**12**	**.333**	**27**	**17**	**15**	**0**	**1**	**179^1**	**184**	**128**	**65**	**2**	**5**	**38**	**56**	**1.210**	**3.26**	**99**	**....**	**.252**	**257**	**.255**	**-6**	**25**	**-1.6**
• REDDING, Phil				Philip Hayden Redding b: 1/25/1890, Crystal Springs, MS d: 3/31/1928, Greenwood, MS BL/TR, 5'11.5", 190 lbs. Deb: 9/14/1912																						
1912 StL-N	2	1	.667	3	3	2	0	0	25^1	31	17	14	2	0	11	9	1.658	4.97	69	5.40	.313	0	.000	-5	1	-0.5
1913 StL-N	0	0	....	1	0	0	0	0	2^2	2	2	2	0	0	1	1	1.125	6.75	48	2.18	.286	0	.000	-1	0	-0.1
Total 2	**2**	**1**	**.667**	**4**	**3**	**2**	**0**	**0**	**28**	**33**	**19**	**16**	**2**	**0**	**12**	**10**	**1.607**	**5.14**	**66**	**5.09**	**.311**	**0**	**.000**	**-6**	**1**	**-0.7**
• REDDING, Tim				Timothy J. Redding b: 2/12/1978, Rochester, NY BR/TR, 6', 180 lbs. Deb: 6/24/2001																						
2001 Hou-N	3	1	.750	13	9	0	0	0	55^2	62	38	34	11	3	24	55	1.545	5.50	83	5.87	.286	3	.214	-6	2	-0.6
2002 Hou-N	3	6	.333	18	14	0	0	0	73^1	78	49	44	10	0	35	63	1.541	5.40	79	4.96	.276	2	.100	-9	1	-1.0

YEAR TM-L	W	L	PCT	G	GS	CG	SH	SV	IP	H	R	ER	HR	HB	BB	SO	RAT	ERA	ERA+	CERA	OAV	BH	AVG	PR+	WS	TPW
2003 Hou-N	10	14	.417	33	32	0	0	0	176	179	85	72	16	7	65	116	1.386	3.68	120	4.07	.261	10	.200	11	10	1.2
Total 3	16	21	.432	64	55	0	0	0	305	319	172	150	37	10	124	234	1.452	4.43	100	4.61	.269	15	.179	-4	13	-0.3
• REDFERN, Pete	Peter Irvine Redfern b: 8/25/1954, Glendale, CA BR/TR, 6'2", 195 lbs. Deb: 5/15/1976																									
1976 Min-A	8	8	.500	23	23	1	1	0	118	105	61	46	6	3	63	74	1.424	3.51	103	3.76	.241	0	....	1	5	0.1
1977 Min-A	6	9	.400	30	28	1	0	0	137^1	164	89	79	13	4	66	73	1.675	5.18	77	5.71	.304	0	....	-18	3	-1.8
1978 Min-A	0	2	.000	3	2	0	0	0	9^2	10	12	7	2	0	6	4	1.655	6.52	59	6.01	.294	0	....	-3	0	-0.3
1979 Min-A	7	3	.700	40	6	0	0	1	108^1	106	45	42	8	1	35	85	1.302	3.49	126	3.54	.258	0	....	11	9	1.1
1980 Min-A	7	7	.500	23	16	2	0	2	104^2	117	58	53	11	0	33	73	1.433	4.56	96	4.38	.283	0	....	-3	6	-0.3
1981 Min-A	9	8	.529	24	23	3	0	0	141^2	140	70	64	12	2	52	77	1.355	4.07	97	3.86	.261	0	....	-1	8	-0.1
1982 Min-A	5	11	.313	27	13	2	0	0	94^1	122	74	69	16	1	51	40	1.834	6.58	64	7.13	.322	0	....	-26	0	-2.6
Total 7	42	48	.467	170	111	9	1	3	714	764	409	360	68	11	306	426	1.499	4.54	89	4.69	.278	0	....	-38	31	-3.9
• REDMAN, Mark	Mark Allen Redman b: 1/5/1974, San Diego, CA BL/TL, 6'5", 220 lbs. Deb: 7/24/1999																									
1999 Min-A	1	0	1.000	5	1	0	0	0	12^2	17	13	12	3	1	7	11	1.895	8.53	60	7.86	.298	0	....	-5	0	-0.4
2000 Min-A	12	9	.571	32	24	0	0	0	151^1	168	81	80	22	3	45	117	1.407	4.76	108	4.73	.281	0	.000	9	10	0.8
2001 Min-A	2	4	.333	9	9	0	0	0	49	57	26	23	6	0	19	29	1.551	4.22	109	5.11	.286	0	....	2	3	0.2
Det-A	0	2	.000	2	2	0	0	0	9	11	6	6	1	1	4	4	1.667	6.00	72	6.12	.306	0	....	-2	0	-0.1
Yr.	2	6	.250	11	11	0	0	0	58	68	32	29	7	1	23	33	1.569	4.50	101	5.27	.289	0	....	1	3	0.1
2002 Det-A	8	15	.348	30	30	3	0	0	203	211	107	95	15	6	51	109	1.291	4.21	102	3.64	.268	1	.200	3	10	0.3
2003★ Fla-N	14	9	.609	29	29	3	0	0	190^2	172	82	76	16	5	61	151	1.222	3.59	114	3.17	.239	1	.016	10	12	0.4
Total 5	37	39	.487	107	95	6	0	0	615^2	636	315	292	63	16	187	421	1.337	4.27	105	4.00	.265	2	.029	18	35	1.1
• REED, Bob	Robert Edward Reed b: 1/12/1945, Boston, MA BR/TR, 5'10", 175 lbs. Deb: 9/5/1969																									
1969 Det-A	0	0	....	8	1	0	0	0	14^2	9	3	3	0	0	8	9	1.159	1.84	203	2.05	.184	1	.500	3	2	0.4
1970 Det-A	2	4	.333	16	4	0	0	2	46^1	54	25	25	5	0	14	26	1.468	4.86	77	4.72	.292	1	.083	-4	2	-0.5
Total 2	2	4	.333	24	5	0	0	2	61	63	28	28	5	0	22	35	1.393	4.13	90	4.08	.269	2	.143	-1	4	-0.2
• REED, Howie	Howard Dean "Diz" Reed b: 12/21/1936, Dallas, TX d: 12/7/1984, Corpus Christi, TX BR/TR, 6'1", 210 lbs. Deb: 9/13/1958																									
1958 KC-A	1	0	1.000	3	1	1	0	0	10^1	5	1	1	0	0	4	5	.871	0.87	449	1.10	.132	0	.000	4	2	0.4
1959 KC-A	0	3	.000	6	3	0	0	0	20^2	26	19	17	3	0	10	11	1.742	7.40	54	6.22	.313	0	.000	-8	0	-0.8
1960 KC-A	0	0	....	1	0	0	0	0	1^2	2	1	0	1	0	0	1	1.200	0.00	....	6.66	.286	0	....	1	0	0.1
1964 LA-N	3	4	.429	26	7	0	0	1	90	79	34	32	4	0	36	52	1.278	3.20	101	2.89	.236	2	.100	1	5	0.0
1965★ LA-N	7	5	.583	38	5	0	0	1	78	73	31	27	6	3	27	47	1.282	3.12	105	3.34	.243	0	.000	0	5	0.0
1966 LA-N	0	0	....	1	0	0	0	0	1^2	1	0	0	0	0	0	0	.600	0.00	....	0.75	.167	0	.000	1	0	0.1
Cal-A	0	1	.000	19	1	0	0	1	43	39	14	14	5	0	15	17	1.256	2.93	115	3.47	.247	0	.000	2	3	0.1
1967 Hou-N	1	1	.500	4	2	0	0	0	18^1	19	8	7	0	0	2	9	1.145	3.44	96	2.55	.268	0	.000	0	1	0.0
1969 Mon-N	6	7	.462	31	15	2	1	1	106	119	59	57	7	2	50	59	1.594	4.84	76	4.82	.290	4	.125	-13	3	-1.3
1970 Mon-N	6	5	.545	57	1	0	0	5	89	81	34	31	7	2	40	42	1.360	3.13	131	3.78	.252	0	.000	9	9	0.9
1971 Mon-N	2	3	.400	43	0	0	0	0	56^2	66	28	27	8	0	24	25	1.588	4.29	82	5.25	.296	0	.000	-5	2	-0.5
Total 10	26	29	.473	229	35	3	1	9	515^1	510	229	213	41	7	208	268	1.393	3.72	96	3.91	.261	6	.066	-9	30	-1.0
• REED, Jerry	Jerry Maxwell Reed b: 10/8/1955, Bryson City, NC BR/TR, 6'1", 190 lbs. Deb: 9/11/1981																									
1981 Phi-N	0	1	.000	4	0	0	0	0	4^2	7	4	4	0	0	6	5	2.786	7.71	47	9.82	.333	0	....	-2	0	-0.2
1982 Phi-N	1	0	1.000	7	0	0	0	0	8^2	11	6	5	0	1	3	1	1.615	5.19	71	5.39	.324	0	....	-1	0	-0.2
Cle-A	1	1	.500	6	1	0	0	0	15^2	15	6	6	1	0	3	10	1.149	3.45	118	2.87	.250	0	....	1	1	0.1
1983 Cle-A	0	0	....	7	0	0	0	0	21^1	26	19	17	4	0	9	11	1.641	7.17	59	6.17	.310	0	....	-7	0	-0.7
1985 Cle-A	3	5	.375	33	5	0	0	8	72^1	67	41	33	12	3	19	37	1.189	4.11	101	3.68	.245	0	....	0	5	0.0
1986 Sea-A	4	0	1.000	11	4	0	0	0	34^2	38	13	12	3	0	13	16	1.471	3.12	136	4.41	.273	0	....	4	4	0.4
1987 Sea-A	1	2	.333	39	1	0	0	7	81^2	79	32	31	7	3	24	51	1.261	3.42	138	3.52	.255	0	....	11	9	1.1
1988 Sea-A	1	1	.500	46	0	0	0	1	86^1	82	42	38	8	2	33	48	1.332	3.96	105	3.70	.256	0	....	2	5	0.2
1989 Sea-A	7	7	.500	52	1	0	0	0	101^2	89	44	36	10	1	43	50	1.298	3.19	126	3.33	.235	0	....	9	7	0.9
1990 Sea-A	0	1	.000	4	0	0	0	0	7^1	8	4	4	1	0	3	2	1.500	4.91	81	5.13	.286	0	....	-1	0	-0.1
Bos-A	2	1	.667	29	0	0	0	2	45	55	27	24	1	0	16	17	1.578	4.80	85	4.46	.302	0	....	-3	2	-0.3
Yr.	2	2	.500	33	0	0	0	2	52^1	63	31	28	2	0	19	19	1.567	4.82	84	4.55	.300	0	....	-4	2	-0.4
Total 9	20	19	.513	238	12	0	0	18	479^1	477	238	210	47	10	172	248	1.354	3.94	106	3.91	.261	0	....	15	33	1.4
• REED, Rick	Richard Allen Reed b: 8/16/1964, Huntington, WV BR/TR, 6', 205 lbs. Deb: 8/8/1988																									
1988 Pit-N	1	0	1.000	2	2	0	0	0	12	10	4	4	1	0	2	6	1.000	3.00	113	2.26	.233	0	.000	0	1	0.0
1989 Pit-N	1	4	.200	15	7	0	0	0	54^2	62	35	34	5	2	11	34	1.335	5.60	60	4.07	.290	1	.077	-14	0	-1.5
1990 Pit-N	2	3	.400	13	8	1	1	1	53^2	62	32	26	6	1	12	27	1.379	4.36	83	4.08	.279	4	.250	-5	1	-0.4
1991 Pit-N	0	0	....	1	1	0	0	0	4^1	8	6	5	1	0	1	2	2.077	10.38	34	10.07	.400	1	.500	-3	0	-0.3
1992 KC-A	3	7	.300	19	18	1	1	0	100^1	105	47	41	10	5	20	49	1.246	3.68	110	3.73	.271	0	....	6	5	0.6
1993 KC-A	0	0	....	1	0	0	0	0	3^2	6	4	4	0	1	1	3	1.909	9.82	47	7.97	.375	0	....	-2	0	-0.2
Tex-A	1	0	1.000	2	0	0	0	0	4	6	1	1	1	1	1	2	1.750	2.25	184	9.70	.375	0	....	1	1	0.1
Yr.	1	0	1.000	3	0	0	0	0	7^2	12	5	5	1	2	2	5	1.826	5.87	76	8.88	.375	0	....	-1	1	-0.1
1994 Tex-A	1	1	.500	4	3	0	0	0	16^2	17	13	11	3	1	7	12	1.440	5.94	81	4.98	.254	0	....	-2	0	-0.2
1995 Cin-N	0	0	....	4	3	0	0	0	17	18	12	11	5	0	3	10	1.235	5.82	71	4.84	.273	0	.000	-4	0	-0.4
1997 NY-N	13	9	.591	33	31	2	0	0	208^1	186	76	67	19	5	31	113	1.042	2.89	140	2.61	.239	10	.175	22	17	2.5
1998 NY-N★	16	11	.593	31	31	2	1	0	212^1	208	84	82	30	6	29	153	1.116	3.48	119	3.39	.261	8	.125	15	16	1.4
1999★ NY-N	11	5	.688	26	26	1	1	0	149^1	163	77	76	23	1	47	104	1.406	4.58	96	4.71	.281	11	.244	-4	8	-0.2
2000★ NY-N	11	5	.688	30	30	0	0	0	184	192	90	84	28	5	34	121	1.228	4.11	107	3.90	.266	10	.204	7	11	0.8
2001 NY-N★	8	6	.571	20	20	3	1	0	134^2	119	53	52	16	1	17	99	1.010	3.48	119	2.55	.236	5	.125	9	11	0.8
Min-A	4	6	.400	12	12	0	0	0	67^2	92	45	39	12	4	14	43	1.567	5.19	89	6.30	.325	0	....	-4	2	-0.4
2002★ Min-A	15	7	.682	33	32	2	1	0	188	192	89	79	32	6	26	121	1.160	3.78	119	3.72	.259	1	.250	15	14	1.5
2003★ Min-A	6	12	.333	27	21	2	1	0	135	155	80	76	21	5	29	71	1.363	5.07	90	4.68	.285	0	....	-5	5	-0.5
Total 15	93	76	.550	273	245	14	7	1	1545^2	1601	748	692	213	44	285	970	1.220	4.03	105	3.82	.267	51	.172	32	92	3.6
• REED, Ron	Ronald Lee Reed b: 11/2/1942, La Porte, IN BR/TR, 6'6", 215 lbs. Deb: 9/26/1966																									
1966 Atl-N	1	1	.500	2	2	0	0	0	8^1	7	2	2	1	0	4	6	1.320	2.16	168	3.68	.226	0	.000	1	1	0.1
1967 Atl-N	1	1	.500	3	3	0	0	0	21^1	21	8	7	1	2	3	11	1.125	2.95	112	2.98	.263	0	.000	1	1	0.0
1968 Atl-N★	11	10	.524	35	28	6	1	0	201^2	189	87	75	10	6	49	111	1.180	3.35	89	2.82	.246	10	.161	-9	8	-0.9
1969★ Atl-N	18	10	.643	36	33	7	1	0	241^1	227	103	93	24	6	56	160	1.173	3.47	104	3.14	.246	10	.125	5	16	0.3
1970 Atl-N	7	10	.412	21	18	6	0	0	134^2	140	69	66	16	2	39	68	1.329	4.41	97	4.00	.266	4	.091	2	7	-0.1
1971 Atl-N	13	14	.481	32	32	8	1	0	222^1	221	105	92	26	2	54	129	1.237	3.72	100	3.51	.261	11	.149	1	13	-0.1
1972 Atl-N	11	15	.423	31	30	11	1	0	213	222	109	93	18	6	60	111	1.324	3.93	96	3.77	.270	13	.178	-0	10	-0.1
1973 Atl-N	4	11	.267	20	19	2	0	1	116^1	133	71	57	7	3	31	64	1.410	4.41	89	4.06	.287	9	.200	-5	4	-0.5
1974 Atl-N	10	11	.476	28	28	6	2	0	186	171	76	70	16	2	41	78	1.140	3.39	111	2.87	.243	6	.105	5	11	0.2
1975 Atl-N	4	5	.444	10	10	1	0	0	74^2	93	39	35	1	0	16	40	1.460	4.22	89	4.01	.304	6	.231	-2	3	-0.1
StL-N	9	8	.529	24	24	7	2	0	175^2	181	79	63	4	4	37	99	1.241	3.23	116	3.01	.263	9	.161	15	10	1.5
Yr.	13	13	.500	34	34	8	2	0	250^1	274	118	98	5	4	53	139	1.306	3.52	107	3.31	.276	15	.183	13	13	1.5
1976★ Phi-N	8	7	.533	59	4	1	0	14	128	88	39	35	8	2	32	96	.938	2.46	144	1.73	.193	4	.167	14	15	1.4
1977★ Phi-N	7	5	.583	60	3	0	0	15	124^1	101	41	38	9	1	37	84	1.110	2.75	145	2.51	.223	2	.111	15	14	1.5
1978★ Phi-N	3	4	.429	66	0	0	0	17	108^2	87	32	27	6	5	23	85	1.012	2.24	160	2.23	.223	0	.000	14	14	1.4
1979 Phi-N	13	8	.619	61	0	0	0	5	102	110	52	47	9	2	32	58	1.392	4.15	92	4.04	.278	3	.300	-5	8	-0.4
1980★ Phi-N	7	5	.583	55	0	0	0	9	91^1	88	45	41	4	1	30	54	1.292	4.04	94	3.07	.253	3	.300	-2	7	-0.2
1981★ Phi-N	5	3	.625	39	0	0	0	8	61^1	54	26	21	6	1	17	40	1.158	3.08	118	2.83	.237	3	.500	3	7	0.5
1982 Phi-N	5	5	.500	57	2	0	0	14	98	85	30	29	4	3	24	57	1.112	2.66	138	2.44	.235	4	.333	11	14	1.3
1983★ Phi-N	9	1	.900	61	0	0	0	8	95^2	89	42	37	5	1	34	73	1.286	3.48	102	3.01	.248	1	.167	2	9	0.2

YEAR TM-L	W	L	PCT	G	GS	CG	SH	SV	IP	H	R	ER	HR	HB	BB	SO	RAT	ERA	ERA+	CERA	OAV	BH	AVG	PR+	WS	TPW
1984 Chi-A	0	6	.000	51	0	0	0	12	73	67	29	25	7	1	14	57	1.110	3.08	135	2.85	.248	0	.000	8	9	0.8
Total 19	146	140	.510	751	236	55	8	103	2477^2	2374	1084	953	182	50	633	1481	1.214	3.46	107	3.13	.252	98	.158	73	181	7.0

• REED, Steve Steven Vincent Reed b: 3/11/1966, Los Angeles, CA BR/TR, 6'2", 202 lbs. Deb: 8/30/1992

YEAR TM-L	W	L	PCT	G	GS	CG	SH	SV	IP	H	R	ER	HR	HB	BB	SO	RAT	ERA	ERA+	CERA	OAV	BH	AVG	PR+	WS	TPW
1992 SF-N	1	0	1.000	18	0	0	0	0	15^2	13	5	4	2	1	3	11	1.021	2.30	144	2.80	.220	0	....	1	1	0.2
1993 Col-N	9	5	.643	64	0	0	0	3	84^1	80	47	42	13	3	30	51	1.304	4.48	106	4.19	.259	0	.000	5	8	0.4
1994 Col-N	3	2	.600	**61**	0	0	0	3	64	79	33	28	9	6	26	51	1.641	3.94	126	6.09	.306	0	.000	9	6	0.9
1995* Col-N	5	2	.714	71	0	0	0	3	84	61	24	20	8	1	21	79	.976	2.14	251	2.11	.203	1	.333	33	12	3.2
1996 Col-N	4	3	.571	70	0	0	0	0	75	66	38	33	11	6	19	51	1.133	3.96	132	3.52	.239	1	.333	12	8	1.2
1997 Col-N	4	6	.400	63	0	0	0	6	62^1	49	28	28	10	5	27	43	1.219	4.04	128	3.78	.219	0	.000	9	7	0.8
1998 SF-N	2	1	.667	50	0	0	0	1	54^2	30	10	9	4	4	19	50	.896	1.48	268	1.64	.160	1	.333	15	7	1.5
* Cle-A	2	2	.500	20	0	0	0	0	25^2	26	19	19	4	1	8	23	1.325	6.66	72	4.38	.260	0	....	-5	1	-0.5
1999* Cle-A	3	2	.600	63	0	0	0	0	61^2	69	33	29	10	3	20	44	1.443	4.23	119	4.91	.285	0	....	6	4	0.5
2000 Cle-A	2	0	1.000	57	0	0	0	0	56	58	30	27	7	1	21	39	1.411	4.34	114	4.31	.269	0	....	4	4	0.4
2001 Cle-A	1	1	.500	31	0	0	0	0	27^1	22	11	11	3	2	10	21	1.171	3.62	125	3.06	.212	0	....	3	2	0.3
* Atl-N	2	2	.500	39	0	0	0	1	31	30	14	12	3	1	13	25	1.387	3.48	126	3.92	.259	0	....	3	3	0.3
2002 SD-N	2	4	.333	40	0	0	0	1	41	33	9	9	2	6	10	36	1.049	1.98	191	2.65	.228	0	.000	9	4	0.8
NY-N	0	1	.000	24	0	0	0	0	26	23	6	6	0	2	4	14	1.038	2.08	191	2.22	.240	0	.000	6	3	0.6
Yr.	2	5	.286	64	0	0	0	1	67	56	15	15	2	8	14	50	1.045	2.01	191	2.48	.232	0	.000	14	7	1.4
2003 Col-N	5	3	.625	67	0	0	0	0	63^1	59	24	23	9	8	26	39	1.342	3.27	150	4.61	.254	0	....	13	7	1.2
Total 12	45	34	.570	738	0	0	0	18	772	698	331	300	95	50	257	577	1.237	3.50	138	3.72	.244	3	.130	123	77	12.0

• REEDER, Bill William Edgar Reeder b: 2/20/1922, Dike, TX d: 3/12/2001, Sulphur Springs, TX BR/TR, 6'5", 205 lbs. Deb: 4/23/1949

YEAR TM-L	W	L	PCT	G	GS	CG	SH	SV	IP	H	R	ER	HR	HB	BB	SO	RAT	ERA	ERA+	CERA	OAV	BH	AVG	PR+	WS	TPW
1949 StL-N	1	1	.500	21	1	0	0	0	33^2	33	22	19	2	1	30	21	1.871	5.08	82	5.55	.270	0	.000	-4	1	-0.4

• REES, Stan Stanley Milton "Nellie" Rees b: 2/25/1899, Cynthiana, KY d: 8/30/1937, Lexington, KY BL/TL, 6'3", 190 lbs. Deb: 6/12/1918

YEAR TM-L	W	L	PCT	G	GS	CG	SH	SV	IP	H	R	ER	HR	HB	BB	SO	RAT	ERA	ERA+	CERA	OAV	BH	AVG	PR+	WS	TPW
1918 Was-A	1	0	1.000	2	0	0	0	0	2	3	0	0	0	0	4	1	3.500	0.00	....	15.98	.500	0	....	1	1	0.1

• REGAN, Mike Michael John Regan b: 11/19/1887, Phoenix, NY d: 5/22/1961, Albany, NY BR/TR, 5'11", 160 lbs. Deb: 5/13/1917

YEAR TM-L	W	L	PCT	G	GS	CG	SH	SV	IP	H	R	ER	HR	HB	BB	SO	RAT	ERA	ERA+	CERA	OAV	BH	AVG	PR+	WS	TPW
1917 Cin-N	11	10	.524	32	26	16	1	0	216	228	106	65	4	4	41	50	1.245	2.71	96	3.02	.273	15	.200	-2	8	0.0
1918 Cin-N	5	5	.500	22	6	4	3	2	80	77	38	29	0	0	29	15	1.325	3.26	82	2.98	.262	8	.296	-6	4	-0.4
1919 Cin-N	0	0	....	1	0	0	0	0	2^1	1	1	0	0	0	0	1	....	0.00	....	0.40	.143	0	.000	1	0	0.1
Total 3	16	15	.516	55	32	20	4	2	298^1	306	145	94	4	4	70	66	1.260	2.84	93	2.99	.269	23	.223	-7	12	-0.4

• REGAN, Phil Philip Raymond "The Vulture" Regan b: 4/6/1937, Otsego, MI BR/TR, 6'3", 200 lbs. Deb: 7/19/1960 M/C

YEAR TM-L	W	L	PCT	G	GS	CG	SH	SV	IP	H	R	ER	HR	HB	BB	SO	RAT	ERA	ERA+	CERA	OAV	BH	AVG	PR+	WS	TPW
1960 Det-A	0	4	.000	17	7	0	0	1	68	70	39	34	11	2	25	38	1.397	4.50	92	4.65	.267	1	.059	-3	2	-0.4
1961 Det-A	10	7	.588	32	16	6	0	2	120	134	70	70	19	1	41	46	1.458	5.25	78	4.94	.281	3	.075	-16	4	-1.7
1962 Det-A	11	9	.550	35	23	6	0	0	171^1	169	89	77	23	1	64	87	1.360	4.04	101	4.11	.254	13	.206	2	9	0.3
1963 Det-A	15	9	.625	38	27	5	1	1	189	179	95	81	33	7	59	115	1.259	3.86	97	3.97	.245	9	.143	-3	9	-0.3
1964 Det-A	5	10	.333	32	21	2	0	1	146^2	162	87	82	21	5	49	91	1.439	5.03	73	4.81	.282	13	.317	-23	3	-1.9
1965 Det-A	1	5	.167	16	7	1	0	0	51^2	57	31	29	6	0	20	37	1.490	5.05	69	4.67	.282	1	.083	-9	0	-1.0
1966* LA-N★	14	1	.933	65	0	0	0	**21**	116^2	85	24	21	6	0	24	88	.934	1.62	203	1.67	.207	3	.143	21	23	2.3
1967 LA-N	6	9	.400	55	3	0	0	6	96^1	108	38	32	2	2	32	53	1.453	2.99	104	3.61	.284	1	.100	2	7	0.2
1968 LA-N	2	0	1.000	5	0	0	0	0	7^2	10	3	3	1	0	1	7	1.435	3.52	78	4.82	.313	0	.000	-1	1	-0.1
Chi-N	10	5	.667	68	0	0	0	25	127	109	36	31	9	2	24	60	1.047	2.20	144	2.36	.232	3	.150	14	19	1.6
Yr.	12	5	.706	73	0	0	0	**25**	134^2	119	39	34	10	2	25	67	1.069	2.27	137	2.50	.237	3	.143	13	20	1.5
1969 Chi-N	12	6	.667	71	0	0	0	17	112	120	49	46	6	2	35	56	1.384	3.70	109	3.74	.282	1	.067	4	12	0.4
1970 Chi-N	5	9	.357	54	0	0	0	12	75^2	81	43	40	8	1	32	31	1.493	4.76	95	4.65	.287	0	.000	-2	6	-0.3
1971 Chi-N	5	5	.500	48	1	0	0	6	73^1	84	37	32	4	2	33	28	1.595	3.93	100	4.63	.301	0	.000	1	5	0.1
1972 Chi-N	0	1	.000	5	0	0	0	0	4	6	1	1	0	0	2	2	2.000	2.25	169	7.72	.400	0	....	1	0	0.1
Chi-A	0	1	.000	10	0	0	0	0	13^1	18	7	6	1	1	6	4	1.800	4.05	77	6.45	.346	1	1.000	-1	0	-0.1
Total 13	96	81	.542	551	105	20	1	92	1372^2	1392	649	585	150	26	447	743	1.340	3.84	99	3.95	.265	49	.153	-11	100	-0.8

• REICHERT, Dan Daniel Robert Reichert b: 7/12/1976, Monterey, CA BR/TR, 6'3", 175 lbs. Deb: 7/16/1999

YEAR TM-L	W	L	PCT	G	GS	CG	SH	SV	IP	H	R	ER	HR	HB	BB	SO	RAT	ERA	ERA+	CERA	OAV	BH	AVG	PR+	WS	TPW
1999 KC-A	2	2	.500	8	8	0	0	0	36^2	48	38	37	2	2	32	20	2.182	9.08	55	7.91	.327	1	.333	-17	0	-1.6
2000 KC-A	8	10	.444	44	18	1	1	2	153^1	157	92	80	15	7	91	94	1.617	4.70	109	5.22	.271	0	.000	4	9	0.4
2001 KC-A	8	8	.500	27	19	0	0	0	123	131	83	77	14	8	67	77	1.610	5.63	87	5.46	.278	0	.000	-13	4	-1.3
2002 KC-A	3	5	.375	30	6	0	0	0	66	77	48	39	10	4	25	36	1.545	5.32	94	5.70	.306	0	....	-2	3	-0.2
2003 Tor-A	0	0	....	15	0	0	0	0	16^1	28	12	11	2	2	8	13	2.204	6.06	76	9.67	.389	0	....	-2	0	-0.2
Total 5	21	25	.457	124	51	1	1	2	395^1	441	273	244	43	23	223	240	1.680	5.55	90	5.81	.290	1	.111	-31	16	-2.9

• REID, Earl Earl Percy Reid b: 6/8/1913, Bangor, AL d: 5/11/1984, Cullman, AL BL/TR, 6'3", 190 lbs. Deb: 5/8/1946

YEAR TM-L	W	L	PCT	G	GS	CG	SH	SV	IP	H	R	ER	HR	HB	BB	SO	RAT	ERA	ERA+	CERA	OAV	BH	AVG	PR+	WS	TPW
1946 Bos-N	1	0	1.000	2	0	0	0	0	3	4	3	1	0	0	3	2	2.333	3.00	114	7.17	.308	0	....	0	0	0.0

• REIDY, Bill William Joseph Reidy b: 10/9/1873, Cleveland, OH d: 10/14/1915, Cleveland, OH BR/TR, 5'10", 175 lbs. Deb: 7/21/1896

YEAR TM-L	W	L	PCT	G	GS	CG	SH	SV	IP	H	R	ER	HR	HB	BB	SO	RAT	ERA	ERA+	CERA	OAV	BH	AVG	PR+	WS	TPW
1896 NY-N	0	1	.000	2	1	1	0	0	13	24	11	11	0	3	2	1	2.000	7.62	55	8.28	.392	0	.000	-5	0	-0.5
1899 Bro-N	1	0	1.000	2	1	1	0	1	7	9	2	2	0	0	2	2	1.571	2.57	152	4.43	.312	0	.000	1	1	0.0
1901 Mil-A	16	20	.444	37	33	28	2	0	301^1	364	183	141	14	9	62	50	1.414	4.21	85	4.16	.295	16	.143	-16	14	-2.0
1902 StL-A	3	5	.375	12	9	7	0	0	95	111	52	47	0	8	13	16	1.305	4.45	79	3.56	.292	8	.195	-11	5	-1.1
1903 StL-A	1	4	.200	5	5	5	1	0	43	53	31	19	1	3	7	8	1.395	3.98	73	3.93	.302	1	.067	-5	0	-0.7
Bro-N	6	7	.462	15	13	11	0	0	104	130	54	40	0	6	14	21	1.385	3.46	92	4.08	.315	9	.243	10	6	1.1
1904 Bro-N	0	4	.000	6	4	2	0	1	38^1	49	33	19	0	2	6	11	1.435	4.46	61	3.92	.293	5	.156	-7	0	-1.1
Total 6	27	41	.397	79	66	55	3	2	601^2	740	366	279	15	31	106	109	1.406	4.17	82	4.11	.301	39	.159	-33	26	-4.3

• REINHART, Art Arthur Conrad Reinhart b: 5/29/1899, Ackley, IA d: 11/11/1946, Houston, TX BL/TL, 6'1", 170 lbs. Deb: 4/26/1919

YEAR TM-L	W	L	PCT	G	GS	CG	SH	SV	IP	H	R	ER	HR	HB	BB	SO	RAT	ERA	ERA+	CERA	OAV	BH	AVG	PR+	WS	TPW
1919 StL-N	0	0	....	1	0	0	0	0	0	0	0	0	0	1	0	0	....	....	....	∞	.000	0	....	0	0	0.0
1925 StL-N	11	5	.688	20	16	15	1	0	144^2	149	61	49	7	4	47	26	1.355	3.05	142	3.68	.278	22	.328	20	14	2.3
1926* StL-N	10	5	.667	27	11	9	0	0	143	159	75	67	5	3	47	26	1.441	4.22	93	3.97	.295	20	.317	-6	9	-0.2
1927 StL-N	5	2	.714	21	9	4	2	1	81^2	82	47	38	5	0	36	15	1.445	4.19	94	3.96	.267	10	.313	-4	5	-0.2
1928 StL-N	4	6	.400	23	9	3	1	2	75^1	80	39	24	3	0	27	12	1.420	2.87	139	3.69	.272	4	.167	9	5	0.8
Total 5	30	18	.625	92	45	31	4	3	444^2	470	222	178	20	8	157	79	1.410	3.60	112	3.83	.280	56	.301	19	33	2.8

• REIS, Bobby Robert Joseph Thomas Reis b: 1/2/1909, Woodside, NY d: 5/1/1973, St. Paul, MN BR/TR, 6'1", 175 lbs. Deb: 9/19/1931 ♦

YEAR TM-L	W	L	PCT	G	GS	CG	SH	SV	IP	H	R	ER	HR	HB	BB	SO	RAT	ERA	ERA+	CERA	OAV	BH	AVG	PR+	WS	TPW
1935 Bro-N	3	2	.600	14	2	1	0	2	41^1	46	26	13	0	1	24	7	1.694	2.83	140	4.48	.277	21	.247	5	4	0.5
1936 Bos-N	6	5	.545	35	5	3	0	0	138^2	152	77	69	7	5	74	25	1.630	4.48	86	4.72	.283	13	.217	-11	6	-1.1
1937 Bos-N	0	0	....	4	0	0	0	0	5	3	1	1	0	0	5	0	1.600	1.80	199	2.88	.158	21	.244	1	3	-0.2
1938 Bos-N	1	6	.143	16	2	1	0	0	57^2	61	35	32	5	6	41	20	1.769	4.99	69	5.64	.271	9	.184	-10	0	-1.6
Total 4	10	13	.435	69	9	5	0	2	242^2	262	139	115	12	12	144	52	1.673	4.27	87	4.86	.277	70	.233	-16	13	-2.4

• REIS, Jack Harrie Crane Reis b: 6/14/1890, Cincinnati, OH d: 7/20/1939, Cincinnati, OH BR/TR, 5'10.5", 160 lbs. Deb: 9/9/1911

YEAR TM-L	W	L	PCT	G	GS	CG	SH	SV	IP	H	R	ER	HR	HB	BB	SO	RAT	ERA	ERA+	CERA	OAV	BH	AVG	PR+	WS	TPW
1911 StL-N	0	0	....	3	0	0	0	0	9^1	5	3	1	0	0	8	4	1.393	0.96	349	2.38	.156	0	.000	2	1	0.2

• REIS, Laurie Lawrence P. Reis b: 11/20/1858, Chicago, IL d: 1/24/1921, Chicago, IL BB/TR, 160 lbs. Deb: 10/1/1877

YEAR TM-L	W	L	PCT	G	GS	CG	SH	SV	IP	H	R	ER	HR	HB	BB	SO	RAT	ERA	ERA+	CERA	OAV	BH	AVG	PR+	WS	TPW
1877 Chi-N	3	1	.750	4	4	4	1	0	36	29	8	3	1	....	6	11	.972	0.75	396	....	.208	2	.125	9	3	0.7
1878 Chi-N	1	3	.250	4	4	4	0	0	36	55	34	13	0	....	4	8	1.639	3.25	74	....	.334	3	.150	-4	1	-0.5
Total 2	4	4	.500	8	8	8	1	0	72	84	42	16	1	....	10	19	1.306	2.00	125	....	.276	5	.139	5	4	0.2

• REIS, Tommy Thomas Edward Reis b: 8/6/1914, Newport, KY BR/TR, 6'2", 180 lbs. Deb: 4/27/1938

YEAR TM-L	W	L	PCT	G	GS	CG	SH	SV	IP	H	R	ER	HR	HB	BB	SO	RAT	ERA	ERA+	CERA	OAV	BH	AVG	PR+	WS	TPW
1938 Phi-N	0	1	.000	4	0	0	0	0	4^2	8	11	10	0	0	8	2	3.429	19.29	21	12.12	.364	0	.000	-8	0	-0.8
Bos-N	0	0	....	4	0	0	0	0	6^1	8	5	5	1	0	1	4	1.421	7.11	48	4.85	.296	0	....	-3	0	-0.3
Yr.	0	1	.000	8	0	0	0	0	11	16	16	15	1	0	9	6	2.273	12.27	31	7.94	.327	0	.000	-10	0	-1.1

YEAR TM-L	W	L	PCT	G	GS	CG	SH	SV	IP	H	R	ER	HR	HB	BB	SO	RAT	ERA	ERA+	CERA	OAV	BH	AVG	PR+	WS	TPW
• REISIGL, Bugs	Jacob Reisigl b: 12/12/1887, Brooklyn, NY d: 2/24/1957, Amsterdam, NY BR/TR, 5'10.5", 175 lbs. Deb: 9/20/1911																									
1911 Cle-A	0	1	.000	2	1	1	0	0	13	13	9	9	1	0	3	6	1.231	6.23	55	3.43	.271	0	.000	-4	0	-0.5
• REISLING, Doc	Frank Carl Reisling b: 7/25/1874, Martins Ferry, OH d: 3/4/1955, Tulsa, OK BR/TR, 5'10", 180 lbs. Deb: 9/10/1904																									
1904 Bro-N	3	4	.429	7	7	6	1	0	51	45	16	12	0	9	10	19	1.078	2.12	129	2.66	.238	2	.154	4	4	0.4
1905 Bro-N	0	1	.000	2	0	0	0	0	3	3	1	1	0	0	4	2	2.333	3.00	96	6.79	.273	0	.000	0	0	0.0
1909 Was-A	2	4	.333	10	6	6	1	0	66^{2}	70	29	18	0	0	17	22	1.305	2.43	100	3.11	.270	4	.167	1	2	0.1
1910 Was-A	10	10	.500	30	20	13	2	1	191	185	77	54	3	5	44	57	1.199	2.54	98	2.93	.264	12	.200	-5	11	-0.3
Total 4	**15**	**19**	**.441**	**49**	**33**	**25**	**4**	**1**	**311^{2}**	**303**	**123**	**85**	**3**	**14**	**75**	**100**	**1.213**	**2.45**	**102**	**2.96**	**.261**	**18**	**.184**	**-1**	**17**	**0.3**
• REITH, Brian	Brian Eric Reith b: 2/28/1978, Fort Wayne, IN BR/TR, 6'5", 190 lbs. Deb: 5/16/2001																									
2001 Cin-N	0	7	.000	9	8	0	0	0	40^{1}	56	37	35	13	2	16	22	1.785	7.81	58	8.42	.333	3	.250	-14	0	-1.3
2003 Cin-N	2	3	.400	42	1	0	0	1	61^{1}	61	32	28	8	1	36	39	1.582	4.11	104	4.89	.263	0	.000	1	3	0.0
Total 2	**2**	**10**	**.167**	**51**	**9**	**0**	**0**	**1**	**101^{2}**	**117**	**69**	**63**	**21**	**3**	**52**	**61**	**1.662**	**5.58**	**79**	**6.29**	**.293**	**3**	**.158**	**-13**	**3**	**-1.3**
• REITSMA, Chris	Christopher Michael Reitsma b: 12/31/1977, Minneapolis, MN BR/TR, 6'5", 214 lbs. Deb: 4/4/2001																									
2001 Cin-N	7	15	.318	36	29	0	0	0	182	209	121	107	23	5	49	96	1.418	5.29	86	4.59	.288	5	.104	-12	3	-1.3
2002 Cin-N	6	12	.333	32	21	1	1	0	138^{1}	144	73	56	17	5	45	84	1.366	3.64	116	4.24	.267	3	.100	9	7	0.8
2003 Cin-N	9	5	.643	57	3	0	0	12	84	92	41	40	14	0	19	53	1.321	4.29	99	4.33	.281	1	.125	0	8	0.0
Total 3	**22**	**32**	**.407**	**125**	**53**	**1**	**1**	**12**	**404^{1}**	**445**	**235**	**203**	**54**	**10**	**113**	**233**	**1.380**	**4.52**	**97**	**4.41**	**.280**	**9**	**.105**	**-3**	**18**	**-0.5**
• REKAR, Bryan	Bryan Robert Rekar b: 6/3/1972, Oaklawn, IL BR/TR, 6'3", 205 lbs. Deb: 7/19/1995																									
1995 Col-N	4	6	.400	15	14	1	0	0	85	95	51	47	11	3	24	60	1.400	4.98	108	4.50	.282	1	.038	6	4	0.4
1996 Col-N	2	4	.333	14	11	0	0	0	58^{1}	87	61	58	11	5	26	25	1.937	8.95	58	8.31	.345	4	.267	-23	0	-2.1
1997 Col-N	1	0	1.000	2	2	0	0	0	9^{1}	11	7	6	3	0	6	4	1.821	5.79	90	7.63	.282	1	.250	-1	0	0.0
1998 TB-A	2	8	.200	16	15	1	0	0	86^{2}	95	56	48	16	2	21	55	1.338	4.98	96	4.69	.282	0	....	-5	3	-0.5
1999 TB-A	6	6	.500	27	12	0	0	0	94^{2}	121	68	61	14	5	41	55	1.711	5.80	86	6.49	.313	1	.200	-8	3	-0.8
2000 TB-A	7	10	.412	30	27	2	0	0	173^{1}	200	92	85	22	4	39	95	1.379	4.41	112	4.56	.291	1	.333	7	11	0.7
2001 TB-A	3	13	.188	25	25	0	0	0	140^{2}	167	104	92	21	6	45	87	1.507	5.89	76	5.31	.294	0	.000	-22	1	-2.2
2002 KC-A	0	2	.000	2	2	0	0	0	7	12	12	12	1	0	6	2	2.571	15.43	33	11.14	.387	0	....	-8	0	-0.8
Total 8	**25**	**49**	**.338**	**131**	**108**	**4**	**0**	**0**	**655**	**788**	**451**	**409**	**99**	**25**	**208**	**383**	**1.521**	**5.62**	**87**	**5.46**	**.299**	**8**	**.145**	**-54**	**22**	**-5.2**
• REMLINGER, Mike	Michael John Remlinger b: 3/23/1966, Middletown, NY BL/TL, 6', 195 lbs. Deb: 6/15/1991																									
1991 SF-N	2	1	.667	8	6	1	1	0	35	36	17	17	5	0	20	19	1.600	4.37	82	5.30	.271	0	.000	-3	1	-0.4
1994 NY-N	1	5	.167	10	9	0	0	0	54^{2}	55	30	28	9	1	35	33	1.646	4.61	91	5.46	.261	0	.000	-3	1	-0.4
1995 NY-N	0	1	.000	5	0	0	0	0	5^{2}	7	5	4	1	0	2	6	1.588	6.35	64	5.47	.292	0	.000	-1	0	-0.2
Cin-N	0	0	....	2	0	0	0	0	1	2	1	1	0	0	3	1	5.000	9.00	46	24.60	.500	0	....	-1	0	-0.1
Yr.	0	1	.000	7	0	0	0	0	6^{2}	9	6	5	1	0	5	7	2.100	6.75	60	8.34	.321	0	.000	-2	0	-0.2
1996 Cin-N	0	1	.000	19	4	0	0	0	27^{1}	24	17	17	4	3	19	19	1.573	5.60	74	5.23	.242	1	.143	-5	0	-0.4
1997 Cin-N	8	8	.500	69	12	2	0	2	124	100	61	57	11	7	60	145	1.290	4.14	104	3.43	.223	2	.095	2	9	0.2
1998 Cin-N	8	15	.348	35	28	1	1	0	164^{1}	164	96	88	23	5	87	144	1.527	4.82	89	5.04	.266	5	.106	-10	5	-1.1
1999* Atl-N	10	1	.909	73	0	0	0	1	83^{2}	66	24	22	9	1	35	81	1.207	2.37	190	3.03	.215	0	.000	21	12	1.9
2000* Atl-N	5	3	.625	71	0	0	0	12	72^{2}	55	29	28	6	3	37	72	1.266	3.47	132	3.15	.207	0	.000	9	12	0.9
2001* Atl-N	3	3	.500	74	0	0	0	1	75	67	25	23	9	2	23	93	1.200	2.76	160	3.27	.234	0	.000	13	9	1.3
2002* Atl-N★	7	3	.700	73	0	0	0	0	68	48	17	15	3	1	28	69	1.118	1.99	206	2.24	.198	0	.000	15	11	1.5
2003* Chi-N	6	5	.545	73	0	0	0	0	69	54	30	28	11	2	39	83	1.348	3.65	115	3.88	.211	0	.000	4	6	0.4
Total 11	**50**	**46**	**.521**	**512**	**59**	**4**	**2**	**16**	**780^{1}**	**678**	**352**	**328**	**91**	**25**	**388**	**765**	**1.366**	**3.78**	**112**	**3.95**	**.234**	**8**	**.073**	**42**	**66**	**3.6**
• REMMERSWAAL, Win	Wilhelmus Abraham Remmerswaal b: 3/8/1954, The Hague, Holland BR/TR, 6'2", 160 lbs. Deb: 8/3/1979																									
1979 Bos-A	1	0	1.000	8	0	0	0	0	20^{1}	26	16	16	1	1	12	16	1.869	7.08	62	6.24	.317	0	....	-6	0	-0.6
1980 Bos-A	2	1	.667	14	0	0	0	0	35^{1}	39	18	18	4	0	9	20	1.358	4.58	92	4.35	.295	0	....	-2	2	-0.2
Total 2	**3**	**1**	**.750**	**22**	**0**	**0**	**0**	**0**	**55^{2}**	**65**	**34**	**34**	**5**	**1**	**21**	**36**	**1.545**	**5.50**	**78**	**5.04**	**.304**	**0**	**....**	**-7**	**2**	**-0.7**
• REMNEAS, Alex	Alexander Norman Remneas b: 2/21/1886, Minneapolis, MN d: 8/27/1975, Phoenix, AZ BR/TR, 6'1", 180 lbs. Deb: 4/15/1912																									
1912 Det-A	0	0	....	1	0	0	0	0	1^{2}	5	5	5	0	0	0	0	3.000	27.00	12	13.15	.455	0	....	-4	0	-0.4
1915 StL-A	0	0	....	2	0	0	0	0	6	3	4	1	0	1	3	5	1.000	1.50	191	1.59	.136	0	.000	1	0	0.1
Total 2	**0**	**0**	**....**	**3**	**0**	**0**	**0**	**0**	**7^{2}**	**8**	**9**	**6**	**0**	**1**	**3**	**5**	**1.435**	**7.04**	**45**	**4.10**	**.242**	**0**	**.000**	**-4**	**0**	**-0.3**
• RENFER, Erwin	Erwin Arthur Renfer b: 12/11/1895, Elgin, IL d: 10/26/1958, Sycamore, IL BR/TR, 6', 180 lbs. Deb: 9/18/1913																									
1913 Det-A	0	1	.000	1	1	0	0	0	6	5	5	4	0	1	3	1	1.333	6.00	49	3.33	.227	0	.000	-2	0	-0.2
• RENFROE, Laddie	Cohen Williams Renfroe b: 5/9/1962, Natchez, MS BB/TR, 5'11", 200 lbs. Deb: 7/3/1991																									
1991 Chi-N	0	1	.000	4	0	0	0	0	4^{2}	11	7	7	1	0	2	4	2.786	13.50	29	13.64	.440	0	.000	-5	0	-0.5
• RENFROE, Marshall	Marshall Daniel Renfroe b: 5/25/1936, Century, FL d: 12/10/1970, Pensacola, FL BL/TL, 6', 180 lbs. Deb: 9/27/1959																									
1959 SF-N	0	0	....	1	1	0	0	0	2	3	6	6	1	0	3	3	3.000	27.00	14	16.26	.333	0	.000	-5	0	-0.5
• RENIFF, Hal	Harold Eugene "Porky" Reniff b: 7/2/1938, Warren, OH BR/TR, 6', 215 lbs. Deb: 6/8/1961																									
1961 NY-A	2	0	1.000	25	0	0	0	2	45^{1}	31	14	13	1	0	31	21	1.368	2.58	144	2.86	.197	0	.000	4	4	0.4
1962 NY-A	0	0	....	2	0	0	0	0	3^{2}	6	3	3	0	1	5	1	3.000	7.36	51	11.10	.400	0	....	-2	0	-0.2
1963* NY-A	4	3	.571	48	0	0	0	18	89^{1}	63	31	26	3	2	42	56	1.175	2.62	134	2.38	.202	0	.000	7	12	0.6
1964* NY-A	6	4	.600	41	0	0	0	9	69^{1}	47	26	24	3	0	30	38	1.111	3.12	116	2.13	.199	1	.100	3	8	0.3
1965 NY-A	3	4	.429	51	0	0	0	3	85^{1}	74	40	36	4	5	48	74	1.430	3.80	90	3.65	.232	0	.000	-3	4	-0.4
1966 NY-A	3	7	.300	56	0	0	0	9	95^{1}	80	37	34	2	5	49	79	1.353	3.21	104	3.12	.229	4	.286	2	7	0.3
1967 NY-A	0	2	.000	24	0	0	0	0	40	40	22	19	0	3	14	24	1.350	4.28	73	3.29	.256	0	.000	-5	0	-0.5
NY-N	3	3	.500	29	0	0	0	4	43	42	20	16	1	1	23	21	1.512	3.35	101	3.82	.266	0	.000	0	3	0.0
Total 7	**21**	**23**	**.477**	**276**	**0**	**0**	**0**	**45**	**471^{1}**	**383**	**193**	**171**	**14**	**17**	**242**	**314**	**1.326**	**3.27**	**105**	**3.05**	**.225**	**5**	**.096**	**7**	**38**	**0.5**
• RENINGER, Jim	James David Reninger b: 3/7/1915, Aurora, IL d: 8/23/1993, North Fort Myers, FL BR/TR, 6'3", 210 lbs. Deb: 9/17/1938																									
1938 Phi-A	0	2	.000	4	4	1	0	0	22^{2}	28	18	18	3	0	14	9	1.853	7.15	68	6.30	.295	0	.000	-5	0	-0.5
1939 Phi-A	0	2	.000	4	2	0	0	0	16^{1}	24	15	14	3	0	12	3	2.204	7.71	61	9.08	.369	1	.167	-5	0	-0.5
Total 2	**0**	**4**	**.000**	**8**	**6**	**1**	**0**	**0**	**39**	**52**	**33**	**32**	**6**	**0**	**26**	**12**	**2.000**	**7.38**	**65**	**7.46**	**.325**	**1**	**.077**	**-10**	**0**	**-1.0**
• RENKO, Steve	Steven Renko b: 12/10/1944, Kansas City, KS BR/TR, 6'5", 230 lbs. Deb: 6/27/1969																									
1969 Mon-N	6	7	.462	18	15	4	0	0	103^{1}	94	54	46	14	2	50	68	1.394	4.01	92	4.15	.243	6	.167	-3	4	-0.3
1970 Mon-N	13	11	.542	41	33	7	1	1	222^{2}	203	121	107	27	6	104	142	1.379	4.32	95	4.05	.241	16	.200	-7	11	-0.4
1971 Mon-N	15	14	.517	40	37	9	3	0	275^{2}	256	128	115	24	3	135	129	1.418	3.75	94	3.92	.247	21	.210	-6	15	-0.2
1972 Mon-N	1	10	.091	30	12	0	0	0	97	96	60	56	11	0	67	66	1.680	5.20	68	5.16	.262	7	.292	-17	0	-1.7
1973 Mon-N	15	11	.577	36	34	9	0	1	249^{2}	201	94	78	26	1	108	164	1.238	2.81	136	3.10	.218	24	.273	27	22	3.7
1974 Mon-N	12	16	.429	37	35	8	1	0	227^{2}	222	115	102	17	0	81	138	1.331	4.03	95	3.56	.257	17	.210	-4	11	-0.1
1975 Mon-N	6	12	.333	31	25	3	1	1	170^{1}	175	89	77	20	1	76	99	1.474	4.07	94	4.47	.265	15	.278	-5	9	0.0
1976 Mon-N	0	1	.000	5	1	0	0	0	13	15	8	8	2	0	3	4	1.385	5.54	67	4.63	.288	1	.333	-3	0	-0.3
Chi-N	8	11	.421	28	27	4	1	0	163^{1}	164	79	70	12	0	43	112	1.267	3.86	100	3.30	.258	5	.094	3	8	0.0
Yr.	8	12	.400	33	28	4	1	0	176^{1}	179	87	78	14	0	46	116	1.276	3.98	97	3.40	.260	6	.107	0	8	-0.3
1977 Chi-N	2	2	.500	13	8	0	0	1	51^{1}	51	32	26	10	1	21	34	1.403	4.56	96	4.65	.258	2	.167	0	2	0.0
Chi-A	5	0	1.000	8	8	0	0	0	53^{1}	55	23	21	3	1	17	36	1.350	3.54	115	3.80	.274	0	....	5	4	0.5
1978 Oak-A	6	12	.333	27	25	3	1	0	151	152	77	72	10	2	67	89	1.450	4.29	85	4.04	.265	0	....	-8	6	-0.9
1979 Bos-A	11	9	.550	27	27	4	1	0	171	174	86	78	22	2	53	99	1.327	4.11	107	4.04	.260	0	....	7	11	0.7
1980 Bos-A	9	9	.500	32	23	1	0	0	165^{1}	180	86	77	17	1	56	90	1.427	4.19	101	4.47	.281	0	....	0	9	0.0
1981 Cal-A	8	4	.667	22	15	0	0	1	102	93	40	39	7	1	42	50	1.324	3.44	106	3.53	.250	0	....	2	6	0.2
1982 Cal-A	11	6	.647	31	23	4	0	0	156	163	78	77	17	1	51	81	1.372	4.44	91	4.15	.269	0	....	-9	8	-0.9

YEAR TM-L	W	L	PCT	G	GS	CG	SH	SV	IP	H	R	ER	HR	HB	BB	SO	RAT	ERA	ERA+	CERA	OAV	BH	AVG	PR+	WS	TPW
1983 KC-A	6	11	.353	25	17	1	0	1	121^{1}	144	63	58	9	0	36	54	1.484	4.30	95	4.48	.293	0	....	-2	5	-0.2
Total 15	134	146	.479	451	365	57	9	6	2494	2438	1233	1107	248	22	1010	1455	1.383	3.99	97	3.96	.256	114	.215	-21	131	0.2
• REPLOGLE, Andy	Andrew David Replogle b: 10/7/1953, South Bend, IN BR/TR, 6'5", 205 lbs. Deb: 4/11/1978																									
1978 Mil-A	9	5	.643	32	18	3	2	0	149^{1}	177	75	65	14	1	47	41	1.500	3.92	96	4.85	.301	0	....	-3	7	-0.3
1979 Mil-A	0	0	....	3	0	0	0	0	8	13	5	5	0	0	2	2	1.875	5.63	74	6.77	.382	0	....	-1	0	-0.1
Total 2	9	5	.643	35	18	3	2	0	157^{1}	190	80	70	14	1	49	43	1.519	4.00	95	4.94	.305	0	....	-4	7	-0.5
• RESCIGNO, Xavier	Xavier Frederick "Mr. X" Rescigno b: 10/13/1913, New York, NY BR/TR, 5'10.5", 175 lbs. Deb: 4/22/1943																									
1943 Pit-N	6	9	.400	37	14	5	1	2	132^{2}	125	52	44	6	2	45	41	1.281	2.98	116	3.16	.252	5	.143	7	8	0.8
1944 Pit-N	10	8	.556	48	6	2	0	5	124	146	69	60	9	1	34	45	1.452	4.35	85	4.28	.291	2	.091	-8	6	-0.8
1945 Pit-N	3	5	.375	44	1	0	0	9	78^{2}	95	57	50	6	1	34	29	1.640	5.72	69	5.21	.303	2	.133	-15	1	-1.5
Total 3	19	22	.463	129	21	7	1	16	335^{1}	366	178	154	21	4	113	115	1.428	4.13	90	4.05	.279	9	.125	-15	15	-1.5
• RETTGER, George	George Edward Rettger b: 7/29/1868, Cleveland, OH d: 6/5/1921, Lakewood, OH BR/TR, 5'11", 175 lbs. Deb: 8/13/1891																									
1891 StL-a	7	3	.700	14	12	10	1	1	92^{2}	85	63	35	4	8	51	49	1.468	3.40	124	....	.236	3	.071	7	7	0.3
1892 Cle-N	1	3	.250	6	5	3	0	0	38	32	27	18	2	1	31	12	1.658	4.26	79	4.32	.219	2	.133	-4	1	-0.3
Cin-N	1	0	1.000	1	1	1	0	0	9	8	5	4	0	1	10	1	2.000	4.00	82	5.44	.229	1	.125	-1	1	-0.1
Yr.	2	3	.400	7	6	4	0	0	47	40	32	22	2	2	41	13	1.723	4.21	80	4.53	.221	3	.130	-4	2	-0.5
Total 2	9	6	.600	21	18	14	1	1	139^{2}	125	95	57	6	10	92	62	1.554	3.67	104	1.52	.231	6	.092	3	9	-0.1
• RETTIG, Otto	Adolph John Rettig b: 1/29/1894, New York, NY d: 6/16/1977, Stuart, FL BR/TR, 5'11", 165 lbs. Deb: 7/19/1922																									
1922 Phi-A	1	2	.333	4	4	1	0	0	18^{1}	18	11	10	0	1	12	3	1.636	4.91	86	4.04	.265	0	.000	-1	1	-0.2
• REULBACH, Ed	Edward Marvin "Big Ed" Reulbach b: 12/1/1882, Detroit, MI d: 7/17/1961, Glens Falls, NY BR/TR, 6'1", 190 lbs. Deb: 5/16/1905																									
1905 Chi-N	18	14	.563	34	29	28	5	1	291^{2}	208	71	46	1	18	73	152	.963	1.42	209	1.68	**.201**	14	.127	40	29	3.6
1906* Chi-N	19	4	.826	33	24	20	6	3	218	129	51	40	2	13	92	94	1.014	1.65	159	1.68	**.175**	13	.157	19	23	1.8
1907* Chi-N	17	4	.810	27	22	16	4	0	192	147	48	36	1	9	64	96	1.099	1.69	147	2.14	.217	11	.175	12	21	1.4
1908* Chi-N	24	7	.774	46	35	25	7	1	297^{2}	227	81	67	4	12	106	133	1.119	2.03	115	2.21	.214	23	.232	7	27	1.6
1909 Chi-N	19	10	.655	35	32	23	6	0	262^{2}	194	69	52	1	11	82	105	1.051	1.78	142	1.93	.212	12	.140	20	21	2.2
1910* Chi-N	12	8	.600	24	23	14	1	0	173^{1}	161	76	60	1	9	49	55	1.212	3.12	92	2.76	.251	6	.107	-6	9	-1.0
1911 Chi-N	16	9	.640	33	29	15	2	0	221^{2}	191	97	73	3	4	103	79	1.326	2.96	111	2.94	.236	6	.090	4	14	0.3
1912 Chi-N	10	6	.625	39	19	8	0	4	169	161	86	71	7	8	60	75	1.308	3.78	88	3.39	.259	6	.109	-13	10	-1.5
1913 Chi-N	1	3	.250	10	3	1	0	0	38^{2}	41	27	19	1	1	21	10	1.603	4.42	72	4.39	.281	3	.250	-6	0	-0.6
Bro-N	7	6	.538	15	12	8	2	0	110	77	34	25	3	4	34	46	1.009	2.05	160	1.84	.202	3	.103	14	10	1.5
Yr.	8	9	.471	25	15	9	2	0	148^{2}	118	61	44	4	5	55	56	1.164	2.66	121	2.50	.224	6	.146	8	10	0.9
1914 Bro-N	11	18	.379	44	29	14	3	3	256	228	108	75	5	10	83	119	1.215	2.64	108	2.73	.242	9	.122	5	14	0.6
1915 New-F	21	10	.677	33	30	23	4	1	270	233	88	67	3	3	69	117	1.119	2.23	127	2.26	.236	18	.196	17	22	1.8
1916 Bos-N	7	6	.538	21	11	6	0	0	109^{1}	99	38	30	1	4	41	47	1.280	2.47	99	2.98	.251	3	.091	-0	5	-0.2
1917 Bos-N	0	1	.000	5	2	0	0	0	22^{1}	21	13	7	0	1	15	9	1.612	2.82	90	3.94	.256	0	.000	-0	1	0.0
Total 13	182	106	.632	399	300	201	40	13	2632^{1}	2117	887	668	33	107	892	1137	1.143	2.28	123	2.37	.224	127	.147	113	206	11.5
• REUSCHEL, Paul	Paul Richard Reuschel b: 1/12/1947, Quincy, IL BR/TR, 6'4", 225 lbs. Deb: 7/25/1975																									
1975 Chi-N	1	3	.250	28	0	0	0	5	36	44	15	14	1	1	13	12	1.583	3.50	110	4.72	.312	0	.000	3	3	0.3
1976 Chi-N	4	2	.667	50	2	0	0	3	87	94	46	44	12	1	33	55	1.460	4.55	85	4.75	.278	2	.154	-5	4	-0.6
1977 Chi-N	5	6	.455	69	0	0	0	4	107	105	58	52	9	0	40	62	1.355	4.37	100	3.68	.262	0	.000	2	7	0.1
1978 Chi-N	2	0	1.000	16	0	0	0	0	28	29	16	16	4	1	13	13	1.500	5.14	78	4.91	.269	0	.000	-3	1	-0.4
Cle-A	2	4	.333	18	6	1	0	0	89^{2}	95	33	31	5	2	22	24	1.305	3.11	120	3.55	.271	0	....	7	6	0.7
1979 Cle-A	2	1	.667	17	1	0	0	1	45^{1}	73	43	40	7	0	11	22	1.853	7.94	54	7.68	.365	0	....	-18	0	-1.7
Total 5	16	16	.500	198	9	1	0	13	393	440	211	197	38	5	132	188	1.455	4.51	90	4.53	.286	2	.063	-14	21	-1.6
• REUSCHEL, Rick	Rickey Eugene "Big Daddy" Reuschel b: 5/16/1949, Quincy, IL BR/TR, 6'3", 235 lbs. Deb: 6/19/1972																									
1972 Chi-N	10	8	.556	21	18	5	4	0	129	127	46	42	3	2	29	87	1.209	2.93	130	2.85	.259	6	.136	13	10	1.3
1973 Chi-N	14	15	.483	36	36	7	3	0	237	244	95	79	15	5	62	168	1.291	3.00	131	3.48	.263	9	.123	30	20	2.8
1974 Chi-N	13	12	.520	41	38	8	2	0	240^{2}	262	130	115	18	6	83	160	1.434	4.30	89	4.14	.276	19	.221	-1	12	0.1
1975 Chi-N	11	17	.393	38	37	6	0	1	234	244	116	97	17	7	67	155	1.329	3.73	103	3.70	.268	16	.208	11	14	1.3
1976 Chi-N	14	12	.538	38	37	9	2	1	260	260	117	100	17	8	64	146	1.246	3.46	111	3.38	.265	19	.229	16	19	2.1
1977 Chi-N★	20	10	.667	39	37	8	4	1	252	233	84	78	13	5	74	166	1.218	2.79	157	3.01	.247	18	.207	**50**	**26**	**5.2**
1978 Chi-N	14	15	.483	35	35	9	1	0	242^{2}	235	98	92	16	5	54	115	1.191	3.41	118	3.01	.254	10	.137	18	18	1.9
1979 Chi-N	18	12	.600	36	36	5	1	0	239	251	104	96	16	10	75	125	1.364	3.62	114	3.93	.274	13	.165	17	17	1.9
1980 Chi-N	11	13	.458	38	**38**	6	0	0	257	281	111	97	13	4	76	140	1.389	3.40	115	3.89	.286	13	.159	18	15	1.9
1981 Chi-N	4	7	.364	13	13	1	0	0	85^{2}	87	40	33	4	4	23	53	1.284	3.47	107	3.45	.267	2	.080	4	4	0.3
*NY-A	4	4	.500	12	11	3	0	0	70^{2}	75	24	21	4	1	10	22	1.203	2.67	134	3.31	.280	0	....	7	5	0.7
1983 Chi-N	1	1	.500	4	4	0	0	0	20^{2}	18	9	9	1	0	10	9	1.355	3.92	97	3.19	.234	1	.143	0	1	0.0
1984 Chi-N	5	5	.500	19	14	1	0	0	92^{1}	123	57	53	7	3	23	43	1.581	5.17	76	5.50	.339	7	.241	-12	3	-1.0
1985 Pit-N	14	8	.636	31	26	9	1	1	194	153	58	49	7	3	52	138	1.057	2.27	157	2.10	.215	10	.169	31	20	3.5
1986 Pit-N	9	16	.360	35	34	4	2	0	215^{2}	232	106	95	20	8	57	125	1.340	3.96	97	4.01	.274	11	.157	-3	8	-0.3
1987 Pit-N★	8	6	.571	25	25	9	3	0	177	163	63	54	12	6	35	80	1.119	2.75	150	2.83	.246	9	.150	24	15	2.5
*SF-N	5	3	.625	9	8	3	1	0	50	44	28	24	1	2	7	27	1.020	4.32	89	2.02	.230	2	.105	-3	2	-0.3
Yr.	13	9	.591	34	33	**12**	**4**	0	227	207	91	78	13	8	42	107	1.097	3.09	130	2.65	.242	11	.139	20	17	2.2
1988 SF-N	19	11	.633	36	**36**	7	2	0	245	242	88	85	11	6	42	92	1.159	3.12	104	2.84	.260	8	.110	4	15	0.2
1989* SF-N★	17	8	.680	32	32	2	0	0	208^{1}	195	75	68	18	2	54	111	1.195	2.94	115	3.11	.247	10	.164	5	13	0.7
1990 SF-N	3	6	.333	15	13	0	0	1	87	102	40	38	8	1	31	49	1.529	3.93	93	4.64	.297	4	.154	-3	3	-0.4
1991 SF-N	0	2	.000	4	1	0	0	0	10^{2}	17	5	5	0	0	7	4	2.250	4.22	85	7.82	.370	0	.000	-1	0	-0.1
Total 19	214	191	.528	557	529	102	26	5	3548^{1}	3588	1494	1330	221	88	935	2015	1.275	3.37	113	3.43	.264	187	.168	223	240	24.3
• REUSS, Jerry	Jerry Reuss b: 6/19/1949, St. Louis, MO BL/TL, 6'5", 217 lbs. Deb: 9/27/1969																									
1969 StL-N	1	0	1.000	1	1	0	0	0	7	2	0	0	0	2	3	3	.714	0.00	....	1.26	.091	1	.333	3	1	0.3
1970 StL-N	7	8	.467	20	20	5	2	0	127^{1}	132	62	58	9	1	49	74	1.421	4.10	100	4.05	.271	2	.050	2	6	0.0
1971 StL-N	14	14	.500	36	35	7	2	0	211	228	125	112	15	7	109	131	**1.597**	4.78	75	4.84	.279	8	.123	-23	4	-2.4
1972 Hou-N	9	13	.409	33	30	4	1	1	192	177	101	89	14	10	83	174	1.354	4.17	81	3.73	.246	7	.106	-17	5	-1.9
1973 Hou-N	16	13	.552	41	**40**	12	3	0	279^{1}	271	123	116	17	3	117	177	1.389	3.74	97	3.73	.256	13	.137	-3	15	-0.4
1974* Pit-N	16	11	.593	35	35	14	1	0	260	259	115	101	20	1	101	105	1.385	3.50	99	3.73	.261	13	.151	-3	13	-0.3
1975* Pit-N★	18	11	.621	32	32	15	6	0	237^{1}	224	73	67	10	0	78	131	1.272	2.54	139	3.09	.253	14	.197	26	20	3.0
1976 Pit-N	14	9	.609	31	29	11	3	2	209^{1}	209	98	82	16	2	51	108	1.242	3.53	99	3.24	.256	16	.242	-2	13	0.4
1977 Pit-N	10	13	.435	33	33	8	2	0	208	225	109	95	11	4	71	116	1.423	4.11	97	4.07	.280	12	.171	-6	9	-0.5
1978 Pit-N	3	2	.600	23	12	3	1	0	82^{2}	97	48	45	5	3	23	42	1.452	4.90	76	4.43	.297	5	.185	-10	2	-1.0
1979 LA-N	7	14	.333	39	21	4	1	3	160	178	88	63	4	3	60	83	1.488	3.54	103	4.01	.282	7	.167	4	7	0.5
1980 LA-N★	18	6	.750	37	29	10	**6**	3	229^{1}	193	74	64	12	0	40	111	1.016	2.51	139	**2.08**	.227	6	.088	22	21	2.2
1981* LA-N	10	4	.714	22	22	8	2	0	152^{2}	138	44	39	6	4	27	51	1.081	2.30	144	2.46	.243	10	.196	18	13	1.9
1982 LA-N	18	11	.621	39	37	8	4	0	254^{2}	232	98	88	11	2	50	138	1.107	3.11	112	2.44	.240	17	.221	12	17	1.6
1983* LA-N	12	11	.522	32	31	7	0	0	223^{1}	233	94	73	12	2	50	143	1.267	2.94	122	3.32	.271	20	.282	21	15	2.7
1984 LA-N	5	7	.417	30	15	2	0	1	99	102	51	42	4	0	31	44	1.343	3.82	92	3.31	.266	4	.167	-2	4	-0.1
1985* LA-N	14	10	.583	34	33	5	3	0	212^{2}	210	78	69	13	3	58	84	1.260	2.92	119	3.29	.260	10	.135	13	13	1.2
1986 LA-N	2	6	.250	19	13	0	0	1	74	96	57	48	13	2	17	29	1.527	5.84	59	5.67	.313	5	.250	-18	0	-1.7
1987 LA-N	0	0	....	1	0	0	0	0	2	2	1	1	0	0	0	2	1.000	4.50	88	1.95	.333	0	....	-0	0	0.0
Cin-N	0	5	.000	7	7	0	0	0	34^{2}	52	31	30	2	1	12	10	1.846	7.79	54	6.60	.351	1	.125	-14	0	-1.4
Yr.	0	5	.000	8	7	0	0	0	36^{2}	54	32	31	2	1	12	12	1.800	7.61	56	6.34	.351	1	.125	-14	0	-1.4
Cal-A	4	5	.444	17	16	1	1	0	82^{1}	112	60	48	16	2	17	37	1.567	5.25	82	6.22	.327	0	....	-9	2	-0.8
1988 Chi-A	13	9	.591	32	29	2	0	0	183	183	79	70	15	3	43	73	1.235	3.44	115	3.43	.263	0	....	8	12	0.8

YEAR	TM-L	W	L	PCT	G	GS	CG	SH	SV	IP	H	R	ER	HR	HB	BB	SO	RAT	ERA	ERA+	CERA	OAV	BH	AVG	PR+	WS	TPW
1989	Chi-A	8	5	.615	23	19	1	1	0	106^{2}	135	65	60	12	3	21	27	1.463	5.06	75	4.95	.308	0	....	-15	2	-1.5
	Mil-A	1	4	.200	7	7	0	0	0	33^{2}	36	23	20	7	1	13	13	1.455	5.35	72	5.31	.273	0	....	-6	0	-0.6
	Yr.	9	9	.500	30	26	1	1	0	140^{1}	171	88	80	19	4	34	40	1.461	5.13	74	5.04	.300	0	....	-21	2	-2.1
1990	Pit-N	0	0	....	4	1	0	0	0	7^{2}	8	3	3	1	0	3	1	1.435	3.52	103	4.19	.267	0	....	-0	0	0.0
Total	**22**	**220**	**191**	**.535**	**628**	**547**	**127**	**39**	**11**	**3669^{2}**	**3734**	**1700**	**1483**	**245**	**59**	**1127**	**1907**	**1.325**	**3.64**	**100**	**3.63**	**.265**	**171**	**.167**	**1**	**194**	**1.8**

• REVENIG, Todd — Todd Michael Revenig b: 6/28/1969, Brainerd, MN BR/TR, 6'1", 185 lbs. Deb: 8/24/1992

YEAR	TM-L	W	L	PCT	G	GS	CG	SH	SV	IP	H	R	ER	HR	HB	BB	SO	RAT	ERA	ERA+	CERA	OAV	BH	AVG	PR+	WS	TPW
1992	Oak-A	0	0	....	2	0	0	0	0	2	2	0	0	0	0	0	1	1.000	0.00	....	2.31	.286	0	....	1	0	0.1

• REYES, Al — Rafael Alberto Reyes b: 4/10/1971, San Cristobal, Dominican Republic BR/TR, 6'1", 195 lbs. Deb: 4/27/1995

YEAR	TM-L	W	L	PCT	G	GS	CG	SH	SV	IP	H	R	ER	HR	HB	BB	SO	RAT	ERA	ERA+	CERA	OAV	BH	AVG	PR+	WS	TPW
1995	Mil-A	1	1	.500	27	0	0	0	1	33^{1}	19	9	9	3	3	18	29	1.110	2.43	205	2.51	.167	0	....	9	4	0.8
1996	Mil-A	1	0	1.000	5	0	0	0	0	5^{2}	8	5	5	1	0	2	2	1.765	7.94	65	6.79	.320	0	....	-2	0	-0.2
1997	Mil-A	1	2	.333	19	0	0	0	1	29^{2}	32	19	18	4	3	9	28	1.382	5.46	85	4.76	.274	0	....	-4	1	-0.4
1998	Mil-N	5	1	.833	50	0	0	0	0	57	55	26	25	9	2	31	58	1.509	3.95	108	5.01	.253	1	.200	1	4	0.1
1999	Mil-N	2	0	1.000	26	0	0	0	0	36	27	17	17	5	3	25	39	1.444	4.25	107	4.35	.206	0	.000	2	3	0.1
	Bal-A	2	3	.400	27	0	0	0	0	29^{2}	23	16	16	4	3	16	28	1.315	4.85	97	3.99	.225	0	....	-1	2	-0.1
2000	Bal-A	1	0	1.000	13	0	0	0	0	13	13	10	10	2	0	11	10	1.846	6.92	68	6.14	.271	0	....	-3	0	-0.3
	LA-N	0	0	....	6	0	0	0	0	6^{2}	2	0	0	0	0	1	8	.450	0.00	....	0.35	.087	0	....	3	1	0.3
2001	LA-N	2	1	.667	19	0	0	0	1	25^{2}	28	13	11	3	1	13	23	1.597	3.86	104	5.07	.269	1	.333	1	2	0.1
2002	Pit-N	0	0	....	15	0	0	0	0	17	9	5	5	1	2	7	21	.941	2.65	158	1.93	.161	0	....	3	2	0.3
2003	NY-A	0	0	....	13	0	0	0	0	17	13	7	6	1	0	9	9	1.294	3.18	137	2.86	.203	0	....	3	1	0.3
Total	**9**	**15**	**8**	**.652**	**220**	**0**	**0**	**0**	**3**	**270^{2}**	**229**	**127**	**122**	**33**	**17**	**142**	**255**	**1.371**	**4.06**	**111**	**4.13**	**.229**	**2**	**.200**	**11**	**20**	**1.1**

• REYES, Carlos — Carlos Alberto Reyes b: 4/4/1969, Miami, FL BB/TR, 6'1", 190 lbs. Deb: 4/7/1994

YEAR	TM-L	W	L	PCT	G	GS	CG	SH	SV	IP	H	R	ER	HR	HB	BB	SO	RAT	ERA	ERA+	CERA	OAV	BH	AVG	PR+	WS	TPW
1994	Oak-A	0	3	.000	27	9	0	0	1	78	71	38	36	10	2	44	57	1.474	4.15	106	4.50	.242	0	....	1	4	0.1
1995	Oak-A	4	6	.400	40	1	0	0	0	69	71	43	39	10	5	28	48	1.435	5.09	87	4.76	.264	0	....	-5	2	-0.4
1996	Oak-A	7	10	.412	46	10	0	0	0	122^{1}	134	71	65	19	2	61	78	1.594	4.78	102	5.42	.281	0	....	-0	7	0.0
1997	Oak-A	3	4	.429	37	6	0	0	0	77^{1}	101	52	50	13	2	25	43	1.629	5.82	77	6.15	.316	0	....	-9	2	-0.9
1998	SD-N	2	2	.500	22	0	0	0	1	27^{2}	23	11	11	4	2	6	24	1.048	3.58	110	3.14	.235	0	....	1	2	0.1
	Bos-A	1	1	.500	24	0	0	0	0	38^{1}	35	15	15	2	1	14	23	1.278	3.52	134	3.25	.246	0	....	5	3	0.4
1999	SD-N	2	4	.333	65	0	0	0	1	77^{1}	76	38	32	11	0	24	57	1.293	3.72	113	3.76	.254	0	.000	4	5	0.3
2000	Phi-N	0	2	.000	10	0	0	0	0	10^{1}	10	6	6	2	0	5	4	1.452	5.23	89	5.04	.270	0	....	-1	0	-0.1
	SD-N	1	1	.500	12	0	0	0	1	18	15	12	12	5	1	8	13	1.278	6.00	72	4.74	.221	0	.000	-4	0	-0.4
	Yr.	1	3	.250	22	0	0	0	1	28^{1}	25	18	18	7	1	13	17	1.341	5.72	77	4.85	.238	0	.000	-4	0	-0.4
2003	TB-A	0	3	.000	10	3	0	0	0	39^{2}	40	23	23	10	2	5	13	1.134	5.22	87	4.28	.265	0	.000	-4	1	-0.4
Total	**8**	**20**	**36**	**.357**	**293**	**29**	**0**	**0**	**4**	**558**	**576**	**309**	**289**	**86**	**17**	**220**	**360**	**1.427**	**4.66**	**97**	**4.71**	**.267**	**0**	**.000**	**-12**	**26**	**-1.1**

• REYES, Dennys — Dennys (Velarde) Reyes b: 4/19/1977, Higuera de Zaragoza, Mexico BL/TL, 6'3", 246 lbs. Deb: 7/13/1997

YEAR	TM-L	W	L	PCT	G	GS	CG	SH	SV	IP	H	R	ER	HR	HB	BB	SO	RAT	ERA	ERA+	CERA	OAV	BH	AVG	PR+	WS	TPW
1997	LA-N	2	3	.400	14	5	0	0	0	47	51	21	20	4	1	18	36	1.468	3.83	101	4.34	.280	0	.000	1	2	0.0
1998	LA-N	0	4	.000	11	3	0	0	0	28^{2}	27	17	15	1	0	20	33	1.640	4.71	84	4.16	.255	0	.000	-2	0	-0.3
	Cin-N	3	1	.750	8	7	0	0	0	38^{2}	35	19	19	2	1	27	44	1.603	4.42	97	4.54	.255	1	.083	-1	2	-0.1
	Yr.	3	5	.375	19	10	0	0	0	67^{1}	62	36	34	3	1	47	77	1.619	4.54	91	4.38	.255	1	.059	-3	2	-0.4
1999	Cin-N	2	2	.500	65	1	0	0	2	61^{2}	53	30	26	5	3	39	72	1.492	3.79	123	4.16	.232	0	.000	4	5	0.3
2000	Cin-N	2	1	.667	62	0	0	0	0	43^{2}	43	31	22	5	1	29	36	1.649	4.53	104	5.24	.262	0	.000	0	2	0.0
2001	Cin-N	2	6	.250	35	6	0	0	0	53	51	35	29	5	1	35	52	1.623	4.92	92	4.77	.248	2	.182	-1	1	-0.1
2002	Col-N	0	1	.000	43	0	0	0	0	40^{1}	43	19	19	1	0	24	30	1.661	4.24	113	4.55	.279	0	....	3	3	0.3
	Tex-A	4	3	.571	15	5	0	0	0	42^{1}	55	33	30	9	0	21	29	1.795	6.38	74	7.24	.316	0	....	-7	1	-0.7
2003	Pit-N	0	0	....	12	0	0	0	0	10^{1}	10	13	12	1	0	9	11	1.839	10.45	42	5.43	.263	0	....	-7	0	-0.7
	Ari-N	0	0	....	3	0	0	0	0	2^{1}	5	3	3	1	0	1	5	2.571	11.57	40	14.73	.417	0	....	-2	0	-0.2
	Yr.	0	0	....	15	0	0	0	0	12^{2}	15	16	15	2	0	10	16	1.974	10.66	42	7.14	.300	0	....	-9	0	-0.9
Total	**7**	**15**	**21**	**.417**	**268**	**27**	**0**	**0**	**2**	**368**	**373**	**221**	**195**	**34**	**7**	**223**	**348**	**1.620**	**4.77**	**93**	**4.94**	**.266**	**3**	**.070**	**-12**	**16**	**-1.4**

• REYNOLDS, Allie — Allie Pierce "Superchief" Reynolds b: 2/10/1917, Bethany, OK d: 12/26/1994, Oklahoma City, OK BR/TR, 6', 195 lbs. Deb: 9/17/1942

YEAR	TM-L	W	L	PCT	G	GS	CG	SH	SV	IP	H	R	ER	HR	HB	BB	SO	RAT	ERA	ERA+	CERA	OAV	BH	AVG	PR+	WS	TPW
1942	Cle-A	0	0	....	2	0	0	0	0	5	5	1	0	0	0	4	2	1.800	0.00	....	4.49	.250	0	.000	2	1	0.2
1943	Cle-A	11	12	.478	34	21	11	3	3	198^{2}	140	72	66	3	7	109	**151**	1.253	2.99	104	2.54	**.202**	10	.149	-2	10	-0.3
1944	Cle-A	11	8	.579	28	21	5	1	1	158	141	63	58	2	4	91	84	1.468	3.30	100	3.48	.240	7	.123	-2	10	-0.5
1945	Cle-A★	18	12	.600	44	30	16	2	4	247^{1}	227	102	88	7	5	130	112	1.443	3.20	101	3.55	.247	8	.094	3	15	-0.4
1946	Cle-A	11	15	.423	31	28	9	3	0	183^{1}	180	93	79	10	1	108	107	1.571	3.88	85	4.27	.259	14	.222	-11	6	-1.0
1947*	NY-A	19	8	.704	34	30	17	4	2	241^{2}	207	94	86	23	4	123	129	1.366	3.20	110	3.58	.227	13	.146	8	16	0.6
1948	NY-A	16	7	.696	39	31	11	1	3	236^{1}	240	108	99	17	4	111	101	1.485	3.77	108	4.28	.268	16	.193	5	16	0.5
1949*	NY-A★	17	6	.739	35	31	4	2	1	213^{2}	200	102	95	15	4	123	105	1.512	4.00	101	4.14	.250	17	.218	-4	14	0.1
1950*	NY-A★	16	12	.571	35	29	14	2	2	240^{2}	215	108	100	12	8	138	160	1.467	3.74	115	3.82	.242	15	.185	12	17	1.2
1951*	NY-A	17	8	.680	40	26	16	**7**	7	221	171	84	75	12	5	100	126	1.226	3.05	125	**2.77**	**.213**	14	.184	16	19	1.6
1952*	NY-A★	20	8	.714	35	29	24	**6**	6	244^{1}	194	70	56	10	7	97	**160**	1.191	**2.06**	**161**	2.63	.218	13	.153	26	24	2.6
1953*	NY-A★	13	7	.650	41	15	5	1	13	145	140	64	55	9	5	61	86	1.386	3.41	108	3.72	.253	5	.122	1	11	0.1
1954	NY-A★	13	4	.765	36	18	5	4	7	157^{1}	133	65	58	13	3	66	100	1.265	3.32	104	3.21	.233	8	.160	-2	11	-0.2
Total	**13**	**182**	**107**	**.630**	**434**	**309**	**137**	**36**	**49**	**2492^{1}**	**2193**	**1026**	**915**	**133**	**57**	**1261**	**1423**	**1.386**	**3.30**	**109**	**3.50**	**.238**	**140**	**.163**	**51**	**170**	**4.3**

• REYNOLDS, Archie — Archie Edward Reynolds b: 1/3/1946, Glendale, CA BR/TR, 6'2", 205 lbs. Deb: 8/15/1968

YEAR	TM-L	W	L	PCT	G	GS	CG	SH	SV	IP	H	R	ER	HR	HB	BB	SO	RAT	ERA	ERA+	CERA	OAV	BH	AVG	PR+	WS	TPW
1968	Chi-N	0	1	.000	7	1	0	0	0	13^{1}	14	10	10	1	1	7	6	1.575	6.75	47	4.84	.259	1	.500	-5	0	-0.5
1969	Chi-N	0	1	.000	2	2	0	0	0	7^{1}	11	5	2	1	0	7	4	2.455	2.45	164	9.96	.379	0	.000	1	1	0.2
1970	Chi-N	0	2	.000	7	1	0	0	0	15	17	11	11	2	1	9	9	1.733	6.60	68	6.57	.298	0	.000	-4	0	-0.3
1971	Cal-A	0	3	.000	15	1	0	0	0	27^{1}	32	15	14	2	0	18	15	1.829	4.61	70	5.70	.305	0	.000	-4	0	-0.5
1972	Mil-A	0	1	.000	5	2	0	0	0	18^{2}	26	18	15	2	0	8	13	1.821	7.23	42	6.57	.338	2	.500	-9	0	-0.9
Total	**5**	**0**	**8**	**.000**	**36**	**7**	**0**	**0**	**0**	**81^{2}**	**100**	**59**	**52**	**8**	**2**	**49**	**47**	**1.824**	**5.73**	**59**	**6.30**	**.311**	**3**	**.273**	**-21**	**1**	**-2.1**

• REYNOLDS, Bob — Robert Allen Reynolds b: 1/21/1947, Seattle, WA BR/TR, 6', 205 lbs. Deb: 9/19/1969

YEAR	TM-L	W	L	PCT	G	GS	CG	SH	SV	IP	H	R	ER	HR	HB	BB	SO	RAT	ERA	ERA+	CERA	OAV	BH	AVG	PR+	WS	TPW
1969	Mon-N	0	0	....	1	1	0	0	0	1^{1}	3	6	3	0	0	3	2	4.500	20.25	18	17.96	.429	0	....	-2	0	-0.3
1971	StL-N	0	0	....	4	0	0	0	0	7	15	8	8	2	1	6	4	3.000	10.29	35	16.69	.441	0	.000	-5	0	-0.6
	Mil-A	0	1	.000	3	0	0	0	0	6	4	2	2	0	0	3	4	1.167	3.00	116	2.37	.222	0	.000	0	0	0.0
1972	Bal-A	0	0	....	3	0	0	0	0	9^{2}	8	2	2	0	0	7	5	1.552	1.86	165	3.64	.258	0	.000	1	1	0.1
1973*	Bal-A	7	5	.583	42	1	0	0	9	111	88	27	24	3	0	31	77	1.072	1.95	192	2.05	.219	0	....	17	14	1.8
1974*	Bal-A	7	5	.583	54	0	0	0	7	69^{1}	75	23	21	4	1	14	43	1.284	2.73	127	3.48	.278	0	....	5	7	0.5
1975	Bal-A	0	1	.000	7	0	0	0	0	6	11	6	6	1	0	1	1	2.000	9.00	39	8.93	.423	0	....	-4	0	-0.4
	Det-A	0	2	.000	21	0	0	0	3	34^{2}	40	20	18	8	1	14	26	1.558	4.67	86	5.99	.288	0	....	-2	1	-0.2
	Cle-A	0	2	.000	5	0	0	0	2	9^{2}	11	7	5	0	0	3	5	1.448	4.66	81	3.70	.289	0	....	-1	0	-0.1
	Yr.	0	5	.000	33	0	0	0	5	50^{1}	62	33	29	9	1	18	32	1.589	5.19	74	5.90	.305	0	....	-7	1	-0.7
Total	**6**	**14**	**16**	**.467**	**140**	**2**	**0**	**0**	**21**	**254^{2}**	**255**	**101**	**89**	**18**	**3**	**82**	**167**	**1.323**	**3.15**	**116**	**3.75**	**.264**	**0**	**.000**	**9**	**23**	**0.9**

• REYNOLDS, Charlie — Charles E. Reynolds b: 7/31/1857, Allegany, NY d: 5/1/1913, Buffalo, NY Deb: 5/18/1882 ♦

YEAR	TM-L	W	L	PCT	G	GS	CG	SH	SV	IP	H	R	ER	HR	HB	BB	SO	RAT	ERA	ERA+	CERA	OAV	BH	AVG	PR+	WS	TPW
1882	Phi-a	1	1	.500	2	2	1	0	0	12	18	11	7	0	....	3	4	1.750	5.25	57	....	.326	1	.125	-3	0	-0.4

• REYNOLDS, Ken — Kenneth Lee Reynolds b: 1/4/1947, Trevose, PA BL/TL, 6', 180 lbs. Deb: 9/5/1970

YEAR	TM-L	W	L	PCT	G	GS	CG	SH	SV	IP	H	R	ER	HR	HB	BB	SO	RAT	ERA	ERA+	CERA	OAV	BH	AVG	PR+	WS	TPW
1970	Phi-N	0	0	....	4	0	0	0	0	2^{1}	3	0	0	0	0	4	1	3.000	0.00	....	11.05	.333	0	....	1	0	0.1
1971	Phi-N	5	9	.357	35	25	2	1	0	162^{1}	163	89	81	11	6	82	81	1.509	4.49	78	4.50	.269	10	.200	-19	4	-1.9
1972	Phi-N	2	15	.118	33	23	2	0	0	154^{1}	149	76	73	17	1	60	87	1.354	4.26	84	3.92	.258	8	.200	-13	3	-1.3
1973	Mil-A	0	1	.000	2	1	0	0	0	7^{1}	5	7	6	1	1	10	3	2.045	7.36	51	7.18	.200	0	....	-3	0	-0.3
1975	StL-N	0	1	.000	10	0	0	0	0	17	12	4	3	0	0	11	7	1.353	1.59	236	2.74	.214	0	.000	5	2	0.4
1976	SD-N	0	3	.000	19	2	0	0	1	32^{1}	38	27	23	0	0	29	18	2.072	6.40	51	6.23	.309	0	.000	-11	0	-1.3
Total	**6**	**7**	**29**	**.194**	**103**	**51**	**4**	**1**	**1**	**375^{2}**	**370**	**203**	**186**	**29**	**8**	**196**	**197**	**1.507**	**4.46**	**79**	**4.42**	**.265**	**18**	**.186**	**-41**	**9**	**-4.1**

YEAR TM-L	W	L	PCT	G	GS	CG	SH	SV	IP	H	R	ER	HR	HB	BB	SO	RAT	ERA	ERA+	CERA	OAV	BH	AVG	PR+	WS	TPW

• REYNOLDS, Ross Ross Ernest "Doc" Reynolds b: 8/20/1887, Barksdale, TX d: 6/23/1970, Ada, OK BR/TR, 6'2", 185 lbs. Deb: 5/2/1914

YEAR TM-L	W	L	PCT	G	GS	CG	SH	SV	IP	H	R	ER	HR	HB	BB	SO	RAT	ERA	ERA+	CERA	OAV	BH	AVG	PR+	WS	TPW
1914 Det-A	5	3	.625	26	7	3	1	0	78	62	26	18	0	6	39	31	1.295	2.08	135	2.99	.230	1	.048	7	6	0.6
1915 Det-A	0	1	.000	4	2	0	0	0	11^1	17	9	8	0	1	5	2	1.941	6.35	48	7.26	.378	0	.000	-4	0	-0.5
Total 2	5	4	.556	30	9	3	1	0	89^1	79	35	26	0	7	44	33	1.377	2.62	109	3.53	.251	1	.042	3	6	0.1

• REYNOLDS, Shane Richard Shane Reynolds b: 3/26/1968, Bastrop, LA BR/TR, 6'3", 210 lbs. Deb: 7/20/1992

YEAR TM-L	W	L	PCT	G	GS	CG	SH	SV	IP	H	R	ER	HR	HB	BB	SO	RAT	ERA	ERA+	CERA	OAV	BH	AVG	PR+	WS	TPW
1992 Hou-N	1	3	.250	8	5	0	0	0	25^1	42	22	20	2	0	6	10	1.895	7.11	47	7.07	.385	2	.500	-10	0	-1.0
1993 Hou-N	0	0	....	5	1	0	0	0	11	11	4	1	0	0	6	10	1.545	0.82	473	3.72	.256	1	.500	4	1	0.4
1994 Hou-N	8	5	.615	33	14	1	1	0	124	128	46	42	10	6	21	110	1.202	3.05	130	3.38	.263	3	.091	12	9	1.0
1995 Hou-N	10	11	.476	30	30	3	2	0	189^1	196	87	73	15	2	37	175	1.231	3.47	111	3.31	.263	8	.127	12	9	1.0
1996 Hou-N	16	10	.615	35	35	4	1	0	239	227	103	97	20	8	44	204	1.134	3.65	106	2.97	.249	14	.184	10	15	1.3
1997* Hou-N	9	10	.474	30	30	2	0	0	181	189	92	85	19	3	47	152	1.304	4.23	95	3.79	.267	6	.113	-7	7	-0.7
1998* Hou-N	19	8	.704	35	**35**	3	1	0	233^1	257	99	91	25	2	53	209	1.329	3.51	116	4.05	.280	13	.159	13	16	1.4
1999* Hou-N	16	14	.533	35	**35**	4	2	0	231^2	250	108	99	23	1	37	197	1.239	3.85	115	3.58	.275	11	.167	13	16	1.3
2000 Hou-N★	7	8	.467	22	22	0	0	0	131	150	86	76	20	6	45	93	1.489	5.22	93	5.17	.287	9	.225	-3	6	-0.1
2001* Hou-N	14	11	.560	28	28	3	0	0	182^2	208	95	88	24	4	36	102	1.336	4.34	105	4.38	.290	4	.077	4	10	0.2
2002 Hou-N	3	6	.333	13	13	0	0	0	74	80	43	40	13	1	26	47	1.432	4.86	87	4.90	.274	1	.048	-4	2	-0.6
2003 Atl-N	11	9	.550	30	29	0	0	0	167^1	191	104	101	20	8	59	94	1.494	5.43	78	5.07	.293	5	.093	-22	3	-2.4
Total 12	114	95	.545	304	277	20	7	0	1789^2	1929	889	813	191	41	417	1403	1.311	4.09	102	3.98	.275	77	.141	21	94	1.8

• REYNOSO, Armando Armando Martin (Gutierrez) Reynoso b: 5/1/1966, San Luis Potosi, Mexico BR/TR, 6', 196 lbs. Deb: 8/11/1991

YEAR TM-L	W	L	PCT	G	GS	CG	SH	SV	IP	H	R	ER	HR	HB	BB	SO	RAT	ERA	ERA+	CERA	OAV	BH	AVG	PR+	WS	TPW
1991 Atl-N	2	1	.667	6	5	0	0	0	23^1	26	18	16	4	3	10	10	1.543	6.17	63	6.09	.299	0	.000	-6	0	-0.7
1992 Atl-N	1	0	1.000	3	1	0	0	1	7^2	11	4	4	2	1	2	2	1.696	4.70	78	8.83	.393	0	.000	-1	0	-0.1
1993 Col-N	12	11	.522	30	30	4	0	0	189	206	101	84	22	9	63	117	1.423	4.00	119	4.55	.277	8	.127	22	13	2.2
1994 Col-N	3	4	.429	9	9	1	0	0	52^1	54	30	28	5	6	22	25	1.452	4.82	103	4.91	.278	3	.176	3	3	0.2
1995* Col-N	7	7	.500	20	18	0	0	0	93	116	61	55	12	5	36	40	1.634	5.32	101	5.99	.316	4	.133	3	5	0.2
1996 Col-N	8	9	.471	30	30	0	0	0	168^2	195	97	93	27	9	49	88	1.447	4.96	105	5.26	.291	9	.173	9	10	0.9
1997 NY-N	6	3	.667	16	16	1	1	0	91^1	95	47	46	7	6	29	47	1.358	4.53	89	4.08	.275	7	.241	-7	5	-0.4
1998 NY-N	7	3	.700	11	11	0	0	0	68^1	64	31	29	4	5	32	40	1.405	3.82	108	4.01	.256	5	.167	2	5	0.2
1999 Ari-N	10	6	.625	31	27	0	0	0	167	178	90	81	20	6	67	79	1.467	4.37	105	4.71	.276	8	.163	3	8	0.3
2000 Ari-N	11	12	.478	31	30	2	0	0	170^2	179	102	100	22	6	52	89	1.354	5.27	89	4.29	.273	5	.104	-10	7	-1.2
2001 Ari-N	1	6	.143	9	9	0	0	0	46^2	58	32	31	13	4	13	15	1.521	5.98	77	6.77	.312	1	.100	-8	0	-0.8
2002 Ari-N	0	0	....	2	0	0	0	0	1^2	3	2	2	0	0	1	2	2.400	10.80	41	8.83	.375	0	....	-1	0	-0.1
Total 12	68	62	.523	198	186	8	1	1	1079^2	1185	615	569	138	60	376	554	1.446	4.74	99	4.88	.283	50	.148	9	56	0.9

• RHEM, Flint Charles Flint "Shad" Rhem b: 1/24/1901, Rhems, SC d: 7/30/1969, Columbia, SC BR/TR, 6'2", 180 lbs. Deb: 9/6/1924

YEAR TM-L	W	L	PCT	G	GS	CG	SH	SV	IP	H	R	ER	HR	HB	BB	SO	RAT	ERA	ERA+	CERA	OAV	BH	AVG	PR+	WS	TPW
1924 StL-N	2	2	.500	6	3	3	0	1	32^1	31	18	16	1	0	17	20	1.485	4.45	85	3.75	.254	2	.167	-2	1	-0.3
1925 StL-N	8	13	.381	30	24	8	1	1	170	204	114	93	16	4	58	66	1.541	4.92	88	4.97	.299	14	.237	-12	6	-1.0
1926* StL-N	**20**	7	.741	34	34	20	1	0	258	241	121	92	12	1	75	72	1.225	3.21	122	2.90	.250	18	.188	18	18	1.6
1927 StL-N	10	12	.455	27	26	9	2	0	169^1	189	102	83	6	4	54	51	1.435	4.41	89	3.95	.285	4	.068	-12	6	-1.7
1928* StL-N	11	8	.579	28	22	9	0	3	169^2	199	91	78	13	3	71	47	1.591	4.14	97	4.96	.296	11	.164	-4	8	-0.5
1930* StL-N	12	8	.600	26	19	9	0	0	139^2	173	90	69	11	3	37	47	1.504	4.45	113	4.68	.306	12	.231	8	9	0.6
1931* StL-N	11	10	.524	33	26	10	2	1	207^1	214	100	82	17	3	60	72	1.322	3.56	111	3.67	.268	9	.130	8	13	0.4
1932 StL-N	4	2	.667	6	6	5	1	0	50	48	19	17	3	0	10	18	1.160	3.06	129	2.90	.257	3	.188	5	5	0.5
Phi-N	11	7	.611	26	20	10	0	1	168^2	177	79	70	13	0	49	35	1.340	3.74	118	3.68	.269	7	.113	13	13	0.8
Yr.	15	9	.625	32	26	15	1	1	218^2	225	98	87	16	0	59	53	1.299	3.58	120	3.51	.266	10	.128	18	18	1.4
1933 Phi-N	5	14	.263	28	19	3	0	2	125	182	109	92	10	2	33	27	1.720	6.62	58	6.00	.340	4	.087	-39	0	-4.5
1934 StL-N	1	0	1.000	5	1	0	0	1	15^2	26	12	8	0	0	7	6	2.106	4.60	92	7.73	.394	0	.000	-1	0	-0.1
Bos-N	8	8	.500	25	20	5	1	0	152^2	164	71	61	5	0	38	56	1.323	3.60	106	3.36	.273	3	.058	4	8	-0.1
Yr.	9	8	.529	30	21	5	1	1	168^1	190	83	69	5	0	45	62	1.396	3.69	105	3.76	.285	3	.056	3	8	-0.2
1935 Bos-N	0	5	.000	10	6	0	0	0	40^1	61	37	24	4	0	11	10	1.785	5.36	71	6.29	.341	0	.000	-6	0	-0.7
1936 StL-N	2	1	.667	10	4	0	0	0	26^2	49	26	20	2	0	9	7	2.175	6.75	58	8.84	.405	1	.125	-8	0	-0.8
Total 12	105	97	.520	294	230	91	8	10	1725^1	1958	989	805	113	20	529	534	1.441	4.20	97	4.22	.287	88	.144	-28	87	-5.8

• RHINES, Billy William Pearl "Bunker" Rhines b: 3/14/1869, Ridgway, PA d: 1/30/1922, Ridgway, PA BR/TR, 5'11", 168 lbs. Deb: 4/22/1890 U

YEAR TM-L	W	L	PCT	G	GS	CG	SH	SV	IP	H	R	ER	HR	HB	BB	SO	RAT	ERA	ERA+	CERA	OAV	BH	AVG	PR+	WS	TPW
1890 Cin-N	28	17	.622	46	45	45	6	0	401^1	337	163	87	6	15	113	182	1.121	**1.95**	**182**	....	.221	29	.188	65	41	5.4
1891 Cin-N	17	24	.415	48	43	40	1	1	372^2	364	224	119	4	22	124	138	1.309	2.87	117	....	.246	18	.122	19	21	1.0
1892 Cin-N	3	7	.300	11	9	6	0	0	74^2	102	71	47	0	4	36	10	1.848	5.67	58	5.82	.313	5	.185	-21	0	-1.8
1893 Lou-N	1	4	.200	5	5	3	0	0	31	49	37	30	3	3	19	0	2.194	8.71	50	8.79	.348	1	.091	-14	0	-1.3
1895 Cin-N	19	10	.655	38	33	25	0	0	267^2	322	195	143	4	21	76	72	1.487	4.81	103	4.10	.293	25	.221	4	18	0.0
1896 Cin-N	8	6	.571	19	17	11	3	0	143	128	52	39	1	9	48	32	1.231	**2.45**	**188**	**2.79**	**.238**	10	.192	31	16	2.4
1897 Cin-N	21	15	.583	41	32	26	1	0	288^2	311	175	131	4	17	86	65	1.375	4.08	111	3.64	.273	17	.159	15	24	0.8
1898 Pit-N	12	16	.429	31	29	27	2	0	258	289	143	101	0	13	61	48	1.357	3.52	101	3.53	.281	15	.150	0	15	-0.3
1899 Pit-N	4	4	.500	9	9	4	0	0	54	59	42	36	3	4	13	6	1.333	6.00	63	3.88	.278	10	.435	-13	2	-0.8
Total 9	113	103	.523	248	222	187	13	1	1891	1961	1102	733	25	108	576	553	1.342	3.49	114	2.31	.262	130	.177	84	137	5.3

• RHOADS, Bob Barton Emory "Dusty" Rhoads b: 10/4/1879, Wooster, OH d: 2/12/1967, San Bernardino, CA BR/TR, 6'1", 215 lbs. Deb: 4/19/1902

YEAR TM-L	W	L	PCT	G	GS	CG	SH	SV	IP	H	R	ER	HR	HB	BB	SO	RAT	ERA	ERA+	CERA	OAV	BH	AVG	PR+	WS	TPW
1902 Chi-N	4	8	.333	16	12	12	1	1	118	131	66	42	1	6	42	43	1.466	3.20	84	3.95	.281	10	.222	-7	3	-0.7
1903 StL-N	5	8	.385	17	13	12	1	0	129	154	88	66	3	3	47	52	1.558	4.60	71	4.62	.303	7	.140	-22	3	-2.3
Cle-A	2	3	.400	5	5	5	0	0	41	55	34	24	2	2	3	21	1.415	5.27	54	4.33	.320	2	.118	-11	0	-1.3
1904 Cle-A	10	9	.526	22	19	18	0	0	175^1	175	72	56	1	5	48	72	1.272	2.87	88	2.96	.261	18	.196	-7	8	-1.0
1905 Cle-A	16	9	.640	28	26	24	4	0	235	219	96	74	4	10	55	61	1.166	2.83	93	2.66	.249	21	.221	-5	17	-0.1
1906 Cle-A	22	10	.688	38	34	31	7	0	315	259	95	63	5	5	92	89	1.114	1.80	146	2.23	.227	19	.161	22	23	2.1
1907 Cle-A	15	14	.517	35	31	23	5	1	275	258	105	70	0	14	84	76	1.244	2.29	109	2.81	.251	17	.185	1	16	0.0
1908 Cle-A	18	12	.600	37	30	20	1	0	270	229	82	53	2	7	73	62	1.119	1.77	135	2.40	.239	20	.222	16	23	2.2
1909 Cle-A	5	9	.357	20	15	9	2	0	133^1	124	63	43	1	6	50	46	1.305	2.90	88	3.53	.281	7	.163	-6	5	-0.7
Total 8	97	82	.542	218	185	154	21	2	1691^2	1604	701	491	19	58	494	522	1.240	2.61	101	2.94	.256	121	.188	-20	98	-1.8

• RHODEN, Rick Richard Alan Rhoden b: 5/16/1953, Boynton Beach, FL BR/TR, 6'3", 195 lbs. Deb: 7/5/1974

YEAR TM-L	W	L	PCT	G	GS	CG	SH	SV	IP	H	R	ER	HR	HB	BB	SO	RAT	ERA	ERA+	CERA	OAV	BH	AVG	PR+	WS	TPW
1974 LA-N	1	0	1.000	4	0	0	0	0	9	5	2	2	1	0	4	7	1.000	2.00	170	1.94	.161	1	.500	1	1	0.2
1975 LA-N	3	3	.500	26	11	1	0	0	99^1	94	40	34	8	1	32	40	1.268	3.08	110	3.39	.253	2	.071	2	5	0.1
1976 LA-N★	12	3	.800	27	26	10	3	0	181	165	66	60	17	1	53	77	1.204	2.98	113	3.17	.242	20	.308	4	17	1.2
1977* LA-N	16	10	.615	31	31	4	1	0	216^1	223	98	90	20	2	63	122	1.322	3.74	102	3.85	.270	18	.231	-0	13	0.5
1978* LA-N	10	8	.556	30	23	6	3	0	164^2	160	77	67	13	3	51	79	1.281	3.66	96	3.48	.255	7	.135	-4	7	-0.5
1979 Pit-N	0	1	.000	1	1	0	0	0	5	5	4	4	0	0	2	2	1.400	7.20	54	3.46	.263	1	1.000	-2	0	-0.1
1980 Pit-N	7	5	.583	20	19	2	0	0	126^2	133	58	54	9	3	40	70	1.366	3.84	95	3.93	.273	15	.375	-4	9	0.2
1981 Pit-N	9	4	.692	21	21	4	2	0	136^1	147	66	59	6	2	53	76	1.467	3.89	92	4.17	.283	9	.188	-4	6	-0.4
1982 Pit-N	11	14	.440	35	35	6	1	0	230^1	239	115	106	14	2	70	128	1.342	4.14	90	3.61	.267	22	.265	-10	11	-0.1
1983 Pit-N	13	13	.500	36	35	7	2	1	244^1	256	95	84	13	2	68	153	1.326	3.09	120	3.58	.276	13	.151	18	16	1.7
1984 Pit-N	14	9	.609	33	33	6	3	0	238^1	216	81	72	13	1	62	136	1.166	2.72	132	2.82	.243	28	.333	20	**20**	**3.1**
1985 Pit-N	10	15	.400	35	35	2	0	0	213^1	254	119	106	18	6	69	128	**1.514**	4.47	80	4.85	.296	14	.189	-18	6	-1.7
1986 Pit-N★	15	12	.556	34	34	12	1	0	253^2	211	82	80	17	2	76	159	1.131	2.84	135	2.64	.228	25	.278	28	20	3.8
1987 NY-A	16	10	.615	30	29	4	0	0	181^2	184	84	78	22	3	61	107	1.349	3.86	114	4.14	.268	0	....	10	14	0.9
1988 NY-A	12	12	.500	30	30	5	1	0	197	206	107	94	20	8	56	94	1.330	4.29	92	3.99	.269	0	.000	-6	8	-0.6
1989 Hou-N	2	6	.250	20	17	0	0	0	96^2	108	49	46	7	3	41	41	1.541	4.28	79	4.61	.289	6	.207	-9	2	-0.9
Total 16	151	125	.547	413	380	69	17	1	2593^2	2606	1143	1036	198	39	801	1419	1.314	3.59	103	3.66	.264	181	.238	28	155	7.4

• RHODES, Arthur Arthur Lee Rhodes b: 10/24/1969, Waco, TX BL/TL, 6'2", 206 lbs. Deb: 8/21/1991

YEAR TM-L	W	L	PCT	G	GS	CG	SH	SV	IP	H	R	ER	HR	HB	BB	SO	RAT	ERA	ERA+	CERA	OAV	BH	AVG	PR+	WS	TPW
1991 Bal-A	0	3	.000	8	8	0	0	0	36	47	35	32	4	0	23	23	1.944	8.00	49	7.00	.320	0	....	-16	0	-1.6

YEAR	TM-L	W	L	PCT	G	GS	CG	SH	SV	IP	H	R	ER	HR	HB	BB	SO	RAT	ERA	ERA+	CERA	OAV	BH	AVG	PR+	WS	TPW
1992	Bal-A	7	5	.583	15	15	2	1	0	94^1	87	39	38	6	1	38	77	1.325	3.63	111	3.48	.249	0	....	4	7	0.4
1993	Bal-A	5	6	.455	17	17	0	0	0	85^2	91	62	62	16	1	49	49	1.634	6.51	69	5.88	.274	0	....	-21	1	-2.0
1994	Bal-A	3	5	.375	10	10	3	2	0	52^2	51	34	34	8	2	30	47	1.538	5.81	86	5.03	.254	0	....	-5	2	-0.5
1995	Bal-A	2	5	.286	19	9	0	0	0	75^1	68	53	52	13	0	48	77	1.540	6.21	76	4.97	.239	0	....	-13	1	-1.2
1996*	Bal-A	9	1	.900	28	2	0	0	1	53	48	28	24	6	0	23	62	1.340	4.08	121	3.72	.241	0	....	5	5	0.5
1997*	Bal-A	10	3	.769	53	0	0	0	1	95^1	75	32	32	9	4	26	102	1.059	3.02	146	2.58	.218	0	.000	14	10	1.4
1998	Bal-A	4	4	.500	45	0	0	0	4	77	65	30	30	8	1	34	83	1.286	3.51	130	3.47	.233	1	.500	10	7	0.9
1999	Bal-A	3	4	.429	43	0	0	0	3	53	43	37	32	9	0	45	59	1.660	5.43	86	5.07	.221	0	....	-5	2	-0.5
2000*	Sea-A	5	8	.385	72	0	0	0	0	69^1	51	34	33	6	0	29	77	1.154	4.28	106	2.62	.205	0	....	1	6	0.1
2001*	Sea-A	8	0	1.000	71	0	0	0	3	68	46	14	13	5	1	12	83	.853	1.72	241	1.61	.189	0	.000	16	12	1.6
2002	Sea-A	10	4	.714	66	0	0	0	2	69^2	45	18	18	4	0	13	81	.833	2.33	182	1.46	.187	0	....	15	11	1.5
2003	Sea-A	3	3	.500	67	0	0	0	3	54	53	25	25	4	1	18	48	1.315	4.17	104	3.57	.256	0	....	-1	4	0.0
Total	13	69	51	.575	514	61	5	3	17	883^1	770	441	425	98	11	388	868	1.311	4.33	103	3.72	.235	1	.250	4	68	0.3

• RHODES, Bill William Clarence Rhodes b: Pottstown, PA Deb: 6/14/1893

YEAR	TM-L	W	L	PCT	G	GS	CG	SH	SV	IP	H	R	ER	HR	HB	BB	SO	RAT	ERA	ERA+	CERA	OAV	BH	AVG	PR+	WS	TPW
1893	Lou-N	5	12	.294	20	19	17	0	0	151^2	244	173	128	10	0	66	22	**2.044**	7.60	58	7.54	.352	9	.129	-52	0	-4.5

• RHODES, Charlie Charles Anderson "Dusty" Rhodes b: 4/7/1885, Caney, KS d: 10/26/1918, Caney, KS BR/TR, 5'7", 180 lbs. Deb: 7/26/1906

YEAR	TM-L	W	L	PCT	G	GS	CG	SH	SV	IP	H	R	ER	HR	HB	BB	SO	RAT	ERA	ERA+	CERA	OAV	BH	AVG	PR+	WS	TPW
1906	StL-N	3	4	.429	9	6	3	0	0	45	37	21	17	0	6	20	32	1.267	3.40	77	2.89	.223	3	.188	-3	2	-0.4
1908	Cin-N	0	0	....	1	0	0	0	0	4	1	2	0	0	1	2	4	.750	0.00	....	1.07	.077	0	.000	1	0	0.1
	StL-N	1	2	.333	4	4	3	0	0	33	23	14	11	2	1	12	15	1.061	3.00	78	2.26	.200	3	.250	-2	2	-0.1
	Yr.	1	2	.333	5	4	3	0	0	37	24	16	11	2	2	14	19	1.027	2.68	87	2.13	.188	3	.231	-1	2	0.0
1909	StL-N	3	5	.375	12	10	4	0	0	61	55	36	27	0	2	33	25	1.443	3.98	63	3.59	.256	4	.211	-8	1	-0.8
Total	3	7	11	.389	26	20	10	0	0	143	116	73	55	2	10	67	76	1.280	3.46	73	2.99	.228	10	.208	-12	5	-1.2

• RHODES, Gordon John Gordon "Dusty" Rhodes b: 8/11/1907, Winnemucca, NV d: 3/22/1960, Long Beach, CA BR/TR, 6', 187 lbs. Deb: 4/29/1929

YEAR	TM-L	W	L	PCT	G	GS	CG	SH	SV	IP	H	R	ER	HR	HB	BB	SO	RAT	ERA	ERA+	CERA	OAV	BH	AVG	PR+	WS	TPW
1929	NY-A	0	4	.000	10	4	0	0	0	42^2	57	32	23	3	2	16	13	1.711	4.85	79	5.89	.333	3	.300	-5	1	-0.4
1930	NY-A	0	0	....	3	0	0	0	0	2	3	3	2	0	0	4	1	3.500	9.00	48	15.98	.500	0	....	-1	0	-0.1
1931	NY-A	6	3	.667	18	11	4	0	0	87	82	49	33	3	0	52	36	1.540	3.41	116	3.62	.235	6	.214	5	5	0.5
1932	NY-A	1	2	.333	10	2	1	0	0	24	25	22	21	0	0	21	15	1.917	7.88	52	5.03	.275	2	.286	-10	0	-0.9
	Bos-A	1	8	.111	12	11	4	0	0	79^1	79	46	45	5	0	31	22	1.387	5.11	88	3.66	.261	2	.074	-4	3	-0.6
	Yr.	2	10	.167	22	13	5	0	0	103^1	104	68	66	5	0	52	37	1.510	5.75	76	3.97	.264	4	.118	-14	3	-1.5
1933	Bos-A	12	15	.444	34	29	14	0	0	232	242	126	104	13	1	93	85	1.444	4.03	109	3.87	.265	23	.267	9	14	1.3
1934	Bos-A	12	12	.500	44	31	10	0	2	219	247	133	111	10	4	98	79	1.575	4.56	105	4.47	.285	10	.133	8	12	0.4
1935	Bos-A	2	10	.167	34	19	1	0	2	146^1	195	103	88	14	1	60	44	1.743	5.41	88	5.98	.324	7	.146	-11	4	-1.4
1936	Phi-A	9	20	.310	35	28	13	1	1	216^1	266	162	138	26	2	102	61	1.701	5.74	89	5.77	.304	16	.213	-16	8	-1.5
Total	8	43	74	.368	200	135	47	1	5	1048^2	1196	676	565	74	10	477	356	1.595	4.85	95	4.78	.286	69	.194	-25	47	-2.6

• RIBANT, Dennis Dennis Joseph Ribant b: 9/20/1941, Detroit, MI BR/TR, 5'11", 175 lbs. Deb: 8/9/1964

YEAR	TM-L	W	L	PCT	G	GS	CG	SH	SV	IP	H	R	ER	HR	HB	BB	SO	RAT	ERA	ERA+	CERA	OAV	BH	AVG	PR+	WS	TPW
1964	NY-N	1	5	.167	14	7	1	1	1	57^2	65	35	33	8	0	9	35	1.283	5.15	69	4.05	.281	2	.100	-11	0	-1.1
1965	NY-N	1	3	.250	19	1	0	0	3	35^1	29	16	15	5	0	6	13	.991	3.82	92	2.58	.228	0	.000	-1	3	-0.2
1966	NY-N	11	9	.550	39	26	10	1	3	188^1	184	78	67	20	1	40	84	1.189	3.20	114	3.23	.254	12	.197	9	14	1.0
1967	Pit-N	9	8	.529	38	22	2	0	0	172	186	78	78	16	3	40	75	1.314	4.08	82	3.92	.280	16	.267	-16	8	-1.2
1968	Det-A	2	2	.500	14	0	0	0	1	24^1	20	7	6	1	1	10	7	1.233	2.22	136	2.70	.217	1	.200	2	2	0.3
	Chi-A	0	2	.000	17	0	0	0	1	31^1	42	24	21	3	2	17	20	1.883	6.03	50	6.57	.318	0	.000	-10	0	-1.3
	Yr.	2	4	.333	31	0	0	0	2	55^2	62	31	27	4	3	27	27	1.599	4.37	69	4.88	.277	1	.083	-8	2	-1.0
1969	StL-N	0	0	....	1	0	0	0	0	1^1	4	2	2	1	0	1	0	3.750	13.50	26	27.46	.571	0	....	-1	0	-0.2
	Cin-N	0	0	....	7	0	0	0	0	8^1	6	5	1	1	0	3	7	1.080	1.08	348	2.45	.188	0	....	2	1	0.3
	Yr.	0	0	....	8	0	0	0	0	9^2	10	7	3	2	0	4	7	1.448	2.79	130	5.90	.256	0	....	1	1	0.1
Total	6	24	29	.453	149	56	13	2	9	518^2	536	245	223	55	7	126	241	1.276	3.87	89	3.73	.267	31	.195	-26	28	-2.4

• RICCELLI, Frank Frank Joseph Riccelli b: 2/24/1953, Syracuse, NY BL/TL, 6'3", 205 lbs. Deb: 9/11/1976

YEAR	TM-L	W	L	PCT	G	GS	CG	SH	SV	IP	H	R	ER	HR	HB	BB	SO	RAT	ERA	ERA+	CERA	OAV	BH	AVG	PR+	WS	TPW
1976	SF-N	1	1	.500	4	3	0	0	0	16	16	10	10	1	0	5	11	1.313	5.63	64	3.46	.258	1	.167	-3	0	-0.4
1978	Hou-N	0	0	....	2	0	0	0	0	3	1	0	0	0	0	0	1	.333	0.00	....	0.25	.100	0	....	1	1	0.1
1979	Hou-N	2	2	.500	11	2	0	0	0	22	22	11	10	0	0	18	20	1.818	4.09	86	4.95	.262	2	.333	-1	1	0.0
Total	3	3	3	.500	17	5	0	0	0	41	39	21	20	1	0	23	32	1.512	4.39	81	4.02	.250	3	.250	-3	2	-0.3

• RICCI, Chuck Charles Mark Ricci b: 11/20/1968, Abington, PA BR/TR, 6'2", 180 lbs. Deb: 9/8/1995

YEAR	TM-L	W	L	PCT	G	GS	CG	SH	SV	IP	H	R	ER	HR	HB	BB	SO	RAT	ERA	ERA+	CERA	OAV	BH	AVG	PR+	WS	TPW
1995	Phi-N	1	0	1.000	7	0	0	0	0	10	9	2	2	0	1	3	9	1.200	1.80	235	3.04	.273	0	....	3	1	0.3

• RICE, Pat Patrick Edward Rice b: 11/2/1963, Rapid City, SD BR/TR, 6'2", 200 lbs. Deb: 5/18/1991

YEAR	TM-L	W	L	PCT	G	GS	CG	SH	SV	IP	H	R	ER	HR	HB	BB	SO	RAT	ERA	ERA+	CERA	OAV	BH	AVG	PR+	WS	TPW
1991	Sea-A	1	1	.500	7	2	0	0	0	21	18	10	7	3	1	10	12	1.333	3.00	137	3.95	.234	0	....	2	1	0.2

• RICE, Sam Edgar Charles Rice b: 2/20/1890, Morocco, IN d: 10/13/1974, Rossmoor, MD BL/TR, 5'9", 150 lbs. Deb: 8/7/1915 HOF: 1963 ♦

YEAR	TM-L	W	L	PCT	G	GS	CG	SH	SV	IP	H	R	ER	HR	HB	BB	SO	RAT	ERA	ERA+	CERA	OAV	BH	AVG	PR+	WS	TPW
1915	Was-A	1	0	1.000	4	2	1	0	0	18	13	8	4	0	0	9	9	1.222	2.00	148	2.39	.213	3	.375	2	2	0.3
1916	Was-A	0	1	.000	5	1	0	0	0	21^1	18	10	7	0	0	10	3	1.313	2.95	94	2.85	.237	59	.299	-1	8	0.3
Total	2	1	1	.500	9	3	1	0	0	39^1	31	18	11	0	0	19	12	1.271	2.52	113	2.64	.226	2987	.322	1	10	0.5

• RICH, Woody Woodrow Earl Rich b: 3/9/1916, Morganton, NC d: 4/18/1983, Morganton, NC BL/TR, 6'2", 185 lbs. Deb: 4/22/1939

YEAR	TM-L	W	L	PCT	G	GS	CG	SH	SV	IP	H	R	ER	HR	HB	BB	SO	RAT	ERA	ERA+	CERA	OAV	BH	AVG	PR+	WS	TPW
1939	Bos-A	4	3	.571	21	12	3	0	1	77	78	46	42	2	5	35	24	1.468	4.91	96	3.89	.264	7	.259	-1	5	-0.1
1940	Bos-A	1	0	1.000	3	1	1	0	0	11^2	9	3	1	2	0	1	8	.857	0.77	583	2.14	.214	0	.000	5	2	0.4
1941	Bos-A	0	0	....	2	1	0	0	0	3^2	8	7	7	1	0	2	4	2.727	17.18	24	13.85	.421	0	....	-5	0	-0.5
1944	Bos-N	1	1	.500	7	2	1	0	0	25	32	17	16	3	3	12	6	1.760	5.76	66	6.70	.327	1	.125	-5	0	-0.6
Total	4	6	4	.600	33	16	5	0	1	117^1	127	73	66	8	8	50	42	1.509	5.06	87	4.63	.280	8	.205	-7	7	-0.8

• RICHARD, J.R. James Rodney Richard b: 3/7/1950, Vienna, LA BR/TR, 6'8", 222 lbs. Deb: 9/5/1971

YEAR	TM-L	W	L	PCT	G	GS	CG	SH	SV	IP	H	R	ER	HR	HB	BB	SO	RAT	ERA	ERA+	CERA	OAV	BH	AVG	PR+	WS	TPW
1971	Hou-N	2	1	.667	4	4	1	0	0	21	17	9	8	1	0	16	29	1.571	3.43	98	3.92	.215	0	.000	-0	1	-0.1
1972	Hou-N	1	0	1.000	4	1	0	0	0	6	10	9	9	0	2	8	8	3.000	13.50	25	13.41	.385	0	....	-7	0	-0.7
1973	Hou-N	6	2	.750	16	10	2	1	0	72	54	37	32	2	1	38	75	1.278	4.00	91	2.85	.210	5	.179	-3	4	-0.3
1974	Hou-N	2	3	.400	15	9	0	0	0	64^2	58	31	30	3	1	36	42	1.454	4.18	83	3.86	.243	3	.143	-6	2	-0.6
1975	Hou-N	12	10	.545	33	31	7	1	0	203	178	107	99	8	4	138	176	1.557	4.39	77	4.11	.238	15	.203	-25	7	-2.2
1976	Hou-N	20	15	.571	39	39	14	3	0	291	221	105	89	14	4	151	214	1.278	2.75	116	2.93	**.212**	14	.140	14	17	1.5
1977	Hou-N	18	12	.600	36	36	13	3	0	267	212	94	88	18	0	104	214	1.184	2.97	120	2.74	.218	20	.230	19	21	2.5
1978	Hou-N	18	11	.621	36	36	16	3	0	275^1	192	104	95	12	2	141	**303**	1.209	3.11	106	2.53	**.196**	18	.178	12	19	1.3
1979	Hou-N	18	13	.581	38	38	19	4	0	292^1	220	98	88	13	3	98	**313**	1.088	**2.71**	130	**2.23**	**.209**	12	.126	27	23	2.7
1980	Hou-N★	10	4	.714	17	17	4	4	0	113^2	65	31	24	2	0	40	119	.924	1.90	173	1.41	.166	6	.154	17	12	1.9
Total	10	107	71	.601	238	221	76	19	0	1606	1227	625	562	73	17	770	1493	1.243	3.15	108	2.83	.212	93	.168	48	106	5.9

• RICHARDS, Duane Duane Lee Richards b: 12/16/1936, Spartanburg, IN BR/TR, 6'3", 200 lbs. Deb: 9/25/1960

YEAR	TM-L	W	L	PCT	G	GS	CG	SH	SV	IP	H	R	ER	HR	HB	BB	SO	RAT	ERA	ERA+	CERA	OAV	BH	AVG	PR+	WS	TPW
1960	Cin-N	0	0	....	2	0	0	0	0	3	5	4	3	0	0	2	2	2.333	9.00	42	8.24	.385	0	....	-2	0	-0.2

• RICHARDS, Rusty Russell Earl Richards b: 1/27/1965, Houston, TX BL/TR, 6'4", 200 lbs. Deb: 9/20/1989

YEAR	TM-L	W	L	PCT	G	GS	CG	SH	SV	IP	H	R	ER	HR	HB	BB	SO	RAT	ERA	ERA+	CERA	OAV	BH	AVG	PR+	WS	TPW
1989	Atl-N	0	0	....	2	2	0	0	0	9^1	10	5	5	2	1	6	4	1.714	4.82	76	7.06	.278	0	.000	-1	0	-0.2
1990	Atl-N	0	0	....	1	0	0	0	0	1	2	3	3	1	0	1	0	3.000	27.00	15	23.01	.400	0	....	-3	0	-0.3
Total	2	0	0	....	3	2	0	0	0	10^1	12	8	8	3	1	7	4	1.839	6.97	54	8.60	.293	0	.000	-4	0	-0.4

• RICHARDSON, Danny Daniel Richardson b: 1/25/1863, Elmira, NY d: 9/12/1926, New York, NY BR/TR, 5'8", 165 lbs. Deb: 5/22/1884 M ♦

YEAR	TM-L	W	L	PCT	G	GS	CG	SH	SV	IP	H	R	ER	HR	HB	BB	SO	RAT	ERA	ERA+	CERA	OAV	BH	AVG	PR+	WS	TPW
1885	NY-N	7	1	.875	9	8	7	1	0	75	58	30	20	0	....	18	21	1.013	2.40	111	....	.204	52	.263	-1	14	0.5
1886	NY-N	0	2	.000	5	1	1	0	0	25	33	24	16	1	....	11	17	1.760	5.76	55	....	.306	55	.232	-7	5	-1.4

YEAR	TM-L	W	L	PCT	G	GS	CG	SH	SV	IP	H	R	ER	HR	HB	BB	SO	RAT	ERA	ERA+	CERA	OAV	BH	AVG	PR+	WS	TPW
1887	NY-N	0	0	....	1	0	0	0	0	0	1	0	0	0	0	1	0	....	....	....	....	1.000	161	.331	0	14	1.6
Total	3	7	3	.700	15	9	8	1	0	100	92	54	36	1	0	30	38	1.210	3.24	89	....	.234	1165	.260	-9	33	0.7

• RICHARDSON, Gordie Gordon Clark Richardson b: 7/19/1938, Colquitt, GA BR/TL, 6', 185 lbs. Deb: 7/26/1964

YEAR	TM-L	W	L	PCT	G	GS	CG	SH	SV	IP	H	R	ER	HR	HB	BB	SO	RAT	ERA	ERA+	CERA	OAV	BH	AVG	PR+	WS	TPW
1964*	StL-N	4	2	.667	19	6	1	0	1	47	40	18	12	2	1	15	28	1.170	2.30	165	2.71	.231	1	.077	8	5	0.8
1965	NY-N	2	2	.500	35	0	0	0	2	52^1	41	27	22	5	2	16	43	1.089	3.78	93	2.74	.224	0	.000	-1	3	-0.2
1966	NY-N	0	2	.000	15	1	0	0	1	18^2	24	19	19	7	0	6	15	1.607	9.16	40	7.30	.312	0	.000	-12	0	-1.2
Total	3	6	6	.500	69	7	1	0	4	118	105	64	53	14	3	37	86	1.203	4.04	90	3.45	.242	1	.048	-5	8	-0.6

• RICHARDSON, Jack John William Richardson b: 10/3/1891, Central City, IL d: 1/18/1970, Marion, IL BB/TR, 6'3", 197 lbs. Deb: 9/17/1915

YEAR	TM-L	W	L	PCT	G	GS	CG	SH	SV	IP	H	R	ER	HR	HB	BB	SO	RAT	ERA	ERA+	CERA	OAV	BH	AVG	PR+	WS	TPW
1915	Phi-A	0	1	.000	3	3	2	0	0	24	21	13	7	0	1	14	11	1.458	2.63	111	3.65	.253	0	.000	1	0	0.0
1916	Phi-A	0	0	....	1	0	0	0	0	0^2	2	3	3	0	0	1	1	4.500	40.50	7	26.87	.667	0	....	-3	0	-0.3
Total	2	0	1	.000	4	3	2	0	0	24^2	23	16	10	0	1	15	12	1.541	3.65	79	4.28	.267	0	.000	-2	0	-0.3

• RICHARDSON, Jeff Jeffrey Scott Richardson b: 8/29/1963, Wichita, KS BR/TR, 6'3", 185 lbs. Deb: 9/19/1990

YEAR	TM-L	W	L	PCT	G	GS	CG	SH	SV	IP	H	R	ER	HR	HB	BB	SO	RAT	ERA	ERA+	CERA	OAV	BH	AVG	PR+	WS	TPW
1990	Cal-A	0	0	....	1	0	0	0	0	0^1	1	0	0	0	0	0	0	3.000	0.00	....	14.52	.500	0	....	0	0	0.0

• RICHERT, Pete Peter Gerard Richert b: 10/29/1939, Floral Park, NY BL/TL, 5'11", 184 lbs. Deb: 4/12/1962

YEAR	TM-L	W	L	PCT	G	GS	CG	SH	SV	IP	H	R	ER	HR	HB	BB	SO	RAT	ERA	ERA+	CERA	OAV	BH	AVG	PR+	WS	TPW
1962	LA-N	5	4	.556	19	12	1	0	0	81^1	77	35	35	6	1	45	75	1.500	3.87	94	4.23	.249	2	.080	-2	4	-0.4
1963	LA-N	5	3	.625	20	12	1	0	0	78	80	40	39	7	1	28	54	1.385	4.50	67	3.97	.262	4	.182	-12	2	-1.2
1964	LA-N	2	3	.400	8	6	1	1	0	34^2	38	17	16	2	2	18	25	1.615	4.15	78	4.78	.271	1	.091	-3	1	-0.4
1965	Was-A★	15	12	.556	34	29	6	0	0	194	146	64	56	18	2	84	161	1.186	2.60	134	2.85	.210	10	.156	20	16	2.1
1966	Was-A★	14	14	.500	36	34	7	0	0	245^2	196	106	92	36	1	69	195	1.079	3.37	103	2.80	.215	14	.163	0	13	0.2
1967	Was-A	2	6	.250	11	10	1	1	0	54^1	49	29	28	5	1	15	41	1.178	4.64	68	3.01	.237	1	.059	-9	0	-1.1
	Bal-A	7	10	.412	26	19	5	1	2	132^1	107	53	44	11	1	41	90	1.118	2.99	105	2.61	.220	4	.108	-0	6	-0.1
	Yr.	9	16	.360	37	29	6	2	2	186^2	156	82	72	16	2	56	131	1.136	3.47	91	2.73	.225	5	.093	-9	6	-1.2
1968	Bal-A	6	3	.667	36	0	0	0	6	62^1	51	25	24	7	3	12	47	1.011	3.47	84	2.60	.225	2	.200	-5	5	-0.5
1969*	Bal-A	7	4	.636	44	0	0	0	12	57^1	42	17	14	7	0	14	54	.977	2.20	162	2.20	.202	1	.125	7	9	0.7
1970*	Bal-A	7	2	.778	50	0	0	0	13	54^2	36	14	12	5	1	24	66	1.098	1.98	185	2.45	.194	0	.000	9	10	0.9
1971*	Bal-A	3	5	.375	35	0	0	0	4	36^1	26	15	14	3	1	22	35	1.321	3.47	97	3.06	.205	0	.000	-1	3	-0.1
1972	LA-N	2	3	.400	37	0	0	0	6	52	42	17	13	3	1	18	38	1.154	2.25	148	2.52	.219	3	.500	6	6	0.8
1973	LA-N	3	3	.500	39	0	0	0	7	51	44	18	18	5	1	19	31	1.235	3.18	108	3.09	.234	1	.200	1	5	0.1
1974	StL-N	0	0	....	13	0	0	0	1	11^1	10	7	3	1	0	11	4	1.853	2.38	150	5.27	.244	0	....	1	1	0.1
	Phi-N	2	1	.667	21	0	0	0	0	20^1	15	6	5	0	0	4	9	.934	2.21	171	1.40	.205	0	....	3	2	0.3
	Yr.	2	1	.667	34	0	0	0	1	31^2	25	13	8	1	0	15	13	1.263	2.27	163	2.78	.219	0	....	4	3	0.5
Total	13	80	73	.523	429	122	22	3	51	1165^2	959	463	413	116	16	424	925	1.186	3.19	104	2.98	.223	43	.145	15	83	1.4

• RICHIE, Lew Lewis A. Richie b: 8/23/1883, Ambler, PA d: 8/15/1936, Ambler, PA BR/TR, 5'8", 165 lbs. Deb: 5/8/1906

YEAR	TM-L	W	L	PCT	G	GS	CG	SH	SV	IP	H	R	ER	HR	HB	BB	SO	RAT	ERA	ERA+	CERA	OAV	BH	AVG	PR+	WS	TPW
1906	Phi-N	9	11	.450	33	22	14	3	0	205^2	170	86	55	3	6	79	65	1.211	2.41	108	2.54	.230	3	.050	7	9	0.5
1907	Phi-N	6	6	.500	25	12	9	2	0	117	88	37	23	0	5	38	40	1.077	1.77	137	1.99	.215	7	.163	6	9	0.7
1908	Phi-N	7	10	.412	25	15	13	2	1	157^2	125	50	32	1	6	49	58	1.104	1.83	132	2.36	.233	11	.212	9	12	1.2
1909	Phi-N	1	1	.500	11	1	0	0	1	45	40	14	10	0	2	18	11	1.289	2.00	129	3.22	.263	4	.250	2	4	0.4
	Bos-N	7	7	.500	22	13	9	2	2	131^2	118	58	34	2	1	44	42	1.230	2.32	121	2.81	.247	5	.114	7	8	0.6
	Yr.	8	8	.500	33	14	9	2	3	176^2	158	72	44	2	3	62	53	1.245	2.24	123	2.91	.251	9	.150	9	12	0.9
1910	Bos-N	0	3	.000	4	2	0	0	0	16^1	20	11	5	0	0	9	7	1.776	2.76	120	5.35	.317	0	.000	1	0	0.0
	*Chi-N	11	4	.733	30	11	8	3	4	130	117	45	39	1	3	51	53	1.292	2.70	106	3.13	.257	9	.225	1	12	0.4
	Yr.	11	7	.611	34	13	8	3	4	146^1	137	56	44	1	3	60	60	1.346	2.71	108	3.38	.264	9	.205	2	12	0.4
1911	Chi-N	15	11	.577	36	29	18	4	1	253	213	88	65	6	2	103	78	1.249	2.31	143	2.83	.235	14	.154	23	20	2.0
1912	Chi-N	16	8	.667	39	27	15	4	0	238	222	102	78	5	6	74	69	1.244	2.95	113	2.94	.261	10	.132	4	17	0.1
1913	Chi-N	2	4	.333	16	5	0	0	0	65	77	53	42	3	1	30	15	1.646	5.82	55	4.92	.304	2	.118	-19	0	-2.0
Total	8	74	65	.532	241	137	86	20	9	1359^1	1190	544	383	21	32	495	438	1.240	2.54	115	2.85	.246	65	.147	40	91	3.8

• RICHMOND, Beryl Beryl Justice Richmond b: 8/24/1907, Glen Easton, WV d: 4/24/1980, Cameron, WV BB/TL, 6'1", 185 lbs. Deb: 4/21/1933

YEAR	TM-L	W	L	PCT	G	GS	CG	SH	SV	IP	H	R	ER	HR	HB	BB	SO	RAT	ERA	ERA+	CERA	OAV	BH	AVG	PR+	WS	TPW
1933	Chi-N	0	0	....	4	0	0	0	0	4^2	10	1	1	0	0	2	2	2.571	1.93	169	10.66	.455	0	.000	1	0	0.0
1934	Cin-N	1	2	.333	6	2	1	0	0	19^1	23	11	8	0	0	10	9	1.707	3.72	110	4.69	.303	0	.000	1	1	0.0
Total	2	1	2	.333	10	2	1	0	0	24	33	12	9	0	0	12	11	1.875	3.38	118	5.85	.337	0	.000	2	1	0.1

• RICHMOND, Lee J Lee Richmond b: 5/5/1857, Sheffield, OH d: 10/1/1929, Toledo, OH TL, 5'10", 155 lbs. Deb: 9/27/1879 U ♦

YEAR	TM-L	W	L	PCT	G	GS	CG	SH	SV	IP	H	R	ER	HR	HB	BB	SO	RAT	ERA	ERA+	CERA	OAV	BH	AVG	PR+	WS	TPW
1879	Bos-N	1	0	1.000	1	1	1	0	0	9	4	6	2	0	....	1	11	.556	2.00	124	....	.125	2	.333	0	1	0.0
1880	Wor-N	32	32	.500	**74**	66	57	5	**3**	590^2	541	278	141	7	....	74	243	1.041	2.15	121	....	.231	70	.227	17	42	1.3
1881	Wor-N	25	26	.490	53	52	50	3	0	462^1	547	302	174	7	....	68	156	1.330	3.39	89	....	.282	63	.250	-8	26	-0.9
1882	Wor-N	14	33	.298	48	46	44	0	0	411	525	343	171	11	....	88	123	1.491	3.74	83	....	.294	64	.281	-11	13	0.0
1883	Pro-N	3	7	.300	12	12	8	0	0	92	122	67	34	2	....	27	13	1.620	3.33	93	....	.301	55	.284	-6	9	-0.6
1886	Cin-a	0	2	.000	3	2	1	0	0	18	24	22	16	0	2	11	6	1.944	8.00	44	....	.306	8	.276	-9	1	-1.0
Total	6	75	100	.429	191	179	161	8	3	1583	1763	1018	538	27	2	269	552	1.284	3.06	96	....	.268	262	.257	-18	92	-1.2

• RICHMOND, Ray Raymond Sinclair Richmond b: 6/5/1896, Fillmore, IL d: 10/21/1969, DeSoto, MO BR/TR, 6', 175 lbs. Deb: 9/25/1920

YEAR	TM-L	W	L	PCT	G	GS	CG	SH	SV	IP	H	R	ER	HR	HB	BB	SO	RAT	ERA	ERA+	CERA	OAV	BH	AVG	PR+	WS	TPW
1920	StL-A	2	0	1.000	2	2	1	0	0	17	18	12	12	0	0	9	4	1.588	6.35	62	4.09	.273	1	.167	-5	0	-0.5
1921	StL-A	0	1	.000	6	2	0	0	0	14^1	21	19	18	1	3	13	6	2.372	11.30	40	9.05	.362	0	.000	-11	0	-1.1
Total	2	2	1	.667	8	4	1	0	0	31^1	39	31	30	1	3	22	10	1.947	8.62	49	6.36	.315	1	.100	-15	0	-1.5

• RICHTER, Reggie Emil Henry Richter b: 9/14/1888, Dusseldorf, Germany d: 8/2/1934, Winfield, IL BR/TR, 6'2", 180 lbs. Deb: 5/30/1911

YEAR	TM-L	W	L	PCT	G	GS	CG	SH	SV	IP	H	R	ER	HR	HB	BB	SO	RAT	ERA	ERA+	CERA	OAV	BH	AVG	PR+	WS	TPW
1911	Chi-N	1	3	.250	22	5	0	0	2	54^2	62	30	19	1	3	20	34	1.500	3.13	106	4.58	.307	1	.100	-0	2	-0.1

• RICKETTS, Dick Richard James Ricketts b: 12/4/1933, Pottstown, PA d: 3/6/1988, Rochester, NY BL/TR, 6'7", 215 lbs. Deb: 6/14/1959

YEAR	TM-L	W	L	PCT	G	GS	CG	SH	SV	IP	H	R	ER	HR	HB	BB	SO	RAT	ERA	ERA+	CERA	OAV	BH	AVG	PR+	WS	TPW
1959	StL-N	1	6	.143	12	9	0	0	0	55^2	68	42	36	7	0	30	25	1.760	5.82	73	6.02	.301	1	.056	-9	0	-1.1

• RIDDLE, Elmer Elmer Ray Riddle b: 7/31/1914, Columbus, GA d: 5/14/1984, Columbus, GA BR/TR, 5'11.5", 170 lbs. Deb: 10/1/1939

YEAR	TM-L	W	L	PCT	G	GS	CG	SH	SV	IP	H	R	ER	HR	HB	BB	SO	RAT	ERA	ERA+	CERA	OAV	BH	AVG	PR+	WS	TPW
1939	Cin-N	0	0	....	1	0	0	0	0	2	1	0	0	0	0	0	0	.500	0.00	....	0.54	.143	0	....	1	0	0.1
1940*	Cin-N	1	2	.333	15	1	1	0	2	33^2	30	12	7	0	0	17	9	1.396	1.87	202	3.12	.250	1	.143	6	4	0.6
1941	Cin-N	19	4	.826	33	22	15	4	1	216^2	180	68	54	8	5	59	80	1.103	**2.24**	**160**	2.32	.224	16	.225	33	26	3.7
1942	Cin-N	7	11	.389	29	19	7	1	0	158^1	157	74	65	7	4	79	78	1.491	3.69	89	3.96	.260	15	.259	-8	7	-0.6
1943	Cin-N	**21**	11	.656	36	33	19	5	3	260^1	235	87	76	6	2	107	69	1.314	2.63	126	3.04	.245	18	.194	13	23	1.5
1944	Cin-N	2	2	.500	4	4	2	0	0	26^2	25	12	12	0	0	12	6	1.388	4.05	86	3.16	.250	1	.125	-2	1	-0.2
1945	Cin-N	1	4	.200	12	3	0	0	0	29^2	39	27	27	4	0	27	5	2.225	8.19	46	8.51	.333	3	.273	-15	0	-1.4
1947	Cin-N	1	0	1.000	16	3	0	0	0	30^1	42	30	28	5	1	31	8	2.407	8.31	49	9.70	.333	0	.000	-14	0	-1.4
1948	Pit-N★	12	10	.545	28	27	12	3	1	191	184	83	74	20	3	81	63	1.387	3.49	117	3.93	.250	12	.188	11	15	1.3
1949	Pit-N	1	8	.111	16	12	1	0	1	74^1	81	45	44	9	4	45	24	1.695	5.33	79	5.71	.281	3	.136	-9	2	-1.0
Total	10	65	52	.556	190	124	57	13	8	1023	974	438	387	59	19	458	342	1.400	3.40	108	3.75	.252	69	.204	17	78	2.5

• RIDDLEBERGER, Denny Dennis Michael Riddleberger b: 11/22/1945, Clifton Forge, VA BR/TL, 6'3", 195 lbs. Deb: 9/15/1970

YEAR	TM-L	W	L	PCT	G	GS	CG	SH	SV	IP	H	R	ER	HR	HB	BB	SO	RAT	ERA	ERA+	CERA	OAV	BH	AVG	PR+	WS	TPW
1970	Was-A	0	0	....	8	0	0	0	0	9^1	7	2	1	1	0	2	5	.964	0.96	369	2.26	.219	0	....	3	1	0.3
1971	Was-A	3	1	.750	57	0	0	0	1	69^2	67	27	25	9	1	32	56	1.421	3.23	102	4.30	.260	0	.000	0	4	0.1
1972	Cle-A	1	3	.250	38	0	0	0	0	54	45	23	15	5	2	22	34	1.241	2.50	129	3.32	.237	0	.000	4	3	0.4
Total	3	4	4	.500	103	0	0	0	1	133	119	52	41	15	3	56	95	1.316	2.77	118	3.76	.248	0	.000	7	8	0.7

• RIDDLEMOSER, Dorsey Dorsey Lee Riddlemoser b: 3/25/1875, Frederick, MD d: 5/11/1954, Frederick, MD BR/TR Deb: 8/22/1899

YEAR	TM-L	W	L	PCT	G	GS	CG	SH	SV	IP	H	R	ER	HR	HB	BB	SO	RAT	ERA	ERA+	CERA	OAV	BH	AVG	PR+	WS	TPW
1899	Was-N	0	0	....	1	0	0	0	0	2	7	4	4	0	0	2	0	4.500	18.00	22	23.72	.552	0	.000	-3	0	-0.3

• RIDGWAY, Jack Jacob Augustus Ridgway b: 7/23/1888, Philadelphia, PA d: 2/23/1928, Philadelphia, PA BL/TR, 5'11", 174 lbs. Deb: 5/20/1914

YEAR	TM-L	W	L	PCT	G	GS	CG	SH	SV	IP	H	R	ER	HR	HB	BB	SO	RAT	ERA	ERA+	CERA	OAV	BH	AVG	PR+	WS	TPW
1914	Bal-F	0	1	.000	4	1	0	0	0	9	20	11	11	1	1	3	2	2.556	11.00	29	12.32	.444	0	.000	-8	0	-0.8

• RIDZIK, Steve Stephen George Ridzik b: 4/29/1929, Yonkers, NY BR/TR, 5'11", 170 lbs. Deb: 9/4/1950

YEAR	TM-L	W	L	PCT	G	GS	CG	SH	SV	IP	H	R	ER	HR	HB	BB	SO	RAT	ERA	ERA+	CERA	OAV	BH	AVG	PR+	WS	TPW
1950	Phi-N	0	0	....	1	0	0	0	0	3	3	2	2	1	0	1	2	1.333	6.00	67	6.28	.300	0	....	-1	0	-0.1
1952	Phi-N	4	2	.667	24	9	2	0	0	92^2	74	37	31	10	1	37	43	1.198	3.01	121	3.01	.218	3	.136	5	6	0.6
1953	Phi-N	9	6	.600	42	12	1	0	0	124	119	61	52	15	5	48	53	1.347	3.77	112	4.06	.256	7	.194	6	9	0.8
1954	Phi-N	4	5	.444	35	6	0	0	0	80^2	72	42	37	7	0	44	45	1.438	4.13	98	3.71	.233	5	.227	-1	4	0.0
1955	Phi-N	0	1	.000	3	1	0	0	0	11	7	9	3	1	3	8	6	1.364	2.45	162	4.18	.179	0	.000	2	0	0.1
	Cin-N	0	3	.000	13	2	0	0	0	30	35	16	15	4	1	14	6	1.633	4.50	94	5.79	.299	1	.167	-1	1	-0.1
	Yr.	0	4	.000	16	3	0	0	0	41	42	25	18	5	4	22	12	1.561	3.95	106	5.36	.269	1	.100	1	1	0.0
1956	NY-N	6	2	.750	41	5	1	1	0	92^1	80	42	39	7	5	65	53	1.570	3.80	99	4.49	.240	7	.250	0	6	0.1
1957	NY-N	0	2	.000	15	0	0	0	0	26^2	19	14	14	3	2	19	13	1.425	4.73	83	4.23	.213	1	.200	-2	1	-0.2
1958	Cle-A	0	2	.000	6	0	0	0	0	8^2	9	7	2	1	0	5	6	1.615	2.08	176	4.47	.257	0	.000	1	0	0.1
1963	Was-A	5	6	.455	20	10	0	0	1	89^2	82	53	48	16	5	35	47	1.305	4.82	77	4.27	.240	5	.172	-11	2	-1.1
1964	Was-A	5	5	.500	49	3	0	0	2	112	96	46	36	10	7	31	60	1.134	2.89	128	2.96	.236	6	.222	10	9	1.1
1965	Was-A	6	4	.600	63	0	0	0	8	109^2	108	61	49	18	7	43	72	1.377	4.02	86	4.58	.257	3	.167	-6	5	-0.6
1966	Phi-N	0	0	....	2	0	0	0	0	2^1	5	2	2	0	0	1	0	2.571	7.71	47	10.38	.455	0	....	-1	0	-0.1
Total	12	39	38	.506	314	48	4	1	11	782^2	709	392	330	93	36	351	406	1.354	3.79	101	4.00	.243	38	.192	1	43	0.5

• RIEDLING, John John Richard Riedling b: 8/29/1975, Fort Lauderdale, FL BR/TR, 5'11", 190 lbs. Deb: 8/30/2000

YEAR	TM-L	W	L	PCT	G	GS	CG	SH	SV	IP	H	R	ER	HR	HB	BB	SO	RAT	ERA	ERA+	CERA	OAV	BH	AVG	PR+	WS	TPW
2000	Cin-N	3	1	.750	13	0	0	0	1	15^1	11	7	4	1	1	8	18	1.239	2.35	200	3.12	.208	0	.000	4	2	0.3
2001	Cin-N	1	1	.500	29	0	0	0	1	33^2	22	9	9	1	2	14	23	1.069	2.41	189	2.13	.186	0	.000	9	4	0.8
2002	Cin-N	2	4	.333	33	0	0	0	0	46^2	39	16	14	2	3	26	30	1.393	2.70	157	3.40	.234	0	.000	8	5	0.8
2003	Cin-N	2	3	.400	55	8	0	0	1	101	107	61	55	7	3	47	65	1.525	4.90	87	4.50	.270	4	.222	-7	4	-0.6
Total	4	8	9	.471	130	8	0	0	3	196^2	179	93	82	11	9	95	136	1.393	3.75	115	3.73	.244	4	.182	13	15	1.3

• RIEGER, Elmer Elmer Jay Rieger b: 2/25/1889, Perris, CA d: 10/21/1959, Los Angeles, CA BB/TR, 6', 175 lbs. Deb: 4/20/1910

YEAR	TM-L	W	L	PCT	G	GS	CG	SH	SV	IP	H	R	ER	HR	HB	BB	SO	RAT	ERA	ERA+	CERA	OAV	BH	AVG	PR+	WS	TPW
1910	StL-N	0	2	.000	13	1	0	0	0	21^1	26	16	13	1	1	7	9	1.547	5.48	54	5.19	.325	0	.000	-5	0	-0.5

• RIGBY, Brad Bradley Kenneth Rigby b: 5/14/1973, Milwaukee, WI BR/TR, 6'6", 203 lbs. Deb: 6/28/1997

YEAR	TM-L	W	L	PCT	G	GS	CG	SH	SV	IP	H	R	ER	HR	HB	BB	SO	RAT	ERA	ERA+	CERA	OAV	BH	AVG	PR+	WS	TPW
1997	Oak-A	1	7	.125	14	14	0	0	0	77^2	92	44	42	14	2	22	34	1.468	4.87	93	5.36	.302	0	.000	-1	3	-0.1
1999	Oak-A	3	4	.429	29	0	0	0	0	62^1	69	31	30	5	5	26	26	1.524	4.33	107	4.78	.284	0	....	3	4	0.2
	KC-A	1	2	.333	20	0	0	0	0	21^1	33	20	17	6	2	5	10	1.781	7.17	70	8.44	.351	0	....	-6	0	-0.5
	Yr.	4	6	.400	49	0	0	0	0	83^2	102	51	47	11	7	31	36	1.590	5.06	94	5.71	.303	0	....	-3	4	-0.3
2000	KC-A	0	0	....	4	0	0	0	1	8^1	19	16	15	6	1	5	3	2.880	16.20	32	20.21	.422	0	....	-10	0	-1.0
	Mon-N	0	0	....	6	0	0	0	1	5^1	8	5	3	0	1	3	2	2.063	5.06	95	7.82	.348	0	.000	-0	0	0.0
Total	3	5	13	.278	73	14	0	0	2	175	221	116	107	31	11	61	75	1.611	5.50	85	6.31	.311	0	.000	-15	7	-1.4

• RIGDON, Paul Paul David Rigdon b: 11/2/1975, Jacksonville, FL BR/TR, 6'5", 210 lbs. Deb: 5/21/2000

YEAR	TM-L	W	L	PCT	G	GS	CG	SH	SV	IP	H	R	ER	HR	HB	BB	SO	RAT	ERA	ERA+	CERA	OAV	BH	AVG	PR+	WS	TPW
2000	Cle-A	1	1	.500	5	4	0	0	0	17^2	21	15	15	4	0	9	15	1.698	7.64	65	6.73	.300	0	....	-5	0	-0.5
	Mil-N	4	4	.500	12	12	0	0	0	69^2	68	37	35	14	1	26	48	1.349	4.52	101	4.44	.255	3	.188	-1	3	0.1
2001	Mil-N	3	5	.375	15	15	0	0	0	79^1	86	52	51	13	3	46	49	1.664	5.79	74	5.90	.287	4	.200	-14	1	-1.3
Total	2	8	10	.444	32	31	0	0	0	166^2	175	104	101	31	4	81	112	1.536	5.45	82	5.38	.275	7	.194	-19	4	-1.7

• RIGGAN, Jerrod Jerrod Ashley Riggan b: 5/16/1974, Brewster, WA BR/TR, 6'3", 185 lbs. Deb: 8/29/2000

YEAR	TM-L	W	L	PCT	G	GS	CG	SH	SV	IP	H	R	ER	HR	HB	BB	SO	RAT	ERA	ERA+	CERA	OAV	BH	AVG	PR+	WS	TPW
2000	NY-N	0	0	....	1	0	0	0	0	2	3	2	0	0	0	0	1	1.500	0.00	....	3.96	.300	0	....	1	0	0.1
2001	NY-N	3	3	.500	35	0	0	0	0	47^2	42	19	18	5	0	24	41	1.385	3.40	122	3.67	.243	0	.000	4	4	0.3
2002	Cle-A	2	1	.667	29	0	0	0	0	33	53	28	28	3	0	18	22	2.152	7.64	57	8.17	.373	0	....	-12	0	-1.1
2003	Cle-A	0	0	....	2	0	0	0	0	4	7	4	4	0	0	1	2	2.000	9.00	49	7.38	.412	0	....	-2	0	-0.2
Total	4	5	4	.556	67	0	0	0	0	86^2	105	53	50	8	0	43	66	1.708	5.19	83	5.56	.307	0	.000	-9	4	-0.9

• RIGHETTI, Dave David Allan Righetti b: 11/28/1958, San Jose, CA BL/TL, 6'4", 198 lbs. Deb: 9/16/1979 C

YEAR	TM-L	W	L	PCT	G	GS	CG	SH	SV	IP	H	R	ER	HR	HB	BB	SO	RAT	ERA	ERA+	CERA	OAV	BH	AVG	PR+	WS	TPW
1979	NY-A	0	1	.000	3	3	0	0	0	17^1	10	7	7	2	0	10	13	1.154	3.63	112	2.80	.182	0	....	1	1	0.1
1981*	NY-A	8	4	.667	15	15	2	0	0	105^1	75	25	24	1	0	38	89	1.073	2.05	174	1.90	.196	0	....	17	10	1.8
1982	NY-A	11	10	.524	33	27	4	0	1	183	155	88	77	11	6	108	163	1.437	3.79	105	3.74	.229	0	....	5	10	0.5
1983	NY-A	14	8	.636	31	31	7	2	0	217	194	96	83	12	2	67	169	1.203	3.44	113	2.88	.237	0	....	12	15	1.2
1984	NY-A	5	6	.455	64	0	0	0	31	96^1	79	29	25	5	0	37	90	1.204	2.34	162	2.62	.223	0	....	16	16	1.6
1985	NY-A	12	7	.632	74	0	0	0	29	107	96	36	33	5	0	45	92	1.318	2.78	144	3.19	.241	0	....	13	15	1.3
1986	NY-A★	8	8	.500	74	0	0	0	**46**	106^2	88	31	29	4	2	35	83	1.153	2.45	167	2.47	.226	0	....	19	20	1.8
1987	NY-A★	8	6	.571	60	0	0	0	31	95	95	45	37	9	2	44	77	1.463	3.51	125	4.27	.262	0	....	9	13	0.8
1988	NY-A	5	4	.556	60	0	0	0	25	87	86	35	34	5	1	37	70	1.414	3.52	112	3.81	.257	0	....	5	11	0.5
1989	NY-A	2	6	.250	55	0	0	0	25	69	73	32	23	3	1	26	51	1.435	3.00	129	3.82	.277	0	....	6	8	0.7
1990	NY-A	1	1	.500	53	0	0	0	36	53	48	24	21	8	2	26	43	1.396	3.57	111	4.26	.234	0	....	2	7	0.2
1991	SF-N	2	7	.222	61	0	0	0	24	71^2	64	29	27	4	3	28	51	1.284	3.39	106	3.18	.240	0	.000	1	8	0.1
1992	SF-N	2	7	.222	54	4	0	0	3	78^1	79	47	44	4	0	36	47	1.468	5.06	65	3.92	.269	1	.143	-17	0	-1.8
1993	SF-N	1	1	.500	51	0	0	0	1	47^1	58	31	30	11	1	17	31	1.585	5.70	68	6.44	.305	1	1.000	-11	0	-1.0
1994	Oak-A	0	0	....	7	0	0	0	0	7	13	13	13	3	1	9	4	3.143	16.71	26	18.77	.419	0	....	-10	0	-0.9
	Tor-A	0	1	.000	13	0	0	0	0	13^1	9	10	10	2	0	10	10	1.425	6.75	71	3.83	.188	0	....	-3	0	-0.3
	Yr.	0	1	.000	20	0	0	0	0	20^1	22	23	23	5	1	19	14	2.016	10.18	45	8.97	.278	0	....	-12	0	-1.1
1995	Chi-A	3	2	.600	10	9	0	0	0	49^1	65	24	23	6	0	18	29	1.682	4.20	106	6.11	.325	0	....	2	3	0.2
Total	16	82	79	.509	718	89	13	2	252	1403^2	1287	602	540	95	21	591	1112	1.338	3.46	113	3.54	.244	2	.182	69	137	6.8

• RIGHTNOWAR, Ron Ronald Gene Rightnowar b: 9/5/1964, Toledo, OH BR/TR, 6'3", 190 lbs. Deb: 5/20/1995

YEAR	TM-L	W	L	PCT	G	GS	CG	SH	SV	IP	H	R	ER	HR	HB	BB	SO	RAT	ERA	ERA+	CERA	OAV	BH	AVG	PR+	WS	TPW
1995	Mil-A	2	1	.667	34	0	0	0	1	36^2	35	23	22	3	5	18	22	1.445	5.40	92	4.57	.271	0	....	-2	2	-0.2

• RIGNEY, Johnny John Dungan Rigney b: 10/28/1914, Oak Park, IL d: 10/21/1984, Lombard, IL BR/TR, 6'2", 190 lbs. Deb: 4/21/1937

YEAR	TM-L	W	L	PCT	G	GS	CG	SH	SV	IP	H	R	ER	HR	HB	BB	SO	RAT	ERA	ERA+	CERA	OAV	BH	AVG	PR+	WS	TPW
1937	Chi-A	2	5	.286	22	4	0	0	1	90^2	107	65	50	10	3	46	38	1.688	4.96	93	5.48	.290	5	.167	-6	3	-0.5
1938	Chi-A	9	9	.500	38	12	7	1	1	167	164	74	66	16	2	72	84	1.413	3.56	138	3.98	.256	8	.145	25	13	2.0
1939	Chi-A	15	8	.652	35	29	11	2	0	218^2	208	103	90	10	2	84	119	1.335	3.70	128	3.25	.247	16	.200	23	20	2.0
1940	Chi-A	14	18	.438	39	33	19	2	3	280^2	240	117	97	22	2	90	141	1.176	3.11	142	2.82	.230	20	.215	35	24	3.3
1941	Chi-A	13	13	.500	30	29	18	3	0	237	224	116	101	21	2	92	119	1.333	3.84	107	3.60	.249	17	.202	4	13	0.5
1942	Chi-A	3	3	.500	7	7	6	0	0	59	40	23	21	2	1	16	34	.949	3.20	112	1.61	.185	1	.053	2	4	0.1
1946	Chi-A	5	5	.500	15	11	3	2	0	82^2	76	37	37	6	2	35	51	1.343	4.03	85	3.48	.240	4	.154	-6	3	-0.7
1947	Chi-A	2	3	.400	11	7	2	0	0	50^2	42	15	11	3	0	15	19	1.125	1.95	187	2.50	.228	0	.000	10	5	0.8
Total	8	63	64	.496	197	132	66	10	5	1186^1	1101	550	473	90	14	450	605	1.307	3.59	120	3.39	.244	71	.177	86	85	7.5

• RIJO, Jose Jose Antonio (Abreu) Rijo b: 5/13/1965, San Cristobal, Dominican Republic BR/TR, 6'1", 200 lbs. Deb: 4/5/1984

YEAR	TM-L	W	L	PCT	G	GS	CG	SH	SV	IP	H	R	ER	HR	HB	BB	SO	RAT	ERA	ERA+	CERA	OAV	BH	AVG	PR+	WS	TPW
1984	NY-A	2	8	.200	24	5	0	0	2	62^1	74	40	33	5	1	33	47	1.717	4.76	80	5.56	.298	0	....	-6	1	-0.6
1985	Oak-A	6	4	.600	12	9	0	0	0	63^2	57	26	25	6	1	28	65	1.335	3.53	109	3.62	.239	0	....	3	4	0.3
1986	Oak-A	9	11	.450	39	26	4	0	1	193^2	172	116	100	24	4	108	176	1.446	4.65	83	4.21	.237	0	....	-17	5	-1.7
1987	Oak-A	2	7	.222	21	14	1	0	0	82^1	106	67	54	10	2	41	67	1.785	5.90	70	6.32	.305	0	....	-15	0	-1.5
1988	Cin-N	13	8	.619	49	19	0	0	0	162	120	47	43	7	3	63	160	1.130	2.39	150	2.35	.209	2	.054	19	15	1.8
1989	Cin-N	7	6	.538	19	19	1	1	0	111	101	39	35	6	2	48	86	1.342	2.84	127	3.50	.249	8	.211	11	9	1.3
1990*	Cin-N	14	8	.636	29	29	7	1	0	197	151	65	59	10	2	78	152	1.162	2.70	146	2.57	.212	10	.161	24	17	2.5
1991	Cin-N	15	6	.714	30	30	3	1	0	204^1	165	69	57	8	3	55	172	1.077	2.51	151	**2.23**	.219	14	.209	30	17	3.2
1992	Cin-N	15	10	.600	33	33	2	0	0	211	185	67	60	15	3	44	171	1.085	2.56	140	2.62	.238	14	.194	24	19	2.7
1993	Cin-N	14	9	.609	36	**36**	2	1	0	257^1	218	76	71	19	2	62	**227**	1.088	2.48	162	2.55	.230	22	.268	46	**26**	**5.3**
1994	Cin-N★	9	6	.600	26	**26**	2	0	0	172^1	177	73	59	16	4	52	171	1.329	3.08	134	3.88	.265	10	.204	20	11	2.1
1995	Cin-N	5	4	.556	14	14	0	0	0	69	76	33	32	6	0	22	62	1.420	4.17	99	4.26	.285	3	.136	-2	4	-0.2
2001	Cin-N	0	0	....	13	0	0	0	0	17	19	6	4	2	0	9	12	1.647	2.12	215	5.00	.271	0	....	5	2	0.5
2002	Cin-N	5	4	.556	31	9	0	0	0	77	89	48	44	13	1	20	38	1.416	5.14	82	4.82	.283	2	.125	-8	2	-0.8
Total	14	116	91	.560	376	269	22	4	3	1880	1710	772	676	147	28	663	1606	1.262	3.24	120	3.34	.243	85	.191	131	132	14.8

• RILEY, George George Michael Riley b: 10/6/1956, Philadelphia, PA BL/TL, 6'2", 210 lbs. Deb: 9/15/1979

YEAR	TM-L	W	L	PCT	G	GS	CG	SH	SV	IP	H	R	ER	HR	HB	BB	SO	RAT	ERA	ERA+	CERA	OAV	BH	AVG	PR+	WS	TPW
1979	Chi-N	0	1	.000	4	1	0	0	0	13	16	9	8	1	2	6	5	1.692	5.54	74	6.26	.320	0	.000	-2	0	-0.2
1980	Chi-N	0	4	.000	22	0	0	0	0	36	41	29	23	2	2	20	18	1.694	5.75	68	5.15	.293	0	.000	-7	0	-0.7
1984	SF-N	1	0	1.000	5	4	0	0	0	29^1	39	14	13	1	2	7	12	1.568	3.99	88	5.05	.315	1	.100	-1	1	-0.1
1986	Mon-N	0	0	....	10	0	0	0	0	8^2	7	4	4	0	1	8	5	1.731	4.15	89	3.76	.212	0	....	-0	0	0.0
Total	4	1	5	.167	41	5	0	0	0	87	103	56	48	4	7	41	40	1.655	4.97	77	5.15	.297	1	.077	-10	1	-1.1

• RILEY, Matt Matthew Paul Riley b: 8/2/1979, Antioch, CA BL/TL, 6'1", 201 lbs. Deb: 9/9/1999

YEAR	TM-L	W	L	PCT	G	GS	CG	SH	SV	IP	H	R	ER	HR	HB	BB	SO	RAT	ERA	ERA+	CERA	OAV	BH	AVG	PR+	WS	TPW
1999	Bal-A	0	0	....	3	3	0	0	0	11	17	9	9	4	0	13	6	2.727	7.36	64	14.43	.378	0	....	-3	0	-0.3
2003	Bal-A	1	0	1.000	2	2	0	0	0	10	7	2	2	1	0	5	8	1.200	1.80	245	2.88	.194	0	....	3	1	0.3
Total	2	1	0	1.000	5	5	0	0	0	21	24	11	11	5	0	18	14	2.000	4.71	98	8.93	.296	0	....	-1	1	0.0

• RINCON, Andy Andrew John Rincon b: 3/5/1959, Monterey Park, CA BR/TR, 6'3", 195 lbs. Deb: 9/15/1980

YEAR	TM-L	W	L	PCT	G	GS	CG	SH	SV	IP	H	R	ER	HR	HB	BB	SO	RAT	ERA	ERA+	CERA	OAV	BH	AVG	PR+	WS	TPW
1980	StL-N	3	1	.750	4	4	1	0	0	31	23	9	9	1	0	7	22	.968	2.61	141	1.80	.215	3	.250	3	3	0.4
1981	StL-N	3	1	.750	5	5	1	1	0	35^2	27	8	7	0	2	5	13	.897	1.77	201	1.62	.214	3	.231	7	4	0.8
1982	StL-N	2	3	.400	11	6	1	0	0	40	35	22	21	1	0	25	11	1.500	4.73	77	3.80	.241	1	.100	-6	1	-0.6
Total	3	8	5	.615	20	15	3	1	0	106^2	85	39	37	2	2	37	46	1.144	3.12	116	2.49	.225	7	.200	4	8	0.5

• RINCON, Juan Juan Manuel Rincon b: 1/23/1979, Maracaibo, Venezuela BR/TR, 5'11", 187 lbs. Deb: 6/7/2001

YEAR	TM-L	W	L	PCT	G	GS	CG	SH	SV	IP	H	R	ER	HR	HB	BB	SO	RAT	ERA	ERA+	CERA	OAV	BH	AVG	PR+	WS	TPW
2001	Min-A	0	0	....	4	0	0	0	0	5^2	7	5	4	1	0	5	4	2.118	6.35	72	8.33	.318	1	1.000	-1	0	-0.1
2002	Min-A	0	2	.000	10	3	0	0	0	28^2	44	23	20	5	0	9	21	1.849	6.28	71	7.62	.352	0	....	-6	0	-0.5
2003*	Min-A	5	6	.455	58	0	0	0	0	85^2	74	38	35	5	4	38	63	1.307	3.68	124	3.21	.231	0	....	10	7	1.0
Total	3	5	8	.385	72	3	0	0	0	120	125	66	59	11	4	52	88	1.475	4.43	102	4.51	.267	1	1.000	3	7	0.3

• RINCON, Ricardo Ricardo (Espinoza) Rincon b: 4/13/1970, Veracruz, Mexico BL/TL, 6', 190 lbs. Deb: 4/3/1997

YEAR	TM-L	W	L	PCT	G	GS	CG	SH	SV	IP	H	R	ER	HR	HB	BB	SO	RAT	ERA	ERA+	CERA	OAV	BH	AVG	PR+	WS	TPW
1997	Pit-N	4	8	.333	62	0	0	0	4	60	51	26	23	5	2	24	71	1.250	3.45	124	3.10	.230	0	.000	6	7	0.6
1998	Pit-N	0	2	.000	60	0	0	0	14	65	50	31	21	6	0	29	64	1.215	2.91	148	2.88	.208	0	.000	10	9	0.9
1999*	Cle-A	2	3	.400	59	0	0	0	0	44^2	41	22	22	6	1	24	30	1.455	4.43	114	4.38	.248	0	....	3	3	0.3
2000	Cle-A	2	0	1.000	35	0	0	0	0	20	17	7	6	1	1	13	20	1.500	2.70	184	3.89	.224	0	....	5	3	0.5
2001*	Cle-A	2	1	.667	67	0	0	0	2	54	44	18	17	3	0	21	50	1.204	2.83	159	2.62	.223	0	....	11	6	1.1
2002	Cle-A	1	4	.200	46	0	0	0	0	35^2	36	21	19	3	1	8	30	1.234	4.79	92	3.38	.263	0	.000	-1	2	-0.1
	*Oak-A	0	0	....	25	0	0	0	1	20^1	11	7	7	1	0	3	19	.689	3.10	142	1.06	.164	0	....	3	4	0.3
	Yr.	1	4	.200	71	0	0	0	1	56	47	28	26	4	1	11	49	1.036	4.18	105	2.54	.230	0	.000	2	6	0.2
2003*	Oak-A	8	4	.667	64	0	0	0	0	55^1	45	21	20	4	3	32	40	1.392	3.25	139	3.62	.230	0	....	8	6	0.7
Total	7	19	22	.463	418	0	0	0	21	355	295	153	135	29	8	154	324	1.265	3.42	132	3.18	.227	0	.000	45	40	4.3

• RINEER, Jeff Jeffrey Alan Rineer b: 7/3/1955, Lancaster, PA BL/TL, 6'4", 205 lbs. Deb: 9/30/1979

YEAR	TM-L	W	L	PCT	G	GS	CG	SH	SV	IP	H	R	ER	HR	HB	BB	SO	RAT	ERA	ERA+	CERA	OAV	BH	AVG	PR+	WS	TPW
1979	Bal-A	0	0	....	1	0	0	0	0	1	0	0	0	0	0	0	0	.000	0.00	....	0.00	.000	0	....	0	0	0.0

• RING, Jimmy James Joseph Ring b: 2/15/1895, Brooklyn, NY d: 7/6/1965, Queens, NY BR/TR, 6'1", 170 lbs. Deb: 4/13/1917

YEAR	TM-L	W	L	PCT	G	GS	CG	SH	SV	IP	H	R	ER	HR	HB	BB	SO	RAT	ERA	ERA+	CERA	OAV	BH	AVG	PR+	WS	TPW
1917	Cin-N	3	7	.300	24	7	3	0	2	88	90	47	43	2	1	35	33	1.420	4.40	59	3.65	.272	2	.077	-17	1	-2.2
1918	Cin-N	9	5	.643	21	18	13	4	0	142^1	130	57	45	5	3	48	26	1.251	2.85	94	2.97	.247	6	.120	-4	7	-0.8
1919*	Cin-N	10	9	.526	32	18	12	2	3	183	150	53	46	1	3	51	61	1.098	2.26	122	2.19	.232	6	.097	7	14	0.2
1920	Cin-N	17	16	.515	42	33	18	1	1	266^2	268	134	105	4	5	92	73	1.350	3.54	86	3.36	.264	19	.198	-16	8	-1.8
1921	Phi-N	10	19	.345	34	30	21	0	1	246	258	161	116	8	5	88	88	1.407	4.24	100	3.66	.274	12	.145	4	11	0.0
1922	Phi-N	12	18	.400	40	33	17	0	1	249^1	292	160	127	19	3	103	116	1.584	4.58	102	4.88	.297	13	.148	3	13	-0.1
1923	Phi-N	18	16	.529	39	36	23	0	1	304^1	336	151	131	13	1	115	112	1.482	3.87	119	4.07	.283	12	.106	33	20	2.4
1924	Phi-N	10	12	.455	32	31	16	1	0	215^1	236	123	95	9	4	108	72	1.598	3.97	112	4.55	.286	17	.230	17	13	1.7
1925	Phi-N	14	16	.467	38	37	21	1	0	270	325	166	131	14	1	119	93	1.644	4.37	109	4.88	.297	11	.109	23	17	1.5
1926	NY-N	11	10	.524	39	23	5	0	2	183^1	207	114	93	12	1	74	76	1.533	4.57	82	4.48	.290	8	.143	-19	5	-2.2
1927	StL-N	0	4	.000	13	3	1	0	0	33	39	28	24	3	1	17	13	1.697	6.55	60	5.36	.300	3	.375	-10	0	-0.9
1928	Phi-N	4	17	.190	35	25	4	0	1	176	220	135	123	14	2	103	70	**1.835**	6.29	67	6.30	....	11	.183	-38	1	-3.8
Total	12	118	149	.442	389	294	154	9	11	2357^1	2551	1329	1079	104	30	953	833	1.486	4.12	95	4.16	.304	120	.147	-16	110	-5.8

• RIOS, Danny Daniel Rios b: 11/11/1972, Madrid, Spain BR/TR, 6'2", 190 lbs. Deb: 5/30/1997

YEAR	TM-L	W	L	PCT	G	GS	CG	SH	SV	IP	H	R	ER	HR	HB	BB	SO	RAT	ERA	ERA+	CERA	OAV	BH	AVG	PR+	WS	TPW
1997	NY-A	0	0	....	2	0	0	0	0	2^1	9	5	5	3	1	2	1	4.714	19.29	23	45.88	.563	0	....	-4	0	-0.4
1998	KC-A	0	1	.000	5	0	0	0	0	7^1	9	8	5	1	1	6	6	2.045	6.14	79	7.92	.300	0	....	-1	0	-0.1
Total	2	0	1	.000	7	0	0	0	0	9^2	18	13	10	4	2	8	7	2.690	9.31	50	17.08	.391	0	....	-5	0	-0.5

• RIPLEY, Allen Allen Stevens Ripley b: 10/18/1952, Norwood, MA BR/TR, 6'3", 190 lbs. Deb: 4/10/1978

YEAR	TM-L	W	L	PCT	G	GS	CG	SH	SV	IP	H	R	ER	HR	HB	BB	SO	RAT	ERA	ERA+	CERA	OAV	BH	AVG	PR+	WS	TPW
1978	Bos-A	2	5	.286	15	11	1	0	0	73	92	49	45	10	3	22	26	1.562	5.55	74	5.64	.311	0	....	-12	0	-1.3
1979	Bos-A	3	1	.750	16	3	0	0	1	64^2	77	42	37	9	2	25	34	1.577	5.15	86	5.49	.295	0	....	-5	3	-0.5
1980	SF-N	9	10	.474	23	20	2	0	0	112^2	119	59	52	10	4	36	65	1.376	4.15	85	4.05	.274	6	.150	-5	4	-0.6
1981	SF-N	4	4	.500	19	14	1	0	0	90^2	103	45	41	5	3	27	47	1.434	4.07	84	4.21	.289	4	.133	-6	2	-0.7
1982	Chi-N	5	7	.417	28	19	0	0	0	122^2	130	61	57	12	2	38	57	1.370	4.18	89	4.16	.285	5	.132	-5	5	-0.7
Total	5	23	27	.460	101	67	4	0	1	463^2	521	256	232	46	15	148	229	1.443	4.50	84	4.56	.289	15	.139	-33	14	-3.7

• RIPLEY, Walt Walter Franklin Ripley b: 11/26/1916, Worcester, MA d: 10/7/1990, Attleboro, MA BR/TR, 6', 168 lbs. Deb: 8/17/1935

YEAR	TM-L	W	L	PCT	G	GS	CG	SH	SV	IP	H	R	ER	HR	HB	BB	SO	RAT	ERA	ERA+	CERA	OAV	BH	AVG	PR+	WS	TPW
1935	Bos-A	0	0	....	2	0	0	0	0	4	7	4	4	0	0	3	0	2.500	9.00	53	9.34	.412	0	....	-2	0	-0.2

• RIPPELMEYER, Ray Raymond Roy Rippelmeyer b: 7/9/1933, Valmeyer, IL BR/TR, 6'3", 200 lbs. Deb: 4/14/1962 C

YEAR	TM-L	W	L	PCT	G	GS	CG	SH	SV	IP	H	R	ER	HR	HB	BB	SO	RAT	ERA	ERA+	CERA	OAV	BH	AVG	PR+	WS	TPW
1962	Was-A	1	2	.333	18	1	0	0	0	39^1	47	24	24	7	0	17	17	1.627	5.49	74	5.82	.294	3	.500	-6	1	-0.4

• RIPPLE, Charlie Charles Dawson Ripple b: 12/1/1921, Bolton, NC d: 5/6/1979, Wilmington, NC BL/TL, 6'2", 210 lbs. Deb: 9/25/1944

YEAR	TM-L	W	L	PCT	G	GS	CG	SH	SV	IP	H	R	ER	HR	HB	BB	SO	RAT	ERA	ERA+	CERA	OAV	BH	AVG	PR+	WS	TPW
1944	Phi-N	0	0	....	1	1	0	0	0	2^1	6	4	4	0	0	4	2	4.286	15.43	23	20.18	.500	1	1.000	-3	0	-0.3
1945	Phi-N	0	1	.000	4	0	0	0	0	7^2	7	6	6	0	0	10	5	2.217	7.04	54	5.71	.241	0	.000	-3	0	-0.3
1946	Phi-N	1	0	1.000	6	0	0	0	0	3^1	5	4	4	0	0	6	3	3.300	10.80	32	12.62	.385	0	....	-3	0	-0.3
Total	3	1	1	.500	11	1	0	0	0	13^1	18	14	14	0	0	20	10	2.850	9.45	39	9.97	.333	1	.500	-8	0	-0.8

• RISKE, David David Richard Riske b: 10/23/1976, Renton, WA BR/TR, 6'2", 180 lbs. Deb: 8/14/1999

YEAR	TM-L	W	L	PCT	G	GS	CG	SH	SV	IP	H	R	ER	HR	HB	BB	SO	RAT	ERA	ERA+	CERA	OAV	BH	AVG	PR+	WS	TPW
1999	Cle-A	1	1	.500	12	0	0	0	0	14	20	15	13	2	0	6	16	1.857	8.36	60	6.96	.333	0	....	-5	0	-0.5
2001*	Cle-A	2	0	1.000	26	0	0	0	1	27^1	20	7	6	3	2	18	29	1.390	1.98	229	3.81	.206	0	....	8	3	0.8
2002	Cle-A	2	2	.500	51	0	0	0	1	51^1	49	32	30	8	4	35	65	1.636	5.26	83	5.55	.257	0	....	-4	2	-0.4
2003	Cle-A	2	2	.500	68	0	0	0	8	74^2	52	21	19	9	3	20	82	.964	2.29	193	2.26	.196	0	....	16	10	1.5
Total	4	7	5	.583	157	0	0	0	10	167^1	141	75	68	22	9	79	192	1.315	3.66	124	3.91	.230	0	....	15	15	1.4

• RISLEY, Bill William Charles Risley b: 5/29/1967, Chicago, IL BR/TR, 6'2", 215 lbs. Deb: 7/8/1992

YEAR	TM-L	W	L	PCT	G	GS	CG	SH	SV	IP	H	R	ER	HR	HB	BB	SO	RAT	ERA	ERA+	CERA	OAV	BH	AVG	PR+	WS	TPW
1992	Mon-N	1	0	1.000	1	1	0	0	0	5	4	1	1	0	0	1	2	1.000	1.80	192	1.82	.235	0	.000	1	1	0.1
1993	Mon-N	0	0	....	2	0	0	0	0	3	2	3	2	1	1	2	2	1.333	6.00	69	6.25	.200	0	....	-1	0	-0.1
1994	Sea-A	9	6	.600	37	0	0	0	0	52^1	31	20	20	7	0	19	61	.955	3.44	142	1.99	.170	0	....	9	6	0.8
1995*	Sea-A	2	1	.667	45	0	0	0	1	60^1	55	21	21	7	1	18	65	1.210	3.13	151	3.37	.244	0	....	12	6	1.1
1996	Tor-A	0	1	.000	25	0	0	0	0	41^2	33	20	18	7	0	25	29	1.392	3.89	129	4.25	.221	0	....	4	3	0.4
1997	Tor-A	0	1	.000	3	0	0	0	0	4^1	3	4	4	2	0	2	2	1.154	8.31	55	4.84	.188	0	....	-2	0	-0.2
1998	Tor-A	3	4	.429	44	0	0	0	0	54^2	52	37	32	7	4	34	42	1.573	5.27	89	5.14	.259	0	....	-4	2	-0.4
Total	7	15	13	.536	157	1	0	0	1	221^1	180	106	98	31	6	101	203	1.270	3.98	119	3.68	.225	0	.000	20	18	1.9

• RITCHIE, Jay Jay Seay Ritchie b: 11/20/1936, Salisbury, NC BR/TR, 6'4", 190 lbs. Deb: 8/4/1964

YEAR	TM-L	W	L	PCT	G	GS	CG	SH	SV	IP	H	R	ER	HR	HB	BB	SO	RAT	ERA	ERA+	CERA	OAV	BH	AVG	PR+	WS	TPW
1964	Bos-A	1	1	.500	21	0	0	0	0	46	43	21	14	4	0	14	35	1.239	2.74	141	3.13	.249	1	.111	7	3	0.7
1965	Bos-A	1	2	.333	44	0	0	0	2	71	83	30	25	3	1	26	55	1.535	3.17	117	4.48	.302	1	.200	6	4	0.6
1966	Atl-N	0	1	.000	22	0	0	0	4	35^1	32	17	16	3	0	12	33	1.245	4.08	89	2.99	.241	2	.500	-2	2	-0.1
1967	Atl-N	4	6	.400	52	0	0	0	2	82^1	75	32	29	6	4	29	57	1.263	3.17	105	3.16	.245	3	.300	1	6	0.2

YEAR	TM-L	W	L	PCT	G	GS	CG	SH	SV	IP	H	R	ER	HR	HB	BB	SO	RAT	ERA	ERA+	CERA	OAV	BH	AVG	PR+	WS	TPW
1968	Cin-N	2	3	.400	28	2	0	0	0	56^{2}	68	32	29	7	1	13	32	1.429	4.61	69	4.62	.293	0	.000	-9	1	-1.1
Total	**5**	**8**	**13**	**.381**	**167**	**2**	**0**	**0**	**8**	**291^{1}**	**301**	**132**	**113**	**23**	**6**	**94**	**212**	**1.356**	**3.49**	**99**	**3.74**	**.269**	**7**	**.200**	**3**	**16**	**0.3**

• RITCHIE, Todd Todd Everett Ritchie b: 11/7/1971, Portsmouth, VA BR/TR, 6'3", 205 lbs. Deb: 4/3/1997

YEAR	TM-L	W	L	PCT	G	GS	CG	SH	SV	IP	H	R	ER	HR	HB	BB	SO	RAT	ERA	ERA+	CERA	OAV	BH	AVG	PR+	WS	TPW
1997	Min-A	2	3	.400	42	0	0	0	0	74^{2}	87	41	38	11	2	28	44	1.540	4.58	102	5.44	.290	0	.000	1	3	0.0
1998	Min-A	0	0	....	15	0	0	0	0	24	30	17	15	1	0	9	21	1.625	5.63	85	4.75	.288	0	....	-2	0	-0.2
1999	Pit-N	15	9	.625	28	26	2	0	0	172^{2}	169	79	67	17	4	54	107	1.292	3.49	131	3.75	.259	8	.151	21	14	1.9
2000	Pit-N	9	8	.529	31	31	1	1	0	187	208	111	100	26	3	51	124	1.385	4.81	95	4.55	.282	13	.217	-2	8	0.0
2001	Pit-N	11	15	.423	33	33	4	2	0	207^{1}	211	118	103	23	7	52	124	1.268	4.47	100	3.68	.259	9	.153	1	10	0.1
2002	Chi-A	5	15	.250	26	23	0	0	0	133^{2}	176	104	90	18	5	52	77	1.706	6.06	75	6.27	.318	1	.250	-23	0	-2.2
2003	Mil-N	1	2	.333	5	5	0	0	0	28^{1}	36	17	16	4	4	10	15	1.624	5.08	84	6.45	.319	2	.222	-2	1	-0.2
Total	**7**	**43**	**52**	**.453**	**180**	**118**	**7**	**3**	**0**	**827^{2}**	**917**	**487**	**429**	**100**	**25**	**256**	**512**	**1.417**	**4.66**	**98**	**4.59**	**.280**	**33**	**.176**	**-7**	**36**	**-0.5**

• RITCHIE, Wally Wallace Reid Ritchie b: 7/12/1965, Glendale, CA BL/TL, 6'2", 180 lbs. Deb: 5/1/1987

YEAR	TM-L	W	L	PCT	G	GS	CG	SH	SV	IP	H	R	ER	HR	HB	BB	SO	RAT	ERA	ERA+	CERA	OAV	BH	AVG	PR+	WS	TPW
1987	Phi-N	3	2	.600	49	0	0	0	3	62^{1}	60	27	26	8	1	29	45	1.428	3.75	113	4.07	.254	1	.250	3	5	0.3
1988	Phi-N	0	0	....	19	0	0	0	0	26	19	14	9	1	1	17	8	1.385	3.12	114	3.07	.207	0	....	2	1	0.2
1991	Phi-N	1	2	.333	39	0	0	0	0	50^{1}	44	17	14	4	2	17	26	1.212	2.50	146	2.97	.234	0	.000	7	4	0.7
1992	Phi-N	2	1	.667	40	0	0	0	1	39	44	17	13	3	0	17	19	1.564	3.00	116	4.64	.288	0	.000	2	2	0.3
Total	**4**	**6**	**5**	**.545**	**147**	**0**	**0**	**0**	**4**	**177^{2}**	**167**	**75**	**62**	**16**	**4**	**80**	**98**	**1.390**	**3.14**	**122**	**3.74**	**.250**	**1**	**.125**	**13**	**12**	**1.4**

• RITTER, Hank William Herbert Ritter b: 10/12/1893, McCoysville, PA d: 9/3/1964, Akron, OH BR/TR, 6', 180 lbs. Deb: 8/3/1912

YEAR	TM-L	W	L	PCT	G	GS	CG	SH	SV	IP	H	R	ER	HR	HB	BB	SO	RAT	ERA	ERA+	CERA	OAV	BH	AVG	PR+	WS	TPW
1912	Phi-N	0	0	....	3	0	0	0	0	6	5	5	3	0	0	5	1	1.667	4.50	80	3.17	.192	0	.000	-1	0	-0.1
1914	NY-N	1	0	1.000	1	0	0	0	0	8	4	1	1	0	0	4	4	1.000	1.13	236	1.43	.160	0	.000	1	1	0.1
1915	NY-N	2	1	.667	22	2	0	0	2	58^{1}	66	38	30	4	5	15	35	1.389	4.63	55	4.22	.291	2	.125	-13	0	-1.5
1916	NY-N	1	0	1.000	3	0	0	0	0	5	3	0	0	0	1	0	3	.600	0.00	....	1.22	.200	0	....	1	1	0.1
Total	**4**	**4**	**1**	**.800**	**29**	**2**	**0**	**0**	**2**	**77^{1}**	**78**	**44**	**34**	**4**	**6**	**24**	**43**	**1.319**	**3.96**	**66**	**3.66**	**.266**	**2**	**.100**	**-11**	**2**	**-1.3**

• RITTER, Reggie Reggie Blake Ritter b: 1/23/1960, Malvern, AR BL/TR, 6'2", 195 lbs. Deb: 5/17/1986

YEAR	TM-L	W	L	PCT	G	GS	CG	SH	SV	IP	H	R	ER	HR	HB	BB	SO	RAT	ERA	ERA+	CERA	OAV	BH	AVG	PR+	WS	TPW
1986	Cle-A	0	0	....	5	0	0	0	0	10	14	10	7	1	1	4	6	1.800	6.30	66	6.88	.341	0	....	-2	0	-0.2
1987	Cle-A	1	1	.500	14	0	0	0	0	26^{2}	33	21	18	5	0	16	11	1.838	6.08	74	6.75	.300	0	....	-4	0	-0.4
Total	**2**	**1**	**1**	**.500**	**19**	**0**	**0**	**0**	**0**	**36^{2}**	**47**	**31**	**25**	**6**	**1**	**20**	**17**	**1.827**	**6.14**	**72**	**6.79**	**.311**	**0**	**....**	**-7**	**0**	**-0.6**

• RITTWAGE, Jim James Michael Rittwage b: 10/23/1944, Cleveland, OH BR/TR, 6'3", 190 lbs. Deb: 9/7/1970

YEAR	TM-L	W	L	PCT	G	GS	CG	SH	SV	IP	H	R	ER	HR	HB	BB	SO	RAT	ERA	ERA+	CERA	OAV	BH	AVG	PR+	WS	TPW
1970	Cle-A	1	1	.500	8	3	1	0	0	26	18	12	12	0	0	21	16	1.500	4.15	95	3.15	.194	3	.375	-1	2	0.0

• RITZ, Kevin Kevin D Ritz b: 6/8/1965, Eatontown, NJ BR/TR, 6'4", 220 lbs. Deb: 7/15/1989

YEAR	TM-L	W	L	PCT	G	GS	CG	SH	SV	IP	H	R	ER	HR	HB	BB	SO	RAT	ERA	ERA+	CERA	OAV	BH	AVG	PR+	WS	TPW
1989	Det-A	4	6	.400	12	12	1	0	0	74	75	41	36	2	1	44	56	1.608	4.38	87	4.29	.265	0	....	-4	3	-0.4
1990	Det-A	0	4	.000	4	4	0	0	0	7^{1}	14	12	9	0	0	14	3	3.818	11.05	36	14.21	.400	0	....	-6	0	-0.6
1991	Det-A	0	3	.000	11	5	0	0	0	15^{1}	17	22	20	1	2	22	9	2.543	11.74	35	9.04	.288	0	....	-13	0	-1.3
1992	Det-A	2	5	.286	23	11	0	0	0	80^{1}	88	52	50	4	3	44	57	1.643	5.60	71	4.87	.278	0	....	-14	1	-1.4
1994	Col-N	5	6	.455	15	15	0	0	0	73^{2}	88	49	46	5	4	35	53	1.670	5.62	89	5.47	.303	0	.000	-3	3	-0.5
1995*	Col-N	11	11	.500	31	28	0	0	2	173^{1}	171	91	81	16	6	65	120	1.362	4.21	128	3.98	.259	9	.188	28	13	2.8
1996	Col-N	17	11	.607	35	35	2	0	0	213	236	135	125	24	12	105	105	1.601	5.28	99	5.40	.282	15	.231	3	14	0.7
1997	Col-N	6	8	.429	18	18	1	0	0	107^{1}	142	72	70	16	1	46	56	1.752	5.87	88	6.69	.330	2	.057	-7	4	-0.8
1998	Col-N	0	2	.000	2	2	0	0	0	9	17	11	11	1	1	2	3	2.111	11.00	47	9.49	.395	1	.333	-6	0	-0.6
Total	**9**	**45**	**56**	**.446**	**151**	**130**	**4**	**0**	**2**	**753^{1}**	**848**	**485**	**448**	**69**	**30**	**377**	**462**	**1.626**	**5.35**	**90**	**5.31**	**.287**	**27**	**.158**	**-21**	**38**	**-2.2**

• RIVERA, Ben Bienvenido Santana Rivera b: 1/11/1968, San Pedro de Macoris, Dominican Republic BR/TR, 6'6", 210 lbs. Deb: 4/9/1992

YEAR	TM-L	W	L	PCT	G	GS	CG	SH	SV	IP	H	R	ER	HR	HB	BB	SO	RAT	ERA	ERA+	CERA	OAV	BH	AVG	PR+	WS	TPW
1992	Atl-N	0	1	.000	8	0	0	0	0	15^{1}	21	8	8	1	2	13	11	2.217	4.70	78	8.43	.339	0	.000	-2	0	-0.2
	Phi-N	7	3	.700	20	14	4	1	0	102	78	32	32	8	2	32	66	1.078	2.82	124	2.45	.211	3	.094	8	7	0.8
	Yr.	7	4	.636	28	14	4	1	0	117^{1}	99	40	40	9	4	45	77	1.227	3.07	115	3.23	.230	3	.091	6	7	0.6
1993*	Phi-N	13	9	.591	30	28	1	1	0	163	175	99	91	16	6	85	123	**1.595**	5.02	79	5.05	.273	5	.098	-18	5	-2.0
1994	Phi-N	3	4	.429	9	7	0	0	0	38	40	29	29	7	1	22	19	1.632	6.87	63	5.77	.274	0	.000	-11	0	-1.1
Total	**3**	**23**	**17**	**.575**	**67**	**49**	**5**	**2**	**0**	**318^{1}**	**314**	**168**	**160**	**32**	**11**	**152**	**219**	**1.464**	**4.52**	**86**	**4.46**	**.258**	**8**	**.086**	**-22**	**12**	**-2.5**

• RIVERA, Luis Luis (Gutierrez) Rivera b: 6/21/1978, Chihuahua, Mexico BR/TR, 6'3", 163 lbs. Deb: 4/4/2000

YEAR	TM-L	W	L	PCT	G	GS	CG	SH	SV	IP	H	R	ER	HR	HB	BB	SO	RAT	ERA	ERA+	CERA	OAV	BH	AVG	PR+	WS	TPW
2000	Atl-N	1	0	1.000	5	0	0	0	0	6^{2}	4	1	1	0	0	5	5	1.350	1.35	339	2.35	.190	0	....	2	1	0.2
	Bal-A	0	0	....	1	0	0	0	0	0^{2}	1	0	0	0	0	1	0	3.000	0.00	....	10.76	.333	0	....	0	0	0.0

• RIVERA, Mariano Mariano Rivera b: 11/29/1969, Panama City, Panama BR/TR, 6'4", 170 lbs. Deb: 5/23/1995

YEAR	TM-L	W	L	PCT	G	GS	CG	SH	SV	IP	H	R	ER	HR	HB	BB	SO	RAT	ERA	ERA+	CERA	OAV	BH	AVG	PR+	WS	TPW
1995*	NY-A	5	3	.625	19	10	0	0	0	67	71	43	41	11	2	30	51	1.507	5.51	84	5.14	.266	0	....	-7	2	-0.7
1996*	NY-A	8	3	.727	61	0	0	0	5	107^{2}	73	25	25	1	2	34	130	.994	2.09	237	1.65	.189	0	....	36	18	3.3
1997*	NY-A★	6	4	.600	66	0	0	0	43	71^{2}	65	17	15	5	0	20	68	1.186	1.88	236	2.73	.237	0	....	21	15	2.0
1998*	NY-A	3	0	1.000	54	0	0	0	36	61^{1}	48	13	13	3	1	17	36	1.060	1.91	230	2.21	.215	0	....	16	14	1.5
1999*	NY-A★	4	3	.571	66	0	0	0	**45**	69	43	15	14	2	3	18	52	.884	1.83	259	1.47	.176	0	....	23	17	2.1
2000*	NY-A★	7	4	.636	66	0	0	0	36	75^{2}	58	26	24	4	0	25	58	1.097	2.85	169	2.20	.208	0	....	18	16	1.6
2001*	NY-A★	4	6	.400	71	0	0	0	**50**	80^{2}	61	24	21	5	1	12	83	.905	2.34	192	1.74	.209	0	....	21	19	2.0
2002*	NY-A★	1	4	.200	45	0	0	0	28	46	35	16	14	3	2	11	41	1.000	2.74	159	2.08	.203	0	....	10	9	0.9
2003*	NY-A	5	2	.714	64	0	0	0	40	70^{2}	61	15	13	3	4	10	63	1.005	1.66	264	2.29	.235	0	....	23	17	2.2
Total	**9**	**43**	**29**	**.597**	**512**	**10**	**0**	**0**	**283**	**649^{2}**	**515**	**194**	**180**	**37**	**15**	**177**	**582**	**1.065**	**2.49**	**185**	**2.34**	**.215**	**0**	**....**	**160**	**127**	**15.0**

• RIVERA, Roberto Roberto (Diaz) Rivera b: 1/1/1969, Bayamon, Puerto Rico BL/TL, 6', 175 lbs. Deb: 9/3/1995

YEAR	TM-L	W	L	PCT	G	GS	CG	SH	SV	IP	H	R	ER	HR	HB	BB	SO	RAT	ERA	ERA+	CERA	OAV	BH	AVG	PR+	WS	TPW
1995	Chi-N	0	0	....	7	0	0	0	0	5	8	3	3	1	0	2	2	2.000	5.40	76	9.22	.381	0	....	-1	0	-0.1
1999	SD-N	1	2	.333	12	0	0	0	0	7	6	4	3	1	0	3	3	1.286	3.86	109	3.62	.240	0	....	0	0	0.0
Total	**2**	**1**	**2**	**.333**	**19**	**0**	**0**	**0**	**0**	**12**	**14**	**7**	**6**	**2**	**0**	**5**	**5**	**1.583**	**4.50**	**92**	**5.95**	**.304**	**0**	**....**	**-1**	**0**	**-0.1**

• RIVIERE, Tink Arthur Bernard Riviere b: 8/2/1899, Liberty, TX d: 9/27/1965, Liberty, TX BR/TR, 5'10", 167 lbs. Deb: 4/15/1921

YEAR	TM-L	W	L	PCT	G	GS	CG	SH	SV	IP	H	R	ER	HR	HB	BB	SO	RAT	ERA	ERA+	CERA	OAV	BH	AVG	PR+	WS	TPW
1921	StL-N	1	0	1.000	18	2	0	0	0	38^{1}	45	30	26	2	2	20	15	1.696	6.10	60	5.02	.280	3	.375	-10	1	-0.8
1925	Chi-A	0	0	....	3	0	0	0	0	4^{2}	6	7	4	0	1	7	1	2.786	7.71	54	11.25	.429	0	.000	-2	0	-0.2
Total	**2**	**1**	**0**	**1.000**	**21**	**2**	**0**	**0**	**0**	**43**	**51**	**37**	**30**	**2**	**3**	**27**	**16**	**1.814**	**6.28**	**59**	**5.69**	**.292**	**3**	**.333**	**-12**	**1**	**-1.0**

• RIXEY, Eppa Eppa "Jephtha" Rixey b: 5/3/1891, Culpeper, VA d: 2/28/1963, Terrace Park, OH BR/TL, 6'5", 210 lbs. Deb: 6/21/1912 HOF: 1963

YEAR	TM-L	W	L	PCT	G	GS	CG	SH	SV	IP	H	R	ER	HR	HB	BB	SO	RAT	ERA	ERA+	CERA	OAV	BH	AVG	PR+	WS	TPW
1912	Phi-N	10	10	.500	23	20	10	3	0	162	147	57	45	2	2	54	59	1.241	2.50	144	2.84	.256	9	.170	20	14	1.8
1913	Phi-N	9	5	.643	35	19	9	1	2	155^{2}	148	67	54	4	6	56	75	1.310	3.12	106	3.21	.258	9	.191	4	12	0.4
1914	Phi-N	2	11	.154	24	15	2	0	0	103	124	73	50	0	3	45	41	1.641	4.37	67	4.70	.313	1	.038	-13	0	-1.6
1915*	Phi-N	11	12	.478	29	22	10	2	1	176^{2}	163	67	47	2	2	64	88	1.285	2.39	114	2.90	.250	9	.164	7	12	0.7
1916	Phi-N	22	10	.688	38	34	20	3	0	287	239	91	59	2	7	74	134	1.091	1.85	143	2.14	.229	15	.155	26	24	2.7
1917	Phi-N	16	21	.432	39	37	23	4	1	281^{1}	249	102	71	1	5	67	121	1.123	2.27	123	2.28	.241	18	.191	15	20	1.6
1919	Phi-N	6	12	.333	23	18	11	1	0	154	160	88	68	4	3	50	63	1.364	3.97	81	3.52	.278	7	.149	-12	4	-1.5
1920	Phi-N	11	22	.333	41	33	25	0	2	284^{1}	288	137	110	5	4	69	109	1.256	3.48	98	3.02	.274	25	.248	-2	18	0.0
1921	Cin-N	19	18	.514	40	36	21	2	1	301	324	128	93	1	5	66	76	1.296	2.78	129	3.17	.282	13	.129	31	22	2.5
1922	Cin-N	**25**	13	.658	40	**38**	26	2	0	**313^{1}**	337	146	123	13	4	45	80	1.219	3.53	113	3.11	.275	21	.193	8	23	0.7
1923	Cin-N	20	15	.571	42	37	23	3	1	309	334	124	96	3	4	65	97	1.291	2.80	138	3.19	.280	17	.159	36	26	3.0
1924	Cin-N	15	14	.517	35	29	15	**4**	1	238^{1}	219	86	73	3	2	47	57	1.116	2.76	137	2.32	.246	18	.214	27	21	2.7
1925	Cin-N	21	11	.656	39	36	22	2	1	287^{1}	302	109	92	8	7	47	69	1.215	2.88	143	3.04	.273	22	.214	34	26	3.1
1926	Cin-N	14	8	.636	37	29	14	3	0	233	231	104	88	12	2	58	61	1.240	3.40	109	3.14	.265	19	.226	7	14	0.7
1927	Cin-N	12	10	.545	34	29	11	1	1	219^{2}	240	106	85	3	3	43	42	1.288	3.48	109	3.25	.287	20	.247	8	15	1.2
1928	Cin-N	19	18	.514	43	**37**	17	3	2	291^{1}	317	127	111	4	3	67	58	1.318	3.43	115	3.33	.288	18	.173	16	22	1.4
1929	Cin-N	10	13	.435	35	24	11	0	1	201	235	102	93	6	3	60	37	1.468	4.16	109	4.12	.296	15	.231	8	14	0.7
1930	Cin-N	9	13	.409	32	21	5	0	0	164	207	103	93	11	7	47	37	1.549	5.10	95	4.97	.317	11	.200	-4	8	-0.5

YEAR TM-L	W	L	PCT	G	GS	CG	SH	SV	IP	H	R	ER	HR	HB	BB	SO	RAT	ERA	ERA+	CERA	OAV	BH	AVG	PR+	WS	TPW
1931 Cin-N	4	7	.364	22	17	4	0	0	126^{2}	143	71	55	4	0	30	22	1.366	3.91	95	3.61	.291	6	.150	-4	5	-0.4
1932 Cin-N	5	5	.500	25	11	6	2	0	111^{2}	108	50	33	3	4	16	14	1.110	2.66	145	2.54	.254	9	.265	15	9	1.6
1933 Cin-N	6	3	.667	16	12	5	1	0	94^{1}	118	48	33	1	0	12	10	1.378	3.15	108	3.60	.298	9	.257	3	6	0.6
Total 21	266	251	.515	692	554	290	37	14	4494^{2}	4633	1986	1572	92	76	1082	1350	1.272	3.15	115	3.14	.272	291	.191	230	315	21.5

• RIZZO, Todd Todd Michael Rizzo b: 5/24/1971, Media, PA BR/TL, 6'3", 220 lbs. Deb: 4/2/1998

YEAR TM-L	W	L	PCT	G	GS	CG	SH	SV	IP	H	R	ER	HR	HB	BB	SO	RAT	ERA	ERA+	CERA	OAV	BH	AVG	PR+	WS	TPW
1998 Chi-A	0	0	....	9	0	0	0	0	6^{2}	12	12	10	0	0	6	3	2.700	13.50	34	10.16	.387	0	....	-7	0	-0.6
1999 Chi-A	0	2	.000	3	0	0	0	0	1^{1}	4	2	1	0	0	3	2	5.250	6.75	72	21.44	.500	0	....	-0	0	0.0
Total 2	0	2	.000	12	0	0	0	0	8	16	14	11	0	0	9	5	3.125	12.38	37	12.04	.410	0	....	-7	0	-0.7

• ROA, Joe Joseph Rodger Roa b: 10/11/1971, Southfield, MI BR/TR, 6'1", 194 lbs. Deb: 9/20/1995

YEAR TM-L	W	L	PCT	G	GS	CG	SH	SV	IP	H	R	ER	HR	HB	BB	SO	RAT	ERA	ERA+	CERA	OAV	BH	AVG	PR+	WS	TPW
1995 Cle-A	0	1	.000	1	1	0	0	0	6	9	4	4	1	0	2	0	1.833	6.00	78	7.46	.360	0	....	-1	0	-0.1
1996 Cle-A	0	0	....	1	0	0	0	0	1^{2}	4	2	2	0	0	3	0	4.200	10.80	45	20.57	.500	0	....	-1	0	-0.1
1997 SF-N	2	5	.286	28	3	0	0	0	65^{2}	86	40	38	8	2	20	34	1.614	5.21	78	5.85	.333	2	.133	-8	1	-0.8
2002 Phi-N	4	4	.500	14	11	0	0	0	71^{1}	78	33	32	11	1	13	35	1.276	4.04	96	4.14	.279	6	.240	-1	4	0.0
2003 Phi-N	0	2	.000	6	3	0	0	0	19^{1}	28	13	13	3	1	4	16	1.655	6.05	66	6.67	.341	1	.250	-4	0	-0.4
Col-N	0	0	....	4	0	0	0	0	6^{2}	7	3	3	2	0	0	4	1.050	4.05	121	4.06	.269	0	....	1	0	0.1
SD-N	1	1	.500	18	1	0	0	0	25^{1}	34	20	19	5	1	6	18	1.579	6.75	58	6.12	.315	1	.333	-8	0	-0.7
Yr.	1	3	.250	28	4	0	0	0	51^{1}	69	36	35	10	2	10	38	1.539	6.14	66	6.06	.319	2	.286	-11	0	-1.1
Total 5	7	13	.350	72	19	0	0	0	196	246	115	111	30	5	48	107	1.500	5.10	79	5.46	.313	10	.213	-23	5	-2.1

• ROACH, Jason Jason Glenn Roach b: 4/20/1976, Kinston, NC BR/TR, 6'4", 205 lbs. Deb: 6/14/2003

YEAR TM-L	W	L	PCT	G	GS	CG	SH	SV	IP	H	R	ER	HR	HB	BB	SO	RAT	ERA	ERA+	CERA	OAV	BH	AVG	PR+	WS	TPW
2003 NY-N	0	2	.000	2	2	0	0	0	9	14	12	12	3	1	4	2	2.000	12.00	35	10.08	.350	2	1.000	-8	0	-0.7

• ROACH, John John F. Roach b: 11/19/1867, Renovo, PA d: 4/2/1934, Peoria, IL BR/TL, 5'9", 175 lbs. Deb: 5/14/1887

YEAR TM-L	W	L	PCT	G	GS	CG	SH	SV	IP	H	R	ER	HR	HB	BB	SO	RAT	ERA	ERA+	CERA	OAV	BH	AVG	PR+	WS	TPW
1887 NY-N	0	1	.000	1	1	1	0	0	8	22	17	10	0	1	4	3	2.750	11.25	33	....	.482	1	.250	-7	0	-0.6

• ROACH, Skel Rudolph Charles Roach b: 10/20/1871, Danzig, Germany d: 3/9/1958, Oak Park, IL BR/TR, 6'2" Deb: 8/9/1899

YEAR TM-L	W	L	PCT	G	GS	CG	SH	SV	IP	H	R	ER	HR	HB	BB	SO	RAT	ERA	ERA+	CERA	OAV	BH	AVG	PR+	WS	TPW
1899 Chi-N	1	0	1.000	1	1	1	0	0	9	13	3	3	0	0	1	0	1.556	3.00	125	4.69	.337	0	.000	1	1	0.0

• ROBBINS, Bruce Bruce Duane Robbins b: 9/10/1959, Portland, IN BL/TL, 6'1", 190 lbs. Deb: 7/28/1979

YEAR TM-L	W	L	PCT	G	GS	CG	SH	SV	IP	H	R	ER	HR	HB	BB	SO	RAT	ERA	ERA+	CERA	OAV	BH	AVG	PR+	WS	TPW
1979 Det-A	3	3	.500	10	8	0	0	0	46	45	21	20	3	0	21	22	1.435	3.91	111	4.06	.265	0	....	2	3	0.2
1980 Det-A	4	2	.667	15	6	0	0	0	51^{2}	60	40	38	12	0	28	23	1.703	6.62	62	6.56	.287	0	....	-14	0	-1.4
Total 2	7	5	.583	25	14	0	0	0	97^{2}	105	61	58	15	0	49	45	1.577	5.34	78	5.38	.277	0	....	-12	3	-1.2

• ROBERGE, Bert Bertrand Roland Roberge b: 10/3/1954, Lewiston, ME BR/TR, 6'4", 190 lbs. Deb: 5/28/1979

YEAR TM-L	W	L	PCT	G	GS	CG	SH	SV	IP	H	R	ER	HR	HB	BB	SO	RAT	ERA	ERA+	CERA	OAV	BH	AVG	PR+	WS	TPW
1979 Hou-N	3	0	1.000	26	0	0	0	4	32	20	6	6	0	0	17	13	1.156	1.69	208	2.20	.196	0	.000	7	6	0.7
1980 Hou-N	2	0	1.000	14	0	0	0	0	24^{1}	24	16	16	2	2	10	9	1.397	5.92	56	4.19	.261	0	.000	-7	0	-0.8
1982 Hou-N	1	2	.333	22	0	0	0	3	25^{2}	29	12	12	0	0	6	18	1.364	4.21	79	3.24	.284	0	.000	-3	1	-0.3
1984 Chi-A	3	3	.500	21	0	0	0	0	40^{2}	36	18	17	2	3	15	25	1.254	3.76	111	3.23	.240	0	....	2	3	0.2
1985 Mon-N	3	3	.500	42	0	0	0	2	68	58	28	26	5	2	22	34	1.176	3.44	99	2.84	.232	0	.000	-1	4	-0.1
1986 Mon-N	0	4	.000	21	0	0	0	1	28^{2}	33	20	20	2	1	10	20	1.500	6.28	59	4.43	.295	0	.000	-8	0	-0.9
Total 6	12	12	.500	146	0	0	0	10	219^{1}	200	100	97	11	8	80	119	1.277	3.98	89	3.22	.248	0	.000	-11	14	-1.3

• ROBERSON, Sid Sidney Dean Roberson b: 9/7/1971, Jacksonville, FL BL/TL, 5'9", 170 lbs. Deb: 5/20/1995

YEAR TM-L	W	L	PCT	G	GS	CG	SH	SV	IP	H	R	ER	HR	HB	BB	SO	RAT	ERA	ERA+	CERA	OAV	BH	AVG	PR+	WS	TPW
1995 Mil-A	6	4	.600	26	13	0	0	0	84^{1}	102	55	54	16	8	37	40	1.648	5.76	86	6.75	.307	0	....	-9	3	-0.8

• ROBERTS, Dale Dale "Mountain Man" Roberts b: 4/12/1942, Owenton, KY BR/TL, 6'4", 180 lbs. Deb: 9/9/1967

YEAR TM-L	W	L	PCT	G	GS	CG	SH	SV	IP	H	R	ER	HR	HB	BB	SO	RAT	ERA	ERA+	CERA	OAV	BH	AVG	PR+	WS	TPW
1967 NY-A	0	0	....	2	0	0	0	0	2	3	2	2	0	2	2	0	2.500	9.00	35	12.65	.429	0	....	-1	0	-0.1

• ROBERTS, Dave David Arthur Roberts b: 9/11/1944, Gallipolis, OH BL/TL, 6'3", 197 lbs. Deb: 7/6/1969

YEAR TM-L	W	L	PCT	G	GS	CG	SH	SV	IP	H	R	ER	HR	HB	BB	SO	RAT	ERA	ERA+	CERA	OAV	BH	AVG	PR+	WS	TPW
1969 SD-N	0	3	.000	22	5	0	0	1	48^{2}	65	30	26	5	3	19	19	1.726	4.81	74	6.29	.322	4	.267	-6	1	-0.6
1970 SD-N	8	14	.364	43	21	3	2	1	181^{2}	182	80	77	16	1	43	102	1.239	3.81	104	3.32	.261	9	.153	3	9	0.4
1971 SD-N	14	17	.452	37	34	14	2	0	269^{2}	238	79	63	9	5	61	135	1.109	2.10	157	2.43	.240	19	.221	38	24	4.3
1972 Hou-N	12	7	.632	35	28	7	3	2	192	227	100	96	18	2	57	111	**1.479**	4.50	75	4.70	.296	16	.239	-24	7	-2.0
1973 Hou-N	17	11	.607	39	36	12	6	0	249^{1}	264	92	79	15	2	62	119	1.307	2.85	127	3.52	.271	11	.129	22	20	2.0
1974 Hou-N	10	12	.455	34	30	8	2	1	204	216	83	77	6	3	65	72	1.377	3.40	102	3.66	.276	16	.219	-1	13	0.3
1975 Hou-N	8	14	.364	32	27	7	0	1	198^{1}	182	98	94	16	2	73	101	1.286	4.27	79	3.35	.244	9	.143	-21	6	-2.2
1976 Det-A	16	17	.485	36	36	18	4	0	252	254	122	112	16	4	63	79	1.258	4.00	93	3.36	.264	0	....	-5	14	-0.6
1977 Det-A	4	10	.286	22	22	5	0	0	129^{1}	143	88	74	20	2	41	46	1.423	5.15	83	4.70	.274	0	....	-12	3	-1.2
Chi-N	1	1	.500	17	6	1	0	1	53	55	22	19	1	1	12	23	1.264	3.23	136	2.91	.275	1	.059	8	4	0.6
1978 Chi-N	6	8	.429	35	20	2	1	1	142^{1}	159	87	83	17	3	56	54	1.511	5.25	77	4.80	.288	17	.327	-18	5	-1.3
1979 SF-N	0	2	.000	26	1	0	0	3	42	42	15	12	3	1	18	23	1.429	2.57	136	3.98	.263	0	.000	5	3	0.4
*Pit-N	5	2	.714	21	3	0	0	1	38^{2}	47	18	14	1	1	12	15	1.526	3.26	119	4.37	.318	0	.000	2	3	0.2
Yr.	5	4	.556	47	4	0	0	4	80^{2}	89	33	26	4	2	30	38	1.475	2.90	127	4.17	.289	0	.000	7	6	0.6
1980 Pit-N	0	1	.000	2	0	0	0	0	2^{1}	2	1	1	0	0	1	1	1.286	3.86	94	3.03	.250	0	....	-0	0	0.0
Sea-A	2	3	.400	37	4	0	0	3	80^{1}	86	46	39	7	1	27	47	1.407	4.37	95	3.93	.270	0	....	-1	4	-0.1
1981 NY-N	0	3	.000	7	4	0	0	0	15^{1}	26	18	16	5	0	5	10	2.022	9.39	37	9.99	.366	1	.250	-10	0	-1.0
Total 13	103	125	.452	445	277	77	20	15	2099	2188	979	882	155	31	615	957	1.335	3.78	97	3.74	.270	103	.194	-22	116	-0.8

• ROBERTS, Grant Grant William Roberts b: 9/13/1977, El Cajon, CA BR/TR, 6'3", 205 lbs. Deb: 7/27/2000

YEAR TM-L	W	L	PCT	G	GS	CG	SH	SV	IP	H	R	ER	HR	HB	BB	SO	RAT	ERA	ERA+	CERA	OAV	BH	AVG	PR+	WS	TPW
2000 NY-N	0	0	....	4	1	0	0	0	7	11	10	9	0	0	4	6	2.143	11.57	38	6.53	.344	0	....	-6	0	-0.5
2001 NY-N	1	0	1.000	16	0	0	0	0	26	24	11	11	2	0	8	29	1.231	3.81	108	3.03	.240	0	.000	1	2	0.0
2002 NY-N	3	1	.750	34	0	0	0	0	45	43	12	11	3	1	16	31	1.311	2.20	180	3.25	.253	1	1.000	9	5	1.0
2003 NY-N	0	3	.000	18	0	0	0	1	19	19	9	8	0	1	3	10	1.158	3.79	110	2.60	.257	0	....	1	1	0.1
Total 4	4	4	.500	72	1	0	0	1	97	97	42	39	5	2	31	76	1.320	3.62	115	3.30	.258	1	.250	5	8	0.6

• ROBERTS, Jim James Newsom "Big Jim" Roberts b: 10/13/1895, Artesia, MS d: 6/24/1984, Columbus, MS BR/TR, 6'3", 205 lbs. Deb: 7/27/1924

YEAR TM-L	W	L	PCT	G	GS	CG	SH	SV	IP	H	R	ER	HR	HB	BB	SO	RAT	ERA	ERA+	CERA	OAV	BH	AVG	PR+	WS	TPW
1924 Bro-N	0	3	.000	11	5	0	0	0	25^{1}	41	28	21	1	2	8	10	1.934	7.46	50	7.12	.360	1	.143	-10	0	-1.0
1925 Bro-N	0	0	....	1	0	0	0	0	1	1	1	0	0	0	0	0	1.000	0.00	....	1.95	.500	0	....	0	0	0.0
Total 2	0	3	.000	12	5	0	0	0	26^{1}	42	29	21	1	2	8	10	1.899	7.18	52	6.92	.362	1	.143	-9	0	-0.9

• ROBERTS, Ray Raymond Roberts b: 8/25/1895, Cruger, MS d: 1/30/1962, Cruger, MS BL/TR, 5'11", 180 lbs. Deb: 9/12/1919

YEAR TM-L	W	L	PCT	G	GS	CG	SH	SV	IP	H	R	ER	HR	HB	BB	SO	RAT	ERA	ERA+	CERA	OAV	BH	AVG	PR+	WS	TPW
1919 Phi-A	0	2	.000	3	2	0	0	0	14	21	14	12	0	0	3	2	1.714	7.71	44	5.84	.368	1	.250	-6	0	-0.6

• ROBERTS, Robin Robin Evan Roberts b: 9/30/1926, Springfield, IL BB/TR, 6', 190 lbs. Deb: 6/18/1948 HOF: 1976

YEAR TM-L	W	L	PCT	G	GS	CG	SH	SV	IP	H	R	ER	HR	HB	BB	SO	RAT	ERA	ERA+	CERA	OAV	BH	AVG	PR+	WS	TPW
1948 Phi-N	7	9	.438	20	20	9	0	0	146^{2}	148	63	52	10	4	61	84	1.425	3.19	123	4.21	.278	11	.250	13	12	1.7
1949 Phi-N	15	15	.500	43	31	11	3	4	226^{2}	229	101	93	15	5	75	95	1.341	3.69	107	3.79	.273	5	.075	4	16	0.1
1950* Phi-N★	20	11	.645	40	**39**	21	**5**	1	304^{1}	282	112	102	29	2	77	146	1.180	3.02	134	3.12	.248	12	.118	34	**26**	3.0
1951 Phi-N★	21	15	.583	44	**39**	22	6	2	**315**	284	115	106	20	3	64	127	1.105	3.03	127	**2.57**	.237	15	.172	29	**28**	**3.5**
1952 Phi-N★	**28**	7	.800	39	**37**	**30**	3	2	**330**	292	104	95	22	5	45	148	1.021	2.59	141	2.31	.234	14	.125	**34**	**32**	3.7
1953 Phi-N★	**23**	16	.590	44	**41**	**33**	5	2	**346^{2}**	324	119	106	30	2	61	**198**	1.111	2.75	153	2.75	.242	22	.179	**56**	**35**	**5.6**
1954 Phi-N★	**23**	15	.605	45	**38**	**29**	4	4	**336^{2}**	289	116	111	35	5	56	**185**	1.025	2.97	136	**2.51**	.231	15	.123	39	**31**	3.5
1955 Phi-N★	**23**	14	.622	41	**38**	**26**	1	3	**305**	292	137	111	41	2	53	160	1.131	3.28	121	3.15	.246	27	.252	20	**27**	3.4
1956 Phi-N★	19	18	.514	43	37	**22**	1	3	297^{1}	328	155	147	46	2	40	157	1.238	4.45	84	4.01	.282	20	.200	-17	12	-1.4
1957 Phi-N	10	22	.313	39	32	14	2	2	249^{2}	246	122	113	40	1	43	128	1.158	4.07	93	3.37	.252	13	.163	-6	12	-0.6
1958 Phi-N	17	14	.548	35	34	21	1	0	269^{2}	270	112	97	30	2	51	130	1.190	3.24	122	3.32	.259	20	.202	26	20	**3.0**
1959 Phi-N	15	17	.469	35	35	19	2	0	257^{1}	267	137	122	34	5	35	137	1.174	4.27	96	3.45	.263	17	.191	-4	13	-0.1
1960 Phi-N	12	16	.429	35	33	13	2	1	237^{1}	256	113	106	31	2	34	122	1.222	4.02	97	3.70	.275	12	.152	-5	13	-0.5
1961 Phi-N	1	10	.091	26	18	2	0	0	117	154	85	76	19	2	23	54	1.513	5.85	70	5.60	.326	3	.091	-25	0	-2.7
1962 Bal-A	10	9	.526	27	25	6	0	0	191^{1}	176	63	59	17	4	41	102	1.134	2.78	135	2.92	.244	10	.192	19	16	2.2

YEAR TM-L	W	L	PCT	G	GS	CG	SH	SV	IP	H	R	ER	HR	HB	BB	SO	RAT	ERA	ERA+	CERA	OAV	BH	AVG	PR+	WS	TPW
1963 Bal-A	14	13	.519	35	35	9	2	0	251^{1}	230	100	93	35	3	40	124	1.074	3.33	106	2.93	.240	16	.203	6	15	0.8
1964 Bal-A	13	7	.650	31	31	8	4	0	204	203	69	66	18	3	52	109	1.250	2.91	123	3.45	.261	9	.132	10	15	0.9
1965 Bal-A	5	7	.417	20	15	5	1	0	114^{2}	110	51	43	17	1	20	63	1.134	3.38	103	3.27	.252	6	.171	-1	5	0.0
Hou-N	5	2	.714	10	10	3	2	0	76	61	22	16	1	0	10	34	.934	1.89	177	1.63	.216	5	.238	14	8	1.8
1966 Hou-N	3	5	.375	13	12	1	1	1	63^{2}	79	31	27	7	1	10	26	1.398	3.82	90	4.62	.307	1	.063	-2	3	-0.3
Chi-N	2	3	.400	11	9	1	0	0	48^{1}	62	35	33	8	0	11	28	1.510	6.14	60	5.59	.313	2	.200	-13	0	-1.3
Yr.	5	8	.385	24	21	2	1	1	112	141	66	60	15	1	21	54	1.446	4.82	74	5.04	.310	3	.115	-15	3	-1.5
Total 19	286	245	.539	676	609	305	45	25	4688^{2}	4582	1962	1774	505	54	902	2357	1.170	3.41	113	3.24	.255	255	.167	231	339	26.5

• ROBERTS, Willis Willis Augusto (DeLeon) Roberts b: 6/19/1975, San Cristobal, Dominican Republic BR/TR, 6'3", 175 lbs. Deb: 7/2/1999

YEAR TM-L	W	L	PCT	G	GS	CG	SH	SV	IP	H	R	ER	HR	HB	BB	SO	RAT	ERA	ERA+	CERA	OAV	BH	AVG	PR+	WS	TPW
1999 Det-A	0	0	....	1	0	0	0	0	1^{1}	3	4	2	0	1	0	0	2.250	13.50	37	12.64	.500	0	....	-1	0	-0.1
2001 Bal-A	9	10	.474	46	18	1	0	6	132	142	75	72	15	11	55	95	1.492	4.91	87	4.98	.274	1	.250	-10	6	-1.0
2002 Bal-A	5	4	.556	66	0	0	0	1	75	79	34	28	5	4	32	51	1.480	3.36	127	4.35	.270	0	....	7	6	0.7
2003 Bal-A	3	1	.750	26	0	0	0	0	39^{1}	41	26	25	7	7	16	26	1.449	5.72	77	5.72	.273	0	....	-6	1	-0.5
Total 4	17	15	.531	139	18	1	0	7	247^{2}	265	139	127	27	23	103	172	1.486	4.62	94	4.95	.274	1	.250	-11	13	-1.0

• ROBERTSON, Charlie Charles Culbertson Robertson b: 1/31/1896, Dexter, TX d: 8/23/1984, Fort Worth, TX BL/TR, 6', 175 lbs. Deb: 5/13/1919

YEAR TM-L	W	L	PCT	G	GS	CG	SH	SV	IP	H	R	ER	HR	HB	BB	SO	RAT	ERA	ERA+	CERA	OAV	BH	AVG	PR+	WS	TPW
1919 Chi-A	0	1	.000	1	1	0	0	0	2	5	2	2	0	0	0	1	2.500	9.00	35	13.40	.556	0	....	-1	0	-0.1
1922 Chi-A	14	15	.483	37	34	21	3	0	272	294	124	110	9	4	89	83	1.408	3.64	112	3.77	.286	16	.184	10	17	0.8
1923 Chi-A	13	18	.419	38	34	18	1	0	255	262	126	108	8	5	104	91	1.435	3.81	104	3.73	.272	21	.247	5	14	0.5
1924 Chi-A	4	10	.286	17	14	5	0	0	97^{1}	108	65	54	2	0	54	29	1.664	4.99	82	4.24	.293	6	.182	-9	2	-0.9
1925 Chi-A	8	12	.400	24	23	6	2	0	137	181	96	80	8	2	47	27	1.664	5.26	79	5.32	.327	10	.222	-17	4	-1.6
1926 StL-A	1	2	.333	8	7	1	0	0	28	38	27	26	4	2	21	13	2.107	8.36	51	8.16	.333	3	.300	-13	0	-1.2
1927 Bos-N	7	17	.292	28	21	6	0	0	154^{1}	188	90	81	2	4	46	49	1.516	4.72	79	4.22	.308	12	.240	-14	4	-1.4
1928 Bos-N	2	5	.286	13	7	3	0	1	59^{1}	73	40	35	5	0	16	17	1.500	5.31	74	4.70	.308	0	.000	-7	1	-0.8
Total 8	49	80	.380	166	141	60	6	1	1005	1149	570	496	38	17	377	310	1.518	4.44	90	4.28	.296	68	.208	-47	42	-4.7

• ROBERTSON, Dick Preston Robertson b: 1891, Washington, DC d: 10/2/1944, New Orleans, LA BR/TR, 5'9", 160 lbs. Deb: 9/16/1913

YEAR TM-L	W	L	PCT	G	GS	CG	SH	SV	IP	H	R	ER	HR	HB	BB	SO	RAT	ERA	ERA+	CERA	OAV	BH	AVG	PR+	WS	TPW
1913 Cin-N	0	1	.000	2	1	1	0	0	10	13	9	8	0	0	9	1	2.200	7.20	45	7.36	.342	0	.000	-4	0	-0.5
1918 Bro-N	3	6	.333	13	9	7	1	0	87	87	34	25	0	0	28	18	1.322	2.59	108	3.15	.272	9	.300	2	6	0.4
1919 Was-A	0	1	.000	7	4	0	0	0	27^{2}	25	11	7	1	0	9	7	1.229	2.28	141	2.99	.253	0	.000	3	1	0.2
Total 3	3	8	.273	22	14	8	1	0	124^{2}	125	54	40	1	0	46	26	1.372	2.89	102	3.45	.274	9	.225	1	7	0.1

• ROBERTSON, Jeriome Jeriome Paul Robertson b: 3/30/1977, San Jose, CA BL/TL, 6'1", 190 lbs. Deb: 9/2/2002

YEAR TM-L	W	L	PCT	G	GS	CG	SH	SV	IP	H	R	ER	HR	HB	BB	SO	RAT	ERA	ERA+	CERA	OAV	BH	AVG	PR+	WS	TPW
2002 Hou-N	0	2	.000	11	1	0	0	0	9^{2}	13	8	7	4	0	5	6	1.862	6.52	65	8.70	.394	0	....	-2	0	-0.2
2003 Hou-N	15	9	.625	32	31	0	0	0	160^{2}	180	98	91	23	6	64	99	1.519	5.10	87	5.19	.287	8	.154	-16	5	-1.6
Total 2	15	11	.577	43	32	0	0	0	170^{1}	193	106	98	27	6	69	105	1.538	5.18	85	5.39	.292	8	.154	-18	5	-1.8

• ROBERTSON, Jerry Jerry Lee Robertson b: 10/13/1943, Winchester, KS d: 3/24/1996, Burlington, KS BB/TR, 6'2", 205 lbs. Deb: 4/8/1969

YEAR TM-L	W	L	PCT	G	GS	CG	SH	SV	IP	H	R	ER	HR	HB	BB	SO	RAT	ERA	ERA+	CERA	OAV	BH	AVG	PR+	WS	TPW
1969 Mon-N	5	16	.238	38	27	3	0	1	179^{2}	186	87	79	17	4	81	133	1.486	3.96	93	4.45	.272	5	.089	-5	7	-0.8
1970 Det-A	0	0	....	11	0	0	0	0	14^{2}	19	8	6	1	0	5	11	1.636	3.68	101	4.97	.306	0	....	1	1	0.1
Total 2	5	16	.238	49	27	3	0	1	194^{1}	205	95	85	18	4	86	144	1.497	3.94	93	4.49	.274	5	.089	-4	8	-0.7

• ROBERTSON, Nate Nathan Daniel Robertson b: 9/3/1977, Wichita, KS BR/TL, 6'2", 215 lbs. Deb: 9/7/2002

YEAR TM-L	W	L	PCT	G	GS	CG	SH	SV	IP	H	R	ER	HR	HB	BB	SO	RAT	ERA	ERA+	CERA	OAV	BH	AVG	PR+	WS	TPW
2002 Fla-N	0	1	.000	6	1	0	0	0	8^{1}	15	11	11	3	2	4	3	2.280	11.88	33	12.69	.375	0	.000	-7	0	-0.8
2003 Det-A	1	2	.333	8	8	0	0	0	44^{2}	55	27	27	6	0	23	33	1.746	5.44	79	6.24	.306	0	....	-6	1	-0.5
Total 2	1	3	.250	14	9	0	0	0	53	70	38	38	9	2	27	36	1.830	6.45	65	7.26	.318	0	.000	-13	1	-1.3

• ROBERTSON, Rich Richard Wayne Robertson b: 9/15/1968, Nacogdoches, TX BL/TL, 6'4", 175 lbs. Deb: 4/30/1993

YEAR TM-L	W	L	PCT	G	GS	CG	SH	SV	IP	H	R	ER	HR	HB	BB	SO	RAT	ERA	ERA+	CERA	OAV	BH	AVG	PR+	WS	TPW
1993 Pit-N	0	1	.000	9	0	0	0	0	9	15	6	6	0	0	4	5	2.111	6.00	67	7.64	.385	0	....	-2	0	-0.2
1994 Pit-N	0	0	....	8	0	0	0	0	15^{2}	20	12	12	2	0	10	8	1.915	6.89	63	6.38	.313	1	.250	-5	0	-0.4
1995 Min-A	2	0	1.000	25	4	1	0	0	51^{2}	48	28	22	4	0	31	38	1.529	3.83	124	4.18	.253	0	....	5	3	0.5
1996 Min-A	7	17	.292	36	31	5	**3**	0	186^{1}	197	113	106	22	9	116	114	**1.680**	5.12	100	5.69	.273	0	....	-2	8	-0.2
1997 Min-A	8	12	.400	31	26	0	0	0	147	169	105	93	19	6	70	69	1.626	5.69	82	5.66	.292	1	.200	-17	3	-1.6
1998 Ana-A	0	0	....	5	0	0	0	0	5^{2}	11	11	10	3	0	2	3	2.294	15.88	30	13.25	.393	0	....	-7	0	-0.7
Total 6	17	30	.362	114	61	6	3	0	415^{1}	460	275	249	50	15	233	237	1.669	5.40	89	5.66	.284	2	.222	-27	14	-2.6

• ROBERTSON, Rich Richard Paul Robertson b: 10/14/1944, Albany, CA BR/TR, 6'2", 210 lbs. Deb: 9/10/1966

YEAR TM-L	W	L	PCT	G	GS	CG	SH	SV	IP	H	R	ER	HR	HB	BB	SO	RAT	ERA	ERA+	CERA	OAV	BH	AVG	PR+	WS	TPW
1966 SF-N	0	0	....	1	0	0	0	0	2^{1}	3	3	2	0	0	2	2	2.143	7.71	48	6.63	.300	0	....	-1	0	-0.1
1967 SF-N	0	0	....	1	0	0	0	0	2	3	1	1	0	0	0	1	1.500	4.50	73	4.47	.333	0	....	-0	0	0.0
1968 SF-N	2	0	1.000	3	1	0	0	0	9	9	6	6	0	0	3	8	1.333	6.00	49	3.15	.265	1	.500	-3	0	-0.3
1969 SF-N	1	3	.250	17	7	1	1	0	44^{1}	53	32	27	4	1	21	20	1.669	5.48	64	5.38	.298	0	.000	-9	0	-1.1
1970 SF-N	8	9	.471	41	26	6	0	1	183^{2}	199	113	99	22	1	96	121	**1.606**	4.85	82	5.18	.277	6	.102	-14	5	-1.5
1971 SF-N	2	2	.500	23	6	1	0	1	61	66	40	31	5	2	31	32	1.590	4.57	74	4.74	.267	1	.067	-8	0	-0.9
Total 6	13	14	.481	86	40	8	1	2	302^{1}	333	195	166	31	4	153	184	1.607	4.94	75	5.07	.278	8	.093	-35	5	-3.9

• ROBINSON, Bill William Robinson b: Taylorsville, KY Deb: 8/12/1889

YEAR TM-L	W	L	PCT	G	GS	CG	SH	SV	IP	H	R	ER	HR	HB	BB	SO	RAT	ERA	ERA+	CERA	OAV	BH	AVG	PR+	WS	TPW
1889 Lou-a	0	1	.000	1	1	1	0	0	8	10	10	9	2	0	6	2	2.000	10.13	38	....	.297	1	.333	-5	0	-0.5

• ROBINSON, Dewey Dewey Everett Robinson b: 4/28/1955, Evanston, IL BR/TR, 6', 180 lbs. Deb: 4/6/1979 C

YEAR TM-L	W	L	PCT	G	GS	CG	SH	SV	IP	H	R	ER	HR	HB	BB	SO	RAT	ERA	ERA+	CERA	OAV	BH	AVG	PR+	WS	TPW
1979 Chi-A	0	1	.000	11	0	0	0	0	14^{1}	11	12	10	1	0	9	5	1.395	6.28	68	3.28	.212	0	....	-3	0	-0.3
1980 Chi-A	1	1	.500	15	0	0	0	0	35	26	13	12	2	0	16	28	1.200	3.09	130	2.72	.215	0	....	4	3	0.4
1981 Chi-A	1	0	1.000	4	0	0	0	0	4	5	2	2	1	0	3	2	2.000	4.50	80	8.59	.357	0	....	-0	0	0.0
Total 3	2	2	.500	30	0	0	0	0	53^{1}	42	27	24	4	0	28	35	1.313	4.05	101	3.31	.225	0	....	0	3	0.0

• ROBINSON, Don Don Allen "Caveman" Robinson b: 6/8/1957, Ashland, KY BR/TR, 6'4", 231 lbs. Deb: 4/10/1978

YEAR TM-L	W	L	PCT	G	GS	CG	SH	SV	IP	H	R	ER	HR	HB	BB	SO	RAT	ERA	ERA+	CERA	OAV	BH	AVG	PR+	WS	TPW
1978 Pit-N	14	6	.700	35	32	9	1	1	228^{1}	203	98	88	20	3	57	135	1.139	3.47	107	2.84	.236	20	.235	9	15	1.2
1979* Pit-N	8	8	.500	29	25	4	0	0	160^{2}	171	74	69	12	4	52	96	1.388	3.87	100	4.07	.277	10	.204	-1	8	0.0
1980 Pit-N	7	10	.412	29	24	3	2	1	160^{1}	157	74	71	14	5	45	103	1.260	3.99	91	3.51	.257	19	.333	-8	9	-0.2
1981 Pit-N	0	3	.000	16	2	0	0	2	38^{1}	47	27	25	4	0	23	17	1.826	5.87	61	6.02	.313	3	.250	-10	0	-1.0
1982 Pit-N	15	13	.536	38	30	6	0	0	227	213	123	108	26	3	103	165	1.392	4.28	87	4.03	.250	24	.282	-13	10	-0.5
1983 Pit-N	2	2	.500	9	6	0	0	0	36^{1}	43	21	18	5	0	21	28	1.761	4.46	83	6.08	.297	2	.154	-3	1	-0.2
1984 Pit-N	5	6	.455	51	1	0	0	10	122	99	45	41	6	0	49	110	1.213	3.02	119	2.72	.226	9	.290	6	11	1.0
1985 Pit-N	5	11	.313	44	6	0	0	3	95^{1}	95	49	41	6	2	42	65	1.437	3.87	92	3.81	.255	5	.238	-2	5	0.1
1986 Pit-N	3	4	.429	50	0	0	0	14	69^{1}	61	27	26	5	2	27	53	1.269	3.38	114	3.20	.237	4	.667	4	8	0.6
1987 Pit-N	6	6	.500	42	0	0	0	12	65^{1}	66	29	28	6	0	22	53	1.347	3.86	107	3.79	.267	1	.143	1	7	0.1
* SF-N	5	1	.833	25	0	0	0	7	42^{2}	39	13	13	1	0	18	26	1.336	2.74	140	3.00	.239	3	.273	5	7	0.7
Yr.	11	7	.611	67	0	0	0	19	108	105	42	41	7	0	40	79	1.343	3.42	118	3.48	.256	4	.222	5	14	0.7
1988 SF-N	10	5	.667	51	19	3	2	6	176^{2}	152	63	48	11	3	49	122	1.138	2.45	133	2.58	.231	9	.173	16	14	2.0
1989* SF-N	12	11	.522	34	32	5	1	0	197	184	80	75	22	2	37	96	1.122	3.43	98	3.01	.248	15	.185	-6	10	-0.2
1990 SF-N	10	7	.588	26	25	4	0	0	157^{2}	173	84	80	18	1	41	78	1.357	4.57	80	4.15	.280	9	.143	-17	5	-1.7
1991 SF-N	5	9	.357	34	16	0	0	1	121^{1}	123	64	59	12	1	50	78	1.426	4.38	82	4.14	.265	6	.150	-12	3	-1.2
1992 Cal-A	1	0	1.000	3	3	0	0	0	16^{1}	19	4	4	1	0	3	9	1.347	2.20	181	3.89	.292	0	....	3	2	0.3
Phi-N	1	4	.200	8	8	0	0	0	43^{2}	49	32	30	6	1	4	17	1.214	6.18	56	3.83	.290	7	.389	-13	1	-1.0
Total 15	109	106	.507	524	229	34	6	57	1958^{1}	1894	907	824	175	27	643	1251	1.295	3.79	96	3.55	.255	146	.231	-41	116	-0.1

• ROBINSON, Hank John Henry "Rube" Robinson b: 8/16/1889, Floyd, AR d: 7/3/1965, North Little Rock, AR BR/TL, 5'11.5", 160 lbs. Deb: 9/2/1911

YEAR TM-L	W	L	PCT	G	GS	CG	SH	SV	IP	H	R	ER	HR	HB	BB	SO	RAT	ERA	ERA+	CERA	OAV	BH	AVG	PR+	WS	TPW
1911 Pit-N	0	1	.000	5	0	0	0	0	13	13	7	4	0	1	5	8	1.385	2.77	124	3.83	.283	0	.000	1	0	0.0
1912 Pit-N	12	7	.632	33	16	11	0	2	175	146	54	44	3	10	30	79	1.006	2.26	144	**2.12**	.237	15	.254	17	17	1.9
1913 Pit-N	14	9	.609	43	23	8	1	0	196^{1}	184	72	52	1	7	41	50	1.146	2.38	126	2.54	.255	11	.180	15	14	1.5

YEAR TM-L	W	L	PCT	G	GS	CG	SH	SV	IP	H	R	ER	HR	HB	BB	SO	RAT	ERA	ERA+	CERA	OAV	BH	AVG	PR+	WS	TPW
1914 StL-N	7	8	.467	26	16	6	1	0	126	128	61	42	1	4	32	30	1.270	3.00	93	3.05	.274	6	.171	-4	6	-0.4
1915 StL-N	7	8	.467	32	15	6	1	0	143	128	54	39	1	7	35	57	1.140	2.45	113	2.46	.245	5	.106	7	8	0.5
1918 NY-A	2	4	.333	11	3	1	0	0	48	47	21	16	0	3	16	14	1.313	3.00	94	3.23	.269	0	.000	-2	2	-0.5
Total 6	42	37	.532	150	73	32	3	2	701^1	646	269	197	6	32	159	238	1.148	2.53	117	2.58	.254	37	.170	34	47	3.1

• ROBINSON, Humberto Humberto Valentino Robinson b: 6/25/1930, Colon, Panama BR/TR, 6'1", 155 lbs. Deb: 4/20/1955

YEAR TM-L	W	L	PCT	G	GS	CG	SH	SV	IP	H	R	ER	HR	HB	BB	SO	RAT	ERA	ERA+	CERA	OAV	BH	AVG	PR+	WS	TPW
1955 Mil-N	3	1	.750	13	2	1	0	2	38	31	13	13	1	4	25	19	1.474	3.08	122	3.96	.235	1	.077	3	3	0.2
1956 Mil-N	0	0	....	1	0	0	0	0	2	1	0	0	0	0	2	0	1.500	0.00	....	2.80	.167	0	....	1	0	0.1
1958 Mil-N	2	4	.333	19	0	0	0	1	41^2	30	15	14	4	2	13	26	1.032	3.02	116	2.40	.203	1	.167	2	3	0.2
1959 Cle-A	1	0	1.000	5	0	0	0	0	8^2	9	4	4	0	0	4	6	1.500	4.15	89	3.72	.281	0	....	-1	1	-0.1
Phi-N	2	4	.333	31	4	1	0	1	73	70	36	27	6	0	24	32	1.288	3.33	123	3.29	.251	3	.231	7	5	0.8
1960 Phi-N	0	4	.000	33	1	0	0	0	49^2	48	24	19	6	0	22	31	1.409	3.44	113	4.03	.255	1	.167	2	3	0.2
Total 5	8	13	.381	102	7	2	0	4	213	189	92	77	17	6	90	114	1.310	3.25	118	3.42	.241	6	.158	14	15	1.4

• ROBINSON, Jack John Edward Robinson b: 2/20/1921, Orange, NJ d: 3/2/2000, Ormond Beach, FL BR/TR, 6', 175 lbs. Deb: 5/4/1949

YEAR TM-L	W	L	PCT	G	GS	CG	SH	SV	IP	H	R	ER	HR	HB	BB	SO	RAT	ERA	ERA+	CERA	OAV	BH	AVG	PR+	WS	TPW
1949 Bos-A	0	0	....	3	0	0	0	0	4	4	1	1	0	1	1	1	1.250	2.25	194	3.74	.267	0	....	1	0	0.1

• ROBINSON, Jeff Jeffrey Daniel Robinson b: 12/13/1960, Santa Ana, CA BR/TR, 6'4", 200 lbs. Deb: 4/7/1984

YEAR TM-L	W	L	PCT	G	GS	CG	SH	SV	IP	H	R	ER	HR	HB	BB	SO	RAT	ERA	ERA+	CERA	OAV	BH	AVG	PR+	WS	TPW
1984 SF-N	7	15	.318	34	33	1	1	0	171^2	195	99	87	12	7	52	102	1.439	4.56	77	4.38	.288	7	.115	-16	3	-1.8
1985 SF-N	0	0	....	8	0	0	0	0	12^1	16	11	7	2	0	10	8	2.108	5.11	67	8.38	.333	0	....	-2	0	-0.2
1986 SF-N	6	3	.667	64	1	0	0	8	104^1	92	46	39	8	1	32	90	1.188	3.36	105	2.86	.234	1	.067	0	7	-0.1
1987 SF-N	6	8	.429	63	0	0	0	10	96^2	69	34	30	10	1	48	82	1.210	2.79	138	2.87	.207	2	.111	10	10	0.9
Pit-N	2	1	.667	18	0	0	0	4	26^2	20	9	9	1	0	6	19	.975	3.04	135	1.86	.215	1	.250	3	5	0.4
Yr.	8	9	.471	81	0	0	0	14	123^1	89	43	39	11	1	54	101	1.159	2.85	137	2.65	.209	3	.136	13	15	1.3
1988 Pit-N	11	5	.688	75	0	0	0	9	124^2	113	44	42	6	3	39	87	1.219	3.03	112	2.96	.244	3	.188	4	12	0.5
1989 Pit-N	7	13	.350	50	19	0	0	4	141^1	161	92	72	14	1	59	95	1.557	4.58	73	4.73	.283	8	.229	-19	1	-1.9
1990 NY-A	3	6	.333	54	4	1	0	0	88^2	82	35	34	8	1	34	43	1.308	3.45	115	3.56	.248	0	....	5	6	0.5
1991 Cal-A	0	3	.000	39	0	0	0	3	57	56	34	34	9	2	29	57	1.491	5.37	76	4.87	.259	0	....	-9	1	-0.9
1992 Chi-N	4	3	.571	49	5	0	0	1	78	76	29	26	5	2	40	46	1.487	3.00	120	4.18	.263	0	.000	5	6	0.4
Total 9	46	57	.447	454	62	2	1	39	901^1	880	433	380	75	18	349	629	1.364	3.79	95	3.81	.258	22	.137	-19	51	-2.2

• ROBINSON, Jeff Jeffrey Mark Robinson b: 12/14/1961, Ventura, CA BR/TR, 6'6", 240 lbs. Deb: 4/12/1987

YEAR TM-L	W	L	PCT	G	GS	CG	SH	SV	IP	H	R	ER	HR	HB	BB	SO	RAT	ERA	ERA+	CERA	OAV	BH	AVG	PR+	WS	TPW
1987* Det-A	9	6	.600	29	21	2	1	0	127^1	132	86	76	16	7	54	98	1.461	5.37	79	4.69	.262	0	....	-17	4	-1.6
1988 Det-A	13	6	.684	24	23	6	2	0	172	121	61	57	19	3	72	114	1.122	2.98	128	2.68	**.197**	0	....	15	14	1.5
1989 Det-A	4	5	.444	16	16	1	1	0	78	76	47	41	10	1	46	40	1.564	4.73	81	4.96	.259	0	....	-7	2	-0.7
1990 Det-A	10	9	.526	27	27	1	1	0	145	141	101	96	23	6	88	76	1.579	5.96	66	5.27	.255	0	....	-36	1	-3.6
1991 Bal-A	4	9	.308	21	19	0	0	0	104^1	119	62	60	12	6	51	65	1.629	5.18	76	5.65	.289	0	....	-15	2	-1.5
1992 Tex-A	4	4	.500	16	4	0	0	0	45^2	50	30	29	6	0	21	18	1.555	5.72	66	5.07	.281	0	....	-9	1	-0.9
Pit-N	3	1	.750	8	7	0	0	0	36^1	33	18	18	2	1	15	14	1.321	4.46	77	3.49	.244	1	.091	-4	1	-0.5
Total 6	47	40	.540	141	117	10	5	0	708^2	672	405	377	88	24	347	425	1.438	4.79	82	4.46	.250	1	.091	-73	25	-7.4

• ROBINSON, Kenny Kenneth Neal Robinson b: 11/3/1969, Barberton, OH d: 2/28/1999, Tucson, AZ BR/TR, 5'9", 175 lbs. Deb: 7/20/1995

YEAR TM-L	W	L	PCT	G	GS	CG	SH	SV	IP	H	R	ER	HR	HB	BB	SO	RAT	ERA	ERA+	CERA	OAV	BH	AVG	PR+	WS	TPW
1995 Tor-A	1	2	.333	21	0	0	0	0	39	25	21	16	7	2	22	31	1.205	3.69	127	3.36	.179	0	....	4	2	0.4
1996 KC-A	1	0	1.000	5	0	0	0	0	6	9	4	4	0	0	3	5	2.000	6.00	84	6.14	.346	0	....	-1	0	-0.1
1997 Tor-A	0	0	....	3	0	0	0	0	3^1	1	1	1	1	0	1	4	.600	2.70	170	1.52	.100	0	....	1	0	0.1
Total 3	2	2	.500	29	0	0	0	0	48^1	35	26	21	8	2	26	40	1.262	3.91	122	3.58	.199	0	....	4	2	0.4

• ROBINSON, Ron Ronald Dean Robinson b: 3/24/1962, Exeter, CA BR/TR, 6'4", 235 lbs. Deb: 8/14/1984

YEAR TM-L	W	L	PCT	G	GS	CG	SH	SV	IP	H	R	ER	HR	HB	BB	SO	RAT	ERA	ERA+	CERA	OAV	BH	AVG	PR+	WS	TPW
1984 Cin-N	1	2	.333	12	5	1	0	0	39^2	35	18	12	3	0	13	24	1.210	2.72	139	2.85	.232	0	.000	5	3	0.4
1985 Cin-N	7	7	.500	33	12	0	0	1	108^1	107	53	48	11	1	32	76	1.283	3.99	95	3.63	.259	2	.091	-3	5	-0.5
1986 Cin-N	10	3	.769	70	0	0	0	14	116^2	110	44	42	10	2	43	117	1.311	3.24	119	3.57	.253	1	.071	9	13	0.8
1987 Cin-N	7	5	.583	48	18	0	0	4	154	148	71	63	14	1	43	99	1.240	3.68	115	3.30	.256	7	.194	9	11	0.9
1988 Cin-N	3	7	.300	17	16	0	0	0	78^2	88	47	36	5	2	26	38	1.449	4.12	87	4.18	.285	5	.200	-6	1	-0.6
1989 Cin-N	5	3	.625	15	15	0	0	0	83^1	80	36	31	8	2	28	36	1.296	3.35	107	3.63	.252	6	.214	3	5	0.5
1990 Cin-N	2	2	.500	6	5	0	0	0	31^1	36	18	17	2	0	14	14	1.596	4.88	81	4.99	.295	1	.091	-4	1	-0.5
Mil-A	12	5	.706	22	22	7	2	0	148^1	158	60	48	5	6	37	57	1.315	2.91	133	3.57	.275	0	....	17	10	1.8
1991 Mil-A	0	1	.000	1	1	0	0	0	4^1	6	3	3	0	1	3	0	2.077	6.23	64	7.73	.353	0	....	-1	0	-0.1
1992 Mil-A	1	4	.200	8	8	0	0	0	35^1	51	26	23	3	2	14	12	1.840	5.86	65	6.75	.331	0	....	-9	0	-0.9
Total 9	48	39	.552	232	102	8	2	19	800	819	376	323	61	17	253	473	1.340	3.63	106	3.78	.267	22	.153	20	49	1.9

• ROBINSON, Yank William H. Robinson b: 9/19/1859, Philadelphia, PA d: 8/25/1894, St. Louis, MO BR/TR, 5'6.5", 170 lbs. Deb: 8/24/1882 ♦

YEAR TM-L	W	L	PCT	G	GS	CG	SH	SV	IP	H	R	ER	HR	HB	BB	SO	RAT	ERA	ERA+	CERA	OAV	BH	AVG	PR+	WS	TPW
1882 Det-N	0	0	....	1	0	0	0	0	2	0	0	0	0	....	1	0	.500	0.00	....	....	.000	7	.179	1	0	-0.2
1884 Bal-U	3	3	.500	11	3	3	0	0	75	96	61	29	1	....	18	61	1.520	3.48	96	....	.292	111	.267	-2	24	2.1
1886* StL-a	0	1	.000	1	1	1	0	0	9	10	11	3	0	0	7	1	1.889	3.00	114	....	.269	132	.274	0	20	3.0
1887* StL-a	0	0	....	1	0	0	0	1	3	6	2	1	0	1	3	0	2.000	3.00	151	....	.401	223	.427	0	20	2.3
Total 4	3	4	.429	14	4	4	0	1	89	112	74	33	1	1	29	62	1.551	3.34	101	....	.294	917	.261	-1	64	7.1

• ROBITAILLE, Chick Joseph Anthony Robitaille b: 3/2/1879, Whitehall, NY d: 7/30/1947, Waterford, NY BR/TR, 5'8", 150 lbs. Deb: 9/2/1904

YEAR TM-L	W	L	PCT	G	GS	CG	SH	SV	IP	H	R	ER	HR	HB	BB	SO	RAT	ERA	ERA+	CERA	OAV	BH	AVG	PR+	WS	TPW
1904 Pit-N	4	3	.571	9	8	8	0	0	66	52	22	14	1	1	13	34	.985	1.91	143	1.73	.208	2	.095	6	5	0.4
1905 Pit-N	8	5	.615	17	12	10	0	0	120^1	126	54	39	1	3	28	32	1.280	2.92	103	3.25	.276	6	.133	-1	8	-0.4
Total 2	12	8	.600	26	20	18	0	0	186^1	178	76	53	2	4	41	66	1.175	2.56	114	2.71	.252	8	.121	4	13	0.1

• ROCHE, Armando Armando (Baez) Roche b: 12/7/1926, Havana, Cuba d: 6/27/1997, Chicago, IL BR/TR, 6', 190 lbs. Deb: 5/10/1945

YEAR TM-L	W	L	PCT	G	GS	CG	SH	SV	IP	H	R	ER	HR	HB	BB	SO	RAT	ERA	ERA+	CERA	OAV	BH	AVG	PR+	WS	TPW
1945 Was-A	0	0	....	2	0	0	0	0	6	10	4	4	0	0	2	0	2.000	6.00	52	7.23	.400	0	.000	-2	0	-0.2

• ROCHFORD, Mike Michael Joseph Rochford b: 3/14/1963, Methuen, MA BL/TL, 6'4", 205 lbs. Deb: 9/3/1988

YEAR TM-L	W	L	PCT	G	GS	CG	SH	SV	IP	H	R	ER	HR	HB	BB	SO	RAT	ERA	ERA+	CERA	OAV	BH	AVG	PR+	WS	TPW
1988 Bos-A	0	0	....	2	0	0	0	0	2^1	4	0	0	0	0	1	1	2.143	0.00	....	7.52	.364	0	....	1	0	0.1
1989 Bos-A	0	0	....	4	0	0	0	0	4	4	7	3	1	0	4	1	2.000	6.75	61	7.17	.267	0	....	-1	0	-0.1
1990 Bos-A	0	1	.000	2	1	0	0	0	4	10	10	8	1	0	4	0	3.500	18.00	23	19.41	.526	0	....	-6	0	-0.6
Total 3	0	1	.000	8	1	0	0	0	10^1	18	17	11	2	0	9	2	2.613	9.58	43	11.99	.400	0	....	-6	0	-0.6

• ROCKER, John John Loy Rocker b: 10/17/1974, Statesboro, GA BR/TL, 6'4", 225 lbs. Deb: 5/5/1998

YEAR TM-L	W	L	PCT	G	GS	CG	SH	SV	IP	H	R	ER	HR	HB	BB	SO	RAT	ERA	ERA+	CERA	OAV	BH	AVG	PR+	WS	TPW
1998* Atl-N	1	3	.250	47	0	0	0	2	38	22	10	9	4	3	22	42	1.158	2.13	195	2.73	.172	0	....	8	5	0.8
1999* Atl-N	4	5	.444	74	0	0	0	38	72^1	47	24	20	5	1	37	104	1.161	2.49	181	2.38	.180	0	....	17	16	1.6
2000* Atl-N	1	2	.333	59	0	0	0	24	53	42	25	17	5	2	48	77	1.698	2.89	159	4.72	.210	0	....	10	8	1.0
2001 Atl-N	2	2	.500	30	0	0	0	19	32	25	13	11	2	2	16	36	1.281	3.09	142	3.23	.216	0	....	4	6	0.4
*Cle-A	3	7	.300	38	0	0	0	4	34^2	33	23	21	2	3	25	43	1.673	5.45	83	4.79	.250	0	....	-3	2	-0.3
2002 Tex-A	2	3	.400	30	0	0	0	1	24^1	29	19	18	5	0	13	30	1.726	6.66	71	6.43	.299	0	....	-5	0	-0.5
2003 TB-A	0	0	....	2	0	0	0	0	1	2	1	1	0	1	3	0	5.000	9.00	50	29.64	.500	0	....	-1	0	0.0
Total 6	13	22	.371	280	0	0	0	88	255^1	200	115	97	23	12	164	332	1.426	3.42	132	3.85	.213	0	....	31	37	3.0

• RODAS, Rich Richard Martin Rodas b: 11/7/1959, Roseville, CA BL/TL, 6'2", 180 lbs. Deb: 9/6/1983

YEAR TM-L	W	L	PCT	G	GS	CG	SH	SV	IP	H	R	ER	HR	HB	BB	SO	RAT	ERA	ERA+	CERA	OAV	BH	AVG	PR+	WS	TPW
1983 LA-N	0	0	....	7	0	0	0	0	4^2	4	1	1	0	0	3	5	1.500	1.93	186	3.03	.222	0	....	1	0	0.1
1984 LA-N	0	0	....	3	0	0	0	0	5	5	3	3	2	0	1	1	1.200	5.40	65	5.11	.250	0	.000	-1	0	-0.1
Total 2	0	0	....	10	0	0	0	0	9^2	9	4	4	2	0	4	6	1.345	3.72	95	4.11	.237	0	.000	-0	0	0.0

• RODNEY, Fernando Fernando Rodney b: 3/17/1977, Santo Domingo, Dominican Republic BR/TR, 5'11", 170 lbs. Deb: 5/4/2002

YEAR TM-L	W	L	PCT	G	GS	CG	SH	SV	IP	H	R	ER	HR	HB	BB	SO	RAT	ERA	ERA+	CERA	OAV	BH	AVG	PR+	WS	TPW
2002 Det-A	1	3	.250	20	0	0	0	0	18	25	15	12	2	0	10	10	1.944	6.00	72	6.77	.329	0	....	-3	0	-0.3
2003 Det-A	1	3	.250	27	0	0	0	3	29^2	35	20	20	2	1	17	33	1.753	6.07	71	5.46	.294	0	....	-6	1	-0.6
Total 2	2	6	.250	47	0	0	0	3	47^2	60	35	32	4	1	27	43	1.825	6.04	71	5.95	.308	0	....	-9	1	-0.9

• RODRIGUEZ, Eduardo Eduardo (Reyes) Rodriguez b: 3/6/1952, Barceloneta, Puerto Rico BR/TR, 6', 185 lbs. Deb: 6/20/1973

YEAR TM-L	W	L	PCT	G	GS	CG	SH	SV	IP	H	R	ER	HR	HB	BB	SO	RAT	ERA	ERA+	CERA	OAV	BH	AVG	PR+	WS	TPW
1973 Mil-A	9	7	.563	30	6	2	0	5	76^1	71	33	28	6	2	47	49	1.546	3.30	114	4.30	.247	1	1.000	4	6	0.6
1974 Mil-A	7	4	.636	43	6	0	0	4	111^2	97	49	45	7	5	51	58	1.325	3.63	100	3.44	.240	0	....	-1	7	-0.1
1975 Mil-A	7	0	1.000	43	1	0	0	7	87^2	77	37	34	9	5	44	65	1.380	3.49	110	3.83	.235	0	....	4	8	0.4
1976 Mil-A	5	13	.278	45	12	3	0	8	136	124	68	55	10	3	65	77	1.390	3.64	96	3.74	.249	0	....	-2	6	-0.3
1977 Mil-A	5	6	.455	42	5	1	1	4	142^2	126	70	69	15	3	56	104	1.276	4.35	93	3.45	.236	0	....	-6	8	-0.6
1978 Mil-A	5	5	.500	32	8	0	0	2	105^1	107	49	46	9	2	26	51	1.263	3.93	96	3.44	.262	0	....	-2	6	-0.3
1979 KC-A	4	1	.800	29	1	1	0	2	74^1	79	42	40	9	3	34	26	1.520	4.84	88	4.92	.276	0	....	-6	4	-0.5
Total 7	42	36	.538	264	39	7	1	32	734	681	348	317	65	23	323	430	1.368	3.89	98	3.78	.248	1	1.000	-9	45	-0.7

• RODRIGUEZ, Felix Felix Antonio Rodriguez b: 12/5/1972, Monte Cristi, Dominican Republic BR/TR, 6'1", 170 lbs. Deb: 5/13/1995

YEAR TM-L	W	L	PCT	G	GS	CG	SH	SV	IP	H	R	ER	HR	HB	BB	SO	RAT	ERA	ERA+	CERA	OAV	BH	AVG	PR+	WS	TPW
1995 LA-N	1	1	.500	11	0	0	0	0	10^2	11	3	3	2	0	5	5	1.500	2.53	150	5.43	.275	0	....	1	1	0.1
1997 Cin-N	0	0	....	26	1	0	0	0	46	48	23	22	2	6	28	34	1.652	4.30	100	5.22	.271	0	.000	-0	2	0.0
1998 Ari-N	0	2	.000	43	0	0	0	5	44	44	31	30	5	1	29	36	1.659	6.14	69	5.11	.259	0	....	-9	1	-0.9
1999 SF-N	2	3	.400	47	0	0	0	0	66^1	67	32	28	6	2	29	55	1.447	3.80	111	4.25	.262	2	.333	3	4	0.5
2000* SF-N	4	2	.667	76	0	0	0	3	81^2	65	29	24	5	3	42	95	1.310	2.64	160	3.26	.220	0	.000	14	9	1.3
2001 SF-N	9	1	.900	80	0	0	0	0	80^1	53	16	15	5	1	27	91	.996	1.68	237	1.92	.188	0	....	20	12	2.0
2002* SF-N	8	6	.571	71	0	0	0	0	69	53	33	32	5	4	29	58	1.188	4.17	93	2.92	.212	1	1.000	-3	5	-0.3
2003* SF-N	8	2	.800	68	0	0	0	2	61	59	21	21	5	4	29	46	1.443	3.10	132	4.33	.259	1	1.000	5	8	0.6
Total 8	32	17	.653	422	1	0	0	10	459	400	188	175	35	21	218	420	1.346	3.43	120	3.69	.235	4	.267	32	42	3.3

• RODRIGUEZ, Francisco Francisco Jose Rodriguez b: 1/7/1982, Caracas, Venezuela BR/TR, 6', 175 lbs. Deb: 9/18/2002

YEAR TM-L	W	L	PCT	G	GS	CG	SH	SV	IP	H	R	ER	HR	HB	BB	SO	RAT	ERA	ERA+	CERA	OAV	BH	AVG	PR+	WS	TPW
2002* Ana-A	0	0	....	5	0	0	0	0	5^2	3	0	0	0	1	2	13	.882	0.00	....	1.52	.167	0	....	3	1	0.3
2003 Ana-A	8	3	.727	59	0	0	0	2	86	50	30	29	12	2	35	95	.988	3.03	142	2.25	.172	0	....	11	9	1.1
Total 2	8	3	.727	64	0	0	0	2	91^2	53	30	29	12	3	37	108	.982	2.85	151	2.20	.172	0	....	14	10	1.3

• RODRIGUEZ, Frank Francisco Rodriguez b: 12/11/1972, Brooklyn, NY BR/TR, 6', 190 lbs. Deb: 4/26/1995

YEAR TM-L	W	L	PCT	G	GS	CG	SH	SV	IP	H	R	ER	HR	HB	BB	SO	RAT	ERA	ERA+	CERA	OAV	BH	AVG	PR+	WS	TPW
1995 Bos-A	0	2	.000	9	2	0	0	0	15^1	21	19	18	3	0	10	14	2.022	10.57	46	8.13	.323	0	....	-10	0	-0.9
Min-A	5	6	.455	16	16	0	0	0	90^1	93	64	54	8	5	47	45	1.550	5.38	89	4.91	.269	0	....	-6	3	-0.6
Yr.	5	8	.385	25	18	0	0	0	105^2	114	83	72	11	5	57	59	1.618	6.13	78	5.38	.277	0	....	-16	3	-1.5
1996 Min-A	13	14	.481	38	33	3	0	2	206^2	218	129	116	27	5	78	110	1.432	5.05	101	4.62	.272	0	....	-0	11	0.0
1997 Min-A	3	6	.333	43	15	0	0	0	142^1	147	82	73	12	4	60	65	1.454	4.62	101	4.32	.271	0	.000	1	6	0.0
1998 Min-A	4	6	.400	20	11	0	0	0	70	88	58	51	6	3	30	62	1.686	6.56	73	5.65	.303	0	....	-13	0	-1.2
1999 Sea-A	2	4	.333	28	5	0	0	3	73^1	94	47	46	11	4	30	47	1.691	5.65	88	6.48	.314	1	.333	-5	3	-0.5
2000 Sea-A	2	1	.667	23	0	0	0	0	47^1	60	33	33	8	0	22	19	1.732	6.27	72	6.60	.317	0	.000	-10	1	-0.9
2001 Cin-N	0	0	....	7	0	0	0	0	8^2	16	12	11	1	0	5	9	2.423	11.42	40	9.65	.400	0	.000	-6	0	-0.6
Total 7	29	39	.426	184	82	3	0	5	654	737	444	402	76	21	282	371	1.558	5.53	88	5.21	.286	1	.167	-50	24	-4.7

• RODRIGUEZ, Freddy Fernando Pedro (Borrego) Rodriguez b: 4/29/1924, Havana, Cuba BR/TR, 6', 180 lbs. Deb: 4/18/1958

YEAR TM-L	W	L	PCT	G	GS	CG	SH	SV	IP	H	R	ER	HR	HB	BB	SO	RAT	ERA	ERA+	CERA	OAV	BH	AVG	PR+	WS	TPW
1958 Chi-N	0	0	....	7	0	0	0	2	7^1	8	6	6	2	1	5	5	1.773	7.36	53	7.64	.267	0	.000	-3	0	-0.3
1959 Phi-N	0	0	....	1	0	0	0	0	2	4	3	3	1	1	0	1	2.000	13.50	30	14.72	.400	0	....	-2	0	-0.2
Total 2	0	0	....	8	0	0	0	2	9^1	12	9	9	3	2	5	6	1.821	8.68	46	9.16	.300	0	.000	-5	0	-0.5

• RODRIGUEZ, Jose Jose Ilich Rodriguez b: 12/18/1974, Cayey, Puerto Rico BL/TL, 6'1", 215 lbs. Deb: 5/18/2000

YEAR TM-L	W	L	PCT	G	GS	CG	SH	SV	IP	H	R	ER	HR	HB	BB	SO	RAT	ERA	ERA+	CERA	OAV	BH	AVG	PR+	WS	TPW
2000 StL-N	0	0	....	6	0	0	0	0	4	2	2	0	0	1	3	2	1.250	0.00	....	2.62	.143	0	.000	2	1	0.2
2002 StL-N	0	0	....	2	0	0	0	0	0^1	4	2	2	0	0	2	0	18.00	54.00	7	128.76	.800	0	....	-2	0	-0.2
Min-A	0	1	.000	4	0	0	0	0	3^2	8	6	6	0	0	4	1	3.273	14.73	30	13.03	.421	0	....	-4	0	-0.4
Total 2	0	1	.000	12	0	0	0	0	8	14	10	8	0	1	9	3	2.875	9.00	48	12.65	.368	0	.000	-4	1	-0.4

• RODRIGUEZ, Nerio Nerio Rodriguez b: 3/4/1971, San Pedro de Macoris, Dominican Republic BR/TR, 6'1", 195 lbs. Deb: 8/16/1996

YEAR TM-L	W	L	PCT	G	GS	CG	SH	SV	IP	H	R	ER	HR	HB	BB	SO	RAT	ERA	ERA+	CERA	OAV	BH	AVG	PR+	WS	TPW
1996 Bal-A	0	1	.000	8	1	0	0	0	16^2	18	11	8	2	1	7	12	1.500	4.32	114	4.81	.265	0	....	1	1	0.1
1997 Bal-A	2	1	.667	6	2	0	0	0	22	21	15	12	2	1	8	11	1.318	4.91	90	3.62	.250	0	....	-1	1	-0.1
1998 Bal-A	1	3	.250	6	4	0	0	0	19	25	17	17	0	0	9	8	1.789	8.05	57	5.41	.321	0	....	-7	0	-0.7
Tor-A	1	0	1.000	7	0	0	0	0	8^1	10	9	9	1	1	8	3	2.160	9.72	48	8.14	.286	0	....	-5	0	-0.4
Yr.	2	3	.400	13	4	0	0	0	27^1	35	26	26	1	1	17	11	1.902	8.56	54	6.24	.310	0	....	-12	0	-1.1
1999 Tor-A	0	1	.000	2	0	0	0	0	2	2	3	3	2	0	2	2	2.000	13.50	36	14.27	.250	0	....	-2	0	-0.2
2002 Cle-A	0	0	....	1	0	0	0	0	0^1	0	0	0	0	0	0	0	.000	0.00	....	0.00	.000	0	....	0	0	0.0
StL-N	0	0	....	2	0	0	0	0	4^1	4	3	2	1	0	1	2	1.154	4.15	95	3.52	.222	0	.000	-0	0	0.0
Total 5	4	6	.400	32	7	0	0	0	72^2	80	58	51	8	3	35	38	1.583	6.32	73	5.15	.275	0	.000	-14	2	-1.3

• RODRIGUEZ, Ricardo Ricardo Antonio Rodriguez b: 5/21/1979, Guayubin, Dominican Republic BR/TR, 6'3", 165 lbs. Deb: 8/21/2002

YEAR TM-L	W	L	PCT	G	GS	CG	SH	SV	IP	H	R	ER	HR	HB	BB	SO	RAT	ERA	ERA+	CERA	OAV	BH	AVG	PR+	WS	TPW
2002 Cle-A	2	2	.500	7	7	0	0	0	41^1	40	27	26	5	8	18	24	1.403	5.66	78	4.92	.255	0	....	-5	1	-0.5
2003 Cle-A	3	9	.250	15	15	0	0	0	81^2	89	57	52	16	3	28	41	1.433	5.73	77	5.14	.275	0	.000	-14	1	-1.3
Total 2	5	11	.313	22	22	0	0	0	123	129	84	78	21	11	46	65	1.423	5.71	77	5.07	.268	0	.000	-19	2	-1.8

• RODRIGUEZ, Rich Richard Anthony Rodriguez b: 3/1/1963, Downey, CA BL/TL, 5'10", 200 lbs. Deb: 6/30/1990

YEAR TM-L	W	L	PCT	G	GS	CG	SH	SV	IP	H	R	ER	HR	HB	BB	SO	RAT	ERA	ERA+	CERA	OAV	BH	AVG	PR+	WS	TPW
1990 SD-N	1	1	.500	32	0	0	0	1	47^2	52	17	15	2	1	16	22	1.427	2.83	135	3.99	.287	0	.000	5	4	0.5
1991 SD-N	3	1	.750	64	1	0	0	0	80	66	31	29	8	0	44	40	1.375	3.26	116	3.63	.234	0	.000	4	6	0.4
1992 SD-N	6	3	.667	61	1	0	0	0	91	77	28	24	4	0	29	64	1.165	2.37	151	2.56	.229	0	.000	12	9	1.3
1993 SD-N	2	3	.400	34	0	0	0	2	30	34	15	11	2	1	9	22	1.433	3.30	125	4.08	.281	0	....	3	2	0.3
Fla-N	0	1	.000	36	0	0	0	1	46	39	23	21	8	1	24	21	1.370	4.11	105	4.14	.229	0	.000	2	2	0.2
Yr.	2	4	.333	70	0	0	0	3	76	73	38	32	10	2	33	43	1.395	3.79	112	4.12	.251	0	.000	5	4	0.5
1994 StL-N	3	5	.375	56	0	0	0	0	60^1	62	30	27	6	1	26	43	1.459	4.03	103	4.38	.270	0	.000	1	4	0.1
1995 StL-N	0	0	....	1	0	0	0	0	1^2	0	0	0	0	0	0	0	.000	0.00	....	0.00	.000	0	....	1	0	0.1
1997* SF-N	4	3	.571	71	0	0	0	1	65^1	65	24	23	7	1	21	32	1.316	3.17	128	3.85	.264	1	.333	7	6	0.7
1998 SF-N	4	0	1.000	68	0	0	0	2	65^2	69	28	27	7	0	20	44	1.355	3.70	107	3.94	.272	1	.167	2	5	0.2
1999 SF-N	3	0	1.000	62	0	0	0	0	56^2	60	33	33	8	1	28	44	1.553	5.24	80	4.98	.274	1	1.000	-7	3	-0.6
2000 NY-N	0	1	.000	32	0	0	0	0	37	59	40	32	7	3	15	18	2.000	7.78	57	8.86	.364	0	.000	-14	0	-1.3
2001 Cle-A	2	2	.500	53	0	0	0	0	39	41	24	18	2	2	17	31	1.487	4.15	109	4.19	.270	0	....	2	2	0.2
2002 Tex-A	3	2	.600	36	0	0	0	1	16^2	14	10	10	1	1	11	12	1.500	5.40	87	4.17	.237	0	....	-1	1	-0.1
2003 Ana-A	0	0	....	3	0	0	0	0	3^2	4	1	1	0	0	1	3	1.364	2.45	176	3.55	.308	0	....	1	0	0.1
Total 13	31	22	.585	609	2	0	0	8	640^2	642	304	271	62	12	261	396	1.409	3.81	108	4.15	.265	3	.107	19	44	2.1

• RODRIGUEZ, Rick Ricardo Rodriguez b: 9/21/1960, Oakland, CA BR/TR, 6'3", 190 lbs. Deb: 9/17/1986

YEAR TM-L	W	L	PCT	G	GS	CG	SH	SV	IP	H	R	ER	HR	HB	BB	SO	RAT	ERA	ERA+	CERA	OAV	BH	AVG	PR+	WS	TPW
1986 Oak-A	1	2	.333	3	3	0	0	0	16^1	17	12	12	4	0	7	2	1.469	6.61	58	5.44	.262	0	....	-5	0	-0.5
1987 Oak-A	1	0	1.000	15	0	0	0	0	24^1	32	8	8	1	1	15	9	1.932	2.96	139	6.82	.337	0	....	3	2	0.3
1988 Cle-A	1	2	.333	10	5	0	0	0	33	43	28	26	4	1	17	9	1.818	7.09	58	6.62	.323	0	....	-10	0	-1.0
1990 SF-N	0	0	....	3	0	0	0	0	3^1	5	3	3	0	0	2	2	2.100	8.10	45	7.36	.357	0	....	-2	0	-0.2
Total 4	3	4	.429	31	8	0	0	0	77	97	51	49	9	2	41	22	1.792	5.73	70	6.47	.316	0	....	-14	2	-1.4

• RODRIGUEZ, Roberto Roberto (Munoz) Rodriguez b: 11/29/1941, Caracas, Venezuela BR/TR, 6'3", 185 lbs. Deb: 5/13/1967

YEAR TM-L	W	L	PCT	G	GS	CG	SH	SV	IP	H	R	ER	HR	HB	BB	SO	RAT	ERA	ERA+	CERA	OAV	BH	AVG	PR+	WS	TPW
1967 KC-A	1	1	.500	15	5	0	0	2	40^1	42	17	16	4	1	14	29	1.388	3.57	89	4.10	.268	0	.000	-2	2	-0.3
1970 Oak-A	0	0	....	6	0	0	0	0	12^1	10	5	4	2	0	3	8	1.054	2.92	121	2.95	.227	0	.000	1	1	0.1
SD-N	0	0	....	10	0	0	0	3	16^1	26	16	12	1	0	5	8	1.898	6.61	60	7.05	.366	0	.000	-5	0	-0.5
Chi-N	3	2	.600	26	0	0	0	2	43^1	50	33	28	6	0	15	46	1.500	5.82	77	4.88	.289	1	.125	-6	1	-0.6
Yr.	3	2	.600	36	0	0	0	5	59^2	76	49	40	7	0	20	54	1.609	6.03	72	5.47	.311	1	.091	-11	1	-1.1
Total 2	4	3	.571	57	5	0	0	7	112^1	128	71	60	13	1	37	91	1.469	4.81	81	4.70	.288	1	.048	-12	4	-1.3

• RODRIGUEZ, Rosario Rosario Isabel (Echavarria) Rodriguez b: 7/8/1969, Los Mochis, Mexico BR/TL, 6', 185 lbs. Deb: 9/1/1989

YEAR TM-L	W	L	PCT	G	GS	CG	SH	SV	IP	H	R	ER	HR	HB	BB	SO	RAT	ERA	ERA+	CERA	OAV	BH	AVG	PR+	WS	TPW
1989 Cin-N	1	1	.500	7	0	0	0	0	4^1	3	2	2	0	0	3	0	1.385	4.15	87	2.37	.188	0	....	-0	0	0.0

YEAR TM-L	W	L	PCT	G	GS	CG	SH	SV	IP	H	R	ER	HR	HB	BB	SO	RAT	ERA	ERA+	CERA	OAV	BH	AVG	PR+	WS	TPW
1990 Cin-N	0	0	....	9	0	0	0	0	10^{1}	15	7	7	3	1	2	8	1.645	6.10	65	8.03	.357	0	....	-3	0	-0.3
1991* Pit-N	1	1	.500	18	0	0	0	6	15^{1}	14	7	7	1	1	8	10	1.435	4.11	87	4.10	.246	0	.000	-1	1	-0.1
Total 3	2	2	.500	34	0	0	0	6	30	32	16	16	4	2	13	18	1.500	4.80	78	5.20	.278	0	.000	-4	1	-0.4
• RODRIGUEZ, Wilfredo	Wilfredo Jose Rodriguez b: 3/20/1979, Ciudad Bolivar, Venezuela BL/TL, 6'3", 180 lbs. Deb: 9/21/2001																									
2001 Hou-N	0	0	....	2	0	0	0	0	3	6	5	5	2	0	1	3	2.333	15.00	30	15.38	.429	0	....	-3	0	-0.3
• ROE, Clay	James Clay "Shad" Roe b: 1/7/1904, Green Brier, TN d: 4/3/1956, Cleveland, MS BL/TL, 6'1", 180 lbs. Deb: 10/3/1923																									
1923 Was-A	0	1	.000	1	1	0	0	0	1^{2}	0	4	0	0	0	6	2	3.600	0.00	....	7.14	.000	0	....	1	0	0.1
• ROE, Preacher	Elwin Charles Roe b: 2/26/1915, Ash Flat, AR BR/TL, 6'2", 170 lbs. Deb: 8/22/1938																									
1938 StL-N	0	0	....	1	0	0	0	0	2^{2}	6	4	4	0	0	2	1	3.000	13.50	29	12.35	.429	0	.000	-3	0	-0.3
1944 Pit-N	13	11	.542	39	25	7	1	1	185^{1}	182	82	64	7	2	59	88	1.300	3.11	120	3.15	.253	7	.132	14	13	1.2
1945 Pit-N★	14	13	.519	33	31	15	3	1	235	228	77	75	11	1	46	**148**	1.166	2.87	137	2.86	.259	8	.107	**30**	20	2.7
1946 Pit-N	3	8	.273	21	10	1	0	2	70	83	50	40	5	2	25	28	1.543	5.14	69	4.73	.294	1	.067	-12	0	-1.3
1947 Pit-N	4	15	.211	38	22	4	1	2	144	156	93	84	19	0	63	59	1.521	5.25	80	4.84	.276	5	.125	-15	3	-1.7
1948 Bro-N	12	8	.600	34	22	8	2	2	177^{2}	156	60	52	14	2	33	86	1.064	2.63	152	2.49	.233	5	.098	23	16	2.1
1949* Bro-N★	15	6	.714	30	27	13	3	1	212^{2}	201	69	66	25	2	44	109	1.152	2.79	147	3.22	.252	8	.114	27	19	2.5
1950 Bro-N★	19	11	.633	36	32	16	2	1	250^{2}	245	96	92	34	4	66	125	1.241	3.30	124	3.73	.257	14	.154	16	21	1.3
1951 Bro-N★	22	3	.880	34	33	19	2	0	257^{2}	247	91	87	30	0	64	113	1.207	3.04	129	3.44	.258	10	.112	20	21	1.5
1952* Bro-N★	11	2	.846	27	25	8	2	0	158^{2}	163	59	55	16	3	39	83	1.273	3.12	117	3.75	.270	4	.070	8	12	0.5
1953* Bro-N	11	3	.786	25	24	9	1	0	157	171	78	76	27	1	40	85	1.344	4.36	98	4.52	.278	3	.053	-4	9	-0.8
1954 Bro-N	3	4	.429	15	10	1	0	0	63	69	40	35	11	0	23	31	1.460	5.00	82	4.93	.279	3	.143	-6	2	-0.6
Total 12	127	84	.602	333	261	101	17	10	1914^{1}	1907	799	730	199	17	504	956	1.259	3.43	116	3.59	.261	68	.110	98	136	7.1
• ROEBUCK, Ed	Edward Jack Roebuck b: 7/3/1931, East Millsboro, PA BR/TR, 6'2", 185 lbs. Deb: 4/18/1955																									
1955* Bro-N	5	6	.455	47	0	0	0	12	84	96	51	44	14	3	24	33	1.429	4.71	86	4.95	.288	2	.111	-7	4	-0.8
1956* Bro-N	5	4	.556	43	0	0	0	1	89^{1}	83	49	39	15	2	29	60	1.254	3.93	101	3.95	.251	6	.333	-1	5	0.0
1957 Bro-N	8	2	.800	44	1	0	0	8	96^{1}	70	37	29	9	2	46	73	1.204	2.71	154	2.89	.205	5	.238	16	12	1.9
1958 LA-N	0	1	.000	32	0	0	0	5	44	45	22	17	9	2	15	26	1.364	3.48	118	4.84	.271	2	.500	3	4	0.4
1960 LA-N	8	3	.727	58	0	0	0	8	116^{2}	109	42	36	13	0	38	77	1.260	2.78	143	3.48	.256	4	.167	14	13	1.5
1961 LA-N	2	0	1.000	5	0	0	0	0	9	12	5	5	1	0	2	9	1.556	5.00	87	5.53	.324	0	.000	-1	1	-0.1
1962 LA-N	10	2	.833	64	0	0	0	9	119^{1}	102	60	41	11	6	54	72	1.307	3.09	117	3.52	.232	6	.214	7	9	0.7
1963 LA-N	2	4	.333	29	0	0	0	0	40^{1}	54	25	19	4	2	21	26	1.860	4.24	71	6.43	.321	1	.250	-5	0	-0.5
Was-A	2	1	.667	26	0	0	0	4	57^{1}	63	27	21	5	2	29	25	1.605	3.30	113	5.07	.284	2	.182	3	4	0.3
1964 Was-A	0	0	....	2	0	0	0	0	1	0	1	1	0	0	2	0	2.000	9.00	41	2.80	.000	0	....	-1	0	-0.1
Phi-N	5	3	.625	60	0	0	0	12	77^{1}	55	21	19	7	4	25	42	1.034	2.21	157	2.29	.196	0	.000	10	11	1.0
1965 Phi-N	5	3	.625	44	0	0	0	3	50^{1}	55	27	19	2	5	15	29	1.391	3.40	102	3.95	.288	0	.000	0	4	0.0
1966 Phi-N	0	2	.000	6	0	0	0	0	6	9	7	4	0	0	2	5	1.833	6.00	60	5.39	.333	0	....	-2	0	-0.2
Total 11	52	31	.627	460	1	0	0	62	791	753	374	294	90	28	302	477	1.334	3.35	113	3.92	.254	28	.204	38	67	4.2
• ROESLER, Mike	Michael Joseph Roesler b: 9/12/1963, Fort Wayne, IN BR/TR, 6'5", 195 lbs. Deb: 8/9/1989																									
1989 Cin-N	0	1	.000	17	0	0	0	0	25	22	11	11	4	0	9	14	1.240	3.96	91	3.69	.239	0	....	-1	1	-0.1
1990 Pit-N	1	0	1.000	5	0	0	0	0	6	5	2	2	1	0	2	4	1.167	3.00	121	3.28	.217	0	.000	0	1	0.0
Total 2	1	1	.500	22	0	0	0	0	31	27	13	13	5	0	11	18	1.226	3.77	95	3.61	.235	0	.000	-0	2	-0.1
• ROETTGER, Oscar	Oscar Frederick Louis "Okkie" Roettger b: 2/19/1900, St. Louis, MO d: 7/4/1986, St. Louis, MO BR/TR, 6', 170 lbs. Deb: 7/7/1923 ♦																									
1923 NY-A	0	0	....	5	0	0	0	1	11^{2}	16	15	11	3	0	12	7	2.400	8.49	46	10.38	.340	0	.000	-6	0	-0.6
1924 NY-A	0	0	....	1	0	0	0	0	0	1	0	0	0	0	2	0	....	....	....	∞	1.000	0	....	0	0	0.0
Total 2	0	0	....	6	0	0	0	1	11^{2}	17	15	11	3	0	14	7	2.657	8.49	46	10.38	.354	14	.212	-6	0	-0.6
• ROGALSKI, Joe	Joseph Anthony Rogalski b: 7/15/1912, Ashland, WI d: 11/20/1951, Ashland, WI BR/TR, 6'2", 187 lbs. Deb: 9/14/1938																									
1938 Det-A	0	0	....	2	0	0	0	0	7	12	4	2	0	0	0	2	1.714	2.57	195	6.33	.400	0	.000	2	1	0.1
• ROGERS, Buck	Orlin Woodrow "Lefty" Rogers b: 11/5/1912, Spring Garden, VA d: 2/20/1999, Winston-Salem, NC BR/TL, 5'8.5", 164 lbs. Deb: 9/15/1935																									
1935 Was-A	0	1	.000	2	1	0	0	0	10	16	15	8	0	0	6	7	2.200	7.20	60	7.18	.340	0	.000	-3	0	-0.3
• ROGERS, Jimmy	James Randall Rogers b: 1/3/1967, Tulsa, OK BR/TR, 6'2", 190 lbs. Deb: 7/30/1995																									
1995 Tor-A	2	4	.333	19	0	0	0	0	23^{2}	21	15	15	4	0	18	13	1.648	5.70	82	4.98	.239	0	....	-3	1	-0.3
• ROGERS, Kenny	Kenneth Scott Rogers b: 11/10/1964, Savannah, GA BL/TL, 6'1", 205 lbs. Deb: 4/6/1989																									
1989 Tex-A	3	4	.429	73	0	0	0	2	73^{2}	60	28	24	2	4	42	63	1.385	2.93	135	3.26	.232	0	....	9	7	0.9
1990 Tex-A	10	6	.625	69	3	0	0	15	97^{2}	93	40	34	6	1	42	74	1.382	3.13	125	3.53	.249	0	....	8	12	0.8
1991 Tex-A	10	10	.500	63	9	0	0	5	109^{2}	121	80	66	14	6	61	73	1.660	5.42	74	5.57	.281	0	....	-15	2	-1.5
1992 Tex-A	3	6	.333	**81**	0	0	0	6	78^{2}	80	32	27	7	0	26	70	1.347	3.09	123	3.63	.261	0	....	8	7	0.8
1993 Tex-A	16	10	.615	35	33	5	0	0	208^{1}	210	108	95	18	4	71	140	1.349	4.10	101	3.88	.263	0	....	5	11	0.5
1994 Tex-A	11	8	.579	24	24	6	2	0	167^{1}	169	93	83	24	3	52	120	1.321	4.46	108	4.12	.260	0	....	11	9	1.0
1995 Tex-A★	17	7	.708	31	31	3	1	0	208	192	87	78	26	2	76	140	1.288	3.38	143	3.72	.243	0	....	34	21	3.2
1996* NY-A	12	8	.600	30	30	2	1	0	179	179	97	93	16	8	83	92	1.464	4.68	106	4.43	.261	0	....	9	11	0.8
1997 NY-A	6	7	.462	31	22	1	0	0	145	161	100	91	18	7	62	78	1.538	5.65	79	5.18	.280	0	.000	-18	2	-1.7
1998 Oak-A	16	8	.667	34	34	7	1	0	238^{2}	215	96	84	19	7	67	138	1.182	3.17	144	3.13	.242	0	.000	40	19	3.7
1999 Oak-A	5	3	.625	19	19	3	0	0	119^{1}	135	66	57	8	9	41	68	1.475	4.30	108	4.68	.288	0	.000	5	7	0.5
* NY-N	5	1	.833	12	12	2	1	0	76	71	35	34	8	4	28	58	1.303	4.03	109	3.91	.253	3	.120	2	5	0.2
2000 Tex-A	13	13	.500	34	34	2	0	0	227^{1}	257	126	115	20	11	78	127	1.474	4.55	110	4.72	.285	2	.500	16	15	1.5
2001 Tex-A	5	7	.417	20	20	0	0	0	120^{2}	150	88	83	18	8	49	74	1.649	6.19	75	6.22	.307	0	.000	-19	2	-1.9
2002 Tex-A	13	8	.619	33	33	2	1	0	210^{2}	212	101	90	21	6	70	107	1.339	3.84	123	3.99	.261	2	.667	23	15	2.3
2003* Min-A	13	8	.619	33	31	0	0	0	195	227	108	99	22	11	50	116	1.421	4.57	99	4.73	.292	0	.000	3	11	0.3
Total 15	158	114	.581	622	335	33	7	28	2455	2532	1285	1153	247	91	898	1538	1.397	4.23	107	4.27	.267	7	.146	120	156	11.4
• ROGERS, Kevin	Charles Kevin Rogers b: 8/20/1968, Cleveland, MS BB/TL, 6'2", 190 lbs. Deb: 9/4/1992																									
1992 SF-N	0	2	.000	6	6	0	0	0	34	37	17	16	4	1	13	26	1.471	4.24	78	4.77	.280	2	.222	-4	0	-0.4
1993 SF-N	2	2	.500	64	0	0	0	0	80^{2}	71	28	24	3	4	28	62	1.227	2.68	146	2.94	.236	0	.000	9	7	0.8
1994 SF-N	0	0	....	9	0	0	0	0	10^{1}	10	4	4	1	0	6	7	1.548	3.48	115	4.58	.250	0	....	0	1	0.0
Total 3	2	4	.333	79	6	0	0	0	125	118	49	44	8	5	47	95	1.320	3.17	116	3.57	.249	2	.167	5	8	0.4
• ROGERS, Lee	Lee Otis "Buck,Lefty" Rogers b: 10/8/1913, Tuscaloosa, AL d: 11/23/1995, Little Rock, AR BR/TL, 5'11", 170 lbs. Deb: 4/27/1938																									
1938 Bos-A	1	1	.500	14	2	0	0	0	27^{2}	32	24	20	4	0	18	7	1.807	6.51	76	6.20	.302	0	.000	-5	0	-0.5
Bro-N	0	2	.000	12	2	0	0	0	23^{2}	23	16	15	0	1	10	11	1.394	5.70	68	3.28	.256	0	.000	-5	0	-0.4
• ROGERS, Steve	Stephen Douglas Rogers b: 10/26/1949, Jefferson City, MO BR/TR, 6'2", 182 lbs. Deb: 7/18/1973																									
1973 Mon-N	10	5	.667	17	17	7	3	0	134	93	28	23	5	1	49	64	1.060	1.54	247	2.04	.199	4	.098	34	15	3.4
1974 Mon-N★	15	22	.405	38	38	11	1	0	253^{2}	255	139	126	19	5	80	154	1.321	4.47	86	3.69	.265	11	.139	-17	8	-1.9
1975 Mon-N	11	12	.478	35	35	12	3	0	251^{2}	248	104	92	13	4	88	137	1.335	3.29	116	3.49	.260	13	.169	15	19	1.7
1976 Mon-N	7	17	.292	33	32	8	4	1	230	212	93	82	10	4	69	150	1.222	3.21	116	2.96	.250	11	.149	13	14	1.3
1977 Mon-N	17	16	.515	40	40	17	4	0	301^{2}	272	122	104	16	5	81	206	1.170	3.10	123	2.81	.242	10	.104	22	21	1.8
1978 Mon-N★	13	10	.565	30	29	11	1	1	219	186	64	60	12	2	64	126	1.142	2.47	143	2.68	.235	8	.113	19	17	1.7
1979 Mon-N★	13	12	.520	37	37	13	**5**	0	248^{2}	232	97	83	14	4	78	143	1.247	3.00	122	3.12	.251	12	.156	17	16	1.8
1980 Mon-N	16	11	.593	37	37	**14**	4	0	281	247	101	93	16	3	85	147	1.181	2.98	120	2.80	.238	13	.160	20	20	2.2
1981* Mon-N	12	8	.600	22	22	7	3	0	160^{2}	149	64	61	7	2	41	87	1.183	3.42	102	2.83	.248	8	.145	1	9	0.0
1982 Mon-N★	19	8	.704	35	35	14	4	0	277	245	84	74	12	6	65	179	1.119	**2.40**	**151**	2.54	.237	11	.129	**37**	24	**3.9**
1983 Mon-N★	17	12	.586	36	36	13	**5**	0	273	258	108	98	14	5	78	146	1.231	3.23	111	3.06	.252	12	.146	7	17	0.6

YEAR	TM-L	W	L	PCT	G	GS	CG	SH	SV	IP	H	R	ER	HR	HB	BB	SO	RAT	ERA	ERA+	CERA	OAV	BH	AVG	PR+	WS	TPW
1984	Mon-N	6	15	.286	31	28	1	0	0	169^{1}	171	93	81	12	2	78	64	1.470	4.31	80	4.22	.267	7	.143	-19	2	-1.9
1985	Mon-N	2	4	.333	8	7	1	0	0	38	51	25	24	1	0	20	18	1.868	5.68	60	6.02	.329	2	.143	-10	0	-1.0
Total	13	158	152	.510	399	393	129	37	2	2837^{2}	2619	1122	1001	151	43	876	1621	1.232	3.17	115	3.07	.248	122	.138	139	182	13.6
• ROGERS, Tom		Thomas Andrew "Shotgun" Rogers	b: 2/12/1892, Sparta, TN	d: 3/7/1936, Nashville, TN	BR/TR, 6'.5", 180 lbs.	Deb: 4/14/1917																					
1917	StL-A	3	6	.333	24	8	3	0	0	108^{2}	112	58	47	2	3	44	27	1.436	3.89	67	3.83	.277	5	.172	-16	2	-1.8
1918	StL-A	8	10	.444	29	16	11	0	2	154	148	66	56	3	3	49	29	1.279	3.27	84	3.12	.267	13	.245	-10	8	-0.9
1919	StL-A	0	1	.000	2	0	0	0	0	1	7	3	3	0	0	0	1	7.000	27.00	12	48.70	.700	0	....	-3	0	-0.3
	Phi-A	4	12	.250	23	18	7	1	0	140	152	85	67	9	3	60	37	1.514	4.31	79	4.70	.292	11	.224	-8	4	-0.8
	Yr.	4	13	.235	25	18	7	1	0	141	159	88	70	9	3	60	38	1.553	4.47	76	5.01	.300	11	.224	-10	4	-1.1
1921*	NY-A	0	1	.000	5	0	0	0	1	11	12	9	9	1	1	9	0	1.909	7.36	58	6.44	.300	1	.333	-4	0	-0.4
Total	4	15	30	.333	83	42	21	1	3	414^{2}	431	221	182	15	10	162	94	1.430	3.95	75	4.04	.282	30	.224	-40	14	-4.1
• ROGGE, Clint		Francis Clinton Rogge	b: 7/19/1889, Memphis, MI	d: 1/6/1969, Mount Clemens, MI	BL/TR, 5'10", 185 lbs.	Deb: 4/11/1915																					
1915	Pit-F	17	11	.607	37	31	17	5	0	254^{1}	240	96	72	6	9	93	93	1.309	2.55	122	3.31	.257	14	.173	16	19	1.7
1921	Cin-N	1	2	.333	6	2	0	0	0	35^{1}	43	19	16	2	0	9	12	1.472	4.08	88	4.42	.307	1	.100	-1	2	-0.1
Total	2	18	13	.581	43	33	17	5	0	289^{2}	283	115	88	8	9	102	105	1.329	2.73	116	3.44	.264	15	.165	15	21	1.6
• ROGGENBURK, Garry		Garry Earl Roggenburk	b: 4/16/1940, Cleveland, OH	BR/TL, 6'6", 195 lbs.	Deb: 4/20/1963																						
1963	Min-A	2	4	.333	36	2	0	0	4	50	47	26	12	3	5	22	24	1.380	2.16	169	3.90	.253	1	.143	8	3	0.9
1965	Min-A	1	0	1.000	12	0	0	0	2	21	21	10	8	1	0	12	6	1.571	3.43	104	4.13	.266	0	.000	0	1	0.0
1966	Min-A	1	2	.333	12	0	0	0	1	12^{1}	14	8	8	4	0	10	3	1.946	5.84	62	8.49	.292	0	....	-3	0	-0.3
	Bos-A	0	0	....	1	0	0	0	0	0^{1}	1	0	0	0	0	1	0	6.000	0.00	....	29.63	.500	0	....	0	0	0.0
	Yr.	1	2	.333	13	0	0	0	1	12^{2}	15	8	8	4	0	11	3	2.053	5.68	63	9.05	.300	0	....	-3	0	-0.3
1968	Bos-A	0	0	....	4	0	0	0	0	8^{1}	9	2	2	0	0	3	4	1.440	2.16	146	3.44	.257	0	....	1	1	0.1
1969	Bos-A	0	1	.000	7	0	0	0	0	9^{2}	13	9	9	1	1	5	8	1.862	8.38	45	7.43	.342	0	.000	-5	0	-0.5
	Sea-A	2	2	.500	7	4	1	0	0	24^{1}	27	12	12	6	1	11	11	1.562	4.44	82	6.14	.276	1	.125	-1	1	-0.2
	Yr.	2	3	.400	14	4	1	0	0	34	40	21	21	7	2	16	19	1.647	5.56	67	6.50	.294	1	.100	-6	1	-0.7
Total	5	6	9	.400	79	6	1	0	7	126	132	67	51	15	7	64	56	1.556	3.64	100	5.13	.272	2	.100	0	6	0.0
• ROGOVIN, Saul		Saul Walter Rogovin	b: 10/10/1923, Brooklyn, NY	d: 1/23/1995, New York, NY	BR/TR, 6'2", 205 lbs.	Deb: 4/28/1949																					
1949	Det-A	0	1	.000	5	0	0	0	0	5^{2}	13	9	9	1	0	7	2	3.529	14.29	29	17.85	.464	0	....	-6	0	-0.6
1950	Det-A	2	1	.667	11	5	1	0	0	40	39	21	20	5	2	26	11	1.625	4.50	104	5.16	.258	3	.188	1	3	0.1
1951	Det-A	1	1	.500	5	4	0	0	0	24	23	15	14	4	0	7	5	1.250	5.25	79	3.80	.247	2	.286	-3	1	-0.2
	Chi-A	11	7	.611	22	22	17	3	0	192^{2}	166	64	53	11	1	67	77	1.209	2.48	163	2.83	.234	15	.203	30	17	3.0
	Yr.	12	8	.600	27	26	17	3	0	216^{2}	189	79	67	15	1	74	82	1.214	**2.78**	**146**	2.94	.235	17	.210	28	18	2.8
1952	Chi-A	14	9	.609	33	30	12	3	1	231^{2}	224	104	99	14	3	79	121	1.308	3.85	95	3.36	.255	17	.202	-7	13	-0.5
1953	Chi-A	7	12	.368	22	19	4	1	1	131	151	82	76	17	2	48	62	1.519	5.22	77	4.98	.289	5	.135	-18	2	-1.8
1955	Bal-A	1	8	.111	14	12	1	0	0	71	79	42	36	5	2	27	35	1.493	4.56	84	4.55	.288	2	.091	-5	1	-0.7
	Phi-N	5	3	.625	12	11	5	2	0	73	60	25	25	3	0	17	27	1.055	3.08	129	2.23	.230	6	.250	6	7	0.9
1956	Phi-N	7	6	.538	22	18	3	0	0	106^{2}	122	65	59	22	0	27	48	1.397	4.98	75	4.95	.282	4	.111	-13	2	-1.6
1957	Phi-N	0	0	....	4	0	0	0	0	8	11	8	8	1	0	3	0	1.750	9.00	42	6.01	.333	0	....	-5	0	-0.5
Total	8	48	48	.500	150	121	43	9	2	883^{2}	888	435	399	83	10	308	388	1.353	4.06	96	3.89	.262	54	.180	-19	46	-1.8
• ROHR, Billy		William Joseph Rohr	b: 7/1/1945, San Diego, CA	BL/TL, 6'3", 170 lbs.	Deb: 4/14/1967																						
1967	Bos-A	2	3	.400	10	8	2	1	0	42^{1}	43	27	24	4	2	22	16	1.535	5.10	68	4.56	.256	0	.000	-7	0	-0.9
1968	Cle-A	1	0	1.000	17	0	0	0	1	18^{1}	18	16	14	5	0	10	5	1.527	6.87	43	5.68	.265	0	.000	-8	0	-0.9
Total	2	3	3	.500	27	8	2	1	1	60^{2}	61	43	38	9	2	32	21	1.533	5.64	58	4.90	.258	0	.000	-16	0	-1.8
• ROHR, Les		Leslie Norvin Rohr	b: 3/5/1946, Lowestoft, England	BL/TL, 6'5", 205 lbs.	Deb: 9/19/1967																						
1967	NY-N	2	1	.667	3	3	0	0	0	17	13	7	4	1	0	9	15	1.294	2.12	160	3.05	.224	0	.000	2	2	0.2
1968	NY-N	0	2	.000	2	1	0	0	0	6	9	4	3	0	0	7	5	2.667	4.50	67	8.12	.333	0	....	-1	0	-0.1
1969	NY-N	0	0	....	1	0	0	0	0	1^{1}	5	4	3	0	0	1	0	4.500	20.25	18	24.33	.625	0	....	-2	0	-0.3
Total	3	2	3	.400	6	4	0	0	0	24^{1}	27	15	10	1	0	17	20	1.808	3.70	90	5.46	.290	0	.000	-1	2	-0.2
• ROJAS, Mel		Melquiades (Medrano) Rojas	b: 12/10/1966, Haina, Dominican Republic	BR/TR, 5'11", 185 lbs.	Deb: 8/1/1990																						
1990	Mon-N	3	1	.750	23	0	0	0	1	40	34	17	16	5	2	24	26	1.450	3.60	101	4.32	.234	0	.000	0	3	0.0
1991	Mon-N	3	3	.500	37	0	0	0	6	48	42	21	20	4	1	13	37	1.146	3.75	96	2.80	.228	0	.000	-1	4	-0.2
1992	Mon-N	7	1	.875	68	0	0	0	10	100^{2}	71	17	16	2	2	34	70	1.043	1.43	242	1.83	.199	1	.067	23	16	2.4
1993	Mon-N	5	8	.385	66	0	0	0	10	88^{1}	80	39	29	6	4	30	48	1.245	2.95	141	3.17	.242	1	.083	12	9	1.1
1994	Mon-N	3	2	.600	58	0	0	0	16	84	71	35	31	11	4	21	84	1.095	3.32	127	3.06	.227	2	.200	9	11	0.8
1995	Mon-N	1	4	.200	59	0	0	0	30	67^{2}	69	32	31	2	7	29	61	1.448	4.12	104	4.06	.262	0	.000	2	8	0.1
1996	Mon-N	7	4	.636	74	0	0	0	36	81	56	30	29	5	2	28	92	1.037	3.22	134	2.07	.193	3	.375	10	18	1.1
1997	Chi-N	0	4	.000	54	0	0	0	13	59	54	30	29	11	5	30	61	1.424	4.42	97	5.01	.244	0	.000	-1	5	-0.1
	NY-N	0	2	.000	23	0	0	0	2	26^{1}	24	17	15	4	2	6	32	1.139	5.13	79	3.43	.235	0	....	-4	1	-0.4
	Yr.	0	6	.000	77	0	0	0	15	85^{1}	78	47	44	15	7	36	93	1.336	4.64	91	4.52	.241	0	.000	-4	6	-0.4
1998	NY-N	5	2	.714	50	0	0	0	2	58	68	39	39	9	3	30	41	1.690	6.05	68	6.24	.305	0	....	-13	1	-1.2
1999	LA-N	0	0	....	5	0	0	0	0	5	5	7	7	3	0	3	3	1.600	12.60	34	8.23	.250	0	....	-5	0	-0.4
	Det-A	0	0	....	5	0	0	0	0	6^{1}	12	16	16	3	3	4	6	2.526	22.74	22	16.51	.387	0	....	-13	0	-1.2
	Mon-N	0	0	....	3	0	0	0	0	2^{2}	5	5	5	0	2	2	1	2.625	16.88	27	13.42	.417	0	....	-4	0	-0.3
	Yr.	0	0	....	8	0	0	0	0	7^{2}	10	12	12	3	2	5	4	1.957	14.09	31	10.03	.313	0	....	-8	0	-0.8
Total	10	34	31	.523	525	0	0	0	126	667	591	305	283	65	37	254	562	1.267	3.82	108	3.60	.237	7	.119	17	76	1.7
• ROJAS, Minnie		Minervino Alejandro (Landin) Rojas	b: 11/26/1933, Remedios Las Villas, Cuba	d: 3/24/2002, Los Angeles, CA	BR/TR, 6'1", 170 lbs.	Deb: 5/30/1966																					
1966	Cal-A	7	4	.636	47	2	0	0	10	84^{1}	83	28	27	9	1	15	37	1.162	2.88	117	3.27	.262	1	.071	4	9	0.4
1967	Cal-A	12	9	.571	72	0	0	0	**27**	121^{2}	106	45	34	7	3	38	83	1.184	2.52	125	2.60	.232	1	.059	7	16	0.7
1968	Cal-A	4	3	.571	38	0	0	0	6	55	55	29	26	11	0	15	33	1.273	4.25	68	4.04	.252	1	.100	-9	2	-1.1
Total	3	23	16	.590	157	2	0	0	43	261	244	102	87	27	4	68	153	1.195	3.00	104	3.12	.246	3	.073	2	27	0.0
• ROLAND, Jim		James Ivan Roland	b: 12/14/1942, Franklin, NC	BR/TL, 6'3", 190 lbs.	Deb: 9/20/1962																						
1962	Min-A	0	0	....	1	0	0	0	0	2	1	0	0	0	0	0	1	.500	0.00	....	0.54	.143	0	....	1	0	0.1
1963	Min-A	4	1	.800	10	7	2	1	0	49	32	17	14	4	0	27	34	1.204	2.57	142	2.65	.185	0	.000	6	4	0.4
1964	Min-A	2	6	.250	30	13	1	0	3	94^{1}	76	48	43	12	4	55	63	1.389	4.10	87	3.99	.218	4	.148	-4	3	-0.5
1966	Min-A	0	0	....	1	0	0	0	0	2	0	0	0	0	0	0	1	.000	0.00	....	0.00	.000	0	....	1	0	0.1
1967	Min-A	0	1	.000	25	0	0	0	2	35^{2}	33	12	12	3	0	17	16	1.402	3.03	114	3.53	.244	0	.000	2	3	0.2
1968	Min-A	4	1	.800	28	4	1	0	0	61^{2}	55	33	24	3	2	24	36	1.281	3.50	88	3.15	.238	0	.000	-2	2	-0.3
1969	Oak-A	5	1	.833	39	3	2	0	1	86^{1}	59	24	21	2	6	46	48	1.216	2.19	157	2.55	.197	2	.095	12	8	1.2
1970	Oak-A	3	3	.500	28	2	0	0	2	43^{1}	28	14	13	2	0	23	26	1.177	2.70	131	2.28	.181	0	.000	4	4	0.3
1971	Oak-A	1	3	.250	31	0	0	0	1	45^{1}	34	18	16	4	5	19	30	1.169	3.18	105	3.05	.214	0	.000	-0	2	0.0
1972	Oak-A	0	0	....	2	0	0	0	0	2^{1}	5	2	1	0	0	0	0	2.143	3.86	74	8.42	.455	0	....	-0	0	0.0
	NY-A	0	1	.000	16	0	0	0	0	25	27	14	14	3	1	16	13	1.720	5.04	58	5.78	.287	0	.000	-6	0	-0.7
	Tex-A	0	0	....	5	0	0	0	0	3^{1}	7	3	3	1	1	2	4	2.700	8.10	37	14.81	.412	0	....	-2	0	-0.2
	Yr.	0	1	.000	23	0	0	0	0	30^{2}	39	19	18	4	2	18	17	1.859	5.28	56	6.96	.320	0	.000	-8	0	-0.9
Total	10	19	17	.528	216	29	6	1	9	450^{1}	357	185	161	34	19	229	272	1.301	3.22	105	3.33	.219	6	.071	11	26	0.6
• ROMAN, Jose		Jose Rafael (Sarita) Roman	b: 5/21/1963, Puerto Plata, Dominican Republic	BR/TR, 6', 175 lbs.	Deb: 9/5/1984																						
1984	Cle-A	0	2	.000	3	2	0	0	0	6	9	12	12	1	0	11	3	3.333	18.00	23	14.57	.391	0	....	-9	0	-0.9
1985	Cle-A	0	4	.000	5	3	0	0	0	16^{1}	13	17	12	3	0	14	12	1.653	6.61	63	5.03	.200	0	....	-4	0	-0.4
1986	Cle-A	1	2	.333	6	5	0	0	0	22	23	20	16	3	1	17	9	1.818	6.55	63	6.32	.280	0	....	-6	0	-0.6
Total	3	1	8	.111	14	10	0	0	0	44^{1}	45	49	40	7	1	42	24	1.962	8.12	51	6.96	.265	0	....	-19	0	-1.9

YEAR	TM-L	W	L	PCT	G	GS	CG	SH	SV	IP	H	R	ER	HR	HB	BB	SO	RAT	ERA	ERA+	CERA	OAV	BH	AVG	PR+	WS	TPW
• ROMANICK, Ron					Ronald James Romanick b: 11/6/1960, Burley, ID BR/TR, 6'4", 195 lbs. Deb: 4/5/1984																						
1984	Cal-A	12	12	.500	33	33	8	2	0	229^2	240	107	96	23	4	61	87	1.311	3.76	105	3.85	.270	0	....	4	14	0.4
1985	Cal-A	14	9	.609	31	31	6	1	0	195	210	101	89	29	4	62	64	1.395	4.11	100	4.68	.280	0	....	-6	10	-0.6
1986	Cal-A	5	8	.385	18	18	1	1	0	106^1	124	68	65	13	0	44	38	1.580	5.50	75	5.34	.297	0	....	-19	2	-1.8
Total	3	31	29	.517	82	82	15	4	0	531	574	276	250	65	8	167	189	1.395	4.24	96	4.45	.279	0	....	-20	26	-2.0
• ROMANO, Jim					James King Romano b: 4/6/1927, Brooklyn, NY d: 9/12/1990, New York, NY BR/TR, 6'4", 190 lbs. Deb: 9/21/1950																						
1950	Bro-N	0	0	....	3	1	0	0	0	6^1	8	6	4	0	0	2	8	1.579	5.68	72	4.12	.296	0	.000	-1	0	-0.1
• ROMANO, Mike					Michael Desport Romano b: 3/3/1972, New Orleans, LA BR/TR, 6'2", 195 lbs. Deb: 9/5/1999																						
1999	Tor-A	0	0	....	3	0	0	0	0	5^1	8	8	7	1	0	5	3	2.438	11.81	42	10.55	.364	0	....	-4	0	-0.4
• ROMBERGER, Dutch					Allen Isaiah Romberger b: 5/26/1927, Klingerstown, PA d: 5/26/1983, Weikert, PA BR/TR, 6', 185 lbs. Deb: 5/31/1954																						
1954	Phi-A	1	1	.500	10	0	0	0	0	15^2	28	20	20	3	0	12	6	2.553	11.49	34	11.71	.406	0	.000	-13	0	-1.3
• ROMERO, J.C.					Juan Carlos Romero b: 6/4/1976, Rio Piedras, Puerto Rico BB/TL, 5'11", 195 lbs. Deb: 9/15/1999																						
1999	Min-A	0	0	....	5	0	0	0	0	9^2	13	4	4	0	0	0	4	1.345	3.72	136	3.95	.333	0	....	2	1	0.1
2000	Min-A	2	7	.222	12	11	0	0	0	57^2	72	51	45	8	1	30	50	1.769	7.02	73	6.48	.312	0	....	-11	0	-1.0
2001	Min-A	1	4	.200	14	11	0	0	0	65	71	48	45	10	1	24	39	1.462	6.23	74	4.89	.277	1	.500	-11	1	-1.0
2002*	Min-A	9	2	.818	81	0	0	0	1	81	62	17	17	3	4	36	76	1.210	1.89	238	2.74	.213	0	....	23	14	2.3
2003*	Min-A	2	0	1.000	73	0	0	0	0	63	66	37	35	7	6	42	50	1.714	5.00	91	5.72	.272	0	.000	-2	3	-0.2
Total	5	14	13	.519	185	22	0	0	1	276^1	284	157	146	28	12	132	219	1.505	4.76	100	4.75	.268	1	.333	0	19	0.1
• ROMERO, Ramon					Ramon (De Los Santos) Romero b: 1/8/1959, San Pedro de Macoris, Dominican Republic BL/TL, 6'4", 170 lbs. Deb: 9/18/1984																						
1984	Cle-A	0	0	....	1	0	0	0	0	3	0	0	0	0	1	0	3	.000	0.00	....	0.13	.000	0	....	1	0	0.1
1985	Cle-A	2	3	.400	19	10	0	0	0	64^1	69	48	47	13	5	38	38	1.663	6.58	63	6.50	.276	0	....	-17	0	-1.7
Total	2	2	3	.400	20	10	0	0	0	67^1	69	48	47	13	6	38	41	1.589	6.28	66	6.22	.276	0	....	-16	0	-1.6
• ROMMEL, Eddie					Edwin Americus Rommel b: 9/13/1897, Baltimore, MD d: 8/26/1970, Baltimore, MD BR/TR, 6'2", 197 lbs. Deb: 4/19/1920 C/U																						
1920	Phi-A	7	7	.500	33	12	8	2	1	173^2	165	68	55	5	4	43	43	1.198	2.85	141	2.84	.259	11	.216	26	14	2.5
1921	Phi-A	16	23	.410	46	32	20	0	3	285^1	312	155	125	21	1	87	71	1.398	3.94	113	3.97	.284	18	.191	22	19	1.8
1922	Phi-A	**27**	13	.675	**51**	33	22	3	2	294	294	128	107	21	5	63	54	1.214	3.28	130	3.24	.267	17	.181	34	27	3.1
1923	Phi-A	18	19	.486	**56**	31	19	3	5	297^2	306	141	108	14	3	108	76	1.391	3.27	126	3.62	.271	24	.238	**35**	25	**3.5**
1924	Phi-A	18	15	.545	43	34	21	3	1	278	302	139	122	8	3	94	72	1.424	3.95	108	3.91	.284	15	.158	13	21	0.7
1925	Phi-A	**21**	10	.677	52	28	14	1	3	261	285	127	107	10	7	95	67	1.456	3.69	126	3.96	.281	15	.185	30	21	2.7
1926	Phi-A	11	11	.500	37	26	12	3	0	219	225	91	75	10	2	54	52	1.274	3.08	135	3.21	.268	6	.098	26	18	2.2
1927	Phi-A	11	3	.786	30	17	8	2	1	146^2	166	83	71	6	3	48	33	1.459	4.36	98	4.09	.286	8	.157	0	8	-0.2
1928	Phi-A	13	5	.722	43	11	6	0	4	173^2	177	70	59	11	2	26	37	1.169	3.06	131	2.99	.266	12	.255	19	17	2.1
1929*	Phi-A	12	2	.857	32	6	4	0	4	113^2	135	52	36	10	1	34	25	1.487	2.85	148	4.57	.294	8	.205	17	12	1.6
1930	Phi-A	9	4	.692	35	9	5	0	3	130^1	142	66	62	11	1	27	35	1.297	4.28	109	3.68	.277	10	.263	5	12	0.8
1931*	Phi-A	7	5	.583	25	10	8	1	0	118	136	50	39	5	1	27	18	1.381	2.97	151	3.90	.291	14	.259	17	12	1.6
1932	Phi-A	1	2	.333	17	0	0	0	2	65^1	84	43	40	6	0	18	16	1.561	5.51	82	5.07	.315	6	.300	-7	3	-0.5
Total	13	171	119	.590	500	249	147	18	29	2556^1	2729	1213	1006	138	33	724	599	1.351	3.54	122	3.67	.277	164	.199	237	209	21.9
• ROMO, Enrique					Enrique (Navarro) Romo b: 7/15/1947, Santa Rosalia, Mexico BR/TR, 5'11", 185 lbs. Deb: 4/7/1977																						
1977	Sea-A	8	10	.444	58	3	0	0	16	114^1	93	40	36	8	5	39	105	1.155	2.83	145	2.81	.227	0	....	14	15	1.4
1978	Sea-A	11	7	.611	56	0	0	0	10	107^1	88	46	44	12	5	39	62	1.183	3.69	103	3.14	.227	0	....	2	10	0.2
1979*	Pit-N	10	5	.667	84	0	0	0	5	129^1	122	50	43	11	3	43	106	1.276	2.99	130	3.44	.253	2	.167	11	11	1.2
1980	Pit-N	5	5	.500	74	0	0	0	11	123^2	117	53	45	10	1	28	82	1.173	3.27	111	2.98	.252	5	.455	4	12	0.8
1981	Pit-N	1	3	.250	33	0	0	0	9	41^2	47	27	21	5	0	18	23	1.560	4.54	79	4.79	.288	0	.000	-4	1	-0.5
1982	Pit-N	9	3	.750	45	0	0	0	1	86^2	81	43	42	11	1	36	58	1.350	4.36	85	3.87	.245	3	.300	-6	5	-0.5
Total	6	44	33	.571	350	3	0	0	52	603	548	259	231	57	15	203	436	1.245	3.45	110	3.33	.245	10	.270	22	54	2.5
• ROMO, Vicente					Vicente (Navarro) "Huevo" Romo b: 4/12/1943, Santa Rosalia, Mexico BR/TR, 6'1", 195 lbs. Deb: 4/11/1968																						
1968	LA-N	0	0	....	1	0	0	0	0	1	1	1	0	0	0	0	0	1.000	0.00	....	1.51	.250	0	....	0	0	0.0
	Cle-A	5	3	.625	40	1	0	0	12	83^1	43	15	15	5	2	32	54	.900	1.62	183	1.48	.154	2	.143	12	14	1.3
1969	Cle-A	1	1	.500	3	0	0	0	0	8	7	3	2	0	0	3	7	1.250	2.25	167	2.31	.233	1	.500	1	1	0.2
	Bos-A	7	9	.438	52	11	4	1	11	127^1	116	51	45	14	1	50	89	1.304	3.18	120	3.62	.247	4	.129	12	11	1.1
	Yr.	8	10	.444	55	11	4	1	11	135^1	123	54	47	14	1	53	96	1.300	3.13	122	3.54	.246	5	.152	13	12	1.3
1970	Bos-A	7	3	.700	48	10	0	0	6	108	115	51	49	14	0	43	71	1.463	4.08	97	4.58	.273	4	.148	1	7	0.1
1971	Chi-A	1	7	.125	45	2	0	0	5	72	52	27	27	5	0	37	48	1.236	3.38	106	2.67	.202	4	.364	3	6	0.5
1972	Chi-A	3	0	1.000	28	0	0	0	1	51^2	47	19	19	5	1	18	46	1.258	3.31	94	3.39	.246	0	.000	0	3	-0.1
1973	SD-N	2	3	.400	49	1	0	0	7	87^2	85	43	36	11	0	46	51	1.494	3.70	94	4.45	.260	2	.125	-2	5	-0.2
1974	SD-N	5	5	.500	54	1	0	0	9	71	78	47	36	6	2	37	26	1.620	4.56	78	4.77	.290	0	.000	-6	3	-0.7
1982	LA-N	1	2	.333	15	6	0	0	1	35^2	25	12	12	1	2	14	24	1.093	3.03	115	2.21	.195	1	.200	2	2	0.2
Total	8	32	33	.492	335	32	4	1	52	645^2	569	269	241	61	8	280	416	1.315	3.36	106	3.52	.239	18	.149	23	52	2.4
• ROMONOSKY, John					John Romonosky b: 7/7/1929, Harrisburg, IL BR/TR, 6'2", 195 lbs. Deb: 9/6/1953																						
1953	StL-N	0	0	....	2	2	0	0	0	7^2	9	6	4	1	1	4	3	1.696	4.70	91	6.05	.281	0	.000	-0	0	-0.1
1958	Was-A	2	4	.333	18	5	1	0	0	55^1	52	42	40	6	0	28	38	1.446	6.51	59	3.98	.243	4	.308	-15	1	-1.3
1959	Was-A	1	0	1.000	12	2	0	0	0	38^1	36	15	14	4	3	19	22	1.435	3.29	119	4.55	.254	2	.182	4	3	0.4
Total	3	3	4	.429	32	9	1	0	0	101^1	97	63	58	11	4	51	63	1.461	5.15	75	4.35	.250	6	.231	-11	4	-0.9
• RONDON, Gilberto					Gilberto Rondon b: 11/18/1953, Bronx, NY BR/TR, 6'2", 200 lbs. Deb: 4/10/1976																						
1976	Hou-N	2	2	.500	19	7	0	0	0	53^2	70	37	34	6	0	39	21	2.031	5.70	56	7.38	.315	4	.286	-15	0	-1.5
1979	Chi-A	0	0	....	4	0	0	0	0	9^2	11	5	4	2	0	6	3	1.759	3.72	114	6.50	.282	0	....	1	1	0.1
Total	2	2	2	.500	23	7	0	0	0	63^1	81	42	38	8	0	45	24	1.989	5.40	61	7.25	.310	4	.286	-14	1	-1.4
• RONEY, Matt					Matthew S. Roney b: 1/10/1980, Tulsa, OK BR/TR, 6'3", 230 lbs. Deb: 4/2/2003																						
2003	Det-A	1	9	.100	45	11	0	0	0	100^2	102	67	61	17	4	48	47	1.490	5.45	79	5.03	.262	1	.500	-13	2	-1.2
• ROOKER, Jim					James Phillip Rooker b: 9/23/1942, Lakeview, OR BR/TL, 6', 201 lbs. Deb: 6/30/1968																						
1968	Det-A	0	0	....	2	0	0	0	0	4^2	4	2	2	0	0	1	4	1.071	3.86	78	2.13	.235	0	.000	-0	0	-0.1
1969	KC-A	4	16	.200	28	22	8	1	0	158^1	136	80	66	13	1	73	108	1.320	3.75	98	3.37	.229	16	.281	1	8	0.9
1970	KC-A	10	15	.400	38	29	6	3	1	203^2	190	99	80	11	1	102	117	1.434	3.54	106	3.78	.252	14	.200	3	10	0.6
1971	KC-A	2	7	.222	20	7	1	1	0	54	59	35	32	2	1	24	31	1.537	5.33	64	4.35	.284	0	.000	-11	0	-1.2
1972	KC-A	5	6	.455	18	10	4	2	0	72	78	37	35	3	1	24	44	1.417	4.38	69	3.94	.280	2	.100	-10	1	-1.2
1973	Pit-N	10	6	.625	41	18	6	3	5	170^1	143	59	54	12	2	52	122	1.145	2.85	123	2.64	.229	12	.245	13	12	1.6
1974*	Pit-N	15	11	.577	33	33	15	1	0	262^2	228	93	81	11	4	83	139	1.184	2.78	124	2.74	.238	29	.305	18	21	2.9
1975*	Pit-N	13	11	.542	28	28	7	1	0	196^2	177	80	65	16	3	76	102	1.286	2.97	119	3.26	.238	6	.095	12	12	1.0
1976	Pit-N	15	8	.652	30	29	10	1	1	198^2	201	83	74	12	2	72	92	1.374	3.35	104	3.72	.263	16	.216	2	13	0.6
1977	Pit-N	14	9	.609	30	30	7	2	0	204^1	196	87	70	24	0	64	89	1.272	3.08	129	3.61	.253	13	.186	17	15	1.8
1978	Pit-N	9	11	.450	28	28	1	0	0	163^1	160	94	77	13	3	81	76	1.476	4.24	87	4.23	.259	9	.161	-8	4	-0.8
1979*	Pit-N	4	7	.364	19	17	1	0	0	103^2	106	58	53	11	0	39	44	1.399	4.60	84	4.10	.266	4	.121	-9	2	-1.1
1980	Pit-N	2	2	.500	4	4	0	0	0	18	16	7	7	0	0	12	8	1.556	3.50	104	4.03	.262	1	.143	0	2	0.1
Total	13	103	109	.486	319	255	66	15	7	1810^1	1694	814	696	128	18	703	976	1.324	3.46	104	3.49	.249	122	.201	28	100	5.1
• ROOT, Charley					Charles Henry "Chinski" Root b: 3/17/1899, Middletown, OH d: 11/5/1970, Hollister, CA BR/TR, 5'10.5", 190 lbs. Deb: 4/18/1923 C																						
1923	StL-A	0	4	.000	27	2	0	0	0	60	68	45	38	4	6	18	27	1.433	5.70	73	4.54	.302	1	.077	-11	0	-1.2
1926	Chi-N	18	17	.514	42	32	21	2	2	271^1	267	104	85	10	6	62	127	1.213	2.82	136	2.99	.264	13	.143	25	22	2.1
1927	Chi-N	**26**	15	.634	**48**	36	21	4	2	**309**	296	148	129	16	9	117	145	1.337	3.76	103	3.45	.254	27	.221	-3	21	0.0

YEAR TM-L	W	L	PCT	G	GS	CG	SH	SV	IP	H	R	ER	HR	HB	BB	SO	RAT	ERA	ERA+	CERA	OAV	BH	AVG	PR+	WS	TPW
1928 Chi-N	14	18	.438	40	30	13	1	2	237	214	109	94	15	7	73	122	1.211	3.57	108	2.97	.242	13	.178	-1	16	-0.1
1929* Chi-N	19	6	.760	43	31	19	4	5	272	286	120	105	12	3	83	124	1.357	3.47	133	3.58	.275	15	.156	30	23	2.7
1930 Chi-N	16	14	.533	37	30	15	**4**	3	220^{1}	247	122	106	17	7	63	124	1.407	4.33	113	4.14	.281	21	.263	15	17	1.7
1931 Chi-N	17	14	.548	39	31	19	3	2	251	240	109	97	7	7	71	131	1.239	3.48	111	2.96	.252	20	.222	13	17	1.6
1932* Chi-N	15	10	.600	39	23	11	0	3	216^{1}	211	99	86	10	5	55	96	1.230	3.58	105	3.02	.253	13	.171	1	16	-0.1
1933 Chi-N	15	10	.600	35	30	20	2	0	242^{1}	232	85	70	14	10	61	86	1.209	2.60	126	3.09	.252	8	.094	13	17	0.9
1934 Chi-N	4	7	.364	34	9	2	0	0	117^{2}	141	62	56	8	5	53	46	1.649	4.28	91	5.23	.298	7	.175	-6	6	-0.5
1935* Chi-N	15	8	.652	38	18	11	1	2	201^{1}	193	85	69	15	3	47	94	1.192	3.08	127	3.07	.252	14	.203	12	16	1.3
1936 Chi-N	3	6	.333	33	4	0	0	1	73^{2}	81	34	34	3	2	20	32	1.371	4.15	96	3.76	.280	5	.333	-3	5	-0.1
1937 Chi-N	13	5	.722	43	15	5	0	5	178^{2}	173	71	67	18	4	32	74	1.147	3.38	118	3.11	.253	12	.179	11	16	1.1
1938* Chi-N	8	7	.533	44	11	5	0	8	160^{2}	163	62	51	10	2	30	70	1.201	2.86	134	3.04	.258	8	.167	16	15	1.6
1939 Chi-N	8	8	.500	35	16	8	0	4	167^{1}	189	83	75	11	2	34	65	1.333	4.03	98	3.79	.286	10	.175	3	10	0.5
1940 Chi-N	2	4	.333	36	8	1	0	1	112	118	61	48	9	1	33	50	1.348	3.86	97	3.68	.265	4	.129	-1	4	-0.2
1941 Chi-N	8	7	.533	19	15	6	0	0	106^{2}	133	68	64	8	0	37	46	1.594	5.40	65	4.94	.306	5	.152	-19	2	-1.8
Total 17	201	160	.557	632	341	177	21	40	3197^{1}	3252	1467	1274	187	79	889	1459	1.295	3.59	110	3.45	.264	196	.180	93	223	9.4
• ROPER, John	John Christopher Roper b: 11/21/1971, Southern Pines, NC BR/TR, 6', 175 lbs. Deb: 5/16/1993																									
1993 Cin-N	2	5	.286	16	15	0	0	0	80	92	51	50	10	4	36	54	1.600	5.63	72	5.54	.295	5	.179	-14	1	-1.4
1994 Cin-N	6	2	.750	16	15	0	0	0	92	90	49	46	16	4	30	51	1.304	4.50	92	4.37	.255	6	.182	-4	4	-0.3
1995 Cin-N	0	0	....	2	2	0	0	0	7	13	9	8	3	0	4	6	2.429	10.29	40	13.67	.406	0	.000	-5	0	-0.5
SF-N	0	0	....	1	0	0	0	0	1	2	3	3	0	0	2	0	4.000	27.00	15	16.69	.500	0	....	-3	0	-0.3
Yr.	0	0	....	3	2	0	0	0	8	15	12	11	3	0	6	6	2.625	12.38	33	14.05	.417	0	.000	-8	0	-0.8
Total 3	8	7	.533	35	32	0	0	0	180	197	112	107	29	8	72	111	1.494	5.35	76	5.32	.281	11	.177	-25	5	-2.5
• ROQUE, Rafael	Rafael Antonio Roque b: 1/1/1972, Cotui, Dominican Republic BL/TL, 6'4", 189 lbs. Deb: 8/1/1998																									
1998 Mil-N	4	2	.667	9	9	0	0	0	48	42	28	26	9	1	24	34	1.375	4.88	88	4.50	.237	1	.077	-4	2	-0.5
1999 Mil-N	1	6	.143	43	9	0	0	1	84^{1}	96	52	50	16	4	42	66	1.636	5.34	85	6.17	.286	1	.059	-7	2	-0.7
2000 Mil-N	0	0	....	4	0	0	0	0	5^{1}	7	6	6	1	0	7	4	2.625	10.13	45	10.54	.333	0	....	-3	0	-0.3
Total 3	5	8	.385	56	18	0	0	1	137^{2}	145	86	82	26	5	73	104	1.584	5.36	83	5.76	.272	2	.067	-14	4	-1.5
• ROSADO, Jose	Jose Antonio Rosado b: 11/9/1974, Newark, NJ BL/TL, 6', 175 lbs. Deb: 6/12/1996																									
1996 KC-A	8	6	.571	16	16	2	1	0	106^{2}	101	39	38	7	4	26	64	1.191	3.21	156	3.10	.249	0	....	21	11	2.0
1997 KC-A★	9	12	.429	33	33	2	0	0	203^{1}	208	117	106	26	4	73	129	1.382	4.69	101	4.27	.264	0	.000	-2	9	-0.2
1998 KC-A	8	11	.421	38	25	2	1	1	174^{2}	180	106	91	25	5	57	135	1.357	4.69	103	4.31	.260	1	.500	5	10	0.5
1999 KC-A★	10	14	.417	33	33	5	0	0	208	197	103	89	24	5	72	141	1.293	3.85	130	3.76	.248	0	.000	22	13	2.0
2000 KC-A	2	2	.500	5	5	0	0	0	27^{2}	29	18	18	4	4	9	15	1.373	5.86	87	4.98	.271	0	....	-3	1	-0.3
Total 5	37	45	.451	125	112	11	2	1	720^{1}	715	383	342	86	22	237	484	1.322	4.27	114	3.99	.257	1	.111	44	44	4.0
• ROSARIO, Rodrigo	Rodrigo Rosario b: 12/14/1977, La Romana, Dominican Republic BR/TR, 6'2", 165 lbs. Deb: 6/21/2003																									
2003 Hou-N	1	0	1.000	2	2	0	0	0	8	5	2	1	0	1	3	6	1.000	1.13	394	1.67	.172	0	....	3	1	0.3
• ROSE, Brian	Brian Leonard Rose b: 2/13/1976, New Bedford, MA BR/TR, 6'3", 215 lbs. Deb: 7/25/1997																									
1997 Bos-A	0	0	....	1	1	0	0	0	3	5	4	4	0	0	2	3	2.333	12.00	39	8.24	.357	0	....	-2	0	-0.2
1998 Bos-A	1	4	.200	8	8	0	0	0	37^{2}	43	32	29	9	2	14	18	1.513	6.93	68	6.07	.285	0	....	-10	0	-0.9
1999 Bos-A	7	6	.538	22	18	0	0	0	98^{1}	112	59	53	19	2	29	51	1.439	4.87	102	5.13	.280	0	.000	1	5	0.1
2000 Bos-A	3	5	.375	15	12	0	0	0	53	58	37	36	11	3	21	24	1.491	6.11	82	5.47	.274	0	.000	-6	1	-0.6
Col-N	4	5	.444	12	12	0	0	0	63^{2}	72	41	39	10	3	30	40	1.602	5.51	105	5.52	.281	1	.048	2	3	0.0
2001 NY-N	0	1	.000	3	0	0	0	0	8^{2}	10	4	4	3	0	2	4	1.385	4.15	99	5.86	.286	0	.000	-0	0	0.0
TB-A	0	2	.000	7	3	0	0	0	20^{1}	31	20	20	4	0	12	11	2.115	8.85	51	9.07	.356	0	....	-10	0	-1.0
Total 5	15	23	.395	68	54	0	0	0	284^{1}	331	197	185	56	10	110	151	1.551	5.86	85	5.74	.287	1	.037	-26	9	-2.6
• ROSE, Chuck	Charles Alfred Rose b: 9/1/1885, Macon, MO d: 8/4/1961, Salina, KS BL/TL, 5'8.5", 158 lbs. Deb: 9/13/1909																									
1909 StL-A	1	2	.333	3	3	3	0	0	25	32	17	15	1	3	7	6	1.560	5.40	45	5.51	.330	0	.000	-8	0	-1.0
• ROSE, Don	Donald Gary Rose b: 3/19/1947, Covina, CA BR/TR, 6'3", 195 lbs. Deb: 9/15/1971																									
1971 NY-N	0	0	....	1	0	0	0	0	2	2	0	0	0	0	0	1	1.000	0.00	....	2.31	.286	0	....	1	0	0.1
1972 Cal-A	1	4	.200	16	4	0	0	0	42^{2}	49	25	20	9	0	19	39	1.594	4.22	69	5.69	.283	2	.200	-7	0	-0.6
1974 SF-N	0	0	....	2	0	0	0	0	1	4	1	1	0	0	1	0	5.000	9.00	42	31.76	.667	0	....	-1	0	-0.1
Total 3	1	4	.200	19	4	0	0	0	45^{2}	55	26	21	9	0	20	40	1.642	4.14	71	6.11	.296	2	.200	-6	0	-0.6
• ROSEBRAUGH, Zeke	Eli Ethelbert Rosebraugh b: 9/8/1870, Charleston, IL d: 7/16/1930, Fresno, CA TL Deb: 9/21/1898																									
1898 Pit-N	0	2	.000	4	2	2	0	0	21^{2}	23	14	8	0	3	9	6	1.477	3.32	107	4.12	.270	3	.375	1	1	0.1
1899 Pit-N	0	1	.000	2	2	0	0	0	6	14	8	6	0	1	3	2	2.833	9.00	42	12.93	.451	0	.000	-3	0	-0.3
Total 2	0	3	.000	6	4	2	0	0	27^{2}	37	22	14	0	4	12	8	1.771	4.55	80	6.03	.319	3	.300	-3	1	-0.2
• ROSENBERG, Steve	Steven Allen Rosenberg b: 10/31/1964, Brooklyn, NY BL/TL, 6', 186 lbs. Deb: 6/4/1988																									
1988 Chi-A	0	1	.000	33	0	0	0	1	46	53	22	22	5	0	19	28	1.565	4.30	92	5.13	.298	0	....	-2	2	-0.2
1989 Chi-A	4	13	.235	38	21	2	0	0	142	148	92	78	14	1	58	77	1.451	4.94	77	4.37	.273	0	....	-18	1	-1.8
1990 Chi-A	1	0	1.000	6	0	0	0	0	10	10	6	6	2	0	5	4	1.500	5.40	71	5.23	.256	0	....	-2	0	-0.2
1991 SD-N	1	1	.500	10	0	0	0	0	11^{2}	11	9	9	3	0	5	6	1.371	6.94	55	4.95	.250	0	.000	-4	0	-0.4
Total 4	6	15	.286	87	21	2	0	1	209^{2}	222	129	115	24	1	87	115	1.474	4.94	78	4.61	.276	0	.000	-27	3	-2.7
• ROSENTHAL, Wayne	Wayne Scott Rosenthal b: 2/19/1965, Brooklyn, NY BR/TR, 6'5", 220 lbs. Deb: 6/26/1991 C																									
1991 Tex-A	1	4	.200	36	0	0	0	1	70^{1}	72	43	41	9	1	36	61	1.536	5.25	77	4.77	.257	0	....	-8	1	-0.8
1992 Tex-A	0	0	....	6	0	0	0	0	4^{2}	7	4	4	1	0	2	1	1.929	7.71	49	7.67	.333	0	....	-2	0	-0.2
Total 2	1	4	.200	42	0	0	0	1	75	79	47	45	10	1	38	62	1.560	5.40	74	4.95	.262	0	....	-10	1	-1.0
• ROSER, Steve	Emerson Corey Roser b: 1/25/1918, Rome, NY d: 2/8/2002, Utica, NY BR/TR, 6'4", 220 lbs. Deb: 5/5/1944																									
1944 NY-A	4	3	.571	16	6	1	0	1	84	80	39	36	3	0	34	34	1.357	3.86	90	3.36	.256	3	.100	-5	4	-0.7
1945 NY-A	0	0	....	11	0	0	0	0	27	27	15	11	1	0	8	11	1.296	3.67	94	3.23	.262	1	.125	-1	1	-0.2
1946 NY-A	1	1	.500	4	1	0	0	0	3^{1}	7	6	6	0	0	4	1	3.300	16.20	21	13.87	.438	0	....	-5	0	-0.5
Bos-N	1	1	.500	14	1	0	0	1	35	33	15	14	1	0	18	18	1.457	3.60	95	3.54	.250	0	.000	-0	2	-0.1
Total 3	6	5	.545	45	8	1	0	2	149^{1}	147	75	67	5	0	64	64	1.413	4.04	86	3.61	.261	4	.093	-11	7	-1.5
• ROSS, Bob	Floyd Robert Ross b: 11/2/1928, Fullerton, CA BR/TL, 6', 165 lbs. Deb: 6/16/1950																									
1950 Was-A	0	1	.000	6	2	0	0	0	12^{2}	15	12	12	1	0	15	2	2.368	8.53	53	7.57	.300	0	.000	-6	0	-0.6
1951 Was-A	0	1	.000	11	1	0	0	0	31^{2}	36	25	23	3	0	21	23	1.800	6.54	63	5.78	.295	1	.111	-8	0	-0.8
1956 Phi-N	0	0	....	3	0	0	0	0	3^{1}	4	3	3	1	0	2	4	1.800	8.10	46	7.57	.333	0	....	-2	0	-0.2
Total 3	0	2	.000	20	3	0	0	0	47^{2}	55	40	38	5	0	38	29	1.951	7.17	58	6.38	.299	1	.083	-15	0	-1.6
• ROSS, Buck	Lee Ravon Ross b: 2/2/1915, Norwood, NC d: 11/23/1978, Charlotte, NC BR/TR, 6'2", 170 lbs. Deb: 5/7/1936																									
1936 Phi-A	9	14	.391	30	27	12	1	0	200^{2}	253	146	130	17	0	83	47	1.674	5.83	88	5.35	.304	12	.169	-16	8	-1.6
1937 Phi-A	5	10	.333	28	22	7	1	0	147^{1}	183	102	80	12	2	63	37	1.670	4.89	96	5.40	.306	5	.102	-3	5	-0.5
1938 Phi-A	9	16	.360	29	28	10	0	0	184^{1}	218	132	109	23	0	80	54	1.617	5.32	91	5.23	.289	12	.190	-5	7	-0.5
1939 Phi-A	6	14	.300	29	28	6	1	0	174	216	143	116	17	0	95	43	1.787	6.00	78	5.77	.302	12	.207	-19	3	-1.8
1940 Phi-A	5	10	.333	24	19	10	0	1	156^{1}	160	91	76	15	0	60	43	1.407	4.38	102	3.92	.256	7	.132	4	7	0.2
1941 Phi-A	0	1	.000	1	1	0	0	0	4	10	9	8	2	0	2	0	3.000	18.00	23	17.81	.435	0	.000	-6	0	-0.6
Chi-A	3	8	.273	20	11	7	0	0	108^{1}	99	51	38	6	1	43	30	1.311	3.16	130	3.17	.239	7	.219	10	7	1.1
Yr.	3	9	.250	21	12	7	0	0	112^{1}	109	60	46	8	1	45	30	1.371	3.69	112	3.69	.249	7	.212	4	7	0.4
1942 Chi-A	5	7	.417	22	14	4	2	1	113^{1}	118	63	63	6	0	39	37	1.385	5.00	72	3.65	.264	6	.158	-18	2	-1.9

YEAR	TM-L	W	L	PCT	G	GS	CG	SH	SV	IP	H	R	ER	HR	HB	BB	SO	RAT	ERA	ERA+	CERA	OAV	BH	AVG	PR+	WS	TPW
1943	Chi-A	11	7	.611	21	21	7	1	0	149^1	140	61	53	6	2	56	41	1.313	3.19	104	3.22	.253	4	.087	2	9	0.1
1944	Chi-A	2	7	.222	20	9	2	0	0	90^1	97	56	52	7	2	35	20	1.461	5.18	66	4.34	.280	2	.077	-18	0	-2.1
1945	Chi-A	1	1	.500	13	2	0	0	0	37^1	51	28	24	3	0	17	8	1.821	5.79	57	6.30	.327	2	.182	-10	0	-1.1
Total	**10**	**56**	**95**	**.371**	**237**	**182**	**65**	**6**	**2**	1365^1	**1545**	**882**	**749**	**114**	**7**	**573**	**360**	**1.551**	**4.94**	**87**	**4.68**	**.283**	**69**	**.154**	**-81**	**48**	**-8.8**

• ROSS, Buster Chester Franklin Ross b: 3/11/1903, Kuttawa, KY d: 4/24/1982, Mayfield, KY BL/TL, 6'1", 195 lbs. Deb: 6/15/1924

YEAR	TM-L	W	L	PCT	G	GS	CG	SH	SV	IP	H	R	ER	HR	HB	BB	SO	RAT	ERA	ERA+	CERA	OAV	BH	AVG	PR+	WS	TPW
1924	Bos-A	4	3	.571	30	2	1	1	1	93^1	109	49	36	3	0	30	16	1.489	3.47	126	4.16	.307	5	.200	10	6	1.0
1925	Bos-A	3	8	.273	33	8	0	0	0	94^1	119	86	65	9	5	40	15	1.686	6.20	73	5.61	.313	3	.125	-15	0	-1.5
1926	Bos-A	0	1	.000	1	0	0	0	0	2^2	5	7	5	0	0	4	0	3.375	16.88	24	12.07	.385	0	.000	-4	0	-0.4
Total	**3**	**7**	**12**	**.368**	**64**	**10**	**1**	**1**	**1**	190^1	**233**	**142**	**106**	**12**	**5**	**74**	**31**	**1.613**	**5.01**	**89**	**4.99**	**.311**	**8**	**.160**	**-8**	**6**	**-0.9**

• ROSS, Cliff Clifford Davis Ross b: 8/3/1928, Philadelphia, PA d: 4/13/1999, Philadelphia, PA BL/TL, 6'4", 195 lbs. Deb: 9/11/1954

YEAR	TM-L	W	L	PCT	G	GS	CG	SH	SV	IP	H	R	ER	HR	HB	BB	SO	RAT	ERA	ERA+	CERA	OAV	BH	AVG	PR+	WS	TPW
1954	Cin-N	0	0	....	4	0	0	0	1	2^2	0	0	0	0	0	0	1	.000	0.00	....	0.00	.000	0	....	1	1	0.1

• ROSS, Ernie Ernest Bertram "Curly" Ross b: 3/31/1880, Toronto, Canada d: 3/28/1950, Toronto, Canada BL/TL, 5'8", 150 lbs. Deb: 9/17/1902

YEAR	TM-L	W	L	PCT	G	GS	CG	SH	SV	IP	H	R	ER	HR	HB	BB	SO	RAT	ERA	ERA+	CERA	OAV	BH	AVG	PR+	WS	TPW
1902	Bal-A	1	1	.500	2	2	2	0	0	17	20	18	14	0	1	12	2	1.882	7.41	51	5.37	.294	0	.000	-6	0	-0.7

• ROSS, Gary Gary Douglas Ross b: 9/16/1947, McKeesport, PA BR/TR, 6'1", 190 lbs. Deb: 6/28/1968

YEAR	TM-L	W	L	PCT	G	GS	CG	SH	SV	IP	H	R	ER	HR	HB	BB	SO	RAT	ERA	ERA+	CERA	OAV	BH	AVG	PR+	WS	TPW
1968	Chi-N	1	1	.500	13	5	1	0	0	41	44	22	19	1	0	25	31	1.683	4.17	76	4.67	.288	1	.091	-5	1	-0.6
1969	Chi-N	0	0	....	2	1	0	0	0	2	1	3	3	0	0	2	2	1.500	13.50	30	2.80	.143	0	....	-2	0	-0.2
	SD-N	3	12	.200	46	7	0	0	3	109^2	104	58	51	5	5	56	58	1.459	4.19	84	3.88	.252	0	.000	-7	4	-0.9
	Yr.	3	12	.200	48	8	0	0	3	111^2	105	61	54	5	5	58	60	1.460	4.35	82	3.86	.250	0	.000	-9	4	-1.1
1970	SD-N	2	3	.400	33	2	0	0	1	62^1	72	37	36	8	3	36	39	1.733	5.20	76	6.04	.305	4	.500	-8	2	-0.7
1971	SD-N	1	3	.250	13	0	0	0	0	24^1	27	10	8	0	1	11	13	1.562	2.96	111	4.17	.300	0	.000	1	1	0.1
1972	SD-N	4	3	.571	60	0	0	0	3	91^2	87	35	25	2	4	49	46	1.484	2.45	134	3.74	.261	2	.154	10	7	1.0
1973	SD-N	4	4	.500	58	0	0	0	0	76^1	93	51	46	8	4	33	44	1.651	5.42	64	5.52	.304	0	.000	-16	1	-1.7
1974	SD-N	0	0	....	9	0	0	0	0	18	23	10	9	1	0	6	11	1.611	4.50	79	4.61	.315	0	.000	-1	1	-0.2
1975	Cal-A	0	1	.000	1	1	0	0	0	5	6	3	3	1	0	1	4	1.400	5.40	66	4.76	.273	0	....	-1	0	-0.1
1976	Cal-A	8	16	.333	34	31	7	2	0	225	224	89	75	12	5	58	100	1.253	3.00	111	3.22	.258	0	....	9	13	1.0
1977	Cal-A	2	4	.333	14	12	0	0	0	58^1	83	41	36	10	2	11	30	1.611	5.55	70	6.50	.337	0	....	-10	0	-1.0
Total	**10**	**25**	**47**	**.347**	**283**	**59**	**8**	**2**	**7**	713^2	**764**	**359**	**311**	**48**	**24**	**288**	**378**	**1.474**	**3.92**	**89**	**4.31**	**.278**	**7**	**.115**	**-30**	**30**	**-3.2**

• ROSS, George George Sidney Ross b: 6/27/1892, San Rafael, CA d: 4/22/1935, Amityville, NY BL/TL, 5'10.5", 175 lbs. Deb: 6/27/1918

YEAR	TM-L	W	L	PCT	G	GS	CG	SH	SV	IP	H	R	ER	HR	HB	BB	SO	RAT	ERA	ERA+	CERA	OAV	BH	AVG	PR+	WS	TPW
1918	NY-N	0	0	....	1	0	0	0	1	2^1	2	0	0	0	0	3	2	2.143	0.00	....	5.32	.222	0	.000	1	0	0.1

• ROSS, Mark Mark Joseph Ross b: 8/8/1954, Galveston, TX BR/TR, 6', 195 lbs. Deb: 9/12/1982

YEAR	TM-L	W	L	PCT	G	GS	CG	SH	SV	IP	H	R	ER	HR	HB	BB	SO	RAT	ERA	ERA+	CERA	OAV	BH	AVG	PR+	WS	TPW
1982	Hou-N	0	0	....	4	0	0	0	0	6	3	1	1	0	0	0	4	.500	1.50	221	0.54	.143	0	....	1	1	0.1
1984	Hou-N	1	0	1.000	2	0	0	0	0	2^1	1	0	0	0	0	0	1	.429	0.00	....	0.40	.125	0	....	1	1	0.1
1985	Hou-N	0	2	.000	8	0	0	0	1	13	12	7	7	2	0	2	3	1.077	4.85	71	3.06	.240	0	.000	-2	0	-0.2
1987	Pit-N	0	0	....	1	0	0	0	0	1	1	1	1	1	0	0	0	1.000	9.00	46	7.45	.250	0	....	-1	0	-0.1
1988	Tor-A	0	0	....	3	0	0	0	0	7^1	5	6	4	0	0	4	4	1.227	4.91	80	1.95	.185	0	....	-1	0	-0.1
1990	Pit-N	1	0	1.000	9	0	0	0	0	12^2	11	5	5	2	0	4	5	1.184	3.55	102	3.34	.244	0	.000	-0	1	0.0
Total	**6**	**2**	**2**	**.500**	**27**	**0**	**0**	**0**	**1**	42^1	**33**	**20**	**18**	**5**	**0**	**10**	**17**	**1.016**	**3.83**	**95**	**2.55**	**.213**	**0**	**.000**	**-2**	**3**	**-0.2**

• ROSSELLI, Joe Joseph Donald Rosselli b: 5/28/1972, Burbank, CA BR/TL, 6'1", 170 lbs. Deb: 4/30/1995

YEAR	TM-L	W	L	PCT	G	GS	CG	SH	SV	IP	H	R	ER	HR	HB	BB	SO	RAT	ERA	ERA+	CERA	OAV	BH	AVG	PR+	WS	TPW
1995	SF-N	2	1	.667	9	5	0	0	0	30	39	29	29	5	0	20	7	1.967	8.70	47	7.77	.342	2	.200	-16	0	-1.5

• ROSSO, Frank Francis James Rosso b: 3/1/1921, Agawam, MA d: 1/26/1980, Springfield, MA BR/TR, 5'11", 180 lbs. Deb: 9/15/1944

YEAR	TM-L	W	L	PCT	G	GS	CG	SH	SV	IP	H	R	ER	HR	HB	BB	SO	RAT	ERA	ERA+	CERA	OAV	BH	AVG	PR+	WS	TPW
1944	NY-N	0	0	....	2	0	0	0	0	4	11	5	4	0	0	3	1	3.500	9.00	41	17.44	.550	0	....	-2	0	-0.2

• ROTBLATT, Marv Marvin "Rotty" Rotblatt b: 10/18/1927, Chicago, IL BB/TL, 5'7", 160 lbs. Deb: 7/4/1948

YEAR	TM-L	W	L	PCT	G	GS	CG	SH	SV	IP	H	R	ER	HR	HB	BB	SO	RAT	ERA	ERA+	CERA	OAV	BH	AVG	PR+	WS	TPW
1948	Chi-A	0	1	.000	7	2	0	0	0	18^1	19	16	16	0	1	23	4	2.291	7.85	54	6.69	.271	0	.000	-8	0	-0.8
1950	Chi-A	0	0	....	2	0	0	0	0	8^2	11	7	6	2	0	5	6	1.846	6.23	72	7.99	.344	0	.000	-2	0	-0.2
1951	Chi-A	4	2	.667	26	2	0	0	2	47^2	44	21	18	4	1	23	20	1.406	3.40	119	3.84	.244	0	.000	3	4	0.1
Total	**3**	**4**	**3**	**.571**	**35**	**4**	**0**	**0**	**2**	74^2	**74**	**44**	**40**	**6**	**2**	**51**	**30**	**1.674**	**4.82**	**87**	**5.02**	**.262**	**0**	**.000**	**-7**	**4**	**-0.9**

• ROTHSCHILD, Larry Lawrence Lee Rothschild b: 3/12/1954, Chicago, IL BL/TR, 6'2", 180 lbs. Deb: 9/11/1981 M/C

YEAR	TM-L	W	L	PCT	G	GS	CG	SH	SV	IP	H	R	ER	HR	HB	BB	SO	RAT	ERA	ERA+	CERA	OAV	BH	AVG	PR+	WS	TPW
1981	Det-A	0	0	....	5	0	0	0	1	5^2	4	1	1	0	0	6	1	1.765	1.59	238	3.72	.200	0	....	1	1	0.1
1982	Det-A	0	0	....	2	0	0	0	0	2^2	4	4	4	1	0	2	0	2.250	13.50	30	11.06	.333	0	....	-3	0	-0.3
Total	**2**	**0**	**0**	**....**	**7**	**0**	**0**	**0**	**1**	8^1	**8**	**5**	**5**	**1**	**0**	**8**	**1**	**1.920**	**5.40**	**74**	**6.06**	**.250**	**0**	**....**	**-2**	**1**	**-0.2**

• ROUNSAVILLE, Gene Virle Gene Rounsaville b: 9/27/1944, Konawa, OK BR/TR, 6'3", 205 lbs. Deb: 4/7/1970

YEAR	TM-L	W	L	PCT	G	GS	CG	SH	SV	IP	H	R	ER	HR	HB	BB	SO	RAT	ERA	ERA+	CERA	OAV	BH	AVG	PR+	WS	TPW
1970	Chi-A	0	1	.000	8	0	0	0	0	6^1	10	8	7	1	0	2	3	1.895	9.95	39	7.54	.357	0	....	-4	0	-0.4

• ROWAN, Jack John Albert Rowan b: 6/16/1887, New Castle, PA d: 9/29/1966, Dayton, OH BR/TR, 6'1", 210 lbs. Deb: 9/6/1906

YEAR	TM-L	W	L	PCT	G	GS	CG	SH	SV	IP	H	R	ER	HR	HB	BB	SO	RAT	ERA	ERA+	CERA	OAV	BH	AVG	PR+	WS	TPW
1906	Det-A	0	1	.000	1	1	1	0	0	9	15	13	11	0	0	6	0	2.333	11.00	25	7.67	.374	1	.250	-8	0	-0.9
1908	Cin-N	3	3	.500	8	7	4	1	0	49^1	46	17	10	0	0	16	24	1.257	1.82	125	2.81	.253	1	.071	3	3	0.3
1909	Cin-N	11	12	.478	38	23	14	0	0	225^2	185	86	70	0	3	104	81	1.281	2.79	93	2.77	.233	6	.092	-7	10	-0.9
1910	Cin-N	14	13	.519	42	30	18	4	1	261	242	122	85	4	9	105	108	1.330	2.93	99	3.29	.254	19	.229	2	14	0.5
1911	Phi-N	2	4	.333	12	6	2	0	0	45^2	59	35	24	3	1	20	17	1.730	4.73	73	5.75	.316	1	.077	-7	0	-0.8
	Chi-N	0	0	....	1	0	0	0	0	2	1	4	1	0	1	2	0	1.500	4.50	73	4.02	.143	0	.000	-0	0	0.0
	Yr.	2	4	.333	13	6	2	0	0	47^2	60	39	25	3	2	22	17	1.720	4.72	73	5.67	.310	1	.071	-7	0	-0.8
1913	Cin-N	0	4	.000	5	5	5	0	0	39	37	14	13	0	1	9	21	1.179	3.00	108	2.66	.264	2	.182	1	3	0.2
1914	Cin-N	1	3	.250	12	2	0	0	2	39	38	22	15	1	0	10	16	1.231	3.46	85	2.88	.262	0	.000	-2	1	-0.3
Total	**7**	**31**	**40**	**.437**	**119**	**74**	**44**	**5**	**3**	670^2	**623**	**313**	**229**	**8**	**15**	**272**	**267**	**1.334**	**3.07**	**92**	**3.25**	**.255**	**30**	**.151**	**-18**	**31**	**-1.8**

• ROWE, Don Donald Howard Rowe b: 4/3/1936, Brawley, CA BL/TL, 6', 180 lbs. Deb: 4/9/1963 C

YEAR	TM-L	W	L	PCT	G	GS	CG	SH	SV	IP	H	R	ER	HR	HB	BB	SO	RAT	ERA	ERA+	CERA	OAV	BH	AVG	PR+	WS	TPW
1963	NY-N	0	0	....	26	1	0	0	0	54^2	59	27	26	6	1	21	27	1.463	4.28	81	4.67	.280	3	.231	-4	2	-0.4

• ROWE, Ken Kenneth Darrell Rowe b: 12/31/1933, Ferndale, MI BR/TR, 6'2", 185 lbs. Deb: 4/14/1963 C

YEAR	TM-L	W	L	PCT	G	GS	CG	SH	SV	IP	H	R	ER	HR	HB	BB	SO	RAT	ERA	ERA+	CERA	OAV	BH	AVG	PR+	WS	TPW
1963	LA-N	1	1	.500	14	0	0	0	1	27^2	28	16	9	2	1	11	12	1.410	2.93	103	3.83	.264	0	.000	1	1	0.0
1964	Bal-A	1	0	1.000	6	0	0	0	0	4^1	10	10	4	1	0	1	4	2.538	8.31	43	12.39	.455	0	....	-2	0	-0.3
1965	Bal-A	0	0	....	6	0	0	0	0	13^1	17	5	5	0	0	2	3	1.425	3.38	103	3.62	.321	1	1.000	-0	1	0.0
Total	**3**	**2**	**1**	**.667**	**26**	**0**	**0**	**0**	**1**	45^1	**55**	**31**	**18**	**3**	**1**	**14**	**19**	**1.522**	**3.57**	**91**	**4.59**	**.304**	**1**	**.167**	**-2**	**2**	**-0.2**

• ROWE, Schoolboy Lynwood Thomas Rowe b: 1/11/1910, Waco, TX d: 1/8/1961, El Dorado, AR BR/TR, 6'4.5", 210 lbs. Deb: 4/15/1933 C

YEAR	TM-L	W	L	PCT	G	GS	CG	SH	SV	IP	H	R	ER	HR	HB	BB	SO	RAT	ERA	ERA+	CERA	OAV	BH	AVG	PR+	WS	TPW
1933	Det-A	7	4	.636	19	15	8	1	0	123^1	129	60	49	7	1	31	75	1.297	3.58	121	3.42	.269	11	.220	9	9	0.8
1934*	Det-A	24	8	.750	45	30	20	3	1	266	259	110	102	12	1	81	149	1.278	3.45	127	3.15	.256	33	.303	26	28	3.4
1935*	Det-A★	19	13	.594	42	34	21	**6**	3	275^2	272	121	113	11	2	68	140	1.233	3.69	113	2.99	.255	34	.312	12	23	2.4
1936	Det-A★	19	10	.655	41	35	19	4	3	245^1	266	134	123	15	2	64	115	1.345	4.51	110	3.69	.275	23	.256	14	21	1.9
1937	Det-A	1	4	.200	10	2	1	0	0	31^1	49	32	30	7	1	9	6	1.851	8.62	54	7.98	.350	2	.200	-13	0	-1.2
1938	Det-A	0	2	.000	4	3	0	0	0	21	20	11	7	1	0	11	4	1.476	3.00	167	3.73	.256	1	.167	5	2	0.4
1939	Det-A	10	12	.455	28	24	8	1	0	164	192	113	91	17	2	61	51	1.543	4.99	98	4.89	.291	15	.246	-2	8	0.0
1940*	Det-A	16	3	.842	27	23	11	1	0	169	170	68	65	15	1	43	61	1.260	3.46	137	3.43	.259	18	.269	27	18	3.0
1941	Det-A	8	6	.571	27	14	4	0	1	139	155	70	64	6	0	33	54	1.353	4.14	110	3.57	.278	15	.273	10	12	1.5
1942	Det-A	1	0	1.000	2	1	0	0	0	10^1	9	2	0	0	0	2	7	1.065	0.00	....	1.89	.220	0	.000	5	2	0.4
	Bro-N	1	0	1.000	9	2	0	0	0	30^1	36	19	18	2	1	12	6	1.582	5.34	61	4.80	.288	4	.211	-7	0	-0.8
1943	Phi-N	14	8	.636	27	25	11	3	1	199	196	73	65	7	3	29	52	1.131	2.94	115	2.58	.249	36	.300	12	19	3.1
1946	Phi-N	11	4	.733	17	16	9	2	0	136	112	39	32	3	6	21	51	.978	2.12	162	1.92	.224	11	.180	20	14	2.4
1947	Phi-N★	14	10	.583	31	28	15	1	1	195^2	232	106	94	22	3	45	74	1.416	4.32	93	4.52	.292	22	.278	-8	13	0.2
1948	Phi-N	10	10	.500	30	20	8	0	2	148	167	74	67	5	2	31	46	1.338	4.07	97	3.53	.281	10	.192	-2	9	0.0

YEAR	TM-L	W	L	PCT	G	GS	CG	SH	SV	IP	H	R	ER	HR	HB	BB	SO	RAT	ERA	ERA+	CERA	OAV	BH	AVG	PR+	WS	TPW
1949	Phi-N	3	7	.300	23	6	2	0	0	65^{1}	68	43	35	2	2	17	22	1.301	4.82	82	3.61	.300	4	.235	-7	2	-0.5
Total	**15**	**158**	**101**	**.610**	**382**	**278**	**137**	**22**	**12**	**2219^{1}**	**2332**	**1075**	**955**	**132**	**27**	**558**	**913**	**1.302**	**3.87**	**110**	**3.51**	**.269**	**239**	**.263**	**100**	**180**	**17.1**
• ROWLAND, Mike	Michael Evan Rowland b: 1/31/1953, Chicago, IL BR/TR, 6'3", 205 lbs. Deb: 7/25/1980																										
1980	SF-N	1	1	.500	19	0	0	0	0	27	20	8	7	2	1	8	8	1.037	2.33	152	2.20	.206	0	....	4	2	0.4
1981	SF-N	0	1	.000	9	1	0	0	0	15^{2}	13	7	6	1	1	6	8	1.213	3.45	100	2.88	.232	1	1.000	0	1	0.1
Total	**2**	**1**	**2**	**.333**	**28**	**1**	**0**	**0**	**0**	**42^{2}**	**33**	**15**	**13**	**3**	**2**	**14**	**16**	**1.102**	**2.74**	**127**	**2.45**	**.216**	**1**	**1.000**	**4**	**3**	**0.5**
• ROY, Charlie	Charles Robert Roy b: 6/22/1884, Beauleau, MN d: 2/10/1950, Blackfoot, ID BR/TR, 5'10", 190 lbs. Deb: 6/27/1906																										
1906	Phi-N	0	1	.000	7	1	0	0	0	18^{1}	24	12	10	0	1	5	6	1.582	4.91	53	4.77	.316	0	.000	-4	0	-0.6
• ROY, Emil	Emil Arthur Roy b: 5/26/1907, Brighton, MA d: 1/5/1997, Crystal River, FL BR/TR, 5'11", 180 lbs. Deb: 9/30/1933																										
1933	Phi-A	0	1	.000	1	1	0	0	0	2^{1}	4	7	7	0	0	4	3	3.429	27.00	16	12.54	.364	0	....	-6	0	-0.6
• ROY, Jean-Pierre	Jean-Pierre Roy b: 6/26/1920, Montreal, Canada BB/TR, 5'10", 160 lbs. Deb: 5/5/1946																										
1946	Bro-N	0	0	....	3	1	0	0	0	6^{1}	5	7	7	2	0	5	6	1.579	9.95	34	5.52	.200	0	.000	-5	0	-0.5
• ROY, Luther	Luther Franklin Roy b: 7/29/1902, Ooletewah, TN d: 7/24/1963, Grand Rapids, MI BR/TR, 5'10.5", 161 lbs. Deb: 6/12/1924																										
1924	Cle-A	0	5	.000	16	5	2	0	0	48^{2}	62	48	42	3	0	31	14	1.911	7.77	55	6.04	.318	4	.267	-18	0	-1.7
1925	Cle-A	0	0	....	6	1	0	0	0	10	14	7	4	1	0	11	1	2.500	3.60	123	9.93	.368	0	.000	1	0	0.1
1927	Chi-N	3	1	.750	11	0	0	0	0	19^{2}	14	9	5	0	1	11	5	1.271	2.29	169	2.54	.209	1	.333	3	2	0.3
1929	Phi-N	3	6	.333	21	11	1	0	0	88^{2}	137	91	83	11	3	37	16	1.962	8.42	62	7.56	.350	9	.281	-30	0	-2.5
	Bro-N	0	0	....	2	0	0	0	0	3^{2}	4	2	2	0	0	2	0	1.636	4.91	94	4.13	.286	0	.000	-0	0	0.0
	Yr.	3	6	.333	23	11	1	0	0	92^{1}	141	93	85	11	3	39	16	1.949	8.29	62	7.43	.348	9	.273	-30	0	-2.5
Total	**4**	**6**	**12**	**.333**	**56**	**17**	**3**	**0**	**0**	**170^{2}**	**231**	**157**	**136**	**15**	**4**	**92**	**36**	**1.893**	**7.17**	**67**	**6.61**	**.327**	**14**	**.264**	**-45**	**2**	**-3.9**
• ROY, Normie	Norman Brooks "Jumbo" Roy b: 11/15/1928, Newton, MA BR/TR, 6', 200 lbs. Deb: 4/23/1950																										
1950	Bos-N	4	3	.571	19	6	2	0	1	59^{2}	72	38	34	7	2	39	25	1.860	5.13	75	6.59	.305	3	.167	-8	1	-0.8
• ROZEK, Dick	Richard Louis Rozek b: 3/27/1927, Cedar Rapids, IA d: 9/27/2001, La Quinta, CA BL/TL, 6'.5", 190 lbs. Deb: 4/29/1950																										
1950	Cle-A	0	0	....	12	2	0	0	0	25^{1}	28	15	14	3	0	19	14	1.855	4.97	87	6.12	.283	0	.000	-2	1	-0.3
1951	Cle-A	0	0	....	7	1	0	0	0	15^{1}	18	12	5	1	1	11	5	1.891	2.93	129	5.90	.286	1	.333	1	0	0.2
1952	Cle-A	1	0	1.000	10	1	0	0	0	12^{2}	11	8	7	0	0	13	5	1.895	4.97	67	4.52	.224	0	.000	-2	0	-0.3
1953	Phi-A	0	0	....	2	0	0	0	0	10^{2}	8	6	6	3	0	9	2	1.594	5.06	85	5.84	.222	0	.000	-1	0	-0.1
1954	Phi-A	0	0	....	2	0	0	0	0	1^{1}	0	1	1	0	1	3	0	2.250	6.75	58	5.14	.000	0	....	-0	0	0.0
Total	**5**	**1**	**0**	**1.000**	**33**	**4**	**0**	**0**	**0**	**65^{1}**	**65**	**42**	**33**	**7**	**2**	**55**	**26**	**1.837**	**4.55**	**87**	**5.69**	**.263**	**1**	**.083**	**-4**	**1**	**-0.5**
• ROZEMA, Dave	David Scott Rozema b: 8/5/1956, Grand Rapids, MI BR/TR, 6'4", 200 lbs. Deb: 4/11/1977																										
1977	Det-A	15	7	.682	28	28	16	1	0	218^{1}	222	87	75	25	7	34	92	1.173	3.09	139	3.46	.265	0	....	30	18	2.9
1978	Det-A	9	12	.429	28	28	11	2	0	209^{1}	205	83	73	17	2	41	57	1.175	3.14	123	3.14	.260	0	....	14	15	1.4
1979	Det-A	4	4	.500	16	16	4	1	0	97^{1}	101	52	38	12	6	30	33	1.346	3.51	123	4.26	.270	0	....	8	5	0.8
1980	Det-A	6	9	.400	42	13	2	1	4	144^{2}	152	68	63	11	5	49	49	1.389	3.92	105	3.97	.277	0	....	5	9	0.5
1981	Det-A	5	5	.500	28	9	2	2	3	104	99	42	42	12	3	25	46	1.192	3.63	104	3.40	.256	0	....	-1	6	-0.1
1982	Det-A	3	0	1.000	8	2	0	0	1	27^{2}	17	5	5	2	1	7	15	.867	1.63	250	1.58	.179	0	....	7	4	0.7
1983	Det-A	8	3	.727	29	16	1	0	2	105	100	50	40	10	1	29	63	1.229	3.43	114	3.22	.248	0	....	4	7	0.4
1984	Det-A	7	6	.538	29	16	0	0	0	101	110	49	42	13	2	18	48	1.267	3.74	105	3.91	.274	0	....	1	5	0.1
1985	Tex-A	3	7	.300	34	4	0	0	7	88	100	45	41	10	2	22	42	1.386	4.19	101	4.45	.287	0	....	2	7	0.2
1986	Tex-A	0	0	....	6	0	0	0	0	10^{2}	19	9	7	1	0	3	3	2.063	5.91	73	8.49	.404	0	....	-2	0	-0.2
Total	**10**	**60**	**53**	**.531**	**248**	**132**	**36**	**7**	**17**	**1106**	**1125**	**490**	**426**	**113**	**29**	**258**	**448**	**1.250**	**3.47**	**117**	**3.63**	**.266**	**0**	**....**	**68**	**76**	**6.8**
• RUBIO, Jorge	Jorge Jesus (Chavez) Rubio b: 4/23/1945, Mexicali, Mexico BR/TR, 6'3", 200 lbs. Deb: 4/21/1966																										
1966	Cal-A	2	1	.667	7	4	1	1	0	27^{1}	22	10	9	2	1	16	27	1.390	2.96	113	3.55	.220	0	.000	1	2	0.0
1967	Cal-A	0	2	.000	3	3	0	0	0	15	18	7	6	2	4	9	4	1.800	3.60	87	8.01	.316	1	.333	-1	1	0.0
Total	**2**	**2**	**3**	**.400**	**10**	**7**	**1**	**1**	**0**	**42^{1}**	**40**	**17**	**15**	**4**	**5**	**25**	**31**	**1.535**	**3.19**	**102**	**5.13**	**.255**	**1**	**.091**	**0**	**3**	**0.0**
• RUCKER, Dave	David Michael Rucker b: 9/1/1957, San Bernardino, CA BL/TL, 6'1", 190 lbs. Deb: 4/12/1981																										
1981	Det-A	0	0	....	2	0	0	0	0	4	3	4	3	0	1	1	2	1.000	6.75	56	2.23	.188	0	....	-1	0	-0.1
1982	Det-A	5	6	.455	27	4	1	0	0	64	62	26	24	4	2	23	31	1.328	3.38	120	3.52	.251	0	....	3	5	0.3
1983	Det-A	1	2	.333	4	3	0	0	0	9	18	17	17	2	1	8	6	2.889	17.00	23	15.03	.419	0	....	-13	0	-1.3
	StL-N	5	3	.625	34	0	0	0	0	37	36	14	11	1	1	18	22	1.459	2.68	135	3.95	.263	0	.000	4	4	0.4
1984	StL-N	2	3	.400	50	0	0	0	0	73	62	23	17	0	1	34	38	1.315	2.10	166	2.89	.237	1	.143	10	6	1.0
1985	Phi-N	3	2	.600	39	3	0	0	1	79^{1}	83	42	38	6	2	40	41	1.550	4.31	85	4.61	.279	4	.333	-4	3	-0.3
1986	Phi-N	0	2	.000	19	0	0	0	0	25	34	19	16	4	0	14	14	1.920	5.76	67	7.27	.340	0	.000	-5	0	-0.6
1988	Pit-N	0	2	.000	31	0	0	0	0	28^{1}	39	19	15	2	0	9	16	1.694	4.76	71	5.60	.328	0	.000	-4	0	-0.5
Total	**7**	**16**	**20**	**.444**	**206**	**10**	**1**	**0**	**1**	**319^{2}**	**337**	**164**	**141**	**19**	**8**	**147**	**170**	**1.514**	**3.97**	**94**	**4.48**	**.276**	**5**	**.192**	**-11**	**18**	**-1.1**
• RUCKER, Nap	George Rucker b: 9/30/1884, Crabapple, GA d: 12/19/1970, Alpharetta, GA BR/TL, 5'11", 190 lbs. Deb: 4/15/1907																										
1907	Bro-N	15	13	.536	37	30	26	4	0	275^{1}	242	94	63	3	8	80	131	1.169	2.06	113	2.51	.242	15	.155	11	18	1.2
1908	Bro-N	17	19	.472	42	37	30	6	1	333^{1}	265	107	77	1	19	125	199	1.170	2.08	112	2.45	.231	21	.179	7	23	0.8
1909	Bro-N	13	19	.406	38	33	28	6	1	309^{1}	245	95	77	6	14	101	201	1.119	2.24	115	2.37	.228	12	.119	15	22	1.2
1910	Bro-N	17	18	.486	41	**39**	**27**	**6**	0	**320**^{1}	293	112	92	5	9	84	147	1.177	2.58	117	2.66	.251	23	.209	13	23	1.3
1911	Bro-N	22	18	.550	48	33	23	5	4	315^{2}	255	102	95	12	8	110	190	1.156	2.71	123	2.53	.226	21	.202	23	31	2.5
1912	Bro-N	18	21	.462	45	34	23	**6**	4	297^{2}	272	101	73	6	3	72	151	1.156	2.21	151	2.53	.250	25	.245	41	24	4.3
1913	Bro-N	14	15	.483	41	33	16	4	3	260	236	99	83	3	7	67	111	1.165	2.87	114	2.58	.249	21	.241	9	19	1.1
1914	Bro-N	7	6	.538	16	16	5	0	0	103^{2}	113	57	39	2	2	27	35	1.350	3.39	84	3.42	.275	9	.265	-7	4	-0.5
1915	Bro-N	9	4	.692	19	15	7	1	1	122^{2}	134	42	33	3	2	28	38	1.321	2.42	115	3.40	.279	9	.214	4	10	0.6
1916*	Bro-N	2	1	.667	9	3	1	0	0	37^{1}	34	14	7	0	1	7	14	1.098	1.69	158	2.28	.241	1	.091	3	3	0.3
Total	**10**	**134**	**134**	**.500**	**336**	**273**	**186**	**38**	**14**	**2375^{1}**	**2089**	**823**	**639**	**41**	**73**	**701**	**1217**	**1.175**	**2.42**	**118**	**2.60**	**.243**	**157**	**.195**	**120**	**177**	**12.7**
• RUDOLPH, Dick	Richard "Baldy" Rudolph b: 8/25/1887, New York, NY d: 10/20/1949, Bronx, NY BR/TR, 5'9.5", 160 lbs. Deb: 9/30/1910 C																										
1910	NY-N	0	1	.000	3	1	1	0	2	12	21	11	10	0	0	2	9	1.917	7.50	39	6.23	.350	1	.250	-6	0	-0.6
1911	NY-N	0	0	....	1	0	0	0	0	2	2	2	2	0	0	0	0	1.000	9.00	37	1.95	.250	1	1.000	-1	0	-0.1
1913	Bos-N	14	13	.519	33	22	17	2	0	249^{1}	258	101	81	4	2	59	109	1.271	2.92	112	3.09	.276	21	.239	14	16	1.9
1914*	Bos-N	26	10	.722	42	36	31	6	0	336^{1}	288	105	88	9	4	61	138	1.038	2.35	117	2.16	.238	15	.125	2	29	0.1
1915	Bos-N	22	19	.537	44	**43**	30	3	1	341^{1}	304	125	90	4	6	64	147	1.078	2.37	113	2.21	.242	23	.198	7	24	1.5
1916	Bos-N	19	12	.613	41	38	27	5	3	312	266	93	75	7	3	38	133	.974	2.16	113	1.89	.235	16	.158	10	21	1.3
1917	Bos-N	13	14	.481	31	30	22	5	0	242^{2}	252	104	92	1	4	54	96	1.261	3.41	75	2.98	.272	20	.230	-21	9	-2.0
1918	Bos-N	9	10	.474	21	20	15	3	0	154	144	63	44	2	0	30	48	1.130	2.57	104	2.42	.255	10	.185	5	7	0.5
1919	Bos-N	13	18	.419	37	32	24	2	2	273^{2}	282	95	66	2	3	54	76	1.228	2.17	132	2.88	.276	17	.193	21	20	2.7
1920	Bos-N	4	8	.333	18	11	3	0	0	89	104	57	40	4	4	24	24	1.438	4.04	75	4.16	.294	5	.185	-11	1	-1.2
1922	Bos-N	0	2	.000	3	3	1	0	0	16	22	10	9	2	0	5	3	1.688	5.06	79	5.97	.328	2	.400	-2	1	-0.1
1923	Bos-N	1	2	.333	4	4	1	1	0	19^{1}	27	12	8	0	1	10	3	1.914	3.72	107	6.17	.333	0	.000	1	1	0.0
1927	Bos-N	0	0	....	1	0	0	0	0	1^{1}	1	0	0	0	0	1	0	1.500	0.00	....	3.02	.200	0	....	1	0	0.1
Total	**13**	**121**	**109**	**.526**	**279**	**240**	**172**	**27**	**8**	**2049**	**1971**	**778**	**605**	**35**	**27**	**402**	**786**	**1.158**	**2.66**	**104**	**2.63**	**.259**	**131**	**.188**	**20**	**129**	**3.8**
• RUDOLPH, Don	Frederick Donald Rudolph b: 8/16/1931, Baltimore, MD d: 9/12/1968, Granada Hills, CA BL/TL, 5'11", 195 lbs. Deb: 9/21/1957																										
1957	Chi-A	1	0	1.000	5	0	0	0	0	12	6	3	3	2	0	2	2	.667	2.25	166	1.33	.146	1	.500	2	1	0.2
1958	Chi-A	1	0	1.000	7	0	0	0	1	7	4	2	2	0	0	5	2	1.286	2.57	141	2.43	.190	0	....	1	1	0.1
1959	Chi-A	0	0	....	4	0	0	0	1	3	4	0	0	0	0	2	0	2.000	0.00	....	5.90	.333	0	....	1	1	0.1
	Cin-N	0	0	....	5	0	0	0	0	7^{1}	13	4	4	1	0	3	8	2.182	4.91	83	9.30	.394	0	.000	-1	0	-0.1

YEAR	TM-L	W	L	PCT	G	GS	CG	SH	SV	IP	H	R	ER	HR	HB	BB	SO	RAT	ERA	ERA+	CERA	OAV	BH	AVG	PR+	WS	TPW
1962	Cle-A	0	0	....	1	0	0	0	0	0^1	1	0	0	0	0	0	0	3.000	0.00	....	14.91	1.000	0	....	0	0	0.0
	Was-A	8	10	.444	37	23	6	2	0	176^1	187	84	71	13	3	42	68	1.299	3.62	111	3.65	.274	10	.175	8	11	1.0
	Yr.	8	10	.444	38	23	6	2	0	176^2	188	84	71	13	3	42	68	1.302	3.62	112	3.67	.275	10	.175	8	11	1.0
1963	Was-A	7	19	.269	37	26	4	0	1	174	189	98	88	28	6	36	70	1.293	4.55	82	4.27	.275	8	.178	-16	5	-1.5
1964	Was-A	1	3	.250	28	8	0	0	0	70^1	81	36	32	10	0	12	32	1.322	4.09	90	4.25	.290	1	.067	-3	2	-0.4
Total	6	18	32	.360	124	57	10	2	3	450^1	485	227	200	54	9	102	182	1.303	4.00	96	4.02	.276	20	.167	-8	21	-0.6
• RUDOLPH, Ernie	Ernest William Rudolph b: 2/13/1909, Black River Falls, WI d: 1/13/2003, Black River Falls, WI BL/TR, 5'8", 165 lbs. Deb: 6/16/1945																										
1945	Bro-N	1	0	1.000	7	0	0	0	0	8^2	12	10	5	1	0	7	3	2.192	5.19	72	7.85	.333	0	....	-1	0	-0.1
• RUEBEL, Matt	Matthew Alexander Ruebel b: 10/16/1969, Cincinnati, OH BL/TL, 6'2", 180 lbs. Deb: 5/21/1996																										
1996	Pit-N	1	1	.500	26	7	0	0	1	58^2	64	38	30	7	6	25	22	1.517	4.60	95	5.27	.277	3	.231	-1	2	0.0
1997	Pit-N	3	2	.600	44	0	0	0	0	62^2	77	50	44	8	5	27	50	1.660	6.32	68	5.88	.301	0	.000	-14	0	-1.4
1998	TB-A	0	2	.000	7	1	0	0	0	8^2	11	7	6	3	0	4	6	1.731	6.23	77	8.17	.314	0	....	-2	0	-0.2
Total	3	4	5	.444	77	8	0	0	1	130	152	95	80	18	11	56	78	1.600	5.54	79	5.76	.291	3	.150	-16	2	-1.6
• RUETER, Kirk	Kirk Wesley Rueter b: 12/1/1970, Hoyleton, IL BL/TL, 6'3", 195 lbs. Deb: 7/7/1993																										
1993	Mon-N	8	0	1.000	14	14	1	0	0	85^2	85	33	26	5	0	18	31	1.202	2.73	153	3.14	.264	2	.077	14	8	1.3
1994	Mon-N	7	3	.700	20	20	0	0	0	92^1	106	60	53	11	2	23	50	1.397	5.17	82	4.54	.294	4	.118	-10	2	-1.0
1995	Mon-N	5	3	.625	9	9	1	1	0	47^1	38	17	17	3	1	9	28	.993	3.23	133	2.19	.224	0	.000	6	4	0.4
1996	Mon-N	5	6	.455	16	16	0	0	0	78^2	91	44	40	12	2	22	30	1.436	4.58	95	5.06	.294	3	.120	-2	3	-0.3
	SF-N	1	2	.333	4	3	0	0	0	23^1	18	6	5	0	0	5	16	.986	1.93	212	1.66	.207	1	.143	5	2	0.5
	Yr.	6	8	.429	20	19	0	0	0	102	109	50	45	12	2	27	46	1.333	3.97	108	4.28	.275	4	.125	4	5	0.3
1997*	SF-N	13	6	.684	32	32	0	0	0	190^2	194	83	73	17	1	51	115	1.285	3.45	117	3.54	.264	9	.138	14	12	1.3
1998	SF-N	16	9	.640	33	33	1	0	0	187^2	193	100	91	27	7	57	102	1.332	4.36	91	4.27	.265	14	.209	-8	8	-0.7
1999	SF-N	15	10	.600	33	33	1	0	0	184^2	219	118	111	28	2	55	94	1.484	5.41	78	5.19	.297	9	.155	-25	5	-2.3
2000*	SF-N	11	9	.550	32	31	0	0	0	184	205	92	81	23	2	62	71	1.451	3.96	107	4.68	.290	12	.200	5	9	0.7
2001	SF-N	14	12	.538	34	34	0	0	0	195^1	213	105	96	25	4	66	83	1.428	4.42	90	4.65	.283	10	.172	-10	7	-0.8
2002*	SF-N	14	8	.636	33	33	0	0	0	203^2	204	83	73	22	1	54	76	1.267	3.23	120	3.61	.262	11	.177	12	12	1.3
2003*	SF-N	10	5	.667	27	27	0	0	0	147	170	77	74	14	1	47	41	1.476	4.53	91	4.72	.297	7	.132	-10	6	-1.1
Total	11	119	73	.620	287	285	4	1	0	1620^1	1736	818	740	187	23	469	737	1.361	4.11	100	4.24	.277	82	.154	-8	78	-0.8
• RUETHER, Dutch	Walter Henry Ruether b: 9/13/1893, Alameda, CA d: 5/16/1970, Phoenix, AZ BL/TL, 6'1.5", 180 lbs. Deb: 4/13/1917																										
1917	Chi-N	2	0	1.000	10	4	1	0	0	36^1	37	12	10	0	3	12	23	1.349	2.48	117	3.52	.285	12	.273	2	5	0.7
	Cin-N	1	2	.333	7	4	1	1	0	35^2	43	17	14	0	2	14	12	1.598	3.53	74	4.82	.323	5	.208	-4	1	-0.2
	Yr.	3	2	.600	17	8	2	1	0	72	80	29	24	0	5	26	35	1.472	3.00	91	4.16	.304	17	.250	-1	6	0.5
1918	Cin-N	0	1	.000	2	2	1	0	0	10	10	9	3	0	1	3	10	1.300	2.70	99	2.94	.244	0	.000	-0	0	-0.1
1919*	Cin-N	19	6	.760	33	29	20	3	0	242^2	195	69	49	1	7	83	78	1.146	1.82	152	2.27	.223	24	.261	21	26	3.0
1920	Cin-N	16	12	.571	37	33	23	5	3	265^2	235	87	73	2	9	96	99	1.246	2.47	123	2.80	.247	20	.192	16	18	1.6
1921	Bro-N	10	13	.435	36	27	12	1	2	211^1	247	116	100	7	7	67	78	1.486	4.26	91	4.23	.299	34	.351	-8	15	0.4
1922	Bro-N	21	12	.636	35	35	26	2	0	267^1	290	123	105	11	6	92	89	1.429	3.53	115	3.93	.282	26	.208	18	20	2.2
1923	Bro-N	15	14	.517	34	34	20	0	0	275	308	157	129	11	6	86	87	1.433	4.22	92	4.00	.287	32	.274	-10	15	-0.4
1924	Bro-N	8	13	.381	30	21	13	2	3	168	190	92	73	4	5	45	63	1.399	3.91	96	3.74	.282	15	.242	1	9	0.3
1925*	Was-A	18	7	.720	30	29	16	1	0	223^1	241	105	96	5	8	105	68	1.549	3.87	109	4.23	.281	36	.333	3	20	1.2
1926	Was-A	12	6	.667	23	23	9	0	0	169^1	214	100	91	5	4	66	48	1.654	4.84	80	4.94	.311	23	.250	-19	7	-1.4
	*NY-A	2	3	.400	5	5	1	0	0	36	32	14	14	0	1	18	8	1.389	3.50	110	3.17	.248	2	.095	2	2	0.0
	Yr.	14	9	.609	28	28	10	0	0	205^1	246	114	105	5	5	84	56	1.607	4.60	84	4.63	.301	25	.221	-17	9	-1.4
1927	NY-A	13	6	.684	27	26	12	3	0	184	202	88	69	8	7	52	45	1.380	3.38	114	3.88	.287	21	.263	9	13	1.3
Total	11	137	95	.591	309	272	155	18	8	2124^2	2244	989	826	54	66	739	708	1.404	3.50	105	3.72	.277	250	.258	32	151	8.6
• RUFFCORN, Scott	Scott Patrick Ruffcorn b: 12/29/1969, New Braunfels, TX BR/TR, 6'4", 210 lbs. Deb: 6/19/1993																										
1993	Chi-A	0	2	.000	3	2	0	0	0	10	9	11	9	2	0	10	2	1.900	8.10	52	7.08	.265	0	....	-4	0	-0.4
1994	Chi-A	0	2	.000	2	2	0	0	0	6^1	15	11	9	1	0	5	3	3.158	12.79	36	15.47	.455	0	....	-6	0	-0.5
1995	Chi-A	0	0	....	4	0	0	0	0	8	10	7	7	0	2	13	5	2.875	7.88	57	11.41	.333	0	....	-3	0	-0.3
1996	Chi-A	0	1	.000	3	1	0	0	0	6^1	10	8	8	1	0	6	3	2.526	11.37	42	10.79	.370	0	....	-5	0	-0.4
1997	Phi-N	0	3	.000	18	4	0	0	0	39^2	42	40	34	4	7	36	33	1.966	7.71	55	7.10	.275	0	.000	-15	0	-1.5
Total	5	0	8	.000	30	9	0	0	0	70^1	86	77	67	8	9	70	46	2.218	8.57	51	8.67	.310	0	.000	-33	0	-3.2
• RUFFIN, Bruce	Bruce Wayne Ruffin b: 10/4/1963, Lubbock, TX BB/TL, 6'2", 209 lbs. Deb: 6/28/1986																										
1986	Phi-N	9	4	.692	21	21	6	0	0	146^1	138	53	40	6	1	44	70	1.244	2.46	156	3.02	.251	4	.073	23	12	2.0
1987	Phi-N	11	14	.440	35	35	3	1	0	204^2	236	118	99	17	2	73	93	1.510	4.35	97	4.78	.298	4	.055	-5	8	-0.9
1988	Phi-N	6	10	.375	55	15	3	0	3	144^1	151	86	71	7	3	80	82	1.600	4.43	80	4.61	.275	4	.121	-12	3	-1.3
1989	Phi-N	6	10	.375	24	23	1	0	0	125^2	152	69	62	10	0	62	70	1.703	4.44	80	5.44	.301	6	.176	-12	3	-1.0
1990	Phi-N	6	13	.316	32	25	2	1	0	149	178	99	89	14	1	62	79	1.611	5.38	71	5.12	.297	3	.068	-28	0	-3.0
1991	Phi-N	4	7	.364	31	15	1	1	0	119	125	52	50	6	1	38	85	1.370	3.78	97	3.70	.272	0	.000	-1	6	-0.2
1992	Mil-A	1	6	.143	25	6	1	0	0	58	66	43	43	7	0	41	45	1.845	6.67	58	6.28	.293	0	....	-19	0	-2.0
1993	Col-N	6	5	.545	59	12	0	0	2	139^2	145	71	60	10	1	69	126	1.532	3.87	123	4.38	.269	2	.080	19	11	1.8
1994	Col-N	4	5	.444	56	0	0	0	16	55^2	55	28	25	6	1	30	65	1.527	4.04	123	4.53	.253	1	.250	7	9	0.8
1995*	Col-N	0	1	.000	37	0	0	0	11	34	26	8	8	1	0	19	23	1.324	2.12	254	2.98	.222	0	.000	13	8	1.3
1996	Col-N	7	5	.583	71	0	0	0	24	69^2	55	35	31	5	0	29	74	1.206	4.00	130	2.72	.212	0	.000	11	14	1.1
1997	Col-N	0	2	.000	23	0	0	0	7	22	18	15	13	3	0	18	31	1.636	5.32	97	4.86	.220	0	....	-0	2	0.0
Total	12	60	82	.423	469	152	17	3	63	1268	1345	677	591	92	10	565	843	1.506	4.19	96	4.41	.275	24	.081	-4	76	-1.5
• RUFFIN, Johnny	Johnny Renando Ruffin b: 7/29/1971, Butler, AL BR/TR, 6'3", 172 lbs. Deb: 8/8/1993																										
1993	Cin-N	2	1	.667	21	0	0	0	2	37^2	36	16	15	4	1	11	30	1.248	3.58	112	3.49	.247	1	.333	2	3	0.2
1994	Cin-N	7	2	.778	51	0	0	0	1	70	57	26	24	7	0	27	44	1.200	3.09	134	2.99	.223	0	.000	8	7	0.7
1995	Cin-N	0	0	....	10	0	0	0	0	13^1	4	3	2	0	0	11	11	1.125	1.35	305	1.49	.093	0	.000	4	2	0.3
1996	Cin-N	1	3	.250	49	0	0	0	0	62^1	71	42	38	10	2	37	69	1.733	5.49	76	6.19	.292	2	.500	-10	1	-0.9
2000	Ari-N	0	0	....	5	0	0	0	0	9	14	9	9	4	0	3	5	1.889	9.00	52	9.93	.350	0	....	-4	0	-0.4
2001	Fla-N	0	0	....	3	0	0	0	0	3^2	5	4	2	0	1	4	4	2.455	4.91	86	8.59	.313	0	....	-0	0	0.0
Total	6	10	6	.625	139	0	0	0	3	196	187	100	90	25	4	93	163	1.429	4.13	101	4.42	.251	3	.176	-0	13	0.0
• RUFFING, Red	Charles Herbert Ruffing b: 5/3/1904, Granville, IL d: 2/17/1986, Mayfield Heights, OH BR/TR, 6'1.5", 205 lbs. Deb: 5/31/1924 C HOF: 1967																										
1924	Bos-A	0	0	....	8	2	0	0	0	23	29	17	17	0	3	9	10	1.652	6.65	66	5.10	.333	1	.143	-6	0	-0.5
1925	Bos-A	9	18	.333	37	27	13	3	1	217^1	253	135	121	10	2	75	64	1.509	5.01	91	4.35	.299	17	.215	-5	9	-0.4
1926	Bos-A	6	15	.286	37	22	6	0	2	166	169	96	81	4	5	68	58	1.428	4.39	93	3.67	.274	10	.196	-3	8	-0.3
1927	Bos-A	5	13	.278	26	18	10	0	2	158^1	160	94	82	7	4	87	77	1.560	4.66	90	4.29	.277	14	.255	-6	8	-0.4
1928	Bos-A	10	25	.286	42	34	**25**	1	2	289^1	303	147	125	8	10	96	118	1.379	3.89	106	3.52	.275	38	.314	6	21	1.7
1929	Bos-A	9	22	.290	35	32	18	1	1	244^1	280	162	132	17	2	118	109	1.629	4.86	88	4.89	.297	35	.307	-15	11	-0.6
1930	Bos-A	0	3	.000	4	3	1	0	0	24	32	19	17	1	1	6	14	1.583	6.38	72	4.77	.323	3	.273	-5	0	-0.4
	NY-A	15	5	.750	34	25	12	2	1	197^2	200	106	91	10	2	62	117	1.325	4.14	104	3.39	.260	37	.374	5	16	2.0
	Yr.	15	8	.652	38	28	13	2	1	221^2	232	125	108	11	3	68	131	1.353	4.38	99	3.54	.267	40	.364	0	16	1.6
1931	NY-A	16	14	.533	37	30	19	1	2	237	240	130	116	11	6	87	132	1.380	4.41	90	3.56	.256	36	.330	-13	15	-0.1
1932*	NY-A	18	7	.720	35	29	22	3	2	259	219	102	89	16	3	115	**190**	1.290	3.09	132	3.06	**.226**	38	.306	29	26	3.8
1933	NY-A	9	14	.391	35	28	18	0	3	235	230	118	102	7	4	93	122	1.374	3.91	99	3.42	.258	29	.252	3	15	0.9
1934	NY-A★	19	11	.633	36	31	19	5	0	256^1	232	134	112	18	1	104	149	1.311	3.93	103	3.24	.236	28	.248	-0	17	0.5
1935	NY-A	16	11	.593	30	29	19	2	0	222	201	88	77	17	1	76	81	1.248	3.12	130	3.13	.239	37	.339	19	22	3.0
1936*	NY-A	20	12	.625	33	33	25	3	0	271	274	133	116	22	3	90	102	1.343	3.85	121	3.72	.263	37	.291	22	23	3.2
1937*	NY-A	20	7	.741	31	31	22	4	0	256^1	242	101	85	17	1	68	131	1.209	2.98	149	3.00	.247	26	.202	38	24	3.6
1938*	NY-A★	**21**	7	.750	31	31	22	3	0	247^1	246	104	91	16	0	82	127	1.326	3.31	137	3.48	.258	24	.224	32	**25**	3.7

YEAR TM-L	W	L	PCT	G	GS	CG	SH	SV	IP	H	R	ER	HR	HB	BB	SO	RAT	ERA	ERA+	CERA	OAV	BH	AVG	PR+	WS	TPW
1939* NY-A★	21	7	.750	28	28	22	**5**	0	233^1	211	88	76	15	2	75	95	1.226	2.93	149	2.98	.240	35	.307	28	22	3.3
1940 NY-A★	15	12	.556	30	30	20	3	0	226	218	98	85	24	3	76	97	1.301	3.38	119	3.65	.252	11	.124	13	16	1.0
1941* NY-A★	15	6	.714	23	23	13	2	0	185^2	177	87	73	13	1	54	60	1.244	3.54	111	3.17	.252	27	.303	1	15	1.2
1942* NY-A★	14	7	.667	24	24	16	4	0	193^2	183	72	69	10	3	41	80	1.157	3.21	107	2.80	.250	20	.250	-3	15	0.3
1945 NY-A	7	3	.700	11	11	8	1	0	87^1	85	32	28	2	1	20	24	1.202	2.89	120	2.74	.251	10	.217	4	7	0.4
1946 NY-A	5	1	.833	8	8	4	2	0	61	37	13	12	2	0	23	19	.984	1.77	195	1.56	.171	3	.120	10	7	0.9
1947 Chi-A	3	5	.375	9	9	1	0	0	53	63	39	36	7	0	16	11	1.491	6.11	60	4.87	.290	5	.208	-14	0	-1.5
Total 22	273	225	.548	624	538	335	45	16	4344	4284	2115	1833	254	58	1541	1987	1.341	3.80	109	3.50	.258	521	.269	139	322	25.5

• RUHLE, Vern Vernon Gerald Ruhle b: 1/25/1951, Coleman, MI BR/TR, 6'1", 187 lbs. Deb: 9/9/1974 C

YEAR TM-L	W	L	PCT	G	GS	CG	SH	SV	IP	H	R	ER	HR	HB	BB	SO	RAT	ERA	ERA+	CERA	OAV	BH	AVG	PR+	WS	TPW
1974 Det-A	2	0	1.000	5	3	1	0	0	33	35	13	10	1	1	6	10	1.242	2.73	139	3.21	.273	0	....	4	3	0.4
1975 Det-A	11	12	.478	32	31	8	3	0	190	199	104	85	17	7	65	67	1.389	4.03	100	4.09	.266	0	....	4	11	0.4
1976 Det-A	9	12	.429	32	32	5	1	0	199^2	227	99	87	19	4	59	88	1.432	3.92	94	4.47	.288	0	....	-2	10	-0.3
1977 Det-A	3	5	.375	14	10	0	0	0	66^1	83	44	42	9	3	15	27	1.477	5.70	75	5.26	.305	0	....	-10	1	-1.0
1978 Hou-N	3	3	.500	13	10	2	2	0	68	57	17	16	0	1	20	27	1.132	2.12	156	2.21	.224	1	.056	10	6	1.0
1979 Hou-N	2	6	.250	13	10	2	2	0	66^1	64	33	30	9	2	8	33	1.085	4.07	86	3.14	.249	1	.053	-4	1	-0.5
1980* Hou-N	12	4	.750	28	22	6	2	0	159^1	148	51	42	7	3	29	55	1.111	2.37	139	2.62	.251	12	.245	16	15	2.1
1981* Hou-N	4	6	.400	20	15	1	0	1	102	97	36	33	6	1	20	39	1.147	2.91	113	2.83	.250	6	.250	4	7	0.8
1982 Hou-N	9	13	.409	31	21	3	2	1	149	169	81	65	12	4	24	56	1.295	3.93	84	3.85	.289	4	.098	-11	4	-1.3
1983 Hou-N	8	5	.615	41	9	0	0	3	114^2	107	49	47	13	3	36	43	1.247	3.69	92	3.48	.249	2	.105	-5	6	-0.6
1984 Hou-N	1	9	.100	40	6	0	0	2	90^1	112	58	46	5	3	29	60	1.561	4.58	72	4.80	.309	1	.083	-14	0	-1.5
1985 Cle-A	2	10	.167	42	16	1	0	3	125	139	65	60	16	2	30	54	1.352	4.32	96	4.27	.283	0	....	-2	5	-0.2
1986* Cal-A	1	3	.250	16	3	0	0	1	47^2	46	25	22	5	1	7	23	1.112	4.15	99	2.96	.247	0	....	-1	2	-0.1
Total 13	67	88	.432	327	188	29	12	11	1411^1	1483	675	585	119	35	348	582	1.297	3.73	98	3.74	.270	27	.148	-13	71	-0.7

• RUNYAN, Sean Sean David Runyan b: 6/21/1974, Fort Smith, AR BL/TL, 6'3", 210 lbs. Deb: 3/31/1998

YEAR TM-L	W	L	PCT	G	GS	CG	SH	SV	IP	H	R	ER	HR	HB	BB	SO	RAT	ERA	ERA+	CERA	OAV	BH	AVG	PR+	WS	TPW
1998 Det-A	1	4	.200	**88**	0	0	0	1	50^1	47	23	20	7	2	28	39	1.490	3.58	132	4.67	.255	0	....	6	4	0.5
1999 Det-A	0	1	.000	12	0	0	0	0	10^2	9	4	4	2	1	3	6	1.125	3.38	146	3.49	.237	0	....	2	1	0.2
2000 Det-A	0	0	....	3	0	0	0	0	3	2	2	2	0	0	2	1	1.333	6.00	80	2.79	.222	0	....	-0	0	0.0
Total 3	1	5	.167	103	0	0	0	1	64	58	29	26	9	3	33	46	1.422	3.66	130	4.39	.251	0	....	7	5	0.7

• RUPE, Ryan Ryan Kittman Rupe b: 3/31/1975, Houston, TX BR/TR, 6'6", 230 lbs. Deb: 5/5/1999

YEAR TM-L	W	L	PCT	G	GS	CG	SH	SV	IP	H	R	ER	HR	HB	BB	SO	RAT	ERA	ERA+	CERA	OAV	BH	AVG	PR+	WS	TPW
1999 TB-A	8	9	.471	24	24	0	0	0	142^1	136	81	72	17	12	57	97	1.356	4.55	109	4.32	.253	0	.000	7	8	0.6
2000 TB-A	5	6	.455	18	18	0	0	0	91	121	75	70	19	9	31	61	1.670	6.92	71	7.02	.321	0	.000	-21	1	-2.0
2001 TB-A	5	12	.294	28	26	0	0	0	143^1	161	111	105	30	11	48	123	1.458	6.59	68	5.67	.283	1	.333	-34	1	-3.2
2002 TB-A	5	10	.333	15	15	2	0	0	90	83	60	56	11	10	25	67	1.200	5.60	80	3.74	.243	0	.000	-13	2	-1.2
2003 Bos-A	1	1	.500	4	1	0	0	0	10	13	9	7	4	0	1	7	1.400	6.30	72	6.40	.302	0	....	-2	0	-0.2
Total 5	24	38	.387	89	84	2	0	0	476^2	514	336	310	81	42	162	355	1.418	5.85	80	5.17	.275	1	.111	-63	12	-6.0

• RUSCH, Glendon Glendon James Rusch b: 11/7/1974, Seattle, WA BL/TL, 6'2", 170 lbs. Deb: 4/6/1997

YEAR TM-L	W	L	PCT	G	GS	CG	SH	SV	IP	H	R	ER	HR	HB	BB	SO	RAT	ERA	ERA+	CERA	OAV	BH	AVG	PR+	WS	TPW
1997 KC-A	6	9	.400	30	27	1	0	0	170^1	206	111	104	28	7	52	116	1.515	5.50	86	5.56	.301	0	.000	-16	5	-1.6
1998 KC-A	6	15	.286	29	24	1	1	1	154^2	191	104	101	22	4	50	94	1.558	5.88	82	5.62	.304	0	.000	-16	5	-1.6
1999 KC-A	0	1	.000	3	0	0	0	0	4	7	7	7	1	1	3	4	2.500	15.75	32	12.89	.368	0	....	-5	0	-0.4
NY-N	0	0	....	1	0	0	0	0	1	1	0	0	0	0	0	0	1.000	0.00	....	2.02	.333	0	....	0	0	0.0
2000* NY-N	11	11	.500	31	30	2	0	0	190^2	196	91	85	18	6	44	157	1.259	4.01	110	3.64	.267	3	.060	9	11	0.6
2001 NY-N	8	12	.400	33	33	1	0	0	179	216	101	92	23	7	43	156	1.447	4.63	89	4.97	.300	3	.056	-11	6	-1.4
2002 Mil-N	10	16	.385	34	34	4	1	0	210^2	227	118	110	30	5	76	140	1.438	4.70	87	4.80	.279	19	.288	-13	7	-0.8
2003 Mil-N	1	12	.077	32	19	1	0	1	123^1	171	93	88	11	4	45	93	1.751	6.42	66	6.27	.331	7	.206	-27	0	-2.6
Total 7	42	76	.356	193	167	10	2	2	1033^2	1215	625	587	133	34	313	760	1.478	5.11	86	5.07	.295	32	.152	-79	34	-7.8

• RUSH, Andy Jesse Howard Rush b: 12/26/1889, Longton, KS d: 3/16/1969, Fresno, CA BR/TR, 6'3", 180 lbs. Deb: 4/16/1925

YEAR TM-L	W	L	PCT	G	GS	CG	SH	SV	IP	H	R	ER	HR	HB	BB	SO	RAT	ERA	ERA+	CERA	OAV	BH	AVG	PR+	WS	TPW
1925 Bro-N	0	1	.000	4	2	0	0	0	9^2	16	14	10	3	0	5	4	2.172	9.31	45	10.01	.364	0	.000	-5	0	-0.5

• RUSH, Bob Robert Ransom Rush b: 12/21/1925, Battle Creek, MI BR/TR, 6'4", 205 lbs. Deb: 4/22/1948

YEAR TM-L	W	L	PCT	G	GS	CG	SH	SV	IP	H	R	ER	HR	HB	BB	SO	RAT	ERA	ERA+	CERA	OAV	BH	AVG	PR+	WS	TPW
1948 Chi-N	5	11	.313	36	16	4	0	0	133^1	153	70	58	8	1	37	72	1.425	3.92	100	4.08	.287	5	.128	1	6	-0.1
1949 Chi-N	10	18	.357	35	27	9	1	4	201	197	104	91	10	0	79	80	1.373	4.07	99	3.49	.255	2	.032	3	11	-0.4
1950 Chi-N★	13	20	.394	39	34	19	1	1	254^2	261	124	105	11	6	93	93	1.390	3.71	113	3.69	.265	15	.167	21	17	2.0
1951 Chi-N	11	12	.478	37	29	12	2	2	211^1	212	108	90	16	3	68	129	1.325	3.83	107	3.50	.254	13	.191	8	13	0.8
1952 Chi-N★	17	13	.567	34	32	17	4	0	250^1	205	99	75	14	6	81	157	1.142	2.70	143	2.50	.216	28	.292	33	23	**4.2**
1953 Chi-N	9	14	.391	29	28	8	1	0	166^2	177	97	84	17	5	66	84	1.458	4.54	98	4.43	.270	6	.111	3	9	0.1
1954 Chi-N	13	15	.464	33	32	11	0	0	236^1	213	102	99	12	5	103	124	1.337	3.77	111	3.31	.243	23	.277	14	16	2.1
1955 Chi-N	13	11	.542	33	33	14	3	0	234	204	95	91	19	2	73	130	1.184	3.50	117	2.95	.234	9	.110	14	18	1.1
1956 Chi-N	13	10	.565	32	32	13	1	0	239^2	210	101	85	30	2	59	104	1.122	3.19	118	2.96	.233	8	.098	11	15	0.8
1957 Chi-N	6	16	.273	31	29	5	0	0	205^1	211	111	100	16	2	66	103	1.349	4.38	88	3.71	.265	14	.203	-9	7	-0.7
1958* Mil-N	10	6	.625	28	20	5	2	0	147^1	142	59	56	13	1	31	84	1.174	3.42	103	3.06	.253	9	.200	0	9	0.1
1959 Mil-N	5	6	.455	31	9	1	1	0	101^1	102	39	27	5	1	23	64	1.234	2.40	148	3.07	.257	6	.188	13	7	1.4
1960 Mil-N	2	0	1.000	10	0	0	0	1	15	24	9	7	2	0	5	8	1.933	4.20	82	7.39	.369	1	.333	-1	1	0.0
Chi-A	0	0	....	9	0	0	0	0	14^1	16	10	9	4	0	5	12	1.465	5.65	67	5.78	.302	1	1.000	-3	0	-0.3
Total 13	127	152	.455	417	321	118	16	8	2410^2	2327	1128	977	177	34	789	1244	1.293	3.65	109	3.40	.251	140	.173	109	152	11.1

• RUSIE, Amos Amos Wilson "The Hoosier Thunderbolt" Rusie b: 5/30/1871, Mooresville, IN d: 12/6/1942, Seattle, WA BR/TR, 6'1", 200 lbs. Deb: 5/9/1889 HOF: 1977

YEAR TM-L	W	L	PCT	G	GS	CG	SH	SV	IP	H	R	ER	HR	HB	BB	SO	RAT	ERA	ERA+	CERA	OAV	BH	AVG	PR+	WS	TPW
1889 Ind-N	12	10	.545	33	22	19	1	0	225	246	181	133	12	9	116	109	1.609	5.32	79	....	.269	18	.175	-32	10	-2.9
1890 NY-N	29	34	.460	67	63	56	4	1	548^2	436	300	156	3	26	289	**341**	1.321	2.56	136	....	**.212**	79	.278	54	40	5.6
1891 NY-N	33	20	.623	61	57	52	**6**	1	500^1	391	244	142	6	18	262	**337**	1.305	2.55	125	....	**.207**	54	.245	29	36	3.0
1892 NY-N	32	31	.508	64	61	59	2	0	541	410	290	170	7	12	270	304	1.257	2.83	114	2.55	.202	54	.211	30	32	2.7
1893 NY-N	33	21	.611	**56**	**52**	**50**	**4**	1	**482**	451	260	173	15	16	218	**208**	1.388	3.23	144	3.45	**.240**	57	.269	71	41	**6.1**
1894* NY-N	**36**	13	.735	54	**50**	45	**3**	1	444	426	228	137	10	5	200	**195**	1.410	**2.78**	**189**	**3.43**	**.250**	52	.280	**117**	**56**	**9.2**
1895 NY-N	23	23	.500	49	47	42	**4**	0	393^1	384	248	163	9	7	159	**201**	1.381	3.73	124	3.39	.252	44	.246	37	28	2.5
1897 NY-N	28	10	.737	38	37	35	2	0	322^1	314	143	91	6	10	87	135	1.244	**2.54**	163	2.95	.254	40	.278	57	31	5.1
1898 NY-N	20	11	.645	37	36	33	4	1	300	288	149	101	6	9	103	114	1.303	3.03	115	3.13	.251	29	.210	15	19	1.2
1901 Cin-N	0	1	.000	3	2	2	0	0	22	43	25	21	1	0	3	6	2.091	8.59	37	8.57	.406	1	.125	-13	0	-1.3
Total 10	246	174	.586	462	427	393	30	5	3778^2	3389	2068	1287	75	112	1707	1950	1.349	3.07	127	2.11	.234	428	.247	366	293	31.3

• RUSKIN, Scott Scott Drew Ruskin b: 6/8/1963, Jacksonville, FL BR/TL, 6'2", 185 lbs. Deb: 4/9/1990

YEAR TM-L	W	L	PCT	G	GS	CG	SH	SV	IP	H	R	ER	HR	HB	BB	SO	RAT	ERA	ERA+	CERA	OAV	BH	AVG	PR+	WS	TPW
1990 Pit-N	2	2	.500	44	0	0	0	2	47^2	50	21	16	2	2	28	34	1.636	3.02	120	4.62	.269	2	.333	3	3	0.4
Mon-N	1	0	1.000	23	0	0	0	0	27^2	25	7	7	2	0	10	23	1.265	2.28	160	3.08	.243	0	.000	4	3	0.4
Yr.	3	2	.600	67	0	0	0	2	75^1	75	28	23	4	2	38	57	1.500	2.75	132	4.06	.260	2	.250	7	6	0.8
1991 Mon-N	4	4	.500	64	0	0	0	6	63^2	57	31	30	4	3	30	46	1.366	4.24	85	3.64	.241	0	.000	-5	4	-0.5
1992 Cin-N	4	3	.571	57	0	0	0	0	53^2	56	31	30	6	1	20	43	1.416	5.03	71	4.23	.275	0	.000	-9	1	-1.0
1993 Cin-N	0	0	....	4	0	0	0	0	1	3	2	2	1	0	2	0	5.000	18.00	22	38.33	.500	0	....	-2	0	-0.2
Total 4	11	9	.550	192	0	0	0	8	193^2	191	92	85	15	6	90	146	1.451	3.95	92	4.14	.260	2	.154	-9	11	-0.8

• RUSSELL, Allan Allan E. "Rubberarm" Russell b: 7/31/1893, Baltimore, MD d: 10/20/1972, Baltimore, MD BB/TR, 5'11", 165 lbs. Deb: 9/13/1915

YEAR TM-L	W	L	PCT	G	GS	CG	SH	SV	IP	H	R	ER	HR	HB	BB	SO	RAT	ERA	ERA+	CERA	OAV	BH	AVG	PR+	WS	TPW
1915 NY-A	1	2	.333	5	3	1	0	0	27	21	10	8	1	1	21	21	1.556	2.67	110	4.01	.228	2	.250	0	2	0.0
1916 NY-A	6	10	.375	34	19	8	1	6	171^1	138	83	61	8	7	75	104	1.243	3.20	90	3.06	.232	2	.044	-8	7	-1.2
1917 NY-A	7	8	.467	25	10	6	0	2	104^1	89	42	26	3	7	39	55	1.227	2.24	120	2.98	.236	10	.323	5	9	0.9
1918 NY-A	7	11	.389	27	18	7	2	4	141	139	68	51	6	5	73	54	1.504	3.26	87	4.09	.267	7	.167	-11	4	-1.3
1919 NY-A	5	5	.500	23	9	4	1	1	90^2	89	48	35	6	2	32	50	1.335	3.47	92	3.54	.251	7	.233	-6	4	-0.6
Bos-A	10	4	.714	21	11	9	1	4	121^1	105	38	34	0	1	39	63	1.187	2.52	120	2.58	.246	5	.122	5	11	0.4
Yr.	15	9	.625	44	20	13	2	**5**	212	194	86	69	6	3	71	113	1.250	2.93	106	2.99	.248	12	.169	-1	15	-0.2

YEAR	TM-L	W	L	PCT	G	GS	CG	SH	SV	IP	H	R	ER	HR	HB	BB	SO	RAT	ERA	ERA+	CERA	OAV	BH	AVG	PR+	WS	TPW
1920	Bos-A	5	6	.455	16	10	7	0	1	107^{2}	100	44	36	3	3	38	53	1.282	3.01	121	3.16	.251	5	.122	6	8	0.4
1921	Bos-A	6	11	.353	39	14	7	0	3	173	204	92	79	10	9	77	60	1.624	4.11	103	5.06	.303	7	.123	-2	9	-0.6
1922	Bos-A	6	7	.462	34	11	1	0	2	125^{2}	152	81	70	6	5	57	34	1.663	5.01	82	5.16	.314	3	.079	-11	4	-1.3
1923	Was-A	10	7	.588	52	5	4	0	**9**	181^{1}	177	81	61	9	2	77	67	1.401	3.03	124	3.67	.270	10	.200	9	13	1.0
1924*	Was-A	5	1	.833	37	0	0	0	8	82^{1}	83	49	40	1	1	45	17	1.555	4.37	92	3.99	.282	5	.278	-5	6	-0.3
1925	Was-A	2	4	.333	32	2	0	0	2	68^{2}	85	57	44	6	1	37	25	1.777	5.77	73	5.87	.315	2	.143	-14	0	-1.3
Total	11	70	76	.479	345	112	54	5	42	1394^{1}	1382	693	545	59	44	610	603	1.429	3.52	99	3.88	.269	65	.157	-31	77	-4.0

• RUSSELL, Jack Jack Erwin Russell b: 10/24/1905, Paris, TX d: 11/3/1990, Clearwater, FL BR/TR, 6'1.5", 178 lbs. Deb: 5/5/1926

YEAR	TM-L	W	L	PCT	G	GS	CG	SH	SV	IP	H	R	ER	HR	HB	BB	SO	RAT	ERA	ERA+	CERA	OAV	BH	AVG	PR+	WS	TPW
1926	Bos-A	0	5	.000	36	5	1	0	0	98	94	40	39	2	1	24	17	1.204	3.58	114	2.85	.268	4	.190	7	7	0.7
1927	Bos-A	4	9	.308	34	15	4	1	0	147	172	80	67	5	5	40	25	1.442	4.10	103	4.05	.298	6	.125	4	8	0.0
1928	Bos-A	11	14	.440	32	26	10	2	0	201^{1}	233	102	86	6	4	41	27	1.361	3.84	107	3.72	.294	13	.210	5	13	0.5
1929	Bos-A	6	18	.250	35	32	13	0	0	227^{1}	263	132	99	12	3	40	37	1.333	3.92	109	3.69	.290	9	.129	10	11	0.5
1930	Bos-A	9	20	.310	35	30	15	0	0	229^{2}	302	162	139	11	3	53	35	1.546	5.45	85	4.78	.321	14	.177	-24	6	-2.4
1931	Bos-A	10	18	.357	36	31	13	0	0	232	298	145	133	7	2	65	45	1.565	5.16	83	4.63	.310	16	.195	-21	10	-2.0
1932	Bos-A	1	7	.125	11	6	1	0	0	39^{2}	61	35	30	2	0	15	7	1.916	6.81	66	6.56	.343	1	.091	-10	0	-1.0
	Cle-A	5	7	.417	18	11	6	0	1	113	146	67	59	5	1	27	27	1.531	4.70	101	4.62	.310	12	.300	3	7	0.5
	Yr.	6	14	.300	29	17	7	0	1	152^{2}	207	102	89	7	1	42	34	1.631	5.25	89	5.12	.319	13	.255	-7	7	-0.5
1933*	Was-A	12	6	.667	50	3	2	0	**13**	124	119	45	37	3	1	32	28	1.218	2.69	156	2.83	.255	5	.147	18	15	1.6
1934	Was-A★	5	10	.333	**54**	9	3	0	**7**	157^{2}	179	86	73	6	2	56	38	1.490	4.17	104	4.17	.287	7	.159	3	11	0.6
1935	Was-A	4	9	.308	43	7	2	0	3	126	170	88	80	10	2	37	30	1.643	5.71	76	5.45	.324	7	.200	-19	3	-1.7
1936	Was-A	3	2	.600	18	5	1	0	3	49^{2}	66	46	35	3	0	25	6	1.832	6.34	75	5.88	.317	0	.000	-9	1	-1.0
	Bos-A	0	3	.000	23	2	0	0	0	40	57	27	25	2	0	16	9	1.825	5.63	94	6.13	.345	2	.286	-2	2	-0.1
	Yr.	3	5	.375	41	7	1	0	3	89^{2}	123	73	60	5	0	41	15	1.829	6.02	83	5.99	.330	2	.091	-11	3	-1.1
1937	Det-A	2	5	.286	25	0	0	0	4	40^{1}	63	35	34	4	1	20	10	2.058	7.59	62	8.06	.362	0	.000	-13	0	-1.2
1938*	Chi-N	6	1	.857	42	0	0	0	3	102^{1}	100	43	38	1	1	30	29	1.270	3.34	114	2.91	.258	7	.219	5	8	0.6
1939	Chi-N	4	3	.571	39	0	0	0	3	68^{2}	78	32	28	3	0	24	32	1.485	3.67	107	4.03	.282	0	.000	4	5	0.1
1940	StL-N	3	4	.429	26	0	0	0	1	54	53	22	15	1	0	26	16	1.463	2.50	160	3.47	.252	0	.000	10	5	0.8
Total	15	85	141	.376	557	182	71	3	38	2050^{2}	2454	1187	1017	83	26	571	418	1.475	4.46	97	4.26	.299	103	.167	-30	112	-3.3

• RUSSELL, Jeff Jeffrey Lee Russell b: 9/2/1961, Cincinnati, OH BR/TR, 6'4", 210 lbs. Deb: 8/13/1983

YEAR	TM-L	W	L	PCT	G	GS	CG	SH	SV	IP	H	R	ER	HR	HB	BB	SO	RAT	ERA	ERA+	CERA	OAV	BH	AVG	PR+	WS	TPW
1983	Cin-N	4	5	.444	10	10	2	0	0	68^{1}	58	30	23	7	0	22	40	1.171	3.03	126	2.90	.233	3	.143	6	5	0.7
1984	Cin-N	6	18	.250	33	30	4	2	0	181^{2}	186	97	86	15	4	65	101	1.382	4.26	89	3.91	.263	8	.140	-8	6	-0.8
1985	Tex-A	3	6	.333	13	13	0	0	0	62	85	55	52	10	2	27	44	1.806	7.55	56	7.02	.324	0	....	-22	0	-2.2
1986	Tex-A	5	2	.714	37	0	0	0	2	82	74	40	31	11	1	31	54	1.280	3.40	126	3.79	.244	0	....	8	6	0.8
1987	Tex-A	5	4	.556	52	2	0	0	3	97^{1}	109	56	48	9	2	52	56	1.654	4.44	101	5.28	.285	0	....	1	5	0.1
1988	Tex-A★	10	9	.526	34	24	5	0	0	188^{2}	183	86	80	15	7	66	88	1.320	3.82	107	3.76	.257	0	.000	5	12	0.4
1989	Tex-A★	6	4	.600	71	0	0	0	**38**	72^{2}	45	21	16	4	3	24	77	.950	1.98	200	1.76	.182	0	....	16	16	1.7
1990	Tex-A	1	5	.167	27	0	0	0	10	25^{1}	23	15	12	1	0	16	16	1.539	4.26	92	3.72	.253	0	....	-1	2	-0.1
1991	Tex-A	6	4	.600	68	0	0	0	30	79^{1}	71	36	29	11	1	26	52	1.223	3.29	122	3.43	.235	0	....	8	10	0.8
1992	Tex-A	2	3	.400	51	0	0	0	28	56^{2}	51	14	12	3	2	22	43	1.288	1.91	199	3.20	.238	0	....	13	10	1.3
	*Oak-A	2	0	1.000	8	0	0	0	2	9^{2}	4	0	0	0	0	3	5	.724	0.00	....	0.86	.125	0	....	4	3	0.4
	Yr.	4	3	.571	59	0	0	0	30	66^{1}	55	14	12	3	2	25	48	1.206	1.63	233	2.86	.224	0	....	17	13	1.7
1993	Bos-A	1	4	.200	51	0	0	0	33	46^{2}	39	16	14	1	1	14	45	1.136	2.70	171	2.41	.231	0	....	10	10	0.9
1994	Bos-A	0	5	.000	29	0	0	0	12	28	30	17	16	3	1	13	18	1.536	5.14	98	4.74	.270	0	....	-1	3	-0.1
	Cle-A	1	1	.500	13	0	0	0	5	12^{2}	13	8	7	2	0	3	10	1.263	4.97	95	4.05	.265	0	....	-0	2	0.0
	Yr.	1	6	.143	42	0	0	0	17	40^{2}	43	25	23	5	1	16	28	1.451	5.09	97	4.52	.269	0	....	-1	5	-0.1
1995	Tex-A	1	0	1.000	37	0	0	0	20	32^{2}	36	12	11	3	0	9	21	1.378	3.03	159	4.08	.277	0	....	7	7	0.6
1996*	Tex-A	3	3	.500	55	0	0	0	3	56	58	22	21	5	4	22	23	1.429	3.38	155	4.31	.269	0	....	12	7	1.0
Total	14	56	73	.434	589	79	11	2	186	1099^{2}	1065	525	458	100	28	415	693	1.346	3.75	111	3.85	.255	11	.139	57	104	5.7

• RUSSELL, John John Albert Russell b: 10/20/1895, San Mateo, CA d: 11/20/1930, Ely, NV BL/TL, 6'2", 195 lbs. Deb: 7/4/1917

YEAR	TM-L	W	L	PCT	G	GS	CG	SH	SV	IP	H	R	ER	HR	HB	BB	SO	RAT	ERA	ERA+	CERA	OAV	BH	AVG	PR+	WS	TPW
1917	Bro-N	0	1	.000	5	1	1	0	0	16	12	8	8	1	0	6	1	1.125	4.50	62	2.54	.222	1	.250	-3	0	-0.3
1918	Bro-N	0	0	....	1	0	0	0	0	1	2	2	2	0	0	1	0	3.000	18.00	15	11.63	.500	0	....	-2	0	-0.2
1921	Chi-A	2	5	.286	11	9	4	0	0	66^{1}	82	42	39	3	1	35	15	1.764	5.29	80	5.51	.314	10	.400	-8	4	-0.4
1922	Chi-A	0	1	.000	4	1	0	0	1	6^{2}	7	5	5	0	0	4	3	1.650	6.75	60	4.10	.280	0	.000	-2	0	-0.2
Total	4	2	7	.222	21	11	5	0	1	90	103	57	54	4	1	46	19	1.656	5.40	71	4.95	.299	11	.367	-15	4	-1.2

• RUSSELL, Lefty Clarence Dickson Russell b: 7/8/1890, Baltimore, MD d: 1/22/1962, Baltimore, MD BL/TL, 6'1", 165 lbs. Deb: 10/1/1910

YEAR	TM-L	W	L	PCT	G	GS	CG	SH	SV	IP	H	R	ER	HR	HB	BB	SO	RAT	ERA	ERA+	CERA	OAV	BH	AVG	PR+	WS	TPW
1910	Phi-A	1	0	1.000	1	1	1	1	0	9	8	0	0	0	0	2	5	1.111	0.00	....	2.44	.258	0	.000	2	1	0.2
1911	Phi-A	0	3	.000	7	2	0	0	0	31^{2}	45	32	27	1	5	18	7	1.989	7.67	41	7.69	.357	5	.385	-16	1	-1.5
1912	Phi-A	0	2	.000	5	2	1	0	0	17^{1}	18	20	14	1	3	14	9	1.846	7.27	43	5.99	.265	0	.000	-8	0	-0.9
Total	3	1	5	.167	13	5	2	1	0	58	71	52	41	2	8	34	21	1.810	6.36	49	6.37	.316	5	.250	-22	2	-2.1

• RUSSELL, Reb Ewell Albert Russell b: 4/12/1889, Jackson, MS d: 9/30/1973, Indianapolis, IN BL/TL, 5'11", 185 lbs. Deb: 4/18/1913 ♦

YEAR	TM-L	W	L	PCT	G	GS	CG	SH	SV	IP	H	R	ER	HR	HB	BB	SO	RAT	ERA	ERA+	CERA	OAV	BH	AVG	PR+	WS	TPW
1913	Chi-A	22	16	.579	**52**	36	26	8	4	316^{2}	250	89	67	2	7	79	122	1.039	1.90	153	1.97	.210	20	.189	35	32	4.0
1914	Chi-A	7	12	.368	38	23	8	1	1	167^{1}	168	80	54	3	3	33	79	1.201	2.90	92	2.95	.260	17	.266	-4	9	0.0
1915	Chi-A	11	10	.524	41	25	10	3	2	229^{1}	215	90	66	0	6	47	90	1.142	2.59	115	2.48	.240	21	.244	12	16	1.7
1916	Chi-A	18	11	.621	56	25	16	5	3	264^{1}	207	88	71	1	1	42	112	.942	2.42	114	**1.65**	.220	13	.143	7	20	0.3
1917*	Chi-A	15	5	.750	35	24	11	5	3	189^{1}	170	61	41	1	1	32	54	1.067	1.95	136	2.19	.240	19	.279	16	18	2.3
1918	Chi-A	7	5	.583	19	15	10	2	0	124^{2}	117	45	36	0	0	33	38	1.203	2.60	105	2.57	.250	7	.140	4	7	0.1
1919	Chi-A	0	0	....	1	0	0	0	0	0	1	0	0	0	0	1	0	....	....	....	∞	1.000	0	....	0	0	0.0
Total	7	80	59	.576	242	148	81	24	13	1291^{2}	1128	453	335	7	18	267	495	1.080	2.33	120	2.21	.233	262	.268	70	102	8.5

• RUSSO, Marius Marius Ugo "Lefty" Russo b: 7/19/1914, Brooklyn, NY BR/TL, 6'1", 190 lbs. Deb: 6/6/1939

YEAR	TM-L	W	L	PCT	G	GS	CG	SH	SV	IP	H	R	ER	HR	HB	BB	SO	RAT	ERA	ERA+	CERA	OAV	BH	AVG	PR+	WS	TPW
1939	NY-A	8	3	.727	21	11	9	2	2	116	86	37	31	6	1	41	55	1.095	2.41	181	2.25	.210	10	.244	21	12	2.0
1940	NY-A	14	8	.636	30	24	15	0	1	189^{1}	181	79	69	17	1	55	87	1.246	3.28	123	3.31	.249	12	.188	13	16	1.5
1941*	NY-A★	14	10	.583	28	27	17	3	1	209^{2}	195	85	72	8	1	87	105	1.345	3.09	127	3.27	.247	18	.231	12	16	1.3
1942	NY-A	4	1	.800	9	5	2	0	0	45^{1}	41	15	14	2	1	14	15	1.213	2.78	124	2.93	.244	4	.235	1	4	0.2
1943*	NY-A	5	10	.333	24	14	5	1	1	101^{2}	89	53	42	7	2	45	42	1.318	3.72	86	3.32	.235	6	.194	-7	3	-0.7
1946	NY-A	0	2	.000	8	3	0	0	0	18^{2}	26	9	9	1	0	11	7	1.982	4.34	80	6.80	.333	0	.000	-2	0	-0.3
Total	6	45	34	.570	120	84	48	6	5	680^{2}	618	278	237	41	6	253	311	1.280	3.13	121	3.19	.242	50	.213	38	51	4.0

• RUSTECK, Dick Richard Frank Rusteck b: 7/12/1941, Chicago, IL BR/TL, 6'1", 175 lbs. Deb: 6/10/1966

YEAR	TM-L	W	L	PCT	G	GS	CG	SH	SV	IP	H	R	ER	HR	HB	BB	SO	RAT	ERA	ERA+	CERA	OAV	BH	AVG	PR+	WS	TPW
1966	NY-N	1	2	.333	8	3	1	1	0	24	24	10	8	1	0	8	9	1.333	3.00	121	3.66	.276	0	.000	2	2	0.1

• RUTH, Babe George Herman "The Bambino,The Sultan Of Swat" Ruth
b: 2/6/1895, Baltimore, MD d: 8/16/1948, New York, NY BL/TL, 6'2", 215 lbs. Deb: 7/11/1914 C HOF: 1936 ♦

YEAR	TM-L	W	L	PCT	G	GS	CG	SH	SV	IP	H	R	ER	HR	HB	BB	SO	RAT	ERA	ERA+	CERA	OAV	BH	AVG	PR+	WS	TPW
1914	Bos-A	2	1	.667	4	3	1	0	0	23	21	12	10	1	0	7	3	1.217	3.91	69	2.64	.236	2	.200	-4	1	-0.4
1915*	Bos-A	18	8	.692	32	28	16	1	0	217^{2}	166	80	59	3	6	85	112	1.153	2.44	114	2.24	.212	29	.315	7	23	2.3
1916*	Bos-A	23	12	.657	44	**41**	23	**9**	1	323^{2}	230	83	63	0	8	118	170	1.075	**1.75**	**158**	1.85	**.201**	37	.272	**41**	**37**	**6.0**
1917	Bos-A	24	13	.649	41	38	**35**	6	2	326^{1}	244	93	73	2	11	108	128	1.079	2.01	128	1.99	.211	40	.325	18	**36**	3.9
1918*	Bos-A	13	7	.650	20	19	18	1	0	166^{1}	125	51	41	1	2	49	40	1.046	2.22	121	1.84	.214	95	.300	8	**40**	5.3
1919	Bos-A	9	5	.643	17	15	12	0	1	133^{1}	148	59	44	2	2	58	30	1.545	2.97	102	4.16	.290	139	.322	-1	43	8.9
1920	NY-A	1	0	1.000	1	1	0	0	0	4	3	4	2	0	0	2	0	1.250	4.50	85	2.29	.200	172	.376	-0	51	10.0
1921*	NY-A	2	0	1.000	2	1	0	0	0	9	14	10	9	1	0	9	2	2.556	9.00	47	9.93	.350	204	.378	-5	53	9.8
1930	NY-A	1	0	1.000	1	1	1	0	0	9	11	3	3	0	0	2	3	1.444	3.00	143	3.85	.306	186	.359	1	38	7.8
1933	NY-A★	1	0	1.000	1	1	1	0	0	9	12	5	5	0	0	3	0	1.667	5.00	78	4.74	.308	138	.301	-1	29	4.9
Total	10	94	46	.671	163	148	107	17	4	1221^{1}	974	400	309	10	29	441	488	1.159	2.28	123	2.32	.222	2873	.342	64	351	58.5

• RUTHERFORD, Johnny John William "Doc" Rutherford b: 5/5/1925, Belleville, Canada BL/TR, 5'10.5", 170 lbs. Deb: 4/30/1952

YEAR TM-L	W	L	PCT	G	GS	CG	SH	SV	IP	H	R	ER	HR	HB	BB	SO	RAT	ERA	ERA+	CERA	OAV	BH	AVG	PR+	WS	TPW
1952★ Bro-N	7	7	.500	22	11	4	0	2	97^{1}	97	51	46	9	2	29	29	1.295	4.25	85	3.65	.262	9	.290	-8	5	-0.5

• RUTHVEN, Dick Richard David Ruthven b: 3/27/1951, Sacramento, CA BR/TR, 6'3", 190 lbs. Deb: 4/17/1973

YEAR TM-L	W	L	PCT	G	GS	CG	SH	SV	IP	H	R	ER	HR	HB	BB	SO	RAT	ERA	ERA+	CERA	OAV	BH	AVG	PR+	WS	TPW
1973 Phi-N	6	9	.400	25	23	3	1	1	128^{1}	125	69	60	10	3	75	98	1.558	4.21	90	4.52	.257	5	.132	-7	5	-0.9
1974 Phi-N	9	13	.409	35	35	6	0	0	212^{2}	182	106	95	11	3	116	153	1.401	4.02	94	3.49	.231	13	.191	-10	10	-1.2
1975 Phi-N	2	2	.500	11	7	0	0	0	40^{2}	37	22	19	2	1	22	26	1.451	4.20	89	3.87	.243	2	.154	-3	1	-0.4
1976 Atl-N★	14	17	.452	36	36	8	4	0	240^{1}	255	112	112	14	8	90	142	1.436	4.19	90	4.13	.275	13	.171	-5	14	-0.5
1977 Atl-N	7	13	.350	25	23	6	2	0	151	158	86	71	14	1	62	84	1.457	4.23	105	4.24	.267	12	.267	8	9	1.2
1978 Atl-N	2	6	.250	13	13	2	1	0	81	78	43	37	8	0	28	45	1.309	4.11	98	3.61	.257	2	.083	1	3	-0.1
★ Phi-N	13	5	.722	20	20	9	2	0	150^{2}	136	52	50	13	1	28	75	1.088	2.99	119	2.74	.248	15	.283	7	13	1.2
Yr.	15	11	.577	33	33	11	3	0	231^{2}	214	95	87	21	1	56	120	1.165	3.38	111	3.05	.251	17	.221	7	16	1.1
1979 Phi-N	7	5	.583	20	20	3	2	0	122^{1}	121	59	58	10	2	37	58	1.292	4.27	90	3.49	.256	6	.146	-7	6	-0.8
1980★ Phi-N	17	10	.630	33	33	6	1	0	223^{1}	241	99	88	9	3	74	86	1.410	3.55	107	3.91	.283	16	.235	6	14	1.0
1981★ Phi-N★	12	7	.632	23	22	5	0	0	146^{2}	162	94	84	10	3	54	80	1.473	5.15	70	4.31	.281	7	.140	-26	2	-2.8
1982 Phi-N	11	11	.500	33	31	8	2	0	204^{1}	189	99	86	18	6	59	115	1.214	3.79	97	3.21	.246	7	.109	-3	10	-0.6
1983 Phi-N	1	3	.250	7	7	0	0	0	33^{2}	46	23	21	5	0	10	26	1.663	5.61	64	6.25	.333	1	.111	-7	0	-0.8
Chi-N	12	9	.571	25	25	5	2	0	149^{1}	156	78	68	17	3	28	73	1.232	4.10	92	3.63	.269	12	.226	-3	7	-0.1
Yr.	13	12	.520	32	32	5	2	0	183	202	101	89	22	3	38	99	1.311	4.38	85	4.11	.281	13	.210	-10	7	-0.9
1984 Chi-N	6	10	.375	23	22	0	0	0	126^{2}	154	75	71	14	4	41	55	1.539	5.04	77	5.21	.302	7	.159	-14	3	-1.5
1985 Chi-N	4	7	.364	20	15	0	0	0	87^{1}	103	49	44	6	0	37	26	1.603	4.53	88	4.91	.299	5	.208	-4	3	-0.5
1986 Chi-N	0	0	....	6	0	0	0	0	10^{2}	12	9	6	4	0	6	3	1.688	5.06	80	8.01	.293	0	.000	-1	0	-0.1
Total 14	123	127	.492	355	332	61	17	1	2109	2155	1075	970	165	38	767	1145	1.385	4.14	92	3.95	.267	123	.183	-70	100	-6.8

• RYAN, B.J. Robert Victor Ryan b: 12/28/1975, Bossier City, LA BL/TL, 6'6", 230 lbs. Deb: 7/28/1999

YEAR TM-L	W	L	PCT	G	GS	CG	SH	SV	IP	H	R	ER	HR	HB	BB	SO	RAT	ERA	ERA+	CERA	OAV	BH	AVG	PR+	WS	TPW
1999 Cin-N	0	0	....	1	0	0	0	0	2	4	1	1	0	0	1	1	2.500	4.50	104	12.01	.500	0	....	-0	0	0.0
Bal-A	1	0	1.000	13	0	0	0	0	18^{1}	9	6	6	0	0	12	28	1.145	2.95	159	1.73	.150	0	....	3	2	0.3
2000 Bal-A	2	3	.400	42	0	0	0	0	42^{2}	36	29	28	7	0	31	41	1.570	5.91	80	4.87	.225	0	....	-5	2	-0.5
2001 Bal-A	2	4	.333	61	0	0	0	2	53	47	31	25	6	2	30	54	1.453	4.25	101	4.13	.233	0	.000	-0	3	0.0
2002 Bal-A	2	1	.667	67	0	0	0	1	57^{2}	51	31	30	7	4	33	56	1.457	4.68	91	4.48	.241	0	.000	-3	3	-0.3
2003 Bal-A	4	1	.800	76	0	0	0	0	50^{1}	42	19	19	1	3	27	63	1.371	3.40	130	3.33	.227	0	....	6	6	0.5
Total 5	11	9	.550	260	0	0	0	3	224	189	117	109	21	9	134	243	1.442	4.38	101	4.06	.229	0	.000	-0	16	0.0

• RYAN, Cyclone Daniel R. Ryan b: 1866, Capperwhite, Ireland d: 1/30/1917, Medfield, MA TR, 6', 200 lbs. Deb: 8/8/1887 ♦

YEAR TM-L	W	L	PCT	G	GS	CG	SH	SV	IP	H	R	ER	HR	HB	BB	SO	RAT	ERA	ERA+	CERA	OAV	BH	AVG	PR+	WS	TPW
1887 NY-a	0	1	.000	2	1	0	0	0	2^{1}	11	9	6	1	0	6	0	4.714	23.14	18	....	.613	10	.286	-5	0	-0.6
1891 Bos-N	0	0	....	1	0	0	0	0	3	2	0	0	0	0	1	0	1.000	0.00	....	....	.182	0	.000	1	1	0.1
Total 2	0	1	.000	3	1	0	0	0	5^{1}	13	9	6	1	0	7	0	2.625	10.13	42	....	.449	10	.278	-4	1	-0.5

• RYAN, Jack Jack "Gulfport" Ryan b: 9/19/1884, Lawrenceville, IL d: 10/16/1949, Mondsboro, MS BR/TR, 5'10", 165 lbs. Deb: 7/2/1908

YEAR TM-L	W	L	PCT	G	GS	CG	SH	SV	IP	H	R	ER	HR	HB	BB	SO	RAT	ERA	ERA+	CERA	OAV	BH	AVG	PR+	WS	TPW
1908 Cle-A	1	1	.500	8	1	1	0	1	35^{2}	27	12	9	3	1	2	7	.813	2.27	105	1.78	.220	1	.091	0	3	0.1
1909 Bos-A	3	3	.500	13	8	2	0	0	59^{1}	64	34	22	0	4	20	24	1.416	3.34	75	3.78	....	4	.211	-7	2	-0.7
1911 Bro-N	0	1	.000	3	1	0	0	0	6	9	7	2	1	1	4	1	2.167	3.00	111	10.21	.375	0	.000	0	0	0.0
Total 3	4	5	.444	24	10	3	0	1	101	100	53	33	4	6	26	32	1.248	2.94	85	3.45	.682	5	.161	-6	5	-0.6

• RYAN, Jay Jason Paul Ryan b: 1/21/1976, Long Branch, NJ BB/TR, 6'3", 195 lbs. Deb: 8/24/1999

YEAR TM-L	W	L	PCT	G	GS	CG	SH	SV	IP	H	R	ER	HR	HB	BB	SO	RAT	ERA	ERA+	CERA	OAV	BH	AVG	PR+	WS	TPW
1999 Min-A	1	4	.200	8	8	1	0	0	40^{2}	46	23	22	9	3	17	15	1.549	4.87	104	6.23	.286	0	....	1	2	0.1
2000 Min-A	0	1	.000	16	1	0	0	0	26	37	24	22	8	1	10	19	1.808	7.62	68	8.35	.330	0	....	-7	0	-0.6
Total 2	1	5	.167	24	9	1	0	0	66^{2}	83	47	44	17	4	27	34	1.650	5.94	86	7.06	.304	0	....	-6	2	-0.5

• RYAN, Jimmy James Edward "Pony" Ryan b: 2/11/1863, Clinton, MA d: 10/26/1923, Chicago, IL BR/TL, 5'9", 162 lbs. Deb: 10/8/1885 U ♦

YEAR TM-L	W	L	PCT	G	GS	CG	SH	SV	IP	H	R	ER	HR	HB	BB	SO	RAT	ERA	ERA+	CERA	OAV	BH	AVG	PR+	WS	TPW
1886★ Chi-N	0	0	....	5	0	0	0	1	23^{1}	19	13	12	2	....	13	15	1.371	4.63	78	....	.214	100	.306	-4	14	0.1
1887 Chi-N	2	1	.667	8	3	2	0	0	45	70	36	21	3	6	17	14	1.556	4.20	106	....	.345	198	.353	1	18	0.1
1888 Chi-N	4	0	1.000	8	2	1	0	0	38^{1}	47	29	13	2	0	12	11	1.539	3.05	99	....	.291	182	.332	-1	34	4.4
1891 Chi-N	0	0	....	2	0	0	0	1	5^{2}	11	7	1	0	0	2	2	2.294	1.59	209	....	.394	140	.277	1	22	1.8
1893 Chi-N	0	0	....	1	0	0	0	0	4^{2}	3	0	0	0	0	0	1	.643	0.00	....	0.88	.179	102	.299	2	12	0.7
Total 5	6	1	.857	24	5	3	0	2	117	150	85	47	7	6	44	43	1.513	3.62	103	0.03	.301	2556	.311	0	100	7.1

• RYAN, John John A. Ryan b: Birmingham, MI BL/TR Deb: 6/11/1884

YEAR TM-L	W	L	PCT	G	GS	CG	SH	SV	IP	H	R	ER	HR	HB	BB	SO	RAT	ERA	ERA+	CERA	OAV	BH	AVG	PR+	WS	TPW
1884 Bal-U	3	2	.600	6	6	5	0	0	51	61	42	19	1	....	16	33	1.510	3.35	100	....	.278	2	.080	-1	3	-0.3

• RYAN, Johnny John Joseph Ryan b: 10/1853, Philadelphia, PA d: 3/22/1902, Philadelphia, PA, 5'7.5", 150 lbs. Deb: 8/19/1873 ♦

YEAR TM-L	W	L	PCT	G	GS	CG	SH	SV	IP	H	R	ER	HR	HB	BB	SO	RAT	ERA	ERA+	CERA	OAV	BH	AVG	PR+	WS	TPW
1874 Bal-n	0	0	....	1	0	0	0	0	3^{1}	13	8	6	0	....	0	0	3.900	16.20	38	....	.540	35	.193	-2	....	0.3
1875 NH-n	1	5	.167	10	6	4	0	0	59^{1}	69	55	21	1	....	9	11	1.315	3.19	69	....	.265	23	.158	-4	....	-1.1
1876 Lou-N	0	0	....	1	0	0	0	0	8	22	20	5	0	....	0	1	2.750	5.63	48	....	.469	61	.247	-3	5	-1.6
Total 2 n	1	5	.167	11	6	4	0	0	62^{2}	82	63	27	1	....	9	11	1.452	3.88	66	....	.288	60	.179	-6	....	-0.9

• RYAN, Ken Kenneth Frederick Ryan b: 10/24/1968, Pawtucket, RI BR/TR, 6'3", 230 lbs. Deb: 8/31/1992

YEAR TM-L	W	L	PCT	G	GS	CG	SH	SV	IP	H	R	ER	HR	HB	BB	SO	RAT	ERA	ERA+	CERA	OAV	BH	AVG	PR+	WS	TPW
1992 Bos-A	0	0	....	7	0	0	0	1	7	4	5	5	2	0	5	5	1.286	6.43	66	4.13	.174	0	....	-2	0	-0.2
1993 Bos-A	7	2	.778	47	0	0	0	1	50	43	23	20	2	3	29	49	1.440	3.60	128	3.56	.235	0	....	5	5	0.5
1994 Bos-A	2	3	.400	42	0	0	0	13	48	46	14	13	1	1	17	32	1.313	2.44	206	3.14	.256	0	....	13	9	1.2
1995 Bos-A	0	4	.000	28	0	0	0	7	32^{2}	34	20	18	4	1	24	34	1.776	4.96	98	5.64	.268	0	....	-0	2	0.0
1996 Phi-N	3	5	.375	62	0	0	0	8	89	71	32	24	4	1	45	70	1.303	2.43	178	2.97	.223	1	.143	18	11	1.8
1997 Phi-N	1	0	1.000	22	0	0	0	0	20^{2}	31	23	22	5	2	13	10	2.129	9.58	44	9.58	.344	0	....	-12	0	-1.2
1998 Phi-N	0	0	....	17	1	0	0	0	22^{2}	21	12	11	1	1	20	16	1.809	4.37	99	5.17	.253	0	.000	-0	1	0.0
1999 Phi-N	1	2	.333	15	0	0	0	0	15^{2}	16	11	11	2	0	11	9	1.723	6.32	75	5.51	.267	0	....	-3	0	-0.3
Total 8	14	16	.467	240	1	0	0	30	285^{2}	266	140	124	21	9	164	225	1.505	3.91	116	4.23	.250	1	.125	19	28	1.8

• RYAN, Nolan Lynn Nolan Ryan b: 1/31/1947, Refugio, TX BR/TR, 6'2", 195 lbs. Deb: 9/11/1966 HOF: 1999

YEAR TM-L	W	L	PCT	G	GS	CG	SH	SV	IP	H	R	ER	HR	HB	BB	SO	RAT	ERA	ERA+	CERA	OAV	BH	AVG	PR+	WS	TPW
1966 NY-N	0	1	.000	2	1	0	0	0	3	5	5	5	1	0	3	6	2.667	15.00	24	12.35	.357	0	....	-4	0	-0.4
1968 NY-N	6	9	.400	21	18	3	0	0	134	93	50	46	12	4	75	133	1.254	3.09	98	3.06	.200	5	.114	-2	6	-0.4
1969★ NY-N	6	3	.667	25	10	2	0	1	89^{1}	60	38	35	3	1	53	92	1.265	3.53	104	2.59	.189	3	.103	-1	6	-0.3
1970 NY-N	7	11	.389	27	19	5	2	1	131^{2}	86	59	50	10	4	97	125	1.390	3.42	118	3.39	.188	8	.178	7	8	0.6
1971 NY-N	10	14	.417	30	26	3	0	0	152	125	78	67	8	15	116	137	1.586	3.97	86	4.39	.219	6	.128	-11	4	-1.2
1972 Cal-A★	19	16	.543	39	39	20	**9**	0	284	166	80	72	14	10	157	**329**	1.137	2.28	127	2.28	**.171**	13	.135	17	24	2.0
1973 Cal-A★	21	16	.568	41	39	26	4	1	326	238	113	104	18	7	162	**383**	1.227	2.87	123	2.78	.203	0	....	28	28	2.9
1974 Cal-A	22	16	.579	42	41	26	3	0	**332^{2}**	221	127	107	18	9	202	**367**	1.272	2.89	119	2.86	**.190**	0	....	23	21	2.4
1975 Cal-A★	14	12	.538	28	28	10	5	0	198	152	90	76	13	7	132	186	1.434	3.45	103	3.72	.213	0	....	3	12	0.3
1976 Cal-A	17	18	.486	39	39	21	**7**	0	284^{1}	193	117	106	13	5	183	**327**	1.322	3.36	99	2.98	**.195**	0	....	1	17	0.1
1977 Cal-A★	19	16	.543	37	37	**22**	4	0	299	198	110	92	12	9	204	**341**	1.344	2.77	141	3.00	**.193**	0	....	**40**	22	**4.0**
1978 Cal-A	10	13	.435	31	31	14	3	0	234^{2}	183	106	97	12	3	148	**260**	1.411	3.72	97	3.43	.220	0	....	-1	12	-0.1
1979★ Cal-A★	16	14	.533	34	34	17	**5**	0	222^{2}	169	104	89	15	6	114	**223**	1.271	3.60	113	3.07	**.212**	0	....	13	13	1.2
1980★ Hou-N	11	10	.524	35	35	4	2	0	233^{2}	205	100	87	10	3	98	200	1.297	3.35	98	3.15	.236	6	.086	-2	11	-0.4
1981★ Hou-N★	11	5	.688	21	21	5	3	0	149	99	34	28	2	1	68	140	1.121	**1.69**	**195**	**2.02**	**.188**	11	.216	**26**	15	**3.1**
1982 Hou-N	16	12	.571	35	35	10	3	0	250^{1}	196	100	88	20	8	109	245	1.218	3.16	105	2.99	**.213**	10	.120	2	16	0.1
1983 Hou-N	14	9	.609	29	29	5	2	0	196^{1}	134	74	65	9	4	101	183	1.197	2.98	114	2.56	**.195**	5	.072	6	12	0.2
1984 Hou-N	12	11	.522	30	30	5	2	0	183^{2}	143	78	62	12	4	69	197	1.154	3.04	109	2.63	.211	6	.098	3	9	0.2
1985 Hou-N★	10	12	.455	35	35	4	0	0	232	205	108	98	12	9	95	209	1.293	3.80	91	3.25	.239	7	.111	-11	7	-1.3
1986★ Hou-N	12	8	.600	30	30	1	0	0	178	119	72	66	14	4	82	194	1.129	3.34	108	2.46	.188	6	.102	5	11	0.2
1987 Hou-N	8	16	.333	34	34	0	0	0	211^{2}	154	75	65	14	4	87	**270**	1.139	**2.76**	**142**	**2.50**	**.199**	4	.062	28	15	2.5
1988 Hou-N	12	11	.522	33	33	4	1	0	220	186	98	86	18	7	87	**228**	1.241	3.52	94	3.15	.227	4	.057	-4	9	-0.7

YEAR TM-L	W	L	PCT	G	GS	CG	SH	SV	IP	H	R	ER	HR	HB	BB	SO	RAT	ERA	ERA+	CERA	OAV	BH	AVG	PR+	WS	TPW
1989 Tex-A★	16	10	.615	32	32	6	2	0	239^1	162	96	85	17	9	98	**301**	1.086	3.20	124	2.31	**.187**	0	....	22	18	2.2
1990 Tex-A	13	9	.591	30	30	5	2	0	204	137	86	78	18	7	74	**232**	1.034	3.44	114	**2.28**	**.188**	0	....	10	15	1.0
1991 Tex-A	12	6	.667	27	27	2	2	0	173	102	58	56	12	5	72	203	1.006	2.91	138	**1.98**	**.172**	0	....	24	13	2.4
1992 Tex-A	5	9	.357	27	27	2	0	0	157^1	138	75	65	9	12	69	157	1.316	3.72	102	3.55	.238	0	....	4	8	0.4
1993 Tex-A	5	5	.500	13	13	0	0	0	66^1	54	47	36	5	1	40	46	1.417	4.88	85	3.67	.220	0	....	-4	2	-0.4
Total 27	324	292	.526	807	773	222	61	3	5386	3923	2178	1911	321	158	2795	5714	1.247	3.19	111	2.90	.204	94	.110	222	334	20.6

• RYAN, Rosy Wilfred Patrick Dolan Ryan b: 3/15/1898, Worcester, MA d: 12/10/1980, Scottsdale, AZ BL/TR, 6', 185 lbs. Deb: 9/7/1919

YEAR TM-L	W	L	PCT	G	GS	CG	SH	SV	IP	H	R	ER	HR	HB	BB	SO	RAT	ERA	ERA+	CERA	OAV	BH	AVG	PR+	WS	TPW
1919 NY-N	1	2	.333	4	3	1	0	0	20^1	20	9	7	0	1	9	7	1.426	3.10	90	3.53	.260	0	.000	-1	1	-0.2
1920 NY-N	0	1	.000	3	1	1	0	0	15^1	14	6	3	1	0	4	5	1.174	1.76	170	2.90	.259	0	.000	2	1	0.1
1921 NY-N	7	10	.412	36	16	5	0	3	147^1	140	72	61	6	1	32	58	1.167	3.73	98	2.75	.255	9	.200	-5	8	-0.5
1922* NY-N	17	12	.586	46	22	12	1	3	191^2	194	87	64	5	2	74	75	1.398	3.01	133	3.55	.269	12	.194	15	16	1.5
1923* NY-N	16	5	.762	**45**	15	7	0	4	172^2	169	77	67	8	2	46	58	1.245	3.49	109	3.06	.257	11	.208	4	15	0.4
1924* NY-N	8	6	.571	37	9	2	0	5	124^2	137	64	59	1	2	37	36	1.396	4.26	86	3.57	.285	5	.139	-9	5	-1.0
1925 Bos-N	2	8	.200	37	7	1	0	2	122^2	152	103	86	7	0	52	48	1.663	6.31	63	5.03	.303	11	.282	-33	1	-2.8
1926 Bos-N	0	2	.000	7	2	0	0	0	19	29	19	16	1	0	7	1	1.895	7.58	47	6.83	.392	1	.200	-8	0	-0.8
1928 NY-A	0	0	....	3	0	0	0	0	6	17	11	11	1	0	1	5	3.000	16.50	23	15.87	.486	0	.000	-8	0	-0.9
1933 Bro-N	1	1	.500	30	0	0	0	2	61^1	69	38	31	3	3	16	22	1.386	4.55	71	3.81	.276	2	.154	-8	1	-0.8
Total 10	52	47	.525	248	75	29	1	19	881	941	486	405	33	11	278	315	1.384	4.14	90	3.69	.277	51	.190	-51	48	-5.0

• RYBA, Mike Dominic Joseph Ryba b: 6/9/1903, DeLancey, PA d: 12/13/1971, Brookline Station, MO BR/TR, 5'11.5", 195 lbs. Deb: 9/22/1935 C

YEAR TM-L	W	L	PCT	G	GS	CG	SH	SV	IP	H	R	ER	HR	HB	BB	SO	RAT	ERA	ERA+	CERA	OAV	BH	AVG	PR+	WS	TPW
1935 StL-N	1	1	.500	2	1	1	0	0	16	15	6	6	0	0	1	6	1.000	3.38	121	1.86	.242	2	.400	1	1	0.2
1936 StL-N	5	1	.833	14	0	0	0	0	45	55	33	27	3	2	16	25	1.578	5.40	73	4.79	.294	3	.167	-7	1	-0.8
1937 StL-N	9	6	.600	38	8	5	0	0	135	152	76	62	8	2	40	57	1.422	4.13	96	4.06	.284	15	.313	-1	8	0.3
1938 StL-N	1	1	.500	3	0	0	0	0	5	8	3	3	0	0	1	0	1.800	5.40	73	5.54	.348	0	....	-1	0	-0.1
1941 Bos-A	7	3	.700	40	3	0	0	6	121	143	72	60	14	0	42	54	1.529	4.46	93	4.94	.297	8	.216	-3	7	-0.1
1942 Bos-A	3	3	.500	18	0	0	0	3	44^1	49	25	19	5	1	13	16	1.398	3.86	97	4.29	.278	5	.294	-2	3	-0.1
1943 Bos-A	7	5	.583	40	8	4	1	2	143^2	142	57	52	4	0	57	50	1.385	3.26	102	3.45	.262	8	.186	0	9	0.0
1944 Bos-A	12	7	.632	42	7	2	0	2	138	119	57	51	7	0	39	50	1.145	3.33	102	2.56	.233	6	.146	1	9	0.0
1945 Bos-A	7	6	.538	34	9	4	1	2	123	122	45	34	5	2	33	44	1.260	2.49	137	3.08	.259	9	.250	12	11	1.4
1946* Bos-A	0	1	.000	9	0	0	0	1	12^2	12	7	5	1	0	5	5	1.342	3.55	103	3.59	.261	2	1.000	0	1	0.1
Total 10	52	34	.605	240	36	16	2	16	783^2	817	381	319	47	7	247	307	1.358	3.66	101	3.68	.269	58	.235	-0	50	0.9

• RYERSON, Gary Gary Lawrence Ryerson b: 6/17/1948, Los Angeles, CA BR/TL, 6'1", 175 lbs. Deb: 6/28/1972

YEAR TM-L	W	L	PCT	G	GS	CG	SH	SV	IP	H	R	ER	HR	HB	BB	SO	RAT	ERA	ERA+	CERA	OAV	BH	AVG	PR+	WS	TPW
1972 Mil-A	3	8	.273	20	14	4	1	0	102	119	48	41	9	0	21	45	1.373	3.62	84	4.02	.290	1	.042	-7	3	-0.9
1973 Mil-A	0	1	.000	9	4	0	0	0	23	32	23	20	0	0	7	10	1.696	7.83	48	4.91	.327	0	....	-10	0	-1.1
Total 2	3	9	.250	29	18	4	1	0	125	151	71	61	9	0	28	55	1.432	4.39	74	4.18	.297	1	.042	-17	3	-2.0

• SAARLOOS, Kirk Kirk Craig Saarloos b: 5/23/1979, Long Beach, CA BR/TR, 6', 185 lbs. Deb: 6/18/2002

YEAR TM-L	W	L	PCT	G	GS	CG	SH	SV	IP	H	R	ER	HR	HB	BB	SO	RAT	ERA	ERA+	CERA	OAV	BH	AVG	PR+	WS	TPW
2002 Hou-N	6	7	.462	17	17	1	1	0	85^1	100	59	57	12	6	27	54	1.488	6.01	71	5.35	.301	2	.067	-16	0	-1.8
2003 Hou-N	2	1	.667	36	4	0	0	0	49^1	55	31	27	4	3	17	43	1.459	4.93	90	4.51	.281	0	.000	-4	1	-0.4
Total 2	8	8	.500	53	21	1	1	0	134^2	155	90	84	16	9	44	97	1.478	5.61	77	5.04	.294	2	.057	-20	1	-2.2

• SABATHIA, C.C. Carsten Charles Sabathia b: 7/21/1980, Vallejo, CA BL/TL, 6'7", 250 lbs. Deb: 4/8/2001

YEAR TM-L	W	L	PCT	G	GS	CG	SH	SV	IP	H	R	ER	HR	HB	BB	SO	RAT	ERA	ERA+	CERA	OAV	BH	AVG	PR+	WS	TPW
2001* Cle-A	17	5	.773	33	33	0	0	0	180^1	149	93	88	19	7	95	171	1.353	4.39	103	3.86	.228	0	.000	6	12	0.5
2002 Cle-A	13	11	.542	33	33	2	0	0	210	198	109	102	17	1	88	149	1.362	4.37	100	3.74	.252	1	.200	3	13	0.3
2003 Cle-A★	13	9	.591	30	30	2	1	0	197^2	190	85	79	19	6	66	141	1.295	3.60	123	3.70	.255	3	.500	14	13	1.4
Total 3	43	25	.632	96	96	4	1	0	588	537	287	269	55	14	249	461	1.337	4.12	108	3.76	.246	4	.267	23	38	2.3

• SABEL, Erik Erik Douglas Sabel b: 10/14/1974, Lafayette, IN BR/TR, 6'3", 185 lbs. Deb: 7/9/1999

YEAR TM-L	W	L	PCT	G	GS	CG	SH	SV	IP	H	R	ER	HR	HB	BB	SO	RAT	ERA	ERA+	CERA	OAV	BH	AVG	PR+	WS	TPW
1999 Ari-N	0	0	....	7	0	0	0	0	9^2	12	7	7	1	2	6	6	1.862	6.52	70	6.89	.300	0	.000	-2	0	-0.2
2001 Ari-N	3	2	.600	42	0	0	0	0	51^1	57	26	25	8	3	12	25	1.344	4.38	104	4.65	.282	0	....	0	3	0.0
2002 Det-A	0	0	....	1	0	0	0	0	0	2	2	2	1	0	0	0		∞	....	∞	1.000	0	....	-2	0	-0.2
Total 3	3	2	.600	50	0	0	0	0	61	71	35	34	10	5	18	31	1.459	5.02	97	5.00	.291	0	.000	-4	3	-0.4

• SABERHAGEN, Bret Bret William Saberhagen b: 4/11/1964, Chicago Heights, IL BR/TR, 6'1", 195 lbs. Deb: 4/4/1984

YEAR TM-L	W	L	PCT	G	GS	CG	SH	SV	IP	H	R	ER	HR	HB	BB	SO	RAT	ERA	ERA+	CERA	OAV	BH	AVG	PR+	WS	TPW
1984* KC-A	10	11	.476	38	18	2	1	1	157^2	138	71	61	13	2	36	73	1.104	3.48	116	2.69	.237	0	....	8	10	0.8
1985* KC-A	20	6	.769	32	32	10	1	0	235^1	211	79	75	19	1	38	158	1.058	2.87	145	**2.56**	.241	0	....	37	**24**	3.6
1986 KC-A	7	12	.368	30	25	4	2	0	156	165	77	72	15	2	29	112	1.244	4.15	102	3.56	.268	0	....	4	8	0.3
1987 KC-A★	18	10	.643	33	33	15	4	0	257	246	99	96	27	6	53	163	1.163	3.36	135	3.24	.252	0	....	37	23	3.6
1988 KC-A	14	16	.467	35	35	9	0	0	260^2	271	122	110	18	4	59	171	1.266	3.80	105	3.45	.269	0	....	10	15	1.0
1989 KC-A	**23**	6	.793	36	35	**12**	4	0	**262**^{1}	209	74	63	13	2	43	193	.961	**2.16**	**178**	**1.89**	.217	0	....	**53**	**28**	**5.4**
1990 KC-A★	5	9	.357	20	20	5	0	0	135	146	52	49	9	1	28	87	1.289	3.27	117	3.61	.279	0	....	12	7	1.2
1991 KC-A	13	8	.619	28	28	7	2	0	196^1	165	76	67	12	9	45	136	1.070	3.07	134	2.51	.228	0	....	29	16	2.9
1992 NY-N	3	5	.375	17	15	1	1	0	97^2	84	39	38	6	4	27	81	1.137	3.50	99	2.78	.233	3	.107	1	5	0.0
1993 NY-N	7	7	.500	19	19	4	1	0	139^1	131	55	51	11	3	17	93	1.062	3.29	122	2.64	.250	5	.111	10	9	1.0
1994 NY-N★	14	4	.778	24	24	4	0	0	177^1	169	58	54	13	4	13	143	1.026	2.74	152	2.56	.254	10	.172	28	16	2.9
1995 NY-N	5	5	.500	16	16	3	0	0	110	105	45	41	13	5	20	71	1.136	3.35	121	3.25	.251	4	.114	8	7	0.7
* Col-N	2	1	.667	9	9	0	0	0	43	60	33	30	8	5	13	29	1.698	6.28	86	7.05	.323	1	.071	-3	1	-0.4
Yr.	7	6	.538	25	25	3	0	0	153	165	78	71	21	10	33	100	1.294	4.18	108	4.32	.273	5	.102	5	8	0.3
1997 Bos-A	0	1	.000	6	6	0	0	0	26	30	20	19	5	2	10	14	1.538	6.58	70	5.79	.288	0	.000	-6	0	-0.5
1998* Bos-A	15	8	.652	31	31	0	0	0	175	181	82	77	22	6	29	100	1.200	3.96	119	3.65	.264	0	.000	13	12	1.2
1999* Bos-A	10	6	.625	22	22	0	0	0	119	122	43	39	11	2	11	81	1.118	2.95	168	3.07	.265	0	.000	27	12	2.5
2001 Bos-A	1	2	.333	3	3	0	0	0	15	19	11	10	3	1	0	10	1.267	6.00	75	4.90	.302	0	....	-2	0	-0.2
Total 16	167	117	.588	399	371	76	16	1	2562^2	2452	1036	952	218	59	471	1715	1.141	3.34	125	3.03	.252	23	.121	267	193	26.1

• SACKINSKY, Brian Brian Walter Sackinsky b: 6/22/1971, Pittsburgh, PA BR/TR, 6'4", 220 lbs. Deb: 4/20/1996

YEAR TM-L	W	L	PCT	G	GS	CG	SH	SV	IP	H	R	ER	HR	HB	BB	SO	RAT	ERA	ERA+	CERA	OAV	BH	AVG	PR+	WS	TPW
1996 Bal-A	0	0	....	3	0	0	0	0	4^2	6	2	2	1	0	3	2	1.929	3.86	128	7.98	.316	0	....	1	0	0.1

• SADECKI, Ray Raymond Michael Sadecki b: 12/26/1940, Kansas City, KS BL/TL, 5'11", 180 lbs. Deb: 5/19/1960

YEAR TM-L	W	L	PCT	G	GS	CG	SH	SV	IP	H	R	ER	HR	HB	BB	SO	RAT	ERA	ERA+	CERA	OAV	BH	AVG	PR+	WS	TPW
1960 StL-N	9	9	.500	26	26	7	1	0	157^1	148	76	66	15	1	86	95	**1.487**	3.78	108	4.31	.249	12	.211	6	10	0.7
1961 StL-N	14	10	.583	31	31	13	0	0	222^2	196	100	92	28	3	102	114	1.338	3.72	118	3.86	.238	22	.253	16	18	1.8
1962 StL-N	6	8	.429	22	17	4	1	1	102^1	121	74	63	13	3	43	50	1.603	5.54	77	5.45	.296	3	.081	-15	1	-1.7
1963 StL-N	10	10	.500	36	28	4	1	1	193^1	198	100	88	25	4	78	136	1.428	4.10	87	4.54	.266	9	.141	-13	6	-1.5
1964* StL-N	20	11	.645	37	32	9	2	1	220	232	104	90	16	1	60	119	1.327	3.68	103	3.67	.273	12	.160	2	15	0.5
1965 StL-N	6	15	.286	36	28	4	0	1	172^2	192	107	100	26	0	64	122	**1.483**	5.21	74	4.95	.284	11	.200	-27	2	-2.6
1966 StL-N	2	1	.667	5	3	1	0	0	24^1	16	9	6	2	0	9	21	1.027	2.22	162	2.12	.188	3	.429	4	3	0.6
SF-N	3	7	.300	26	19	3	1	0	105	125	82	63	20	4	39	62	1.562	5.40	68	5.84	.293	11	.324	-20	2	-1.6
Yr.	5	8	.385	31	22	4	1	0	129^1	141	91	69	22	4	48	83	1.461	4.80	76	5.14	.276	14	.341	-17	5	-1.0
1967 SF-N	12	6	.667	35	24	10	2	0	188	165	65	58	8	4	58	145	1.186	2.78	118	2.75	.238	18	.247	10	15	1.6
1968 SF-N	12	18	.400	38	36	13	6	0	254	225	94	82	14	3	70	206	1.161	2.91	101	2.66	.237	8	.094	3	12	0.2
1969 SF-N	5	8	.385	29	17	4	3	0	138^1	137	73	65	18	2	53	104	1.373	4.23	83	4.16	.259	5	.125	-10	4	-0.9
1970 NY-N	8	4	.667	28	19	4	0	0	138^2	134	67	60	18	0	52	89	1.341	3.89	103	3.88	.255	8	.205	-0	8	0.0
1971 NY-N	7	7	.500	34	20	5	2	0	163^1	139	56	53	10	4	44	120	1.120	2.92	117	2.60	.229	10	.200	7	11	0.9
1972 NY-N	2	1	.667	34	2	0	0	0	75^2	73	33	26	3	2	31	38	1.374	3.09	109	3.44	.257	2	.154	3	4	0.3
1973* NY-N	5	4	.556	31	11	1	0	1	116^2	109	47	44	11	1	41	87	1.286	3.39	107	3.50	.248	7	.226	2	7	0.3
1974 NY-N	8	8	.500	34	10	3	1	0	103	107	49	39	7	2	35	46	1.379	3.41	105	3.84	.274	7	.259	1	7	0.3

YEAR	TM-L	W	L	PCT	G	GS	CG	SH	SV	IP	H	R	ER	HR	HB	BB	SO	RAT	ERA	ERA+	CERA	OAV	BH	AVG	PR+	WS	TPW
1975	StL-N	1	0	1.000	8	0	0	0	0	11	13	7	4	0	0	7	8	1.818	3.27	115	4.59	.289	0	....	1	1	0.1
	Atl-N	2	3	.400	25	5	0	0	1	66^1	73	39	31	3	4	21	24	1.417	4.21	90	4.01	.286	3	.200	-2	2	-0.1
	Yr.	3	3	.500	33	5	0	0	1	77^1	86	46	35	3	4	28	32	1.474	4.07	93	4.09	.287	3	.200	-1	3	0.0
	KC-A	1	0	1.000	5	0	0	0	0	3	5	2	1	0	0	3	0	2.667	3.00	128	9.13	.333	0	....	0	0	0.0
1976	KC-A	0	0	....	3	0	0	0	0	4^2	7	0	0	0	0	3	1	2.143	0.00	....	7.77	.368	0	....	2	1	0.2
	Mil-A	2	0	1.000	36	0	0	0	1	37^1	38	20	18	2	3	20	27	1.554	4.34	80	4.61	.262	0	....	-4	1	-0.4
	Yr.	2	0	1.000	39	0	0	0	1	42	45	20	18	2	3	23	28	1.619	3.86	91	4.96	.274	0	....	-2	2	-0.2
1977	NY-N	0	1	.000	4	0	0	0	0	3	3	2	2	1	0	3	0	2.000	6.00	62	9.05	.300	0	....	-1	0	-0.1
Total	**18**	**135**	**131**	**.508**	**563**	**328**	**85**	**20**	**7**	**2500^2**	**2456**	**1206**	**1051**	**240**	**41**	**922**	**1614**	**1.351**	**3.78**	**97**	**3.87**	**.258**	**151**	**.191**	**-33**	**130**	**-1.5**
• SADLER, Carl	William Carl Sadler b: 10/11/1976, Gainesville, FL BL/TL, 6'2", 180 lbs. Deb: 7/31/2002																										
2002	Cle-A	1	2	.333	24	0	0	0	0	20^1	15	10	10	2	0	11	23	1.279	4.43	99	3.34	.211	0	....	0	2	0.0
2003	Cle-A	0	0	....	18	0	0	0	0	9^2	11	2	2	0	2	5	10	1.655	1.86	237	5.48	.306	0	....	3	1	0.2
Total	**2**	**1**	**2**	**.333**	**42**	**0**	**0**	**0**	**0**	**30**	**26**	**12**	**12**	**2**	**2**	**16**	**33**	**1.400**	**3.60**	**122**	**4.03**	**.243**	**0**	**....**	**3**	**3**	**0.3**
• SADOWSKI, Bob	Robert Sadowski b: 2/19/1938, Pittsburgh, PA BR/TR, 6'2", 195 lbs. Deb: 6/19/1963																										
1963	Mil-N	5	7	.417	19	18	5	1	0	116^2	99	36	34	8	5	30	72	1.106	2.62	123	2.66	.231	2	.057	6	8	0.4
1964	Mil-N	9	10	.474	51	18	5	0	5	166^2	159	85	76	18	7	56	96	1.290	4.10	86	3.74	.251	8	.154	-11	6	-1.2
1965	Mil-N	5	9	.357	34	13	3	0	3	123	117	62	59	11	3	35	78	1.236	4.32	82	3.35	.250	3	.086	-12	4	-1.4
1966	Bos-A	1	1	.500	11	5	0	0	0	33^1	41	26	20	4	1	9	11	1.500	5.40	70	5.04	.311	0	.000	-6	0	-0.7
Total	**4**	**20**	**27**	**.426**	**115**	**54**	**13**	**1**	**8**	**439^2**	**416**	**209**	**189**	**41**	**16**	**130**	**257**	**1.242**	**3.87**	**90**	**3.44**	**.250**	**13**	**.101**	**-23**	**18**	**-2.8**
• SADOWSKI, Jim	James Michael Sadowski b: 8/7/1951, Pittsburgh, PA BR/TR, 6'3", 195 lbs. Deb: 4/27/1974																										
1974	Pit-N	0	1	.000	4	0	0	0	0	9	7	6	6	1	0	9	1	1.778	6.00	57	5.13	.233	0	.000	-3	0	-0.2
• SADOWSKI, Ted	Theodore Sadowski b: 4/1/1936, Pittsburgh, PA d: 7/18/1993, Pittsburgh, PA BR/TR, 6'1.5", 190 lbs. Deb: 9/2/1960																										
1960	Was-A	1	0	1.000	9	1	0	0	1	17^1	17	10	10	4	1	9	12	1.500	5.19	76	5.59	.258	0	.000	-2	1	-0.2
1961	Min-A	0	2	.000	15	1	0	0	0	33	49	29	25	6	1	11	12	1.818	6.82	62	7.39	.348	0	.000	-9	0	-0.9
1962	Min-A	1	1	.500	19	0	0	0	0	34	37	19	19	6	1	11	15	1.412	5.03	81	5.29	.301	2	.500	-4	1	-0.3
Total	**3**	**2**	**3**	**.400**	**43**	**2**	**0**	**0**	**1**	**84^1**	**103**	**58**	**54**	**16**	**3**	**31**	**39**	**1.589**	**5.76**	**72**	**6.17**	**.312**	**2**	**.154**	**-15**	**2**	**-1.5**
• SAGER, A.J.	Anthony Joseph Sager b: 3/3/1965, Columbus, OH BR/TR, 6'4", 220 lbs. Deb: 4/4/1994																										
1994	SD-N	1	4	.200	22	3	0	0	0	46^2	62	34	31	4	2	16	26	1.671	5.98	69	5.58	.325	1	.100	-9	0	-0.8
1995	Col-N	0	0	....	10	0	0	0	0	14^2	19	16	12	1	0	7	10	1.773	7.36	73	5.60	.311	0	.000	-3	0	-0.3
1996	Det-A	4	5	.444	22	9	0	0	0	79	91	46	44	10	2	29	52	1.519	5.01	101	5.14	.294	0	....	2	3	0.2
1997	Det-A	3	4	.429	38	1	0	0	3	84	81	43	39	10	1	24	53	1.250	4.18	110	3.51	.258	0	....	3	6	0.3
1998	Det-A	4	2	.667	31	3	0	0	2	59^1	79	47	43	7	1	23	23	1.719	6.52	72	6.09	.325	0	.000	-13	1	-1.2
Total	**5**	**12**	**15**	**.444**	**123**	**16**	**0**	**0**	**5**	**283^2**	**332**	**186**	**169**	**32**	**6**	**99**	**164**	**1.519**	**5.36**	**87**	**4.95**	**.297**	**1**	**.071**	**-19**	**10**	**-1.9**
• SAIN, Johnny	John Franklin Sain b: 9/25/1917, Havana, AR BR/TR, 6'2", 200 lbs. Deb: 4/24/1942 C																										
1942	Bos-N	4	7	.364	40	3	0	0	6	97	79	54	42	8	5	63	68	1.464	3.90	86	3.96	.228	2	.074	-5	3	-0.8
1946	Bos-N	20	14	.588	37	34	**24**	3	2	265	225	80	65	8	2	87	129	1.177	2.21	156	**2.51**	.230	28	.298	**38**	26	**4.6**
1947	Bos-N★	21	12	.636	38	35	22	3	1	266	265	117	104	19	4	79	132	1.293	3.52	111	3.42	.255	37	.346	14	24	2.5
1948★	Bos-N★	**24**	15	.615	42	**39**	**28**	4	1	**314^2**	297	105	91	19	5	83	137	1.208	2.60	147	2.96	.245	25	.217	41	**28**	4.3
1949	Bos-N	10	17	.370	37	36	16	1	0	243	285	150	130	15	4	75	73	1.481	4.81	78	4.38	.291	20	.206	-27	6	-2.6
1950	Bos-N	20	13	.606	37	37	25	3	0	278^1	294	139	122	34	2	70	96	1.308	3.94	98	3.92	.269	21	.206	-1	15	0.2
1951	Bos-N	5	13	.278	26	22	6	1	1	160^1	195	88	75	16	3	45	63	1.497	4.21	87	4.81	.299	11	.212	-8	5	-0.5
	★NY-A	2	1	.667	7	4	1	0	1	37	41	17	17	5	0	8	21	1.324	4.14	93	4.19	.281	4	.286	-2	2	-0.1
1952★	NY-A	11	6	.647	35	16	8	0	7	148^1	149	70	57	15	2	38	57	1.261	3.46	96	3.55	.261	19	.268	-7	10	-0.1
1953★	NY-A★	14	7	.667	40	19	10	1	9	189	189	68	63	16	3	45	84	1.238	3.00	123	3.39	.262	17	.250	10	16	1.4
1954	NY-A	6	6	.500	45	0	0	0	**22**	77	66	27	27	11	0	15	33	1.052	3.16	109	2.73	.229	6	.353	1	11	0.3
1955	NY-A	0	0	....	3	0	0	0	0	5^1	6	4	4	4	0	1	5	1.313	6.75	55	8.59	.300	0	.000	-2	0	-0.2
	KC-A	2	5	.286	25	0	0	0	1	44^2	54	28	27	10	0	10	12	1.433	5.44	77	5.21	.297	0	.000	-6	1	-0.7
	Yr.	2	5	.286	28	0	0	0	1	50	60	32	31	14	0	11	17	1.420	5.58	74	5.57	.297	0	.000	-8	1	-0.9
Total	**11**	**139**	**116**	**.545**	**412**	**245**	**140**	**16**	**51**	**2125^2**	**2145**	**947**	**824**	**180**	**30**	**619**	**910**	**1.300**	**3.49**	**106**	**3.59**	**.261**	**190**	**.245**	**45**	**147**	**8.3**
• SAIPE, Mike	Michael Eric Saipe b: 9/10/1973, San Diego, CA BR/TR, 6'1" Deb: 6/25/1998																										
1998	Col-N	0	1	.000	2	2	0	0	0	10	22	12	12	5	2	0	2	2.200	10.80	48	14.60	.431	0	.000	-6	0	-0.6
• SALE, Freddy	Frederick Link Sale b: 5/2/1902, Chester, SC d: 5/27/1956, Hermosa Beach, CA BR/TR, 5'9", 160 lbs. Deb: 6/30/1924																										
1924	Pit-N	0	0	....	1	0	0	0	0	1	2	0	0	0	0	0	0	2.000	0.00	....	9.49	.500	0	....	0	0	0.0
• SALISBURY, Bill	William Ansel "Solly" Salisbury b: 11/12/1876, Algona, IA d: 1/17/1952, Rowena, OR BR/TR, 6', 180 lbs. Deb: 4/19/1902																										
1902	Phi-N	0	0	....	2	1	0	0	0	6	15	10	9	1	1	2	0	2.833	13.50	21	15.30	.468	0	.000	-7	0	-0.7
• SALISBURY, Harry	Henry H. Salisbury b: 5/15/1855, Providence, RI d: 3/29/1933, Chicago, IL BL, 5'8.5", 162 lbs. Deb: 8/28/1879																										
1879	Tro-N	4	6	.400	10	10	9	0	0	89	103	72	22	0	....	11	31	1.281	2.22	112	....	.272	2	.056	5	2	0.1
1882	Pit-a	20	18	.526	38	38	38	1	0	335	315	188	98	1	....	37	135	1.051	2.63	99	....	.232	22	.152	1	19	-0.2
Total	**2**	**24**	**24**	**.500**	**48**	**48**	**47**	**1**	**0**	**424**	**418**	**260**	**120**	**1**	**....**	**48**	**166**	**1.099**	**2.55**	**102**	**....**	**.241**	**24**	**.133**	**6**	**21**	**-0.1**
• SALKELD, Roger	Roger William Salkeld b: 3/6/1971, Burbank, CA BR/TR, 6'5", 215 lbs. Deb: 9/8/1993																										
1993	Sea-A	0	0	....	3	2	0	0	0	14^1	13	4	4	0	1	4	13	1.186	2.51	175	2.65	.232	0	....	3	1	0.3
1994	Sea-A	2	5	.286	13	13	0	0	0	59	76	47	47	7	1	45	46	2.051	7.17	68	7.57	.314	0	....	-14	0	-1.3
1996	Cin-N	8	5	.615	29	19	1	1	0	116	114	69	67	18	6	54	82	1.448	5.20	80	4.84	.261	1	.031	-14	4	-1.7
Total	**3**	**10**	**10**	**.500**	**45**	**34**	**1**	**1**	**0**	**189^1**	**203**	**120**	**118**	**25**	**8**	**103**	**141**	**1.616**	**5.61**	**79**	**5.53**	**.277**	**1**	**.031**	**-26**	**5**	**-2.7**
• SALLEE, Slim	Harry Franklin "Scatter" Sallee b: 2/3/1885, Higginsport, OH d: 3/22/1950, Higginsport, OH BL/TL, 6'3", 180 lbs. Deb: 4/16/1908																										
1908	StL-N	3	8	.273	25	12	7	1	0	128^2	144	65	45	1	3	36	39	1.399	3.15	74	3.57	.274	2	.049	-8	3	-1.3
1909	StL-N	10	11	.476	32	27	12	1	0	219	223	107	59	3	5	59	55	1.288	2.42	104	3.16	.264	8	.113	8	6	0.7
1910	StL-N	7	8	.467	18	13	9	1	2	115	112	44	38	4	1	24	46	1.183	2.97	100	2.77	.251	4	.108	3	6	0.1
1911	StL-N	15	9	.625	36	30	18	1	3	245	234	102	75	6	5	64	74	1.216	2.76	122	2.94	.257	15	.169	16	18	1.4
1912	StL-N	16	17	.485	48	32	20	3	**6**	294	289	122	85	6	6	72	108	1.228	2.60	131	2.94	.266	14	.136	25	21	2.1
1913	StL-N	19	15	.559	50	29	18	3	5	276	257	98	83	11	5	60	106	1.149	2.71	119	2.70	.255	20	.211	15	22	1.8
1914	StL-N	18	17	.514	46	29	18	3	**6**	282^1	252	92	66	5	9	72	105	1.148	2.10	133	2.50	.246	21	.231	20	25	2.4
1915	StL-N	13	17	.433	46	33	17	2	3	275^1	245	121	87	6	3	57	91	1.097	2.84	98	2.24	.238	11	.120	1	13	-0.2
1916	StL-N	5	5	.500	16	7	4	2	1	70	75	28	27	2	2	23	28	1.400	3.47	76	3.87	.290	3	.167	-6	3	-0.7
	NY-N	9	4	.692	15	11	7	2	0	111^2	96	24	17	2	0	10	35	.949	1.37	177	1.78	.234	9	.257	11	12	1.5
	Yr.	14	9	.609	31	18	11	4	1	181^2	171	52	44	4	2	33	63	1.163	2.18	117	2.59	.256	12	.226	5	15	0.8
1917★	NY-N	18	7	.720	34	24	18	1	**4**	215^2	199	70	52	4	1	34	54	1.080	2.17	117	2.26	.249	17	.221	7	17	0.8
1918	NY-N	8	8	.500	18	16	12	1	2	132	122	44	33	3	0	12	33	1.015	2.25	117	2.01	.241	5	.122	5	9	0.4
1919★	Cin-N	21	7	.750	29	28	22	4	0	227^2	221	63	52	4	1	20	24	1.059	2.06	135	2.30	.258	14	.189	14	22	1.7
1920	Cin-N	5	6	.455	21	12	6	0	2	116	129	57	43	4	2	16	13	1.250	3.34	91	3.28	.293	6	.171	-4	4	-0.5
	NY-N	1	0	1.000	5	2	1	0	0	17	16	7	3	0	0	0	2	.941	1.59	189	1.70	.239	1	.333	2	2	0.3
	Yr.	6	6	.500	26	14	7	0	2	133	145	64	46	4	2	16	15	1.211	3.11	97	3.08	.286	7	.184	-2	6	-0.2
1921	NY-N	6	4	.600	37	0	0	0	2	96^1	115	48	39	7	0	14	23	1.339	3.64	101	3.97	.307	8	.364	-3	6	-0.1
Total	**14**	**174**	**143**	**.549**	**476**	**305**	**189**	**25**	**36**	**2821^2**	**2729**	**1092**	**804**	**68**	**43**	**573**	**836**	**1.170**	**2.56**	**113**	**2.71**	**.258**	**158**	**.171**	**106**	**189**	**10.4**
• SALMON, Roger	Roger Elliott Salmon b: 5/11/1891, Newark, NJ d: 6/17/1974, Belfast, ME BL/TL, 6'2", 170 lbs. Deb: 5/3/1912																										
1912	Phi-A	1	0	1.000	2	1	0	0	0	5	7	7	5	0	0	4	5	2.200	9.00	34	6.84	.318	0	.000	-3	0	-0.4

• SALVE, Gus
Augustus William Salve b: 12/29/1885, Boston, MA d: 3/29/1971, Providence, RI BL/TL, 6', 190 lbs. Deb: 9/14/1908

YEAR	TM-L	W	L	PCT	G	GS	CG	SH	SV	IP	H	R	ER	HR	HB	BB	SO	RAT	ERA	ERA+	CERA	OAV	BH	AVG	PR+	WS	TPW
1908	Phi-A	0	1	.000	2	1	1	0	0	15^1	17	7	7	1	1	9	6	1.696	4.11	62	5.05	.266	0	.000	-2	0	-0.3

• SALVESON, Jack
John Theodore Salveson b: 1/5/1914, Fullerton, CA d: 12/28/1974, Norwalk, CA BR/TR, 6'.5", 180 lbs. Deb: 6/3/1933

YEAR	TM-L	W	L	PCT	G	GS	CG	SH	SV	IP	H	R	ER	HR	HB	BB	SO	RAT	ERA	ERA+	CERA	OAV	BH	AVG	PR+	WS	TPW
1933	NY-N	0	2	.000	8	2	2	0	0	30^2	30	17	13	4	0	14	8	1.435	3.82	84	4.25	.252	1	.111	-3	0	-0.3
1934	NY-N	3	1	.750	12	4	0	0	0	38^1	43	16	15	2	0	13	18	1.461	3.52	110	4.06	.281	3	.300	1	3	0.1
1935	Pit-N	0	1	.000	5	0	0	0	0	7	11	12	7	1	1	5	2	2.286	9.00	46	8.59	.306	0	.000	-4	0	-0.4
	Chi-A	1	2	.333	20	2	2	0	1	66^2	79	39	36	6	0	23	22	1.530	4.86	95	4.75	.298	6	.300	-2	4	0.0
1943	Cle-A	5	3	.625	23	11	4	3	3	86	87	36	32	5	1	26	24	1.314	3.35	93	3.56	.266	6	.231	-4	5	-0.3
1945	Cle-A	0	0	....	19	0	0	0	0	44	52	23	18	3	1	6	11	1.318	3.68	88	3.90	.294	4	.400	-2	2	0.1
Total	**5**	**9**	**9**	**.500**	**87**	**19**	**8**	**3**	**4**	**272^2**	**302**	**143**	**121**	**21**	**3**	**87**	**85**	**1.427**	**3.99**	**91**	**4.18**	**.280**	**20**	**.260**	**-14**	**14**	**-0.7**

• SALVO, Manny
Manuel "Gyp" Salvo b: 6/30/1912, Sacramento, CA d: 2/7/1997, Vallejo, CA BR/TR, 6'4", 210 lbs. Deb: 4/22/1939

YEAR	TM-L	W	L	PCT	G	GS	CG	SH	SV	IP	H	R	ER	HR	HB	BB	SO	RAT	ERA	ERA+	CERA	OAV	BH	AVG	PR+	WS	TPW
1939	NY-N	4	10	.286	32	18	4	0	1	136	150	84	70	11	5	75	69	1.654	4.63	85	5.09	.285	4	.098	-11	3	-1.3
1940	Bos-N	10	9	.526	21	20	14	**5**	0	160^2	151	63	55	9	2	43	60	1.207	3.08	121	2.96	.248	6	.103	8	12	0.5
1941	Bos-N	7	16	.304	35	27	11	2	0	195	192	103	88	9	4	93	67	1.462	4.06	88	3.81	.255	7	.113	-12	7	-1.3
1942	Bos-N	7	8	.467	25	14	6	1	0	130^2	129	52	44	7	4	41	25	1.301	3.03	110	3.37	.260	5	.122	5	8	0.4
1943	Bos-N	0	1	.000	1	1	0	0	0	5	5	4	4	0	0	6	1	2.200	7.20	47	6.12	.263	2	1.000	-2	6	-0.1
	Phi-N	0	0	....	1	0	0	0	0	0^1	2	1	1	0	0	1	0	9.000	27.00	12	54.30	.667	0	....	-1	0	-0.1
	Bos-N	5	6	.455	20	13	5	1	0	93^2	94	45	34	6	1	25	25	1.270	3.27	104	3.33	.260	6	.214	0	0	0.1
	Yr.	5	7	.417	22	14	5	1	0	99	101	50	39	6	1	32	26	1.343	3.55	96	3.64	.264	8	.267	-3	6	-0.1
Total	**5**	**33**	**50**	**.398**	**135**	**93**	**40**	**9**	**1**	**721^1**	**723**	**352**	**296**	**42**	**16**	**284**	**247**	**1.396**	**3.69**	**98**	**3.76**	**.261**	**30**	**.129**	**-12**	**36**	**-1.6**

• SAMBITO, Joe
Joseph Charles Sambito b: 6/28/1952, Brooklyn, NY BL/TL, 6'1", 190 lbs. Deb: 7/20/1976

YEAR	TM-L	W	L	PCT	G	GS	CG	SH	SV	IP	H	R	ER	HR	HB	BB	SO	RAT	ERA	ERA+	CERA	OAV	BH	AVG	PR+	WS	TPW
1976	Hou-N	3	2	.600	20	4	1	1	1	53^1	45	21	21	4	0	14	26	1.106	3.54	90	2.68	.237	2	.222	-2	3	-0.1
1977	Hou-N	5	5	.500	54	1	0	0	7	89	77	34	23	6	0	24	67	1.135	2.33	153	2.67	.235	2	.154	13	9	1.2
1978	Hou-N	4	9	.308	62	0	0	0	11	88	85	32	30	5	0	32	96	1.330	3.07	108	3.35	.260	1	.167	4	8	0.5
1979	Hou-N★	8	7	.533	63	0	0	0	22	91^1	80	20	18	8	4	23	83	1.128	1.77	198	2.86	.235	2	.286	18	18	2.1
1980*	Hou-N	8	4	.667	64	0	0	0	17	90^1	65	26	22	3	2	22	75	.963	2.19	150	1.74	.200	0	.000	11	14	1.1
1981*	Hou-N	5	5	.500	49	0	0	0	10	63^2	43	17	13	4	2	22	41	1.021	1.84	179	1.98	.192	0	.000	10	8	1.0
1982	Hou-N	0	0	....	9	0	0	0	4	12^2	7	2	1	0	0	2	7	.711	0.71	467	0.80	.159	0	.000	4	3	0.4
1984	Hou-N	0	0	....	32	0	0	0	0	47^2	39	16	16	5	0	16	26	1.154	3.02	110	2.90	.228	0	.000	1	3	0.1
1985	NY-N	0	0	....	8	0	0	0	0	10^2	21	18	15	1	0	8	3	2.719	12.66	27	11.83	.420	0	....	-11	0	-1.1
1986*	Bos-A	2	0	1.000	53	0	0	0	12	44^2	54	26	24	4	2	16	30	1.567	4.84	86	5.13	.298	0	....	-3	3	-0.3
1987	Bos-A	2	6	.250	47	0	0	0	0	37^2	46	29	29	8	0	16	35	1.646	6.93	65	6.22	.301	0	....	-10	0	-0.9
Total	**11**	**37**	**38**	**.493**	**461**	**5**	**1**	**1**	**84**	**629**	**562**	**241**	**212**	**48**	**10**	**195**	**489**	**1.203**	**3.03**	**117**	**3.11**	**.241**	**7**	**.135**	**34**	**69**	**3.9**

• SAMPEN, Bill
William Albert Sampen b: 1/18/1963, Lincoln, IL BR/TR, 6'1", 195 lbs. Deb: 4/10/1990

YEAR	TM-L	W	L	PCT	G	GS	CG	SH	SV	IP	H	R	ER	HR	HB	BB	SO	RAT	ERA	ERA+	CERA	OAV	BH	AVG	PR+	WS	TPW
1990	Mon-N	12	7	.632	59	4	0	0	2	90^1	94	34	30	7	2	33	69	1.406	2.99	122	3.95	.268	0	.000	6	8	0.6
1991	Mon-N	9	5	.643	43	8	0	0	0	92^1	96	49	41	13	3	46	52	1.538	4.00	91	5.06	.273	3	.231	-5	4	-0.5
1992	Mon-N	1	4	.200	44	1	0	0	0	63^1	62	22	22	4	1	29	23	1.437	3.13	111	3.97	.268	0	.000	2	3	0.2
	KC-A	0	2	.000	8	1	0	0	0	19^2	21	10	8	0	3	3	14	1.220	3.66	111	3.45	.292	0	....	1	1	0.1
1993	KC-A	2	2	.500	18	0	0	0	0	18^1	25	12	12	1	4	9	9	1.855	5.89	78	7.33	.338	0	....	-3	1	-0.3
1994	Cal-A	1	1	.500	10	0	0	0	0	15^1	14	11	11	1	3	13	9	1.761	6.46	76	5.79	.241	0	....	-3	0	-0.3
Total	**5**	**25**	**21**	**.543**	**182**	**14**	**0**	**0**	**2**	**299^1**	**312**	**138**	**124**	**26**	**16**	**133**	**176**	**1.487**	**3.73**	**102**	**4.56**	**.274**	**3**	**.111**	**-0**	**17**	**-0.1**

• SAMPSON, Benj
Benjamin Damon Sampson b: 4/27/1975, Des Moines, IA BR/TL, 6'2", 210 lbs. Deb: 9/9/1998

YEAR	TM-L	W	L	PCT	G	GS	CG	SH	SV	IP	H	R	ER	HR	HB	BB	SO	RAT	ERA	ERA+	CERA	OAV	BH	AVG	PR+	WS	TPW
1998	Min-A	1	0	1.000	5	2	0	0	0	17^1	10	3	3	0	0	6	16	.923	1.56	306	1.35	.169	0	....	6	2	0.6
1999	Min-A	3	2	.600	30	4	0	0	0	71	107	65	64	17	0	34	56	1.986	8.11	63	8.68	.351	0	.000	-24	0	-2.2
Total	**2**	**4**	**2**	**.667**	**35**	**6**	**0**	**0**	**0**	**88^1**	**117**	**68**	**67**	**17**	**0**	**40**	**72**	**1.777**	**6.83**	**74**	**7.24**	**.321**	**0**	**.000**	**-17**	**2**	**-1.6**

• SAMUELS, Joe
Joseph Jonas "Skabotch" Samuels b: 3/21/1905, Scranton, PA d: 10/28/1996, Bath, NY BR/TR, 6'1.5", 196 lbs. Deb: 4/23/1930

YEAR	TM-L	W	L	PCT	G	GS	CG	SH	SV	IP	H	R	ER	HR	HB	BB	SO	RAT	ERA	ERA+	CERA	OAV	BH	AVG	PR+	WS	TPW
1930	Det-A	0	0	....	2	0	0	0	0	6	10	11	11	1	0	6	1	2.667	16.50	29	12.19	.417	0	.000	-8	0	-0.7

• SAMUELS, Roger
Roger Howard Samuels b: 1/5/1961, San Jose, CA BL/TL, 6'5", 210 lbs. Deb: 7/20/1988

YEAR	TM-L	W	L	PCT	G	GS	CG	SH	SV	IP	H	R	ER	HR	HB	BB	SO	RAT	ERA	ERA+	CERA	OAV	BH	AVG	PR+	WS	TPW
1988	SF-N	1	2	.333	15	0	0	0	0	23^1	17	10	9	4	1	7	22	1.029	3.47	94	2.92	.202	0	.000	-1	1	-0.1
1989	Pit-N	0	0	....	5	0	0	0	0	3^2	9	4	4	1	0	4	2	3.545	9.82	34	19.88	.474	0	....	-3	0	-0.3
Total	**2**	**1**	**2**	**.333**	**20**	**0**	**0**	**0**	**0**	**27**	**26**	**14**	**13**	**5**	**1**	**11**	**24**	**1.370**	**4.33**	**76**	**5.23**	**.252**	**0**	**.000**	**-3**	**1**	**-0.4**

• SANCHEZ, Alex
Alex Anthony Sanchez b: 4/8/1966, Concord, CA BR/TR, 6'2", 185 lbs. Deb: 5/23/1989

YEAR	TM-L	W	L	PCT	G	GS	CG	SH	SV	IP	H	R	ER	HR	HB	BB	SO	RAT	ERA	ERA+	CERA	OAV	BH	AVG	PR+	WS	TPW
1989	Tor-A	0	1	.000	4	3	0	0	0	11^2	16	13	13	1	0	14	4	2.571	10.03	36	10.12	.356	0	....	-8	0	-0.8

• SANCHEZ, Duaner
Duaner Sanchez b: 10/14/1979, Cotui, Dominican Republic BR/TR, 6', 190 lbs. Deb: 6/14/2002

YEAR	TM-L	W	L	PCT	G	GS	CG	SH	SV	IP	H	R	ER	HR	HB	BB	SO	RAT	ERA	ERA+	CERA	OAV	BH	AVG	PR+	WS	TPW
2002	Ari-N	0	0	....	6	0	0	0	0	3^2	3	2	2	1	0	5	4	2.182	4.91	90	8.32	.214	0	....	-0	0	0.0
	Pit-N	0	0	....	3	0	0	0	0	2^1	3	4	4	1	0	2	2	2.143	15.43	27	10.55	.300	0	....	-3	0	-0.3
	Yr.	0	0	....	9	0	0	0	0	6	6	6	6	2	0	7	6	2.167	9.00	47	9.19	.250	0	....	-3	0	-0.3
2003	Pit-N	1	0	1.000	6	0	0	0	0	6	15	11	11	2	2	1	3	2.667	16.50	27	17.96	.500	0	....	-8	0	-0.8
Total	**2**	**1**	**0**	**1.000**	**15**	**0**	**0**	**0**	**0**	**12**	**21**	**17**	**17**	**4**	**2**	**8**	**9**	**2.417**	**12.75**	**34**	**13.57**	**.389**	**0**	**....**	**-11**	**0**	**-1.1**

• SANCHEZ, Felix
Felix Antonio Sanchez b: 8/3/1981, Puerto Plata, Dominican Republic BR/TL, 6'3", 180 lbs. Deb: 9/3/2003

YEAR	TM-L	W	L	PCT	G	GS	CG	SH	SV	IP	H	R	ER	HR	HB	BB	SO	RAT	ERA	ERA+	CERA	OAV	BH	AVG	PR+	WS	TPW
2003	Chi-N	0	0	....	3	0	0	0	0	1^2	2	2	2	1	0	3	2	3.000	10.80	39	18.51	.333	0	....	-1	0	-0.1

• SANCHEZ, Israel
Israel (Matos) Sanchez b: 8/20/1963, Falcon Lasvias, Cuba BL/TL, 5'9", 170 lbs. Deb: 7/7/1988

YEAR	TM-L	W	L	PCT	G	GS	CG	SH	SV	IP	H	R	ER	HR	HB	BB	SO	RAT	ERA	ERA+	CERA	OAV	BH	AVG	PR+	WS	TPW
1988	KC-A	3	2	.600	19	1	0	0	1	35^2	36	20	18	0	0	18	14	1.514	4.54	88	3.71	.265	0	....	-2	2	-0.2
1990	KC-A	0	0	....	11	0	0	0	0	9^2	16	9	9	1	1	3	5	1.966	8.38	46	8.38	.381	0	....	-5	0	-0.5
Total	**2**	**3**	**2**	**.600**	**30**	**1**	**0**	**0**	**1**	**45^1**	**52**	**29**	**27**	**1**	**1**	**21**	**19**	**1.610**	**5.36**	**73**	**4.70**	**.292**	**0**	**....**	**-6**	**2**	**-0.6**

• SANCHEZ, Jesus
Jesus Paulino Sanchez b: 10/11/1974, Nizao, Dominican Republic BL/TL, 5'10", 155 lbs. Deb: 3/31/1998

YEAR	TM-L	W	L	PCT	G	GS	CG	SH	SV	IP	H	R	ER	HR	HB	BB	SO	RAT	ERA	ERA+	CERA	OAV	BH	AVG	PR+	WS	TPW
1998	Fla-N	7	9	.438	35	29	0	0	0	173	178	98	86	18	4	91	137	1.555	4.47	92	4.91	.272	7	.135	-6	4	-0.7
1999	Fla-N	5	7	.417	59	10	0	0	0	76^1	84	53	51	16	4	60	62	1.886	6.01	72	7.28	.291	1	.083	-14	1	-1.4
2000	Fla-N	9	12	.429	32	32	2	2	0	182	197	118	108	32	4	76	123	1.500	5.34	83	5.24	.280	13	.232	-17	6	-1.5
2001	Fla-N	2	4	.333	16	9	0	0	0	62^2	61	33	33	7	2	31	46	1.468	4.74	89	4.49	.256	4	.235	-4	2	-0.3
2002	Chi-N	0	0	....	8	0	0	0	0	8^1	15	12	12	4	1	10	6	3.000	12.96	31	17.13	.395	0	.000	-8	0	-0.8
2003	Col-N	0	0	....	9	0	0	0	0	8	11	8	8	1	0	4	2	1.875	9.00	55	6.48	.324	0	....	-3	0	-0.3
Total	**6**	**23**	**32**	**.418**	**159**	**80**	**2**	**2**	**0**	**510^1**	**546**	**322**	**298**	**78**	**15**	**272**	**376**	**1.603**	**5.26**	**82**	**5.56**	**.279**	**25**	**.181**	**-53**	**13**	**-5.0**

• SANCHEZ, Luis
Luis Mercedes Escoba Sanchez b: 8/24/1953, Cariaco, Venezuela BR/TR, 6'2", 210 lbs. Deb: 4/10/1981

YEAR	TM-L	W	L	PCT	G	GS	CG	SH	SV	IP	H	R	ER	HR	HB	BB	SO	RAT	ERA	ERA+	CERA	OAV	BH	AVG	PR+	WS	TPW
1981	Cal-A	0	2	.000	17	0	0	0	2	33^2	39	16	11	4	1	11	13	1.485	2.94	124	4.90	.287	0	....	2	1	0.3
1982*	Cal-A	7	4	.636	46	0	0	0	5	92^2	89	36	33	3	7	34	58	1.327	3.21	127	3.59	.259	0	....	7	9	0.7
1983	Cal-A	10	8	.556	56	1	0	0	7	98^1	92	42	40	6	3	40	49	1.342	3.66	110	3.41	.254	0	....	4	9	0.4
1984	Cal-A	9	7	.563	49	0	0	0	11	83^2	84	34	31	10	3	33	62	1.398	3.33	119	4.24	.268	0	....	6	9	0.6
1985	Cal-A	2	0	1.000	26	0	0	0	2	61^1	67	41	39	9	1	27	34	1.533	5.72	72	5.20	.283	0	....	-13	1	-1.3
Total	**5**	**28**	**21**	**.571**	**194**	**1**	**0**	**0**	**27**	**369^2**	**371**	**169**	**154**	**32**	**15**	**145**	**216**	**1.396**	**3.75**	**107**	**4.07**	**.267**	**0**	**....**	**6**	**29**	**0.7**

• SANCHEZ, Raul
Raul Guadalupe (Rodriguez) Sanchez b: 12/12/1930, Marianao, Cuba BR/TR, 6', 150 lbs. Deb: 4/17/1952

YEAR	TM-L	W	L	PCT	G	GS	CG	SH	SV	IP	H	R	ER	HR	HB	BB	SO	RAT	ERA	ERA+	CERA	OAV	BH	AVG	PR+	WS	TPW
1952	Was-A	1	1	.500	3	2	1	1	0	12^2	13	5	5	0	0	7	6	1.579	3.55	100	3.89	.260	0	.000	0	1	-0.1
1957	Cin-N	3	2	.600	38	0	0	0	5	62^1	61	37	33	7	4	25	37	1.380	4.76	86	4.24	.262	2	.286	-5	4	-0.4
1960	Cin-N	1	0	1.000	8	0	0	0	0	14^2	12	9	8	1	3	11	5	1.568	4.91	78	4.87	.226	1	.500	-2	0	-0.2
Total	**3**	**5**	**3**	**.625**	**49**	**2**	**1**	**1**	**5**	**89^2**	**86**	**51**	**46**	**8**	**7**	**43**	**48**	**1.439**	**4.62**	**86**	**4.29**	**.256**	**3**	**.214**	**-6**	**5**	**-0.6**

YEAR TM-L	W	L	PCT	G	GS	CG	SH	SV	IP	H	R	ER	HR	HB	BB	SO	RAT	ERA	ERA+	CERA	OAV	BH	AVG	PR+	WS	TPW
• **SANDERS, Ben**	Alexander Bennett Sanders b: 2/16/1865, Catharpin, VA d: 8/29/1930, Memphis, TN BR/TR, 6', 210 lbs. Deb: 6/6/1888 U ♦																									
1888 Phi-N	19	10	.655	31	29	28	**8**	0	275^{1}	240	100	58	3	3	33	121	.992	1.90	156	....	.226	58	.246	36	35	4.0
1889 Phi-N	19	18	.514	44	39	34	1	1	349^{2}	406	217	138	9	4	96	123	1.436	3.55	123	....	.281	47	.278	44	28	4.4
1890 Phi-P	19	18	.514	43	40	37	2	1	346^{2}	412	237	145	13	10	69	107	1.388	3.76	114	....	.283	59	.312	20	28	2.3
1891 Phi-a	11	5	.688	19	18	15	0	0	145	157	85	61	3	8	37	40	1.338	3.79	101	....	.267	39	.250	1	13	-0.3
1892 Lou-N	12	19	.387	31	31	30	3	0	268^{1}	281	150	96	6	2	62	77	1.278	3.22	95	3.14	.259	54	.273	-7	22	0.5
Total 5	80	70	.533	168	157	144	14	2	1385	1496	789	498	34	27	297	468	1.295	3.24	116	0.61	.266	257	.271	94	126	11.0
• **SANDERS, David**	David Andrew Sanders b: 8/29/1979, Oklahoma City, OK BL/TL, 6', 200 lbs. Deb: 4/23/2003																									
2003 Chi-A	0	0	....	20	0	0	0	0	22	25	16	15	5	1	11	14	1.636	6.14	73	6.39	.281	0	....	-4	0	-0.4
• **SANDERS, Dee**	Dee Wilman Sanders b: 4/8/1921, Quitman, TX BR/TR, 6'3", 195 lbs. Deb: 8/12/1945																									
1945 StL-A	0	0	....	2	0	0	0	0	1^{1}	7	7	6	0	0	1	1	6.000	40.50	9	36.76	.700	0	....	-5	0	-0.6
• **SANDERS, Ken**	Kenneth George "Daffy,Bulldog" Sanders b: 7/8/1941, St. Louis, MO BR/TR, 5'11", 185 lbs. Deb: 8/6/1964																									
1964 KC-A	0	2	.000	21	0	0	0	1	27	23	12	11	2	1	17	18	1.481	3.67	104	3.82	.232	0	....	1	2	0.1
1966 Bos-A	3	6	.333	24	0	0	0	2	47^{1}	36	22	20	2	2	28	33	1.352	3.80	100	2.95	.214	0	.000	0	3	0.0
KC-A	3	4	.429	38	1	0	0	1	65^{1}	59	28	27	7	1	48	41	1.638	3.72	91	4.87	.250	2	.250	-3	3	-0.3
Yr.	6	10	.375	62	1	0	0	3	112^{2}	95	50	47	9	3	76	74	1.518	3.75	95	4.06	.235	2	.143	-2	6	-0.2
1968 Oak-A	0	1	.000	7	0	0	0	0	10^{2}	8	5	4	1	0	8	6	1.500	3.38	83	3.86	.229	0	....	-1	0	-0.1
1970 Mil-A	5	2	.714	50	0	0	0	13	92^{1}	64	19	18	1	4	25	64	.964	1.75	216	1.65	.201	3	.231	23	15	2.5
1971 Mil-A	7	12	.368	**83**	0	0	0	**31**	136^{1}	111	35	29	9	4	34	80	1.064	1.91	181	2.39	.227	0	.000	22	21	2.3
1972 Mil-A	2	9	.182	62	0	0	0	17	92^{1}	88	38	32	10	2	31	51	1.289	3.12	97	3.42	.245	1	.143	-1	6	-0.1
1973 Min-A	2	4	.333	27	0	0	0	8	44^{1}	53	31	30	4	2	21	19	1.669	6.09	65	5.50	.299	0	....	-10	1	-1.1
Cle-A	5	1	.833	15	0	0	0	5	27^{1}	18	6	5	2	0	9	14	.988	1.65	238	1.84	.188	0	....	7	6	0.7
Yr.	7	5	.583	42	0	0	0	13	71^{2}	71	37	35	6	2	30	33	1.409	4.40	90	4.10	.260	0	....	-3	7	-0.3
1974 Cle-A	0	1	.000	9	0	0	0	1	11	21	12	12	5	0	5	4	2.364	9.82	37	13.14	.404	0	....	-8	0	-0.8
Cal-A	0	0	....	9	0	0	0	1	9^{2}	10	5	3	0	0	3	4	1.345	2.79	123	3.14	.278	0	....	1	0	0.1
Yr.	0	1	.000	18	0	0	0	2	20^{2}	31	17	15	5	0	8	8	1.887	6.53	55	8.46	.352	0	....	-7	0	-0.7
1975 NY-N	1	1	.500	29	0	0	0	5	43	31	11	11	2	0	14	8	1.047	2.30	150	1.82	.205	0	.000	5	5	0.5
1976 NY-N	1	2	.333	31	0	0	0	1	47	39	16	15	4	1	12	16	1.085	2.87	115	2.53	.231	0	.000	2	3	0.2
KC-A	0	0	....	3	0	0	0	0	3	3	0	0	0	0	3	2	2.000	0.00	....	5.91	.273	0	....	1	0	0.1
Total 10	29	45	.392	408	1	0	0	86	656^{2}	564	240	217	49	17	258	360	1.252	2.97	118	3.17	.235	6	.115	40	65	4.2
• **SANDERS, Roy**	Roy Garvin "Butch,Pepe" Sanders b: 8/1/1892, Stafford, KS d: 1/17/1950, Kansas City, MO BR/TR, 6'.5", 195 lbs. Deb: 4/16/1917																									
1917 Cin-N	0	1	.000	2	2	1	0	0	14	12	7	7	0	1	16	3	2.000	4.50	58	5.60	.273	0	.000	-3	0	-0.4
1918 Pit-N	7	9	.438	28	14	6	1	1	156	135	59	45	1	2	52	55	1.199	2.60	111	2.47	.239	8	.151	-0	9	-0.1
Total 2	7	10	.412	30	16	7	1	1	170	147	66	52	1	3	68	58	1.265	2.75	103	2.73	.241	8	.136	-3	9	-0.5
• **SANDERS, Roy**	Roy Lee "Simon" Sanders b: 6/10/1894, MO d: 7/8/1963, Louisville, KY BR/TR, 6', 185 lbs. Deb: 8/6/1918																									
1918 NY-A	0	2	.000	6	2	0	0	0	25^{2}	28	15	12	0	2	16	8	1.714	4.21	67	5.12	.301	0	.000	-5	0	-0.6
1920 StL-A	1	1	.500	8	1	0	0	0	17^{1}	20	10	10	1	1	17	2	2.135	5.19	75	7.46	.313	0	.000	-3	1	-0.3
Total 2	1	3	.250	14	3	0	0	0	43	48	25	22	1	3	33	10	1.884	4.60	70	6.07	.306	0	.000	-7	1	-1.0
• **SANDERS, Scott**	Scott Gerald Sanders b: 3/25/1969, Hannibal, MO BR/TR, 6'4", 220 lbs. Deb: 8/6/1993																									
1993 SD-N	3	3	.500	9	9	0	0	0	52^{1}	54	32	24	4	1	23	37	1.471	4.13	100	4.26	.265	1	.063	0	2	-0.1
1994 SD-N	4	8	.333	23	20	0	0	1	111	103	63	59	10	5	48	109	1.360	4.78	86	3.79	.245	4	.125	-5	4	-0.6
1995 SD-N	5	5	.500	17	15	1	0	0	90	79	46	43	14	2	31	88	1.222	4.30	93	3.50	.228	8	.296	-4	5	-0.2
1996* SD-N	9	5	.643	46	16	0	0	0	144	117	58	54	10	2	48	157	1.146	3.38	117	2.61	.221	7	.194	10	10	1.1
1997 Sea-A	3	6	.333	33	6	0	0	2	65^{1}	73	48	47	16	3	38	62	1.699	6.47	70	6.60	.280	0	....	-14	1	-1.3
Det-A	3	8	.273	14	14	1	1	0	74^{1}	79	44	44	14	1	24	58	1.386	5.33	86	4.84	.276	0	....	-7	3	-0.7
Yr.	6	14	.300	47	20	1	1	2	139^{2}	152	92	91	30	4	62	120	1.532	5.86	77	5.66	.278	0	....	-21	4	-2.0
1998 Det-A	0	2	.000	3	2	0	0	0	9^{2}	24	19	19	1	0	6	6	3.103	17.69	27	14.87	.471	0	....	-14	0	-1.3
SD-N	3	1	.750	23	0	0	0	0	30^{2}	33	20	14	5	0	5	26	1.239	4.11	96	3.81	.270	0	....	-1	1	-0.1
1999 Chi-N	4	7	.364	67	6	0	0	2	104^{1}	112	69	64	19	0	53	89	1.581	5.52	82	5.41	.277	5	.278	-10	5	-0.8
Total 7	34	45	.430	235	88	2	1	5	681^{2}	674	399	368	93	14	276	632	1.394	4.86	88	4.33	.257	25	.194	-45	31	-3.9
• **SANDERS, War**	Warren Williams Sanders b: 8/2/1877, Maynardville, TN d: 8/3/1962, Chattanooga, TN BR/TL, 5'10", 160 lbs. Deb: 4/18/1903																									
1903 StL-N	1	6	.143	8	6	3	0	0	40	48	37	27	0	2	21	9	1.725	6.08	54	4.84	.286	1	.067	-13	0	-1.4
1904 StL-N	1	2	.333	4	3	1	0	0	19	25	15	10	1	1	1	11	1.368	4.74	57	4.10	.298	0	.000	-4	0	-0.5
Total 2	2	8	.200	12	9	4	0	0	59	73	52	37	1	3	22	20	1.610	5.64	55	4.60	.290	1	.048	-17	0	-1.9
• **SANDERSON, Scott**	Scott Douglas Sanderson b: 7/22/1956, Dearborn, MI BR/TR, 6'5", 200 lbs. Deb: 8/6/1978																									
1978 Mon-N	4	2	.667	10	9	1	1	0	61	52	20	17	3	1	21	50	1.197	2.51	140	2.82	.232	2	.105	5	4	0.4
1979 Mon-N	9	8	.529	34	24	5	3	1	168	148	69	64	16	3	54	138	1.202	3.43	107	3.13	.236	8	.160	4	10	0.3
1980 Mon-N	16	11	.593	33	33	7	3	0	211^{1}	206	76	73	18	3	56	125	1.240	3.11	115	3.38	.258	5	.078	12	14	0.9
1981* Mon-N	9	7	.563	22	22	4	1	0	137^{1}	122	50	45	10	1	31	77	1.114	2.95	119	2.64	.236	4	.114	8	10	1.0
1982 Mon-N	12	12	.500	32	32	7	0	0	224	212	98	86	24	3	58	158	1.205	3.46	105	3.33	.251	8	.140	4	12	0.5
1983 Mon-N	6	7	.462	18	16	0	0	1	81^{1}	98	50	42	12	0	20	55	1.451	4.65	77	5.10	.303	4	.143	-11	1	-1.1
1984* Chi-N	8	5	.615	24	24	3	0	0	140^{2}	140	54	49	5	2	24	76	1.166	3.14	125	2.82	.264	5	.119	14	11	1.4
1985 Chi-N	5	6	.455	19	19	2	0	0	121	100	49	42	13	0	27	80	1.050	3.12	128	2.52	.228	2	.065	13	9	1.2
1986 Chi-N	9	11	.450	37	28	1	1	1	169^{2}	165	85	79	21	2	37	124	1.191	4.19	96	3.42	.255	3	.059	0	9	-0.3
1987 Chi-N	8	9	.471	32	22	0	0	2	144^{2}	156	72	69	23	3	50	106	1.424	4.29	100	4.74	.274	3	.075	3	9	0.2
1988 Chi-N	1	2	.333	11	0	0	0	0	15^{1}	13	9	9	1	0	3	6	1.043	5.28	68	2.18	.232	0	....	-3	0	-0.3
1989* Chi-N	11	9	.550	37	23	2	0	0	146^{1}	155	69	64	16	2	31	86	1.271	3.94	95	3.74	.273	2	.047	-2	7	-0.5
1990* Oak-A	17	11	.607	34	34	2	1	0	206^{1}	205	99	89	27	4	66	128	1.313	3.88	96	3.95	.255	0	....	-8	9	-0.9
1991 NY-A★	16	10	.615	34	34	2	2	0	208	200	95	88	22	3	29	130	1.101	3.81	109	2.98	.252	0	....	8	13	0.8
1992 NY-A	12	11	.522	33	33	2	1	0	193^{1}	220	116	106	28	4	64	104	1.469	4.93	79	4.94	.286	0	....	-22	5	-2.3
1993 Cal-A	7	11	.389	21	21	4	1	0	135^{1}	153	77	67	15	5	27	66	1.330	4.46	101	4.20	.289	0	....	-1	6	-0.1
SF-N	4	2	.667	11	8	0	0	0	48^{2}	48	20	19	12	1	7	36	1.130	3.51	111	3.89	.255	0	.000	1	3	0.0
1994 Chi-A	8	4	.667	18	14	1	0	0	92	110	57	52	20	2	12	36	1.326	5.09	92	5.02	.296	0	....	-4	4	-0.4
1995 Cal-A	1	3	.250	7	7	0	0	0	39^{1}	48	23	18	6	2	4	23	1.322	4.12	114	4.61	.298	0	....	2	2	0.2
1996 Cal-A	0	2	.000	5	4	0	0	0	18	39	21	15	5	2	4	7	2.389	7.50	65	13.02	.433	0	....	-5	0	-0.5
Total 19	163	143	.533	472	407	43	14	5	2561^{2}	2590	1209	1093	297	43	625	1611	1.255	3.84	102	3.71	.263	46	.097	17	138	0.8
• **SANFORD, Fred**	John Frederick Sanford b: 8/9/1919, Garfield, UT BB/TR, 6'1", 200 lbs. Deb: 5/5/1943																									
1943 StL-A	0	0	....	3	0	0	0	0	9^{1}	7	2	2	0	0	4	2	1.179	1.93	172	2.23	.219	0	....	2	1	0.2
1946 StL-A	2	1	.667	3	3	2	2	0	22	19	7	5	0	0	9	8	1.273	2.05	182	2.65	.235	2	.286	4	3	0.5
1947 StL-A	7	16	.304	34	23	9	0	4	186^{2}	186	89	77	17	0	76	62	1.404	3.71	105	3.93	.261	11	.204	6	12	0.5
1948 StL-A	12	21	.364	42	33	9	1	2	227	250	123	117	19	2	91	79	1.502	4.64	98	4.48	.279	11	.151	2	13	0.0
1949 NY-A	7	3	.700	29	11	3	0	0	95^{1}	100	53	41	9	0	57	51	1.647	3.87	105	4.94	.270	4	.118	-0	4	-0.3
1950 NY-A	5	4	.556	26	12	2	0	0	112^{2}	103	60	57	9	1	79	54	1.615	4.55	94	4.53	.252	8	.229	-5	5	-0.4
1951 NY-A	0	3	.000	11	2	0	0	0	26^{2}	15	11	11	2	0	25	10	1.500	3.71	103	3.31	.169	0	.000	-0	1	-0.1
Was-A	2	3	.400	7	7	0	0	0	37	51	27	27	5	0	27	12	2.108	6.57	62	7.99	.329	1	.071	-10	0	-1.1
StL-A	2	4	.333	9	7	1	0	0	27^{1}	37	33	31	6	0	23	7	2.195	10.21	43	8.68	.308	2	.286	-17	0	-1.6
Yr.	4	10	.286	27	16	1	0	0	91	103	71	69	13	0	75	29	1.956	6.82	61	6.83	.283	3	.115	-27	1	-2.7
Total 7	37	55	.402	164	98	26	3	6	744	768	405	368	67	3	391	285	1.558	4.45	95	4.61	.268	39	.170	-18	39	-2.1
• **SANFORD, Jack**	John Stanley Sanford b: 5/18/1929, Wellesley Hills, MA d: 3/7/2000, Beckley, WV BR/TR, 6', 190 lbs. Deb: 9/16/1956 C																									
1956 Phi-N	1	0	1.000	3	1	0	0	0	13	7	2	2	0	1	13	6	1.538	1.38	269	3.66	.184	1	.333	4	2	0.4

YEAR	TM-L	W	L	PCT	G	GS	CG	SH	SV	IP	H	R	ER	HR	HB	BB	SO	RAT	ERA	ERA+	CERA	OAV	BH	AVG	PR+	WS	TPW
1957	Phi-N★	19	8	.704	33	33	15	3	0	236^2	194	94	81	22	3	94	**188**	1.217	3.08	123	3.06	**.221**	15	.169	20	20	1.9
1958	Phi-N	10	13	.435	38	27	7	2	0	186^1	197	103	92	15	3	81	106	1.492	4.44	89	4.42	.274	10	.169	-7	7	-0.6
1959	SF-N	15	12	.556	36	31	10	0	1	222^1	198	90	78	22	7	70	132	1.205	3.16	121	3.21	.235	8	.111	17	15	1.6
1960	SF-N	12	14	.462	37	34	11	**6**	0	219	199	111	93	11	2	99	125	1.361	3.82	91	3.41	.243	13	.176	-6	8	-0.5
1961	SF-N	13	9	.591	38	33	6	0	0	217^1	203	114	102	22	5	87	112	1.334	4.22	90	3.78	.249	16	.216	-8	11	-0.3
1962*	SF-N	24	7	.774	39	38	13	2	0	265^1	233	110	101	23	3	92	147	1.225	3.43	111	3.16	.234	15	.153	11	20	1.1
1963	SF-N	16	13	.552	42	**42**	11	0	0	284^1	273	123	111	21	5	76	158	1.227	3.51	91	3.20	.251	13	.138	-5	13	-0.2
1964	SF-N	5	7	.417	18	17	3	1	1	106^1	91	44	39	7	4	37	64	1.204	3.30	108	2.94	.228	4	.133	2	7	0.3
1965	SF-N	4	5	.444	23	16	0	0	2	91	92	50	40	11	7	30	43	1.341	3.96	91	4.09	.256	3	.120	-2	3	-0.3
	Cal-A	1	2	.333	9	5	0	0	1	29^1	35	16	15	2	0	10	13	1.534	4.60	74	4.94	.324	1	.143	-4	0	-0.4
1966	Cal-A	13	7	.650	50	6	0	0	5	108	108	51	46	11	4	27	54	1.250	3.83	88	3.63	.271	3	.136	-7	8	-0.7
1967	Cal-A	3	2	.600	12	9	0	0	1	48^1	53	26	24	6	0	7	21	1.241	4.47	70	3.84	.288	3	.200	-8	1	-0.7
	KC-A	1	2	.333	10	1	0	0	0	22	24	18	16	1	2	14	13	1.727	6.55	49	5.21	.296	0	.000	-8	0	-0.9
	Yr.	4	4	.500	22	10	0	0	1	70^1	77	44	40	7	2	21	34	1.393	5.12	62	4.27	.291	3	.167	-16	1	-1.6
Total	12	137	101	.576	388	293	76	14	11	2049^1	1907	952	840	174	46	737	1182	1.290	3.69	98	3.49	.247	105	.158	-1	115	0.7

• SANFORD, Mo Meredith Leroy Sanford b: 12/24/1966, Americus, GA BR/TR, 6'6", 220 lbs. Deb: 8/9/1991

YEAR	TM-L	W	L	PCT	G	GS	CG	SH	SV	IP	H	R	ER	HR	HB	BB	SO	RAT	ERA	ERA+	CERA	OAV	BH	AVG	PR+	WS	TPW
1991	Cin-N	1	2	.333	5	5	0	0	0	28	19	14	12	3	1	15	31	1.214	3.86	99	2.96	.186	0	.000	-0	1	-0.1
1993	Col-N	1	2	.333	11	6	0	0	0	35^2	37	25	21	4	0	27	36	1.794	5.30	90	5.88	.278	0	.000	-1	1	-0.1
1995	Min-A	0	0	....	11	0	0	0	0	18^2	16	11	11	7	2	16	17	1.714	5.30	90	7.74	.225	0	....	-1	1	-0.1
Total	3	2	4	.333	27	11	0	0	0	82^1	72	50	44	14	3	58	84	1.579	4.81	93	5.31	.235	0	.000	-2	3	-0.3

• SANTANA, Johan Johan Alexander Santana b: 3/13/1979, Merida, Venezuela BL/TL, 6', 195 lbs. Deb: 4/3/2000

YEAR	TM-L	W	L	PCT	G	GS	CG	SH	SV	IP	H	R	ER	HR	HB	BB	SO	RAT	ERA	ERA+	CERA	OAV	BH	AVG	PR+	WS	TPW
2000	Min-A	2	3	.400	30	5	0	0	0	86	102	64	62	11	2	54	64	1.814	6.49	79	6.59	.302	0	.000	-11	2	-1.1
2001	Min-A	1	0	1.000	15	4	0	0	0	43^2	50	25	23	6	3	16	28	1.511	4.74	97	5.36	.292	0	....	-0	2	0.0
2002*	Min-A	8	6	.571	27	14	0	0	1	108^1	84	41	36	7	1	49	137	1.228	2.99	150	2.86	.212	1	.250	18	10	1.8
2003*	Min-A	12	3	.800	45	18	0	0	0	158^1	127	56	54	17	3	47	169	1.099	3.07	148	2.73	.216	1	.333	29	16	2.8
Total	4	23	12	.657	117	41	0	0	1	396^1	363	186	175	41	9	166	398	1.335	3.97	119	3.90	.243	2	.250	35	30	3.5

• SANTANA, Julio Julio Franklin Santana b: 1/20/1973, San Pedro de Macoris, Dominican Republic BR/TR, 6', 175 lbs. Deb: 4/6/1997

YEAR	TM-L	W	L	PCT	G	GS	CG	SH	SV	IP	H	R	ER	HR	HB	BB	SO	RAT	ERA	ERA+	CERA	OAV	BH	AVG	PR+	WS	TPW
1997	Tex-A	4	6	.400	30	14	0	0	0	104	141	86	78	16	4	49	64	1.827	6.75	71	7.06	.323	1	.500	-21	0	-2.0
1998	Tex-A	0	0	....	3	0	0	0	0	5^1	7	5	5	0	0	4	1	2.063	8.44	57	5.97	.304	0	....	-2	0	-0.2
	TB-A	5	6	.455	32	19	1	0	0	140^1	144	72	66	18	5	58	60	1.439	4.23	113	4.70	.270	0	.000	3	8	0.3
	Yr.	5	6	.455	35	19	1	0	0	145^2	151	77	71	18	5	62	61	1.462	4.39	109	4.75	.272	0	.000	1	8	0.1
1999	TB-A	1	4	.200	22	5	0	0	0	55^1	66	49	45	10	7	32	34	1.771	7.32	68	7.29	.300	1	1.000	-14	0	-1.3
2000	Mon-N	1	5	.167	36	4	0	0	0	66^2	69	45	42	11	2	33	58	1.530	5.67	85	5.31	.271	0	.000	-6	1	-0.6
2002	Det-A	3	5	.375	38	0	0	0	0	57	49	19	18	8	2	28	38	1.351	2.84	151	4.13	.238	0	....	10	5	0.9
Total	5	14	26	.350	161	42	1	0	0	428^2	476	276	254	63	20	204	255	1.586	5.33	90	5.64	.284	2	.143	-31	14	-2.9

• SANTANA, Marino Marino (Castro) Santana b: 5/10/1972, San Jose de Los Llanos, Dominican Republic BR/TR, 6'1", 175 lbs. Deb: 9/4/1998

YEAR	TM-L	W	L	PCT	G	GS	CG	SH	SV	IP	H	R	ER	HR	HB	BB	SO	RAT	ERA	ERA+	CERA	OAV	BH	AVG	PR+	WS	TPW
1998	Det-A	0	0	....	7	0	0	0	0	7^1	9	3	3	1	1	8	10	2.318	3.68	128	8.74	.310	0	....	1	1	0.1
1999	Bos-A	0	0	....	3	0	0	0	0	4	8	7	7	3	0	3	4	2.750	15.75	32	19.63	.444	0	....	-5	0	-0.4
Total	2	0	0	....	10	0	0	0	0	11^1	17	10	10	4	1	11	14	2.471	7.94	62	12.58	.362	0	....	-4	1	-0.4

• SANTIAGO, Jose Jose Guillermo (Guzman) "Pantalones" Santiago b: 9/4/1928, Coamo, Puerto Rico BR/TR, 5'10", 175 lbs. Deb: 4/17/1954

YEAR	TM-L	W	L	PCT	G	GS	CG	SH	SV	IP	H	R	ER	HR	HB	BB	SO	RAT	ERA	ERA+	CERA	OAV	BH	AVG	PR+	WS	TPW
1954	Cle-A	0	0	....	1	0	0	0	0	1^2	0	1	0	0	0	2	1	1.200	0.00	....	0.96	.000	0	....	1	0	0.1
1955	Cle-A	2	0	1.000	17	0	0	0	0	32^2	31	11	9	1	5	14	19	1.378	2.48	161	3.89	.256	2	.500	5	4	0.6
1956	KC-A	1	2	.333	9	5	0	0	0	21^2	36	26	20	8	5	17	9	2.446	8.31	52	14.28	.387	2	.400	-10	0	-0.9
Total	3	3	2	.600	27	5	0	0	0	56	67	38	29	9	10	33	29	1.786	4.66	90	7.82	.313	4	.444	-4	4	-0.2

• SANTIAGO, Jose Jose Rafael (Alfonso) "Palillo" Santiago b: 8/15/1940, Juana Diaz, Puerto Rico BR/TR, 6'2", 185 lbs. Deb: 9/9/1963

YEAR	TM-L	W	L	PCT	G	GS	CG	SH	SV	IP	H	R	ER	HR	HB	BB	SO	RAT	ERA	ERA+	CERA	OAV	BH	AVG	PR+	WS	TPW
1963	KC-A	1	0	1.000	4	0	0	0	0	7	8	7	7	4	0	2	6	1.429	9.00	43	7.66	.276	0	....	-4	0	-0.4
1964	KC-A	0	6	.000	34	8	0	0	0	83^2	84	53	44	9	4	35	64	1.422	4.73	81	4.32	.258	0	.000	-7	1	-0.9
1965	KC-A	0	0	....	4	0	0	0	0	5	8	5	5	1	0	4	8	2.400	9.00	39	9.08	.364	0	....	-3	0	-0.3
1966	Bos-A	12	13	.480	35	28	7	1	2	172	155	87	70	17	2	58	119	1.238	3.66	104	3.30	.238	11	.196	4	9	0.5
1967*	Bos-A	12	4	.750	50	11	2	0	5	145^1	138	61	58	14	2	47	109	1.273	3.59	97	3.54	.251	8	.190	-1	11	0.1
1968	Bos-A★	9	4	.692	18	18	7	2	0	124	96	34	31	9	3	42	86	1.113	2.25	140	2.62	.215	7	.163	13	11	1.6
1969	Bos-A	0	0	....	10	0	0	0	0	7^2	11	5	3	2	0	4	4	1.957	3.52	108	8.20	.324	0	....	0	0	0.0
1970	Bos-A	0	2	.000	8	0	0	0	1	11^1	18	13	13	0	0	8	8	2.294	10.32	38	7.85	.353	2	.667	-8	0	-0.7
Total	8	34	29	.540	163	65	16	3	8	556	518	265	231	56	11	200	404	1.291	3.74	97	3.63	.246	28	.173	-6	32	-0.1

• SANTIAGO, Jose Jose Rafael (Fuentes) Santiago b: 11/5/1974, Fajardo, Puerto Rico BR/TR, 6'3", 200 lbs. Deb: 6/7/1997

YEAR	TM-L	W	L	PCT	G	GS	CG	SH	SV	IP	H	R	ER	HR	HB	BB	SO	RAT	ERA	ERA+	CERA	OAV	BH	AVG	PR+	WS	TPW
1997	KC-A	0	0	....	4	0	0	0	0	4^2	7	2	1	0	1	2	1	1.929	1.93	245	6.62	.333	0	....	1	0	0.1
1998	KC-A	0	0	....	2	0	0	0	0	2	4	2	2	0	0	0	2	2.000	9.00	54	8.38	.444	0	....	-1	0	-0.1
1999	KC-A	3	4	.429	34	0	0	0	2	47^1	46	23	18	7	2	14	15	1.268	3.42	146	3.87	.251	0	....	7	4	0.7
2000	KC-A	8	6	.571	45	0	0	0	2	69	70	33	30	7	3	26	44	1.391	3.91	131	4.14	.260	0	....	8	7	0.7
2001	KC-A	2	2	.500	20	0	0	0	0	29^1	40	22	22	2	1	9	15	1.670	6.75	73	5.60	.333	0	....	-7	0	-0.6
	Phi-N	2	4	.333	53	0	0	0	0	62^1	66	25	25	3	2	13	28	1.267	3.61	118	3.42	.272	0	.000	4	5	0.4
2002	Phi-N	1	3	.250	42	0	0	0	0	47	56	35	35	7	3	15	30	1.511	6.70	58	5.34	.290	0	.000	-15	0	-1.5
2003	Cle-A	1	3	.250	25	0	0	0	0	31^2	37	11	10	2	0	14	15	1.611	2.84	155	4.94	.298	0	....	5	2	0.5
Total	7	17	22	.436	225	0	0	0	4	293^1	326	153	143	28	12	93	150	1.428	4.39	103	4.44	.281	0	.000	3	18	0.1

• SANTORINI, Al Alan Joel Santorini b: 5/19/1948, Irvington, NJ BR/TR, 6', 190 lbs. Deb: 9/10/1968

YEAR	TM-L	W	L	PCT	G	GS	CG	SH	SV	IP	H	R	ER	HR	HB	BB	SO	RAT	ERA	ERA+	CERA	OAV	BH	AVG	PR+	WS	TPW
1968	Atl-N	0	1	.000	1	1	0	0	0	3	4	4	0	1	0	0	0	1.333	0.00	....	5.36	.286	0	....	1	0	0.1
1969	SD-N	8	14	.364	32	30	2	1	0	184^2	194	95	81	11	7	73	111	1.446	3.95	90	4.08	.270	7	.111	-6	8	-0.8
1970	SD-N	1	8	.111	21	12	0	0	1	75^2	91	56	51	11	3	43	41	1.771	6.07	66	6.27	.294	0	.000	-17	0	-1.9
1971	SD-N	0	2	.000	18	3	0	0	0	38^1	43	19	16	4	0	11	21	1.409	3.76	88	4.31	.285	2	.400	-2	1	-0.1
	StL-N	0	2	.000	19	5	0	0	2	49^2	51	21	21	2	1	19	21	1.409	3.81	95	3.81	.270	3	.300	-0	3	0.1
	Yr.	0	4	.000	37	8	0	0	2	88	94	40	37	6	1	30	42	1.409	3.78	91	4.03	.276	5	.333	-2	4	-0.1
1972	StL-N	8	11	.421	30	19	3	3	0	133^2	136	63	61	6	1	46	72	1.362	4.11	83	3.54	.263	3	.075	-11	6	-1.3
1973	StL-N	0	0	....	6	0	0	0	0	8^1	14	5	5	1	1	2	2	1.920	5.40	67	8.51	.400	0	.000	-2	0	-0.2
Total	6	17	38	.309	127	70	5	4	3	493^1	533	263	235	36	13	194	268	1.474	4.29	83	4.34	.276	15	.109	-36	18	-4.1

• SANTOS, Victor Victor Irving Santos b: 10/2/1976, San Pedro de Macoris, Dominican Republic BR/TR, 6'3", 175 lbs. Deb: 4/9/2001

YEAR	TM-L	W	L	PCT	G	GS	CG	SH	SV	IP	H	R	ER	HR	HB	BB	SO	RAT	ERA	ERA+	CERA	OAV	BH	AVG	PR+	WS	TPW
2001	Det-A	2	2	.500	33	7	0	0	0	76^1	62	33	28	9	3	49	52	1.454	3.30	131	4.18	.222	0	....	10	5	1.0
2002	Col-N	0	4	.000	24	2	0	0	0	26	41	30	30	3	0	22	25	2.423	10.38	46	9.37	.360	1	.500	-16	0	-1.6
2003	Tex-A	0	2	.000	8	4	0	0	0	25^2	29	21	20	5	1	16	15	1.753	7.01	71	6.82	.296	0	.000	-6	0	-0.5
Total	3	2	8	.200	65	13	0	0	0	128	132	84	78	17	4	87	92	1.711	5.48	85	5.76	.269	1	.250	-11	5	-1.1

• SARMIENTO, Manny Manuel Eduardo (Aponte) Sarmiento b: 2/2/1956, Cagua, Venezuela BR/TR, 6', 170 lbs. Deb: 7/30/1976

YEAR	TM-L	W	L	PCT	G	GS	CG	SH	SV	IP	H	R	ER	HR	HB	BB	SO	RAT	ERA	ERA+	CERA	OAV	BH	AVG	PR+	WS	TPW
1976*	Cin-N	5	1	.833	22	0	0	0	0	43^2	36	14	10	1	1	12	20	1.099	2.06	170	2.19	.222	0	.000	7	4	0.6
1977	Cin-N	0	0	....	24	0	0	0	1	40^1	28	13	11	6	0	11	23	.967	2.45	160	2.25	.196	0	.000	6	4	0.6
1978	Cin-N	9	7	.563	63	4	0	0	5	127^1	109	65	62	16	1	54	72	1.280	4.38	81	3.45	.234	0	.000	-10	6	-1.2
1979	Cin-N	0	4	.000	23	1	0	0	0	38^2	47	21	20	2	1	7	23	1.397	4.66	80	4.18	.311	0	.000	-4	1	-0.5
1980	Sea-A	0	1	.000	9	0	0	0	1	14^2	14	7	6	2	0	6	15	1.364	3.68	112	3.98	.255	0	....	1	1	0.1
1982	Pit-N	9	4	.692	35	17	4	0	1	164^2	153	69	62	7	0	46	81	1.209	3.39	109	2.83	.246	9	.191	7	10	0.8
1983	Pit-N	3	5	.375	52	0	0	0	4	84^1	74	35	28	8	0	36	49	1.304	2.99	124	3.33	.243	0	.000	7	6	0.7
Total	7	26	22	.542	228	22	4	0	12	513^2	461	224	199	42	3	172	283	1.232	3.49	105	3.10	.242	9	.103	14	32	1.1

YEAR	TM-L	W	L	PCT	G	GS	CG	SH	SV	IP	H	R	ER	HR	HB	BB	SO	RAT	ERA	ERA+	CERA	OAV	BH	AVG	PR+	WS	TPW
• SASAKI, Kazuhiro	Kazuhiro Sasaki b: 2/22/1968, Tokyo, Japan BR/TR, 6'4", 209 lbs. Deb: 4/5/2000																										
2000*	Sea-A	2	5	.286	63	0	0	0	37	62^{2}	42	25	22	10	2	31	78	1.165	3.16	144	2.98	.184	0	....	9	11	0.8
2001*	Sea-A★	0	4	.000	69	0	0	0	45	66^{2}	48	24	24	6	4	11	62	.885	3.24	128	1.90	.195	0	....	5	12	0.5
2002	Sea-A★	4	5	.444	61	0	0	0	37	60^{2}	44	24	17	6	2	20	73	1.055	2.52	167	2.35	.201	0	....	12	11	1.1
2003	Sea-A	1	2	.333	35	0	0	0	10	33^{1}	31	17	15	2	1	15	29	1.380	4.05	107	3.45	.238	0	....	0	4	0.0
Total	4	7	16	.304	228	0	0	0	129	223^{1}	165	90	78	24	9	77	242	1.084	3.14	137	2.55	.200	0	....	26	38	2.5
• SAUCIER, Kevin	Kevin Andrew Saucier b: 8/9/1956, Pensacola, FL BR/TL, 6'1", 196 lbs. Deb: 10/1/1978																										
1978	Phi-N	0	1	.000	1	0	0	0	0	2	4	4	4	0	1	1	2	2.500	18.00	20	12.01	.400	0	....	-3	0	-0.3
1979	Phi-N	1	4	.200	29	2	0	0	1	62^{1}	68	31	29	4	3	33	21	1.620	4.19	91	5.09	.291	1	.100	-3	3	-0.4
1980*	Phi-N	7	3	.700	40	0	0	0	0	50	50	21	19	2	4	20	25	1.400	3.42	111	3.92	.281	0	.000	2	4	0.1
1981	Det-A	4	2	.667	38	0	0	0	13	49	26	11	9	1	5	21	23	.959	1.65	228	1.68	.160	0	....	10	10	1.1
1982	Det-A	3	1	.750	31	1	0	0	5	40^{1}	35	15	14	0	2	29	23	1.587	3.12	130	4.06	.254	0	....	3	4	0.3
Total	5	15	11	.577	139	3	0	0	19	203^{2}	183	82	75	7	15	104	94	1.409	3.31	116	3.85	.253	1	.056	9	21	0.8
• SAUERBECK, Scott	Scott William Sauerbeck b: 11/9/1971, Cincinnati, OH BR/TL, 6'3", 197 lbs. Deb: 4/5/1999																										
1999	Pit-N	4	1	.800	65	0	0	0	2	67^{2}	53	19	15	6	4	38	55	1.345	2.00	229	3.60	.220	0	.000	20	9	1.8
2000	Pit-N	5	4	.556	75	0	0	0	1	75^{2}	76	36	34	4	1	61	83	1.811	4.04	114	5.31	.270	0	.000	6	6	0.5
2001	Pit-N	2	2	.500	70	0	0	0	2	62^{2}	61	41	39	4	2	40	79	1.612	5.60	80	4.60	.257	0	.000	-8	3	-0.8
2002	Pit-N	5	4	.556	78	0	0	0	0	62^{2}	50	18	16	4	1	27	70	1.229	2.30	181	2.91	.220	0	.000	13	9	1.2
2003	Pit-N	3	4	.429	53	0	0	0	0	40	30	20	18	5	1	25	32	1.375	4.05	108	3.75	.207	0	.000	2	3	0.1
	*Bos-A	0	1	.000	26	0	0	0	0	16^{2}	17	14	12	1	4	18	18	2.100	6.48	70	7.20	.266	0	....	-3	0	-0.3
Total	5	19	16	.543	367	0	0	0	5	325^{1}	287	148	134	24	13	209	337	1.525	3.71	121	4.26	.240	0	.000	28	30	2.7
• SAUNDERS, Dennis	Dennis James Saunders b: 1/4/1949, Alhambra, CA BB/TR, 6'3", 195 lbs. Deb: 5/21/1970																										
1970	Det-A	1	1	.500	8	0	0	0	1	14	16	5	5	1	1	5	8	1.500	3.21	116	4.55	.286	0	.000	1	1	0.1
• SAUNDERS, Tony	Anthony Scott Saunders b: 4/29/1974, Baltimore, MD BL/TL, 6'2", 205 lbs. Deb: 4/5/1997																										
1997*	Fla-N	4	6	.400	22	21	0	0	0	111^{1}	99	62	57	12	2	64	102	1.464	4.61	88	4.31	.244	3	.081	-8	3	-0.8
1998	TB-A	6	15	.286	31	31	2	0	0	192^{1}	191	95	88	15	7	111	172	1.570	4.12	116	4.78	.265	2	1.000	7	12	0.7
1999	TB-A	3	3	.500	9	9	0	0	0	42	53	39	30	6	4	29	30	1.952	6.43	77	7.78	.315	0	....	-7	0	-0.6
Total	3	13	24	.351	62	61	2	0	0	345^{2}	343	196	175	33	13	204	304	1.582	4.56	100	4.99	.265	5	.128	-8	15	-0.7
• SAUVEUR, Rich	Richard Daniel Sauveur b: 11/23/1963, Arlington, VA BL/TL, 6'4", 170 lbs. Deb: 7/1/1986																										
1986	Pit-N	0	0	....	3	3	0	0	0	12	17	8	8	3	2	6	6	1.917	6.00	64	9.57	.354	1	.333	-3	0	-0.3
1988	Mon-N	0	0	....	4	0	0	0	0	3	3	2	2	1	0	2	3	1.667	6.00	60	6.85	.250	0	....	-1	0	-0.1
1991	NY-N	0	0	....	6	0	0	0	0	3^{1}	7	4	4	1	0	2	4	2.700	10.80	34	14.00	.467	0	....	-3	0	-0.3
1992	KC-A	0	1	.000	8	0	0	0	0	14^{1}	15	7	7	1	2	8	7	1.605	4.40	92	5.29	.273	0	....	-0	0	0.0
1996	Chi-A	0	0	....	3	0	0	0	0	3	3	5	5	1	1	5	1	2.667	15.00	32	15.92	.333	0	....	-3	0	-0.3
2000	Oak-A	0	0	....	10	0	0	0	0	10^{1}	13	5	5	3	0	1	7	1.355	4.35	109	5.79	.310	0	....	1	1	0.1
Total	6	0	1	.000	34	3	0	0	0	46	58	31	31	10	5	24	28	1.783	6.07	67	7.95	.320	1	.333	-9	1	-0.9
• SAVAGE, Bob	John Robert Savage b: 12/1/1921, Manchester, NH BR/TR, 6'2", 180 lbs. Deb: 6/24/1942																										
1942	Phi-A	0	1	.000	8	3	0	0	0	30^{2}	24	16	11	0	0	31	10	1.793	3.23	117	4.19	.220	1	.111	3	1	0.3
1946	Phi-A	3	15	.167	40	19	7	1	2	164	164	80	74	5	2	93	78	1.567	4.06	87	4.02	.259	5	.122	-8	6	-0.7
1947	Phi-A	8	10	.444	44	8	2	1	2	146	135	71	61	8	0	55	56	1.301	3.76	102	3.19	.245	2	.050	-3	7	-0.7
1948	Phi-A	5	1	.833	33	1	1	0	5	75^{1}	98	55	52	9	0	33	26	1.739	6.21	69	6.09	.318	1	.077	-17	1	-1.7
1949	StL-A	0	0	....	4	0	0	0	0	7	12	5	5	1	0	3	1	2.143	6.43	70	8.96	.400	0	.000	-1	0	-0.1
Total	5	16	27	.372	129	31	10	2	9	423	433	227	203	23	2	215	171	1.532	4.32	89	4.20	.265	9	.087	-27	15	-3.0
• SAVAGE, Jack	John Joseph Savage b: 4/22/1964, Louisville, KY BR/TR, 6'3", 190 lbs. Deb: 9/14/1987																										
1987	LA-N	0	0	....	3	0	0	0	0	3^{1}	4	1	1	0	0	0	0	1.200	2.70	147	2.89	.286	0	....	0	0	0.0
1990	Min-A	0	2	.000	17	0	0	0	1	26	37	26	24	3	0	11	12	1.846	8.31	50	6.89	.339	0	....	-12	0	-1.2
Total	2	0	2	.000	20	0	0	0	1	29^{1}	41	27	25	3	0	11	12	1.773	7.67	54	6.44	.333	0	....	-12	0	-1.2
• SAVIDGE, Don	Donald Snyder Savidge b: 8/28/1908, Berwick, PA d: 3/22/1983, Santa Barbara, CA BR/TR, 6'1", 180 lbs. Deb: 8/6/1929																										
1929	Was-A	0	0	....	3	0	0	0	0	6	12	7	6	1	0	2	2	2.333	9.00	47	10.46	.414	0	....	-3	0	-0.3
• SAVIDGE, Ralph	Ralph Austin "Human Ripcord" Savidge b: 2/3/1879, Jerseytown, PA d: 7/22/1959, Berwick, PA BR/TR, 6'2", 210 lbs. Deb: 9/22/1908																										
1908	Cin-N	0	1	.000	4	1	1	0	0	21	18	9	6	0	0	8	7	1.238	2.57	89	2.73	.247	0	.000	-0	1	-0.1
1909	Cin-N	0	0	....	1	0	0	0	0	4	10	12	10	1	1	3	2	3.250	22.50	12	20.69	.588	0	.000	-9	0	-1.0
Total	2	0	1	.000	5	1	1	0	0	25	28	21	16	1	1	11	9	1.560	5.76	43	5.60	.312	0	.000	-9	1	-1.1
• SAVRANSKY, Moe	Morris Savransky b: 1/13/1929, Cleveland, OH BL/TL, 5'11", 175 lbs. Deb: 4/23/1954																										
1954	Cin-N	0	2	.000	16	0	0	0	0	24	23	13	13	6	2	8	7	1.292	4.88	86	4.76	.247	1	.500	-2	1	-0.1
• SAWYER, Rick	Richard Clyde Sawyer b: 4/7/1948, Bakersfield, CA BR/TR, 6'2", 205 lbs. Deb: 4/28/1974																										
1974	NY-A	0	0	....	1	0	0	0	0	1^{2}	2	3	3	0	0	1	1	1.800	16.20	22	5.10	.500	0	....	-2	0	-0.2
1975	NY-A	0	0	....	4	0	0	0	0	6	7	4	2	0	0	2	3	1.500	3.00	121	4.27	.304	0	....	0	0	0.0
1976	SD-N	5	3	.625	13	11	4	2	0	81^{2}	84	24	23	2	1	38	33	1.494	2.53	129	3.88	.272	5	.208	7	7	0.8
1977	SD-N	7	6	.538	56	9	0	0	0	111	136	77	72	15	7	55	45	1.721	5.84	61	6.30	.316	3	.150	-28	1	-2.7
Total	4	12	9	.571	74	20	4	2	0	200^{1}	229	108	100	17	8	96	82	1.622	4.49	77	5.25	.299	8	.182	-23	8	-2.1
• SAWYER, Will	Willard Newton Sawyer b: 7/29/1864, Brimfield, OH d: 1/5/1936, Kent, OH BL/TL Deb: 7/21/1883																										
1883	Cle-N	4	10	.286	17	15	15	0	0	141	119	79	37	1	....	47	76	1.177	2.36	133	....	**.215**	1	.021	7	11	0.1
• SAYLES, Bill	William Nisbeth Sayles b: 7/27/1917, Portland, OR d: 11/20/1996, Lincoln City, OR BR/TR, 6'2", 175 lbs. Deb: 7/17/1939																										
1939	Bos-A	0	0	....	5	0	0	0	0	14	14	13	11	1	0	13	9	1.929	7.07	67	5.72	.264	1	.143	-4	0	-0.4
1943	NY-N	1	3	.250	18	3	1	0	0	53	60	29	28	1	0	23	38	1.566	4.75	72	4.16	.284	4	.308	-7	2	-0.7
	Bro-N	0	0	....	5	0	0	0	0	11^{2}	13	14	10	0	0	10	5	1.971	7.71	43	5.34	.271	1	.500	-5	0	-0.5
	Yr.	1	3	.250	23	3	1	0	0	64^{2}	73	43	38	1	0	33	43	1.639	5.29	65	4.37	.282	5	.333	-13	2	-1.2
Total	2	1	3	.250	28	3	1	0	0	78^{2}	87	56	49	2	0	46	52	1.691	5.61	65	4.61	.279	6	.273	-16	2	-1.6
• SAYLOR, Phil	Philip Andrew "Lefty" Saylor b: 1/2/1871, Van Wert County, OH d: 7/23/1937, West Alexandria, OH TL Deb: 7/11/1891																										
1891	Phi-N	0	0	....	1	0	0	0	0	3	2	2	2	1	0	0	0	.667	6.00	57	....	.182	0	.000	-1	0	-0.1
• SCANLAN, Bob	Robert Guy Scanlan b: 8/9/1966, Los Angeles, CA BR/TR, 6'7", 210 lbs. Deb: 5/7/1991																										
1991	Chi-N	7	8	.467	40	13	0	0	1	111	114	60	48	5	3	40	44	1.387	3.89	100	3.72	.268	1	.042	2	5	0.0
1992	Chi-N	3	6	.333	69	0	0	0	14	87^{1}	76	32	28	4	1	30	42	1.214	2.89	125	2.77	.235	0	.000	7	10	0.7
1993	Chi-N	4	5	.444	70	0	0	0	0	75^{1}	79	41	38	6	3	28	44	1.420	4.54	88	4.17	.278	1	.500	-5	5	-0.5
1994	Mil-A	2	6	.250	30	12	0	0	2	103	117	53	47	11	4	28	65	1.408	4.11	122	4.59	.288	0	....	8	7	0.7
1995	Mil-A	4	7	.364	17	14	0	0	0	83^{1}	101	66	61	9	7	44	29	1.740	6.59	76	6.26	.304	0	....	-16	1	-1.5
1996	Det-A	0	0	....	8	0	0	0	0	11	16	15	13	1	1	9	3	2.273	10.64	48	8.90	.348	0	....	-7	0	-0.6
	KC-A	0	1	.000	9	0	0	0	0	11^{1}	13	4	4	1	1	3	3	1.412	3.18	158	4.68	.295	0	....	2	1	0.2
	Yr.	0	1	.000	17	0	0	0	0	22^{1}	29	19	17	2	2	12	6	1.836	6.85	74	6.76	.322	0	....	-4	1	-0.4
1998	Hou-N	0	1	.000	27	0	0	0	0	26^{1}	24	12	9	4	1	13	9	1.405	3.08	132	4.33	.245	0	....	3	2	0.3
2000	Mil-N	0	0	....	2	0	0	0	0	1^{2}	6	6	5	0	1	0	1	3.600	27.00	17	20.55	.600	0	....	-4	0	-0.4
2001	Mon-N	0	0	....	18	0	0	0	0	26^{1}	37	23	23	0	1	14	5	1.937	7.86	57	6.40	.339	0	....	-9	0	-0.9
Total	9	20	34	.370	290	39	0	0	17	536^{2}	583	312	276	41	23	209	245	1.476	4.63	95	4.53	.281	2	.067	-21	31	-2.1

YEAR	TM-L	W	L	PCT	G	GS	CG	SH	SV	IP	H	R	ER	HR	HB	BB	SO	RAT	ERA	ERA+	CERA	OAV	BH	AVG	PR+	WS	TPW
• SCANLAN, Doc		William Dennis Scanlan b: 3/7/1881, Syracuse, NY d: 5/29/1949, Brooklyn, NY BL/TR, 5'8", 165 lbs. Deb: 9/24/1903																									
1903	Pit-N	0	1	.000	1	1	1	0	0	9	5	7	4	0	0	6	0	1.222	4.00	81	2.02	.167	0	.000	-1	0	-0.1
1904	Pit-N	1	3	.250	4	3	1	0	0	22	21	18	12	0	2	20	10	1.864	4.91	56	4.81	.236	0	.000	-5	0	-0.6
	Bro-N	6	6	.500	13	12	11	3	0	104	94	39	25	0	2	40	40	1.288	2.16	126	2.86	.242	5	.143	7	7	0.6
	Yr.	7	9	.438	17	15	12	3	0	126	115	57	37	0	4	60	50	1.389	2.64	103	3.20	.241	5	.122	2	7	0.0
1905	Bro-N	14	12	.538	33	28	22	2	0	249^2	220	119	81	4	8	104	135	1.298	2.92	99	2.99	.237	16	.167	5	12	0.4
1906	Bro-N	18	13	.581	38	33	28	6	2	288	230	128	102	5	6	127	120	1.240	3.19	79	2.57	.214	18	.186	-19	11	-1.7
1907	Bro-N	6	8	.429	17	15	10	2	0	107	90	50	38	1	3	61	59	1.411	3.20	73	3.36	.239	9	.265	-9	5	-0.4
1909	Bro-N	8	7	.533	19	17	12	2	0	141^1	125	53	46	2	4	65	72	1.344	2.93	88	3.32	.252	12	.273	-4	10	0.2
1910	Bro-N	9	11	.450	34	25	14	0	2	217^1	175	76	63	1	5	116	103	1.339	2.61	116	3.05	.234	14	.203	8	16	1.0
1911	Bro-N	3	10	.231	22	15	3	0	1	113^2	101	67	46	2	6	69	45	1.496	3.64	91	3.99	.256	4	.121	-4	4	-0.6
Total	8	65	71	.478	181	149	102	15	5	1252	1061	557	417	15	36	608	584	1.333	3.00	91	3.07	.234	78	.188	-21	65	-1.2
• SCANLAN, Frank		Frank Aloysius Scanlan b: 4/28/1890, Syracuse, NY d: 4/9/1969, Brooklyn, NY BL/TL, 6'1.5", 175 lbs. Deb: 8/6/1909																									
1909	Phi-N	0	0	....	6	0	0	0	1	11	8	3	2	0	0	5	5	1.182	1.64	158	2.24	.211	0	.000	1	1	0.1
• SCANTLEBURY, Pat		Patricio Athelstan Scantlebury b: 11/11/1917, Gatun, Panama d: 5/24/1991, Glen Ridge, NJ BL/TL, 6'1", 180 lbs. Deb: 4/19/1956																									
1956	Cin-N	0	1	.000	6	2	0	0	0	19	24	14	14	5	0	5	10	1.526	6.63	60	6.04	.293	0	.000	-5	0	-0.6
• SCARBERY, Randy		Randy James Scarbery b: 6/22/1952, Fresno, CA BB/TR, 6'1", 185 lbs. Deb: 4/16/1979																									
1979	Chi-A	2	8	.200	45	5	0	0	4	101^1	102	56	52	9	3	34	45	1.342	4.62	92	3.83	.262	0	....	-5	4	-0.4
1980	Chi-A	1	2	.333	15	0	0	0	2	28^2	24	14	13	1	2	7	18	1.081	4.08	99	2.50	.238	0	....	0	2	0.0
Total	2	3	10	.231	60	5	0	0	6	130	126	70	65	10	5	41	63	1.285	4.50	93	3.54	.257	0	....	-4	6	-0.4
• SCARBOROUGH, Ray		Ray Wilson Scarborough b: 7/23/1917, Mount Gilead, NC d: 7/1/1982, Mount Olive, NC BR/TR, 6', 185 lbs. Deb: 6/26/1942 C																									
1942	Was-A	2	1	.667	17	5	1	1	0	63^1	68	32	29	2	0	32	16	1.579	4.12	89	4.25	.272	4	.190	-1	2	-0.1
1943	Was-A	4	4	.500	24	6	2	0	3	86	93	42	27	2	0	46	43	1.616	2.83	113	4.27	.273	8	.333	4	5	0.7
1946	Was-A	7	11	.389	32	20	6	1	1	155^2	176	85	70	8	1	74	46	**1.606**	4.05	83	4.70	.286	7	.140	-9	4	-1.2
1947	Was-A	6	13	.316	33	18	8	2	0	161	165	74	61	5	1	67	63	1.441	3.41	109	3.73	.267	6	.120	8	10	0.6
1948	Was-A	15	8	.652	31	26	9	0	1	185^1	166	71	58	10	3	72	76	1.284	2.82	154	3.08	.233	14	.219	35	18	3.4
1949	Was-A	13	11	.542	34	27	11	1	0	199^2	204	115	102	10	7	88	81	1.462	4.60	93	3.98	.265	13	.194	-0	9	0.0
1950	Was-A	3	5	.375	8	8	4	2	0	58^1	62	30	26	1	2	22	24	1.440	4.01	112	3.75	.276	2	.100	3	4	0.2
	Chi-A★	10	13	.435	27	23	8	1	1	149^1	160	95	88	10	4	62	70	1.487	5.30	85	4.29	.274	8	.174	-17	5	-1.7
	Yr.	13	18	.419	35	31	12	3	1	207^2	222	125	114	11	6	84	94	1.474	4.94	91	4.14	.274	10	.152	-13	9	-1.5
1951	Bos-A	12	9	.571	37	22	8	0	0	184	201	106	104	21	14	61	71	1.424	5.09	88	4.62	.275	13	.191	-13	8	-1.5
1952	Bos-A	1	5	.167	28	8	1	1	4	76^2	79	47	41	8	4	35	29	1.487	4.81	82	4.56	.266	4	.222	-8	2	-0.8
	*NY-A	5	1	.833	9	4	1	0	0	34	27	11	11	4	1	15	13	1.235	2.91	114	3.33	.223	5	.357	0	4	0.2
	Yr.	6	6	.500	37	12	2	1	4	110^2	106	58	52	12	5	50	42	1.410	4.23	90	4.18	.254	9	.281	-7	6	-0.6
1953	NY-A	2	2	.500	25	1	0	0	0	54^2	52	23	20	4	4	26	20	1.427	3.29	112	4.06	.250	1	.083	1	3	0.1
	Det-A	0	2	.000	13	0	0	0	2	20^2	34	24	19	3	3	11	12	2.177	8.27	49	9.22	.354	0	.000	-9	0	-0.9
	Yr.	2	4	.333	38	1	0	0	2	75^1	86	47	39	7	7	37	32	1.633	4.66	83	5.48	.283	1	.071	-8	3	-0.9
Total	10	80	85	.485	318	168	59	9	12	1428^2	1487	755	656	88	44	611	564	1.469	4.13	97	4.14	.267	85	.186	-5	74	-1.0
• SCARCE, Mac		Guerrant McCurdy Scarce b: 4/8/1949, Danville, VA BL/TL, 6'3", 200 lbs. Deb: 7/10/1972																									
1972	Phi-N	1	2	.333	31	0	0	0	4	36^2	30	14	14	6	2	20	40	1.364	3.44	104	4.18	.222	0	.000	0	3	0.0
1973	Phi-N	1	8	.111	52	0	0	0	12	70^2	54	23	19	3	1	47	57	1.429	2.42	157	3.19	.220	0	.000	10	9	1.0
1974	Phi-N	3	8	.273	58	0	0	0	5	70^1	72	40	39	6	2	35	50	1.521	4.99	76	4.51	.275	0	.000	-11	2	-1.2
1975	NY-N	0	0	....	1	0	0	0	0	0	1	0	0	0	0	0	0	....	....	....	∞	1.000	0	....	0	0	0.0
1978	Min-A	1	1	.500	17	0	0	0	0	32	35	19	14	5	3	15	17	1.563	3.94	97	5.84	.292	0	....	-1	1	-0.1
Total	5	6	19	.240	159	0	0	0	21	209^2	192	96	86	20	8	117	164	1.474	3.69	102	4.21	.251	0	.000	-1	15	-0.3
• SCHACHT, Al		Alexander Schacht b: 11/11/1892, New York, NY d: 7/14/1984, Waterbury, CT BR/TR, 5'11", 142 lbs. Deb: 9/18/1919 C																									
1919	Was-A	2	0	1.000	2	2	1	0	0	15	14	5	4	0	0	4	4	1.200	2.40	133	2.40	.233	0	.000	1	1	0.2
1920	Was-A	6	4	.600	22	11	5	1	1	99^1	130	60	49	2	1	30	19	1.611	4.44	84	4.92	.319	5	.192	-7	4	-0.6
1921	Was-A	6	6	.500	29	5	2	0	1	82^2	110	59	45	2	2	27	15	1.657	4.90	84	5.14	.332	5	.227	-8	3	-0.7
Total	3	14	10	.583	53	18	8	1	2	197	254	124	98	4	3	61	38	1.599	4.48	86	4.82	.318	10	.196	-14	8	-1.1
• SCHACHT, Sid		Sidney Schacht b: 2/3/1918, Bogota, NJ d: 3/30/1991, Fort Lauderdale, FL BR/TR, 5'11", 170 lbs. Deb: 4/23/1950																									
1950	StL-A	0	0	....	8	1	0	0	0	10^2	24	22	19	5	0	14	7	3.563	16.03	31	20.36	.429	0	.000	-13	0	-1.2
1951	StL-A	0	0	....	6	0	0	0	1	6	14	15	14	1	0	5	4	3.167	21.00	21	15.63	.452	0	....	-11	0	-1.1
	Bos-N	0	2	.000	5	0	0	0	0	4^2	6	4	1	0	0	2	1	1.714	1.93	191	4.81	.300	0	....	1	0	0.1
Total	2	0	2	.000	19	1	0	0	1	21^1	44	41	34	6	0	21	12	3.047	14.34	32	15.63	.411	0	.000	-23	0	-2.2
• SCHACKER, Hal		Harold Schacker b: 4/6/1925, Brooklyn, NY BR/TR, 6', 190 lbs. Deb: 5/9/1945																									
1945	Bos-N	0	1	.000	6	0	0	0	0	15^1	14	12	9	2	0	9	6	1.500	5.28	72	4.29	.241	0	.000	-3	0	-0.2
• SCHAEFFER, Harry		Harry Edward "Lefty" Schaeffer b: 6/23/1924, Reading, PA BL/TL, 6'2.5", 175 lbs. Deb: 7/28/1952																									
1952	NY-A	0	1	.000	5	2	0	0	0	17	18	14	10	2	0	18	15	2.118	5.29	63	6.87	.265	0	.000	-4	0	-0.5
• SCHAEFFER, Mark		Mark Philip Schaeffer b: 6/5/1948, Santa Monica, CA BL/TL, 6'5", 215 lbs. Deb: 4/18/1972																									
1972	SD-N	2	0	1.000	41	0	0	0	1	41	52	21	21	3	2	28	25	1.951	4.61	71	6.77	.319	0	.000	-5	1	-0.6
• SCHAFFERNOTH, Joe		Joseph Arthur Schaffernoth b: 8/6/1937, Trenton, NJ BR/TR, 6'4.5", 195 lbs. Deb: 4/15/1959																									
1959	Chi-N	1	0	1.000	5	1	0	0	0	7^2	11	7	7	1	0	4	3	1.957	8.22	48	7.74	.355	0	.000	-4	0	-0.4
1960	Chi-N	2	3	.400	33	0	0	0	3	55	46	21	17	2	1	17	33	1.145	2.78	136	2.53	.235	2	.286	6	5	0.7
1961	Chi-N	0	4	.000	21	0	0	0	0	38^1	43	29	27	7	1	18	23	1.591	6.34	66	5.83	.293	0	.000	-9	0	-0.9
	Cle-A	0	1	.000	15	0	0	0	0	17	16	11	9	2	1	14	9	1.765	4.76	83	5.56	.242	0	.000	-2	0	-0.2
Total	3	3	8	.273	74	1	0	0	3	118	116	68	60	12	3	53	68	1.432	4.58	87	4.38	.264	2	.125	-8	5	-0.8
• SCHALLOCK, Art		Arthur Lawrence Schallock b: 4/25/1924, Mill Valley, CA BL/TL, 5'9", 160 lbs. Deb: 7/16/1951																									
1951	NY-A	3	1	.750	11	6	1	0	0	46^1	50	20	20	3	1	20	19	1.511	3.88	99	4.31	.272	5	.294	-1	3	0.0
1952	NY-A	0	0	....	2	0	0	0	0	2	3	2	2	0	0	2	1	2.500	9.00	37	9.12	.375	0	....	-1	0	-0.1
1953*	NY-A	0	0	....	7	1	0	0	1	21^1	30	12	7	2	1	15	13	2.109	2.95	125	8.02	.345	2	.333	1	1	0.2
1954	NY-A	0	1	.000	6	1	1	0	0	17^1	20	10	8	3	1	11	9	1.788	4.15	83	6.52	.282	0	.000	-2	0	-0.2
1955	NY-A	0	0	....	2	0	0	0	0	3	4	2	2	1	0	1	2	1.667	6.00	62	8.06	.333	0	....	-1	0	-0.1
	Bal-A	3	5	.375	30	6	1	0	0	80^1	92	52	37	2	2	42	33	1.668	4.15	92	4.91	.294	2	.105	-2	2	-0.2
	Yr.	3	5	.375	32	6	1	0	0	83^1	96	54	39	3	2	43	35	1.668	4.21	90	5.02	.295	2	.105	-3	2	-0.3
Total	5	6	7	.462	58	14	3	0	1	170^1	199	98	76	11	5	91	77	1.703	4.02	93	5.40	.295	9	.200	-6	6	-0.5
• SCHANZ, Charley		Charles Murrell Schanz b: 6/8/1919, Anacortes, WA d: 5/28/1992, Sacramento, CA BR/TR, 6'3.5", 215 lbs. Deb: 4/20/1944																									
1944	Phi-N	13	16	.448	40	30	13	1	3	241^1	231	108	89	6	6	103	84	1.384	3.32	109	3.40	.254	12	.148	8	16	0.8
1945	Phi-N	4	15	.211	35	21	5	1	5	144^2	165	99	70	5	9	87	56	1.742	4.35	88	5.15	.285	6	.154	-5	4	-0.5
1946	Phi-N	6	6	.500	32	15	4	0	4	116^1	130	82	75	8	5	71	47	1.728	5.80	59	5.42	.286	3	.083	-30	0	-3.5
1947	Phi-N	2	4	.333	34	6	1	0	2	101^2	107	59	47	7	3	47	42	1.515	4.16	96	4.72	.295	4	.148	-2	4	-0.3
1950	Bos-A	3	2	.600	14	0	0	0	0	22^2	25	21	21	3	1	24	14	2.162	8.34	59	7.58	.281	1	.091	-9	0	-0.9
Total	5	28	43	.394	155	72	23	2	14	626^2	658	369	302	29	24	332	243	1.580	4.34	86	4.54	.275	26	.134	-38	24	-4.3
• SCHAPPERT, John		John Schappert b: Brooklyn, NY d: 7/29/1916, Rockaway Beach, NY BR/TR, 5'10", 170 lbs. Deb: 5/3/1882																									
1882	StL-a	8	7	.533	15	14	13	0	0	128	131	99	50	2	....	32	38	1.273	3.52	80	....	.248	9	.180	-8	6	-0.7

YEAR	TM-L	W	L	PCT	G	GS	CG	SH	SV	IP	H	R	ER	HR	HB	BB	SO	RAT	ERA	ERA+	CERA	OAV	BH	AVG	PR+	WS	TPW
• SCHARDT, Bill	Wilburt "Big Bill" Schardt b: 1/20/1886, Cleveland, OH d: 7/20/1964, Vermilion, OH BR/TR, 6'4", 210 lbs. Deb: 4/14/1911																										
1911	Bro-N	5	15	.250	39	22	10	1	4	195^1	190	102	78	4	8	91	77	1.439	3.59	92	3.84	.266	10	.169	-5	9	-0.5
1912	Bro-N	0	1	.000	7	0	0	0	1	20^2	25	13	10	1	2	6	7	1.500	4.35	77	4.84	.321	0	.000	-2	0	-0.3
Total	**2**	**5**	**16**	**.238**	**46**	**22**	**10**	**1**	**5**	**216**	**215**	**115**	**88**	**5**	**10**	**97**	**84**	**1.444**	**3.67**	**91**	**3.94**	**.271**	**10**	**.154**	**-7**	**9**	**-0.8**
• SCHATTINGER, Jeff	Jeffrey Charles Schattinger b: 10/25/1955, Fresno, CA BL/TR, 6'5", 200 lbs. Deb: 9/21/1981																										
1981	KC-A	0	0	....	1	0	0	0	0	3	2	0	0	0	2	1	1	1.000	0.00	....	3.63	.182	0	....	1	0	0.1
• SCHATZEDER, Dan	Daniel Ernest Schatzeder b: 12/1/1954, Elmhurst, IL BL/TL, 6', 195 lbs. Deb: 9/4/1977																										
1977	Mon-N	2	1	.667	6	3	1	1	0	21^2	16	6	6	0	0	13	14	1.338	2.49	153	2.70	.203	2	.333	3	3	0.4
1978	Mon-N	7	7	.500	29	18	2	0	0	143^2	108	54	49	10	2	68	69	1.225	3.07	115	2.89	.213	10	.222	3	9	0.6
1979	Mon-N	10	5	.667	32	21	3	0	1	162	136	57	51	17	1	59	106	1.204	2.83	129	3.07	.225	11	.216	14	14	1.9
1980	Det-A	11	13	.458	32	26	9	2	0	192^2	178	88	86	23	3	58	94	1.225	4.02	102	3.44	.246	0	....	4	11	0.4
1981	Det-A	6	8	.429	17	14	1	0	0	71^1	74	49	48	13	2	29	20	1.444	6.06	62	4.91	.265	0	....	-20	0	-2.1
1982	SF-N	1	4	.200	13	3	0	0	0	33^1	47	30	27	3	0	12	18	1.770	7.29	49	6.05	.333	1	.125	-13	0	-1.4
	Mon-N	0	2	.000	26	1	0	0	0	36	37	16	14	1	2	12	15	1.361	3.50	104	3.53	.276	2	.400	0	2	0.1
	Yr.	1	6	.143	39	4	0	0	0	69^1	84	46	41	4	2	24	33	1.558	5.32	68	4.74	.305	3	.231	-13	2	-1.3
1983	Mon-N	5	2	.714	58	2	0	0	2	87	88	34	31	3	5	25	48	1.299	3.21	112	3.38	.265	2	.200	2	6	0.3
1984	Mon-N	7	7	.500	36	14	1	1	1	136	112	44	41	13	2	36	89	1.088	2.71	126	2.66	.224	11	.314	9	12	1.5
1985	Mon-N	3	5	.375	24	15	1	0	0	104^1	101	52	44	13	0	31	64	1.265	3.80	89	3.72	.259	6	.194	-6	4	-0.3
1986	Mon-N	3	2	.600	30	1	0	0	1	59	53	29	21	6	0	19	33	1.220	3.20	115	3.19	.240	9	.429	3	6	1.0
	Phi-N	3	3	.500	25	0	0	0	1	29^1	28	14	11	3	0	16	14	1.500	3.38	114	3.94	.252	1	.200	2	2	0.2
	Yr.	6	5	.545	55	1	0	0	2	88^1	81	43	32	9	0	35	47	1.313	3.26	115	3.44	.244	10	.385	5	8	1.2
1987	Phi-N	3	1	.750	26	0	0	0	0	37^2	40	21	17	4	0	14	28	1.434	4.06	104	4.03	.278	2	.167	0	2	0.0
	* Min-A	3	1	.750	30	1	0	0	0	43^2	64	37	31	8	1	18	30	1.878	6.39	72	7.66	.342	0	....	-9	0	-0.8
1988	Cle-A	0	2	.000	15	0	0	0	3	16	26	19	17	6	1	2	10	1.750	9.56	43	9.05	.351	0	....	-9	0	-0.9
	Min-A	0	1	.000	10	0	0	0	0	10^1	8	2	2	1	1	5	7	1.258	1.74	234	3.37	.216	0	....	3	1	0.3
	Yr.	0	3	.000	25	0	0	0	3	26^1	34	21	19	7	2	7	17	1.557	6.49	63	6.82	.306	0	....	-7	1	-0.7
1989	Hou-N	4	1	.800	36	0	0	0	1	56^2	64	33	28	2	3	28	46	1.624	4.45	76	4.70	.287	0	.000	-6	2	-0.8
1990	Hou-N	1	3	.250	45	2	0	0	0	64	61	23	17	2	0	23	37	1.313	2.39	155	3.18	.261	1	.250	9	5	1.0
	NY-N	0	0	....	6	0	0	0	0	5^2	5	0	0	0	0	0	2	.882	0.00	....	1.77	.263	0	....	1	1	0.3
	Yr.	1	3	.250	51	2	0	0	0	69^2	66	23	17	2	0	23	39	1.278	2.20	169	3.07	.261	1	.250	12	6	1.2
1991	KC-A	0	0	....	8	0	0	0	0	6^2	11	9	7	0	0	7	4	2.700	9.45	44	9.72	.367	0	....	-4	0	-0.4
Total	**15**	**69**	**68**	**.504**	**504**	**121**	**18**	**4**	**10**	**1317**	**1257**	**617**	**548**	**128**	**23**	**475**	**748**	**1.315**	**3.74**	**100**	**3.70**	**.253**	**58**	**.240**	**-11**	**80**	**1.2**
• SCHAUER, Rube	Alexander John Schauer b: 3/19/1891, Odessa, Ukraine d: 4/15/1957, Minneapolis, MN BR/TR, 6'2", 192 lbs. Deb: 8/27/1913																										
1913	NY-N	0	1	.000	3	1	1	0	0	12	14	11	10	0	0	9	7	1.917	7.50	42	5.36	.292	0	.000	-6	0	-0.6
1914	NY-N	0	0	....	6	0	0	0	0	22^1	16	10	8	2	0	8	6	1.075	3.22	82	2.33	.205	1	.143	-1	1	-0.2
1915	NY-N	2	8	.200	32	7	4	0	0	105^1	101	56	41	4	2	35	65	1.291	3.50	73	3.15	.258	2	.077	-10	2	-1.3
1916	NY-N	1	4	.200	19	3	1	0	0	45^2	44	22	15	0	2	16	24	1.314	2.96	82	3.07	.257	2	.222	-3	1	-0.3
1917	Phi-A	7	16	.304	33	21	10	0	1	215	209	116	75	6	3	69	62	1.293	3.14	88	3.16	.263	11	.145	-6	5	-0.9
Total	**5**	**10**	**29**	**.256**	**93**	**32**	**16**	**0**	**1**	**400^1**	**384**	**215**	**149**	**12**	**7**	**137**	**164**	**1.301**	**3.35**	**80**	**3.17**	**.259**	**16**	**.132**	**-27**	**9**	**-3.4**
• SCHEETZ, Owen	Owen Franklin Scheetz b: 12/24/1913, New Bedford, OH d: 9/28/1994, Kirkersville, OH BR/TR, 6', 200 lbs. Deb: 4/22/1943																										
1943	Was-A	0	0	....	6	0	0	0	1	9	16	7	7	0	0	4	5	2.222	7.00	46	8.04	.381	0	.000	-4	0	-0.4
• SCHEFFER, Aaron	Aaron Alvin Marcus Scheffer b: 10/15/1975, Ypsilanti, MI BL/TR, 6'2", 165 lbs. Deb: 6/13/1999																										
1999	Sea-A	0	0	....	4	0	0	0	0	4^2	6	5	1	0	1	3	4	1.929	1.93	258	6.63	.353	0	....	2	0	0.1
• SCHEGG, Lefty	Gilbert Eugene Schegg b: 8/28/1889, Leesville, OH d: 2/27/1963, Niles, OH BL/TL, 5'11", 180 lbs. Deb: 8/20/1912																										
1912	Was-A	0	0	....	2	1	0	0	0	5^1	7	5	2	0	0	4	3	2.063	3.38	99	6.66	.333	0	.000	-0	0	-0.1
• SCHEIB, Carl	Carl Alvin Scheib b: 1/1/1927, Gratz, PA BR/TR, 6'1", 192 lbs. Deb: 9/6/1943																										
1943	Phi-A	0	1	.000	6	0	0	0	0	18^2	24	14	9	4	1	3	3	1.446	4.34	78	5.55	.308	0	.000	-1	0	-0.2
1944	Phi-A	0	0	....	15	0	0	0	0	36^1	36	18	17	1	4	11	13	1.294	4.21	83	3.47	.257	3	.300	-3	2	-0.2
1945	Phi-A	0	0	....	4	0	0	0	0	8^2	6	3	3	0	0	4	2	1.154	3.12	110	2.07	.207	0	.000	0	1	0.0
1947	Phi-A	4	6	.400	21	12	6	2	0	116	121	68	65	11	2	55	26	1.517	5.04	76	4.61	.274	6	.133	-19	1	-2.2
1948	Phi-A	14	8	.636	32	24	15	1	0	198^2	219	90	87	14	1	76	44	1.485	3.94	109	4.39	.286	31	.298	6	20	1.7
1949	Phi-A	9	12	.429	38	23	11	2	0	182^2	191	117	104	16	2	118	43	**1.692**	5.12	80	5.22	.275	17	.236	-25	5	-2.1
1950	Phi-A	3	10	.231	43	8	1	0	3	106	138	96	85	13	0	70	37	1.962	7.22	63	6.98	.317	13	.250	-31	0	-2.7
1951	Phi-A	1	12	.077	46	11	3	0	10	143	132	78	71	7	8	71	49	1.420	4.47	96	3.78	.250	21	.396	-5	10	0.3
1952	Phi-A	11	7	.611	30	19	8	1	2	158	153	82	77	21	4	50	42	1.285	4.39	90	3.82	.253	18	.220	-5	9	-0.6
1953	Phi-A	3	7	.300	28	8	3	0	2	96	99	57	52	9	7	29	25	1.333	4.88	88	3.92	.261	8	.195	-6	4	-0.7
1954	Phi-A	0	1	.000	1	1	0	0	0	2	5	5	5	0	1	1	1	3.000	22.50	17	16.59	.500	0	....	-4	0	-0.4
	StL-N	0	1	.000	3	1	0	0	0	4^2	6	6	6	3	0	5	5	2.357	11.57	36	13.36	.300	0	.000	-4	0	-0.4
Total	**11**	**45**	**65**	**.409**	**267**	**107**	**47**	**6**	**17**	**1070^2**	**1130**	**634**	**581**	**99**	**30**	**493**	**290**	**1.516**	**4.88**	**85**	**4.64**	**.274**	**117**	**.250**	**-97**	**52**	**-7.5**
• SCHEIBLE, Jack	John G. Scheible b: 2/16/1866, Youngstown, OH d: 8/9/1897, Youngstown, OH TL Deb: 9/8/1893																										
1893	Cle-N	1	1	.500	2	2	2	1	0	18	15	9	4	0	0	11	1	1.444	2.00	244	3.20	.220	1	.143	6	2	0.4
1894	Phi-N	0	1	.000	1	1	0	0	0	0^1	6	10	7	0	1	2	0	24.00	189.00	3	201.98	.862	0	....	-7	0	-0.5
Total	**2**	**1**	**2**	**.333**	**3**	**3**	**2**	**1**	**0**	**18^1**	**21**	**19**	**11**	**0**	**1**	**13**	**1**	**1.855**	**5.40**	**93**	**6.81**	**.279**	**1**	**.143**	**-1**	**2**	**-0.1**
• SCHEID, Rich	Richard Paul Scheid b: 2/3/1965, Staten Island, NY BL/TL, 6'3", 185 lbs. Deb: 9/11/1992																										
1992	Hou-N	0	1	.000	7	1	0	0	0	12	14	8	8	2	0	6	8	1.667	6.00	56	5.69	.280	0	.000	-3	0	-0.4
1994	Fla-N	1	3	.250	8	5	0	0	0	32^1	35	18	12	6	2	8	17	1.330	3.34	131	4.68	.269	0	.000	3	2	0.2
1995	Fla-N	0	0	....	6	0	0	0	0	10^1	14	7	7	1	0	7	10	2.032	6.10	69	7.49	.341	0	.000	-2	0	-0.2
Total	**3**	**1**	**4**	**.200**	**21**	**6**	**0**	**0**	**0**	**54^2**	**63**	**33**	**27**	**9**	**2**	**21**	**35**	**1.537**	**4.45**	**89**	**5.43**	**.285**	**0**	**.000**	**-2**	**2**	**-0.4**
• SCHELLE, Jim	Gerard Anthony Schelle b: 4/13/1917, Baltimore, MD d: 5/4/1990, Weymouth, MA BR/TR, 6'3", 204 lbs. Deb: 7/23/1939																										
1939	Phi-A	0	0	....	1	0	0	0	0	0	1	3	3	0	1	3	0	....	∞	....	∞	1.000	0	....	-3	0	-0.3
• SCHEMANSKE, Fred	Frederick George "Buck" Schemanske b: 4/28/1903, Detroit, MI d: 2/18/1960, Detroit, MI BR/TR, 6'2", 190 lbs. Deb: 9/15/1923																										
1923	Was-A	0	0	....	1	0	0	0	0	1	3	3	3	0	0	0	0	3.000	27.00	14	14.52	.600	2	1.000	-3	1	-0.1
• SCHENEBERG, John	John Bluford Scheneberg b: 11/20/1887, Guyandotte, WV d: 9/26/1950, Huntington, WV BB/TR, 6'1", 180 lbs. Deb: 9/23/1913																										
1913	Pit-N	0	1	.000	1	1	0	0	0	6	10	5	4	0	0	2	1	2.000	6.00	50	6.96	.400	1	.500	-2	0	-0.2
1920	StL-A	0	0	....	1	0	0	0	0	2	7	7	6	0	0	1	0	4.000	27.00	14	22.41	.583	0	....	-5	0	-0.5
Total	**2**	**0**	**1**	**.000**	**2**	**1**	**0**	**0**	**0**	**8**	**17**	**12**	**10**	**0**	**0**	**3**	**1**	**2.500**	**11.25**	**31**	**10.82**	**.459**	**1**	**.500**	**-7**	**0**	**-0.7**
• SCHERMAN, Fred	Frederick John Scherman b: 7/25/1944, Dayton, OH BL/TL, 6'1", 195 lbs. Deb: 4/26/1969																										
1969	Det-A	1	0	1.000	4	0	0	0	0	4	6	3	3	2	0	0	3	1.500	6.75	55	8.13	.333	0	....	-1	0	-0.1
1970	Det-A	4	4	.500	48	0	0	0	1	69^2	61	28	25	5	1	28	58	1.278	3.23	115	3.25	.237	2	.167	6	6	0.6
1971	Det-A	11	6	.647	69	1	0	0	20	113	91	38	34	11	5	49	46	1.239	2.71	133	3.29	.226	5	.208	11	15	1.3
1972*	Det-A	7	3	.700	57	3	0	0	12	94	91	43	38	5	5	53	53	1.532	3.64	86	4.36	.269	2	.091	-6	5	-0.8
1973	Det-A	2	2	.500	34	0	0	0	0	61^2	59	30	29	6	3	30	28	1.443	4.23	97	4.33	.258	0	....	-1	3	-0.1
1974	Hou-N	2	5	.286	53	0	0	0	4	61^1	67	33	28	5	7	26	35	1.516	4.11	84	4.87	.284	0	.000	-5	2	-0.6
1975	Hou-N	0	1	.000	16	0	0	0	0	16^1	21	11	9	4	1	4	13	1.531	4.96	68	6.31	.318	0	.000	-3	0	-0.3
	Mon-N	4	3	.571	34	7	0	0	0	76^1	84	37	30	3	5	41	43	1.638	3.54	108	4.80	.283	1	.063	2	5	0.2
	Yr.	4	4	.500	50	7	0	0	0	92^2	105	48	39	7	6	45	56	1.619	3.79	98	5.06	.289	1	.059	-1	5	-0.2
1976	Mon-N	2	2	.500	31	0	0	0	1	40	42	25	22	5	3	14	18	1.400	4.95	75	4.35	.261	1	.250	-5	1	-0.6
Total	**8**	**33**	**26**	**.559**	**346**	**11**	**1**	**0**	**39**	**536^1**	**522**	**248**	**218**	**46**	**30**	**245**	**297**	**1.430**	**3.66**	**98**	**4.19**	**.260**	**11**	**.134**	**-2**	**37**	**-0.4**

YEAR	TM-L	W	L	PCT	G	GS	CG	SH	SV	IP	H	R	ER	HR	HB	BB	SO	RAT	ERA	ERA+	CERA	OAV	BH	AVG	PR+	WS	TPW
• SCHERRER, Bill					William Joseph Scherrer b: 1/20/1958, Tonawanda, NY BL/TL, 6'4", 180 lbs. Deb: 9/7/1982																						
1982	Cin-N	0	1	.000	5	2	0	0	0	17^1	17	7	5	0	0	0	7	.981	2.60	142	1.87	.250	1	.500	2	1	0.3
1983	Cin-N	2	3	.400	73	0	0	0	10	92	73	31	28	6	0	33	57	1.152	2.74	139	2.58	.225	1	.091	11	11	1.1
1984	Cin-N	1	1	.500	36	0	0	0	1	52^1	64	31	29	6	0	15	35	1.510	4.99	76	4.88	.300	0	.000	-7	1	-0.7
	*Det-A	1	0	1.000	18	0	0	0	0	19	14	4	4	1	0	8	16	1.158	1.89	207	2.42	.206	0	....	4	2	0.4
1985	Det-A	3	2	.600	48	0	0	0	0	66	62	35	32	10	1	41	46	1.561	4.36	93	4.65	.248	0	....	-2	3	-0.2
1986	Det-A	0	1	.000	13	0	0	0	0	21	19	19	17	3	1	22	16	1.952	7.29	57	6.29	.244	0	....	-8	0	-0.7
1987	Cin-N	1	1	.500	23	0	0	0	0	33	43	17	16	3	0	16	24	1.788	4.36	97	6.06	.328	0	.000	-1	2	-0.1
1988	Bal-A	0	1	.000	4	0	0	0	0	4	8	6	6	2	0	3	3	2.750	13.50	29	16.12	.400	0	....	-4	0	-0.4
	Phi-N	0	0	....	8	0	0	0	0	6^2	7	4	4	0	0	2	3	1.350	5.40	66	3.32	.269	0	....	-1	0	-0.1
Total	**7**	**8**	**10**	**.444**	**228**	**2**	**0**	**0**	**11**	**311^1**	**307**	**154**	**141**	**31**	**2**	**140**	**207**	**1.436**	**4.08**	**97**	**4.17**	**.260**	**2**	**.118**	**-5**	**20**	**-0.5**
• SCHESLER, Dutch					Charles Schesler b: 6/1/1900, Frankfurt, Germany d: 11/19/1953, Harrisburg, PA BR/TR, 6'2", 185 lbs. Deb: 4/16/1931																						
1931	Phi-N	0	0	....	17	0	0	0	0	38^1	65	39	31	4	4	18	14	2.165	7.28	58	9.21	.385	1	.111	-12	0	-1.3
• SCHETTLER, Lou					Louis Martin Schettler b: 6/12/1886, Pittsburgh, PA d: 5/1/1960, Youngstown, OH BR/TR, 5'11", 160 lbs. Deb: 4/25/1910																						
1910	Phi-N	2	6	.250	27	7	3	0	1	107	96	53	38	2	2	51	62	1.374	3.20	98	3.33	.247	7	.171	-2	4	-0.3
• SCHILLING, Curt					Curtis Montague Schilling b: 11/14/1966, Anchorage, AK BR/TR, 6'5", 215 lbs. Deb: 9/7/1988																						
1988	Bal-A	0	3	.000	4	4	0	0	0	14^2	22	19	16	3	1	10	4	2.182	9.82	40	9.43	.355	0	....	-10	0	-1.0
1989	Bal-A	0	1	.000	5	1	0	0	0	8^2	10	6	6	2	0	3	6	1.500	6.23	61	5.74	.286	0	....	-2	0	-0.2
1990	Bal-A	1	2	.333	35	0	0	0	3	46	38	13	13	1	0	19	32	1.239	2.54	149	2.68	.229	0	....	6	5	0.6
1991	Hou-N	3	5	.375	56	0	0	0	8	75^2	79	35	32	2	0	39	71	1.559	3.81	92	4.08	.271	1	.333	-3	5	-0.3
1992	Phi-N	14	11	.560	42	26	10	4	2	226^1	165	67	59	11	1	59	147	.990	2.35	149	**1.86**	**.201**	10	.156	30	17	3.3
1993*	Phi-N	16	7	.696	34	34	7	2	0	235^1	234	114	105	23	4	57	186	1.237	4.02	99	3.44	.259	11	.147	0	13	-0.1
1994	Phi-N	2	8	.200	13	13	1	0	0	82^1	87	42	41	10	3	28	58	1.397	4.48	96	4.36	.270	3	.107	-1	2	-0.2
1995	Phi-N	7	5	.583	17	17	1	0	0	116	96	52	46	12	3	26	114	1.052	3.57	118	2.55	.220	7	.175	8	8	0.7
1996	Phi-N	9	10	.474	26	26	**8**	2	0	183^1	149	69	65	16	3	50	182	1.085	3.19	135	2.59	.223	11	.175	22	14	2.1
1997	Phi-N★	17	11	.607	35	**35**	7	2	0	254^1	208	96	84	25	5	58	**319**	1.046	2.97	143	2.55	.224	14	.173	37	22	3.7
1998	Phi-N★	15	14	.517	35	**35**	**15**	2	0	**268^2**	236	101	97	23	6	61	**300**	1.105	3.25	133	2.75	.236	10	.132	32	22	3.0
1999	Phi-N★	15	6	.714	24	24	8	1	0	180^1	159	74	71	25	5	44	152	1.126	3.54	133	3.20	.237	5	.100	21	15	2.0
2000	Phi-N	6	6	.500	16	16	4	1	0	112^2	110	49	49	17	1	32	96	1.260	3.91	119	3.79	.253	5	.167	9	8	0.9
	Ari-N	5	6	.455	13	13	4	1	0	97^2	94	41	40	10	0	13	72	1.096	3.69	128	2.91	.257	8	.258	11	8	1.2
	Yr.	11	12	.478	29	29	**8**	2	0	210^1	204	90	89	27	1	45	168	1.184	3.81	123	3.38	.255	13	.213	20	16	2.1
2001*	Ari-N★	**22**	6	.786	35	**35**	**6**	1	0	**256^2**	237	86	85	37	1	39	293	1.075	2.98	154	3.03	.245	11	.133	42	24	3.9
2002*	Ari-N★	23	7	.767	36	35	5	1	0	259^1	218	95	93	29	3	33	316	.968	3.23	137	2.33	.224	15	.174	38	24	3.8
2003	Ari-N	8	9	.471	24	24	3	2	0	168	144	58	55	17	3	32	194	1.048	2.95	158	2.59	.230	3	.058	34	15	3.0
Total	**16**	**163**	**117**	**.582**	**450**	**338**	**79**	**19**	**13**	**2586**	**2286**	**1017**	**957**	**263**	**39**	**603**	**2542**	**1.117**	**3.33**	**128**	**2.89**	**.236**	**114**	**.150**	**273**	**202**	**26.3**
• SCHILLINGS, Red					Elbert Isaiah Schillings b: 3/29/1900, Deport, TX d: 1/7/1954, Oklahoma City, OK BR/TR, 5'10", 180 lbs. Deb: 9/11/1922																						
1922	Phi-A	0	0	....	4	0	0	0	0	8	10	6	6	1	0	11	4	2.625	6.75	63	9.33	.313	0	.000	-2	0	-0.2
• SCHIRALDI, Calvin					Calvin Drew Schiraldi b: 6/16/1962, Houston, TX BR/TR, 6'5", 200 lbs. Deb: 9/1/1984																						
1984	NY-N	0	2	.000	5	3	0	0	0	17^1	20	13	11	3	0	10	16	1.731	5.71	62	6.31	.286	0	.000	-4	0	-0.5
1985	NY-N	2	1	.667	10	4	0	0	0	26^1	43	27	26	4	3	11	21	2.051	8.89	39	9.20	.368	1	.125	-16	0	-1.7
1986*	Bos-A	4	2	.667	25	0	0	0	9	51	36	8	8	5	1	15	55	1.000	1.41	295	2.23	.201	0	....	16	10	1.6
1987	Bos-A	8	5	.615	62	1	0	0	6	83^2	75	45	41	15	1	40	93	1.375	4.41	103	4.30	.240	0	....	2	7	0.2
1988	Chi-N	9	13	.409	29	27	2	1	1	166^1	166	87	81	13	2	63	140	1.377	4.38	82	3.79	.257	6	.100	-11	5	-1.4
1989	Chi-N	3	6	.333	54	0	0	0	4	78^2	60	34	33	7	1	50	54	1.398	3.78	99	3.58	.209	0	.000	0	5	-0.1
	SD-N	3	1	.750	5	4	0	0	0	21^1	12	6	6	1	0	13	17	1.172	2.53	138	2.24	.162	1	.143	2	2	0.3
	Yr.	6	7	.462	59	4	0	0	4	100	72	40	39	8	1	63	71	1.350	3.51	106	3.30	.199	1	.063	2	7	0.2
1990	SD-N	3	8	.273	42	8	0	0	1	104	105	59	51	11	1	60	74	1.587	4.41	87	4.81	.264	4	.190	-7	3	-0.5
1991	Tex-A	0	1	.000	3	0	0	0	0	4^2	5	6	6	3	0	5	1	2.143	11.57	35	11.56	.263	0	....	-4	0	-0.4
Total	**8**	**32**	**39**	**.451**	**235**	**47**	**2**	**1**	**21**	**553^1**	**522**	**285**	**263**	**62**	**9**	**267**	**471**	**1.426**	**4.28**	**89**	**4.23**	**.248**	**12**	**.111**	**-22**	**32**	**-2.5**
• SCHLITZER, Biff					Victor Joseph Schlitzer b: 12/4/1884, Rochester, NY d: 1/4/1948, Wellesley Hills, MA BR/TR, 5'11", 175 lbs. Deb: 4/17/1908																						
1908	Phi-A	6	8	.429	24	18	11	2	0	131	110	56	46	1	2	45	57	1.183	3.16	81	2.51	.234	9	.196	-6	6	-0.7
1909	Phi-A	0	3	.000	4	3	0	0	0	13^1	13	9	8	0	3	7	6	1.500	5.40	44	4.19	.245	1	.250	-5	0	-0.5
	Bos-A	4	4	.500	13	8	5	0	1	69^2	68	34	27	0	1	17	23	1.220	3.49	71	2.15	.234	5	.185	-9	3	-1.0
	Yr.	4	7	.364	17	11	5	0	1	83	81	43	35	0	4	24	29	1.265	3.80	65	2.47	.236	6	.194	-13	3	-1.5
1914	Buf-F	0	0	....	3	0	0	0	0	3^1	7	8	6	3	0	2	1	2.700	16.20	21	20.56	.438	1	1.000	-5	0	-0.5
Total	**3**	**10**	**15**	**.400**	**44**	**29**	**16**	**2**	**1**	**217^1**	**198**	**107**	**87**	**4**	**6**	**71**	**87**	**1.238**	**3.60**	**71**	**2.78**	**.239**	**16**	**.205**	**-24**	**9**	**-2.6**
• SCHMACK, Brian					Brian Robert Schmack b: 12/7/1973, Chicago, IL BR/TR, 6'2", 190 lbs. Deb: 8/24/2003																						
2003	Det-A	1	0	1.000	11	0	0	0	0	13	14	6	5	1	1	4	4	1.385	3.46	125	4.43	.292	0	....	1	1	0.1
• SCHMELZ, Al					Alan George Schmelz b: 11/12/1943, Whittier, CA BR/TR, 6'4", 210 lbs. Deb: 9/7/1967																						
1967	NY-N	0	0	....	2	0	0	0	0	3	4	1	1	1	0	1	2	1.667	3.00	113	8.78	.364	0	....	0	0	0.0
• SCHMIDT, Bill					Frederick William Schmidt b: 4/1861, New Orleans, LA d: 5/24/1928, New Orleans, LA TR, 5'8", 152 lbs. Deb: 7/6/1886																						
1886	Det-N	5	4	.556	9	9	9	0	0	77	81	47	35	0	....	30	36	1.442	4.09	80	....	.260	7	.184	-8	4	-0.8
• SCHMIDT, Curt					Curtis Allen Schmidt b: 3/16/1970, Miles City, MT BR/TR, 6'5", 200 lbs. Deb: 4/28/1995																						
1995	Mon-N	0	0	....	11	0	0	0	0	10^1	15	8	8	1	2	9	7	2.323	6.97	62	10.07	.357	0	....	-3	0	-0.3
• SCHMIDT, Dave					David Joseph Schmidt b: 4/22/1957, Niles, MI BR/TR, 6'1", 185 lbs. Deb: 5/1/1981																						
1981	Tex-A	0	1	.000	14	1	0	0	1	31^2	31	11	11	1	1	11	13	1.326	3.13	111	3.34	.258	0	....	1	2	0.1
1982	Tex-A	4	6	.400	33	8	0	0	6	109^2	118	45	39	5	5	25	69	1.304	3.20	121	3.59	.279	0	....	9	10	0.9
1983	Tex-A	3	3	.500	31	0	0	0	2	46^1	42	20	20	3	1	14	29	1.209	3.88	103	3.04	.241	0	....	1	3	0.1
1984	Tex-A	6	6	.500	43	0	0	0	12	70^1	69	30	20	3	0	20	46	1.265	2.56	162	2.96	.262	0	....	13	9	1.3
1985	Tex-A	7	6	.538	51	4	1	1	5	85^2	81	36	30	6	0	22	46	1.202	3.15	134	2.87	.246	0	....	12	9	1.2
1986	Chi-A	3	6	.333	49	1	0	0	8	92^1	94	37	34	10	5	27	67	1.310	3.31	130	3.91	.264	0	....	8	8	0.8
1987	Bal-A	10	5	.667	35	14	2	2	1	124	128	57	52	13	1	26	70	1.242	3.77	117	3.56	.263	0	....	9	10	0.8
1988	Bal-A	8	5	.615	41	9	0	0	2	129^2	129	58	49	14	3	38	67	1.288	3.40	115	3.77	.262	0	....	6	9	0.6
1989	Bal-A	10	13	.435	38	26	2	0	0	156^2	196	102	99	24	2	36	46	1.481	5.69	67	5.27	.310	0	....	-34	1	-3.5
1990	Mon-N	3	3	.500	34	0	0	0	13	48	58	26	23	3	0	13	22	1.479	4.31	85	4.23	.297	0	.000	-4	3	-0.4
1991	Mon-N	0	1	.000	4	0	0	0	0	4^1	9	5	5	2	0	2	3	2.538	10.38	35	14.73	.429	0	....	-3	0	-0.3
1992	Sea-A	0	0	....	3	0	0	0	0	3^1	7	7	7	1	0	3	1	3.000	18.90	21	16.41	.438	0	....	-6	0	-0.6
Total	**12**	**54**	**55**	**.495**	**376**	**63**	**5**	**3**	**50**	**902**	**962**	**434**	**389**	**85**	**18**	**237**	**479**	**1.329**	**3.88**	**102**	**3.92**	**.274**	**0**	**.000**	**12**	**64**	**1.0**
• SCHMIDT, Freddy					Frederick Albert Schmidt b: 2/9/1916, Hartford, CT BR/TR, 6'1", 185 lbs. Deb: 4/25/1944																						
1944*	StL-N	7	3	.700	37	9	3	2	5	114^1	94	48	40	5	1	58	58	1.329	3.15	112	3.02	.222	7	.206	2	8	0.2
1946	StL-N	1	0	1.000	16	0	0	0	0	27^1	27	11	10	0	3	15	14	1.537	3.29	105	4.18	.276	0	.000	0	2	0.0
1947	StL-N	0	0	....	2	0	0	0	0	4	5	2	1	1	0	1	2	1.500	2.25	184	6.61	.333	0	....	1	0	0.1
	Phi-N	5	8	.385	29	5	0	0	0	76^2	76	44	40	4	4	43	24	1.552	4.70	85	4.69	.285	1	.050	-6	3	-0.8
	Chi-N	0	0	....	1	1	0	0	0	3	4	3	3	0	0	5	0	3.000	9.00	44	9.16	.333	0	.000	-2	0	-0.2
	Yr.	5	8	.385	32	6	0	0	0	83^2	85	49	44	5	4	49	26	1.602	4.73	85	4.94	.289	1	.045	-7	3	-0.9
Total	**3**	**13**	**11**	**.542**	**85**	**15**	**3**	**2**	**5**	**225^1**	**206**	**108**	**94**	**10**	**8**	**122**	**98**	**1.456**	**3.75**	**99**	**3.88**	**.252**	**8**	**.140**	**-5**	**13**	**-0.7**
• SCHMIDT, Henry					Henry Martin Schmidt b: 6/26/1873, Brownsville, TX d: 4/23/1926, Nashville, TN BR/TR, 5'11", 170 lbs. Deb: 4/17/1903 U																						
1903	Bro-N	22	13	.629	40	36	29	5	2	301	321	167	128	5	21	120	96	1.465	3.83	83	4.05	.280	21	.196	18	18	2.1

YEAR	TM-L	W	L	PCT	G	GS	CG	SH	SV	IP	H	R	ER	HR	HB	BB	SO	RAT	ERA	ERA+	CERA	OAV	BH	AVG	PR+	WS	TPW
• SCHMIDT, Jason	Jason David Schmidt b: 1/29/1973, Lewiston, ID BR/TR, 6'5", 185 lbs. Deb: 4/28/1995																										
1995	Atl-N	2	2	.500	9	2	0	0	0	25	27	17	16	2	1	18	19	1.800	5.76	74	5.56	.287	1	.200	-4	0	-0.3
1996	Atl-N	3	4	.429	13	11	0	0	0	58^2	69	48	44	8	0	32	48	1.722	6.75	65	5.92	.296	0	.000	-14	0	-1.6
	Pit-N	2	2	.500	6	6	1	0	0	37^2	39	19	17	2	2	21	26	1.593	4.06	107	4.75	.271	1	.083	2	2	0.1
	Yr.	5	6	.455	19	17	1	0	0	96^1	108	67	61	10	2	53	74	1.671	5.70	77	5.46	.286	1	.032	-13	2	-1.5
1997	Pit-N	10	9	.526	32	32	2	0	0	187^2	193	106	96	16	9	76	136	1.433	4.60	93	4.31	.265	6	.107	-5	8	-0.6
1998	Pit-N	11	14	.440	33	33	0	0	0	214^1	228	106	97	24	4	71	158	1.395	4.07	106	4.35	.275	6	.097	4	11	0.2
1999	Pit-N	13	11	.542	33	33	2	0	0	212^2	219	110	99	24	3	85	148	1.429	4.19	109	4.30	.262	5	.083	10	13	0.7
2000	Pit-N	2	5	.286	11	11	0	0	0	63^1	71	43	38	6	1	41	51	1.768	5.40	85	5.77	.284	0	.000	-5	1	-0.6
2001	Pit-N	6	6	.500	14	14	1	0	0	84	81	46	43	11	7	28	77	1.298	4.61	97	4.17	.256	4	.174	-1	4	0.0
	SF-N	7	1	.875	11	11	0	0	0	66^1	57	29	25	2	0	33	65	1.357	3.39	117	3.16	.230	4	.154	4	5	0.5
	Yr.	13	7	.650	25	25	1	0	0	150^1	138	75	68	13	7	61	142	1.324	4.07	105	3.72	.244	8	.163	3	9	0.5
2002*	SF-N	13	8	.619	29	29	2	2	0	185^1	148	78	71	15	2	73	196	1.192	3.45	112	2.87	.218	7	.125	7	10	0.6
2003*	SF-N★	17	5	.773	29	29	5	**3**	0	207^2	152	56	54	14	5	46	208	.953	**2.34**	**175**	**1.93**	**.200**	4	.066	36	22	3.2
Total	9	86	67	.562	220	211	13	5	0	1342^2	1284	658	600	124	34	524	1132	1.347	4.02	107	3.86	.251	38	.095	34	76	2.1
• SCHMIDT, Jeff	Jeffrey Thomas Schmidt b: 2/21/1971, Northfield, MN BR/TR, 6'5", 205 lbs. Deb: 5/17/1996																										
1996	Cal-A	2	0	1.000	9	0	0	0	0	8	13	9	7	2	0	8	2	2.625	7.88	62	12.88	.394	0	....	-3	0	-0.2
• SCHMIDT, Pete	Friedrich Christoph Herman Schmidt b: 7/23/1890, Lowden, IA d: 3/11/1973, Pembroke, Canada BR/TR, 5'11", 175 lbs. Deb: 7/14/1913																										
1913	StL-A	0	0	....	1	0	0	0	1	2	3	1	1	0	0	2	0	2.500	4.50	65	8.24	.333	0	....	-0	0	0.0
• SCHMIDT, Willard	Willard Raymond Schmidt b: 5/29/1928, Hays, KS BR/TR, 6'1", 187 lbs. Deb: 4/19/1952																										
1952	StL-N	2	3	.400	18	3	0	0	1	34^2	36	20	20	6	2	18	30	1.558	5.19	71	5.36	.267	1	.125	-6	1	-0.6
1953	StL-N	0	2	.000	6	2	0	0	0	17^2	21	20	18	1	1	13	11	1.925	9.17	46	5.96	.288	0	.000	-9	0	-1.0
1955	StL-N	7	6	.538	20	15	8	1	0	129^2	89	40	40	7	3	57	86	1.126	2.78	146	2.34	.197	5	.119	20	13	1.7
1956	StL-N	6	8	.429	33	21	2	0	1	147^2	131	69	63	18	1	78	52	1.415	3.84	99	4.13	.246	10	.233	-1	8	0.1
1957	StL-N	10	3	.769	40	8	1	0	0	116^2	146	67	62	13	2	49	63	1.671	4.78	83	5.79	.312	7	.212	-10	5	-1.0
1958	Cin-N	3	5	.375	41	2	0	0	0	69^1	60	29	22	8	1	33	41	1.341	2.86	145	3.55	.235	1	.091	10	5	0.9
1959	Cin-N	3	2	.600	36	4	0	0	0	70^2	80	36	31	4	1	30	40	1.557	3.95	103	4.70	.296	1	.083	1	4	0.1
Total	7	31	29	.517	194	55	11	1	2	586^1	563	281	256	57	11	278	323	1.434	3.93	101	4.19	.258	25	.163	4	36	0.2
• SCHMIT, Crazy	Frederick M. "Germany" Schmit b: 2/13/1866, Chicago, IL d: 10/5/1940, Chicago, IL BL/TL, 5'10.5", 165 lbs. Deb: 4/21/1890																										
1890	Pit-N	1	9	.100	11	10	9	1	0	83^1	108	98	54	3	8	42	35	1.800	5.83	56	....	.305	2	.061	-19	0	-1.9
1892	Bal-N	1	4	.200	6	6	6	0	0	47^1	37	26	17	0	0	26	17	1.331	3.23	106	2.66	.207	2	.105	3	2	0.2
1893	Bal-N	3	2	.600	9	6	4	0	0	49	67	51	36	1	2	22	10	1.816	6.61	72	5.83	.316	5	.238	-9	1	-0.7
	NY-N	0	2	.000	4	4	1	0	0	20^2	30	25	17	0	2	17	5	2.274	7.40	63	7.83	.329	4	.444	-7	0	-0.4
	Yr.	3	4	.429	13	10	5	0	0	69^2	97	76	53	1	4	39	15	1.952	6.85	69	6.42	.320	9	.300	-16	1	-1.2
1899	Cle-N	2	17	.105	20	19	16	0	0	138^1	197	138	90	3	14	62	24	1.872	5.86	63	6.42	.334	11	.157	-27	3	-2.8
1901	Bal-A	0	2	.000	4	3	1	0	0	22^2	25	20	5	0	0	16	2	1.809	1.99	194	4.88	.277	2	.222	5	1	0.5
Total	5	7	36	.163	54	48	37	1	0	361^1	464	358	219	7	26	185	93	1.796	5.45	69	4.35	.306	26	.161	-53	7	-5.1
• SCHMITZ, Johnny	John Albert "Bear Tracks" Schmitz b: 11/27/1920, Wausau, WI BR/TL, 6', 170 lbs. Deb: 9/6/1941																										
1941	Chi-N	2	0	1.000	5	3	1	0	0	20^2	12	5	3	0	1	9	11	1.016	1.31	269	1.65	.182	4	.571	6	3	0.7
1942	Chi-N	3	7	.300	23	10	1	0	2	86^2	70	41	33	3	3	45	51	1.327	3.43	93	3.09	.230	4	.154	-1	4	-0.2
1946	Chi-N★	11	11	.500	41	31	14	2	2	224^1	184	77	65	6	2	94	**135**	1.239	2.61	127	2.60	**.221**	9	.129	22	16	2.1
1947	Chi-N	13	18	.419	38	28	10	3	4	207	209	91	74	8	2	80	97	1.396	3.22	123	3.57	.262	9	.132	17	18	1.5
1948	Chi-N★	18	13	.581	34	30	18	2	1	242	186	92	71	11	2	97	100	1.169	2.64	148	2.47	**.215**	11	.131	36	22	3.4
1949	Chi-N	11	13	.458	36	31	9	3	3	207	227	117	100	11	2	92	75	1.541	4.35	93	4.49	.287	10	.143	-3	10	-0.4
1950	Chi-N	10	16	.385	39	27	8	3	0	193	217	122	107	23	4	91	75	1.596	4.99	84	5.17	.284	8	.119	-12	6	-1.5
1951	Chi-N	1	2	.333	8	3	0	0	0	18	22	16	16	1	0	15	6	2.056	8.00	51	6.38	.301	1	.167	-8	0	-0.8
	Bro-N	1	4	.200	16	7	0	0	0	55^2	55	37	33	4	2	28	20	1.491	5.34	74	4.23	.259	4	.222	-10	1	-0.8
	Yr.	2	6	.250	24	10	0	0	0	73^2	77	53	49	5	2	43	26	1.629	5.99	66	4.76	.270	5	.208	-18	1	-1.6
1952	Bro-N	1	1	.500	10	3	1	0	0	33^1	29	16	16	3	1	18	11	1.410	4.32	84	3.86	.238	1	.125	-3	1	-0.3
	NY-A	1	1	.500	5	2	1	0	1	15	15	7	6	0	1	9	3	1.600	3.60	92	4.25	.263	3	.600	-1	1	0.1
	Cin-N	1	0	1.000	3	0	0	0	0	5	3	0	0	0	0	3	3	1.200	0.00	....	2.02	.188	0	....	2	1	0.2
	Yr.	2	1	.667	13	3	1	0	0	38^1	32	16	16	3	1	21	14	1.383	3.76	97	3.62	.232	1	.125	-1	2	-0.1
1953	NY-A	0	0	....	3	0	0	0	2	4^1	2	1	1	1	0	3	0	1.154	2.08	178	3.17	.143	0	....	1	0	0.1
	Was-A	2	7	.222	24	13	5	0	4	107^2	118	52	44	9	4	37	39	1.440	3.68	106	4.38	.286	2	.059	2	4	-0.2
	Yr.	2	7	.222	27	13	5	0	6	112	120	53	45	10	4	40	39	1.429	3.62	108	4.33	.282	2	.059	3	4	-0.1
1954	Was-A	11	8	.579	29	23	12	2	1	185^1	176	66	60	6	3	64	56	1.295	2.91	122	3.16	.255	7	.117	16	14	1.4
1955	Was-A	7	10	.412	32	21	6	1	1	165	187	76	68	8	7	54	49	1.461	3.71	103	4.31	.291	10	.185	7	8	0.7
1956	Bos-A	0	0	....	2	0	0	0	0	4^1	5	2	0	0	0	4	0	2.077	0.00	....	6.09	.278	0	.000	2	0	0.2
	Bal-A	0	3	.000	18	3	0	0	0	38^1	49	23	17	3	1	14	15	1.643	3.99	98	5.44	.318	0	.000	-0	1	-0.1
	Yr.	0	3	.000	20	3	0	0	0	42^2	54	25	17	3	1	18	15	1.688	3.59	109	5.51	.314	0	.000	2	1	0.1
Total	13	93	114	.449	366	235	86	16	21	1812^2	1766	841	714	97	35	757	746	1.392	3.55	108	3.71	.258	83	.141	74	110	6.1
• SCHMUTZ, Charlie	Charles Otto "King" Schmutz b: 1/1/1892, San Diego, CA d: 6/27/1962, Seattle, WA BR/TR, 6'1.5", 195 lbs. Deb: 5/13/1914																										
1914	Bro-N	1	3	.250	18	5	1	0	0	57^1	57	29	21	1	1	13	21	1.221	3.30	87	2.89	.265	3	.188	-3	2	-0.3
1915	Bro-N	0	0	....	1	0	0	0	0	4	7	5	3	0	0	1	1	2.000	6.75	41	7.73	.438	0	.000	-2	0	-0.2
Total	2	1	3	.250	19	5	1	0	0	61^1	64	34	24	1	1	14	22	1.272	3.52	81	3.21	.277	3	.176	-5	2	-0.5
• SCHNEIBERG, Frank	Frank Frederick Schneiberg b: 3/12/1882, Milwaukee, WI d: 5/18/1948, Milwaukee, WI TR Deb: 6/8/1910																										
1910	Bro-N	0	0	....	1	0	0	0	0	1	5	8	7	0	0	4	0	9.000	63.00	5	49.96	.625	0	....	-7	0	-0.7
• SCHNEIDER, Dan	Daniel Louis Schneider b: 8/29/1942, Evansville, IN BL/TL, 6'3", 170 lbs. Deb: 5/12/1963																										
1963	Mil-N	1	0	1.000	30	3	0	0	0	43^2	36	20	15	2	0	20	19	1.282	3.09	104	2.80	.225	0	.000	-0	2	-0.1
1964	Mil-N	1	2	.333	13	5	0	0	0	36^1	38	25	22	6	0	13	14	1.404	5.45	65	4.47	.270	0	.000	-8	0	-0.9
1966	Atl-N	0	0	....	14	0	0	0	0	26^1	35	13	10	1	1	5	11	1.519	3.42	106	4.82	.324	4	.500	1	2	0.2
1967	Hou-N	0	2	.000	54	0	0	0	2	52^2	60	33	29	5	2	27	39	1.652	4.96	67	5.18	.296	1	.200	-9	0	-0.9
1969	Hou-N	0	1	.000	6	0	0	0	0	7^1	16	12	11	2	0	5	3	2.864	13.50	26	14.09	.485	0	.000	-8	0	-0.9
Total	5	2	5	.286	117	8	0	0	2	166^1	185	103	87	16	3	70	86	1.533	4.71	72	4.73	.287	5	.172	-24	4	-2.6
• SCHNEIDER, Jeff	Jeffrey Theodore Schneider b: 12/6/1952, Bremerton, WA BB/TL, 6'3", 195 lbs. Deb: 8/12/1981																										
1981	Bal-A	0	0	....	11	0	0	0	1	24	27	15	13	4	1	12	17	1.625	4.88	74	5.86	.290	0	....	-3	0	-0.3
• SCHNEIDER, Pete	Peter Joseph Schneider b: 8/20/1895, Los Angeles, CA d: 6/1/1957, Los Angeles, CA BR/TR, 6'1", 194 lbs. Deb: 6/20/1914																										
1914	Cin-N	5	13	.278	29	15	11	1	1	144^1	143	71	45	1	7	56	62	1.379	2.81	104	3.42	.269	8	.178	2	7	0.4
1915	Cin-N	14	19	.424	48	35	16	5	2	275^2	254	110	76	4	7	104	108	1.299	2.48	115	3.02	.251	23	.245	5	18	1.2
1916	Cin-N	10	19	.345	44	31	16	2	1	274^1	259	112	82	4	13	82	117	1.243	2.69	96	2.96	.255	21	.236	-6	13	-0.3
1917	Cin-N	20	19	.513	46	42	24	0	0	333^2	311	128	78	4	11	117	138	1.283	2.10	124	2.92	.255	19	.167	20	18	2.3
1918	Cin-N	10	15	.400	33	30	17	2	0	217	213	106	85	2	11	117	51	**1.521**	3.53	76	3.99	.272	24	.289	-22	8	-1.8
1919	NY-A	0	1	.000	7	4	0	0	0	29	19	14	11	1	3	22	11	1.414	3.41	93	3.35	.192	1	.111	-2	1	-0.3
Total	6	59	86	.407	207	157	84	10	4	1274	1199	541	377	16	52	498	487	1.332	2.66	102	3.20	.257	96	.221	-2	65	1.4
• SCHNELL, Karl	Karl Otto Schnell b: 9/20/1899, Los Angeles, CA d: 5/31/1992, Palo Alto, CA BR/TR, 6'1", 176 lbs. Deb: 4/24/1922																										
1922	Cin-N	0	0	....	10	0	0	0	0	20	21	10	6	0	0	18	5	1.950	2.70	148	5.55	.300	1	.250	2	1	0.2
1923	Cin-N	0	0	....	1	0	0	0	0	1	2	4	4	0	0	2	0	4.000	36.00	11	15.81	.667	0	....	-4	0	-0.3
Total	2	0	0	....	11	0	0	0	0	21	23	14	10	0	0	20	5	2.048	4.29	92	6.03	.315	1	.250	-1	1	-0.1

YEAR	TM-L	W	L	PCT	G	GS	CG	SH	SV	IP	H	R	ER	HR	HB	BB	SO	RAT	ERA	ERA+	CERA	OAV	BH	AVG	PR+	WS	TPW
• SCHOEN, Gerry	Gerald Thomas Schoen b: 1/15/1947, New Orleans, LA BR/TR, 6'3", 215 lbs. Deb: 9/14/1968																										
1968	Was-A	0	1	.000	1	1	0	0	0	3^2	6	3	3	1	0	1	1	1.909	7.36	40	9.86	.400	0	.000	-2	0	-0.2
• SCHOENEWEIS, Scott	Scott David Schoeneweis b: 10/2/1973, Long Branch, NJ BL/TL, 6', 185 lbs. Deb: 4/7/1999																										
1999	Ana-A	1	1	.500	31	0	0	0	0	39^1	47	27	24	4	0	14	22	1.551	5.49	88	4.99	.294	0	....	-3	1	-0.3
2000	Ana-A	7	10	.412	27	27	1	1	0	170	183	112	103	21	6	67	78	1.471	5.45	93	4.84	.276	1	.333	-11	6	-1.0
2001	Ana-A	10	11	.476	32	32	1	0	0	205^1	227	122	116	21	14	77	104	1.481	5.08	90	4.87	.281	0	....	-13	9	-1.2
2002*	Ana-A	9	8	.529	54	15	0	0	1	118	119	68	64	17	5	49	65	1.424	4.88	91	4.68	.264	0	.000	-10	5	-1.0
2003	Ana-A	1	1	.500	39	0	0	0	0	38^2	37	19	17	2	3	10	29	1.216	3.96	109	3.14	.250	0	....	1	2	0.1
	Chi-A	2	1	.667	20	0	0	0	0	26	26	16	13	1	1	9	27	1.346	4.50	99	3.41	.255	0	....	-0	1	0.0
	Yr.	3	2	.600	59	0	0	0	0	64^2	63	35	30	3	4	19	56	1.268	4.18	105	3.25	.252	0	....	1	3	0.1
Total	5	30	32	.484	203	74	2	1	1	597^1	639	364	337	66	29	226	325	1.448	5.08	92	4.66	.274	1	.200	-37	24	-3.4
• SCHOOLER, Mike	Michael Ralph Schooler b: 8/10/1962, Anaheim, CA BR/TR, 6'3", 220 lbs. Deb: 6/10/1988																										
1988	Sea-A	5	8	.385	40	0	0	0	15	48^1	45	21	19	4	1	24	54	1.428	3.54	118	3.81	.245	0	....	4	6	0.4
1989	Sea-A	1	7	.125	67	0	0	0	33	77	81	27	24	2	2	19	69	1.299	2.81	144	3.26	.266	0	....	10	11	1.0
1990	Sea-A	1	4	.200	49	0	0	0	30	56	47	18	14	5	1	16	45	1.125	2.25	176	2.65	.227	0	.000	11	10	1.1
1991	Sea-A	3	3	.500	34	0	0	0	7	34^1	25	14	14	2	0	10	31	1.019	3.67	112	1.99	.198	0	....	1	5	0.1
1992	Sea-A	2	7	.222	53	0	0	0	13	51^2	55	29	27	7	1	24	33	1.529	4.70	84	4.80	.275	0	....	-4	3	-0.4
1993	Tex-A	3	0	1.000	17	0	0	0	0	24^1	30	17	15	3	0	10	16	1.644	5.55	75	5.55	.303	0	....	-3	1	-0.3
Total	6	15	29	.341	260	0	0	0	98	291^2	283	126	113	23	5	103	248	1.323	3.49	116	3.55	.253	0	.000	18	36	1.9
• SCHORR, Ed	Edward Walter Schorr b: 2/14/1891, Bremen, OH d: 9/12/1969, Atlantic City, NJ BR/TR, 6'2.5", 180 lbs. Deb: 4/26/1915																										
1915	Chi-N	0	0	....	2	0	0	0	0	6	9	5	5	0	0	5	3	2.333	7.50	37	8.44	.409	1	.500	-3	0	-0.3
• SCHOTT, Gene	Arthur Eugene Schott b: 7/14/1913, Batavia, OH d: 11/16/1992, Sun City Center, FL BR/TR, 6'2", 185 lbs. Deb: 4/16/1935																										
1935	Cin-N	8	11	.421	33	19	9	1	0	159	153	84	69	5	1	64	49	1.365	3.91	102	3.31	.253	12	.200	3	9	0.4
1936	Cin-N	11	11	.500	31	22	8	0	1	180	184	93	76	7	4	73	65	1.428	3.80	101	3.68	.262	18	.300	2	13	0.8
1937	Cin-N	4	13	.235	37	16	7	2	1	154^1	150	69	51	2	1	48	56	1.283	2.97	125	2.91	.253	7	.143	14	8	1.2
1938	Cin-N	5	5	.500	31	4	0	0	2	83	89	47	41	8	1	32	21	1.458	4.45	82	4.40	.279	3	.125	-9	3	-1.0
1939	Phi-N	0	1	.000	4	0	0	0	0	11	14	7	6	0	2	5	1	1.727	4.91	80	5.47	.326	2	.333	-1	0	0.0
Total	5	28	41	.406	136	61	24	3	4	587^1	590	300	243	22	9	222	192	1.383	3.72	102	3.52	.261	42	.211	8	33	1.4
• SCHOUREK, Pete	Peter Alan Schourek b: 5/10/1969, Austin, TX BL/TL, 6'5", 205 lbs. Deb: 4/9/1991																										
1991	NY-N	5	4	.556	35	8	1	1	2	86^1	82	49	41	7	2	43	67	1.448	4.27	85	3.97	.248	3	.136	-4	4	-0.4
1992	NY-N	6	8	.429	22	21	0	0	0	136	137	60	55	9	2	44	60	1.331	3.64	95	3.58	.261	2	.048	-1	6	-0.4
1993	NY-N	5	12	.294	41	18	0	0	0	128^1	168	90	85	13	3	45	72	1.660	5.96	67	5.71	.319	7	.219	-29	0	-2.7
1994	Cin-N	7	2	.778	22	10	0	0	0	81^1	90	39	37	11	3	29	69	1.463	4.09	101	4.90	.287	4	.174	0	4	0.1
1995*	Cin-N	18	7	.720	29	29	2	0	0	190^1	158	72	68	17	8	45	160	1.067	3.22	128	2.70	.228	13	.220	15	16	1.6
1996	Cin-N	4	5	.444	12	12	0	0	0	67^1	79	48	45	7	3	24	54	1.530	6.01	69	5.03	.293	5	.263	-14	1	-1.3
1997	Cin-N	5	8	.385	18	17	0	0	0	84^2	78	59	51	18	4	38	59	1.370	5.42	79	4.76	.241	4	.167	-11	1	-1.0
1998	Hou-N	7	6	.538	15	15	0	0	0	80	82	43	40	10	4	36	59	1.475	4.50	90	4.81	.269	4	.211	-4	3	-0.3
	*Bos-A	1	3	.250	10	8	0	0	0	44	45	21	21	7	1	14	36	1.341	4.30	110	4.48	.273	0	....	2	2	0.2
1999	Pit-N	4	7	.364	30	17	0	0	0	113	128	75	67	20	5	49	94	1.566	5.34	86	5.66	.287	0	.000	-9	3	-1.1
2000	Bos-A	3	10	.231	21	21	0	0	0	107^1	116	67	61	17	3	38	63	1.435	5.11	98	4.91	.278	2	.500	-1	4	0.0
2001	Bos-A	1	5	.167	33	0	0	0	0	30^1	35	19	15	4	1	15	20	1.648	4.45	101	5.64	.292	0	....	1	1	0.1
Total	11	66	77	.462	288	176	3	1	2	1149	1198	642	586	140	39	420	813	1.408	4.59	91	4.47	.270	44	.164	-56	45	-5.3
• SCHREIBER, Barney	David Henry Schreiber b: 5/8/1882, Waverly, OH d: 10/6/1964, Chillicothe, OH BL/TL, 6', 185 lbs. Deb: 5/15/1911																										
1911	Cin-N	0	0	....	3	0	0	0	1	10	19	11	6	2	0	2	5	2.100	5.40	61	10.09	.413	0	.000	-2	0	-0.2
• SCHREIBER, Paul	Paul Frederick "Von" Schreiber b: 10/8/1902, Jacksonville, FL d: 1/28/1982, Sarasota, FL BR/TR, 6'2", 180 lbs. Deb: 9/2/1922 C																										
1922	Bro-N	0	0	....	1	0	0	0	0	1	2	0	0	0	0	0	0	2.000	0.00	....	9.49	.500	0	....	0	0	0.0
1923	Bro-N	0	0	....	9	0	0	0	1	15	16	9	7	1	2	8	4	1.600	4.20	92	4.95	.276	0	.000	-1	1	-0.1
1945	NY-A	0	0	....	2	0	0	0	0	4^1	4	2	2	0	0	2	1	1.385	4.15	83	3.19	.267	0	.000	-0	0	-0.1
Total	3	0	0	....	12	0	0	0	1	20^1	22	11	9	1	2	10	5	1.574	3.98	95	4.80	.286	0	.000	-0	1	-0.1
• SCHRENK, Steve	Steven Wayne Schrenk b: 11/20/1968, Chicago, IL BR/TR, 6'3", 215 lbs. Deb: 7/3/1999																										
1999	Phi-N	1	3	.250	32	2	0	0	1	50^1	41	24	24	6	7	14	36	1.093	4.29	110	3.15	.223	0	.000	2	3	0.1
2000	Phi-N	2	3	.400	20	0	0	0	0	23^1	25	20	19	3	1	13	19	1.629	7.33	64	5.39	.269	0	....	-7	0	-0.7
Total	2	3	6	.333	52	2	0	0	1	73^2	66	44	43	9	8	27	55	1.262	5.25	89	3.86	.238	0	.000	-5	3	-0.5
• SCHROLL, Al	Albert Bringhurst "Bull" Schroll b: 3/22/1932, New Orleans, LA d: 11/30/1999, Alexandria, LA BR/TR, 6'2", 210 lbs. Deb: 4/20/1958																										
1958	Bos-A	0	0	....	5	0	0	0	0	10	6	5	5	1	0	4	7	1.000	4.50	89	2.07	.176	1	1.000	-0	1	0.0
1959	Phi-N	1	1	.500	3	0	0	0	0	9^1	12	9	9	1	0	6	4	1.929	8.68	47	7.38	.353	1	.250	-5	0	-0.4
	Bos-A	1	4	.200	14	5	1	0	0	46	47	29	24	3	1	22	26	1.500	4.70	86	4.31	.269	1	.111	-3	1	-0.3
1960	Chi-N	0	0	....	2	0	0	0	0	2^2	3	3	3	1	0	5	2	3.000	10.13	37	13.94	.273	1	1.000	-2	0	-0.1
1961	Min-A	4	4	.500	11	8	2	0	0	50	53	36	29	5	2	27	24	1.600	5.22	81	5.08	.266	5	.278	-4	2	-0.2
Total	4	6	9	.400	35	13	3	0	0	118	121	82	70	11	3	64	63	1.568	5.34	77	4.90	.267	9	.273	-15	4	-1.1
• SCHROM, Ken	Kenneth Marvin Schrom b: 11/23/1954, Grangeville, ID BR/TR, 6'2", 195 lbs. Deb: 8/8/1980																										
1980	Tor-A	1	0	1.000	17	0	0	0	1	31	32	18	18	2	0	19	13	1.645	5.23	82	4.68	.274	0	....	-3	1	-0.3
1982	Tor-A	1	0	1.000	6	0	0	0	0	15^1	13	11	10	3	0	15	8	1.826	5.87	76	6.05	.232	0	....	-2	0	-0.2
1983	Min-A	15	8	.652	33	28	6	1	0	196^1	196	92	81	14	9	80	80	1.406	3.71	114	4.11	.266	0	....	9	13	0.9
1984	Min-A	5	11	.313	25	21	3	0	0	137	156	75	68	15	1	41	49	1.438	4.47	94	4.53	.285	0	....	-7	6	-0.7
1985	Min-A	9	12	.429	29	26	6	0	0	160^2	164	95	89	28	0	59	74	1.388	4.99	88	4.66	.272	0	....	-10	7	-1.0
1986	Cle-A★	14	7	.667	34	33	3	1	0	206	217	118	104	34	12	49	87	1.291	4.54	91	4.36	.271	0	....	-8	10	-0.8
1987	Cle-A	6	13	.316	32	29	4	1	0	153^2	185	126	111	29	3	57	61	1.575	6.50	70	5.85	.298	0	....	-31	1	-3.0
Total	7	51	51	.500	176	137	22	3	1	900	963	535	481	125	25	320	372	1.426	4.81	90	4.68	.276	0	....	-53	38	-5.2
• SCHUELER, Ron	Ronald Richard Schueler b: 4/14/1948, Catherine, KS BR/TR, 6'4", 205 lbs. Deb: 4/16/1972 C																										
1972	Atl-N	5	8	.385	37	18	3	0	2	144^2	122	68	59	16	2	60	96	1.258	3.67	103	3.36	.227	8	.190	4	8	0.5
1973	Atl-N	8	7	.533	39	20	4	2	2	186	179	91	80	24	0	66	124	1.317	3.87	102	3.85	.255	11	.177	3	10	0.3
1974	Phi-N	11	16	.407	44	27	5	0	1	203^1	202	91	84	17	4	98	109	1.475	3.72	102	4.43	.264	6	.118	-3	12	-0.5
1975	Phi-N	4	4	.500	46	6	1	0	0	92^2	88	55	54	6	1	40	69	1.381	5.24	71	3.72	.258	2	.154	-18	2	-1.9
1976	Phi-N	1	0	1.000	35	0	0	0	3	49^2	44	18	16	4	2	16	43	1.208	2.90	122	3.20	.243	0	.000	3	4	0.3
1977	Min-A	8	7	.533	52	7	0	0	3	134^2	131	74	66	16	6	61	77	1.426	4.41	90	4.40	.260	0	....	-6	7	-0.6
1978	Chi-A	3	5	.375	30	7	0	0	0	81^2	76	50	39	10	7	39	39	1.408	4.30	88	4.43	.251	0	....	-4	2	-0.4
1979	Chi-A	0	1	.000	8	1	0	0	0	19^2	19	16	16	3	2	13	6	1.627	7.32	58	5.73	.264	0	....	-7	0	-0.7
Total	8	40	48	.455	291	86	13	2	11	912^1	861	463	414	96	24	393	563	1.374	4.08	94	3.98	.253	27	.159	-28	45	-3.1
• SCHULER, Dave	David Paul Schuler b: 10/4/1953, Framingham, MA BR/TL, 6'4", 210 lbs. Deb: 9/17/1979																										
1979	Cal-A	0	0	....	1	0	0	0	0	1^2	2	2	2	1	0	0	0	1.200	10.80	38	6.66	.333	0	....	-1	0	-0.1
1980	Cal-A	0	1	.000	8	0	0	0	0	12^2	13	5	5	3	0	2	7	1.184	3.55	111	3.95	.271	0	....	1	1	0.1
1985	Atl-N	0	0	....	9	0	0	0	0	10^2	19	8	8	4	0	3	10	2.063	6.75	57	11.57	.404	0	....	-3	0	-0.4
Total	3	0	1	.000	18	0	0	0	0	25	34	15	15	8	0	5	17	1.560	5.40	72	7.38	.337	0	....	-4	1	-0.4
• SCHULLSTROM, Erik	Erik Paul Schullstrom b: 3/25/1969, San Diego, CA BR/TR, 6'5", 220 lbs. Deb: 7/18/1994																										
1994	Min-A	0	0	....	9	0	0	0	1	13	13	7	4	0	1	5	13	1.385	2.77	176	3.57	.260	0	....	3	1	0.3

YEAR TM-L	W	L	PCT	G	GS	CG	SH	SV	IP	H	R	ER	HR	HB	BB	SO	RAT	ERA	ERA+	CERA	OAV	BH	AVG	PR+	WS	TPW
1995 Min-A	0	0	....	37	0	0	0	0	47	66	36	36	8	1	22	21	1.872	6.89	69	7.44	.332	0	....	-11	0	-1.0
Total 2	0	0	....	46	0	0	0	1	60	79	43	40	8	2	27	34	1.767	6.00	80	6.60	.317	0	....	-8	1	-0.7
• SCHULTZ, Barney	George Warren Schultz b: 8/15/1926, Beverly, NJ BR/TR, 6'2", 200 lbs. Deb: 4/12/1955 C																									
1955 StL-N	1	2	.333	19	0	0	0	4	29^2	28	27	26	5	4	15	19	1.449	7.89	51	5.06	.259	0	.000	-12	0	-1.3
1959 Det-A	1	2	.333	13	0	0	0	0	18^1	17	12	9	1	1	14	17	1.691	4.42	92	4.85	.254	2	1.000	-1	1	0.0
1961 Chi-N	7	6	.538	41	0	0	0	7	66^2	57	32	20	6	4	25	59	1.230	2.70	155	3.19	.228	1	.100	12	7	1.1
1962 Chi-N	5	5	.500	51	0	0	0	5	77^2	66	36	33	7	4	23	58	1.146	3.82	108	2.91	.231	0	.000	3	7	0.2
1963 Chi-N	1	0	1.000	15	0	0	0	2	27^1	25	11	11	5	0	9	18	1.244	3.62	97	3.97	.263	0	.000	-1	2	-0.1
StL-N	2	0	1.000	24	0	0	0	1	35^1	36	15	14	5	2	8	26	1.245	3.57	99	3.86	.263	0	....	-0	2	0.0
Yr.	3	0	1.000	39	0	0	0	3	62^2	61	26	25	10	2	17	44	1.245	3.59	98	3.90	.263	0	.000	-1	4	-0.1
1964* StL-N	1	3	.250	30	0	0	0	14	49^1	35	14	9	1	0	11	29	.932	1.64	231	1.52	.201	1	.167	12	10	1.2
1965 StL-N	2	2	.500	34	0	0	0	2	42^1	39	22	18	8	0	11	38	1.181	3.83	100	3.55	.242	0	.000	-0	2	0.0
Total 7	20	20	.500	227	0	0	0	35	346^2	303	169	140	38	15	116	264	1.209	3.63	109	3.31	.237	4	.121	12	31	1.2
• SCHULTZ, Bob	Robert Duffy Schultz b: 11/27/1923, Louisville, KY d: 3/31/1979, Nashville, TN BR/TL, 6'3", 200 lbs. Deb: 4/20/1951																									
1951 Chi-N	3	6	.333	17	10	2	0	0	77^1	75	51	45	9	2	51	27	1.629	5.24	78	4.93	.251	4	.138	-9	1	-1.0
1952 Chi-N	6	3	.667	29	5	1	0	0	74	63	34	33	3	2	51	31	1.541	4.01	96	3.84	.232	4	.222	-1	5	-0.1
1953 Chi-N	0	2	.000	7	2	0	0	0	11^2	13	10	7	2	1	11	4	2.057	5.40	82	7.65	.289	0	.000	-1	0	-0.1
Pit-N	0	2	.000	11	2	0	0	0	18^2	26	19	17	3	2	10	5	1.929	8.20	55	7.73	.321	0	.000	-8	0	-0.7
Yr.	0	4	.000	18	4	0	0	0	30^1	39	29	24	5	3	21	9	1.978	7.12	63	7.70	.310	0	.000	-9	0	-0.9
1955 Det-A	0	0	....	1	0	0	0	0	1^1	2	3	3	0	0	2	0	3.000	20.25	19	10.76	.333	0	....	-2	0	-0.2
Total 4	9	13	.409	65	19	3	0	0	183	179	117	105	17	7	125	67	1.661	5.16	79	4.99	.255	8	.154	-21	6	-2.2
• SCHULTZ, Buddy	Charles Budd Schultz b: 9/19/1950, Cleveland, OH BR/TL, 6', 175 lbs. Deb: 9/3/1975																									
1975 Chi-N	2	0	1.000	6	0	0	0	0	5^2	11	6	4	0	0	5	4	2.824	6.35	60	9.99	.367	0	....	-1	0	-0.1
1976 Chi-N	1	1	.500	29	0	0	0	2	23^2	37	19	16	3	0	9	15	1.944	6.08	63	7.45	.356	0	.000	-5	0	-0.6
1977 StL-N	6	1	.857	40	3	0	0	1	85^1	76	26	22	5	0	24	66	1.172	2.32	166	2.84	.245	2	.167	13	8	1.3
1978 StL-N	2	4	.333	62	0	0	0	6	83	68	36	35	6	0	36	70	1.253	3.80	93	2.97	.226	1	.200	-3	5	-0.2
1979 StL-N	4	3	.571	31	0	0	0	3	42^1	40	21	21	7	0	14	38	1.276	4.46	84	3.75	.256	0	.000	-4	3	-0.5
Total 5	15	9	.625	168	3	0	0	12	240	232	108	98	21	0	88	193	1.333	3.68	101	3.67	.257	3	.120	-2	16	-0.2
• SCHULTZ, Mike	William Michael Schultz b: 12/17/1920, Syracuse, NY BL/TL, 6'1", 175 lbs. Deb: 4/20/1947																									
1947 Cin-N	0	0	....	1	0	0	0	0	2	4	2	1	0	0	2	0	3.000	4.50	91	12.74	.444	0	....	-0	0	0.0
• SCHULTZ, Webb	Wilbert Carl Schultz b: 1/31/1898, Wautoma, WI d: 7/26/1986, Delavan, WI BR/TR, 5'11", 172 lbs. Deb: 8/3/1924																									
1924 Chi-A	0	0	....	1	0	0	0	0	1	1	1	1	0	0	0	0	1.000	9.00	46	1.95	.250	0	....	-1	0	-0.1
• SCHULTZE, John	John F. Schultze b: Burlington, NJ, 6'.5", 165 lbs. Deb: 5/6/1891																									
1891 Phi-N	0	1	.000	6	1	0	0	0	15	18	15	11	1	0	11	4	1.933	6.60	51	....	.287	1	.167	-5	0	-0.5
• SCHULZ, Al	Albert Christopher Schulz b: 5/12/1889, Toledo, OH d: 12/13/1931, Gallipolis, OH BR/TL, 6', 182 lbs. Deb: 9/25/1912																									
1912 NY-A	1	1	.500	3	1	1	0	0	16^1	11	8	4	0	0	11	8	1.347	2.20	164	2.43	.183	0	.000	3	1	0.3
1913 NY-A	7	14	.333	38	22	9	0	0	193	197	110	80	4	5	69	77	1.378	3.73	80	3.53	.266	11	.175	-16	6	-1.7
1914 NY-A	1	3	.250	6	4	1	0	0	28^1	27	17	15	0	2	10	18	1.306	4.76	58	2.97	.237	0	.000	-7	0	-0.8
Buf-F	9	12	.429	27	23	10	0	2	171	160	80	64	3	2	77	87	1.386	3.37	99	3.47	.259	10	.179	-3	10	-0.3
1915 Buf-F	21	14	.600	42	38	25	5	0	309^2	264	125	106	8	6	149	160	1.334	3.08	99	3.18	.238	18	.165	0	21	-0.2
1916 Cin-N	8	19	.296	44	22	10	0	2	215	208	100	75	4	5	93	95	**1.400**	3.14	82	3.55	.268	8	.125	-15	7	-2.1
Total 5	47	63	.427	160	110	56	5	4	933^1	867	440	344	19	20	409	445	1.367	3.32	89	3.37	.254	47	.155	-37	45	-4.7
• SCHULZ, Walt	Walter Frederick Schulz b: 8/16/1900, St. Louis, MO d: 2/27/1928, Prescott, AR BR/TR, 6', 170 lbs. Deb: 7/8/1920																									
1920 StL-N	0	0	....	2	0	0	0	0	6	10	5	4	0	0	2	0	2.000	6.00	51	6.71	.370	0	.000	-2	0	-0.2
• SCHULZE, Don	Donald Arthur Schulze b: 9/27/1962, Roselle, IL BR/TR, 6'3", 225 lbs. Deb: 9/13/1983																									
1983 Chi-N	0	1	.000	4	3	0	0	0	14	19	11	11	1	1	7	8	1.857	7.07	54	6.73	.322	0	.000	-5	0	-0.5
1984 Chi-N	0	0	....	1	1	0	0	0	3	8	4	4	0	0	1	2	3.000	12.00	33	15.46	.571	0	....	-3	0	-0.3
Cle-A	3	6	.333	19	14	2	0	0	85^2	105	53	46	9	0	27	39	1.541	4.83	85	5.07	.302	0	....	-8	2	-0.8
1985 Cle-A	4	10	.286	19	18	1	0	0	94^1	128	75	63	10	4	19	37	1.558	6.01	69	5.46	.322	0	....	-19	0	-1.9
1986 Cle-A	4	4	.500	19	13	1	0	0	84^2	88	48	47	9	5	34	33	1.441	5.00	83	4.61	.266	0	....	-7	3	-0.7
1987 NY-N	1	2	.333	5	4	0	0	0	21^2	24	15	15	4	1	6	5	1.385	6.23	61	5.17	.296	0	.000	-6	0	-0.5
1989 NY-A	1	1	.500	2	2	0	0	0	11	12	5	5	1	1	5	5	1.545	4.09	95	5.21	.300	0	....	-0	1	0.0
SD-N	2	1	.667	7	4	0	0	0	24^1	38	20	15	6	0	6	15	1.808	5.55	63	7.78	.352	0	.000	-6	0	-0.7
Total 6	15	25	.375	76	59	4	0	0	338^2	422	231	206	40	12	105	144	1.556	5.47	73	5.43	.306	0	.000	-54	6	-5.4
• SCHUMACHER, Hal	Harold Henry "Prince Hal" Schumacher b: 11/23/1910, Hinckley, NY d: 4/21/1993, Cooperstown, NY BR/TR, 6', 190 lbs. Deb: 4/15/1931																									
1931 NY-N	1	1	.500	8	2	1	0	1	18^1	31	23	22	3	0	14	11	2.455	10.80	34	10.74	.387	1	.143	-15	0	-1.5
1932 NY-N	5	6	.455	27	13	2	1	0	101^1	119	60	40	3	2	39	38	1.559	3.55	105	4.40	.288	7	.226	4	4	0.4
1933* NY-N★	19	12	.613	35	33	21	7	1	258^2	199	71	62	9	1	84	96	1.094	2.16	149	2.18	**.214**	21	.214	26	23	2.8
1934 NY-N	23	10	.697	41	36	18	2	0	297	299	131	105	16	2	89	112	1.306	3.18	122	3.36	.259	28	.239	20	24	2.8
1935 NY-N★	19	9	.679	33	33	19	3	0	261^2	235	100	84	11	5	70	79	1.166	2.89	133	2.67	.238	21	.196	27	23	2.8
1936* NY-N	11	13	.458	35	30	9	3	1	215^1	234	103	83	15	1	69	75	1.407	3.47	112	4.01	.280	16	.216	3	15	0.5
1937* NY-N	13	12	.520	38	29	10	1	1	217^2	222	100	87	11	0	89	100	1.429	3.60	108	3.77	.264	18	.222	3	15	0.6
1938 NY-N	13	8	.619	28	28	12	3	0	185	178	81	72	12	2	50	54	1.232	3.50	107	3.09	.248	16	.239	5	15	0.9
1939 NY-N	13	10	.565	29	27	8	0	0	181^2	199	106	97	14	3	89	58	1.585	4.81	82	4.67	.276	14	.203	-18	7	-1.7
1940 NY-N	13	13	.500	34	30	12	1	1	227	218	93	82	14	0	96	123	1.383	3.25	119	3.57	.251	15	.192	17	17	2.0
1941 NY-N	12	10	.545	30	26	12	3	1	206	187	81	77	11	5	79	63	1.291	3.36	110	3.22	.243	10	.152	6	16	0.6
1942 NY-N	12	13	.480	29	29	12	3	0	216	208	81	73	12	3	82	49	1.343	3.04	110	3.42	.251	13	.173	6	14	0.7
1946 NY-N	4	4	.500	24	13	2	0	1	96^2	95	50	42	8	0	52	48	1.521	3.91	88	4.21	.255	1	.038	-4	3	-0.6
Total 13	158	121	.566	391	329	138	27	7	2482^1	2424	1080	926	139	24	902	906	1.340	3.36	111	3.47	.255	181	.202	79	176	10.1
• SCHUMANN, Hack	Carl J. Schumann b: 8/13/1884, Buffalo, NY d: 3/25/1946, Millgrove, NY TR, 6'2", 230 lbs. Deb: 9/19/1906																									
1906 Phi-A	0	2	.000	4	2	1	0	0	18	21	13	8	0	2	8	9	1.611	4.00	68	4.72	.294	0	.000	-3	0	-0.4
• SCHUPP, Ferdie	Ferdinand Maurice Schupp b: 1/16/1891, Louisville, KY d: 12/16/1971, Los Angeles, CA BR/TL, 5'10", 150 lbs. Deb: 4/19/1913																									
1913 NY-N	0	0	....	5	1	0	0	0	12	10	3	1	0	0	3	2	1.083	0.75	415	2.17	.244	1	.333	3	2	0.4
1914 NY-N	0	0	....	8	0	0	0	1	17	19	11	11	0	2	9	9	1.647	5.82	46	5.12	.306	0	.000	-6	0	-0.7
1915 NY-N	1	0	1.000	23	1	0	0	0	54^2	57	37	31	1	3	29	28	1.573	5.10	50	4.30	.281	2	.200	-15	0	-1.6
1916 NY-N	9	3	.750	30	11	8	4	1	140^1	79	22	14	1	5	37	86	.827	0.90	270	1.23	.167	4	.098	22	15	2.2
1917* NY-N	21	7	.750	36	32	25	6	0	272	202	69	59	7	4	70	147	1.000	1.95	130	1.82	**.209**	15	.161	15	23	1.8
1918 NY-N	0	1	.000	10	2	1	0	0	33^1	42	34	28	1	3	27	22	2.070	7.56	35	6.93	.328	1	.111	-18	0	-2.1
1919 NY-N	1	3	.250	9	4	0	0	1	32	32	24	20	2	0	18	17	1.563	5.63	50	4.31	.269	2	.333	-11	0	-1.1
StL-N	4	4	.500	10	10	6	0	0	69^2	55	31	29	2	1	30	37	1.220	3.75	74	2.57	.221	1	.050	-8	2	-0.9
Yr.	5	7	.417	19	14	6	0	1	101^2	87	55	49	4	1	48	54	1.328	4.34	64	3.12	.237	3	.115	-19	2	-2.1
1920 StL-N	16	13	.552	38	37	17	0	0	250^2	246	118	98	5	9	127	119	1.488	3.52	87	3.84	.265	22	.256	-13	13	-0.9
1921 StL-N	2	0	1.000	9	4	1	0	1	37^1	42	26	17	5	2	21	22	1.688	4.10	89	5.54	.276	4	.286	-2	1	-0.2
Bro-N	3	4	.429	20	7	1	0	2	61	75	34	31	2	2	27	26	1.672	4.57	85	5.07	.310	1	.083	-4	3	-0.5
Yr.	5	4	.556	29	11	2	0	3	98^1	117	60	48	7	4	48	48	1.678	4.39	86	5.25	.297	5	.192	-6	4	-0.6
1922 Chi-A	4	4	.500	18	12	3	1	0	74	79	61	50	4	2	66	38	1.959	6.08	67	5.97	.284	5	.217	-17	0	-1.7
Total 10	61	39	.610	216	121	62	11	6	1054	938	470	389	30	33	464	553	1.330	3.32	90	3.30	.244	58	.182	-56	59	-5.3

YEAR	TM-L	W	L	PCT	G	GS	CG	SH	SV	IP	H	R	ER	HR	HB	BB	SO	RAT	ERA	ERA+	CERA	OAV	BH	AVG	PR+	WS	TPW
• SCHURR, Wayne	Wayne Allen Schurr b: 8/6/1937, Garrett, IN BR/TR, 6'4", 185 lbs. Deb: 4/15/1964																										
1964	Chi-N	0	0	....	26	0	0	0	0	48^1	57	22	20	3	0	11	29	1.407	3.72	100	4.17	.298	0	.000	0	3	0.0
• SCHUTZ, Carl	Carl James Schutz b: 8/22/1971, Hammond, LA BL/TL, 5'11", 208 lbs. Deb: 9/3/1996																										
1996	Atl-N	0	0	....	3	0	0	0	0	3^1	3	1	1	0	0	2	5	1.500	2.70	163	3.50	.273	0	....	1	0	0.1
• SCHWABE, Mike	Michael Scott Schwabe b: 7/12/1964, Fort Dodge, IA BR/TR, 6'4", 200 lbs. Deb: 5/27/1989																										
1989	Det-A	2	4	.333	13	4	0	0	0	44^2	58	33	30	6	1	16	13	1.657	6.04	63	5.67	.307	0	....	-11	0	-1.1
1990	Det-A	0	0	....	1	0	0	0	0	3^2	5	1	1	0	0	0	1	1.364	2.45	161	4.01	.357	0	....	1	0	0.1
Total	2	2	4	.333	14	4	0	0	0	48^1	63	34	31	6	1	16	14	1.634	5.77	66	5.54	.310	0	....	-10	0	-1.0
• SCHWALL, Don	Donald Bernard Schwall b: 3/2/1936, Wilkes-Barre, PA BR/TR, 6'6", 200 lbs. Deb: 5/21/1961																										
1961	Bos-A★	15	7	.682	25	25	10	2	0	178^2	167	76	64	8	6	110	91	1.550	3.22	129	4.35	.255	11	.180	19	15	1.9
1962	Bos-A	9	15	.375	33	32	5	1	0	182^1	180	118	100	18	10	121	89	**1.651**	4.94	84	5.26	.260	9	.136	-17	4	-1.9
1963	Pit-N	6	12	.333	33	24	3	2	0	167^2	158	72	62	13	6	74	86	1.384	3.33	99	3.81	.255	8	.160	-2	7	-0.2
1964	Pit-N	4	3	.571	15	9	0	0	0	49^2	53	28	24	1	0	15	36	1.369	4.35	81	3.44	.269	5	.263	-4	2	-0.3
1965	Pit-N	9	6	.600	43	1	0	0	4	77	77	37	25	5	2	30	55	1.390	2.92	120	3.90	.269	0	.000	3	6	0.2
1966	Pit-N	3	2	.600	11	4	0	0	0	41^2	31	13	10	3	1	21	24	1.248	2.16	165	2.98	.209	1	.100	6	4	0.6
	Atl-N	3	3	.500	11	8	0	0	0	45^1	44	23	22	2	2	19	27	1.390	4.37	83	3.70	.256	0	.000	-4	1	-0.6
	Yr.	6	5	.545	22	12	0	0	0	87	75	36	32	5	3	40	51	1.322	3.31	109	3.35	.234	1	.043	2	5	0.0
1967	Atl-N	0	0	....	1	0	0	0	0	0^2	0	0	0	0	0	1	0	1.500	0.00	....	0.00	.000	0	....	0	0	0.0
Total	7	49	48	.505	172	103	18	5	4	743	710	367	307	50	27	391	408	1.482	3.72	102	4.22	.257	34	.145	2	39	-0.3
• SCHWAMB, Blackie	Ralph Richard Schwamb b: 8/6/1926, Los Angeles, CA d: 12/21/1989, Lancaster, CA BR/TR, 6'5.5", 198 lbs. Deb: 7/25/1948																										
1948	StL-A	1	1	.500	12	5	0	0	0	31^2	44	34	30	3	0	21	7	2.053	8.53	53	7.31	.331	3	.300	-13	0	-1.2
• SCHWARZ, Jeff	Jeffrey William Schwarz b: 5/20/1964, Fort Pierce, FL BR/TR, 6'5", 190 lbs. Deb: 4/24/1993																										
1993	Chi-A	2	2	.500	41	0	0	0	0	51	35	21	21	1	3	38	41	1.431	3.71	113	3.34	.201	0	....	3	4	0.3
1994	Chi-A	0	0	....	9	0	0	0	0	11^1	9	10	8	0	0	16	14	2.206	6.35	73	5.73	.205	0	....	-2	0	-0.2
	Cal-A	0	0	....	4	0	0	0	0	6^2	5	3	3	0	0	6	4	1.650	4.05	121	4.18	.250	0	....	1	1	0.1
	Yr.	0	0	....	13	0	0	0	0	18	14	13	11	0	0	22	18	2.000	5.50	86	5.16	.219	0	....	-1	1	-0.1
Total	2	2	2	.500	54	0	0	0	0	69	49	34	32	1	3	60	59	1.580	4.17	104	3.81	.206	0	....	1	5	0.1
• SCHWENCK, Rudy	Rudolph Christian Schwenck b: 4/6/1884, Louisville, KY d: 11/27/1941, Anchorage, KY BL/TL, 6', 174 lbs. Deb: 9/23/1909																										
1909	Chi-N	1	1	.500	3	2	0	0	0	4	16	7	6	0	1	3	3	4.750	13.50	19	15.33	.308	1	.250	-5	0	-0.5
• SCHWENK, Hal	Harold Edward Schwenk b: 8/23/1890, Schuykill, PA d: 9/3/1955, Kansas City, MO BL/TL, 6', 185 lbs. Deb: 9/4/1913																										
1913	StL-A	1	0	1.000	1	1	1	0	0	11	12	4	4	0	0	4	3	1.455	3.27	89	4.45	.333	1	.333	-1	1	0.0
• SCOGGINS, Jim	Lynn J. "Lefty" Scoggins b: 7/19/1891, Killeen, TX d: 8/16/1923, Columbia, SC BL/TL, 5'11", 165 lbs. Deb: 8/26/1913																										
1913	Chi-A	0	1	.000	1	1	0	0	0	0	0	0	0	0	0	1	0	....	....	....	∞	.000	0	....	0	0	0.0
• SCORE, Herb	Herbert Jude Score b: 6/7/1933, Rosedale, NY BL/TL, 6'2", 185 lbs. Deb: 4/15/1955																										
1955	Cle-A★	16	10	.615	33	32	11	2	0	227^1	158	85	72	18	1	154	**245**	1.372	2.85	140	3.33	.194	10	.119	28	19	2.4
1956	Cle-A★	20	9	.690	35	33	16	**5**	0	249^1	162	82	70	18	2	129	**263**	1.167	2.53	**166**	**2.52**	**.186**	16	.184	**47**	25	4.7
1957	Cle-A	2	1	.667	5	5	3	1	0	36	18	9	8	0	1	26	39	1.222	2.00	186	2.00	.149	1	.091	7	4	0.7
1958	Cle-A	2	3	.400	12	5	2	1	3	41	29	19	18	1	0	34	48	1.537	3.95	92	3.49	.197	1	.091	-2	2	-0.2
1959	Cle-A	9	11	.450	30	25	9	1	0	160^2	123	93	84	28	1	115	147	**1.481**	4.71	78	4.53	**.210**	5	.096	-19	3	-2.3
1960	Chi-A	5	10	.333	23	22	5	1	0	113^2	91	54	47	10	2	87	78	1.566	3.72	102	4.39	.226	3	.100	-1	5	-0.1
1961	Chi-A	1	2	.333	8	5	1	0	0	24^1	22	19	18	3	0	24	14	1.890	6.66	59	5.84	.259	0	.000	-7	0	-0.8
1962	Chi-A	0	0	....	4	0	0	0	0	6	6	3	3	1	0	4	3	1.667	4.50	87	5.76	.261	0	....	-0	0	0.0
Total	8	55	46	.545	150	127	47	11	3	858^1	609	364	320	79	7	573	837	1.377	3.36	116	3.50	.200	36	.128	54	58	4.4
• SCOTT, Darryl	Darryl Nelson Scott b: 8/6/1968, Fresno, CA BR/TR, 6'1", 185 lbs. Deb: 5/31/1993																										
1993	Cal-A	1	2	.333	16	0	0	0	0	20	19	13	13	1	1	11	13	1.500	5.85	77	4.06	.250	0	....	-3	1	-0.3
• SCOTT, Dick	Amos Richard Scott b: 2/5/1883, Bethel, OH d: 1/18/1911, Chicago, IL BR/TR, 6', 180 lbs. Deb: 6/26/1901																										
1901	Cin-N	0	2	.000	3	2	2	0	0	21	26	15	12	2	3	9	7	1.667	5.14	62	5.99	.302	0	.000	-4	0	-0.5
• SCOTT, Dick	Richard Lewis Scott b: 3/15/1933, Portsmouth, NH BR/TL, 6'2", 185 lbs. Deb: 5/8/1963																										
1963	LA-N	0	0	....	9	0	0	0	2	12	17	10	9	6	0	3	6	1.667	6.75	45	9.25	.340	0	....	-5	0	-0.5
1964	Chi-N	0	0	....	3	0	0	0	0	4^1	10	6	6	2	0	1	1	2.538	12.46	30	14.62	.417	0	....	-4	0	-0.4
Total	2	0	0	....	12	0	0	0	2	16^1	27	16	15	8	0	4	7	1.898	8.27	39	10.68	.365	0	....	-9	0	-1.0
• SCOTT, Ed	Edward Scott b: 8/12/1870, Walbridge, OH d: 11/1/1933, Toledo, OH BR/TR, 6'3" Deb: 4/19/1900																										
1900	Cin-N	17	20	.459	42	35	31	0	1	315	370	192	135	10	14	65	87	1.381	3.86	95	3.93	.292	19	.154	-7	14	-1.0
1901	Cle-A	6	6	.500	17	16	11	0	1	124^2	149	82	61	2	7	38	23	1.500	4.40	81	4.31	.293	10	.208	-11	6	-0.9
Total	2	23	26	.469	59	51	42	0	2	439^2	519	274	196	12	21	103	110	1.415	4.01	90	4.04	.292	29	.170	-18	20	-2.0
• SCOTT, George	George William Scott b: 11/17/1896, Trenton, MO d: 12/3/1962, Philomath, OR BR/TR, 6'1", 175 lbs. Deb: 8/17/1920																										
1920	StL-N	0	0	....	2	0	0	0	0	6	4	3	3	0	0	3	1	1.167	4.50	68	1.91	.200	0	.000	-1	0	-0.1
• SCOTT, Jack	John William Scott b: 4/18/1892, Ridgeway, NC d: 11/30/1959, Durham, NC BL/TR, 6'2.5", 199 lbs. Deb: 9/6/1916																										
1916	Pit-N	0	0	....	1	0	0	0	0	5	5	6	6	1	0	3	4	1.600	10.80	25	5.92	.278	0	.000	-4	0	-0.5
1917	Bos-N	1	2	.333	7	3	3	0	0	39^2	36	12	8	0	3	5	21	1.034	1.82	140	2.22	.255	2	.125	4	2	0.3
1919	Bos-N	6	6	.500	19	12	7	0	1	103^2	109	47	36	3	1	39	44	1.428	3.13	91	3.74	.275	7	.175	-3	5	-0.5
1920	Bos-N	10	21	.323	44	32	22	3	1	291	308	148	114	6	13	85	94	1.351	3.53	86	3.53	.277	21	.212	-19	11	-2.0
1921	Bos-N	15	13	.536	**47**	29	16	2	3	233^2	258	108	96	9	7	57	83	1.348	3.70	99	3.68	.283	30	.341	-3	17	0.7
1922	Cin-N	0	0	....	1	0	0	0	0	1	2	1	1	0	0	1	0	3.000	9.00	44	11.63	.500	0	.000	-1	0	-0.1
	*NY-N	8	2	.800	17	10	5	0	2	79^2	83	42	39	7	2	23	37	1.331	4.41	91	3.76	.265	8	.267	-6	5	-0.5
	Yr.	8	2	.800	18	10	5	0	2	80^2	85	43	40	7	2	24	37	1.351	4.46	90	3.85	.268	8	.258	-7	5	-0.6
1923*	NY-N	16	7	.696	40	25	9	3	1	220	223	104	95	15	4	65	79	1.309	3.89	98	3.53	.267	25	.316	-4	17	0.2
1925	NY-N	14	15	.483	36	28	18	2	3	239^2	251	98	84	10	4	55	87	1.277	3.15	128	3.25	.269	21	.241	24	25	2.8
1926	NY-N	13	15	.464	**50**	22	13	0	5	226	242	118	109	13	3	53	82	1.305	4.34	86	3.52	.276	28	.337	-18	15	-0.9
1927	Phi-N	9	21	.300	**48**	25	17	1	1	233^1	304	154	132	15	4	69	69	1.599	5.09	81	5.17	.330	33	.289	-21	9	-1.1
1928	NY-N	4	1	.800	16	3	3	0	1	50^1	59	22	20	3	2	11	17	1.391	3.58	109	4.15	.295	4	.267	1	4	0.2
1929	NY-N	7	6	.538	30	6	2	0	1	91^2	89	44	36	12	0	27	40	1.265	3.53	129	3.67	.260	8	.308	9	8	1.1
Total	12	103	109	.486	356	195	115	11	19	1814^2	1969	904	776	94	43	493	657	1.357	3.85	95	3.75	.281	187	.275	-40	118	-0.1
• SCOTT, Jim	James "Death Valley Jim" Scott b: 4/23/1888, Deadwood, SD d: 4/7/1957, Jacumba, CA BR/TR, 6'1", 235 lbs. Deb: 4/25/1909																										
1909	Chi-A	12	12	.500	36	29	20	4	0	250^1	194	86	64	0	16	93	135	1.146	2.30	102	2.44	.223	9	.106	1	13	0.0
1910	Chi-A	8	18	.308	41	23	14	2	1	229^2	182	99	62	5	4	86	135	1.167	2.43	99	2.51	.226	15	.203	0	10	0.2
1911	Chi-A	14	11	.560	39	26	13	3	0	222	195	82	59	3	4	81	128	1.243	2.39	135	2.79	.240	11	.155	21	16	1.9
1912	Chi-A	2	2	.500	6	4	2	1	0	37^2	36	16	9	0	1	15	23	1.354	2.15	150	3.35	.265	0	.000	5	3	0.3
1913	Chi-A	20	21	.488	48	**38**	25	4	1	312^1	252	96	66	2	9	86	158	1.082	1.90	153	2.20	.221	7	.072	35	27	3.0
1914	Chi-A	14	18	.438	43	33	12	2	1	253^1	228	109	80	5	5	75	138	1.196	2.84	94	2.75	.246	14	.163	-4	14	-0.6
1915	Chi-A	24	11	.686	48	35	23	**7**	2	296^1	256	98	67	3	5	78	120	1.127	2.03	146	2.39	.238	12	.126	34	23	3.1
1916	Chi-A	7	14	.333	32	21	8	1	3	165^1	155	63	50	3	3	53	71	1.258	2.72	101	3.06	.258	6	.115	-1	9	-0.5
1917	Chi-A	6	7	.462	24	17	6	2	1	125	126	37	26	0	6	42	37	1.344	1.87	142	3.41	.272	5	.119	12	9	1.1
Total	9	107	114	.484	317	226	123	26	9	1892	1624	686	483	21	53	609	945	1.180	2.30	119	2.62	.238	79	.129	102	124	8.5

YEAR TM-L	W	L	PCT	G	GS	CG	SH	SV	IP	H	R	ER	HR	HB	BB	SO	RAT	ERA	ERA+	CERA	OAV	BH	AVG	PR+	WS	TPW
• SCOTT, Lefty	Marshall Scott b: 7/15/1915, Roswell, NM d: 3/3/1964, Houston, TX BR/TL, 6'.5", 165 lbs. Deb: 6/15/1945																									
1945 Phi-N	0	2	.000	8	2	0	0	0	22^{1}	29	13	11	1	0	12	5	1.836	4.43	86	5.64	.312	0	.000	-1	1	-0.1
• SCOTT, Mickey	Ralph Robert Scott b: 7/25/1947, Weimer, Germany BL/TL, 6'1", 165 lbs. Deb: 5/6/1972																									
1972 Bal-A	0	1	.000	15	0	0	0	0	23	23	7	7	2	1	5	11	1.217	2.74	112	3.63	.277	0	.000	0	2	0.1
1973 Bal-A	0	0	....	1	0	0	0	0	1^{2}	2	1	1	1	0	2	2	2.400	5.40	69	13.35	.286	0	....	-0	0	0.0
Mon-N	1	2	.333	22	0	0	0	0	24	27	14	14	3	2	9	11	1.500	5.25	73	5.20	.287	0	.000	-4	0	-0.4
1975 Cal-A	4	2	.667	50	0	0	0	1	68^{1}	59	34	25	8	1	18	31	1.127	3.29	108	2.83	.233	0	....	2	4	0.2
1976 Cal-A	3	0	1.000	33	0	0	0	3	39	47	17	14	3	0	12	10	1.513	3.23	103	4.53	.307	0	....	1	3	0.1
1977 Cal-A	0	2	.000	12	0	0	0	0	16	19	16	10	1	0	4	5	1.438	5.63	70	4.02	.302	0	....	-3	0	-0.3
Total 5	8	7	.533	133	0	0	0	4	172	177	89	71	18	4	50	70	1.320	3.72	95	3.86	.271	0	.000	-4	9	-0.4
• SCOTT, Mike	Michael Warren Scott b: 4/26/1955, Santa Monica, CA BR/TR, 6'2", 215 lbs. Deb: 4/18/1979																									
1979 NY-N	1	3	.250	18	9	0	0	0	52^{1}	59	35	31	4	0	20	21	1.510	5.33	68	4.49	.289	0	.000	-10	0	-1.2
1980 NY-N	1	1	.500	6	6	1	1	0	29^{1}	40	14	14	1	0	8	13	1.636	4.30	83	5.13	.331	1	.111	-2	1	-0.2
1981 NY-N	5	10	.333	23	23	1	0	0	136	130	65	59	11	1	34	54	1.206	3.90	89	3.23	.261	3	.073	-5	4	-0.7
1982 NY-N	7	13	.350	37	22	1	0	3	147	185	100	84	13	2	60	63	1.667	5.14	71	5.57	.321	7	.146	-23	0	-2.4
1983 Hou-N	10	6	.625	24	24	2	2	0	145	143	67	60	8	5	46	73	1.303	3.72	91	3.53	.258	8	.167	-7	6	-0.7
1984 Hou-N	5	11	.313	31	29	0	0	0	154	179	96	80	7	3	43	83	1.442	4.68	71	4.13	.293	6	.128	-25	0	-2.7
1985 Hou-N	18	8	.692	36	35	4	2	0	221^{2}	194	91	81	20	3	80	137	1.236	3.29	105	3.22	.235	11	.153	2	12	0.5
1986* Hou-N★	18	10	.643	37	37	7	**5**	0	**275^{1}**	182	73	68	17	2	72	**306**	.923	**2.22**	**162**	**1.67**	**.186**	12	.126	**41**	**27**	**4.1**
1987 Hou-N★	16	13	.552	36	**36**	8	3	0	247^{2}	199	94	89	21	4	79	233	1.122	3.23	121	2.65	.217	10	.125	20	18	1.8
1988 Hou-N	14	8	.636	32	32	8	5	0	218^{2}	162	74	71	19	8	53	190	.983	2.92	114	2.15	.204	6	.085	11	14	0.9
1989 Hou-N★	**20**	10	.667	33	32	9	2	0	229	180	87	79	23	3	62	172	1.057	3.10	109	2.43	.212	10	.133	9	15	0.8
1990 Hou-N	9	13	.409	32	32	4	2	0	205^{2}	194	102	87	27	1	66	121	1.264	3.81	98	3.59	.246	7	.130	-3	8	-0.3
1991 Hou-N	0	2	.000	2	2	0	0	0	7	11	10	10	2	1	4	3	2.143	12.86	27	10.85	.367	0	.000	-7	0	-0.8
Total 13	124	108	.534	347	319	45	22	3	2068^{2}	1858	908	813	173	33	627	1469	1.201	3.54	100	3.12	.240	81	.124	-1	105	-0.9
• SCOTT, Tim	Timothy Dale Scott b: 11/16/1966, Hanford, CA BR/TR, 6'2", 205 lbs. Deb: 6/25/1991																									
1991 SD-N	0	0	....	2	0	0	0	0	1	2	2	1	0	0	0	1	2.000	9.00	42	7.48	.400	0	....	-1	0	-0.1
1992 SD-N	4	1	.800	34	0	0	0	0	37^{2}	39	24	22	4	1	21	30	1.593	5.26	68	4.69	.267	0	....	-7	1	-0.7
1993 SD-N	2	0	1.000	24	0	0	0	0	37^{2}	38	13	10	1	4	15	30	1.407	2.39	173	3.91	.260	0	.000	7	3	0.7
Mon-N	5	2	.714	32	0	0	0	1	34	31	15	14	3	0	19	35	1.471	3.71	112	4.04	.242	0	.000	2	3	0.1
Yr.	7	2	.778	56	0	0	0	1	71^{2}	69	28	24	4	4	34	65	1.437	3.01	138	3.98	.252	0	.000	9	6	0.9
1994 Mon-N	5	2	.714	40	0	0	0	1	53^{1}	51	17	16	0	2	18	37	1.294	2.70	156	3.01	.251	0	.000	9	6	0.9
1995 Mon-N	2	0	1.000	62	0	0	0	2	63^{1}	52	30	28	6	6	23	57	1.184	3.98	108	3.21	.222	1	.250	3	5	0.3
1996 Mon-N	3	5	.375	45	0	0	0	1	46^{1}	41	18	16	3	2	21	37	1.338	3.11	139	3.51	.238	0	.000	6	5	0.6
SF-N	2	2	.500	20	0	0	0	0	19^{2}	24	18	18	5	1	9	10	1.678	8.24	50	7.15	.316	0	.000	-9	0	-0.9
Yr.	5	7	.417	65	0	0	0	1	66	65	36	34	8	3	30	47	1.439	4.64	91	4.60	.262	0	.000	-3	5	-0.3
1997 SD-N	1	1	.500	14	0	0	0	0	18^{1}	25	17	16	2	3	5	14	1.636	7.85	49	6.38	.321	0	....	-8	0	-0.8
Col-N	0	0	....	3	0	0	0	0	2^{2}	5	3	3	0	0	2	2	2.625	10.13	51	10.75	.455	0	....	-1	0	-0.1
Yr.	1	1	.500	17	0	0	0	0	21	30	20	19	2	3	7	16	1.762	8.14	49	6.94	.337	0	....	-9	0	-0.9
Total 7	24	13	.649	276	0	0	0	5	314	308	157	144	24	19	133	253	1.404	4.13	99	4.08	.257	1	.067	1	23	0.0
• SCUDDER, Scott	William Scott Scudder b: 2/14/1968, Paris, TX BR/TR, 6'2", 185 lbs. Deb: 6/6/1989																									
1989 Cin-N	4	9	.308	23	17	0	0	0	100^{1}	91	54	50	14	1	61	66	1.515	4.49	80	4.44	.239	4	.167	-9	2	-0.8
1990* Cin-N	5	5	.500	21	10	0	0	0	71^{2}	74	41	39	12	3	30	42	1.451	4.90	81	4.89	.265	1	.056	-9	2	-1.0
1991 Cin-N	6	9	.400	27	14	0	0	1	101^{1}	91	52	49	6	6	56	51	1.451	4.35	87	4.00	.246	3	.103	-6	4	-0.7
1992 Cle-A	6	10	.375	23	22	0	0	0	109	134	80	64	10	2	55	66	1.734	5.28	74	5.82	.303	0	....	-16	1	-1.6
1993 Cle-A	0	1	.000	2	1	0	0	0	4	5	4	4	0	1	4	1	2.250	9.00	48	8.87	.333	0	....	-2	0	-0.2
Total 5	21	34	.382	96	64	0	0	1	386^{1}	395	231	206	42	13	206	226	1.556	4.80	80	4.85	.266	8	.113	-42	9	-4.3
• SCURRY, Rod	Rodney Grant Scurry b: 3/17/1956, Sacramento, CA d: 11/5/1992, Reno, NV BL/TL, 6'2", 180 lbs. Deb: 4/17/1980																									
1980 Pit-N	0	2	.000	20	0	0	0	0	37^{2}	23	12	9	2	2	17	28	1.062	2.15	169	2.03	.176	1	.250	6	3	0.6
1981 Pit-N	4	5	.444	27	7	0	0	7	74	74	33	31	6	3	40	65	1.541	3.77	95	4.64	.261	3	.158	-1	4	-0.1
1982 Pit-N	4	5	.444	76	0	0	0	14	103^{2}	79	26	20	3	4	64	94	1.379	1.74	214	3.14	.212	5	.238	23	13	2.6
1983 Pit-N	4	9	.308	61	0	0	0	7	68	63	45	42	6	4	53	67	1.706	5.56	67	5.10	.249	0	.000	-14	0	-1.5
1984 Pit-N	5	6	.455	43	0	0	0	4	46^{1}	28	14	13	1	0	22	48	1.079	2.53	143	1.76	.175	0	.000	5	5	0.5
1985 Pit-N	0	1	.000	30	0	0	0	2	47^{2}	42	22	17	4	0	28	43	1.469	3.21	111	3.96	.236	0	.000	3	3	0.2
NY-A	1	0	1.000	5	0	0	0	1	12^{2}	5	4	4	2	0	10	17	1.184	2.84	141	2.68	.125	0	....	1	1	0.1
1986 NY-A	1	2	.333	31	0	0	0	2	39^{1}	38	18	16	1	2	22	36	1.525	3.66	112	4.07	.252	0	....	2	3	0.2
1988 Sea-A	0	2	.000	39	0	0	0	2	31^{1}	32	16	14	6	4	18	33	1.596	4.02	103	5.69	.258	0	....	1	1	0.1
Total 8	19	32	.373	332	7	0	0	39	460^{2}	384	190	166	31	19	274	431	1.428	3.24	115	3.77	.227	9	.164	26	33	2.7
• SEALE, Johnnie	Johnny Ray "Durango Kid" Seale b: 11/14/1938, Edgewater, CO BL/TL, 5'10", 155 lbs. Deb: 9/20/1964																									
1964 Det-A	1	0	1.000	4	0	0	0	0	10	6	4	4	1	0	4	5	1.000	3.60	102	2.00	.171	0	.000	0	1	0.0
1965 Det-A	0	0	....	4	0	0	0	0	3	7	4	4	1	0	2	3	3.000	12.00	29	16.51	.500	0	....	-3	0	-0.3
Total 2	1	0	1.000	8	0	0	0	0	13	13	8	8	2	0	6	8	1.462	5.54	64	5.35	.265	0	.000	-3	1	-0.3
• SEAMAN, Kim	Kim Michael Seaman b: 5/6/1957, Pascagoula, MS BL/TL, 6'4", 205 lbs. Deb: 9/28/1979																									
1979 StL-N	0	0	....	1	0	0	0	0	2	0	0	0	0	0	2	3	1.000	0.00	....	0.95	.000	0	....	1	0	0.1
1980 StL-N	3	2	.600	26	0	0	0	4	23^{2}	16	9	9	2	0	13	10	1.225	3.42	108	2.72	.188	0	.000	0	3	0.0
Total 2	3	2	.600	27	0	0	0	4	25^{2}	16	9	9	2	0	15	13	1.208	3.16	117	2.59	.188	0	.000	1	3	0.1
• SEANEZ, Rudy	Rudy Caballero Seanez b: 10/20/1968, Brawley, CA BR/TR, 5'10", 185 lbs. Deb: 9/7/1989																									
1989 Cle-A	0	0	....	5	0	0	0	0	5	1	2	2	0	0	4	7	1.000	3.60	110	0.94	.071	0	....	0	0	0.0
1990 Cle-A	2	1	.667	24	0	0	0	0	27^{1}	22	17	17	2	1	25	24	1.720	5.60	70	4.85	.220	0	....	-5	1	-0.5
1991 Cle-A	0	0	....	5	0	0	0	0	5	10	12	9	2	0	7	7	3.400	16.20	26	17.96	.385	0	....	-7	0	-0.7
1993 SD-N	0	0	....	3	0	0	0	0	3^{1}	8	6	5	1	0	2	1	3.000	13.50	31	16.31	.471	0	....	-3	0	-0.3
1994 LA-N	1	1	.500	17	0	0	0	0	23^{2}	24	7	7	2	1	9	18	1.394	2.66	147	4.01	.273	0	.000	3	2	0.3
1995 LA-N	1	3	.250	37	0	0	0	3	34^{2}	39	27	26	5	1	18	29	1.644	6.75	56	5.57	.285	0	.000	-11	0	-1.1
1998* Atl-N	4	1	.800	34	0	0	0	2	36	25	13	11	2	1	16	50	1.139	2.75	151	2.44	.195	0	.000	5	5	0.5
1999 Atl-N	6	1	.857	56	0	0	0	3	53^{2}	47	21	20	3	1	21	41	1.267	3.35	134	3.12	.234	0	.000	7	7	0.7
2000 Atl-N	2	4	.333	23	0	0	0	2	21	15	11	10	3	1	9	20	1.143	4.29	107	2.95	.192	0	....	1	2	0.1
2001 SD-N	0	2	.000	26	0	0	0	1	24	15	8	7	3	1	15	24	1.250	2.63	152	3.21	.176	0	....	4	2	0.4
* Atl-N	0	0	....	12	0	0	0	0	12	8	4	4	1	0	4	17	1.000	3.00	147	1.99	.182	0	....	2	1	0.2
Yr.	0	2	.000	38	0	0	0	1	36	23	12	11	4	1	19	41	1.167	2.75	150	2.80	.178	0	....	6	3	0.6
2002 Tex-A	1	3	.250	33	0	0	0	0	33	28	25	21	5	0	24	40	1.576	5.73	82	4.77	.230	0	....	-3	1	-0.3
2003 Bos-A	0	1	.000	9	0	0	0	0	8^{2}	11	7	6	2	0	6	9	1.962	6.23	73	7.45	.297	0	....	-1	0	-0.1
Total 12	17	17	.500	284	0	0	0	11	287^{1}	253	160	145	31	7	160	287	1.437	4.54	92	4.21	.235	0	.000	-8	21	-0.9
• SEARAGE, Ray	Raymond Mark Searage b: 5/1/1955, Freeport, NY BL/TL, 6'1", 180 lbs. Deb: 6/11/1981																									
1981 NY-N	1	0	1.000	26	0	0	0	1	36^{2}	34	16	15	2	0	17	16	1.391	3.68	95	3.51	.252	1	1.000	-0	2	0.0
1984 Mil-A	2	1	.667	21	0	0	0	6	38^{1}	20	3	3	0	1	16	29	.939	0.70	547	1.32	.155	0	....	14	7	1.4
1985 Mil-A	1	4	.200	33	0	0	0	1	38	54	27	25	2	0	24	36	2.053	5.92	70	6.91	.338	0	....	-7	0	-0.7
1986 Mil-A	0	1	.000	17	0	0	0	1	22	29	17	17	6	1	9	10	1.727	6.95	62	7.51	.315	0	....	-6	0	-0.6
Chi-A	1	0	1.000	29	0	0	0	0	29	15	3	2	1	0	19	26	1.172	0.62	694	1.98	.156	0	....	11	4	1.1
Yr.	1	1	.500	46	0	0	0	1	51	44	20	19	7	1	28	36	1.412	3.35	129	4.36	.234	0	....	5	4	0.5
1987 Chi-A	2	3	.400	58	0	0	0	2	55^{2}	56	28	26	9	1	24	33	1.437	4.20	109	4.73	.264	0	....	1	4	0.1
1989 LA-N	3	4	.429	41	0	0	0	0	35^{2}	29	15	14	1	0	18	24	1.318	3.53	97	2.68	.225	0	....	-1	2	-0.1

YEAR	TM-L	W	L	PCT	G	GS	CG	SH	SV	IP	H	R	ER	HR	HB	BB	SO	RAT	ERA	ERA+	CERA	OAV	BH	AVG	PR+	WS	TPW
1990	LA-N	1	0	1.000	29	0	0	0	0	32^{1}	30	11	10	1	0	10	19	1.237	2.78	131	2.84	.250	0	.000	3	2	0.3
Total	7	11	13	.458	254	0	0	0	11	287^{2}	267	120	112	22	3	137	193	1.404	3.50	114	3.88	.249	1	.333	14	21	1.4

• SEARCY, Steve William Steven Searcy b: 6/4/1964, Knoxville, TN BL/TL, 6'1", 185 lbs. Deb: 8/29/1988

YEAR	TM-L	W	L	PCT	G	GS	CG	SH	SV	IP	H	R	ER	HR	HB	BB	SO	RAT	ERA	ERA+	CERA	OAV	BH	AVG	PR+	WS	TPW
1988	Det-A	0	2	.000	2	2	0	0	0	8	8	6	5	3	0	4	5	1.500	5.63	68	6.19	.242	0	....	-2	0	-0.2
1989	Det-A	1	1	.500	8	2	0	0	0	22^{1}	27	16	15	3	0	12	11	1.746	6.04	63	6.30	.307	0	....	-5	0	-0.5
1990	Det-A	2	7	.222	16	12	1	0	0	75^{1}	76	44	39	9	0	51	66	1.686	4.66	85	5.39	.270	0	....	-8	2	-0.8
1991	Det-A	1	2	.333	16	5	0	0	0	40^{2}	52	40	38	8	0	30	32	2.016	8.41	49	7.97	.313	0	....	-19	0	-1.9
	Phi-N	2	1	.667	18	0	0	0	0	30^{1}	29	16	14	2	0	14	21	1.418	4.15	88	3.68	.252	0	.000	-2	1	-0.2
1992	Phi-N	0	0	....	10	0	0	0	0	10^{1}	13	9	7	0	0	8	5	2.032	6.10	57	6.39	.325	0	....	-3	0	-0.3
Total	5	6	13	.316	70	21	1	0	0	187	205	131	118	25	0	119	140	1.733	5.68	69	5.87	.283	0	.000	-38	3	-3.9

• SEATON, Tom Thomas Gordon Seaton b: 8/30/1887, Blair, NE d: 4/10/1940, El Paso, TX BB/TR, 6', 175 lbs. Deb: 4/13/1912

YEAR	TM-L	W	L	PCT	G	GS	CG	SH	SV	IP	H	R	ER	HR	HB	BB	SO	RAT	ERA	ERA+	CERA	OAV	BH	AVG	PR+	WS	TPW
1912	Phi-N	16	12	.571	44	27	16	2	2	255	246	126	93	8	9	106	118	1.380	3.28	110	3.56	.261	18	.217	9	17	0.8
1913	Phi-N	**27**	12	.692	52	35	21	5	1	**322^{1}**	262	117	93	6	10	136	**168**	1.235	2.60	128	2.68	.226	12	.109	27	29	2.3
1914	Bro-F	25	14	.641	44	38	26	7	2	302^{2}	299	130	102	6	13	102	172	1.325	3.03	107	3.35	.259	22	.206	10	22	1.5
1915	Bro-F	11	11	.500	32	24	13	0	3	189^{1}	199	126	96	6	3	99	86	1.574	4.56	65	4.26	.273	16	.242	-35	4	-3.3
	New-F	2	6	.250	12	10	7	0	1	75	61	26	19	1	2	21	28	1.093	2.28	125	2.17	.224	4	.154	4	5	0.5
	Yr.	13	17	.433	44	34	20	0	4	264^{1}	260	152	115	7	5	120	114	1.438	3.92	75	3.67	.260	20	.217	-30	9	-2.8
1916	Chi-N	6	6	.500	31	12	4	0	1	121	108	54	44	3	4	43	45	1.248	3.27	89	2.88	.246	7	.184	-3	7	-0.3
1917	Chi-N	5	4	.556	16	9	3	1	1	74^{2}	60	30	21	0	1	23	27	1.112	2.53	114	2.13	.227	5	.238	4	5	0.6
Total	6	92	65	.586	231	155	90	15	11	1340	1235	609	468	30	42	530	644	1.317	3.14	102	3.18	.249	84	.186	16	89	2.1

• SEATS, Tom Thomas Edward Seats b: 9/24/1910, Farmington, NC d: 5/10/1992, San Ramon, CA BR/TL, 5'11", 190 lbs. Deb: 5/4/1940

YEAR	TM-L	W	L	PCT	G	GS	CG	SH	SV	IP	H	R	ER	HR	HB	BB	SO	RAT	ERA	ERA+	CERA	OAV	BH	AVG	PR+	WS	TPW
1940	Det-A	2	2	.500	26	2	0	0	1	55^{2}	67	43	29	4	0	21	25	1.581	4.69	101	4.70	.290	1	.083	1	2	0.0
1945	Bro-N	10	7	.588	31	18	6	2	0	121^{2}	127	71	59	8	5	37	44	1.348	4.36	86	3.70	.261	9	.209	-8	5	-0.7
Total	2	12	9	.571	57	20	6	2	1	177^{1}	194	114	88	12	5	58	69	1.421	4.47	90	4.01	.271	10	.182	-6	7	-0.7

• SEAVER, Tom George Thomas "Tom Terrific" Seaver b: 11/17/1944, Fresno, CA BR/TR, 6'1", 206 lbs. Deb: 4/13/1967 HOF: 1992

YEAR	TM-L	W	L	PCT	G	GS	CG	SH	SV	IP	H	R	ER	HR	HB	BB	SO	RAT	ERA	ERA+	CERA	OAV	BH	AVG	PR+	WS	TPW
1967	NY-N★	16	13	.552	35	34	18	2	0	251	224	85	77	19	5	78	170	1.203	2.76	123	3.07	.241	11	.143	17	21	2.1
1968	NY-N★	16	12	.571	36	35	14	5	1	277^{2}	224	73	68	15	8	48	205	.980	2.20	137	2.07	.222	15	.158	22	23	2.6
1969*	NY-N★	**25**	7	.781	36	35	18	5	0	273^{1}	202	75	67	24	7	82	208	1.039	2.21	166	2.34	**.207**	11	.121	37	32	3.9
1970	NY-N★	18	12	.600	37	36	19	2	0	290^{2}	230	103	91	21	4	83	**283**	1.077	**2.82**	**143**	**2.39**	.214	17	.179	34	25	3.8
1971	NY-N★	20	10	.667	36	35	21	4	0	286^{1}	210	61	56	18	4	61	**289**	.946	**1.76**	**193**	**1.90**	.206	18	.196	**50**	32	5.7
1972	NY-N★	21	12	.636	35	35	13	3	0	262	215	92	85	23	5	77	249	1.115	2.92	115	2.72	.224	13	.146	15	22	2.0
1973*	NY-N★	19	10	.655	36	36	**18**	3	0	290	219	74	67	23	4	64	**251**	.976	**2.08**	**174**	**2.05**	**.206**	15	.161	**48**	**29**	**5.3**
1974	NY-N	11	11	.500	32	32	12	5	0	236	199	89	84	19	3	75	201	1.161	3.20	111	2.83	.230	7	.099	9	16	0.7
1975	NY-N★	**22**	9	.710	36	36	15	5	0	280^{1}	217	81	74	11	4	88	**243**	1.088	2.38	145	2.26	.214	17	.179	30	26	3.4
1976	NY-N★	14	11	.560	35	34	13	5	0	271	211	83	78	14	4	77	**235**	1.063	2.59	127	2.23	.213	7	.085	20	20	1.9
1977	NY-N	7	3	.700	13	13	5	3	0	96	79	33	32	7	0	28	72	1.115	3.00	125	2.51	.221	5	.161	8	8	0.8
	Cin-N★	14	3	.824	20	20	14	4	0	165^{1}	120	45	43	12	0	38	124	.956	2.34	168	1.89	.201	12	.218	28	17	3.2
	Yr.	21	6	.778	33	33	19	**7**	0	261^{1}	199	78	75	19	0	66	196	1.014	2.58	149	**2.12**	**.209**	17	.198	36	25	4.0
1978	Cin-N★	16	14	.533	36	36	8	1	0	259^{2}	218	97	83	26	0	89	226	1.182	2.88	123	2.91	.227	9	.122	24	19	2.5
1979*	Cin-N	16	6	.727	32	32	9	**5**	0	215	187	85	75	16	0	61	131	1.153	3.14	119	2.77	.236	12	.158	14	16	1.6
1980	Cin-N	10	8	.556	26	26	5	1	0	168	140	74	68	24	1	59	101	1.185	3.64	98	3.26	.225	6	.130	1	9	0.2
1981	Cin-N★	**14**	2	.875	23	23	6	1	0	166^{1}	120	51	47	10	3	66	87	1.118	2.54	140	2.38	.205	11	.200	17	**17**	2.2
1982	Cin-N	5	13	.278	21	21	0	0	0	111^{1}	136	75	68	14	3	44	62	1.617	5.50	67	5.65	.302	6	.176	-23	0	-2.3
1983	NY-N	9	14	.391	34	34	5	2	0	231	201	104	91	18	4	86	135	1.242	3.55	102	3.17	.235	10	.156	-1	12	0.2
1984	Chi-A	15	11	.577	34	33	10	4	0	236^{2}	216	108	104	27	2	61	131	1.170	3.95	105	3.14	.240	0	....	4	16	0.4
1985	Chi-A	16	11	.593	35	33	6	1	0	238^{2}	223	103	84	22	8	69	134	1.223	3.17	136	3.34	.248	0	....	29	18	2.9
1986	Chi-A	2	6	.250	12	12	1	0	0	72	66	37	35	9	5	27	31	1.292	4.38	99	3.92	.242	0	....	-2	3	-0.2
	Bos-A	5	7	.417	16	16	1	0	0	104^{1}	114	46	44	8	2	29	72	1.371	3.80	110	3.99	.278	0	....	5	7	0.5
	Yr.	7	13	.350	28	28	2	0	0	176^{1}	180	83	79	17	7	56	103	1.338	4.03	105	3.96	.264	0	....	3	10	0.3
Total	20	311	205	.603	656	647	231	61	1	4782^{2}	3971	1674	1521	380	76	1390	3640	1.121	2.86	127	2.69	.226	202	.154	384	388	43.2

• SEAY, Bobby Robert Michael Seay b: 6/20/1978, Sarasota, FL BL/TL, 6'2", 221 lbs. Deb: 8/14/2001

YEAR	TM-L	W	L	PCT	G	GS	CG	SH	SV	IP	H	R	ER	HR	HB	BB	SO	RAT	ERA	ERA+	CERA	OAV	BH	AVG	PR+	WS	TPW
2001	TB-A	1	1	.500	12	0	0	0	0	13	13	11	9	3	1	5	12	1.385	6.23	72	5.03	.260	0	....	-3	0	-0.2
2003	TB-A	0	0	....	12	0	0	0	0	9	7	3	3	0	0	6	5	1.444	3.00	151	3.17	.226	0	....	1	1	0.1
Total	2	1	1	.500	24	0	0	0	0	22	20	14	12	3	1	11	17	1.409	4.91	92	4.27	.247	0	....	-1	1	-0.1

• SEBRA, Bob Robert Bush Sebra b: 12/11/1961, Ridgewood, NJ BR/TR, 6'2", 200 lbs. Deb: 6/26/1985

YEAR	TM-L	W	L	PCT	G	GS	CG	SH	SV	IP	H	R	ER	HR	HB	BB	SO	RAT	ERA	ERA+	CERA	OAV	BH	AVG	PR+	WS	TPW
1985	Tex-A	0	2	.000	7	4	0	0	0	20^{1}	26	17	17	4	1	14	13	1.967	7.52	56	7.64	.306	0	....	-7	0	-0.7
1986	Mon-N	5	5	.500	17	13	3	1	0	91^{1}	82	39	36	9	3	25	66	1.172	3.55	104	3.12	.239	6	.207	1	5	0.2
1987	Mon-N	6	15	.286	36	27	4	1	0	177^{1}	184	99	87	15	3	67	156	1.415	4.42	95	4.18	.272	8	.157	-2	6	-0.2
1988	Phi-N	1	2	.333	3	3	0	0	0	11^{1}	15	11	10	0	0	10	7	2.206	7.94	45	6.84	.333	0	.000	-5	0	-0.6
1989	Phi-N	2	3	.400	6	5	0	0	0	34^{1}	41	20	17	6	4	10	21	1.485	4.46	80	5.61	.295	0	.000	-3	1	-0.4
	Cin-N	0	0	....	15	0	0	0	1	21	24	16	15	2	3	18	14	2.000	6.43	56	7.24	.296	0	.000	-6	0	-0.7
	Yr.	2	3	.400	21	5	0	0	1	55^{1}	65	36	32	8	7	28	35	1.681	5.20	69	6.23	.295	0	.000	-10	1	-1.1
1990	Mil-A	1	2	.333	10	0	0	0	0	11	20	10	10	1	1	5	4	2.273	8.18	47	9.38	.408	0	....	-5	0	-0.5
Total	6	15	29	.341	94	52	7	2	1	366^{2}	392	212	192	37	15	149	281	1.475	4.71	83	4.66	.276	14	.146	-28	12	-2.9

• SECHRIST, Doc Theodore O'Hara Sechrist b: 2/10/1876, Williamstown, KY d: 4/2/1950, Louisville, KY BR/TR, 5'9", 160 lbs. Deb: 4/28/1899

YEAR	TM-L	W	L	PCT	G	GS	CG	SH	SV	IP	H	R	ER	HR	HB	BB	SO	RAT	ERA	ERA+	CERA	OAV	BH	AVG	PR+	WS	TPW
1899	NY-N	0	0	....	1	0	0	0	0	0	0	0	0	0	0	2	0	....	....	....	∞	-1.000	0		0	0	0.0

• SECRIST, Don Donald Laverne Secrist b: 2/26/1944, Seattle, WA BL/TL, 6'2", 195 lbs. Deb: 4/11/1969

YEAR	TM-L	W	L	PCT	G	GS	CG	SH	SV	IP	H	R	ER	HR	HB	BB	SO	RAT	ERA	ERA+	CERA	OAV	BH	AVG	PR+	WS	TPW
1969	Chi-A	0	1	.000	19	0	0	0	0	40	35	28	27	7	1	14	23	1.225	6.08	64	3.64	.227	1	.143	-9	0	-1.0
1970	Chi-A	0	0	....	9	0	0	0	0	14^{2}	19	9	9	2	0	12	9	2.114	5.52	71	8.24	.333	0	....	-2	0	-0.2
Total	2	0	1	.000	28	0	0	0	0	54^{2}	54	37	36	9	1	26	32	1.463	5.93	65	4.87	.256	1	.143	-12	0	-1.2

• SEDGWICK, Duke Harry Kenneth Sedgwick b: 6/1/1898, Martins Ferry, OH d: 12/4/1982, Clearwater, FL BR/TR, 6', 175 lbs. Deb: 7/12/1921

YEAR	TM-L	W	L	PCT	G	GS	CG	SH	SV	IP	H	R	ER	HR	HB	BB	SO	RAT	ERA	ERA+	CERA	OAV	BH	AVG	PR+	WS	TPW
1921	Phi-N	1	3	.250	16	5	1	0	0	71^{1}	81	48	39	3	4	32	21	1.584	4.92	86	4.52	.283	5	.208	-4	2	-0.5
1923	Was-A	0	1	.000	5	2	1	0	0	16	27	17	14	1	0	6	4	2.063	7.88	48	8.33	.415	0	.000	-8	0	-0.8
Total	2	1	4	.200	21	7	2	0	0	87^{1}	108	65	53	4	4	38	25	1.672	5.46	75	5.22	.307	5	.172	-12	2	-1.3

• SEDLACEK, Shawn Shawn Patrick Sedlacek b: 6/29/1977, Cedar Rapids, IA BR/TR, 6'4", 200 lbs. Deb: 6/18/2002

YEAR	TM-L	W	L	PCT	G	GS	CG	SH	SV	IP	H	R	ER	HR	HB	BB	SO	RAT	ERA	ERA+	CERA	OAV	BH	AVG	PR+	WS	TPW
2002	KC-A	3	5	.375	16	14	0	0	0	84^{1}	99	64	63	16	6	36	52	1.601	6.72	75	6.24	.303	0	.000	-16	1	-1.6

• SEELBACH, Chris Christopher Don Seelbach b: 12/18/1972, Lufkin, TX BR/TR, 6'4", 180 lbs. Deb: 9/9/2000

YEAR	TM-L	W	L	PCT	G	GS	CG	SH	SV	IP	H	R	ER	HR	HB	BB	SO	RAT	ERA	ERA+	CERA	OAV	BH	AVG	PR+	WS	TPW
2000	Atl-N	0	1	.000	2	0	0	0	0	1^{2}	3	2	2	0	0	0	1	1.800	10.80	42	7.19	.500	0	....	-1	0	-0.1
2001	Atl-N	0	0	....	5	0	0	0	0	8	9	7	7	3	0	5	8	1.750	7.88	56	7.57	.273	0	....	-3	0	-0.3
Total	2	0	1	.000	7	0	0	0	0	9^{2}	12	9	9	3	0	5	9	1.759	8.38	53	7.51	.308	0	....	-4	0	-0.4

• SEELBACH, Chuck Charles Frederick Seelbach b: 3/20/1948, Lakewood, OH BR/TR, 6', 180 lbs. Deb: 6/29/1971

YEAR	TM-L	W	L	PCT	G	GS	CG	SH	SV	IP	H	R	ER	HR	HB	BB	SO	RAT	ERA	ERA+	CERA	OAV	BH	AVG	PR+	WS	TPW
1971	Det-A	0	0	....	5	0	0	0	0	4	6	6	6	2	1	7	1	3.250	13.50	27	20.53	.375	0	....	-4	0	-0.5
1972*	Det-A	9	8	.529	61	3	0	0	14	112	96	39	36	6	3	39	76	1.205	2.89	109	2.93	.238	3	.143	2	12	0.4
1973	Det-A	1	0	1.000	5	0	0	0	0	7	7	3	3	1	0	2	2	1.286	3.86	106	3.48	.250	0	....	0	1	0.0
1974	Det-A	0	0	....	4	0	0	0	0	7^{2}	9	4	4	2	1	3	0	1.565	4.70	81	7.15	.300	0	....	-1	0	-0.1
Total	4	10	8	.556	75	3	0	0	14	130^{2}	118	52	49	11	5	51	79	1.293	3.38	97	3.75	.247	3	.143	-3	13	-0.2

YEAR TM-L	W	L	PCT	G	GS	CG	SH	SV	IP	H	R	ER	HR	HB	BB	SO	RAT	ERA	ERA+	CERA	OAV	BH	AVG	PR+	WS	TPW
• SEGELKE, Herman	Herman Neils Segelke b: 4/24/1958, San Mateo, CA BR/TR, 6'4", 200 lbs. Deb: 4/7/1982																									
1982 Chi-N	0	0	....	3	0	0	0	0	4^{1}	6	4	4	1	0	6	4	2.769	8.31	45	11.91	.316	0	....	-2	0	-0.2
• SEGUI, Diego	Diego Pablo (Gonzalez) Segui b: 8/17/1937, Holguin, Cuba BR/TR, 6', 190 lbs. Deb: 4/12/1962																									
1962 KC-A	8	5	.615	37	13	2	0	6	116^{2}	89	53	50	16	1	46	71	1.157	3.86	108	3.05	.211	8	.235	5	11	0.7
1963 KC-A	9	6	.600	38	23	4	1	0	167	173	84	70	17	2	73	116	**1.473**	3.77	102	4.37	.267	12	.218	3	10	0.4
1964 KC-A	8	17	.320	40	35	5	2	0	217	219	118	110	30	1	94	155	1.442	4.56	84	4.52	.260	11	.155	-14	7	-1.4
1965 KC-A	5	15	.250	40	25	5	1	0	163	166	102	84	18	2	67	119	1.429	4.64	75	4.29	.261	9	.191	-20	2	-1.9
1966 Was-A	3	7	.300	21	13	1	1	0	72	82	42	40	8	0	24	54	1.472	5.00	69	4.71	.291	2	.111	-13	0	-1.4
1967 KC-A	3	4	.429	36	3	0	0	1	70	62	30	24	4	2	31	52	1.329	3.09	103	3.27	.238	0	.000	1	4	0.0
1968 Oak-A	6	5	.545	52	0	0	0	6	83	51	25	22	7	0	32	72	1.000	2.39	118	1.83	.173	1	.111	4	8	0.4
1969 Sea-A	12	6	.667	66	8	2	0	12	142^{1}	127	62	53	14	2	61	113	1.321	3.35	108	3.50	.238	4	.148	8	12	0.9
1970 Oak-A	10	10	.500	47	19	3	2	2	162	130	54	46	9	2	68	95	1.222	**2.56**	**138**	2.84	.222	5	.116	16	13	1.5
1971* Oak-A	10	8	.556	26	21	5	0	0	146^{1}	122	59	51	13	4	63	81	1.264	3.14	106	3.33	.229	4	.085	1	8	-0.1
1972 Oak-A	0	1	.000	7	3	0	0	0	22^{2}	25	10	9	2	0	7	11	1.412	3.57	80	4.28	.287	1	.143	-2	0	-0.3
StL-N	3	1	.750	33	0	0	0	9	55^{2}	47	23	19	2	0	32	54	1.419	3.07	111	3.09	.229	1	.143	2	7	0.2
1973 StL-N	7	6	.538	65	0	0	0	17	100^{1}	78	35	31	6	0	53	93	1.306	2.78	131	2.86	.211	0	.000	10	10	0.9
1974 Bos-A	6	8	.429	58	0	0	0	10	108	106	54	48	9	1	49	76	1.435	4.00	96	3.93	.257	0	....	-1	7	-0.1
1975* Bos-A	2	5	.286	33	1	1	0	6	71	71	41	38	10	0	43	45	1.606	4.82	85	5.21	.270	0	....	-6	3	-0.6
1977 Sea-A	0	7	.000	40	7	0	0	2	110^{2}	108	75	70	20	1	43	91	1.364	5.69	72	4.37	.251	0	....	-21	1	-2.1
Total 15	92	111	.453	639	171	28	7	71	1807^{2}	1656	867	765	185	18	786	1298	1.351	3.81	96	3.74	.243	58	.151	-28	103	-2.9
• SEGURA, Jose	Jose Altagracia (Mota) Segura b: 1/26/1963, Fundacion, Dominican Republic BR/TR, 5'11", 180 lbs. Deb: 4/10/1988																									
1988 Chi-A	0	0	....	4	0	0	0	0	8^{2}	19	17	13	1	0	8	2	3.115	13.50	29	14.62	.432	0	....	-9	0	-0.9
1989 Chi-A	0	1	.000	7	0	0	0	0	6	13	11	10	2	0	3	4	2.667	15.00	25	13.93	.464	0	....	-7	0	-0.8
1991 SF-N	0	1	.000	11	0	0	0	0	16^{1}	20	11	8	1	0	5	10	1.531	4.41	81	4.72	.303	0	....	-2	0	-0.2
Total 3	0	2	.000	22	0	0	0	0	31	52	39	31	4	0	16	16	2.194	9.00	42	9.27	.377	0	....	-18	0	-1.9
• SEIBOLD, Socks	Harry Seibold b: 4/3/1896, Philadelphia, PA d: 9/21/1965, Philadelphia, PA BR/TR, 5'8.5", 162 lbs. Deb: 9/18/1915 ♦																									
1916 Phi-A	1	1	.500	3	2	1	1	0	21^{2}	22	12	10	0	0	9	5	1.431	4.15	69	3.57	.272	2	.167	-3	0	-0.3
1917 Phi-A	4	16	.200	33	15	9	1	1	160	141	86	70	1	3	85	55	1.413	3.94	70	3.20	.243	13	.220	-19	3	-1.9
1919 Phi-A	2	3	.400	14	4	1	0	0	45^{2}	58	34	27	2	4	26	19	1.839	5.32	64	6.37	.322	2	.154	-8	0	-0.9
1929 Bos-N	12	17	.414	33	27	16	1	1	205^{2}	228	119	108	17	2	80	54	1.498	4.73	99	4.48	.285	20	.286	-0	13	0.4
1930 Bos-N	15	16	.484	36	33	20	1	2	251	288	135	115	16	2	85	70	1.486	4.12	120	4.32	.290	19	.211	23	20	2.0
1931 Bos-N	10	18	.357	33	29	10	3	0	206^{1}	226	122	107	12	3	65	50	1.410	4.67	81	3.94	.279	9	.129	-19	5	-2.3
1932 Bos-N	3	10	.231	28	20	6	1	0	136^{2}	173	91	71	12	2	41	33	1.566	4.68	80	5.08	.309	7	.152	-14	0	-1.6
1933 Bos-N	1	4	.200	11	5	1	0	1	36^{2}	43	18	15	0	0	14	10	1.555	3.68	83	4.10	.295	1	.111	-2	1	-0.2
Total 8	48	85	.361	191	135	64	8	5	1063^{2}	1179	617	523	60	16	405	296	1.489	4.43	87	4.27	.284	76	.192	-42	42	-4.7
• SELE, Aaron	Aaron Helmer Sele b: 6/25/1970, Golden Valley, MN BR/TR, 6'5", 218 lbs. Deb: 6/23/1993																									
1993 Bos-A	7	2	.778	18	18	0	0	0	111^{2}	100	42	34	5	7	48	93	1.325	2.74	168	3.40	.237	0	....	22	11	2.2
1994 Bos-A	8	7	.533	22	22	2	0	0	143^{1}	140	68	61	13	9	60	105	1.395	3.83	131	4.26	.261	0	....	18	11	1.6
1995 Bos-A	3	1	.750	6	6	0	0	0	32^{1}	32	14	11	3	3	14	21	1.423	3.06	159	4.35	.252	0	....	6	3	0.6
1996 Bos-A	7	11	.389	29	29	1	0	0	157^{1}	192	110	93	14	8	67	137	1.646	5.32	95	5.56	.303	0	....	-1	6	-0.1
1997 Bos-A	13	12	.520	33	33	1	0	0	177^{1}	196	115	106	25	15	80	122	1.556	5.38	86	5.47	.279	0	.000	-14	7	-1.4
1998* Tex-A★	19	11	.633	33	33	3	2	0	212^{2}	239	116	100	14	13	84	167	1.519	4.23	114	4.69	.283	1	.250	17	14	1.6
1999* Tex-A	18	9	.667	33	33	2	2	0	205	244	115	109	21	12	70	186	1.532	4.79	106	5.17	.293	0	.000	9	13	0.9
2000* Sea-A★	17	10	.630	34	34	2	2	0	211^{2}	221	110	106	17	5	74	137	1.394	4.51	101	4.06	.271	0	.000	-1	12	-0.1
2001* Sea-A	15	5	.750	34	33	2	1	0	215	216	93	86	25	7	51	114	1.242	3.60	115	3.70	.261	1	.167	7	14	0.7
2002 Ana-A	8	9	.471	26	26	1	1	0	160	190	92	87	21	7	49	82	1.494	4.89	90	5.20	.299	1	.500	-13	5	-1.3
2003 Ana-A	7	11	.389	25	25	0	0	0	121^{2}	135	82	78	17	12	58	53	1.586	5.77	75	5.77	.284	1	.333	-21	2	-2.0
Total 11	122	88	.581	293	292	14	8	0	1748	1905	957	871	175	98	655	1217	1.465	4.48	104	4.70	.278	4	.167	29	98	2.7
• SELL, Epp	Lester Elwood Sell b: 4/26/1897, Llewellyn, PA d: 2/19/1961, Reading, PA BR/TR, 6', 175 lbs. Deb: 9/1/1922																									
1922 StL-N	4	2	.667	7	5	0	0	0	33	47	26	25	2	2	6	5	1.606	6.82	57	5.60	.338	4	.333	-10	1	-0.8
1923 StL-N	0	1	.000	5	1	0	0	0	15	16	10	10	1	0	8	2	1.600	6.00	65	4.78	.291	0	.000	-3	0	-0.4
Total 2	4	3	.571	12	6	0	0	0	48	63	36	35	3	2	14	7	1.604	6.56	59	5.34	.325	4	.211	-13	1	-1.3
• SELLERS, Jeff	Jeffrey Doyle Sellers b: 5/11/1964, Compton, CA BR/TR, 6'1", 175 lbs. Deb: 9/15/1985																									
1985 Bos-A	2	0	1.000	4	4	1	0	0	22^{1}	24	10	9	1	0	7	6	1.388	3.63	118	3.64	.273	0	....	2	2	0.2
1986 Bos-A	3	7	.300	14	13	1	0	0	82	90	56	45	13	3	40	51	1.585	4.94	84	5.65	.282	0	....	-6	2	-0.6
1987 Bos-A	7	8	.467	25	22	4	2	0	139^{2}	161	85	82	10	3	61	99	1.589	5.28	86	5.05	.298	0	....	-11	6	-1.0
1988 Bos-A	1	7	.125	18	12	1	0	0	85^{2}	89	49	46	9	3	56	70	1.693	4.83	85	5.48	.268	0	....	-6	2	-0.6
Total 4	13	22	.371	61	51	7	2	0	329^{2}	364	200	182	33	9	164	226	1.602	4.97	87	5.22	.285	0	....	-21	12	-2.0
• SELLS, Dave	David Wayne Sells b: 9/18/1946, Vacaville, CA BR/TR, 5'11", 175 lbs. Deb: 8/2/1972																									
1972 Cal-A	2	0	1.000	10	0	0	0	0	16	11	6	5	0	0	5	2	1.000	2.81	103	1.58	.196	0	....	0	1	0.0
1973 Cal-A	7	2	.778	51	0	0	0	10	68	72	30	28	2	5	35	25	1.574	3.71	96	4.46	.277	0	....	-0	6	0.0
1974 Cal-A	2	3	.400	20	0	0	0	2	39	48	19	16	3	3	16	14	1.641	3.69	93	5.62	.312	0	....	-1	1	-0.1
1975 Cal-A	0	0	....	4	0	0	0	0	8^{1}	9	10	8	3	0	8	7	2.040	8.64	41	8.33	.250	0	....	-5	0	-0.5
LA-N	0	2	.000	5	0	0	0	0	7	6	3	3	2	0	3	1	1.286	3.86	88	4.56	.222	1	1.000	-0	0	0.0
Total 4	11	7	.611	90	0	0	0	12	138^{1}	146	68	60	10	8	67	49	1.540	3.90	88	4.69	.274	1	1.000	-6	8	-0.6
• SELMA, Dick	Richard Jay "Mortimer Snerd" Selma b: 11/4/1943, Santa Ana, CA d: 8/29/2001, Clovis, CA BR/TR, 5'11", 175 lbs. Deb: 9/2/1965																									
1965 NY-N	2	1	.667	4	4	1	1	0	26^{2}	22	11	11	2	1	9	26	1.163	3.71	95	2.95	.229	2	.222	-0	2	0.0
1966 NY-N	4	6	.400	30	7	0	0	1	80^{2}	84	47	38	11	3	39	58	1.525	4.24	86	5.04	.274	1	.071	-6	3	-0.5
1967 NY-N	2	4	.333	38	4	0	0	2	81^{1}	71	29	25	3	2	36	52	1.316	2.77	122	3.14	.241	2	.091	5	6	0.5
1968 NY-N	9	10	.474	33	23	4	3	0	169^{2}	148	63	52	11	5	54	117	1.191	2.76	110	2.91	.233	12	.207	3	10	0.6
1969 SD-N	2	2	.500	4	3	1	0	0	22	19	10	10	3	0	9	20	1.273	4.09	86	3.62	.229	2	.286	-1	2	-0.1
Chi-N	10	8	.556	36	25	4	2	1	168^{2}	137	74	68	13	3	72	161	1.239	3.63	111	3.05	.222	8	.154	8	11	0.8
Yr.	12	10	.545	40	28	5	2	1	190^{2}	156	84	78	16	3	81	181	1.243	3.68	107	3.11	.223	10	.169	7	13	0.7
1970 Phi-N	8	9	.471	73	0	0	0	22	134^{1}	108	42	41	8	4	59	153	1.243	2.75	145	2.98	.226	3	.150	20	21	1.9
1971 Phi-N	0	2	.000	17	0	0	0	1	24^{2}	21	9	9	2	2	8	15	1.176	3.28	107	3.20	.231	1	1.000	0	2	0.1
1972 Phi-N	2	9	.182	46	10	1	0	3	98^{2}	91	67	61	13	5	73	58	1.662	5.56	65	5.22	.249	4	.200	-23	0	-2.4
1973 Phi-N	1	1	.500	6	0	0	0	0	8	6	5	5	1	0	5	4	1.375	5.63	67	3.84	.240	0	....	-2	0	-0.2
1974 Cal-A	2	2	.500	18	0	0	0	1	23	22	13	13	2	1	17	15	1.696	5.09	68	5.34	.272	0	....	-4	0	-0.4
Mil-A	0	0	....	2	0	0	0	0	2^{1}	5	5	5	0	1	0	2	2.143	19.29	19	10.38	.455	0	....	-4	0	-0.4
Yr.	2	2	.500	20	0	0	0	1	25^{1}	27	18	18	2	2	17	17	1.737	6.39	54	5.80	.293	0	....	-8	0	-0.8
Total 10	42	54	.438	307	76	11	6	31	840	734	375	338	69	27	381	681	1.327	3.62	99	3.57	.238	35	.172	-3	57	-0.2
• SEMBERA, Carroll	Carroll William Sembera b: 7/26/1941, Shiner, TX BR/TR, 6', 155 lbs. Deb: 9/28/1965																									
1965 Hou-N	0	1	.000	2	1	0	0	0	7^{1}	5	3	3	0	0	3	4	1.091	3.68	91	1.82	.185	0	.000	-0	0	0.0
1966 Hou-N	1	2	.333	24	0	0	0	1	33	36	11	11	3	0	16	21	1.576	3.00	114	5.00	.288	0	.000	2	2	0.2
1967 Hou-N	2	6	.250	45	0	0	0	3	59^{2}	66	39	32	7	1	19	48	1.425	4.83	69	4.25	.269	1	.143	-9	1	-1.0
1969 Mon-N	0	2	.000	23	0	0	0	2	33	28	14	13	1	2	24	15	1.576	3.55	104	4.08	.246	1	.250	1	2	0.1
1970 Mon-N	0	0	....	5	0	0	0	0	6^{2}	14	14	14	2	1	11	6	3.750	18.90	22	18.95	.424	0	....	-11	0	-1.1
Total 5	3	11	.214	99	1	0	0	6	139^{2}	149	81	73	13	4	73	94	1.589	4.70	75	4.96	.274	2	.133	-17	5	-1.8
• SEMINARA, Frank	Frank Peter Seminara b: 5/16/1967, Brooklyn, NY BR/TR, 6'2", 205 lbs. Deb: 6/2/1992																									
1992 SD-N	9	4	.692	19	18	0	0	0	100^{1}	98	46	41	5	3	46	61	1.435	3.68	97	3.91	.257	4	.118	-1	6	-0.2

YEAR	TM-L	W	L	PCT	G	GS	CG	SH	SV	IP	H	R	ER	HR	HB	BB	SO	RAT	ERA	ERA+	CERA	OAV	BH	AVG	PR+	WS	TPW
1993	SD-N	3	3	.500	18	7	0	0	0	46^1	53	30	23	5	3	21	22	1.597	4.47	93	5.31	.294	2	.200	-2	1	-0.1
1994	NY-N	0	2	.000	10	1	0	0	0	17	20	12	11	2	0	8	7	1.647	5.82	72	5.71	.303	0	.000	-3	0	-0.3
Total	**3**	**12**	**9**	**.571**	**47**	**26**	**0**	**0**	**0**	**163^2**	**171**	**88**	**75**	**12**	**6**	**75**	**90**	**1.503**	**4.12**	**93**	**4.49**	**.273**	**6**	**.128**	**-5**	**7**	**-0.7**
• SEMPROCH, Ray	Roman Anthony "Baby" Semproch b: 1/7/1931, Cleveland, OH BR/TR, 5'11", 180 lbs. Deb: 4/15/1958																										
1958	Phi-N	13	11	.542	36	30	12	2	0	204^1	211	105	89	25	6	58	92	1.316	3.92	101	4.05	.264	7	.095	4	10	0.0
1959	Phi-N	3	10	.231	30	18	2	0	3	111^2	119	76	67	12	3	59	54	1.594	5.40	76	5.14	.277	6	.176	-16	1	-1.6
1960	Det-A	3	0	1.000	17	0	0	0	0	27	29	17	12	2	0	16	9	1.667	4.00	103	4.99	.269	0	.000	0	2	0.0
1961	LA-A	0	0	....	2	0	0	0	0	1	1	2	1	0	0	3	1	4.000	9.00	50	13.82	.333	0	....	-0	0	0.0
Total	**4**	**19**	**21**	**.475**	**85**	**48**	**14**	**2**	**3**	**344**	**360**	**200**	**169**	**39**	**9**	**136**	**156**	**1.442**	**4.42**	**91**	**4.51**	**.269**	**13**	**.116**	**-11**	**13**	**-1.7**
• SENTENEY, Steve	Stephen Leonard Senteney b: 8/7/1955, Indianapolis, IN d: 6/18/1989, Colusa, CA BR/TR, 6'2", 205 lbs. Deb: 6/6/1982																										
1982	Tor-A	0	0	....	11	0	0	0	0	22	23	16	12	5	0	6	20	1.318	4.91	91	4.27	.247	0	....	-1	0	-0.1
• SEO, Jae Weong	Jae Weong Seo b: 5/24/1977, Kwangju, South Korea BR/TR, 6'1", 215 lbs. Deb: 7/21/2002																										
2002	NY-N	0	0	....	1	0	0	0	0	1	0	0	0	0	0	0	1	.000	0.00	....	0.00	.000	0	....	0	0	0.0
2003	NY-N	9	12	.429	32	31	0	0	0	188^1	193	94	80	18	6	46	110	1.269	3.82	109	3.54	.260	5	.098	8	9	0.6
Total	**2**	**9**	**12**	**.429**	**33**	**31**	**0**	**0**	**0**	**189^1**	**193**	**94**	**80**	**18**	**6**	**46**	**111**	**1.262**	**3.80**	**109**	**3.52**	**.260**	**5**	**.098**	**8**	**9**	**0.7**
• SEOANE, Manny	Manuel Modesto Seoane b: 6/26/1955, Tampa, FL BR/TR, 6'3", 187 lbs. Deb: 9/18/1977																										
1977	Phi-N	0	0	....	2	1	0	0	0	6	11	4	4	0	0	3	4	2.333	6.00	67	9.22	.407	1	.500	-1	0	-0.1
1978	Chi-N	1	0	1.000	7	1	0	0	0	8^1	11	6	5	0	0	6	5	2.040	5.40	75	5.64	.297	0	....	-1	0	-0.1
Total	**2**	**1**	**0**	**1.000**	**9**	**2**	**0**	**0**	**0**	**14^1**	**22**	**10**	**9**	**0**	**0**	**9**	**9**	**2.163**	**5.65**	**71**	**7.14**	**.344**	**1**	**.500**	**-3**	**0**	**-0.2**
• SERAD, Billy	William I. Serad b: 1863, Philadelphia, PA d: 11/1/1925, Chester, PA BR/TR, 5'7", 156 lbs. Deb: 5/5/1884 U																										
1884	Buf-N	16	20	.444	37	37	34	2	0	308	373	285	146	21	....	111	150	**1.571**	4.27	74	....	.284	24	.175	-33	9	-3.5
1885	Buf-N	7	21	.250	30	29	27	0	0	241^1	299	194	110	5	....	80	90	**1.570**	4.10	73	....	.290	16	.154	-15	5	-1.8
1887	Cin-a	10	11	.476	22	21	20	2	1	187^1	281	139	85	7	8	80	34	1.500	4.08	106	....	.335	17	.207	-3	15	-0.5
1888	Cin-a	2	3	.400	6	5	5	0	0	50^2	62	43	20	1	6	19	4	1.599	3.55	89	....	.291	3	.130	-3	1	-0.4
Total	**4**	**35**	**55**	**.389**	**95**	**92**	**86**	**4**	**1**	**787^1**	**1015**	**661**	**361**	**34**	**14**	**290**	**278**	**1.556**	**4.13**	**80**	**....**	**.299**	**60**	**.173**	**-54**	**30**	**-6.3**
• SERAFINI, Dan	Daniel Joseph Serafini b: 1/25/1974, San Francisco, CA BB/TL, 6'1", 185 lbs. Deb: 6/25/1996																										
1996	Min-A	0	1	.000	1	1	0	0	0	4^1	7	5	5	1	1	2	1	2.077	10.38	49	10.22	.368	0	....	-3	0	-0.2
1997	Min-A	2	1	.667	6	4	1	0	0	26^1	27	11	10	1	0	11	15	1.443	3.42	136	3.98	.273	0	....	4	2	0.3
1998	Min-A	7	4	.636	28	9	0	0	0	75	95	58	54	10	1	29	46	1.653	6.48	74	5.82	.310	0	.000	-13	2	-1.2
1999	Chi-N	3	2	.600	42	4	0	0	1	62^1	86	51	48	9	1	32	17	1.893	6.93	65	7.11	.333	1	.083	-16	0	-1.5
2000	SD-N	0	0	....	3	0	0	0	0	3	9	6	6	2	0	2	3	3.667	18.00	24	25.94	.500	0	....	-5	0	-0.4
	Pit-N	2	5	.286	11	11	0	0	0	62^1	70	35	34	9	4	26	32	1.540	4.91	94	5.44	.292	2	.083	-1	2	-0.3
	Yr.	2	5	.286	14	11	0	0	0	65^1	79	41	40	11	4	28	35	1.638	5.51	83	6.38	.306	2	.083	-6	2	-0.7
2003	Cin-N	1	3	.250	10	4	0	0	0	30	41	23	18	5	0	14	13	1.833	5.40	79	7.08	.336	0	.000	-4	0	-0.4
Total	**6**	**15**	**16**	**.484**	**101**	**33**	**1**	**0**	**1**	**263^1**	**335**	**189**	**175**	**37**	**7**	**116**	**127**	**1.713**	**5.98**	**77**	**6.30**	**.315**	**3**	**.070**	**-38**	**6**	**-3.8**
• SERRANO, Wascar	Wascar Radames Serrano b: 6/2/1978, Santo Domingo, Dominican Republic BR/TR, 6'2", 178 lbs. Deb: 5/12/2001																										
2001	SD-N	3	3	.500	20	5	0	0	0	46^2	60	37	34	7	2	21	39	1.736	6.56	61	6.39	.313	1	.111	-12	0	-1.3
• SERUM, Gary	Gary Wayne Serum b: 10/24/1956, Fargo, ND BR/TR, 6'1", 180 lbs. Deb: 7/22/1977																										
1977	Min-A	0	0	....	8	0	0	0	0	22^2	22	11	11	4	2	10	14	1.412	4.37	91	5.08	.268	0	....	-1	1	-0.1
1978	Min-A	9	9	.500	34	23	6	1	1	184^1	188	88	84	14	3	44	80	1.259	4.10	93	3.43	.266	0	....	-6	8	-0.7
1979	Min-A	1	3	.250	20	5	0	0	0	64	93	47	47	10	0	20	31	1.766	6.61	66	7.10	.354	0	....	-16	0	-1.5
Total	**3**	**10**	**12**	**.455**	**62**	**28**	**6**	**1**	**1**	**271**	**303**	**146**	**142**	**28**	**5**	**74**	**125**	**1.391**	**4.72**	**85**	**4.44**	**.288**	**0**	**....**	**-23**	**9**	**-2.3**
• SERVICE, Scott	Scott David Service b: 2/26/1967, Cincinnati, OH BR/TR, 6'6", 226 lbs. Deb: 9/5/1988																										
1988	Phi-N	0	0	....	5	0	0	0	0	5^1	7	1	1	0	1	1	6	1.500	1.69	211	5.34	.333	0	....	1	1	0.1
1992	Mon-N	0	0	....	5	0	0	0	0	7	15	11	11	1	0	5	11	2.857	14.14	24	13.24	.417	0	.000	-8	0	-0.9
1993	Col-N	0	0	....	3	0	0	0	0	4^2	8	5	5	1	1	1	3	1.929	9.64	49	9.48	.400	0	....	-2	0	-0.2
	Cin-N	2	2	.500	26	0	0	0	2	41^1	36	19	17	5	1	15	40	1.234	3.70	109	3.31	.235	1	.143	2	3	0.2
	Yr.	2	2	.500	29	0	0	0	2	46	44	24	22	6	2	16	43	1.304	4.30	97	3.94	.254	1	.143	-1	3	-0.1
1994	Cin-N	1	2	.333	6	0	0	0	0	7^1	8	9	6	2	0	3	5	1.500	7.36	56	5.42	.267	0	....	-3	0	-0.3
1995	SF-N	3	1	.750	28	0	0	0	0	31	18	11	11	4	2	20	30	1.226	3.19	128	3.04	.176	0	.000	3	3	0.3
1996	Cin-N	1	0	1.000	34	1	0	0	0	48	51	21	21	7	6	18	46	1.438	3.94	106	5.07	.277	0	.000	1	3	0.0
1997	Cin-N	0	0	....	4	0	0	0	0	5^1	11	7	7	1	0	1	3	2.250	11.81	36	11.35	.458	0	....	-4	0	-0.4
	KC-A	0	3	.000	12	0	0	0	0	17	17	9	9	1	0	5	19	1.294	4.76	99	3.53	.274	0	....	-0	1	0.0
1998	KC-A	6	4	.600	73	0	0	0	4	82^2	70	35	32	7	9	34	95	1.258	3.48	138	3.52	.231	0	.000	13	11	1.2
1999	KC-A	5	5	.500	68	0	0	0	8	75^1	87	51	51	13	3	42	68	1.712	6.09	82	6.14	.294	0	....	-11	3	-1.0
2000	Oak-A	1	2	.333	20	0	0	0	1	36^2	45	31	26	5	1	19	35	1.745	6.38	74	6.22	.302	0	....	-6	0	-0.6
2003	Ari-N	0	2	.000	18	0	0	0	1	18^1	21	10	10	1	0	2	18	1.255	4.91	95	3.32	.288	0	....	-0	1	0.0
	Tor-A	0	0	....	15	0	0	0	0	16	17	8	8	3	0	6	17	1.438	4.50	102	5.00	.274	0	....	0	1	0.0
Total	**11**	**19**	**21**	**.475**	**317**	**1**	**0**	**0**	**16**	**396**	**411**	**228**	**215**	**51**	**24**	**172**	**396**	**1.472**	**4.89**	**92**	**4.86**	**.271**	**1**	**.063**	**-15**	**27**	**-1.6**
• SETTLEMIRE, Merle	Edgar Merle "Lefty" Settlemire b: 1/19/1903, Santa Fe, OH d: 6/12/1988, Russells Point, OH BL/TL, 5'9", 156 lbs. Deb: 4/13/1928																										
1928	Bos-A	0	6	.000	30	9	0	0	0	82^1	116	62	50	2	6	34	12	1.822	5.47	75	6.05	.345	3	.176	-13	0	-1.3
• SEVERINSEN, Al	Albert Henry Severinsen b: 11/9/1944, Brooklyn, NY BR/TR, 6'3", 220 lbs. Deb: 7/1/1969																										
1969	Bal-A	1	1	.500	12	0	0	0	0	19^2	14	6	5	2	0	10	13	1.220	2.29	156	2.79	.206	1	.333	2	2	0.2
1971	SD-N	2	5	.286	59	0	0	0	8	70	77	30	27	4	2	30	31	1.529	3.47	95	4.36	.292	0	.000	-1	4	-0.1
1972	SD-N	0	1	.000	17	0	0	0	1	21^1	13	8	6	1	2	7	9	.938	2.53	130	1.78	.173	0	.000	2	2	0.2
Total	**3**	**3**	**7**	**.300**	**88**	**0**	**0**	**0**	**9**	**111**	**104**	**44**	**38**	**7**	**4**	**47**	**53**	**1.360**	**3.08**	**108**	**3.59**	**.256**	**1**	**.200**	**3**	**8**	**0.4**
• SEWARD, Ed	Edward William Seward b: 6/29/1867, Cleveland, OH d: 7/30/1947, Cleveland, OH TR, 5'7", 175 lbs. Deb: 9/30/1885 U ♦																										
1885	Pro-N	0	0	....	1	0	0	0	0	6	2	0	0	0	....	0	1	.333	0.00	....	....	.099	0	.000	2	1	0.1
1887	Phi-a	25	25	.500	55	52	52	3	0	470^2	585	293	216	7	24	140	155	1.243	4.13	104	....	.294	66	.234	4	33	-0.5
1888	Phi-a	35	19	.648	57	57	57	**6**	0	518^2	388	203	116	4	22	127	**272**	.993	2.01	148	....	.201	32	.142	54	42	4.6
1889	Phi-a	21	15	.583	39	38	35	3	0	320	353	212	141	8	13	101	102	1.419	3.97	95	....	.271	31	.217	-18	21	-1.0
1890	Phi-a	6	12	.333	21	19	15	1	0	154	165	105	81	4	7	72	55	1.539	4.73	81	....	.266	10	.139	-7	6	-0.7
1891	Cle-N	2	1	.667	3	3	0	0	0	16^1	16	10	7	0	0	11	4	1.653	3.86	90	....	.247	4	.211	-1	1	-0.1
Total	**6**	**89**	**72**	**.553**	**176**	**169**	**159**	**13**	**0**	**1485^2**	**1509**	**823**	**561**	**23**	**66**	**451**	**589**	**1.225**	**3.40**	**110**	**....**	**.255**	**143**	**.192**	**35**	**104**	**2.5**
• SEWARD, Frank	Frank Martin Seward b: 4/7/1921, Pennsauken, NJ BR/TR, 6'3", 200 lbs. Deb: 9/28/1943																										
1943	NY-N	0	1	.000	1	1	1	0	0	9	12	3	3	0	0	5	2	1.889	3.00	115	5.83	.324	0	.000	1	0	0.0
1944	NY-N	3	2	.600	25	7	2	0	0	78^1	98	51	47	8	2	32	16	1.660	5.40	68	5.56	.306	2	.083	-16	1	-1.8
Total	**2**	**3**	**3**	**.500**	**26**	**8**	**3**	**0**	**0**	**87^1**	**110**	**54**	**50**	**8**	**2**	**37**	**18**	**1.683**	**5.15**	**71**	**5.58**	**.308**	**2**	**.071**	**-15**	**1**	**-1.8**
• SEWELL, Rip	Truett Banks Sewell b: 5/11/1907, Decatur, AL d: 9/3/1989, Plant City, FL BL/TR, 6'1", 180 lbs. Deb: 6/14/1932 C																										
1932	Det-A	0	0	....	5	0	0	0	0	10^2	19	15	15	2	0	8	2	2.531	12.66	37	10.99	.388	1	.500	-10	0	-0.9
1938	Pit-N	0	1	.000	17	0	0	0	1	38^1	41	27	18	3	2	21	17	1.617	4.23	90	4.91	.275	1	.083	-2	0	-0.4
1939	Pit-N	10	9	.526	52	12	5	1	2	176^1	177	93	80	10	1	73	69	1.418	4.08	94	3.76	.265	11	.200	-1	10	0.0
1940	Pit-N	16	5	.762	33	23	14	2	1	189^2	169	71	59	6	3	67	60	1.244	2.80	136	2.84	.238	14	.192	27	15	2.9
1941	Pit-N	14	17	.452	39	32	18	2	2	249	225	126	103	18	3	84	76	1.241	3.72	97	3.04	.235	16	.174	-0	12	0.0
1942	Pit-N	17	15	.531	40	33	18	5	2	248	259	117	94	13	2	72	69	1.335	3.41	99	3.47	.265	13	.149	2	13	0.1
1943	Pit-N★	**21**	9	.700	35	31	**25**	2	3	265^1	267	94	75	6	2	75	65	1.289	2.54	137	3.10	.260	30	.286	28	23	**3.6**
1944	Pit-N★	21	12	.636	38	33	24	3	2	286	263	112	101	15	3	99	87	1.266	3.18	117	3.01	.240	25	.223	20	24	2.3

YEAR TM-L	W	L	PCT	G	GS	CG	SH	SV	IP	H	R	ER	HR	HB	BB	SO	RAT	ERA	ERA+	CERA	OAV	BH	AVG	PR+	WS	TPW
1945 Pit-N★	11	9	.550	33	24	9	1	1	188	212	116	85	9	2	91	60	1.612	4.07	97	4.57	.279	20	.313	-1	10	0.6
1946 Pit-N★	8	12	.400	25	20	11	2	0	149^1	140	68	61	6	1	53	33	1.292	3.68	96	3.03	.245	9	.180	-0	8	0.0
1947 Pit-N	6	4	.600	24	12	4	1	0	121	121	58	48	11	3	36	36	1.298	3.57	118	3.70	.263	5	.125	10	7	0.8
1948 Pit-N	13	3	.813	21	17	7	0	0	121^2	126	51	47	9	1	37	36	1.340	3.48	117	3.64	.263	6	.143	7	11	0.9
1949 Pit-N	6	1	.857	28	6	2	1	1	76	82	35	33	8	0	32	26	1.500	3.91	108	4.61	.280	1	.063	3	6	0.3
Total 13	143	97	.596	390	243	137	20	15	2119^1	2101	983	819	116	23	748	636	1.344	3.48	108	3.47	.256	152	.203	82	139	10.2
• SEXAUER, Elmer	Elmer George Sexauer b: 5/21/1926, St. Louis County, MO BR/TR, 6'4", 220 lbs. Deb: 9/6/1948																									
1948 Bro-N	0	0	....	2	0	0	0	0	0^2	0	1	1	0	0	2	0	3.000	13.50	30	5.85	.000	0	....	-1	0	-0.1
• SEXTON, Frank	Frank Joseph Sexton b: 7/8/1872, Brockton, MA d: 1/4/1938, Brighton, MA, 160 lbs. Deb: 6/21/1895																									
1895 Bos-N	1	5	.167	7	5	4	0	0	49	59	39	31	2	2	22	14	1.653	5.69	88	5.03	.294	5	.227	-4	2	-0.4
• SEYFRIED, Gordon	Gordon Clay Seyfried b: 7/4/1937, Long Beach, CA BR/TR, 6', 185 lbs. Deb: 9/13/1963																									
1963 Cle-A	0	1	.000	3	1	0	0	0	7^1	9	2	1	0	0	3	1	1.636	1.23	295	4.28	.300	0	.000	2	1	0.2
1964 Cle-A	0	0	....	2	0	0	0	0	2^1	4	0	0	0	0	0	0	1.714	0.00	....	6.33	.444	0	....	1	0	0.1
Total 2	0	1	.000	5	1	0	0	0	9^2	13	2	1	0	0	3	1	1.655	0.93	389	4.78	.333	0	.000	3	1	0.3
• SEYMOUR, Cy	James Bentley Seymour b: 12/9/1872, Albany, NY d: 9/20/1919, New York, NY BL/TL, 6', 200 lbs. Deb: 4/22/1896 ♦																									
1896 NY-N	2	4	.333	11	8	4	0	0	70^1	75	75	50	8	0	51	33	1.791	6.40	66	5.70	.271	7	.219	-18	0	-1.6
1897 NY-N	18	14	.563	38	33	28	2	1	277^2	254	161	104	4	21	164	**156**	1.505	3.37	123	3.82	**.242**	34	.241	24	21	2.0
1898 NY-N	25	19	.568	45	43	39	4	0	356^2	313	199	126	4	32	213	**239**	1.475	3.18	109	3.66	.234	82	.276	12	26	1.2
1899 NY-N	14	18	.438	32	32	31	0	0	268^1	247	139	106	5	21	170	142	1.554	3.56	105	4.03	.245	52	.327	3	21	1.0
1900 NY-N	2	1	.667	13	7	2	0	0	53	58	54	41	4	10	54	19	2.113	6.96	52	7.38	.278	12	.300	-20	1	-1.8
1902 Cin-N	0	0	....	1	0	0	0	0	3	4	3	3	0	0	3	2	2.333	9.00	33	7.37	.319	83	.340	-2	10	0.6
Total 6	61	56	.521	140	123	104	6	1	1029	951	631	430	25	84	655	591	1.561	3.76	100	4.14	.244	1724	.303	-1	79	1.4
• SEYMOUR, Jake	Jacob Seymour b: 1854, Pittsburgh, PA d: 8/1/1897, Allegheny, PA Deb: 9/23/1882																									
1882 Pit-a	0	1	.000	1	1	1	0	0	8	16	13	7	0	....	2	2	2.250	7.88	33	....	.392	0	.000	-5	0	-0.5
• SHAFFER, John	John W. "Cannon Ball" Shaffer b: 2/18/1864, Lock Haven, PA d: 11/21/1926, Endicott, NY, 5'10" Deb: 9/13/1886																									
1886 NY-a	5	3	.625	8	8	8	1	0	69	40	29	15	0	1	29	36	1.000	1.96	174	....	.161	6	.240	10	7	1.0
1887 NY-a	2	11	.154	13	13	13	0	0	112	201	119	77	3	11	53	22	1.795	6.19	69	....	.376	9	.184	-21	1	-1.9
Total 2	7	14	.333	21	21	21	1	0	181	241	148	92	3	12	82	58	1.492	4.57	89	....	.308	15	.203	-11	8	-0.9
• SHALLIX, Gus	August Shallix b: 3/29/1858, Paderborn, Germany d: 10/28/1937, Cincinnati, OH BR/TR, 5'11", 165 lbs. Deb: 6/22/1884																									
1884 Cin-a	11	10	.524	23	23	23	0	0	199^2	163	113	82	6	26	53	78	1.082	3.70	90	....	.211	3	.036	-12	10	-2.0
1885 Cin-a	6	4	.600	13	12	7	0	0	91^1	95	59	33	1	13	33	15	1.401	3.25	100	....	.257	5	.128	-1	6	-0.3
Total 2	17	14	.548	36	35	30	0	0	291	258	172	115	7	39	86	93	1.182	3.56	93	....	.226	8	.065	-13	16	-2.2
• SHANAHAN, Greg	Paul Gregory Shanahan b: 12/11/1947, Eureka, CA BR/TR, 6'2", 190 lbs. Deb: 9/4/1973																									
1973 LA-N	0	0	....	7	0	0	0	1	15^2	14	6	6	2	0	4	11	1.149	3.45	100	3.01	.230	0	.000	-0	1	0.0
1974 LA-N	0	0	....	4	0	0	0	0	7	7	3	3	1	0	5	2	1.714	3.86	88	5.37	.259	0	....	-0	0	0.0
Total 2	0	0	....	11	0	0	0	1	22^2	21	9	9	3	0	9	13	1.324	3.57	96	3.74	.239	0	.000	-1	1	0.0
• SHANK, Harvey	Harvey Tillman Shank b: 7/29/1946, Toronto, Canada BR/TR, 6'4", 220 lbs. Deb: 5/16/1970																									
1970 Cal-A	0	0	....	1	0	0	0	0	3	2	0	0	0	0	2	1	1.333	0.00	....	2.54	.182	0	....	1	0	0.1
• SHANNER, Bill	Wilfred William Shanner b: 11/4/1894, Oakland City, IN d: 12/18/1986, Evansville, IN BL/TR Deb: 10/1/1920																									
1920 Phi-A	0	0	....	1	0	0	0	0	4	6	4	3	2	0	1	1	1.750	6.75	60	9.99	.353	0	.000	-1	0	-0.1
• SHANTZ, Bobby	Robert Clayton Shantz b: 9/26/1925, Pottstown, PA BR/TL, 5'6", 142 lbs. Deb: 5/1/1949																									
1949 Phi-A	6	8	.429	33	7	4	1	2	127	100	50	48	9	3	74	58	1.370	3.40	121	3.42	.221	7	.189	7	11	0.8
1950 Phi-A	8	14	.364	36	23	6	1	0	214^2	251	122	110	18	7	85	93	1.565	4.61	99	4.97	.294	11	.167	-0	10	0.0
1951 Phi-A★	18	10	.643	32	25	13	3	0	205^1	213	96	90	15	5	70	77	1.378	3.94	108	3.95	.270	18	.250	4	15	0.6
1952 Phi-A★	**24**	7	.774	33	33	27	5	0	279^2	230	87	77	21	4	63	152	1.048	2.48	160	2.39	.225	19	.198	**50**	**33**	**5.3**
1953 Phi-A	5	9	.357	16	16	6	0	0	105^2	107	52	48	10	0	26	58	1.259	4.09	105	3.49	.263	9	.237	3	7	0.4
1954 Phi-A	1	0	1.000	2	1	0	0	0	8	12	7	7	2	1	3	3	1.875	7.88	50	9.00	.364	1	.333	-3	0	-0.3
1955 KC-A	5	10	.333	23	17	4	1	0	125	124	70	63	8	1	66	58	1.520	4.54	92	4.18	.264	6	.146	-4	5	-0.6
1956 KC-A	2	7	.222	45	2	1	0	9	101^1	95	51	49	12	3	37	67	1.303	4.35	99	3.83	.248	2	.091	-1	7	-0.3
1957* NY-A★	11	5	.688	30	21	9	1	5	173	157	58	47	15	6	40	72	1.139	**2.45**	**147**	3.08	.248	10	.179	20	15	2.3
1958 NY-A	7	6	.538	33	13	3	0	0	126	127	52	47	8	2	35	80	1.286	3.36	105	3.37	.262	8	.229	0	7	0.2
1959 NY-A	7	3	.700	33	4	2	2	3	94^2	64	33	25	4	0	33	66	1.025	2.38	153	1.82	.189	5	.217	13	9	1.5
1960* NY-A	5	4	.556	42	0	0	0	11	67^2	57	24	21	5	2	24	54	1.197	2.79	128	2.92	.235	1	.100	4	8	0.4
1961 Pit-N	6	3	.667	43	6	2	1	2	89^1	91	38	33	5	4	26	61	1.310	3.32	120	3.56	.271	7	.438	6	8	1.0
1962 Hou-N	1	1	.500	3	3	1	0	0	20^2	15	4	3	1	0	5	14	.968	1.31	286	1.90	.208	0	.000	6	2	0.5
StL-N	5	3	.625	28	0	0	0	4	57^2	45	22	14	7	1	20	47	1.127	2.18	195	2.84	.211	2	.154	13	7	1.2
Yr.	6	4	.600	31	3	1	0	4	78^1	60	26	17	8	1	25	61	1.085	1.95	213	2.59	.211	2	.095	19	9	1.7
1963 StL-N	6	4	.600	55	0	0	0	11	79^1	55	28	23	6	2	17	70	.908	2.61	136	1.70	.192	1	.143	8	11	0.9
1964 StL-N	1	3	.250	16	0	0	0	0	17^1	14	6	6	2	0	7	12	1.212	3.12	122	2.89	.226	0	....	1	1	0.2
Chi-N	0	1	.000	20	0	0	0	1	11^1	15	7	7	2	0	6	12	1.853	5.56	67	6.68	.319	0	....	-2	0	-0.2
Phi-N	1	1	.500	14	0	0	0	0	32	23	10	8	1	0	6	18	.906	2.25	154	1.47	.204	0	.000	4	3	0.4
Yr.	2	5	.286	50	0	0	0	1	60^2	52	23	21	5	0	19	42	1.170	3.12	117	2.85	.234	0	.000	3	4	0.4
Total 16	119	99	.546	537	171	78	15	48	1935^2	1795	817	726	151	41	643	1072	1.260	3.38	120	3.35	.248	107	.195	128	159	14.3
• SHARROTT, George	George Oscar Sharrott b: 11/2/1869, West New Brighton, NY d: 1/6/1932, Jamaica, NY BL/TL, 5'8", 164 lbs. Deb: 7/27/1893																									
1893 Bro-N	4	6	.400	13	10	10	0	1	95	114	80	62	3	8	58	24	1.811	5.87	75	5.68	.289	9	.231	-14	3	-1.1
1894 Bro-N	0	1	.000	3	3	2	0	0	18	25	21	7	0	5	5	7	1.667	3.50	141	6.03	.326	1	.333	3	0	0.2
Total 2	4	7	.364	16	13	12	0	1	113	139	101	69	3	13	63	31	1.788	5.50	81	5.74	.295	10	.238	-11	3	-0.9
• SHARROTT, Jack	John Henry Sharrott b: 8/13/1869, Bangor, ME d: 12/31/1927, Los Angeles, CA BR/TR, 5'9", 165 lbs. Deb: 4/22/1890 ♦																									
1890 NY-N	11	10	.524	25	19	18	0	0	184	162	107	59	3	9	88	84	1.359	2.89	121	....	.230	22	.202	11	11	0.4
1891 NY-N	5	5	.500	10	9	6	0	1	69^1	47	32	20	2	4	35	41	1.183	2.60	123	....	.185	10	.333	4	6	0.7
1892 NY-N	0	0	....	1	0	0	0	0	2	2	1	1	0	0	1	1	1.500	4.50	71	3.61	.250	1	.125	-0	0	-0.2
1893 Phi-N	4	2	.667	12	4	2	0	0	56	53	43	28	1	4	33	11	1.536	4.50	102	3.99	.242	38	.250	-0	4	-0.9
Total 4	20	17	.541	48	32	26	0	1	311^1	264	183	108	6	17	157	137	1.352	3.12	117	0.74	.222	71	.237	14	21	0.0
• SHAUTE, Joe	Joseph Benjamin "Lefty" Shaute b: 8/1/1899, Peckville, PA d: 2/21/1970, Scranton, PA BL/TL, 6', 190 lbs. Deb: 7/6/1922																									
1922 Cle-A	0	0	....	2	0	0	0	0	3^2	7	8	8	2	0	3	3	2.727	19.64	20	15.96	.389	0	.000	-6	0	-0.8
1923 Cle-A	10	8	.556	33	16	7	0	0	172	176	93	67	4	1	53	61	1.331	3.51	113	3.33	.275	11	.162	10	9	0.7
1924 Cle-A	20	17	.541	46	34	21	2	2	283	317	138	118	8	6	83	68	1.413	3.75	114	3.81	.287	34	.318	20	22	2.7
1925 Cle-A	4	12	.250	26	17	10	1	4	131	160	91	79	6	1	44	34	1.557	5.43	81	4.57	.304	16	.302	-14	6	-1.0
1926 Cle-A	14	10	.583	34	25	15	1	1	206^2	215	92	81	9	3	65	47	1.355	3.53	115	3.68	.278	20	.274	7	16	1.1
1927 Cle-A	9	16	.360	45	28	14	0	2	230^1	255	140	108	9	2	75	63	1.433	4.22	99	3.88	.286	27	.325	1	13	0.6
1928 Cle-A	13	17	.433	36	31	21	1	2	253^2	295	145	114	9	6	68	81	1.431	4.04	102	3.98	.299	21	.228	4	15	0.8
1929 Cle-A	8	8	.500	26	24	8	0	0	162	211	100	77	6	1	52	43	1.623	4.28	104	4.96	.320	17	.293	4	10	0.7
1930 Cle-A	0	0	....	4	0	0	0	0	4^2	8	10	8	0	0	4	2	2.571	15.43	31	8.40	.333	0	....	-5	0	-0.5
1931 Bro-N	11	8	.579	25	19	6	0	0	128^2	162	87	69	9	1	32	50	1.508	4.83	79	4.68	.305	8	.178	-13	4	-1.3
1932 Bro-N	7	7	.500	34	9	1	0	4	117	147	67	59	8	2	21	32	1.436	4.54	84	4.36	.301	9	.200	-10	6	-0.8
1933 Bro-N	3	4	.429	41	4	0	0	2	108^1	125	63	42	4	1	31	26	1.440	3.49	92	3.94	.287	6	.222	-1	4	0.1

YEAR TM-L	W	L	PCT	G	GS	CG	SH	SV	IP	H	R	ER	HR	HB	BB	SO	RAT	ERA	ERA+	CERA	OAV	BH	AVG	PR+	WS	TPW
1934 Cin-N	0	2	.000	8	1	0	0	1	17^1	19	9	8	1	0	3	2	1.269	4.15	98	3.31	.268	1	.250	0	1	0.0
Total 13	99	109	.476	360	208	103	5	18	1818^1	2097	1043	838	75	24	534	512	1.447	4.15	98	4.08	.293	170	.258	-2	106	2.2
• SHAVER, Jeff	Jeffrey Thomas Shaver b: 7/30/1963, Beaver, PA BR/TR, 6'3", 195 lbs. Deb: 7/6/1988																									
1988 Oak-A	0	0	....	1	0	0	0	0	1	0	0	0	0	1	0	0	.000	0.00	....	0.95	.000	0	....	0	0	0.0
• SHAW, Bob	Robert John Shaw b: 6/29/1933, Bronx, NY BR/TR, 6'2", 195 lbs. Deb: 8/11/1957 C																									
1957 Det-A	0	1	.000	7	0	0	0	0	9^2	11	9	8	2	0	7	4	1.862	7.45	52	6.92	.289	0	.000	-4	0	-0.4
1958 Det-A	1	2	.333	11	2	0	0	0	26^2	32	16	15	2	0	13	17	1.688	5.06	80	5.24	.302	3	.375	-3	1	-0.2
Chi-A	4	2	.667	29	3	0	0	1	64	67	33	33	8	2	28	18	1.484	4.64	78	4.77	.271	0	.000	-8	2	-0.9
Yr.	5	4	.556	40	5	0	0	1	90^2	99	49	48	10	2	41	35	1.544	4.76	79	4.91	.280	3	.136	-11	3	-1.2
1959* Chi-A	18	6	.750	47	26	8	3	3	230^2	217	72	69	15	6	54	89	1.175	2.69	139	2.97	.249	9	.123	23	22	2.1
1960 Chi-A	13	13	.500	36	32	7	1	0	192^2	221	97	87	16	3	62	46	1.469	4.06	93	4.54	.292	8	.138	-9	9	-0.9
1961 Chi-A	3	4	.429	14	10	3	0	0	71^1	85	40	30	11	1	20	31	1.472	3.79	103	5.06	.302	0	.000	1	3	0.0
KC-A	9	10	.474	26	24	6	0	0	150^1	165	87	72	13	7	58	60	1.483	4.31	96	4.59	.281	11	.200	-2	7	-0.2
Yr.	12	14	.462	40	34	9	0	0	221^2	250	127	102	24	8	78	91	1.480	4.14	98	4.74	.288	11	.151	-0	10	-0.2
1962 Mil-N★	15	9	.625	38	29	12	3	2	225	223	80	70	20	12	44	124	1.187	2.80	135	3.32	.260	10	.137	24	20	2.5
1963 Mil-N	7	11	.389	48	16	3	3	13	159	144	51	47	10	4	55	105	1.252	2.66	121	3.10	.243	5	.122	7	13	0.8
1964 SF-N	7	6	.538	61	1	0	0	11	93^1	105	43	39	5	5	31	57	1.457	3.76	95	4.27	.286	0	.000	-3	7	-0.4
1965 SF-N	16	9	.640	42	33	6	1	2	235	213	85	69	17	3	53	148	1.132	2.64	136	2.71	.236	8	.101	28	19	2.7
1966 SF-N	1	4	.200	13	6	0	0	0	31^2	45	23	22	9	0	7	21	1.642	6.25	59	6.99	.324	0	.000	-9	0	-1.0
NY-N	11	10	.524	26	25	7	2	0	167^2	171	85	73	12	7	42	104	1.270	3.92	93	3.55	.261	13	.260	-6	9	-0.3
Yr.	12	14	.462	39	31	7	2	0	199^1	216	108	95	21	7	49	125	1.329	4.29	85	4.10	.272	13	.232	-15	9	-1.3
1967 NY-N	3	9	.250	23	13	3	1	0	98^2	105	54	47	9	2	28	49	1.348	4.29	79	3.87	.273	1	.040	-10	2	-1.3
Chi-N	0	2	.000	9	3	0	0	0	22^1	33	16	15	0	4	9	7	1.881	6.04	59	6.44	.351	1	.250	-6	0	-0.6
Yr.	3	11	.214	32	16	3	1	0	121	138	70	62	9	6	37	56	1.446	4.61	74	4.34	.289	2	.069	-17	2	-1.9
Total 11	108	98	.524	430	223	55	14	32	1778	1837	791	696	149	56	511	880	1.321	3.52	105	3.79	.267	69	.133	24	114	1.7
• SHAW, Don	Donald Wellington Shaw b: 2/23/1944, Pittsburgh, PA BL/TL, 6', 185 lbs. Deb: 4/11/1967																									
1967 NY-N	4	5	.444	40	0	0	0	3	51^1	40	19	17	5	0	23	44	1.227	2.98	114	2.86	.219	0	.000	2	5	0.3
1968 NY-N	0	0	....	7	0	0	0	0	12^1	3	1	1	1	0	5	11	.649	0.73	414	0.92	.086	0	....	3	2	0.3
1969 Mon-N	2	5	.286	35	1	0	0	1	65^2	61	43	38	9	2	37	45	1.492	5.21	71	4.65	.254	0	.000	-11	1	-1.2
1971 StL-N	7	2	.778	45	0	0	0	2	51	45	19	15	1	1	31	19	1.490	2.65	136	3.47	.237	0	.000	7	5	0.7
1972 StL-N	0	1	.000	8	0	0	0	0	3	5	3	3	1	0	3	0	2.667	9.00	38	14.00	.417	0	.000	-2	0	-0.2
Oak-A	0	1	.000	3	0	0	0	0	5^1	12	10	10	2	0	2	4	2.625	16.88	17	15.25	.500	0	....	-8	0	-1.0
Total 5	13	14	.481	138	1	0	0	6	188^2	166	95	84	19	3	101	123	1.415	4.01	86	4.05	.243	0	.000	-9	13	-1.0
• SHAW, Dupee	Frederick Lander Shaw b: 5/31/1859, Charlestown, MA d: 6/11/1938, Wakefield, MA BL/TL, 5'8", 165 lbs. Deb: 6/18/1883																									
1883 Det-N	10	15	.400	26	25	23	1	0	227	238	135	63	3	....	44	73	1.242	2.50	124	....	.254	29	.206	19	12	1.2
1884 Det-N	9	18	.333	28	28	25	0	0	227^2	219	153	77	8	....	72	142	1.278	3.04	95	....	.239	26	.191	4	9	0.1
Bos-U	21	15	.583	39	38	35	5	0	315^2	227	128	62	1	....	37	309	.836	1.77	168	....	.188	37	.242	38	31	3.4
1885 Pro-N	23	26	.469	49	49	47	6	0	399^2	343	209	114	7	....	99	194	1.106	2.57	103	....	.221	22	.133	4	23	-0.5
1886 Was-N	13	31	.295	45	44	43	1	0	385^2	384	224	143	12	....	91	177	1.232	3.34	98	....	.250	13	.088	-2	15	-1.0
1887 Was-N	7	13	.350	21	20	20	0	0	181^1	309	177	130	8	3	46	47	**1.704**	6.45	63	....	.366	21	.269	-45	3	-3.9
1888 Was-N	0	3	.000	3	3	3	0	0	25	36	24	18	2	0	7	8	1.720	6.48	43	....	.325	0	.000	-10	0	-1.1
Total 6	83	121	.407	211	207	196	13	0	1762	1756	1050	607	41	3	396	950	1.195	3.10	101	....	.247	148	.178	7	93	-1.9
• SHAW, Jeff	Jeffrey Lee Shaw b: 7/7/1966, Washington Court House, OH BR/TR, 6'2", 200 lbs. Deb: 4/30/1990																									
1990 Cle-A	3	4	.429	12	9	0	0	0	48^2	73	38	36	11	0	20	25	1.911	6.66	59	8.42	.356	0	....	-14	0	-1.4
1991 Cle-A	0	5	.000	29	1	0	0	1	72^1	72	34	27	6	4	27	31	1.369	3.36	124	3.96	.262	0	....	8	4	0.8
1992 Cle-A	0	1	.000	2	1	0	0	0	7^2	7	7	7	2	0	4	3	1.435	8.22	48	5.29	.259	0	....	-4	0	-0.4
1993 Mon-N	2	7	.222	55	8	0	0	0	95^2	91	47	44	12	7	32	50	1.286	4.14	101	4.03	.254	1	.067	0	4	-0.1
1994 Mon-N	5	2	.714	46	0	0	0	1	67^1	67	32	29	8	2	15	47	1.218	3.88	109	3.46	.254	2	.286	3	5	0.3
1995 Mon-N	1	6	.143	50	0	0	0	3	62^1	58	35	32	4	3	26	45	1.348	4.62	93	3.59	.250	0	.000	-2	3	-0.2
Chi-A	0	0	....	9	0	0	0	0	9^2	12	7	7	2	1	1	6	1.345	6.52	68	5.61	.316	0	....	-2	0	-0.2
1996 Cin-N	8	6	.571	78	0	0	0	4	104^2	99	34	29	8	2	29	69	1.223	2.49	167	3.08	.252	0	.000	18	12	1.8
1997 Cin-N	4	2	.667	78	0	0	0	**42**	94^2	79	26	25	7	1	12	74	.961	2.38	181	2.08	.227	0	.000	20	21	1.9
1998 Cin-N	2	4	.333	39	0	0	0	23	49^2	40	11	10	2	1	12	29	1.047	1.81	237	2.17	.231	0	.000	14	10	1.3
LA-N★	1	4	.200	34	0	0	0	25	35^1	35	11	10	6	0	7	26	1.189	2.55	156	3.60	.252	0	....	6	6	0.6
Yr.	3	8	.273	73	0	0	0	48	85	75	22	20	8	1	19	55	1.106	2.12	195	2.76	.240	0	.000	19	16	1.9
1999 LA-N	2	4	.333	64	0	0	0	34	68	64	25	21	6	1	15	43	1.162	2.78	154	2.96	.242	0	....	12	12	1.1
2000 LA-N	3	4	.429	60	0	0	0	27	57^1	61	29	27	7	1	16	39	1.343	4.24	102	4.02	.265	0	....	1	7	0.1
2001 LA-N★	3	5	.375	77	0	0	0	43	74^2	63	32	30	10	2	18	58	1.085	3.62	111	2.79	.227	0	....	4	13	0.4
Total 12	34	54	.386	633	19	0	0	203	848	821	368	334	91	25	234	545	1.244	3.54	117	3.57	.255	3	.079	63	97	6.0
• SHAW, Jim	James Aloysius "Grunting Jim" Shaw b: 8/19/1893, Pittsburgh, PA d: 1/27/1962, Washington, DC BR/TR, 6', 180 lbs. Deb: 9/15/1913																									
1913 Was-A	0	1	.000	2	1	0	0	0	13	8	4	3	0	1	7	14	1.154	2.08	142	2.44	.205	0	.000	1	1	0.1
1914 Was-A	15	17	.469	48	31	15	5	**4**	257	198	99	77	3	8	137	164	1.304	2.70	104	2.81	.216	10	.118	2	14	-0.2
1915 Was-A	6	11	.353	25	18	7	1	1	133	102	50	37	2	2	76	78	1.338	2.50	118	2.95	.220	10	.233	5	10	0.7
1916 Was-A	3	8	.273	26	9	5	2	1	106^1	86	36	31	1	2	50	44	1.279	2.62	106	2.78	.227	5	.156	1	6	0.1
1917 Was-A	15	14	.517	47	31	15	2	1	266^1	233	118	95	1	1	123	118	1.337	3.21	82	2.99	.242	14	.154	-20	11	-2.5
1918 Was-A	16	12	.571	41	30	14	4	1	241^1	201	88	65	2	1	90	129	1.206	2.42	112	2.45	.228	11	.133	0	15	-0.5
1919 Was-A	17	17	.500	**45**	37	23	3	**5**	**306^2**	274	118	93	5	5	101	128	1.223	2.73	117	2.78	.244	17	.160	19	18	2.0
1920 Was-A	11	18	.379	38	32	17	0	1	236^1	285	127	112	12	4	87	88	1.574	4.27	87	5.01	.314	14	.189	-12	9	-1.2
1921 Was-A	1	0	1.000	15	4	0	0	3	40^1	59	37	33	2	0	17	4	1.884	7.36	56	6.37	.345	5	.417	-15	1	-1.2
Total 9	84	98	.462	287	193	96	17	17	1600^1	1446	677	546	28	24	688	767	1.333	3.07	99	3.20	.247	86	.163	-19	85	-2.6
• SHAW, Sam	Samuel E. Shaw b: 5/1864, Baltimore, MD BR/TR, 5'5", 140 lbs. Deb: 5/3/1888																									
1888 Bal-a	2	4	.333	6	6	6	0	0	53	65	37	20	2	4	15	22	1.509	3.40	88	....	.291	3	.150	-1	2	-0.2
1893 Chi-N	1	0	1.000	2	2	1	0	0	16	12	12	10	2	9	13	1	1.563	5.63	82	6.31	.202	2	.286	-2	1	-0.1
Total 2	3	4	.429	8	8	7	0	0	69	77	49	30	4	13	28	23	1.522	3.91	86	1.46	.273	5	.185	-3	3	-0.3
• SHAWKEY, Bob	James Robert Shawkey b: 12/4/1890, Sigel, PA d: 12/31/1980, Syracuse, NY BR/TR, 5'11", 168 lbs. Deb: 7/16/1913 M/C																									
1913 Phi-A	6	5	.545	18	15	8	1	0	111^1	92	41	29	2	3	50	52	1.275	2.34	118	2.57	.207	6	.136	5	6	0.3
1914* Phi-A	15	8	.652	38	31	18	5	2	237	223	88	72	4	2	75	89	1.257	2.73	95	3.08	.262	17	.205	-5	14	-0.3
1915 Phi-A	6	6	.500	17	13	7	1	0	100	103	57	45	3	1	38	56	1.410	4.05	72	3.83	.278	4	.129	-12	2	-1.3
NY-A	4	7	.364	16	9	5	1	0	85^2	78	38	31	2	2	35	31	1.319	3.26	90	3.44	.265	7	.241	-4	5	-0.3
Yr.	10	13	.435	33	22	12	2	0	185^2	181	95	76	5	3	73	87	1.368	3.68	79	3.65	.272	11	.183	-16	7	-1.6
1916 NY-A	24	14	.632	53	27	21	4	**8**	276^2	204	78	68	4	6	81	122	1.030	2.21	131	1.92	.209	17	.183	18	27	1.8
1917 NY-A	13	15	.464	32	26	16	2	0	236^1	207	81	64	2	6	72	97	1.181	2.44	110	2.63	.243	16	.190	6	17	0.6
1918 NY-A	1	1	.500	3	2	1	1	0	16	7	2	2	0	0	10	3	1.063	1.13	251	1.50	.143	3	.750	3	2	0.5
1919 NY-A	20	11	.645	41	27	22	3	**5**	261^1	218	94	79	7	5	92	122	1.186	2.72	117	2.64	.231	22	.234	5	24	0.6
1920 NY-A	20	13	.606	38	31	20	5	2	267^2	246	88	73	10	1	85	126	1.237	**2.45**	**155**	2.88	.248	23	.230	**40**	27	3.9
1921* NY-A	18	12	.600	38	31	18	3	2	245	245	131	111	15	7	86	126	1.351	4.08	104	3.62	.263	27	.300	1	17	0.5
1922* NY-A	20	12	.625	39	34	22	3	1	299^2	286	112	97	16	0	98	130	1.281	2.91	137	3.17	.256	21	.183	34	27	3.0
1923* NY-A	16	11	.593	36	31	17	1	1	258^2	232	114	101	17	4	102	125	1.291	3.51	112	3.28	**.246**	20	.202	10	19	0.7
1924 NY-A	16	11	.593	38	25	10	1	0	207^2	226	107	95	11	3	74	114	1.445	4.12	101	4.09	.286	22	.319	-0	15	0.7
1925 NY-A	6	14	.300	33	19	9	1	0	186	209	101	85	12	5	67	81	1.484	4.11	104	4.47	.294	10	.147	4	9	0.0
1926* NY-A	8	7	.533	29	10	3	1	3	104^1	102	49	42	8	2	37	63	1.332	3.62	106	3.59	.263	9	.257	4	8	0.6

YEAR TM-L	W	L	PCT	G	GS	CG	SH	SV	IP	H	R	ER	HR	HB	BB	SO	RAT	ERA	ERA+	CERA	OAV	BH	AVG	PR+	WS	TPW
1927 NY-A	2	3	.400	19	2	0	0	4	43^2	44	19	14	1	1	16	23	1.374	2.89	133	3.39	.262	1	.091	5	4	0.3
Total 15	195	150	.565	488	333	197	33	28	2937	2722	1200	1008	114	48	1018	1360	1.273	3.09	113	3.14	.252	225	.214	113	223	11.5
• SHEA, John	John Michael Joseph "Lefty" Shea b: 12/27/1904, Everett, MA d: 11/30/1956, Malden, MA BL/TL, 5'10.5", 171 lbs. Deb: 6/30/1928																									
1928 Bos-A	0	0	....	1	0	0	0	0	1	1	2	2	0	0	1	0	2.000	18.00	23	5.17	.250	0	....	-2	0	-0.1
• SHEA, Mike	Michael Joseph Shea b: 3/10/1867, New Orleans, LA d: 8/22/1927, New Orleans, LA TR, 5'10", 170 lbs. Deb: 4/20/1887																									
1887 Cin-a	1	1	.500	2	2	2	0	0	16^2	36	25	13	0	0	10	0	2.160	7.02	62	....	.420	3	.333	-6	0	-0.5
• SHEA, Red	Patrick Henry Shea b: 11/29/1898, Ware, MA d: 11/17/1981, Stafford Springs, CT BR/TR, 6', 165 lbs. Deb: 5/6/1918																									
1918 Phi-A	0	0	....	3	0	0	0	0	9	14	8	4	0	0	2	2	1.778	4.00	73	6.25	.378	0	.000	-1	0	-0.2
1921 NY-N	5	2	.714	9	2	1	0	0	32	28	13	11	2	3	2	10	.938	3.09	118	2.30	.239	1	.111	1	3	0.0
1922 NY-N	0	3	.000	11	2	0	0	0	23	22	14	12	2	0	11	5	1.435	4.70	85	3.87	.256	0	.000	-2	0	-0.3
Total 3	5	5	.500	23	4	1	0	0	64	64	35	27	4	3	15	17	1.234	3.80	97	3.42	.267	1	.053	-3	3	-0.5
• SHEA, Spec	Francis Joseph "The Naugatuck Nugget" Shea b: 10/2/1920, Naugatuck, CT d: 7/19/2002, New Haven, CT BR/TR, 6', 195 lbs. Deb: 4/19/1947																									
1947* NY-A★	14	5	.737	27	23	13	3	1	178^2	127	63	61	10	4	89	89	1.209	3.07	115	**2.62**	**.200**	11	.196	8	14	1.0
1948 NY-A	9	10	.474	28	22	8	3	1	155^2	117	66	59	10	2	87	71	1.310	3.41	120	2.99	**.208**	7	.149	10	11	1.0
1949 NY-A	1	1	.500	20	3	0	0	1	52^1	48	36	31	5	0	43	22	1.739	5.33	76	5.09	.250	3	.250	-9	1	-0.8
1951 NY-A	5	5	.500	25	11	2	2	0	95^2	112	59	46	11	4	50	38	1.693	4.33	89	5.88	.300	6	.214	-7	3	-0.6
1952 Was-A	11	7	.611	22	21	12	2	0	169	144	62	55	6	2	92	65	1.396	2.93	121	3.30	.231	15	.238	13	15	1.6
1953 Was-A	12	7	.632	23	23	11	1	0	164^2	151	82	72	11	4	75	38	1.372	3.94	99	3.59	.244	11	.177	-2	7	-0.3
1954 Was-A	2	9	.182	23	11	1	0	0	71^1	97	54	49	9	2	34	22	1.836	6.18	58	6.85	.340	1	.050	-20	0	-2.2
1955 Was-A	2	2	.500	27	4	1	1	2	56^1	53	31	25	4	1	27	16	1.420	3.99	96	3.89	.251	4	.400	0	3	0.2
Total 8	56	46	.549	195	118	48	12	5	943^2	849	453	398	66	19	497	361	1.426	3.80	99	3.83	.243	58	.195	-6	54	0.0
• SHEA, Steve	Steven Francis Shea b: 12/5/1942, Worcester, MA BR/TR, 6'3", 215 lbs. Deb: 7/14/1968																									
1968 Hou-N	4	4	.500	30	0	0	0	6	34^2	27	14	13	0	3	11	15	1.096	3.38	88	2.35	.229	0	.000	-1	4	-0.2
1969 Mon-N	0	0	....	10	0	0	0	0	15^2	18	8	5	2	0	8	11	1.660	2.87	128	5.40	.300	0	....	1	1	0.2
Total 2	4	4	.500	40	0	0	0	6	50^1	45	22	18	2	3	19	26	1.272	3.22	97	3.30	.253	0	.000	1	5	0.0
• SHEALY, Al	Albert Berley Shealy b: 3/20/1900, Chapin, SC d: 3/7/1967, Hagerstown, MD BR/TR, 5'11", 175 lbs. Deb: 4/13/1928																									
1928 NY-A	8	6	.571	23	12	3	0	2	96	124	64	54	4	1	42	39	1.729	5.06	74	5.27	.308	9	.237	-13	3	-1.0
1930 Chi-N	0	0	....	24	0	0	0	0	27	37	24	24	2	0	14	14	1.889	8.00	61	6.46	.327	3	.600	-9	0	-0.7
Total 2	8	6	.571	47	12	3	0	2	123	161	88	78	6	1	56	53	1.764	5.71	71	5.53	.312	12	.279	-22	3	-1.7
• SHEARON, John	John M. Shearon b: 1870, Pittsburgh, PA d: 2/1/1923, Bradford, PA Deb: 7/28/1891 ♦																									
1891 Cle-N	1	3	.250	6	5	4	0	0	46	57	39	18	2	1	24	19	1.761	3.52	98	....	.293	30	.242	0	2	-0.7
• SHEARS, George	George Penfield Shears b: 4/13/1890, Marshall, MO d: 11/12/1978, Loveland, CO BR/TL, 6'3", 180 lbs. Deb: 4/24/1912																									
1912 NY-A	0	0	....	4	0	0	0	0	15	24	18	9	1	0	11	9	2.333	5.40	67	8.84	.364	1	.167	-2	0	-0.2
• SHEEHAN, Tom	Thomas Clancy Sheehan b: 3/31/1894, Grand Ridge, IL d: 10/29/1982, Chillicothe, OH BR/TR, 6'2.5", 190 lbs. Deb: 7/14/1915 M/C																									
1915 Phi-A	4	9	.308	15	13	8	1	0	102	131	73	47	1	1	38	22	1.657	4.15	70	5.28	.335	4	.118	-13	1	-1.7
1916 Phi-A	1	16	.059	38	17	8	0	0	188	197	111	77	2	2	94	54	**1.548**	3.69	77	4.29	.287	7	.125	-13	2	-1.7
1921 NY-A	1	0	1.000	12	1	0	0	1	33	43	23	20	1	1	19	7	1.879	5.45	78	6.13	.326	5	.625	-5	2	-0.3
1924 Cin-N	9	11	.450	39	16	8	2	1	166^2	170	72	60	5	1	54	52	1.344	3.24	116	3.37	.269	18	.310	10	13	1.3
1925 Cin-N	1	0	1.000	10	3	1	0	1	29	37	31	26	3	0	12	5	1.690	8.07	51	5.52	.298	1	.200	-13	0	-1.2
Pit-N	1	1	.500	23	0	0	0	2	57^1	63	25	17	2	0	13	13	1.326	2.67	167	3.45	.286	3	.150	10	5	0.8
Yr.	2	1	.667	33	3	1	0	3	86^1	100	56	43	5	0	25	18	1.448	4.48	95	4.15	.290	4	.160	-3	5	-0.3
1926 Pit-N	0	2	.000	9	4	1	0	0	31	36	24	23	0	2	12	16	1.548	6.68	59	4.33	.298	1	.111	-10	0	-1.1
Total 6	17	39	.304	146	54	26	3	5	607	677	359	270	14	7	242	169	1.514	4.00	85	4.28	.294	39	.205	-35	23	-3.7
• SHEETS, Ben	Ben M. Sheets b: 7/18/1978, Baton Rouge, LA BR/TR, 6'1", 195 lbs. Deb: 4/5/2001																									
2001 Mil-N★	11	10	.524	25	25	1	1	0	151^1	166	89	80	23	5	48	94	1.414	4.76	90	4.78	.283	3	.071	-9	6	-1.0
2002 Mil-N	11	16	.407	34	34	1	0	0	216^2	237	105	100	21	10	70	170	1.417	4.15	98	4.45	.281	6	.088	-1	8	-0.3
2003 Mil-N	11	13	.458	34	34	1	0	0	220^2	232	122	109	29	6	43	157	1.246	4.45	95	3.83	.268	5	.076	-1	10	-0.5
Total 3	33	39	.458	93	93	3	1	0	588^2	635	316	289	73	21	161	421	1.352	4.42	95	4.30	.277	14	.080	-10	24	-1.8
• SHELDON, Rollie	Roland Frank Sheldon b: 12/17/1936, Putnam, CT BR/TR, 6'4", 190 lbs. Deb: 4/23/1961																									
1961 NY-A	11	5	.688	35	21	6	2	0	162^2	149	70	65	17	2	55	84	1.254	3.60	103	3.50	.246	7	.125	-3	9	-0.5
1962 NY-A	7	8	.467	34	16	2	0	1	118	136	78	72	12	1	28	54	1.390	5.49	68	4.25	.289	2	.077	-24	0	-2.4
1964* NY-A	5	2	.714	19	12	3	0	1	102^1	92	43	41	18	1	18	57	1.075	3.61	100	3.21	.243	3	.088	-1	5	-0.3
1965 NY-A	0	0	....	3	0	0	0	0	6^1	5	1	1	0	0	1	7	.947	1.42	240	1.64	.238	0	.000	1	1	0.1
KC-A	10	8	.556	32	29	4	1	0	186^2	180	86	82	22	7	56	105	1.264	3.95	88	3.73	.251	4	.078	-8	7	-1.2
Yr.	10	8	.556	35	29	4	1	0	193	185	87	83	22	7	57	112	1.254	3.87	90	3.66	.251	4	.077	-7	8	-1.1
1966 KC-A	4	7	.364	14	13	1	1	0	69	73	31	24	3	1	26	26	1.435	3.13	108	3.86	.275	2	.087	2	3	0.0
Bos-A	1	6	.143	23	10	1	0	0	79^2	106	49	44	15	2	23	38	1.619	4.97	77	6.28	.320	2	.111	-10	1	-1.2
Yr.	5	13	.278	37	23	2	1	0	148^2	179	80	68	18	3	49	64	1.534	4.12	89	5.16	.300	4	.098	-8	4	-1.1
Total 5	38	36	.514	160	101	17	4	2	724^2	741	358	329	87	14	207	371	1.308	4.09	89	3.96	.266	20	.096	-43	26	-5.4
• SHELLENBACK, Frank	Frank Victor Shellenback b: 12/16/1898, Joplin, MO d: 8/17/1969, Newton, MA BR/TR, 6'2", 192 lbs. Deb: 5/8/1918 C																									
1918 Chi-A	9	12	.429	28	21	10	2	2	182^2	180	77	54	1	4	74	47	1.391	2.66	103	3.37	.262	7	.130	4	9	0.3
1919 Chi-A	1	3	.250	8	4	2	0	0	35	40	24	20	1	0	16	10	1.600	5.14	62	4.76	.303	1	.091	-8	0	-0.9
Total 2	10	15	.400	36	25	12	2	2	217^2	220	101	74	2	4	90	57	1.424	3.06	93	3.59	.269	8	.123	-4	9	-0.6
• SHELLENBACK, Jim	James Philip Shellenback b: 11/18/1943, Riverside, CA BL/TL, 6'2", 200 lbs. Deb: 9/15/1966 C																									
1966 Pit-N	0	0	....	2	0	0	0	0	3	3	3	3	2	0	3	0	2.000	9.00	40	12.40	.300	0	....	-2	0	-0.2
1967 Pit-N	1	1	.500	6	2	1	0	0	23^1	23	12	7	1	1	12	11	1.500	2.70	125	4.05	.250	1	.167	1	1	0.1
1969 Pit-N	0	0	....	8	0	0	0	0	16^2	14	8	6	1	0	4	7	1.080	3.24	108	2.39	.233	0	.000	1	1	0.0
Was-A	4	7	.364	30	11	2	0	1	84^2	87	43	38	8	1	48	50	1.594	4.04	86	4.85	.268	5	.185	-6	2	-0.6
1970 Was-A	6	7	.462	39	14	2	1	0	117^1	107	57	48	6	0	51	57	1.347	3.68	97	3.39	.246	2	.067	-3	5	-0.5
1971 Was-A	3	11	.214	40	15	3	1	0	120	123	56	47	10	3	49	47	1.433	3.53	94	4.15	.267	5	.167	-3	4	-0.3
1972 Tex-A	2	4	.333	22	6	0	0	1	57	46	24	22	6	2	16	30	1.088	3.47	87	2.81	.221	1	.100	-2	2	-0.2
1973 Tex-A	0	0	....	2	0	0	0	0	1^2	0	0	0	0	0	0	3	.000	0.00	....	0.00	.000	0	....	1	0	0.1
1974 Tex-A	0	0	....	11	0	0	0	0	24^2	30	18	16	5	1	12	14	1.703	5.84	61	6.86	.306	0	....	-6	0	-0.7
1977 Min-A	0	0	....	5	0	0	0	0	5^2	10	7	5	1	0	5	3	2.647	7.94	50	11.66	.385	0	....	-2	0	-0.2
Total 9	16	30	.348	165	48	8	2	2	454	443	228	192	40	8	200	222	1.416	3.81	89	4.13	.258	14	.135	-22	15	-2.5
• SHEPARD, Bert	Bert Robert Shepard b: 6/28/1920, Dana, IN BL/TL, 5'11", 185 lbs. Deb: 8/4/1945 C																									
1945 Was-A	0	0	....	1	0	0	0	0	5^1	3	1	1	0	1	1	2	.750	1.69	184	1.36	.167	0	.000	1	0	0.0
• SHEPHERD, Keith	Keith Wayne Shepherd b: 1/21/1968, Wabash, IN BR/TR, 6'2", 205 lbs. Deb: 9/6/1992																									
1992 Phi-N	1	1	.500	12	0	0	0	2	22	19	10	8	0	0	6	10	1.136	3.27	107	2.14	.244	0	....	1	2	0.1
1993 Col-N	1	3	.250	14	1	0	0	1	19^1	26	16	15	4	1	4	7	1.552	6.98	68	6.50	.333	0	.000	-4	0	-0.4
1995 Bos-A	0	0	....	2	0	0	0	0	1	4	4	4	0	0	2	0	6.000	36.00	14	32.97	.571	0	....	-3	0	-0.3
1996 Bal-A	0	1	.000	13	0	0	0	0	20^2	31	27	20	6	0	18	17	2.371	8.71	57	10.74	.341	0	....	-9	0	-0.8
Total 4	2	5	.286	41	1	0	0	3	63	80	57	47	10	1	30	34	1.746	6.71	68	6.79	.315	0	.000	-16	2	-1.5
• SHERDEL, Bill	William Henry "Wee Willie" Sherdel b: 8/15/1896, McSherrystown, PA d: 11/14/1968, McSherrystown, PA BL/TL, 5'10", 160 lbs. Deb: 4/22/1918																									
1918 StL-N	6	12	.333	35	16	9	1	0	182^1	174	78	55	3	3	49	40	1.223	2.71	100	2.83	.259	15	.242	-1	9	0.3

YEAR	TM-L	W	L	PCT	G	GS	CG	SH	SV	IP	H	R	ER	HR	HB	BB	SO	RAT	ERA	ERA+	CERA	OAV	BH	AVG	PR+	WS	TPW
1919	StL-N	5	9	.357	36	10	7	0	1	137^{1}	137	66	53	3	2	42	52	1.303	3.47	80	3.23	.270	13	.271	-12	5	-1.0
1920	StL-N	11	10	.524	43	7	4	0	**6**	170	183	72	62	1	11	40	74	1.312	3.28	93	3.55	.297	14	.222	-5	10	-0.3
1921	StL-N	9	8	.529	38	8	5	1	1	144^{1}	137	62	51	7	3	38	57	1.212	3.18	115	2.88	.247	5	.114	7	9	0.5
1922	StL-N	17	13	.567	47	31	15	3	2	242	298	132	104	12	5	62	79	1.488	3.87	100	4.37	.303	17	.193	5	16	0.5
1923	StL-N	15	13	.536	39	26	14	0	2	225	270	127	108	15	6	59	78	1.462	4.32	90	4.39	.296	28	.337	-9	14	0.0
1924	StL-N	8	9	.471	35	10	6	0	1	168^{2}	188	77	64	9	5	38	57	1.340	3.42	111	3.82	.291	15	.200	7	11	0.9
1925	StL-N	15	6	.714	32	21	17	2	1	200	216	77	69	8	3	42	53	1.290	3.11	139	3.40	.277	15	.205	26	19	2.6
1926*	StL-N	16	12	.571	34	29	17	3	0	234^{2}	255	103	91	15	5	49	59	1.295	3.49	112	3.59	.278	22	.244	9	17	1.1
1927	StL-N	17	12	.586	39	28	18	0	**6**	232^{1}	241	109	91	17	3	48	59	1.244	3.53	112	3.34	.269	14	.194	7	18	0.8
1928*	StL-N	21	10	.677	38	27	20	0	**5**	248^{2}	251	96	79	17	2	56	72	1.235	2.86	140	3.19	.261	19	.226	30	24	3.3
1929	StL-N	10	15	.400	33	22	11	1	0	195^{2}	278	144	129	14	2	58	69	**1.717**	5.93	79	5.82	.337	16	.229	-27	5	-2.3
1930	StL-N	3	2	.600	13	7	1	0	0	64	86	34	33	5	1	13	29	1.547	4.64	108	5.13	.325	2	.105	2	4	0.1
	Bos-N	6	5	.545	21	14	7	0	1	119^{1}	131	73	63	10	2	30	26	1.349	4.75	104	3.85	.283	4	.095	2	7	-0.1
	Yr.	9	7	.563	34	21	8	0	1	183^{1}	217	107	96	15	3	43	55	1.418	4.71	105	4.30	.298	6	.098	5	11	0.0
1931	Bos-N	6	10	.375	27	16	8	0	0	137^{2}	163	70	65	13	1	35	34	1.438	4.25	89	4.41	.294	14	.304	-6	8	-0.3
1932	Bos-N	0	0	....	1	0	0	0	0	1^{2}	3	3	0	0	0	1	0	2.400	0.00	....	8.62	.375	0	....	1	0	0.1
	StL-N	0	0	....	3	0	0	0	0	5^{2}	7	3	3	0	0	1	1	1.412	4.76	83	3.66	.304	1	1.000	-0	1	0.0
	Yr.	0	0	....	4	0	0	0	0	7^{1}	10	6	3	0	0	2	1	1.636	3.68	107	4.78	.322	1	1.000	0	1	0.1
Total	15	165	146	.531	514	272	159	11	26	2709^{1}	3018	1326	1120	149	54	661	839	1.358	3.72	103	3.81	.285	214	.223	36	177	6.2

• SHERID, Roy — Royden Richard Sherid b: 1/25/1907, Norristown, PA d: 2/28/1982, Parker Ford, PA BR/TR, 6'2", 185 lbs. Deb: 5/11/1929

YEAR	TM-L	W	L	PCT	G	GS	CG	SH	SV	IP	H	R	ER	HR	HB	BB	SO	RAT	ERA	ERA+	CERA	OAV	BH	AVG	PR+	WS	TPW
1929	NY-A	6	6	.500	33	15	9	0	1	154^{2}	165	81	62	6	5	55	51	1.422	3.61	107	3.90	.277	9	.180	3	8	0.2
1930	NY-A	12	13	.480	37	21	8	0	4	184	214	122	107	13	5	87	59	1.636	5.23	82	4.99	.289	7	.101	-17	6	-2.1
1931	NY-A	5	5	.500	17	8	3	0	2	74^{1}	94	52	47	4	3	24	39	1.587	5.69	70	5.02	.306	10	.333	-15	2	-1.2
Total	3	23	24	.489	87	44	20	0	7	413	473	255	216	23	13	166	149	1.547	4.71	87	4.59	.288	26	.174	-29	16	-3.1

• SHERMAN, Dan — Lester Daniel "Babe,General" Sherman b: 11/26/1890, Hubbardsville, NY d: 9/16/1955, Highland Park, MI BR/TR, 5'6", 145 lbs. Deb: 6/4/1914

YEAR	TM-L	W	L	PCT	G	GS	CG	SH	SV	IP	H	R	ER	HR	HB	BB	SO	RAT	ERA	ERA+	CERA	OAV	BH	AVG	PR+	WS	TPW
1914	Chi-F	0	1	.000	1	1	0	0	0	0^{1}	0	2	0	0	0	2	0	6.000	0.00	....	16.98	.000	0	....	0	0	0.0

• SHERMAN, Joe — Joel Powers Sherman b: 11/4/1890, Yarmouth, MA d: 12/21/1987, Cape Coral, FL BR/TR, 6', 165 lbs. Deb: 9/24/1915

YEAR	TM-L	W	L	PCT	G	GS	CG	SH	SV	IP	H	R	ER	HR	HB	BB	SO	RAT	ERA	ERA+	CERA	OAV	BH	AVG	PR+	WS	TPW
1915	Phi-A	1	0	1.000	2	1	1	0	0	15	15	4	4	0	2	1	5	1.067	2.40	122	2.66	.259	2	.333	1	1	0.1

• SHERRILL, Tim — Timothy Shawn Sherrill b: 9/10/1965, Harrison, AR BL/TL, 5'11", 170 lbs. Deb: 8/14/1990

YEAR	TM-L	W	L	PCT	G	GS	CG	SH	SV	IP	H	R	ER	HR	HB	BB	SO	RAT	ERA	ERA+	CERA	OAV	BH	AVG	PR+	WS	TPW
1990	StL-N	0	0	....	8	0	0	0	0	4^{1}	10	5	3	0	0	3	3	3.000	6.23	61	13.32	.476	0	....	-1	0	-0.1
1991	StL-N	0	0	....	10	0	0	0	0	14^{1}	20	13	13	2	2	3	4	1.605	8.16	46	6.34	.339	0	....	-7	0	-0.8
Total	2	0	0	....	18	0	0	0	0	18^{2}	30	18	16	2	2	6	7	1.929	7.71	48	7.96	.375	0	....	-8	0	-0.9

• SHERRY, Fred — Fred Peter Sherry b: 1/13/1889, Honesdale, PA d: 7/27/1975, Honesdale, PA BR/TR, 6', 170 lbs. Deb: 4/25/1911

YEAR	TM-L	W	L	PCT	G	GS	CG	SH	SV	IP	H	R	ER	HR	HB	BB	SO	RAT	ERA	ERA+	CERA	OAV	BH	AVG	PR+	WS	TPW
1911	Was-A	0	4	.000	10	3	2	0	0	52^{1}	63	40	25	1	0	19	20	1.567	4.30	76	4.64	.310	3	.158	-6	0	-0.6

• SHERRY, Larry — Lawrence Sherry b: 7/25/1935, Los Angeles, CA BR/TR, 6'2", 204 lbs. Deb: 4/17/1958 C

YEAR	TM-L	W	L	PCT	G	GS	CG	SH	SV	IP	H	R	ER	HR	HB	BB	SO	RAT	ERA	ERA+	CERA	OAV	BH	AVG	PR+	WS	TPW
1958	LA-N	0	0	....	5	0	0	0	0	4^{1}	10	7	6	0	1	7	2	3.923	12.46	33	18.89	.476	0	....	-4	0	-0.4
1959*	LA-N	7	2	.778	23	9	1	1	3	94^{1}	75	27	23	9	2	43	72	1.251	2.19	193	3.18	.218	7	.219	21	12	2.4
1960	LA-N	14	10	.583	57	3	1	0	7	142^{1}	125	65	60	14	6	82	114	1.454	3.79	105	4.09	.238	6	.162	1	11	0.2
1961	LA-N	4	4	.500	53	1	0	0	15	94^{2}	90	48	41	10	4	39	79	1.363	3.90	111	3.95	.252	2	.154	4	10	0.4
1962	LA-N	7	3	.700	58	0	0	0	11	90	81	40	32	8	6	44	71	1.389	3.20	113	3.92	.241	2	.118	4	7	0.4
1963	LA-N	2	6	.250	36	3	0	0	3	79^{2}	82	43	33	8	4	24	47	1.331	3.73	81	3.88	.265	1	.111	-6	2	-0.5
1964	Det-A	7	5	.583	38	0	0	0	11	66^{1}	52	29	27	7	3	37	58	1.342	3.66	100	3.64	.216	0	.000	-0	7	-0.2
1965	Det-A	3	6	.333	39	0	0	0	5	78^{1}	71	30	27	5	1	40	46	1.417	3.10	112	3.63	.254	3	.300	4	7	0.6
1966	Det-A	8	5	.615	55	0	0	0	20	77^{2}	66	38	33	8	3	36	63	1.313	3.82	91	3.63	.232	4	.400	-3	9	-0.2
1967	Det-A	0	1	.000	20	0	0	0	1	28	35	22	20	3	1	7	20	1.500	6.43	51	4.73	.289	0	.000	-10	0	-1.1
	Hou-N	1	2	.333	29	0	0	0	6	40^{2}	53	26	22	4	1	13	32	1.623	4.87	68	5.44	.327	0	.000	-6	0	-0.7
1968	Cal-A	0	0	....	3	0	0	0	0	3	7	2	2	2	0	2	2	3.000	6.00	48	21.40	.467	0	....	-1	0	-0.1
Total	11	53	44	.546	416	16	2	1	82	799^{1}	747	377	326	78	32	374	606	1.402	3.67	99	4.04	.249	25	.169	4	65	0.7

• SHIELDS, Ben — Benjamin Cowan "Lefty,Big Ben" Shields b: 6/17/1903, Huntersville, NC d: 1/24/1982, Woodruff, SC BR/TL, 6'1.5", 195 lbs. Deb: 4/17/1924

YEAR	TM-L	W	L	PCT	G	GS	CG	SH	SV	IP	H	R	ER	HR	HB	BB	SO	RAT	ERA	ERA+	CERA	OAV	BH	AVG	PR+	WS	TPW
1924	NY-A	0	0	....	2	0	0	0	0	2	6	6	6	0	0	2	3	4.000	27.00	15	20.63	.545	0	....	-5	0	-0.5
1925	NY-A	3	0	1.000	4	2	2	0	0	24	24	13	13	2	2	12	5	1.500	4.88	87	4.64	.267	1	.125	-2	2	-0.2
1930	Bos-A	0	0	....	3	0	0	0	0	10	16	11	10	0	0	6	1	2.200	9.00	51	7.99	.400	0	.000	-5	0	-0.5
1931	Phi-N	1	0	1.000	4	0	0	0	0	5^{1}	9	9	9	1	0	7	0	3.000	15.19	28	12.79	.391	0	.000	-6	0	-0.7
Total	4	4	0	1.000	13	2	2	0	0	41^{1}	55	39	38	3	2	27	9	1.984	8.27	52	7.28	.336	1	.077	-18	2	-1.9

• SHIELDS, Charlie — Charles Jessamine Shields b: 12/10/1879, Jackson, TN d: 8/27/1953, Memphis, TN BL/TL, 5'8" Deb: 4/23/1902

YEAR	TM-L	W	L	PCT	G	GS	CG	SH	SV	IP	H	R	ER	HR	HB	BB	SO	RAT	ERA	ERA+	CERA	OAV	BH	AVG	PR+	WS	TPW
1902	Bal-A	4	11	.267	23	15	10	1	1	142^{1}	201	102	67	7	2	32	28	1.637	4.24	89	5.37	.333	8	.167	0	4	-0.1
	StL-A	3	0	1.000	4	4	3	0	0	30	37	16	11	1	0	7	6	1.467	3.30	107	4.20	.303	6	.462	0	3	0.3
	Yr.	7	11	.389	27	19	13	1	1	172^{1}	238	118	78	8	2	39	34	1.607	4.07	92	5.17	.328	14	.230	1	7	0.2
1907	StL-N	0	2	.000	3	2	0	0	0	6^{2}	12	11	7	0	2	7	1	2.850	9.45	26	13.36	.444	0	.000	-5	0	-0.6
Total	2	7	13	.350	30	21	13	1	1	179	250	129	85	8	4	46	35	1.654	4.27	84	5.47	.332	14	.222	-5	7	-0.4

• SHIELDS, Scot — Robert Scot Shields b: 7/22/1975, Fort Lauderdale, FL BR/TR, 6'1", 175 lbs. Deb: 5/26/2001

YEAR	TM-L	W	L	PCT	G	GS	CG	SH	SV	IP	H	R	ER	HR	HB	BB	SO	RAT	ERA	ERA+	CERA	OAV	BH	AVG	PR+	WS	TPW
2001	Ana-A	0	0	....	8	0	0	0	0	11	8	1	0	0	1	7	7	1.364	0.00	....	3.10	.200	0	....	6	2	0.5
2002*	Ana-A	5	3	.625	29	1	0	0	0	49	31	13	12	4	1	21	30	1.061	2.20	201	2.35	.188	0	....	11	6	1.0
2003	Ana-A	5	6	.455	44	13	0	0	1	148^{1}	138	56	47	12	5	38	111	1.187	2.85	151	3.12	.247	0	....	22	12	2.1
Total	3	10	9	.526	81	14	0	0	1	208^{1}	177	70	59	16	7	66	148	1.166	2.55	170	2.94	.232	0	....	38	20	3.6

• SHIELDS, Steve — Stephen Mack Shields b: 11/30/1958, Gadsden, AL BR/TR, 6'5", 230 lbs. Deb: 6/1/1985

YEAR	TM-L	W	L	PCT	G	GS	CG	SH	SV	IP	H	R	ER	HR	HB	BB	SO	RAT	ERA	ERA+	CERA	OAV	BH	AVG	PR+	WS	TPW
1985	Atl-N	1	2	.333	23	6	0	0	0	68	86	46	39	9	1	32	29	1.735	5.16	74	6.18	.320	2	.111	-9	1	-1.0
1986	Atl-N	0	0	....	6	0	0	0	0	12^{2}	13	10	10	4	0	7	6	1.579	7.11	56	6.73	.271	0	.000	-4	0	-0.5
	KC-A	0	0	....	3	0	0	0	0	8^{2}	3	3	2	1	0	4	2	.808	2.08	205	1.23	.111	0	....	2	1	0.2
1987	Sea-A	2	0	1.000	20	0	0	0	3	30	43	25	22	7	0	12	22	1.833	6.60	71	7.61	.333	0	....	-6	0	-0.6
1988	NY-A	5	5	.500	39	0	0	0	0	82^{1}	96	44	40	8	2	30	55	1.530	4.37	90	4.95	.298	0	....	-3	3	-0.3
1989	Min-A	0	1	.000	11	0	0	0	0	17^{1}	28	18	15	3	0	6	12	1.962	7.79	53	7.94	.354	0	....	-7	0	-0.7
Total	5	8	8	.500	102	6	0	0	3	219	269	146	128	32	3	91	126	1.644	5.26	77	5.89	.308	2	.105	-28	5	-2.9

• SHIELDS, Vince — Vincent William Shields b: 11/18/1900, Fredericton, Canada d: 10/17/1952, Plaster Rock, Canada BL/TR, 5'11", 185 lbs. Deb: 9/20/1924

YEAR	TM-L	W	L	PCT	G	GS	CG	SH	SV	IP	H	R	ER	HR	HB	BB	SO	RAT	ERA	ERA+	CERA	OAV	BH	AVG	PR+	WS	TPW
1924	StL-N	1	1	.500	2	1	0	0	0	12	10	5	4	1	3	3	4	1.083	3.00	126	3.31	.227	2	.400	1	1	0.1

• SHIELL, Jason — Jason Alexander Shiell b: 10/19/1976, Savannah, GA BR/TR, 6', 180 lbs. Deb: 9/8/2002

YEAR	TM-L	W	L	PCT	G	GS	CG	SH	SV	IP	H	R	ER	HR	HB	BB	SO	RAT	ERA	ERA+	CERA	OAV	BH	AVG	PR+	WS	TPW
2002	SD-N	0	0	....	3	0	0	0	0	1^{1}	7	4	4	0	0	3	1	7.500	27.00	14	48.76	.700	0	....	-3	0	-0.3
2003	Bos-A	2	0	1.000	17	0	0	0	1	23^{1}	23	13	12	4	2	17	23	1.714	4.63	99	6.06	.253	0	....	0	2	0.0
Total	2	2	0	1.000	20	0	0	0	1	24^{2}	30	17	16	4	2	20	24	2.027	5.84	74	8.37	.297	0	....	-3	2	-0.3

• SHIFFLETT, Garland — Garland Jessie "Duck" Shifflett b: 3/28/1935, Elkton, VA BR/TR, 5'10.5", 165 lbs. Deb: 4/22/1957

YEAR	TM-L	W	L	PCT	G	GS	CG	SH	SV	IP	H	R	ER	HR	HB	BB	SO	RAT	ERA	ERA+	CERA	OAV	BH	AVG	PR+	WS	TPW
1957	Was-A	0	0	....	6	1	0	0	0	8	6	9	9	0	0	10	2	2.000	10.13	38	5.12	.222	0	....	-5	0	-0.6
1964	Min-A	0	2	.000	10	0	0	0	1	17^{2}	22	9	9	1	1	7	8	1.642	4.58	78	5.17	.297	0	.000	-2	0	-0.2
Total	2	0	2	.000	16	1	0	0	1	25^{2}	28	18	18	1	1	17	10	1.753	6.31	59	5.15	.277	0	.000	-7	0	-0.8

• SHIFFLETT, Steve — Stephen Earl Shifflett b: 1/5/1966, Kansas City, MO BR/TR, 6'1", 205 lbs. Deb: 7/3/1992

YEAR	TM-L	W	L	PCT	G	GS	CG	SH	SV	IP	H	R	ER	HR	HB	BB	SO	RAT	ERA	ERA+	CERA	OAV	BH	AVG	PR+	WS	TPW
1992	KC-A	1	4	.200	34	0	0	0	0	52	55	15	15	6	2	17	25	1.385	2.60	156	4.27	.279	0	....	9	4	0.9

YEAR	TM-L	W	L	PCT	G	GS	CG	SH	SV	IP	H	R	ER	HR	HB	BB	SO	RAT	ERA	ERA+	CERA	OAV	BH	AVG	PR+	WS	TPW
• SHINALL, Zak	Zakary Sebastien Shinall b: 10/14/1968, St. Louis, MO BR/TR, 6'3", 215 lbs. Deb: 5/12/1993																										
1993	Sea-A	0	0	....	1	0	0	0	0	2^2	4	1	1	1	0	2	0	2.250	3.38	130	11.06	.333	0	....	0	0	0.0
• SHIPANOFF, Dave	David Noel Shipanoff b: 11/13/1959, Edmonton, Canada BR/TR, 6'2", 185 lbs. Deb: 8/9/1985																										
1985	Phi-N	1	2	.333	26	0	0	0	3	36^1	33	15	13	3	1	16	26	1.349	3.22	114	3.42	.231	0	.000	2	3	0.2
• SHIPLEY, Joe	Joseph Clark "Moses" Shipley b: 5/9/1935, Morristown, TN BR/TR, 6'4", 210 lbs. Deb: 7/14/1958																										
1958	SF-N	0	0	....	1	0	0	0	0	1^1	3	5	5	0	2	3	0	4.500	33.75	11	27.12	.429	0	....	-4	0	-0.4
1959	SF-N	0	0	....	10	1	0	0	0	18	16	11	9	2	1	17	11	1.833	4.50	85	5.86	.239	0	.000	-1	0	-0.2
1960	SF-N	0	0	....	15	0	0	0	0	20	20	13	12	2	3	9	9	1.450	5.40	64	4.97	.274	0	....	-4	0	-0.4
1963	Chi-A	0	1	.000	3	0	0	0	0	4^2	9	7	3	0	0	6	3	3.214	5.79	61	13.30	.409	0	.000	-1	0	-0.2
Total	4	0	1	.000	29	1	0	0	0	44	48	36	29	4	6	35	23	1.886	5.93	61	6.89	.284	0	.000	-11	0	-1.2
• SHIREY, Duke	Clair Lee Shirey b: 6/20/1898, Jersey Shore, PA d: 9/1/1962, Hagerstown, MD BR/TR, 6'1", 175 lbs. Deb: 9/28/1920																										
1920	Was-A	0	1	.000	2	1	0	0	0	4	5	4	3	0	1	2	0	1.750	6.75	55	6.08	.313	0	.000	-1	0	-0.1
• SHIRLEY, Bob	Robert Charles Shirley b: 6/25/1954, Cushing, OK BR/TL, 5'11", 185 lbs. Deb: 4/10/1977																										
1977	SD-N	12	18	.400	39	35	1	0	0	214	215	107	88	22	4	100	146	1.472	3.70	96	4.31	.259	9	.122	-3	6	-0.5
1978	SD-N	8	11	.421	50	20	2	0	5	166	164	75	68	10	3	61	102	1.355	3.69	90	3.58	.262	5	.125	-7	7	-0.7
1979	SD-N	8	16	.333	49	25	4	1	0	205	196	89	77	15	6	59	117	1.244	3.38	104	3.35	.257	5	.091	2	11	0.0
1980	SD-N	11	12	.478	59	12	3	0	7	137	143	58	54	12	0	54	67	1.438	3.55	97	4.11	.276	1	.033	-4	8	-0.6
1981	StL-N	6	4	.600	28	11	1	0	1	79^1	78	42	36	6	1	34	36	1.412	4.08	87	3.93	.260	3	.136	-6	3	-0.7
1982	Cin-N	8	13	.381	41	20	1	0	0	152^2	138	74	61	17	3	73	89	1.382	3.60	103	3.94	.248	6	.143	1	7	0.0
1983	NY-A	5	8	.385	25	17	1	1	0	108	122	71	61	10	0	36	53	1.463	5.08	77	4.49	.293	0	....	-14	2	-1.4
1984	NY-A	3	3	.500	41	7	1	0	0	114^1	119	47	43	8	0	38	48	1.373	3.38	112	3.91	.274	0	....	6	6	0.6
1985	NY-A	5	5	.500	48	8	2	0	2	109	103	34	32	5	0	26	55	1.183	2.64	152	2.80	.251	0	....	15	9	1.5
1986	NY-A	0	4	.000	39	6	0	0	3	105^1	108	60	59	13	3	40	64	1.405	5.04	81	4.44	.271	0	....	-12	3	-1.2
1987	NY-A	1	0	1.000	12	1	0	0	0	34	36	20	17	4	0	16	12	1.529	4.50	97	4.78	.277	0	....	-1	2	-0.1
	KC-A	0	0	....	3	0	0	0	0	7^1	10	12	12	5	0	6	1	2.182	14.73	31	13.63	.323	0	....	-8	0	-0.8
	Yr.	1	0	1.000	15	1	0	0	0	41^1	46	32	29	9	0	22	13	1.645	6.31	71	6.35	.286	0	....	-9	2	-0.8
Total	11	67	94	.416	434	162	16	2	18	1432	1432	689	608	127	20	543	790	1.379	3.82	96	3.94	.264	29	.110	-30	64	-3.9
• SHIRLEY, Steve	Steven Brian Shirley b: 10/12/1956, San Francisco, CA BL/TL, 6', 185 lbs. Deb: 6/21/1982																										
1982	LA-N	1	1	.500	11	0	0	0	0	12^2	15	6	6	0	0	7	8	1.737	4.26	81	4.71	.300	1	1.000	-1	1	-0.1
• SHIRLEY, Tex	Alvis Newman Shirley b: 4/25/1918, Birthright, TX d: 11/7/1993, DeSoto, TX BB/TR, 6'1", 175 lbs. Deb: 9/6/1941																										
1941	Phi-A	0	1	.000	5	0	0	0	1	7^1	8	4	2	1	0	6	1	1.909	2.45	171	6.42	.286	0	.000	1	1	0.1
1942	Phi-A	0	1	.000	15	1	0	0	1	35^2	37	30	21	0	2	22	10	1.654	5.30	71	4.45	.272	0	.000	-5	0	-0.7
1944*	StL-A	5	4	.556	23	11	2	1	0	80^1	59	45	37	4	1	64	35	1.531	4.15	87	3.55	.203	4	.143	-3	3	-0.5
1945	StL-A	8	12	.400	32	24	10	2	0	183^2	191	79	74	8	1	93	77	**1.546**	3.63	97	4.24	.274	20	.286	-2	12	0.1
1946	StL-A	6	12	.333	27	18	7	0	0	139^2	148	89	77	7	1	105	45	1.811	4.96	75	5.25	.273	10	.196	-19	2	-2.0
Total	5	19	30	.388	102	54	19	3	2	446^2	443	247	211	20	5	290	168	1.641	4.25	86	4.48	.261	34	.214	-28	18	-2.9
• SHOCKER, Urban	Urban James Shocker b: 9/22/1892, Cleveland, OH d: 9/9/1928, Denver, CO BR/TR, 5'10", 170 lbs. Deb: 4/24/1916																										
1916	NY-A	4	3	.571	12	9	4	1	0	82^1	67	25	24	2	6	32	43	1.202	2.62	110	2.85	.230	4	.190	1	6	0.3
1917	NY-A	8	5	.615	26	13	7	0	1	145	124	59	42	4	0	46	68	1.172	2.61	103	2.62	.241	8	.178	1	9	0.0
1918	StL-A	6	5	.545	14	9	7	0	2	94^2	69	26	19	0	1	40	33	1.151	1.81	151	2.12	.209	11	.324	9	11	1.5
1919	StL-A	13	11	.542	30	25	14	5	0	211	193	75	63	6	4	55	86	1.175	2.69	123	2.71	.244	8	.138	13	17	1.3
1920	StL-A	20	10	.667	38	28	22	5	**5**	245^2	224	97	74	10	4	70	107	1.197	2.71	144	2.89	.248	18	.225	32	24	3.4
1921	StL-A	**27**	12	.692	47	38	30	4	4	326^2	345	151	129	21	6	86	132	1.319	3.55	126	3.57	.270	27	.260	35	30	3.7
1922	StL-A	24	17	.585	48	38	29	2	3	348	365	141	115	22	4	57	**149**	1.213	2.97	139	3.19	.272	22	.191	36	29	3.7
1923	StL-A	20	12	.625	43	35	24	3	5	277^1	292	122	105	12	3	49	109	1.230	3.41	122	3.12	.272	16	.200	20	25	2.1
1924	StL-A	16	13	.552	40	33	17	4	1	246^1	270	128	115	11	3	52	88	1.307	4.20	107	3.42	.277	16	.239	6	20	1.2
1925	NY-A	12	12	.500	41	30	15	2	2	244^1	278	108	99	17	3	58	74	1.375	3.65	117	4.05	.294	11	.172	17	19	2.0
1926*	NY-A	19	11	.633	41	32	18	0	2	258^1	272	113	97	13	2	71	59	1.328	3.38	114	3.46	.269	13	.171	18	19	1.8
1927	NY-A	18	6	.750	31	27	13	2	0	200	207	86	63	8	1	41	35	1.240	2.84	136	3.06	.268	13	.241	22	16	2.4
1928	NY-A	0	0	....	1	0	0	0	0	2	3	0	0	0	0	0	0	1.500	0.00	....	5.90	.429	0	....	1	0	0.1
Total	13	187	117	.615	412	317	200	28	25	2681^2	2709	1131	945	126	37	657	983	1.255	3.17	124	3.20	.265	167	.209	213	225	23.6
• SHOFFNER, Milt	Milburn James Shoffner b: 11/13/1905, Sherman, TX d: 1/19/1978, Madison, OH BL/TL, 6'1.5", 184 lbs. Deb: 7/20/1929																										
1929	Cle-A	2	3	.400	11	3	1	0	0	44^2	46	28	25	4	3	22	15	1.522	5.04	88	4.74	.284	0	.000	-3	2	-0.5
1930	Cle-A	3	4	.429	24	10	1	0	0	84^2	129	86	75	8	1	50	17	2.114	7.97	60	8.00	.362	7	.212	-28	0	-2.4
1931	Cle-A	2	3	.400	12	4	1	0	0	41	55	34	33	4	2	26	12	1.976	7.24	64	7.06	.320	1	.077	-11	0	-1.1
1937	Bos-N	3	1	.750	6	5	3	1	1	42^2	38	14	12	1	1	9	13	1.102	2.53	142	2.33	.239	2	.125	4	4	0.5
1938	Bos-N	8	7	.533	26	15	9	1	1	139^2	147	60	55	7	2	36	49	1.310	3.54	97	3.43	.270	12	.211	-3	9	0.0
1939	Bos-N	4	6	.400	25	11	7	0	1	132^1	133	56	46	4	1	42	51	1.322	3.13	118	3.25	.265	7	.159	6	8	0.6
	Cin-N	2	2	.500	10	3	0	0	0	37^2	43	18	14	3	2	11	6	1.434	3.35	115	4.37	.289	1	.091	1	2	0.0
	Yr.	6	8	.429	35	14	7	0	1	170	176	74	60	7	3	53	57	1.347	3.18	117	3.50	.271	8	.145	7	10	0.6
1940	Cin-N	1	0	1.000	20	0	0	0	0	54^1	56	35	34	3	0	18	17	1.362	5.63	67	3.58	.268	2	.125	-13	0	-1.4
Total	7	25	26	.490	134	51	22	2	3	577	647	331	294	34	12	214	180	1.492	4.59	88	4.41	.287	32	.156	-46	25	-4.3
• SHORE, Ernie	Ernest Grady Shore b: 3/24/1891, East Bend, NC d: 9/24/1980, Winston-Salem, NC BR/TR, 6'4", 220 lbs. Deb: 6/20/1912																										
1912	NY-N	0	0	....	1	0	0	0	1	1	8	10	3	1	0	1	1	9.000	27.00	13	73.30	.667	0	....	-3	0	-0.3
1914	Bos-A	10	5	.667	20	16	10	1	1	139^2	103	45	31	1	5	34	51	.981	2.00	134	1.65	.204	5	.102	8	11	0.6
1915*	Bos-A	19	8	.704	38	32	17	4	0	247	207	75	45	3	4	66	102	1.105	1.64	169	2.24	.228	8	.101	29	22	2.8
1916*	Bos-A	16	10	.615	38	28	10	3	1	225^2	221	83	66	1	4	49	62	1.196	2.63	105	2.75	.259	7	.091	6	14	0.2
1917	Bos-A	13	10	.565	29	27	14	1	1	226^2	201	76	56	1	12	55	57	1.129	2.22	116	2.48	.240	13	.167	8	17	0.7
1919	NY-A	5	8	.385	20	13	3	0	0	95	105	50	44	4	1	44	24	1.568	4.17	76	4.58	.288	4	.143	-13	3	-1.5
1920	NY-A	2	2	.500	14	5	2	0	1	44^1	61	31	24	1	1	21	12	1.850	4.87	78	6.07	.333	2	.182	-5	1	-0.5
Total	7	65	43	.602	160	121	56	9	5	979^1	906	370	269	12	27	270	309	1.201	2.47	115	2.80	.247	39	.121	30	68	1.9
• SHORE, Ray	Raymond Everett Shore b: 6/9/1921, Cincinnati, OH d: 8/13/1996, St. Louis, MO BR/TR, 6'3", 210 lbs. Deb: 9/21/1946 C																										
1946	StL-A	0	0	....	1	0	0	0	0	1	3	2	2	0	0	1	1	4.000	18.00	21	19.12	.500	0	....	-2	0	-0.2
1948	StL-A	1	2	.333	17	4	0	0	0	38	40	30	27	2	4	35	12	1.974	6.39	71	6.15	.270	0	.000	-7	0	-0.8
1949	StL-A	0	1	.000	13	0	0	0	0	23^1	27	30	28	3	2	31	13	2.486	10.80	42	9.28	.297	0	.000	-15	0	-1.6
Total	3	1	3	.250	31	4	0	0	0	62^1	70	62	57	5	6	67	26	2.198	8.23	55	7.53	.286	0	.000	-24	0	-2.6
• SHORES, Bill	William David Shores b: 5/26/1904, Abilene, TX d: 2/19/1984, Purcell, OK BR/TR, 6', 185 lbs. Deb: 4/11/1928																										
1928	Phi-A	1	1	.500	3	2	1	0	0	14	13	7	5	0	0	7	5	1.429	3.21	125	3.20	.250	0	.000	1	1	0.0
1929	Phi-A	11	6	.647	39	13	5	1	7	152^2	150	71	61	9	3	59	49	1.369	3.60	118	3.63	.262	5	.125	10	13	0.8
1930*	Phi-A	12	4	.750	31	19	7	1	0	159	169	86	74	11	3	70	48	1.503	4.19	111	4.34	.276	11	.193	8	11	0.5
1931	Phi-A	0	3	.000	6	2	0	0	0	16	26	18	9	3	0	10	2	2.250	5.06	89	9.47	.361	1	.333	-1	0	-0.1
1933	NY-N	2	1	.667	8	3	1	0	0	36^2	41	18	16	4	0	14	20	1.500	3.93	82	4.72	.291	3	.273	-4	2	-0.3
1936	Chi-A	0	0	....	9	0	0	0	0	17	26	18	18	1	0	8	5	2.000	9.53	55	7.00	.356	1	.200	-8	0	-0.8
Total	6	26	15	.634	96	39	14	2	7	395^1	425	218	183	28	6	168	129	1.500	4.17	105	4.38	.279	21	.174	6	27	0.2
• SHORT, Bill	William Ross Short b: 11/27/1937, Kingston, NY BL/TL, 5'9", 170 lbs. Deb: 4/23/1960																										
1960	NY-A	3	5	.375	10	10	2	0	0	47	49	25	25	5	1	30	14	1.681	4.79	75	5.55	.282	3	.200	-8	1	-0.7
1962	Bal-A	0	0	....	5	0	0	0	0	4	8	7	7	0	1	6	3	3.500	15.75	24	14.94	.381	0	.000	-5	0	-0.6

YEAR	TM-L	W	L	PCT	G	GS	CG	SH	SV	IP	H	R	ER	HR	HB	BB	SO	RAT	ERA	ERA+	CERA	OAV	BH	AVG	PR+	WS	TPW
1966	Bal-A	2	3	.400	6	6	1	1	0	37^2	34	15	12	2	0	10	27	1.168	2.87	116	2.73	.239	1	.091	2	2	0.1
	Bos-A	0	0	....	8	0	0	0	0	8^1	10	6	4	1	0	2	2	1.440	4.32	88	4.74	.294	0	.000	-0	0	-0.1
	Yr.	2	3	.400	14	6	1	1	0	46	44	21	16	3	0	12	29	1.217	3.13	110	3.09	.250	1	.083	1	2	0.1
1967	Pit-N	0	0	....	6	0	0	0	1	2^1	1	1	1	0	0	1	1	.857	3.86	87	1.08	.143	0	.000	-0	0	0.0
1968	NY-N	0	3	.000	34	0	0	0	1	30^1	24	17	16	0	1	14	24	1.253	4.75	64	2.57	.220	0	.000	-6	0	-0.7
1969	Cin-N	0	0	....	4	0	0	0	0	2^1	4	4	4	0	0	1	0	2.143	15.43	24	8.25	.400	0	.000	-3	0	-0.3
Total	6	5	11	.313	73	16	3	1	2	132	130	75	69	8	3	64	71	1.470	4.70	73	4.26	.262	4	.125	-21	3	-2.3

• SHORT, Chris Christopher Joseph Short b: 9/19/1937, Milford, DE d: 8/1/1991, Wilmington, DE BR/TL, 6'4", 205 lbs. Deb: 4/19/1959

YEAR	TM-L	W	L	PCT	G	GS	CG	SH	SV	IP	H	R	ER	HR	HB	BB	SO	RAT	ERA	ERA+	CERA	OAV	BH	AVG	PR+	WS	TPW
1959	Phi-N	0	0	....	3	2	0	0	0	14^1	19	13	13	3	1	10	8	2.023	8.16	50	8.52	.317	0	.000	-6	0	-0.7
1960	Phi-N	6	9	.400	42	10	2	0	3	107^1	101	55	47	8	3	52	54	1.425	3.94	98	3.93	.249	0	.000	-1	6	-0.4
1961	Phi-N	6	12	.333	39	16	1	0	1	127^1	157	94	84	12	3	71	80	1.791	5.94	69	5.95	.304	6	.162	-28	0	-2.9
1962	Phi-N	11	9	.550	47	12	4	0	3	142	149	66	54	13	8	56	91	1.444	3.42	113	4.45	.272	8	.222	6	11	0.7
1963	Phi-N	9	12	.429	38	27	6	3	0	198	185	77	65	12	3	69	160	1.283	2.95	109	3.29	.248	7	.106	3	11	0.1
1964	Phi-N★	17	9	.654	42	31	12	4	2	220^2	174	63	54	10	4	51	181	1.020	2.20	157	2.10	.217	7	.108	30	21	3.0
1965	Phi-N	18	11	.621	47	40	15	5	2	297^1	260	102	93	18	5	89	237	1.174	2.82	123	2.81	.235	13	.131	21	24	2.0
1966	Phi-N	20	10	.667	42	39	19	4	0	272	257	120	107	28	9	68	177	1.195	3.54	101	3.37	.250	22	.208	1	17	0.2
1967	Phi-N★	9	11	.450	29	26	8	2	1	199^1	163	55	53	9	4	74	142	1.189	2.39	142	2.69	.225	6	.091	23	16	2.2
1968	Phi-N	19	13	.594	42	36	9	2	1	269^2	236	99	88	25	9	81	202	1.176	2.94	102	3.08	.236	12	.152	5	18	0.6
1969	Phi-N	0	0	....	2	2	0	0	0	10	11	8	8	2	1	4	5	1.500	7.20	49	5.83	.282	0	.000	-4	0	-0.5
1970	Phi-N	9	16	.360	36	34	7	2	1	199	211	100	95	13	6	66	133	1.392	4.30	93	3.98	.272	3	.049	-5	9	-1.0
1971	Phi-N	7	14	.333	31	26	5	2	1	173	182	85	74	22	3	63	95	1.416	3.85	91	4.51	.274	4	.083	-8	7	-1.0
1972	Phi-N	1	1	.500	19	0	0	0	1	23	24	12	10	3	0	8	20	1.391	3.91	92	4.14	.267	0	....	-1	1	-0.1
1973	Mil-A	3	5	.375	42	7	0	0	2	72	86	42	41	5	2	44	44	1.806	5.13	73	5.83	.299	0	....	-11	1	-1.1
Total	15	135	132	.506	501	308	88	24	18	2325	2215	991	886	183	61	806	1629	1.299	3.43	104	3.58	.252	88	.126	24	142	1.1

• SHOUN, Clyde Clyde Mitchell "Hardrock" Shoun b: 3/20/1912, Mountain City, TN d: 3/20/1968, Mountain Home, TN BL/TL, 6'1", 188 lbs. Deb: 8/7/1935

YEAR	TM-L	W	L	PCT	G	GS	CG	SH	SV	IP	H	R	ER	HR	HB	BB	SO	RAT	ERA	ERA+	CERA	OAV	BH	AVG	PR+	WS	TPW
1935	Chi-N	1	0	1.000	5	1	0	0	0	12^2	14	4	4	2	0	5	5	1.500	2.84	138	5.27	.298	0	.000	1	1	0.1
1936	Chi-N	0	0	....	4	0	0	0	0	4^1	3	6	6	0	0	6	1	2.077	12.46	32	4.96	.200	0	....	-4	0	-0.4
1937	Chi-N	7	7	.500	37	9	2	0	0	93	118	65	58	9	0	45	43	1.753	5.61	71	5.75	.309	4	.138	-17	1	-1.8
1938	StL-N	6	6	.500	40	12	3	0	1	117^1	130	58	54	8	1	43	37	1.474	4.14	95	4.31	.283	8	.258	-2	7	-0.2
1939	StL-N	3	1	.750	**53**	2	0	0	**9**	103	98	51	43	4	2	42	50	1.359	3.76	109	3.31	.248	3	.115	3	8	0.2
1940	StL-N	13	11	.542	**54**	19	13	1	5	197^1	193	96	86	13	2	46	82	1.211	3.92	102	3.08	.255	12	.190	5	13	0.4
1941	StL-N	3	5	.375	26	6	0	0	0	70	98	48	44	9	0	20	34	1.686	5.66	67	6.12	.337	4	.182	-16	0	-1.6
1942	StL-N	0	0	....	2	0	0	0	0	1^2	1	0	0	0	0	0	0	.600	0.00	....	0.65	.167	0	....	1	0	0.1
	Cin-N	1	3	.250	34	0	0	0	0	72^2	55	23	18	2	0	24	32	1.087	2.23	147	2.11	.216	4	.308	8	6	1.0
	Yr.	1	3	.250	36	0	0	0	0	74^1	56	23	18	2	0	24	32	1.076	2.18	151	2.08	.215	4	.308	9	6	1.0
1943	Cin-N	14	5	.737	45	5	2	0	7	147	131	52	50	5	0	46	61	1.204	3.06	108	2.69	.241	13	.310	0	15	0.4
1944	Cin-N	13	10	.565	38	21	12	1	2	202^2	193	83	68	10	3	42	55	1.160	3.02	115	2.75	.248	15	.224	6	15	0.7
1946	Cin-N	1	6	.143	27	5	0	0	0	79	87	42	36	3	1	26	20	1.430	4.10	82	4.00	.292	2	.095	-9	1	-1.1
1947	Cin-N	0	0	....	10	0	0	0	0	14^1	16	8	8	2	1	5	7	1.465	5.02	82	5.65	.320	0	....	-1	0	-0.1
	Bos-N	5	3	.625	26	3	1	1	1	73^2	73	41	36	6	0	21	23	1.276	4.40	89	3.35	.254	3	.158	-3	3	-0.4
	Yr.	5	3	.625	36	3	1	1	1	88	89	49	44	8	1	26	30	1.307	4.50	87	3.72	.264	3	.158	-5	3	-0.5
1948	Bos-N	5	1	.833	36	2	1	0	4	74	77	37	33	7	0	20	25	1.311	4.01	95	3.73	.267	4	.190	-2	5	-0.2
1949	Bos-N	0	0	....	1	0	0	0	0	1	1	0	0	0	0	0	0	1.000	0.00	....	1.95	.250	0	....	0	0	0.0
	Chi-A	1	1	.500	16	0	0	0	0	23^1	37	17	15	1	0	13	8	2.143	5.79	72	7.74	.370	1	.200	-4	0	-0.4
Total	14	73	59	.553	454	85	34	3	29	1287	1325	631	559	81	10	404	483	1.343	3.91	96	3.66	.267	73	.202	-35	75	-3.4

• SHOUSE, Brian Brian Douglas Shouse b: 9/26/1968, Effingham, IL BL/TL, 5'11", 180 lbs. Deb: 7/31/1993

YEAR	TM-L	W	L	PCT	G	GS	CG	SH	SV	IP	H	R	ER	HR	HB	BB	SO	RAT	ERA	ERA+	CERA	OAV	BH	AVG	PR+	WS	TPW
1993	Pit-N	0	0	....	6	0	0	0	0	4	7	4	4	1	0	2	3	2.250	9.00	45	9.92	.368	0	....	-2	0	-0.2
1998	Bos-A	0	1	.000	7	0	0	0	0	8	9	5	5	2	0	4	5	1.625	5.63	84	6.42	.281	0	....	-1	0	-0.1
2002	KC-A	0	0	....	23	0	0	0	0	14^2	15	10	10	3	2	9	11	1.636	6.14	82	6.11	.259	0	....	-2	0	-0.2
2003	Tex-A	0	1	.000	62	0	0	0	1	61	62	24	21	1	4	14	40	1.246	3.10	160	3.10	.267	0	....	13	6	1.3
Total	4	0	2	.000	98	0	0	0	1	87^2	93	43	40	7	6	29	59	1.392	4.11	118	4.22	.273	0	....	9	6	0.8

• SHOW, Eric Eric Vaughn Show b: 5/19/1956, Riverside, CA d: 3/16/1994, Dulzura, CA BR/TR, 6'1", 185 lbs. Deb: 9/2/1981

YEAR	TM-L	W	L	PCT	G	GS	CG	SH	SV	IP	H	R	ER	HR	HB	BB	SO	RAT	ERA	ERA+	CERA	OAV	BH	AVG	PR+	WS	TPW
1981	SD-N	1	3	.250	15	0	0	0	3	23	17	9	8	2	1	9	22	1.130	3.13	104	2.63	.213	0	....	0	2	0.0
1982	SD-N	10	6	.625	47	14	2	2	3	150	117	49	44	10	5	48	88	1.100	2.64	130	2.50	.217	6	.146	12	11	1.1
1983	SD-N	15	12	.556	35	33	4	2	0	200^2	201	97	93	25	6	74	120	1.370	4.17	84	4.27	.263	11	.172	-19	8	-1.9
1984*	SD-N	15	9	.625	32	32	3	1	0	206^2	175	88	78	18	4	88	104	1.273	3.40	105	3.33	.234	17	.246	-0	12	0.6
1985	SD-N	12	11	.522	35	35	5	2	0	233	212	95	80	27	5	87	141	1.283	3.09	114	3.65	.243	10	.127	7	13	0.6
1986	SD-N	9	5	.643	24	22	2	0	0	136^1	109	47	45	11	4	69	94	1.306	2.97	123	3.39	.225	7	.163	11	10	1.1
1987	SD-N	8	16	.333	34	34	5	3	0	206^1	188	99	88	26	9	85	117	1.323	3.84	103	3.91	.241	5	.071	1	9	-0.3
1988	SD-N	16	11	.593	32	32	13	1	0	234^2	201	86	85	22	6	53	144	1.082	3.26	104	2.73	.231	12	.148	0	14	0.0
1989	SD-N	8	6	.571	16	16	1	0	0	106^1	113	59	50	9	2	39	66	1.429	4.23	83	4.20	.274	8	.235	-10	4	-0.9
1990	SD-N	6	8	.429	39	12	0	0	1	106^1	131	74	68	16	4	41	55	1.618	5.76	66	5.79	.306	5	.200	-23	0	-2.3
1991	Oak-A	1	2	.333	23	5	0	0	0	51^2	62	36	34	5	0	17	20	1.529	5.92	65	4.83	.298	0	....	-12	0	-1.2
Total	11	101	89	.532	332	235	35	11	7	1655	1526	739	673	171	46	610	971	1.291	3.66	98	3.66	.247	81	.160	-33	83	-3.1

• SHREVE, Lev Leven Lawrence Shreve b: 1/14/1869, Louisville, KY d: 10/18/1942, Detroit, MI BR/TR, 5'11", 150 lbs. Deb: 5/2/1887

YEAR	TM-L	W	L	PCT	G	GS	CG	SH	SV	IP	H	R	ER	HR	HB	BB	SO	RAT	ERA	ERA+	CERA	OAV	BH	AVG	PR+	WS	TPW
1887	Bal-a	3	1	.750	5	5	4	1	0	38	52	26	16	0	1	19	13	1.368	3.79	108	....	.315	5	.200	2	2	0.1
	Ind-N	5	9	.357	14	14	14	1	0	122	206	100	64	5	4	65	22	1.689	4.72	87	....	.364	16	.308	-9	4	-0.7
1888	Ind-N	11	24	.314	35	35	34	1	0	297^2	352	208	153	23	8	93	101	**1.495**	4.63	64	....	.284	21	.183	-51	5	-5.1
1889	Ind-N	0	3	.000	3	3	1	0	0	15^2	25	27	24	3	1	12	5	2.362	13.79	30	....	.350	0	.000	-17	0	-1.5
Total	3	19	37	.339	57	57	53	3	0	473^1	635	361	257	31	14	189	141	1.563	4.89	68	....	.311	42	.211	-75	11	-7.2

• SHRIVER, Harry Harry Graydon "Pop" Shriver b: 9/2/1896, Wadestown, WV d: 1/21/1970, Morgantown, WV BR/TR, 6'2", 180 lbs. Deb: 4/14/1922

YEAR	TM-L	W	L	PCT	G	GS	CG	SH	SV	IP	H	R	ER	HR	HB	BB	SO	RAT	ERA	ERA+	CERA	OAV	BH	AVG	PR+	WS	TPW
1922	Bro-N	4	6	.400	25	13	4	2	0	108^1	114	49	36	5	2	48	38	1.495	2.99	136	4.19	.287	1	.037	14	7	1.0
1923	Bro-N	0	0	....	1	1	0	0	0	4	8	3	3	0	0	0	1	2.000	6.75	57	7.91	.444	0	.000	-1	0	-0.1
Total	2	4	6	.400	26	14	4	2	0	112^1	122	52	39	5	2	48	39	1.513	3.12	130	4.33	.294	1	.036	12	7	0.9

• SHUEY, Paul Paul Kenneth Shuey b: 9/16/1970, Lima, OH BR/TR, 6'3", 215 lbs. Deb: 5/8/1994

YEAR	TM-L	W	L	PCT	G	GS	CG	SH	SV	IP	H	R	ER	HR	HB	BB	SO	RAT	ERA	ERA+	CERA	OAV	BH	AVG	PR+	WS	TPW
1994	Cle-A	0	1	.000	14	0	0	0	5	11^2	14	11	11	1	0	12	16	2.229	8.49	56	7.28	.280	0	....	-5	0	-0.5
1995	Cle-A	0	2	.000	7	0	0	0	0	6^1	5	4	3	0	0	5	5	1.579	4.26	110	3.70	.238	0	....	0	0	0.0
1996*	Cle-A	5	2	.714	42	0	0	0	4	53^2	45	19	17	6	0	26	44	1.323	2.85	172	3.56	.231	0	....	12	7	1.1
1997	Cle-A	4	2	.667	40	0	0	0	2	45	52	31	31	5	1	28	46	1.778	6.20	76	5.92	.294	0	.000	-7	1	-0.7
1998*	Cle-A	5	4	.556	43	0	0	0	2	51	44	19	17	6	3	25	58	1.353	3.00	159	3.83	.229	0	.000	10	6	1.0
1999*	Cle-A	8	5	.615	72	0	0	0	6	81^2	68	37	32	8	1	40	103	1.322	3.53	143	3.36	.223	0	....	14	10	1.3
2000	Cle-A	4	2	.667	57	0	0	0	0	63^2	51	25	24	4	3	30	69	1.272	3.39	146	3.11	.219	0	....	12	8	1.1
2001*	Cle-A	5	3	.625	47	0	0	0	2	54^1	53	25	17	1	1	26	70	1.454	2.82	160	3.46	.251	0	....	11	6	1.1
2002	Cle-A	3	0	1.000	39	0	0	0	0	37^1	31	11	10	1	0	10	39	1.098	2.41	182	2.21	.225	0	....	9	5	0.8
	LA-N	5	2	.714	28	0	0	0	1	30^2	25	18	15	2	1	21	24	1.500	4.40	87	3.89	.217	1	.333	-2	2	-0.2
2003	LA-N	6	4	.600	62	0	0	0	0	69	50	24	23	6	4	33	60	1.203	3.00	134	3.06	.207	0	.000	7	7	0.6
Total	10	45	27	.625	451	0	0	0	22	504^1	438	224	200	40	14	256	534	1.376	3.57	129	3.64	.233	1	.143	61	52	5.7

• SHULTZ, Toots Wallace Luther Shultz b: 10/10/1888, Homestead, PA d: 1/30/1959, McKeesport, PA BR/TR, 5'10", 175 lbs. Deb: 5/5/1911

YEAR	TM-L	W	L	PCT	G	GS	CG	SH	SV	IP	H	R	ER	HR	HB	BB	SO	RAT	ERA	ERA+	CERA	OAV	BH	AVG	PR+	WS	TPW
1911	Phi-N	0	3	.000	5	3	2	0	0	25	30	28	26	5	4	15	9	1.800	9.36	37	7.62	.300	2	.250	-16	0	-1.6
1912	Phi-N	1	4	.200	22	4	1	0	1	59	75	44	30	2	3	35	20	1.864	4.58	79	6.13	.333	5	.238	-6	1	-0.6
Total	2	1	7	.125	27	7	3	0	1	84	105	72	56	7	7	50	29	1.845	6.00	59	6.57	.323	7	.241	-23	1	-2.3

YEAR	TM-L	W	L	PCT	G	GS	CG	SH	SV	IP	H	R	ER	HR	HB	BB	SO	RAT	ERA	ERA+	CERA	OAV	BH	AVG	PR+	WS	TPW
• SHUMAKER, Anthony	Anthony Warren Shumaker b: 5/14/1973, Tucson, AZ BL/TL, 6'5", 219 lbs. Deb: 7/23/1999																										
1999	Phi-N	0	3	.000	8	4	0	0	0	22^{2}	23	17	15	3	1	14	17	1.632	5.96	79	5.39	.261	1	.200	-3	0	-0.3
• SHUMAN, Harry	Harry Shuman b: 3/5/1915, Philadelphia, PA d: 10/25/1996, Philadelphia, PA BR/TR, 6'2", 195 lbs. Deb: 9/14/1942																										
1942	Pit-N	0	0	....	1	0	0	0	0	2	0	0	0	0	0	1	1	.500	0.00	....	0.23	.000	0	....	1	0	0.1
1943	Pit-N	0	0	....	11	0	0	0	0	22	30	20	13	0	2	8	5	1.727	5.32	65	5.52	.337	0	.000	-4	0	-0.5
1944	Phi-N	0	0	....	18	0	0	0	0	26^{2}	26	15	12	1	0	11	4	1.388	4.05	89	3.32	.245	0	.000	-1	1	-0.1
Total	3	0	0	....	30	0	0	0	0	50^{2}	56	35	25	1	2	20	10	1.500	4.44	80	4.16	.287	0	.000	-5	1	-0.6
• SIEBERT, Paul	Paul Edward Siebert b: 6/5/1953, Minneapolis, MN BL/TL, 6'2", 205 lbs. Deb: 9/7/1974																										
1974	Hou-N	1	1	.500	5	5	1	1	0	25^{1}	21	12	10	3	0	11	10	1.263	3.55	97	3.44	.236	0	.000	-1	1	-0.1
1975	Hou-N	0	2	.000	7	2	0	0	2	18^{1}	20	7	6	0	1	6	6	1.418	2.95	114	3.86	.294	0	.000	1	1	0.0
1976	Hou-N	0	2	.000	19	0	0	0	0	25^{2}	29	10	9	0	1	18	10	1.831	3.16	101	4.75	.296	0	.000	0	1	0.0
1977	SD-N	0	0	....	4	0	0	0	0	3^{2}	3	4	1	1	0	4	1	1.909	2.45	144	6.20	.214	0	....	0	0	0.0
	NY-N	2	1	.667	25	0	0	0	0	28	27	12	12	0	1	13	20	1.429	3.86	97	3.27	.257	0	.000	-0	2	-0.1
	Yr.	2	1	.667	29	0	0	0	0	31^{2}	30	16	13	1	1	17	21	1.484	3.69	101	3.61	.252	0	.000	0	2	0.0
1978	NY-N	0	2	.000	27	0	0	0	1	28	30	16	16	2	1	21	12	1.821	5.14	68	5.60	.283	0	.000	-5	0	-0.6
Total	5	3	8	.273	87	7	1	1	3	129	130	61	54	6	4	73	59	1.574	3.77	92	4.27	.271	0	.000	-5	5	-0.7
• SIEBERT, Sonny	Wilfred Charles Siebert b: 1/14/1937, St. Mary, MO BR/TR, 6'3", 198 lbs. Deb: 4/26/1964 C																										
1964	Cle-A	7	9	.438	41	14	3	1	3	156	142	61	56	15	2	57	144	1.276	3.23	112	3.45	.243	13	.265	10	12	1.6
1965	Cle-A	16	8	.667	39	27	4	1	1	188^{2}	139	58	51	14	5	46	191	.981	2.43	143	2.09	.206	7	.106	22	17	2.2
1966	Cle-A★	16	8	.667	34	32	11	1	1	241	193	89	75	25	6	62	163	1.058	2.80	123	2.63	.221	11	.129	21	20	2.0
1967	Cle-A	10	12	.455	34	26	7	1	4	185^{1}	136	59	49	17	6	54	136	1.025	2.38	137	2.33	.202	7	.135	20	15	2.4
1968	Cle-A	12	10	.545	31	30	8	4	0	206	145	76	68	12	8	88	146	1.131	2.97	100	2.43	.198	11	.157	-2	11	-0.1
1969	Cle-A	0	1	.000	2	2	0	0	0	14	10	5	5	1	0	8	6	1.286	3.21	117	2.93	.196	1	.250	1	1	0.1
	Bos-A	14	10	.583	43	22	2	0	5	163^{1}	151	93	69	21	4	68	127	1.341	3.80	100	4.01	.245	8	.151	4	9	0.5
	Yr.	14	11	.560	45	24	2	0	5	177^{1}	161	98	74	22	4	76	133	1.336	3.76	101	3.93	.241	9	.158	4	10	0.6
1970	Bos-A	15	8	.652	33	33	7	2	0	222^{2}	207	98	85	29	6	60	142	1.199	3.44	115	3.51	.248	10	.130	17	14	1.7
1971	Bos-A★	16	10	.615	32	32	12	4	0	235^{1}	220	84	76	20	3	60	131	1.190	2.91	127	3.07	.245	21	.266	24	22	3.6
1972	Bos-A	12	12	.500	32	30	7	3	0	196^{1}	204	105	83	17	7	59	123	1.340	3.80	84	3.86	.264	17	.236	-9	7	-0.4
1973	Bos-A	0	1	.000	2	0	0	0	0	2^{1}	5	2	2	1	0	1	5	2.571	7.71	52	14.73	.417	0	....	-1	0	-0.1
	Tex-A	7	11	.389	25	20	1	1	2	119^{2}	120	68	53	11	3	37	76	1.312	3.99	93	3.74	.258	0	....	-0	5	0.0
	Yr.	7	12	.368	27	20	1	1	2	122	125	70	55	12	3	38	81	1.336	4.06	92	3.95	.262	0	....	-1	5	-0.1
1974	StL-N	8	8	.500	28	20	5	3	0	133^{2}	150	66	57	8	3	51	68	1.504	3.84	93	4.35	.288	5	.114	-6	6	-0.8
1975	SD-N	3	2	.600	6	6	0	0	0	26^{2}	37	15	13	2	1	10	10	1.763	4.39	79	5.89	.330	3	.375	-2	2	0.0
	Oak-A	4	4	.500	17	13	0	0	0	61	60	28	25	4	0	31	44	1.492	3.69	98	3.95	.252	0	.000	-1	3	-0.1
Total	12	140	114	.551	399	307	67	21	16	2152	1919	907	767	197	54	692	1512	1.213	3.21	109	3.22	.238	114	.173	97	144	12.4
• SIEBLER, Dwight	Dwight Leroy Siebler b: 8/5/1937, Columbus, NE BR/TR, 6'2", 184 lbs. Deb: 8/26/1963																										
1963	Min-A	2	1	.667	7	5	2	0	0	38^{2}	25	13	12	6	1	12	22	.957	2.79	131	2.38	.182	2	.133	4	3	0.4
1964	Min-A	0	0	....	9	0	0	0	0	11	10	6	6	1	0	6	10	1.455	4.91	73	4.11	.256	0	....	-1	0	-0.2
1965	Min-A	0	0	....	7	1	0	0	0	15	11	7	7	2	0	11	15	1.467	4.20	85	3.97	.193	0	.000	-1	0	-0.1
1966	Min-A	2	2	.500	23	2	0	0	1	49^{2}	47	26	19	6	1	14	24	1.228	3.44	104	3.42	.253	0	.000	1	2	0.1
1967	Min-A	0	0	....	2	0	0	0	0	3	4	1	1	0	0	1	0	1.667	3.00	115	5.24	.364	0	....	0	0	0.0
Total	5	4	3	.571	48	8	2	0	1	117^{1}	97	53	45	15	2	44	71	1.202	3.45	104	3.26	.226	2	.074	2	5	0.1
• SIERRA, Candy	Ulises (Pizarro) Sierra b: 3/27/1967, Rio Piedras, Puerto Rico BR/TR, 6'2", 190 lbs. Deb: 4/6/1988																										
1988	SD-N	0	1	.000	15	0	0	0	0	23^{2}	36	15	15	2	0	11	20	1.986	5.70	60	7.66	.379	0	.000	-6	0	-0.7
	Cin-N	0	0	....	1	0	0	0	0	4	5	2	2	0	0	1	4	1.500	4.50	80	4.05	.294	0	.000	-0	0	-0.1
	Yr.	0	1	.000	16	0	0	0	0	27^{2}	41	17	17	2	0	12	24	1.916	5.53	62	7.14	.366	0	.000	-7	0	-0.8
• SIEVER, Ed	Edward Tilden Siever b: 4/2/1877, Goddard, KS d: 2/5/1920, Detroit, MI BL/TL, 5'11.5", 190 lbs. Deb: 4/26/1901 U																										
1901	Det-A	18	14	.563	38	33	30	2	0	288^{2}	334	166	104	9	8	65	85	1.382	3.24	119	3.83	.286	18	.168	16	22	1.0
1902	Det-A	8	11	.421	25	23	17	4	1	188^{1}	166	73	40	0	2	32	36	1.051	**1.91**	**191**	2.02	.237	10	.152	34	16	2.9
1903	StL-A	13	14	.481	31	27	24	1	0	254	245	102	70	6	5	39	90	1.118	2.48	117	2.50	.253	13	.140	12	17	0.8
1904	StL-A	10	15	.400	29	24	19	2	0	217	235	112	64	3	3	65	77	1.382	2.65	93	3.46	.277	11	.155	-1	8	-0.3
1906	Det-A	14	11	.560	30	25	20	1	0	222^{2}	240	95	67	5	10	45	71	1.280	2.71	102	3.33	.278	12	.156	1	16	-0.2
1907*	Det-A	18	11	.621	39	33	22	3	1	274^{2}	256	89	66	1	11	52	88	1.121	2.16	120	2.39	.250	15	.160	14	18	1.2
1908	Det-A	2	6	.250	11	9	4	1	0	61^{2}	74	37	24	0	0	13	23	1.411	3.50	69	3.81	.302	3	.167	-6	0	-0.8
Total	7	83	82	.503	203	174	136	14	2	1507	1550	674	435	24	39	311	470	1.235	2.60	114	2.99	.266	82	.156	69	97	4.7
• SIGNER, Walter	Walter Donald Aloysius Signer b: 10/12/1910, New York, NY d: 7/23/1974, Greenwich, CT BR/TR, 6', 185 lbs. Deb: 9/18/1943																										
1943	Chi-N	2	1	.667	4	2	1	0	0	25	24	8	8	3	0	4	5	1.120	2.88	116	2.93	.245	2	.250	2	2	0.2
1945	Chi-N	0	0	....	6	0	0	0	1	8	11	6	3	1	0	5	0	2.000	3.38	108	5.85	.256	0	.000	0	0	0.0
Total	2	2	1	.667	10	2	1	0	1	33	35	14	11	4	0	9	5	1.333	3.00	114	3.64	.248	2	.222	2	2	0.2
• SIGSBY, Seth	Seth De Witt Sigsby b: 4/30/1874, Cobleskill, NY d: 9/15/1953, Schenectady, NY, 6', 175 lbs. Deb: 6/27/1893																										
1893	NY-N	0	0	....	1	0	0	0	0	3	1	4	3	0	1	4	2	1.667	9.00	52	3.74	.101	0	.000	-1	0	-0.1
• SIKORSKI, Brian	Brian Patrick Sikorski b: 7/27/1974, Detroit, MI BR/TR, 6'1", 200 lbs. Deb: 8/16/2000																										
2000	Tex-A	1	3	.250	10	5	0	0	0	37^{2}	46	31	24	9	1	25	32	1.885	5.73	87	7.48	.288	0	....	-2	1	-0.2
• SILVA, Carlos	Carlos Silva b: 4/23/1979, Bolivar, Venezuela BR/TR, 6'4", 225 lbs. Deb: 4/1/2002																										
2002	Phi-N	5	0	1.000	68	0	0	0	1	84	88	34	30	4	4	22	41	1.310	3.21	121	3.60	.282	0	.000	6	7	0.6
2003	Phi-N	3	1	.750	62	1	0	0	1	87^{1}	92	43	43	7	8	37	48	1.477	4.43	90	4.71	.280	2	.222	-4	5	-0.4
Total	2	8	1	.889	130	1	0	0	2	171^{1}	180	77	73	11	12	59	89	1.395	3.83	103	4.17	.281	2	.182	2	12	0.3
• SILVA, Jose	Jose Leonel Silva b: 12/19/1973, Tijuana, Mexico BR/TR, 6'5", 210 lbs. Deb: 9/10/1996																										
1996	Tor-A	0	0	....	2	0	0	0	0	2	5	3	3	1	0	0	0	2.500	13.50	37	15.86	.455	0	....	-2	0	-0.2
1997	Pit-N	2	1	.667	11	4	0	0	0	36^{1}	52	26	24	4	1	16	30	1.872	5.94	72	6.88	.347	1	.143	-6	1	-0.6
1998	Pit-N	6	7	.462	18	18	1	0	0	100^{1}	104	55	49	7	1	30	64	1.336	4.40	98	3.70	.271	1	.037	-2	4	-0.3
1999	Pit-N	2	8	.200	34	12	0	0	4	97^{1}	108	70	62	10	3	39	77	1.510	5.73	80	4.84	.281	2	.100	-12	2	-1.3
2000	Pit-N	11	9	.550	51	19	1	0	0	136	178	96	84	16	5	50	98	1.676	5.56	83	5.91	.317	6	.176	-13	4	-1.2
2001	Pit-N	3	3	.500	26	0	0	0	0	32	35	24	24	6	0	9	23	1.375	6.75	66	4.59	.271	0	.000	-8	0	-0.8
2002	Cin-N	1	0	1.000	12	0	0	0	0	23^{1}	25	11	11	3	3	10	6	1.500	4.24	100	5.37	.294	0	....	-0	1	0.0
Total	7	25	28	.472	154	53	2	0	4	427^{1}	507	285	257	47	13	154	298	1.547	5.41	83	5.15	.297	10	.111	-43	12	-4.4
• SIMA, Al	Albert Sima b: 10/7/1921, Mahwah, NJ d: 8/17/1993, Suffern, NY BR/TL, 6', 187 lbs. Deb: 6/28/1950																										
1950	Was-A	4	5	.444	17	9	1	0	0	77	89	49	41	9	1	26	23	1.494	4.79	94	4.76	.291	3	.115	-2	3	-0.5
1951	Was-A	3	7	.300	18	8	1	0	0	77	79	51	41	5	0	41	26	1.558	4.79	86	4.27	.261	3	.176	-5	2	-0.4
1953	Was-A	2	3	.400	31	5	1	0	1	68^{1}	63	31	26	7	3	31	25	1.376	3.42	114	3.99	.249	2	.118	3	3	0.2
1954	Chi-A	0	1	.000	5	1	0	0	1	7	11	5	4	1	0	2	1	1.857	5.14	73	7.38	.393	0	.000	-1	0	-0.1
	Phi-A	2	5	.286	29	7	1	0	2	79^{1}	101	51	46	9	0	32	36	1.676	5.22	75	5.69	.309	1	.050	-10	2	-1.3
	Yr.	2	6	.250	34	8	1	0	3	86^{1}	112	56	50	10	0	34	37	1.691	5.21	75	5.83	.315	1	.045	-12	2	-1.4
Total	4	11	21	.344	100	30	4	0	4	308^{2}	343	187	158	31	4	132	111	1.539	4.61	89	4.77	.282	9	.110	-16	10	-2.1
• SIMAS, Bill	William Anthony Simas b: 11/28/1971, Hanford, CA BL/TR, 6'3", 220 lbs. Deb: 8/15/1995																										
1995	Chi-A	1	1	.500	14	0	0	0	0	14	15	5	4	1	1	10	16	1.786	2.57	173	5.58	.273	0	....	3	1	0.3
1996	Chi-A	2	8	.200	64	0	0	0	2	72^{2}	75	39	37	5	3	39	65	1.569	4.58	104	4.57	.265	0	....	2	4	0.2
1997	Chi-A	3	1	.750	40	0	0	0	1	41^{1}	46	23	19	6	2	24	38	1.694	4.14	106	5.85	.279	0	....	2	2	0.2

YEAR	TM-L	W	L	PCT	G	GS	CG	SH	SV	IP	H	R	ER	HR	HB	BB	SO	RAT	ERA	ERA+	CERA	OAV	BH	AVG	PR+	WS	TPW
1998	Chi-A	4	3	.571	60	0	0	0	18	70^2	54	29	28	12	1	22	56	1.075	3.57	128	2.87	.206	0	....	8	10	0.7
1999	Chi-A	6	3	.667	70	0	0	0	2	72	73	36	30	6	6	32	41	1.458	3.75	130	4.33	.263	0	....	9	6	0.9
2000*	Chi-A	2	3	.400	60	0	0	0	0	67^2	69	27	26	9	1	22	49	1.345	3.46	144	4.13	.276	0	....	10	6	1.0
Total	**6**	**18**	**19**	**.486**	**308**	**0**	**0**	**0**	**23**	**338^1**	**332**	**159**	**144**	**39**	**14**	**149**	**265**	**1.422**	**3.83**	**123**	**4.27**	**.257**	**0**	**....**	**34**	**29**	**3.2**

• SIMMONS, Curt — Curtis Thomas Simmons b: 5/19/1929, Egypt, PA BL/TL, 5'11", 187 lbs. Deb: 9/28/1947

YEAR	TM-L	W	L	PCT	G	GS	CG	SH	SV	IP	H	R	ER	HR	HB	BB	SO	RAT	ERA	ERA+	CERA	OAV	BH	AVG	PR+	WS	TPW
1947	Phi-N	1	0	1.000	1	1	1	0	0	9	5	1	1	0	0	6	9	1.222	1.00	401	1.95	.161	1	.500	3	2	0.3
1948	Phi-N	7	13	.350	31	22	7	0	0	170	169	110	92	8	2	108	86	**1.629**	4.87	81	4.52	.266	7	.137	-17	3	-1.8
1949	Phi-N	4	10	.286	38	14	2	0	1	131^1	133	72	67	7	1	55	83	1.431	4.59	86	3.96	.275	7	.171	-11	5	-1.1
1950	Phi-N	17	8	.680	31	27	11	2	1	214^2	178	93	81	19	2	88	146	1.239	3.40	119	3.05	.223	12	.156	15	16	1.4
1952	Phi-N★	14	8	.636	28	28	15	**6**	0	201^1	170	72	63	11	1	70	141	1.192	2.82	130	2.69	.227	11	.164	16	17	1.8
1953	Phi-N★	16	13	.552	32	30	19	4	0	238	211	102	85	17	3	82	138	1.231	3.21	131	3.02	.236	13	.140	26	19	2.3
1954	Phi-N	14	15	.483	34	33	21	3	1	253	226	101	79	14	5	98	125	1.281	2.81	144	3.10	.239	16	.176	34	21	3.2
1955	Phi-N	8	8	.500	25	22	3	0	0	130	148	76	71	15	3	50	58	1.523	4.92	81	5.05	.290	8	.174	-15	4	-1.6
1956	Phi-N	15	10	.600	33	27	14	0	0	198	186	95	74	17	3	65	88	1.268	3.36	111	3.36	.248	17	.236	12	13	1.6
1957	Phi-N★	12	11	.522	32	29	9	2	0	212	214	92	81	11	2	50	92	1.245	3.44	111	3.13	.264	17	.239	9	15	1.3
1958	Phi-N	7	14	.333	29	27	7	1	1	168^1	196	92	82	11	3	40	78	1.402	4.38	90	4.14	.293	12	.203	-5	6	-0.5
1959	Phi-N	0	0	....	7	0	0	0	0	10	16	5	5	2	1	0	4	1.600	4.50	91	7.93	.400	0	....	-0	0	0.0
1960	Phi-N	0	0	....	4	2	0	0	0	4	13	8	8	3	0	6	4	4.750	18.00	22	34.20	.542	0	....	-6	0	-0.6
	StL-N	7	4	.636	23	17	3	1	0	152	149	50	45	11	0	31	63	1.184	2.66	154	3.02	.257	10	.213	25	15	2.7
	Yr.	7	4	.636	27	19	3	1	0	156	162	58	53	14	0	37	67	1.276	3.06	133	3.82	.269	10	.213	19	15	2.1
1961	StL-N	9	10	.474	30	29	6	2	0	195^2	203	91	68	14	4	64	99	1.365	3.13	**140**	3.83	.269	20	.303	27	17	**3.2**
1962	StL-N	10	10	.500	31	22	9	4	0	154	167	78	60	18	3	32	74	1.292	3.51	122	4.03	.280	8	.160	12	9	1.2
1963	StL-N	15	9	.625	32	32	11	6	0	232^2	209	82	64	13	6	48	127	1.105	2.48	143	2.61	.239	13	.160	27	18	3.0
1964*	StL-N	18	9	.667	34	34	12	3	0	244	233	106	93	24	5	49	104	1.156	3.43	111	3.11	.249	10	.106	9	16	0.7
1965	StL-N	9	15	.375	34	32	5	0	0	203	229	104	92	19	4	54	96	1.394	4.08	94	4.21	.283	3	.047	-6	7	-1.1
1966	StL-N	1	1	.500	10	5	1	0	0	33^1	35	17	17	3	0	14	14	1.470	4.59	78	4.22	.269	1	.125	-4	1	-0.4
	Chi-N	4	7	.364	19	10	3	1	0	77^1	79	39	35	7	1	21	24	1.293	4.07	90	3.67	.268	2	.111	-2	3	-0.3
	Yr.	5	8	.385	29	15	4	1	0	110^2	114	56	52	10	1	35	38	1.346	4.23	86	3.84	.268	3	.115	-6	4	-0.7
1967	Chi-N	3	7	.300	17	14	3	0	0	82	100	54	45	10	2	23	31	1.500	4.94	72	4.92	.300	4	.143	-14	0	-1.5
	Cal-A	2	1	.667	14	4	1	1	1	34^2	44	11	10	1	2	9	13	1.529	2.60	121	4.81	.321	2	.222	2	3	0.3
Total	**20**	**193**	**183**	**.513**	**569**	**461**	**163**	**36**	**5**	**3348^1**	**3313**	**1551**	**1318**	**255**	**53**	**1063**	**1697**	**1.307**	**3.54**	**110**	**3.57**	**.259**	**194**	**.171**	**136**	**210**	**14.0**

• SIMMONS, Pat — Patrick Clement Simmons b: 11/29/1908, Watervliet, NY d: 7/3/1968, Albany, NY BR/TR, 5'11", 172 lbs. Deb: 4/18/1928

YEAR	TM-L	W	L	PCT	G	GS	CG	SH	SV	IP	H	R	ER	HR	HB	BB	SO	RAT	ERA	ERA+	CERA	OAV	BH	AVG	PR+	WS	TPW
1928	Bos-A	0	2	.000	31	3	0	0	1	69	69	38	31	4	1	38	16	1.551	4.04	102	4.40	.271	2	.133	0	3	-0.1
1929	Bos-A	0	0	....	2	0	0	0	1	7	6	0	0	0	0	3	2	1.286	0.00	....	2.68	.231	0	.000	3	2	0.3
Total	**2**	**0**	**2**	**.000**	**33**	**3**	**0**	**0**	**2**	**76**	**75**	**38**	**31**	**4**	**1**	**41**	**18**	**1.526**	**3.67**	**112**	**4.25**	**.267**	**2**	**.125**	**4**	**5**	**0.2**

• SIMONS, Doug — Douglas Eugene Simons b: 9/15/1966, Bakersfield, CA BL/TL, 6', 170 lbs. Deb: 4/9/1991

YEAR	TM-L	W	L	PCT	G	GS	CG	SH	SV	IP	H	R	ER	HR	HB	BB	SO	RAT	ERA	ERA+	CERA	OAV	BH	AVG	PR+	WS	TPW
1991	NY-N	2	3	.400	42	1	0	0	1	60^2	55	40	35	5	2	19	38	1.220	5.19	70	3.05	.246	0	.000	-9	1	-1.0
1992	Mon-N	0	0	....	7	0	0	0	0	5^1	15	14	14	3	1	2	6	3.188	23.63	15	21.80	.500	0	....	-12	0	-1.3
Total	**2**	**2**	**3**	**.400**	**49**	**1**	**0**	**0**	**1**	**66**	**70**	**54**	**49**	**8**	**3**	**21**	**44**	**1.379**	**6.68**	**54**	**4.57**	**.276**	**0**	**.000**	**-21**	**1**	**-2.3**

• SIMONTACCHI, Jason — Jason William Simontacchi b: 11/13/1973, Mountain View, CA BR/TR, 6'2", 185 lbs. Deb: 5/4/2002

YEAR	TM-L	W	L	PCT	G	GS	CG	SH	SV	IP	H	R	ER	HR	HB	BB	SO	RAT	ERA	ERA+	CERA	OAV	BH	AVG	PR+	WS	TPW
2002	StL-N	11	5	.688	24	24	0	0	0	143^1	134	68	64	18	6	54	72	1.312	4.02	98	4.01	.253	12	.240	-3	8	-0.1
2003	StL-N	9	5	.643	46	16	1	0	1	126^1	153	82	78	21	5	41	74	1.536	5.56	73	5.68	.299	5	.132	-21	2	-2.2
Total	**2**	**20**	**10**	**.667**	**70**	**40**	**1**	**0**	**1**	**269^2**	**287**	**150**	**142**	**39**	**11**	**95**	**146**	**1.417**	**4.74**	**85**	**4.79**	**.276**	**17**	**.193**	**-24**	**10**	**-2.3**

• SIMPSON, Duke — Thomas Leo Simpson b: 9/15/1927, Columbus, OH BR/TR, 6'1.5", 190 lbs. Deb: 5/6/1953

YEAR	TM-L	W	L	PCT	G	GS	CG	SH	SV	IP	H	R	ER	HR	HB	BB	SO	RAT	ERA	ERA+	CERA	OAV	BH	AVG	PR+	WS	TPW
1953	Chi-N	1	2	.333	30	1	0	0	0	45	60	47	40	8	1	25	21	1.889	8.00	56	7.10	.314	2	.250	-16	0	-1.6

• SIMPSON, Steve — Steven Edward Simpson b: 8/30/1948, St. Joseph, MO d: 11/2/1989, Omaha, NE BR/TR, 6'3", 200 lbs. Deb: 9/10/1972

YEAR	TM-L	W	L	PCT	G	GS	CG	SH	SV	IP	H	R	ER	HR	HB	BB	SO	RAT	ERA	ERA+	CERA	OAV	BH	AVG	PR+	WS	TPW
1972	SD-N	0	2	.000	9	0	0	0	2	11^1	10	6	6	0	0	8	9	1.588	4.76	69	3.67	.238	0	....	-2	0	-0.2

• SIMPSON, Wayne — Wayne Kirby Simpson b: 12/2/1948, Los Angeles, CA BR/TR, 6'3", 220 lbs. Deb: 4/9/1970

YEAR	TM-L	W	L	PCT	G	GS	CG	SH	SV	IP	H	R	ER	HR	HB	BB	SO	RAT	ERA	ERA+	CERA	OAV	BH	AVG	PR+	WS	TPW
1970	Cin-N★	14	3	.824	26	26	10	2	0	176	125	73	59	15	9	81	119	1.170	3.02	138	2.83	**.198**	6	.094	22	14	1.8
1971	Cin-N	4	7	.364	22	21	1	0	0	117^1	106	66	62	9	3	77	61	1.560	4.76	68	4.37	.244	1	.031	-22	0	-2.6
1972	Cin-N	8	5	.615	24	22	1	0	0	130^1	124	63	60	17	2	49	70	1.327	4.14	77	3.93	.247	3	.063	-16	3	-2.0
1973	KC-A	3	4	.429	16	10	1	0	0	59^2	66	39	38	1	1	35	29	1.693	5.73	72	4.87	.284	0	....	-10	1	-1.0
1975	Phi-N	1	0	1.000	7	5	0	0	0	30^2	31	11	11	1	1	11	19	1.370	3.23	116	3.63	.263	2	.222	1	2	0.1
1977	Cal-A	6	12	.333	27	23	0	0	0	122	154	90	79	14	7	62	55	1.770	5.83	67	6.39	.308	0	....	-25	0	-2.5
Total	**6**	**36**	**31**	**.537**	**122**	**107**	**13**	**2**	**0**	**636**	**606**	**342**	**309**	**57**	**23**	**315**	**353**	**1.448**	**4.37**	**84**	**4.25**	**.251**	**12**	**.078**	**-50**	**20**	**-6.2**

• SIMS, Pete — Clarence Sims b: 5/24/1891, Crown City, OH d: 12/2/1968, Dallas, TX BR/TR, 5'11.5", 165 lbs. Deb: 9/16/1915

YEAR	TM-L	W	L	PCT	G	GS	CG	SH	SV	IP	H	R	ER	HR	HB	BB	SO	RAT	ERA	ERA+	CERA	OAV	BH	AVG	PR+	WS	TPW
1915	StL-A	1	0	1.000	3	2	0	0	0	8^1	6	4	4	0	0	6	4	1.440	4.32	66	3.08	.214	1	1.000	-1	1	-0.1

• SINCLAIR, Steve — Steven Scott Sinclair b: 8/2/1971, Victoria, Canada BL/TL, 6'2", 190 lbs. Deb: 4/25/1998

YEAR	TM-L	W	L	PCT	G	GS	CG	SH	SV	IP	H	R	ER	HR	HB	BB	SO	RAT	ERA	ERA+	CERA	OAV	BH	AVG	PR+	WS	TPW
1998	Tor-A	0	2	.000	24	0	0	0	0	15	13	7	6	0	0	5	8	1.200	3.60	130	2.51	.232	0	....	2	1	0.2
1999	Tor-A	0	0	....	3	0	0	0	0	5^2	7	8	8	4	1	4	3	1.941	12.71	39	13.32	.304	0	....	-5	0	-0.5
	Sea-A	0	1	.000	18	0	0	0	0	13^2	15	8	6	1	1	10	15	1.829	3.95	126	5.63	.268	0	....	2	1	0.1
	Yr.	0	1	.000	21	0	0	0	0	19^1	22	16	14	5	2	14	18	1.862	6.52	76	7.89	.278	0	....	-3	1	-0.3
Total	**2**	**0**	**3**	**.000**	**45**	**0**	**0**	**0**	**0**	**34^1**	**35**	**23**	**20**	**5**	**2**	**19**	**26**	**1.573**	**5.24**	**93**	**5.54**	**.259**	**0**	**....**	**-2**	**2**	**-0.1**

• SINCOCK, Bert — Herbert Sylvester Sincock b: 9/8/1887, Barkerville, Canada d: 8/1/1946, Houghton, MI BL/TL, 5'10.5", 165 lbs. Deb: 6/25/1908

YEAR	TM-L	W	L	PCT	G	GS	CG	SH	SV	IP	H	R	ER	HR	HB	BB	SO	RAT	ERA	ERA+	CERA	OAV	BH	AVG	PR+	WS	TPW
1908	Cin-N	0	0	....	1	0	0	0	0	4^2	3	2	2	0	0	0	1	.643	3.86	59	0.77	.176	0	.000	-1	0	-0.1

• SINGER, Bill — William Robert "Sing Sing,The Singer Throwing Machine" Singer b: 4/24/1944, Los Angeles, CA BR/TR, 6'4", 200 lbs. Deb: 9/24/1964

YEAR	TM-L	W	L	PCT	G	GS	CG	SH	SV	IP	H	R	ER	HR	HB	BB	SO	RAT	ERA	ERA+	CERA	OAV	BH	AVG	PR+	WS	TPW
1964	LA-N	0	1	.000	2	2	0	0	0	14	11	5	5	0	0	12	3	1.643	3.21	101	3.70	.216	1	.167	0	1	0.0
1965	LA-N	0	0	....	2	0	0	0	0	1	2	0	0	0	0	2	1	4.000	0.00	....	16.69	.400	0	....	0	0	0.0
1966	LA-N	0	0	....	3	0	0	0	0	4	4	0	0	0	0	2	4	1.500	0.00	....	4.15	.286	0	....	1	1	0.2
1967	LA-N	12	8	.600	32	29	7	3	0	204^1	185	68	60	5	8	61	169	1.204	2.64	117	2.73	.239	6	.090	13	15	1.0
1968	LA-N	13	17	.433	37	36	12	6	0	256^1	227	97	82	14	5	78	227	1.190	2.88	96	2.81	.237	12	.148	-5	12	-0.3
1969	LA-N★	20	12	.625	41	40	16	2	1	315^2	244	96	82	22	10	74	247	1.007	2.34	142	2.19	.210	11	.102	32	26	2.9
1970	LA-N	8	5	.615	16	16	5	3	0	106^1	79	39	37	10	2	32	93	1.044	3.13	122	2.35	.203	5	.132	6	7	0.6
1971	LA-N	10	17	.370	31	31	8	1	0	203^1	195	103	94	19	4	71	144	1.308	4.16	78	3.67	.252	6	.103	-22	4	-2.4
1972	LA-N	6	16	.273	26	25	4	3	0	169^1	148	84	69	8	5	60	101	1.228	3.67	91	2.94	.237	4	.073	-7	3	-1.0
1973	Cal-A★	20	14	.588	40	40	19	2	0	315^2	280	124	113	15	9	130	241	1.299	3.22	110	3.20	.235	0	....	15	23	1.6
1974	Cal-A	7	4	.636	14	14	8	0	0	108^2	102	48	36	3	1	43	77	1.334	2.98	115	3.26	.250	0	....	6	6	0.7
1975	Cal-A	7	15	.318	29	27	8	0	1	179	171	107	99	18	6	81	78	1.408	4.98	71	4.17	.257	0	....	-28	3	-2.8
1976	Tex-A	4	1	.800	10	10	2	1	0	64^2	56	31	25	4	5	27	34	1.284	3.48	103	3.47	.239	0	....	0	4	0.0
	Min-A	9	9	.500	26	26	5	3	0	172	177	88	72	9	6	69	63	1.430	3.77	96	4.08	.274	0	....	-4	7	-0.4
	Yr.	13	10	.565	36	36	7	4	0	236^2	233	119	97	13	11	96	97	1.390	3.69	97	3.92	.264	0	....	-3	11	-0.3
1977	Tor-A	2	8	.200	13	12	0	0	0	59^2	71	54	45	5	2	39	33	1.844	6.79	62	6.09	.296	0	....	-16	0	-1.6
Total	**14**	**118**	**127**	**.482**	**322**	**308**	**94**	**24**	**2**	**2174**	**1952**	**944**	**819**	**132**	**63**	**781**	**1515**	**1.257**	**3.39**	**100**	**3.20**	**.240**	**45**	**.109**	**-6**	**112**	**-1.5**

• SINGLETON, Elmer — Bert Elmer "Smoky" Singleton b: 6/26/1918, Ogden, UT d: 1/5/1996, Ogden, UT BR/TR, 6'2", 174 lbs. Deb: 8/20/1945

YEAR	TM-L	W	L	PCT	G	GS	CG	SH	SV	IP	H	R	ER	HR	HB	BB	SO	RAT	ERA	ERA+	CERA	OAV	BH	AVG	PR+	WS	TPW
1945	Bos-N	1	4	.200	7	5	1	0	0	37^1	35	22	20	1	1	14	14	1.313	4.82	79	3.15	.248	0	.000	-4	1	-0.6
1946	Bos-N	0	1	.000	15	2	0	0	1	33^2	27	20	14	3	1	21	17	1.426	3.74	92	3.74	.221	0	.000	-1	1	-0.2
1947	Pit-N	2	2	.500	36	3	0	0	1	67	70	49	47	9	2	39	24	1.627	6.31	67	5.21	.267	4	.308	-15	1	-1.4
1948	Pit-N	4	6	.400	38	5	1	0	2	92^1	90	52	51	11	1	40	53	1.408	4.97	82	4.08	.253	2	.087	-10	4	-1.2
1950	Was-A	1	2	.333	21	1	0	0	0	36^1	39	23	21	4	0	17	19	1.541	5.20	86	4.87	.291	3	.429	-3	2	-0.1

YEAR TM-L	W	L	PCT	G	GS	CG	SH	SV	IP	H	R	ER	HR	HB	BB	SO	RAT	ERA	ERA+	CERA	OAV	BH	AVG	PR+	WS	TPW
1957 Chi-N	0	1	.000	5	2	0	0	0	13^1	20	11	10	3	0	2	6	1.650	6.75	57	6.81	.333	0	.000	-4	0	-0.5
1958 Chi-N	1	0	1.000	2	0	0	0	0	4^2	1	0	0	0	0	1	2	.429	0.00	....	0.22	.071	0	.000	2	1	0.2
1959 Chi-N	2	1	.667	21	1	0	0	0	43	40	15	13	2	0	12	25	1.209	2.72	145	2.78	.252	0	.000	6	4	0.5
Total 8	11	17	.393	145	19	2	0	4	327^2	322	192	176	33	5	146	160	1.428	4.83	84	4.14	.258	9	.132	-29	14	-3.2

• SINGLETON, John John Edward "Sheriff" Singleton b: 11/27/1896, Gallipolis, OH d: 10/23/1937, Dayton, OH BR/TR, 5'11", 171 lbs. Deb: 6/8/1922

YEAR TM-L	W	L	PCT	G	GS	CG	SH	SV	IP	H	R	ER	HR	HB	BB	SO	RAT	ERA	ERA+	CERA	OAV	BH	AVG	PR+	WS	TPW
1922 Phi-N	1	10	.091	22	9	3	1	0	93	127	80	61	6	5	38	27	1.774	5.90	79	6.19	.346	5	.139	-12	1	-1.4

• SIROTKA, Mike Michael Robert Sirotka b: 5/13/1971, Houston, TX BL/TL, 6'1", 190 lbs. Deb: 7/19/1995

YEAR TM-L	W	L	PCT	G	GS	CG	SH	SV	IP	H	R	ER	HR	HB	BB	SO	RAT	ERA	ERA+	CERA	OAV	BH	AVG	PR+	WS	TPW
1995 Chi-A	1	2	.333	6	6	0	0	0	34^1	39	16	16	2	0	17	19	1.631	4.19	106	5.04	.298	0	....	1	2	0.1
1996 Chi-A	1	2	.333	15	4	0	0	0	26^1	34	27	21	3	0	12	11	1.747	7.18	66	6.14	.315	0	....	-7	0	-0.6
1997 Chi-A	3	0	1.000	7	4	0	0	0	32	36	9	8	4	1	5	24	1.281	2.25	195	4.24	.290	0	.000	8	4	0.8
1998 Chi-A	14	15	.483	33	33	5	0	0	211^2	255	137	119	30	2	47	128	1.427	5.06	90	4.91	.300	0	.000	-13	7	-1.2
1999 Chi-A	11	13	.458	32	32	3	1	0	209	236	108	93	24	3	57	125	1.402	4.00	122	4.41	.283	2	.250	22	13	2.0
2000* Chi-A	15	10	.600	32	32	1	0	0	197	203	101	83	23	1	69	128	1.381	3.79	131	4.26	.269	0	.000	23	14	2.1
Total 6	45	42	.517	125	111	9	1	0	710^1	803	398	340	86	7	207	435	1.422	4.31	110	4.61	.286	2	.118	34	40	3.2

• SISK, Doug Douglas Randall Sisk b: 9/26/1957, Renton, WA BR/TR, 6'2", 210 lbs. Deb: 9/6/1982

YEAR TM-L	W	L	PCT	G	GS	CG	SH	SV	IP	H	R	ER	HR	HB	BB	SO	RAT	ERA	ERA+	CERA	OAV	BH	AVG	PR+	WS	TPW
1982 NY-N	0	1	.000	8	0	0	0	1	8^2	5	1	1	1	1	4	4	1.038	1.04	349	2.41	.172	0	....	3	1	0.3
1983 NY-N	5	4	.556	67	0	0	0	11	104^1	88	38	26	1	4	59	33	1.409	2.24	162	3.29	.235	3	.500	15	12	1.7
1984 NY-N	1	3	.250	50	0	0	0	15	77^2	57	24	18	1	3	54	32	1.429	2.09	169	3.26	.215	1	.091	13	9	1.3
1985 NY-N	4	5	.444	42	0	0	0	2	73	86	48	43	3	2	40	26	1.726	5.30	65	5.26	.291	0	.000	-15	0	-1.7
1986* NY-N	4	2	.667	41	0	0	0	1	70^2	77	31	24	0	5	31	31	1.528	3.06	116	4.21	.282	0	.000	4	4	0.3
1987 NY-N	3	1	.750	55	0	0	0	3	78	83	38	30	5	3	22	37	1.346	3.46	109	3.73	.270	0	.000	4	5	0.3
1988 Bal-A	3	3	.500	52	0	0	0	0	94^1	109	43	39	3	2	45	26	1.633	3.72	105	4.96	.306	0	....	1	6	0.1
1990 Atl-N	0	0	....	3	0	0	0	0	2^1	1	1	1	0	0	4	1	2.143	3.86	105	4.42	.143	0	....	0	0	0.0
1991 Atl-N	2	1	.667	14	0	0	0	0	14^1	21	14	8	1	0	8	5	2.023	5.02	77	6.74	.333	0	....	-2	0	-0.2
Total 9	22	20	.524	332	0	0	0	33	523^1	527	238	190	15	20	267	195	1.517	3.27	112	4.14	.268	4	.105	22	37	2.1

• SISK, Tommie Tommie Wayne Sisk b: 4/12/1942, Ardmore, OK BR/TR, 6'3", 195 lbs. Deb: 7/19/1962

YEAR TM-L	W	L	PCT	G	GS	CG	SH	SV	IP	H	R	ER	HR	HB	BB	SO	RAT	ERA	ERA+	CERA	OAV	BH	AVG	PR+	WS	TPW
1962 Pit-N	0	2	.000	5	3	1	0	0	17^2	18	9	8	1	1	8	6	1.472	4.08	96	4.15	.257	1	.200	-0	1	0.0
1963 Pit-N	1	3	.250	57	4	1	0	1	108	85	42	35	6	1	45	73	1.204	2.92	113	2.69	.222	1	.063	4	6	0.4
1964 Pit-N	1	4	.200	42	1	0	0	0	61^1	91	47	42	4	3	29	35	1.957	6.16	57	7.21	.364	0	.000	-17	0	-1.9
1965 Pit-N	7	3	.700	38	12	1	1	0	111^1	103	48	42	6	1	50	66	1.374	3.40	103	3.47	.248	2	.061	-1	6	-0.3
1966 Pit-N	10	5	.667	34	23	4	1	1	150	146	74	69	14	4	52	60	1.320	4.14	86	3.76	.256	5	.098	-12	6	-1.4
1967 Pit-N	13	13	.500	37	31	11	2	1	207^2	196	88	77	6	3	78	85	1.319	3.34	101	3.20	.253	7	.101	-2	10	-0.5
1968 Pit-N	5	5	.500	33	11	0	0	1	96	101	40	35	3	3	35	41	1.417	3.28	89	3.86	.282	2	.083	-5	3	-0.6
1969 SD-N	2	13	.133	53	13	1	0	6	143	160	81	76	11	1	48	59	1.455	4.78	74	4.23	.285	3	.120	-18	4	-1.8
1970 Chi-A	1	1	.500	17	1	0	0	0	33^1	37	28	20	6	0	13	16	1.500	5.40	72	4.88	.276	1	.250	-5	0	-0.5
Total 9	40	49	.449	316	99	19	4	10	928^1	937	457	404	57	17	358	441	1.395	3.92	88	3.83	.266	22	.094	-57	36	-6.8

• SISLER, Dave David Michael Sisler b: 10/16/1931, St. Louis, MO BR/TR, 6'4", 200 lbs. Deb: 4/21/1956

YEAR TM-L	W	L	PCT	G	GS	CG	SH	SV	IP	H	R	ER	HR	HB	BB	SO	RAT	ERA	ERA+	CERA	OAV	BH	AVG	PR+	WS	TPW
1956 Bos-A	9	8	.529	39	14	3	0	3	142^1	120	81	73	13	7	72	93	1.349	4.62	100	3.69	.227	5	.119	0	8	-0.2
1957 Bos-A	7	8	.467	22	19	5	0	1	122^1	135	68	64	15	2	61	55	1.602	4.71	85	5.28	.280	7	.167	-8	5	-0.8
1958 Bos-A	8	9	.471	30	25	4	1	0	149^1	157	94	82	22	1	79	71	1.580	4.94	81	5.29	.276	9	.196	-13	4	-1.3
1959 Bos-A	0	0	....	3	0	0	0	0	6^2	9	5	5	3	0	1	3	1.500	6.75	60	7.51	.310	1	.500	-2	0	-0.2
Det-A	1	3	.250	32	0	0	0	7	51^2	46	28	23	4	1	36	29	1.587	4.01	101	4.51	.242	1	.200	0	4	0.0
Yr.	1	3	.250	35	0	0	0	7	58^1	55	33	28	7	1	37	32	1.577	4.32	94	4.85	.251	2	.286	-2	4	-0.2
1960 Det-A	7	5	.583	41	0	0	0	6	80	56	23	22	3	2	45	47	1.263	2.48	167	2.76	.199	2	.125	15	10	1.5
1961 Was-A	2	8	.200	45	1	0	0	11	60^1	55	34	28	6	3	48	30	1.707	4.18	94	5.28	.251	0	.000	-2	3	-0.2
1962 Cin-N	4	3	.571	35	0	0	0	1	43^2	44	19	19	4	0	26	27	1.603	3.92	103	4.73	.270	0	....	0	3	0.0
Total 7	38	44	.463	247	59	12	1	29	656^1	622	352	316	70	16	368	355	1.508	4.33	95	4.55	.253	25	.157	-9	37	-1.1

• SISLER, George George Harold "Gorgeous George" Sisler
b: 3/24/1893, Manchester, OH d: 3/26/1973, Richmond Heights, MO BL/TL, 5'11", 170 lbs. Deb: 6/28/1915 M/C HOF: 1939 ♦

YEAR TM-L	W	L	PCT	G	GS	CG	SH	SV	IP	H	R	ER	HR	HB	BB	SO	RAT	ERA	ERA+	CERA	OAV	BH	AVG	PR+	WS	TPW
1915 StL-A	4	4	.500	15	8	6	0	0	70	62	26	22	0	4	38	41	1.429	2.83	101	3.51	.247	78	.285	-1	10	-0.8
1916 StL-A	1	2	.333	3	3	3	1	0	27	18	4	3	0	1	6	12	.889	1.00	274	1.49	.198	177	.305	5	25	1.7
1918 StL-A	0	0	....	2	1	0	0	1	8	10	6	4	0	1	4	4	1.750	4.50	61	5.01	.286	154	.341	-2	22	4.6
1920 StL-A	0	0	....	1	0	0	0	1	1	0	0	0	0	0	0	2	.000	0.00	....	0.00	.000	257	.407	0	33	7.6
1925 StL-A	0	0	....	1	0	0	0	0	2	1	0	0	0	0	1	1	1.000	0.00	....	1.54	.167	224	.345	1	19	-0.5
1926 StL-A	0	0	....	1	0	0	0	1	2	0	0	0	0	0	2	3	1.000	0.00	....	0.92	.000	178	.290	1	11	-3.4
1928 Bos-N	0	0	....	1	0	0	0	0	1	0	0	0	0	0	1	0	1.000	0.00	....	0.82	.000	167	.340	0	15	1.3
Total 7	5	6	.455	24	12	9	1	3	111	91	36	29	0	6	52	63	1.288	2.35	120	2.99	.238	2812	.340	5	135	10.5

• SITTON, Carl Carl Vetter Sitton b: 9/22/1882, Pendleton, SC d: 9/11/1931, Valdosta, GA BR/TR, 5'10.5", 170 lbs. Deb: 4/24/1909

YEAR TM-L	W	L	PCT	G	GS	CG	SH	SV	IP	H	R	ER	HR	HB	BB	SO	RAT	ERA	ERA+	CERA	OAV	BH	AVG	PR+	WS	TPW
1909 Cle-A	3	2	.600	14	5	3	0	0	50	50	22	16	1	2	16	16	1.320	2.88	89	3.37	.263	2	.154	-2	3	-0.2

• SIVESS, Pete Peter Sivess b: 9/23/1913, South River, NJ d: 6/1/2003, Candler, NC BR/TR, 6'3.5", 195 lbs. Deb: 6/13/1936

YEAR TM-L	W	L	PCT	G	GS	CG	SH	SV	IP	H	R	ER	HR	HB	BB	SO	RAT	ERA	ERA+	CERA	OAV	BH	AVG	PR+	WS	TPW
1936 Phi-N	3	4	.429	17	6	2	0	0	65	84	40	33	6	1	36	22	1.846	4.57	99	6.17	.310	3	.120	2	3	0.0
1937 Phi-N	1	1	.500	6	2	1	0	0	23	30	18	18	5	0	11	4	1.783	7.04	61	7.38	.330	0	.000	-7	0	-0.7
1938 Phi-N	3	6	.333	39	8	2	0	3	116	143	78	71	12	1	69	32	1.828	5.51	73	6.16	.306	6	.188	-16	2	-1.7
Total 3	7	11	.389	62	16	5	0	3	204	257	136	122	23	2	116	58	1.828	5.38	78	6.30	.310	9	.143	-21	5	-2.4

• SIWY, Jim James Gerard Siwy b: 9/20/1958, Pawtucket, RI BR/TR, 6'4", 200 lbs. Deb: 8/20/1982

YEAR TM-L	W	L	PCT	G	GS	CG	SH	SV	IP	H	R	ER	HR	HB	BB	SO	RAT	ERA	ERA+	CERA	OAV	BH	AVG	PR+	WS	TPW
1982 Chi-A	0	0	....	2	1	0	0	0	7	10	8	8	1	0	5	3	2.143	10.29	39	9.33	.385	0	....	-5	0	-0.5
1984 Chi-A	0	0	....	1	0	0	0	0	4^1	3	1	1	0	0	2	1	1.154	2.08	200	2.17	.231	0	....	1	1	0.1
Total 2	0	0	....	3	1	0	0	0	11^1	13	9	9	1	0	7	4	1.765	7.15	57	6.59	.333	0	....	-4	1	-0.4

• SKALSKI, Joe Joseph Douglas Skalski b: 9/26/1964, Burnham, IL BR/TR, 6'3", 190 lbs. Deb: 4/10/1989

YEAR TM-L	W	L	PCT	G	GS	CG	SH	SV	IP	H	R	ER	HR	HB	BB	SO	RAT	ERA	ERA+	CERA	OAV	BH	AVG	PR+	WS	TPW
1989 Cle-A	0	2	.000	2	1	0	0	0	6^2	7	6	5	0	2	4	3	1.650	6.75	59	5.39	.259	0	....	-2	0	-0.2

• SKAUGSTAD, Dave David Wendell Skaugstad b: 1/10/1940, Algona, IA BL/TL, 6'1", 179 lbs. Deb: 9/25/1957

YEAR TM-L	W	L	PCT	G	GS	CG	SH	SV	IP	H	R	ER	HR	HB	BB	SO	RAT	ERA	ERA+	CERA	OAV	BH	AVG	PR+	WS	TPW
1957 Cin-N	0	0	....	2	0	0	0	0	5^2	4	1	1	0	0	6	4	1.765	1.59	259	4.04	.190	0	.000	2	1	0.2

• SKEELS, Dave David Skeels b: 12/9/1892, Addy, WA d: 12/2/1926, Spokane, WA BL/TR, 6'1", 187 lbs. Deb: 9/14/1910

YEAR TM-L	W	L	PCT	G	GS	CG	SH	SV	IP	H	R	ER	HR	HB	BB	SO	RAT	ERA	ERA+	CERA	OAV	BH	AVG	PR+	WS	TPW
1910 Det-A	0	0	....	1	1	0	0	0	6	9	8	8	0	1	4	2	2.167	12.00	22	7.60	.333	0	.000	-6	0	-0.7

• SKOK, Craig Craig Richard Skok b: 9/1/1947, Dobbs Ferry, NY BR/TL, 6', 190 lbs. Deb: 5/4/1973

YEAR TM-L	W	L	PCT	G	GS	CG	SH	SV	IP	H	R	ER	HR	HB	BB	SO	RAT	ERA	ERA+	CERA	OAV	BH	AVG	PR+	WS	TPW
1973 Bos-A	0	1	.000	11	0	0	0	1	28^2	35	22	20	2	0	11	22	1.605	6.28	64	4.93	.304	0	....	-7	0	-0.8
1976 Tex-A	0	1	.000	9	0	0	0	0	5	13	7	7	2	0	3	5	3.200	12.60	28	19.68	.481	0	....	-5	0	-0.5
1978 Atl-N	3	2	.600	43	0	0	0	2	62	64	38	30	8	0	27	28	1.468	4.35	93	4.36	.266	2	.250	-1	3	-0.1
1979 Atl-N	1	3	.250	44	0	0	0	2	54^1	58	26	24	7	3	17	30	1.380	3.98	102	4.56	.282	0	.000	2	3	0.2
Total 4	4	7	.364	107	0	0	0	5	150	170	93	81	19	3	58	85	1.520	4.86	82	5.05	.289	2	.182	-12	6	-1.2

• SKOPEC, John John S. "Buckshot" Skopec b: 5/8/1880, Chicago, IL d: 10/20/1912, Chicago, IL BR/TL, 5'10", 190 lbs. Deb: 4/25/1901

YEAR TM-L	W	L	PCT	G	GS	CG	SH	SV	IP	H	R	ER	HR	HB	BB	SO	RAT	ERA	ERA+	CERA	OAV	BH	AVG	PR+	WS	TPW
1901 Chi-A	6	3	.667	9	9	6	0	0	68^1	62	39	24	1	8	45	24	1.566	3.16	110	4.14	.239	10	.333	2	6	0.5
1903 Det-A	2	2	.500	6	5	3	0	0	39^1	46	22	15	0	2	13	14	1.500	3.43	85	4.08	.291	2	.154	-2	1	-0.3
Total 2	8	5	.615	15	14	9	0	0	107^2	108	61	39	1	10	58	38	1.542	3.26	99	4.12	.259	12	.279	0	7	0.2

YEAR TM-L	W	L	PCT	G	GS	CG	SH	SV	IP	H	R	ER	HR	HB	BB	SO	RAT	ERA	ERA+	CERA	OAV	BH	AVG	PR+	WS	TPW
• SKRMETTA, Matt	Matthew Leland Skrmetta b: 11/6/1972, Biloxi, MS BB/TR, 6'3", 220 lbs. Deb: 6/6/2000																									
2000 Mon-N	0	0	....	6	0	0	0	0	5^1	6	10	9	1	0	6	4	2.250	15.19	32	8.17	.273	0	....	-6	0	-0.6
Pit-N	2	2	.500	8	0	0	0	0	9^1	13	12	10	2	1	3	7	1.714	9.64	48	7.50	.333	0	.000	-5	0	-0.5
Yr.	2	2	.500	14	0	0	0	0	14^2	19	22	19	3	1	9	11	1.909	11.66	40	7.75	.311	0	.000	-11	0	-1.1
• SLAGLE, John	John A. Slagle b: Lawrence, IN BL/TR, 5'10.5" Deb: 4/30/1891																									
1891 Cin-a	0	0	....	1	0	0	0	1	1^1	3	0	0	0	0	1	1	3.000	0.00	....	....	.431	0	.000	1	0	0.0
• SLAGLE, Roger	Roger Lee Slagle b: 11/4/1953, Wichita, KS BR/TR, 6'3", 190 lbs. Deb: 9/7/1979																									
1979 NY-A	0	0	....	1	0	0	0	0	2	0	0	0	0	0	0	2	.000	0.00	....	0.00	.000	0	....	1	0	0.1
• SLAGLE, Walt	Walter Jennings Slagle b: 12/15/1878, Kenton, OH d: 6/14/1974, San Gabriel, CA BB/TR, 6', 165 lbs. Deb: 5/4/1910																									
1910 Cin-N	0	0	....	1	0	0	0	0	1	0	1	1	0	1	3	0	3.000	9.00	32	9.21	.000	0	....	-1	0	-0.1
• SLAPNICKA, Cy	Cyril Charles Slapnicka b: 3/23/1886, Cedar Rapids, IA d: 10/20/1979, Cedar Rapids, IA BB/TR, 5'10", 165 lbs. Deb: 9/26/1911																									
1911 Chi-N	0	2	.000	3	2	1	0	0	24	21	12	9	0	3	7	10	1.167	3.38	98	2.75	.236	2	.222	-1	1	-0.1
1918 Pit-N	1	4	.200	7	6	4	0	1	49^1	50	34	26	2	5	22	3	1.459	4.74	61	4.14	.269	1	.071	-12	0	-1.4
Total 2	**1**	**6**	**.143**	**10**	**8**	**5**	**0**	**1**	**73^1**	**71**	**46**	**35**	**2**	**8**	**29**	**13**	**1.364**	**4.30**	**69**	**3.68**	**.258**	**3**	**.130**	**-13**	**1**	**-1.5**
• SLAPPEY, John	John Henry Slappey b: 8/8/1898, Albany, GA d: 6/10/1957, Marietta, GA BL/TL, 6'4", 170 lbs. Deb: 8/23/1920																									
1920 Phi-A	0	1	.000	3	1	0	0	0	6^1	15	12	5	0	0	4	1	3.000	7.11	57	12.69	.441	1	.500	-2	0	-0.1
• SLATON, Jim	James Michael Slaton b: 6/19/1950, Long Beach, CA BR/TR, 6', 185 lbs. Deb: 4/14/1971																									
1971 Mil-A	10	8	.556	26	23	5	4	0	147^2	140	67	62	16	1	71	63	1.429	3.78	92	4.16	.253	5	.109	-6	7	-0.8
1972 Mil-A	1	6	.143	9	8	0	0	0	44	50	31	27	3	1	21	17	1.614	5.52	55	4.90	.287	1	.091	-12	0	-1.5
1973 Mil-A	13	15	.464	38	38	13	3	0	276^1	266	127	114	30	1	99	134	1.321	3.71	101	3.76	.251	0	....	3	13	0.3
1974 Mil-A	13	16	.448	40	35	10	3	0	250	255	117	109	22	3	102	126	1.428	3.92	92	4.20	.268	0	....	-10	12	-1.0
1975 Mil-A	11	18	.379	37	33	10	3	0	217	238	129	109	28	2	90	119	1.512	4.52	85	4.84	.276	0	....	-15	6	-1.6
1976 Mil-A	14	15	.483	38	38	12	2	0	292^2	287	126	112	14	6	94	138	1.302	3.44	101	3.33	.259	0	....	1	15	0.1
1977 Mil-A★	10	14	.417	32	31	7	1	0	221	223	104	88	25	11	77	104	1.357	3.58	114	4.23	.266	0	....	10	14	1.0
1978 Det-A	17	11	.607	35	34	11	2	0	233^2	235	117	107	27	8	85	92	1.369	4.12	94	4.23	.263	0	....	-10	13	-1.0
1979 Mil-A	15	9	.625	32	31	12	3	0	213	229	95	86	15	2	54	80	1.329	3.63	115	3.79	.278	0	....	14	16	1.3
1980 Mil-A	1	1	.500	3	3	0	0	0	16^1	17	10	8	3	0	5	4	1.347	4.41	88	4.63	.270	0	....	-1	0	-0.1
1981* Mil-A	5	7	.417	24	21	0	0	0	117^1	120	60	57	10	2	50	47	1.449	4.37	78	4.36	.273	0	....	-14	3	-1.4
1982* Mil-A	10	6	.625	39	7	0	0	6	117^2	117	48	43	14	1	41	59	1.343	3.29	115	4.04	.264	0	....	5	8	0.5
1983 Mil-A	14	6	.700	46	0	0	0	5	112^1	112	57	54	12	3	56	38	1.496	4.33	86	4.60	.272	0	....	-7	7	-0.7
1984 Cal-A	7	10	.412	32	22	5	1	0	163	192	95	90	22	2	56	67	1.521	4.97	80	5.14	.295	0	....	-19	4	-1.9
1985 Cal-A	6	10	.375	29	24	1	0	1	148^1	162	82	72	22	2	63	60	1.517	4.37	94	5.22	.284	0	....	-9	6	-0.9
1986 Cal-A	4	6	.400	14	12	0	0	0	73^1	84	52	46	9	2	29	31	1.541	5.65	73	5.23	.295	0	....	-14	0	-1.4
Det-A	0	0	....	22	0	0	0	2	40	46	18	18	5	1	11	12	1.425	4.05	102	4.59	.288	0	....	-0	2	0.0
Yr.	4	6	.400	36	12	0	0	2	113^1	130	70	64	14	3	40	43	1.500	5.08	81	5.01	.292	0	....	-14	2	-1.4
Total 16	**151**	**158**	**.489**	**496**	**360**	**86**	**22**	**14**	**2683^2**	**2773**	**1335**	**1202**	**277**	**48**	**1004**	**1191**	**1.407**	**4.03**	**94**	**4.26**	**.270**	**6**	**.105**	**-85**	**126**	**-9.1**
• SLATTERY, Phil	Philip Ryan Slattery b: 2/25/1893, Harper, IA d: 3/2/1968, Long Beach, CA BR/TL, 5'11", 160 lbs. Deb: 9/16/1915																									
1915 Pit-N	0	0	....	3	0	0	0	0	8	5	0	0	0	2	1	1	.750	0.00	....	1.53	.185	0	.000	2	1	0.3
• SLAUGHTER, Barney	Byron Atkins Slaughter b: 10/6/1884, Smyrna, DE d: 5/17/1961, Philadelphia, PA BR/TR, 5'11.5", 165 lbs. Deb: 8/9/1910																									
1910 Phi-N	0	1	.000	8	1	0	0	1	18	21	12	11	0	0	11	7	1.778	5.50	57	5.40	.318	1	.200	-5	0	-0.5
• SLAUGHTER, Sterling	Sterling Feore Slaughter b: 11/18/1941, Danville, IL BR/TR, 5'11", 165 lbs. Deb: 4/19/1964																									
1964 Chi-N	2	4	.333	20	6	1	0	0	51^2	64	35	33	8	0	32	32	1.858	5.75	64	6.59	.305	1	.083	-11	0	-1.2
• SLAYBACK, Bill	William Grover Slayback b: 2/21/1948, Hollywood, CA BR/TR, 6'4", 200 lbs. Deb: 6/26/1972																									
1972 Det-A	5	6	.455	23	13	3	1	0	81^2	74	36	29	4	1	25	65	1.212	3.20	98	2.89	.239	4	.174	-1	4	-0.2
1973 Det-A	0	0	....	3	0	0	0	0	2	5	4	1	0	1	0	1	2.500	4.50	91	12.20	.417	0	....	-0	0	0.0
1974 Det-A	1	3	.250	16	4	0	0	0	54^2	57	34	29	1	3	26	23	1.518	4.77	80	4.12	.273	0	....	-6	1	-0.6
Total 3	**6**	**9**	**.400**	**42**	**17**	**3**	**1**	**0**	**138^1**	**136**	**74**	**59**	**5**	**5**	**51**	**89**	**1.352**	**3.84**	**90**	**3.51**	**.256**	**4**	**.174**	**-7**	**5**	**-0.8**
• SLAYTON, Steve	Foster Herbert Slayton b: 4/26/1902, Barre, VT d: 12/20/1984, Manchester, NH BR/TR, 6', 163 lbs. Deb: 7/21/1928																									
1928 Bos-A	0	0	....	3	0	0	0	0	7	6	3	3	0	0	3	2	1.286	3.86	106	2.68	.240	0	.000	0	0	0.0
• SLEATER, Lou	Louis Mortimer Sleater b: 9/8/1926, St. Louis, MO BL/TL, 5'10", 185 lbs. Deb: 4/25/1950																									
1950 StL-A	0	0	....	1	0	0	0	0	1	0	0	0	0	0	0	1	.000	0.00	....	0.00	.000	0	....	1	0	0.1
1951 StL-A	1	9	.100	20	8	4	0	1	81	88	53	46	7	5	53	33	1.741	5.11	86	5.48	.271	7	.226	-5	2	-0.4
1952 StL-A	0	1	.000	4	2	0	0	0	8^2	9	8	7	1	0	5	1	1.615	7.27	54	4.84	.265	0	.000	-3	0	-0.4
Was-A	4	2	.667	14	9	3	1	0	57	56	29	23	4	2	30	22	1.509	3.63	98	4.34	.260	1	.050	-0	3	-0.2
Yr.	4	3	.571	18	11	3	1	0	65^2	65	37	30	5	2	35	23	1.523	4.11	88	4.41	.261	1	.045	-3	3	-0.6
1955 KC-A	1	1	.500	16	1	0	0	0	25^2	33	22	22	3	0	21	11	2.104	7.71	54	7.78	.324	2	.154	-10	0	-1.1
1956 Mil-N	2	2	.500	25	1	0	0	2	45^2	42	22	16	6	0	27	32	1.511	3.15	110	4.10	.240	5	.500	1	4	0.3
1957 Det-A	3	3	.500	41	0	0	0	2	69^1	61	33	29	9	1	28	43	1.284	3.76	102	3.48	.237	5	.250	0	5	0.4
1958 Det-A	0	0	....	4	0	0	0	0	5^1	3	4	4	2	0	6	4	1.688	6.75	60	6.49	.158	1	1.000	-2	1	0.0
Bal-A	1	0	1.000	6	0	0	0	0	7	14	10	10	0	0	2	5	2.286	12.86	28	9.29	.438	0	.000	-7	0	-0.8
Yr.	1	0	1.000	10	0	0	0	0	12^1	17	14	14	2	0	8	9	2.027	10.22	36	8.08	.333	1	.143	-9	1	-0.9
Total 7	**12**	**18**	**.400**	**131**	**21**	**7**	**1**	**5**	**300^2**	**306**	**181**	**157**	**32**	**8**	**172**	**152**	**1.590**	**4.70**	**84**	**4.86**	**.264**	**21**	**.204**	**-25**	**15**	**-2.2**
• SLOAT, Lefty	Dwain Clifford Sloat b: 12/1/1918, Nokomis, IL d: 4/18/2003, St. Paul, MN BR/TL, 6', 168 lbs. Deb: 4/24/1948																									
1948 Bro-N	0	1	.000	4	1	0	0	0	7^1	7	5	5	0	0	8	1	2.045	6.14	65	5.73	.280	0	.000	-2	0	-0.2
1949 Chi-N	0	0	....	5	1	0	0	0	9	14	7	7	0	0	3	3	1.889	7.00	58	6.35	.400	0	....	-3	0	-0.3
Total 2	**0**	**1**	**.000**	**9**	**2**	**0**	**0**	**0**	**16^1**	**21**	**12**	**12**	**0**	**0**	**11**	**4**	**1.959**	**6.61**	**61**	**6.07**	**.350**	**0**	**.000**	**-5**	**0**	**-0.5**
• SLOCUMB, Heathcliff	Heath Slocumb b: 6/7/1966, Jamaica, NY BR/TR, 6'3", 220 lbs. Deb: 4/11/1991																									
1991 Chi-N	2	1	.667	52	0	0	0	1	62^2	53	29	24	3	3	30	34	1.324	3.45	113	3.12	.231	0	.000	4	4	0.4
1992 Chi-N	0	3	.000	30	0	0	0	1	36	52	27	26	3	1	21	27	2.028	6.50	55	7.53	.351	0	.000	-12	0	-1.3
1993 Chi-N	1	0	1.000	10	0	0	0	0	10^2	7	5	4	0	0	4	4	1.031	3.38	118	1.67	.189	0	.000	1	1	0.0
Cle-A	3	1	.750	20	0	0	0	0	27^1	28	14	13	3	0	16	18	1.610	4.28	101	4.96	.272	0	....	0	1	0.0
1994 Phi-N	5	1	.833	52	0	0	0	0	72^1	75	32	23	0	2	28	58	1.424	2.86	150	3.43	.262	1	.250	12	7	1.2
1995 Phi-N★	5	6	.455	61	0	0	0	32	65^1	64	26	21	2	1	35	63	1.515	2.89	146	3.96	.257	0	.000	9	11	0.9
1996 Bos-A	5	5	.500	75	0	0	0	31	83^1	68	31	28	2	3	55	88	1.476	3.02	168	3.53	.222	0	....	21	15	1.9
1997 Bos-A	0	5	.000	49	0	0	0	17	46^2	58	32	30	4	3	34	36	1.971	5.79	80	6.95	.312	0	....	-6	1	-0.6
*Sea-A	0	4	.000	27	0	0	0	10	28^1	26	13	13	2	1	15	28	1.447	4.13	109	3.92	.241	0	....	1	3	0.1
Yr.	0	9	.000	76	0	0	0	27	75	84	45	43	6	4	49	64	1.773	5.16	89	5.81	.286	0	....	-4	4	-0.4
1998 Sea-A	2	5	.286	57	0	0	0	3	67^2	72	40	40	5	1	44	51	1.714	5.32	87	5.27	.275	0	....	-4	3	-0.4
1999 Bal-A	0	0	....	10	0	0	0	0	8^2	15	12	12	2	2	9	12	2.769	12.46	38	14.14	.395	0	....	-8	0	-0.7
StL-N	3	2	.600	40	0	0	0	2	53^1	49	16	14	3	1	30	48	1.481	2.36	193	3.79	.243	0	....	13	7	1.2
2000 StL-N	2	3	.400	43	0	0	0	1	49^2	50	32	30	9	1	24	34	1.490	5.44	85	5.13	.266	0	.000	-5	2	-0.5
SD-N	0	1	.000	22	0	0	0	0	19	19	11	8	0	2	13	12	1.684	3.79	114	4.39	.264	0	....	1	1	0.1
Yr.	2	4	.333	65	0	0	0	1	68^2	69	43	38	9	3	37	46	1.544	4.98	91	4.92	.265	0	.000	-4	3	-0.4
Total 10	**28**	**37**	**.431**	**548**	**0**	**0**	**0**	**98**	**631**	**636**	**320**	**286**	**38**	**21**	**358**	**513**	**1.575**	**4.08**	**107**	**4.56**	**.263**	**1**	**.083**	**28**	**56**	**2.5**
• SLUSARSKI, Joe	Joseph Andrew Slusarski b: 12/19/1966, Indianapolis, IN BR/TR, 6'4", 195 lbs. Deb: 4/11/1991																									
1991 Oak-A	5	7	.417	20	19	1	0	0	109^1	121	69	64	14	4	52	60	1.582	5.27	73	5.44	.283	0	....	-17	2	-1.7
1992 Oak-A	5	5	.500	15	14	0	0	0	76	85	52	46	15	6	27	38	1.474	5.45	69	5.64	.284	0	....	-15	0	-1.5

YEAR	TM-L	W	L	PCT	G	GS	CG	SH	SV	IP	H	R	ER	HR	HB	BB	SO	RAT	ERA	ERA+	CERA	OAV	BH	AVG	PR+	WS	TPW
1993	Oak-A	0	0	....	2	1	0	0	0	8^{2}	9	5	5	1	0	11	1	2.308	5.19	78	7.64	.300	0	....	-1	0	-0.1
1995	Mil-A	1	1	.500	12	0	0	0	0	15	21	11	9	3	2	6	6	1.800	5.40	92	7.71	.333	0	....	-1	0	-0.1
1999	Hou-N	0	0	....	3	0	0	0	0	3^{2}	1	0	0	0	0	3	3	1.091	0.00	....	1.10	.083	0	....	2	1	0.2
2000	Hou-N	2	7	.222	54	0	0	0	3	77	80	36	36	8	3	22	54	1.325	4.21	115	3.99	.268	1	.111	7	6	0.6
2001	Atl-N	0	0	....	4	0	0	0	0	6	9	6	6	2	0	1	5	1.667	9.00	49	7.74	.346	0	....	-3	0	-0.3
	Hou-N	0	1	.000	8	0	0	0	0	10	16	10	10	2	0	3	6	1.900	9.00	51	8.15	.364	0	....	-5	0	-0.5
	Yr.	0	1	.000	12	0	0	0	0	16	25	16	16	4	0	4	11	1.813	9.00	50	7.99	.357	0	....	-8	0	-0.8
Total	7	13	21	.382	118	34	1	0	3	305^{2}	342	189	176	45	15	125	173	1.528	5.18	79	5.38	.285	1	.111	-34	9	-3.5

• SMALL, Aaron Aaron James Small b: 11/23/1971, Oxnard, CA BR/TR, 6'5", 200 lbs. Deb: 6/11/1994

YEAR	TM-L	W	L	PCT	G	GS	CG	SH	SV	IP	H	R	ER	HR	HB	BB	SO	RAT	ERA	ERA+	CERA	OAV	BH	AVG	PR+	WS	TPW
1994	Tor-A	0	0	....	1	0	0	0	0	2	5	2	2	1	0	2	0	3.500	9.00	54	21.61	.500	0	....	-1	0	-0.1
1995	Fla-N	1	0	1.000	7	0	0	0	0	6^{1}	7	2	1	1	0	6	5	2.053	1.42	296	7.30	.269	0	....	2	1	0.2
1996	Oak-A	1	3	.250	12	3	0	0	0	28^{2}	37	28	26	3	1	22	17	2.058	8.16	60	7.42	.308	0	....	-11	0	-1.0
1997	Oak-A	9	5	.643	71	0	0	0	4	96^{2}	109	50	46	6	3	40	57	1.541	4.28	105	4.67	.294	0	.000	5	7	0.4
1998	Oak-A	1	1	.500	24	0	0	0	0	36	51	34	29	3	3	14	19	1.806	7.25	63	6.49	.333	0	....	-10	0	-1.0
	Ari-N	3	1	.750	23	0	0	0	0	31^{2}	32	14	13	5	1	8	14	1.263	3.69	114	4.14	.269	0	....	2	2	0.2
2002	Atl-N	0	0	....	1	0	0	0	0	0^{1}	2	1	1	0	0	2	1	12.00	27.00	15	71.88	.667	0	....	-1	0	-0.1
Total	6	15	10	.600	139	3	0	0	4	201^{2}	243	131	118	19	8	94	113	1.671	5.27	87	5.66	.303	0	.000	-14	10	-1.3

• SMALL, Mark Mark Allen Small b: 11/12/1967, Portland, OR BR/TR, 6'3", 205 lbs. Deb: 4/5/1996

YEAR	TM-L	W	L	PCT	G	GS	CG	SH	SV	IP	H	R	ER	HR	HB	BB	SO	RAT	ERA	ERA+	CERA	OAV	BH	AVG	PR+	WS	TPW
1996	Hou-N	0	1	.000	16	0	0	0	0	24^{1}	33	23	16	1	1	13	16	1.890	5.92	65	5.92	.308	0	.000	-5	0	-0.5

• SMALLWOOD, Walt Walter Clayton Smallwood b: 4/24/1893, Dayton, MD d: 4/29/1967, Baltimore, MD BR/TR, 6'2", 190 lbs. Deb: 9/19/1917

YEAR	TM-L	W	L	PCT	G	GS	CG	SH	SV	IP	H	R	ER	HR	HB	BB	SO	RAT	ERA	ERA+	CERA	OAV	BH	AVG	PR+	WS	TPW
1917	NY-A	0	0	....	2	0	0	0	0	2	1	0	0	0	0	1	1	1.000	0.00	....	1.54	.167	0	....	1	0	0.1
1919	NY-A	0	0	....	6	0	0	0	0	21^{2}	20	12	12	1	2	9	6	1.338	4.98	64	3.88	.263	0	.000	-5	0	-0.6
Total	2	0	0	....	8	0	0	0	0	23^{2}	21	12	12	1	2	10	7	1.310	4.56	70	3.68	.256	0	.000	-4	0	-0.5

• SMART, J.D. Jon David Smart b: 11/12/1973, San Saba, TX BR/TR, 6'2", 180 lbs. Deb: 4/6/1999

YEAR	TM-L	W	L	PCT	G	GS	CG	SH	SV	IP	H	R	ER	HR	HB	BB	SO	RAT	ERA	ERA+	CERA	OAV	BH	AVG	PR+	WS	TPW
1999	Mon-N	0	1	.000	29	0	0	0	0	52	56	30	29	4	0	17	21	1.404	5.02	89	4.08	.276	0	.000	-2	2	-0.2
2001	Tex-A	1	2	.333	15	0	0	0	0	15^{1}	19	11	11	3	0	4	10	1.500	6.46	72	5.55	.306	0	....	-3	0	-0.3
Total	2	1	3	.250	44	0	0	0	0	67^{1}	75	41	40	7	0	21	31	1.426	5.35	85	4.41	.283	0	.000	-5	2	-0.5

• SMILEY, John John Patrick Smiley b: 3/17/1965, Phoenixville, PA BL/TL, 6'4", 200 lbs. Deb: 9/1/1986

YEAR	TM-L	W	L	PCT	G	GS	CG	SH	SV	IP	H	R	ER	HR	HB	BB	SO	RAT	ERA	ERA+	CERA	OAV	BH	AVG	PR+	WS	TPW
1986	Pit-N	1	0	1.000	12	0	0	0	0	11^{2}	4	6	5	2	0	4	9	.686	3.86	99	1.28	.105	0	....	-0	1	0.0
1987	Pit-N	5	5	.500	63	0	0	0	4	75	69	49	48	7	0	50	58	1.587	5.76	71	4.44	.244	1	.143	-15	2	-1.5
1988	Pit-N	13	11	.542	34	32	5	1	0	205	185	81	74	15	3	46	129	1.127	3.25	105	2.74	.241	5	.079	2	12	0.0
1989	Pit-N	12	8	.600	28	28	8	1	0	205^{1}	174	78	64	22	4	49	123	1.086	2.81	120	2.72	.226	9	.138	12	12	1.4
1990*	Pit-N	9	10	.474	26	25	2	0	0	149^{1}	161	83	77	15	2	36	86	1.319	4.64	78	3.94	.275	6	.122	-19	3	-2.0
1991*	Pit-N★	**20**	8	.714	33	32	2	1	0	207^{2}	194	78	71	17	3	44	129	1.146	3.08	116	2.99	.251	7	.100	10	14	0.8
1992	Min-A	16	9	.640	34	34	5	2	0	241	205	93	86	17	6	65	163	1.120	3.21	126	2.74	.231	0	....	21	18	2.1
1993	Cin-N	3	9	.250	18	18	2	0	0	105^{2}	117	69	66	15	2	31	60	1.401	5.62	72	4.66	.286	8	.250	-18	2	-1.6
1994	Cin-N	11	10	.524	24	24	1	1	0	158^{2}	169	80	68	18	4	37	112	1.298	3.86	107	3.94	.275	11	.200	5	8	0.7
1995*	Cin-N★	12	5	.706	28	27	1	0	0	176^{2}	173	72	68	11	4	39	124	1.200	3.46	119	3.13	.263	9	.164	9	13	1.1
1996	Cin-N	13	14	.481	35	34	2	2	0	217^{1}	207	100	88	20	4	54	171	1.201	3.64	114	3.26	.256	13	.191	11	14	1.2
1997	Cin-N	9	10	.474	20	20	0	0	0	117	139	76	68	17	6	31	94	1.453	5.23	82	5.12	.296	4	.100	-12	3	-1.4
	Cle-A	2	4	.333	6	6	0	0	0	37^{1}	45	23	23	9	1	10	26	1.473	5.54	85	6.06	.304	0	....	-3	1	-0.3
Total	12	126	103	.550	361	280	28	8	4	1907^{2}	1842	888	806	185	39	496	1284	1.226	3.80	102	3.43	.255	73	.145	1	103	0.5

• SMITH, Smith Deb: 6/5/1884

YEAR	TM-L	W	L	PCT	G	GS	CG	SH	SV	IP	H	R	ER	HR	HB	BB	SO	RAT	ERA	ERA+	CERA	OAV	BH	AVG	PR+	WS	TPW
1884	Bal-U	0	0	....	1	1	0	0	0	6	12	11	6	0	....	2	2	2.333	9.00	37	....	.391	1	.200	-4	0	-0.4

• SMITH, Smith Deb: 5/31/1886

YEAR	TM-L	W	L	PCT	G	GS	CG	SH	SV	IP	H	R	ER	HR	HB	BB	SO	RAT	ERA	ERA+	CERA	OAV	BH	AVG	PR+	WS	TPW
1886	Cin-a	0	1	.000	1	1	1	0	0	9	8	8	4	0	0	10	1	2.000	4.00	88	....	.227	1	.250	-1	0	-0.1

• SMITH, Al Alfred Kendricks Smith b: 12/13/1903, Norristown, PA d: 8/11/1995, San Diego, CA BR/TR, 6', 170 lbs. Deb: 6/18/1926

YEAR	TM-L	W	L	PCT	G	GS	CG	SH	SV	IP	H	R	ER	HR	HB	BB	SO	RAT	ERA	ERA+	CERA	OAV	BH	AVG	PR+	WS	TPW
1926	NY-N	0	0	....	1	0	0	0	0	2	4	2	2	0	0	2	0	3.000	9.00	42	12.74	.444	0	....	-1	0	-0.1

• SMITH, Al Alfred John Smith b: 10/12/1907, Belleville, IL d: 4/28/1977, Brownsville, TX BL/TL, 5'11", 180 lbs. Deb: 5/5/1934 C

YEAR	TM-L	W	L	PCT	G	GS	CG	SH	SV	IP	H	R	ER	HR	HB	BB	SO	RAT	ERA	ERA+	CERA	OAV	BH	AVG	PR+	WS	TPW
1934	NY-N	3	5	.375	30	4	0	0	5	66^{2}	70	40	32	2	0	21	27	1.365	4.32	90	3.40	.266	4	.286	-4	3	-0.3
1935	NY-N	10	8	.556	40	10	4	1	5	124	125	50	47	6	7	32	44	1.266	3.41	113	3.39	.263	4	.118	6	11	0.5
1936*	NY-N	14	13	.519	43	30	9	**4**	2	209^{1}	217	116	88	16	4	69	89	1.366	3.78	103	3.97	.274	10	.137	-4	11	-0.6
1937*	NY-N	5	4	.556	33	9	2	0	0	85^{2}	91	45	40	8	2	30	41	1.412	4.20	92	4.24	.275	3	.120	-5	4	-0.6
1938	Phi-N	1	4	.200	37	1	0	0	1	86	115	70	60	7	0	40	46	1.802	6.28	64	6.03	.320	0	.000	-19	0	-2.1
1939	Phi-N	0	0	....	5	0	0	0	0	9	11	5	4	1	2	5	2	1.778	4.00	99	7.18	.314	0	.000	-0	0	0.0
1940	Cle-A	15	7	.682	31	24	11	1	2	183	187	79	70	12	6	55	46	1.322	3.44	122	3.72	.270	19	.306	11	16	1.7
1941	Cle-A	12	13	.480	29	27	13	2	0	206^{2}	204	95	88	12	1	75	76	1.350	3.83	103	3.49	.256	11	.155	1	13	0.4
1942	Cle-A	10	15	.400	30	24	7	1	0	168^{1}	163	96	74	9	5	71	66	1.390	3.96	87	3.58	.251	15	.250	-12	6	-1.0
1943	Cle-A★	17	7	.708	29	27	14	3	1	208^{1}	186	74	59	7	0	72	72	1.238	2.55	122	2.79	.239	14	.206	8	15	1.3
1944	Cle-A	7	13	.350	28	26	7	1	0	181^{2}	197	83	69	6	3	69	44	1.464	3.42	97	3.96	.280	10	.156	-5	8	-0.7
1945	Cle-A	5	12	.294	21	19	8	3	1	133^{2}	141	74	57	8	2	48	34	1.414	3.84	84	3.92	.275	12	.293	-8	5	-0.4
Total	12	99	101	.495	356	201	75	16	17	1662^{1}	1707	827	688	94	32	587	587	1.380	3.72	99	3.76	.267	102	.191	-31	92	-1.8

• SMITH, Art Arthur Laird Smith b: 6/21/1906, Boston, MA d: 11/22/1995, Norwalk, CT BR/TR, 6', 175 lbs. Deb: 6/9/1932

YEAR	TM-L	W	L	PCT	G	GS	CG	SH	SV	IP	H	R	ER	HR	HB	BB	SO	RAT	ERA	ERA+	CERA	OAV	BH	AVG	PR+	WS	TPW
1932	Chi-A	0	1	.000	3	2	0	0	0	7	17	13	9	1	0	4	1	3.000	11.57	37	15.59	.500	0	.000	-6	0	-0.5

• SMITH, Bill William Garland Smith b: 6/8/1934, Washington, DC d: 3/30/1997, Clinton, MD BL/TL, 6', 190 lbs. Deb: 9/13/1958

YEAR	TM-L	W	L	PCT	G	GS	CG	SH	SV	IP	H	R	ER	HR	HB	BB	SO	RAT	ERA	ERA+	CERA	OAV	BH	AVG	PR+	WS	TPW
1958	StL-N	0	1	.000	2	1	0	0	0	9^{2}	12	7	7	0	0	4	4	1.655	6.52	63	4.99	.324	0	.000	-3	0	-0.3
1959	StL-N	0	0	....	6	0	0	0	1	8^{1}	11	3	1	0	0	3	4	1.680	1.08	392	5.07	.333	0	.000	3	1	0.3
1962	Phi-N	1	5	.167	24	5	0	0	0	50^{1}	59	32	24	8	1	10	26	1.371	4.29	90	4.63	.295	2	.182	-3	1	-0.2
Total	3	1	6	.143	32	6	0	0	1	68^{1}	82	42	32	8	1	17	34	1.449	4.21	93	4.73	.304	2	.143	-2	2	-0.2

• SMITH, Billy Billy Lavern Smith b: 9/13/1954, LaMarque, TX BR/TR, 6'7", 200 lbs. Deb: 6/9/1981

YEAR	TM-L	W	L	PCT	G	GS	CG	SH	SV	IP	H	R	ER	HR	HB	BB	SO	RAT	ERA	ERA+	CERA	OAV	BH	AVG	PR+	WS	TPW
1981*	Hou-N	1	1	.500	10	1	0	0	1	20^{2}	20	7	7	3	0	3	3	1.113	3.05	108	3.25	.263	0	.000	0	1	0.0

• SMITH, Bob Robert Eldridge Smith b: 4/22/1895, Rogersville, TN d: 7/19/1987, Waycross, GA BR/TR, 5'10", 175 lbs. Deb: 4/19/1923 ♦

YEAR	TM-L	W	L	PCT	G	GS	CG	SH	SV	IP	H	R	ER	HR	HB	BB	SO	RAT	ERA	ERA+	CERA	OAV	BH	AVG	PR+	WS	TPW
1925	Bos-N	5	3	.625	13	10	6	0	0	92^{2}	110	51	46	6	0	36	19	1.576	4.47	90	4.79	.304	49	.282	-6	8	-0.6
1926	Bos-N	10	13	.435	33	23	14	4	1	201^{1}	199	91	84	10	0	75	44	1.361	3.75	94	3.53	.269	25	.298	-2	14	0.5
1927	Bos-N	10	18	.357	41	32	16	1	3	260^{2}	297	132	109	9	2	75	81	1.427	3.76	99	3.98	.301	27	.248	3	14	0.8
1928	Bos-N	13	17	.433	38	25	14	0	2	244^{1}	274	138	105	11	2	74	59	1.424	3.87	101	3.95	.289	23	.250	10	10	1.3
1929	Bos-N	11	17	.393	34	29	19	1	3	231	256	135	120	20	1	71	65	1.416	4.68	100	4.21	.285	17	.172	1	13	0.0
1930	Bos-N	10	14	.417	38	24	14	2	5	219^{2}	247	115	104	25	3	85	84	1.511	4.26	116	4.80	.290	19	.235	16	17	1.4
1931	Chi-N	15	12	.556	36	29	18	2	2	240^{1}	239	101	86	10	1	62	63	1.252	3.22	120	3.06	.256	19	.218	19	17	2.1
1932*	Chi-N	4	3	.571	34	11	4	1	2	119	148	64	61	4	3	36	35	1.546	4.61	82	4.53	.303	10	.238	-13	6	-1.0
1933	Cin-N	4	4	.500	16	6	4	0	0	73^{2}	75	27	18	3	0	11	18	1.167	2.20	154	2.78	.260	5	.200	10	6	1.1
	Bos-N	4	3	.571	14	4	3	1	1	58^{2}	68	24	21	3	0	7	16	1.278	3.22	95	3.54	.296	4	.200	-1	4	0.0
	Yr.	8	7	.533	30	10	7	1	1	132^{1}	143	51	39	6	0	18	34	1.217	2.65	121	3.12	.276	9	.200	10	10	1.1
1934	Bos-N	6	9	.400	39	5	3	0	5	121^{2}	133	69	63	9	0	36	26	1.389	4.66	82	3.90	.277	9	.250	-11	5	-1.0
1935	Bos-N	8	18	.308	46	20	8	2	5	203^{1}	232	105	89	13	3	61	58	1.441	3.94	96	4.15	.285	17	.270	4	9	0.6
1936	Bos-N	6	7	.462	35	11	5	2	8	136	142	65	57	3	1	35	36	1.301	3.77	102	3.14	.264	10	.222	-0	10	0.0
1937	Bos-N	0	1	.000	18	0	0	0	3	44	52	22	20	6	2	6	14	1.318	4.09	88	4.52	.295	2	.200	-3	2	-0.3
Total	13	106	139	.433	435	229	128	16	40	2246^{1}	2472	1139	983	132	18	670	618	1.399	3.94	100	3.93	.283	409	.242	27	135	4.7

YEAR	TM-L	W	L	PCT	G	GS	CG	SH	SV	IP	H	R	ER	HR	HB	BB	SO	RAT	ERA	ERA+	CERA	OAV	BH	AVG	PR+	WS	TPW
• SMITH, Bob	Robert Gilchrist Smith b: 2/1/1931, Woodsville, NH BR/TL, 6'1.5", 190 lbs. Deb: 4/29/1955																										
1955	Bos-A	0	0	....	1	0	0	0	0	1^2	1	0	0	0	0	1	1	1.200	0.00	....	2.46	.200	0	....	1	0	0.1
1957	StL-N	0	0	....	6	0	0	0	1	9^2	12	10	5	0	1	6	11	1.862	4.66	85	5.04	.267	0	.000	-1	0	-0.1
	Pit-N	2	4	.333	20	4	2	0	0	55	48	22	19	2	1	25	35	1.327	3.11	122	3.09	.229	1	.077	4	3	0.3
	Yr.	2	4	.333	26	4	2	0	1	64^2	60	32	24	2	2	31	46	1.407	3.34	114	3.38	.235	1	.067	3	3	0.2
1958	Pit-N	2	2	.500	35	4	0	0	1	61	61	39	30	6	2	31	24	1.508	4.43	87	4.37	.262	1	.091	-5	1	-0.6
1959	Pit-N	0	0	....	20	0	0	0	0	28^1	32	16	11	1	0	17	12	1.729	3.49	111	5.15	.291	0	.000	1	1	0.1
	Det-A	0	3	.000	9	0	0	0	0	11	20	15	10	5	0	3	10	2.091	8.18	50	12.11	.417	0	.000	-5	0	-0.5
Total	4	4	9	.308	91	8	2	0	2	166^2	174	102	75	14	4	83	93	1.542	4.05	96	4.61	.267	2	.069	-6	5	-0.8
• SMITH, Bob	Robert Walkup "Riverboat" Smith b: 5/13/1928, Clarence, MO d: 6/23/2003, Clarence, MO BL/TL, 6', 185 lbs. Deb: 4/22/1958																										
1958	Bos-A	4	3	.571	17	7	1	0	0	66^2	61	32	28	4	0	45	43	1.590	3.78	106	4.35	.248	2	.105	3	4	0.2
1959	Chi-N	0	0	....	1	0	0	0	0	0^2	5	6	6	0	0	2	0	10.50	81.00	5	63.96	.833	0	....	-6	0	-0.6
	Cle-A	0	1	.000	12	3	0	0	0	29^1	31	19	17	2	0	12	17	1.466	5.22	71	4.17	.282	0	.000	-5	0	-0.6
Total	2	4	4	.500	30	10	1	0	0	96^2	97	57	51	6	0	59	60	1.614	4.75	82	4.71	.268	2	.080	-8	4	-1.0
• SMITH, Bob	Robert Ashley Smith b: 7/20/1890, Woodbury, VT d: 12/27/1965, West Los Angeles, CA BR/TR, 5'11", 160 lbs. Deb: 4/19/1913																										
1913	Chi-A	0	0	....	1	0	0	0	0	2	3	3	3	0	0	3	1	3.000	13.50	22	8.65	.273	0	....	-2	0	-0.3
1914	Buf-F	0	0	....	15	1	0	0	3	36^2	39	16	14	3	0	16	13	1.500	3.44	97	4.35	.281	2	.222	-1	3	-0.1
1915	Buf-F	0	0	....	1	0	0	0	0	1	1	2	2	0	1	2	0	3.000	18.00	17	12.85	.333	0	....	-2	0	-0.2
Total	3	0	0	....	17	1	0	0	3	39^2	43	21	19	3	1	21	14	1.613	4.31	75	4.78	.281	2	.222	-5	3	-0.5
• SMITH, Brian	Randall Brian Smith b: 7/19/1972, Salisbury, NC BR/TR, 5'11", 190 lbs. Deb: 9/11/2000																										
2000	Pit-N	0	0	....	3	0	0	0	0	4^1	6	5	5	1	0	2	3	1.846	10.38	44	7.97	.375	0	....	-3	0	-0.3
• SMITH, Bryn	Bryn Nelson Smith b: 8/11/1955, Marietta, GA BR/TR, 6'2", 205 lbs. Deb: 9/8/1981																										
1981	Mon-N	1	0	1.000	7	0	0	0	0	13	14	4	4	1	0	3	9	1.308	2.77	126	3.83	.280	0	.000	1	1	0.1
1982	Mon-N	2	4	.333	47	1	0	0	3	79^1	81	43	37	5	0	23	50	1.311	4.20	87	3.41	.264	0	.000	-5	3	-0.6
1983	Mon-N	6	11	.353	49	12	5	3	3	155^1	142	51	43	13	5	43	101	1.191	2.49	144	3.14	.248	5	.167	17	13	1.8
1984	Mon-N	12	13	.480	28	28	4	2	0	179	178	72	66	15	3	51	101	1.279	3.32	103	3.51	.259	7	.132	-0	10	0.1
1985	Mon-N	18	5	.783	32	32	4	2	0	222^1	193	85	72	12	1	41	127	1.052	2.91	116	2.29	.232	14	.194	10	16	1.4
1986	Mon-N	10	8	.556	30	30	1	0	0	187^1	182	101	82	15	6	63	105	1.308	3.94	94	3.55	.251	8	.138	-5	7	-0.5
1987	Mon-N	10	9	.526	26	26	2	0	0	150^1	164	81	73	16	2	31	94	1.297	4.37	96	3.81	.274	6	.136	-1	7	-0.1
1988	Mon-N	12	10	.545	32	32	1	0	0	198	179	79	66	15	10	32	122	1.066	3.00	120	2.73	.243	6	.109	10	11	1.0
1989	Mon-N	10	11	.476	33	32	3	1	0	215^2	177	76	68	16	4	54	129	1.071	2.84	124	2.47	.223	4	.065	18	15	1.7
1990	StL-N	9	8	.529	26	25	0	0	0	141^1	160	81	67	11	4	30	78	1.344	4.27	89	4.02	.286	10	.256	-7	7	-0.3
1991	StL-N	12	9	.571	31	31	3	0	0	198^2	188	95	85	16	7	45	94	1.173	3.85	97	3.12	.251	16	.246	-5	9	-0.2
1992	StL-N	4	2	.667	13	1	0	0	0	21^1	20	11	11	3	3	5	9	1.172	4.64	73	3.80	.247	0	.000	-3	1	-0.4
1993	Col-N	2	4	.333	11	5	0	0	0	29^2	47	29	28	2	3	11	9	1.955	8.49	56	7.42	.362	0	.000	-11	0	-1.1
Total	13	108	94	.535	365	255	23	8	6	1791^1	1725	808	702	140	48	432	1028	1.204	3.53	104	3.21	.253	76	.153	18	100	2.8
• SMITH, Bud	Robert Allan Smith b: 10/23/1979, Torrance, CA BL/TL, 6', 170 lbs. Deb: 6/10/2001																										
2001*	StL-N	6	3	.667	16	14	1	1	0	84^2	79	40	36	12	1	24	59	1.217	3.83	111	3.50	.250	4	.160	2	5	0.2
2002	StL-N	1	5	.167	11	10	0	0	0	48	67	39	37	4	3	22	22	1.854	6.94	57	6.78	.338	3	.214	-17	0	-1.6
Total	2	7	8	.467	27	24	1	1	0	132^2	146	79	73	16	4	46	81	1.447	4.95	83	4.69	.284	7	.179	-14	5	-1.4
• SMITH, Charlie	Charles Edwin Smith b: 4/20/1880, Cleveland, OH d: 1/3/1929, Wickliffe, OH BR/TR, 6'1", 185 lbs. Deb: 8/6/1902																										
1902	Cle-A	2	1	.667	3	3	2	1	0	20	23	9	9	0	0	5	5	1.400	4.05	85	3.56	.289	1	.125	-1	1	-0.2
1906	Was-A	9	16	.360	33	22	17	2	0	235^1	250	113	76	2	8	75	105	1.381	2.91	91	3.51	.275	16	.184	-3	6	-0.4
1907	Was-A	10	20	.333	36	31	21	3	0	258^2	254	103	75	0	1	51	119	1.179	2.61	93	2.49	.259	12	.143	4	7	0.1
1908	Was-A	9	13	.409	26	23	14	1	1	183	166	76	49	2	3	60	83	1.235	2.41	95	2.81	....	8	.123	-3	8	-0.7
1909	Was-A	3	12	.200	23	15	7	1	0	145^2	140	73	53	4	5	37	72	1.215	3.27	74	2.92	.250	7	.156	-12	3	-1.4
	Bos-A	3	0	1.000	3	3	2	0	0	25	23	6	6	2	1	2	11	1.000	2.16	115	2.44	.237	3	.300	1	3	0.1
	Yr.	6	12	.333	26	18	9	1	0	170^2	163	79	59	6	6	39	83	1.184	3.11	78	2.85	.248	10	.182	-12	6	-1.3
1910	Bos-A	11	6	.647	24	18	11	0	1	156^1	141	57	40	4	2	35	53	1.126	2.30	111	2.57	.248	5	.114	5	10	0.3
1911	Bos-A	0	0	....	1	1	0	0	0	2	2	3	2	1	0	1	0	1.500	9.00	36	7.17	.250	0	....	-1	0	-0.1
	Chi-N	3	2	.600	7	5	3	1	0	38	31	11	6	0	1	7	11	1.000	1.42	232	1.90	.228	1	.077	7	4	0.6
1912	Chi-N	7	4	.636	20	5	1	0	1	94	92	56	44	2	3	31	47	1.309	4.21	79	3.21	.269	9	.257	-12	5	-1.1
1913	Chi-N	7	9	.438	20	17	8	1	0	137^2	138	53	39	2	4	34	47	1.249	2.55	124	3.07	.274	4	.089	9	9	0.6
1914	Chi-N	2	4	.333	16	5	1	0	0	53^2	49	27	23	3	1	15	17	1.193	3.86	72	2.94	.251	1	.091	-5	1	-0.7
Total	10	66	87	.431	212	148	87	10	3	1349^1	1309	587	422	22	29	353	570	1.232	2.81	94	2.90	.299	67	.150	-13	57	-2.8
• SMITH, Chick	John William Smith b: 12/2/1892, Dayton, KY d: 10/11/1935, Dayton, KY BL/TL, 5'8", 165 lbs. Deb: 4/12/1913																										
1913	Cin-N	0	1	.000	5	1	0	0	0	17^2	15	8	7	1	0	11	11	1.472	3.57	91	3.64	.238	0	.000	-1	1	-0.1
• SMITH, Chuck	Charles Edward Smith b: 10/21/1969, Memphis, TN BR/TR, 6'1", 185 lbs. Deb: 6/13/2000																										
2000	Fla-N	6	6	.500	19	19	1	0	0	122^2	111	53	44	6	3	54	118	1.345	3.23	137	3.51	.248	4	.100	17	10	1.4
2001	Fla-N	5	5	.500	15	15	0	0	0	88	89	47	46	10	6	35	71	1.409	4.70	90	4.43	.265	5	.192	-5	4	-0.5
Total	2	11	11	.500	34	34	1	0	0	210^2	200	100	90	16	9	89	189	1.372	3.84	112	3.90	.255	9	.136	12	14	0.9
• SMITH, Clay	Clay Jamieson Smith b: 9/11/1914, Cambridge, KS d: 3/5/2002, Winfield, KS BR/TR, 6'2", 190 lbs. Deb: 9/13/1938																										
1938	Cle-A	0	0	....	4	0	0	0	0	11	18	10	8	1	0	2	3	1.818	6.55	71	6.98	.367	0	.000	-2	0	-0.2
1940*	Det-A	1	1	.500	14	1	0	0	0	28^1	32	18	16	3	1	13	14	1.588	5.08	94	5.12	.283	0	.000	-1	1	-0.1
Total	2	1	1	.500	18	1	0	0	0	39^1	50	28	24	4	1	15	17	1.653	5.49	86	5.64	.309	0	.000	-3	1	-0.4
• SMITH, Dan	Daniel Scott Smith b: 4/20/1969, St. Paul, MN BL/TL, 6'5", 190 lbs. Deb: 9/12/1992																										
1992	Tex-A	0	3	.000	4	2	0	0	0	14^1	18	8	8	1	0	8	5	1.814	5.02	76	5.89	.321	0	....	-2	0	-0.2
1994	Tex-A	1	2	.333	13	0	0	0	0	14^2	18	11	7	2	0	12	9	2.045	4.30	112	7.12	.281	0	....	1	1	0.1
Total	2	1	5	.167	17	2	0	0	0	29	36	19	15	3	0	20	14	1.931	4.66	90	6.51	.300	0	....	-0	1	-0.1
• SMITH, Dan	Daniel Charles Smith b: 9/15/1975, Flemington, NJ BR/TR, 6'3", 210 lbs. Deb: 6/8/1999																										
1999	Mon-N	4	9	.308	20	17	0	0	0	89^2	104	64	60	12	4	39	72	1.595	6.02	74	5.59	.293	2	.083	-14	2	-1.3
2000	Bos-A	0	0	....	2	0	0	0	0	3^1	2	3	3	0	0	3	1	1.500	8.10	62	2.96	.250	0	....	-1	0	-0.1
2002	Mon-N	1	1	.500	33	0	0	0	2	46^2	34	18	18	6	1	21	34	1.179	3.47	123	3.17	.210	0	.000	4	4	0.4
2003	Mon-N	2	2	.500	32	0	0	0	0	37^2	42	23	22	11	2	18	35	1.593	5.26	96	6.75	.280	0	.000	-1	2	-0.1
Total	4	7	12	.368	87	17	0	0	2	177^1	182	108	103	29	7	81	142	1.483	5.23	87	5.15	.270	2	.069	-11	8	-1.2
• SMITH, Daryl	Daryl Clinton Smith b: 7/29/1960, Baltimore, MD BR/TR, 6'4", 185 lbs. Deb: 9/18/1990																										
1990	KC-A	0	1	.000	2	1	0	0	0	6^2	5	3	3	0	0	4	6	1.350	4.05	95	2.96	.238	0	....	0	0	0.0
• SMITH, Dave	David Wayne Smith b: 8/30/1957, Tomball, TX BR/TR, 6'1", 190 lbs. Deb: 9/18/1984																										
1984	Cal-A	0	0	....	1	0	0	0	0	1	4	2	2	1	0	0	0	4.000	18.00	22	34.98	.571	0	....	-2	0	-0.2
1985	Cal-A	0	0	....	4	0	0	0	0	5	5	4	4	1	0	1	3	1.200	7.20	57	4.08	.278	0	....	-2	0	-0.2
Total	2	0	0	....	5	0	0	0	0	6	9	6	6	2	0	1	3	1.667	9.00	45	9.23	.360	0	....	-3	0	-0.3
• SMITH, Dave	David Merwin Smith b: 12/17/1914, Sellers, SC d: 4/1/1998, Whiteville, NC BR/TR, 5'10", 170 lbs. Deb: 6/16/1938																										
1938	Phi-A	2	1	.667	21	0	0	0	0	44^1	50	29	25	0	1	28	13	1.759	5.08	95	4.83	.284	0	.000	-0	2	-0.1
1939	Phi-A	0	0	....	1	0	0	0	0	0	1	0	0	0	0	2	0	....	....	....	∞	1.000	0	....	0	0	0.0
Total	2	2	1	.667	22	0	0	0	0	44^1	51	29	25	0	1	30	13	1.827	5.08	95	4.83	.288	0	.000	-0	2	-0.1

• SMITH, Dave David Stanley Smith b: 1/21/1955, Richmond, CA BR/TR, 6'1", 195 lbs. Deb: 4/11/1980 C

YEAR TM-L	W	L	PCT	G	GS	CG	SH	SV	IP	H	R	ER	HR	HB	BB	SO	RAT	ERA	ERA+	CERA	OAV	BH	AVG	PR+	WS	TPW
1980* Hou-N	7	5	.583	57	0	0	0	10	102^2	90	24	22	1	4	32	85	1.188	1.93	171	2.56	.237	0	.000	15	13	1.5
1981* Hou-N	5	3	.625	42	0	0	0	8	75	54	26	23	2	2	23	52	1.027	2.76	119	1.83	.198	2	.250	4	7	0.5
1982 Hou-N	5	4	.556	49	1	0	0	11	63^1	69	30	27	4	0	31	28	1.579	3.84	86	4.51	.285	0	.000	-4	4	-0.5
1983 Hou-N	3	1	.750	42	0	0	0	6	72^2	72	32	25	2	0	36	41	1.486	3.10	110	3.71	.258	0	.000	1	5	0.1
1984 Hou-N	5	4	.556	53	0	0	0	5	77^1	60	22	19	5	1	20	45	1.034	2.21	150	2.21	.214	0	.000	8	8	0.9
1985 Hou-N	9	5	.643	64	0	0	0	27	79^1	69	26	20	3	1	17	40	1.084	2.27	152	2.31	.235	0	.000	10	13	1.0
1986* Hou-N★	4	7	.364	54	0	0	0	33	56	39	17	17	5	1	22	46	1.089	2.73	132	2.43	.200	0	.000	5	11	0.5
1987 Hou-N	2	3	.400	50	0	0	0	24	60	39	13	11	0	1	21	73	1.000	1.65	237	1.47	.182	1	.500	15	15	1.6
1988 Hou-N	4	5	.444	51	0	0	0	27	57^1	60	26	17	1	1	19	38	1.378	2.67	124	3.28	.268	0	.000	4	7	0.5
1989 Hou-N	3	4	.429	52	0	0	0	25	58	49	20	17	1	1	19	31	1.172	2.64	128	2.33	.233	0	.000	5	10	0.5
1990 Hou-N★	6	6	.500	49	0	0	0	23	60^1	45	18	16	4	0	20	50	1.077	2.39	156	2.24	.210	0	.000	9	12	0.9
1991 Chi-N	0	6	.000	35	0	0	0	17	33	39	22	22	6	1	19	16	1.758	6.00	65	6.54	.302	0	.000	-7	0	-0.8
1992 Chi-N	0	0	....	11	0	0	0	0	14^1	15	4	4	0	0	4	3	1.326	2.51	143	2.94	.273	0	....	2	1	0.2
Total 13	53	53	.500	609	1	0	0	216	809^1	700	280	240	34	13	283	548	1.215	2.67	130	2.78	.234	3	.068	68	106	6.9

• SMITH, Doug Douglass Weldon Smith b: 5/25/1892, Millers Falls, MA d: 9/18/1973, Greenfield, MA BL/TL, 5'10", 168 lbs. Deb: 7/10/1912

YEAR TM-L	W	L	PCT	G	GS	CG	SH	SV	IP	H	R	ER	HR	HB	BB	SO	RAT	ERA	ERA+	CERA	OAV	BH	AVG	PR+	WS	TPW
1912 Bos-A	0	0	....	1	0	0	0	0	3	4	1	1	0	0	0	1	1.333	3.00	114	4.31	.364	0	....	0	0	0.0

• SMITH, Ed Ed Smith Deb: 4/18/1884

YEAR TM-L	W	L	PCT	G	GS	CG	SH	SV	IP	H	R	ER	HR	HB	BB	SO	RAT	ERA	ERA+	CERA	OAV	BH	AVG	PR+	WS	TPW
1884 Bal-U	3	4	.429	9	8	5	0	0	62	86	61	24	2	....	17	13	1.661	3.48	96	....	.309	5	.147	-2	2	-0.4

• SMITH, Ed Rhesa Edward Smith b: 2/21/1879, Mentone, IN d: 3/20/1955, Tarpon Springs, FL BR/TR, 5'11", 170 lbs. Deb: 4/27/1906

YEAR TM-L	W	L	PCT	G	GS	CG	SH	SV	IP	H	R	ER	HR	HB	BB	SO	RAT	ERA	ERA+	CERA	OAV	BH	AVG	PR+	WS	TPW
1906 StL-A	8	11	.421	19	18	13	0	0	154^2	153	90	64	3	9	53	45	1.332	3.72	69	3.36	.261	11	.204	-20	3	-1.9

• SMITH, Eddie Edgar Smith b: 12/14/1913, Mansfield, NJ d: 1/2/1994, Willingboro, NJ BB/TL, 5'10", 174 lbs. Deb: 9/20/1936

YEAR TM-L	W	L	PCT	G	GS	CG	SH	SV	IP	H	R	ER	HR	HB	BB	SO	RAT	ERA	ERA+	CERA	OAV	BH	AVG	PR+	WS	TPW
1936 Phi-A	1	1	.500	2	2	2	0	0	19	22	10	4	3	0	8	7	1.579	1.89	269	5.21	.275	1	.125	7	2	0.5
1937 Phi-A	4	17	.190	38	23	14	1	5	196^2	178	100	86	18	4	90	79	1.363	3.94	120	3.66	.242	17	.233	17	13	1.7
1938 Phi-A	3	10	.231	43	7	0	0	4	130^2	151	102	86	13	4	76	78	1.737	5.92	82	5.62	.287	12	.286	-12	4	-0.9
1939 Phi-A	1	0	1.000	3	0	0	0	0	3^2	7	4	4	0	0	2	3	2.455	9.82	48	9.13	.412	0	....	-2	0	-0.2
Chi-A	9	11	.450	29	22	7	1	0	176^2	161	83	72	11	4	90	67	1.421	3.67	129	3.73	.247	6	.115	19	15	1.6
Yr.	10	11	.476	32	22	7	1	0	180^1	168	87	76	11	4	92	70	1.442	3.79	125	3.83	.251	6	.115	17	15	1.5
1940 Chi-A	14	9	.609	32	28	12	0	0	207^1	179	92	74	16	3	95	119	1.322	3.21	138	3.29	.228	15	.217	23	18	2.4
1941 Chi-A★	13	17	.433	34	33	21	1	1	263^1	243	107	93	13	5	114	111	1.356	3.18	129	3.40	.246	19	.216	24	20	2.6
1942 Chi-A★	7	20	.259	29	28	18	2	1	215	223	112	95	17	4	86	78	1.437	3.98	90	4.11	.269	9	.123	-10	7	-1.3
1943 Chi-A	11	11	.500	25	25	14	2	0	187^2	197	85	77	2	5	76	66	1.455	3.69	90	3.77	.277	11	.159	-8	8	-1.0
1946 Chi-A	8	11	.421	24	21	3	1	1	145^1	135	71	46	9	4	60	59	1.342	2.85	120	3.43	.246	8	.178	8	8	0.9
1947 Chi-A	1	3	.250	15	5	0	0	0	33^1	40	36	27	1	0	24	12	1.920	7.29	50	5.53	.299	1	.167	-13	0	-1.4
Bos-A	1	3	.250	8	3	0	0	0	17	18	14	14	3	0	18	15	2.118	7.41	52	7.41	.269	1	.167	-7	0	-0.7
Yr.	2	6	.250	23	8	0	0	0	50^1	58	50	41	4	0	42	27	1.987	7.33	51	6.17	.289	2	.167	-20	0	-2.1
Total 10	73	113	.392	282	197	91	8	12	1595^2	1554	816	678	106	33	739	694	1.437	3.82	107	3.90	.256	100	.188	44	95	4.3

• SMITH, Edgar Edgar Eugene Smith b: 6/12/1862, Providence, RI d: 11/3/1892, Providence, RI BR/TR, 5'10", 160 lbs. Deb: 5/25/1883 U ♦

YEAR TM-L	W	L	PCT	G	GS	CG	SH	SV	IP	H	R	ER	HR	HB	BB	SO	RAT	ERA	ERA+	CERA	OAV	BH	AVG	PR+	WS	TPW
1883 Phi-N	0	1	.000	1	1	0	0	0	7	18	17	12	0	....	3	2	3.000	15.43	20	....	.455	3	.750	-9	1	-0.7
1884 Was-a	0	2	.000	3	2	2	0	0	22	27	23	12	0	1	5	4	1.455	4.91	62	....	.287	5	.088	-3	0	-0.6
1885 Pro-N	1	0	1.000	1	1	1	0	0	9	9	3	1	0	....	0	1	1.000	1.00	265	....	.248	1	.250	2	1	0.2
1890 Cle-N	1	4	.200	6	6	5	0	0	44	42	24	21	1	1	10	11	1.182	4.30	83	....	.244	7	.292	-4	3	-0.1
Total 4	2	7	.222	11	10	8	0	0	82	96	67	46	1	2	18	18	1.390	5.05	65	....	.281	18	.184	-14	5	-1.3

• SMITH, Elmer Elmer Ellsworth Smith b: 3/23/1868, Pittsburgh, PA d: 11/5/1945, Pittsburgh, PA BL/TL, 5'11", 178 lbs. Deb: 9/10/1886 ♦

YEAR TM-L	W	L	PCT	G	GS	CG	SH	SV	IP	H	R	ER	HR	HB	BB	SO	RAT	ERA	ERA+	CERA	OAV	BH	AVG	PR+	WS	TPW
1886 Cin-a	4	4	.500	9	9	8	0	0	72^2	57	54	30	1	3	44	40	1.390	3.72	95	....	.206	8	.286	-2	5	0.2
1887 Cin-a	34	17	.667	52	52	49	3	0	447^1	526	224	146	5	9	126	176	1.176	**2.94**	**148**	....	.283	58	.294	51	**54**	4.5
1888 Cin-a	22	17	.564	40	40	37	5	0	348^1	309	167	106	1	19	89	154	1.143	2.74	116	....	.229	29	.225	8	30	1.2
1889 Cin-a	9	12	.429	29	22	16	0	0	203	253	171	110	11	7	101	104	**1.744**	4.88	80	....	.296	23	.277	-24	9	-1.5
1892 Pit-N	6	7	.462	17	13	12	1	0	134	140	94	54	2	1	58	51	1.478	3.63	91	3.76	.259	140	.274	-9	31	0.3
1894 Pit-N	0	0	....	1	0	0	0	0	4	6	2	2	0	1	1	0	1.750	4.50	116	6.50	.343	175	.357	0	19	1.6
1898 Cin-N	0	0	....	1	0	0	0	0	1	2	2	2	0	0	3	0	5.000	18.00	21	20.55	.411	166	.342	-2	27	1.2
Total 7	75	57	.568	149	136	122	9	0	1210^1	1293	714	450	20	40	422	525	1.313	3.35	111	0.45	.264	1467	.312	22	175	7.5

• SMITH, Frank Frank Elmer "Piano Mover,Nig" Smith b: 10/28/1879, Pittsburgh, PA d: 11/3/1952, Pittsburgh, PA BR/TR, 5'10.5", 194 lbs. Deb: 4/22/1904

YEAR TM-L	W	L	PCT	G	GS	CG	SH	SV	IP	H	R	ER	HR	HB	BB	SO	RAT	ERA	ERA+	CERA	OAV	BH	AVG	PR+	WS	TPW
1904 Chi-A	16	9	.640	26	23	22	4	0	202^1	157	62	47	0	12	58	107	1.063	2.09	117	2.02	.215	18	.250	4	17	0.9
1905 Chi-A	19	13	.594	39	31	27	4	0	291^2	215	97	69	0	8	107	171	1.104	2.13	116	1.99	.208	24	.226	2	22	1.0
1906 Chi-A	5	5	.500	20	13	8	1	1	122	124	58	46	3	5	37	53	1.320	3.39	75	3.35	.267	12	.293	-13	6	-0.9
1907 Chi-A	23	10	.697	41	37	29	3	0	310	280	105	85	3	2	111	139	1.261	2.47	97	2.74	.244	18	.196	0	24	0.6
1908 Chi-A	16	17	.485	41	35	24	3	1	297^2	213	92	67	2	2	73	129	.961	2.03	114	1.61	.203	20	.189	13	21	1.7
1909 Chi-A	25	17	.595	**51**	**40**	**37**	7	1	**365**	278	104	73	1	6	70	**177**	.953	1.80	130	1.60	.214	22	.173	22	**31**	3.2
1910 Chi-A	4	9	.308	19	15	9	3	0	128^2	91	43	29	1	2	40	50	1.018	2.03	118	1.80	.204	8	.186	6	8	0.9
Bos-A	1	2	.333	4	3	2	0	0	28	22	19	15	0	1	11	8	1.179	4.82	53	2.56	.234	1	.111	-7	0	-0.8
Yr.	5	11	.313	23	18	11	3	0	156^2	113	62	44	1	3	51	58	1.047	2.53	97	1.94	.209	9	.173	-1	8	0.1
1911 Bos-A	0	0	....	1	1	0	0	0	2^1	6	4	4	0	0	3	1	3.857	15.43	21	18.25	.500	0	....	-3	0	-0.3
Cin-N	10	14	.417	34	18	10	0	1	176^1	198	112	78	1	3	55	67	1.435	3.98	83	3.86	.289	12	.214	-13	5	-1.0
1912 Cin-N	1	1	.500	7	3	1	0	0	22^2	34	25	16	1	0	15	5	2.162	6.35	53	7.70	.370	0	.000	-7	0	-0.7
1914 Bal-F	10	8	.556	39	22	9	1	2	174^2	180	86	58	8	0	47	83	1.300	2.99	106	3.27	.259	12	.203	8	11	0.9
1915 Bal-F	4	4	.500	17	9	2	0	0	88^2	108	53	46	5	0	31	37	1.568	4.67	72	4.71	.312	5	.172	-11	2	-1.1
Bro-F	5	2	.714	15	5	4	1	0	63	69	31	22	2	0	18	24	1.381	3.14	95	3.62	.290	4	.200	-2	4	-0.1
Yr.	9	6	.600	32	14	6	1	0	151^2	177	84	68	7	0	49	61	1.490	4.04	80	4.26	.303	9	.184	-13	6	-1.2
Total 11	139	111	.556	354	255	184	27	6	2273	1975	891	655	27	41	676	1051	1.166	2.59	102	2.52	.237	156	.204	-2	151	4.3

• SMITH, Frank Frank Thomas Smith b: 4/4/1928, Pierrepont Manor, NY BR/TR, 6'3", 200 lbs. Deb: 4/18/1950

YEAR TM-L	W	L	PCT	G	GS	CG	SH	SV	IP	H	R	ER	HR	HB	BB	SO	RAT	ERA	ERA+	CERA	OAV	BH	AVG	PR+	WS	TPW
1950 Cin-N	2	7	.222	38	4	0	0	3	90^2	73	43	39	12	8	39	55	1.235	3.87	109	3.49	.216	2	.095	5	6	0.3
1951 Cin-N	5	5	.500	50	0	0	0	11	76	65	33	27	7	4	22	34	1.145	3.20	128	2.93	.230	0	.000	8	9	0.7
1952 Cin-N	12	11	.522	53	2	1	0	7	122^1	109	56	51	13	7	41	77	1.226	3.75	100	3.41	.242	5	.172	-0	10	0.0
1953 Cin-N	8	1	.889	50	1	0	0	2	83^2	89	64	51	15	3	25	42	1.363	5.49	79	4.60	.272	2	.154	-12	3	-1.2
1954 Cin-N	5	8	.385	50	0	0	0	20	81	60	29	24	15	3	29	51	1.099	2.67	157	3.14	.211	1	.100	13	13	1.4
1955 StL-N	3	1	.750	28	0	0	0	1	39	27	18	14	3	5	23	17	1.282	3.23	126	3.33	.205	0	.000	4	4	0.3
1956 Cin-N	0	0	....	2	0	0	0	0	3	3	4	4	2	0	2	1	1.667	12.00	33	10.24	.300	0	....	-3	0	-0.3
Total 7	35	33	.515	271	7	1	0	44	495^2	426	247	210	67	30	181	277	1.225	3.81	108	3.54	.234	10	.115	14	45	1.2

• SMITH, Fred Frederick Smith b: 11/24/1878, New Diggings, WI d: 2/4/1964, Los Angeles, CA BL/TR, 6', 186 lbs. Deb: 6/14/1907

YEAR TM-L	W	L	PCT	G	GS	CG	SH	SV	IP	H	R	ER	HR	HB	BB	SO	RAT	ERA	ERA+	CERA	OAV	BH	AVG	PR+	WS	TPW
1907 Cin-N	2	7	.222	18	9	5	0	1	85^1	90	44	27	3	4	24	19	1.336	2.85	91	3.68	.274	3	.107	-3	1	-0.6

• SMITH, Fred Frederick C. Smith b: 3/25/1863, Greene, NY d: 1/9/1941, Syracuse, NY BL/TR, 5'11", 156 lbs. Deb: 4/18/1890 U

YEAR TM-L	W	L	PCT	G	GS	CG	SH	SV	IP	H	R	ER	HR	HB	BB	SO	RAT	ERA	ERA+	CERA	OAV	BH	AVG	PR+	WS	TPW
1890 Tol-a	19	13	.594	35	34	31	2	0	286	273	155	104	13	13	90	116	1.269	3.27	121	....	.244	21	.167	15	22	1.1

• SMITH, George George Allen "Columbia George" Smith b: 5/31/1892, Byram, CT d: 1/7/1965, Greenwich, CT BR/TR, 6'2", 163 lbs. Deb: 8/9/1916

YEAR TM-L	W	L	PCT	G	GS	CG	SH	SV	IP	H	R	ER	HR	HB	BB	SO	RAT	ERA	ERA+	CERA	OAV	BH	AVG	PR+	WS	TPW
1916 NY-N	3	0	1.000	9	1	0	0	0	20^2	14	8	6	0	1	6	9	.968	2.61	93	1.59	.197	0	.000	-1	2	-0.1
1917 NY-N	0	3	.000	14	1	1	0	0	38	38	13	12	1	1	11	16	1.289	2.84	90	3.21	.270	0	.000	-2	1	-0.3
1918 Cin-N	2	3	.400	10	6	4	1	0	55^1	71	36	25	3	0	11	19	1.482	4.07	66	4.57	.329	0	.000	-9	0	-1.2
NY-N	2	3	.400	5	2	1	0	0	26^2	26	12	12	0	1	6	4	1.200	4.05	65	2.69	.255	2	.250	-4	1	-0.5
Bro-N	4	1	.800	8	5	4	0	0	50	43	14	13	0	2	5	18	.960	2.34	119	1.94	.249	3	.200	2	5	0.3
Yr.	8	7	.533	23	13	9	1	0	132	140	62	50	3	3	22	41	1.227	3.41	79	3.19	.285	5	.125	-11	6	-1.4

YEAR	TM-L	W	L	PCT	G	GS	CG	SH	SV	IP	H	R	ER	HR	HB	BB	SO	RAT	ERA	ERA+	CERA	OAV	BH	AVG	PR+	WS	TPW
1919	NY-N	0	2	.000	3	2	0	0	0	11	18	8	7	1	0	4	0	2.000	5.73	49	7.90	.383	0	.000	-4	0	-0.5
	Phi-N	5	11	.313	31	19	11	1	0	184^2	194	94	66	7	3	46	42	1.300	3.22	100	3.39	.278	8	.133	1	6	-0.2
	Yr.	5	13	.278	34	21	11	1	0	195^2	212	102	73	8	3	50	42	1.339	3.36	94	3.65	.285	8	.127	-3	6	-0.7
1920	Phi-N	13	18	.419	43	28	10	1	2	250^2	265	115	96	10	6	51	51	1.261	3.45	99	3.31	.283	7	.097	-1	15	-0.6
1921	Phi-N	4	20	.167	39	28	12	1	1	221^1	303	166	117	12	3	52	45	**1.604**	4.76	89	5.20	.335	4	.056	-9	5	-1.6
1922	Phi-N	5	14	.263	42	16	6	1	0	194	250	124	103	16	6	35	44	1.469	4.78	98	4.81	.316	5	.076	-2	9	-0.8
1923	Bro-N	3	6	.333	25	7	3	0	1	91	99	53	37	4	3	28	15	1.396	3.66	106	3.84	.278	5	.192	2	4	0.1
Total	8	41	81	.336	229	115	52	5	4	1143^1	1321	643	494	54	26	255	263	1.378	3.89	93	3.98	.298	34	.097	-25	48	-5.4

• SMITH, George George Shelby Smith b: 10/27/1901, Louisville, KY d: 5/26/1981, Richmond, VA BR/TR, 6'1", 175 lbs. Deb: 4/21/1926

YEAR	TM-L	W	L	PCT	G	GS	CG	SH	SV	IP	H	R	ER	HR	HB	BB	SO	RAT	ERA	ERA+	CERA	OAV	BH	AVG	PR+	WS	TPW
1926	Det-A	1	2	.333	23	1	0	0	0	44	55	37	34	3	2	33	15	2.000	6.95	58	6.75	.318	0	.000	-14	0	-1.4
1927	Det-A	4	1	.800	29	0	0	0	0	71^1	62	38	31	3	2	50	32	1.570	3.91	108	4.02	.240	7	.368	3	5	0.6
1928	Det-A	1	1	.500	39	2	0	0	3	106	103	55	52	3	0	50	54	1.443	4.42	93	3.51	.263	3	.111	-4	5	-0.5
1929	Det-A	3	2	.600	14	2	1	0	0	35^2	42	33	23	1	0	36	13	2.187	5.80	74	6.79	.307	5	.417	-5	1	-0.3
1930	Bos-A	1	2	.333	27	2	0	0	0	73^2	92	62	54	7	1	49	21	1.914	6.60	70	6.44	.317	8	.333	-17	0	-1.4
Total	5	10	8	.556	132	7	1	0	3	330^2	354	225	194	17	5	218	135	1.730	5.28	81	5.06	.283	23	.264	-36	11	-3.0

• SMITH, Hal Harold Laverne Smith b: 6/30/1902, Creston, IA d: 9/27/1992, Fort Lauderdale, FL BR/TR, 6'3", 195 lbs. Deb: 9/14/1932

YEAR	TM-L	W	L	PCT	G	GS	CG	SH	SV	IP	H	R	ER	HR	HB	BB	SO	RAT	ERA	ERA+	CERA	OAV	BH	AVG	PR+	WS	TPW
1932	Pit-N	1	0	1.000	2	1	1	1	0	12	9	1	1	0	0	2	4	.917	0.75	508	1.48	.209	0	.000	4	2	0.4
1933	Pit-N	8	7	.533	28	19	8	2	1	145	149	66	46	5	5	31	40	1.241	2.86	116	3.11	.261	6	.128	7	8	0.5
1934	Pit-N	3	4	.429	20	5	1	0	0	50	72	44	40	3	4	18	15	1.800	7.20	57	6.33	.343	1	.059	-17	0	-1.8
1935	Pit-N	0	0	....	1	0	0	0	0	3	2	1	1	0	0	1	0	1.000	3.00	137	1.66	.200	0	....	0	0	0.0
Total	4	12	11	.522	51	25	10	3	1	210	232	112	88	8	9	52	59	1.352	3.77	97	3.77	.278	7	.104	-6	10	-0.9

• SMITH, Harry Harrison Morton Smith b: 8/15/1889, Union, NE d: 7/26/1964, Dunbar, NE BR/TR, 5'9", 160 lbs. Deb: 10/6/1912

YEAR	TM-L	W	L	PCT	G	GS	CG	SH	SV	IP	H	R	ER	HR	HB	BB	SO	RAT	ERA	ERA+	CERA	OAV	BH	AVG	PR+	WS	TPW
1912	Chi-A	1	0	1.000	1	1	0	0	0	5	6	1	1	0	0	0	1	1.200	1.80	179	3.46	.333	0	.000	1	1	0.1

• SMITH, Jack Jack Hatfield Smith b: 11/15/1935, Pikeville, KY BR/TR, 6', 185 lbs. Deb: 9/10/1962

YEAR	TM-L	W	L	PCT	G	GS	CG	SH	SV	IP	H	R	ER	HR	HB	BB	SO	RAT	ERA	ERA+	CERA	OAV	BH	AVG	PR+	WS	TPW
1962	LA-N	0	0	....	8	0	0	0	1	10	10	6	5	0	0	4	7	1.400	4.50	81	3.21	.263	0	.000	-1	0	-0.1
1963	LA-N	0	0	....	4	0	0	0	0	8^1	10	7	7	2	2	2	5	1.440	7.56	40	6.53	.303	0	.000	-4	0	-0.5
1964	Mil-N	2	2	.500	22	0	0	0	0	31	28	15	13	3	0	11	19	1.258	3.77	93	3.04	.237	1	.333	-1	1	-0.1
Total	3	2	2	.500	34	0	0	0	1	49^1	48	28	25	5	2	17	31	1.318	4.56	74	3.66	.254	1	.167	-6	1	-0.6

• SMITH, Jake Jacob Smith b: 6/10/1887, Dravosburg, PA d: 11/7/1948, East McKeesport, PA BB/TL, 6'5", 200 lbs. Deb: 10/3/1911

YEAR	TM-L	W	L	PCT	G	GS	CG	SH	SV	IP	H	R	ER	HR	HB	BB	SO	RAT	ERA	ERA+	CERA	OAV	BH	AVG	PR+	WS	TPW
1911	Phi-N	0	0	....	2	0	0	0	0	5	3	0	0	0	0	2	1	1.000	0.00	....	1.53	.176	0	.000	2	1	0.1

• SMITH, Lee Lee Arthur Smith b: 12/4/1957, Jamestown, LA BR/TR, 6'5", 225 lbs. Deb: 9/1/1980

YEAR	TM-L	W	L	PCT	G	GS	CG	SH	SV	IP	H	R	ER	HR	HB	BB	SO	RAT	ERA	ERA+	CERA	OAV	BH	AVG	PR+	WS	TPW
1980	Chi-N	2	0	1.000	18	0	0	0	0	21^2	21	9	7	0	0	14	17	1.615	2.91	135	3.71	.259	0	....	3	2	0.3
1981	Chi-N	3	6	.333	40	1	0	0	1	66^2	57	31	26	2	1	31	50	1.320	3.51	105	2.96	.239	0	.000	3	4	0.2
1982	Chi-N	2	5	.286	72	5	0	0	17	117	105	38	35	5	3	37	99	1.214	2.69	139	2.90	.245	1	.063	15	13	1.5
1983	Chi-N★	4	10	.286	66	0	0	0	**29**	103^1	70	23	19	5	1	41	91	1.074	1.65	229	1.95	.194	1	.111	26	19	2.7
1984*	Chi-N	9	7	.563	69	0	0	0	33	101	98	42	41	6	0	35	86	1.317	3.65	107	3.31	.255	1	.077	4	15	0.3
1985	Chi-N	7	4	.636	65	0	0	0	33	97^2	87	35	33	9	1	32	112	1.218	3.04	131	3.18	.242	0	.000	11	17	1.2
1986	Chi-N	9	9	.500	66	0	0	0	31	90^1	69	32	31	7	0	42	93	1.229	3.09	131	2.76	.215	0	.000	11	17	1.1
1987	Chi-N★	4	10	.286	62	0	0	0	36	83^2	84	30	29	4	0	32	96	1.386	3.12	137	3.55	.259	0	.000	13	15	1.2
1988*	Bos-A	4	5	.444	64	0	0	0	29	83^2	72	34	26	7	1	37	96	1.303	2.80	147	3.20	.225	0	....	13	12	1.4
1989	Bos-A	6	1	.857	64	0	0	0	25	70^2	53	30	28	6	0	33	96	1.217	3.57	115	2.80	.209	0	....	5	11	0.5
1990	Bos-A	2	1	.667	11	0	0	0	4	14^1	13	4	3	0	0	9	17	1.535	1.88	216	3.42	.236	0	....	4	3	0.4
	StL-N	3	4	.429	53	0	0	0	27	68^2	58	20	16	3	0	20	70	1.136	2.10	182	2.38	.227	0	.000	13	14	1.4
1991	StL-N★	6	3	.667	67	0	0	0	**47**	73	70	19	19	5	0	13	67	1.137	2.34	159	2.68	.249	0	....	10	15	1.1
1992	StL-N★	4	9	.308	70	0	0	0	**43**	75	62	28	26	4	0	26	60	1.173	3.12	109	2.55	.221	0	....	1	12	0.1
1993	StL-N★	2	4	.333	55	0	0	0	43	50	49	25	25	11	0	9	49	1.160	4.50	88	3.80	.251	0	.000	-3	7	-0.3
	NY-A	0	0	....	8	0	0	0	3	8	4	0	0	0	0	5	11	1.125	0.00	....	1.54	.148	0	....	4	2	0.4
1994	Bal-A★	1	4	.200	41	0	0	0	**33**	38^1	34	16	14	6	0	11	42	1.174	3.29	152	3.29	.239	0	....	7	8	0.6
1995	Cal-A★	0	5	.000	52	0	0	0	37	49^1	42	19	19	3	1	25	43	1.358	3.47	135	3.39	.237	0	....	6	8	0.6
1996	Cal-A	0	0	....	11	0	0	0	0	11	8	4	3	0	0	3	6	1.000	2.45	200	1.63	.205	0	....	3	1	0.3
	Cin-N	3	4	.429	43	0	0	0	2	44^1	49	20	20	4	1	23	35	1.624	4.06	102	5.02	.277	0	....	0	3	0.0
1997	Mon-N	0	1	.000	25	0	0	0	5	21^2	28	16	14	2	1	8	15	1.662	5.82	72	5.77	.308	0	....	-4	0	-0.4
Total	18	71	92	.436	1022	6	0	0	478	1289^1	1133	475	434	89	10	486	1251	1.256	3.03	131	3.05	.237	3	.047	146	198	14.5

• SMITH, Mark Mark Christopher Smith b: 11/23/1955, Alexandria, VA BR/TR, 6'2", 215 lbs. Deb: 8/12/1983

YEAR	TM-L	W	L	PCT	G	GS	CG	SH	SV	IP	H	R	ER	HR	HB	BB	SO	RAT	ERA	ERA+	CERA	OAV	BH	AVG	PR+	WS	TPW
1983	Oak-A	1	0	1.000	8	1	0	0	0	14^2	24	11	11	0	1	6	10	2.045	6.75	57	7.64	.387	0	....	-5	0	-0.5

• SMITH, Mike Michael Anthony Smith b: 9/19/1977, Norwood, MA BR/TR, 5'11", 195 lbs. Deb: 4/26/2002

YEAR	TM-L	W	L	PCT	G	GS	CG	SH	SV	IP	H	R	ER	HR	HB	BB	SO	RAT	ERA	ERA+	CERA	OAV	BH	AVG	PR+	WS	TPW
2002	Tor-A	0	3	.000	14	6	0	0	0	35^1	43	28	26	3	7	20	16	1.783	6.62	70	6.66	.301	0	....	-8	0	-0.7

• SMITH, Mike Michael Anthony Smith b: 2/23/1961, Jackson, MS BR/TR, 6', 195 lbs. Deb: 4/6/1984

YEAR	TM-L	W	L	PCT	G	GS	CG	SH	SV	IP	H	R	ER	HR	HB	BB	SO	RAT	ERA	ERA+	CERA	OAV	BH	AVG	PR+	WS	TPW
1984	Cin-N	1	0	1.000	8	0	0	0	0	10^1	12	6	6	1	0	5	7	1.645	5.23	72	5.31	.286	0	....	-2	0	-0.2
1985	Cin-N	0	0	....	2	0	0	0	0	3^1	2	2	2	2	0	1	2	.900	5.40	70	4.23	.167	0	....	-1	0	-0.1
1986	Cin-N	0	0	....	2	1	0	0	0	3^1	7	5	5	0	0	1	1	2.400	13.50	29	9.49	.412	0	....	-4	0	-0.4
1988	Mon-N	0	0	....	5	0	0	0	1	8^2	6	3	3	0	0	5	4	1.269	3.12	115	2.54	.207	0	.000	0	1	0.0
1989	Pit-N	0	1	.000	16	0	0	0	0	24	28	12	10	1	0	10	12	1.583	3.75	89	4.60	.301	0	.000	-1	1	-0.1
Total	5	1	1	.500	33	1	0	0	1	49^2	55	28	26	4	0	22	26	1.550	4.71	76	4.69	.285	0	.000	-6	2	-0.7

• SMITH, Mike Michael Anthony Smith b: 10/31/1963, San Antonio, TX BR/TR, 6'3", 180 lbs. Deb: 6/30/1989

YEAR	TM-L	W	L	PCT	G	GS	CG	SH	SV	IP	H	R	ER	HR	HB	BB	SO	RAT	ERA	ERA+	CERA	OAV	BH	AVG	PR+	WS	TPW
1989	Bal-A	2	0	1.000	13	1	0	0	0	20	25	19	17	3	0	14	12	1.950	7.65	50	7.03	.313	0	....	-9	0	-0.9
1990	Bal-A	0	0	....	2	0	0	0	0	3	4	4	4	2	0	1	2	1.667	12.00	32	10.06	.308	0	....	-3	0	-0.3
Total	2	2	0	1.000	15	1	0	0	0	23	29	23	21	5	0	15	14	1.913	8.22	46	7.43	.312	0	....	-11	0	-1.2

• SMITH, Pete Peter Luke Smith b: 3/19/1940, Natick, MA BR/TR, 6'2", 190 lbs. Deb: 9/13/1962

YEAR	TM-L	W	L	PCT	G	GS	CG	SH	SV	IP	H	R	ER	HR	HB	BB	SO	RAT	ERA	ERA+	CERA	OAV	BH	AVG	PR+	WS	TPW
1962	Bos-A	0	1	.000	1	1	0	0	0	3^2	7	8	8	3	0	2	1	2.455	19.64	21	18.35	.438	0	.000	-6	0	-0.6
1963	Bos-A	0	0	....	6	1	0	0	0	15	11	6	6	2	0	6	6	1.133	3.60	105	2.74	.212	0	.000	0	1	0.0
Total	2	0	1	.000	7	2	0	0	0	18^2	18	14	14	5	0	8	7	1.393	6.75	59	5.81	.265	0	.000	-6	1	-0.6

• SMITH, Pete Peter John Smith b: 2/27/1966, Abington, MA BR/TR, 6'2", 200 lbs. Deb: 9/8/1987

YEAR	TM-L	W	L	PCT	G	GS	CG	SH	SV	IP	H	R	ER	HR	HB	BB	SO	RAT	ERA	ERA+	CERA	OAV	BH	AVG	PR+	WS	TPW
1987	Atl-N	1	2	.333	6	6	0	0	0	31^2	39	21	17	3	0	14	11	1.674	4.83	90	5.63	.307	1	.091	-2	1	-0.2
1988	Atl-N	7	15	.318	32	32	5	3	0	195^1	183	89	80	15	1	88	124	1.387	3.69	100	3.77	.250	6	.113	2	9	0.1
1989	Atl-N	5	14	.263	28	27	1	0	0	142	144	83	75	13	0	57	115	1.415	4.75	77	4.08	.263	4	.098	-16	2	-1.7
1990	Atl-N	5	6	.455	13	13	3	0	0	77	77	45	41	11	0	24	56	1.312	4.79	84	3.96	.260	2	.087	-5	3	-0.6
1991	Atl-N	1	3	.250	14	10	0	0	0	48	48	33	27	5	0	22	29	1.458	5.06	77	4.20	.262	2	.167	-6	0	-0.6
1992*	Atl-N	7	0	1.000	12	11	2	1	0	79	63	19	18	3	0	28	43	1.152	2.05	178	2.40	.217	1	.038	14	9	1.3
1993	Atl-N	4	8	.333	20	14	0	0	0	90^2	92	45	44	15	2	36	53	1.412	4.37	92	4.70	.270	6	.222	-4	4	-0.3
1994	NY-N	4	10	.286	21	21	1	0	0	131^1	145	83	81	25	2	42	62	1.424	5.55	75	5.07	.285	5	.135	-20	1	-1.9
1995	Cin-N	1	2	.333	11	2	0	0	0	24^1	30	19	18	8	1	7	14	1.521	6.66	62	6.99	.319	0	.000	-7	0	-0.7
1997	SD-N	7	6	.538	37	15	0	0	1	118	120	66	63	16	1	52	68	1.458	4.81	80	4.65	.267	5	.167	-11	3	-1.0
1998	SD-N	3	2	.600	10	8	0	0	0	43^1	45	23	23	5	3	18	36	1.454	4.78	82	4.67	.266	1	.071	-4	2	-0.4
	Bal-A	2	3	.400	27	4	0	0	0	45	57	31	31	7	0	16	29	1.622	6.20	73	5.82	.311	0	.000	-8	1	-0.8
Total	11	47	71	.398	231	163	12	4	1	1025^2	1043	557	518	126	10	404	640	1.411	4.55	86	4.35	.266	33	.118	-67	35	-6.8

YEAR TM-L	W	L	PCT	G	GS	CG	SH	SV	IP	H	R	ER	HR	HB	BB	SO	RAT	ERA	ERA+	CERA	OAV	BH	AVG	PR+	WS	TPW
• SMITH, Phenomenal	John Francis Smith b: 12/12/1864, Philadelphia, PA d: 4/3/1952, Manchester, NH BL/TL, 5'6.5", 161 lbs. Deb: 8/14/1884 U																									
1884 Phi-a	0	1	.000	1	1	1	0	0	9	14	6	4	0	0	1	3	1.667	4.00	84	....	.337	1	.250	-1	0	-0.1
Pit-a	0	1	.000	1	1	1	0	0	8	11	10	8	0	1	2	4	1.625	9.00	37	....	.310	0	.000	-5	0	-0.5
Yr.	0	2	.000	2	2	2	0	0	17	25	16	12	0	1	3	7	1.647	6.35	53	....	.325	1	.125	-5	0	-0.5
1885 Bro-a	0	1	.000	1	1	1	0	0	8	12	18	11	0	1	6	2	2.250	12.38	27	....	.333	1	.333	-8	0	-0.7
Phi-a	0	1	.000	1	1	0	0	0	4	7	9	4	0	1	4	7	2.750	9.00	38	....	.368	0	.000	-2	0	-0.2
Yr.	0	2	.000	2	2	1	0	0	12	19	27	15	0	2	10	9	2.417	11.25	30	....	.345	1	.200	-10	0	-1.0
1886 Det-N	1	1	.500	3	3	3	0	0	25	16	9	6	0	....	8	15	.960	2.16	152	....	.176	1	.111	3	2	0.2
1887 Bal-a	25	30	.455	58	55	54	1	0	491^1	702	369	207	7	14	176	206	1.429	3.79	108	....	.324	74	.320	29	32	3.0
1888 Bal-a	14	19	.424	35	32	31	0	0	292	249	170	117	5	24	137	152	1.322	3.61	83	....	.222	27	.248	-15	18	-0.6
Phi-a	2	1	.667	3	3	3	0	0	22	21	15	7	0	0	10	19	1.409	2.86	104	....	.243	3	.333	0	2	0.1
Yr.	16	20	.444	38	35	34	0	0	314	270	185	124	5	24	147	171	1.328	3.55	84	....	.224	30	.254	-15	20	-0.4
1889 Phi-a	2	3	.400	5	5	5	0	0	43	53	31	21	2	3	25	12	1.814	4.40	86	....	.294	3	.188	-4	2	-0.3
1890 Phi-N	8	12	.400	24	20	19	1	0	204	209	125	97	5	8	89	81	1.461	4.28	85	....	.257	24	.279	-17	13	-1.1
Pit-N	1	3	.250	5	5	5	0	0	44	39	25	15	0	1	13	15	1.182	3.07	107	....	.231	7	.412	3	1	0.6
Yr.	9	15	.375	29	25	24	1	0	248	248	150	112	5	9	102	96	1.411	4.06	88	....	.253	31	.301	-14	14	-0.6
1891 Phi-N	1	1	.500	3	2	0	0	0	19	20	15	9	1	0	8	3	1.474	4.26	80	....	.261	3	.375	-2	1	-0.1
Total 8	**54**	**74**	**.422**	**140**	**129**	**123**	**2**	**0**	**1169^1**	**1353**	**802**	**506**	**20**	**53**	**479**	**519**	**1.416**	**3.89**	**92**	**....**	**.280**	**144**	**.289**	**-19**	**71**	**0.2**
• SMITH, Pop-Boy	Charles Ossie Smith b: 5/23/1892, Newport, TN d: 2/16/1924, Sweetwater, TX BR/TR, 6'1", 176 lbs. Deb: 4/19/1913																									
1913 Chi-A	0	1	.000	15	2	0	0	0	32	31	15	12	0	3	11	13	1.313	3.38	86	3.37	.261	0	.000	-2	1	-0.2
1916 Cle-A	1	2	.333	5	3	0	0	1	25^2	25	15	11	1	1	11	4	1.403	3.86	78	3.66	.253	2	.286	-2	1	-0.3
1917 Cle-A	0	1	.000	6	0	0	0	0	8^2	14	11	8	0	1	4	3	2.077	8.31	34	8.32	.368	0	.000	-6	0	-0.6
Total 3	**1**	**4**	**.200**	**26**	**5**	**0**	**0**	**1**	**66^1**	**70**	**41**	**31**	**1**	**5**	**26**	**20**	**1.447**	**4.21**	**69**	**4.13**	**.274**	**2**	**.154**	**-10**	**2**	**-1.1**
• SMITH, Rex	Reginald Smith b: 1864, Louisville, KY d: 6/21/1895, Louisville, KY Deb: 7/11/1886																									
1886 Phi-a	0	1	.000	1	1	1	0	0	9	15	13	7	0	0	5	4	2.222	7.00	50	....	.355	0	.000	-3	0	-0.4
• SMITH, Roy	Walter Roy Smith b: 5/18/1976, St. Petersburg, FL BR/TR, 6'6", 235 lbs. Deb: 5/26/2001																									
2001 Cle-A	0	0	....	9	0	0	0	0	16^1	16	14	11	3	2	13	17	1.776	6.06	75	6.49	.246	0	....	-2	0	-0.2
2002 Cle-A	0	0	....	4	1	0	0	0	6	9	4	2	1	1	5	2	2.333	3.00	146	9.63	.310	0	....	1	0	0.1
Total 2	**0**	**0**	**....**	**13**	**1**	**0**	**0**	**0**	**22^1**	**25**	**18**	**13**	**4**	**3**	**18**	**19**	**1.925**	**5.24**	**86**	**7.34**	**.266**	**0**	**....**	**-1**	**0**	**-0.1**
• SMITH, Roy	Le Roy Purdy Smith b: 9/6/1961, Mount Vernon, NY BR/TR, 6'3", 200 lbs. Deb: 6/23/1984																									
1984 Cle-A	5	5	.500	22	14	0	0	0	86^1	91	49	44	14	1	40	55	1.517	4.59	89	5.06	.270	0	....	-5	3	-0.5
1985 Cle-A	1	4	.200	12	11	1	0	0	62^1	84	40	37	8	1	17	28	1.620	5.34	77	5.82	.321	0	....	-8	1	-0.8
1986 Min-A	0	2	.000	5	0	0	0	0	10^1	13	8	8	1	1	5	8	1.742	6.97	62	5.98	.295	0	....	-3	0	-0.3
1987 Min-A	1	0	1.000	7	1	0	0	0	16^1	20	10	9	3	2	6	8	1.592	4.96	93	6.19	.290	0	....	-1	1	-0.1
1988 Min-A	3	0	1.000	9	4	0	0	0	37	29	12	11	3	1	12	17	1.108	2.68	152	2.56	.210	0	....	6	4	0.6
1989 Min-A	10	6	.625	32	26	2	0	1	172^1	180	82	75	22	5	51	92	1.340	3.92	106	4.20	.269	0	....	5	10	0.5
1990 Min-A	5	10	.333	32	23	1	1	0	153^1	191	91	82	20	0	47	87	1.552	4.81	86	5.40	.313	0	....	-11	5	-1.2
1991 Bal-A	5	4	.556	17	14	0	0	0	80^1	99	52	50	9	1	24	25	1.531	5.60	70	5.29	.311	0	....	-15	1	-1.5
Total 8	**30**	**31**	**.492**	**136**	**93**	**4**	**1**	**1**	**618^1**	**707**	**344**	**316**	**80**	**12**	**202**	**320**	**1.470**	**4.60**	**90**	**4.91**	**.289**	**0**	**....**	**-33**	**25**	**-3.3**
• SMITH, Rufus	Rufus Frazier "Shirt" Smith b: 1/24/1905, Guilford College, NC d: 8/21/1984, Aiken, SC BR/TL, 5'8", 165 lbs. Deb: 10/2/1927																									
1927 Det-A	0	0	....	1	1	0	0	0	8	8	4	3	0	1	3	2	1.375	3.38	125	3.39	.242	0	.000	1	1	0.0
• SMITH, Sherry	Sherrod Malone Smith b: 2/18/1891, Monticello, GA d: 9/12/1949, Reidsville, GA BR/TL, 6'1", 170 lbs. Deb: 5/11/1911																									
1911 Pit-N	0	0	....	1	0	0	0	0	0^2	4	5	4	0	0	1	0	7.500	54.00	6	47.10	.667	0	....	-4	0	-0.4
1912 Pit-N	0	0	....	3	0	0	0	1	4	6	3	3	0	0	1	3	1.750	6.75	48	5.72	.600	0	....	-2	0	-0.2
1915 Bro-N	14	8	.636	29	20	11	2	2	173^2	169	71	50	3	5	42	52	1.215	2.59	107	2.87	.264	14	.246	3	13	0.6
1916* Bro-N	14	10	.583	36	25	15	4	1	219	193	76	57	5	3	45	67	1.087	2.34	114	2.26	.239	21	.273	4	17	1.1
1917 Bro-N	12	12	.500	38	23	15	0	3	211^1	210	103	78	5	2	51	58	1.235	3.32	84	2.93	.265	15	.195	-15	9	-1.4
1919 Bro-N	7	12	.368	30	19	13	2	1	173	181	63	43	3	4	29	40	1.214	2.24	133	3.01	.278	8	.148	18	11	1.8
1920* Bro-N	11	9	.550	33	12	6	2	3	136^1	134	42	28	1	2	27	33	1.181	1.85	173	2.67	.264	10	.233	22	15	2.6
1921 Bro-N	7	11	.389	35	17	9	0	4	175^1	232	95	76	4	1	34	36	1.517	3.90	100	4.43	.319	13	.228	0	11	0.2
1922 Bro-N	4	8	.333	28	9	3	1	2	108^2	128	71	55	6	7	35	15	1.500	4.56	89	4.64	.309	9	.257	-5	4	-0.3
Cle-A	1	0	1.000	2	2	1	0	0	15^2	18	7	6	0	0	3	4	1.340	3.45	116	3.44	.295	2	.333	1	2	0.2
1923 Cle-A	9	6	.600	30	16	10	1	1	124	129	62	45	4	2	37	23	1.339	3.27	121	3.44	.269	11	.244	11	9	1.1
1924 Cle-A	12	14	.462	39	27	20	2	1	247^2	267	110	83	5	7	42	34	1.248	3.02	142	3.09	.277	18	.202	38	18	3.4
1925 Cle-A	11	14	.440	31	30	**22**	1	1	237	296	151	128	11	5	48	30	1.451	4.86	91	4.28	.306	28	.304	-11	13	-0.4
1926 Cle-A	11	10	.524	27	24	16	1	0	188^1	214	80	78	8	4	31	25	1.301	3.73	109	3.60	.292	14	.215	3	14	0.4
1927 Cle-A	1	4	.200	11	2	1	0	1	38	53	25	23	2	0	14	8	1.763	5.45	77	5.85	.342	2	.167	-5	1	-0.5
Total 14	**114**	**118**	**.491**	**373**	**226**	**142**	**16**	**21**	**2052^2**	**2234**	**964**	**757**	**57**	**42**	**440**	**428**	**1.303**	**3.32**	**108**	**3.41**	**.282**	**165**	**.233**	**58**	**137**	**8.2**
• SMITH, Tom	Thomas Edward Smith b: 12/5/1871, Boston, MA d: 3/2/1929, Dorchester, MA BR/TR, 5'7.5", 165 lbs. Deb: 6/6/1894																									
1894 Bos-N	0	0	....	2	0	0	0	1	6	8	14	10	2	4	6	2	2.333	15.00	39	13.73	.317	0	.000	-6	0	-0.5
1895 Phi-N	2	3	.400	11	7	4	0	0	68	76	67	52	1	7	53	21	1.897	6.88	70	5.73	.278	8	.242	-16	2	-1.3
1896 Lou-N	2	3	.400	11	5	4	0	0	55	73	55	33	2	4	25	14	1.782	5.40	80	5.86	.316	8	.205	-5	1	-0.6
1898 StL-N	0	1	.000	1	1	1	0	0	9	9	8	2	0	2	5	1	1.556	2.00	189	4.55	.259	1	.500	2	1	0.3
Total 4	**4**	**7**	**.364**	**25**	**13**	**9**	**0**	**1**	**138**	**166**	**144**	**97**	**5**	**17**	**89**	**38**	**1.848**	**6.33**	**74**	**6.05**	**.295**	**17**	**.224**	**-25**	**4**	**-2.1**
• SMITH, Travis	Travis William Smith b: 11/7/1972, Springfield, OR BR/TR, 5'10" Deb: 6/21/1998																									
1998 Mil-N	0	0	....	1	0	0	0	0	2	1	0	0	0	0	0	1	.500	0.00	....	0.54	.143	0	.000	1	0	0.1
2002 StL-N	4	2	.667	12	10	0	0	0	54	69	44	43	10	3	20	32	1.648	7.17	55	6.63	.322	3	.167	-20	0	-2.0
Total 2	**4**	**2**	**.667**	**13**	**10**	**0**	**0**	**0**	**56**	**70**	**44**	**43**	**10**	**3**	**20**	**33**	**1.607**	**6.91**	**57**	**6.41**	**.317**	**3**	**.158**	**-19**	**0**	**-2.0**
• SMITH, Willie	Willie Everett Smith b: 8/27/1967, Savannah, GA BR/TR, 6'6", 250 lbs. Deb: 4/25/1994																									
1994 StL-N	1	1	.500	8	0	0	0	0	7	9	7	7	4	0	3	7	1.714	9.00	46	9.49	.300	0	....	-4	0	-0.4
• SMITH, Willie	Willie Smith b: 2/11/1939, Anniston, AL BL/TL, 6', 190 lbs. Deb: 6/18/1963 ♦																									
1963 Det-A	1	0	1.000	11	2	0	0	2	21^2	24	13	11	2	0	13	16	1.708	4.57	82	5.32	.300	1	.125	-2	1	-0.3
1964 LA-A	1	4	.200	15	1	0	0	0	31^2	34	13	10	5	1	10	20	1.389	2.84	116	4.76	.293	108	.301	1	14	0.7
1968 Cle-A	0	0	....	2	0	0	0	0	5	2	0	0	0	0	1	1	.600	0.00	....	0.67	.125	6	.143	2	0	-0.3
Chi-N	0	0	....	1	0	0	0	0	2^2	0	0	0	0	0	0	2	.000	0.00	....	0.00	.000	39	.275	1	7	0.5
Total 3	**2**	**4**	**.333**	**29**	**3**	**0**	**0**	**2**	**61**	**60**	**26**	**21**	**7**	**1**	**24**	**39**	**1.377**	**3.10**	**113**	**4.42**	**.283**	**410**	**.248**	**2**	**22**	**0.6**
• SMITH, Zane	Zane William Smith b: 12/28/1960, Madison, WI BL/TL, 6'2", 195 lbs. Deb: 9/10/1984																									
1984 Atl-N	1	0	1.000	3	3	0	0	0	20	16	7	5	1	0	13	16	1.450	2.25	171	3.41	.219	5	.556	4	2	0.6
1985 Atl-N	9	10	.474	42	18	2	2	0	147	135	70	62	4	3	80	85	1.463	3.80	101	3.76	.254	6	.162	2	8	0.2
1986 Atl-N	8	16	.333	38	32	3	1	1	204^2	209	109	92	8	5	105	139	1.534	4.05	98	4.35	.275	5	.085	1	9	-0.2
1987 Atl-N	15	10	.600	36	**36**	9	3	0	242	245	130	110	19	5	91	130	1.388	4.09	106	3.98	.266	10	.132	8	14	0.8
1988 Atl-N	5	10	.333	23	22	3	0	0	140^1	159	72	67	8	3	44	59	1.447	4.30	86	4.24	.292	7	.167	-8	5	-0.8
1989 Atl-N	1	12	.077	17	17	0	0	0	99	102	65	49	5	2	33	58	1.364	4.45	82	3.59	.267	5	.179	-8	0	-0.8
Mon-N	0	1	.000	31	0	0	0	2	48	39	11	8	2	1	19	35	1.208	1.50	235	2.58	.220	1	.250	11	6	1.2
Yr.	1	13	.071	48	17	0	0	2	147	141	76	57	7	3	52	93	1.313	3.49	104	3.26	.252	6	.188	3	6	0.4
1990 Mon-N	6	7	.462	22	21	1	0	0	139^1	141	57	50	11	3	41	80	1.306	3.23	113	3.73	.266	7	.175	6	8	0.7
* Pit-N	6	2	.750	11	10	3	2	0	76	55	20	11	4	0	9	50	.842	1.30	278	1.53	.203	4	.143	19	8	2.0
Yr.	12	9	.571	33	31	4	2	0	215^1	196	77	61	15	3	50	130	1.142	2.55	143	2.95	.245	11	.162	25	16	2.7
1991* Pit-N	16	10	.615	35	35	6	3	0	228	234	95	81	15	2	29	120	1.154	3.20	112	3.02	.268	13	.183	8	14	1.1

YEAR TM-L	W	L	PCT	G	GS	CG	SH	SV	IP	H	R	ER	HR	HB	BB	SO	RAT	ERA	ERA+	CERA	OAV	BH	AVG	PR+	WS	TPW
1992 Pit-N	8	8	.500	23	22	4	3	0	141	138	56	48	8	2	19	56	1.113	3.06	112	2.74	.261	6	.122	5	8	0.5
1993 Pit-N	3	7	.300	14	14	1	0	0	83	97	43	42	5	0	22	32	1.434	4.55	89	4.24	.298	2	.080	-5	3	-0.7
1994 Pit-N	10	8	.556	25	24	2	1	0	157	162	67	57	18	0	34	57	1.248	3.27	132	3.62	.270	12	.211	17	13	1.7
1995* Bos-A	8	8	.500	24	21	0	0	0	110^{2}	144	78	69	7	1	23	47	1.509	5.61	87	4.83	.316	0	....	-10	4	-0.9
1996 Pit-N	4	6	.400	16	16	1	1	0	83^{1}	104	53	47	7	4	21	47	1.500	5.08	86	4.93	.309	4	.154	-5	3	-0.6
Total 13	100	115	.465	360	291	35	16	3	1919^{1}	1980	933	798	122	31	583	1011	1.335	3.74	106	3.71	.271	87	.158	44	105	4.7

• SMITHBERG, Roger Roger Craig Smithberg b: 3/21/1966, Elgin, IL BR/TR, 6'3", 205 lbs. Deb: 9/1/1993

YEAR TM-L	W	L	PCT	G	GS	CG	SH	SV	IP	H	R	ER	HR	HB	BB	SO	RAT	ERA	ERA+	CERA	OAV	BH	AVG	PR+	WS	TPW
1993 Oak-A	1	2	.333	13	0	0	0	3	19^{2}	13	7	6	2	1	7	4	1.017	2.75	148	2.32	.197	0	....	3	2	0.3
1994 Oak-A	0	0	....	2	0	0	0	0	2^{1}	6	4	4	1	0	1	3	3.000	15.43	29	19.60	.500	0	....	-3	0	-0.3
Total 2	1	2	.333	15	0	0	0	3	22	19	11	10	3	1	8	7	1.227	4.09	103	4.15	.244	0	....	0	2	0.0

• SMITHSON, Mike Billy Mike Smithson b: 1/21/1955, Centerville, TN BL/TR, 6'8", 215 lbs. Deb: 8/27/1982

YEAR TM-L	W	L	PCT	G	GS	CG	SH	SV	IP	H	R	ER	HR	HB	BB	SO	RAT	ERA	ERA+	CERA	OAV	BH	AVG	PR+	WS	TPW
1982 Tex-A	3	4	.429	8	8	3	0	0	46^{2}	51	26	26	5	3	13	24	1.371	5.01	77	4.44	.282	0	....	-6	2	-0.6
1983 Tex-A	10	14	.417	33	33	10	0	0	223^{1}	233	102	97	14	8	71	135	1.361	3.91	102	3.86	.269	0	....	3	11	0.3
1984 Min-A	15	13	.536	36	**36**	10	1	0	252	246	113	103	35	8	54	144	1.190	3.68	114	3.55	.252	0	....	9	18	0.9
1985 Min-A	15	14	.517	37	**37**	8	3	0	257	264	134	124	25	15	78	127	1.331	4.34	102	4.12	.270	0	....	2	15	0.2
1986 Min-A	13	14	.481	34	33	8	1	0	198	234	123	105	26	14	57	114	1.470	4.77	90	5.15	.294	0	....	-8	9	-0.8
1987 Min-A	4	7	.364	21	20	0	0	0	109	126	76	72	17	9	38	53	1.505	5.94	78	5.42	.286	0	....	-16	2	-1.6
1988* Bos-A	9	6	.600	31	18	1	0	0	126^{2}	149	87	84	25	6	37	73	1.468	5.97	69	5.54	.292	0	....	-24	2	-2.5
1989 Bos-A	7	14	.333	40	19	1	1	2	143^{2}	170	84	79	21	10	35	61	1.427	4.95	83	5.06	.297	0	....	-12	4	-1.2
Total 8	76	86	.469	240	204	41	6	2	1356^{1}	1473	745	690	168	73	383	731	1.368	4.58	92	4.47	.277	0	....	-53	63	-5.3

• SMOLL, Lefty Clyde Hetrick Smoll b: 4/17/1914, Quakertown, PA d: 8/31/1985, Quakertown, PA BB/TL, 5'10", 175 lbs. Deb: 4/26/1940

YEAR TM-L	W	L	PCT	G	GS	CG	SH	SV	IP	H	R	ER	HR	HB	BB	SO	RAT	ERA	ERA+	CERA	OAV	BH	AVG	PR+	WS	TPW
1940 Phi-N	2	8	.200	33	9	0	0	0	109	145	77	65	6	4	36	31	1.661	5.37	73	5.42	.322	5	.161	-18	0	-1.9

• SMOLTZ, John John Andrew Smoltz b: 5/15/1967, Detroit, MI BR/TR, 6'3", 210 lbs. Deb: 7/23/1988

YEAR TM-L	W	L	PCT	G	GS	CG	SH	SV	IP	H	R	ER	HR	HB	BB	SO	RAT	ERA	ERA+	CERA	OAV	BH	AVG	PR+	WS	TPW
1988 Atl-N	2	7	.222	12	12	0	0	0	64	74	40	39	10	2	33	37	1.672	5.48	67	5.86	.285	2	.118	-12	0	-1.3
1989 Atl-N★	12	11	.522	29	29	5	0	0	208	160	79	68	15	2	72	168	1.115	2.94	124	2.50	.212	7	.113	19	15	2.1
1990 Atl-N	14	11	.560	34	34	6	2	0	231^{1}	206	109	99	20	1	90	170	1.280	3.85	105	3.37	.240	12	.162	10	14	1.2
1991* Atl-N	14	13	.519	36	36	5	0	0	229^{2}	206	101	97	16	3	77	148	1.232	3.80	102	3.15	.243	7	.108	2	13	0.2
1992* Atl-N★	15	12	.556	35	**35**	9	3	0	246^{2}	206	90	78	17	5	80	**215**	1.159	2.85	128	2.73	.224	12	.160	21	18	2.5
1993* Atl-N★	15	11	.577	35	35	3	1	0	243^{2}	208	104	98	23	6	100	208	1.264	3.62	111	3.29	.230	13	.183	8	16	1.1
1994 Atl-N	6	10	.375	21	21	1	0	0	134^{2}	120	69	62	15	4	48	113	1.248	4.14	102	3.44	.239	6	.162	3	6	0.5
1995* Atl-N	12	7	.632	29	29	2	1	0	192^{2}	166	76	68	15	4	72	193	1.235	3.18	134	3.08	.232	6	.107	26	17	2.4
1996* Atl-N★	**24**	8	.750	35	35	6	2	0	**253^{2}**	199	93	83	19	2	55	**276**	1.001	2.94	150	2.17	.216	17	.218	45	**27**	4.7
1997* Atl-N	15	12	.556	35	**35**	7	2	0	**256**	234	97	86	21	1	63	241	1.160	3.02	139	2.89	.242	18	.228	32	21	3.7
1998* Atl-N	17	3	.850	26	26	2	2	0	167^{2}	145	58	54	10	4	44	173	1.127	2.90	144	2.67	.231	10	.196	22	16	2.5
1999* Atl-N	11	8	.579	29	29	1	1	0	186^{1}	168	70	66	14	4	40	156	1.116	3.19	141	2.81	.245	17	.274	29	18	3.4
2001* Atl-N	3	3	.500	36	5	0	0	10	59	53	24	22	7	2	10	57	1.068	3.36	131	2.85	.238	0	.000	7	8	0.6
2002* Atl-N★	3	2	.600	75	0	0	0	**55**	80^{1}	59	30	29	4	0	24	85	1.033	3.25	126	2.06	.206	0	.000	6	17	0.6
2003* Atl-N★	0	2	.000	62	0	0	0	45	64^{1}	48	9	8	2	0	8	73	.870	1.12	377	1.50	.204	0	.000	22	16	2.2
Total 15	163	120	.576	529	361	47	14	110	2618	2252	1049	957	208	40	816	2313	1.172	3.29	123	2.91	.232	127	.172	240	222	26.4

• SMYTH, Steve Steven Delton Smyth b: 6/3/1978, Brawley, CA BL/TL, 6'1", 195 lbs. Deb: 8/6/2002

YEAR TM-L	W	L	PCT	G	GS	CG	SH	SV	IP	H	R	ER	HR	HB	BB	SO	RAT	ERA	ERA+	CERA	OAV	BH	AVG	PR+	WS	TPW
2002 Chi-N	1	3	.250	8	7	0	0	0	26	34	28	27	9	1	10	16	1.692	9.35	43	7.88	.321	2	.222	-15	0	-1.5

• SMYTHE, Harry William Henry Smythe b: 10/24/1904, Augusta, GA d: 8/28/1980, Augusta, GA BL/TL, 5'10.5", 179 lbs. Deb: 7/21/1929

YEAR TM-L	W	L	PCT	G	GS	CG	SH	SV	IP	H	R	ER	HR	HB	BB	SO	RAT	ERA	ERA+	CERA	OAV	BH	AVG	PR+	WS	TPW
1929 Phi-N	4	6	.400	19	7	2	0	1	68^{2}	94	47	40	3	1	15	12	1.587	5.24	99	5.07	.330	5	.192	1	4	0.0
1930 Phi-N	0	3	.000	25	3	0	0	2	49^{2}	84	60	43	3	3	31	9	2.315	7.79	70	8.91	.368	4	.286	-12	0	-1.0
1934 NY-A	0	2	.000	8	0	0	0	1	15	24	16	13	1	0	8	7	2.133	7.80	52	8.02	.381	1	.200	-6	0	-0.6
Bro-N	1	1	.500	8	0	0	0	0	21^{1}	30	19	14	3	1	8	5	1.781	5.91	66	6.86	.337	3	.333	-5	1	-0.3
Total 3	5	12	.294	60	10	2	0	4	154^{2}	232	142	110	10	5	62	33	1.901	6.40	77	6.84	.349	13	.241	-22	5	-1.9

• SNELL, Nate Nathaniel Snell b: 9/2/1952, Orangeburg, SC BR/TR, 6'4", 190 lbs. Deb: 9/20/1984

YEAR TM-L	W	L	PCT	G	GS	CG	SH	SV	IP	H	R	ER	HR	HB	BB	SO	RAT	ERA	ERA+	CERA	OAV	BH	AVG	PR+	WS	TPW
1984 Bal-A	1	1	.500	5	0	0	0	0	7^{2}	8	2	2	1	0	1	7	1.174	2.35	165	3.26	.258	0	....	1	1	0.1
1985 Bal-A	3	2	.600	43	0	0	0	5	100^{1}	100	44	30	4	1	30	41	1.296	2.69	150	3.24	.260	0	....	16	8	1.6
1986 Bal-A	2	1	.667	34	0	0	0	0	72^{1}	69	36	31	9	1	22	29	1.258	3.86	107	3.67	.257	0	....	3	4	0.3
1987 Det-A	1	2	.333	22	2	0	0	0	38^{2}	39	20	17	5	0	19	19	1.500	3.96	107	4.64	.267	0	....	1	2	0.1
Total 4	7	6	.538	104	2	0	0	5	219	216	102	80	19	2	72	96	1.315	3.29	125	3.63	.260	0	....	21	15	2.0

• SNOOK, Frank Frank Walter Snook b: 3/28/1949, Somerville, NJ BR/TR, 6'2", 180 lbs. Deb: 7/13/1973

YEAR TM-L	W	L	PCT	G	GS	CG	SH	SV	IP	H	R	ER	HR	HB	BB	SO	RAT	ERA	ERA+	CERA	OAV	BH	AVG	PR+	WS	TPW
1973 SD-N	0	2	.000	18	0	0	0	1	27^{1}	19	15	11	4	0	18	13	1.354	3.62	96	3.68	.200	0	.000	-0	1	-0.1

• SNOVER, Colonel Colonel Lester "Bosco" Snover b: 5/16/1895, Hallstead, PA d: 4/30/1969, Rochester, NY BL/TL, 6'.5", 200 lbs. Deb: 9/18/1919

YEAR TM-L	W	L	PCT	G	GS	CG	SH	SV	IP	H	R	ER	HR	HB	BB	SO	RAT	ERA	ERA+	CERA	OAV	BH	AVG	PR+	WS	TPW
1919 NY-N	0	1	.000	2	1	0	0	0	9	7	5	1	0	1	3	4	1.111	1.00	280	2.25	.212	0	.000	2	0	0.2

• SNYDER, Bill William Nicholas Snyder b: 1/28/1898, Mansfield, OH d: 10/8/1934, Vicksburg, MI BR/TR Deb: 9/4/1919

YEAR TM-L	W	L	PCT	G	GS	CG	SH	SV	IP	H	R	ER	HR	HB	BB	SO	RAT	ERA	ERA+	CERA	OAV	BH	AVG	PR+	WS	TPW
1919 Was-A	0	1	.000	2	1	0	0	0	8	6	4	1	0	0	3	5	1.125	1.13	285	1.93	.200	0	.000	2	0	0.2
1920 Was-A	2	1	.667	16	4	1	0	1	54	59	33	25	1	6	28	17	1.611	4.17	89	4.79	.280	6	.316	-2	2	-0.1
Total 2	2	2	.500	18	5	1	0	1	62	65	37	26	1	6	31	22	1.548	3.77	98	4.42	.270	6	.286	-0	2	0.1

• SNYDER, Brian Brian Robert Snyder b: 2/20/1958, Flemington, NJ BL/TL, 6'3", 185 lbs. Deb: 5/25/1985

YEAR TM-L	W	L	PCT	G	GS	CG	SH	SV	IP	H	R	ER	HR	HB	BB	SO	RAT	ERA	ERA+	CERA	OAV	BH	AVG	PR+	WS	TPW
1985 Sea-A	1	2	.333	15	6	0	0	1	35^{1}	44	28	25	2	1	19	23	1.783	6.37	66	5.74	.306	0	....	-8	0	-0.8
1989 Oak-A	0	0	....	2	0	0	0	0	0^{2}	2	2	2	1	0	2	1	6.000	27.00	14	51.61	.500	0	....	-2	0	-0.2
Total 2	1	2	.333	17	6	0	0	1	36	46	30	27	3	1	21	24	1.861	6.75	62	6.59	.311	0	....	-10	0	-1.0

• SNYDER, Gene Gene Walter Snyder b: 3/31/1931, York, PA d: 6/2/1996, York, PA BR/TL, 5'11", 175 lbs. Deb: 4/26/1959

YEAR TM-L	W	L	PCT	G	GS	CG	SH	SV	IP	H	R	ER	HR	HB	BB	SO	RAT	ERA	ERA+	CERA	OAV	BH	AVG	PR+	WS	TPW
1959 LA-N	1	1	.500	11	2	0	0	0	26^{1}	32	19	16	1	0	20	20	1.975	5.47	77	6.14	.299	0	.000	-4	0	-0.4

• SNYDER, George George T. Snyder b: 8/1848, Philadelphia, PA d: 8/2/1905, Philadelphia, PA Deb: 9/30/1882

YEAR TM-L	W	L	PCT	G	GS	CG	SH	SV	IP	H	R	ER	HR	HB	BB	SO	RAT	ERA	ERA+	CERA	OAV	BH	AVG	PR+	WS	TPW
1882 Phi-a	1	0	1.000	1	1	1	0	0	9	4	3	0	0	....	2	0	.667	0.00	....	....	.125	1	.333	3	1	0.3

• SNYDER, John John Michael Snyder b: 8/16/1974, Southfield, MI BR/TR, 6'3", 200 lbs. Deb: 6/30/1998

YEAR TM-L	W	L	PCT	G	GS	CG	SH	SV	IP	H	R	ER	HR	HB	BB	SO	RAT	ERA	ERA+	CERA	OAV	BH	AVG	PR+	WS	TPW
1998 Chi-A	7	2	.778	15	14	1	0	0	86^{1}	96	49	46	14	2	23	52	1.378	4.80	95	4.76	.286	0	....	-3	4	-0.2
1999 Chi-A	9	12	.429	25	25	1	0	0	129^{1}	167	103	96	27	6	49	67	1.670	6.68	73	6.71	.311	0	....	-25	1	-2.3
2000 Mil-N	3	10	.231	23	23	0	0	0	127	147	95	87	8	9	77	69	1.764	6.17	74	5.71	.296	3	.079	-25	0	-2.5
Total 3	19	24	.442	63	62	2	0	0	342^{2}	410	247	229	49	17	149	188	1.631	6.01	78	5.85	.299	3	.079	-52	5	-5.0

• SNYDER, Kyle Kyle Ehren Snyder b: 9/9/1977, Houston, TX BB/TR, 6'8", 220 lbs. Deb: 5/1/2003

YEAR TM-L	W	L	PCT	G	GS	CG	SH	SV	IP	H	R	ER	HR	HB	BB	SO	RAT	ERA	ERA+	CERA	OAV	BH	AVG	PR+	WS	TPW
2003 KC-A	1	6	.143	15	15	0	0	0	85^{1}	94	52	49	11	2	21	39	1.348	5.17	100	4.29	.283	0	.000	0	4	0.0

• SOBKOWIAK, Scott Scott Sobkowiak b: 10/26/1977, Woodstock, IL BR/TR, 6'5", 230 lbs. Deb: 10/7/2001

YEAR TM-L	W	L	PCT	G	GS	CG	SH	SV	IP	H	R	ER	HR	HB	BB	SO	RAT	ERA	ERA+	CERA	OAV	BH	AVG	PR+	WS	TPW
2001 Atl-N	0	0	....	1	0	0	0	0	1	2	1	1	0	0	0	0	2.000	9.00	49	7.48	.400	0	.000	-1	0	-0.1

• SODERSTROM, Steve Stephen Andrew Soderstrom b: 4/3/1972, Turlock, CA BR/TR, 6'3", 215 lbs. Deb: 9/17/1996

YEAR TM-L	W	L	PCT	G	GS	CG	SH	SV	IP	H	R	ER	HR	HB	BB	SO	RAT	ERA	ERA+	CERA	OAV	BH	AVG	PR+	WS	TPW
1996 SF-N	2	0	1.000	3	3	0	0	0	13^{2}	16	11	8	1	2	6	9	1.610	5.27	78	5.66	.302	0	.000	-2	0	-0.2

• SODOWSKY, Clint Clint Rea Sodowsky b: 7/13/1972, Ponca City, OK BL/TR, 6'3", 180 lbs. Deb: 9/4/1995

YEAR TM-L	W	L	PCT	G	GS	CG	SH	SV	IP	H	R	ER	HR	HB	BB	SO	RAT	ERA	ERA+	CERA	OAV	BH	AVG	PR+	WS	TPW
1995 Det-A	2	2	.500	6	6	0	0	0	23^{1}	24	15	13	4	0	18	14	1.800	5.01	95	6.19	.258	0	....	-0	1	0.0
1996 Det-A	1	3	.250	7	7	0	0	0	24^{1}	40	34	32	5	3	20	9	2.466	11.84	43	11.76	.370	0	....	-18	0	-1.6
1997 Pit-N	2	2	.500	45	0	0	0	0	52	49	22	21	6	2	34	51	1.596	3.63	118	4.78	.249	1	.500	4	4	0.5

YEAR TM-L	W	L	PCT	G	GS	CG	SH	SV	IP	H	R	ER	HR	HB	BB	SO	RAT	ERA	ERA+	CERA	OAV	BH	AVG	PR+	WS	TPW
1998 Ari-N	3	6	.333	45	6	0	0	0	77^2	86	56	49	5	7	39	42	1.609	5.68	74	5.06	.283	3	.300	-13	1	-1.2
1999 StL-N	0	1	.000	3	1	0	0	0	6^1	15	11	11	1	0	6	2	3.316	15.63	29	16.70	.455	0	.000	-8	0	-0.7
Total 5	8	14	.364	106	20	0	0	0	183^2	214	138	126	21	12	117	118	1.802	6.17	73	6.41	.291	4	.308	-34	6	-3.1
• SOFF, Ray	Raymond John Soff b: 10/31/1958, Adrian, MI BR/TR, 6', 185 lbs. Deb: 7/17/1986																									
1986 StL-N	4	2	.667	30	0	0	0	0	38^1	37	17	14	4	0	13	22	1.304	3.29	111	3.63	.255	0	.000	0	3	0.0
1987 StL-N	1	0	1.000	12	0	0	0	0	15^1	18	11	11	3	1	5	9	1.500	6.46	64	5.70	.295	0	.000	-4	0	-0.4
Total 2	5	2	.714	42	0	0	0	0	53^2	55	28	25	7	1	18	31	1.360	4.19	92	4.22	.267	0	.000	-4	3	-0.4
• SOLANO, Julio	Julio Cesar Solano b: 1/8/1960, Aqua Blanca, Dominican Republic BR/TR, 6'1", 160 lbs. Deb: 4/5/1983																									
1983 Hou-N	0	2	.000	4	0	0	0	0	6	5	5	4	1	0	4	3	1.500	6.00	57	4.29	.217	0	....	-2	0	-0.2
1984 Hou-N	1	3	.250	31	0	0	0	0	50^2	31	13	11	3	0	18	33	.967	1.95	170	1.71	.179	1	.333	7	4	0.8
1985 Hou-N	2	2	.500	20	0	0	0	0	33^2	34	13	13	5	0	13	17	1.396	3.48	100	4.36	.262	0	.000	-0	2	-0.1
1986 Hou-N	3	1	.750	16	1	0	0	0	32	39	28	27	5	3	22	21	1.906	7.59	47	7.41	.310	0	.000	-14	0	-1.6
1987 Hou-N	0	0	....	11	0	0	0	0	20	25	17	17	5	0	9	12	1.700	7.65	51	6.79	.298	0	.000	-8	0	-0.8
1988 Sea-A	0	0	....	17	0	0	0	3	22	22	13	10	3	0	12	10	1.545	4.09	102	4.76	.268	0	....	0	1	0.0
1989 Sea-A	0	0	....	7	0	0	0	0	9^2	6	8	6	1	1	4	6	1.034	5.59	72	2.58	.176	0	....	-2	0	-0.2
Total 7	6	8	.429	106	1	0	0	3	174	162	97	88	23	4	82	102	1.402	4.55	81	4.38	.248	1	.077	-19	7	-2.0
• SOLIS, Marcelino	Marcelino Solis b: 7/19/1930, San Luis Potosi, Mexico BL/TL, 6'1", 185 lbs. Deb: 7/16/1958																									
1958 Chi-N	3	3	.500	15	4	0	0	0	52	74	41	35	5	4	20	15	1.808	6.06	65	6.93	.339	5	.250	-12	0	-1.1
• SOLOMON, Eddie	Eddie "Buddy J" Solomon b: 2/9/1951, Perry, GA d: 1/12/1986, Macon, GA BR/TR, 6'2", 190 lbs. Deb: 9/2/1973																									
1973 LA-N	0	0	....	4	0	0	0	0	6^1	10	5	5	3	1	4	6	2.211	7.11	48	13.20	.357	0	.000	-3	0	-0.3
1974* LA-N	0	0	....	4	0	0	0	1	6	5	1	1	1	0	2	2	1.167	1.50	227	3.28	.217	0	....	1	1	0.1
1975 Chi-N	0	0	....	6	0	0	0	0	6^2	7	6	1	1	0	6	3	1.950	1.35	284	5.89	.269	0	....	2	0	0.2
1976 StL-N	1	1	.500	26	2	0	0	0	37	45	24	20	2	1	16	19	1.649	4.86	73	5.13	.306	2	.400	-6	1	-0.5
1977 Atl-N	6	6	.500	18	16	0	0	0	88^2	110	64	45	10	2	34	54	1.624	4.57	97	5.56	.305	4	.129	1	3	0.1
1978 Atl-N	4	6	.400	37	8	0	0	2	106	98	52	48	12	2	50	64	1.396	4.08	99	3.93	.247	4	.138	1	6	0.1
1979 Atl-N	7	14	.333	31	30	4	0	0	186	184	98	87	19	6	51	96	1.263	4.21	96	3.59	.254	13	.203	2	9	0.3
1980 Pit-N	7	3	.700	26	12	2	0	0	100^1	96	44	30	8	4	37	35	1.326	2.69	135	3.66	.253	7	.219	10	7	1.1
1981 Pit-N	8	6	.571	22	17	2	0	1	127	133	49	44	10	3	27	38	1.260	3.12	115	3.61	.278	7	.163	7	8	0.7
1982 Pit-N	2	6	.250	11	10	0	0	0	46^2	69	38	35	9	1	18	18	1.864	6.75	55	7.86	.347	2	.133	-15	0	-1.7
Chi-A	1	0	1.000	6	0	0	0	0	7^1	7	5	3	1	0	2	2	1.227	3.68	110	3.50	.241	0	....	0	0	0.0
Total 10	36	42	.462	191	95	8	0	4	718	764	386	319	76	20	247	337	1.408	4.00	98	4.35	.274	39	.177	1	35	0.2
• SOMMER, Joe	Joseph John Sommer b: 11/20/1858, Covington, KY d: 1/16/1938, Cincinnati, OH BR/TR Deb: 7/8/1880 U ♦																									
1883 Cin-a	0	0	....	1	0	0	0	0	5	9	6	3	0	....	1	2	2.000	5.40	60	....	.367	115	.278	-1	13	-0.5
1885 Bal-a	0	0	....	2	0	0	0	1	3	6	3	3	0	0	0	0	2.000	9.00	36	....	.399	118	.251	-2	10	0.3
1886 Bal-a	0	0	....	1	0	0	0	0	4	14	12	8	0	0	3	1	4.250	18.00	19	....	.537	117	.209	-6	9	-2.8
1887 Bal-a	0	0	....	1	0	0	0	0	1	3	1	1	0	0	1	0	3.000	9.00	45	....	.501	186	.354	-1	13	-0.6
1890 Cle-N	0	0	....	1	0	0	0	0	1	2	3	0	1	0	2	0	4.000	0.00	....	....	.404	8	.229	0	0	-0.3
Total 5	0	0	....	6	0	0	0	1	14	34	25	15	1	0	7	3	2.857	9.64	35	....	.444	974	.261	-10	45	-4.0
• SOMMERS, Rudy	Rudolph Sommers b: 10/30/1888, Cincinnati, OH d: 3/18/1949, Louisville, KY BB/TL, 5'11", 165 lbs. Deb: 9/8/1912																									
1912 Chi-N	0	1	.000	1	0	0	0	0	3	4	1	1	0	0	2	2	2.000	3.00	111	5.94	.333	0	.000	0	0	0.0
1914 Bro-F	2	7	.222	23	8	2	0	2	82	88	54	37	2	3	34	40	1.488	4.06	80	4.19	.282	6	.250	-7	2	-0.4
1926 Bos-A	0	0	....	2	0	0	0	0	2	3	3	3	0	0	3	0	3.000	13.50	30	10.19	.333	0	....	-2	0	-0.2
1927 Bos-A	0	0	....	7	0	0	0	0	14	18	15	13	2	0	14	2	2.286	8.36	50	8.87	.353	1	.500	-6	0	-0.6
Total 4	2	8	.200	33	8	2	0	2	101	113	73	54	4	3	53	44	1.644	4.81	72	5.01	.294	7	.259	-15	2	-1.2
• SOMMERVILLE, Andy	Andrew Henry Sommerville b: 2/6/1876, Brooklyn, NY d: 6/16/1931, Richmond Hill, NY Deb: 8/8/1894																									
1894 Bro-N	0	1	.000	1	1	0	0	0	0^1	1	6	6	0	0	5	0	18.00	162.00	3	82.33	.511	0	....	-6	0	-0.4
• SONGER, Don	Donald C. Songer b: 1/31/1900, Walnut, KS d: 10/3/1962, Kansas City, MO BL/TL, 6', 165 lbs. Deb: 9/21/1924																									
1924 Pit-N	0	0	....	4	1	0	0	1	9^1	14	7	7	1	0	3	3	1.821	6.75	57	6.55	.333	0	.000	-3	0	-0.4
1925 Pit-N	0	1	.000	8	0	0	0	0	11^2	14	7	3	0	0	8	4	1.886	2.31	193	5.23	.298	0	.000	3	1	0.2
1926 Pit-N	7	8	.467	35	15	5	1	2	126^1	118	60	44	4	11	52	27	1.346	3.13	126	3.48	.252	4	.105	9	9	0.7
1927 Pit-N	0	0	....	2	0	0	0	0	4^2	10	10	6	0	1	4	1	3.000	11.57	35	13.95	.526	0	.000	-4	0	-0.4
NY-N	3	5	.375	22	1	0	0	1	50^1	48	22	16	4	1	31	9	1.570	2.86	135	4.37	.261	3	.300	6	4	0.7
Yr.	3	5	.375	24	1	0	0	1	55	58	32	22	4	2	35	10	1.691	3.60	109	5.18	.286	3	.273	2	4	0.3
Total 4	10	14	.417	71	17	5	1	4	202^1	204	106	76	9	13	98	44	1.493	3.38	117	4.19	.268	7	.132	10	14	0.8
• SORENSEN, Lary	Lary Alan Sorensen b: 10/4/1955, Detroit, MI BR/TR, 6'2", 210 lbs. Deb: 6/7/1977																									
1977 Mil-A	7	10	.412	23	20	9	0	0	142^1	147	72	69	10	1	36	57	1.286	4.36	93	3.50	.270	0	....	-6	7	-0.6
1978 Mil-A★	18	12	.600	37	36	17	3	1	280^2	277	111	100	14	5	50	78	1.165	3.21	117	2.89	.259	0	....	16	20	1.7
1979 Mil-A	15	14	.517	34	34	16	2	0	235^1	250	113	104	30	4	42	63	1.241	3.98	105	3.85	.275	0	....	6	15	0.6
1980 Mil-A	12	10	.545	35	29	8	2	1	195^2	242	91	80	13	2	45	54	1.467	3.68	105	4.59	.311	0	....	2	10	0.2
1981 StL-N	7	7	.500	23	23	3	1	0	140^1	149	59	51	3	1	26	52	1.247	3.27	109	3.10	.271	3	.065	2	7	-0.1
1982 Cle-A	10	15	.400	32	30	6	1	0	189^1	251	130	118	19	3	55	62	**1.616**	5.61	73	5.60	.322	0	....	-30	3	-3.0
1983 Cle-A	12	11	.522	36	34	8	1	0	222^2	238	112	105	21	2	65	76	1.361	4.24	100	4.02	.276	0	....	2	13	0.2
1984 Oak-A	6	13	.316	46	21	2	0	1	183^1	240	117	100	21	6	44	63	**1.549**	4.91	76	5.44	.316	0	....	-24	3	-2.4
1985 Chi-N	3	7	.300	45	3	0	0	0	82^1	86	44	39	8	4	24	34	1.336	4.26	94	3.85	.274	0	.000	-2	3	-0.2
1987 Mon-N	3	4	.429	23	5	0	0	1	47^2	56	32	25	7	3	12	21	1.427	4.72	89	4.90	.286	0	.000	-2	1	-0.3
1988 SF-N	0	0	....	12	0	0	0	2	16^2	24	13	9	1	0	3	9	1.620	4.86	67	5.22	.329	0	.000	-3	0	-0.3
Total 11	93	103	.474	346	235	69	10	6	1736^1	1960	894	800	147	31	402	569	1.360	4.15	95	4.11	.287	3	.049	-39	82	-4.3
• SORIANO, Rafael	Rafael Soriano b: 12/19/1979, San Jose, Dominican Republic BR/TR, 6'1", 175 lbs. Deb: 5/10/2002																									
2002 Sea-A	0	3	.000	10	8	0	0	1	47^1	45	25	24	8	0	16	32	1.289	4.56	93	3.93	.243	0	.000	-1	1	-0.2
2003 Sea-A	3	0	1.000	40	0	0	0	1	53	30	9	9	2	3	12	68	.792	1.53	283	1.32	.162	0	....	15	7	1.4
Total 2	3	3	.500	50	8	0	0	2	100^1	75	34	33	10	3	28	100	1.027	2.96	144	2.55	.203	0	.000	14	8	1.3
• SORRELL, Vic	Victor Garland Sorrell b: 4/9/1901, Morrisville, NC d: 5/4/1972, Raleigh, NC BR/TR, 5'10", 180 lbs. Deb: 4/22/1928																									
1928 Det-A	8	11	.421	29	23	8	0	0	171	182	106	91	9	5	83	67	1.550	4.79	86	4.33	.277	6	.109	-13	6	-1.7
1929 Det-A	14	15	.483	36	31	13	1	1	226	270	152	130	15	2	106	81	**1.664**	5.18	83	5.11	.302	12	.145	-15	7	-1.9
1930 Det-A	16	11	.593	35	30	14	2	1	233^1	245	116	100	13	0	106	97	1.504	3.86	124	4.16	.274	15	.188	24	19	1.9
1931 Det-A	13	14	.481	35	32	19	1	1	245	267	131	113	8	1	114	99	1.555	4.15	110	4.20	.278	14	.159	12	17	0.7
1932 Det-A	14	14	.500	32	31	13	1	0	234^1	234	124	105	11	3	77	84	1.327	4.03	117	3.38	.259	9	.118	14	14	1.0
1933 Det-A	11	15	.423	36	28	13	1	1	232^2	233	112	98	18	2	78	75	1.337	3.79	114	3.59	.260	11	.149	11	15	0.8
1934 Det-A	6	9	.400	28	19	6	1	2	129^2	146	76	69	13	3	45	46	1.473	4.79	92	4.59	.283	4	.108	-7	6	-0.7
1935 Det-A	4	3	.571	12	6	4	0	0	51^1	65	28	23	2	2	25	22	1.753	4.03	103	5.64	.319	0	.000	0	3	-0.3
1936 Det-A	6	7	.462	30	14	5	1	3	131^1	153	86	77	9	2	64	37	1.652	5.28	94	5.09	.294	6	.154	-4	7	-0.3
1937 Det-A	0	2	.000	7	2	0	0	1	17	25	18	17	3	0	8	11	1.941	9.00	52	7.66	.338	0	.000	-8	0	-0.8
Total 10	92	101	.477	280	216	95	8	10	1671^2	1820	949	823	101	20	706	619	1.511	4.43	101	4.31	.279	77	.139	15	94	-1.2
• SOSA, Elias	Elias (Martinez) Sosa b: 6/10/1950, La Vega, Dominican Republic BR/TR, 6'2", 190 lbs. Deb: 9/8/1972																									
1972 SF-N	0	1	.000	8	0	0	0	3	15^2	10	4	4	0	0	12	10	1.404	2.30	152	2.81	.189	0	.000	2	2	0.2
1973 SF-N	10	4	.714	71	1	0	0	18	107	95	42	39	7	4	41	70	1.271	3.28	116	3.21	.241	1	.071	7	13	0.7
1974 SF-N	9	7	.563	68	0	0	0	6	101	94	54	39	8	1	45	48	1.376	3.48	109	3.67	.252	1	.067	4	7	0.3

YEAR TM-L	W	L	PCT	G	GS	CG	SH	SV	IP	H	R	ER	HR	HB	BB	SO	RAT	ERA	ERA+	CERA	OAV	BH	AVG	PR+	WS	TPW
1975 StL-N	0	3	.000	14	1	0	0	0	27^1	22	14	12	3	1	14	15	1.317	3.95	95	3.56	.227	1	.125	0	1	0.0
Atl-N	2	2	.500	43	0	0	0	2	62^1	70	35	31	3	3	29	31	1.588	4.48	84	4.69	.294	1	.143	-3	2	-0.4
Yr.	2	5	.286	57	1	0	0	2	89^2	92	49	43	6	4	43	46	1.506	4.32	87	4.35	.275	2	.133	-3	3	-0.4
1976 Atl-N	4	4	.500	21	0	0	0	3	35^1	41	26	21	3	1	13	32	1.528	5.35	71	4.65	.287	1	.143	-5	1	-0.6
LA-N	2	4	.333	24	0	0	0	1	33^2	30	16	13	0	0	12	20	1.248	3.48	97	2.46	.242	0	....	-1	2	-0.1
Yr.	6	8	.429	45	0	0	0	4	69	71	42	34	3	1	25	52	1.391	4.43	82	3.58	.266	1	.143	-6	3	-0.7
1977* LA-N	2	2	.500	44	0	0	0	1	63^2	42	15	14	7	1	12	47	.848	1.98	193	1.70	.189	1	.250	12	7	1.3
1978 Oak-A	8	2	.800	68	0	0	0	14	109	106	37	32	5	1	44	61	1.376	2.64	138	3.50	.262	0	....	14	14	1.4
1979 Mon-N	8	7	.533	62	0	0	0	18	96^2	77	24	21	2	2	37	59	1.179	1.96	187	2.35	.219	2	.154	18	16	1.8
1980 Mon-N	9	6	.600	67	0	0	0	9	93^2	104	33	32	5	1	19	58	1.313	3.07	116	3.61	.286	1	.091	6	9	0.5
1981* Mon-N	1	2	.333	32	0	0	0	3	39^1	46	16	16	3	1	8	18	1.373	3.66	95	4.16	.297	2	1.000	-1	2	0.0
1982 Det-A	3	3	.500	38	0	0	0	4	61	64	31	30	11	2	18	24	1.344	4.43	92	4.58	.270	0	....	-4	3	-0.4
1983 SD-N	1	4	.200	41	1	0	0	1	72^1	72	41	35	7	3	30	45	1.410	4.35	80	4.15	.268	1	.143	-8	1	-0.9
Total 12	59	51	.536	601	3	0	0	83	918	873	388	339	64	21	334	538	1.315	3.32	111	3.48	.255	12	.130	41	80	3.9

• SOSA, Jorge Jorge Bolivar Sosa b: 4/28/1978, Santo Domingo, Dominican Republic BB/TR, 6'2", 177 lbs. Deb: 4/4/2002

YEAR TM-L	W	L	PCT	G	GS	CG	SH	SV	IP	H	R	ER	HR	HB	BB	SO	RAT	ERA	ERA+	CERA	OAV	BH	AVG	PR+	WS	TPW
2002 TB-A	2	7	.222	31	14	0	0	0	99^1	88	63	61	16	2	54	48	1.430	5.53	81	4.51	.236	0	....	-13	2	-1.3
2003 TB-A	5	12	.294	29	19	1	1	0	128^2	137	71	66	14	4	60	72	1.531	4.62	98	4.93	.278	0	....	-4	5	-0.4
Total 2	7	19	.269	60	33	1	1	0	228	225	134	127	30	6	114	120	1.487	5.01	90	4.75	.260	0	....	-18	7	-1.7

• SOSA, Jose Jose Ynocencio Sosa b: 12/28/1952, Santo Domingo, Dominican Republic BR/TR, 5'11", 158 lbs. Deb: 7/22/1975

YEAR TM-L	W	L	PCT	G	GS	CG	SH	SV	IP	H	R	ER	HR	HB	BB	SO	RAT	ERA	ERA+	CERA	OAV	BH	AVG	PR+	WS	TPW
1975 Hou-N	1	3	.250	25	2	0	0	1	47	51	21	21	5	1	23	31	1.574	4.02	84	5.04	.291	3	.333	-4	2	-0.2
1976 Hou-N	0	0	....	9	0	0	0	0	11^2	16	9	9	0	3	6	5	1.886	6.94	46	6.44	.340	0	....	-5	0	-0.5
Total 2	1	3	.250	34	2	0	0	1	58^2	67	30	30	5	4	29	36	1.636	4.60	72	5.32	.302	3	.333	-9	2	-0.7

• SOTHORON, Allen Allen Sutton Sothoron b: 4/27/1893, Bradford, OH d: 6/17/1939, St. Louis, MO BB/TR, 5'11", 182 lbs. Deb: 9/17/1914 M/C

YEAR TM-L	W	L	PCT	G	GS	CG	SH	SV	IP	H	R	ER	HR	HB	BB	SO	RAT	ERA	ERA+	CERA	OAV	BH	AVG	PR+	WS	TPW
1914 StL-A	0	0	....	1	0	0	0	0	6	6	4	4	0	0	4	3	1.667	6.00	45	4.22	.261	0	.000	-2	0	-0.3
1915 StL-A	0	1	.000	3	1	0	0	0	3^2	8	10	3	0	0	5	2	3.545	7.36	39	13.88	.400	0	.000	-2	0	-0.2
1917 StL-A	14	19	.424	48	32	17	3	4	276^2	259	135	87	2	9	96	85	1.283	2.83	92	2.99	.251	20	.217	-7	10	-0.4
1918 StL-A	12	12	.500	29	24	14	2	0	209	152	64	45	3	3	67	71	1.048	1.94	141	1.86	**.205**	10	.159	18	17	1.7
1919 StL-A	20	12	.625	40	30	21	3	3	270	256	101	66	4	10	87	106	1.270	2.20	151	2.98	.246	17	.175	31	24	3.0
1920 StL-A	8	15	.348	36	26	12	1	2	218^1	263	151	114	6	6	89	81	**1.612**	4.70	83	4.79	.307	16	.222	-20	7	-2.0
1921 StL-A	1	2	.333	5	4	1	0	0	27^2	33	19	16	0	1	8	9	1.482	5.20	86	4.05	.314	1	.111	-2	1	-0.3
Bos-A	0	2	.000	2	2	0	0	0	6	15	10	9	0	0	5	2	3.333	13.50	31	14.15	.455	1	.500	-6	0	-0.5
Cle-A	12	4	.750	22	16	10	2	0	144^2	146	60	52	0	7	58	61	1.410	3.24	132	3.54	.279	16	.276	17	13	1.7
Yr.	13	8	.619	29	22	11	2	0	178^1	194	89	77	0	8	71	72	1.486	3.89	111	3.98	.293	18	.261	8	14	0.9
1922 Cle-A	1	3	.250	6	4	2	0	0	25^1	26	22	18	1	2	14	8	1.579	6.39	62	4.42	.274	4	.444	-6	1	-0.5
1924 StL-N	10	16	.385	29	28	16	**4**	0	196^2	209	102	78	9	10	84	62	1.490	3.57	106	4.15	.275	14	.194	5	9	0.3
1925 StL-N	10	10	.500	28	23	8	2	0	155^2	173	86	70	7	6	63	67	1.516	4.05	107	4.30	.280	11	.196	4	9	0.3
1926 StL-N	3	3	.500	15	4	1	0	0	42^2	37	22	20	2	0	16	19	1.242	4.22	93	2.84	.247	3	.231	-2	2	-0.2
Total 11	91	99	.479	264	194	102	17	9	1582^1	1583	786	582	34	54	596	576	1.377	3.31	106	3.52	.264	113	.207	27	93	2.7

• SOTO, Mario Mario Melvin Soto b: 7/12/1956, Bani, Dominican Republic BR/TR, 6', 185 lbs. Deb: 7/21/1977

YEAR TM-L	W	L	PCT	G	GS	CG	SH	SV	IP	H	R	ER	HR	HB	BB	SO	RAT	ERA	ERA+	CERA	OAV	BH	AVG	PR+	WS	TPW
1977 Cin-N	2	6	.250	12	10	2	1	0	60^2	60	38	36	12	3	26	44	1.418	5.34	74	4.92	.258	1	.077	-10	0	-1.0
1978 Cin-N	1	0	1.000	5	1	0	0	0	18	13	5	5	1	0	13	13	1.444	2.50	142	3.15	.197	0	.000	2	2	0.2
1979* Cin-N	3	2	.600	25	0	0	0	0	37^1	33	25	22	2	1	30	32	1.688	5.30	70	4.73	.243	4	.571	-7	1	-0.5
1980 Cin-N	10	8	.556	53	12	3	1	4	190^1	126	72	65	11	2	84	182	1.103	3.07	116	2.15	**.187**	2	.043	13	14	0.9
1981 Cin-N	12	9	.571	25	**25**	10	3	0	175	142	69	64	13	3	61	151	1.160	3.29	108	2.76	.220	4	.068	3	11	-0.1
1982 Cin-N★	14	13	.519	35	34	13	2	0	257^2	202	88	80	19	4	71	274	1.060	2.79	132	2.37	.215	14	.167	24	20	2.7
1983 Cin-N★	17	13	.567	34	34	**18**	3	0	273^2	207	96	82	28	5	95	242	1.104	2.70	141	2.63	.208	11	.125	34	**25**	3.3
1984 Cin-N★	18	7	.720	33	33	**13**	0	0	237^1	181	102	93	26	5	87	185	1.129	3.53	107	2.79	.209	18	.207	9	18	1.3
1985 Cin-N	12	15	.444	36	36	9	1	0	256^2	196	109	102	30	2	104	214	1.169	3.58	106	2.95	.211	11	.133	3	14	0.2
1986 Cin-N	5	10	.333	19	19	1	1	0	105	113	61	55	15	1	46	67	1.514	4.71	82	4.97	.280	3	.111	-9	2	-1.0
1987 Cin-N	3	2	.600	6	6	0	0	0	31^2	34	18	18	7	0	12	11	1.453	5.12	83	5.24	.279	1	.083	-3	1	-0.4
1988 Cin-N	3	7	.300	14	14	3	1	0	87	88	49	45	8	2	28	34	1.333	4.66	77	3.86	.267	1	.045	-12	1	-1.4
Total 12	100	92	.521	297	224	72	13	4	1730^1	1395	732	667	172	28	657	1449	1.186	3.47	108	3.00	.220	70	.132	48	109	4.2

• SOUZA, Mark Kenneth Mark Souza b: 2/1/1954, Redwood City, CA BL/TL, 6', 180 lbs. Deb: 4/22/1980

YEAR TM-L	W	L	PCT	G	GS	CG	SH	SV	IP	H	R	ER	HR	HB	BB	SO	RAT	ERA	ERA+	CERA	OAV	BH	AVG	PR+	WS	TPW
1980 Oak-A	0	0	....	5	0	0	0	0	7	9	6	6	1	0	5	2	2.000	7.71	49	7.54	.310	0	....	-3	0	-0.3

• SOWDERS, Bill William Jefferson "Little Bill" Sowders b: 11/29/1864, Louisville, KY d: 2/2/1951, Indianapolis, IN BR/TR, 6', 155 lbs. Deb: 4/24/1888

YEAR TM-L	W	L	PCT	G	GS	CG	SH	SV	IP	H	R	ER	HR	HB	BB	SO	RAT	ERA	ERA+	CERA	OAV	BH	AVG	PR+	WS	TPW
1888 Bos-N	19	15	.559	36	35	34	2	0	317	278	155	73	3	9	73	132	1.107	2.07	139	....	.227	18	.148	25	21	2.1
1889 Bos-N	1	2	.333	7	4	3	0	2	42	53	35	24	3	2	23	10	1.810	5.14	81	....	.298	4	.235	-4	1	-0.4
Pit-N	6	5	.545	13	11	9	0	0	52^2	94	55	43	1	4	29	33	2.335	7.35	51	....	.376	13	.271	-21	1	-1.6
Yr.	7	7	.500	20	15	12	0	**2**	94^2	147	90	67	4	6	52	43	2.102	6.37	61	....	.343	17	.262	-25	2	-2.0
1890 Pit-N	3	8	.273	15	11	9	0	0	106	117	77	52	1	2	24	30	1.330	4.42	74	....	.272	9	.180	-7	2	-0.9
Total 3	29	30	.492	71	61	55	2	2	517^2	542	322	192	8	17	149	205	1.335	3.34	99	....	.260	44	.186	-8	25	-0.8

• SOWDERS, John John Sowders b: 12/10/1866, Louisville, KY d: 7/29/1939, Indianapolis, IN BR/TL, 6' Deb: 6/28/1887

YEAR TM-L	W	L	PCT	G	GS	CG	SH	SV	IP	H	R	ER	HR	HB	BB	SO	RAT	ERA	ERA+	CERA	OAV	BH	AVG	PR+	WS	TPW
1887 Ind-N	0	0	....	1	0	0	0	0	3	16	13	7	0	....	5	0	5.333	21.00	20	....	.644	0	.000	-6	0	-0.5
1889 KC-a	6	16	.273	25	23	20	0	1	185	204	181	99	9	7	105	104	1.670	4.82	87	....	.271	19	.218	-7	6	-0.8
1890 Bro-P	19	16	.543	39	37	28	1	0	309	358	233	131	3	11	161	91	1.680	3.82	117	....	.278	25	.189	19	22	1.2
Total 3	25	32	.439	65	60	48	1	1	497	578	427	237	12	18	271	195	1.698	4.29	101	....	.280	44	.199	6	28	-0.1

• SPADE, Bob Robert Spade b: 1/4/1877, Akron, OH d: 9/7/1924, Cincinnati, OH BR/TR, 5'10", 190 lbs. Deb: 9/22/1907

YEAR TM-L	W	L	PCT	G	GS	CG	SH	SV	IP	H	R	ER	HR	HB	BB	SO	RAT	ERA	ERA+	CERA	OAV	BH	AVG	PR+	WS	TPW
1907 Cin-N	1	2	.333	3	3	3	1	0	27	21	5	3	0	1	9	7	1.111	1.00	259	2.19	.219	2	.286	4	3	0.6
1908 Cin-N	17	12	.586	35	28	22	2	1	249^1	230	111	76	2	5	85	74	1.263	2.74	83	2.93	.250	17	.195	-9	13	-0.9
1909 Cin-N	5	5	.500	14	13	8	0	0	98	91	38	31	0	4	39	31	1.327	2.85	91	3.12	.236	10	.294	-4	6	0.0
1910 Cin-N	1	2	.333	3	3	1	0	0	17^1	35	19	13	1	1	9	1	2.538	6.75	43	12.47	.479	0	.000	-7	0	-0.8
StL-A	1	3	.250	7	5	2	1	0	34^2	34	24	17	1	1	17	8	1.471	4.41	56	4.03	.270	3	.273	-7	1	-0.6
Total 4	25	24	.510	62	52	36	4	1	426^1	411	197	140	4	12	159	121	1.337	2.96	82	3.40	.257	32	.222	-22	23	-1.7

• SPAHN, Warren Warren Edward Spahn b: 4/23/1921, Buffalo, NY d: 11/24/2003, Broken Arrow, OK BL/TL, 6', 175 lbs. Deb: 4/19/1942 C HOF: 1973

YEAR TM-L	W	L	PCT	G	GS	CG	SH	SV	IP	H	R	ER	HR	HB	BB	SO	RAT	ERA	ERA+	CERA	OAV	BH	AVG	PR+	WS	TPW
1942 Bos-N	0	0	....	4	2	1	0	0	15^2	25	15	10	0	0	11	7	2.298	5.74	58	8.12	.368	1	.167	-4	0	-0.5
1946 Bos-N	8	5	.615	24	16	8	0	1	125^2	107	46	41	6	1	36	67	1.138	2.94	117	2.48	.228	7	.163	8	9	0.8
1947 Bos-N★	21	10	.677	40	35	22	**7**	3	**289^2**	245	87	75	15	1	84	123	1.136	**2.33**	**167**	**2.50**	.226	16	.163	**53**	**32**	**5.3**
1948* Bos-N	15	12	.556	36	35	16	3	1	257	237	115	106	19	1	77	114	1.222	3.71	103	3.05	.242	15	.167	2	14	0.3
1949 Bos-N★	**21**	14	.600	38	**38**	**25**	4	0	**302^1**	283	125	103	27	3	86	**151**	1.221	3.07	123	3.18	.245	18	.162	25	**24**	2.5
1950 Bos-N★	**21**	17	.553	41	**39**	25	1	1	293	248	123	103	22	1	111	**191**	1.225	3.16	122	2.93	.227	23	.217	24	21	2.7
1951 Bos-N★	22	14	.611	39	36	**26**	**7**	0	310^2	278	111	103	20	1	109	**164**	1.246	2.98	123	3.03	.238	22	.190	27	26	3.1
1952 Bos-N★	14	19	.424	40	35	19	5	3	290	263	109	96	19	6	73	**183**	1.159	2.98	121	2.81	.240	18	.161	25	22	2.9
1953 Mil-N★	**23**	7	.767	35	32	24	5	3	265^2	211	75	62	14	1	70	148	1.058	**2.10**	**187**	**2.19**	**.217**	23	.219	51	31	5.3
1954 Mil-N★	21	12	.636	39	34	23	1	3	283^1	262	107	99	24	1	86	136	1.228	3.14	118	3.14	.245	21	.208	15	23	2.0
1955 Mil-N	17	14	.548	39	32	16	1	1	245^2	249	99	89	25	2	65	110	1.278	3.26	115	3.67	.265	17	.210	14	19	1.8
1956 Mil-N★	20	11	.645	39	35	20	3	3	281^1	249	92	87	25	3	52	128	1.070	2.78	124	2.61	.238	22	.210	19	24	2.5
1957* Mil-N★	**21**	11	.656	39	35	**18**	4	3	271	241	94	81	23	2	78	111	1.177	2.69	130	2.97	.237	13	.138	20	**22**	2.1
1958* Mil-N★	**22**	11	.667	38	36	**23**	2	1	**290**	257	106	99	29	2	76	150	1.148	3.07	115	2.96	.237	36	.333	11	**28**	2.9
1959 Mil-N★	**21**	15	.583	40	36	**21**	**4**	0	**292**	282	106	96	21	1	70	143	1.205	2.96	120	3.07	.253	24	.231	21	23	2.7
1960 Mil-N	**21**	10	.677	40	33	**18**	4	2	267^2	254	114	104	24	4	74	154	1.225	3.50	98	3.27	.250	14	.147	2	16	0.4
1961 Mil-N★	**21**	13	.618	38	34	**21**	**4**	0	262^2	236	96	88	24	4	64	115	1.142	**3.02**	124	**2.96**	.243	21	.223	22	**25**	3.1

YEAR	TM-L	W	L	PCT	G	GS	CG	SH	SV	IP	H	R	ER	HR	HB	BB	SO	RAT	ERA	ERA+	CERA	OAV	BH	AVG	PR+	WS	TPW
1962	Mil-N★	18	14	.563	34	34	**22**	0	0	269^1	248	97	91	25	3	55	118	1.125	3.04	125	2.90	.246	18	.184	22	23	2.5
1963	Mil-N★	23	7	.767	33	33	**22**	7	0	259^2	241	85	75	23	0	49	102	1.117	2.60	124	2.84	.248	16	.178	13	22	2.0
1964	Mil-N	6	13	.316	38	25	4	1	4	173^2	204	110	102	23	2	52	78	**1.474**	5.29	67	4.94	.297	11	.186	-34	1	-3.5
1965	NY-N	4	12	.250	20	19	5	0	0	126	140	70	61	18	2	35	56	1.389	4.36	81	4.57	.281	4	.114	-11	4	-1.1
	SF-N	3	4	.429	16	11	3	0	0	71^2	70	34	27	8	1	21	34	1.270	3.39	106	3.61	.256	3	.143	3	3	0.3
	Yr.	7	16	.304	36	30	8	0	0	197^2	210	104	88	26	3	56	90	1.346	4.01	89	4.23	.272	7	.125	-9	7	-0.8
Total	21	363	245	.597	750	665	382	63	29	5243^2	4830	2016	1798	434	42	1434	2583	1.195	3.09	118	3.06	.244	363	.194	326	412	40.2
• SPALDING, Al	Albert Goodwill Spalding b: 9/2/1850, Byron, IL d: 9/9/1915, San Diego, CA BR/TR, 6'1", 170 lbs. Deb: 5/5/1871 M HOF: 1939 ♦																										
1871	Bos-n	**19**	10	.655	31	31	22	**1**	0	257^1	333	272	96	2	....	38	23	1.442	3.36	124	....	.274	39	.271	18	....	1.2
1872	Bos-n	**38**	8	.826	48	48	41	**3**	0	404^2	417	224	84	0	....	27	28	1.097	1.87	**200**	....	.232	84	.354	**48**	....	**4.5**
1873	Bos-n	**41**	14	.745	**60**	**54**	46	1	2	**497^2**	643	413	136	5	....	28	50	1.348	2.46	135	....	.278	106	.329	**47**	....	**4.4**
1874	Bos-n	**52**	16	.765	**71**	**69**	**65**	**4**	0	**617^1**	755	402	132	1	....	23	31	1.260	1.92	**154**	....	.269	119	.329	**69**	....	**6.7**
1875	Bos-n	**54**	5	.915	**72**	62	52	**7**	**8**	570	573	241	101	1	....	14	75	1.030	1.59	149	....	.238	107	.312	25	....	**3.5**
1876	Chi-N	**47**	12	.797	61	60	53	8	0	528^1	542	226	103	6	....	26	39	1.075	1.75	139	....	.245	91	.305	16	**57**	2.1
1877	Chi-N	1	0	1.000	4	1	0	0	1	11	17	12	4	0	....	0	2	1.545	3.27	91	....	.335	65	.256	-0	5	-0.3
Total	5 n	204	53	.794	282	264	226	16	10	2347	2721	1552	549	9	....	130	207	1.215	2.11	150	....	.258	455	.323	207	....	20.3
Total	2	48	12	.800	65	61	53	8	1	539^1	559	238	107	6	....	26	41	1.085	1.79	138	....	.247	158	.284	15	62	1.8
• SPANSWICK, Bill	William Henry Spanswick b: 7/8/1938, Springfield, MA BL/TL, 6'3", 195 lbs. Deb: 4/18/1964																										
1964	Bos-A	2	3	.400	29	7	0	0	0	65^1	75	51	50	9	3	44	55	1.821	6.89	56	6.78	.306	4	.286	-21	0	-2.0
• SPARKS, Jeff	James Jeffrey Sparks b: 4/4/1972, Houston, TX BR/TR, 6'3", 220 lbs. Deb: 9/12/1999																										
1999	TB-A	0	0	....	8	0	0	0	1	10	6	6	6	1	1	12	17	1.800	5.40	92	4.98	.171	0	....	-0	1	0.0
2000	TB-A	0	1	.000	15	0	0	0	0	20^1	13	8	8	2	2	18	24	1.525	3.54	139	4.32	.186	0	....	3	2	0.3
Total	2	0	1	.000	23	0	0	0	1	30^1	19	14	14	3	3	30	41	1.615	4.15	119	4.53	.181	0	....	2	3	0.2
• SPARKS, Steve	Stephen Lanier Sparks b: 3/28/1975, Mobile, AL BR/TR, 6'4", 210 lbs. Deb: 7/19/2000																										
2000	Pit-N	0	0	....	3	0	0	0	0	4	4	3	3	0	0	5	2	2.250	6.75	68	6.80	.267	0	....	-1	0	-0.1
• SPARKS, Steve	Steven William Sparks b: 7/2/1965, Tulsa, OK BR/TR, 6', 180 lbs. Deb: 4/28/1995																										
1995	Mil-A	9	11	.450	33	27	3	0	0	202	210	111	104	17	5	86	96	1.465	4.63	108	4.44	.274	0	....	4	11	0.4
1996	Mil-A	4	7	.364	20	13	1	0	0	88^2	103	66	65	19	3	52	21	1.748	6.60	79	7.03	.297	0	....	-16	2	-1.4
1998	Ana-A	9	4	.692	22	20	0	0	0	128^2	130	66	62	14	5	58	90	1.461	4.34	108	4.60	.263	0	.000	6	8	0.6
1999	Ana-A	5	11	.313	28	26	0	0	0	147^2	165	101	89	21	9	82	73	1.673	5.42	89	5.94	.281	1	.333	-11	5	-0.9
2000	Det-A	7	5	.583	20	15	1	1	1	104	108	55	47	7	4	29	53	1.317	4.07	118	3.71	.263	0	....	9	7	0.8
2001	Det-A	14	9	.609	35	33	**8**	1	0	232	244	110	94	22	6	64	116	1.328	3.65	119	3.97	.271	0	.000	22	16	2.0
2002	Det-A	8	16	.333	32	30	3	0	0	189	238	134	116	23	12	67	98	**1.614**	5.52	78	5.78	.306	0	.000	-24	3	-2.4
2003	Det-A	0	6	.000	42	0	0	0	2	89^2	95	57	47	11	3	34	49	1.439	4.72	91	4.64	.278	0	....	-4	3	-0.4
	* Oak-A	0	0	....	9	0	0	0	0	17^1	19	11	11	2	0	3	5	1.269	5.71	79	3.73	.271	0	....	-2	0	-0.2
	Yr.	0	6	.000	51	0	0	0	2	107	114	68	58	13	3	37	54	1.411	4.88	89	4.49	.277	0	....	-7	3	-0.6
Total	8	56	69	.448	241	164	16	2	3	1199	1312	711	635	136	47	475	601	1.490	4.77	97	4.90	.279	1	.100	-16	55	-1.5
• SPARKS, Tully	Thomas Frank Sparks b: 12/12/1874, Etna, GA d: 7/15/1937, Anniston, AL BR/TR, 5'10" Deb: 9/15/1897																										
1897	Phi-N	0	1	.000	1	1	1	0	0	8	12	9	9	0	0	4	0	2.000	10.13	41	6.16	.343	0	.000	-5	0	-0.5
1899	Pit-N	8	6	.571	28	17	8	0	0	170	180	101	73	1	10	82	53	1.541	3.86	98	4.11	.272	8	.129	-2	9	-0.3
1901	Mil-A	7	17	.292	29	26	18	0	0	210	228	157	82	5	14	93	62	**1.529**	3.51	102	4.29	.274	12	.169	5	8	0.4
1902	NY-N	4	10	.286	16	14	12	0	1	123^1	142	72	48	2	4	41	42	1.484	3.50	80	4.09	.288	5	.135	-9	4	-1.0
	Bos-A	7	9	.438	17	15	15	1	0	142^2	151	83	55	4	7	40	37	1.339	3.47	103	3.55	.272	8	.154	-2	7	-0.3
1903	Phi-N	11	15	.423	28	28	27	0	0	248	248	109	75	3	8	56	88	1.226	2.72	120	2.98	.263	10	.109	11	14	0.6
1904	Phi-N	7	16	.304	26	25	19	3	0	200^2	208	109	59	1	5	43	67	1.251	2.65	101	2.74	.260	8	.105	4	5	0.0
1905	Phi-N	14	11	.560	34	26	20	3	1	259^2	217	86	63	2	9	73	98	1.117	2.18	133	2.40	.236	12	.128	17	21	1.5
1906	Phi-N	19	16	.543	42	37	29	6	3	316^2	244	99	76	4	10	62	114	.966	2.16	121	1.75	.211	16	.154	19	21	2.2
1907	Phi-N	22	8	.733	33	31	24	3	1	265	221	78	59	2	7	51	90	1.026	2.00	121	2.01	.228	3	.034	8	24	0.0
1908	Phi-N	16	15	.516	33	31	24	2	2	263^1	251	98	76	3	8	51	85	1.147	2.60	93	2.67	.257	4	.052	-8	13	-1.5
1909	Phi-N	6	11	.353	24	16	6	1	0	121^2	126	54	40	4	3	32	40	1.299	2.96	87	3.54	.280	5	.139	-7	5	-0.9
1910	Phi-N	0	2	.000	3	3	0	0	0	15	22	12	10	2	2	2	4	1.600	6.00	52	6.23	.324	0	.000	-5	0	-0.6
Total	12	121	137	.469	314	270	203	19	8	2344	2250	1067	725	33	87	630	780	1.229	2.78	105	2.94	.254	91	.114	26	131	-0.4
• SPARMA, Joe	Joseph Blase Sparma b: 2/4/1942, Massillon, OH d: 5/14/1986, Columbus, OH BR/TR, 6'1", 195 lbs. Deb: 5/20/1964																										
1964	Det-A	5	6	.455	21	11	3	2	0	84	62	33	28	4	3	45	71	1.274	3.00	122	2.95	.207	4	.160	6	6	0.7
1965	Det-A	13	8	.619	30	28	6	0	0	167	142	69	59	13	3	75	127	1.299	3.18	109	3.29	.228	7	.135	6	11	0.7
1966	Det-A	2	7	.222	29	13	0	0	0	91^2	103	57	54	14	3	52	61	1.691	5.30	66	6.09	.288	5	.217	-19	0	-2.0
1967	Det-A	16	9	.640	37	37	11	5	0	217^2	186	103	91	20	8	85	153	1.245	3.76	87	3.30	.227	4	.054	-14	8	-2.1
1968*	Det-A	10	10	.500	34	31	7	1	0	182^1	169	81	75	14	7	77	110	**1.349**	3.70	81	3.73	.246	8	.133	-15	5	-1.8
1969	Det-A	6	8	.429	23	16	3	2	0	92^2	78	55	49	5	1	77	41	1.673	4.76	78	4.57	.231	4	.138	-11	2	-1.2
1970	Mon-N	0	4	.000	9	6	1	0	0	29^1	34	25	23	7	2	25	23	2.011	7.06	58	8.22	.296	0	.000	-10	0	-1.0
Total	7	52	52	.500	183	142	31	10	0	864^2	774	423	379	77	27	436	586	1.399	3.94	86	3.95	.239	32	.119	-56	32	-6.7
• SPECK, Cliff	Robert Clifford Speck b: 8/8/1956, Portland, OR BR/TR, 6'4", 195 lbs. Deb: 7/30/1986																										
1986	Atl-N	2	1	.667	13	1	0	0	0	28^1	25	13	13	2	1	15	21	1.412	4.13	96	3.86	.238	0	.000	-0	2	0.0
• SPEECE, By	Byron Franklin Speece b: 1/6/1897, West Baden, IN d: 9/29/1974, Elgin, OR BR/TR, 5'11", 170 lbs. Deb: 4/21/1924																										
1924*	Was-A	2	1	.667	21	1	0	0	0	54^1	60	30	16	0	2	27	15	1.601	2.65	152	4.34	.303	3	.150	7	4	0.6
1925	Cle-A	3	5	.375	28	3	3	0	1	90^1	106	48	43	0	3	28	26	1.483	4.28	103	3.93	.297	5	.161	2	5	0.0
1926	Cle-A	0	0	....	2	0	0	0	0	3	1	1	0	0	0	2	1	1.000	0.00	....	1.40	.125	0	....	1	0	0.1
1930	Phi-N	0	0	....	11	0	0	0	0	19^2	41	30	29	1	0	4	9	2.288	13.27	41	9.27	.432	1	.333	-17	0	-1.5
Total	4	5	6	.455	62	4	3	0	1	167^1	208	109	88	1	5	61	51	1.608	4.73	98	4.64	.316	9	.167	-7	9	-0.7
• SPEER, Floyd	Floyd Vernie Speer b: 1/27/1913, Booneville, AR d: 3/22/1969, Little Rock, AR BR/TR, 6', 180 lbs. Deb: 4/25/1943																										
1943	Chi-A	0	0	....	1	0	0	0	0	1	1	1	1	0	0	2	1	3.000	9.00	37	8.74	.250	0	....	-1	0	-0.1
1944	Chi-A	0	0	....	2	0	0	0	0	2	4	2	2	0	0	0	1	2.000	9.00	38	8.38	.500	0	....	-1	0	-0.1
Total	2	0	0	....	3	0	0	0	0	3	5	3	3	0	0	2	2	2.333	9.00	38	8.50	.417	0	....	-2	0	-0.2
• SPEER, Kid	George Nathan Speer b: 6/16/1886, Corning, MO d: 1/13/1946, Edmonton, Canada BL/TL, 5'9", 152 lbs. Deb: 4/24/1909																										
1909	Det-A	4	4	.500	12	8	4	0	1	76^1	88	39	24	2	4	13	12	1.323	2.83	89	3.77	.293	3	.120	-3	3	-0.4
• SPEIER, Justin	Justin James Speier b: 11/6/1973, Daly City, CA BR/TR, 6'4", 205 lbs. Deb: 5/27/1998																										
1998	Chi-N	0	0	....	1	0	0	0	0	1^1	2	2	2	0	0	1	2	2.250	13.50	33	7.52	.333	0	....	-1	0	-0.1
	Fla-N	0	3	.000	18	0	0	0	0	19^1	25	18	18	7	0	12	15	1.914	8.38	49	9.02	.325	0	....	-9	0	-0.9
	Yr.	0	3	.000	19	0	0	0	0	20^2	27	20	20	7	0	13	17	1.935	8.71	47	8.93	.325	0	....	-10	0	-1.0
1999	Atl-N	0	0	....	19	0	0	0	0	28^2	28	18	18	8	0	13	22	1.430	5.65	80	5.27	.248	1	.333	-3	1	-0.3
2000	Cle-A	5	2	.714	47	0	0	0	0	68^1	57	27	25	9	4	28	69	1.244	3.29	151	3.56	.226	1	.500	13	7	1.3
2001	Cle-A	2	0	1.000	12	0	0	0	0	20^2	24	16	16	5	3	8	15	1.548	6.97	65	6.61	.293	0	....	-5	0	-0.5
	Col-N	4	3	.571	42	0	0	0	0	56	47	24	23	8	5	12	47	1.054	3.70	144	3.04	.229	0	.000	10	5	0.9
2002	Col-N	5	1	.833	63	0	0	0	1	62^1	51	31	30	9	3	19	47	1.123	4.33	110	3.06	.216	1	.333	4	6	0.4
2003	Col-N	3	1	.750	72	0	0	0	9	73^1	73	37	33	11	7	23	66	1.309	4.05	121	4.27	.257	0	.000	8	8	0.8
Total	6	19	10	.655	274	0	0	0	10	330	307	173	165	57	22	116	283	1.282	4.50	105	4.21	.245	3	.188	16	27	1.5
• SPENCER, George	George Elwell Spencer b: 7/7/1926, Columbus, OH BR/TR, 6'1", 215 lbs. Deb: 8/17/1950																										
1950	NY-N	1	0	1.000	10	1	1	0	0	25^1	12	7	7	3	0	7	5	.750	2.49	165	1.30	.141	0	.000	4	3	0.3

YEAR TM-L	W	L	PCT	G	GS	CG	SH	SV	IP	H	R	ER	HR	HB	BB	SO	RAT	ERA	ERA+	CERA	OAV	BH	AVG	PR+	WS	TPW
1951* NY-N	10	4	.714	57	4	2	0	6	132	125	62	55	21	1	56	36	1.371	3.75	104	4.31	.254	4	.125	2	10	0.1
1952 NY-N	3	5	.375	35	4	0	0	3	60	57	39	37	13	3	21	27	1.300	5.55	67	4.51	.251	2	.200	-12	1	-1.3
1953 NY-N	0	0	....	1	0	0	0	0	2^1	3	2	2	0	0	2	1	2.143	7.71	56	6.35	.300	0	....	-1	0	-0.1
1954 NY-N	1	0	1.000	6	0	0	0	0	12^1	9	5	5	1	0	8	4	1.378	3.65	111	3.33	.209	0	.000	0	1	0.0
1955 NY-N	0	0	....	1	0	0	0	0	1^2	1	1	1	1	0	3	0	2.400	5.40	75	12.02	.167	0	....	-0	0	0.0
1958 Det-A	1	0	1.000	7	0	0	0	0	10	11	4	3	0	0	4	5	1.500	2.70	150	3.90	.289	0	....	1	1	0.1
1960 Det-A	0	1	.000	5	0	0	0	0	7^2	10	3	3	1	0	5	4	1.957	3.52	117	6.98	.323	0	.000	1	0	0.0
Total 8	16	10	.615	122	9	3	0	9	251^1	228	123	113	40	4	106	82	1.329	4.05	96	4.14	.245	6	.120	-5	16	-0.7

• SPENCER, Glenn Glenn Edward Spencer b: 9/11/1905, Corning, NY d: 12/30/1958, Binghamton, NY BR/TR, 5'11", 155 lbs. Deb: 4/11/1928

YEAR TM-L	W	L	PCT	G	GS	CG	SH	SV	IP	H	R	ER	HR	HB	BB	SO	RAT	ERA	ERA+	CERA	OAV	BH	AVG	PR+	WS	TPW
1928 Pit-N	0	0	....	4	0	0	0	0	5^2	4	3	1	0	0	3	2	1.235	1.59	255	2.06	.200	0	.000	2	1	0.1
1930 Pit-N	8	9	.471	41	10	5	0	4	156^2	185	110	94	16	2	63	60	1.583	5.40	92	5.12	.305	6	.113	-7	7	-1.0
1931 Pit-N	11	12	.478	38	18	11	1	3	186^2	180	83	71	8	5	65	51	1.313	3.42	112	3.35	.260	5	.096	6	13	0.3
1932 Pit-N	4	8	.333	39	13	5	1	1	137^2	167	104	76	10	3	44	35	1.533	4.97	77	4.58	.288	6	.162	-19	1	-1.9
1933 NY-N	0	2	.000	17	3	1	0	0	47^1	52	33	27	3	1	26	14	1.648	5.13	62	4.88	.284	2	.167	-11	0	-1.2
Total 5	23	31	.426	139	44	22	2	8	534	588	333	269	37	11	201	162	1.478	4.53	90	4.31	.282	19	.123	-30	22	-3.7

• SPENCER, Hack Fred Calvin Spencer b: 4/25/1885, Minneapolis, MN d: 2/5/1969, St. Anthony, MN BR/TR, 5'7", 172 lbs. Deb: 4/18/1912

YEAR TM-L	W	L	PCT	G	GS	CG	SH	SV	IP	H	R	ER	HR	HB	BB	SO	RAT	ERA	ERA+	CERA	OAV	BH	AVG	PR+	WS	TPW
1912 StL-A	0	0	....	1	0	0	0	0	1^2	2	2	0	0	0	0	0	1.200	0.00	....	2.89	.286	0	....	1	0	0.1

• SPENCER, Sean Sean James Spencer b: 5/29/1975, Seattle, WA BL/TL, 5'11", 185 lbs. Deb: 5/6/1999

YEAR TM-L	W	L	PCT	G	GS	CG	SH	SV	IP	H	R	ER	HR	HB	BB	SO	RAT	ERA	ERA+	CERA	OAV	BH	AVG	PR+	WS	TPW
1999 Sea-A	0	0	....	2	0	0	0	0	1^2	5	4	4	0	0	3	2	4.800	21.60	23	25.59	.556	0	....	-3	0	-0.3
2000 Mon-N	0	0	....	8	0	0	0	0	6^2	7	4	4	2	0	3	6	1.500	5.40	89	6.38	.292	0	....	-0	0	0.0
Total 2	0	0	....	10	0	0	0	0	8^1	12	8	8	2	0	6	8	2.160	8.64	57	10.22	.364	0	....	-3	0	-0.3

• SPENCER, Stan Stanley Roger Spencer b: 8/2/1968, Vancouver, WA BR/TR, 6'4", 223 lbs. Deb: 8/27/1998

YEAR TM-L	W	L	PCT	G	GS	CG	SH	SV	IP	H	R	ER	HR	HB	BB	SO	RAT	ERA	ERA+	CERA	OAV	BH	AVG	PR+	WS	TPW
1998 SD-N	1	0	1.000	6	5	0	0	0	30^2	29	16	16	5	1	4	31	1.076	4.70	84	3.25	.244	1	.111	-3	1	-0.3
1999 SD-N	0	7	.000	9	8	0	0	0	38^1	56	44	39	11	1	11	36	1.748	9.16	46	7.78	.335	0	.000	-21	0	-2.1
2000 SD-N	2	2	.500	8	8	0	0	0	49^2	44	22	18	7	2	19	40	1.268	3.26	132	3.83	.239	4	.333	5	3	0.6
Total 3	3	9	.250	23	21	0	0	0	118^2	129	82	73	23	4	34	107	1.374	5.54	75	4.96	.274	5	.161	-19	4	-1.8

• SPICER, Bob Robert Oberton Spicer b: 4/11/1925, Richmond, VA BL/TR, 5'10", 173 lbs. Deb: 4/17/1955

YEAR TM-L	W	L	PCT	G	GS	CG	SH	SV	IP	H	R	ER	HR	HB	BB	SO	RAT	ERA	ERA+	CERA	OAV	BH	AVG	PR+	WS	TPW
1955 KC-A	0	0	....	2	0	0	0	0	2^2	9	10	10	2	1	4	2	4.875	33.75	12	37.54	.529	0	.000	-9	0	-0.9
1956 KC-A	0	0	....	2	0	0	0	0	2^1	6	5	5	1	1	1	0	3.000	19.29	22	23.80	.545	0	....	-4	0	-0.4
Total 2	0	0	....	4	0	0	0	0	5	15	15	15	3	2	5	2	4.000	27.00	16	31.13	.536	0	.000	-13	0	-1.3

• SPILLNER, Dan Daniel Ray Spillner b: 11/27/1951, Casper, WY BR/TR, 6'1", 190 lbs. Deb: 5/21/1974

YEAR TM-L	W	L	PCT	G	GS	CG	SH	SV	IP	H	R	ER	HR	HB	BB	SO	RAT	ERA	ERA+	CERA	OAV	BH	AVG	PR+	WS	TPW
1974 SD-N	9	11	.450	30	25	5	2	0	148	153	78	66	15	0	70	95	1.507	4.01	89	4.53	.267	1	.023	-3	6	-0.8
1975 SD-N	5	13	.278	37	25	3	0	1	166^2	194	93	79	14	2	63	104	1.542	4.27	81	4.75	.293	6	.133	-13	4	-1.2
1976 SD-N	2	11	.154	32	14	0	0	0	106^2	120	70	60	11	0	55	57	1.641	5.06	65	5.16	.291	1	.040	-21	0	-2.4
1977 SD-N	7	6	.538	76	0	0	0	6	123	130	61	51	12	1	60	74	1.545	3.73	95	4.63	.280	2	.118	-2	5	-0.1
1978 SD-N	1	0	1.000	17	0	0	0	0	25^2	32	15	13	2	0	7	16	1.519	4.56	73	4.91	.317	0	....	-4	0	-0.3
Cle-A	3	1	.750	36	0	0	0	3	56^1	54	26	23	2	1	21	48	1.331	3.67	102	3.26	.254	0	....	1	4	0.1
1979 Cle-A	9	5	.643	49	13	3	0	1	157^2	153	82	81	16	3	64	97	1.376	4.62	92	3.97	.256	0	....	-3	9	-0.3
1980 Cle-A	16	11	.593	34	30	7	1	0	194^1	225	122	114	23	3	74	100	1.539	5.28	77	5.09	.288	0	....	-25	7	-2.5
1981 Cle-A	4	4	.500	32	5	1	0	7	97^1	86	41	34	3	0	39	59	1.284	3.14	115	2.92	.240	0	....	9	8	0.9
1982 Cle-A	12	10	.545	65	0	0	0	21	133^2	117	44	37	9	0	45	90	1.212	2.49	164	2.85	.235	0	....	25	21	2.5
1983 Cle-A	2	9	.182	60	0	0	0	8	92^1	117	54	52	7	2	38	48	1.679	5.07	83	5.49	.315	0	....	-8	3	-0.8
1984 Cle-A	0	5	.000	14	8	0	0	1	51	70	36	32	3	0	22	23	1.804	5.65	72	5.96	.332	0	....	-9	0	-0.9
Chi-A	1	0	1.000	22	0	0	0	1	48^1	51	25	22	7	1	14	26	1.345	4.10	102	4.43	.276	0	....	0	3	0.0
Yr.	1	5	.167	36	8	0	0	2	99^1	121	61	54	10	1	36	49	1.581	4.89	84	5.21	.306	0	....	-9	3	-0.9
1985 Chi-A	4	3	.571	52	3	0	0	1	91^2	83	39	35	10	0	33	41	1.265	3.44	126	3.49	.245	0	....	9	7	0.9
Total 12	75	89	.457	556	123	19	3	50	1492^2	1585	786	699	134	13	605	878	1.467	4.21	91	4.37	.275	10	.077	-45	77	-4.9

• SPINKS, Scipio Scipio Ronald Spinks b: 7/12/1947, Chicago, IL BR/TR, 6'1", 185 lbs. Deb: 9/16/1969

YEAR TM-L	W	L	PCT	G	GS	CG	SH	SV	IP	H	R	ER	HR	HB	BB	SO	RAT	ERA	ERA+	CERA	OAV	BH	AVG	PR+	WS	TPW
1969 Hou-N	0	0	....	1	0	0	0	0	2	1	1	0	0	0	1	4	1.000	0.00	....	1.41	.143	0	....	1	0	0.1
1970 Hou-N	0	1	.000	5	2	0	0	0	13^2	17	15	15	5	0	9	6	1.902	9.88	39	8.70	.293	0	.000	-9	0	-0.9
1971 Hou-N	1	0	1.000	5	3	1	0	0	29^1	22	12	12	2	1	13	26	1.193	3.68	91	2.84	.210	2	.222	-1	1	-0.1
1972 StL-N	5	5	.500	16	16	6	0	0	118	96	39	35	5	2	59	93	1.314	2.67	127	3.11	.221	7	.167	10	10	0.9
1973 StL-N	1	5	.167	8	8	0	0	0	38^2	39	25	21	4	0	25	25	1.655	4.89	74	5.11	.269	2	.182	-5	0	-0.4
Total 5	7	11	.389	35	29	7	0	0	201^2	175	92	83	16	3	107	154	1.398	3.70	95	3.82	.234	11	.169	-5	11	-0.5

• SPLITTORFF, Paul Paul William Splittorff b: 10/8/1946, Evansville, IN BL/TL, 6'3", 210 lbs. Deb: 9/23/1970

YEAR TM-L	W	L	PCT	G	GS	CG	SH	SV	IP	H	R	ER	HR	HB	BB	SO	RAT	ERA	ERA+	CERA	OAV	BH	AVG	PR+	WS	TPW
1970 KC-A	0	1	.000	2	1	0	0	0	8^2	16	9	7	1	0	5	10	2.423	7.27	51	10.40	.390	1	.500	-3	0	-0.3
1971 KC-A	8	9	.471	22	22	6	3	0	144^1	129	49	43	4	4	35	80	1.136	2.68	128	2.59	.243	5	.104	13	10	1.2
1972 KC-A	12	12	.500	35	33	12	2	0	216	189	81	75	11	4	67	140	1.185	3.13	97	2.86	.241	16	.225	0	12	0.5
1973 KC-A	20	11	.645	38	38	12	3	0	262	279	135	116	19	5	78	110	1.363	3.98	103	3.89	.272	0	....	7	17	0.7
1974 KC-A	13	19	.406	36	36	8	1	0	226	252	122	103	23	1	75	90	1.447	4.10	93	4.42	.285	0	....	-4	9	-0.4
1975 KC-A	9	10	.474	35	23	6	3	1	159	156	75	56	10	1	56	76	1.333	3.17	121	3.45	.257	0	....	14	11	1.5
1976* KC-A	11	8	.579	26	23	5	1	0	158^2	169	79	70	11	3	59	59	1.437	3.97	88	4.22	.277	0	....	-9	6	-0.9
1977* KC-A	16	6	.727	37	37	6	2	0	229	243	104	94	11	2	83	99	1.424	3.69	109	3.98	.278	0	....	7	15	0.7
1978* KC-A	19	13	.594	39	38	13	2	0	262	244	113	99	22	3	60	76	1.160	3.40	112	3.00	.247	0	....	10	16	1.1
1979 KC-A	15	17	.469	36	35	11	0	0	240	248	137	113	25	5	77	77	1.354	4.24	101	4.06	.268	0	....	-2	12	-0.2
1980* KC-A	14	11	.560	34	33	4	0	0	204	236	101	94	17	1	43	53	1.368	4.15	98	4.16	.296	0	....	-2	11	-0.2
1981 KC-A	5	5	.500	21	15	1	0	0	99	111	48	48	12	1	23	48	1.354	4.36	83	4.26	.294	0	....	-8	4	-0.8
1982 KC-A	10	10	.500	29	28	0	0	0	162	166	83	77	14	3	57	74	1.377	4.28	95	4.02	.266	0	....	-3	7	-0.3
1983 KC-A	13	8	.619	27	27	4	0	0	156	159	77	63	9	1	52	61	1.353	3.63	112	3.62	.262	0	....	9	10	0.9
1984 KC-A	1	3	.250	12	3	0	0	0	28	47	30	24	3	0	10	4	2.036	7.71	52	8.13	.376	0	....	-12	0	-1.2
Total 15	166	143	.537	429	392	88	17	1	2554^2	2644	1243	1082	192	34	780	1057	1.340	3.81	101	3.80	.270	22	.182	18	140	2.2

• SPOLJARIC, Paul Paul Nikola Spoljaric b: 9/24/1970, Kelowna, Canada BR/TL, 6'3", 205 lbs. Deb: 4/6/1994

YEAR TM-L	W	L	PCT	G	GS	CG	SH	SV	IP	H	R	ER	HR	HB	BB	SO	RAT	ERA	ERA+	CERA	OAV	BH	AVG	PR+	WS	TPW
1994 Tor-A	0	1	.000	2	1	0	0	0	2^1	5	10	10	3	0	9	2	6.000	38.57	12	44.17	.417	0	....	-9	0	-0.8
1996 Tor-A	2	2	.500	28	0	0	0	1	38	30	17	13	6	2	19	38	1.289	3.08	163	3.84	.214	0	....	7	4	0.7
1997 Tor-A	0	3	.000	37	0	0	0	3	48	37	17	17	3	2	21	43	1.208	3.19	144	2.81	.215	0	.000	7	5	0.6
*Sea-A	0	0	....	20	0	0	0	0	22^2	24	13	12	1	1	15	27	1.721	4.76	94	5.10	.276	0	....	-0	1	0.0
Yr.	0	3	.000	57	0	0	0	3	70^2	61	30	29	4	3	36	70	1.373	3.69	123	3.55	.236	0	.000	6	6	0.6
1998 Sea-A	4	6	.400	53	6	0	0	0	83^1	85	67	60	14	1	55	89	1.680	6.48	71	5.69	.263	0	....	-16	1	-1.5
1999 Phi-N	0	3	.000	5	3	0	0	0	11^1	23	24	19	1	1	7	10	2.647	15.09	31	11.98	.426	0	.000	-13	0	-1.3
Tor-A	2	2	.500	37	2	0	0	0	62	62	41	32	9	2	32	63	1.516	4.65	106	4.83	.258	0	....	2	3	0.2
2000 KC-A	0	0	....	13	0	0	0	0	9^2	9	7	7	4	0	5	6	1.448	6.52	79	6.81	.265	0	....	-2	0	-0.2
Total 6	8	17	.320	195	12	0	0	4	277^1	275	196	170	41	9	163	278	1.579	5.52	86	5.32	.259	0	.000	-24	14	-2.3

• SPONGBERG, Carl Carl Gustav Spongberg b: 5/21/1884, Idaho Falls, ID d: 7/21/1938, Los Angeles, CA BR/TR, 6'2", 208 lbs. Deb: 8/1/1908

YEAR TM-L	W	L	PCT	G	GS	CG	SH	SV	IP	H	R	ER	HR	HB	BB	SO	RAT	ERA	ERA+	CERA	OAV	BH	AVG	PR+	WS	TPW
1908 Chi-N	0	0	....	1	0	0	0	0	7	9	7	7	1	2	6	4	2.143	9.00	26	9.33	.321	2	.667	-5	0	-0.5

• SPOONER, Karl Karl Benjamin Spooner b: 6/23/1931, Oriskany Falls, NY d: 4/10/1984, Vero Beach, FL BR/TL, 6', 185 lbs. Deb: 9/22/1954

YEAR TM-L	W	L	PCT	G	GS	CG	SH	SV	IP	H	R	ER	HR	HB	BB	SO	RAT	ERA	ERA+	CERA	OAV	BH	AVG	PR+	WS	TPW
1954 Bro-N	2	0	1.000	2	2	2	2	0	18	7	0	0	0	0	6	27	.722	0.00	....	0.76	.113	1	.167	8	4	0.8
1955* Bro-N	8	6	.571	29	14	2	1	2	98^2	79	50	40	8	5	41	78	1.216	3.65	111	3.05	.215	8	.286	4	8	0.7
Total 2	10	6	.625	31	16	4	3	2	116^2	86	50	40	8	5	47	105	1.140	3.09	132	2.70	.200	9	.265	12	12	1.5

YEAR TM-L	W	L	PCT	G	GS	CG	SH	SV	IP	H	R	ER	HR	HB	BB	SO	RAT	ERA	ERA+	CERA	OAV	BH	AVG	PR+	WS	TPW
• SPOONEYBARGER, Tim	Timothy Floyd Spooneybarger b: 10/21/1979, San Diego, CA BR/TR, 6'3", 190 lbs. Deb: 9/5/2001																									
2001 Atl-N	0	1	.000	4	0	0	0	0	4	5	1	1	0	0	2	3	1.750	2.25	196	4.53	.313	0	....	1	0	0.1
2002 Atl-N	1	0	1.000	51	0	0	0	1	51^1	38	16	15	4	2	26	33	1.247	2.63	156	2.96	.207	0	.000	7	6	0.7
2003 Fla-N	1	2	.333	33	0	0	0	0	42	27	21	19	1	1	11	32	.905	4.07	101	1.55	.190	0	.000	-0	2	0.0
Total 3	2	3	.400	88	0	0	0	1	97^1	70	38	35	5	3	39	68	1.120	3.24	127	2.42	.205	0	.000	8	8	0.8
• SPRADLIN, Jerry	Jerry Carl Spradlin b: 6/14/1967, Fullerton, CA BB/TR, 6'7", 230 lbs. Deb: 7/2/1993																									
1993 Cin-N	2	1	.667	37	0	0	0	2	49	44	20	19	4	0	9	24	1.082	3.49	115	2.67	.249	0	.000	3	4	0.3
1994 Cin-N	0	0	....	6	0	0	0	0	8	12	11	9	2	0	2	4	1.750	10.13	41	7.48	.353	0	....	-5	0	-0.5
1996 Cin-N	0	0	....	1	0	0	0	0	0^1	0	0	0	0	0	0	0	.000	0.00	....	0.00	.000	0	....	0	0	0.0
1997 Phi-N	4	8	.333	76	0	0	0	1	81^2	86	45	43	9	1	27	67	1.384	4.74	90	4.25	.274	0	.000	-4	4	-0.4
1998 Phi-N	4	4	.500	69	0	0	0	1	81^2	63	34	32	9	2	20	76	1.016	3.53	123	2.50	.216	1	1.000	7	8	0.8
1999 Cle-A	0	0	....	4	0	0	0	0	3	6	6	6	1	0	3	2	3.000	18.00	28	15.68	.400	0	....	-4	0	-0.4
SF-N	3	1	.750	59	0	0	0	0	58	59	31	27	4	10	29	52	1.517	4.19	100	4.78	.259	0	.000	0	3	0.0
2000 KC-A	4	4	.500	50	0	0	0	7	75	81	49	46	9	3	27	54	1.440	5.52	93	4.77	.283	0	....	-5	5	-0.4
Chi-N	0	1	.000	8	1	0	0	0	15	20	15	14	2	1	5	13	1.667	8.40	54	6.13	.328	0	.000	-6	0	-0.6
Total 7	17	19	.472	310	1	0	0	11	371^2	371	211	196	40	17	122	292	1.326	4.75	94	4.08	.264	1	.167	-14	24	-1.3
• SPRAGINS, Homer	Homer Franklin Spragins b: 11/9/1920, Grenada, MS d: 12/10/2002, Minter City, MS BR/TR, 6'1", 190 lbs. Deb: 9/13/1947																									
1947 Phi-N	0	0	....	4	0	0	0	0	5^1	3	4	4	0	0	3	3	1.125	6.75	59	1.65	.158	0	....	-2	0	-0.2
• SPRAGUE, Charlie	Charles Wellington Sprague b: 10/10/1864, Cleveland, OH d: 12/31/1912, Des Moines, IA BL/TL, 5'11", 150 lbs. Deb: 9/17/1887 U ♦																									
1887 Chi-N	1	0	1.000	3	3	2	0	0	22	37	16	12	1	4	13	9	1.682	4.91	91	....	.363	2	.154	-1	1	-0.2
1889 Cle-N	0	2	.000	2	2	2	0	0	17	27	31	16	0	2	10	8	2.176	8.47	48	....	.349	1	.143	-9	0	-0.8
1890 Tol-a	9	5	.643	19	12	9	0	0	122^2	111	83	53	0	18	78	59	1.541	3.89	101	....	.234	47	.236	-2	11	-0.4
Total 3	10	7	.588	24	17	13	0	0	161^2	175	130	81	1	24	101	76	1.627	4.51	89	....	.268	50	.228	-12	12	-1.4
• SPRAGUE, Ed	Edward Nelson Sprague, Sr. b: 9/16/1945, Boston, MA BR/TR, 6'4", 195 lbs. Deb: 4/10/1968																									
1968 Oak-A	3	4	.429	47	1	0	0	4	68^2	51	29	25	5	2	34	34	1.238	3.28	86	2.94	.209	0	.000	-4	3	-0.5
1969 Oak-A	1	1	.500	27	0	0	0	2	46^1	47	24	23	4	2	31	20	1.683	4.47	77	5.17	.267	1	.200	-5	1	-0.5
1971 Cin-N	1	0	1.000	7	0	0	0	0	11	8	2	0	0	0	1	7	.818	0.00	....	1.22	.195	0	.000	4	2	0.4
1972 Cin-N	3	3	.500	33	1	0	0	0	56^2	55	33	26	6	3	26	25	1.429	4.13	78	4.38	.261	0	.000	-7	1	-0.8
1973 Cin-N	1	3	.250	28	0	0	0	1	38^2	35	22	22	3	2	22	19	1.474	5.12	66	3.91	.246	0	.000	-8	0	-0.9
StL-N	0	0	....	8	0	0	0	0	8	8	2	2	1	0	4	2	1.500	2.25	162	4.85	.276	0	....	1	1	0.1
Yr.	1	3	.250	36	0	0	0	1	46^2	43	24	24	4	2	26	21	1.479	4.63	74	4.07	.251	0	.000	-7	1	-0.7
Mil-A	0	1	.000	7	0	0	0	1	9^2	13	11	10	0	2	14	3	2.793	9.31	40	8.90	.317	0	....	-6	0	-0.6
1974 Mil-A	7	2	.778	20	10	3	0	0	94	94	32	25	3	4	31	57	1.330	2.39	151	3.57	.266	0	....	12	9	1.3
1975 Mil-A	1	7	.125	18	11	0	0	1	67^1	81	46	35	5	2	40	21	1.797	4.68	82	5.84	.297	0	....	-6	1	-0.6
1976 Mil-A	0	2	.000	3	0	0	0	0	7^2	14	7	6	0	0	3	0	2.217	7.04	50	8.48	.438	0	....	-3	0	-0.3
Total 8	17	23	.425	198	23	3	0	9	408	406	208	174	27	17	206	188	1.500	3.84	89	4.34	.263	1	.045	-22	18	-2.5
• SPRING, Jack	Jack Russell Spring b: 3/11/1933, Spokane, WA BR/TL, 6'1", 180 lbs. Deb: 4/16/1955																									
1955 Phi-N	0	1	.000	2	0	0	0	0	2^2	2	2	2	2	0	1	2	1.125	6.75	59	6.51	.200	0	.000	-1	0	-0.1
1957 Bos-A	0	0	....	1	0	0	0	0	1	0	0	0	0	0	0	2	.000	0.00	....	0.00	.000	0	....	0	0	0.0
1958 Was-A	0	0	....	3	1	0	0	0	7	16	11	11	1	0	7	1	3.286	14.14	27	14.95	.457	0	.000	-8	0	-0.8
1961 LA-A	3	0	1.000	18	4	0	0	0	38	35	19	18	4	3	15	27	1.316	4.26	106	3.81	.243	0	.000	1	3	0.1
1962 LA-A	4	2	.667	57	0	0	0	6	65	66	32	29	7	2	30	31	1.477	4.02	96	4.33	.270	1	.091	-1	4	-0.1
1963 LA-A	3	0	1.000	45	0	0	0	2	38^1	40	18	13	3	0	9	13	1.278	3.05	112	3.52	.268	1	.333	2	3	0.2
1964 LA-A	1	0	1.000	6	0	0	0	0	3^1	3	1	1	1	0	3	0	1.800	2.70	122	6.91	.273	0	....	0	1	0.0
Chi-N	0	0	....	7	0	0	0	0	6	4	5	4	0	0	2	1	1.000	6.00	62	1.57	.200	0	....	-1	0	-0.2
StL-N	0	0	....	2	0	0	0	0	3	8	9	1	1	0	1	0	3.000	3.00	127	14.80	.471	0	....	0	0	0.0
Yr.	0	0	....	9	0	0	0	0	9	12	14	5	1	0	3	1	1.667	5.00	75	5.98	.324	0	....	-1	0	-0.1
1965 Cle-A	1	2	.333	14	0	0	0	0	21^2	21	9	9	2	0	10	9	1.431	3.74	93	4.01	.259	1	.333	-1	1	0.0
Total 8	12	5	.706	155	5	0	0	8	186	195	106	88	21	5	78	86	1.468	4.26	90	4.55	.274	3	.107	-7	12	-0.9
• SPRINGER, Brad	Bradford Louis Springer b: 5/9/1904, Detroit, MI d: 1/4/1970, Birmingham, MI BL/TL, 6', 155 lbs. Deb: 5/1/1925																									
1925 StL-A	0	0	....	2	0	0	0	0	3	1	2	1	0	0	7	0	2.667	3.00	156	6.55	.200	0	....	1	0	0.0
1926 Cin-N	0	0	....	1	0	0	0	0	1^1	2	3	1	0	1	2	1	3.000	6.75	55	11.79	.286	0	.000	-0	0	-0.1
Total 2	0	0	....	3	0	0	0	0	4^1	3	5	2	0	1	9	1	2.769	4.15	99	8.16	.250	0	.000	0	0	0.0
• SPRINGER, Dennis	Dennis Leroy Springer b: 2/12/1965, Fresno, CA BR/TR, 5'10", 185 lbs. Deb: 9/14/1995																									
1995 Phi-N	0	3	.000	4	4	0	0	0	22^1	21	15	12	3	1	9	15	1.343	4.84	87	4.20	.256	1	.125	-2	0	-0.2
1996 Cal-A	5	6	.455	20	15	2	1	0	94^2	91	65	58	24	6	43	64	1.415	5.51	89	5.49	.251	0	....	-6	3	-0.6
1997 Ana-A	9	9	.500	32	28	3	1	0	194^2	199	118	112	32	10	73	75	1.397	5.18	89	4.79	.267	0	.000	-13	8	-1.3
1998 TB-A	3	11	.214	29	17	1	0	0	115^2	120	77	70	21	12	60	46	1.556	5.45	88	5.94	.271	0	.000	-13	3	-1.2
1999 Fla-N	6	16	.273	38	29	3	2	1	196^1	231	121	106	23	7	64	83	1.503	4.86	90	5.14	.303	6	.120	-10	6	-1.2
2000 NY-N	0	1	.000	2	2	0	0	0	11^1	20	11	11	2	1	5	5	2.206	8.74	50	10.14	.377	0	.000	-5	0	-0.6
2001 LA-N	1	1	.500	4	3	0	0	0	19	19	7	7	3	3	2	7	1.105	3.32	121	4.19	.275	0	.000	2	1	0.1
2002 LA-N	0	1	.000	1	0	0	0	0	1^1	1	1	1	0	0	2	1	2.250	6.75	57	5.91	.200	0	....	-0	0	0.0
Total 8	24	48	.333	130	98	9	4	1	655^1	702	415	377	108	40	258	296	1.465	5.18	88	5.26	.278	7	.097	-49	21	-5.0
• SPRINGER, Ed	Edward H. Springer b: 2/9/1861, CA d: 4/24/1926, Los Angeles, CA, 6'2", 187 lbs. Deb: 7/12/1889																									
1889 Lou-a	0	1	.000	1	1	1	0	0	5	8	8	5	0	2	2	1	2.000	9.00	43	....	.351	0	.000	-3	0	-0.3
• SPRINGER, Russ	Russell Paul Springer b: 11/7/1968, Alexandria, LA BR/TR, 6'4", 195 lbs. Deb: 4/17/1992																									
1992 NY-A	0	0	....	14	0	0	0	0	16	18	11	11	0	1	10	12	1.750	6.19	63	5.15	.281	0	....	-4	0	-0.4
1993 Cal-A	1	6	.143	14	9	1	0	0	60	73	48	48	11	3	32	31	1.750	7.20	63	6.87	.303	0	....	-19	0	-1.8
1994 Cal-A	2	2	.500	18	5	0	0	2	45^2	53	28	28	9	0	14	28	1.467	5.52	88	5.38	.291	0	....	-3	3	-0.3
1995 Cal-A	1	2	.333	19	6	0	0	1	51^2	60	37	35	11	5	25	38	1.645	6.10	77	6.69	.290	0	....	-8	1	-0.8
Phi-N	0	0	....	14	0	0	0	0	26^2	22	11	11	5	2	10	32	1.200	3.71	114	3.73	.227	0	.000	1	2	0.1
1996 Phi-N	3	10	.231	51	7	0	0	0	96^2	106	60	50	12	1	38	94	1.490	4.66	93	4.57	.272	1	.059	-4	3	-0.5
1997* Hou-N	3	3	.500	54	0	0	0	3	55^1	48	28	26	4	4	27	74	1.355	4.23	95	3.69	.232	0	.000	-2	3	-0.2
1998 Ari-N	4	3	.571	26	0	0	0	0	32^2	29	16	15	4	1	14	37	1.316	4.13	102	3.77	.232	0	.000	0	2	0.0
Atl-N	1	1	.500	22	0	0	0	0	20	22	10	9	0	0	16	19	1.900	4.05	103	5.36	.301	0	....	0	1	0.0
Yr.	5	4	.556	48	0	0	0	0	52^2	51	26	24	4	1	30	56	1.538	4.10	102	4.37	.258	0	.000	0	3	0.0
1999* Atl-N	2	1	.667	49	0	0	0	1	47^1	31	20	18	5	2	22	49	1.120	3.42	131	2.63	.185	0	....	6	5	0.6
2000 Ari-N	2	4	.333	52	0	0	0	0	62	63	36	35	11	2	34	59	1.565	5.08	93	5.25	.261	1	.200	-2	3	-0.2
2001 Ari-N	0	0	....	18	0	0	0	1	17^2	20	16	14	5	0	4	12	1.358	7.13	64	5.13	.274	0	....	-5	0	-0.5
2003 StL-N	1	1	.500	17	0	0	0	0	17^1	19	16	16	8	1	6	11	1.442	8.31	49	7.27	.271	0	.000	-8	0	-0.8
Total 11	20	33	.377	368	27	1	0	8	549	564	337	316	85	22	252	496	1.486	5.18	85	4.97	.264	2	.077	-49	23	-4.9
• SPROULL, Charlie	Charles William Sproull b: 1/9/1919, Taylorsville, GA d: 1/13/1980, Rockford, IL BR/TR, 6'3", 185 lbs. Deb: 4/19/1945																									
1945 Phi-N	4	10	.286	34	19	2	0	1	130^1	158	102	86	10	0	80	47	1.826	5.94	64	5.75	.298	5	.143	-27	0	-2.8
• SPROUT, Bob	Robert Samuel Sprout b: 12/5/1941, Florin, PA BL/TL, 6', 165 lbs. Deb: 9/27/1961																									
1961 LA-A	0	0	....	1	1	0	0	0	4	4	3	2	0	0	3	2	1.750	4.50	100	4.82	.267	0	....	0	0	0.0
• SPROWL, Bobby	Robert John Sprowl b: 4/14/1956, Sandusky, OH BL/TL, 6'2", 190 lbs. Deb: 9/5/1978																									
1978 Bos-A	0	2	.000	3	3	0	0	0	12^2	12	10	9	3	0	10	10	1.737	6.39	64	6.42	.245	0	....	-3	0	-0.3
1979 Hou-N	0	0	....	3	0	0	0	0	4	1	0	0	0	0	2	3	.750	0.00	....	0.81	.083	0	....	2	1	0.2
1980 Hou-N	0	0	....	1	0	0	0	0	1	1	0	0	0	0	1	3	2.000	0.00	....	5.48	.250	0	....	0	0	0.0

YEAR TM-L	W	L	PCT	G	GS	CG	SH	SV	IP	H	R	ER	HR	HB	BB	SO	RAT	ERA	ERA+	CERA	OAV	BH	AVG	PR+	WS	TPW
1981 Hou-N	0	1	.000	15	1	0	0	0	28^2	40	20	19	1	0	14	18	1.884	5.97	55	6.12	.333	1	.167	-9	0	-0.9
Total 4	0	3	.000	22	4	0	0	0	46^1	54	30	28	4	0	27	34	1.748	5.44	65	5.73	.292	1	.167	-10	1	-1.1
• SPURGEON, Jay	Jay Aaron Spurgeon b: 7/5/1976, West Covina, CA BR/TR, 6'6", 211 lbs. Deb: 8/15/2000																									
2000 Bal-A	1	1	.500	7	4	0	0	0	24	26	16	16	5	2	15	11	1.708	6.00	79	6.88	.283	0	....	-3	1	-0.3
• SPURLING, Chris	Christopher Michael Spurling b: 6/28/1977, Dayton, OH BR/TR, 6'6", 228 lbs. Deb: 4/2/2003																									
2003 Det-A	1	3	.250	66	0	0	0	3	77	78	42	40	9	3	22	38	1.299	4.68	92	3.97	.266	0	....	-3	4	-0.3
• ST. CLAIRE, Randy	Randy Anthony St. Claire b: 8/23/1960, Glens Falls, NY BR/TR, 6'3", 190 lbs. Deb: 9/11/1984																									
1984 Mon-N	0	0	....	4	0	0	0	0	8	11	4	4	0	1	2	4	1.625	4.50	76	5.00	.344	0	....	-1	0	-0.1
1985 Mon-N	5	3	.625	42	0	0	0	0	68^2	69	32	30	3	1	26	25	1.383	3.93	86	3.53	.265	1	.200	-5	3	-0.4
1986 Mon-N	2	0	1.000	11	0	0	0	1	19	13	5	5	2	0	6	21	1.000	2.37	156	2.07	.186	0	.000	3	3	0.3
1987 Mon-N	3	3	.500	44	0	0	0	7	67	64	31	30	9	1	20	43	1.254	4.03	104	3.61	.249	2	.333	2	6	0.3
1988 Mon-N	0	0	....	6	0	0	0	0	7^1	11	5	5	2	0	5	6	2.182	6.14	59	9.47	.344	0	....	-2	0	-0.2
Cin-N	1	0	1.000	10	0	0	0	0	13^2	13	8	4	3	0	5	8	1.317	2.63	136	4.09	.241	0	.000	1	1	0.1
Yr.	1	0	1.000	16	0	0	0	0	21	24	13	9	5	0	10	14	1.619	3.86	93	5.97	.279	0	.000	-1	1	-0.1
1989 Min-A	1	0	1.000	14	0	0	0	1	22^1	19	13	13	4	2	10	14	1.299	5.24	79	4.10	.226	0	....	-3	1	-0.3
1991* Atl-N	0	0	....	19	0	0	0	0	28^2	31	17	13	4	0	9	30	1.395	4.08	95	4.32	.282	1	.500	-1	1	0.0
1992 Atl-N	0	0	....	10	0	0	0	0	15^1	17	11	10	1	0	8	7	1.630	5.87	62	4.67	.283	0	....	-4	0	-0.4
1994 Tor-A	0	0	....	2	0	0	0	0	2	4	4	2	0	0	2	2	3.000	9.00	54	10.75	.444	0	....	-1	0	-0.1
Total 9	12	6	.667	162	0	0	0	9	252	252	130	116	28	5	93	160	1.369	4.14	91	3.96	.260	4	.267	-10	15	-0.9
• ST. VRAIN, Jim	James Marcellin St. Vrain b: 6/6/1883, Ralls County, MO d: 6/12/1937, Butte, MT BR/TL, 5'9", 175 lbs. Deb: 4/20/1902																									
1902 Chi-N	4	6	.400	12	11	10	1	0	95	88	36	22	0	5	25	51	1.189	2.08	129	2.64	.246	3	.097	6	6	0.5
• STABLEIN, George	George Charles Stablein b: 10/29/1957, Inglewood, CA BR/TR, 6'4", 185 lbs. Deb: 9/20/1980																									
1980 SD-N	0	1	.000	4	2	0	0	0	11^2	16	4	4	0	0	3	4	1.629	3.09	111	5.06	.340	0	.000	0	1	0.0
• STACK, Eddie	William Edward Stack b: 10/24/1887, Chicago, IL d: 8/28/1958, Chicago, IL BR/TR, 6', 175 lbs. Deb: 6/7/1910 U																									
1910 Phi-N	6	7	.462	20	16	8	1	0	117	115	61	52	7	4	34	48	1.274	4.00	78	3.54	.266	3	.083	-12	3	-1.6
1911 Phi-N	5	5	.500	13	10	5	0	0	77^2	67	48	31	3	6	41	36	1.391	3.59	95	3.59	.234	2	.083	-1	3	-0.3
1912 Bro-N	7	5	.583	28	17	4	0	1	142	139	80	53	3	9	55	45	1.366	3.36	99	3.54	.264	7	.135	2	6	-0.1
1913 Bro-N	4	4	.500	23	9	4	1	0	87	79	30	23	0	1	32	34	1.276	2.38	138	2.84	.250	4	.160	8	7	0.7
Chi-N	4	2	.667	11	7	3	1	1	51	56	29	24	1	2	15	28	1.392	4.24	75	3.72	.280	1	.063	-6	2	-0.8
Yr.	8	6	.571	34	16	7	2	1	138	135	59	47	1	3	47	62	1.319	3.07	105	3.17	.262	5	.122	1	9	-0.1
1914 Chi-N	0	1	.000	7	1	0	0	0	16^1	13	11	9	0	0	11	9	1.469	4.96	56	3.12	.220	0	.000	-4	0	-0.4
Total 5	26	24	.520	102	60	24	3	2	491	469	259	192	14	22	188	200	1.338	3.52	92	3.43	.258	17	.108	-15	21	-2.5
• STAFFORD, Bill	William Charles Stafford b: 8/13/1939, Catskill, NY d: 9/19/2001, Wayne, MI BR/TR, 6'1", 193 lbs. Deb: 4/17/1960																									
1960* NY-A	3	1	.750	11	8	2	1	0	60	50	17	15	3	1	18	36	1.133	2.25	159	2.55	.226	1	.045	7	5	0.5
1961* NY-A	14	9	.609	36	25	8	3	2	195	168	65	58	13	5	59	101	1.164	2.68	139	2.84	.232	12	.179	16	17	1.8
1962* NY-A	14	9	.609	35	33	7	2	0	213^1	188	95	87	23	4	77	109	1.242	3.67	102	3.33	.233	17	.218	-0	12	0.2
1963 NY-A	4	8	.333	28	14	0	0	3	89^2	104	64	60	16	3	42	52	1.628	6.02	58	5.91	.287	7	.292	-27	1	-2.5
1964 NY-A	5	0	1.000	31	1	0	0	4	60^2	50	19	18	4	2	22	39	1.187	2.67	136	2.79	.231	1	.077	6	6	0.6
1965 NY-A	3	8	.273	22	15	1	0	0	111^1	93	45	44	16	2	31	71	1.114	3.56	96	3.05	.229	0	.000	-1	5	-0.5
1966 KC-A	0	4	.000	9	8	0	0	0	39^2	42	28	22	2	2	12	31	1.361	4.99	68	3.75	.273	0	.000	-7	0	-0.9
1967 KC-A	0	1	.000	14	0	0	0	0	16	12	4	3	0	0	9	10	1.313	1.69	189	2.49	.214	0	.000	3	1	0.3
Total 8	43	40	.518	186	104	18	6	9	785^2	707	337	307	77	19	270	449	1.244	3.52	102	3.37	.240	38	.155	-3	47	-0.6
• STAFFORD, General	James Joseph "Jamsey" Stafford b: 7/9/1868, Webster, MA d: 9/18/1923, Worcester, MA BR/TR, 5'8", 165 lbs. Deb: 8/27/1890 ♦																									
1890 Buf-P	3	9	.250	12	12	11	0	0	98	123	89	56	8	1	43	21	1.694	5.14	80	....	.294	7	.143	-10	2	-1.1
• STALEY, Gerry	Gerald Lee Staley b: 8/21/1920, Brush Prairie, WA BR/TR, 6', 195 lbs. Deb: 4/20/1947																									
1947 StL-N	1	0	1.000	18	1	1	0	0	29^1	33	11	9	2	1	8	14	1.398	2.76	150	4.15	.287	0	.000	4	2	0.4
1948 StL-N	4	4	.500	31	3	0	0	0	52	61	44	40	5	0	21	23	1.577	6.92	59	4.85	.288	2	.222	-16	0	-1.5
1949 StL-N	10	10	.500	45	17	5	2	6	171^1	154	65	52	7	3	41	55	1.138	2.73	152	**2.56**	**.238**	5	.122	26	17	2.6
1950 StL-N	13	13	.500	42	22	7	1	3	169^2	201	101	94	14	7	61	62	1.544	4.99	86	5.01	.300	8	.145	-12	7	-1.3
1951 StL-N	19	13	.594	42	30	10	4	3	227	244	108	96	14	8	74	67	1.401	3.81	104	4.02	.275	13	.160	1	15	-0.1
1952 StL-N★	17	14	.548	35	33	15	0	0	239^2	238	101	87	21	7	52	93	1.210	3.27	114	3.31	.256	13	.153	11	15	1.0
1953 StL-N★	18	9	.667	40	32	10	1	4	230	243	118	102	31	17	54	88	1.291	3.99	107	4.22	.269	8	.103	10	15	0.5
1954 StL-N	7	13	.350	48	20	3	1	2	155^2	198	107	91	21	6	47	50	1.574	5.26	78	5.51	.308	5	.139	-19	2	-1.9
1955 Cin-N	5	8	.385	30	18	2	0	0	119^2	146	72	62	22	3	28	40	1.454	4.66	91	5.40	.309	2	.056	-6	4	-0.9
NY-A	0	0	....	2	0	0	0	0	2	5	5	3	1	0	1	0	3.000	13.50	28	17.28	.417	0	....	-2	0	-0.2
1956 NY-A	0	0	....	1	0	0	0	0	0^1	4	4	4	0	0	0	1	12.00	108.00	4	95.94	.800	0	.000	-4	0	-0.4
Chi-A	8	3	.727	26	10	5	0	0	101^2	98	37	33	11	6	20	25	1.161	2.92	140	3.34	.251	3	.094	13	9	1.0
Yr.	8	3	.727	27	10	5	0	0	102	102	41	37	11	6	20	26	1.196	3.26	125	3.64	.258	3	.091	9	9	0.6
1957 Chi-A	5	1	.833	47	0	0	0	7	105	95	27	24	7	0	27	44	1.162	2.06	182	2.73	.244	1	.045	17	12	1.7
1958 Chi-A	4	5	.444	50	0	0	0	8	85^1	81	36	30	10	0	24	27	1.230	3.16	115	3.46	.259	0	.000	3	7	0.2
1959* Chi-A	8	5	.615	**67**	0	0	0	14	116^1	111	39	29	5	0	25	54	1.169	2.24	167	2.68	.259	2	.154	17	16	1.8
1960 Chi-A★	13	8	.619	64	0	0	0	10	115^1	94	40	31	8	3	25	52	1.032	2.42	156	2.25	.227	4	.235	16	14	1.7
1961 Chi-A	0	3	.000	16	0	0	0	0	18	17	10	10	3	0	5	8	1.222	5.00	78	3.63	.246	0	....	-2	0	-0.2
KC-A	1	1	.500	23	0	0	0	2	30	32	15	12	4	2	10	16	1.400	3.60	114	4.61	.278	0	.000	2	2	0.2
Det-A	1	1	.500	13	0	0	0	2	13^1	15	6	5	1	0	6	8	1.575	3.38	122	4.64	.288	0	.000	1	1	0.1
Yr.	2	5	.286	52	0	0	0	4	61^1	64	31	27	8	2	21	32	1.386	3.96	102	4.33	.271	0	.000	1	3	0.1
Total 15	134	111	.547	640	186	58	9	61	1981^2	2070	946	814	187	63	529	727	1.312	3.70	109	3.87	.270	66	.126	61	138	4.6
• STALEY, Harry	Henry Eli Staley b: 11/3/1866, Jacksonville, IL d: 1/12/1910, Battle Creek, MI BR/TR, 5'10", 175 lbs. Deb: 6/23/1888 U																									
1888 Pit-N	12	12	.500	25	24	24	2	0	207^1	185	104	62	6	7	53	89	1.148	2.69	98	....	.230	11	.129	0	12	-0.3
1889 Pit-N	21	26	.447	49	47	46	1	1	420	433	254	164	11	8	116	159	1.307	3.51	107	....	.258	30	.161	10	22	0.4
1890 Pit-P	21	25	.457	46	46	44	3	0	387^2	392	246	139	5	11	74	145	1.202	3.23	121	....	.251	34	.207	40	27	3.3
1891 Pit-N	4	5	.444	9	7	6	0	0	71^2	77	49	23	4	2	11	25	1.228	2.89	113	....	.264	7	.226	4	4	0.4
Bos-N	20	8	.714	31	30	26	1	0	252^1	236	111	70	11	4	69	114	1.209	2.50	146	....	.238	17	.167	33	25	2.8
Yr.	24	13	.649	40	37	32	1	0	324	313	160	93	15	6	80	139	1.213	2.58	137	....	.244	24	.180	36	29	3.3
1892* Bos-N	22	10	.688	37	35	31	3	0	299^2	273	144	101	10	3	97	93	1.235	3.03	116	2.84	.233	16	.131	7	29	0.1
1893 Bos-N	18	10	.643	36	31	23	0	0	263	344	224	150	22	6	81	61	1.616	5.13	96	5.62	.307	30	.265	-9	15	-0.5
1894 Bos-N	12	10	.545	27	21	18	0	0	208^2	305	204	158	15	5	61	32	1.754	6.81	87	6.36	.337	20	.235	-27	12	-2.1
1895 StL-N	6	13	.316	23	16	13	0	0	158^2	223	136	92	8	2	39	28	1.651	5.22	93	5.57	.327	9	.134	-2	6	-0.7
Total 8	136	119	.533	283	257	231	10	1	2269	2468	1472	959	92	48	601	746	1.353	3.80	108	2.00	.268	174	.182	55	152	3.6
• STALLARD, Tracy	Evan Tracy Stallard b: 8/31/1937, Coeburn, VA BR/TR, 6'5", 205 lbs. Deb: 9/24/1960																									
1960 Bos-A	0	0	....	4	0	0	0	0	4	0	0	0	0	0	2	6	.500	0.00	....	0.25	.000	0	....	2	1	0.2
1961 Bos-A	2	7	.222	43	14	1	0	2	132^2	110	75	72	15	1	96	109	1.553	4.88	85	4.53	.229	3	.083	-10	4	-1.3
1962 Bos-A	0	0	....	1	0	0	0	0	1	0	0	0	0	0	0	0	.000	0.00	....	0.00	.000	0	....	0	0	0.0
1963 NY-N	6	17	.261	39	23	5	0	1	154^2	156	89	81	23	1	77	110	1.506	4.71	74	4.83	.262	3	.063	-19	3	-2.4
1964 NY-N	10	20	.333	36	34	11	2	0	225^2	213	111	95	20	6	73	118	1.267	3.79	94	3.50	.252	15	.190	-7	8	-0.5
1965 StL-N	11	8	.579	40	26	4	1	0	194^1	172	83	73	25	6	70	99	1.245	3.38	114	3.53	.235	6	.088	9	12	0.6
1966 StL-N	1	5	.167	20	7	0	0	1	52^1	65	40	33	9	2	25	35	1.720	5.68	63	6.41	.305	0	.000	-13	0	-1.5
Total 7	30	57	.345	183	104	21	3	4	764^2	716	398	354	92	16	343	477	1.385	4.17	89	4.13	.250	27	.110	-38	28	-4.9

YEAR TM-L	W	L	PCT	G	GS	CG	SH	SV	IP	H	R	ER	HR	HB	BB	SO	RAT	ERA	ERA+	CERA	OAV	BH	AVG	PR+	WS	TPW
• STANCEU, Charley	Charles Stanceu b: 1/9/1916, Canton, OH d: 4/3/1969, Canton, OH BR/TR, 6'2", 190 lbs. Deb: 4/16/1941																									
1941 NY-A	3	3	.500	22	2	0	0	0	48	58	41	30	3	1	35	21	1.938	5.63	70	5.96	.296	0	.000	-11	0	-1.2
1946 NY-A	0	0	....	3	0	0	0	0	4	6	4	4	0	0	5	3	2.750	9.00	38	8.80	.316	0	....	-3	0	-0.3
Phi-N	2	4	.333	14	11	1	0	0	70^1	71	35	33	4	0	39	23	1.564	4.22	81	4.37	.270	0	.000	-6	2	-0.8
Total 2	**5**	**7**	**.417**	**39**	**13**	**1**	**0**	**0**	**122^1**	**135**	**80**	**67**	**7**	**1**	**79**	**47**	**1.749**	**4.93**	**74**	**5.14**	**.282**	**0**	**.000**	**-19**	**2**	**-2.3**
• STANDRIDGE, Jason	Jason Wayne Standridge b: 11/9/1978, Birmingham, AL BR/TR, 6'4", 205 lbs. Deb: 7/29/2001																									
2001 TB-A	0	0	....	9	1	0	0	0	19^1	19	10	10	5	0	14	9	1.707	4.66	96	6.63	.260	0	....	-0	1	0.0
2002 TB-A	0	0	....	1	0	0	0	0	3	7	3	3	1	0	4	1	3.667	9.00	50	22.36	.500	0	....	-2	0	-0.2
2003 TB-A	0	5	.000	8	7	1	0	0	35^1	38	25	25	7	1	16	20	1.528	6.37	71	5.60	.275	0	....	-8	0	-0.8
Total 3	**0**	**5**	**.000**	**18**	**8**	**1**	**0**	**0**	**57^2**	**64**	**38**	**38**	**13**	**1**	**34**	**30**	**1.699**	**5.93**	**76**	**6.82**	**.284**	**0**	**....**	**-10**	**1**	**-1.0**
• STANDRIDGE, Pete	Alfred Peter Standridge b: 4/25/1891, Black Diamond, WA d: 8/2/1963, San Francisco, CA BR/TR, 5'10.5", 165 lbs. Deb: 9/19/1911																									
1911 StL-N	0	0	....	2	0	0	0	0	4^2	10	10	5	0	1	4	3	3.000	9.64	35	13.43	.435	0	.000	-3	0	-0.3
1915 Chi-N	4	1	.800	29	3	2	0	0	112^1	120	56	45	2	2	36	42	1.389	3.61	77	3.50	.274	9	.225	-9	5	-0.7
Total 2	**4**	**1**	**.800**	**31**	**3**	**2**	**0**	**0**	**117**	**130**	**66**	**50**	**2**	**3**	**40**	**45**	**1.453**	**3.85**	**73**	**3.89**	**.282**	**9**	**.220**	**-12**	**5**	**-1.1**
• STANEK, Al	Albert Wilfred "Lefty" Stanek b: 12/24/1943, Springfield, MA BL/TL, 5'11.5", 190 lbs. Deb: 4/26/1963																									
1963 SF-N	0	0	....	11	0	0	0	0	13^1	10	7	7	1	0	12	5	1.650	4.73	68	4.12	.217	0	.000	-2	0	-0.2
• STANFIELD, Kevin	Kevin Bruce Stanfield b: 12/19/1955, Huron, SD BL/TL, 6', 190 lbs. Deb: 9/14/1979																									
1979 Min-A	0	0	....	3	0	0	0	0	3	2	2	2	0	0	0	0	.667	6.00	73	1.01	.200	0	....	-1	0	-0.1
• STANFORD, Jason	Jason John Stanford b: 1/23/1977, Tucson, AZ BL/TL, 6'2", 200 lbs. Deb: 7/6/2003																									
2003 Cle-A	1	3	.250	13	8	0	0	0	50	48	20	20	5	1	16	30	1.280	3.60	123	3.55	.246	0	....	4	3	0.3
• STANGE, Lee	Albert Lee Stange b: 10/27/1936, Chicago, IL BR/TR, 5'10", 170 lbs. Deb: 4/15/1961 C																									
1961 Min-A	1	0	1.000	7	0	0	0	0	12^1	15	6	4	1	0	10	10	2.027	2.92	145	6.69	.294	0	.000	2	1	0.2
1962 Min-A	4	3	.571	44	6	1	0	3	95	98	57	47	14	1	39	70	1.442	4.45	92	4.64	.271	1	.059	-4	4	-0.5
1963 Min-A	12	5	.706	32	20	7	2	0	164^2	145	53	48	21	0	43	100	1.142	2.62	139	3.05	.233	5	.096	19	12	1.8
1964 Min-A	3	6	.333	14	11	2	0	0	79^2	78	45	42	13	0	19	54	1.218	4.74	75	3.69	.255	1	.040	-9	1	-1.1
Cle-A	4	8	.333	23	14	0	0	0	91^2	98	47	42	14	1	31	78	1.407	4.12	87	4.51	.270	2	.080	-3	3	-0.4
Yr.	7	14	.333	37	25	2	0	0	171^1	176	92	84	27	1	50	132	1.319	4.41	81	4.13	.263	3	.060	-12	4	-1.5
1965 Cle-A	8	4	.667	41	12	4	2	0	132	122	50	49	13	1	26	80	1.121	3.34	104	2.87	.247	3	.107	2	9	0.4
1966 Cle-A	1	0	1.000	8	2	1	0	0	16	17	5	5	1	1	3	8	1.250	2.81	122	3.68	.279	1	.250	1	1	0.2
Bos-A	7	9	.438	28	19	8	2	0	153^1	140	65	57	17	1	43	77	1.193	3.35	114	3.15	.246	3	.063	9	9	0.6
Yr.	8	9	.471	36	21	9	2	0	169^1	157	70	62	18	2	46	85	1.199	3.30	114	3.20	.249	4	.077	10	10	0.8
1967* Bos-A	8	10	.444	35	24	6	2	1	181^2	171	64	56	14	2	32	101	1.117	2.77	126	2.76	.246	3	.061	15	13	1.4
1968 Bos-A	5	5	.500	50	2	1	0	12	103	89	54	45	10	1	25	53	1.107	3.93	80	2.70	.237	2	.133	-8	6	-0.9
1969 Bos-A	6	9	.400	41	15	2	0	3	137	137	70	56	14	6	56	59	1.409	3.68	103	4.15	.256	3	.086	5	7	0.3
1970 Bos-A	2	2	.500	20	0	0	0	2	27^1	34	24	17	5	2	12	14	1.683	5.60	71	6.19	.301	0	.000	-4	0	-0.5
Chi-A	1	0	1.000	16	0	0	0	0	22^1	28	13	13	5	0	5	14	1.478	5.24	74	5.46	.295	0	.000	-3	1	-0.3
Yr.	3	2	.600	36	0	0	0	2	49^2	62	37	30	10	2	17	28	1.591	5.44	72	5.86	.298	0	.000	-7	1	-0.8
Total 10	**62**	**61**	**.504**	**359**	**125**	**32**	**8**	**21**	**1216**	**1172**	**553**	**481**	**142**	**16**	**344**	**718**	**1.247**	**3.56**	**102**	**3.53**	**.252**	**24**	**.079**	**21**	**67**	**1.2**
• STANHOUSE, Don	Donald Joseph Stanhouse b: 2/12/1951, DuQuoin, IL BR/TR, 6'2.5", 195 lbs. Deb: 4/19/1972																									
1972 Tex-A	2	9	.182	24	16	1	0	0	104^2	83	48	44	8	1	73	78	1.490	3.78	80	3.88	.223	4	.129	-7	2	-0.8
1973 Tex-A	1	7	.125	21	5	1	0	1	70	70	41	37	5	2	44	42	1.629	4.76	78	4.83	.262	0	....	-6	1	-0.6
1974 Tex-A	1	1	.500	18	0	0	0	0	31^1	38	20	17	4	2	17	26	1.755	4.88	73	6.39	.302	0	....	-5	0	-0.5
1975 Mon-N	0	0	....	4	3	0	0	0	13	19	12	12	1	0	11	5	2.308	8.31	46	8.34	.345	1	.333	-6	0	-0.7
1976 Mon-N	9	12	.429	34	26	8	1	1	184	182	84	77	7	4	92	79	1.489	3.77	99	3.98	.263	11	.212	-1	11	0.2
1977 Mon-N	10	10	.500	47	16	1	1	10	158^1	147	72	60	12	4	84	89	1.459	3.41	112	4.05	.251	9	.191	6	12	0.8
1978 Bal-A	6	9	.400	56	0	0	0	24	74^2	60	28	24	0	0	52	42	1.500	2.89	121	3.28	.230	0	....	4	10	0.4
1979* Bal-A★	7	3	.700	52	0	0	0	21	72^2	49	24	23	4	1	51	34	1.376	2.85	141	3.10	.202	0	....	8	13	0.8
1980 LA-N	2	2	.500	21	0	0	0	7	25	30	14	14	4	0	16	5	1.840	5.04	69	6.60	.306	0	.000	-5	0	-0.5
1982 Bal-A	0	1	.000	17	0	0	0	0	26^2	29	16	16	3	2	15	8	1.650	5.40	75	5.49	.276	0	....	-4	0	-0.4
Total 10	**38**	**54**	**.413**	**294**	**66**	**11**	**2**	**64**	**760^1**	**707**	**359**	**324**	**48**	**16**	**455**	**408**	**1.528**	**3.84**	**94**	**4.22**	**.252**	**25**	**.185**	**-15**	**49**	**-1.3**
• STANIFER, Rob	Robert Wayne Stanifer b: 3/10/1972, Easley, SC BR/TR, 6'3", 205 lbs. Deb: 5/3/1997																									
1997 Fla-N	1	2	.333	36	0	0	0	1	45	43	23	23	9	3	16	28	1.311	4.60	88	4.76	.261	2	.667	-3	3	-0.2
1998 Fla-N	2	4	.333	38	0	0	0	1	48	54	33	30	5	0	22	30	1.583	5.63	73	4.89	.277	0	.000	-8	1	-0.8
2000 Bos-A	0	0	....	8	0	0	0	0	13	22	19	11	3	0	4	3	2.000	7.62	66	8.60	.355	0	....	-4	0	-0.3
Total 3	**3**	**6**	**.333**	**82**	**0**	**0**	**0**	**2**	**106**	**119**	**75**	**64**	**17**	**3**	**42**	**61**	**1.519**	**5.43**	**77**	**5.29**	**.282**	**2**	**.250**	**-15**	**4**	**-1.3**
• STANKA, Joe	Joe Donald Stanka b: 7/23/1931, Hammon, OK BR/TR, 6'5", 201 lbs. Deb: 9/2/1959																									
1959 Chi-A	1	0	1.000	2	0	0	0	0	5^1	2	2	2	1	0	4	3	1.125	3.38	111	2.37	.111	1	.333	0	1	0.0
• STANLEY, Bob	Robert William Stanley b: 11/10/1954, Portland, ME BR/TR, 6'4", 215 lbs. Deb: 4/16/1977																									
1977 Bos-A	8	7	.533	41	13	3	1	3	151	176	74	67	10	3	43	44	1.450	3.99	112	4.40	.294	0	....	11	11	1.0
1978 Bos-A	15	2	.882	52	3	0	0	10	141^2	142	50	41	5	1	34	38	1.242	2.60	158	3.09	.266	0	....	23	17	2.3
1979 Bos-A★	16	12	.571	40	30	9	4	1	216^2	250	110	96	14	4	44	56	1.357	3.99	111	4.02	.294	0	....	12	15	1.2
1980 Bos-A	10	8	.556	52	17	5	1	14	175	186	75	66	11	7	52	71	1.360	3.39	124	3.94	.278	0	....	16	15	1.6
1981 Bos-A	10	8	.556	35	1	0	0	0	98^2	110	46	42	3	6	38	28	1.500	3.83	101	4.42	.294	0	....	2	6	0.2
1982 Bos-A	12	7	.632	48	0	0	0	14	168^1	161	60	58	11	4	50	83	1.253	3.10	**139**	3.31	.255	0	....	26	20	2.6
1983 Bos-A★	8	10	.444	64	0	0	0	33	145^1	145	56	46	7	3	38	65	1.259	2.85	153	3.18	.266	0	....	25	21	2.5
1984 Bos-A	9	10	.474	57	0	0	0	22	106^2	113	57	42	9	2	23	52	1.275	3.54	118	3.46	.267	0	....	11	12	1.1
1985 Bos-A	6	6	.500	48	0	0	0	10	87^2	76	30	28	7	2	30	46	1.209	2.87	149	2.96	.237	0	....	15	10	1.5
1986* Bos-A	6	6	.500	66	1	0	0	16	82^1	109	48	40	9	0	22	54	1.591	4.37	95	5.37	.322	0	....	-1	6	-0.1
1987 Bos-A	4	15	.211	34	20	4	1	0	152^2	198	96	85	17	1	42	67	1.572	5.01	91	5.38	.321	0	....	-7	5	-0.7
1988* Bos-A	6	4	.600	57	0	0	0	5	101^2	90	41	36	6	7	29	57	1.170	3.19	129	2.94	.242	0	....	12	9	1.2
1989 Bos-A	5	2	.714	43	0	0	0	4	79^1	102	54	43	4	1	26	32	1.613	4.88	84	5.10	.321	0	....	-6	2	-0.6
Total 13	**115**	**97**	**.542**	**637**	**85**	**21**	**7**	**132**	**1707**	**1858**	**797**	**690**	**113**	**41**	**471**	**693**	**1.364**	**3.64**	**118**	**3.93**	**.282**	**0**	**....**	**137**	**149**	**13.8**
• STANLEY, Buck	John Leonard Stanley b: 11/13/1889, Washington, DC d: 8/13/1940, Norfolk, VA BL/TL, 5'10", 160 lbs. Deb: 9/12/1911																									
1911 Phi-N	0	0	....	4	0	0	0	0	11^1	14	11	8	0	0	9	5	2.029	6.35	54	6.43	.326	0	.000	-4	0	-0.4
• STANTON, Mike	Michael Thomas Stanton b: 9/25/1952, Phenix City, AL BB/TR, 6'2", 205 lbs. Deb: 7/9/1975																									
1975 Hou-N	0	2	.000	7	2	0	0	1	17^1	20	14	14	1	0	20	16	2.308	7.27	46	7.84	.290	1	.250	-8	0	-0.8
1980 Cle-A	1	3	.250	51	0	0	0	5	85^2	98	58	52	5	3	44	74	1.658	5.46	74	5.27	.297	0	....	-13	2	-1.3
1981 Cle-A	3	3	.500	24	0	0	0	2	43^1	43	21	21	4	0	18	34	1.408	4.36	83	3.94	.262	0	....	-2	2	-0.2
1982 Sea-A	2	4	.333	56	1	0	0	7	71^1	70	37	33	5	0	21	49	1.276	4.16	102	3.26	.260	0	....	1	5	0.1
1983 Sea-A	2	3	.400	50	0	0	0	7	65	65	26	24	3	1	28	47	1.431	3.32	128	3.88	.273	0	....	7	6	0.7
1984 Sea-A	4	4	.500	54	0	0	0	8	61	55	28	24	3	2	22	55	1.262	3.54	113	3.08	.241	0	....	4	7	0.4
1985 Sea-A	1	2	.333	24	0	0	0	1	29	32	20	17	4	3	21	17	1.828	5.28	80	6.55	.278	0	....	-3	1	-0.3
Chi-A	0	1	.000	11	0	0	0	0	11^2	15	14	12	2	0	8	12	1.971	9.26	47	7.16	.294	0	....	-6	0	-0.6
Yr.	1	3	.250	35	0	0	0	1	40^2	47	34	29	6	3	29	29	1.869	6.42	66	6.73	.283	0	....	-10	1	-1.0
Total 7	**13**	**22**	**.371**	**277**	**3**	**0**	**0**	**31**	**384^1**	**398**	**218**	**197**	**27**	**9**	**182**	**304**	**1.509**	**4.61**	**87**	**4.43**	**.272**	**1**	**.250**	**-20**	**23**	**-2.0**
• STANTON, Mike	William Michael Stanton b: 6/2/1967, Houston, TX BL/TL, 6'1", 190 lbs. Deb: 8/24/1989																									
1989 Atl-N	0	1	.000	20	0	0	0	7	24	17	4	4	0	0	8	27	1.042	1.50	243	1.72	.207	0	....	6	5	0.6
1990 Atl-N	0	3	.000	7	0	0	0	2	7	16	16	14	1	1	4	7	2.857	18.00	22	13.58	.444	0	....	-11	0	-1.1

YEAR TM-L	W	L	PCT	G	GS	CG	SH	SV	IP	H	R	ER	HR	HB	BB	SO	RAT	ERA	ERA+	CERA	OAV	BH	AVG	PR+	WS	TPW
1991* Atl-N	5	5	.500	74	0	0	0	7	78	62	27	25	6	1	21	54	1.064	2.88	135	2.31	.217	3	.500	9	10	1.1
1992* Atl-N	5	4	.556	65	0	0	0	8	63^{2}	59	32	29	6	2	20	44	1.241	4.10	89	3.42	.247	1	.500	-3	5	-0.3
1993* Atl-N	4	6	.400	63	0	0	0	27	52	51	35	27	4	0	29	43	1.538	4.67	86	4.08	.255	0	....	-4	5	-0.4
1994 Atl-N	3	1	.750	49	0	0	0	3	45^{2}	41	18	18	2	3	26	35	1.467	3.55	120	4.01	.248	2	.667	4	5	0.5
1995 Atl-N	1	1	.500	26	0	0	0	1	19^{1}	31	14	12	3	1	6	13	1.914	5.59	76	7.86	.369	0	....	-3	0	-0.3
* Bos-A	1	0	1.000	22	0	0	0	0	21	17	9	7	3	0	8	10	1.190	3.00	162	3.37	.224	0	....	4	2	0.4
1996 Bos-A	4	3	.571	59	0	0	0	1	56^{1}	58	24	24	9	0	23	46	1.438	3.83	132	4.71	.275	0	....	9	6	0.8
* Tex-A	0	1	.000	22	0	0	0	0	22^{1}	20	8	8	2	0	4	14	1.075	3.22	163	2.62	.241	0	....	5	3	0.5
Yr.	4	4	.500	81	0	0	0	1	78^{2}	78	32	32	11	0	27	60	1.335	3.66	140	4.12	.265	0	....	14	9	1.3
1997* NY-A	6	1	.857	64	0	0	0	3	66^{2}	50	19	19	3	3	34	70	1.260	2.57	174	2.88	.205	0	....	15	9	1.4
1998* NY-A	4	1	.800	67	0	0	0	6	79	71	51	48	13	4	26	69	1.228	5.47	80	3.88	.239	0	.000	-11	4	-1.0
1999* NY-A	2	2	.500	73	1	0	0	0	62^{1}	71	30	30	5	1	18	59	1.428	4.33	109	4.23	.289	0	.000	3	4	0.3
2000* NY-A	2	3	.400	69	0	0	0	0	68	68	32	31	5	2	24	75	1.353	4.10	118	3.78	.263	1	1.000	7	6	0.7
2001* NY-A★	9	4	.692	76	0	0	0	0	80^{1}	80	25	23	4	4	29	78	1.357	2.58	174	3.61	.263	0	....	19	10	1.8
2002* NY-A	7	1	.875	79	0	0	0	6	78	73	29	26	4	0	28	44	1.295	3.00	145	3.23	.256	0	.000	14	10	1.3
2003 NY-N	2	7	.222	50	0	0	0	5	45^{1}	37	25	23	6	2	19	34	1.235	4.57	91	3.33	.219	0	.000	-2	3	-0.2
Total 15	55	44	.556	885	1	0	0	76	869	822	398	368	76	24	327	722	1.322	3.81	114	3.67	.252	7	.412	61	87	6.0

• STAPLETON, Dave David Earl Stapleton b: 10/16/1961, Miami, AZ BL/TL, 6'1", 185 lbs. Deb: 9/14/1987

YEAR TM-L	W	L	PCT	G	GS	CG	SH	SV	IP	H	R	ER	HR	HB	BB	SO	RAT	ERA	ERA+	CERA	OAV	BH	AVG	PR+	WS	TPW
1987 Mil-A	2	0	1.000	4	0	0	0	0	14^{2}	13	3	3	0	0	3	14	1.091	1.84	248	2.18	.241	0	....	5	2	0.4
1988 Mil-A	0	0	....	6	0	0	0	0	13^{2}	20	9	9	1	1	9	6	2.122	5.93	67	7.98	.339	0	....	-3	0	-0.3
Total 2	2	0	1.000	10	0	0	0	0	28^{1}	33	12	12	1	1	12	20	1.588	3.81	108	4.98	.292	0	....	1	2	0.1

• STARK, Dennis Dennis Stark b: 10/27/1974, Hicksville, OH BR/TR, 6'2", 210 lbs. Deb: 9/15/1999

YEAR TM-L	W	L	PCT	G	GS	CG	SH	SV	IP	H	R	ER	HR	HB	BB	SO	RAT	ERA	ERA+	CERA	OAV	BH	AVG	PR+	WS	TPW
1999 Sea-A	0	0	....	5	0	0	0	0	6^{1}	10	8	7	0	0	4	4	2.211	9.95	50	8.05	.370	0	....	-3	0	-0.3
2001 Sea-A	1	1	.500	4	3	0	0	0	14^{2}	21	15	15	5	0	4	12	1.705	9.20	45	7.99	.333	0	....	-9	0	-0.8
2002 Col-N	11	4	.733	32	20	0	0	0	128^{1}	108	69	57	25	5	64	64	1.340	4.00	119	4.33	.225	7	.171	12	10	1.3
2003 Col-N	3	3	.500	17	13	0	0	0	78^{2}	98	57	51	12	3	33	30	1.665	5.83	84	6.05	.305	0	.000	-7	2	-0.8
Total 4	15	8	.652	58	36	0	0	0	228	237	149	130	42	8	105	110	1.500	5.13	93	5.26	.266	7	.111	-6	12	-0.6

• STARKEL, Con Conrad Starkel b: 11/16/1880, Germany d: 1/19/1933, Tacoma, WA BR/TR, 6', 200 lbs. Deb: 4/19/1906

YEAR TM-L	W	L	PCT	G	GS	CG	SH	SV	IP	H	R	ER	HR	HB	BB	SO	RAT	ERA	ERA+	CERA	OAV	BH	AVG	PR+	WS	TPW
1906 Was-A	0	0	....	1	0	0	0	0	3	7	6	6	1	0	2	1	3.000	18.00	15	16.69	.455	0	....	-5	0	-0.5

• STARR, Dick Richard Eugene Starr b: 3/2/1921, Kittanning, PA BR/TR, 6'3", 190 lbs. Deb: 9/5/1947

YEAR TM-L	W	L	PCT	G	GS	CG	SH	SV	IP	H	R	ER	HR	HB	BB	SO	RAT	ERA	ERA+	CERA	OAV	BH	AVG	PR+	WS	TPW
1947 NY-A	1	0	1.000	4	1	1	0	0	12^{1}	12	4	2	1	0	8	1	1.622	1.46	242	4.47	.250	1	.333	3	1	0.3
1948 NY-A	0	0	....	1	0	0	0	0	2	0	1	1	0	0	2	2	1.000	4.50	91	0.80	.000	0	....	-0	0	0.0
1949 StL-A	1	7	.125	30	8	1	1	0	83^{1}	96	46	40	6	1	48	44	1.728	4.32	105	5.42	.292	2	.087	5	4	0.4
1950 StL-A	7	5	.583	32	16	4	1	2	123^{2}	140	83	69	11	7	74	30	1.730	5.02	99	5.63	.287	5	.139	3	7	0.1
1951 StL-A	2	5	.286	15	9	0	0	0	62	66	55	51	10	2	42	26	1.742	7.40	59	6.09	.273	4	.222	-19	0	-1.9
Was-A	1	7	.125	11	11	1	0	0	61^{1}	76	41	38	12	0	24	17	1.630	5.58	73	6.14	.304	3	.176	-9	0	-0.9
Yr.	3	12	.200	26	20	1	0	0	123^{1}	142	96	89	22	2	66	43	1.686	6.49	66	6.11	.289	7	.200	-29	0	-2.8
Total 5	12	24	.333	93	45	7	2	2	344^{2}	390	230	201	40	10	198	120	1.706	5.25	86	5.68	.288	15	.155	-18	12	-2.0

• STARR, Ray Raymond Francis "Iron Man" Starr b: 4/23/1906, Nowata, OK d: 2/9/1963, Baylis, IL BR/TR, 6'1", 178 lbs. Deb: 9/11/1932

YEAR TM-L	W	L	PCT	G	GS	CG	SH	SV	IP	H	R	ER	HR	HB	BB	SO	RAT	ERA	ERA+	CERA	OAV	BH	AVG	PR+	WS	TPW
1932 StL-N	1	1	.500	3	2	1	1	0	20	19	7	6	2	1	10	6	1.450	2.70	146	4.79	.284	1	.250	3	2	0.3
1933 NY-N	0	1	.000	6	2	0	0	0	13^{1}	19	11	8	0	1	10	2	2.175	5.40	59	7.20	.339	0	.000	-3	0	-0.4
Bos-N	0	1	.000	9	1	0	0	0	28	32	15	12	4	1	9	15	1.464	3.86	79	5.05	.296	1	.143	-2	0	-0.2
Yr.	0	2	.000	15	3	0	0	0	41^{1}	51	26	20	4	2	19	17	1.694	4.35	72	5.74	.311	1	.100	-6	0	-0.6
1941 Cin-N	3	2	.600	7	4	3	2	0	34	28	10	10	1	1	6	11	1.000	2.65	136	1.96	.219	2	.182	4	3	0.4
1942 Cin-N★	15	13	.536	37	33	17	4	0	276^{2}	228	88	82	10	3	106	83	1.207	2.67	123	2.63	.226	8	.091	17	21	1.4
1943 Cin-N	11	10	.524	36	33	9	2	1	217^{1}	201	93	88	9	5	91	42	1.344	3.64	91	3.33	.248	9	.122	-14	9	-1.9
1944 Pit-N	6	5	.545	27	12	5	0	3	89^{2}	116	60	50	6	1	36	25	1.695	5.02	74	5.46	.314	3	.136	-12	2	-1.1
1945 Pit-N	0	2	.000	4	0	0	0	0	6^{2}	10	7	7	0	0	4	0	2.100	9.45	42	6.93	.370	1	1.000	-4	0	-0.3
Chi-N	1	0	1.000	9	1	0	0	0	13^{1}	17	11	11	1	0	7	5	1.800	7.43	49	5.71	.298	1	.500	-6	0	-0.5
Yr.	1	2	.333	13	1	0	0	0	20	27	18	18	1	0	11	5	1.900	8.10	46	6.11	.321	2	.667	-10	0	-0.9
Total 7	37	35	.514	138	88	35	9	4	699	670	302	274	33	13	279	189	1.358	3.53	96	3.53	.255	26	.123	-17	37	-2.5

• STARRETTE, Herman Herman Paul Starrette b: 11/20/1938, Statesville, NC BR/TR, 6', 175 lbs. Deb: 7/1/1963 C

YEAR TM-L	W	L	PCT	G	GS	CG	SH	SV	IP	H	R	ER	HR	HB	BB	SO	RAT	ERA	ERA+	CERA	OAV	BH	AVG	PR+	WS	TPW
1963 Bal-A	0	1	.000	18	0	0	0	0	26	26	10	10	1	2	7	13	1.269	3.46	102	3.50	.271	0	.000	0	1	0.0
1964 Bal-A	1	0	1.000	5	0	0	0	0	11	9	3	2	0	0	6	5	1.364	1.64	218	3.10	.250	0	.000	2	1	0.2
1965 Bal-A	0	0	....	4	0	0	0	0	9	8	3	1	0	0	3	3	1.222	1.00	347	2.68	.258	0	.000	2	1	0.2
Total 3	1	1	.500	27	0	0	0	0	46	43	16	13	1	2	16	21	1.283	2.54	139	3.24	.264	0	.000	5	3	0.5

• STAUFFER, Ed Charles Edward Stauffer b: 1/10/1898, Emsworth, PA d: 7/2/1979, St. Petersburg, FL BR/TR, 5'11", 185 lbs. Deb: 4/26/1923

YEAR TM-L	W	L	PCT	G	GS	CG	SH	SV	IP	H	R	ER	HR	HB	BB	SO	RAT	ERA	ERA+	CERA	OAV	BH	AVG	PR+	WS	TPW
1923 Chi-N	0	0	....	1	0	0	0	0	2	5	3	3	0	0	1	0	3.000	13.50	30	13.07	.556	0	....	-2	0	-0.2
1925 StL-A	0	1	.000	20	1	0	0	0	30^{1}	34	21	18	1	0	21	13	1.813	5.34	87	5.27	.283	1	.250	-3	1	-0.2
Total 2	0	1	.000	21	1	0	0	0	32^{1}	39	24	21	1	0	22	13	1.887	5.85	78	5.76	.302	1	.250	-5	1	-0.5

• STEARNS, Bill William E. Stearns b: 3/20/1853, Washington, DC d: 12/30/1898, Washington, DC TR Deb: 6/26/1871

YEAR TM-L	W	L	PCT	G	GS	CG	SH	SV	IP	H	R	ER	HR	HB	BB	SO	RAT	ERA	ERA+	CERA	OAV	BH	AVG	PR+	WS	TPW
1871 Oly-n	2	0	1.000	2	2	2	0	0	18	10	11	5	0	....	8	0	1.000	2.50	167	....	.139	0	.000	2	....	0.0
1872 Nat-n	0	11	.000	11	11	11	0	0	99	193	190	68	2	....	3	2	1.980	6.18	68	....	.363	12	.267	-13	....	-1.0
1873 Was-n	7	25	.219	32	32	32	0	0	283	481	395	143	8	....	15	4	1.753	4.55	74	....	.336	24	.180	-35	....	-2.8
1874 Har-n	3	14	.176	22	18	14	0	1	158^{2}	237	194	52	1	....	15	14	1.588	2.95	68	....	.310	21	.159	-21	....	-2.4
1875 Was-n	1	14	.067	17	16	14	0	0	141	246	211	63	1	....	4	3	**1.773**	4.02	49	....	.351	20	.256	-29	....	-2.5
Total 5 n	13	64	.169	84	79	73	0	1	699^{2}	1167	1001	331	12	....	45	23	1.732	4.26	66	....	.333	77	.194	-95	....	-8.6

• STECHER, Charlie William Theodore Stecher b: 10/20/1869, Riverside, NJ d: 12/26/1926, Riverside, NJ Deb: 9/6/1890

YEAR TM-L	W	L	PCT	G	GS	CG	SH	SV	IP	H	R	ER	HR	HB	BB	SO	RAT	ERA	ERA+	CERA	OAV	BH	AVG	PR+	WS	TPW
1890 Phi-a	0	10	.000	10	10	9	0	0	68	111	110	78	1	0	60	18	2.515	10.32	37	....	.356	7	.241	-45	0	-3.9

• STECHSCHULTE, Gene Gene Urban Stechschulte b: 8/12/1973, Lima, OH BR/TR, 6'5", 210 lbs. Deb: 4/20/2000

YEAR TM-L	W	L	PCT	G	GS	CG	SH	SV	IP	H	R	ER	HR	HB	BB	SO	RAT	ERA	ERA+	CERA	OAV	BH	AVG	PR+	WS	TPW
2000 StL-N	1	0	1.000	20	0	0	0	0	25^{2}	24	22	18	6	0	17	12	1.597	6.31	73	5.69	.247	0	....	-5	0	-0.5
2001* StL-N	1	5	.167	67	0	0	0	6	70	71	35	30	10	4	30	51	1.443	3.86	110	4.90	.273	2	.667	2	5	0.4
2002 StL-N	6	2	.750	29	0	0	0	0	32	27	19	17	4	1	17	21	1.375	4.78	83	3.98	.235	0	.000	-3	2	-0.4
Total 3	8	7	.533	116	0	0	0	6	127^{2}	122	76	65	20	5	64	84	1.457	4.58	93	4.82	.258	2	.400	-7	7	-0.5

• STEELE, Bill William Mitchell "Big Bill" Steele b: 10/5/1885, Milford, PA d: 10/19/1949, Overland, MO BR/TR, 5'11", 200 lbs. Deb: 9/10/1910

YEAR TM-L	W	L	PCT	G	GS	CG	SH	SV	IP	H	R	ER	HR	HB	BB	SO	RAT	ERA	ERA+	CERA	OAV	BH	AVG	PR+	WS	TPW
1910 StL-N	4	4	.500	9	8	8	0	1	71^{2}	71	35	26	1	6	24	25	1.326	3.27	91	3.51	.264	8	.258	-0	3	0.1
1911 StL-N	18	19	.486	43	34	23	1	3	287^{1}	287	153	119	8	10	113	115	1.392	3.73	90	3.74	.269	21	.208	-13	15	-0.8
1912 StL-N	9	13	.409	40	25	7	0	2	194	245	143	101	5	7	66	67	1.603	4.69	73	4.88	.322	11	.180	-28	4	-2.6
1913 StL-N	4	4	.500	12	9	2	0	0	54	58	31	30	3	3	18	10	1.407	5.00	64	4.14	.286	1	.056	-11	1	-1.3
1914 StL-N	1	2	.333	17	2	0	0	0	53^{1}	55	30	16	3	3	7	16	1.163	2.70	103	3.12	.274	5	.294	0	2	0.2
Bro-N	1	1	.500	8	1	0	0	1	16^{1}	17	16	10	1	0	7	3	1.469	5.51	52	3.86	.258	1	.333	-5	0	-0.4
Yr.	2	3	.400	25	3	0	0	1	69^{2}	72	46	26	4	3	14	19	1.234	3.36	84	3.30	.270	6	.300	-5	2	-0.2
Total 5	37	43	.463	129	79	40	1	7	676^{2}	733	408	302	21	29	235	236	1.431	4.02	82	4.03	.286	47	.203	-57	25	-4.8

• STEELE, Bob Robert Wesley Steele b: 1/5/1894, Cassburn, Canada d: 1/27/1962, Ocala, FL BB/TL, 5'10.5", 175 lbs. Deb: 4/17/1916

YEAR TM-L	W	L	PCT	G	GS	CG	SH	SV	IP	H	R	ER	HR	HB	BB	SO	RAT	ERA	ERA+	CERA	OAV	BH	AVG	PR+	WS	TPW
1916 StL-N	5	15	.250	29	21	7	1	0	148	156	74	56	6	3	42	67	1.338	3.41	77	3.59	.285	10	.196	-12	4	-1.5
1917 StL-N	1	3	.250	12	6	1	0	0	42	33	18	15	1	0	19	23	1.238	3.21	84	2.55	.223	5	.385	-3	3	-0.1
Pit-N	5	11	.313	27	19	13	1	1	179^{2}	158	70	55	0	5	53	82	1.174	2.76	103	2.40	.237	17	.224	3	9	0.4
Yr.	6	14	.300	39	25	14	1	1	221^{2}	191	88	70	1	5	72	105	1.186	2.84	99	2.43	.234	22	.247	0	12	0.3

YEAR	TM-L	W	L	PCT	G	GS	CG	SH	SV	IP	H	R	ER	HR	HB	BB	SO	RAT	ERA	ERA+	CERA	OAV	BH	AVG	PR+	WS	TPW
1918	Pit-N	2	3	.400	10	4	2	1	1	49	44	25	18	2	2	17	21	1.245	3.31	87	2.93	.240	2	.125	-4	2	-0.5
	NY-N	3	5	.375	12	7	5	1	1	66	56	29	19	1	3	11	24	1.015	2.59	101	1.97	.226	6	.286	0	4	0.2
	Yr.	5	8	.385	22	11	7	2	2	115	100	54	37	3	5	28	45	1.113	2.90	95	2.38	.232	8	.216	-4	6	-0.2
1919	NY-N	0	1	.000	1	0	0	0	0	3	3	3	2	0	0	2	0	1.667	6.00	47	3.74	.250	0	.000	-1	0	-0.1
Total	4	16	38	.296	91	57	28	4	3	487^{2}	450	219	165	10	13	144	217	1.218	3.05	90	2.78	.249	40	.225	-17	22	-1.6
• STEELE, Elmer	Elmer Rae Steele b: 5/17/1886, Muitzes Kill, NY d: 3/9/1966, Poughkeepsie, NY BB/TR, 5'11", 200 lbs. Deb: 9/12/1907																										
1907	Bos-A	0	1	.000	4	1	0	0	0	11^{1}	11	7	2	0	0	1	10	1.059	1.59	162	2.14	.257	0	.000	1	0	0.0
1908	Bos-A	5	7	.417	16	13	9	1	0	118	85	34	24	1	3	13	37	.831	1.83	134	1.43	.209	2	.051	6	7	0.2
1909	Bos-A	4	4	.500	16	8	2	0	1	75^{2}	75	37	24	1	1	15	32	1.189	2.85	87	2.62	.255	5	.227	-4	4	-0.4
1910	Pit-N	0	3	.000	3	3	2	0	0	24	19	9	6	0	0	3	7	.917	2.25	139	1.57	.221	0	.000	2	2	0.2
1911	Pit-N	9	9	.500	31	16	7	2	2	166	153	65	48	5	4	31	52	1.108	2.60	131	2.66	.256	11	.180	12	11	1.2
	Bro-N	0	0	....	5	2	0	0	0	23	24	10	8	0	0	5	9	1.261	3.13	106	2.82	.258	0	.000	1	1	0.0
	Yr.	9	9	.500	36	18	7	2	2	189	177	75	56	5	4	36	61	1.127	2.67	128	2.68	.256	11	.157	13	12	1.1
Total	5	18	24	.429	75	43	20	3	3	418	367	162	112	7	8	68	147	1.041	2.41	121	2.24	.241	18	.127	17	25	1.2
• STEEN, Bill	William John Steen b: 11/11/1887, Pittsburgh, PA d: 3/13/1979, Signal Hill, CA BR/TR, 6'.5", 180 lbs. Deb: 4/15/1912																										
1912	Cle-A	9	8	.529	26	16	6	1	0	143^{1}	163	75	60	3	1	45	61	1.451	3.77	91	4.11	.298	13	.271	-8	9	-0.6
1913	Cle-A	4	5	.444	22	13	7	2	2	128^{1}	113	52	35	3	4	49	57	1.262	2.45	124	2.93	.237	7	.171	6	9	0.7
1914	Cle-A	9	14	.391	30	22	13	1	0	200^{2}	201	74	58	0	4	68	97	1.341	2.60	111	3.35	.272	14	.200	9	11	1.1
1915	Cle-A	1	4	.200	10	7	2	0	0	45^{1}	51	30	25	1	2	15	22	1.456	4.96	61	4.16	.290	3	.188	-9	0	-1.0
	Det-A	5	1	.833	20	7	3	0	4	79^{1}	83	35	24	0	1	22	28	1.324	2.72	111	3.19	.269	5	.179	4	6	0.4
	Yr.	6	5	.545	30	14	5	0	4	124^{2}	134	65	49	1	3	37	50	1.372	3.54	86	3.55	.277	8	.182	-5	6	-0.7
Total	4	28	32	.467	108	65	31	4	6	597	611	266	202	7	12	199	265	1.357	3.05	102	3.48	.272	42	.207	2	35	0.4
• STEENGRAFE, Milt	Milton Henry Steengrafe b: 5/26/1900, San Francisco, CA d: 6/2/1977, Oklahoma City, OK BR/TR, 6', 170 lbs. Deb: 5/5/1924																										
1924	Chi-A	0	0	....	3	0	0	0	0	5^{2}	15	8	8	0	0	4	3	3.353	12.71	32	15.08	.484	0	.000	-5	0	-0.5
1926	Chi-A	1	1	.500	13	1	0	0	0	38^{1}	43	22	17	1	2	19	10	1.617	3.99	97	4.63	.295	0	.000	-1	1	-0.3
Total	2	1	1	.500	16	1	0	0	0	44	58	30	25	1	2	23	13	1.841	5.11	77	5.98	.328	0	.000	-6	1	-0.8
• STEENSTRA, Kennie	Kenneth Gregory Steenstra b: 10/13/1970, Springfield, MO BR/TR, 6'5" Deb: 5/21/1998																										
1998	Chi-N	0	0	....	4	0	0	0	0	3^{1}	7	4	4	2	0	1	4	2.400	10.80	41	15.36	.412	0	....	-2	0	-0.2
• STEEVENS, Morrie	Morris Dale Steevens b: 10/7/1940, Salem, IL BL/TL, 6'2", 175 lbs. Deb: 4/13/1962																										
1962	Chi-N	0	1	.000	12	1	0	0	0	15	10	4	4	0	1	11	5	1.400	2.40	173	2.96	.196	0	.000	3	2	0.3
1964	Phi-N	0	0	....	4	0	0	0	0	2^{2}	5	3	1	0	0	1	3	2.250	3.38	103	8.33	.385	0	....	0	0	0.0
1965	Phi-N	0	1	.000	6	0	0	0	0	2^{2}	5	5	5	1	0	4	3	3.375	16.88	20	18.93	.417	0	....	-4	0	-0.4
Total	3	0	2	.000	22	1	0	0	0	20^{1}	20	12	10	1	1	16	11	1.770	4.43	84	5.76	.263	0	.000	-1	2	-0.1
• STEIN, Blake	William Blake Stein b: 8/3/1973, McComb, MS BR/TR, 6'7", 240 lbs. Deb: 5/10/1998																										
1998	Oak-A	5	9	.357	24	20	1	1	0	117^{1}	117	92	83	22	5	71	89	1.602	6.37	72	5.64	.255	0	.000	-22	0	-2.1
1999	Oak-A	0	0	....	1	1	0	0	0	2^{2}	6	5	5	1	0	6	4	4.500	16.88	27	26.09	.462	0	....	-4	0	-0.3
	KC-A	1	2	.333	12	11	0	0	0	70^{1}	59	33	32	10	7	41	43	1.422	4.09	122	4.63	.230	0	....	6	4	0.5
	Yr.	1	2	.333	13	12	0	0	0	73	65	38	37	11	7	47	47	1.534	4.56	109	5.41	.241	0	....	2	4	0.2
2000	KC-A	8	5	.615	17	17	1	0	0	107^{2}	98	57	56	19	3	57	78	1.440	4.68	109	4.82	.247	0	.000	3	7	0.3
2001	KC-A	7	8	.467	36	15	0	0	1	131	112	73	69	20	3	79	113	1.458	4.74	103	4.57	.233	0	.000	-1	7	-0.1
2002	KC-A	0	4	.000	27	2	0	0	1	46^{2}	59	41	41	6	3	27	42	1.843	7.91	63	6.76	.306	0	....	-15	0	-1.4
Total	5	21	28	.429	117	66	2	1	2	475^{2}	451	301	286	78	21	281	369	1.539	5.41	90	5.23	.251	0	.000	-33	18	-3.2
• STEIN, Ed	Edward F. Stein b: 9/5/1869, Detroit, MI d: 5/10/1928, Detroit, MI BR/TR, 5'11", 170 lbs. Deb: 7/24/1890 U																										
1890	Chi-N	12	6	.667	20	18	14	1	0	160^{2}	147	100	68	9	11	83	65	1.432	3.81	96	....	.236	9	.153	-7	11	-0.7
1891	Chi-N	7	6	.538	14	10	9	1	0	101	99	68	42	7	2	57	38	1.545	3.74	89	....	.247	7	.163	-7	6	-0.7
1892	Bro-N	27	16	.628	48	42	38	6	1	377^{1}	310	166	119	6	15	150	190	1.219	2.84	111	2.62	.215	31	.215	13	30	1.6
1893	Bro-N	19	15	.559	37	34	28	1	0	298^{1}	294	190	125	4	8	119	81	1.384	3.77	117	3.38	.250	25	.212	25	20	1.8
1894	Bro-N	26	14	.650	44	40	37	2	1	350	388	261	180	10	14	170	84	1.594	4.63	107	4.51	.278	38	.259	16	27	1.6
1895	Bro-N	15	13	.536	32	27	24	1	1	255^{1}	282	163	134	9	6	93	55	1.469	4.72	93	4.05	.276	26	.250	-13	18	-0.9
1896	Bro-N	3	6	.333	17	10	6	0	0	90^{1}	130	79	49	6	2	51	16	2.004	4.88	84	7.06	.334	10	.256	-7	2	-0.6
1898	Bro-N	0	2	.000	3	2	2	0	0	23	39	21	14	0	0	9	6	2.087	5.48	65	7.32	.372	4	.400	-5	0	-0.3
Total	8	109	78	.583	215	183	158	12	3	1656	1689	1048	731	51	58	732	535	1.462	3.97	102	3.27	.258	150	.226	16	114	1.9
• STEIN, Irv	Irvin Michael Stein b: 5/21/1911, Madisonville, LA d: 1/7/1981, Covington, LA BR/TR, 6'2", 170 lbs. Deb: 7/7/1932																										
1932	Phi-A	0	0	....	1	0	0	0	0	3	7	4	4	2	0	1	0	2.667	12.00	38	19.21	.500	0	.000	-3	0	-0.2
• STEIN, Randy	William Randolph Stein b: 3/7/1953, Pomona, CA BR/TR, 6'4", 210 lbs. Deb: 4/17/1978																										
1978	Mil-A	3	2	.600	31	1	0	0	1	72^{2}	78	51	43	5	4	39	42	1.610	5.33	71	5.04	.280	0	....	-13	1	-1.3
1979	Sea-A	2	3	.400	23	1	0	0	0	41^{1}	48	29	27	7	1	27	39	1.815	5.88	74	6.51	.291	0	....	-7	1	-0.7
1981	Sea-A	0	1	.000	5	0	0	0	0	9^{1}	18	12	11	1	0	8	6	2.786	10.61	36	12.73	.429	0	....	-7	0	-0.7
1982	Chi-N	0	0	....	6	0	0	0	0	10^{1}	7	4	4	2	0	7	6	1.355	3.48	107	3.84	.200	0	....	0	1	0.0
Total	4	5	6	.455	65	2	0	0	1	133^{2}	151	96	85	15	5	81	93	1.736	5.72	69	5.94	.290	0	....	-26	3	-2.7
• STEINEDER, Ray	Raymond J. Steineder b: 11/13/1895, Salem, NJ d: 8/25/1982, Vineland, NJ BR/TR, 6'.5", 160 lbs. Deb: 7/16/1923																										
1923	Pit-N	2	0	1.000	15	2	1	0	0	55	58	30	29	3	2	18	23	1.382	4.75	84	3.91	.278	7	.467	-5	3	-0.3
1924	Pit-N	0	1	.000	5	0	0	0	0	2^{2}	6	6	4	0	0	5	0	4.125	13.50	28	15.49	.400	0	....	-3	0	-0.3
	Phi-N	1	1	.500	9	0	0	0	0	28^{2}	31	15	14	1	0	16	11	1.640	4.40	101	4.59	.266	3	.300	1	2	0.1
	Yr.	1	2	.333	14	0	0	0	0	31^{1}	37	21	18	1	0	21	11	1.851	5.17	83	5.52	.281	3	.300	-2	2	-0.2
Total	2	3	2	.600	29	2	1	0	0	86^{1}	95	51	47	4	2	39	34	1.552	4.90	84	4.49	.279	10	.400	-8	5	-0.5
• STEIRER, Rick	Ricky Francis Steirer b: 8/27/1956, Baltimore, MD BR/TR, 6'4", 200 lbs. Deb: 8/5/1982																										
1982	Cal-A	1	0	1.000	10	1	0	0	0	26^{1}	25	14	11	2	1	11	14	1.367	3.76	108	3.71	.243	0	....	0	1	0.0
1983	Cal-A	3	2	.600	19	5	0	0	0	61^{2}	77	40	33	3	3	18	25	1.541	4.82	83	4.66	.302	0	....	-5	2	-0.5
1984	Cal-A	0	1	.000	1	1	0	0	0	2^{2}	6	5	5	0	0	2	2	3.000	16.88	24	13.44	.500	0	....	-4	0	-0.4
Total	3	4	3	.571	30	7	0	0	0	90^{2}	108	59	49	5	4	31	41	1.533	4.86	83	4.64	.292	0	....	-9	3	-0.9
• STELLBERGER, Bill	William F. Stellberger b: 4/22/1865, Detroit, MI d: 11/9/1936, Detroit, MI BL/TL Deb: 10/1/1885																										
1885	Pro-N	0	1	.000	1	1	1	0	0	8	14	10	7	0	....	4	0	2.250	7.88	34	....	.366	0	.000	-5	0	-0.5
• STEMBER, Jeff	Jeffrey Alan Stember b: 3/2/1958, Elizabeth, NJ BR/TR, 6'5", 220 lbs. Deb: 8/5/1980																										
1980	SF-N	0	0	....	1	1	0	0	0	3	2	3	1	1	0	2	0	1.333	3.00	118	4.41	.167	0	.000	0	0	0.0
• STEMMEYER, Bill	William "Cannon Ball" Stemmeyer b: 5/6/1865, Cleveland, OH d: 5/3/1945, Cleveland, OH BR/TR, 6'2", 190 lbs. Deb: 10/3/1885																										
1885	Bos-N	1	1	.500	2	2	2	1	0	11	7	7	0	0	....	11	8	1.636	0.00	....	....	.174	3	.429	4	1	0.5
1886	Bos-N	22	18	.550	41	41	41	0	0	348^{2}	300	218	117	11	....	144	239	1.273	3.02	105	....	.223	41	.277	14	23	2.2
1887	Bos-N	6	8	.429	15	14	14	0	**1**	119^{1}	179	107	69	4	2	41	41	1.500	5.20	75	....	.337	15	.300	-19	4	-1.4
1888	Cle-a	0	2	.000	2	2	2	0	0	16	37	42	16	0	5	9	7	2.875	9.00	34	....	.437	4	.400	-10	1	-0.8
Total	4	29	29	.500	60	59	59	1	1	495	523	374	202	15	7	205	295	1.388	3.67	92	....	.262	63	.293	-12	29	0.5
• STENHOUSE, Dave	David Rotchford Stenhouse b: 9/12/1933, Westerly, RI BR/TR, 6', 195 lbs. Deb: 4/18/1962																										
1962	Was-A★	11	12	.478	34	26	9	2	0	197	169	84	80	24	2	90	123	1.315	3.65	110	3.66	.234	3	.052	9	13	0.4
1963	Was-A	3	9	.250	16	16	2	1	0	87	90	46	44	12	1	45	47	1.552	4.55	82	4.91	.260	2	.080	-8	2	-1.0
1964	Was-A	2	7	.222	26	14	1	0	1	88	80	54	47	12	1	39	44	1.352	4.81	77	3.98	.239	6	.300	-11	2	-1.0
Total	3	16	28	.364	76	56	12	3	1	372	339	184	171	48	4	174	214	1.379	4.14	93	4.03	.241	11	.107	-11	17	-1.6

• STEPHEN, Buzz Louis Roberts Stephen b: 7/13/1944, Porterville, CA BR/TR, 6'4", 205 lbs. Deb: 9/20/1968

YEAR	TM-L	W	L	PCT	G	GS	CG	SH	SV	IP	H	R	ER	HR	HB	BB	SO	RAT	ERA	ERA+	CERA	OAV	BH	AVG	PR+	WS	TPW
1968	Min-A	1	1	.500	2	2	0	0	0	11^{1}	11	7	6	0	1	7	4	1.588	4.76	65	4.60	.275	0	.000	-2	0	-0.3

• STEPHENS, Ben George Benjamin Stephens b: 9/28/1867, Romeo, MI d: 8/5/1896, Armada, MI TR, 5'10.5", 170 lbs. Deb: 8/5/1892

YEAR	TM-L	W	L	PCT	G	GS	CG	SH	SV	IP	H	R	ER	HR	HB	BB	SO	RAT	ERA	ERA+	CERA	OAV	BH	AVG	PR+	WS	TPW
1892	Bal-N	1	1	.500	5	2	2	0	1	29	37	22	9	2	1	9	7	1.586	2.79	123	5.13	.299	0	.000	3	1	0.2
1893	Was-N	0	6	.000	9	6	6	0	0	63^{2}	83	58	41	1	4	31	14	1.791	5.80	80	5.63	.306	3	.103	-7	1	-0.8
1894	Was-N	0	0	....	3	2	1	0	0	11	19	16	6	1	1	8	1	2.455	4.91	107	10.20	.375	1	.250	1	0	0.0
Total	3	1	7	.125	17	10	9	0	1	103^{2}	139	96	56	4	6	48	22	1.804	4.86	91	5.97	.312	4	.087	-3	2	-0.6

• STEPHENS, Bryan Bryan Maris Stephens b: 7/14/1920, Fayetteville, AR d: 11/21/1991, Santa Ana, CA BR/TR, 6'4", 175 lbs. Deb: 5/15/1947

YEAR	TM-L	W	L	PCT	G	GS	CG	SH	SV	IP	H	R	ER	HR	HB	BB	SO	RAT	ERA	ERA+	CERA	OAV	BH	AVG	PR+	WS	TPW
1947	Cle-A	5	10	.333	31	5	1	0	1	92	79	46	41	6	2	39	34	1.283	4.01	87	3.10	.230	3	.111	-7	3	-0.9
1948	StL-A	3	6	.333	43	12	2	0	3	122^{2}	141	94	82	14	4	67	35	1.696	6.02	76	6.06	.315	4	.125	-18	2	-1.8
Total	2	8	16	.333	74	17	3	0	4	214^{2}	220	140	123	20	6	106	69	1.519	5.16	80	4.79	.278	7	.119	-25	5	-2.7

• STEPHENS, Clarence Clarence Wright Stephens b: 8/19/1863, Cincinnati, OH d: 2/28/1945, Cincinnati, OH TR Deb: 10/8/1886

YEAR	TM-L	W	L	PCT	G	GS	CG	SH	SV	IP	H	R	ER	HR	HB	BB	SO	RAT	ERA	ERA+	CERA	OAV	BH	AVG	PR+	WS	TPW
1886	Cin-a	1	0	1.000	1	1	1	0	0	8	9	8	5	0	1	5	6	1.750	5.63	62	....	.271	3	.600	-2	1	-0.1
1891	Cin-N	0	1	.000	1	1	1	0	0	8	9	9	7	1	0	3	3	1.500	7.88	43	....	.274	0	.000	-4	0	-0.4
1892	Cin-N	0	1	.000	1	1	0	0	0	7	12	3	1	0	0	4	1	2.286	1.29	254	8.17	.364	0	.000	1	1	0.1
Total	3	1	2	.333	3	3	2	0	0	23	30	20	13	1	1	12	10	1.826	5.09	67	2.49	.303	3	.300	-5	2	-0.4

• STEPHENS, John John M. Stephens b: 11/15/1979, Sydney, Australia BR/TR, 6'1", 204 lbs. Deb: 7/30/2002

YEAR	TM-L	W	L	PCT	G	GS	CG	SH	SV	IP	H	R	ER	HR	HB	BB	SO	RAT	ERA	ERA+	CERA	OAV	BH	AVG	PR+	WS	TPW
2002	Bal-A	2	5	.286	12	11	0	0	0	65	68	44	44	13	3	22	56	1.385	6.09	70	4.97	.271	0	....	-14	1	-1.3

• STEPHENSON, Earl Chester Earl Stephenson b: 7/31/1947, Benson, NC BL/TL, 6'3", 175 lbs. Deb: 4/7/1971

YEAR	TM-L	W	L	PCT	G	GS	CG	SH	SV	IP	H	R	ER	HR	HB	BB	SO	RAT	ERA	ERA+	CERA	OAV	BH	AVG	PR+	WS	TPW
1971	Chi-N	1	0	1.000	16	0	0	0	1	20^{1}	24	10	10	1	0	11	11	1.721	4.43	89	5.54	.316	0	.000	-1	1	-0.1
1972	Mil-A	3	5	.375	35	8	1	0	0	80^{1}	79	32	29	5	3	33	33	1.394	3.25	93	3.84	.262	0	.000	-2	4	-0.4
1977	Bal-A	0	0	....	1	0	0	0	0	3	5	3	3	1	0	0	2	1.667	9.00	42	8.04	.357	0	....	-2	0	-0.2
1978	Bal-A	0	0	....	2	0	0	0	0	9^{2}	10	3	3	0	0	5	4	1.552	2.79	125	4.32	.294	0	....	1	1	0.1
Total	4	4	5	.444	54	8	1	0	1	113^{1}	118	48	45	7	3	49	50	1.474	3.57	91	4.30	.277	0	.000	-4	6	-0.7

• STEPHENSON, Garrett Garrett Charles Stephenson b: 1/2/1972, Takoma Park, MD BR/TR, 6'4", 185 lbs. Deb: 7/25/1996

YEAR	TM-L	W	L	PCT	G	GS	CG	SH	SV	IP	H	R	ER	HR	HB	BB	SO	RAT	ERA	ERA+	CERA	OAV	BH	AVG	PR+	WS	TPW
1996	Bal-A	0	1	.000	3	0	0	0	0	6^{1}	13	9	9	1	1	3	3	2.526	12.79	39	12.31	.433	0	....	-6	0	-0.5
1997	Phi-N	8	6	.571	20	18	2	0	0	117	104	45	41	11	3	38	81	1.214	3.15	135	3.35	.244	3	.094	15	10	1.3
1998	Phi-N	0	2	.000	6	6	0	0	0	23	31	24	23	3	0	19	17	2.174	9.00	48	8.16	.316	1	.167	-12	0	-1.2
1999	StL-N	6	3	.667	18	12	0	0	0	85^{1}	90	43	40	11	5	29	59	1.395	4.22	108	4.58	.275	2	.074	4	5	0.2
2000*	StL-N	16	9	.640	32	31	3	2	0	200^{1}	209	105	100	31	7	63	123	1.358	4.49	103	4.53	.270	3	.051	0	11	-0.3
2002	StL-N	2	5	.286	12	10	0	0	0	45	48	27	27	4	5	25	34	1.622	5.40	73	5.54	.282	0	.000	-8	0	-0.9
2003	StL-N	7	13	.350	32	27	1	0	0	174^{1}	167	94	89	30	13	60	91	1.302	4.59	88	4.40	.255	9	.205	-11	5	-0.9
Total	7	39	39	.500	123	104	6	2	0	651^{1}	662	347	329	91	34	237	408	1.380	4.55	95	4.56	.267	18	.100	-18	31	-2.2

• STEPHENSON, Jerry Jerry Joseph Stephenson b: 10/6/1943, Detroit, MI BL/TR, 6'2", 185 lbs. Deb: 4/14/1963

YEAR	TM-L	W	L	PCT	G	GS	CG	SH	SV	IP	H	R	ER	HR	HB	BB	SO	RAT	ERA	ERA+	CERA	OAV	BH	AVG	PR+	WS	TPW
1963	Bos-A	0	0	....	1	1	0	0	0	2^{1}	5	2	2	0	0	2	3	3.000	7.71	49	13.37	.556	0	.000	-1	0	-0.1
1965	Bos-A	1	5	.167	15	8	0	0	0	52	62	41	36	7	1	33	49	1.827	6.23	60	6.36	.287	3	.231	-14	0	-1.4
1966	Bos-A	2	5	.286	15	11	1	0	0	66^{1}	68	51	43	6	1	44	50	1.688	5.83	65	5.18	.264	2	.118	-15	0	-1.7
1967*	Bos-A	3	1	.750	8	6	0	0	1	39^{2}	32	18	17	4	1	16	24	1.210	3.86	90	3.16	.227	4	.250	-1	2	-0.1
1968	Bos-A	2	8	.200	23	7	2	0	0	68^{2}	81	51	43	4	2	42	51	1.791	5.64	56	5.59	.295	6	.353	-19	0	-1.9
1969	Sea-A	0	0	....	2	0	0	0	0	2^{2}	6	4	3	0	1	3	1	3.375	10.13	36	16.21	.429	0	....	-2	0	-0.2
1970	LA-N	0	0	....	3	0	0	0	0	6^{2}	11	7	7	0	0	5	6	2.400	9.45	41	9.02	.379	0	.000	-4	0	-0.4
Total	7	8	19	.296	67	33	3	0	1	238^{1}	265	174	151	21	6	145	184	1.720	5.70	62	5.53	.281	15	.231	-55	2	-5.8

• STERLING, John John A. Sterling b: Philadelphia, PA, 6'1" Deb: 10/12/1890

YEAR	TM-L	W	L	PCT	G	GS	CG	SH	SV	IP	H	R	ER	HR	HB	BB	SO	RAT	ERA	ERA+	CERA	OAV	BH	AVG	PR+	WS	TPW
1890	Phi-a	0	1	.000	1	1	1	0	0	5	16	12	12	1	1	4	1	4.000	21.60	18	....	.520	0	.000	-10	0	-0.9

• STERLING, Randy Randall Wayne Sterling b: 4/21/1951, Key West, FL BB/TR, 6'2", 195 lbs. Deb: 9/16/1974

YEAR	TM-L	W	L	PCT	G	GS	CG	SH	SV	IP	H	R	ER	HR	HB	BB	SO	RAT	ERA	ERA+	CERA	OAV	BH	AVG	PR+	WS	TPW
1974	NY-N	1	1	.500	3	2	0	0	0	9^{1}	13	8	5	0	1	3	2	1.714	4.82	74	5.68	.351	0	.000	-1	0	-0.1

• STEVENS, Dave David James Stevens b: 3/4/1970, Fullerton, CA BR/TR, 6'3", 210 lbs. Deb: 5/20/1994

YEAR	TM-L	W	L	PCT	G	GS	CG	SH	SV	IP	H	R	ER	HR	HB	BB	SO	RAT	ERA	ERA+	CERA	OAV	BH	AVG	PR+	WS	TPW
1994	Min-A	5	2	.714	24	0	0	0	0	45	55	35	34	6	1	23	24	1.733	6.80	72	6.16	.302	0	....	-9	1	-0.8
1995	Min-A	5	4	.556	56	0	0	0	10	65^{2}	74	40	37	14	1	32	47	1.614	5.07	94	5.98	.285	0	....	-2	4	-0.2
1996	Min-A	3	3	.500	49	0	0	0	11	58	58	31	30	12	0	25	29	1.431	4.66	110	4.93	.264	0	....	2	6	0.2
1997	Min-A	1	3	.250	6	6	0	0	0	23	41	23	23	8	0	17	16	2.522	9.00	52	13.14	.383	0	....	-11	0	-1.1
	Chi-N	0	2	.000	10	0	0	0	0	9^{1}	13	11	10	0	1	9	13	2.357	9.64	45	8.36	.333	0	.000	-6	0	-0.6
1998	Chi-N	1	2	.333	31	0	0	0	0	38	42	20	20	6	1	17	31	1.553	4.74	93	5.23	.288	1	.250	-1	2	-0.1
1999	Cle-A	0	0	....	5	0	0	0	0	9	10	10	10	1	0	8	6	2.000	10.00	50	6.61	.286	0	....	-5	0	-0.5
2000	Atl-N	0	0	....	2	0	0	0	0	3	5	4	4	2	0	1	4	2.000	12.00	38	12.68	.357	0	.000	-2	0	-0.2
Total	7	15	16	.484	183	6	0	0	21	251	298	174	168	49	4	132	170	1.713	6.02	79	6.50	.297	1	.167	-33	13	-3.2

• STEVENS, Jim James Arthur "Steve" Stevens b: 8/25/1889, Williamsburg, MD d: 9/25/1966, Baltimore, MD BR/TR, 5'11", 180 lbs. Deb: 8/24/1914

YEAR	TM-L	W	L	PCT	G	GS	CG	SH	SV	IP	H	R	ER	HR	HB	BB	SO	RAT	ERA	ERA+	CERA	OAV	BH	AVG	PR+	WS	TPW
1914	Was-A	0	0	....	2	0	0	0	0	3	4	3	3	0	1	2	0	2.000	9.00	31	8.28	.364	0	.000	-2	0	-0.2

• STEWART, Bunky Veston Goff Stewart b: 1/7/1931, Jasper, NC BL/TL, 6', 155 lbs. Deb: 5/4/1952

YEAR	TM-L	W	L	PCT	G	GS	CG	SH	SV	IP	H	R	ER	HR	HB	BB	SO	RAT	ERA	ERA+	CERA	OAV	BH	AVG	PR+	WS	TPW
1952	Was-A	0	0	....	1	0	0	0	0	1	2	2	2	0	0	1	1	3.000	18.00	20	14.07	.500	0	....	-2	0	-0.2
1953	Was-A	0	2	.000	2	2	1	0	0	15^{1}	17	9	8	1	1	11	3	1.826	4.70	83	5.85	.283	1	.200	-1	0	-0.2
1954	Was-A	0	2	.000	29	2	0	0	1	50^{2}	67	52	43	3	4	27	27	1.855	7.64	47	6.16	.324	0	.000	-22	0	-2.3
1955	Was-A	0	0	....	7	1	0	0	0	15^{1}	18	7	7	0	0	6	10	1.565	4.11	93	4.12	.295	0	.000	-0	1	0.0
1956	Was-A	5	7	.417	33	9	1	0	2	105	111	77	65	15	5	82	36	1.838	5.57	78	6.46	.276	7	.250	-11	3	-1.1
Total	5	5	11	.313	72	14	2	0	3	187^{1}	215	147	125	19	10	127	77	1.826	6.01	66	6.18	.293	8	.211	-37	4	-3.7

• STEWART, Dave David Keith Stewart b: 2/19/1957, Oakland, CA BR/TR, 6'2", 200 lbs. Deb: 9/22/1978 C

YEAR	TM-L	W	L	PCT	G	GS	CG	SH	SV	IP	H	R	ER	HR	HB	BB	SO	RAT	ERA	ERA+	CERA	OAV	BH	AVG	PR+	WS	TPW
1978	LA-N	0	0	....	1	0	0	0	0	2	1	0	0	0	0	0	1	.500	0.00	....	0.55	.167	0	....	1	0	0.1
1981*	LA-N	4	3	.571	32	0	0	0	6	43^{1}	40	13	12	3	0	14	29	1.246	2.49	133	2.92	.250	2	.400	4	6	0.6
1982	LA-N	9	8	.529	45	14	0	0	1	146^{1}	137	72	62	14	2	49	80	1.271	3.81	91	3.37	.249	7	.179	-4	6	-0.4
1983	LA-N	5	2	.714	46	1	0	0	8	76	67	28	25	4	2	33	54	1.316	2.96	121	3.13	.237	1	.143	7	8	0.7
	Tex-A	5	2	.714	8	8	2	0	0	59	50	15	14	2	2	17	24	1.136	2.14	188	2.61	.233	0	....	12	6	1.2
1984	Tex-A	7	14	.333	32	27	3	0	0	192^{1}	193	106	101	26	4	87	119	1.456	4.73	88	4.59	.258	0	....	-10	6	-1.0
1985	Tex-A	0	6	.000	42	5	0	0	4	81^{1}	86	53	49	13	2	37	64	1.512	5.42	78	5.07	.273	0	....	-9	2	-0.9
	Phi-N	0	0	....	4	0	0	0	0	4^{1}	5	4	3	0	0	4	2	2.077	6.23	59	6.09	.278	0	....	-1	0	-0.1
1986	Phi-N	0	0	....	8	0	0	0	0	12^{1}	15	9	9	1	0	4	9	1.541	6.57	59	4.75	.306	0	....	-4	0	-0.4
	Oak-A	9	5	.643	29	17	4	1	0	149^{1}	137	67	62	15	3	65	102	1.353	3.74	103	3.81	.241	0	....	2	8	0.2
1987	Oak-A	**20**	13	.606	37	37	8	1	0	261^{1}	224	121	107	24	6	105	205	1.259	3.68	112	3.31	.229	0	....	16	17	1.5
1988*	Oak-A	21	12	.636	37	**37**	**14**	2	0	**275^{2}**	240	111	99	14	3	110	192	1.270	3.23	117	3.06	.234	0	....	13	18	1.3
1989*	Oak-A★	21	9	.700	36	**36**	8	0	0	257^{2}	260	105	95	23	6	69	155	1.277	3.32	111	3.65	.263	0	....	6	16	0.7
1990*	Oak-A	22	11	.667	36	**36**	**11**	**4**	0	**267**	226	84	76	16	5	83	166	1.157	2.56	145	2.75	.231	0	....	28	21	2.9
1991	Oak-A	11	11	.500	35	**35**	2	1	0	226	245	135	130	24	9	105	144	**1.549**	5.18	74	5.02	.278	0	....	-34	5	-3.4
1992*	Oak-A	12	10	.545	31	31	2	0	0	199^{1}	175	96	81	25	8	79	130	1.274	3.66	102	3.74	.237	0	....	0	9	0.0
1993*	Tor-A	12	8	.600	26	26	0	0	0	162	146	86	80	23	4	72	96	1.346	4.44	97	4.14	.242	0	....	-1	9	-0.1
1994	Tor-A	7	8	.467	22	22	1	0	0	133^{1}	151	89	87	26	4	62	111	1.598	5.87	82	5.93	.285	0	....	-14	4	-1.3
1995	Oak-A	3	7	.300	16	16	0	0	0	81	101	65	62	11	2	39	58	1.728	6.89	64	6.15	.305	0	....	-22	0	-2.0
Total	16	168	129	.566	523	348	55	9	19	2629^{2}	2499	1259	1154	264	62	1034	1741	1.344	3.95	100	3.87	.251	10	.196	-10	141	-0.5

YEAR	TM-L	W	L	PCT	G	GS	CG	SH	SV	IP	H	R	ER	HR	HB	BB	SO	RAT	ERA	ERA+	CERA	OAV	BH	AVG	PR+	WS	TPW
• STEWART, Frank	Frank "Stewy" Stewart b: 9/8/1906, Minneapolis, MN d: 4/30/2001, Stillwater, MN BR/TR, 6'1.5", 180 lbs. Deb: 10/2/1927																										
1927	Chi-A	0	1	.000	1	1	0	0	0	4	5	4	4	0	0	4	0	2.250	9.00	45	7.42	.357	0	.000	-2	0	-0.2
• STEWART, Joe	Joseph Lawrence "Ace" Stewart b: 3/11/1879, Monroe, NC d: 2/9/1913, Youngstown, OH TR, 5'11", 175 lbs. Deb: 6/9/1904																										
1904	Bos-N	0	0	....	2	0	0	0	0	9^1	12	11	10	0	1	4	1	1.714	9.64	28	4.94	.286	1	.200	-7	0	-0.7
• STEWART, Josh	Joshua Craig Stewart b: 12/5/1978, Paducah, KY BL/TL, 6'3", 205 lbs. Deb: 4/6/2003																										
2003	Chi-A	1	2	.333	5	5	0	0	0	25^2	28	18	17	4	0	16	13	1.714	5.96	75	5.82	.272	0	....	-5	0	-0.4
• STEWART, Lefty	Walter Cleveland Stewart b: 9/23/1900, Sparta, TN d: 9/26/1974, Knoxville, TN BR/TL, 5'10", 160 lbs. Deb: 4/20/1921																										
1921	Det-A	0	0	....	5	0	0	0	1	9	20	12	12	0	0	5	4	2.778	12.00	36	11.32	.455	0	.000	-8	0	-0.7
1927	StL-A	8	11	.421	27	19	11	0	1	155^2	187	83	74	7	2	43	43	1.478	4.28	102	4.36	.310	15	.306	0	11	0.3
1928	StL-A	7	9	.438	29	17	7	1	3	142^2	173	81	74	5	2	32	25	1.437	4.67	90	4.08	.310	14	.275	-8	9	-0.4
1929	StL-A	9	6	.600	23	18	8	1	0	149^2	137	67	54	11	4	49	47	1.243	3.25	136	3.18	.246	6	.118	18	12	1.4
1930	StL-A	20	12	.625	35	33	23	1	0	271	281	119	104	21	1	70	79	1.295	3.45	141	3.53	.268	22	.244	40	28	3.9
1931	StL-A	14	17	.452	36	33	20	1	0	258	287	155	126	17	3	85	89	1.442	4.40	105	4.10	.277	22	.250	6	17	1.2
1932	StL-A	15	19	.441	41	32	18	2	1	259^2	269	148	133	22	3	99	86	1.417	4.61	105	4.08	.270	12	.146	6	17	0.5
1933*	Was-A	15	6	.714	34	31	11	1	0	230^2	227	116	98	19	1	60	69	1.244	3.82	109	3.30	.256	11	.143	4	14	0.4
1934	Was-A	7	11	.389	24	22	7	1	0	152	184	74	68	8	1	36	36	1.447	4.03	107	4.29	.303	7	.156	5	9	0.4
1935	Was-A	0	1	.000	1	1	0	0	0	2^2	8	9	4	1	0	2	1	3.750	13.50	32	22.56	.533	0	.000	-3	0	-0.3
	Cle-A	6	6	.500	24	10	2	0	2	91	122	68	55	6	1	17	24	1.527	5.44	83	4.75	.312	6	.200	-8	2	-0.9
	Yr.	6	7	.462	25	11	2	0	2	93^2	130	77	59	7	1	19	25	1.591	5.67	79	5.26	.320	6	.194	-11	2	-1.1
Total	**10**	**101**	**98**	**.508**	**279**	**216**	**107**	**8**	**8**	**1722**	**1895**	**932**	**802**	**117**	**18**	**498**	**503**	**1.390**	**4.19**	**108**	**3.96**	**.281**	**115**	**.204**	**53**	**119**	**5.6**
• STEWART, Mack	William Macklin Stewart b: 9/23/1914, Stevenson, AL d: 3/21/1960, Macon, GA BR/TR, 6', 167 lbs. Deb: 7/7/1944																										
1944	Chi-N	0	0	....	8	0	0	0	0	12^1	11	2	2	1	0	4	3	1.216	1.46	242	3.08	.239	0	.000	3	1	0.3
1945	Chi-N	0	1	.000	16	1	0	0	0	28^1	37	16	15	0	0	14	9	1.800	4.76	77	5.42	.322	1	.333	-4	0	-0.4
Total	**2**	**0**	**1**	**.000**	**24**	**1**	**0**	**0**	**0**	40^2	**48**	**18**	**17**	**1**	**0**	**18**	**12**	**1.623**	**3.76**	**97**	**4.71**	**.298**	**1**	**.250**	**-1**	**1**	**-0.1**
• STEWART, Sammy	Samuel Lee Stewart b: 10/28/1954, Asheville, NC BR/TR, 6'3", 208 lbs. Deb: 9/1/1978																										
1978	Bal-A	1	1	.500	2	2	0	0	0	11^1	10	5	4	0	0	3	11	1.147	3.18	110	2.32	.238	0	....	0	1	0.0
1979*	Bal-A	8	5	.615	31	3	1	0	1	117^2	96	47	46	11	5	71	71	1.419	3.52	114	4.05	.232	0	....	5	9	0.4
1980	Bal-A	7	7	.500	33	3	2	0	3	118^2	103	51	47	9	2	60	78	1.374	3.56	111	3.57	.235	0	....	3	8	0.3
1981	Bal-A	4	8	.333	29	3	0	0	4	112^1	89	33	29	8	3	57	57	1.300	**2.32**	**156**	3.32	.225	0	....	17	11	1.8
1982	Bal-A	10	9	.526	38	12	1	1	5	139	140	68	64	9	2	62	69	1.453	4.14	97	4.06	.263	0	....	-2	9	-0.2
1983*	Bal-A	9	4	.692	58	1	0	0	7	144^1	138	60	58	7	1	67	95	1.420	3.62	109	3.70	.252	0	....	6	11	0.6
1984	Bal-A	7	4	.636	60	0	0	0	13	93	81	42	34	7	1	47	56	1.376	3.29	118	3.57	.241	0	....	4	9	0.4
1985	Bal-A	5	7	.417	56	1	0	0	9	129^2	117	60	52	15	1	66	77	1.411	3.61	112	4.01	.246	0	....	7	9	0.7
1986	Bos-A	4	1	.800	27	0	0	0	0	63^2	64	33	31	7	0	48	47	1.759	4.38	95	5.58	.266	0	....	-1	4	-0.1
1987	Cle-A	4	2	.667	25	0	0	0	3	27	25	22	17	4	1	21	25	1.704	5.67	80	5.40	.234	0	....	-3	1	-0.3
Total	**10**	**59**	**48**	**.551**	**359**	**25**	**4**	**1**	**45**	956^2	**863**	**421**	**382**	**77**	**16**	**502**	**586**	**1.427**	**3.59**	**111**	**3.92**	**.245**	**0**	**....**	**35**	**72**	**3.6**
• STEWART, Scott	Scott Edward Stewart b: 8/14/1975, Stoughton, MA BR/TL, 6'2", 225 lbs. Deb: 4/5/2001																										
2001	Mon-N	3	1	.750	62	0	0	0	3	47^2	43	20	20	5	3	13	39	1.175	3.78	118	3.31	.243	0	....	5	6	0.4
2002	Mon-N	4	2	.667	67	0	0	0	17	64	49	29	22	4	1	22	67	1.109	3.09	138	2.30	.207	0	.000	8	12	0.8
2003	Mon-N	3	1	.750	51	0	0	0	0	43	52	22	19	5	1	13	29	1.512	3.98	127	5.08	.306	0	.000	5	4	0.5
Total	**3**	**10**	**4**	**.714**	**180**	**0**	**0**	**0**	**20**	154^2	**144**	**71**	**61**	**14**	**5**	**48**	**135**	**1.241**	**3.55**	**128**	**3.38**	**.247**	**0**	**.000**	**18**	**22**	**1.7**
• STIDHAM, Phil	Phillip Wayne Stidham b: 11/18/1968, Tulsa, OK BR/TR, 6', 180 lbs. Deb: 6/4/1994																										
1994	Det-A	0	0	....	5	0	0	0	0	4^1	12	12	12	3	0	4	4	3.692	24.92	19	28.09	.571	0	....	-10	0	-0.9
• STIEB, Dave	David Andrew Stieb b: 7/22/1957, Santa Ana, CA BR/TR, 6', 195 lbs. Deb: 6/29/1979																										
1979	Tor-A	8	8	.500	18	18	7	1	0	129^1	139	70	62	11	4	48	52	1.446	4.31	101	4.39	.276	0	....	-0	8	0.0
1980	Tor-A★	12	15	.444	34	32	14	4	0	242^2	232	108	100	12	6	83	108	1.298	3.71	116	3.41	.260	0	.000	14	16	1.3
1981	Tor-A★	11	10	.524	25	25	11	2	0	183^2	148	70	65	10	11	61	89	1.138	3.19	124	2.74	.223	0	....	17	15	1.7
1982	Tor-A	17	14	.548	38	38	**19**	**5**	0	$\mathbf{288^1}$	271	116	104	27	5	75	141	1.200	3.25	138	3.24	.248	0	....	**42**	**25**	**4.2**
1983	Tor-A★	17	12	.586	36	36	14	4	0	278	223	105	94	21	14	93	187	1.137	3.04	141	2.78	.219	0	....	**38**	**24**	**3.8**
1984	Tor-A★	16	8	.667	35	35	11	2	0	**267**	215	87	84	19	11	88	198	1.135	2.83	**145**	2.77	**.221**	0	....	**36**	**25**	**3.6**
1985*	Tor-A★	14	13	.519	36	36	8	2	0	265	206	89	73	22	9	96	167	1.140	**2.48**	**170**	2.75	**.213**	0	....	**47**	**24**	**4.6**
1986	Tor-A	7	12	.368	37	34	1	1	1	205	239	128	108	29	15	87	127	1.590	4.74	89	5.86	.297	0	....	-12	6	-1.1
1987	Tor-A	13	9	.591	33	31	3	1	0	185	164	92	84	16	7	87	115	1.357	4.09	110	3.78	.239	0	....	6	11	0.6
1988	Tor-A★	16	8	.667	32	31	8	4	0	207^1	157	76	70	15	13	79	147	1.138	3.04	129	2.81	.210	0	....	19	16	2.0
1989*	Tor-A	17	8	.680	33	33	3	2	0	206^2	164	83	77	12	13	76	101	1.161	3.35	108	2.83	.219	0	....	6	13	0.6
1990	Tor-A★	18	6	.750	33	33	2	2	0	208^2	179	73	68	11	10	64	125	1.165	2.93	139	2.84	.230	0	....	27	18	2.8
1991	Tor-A	4	3	.571	9	9	1	0	0	59^2	52	22	21	4	2	23	29	1.257	3.17	133	3.34	.243	0	....	7	5	0.7
1992	Tor-A	4	6	.400	21	14	1	0	0	96^1	98	58	54	9	4	43	45	1.464	5.04	81	4.54	.275	0	....	-10	2	-1.0
1993	Chi-A	1	3	.250	4	4	0	0	0	22^1	27	17	15	1	0	14	11	1.836	6.04	69	5.68	.300	0	....	-5	0	-0.5
1998	Tor-A	1	2	.333	19	3	0	0	2	50^1	58	31	27	6	5	17	27	1.490	4.83	97	5.16	.284	0	.000	-1	2	-0.1
Total	**16**	**176**	**137**	**.562**	**443**	**412**	**103**	**30**	**3**	2895^1	**2572**	**1225**	**1106**	**225**	**129**	**1034**	**1669**	**1.245**	**3.44**	**122**	**3.37**	**.239**	**0**	**.000**	**231**	**210**	**23.2**
• STIELY, Fred	Fred Warren "Lefty" Stiely b: 6/1/1901, Pillow, PA d: 1/6/1981, Valley View, PA BL/TL, 5'8", 170 lbs. Deb: 10/6/1929																										
1929	StL-A	1	0	1.000	1	1	1	0	0	9	11	2	0	0	1	3	2	1.556	0.00	....	4.63	.297	2	.667	4	2	0.5
1930	StL-A	0	1	.000	4	2	1	0	0	19	27	21	18	4	1	8	5	1.842	8.53	57	7.46	.346	3	.429	-8	0	-0.6
1931	StL-A	0	0	....	4	0	0	0	0	6^2	7	5	5	0	1	3	2	1.500	6.75	69	4.25	.269	0	....	-2	0	-0.1
Total	**3**	**1**	**1**	**.500**	**9**	**3**	**2**	**0**	**0**	34^2	**45**	**28**	**23**	**4**	**3**	**14**	**9**	**1.702**	**5.97**	**81**	**6.11**	**.319**	**5**	**.500**	**-5**	**2**	**-0.2**
• STIGMAN, Dick	Richard Lewis Stigman b: 1/24/1936, Nimrod, MN BR/TL, 6'3", 200 lbs. Deb: 4/22/1960																										
1960	Cle-A★	5	11	.313	41	18	3	0	9	133^2	118	78	67	13	0	87	104	1.534	4.51	83	4.34	.238	8	.222	-12	5	-1.0
1961	Cle-A	2	5	.286	22	6	0	0	0	64^1	65	35	33	9	0	25	48	1.399	4.62	85	4.32	.264	2	.125	-5	2	-0.6
1962	Min-A	12	5	.706	40	15	6	0	3	142^2	122	60	58	19	2	64	116	1.304	3.66	112	3.78	.233	2	.044	6	11	0.2
1963	Min-A	15	15	.500	33	33	15	3	0	241	210	90	87	32	0	81	193	1.207	3.25	112	3.33	.231	9	.107	11	14	1.0
1964	Min-A	6	15	.286	32	29	5	1	0	190	160	94	85	31	5	70	159	1.211	4.03	89	3.54	.225	7	.101	-7	5	-1.0
1965	Min-A	4	2	.667	33	8	0	0	4	70	59	34	34	14	0	33	70	1.314	4.37	81	4.11	.227	2	.133	-7	3	-0.8
1966	Bos-A	2	1	.667	34	10	1	1	0	81	85	51	49	15	1	46	65	1.617	5.44	70	5.59	.268	2	.118	-14	1	-1.6
Total	**7**	**46**	**54**	**.460**	**235**	**119**	**30**	**5**	**16**	922^2	**819**	**442**	**413**	**133**	**8**	**406**	**755**	**1.328**	**4.03**	**93**	**3.91**	**.237**	**32**	**.113**	**-28**	**41**	**-3.8**
• STILES, Rollie	Rolland Mays "Lena" Stiles b: 11/17/1906, Ratcliff, AR BR/TR, 6'1.5", 180 lbs. Deb: 6/19/1930																										
1930	StL-A	3	6	.333	20	7	3	0	0	102	136	77	67	10	1	41	25	1.735	5.91	82	6.00	.337	10	.270	-13	4	-1.1
1931	StL-A	3	1	.750	34	2	0	0	0	81	112	72	65	2	2	60	32	2.123	7.22	64	7.43	.352	1	.045	-24	0	-2.4
1933	StL-A	3	7	.300	31	9	6	1	1	115	154	83	64	4	2	47	29	1.748	5.01	93	5.56	.327	2	.061	-7	4	-0.9
Total	**3**	**9**	**14**	**.391**	**85**	**18**	**9**	**1**	**1**	**298**	**402**	**232**	**196**	**16**	**5**	**148**	**86**	**1.846**	**5.92**	**80**	**6.22**	**.337**	**13**	**.141**	**-43**	**8**	**-4.5**
• STIMMEL, Archie	Archibald May "Lumbago" Stimmel b: 5/30/1873, Woodsboro, MD d: 8/18/1958, Frederick, MD BR/TR, 6', 175 lbs. Deb: 7/3/1900																										
1900	Cin-N	1	1	.500	2	1	1	0	0	13	18	11	10	1	0	4	2	1.692	6.92	53	5.70	.327	1	.200	-5	0	-0.4
1901	Cin-N	4	14	.222	20	18	14	1	0	153^1	170	96	70	10	12	44	55	1.396	4.11	78	4.22	.279	5	.081	-12	5	-1.7
1902	Cin-N	0	4	.000	4	3	3	0	0	26	37	16	10	1	2	12	7	1.885	3.46	86	6.56	.334	2	.200	-2	1	-0.2
Total	**3**	**5**	**19**	**.208**	**26**	**22**	**18**	**1**	**0**	192^1	**225**	**123**	**90**	**12**	**14**	**60**	**64**	**1.482**	**4.21**	**76**	**4.63**	**.290**	**8**	**.104**	**-19**	**6**	**-2.4**
• STIMSON, Carl	Carl Remus Stimson b: 7/18/1894, Hamburg, IA d: 11/9/1936, Omaha, NE BB/TR, 6'5", 190 lbs. Deb: 6/6/1923																										
1923	Bos-A	0	0	....	2	0	0	0	0	4	12	10	10	0	1	5	1	4.250	22.50	18	26.87	.750	0	.000	-8	0	-0.8

YEAR TM-L	W	L	PCT	G	GS	CG	SH	SV	IP	H	R	ER	HR	HB	BB	SO	RAT	ERA	ERA+	CERA	OAV	BH	AVG	PR+	WS	TPW
• STINE, Harry	Harry C. Stine b: 2/20/1864, Shenandoah, PA d: 6/5/1924, Niagara Falls, NY TL, 5'6", 150 lbs. Deb: 7/22/1890																									
1890 Phi-a	0	1	.000	1	1	1	0	0	8	17	9	8	0	0	4	1	2.625	9.00	42	....	.418	0	.000	-4	0	-0.4
• STINE, Lee	Lee Elbert Stine b: 11/17/1913, Stillwater, OK BR/TR, 5'11", 185 lbs. Deb: 4/17/1934																									
1934 Chi-A	0	0	....	4	0	0	0	0	11	11	10	10	2	1	10	8	1.909	8.18	58	7.19	.268	0	.000	-4	0	-0.3
1935 Chi-A	0	0	....	1	0	0	0	0	2	2	2	2	1	0	3	1	2.500	9.00	51	13.17	.286	0	....	-1	0	-0.1
1936 Cin-N	3	8	.273	40	13	5	1	2	121^2	157	79	68	6	8	41	26	1.627	5.03	76	5.25	.318	8	.296	-16	4	-1.2
1938 NY-A	0	0	....	4	0	0	0	0	8^2	9	1	1	0	0	1	4	1.154	1.04	437	3.21	.333	1	.500	3	1	0.3
Total 4	3	8	.273	49	13	5	1	2	143^1	179	92	81	9	9	55	39	1.633	5.09	77	5.39	.315	9	.300	-17	5	-1.3
• STIVETTS, Jack	John Elmer "Happy Jack" Stivetts b: 3/31/1868, Ashland, PA d: 4/18/1930, Ashland, PA BR/TR, 6'2", 185 lbs. Deb: 6/26/1889 U ♦																									
1889 StL-a	12	7	.632	26	20	18	2	1	191^2	153	85	48	4	5	68	143	1.153	**2.25**	**187**	....	**.212**	18	.228	38	21	3.1
1890 StL-a	27	21	.563	54	46	41	3	0	419^1	399	255	164	14	17	179	289	1.378	3.52	122	....	.243	65	.288	35	41	4.5
1891 StL-a	33	22	.600	**64**	56	40	3	1	440	357	237	140	15	18	232	**259**	1.339	2.86	147	....	.214	92	.305	**60**	**46**	**6.1**
1892* Bos-N	35	16	.686	54	48	45	3	1	415^2	346	223	140	12	10	171	180	1.244	3.03	116	2.75	.217	71	.296	10	**49**	2.3
1893 Bos-N	20	12	.625	38	34	29	1	1	283^2	315	194	139	17	10	115	61	1.516	4.41	112	4.46	.273	51	.297	13	25	1.5
1894 Bos-N	26	14	.650	45	39	30	0	0	338	429	278	184	27	13	127	76	1.645	4.90	121	5.44	.306	80	.328	28	33	2.7
1895 Bos-N	17	17	.500	38	34	30	0	0	291	341	219	150	15	12	89	111	1.478	4.64	108	4.40	.288	30	.190	9	18	-0.1
1896 Bos-N	22	14	.611	42	36	31	2	0	329	353	219	150	20	7	99	71	1.374	4.10	111	3.84	.272	76	.344	7	29	1.5
1897* Bos-N	11	4	.733	18	15	10	0	0	129^1	147	75	49	5	5	43	27	1.469	3.41	131	4.20	.284	73	.367	12	20	2.0
1898 Bos-N	0	1	.000	2	1	1	0	0	12	17	12	11	2	0	7	1	2.000	8.25	45	7.81	.331	28	.252	-6	2	-1.1
1899 Cle-N	0	4	.000	7	4	3	0	0	38	48	39	24	0	2	25	5	1.921	5.68	65	5.84	.308	8	.205	-7	1	-0.7
Total 11	203	132	.606	388	333	278	14	4	2887^2	2905	1836	1199	131	99	1155	1223	1.406	3.74	121	2.65	.255	592	.297	199	285	21.9
• STOBBS, Chuck	Charles Klein Stobbs b: 7/2/1929, Wheeling, WV BL/TL, 6'1", 185 lbs. Deb: 9/15/1947																									
1947 Bos-A	0	1	.000	4	1	0	0	0	9	10	6	6	0	0	10	5	2.222	6.00	65	6.52	.294	0	.000	-2	0	-0.2
1948 Bos-A	0	0	....	6	0	0	0	0	7	9	5	5	0	0	7	4	2.286	6.43	68	7.30	.321	0	.000	-2	0	-0.2
1949 Bos-A	11	6	.647	26	19	10	0	0	152	145	72	68	10	2	75	70	1.447	4.03	108	3.93	.254	11	.208	3	11	0.3
1950 Bos-A	12	7	.632	32	21	6	0	1	169^1	158	104	96	17	5	88	78	1.453	5.10	96	4.18	.250	14	.246	-3	10	0.0
1951 Bos-A	10	9	.526	34	25	6	0	0	170	180	100	90	16	5	74	75	1.494	4.76	94	4.49	.271	11	.180	-6	8	-0.7
1952 Chi-A	7	12	.368	38	17	2	0	1	135	118	54	47	9	5	72	73	1.407	3.13	116	3.68	.237	3	.079	7	8	0.5
1953 Was-A	11	8	.579	27	20	8	0	0	153	146	64	56	11	1	44	67	1.242	3.29	118	3.15	.246	10	.227	9	10	1.0
1954 Was-A	11	11	.500	31	24	10	3	0	182	189	87	83	6	1	67	67	1.407	4.10	87	3.60	.270	7	.137	-8	8	-0.8
1955 Was-A	4	14	.222	41	16	2	0	3	140^1	169	90	78	13	1	57	60	1.610	5.00	77	5.15	.302	6	.171	-15	3	-1.2
1956 Was-A	15	15	.500	37	33	15	1	1	240	264	115	96	29	1	54	97	1.325	3.60	120	4.04	.279	15	.179	27	19	2.4
1957 Was-A	8	20	.286	42	31	5	2	1	211^2	235	140	126	28	5	80	114	1.488	5.36	73	4.80	.279	16	.211	-29	3	-2.9
1958 Was-A	2	6	.250	19	8	0	0	0	56^2	87	44	38	7	2	16	23	1.818	6.04	63	7.18	.369	0	.000	-13	0	-1.5
StL-N	1	3	.250	17	0	0	0	1	39^2	40	16	16	4	0	14	25	1.361	3.63	114	3.86	.261	1	.250	2	3	0.3
1959 Was-A	1	8	.111	41	7	0	0	7	90^2	82	42	30	13	2	24	50	1.169	2.98	131	3.28	.238	2	.105	13	7	1.1
1960 Was-A	12	7	.632	40	13	1	1	2	119^1	115	54	44	13	3	38	72	1.282	3.32	119	3.61	.252	3	.088	10	9	0.8
1961 Min-A	2	3	.400	24	3	0	0	2	44^2	56	37	37	8	2	15	17	1.590	7.46	57	6.00	.311	3	.375	-15	0	-1.4
Total 15	107	130	.451	459	238	65	7	19	1920^1	2003	1030	916	184	35	735	897	1.426	4.29	95	4.21	.269	102	.176	-22	99	-2.4
• STOCK, Wes	Wesley Gay Stock b: 4/10/1934, Longview, WA BR/TR, 6'2", 188 lbs. Deb: 4/19/1959 C																									
1959 Bal-A	0	0	....	7	0	0	0	1	12^2	16	6	5	1	0	2	8	1.421	3.55	107	4.42	.302	0	.000	0	1	0.0
1960 Bal-A	2	2	.500	17	0	0	0	2	34^1	26	11	11	2	1	14	23	1.165	2.88	132	2.72	.218	0	.000	3	3	0.2
1961 Bal-A	5	0	1.000	35	1	0	0	3	71^2	58	24	24	3	2	27	47	1.186	3.01	130	2.69	.225	0	.000	6	8	0.5
1962 Bal-A	3	2	.600	53	0	0	0	3	65	50	33	32	7	1	36	34	1.323	4.43	85	3.41	.217	0	.000	-5	3	-0.5
1963 Bal-A	7	0	1.000	47	0	0	0	1	75^1	69	41	33	11	0	31	55	1.327	3.94	89	3.84	.246	0	.000	-3	3	-0.5
1964 Bal-A	2	0	1.000	14	0	0	0	0	20^2	17	9	9	5	0	8	14	1.210	3.92	91	3.99	.233	0	.000	-1	1	-0.2
KC-A	6	3	.667	50	0	0	0	5	93	69	21	20	10	4	34	101	1.108	1.94	197	2.76	.213	3	.200	21	12	2.2
Yr.	8	3	.727	64	0	0	0	5	113^2	86	30	29	15	4	42	115	1.126	2.30	163	2.98	.217	3	.158	20	13	2.1
1965 KC-A	0	4	.000	62	2	0	0	4	99^2	96	62	58	18	4	40	52	1.365	5.24	67	4.51	.251	0	.000	-19	1	-2.1
1966 KC-A	2	2	.500	35	0	0	0	3	44	30	15	13	3	3	21	31	1.159	2.66	128	2.65	.199	0	.000	3	4	0.3
1967 KC-A	0	0	....	1	0	0	0	0	1	3	2	2	0	0	2	0	5.000	18.00	18	24.59	.500	0	....	-2	0	-0.2
Total 9	27	13	.675	321	3	0	0	22	517^1	434	224	207	60	15	215	365	1.255	3.60	101	3.44	.231	3	.051	3	36	-0.2
• STOCKSDALE, Otis	Otis Hinkley "Old Gray Fox" Stocksdale b: 8/7/1871, Arcadia, MD d: 3/15/1933, Pennsville, NJ BL/TR, 5'10.5", 180 lbs. Deb: 7/24/1893 U																									
1893 Was-N	2	8	.200	11	11	7	0	0	69	111	82	63	4	5	32	12	2.072	8.22	56	7.88	.352	12	.300	-26	1	-2.0
1894 Was-N	5	9	.357	18	14	11	0	0	117^1	176	115	66	10	14	42	10	1.858	5.06	104	7.18	.343	23	.324	5	5	0.4
1895 Was-N	6	11	.353	20	17	11	0	1	136	199	143	92	7	8	52	23	1.846	6.09	79	6.50	.336	23	.311	-17	4	-1.2
Bos-N	2	2	.500	4	4	1	0	0	23	31	22	15	2	0	8	2	1.696	5.87	85	5.72	.318	4	.267	-2	1	-0.2
Yr.	8	13	.381	24	21	12	0	1	159	230	165	107	9	8	60	25	1.824	6.06	80	6.39	.333	27	.303	-20	5	-1.5
1896 Bal-N	0	1	.000	1	0	0	0	0	1^2	4	4	3	0	1	2	1	3.600	16.20	26	18.48	.456	1	.333	-2	0	-0.1
Total 4	15	31	.326	54	46	30	0	1	347	521	366	239	23	28	136	48	1.893	6.20	79	7.01	.341	63	.310	-42	11	-3.2
• STODDARD, Bob	Robert Lyle Stoddard b: 3/8/1957, San Jose, CA BR/TR, 6'1", 200 lbs. Deb: 9/4/1981																									
1981 Sea-A	2	1	.667	5	5	1	0	0	34^2	35	10	10	3	1	9	22	1.269	2.60	148	3.75	.269	0	....	5	3	0.6
1982 Sea-A	3	3	.500	9	9	2	1	0	67^1	48	22	18	7	3	18	24	.980	2.41	176	2.38	.205	0	....	14	7	1.4
1983 Sea-A	9	17	.346	35	23	2	1	0	175^2	182	95	86	29	4	58	87	1.366	4.41	97	4.66	.274	0	....	-3	8	-0.3
1984 Sea-A	2	3	.400	27	6	0	0	0	79	86	51	45	10	2	37	39	1.557	5.13	78	5.13	.278	0	....	-8	2	-0.8
1985 Det-A	0	0	....	8	0	0	0	1	13^1	15	11	10	3	0	5	11	1.500	6.75	60	5.39	.268	0	....	-4	0	-0.4
1986 SD-N	1	0	1.000	18	0	0	0	1	23^1	20	7	6	1	1	11	17	1.329	2.31	158	3.18	.227	0	.000	4	2	0.4
1987 KC-A	1	3	.250	17	2	0	0	1	40	51	26	19	3	3	22	23	1.825	4.28	107	6.39	.313	0	....	2	2	0.2
Total 7	18	27	.400	119	45	5	2	3	433^1	437	222	194	56	14	160	223	1.378	4.03	103	4.42	.266	0	.000	10	24	1.0
• STODDARD, Tim	Timothy Paul Stoddard b: 1/24/1953, East Chicago, IN BR/TR, 6'7", 250 lbs. Deb: 9/7/1975																									
1975 Chi-A	0	0	....	1	0	0	0	0	1	2	1	1	1	0	0	0	2.000	9.00	43	16.28	.400	0	....	-1	0	-0.1
1978 Bal-A	0	1	.000	8	0	0	0	0	18	22	17	12	3	2	8	14	1.667	6.00	58	6.48	.301	0	....	-5	0	-0.5
1979* Bal-A	3	1	.750	29	0	0	0	3	58	44	12	11	3	0	19	47	1.086	1.71	235	2.27	.212	0	....	14	8	1.4
1980 Bal-A	5	3	.625	64	0	0	0	26	86	72	27	24	2	1	38	64	1.279	2.51	157	2.96	.233	0	....	12	14	1.2
1981 Bal-A	4	2	.667	31	0	0	0	7	37^1	38	16	16	6	2	18	32	1.500	3.86	94	5.34	.268	0	....	-1	3	-0.1
1982 Bal-A	3	4	.429	50	0	0	0	12	56	53	26	25	4	1	29	42	1.464	4.02	100	3.85	.249	0	....	0	5	0.0
1983 Bal-A	4	3	.571	47	0	0	0	9	57^2	65	39	39	10	1	29	50	1.630	6.09	65	5.78	.291	0	....	-14	1	-1.4
1984* Chi-N	10	6	.625	58	0	0	0	7	92	77	41	39	9	1	57	87	1.457	3.82	102	3.90	.236	1	.091	2	8	0.2
1985 SD-N	1	6	.143	44	0	0	0	1	60	63	35	31	3	0	37	42	1.667	4.65	76	4.52	.269	0	.000	-8	1	-0.9
1986 SD-N	1	3	.250	30	0	0	0	0	45^1	33	20	19	6	0	34	47	1.478	3.77	97	3.84	.200	1	.250	-1	2	0.1
NY-A	4	1	.800	24	0	0	0	0	49^1	41	23	21	6	0	23	34	1.297	3.83	107	3.46	.232	0	....	1	3	0.1
1987 NY-A	4	3	.571	57	0	0	0	8	92^2	83	38	36	13	0	30	78	1.219	3.50	125	3.42	.235	0	....	9	10	0.8
1988 NY-A	2	2	.500	28	0	0	0	3	55	62	41	39	5	2	27	33	1.618	6.38	62	5.16	.286	0	....	-14	0	-1.5
1989 Cle-A	0	0	....	14	0	0	0	0	21^1	25	7	7	1	0	7	12	1.500	2.95	134	4.44	.313	0	....	2	2	0.3
Total 13	41	35	.539	485	0	0	0	76	729^2	680	343	320	72	10	356	582	1.420	3.95	99	4.03	.250	2	.100	-3	57	-0.5
• STOKES, Art	Arthur Milton Stokes b: 9/13/1896, Emmitsburg, MD d: 6/3/1962, Titusville, PA BR/TR, 5'10.5", 155 lbs. Deb: 5/5/1925																									
1925 Phi-A	1	1	.500	12	0	0	0	0	24^1	24	15	11	0	2	10	7	1.397	4.07	114	3.64	.270	0	.000	2	1	0.1
• STONE, Arnie	Edwin Arnold Stone b: 10/9/1892, North Creek, NY d: 7/29/1948, Hudson Falls, NY BR/TL, 6', 180 lbs. Deb: 7/30/1923																									
1923 Pit-N	0	1	.000	9	0	0	0	0	12^1	19	12	11	0	0	4	2	1.865	8.03	50	6.13	.352	0	.000	-6	0	-0.6
1924 Pit-N	4	2	.667	26	2	1	0	0	64	57	27	21	0	0	15	7	1.125	2.95	130	2.32	.259	2	.133	4	5	0.3
Total 2	4	3	.571	35	2	1	0	0	76^1	76	39	32	0	0	19	9	1.245	3.77	103	2.93	.277	2	.125	-2	5	-0.3

• STONE, Dean

Darrah Dean Stone b: 9/1/1930, Moline, IL BL/TL, 6'4", 205 lbs. Deb: 9/13/1953

YEAR	TM-L	W	L	PCT	G	GS	CG	SH	SV	IP	H	R	ER	HR	HB	BB	SO	RAT	ERA	ERA+	CERA	OAV	BH	AVG	PR+	WS	TPW
1953	Was-A	0	1	.000	3	1	0	0	0	8^2	13	8	8	0	0	5	5	2.077	8.31	47	6.78	.361	0	.000	-4	0	-0.5
1954	Was-A★	12	10	.545	31	23	10	2	0	178^2	161	76	64	7	1	69	87	1.287	3.22	110	3.00	.240	5	.096	10	11	1.0
1955	Was-A	6	13	.316	43	24	5	1	1	180	180	98	83	14	3	114	84	**1.633**	4.15	92	4.88	.267	2	.043	-2	6	-0.5
1956	Was-A	5	7	.417	41	21	2	0	3	132	148	107	92	10	7	93	86	1.826	6.27	69	5.97	.282	3	.088	-25	1	-2.5
1957	Was-A	0	0	....	3	0	0	0	0	3^1	5	3	3	0	0	2	3	2.100	8.10	48	6.27	.357	0	....	-1	0	-0.2
	Bos-A	1	3	.250	17	8	0	0	1	51^1	56	42	29	5	0	35	32	1.773	5.08	78	5.74	.284	0	.000	-5	0	-0.7
	Yr.	1	3	.250	20	8	0	0	1	54^2	61	45	32	5	0	37	35	1.793	5.27	76	5.77	.289	0	.000	-7	0	-0.8
1959	StL-N	0	1	.000	18	1	0	0	1	30	30	15	14	4	0	16	17	1.533	4.20	101	4.67	.273	0	.000	0	2	0.0
1962	Hou-N	3	2	.600	15	7	2	2	0	52^1	61	31	26	4	1	20	31	1.548	4.47	84	4.91	.295	4	.250	-3	2	-0.2
	Chi-A	1	0	1.000	27	0	0	0	5	30^1	28	11	11	3	1	9	23	1.220	3.26	120	3.33	.255	1	.500	2	4	0.3
1963	Bal-A	1	2	.333	17	0	0	0	1	19^1	23	11	11	0	0	10	12	1.707	5.12	69	4.65	.307	0	....	-3	0	-0.4
Total	8	29	39	.426	215	85	19	5	12	686	705	402	341	47	13	373	380	1.571	4.47	87	4.61	.269	15	.088	-32	26	-3.7

• STONE, Dick

Charles Richard Stone b: 12/5/1911, Oklahoma City, OK d: 2/18/1980, Oklahoma City, OK BL/TL, 5'9", 153 lbs. Deb: 8/26/1945

YEAR	TM-L	W	L	PCT	G	GS	CG	SH	SV	IP	H	R	ER	HR	HB	BB	SO	RAT	ERA	ERA+	CERA	OAV	BH	AVG	PR+	WS	TPW
1945	Was-A	0	0	....	3	0	0	0	0	5	6	0	0	0	0	2	0	1.600	0.00	....	4.45	.316	0	....	2	1	0.2

• STONE, Dwight

Dwight Ely Stone b: 8/2/1886, Holt County, NE d: 6/3/1976, Glendale, CA BR/TR, 6'1.5", 170 lbs. Deb: 4/13/1913

YEAR	TM-L	W	L	PCT	G	GS	CG	SH	SV	IP	H	R	ER	HR	HB	BB	SO	RAT	ERA	ERA+	CERA	OAV	BH	AVG	PR+	WS	TPW
1913	StL-A	2	6	.250	18	7	4	1	0	91	94	45	36	0	7	46	37	1.538	3.56	82	4.11	.267	9	.273	-8	3	-0.7
1914	KC-F	8	14	.364	39	22	6	0	0	186^2	205	110	90	8	8	77	88	1.511	4.34	71	4.40	.281	7	.121	-27	3	-3.1
Total	2	10	20	.333	57	29	10	1	0	277^2	299	155	126	8	15	123	125	1.520	4.08	74	4.30	.276	16	.176	-35	6	-3.7

• STONE, George

George Heard Stone b: 7/9/1946, Ruston, LA BL/TL, 6'3", 205 lbs. Deb: 9/15/1967

YEAR	TM-L	W	L	PCT	G	GS	CG	SH	SV	IP	H	R	ER	HR	HB	BB	SO	RAT	ERA	ERA+	CERA	OAV	BH	AVG	PR+	WS	TPW
1967	Atl-N	0	0	....	2	1	0	0	0	7^1	8	4	4	0	0	1	5	1.227	4.91	68	2.82	.267	0	.000	-1	0	-0.2
1968	Atl-N	7	4	.636	17	10	2	0	0	75	63	27	23	9	0	19	52	1.093	2.76	108	2.69	.222	9	.333	2	7	0.5
1969*	Atl-N	13	10	.565	36	20	3	0	3	165^1	166	82	67	20	5	48	102	1.294	3.65	99	3.87	.260	11	.186	-0	10	0.1
1970	Atl-N	11	11	.500	35	30	9	2	0	207^1	218	111	89	27	6	50	131	1.293	3.86	111	3.94	.267	17	.236	15	13	1.9
1971	Atl-N	6	8	.429	27	24	4	2	0	172^2	186	80	69	19	6	35	110	1.280	3.60	103	3.85	.274	11	.177	3	10	0.3
1972	Atl-N	6	11	.353	31	16	2	1	1	111	143	72	68	18	4	44	63	1.685	5.51	69	6.24	.315	5	.200	-20	1	-1.9
1973*	NY-N	12	3	.800	27	20	2	0	1	148	157	53	46	16	0	31	77	1.270	2.80	129	3.68	.274	13	.271	13	13	1.5
1974	NY-N	2	7	.222	15	13	1	0	0	77	103	57	43	10	0	21	29	1.610	5.03	71	5.63	.322	3	.115	-13	0	-1.5
1975	NY-N	3	3	.500	13	11	1	0	0	57	75	38	32	3	0	21	21	1.684	5.05	68	5.32	.323	3	.167	-11	0	-1.1
Total	9	60	57	.513	203	145	24	5	5	1020^2	1119	524	441	122	21	270	590	1.361	3.89	95	4.23	.278	72	.212	-12	54	-0.3

• STONE, Ricky

Ricky L. Stone b: 2/28/1975, Hamilton, OH BR/TR, 6'1", 168 lbs. Deb: 9/21/2001

YEAR	TM-L	W	L	PCT	G	GS	CG	SH	SV	IP	H	R	ER	HR	HB	BB	SO	RAT	ERA	ERA+	CERA	OAV	BH	AVG	PR+	WS	TPW
2001	Hou-N	0	0	....	6	0	0	0	0	7^2	8	3	2	1	0	2	4	1.304	2.35	195	3.69	.258	0	....	2	1	0.2
2002	Hou-N	3	3	.500	78	0	0	0	1	77^1	78	36	31	9	1	34	63	1.448	3.61	118	4.43	.266	0	.000	6	5	0.6
2003	Hou-N	6	4	.600	65	0	0	0	1	83	76	36	34	11	6	31	47	1.289	3.69	120	4.00	.247	0	.000	5	6	0.5
Total	3	9	7	.563	149	0	0	0	2	168	162	75	67	21	7	67	114	1.363	3.59	121	4.18	.256	0	.000	13	12	1.2

• STONE, Rocky

John Vernon Stone b: 8/23/1918, Redding, CA d: 11/12/1986, Fountain Valley, CA BR/TR, 6', 200 lbs. Deb: 5/2/1943

YEAR	TM-L	W	L	PCT	G	GS	CG	SH	SV	IP	H	R	ER	HR	HB	BB	SO	RAT	ERA	ERA+	CERA	OAV	BH	AVG	PR+	WS	TPW
1943	Cin-N	0	1	.000	13	0	0	0	0	24^2	23	14	12	0	0	8	11	1.257	4.38	76	2.62	.237	1	.250	-4	0	-0.4

• STONE, Steve

Steven Michael Stone b: 7/14/1947, Euclid, OH BR/TR, 5'10", 175 lbs. Deb: 4/8/1971

YEAR	TM-L	W	L	PCT	G	GS	CG	SH	SV	IP	H	R	ER	HR	HB	BB	SO	RAT	ERA	ERA+	CERA	OAV	BH	AVG	PR+	WS	TPW
1971	SF-N	5	9	.357	24	19	2	2	0	110^2	110	56	51	9	3	55	63	1.491	4.15	82	4.37	.259	0	.000	-9	3	-1.2
1972	SF-N	6	8	.429	27	16	4	1	0	123^2	97	48	41	11	2	49	85	1.181	2.98	117	2.90	.218	4	.118	7	7	0.6
1973	Chi-A	6	11	.353	36	22	3	0	1	176^1	163	87	83	11	7	82	138	1.389	4.24	93	3.83	.245	0	....	-3	8	-0.3
1974	Chi-N	8	6	.571	38	23	1	0	0	169^2	185	92	78	19	4	64	90	1.468	4.14	92	4.59	.278	7	.121	2	8	0.0
1975	Chi-N	12	8	.600	33	32	6	1	0	214^1	198	103	94	24	5	80	139	1.297	3.95	97	3.69	.245	8	.111	5	13	0.3
1976	Chi-N	3	6	.333	17	15	1	1	0	75	70	36	34	6	3	21	33	1.213	4.08	95	3.26	.250	3	.143	-1	3	-0.1
1977	Chi-A	15	12	.556	31	31	8	0	0	207^1	228	115	104	25	5	80	124	1.486	4.51	90	4.80	.281	0	....	-4	9	-0.4
1978	Chi-A	12	12	.500	30	30	6	1	0	212	196	110	103	19	3	84	118	1.321	4.37	87	3.63	.247	0	....	-12	9	-1.2
1979*	Bal-A	11	7	.611	32	32	3	0	0	186	173	91	78	31	1	73	96	1.323	3.77	106	4.18	.248	0	....	2	11	0.2
1980	Bal-A★	**25**	7	.781	37	37	9	1	0	250^2	224	103	90	22	6	101	149	1.297	3.23	122	3.55	.240	0	....	15	20	1.5
1981	Bal-A	4	7	.364	15	12	0	0	0	62^2	63	39	32	7	1	27	30	1.436	4.60	79	4.43	.266	0	....	-6	1	-0.7
Total	11	107	93	.535	320	269	43	7	1	1788^1	1707	880	788	184	40	716	1065	1.355	3.97	97	3.94	.253	22	.100	-4	92	-1.3

• STONEMAN, Bill

William Hambly Stoneman b: 4/7/1944, Oak Park, IL BR/TR, 5'10", 170 lbs. Deb: 7/16/1967

YEAR	TM-L	W	L	PCT	G	GS	CG	SH	SV	IP	H	R	ER	HR	HB	BB	SO	RAT	ERA	ERA+	CERA	OAV	BH	AVG	PR+	WS	TPW
1967	Chi-N	2	4	.333	28	2	0	0	4	63	51	24	23	7	0	22	52	1.159	3.29	108	2.84	.223	0	.000	1	4	0.0
1968	Chi-N	0	1	.000	18	0	0	0	0	29^1	35	19	18	6	1	14	18	1.670	5.52	57	6.65	.310	0	.000	-8	0	-0.9
1969	Mon-N	11	19	.367	42	36	8	5	0	235^2	233	133	115	26	12	123	185	1.511	4.39	84	4.78	.261	4	.055	-18	7	-2.2
1970	Mon-N	7	15	.318	40	30	5	3	0	207^2	209	118	106	26	14	109	176	1.531	4.59	89	5.04	.263	6	.100	-13	7	-1.5
1971	Mon-N	17	16	.515	39	**39**	20	3	0	294^2	243	112	103	20	5	146	251	1.320	3.15	112	3.30	.225	12	.129	13	20	1.4
1972	Mon-N★	12	14	.462	36	35	13	4	0	250^2	213	93	83	15	3	102	171	1.257	2.98	119	3.00	.229	6	.080	17	18	1.4
1973	Mon-N	4	8	.333	29	17	0	0	1	96^2	120	77	73	12	6	55	48	1.810	6.80	56	6.52	.310	1	.050	-32	0	-3.4
1974	Cal-A	1	8	.111	13	11	0	0	0	58^2	78	41	40	8	2	31	33	1.858	6.14	56	7.11	.322	0	....	-17	0	-1.8
Total	8	54	85	.388	245	170	46	15	5	1236^1	1182	617	561	120	43	602	934	1.443	4.08	90	4.30	.253	29	.086	-55	56	-7.0

• STONER, Lil

Ulysses Simpson Grant Stoner b: 2/28/1899, Bowie, TX d: 6/26/1966, Enid, OK BR/TR, 5'9.5", 180 lbs. Deb: 4/15/1922

YEAR	TM-L	W	L	PCT	G	GS	CG	SH	SV	IP	H	R	ER	HR	HB	BB	SO	RAT	ERA	ERA+	CERA	OAV	BH	AVG	PR+	WS	TPW
1922	Det-A	4	4	.500	17	7	2	0	0	62^2	76	53	49	3	3	35	18	1.771	7.04	55	5.69	.315	2	.100	-21	0	-2.1
1924	Det-A	11	11	.500	36	25	10	1	0	215^2	271	130	113	13	5	65	66	1.558	4.72	87	4.86	.316	15	.195	-14	10	-1.3
1925	Det-A	10	9	.526	34	18	8	0	1	152	166	79	72	6	9	53	51	1.441	4.26	101	4.10	.283	16	.291	0	11	0.4
1926	Det-A	7	10	.412	32	22	7	0	0	159^2	179	115	97	11	3	63	57	1.516	5.47	74	4.50	.291	9	.170	-23	2	-2.4
1927	Det-A	10	13	.435	38	24	13	0	5	215	251	118	95	9	3	77	63	1.526	3.98	106	4.42	.301	8	.108	8	12	0.1
1928	Det-A	5	8	.385	36	11	4	0	4	126^1	151	75	61	16	3	42	29	1.528	4.35	94	4.87	.296	7	.179	-3	6	-0.4
1929	Det-A	3	3	.500	24	3	1	0	4	53	57	37	31	2	2	31	12	1.660	5.26	81	4.76	.288	1	.067	-4	2	-0.6
1930	Pit-N	0	0	....	5	0	0	0	0	5^2	7	3	3	2	0	3	1	1.765	4.76	104	8.42	.318	0	....	0	0	0.0
1931	Phi-N	0	0	....	7	1	0	0	0	13^2	22	13	10	0	0	5	2	1.976	6.59	64	6.70	.373	0	.000	-3	0	-0.4
Total	9	50	58	.463	229	111	45	1	14	1003^2	1180	623	531	62	28	374	299	1.548	4.76	87	4.69	.301	58	.172	-61	43	-6.7

• STOOPS, Jim

James Wellington Stoops b: 6/30/1972, Edison, NJ BR/TR, 6'2" Deb: 9/9/1998

YEAR	TM-L	W	L	PCT	G	GS	CG	SH	SV	IP	H	R	ER	HR	HB	BB	SO	RAT	ERA	ERA+	CERA	OAV	BH	AVG	PR+	WS	TPW
1998	Col-N	1	0	1.000	3	0	0	0	0	4	5	1	1	1	1	3	0	2.000	2.25	230	11.67	.385	0	....	1	1	0.1

• STOTTLEMYRE, Mel

Melvin Leon Stottlemyre, Jr. b: 12/28/1963, Prosser, WA BR/TR, 6', 190 lbs. Deb: 7/17/1990

YEAR	TM-L	W	L	PCT	G	GS	CG	SH	SV	IP	H	R	ER	HR	HB	BB	SO	RAT	ERA	ERA+	CERA	OAV	BH	AVG	PR+	WS	TPW
1990	KC-A	0	1	.000	13	2	0	0	0	31^1	35	18	17	3	0	12	14	1.500	4.88	78	4.58	.280	0	....	-3	0	-0.3

• STOTTLEMYRE, Mel

Melvin Leon Stottlemyre, Sr. b: 11/13/1941, Hazleton, MO BR/TR, 6'1", 190 lbs. Deb: 8/12/1964 C

YEAR	TM-L	W	L	PCT	G	GS	CG	SH	SV	IP	H	R	ER	HR	HB	BB	SO	RAT	ERA	ERA+	CERA	OAV	BH	AVG	PR+	WS	TPW
1964*	NY-A	9	3	.750	13	12	5	2	0	96	77	26	22	3	2	35	49	1.167	2.06	176	2.52	.219	9	.243	16	10	1.9
1965	NY-A★	20	9	.690	37	37	**18**	4	0	**291**	250	99	85	18	7	88	155	1.162	2.63	130	2.81	.233	13	.131	27	23	2.9
1966	NY-A★	12	20	.375	37	35	9	3	1	251	239	116	106	18	1	82	146	1.279	3.80	87	3.36	.253	11	.138	-12	9	-1.2
1967	NY-A	15	15	.500	36	36	10	4	0	255	235	96	84	20	2	88	151	1.267	2.96	105	3.28	.248	8	.098	8	16	0.5
1968	NY-A★	21	12	.636	36	36	19	6	0	278^2	243	86	76	21	3	65	140	1.105	2.45	118	2.63	.234	13	.143	17	22	2.1
1969	NY-A★	20	14	.588	39	39	**24**	3	0	303	267	105	95	19	6	97	113	1.201	2.82	123	2.94	.239	18	.178	21	26	2.6
1970	NY-A★	15	13	.536	37	37	14	0	0	271	262	110	93	23	6	84	126	1.277	3.09	114	3.50	.255	16	.188	12	18	2.2
1971	NY-A	16	12	.571	35	35	19	7	0	269^2	234	100	86	16	4	69	132	1.124	2.87	113	2.61	.233	16	.170	12	19	1.5
1972	NY-A	14	18	.438	36	36	9	7	0	260	250	99	93	13	4	85	110	1.288	3.22	92	3.25	.254	16	.200	-8	11	-0.6
1973	NY-A	16	16	.500	38	38	19	4	0	273	259	112	93	13	5	79	95	1.238	3.07	120	3.13	.253	0	....	15	18	1.6
1974	NY-A	6	7	.462	16	15	6	0	0	113	119	54	45	7	4	37	40	1.381	3.58	97	3.94	.272	0	....	-3	5	-0.3
Total	11	164	139	.541	360	356	152	40	1	2661^1	2435	1003	878	171	44	809	1257	1.219	2.97	111	3.07	.245	120	.160	104	177	13.1

YEAR TM-L	W	L	PCT	G	GS	CG	SH	SV	IP	H	R	ER	HR	HB	BB	SO	RAT	ERA	ERA+	CERA	OAV	BH	AVG	PR+	WS	TPW
• STOTTLEMYRE, Todd	Todd Vernon Stottlemyre b: 5/20/1965, Sunnyside, WA BL/TR, 6'3", 195 lbs. Deb: 4/6/1988																									
1988 Tor-A	4	8	.333	28	16	0	0	0	98	109	70	62	15	4	46	67	1.582	5.69	69	5.49	.283	0	....	-20	0	-2.0
1989* Tor-A	7	7	.500	27	18	0	0	0	127^2	137	56	55	11	5	44	63	1.418	3.88	93	4.37	.282	0	....	-4	6	-0.4
1990 Tor-A	13	17	.433	33	33	4	0	0	203	214	101	98	18	8	69	115	1.394	4.34	94	4.27	.274	0	....	-5	9	-0.5
1991* Tor-A	15	8	.652	34	34	1	0	0	219	194	97	92	21	12	75	116	1.228	3.78	111	3.39	.235	0	....	11	15	1.1
1992* Tor-A	12	11	.522	28	27	6	2	0	174	175	99	87	20	10	63	98	1.368	4.50	91	4.25	.262	0	....	-7	7	-0.8
1993* Tor-A	11	12	.478	30	28	1	1	0	176^2	204	107	95	11	3	69	98	1.545	4.84	89	4.67	.292	0	....	-9	7	-0.9
1994 Tor-A	7	7	.500	26	19	3	1	1	140^2	149	67	66	19	7	48	105	1.400	4.22	114	4.67	.275	0	....	11	10	1.0
1995 Oak-A	14	7	.667	31	31	2	0	0	209^2	228	117	106	26	6	80	205	1.469	4.55	98	4.75	.276	0	.000	-2	10	-0.2
1996* StL-N	14	11	.560	34	33	5	2	0	223^1	191	100	96	30	4	93	194	1.272	3.87	108	3.58	.231	15	.227	3	14	0.6
1997 StL-N	12	9	.571	28	28	0	0	0	181	155	86	78	16	12	65	160	1.215	3.88	107	3.29	.231	13	.236	5	11	1.1
1998 StL-N	9	9	.500	23	23	3	0	0	161^1	146	74	63	20	4	51	147	1.221	3.51	119	3.48	.240	12	.226	13	10	1.5
* Tex-A	5	4	.556	10	10	0	0	0	60^1	68	33	29	5	0	30	57	1.624	4.33	112	4.99	.282	0	....	4	4	0.4
1999* Ari-N	6	3	.667	17	17	0	0	0	101^1	106	51	46	12	6	40	74	1.441	4.09	112	4.67	.268	4	.125	5	6	0.5
2000 Ari-N	9	6	.600	18	18	0	0	0	95^1	98	55	52	18	2	36	76	1.406	4.91	96	4.90	.268	6	.194	-2	6	0.0
2002 Ari-N	0	2	.000	5	4	0	0	0	20^1	26	17	17	4	0	7	12	1.623	7.52	59	6.22	.313	0	.000	-7	0	-0.7
Total 14	**138**	**121**	**.533**	**372**	**339**	**25**	**6**	**1**	**2191^2**	**2200**	**1130**	**1042**	**246**	**83**	**816**	**1587**	**1.376**	**4.28**	**99**	**4.22**	**.262**	**50**	**.207**	**-4**	**115**	**0.9**
• STOUT, Allyn	Allyn McClelland "Fish Hook" Stout b: 10/31/1904, Peoria, IL d: 12/22/1974, Sikeston, MO BR/TR, 5'10", 167 lbs. Deb: 5/16/1931																									
1931 StL-N	6	0	1.000	30	3	1	0	3	72^2	87	40	34	2	1	34	40	1.665	4.21	93	4.96	.305	2	.105	-2	5	-0.4
1932 StL-N	4	5	.444	36	3	1	0	1	73^2	87	40	36	5	4	28	32	1.561	4.40	89	4.95	.305	2	.100	-3	3	-0.5
1933 StL-N	0	0	....	1	0	0	0	0	2	1	0	0	0	0	1	1	1.000	0.00	....	1.54	.167	0	....	1	0	0.1
Cin-N	2	3	.400	23	5	2	0	0	71^1	85	36	30	3	0	26	29	1.556	3.79	90	4.50	.295	4	.182	-2	3	-0.3
Yr.	2	3	.400	24	5	2	0	0	73^1	86	36	30	3	0	27	30	1.541	3.68	92	4.42	.292	4	.182	-2	3	-0.2
1934 Cin-N	6	8	.429	41	16	4	0	1	140^2	170	85	76	10	4	47	51	1.543	4.86	84	4.76	.297	8	.186	-9	5	-0.8
1935 NY-N	1	4	.200	40	2	0	0	5	88	99	58	48	7	4	37	29	1.545	4.91	79	4.77	.289	2	.133	-11	2	-1.0
1943 Bos-N	1	0	1.000	9	0	0	0	1	9^1	17	12	7	1	0	4	3	2.250	6.75	51	9.08	.378	0	.000	-4	0	-0.4
Total 6	**20**	**20**	**.500**	**180**	**29**	**8**	**0**	**11**	**457^2**	**546**	**271**	**231**	**28**	**13**	**177**	**185**	**1.580**	**4.54**	**85**	**4.86**	**.299**	**18**	**.149**	**-30**	**18**	**-3.3**
• STOVALL, Jesse	Jesse Cramer "Scout" Stovall b: 7/24/1875, Leeds, MO d: 7/12/1955, San Diego, CA BL/TR, 6', 175 lbs. Deb: 8/31/1903																									
1903 Cle-A	5	1	.833	6	6	6	2	0	57	44	17	13	0	3	21	12	1.140	2.05	139	2.23	.213	1	.045	4	5	0.2
1904 Det-A	2	13	.133	22	17	13	1	0	146^2	170	97	72	3	16	45	41	1.466	4.42	58	4.35	.291	11	.196	-32	0	-3.6
Total 2	**7**	**14**	**.333**	**28**	**23**	**19**	**3**	**0**	**203^2**	**214**	**114**	**85**	**3**	**19**	**66**	**53**	**1.375**	**3.76**	**69**	**3.76**	**.270**	**12**	**.154**	**-28**	**5**	**-3.4**
• STOWE, Hal	Harold Rudolph Stowe b: 8/29/1937, Gastonia, NC BL/TL, 6', 170 lbs. Deb: 9/30/1960																									
1960 NY-A	0	0	....	1	0	0	0	0	1	0	1	1	0	0	1	0	1.000	9.00	40	0.95	.000	0	....	-1	0	-0.1
• STRAHLER, Mike	Michael Wayne Strahler b: 3/14/1947, Chicago, IL BR/TR, 6'4", 180 lbs. Deb: 9/12/1970																									
1970 LA-N	1	1	.500	6	0	0	0	1	18^2	13	6	3	1	0	10	11	1.232	1.45	265	2.69	.194	2	.250	5	2	0.5
1971 LA-N	0	0	....	6	0	0	0	0	12^2	10	4	4	1	0	8	7	1.421	2.84	114	3.65	.217	0	.000	1	1	0.0
1972 LA-N	1	2	.333	19	2	1	0	0	47	42	25	17	5	1	22	25	1.362	3.26	102	3.74	.237	2	.182	0	2	0.1
1973 Det-A	4	5	.444	22	11	1	0	0	80^1	84	45	39	7	1	39	37	1.531	4.37	94	4.71	.273	0	....	-2	3	-0.2
Total 4	**6**	**8**	**.429**	**53**	**13**	**2**	**0**	**1**	**158^2**	**149**	**80**	**63**	**14**	**2**	**79**	**80**	**1.437**	**3.57**	**106**	**4.10**	**.249**	**4**	**.200**	**3**	**8**	**0.5**
• STRAHS, Dick	Richard Bernard Strahs b: 12/4/1923, Evanston, IL d: 5/26/1988, Las Vegas, NV BL/TR, 6', 192 lbs. Deb: 7/24/1954																									
1954 Chi-A	0	0	....	9	0	0	0	1	14^1	16	10	9	0	0	8	8	1.674	5.65	66	4.24	.271	0	.000	-3	0	-0.3
• STRAKER, Les	Lester Paul (Bolnalda) Straker b: 10/10/1959, Ciudad Bolivar, Venezuela BR/TR, 6'1", 193 lbs. Deb: 4/11/1987																									
1987* Min-A	8	10	.444	31	26	1	0	0	154^1	150	79	75	24	2	59	76	1.354	4.37	106	4.26	.257	0	....	4	9	0.3
1988 Min-A	2	5	.286	16	14	1	1	1	82^2	86	39	36	8	0	25	23	1.343	3.92	104	4.01	.276	0	....	1	4	0.1
Total 2	**10**	**15**	**.400**	**47**	**40**	**2**	**1**	**1**	**237**	**236**	**118**	**111**	**32**	**2**	**84**	**99**	**1.350**	**4.22**	**105**	**4.17**	**.264**	**0**	**....**	**5**	**13**	**0.5**
• STRAMPE, Bob	Robert Edwin Strampe b: 6/13/1950, Janesville, WI BB/TR, 6'1", 185 lbs. Deb: 5/10/1972																									
1972 Det-A	0	0	....	7	0	0	0	0	4^2	6	6	6	0	0	7	4	2.786	11.57	27	8.78	.300	0	....	-4	0	-0.5
• STRAND, Paul	Paul Edward Strand b: 12/19/1893, Carbonado, WA d: 7/2/1974, Salt Lake City, UT BL/TL, 6'.5", 190 lbs. Deb: 5/15/1913 ♦																									
1913 Bos-N	0	0	....	7	0	0	0	0	17	22	9	4	1	0	12	6	2.000	2.12	155	7.85	.393	1	.167	2	1	0.2
1914 Bos-N	6	2	.750	16	3	1	0	1	55^1	47	23	15	1	1	23	33	1.265	2.44	113	2.77	.235	8	.333	-0	5	0.2
1915 Bos-N	1	1	.500	6	2	2	0	1	22^2	26	12	6	0	0	3	13	1.279	2.38	112	4.25	.295	2	.091	0	1	-0.2
Total 3	**7**	**3**	**.700**	**29**	**5**	**3**	**0**	**2**	**95**	**95**	**44**	**25**	**2**	**1**	**38**	**52**	**1.400**	**2.37**	**118**	**4.03**	**.276**	**49**	**.224**	**3**	**7**	**0.2**
• STRANGE, Pat	Patrick Martin Strange b: 8/23/1980, Springfield, MA BR/TR, 6'5", 243 lbs. Deb: 9/13/2002																									
2002 NY-N	0	0	....	5	0	0	0	0	8	6	1	1	0	0	1	4	.875	1.13	352	1.32	.207	0	....	3	1	0.3
2003 NY-N	0	0	....	6	0	0	0	0	9	13	11	11	4	0	11	5	2.667	11.00	38	14.67	.351	0	.000	-7	0	-0.7
Total 2	**0**	**0**	**....**	**11**	**0**	**0**	**0**	**0**	**17**	**19**	**12**	**12**	**4**	**0**	**12**	**9**	**1.824**	**6.35**	**65**	**8.39**	**.288**	**0**	**.000**	**-4**	**1**	**-0.4**
• STRATTON, Ed	William Edward Stratton b: Baltimore, MD Deb: 5/14/1873																									
1873 Mar-n	0	3	.000	3	3	3	0	0	27	75	....	25	3	....	0	0	2.778	8.33	39	....	.452	2	.125	-9	....	-0.7
• STRATTON, Monty	Monty Franklin Pierce "Gander" Stratton b: 5/21/1912, Celeste, TX d: 9/29/1982, Greenville, TX BR/TR, 6'5", 180 lbs. Deb: 6/2/1934 C																									
1934 Chi-A	0	0	....	1	0	0	0	0	3^1	4	2	2	0	0	1	0	1.500	5.40	88	4.57	.333	0	.000	-0	0	0.0
1935 Chi-A	1	2	.333	5	5	2	0	0	38	40	17	17	0	2	9	8	1.289	4.03	115	3.23	.274	2	.143	2	3	0.1
1936 Chi-A	5	7	.417	16	14	3	0	0	95	117	66	55	8	1	46	37	1.716	5.21	100	5.62	.305	8	.216	-1	5	0.0
1937 Chi-A★	15	5	.750	22	21	14	5	0	164^2	142	55	44	6	2	37	69	1.087	2.40	**191**	**2.36**	.234	12	.200	37	19	3.3
1938 Chi-A	15	9	.625	26	22	17	0	2	186^1	186	95	83	18	7	56	82	1.299	4.01	122	3.69	.255	21	.266	19	15	2.2
Total 5	**36**	**23**	**.610**	**70**	**62**	**36**	**5**	**2**	**487^1**	**489**	**235**	**201**	**32**	**12**	**149**	**196**	**1.309**	**3.71**	**131**	**3.59**	**.261**	**43**	**.224**	**56**	**42**	**5.6**
• STRATTON, Scott	C. Scott Stratton b: 10/2/1869, Campbellsburg, KY d: 3/8/1939, Louisville, KY BL/TR, 6', 180 lbs. Deb: 4/21/1888 ♦																									
1888 Lou-a	10	17	.370	33	28	28	2	0	269^2	287	196	109	7	15	53	97	1.261	3.64	84	....	.263	64	.257	-10	11	-0.6
1889 Lou-a	3	13	.188	19	17	13	0	1	133^2	157	126	48	6	7	42	42	1.489	3.23	119	....	.284	66	.288	11	7	1.6
1890* Lou-a	34	14	.708	50	49	44	4	0	431	398	186	113	3	13	61	207	1.065	**2.36**	**163**	....	.238	61	.323	**69**	**51**	**7.6**
1891 Pit-N	0	2	.000	2	2	2	0	0	18^1	16	9	5	0	7	5	5	1.145	2.45	133	....	.226	1	.125	2	1	0.1
Lou-a	6	13	.316	20	20	20	1	0	172	204	112	78	10	0	34	52	1.384	4.08	89	....	.285	27	.235	-9	9	-0.9
1892 Lou-N	21	19	.525	42	40	39	2	0	351^2	342	188	114	1	9	70	93	1.172	2.92	105	2.60	.245	56	.256	3	29	1.4
1893 Lou-N	12	23	.343	37	35	34	1	0	314^2	445	253	190	8	8	100	43	1.732	5.43	81	5.59	.324	50	.226	-32	16	-2.7
1894 Lou-N	1	5	.167	7	5	4	0	0	43	72	50	40	3	3	13	3	1.977	8.37	61	7.74	.368	12	.324	-16	1	-1.0
Chi-N	8	5	.615	16	13	12	0	0	128^1	205	131	80	5	3	42	24	1.925	5.61	100	6.88	.357	37	.374	3	8	0.8
Yr.	9	10	.474	23	18	16	0	0	171^1	277	181	120	8	6	55	27	1.938	6.30	86	7.09	.360	49	.360	-13	9	-0.2
1895 Chi-N	2	3	.400	5	5	3	0	0	30	51	42	32	1	4	14	4	2.167	9.60	53	8.51	.370	7	.292	-15	1	-1.2
Total 8	**97**	**114**	**.460**	**231**	**214**	**199**	**10**	**1**	**1892^1**	**2177**	**1293**	**809**	**44**	**69**	**434**	**570**	**1.380**	**3.85**	**101**	**2.19**	**.280**	**381**	**.274**	**5**	**134**	**5.2**
• STREIT, Oscar	Oscar William Streit b: 7/7/1873, Florence, AL d: 10/10/1935, Birmingham, AL BL/TL, 6'5", 190 lbs. Deb: 4/21/1899																									
1899 Bos-N	1	0	1.000	2	1	1	0	0	14^2	15	17	11	1	2	15	0	2.045	6.75	62	6.67	.265	0	.000	-5	0	-0.5
1902 Cle-A	0	7	.000	8	7	4	0	0	51^2	72	54	30	3	3	25	10	1.877	5.23	66	6.52	.330	4	.211	-10	0	-0.9
Total 2	**1**	**7**	**.125**	**10**	**8**	**5**	**0**	**0**	**66^1**	**87**	**71**	**41**	**4**	**5**	**40**	**10**	**1.915**	**5.56**	**65**	**6.55**	**.316**	**4**	**.154**	**-15**	**0**	**-1.4**
• STRELECKI, Ed	Edward Harold Strelecki b: 4/10/1905, Newark, NJ d: 1/9/1968, Newark, NJ BR/TR, 5'11.5", 180 lbs. Deb: 4/16/1928																									
1928 StL-A	0	2	.000	22	2	1	0	1	50^1	49	27	24	4	1	17	8	1.311	4.29	98	3.53	.269	2	.200	-1	3	0.0
1929 StL-A	1	1	.500	7	0	0	0	0	11	12	8	6	1	1	6	2	1.636	4.91	90	5.17	.279	0	.000	-1	0	-0.1

YEAR TM-L	W	L	PCT	G	GS	CG	SH	SV	IP	H	R	ER	HR	HB	BB	SO	RAT	ERA	ERA+	CERA	OAV	BH	AVG	PR+	WS	TPW
1931 Cin-N	0	0	....	13	0	0	0	0	24^1	37	25	25	2	3	9	3	1.890	9.25	40	7.77	.394	1	.200	-15	0	-1.5
Total 3	1	3	.250	42	2	1	0	1	85^2	98	60	55	7	5	32	13	1.518	5.78	69	4.94	.307	3	.176	-16	3	-1.6
• STREMMEL, Phil	Philip Stremmel b: 4/16/1880, Zanesville, OH d: 12/26/1947, Chicago, IL BR/TR, 6', 175 lbs. Deb: 9/16/1909																									
1909 StL-A	0	2	.000	2	2	2	0	0	18	20	9	9	0	1	4	6	1.333	4.50	54	3.85	.308	0	.000	-4	0	-0.6
1910 StL-A	0	2	.000	5	2	2	0	0	29	31	19	12	0	0	16	7	1.621	3.72	66	4.41	.287	1	.125	-4	0	-0.4
Total 2	0	4	.000	7	4	4	0	0	47	51	28	21	0	1	20	13	1.511	4.02	61	4.19	.295	1	.071	-8	0	-1.0
• STRICKER, Cub	John A. Stricker b: 6/8/1859, Philadelphia, PA d: 11/19/1937, Philadelphia, PA BR/TR, 5'3", 138 lbs. Deb: 5/2/1882 M/U ♦																									
1882 Phi-a	1	0	1.000	2	0	0	0	0	7	3	1	1	0	....	1	2	.571	1.29	232	....	.121	59	.217	1	7	1.1
1884 Phi-a	0	0	....	1	0	0	0	0	3	6	2	2	0	0	1	1	2.333	6.00	56	....	.396	92	.231	-1	7	-3.7
1887 Cle-a	0	0	....	3	0	0	0	1	5^2	12	5	2	0	0	7	2	2.118	3.18	136	....	.415	194	.330	1	12	-0.9
1888 Cle-a	1	0	1.000	2	0	0	0	0	12	16	6	6	0	1	2	5	1.500	4.50	69	....	.309	115	.233	-2	15	1.1
Total 4	2	0	1.000	8	0	0	0	1	27^2	37	14	11	0	1	11	10	1.482	3.58	92	....	.307	1159	.247	-1	41	-2.5
• STRICKLAND, Bill	William Goss Strickland b: 3/29/1908, Ray City, GA d: 1/26/2000, Lakeland, FL BR/TR, 6'2", 170 lbs. Deb: 7/16/1937																									
1937 StL-A	0	0	....	9	0	0	0	0	21^1	28	18	14	2	2	15	6	2.016	5.91	82	7.84	.341	1	.167	-2	0	-0.2
• STRICKLAND, Jim	James Michael Strickland b: 6/12/1946, Los Angeles, CA BL/TL, 6', 175 lbs. Deb: 5/19/1971																									
1971 Min-A	1	0	1.000	24	0	0	0	1	31^1	20	14	5	2	2	18	21	1.213	1.44	247	2.66	.183	0	.000	8	3	0.9
1972 Min-A	3	1	.750	25	0	0	0	3	36	28	16	10	7	0	19	30	1.306	2.50	128	3.92	.214	1	.333	3	3	0.4
1973 Min-A	0	1	.000	7	0	0	0	0	5^1	11	8	7	0	0	5	6	3.000	11.81	34	12.58	.440	0	....	-5	0	-0.5
1975 Cle-A	0	0	....	4	0	0	0	1	4^2	4	1	1	0	1	2	3	1.286	1.93	196	3.39	.222	0	....	1	1	0.1
Total 4	4	2	.667	60	0	0	0	5	77^1	63	39	23	9	3	44	60	1.384	2.68	131	3.97	.223	1	.250	7	7	0.8
• STRICKLAND, Scott	Scott Michael Strickland b: 4/26/1976, Houston, TX BR/TR, 5'11", 180 lbs. Deb: 8/14/1999																									
1999 Mon-N	0	1	.000	17	0	0	0	0	18	15	10	9	3	0	11	23	1.444	4.50	100	4.48	.231	0	....	0	1	0.0
2000 Mon-N	4	3	.571	49	0	0	0	9	48	38	18	16	3	1	16	48	1.125	3.00	160	2.44	.215	0	.000	10	8	0.9
2001 Mon-N	2	6	.250	77	0	0	0	9	81^1	67	36	29	9	4	41	85	1.328	3.21	139	3.65	.222	0	.000	13	10	1.2
2002 Mon-N	0	0	....	1	0	0	0	0	1	0	0	0	0	0	0	2	.000	0.00	....	0.00	.000	0	....	0	0	0.0
NY-N	6	9	.400	68	0	0	0	2	67^2	61	29	27	7	2	33	67	1.389	3.59	110	3.74	.236	0	....	3	5	0.3
Yr.	6	9	.400	69	0	0	0	2	68^2	61	29	27	7	2	33	69	1.369	3.54	112	3.69	.236	0	....	4	5	0.4
2003 NY-N	0	2	.000	19	0	0	0	0	20	16	6	5	1	1	10	16	1.300	2.25	185	3.19	.219	0	.000	4	2	0.4
Total 5	12	21	.364	231	0	0	0	20	236	197	99	86	23	8	111	241	1.305	3.28	132	3.44	.225	0	.000	31	26	3.0
• STRICKLETT, Elmer	Elmer Griffin "Spitball" Stricklett b: 8/29/1876, Glasco, KS d: 6/7/1964, Santa Cruz, CA BR/TR, 5'6", 140 lbs. Deb: 4/22/1904 U																									
1904 Chi-A	0	1	.000	1	1	0	0	0	7	12	10	8	0	0	2	3	2.000	10.29	24	7.04	.377	0	.000	-6	0	-0.7
1905 Bro-N	9	18	.333	33	28	25	1	1	237^1	259	143	88	0	14	71	77	1.390	3.34	86	3.73	.282	13	.148	-6	8	-0.7
1906 Bro-N	14	18	.438	41	35	28	5	5	291^2	273	128	88	2	5	77	88	1.200	2.72	93	2.73	.253	20	.206	-3	13	0.2
1907 Bro-N	12	14	.462	29	26	25	4	0	229^2	211	85	58	1	8	65	69	1.202	2.27	103	2.81	.255	12	.148	4	14	0.5
Total 4	35	51	.407	104	90	78	10	6	765^2	755	366	242	3	27	215	237	1.267	2.84	91	3.10	.264	45	.167	-12	35	-0.7
• STRIKE, John	John Strike b: 1865, Philadelphia, PA Deb: 9/24/1886 ♦																									
1886 Phi-N	1	1	.500	2	2	1	0	0	15	19	10	8	1	....	7	11	1.733	4.80	68	....	.298	0	.000	-2	0	-0.3
• STRIKER, Jake	Wilbur Scott Striker b: 10/23/1933, New Washington, OH BL/TL, 6'2", 200 lbs. Deb: 9/25/1959																									
1959 Cle-A	1	0	1.000	1	1	0	0	0	6^2	8	2	2	0	0	4	5	1.800	2.70	136	5.10	.296	0	.000	1	1	0.1
1960 Chi-A	0	0	....	2	0	0	0	0	3^2	5	3	2	1	1	1	1	1.636	4.91	77	9.26	.357	0	....	-1	0	-0.1
Total 2	1	0	1.000	3	1	0	0	0	10^1	13	5	4	1	1	5	6	1.742	3.48	107	6.58	.317	0	.000	0	1	0.1
• STRINCEVICH, Nick	Nicholas "Jumbo" Strincevich b: 3/1/1915, Gary, IN BR/TR, 6'1", 180 lbs. Deb: 4/23/1940																									
1940 Bos-N	4	8	.333	32	14	5	0	1	128^2	142	89	79	17	8	63	54	1.593	5.53	67	5.38	.278	5	.116	-29	0	-3.1
1941 Bos-N	0	0	....	3	0	0	0	0	3^1	7	5	4	0	1	6	1	3.900	10.80	33	16.99	.412	0	....	-3	0	-0.3
Pit-N	1	2	.333	12	3	0	0	0	31	35	23	18	4	1	13	12	1.548	5.23	69	4.96	.280	3	.429	-5	0	-0.4
Yr.	1	2	.333	15	3	0	0	0	34^1	42	28	22	4	2	19	13	1.777	5.77	62	6.13	.296	3	.429	-8	0	-0.7
1942 Pit-N	0	0	....	7	1	0	0	0	22^1	19	7	7	2	1	9	10	1.254	2.82	120	3.32	.229	0	.000	2	2	0.1
1944 Pit-N	14	7	.667	40	26	11	0	2	190	190	86	65	5	4	37	47	1.195	3.08	121	2.77	.257	9	.158	15	14	1.4
1945 Pit-N	16	10	.615	36	29	18	1	2	228^1	235	94	84	7	3	49	74	1.244	3.31	119	3.00	.260	17	.202	18	18	1.9
1946 Pit-N	10	15	.400	32	22	11	3	1	176	185	77	70	7	4	44	49	1.301	3.58	99	3.38	.268	8	.154	1	11	0.2
1947 Pit-N	1	6	.143	32	7	1	0	0	89	111	59	52	9	2	37	22	1.663	5.26	80	5.72	.316	1	.048	-10	1	-1.1
1948 Pit-N	0	0	....	3	0	0	0	0	4^1	8	4	4	0	0	2	1	2.308	8.31	49	9.71	.444	0	....	-2	0	-0.2
Phi-N	0	1	.000	6	1	0	0	0	16^2	26	18	17	1	0	10	4	2.160	9.18	43	7.63	.342	0	.000	-10	0	-1.0
Yr.	0	1	.000	9	1	0	0	0	21	34	22	21	1	0	12	5	2.190	9.00	44	8.06	.362	0	.000	-12	0	-1.2
Total 8	46	49	.484	203	103	46	4	6	889^2	958	462	400	52	24	270	274	1.380	4.05	94	3.89	.273	43	.158	-21	46	-2.5
• STROHMAYER, John	John Emery Strohmayer b: 10/13/1946, Belle Fourche, SD BR/TR, 6'1", 181 lbs. Deb: 4/29/1970																									
1970 Mon-N	3	1	.750	42	0	0	0	0	76	85	48	41	7	2	39	74	1.632	4.86	85	5.14	.279	1	.167	-7	2	-0.7
1971 Mon-N	7	5	.583	27	14	2	0	1	114	124	63	55	16	4	31	56	1.360	4.34	81	4.54	.281	8	.229	-10	4	-1.0
1972 Mon-N	1	2	.333	48	0	0	0	3	76^2	73	32	30	6	1	31	50	1.357	3.52	101	3.73	.256	0	.000	1	5	0.1
1973 Mon-N	0	1	.000	17	3	0	0	0	34^2	34	20	20	4	1	22	15	1.615	5.19	73	5.08	.260	1	.200	-5	0	-0.5
NY-N	0	0	....	7	0	0	0	0	10	13	10	9	2	0	4	5	1.700	8.10	45	6.45	.310	0	....	-5	0	-0.5
Yr.	0	1	.000	24	3	0	0	0	44^2	47	30	29	6	1	26	20	1.634	5.84	64	5.39	.272	1	.200	-10	0	-1.1
1974 NY-N	0	0	....	1	0	0	0	0	1	0	0	0	0	0	1	0	1.000	0.00	....	0.95	.000	0	....	0	0	0.0
Total 5	11	9	.550	142	17	2	0	4	312^1	329	173	155	35	8	128	200	1.463	4.47	83	4.60	.273	10	.200	-26	11	-2.7
• STROM, Brent	Brent Terry Strom b: 10/14/1948, San Diego, CA BR/TL, 6'3", 190 lbs. Deb: 7/31/1972 C																									
1972 NY-N	0	3	.000	11	5	0	0	0	30^1	34	25	23	7	0	15	20	1.615	6.82	49	6.27	.296	0	.000	-11	0	-1.3
1973 Cle-A	2	10	.167	27	18	2	0	0	123	134	73	63	18	3	47	91	1.472	4.61	85	4.91	.278	0	....	-9	3	-0.9
1975 SD-N	8	8	.500	18	16	6	2	0	120^1	103	42	34	6	2	33	56	1.130	2.54	136	2.57	.233	3	.100	14	11	1.4
1976 SD-N	12	16	.429	36	33	8	1	0	210^2	188	100	77	15	2	73	103	1.239	3.29	99	3.08	.239	4	.063	-0	8	-0.3
1977 SD-N	0	2	.000	8	3	0	0	0	16^2	23	25	23	5	0	12	8	2.100	12.42	28	9.11	.329	1	.333	-16	0	-1.6
Total 5	22	39	.361	100	75	16	3	0	501	482	265	220	51	7	180	278	1.321	3.95	89	3.80	.254	8	.078	-23	22	-2.7
• STROMME, Floyd	Floyd Marvin "Rock" Stromme b: 8/1/1916, Cooperstown, ND d: 2/7/1993, Wenatchee, WA BR/TR, 5'11", 170 lbs. Deb: 7/5/1939																									
1939 Cle-A	0	1	.000	5	0	0	0	0	13	13	8	7	1	0	13	4	2.000	4.85	91	5.95	.265	1	.333	-1	0	0.0
• STRONG, Joe	Joseph Benjamin Strong b: 9/9/1962, Fairfield, CA BB/TR, 6', 200 lbs. Deb: 5/11/2000																									
2000 Fla-N	1	1	.500	18	0	0	0	1	19^2	26	16	16	3	2	12	18	1.932	7.32	61	7.85	.325	0	.000	-6	0	-0.6
2001 Fla-N	0	0	....	5	0	0	0	0	6^2	3	1	1	1	0	3	4	.900	1.35	312	1.86	.136	0	.000	2	1	0.2
Total 2	1	1	.500	23	0	0	0	1	26^1	29	17	17	4	2	15	22	1.671	5.81	76	6.33	.284	0	.000	-4	1	-0.4
• STROUD, Sailor	Ralph Vivian Stroud b: 3/15/1885, Ironia, NJ d: 4/11/1970, Stockton, CA BR/TR, 6', 160 lbs. Deb: 4/29/1910																									
1910 Det-A	5	9	.357	28	15	7	3	1	130^1	123	54	47	9	7	41	63	1.258	3.25	81	3.53	.257	1	.026	-9	5	-1.4
1915 NY-N	12	9	.571	32	22	8	0	1	184	194	76	57	3	6	35	62	1.245	2.79	92	3.15	.281	9	.161	-3	8	-0.4
1916 NY-N	3	2	.600	10	4	0	0	1	46^2	47	18	14	1	1	9	16	1.200	2.70	90	2.82	.266	1	.071	-2	2	-0.3
Total 3	20	20	.500	70	41	15	3	3	361	364	148	118	13	14	85	141	1.244	2.94	87	3.25	.270	11	.101	-14	15	-2.1
• STRUSS, Steamboat	Clarence Herbert Struss b: 2/24/1909, Riverdale, IL d: 9/12/1985, Grand Rapids, MI BR/TR, 5'11", 163 lbs. Deb: 9/30/1934																									
1934 Pit-N	0	1	.000	1	1	0	0	0	7	7	6	5	0	0	6	3	1.857	6.43	64	4.68	.250	1	.333	-2	0	-0.1

YEAR	TM-L	W	L	PCT	G	GS	CG	SH	SV	IP	H	R	ER	HR	HB	BB	SO	RAT	ERA	ERA+	CERA	OAV	BH	AVG	PR+	WS	TPW
• STRYKER, Dutch	Sterling Alpa Stryker b: 7/29/1885, Atlantic Highlands, NJ d: 11/5/1964, Red Bank, NJ BR/TR, 5'11.5", 180 lbs. Deb: 4/16/1924																										
1924	Bos-N	3	8	.273	20	10	2	0	0	73^1	90	56	49	4	1	22	22	1.527	6.01	64	4.74	.314	5	.217	-17	0	-1.7
1926	Bro-N	0	0	....	2	0	0	0	0	2	8	8	6	0	0	1	0	4.500	27.00	14	24.85	.571	0	....	-5	0	-0.5
Total	2	3	8	.273	22	10	2	0	0	75^1	98	64	55	4	1	23	22	1.606	6.57	58	5.28	.326	5	.217	-22	0	-2.2
• STUART, Johnny	John Davis "Stud" Stuart b: 4/27/1901, Clinton, TN d: 5/13/1970, Charleston, WV BR/TR, 5'11", 170 lbs. Deb: 7/27/1922																										
1922	StL-N	0	0	....	2	1	0	0	0	2	2	4	2	0	1	2	1	2.000	9.00	43	6.30	.222	0	....	-1	0	-0.1
1923	StL-N	9	5	.643	37	10	7	1	3	149^2	139	82	71	11	9	70	55	1.396	4.27	91	3.88	.252	14	.246	-5	8	-0.4
1924	StL-N	9	11	.450	28	22	13	0	0	159	167	100	84	12	5	60	54	1.428	4.75	80	4.10	.273	11	.204	-17	4	-1.8
1925	StL-N	2	2	.500	15	1	1	0	0	47	52	41	32	6	2	24	14	1.617	6.13	70	5.30	.278	4	.250	-10	0	-0.8
Total	4	20	18	.526	82	34	21	1	3	357^2	360	227	189	29	17	156	124	1.443	4.76	82	4.18	.265	29	.228	-33	12	-3.2
• STUART, Marlin	Marlin Henry Stuart b: 8/8/1918, Paragould, AR d: 6/16/1994, Paragould, AR BL/TR, 6'2", 185 lbs. Deb: 4/26/1949																										
1949	Det-A	0	2	.000	14	2	0	0	0	29^2	39	33	30	3	0	35	14	2.494	9.10	46	9.75	.348	2	.333	-16	0	-1.5
1950	Det-A	3	1	.750	19	1	0	0	2	43^2	59	32	27	6	1	22	19	1.855	5.56	84	6.98	.330	1	.083	-5	1	-0.5
1951	Det-A	4	6	.400	29	15	5	0	1	124	119	60	52	9	7	71	46	1.532	3.77	111	4.43	.258	10	.233	7	9	0.8
1952	Det-A	3	2	.600	30	9	2	0	1	91^1	91	60	50	8	3	48	32	1.522	4.93	77	4.46	.265	2	.087	-10	1	-1.1
	StL-A	1	2	.333	12	2	0	0	1	26	26	18	12	3	0	9	13	1.346	4.15	94	3.80	.260	0	.000	-1	1	-0.1
	Yr.	4	4	.500	42	11	2	0	2	117^1	117	78	62	11	3	57	45	1.483	4.76	80	4.32	.264	2	.069	-10	2	-1.2
1953	StL-A	8	2	.800	60	2	0	0	7	114^1	136	62	50	6	1	44	46	1.574	3.94	107	4.70	.300	5	.192	4	9	0.4
1954	Bal-A	1	2	.333	22	0	0	0	2	38^1	46	23	19	2	2	15	13	1.591	4.46	80	4.82	.303	0	.000	-3	1	-0.4
	NY-A	3	0	1.000	10	0	0	0	1	18^1	28	12	11	0	0	12	2	2.182	5.40	64	7.08	.350	2	.333	-4	1	-0.4
	Yr.	4	2	.667	32	0	0	0	3	56^2	74	35	30	2	2	27	15	1.782	4.76	74	5.55	.319	2	.222	-8	2	-0.8
Total	6	23	17	.575	196	31	7	0	15	485^2	544	300	251	37	14	256	185	1.647	4.65	87	5.15	.289	22	.176	-28	23	-2.9
• STUELAND, George	George Anton Stueland b: 3/2/1899, Algona, IA d: 9/9/1964, Onawa, IA BB/TR, 6'1.5", 174 lbs. Deb: 9/15/1921																										
1921	Chi-N	0	1	.000	2	1	0	0	0	11	11	7	7	0	0	7	4	1.636	5.73	67	4.13	.282	1	.333	-2	0	-0.2
1922	Chi-N	9	4	.692	35	11	4	0	0	113	129	81	73	9	5	49	44	1.575	5.81	72	5.02	.297	4	.129	-21	2	-2.2
1923	Chi-N	0	1	.000	6	0	0	0	0	8	11	7	5	0	0	5	2	2.000	5.63	71	6.21	.478	0	....	-2	0	-0.2
1925	Chi-N	0	0	....	2	0	0	0	0	3	2	1	1	0	0	3	2	1.667	3.00	144	3.36	.182	1	1.000	0	1	0.1
Total	4	9	6	.600	45	12	4	0	0	135	153	96	86	9	5	64	52	1.607	5.73	72	4.98	.302	6	.171	-25	3	-2.5
• STUFFEL, Paul	Paul Harrington "Stu" Stuffel b: 3/22/1927, Canton, OH BR/TR, 6'2", 185 lbs. Deb: 9/16/1950																										
1950	Phi-N	0	0	....	3	0	0	0	0	5	4	1	1	0	1	1	3	1.000	1.80	225	2.23	.211	0	....	1	1	0.1
1952	Phi-N	1	0	1.000	2	1	0	0	0	6	5	3	2	0	0	7	3	2.000	3.00	122	4.61	.217	0	.000	0	1	0.0
1953	Phi-N	0	0	....	2	0	0	0	0	0	0	4	0	0	0	4	0	....	....	....	∞	1.000	0	....	0	0	0.0
Total	3	1	0	1.000	7	1	0	0	0	11	9	8	3	0	1	12	6	1.909	2.45	154	3.53	.214	0	.000	2	2	0.1
• STULL, Everett	Everett James Stull b: 8/24/1971, Fort Riley, KS BR/TR, 6'3", 200 lbs. Deb: 4/14/1997																										
1997	Mon-N	0	1	.000	3	0	0	0	0	3^1	7	7	6	1	0	4	2	3.300	16.20	26	17.12	.438	0	....	-4	0	-0.4
1999	Atl-N	0	0	....	1	0	0	0	0	0^2	2	3	1	0	0	2	0	6.000	13.50	33	25.31	.500	0	....	-1	0	-0.1
2000	Mil-N	2	3	.400	20	4	0	0	0	43^1	41	30	28	7	4	30	33	1.638	5.82	78	5.72	.256	0	.000	-7	1	-0.7
2002	Mil-N	0	1	.000	2	2	0	0	0	10	15	7	7	0	1	9	7	2.400	6.30	65	8.45	.357	1	.333	-2	0	-0.2
Total	4	2	5	.286	26	6	0	0	0	57^1	65	47	42	8	5	45	42	1.919	6.59	67	7.09	.293	1	.083	-14	1	-1.4
• STULTZ, George	George Irvin Stultz b: 6/30/1873, Louisville, KY d: 3/19/1955, Louisville, KY, 5'10", 150 lbs. Deb: 9/22/1894																										
1894	Bos-N	1	0	1.000	1	1	1	0	0	9	4	2	0	0	0	5	1	1.000	0.00	....	1.32	.134	1	.333	6	1	0.4
• STUMP, Jim	James Gilbert Stump b: 2/10/1932, Lansing, MI BR/TR, 6', 188 lbs. Deb: 8/29/1957																										
1957	Det-A	1	0	1.000	6	0	0	0	0	13^1	11	4	3	0	0	8	2	1.425	2.03	190	2.97	.220	1	.500	3	2	0.3
1959	Det-A	0	0	....	5	0	0	0	0	11^1	12	3	3	1	0	4	6	1.412	2.38	171	4.23	.279	1	1.000	2	2	0.3
Total	2	1	0	1.000	11	0	0	0	0	24^2	23	7	6	1	0	12	8	1.419	2.19	181	3.55	.247	2	.667	5	4	0.6
• STUPER, John	John Anton Stuper b: 5/9/1957, Butler, PA BR/TR, 6'2", 200 lbs. Deb: 6/1/1982																										
1982*	StL-N	9	7	.563	23	21	2	0	0	136^2	137	55	51	8	0	55	53	1.405	3.36	108	3.83	.266	5	.119	1	8	0.0
1983	StL-N	12	11	.522	40	30	6	1	1	198	202	95	81	15	2	71	81	1.379	3.68	98	3.90	.265	8	.136	-0	10	-0.1
1984	StL-N	3	5	.375	15	12	0	0	0	61^1	73	39	36	4	2	20	19	1.516	5.28	66	4.69	.297	1	.063	-13	0	-1.5
1985	Cin-N	8	5	.615	33	13	1	0	0	99	116	60	50	8	0	37	38	1.545	4.55	83	4.85	.303	1	.059	-9	3	-1.0
Total	4	32	28	.533	111	76	9	1	1	495	528	249	218	35	4	183	191	1.436	3.96	92	4.17	.277	15	.112	-22	21	-2.6
• STURDIVANT, Tom	Thomas Virgil "Smoke,Snake" Sturdivant b: 4/28/1930, Gordon, KS BL/TR, 6'.5", 186 lbs. Deb: 4/14/1955																										
1955*	NY-A	1	3	.250	33	1	0	0	0	68^1	48	24	24	6	2	42	48	1.317	3.16	118	3.37	.203	1	.083	2	4	0.1
1956*	NY-A	16	8	.667	32	17	6	2	5	158^1	134	63	58	15	4	52	110	1.175	3.30	117	2.99	.224	20	.313	6	14	1.0
1957*	NY-A	16	6	.727	28	28	7	2	0	201^2	170	65	57	14	4	80	118	1.240	2.54	141	3.14	.232	13	.183	21	16	2.2
1958	NY-A	3	6	.333	15	10	0	0	0	70^2	77	37	33	6	3	38	41	1.627	4.20	84	5.16	.274	4	.190	-7	2	-0.7
1959	NY-A	0	2	.000	7	3	0	0	0	25^1	20	16	14	4	0	9	16	1.145	4.97	73	3.16	.222	0	.000	-4	0	-0.5
	KC-A	2	6	.250	36	3	0	0	5	71^2	70	45	37	9	6	34	57	1.451	4.65	86	4.59	.258	1	.059	-5	2	-0.7
	Yr.	2	8	.200	43	6	0	0	5	97	90	61	51	13	6	43	73	1.371	4.73	82	4.21	.249	1	.043	-8	2	-1.1
1960	Bos-A	3	3	.500	40	3	0	0	1	101^1	106	58	56	16	2	45	67	1.490	4.97	81	4.99	.279	4	.182	-8	4	-0.8
1961	Was-A	2	6	.250	15	10	1	1	0	80	67	42	41	6	3	40	39	1.338	4.61	85	3.52	.233	2	.077	-6	2	-0.8
	Pit-N	5	2	.714	13	11	6	1	1	85^2	81	29	27	6	1	17	45	1.144	2.84	140	2.82	.249	8	.250	11	8	1.1
1962	Pit-N	9	5	.643	49	12	2	1	2	125^1	120	62	52	12	3	39	76	1.269	3.73	105	3.50	.260	6	.182	2	8	0.2
1963	Pit-N	0	0	....	3	0	0	0	0	8^1	8	6	6	1	0	4	6	1.440	6.48	51	4.34	.267	0	.000	-3	0	-0.3
	Det-A	1	2	.333	28	0	0	0	2	55	43	26	23	7	1	24	36	1.218	3.76	99	3.20	.221	0	.000	-0	3	-0.1
	KC-A	1	2	.333	17	3	0	0	0	53	47	24	22	3	1	17	26	1.208	3.74	103	2.91	.237	0	.000	1	3	0.0
	Yr.	2	4	.333	45	3	0	0	2	108	90	50	45	10	2	41	62	1.213	3.75	101	3.05	.229	0	.000	1	6	-0.1
1964	KC-A	0	0	....	3	0	0	0	0	3^2	4	4	4	0	2	1	1	1.364	9.82	39	6.04	.308	1	1.000	-2	0	-0.2
	NY-N	0	0	....	16	0	0	0	1	28^2	34	20	19	2	2	7	18	1.430	5.97	60	4.61	.306	0	.000	-8	0	-0.8
Total	10	59	51	.536	335	101	22	7	17	1137	1029	521	473	107	34	449	704	1.300	3.74	102	3.60	.244	60	.183	-1	66	-0.4
• STURTZE, Tanyon	Tanyon James Sturtze b: 10/12/1970, Worcester, MA BR/TR, 6'5", 190 lbs. Deb: 5/3/1995																										
1995	Chi-N	0	0	....	2	0	0	0	0	2	2	2	2	1	0	1	0	1.500	9.00	46	7.30	.250	0	....	-1	0	-0.1
1996	Chi-N	1	0	1.000	6	0	0	0	0	11	16	11	11	3	0	5	7	1.909	9.00	48	8.87	.348	0	.000	-6	0	-0.6
1997	Tex-A	1	1	.500	9	5	0	0	0	32^2	45	30	30	6	0	18	18	1.929	8.27	58	7.84	.338	0	....	-12	0	-1.2
1999	Chi-A	0	0	....	1	1	0	0	0	6	4	0	0	0	0	2	2	1.000	0.00	....	1.73	.200	0	....	3	1	0.3
2000	Chi-A	1	2	.333	10	1	0	0	0	15^2	25	23	21	4	2	15	6	2.553	12.06	41	12.84	.379	0	....	-13	0	-1.2
	TB-A	4	0	1.000	19	5	0	0	0	52^2	47	16	15	4	1	14	38	1.158	2.56	193	2.89	.236	0	....	13	6	1.2
	Yr.	5	2	.714	29	6	0	0	0	68^1	72	39	36	8	3	29	44	1.478	4.74	105	5.18	.272	0	....	1	6	0.0
2001	TB-A	11	12	.478	39	27	0	0	1	195^1	200	98	96	23	9	79	110	1.428	4.42	101	4.65	.271	1	.125	1	11	0.0
2002	TB-A	4	18	.182	33	33	4	0	0	224	271	141	129	33	9	89	137	1.607	5.18	86	5.87	.302	0	.000	-22	6	-2.1
2003	Tor-A	7	6	.538	40	8	0	0	0	89^1	107	67	59	14	7	43	54	1.679	5.94	77	6.30	.296	0	....	-12	2	-1.1
Total	8	29	39	.426	159	80	4	0	1	628^2	717	388	363	88	28	266	372	1.564	5.20	88	5.60	.291	1	.077	-48	26	-4.7
• SUCH, Dick	Richard Stanley Such b: 10/15/1944, Sanford, NC BL/TR, 6'4", 190 lbs. Deb: 4/6/1970 C																										
1970	Was-A	1	5	.167	21	5	0	0	0	50	48	42	42	8	3	45	41	1.860	7.56	47	6.47	.258	3	.231	-23	0	-2.3
• SUCHE, Charley	Charles Morris Suche b: 8/15/1915, Cranes Mills, TX d: 2/11/1984, San Antonio, TX BR/TL, 6'2", 190 lbs. Deb: 9/18/1938																										
1938	Cle-A	0	0	....	1	0	0	0	0	1^1	4	4	4	0	0	3	1	5.250	27.00	17	27.28	.571	1	1.000	-3	0	-0.2

• SUCHECKI, Jim James Joseph Suchecki b: 8/25/1927, Chicago, IL d: 7/20/2000, Crofton, MD BR/TR, 6', 185 lbs. Deb: 5/20/1950

YEAR TM-L	W	L	PCT	G	GS	CG	SH	SV	IP	H	R	ER	HR	HB	BB	SO	RAT	ERA	ERA+	CERA	OAV	BH	AVG	PR+	WS	TPW
1950 Bos-A	0	0	....	4	0	0	0	0	4	3	2	2	0	0	4	3	1.750	4.50	109	4.03	.231	0	....	0	0	0.0
1951 StL-A	0	6	.000	29	6	0	0	0	89^2	113	64	54	8	1	42	47	1.729	5.42	81	5.52	.299	2	.100	-8	1	-1.0
1952 Pit-N	0	0	....	5	0	0	0	0	10	14	7	6	1	1	4	6	1.800	5.40	74	6.58	.326	0	.000	-1	0	-0.1
Total 3	0	6	.000	38	6	0	0	0	103^2	130	73	62	9	2	50	56	1.736	5.38	81	5.56	.300	2	.091	-9	1	-1.1

• SUDHOFF, Willie John William "Wee Willie" Sudhoff b: 9/17/1874, St. Louis, MO d: 5/25/1917, St. Louis, MO BR/TR, 5'7", 165 lbs. Deb: 8/20/1897 ♦

YEAR TM-L	W	L	PCT	G	GS	CG	SH	SV	IP	H	R	ER	HR	HB	BB	SO	RAT	ERA	ERA+	CERA	OAV	BH	AVG	PR+	WS	TPW
1897 StL-N	2	7	.222	11	9	9	0	0	92^2	126	72	46	8	0	21	19	1.586	4.47	98	5.31	.322	10	.238	3	2	0.2
1898 StL-N	11	27	.289	41	38	35	0	1	315	355	205	152	11	27	102	65	1.451	4.34	87	4.25	.282	19	.158	-9	14	-1.3
1899 Cle-N	3	8	.273	11	10	8	0	0	86^1	131	85	67	3	7	25	10	1.807	6.98	53	6.41	.348	2	.065	-27	2	-2.7
StL-N	12	10	.545	25	23	16	0	0	178^1	193	109	76	6	15	62	29	1.430	3.84	104	4.07	.276	13	.203	1	14	0.1
Yr.	15	18	.455	36	33	24	0	0	264^2	324	194	143	9	22	87	39	1.553	4.86	79	4.84	.301	15	.158	-26	16	-2.5
1900 StL-N	6	8	.429	16	14	13	2	0	127	128	62	39	3	8	37	29	1.299	2.76	131	3.34	.262	20	.189	14	9	0.9
1901 StL-N	17	11	.607	38	26	25	1	2	276^1	281	142	108	4	18	92	78	1.350	3.52	90	3.46	.262	19	.176	-17	14	-1.3
1902 StL-A	12	12	.500	30	25	20	0	0	220	213	99	70	6	12	67	42	1.273	2.86	123	3.17	.255	13	.169	13	19	1.1
1903 StL-A	21	15	.583	38	35	30	5	0	293^2	262	100	74	4	9	56	104	1.083	2.27	128	2.21	.238	20	.182	21	25	2.0
1904 StL-A	8	15	.348	27	24	20	1	0	222^1	232	121	93	8	10	54	63	1.286	3.76	66	3.35	.270	14	.165	-29	4	-3.3
1905 StL-A	10	20	.333	32	30	23	1	0	244	222	121	81	8	13	78	70	1.230	2.99	85	2.96	.245	16	.186	-8	8	-0.7
1906 Was-A	0	2	.000	9	5	0	0	0	19^2	30	25	20	1	2	9	7	1.983	9.15	29	7.36	.353	3	.429	-14	0	-1.4
Total 10	102	135	.430	278	239	199	10	3	2075^1	2173	1141	826	62	121	603	516	1.338	3.58	90	3.59	.269	149	.178	-52	111	-6.4

• SUGGS, George George Franklin Suggs b: 7/7/1882, Kinston, NC d: 4/4/1949, Kinston, NC BR/TR, 5'7.5", 168 lbs. Deb: 4/21/1908

YEAR TM-L	W	L	PCT	G	GS	CG	SH	SV	IP	H	R	ER	HR	HB	BB	SO	RAT	ERA	ERA+	CERA	OAV	BH	AVG	PR+	WS	TPW
1908 Det-A	1	1	.500	6	1	1	0	1	27	32	8	5	0	0	2	8	1.259	1.67	145	3.26	.299	2	.200	3	2	0.4
1909 Det-A	1	3	.250	9	4	2	0	1	44^1	34	12	10	1	3	10	18	.992	2.03	124	2.18	.228	1	.067	2	3	0.2
1910 Cin-N	20	12	.625	35	30	23	2	3	266	248	96	71	6	14	48	91	1.113	2.40	121	2.67	.253	14	.165	18	20	2.1
1911 Cin-N	15	13	.536	36	29	17	1	0	260^2	258	110	87	3	10	79	91	1.293	3.00	110	3.29	.268	23	.256	9	17	1.6
1912 Cin-N	19	16	.543	42	36	25	5	3	303	320	132	99	6	11	56	104	1.241	2.94	114	3.14	.278	17	.160	18	22	1.7
1913 Cin-N	8	15	.348	36	22	9	2	2	199	220	110	89	6	7	35	73	1.281	4.03	80	3.47	.292	17	.254	-18	7	-1.6
1914 Bal-F	24	14	.632	46	38	26	6	4	319^1	322	118	103	6	10	57	132	1.187	2.90	109	2.92	.266	21	.212	17	28	2.2
1915 Bal-F	11	17	.393	35	25	12	0	3	232^2	288	134	107	12	7	68	71	1.530	4.14	82	4.98	.318	17	.221	-16	8	-1.5
Total 8	99	91	.521	245	185	115	16	17	1652	1722	720	571	40	62	355	588	1.257	3.11	103	3.32	.277	112	.204	33	107	5.0

• SUKLA, Ed Edward Anthony Sukla b: 3/3/1943, Long Beach, CA BR/TR, 5'11", 170 lbs. Deb: 9/17/1964

YEAR TM-L	W	L	PCT	G	GS	CG	SH	SV	IP	H	R	ER	HR	HB	BB	SO	RAT	ERA	ERA+	CERA	OAV	BH	AVG	PR+	WS	TPW
1964 LA-A	0	1	.000	2	0	0	0	0	2^2	2	2	2	1	0	1	3	1.125	6.75	49	4.26	.200	0	....	-1	0	-0.1
1965 Cal-A	2	3	.400	25	0	0	0	3	32	32	16	16	3	1	10	15	1.313	4.50	76	3.72	.264	0	....	-4	1	-0.4
1966 Cal-A	1	1	.500	12	0	0	0	1	16^2	18	12	12	4	0	6	8	1.440	6.48	52	5.51	.281	0	.000	-6	0	-0.6
Total 3	3	5	.375	39	0	0	0	4	51^1	52	30	30	8	1	17	26	1.344	5.26	64	4.33	.267	0	.000	-11	1	-1.2

• SULLIVAN, Bill William F. Sullivan b: 12/1868, Providence, RI d: 10/8/1905, Providence, RI BR/TR Deb: 4/19/1890

YEAR TM-L	W	L	PCT	G	GS	CG	SH	SV	IP	H	R	ER	HR	HB	BB	SO	RAT	ERA	ERA+	CERA	OAV	BH	AVG	PR+	WS	TPW
1890 Syr-a	1	4	.200	6	6	4	0	0	42	51	50	37	2	6	27	13	1.857	7.93	44	....	.291	2	.091	-20	0	-1.9

• SULLIVAN, Charlie Charles Edward Sullivan b: 5/23/1903, Yadkin Valley, NC d: 5/28/1935, Maiden, NC BL/TR, 6'1", 185 lbs. Deb: 4/21/1928

YEAR TM-L	W	L	PCT	G	GS	CG	SH	SV	IP	H	R	ER	HR	HB	BB	SO	RAT	ERA	ERA+	CERA	OAV	BH	AVG	PR+	WS	TPW
1928 Det-A	0	2	.000	3	2	0	0	0	12^1	18	12	9	1	0	6	2	1.946	6.57	62	6.98	.360	0	.000	-3	0	-0.4
1930 Det-A	1	5	.167	40	3	2	0	5	93^2	112	72	68	9	1	53	38	1.762	6.53	73	5.80	.311	7	.292	-18	3	-1.5
1931 Det-A	3	2	.600	31	4	2	0	0	95	109	60	52	6	1	46	28	1.632	4.93	93	4.85	.288	4	.167	-4	5	-0.4
Total 3	4	9	.308	74	9	4	0	5	201	239	144	129	16	2	105	68	1.711	5.78	81	5.42	.303	11	.212	-25	8	-2.3

• SULLIVAN, Fleury Florence P. Sullivan b: 1862, East St. Louis, IL d: 2/15/1897, East St. Louis, IL Deb: 5/3/1884

YEAR TM-L	W	L	PCT	G	GS	CG	SH	SV	IP	H	R	ER	HR	HB	BB	SO	RAT	ERA	ERA+	CERA	OAV	BH	AVG	PR+	WS	TPW
1884 Pit-a	16	35	.314	51	51	51	2	0	441	496	328	206	15	20	96	189	1.342	4.20	80	....	.269	29	.153	-27	16	-3.4

• SULLIVAN, Frank Franklin Leal Sullivan b: 1/23/1930, Hollywood, CA BR/TR, 6'6.5", 215 lbs. Deb: 7/31/1953

YEAR TM-L	W	L	PCT	G	GS	CG	SH	SV	IP	H	R	ER	HR	HB	BB	SO	RAT	ERA	ERA+	CERA	OAV	BH	AVG	PR+	WS	TPW
1953 Bos-A	1	1	.500	14	0	0	0	0	25^2	24	16	16	3	1	11	17	1.364	5.61	75	4.28	.264	1	.250	-4	1	-0.4
1954 Bos-A	15	12	.556	36	26	11	3	1	206^1	185	81	72	18	6	66	124	1.216	3.14	131	3.17	.240	7	.103	25	15	2.3
1955 Bos-A★	**18**	13	.581	35	**35**	16	3	0	**260**	235	103	84	23	2	100	129	1.288	2.91	148	3.40	.241	10	.112	**43**	22	3.9
1956 Bos-A★	14	7	.667	34	33	12	1	0	242	253	112	92	22	8	82	116	1.384	3.42	135	4.11	.268	12	.141	33	19	2.7
1957 Bos-A	14	11	.560	31	30	14	3	0	240^2	206	76	73	16	7	48	127	1.055	2.73	146	**2.46**	.230	13	.165	**37**	23	**3.7**
1958 Bos-A	13	9	.591	32	29	10	2	3	199^1	216	91	79	12	3	49	103	1.329	3.57	112	3.78	.278	11	.164	13	14	1.3
1959 Bos-A	9	11	.450	30	26	5	2	1	177^2	172	86	78	17	7	67	107	1.345	3.95	103	3.99	.258	12	.200	2	10	0.1
1960 Bos-A	6	16	.273	40	22	4	0	1	153^2	164	94	87	12	6	52	98	1.406	5.10	79	4.07	.269	5	.125	-14	4	-1.5
1961 Phi-N	3	16	.158	49	18	1	1	6	159^1	161	93	76	19	5	55	114	1.356	4.29	95	4.11	.262	5	.152	-6	6	-0.6
1962 Phi-N	0	2	.000	19	0	0	0	0	23	38	21	16	2	2	12	12	2.174	6.26	62	9.00	.396	0	....	-6	0	-0.6
Min-A	4	1	.800	21	0	0	0	5	33^1	33	17	12	3	0	13	10	1.380	3.24	126	3.85	.258	0	.000	3	4	0.3
1963 Min-A	0	1	.000	10	0	0	0	1	11	15	7	7	1	0	4	2	1.727	5.73	64	6.06	.349	0	....	-3	0	-0.3
Total 11	97	100	.492	351	219	73	15	18	1732	1702	797	692	148	47	559	959	1.305	3.60	115	3.68	.257	76	.144	122	118	10.9

• SULLIVAN, Harry Harry Andrew Sullivan b: 4/22/1888, Rockford, IL d: 9/22/1919, Rockford, IL BL/TL Deb: 8/11/1909

YEAR TM-L	W	L	PCT	G	GS	CG	SH	SV	IP	H	R	ER	HR	HB	BB	SO	RAT	ERA	ERA+	CERA	OAV	BH	AVG	PR+	WS	TPW
1909 StL-N	0	0	....	2	1	0	0	0	1	4	6	4	1	0	2	1	6.000	36.00	7	41.89	.500	0	.000	-4	0	-0.4

• SULLIVAN, Jim James E. Sullivan b: 4/25/1869, Charlestown, MA d: 11/30/1901, Roxbury, MA BR/TR, 5'10", 155 lbs. Deb: 4/22/1891 U

YEAR TM-L	W	L	PCT	G	GS	CG	SH	SV	IP	H	R	ER	HR	HB	BB	SO	RAT	ERA	ERA+	CERA	OAV	BH	AVG	PR+	WS	TPW
1891 Bos-N	0	0	....	1	0	0	0	0	0^1	2	4	3	0	0	5	0	21.00	81.00	5	....	.668	0	....	-3	0	-0.3
Col-a	0	1	.000	1	1	1	0	0	9	10	9	4	1	1	5	1	1.667	4.00	86	....	.272	0	.000	-1	0	-0.1
1895 Bos-N	11	9	.550	21	19	16	0	0	179^1	236	133	96	10	16	58	46	1.639	4.82	104	5.52	.312	15	.176	2	11	-0.3
1896 Bos-N	11	12	.478	31	26	21	1	1	225^1	268	148	101	12	6	68	33	1.491	4.03	112	4.45	.293	19	.216	7	15	0.4
1897★ Bos-N	4	5	.444	13	9	8	1	2	89	91	56	39	1	2	26	17	1.315	3.94	113	3.19	.263	6	.182	3	6	0.0
Total 4	26	27	.491	67	55	46	2	3	503	607	350	243	24	25	162	97	1.529	4.35	107	4.53	.295	40	.190	8	32	-0.2

• SULLIVAN, Jim James Richard Sullivan b: 4/5/1894, Mine Run, VA d: 2/12/1972, Burtonsville, MD BR/TR, 5'11", 165 lbs. Deb: 9/27/1921

YEAR TM-L	W	L	PCT	G	GS	CG	SH	SV	IP	H	R	ER	HR	HB	BB	SO	RAT	ERA	ERA+	CERA	OAV	BH	AVG	PR+	WS	TPW
1921 Phi-A	0	2	.000	2	2	2	0	0	17	20	13	6	0	0	7	8	1.588	3.18	140	4.08	.294	0	.000	3	1	0.2
1922 Phi-A	0	2	.000	20	2	1	0	0	51^1	76	43	31	3	1	25	15	1.968	5.44	78	7.07	.373	1	.091	-6	0	-0.7
1923 Cle-A	0	1	.000	3	0	0	0	0	5	10	10	8	0	1	5	4	3.000	14.40	28	13.86	.476	0	.000	-6	0	-0.6
Total 3	0	5	.000	25	4	3	0	0	73^1	106	66	45	3	2	37	27	1.950	5.52	76	6.84	.362	1	.056	-9	1	-1.1

• SULLIVAN, Joe Joe Sullivan b: 9/26/1910, Mason City, IL d: 4/8/1985, Sequim, WA BL/TL, 5'11", 175 lbs. Deb: 4/20/1935

YEAR TM-L	W	L	PCT	G	GS	CG	SH	SV	IP	H	R	ER	HR	HB	BB	SO	RAT	ERA	ERA+	CERA	OAV	BH	AVG	PR+	WS	TPW
1935 Det-A	6	6	.500	25	12	5	0	0	125^2	119	66	49	4	3	71	53	1.512	3.51	119	3.78	.244	7	.163	8	7	0.7
1936 Det-A	2	5	.286	26	4	1	0	1	79^2	111	70	60	4	2	40	32	1.895	6.78	73	6.39	.331	5	.179	-15	0	-1.4
1939 Bos-N	6	9	.400	31	11	7	0	2	113^2	114	57	46	3	2	50	46	1.443	3.64	101	3.66	.266	12	.300	-1	7	0.2
1940 Bos-N	10	14	.417	36	22	7	0	1	177^1	157	89	70	9	8	89	64	1.387	3.55	105	3.54	.240	14	.197	-1	10	-0.1
1941 Bos-N	2	2	.500	16	2	0	0	0	52^1	60	26	24	3	2	26	11	1.643	4.13	86	4.99	.290	1	.067	-4	2	-0.5
Pit-N	4	1	.800	16	4	0	0	1	39^1	40	26	13	2	0	22	10	1.576	2.97	121	4.22	.258	4	.364	3	3	0.4
Yr.	6	3	.667	32	6	0	0	1	91^2	100	52	37	5	2	48	21	1.615	3.63	99	4.66	.276	5	.192	-0	5	-0.1
Total 5	30	37	.448	150	55	20	0	5	588	601	334	262	25	17	298	216	1.529	4.01	100	4.18	.265	43	.207	-10	29	-0.7

• SULLIVAN, John John Jeremiah "Lefty" Sullivan b: 5/31/1894, Chicago, IL d: 7/7/1958, Chicago, IL BL/TL, 5'11", 165 lbs. Deb: 7/18/1919

YEAR TM-L	W	L	PCT	G	GS	CG	SH	SV	IP	H	R	ER	HR	HB	BB	SO	RAT	ERA	ERA+	CERA	OAV	BH	AVG	PR+	WS	TPW
1919 Chi-A	0	1	.000	4	2	1	0	0	15	24	15	7	0	1	8	9	2.133	4.20	76	7.65	.364	0	.000	-2	0	-0.2

• SULLIVAN, Lefty Paul Thomas Sullivan b: 9/7/1916, Nashville, TN d: 11/1/1988, Scottsdale, AZ BL/TL, 6'3", 204 lbs. Deb: 5/6/1939

YEAR TM-L	W	L	PCT	G	GS	CG	SH	SV	IP	H	R	ER	HR	HB	BB	SO	RAT	ERA	ERA+	CERA	OAV	BH	AVG	PR+	WS	TPW
1939 Cle-A	0	1	.000	7	1	0	0	0	12^2	9	8	6	0	1	9	4	1.421	4.26	103	3.14	.214	0	.000	0	0	0.0

• SULLIVAN, Mike Michael Joseph "Big Mike" Sullivan b: 10/23/1866, Boston, MA d: 6/14/1906, Boston, MA BL, 6'1", 210 lbs. Deb: 6/17/1889 U

YEAR TM-L	W	L	PCT	G	GS	CG	SH	SV	IP	H	R	ER	HR	HB	BB	SO	RAT	ERA	ERA+	CERA	OAV	BH	AVG	PR+	WS	TPW
1889 Was-N	0	3	.000	9	3	3	0	0	41	47	47	33	2	3	32	15	1.927	7.24	55	....	.279	1	.053	-14	0	-1.4
1890 Chi-N	5	6	.455	12	12	10	0	0	96	108	77	49	3	4	58	33	1.729	4.59	79	....	.276	5	.125	-12	4	-1.4

YEAR	TM-L	W	L	PCT	G	GS	CG	SH	SV	IP	H	R	ER	HR	HB	BB	SO	RAT	ERA	ERA+	CERA	OAV	BH	AVG	PR+	WS	TPW
1891	Phi-a	0	2	.000	2	2	2	0	0	18	17	13	7	2	3	10	7	1.500	3.50	109	....	.241	0	.000	1	1	0.0
	NY-N	1	2	.333	3	3	3	0	0	24	24	19	9	0	1	8	11	1.333	3.38	95	....	.251	2	.200	-1	1	-0.1
1892	Cin-N	12	4	.750	21	16	15	0	0	166^{1}	179	90	57	8	9	74	56	1.521	3.08	106	4.39	.264	13	.176	0	12	-0.2
1893	Cin-N	8	11	.421	27	18	14	0	1	183^{2}	200	146	103	5	17	103	40	1.650	5.05	95	4.84	.269	16	.203	-8	10	-0.9
1894	Was-N	2	10	.167	20	12	11	0	1	117^{2}	166	134	86	10	8	74	21	2.040	6.58	80	7.49	.329	9	.158	-14	2	-1.4
	Cle-N	6	5	.545	13	11	9	0	0	90^{2}	128	82	64	4	3	47	19	1.930	6.35	86	6.55	.329	13	.295	-9	6	-0.7
	Yr.	8	15	.348	33	23	20	0	1	208^{1}	294	216	150	14	11	121	40	1.992	6.48	82	7.08	.329	22	.218	-23	8	-2.1
1895	Cle-N	1	2	.333	4	3	2	0	0	31	42	34	29	1	1	16	5	1.871	8.42	59	6.08	.319	2	.133	-12	0	-1.1
1896	NY-N	10	13	.435	25	22	18	0	0	185^{1}	188	131	96	3	13	71	42	1.397	4.66	90	3.65	.261	16	.208	-11	9	-1.2
1897	NY-N	8	7	.533	23	16	11	1	2	148^{2}	183	113	84	6	14	71	35	1.709	5.09	82	5.49	.300	18	.273	-16	7	-1.3
1898	Bos-N	0	1	.000	3	2	0	0	0	12	19	16	16	1	1	9	1	2.333	12.00	31	9.19	.356	1	.333	-11	0	-1.1
1899	Bos-N	1	0	1.000	1	1	1	0	0	9	10	6	5	1	1	4	1	1.556	5.00	83	5.30	.281	1	.333	-1	1	-0.1
Total	11	54	66	.450	163	121	99	1	4	1123^{1}	1311	908	638	46	78	577	286	1.681	5.11	84	4.39	.286	97	.196	-109	53	-10.8

• SULLIVAN, Scott

William Scott Sullivan b: 3/13/1971, Tuscaloosa, AL BR/TR, 6'3", 210 lbs. Deb: 5/6/1995

YEAR	TM-L	W	L	PCT	G	GS	CG	SH	SV	IP	H	R	ER	HR	HB	BB	SO	RAT	ERA	ERA+	CERA	OAV	BH	AVG	PR+	WS	TPW
1995	Cin-N	0	0	....	3	0	0	0	0	3^{2}	4	2	2	0	0	2	2	1.636	4.91	84	4.28	.286	0	.000	-0	0	-0.1
1996	Cin-N	0	0	....	7	0	0	0	0	8	7	2	2	0	1	5	3	1.500	2.25	185	4.11	.250	0	.000	2	1	0.1
1997	Cin-N	5	3	.625	59	0	0	0	1	97^{1}	79	36	35	12	7	30	96	1.120	3.24	133	3.01	.220	0	.000	11	9	1.0
1998	Cin-N	5	5	.500	67	0	0	0	1	102	98	62	59	14	9	36	86	1.314	5.21	82	4.22	.253	1	.091	-10	3	-1.1
1999	Cin-N	5	4	.556	79	0	0	0	3	113^{2}	88	41	38	10	8	47	78	1.188	3.01	155	3.08	.216	0	.000	17	11	1.5
2000	Cin-N	3	6	.333	79	0	0	0	3	106^{1}	87	44	41	14	9	38	96	1.176	3.47	135	3.40	.226	2	.286	13	10	1.3
2001	Cin-N	7	1	.875	79	0	0	0	0	103^{1}	94	44	38	10	8	36	82	1.258	3.31	138	3.55	.243	0	.000	16	9	1.5
2002	Cin-N	6	5	.545	71	0	0	0	1	78^{2}	93	60	53	15	5	31	78	1.576	6.06	70	5.83	.294	1	.333	-16	1	-1.6
2003	Cin-N	6	0	1.000	50	0	0	0	0	49^{2}	39	22	20	4	5	26	43	1.309	3.62	118	3.42	.211	0	....	4	5	0.4
	Chi-A	0	0	....	15	0	0	0	0	14^{1}	9	6	6	2	1	6	13	1.047	3.77	119	2.71	.184	0	....	1	1	0.1
Total	9	37	24	.607	509	0	0	0	9	677	598	319	294	81	53	257	577	1.263	3.91	113	3.72	.237	4	.083	37	50	3.2

• SULLIVAN, Suter

Suter G. Sullivan b: 10/14/1872, Baltimore, MD d: 4/19/1925, Baltimore, MD, 6', 170 lbs. Deb: 7/24/1898 ♦

YEAR	TM-L	W	L	PCT	G	GS	CG	SH	SV	IP	H	R	ER	HR	HB	BB	SO	RAT	ERA	ERA+	CERA	OAV	BH	AVG	PR+	WS	TPW
1898	StL-N	0	0	....	1	0	0	0	0	6	10	4	1	0	0	4	3	2.333	1.50	252	8.24	.368	32	.222	2	1	-1.5

• SULLIVAN, Tom

Thomas Sullivan b: 3/1/1860, New York, NY d: 4/12/1947, Cincinnati, OH Deb: 9/27/1884

YEAR	TM-L	W	L	PCT	G	GS	CG	SH	SV	IP	H	R	ER	HR	HB	BB	SO	RAT	ERA	ERA+	CERA	OAV	BH	AVG	PR+	WS	TPW
1884	Col-a	2	2	.500	4	4	4	0	0	31	42	22	14	2	0	3	12	1.452	4.06	74	....	.307	1	.091	-4	1	-0.5
1886	Lou-a	2	7	.222	9	9	8	0	0	75	94	70	33	6	2	33	27	1.693	3.96	92	....	.293	3	.111	-4	2	-0.5
1888	KC-a	8	16	.333	24	24	24	0	0	214^{2}	227	146	81	2	24	68	84	1.374	3.40	101	....	.262	10	.109	0	12	-0.5
1889	KC-a	2	8	.200	10	10	10	0	0	87^{1}	111	88	55	2	6	48	24	1.821	5.67	74	....	.300	5	.152	-12	2	-1.0
Total	4	14	33	.298	47	47	46	0	0	408	474	326	183	12	32	152	147	1.534	4.04	90	....	.280	19	.117	-20	17	-2.5

• SULLIVAN, Tom

Thomas Augustin Sullivan b: 10/18/1895, Boston, MA d: 9/23/1962, Boston, MA BL/TL, 5'11", 178 lbs. Deb: 5/15/1922

YEAR	TM-L	W	L	PCT	G	GS	CG	SH	SV	IP	H	R	ER	HR	HB	BB	SO	RAT	ERA	ERA+	CERA	OAV	BH	AVG	PR+	WS	TPW
1922	Phi-N	0	0	....	3	0	0	0	0	8	16	11	10	0	1	5	2	2.625	11.25	41	10.84	.410	1	.250	-6	0	-0.5

• SUMMERS, Ed

Oron Edgar "Kickapoo Ed,Chief" Summers b: 12/5/1884, Ladoga, IN d: 5/12/1953, Indianapolis, IN BB/TR, 6'2", 180 lbs. Deb: 4/16/1908

YEAR	TM-L	W	L	PCT	G	GS	CG	SH	SV	IP	H	R	ER	HR	HB	BB	SO	RAT	ERA	ERA+	CERA	OAV	BH	AVG	PR+	WS	TPW
1908*	Det-A	24	12	.667	40	32	23	5	1	301	271	112	55	3	20	55	103	1.083	1.64	147	2.43	.242	14	.124	31	21	2.8
1909*	Det-A	19	9	.679	35	32	24	3	1	281^{2}	243	91	70	4	10	52	107	1.047	2.24	112	2.11	.227	10	.106	8	21	0.5
1910	Det-A	13	12	.520	30	25	18	1	0	220^{1}	211	83	62	8	5	60	82	1.230	2.53	104	3.04	.254	14	.184	3	14	0.3
1911	Det-A	11	11	.500	30	20	13	0	1	179^{1}	189	108	73	3	11	51	65	1.338	3.66	94	3.60	.274	16	.254	-2	11	-0.1
1912	Det-A	1	1	.500	3	3	1	0	0	16^{2}	16	10	9	1	0	3	5	1.140	4.86	67	2.77	.250	3	.500	-3	1	-0.2
Total	5	68	45	.602	138	112	79	9	3	999	930	404	269	19	46	221	362	1.152	2.42	113	2.69	.246	57	.162	37	68	3.4

• SUNDIN, Gordie

Gordon Vincent Sundin b: 10/10/1937, Minneapolis, MN BR/TR, 6'4", 215 lbs. Deb: 9/19/1956

YEAR	TM-L	W	L	PCT	G	GS	CG	SH	SV	IP	H	R	ER	HR	HB	BB	SO	RAT	ERA	ERA+	CERA	OAV	BH	AVG	PR+	WS	TPW
1956	Bal-A	0	0	....	1	0	0	0	0	0	0	1	1	0	0	2	0	....	∞	....	∞	1.000	0	....	-1	0	-0.1

• SUNDRA, Steve

Stephen Richard "Smokey" Sundra b: 3/27/1910, Luxor, PA d: 3/23/1952, Cleveland, OH BR/TR, 6'2", 190 lbs. Deb: 4/17/1936

YEAR	TM-L	W	L	PCT	G	GS	CG	SH	SV	IP	H	R	ER	HR	HB	BB	SO	RAT	ERA	ERA+	CERA	OAV	BH	AVG	PR+	WS	TPW
1936	NY-A	0	0	....	1	0	0	0	0	2	2	0	0	0	0	2	1	2.000	0.00	....	5.81	.286	0	.000	1	0	0.1
1938	NY-A	6	4	.600	25	8	3	0	0	93^{2}	107	61	50	7	0	43	33	1.601	4.80	94	4.88	.291	6	.182	-4	5	-0.2
1939*	NY-A	11	1	.917	24	11	8	1	0	120^{2}	110	43	37	7	0	56	27	1.376	2.76	158	3.40	.240	13	.265	17	12	1.8
1940	NY-A	4	6	.400	27	8	2	0	2	99^{1}	121	68	61	11	1	42	26	1.641	5.53	73	5.37	.299	4	.138	-18	2	-1.8
1941	Was-A	9	13	.409	28	23	11	0	0	168^{1}	203	108	99	11	1	61	50	1.568	5.29	76	4.72	.294	13	.217	-21	5	-1.8
1942	Was-A	1	3	.250	6	4	2	0	0	33^{2}	43	24	21	1	1	15	5	1.723	5.61	65	5.24	.305	2	.167	-6	0	-0.6
	StL-A	8	3	.727	20	13	6	0	0	110^{2}	122	56	47	2	0	29	26	1.364	3.82	97	3.44	.275	9	.225	-0	7	0.2
	Yr.	9	6	.600	26	17	8	0	0	144^{1}	165	80	68	3	1	44	31	1.448	4.24	87	3.86	.282	11	.212	-6	7	-0.4
1943	StL-A	15	11	.577	32	29	13	3	0	208	212	89	75	10	0	66	44	1.337	3.25	102	3.42	.266	16	.219	5	13	0.7
1944	StL-A	2	0	1.000	3	3	2	0	0	19	15	3	3	1	0	4	1	1.000	1.42	253	1.97	.211	0	.000	5	3	0.5
1946	StL-A	0	0	....	2	0	0	0	0	4	9	9	5	0	0	3	1	3.000	11.25	33	11.36	.409	0	....	-3	0	-0.3
Total	9	56	41	.577	168	99	47	4	2	859^{1}	944	461	398	50	3	321	214	1.472	4.17	93	4.14	.277	63	.209	-25	47	-1.5

• SUNKEL, Tom

Thomas Jacob "Lefty" Sunkel b: 8/9/1912, Paris, IL d: 4/6/2002, Paris, IL BL/TL, 6'1", 190 lbs. Deb: 8/26/1937

YEAR	TM-L	W	L	PCT	G	GS	CG	SH	SV	IP	H	R	ER	HR	HB	BB	SO	RAT	ERA	ERA+	CERA	OAV	BH	AVG	PR+	WS	TPW
1937	StL-N	0	0	....	9	1	0	0	1	29^{1}	24	11	9	0	0	11	9	1.193	2.76	144	2.19	.214	1	.111	4	3	0.3
1939	StL-N	4	4	.500	20	11	2	1	0	85^{1}	79	47	40	4	1	56	54	1.582	4.22	97	4.02	.242	9	.321	-2	5	0.0
1941	NY-N	1	1	.500	2	2	1	1	0	15^{1}	7	5	5	0	1	12	14	1.239	2.93	126	2.01	.140	2	.333	1	2	0.2
1942	NY-N	3	6	.333	19	11	3	0	0	63^{2}	65	40	34	5	0	41	29	1.665	4.81	70	4.90	.269	2	.105	-11	0	-1.3
1943	NY-N	0	1	.000	1	1	0	0	0	2^{2}	4	3	3	1	0	3	0	2.625	10.13	34	11.75	.308	0	....	-2	0	-0.2
1944	Bro-N	1	3	.250	12	3	0	0	1	24	39	20	20	1	0	10	6	2.042	7.50	47	7.34	.368	0	.000	-10	0	-1.1
Total	6	9	15	.375	63	29	6	2	2	220^{1}	218	126	111	11	2	133	112	1.593	4.53	82	4.35	.256	14	.212	-19	10	-2.0

• SUPPAN, Jeff

Jeffrey Scot Suppan b: 1/2/1975, Oklahoma City, OK BR/TR, 6'1", 200 lbs. Deb: 7/17/1995

YEAR	TM-L	W	L	PCT	G	GS	CG	SH	SV	IP	H	R	ER	HR	HB	BB	SO	RAT	ERA	ERA+	CERA	OAV	BH	AVG	PR+	WS	TPW
1995	Bos-A	1	2	.333	8	3	0	0	0	22^{2}	29	15	15	4	0	5	19	1.500	5.96	82	5.43	.312	0	....	-3	1	-0.3
1996	Bos-A	1	1	.500	8	4	0	0	0	22^{2}	29	19	19	3	1	13	13	1.853	7.54	67	7.03	.330	0	....	-6	0	-0.5
1997	Bos-A	7	3	.700	23	22	0	0	0	112^{1}	140	75	71	12	4	36	67	1.567	5.69	82	5.39	.305	0	.000	-13	4	-1.3
1998	Ari-N	1	7	.125	13	13	1	0	0	66	82	55	49	12	1	21	39	1.561	6.68	63	5.73	.301	6	.273	-18	0	-1.6
	KC-A	0	0	....	4	1	0	0	0	12^{2}	9	1	1	1	0	1	12	.789	0.71	679	1.51	.200	0	....	6	2	0.6
1999	KC-A	10	12	.455	32	32	4	1	0	208^{2}	222	113	105	28	3	62	103	1.361	4.53	111	4.33	.274	1	.200	7	12	0.6
2000	KC-A	10	9	.526	35	33	3	1	0	217	240	121	119	36	7	84	128	1.493	4.94	104	5.31	.284	0	.000	-0	12	0.0
2001	KC-A	10	14	.417	34	34	1	0	0	218^{1}	227	120	106	26	12	74	120	1.379	4.37	112	4.40	.267	2	.400	7	12	0.8
2002	KC-A	9	16	.360	33	33	3	1	0	208	229	134	123	32	7	68	109	1.428	5.32	94	4.84	.279	0	.000	-6	9	-0.6
2003	Pit-N	10	7	.588	21	21	3	2	0	141	147	57	56	11	6	31	78	1.262	3.57	122	3.55	.268	12	.293	13	11	1.6
	Bos-A	3	4	.429	11	10	0	0	0	63	70	41	39	12	2	20	32	1.429	5.57	82	5.15	.281	0	.000	-6	2	-0.6
Total	9	62	75	.453	222	206	15	5	0	1292^{1}	1424	751	703	177	43	415	720	1.423	4.90	99	4.75	.280	21	.259	-19	65	-1.3

• SURHOFF, Rick

Richard Clifford Surhoff b: 10/3/1962, Bronx, NY BR/TR, 6'3", 210 lbs. Deb: 9/8/1985

YEAR	TM-L	W	L	PCT	G	GS	CG	SH	SV	IP	H	R	ER	HR	HB	BB	SO	RAT	ERA	ERA+	CERA	OAV	BH	AVG	PR+	WS	TPW
1985	Phi-N	1	0	1.000	2	0	0	0	0	1	2	0	0	0	0	0	1	2.000	0.00	....	9.49	.500	0	....	0	0	0.0
	Tex-A	0	1	.000	7	0	0	0	2	8^{1}	12	7	7	2	0	3	8	1.800	7.56	56	7.74	.343	0	....	-3	0	-0.3

• SURKONT, Max

Matthew Constantine Surkont b: 6/16/1922, Central Falls, RI d: 10/8/1986, Largo, FL BR/TR, 6'1", 205 lbs. Deb: 4/19/1949

YEAR	TM-L	W	L	PCT	G	GS	CG	SH	SV	IP	H	R	ER	HR	HB	BB	SO	RAT	ERA	ERA+	CERA	OAV	BH	AVG	PR+	WS	TPW
1949	Chi-A	3	5	.375	44	2	0	0	4	96	92	61	51	9	3	60	38	1.583	4.78	87	4.61	.255	1	.045	-7	3	-0.8
1950	Bos-N	5	2	.714	9	6	2	0	0	55^{2}	63	29	20	5	2	20	21	1.491	3.23	119	4.64	.285	10	.435	4	5	0.9
1951	Bos-N	12	16	.429	37	33	11	2	1	237	230	119	105	21	7	89	110	1.346	3.99	92	3.73	.252	11	.151	-6	10	-0.6
1952	Bos-N	12	13	.480	31	29	12	3	0	215	201	95	90	19	3	76	125	1.288	3.77	96	3.40	.245	7	.111	-0	11	-0.1
1953	Mil-N	11	5	.688	28	24	11	2	0	170	168	82	79	22	0	64	83	1.365	4.18	94	4.00	.255	16	.286	-7	11	0.0
1954	Pit-N	9	18	.333	33	29	11	0	0	208^{1}	216	124	102	25	4	78	78	1.411	4.41	95	4.24	.268	10	.167	-0	9	0.0
1955	Pit-N	7	14	.333	35	22	5	0	2	166^{1}	194	109	103	23	3	78	84	**1.635**	5.57	74	5.75	.298	7	.140	-25	2	-2.6

YEAR	TM-L	W	L	PCT	G	GS	CG	SH	SV	IP	H	R	ER	HR	HB	BB	SO	RAT	ERA	ERA+	CERA	OAV	BH	AVG	PR+	WS	TPW
1956	Pit-N	0	0	....	1	0	0	0	0	2	2	1	1	0	0	3	1	2.500	4.50	84	7.45	.333	0	....	-0	0	0.0
	StL-N	0	0	....	5	0	0	0	0	5^{2}	10	6	6	3	0	2	5	2.118	9.53	40	13.29	.417	0	.000	-4	0	-0.4
	NY-N	2	2	.500	8	4	1	0	1	32	24	17	17	5	0	9	18	1.031	4.78	79	2.57	.202	1	.111	-3	1	-0.4
	Yr.	2	2	.500	14	4	1	0	1	39^{2}	36	24	24	8	0	14	24	1.261	5.45	69	4.35	.242	1	.100	-7	1	-0.8
1957	NY-N	0	1	.000	5	0	0	0	0	6^{1}	9	7	7	2	0	2	8	1.737	9.95	40	7.81	.321	0	....	-4	0	-0.4
Total	9	61	76	.445	236	149	53	7	8	1194^{1}	1209	650	581	134	22	481	571	1.415	4.38	89	4.23	.262	63	.176	-52	52	-4.4

• SUSCE, George

George Daniel Susce b: 9/13/1931, Pittsburgh, PA BR/TR, 6'1", 180 lbs. Deb: 4/15/1955 C

YEAR	TM-L	W	L	PCT	G	GS	CG	SH	SV	IP	H	R	ER	HR	HB	BB	SO	RAT	ERA	ERA+	CERA	OAV	BH	AVG	PR+	WS	TPW
1955	Bos-A	9	7	.563	29	15	6	1	1	144^{1}	123	54	49	12	8	49	60	1.192	3.06	140	3.12	.232	7	.143	21	12	1.9
1956	Bos-A	2	4	.333	21	6	0	0	0	69^{2}	71	54	48	14	4	44	26	1.651	6.20	75	6.07	.262	4	.222	-12	1	-1.1
1957	Bos-A	7	3	.700	29	5	0	0	1	88^{1}	93	45	42	6	3	41	40	1.517	4.28	93	4.46	.274	3	.120	-1	5	-0.2
1958	Bos-A	0	0	....	2	0	0	0	0	2	6	4	4	1	0	1	0	3.500	18.00	22	24.92	.600	0	....	-3	0	-0.3
	Det-A	4	3	.571	27	10	2	0	1	90^{2}	90	45	37	7	3	26	42	1.279	3.67	110	3.53	.259	3	.125	3	5	0.2
	Yr.	4	3	.571	29	10	2	0	1	92^{2}	96	49	41	8	3	27	42	1.327	3.98	101	3.99	.269	3	.125	-0	5	-0.1
1959	Det-A	0	0	....	9	0	0	0	0	14^{2}	24	22	21	4	2	9	9	2.250	12.89	32	10.91	.358	0	.000	-14	0	-1.5
Total	5	22	17	.564	117	36	8	1	3	409^{2}	407	224	201	44	20	170	177	1.408	4.42	95	4.39	.260	17	.145	-7	23	-0.9

• SUTCLIFFE, Rick

Richard Lee "Red Baron" Sutcliffe b: 6/21/1956, Independence, MO BL/TR, 6'7", 215 lbs. Deb: 9/29/1976

YEAR	TM-L	W	L	PCT	G	GS	CG	SH	SV	IP	H	R	ER	HR	HB	BB	SO	RAT	ERA	ERA+	CERA	OAV	BH	AVG	PR+	WS	TPW
1976	LA-N	0	0	....	1	1	0	0	0	5	2	0	0	0	0	1	3	.600	0.00	....	0.67	.125	0	.000	2	1	0.2
1978	LA-N	0	0	....	2	0	0	0	0	1^{2}	2	0	0	0	1	1	0	1.800	0.00	....	7.49	.286	0	....	1	0	0.1
1979	LA-N	17	10	.630	39	30	5	1	0	242	217	104	93	16	2	97	117	1.298	3.46	105	3.30	.243	21	.247	8	16	1.3
1980	LA-N	3	9	.250	42	10	1	1	5	110	122	73	68	10	1	55	59	1.609	5.56	63	5.10	.285	4	.148	-27	0	-2.8
1981	LA-N	2	2	.500	14	6	0	0	0	47	41	24	21	5	2	20	16	1.298	4.02	83	3.68	.238	2	.182	-4	1	-0.3
1982	Cle-A	14	8	.636	34	27	6	1	1	216	174	81	71	16	4	98	142	1.259	**2.96**	138	3.19	**.226**	0	....	29	20	2.9
1983	Cle-A★	17	11	.607	36	35	10	2	0	243^{1}	251	131	116	23	6	102	160	1.451	4.29	99	4.37	.268	0	....	0	14	0.0
1984	Cle-A	4	5	.444	15	15	2	0	0	94^{1}	111	60	54	7	2	46	58	1.664	5.15	79	5.33	.298	0	....	-12	2	-1.2
	*Chi-N	16	1	.941	20	20	7	3	0	150^{1}	123	53	45	9	1	39	155	1.078	2.69	145	2.39	.220	14	.250	22	16	2.6
1985	Chi-N	8	8	.500	20	20	6	3	0	130	119	51	46	12	3	44	102	1.254	3.18	125	3.35	.240	10	.233	13	11	1.6
1986	Chi-N	5	14	.263	28	27	4	1	0	176^{2}	166	92	91	18	1	96	122	1.483	4.64	87	4.34	.252	11	.208	-9	7	-0.6
1987	Chi-N★	**18**	10	.643	34	34	6	1	0	237^{1}	223	106	97	24	4	106	174	1.386	3.68	116	3.95	.252	12	.148	21	19	2.4
1988	Chi-N	13	14	.481	32	32	12	2	0	226	232	97	97	18	2	70	144	1.336	3.86	93	3.72	.269	12	.160	-1	14	0.2
1989*	Chi-N★	16	11	.593	35	34	5	1	0	229	202	98	93	18	2	69	153	1.183	3.66	103	2.93	.240	10	.143	4	14	0.6
1990	Chi-N	0	2	.000	5	5	0	0	0	21^{1}	25	14	14	2	0	12	7	1.734	5.91	69	5.80	.305	0	.000	-4	0	-0.4
1991	Chi-N	6	5	.545	19	18	0	0	0	96^{2}	96	52	44	4	0	45	52	1.459	4.10	95	3.83	.264	3	.094	-1	4	-0.2
1992	Bal-A	16	15	.516	36	**36**	5	2	0	237^{1}	251	123	118	20	7	74	109	1.369	4.47	90	4.04	.273	0	....	-13	10	-1.4
1993	Bal-A	10	10	.500	29	28	3	0	0	166	212	112	106	23	6	74	80	**1.723**	5.75	78	6.39	.314	0	....	-26	4	-2.5
1994	StL-N	6	4	.600	16	14	0	0	0	67^{2}	93	53	49	11	2	32	26	1.847	6.52	64	7.31	.331	3	.130	-18	0	-1.8
Total	18	171	139	.552	457	392	72	18	6	2697^{2}	2662	1324	1223	236	46	1081	1679	1.387	4.08	97	4.01	.260	102	.181	-14	153	0.8

• SUTER, Harry

Harry Richard "Handsome Harry,Rube" Suter b: 9/15/1887, Independence, MO d: 7/24/1971, Topeka, KS BL/TL, 5'10", 190 lbs. Deb: 4/16/1909

YEAR	TM-L	W	L	PCT	G	GS	CG	SH	SV	IP	H	R	ER	HR	HB	BB	SO	RAT	ERA	ERA+	CERA	OAV	BH	AVG	PR+	WS	TPW
1909	Chi-A	2	3	.400	18	7	3	1	1	87^{1}	72	34	24	2	4	28	53	1.145	2.47	94	2.67	.199	3	.094	-1	4	-0.3

• SUTHERLAND, Darrell

Darrell Wayne Sutherland b: 11/14/1941, Glendale, CA BR/TR, 6'4", 169 lbs. Deb: 6/28/1964

YEAR	TM-L	W	L	PCT	G	GS	CG	SH	SV	IP	H	R	ER	HR	HB	BB	SO	RAT	ERA	ERA+	CERA	OAV	BH	AVG	PR+	WS	TPW
1964	NY-N	0	3	.000	10	4	0	0	0	26^{2}	32	26	23	1	2	12	9	1.650	7.76	46	5.07	.302	1	.200	-13	0	-1.3
1965	NY-N	3	1	.750	18	2	0	0	0	48	33	16	15	4	4	17	16	1.042	2.81	125	2.48	.199	2	.154	4	5	0.5
1966	NY-N	2	0	1.000	31	0	0	0	1	44^{1}	60	25	24	6	2	25	23	1.917	4.87	75	7.32	.339	2	.667	-6	2	-0.6
1968	Cle-A	0	0	....	3	0	0	0	0	3^{1}	6	3	3	0	0	4	2	3.000	8.10	37	10.76	.375	0	....	-2	0	-0.2
Total	4	5	4	.556	62	6	0	0	1	122^{1}	131	70	65	11	8	58	50	1.545	4.78	74	5.02	.282	5	.238	-17	7	-1.6

• SUTHERLAND, Dizzy

Howard Alvin Sutherland b: 4/9/1922, Washington, DC d: 8/26/1979, Washington, DC BL/TL, 6', 200 lbs. Deb: 9/20/1949

YEAR	TM-L	W	L	PCT	G	GS	CG	SH	SV	IP	H	R	ER	HR	HB	BB	SO	RAT	ERA	ERA+	CERA	OAV	BH	AVG	PR+	WS	TPW
1949	Was-A	0	1	.000	1	1	0	0	0	1	2	5	5	0	0	6	0	8.000	45.00	9	32.72	.400	0	....	-4	0	-0.4

• SUTHERLAND, Suds

Harvey Scott Sutherland b: 2/20/1894, Beaverton, OR d: 5/11/1972, Portland, OR BR/TR, 6', 180 lbs. Deb: 4/14/1921

YEAR	TM-L	W	L	PCT	G	GS	CG	SH	SV	IP	H	R	ER	HR	HB	BB	SO	RAT	ERA	ERA+	CERA	OAV	BH	AVG	PR+	WS	TPW
1921	Det-A	6	2	.750	13	8	3	0	0	58	80	43	32	1	0	18	18	1.690	4.97	86	5.07	.328	11	.407	-3	3	0.0

• SUTTER, Bruce

Howard Bruce Sutter b: 1/8/1953, Lancaster, PA BR/TR, 6'2", 190 lbs. Deb: 5/9/1976

YEAR	TM-L	W	L	PCT	G	GS	CG	SH	SV	IP	H	R	ER	HR	HB	BB	SO	RAT	ERA	ERA+	CERA	OAV	BH	AVG	PR+	WS	TPW
1976	Chi-N	6	3	.667	52	0	0	0	10	83^{1}	63	27	25	4	0	26	73	1.068	2.70	143	2.05	.209	0	.000	12	12	1.2
1977	Chi-N★	7	3	.700	62	0	0	0	31	107^{1}	69	21	16	5	1	23	129	.857	1.34	327	1.41	.183	3	.150	38	27	3.9
1978	Chi-N★	8	10	.444	64	0	0	0	27	99	82	44	35	10	1	34	106	1.172	3.18	127	2.82	.220	1	.077	10	16	1.0
1979	Chi-N★	6	6	.500	62	0	0	0	**37**	101^{1}	67	29	25	3	0	32	110	.977	2.22	185	1.59	.186	3	.250	23	22	2.4
1980	Chi-N★	5	8	.385	60	0	0	0	**28**	102^{1}	90	35	30	5	1	34	76	1.212	2.64	148	2.76	.242	1	.111	16	16	1.6
1981	StL-N★	3	5	.375	48	0	0	0	**25**	82^{1}	64	24	24	5	1	24	57	1.069	2.62	136	2.20	.218	0	.000	7	13	0.7
1982*	StL-N	9	8	.529	70	0	0	0	**36**	102^{1}	88	38	33	8	3	34	61	1.192	2.90	125	2.84	.235	1	.125	6	17	0.6
1983	StL-N	9	10	.474	60	0	0	0	21	89^{1}	90	45	42	8	1	30	64	1.343	4.23	86	3.55	.262	0	.000	-6	9	-0.7
1984	StL-N★	5	7	.417	71	0	0	0	**45**	122^{2}	109	26	21	9	1	23	77	1.076	1.54	225	2.61	.245	0	.000	24	23	2.5
1985	Atl-N	7	7	.500	58	0	0	0	23	88^{1}	91	46	44	13	3	29	52	1.358	4.48	86	4.33	.267	0	.000	-6	8	-0.6
1986	Atl-N	2	0	1.000	16	0	0	0	3	18^{2}	17	9	9	3	0	9	16	1.393	4.34	92	4.18	.243	0	.000	-1	2	-0.1
1988	Atl-N	1	4	.200	38	0	0	0	14	45^{1}	49	26	24	4	1	11	40	1.324	4.76	77	3.80	.275	0	.000	-5	3	-0.5
Total	12	68	71	.489	661	0	0	0	300	1042^{1}	879	370	328	77	13	309	861	1.140	2.83	134	2.68	.230	9	.088	120	168	12.0

• SUTTHOFF, Jack

John Gerhard "Sunny Jack" Sutthoff b: 6/29/1873, Cincinnati, OH d: 8/3/1942, Cincinnati, OH BL/TR, 5'9", 175 lbs. Deb: 9/15/1898

YEAR	TM-L	W	L	PCT	G	GS	CG	SH	SV	IP	H	R	ER	HR	HB	BB	SO	RAT	ERA	ERA+	CERA	OAV	BH	AVG	PR+	WS	TPW
1898	Was-N	0	0	....	2	1	0	0	0	8^{1}	16	13	12	1	0	8	3	2.880	12.96	28	12.52	.401	1	.333	-8	0	-0.7
1899	StL-N	1	2	.333	2	3	3	3	0	24	29	25	15	0	0	15	8	1.833	5.63	71	5.21	.298	1	.100	-5	0	-0.5
1901	Cin-N	1	6	.143	10	4	4	0	0	70^{1}	82	55	43	2	2	39	12	1.720	5.50	58	5.04	.289	3	.107	-16	0	-1.9
1903	Cin-N	16	9	.640	30	27	21	3	0	224^{2}	207	104	70	2	16	79	76	1.273	2.80	127	3.08	.246	12	.143	19	16	1.6
1904	Cin-N	5	6	.455	12	10	8	0	0	90	83	49	23	1	3	43	27	1.400	2.30	127	3.51	.255	6	.182	4	5	0.4
	Phi-N	6	13	.316	19	18	17	0	0	163^{2}	172	90	67	2	9	71	46	1.485	3.68	72	4.01	.272	10	.164	-15	3	-1.7
	Yr.	11	19	.367	31	28	25	0	0	253^{2}	255	139	90	3	12	114	73	1.455	3.19	85	3.83	.266	16	.170	-12	8	-1.3
1905	Phi-N	3	4	.429	13	6	4	1	0	77^{2}	82	46	33	2	4	36	26	1.519	3.82	76	4.49	.290	2	.080	-9	2	-1.0
Total	6	32	40	.444	88	69	57	7	0	658^{2}	671	382	263	10	34	291	198	1.461	3.59	87	3.94	.268	35	.143	-31	26	-3.8

• SUTTON, Don

Donald Howard Sutton b: 4/2/1945, Clio, AL BR/TR, 6'1", 185 lbs. Deb: 4/14/1966 HOF: 1998

YEAR	TM-L	W	L	PCT	G	GS	CG	SH	SV	IP	H	R	ER	HR	HB	BB	SO	RAT	ERA	ERA+	CERA	OAV	BH	AVG	PR+	WS	TPW
1966	LA-N	12	12	.500	37	35	6	2	0	225^{2}	192	82	75	19	3	52	209	1.081	2.99	110	2.54	.228	15	.183	7	14	0.8
1967	LA-N	11	15	.423	37	34	11	3	1	232^{2}	223	106	102	18	6	57	169	1.203	3.95	79	3.16	.250	10	.133	-19	7	-2.1
1968	LA-N	11	15	.423	35	27	7	2	1	207^{2}	179	64	60	6	2	59	162	1.146	2.60	106	2.40	.232	11	.177	2	13	0.3
1969	LA-N	17	18	.486	41	41	11	4	0	293^{1}	269	123	113	25	3	91	217	1.227	3.47	96	3.17	.242	15	.153	-7	14	-0.9
1970	LA-N	15	13	.536	38	38	10	4	0	260^{1}	251	127	118	38	10	78	201	1.264	4.08	94	3.86	.249	13	.155	-12	11	-0.9
1971	LA-N	17	12	.586	38	37	12	4	1	265^{1}	231	85	75	10	5	55	194	1.078	2.54	127	2.36	.238	19	.216	20	21	2.4
1972	LA-N★	19	9	.679	33	33	18	**9**	0	272^{2}	186	78	63	13	4	63	207	.913	2.08	160	**1.63**	**.189**	13	.143	37	24	3.8
1973	LA-N★	18	10	.643	33	33	14	3	0	256^{1}	196	78	69	18	5	56	200	.983	2.42	142	2.08	.209	10	.119	26	22	2.5
1974*	LA-N	19	9	.679	40	**40**	10	5	0	276	241	111	99	23	6	80	179	1.163	3.23	105	2.90	.229	18	.184	7	15	0.8
1975	LA-N★	16	13	.552	35	35	11	4	0	254^{1}	202	87	81	17	3	62	175	1.038	2.87	119	**2.20**	.213	11	.138	12	17	1.2
1976	LA-N	21	10	.677	35	34	15	4	0	267^{2}	231	98	91	22	3	82	161	1.169	3.06	110	2.90	.234	7	.083	4	20	0.1
1977*	LA-N★	14	8	.636	33	33	9	3	0	240^{1}	207	93	85	23	3	69	150	1.148	3.18	120	2.93	.233	11	.151	15	17	1.6
1978*	LA-N	15	11	.577	34	34	12	2	0	238^{1}	228	109	94	29	5	54	154	1.183	3.55	99	3.32	.250	6	.083	-3	11	-0.6
1979	LA-N	12	15	.444	33	32	6	1	1	226	201	109	96	21	1	61	146	1.159	3.82	95	2.91	.239	11	.143	-2	10	-0.4
1980	LA-N	13	5	.722	32	31	4	2	1	212^{1}	163	56	52	20	2	47	128	.989	**2.20**	159	2.20	.211	5	.078	28	20	2.5
1981	Hou-N	11	9	.550	23	23	6	3	0	158^{2}	132	51	46	6	1	29	104	1.015	2.61	126	2.05	.230	7	.137	11	11	1.3
1982	Hou-N	13	8	.619	27	27	4	0	0	195	169	75	65	10	1	46	139	1.103	3.00	111	2.47	.232	11	.162	5	14	0.5
	*Mil-A	4	1	.800	7	7	2	1	0	54^{2}	55	21	20	8	0	18	36	1.335	3.29	115	4.24	.263	0	....	2	3	0.2

YEAR	TM-L	W	L	PCT	G	GS	CG	SH	SV	IP	H	R	ER	HR	HB	BB	SO	RAT	ERA	ERA+	CERA	OAV	BH	AVG	PR+	WS	TPW
1983	Mil-A	8	13	.381	31	31	4	0	0	220^{1}	209	109	100	21	5	54	134	1.194	4.08	91	3.19	.246	0	....	-8	9	-0.8
1984	Mil-A	14	12	.538	33	33	1	0	0	212^{2}	224	103	89	24	3	51	143	1.293	3.77	102	3.80	.266	0	....	4	11	0.4
1985	Oak-A	13	8	.619	29	29	1	1	0	194^{1}	194	88	84	19	0	51	91	1.261	3.89	99	3.48	.256	0	....	1	9	0.1
	Cal-A	2	2	.500	5	5	0	0	0	31^{2}	27	13	13	6	0	8	16	1.105	3.69	111	3.39	.233	0	....	0	2	0.0
	Yr.	15	10	.600	34	34	1	1	0	226	221	101	97	25	0	59	107	1.239	3.86	101	3.47	.253	0	....	1	11	0.1
1986*	Cal-A	15	11	.577	34	34	3	1	0	207	192	93	86	31	3	49	116	1.164	3.74	110	3.40	.242	0	....	4	13	0.4
1987	Cal-A	11	11	.500	35	34	1	0	0	191^{2}	199	101	100	38	7	41	99	1.252	4.70	92	4.43	.269	0	....	-9	9	-0.8
1988	LA-N	3	6	.333	16	16	0	0	0	87^{1}	91	44	38	7	1	30	44	1.385	3.92	85	3.83	.270	2	.087	-5	2	-0.6
Total	23	324	256	.559	774	756	178	58	5	5282^{1}	4692	2104	1914	472	82	1343	3574	1.142	3.26	108	2.90	.236	195	.144	122	319	11.8

• SUTTON, John Johnny Ike Sutton b: 11/13/1952, Dallas, TX BR/TR, 5'11", 185 lbs. Deb: 4/7/1977

YEAR	TM-L	W	L	PCT	G	GS	CG	SH	SV	IP	H	R	ER	HR	HB	BB	SO	RAT	ERA	ERA+	CERA	OAV	BH	AVG	PR+	WS	TPW
1977	StL-N	2	1	.667	14	0	0	0	0	24^{1}	28	10	7	1	0	9	9	1.521	2.59	149	4.62	.315	0	.000	3	2	0.3
1978	Min-A	0	0	....	17	0	0	0	0	44^{1}	46	19	17	3	1	15	18	1.376	3.45	111	3.79	.264	0	....	2	2	0.2
Total	2	2	1	.667	31	0	0	0	0	68^{2}	74	29	24	4	1	24	27	1.427	3.15	122	4.08	.281	0	.000	5	4	0.5

• SUZUKI, Mac Makoto Suzuki b: 5/31/1975, Kobe, Japan BR/TR, 6'3", 195 lbs. Deb: 7/7/1996

YEAR	TM-L	W	L	PCT	G	GS	CG	SH	SV	IP	H	R	ER	HR	HB	BB	SO	RAT	ERA	ERA+	CERA	OAV	BH	AVG	PR+	WS	TPW
1996	Sea-A	0	0	....	1	0	0	0	0	1^{1}	2	3	3	0	0	2	1	3.000	20.25	24	8.87	.333	0	....	-2	0	-0.2
1998	Sea-A	1	2	.333	6	5	0	0	0	26^{1}	34	23	21	3	0	15	19	1.861	7.18	65	6.52	.304	0	....	-7	0	-0.7
1999	Sea-A	0	2	.000	16	4	0	0	0	42	47	47	44	7	4	34	32	1.929	9.43	53	7.34	.283	0	....	-21	0	-1.9
	KC-A	2	3	.400	22	9	0	0	0	68	77	45	39	9	3	30	36	1.574	5.16	97	5.49	.287	0	....	-3	3	-0.2
	Yr.	2	5	.286	38	13	0	0	0	110	124	92	83	16	7	64	68	1.709	6.79	74	6.20	.286	0	....	-23	3	-2.1
2000	KC-A	8	10	.444	32	29	1	1	0	188^{2}	195	100	91	26	3	94	135	1.532	4.34	118	4.96	.265	1	.200	12	12	1.1
2001	KC-A	2	5	.286	15	9	0	0	0	56	61	38	33	12	3	25	37	1.536	5.30	92	5.85	.277	0	....	-4	2	-0.4
	Col-N	0	2	.000	3	1	0	0	0	6^{1}	9	12	11	3	1	11	5	3.158	15.63	34	17.88	.333	0	.000	-7	0	-0.7
	Mil-N	3	5	.375	15	9	0	0	0	56	52	37	33	5	4	37	47	1.589	5.30	81	4.87	.251	0	.000	-7	1	-0.8
	Yr.	3	7	.300	18	10	0	0	0	62^{1}	61	49	44	8	5	48	52	1.749	6.35	71	6.19	.261	0	.000	-14	1	-1.5
2002	KC-A	0	2	.000	7	1	0	0	0	21	24	21	21	2	0	17	15	1.952	9.00	56	6.48	.296	1	.500	-9	0	-0.9
Total	6	16	31	.340	117	67	1	1	0	465^{2}	501	326	296	67	18	265	327	1.645	5.72	86	5.69	.275	2	.080	-47	18	-4.6

• SWABACH, Bill William Swabach b: 10/1867, New York, NY d: 5/17/1949, Stamford, CT Deb: 7/9/1887

YEAR	TM-L	W	L	PCT	G	GS	CG	SH	SV	IP	H	R	ER	HR	HB	BB	SO	RAT	ERA	ERA+	CERA	OAV	BH	AVG	PR+	WS	TPW
1887	NY-N	0	2	.000	2	2	2	0	0	16	33	23	9	1	1	6	6	2.063	5.06	74	....	.411	0	.000	-3	0	-0.3

• SWAGGERTY, Bill William David Swaggerty b: 12/5/1956, Sanford, FL BR/TR, 6'2", 186 lbs. Deb: 8/13/1983

YEAR	TM-L	W	L	PCT	G	GS	CG	SH	SV	IP	H	R	ER	HR	HB	BB	SO	RAT	ERA	ERA+	CERA	OAV	BH	AVG	PR+	WS	TPW
1983	Bal-A	1	1	.500	7	2	0	0	0	21^{2}	23	8	7	1	0	6	7	1.338	2.91	136	3.56	.267	0	....	3	2	0.3
1984	Bal-A	3	2	.600	23	6	0	0	0	57	68	41	33	7	0	21	18	1.561	5.21	74	5.21	.302	0	....	-10	0	-1.0
1985	Bal-A	0	0	....	1	0	0	0	0	1^{2}	3	1	1	0	0	2	2	3.000	5.40	75	10.00	.375	0	....	-0	0	0.0
1986	Bal-A	0	0	....	1	0	0	0	0	1	6	2	2	0	0	1	1	7.000	18.00	23	46.35	.750	0	....	-2	0	-0.2
Total	4	4	3	.571	32	8	0	0	0	81^{1}	100	52	43	8	0	30	28	1.598	4.76	82	5.38	.306	0		-9	2	-0.9

• SWAIM, Cy John Hillary Swaim b: 3/11/1874, Cadwallader, OH d: 12/27/1945, Eustis, FL, 6'6", 180 lbs. Deb: 5/3/1897

YEAR	TM-L	W	L	PCT	G	GS	CG	SH	SV	IP	H	R	ER	HR	HB	BB	SO	RAT	ERA	ERA+	CERA	OAV	BH	AVG	PR+	WS	TPW
1897	Was-N	10	11	.476	26	19	14	0	0	184	219	129	95	5	10	59	52	1.511	4.65	93	4.42	.293	16	.225	-9	9	-1.0
1898	Was-N	3	11	.214	16	13	9	0	1	101^{1}	119	77	48	4	4	28	30	1.451	4.26	86	4.21	.291	5	.143	-5	3	-0.7
Total	2	13	22	.371	42	32	23	0	1	285^{1}	338	206	143	9	14	87	82	1.489	4.51	90	4.35	.292	21	.198	-14	12	-1.7

• SWAN, Craig Craig Steven Swan b: 11/30/1950, Van Nuys, CA BR/TR, 6'3", 215 lbs. Deb: 9/3/1973

YEAR	TM-L	W	L	PCT	G	GS	CG	SH	SV	IP	H	R	ER	HR	HB	BB	SO	RAT	ERA	ERA+	CERA	OAV	BH	AVG	PR+	WS	TPW
1973	NY-N	0	1	.000	3	1	0	0	0	8^{1}	16	9	8	2	0	2	4	2.160	8.64	42	10.49	.432	0	.000	-5	0	-0.5
1974	NY-N	1	3	.250	7	5	0	0	0	30^{1}	28	19	15	1	0	21	10	1.615	4.45	80	4.05	.255	4	.364	-3	1	-0.2
1975	NY-N	1	3	.250	6	6	0	0	0	31	38	22	22	4	1	13	19	1.645	6.39	54	5.71	.302	0	.000	-11	0	-1.2
1976	NY-N	6	9	.400	23	22	2	1	0	132^{1}	129	64	52	11	5	44	89	1.307	3.54	93	3.63	.254	4	.103	-4	4	-0.5
1977	NY-N	9	10	.474	26	24	2	1	0	146^{2}	153	76	69	10	1	56	71	1.425	4.23	88	4.00	.268	9	.188	-8	6	-0.9
1978	NY-N	9	6	.600	29	28	5	1	0	207^{1}	164	62	56	12	2	58	125	1.071	**2.43**	**143**	2.31	.219	10	.154	23	17	2.3
1979	NY-N	14	13	.519	35	35	10	3	0	251^{1}	241	102	92	20	2	57	145	1.186	3.29	110	3.06	.255	10	.123	7	15	0.6
1980	NY-N	5	9	.357	21	21	4	1	0	128^{1}	117	59	51	20	0	30	79	1.145	3.58	99	3.30	.247	7	.219	-1	6	0.1
1981	NY-N	0	2	.000	5	3	0	0	0	13^{2}	10	6	5	0	0	1	9	.805	3.29	106	1.27	.204	0	.000	0	0	0.0
1982	NY-N	11	7	.611	37	21	2	0	1	166^{1}	165	70	62	13	0	37	67	1.214	3.35	108	3.15	.256	8	.182	7	12	1.1
1983	NY-N	2	8	.200	27	18	0	0	1	96^{1}	112	63	59	14	0	42	43	1.599	5.51	66	5.59	.299	2	.077	-21	0	-2.4
1984	NY-N	1	0	1.000	10	0	0	0	0	18^{2}	18	17	17	5	0	7	10	1.339	8.20	43	4.83	.247	0	....	-10	0	-1.0
	Cal-A	0	1	.000	2	1	0	0	0	5	8	6	6	3	0	0	2	1.600	10.80	37	9.62	.348	0	....	-4	0	-0.4
Total	12	59	72	.450	231	185	25	7	2	1235^{2}	1199	575	514	115	11	368	673	1.268	3.74	95	3.51	.256	54	.151	-30	61	-3.0

• SWAN, Ducky Harry Gordon Swan b: 8/11/1887, Lancaster, PA d: 5/9/1946, Pittsburgh, PA BR/TR, 5'10", 165 lbs. Deb: 4/28/1914

YEAR	TM-L	W	L	PCT	G	GS	CG	SH	SV	IP	H	R	ER	HR	HB	BB	SO	RAT	ERA	ERA+	CERA	OAV	BH	AVG	PR+	WS	TPW
1914	KC-F	0	0	....	1	0	0	0	0	1	0	0	0	0	0	1	1	1.000	0.00	....	0.82	.000	0	....	0	0	0.0

• SWAN, Russ Russell Howard Swan b: 1/3/1964, Fremont, CA BL/TL, 6'4", 215 lbs. Deb: 8/3/1989

YEAR	TM-L	W	L	PCT	G	GS	CG	SH	SV	IP	H	R	ER	HR	HB	BB	SO	RAT	ERA	ERA+	CERA	OAV	BH	AVG	PR+	WS	TPW
1989	SF-N	0	2	.000	2	2	0	0	0	6^{2}	11	10	8	4	0	4	2	2.250	10.80	31	13.91	.393	0	.000	-6	0	-0.6
1990	SF-N	0	1	.000	2	1	0	0	0	2^{1}	6	4	1	0	0	4	1	4.286	3.86	94	18.60	.429	0	.000	-0	0	0.0
	Sea-A	2	3	.400	11	8	0	0	0	47	42	22	19	3	0	18	15	1.277	3.64	109	3.16	.244	0	....	2	3	0.2
1991	Sea-A	6	2	.750	63	0	0	0	2	78^{2}	81	35	30	8	0	28	33	1.386	3.43	120	3.96	.269	0	....	5	6	0.5
1992	Sea-A	3	10	.231	55	9	1	0	9	104^{1}	104	60	55	8	3	45	45	1.428	4.74	84	3.99	.262	0	....	-9	4	-0.9
1993	Sea-A	3	3	.500	23	0	0	0	0	19^{2}	25	20	20	2	2	18	10	2.186	9.15	48	8.39	.316	0	....	-10	0	-1.0
1994	Cle-A	0	1	.000	12	0	0	0	0	8	13	11	10	1	0	7	2	2.500	11.25	42	10.07	.382	0	....	-6	0	-0.5
Total	6	14	22	.389	168	20	1	0	11	266^{2}	282	162	143	26	5	124	108	1.523	4.83	84	4.72	.275	0	.000	-24	13	-2.4

• SWANSON, Red Arthur Leonard Swanson b: 10/15/1936, Baton Rouge, LA BR/TR, 6'1.5", 175 lbs. Deb: 9/10/1955

YEAR	TM-L	W	L	PCT	G	GS	CG	SH	SV	IP	H	R	ER	HR	HB	BB	SO	RAT	ERA	ERA+	CERA	OAV	BH	AVG	PR+	WS	TPW
1955	Pit-N	0	0	....	1	0	0	0	0	2	2	4	4	1	0	3	0	2.500	18.00	23	13.74	.286	0	....	-3	0	-0.3
1956	Pit-N	0	0	....	9	0	0	0	0	11^{2}	21	13	13	1	0	8	5	2.486	10.03	38	10.03	.438	0	....	-8	0	-0.8
1957	Pit-N	3	3	.500	32	8	1	0	0	72^{2}	68	35	30	9	1	31	29	1.362	3.72	102	4.02	.248	0	.000	-0	3	-0.2
Total	3	3	3	.500	42	8	1	0	0	86^{1}	91	52	47	11	1	42	34	1.541	4.90	78	5.05	.277	0	.000	-11	3	-1.3

• SWARTZ, Bud Sherwin Merle Swartz b: 6/13/1929, Tulsa, OK d: 6/24/1991, Los Angeles, CA BL/TL, 6'2.5", 180 lbs. Deb: 7/12/1947

YEAR	TM-L	W	L	PCT	G	GS	CG	SH	SV	IP	H	R	ER	HR	HB	BB	SO	RAT	ERA	ERA+	CERA	OAV	BH	AVG	PR+	WS	TPW
1947	StL-A	0	0	....	5	0	0	0	0	5^{1}	9	6	4	1	0	7	1	3.000	6.75	57	12.79	.360	1	1.000	-2	0	-0.1

• SWARTZ, Monty Vernon Monroe "Dazzy" Swartz b: 1/1/1897, Farmersville, OH d: 1/13/1980, Germantown, OH BR/TR, 5'11", 182 lbs. Deb: 10/3/1920

YEAR	TM-L	W	L	PCT	G	GS	CG	SH	SV	IP	H	R	ER	HR	HB	BB	SO	RAT	ERA	ERA+	CERA	OAV	BH	AVG	PR+	WS	TPW
1920	Cin-N	0	1	.000	1	1	1	0	0	12	17	6	6	0	0	2	2	1.583	4.50	67	4.80	.333	2	.500	-2	0	-0.1

• SWARTZBAUGH, Dave David Theodore Swartzbaugh b: 2/11/1968, Middletown, OH BR/TR, 6'2", 195 lbs. Deb: 9/3/1995

YEAR	TM-L	W	L	PCT	G	GS	CG	SH	SV	IP	H	R	ER	HR	HB	BB	SO	RAT	ERA	ERA+	CERA	OAV	BH	AVG	PR+	WS	TPW
1995	Chi-N	0	0	....	7	0	0	0	0	7^{1}	5	2	0	0	0	3	5	1.091	0.00	....	1.88	.208	0	....	3	1	0.3
1996	Chi-N	0	2	.000	6	5	0	0	0	24	26	17	17	3	0	14	13	1.667	6.38	68	5.39	.277	0	.000	-6	0	-0.6
1997	Chi-N	0	1	.000	2	2	0	0	0	8	12	8	8	1	1	7	4	2.375	9.00	48	10.33	.364	0	.000	-4	0	-0.5
Total	3	0	3	.000	15	7	0	0	0	39^{1}	43	27	25	4	1	24	22	1.703	5.72	76	5.74	.285	0	.000	-7	1	-0.7

• SWARTZEL, Park Parke B. Swartzel b: 11/21/1865, Knightstown, IN d: 1/3/1940, Los Angeles, CA BR/TR, 5'10" Deb: 4/17/1889

YEAR	TM-L	W	L	PCT	G	GS	CG	SH	SV	IP	H	R	ER	HR	HB	BB	SO	RAT	ERA	ERA+	CERA	OAV	BH	AVG	PR+	WS	TPW
1889	KC-a	19	27	.413	48	47	45	0	1	410^{1}	481	334	197	21	23	117	147	1.457	4.32	97	....	.284	25	.144	6	19	-0.1

• SWEENEY, Bill William J. Sweeney b: 1858, Philadelphia, PA d: 8/2/1903, Philadelphia, PA TR, 5'11", 160 lbs. Deb: 6/27/1882

YEAR	TM-L	W	L	PCT	G	GS	CG	SH	SV	IP	H	R	ER	HR	HB	BB	SO	RAT	ERA	ERA+	CERA	OAV	BH	AVG	PR+	WS	TPW
1882	Phi-a	9	10	.474	20	20	18	0	0	170	178	119	55	4	....	42	48	1.294	2.91	102	....	.252	14	.159	-2	10	-0.6
1884	Bal-U	**40**	21	.656	**62**	**60**	**58**	4	0	**538**	522	294	155	13	....	74	374	1.108	2.59	129	....	.238	71	.240	38	**49**	3.1
Total	2	49	31	.613	82	80	76	4	0	708	700	413	210	17	....	116	422	1.153	2.67	121	....	.241	85	.221	36	59	2.5

• SWEENEY, Brian Brian Edward Sweeney b: 6/13/1974, Yonkers, NY BR/TR, 6'2", 185 lbs. Deb: 8/16/2003

YEAR	TM-L	W	L	PCT	G	GS	CG	SH	SV	IP	H	R	ER	HR	HB	BB	SO	RAT	ERA	ERA+	CERA	OAV	BH	AVG	PR+	WS	TPW
2003	Sea-A	0	0	....	5	0	0	0	0	9^{1}	7	2	2	0	1	1	7	.857	1.93	224	1.66	.212	0	....	2	1	0.2

YEAR TM-L	W	L	PCT	G	GS	CG	SH	SV	IP	H	R	ER	HR	HB	BB	SO	RAT	ERA	ERA+	CERA	OAV	BH	AVG	PR+	WS	TPW
• SWEENEY, Charlie	Charles J. Sweeney b: 4/13/1863, San Francisco, CA d: 4/4/1902, San Francisco, CA BR/TR, 5'10.5", 181 lbs. Deb: 5/11/1882 U ♦																									
1883 Pro-N	7	7	.500	20	18	14	0	0	146^2	142	94	51	3	....	28	48	1.159	3.13	99	....	.239	19	.218	-7	9	-0.7
1884 Pro-N	17	8	.680	27	24	22	4	1	221	153	70	38	4	....	29	145	.824	1.55	182	....	**.184**	50	.298	25	32	2.9
StL-U	24	7	.774	33	32	31	2	0	271	207	112	55	2	....	13	192	.812	1.83	163	....	.197	54	.316	22	35	3.1
1885 StL-N	11	21	.344	35	35	32	2	0	275	276	175	120	6	....	50	84	1.185	3.93	70	....	.249	55	.206	-45	12	-5.1
1886 StL-N	5	6	.455	11	11	11	0	0	93	108	73	43	9	....	39	28	1.581	4.16	77	....	.280	16	.250	-12	3	-1.0
1887 Cle-a	0	3	.000	3	3	3	0	0	24	55	36	22	0	0	13	8	2.292	8.25	53	....	.435	51	.331	-10	2	-1.4
Total 5	64	52	.552	129	123	113	8	1	1030^2	941	560	329	24	0	172	505	1.067	2.87	103	....	.230	245	.268	-26	93	-2.2
• SWEETLAND, Les	Lester Leo Sweetland b: 8/15/1901, St. Ignace, MI d: 3/4/1974, Melbourne, FL BR/TL, 5'11.5", 155 lbs. Deb: 7/4/1927																									
1927 Phi-N	2	10	.167	21	13	6	0	0	103^2	147	77	71	3	3	53	21	1.929	6.16	67	6.51	.348	12	.316	-22	2	-1.7
1928 Phi-N	3	15	.167	37	18	5	0	2	135^1	163	111	99	15	15	97	23	1.921	6.58	65	6.93	.306	9	.191	-33	1	-3.1
1929 Phi-N	13	11	.542	43	25	10	2	2	204^1	255	129	116	23	9	87	47	1.674	5.11	101	5.88	.316	26	.292	6	13	0.9
1930 Phi-N	7	15	.318	34	25	8	1	0	167	271	164	143	24	5	60	36	**1.982**	7.71	71	8.13	.373	16	.281	-37	3	-2.9
1931 Chi-N	8	7	.533	26	14	9	0	0	130^1	156	89	73	3	5	61	32	1.665	5.04	77	4.87	.297	15	.268	-16	4	-1.1
Total 5	33	58	.363	161	95	38	3	4	740^2	992	570	502	68	37	358	159	1.823	6.10	76	6.49	.329	78	.272	-102	23	-7.9
• SWETONIC, Steve	Stephen Albert Swetonic b: 8/13/1903, Mount Pleasant, PA d: 4/22/1974, Canonsburg, PA BR/TR, 5'11", 185 lbs. Deb: 4/17/1929																									
1929 Pit-N	8	10	.444	41	12	3	0	5	143^2	172	87	77	6	5	50	35	1.545	4.82	99	4.58	.299	13	.271	-3	9	0.0
1930 Pit-N	6	6	.500	23	6	3	1	5	96^2	107	53	48	7	0	27	35	1.386	4.47	111	3.88	.276	4	.111	6	8	0.2
1931 Pit-N	0	2	.000	14	0	0	0	1	27^2	28	12	12	0	0	16	8	1.590	3.90	99	3.96	.264	1	.143	-1	1	-0.1
1932 Pit-N	11	6	.647	24	19	11	**4**	0	162^2	134	57	51	11	0	55	39	1.162	2.82	135	2.61	**.221**	5	.093	17	15	1.3
1933 Pit-N	12	12	.500	31	21	8	3	0	164^2	166	78	64	10	2	64	37	1.397	3.50	95	3.74	.260	11	.200	-4	8	-0.4
Total 5	37	36	.507	133	58	25	8	11	595^1	607	287	252	34	7	212	154	1.376	3.81	107	3.67	.262	34	.170	14	41	1.1
• SWIFT, Bill	William Vincent Swift b: 1/10/1908, Elmira, NY d: 2/23/1969, Bartow, FL BR/TR, 6'1.5", 192 lbs. Deb: 4/12/1932																									
1932 Pit-N	14	10	.583	39	23	11	0	4	214^1	205	97	86	15	2	26	64	1.078	3.61	106	2.59	.248	15	.192	3	16	0.2
1933 Pit-N	14	10	.583	37	29	13	2	0	218^1	214	96	76	11	4	36	64	1.145	3.13	106	2.72	.251	20	.244	3	13	0.6
1934 Pit-N	11	13	.458	37	25	13	1	0	212^2	244	107	94	15	8	46	81	1.364	3.98	103	4.01	.284	18	.214	6	12	0.7
1935 Pit-N	15	8	.652	39	22	11	3	1	203^2	193	76	61	6	1	37	74	1.129	2.70	152	2.49	.247	19	.244	33	20	3.5
1936 Pit-N	16	16	.500	45	31	17	0	2	262^1	275	132	117	18	5	63	92	1.288	4.01	101	3.46	.265	31	.295	3	18	1.2
1937 Pit-N	9	10	.474	36	17	9	0	3	164	160	79	72	14	3	34	84	1.183	3.95	98	3.13	.256	9	.167	-3	10	-0.3
1938 Pit-N	7	5	.583	36	9	2	0	4	150	155	65	54	9	4	40	77	1.300	3.24	117	3.51	.271	10	.200	7	11	0.8
1939 Pit-N	5	7	.417	36	8	2	1	4	129^2	150	60	56	6	3	28	56	1.373	3.89	99	3.87	.293	10	.238	2	8	0.4
1940 Bos-N	1	1	.500	4	0	0	0	1	9^1	12	7	3	0	0	7	7	2.036	2.89	128	6.10	.308	0	.000	1	0	0.0
1941 Bro-N	3	0	1.000	9	0	0	0	1	22	26	9	8	4	0	7	9	1.500	3.27	112	5.30	.289	1	.200	1	2	0.1
1943 Chi-A	0	2	.000	18	1	0	0	0	51^1	48	25	24	5	6	27	28	1.461	4.21	79	4.49	.246	1	.100	-5	1	-0.5
Total 11	95	82	.537	336	165	78	7	20	1637^2	1682	753	651	103	36	351	636	1.241	3.58	107	3.28	.263	134	.227	50	111	6.6
• SWIFT, Bill	William Charles Swift b: 10/27/1961, Portland, ME BR/TR, 6', 180 lbs. Deb: 6/7/1985																									
1985 Sea-A	6	10	.375	23	21	0	0	0	120^2	131	71	64	8	5	48	55	1.483	4.77	88	4.41	.279	0	....	-7	4	-0.7
1986 Sea-A	2	9	.182	29	17	1	0	0	115^1	148	85	70	5	7	55	55	1.760	5.46	78	5.92	.319	0	....	-15	2	-1.5
1988 Sea-A	8	12	.400	38	24	6	1	0	174^2	199	99	89	10	8	65	47	1.511	4.59	91	4.73	.294	0	....	-8	7	-0.8
1989 Sea-A	7	3	.700	37	16	0	0	1	130	140	72	64	7	2	38	45	1.369	4.43	91	3.82	.278	0	....	-6	6	-0.6
1990 Sea-A	6	4	.600	55	8	0	0	6	128	135	46	34	4	7	21	42	1.219	2.39	165	3.16	.272	0	....	22	12	2.3
1991 Sea-A	1	2	.333	71	0	0	0	17	90^1	74	22	20	3	1	26	48	1.107	1.99	207	2.32	.224	0	....	20	14	2.0
1992 SF-N	10	4	.714	30	22	3	2	1	164^2	144	41	38	6	3	43	77	1.136	**2.08**	159	2.60	.239	8	.157	19	16	2.1
1993 SF-N	21	8	.724	34	34	1	1	0	232^2	195	82	73	18	6	55	157	1.074	2.82	138	2.57	.226	21	.263	22	19	2.7
1994 SF-N	8	7	.533	17	17	0	0	0	109^1	109	49	41	10	1	31	62	1.280	3.38	119	3.52	.262	6	.188	4	7	0.5
1995★ Col-N	9	3	.750	19	19	0	0	0	105^2	122	62	58	12	1	43	68	1.562	4.94	109	5.21	.296	7	.194	8	7	0.9
1996 Col-N	1	1	.500	7	3	0	0	2	18^1	23	12	11	1	0	5	5	1.527	5.40	97	4.69	.307	2	.333	0	2	0.0
1997 Col-N	4	6	.400	14	13	0	0	0	65^1	85	57	46	11	2	26	29	1.699	6.34	82	6.48	.317	4	.211	-8	1	-0.6
1998 Sea-A	11	9	.550	29	26	0	0	0	144^2	183	103	94	21	10	51	77	1.618	5.85	79	6.05	.306	0	.000	-17	4	-1.7
Total 13	94	78	.547	403	220	11	4	27	1599^2	1688	801	702	116	53	507	767	1.372	3.95	108	4.06	.273	48	.210	33	101	4.7
• SWIGART, Oad	Oadis Vaughn Swigart b: 2/13/1915, Archie, MO d: 8/8/1997, St. Joseph, MO BL/TR, 6', 175 lbs. Deb: 9/14/1939																									
1939 Pit-N	1	1	.500	3	3	1	1	0	24^1	27	14	12	1	0	6	8	1.356	4.44	86	3.77	.293	2	.250	-1	1	-0.1
1940 Pit-N	0	2	.000	7	2	0	0	0	22^1	27	14	11	1	0	10	9	1.657	4.43	86	4.90	.297	1	.200	-1	0	-0.1
Total 2	1	3	.250	10	5	1	1	0	46^2	54	28	23	2	0	16	17	1.500	4.44	86	4.31	.295	3	.231	-2	1	-0.2
• SWIGLER, Ad	Adam William "Doc" Swigler b: 9/21/1895, Philadelphia, PA d: 2/5/1975, Philadelphia, PA BR/TR, 5'10", 180 lbs. Deb: 9/25/1917																									
1917 NY-N	0	1	.000	1	1	0	0	0	6	7	4	4	0	0	8	4	2.500	6.00	42	8.15	.333	0	.000	-2	0	-0.3
• SWINDELL, Greg	Forest Gregory Swindell b: 1/2/1965, Fort Worth, TX BR/TL, 6'2", 225 lbs. Deb: 8/21/1986																									
1986 Cle-A	5	2	.714	9	9	1	0	0	61^2	57	35	29	9	1	15	46	1.168	4.23	98	3.39	.243	0	....	-0	3	0.0
1987 Cle-A	3	8	.273	16	15	4	1	0	102^1	112	62	58	18	1	37	97	1.456	5.10	89	5.12	.283	0	....	-5	4	-0.5
1988 Cle-A	18	14	.563	33	33	12	4	0	242	234	97	86	18	1	45	180	1.153	3.20	128	2.91	.252	0	....	29	19	3.0
1989 Cle-A★	13	6	.684	28	28	5	2	0	184^1	170	71	69	16	0	51	129	1.199	3.37	118	3.14	.246	0	....	13	14	1.3
1990 Cle-A	12	9	.571	34	34	3	0	0	214^2	245	110	105	27	1	47	135	1.360	4.40	89	4.36	.288	0	....	-8	9	-0.8
1991 Cle-A	9	16	.360	33	33	7	0	0	238	241	112	92	21	3	31	169	1.143	3.48	119	3.07	.263	0	....	22	13	2.2
1992 Cin-N	12	8	.600	31	30	5	3	0	213^2	210	72	64	14	2	41	138	1.175	2.70	133	3.01	.260	10	.125	21	16	2.1
1993 Hou-N	12	13	.480	31	30	1	1	0	190^1	215	98	88	24	1	40	124	1.340	4.16	93	4.18	.283	11	.183	-8	8	-0.8
1994 Hou-N	8	9	.471	24	24	1	0	0	148^1	175	80	72	20	1	26	74	1.355	4.37	91	4.52	.302	11	.250	-8	5	-0.5
1995 Hou-N	10	9	.526	33	26	1	1	0	153	180	86	76	21	2	39	96	1.431	4.47	86	4.85	.297	12	.240	-7	6	-0.3
1996 Hou-N	0	3	.000	8	4	0	0	0	23	35	25	20	5	1	11	15	2.000	7.83	49	8.64	.340	2	.333	-10	0	-0.9
Cle-A	1	1	.500	13	2	0	0	0	28^2	31	21	21	8	0	8	21	1.360	6.59	74	5.37	.279	0	....	-5	1	-0.5
1997 Min-A	7	4	.636	65	1	0	0	1	115^2	102	46	46	12	2	25	75	1.098	3.58	130	2.86	.238	0	....	14	10	1.3
1998 Min-A	3	3	.500	52	0	0	0	2	66^1	67	27	27	10	3	18	45	1.281	3.66	130	4.11	.263	0	....	9	7	0.9
★Bos-A	2	3	.400	29	0	0	0	0	24	25	13	9	3	0	13	18	1.583	3.38	140	5.19	.278	0	....	3	2	0.3
Yr.	5	6	.455	81	0	0	0	2	90^1	92	40	36	13	3	31	63	1.362	3.59	133	4.40	.267	0	....	13	9	1.2
1999★ Ari-N	4	0	1.000	63	0	0	0	1	64^2	54	19	18	8	1	21	51	1.160	2.51	183	3.15	.230	0	.000	15	8	1.3
2000 Ari-N	2	6	.250	64	0	0	0	1	76	71	29	27	7	1	20	64	1.197	3.20	147	3.05	.247	0	.000	13	7	1.2
2001★ Ari-N	2	6	.250	64	0	0	0	2	53^2	51	27	27	12	0	8	42	1.099	4.53	101	3.58	.250	0	....	-0	4	0.0
2002★ Ari-N	0	2	.000	34	0	0	0	0	33	38	23	23	9	0	5	23	1.303	6.27	71	4.91	.279	0	....	-6	0	-0.6
Total 17	123	122	.502	664	269	40	12	7	2233^1	2313	1053	957	262	21	501	1542	1.260	3.86	106	3.76	.268	46	.188	81	136	8.6
• SWINDELL, Josh	Joshua Ernest Swindell b: 7/5/1885, Rose Hill, KS d: 3/19/1969, Fruita, CO BR/TR, 6', 180 lbs. Deb: 9/16/1911																									
1911 Cle-A	0	1	.000	4	1	1	0	0	17^1	19	9	4	0	1	4	6	1.327	2.08	164	3.16	.257	1	.250	2	1	0.2
• SWINGLE, Paul	Paul Christopher Swingle b: 12/21/1966, Inglewood, CA BR/TR, 6', 185 lbs. Deb: 9/7/1993																									
1993 Cal-A	0	1	.000	9	0	0	0	0	9^2	15	9	9	2	0	6	6	2.172	8.38	54	9.42	.357	0	....	-4	0	-0.4
• SWITZER, Jon	Jon Michael Switzer b: 8/13/1979, Bowling Green, KY BL/TL, 6'3", 191 lbs. Deb: 8/2/2003																									
2003 TB-A	0	0	....	5	0	0	0	0	9^2	13	8	8	2	4	3	7	1.655	7.45	61	8.88	.342	0	....	-3	0	-0.3
• SWORMSTEDT, Len	Leonard Jordan Swormstedt b: 10/6/1878, Cincinnati, OH d: 7/19/1964, Salem, MA BR/TR, 5'11.5", 165 lbs. Deb: 9/29/1901																									
1901 Cin-N	2	1	.667	3	3	3	0	0	26	19	8	5	2	2	5	13	.923	1.73	185	2.04	.203	0	.000	5	2	0.3
1902 Cin-N	0	2	.000	2	2	2	0	0	18	22	11	8	1	0	5	3	1.500	4.00	75	4.95	.301	0	.000	-2	0	-0.3
1906 Bos-A	1	1	.500	3	2	2	0	0	21	17	6	3	0	1	0	6	.810	1.29	214	1.43	.225	1	.125	4	2	0.3
Total 3	3	4	.429	8	7	7	0	0	65	58	25	16	3	3	10	22	1.046	2.22	135	2.65	.239	1	.043	6	4	0.3

• SYKES, Bob Robert Joseph Sykes b: 12/11/1954, Neptune, NJ BB/TL, 6'1", 200 lbs. Deb: 4/9/1977

YEAR	TM-L	W	L	PCT	G	GS	CG	SH	SV	IP	H	R	ER	HR	HB	BB	SO	RAT	ERA	ERA+	CERA	OAV	BH	AVG	PR+	WS	TPW
1977	Det-A	5	7	.417	32	20	3	0	0	132^{2}	141	74	65	15	2	50	58	1.440	4.41	97	4.44	.271	0	....	-1	6	-0.1
1978	Det-A	6	6	.500	22	10	3	2	2	93^{2}	99	43	41	14	1	34	58	1.420	3.94	98	4.73	.275	0	....	-2	6	-0.2
1979	StL-N	4	3	.571	13	11	0	0	0	67	86	49	46	11	1	34	35	1.791	6.18	61	6.85	.315	2	.095	-19	0	-2.0
1980	StL-N	6	10	.375	27	19	4	3	0	126	134	67	65	12	0	54	50	1.492	4.64	80	4.55	.277	4	.103	-15	3	-1.8
1981	StL-N	2	0	1.000	22	1	0	0	0	37^{1}	37	20	19	2	1	18	14	1.473	4.58	78	4.19	.266	0	.000	-5	1	-0.5
Total	**5**	**23**	**26**	**.469**	**116**	**61**	**10**	**5**	**2**	**456^{2}**	**497**	**253**	**236**	**54**	**5**	**190**	**215**	**1.504**	**4.65**	**83**	**4.86**	**.280**	**6**	**.097**	**-43**	**16**	**-4.7**

• SYLVESTER, Lou Louis J. Sylvester b: 2/14/1855, Springfield, IL d: 5/5/1936, Brooklyn, NY BR/TR, 5'6", 165 lbs. Deb: 4/18/1884 U ♦

YEAR	TM-L	W	L	PCT	G	GS	CG	SH	SV	IP	H	R	ER	HR	HB	BB	SO	RAT	ERA	ERA+	CERA	OAV	BH	AVG	PR+	WS	TPW
1884	Cin-U	0	1	.000	6	1	1	0	1	32^{2}	32	27	13	0	....	6	7	1.163	3.58	89	....	.240	89	.267	-1	13	-0.1

• TABAKA, Jeff Jeffrey Jon Tabaka b: 1/17/1964, Barberton, OH BR/TL, 6'2", 195 lbs. Deb: 4/19/1994

YEAR	TM-L	W	L	PCT	G	GS	CG	SH	SV	IP	H	R	ER	HR	HB	BB	SO	RAT	ERA	ERA+	CERA	OAV	BH	AVG	PR+	WS	TPW
1994	Pit-N	0	0	....	5	0	0	0	0	4	4	8	8	1	0	8	2	3.000	18.00	24	12.25	.250	0	....	-6	0	-0.6
	SD-N	3	1	.750	34	0	0	0	1	37	28	21	16	0	0	19	30	1.270	3.89	106	2.37	.209	1	1.000	2	3	0.3
	Yr.	3	1	.750	39	0	0	0	1	41	32	29	24	1	0	27	32	1.439	5.27	79	3.33	.213	1	1.000	-4	3	-0.3
1995	SD-N	0	0	....	10	0	0	0	0	6^{1}	10	5	5	1	0	5	6	2.368	7.11	56	10.00	.370	0	....	-2	0	-0.2
	Hou-N	1	0	1.000	24	0	0	0	0	24^{1}	17	6	6	1	0	12	19	1.192	2.22	174	2.59	.202	0	.000	5	2	0.5
	Yr.	1	0	1.000	34	0	0	0	0	30^{2}	27	11	11	2	0	17	25	1.435	3.23	122	4.12	.243	0	.000	3	2	0.3
1996	Hou-N	0	2	.000	18	0	0	0	1	20^{1}	28	18	15	5	3	14	18	2.066	6.64	58	9.50	.322	0	.000	-6	0	-0.6
1997	Cin-N	0	0	....	3	0	0	0	0	2	1	1	1	1	2	1	1	1.000	4.50	96	8.87	.143	0	....	-0	0	0.0
1998	Pit-N	2	2	.500	37	0	0	0	0	50^{2}	37	19	17	6	5	22	40	1.164	3.02	142	3.13	.204	0	.000	7	4	0.7
2001	StL-N	0	0	....	8	0	0	0	0	3^{2}	6	3	3	1	0	1	3	1.909	7.36	58	9.25	.375	0	....	-1	0	-0.1
Total	**6**	**6**	**5**	**.545**	**139**	**0**	**0**	**0**	**2**	**148^{1}**	**131**	**81**	**71**	**16**	**10**	**82**	**119**	**1.436**	**4.31**	**95**	**4.49**	**.237**	**1**	**.250**	**-2**	**9**	**-0.1**

• TABER, John John Pardon Taber b: 6/28/1868, Acushnet, MA d: 2/21/1940, Boston, MA BR/TR, 5'8" Deb: 4/30/1890

YEAR	TM-L	W	L	PCT	G	GS	CG	SH	SV	IP	H	R	ER	HR	HB	BB	SO	RAT	ERA	ERA+	CERA	OAV	BH	AVG	PR+	WS	TPW
1890	Bos-N	0	1	.000	2	1	1	0	1	13	11	8	6	0	0	8	3	1.462	4.15	90	....	.223	0	.000	-1	1	-0.1

• TABER, Lefty Edward Timothy Taber b: 1/11/1900, Rock Island, IL d: 11/5/1983, Lincoln, NE BL/TL, 6', 180 lbs. Deb: 9/4/1926

YEAR	TM-L	W	L	PCT	G	GS	CG	SH	SV	IP	H	R	ER	HR	HB	BB	SO	RAT	ERA	ERA+	CERA	OAV	BH	AVG	PR+	WS	TPW
1926	Phi-N	0	0	....	6	0	0	0	0	8^{1}	8	7	7	0	2	5	0	1.560	7.56	55	4.41	.242	0	.000	-3	0	-0.3
1927	Phi-N	0	1	.000	3	1	0	0	0	3^{1}	8	9	7	0	1	5	0	3.900	18.90	22	17.26	.533	0	.000	-5	0	-0.5
Total	**2**	**0**	**1**	**.000**	**9**	**1**	**0**	**0**	**0**	**11^{2}**	**16**	**16**	**14**	**0**	**3**	**10**	**0**	**2.229**	**10.80**	**38**	**8.08**	**.333**	**0**	**.000**	**-8**	**0**	**-0.9**

• TAFF, John John Gallatin Taff b: 6/3/1890, Austin, TX d: 5/15/1961, Houston, TX BR/TR, 6', 170 lbs. Deb: 5/11/1913

YEAR	TM-L	W	L	PCT	G	GS	CG	SH	SV	IP	H	R	ER	HR	HB	BB	SO	RAT	ERA	ERA+	CERA	OAV	BH	AVG	PR+	WS	TPW
1913	Phi-A	0	1	.000	7	1	0	0	1	17^{2}	22	13	13	0	0	5	9	1.528	6.62	42	4.07	.293	1	.200	-8	0	-0.8

• TALBOT, Fred Frederick Lealand "Bubby" Talbot b: 6/28/1941, Washington, DC BR/TR, 6'2", 195 lbs. Deb: 9/28/1963

YEAR	TM-L	W	L	PCT	G	GS	CG	SH	SV	IP	H	R	ER	HR	HB	BB	SO	RAT	ERA	ERA+	CERA	OAV	BH	AVG	PR+	WS	TPW
1963	Chi-A	0	0	....	1	0	0	0	0	3	2	1	1	0	0	4	2	2.000	3.00	117	5.63	.222	0	.000	0	0	0.0
1964	Chi-A	4	5	.444	17	12	3	2	0	75^{1}	83	31	31	7	4	20	34	1.367	3.70	93	4.41	.288	5	.263	-4	4	-0.1
1965	KC-A	10	12	.455	39	33	2	1	0	198	188	96	91	25	6	86	117	1.384	4.14	84	4.21	.251	14	.200	-13	7	-1.0
1966	KC-A	4	4	.500	11	11	0	0	0	67^{2}	65	39	36	6	2	28	37	1.374	4.79	71	3.75	.248	3	.150	-11	1	-1.1
	NY-A	7	7	.500	23	19	3	0	0	124^{1}	123	59	57	16	3	45	48	1.351	4.13	81	4.19	.262	5	.143	-11	4	-1.0
	Yr.	11	11	.500	34	30	3	0	0	192	188	98	93	22	5	73	85	1.359	4.36	77	4.03	.257	8	.145	-21	5	-2.1
1967	NY-A	6	8	.429	29	22	2	0	0	138^{2}	132	78	65	20	6	54	61	1.341	4.22	74	4.13	.252	6	.158	-15	2	-1.3
1968	NY-A	1	9	.100	29	11	1	0	0	99	89	47	37	6	2	42	67	1.323	3.36	86	3.33	.241	2	.118	-4	2	-0.4
1969	NY-A	0	0	....	8	0	0	0	0	12^{1}	13	9	7	1	0	6	7	1.541	5.11	68	4.19	.283	0	.000	-2	0	-0.3
	Sea-A	5	8	.385	25	16	1	1	0	114^{2}	125	58	53	12	4	41	67	1.448	4.16	87	4.53	.278	6	.162	-3	5	-0.1
	Oak-A	1	2	.333	12	2	0	0	1	19	22	11	11	2	0	7	9	1.526	5.21	66	5.03	.297	1	.333	-4	0	-0.4
	Yr.	6	10	.375	45	18	1	1	1	146	160	78	71	15	4	54	83	1.466	4.38	82	4.57	.281	7	.171	-10	5	-0.8
1970	Oak-A	0	1	.000	1	0	0	0	0	1^{2}	2	2	2	1	0	1	0	1.800	10.80	33	10.04	.286	0	....	-1	0	-0.1
Total	**8**	**38**	**56**	**.404**	**195**	**126**	**12**	**4**	**1**	**853^{2}**	**844**	**431**	**391**	**96**	**27**	**334**	**449**	**1.380**	**4.12**	**81**	**4.15**	**.260**	**42**	**.174**	**-68**	**25**	**-5.9**

• TALCOTT, Roy Le Roy Everett Talcott b: 1/16/1920, Brookline, MA d: 12/6/1999, Miami, FL BR/TR, 6'1.5", 180 lbs. Deb: 6/24/1943

YEAR	TM-L	W	L	PCT	G	GS	CG	SH	SV	IP	H	R	ER	HR	HB	BB	SO	RAT	ERA	ERA+	CERA	OAV	BH	AVG	PR+	WS	TPW
1943	Bos-N	0	0	....	1	0	0	0	0	0^{2}	1	2	2	0	0	2	0	4.500	27.00	13	16.18	.333	0	....	-2	0	-0.2

• TALLET, Brian Brian Curtis Tallet b: 9/21/1977, Midwest City, OK BL/TL, 6'7", 208 lbs. Deb: 9/16/2002

YEAR	TM-L	W	L	PCT	G	GS	CG	SH	SV	IP	H	R	ER	HR	HB	BB	SO	RAT	ERA	ERA+	CERA	OAV	BH	AVG	PR+	WS	TPW
2002	Cle-A	1	0	1.000	2	2	0	0	0	12	9	3	2	0	1	4	5	1.083	1.50	293	2.31	.214	0	....	4	2	0.4
2003	Cle-A	0	2	.000	5	3	0	0	0	19	23	14	10	2	1	8	9	1.632	4.74	93	5.65	.303	0	.000	-1	0	-0.1
Total	**2**	**1**	**2**	**.333**	**7**	**5**	**0**	**0**	**0**	**31**	**32**	**17**	**12**	**2**	**2**	**12**	**14**	**1.419**	**3.48**	**127**	**4.35**	**.271**	**0**	**.000**	**3**	**2**	**0.3**

• TAM, Jeff Jeffrey Eugene Tam b: 8/19/1970, Fullerton, CA BR/TR, 6'1", 202 lbs. Deb: 6/30/1998

YEAR	TM-L	W	L	PCT	G	GS	CG	SH	SV	IP	H	R	ER	HR	HB	BB	SO	RAT	ERA	ERA+	CERA	OAV	BH	AVG	PR+	WS	TPW
1998	NY-N	1	1	.500	15	0	0	0	0	14^{1}	13	10	10	2	2	4	8	1.186	6.28	66	3.86	.241	0	.000	-3	0	-0.4
1999	NY-N	0	0	....	9	0	0	0	0	11^{1}	6	4	4	3	0	3	8	.794	3.18	138	2.05	.150	0	....	1	1	0.1
	Cle-A	0	0	....	1	0	0	0	0	0^{1}	2	3	3	0	0	1	0	9.000	81.00	6	44.68	1.000	0	....	-3	0	-0.3
2000*	Oak-A	3	3	.500	72	0	0	0	3	85^{2}	86	30	25	3	1	23	46	1.272	2.63	181	3.14	.268	0	....	21	10	2.0
2001*	Oak-A	2	4	.333	70	0	0	0	3	74^{2}	68	27	25	3	3	29	44	1.299	3.01	147	3.18	.250	0	....	11	8	1.1
2002	Oak-A	1	2	.333	40	0	0	0	0	40^{1}	56	26	23	2	2	13	14	1.711	5.13	86	5.59	.333	0	....	-3	1	-0.3
2003	Tor-A	0	4	.000	44	0	0	0	1	44^{2}	58	30	28	5	1	25	26	1.858	5.64	81	6.37	.314	1	1.000	-4	1	-0.3
Total	**6**	**7**	**14**	**.333**	**251**	**0**	**0**	**0**	**7**	**271^{1}**	**289**	**130**	**118**	**18**	**9**	**98**	**146**	**1.426**	**3.91**	**115**	**4.09**	**.277**	**1**	**.500**	**21**	**21**	**1.9**

• TAMULIS, Vito Vitautis Casimirus Tamulis b: 7/11/1911, Cambridge, MA d: 5/5/1974, Nashville, TN BL/TL, 5'9", 170 lbs. Deb: 9/25/1934

YEAR	TM-L	W	L	PCT	G	GS	CG	SH	SV	IP	H	R	ER	HR	HB	BB	SO	RAT	ERA	ERA+	CERA	OAV	BH	AVG	PR+	WS	TPW
1934	NY-A	1	0	1.000	1	1	1	1	0	9	7	0	0	0	0	1	5	.889	0.00	....	1.46	.219	1	.250	4	2	0.4
1935	NY-A	10	5	.667	30	19	9	3	1	160^{2}	178	80	73	7	2	55	57	1.450	4.09	99	3.97	.280	14	.246	-3	10	0.0
1938	StL-A	0	3	.000	3	2	0	0	0	15^{1}	26	15	13	2	0	10	11	2.348	7.63	65	9.53	.366	2	.400	-5	0	-0.3
	Bro-N	12	6	.667	38	18	9	0	2	159^{2}	181	81	68	11	2	40	70	1.384	3.83	102	4.04	.288	7	.127	3	9	0.0
1939	Bro-N	9	8	.529	39	17	8	1	4	158^{2}	177	81	77	10	8	45	83	1.399	4.37	92	4.12	.287	10	.182	-5	9	-0.6
1940	Bro-N	8	5	.615	41	12	4	1	2	154^{1}	147	60	53	5	3	34	55	1.173	3.09	129	2.67	.244	6	.130	16	13	1.4
1941	Phi-N	0	1	.000	6	1	0	0	0	12	21	13	12	1	1	7	5	2.333	9.00	41	9.53	.382	0	.000	-7	0	-0.7
	Bro-N	0	0	....	12	0	0	0	1	22	21	10	9	1	0	10	8	1.409	3.68	100	3.41	.244	0	.000	-0	1	-0.1
	Yr.	0	1	.000	18	1	0	0	1	34	42	23	21	2	1	17	13	1.735	5.56	66	5.57	.298	0	.000	-7	1	-0.9
Total	**6**	**40**	**28**	**.588**	**170**	**70**	**31**	**6**	**10**	**691^{2}**	**758**	**340**	**305**	**37**	**16**	**202**	**294**	**1.388**	**3.97**	**101**	**3.90**	**.278**	**40**	**.175**	**2**	**44**	**0.0**

• TANANA, Frank Frank Daryl Tanana b: 7/3/1953, Detroit, MI BL/TL, 6'2", 195 lbs. Deb: 9/9/1973

YEAR	TM-L	W	L	PCT	G	GS	CG	SH	SV	IP	H	R	ER	HR	HB	BB	SO	RAT	ERA	ERA+	CERA	OAV	BH	AVG	PR+	WS	TPW
1973	Cal-A	2	2	.500	4	4	2	1	0	26^{1}	20	11	9	2	0	8	22	1.063	3.08	115	2.25	.200	0	....	2	2	0.2
1974	Cal-A	14	19	.424	39	35	12	4	0	268^{2}	262	104	93	27	8	77	180	1.262	3.12	110	3.61	.255	0	....	12	15	1.3
1975	Cal-A	16	9	.640	34	33	16	5	0	257^{1}	211	80	75	21	7	73	**269**	1.104	2.62	135	2.69	.226	0	....	27	22	2.8
1976	Cal-A★	19	10	.655	34	34	23	2	0	288^{1}	212	88	78	24	9	73	261	.988	2.43	137	**2.16**	.203	0	....	30	**27**	3.2
1977	Cal-A★	15	9	.625	31	31	20	**7**	0	241^{1}	201	72	68	19	12	61	205	1.086	**2.54**	**154**	2.70	.227	0	....	39	20	3.9
1978	Cal-A★	18	12	.600	33	33	10	4	0	239	239	108	97	26	9	60	137	1.251	3.65	99	3.62	.258	0	....	0	14	0.0
1979*	Cal-A	7	5	.583	18	17	2	1	0	90^{1}	93	44	39	9	2	25	46	1.306	3.89	105	3.85	.264	0	....	2	5	0.2
1980	Cal-A	11	12	.478	32	31	7	0	0	204	223	107	94	18	8	45	113	1.314	4.15	95	3.96	.277	0	....	-4	9	-0.4
1981	Bos-A	4	10	.286	24	23	5	2	0	141^{1}	142	70	63	17	4	43	78	1.309	4.01	97	3.97	.265	0	....	0	6	0.0
1982	Tex-A	7	18	.280	30	30	7	0	0	194^{1}	199	102	91	16	7	55	87	1.307	4.21	92	3.66	.264	0	....	-6	9	-0.6
1983	Tex-A	7	9	.438	29	22	3	0	0	159^{1}	144	70	56	14	7	49	108	1.211	3.16	127	3.23	.240	0	....	16	10	1.5
1984	Tex-A	15	15	.500	35	35	9	1	0	246^{1}	234	117	89	30	6	81	141	1.279	3.25	128	3.69	.245	0	....	27	15	2.7
1985	Tex-A	2	7	.222	13	13	0	0	0	77^{2}	89	53	51	15	1	23	52	1.442	5.91	72	5.15	.287	0	....	-13	1	-1.3
	Det-A	10	7	.588	20	20	4	0	0	137^{1}	131	59	51	13	2	34	107	1.201	3.34	122	3.20	.250	0	....	11	10	1.1
	Yr.	12	14	.462	33	33	4	0	0	215	220	112	102	28	3	57	159	1.288	4.27	97	3.91	.264	0	....	-2	11	-0.2
1986	Det-A	12	9	.571	32	31	3	1	0	188^{1}	196	95	87	23	3	65	119	1.386	4.16	99	4.23	.268	0	....	-3	9	-0.3
1987*	Det-A	15	10	.600	34	34	5	3	0	218^{2}	216	106	95	27	5	56	146	1.244	3.91	108	3.62	.256	0	....	6	15	0.6
1988	Det-A	14	11	.560	32	32	2	0	0	203	213	105	95	25	4	64	127	1.365	4.21	91	4.18	.267	0	....	-10	9	-1.0

YEAR	TM-L	W	L	PCT	G	GS	CG	SH	SV	IP	H	R	ER	HR	HB	BB	SO	RAT	ERA	ERA+	CERA	OAV	BH	AVG	PR+	WS	TPW
1989	Det-A	10	14	.417	33	33	6	1	0	223^2	227	105	89	21	8	74	147	1.346	3.58	107	3.95	.265	0	....	8	12	0.8
1990	Det-A	9	8	.529	34	29	1	0	1	176^1	190	104	104	25	9	66	114	1.452	5.31	75	4.96	.280	0	....	-30	4	-3.1
1991	Det-A	13	12	.520	33	33	3	2	0	217^1	217	98	91	26	2	78	107	1.357	3.77	110	4.06	.265	0	....	10	13	0.9
1992	Det-A	13	11	.542	32	31	3	0	0	186^2	188	102	91	22	7	90	91	1.489	4.39	90	4.70	.267	0	.000	-7	7	-0.7
1993	NY-N	7	15	.318	29	29	0	0	0	183	198	100	91	26	9	48	104	1.344	4.48	90	4.44	.278	9	.155	-10	6	-1.0
	NY-A	0	2	.000	3	3	0	0	0	19^2	18	10	7	2	0	7	12	1.271	3.20	130	3.13	.222	0	....	2	1	0.2
Total	**21**	**240**	**236**	**.504**	**638**	**616**	**143**	**34**	**1**	**4188^1**	**4063**	**1910**	**1704**	**448**	**129**	**1255**	**2773**	**1.270**	**3.66**	**106**	**3.67**	**.254**	**9**	**.153**	**108**	**241**	**11.0**
• TANKERSLEY, Dennis	Dennis Lee Tankersley b: 2/24/1979, Troy, MO BR/TR, 6'2", 185 lbs. Deb: 5/10/2002																										
2002	SD-N	1	4	.200	17	9	0	0	0	51^1	59	46	46	10	6	40	39	1.929	8.06	47	8.04	.304	4	.308	-24	0	-2.2
2003	SD-N	0	1	.000	1	1	0	0	0	0	3	7	7	0	0	4	0	....	∞	....	∞	1.000	0	....	-7	0	-0.7
Total	**2**	**1**	**5**	**.167**	**18**	**10**	**0**	**0**	**0**	**51^1**	**62**	**53**	**53**	**10**	**6**	**44**	**39**	**2.065**	**9.29**	**47**	**8.04**	**.315**	**4**	**.308**	**-31**	**0**	**-2.9**
• TANNEHILL, Jesse	Jesse Niles "Tanny,Powder" Tannehill b: 7/14/1874, Dayton, KY d: 9/22/1956, Dayton, KY BB/TL, 5'8", 150 lbs. Deb: 6/17/1894 C/U ♦																										
1894	Cin-N	1	1	.500	5	2	1	0	1	29	37	30	23	1	0	16	7	1.828	7.14	78	5.63	.307	0	.000	-5	1	-0.6
1897	Pit-N	9	9	.500	21	16	11	1	1	142	172	97	67	1	7	24	40	1.380	4.25	98	3.83	.297	49	.266	2	14	0.0
1898	Pit-N	25	13	.658	43	38	34	5	2	326^2	338	147	107	2	12	63	93	1.228	2.95	120	2.94	.265	44	.289	21	34	2.9
1899	Pit-N	24	14	.632	41	36	33	3	1	322^1	361	139	95	4	14	52	65	1.281	2.65	143	3.34	.283	34	.250	40	27	4.1
1900	Pit-N	20	6	.769	29	27	23	2	0	234	247	108	75	3	17	43	50	1.239	2.88	126	3.18	.271	37	.336	18	23	2.5
1901	Pit-N	18	10	.643	32	30	25	4	1	252^1	240	94	61	1	10	36	118	1.094	**2.18**	150	2.37	.249	33	.244	27	22	3.0
1902	Pit-N	20	6	.769	26	24	23	2	0	231	203	78	50	0	10	25	100	.987	1.95	140	1.93	.236	43	.291	15	24	2.2
1903	NY-A	15	15	.500	32	31	22	2	0	239^2	258	123	87	3	10	34	106	1.218	3.27	96	2.99	.274	26	.234	-3	15	0.3
1904	Bos-A	21	11	.656	33	31	30	4	0	281^2	256	89	64	5	15	33	116	1.026	2.04	131	2.19	.243	24	.197	19	25	2.4
1905	Bos-A	22	9	.710	37	32	27	6	0	271^2	238	91	75	7	13	59	113	1.093	2.48	108	2.41	.238	21	.226	7	26	1.5
1906	Bos-A	13	11	.542	27	26	18	2	0	196^1	207	91	69	9	10	39	82	1.253	3.16	87	3.38	.274	22	.278	-7	13	-0.1
1907	Bos-A	6	7	.462	18	16	10	2	1	131	131	59	36	3	5	20	29	1.153	2.47	104	2.71	.263	10	.196	-4	7	-0.3
1908	Bos-A	0	0	....	1	1	0	0	0	5	4	2	2	0	0	3	2	1.400	3.60	68	2.67	.200	1	.500	-1	0	0.0
	Was-A	2	4	.333	10	9	5	0	0	71^2	77	36	30	0	6	23	14	1.395	3.77	61	3.51	.278	11	.256	-12	1	-1.1
	Yr.	2	4	.333	11	10	5	0	0	76^2	81	38	32	0	6	26	16	1.396	3.76	61	3.46	.273	12	.267	-13	1	-1.2
1909	Was-A	1	1	.500	3	2	2	1	0	21	19	8	8	1	1	5	8	1.143	3.43	71	3.13	.268	6	.167	-2	1	-0.5
1911	Cin-N	0	0	....	1	0	0	0	0	4^1	6	7	3	0	0	3	1	2.077	6.23	53	6.34	.316	0	.000	-1	0	-0.2
Total	**15**	**197**	**117**	**.627**	**359**	**321**	**264**	**34**	**7**	**2759^2**	**2794**	**1199**	**852**	**40**	**130**	**478**	**944**	**1.186**	**2.78**	**114**	**2.86**	**.263**	**361**	**.255**	**114**	**233**	**16.2**
• TANNER, Bruce	Bruce Matthew Tanner b: 12/9/1961, New Castle, PA BL/TR, 6'3", 220 lbs. Deb: 6/12/1985 C																										
1985	Chi-A	1	2	.333	10	4	0	0	0	27	34	17	16	1	2	13	9	1.741	5.33	81	5.46	.309	0	....	-3	1	-0.3
• TAPANI, Kevin	Kevin Ray Tapani b: 2/18/1964, Des Moines, IA BR/TR, 6', 187 lbs. Deb: 7/4/1989																										
1989	NY-N	0	0	....	3	0	0	0	0	7^1	5	3	3	1	0	4	2	1.227	3.68	89	3.10	.192	0	.000	-0	0	-0.1
	Min-A	2	2	.500	5	5	0	0	0	32^2	34	15	14	2	0	8	21	1.286	3.86	107	3.36	.266	0	....	1	2	0.1
1990	Min-A	12	8	.600	28	28	1	1	0	159^1	164	75	72	12	2	29	101	1.211	4.07	102	3.26	.264	0	....	1	10	0.1
1991*	Min-A	16	9	.640	34	34	4	1	0	244	225	84	81	23	2	40	135	1.086	2.99	143	2.79	.245	0	....	32	21	3.2
1992	Min-A	16	11	.593	34	34	4	1	0	220	226	103	97	17	5	48	138	1.245	3.97	102	3.48	.269	0	....	0	12	0.1
1993	Min-A	12	15	.444	36	35	3	1	0	225^2	243	123	111	21	6	57	150	1.329	4.43	98	3.97	.272	0	....	0	12	0.0
1994	Min-A	11	7	.611	24	24	4	1	0	156	181	86	80	13	4	39	91	1.410	4.62	105	4.40	.291	0	....	7	11	0.7
1995	Min-A	6	11	.353	20	20	3	1	0	133^2	155	79	73	21	4	34	88	1.414	4.92	97	4.93	.290	0	....	-2	6	-0.2
	*LA-N	4	2	.667	13	11	0	0	0	57	72	37	32	8	1	14	43	1.509	5.05	75	5.22	.306	3	.176	-8	1	-0.8
1996	Chi-A	13	10	.565	34	34	1	0	0	225^1	236	123	115	34	3	76	150	1.385	4.59	103	4.47	.268	0	....	5	11	0.5
1997	Chi-N	9	3	.750	13	13	1	1	0	85	77	33	32	7	2	23	55	1.176	3.39	127	3.00	.242	3	.136	9	8	0.9
1998*	Chi-N	19	9	.679	35	34	2	2	0	219	244	120	118	30	5	62	136	1.397	4.85	91	4.59	.284	10	.133	-7	11	-0.6
1999	Chi-N	6	12	.333	23	23	1	0	0	136	151	81	73	12	4	33	73	1.353	4.83	94	4.02	.280	2	.051	-3	6	-0.5
2000	Chi-N	8	12	.400	30	30	2	0	0	195^2	208	113	109	35	8	47	150	1.303	5.01	91	4.52	.271	10	.179	-10	6	-0.8
2001	Chi-N	9	14	.391	29	29	0	0	0	168^1	186	93	84	24	7	40	149	1.343	4.49	92	4.38	.279	12	.240	-4	7	-0.1
Total	**13**	**143**	**125**	**.534**	**361**	**354**	**26**	**9**	**0**	**2265**	**2407**	**1168**	**1094**	**260**	**53**	**554**	**1482**	**1.307**	**4.35**	**101**	**4.01**	**.272**	**40**	**.153**	**23**	**124**	**2.6**
• TATE, Al	Walter Alvin Tate b: 7/1/1918, Coleman, OK d: 5/8/1993, Bountiful, UT BR/TR, 6', 180 lbs. Deb: 9/27/1946																										
1946	Pit-N	0	1	.000	2	1	1	0	0	9	8	5	5	0	0	7	2	1.667	5.00	71	4.16	.267	1	.333	-1	0	-0.1
• TATE, Randy	Randall Lee Tate b: 10/23/1952, Florence, AL BR/TR, 6'3", 190 lbs. Deb: 4/14/1975																										
1975	NY-N	5	13	.278	26	23	2	0	0	137^2	121	73	68	8	5	86	99	1.504	4.45	78	4.11	.240	0	.000	-17	2	-2.3
• TATE, Stu	Stuart Douglas Tate b: 6/17/1962, Huntsville, AL BR/TR, 6'3", 205 lbs. Deb: 9/20/1989																										
1989	SF-N	0	0	....	2	0	0	0	0	2^2	3	3	1	0	0	0	4	1.125	3.38	100	2.27	.250	0	....	-0	0	0.0
• TATIS, Ramon	Ramon Francisco (Medrano) Tatis b: 1/5/1973, Guayubin, Dominican Republic BL/TL, 6'2", 185 lbs. Deb: 4/6/1997																										
1997	Chi-N	1	1	.500	56	0	0	0	0	55^2	66	36	33	13	3	29	33	1.707	5.34	81	6.90	.308	0	.000	-6	1	-0.6
1998	TB-A	0	0	....	22	0	0	0	0	11^2	23	19	18	2	1	16	5	3.343	13.89	35	16.38	.418	0	....	-12	0	-1.2
Total	**2**	**1**	**1**	**.500**	**78**	**0**	**0**	**0**	**0**	**67^1**	**89**	**55**	**51**	**15**	**4**	**45**	**38**	**1.990**	**6.82**	**66**	**8.54**	**.331**	**0**	**.000**	**-19**	**1**	**-1.8**
• TATUM, Ken	Kenneth Ray Tatum b: 4/25/1944, Alexandria, LA BR/TR, 6'2", 205 lbs. Deb: 5/28/1969																										
1969	Cal-A	7	2	.778	45	0	0	0	22	86^1	51	13	13	1	4	39	65	1.042	1.36	257	1.75	.172	6	.286	19	20	2.4
1970	Cal-A	7	4	.636	62	0	0	0	17	88^2	68	35	29	12	5	26	50	1.060	2.94	123	2.75	.208	2	.182	4	11	0.5
1971	Bos-A	2	4	.333	36	1	0	0	9	53^2	50	27	25	3	8	25	21	1.398	4.19	88	4.04	.255	3	.300	-2	4	0.0
1972	Bos-A	0	2	.000	22	0	0	0	4	29^1	32	12	10	3	2	15	15	1.602	3.07	105	5.19	.283	0	.000	1	1	0.1
1973	Bos-A	0	0	....	1	0	0	0	0	4	6	4	4	2	0	3	0	2.250	9.00	45	14.37	.462	0	....	-2	0	-0.2
1974	Chi-A	0	0	....	10	1	0	0	0	20^2	23	12	11	3	0	9	5	1.548	4.79	78	5.08	.274	0	.000	-2	0	-0.2
Total	**6**	**16**	**12**	**.571**	**176**	**2**	**0**	**0**	**52**	**282^2**	**230**	**103**	**92**	**24**	**19**	**117**	**156**	**1.228**	**2.93**	**123**	**3.28**	**.224**	**11**	**.244**	**18**	**36**	**2.6**
• TAUSCHER, Walt	Walter Edward Tauscher b: 11/22/1901, LaSalle, IL d: 11/27/1992, Winter Park, FL BR/TR, 6'1", 186 lbs. Deb: 4/19/1928																										
1928	Pit-N	0	0	....	17	0	0	0	1	29^1	28	20	16	0	3	12	7	1.364	4.91	83	3.53	.280	1	.167	-3	1	-0.3
1931	Was-A	1	0	1.000	6	0	0	0	0	12	24	16	10	2	0	4	5	2.333	7.50	57	10.82	.429	0	....	-4	0	-0.4
Total	**2**	**1**	**0**	**1.000**	**23**	**0**	**0**	**0**	**1**	**41^1**	**52**	**36**	**26**	**2**	**3**	**16**	**12**	**1.645**	**5.66**	**73**	**5.64**	**.333**	**1**	**.167**	**-7**	**1**	**-0.7**
• TAVAREZ, Julian	Julian (Carmen) Tavarez b: 5/22/1973, Santiago, Dominican Republic BR/TR, 6'2", 165 lbs. Deb: 8/7/1993																										
1993	Cle-A	2	2	.500	8	7	0	0	0	37	53	29	27	7	2	13	19	1.784	6.57	66	7.48	.340	0	....	-9	0	-0.9
1994	Cle-A	0	1	.000	1	1	0	0	0	1^2	6	8	4	1	0	1	0	4.200	21.60	22	24.13	.500	0	....	-3	0	-0.3
1995*	Cle-A	10	2	.833	57	0	0	0	0	85	76	36	23	7	3	21	68	1.141	2.44	193	2.93	.235	0	....	22	10	2.0
1996*	Cle-A	4	7	.364	51	4	0	0	0	80^2	101	49	48	9	1	22	46	1.525	5.36	91	5.12	.315	0	....	-4	4	-0.4
1997*	SF-N	6	4	.600	**89**	0	0	0	0	88^1	91	43	38	6	4	34	38	1.415	3.87	104	4.13	.277	0	.000	2	6	0.2
1998	SF-N	5	3	.625	60	0	0	0	1	85^1	96	41	36	5	8	36	52	1.547	3.80	105	4.89	.298	1	.111	2	5	0.1
1999	SF-N	2	0	1.000	47	0	0	0	0	54^2	65	38	36	7	8	25	33	1.646	5.93	71	6.10	.295	1	.200	-10	1	-1.0
2000	Col-N	11	5	.688	51	12	1	0	1	120	124	68	59	11	7	53	62	1.475	4.43	131	4.49	.268	3	.086	18	10	1.4
2001	Chi-N	10	9	.526	34	28	0	0	0	161^1	172	98	81	13	11	69	107	1.494	4.52	92	4.70	.277	5	.122	-4	6	-0.4
2002	Fla-N	10	12	.455	29	27	0	0	0	153^2	188	100	92	9	15	74	67	1.705	5.39	73	5.75	.308	5	.125	-25	2	-2.6
2003	Pit-N	3	3	.500	64	0	0	0	11	83^2	75	37	34	1	5	27	39	1.219	3.66	120	2.72	.244	0	.000	7	10	0.7
Total	**11**	**63**	**48**	**.568**	**491**	**79**	**1**	**0**	**13**	**951^1**	**1047**	**547**	**478**	**76**	**64**	**375**	**531**	**1.495**	**4.52**	**96**	**4.73**	**.284**	**15**	**.111**	**-6**	**54**	**-1.1**
• TAYLOR, Aaron	Aaron Wade Taylor b: 8/20/1977, Valdosta, GA BR/TR, 6'7", 230 lbs. Deb: 9/9/2002																										
2002	Sea-A	0	0	....	5	0	0	0	0	5	8	5	5	2	0	0	6	1.600	9.00	47	8.09	.348	0	....	-3	0	-0.3
2003	Sea-A	0	0	....	10	0	0	0	0	12^2	17	12	12	0	1	6	9	1.816	8.53	51	5.74	.315	0	....	-6	0	-0.6
Total	**2**	**0**	**0**	**....**	**15**	**0**	**0**	**0**	**0**	**17^2**	**25**	**17**	**17**	**2**	**1**	**6**	**15**	**1.755**	**8.66**	**50**	**6.41**	**.325**	**0**	**....**	**-9**	**0**	**-0.9**

YEAR	TM-L	W	L	PCT	G	GS	CG	SH	SV	IP	H	R	ER	HR	HB	BB	SO	RAT	ERA	ERA+	CERA	OAV	BH	AVG	PR+	WS	TPW
• TAYLOR, Arlas	Arlas Walter "Foxy,Lefty" Taylor b: 3/16/1896, Warrick County, IN d: 9/10/1958, Dade City, FL BR/TL, 5'11" Deb: 9/15/1921																										
1921	Phi-A	0	1	.000	1	1	0	0	0	2	7	5	5	1	0	2	1	4.500	22.50	20	29.71	.636	0	....	-4	0	-0.4
• TAYLOR, Ben	Benjamin Harrison Taylor b: 4/2/1889, Paoli, IN d: 11/3/1946, Martin County, IN BR/TR, 5'11", 163 lbs. Deb: 6/28/1912																										
1912	Cin-N	0	0	....	2	0	0	0	0	5^{2}	9	7	2	0	1	3	2	2.118	3.18	105	7.67	.360	0	.000	0	0	0.0
• TAYLOR, Billy	William Henry "Bollicky Bill" Taylor b: 1855, Washington, DC d: 5/14/1900, Jacksonville, FL BR/TR, 5'11.5", 204 lbs. Deb: 5/21/1881 ♦																										
1881	Wor-N	0	1	.000	1	1	1	0	0	8	15	13	7	0	....	6	0	2.625	7.88	38	....	.383	3	.107	-4	0	-0.7
	Cle-N	0	0	....	1	0	0	0	0	3	0	0	0	0	....	1	2	.333	0.00	....	....	.000	25	.243	1	2	-0.6
	Yr.	0	1	.000	2	1	1	0	0	11	15	13	7	0	....	7	2	2.000	5.73	53	....	.383	28	.214	-3	2	-1.3
1882	Pit-a	0	1	.000	1	0	0	0	0	5	11	10	9	0	....	4	1	3.000	16.20	16	....	.415	84	.281	-8	12	0.2
1883	Pit-a	4	7	.364	19	9	8	0	0	127	166	115	76	4	....	34	41	**1.575**	5.39	60	....	.297	96	.260	-28	9	-2.4
1884	StL-U	25	4	.862	33	29	29	2	**4**	263	222	97	49	2	....	40	154	.996	1.68	178	....	.214	68	.366	26	41	**4.3**
	Phi-a	18	12	.600	30	30	30	1	0	260	232	118	73	3	12	44	130	1.062	2.53	134	....	.226	28	.252	25	24	2.6
1885	Phi-a	1	5	.167	6	6	6	0	0	52^{1}	68	35	19	0	1	9	11	1.471	3.27	105	....	.302	4	.190	1	2	0.1
1886	Bal-a	1	6	.143	8	8	8	0	0	72^{1}	87	63	46	1	2	20	37	1.479	5.72	60	....	.285	12	.308	-17	2	-1.3
1887	Phi-a	1	0	1.000	1	1	1	0	0	9	17	5	3	1	0	7	0	1.889	3.00	143	....	.388	1	.250	1	1	0.1
Total	7	50	36	.581	100	84	83	3	4	799^{2}	818	456	282	11	15	165	376	1.221	3.17	102	....	.250	323	.277	-3	93	2.1
• TAYLOR, Billy	William Howell Taylor b: 10/16/1961, Monticello, FL BR/TR, 6'8", 200 lbs. Deb: 4/5/1994																										
1994	Oak-A	1	3	.250	41	0	0	0	1	46^{1}	38	24	18	4	2	18	48	1.209	3.50	127	2.94	.220	0	....	4	3	0.4
1996	Oak-A	6	3	.667	55	0	0	0	17	60^{1}	52	30	29	5	4	25	67	1.276	4.33	113	3.34	.231	0	....	3	10	0.3
1997	Oak-A	3	4	.429	72	0	0	0	23	73	70	32	31	3	5	36	66	1.452	3.82	118	3.86	.254	0	....	7	10	0.7
1998	Oak-A	4	9	.308	70	0	0	0	33	73	71	37	29	7	3	22	58	1.274	3.58	128	3.56	.255	0	....	9	10	0.8
1999	Oak-A	1	5	.167	43	0	0	0	26	43	48	23	19	3	2	14	38	1.442	3.98	117	4.28	.287	0	....	3	5	0.3
	NY-N	0	1	.000	18	0	0	0	0	13^{1}	20	12	12	2	0	9	14	2.175	8.10	54	7.92	.345	0	....	-6	0	-0.5
2000	TB-A	1	3	.250	17	0	0	0	0	13^{2}	13	13	13	2	2	9	13	1.610	8.56	58	5.67	.255	0	....	-6	0	-0.5
2001	Pit-N	0	0	....	1	0	0	0	0	2	2	1	1	1	0	0	3	1.000	4.50	100	4.70	.250	0	....	0	0	0.0
Total	7	16	28	.364	317	0	0	0	100	324^{2}	314	172	152	27	18	133	307	1.377	4.21	110	3.87	.254	0	....	16	38	1.5
• TAYLOR, Bruce	Bruce Bell Taylor b: 4/16/1953, Holden, MA BR/TR, 6', 178 lbs. Deb: 8/5/1977																										
1977	Det-A	1	0	1.000	19	0	0	0	2	29^{1}	23	11	11	2	1	10	19	1.125	3.38	127	2.54	.219	0	....	3	3	0.3
1978	Det-A	0	0	....	1	0	0	0	0	1	0	0	0	0	0	0	0	.000	0.00	....	0.00	.000	0	....	0	0	0.0
1979	Det-A	1	2	.333	10	0	0	0	0	18^{2}	16	13	10	1	2	7	8	1.232	4.82	90	3.05	.242	0	....	-1	0	-0.1
Total	3	2	2	.500	30	0	0	0	2	49	39	24	21	3	3	17	27	1.143	3.86	112	2.68	.228	0	....	2	3	0.2
• TAYLOR, Chuck	Charles Gilbert Taylor b: 4/18/1942, Shelbyville, TN BR/TR, 6'2", 195 lbs. Deb: 5/27/1969																										
1969	StL-N	7	5	.583	27	13	5	1	0	126^{2}	108	39	36	8	3	30	62	1.089	2.56	140	2.56	.235	7	.179	13	11	1.5
1970	StL-N	6	7	.462	56	7	1	1	8	124^{1}	116	47	43	5	2	31	64	1.182	3.11	132	2.78	.256	3	.115	16	12	1.5
1971	StL-N	3	1	.750	43	1	0	0	3	71^{1}	72	32	28	7	1	25	46	1.360	3.53	102	3.90	.267	2	.167	2	5	0.3
1972	NY-N	0	0	....	20	0	0	0	2	31	44	19	19	2	1	9	9	1.710	5.52	61	5.79	.341	0	.000	-7	0	-0.8
	Mil-A	0	0	....	5	0	0	0	1	11^{2}	8	2	2	0	1	3	5	.943	1.54	196	1.79	.200	1	.500	2	2	0.3
1973	Mon-N	2	0	1.000	8	0	0	0	0	20^{1}	17	4	4	3	0	2	10	.934	1.77	215	2.38	.230	0	.000	5	3	0.4
1974	Mon-N	6	2	.750	61	0	0	0	11	107^{2}	101	27	26	8	3	25	43	1.170	2.17	176	2.97	.256	3	.300	20	15	2.2
1975	Mon-N	2	2	.500	54	0	0	0	6	74	72	32	29	6	1	24	29	1.297	3.53	108	3.51	.264	0	.000	2	7	0.2
1976	Mon-N	2	3	.400	31	0	0	0	0	40	38	20	20	4	0	13	14	1.275	4.50	83	3.60	.273	0	.000	-3	1	-0.4
Total	8	28	20	.583	305	21	6	2	31	607	576	222	207	43	12	162	282	1.216	3.07	122	3.16	.258	16	.158	49	56	5.1
• TAYLOR, Dorn	Donald Clyde Taylor b: 8/11/1958, Abington, PA BR/TR, 6'2", 180 lbs. Deb: 4/30/1987																										
1987	Pit-N	2	3	.400	14	8	0	0	0	53^{1}	48	35	34	10	1	28	37	1.425	5.74	72	4.83	.247	3	.167	-11	1	-1.1
1989	Pit-N	1	1	.500	9	0	0	0	0	10^{2}	14	6	6	0	0	5	3	1.781	5.06	66	5.35	.333	0	.000	-2	0	-0.2
1990	Bal-A	0	1	.000	4	0	0	0	0	3^{2}	4	3	1	0	0	2	4	1.636	2.45	154	4.01	.250	0	....	1	0	0.1
Total	3	3	5	.375	27	8	0	0	0	67^{2}	66	44	41	10	1	35	44	1.493	5.45	73	4.87	.262	3	.158	-12	1	-1.2
• TAYLOR, Dummy	Luther Haden Taylor b: 2/21/1875, Oskaloosa, KS d: 8/22/1958, Jacksonville, IL BR/TR, 6'1", 160 lbs. Deb: 8/27/1900																										
1900	NY-N	4	3	.571	11	7	6	0	0	62^{1}	74	31	17	0	5	24	16	1.572	2.45	147	4.51	.294	3	.136	8	5	0.6
1901	NY-N	18	27	.400	**45**	**43**	37	4	0	353^{1}	377	193	125	8	16	112	136	1.384	3.18	104	3.53	.271	18	.132	14	14	0.6
1902	NY-N	7	15	.318	26	25	18	0	0	200^{2}	194	98	51	4	15	55	87	1.241	2.29	123	3.08	.254	6	.092	13	11	0.9
	Cle-A	1	3	.250	4	4	4	1	0	34	37	17	6	0	2	8	8	1.324	1.59	217	3.26	.278	1	.100	7	2	0.6
1903	NY-N	13	13	.500	33	31	18	1	0	244^{2}	306	143	115	6	4	89	94	1.614	4.23	79	4.96	.314	12	.146	-29	11	-3.0
1904	NY-N	21	15	.583	37	36	29	5	0	296^{1}	231	100	77	6	9	75	138	1.033	2.34	116	2.01	.214	16	.157	7	22	0.6
1905	NY-N	16	9	.640	32	28	18	4	0	213^{1}	200	85	63	5	8	51	91	1.177	2.66	110	2.75	.247	9	.130	8	14	0.7
1906	NY-N	17	9	.654	31	27	13	2	0	213	186	81	52	4	6	57	91	1.141	2.20	118	2.46	.233	14	.184	9	16	1.0
1907	NY-N	11	7	.611	28	21	11	3	1	171	145	66	46	1	3	46	56	1.117	2.42	102	2.28	.232	6	.125	7	11	0.7
1908	NY-N	8	5	.615	27	15	6	1	2	127^{2}	127	56	33	5	4	34	50	1.261	2.33	103	3.15	.253	8	.229	2	7	0.5
Total	9	116	106	.523	274	237	160	21	3	1916^{1}	1877	870	585	39	72	551	767	1.267	2.75	107	3.11	.256	93	.144	45	113	3.2
• TAYLOR, Ed	Edgar Ruben "Rube" Taylor b: 3/23/1877, Palestine, TX d: 1/31/1912, Dallas, TX TL Deb: 8/8/1903																										
1903	StL-N	0	0	....	1	0	0	0	0	3	0	0	0	0	0	0	1	.000	0.00	....	0.00	.000	0	.000	1	0	0.1
• TAYLOR, Gary	Gary William Taylor b: 10/19/1945, Detroit, MI BR/TR, 6'2", 190 lbs. Deb: 9/2/1969																										
1969	Det-A	0	1	.000	7	0	0	0	0	10^{1}	10	6	6	2	0	6	3	1.548	5.23	71	5.20	.244	0	.000	-2	0	-0.2
• TAYLOR, Harry	James Harry Taylor b: 5/20/1919, East Glenn, IN d: 11/5/2000, Terre Haute, IN BR/TR, 6'1", 175 lbs. Deb: 9/22/1946																										
1946	Bro-N	0	0	....	4	0	0	0	1	4^{2}	5	2	2	0	0	1	6	1.286	3.86	88	3.34	.313	0	....	-0	0	0.0
1947*	Bro-N	10	5	.667	33	20	10	2	1	162	130	63	56	10	5	83	58	1.315	3.11	133	3.24	**.225**	8	.129	15	13	1.3
1948	Bro-N	2	7	.222	17	13	2	0	0	80^{2}	90	55	48	8	3	61	32	1.872	5.36	75	6.21	.288	6	.273	-14	1	-1.3
1950	Bos-A	2	0	1.000	3	2	2	1	0	19	13	3	3	0	0	8	8	1.105	1.42	345	1.90	.197	2	.286	7	3	0.7
1951	Bos-A	4	9	.308	31	8	1	0	2	81^{1}	100	59	52	6	1	42	22	1.746	5.75	78	5.58	.307	3	.103	-12	1	-1.4
1952	Bos-A	1	0	1.000	2	1	1	0	0	10	6	2	2	1	1	6	1	1.200	1.80	219	3.00	.176	1	.250	2	1	0.2
Total	6	19	21	.475	90	44	16	3	4	357^{2}	344	184	163	25	10	201	127	1.524	4.10	102	4.37	.258	20	.161	-1	19	-0.5
• TAYLOR, Harry	Harry Evans Taylor b: 12/2/1935, San Angelo, TX BR/TR, 6', 185 lbs. Deb: 9/17/1957																										
1957	KC-A	0	0	....	2	0	0	0	0	8^{2}	11	4	3	0	1	4	4	1.731	3.12	127	5.71	.314	1	.250	1	1	0.1
• TAYLOR, Jack	John Budd "Brewery Jack" Taylor b: 5/23/1873, Sandy Hill, MD d: 2/7/1900, Staten Island, NY BR/TR, 6'1", 190 lbs. Deb: 9/16/1891 U																										
1891	NY-N	0	1	.000	1	1	1	0	0	8	4	2	1	1	0	3	3	.875	1.13	284	....	.143	0	.000	2	1	0.2
1892	Phi-N	1	0	1.000	3	3	2	0	0	26	28	19	4	2	0	10	7	1.462	1.38	234	4.20	.264	2	.167	5	2	0.4
1893	Phi-N	10	9	.526	25	16	14	0	1	170	187	113	80	8	10	77	41	1.553	4.24	108	4.35	.271	20	.215	4	11	0.0
1894	Phi-N	23	13	.639	41	34	31	1	1	298	347	201	135	13	17	96	76	1.487	4.08	125	4.21	.288	48	.333	38	23	3.5
1895	Phi-N	26	14	.650	41	37	33	1	1	335	403	233	167	7	15	83	93	1.451	4.49	107	3.99	.293	45	.290	12	25	1.6
1896	Phi-N	20	21	.488	45	41	35	1	1	359	459	282	191	17	20	112	97	1.591	4.79	90	4.85	.308	29	.185	-15	17	-1.9
1897	Phi-N	16	20	.444	40	37	35	2	2	317^{1}	376	204	149	5	28	76	88	1.424	4.23	99	4.14	.292	35	.252	6	18	0.7
1898	StL-N	15	29	.341	**50**	**47**	**42**	0	1	**397^{1}**	465	259	172	14	25	83	89	1.379	3.90	97	4.00	.290	38	.242	8	22	1.2
1899	Cin-N	9	10	.474	25	19	16	2	2	180^{1}	207	110	77	7	11	43	35	1.386	3.84	102	4.02	.288	17	.250	1	10	0.0
Total	9	120	117	.506	271	235	209	7	9	2091	2476	1423	976	74	126	583	529	1.463	4.20	103	4.21	.291	234	.252	60	129	5.8
• TAYLOR, Jack	John W. Taylor b: 1/14/1874, New Straightsville, OH d: 3/4/1938, Columbus, OH BR/TR, 5'10", 170 lbs. Deb: 9/25/1898 U																										
1898	Chi-N	5	0	1.000	5	5	5	0	0	41	32	12	10	0	1	10	11	1.024	2.20	163	1.81	.214	3	.200	6	5	0.7
1899	Chi-N	18	21	.462	41	39	39	1	0	354^{2}	380	223	148	6	22	84	67	1.308	3.76	100	3.43	.274	37	.266	-1	21	0.8
1900	Chi-N	10	17	.370	28	26	25	2	1	222^{1}	226	130	63	4	8	58	57	1.277	2.55	141	3.15	.263	19	.235	30	16	3.0

YEAR	TM-L	W	L	PCT	G	GS	CG	SH	SV	IP	H	R	ER	HR	HB	BB	SO	RAT	ERA	ERA+	CERA	OAV	BH	AVG	PR+	WS	TPW
1901	Chi-N	13	19	.406	33	31	30	0	0	275^2	341	165	103	5	8	44	68	1.397	3.36	96	3.95	.302	23	.217	-1	13	0.1
1902	Chi-N	23	11	.676	36	33	33	**8**	1	324^2	271	86	48	2	10	43	83	.967	**1.33**	**203**	**1.73**	.227	44	.237	**48**	**32**	**5.1**
1903	Chi-N	21	14	.600	37	33	33	1	1	312^1	277	137	85	2	5	57	83	1.069	2.45	128	2.15	.235	28	.222	19	25	2.1
1904	StL-N	20	19	.513	41	39	**39**	2	1	352	297	133	87	5	13	82	103	1.077	2.22	121	2.13	.220	28	.211	25	27	3.2
1905	StL-N	15	21	.417	37	34	34	3	1	309	302	155	118	10	11	85	102	1.252	3.44	86	3.18	.259	23	.190	-5	14	-0.2
1906	StL-N	8	9	.471	17	17	17	1	0	155	133	50	37	3	7	47	27	1.161	2.15	122	2.52	.227	11	.208	10	12	1.4
	Chi-N	12	3	.800	17	16	15	2	0	147^1	116	42	30	1	6	39	34	1.052	1.83	144	2.11	.223	11	.208	10	14	1.3
	Yr.	20	12	.625	34	33	32	3	0	302^1	249	92	67	4	13	86	61	1.108	1.99	132	2.32	.225	22	.208	19	26	2.7
1907	Chi-N	7	5	.583	18	13	8	0	0	123	127	62	45	3	1	33	22	1.301	3.29	76	3.28	.268	9	.191	-14	4	-1.6
Total	**10**	**152**	**139**	**.522**	**310**	**286**	**278**	**20**	**5**	**2617**	**2502**	**1195**	**774**	**41**	**92**	**582**	**657**	**1.178**	**2.66**	**115**	**2.73**	**.250**	**236**	**.223**	**126**	**183**	**15.9**

• TAYLOR, Kerry Kerry Thomas Taylor b: 1/25/1971, Bemidji, MN BR/TR, 6'3", 200 lbs. Deb: 4/13/1993

YEAR	TM-L	W	L	PCT	G	GS	CG	SH	SV	IP	H	R	ER	HR	HB	BB	SO	RAT	ERA	ERA+	CERA	OAV	BH	AVG	PR+	WS	TPW
1993	SD-N	0	5	.000	36	7	0	0	0	68^1	72	53	49	5	4	49	45	1.771	6.45	64	5.62	.277	0	.000	-17	0	-1.9
1994	SD-N	0	0	....	1	1	0	0	0	4^1	9	4	4	1	1	1	3	2.308	8.31	49	12.40	.409	0	.000	-2	0	-0.2
Total	**2**	**0**	**5**	**.000**	**37**	**8**	**0**	**0**	**0**	**72^2**	**81**	**57**	**53**	**6**	**5**	**50**	**48**	**1.803**	**6.56**	**63**	**6.02**	**.287**	**0**	**.000**	**-19**	**0**	**-2.1**

• TAYLOR, Pete Vernon Charles Taylor b: 11/26/1927, Severn, MD BR/TR, 6'1", 170 lbs. Deb: 5/2/1952

YEAR	TM-L	W	L	PCT	G	GS	CG	SH	SV	IP	H	R	ER	HR	HB	BB	SO	RAT	ERA	ERA+	CERA	OAV	BH	AVG	PR+	WS	TPW
1952	StL-A	0	0	....	1	0	0	0	0	2	4	3	3	0	0	3	0	3.500	13.50	29	16.31	.500	0	....	-2	0	-0.2

• TAYLOR, Ron Ronald Wesley Taylor b: 12/13/1937, Toronto, Canada BR/TR, 6'1", 195 lbs. Deb: 4/11/1962

YEAR	TM-L	W	L	PCT	G	GS	CG	SH	SV	IP	H	R	ER	HR	HB	BB	SO	RAT	ERA	ERA+	CERA	OAV	BH	AVG	PR+	WS	TPW
1962	Cle-A	2	2	.500	8	4	1	0	0	33^1	36	23	22	6	1	13	15	1.470	5.94	65	5.11	.281	3	.273	-8	0	-0.8
1963	StL-N	9	7	.563	54	9	2	0	11	133^1	119	44	42	10	4	30	91	1.118	2.84	125	2.75	.243	1	.031	10	13	0.8
1964*	StL-N	8	4	.667	63	2	0	0	7	101^1	109	56	52	15	1	33	69	1.401	4.62	82	4.44	.274	2	.133	-9	6	-1.0
1965	StL-N	2	1	.667	25	0	0	0	1	43^2	43	24	22	6	1	15	26	1.328	4.53	85	4.00	.261	2	.400	-4	2	-0.3
	Hou-N	1	5	.167	32	1	0	0	4	57^2	68	42	41	5	5	16	37	1.457	6.40	52	4.72	.305	0	.000	-18	0	-2.1
	Yr.	3	6	.333	57	1	0	0	5	101^1	111	66	63	11	6	31	63	1.401	5.60	63	4.41	.286	2	.111	-22	2	-2.4
1966	Hou-N	2	3	.400	36	1	0	0	0	64^2	89	47	41	5	5	10	29	1.531	5.71	60	5.30	.333	2	.167	-16	0	-1.6
1967	NY-N	4	6	.400	50	0	0	0	8	73	60	21	19	1	1	23	46	1.137	2.34	145	2.06	.230	0	.000	8	9	0.8
1968	NY-N	1	5	.167	58	0	0	0	13	76^2	64	24	23	4	1	18	49	1.070	2.70	112	2.20	.228	0	.000	2	8	0.1
1969*	NY-N	9	4	.692	59	0	0	0	13	76	61	23	23	7	1	24	42	1.118	2.72	134	2.69	.228	1	.250	6	13	0.6
1970	NY-N	5	4	.556	57	0	0	0	13	66^1	65	31	29	5	0	16	28	1.221	3.93	102	2.96	.265	0	.000	-0	7	-0.1
1971	NY-N	2	2	.500	45	0	0	0	2	69	71	28	28	7	1	11	32	1.188	3.65	93	3.28	.269	1	.250	-3	4	-0.3
1972	SD-N	0	0	....	4	0	0	0	0	5	9	7	7	5	0	0	0	1.800	12.60	26	14.47	.375	0	....	-5	0	-0.5
Total	**11**	**45**	**43**	**.511**	**491**	**17**	**3**	**0**	**72**	**800**	**794**	**370**	**349**	**76**	**21**	**209**	**464**	**1.254**	**3.93**	**91**	**3.49**	**.264**	**12**	**.103**	**-37**	**62**	**-4.3**

• TAYLOR, Scott Rodney Scott Taylor b: 8/2/1967, Defiance, OH BL/TL, 6'1", 185 lbs. Deb: 9/17/1992

YEAR	TM-L	W	L	PCT	G	GS	CG	SH	SV	IP	H	R	ER	HR	HB	BB	SO	RAT	ERA	ERA+	CERA	OAV	BH	AVG	PR+	WS	TPW
1992	Bos-A	1	1	.500	4	1	0	0	0	14^2	13	8	8	4	0	4	7	1.159	4.91	86	4.30	.245	0	....	-1	1	-0.1
1993	Bos-A	0	1	.000	16	0	0	0	0	11	14	10	10	1	1	12	8	2.364	8.18	56	8.31	.311	0	....	-4	0	-0.4
Total	**2**	**1**	**2**	**.333**	**20**	**1**	**0**	**0**	**0**	**25^2**	**27**	**18**	**18**	**5**	**1**	**16**	**15**	**1.675**	**6.31**	**70**	**6.01**	**.276**	**0**	**....**	**-6**	**1**	**-0.6**

• TAYLOR, Scott Scott Michael Taylor b: 10/3/1966, Topeka, KS BR/TR, 6'3", 200 lbs. Deb: 7/28/1995

YEAR	TM-L	W	L	PCT	G	GS	CG	SH	SV	IP	H	R	ER	HR	HB	BB	SO	RAT	ERA	ERA+	CERA	OAV	BH	AVG	PR+	WS	TPW
1995	Tex-A	1	2	.333	3	3	0	0	0	15^1	25	16	16	6	0	5	10	1.957	9.39	51	10.70	.379	0	....	-8	0	-0.7

• TAYLOR, Terry Terry Derrell Taylor b: 7/28/1964, Crestview, FL BR/TR, 6'1", 180 lbs. Deb: 8/19/1988

YEAR	TM-L	W	L	PCT	G	GS	CG	SH	SV	IP	H	R	ER	HR	HB	BB	SO	RAT	ERA	ERA+	CERA	OAV	BH	AVG	PR+	WS	TPW
1988	Sea-A	0	1	.000	5	5	0	0	0	23	26	17	16	2	0	11	9	1.609	6.26	66	5.11	.295	0	....	-5	0	-0.5

• TAYLOR, Wade Wade Eric Taylor b: 10/19/1965, Mobile, AL BR/TR, 6'1", 185 lbs. Deb: 6/2/1991

YEAR	TM-L	W	L	PCT	G	GS	CG	SH	SV	IP	H	R	ER	HR	HB	BB	SO	RAT	ERA	ERA+	CERA	OAV	BH	AVG	PR+	WS	TPW
1991	NY-A	7	12	.368	23	22	0	0	0	116^1	144	85	81	13	7	53	72	1.693	6.27	66	6.20	.314	0	....	-27	0	-2.7

• TAYLOR, Wiley Philip Wiley Taylor b: 3/18/1888, Wamego, KS d: 7/8/1954, Westmoreland, KS BR/TR, 6'1", 175 lbs. Deb: 9/6/1911

YEAR	TM-L	W	L	PCT	G	GS	CG	SH	SV	IP	H	R	ER	HR	HB	BB	SO	RAT	ERA	ERA+	CERA	OAV	BH	AVG	PR+	WS	TPW
1911	Det-A	0	2	.000	3	2	1	0	0	19	18	11	8	0	1	10	9	1.474	3.79	91	3.58	.247	0	.000	-0	1	-0.1
1912	Chi-A	0	1	.000	3	3	0	0	0	20	21	12	11	0	0	14	4	1.750	4.95	65	5.22	.309	0	.000	-3	0	-0.4
1913	StL-A	0	2	.000	5	4	1	0	0	31^2	33	19	17	0	0	16	12	1.547	4.83	61	4.06	.280	0	.000	-7	0	-0.9
1914	StL-A	2	5	.286	16	8	2	1	0	50	41	24	19	0	2	25	20	1.320	3.42	79	2.66	.209	2	.167	-3	2	-0.4
Total	**4**	**2**	**10**	**.167**	**27**	**17**	**4**	**1**	**0**	**120^2**	**113**	**66**	**55**	**0**	**3**	**65**	**45**	**1.475**	**4.10**	**72**	**3.60**	**.248**	**2**	**.061**	**-15**	**3**	**-1.9**

• TEACHOUT, Bud Arthur John Teachout b: 2/27/1904, Los Angeles, CA d: 5/11/1985, Laguna Beach, CA BR/TL, 6'2", 183 lbs. Deb: 5/12/1930

YEAR	TM-L	W	L	PCT	G	GS	CG	SH	SV	IP	H	R	ER	HR	HB	BB	SO	RAT	ERA	ERA+	CERA	OAV	BH	AVG	PR+	WS	TPW
1930	Chi-N	11	4	.733	40	16	6	0	0	153	178	80	69	16	0	48	59	1.477	4.06	120	4.67	.296	17	.270	15	13	1.5
1931	Chi-N	1	2	.333	27	3	1	0	0	61^1	79	40	39	6	1	28	14	1.745	5.72	67	5.67	.305	5	.238	-12	0	-1.3
1932	StL-N	0	0	....	1	0	0	0	0	1	2	1	0	0	0	0	0	2.000	0.00	....	7.48	.400	0	....	0	0	0.0
Total	**3**	**12**	**6**	**.667**	**68**	**19**	**7**	**0**	**0**	**215^1**	**259**	**121**	**108**	**22**	**1**	**76**	**73**	**1.556**	**4.51**	**99**	**4.96**	**.299**	**22**	**.262**	**3**	**13**	**0.3**

• TEDROW, Al Allen Seymour Tedrow b: 12/14/1891, Westerville, OH d: 1/23/1958, Westerville, OH BR/TL, 6', 180 lbs. Deb: 9/15/1914

YEAR	TM-L	W	L	PCT	G	GS	CG	SH	SV	IP	H	R	ER	HR	HB	BB	SO	RAT	ERA	ERA+	CERA	OAV	BH	AVG	PR+	WS	TPW
1914	Cle-A	1	2	.333	4	3	1	0	0	22^1	19	6	3	0	3	14	4	1.478	1.21	238	3.78	.235	1	.167	4	2	0.5

• TEJERA, Michael Michael Tejera b: 10/18/1976, Havana, Cuba BL/TL, 5'9", 175 lbs. Deb: 9/8/1999

YEAR	TM-L	W	L	PCT	G	GS	CG	SH	SV	IP	H	R	ER	HR	HB	BB	SO	RAT	ERA	ERA+	CERA	OAV	BH	AVG	PR+	WS	TPW
1999	Fla-N	0	0	....	3	1	0	0	0	6^1	10	8	8	1	0	5	7	2.368	11.37	38	10.73	.385	0	....	-5	0	-0.5
2002	Fla-N	8	8	.500	47	18	0	0	1	139^2	144	71	69	17	6	60	95	1.461	4.45	89	4.70	.269	7	.189	-8	7	-0.7
2003*	Fla-N	3	4	.429	50	6	0	0	2	81	82	44	42	6	1	36	58	1.457	4.67	88	4.13	.267	1	.067	-6	3	-0.7
Total	**3**	**11**	**12**	**.478**	**100**	**25**	**0**	**0**	**3**	**227**	**236**	**123**	**119**	**24**	**7**	**101**	**160**	**1.485**	**4.72**	**85**	**4.67**	**.272**	**8**	**.154**	**-19**	**10**	**-1.8**

• TEKULVE, Kent Kenton Charles Tekulve b: 3/5/1947, Cincinnati, OH BR/TR, 6'4", 180 lbs. Deb: 5/20/1974

YEAR	TM-L	W	L	PCT	G	GS	CG	SH	SV	IP	H	R	ER	HR	HB	BB	SO	RAT	ERA	ERA+	CERA	OAV	BH	AVG	PR+	WS	TPW
1974	Pit-N	1	1	.500	8	0	0	0	0	9	12	6	6	1	1	5	6	1.889	6.00	57	6.84	.343	0	....	-3	0	-0.3
1975*	Pit-N	1	2	.333	34	0	0	0	5	56	43	20	14	2	1	23	28	1.179	2.25	157	2.36	.215	1	.091	8	5	0.8
1976	Pit-N	5	3	.625	64	0	0	0	9	102^2	91	30	28	3	0	25	68	1.130	2.45	142	2.40	.241	0	.000	11	11	1.1
1977	Pit-N	10	1	.909	72	0	0	0	7	103	89	41	35	5	1	33	59	1.184	3.06	130	2.68	.236	3	.250	9	11	0.9
1978	Pit-N	8	7	.533	**91**	0	0	0	31	135	115	44	35	5	2	55	77	1.259	2.33	159	2.69	.228	2	.095	22	20	2.3
1979*	Pit-N	10	8	.556	**94**	0	0	0	31	134^1	109	46	41	5	2	49	75	1.176	2.75	141	2.39	.222	2	.133	15	20	1.6
1980	Pit-N★	8	12	.400	78	0	0	0	21	93	96	39	35	6	1	40	47	1.462	3.39	107	3.87	.267	0	.000	2	10	0.1
1981	Pit-N	5	5	.500	45	0	0	0	3	65	61	19	18	1	1	17	34	1.200	2.49	144	2.62	.250	0	.000	8	6	0.8
1982	Pit-N	12	8	.600	**85**	0	0	0	20	128^2	113	47	41	7	3	46	66	1.236	2.87	129	2.75	.237	1	.071	13	15	1.2
1983	Pit-N	7	5	.583	76	0	0	0	18	99	78	27	18	1	0	36	52	1.152	1.64	226	2.12	.223	0	.000	23	17	2.3
1984	Pit-N	3	9	.250	72	0	0	0	13	88	86	30	26	4	1	33	36	1.352	2.66	135	3.36	.262	0	.000	8	8	0.8
1985	Pit-N	0	0	....	3	0	0	0	0	3^1	7	7	6	1	0	5	4	3.600	16.20	22	18.73	.467	0	....	-5	0	-0.5
	Phi-N	4	10	.286	58	0	0	0	14	72^1	67	28	24	4	2	25	36	1.272	2.99	123	3.06	.246	0	.000	7	8	0.7
	Yr.	4	10	.286	61	0	0	0	14	75^2	74	35	30	5	2	30	40	1.374	3.57	103	3.75	.258	0	.000	2	8	0.2
1986	Phi-N	11	5	.688	73	0	0	0	4	110	99	35	31	2	0	25	57	1.127	2.54	152	2.26	.240	0	.000	16	12	1.7
1987	Phi-N	6	4	.600	**90**	0	0	0	3	105	96	38	36	8	0	29	60	1.190	3.09	137	2.81	.243	0	.000	12	11	1.2
1988	Phi-N	3	7	.300	70	0	0	0	4	80	87	34	32	3	2	22	43	1.363	3.60	99	3.46	.276	0	.000	1	5	0.1
1989	Cin-N	0	3	.000	37	0	0	0	1	52	56	35	29	5	0	23	31	1.519	5.02	72	4.28	.272	1	.500	-8	0	-0.8
Total	**16**	**94**	**90**	**.511**	**1050**	**0**	**0**	**0**	**184**	**1436^1**	**1305**	**526**	**455**	**63**	**17**	**491**	**779**	**1.250**	**2.85**	**131**	**2.87**	**.244**	**10**	**.083**	**141**	**159**	**14.1**

• TELEMACO, Amaury Amaury (Regalado) Telemaco b: 1/19/1974, Higuey, Dominican Republic BR/TR, 6'4", 220 lbs. Deb: 5/16/1996

YEAR	TM-L	W	L	PCT	G	GS	CG	SH	SV	IP	H	R	ER	HR	HB	BB	SO	RAT	ERA	ERA+	CERA	OAV	BH	AVG	PR+	WS	TPW
1996	Chi-N	5	7	.417	25	17	0	0	0	97^1	108	67	59	20	3	31	64	1.428	5.46	80	5.20	.281	3	.103	-13	1	-1.4
1997	Chi-N	0	3	.000	10	5	0	0	0	38	47	26	26	4	0	11	29	1.526	6.16	70	5.00	.303	2	.222	-8	0	-0.7
1998	Chi-N	1	1	.500	14	0	0	0	0	27^2	23	12	12	5	0	13	18	1.301	3.90	113	3.92	.219	1	.167	2	2	0.2
	Ari-N	6	9	.400	27	18	0	0	0	121	127	63	53	13	4	33	60	1.322	3.94	107	3.98	.271	2	.069	3	6	0.3
	Yr.	7	10	.412	41	18	0	0	0	148^2	150	75	65	18	4	46	78	1.318	3.93	108	3.97	.262	3	.086	5	8	0.4
1999	Ari-N	1	0	1.000	5	0	0	0	0	6	7	5	5	2	0	6	2	2.167	7.50	61	10.24	.333	0	....	-2	0	-0.2
	Phi-N	3	0	1.000	44	0	0	0	0	47	45	29	29	8	2	20	41	1.383	5.55	85	4.45	.250	0	....	-5	2	-0.5
	Yr.	4	0	1.000	49	0	0	0	0	53	52	34	34	10	2	26	43	1.472	5.77	81	5.11	.259	0	....	-7	2	-0.7

YEAR	TM-L	W	L	PCT	G	GS	CG	SH	SV	IP	H	R	ER	HR	HB	BB	SO	RAT	ERA	ERA+	CERA	OAV	BH	AVG	PR+	WS	TPW
2000	Phi-N	1	3	.250	13	2	0	0	0	24^1	25	22	18	6	0	14	22	1.603	6.66	70	6.24	.275	0	.000	-5	0	-0.5
2001	Phi-N	5	5	.500	24	14	1	0	0	89^1	93	59	55	15	9	32	59	1.399	5.54	77	5.07	.274	2	.095	-14	2	-1.4
2003	Phi-N	1	4	.200	8	8	0	0	0	45^1	41	22	20	5	7	11	29	1.147	3.97	101	3.48	.238	4	.286	0	2	0.2
Total	**7**	**23**	**32**	**.418**	**170**	**64**	**1**	**0**	**0**	**496**	**516**	**305**	**277**	**78**	**25**	**171**	**324**	**1.385**	**5.03**	**86**	**4.68**	**.269**	**14**	**.125**	**-42**	**15**	**-4.1**
• TELFORD, Anthony	Anthony Charles Telford b: 3/6/1966, San Jose, CA BR/TR, 6', 175 lbs. Deb: 8/19/1990																										
1990	Bal-A	3	3	.500	8	8	0	0	0	36^1	43	22	20	4	1	19	20	1.706	4.95	77	5.85	.295	0	....	-5	1	-0.5
1991	Bal-A	0	0	....	9	1	0	0	0	26^2	27	12	12	3	0	6	24	1.238	4.05	97	3.56	.265	0	....	-0	1	0.0
1993	Bal-A	0	0	....	3	0	0	0	0	7^1	11	8	8	3	1	1	6	1.636	9.82	46	9.17	.344	0	....	-4	0	-0.4
1997	Mon-N	4	6	.400	65	0	0	0	1	89	77	34	32	11	5	33	61	1.236	3.24	130	3.60	.236	3	.200	9	8	1.0
1998	Mon-N	3	6	.333	77	0	0	0	1	91	85	45	39	9	4	36	59	1.330	3.86	109	3.75	.247	1	.250	5	5	0.5
1999	Mon-N	5	4	.556	79	0	0	0	2	96	112	52	42	3	3	38	69	1.563	3.94	114	4.58	.295	0	.000	8	7	0.7
2000	Mon-N	5	4	.556	64	0	0	0	3	78^1	76	38	33	10	5	23	68	1.264	3.79	126	3.95	.257	0	.000	9	7	0.9
2001	Mon-N	0	1	.000	8	0	0	0	0	7	14	12	8	2	1	5	5	2.714	10.29	43	14.07	.412	0	....	-4	0	-0.4
2002	Tex-A	2	1	.667	20	0	0	0	1	23^2	30	18	17	3	4	15	19	1.901	6.46	73	7.46	.316	0	....	-4	0	-0.4
Total	**9**	**22**	**25**	**.468**	**333**	**9**	**0**	**0**	**8**	**455^1**	**475**	**241**	**211**	**48**	**24**	**176**	**331**	**1.430**	**4.17**	**104**	**4.52**	**.271**	**4**	**.174**	**13**	**29**	**1.2**
• TELGHEDER, Dave	David William Telgheder b: 11/11/1966, Middletown, NY BR/TR, 6'3", 212 lbs. Deb: 6/12/1993																										
1993	NY-N	6	2	.750	24	7	0	0	0	75^2	82	40	40	10	4	21	35	1.361	4.76	84	4.49	.276	1	.067	-7	3	-0.7
1994	NY-N	0	1	.000	6	0	0	0	0	10	11	8	8	2	0	8	4	1.900	7.20	58	6.75	.282	0	....	-3	0	-0.3
1995	NY-N	1	2	.333	7	4	0	0	0	25^2	34	18	16	4	0	7	16	1.597	5.61	72	5.53	.318	2	.333	-5	0	-0.4
1996	Oak-A	4	7	.364	16	14	1	1	0	79^1	92	42	41	12	1	26	43	1.487	4.65	105	5.13	.292	0	....	1	5	0.1
1997	Oak-A	4	6	.400	20	19	0	0	0	101	134	71	68	15	2	35	55	1.673	6.06	74	6.31	.324	0	.000	-15	2	-1.5
1998	Oak-A	0	1	.000	8	2	0	0	0	20	19	12	8	4	2	6	5	1.250	3.60	127	4.18	.235	0	....	2	1	0.2
Total	**6**	**15**	**19**	**.441**	**81**	**46**	**1**	**1**	**0**	**311^2**	**372**	**191**	**181**	**47**	**9**	**103**	**158**	**1.524**	**5.23**	**84**	**5.38**	**.297**	**3**	**.130**	**-26**	**11**	**-2.6**
• TELLMANN, Tom	Thomas John Tellmann b: 3/29/1954, Warren, PA BR/TR, 6'3", 195 lbs. Deb: 6/9/1979																										
1979	SD-N	0	0	....	1	0	0	0	0	2^2	7	5	5	1	0	0	1	2.625	16.88	21	15.60	.467	0	.000	-4	0	-0.4
1980	SD-N	3	0	1.000	6	2	2	0	1	22^1	23	5	4	0	0	8	9	1.388	1.61	213	3.41	.264	1	.125	4	3	0.4
1983	Mil-A	9	4	.692	44	0	0	0	8	99^2	95	34	31	7	2	35	48	1.304	2.80	133	3.51	.259	0	....	10	10	1.0
1984	Mil-A	6	3	.667	50	0	0	0	4	81	82	28	25	6	1	31	28	1.395	2.78	139	3.81	.272	0	....	10	7	1.0
1985	Oak-A	0	0	....	11	0	0	0	0	21^1	33	12	12	3	1	9	8	1.969	5.06	76	7.86	.347	0	....	-3	0	-0.3
Total	**5**	**18**	**7**	**.720**	**112**	**2**	**2**	**0**	**13**	**227**	**240**	**84**	**77**	**17**	**4**	**83**	**94**	**1.423**	**3.05**	**123**	**4.16**	**.277**	**1**	**.111**	**18**	**20**	**1.8**
• TEMPLETON, Chuck	Charles Sherman Templeton b: 6/1/1932, Detroit, MI d: 10/9/1997, Irving, TX BR/TL, 6'3", 210 lbs. Deb: 9/9/1955																										
1955	Bro-N	0	1	.000	4	0	0	0	0	4^2	5	7	6	2	1	5	3	2.143	11.57	35	11.67	.294	0	....	-4	0	-0.4
1956	Bro-N	0	1	.000	6	2	0	0	0	16^1	20	13	12	2	0	10	8	1.837	6.61	60	6.22	.294	0	.000	-5	0	-0.6
Total	**2**	**0**	**2**	**.000**	**10**	**2**	**0**	**0**	**0**	**21**	**25**	**20**	**18**	**4**	**1**	**15**	**11**	**1.905**	**7.71**	**52**	**7.43**	**.294**	**0**	**.000**	**-9**	**0**	**-1.0**
• TENER, John	John Kinley Tener b: 7/25/1863, County Tyrone, Ireland d: 5/19/1946, Pittsburgh, PA BR/TR, 6'4", 180 lbs. Deb: 6/8/1885 U ♦																										
1888	Chi-N	7	5	.583	12	12	11	1	0	102	90	59	31	6	8	25	39	1.127	2.74	110	....	.228	9	.196	1	6	0.1
1889	Chi-N	15	15	.500	35	30	28	1	0	287	302	192	116	16	7	105	105	1.418	3.64	115	....	.262	41	.273	15	18	1.6
1890	Pit-P	3	11	.214	14	14	13	0	0	117	160	147	95	6	5	70	30	1.966	7.31	53	....	.312	12	.190	-41	0	-3.2
Total	**3**	**25**	**31**	**.446**	**61**	**56**	**52**	**2**	**0**	**506**	**552**	**398**	**242**	**28**	**20**	**200**	**174**	**1.486**	**4.30**	**90**	**....**	**.268**	**62**	**.236**	**-26**	**24**	**-1.5**
• TENNANT, Jim	James McDonnell Tennant b: 3/3/1907, Shepherdstown, WV d: 4/16/1967, Trumbull, CT BR/TR, 6'1", 190 lbs. Deb: 9/28/1929																										
1929	NY-N	0	0	....	1	0	0	0	0	1	1	0	0	0	0	0	1	1.000	0.00	....	2.02	.333	0	....	0	0	0.0
• TERLECKI, Bob	Robert Joseph Terlecki b: 2/14/1945, Trenton, NJ BR/TR, 5'8", 185 lbs. Deb: 8/16/1972																										
1972	Phi-N	0	0	....	9	0	0	0	0	13^1	16	9	7	2	0	10	5	1.950	4.73	76	7.10	.308	0	....	-2	0	-0.2
• TERLECKY, Greg	Gregory John Terlecky b: 3/20/1952, Culver City, CA BR/TR, 6'3", 200 lbs. Deb: 6/12/1975																										
1975	StL-N	0	1	.000	20	0	0	0	0	30^1	38	16	15	4	0	12	13	1.648	4.45	84	5.35	.306	1	.333	-2	1	-0.1
• TERPKO, Jeff	Jeffrey Michael Terpko b: 10/16/1950, Sayre, PA BR/TR, 6', 180 lbs. Deb: 9/21/1974																										
1974	Tex-A	0	0	....	3	0	0	0	0	7	6	1	1	0	0	4	3	1.429	1.29	277	3.27	.231	0	....	2	1	0.2
1976	Tex-A	3	3	.500	32	0	0	0	0	52^2	42	15	14	3	0	29	24	1.348	2.39	150	3.26	.223	0	....	7	5	0.7
1977	Mon-N	0	1	.000	13	0	0	0	0	20^2	28	13	13	2	0	15	14	2.081	5.66	67	7.76	.346	0	.000	-4	0	-0.5
Total	**3**	**3**	**4**	**.429**	**48**	**0**	**0**	**0**	**0**	**80^1**	**76**	**29**	**28**	**5**	**0**	**48**	**41**	**1.544**	**3.14**	**117**	**4.42**	**.258**	**0**	**.000**	**4**	**6**	**0.4**
• TERRELL, Walt	Charles Walter Terrell b: 5/11/1958, Jeffersonville, IN BL/TR, 6'2", 205 lbs. Deb: 9/8/1982																										
1982	NY-N	0	3	.000	3	3	0	0	0	21	22	12	8	2	0	14	8	1.714	3.43	106	5.19	.268	2	.400	1	1	0.1
1983	NY-N	8	8	.500	21	20	4	2	0	133^2	123	57	53	7	2	55	59	1.332	3.57	102	3.38	.251	8	.182	-1	8	0.3
1984	NY-N	11	12	.478	33	33	3	1	0	215	232	99	84	16	4	80	114	1.451	3.52	101	4.36	.282	6	.080	0	10	-0.3
1985	Det-A	15	10	.600	34	34	5	3	0	229	221	107	98	9	4	95	130	1.380	3.85	106	3.55	.255	0	....	5	14	0.5
1986	Det-A	15	12	.556	34	33	9	2	0	217^1	199	116	110	30	3	98	93	1.367	4.56	90	4.17	.245	0	....	-13	9	-1.3
1987*	Det-A	17	10	.630	35	35	10	1	0	244^2	254	123	110	30	3	94	143	1.422	4.05	104	4.42	.268	0	....	3	16	0.3
1988	Det-A	7	16	.304	29	29	11	1	0	206^1	199	101	91	20	2	78	84	1.342	3.97	96	3.80	.258	0	....	-5	8	-0.5
1989	SD-N	5	13	.278	19	19	4	1	0	123^1	134	65	55	14	0	26	63	1.297	4.01	87	3.88	.277	4	.100	-9	3	-1.0
	NY-A	6	5	.545	13	13	1	1	0	83	102	52	48	9	2	24	30	1.518	5.20	74	5.21	.307	0	....	-13	2	-1.3
1990	Pit-N	2	7	.222	16	16	0	0	0	82^2	98	59	54	13	4	33	34	1.585	5.88	62	5.73	.295	3	.107	-22	0	-2.3
	Det-A	6	4	.600	13	12	0	0	0	75^1	86	39	38	7	8	24	30	1.460	4.54	87	4.92	.290	0	....	-7	3	-0.7
1991	Det-A	12	14	.462	35	33	8	2	0	218^2	257	115	103	16	2	79	80	1.537	4.24	98	4.78	.301	0	....	-2	10	-0.2
1992	Det-A	7	10	.412	36	14	1	0	0	136^2	163	86	79	14	3	48	61	1.544	5.20	76	4.96	.298	0	....	-18	3	-1.8
Total	**11**	**111**	**124**	**.472**	**321**	**294**	**56**	**14**	**0**	**1986^2**	**2090**	**1031**	**931**	**187**	**37**	**748**	**929**	**1.429**	**4.22**	**92**	**4.31**	**.274**	**23**	**.120**	**-78**	**87**	**-8.1**
• TERRY, Adonis	William H Terry b: 8/7/1864, Westfield, MA d: 2/24/1915, Milwaukee, WI BR/TR, 5'11.5", 168 lbs. Deb: 5/1/1884 U ♦																										
1884	Bro-a	19	35	.352	56	55	54	2	0	476	486	308	188	10	8	72	230	1.172	3.55	93	....	.250	55	.233	-4	29	0.1
1885	Bro-a	6	17	.261	25	23	23	0	1	209	213	147	99	9	4	42	96	1.220	4.26	77	....	.253	45	.170	-21	9	-3.4
1886	Bro-a	18	16	.529	34	34	32	5	0	288^1	263	177	99	1	16	115	162	1.311	3.09	113	....	.232	71	.237	14	26	1.1
1887	Bro-a	16	16	.500	40	35	35	1	**3**	318	430	230	142	10	9	99	138	1.352	4.02	107	....	.312	119	.323	9	27	0.9
1888	Bro-a	13	8	.619	23	23	20	2	0	195	145	79	44	2	9	67	138	1.087	2.03	147	....	**.200**	29	.252	20	21	2.2
1889*	Bro-a	22	15	.595	41	39	35	2	0	326	285	189	119	6	16	126	186	1.261	3.29	113	....	.228	48	.300	16	30	2.3
1890*	Bro-N	26	16	.619	46	44	38	1	0	370	362	200	121	3	15	133	185	1.338	2.94	117	....	.249	101	.278	19	41	3.0
1891	Bro-N	6	16	.273	25	22	18	1	1	194	207	139	91	5	7	80	65	1.479	4.22	78	....	.263	19	.209	-15	9	-1.1
1892	Bal-N	0	1	.000	1	1	1	0	0	9	7	7	4	0	0	7	3	1.556	4.00	86	3.34	.206	0	.000	-0	0	-0.1
	Pit-N	18	7	.720	30	26	24	2	1	240	185	106	67	3	8	106	95	1.213	2.51	131	2.47	.205	16	.160	13	20	1.3
	Yr.	18	8	.692	31	27	25	2	1	249	192	113	71	3	8	113	98	1.225	2.57	128	2.50	.205	16	.154	13	20	1.2
1893	Pit-N	12	8	.600	26	19	14	0	0	170	177	121	84	5	11	99	52	1.624	4.45	102	4.57	.260	18	.254	-3	13	0.0
1894	Pit-N	0	1	.000	1	1	0	0	0	0^2	2	5	5	0	0	4	0	9.000	67.50	8	42.37	.511	0	....	-5	0	-0.4
	Chi-N	5	11	.313	23	21	16	0	0	163^1	232	191	106	12	16	123	39	2.173	5.84	96	8.07	.331	33	.347	-1	8	0.3
	Yr.	5	12	.294	24	22	16	0	0	164	234	196	111	12	16	127	39	**2.201**	6.09	92	8.21	.332	33	.347	-5	8	0.0
1895	Chi-N	21	14	.600	38	34	31	0	0	311^1	346	228	166	4	17	131	88	1.532	4.80	106	4.23	.277	30	.219	11	22	0.3
1896	Chi-N	15	14	.517	30	28	25	1	0	235^2	273	166	116	6	10	88	75	1.532	4.43	102	4.38	.288	26	.263	-1	18	0.2
1897	Chi-N	0	1	.000	1	1	1	0	0	8	11	10	9	0	2	6	1	2.125	10.13	44	7.64	.324	0	.000	-5	0	-0.5
Total	**14**	**197**	**196**	**.501**	**440**	**406**	**367**	**17**	**6**	**3514^1**	**3624**	**2303**	**1460**	**76**	**148**	**1298**	**1553**	**1.372**	**3.74**	**103**	**1.47**	**.258**	**610**	**.254**	**48**	**273**	**6.4**
• TERRY, John	John Burchard Terry b: 11/1/1879, Waterbury, CT d: 4/27/1933, Kansas City, MO Deb: 9/17/1902																										
1902	Det-A	0	1	.000	1	1	1	0	0	5	8	3	2	0	0	1	0	1.800	3.60	101	5.79	.361	0	.000	-0	0	0.0

YEAR TM-L	W	L	PCT	G	GS	CG	SH	SV	IP	H	R	ER	HR	HB	BB	SO	RAT	ERA	ERA+	CERA	OAV	BH	AVG	PR+	WS	TPW
1903 StL-A	1	1	.500	3	1	1	0	0	17^2	21	6	5	0	3	4	2	1.415	2.55	114	4.16	.294	0	.000	1	1	-0.1
Total 2	1	2	.333	4	2	2	0	0	22^2	29	9	7	0	3	5	2	1.500	2.78	111	4.52	.310	0	.000	1	1	-0.1
• TERRY, Ralph	Ralph Willard Terry b: 1/9/1936, Big Cabin, OK BR/TR, 6'3", 195 lbs. Deb: 8/6/1956																									
1956 NY-A	1	2	.333	3	3	0	0	0	13^1	17	15	14	2	0	11	8	2.100	9.45	41	8.60	.347	1	.167	-9	0	-0.9
1957 NY-A	1	1	.500	7	2	1	1	0	20^2	18	7	7	1	0	8	7	1.258	3.05	118	2.97	.240	1	.250	1	2	0.1
KC-A	4	11	.267	21	19	3	1	0	130^2	119	63	49	15	4	47	80	1.270	3.38	117	3.59	.239	6	.143	9	7	0.7
Yr.	5	12	.294	28	21	4	2	0	151^1	137	70	56	16	4	55	87	1.269	3.33	117	3.50	.239	7	.152	10	9	0.9
1958 KC-A	11	13	.458	40	33	8	3	2	216^2	217	111	102	29	2	61	134	1.283	4.24	92	3.89	.262	14	.197	-7	11	-0.8
1959 KC-A	2	4	.333	9	7	2	0	0	46^1	56	29	27	9	1	19	35	1.619	5.24	76	6.29	.308	3	.176	-6	1	-0.7
NY-A	3	7	.300	24	16	5	1	0	127^1	130	55	48	7	2	30	55	1.257	3.39	107	3.28	.270	4	.098	4	6	0.1
Yr.	5	11	.313	33	23	7	1	0	173^2	186	84	75	16	3	49	90	1.353	3.89	97	4.08	.281	7	.121	-3	7	-0.6
1960* NY-A	10	8	.556	35	23	7	3	1	166^2	149	78	63	15	4	52	92	1.206	3.40	105	3.19	.237	6	.122	-1	9	-0.3
1961* NY-A	16	3	.842	31	27	9	2	0	188^1	162	74	66	19	1	42	86	1.083	3.15	118	2.72	.232	15	.227	6	15	0.8
1962* NY-A★	**23**	12	.657	43	**39**	14	3	2	**298^2**	257	123	106	40	3	57	176	1.051	3.19	117	2.79	.231	20	.189	16	21	1.6
1963* NY-A	17	15	.531	40	**37**	**18**	3	1	268	246	103	96	29	4	39	114	1.063	3.22	109	2.78	.242	7	.080	4	17	-0.2
1964* NY-A	7	11	.389	27	14	2	1	4	115	130	60	58	20	1	31	77	1.400	4.54	80	4.78	.283	7	.200	-13	3	-1.2
1965 Cle-A	11	6	.647	30	26	6	2	0	165^2	154	77	68	22	1	23	84	1.068	3.69	94	2.88	.242	7	.143	-4	9	-0.2
1966 KC-A	1	5	.167	15	10	0	0	0	64	65	35	27	7	1	15	33	1.250	3.80	89	3.53	.263	3	.214	-3	2	-0.2
NY-N	0	1	.000	11	1	0	0	1	24^2	27	14	13	1	0	11	14	1.541	4.74	77	4.53	.293	1	.167	-3	1	-0.3
1967 NY-N	0	0	....	2	0	0	0	0	3^1	1	1	0	0	0	0	5	.300	0.00	....	0.21	.091	0	....	1	1	0.1
Total 12	107	99	.519	338	257	75	20	11	1849^1	1748	844	744	216	24	446	1000	1.186	3.62	102	3.34	.249	95	.160	-6	105	-1.3
• TERRY, Scott	Scott Ray Terry b: 11/21/1959, Hobbs, NM BR/TR, 5'11", 195 lbs. Deb: 4/9/1986																									
1986 Cin-N	1	2	.333	28	3	0	0	0	55^2	66	40	38	8	0	32	32	1.760	6.14	63	6.16	.300	1	.250	-14	0	-1.4
1987 StL-N	0	0	....	11	0	0	0	0	13^1	13	5	5	0	0	8	9	1.575	3.38	123	3.74	.260	0	.000	1	1	0.1
1988 StL-N	9	6	.600	51	11	1	0	3	129^1	119	48	42	5	0	34	65	1.183	2.92	119	2.71	.247	7	.250	7	11	0.9
1989 StL-N	8	10	.444	31	24	1	0	2	148^2	142	65	59	14	3	43	69	1.244	3.57	102	3.40	.253	7	.156	-1	8	0.1
1990 StL-N	2	6	.250	50	2	0	0	2	72	75	45	38	7	4	27	35	1.417	4.75	80	4.18	.264	5	.455	-7	2	-0.5
1991 StL-N	4	4	.500	65	0	0	0	1	80^1	76	31	25	1	0	32	52	1.344	2.80	133	2.92	.249	1	.143	7	7	0.8
Total 6	24	28	.462	236	40	2	0	8	499^1	491	234	207	35	7	176	262	1.336	3.73	99	3.57	.258	21	.216	-7	29	0.0
• TERRY, Yank	Lancelot Yank Terry b: 2/11/1911, Bedford, IN d: 11/4/1979, Bloomington, IN BR/TR, 6'1", 180 lbs. Deb: 8/3/1940																									
1940 Bos-A	1	0	1.000	4	1	0	0	0	19^1	24	19	19	2	0	11	9	1.810	8.84	51	5.84	.304	2	.250	-9	0	-0.9
1942 Bos-A	6	5	.545	20	11	3	0	1	85	82	48	37	5	2	43	37	1.471	3.92	95	3.89	.248	3	.111	-4	4	-0.5
1943 Bos-A	7	9	.438	30	22	7	0	1	163^2	147	70	64	8	1	63	63	1.283	3.52	94	3.07	.242	3	.067	-5	8	-0.8
1944 Bos-A	6	10	.375	27	17	3	0	0	132^2	142	72	62	10	3	65	30	1.560	4.21	81	4.64	.276	11	.234	-12	4	-1.1
1945 Bos-A	0	4	.000	12	4	1	0	0	56^2	68	29	26	8	0	14	28	1.447	4.13	82	4.87	.296	2	.111	-5	1	-0.7
Total 5	20	28	.417	93	55	14	0	2	457^1	463	238	208	33	6	196	167	1.441	4.09	86	4.02	.263	21	.145	-35	17	-4.0
• TERWILLIGER, Dick	Richard Martin Terwilliger b: 6/27/1906, Sand Lake, MI d: 1/21/1969, Greenville, MI BR/TR, 5'11", 178 lbs. Deb: 8/18/1932																									
1932 StL-N	0	0	....	1	0	0	0	0	3	1	0	0	0	1	2	2	1.000	0.00	....	1.98	.143	0	.000	1	0	0.1
• TESREAU, Jeff	Charles Monroe Tesreau b: 3/5/1889, Silver Mine, MO d: 9/24/1946, Hanover, NH BR/TR, 6'2", 218 lbs. Deb: 4/12/1912 C																									
1912* NY-N	17	7	.708	36	28	19	3	1	243	177	90	53	2	10	106	119	1.165	**1.96**	**172**	2.22	**.204**	12	.146	38	21	3.5
1913* NY-N	22	13	.629	41	**38**	17	1	0	282	222	98	68	7	7	119	167	1.209	2.17	143	2.56	**.220**	21	.221	28	25	3.1
1914 NY-N	26	10	.722	42	**41**	26	**8**	1	322^1	238	104	85	8	7	128	189	1.135	2.37	112	2.24	**.209**	28	.239	10	26	1.7
1915 NY-N	19	16	.543	43	38	24	8	3	306	235	98	78	4	5	75	176	1.013	2.29	111	1.84	.215	24	.233	12	21	1.9
1916 NY-N	14	14	.500	40	33	23	5	2	268^1	249	103	87	9	6	65	113	1.170	2.92	83	2.73	.250	18	.191	-19	12	-1.9
1917* NY-N	13	8	.619	33	20	11	1	2	183^2	168	71	63	6	3	58	85	1.230	3.09	82	2.87	.249	14	.230	-13	9	-1.3
1918 NY-N	4	4	.500	12	9	3	1	0	73^2	61	27	19	1	0	21	31	1.113	2.32	113	2.15	.227	7	.318	2	5	0.5
Total 7	115	72	.615	247	207	123	27	9	1679	1350	591	453	37	38	572	880	1.145	2.43	111	2.36	.223	124	.216	59	119	7.3
• TESSMER, Jay	Jay Weldon Tessmer b: 12/26/1971, Meadville, PA BR/TR, 6'3", 188 lbs. Deb: 8/27/1998																									
1998 NY-A	1	0	1.000	7	0	0	0	0	8^2	4	3	3	1	0	4	6	.923	3.12	141	1.74	.143	0	....	1	1	0.1
1999 NY-A	0	0	....	6	0	0	0	0	6^2	16	11	11	1	1	4	3	3.000	14.85	32	14.65	.444	0	....	-7	0	-0.7
2000 NY-A	0	0	....	7	0	0	0	0	6^2	9	6	5	3	0	1	5	1.500	6.75	72	7.01	.300	0	....	-1	0	-0.1
2002 NY-A	0	0	....	2	0	0	0	0	1^1	0	1	1	0	0	2	0	1.500	6.75	65	1.96	.000	0	....	-0	0	0.0
Total 4	1	0	1.000	22	0	0	0	0	23^1	29	21	20	5	1	11	14	1.714	7.71	61	6.95	.309	0	....	-8	1	-0.7
• TEUT, Nate	Nathan Mark Teut b: 3/11/1976, Newton, IA BR/TL, 6'7", 225 lbs. Deb: 5/4/2002																									
2002 Fla-N	0	1	.000	2	1	0	0	0	7^1	13	8	8	0	0	3	4	2.182	9.82	40	7.97	.394	0	.000	-5	0	-0.5
• TEWKSBURY, Bob	Robert Alan Tewksbury b: 11/30/1960, Concord, NH BR/TR, 6'4", 200 lbs. Deb: 4/11/1986																									
1986 NY-A	9	5	.643	23	20	2	0	0	130^1	144	58	48	8	5	31	49	1.343	3.31	123	3.91	.282	0	....	10	9	1.0
1987 NY-A	1	4	.200	8	6	0	0	0	33^1	47	26	25	5	1	7	12	1.620	6.75	65	6.34	.338	0	....	-9	0	-0.8
Chi-N	0	4	.000	7	3	0	0	0	18	32	15	13	1	0	13	10	2.500	6.50	66	10.03	.421	0	.000	-4	0	-0.5
1988 Chi-N	0	0	....	1	1	0	0	0	3^1	6	5	3	1	0	2	1	2.400	8.10	45	11.76	.400	0	.000	-2	0	-0.2
1989 StL-N	1	0	1.000	7	4	1	1	0	30	25	12	11	2	2	10	17	1.167	3.30	110	2.80	.225	1	.111	1	2	0.0
1990 StL-N	10	9	.526	28	20	3	2	1	145^1	151	67	56	7	3	15	50	1.142	3.47	110	2.86	.267	7	.171	6	10	0.8
1991 StL-N	11	12	.478	30	30	3	0	0	191	206	86	69	13	5	38	75	1.277	3.25	114	3.63	.281	9	.155	8	10	0.9
1992 StL-N★	16	5	.762	33	32	5	0	0	233	217	63	56	15	3	20	91	1.017	2.16	157	2.40	.248	6	.086	29	21	2.9
1993 StL-N	17	10	.630	32	32	2	0	0	213^2	258	99	91	15	6	20	97	1.301	3.83	103	3.91	.301	14	.203	3	12	0.5
1994 StL-N	12	10	.545	24	24	4	1	0	155^2	190	97	92	19	3	22	79	1.362	5.32	78	4.51	.304	10	.185	-20	5	-1.9
1995 Tex-A	8	7	.533	21	21	4	1	0	129^2	169	75	66	8	3	20	53	1.458	4.58	105	4.64	.319	0	.000	4	8	0.4
1996 SD-N	10	10	.500	36	33	1	0	0	206^2	224	116	99	17	3	43	126	1.292	4.31	92	3.65	.275	2	.031	-7	7	-1.2
1997 Min-A	8	13	.381	26	26	5	2	0	168^2	200	83	79	12	1	31	92	1.370	4.22	110	4.08	.297	1	.200	8	9	0.8
1998 Min-A	7	13	.350	26	25	1	0	0	148^1	174	82	79	19	6	20	60	1.308	4.79	100	4.31	.292	0	.000	2	8	0.2
Total 13	110	102	.519	302	277	31	7	1	1807	2043	884	787	142	41	292	812	1.292	3.92	105	3.83	.287	50	.132	29	101	2.9
• THATCHER, Grant	Ulysses Grant Thatcher b: 2/23/1877, Maytown, PA d: 3/17/1936, Lancaster, PA TR, 5'10.5", 180 lbs. Deb: 9/9/1903																									
1903 Bro-N	3	1	.750	4	4	4	0	0	28	33	12	9	1	0	7	9	1.429	2.89	110	4.01	.292	2	.182	5	2	0.5
1904 Bro-N	1	0	1.000	1	0	0	0	0	9	9	6	4	0	0	2	4	1.222	4.00	68	3.00	.281	1	.250	-1	0	-0.1
Total 2	4	1	.800	5	4	4	0	0	37	42	18	13	1	0	9	13	1.378	3.16	96	3.76	.290	3	.200	3	2	0.3
• THAYER, Greg	Gregory Allen Thayer b: 10/23/1949, Cedar Rapids, IA BR/TR, 5'11", 182 lbs. Deb: 4/7/1978																									
1978 Min-A	1	1	.500	20	0	0	0	0	45	40	19	19	5	3	30	30	1.556	3.80	100	5.07	.258	0	....	-0	2	0.0
• THEIS, Jack	John Louis Theis b: 7/23/1891, Georgetown, OH d: 7/6/1941, Georgetown, OH BR/TR, 6', 190 lbs. Deb: 7/5/1920																									
1920 Cin-N	0	0	....	1	0	0	0	0	2	1	0	0	0	0	3	0	2.000	0.00	....	4.02	.143	0	....	1	0	0.1
• THEISS, Duane	Duane Charles Theiss b: 11/20/1953, Zanesville, OH BR/TR, 6'3", 185 lbs. Deb: 8/5/1977																									
1977 Atl-N	1	1	.500	17	0	0	0	0	20^2	26	16	15	1	1	16	7	2.032	6.53	68	6.45	.338	0	.000	-4	0	-0.4
1978 Atl-N	0	0	....	3	0	0	0	0	6^1	3	1	1	0	1	3	3	.947	1.42	285	1.76	.158	0	.000	2	1	0.2
Total 2	1	1	.500	20	0	0	0	0	27	29	17	16	1	2	19	10	1.778	5.33	83	5.35	.302	0	.000	-2	1	-0.2
• THESENGA, Jug	Arnold Joseph Thesenga b: 4/27/1914, Jefferson, SD d: 12/3/2002, Wichita, KS BR/TR, 6', 200 lbs. Deb: 9/1/1944																									
1944 Was-A	0	0	....	5	1	0	0	0	12^1	18	9	7	0	0	12	2	2.432	5.11	64	8.13	.340	0	.000	-2	0	-0.3
• THIEL, Bert	Maynard Bert Thiel b: 5/4/1926, Marion, WI BR/TR, 5'10", 185 lbs. Deb: 4/17/1952																									
1952 Bos-N	1	1	.500	4	0	0	0	0	7	11	7	6	1	2	4	6	2.143	7.71	47	9.29	.344	0	....	-3	0	-0.3

YEAR TM-L	W	L	PCT	G	GS	CG	SH	SV	IP	H	R	ER	HR	HB	BB	SO	RAT	ERA	ERA+	CERA	OAV	BH	AVG	PR+	WS	TPW
• THIELMAN, Henry	Henry Joseph Thielman b: 10/3/1880, St. Cloud, MN d: 9/2/1942, New York, NY BR/TR, 5'11", 175 lbs. Deb: 4/17/1902 ♦																									
1902 NY-N	0	1	.000	2	2	0	0	0	6	8	10	1	0	0	6	5	2.333	1.50	187	7.37	.319	1	.111	1	0	0.0
Cin-N	9	15	.375	25	23	22	0	1	211	201	111	76	2	19	78	49	1.322	3.24	92	3.30	.251	12	.132	-10	8	-1.6
Yr.	9	16	.360	27	25	22	0	1	217	209	121	77	2	19	84	54	1.350	3.19	94	3.41	.253	13	.130	-9	8	-1.6
1903 Bro-N	0	3	.000	4	3	3	0	0	29	31	20	15	3	2	14	10	1.552	4.66	68	6.01	.330	5	.217	-1	1	-0.1
Total 2	9	19	.321	31	28	25	0	1	246	240	141	92	5	21	98	64	1.374	3.37	90	3.72	.261	18	.146	-10	9	-1.7
• THIELMAN, Jake	John Peter Thielman b: 5/20/1879, St. Cloud, MN d: 1/28/1928, Minneapolis, MN BR/TR, 5'11", 175 lbs. Deb: 4/23/1905																									
1905 StL-N	15	16	.484	32	29	26	0	0	242	265	138	94	4	12	62	87	1.351	3.50	85	3.66	.281	21	.231	-6	12	0.3
1906 StL-N	0	1	.000	1	1	0	0	0	5	5	6	2	0	0	2	0	1.400	3.60	73	3.36	.263	1	.500	-0	0	0.0
1907 Cle-A	11	8	.579	20	18	18	3	0	166	151	60	43	2	7	34	56	1.114	2.33	107	2.45	.245	12	.203	-0	11	0.1
1908 Cle-A	4	3	.571	11	8	5	0	0	61^{2}	59	26	25	2	4	9	15	1.103	3.65	65	2.74	.260	8	.348	-9	5	-0.6
Bos-A	0	0	....	1	0	0	0	0	0^{2}	3	4	3	1	0	0	0	4.500	40.50	6	46.37	.600	0	....	-3	0	-0.3
Yr.	4	3	.571	12	8	5	0	0	62^{1}	62	30	28	3	4	9	15	1.139	4.04	59	3.21	.267	8	.348	-12	5	-0.9
Total 4	30	28	.517	65	56	49	3	0	475^{1}	483	234	167	9	23	107	158	1.241	3.16	86	3.18	.267	42	.240	-18	28	-0.5
• THIES, Dave	David Robert Thies b: 3/21/1937, Minneapolis, MN BR/TR, 6'4", 205 lbs. Deb: 4/20/1963																									
1963 KC-A	0	1	.000	9	2	0	0	0	25^{1}	26	15	13	2	2	12	9	1.500	4.62	83	4.84	.274	2	.333	-2	1	-0.1
• THIES, Jake	Vernon Arthur Thies b: 4/1/1926, St. Louis, MO BR/TR, 5'11", 170 lbs. Deb: 4/24/1954																									
1954 Pit-N	3	9	.250	33	18	3	1	0	130^{1}	120	70	56	13	3	49	57	1.297	3.87	108	3.49	.244	1	.030	8	7	0.6
1955 Pit-N	0	1	.000	1	1	0	0	0	3^{2}	5	5	2	0	1	3	0	2.182	4.91	84	7.46	.357	0	....	-0	0	0.0
Total 2	3	10	.231	34	19	3	1	0	134	125	75	58	13	4	52	57	1.321	3.90	108	3.60	.248	1	.030	7	7	0.6
• THIGPEN, Bobby	Robert Thomas Thigpen b: 7/17/1963, Tallahassee, FL BR/TR, 6'3", 195 lbs. Deb: 8/6/1986																									
1986 Chi-A	2	0	1.000	20	0	0	0	7	35^{2}	26	7	7	1	1	12	20	1.065	1.77	244	2.13	.205	0	....	9	7	0.9
1987 Chi-A	7	5	.583	51	0	0	0	16	89	86	30	27	10	3	24	52	1.236	2.73	168	3.55	.256	0	....	16	12	1.5
1988 Chi-A	5	8	.385	68	0	0	0	34	90	96	38	33	6	4	33	62	1.433	3.30	120	4.15	.273	0	....	5	11	0.5
1989 Chi-A	2	6	.250	61	0	0	0	34	79	62	34	33	10	1	40	47	1.291	3.76	101	3.45	.218	0	....	0	8	0.0
1990 Chi-A★	4	6	.400	**77**	0	0	0	**57**	88^{2}	60	20	18	5	1	32	70	1.038	1.83	209	2.05	.195	0	....	18	21	1.8
1991 Chi-A	7	5	.583	67	0	0	0	30	69^{2}	63	32	27	10	4	38	47	1.450	3.49	114	4.44	.245	0	....	2	8	0.2
1992 Chi-A	1	3	.250	55	0	0	0	22	55	58	29	29	4	3	33	45	1.655	4.75	81	5.03	.275	0	....	-5	3	-0.6
1993 Chi-A	0	0	....	25	0	0	0	1	34^{2}	51	25	22	5	5	12	19	1.817	5.71	73	7.81	.349	0	....	-6	0	-0.6
*Phi-N	3	1	.750	17	0	0	0	0	19^{1}	23	13	13	2	1	9	10	1.655	6.05	65	5.66	.307	0	.000	-4	1	-0.4
1994 Sea-A	0	2	.000	7	0	0	0	0	7^{2}	12	9	8	3	0	5	4	2.217	9.39	52	11.18	.353	0	....	-4	0	-0.3
Total 9	31	36	.463	448	0	0	0	201	568^{2}	537	237	217	56	23	238	376	1.363	3.43	118	4.00	.252	0	.000	31	71	3.1
• THOBE, J.J.	John Joseph Thobe b: 11/19/1970, Covington, KY BR/TR, 6'6", 200 lbs. Deb: 9/18/1995																									
1995 Mon-N	0	0	....	4	0	0	0	0	4	6	4	4	0	0	3	0	2.250	9.00	48	7.52	.333	0	....	-2	0	-0.2
• THOBE, Tom	Thomas Neal Thobe b: 9/3/1969, Covington, KY BL/TL, 6'6", 195 lbs. Deb: 9/12/1995																									
1995 Atl-N	0	0	....	3	0	0	0	0	3^{1}	7	4	4	0	0	0	2	2.100	10.80	39	8.13	.412	0	....	-2	0	-0.2
1996 Atl-N	0	1	.000	4	0	0	0	0	6	5	2	1	1	0	0	1	.833	1.50	294	1.95	.217	0	.000	2	1	0.2
Total 2	0	1	.000	7	0	0	0	0	9^{1}	12	6	5	1	0	0	3	1.286	4.82	89	4.16	.300	0	.000	-0	1	0.0
• THOENEN, Dick	Richard Crispin Thoenen b: 1/9/1944, Mexico, MO BR/TR, 6'6", 215 lbs. Deb: 9/16/1967																									
1967 Phi-N	0	0	....	1	0	0	0	0	1	2	1	1	0	0	0	0	2.000	9.00	38	7.48	.500	0	....	-1	0	-0.1
• THOMAS, Blaine	Blaine M. "Baldy" Thomas b: 8/1888, Glendora, CA d: 8/21/1915, Glendora, CA BR/TR, 5'10", 165 lbs. Deb: 8/25/1911																									
1911 Bos-A	0	0	....	2	2	0	0	0	4^{2}	3	2	0	0	1	7	0	2.143	0.00	....	7.42	.273	1	.500	2	1	0.2
• THOMAS, Brad	Bradley Richard Thomas b: 10/22/1977, Sydney, Australia BL/TL, 6'4", 204 lbs. Deb: 5/26/2001																									
2001 Min-A	0	2	.000	5	5	0	0	0	16^{1}	20	17	17	6	1	14	6	2.082	9.37	49	10.12	.303	0	....	-9	0	-0.8
2003 Min-A	0	1	.000	3	0	0	0	0	4^{2}	6	4	4	1	0	3	2	1.929	7.71	59	7.54	.316	0	....	-2	0	-0.1
Total 2	0	3	.000	8	5	0	0	0	21	26	21	21	7	1	17	8	2.048	9.00	51	9.54	.306	0	....	-10	0	-1.0
• THOMAS, Bud	Luther Baxter Thomas b: 9/9/1910, Faber, VA d: 5/20/2001, North Garden, VA BR/TR, 6', 180 lbs. Deb: 9/13/1932																									
1932 Was-A	0	0	....	2	0	0	0	0	3	1	0	0	0	0	2	1	1.000	0.00	....	1.16	.100	0	....	1	1	0.1
1933 Was-A	0	0	....	2	0	0	0	0	4	11	8	7	1	1	2	1	3.250	15.75	27	21.56	.550	0	.000	-5	0	-0.5
1937 Phi-A	8	15	.348	35	26	6	1	0	169^{2}	208	108	94	15	1	52	54	1.532	4.99	94	4.78	.295	6	.128	-5	6	-0.6
1938 Phi-A	9	14	.391	42	29	7	1	0	212^{1}	259	138	116	23	2	62	48	1.512	4.92	98	4.89	.299	9	.130	4	10	0.1
1939 Phi-A	0	1	.000	2	2	0	0	0	4	8	8	7	2	0	1	0	2.250	15.75	30	13.23	.421	0	.000	-5	0	-0.5
Was-A	0	0	....	4	0	0	0	0	9	11	7	6	0	0	2	0	1.444	6.00	72	3.85	.306	0	.000	-2	0	-0.2
Det-A	7	0	1.000	27	0	0	0	1	47^{1}	45	25	22	7	0	20	14	1.373	4.18	117	4.14	.254	1	.111	4	4	0.3
Yr.	7	1	.875	33	2	0	0	1	60^{1}	64	40	35	9	0	23	14	1.442	5.22	91	4.70	.276	1	.071	-3	4	-0.4
1940 Det-A	0	1	.000	3	0	0	0	0	4	8	5	4	1	0	3	0	2.750	9.00	53	12.64	.421	0	....	-2	0	-0.2
1941 Det-A	1	3	.250	26	1	0	0	2	72^{2}	74	45	34	4	0	22	17	1.321	4.21	108	3.29	.260	2	.105	5	4	0.4
Total 7	25	34	.424	143	58	13	2	3	526	625	344	290	53	4	166	135	1.504	4.96	95	4.77	.292	18	.120	-5	25	-1.1
• THOMAS, Carl	Carl Leslie Thomas b: 5/28/1932, Minneapolis, MN BR/TR, 6'5", 245 lbs. Deb: 4/19/1960																									
1960 Cle-A	1	0	1.000	4	0	0	0	0	9^{2}	8	8	8	1	1	10	5	1.862	7.45	50	6.04	.229	1	.333	-4	0	-0.3
• THOMAS, Claude	Claude Alfred "Lefty" Thomas b: 5/15/1890, Stanberry, MO d: 3/6/1946, Sulpher, OK BL/TL, 6'1", 180 lbs. Deb: 9/14/1916																									
1916 Was-A	1	2	.333	7	4	1	1	0	28^{1}	27	14	13	1	2	12	7	1.376	4.13	67	3.85	.265	1	.100	-4	0	-0.6
• THOMAS, Fay	Fay Wesley "Scow" Thomas b: 10/10/1903, Holyrood, KS d: 8/12/1990, Chatsworth, CA BR/TR, 6'2", 195 lbs. Deb: 6/27/1927																									
1927 NY-N	0	0	....	9	0	0	0	0	16^{1}	19	10	6	3	1	4	11	1.408	3.31	116	5.20	.302	0	.000	1	1	0.1
1931 Cle-A	2	4	.333	16	2	1	0	0	48^{2}	63	34	28	2	1	32	25	1.952	5.18	89	6.43	.323	2	.154	-2	2	-0.2
1932 Bro-N	0	1	.000	7	2	0	0	0	17	22	15	14	0	0	8	9	1.765	7.41	51	5.07	.306	0	.000	-7	0	-0.7
1935 StL-A	7	15	.318	49	19	4	0	1	147	165	95	78	11	3	89	67	1.728	4.78	100	5.36	.289	4	.105	1	8	-0.2
Total 4	9	20	.310	81	23	5	0	1	229	269	154	126	16	5	133	112	1.755	4.95	92	5.56	.299	6	.107	-6	11	-1.0
• THOMAS, Frosty	Forrest Thomas b: 5/23/1881, Faucett, MO d: 3/18/1970, St. Joseph, MO BR/TR, 6', 185 lbs. Deb: 5/1/1905																									
1905 Det-A	0	1	.000	2	1	0	0	0	6	10	8	5	0	1	3	5	2.167	7.50	36	8.24	.372	0	.000	-3	0	-0.4
• THOMAS, Larry	Larry Wayne Thomas b: 10/25/1969, Miami, FL BR/TL, 6'1", 190 lbs. Deb: 8/11/1995																									
1995 Chi-A	0	0	....	17	0	0	0	0	13^{2}	8	2	2	1	0	6	12	1.024	1.32	338	1.86	.167	0	....	5	2	0.5
1996 Chi-A	2	3	.400	57	0	0	0	0	30^{2}	32	11	11	1	3	14	20	1.500	3.23	147	4.40	.281	0	....	5	3	0.5
1997 Chi-A	0	0	....	5	0	0	0	0	3^{1}	3	3	3	1	0	2	0	1.500	8.10	54	5.66	.250	0	....	-1	0	-0.1
Total 3	2	3	.400	79	0	0	0	0	47^{2}	43	16	16	3	3	22	32	1.364	3.02	154	3.76	.247	0	....	9	5	0.8
• THOMAS, Lefty	Clarence Fletcher Thomas b: 10/4/1903, Glade Springs, VA d: 3/21/1952, Charlottesville, VA BL/TL, 6', 183 lbs. Deb: 9/26/1925																									
1925 Was-A	0	2	.000	2	2	1	0	0	13	14	8	3	0	0	7	10	1.615	2.08	204	3.96	.264	0	.000	3	1	0.2
1926 Was-A	0	0	....	6	0	0	0	0	8^{2}	8	7	5	0	0	10	3	2.077	5.19	74	5.25	.267	0	.000	-1	0	-0.1
Total 2	0	2	.000	8	2	1	0	0	21^{2}	22	15	8	0	0	17	13	1.800	3.32	120	4.48	.265	0	.000	1	1	0.0
• THOMAS, Mike	Michael Steven Thomas b: 9/2/1969, Sacramento, CA BL/TL, 6'2", 205 lbs. Deb: 7/12/1995																									
1995 Mil-A	0	0	....	1	0	0	0	0	1^{1}	2	0	0	0	0	1	0	2.250	0.00	....	7.52	.333	0	....	1	0	0.1
• THOMAS, Myles	Myles Lewis Thomas b: 10/22/1897, State College, PA d: 12/12/1963, Toledo, OH BR/TR, 5'9.5", 170 lbs. Deb: 4/18/1926																									
1926* NY-A	6	6	.500	33	13	3	0	0	140^{1}	140	79	66	6	3	65	38	1.461	4.23	91	3.86	.271	5	.116	-4	6	-0.6
1927 NY-A	7	4	.636	21	9	1	0	0	88^{2}	111	58	48	4	1	43	25	1.737	4.87	79	5.54	.322	9	.333	-10	3	-0.8

YEAR	TM-L	W	L	PCT	G	GS	CG	SH	SV	IP	H	R	ER	HR	HB	BB	SO	RAT	ERA	ERA+	CERA	OAV	BH	AVG	PR+	WS	TPW
1928	NY-A	1	0	1.000	12	1	0	0	0	31^2	33	19	12	3	0	9	10	1.326	3.41	110	3.54	.277	4	.400	2	2	0.3
1929	NY-A	0	2	.000	5	1	0	0	0	15	27	21	18	1	0	9	3	2.400	10.80	36	9.52	.409	1	.143	-12	0	-1.2
	Was-A	7	8	.467	22	14	7	0	2	125^1	139	72	49	3	0	48	33	1.492	3.52	120	3.97	.288	14	.292	8	9	1.0
	Yr.	7	10	.412	27	15	7	0	2	140^1	166	93	67	4	0	57	36	1.589	4.30	96	4.56	.303	15	.273	-3	9	-0.2
1930	Was-A	2	2	.500	12	2	0	0	0	33^2	49	35	31	3	0	15	12	1.901	8.29	55	6.79	.358	2	.182	-15	0	-1.4
Total	5	23	22	.511	105	40	11	0	2	434^2	499	284	224	20	4	189	121	1.583	4.64	87	4.63	.300	35	.240	-30	20	-2.8

• THOMAS, Roy Roy Justin Thomas b: 6/22/1953, Quantico, VA BR/TR, 6'5", 200 lbs. Deb: 9/21/1977

YEAR	TM-L	W	L	PCT	G	GS	CG	SH	SV	IP	H	R	ER	HR	HB	BB	SO	RAT	ERA	ERA+	CERA	OAV	BH	AVG	PR+	WS	TPW
1977	Hou-N	0	0	....	4	0	0	0	0	6^1	5	2	2	0	0	3	4	1.263	2.84	125	2.50	.208	0	....	1	0	0.1
1978	StL-N	1	1	.500	16	1	0	0	3	28^1	21	14	12	0	0	16	16	1.306	3.81	92	2.45	.216	1	.250	-1	2	-0.1
1979	StL-N	3	4	.429	26	6	0	0	1	77	66	29	25	9	0	24	44	1.169	2.92	129	3.11	.237	1	.059	5	6	0.5
1980	StL-N	2	3	.400	24	5	0	0	0	55	59	32	29	3	3	25	22	1.527	4.75	78	4.38	.274	2	.154	-7	1	-0.8
1983	Sea-A	3	1	.750	43	0	0	0	1	88^2	95	44	34	3	2	32	77	1.432	3.45	123	3.88	.275	0	....	8	6	0.8
1984	Sea-A	3	2	.600	21	1	0	0	1	49^2	52	33	29	8	4	37	42	1.792	5.26	76	6.67	.280	0	....	-6	1	-0.6
1985	Sea-A	7	0	1.000	40	0	0	0	1	93^2	66	37	35	8	2	48	70	1.217	3.36	125	2.76	.202	0	....	9	8	0.9
1987	Sea-A	1	0	1.000	8	0	0	0	0	20^2	23	12	12	2	1	11	14	1.645	5.23	90	5.62	.299	0	....	-1	1	-0.1
Total	8	20	11	.645	182	13	0	0	7	419^1	387	203	178	33	12	196	289	1.390	3.82	104	3.85	.250	4	.118	8	25	0.6

• THOMAS, Stan Stanley Brown Thomas b: 7/11/1949, Rumford, ME BR/TR, 6'2", 185 lbs. Deb: 7/5/1974

YEAR	TM-L	W	L	PCT	G	GS	CG	SH	SV	IP	H	R	ER	HR	HB	BB	SO	RAT	ERA	ERA+	CERA	OAV	BH	AVG	PR+	WS	TPW
1974	Tex-A	0	0	....	12	0	0	0	0	13^2	22	10	10	1	0	6	8	2.049	6.59	54	7.61	.379	0	....	-5	0	-0.5
1975	Tex-A	4	4	.500	46	1	0	0	3	81^1	72	36	28	2	3	34	46	1.303	3.10	121	3.07	.239	0	....	6	6	0.6
1976	Cle-A	4	4	.500	37	7	2	0	6	105^2	88	33	27	5	4	41	54	1.221	2.30	152	2.92	.229	0	....	14	10	1.4
1977	Sea-A	2	6	.250	13	9	1	0	0	58^1	74	49	39	8	3	25	14	1.697	6.02	68	6.26	.310	0	....	-13	0	-1.3
	NY-A	1	0	1.000	3	0	0	0	0	6^1	7	7	5	0	0	4	1	1.737	7.11	55	4.51	.280	0	....	-2	0	-0.2
	Yr.	3	6	.333	16	9	1	0	0	64^2	81	56	44	8	3	29	15	1.701	6.12	67	6.09	.307	0	....	-16	0	-1.6
Total	4	11	14	.440	111	17	3	0	9	265^1	263	135	109	16	10	110	123	1.406	3.70	103	3.98	.261	0	....	-1	16	0.0

• THOMAS, Tom Thomas R. "Savage Tom" Thomas b: 12/27/1873, Shawnee, OH d: 9/23/1942, Shawnee, OH BR/TR, 6'4", 195 lbs. Deb: 9/20/1894

YEAR	TM-L	W	L	PCT	G	GS	CG	SH	SV	IP	H	R	ER	HR	HB	BB	SO	RAT	ERA	ERA+	CERA	OAV	BH	AVG	PR+	WS	TPW
1894	Cle-N	0	0	....	1	0	0	0	0	0^1	0	1	1	0	0	2	0	6.000	27.00	20	16.54	.000	0	....	-1	0	-0.1
1899	StL-N	1	1	.500	4	2	2	0	0	25	22	14	7	1	0	4	8	1.040	2.52	158	2.19	.237	3	.250	4	2	0.4
1900	StL-N	2	2	.500	5	1	1	0	0	26^1	38	22	11	2	1	4	7	1.595	3.76	97	5.58	.336	1	.091	0	1	0.0
Total	3	3	3	.500	10	3	3	0	0	51^2	60	37	19	3	1	10	15	1.355	3.31	115	4.01	.291	4	.174	3	3	0.3

• THOMAS, Tommy Alphonse Thomas b: 12/23/1899, Baltimore, MD d: 4/27/1988, Dallastown, PA BR/TR, 5'10", 175 lbs. Deb: 4/17/1926

YEAR	TM-L	W	L	PCT	G	GS	CG	SH	SV	IP	H	R	ER	HR	HB	BB	SO	RAT	ERA	ERA+	CERA	OAV	BH	AVG	PR+	WS	TPW
1926	Chi-A	15	12	.556	44	32	13	2	2	249	225	113	105	7	1	110	127	1.345	3.80	102	3.12	**.244**	16	.186	-1	16	-0.2
1927	Chi-A	19	16	.543	40	**36**	24	3	1	**307^2**	271	110	102	16	1	94	107	1.186	2.98	136	2.75	.244	14	.147	31	27	2.7
1928	Chi-A	17	16	.515	36	32	24	3	2	283	277	114	97	14	4	76	129	1.247	3.08	131	2.98	.259	21	.219	29	26	3.1
1929	Chi-A	14	18	.438	36	31	**24**	2	1	259^2	270	127	92	17	0	60	62	1.271	3.19	134	3.33	.269	25	.255	28	20	2.8
1930	Chi-A	5	13	.278	34	27	7	0	0	169	229	125	98	13	1	44	58	1.615	5.22	88	5.20	.323	7	.125	-7	5	-0.9
1931	Chi-A	10	14	.417	43	36	11	2	2	245^1	298	166	129	17	5	69	72	1.496	4.73	90	4.55	.292	21	.241	-9	10	-0.7
1932	Chi-A	3	3	.500	12	3	1	0	0	43^2	55	33	30	6	1	15	11	1.603	6.18	70	5.63	.307	1	.077	-9	0	-0.9
	Was-A	8	7	.533	18	14	7	1	0	117	114	48	46	5	0	46	36	1.368	3.54	122	3.40	.255	10	.238	7	10	0.8
	Yr.	11	10	.524	30	17	8	1	0	160^2	169	81	76	11	1	61	47	1.432	4.26	101	4.01	.270	11	.200	-1	10	-0.1
1933*	Was-A	7	7	.500	35	14	2	0	3	135	149	87	72	9	2	49	35	1.467	4.80	87	4.11	.273	10	.238	-12	5	-1.0
1934	Was-A	8	9	.471	33	18	7	1	1	133^1	154	87	81	9	3	58	42	1.590	5.47	79	4.86	.294	7	.184	-17	5	-1.6
1935	Was-A	0	0	....	1	0	0	0	0	0^1	3	2	2	0	0	0	0	9.000	54.00	8	67.29	.750	0	....	-2	0	-0.2
	Phi-N	0	1	.000	4	1	0	0	0	12	15	9	7	2	0	5	3	1.667	5.25	86	6.11	.313	0	.000	-1	0	-0.1
1936	StL-A	11	9	.550	36	21	8	1	0	179^2	219	132	105	25	4	72	40	1.620	5.26	102	5.57	.297	8	.138	6	10	0.3
1937	StL-A	0	1	.000	17	2	0	0	0	30^2	46	26	24	2	1	10	10	1.826	7.04	69	6.49	.348	0	.000	-7	0	-0.7
	Bos-A	0	2	.000	9	0	0	0	0	11	16	6	5	2	1	4	4	1.818	4.09	116	7.59	.340	1	.250	1	1	0.1
	Yr.	0	3	.000	26	2	0	0	0	41^2	62	32	29	4	2	14	14	1.824	6.26	77	6.78	.346	1	.125	-6	1	-0.6
Total	12	117	128	.478	398	267	128	15	12	2176^1	2341	1185	995	144	24	712	736	1.403	4.11	105	3.93	.275	141	.195	39	135	3.4

• THOMASON, Erskine Melvin Erskine Thomason b: 8/13/1948, Laurens, SC BR/TR, 6'1", 190 lbs. Deb: 9/18/1974

YEAR	TM-L	W	L	PCT	G	GS	CG	SH	SV	IP	H	R	ER	HR	HB	BB	SO	RAT	ERA	ERA+	CERA	OAV	BH	AVG	PR+	WS	TPW
1974	Phi-N	0	0	....	1	0	0	0	0	1	0	0	0	0	0	0	1	.000	0.00	....	0.00	.000	0	....	0	0	0.0

• THOMPSON, Art Arthur J. Thompson Deb: 6/17/1884

YEAR	TM-L	W	L	PCT	G	GS	CG	SH	SV	IP	H	R	ER	HR	HB	BB	SO	RAT	ERA	ERA+	CERA	OAV	BH	AVG	PR+	WS	TPW
1884	Was-U	0	1	.000	1	1	1	0	0	8	10	11	6	0	....	3	8	1.625	6.75	44	....	.287	0	.000	-3	0	-0.3

• THOMPSON, Forrest David Forrest Thompson b: 3/3/1918, Mooresville, NC d: 2/26/1979, Charlotte, NC BL/TL, 5'11", 195 lbs. Deb: 4/26/1948

YEAR	TM-L	W	L	PCT	G	GS	CG	SH	SV	IP	H	R	ER	HR	HB	BB	SO	RAT	ERA	ERA+	CERA	OAV	BH	AVG	PR+	WS	TPW
1948	Was-A	6	10	.375	46	7	0	0	4	131^1	134	71	56	9	1	54	40	1.431	3.84	113	3.84	.262	10	.286	10	10	1.2
1949	Was-A	1	3	.250	9	1	1	0	0	16^1	22	11	8	1	1	9	8	1.898	4.41	97	6.44	.328	3	.600	0	1	0.2
Total	2	7	13	.350	55	8	1	0	4	147^2	156	82	64	10	2	63	48	1.483	3.90	111	4.13	.270	13	.325	10	11	1.4

• THOMPSON, Fuller Fuller Weidner Thompson b: 6/1/1889, Los Angeles, CA d: 2/19/1972, Los Angeles, CA BR/TR, 5'11.5", 164 lbs. Deb: 8/19/1911

YEAR	TM-L	W	L	PCT	G	GS	CG	SH	SV	IP	H	R	ER	HR	HB	BB	SO	RAT	ERA	ERA+	CERA	OAV	BH	AVG	PR+	WS	TPW
1911	Bos-N	0	0	....	3	0	0	0	0	4^2	5	4	2	0	0	2	0	1.500	3.86	99	4.08	.294	0	....	0	0	0.0

• THOMPSON, Gus John Gustav Thompson b: 6/22/1877, Humboldt, IA d: 3/28/1958, Kailspell, MT BR/TR, 6'2", 185 lbs. Deb: 8/31/1903

YEAR	TM-L	W	L	PCT	G	GS	CG	SH	SV	IP	H	R	ER	HR	HB	BB	SO	RAT	ERA	ERA+	CERA	OAV	BH	AVG	PR+	WS	TPW
1903*	Pit-N	2	2	.500	5	4	3	0	0	43	52	30	17	1	1	16	22	1.581	3.56	91	4.57	.295	4	.250	-3	2	-0.3
1906	StL-N	2	11	.154	17	12	8	0	0	103	111	61	49	2	5	25	36	1.320	4.28	61	3.64	.285	6	.176	-18	0	-2.0
Total	2	4	13	.235	22	16	11	0	0	146	163	91	66	3	6	41	58	1.397	4.07	68	3.91	.288	10	.200	-21	2	-2.3

• THOMPSON, Harry Harold Thompson b: 9/9/1889, Nanticoke, PA d: 2/14/1951, Reno, NV BL/TL, 5'8", 150 lbs. Deb: 4/24/1919

YEAR	TM-L	W	L	PCT	G	GS	CG	SH	SV	IP	H	R	ER	HR	HB	BB	SO	RAT	ERA	ERA+	CERA	OAV	BH	AVG	PR+	WS	TPW
1919	Was-A	0	3	.000	12	2	0	0	1	43^1	48	21	17	0	2	8	10	1.292	3.53	91	3.48	.293	8	.250	-1	2	-0.1
	Phi-A	0	1	.000	3	0	0	0	0	12	16	9	9	4	0	3	1	1.583	6.75	51	7.41	.327	0	.000	-4	0	-0.5
	Yr.	0	4	.000	15	2	0	0	1	55^1	64	30	26	4	2	11	11	1.355	4.23	77	4.33	.301	8	.211	-5	2	-0.6

• THOMPSON, Jocko John Samuel Thompson b: 1/17/1917, Beverly, MA d: 2/3/1988, Olney, MD BL/TL, 6', 185 lbs. Deb: 9/21/1948

YEAR	TM-L	W	L	PCT	G	GS	CG	SH	SV	IP	H	R	ER	HR	HB	BB	SO	RAT	ERA	ERA+	CERA	OAV	BH	AVG	PR+	WS	TPW
1948	Phi-N	1	0	1.000	2	2	1	0	0	13	10	4	4	0	0	9	7	1.462	2.77	142	3.35	.233	0	.000	2	1	0.2
1949	Phi-N	1	3	.250	8	5	1	0	0	31^1	38	24	24	6	0	11	12	1.564	6.89	57	5.99	.314	2	.182	-11	0	-1.1
1950	Phi-N	0	0	....	2	0	0	0	0	4	1	1	0	0	0	4	2	1.250	0.00	....	1.50	.077	0	....	2	1	0.2
1951	Phi-N	4	8	.333	29	14	3	2	1	119^1	102	55	51	12	2	59	60	1.349	3.85	100	3.62	.231	4	.103	0	6	-0.1
Total	4	6	11	.353	41	21	5	2	1	167^2	151	84	79	18	2	83	81	1.396	4.24	92	3.99	.244	6	.113	-7	8	-0.8

• THOMPSON, Junior Eugene Earl Thompson b: 6/7/1917, Latham, IL BR/TR, 6'1", 185 lbs. Deb: 4/26/1939

YEAR	TM-L	W	L	PCT	G	GS	CG	SH	SV	IP	H	R	ER	HR	HB	BB	SO	RAT	ERA	ERA+	CERA	OAV	BH	AVG	PR+	WS	TPW
1939*	Cin-N	13	5	.722	42	11	5	3	2	152^1	130	51	43	6	3	55	87	1.214	2.54	151	2.77	.236	11	.229	18	16	1.8
1940*	Cin-N	16	9	.640	33	31	17	3	0	225^1	197	90	83	10	2	96	103	1.300	3.32	114	3.05	.233	18	.228	4	18	0.7
1941	Cin-N	6	6	.500	27	15	4	0	1	109	117	65	59	6	3	57	46	1.596	4.87	74	4.43	.272	7	.233	-15	3	-1.4
1942	Cin-N	4	7	.364	29	10	1	0	0	101^2	86	61	38	5	2	53	35	1.367	3.36	98	3.23	.226	8	.267	-1	3	0.0
1946	NY-N	4	6	.400	39	1	0	0	4	62^2	36	18	9	5	0	40	31	1.213	1.29	267	2.64	.190	1	.143	16	7	1.7
1947	NY-N	4	2	.667	15	0	0	0	0	35^2	36	20	17	3	1	27	13	1.766	4.29	95	5.43	.279	0	.000	-1	2	-0.2
Total	6	47	35	.573	185	68	27	6	7	686^2	602	305	249	35	11	328	315	1.354	3.26	112	3.32	.239	45	.225	20	49	2.6

• THOMPSON, Justin Justin Willard Thompson b: 3/8/1973, San Antonio, TX BL/TL, 6'4", 215 lbs. Deb: 5/27/1996

YEAR	TM-L	W	L	PCT	G	GS	CG	SH	SV	IP	H	R	ER	HR	HB	BB	SO	RAT	ERA	ERA+	CERA	OAV	BH	AVG	PR+	WS	TPW
1996	Det-A	1	6	.143	11	11	0	0	0	59	62	35	30	7	2	31	44	1.576	4.58	111	5.07	.267	0	....	4	2	0.4
1997	Det-A★	15	11	.577	32	32	4	0	0	223^1	188	82	75	20	2	66	151	1.137	3.02	152	2.87	.233	0	.000	36	21	3.4
1998	Det-A	11	15	.423	34	34	5	0	0	222	227	114	100	20	2	79	149	1.378	4.05	116	4.00	.267	1	.143	13	14	1.2
1999	Det-A	9	11	.450	24	24	0	0	0	142^2	152	85	81	24	4	59	83	1.479	5.11	97	5.14	.274	0	.000	-3	7	-0.3
Total	4	36	43	.456	101	101	9	0	0	647	629	316	286	71	10	235	427	1.335	3.98	120	3.96	.257	1	.071	51	44	4.7

YEAR	TM-L	W	L	PCT	G	GS	CG	SH	SV	IP	H	R	ER	HR	HB	BB	SO	RAT	ERA	ERA+	CERA	OAV	BH	AVG	PR+	WS	TPW
• THOMPSON, Lee	John Dudley "Lefty" Thompson b: 2/26/1898, Smithfield, UT d: 2/17/1963, Santa Barbara, CA BL/TL, 6'1", 185 lbs. Deb: 9/4/1921																										
1921	Chi-A	0	3	.000	4	4	0	0	0	20^2	32	21	19	0	0	6	4	1.839	8.27	51	5.52	.333	2	.286	-9	0	-0.9
• THOMPSON, Mark	Mark Radford Thompson b: 4/7/1971, Russellville, KY BR/TR, 6'2", 205 lbs. Deb: 7/26/1994																										
1994	Col-N	1	1	.500	2	2	0	0	0	9	16	9	9	2	1	8	5	2.667	9.00	55	13.62	.400	0	.000	-4	0	-0.4
1995*	Col-N	2	3	.400	21	5	0	0	0	51	73	42	37	7	1	22	30	1.863	6.53	83	7.23	.349	5	.385	-5	1	-0.4
1996	Col-N	9	11	.450	34	28	3	1	0	169^2	189	109	100	25	13	74	99	1.550	5.30	99	5.59	.285	8	.138	2	9	0.1
1997	Col-N	3	3	.500	6	6	0	0	0	29^2	40	27	26	8	4	13	9	1.787	7.89	66	8.17	.323	2	.182	-9	0	-0.8
1998	Col-N	1	2	.333	6	6	0	0	0	23^1	36	22	20	8	5	12	14	2.057	7.71	67	11.65	.379	1	.143	-7	0	-0.7
1999	StL-N	1	3	.250	5	5	0	0	0	29^1	26	12	9	1	2	17	22	1.466	2.76	165	3.85	.241	0	.000	6	2	0.5
2000	StL-N	1	1	.500	20	0	0	0	0	25	24	21	14	4	3	15	19	1.560	5.04	91	5.52	.250	0	.000	-1	0	-0.2
Total	**7**	**18**	**24**	**.429**	**94**	**52**	**3**	**1**	**0**	**337**	**404**	**242**	**215**	**55**	**29**	**161**	**198**	**1.677**	**5.74**	**90**	**6.54**	**.303**	**16**	**.154**	**-17**	**12**	**-1.8**
• THOMPSON, Mike	Michael Wayne Thompson b: 9/6/1949, Denver, CO BR/TR, 6'3", 190 lbs. Deb: 5/19/1971																										
1971	Was-A	1	6	.143	16	12	0	0	0	66^2	53	39	36	3	3	54	41	1.605	4.86	68	4.24	.222	2	.118	-12	0	-1.2
1973	StL-N	0	0	....	2	2	0	0	0	4	1	0	0	0	0	5	3	1.500	0.00	....	2.38	.077	0	.000	2	1	0.2
1974	StL-N	0	3	.000	19	4	0	0	0	38^1	37	24	24	1	2	35	25	1.878	5.63	63	5.66	.274	0	.000	-9	0	-1.1
	Atl-N	0	0	....	1	1	0	0	0	4	7	2	2	0	0	2	2	2.250	4.50	84	8.49	.412	1	1.000	-0	1	0.0
	Yr.	0	3	.000	20	5	0	0	0	42^1	44	26	26	1	2	37	27	1.913	5.53	65	5.92	.289	1	.111	-10	1	-1.1
1975	Atl-N	0	6	.000	16	10	0	0	0	51^2	60	32	27	2	0	32	42	1.781	4.70	80	5.44	.305	1	.071	-4	0	-0.5
Total	**4**	**1**	**15**	**.063**	**54**	**29**	**0**	**0**	**0**	**164^2**	**158**	**97**	**89**	**6**	**5**	**128**	**113**	**1.737**	**4.86**	**72**	**5.00**	**.263**	**4**	**.098**	**-24**	**2**	**-2.7**
• THOMPSON, Rich	Richard Neil Thompson b: 11/1/1958, New York, NY BR/TR, 6'3", 225 lbs. Deb: 4/28/1985																										
1985	Cle-A	3	8	.273	57	0	0	0	5	80	95	63	56	8	6	48	30	1.788	6.30	66	6.19	.303	0	....	-19	0	-1.9
1989	Mon-N	0	2	.000	19	1	0	0	0	33	27	11	8	2	2	11	15	1.152	2.18	162	2.92	.241	0	.000	5	2	0.6
1990	Mon-N	0	0	....	1	0	0	0	0	1	1	0	0	0	0	0	0	1.000	0.00	....	1.95	.250	0	....	0	0	0.0
Total	**3**	**3**	**10**	**.231**	**77**	**1**	**0**	**0**	**5**	**114**	**123**	**74**	**64**	**10**	**8**	**59**	**45**	**1.596**	**5.05**	**80**	**5.20**	**.286**	**0**	**.000**	**-14**	**2**	**-1.3**
• THOMPSON, Tommy	Thomas Carl Thompson b: 11/7/1889, Spring City, TN d: 1/16/1963, La Jolla, CA BR/TR, 5'9.5", 170 lbs. Deb: 6/5/1912																										
1912	NY-A	0	2	.000	7	2	1	0	0	32^2	43	32	22	0	3	13	15	1.714	6.06	60	5.81	.341	3	.300	-7	0	-0.6
• THOMPSON, Will	Will McLain Thompson b: 8/30/1870, Pittsburgh, PA d: 6/9/1962, Pittsburgh, PA BR/TR, 5'11.5", 190 lbs. Deb: 7/9/1892																										
1892	Pit-N	0	1	.000	1	1	0	0	0	3	3	5	1	0	1	5	0	2.667	3.00	110	8.98	.250	0	....	0	0	0.0
• THOMSON, John	John Carl Thomson b: 10/1/1973, Vicksburg, MS BR/TR, 6'3", 175 lbs. Deb: 5/11/1997																										
1997	Col-N	7	9	.438	27	27	2	1	0	166^1	193	94	87	15	5	51	106	1.467	4.71	110	4.74	.296	10	.213	11	10	1.1
1998	Col-N	8	11	.421	26	26	2	0	0	161	174	86	86	21	0	49	106	1.385	4.81	108	4.45	.282	6	.120	6	9	0.4
1999	Col-N	1	10	.091	14	13	1	0	0	62^2	85	62	56	11	1	36	34	1.931	8.04	72	7.60	.324	3	.167	-15	0	-1.4
2001	Col-N	4	5	.444	14	14	1	1	0	93^2	84	46	42	15	4	25	68	1.164	4.04	132	3.52	.239	7	.241	13	7	1.4
2002	Col-N	7	8	.467	21	21	0	0	0	127^1	136	77	69	21	2	27	76	1.280	4.88	98	4.02	.268	6	.176	-0	6	0.0
	NY-N	2	6	.250	9	9	0	0	0	54^1	65	39	26	7	0	17	31	1.509	4.31	92	4.74	.290	5	.278	-2	1	0.0
	Yr.	9	14	.391	30	30	0	0	0	181^2	201	116	95	28	2	44	107	1.349	4.71	96	4.24	.275	11	.212	-2	7	0.0
2003	Tex-A	13	14	.481	35	35	3	1	0	217	234	125	117	27	4	49	136	1.304	4.85	102	4.10	.276	0	.000	5	11	0.5
Total	**6**	**42**	**63**	**.400**	**146**	**145**	**9**	**3**	**0**	**882^1**	**971**	**529**	**483**	**117**	**16**	**254**	**557**	**1.388**	**4.93**	**103**	**4.50**	**.280**	**37**	**.188**	**18**	**44**	**1.9**
• THORMAHLEN, Hank	Herbert Ehler "Lefty" Thormahlen b: 7/5/1896, Jersey City, NJ d: 2/6/1955, Hollywood, CA BL/TL, 6', 180 lbs. Deb: 9/29/1917																										
1917	NY-A	0	1	.000	1	1	0	0	0	8	9	3	2	0	1	4	5	1.625	2.25	119	4.73	.281	0	.000	0	0	0.0
1918	NY-A	7	3	.700	16	12	5	2	0	112^2	85	39	31	1	6	52	22	1.216	2.48	114	2.58	.217	3	.077	1	7	-0.3
1919	NY-A	12	8	.600	30	25	13	2	1	188^2	155	69	55	10	4	61	62	1.145	2.62	121	2.66	.228	11	.186	6	16	0.6
1920	NY-A	9	6	.600	29	15	6	0	1	143^1	178	86	66	5	2	43	35	1.542	4.14	92	4.68	.312	10	.222	-5	7	-0.4
1921	Bos-A	1	7	.125	23	9	3	0	0	96^1	101	56	48	3	6	34	17	1.401	4.48	94	3.82	.277	4	.174	-5	4	-0.5
1925	Bro-N	0	3	.000	5	2	0	0	0	16	22	14	7	0	2	9	7	1.938	3.94	106	6.27	.333	1	.200	1	0	0.1
Total	**6**	**29**	**28**	**.509**	**104**	**64**	**27**	**4**	**2**	**565**	**550**	**267**	**209**	**19**	**21**	**203**	**148**	**1.333**	**3.33**	**106**	**3.49**	**.261**	**29**	**.168**	**-2**	**34**	**-0.4**
• THORMODSGARD, Paul	Paul Gayton Thormodsgard b: 11/10/1953, San Francisco, CA BR/TR, 6'2", 190 lbs. Deb: 4/10/1977																										
1977	Min-A	11	15	.423	37	37	8	1	0	218	236	122	112	25	3	65	94	1.381	4.62	86	4.35	.280	0	....	-15	9	-1.5
1978	Min-A	1	6	.143	12	12	1	0	0	66	81	40	37	7	1	17	23	1.485	5.05	76	4.99	.308	0	....	-9	1	-0.9
1979	Min-A	0	0	....	1	0	0	0	0	1	3	1	1	1	0	0	1	3.000	9.00	49	25.51	.500	0	....	-1	0	0.0
Total	**3**	**12**	**21**	**.364**	**50**	**49**	**9**	**1**	**0**	**285**	**320**	**163**	**150**	**33**	**4**	**82**	**118**	**1.411**	**4.74**	**83**	**4.57**	**.288**	**0**	**....**	**-25**	**10**	**-2.5**
• THORNTON, John	John Thornton b: 1870, Washington, DC BL, 5'10.5", 175 lbs. Deb: 8/14/1889																										
1889	Was-N	0	1	.000	1	1	1	0	0	9	8	11	5	0	0	7	3	1.667	5.00	79	....	.230	0	.000	-1	0	-0.1
1891	Phi-N	15	16	.484	37	32	23	1	2	269	268	161	110	3	10	115	52	1.424	3.68	92	....	.250	17	.138	-10	14	-1.7
1892	Phi-N	0	2	.000	3	2	1	0	0	12	16	19	17	1	0	17	2	2.750	12.75	25	9.88	.308	5	.385	-13	0	-1.2
Total	**3**	**15**	**19**	**.441**	**41**	**35**	**25**	**1**	**2**	**290**	**292**	**191**	**132**	**4**	**10**	**139**	**57**	**1.486**	**4.10**	**83**	**0.41**	**.252**	**22**	**.154**	**-24**	**14**	**-3.0**
• THORNTON, Walter	Walter Miller Thornton b: 2/18/1875, Lewiston, ME d: 7/14/1960, Los Angeles, CA BL/TL, 6'1", 180 lbs. Deb: 7/1/1895 ♦																										
1895	Chi-N	2	0	1.000	7	2	2	0	1	40	58	50	27	3	5	31	13	2.225	6.08	84	8.48	.334	7	.318	-4	1	-0.2
1896	Chi-N	2	1	.667	5	5	2	0	0	23^2	30	26	15	1	0	13	10	1.817	5.70	79	5.64	.307	8	.364	-3	2	-0.1
1897	Chi-N	6	7	.462	16	16	15	0	0	130^1	164	91	68	4	6	51	55	1.650	4.70	95	5.07	.305	85	.321	-2	14	-0.6
1898	Chi-N	13	10	.565	28	25	21	2	0	215^1	226	116	80	4	18	56	56	1.310	3.34	107	3.48	.268	62	.295	4	19	0.8
Total	**4**	**23**	**18**	**.561**	**56**	**48**	**40**	**2**	**1**	**409^1**	**478**	**283**	**190**	**12**	**29**	**151**	**134**	**1.537**	**4.18**	**98**	**4.60**	**.289**	**162**	**.312**	**-5**	**36**	**-0.1**
• THORPE, Bob	Robert Joseph Thorpe b: 6/12/1935, San Diego, CA d: 3/17/1960, San Diego, CA BR/TR, 6'1", 170 lbs. Deb: 4/17/1955																										
1955	Chi-N	0	0	....	2	0	0	0	0	3	4	2	1	0	0	0	0	1.333	3.00	136	3.91	.333	0	....	0	0	0.0
• THROOP, George	George Lynford Throop b: 11/24/1950, Pasadena, CA BR/TR, 6'7", 205 lbs. Deb: 9/7/1975																										
1975	KC-A	0	0	....	7	0	0	0	2	9	8	5	4	1	0	2	8	1.111	4.00	96	2.91	.250	0	....	-0	1	0.0
1977	KC-A	0	0	....	4	0	0	0	1	5^1	1	2	2	1	0	4	1	.938	3.38	120	1.77	.059	0	....	0	1	0.0
1978	KC-A	1	0	1.000	1	0	0	0	0	3	2	0	0	0	0	3	2	1.667	0.00	....	3.96	.222	0	....	1	1	0.1
1979	KC-A	0	0	....	4	0	0	0	0	2^2	7	4	4	0	0	5	1	4.500	13.50	32	18.67	.467	0	....	-3	0	-0.3
	Hou-N	1	0	1.000	14	0	0	0	0	22^1	23	10	8	4	1	11	15	1.522	3.22	109	5.39	.271	0	.000	1	1	0.0
Total	**4**	**2**	**0**	**1.000**	**30**	**0**	**0**	**0**	**3**	**42^1**	**41**	**21**	**18**	**6**	**1**	**25**	**27**	**1.559**	**3.83**	**99**	**5.14**	**.259**	**0**	**.000**	**-0**	**4**	**-0.1**
• THUMAN, Lou	Louis Charles Frank Thuman b: 12/13/1916, Baltimore, MD d: 12/19/2000, Baltimore, MD BR/TR, 6'2", 185 lbs. Deb: 9/8/1939																										
1939	Was-A	0	0	....	3	0	0	0	0	4	5	6	4	0	0	2	1	1.750	9.00	48	4.34	.278	0	....	-2	0	-0.2
1940	Was-A	0	1	.000	2	0	0	0	0	5	10	11	8	0	0	7	0	3.400	14.40	29	12.88	.400	0	.000	-6	0	-0.6
Total	**2**	**0**	**1**	**.000**	**5**	**0**	**0**	**0**	**0**	**9**	**15**	**17**	**12**	**0**	**0**	**9**	**1**	**2.667**	**12.00**	**35**	**9.09**	**.349**	**0**	**.000**	**-8**	**0**	**-0.8**
• THURMAN, Corey	Corey Lamar Thurman b: 11/5/1978, Augusta, GA BR/TR, 6'1", 215 lbs. Deb: 4/5/2002																										
2002	Tor-A	2	3	.400	43	1	0	0	0	68	65	34	33	11	2	45	56	1.618	4.37	106	5.40	.248	0	.000	2	4	0.2
2003	Tor-A	1	1	.500	6	3	0	0	0	15^1	21	11	11	3	0	9	11	1.957	6.46	71	7.61	.313	0	....	-3	0	-0.3
Total	**2**	**3**	**4**	**.429**	**49**	**4**	**0**	**0**	**0**	**83^1**	**86**	**45**	**44**	**14**	**2**	**54**	**67**	**1.680**	**4.75**	**97**	**5.81**	**.261**	**0**	**.000**	**-0**	**4**	**-0.1**
• THURMAN, Mike	Michael Richard Thurman b: 7/22/1973, Corvallis, OR BR/TR, 6'4", 190 lbs. Deb: 9/2/1997																										
1997	Mon-N	1	0	1.000	5	2	0	0	0	11^2	8	9	7	3	1	4	8	1.029	5.40	78	3.42	.186	1	.500	-2	0	-0.1
1998	Mon-N	4	5	.444	14	13	0	0	0	67	60	38	35	7	3	26	32	1.284	4.70	90	3.57	.238	0	.000	-3	2	-0.5
1999	Mon-N	7	11	.389	29	27	0	0	0	146^2	140	84	66	17	7	52	85	1.309	4.05	111	3.89	.251	1	.025	10	8	0.6
2000	Mon-N	4	9	.308	17	17	0	0	0	88^1	112	69	63	9	3	46	52	1.789	6.42	75	6.25	.315	1	.042	-15	0	-1.6
2001	Mon-N	9	11	.450	28	26	0	0	0	147	172	90	87	21	6	50	96	1.510	5.33	84	5.19	.294	1	.024	-11	5	-1.4

YEAR TM-L	W	L	PCT	G	GS	CG	SH	SV	IP	H	R	ER	HR	HB	BB	SO	RAT	ERA	ERA+	CERA	OAV	BH	AVG	PR+	WS	TPW
2002 NY-A	1	0	1.000	12	2	0	0	0	33	45	21	19	2	1	12	23	1.727	5.18	84	5.88	.328	0	....	-2	1	-0.2
Total 6	26	36	.419	105	87	0	0	0	493^2	537	311	277	59	21	190	296	1.473	5.05	89	4.78	.278	4	.031	-23	16	-3.2
• THURMOND, Mark	Mark Anthony Thurmond b: 9/12/1956, Houston, TX BL/TL, 6', 193 lbs. Deb: 5/14/1983																									
1983 SD-N	7	3	.700	21	18	2	0	0	115^1	104	40	34	7	2	33	49	1.188	2.65	131	2.97	.248	2	.054	9	9	0.7
1984★ SD-N	14	8	.636	32	29	1	1	0	178^2	174	70	59	12	0	55	57	1.282	2.97	120	3.33	.256	11	.190	8	12	1.0
1985 SD-N	7	11	.389	36	23	1	1	2	138^1	154	70	61	9	3	44	57	1.431	3.97	89	4.24	.291	3	.088	-9	5	-1.1
1986 SD-N	3	7	.300	17	15	2	1	0	70^2	96	58	51	7	0	27	32	1.741	6.50	56	5.97	.325	6	.250	-22	0	-2.2
Det-A	4	1	.800	25	4	0	0	3	51^2	44	13	11	7	0	17	17	1.181	1.92	215	3.24	.234	0	....	12	6	1.2
1987★ Det-A	0	1	.000	48	0	0	0	5	61^2	83	32	29	5	0	24	21	1.735	4.23	100	5.92	.331	0	....	-0	3	0.0
1988 Bal-A	1	8	.111	43	6	0	0	3	74^2	80	43	38	10	2	27	29	1.433	4.58	85	4.68	.277	0	....	-6	2	-0.6
1989 Bal-A	2	4	.333	49	2	0	0	4	90	102	43	39	6	1	17	34	1.322	3.90	97	3.84	.288	0	....	-2	5	-0.2
1990 SF-N	2	3	.400	43	0	0	0	4	56^2	53	26	21	6	0	18	24	1.253	3.34	109	3.34	.257	0	.000	2	4	0.1
Total 8	40	46	.465	314	97	6	3	21	837^2	890	395	343	69	8	262	320	1.375	3.69	100	4.01	.277	22	.139	-9	46	-1.1
• THURSTON, Sloppy	Hollis John Thurston b: 6/2/1899, Fremont, NE d: 9/14/1973, Los Angeles, CA BR/TR, 5'11", 165 lbs. Deb: 4/19/1923																									
1923 StL-A	0	0	....	2	1	0	0	0	4	8	4	3	0	0	2	0	2.500	6.75	62	9.55	.421	0	....	-1	0	-0.1
Chi-A	7	8	.467	44	12	8	0	4	191^2	223	70	65	11	1	36	55	1.351	3.05	130	3.94	.308	25	.316	20	17	2.5
Yr.	7	8	.467	46	13	8	0	4	195^2	231	74	68	11	1	38	55	1.375	3.13	127	4.06	.311	25	.316	19	17	2.4
1924 Chi-A	20	14	.588	38	36	**28**	1	1	291	330	150	123	17	6	60	37	1.340	3.80	108	3.76	.290	31	.254	11	20	1.6
1925 Chi-A	10	14	.417	36	25	9	0	1	183	250	143	121	14	5	47	35	1.623	5.95	70	5.53	.335	24	.286	-37	4	-2.8
1926 Chi-A	6	8	.429	31	13	6	1	3	134^1	164	85	75	10	1	36	35	1.489	5.02	77	4.56	.311	19	.311	-19	5	-1.3
1927 Was-A	13	13	.500	29	28	13	2	0	205^1	254	118	102	16	2	60	38	1.529	4.47	91	4.78	.308	29	.315	-12	12	-0.2
1930 Bro-N	6	4	.600	24	11	5	2	1	106	110	46	40	4	0	17	26	1.198	3.40	145	2.91	.266	10	.200	15	10	1.3
1931 Bro-N	9	9	.500	24	17	11	0	0	143	175	72	63	3	1	39	23	1.497	3.97	96	4.18	.301	13	.217	-1	9	0.2
1932 Bro-N	12	8	.600	28	20	10	2	0	153	174	81	69	14	1	38	35	1.386	4.06	94	4.19	.287	17	.304	-4	10	0.1
1933 Bro-N	6	8	.429	32	15	5	0	3	131^1	171	70	66	4	6	34	22	1.561	4.52	71	4.82	.319	7	.159	-16	3	-1.8
Total 9	89	86	.509	288	178	95	8	13	1542^2	1859	839	727	93	23	369	306	1.444	4.24	93	4.33	.304	175	.270	-43	90	-0.6
• TIANT, Luis	Luis Clemente (Vega) Tiant b: 11/23/1940, Marianao, Cuba BR/TR, 6', 190 lbs. Deb: 7/19/1964																									
1964 Cle-A	10	4	.714	19	16	9	3	1	127	94	41	40	13	2	47	105	1.110	2.83	127	2.67	.207	5	.111	14	11	1.3
1965 Cle-A	11	11	.500	41	30	10	2	1	196^1	166	88	77	20	3	66	152	1.182	3.53	99	3.04	.228	6	.088	-1	9	-0.3
1966 Cle-A	12	11	.522	46	16	7	**5**	8	155	121	50	48	16	2	50	145	1.103	2.79	123	2.66	.213	4	.111	14	16	1.3
1967 Cle-A	12	9	.571	33	29	9	1	2	213^2	177	76	65	24	1	67	219	1.142	2.74	119	2.91	.221	18	.254	15	17	2.1
1968 Cle-A★	21	9	.700	34	32	19	**9**	0	258^1	152	53	46	16	4	73	264	.871	**1.60**	**185**	**1.51**	**.168**	7	.080	36	28	3.6
1969 Cle-A	9	20	.310	38	37	9	1	0	249^2	229	123	103	37	8	129	156	1.434	3.71	101	4.48	.246	19	.235	3	11	0.9
1970★ Min-A	7	3	.700	18	17	2	1	0	92^2	84	36	35	12	2	41	50	1.349	3.40	109	4.10	.246	13	.406	3	8	0.9
1971 Bos-A	1	7	.125	21	10	1	0	0	72^1	73	42	39	8	1	32	59	1.452	4.85	76	4.33	.259	3	.158	-8	1	-0.9
1972 Bos-A	15	6	.714	43	19	12	6	3	179	128	45	38	7	0	65	123	1.078	**1.91**	**168**	2.08	.202	6	.107	29	19	3.1
1973 Bos-A	20	13	.606	35	35	23	0	0	272	217	105	101	32	7	78	206	1.085	3.34	120	2.78	.219	0	....	19	21	1.9
1974 Bos-A★	22	13	.629	38	38	25	**7**	0	311^1	281	106	101	21	4	82	176	1.166	2.92	132	2.89	.241	0	....	35	29	3.6
1975★ Bos-A	18	14	.563	35	35	18	2	0	260	262	126	116	25	4	72	142	1.285	4.02	101	3.73	.264	0	.000	2	17	0.2
1976 Bos-A★	21	12	.636	38	38	19	3	0	279	274	107	95	25	3	64	131	1.211	3.06	128	3.35	.260	0	.000	29	22	3.1
1977 Bos-A	12	8	.600	32	32	3	3	0	188^2	210	98	95	26	2	51	124	1.383	4.53	99	4.47	.279	0	....	2	12	0.2
1978 Bos-A	13	8	.619	32	31	12	5	0	212^1	185	80	78	26	5	57	114	1.140	3.31	124	3.11	.234	0	....	17	17	1.8
1979 NY-A	13	8	.619	30	30	5	1	0	195^2	190	94	85	22	0	53	104	1.242	3.91	104	3.47	.251	0	....	0	12	0.0
1980 NY-A	8	9	.471	25	25	3	0	0	136^1	139	79	74	10	1	50	84	1.386	4.89	80	3.85	.265	0	....	-14	4	-1.4
1981 Pit-N	2	5	.286	9	9	1	0	0	57^1	54	31	25	3	0	19	32	1.273	3.92	92	3.09	.243	3	.188	-2	2	-0.1
1982 Cal-A	2	2	.500	6	5	0	0	0	29^2	39	20	19	3	0	8	30	1.584	5.76	70	5.29	.310	0	....	-6	0	-0.6
Total 19	229	172	.571	573	484	187	49	15	3486^1	3075	1400	1280	346	49	1104	2416	1.199	3.30	115	3.20	.236	84	.164	186	256	20.8
• TIBBS, Jay	Jay Lindsey Tibbs b: 1/4/1962, Birmingham, AL BR/TR, 6'3", 185 lbs. Deb: 7/15/1984																									
1984 Cin-N	6	2	.750	14	14	3	1	0	100^2	87	34	32	4	0	33	40	1.192	2.86	132	2.76	.238	5	.139	11	9	1.1
1985 Cin-N	10	16	.385	35	34	5	2	0	218	216	111	95	14	0	83	98	1.372	3.92	96	3.65	.262	6	.092	-5	9	-0.9
1986 Mon-N	7	9	.438	35	31	3	2	0	190^1	181	96	84	12	3	70	117	1.319	3.97	93	3.52	.256	7	.130	-6	7	-0.6
1987 Mon-N	4	5	.444	19	12	0	0	0	83	95	55	46	10	0	34	54	1.554	4.99	84	5.11	.289	3	.120	-6	2	-0.6
1988 Bal-A	4	15	.211	30	24	1	0	0	158^2	184	103	95	18	3	63	82	1.557	5.39	72	5.16	.293	0	....	-27	1	-2.8
1989 Bal-A	5	0	1.000	10	8	1	0	0	54^1	62	17	17	2	0	20	30	1.509	2.82	135	4.31	.287	0	....	6	5	0.6
1990 Bal-A	2	7	.222	10	10	0	0	0	50^2	55	34	32	8	0	14	23	1.362	5.68	67	4.47	.279	0	....	-11	0	-1.1
Pit-N	1	0	1.000	5	0	0	0	0	7	7	2	2	0	0	2	4	1.286	2.57	141	3.01	.259	0	....	1	1	0.1
Total 7	39	54	.419	158	133	13	5	0	862^2	887	452	403	68	6	319	448	1.398	4.20	91	4.02	.269	21	.117	-39	34	-4.3
• TIDROW, Dick	Richard William "Dirt" Tidrow b: 5/14/1947, San Francisco, CA BR/TR, 6'4", 213 lbs. Deb: 4/18/1972																									
1972 Cle-A	14	15	.483	39	34	10	3	0	237^1	200	83	73	21	6	70	123	1.138	2.77	116	2.79	.230	7	.100	9	17	0.7
1973 Cle-A	14	16	.467	42	40	13	2	0	274^2	289	150	135	31	8	95	138	1.398	4.42	89	4.29	.270	0	....	-14	12	-1.5
1974 Cle-A	1	3	.250	4	4	0	0	0	19	21	17	15	4	2	13	8	1.789	7.11	51	6.89	.276	0	....	-7	0	-0.8
NY-A	11	9	.550	33	25	5	0	1	190^2	205	99	82	14	4	53	100	1.353	3.87	90	3.88	.279	0	....	-12	8	-1.2
Yr.	12	12	.500	37	29	5	0	1	209^2	226	116	97	18	6	66	108	1.393	4.16	84	4.15	.279	0	....	-19	8	-2.0
1975 NY-A	6	3	.667	37	0	0	0	5	69^1	65	27	24	5	3	31	38	1.385	3.12	117	3.83	.256	0	....	2	6	0.2
1976★ NY-A	4	5	.444	47	2	0	0	10	92^1	80	29	27	5	1	24	65	1.126	2.63	130	2.58	.233	0	....	5	9	0.5
1977★ NY-A	11	4	.733	49	7	0	0	5	151	143	57	53	20	2	41	83	1.219	3.16	125	3.46	.250	0	....	10	13	1.0
1978★ NY-A	7	11	.389	31	25	4	0	0	185^1	191	87	79	13	5	53	73	1.317	3.84	94	3.68	.267	0	....	-6	8	-0.6
1979 NY-A	2	1	.667	14	0	0	0	2	22^2	38	20	20	5	0	4	7	1.853	7.94	51	8.83	.409	0	....	-10	0	-1.0
Chi-N	11	5	.688	63	0	0	0	4	102^2	86	35	31	5	2	42	68	1.247	2.72	151	2.84	.231	2	.200	17	12	1.8
1980 Chi-N	6	5	.545	**84**	0	0	0	6	116	97	44	36	10	5	53	97	1.293	2.79	140	3.24	.229	0	.000	16	11	1.6
1981 Chi-N	3	10	.231	51	0	0	0	9	74^2	73	45	42	6	1	30	39	1.379	5.06	73	3.46	.256	0	.000	-10	3	-1.1
1982 Chi-N	8	3	.727	65	0	0	0	6	103^2	106	45	39	6	3	29	62	1.302	3.39	110	3.39	.265	0	.000	5	9	0.5
1983★ Chi-A	2	4	.333	50	1	0	0	7	91^2	86	50	43	13	1	34	66	1.309	4.22	99	3.72	.242	0	....	-1	5	-0.1
1984 NY-N	0	0	....	11	0	0	0	0	15^2	25	19	16	5	0	7	8	2.043	9.19	38	9.82	.357	0	....	-10	0	-1.0
Total 13	100	94	.515	620	138	32	5	55	1746^2	1705	807	715	163	43	579	975	1.308	3.68	101	3.66	.257	9	.095	-5	113	-0.9
• TIEFENAUER, Bobby	Bobby Gene Tiefenauer b: 10/20/1929, Desloge, MO d: 6/13/2000, Desloge, MO BR/TR, 6'2", 185 lbs. Deb: 7/14/1952 C																									
1952 StL-N	0	0	....	6	0	0	0	0	8	12	8	7	1	0	7	3	2.375	7.88	47	8.97	.343	0	.000	-4	0	-0.4
1955 StL-N	1	4	.200	18	0	0	0	0	32^2	31	19	16	6	4	10	16	1.255	4.41	92	4.34	.261	0	.000	-1	1	-0.1
1960 Cle-A	0	1	.000	6	0	0	0	0	9	8	2	2	0	0	3	2	1.222	2.00	187	2.60	.242	0	.000	2	1	0.2
1961 StL-N	0	0	....	3	0	0	0	0	4^1	9	4	3	0	0	4	3	3.000	6.23	71	13.27	.450	0	....	-1	0	-0.1
1962 Hou-N	2	4	.333	43	0	0	0	1	85	91	42	41	6	2	21	60	1.318	4.34	86	3.73	.277	1	.111	-4	4	-0.4
1963 Mil-N	1	1	.500	12	0	0	0	2	29^2	20	4	4	1	0	4	22	.809	1.21	265	1.34	.194	0	.000	6	4	0.6
1964 Mil-N	4	6	.400	46	0	0	0	13	73	61	33	26	6	3	15	48	1.041	3.21	110	2.46	.225	0	.000	2	6	0.1
1965 Mil-N	0	1	.000	6	0	0	0	0	7	8	7	6	1	1	3	7	1.571	7.71	46	5.37	.286	0	....	-3	0	-0.3
NY-A	1	1	.500	10	0	0	0	2	20^1	19	10	8	3	1	5	15	1.180	3.54	96	3.57	.253	0	.000	-0	1	0.0
Cle-A	0	5	.000	15	0	0	0	4	22^1	24	17	12	3	1	10	13	1.522	4.84	72	4.73	.273	0	.000	-3	0	-0.4
Yr.	1	6	.143	25	0	0	0	6	42^2	43	27	20	6	2	15	28	1.359	4.22	82	4.18	.264	0	.000	-3	1	-0.4
1967 Cle-A	0	1	.000	5	0	0	0	0	11^1	9	3	1	0	0	3	6	1.059	0.79	411	1.86	.225	0	....	3	1	0.4
1968 Chi-N	0	1	.000	9	0	0	0	1	13^1	20	12	9	2	0	2	9	1.650	6.08	52	5.89	.351	0	.000	-4	0	-0.5
Total 10	9	25	.265	179	0	0	0	23	316	312	161	135	29	12	87	204	1.263	3.84	94	3.63	.260	1	.026	-7	18	-0.9
• TIEFENTHALER, Verle	Verle Matthew Tiefenthaler b: 7/11/1937, Brenda, IA BL/TR, 6'1", 190 lbs. Deb: 4/19/1962																									
1962 Chi-A	0	0	....	3	0	0	0	0	3^2	6	4	4	1	0	7	1	3.545	9.82	40	16.81	.353	0	....	-2	0	-0.2

YEAR TM-L	W	L	PCT	G	GS	CG	SH	SV	IP	H	R	ER	HR	HB	BB	SO	RAT	ERA	ERA+	CERA	OAV	BH	AVG	PR+	WS	TPW
• TIERNAN, Mike	Michael Joseph "Silent Mike" Tiernan b: 1/21/1867, Trenton, NJ d: 11/9/1918, New York, NY BL/TL, 5'11", 165 lbs. Deb: 4/30/1887 U ♦																									
1887 NY-N	1	2	.333	5	0	0	0	**1**	19^{2}	40	25	19	2	1	7	3	2.034	8.69	43	....	.408	149	.339	-11	12	-0.4
• TIETJE, Les	Leslie William "Toots" Tietje b: 9/11/1911, Sumner, IA d: 10/2/1996, Rochester, MN BR/TR, 6'.5", 178 lbs. Deb: 9/18/1933																									
1933 Chi-A	2	0	1.000	3	3	1	0	0	22^{1}	16	8	6	1	0	15	9	1.388	2.42	175	3.05	.203	1	.125	5	2	0.5
1934 Chi-A	5	14	.263	34	22	6	1	0	176	174	106	94	20	2	96	81	1.534	4.81	98	4.57	.257	1	.017	3	8	-0.4
1935 Chi-A	9	15	.375	30	21	9	1	0	169^{2}	184	88	81	14	2	81	64	1.562	4.30	107	4.66	.277	12	.197	4	11	0.3
1936 Chi-A	0	0	....	2	0	0	0	0	2^{1}	6	7	7	0	0	5	3	4.714	27.00	19	20.84	.462	0	....	-6	0	-0.5
StL-A	3	5	.375	14	7	2	0	0	50^{1}	65	44	37	2	2	30	16	1.887	6.62	81	5.95	.310	1	.067	-6	1	-0.6
Yr.	3	5	.375	16	7	2	0	0	52^{2}	71	51	44	2	2	35	19	2.013	7.52	71	6.61	.318	1	.067	-12	1	-1.1
1937 StL-A	1	2	.333	5	4	2	0	0	30	32	15	14	0	0	17	5	1.633	4.20	115	4.32	.283	0	.000	2	2	0.1
1938 StL-A	2	5	.286	17	8	2	1	0	62	83	55	52	8	0	38	15	1.952	7.55	66	7.17	.327	2	.111	-18	0	-1.7
Total 6	22	41	.349	105	65	22	3	0	512^{2}	560	323	291	45	6	282	193	1.642	5.11	94	5.04	.279	17	.099	-14	24	-2.3
• TIFT, Ray	Raymond Frank Tift b: 6/21/1884, Fitchburg, MA d: 3/29/1945, Verona, NJ TL Deb: 8/7/1907																									
1907 NY-A	0	0	....	4	1	0	0	0	19	33	14	10	0	0	4	6	1.947	4.74	59	6.74	.383	0	.000	-4	0	-0.5
• TILLMAN, Johnny	John Lawrence "Ducky" Tillman b: 10/6/1893, Bridgeport, CT d: 4/7/1964, Harrisburg, PA BB/TR, 5'11", 170 lbs. Deb: 9/20/1915																									
1915 StL-A	1	0	1.000	2	1	0	0	0	10	6	2	1	0	0	4	6	1.000	0.90	318	1.53	.176	0	.000	2	1	0.2
• TILLOTSON, Thad	Thaddeus Asa Tillotson b: 12/20/1940, Merced, CA BR/TR, 6'2.5", 195 lbs. Deb: 4/14/1967																									
1967 NY-A	3	9	.250	43	5	1	0	2	98^{1}	99	52	44	9	2	39	62	1.403	4.03	78	4.02	.261	1	.063	-9	2	-1.0
1968 NY-A	1	0	1.000	7	0	0	0	0	10^{1}	11	6	5	0	0	7	1	1.742	4.35	67	4.27	.282	0	.000	-2	0	-0.2
Total 2	4	9	.308	50	5	1	0	2	108^{2}	110	58	49	9	2	46	63	1.436	4.06	76	4.05	.263	1	.059	-10	2	-1.2
• TIMBERLAKE, Gary	Gary Dale Timberlake b: 8/8/1948, Laconia, IN BR/TL, 6'2", 205 lbs. Deb: 6/18/1969																									
1969 Sea-A	0	0	....	2	2	0	0	0	6	7	6	5	0	0	9	4	2.667	7.50	48	8.26	.269	0	.000	-2	0	-0.3
• TIMLIN, Mike	Michael August Timlin b: 3/10/1966, Midland, TX BR/TR, 6'4", 210 lbs. Deb: 4/8/1991																									
1991* Tor-A	11	6	.647	63	3	0	0	3	108^{1}	94	43	38	6	1	50	85	1.329	3.16	133	3.14	.233	0	....	13	11	1.3
1992* Tor-A	0	2	.000	26	0	0	0	1	43^{2}	45	23	20	0	1	20	35	1.489	4.12	99	3.68	.271	0	....	-0	2	0.0
1993* Tor-A	4	2	.667	54	0	0	0	1	55^{2}	63	32	29	7	1	27	49	1.617	4.69	92	5.32	.284	0	....	-2	3	-0.2
1994 Tor-A	0	1	.000	34	0	0	0	2	40	41	25	23	5	2	20	38	1.525	5.18	93	5.01	.261	0	....	-1	2	-0.1
1995 Tor-A	4	3	.571	31	0	0	0	5	42	38	13	10	1	2	17	36	1.310	2.14	220	3.04	.242	0	....	12	6	1.1
1996 Tor-A	1	6	.143	59	0	0	0	31	56^{2}	47	25	23	4	2	18	52	1.147	3.65	137	2.74	.229	0	....	7	10	0.7
1997 Tor-A	3	2	.600	38	0	0	0	9	47	41	17	15	6	1	15	36	1.191	2.87	160	3.30	.243	0	....	8	7	0.8
* Sea-A	3	2	.600	26	0	0	0	1	25^{2}	28	13	11	2	0	5	9	1.286	3.86	117	3.59	.280	0	....	2	2	0.2
Yr.	6	4	.600	64	0	0	0	10	72^{2}	69	30	26	8	1	20	45	1.225	3.22	141	3.40	.257	0	....	10	9	1.0
1998 Sea-A	3	3	.500	70	0	0	0	19	79^{1}	78	26	26	5	3	16	60	1.185	2.95	157	3.17	.264	0	....	16	12	1.5
1999 Bal-A	3	9	.250	62	0	0	0	27	63	51	30	25	9	5	23	50	1.175	3.57	131	3.46	.221	0	....	7	9	0.6
2000 Bal-A	2	3	.400	37	0	0	0	11	35	37	22	19	6	2	15	26	1.486	4.89	97	5.08	.276	0	....	-1	3	0.0
* StL-N	3	1	.750	25	0	0	0	1	29^{2}	30	11	11	2	2	20	26	1.685	3.34	138	5.05	.265	0	....	4	3	0.4
2001* StL-N	4	5	.444	67	0	0	0	3	72^{2}	78	35	33	6	3	19	47	1.335	4.09	104	3.95	.277	0	.000	-0	5	0.0
2002 StL-N	1	3	.250	42	1	0	0	0	61	48	19	17	9	4	7	35	.902	2.51	158	2.41	.215	0	.000	9	5	0.8
Phi-N	3	3	.500	30	0	0	0	0	35^{2}	27	16	15	6	1	7	15	.953	3.79	103	2.55	.206	0	....	0	3	0.0
Yr.	4	6	.400	72	1	0	0	0	96^{2}	75	35	32	15	5	14	50	.921	2.98	132	2.46	.212	0	.000	9	8	0.8
2003* Bos-A	6	4	.600	72	0	0	0	2	83^{2}	77	37	33	11	4	9	65	1.028	3.55	128	2.81	.239	0	....	11	8	1.1
Total 13	51	55	.481	736	4	0	0	116	879	823	387	348	85	34	288	664	1.264	3.56	125	3.51	.248	0	.000	85	91	8.1
• TIMMERMANN, Tom	Thomas Henry Timmermann b: 5/12/1940, Breese, IL BR/TR, 6'4", 215 lbs. Deb: 6/18/1969																									
1969 Det-A	4	3	.571	31	1	1	0	1	55^{2}	50	22	17	1	2	26	42	1.365	2.75	136	3.19	.238	1	.111	6	5	0.6
1970 Det-A	6	7	.462	61	0	0	0	27	85^{1}	90	44	39	3	2	34	49	1.453	4.11	91	3.72	.273	0	.000	-1	11	-0.3
1971 Det-A	7	6	.538	52	2	0	0	4	84	82	36	36	6	3	37	51	1.417	3.86	93	4.02	.262	1	.053	-2	5	-0.4
1972 Det-A	8	10	.444	34	25	3	2	0	149^{2}	121	57	48	12	5	41	88	1.082	2.89	109	2.54	.216	6	.136	3	9	0.3
1973 Det-A	1	1	.500	17	1	0	0	1	39	39	17	16	4	0	11	21	1.282	3.69	111	3.61	.258	0	....	2	3	0.2
Cle-A	8	7	.533	29	15	4	0	2	124^{1}	117	73	68	15	3	54	62	1.375	4.92	80	4.09	.251	0	....	-13	5	-1.4
Yr.	9	8	.529	46	16	4	0	3	163^{1}	156	90	84	19	3	65	83	1.353	4.63	85	3.98	.252	0	....	-11	8	-1.2
1974 Cle-A	1	1	.500	4	0	0	0	0	10	9	6	6	1	0	5	2	1.400	5.40	67	4.03	.250	0	....	-2	0	-0.2
Total 6	35	35	.500	228	44	8	2	35	548	508	255	230	42	15	208	315	1.307	3.78	96	3.47	.246	8	.091	-8	38	-1.2
• TINCUP, Ben	Austin Ben Tincup b: 12/14/1890, Adair, OK d: 7/5/1980, Claremore, OK BL/TR, 6'1", 180 lbs. Deb: 5/22/1914 C																									
1914 Phi-N	8	10	.444	28	17	9	3	2	155	165	71	45	0	4	62	108	1.465	2.61	112	3.83	.286	9	.170	10	8	1.0
1915 Phi-N	0	0	....	10	0	0	0	0	31	26	8	7	1	0	9	10	1.129	2.03	135	2.57	.263	0	.000	2	2	0.1
1918 Phi-N	0	1	.000	8	1	0	0	0	16^{2}	24	20	14	0	0	6	6	1.800	7.56	40	5.30	.329	1	.125	-8	0	-1.0
1928 Chi-N	0	0	....	2	0	0	0	0	9	14	7	7	0	0	1	3	1.667	7.00	55	5.33	.378	0	.000	-3	0	-0.4
Total 4	8	11	.421	48	18	9	3	2	211^{2}	229	106	73	1	4	78	127	1.450	3.10	96	3.82	.291	10	.135	1	10	-0.2
• TINNING, Bud	Lyle Forrest Tinning b: 3/12/1906, Pilger, NE d: 1/17/1961, Evansville, IN BB/TR, 5'11", 198 lbs. Deb: 4/20/1932																									
1932* Chi-N	5	3	.625	24	7	2	0	0	93^{1}	93	34	29	3	2	24	30	1.254	2.80	135	3.10	.263	2	.087	9	8	0.8
1933 Chi-N	13	6	.684	32	21	10	3	1	175^{1}	169	73	62	3	4	60	59	1.306	3.18	103	3.12	.255	14	.209	-2	11	-0.2
1934 Chi-N	4	6	.400	39	7	1	1	3	129^{1}	134	59	48	9	1	46	44	1.392	3.34	116	3.80	.269	7	.179	7	9	0.6
1935 StL-N	0	0	....	4	0	0	0	0	7^{2}	9	6	5	1	1	5	2	1.826	5.87	70	6.74	.300	0	.000	-2	0	-0.2
Total 4	22	15	.595	99	35	13	4	4	405^{2}	405	172	144	16	8	135	135	1.331	3.19	112	3.40	.262	23	.177	11	28	1.0
• TIPPLE, Dan	Daniel E. "Rusty,Big Dan" Tipple b: 2/13/1890, Rockford, IL d: 3/26/1960, Omaha, NE BR/TR, 6', 176 lbs. Deb: 9/18/1915																									
1915 NY-A	1	1	.500	3	2	2	0	0	19	14	6	2	1	0	11	14	1.316	0.95	309	2.89	.203	0	.000	4	2	0.3
• TISING, Jack	Johnnie Joseph Tising b: 10/9/1903, High Point, MO d: 9/5/1967, Leadville, CO BL/TR, 6'2", 180 lbs. Deb: 4/24/1936																									
1936 Pit-N	1	3	.250	10	6	1	0	0	47	52	26	22	5	0	24	27	1.617	4.21	96	4.87	.272	3	.273	-0	2	0.0
• TITCOMB, Cannonball	Ledell Titcomb b: 8/21/1866, West Baldwin, ME d: 6/8/1950, Kingston, NH BL/TL, 5'6", 157 lbs. Deb: 5/5/1886																									
1886 Phi-N	0	5	.000	5	5	5	0	0	41	43	45	17	1	....	24	24	1.634	3.73	88	....	.260	1	.063	-1	0	-0.2
1887 Phi-a	1	2	.333	3	3	3	0	0	24	50	30	18	1	0	19	16	2.083	6.75	63	....	.411	2	.167	-7	0	-0.7
NY-N	4	3	.571	9	9	9	0	0	72	105	50	31	3	1	37	34	1.458	3.88	97	....	.331	3	.100	-2	4	-0.5
1888* NY-N	14	8	.636	23	23	22	4	0	197	149	91	49	4	5	46	129	.990	2.24	121	....	.202	10	.122	5	12	0.1
1889 NY-N	1	2	.333	3	3	3	0	0	26	27	26	19	1	2	16	7	1.654	6.58	60	....	.259	1	.083	-8	0	-0.8
1890 Roc-a	10	9	.526	20	19	19	1	0	168^{2}	168	123	70	6	14	97	73	1.571	3.74	95	....	.252	8	.107	-4	6	-0.9
Total 5	30	29	.508	63	62	61	5	0	528^{2}	542	365	204	16	22	239	283	1.371	3.47	98	....	.257	25	.110	-18	22	-3.0
• TOBIK, Dave	David Vance Tobik b: 3/2/1953, Euclid, OH BR/TR, 6'1", 195 lbs. Deb: 8/26/1978																									
1978 Det-A	0	0	....	5	0	0	0	0	12	12	5	5	1	0	3	11	1.250	3.75	103	3.46	.261	0	....	-0	1	0.0
1979 Det-A	3	5	.375	37	0	0	0	3	68^{2}	59	34	33	12	0	25	48	1.223	4.33	100	3.52	.231	0	....	-1	4	-0.1
1980 Det-A	1	0	1.000	17	1	0	0	0	61	61	27	27	7	0	21	34	1.344	3.98	103	3.97	.266	0	....	2	4	0.2
1981 Det-A	2	2	.500	27	0	0	0	1	60^{1}	47	19	18	7	0	33	32	1.326	2.69	141	3.44	.215	0	....	6	5	0.6
1982 Det-A	4	9	.308	51	1	0	0	9	98^{2}	86	45	39	8	1	38	63	1.257	3.56	114	3.17	.241	0	....	3	8	0.3
1983 Tex-A	2	1	.667	27	0	0	0	9	44	36	18	18	2	0	13	30	1.114	3.68	109	2.33	.222	0	....	2	5	0.2
1984 Tex-A	1	6	.143	24	0	0	0	5	42^{1}	44	20	17	5	1	17	30	1.441	3.61	115	4.26	.265	0	....	3	3	0.3
1985 Sea-A	1	0	1.000	8	0	0	0	1	9	10	8	6	2	0	3	8	1.444	6.00	70	5.20	.286	0	....	-2	0	-0.2
Total 8	14	23	.378	196	2	0	0	28	396	355	176	163	44	2	153	256	1.283	3.70	110	3.47	.242	0	....	13	30	1.3

YEAR	TM-L	W	L	PCT	G	GS	CG	SH	SV	IP	H	R	ER	HR	HB	BB	SO	RAT	ERA	ERA+	CERA	OAV	BH	AVG	PR+	WS	TPW
• TOBIN, Jim	James Anthony "Abba Dabba" Tobin b: 12/27/1912, Oakland, CA d: 5/19/1969, Oakland, CA BR/TR, 6', 185 lbs. Deb: 4/30/1937																										
1937	Pit-N	6	3	.667	20	8	7	0	1	87	74	38	29	1	1	28	37	1.172	3.00	129	2.39	.226	15	.441	8	10	1.5
1938	Pit-N	14	12	.538	40	33	14	2	0	241^1	254	109	93	17	6	66	70	1.326	3.47	109	3.69	.270	25	.243	5	17	1.1
1939	Pit-N	9	9	.500	25	19	8	0	0	145^1	194	84	73	7	2	33	43	1.562	4.52	85	4.86	.319	18	.243	-8	7	-0.3
1940	Bos-N	7	3	.700	15	11	9	0	0	96^1	102	41	41	8	0	24	29	1.308	3.83	97	3.58	.264	12	.279	-3	7	0.0
1941	Bos-N	12	12	.500	33	26	20	3	0	238	229	91	82	12	0	60	61	1.214	3.10	115	2.93	.253	19	.184	11	17	1.4
1942	Bos-N	12	21	.364	37	33	**28**	1	0	**287^2**	283	145	127	20	6	96	71	1.317	3.97	84	3.51	.257	28	.246	-18	15	-0.4
1943	Bos-N	14	14	.500	33	30	24	1	0	250	241	96	74	12	2	69	52	1.240	2.66	128	3.00	.251	30	.280	18	24	2.8
1944	Bos-N★	18	19	.486	43	36	**28**	5	3	299^1	271	125	100	18	1	97	83	1.229	3.01	127	2.93	.240	22	.190	26	23	3.3
1945	Bos-N	9	14	.391	27	25	16	0	0	196^2	220	101	84	10	5	56	38	1.403	3.84	100	3.93	.282	11	.143	-1	12	0.5
	*Det-A	4	5	.444	14	6	2	0	1	58^1	61	31	23	2	4	28	14	1.526	3.55	99	4.27	.274	3	.120	-1	3	0.0
Total	9	105	112	.484	287	227	156	12	5	1900	1929	861	726	107	27	557	498	1.308	3.44	106	3.42	.262	183	.230	36	135	9.8
• TOBIN, Pat	Marion Brooks Tobin b: 1/28/1916, Hermitage, AR d: 1/21/1975, Shreveport, LA BR/TR, 6'1", 198 lbs. Deb: 8/21/1941																										
1941	Phi-A	0	0	....	1	0	0	0	0	1	4	5	4	0	0	2	0	6.000	36.00	12	28.70	.571	0	....	-4	0	-0.3
• TODD, Frank	George Franklin Todd b: 10/18/1869, Aberdeen, MD d: 8/11/1919, Havre de Grace, MD TL Deb: 7/14/1898																										
1898	Lou-N	0	2	.000	4	2	0	0	0	11	23	21	17	0	2	8	5	2.818	13.91	26	12.21	.422	1	.200	-13	0	-1.1
• TODD, Jackson	Jackson A. Todd b: 11/20/1951, Tulsa, OK BR/TR, 6'2", 180 lbs. Deb: 5/5/1977																										
1977	NY-N	3	6	.333	19	10	0	0	0	71^2	78	41	38	8	2	20	39	1.367	4.77	78	4.12	.273	1	.059	-8	1	-1.0
1979	Tor-A	0	1	.000	12	1	0	0	0	32^1	40	26	21	7	1	7	14	1.454	5.85	74	5.59	.299	0	....	-6	0	-0.5
1980	Tor-A	5	2	.714	12	12	4	0	0	85	90	40	38	14	2	30	44	1.412	4.02	107	4.88	.276	0	....	2	6	0.2
1981	Tor-A	2	7	.222	21	13	3	0	0	97^2	94	51	43	10	4	31	41	1.280	3.96	99	3.68	.251	0	....	0	4	0.0
Total	4	10	16	.385	64	36	7	0	0	286^2	302	158	140	39	9	88	138	1.360	4.40	92	4.36	.270	1	.059	-12	11	-1.3
• TODD, Jim	James Richard Todd b: 9/21/1947, Lancaster, PA BL/TR, 6'2", 190 lbs. Deb: 4/29/1974																										
1974	Chi-N	4	2	.667	43	6	0	0	3	88	82	45	38	7	3	41	42	1.398	3.89	98	3.96	.252	1	.063	4	5	0.2
1975*	Oak-A	8	3	.727	58	0	0	0	12	122	104	40	31	4	3	33	50	1.123	2.29	159	2.48	.234	0	....	18	13	1.8
1976	Oak-A	7	8	.467	49	0	0	0	4	82^2	87	43	35	6	6	34	22	1.464	3.81	88	4.40	.276	0	....	-3	4	-0.3
1977	Chi-N	1	1	.500	20	0	0	0	0	30^2	47	37	31	1	2	19	17	2.152	9.10	48	7.57	.336	0	.000	-15	0	-1.6
1978	Sea-A	3	4	.429	49	2	0	0	3	106^2	113	52	46	4	0	61	37	1.631	3.88	98	4.67	.280	0	....	-0	6	0.0
1979	Oak-A	2	5	.286	51	0	0	0	2	81	108	66	59	12	2	51	26	1.963	6.56	62	7.40	.329	0	....	-20	0	-2.0
Total	6	25	23	.521	270	8	0	0	24	511	541	283	240	34	16	239	194	1.526	4.23	91	4.59	.277	1	.059	-17	28	-1.8
• TOENES, Hal	William Harrel Toenes b: 10/8/1917, Mobile, AL BR/TR, 5'11.5", 175 lbs. Deb: 9/17/1947																										
1947	Was-A	0	1	.000	3	1	0	0	0	6^2	11	5	5	0	0	2	5	1.950	6.75	55	6.70	.379	0	.000	-2	0	-0.2
• TOLAR, Kevin	Kevin Anthony Tolar b: 1/28/1971, Panama City, FL BR/TL, 6'3", 225 lbs. Deb: 9/11/2000																										
2000	Det-A	0	0	....	5	0	0	0	0	3	1	1	1	0	0	1	3	.667	3.00	161	0.63	.091	0	....	1	0	0.1
2001	Det-A	0	0	....	9	0	0	0	0	10^2	7	8	8	0	0	13	11	1.875	6.75	64	4.35	.189	0	....	-3	0	-0.3
2003	Bos-A	0	0	....	6	0	0	0	0	4	5	5	4	1	0	2	3	1.750	9.00	51	7.44	.313	0	....	-2	0	-0.2
Total	3	0	0	....	20	0	0	0	0	17^2	13	14	13	1	0	16	17	1.642	6.62	67	4.42	.203	0	....	-4	0	-0.4
• TOLIVER, Freddie	Freddie Lee Toliver b: 2/3/1961, Natchez, MS BR/TR, 6'1", 170 lbs. Deb: 9/15/1984																										
1984	Cin-N	0	0	....	3	1	0	0	0	10	7	2	1	0	0	7	4	1.400	0.90	420	2.96	.206	0	.000	3	1	0.3
1985	Phi-N	0	4	.000	11	3	0	0	1	25	27	15	13	2	0	17	23	1.760	4.68	79	5.40	.273	2	.500	-2	0	-0.2
1986	Phi-N	0	2	.000	5	5	0	0	0	25^2	28	14	10	0	0	11	20	1.519	3.51	110	4.01	.286	0	.000	1	1	0.1
1987	Phi-N	1	1	.500	10	4	0	0	0	30^1	34	19	19	2	1	17	25	1.681	5.64	75	5.13	.291	0	.000	-5	0	-0.6
1988	Min-A	7	6	.538	21	19	0	0	0	114^2	116	57	54	8	1	52	69	1.465	4.24	96	4.25	.270	0	....	-2	6	-0.2
1989	Min-A	1	3	.250	7	5	0	0	0	29	39	26	25	2	1	15	11	1.862	7.76	53	6.44	.317	0	....	-12	0	-1.2
	SD-N	0	0	....	9	0	0	0	0	14	17	14	11	5	1	9	14	1.857	7.07	49	9.27	.321	0	....	-6	0	-0.6
1993	Pit-N	1	0	1.000	12	0	0	0	0	21^2	20	10	9	2	2	8	14	1.292	3.74	108	3.99	.267	0	.000	1	2	0.0
Total	7	10	16	.385	78	37	0	0	1	270^1	288	157	142	21	6	136	180	1.568	4.73	84	4.86	.280	2	.111	-22	10	-2.3
• TOLLBERG, Brian	Brian Patrick Tollberg b: 9/16/1972, Tampa, FL BR/TR, 6'3", 195 lbs. Deb: 6/20/2000																										
2000	SD-N	4	5	.444	19	19	1	0	0	118	126	58	47	13	5	35	76	1.364	3.58	120	4.26	.274	3	.094	8	6	0.6
2001	SD-N	10	4	.714	19	19	0	0	0	117^1	133	58	56	15	2	25	71	1.347	4.30	93	4.29	.287	8	.200	-2	6	-0.1
2002	SD-N	1	5	.167	12	11	0	0	0	61^2	88	47	42	11	1	19	33	1.735	6.13	61	6.84	.342	3	.158	-16	0	-1.5
2003	SD-N	0	2	.000	3	3	0	0	0	10^1	9	11	8	1	0	4	2	1.258	6.97	56	3.15	.231	0	.000	-3	0	-0.4
Total	4	15	16	.484	53	52	1	0	0	307^1	356	174	153	40	8	83	182	1.428	4.48	90	4.75	.292	14	.151	-13	12	-1.3
• TOMANEK, Dick	Richard Carl "Bones" Tomanek b: 1/6/1931, Avon Lake, OH BL/TL, 6'1", 175 lbs. Deb: 9/25/1953																										
1953	Cle-A	1	0	1.000	1	1	1	0	0	9	6	3	2	1	1	6	6	1.333	2.00	187	3.39	.176	0	.000	2	1	0.1
1954	Cle-A	0	0	....	1	0	0	0	0	1^2	1	1	1	1	0	1	0	1.200	5.40	68	5.67	.167	0	....	-0	0	0.0
1957	Cle-A	2	1	.667	34	2	0	0	0	69^2	67	51	44	13	1	37	55	1.493	5.68	65	4.96	.248	3	.231	-14	0	-1.4
1958	Cle-A	2	3	.400	18	6	2	0	0	57^2	61	37	36	8	2	28	42	1.543	5.62	65	5.22	.276	2	.118	-13	0	-1.3
	KC-A	5	5	.500	36	2	1	0	5	72^1	69	34	29	5	0	28	50	1.341	3.61	108	3.53	.252	3	.231	3	7	0.4
	Yr.	7	8	.467	54	8	3	0	5	130	130	71	65	13	2	56	92	1.431	4.50	84	4.28	.263	5	.167	-10	7	-0.9
1959	KC-A	0	1	.000	16	0	0	0	2	20^2	27	15	15	6	2	12	13	1.887	6.53	61	8.38	.310	1	.500	-6	0	-0.5
Total	5	10	10	.500	106	11	4	0	7	231	231	141	127	34	6	112	166	1.485	4.95	76	4.83	.259	9	.180	-29	8	-2.9
• TOMASIC, Andy	Andrew John Tomasic b: 12/10/1919, Hokendauqua, PA BR/TR, 6', 175 lbs. Deb: 4/28/1949																										
1949	NY-N	0	1	.000	2	0	0	0	0	5	9	10	10	2	0	5	2	2.800	18.00	22	14.49	.375	0	.000	-8	0	-0.8
• TOMKO, Brett	Brett Daniel Tomko b: 4/7/1973, Cleveland, OH BR/TR, 6'4", 215 lbs. Deb: 5/27/1997																										
1997	Cin-N	11	7	.611	22	19	0	0	0	126	106	50	48	14	4	47	95	1.214	3.43	126	3.31	.233	5	.139	12	10	1.1
1998	Cin-N	13	12	.520	34	34	1	0	0	210^2	198	111	104	22	7	64	162	1.244	4.44	96	3.50	.247	7	.108	-3	9	-0.5
1999	Cin-N	5	7	.417	33	26	1	0	0	172	175	103	94	31	4	60	132	1.366	4.92	95	4.51	.263	10	.213	-10	6	-0.8
2000*	Sea-A	7	5	.583	32	8	0	0	1	92^1	92	53	48	12	3	40	59	1.430	4.68	97	4.49	.264	0	....	-2	5	-0.2
2001	Sea-A	3	1	.750	11	4	0	0	0	34^2	42	24	20	9	0	15	22	1.644	5.19	80	6.31	.288	0	....	-5	1	-0.5
2002	SD-N	10	10	.500	32	32	3	0	0	204^1	212	107	102	31	2	60	126	1.331	4.49	84	4.18	.267	12	.182	-14	6	-1.3
2003	StL-N	13	9	.591	33	32	2	0	0	202^2	252	126	119	35	5	57	114	1.525	5.28	77	5.63	.305	18	.286	-28	6	-2.2
Total	7	62	51	.549	197	155	7	0	1	1042^2	1077	574	535	154	25	343	710	1.362	4.62	91	4.37	.267	52	.188	-51	43	-4.4
• TOMLIN, Dave	David Allen Tomlin b: 6/22/1949, Maysville, KY BL/TL, 6'2", 185 lbs. Deb: 9/2/1972																										
1972	Cin-N	0	0	....	3	0	0	0	0	4	7	4	4	2	0	1	2	2.000	9.00	36	11.38	.412	0	....	-3	0	-0.3
1973*	Cin-N	1	2	.333	16	0	0	0	1	27^2	24	15	15	5	0	15	20	1.410	4.88	70	4.28	.238	0	.000	-5	0	-0.6
1974	SD-N	2	0	1.000	47	0	0	0	2	58	59	29	28	4	2	30	29	1.534	4.34	82	4.20	.271	0	.000	-3	3	-0.4
1975	SD-N	4	2	.667	67	0	0	0	1	83	87	38	30	5	2	31	48	1.422	3.25	107	3.82	.275	1	.200	3	6	0.4
1976	SD-N	0	1	.000	49	1	0	0	0	73	62	24	23	4	1	20	43	1.123	2.84	115	2.52	.235	0	.000	4	4	0.3
1977	SD-N	4	4	.500	76	0	0	0	3	101^2	98	38	34	3	2	32	55	1.279	3.01	117	3.01	.259	2	.286	7	5	0.7
1978	Cin-N	9	1	.900	57	0	0	0	4	62^1	88	54	40	3	3	30	32	1.893	5.78	61	6.23	.326	1	.200	-14	0	-1.5
1979*	Cin-N	2	2	.500	53	0	0	0	1	58^1	59	29	17	3	1	18	30	1.320	2.62	142	3.44	.269	1	.500	7	4	0.8
1980	Cin-N	3	0	1.000	27	0	0	0	0	26	38	17	16	2	0	11	6	1.885	5.54	65	6.43	.355	0	....	-5	1	-0.5
1982	Mon-N	0	0	....	1	0	0	0	0	2	1	1	1	0	0	1	2	1.000	4.50	81	1.62	.167	0	....	-0	0	0.0
1983	Pit-N	0	0	....	5	0	0	0	0	4	6	4	3	0	0	1	5	1.750	6.75	55	5.16	.316	0	....	-1	0	-0.1
1985	Pit-N	0	0	....	1	0	0	0	0	1	1	0	0	0	0	1	0	2.000	0.00	....	6.99	.333	0	....	0	0	0.0
1986	Mon-N	0	0	....	7	0	0	0	0	10^1	13	8	6	1	1	7	6	1.935	5.23	71	6.59	.317	0	....	-2	0	-0.2
Total	13	25	12	.676	409	1	0	0	12	511^1	543	261	217	32	12	198	278	1.449	3.82	92	4.05	.277	5	.147	-13	23	-1.4

YEAR TM-L	W	L	PCT	G	GS	CG	SH	SV	IP	H	R	ER	HR	HB	BB	SO	RAT	ERA	ERA+	CERA	OAV	BH	AVG	PR+	WS	TPW
• TOMLIN, Randy	Randy Leon Tomlin b: 6/14/1966, Bainbridge, MD BL/TL, 5'11", 170 lbs. Deb: 8/6/1990																									
1990 Pit-N	4	4	.500	12	12	2	0	0	77^2	62	24	22	5	1	12	42	.953	2.55	142	2.02	.221	1	.040	8	6	0.7
1991* Pit-N	8	7	.533	31	27	4	2	0	175	170	75	58	9	6	54	104	1.280	2.98	120	3.35	.254	10	.192	10	10	1.2
1992* Pit-N	14	9	.609	35	33	1	1	0	208^2	226	85	79	11	5	42	90	1.284	3.41	101	3.57	.282	9	.138	-1	12	-0.1
1993 Pit-N	4	8	.333	18	18	1	0	0	98^1	109	57	53	11	5	15	44	1.261	4.85	83	4.03	.291	6	.182	-10	3	-0.9
1994 Pit-N	0	3	.000	10	4	0	0	0	20^2	23	9	9	1	0	10	17	1.597	3.92	110	4.89	.291	3	.500	1	1	0.2
Total 5	**30**	**31**	**.492**	**106**	**94**	**8**	**3**	**0**	**580^1**	**590**	**250**	**221**	**37**	**17**	**133**	**297**	**1.246**	**3.43**	**107**	**3.42**	**.268**	**29**	**.160**	**9**	**32**	**1.0**
• TOMPKINS, Chuck	Charles Herbert Tompkins b: 9/1/1889, Prescott, AR d: 9/20/1975, Prescott, AR BR/TR, 6', 185 lbs. Deb: 6/25/1912																									
1912 Cin-N	0	0	....	1	0	0	0	0	3	5	1	0	0	0	0	1	1.667	0.00	....	5.42	.357	1	1.000	1	1	0.2
• TOMPKINS, Ron	Ronald Everett "Stretch" Tompkins b: 11/27/1944, San Diego, CA BR/TR, 6'4", 198 lbs. Deb: 9/9/1965																									
1965 KC-A	0	0	....	5	1	0	0	0	10^1	9	4	4	0	1	3	4	1.161	3.48	100	2.68	.237	0	.000	0	1	0.0
1971 Chi-N	0	2	.000	35	0	0	0	3	39^2	31	18	18	3	3	21	20	1.311	4.08	96	3.36	.214	0	....	0	3	0.0
Total 2	**0**	**2**	**.000**	**40**	**1**	**0**	**0**	**3**	**50**	**40**	**22**	**22**	**3**	**4**	**24**	**24**	**1.280**	**3.96**	**97**	**3.22**	**.219**	**0**	**.000**	**0**	**4**	**0.0**
• TOMS, Tommy	Thomas Howard Toms b: 10/15/1951, Charlottesville, VA BR/TR, 6'4", 195 lbs. Deb: 5/4/1975																									
1975 SF-N	0	1	.000	7	0	0	0	0	10^1	13	8	7	1	0	6	6	1.839	6.10	62	5.48	.317	0	....	-3	0	-0.3
1976 SF-N	0	1	.000	7	0	0	0	1	8^2	13	7	6	1	0	1	4	1.615	6.23	58	5.97	.351	0	....	-2	0	-0.3
1977 SF-N	0	1	.000	4	0	0	0	0	4^1	7	5	1	0	0	2	2	2.077	2.08	188	6.70	.333	0	....	1	0	0.1
Total 3	**0**	**3**	**.000**	**18**	**0**	**0**	**0**	**1**	**23^1**	**33**	**20**	**14**	**2**	**0**	**9**	**12**	**1.800**	**5.40**	**69**	**5.89**	**.333**	**0**	**....**	**-4**	**0**	**-0.4**
• TONEY, Fred	Fred Alexandra Toney b: 12/11/1888, Nashville, TN d: 3/11/1953, Nashville, TN BR/TR, 6'6", 195 lbs. Deb: 4/15/1911																									
1911 Chi-N	1	1	.500	18	4	1	0	0	67	55	36	18	2	5	35	27	1.343	2.42	137	3.33	.229	2	.111	5	3	0.4
1912 Chi-N	1	2	.333	9	2	0	0	0	24	21	19	14	0	1	11	9	1.333	5.25	63	3.05	.247	0	.000	-6	0	-0.6
1913 Chi-N	2	2	.500	7	5	2	0	0	39	52	29	26	1	1	22	12	1.897	6.00	53	6.09	.327	3	.250	-12	0	-1.2
1915 Cin-N	17	6	.739	36	23	18	6	2	222^2	160	46	39	1	3	73	108	1.046	1.58	181	1.80	.207	7	.095	27	23	2.5
1916 Cin-N	14	17	.452	41	38	21	3	1	300	247	98	76	7	8	78	146	1.083	2.28	114	2.26	.231	12	.121	8	18	0.4
1917 Cin-N	24	16	.600	43	42	31	7	1	339^2	300	119	83	4	6	77	123	1.110	2.20	119	2.28	.238	13	.112	16	19	1.2
1918 Cin-N	6	10	.375	21	19	9	1	2	136^2	148	61	44	2	0	31	32	1.310	2.90	92	3.26	.282	9	.214	-5	5	-0.5
NY-N	6	2	.750	11	9	7	1	1	85^1	55	19	16	1	2	7	19	.727	1.69	156	1.12	.192	6	.188	9	9	0.9
Yr.	12	12	.500	32	28	16	2	**3**	222	203	80	60	3	2	38	51	1.086	2.43	109	2.44	.250	15	.203	4	14	0.4
1919 NY-N	13	6	.684	24	20	14	4	1	181	157	47	37	6	2	35	40	1.061	1.84	152	2.23	.235	15	.227	17	16	2.0
1920 NY-N	21	11	.656	42	37	17	4	1	278^1	266	101	82	8	6	57	81	1.160	2.65	113	2.73	.259	23	.240	6	21	1.0
1921* NY-N	18	11	.621	42	32	16	1	3	249^1	274	112	100	14	4	65	63	1.360	3.61	102	3.82	.289	18	.209	-6	16	-0.4
1922 NY-N	5	6	.455	13	12	6	0	0	86^1	91	44	40	5	2	31	10	1.413	4.17	96	3.97	.277	2	.067	-4	4	-0.6
1923 StL-N	11	12	.478	29	28	16	1	0	196^2	211	104	84	8	6	61	48	1.383	3.84	101	3.75	.282	8	.116	3	10	-0.2
Total 12	**139**	**102**	**.577**	**336**	**271**	**158**	**28**	**12**	**2206**	**2037**	**835**	**659**	**59**	**46**	**583**	**718**	**1.188**	**2.69**	**114**	**2.78**	**.251**	**118**	**.159**	**58**	**144**	**4.8**
• TONKIN, Doc	Harry Glenville Tonkin b: 8/11/1881, Concord, NH d: 5/30/1959, Miami, FL BL/TL, 5'9", 165 lbs. Deb: 8/19/1907																									
1907 Was-A	0	0	....	1	0	0	0	0	2^2	6	3	2	0	0	5	0	4.125	6.75	36	15.49	.445	2	1.000	-1	0	0.0
• TOOLE, Steve	Stephen John Toole b: 4/9/1859, New Orleans, LA d: 3/28/1919, Pittsburgh, PA BR/TL, 6', 170 lbs. Deb: 4/20/1886 U																									
1886 Bro-a	6	6	.500	13	12	11	0	0	104	100	92	51	0	8	64	48	1.577	4.41	79	....	.241	20	.351	-10	6	-0.6
1887 Bro-a	14	10	.583	24	24	22	1	0	194	292	133	93	1	12	106	48	1.505	4.31	100	....	.335	27	.255	-1	13	-0.1
1888 KC-a	5	6	.455	12	10	10	0	0	91^2	124	99	68	4	5	50	35	1.898	6.68	51	....	.312	10	.208	-33	1	-3.0
1890 Bro-a	2	4	.333	6	6	6	0	0	53^1	47	32	24	0	4	39	10	1.613	4.05	96	....	.230	6	.300	-1	2	0.1
Total 4	**27**	**26**	**.509**	**55**	**52**	**49**	**1**	**0**	**443**	**563**	**356**	**236**	**5**	**29**	**259**	**141**	**1.616**	**4.79**	**79**	**....**	**.298**	**63**	**.273**	**-45**	**22**	**-3.6**
• TOPPIN, Rupe	Ruperto Toppin b: 12/7/1941, Panama City, Panama BR/TR, 6', 185 lbs. Deb: 7/28/1962																									
1962 KC-A	0	0	....	2	0	0	0	0	2	1	3	3	0	0	5	1	3.000	13.50	31	9.05	.167	1	1.000	-2	0	-0.2
• TORKELSON, Red	Chester Leroy Torkelson b: 3/19/1894, Chicago, IL d: 9/22/1964, Chicago, IL BR/TR, 6', 175 lbs. Deb: 8/29/1917																									
1917 Cle-A	2	1	.667	4	3	0	0	0	22^1	33	25	19	1	2	13	10	2.060	7.66	37	6.86	.333	2	.222	-13	0	-1.4
• TORREALBA, Pablo	Pablo Arnoldo (Torrealba) Torrealba b: 4/28/1948, Barquisimeto, Venezuela BL/TL, 5'10", 175 lbs. Deb: 4/9/1975																									
1975 Atl-N	0	1	.000	6	0	0	0	0	6^2	7	2	1	0	0	3	5	1.500	1.35	280	3.58	.250	1	1.000	2	1	0.3
1976 Atl-N	0	2	.000	36	0	0	0	2	53	67	25	21	0	3	22	33	1.679	3.57	106	4.94	.315	0	.000	3	3	0.2
1977 Oak-A	4	6	.400	41	10	3	0	2	116^2	127	45	34	5	2	38	51	1.414	2.62	153	3.90	.279	0	....	20	9	1.9
1978 Chi-A	2	4	.333	25	3	1	1	1	57^1	69	37	30	6	3	39	23	1.884	4.71	81	6.56	.301	0	....	-5	1	-0.5
1979 Chi-A	0	0	....	3	0	0	0	0	5^2	5	1	1	1	0	2	1	1.235	1.59	268	3.68	.250	0	....	2	1	0.2
Total 5	**6**	**13**	**.316**	**111**	**13**	**4**	**1**	**5**	**239^1**	**275**	**110**	**87**	**12**	**8**	**104**	**113**	**1.584**	**3.27**	**119**	**4.75**	**.291**	**1**	**.200**	**21**	**15**	**2.0**
• TORRES, Angel	Angel Rafael (Ruiz) Torres b: 10/24/1952, Las Cienagas Azua, Dominican Republic BL/TL, 5'11", 168 lbs. Deb: 9/12/1977																									
1977 Cin-N	0	0	....	5	0	0	0	0	8^1	7	2	2	2	0	8	8	1.800	2.16	182	6.35	.233	0	....	2	1	0.2
• TORRES, Dilson	Dilson Dario Torres b: 5/31/1970, Sur Edo Aragua, Venezuela BR/TR, 6'3", 200 lbs. Deb: 4/29/1995																									
1995 KC-A	1	2	.333	24	2	0	0	0	44^1	56	30	30	6	1	17	28	1.647	6.09	79	5.98	.311	0	....	-7	1	-0.7
• TORRES, Salomon	Salomon (Ramirez) Torres b: 3/11/1972, San Pedro de Macoris, Dominican Republic BR/TR, 5'11", 165 lbs. Deb: 8/29/1993																									
1993 SF-N	3	5	.375	8	8	0	0	0	44^2	37	21	20	5	1	27	23	1.433	4.03	97	3.95	.231	3	.231	-2	2	-0.2
1994 SF-N	2	8	.200	16	14	1	0	0	84^1	95	55	51	10	7	34	42	1.530	5.44	74	5.29	.292	4	.154	-17	0	-1.7
1995 SF-N	0	1	.000	4	1	0	0	0	8	13	8	8	4	0	7	2	2.500	9.00	45	15.31	.394	0	.000	-4	0	-0.4
Sea-A	3	8	.273	16	13	1	0	0	72	87	53	48	12	2	42	45	1.792	6.00	79	6.55	.291	0	....	-8	1	-0.8
1996 Sea-A	3	3	.500	10	7	1	1	0	49	44	27	25	5	3	23	36	1.367	4.59	108	3.98	.242	0	....	2	3	0.2
1997 Sea-A	0	0	....	2	0	0	0	0	3^1	7	10	10	0	1	3	0	3.000	27.00	17	13.67	.412	0	....	-8	0	-0.8
Mon-N	0	0	....	12	0	0	0	0	22^1	25	19	18	2	2	12	11	1.657	7.25	58	5.47	.284	0	.000	-8	0	-0.8
2002 Pit-N	2	1	.667	5	5	0	0	0	30	28	10	9	2	3	13	12	1.367	2.70	154	4.07	.257	2	.154	5	3	0.4
2003 Pit-N	7	5	.583	41	16	0	0	2	121	128	65	64	19	7	42	84	1.405	4.76	92	4.88	.276	2	.063	-5	6	-0.6
Total 7	**20**	**31**	**.392**	**114**	**64**	**3**	**1**	**2**	**434^2**	**464**	**268**	**253**	**59**	**26**	**203**	**255**	**1.535**	**5.24**	**83**	**5.27**	**.277**	**11**	**.121**	**-46**	**15**	**-4.6**
• TORREZ, Mike	Michael Augustine Torrez b: 8/28/1946, Topeka, KS BR/TR, 6'5", 220 lbs. Deb: 9/10/1967																									
1967 StL-N	0	1	.000	3	1	0	0	0	5^2	5	2	2	0	1	1	5	1.059	3.18	102	2.68	.238	0	.000	0	0	0.0
1968 StL-N	2	1	.667	5	2	0	0	0	19^1	20	7	6	1	1	12	6	1.655	2.79	104	5.10	.286	2	.286	0	2	0.1
1969 StL-N	10	4	.714	24	15	3	0	0	107^2	96	47	43	7	3	62	61	1.467	3.59	99	4.04	.240	3	.073	-1	6	-0.3
1970 StL-N	8	10	.444	30	28	5	1	0	179^1	168	96	84	12	4	103	100	1.511	4.22	98	4.13	.248	17	.270	1	9	0.4
1971 StL-N	1	2	.333	9	6	0	0	0	36	41	27	24	2	1	30	8	1.972	6.00	60	6.38	.304	1	.143	-9	0	-0.8
Mon-N	0	0	....	1	0	0	0	0	3	4	0	0	0	0	1	2	1.667	0.00	....	4.83	.308	0	....	1	1	0.1
Yr.	1	2	.333	10	6	0	0	0	39	45	27	24	2	1	31	10	1.949	5.54	65	6.26	.304	1	.143	-8	1	-0.7
1972 Mon-N	16	12	.571	34	33	13	0	0	243^1	215	97	90	15	6	103	112	1.307	3.33	107	3.40	.242	15	.176	7	18	0.8
1973 Mon-N	9	12	.429	35	34	3	1	0	208	207	116	103	17	4	115	90	**1.548**	4.46	86	4.54	.262	12	.174	-15	6	-1.6
1974 Mon-N	15	8	.652	32	30	6	1	0	186^1	184	90	74	10	3	84	92	1.438	3.57	107	3.91	.257	8	.125	6	11	0.3
1975 Bal-A	20	9	.690	36	36	16	2	0	270^2	238	103	92	15	5	133	119	1.371	3.06	115	3.56	.239	0	....	5	19	0.5
1976 Oak-A	16	12	.571	39	39	13	4	0	266^1	231	93	74	15	6	87	115	1.194	2.50	134	2.90	.235	0	....	30	20	3.1
1977 Oak-A	3	1	.750	4	4	2	0	0	26^1	23	14	13	3	1	11	12	1.291	4.44	91	3.72	.242	0	....	-1	1	-0.1
* NY-A	14	12	.538	31	31	15	2	0	217	212	99	92	20	6	75	90	1.323	3.82	103	3.83	.259	0	....	-1	12	-0.1
Yr.	17	13	.567	35	35	17	2	0	243^1	235	113	105	23	7	86	102	1.319	3.88	102	3.82	.257	0	....	-2	13	-0.2
1978 Bos-A	16	13	.552	36	36	15	2	0	250	272	122	110	19	3	99	120	1.484	3.96	104	4.40	.281	0	....	2	14	0.2
1979 Bos-A	16	13	.552	36	36	12	1	0	252^1	254	144	126	20	5	121	125	1.486	4.49	98	4.31	.264	0	....	-0	14	0.0
1980 Bos-A	9	16	.360	36	32	6	1	0	207^1	256	124	117	18	1	75	97	1.596	5.08	83	5.20	.313	0	....	-20	6	-2.0
1981 Bos-A	10	3	.769	22	22	2	0	0	127^1	130	61	52	10	0	51	54	1.421	3.68	105	4.09	.267	0	....	5	8	0.5

YEAR	TM-L	W	L	PCT	G	GS	CG	SH	SV	IP	H	R	ER	HR	HB	BB	SO	RAT	ERA	ERA+	CERA	OAV	BH	AVG	PR+	WS	TPW
1982	Bos-A	9	9	.500	31	31	1	0	0	175^2	196	107	102	20	6	74	84	1.537	5.23	82	5.08	.282	0	....	-14	6	-1.4
1983	NY-N	10	17	.370	39	34	5	0	0	222^1	227	120	108	16	1	113	94	1.529	4.37	83	4.41	.271	3	.046	-21	6	-2.7
1984	NY-N	1	5	.167	9	8	0	0	0	37^2	55	25	21	3	2	18	16	1.938	5.02	70	7.63	.369	3	.300	-6	0	-0.5
	Oak-A	0	0	....	2	0	0	0	0	2^1	9	7	7	0	0	3	2	5.143	27.00	14	28.02	.563	0	....	-6	0	-0.6
Total	**18**	**185**	**160**	**.536**	**494**	**458**	**117**	**15**	**0**	**3044**	**3043**	**1501**	**1340**	**223**	**59**	**1371**	**1404**	**1.450**	**3.96**	**98**	**4.18**	**.264**	**64**	**.155**	**-38**	**159**	**-4.2**
• TOST, Lou	Louis Eugene Tost b: 6/1/1911, Cumberland, WA d: 2/21/1967, Santa Clara, CA BL/TL, 6', 175 lbs. Deb: 4/20/1942																										
1942	Bos-N	10	10	.500	35	22	5	1	0	147^2	146	66	58	12	4	52	43	1.341	3.53	94	3.70	.256	9	.176	-2	8	-0.2
1943	Bos-N	0	1	.000	3	1	0	0	0	6^2	10	5	4	2	0	4	3	2.100	5.40	63	10.05	.357	0	.000	-2	0	-0.2
1947	Pit-N	0	0	....	1	0	0	0	0	1	3	1	1	0	0	0	0	3.000	9.00	47	14.52	.600	0	....	-1	0	-0.1
Total	**3**	**10**	**11**	**.476**	**39**	**23**	**5**	**1**	**0**	**155^1**	**159**	**72**	**63**	**14**	**4**	**56**	**46**	**1.384**	**3.65**	**92**	**4.04**	**.263**	**9**	**.173**	**-4**	**8**	**-0.4**
• TOTH, Paul	Paul Louis Toth b: 6/30/1935, McRoberts, KY d: 3/20/1999, Anaheim, CA BR/TR, 6'1", 175 lbs. Deb: 4/22/1962																										
1962	StL-N	1	0	1.000	6	1	1	0	0	16^2	18	10	10	1	0	4	5	1.320	5.40	79	3.77	.295	2	.400	-2	1	-0.2
	Chi-N	3	1	.750	6	4	1	0	0	34	29	17	16	2	2	10	11	1.147	4.24	98	2.86	.240	2	.182	-0	2	0.0
	Yr.	4	1	.800	12	5	2	0	0	50^2	47	27	26	3	2	14	16	1.204	4.62	91	3.16	.258	4	.250	-3	3	-0.2
1963	Chi-N	5	9	.357	27	14	3	2	0	130^2	115	50	45	9	2	35	66	1.148	3.10	113	2.77	.240	1	.026	4	8	0.1
1964	Chi-N	0	2	.000	4	2	0	0	0	10^2	15	10	10	2	0	5	0	1.875	8.44	44	7.69	.341	1	.333	-5	0	-0.6
Total	**3**	**9**	**12**	**.429**	**43**	**21**	**5**	**2**	**0**	**192**	**177**	**87**	**81**	**14**	**4**	**54**	**82**	**1.203**	**3.80**	**98**	**3.14**	**.251**	**6**	**.103**	**-4**	**11**	**-0.6**
• TOUCHSTONE, Clay	Clayland Maffitt Touchstone b: 1/24/1903, Moore Township, PA d: 4/28/1949, Beaumont, TX BR/TR, 5'9", 175 lbs. Deb: 9/4/1928																										
1928	Bos-N	0	0	....	5	0	0	0	0	8	15	8	4	0	1	2	1	2.125	4.50	87	8.64	.417	0	.000	-0	0	-0.1
1929	Bos-N	0	0	....	1	0	0	0	0	2^2	6	5	5	1	0	0	1	2.250	16.88	28	12.67	.429	1	1.000	-4	0	-0.3
1945	Chi-A	0	0	....	6	0	0	0	0	10	14	10	6	1	1	6	4	2.000	5.40	61	7.07	.311	0	.000	-2	0	-0.2
Total	**3**	**0**	**0**	**....**	**12**	**0**	**0**	**0**	**0**	**20^2**	**35**	**23**	**15**	**2**	**2**	**8**	**6**	**2.081**	**6.53**	**59**	**8.40**	**.369**	**1**	**.250**	**-6**	**0**	**-0.6**
• TOWERS, Josh	Joshua Eric Towers b: 2/26/1977, Port Hueneme, CA BR/TR, 6'1", 165 lbs. Deb: 5/2/2001																										
2001	Bal-A	8	10	.444	24	20	1	1	0	140^1	165	74	70	21	6	16	58	1.290	4.49	96	4.51	.296	0	.000	-5	6	-0.5
2002	Bal-A	0	3	.000	5	3	0	0	0	27^1	42	24	24	11	0	5	13	1.720	7.90	54	9.00	.362	0	....	-11	0	-1.1
2003	Tor-A	8	1	.889	14	8	1	0	1	64^1	67	34	32	15	4	7	42	1.150	4.48	103	4.26	.266	0	.000	2	5	0.2
Total	**3**	**16**	**14**	**.533**	**43**	**31**	**2**	**1**	**1**	**232**	**274**	**132**	**126**	**47**	**10**	**28**	**113**	**1.302**	**4.89**	**89**	**4.97**	**.296**	**0**	**.000**	**-14**	**11**	**-1.4**
• TOWNSEND, Happy	John Townsend b: 4/9/1879, Townsend, DE d: 12/21/1963, Wilmington, DE BR/TR, 6', 190 lbs. Deb: 4/19/1901																										
1901	Phi-N	9	6	.600	19	16	14	2	0	143^2	118	73	55	3	5	64	72	1.267	3.45	99	2.78	**.223**	7	.109	-1	8	-0.5
1902	Was-A	9	16	.360	27	26	22	0	0	220^1	233	157	109	12	13	89	71	1.461	4.45	83	4.20	.272	23	.264	-14	9	-1.0
1903	Was-A	2	11	.154	20	13	10	0	0	126^2	145	85	67	3	9	48	54	1.524	4.76	66	4.45	.287	2	.045	-22	1	-2.7
1904	Was-A	5	26	.161	36	34	31	2	0	291^1	319	163	116	3	9	100	143	**1.438**	3.58	74	3.74	.279	20	.168	-22	4	-2.7
1905	Was-A	7	16	.304	34	24	22	0	0	263	247	117	77	2	15	84	102	1.259	2.63	100	2.95	.251	15	.181	-7	14	-0.6
1906	Cle-A	3	7	.300	17	12	8	1	0	92^2	92	45	30	1	6	31	31	1.327	2.91	90	3.32	.262	4	.133	-5	2	-0.7
Total	**6**	**35**	**82**	**.299**	**153**	**125**	**107**	**5**	**0**	**1137^2**	**1154**	**640**	**454**	**24**	**57**	**416**	**473**	**1.380**	**3.59**	**84**	**3.57**	**.264**	**71**	**.166**	**-71**	**38**	**-8.2**
• TOWNSEND, Ira	Ira Dance "Pat" Townsend b: 1/9/1894, Weimer, TX d: 7/21/1965, Schulenburg, TX BR/TR, 6'1", 180 lbs. Deb: 8/25/1920																										
1920	Bos-N	0	0	....	4	1	0	0	0	6^2	10	3	1	0	1	2	1	1.800	1.35	226	6.81	.370	0	.000	1	0	0.1
1921	Bos-N	0	0	....	4	0	0	0	0	7^1	11	7	5	1	2	4	0	2.045	6.14	59	8.61	.344	0	.000	-2	0	-0.2
Total	**2**	**0**	**0**	**....**	**8**	**1**	**0**	**0**	**0**	**14**	**21**	**10**	**6**	**1**	**3**	**6**	**1**	**1.929**	**3.86**	**92**	**7.75**	**.356**	**0**	**.000**	**-1**	**0**	**-0.1**
• TOWNSEND, Leo	Leo Alphonse "Lefty" Townsend b: 1/15/1891, Mobile, AL d: 12/3/1976, Mobile, AL BL/TL, 5'10", 160 lbs. Deb: 9/8/1920																										
1920	Bos-N	2	2	.500	7	1	1	0	0	24^1	18	4	4	1	0	2	0	.822	1.48	206	1.50	.220	1	.167	4	3	0.4
1921	Bos-N	0	1	.000	1	1	0	0	0	1^1	2	4	4	0	0	3	0	3.750	27.00	14	13.16	.400	0	....	-3	0	-0.3
Total	**2**	**2**	**3**	**.400**	**8**	**2**	**1**	**0**	**0**	**25^2**	**20**	**8**	**8**	**1**	**0**	**5**	**0**	**.974**	**2.81**	**118**	**2.10**	**.230**	**1**	**.167**	**0**	**3**	**0.1**
• TOZER, Bill	William Louis Tozer b: 7/3/1882, St. Louis, MO d: 2/23/1955, Belmont, CA BR/TR, 6', 200 lbs. Deb: 4/16/1908																										
1908	Cin-N	0	0	....	4	0	0	0	0	10^2	11	5	2	0	1	4	5	1.406	1.69	136	3.74	.268	0	.000	1	1	0.1
• TRABER, Billy	William Henry Traber b: 9/18/1979, Torrance, CA BL/TL, 6'5", 205 lbs. Deb: 4/4/2003																										
2003	Cle-A	6	9	.400	33	18	1	1	0	111^2	132	67	65	15	5	40	88	1.540	5.24	84	5.31	.293	0	.000	-12	3	-1.2
• TRACHSEL, Steve	Stephen Christopher Trachsel b: 10/31/1970, Oxnard, CA BR/TR, 6'3", 205 lbs. Deb: 9/19/1993																										
1993	Chi-N	0	2	.000	3	3	0	0	0	19^2	16	10	10	4	0	3	14	.966	4.58	87	2.71	.219	1	.167	-2	1	-0.1
1994	Chi-N	9	7	.563	22	22	1	0	0	146	133	57	52	19	3	54	108	1.281	3.21	130	3.74	.242	8	.186	15	10	1.4
1995	Chi-N	7	13	.350	30	29	2	0	0	160^2	174	104	92	25	0	76	117	**1.556**	5.15	80	5.13	.277	13	.265	-20	4	-1.6
1996	Chi-N★	13	9	.591	31	31	3	2	0	205	181	82	69	30	8	62	132	1.185	3.03	143	3.52	.235	7	.106	27	15	2.5
1997	Chi-N	8	12	.400	34	34	0	0	0	201^1	225	110	101	32	5	69	160	1.460	4.51	95	5.04	.287	7	.117	-4	9	-0.4
1998	Chi-N	15	8	.652	33	33	1	0	0	208	204	107	103	27	8	84	149	1.385	4.46	99	4.35	.260	17	.266	3	13	0.9
1999	Chi-N	8	18	.308	34	34	4	0	0	205^2	226	133	127	32	3	64	149	1.410	5.56	81	4.69	.280	7	.111	-21	6	-2.2
2000	TB-A	6	10	.375	23	23	3	1	0	137^2	160	76	70	16	6	49	78	1.518	4.58	108	5.19	.294	1	.250	3	8	0.4
	Tor-A	2	5	.286	11	11	0	0	0	63	72	40	37	10	0	25	32	1.540	5.29	96	5.38	.293	0	....	-2	3	-0.1
	Yr.	8	15	.348	34	34	3	1	0	200^2	232	116	107	26	6	74	110	1.525	4.80	104	5.25	.294	1	.250	2	11	0.2
2001	NY-N	11	13	.458	28	28	1	1	0	173^2	168	90	86	28	3	47	144	1.238	4.46	93	3.80	.254	9	.161	-7	8	-0.7
2002	NY-N	11	11	.500	30	30	1	1	0	173^2	170	80	65	16	0	69	105	1.376	3.37	118	3.88	.258	5	.109	13	10	1.2
2003	NY-N	16	10	.615	33	33	2	2	0	204^2	204	90	86	26	3	65	111	1.314	3.78	110	3.97	.264	11	.190	10	13	1.1
Total	**11**	**106**	**118**	**.473**	**312**	**311**	**18**	**7**	**0**	**1899**	**1933**	**979**	**898**	**265**	**39**	**667**	**1299**	**1.369**	**4.26**	**102**	**4.33**	**.265**	**86**	**.167**	**15**	**100**	**2.2**
• TRAUTMAN, Fred	Frederick Orlando Trautman b: 3/24/1892, Bucyrus, OH d: 2/15/1964, Bucyrus, OH BR/TR, 6'1", 175 lbs. Deb: 4/27/1915																										
1915	New-F	0	0	....	1	0	0	0	0	3	4	3	2	0	1	1	2	1.667	6.00	47	6.11	.364	0	.000	-1	0	-0.1
• TRAUTWEIN, John	John Howard Trautwein b: 8/7/1962, Lafayette Hills, PA BR/TR, 6'3", 205 lbs. Deb: 4/7/1988																										
1988	Bos-A	0	1	.000	9	0	0	0	0	16	26	17	16	2	1	9	8	2.188	9.00	46	9.70	.382	0	....	-8	0	-0.9
• TRAVERS, Allan	Aloysius Joseph "Joe" Travers b: 5/7/1892, Philadelphia, PA d: 4/19/1968, Philadelphia, PA BR/TR, 6'1", 180 lbs. Deb: 5/18/1912																										
1912	Det-A	0	1	.000	1	1	1	0	0	8	26	24	14	0	0	7	1	4.125	15.75	21	23.47	.605	0	.000	-11	0	-1.2
• TRAVERS, Bill	William Edward Travers b: 10/27/1952, Norwood, MA BL/TL, 6'4", 200 lbs. Deb: 5/19/1974																										
1974	Mil-A	2	3	.400	23	1	0	0	0	53	59	29	29	6	1	30	31	1.679	4.92	73	5.57	.296	0	....	-8	1	-0.8
1975	Mil-A	6	11	.353	28	23	5	0	1	136^1	130	78	65	15	11	60	57	1.394	4.29	89	4.35	.252	0	....	-6	5	-0.6
1976	Mil-A★	15	16	.484	34	34	15	3	0	240	211	92	75	21	8	95	120	1.275	2.81	124	3.44	.237	0	....	18	16	1.9
1977	Mil-A	4	12	.250	19	19	2	1	0	121^2	140	75	71	13	7	57	49	1.619	5.25	77	5.42	.291	0	....	-17	2	-1.7
1978	Mil-A	12	11	.522	28	28	8	3	0	175^2	184	93	86	20	6	58	66	1.378	4.41	85	4.28	.268	0	....	-13	7	-1.4
1979	Mil-A	14	8	.636	30	27	9	2	0	187^1	196	89	81	33	3	45	74	1.286	3.89	107	4.31	.270	0	....	7	13	0.7
1980	Mil-A	12	6	.667	29	25	7	1	0	154^1	147	76	67	20	6	47	62	1.257	3.91	99	3.78	.249	0	....	-2	8	-0.2
1981	Cal-A	0	1	.000	4	4	0	0	0	9^2	14	11	9	2	0	4	5	1.862	8.38	44	7.73	.333	0	....	-5	0	-0.5
1983	Cal-A	0	3	.000	10	7	0	0	0	42^2	58	32	28	4	2	19	24	1.805	5.91	68	6.55	.331	0	....	-9	0	-0.9
Total	**9**	**65**	**71**	**.478**	**205**	**168**	**46**	**10**	**1**	**1120^2**	**1139**	**575**	**511**	**134**	**44**	**415**	**488**	**1.387**	**4.10**	**94**	**4.35**	**.265**	**0**	**....**	**-36**	**52**	**-3.6**
• TREKELL, Harry	Harry Roy Trekell b: 11/18/1892, Buda, IL d: 11/4/1965, Spokane, WA BR/TR, 6'1.5", 170 lbs. Deb: 8/16/1913																										
1913	StL-N	0	1	.000	7	1	1	0	0	30	25	20	15	2	2	8	15	1.100	4.50	72	2.55	.221	1	.111	-4	0	-0.5
• TREMEL, Bill	William Leonard "Mumbles" Tremel b: 7/4/1929, Lilly, PA BR/TR, 5'11", 180 lbs. Deb: 6/12/1954																										
1954	Chi-N	1	2	.333	33	0	0	0	4	51^1	45	27	24	3	0	28	21	1.422	4.21	100	3.56	.243	2	.250	1	3	0.1
1955	Chi-N	3	0	1.000	23	0	0	0	2	38^2	33	18	16	2	0	18	13	1.319	3.72	110	3.13	.239	2	.286	1	4	0.2

YEAR	TM-L	W	L	PCT	G	GS	CG	SH	SV	IP	H	R	ER	HR	HB	BB	SO	RAT	ERA	ERA+	CERA	OAV	BH	AVG	PR+	WS	TPW
1956	Chi-N	0	0	....	1	0	0	0	0	1	3	1	1	0	0	0	0	3.000	9.00	42	17.53	.600	0	....	-1	0	-0.1
Total	3	4	2	.667	57	0	0	0	6	91	81	46	41	5	0	46	34	1.396	4.05	102	3.53	.247	4	.267	1	7	0.2

• TRICE, Bob Robert Lee Trice b: 8/28/1926, Newton, GA d: 9/16/1988, Weirton, WV BR/TR, 6'3", 190 lbs. Deb: 9/13/1953

YEAR	TM-L	W	L	PCT	G	GS	CG	SH	SV	IP	H	R	ER	HR	HB	BB	SO	RAT	ERA	ERA+	CERA	OAV	BH	AVG	PR+	WS	TPW
1953	Phi-A	2	1	.667	3	3	1	0	0	23	25	14	14	4	0	6	4	1.348	5.48	78	4.51	.275	1	.143	-3	1	-0.3
1954	Phi-A	7	8	.467	19	18	8	1	0	119	146	86	74	14	0	48	22	1.630	5.60	70	5.42	.305	12	.286	-21	4	-1.6
1955	KC-A	0	0	....	4	0	0	0	0	10	14	13	10	4	0	6	2	2.000	9.00	46	9.59	.326	2	.667	-5	0	-0.5
Total	3	9	9	.500	26	21	9	1	0	152	185	113	98	22	0	60	28	1.612	5.80	69	5.56	.302	15	.288	-29	5	-2.4

• TRIMBLE, Joe Joseph Gerard Trimble b: 10/12/1930, Providence, RI BR/TR, 6'1", 190 lbs. Deb: 4/29/1955

YEAR	TM-L	W	L	PCT	G	GS	CG	SH	SV	IP	H	R	ER	HR	HB	BB	SO	RAT	ERA	ERA+	CERA	OAV	BH	AVG	PR+	WS	TPW
1955	Bos-A	0	0	....	2	0	0	0	0	2	0	0	0	0	0	3	1	1.500	0.00	....	2.28	.000	0	....	1	0	0.1
1957	Pit-N	0	2	.000	5	4	0	0	0	19^2	23	19	18	7	1	13	9	1.831	8.24	46	8.36	.291	1	.143	-10	0	-1.0
Total	2	0	2	.000	7	4	0	0	0	21^2	23	19	18	7	1	16	10	1.800	7.48	51	7.80	.291	1	.143	-9	0	-0.9

• TRINKLE, Ken Kenneth Wayne Trinkle b: 12/15/1919, Paoli, IN d: 5/10/1976, Paoli, IN BR/TR, 6'1.5", 175 lbs. Deb: 4/25/1943

YEAR	TM-L	W	L	PCT	G	GS	CG	SH	SV	IP	H	R	ER	HR	HB	BB	SO	RAT	ERA	ERA+	CERA	OAV	BH	AVG	PR+	WS	TPW
1943	NY-N	1	5	.167	11	6	1	0	0	45^2	51	23	19	3	1	15	10	1.445	3.74	92	4.07	.276	3	.250	-1	2	0.0
1946	NY-N	7	14	.333	**48**	13	2	0	2	151	146	77	65	8	2	74	49	1.457	3.87	89	3.81	.253	3	.079	-5	5	-0.8
1947	NY-N	8	4	.667	**62**	0	0	0	10	93^2	100	47	39	3	1	48	37	1.580	3.75	109	4.34	.278	3	.188	3	8	0.3
1948	NY-N	4	5	.444	53	0	0	0	7	70^2	66	28	25	6	3	41	20	1.514	3.18	124	4.28	.244	2	.250	6	6	0.7
1949	Phi-N	1	1	.500	42	0	0	0	2	74^1	79	37	33	3	3	30	14	1.466	4.00	99	4.34	.299	0	.000	-1	4	-0.2
Total	5	21	29	.420	216	19	3	0	21	435^1	442	212	181	23	10	208	130	1.493	3.74	99	4.12	.267	11	.138	2	25	0.0

• TRLICEK, Ricky Richard Alan Trlicek b: 4/26/1969, Houston, TX BR/TR, 6'3", 200 lbs. Deb: 4/8/1992

YEAR	TM-L	W	L	PCT	G	GS	CG	SH	SV	IP	H	R	ER	HR	HB	BB	SO	RAT	ERA	ERA+	CERA	OAV	BH	AVG	PR+	WS	TPW
1992	Tor-A	0	0	....	2	0	0	0	0	1^2	2	2	2	0	0	2	1	2.400	10.80	38	7.49	.286	0	....	-1	0	-0.1
1993	LA-N	1	2	.333	41	0	0	0	1	64	59	32	29	3	2	21	41	1.250	4.08	93	3.06	.244	1	.250	-2	3	-0.2
1994	Bos-A	1	1	.500	12	1	0	0	0	22^1	32	21	20	5	0	16	7	2.149	8.06	62	8.99	.330	0	....	-8	0	-0.7
1996	NY-N	0	1	.000	5	0	0	0	0	5^1	3	2	2	0	1	3	3	1.125	3.38	119	2.41	.214	0	....	0	0	0.0
1997	Bos-A	3	4	.429	18	0	0	0	0	23^1	26	14	12	2	1	18	10	1.886	4.63	100	6.06	.289	0	....	0	1	0.0
	NY-N	0	0	....	9	0	0	0	0	9	10	9	8	2	0	5	4	1.667	8.00	51	6.69	.303	0	....	-4	0	-0.4
Total	5	5	8	.385	87	1	0	0	1	125^2	132	80	73	12	4	65	66	1.568	5.23	81	4.96	.273	1	.250	-14	4	-1.4

• TROEDSON, Rich Richard La Monte Troedson b: 5/1/1950, Palo Alto, CA BL/TL, 6'1", 170 lbs. Deb: 4/9/1973

YEAR	TM-L	W	L	PCT	G	GS	CG	SH	SV	IP	H	R	ER	HR	HB	BB	SO	RAT	ERA	ERA+	CERA	OAV	BH	AVG	PR+	WS	TPW
1973	SD-N	7	9	.438	50	18	2	0	1	152^1	167	77	72	12	1	59	81	1.484	4.25	82	4.41	.284	7	.175	-12	6	-1.3
1974	SD-N	1	1	.500	15	1	0	0	1	18^2	24	18	18	6	1	8	11	1.714	8.68	41	7.56	.300	0	.000	-10	0	-1.1
Total	2	8	10	.444	65	19	2	0	2	171	191	95	90	18	2	67	92	1.500	4.74	74	4.75	.286	7	.171	-22	6	-2.3

• TROMBLEY, Mike Michael Scott Trombley b: 4/14/1967, Springfield, MA BR/TR, 6'2", 208 lbs. Deb: 8/19/1992

YEAR	TM-L	W	L	PCT	G	GS	CG	SH	SV	IP	H	R	ER	HR	HB	BB	SO	RAT	ERA	ERA+	CERA	OAV	BH	AVG	PR+	WS	TPW
1992	Min-A	3	2	.600	10	7	0	0	0	46^1	43	20	17	5	1	17	38	1.295	3.30	123	3.74	.247	0	....	4	3	0.4
1993	Min-A	6	6	.500	44	10	0	0	2	114^1	131	72	62	15	3	41	85	1.504	4.88	89	5.03	.290	0	....	-6	5	-0.5
1994	Min-A	2	0	1.000	24	0	0	0	0	48^1	56	36	34	10	3	18	32	1.531	6.33	77	5.83	.287	0	....	-7	1	-0.6
1995	Min-A	4	8	.333	20	18	0	0	0	97^2	107	68	61	18	3	42	68	1.526	5.62	85	5.40	.273	0	....	-9	3	-0.8
1996	Min-A	5	1	.833	43	0	0	0	6	68^2	61	24	23	2	5	25	57	1.252	3.01	170	2.93	.236	0	....	15	9	1.4
1997	Min-A	2	3	.400	67	0	0	0	1	82^1	77	43	40	7	2	31	74	1.312	4.37	106	3.55	.248	0	.000	3	5	0.2
1998	Min-A	6	5	.545	77	1	0	0	1	96^2	90	41	39	16	5	41	89	1.355	3.63	131	4.46	.247	0	....	14	9	1.3
1999	Min-A	2	8	.200	75	0	0	0	24	87^1	93	42	42	15	2	28	82	1.385	4.33	117	4.69	.272	0	....	8	10	0.7
2000	Bal-A	4	5	.444	75	0	0	0	4	72	67	34	33	15	4	38	72	1.458	4.13	114	4.96	.247	0	.000	5	6	0.5
2001	Bal-A	3	4	.429	50	0	0	0	6	54^2	38	23	21	4	2	27	45	1.189	3.46	124	2.73	.200	0	....	4	6	0.4
	LA-N	0	4	.000	19	0	0	0	0	23^1	27	17	17	5	0	10	27	1.586	6.56	61	5.56	.290	0	....	-6	0	-0.6
2002	Min-A	0	1	.000	5	0	0	0	0	4	10	7	7	2	0	1	3	2.750	15.75	28	17.32	.455	0	....	-5	0	-0.5
Total	11	37	47	.440	509	36	0	0	44	795^2	800	427	396	114	30	319	672	1.406	4.48	103	4.52	.261	0	.000	19	57	1.7

• TROSKY, Hal Harold Arthur "Hal,Hoot" Trosky, Jr. b: 9/29/1936, Cleveland, OH BR/TR, 6'3", 205 lbs. Deb: 9/25/1958

YEAR	TM-L	W	L	PCT	G	GS	CG	SH	SV	IP	H	R	ER	HR	HB	BB	SO	RAT	ERA	ERA+	CERA	OAV	BH	AVG	PR+	WS	TPW
1958	Chi-A	1	0	1.000	2	0	0	0	0	3	5	3	2	0	0	2	1	2.333	6.00	61	8.83	.385	0	....	-1	0	-0.1

• TROTTER, Bill William Felix Trotter b: 8/10/1908, Cisne, IL d: 8/26/1984, Arlington, MA BR/TR, 6'2", 195 lbs. Deb: 4/23/1937

YEAR	TM-L	W	L	PCT	G	GS	CG	SH	SV	IP	H	R	ER	HR	HB	BB	SO	RAT	ERA	ERA+	CERA	OAV	BH	AVG	PR+	WS	TPW
1937	StL-A	2	9	.182	34	12	3	0	1	122^1	150	88	79	14	7	50	37	1.635	5.81	83	5.64	.304	1	.030	-12	4	-1.3
1938	StL-A	0	1	.000	1	1	1	0	0	8	8	7	5	0	0	0	1	1.000	5.63	88	1.74	.242	0	.000	-1	0	0.0
1939	StL-A	6	13	.316	41	13	4	0	0	156^2	205	120	93	16	5	54	61	1.653	5.34	91	5.73	.318	4	.108	-4	4	-0.5
1940	StL-A	7	6	.538	36	4	1	0	2	98	117	56	41	5	1	31	29	1.510	3.77	122	4.51	.300	1	.045	10	7	0.7
1941	StL-A	4	2	.667	29	0	0	0	0	49^2	68	35	33	2	2	19	17	1.752	5.98	72	5.78	.332	0	.000	-9	1	-0.9
1942	StL-A	0	1	.000	3	0	0	0	0	2	5	5	4	0	0	2	0	3.500	18.00	21	13.16	.385	0	....	-3	0	-0.3
	Was-A	3	1	.750	17	0	0	0	0	40^2	52	29	26	4	0	14	13	1.623	5.75	63	5.26	.304	0	.000	-8	0	-0.8
	Yr.	3	2	.600	20	0	0	0	0	42^2	57	34	30	4	0	16	13	1.711	6.33	58	5.63	.310	0	.000	-11	0	-1.2
1944	StL-N	0	1	.000	2	1	0	0	0	6	14	14	9	5	0	4	0	3.000	13.50	26	21.15	.467	0	.000	-7	0	-0.7
Total	7	22	34	.393	163	31	9	0	3	483^1	619	354	290	46	15	174	158	1.641	5.40	84	5.58	.313	6	.055	-34	16	-3.9

• TROUT, Dizzy Paul Howard Trout b: 6/29/1915, Sandcut, IN d: 2/28/1972, Harvey, IL BR/TR, 6'2.5", 195 lbs. Deb: 4/25/1939

YEAR	TM-L	W	L	PCT	G	GS	CG	SH	SV	IP	H	R	ER	HR	HB	BB	SO	RAT	ERA	ERA+	CERA	OAV	BH	AVG	PR+	WS	TPW
1939	Det-A	9	10	.474	33	22	6	0	2	162	168	82	65	5	4	74	72	1.494	3.61	135	3.96	.270	12	.211	23	13	2.1
1940*	Det-A	3	7	.300	33	10	1	0	2	100^2	125	60	50	4	3	54	64	1.778	4.47	106	5.56	.307	4	.129	5	5	0.3
1941	Det-A	9	9	.500	37	18	6	1	2	151^2	144	76	63	7	2	84	88	1.503	3.74	122	3.89	.252	9	.180	18	13	1.8
1942	Det-A	12	18	.400	35	29	13	1	0	223	214	98	85	15	4	89	91	1.359	3.43	115	3.55	.249	16	.213	16	16	1.9
1943	Det-A	**20**	12	.625	44	30	18	**5**	6	246^2	204	83	68	6	0	101	111	1.236	2.48	142	2.61	.227	20	.220	29	23	3.4
1944	Det-A★	27	14	.659	49	**40**	**33**	**7**	0	**352^1**	314	104	83	9	4	83	144	1.127	**2.12**	**168**	2.42	.237	36	.271	**58**	**42**	**7.3**
1945*	Det-A	18	15	.545	41	31	18	4	2	246^1	252	108	86	8	0	79	97	1.344	3.14	112	3.37	.267	25	.245	9	18	1.4
1946	Det-A	17	13	.567	38	32	23	5	3	276^1	244	85	72	11	3	97	151	1.234	2.34	156	2.84	.238	20	.194	44	27	4.9
1947	Det-A★	10	11	.476	32	26	9	2	2	186^1	186	85	72	6	3	65	74	1.347	3.48	108	3.37	.261	11	.162	10	13	1.4
1948	Det-A	10	14	.417	32	23	11	2	2	183^2	193	87	70	6	2	73	91	1.448	3.43	127	3.79	.269	15	.217	23	15	2.4
1949	Det-A	3	6	.333	33	0	0	0	3	59^1	68	35	29	2	0	21	19	1.500	4.40	95	4.14	.292	2	.143	-1	3	-0.1
1950	Det-A	13	5	.722	34	20	11	1	4	184^2	190	84	77	13	5	64	88	1.375	3.75	125	3.86	.267	12	.190	18	17	1.8
1951	Det-A	9	14	.391	42	22	7	0	5	191^2	172	98	86	13	1	75	89	1.289	4.04	103	3.24	.240	14	.269	5	15	1.0
1952	Det-A	1	5	.167	10	2	0	0	1	27	30	16	16	4	0	19	20	1.815	5.33	71	6.11	.286	3	.333	-4	0	-0.4
	Bos-A	9	8	.529	26	17	2	0	1	133^2	133	62	54	3	3	68	57	1.504	3.64	108	3.85	.263	6	.136	4	8	0.3
	Yr.	10	13	.435	36	19	2	0	2	160^2	163	78	70	7	3	87	77	1.556	3.92	100	4.23	.267	9	.170	-0	8	-0.1
1957	Bal-A	0	0	....	2	0	0	0	0	0^1	4	3	3	0	0	0	0	12.00	81.00	4	95.94	.800	0	....	-3	0	-0.3
Total	15	170	161	.514	521	322	158	28	35	2725^2	2641	1166	979	112	34	1046	1256	1.353	3.23	124	3.42	.255	205	.213	254	228	29.2

• TROUT, Steve Steven Russell Trout b: 7/30/1957, Detroit, MI BL/TL, 6'4", 195 lbs. Deb: 7/1/1978

YEAR	TM-L	W	L	PCT	G	GS	CG	SH	SV	IP	H	R	ER	HR	HB	BB	SO	RAT	ERA	ERA+	CERA	OAV	BH	AVG	PR+	WS	TPW
1978	Chi-A	3	0	1.000	4	3	1	0	0	22^1	19	10	10	0	0	11	11	1.343	4.03	94	2.85	.229	0	....	-0	2	0.0
1979	Chi-A	11	8	.579	34	18	6	2	4	155	165	77	67	10	5	59	76	1.445	3.89	109	4.19	.273	0	....	6	10	0.5
1980	Chi-A	9	16	.360	32	30	7	2	0	199^2	229	102	82	14	9	49	89	1.392	3.70	109	4.22	.290	0	....	9	11	0.9
1981	Chi-A	8	7	.533	20	18	3	0	0	124^2	122	53	48	7	4	38	54	1.283	3.47	103	3.49	.261	0	....	0	7	0.0
1982	Chi-A	6	9	.400	25	19	2	0	0	120^1	130	76	57	9	2	50	62	1.496	4.26	95	4.39	.273	0	....	-2	4	-0.2
1983	Chi-N	10	14	.417	34	32	1	0	0	180	217	105	93	13	2	59	80	1.533	4.65	82	4.82	.305	12	.194	-15	5	-1.4
1984*	Chi-N	13	7	.650	32	31	6	2	0	190	205	80	72	7	2	59	81	1.389	3.41	115	3.81	.285	8	.131	13	14	1.2
1985	Chi-N	9	7	.563	24	24	3	1	0	140^2	142	57	53	8	1	63	44	1.457	3.39	118	4.05	.270	5	.109	11	10	1.0
1986	Chi-N	5	7	.417	37	25	0	0	0	161	184	88	85	6	1	78	69	1.627	4.75	85	4.76	.298	9	.209	-10	6	-0.9
1987	Chi-N	6	3	.667	11	11	3	2	0	75	72	27	25	3	1	27	32	1.320	3.00	142	3.47	.260	4	.154	12	7	1.2
	NY-A	0	4	.000	14	9	0	0	0	46^1	51	36	34	4	1	37	27	1.899	6.60	66	6.23	.274	0	....	-12	0	-1.1
1988	Sea-A	4	7	.364	15	13	0	0	0	56^1	86	53	49	6	5	31	14	2.077	7.83	53	8.54	.361	0	....	-23	0	-2.3

YEAR TM-L	W	L	PCT	G	GS	CG	SH	SV	IP	H	R	ER	HR	HB	BB	SO	RAT	ERA	ERA+	CERA	OAV	BH	AVG	PR+	WS	TPW
1989 Sea-A	4	3	.571	19	3	0	0	0	30	43	27	22	3	0	17	17	2.000	6.60	61	7.19	.333	0	....	-9	0	-0.9
Total 12	88	92	.489	301	236	32	9	4	1501^{1}	1665	791	697	90	33	578	656	1.494	4.18	96	4.46	.286	38	.160	-19	76	-2.0
• TROWBRIDGE, Bob	Robert Trowbridge b: 6/27/1930, Hudson, NY d: 4/3/1980, Hudson, NY BR/TR, 6'1", 190 lbs. Deb: 4/22/1956																									
1956 Mil-N	3	2	.600	19	4	1	0	0	50^{2}	38	15	15	4	2	34	40	1.421	2.66	130	3.70	.210	0	.000	4	4	0.4
1957* Mil-N	7	5	.583	32	16	3	1	1	126	118	57	51	9	1	52	75	1.349	3.64	96	3.55	.248	4	.103	-4	6	-0.6
1958 Mil-N	1	3	.250	27	4	0	0	1	55	53	26	24	4	1	26	31	1.436	3.93	90	3.90	.252	1	.111	-3	2	-0.4
1959 Mil-N	1	0	1.000	16	0	0	0	1	30^{1}	45	25	20	2	0	10	22	1.813	5.93	60	6.10	.344	0	.000	-8	0	-0.8
1960 KC-A	1	3	.250	22	1	0	0	2	68^{1}	70	41	35	6	1	34	33	1.522	4.61	86	4.58	.281	1	.056	-4	2	-0.5
Total 5	13	13	.500	116	25	4	1	5	330^{1}	324	164	145	25	5	156	201	1.453	3.95	91	4.08	.260	6	.078	-15	14	-2.0
• TROY, Bun	Robert Gustave Troy b: 8/27/1888, Bad Wurzach, Germany d: 10/7/1918, Petit Maujouym, France BR/TR, 6'4", 195 lbs. Deb: 9/15/1912																									
1912 Det-A	0	1	.000	1	1	0	0	0	6^{2}	9	4	4	0	1	3	1	1.800	5.40	61	6.43	.346	0	.000	-2	0	-0.2
• TRUCKS, Virgil	Virgil Oliver "Fire" Trucks b: 4/26/1917, Birmingham, AL BR/TR, 5'11", 198 lbs. Deb: 9/27/1941 C																									
1941 Det-A	0	0	....	1	0	0	0	0	2	4	2	2	0	0	0	3	2.000	9.00	50	9.49	.500	0	....	-1	0	-0.1
1942 Det-A	14	8	.636	28	20	8	2	0	167^{2}	147	64	51	3	2	74	91	1.318	2.74	144	2.89	.231	8	.123	25	15	2.2
1943 Det-A	16	10	.615	33	25	10	2	2	202^{2}	170	72	64	11	1	52	118	1.095	2.84	124	2.37	.225	13	.181	16	16	1.6
1945* Det-A	0	0	....	1	1	0	0	0	5^{1}	3	1	1	0	0	2	3	.938	1.69	208	1.43	.176	0	.000	1	0	0.1
1946 Det-A	14	9	.609	32	29	15	2	0	236^{2}	217	94	85	23	3	75	161	1.234	3.23	113	3.24	.241	17	.179	14	16	1.4
1947 Det-A	10	12	.455	36	26	8	2	2	180^{2}	186	105	91	14	2	79	108	1.467	4.53	83	4.10	.263	19	.271	-11	7	-0.9
1948 Det-A	14	13	.519	43	26	7	0	2	211^{2}	190	97	89	14	2	85	123	1.299	3.78	116	3.20	.240	13	.165	19	16	1.5
1949 Det-A★	19	11	.633	41	32	17	**6**	4	275	209	95	86	16	4	124	**153**	1.211	2.81	148	**2.68**	.211	12	.120	44	27	3.6
1950 Det-A	3	1	.750	7	7	2	1	0	48^{1}	45	20	19	6	1	21	25	1.366	3.54	132	3.94	.243	3	.150	6	4	0.5
1951 Det-A	13	8	.619	37	18	6	1	1	153^{2}	153	81	74	9	5	75	89	1.484	4.33	96	4.07	.262	13	.236	-1	10	-0.1
1952 Det-A	5	19	.208	35	29	8	3	1	197	190	99	87	12	7	82	129	1.381	3.97	96	3.66	.251	12	.188	0	8	0.0
1953 StL-A	5	4	.556	16	12	4	2	2	88	83	37	30	4	4	32	47	1.307	3.07	137	3.33	.249	4	.160	12	8	1.1
Chi-A	15	6	.714	24	21	13	3	1	176^{1}	151	60	56	14	3	67	102	1.236	2.86	141	3.10	.232	15	.238	22	17	2.4
Yr.	20	10	.667	40	33	17	5	3	264^{1}	234	97	86	18	7	99	149	1.260	2.93	139	3.18	.238	19	.216	34	**25**	**3.5**
1954 Chi-A★	19	12	.613	40	33	16	**5**	3	264^{2}	224	87	82	13	1	95	152	1.205	2.79	134	2.71	.228	17	.183	25	22	2.5
1955 Chi-A	13	8	.619	32	26	7	3	0	175	176	78	77	19	2	61	91	1.354	3.96	100	3.96	.260	8	.125	-3	10	-0.6
1956 Det-A	6	5	.545	22	16	3	1	1	120	104	56	51	15	6	63	43	1.392	3.83	108	4.19	.239	11	.244	4	7	0.4
1957 KC-A	9	7	.563	48	7	0	0	7	116	106	45	39	12	2	62	55	1.448	3.03	131	4.15	.248	4	.143	13	11	1.2
1958 KC-A	0	1	.000	16	0	0	0	3	22	18	7	5	2	0	15	15	1.500	2.05	191	3.96	.222	0	.000	5	3	0.5
NY-A	2	1	.667	25	0	0	0	1	39^{2}	40	24	20	1	2	24	26	1.613	4.54	78	4.43	.265	2	.250	-5	1	-0.5
Yr.	2	2	.500	41	0	0	0	4	61^{2}	58	31	25	3	2	39	41	1.573	3.65	99	4.27	.250	2	.222	-1	4	-0.1
Total 17	177	135	.567	517	328	124	33	30	2682^{1}	2416	1124	1009	188	47	1088	1534	1.306	3.39	116	3.34	.240	171	.180	183	198	16.5
• TRUJILLO, J.J.	John Trujillo b: 10/9/1975, Corpus Christi, TX BR/TR, 6', 180 lbs. Deb: 6/11/2002																									
2002 SD-N	0	1	.000	4	0	0	0	0	2^{2}	4	3	3	1	1	6	3	3.750	10.13	37	21.78	.364	0	....	-2	0	-0.2
• TRUJILLO, Mike	Michael Andrew Trujillo b: 1/12/1960, Denver, CO BR/TR, 6'1", 180 lbs. Deb: 4/14/1985																									
1985 Bos-A	4	4	.500	27	7	1	0	1	84	112	55	45	7	3	23	19	1.607	4.82	89	5.53	.320	0	....	-4	2	-0.4
1986 Bos-A	0	0	....	3	0	0	0	0	5^{2}	7	6	6	0	0	6	4	2.294	9.53	44	6.36	.304	0	....	-3	0	-0.3
Sea-A	3	2	.600	11	4	1	1	1	41^{1}	32	11	11	5	0	15	19	1.137	2.40	177	2.86	.215	0	....	9	5	0.8
Yr.	3	2	.600	14	4	1	1	1	47	39	17	17	5	0	21	23	1.277	3.26	129	3.28	.227	0	....	5	5	0.5
1987 Sea-A	4	4	.500	28	7	0	0	1	65^{2}	70	46	45	12	2	26	36	1.462	6.17	76	5.27	.277	0	....	-11	2	-1.0
1988 Det-A	0	0	....	6	0	0	0	0	12^{1}	11	7	7	2	0	5	5	1.297	5.11	75	3.67	.234	0	....	-2	0	-0.2
1989 Det-A	1	2	.333	8	4	1	0	0	25^{2}	35	17	17	3	0	13	13	1.870	5.96	64	6.85	.333	0	....	-6	0	-0.6
Total 5	12	12	.500	83	22	3	1	3	234^{2}	267	142	131	29	5	88	96	1.513	5.02	86	5.05	.288	0	....	-17	9	-1.7
• TRUMBULL, Ed	Edward J. Trumbull b: 11/3/1860, Chicopee, MA d: 1/14/1937, Kingston, PA Deb: 5/10/1884 ♦																									
1884 Was-a	1	9	.100	10	10	10	0	0	84	108	90	44	4	1	31	43	1.655	4.71	64	....	.296	10	.116	-11	0	-1.7
• TSAMIS, George	George Alex Tsamis b: 6/14/1967, Campbell, CA BR/TL, 6'2", 190 lbs. Deb: 4/26/1993																									
1993 Min-A	1	2	.333	41	0	0	0	1	68^{1}	86	51	47	9	3	27	30	1.654	6.19	70	5.97	.317	0	....	-13	1	-1.3
• TSAO, Chin-hui	Chin-hui Tsao b: 6/2/1981, Hua-lien, Taiwan BR/TR, 6'2", 177 lbs. Deb: 7/25/2003																									
2003 Col-N	3	3	.500	9	8	0	0	0	43^{1}	48	30	29	11	4	20	29	1.569	6.02	81	6.56	.284	2	.154	-5	1	-0.5
• TSITOURIS, John	John Philip Tsitouris b: 5/4/1936, Monroe, NC BR/TR, 6', 175 lbs. Deb: 6/13/1957																									
1957 Det-A	1	0	1.000	2	0	0	0	0	3^{1}	8	3	3	0	0	2	2	3.000	8.10	48	14.52	.500	0	.000	-2	0	-0.2
1958 KC-A	0	0	....	1	1	0	0	0	3	2	1	1	0	0	2	1	1.333	3.00	130	2.54	.182	0	.000	0	0	0.0
1959 KC-A	4	3	.571	24	10	0	0	0	83^{1}	90	52	46	3	3	35	50	1.500	4.97	81	4.11	.271	3	.150	-8	2	-0.9
1960 KC-A	0	2	.000	14	2	0	0	0	33	38	25	24	3	8	21	12	1.788	6.55	61	6.69	.297	0	.000	-9	0	-1.0
1962 Cin-N	1	0	1.000	4	2	1	1	0	21^{1}	13	2	2	0	3	7	7	.938	0.84	477	1.79	.181	0	.000	7	3	0.7
1963 Cin-N	12	8	.600	30	21	8	3	0	191	167	73	67	20	11	38	113	1.073	3.16	106	2.87	.232	5	.081	4	13	0.0
1964 Cin-N	9	13	.409	37	24	6	1	2	175^{1}	178	90	74	20	5	75	146	1.443	3.80	95	4.39	.263	11	.190	-6	7	-0.5
1965 Cin-N	6	9	.400	31	20	3	0	1	131	134	87	72	18	9	65	91	1.519	4.95	76	5.09	.265	3	.070	-17	1	-2.1
1966 Cin-N	0	0	....	1	0	0	0	0	1	3	2	2	0	0	1	0	4.000	18.00	22	22.91	.750	0	....	-2	0	-0.2
1967 Cin-N	1	0	1.000	2	1	0	0	0	8	4	3	3	1	0	6	4	1.250	3.38	111	2.94	.154	0	....	0	1	0.1
1968 Cin-N	0	3	.000	3	3	0	0	0	12^{2}	16	10	10	6	1	8	6	1.895	7.11	44	10.20	.302	0	.000	-5	0	-0.6
Total 11	34	38	.472	149	84	18	5	3	663	653	348	304	71	40	260	432	1.377	4.13	88	4.25	.257	22	.111	-37	27	-4.5
• TUCKER, T.J.	Thomas John Tucker b: 8/20/1978, Clearwater, FL BR/TR, 6'3", 245 lbs. Deb: 6/3/2000																									
2000 Mon-N	0	1	.000	2	2	0	0	0	7	11	9	9	5	0	3	2	2.000	11.57	41	12.90	.344	1	1.000	-5	0	-0.4
2002 Mon-N	6	3	.667	57	0	0	0	4	61^{1}	69	32	28	5	0	31	42	1.630	4.11	104	4.84	.290	3	.750	1	5	0.2
2003 Mon-N	2	3	.400	45	7	0	0	0	80	90	49	42	8	4	20	47	1.375	4.73	107	4.33	.278	5	.263	3	4	0.4
Total 3	8	7	.533	104	9	0	0	4	148^{1}	170	90	79	18	4	54	91	1.510	4.79	98	4.94	.286	9	.375	-1	9	0.2
• TUCKEY, Tom	Thomas H. "Tabasco Tom" Tuckey b: 10/7/1883, Birmingham, England d: 10/17/1950, New York, NY TL, 6'3" Deb: 8/11/1908																									
1908 Bos-N	3	3	.500	8	8	3	1	0	72	60	21	20	2	4	20	26	1.111	2.50	96	2.94	.265	1	.050	-3	4	-0.5
1909 Bos-N	0	9	.000	17	10	4	0	0	90^{2}	104	59	43	1	3	22	16	1.390	4.27	66	3.87	.295	4	.138	-15	0	-1.8
Total 2	3	12	.200	25	18	7	1	0	162^{2}	164	80	63	3	7	42	42	1.266	3.49	76	3.46	.283	5	.102	-17	4	-2.3
• TUDOR, John	John Thomas Tudor b: 2/2/1954, Schenectady, NY BL/TL, 6', 185 lbs. Deb: 8/16/1979																									
1979 Bos-A	1	2	.333	6	6	1	0	0	28	39	23	20	2	0	9	11	1.714	6.43	69	5.82	.345	0	....	-6	0	-0.6
1980 Bos-A	8	5	.615	16	13	5	0	0	92^{1}	81	35	31	4	3	31	45	1.213	3.02	140	2.92	.238	0	....	12	8	1.2
1981 Bos-A	4	3	.571	18	11	2	0	1	78^{2}	74	44	40	11	3	28	44	1.297	4.58	85	4.02	.252	0	....	-5	3	-0.5
1982 Bos-A	13	10	.565	32	30	6	1	0	195^{2}	215	90	79	20	8	59	146	1.400	3.63	119	4.41	.280	0	....	19	15	1.9
1983 Bos-A	13	12	.520	34	34	7	2	0	242	236	122	110	32	4	81	136	1.310	4.09	106	3.97	.255	0	....	8	14	0.8
1984 Pit-N	12	11	.522	32	32	6	1	0	212	200	81	77	19	1	56	117	1.208	3.27	110	3.16	.248	16	.211	5	13	0.8
1985* StL-N	21	8	.724	36	36	14	**10**	0	275	209	68	59	14	5	49	169	.938	1.93	183	1.84	.209	13	.138	43	27	4.7
1986 StL-N	13	7	.650	30	30	3	0	0	219	197	81	71	22	1	53	107	1.142	2.92	125	2.97	.244	11	.153	10	16	1.0
1987* StL-N	10	2	.833	16	16	0	0	0	96	100	43	41	11	1	32	54	1.375	3.84	108	4.26	.272	7	.200	3	7	0.4
1988 StL-N	6	5	.545	21	21	4	1	0	145^{1}	131	44	37	5	1	31	55	1.115	2.29	152	2.45	.247	5	.109	18	12	1.9
*LA-N	4	3	.571	9	9	1	0	0	52^{1}	58	16	14	5	0	10	32	1.299	2.41	138	3.91	.284	0	.000	6	4	0.5
Yr.	10	8	.556	30	30	5	1	0	197^{2}	189	60	51	10	1	41	87	1.164	2.32	148	2.84	.257	5	.085	24	16	2.4
1989 LA-N	0	0	....	6	3	0	0	0	14^{1}	17	5	5	1	0	6	9	1.605	3.14	109	5.21	.309	0	.000	0	1	0.0
1990 StL-N	12	4	.750	25	22	1	1	0	146^{1}	120	48	39	10	2	30	63	1.025	2.40	159	2.27	.225	7	.152	24	15	2.5
Total 12	117	72	.619	281	263	50	16	1	1797	1677	700	623	156	29	475	988	1.198	3.12	125	3.22	.248	59	.154	136	135	14.4

YEAR TM-L	W	L	PCT	G	GS	CG	SH	SV	IP	H	R	ER	HR	HB	BB	SO	RAT	ERA	ERA+	CERA	OAV	BH	AVG	PR+	WS	TPW
• TUERO, Oscar	Oscar (Monzon) Tuero b: 12/17/1898, Havana, Cuba d: 10/21/1960, Houston, TX BR/TR, 5'8.5", 158 lbs. Deb: 5/30/1918																									
1918 StL-N	1	2	.333	11	3	2	0	0	44^{1}	32	12	5	0	3	10	13	.947	1.02	267	1.65	.208	3	.250	8	4	0.9
1919 StL-N	5	7	.417	**45**	16	4	0	**4**	154^{2}	137	71	55	4	10	42	45	1.157	3.20	87	2.71	.242	8	.205	-9	6	-0.9
1920 StL-N	0	0	....	2	0	0	0	0	0^{2}	5	4	4	0	0	1	0	9.000	54.00	6	60.80	.833	0	....	-4	0	-0.4
Total 3	6	9	.400	58	19	6	0	4	199^{2}	174	87	64	4	13	53	58	1.137	2.88	97	2.67	.240	11	.216	-5	10	-0.3
• TUFTS, Bob	Robert Malcolm Tufts b: 11/2/1955, Medford, MA BL/TL, 6'5", 215 lbs. Deb: 8/10/1981																									
1981 SF-N	0	0	....	11	0	0	0	0	15^{1}	20	9	6	1	1	6	12	1.696	3.52	97	5.59	.308	0	.000	-0	0	0.0
1982 KC-A	2	0	1.000	10	0	0	0	2	20	24	10	10	3	0	3	13	1.350	4.50	91	4.50	.293	0	....	-1	1	-0.1
1983 KC-A	0	0	....	6	0	0	0	0	6^{2}	16	8	6	1	1	5	3	3.150	8.10	50	16.18	.444	0	....	-3	0	-0.3
Total 3	2	0	1.000	27	0	0	0	2	42	60	27	22	5	2	14	28	1.762	4.71	82	6.75	.328	0	.000	-4	1	-0.4
• TUNNELL, Lee	Byron Lee Tunnell b: 10/30/1960, Tyler, TX BR/TR, 6'1", 180 lbs. Deb: 9/4/1982																									
1982 Pit-N	1	1	.500	5	3	0	0	0	18^{1}	17	8	8	1	2	5	4	1.200	3.93	94	3.42	.254	0	.000	-0	1	-0.1
1983 Pit-N	11	6	.647	35	25	5	3	0	177^{2}	167	81	72	15	2	58	95	1.266	3.65	102	3.45	.252	7	.121	2	10	0.1
1984 Pit-N	1	7	.125	26	6	0	0	1	68^{1}	81	44	40	6	0	40	51	1.771	5.27	68	5.68	.298	1	.083	-14	0	-1.5
1985 Pit-N	4	10	.286	24	23	0	0	0	132^{1}	126	70	59	11	1	57	74	1.383	4.01	89	3.82	.251	4	.085	-4	4	-0.7
1987* StL-N	4	4	.500	32	9	0	0	0	74^{1}	90	45	40	5	1	34	49	1.668	4.84	86	5.24	.307	4	.235	-6	2	-0.6
1989 Min-A	1	0	1.000	10	0	0	0	0	12	18	8	8	1	0	6	7	2.000	6.00	69	7.17	.340	0	....	-2	0	-0.2
Total 6	22	28	.440	132	66	5	3	1	483	499	256	227	39	6	200	280	1.447	4.23	88	4.24	.270	16	.116	-25	17	-3.0
• TURBEVILLE, George	George Elkins Turbeville b: 8/24/1914, Turbeville, SC d: 10/5/1983, Salisbury, NC BR/TL, 6'1", 175 lbs. Deb: 7/20/1935																									
1935 Phi-A	0	3	.000	19	6	2	0	0	63^{2}	74	58	54	2	0	69	20	2.246	7.63	60	7.21	.312	2	.105	-21	0	-2.1
1936 Phi-A	2	5	.286	12	6	2	0	0	43^{2}	42	36	31	6	6	32	10	1.695	6.39	80	5.94	.258	2	.143	-6	1	-0.6
1937 Phi-A	0	4	.000	31	3	0	0	0	77^{1}	80	50	41	2	0	56	17	1.759	4.77	99	4.75	.266	6	.231	-1	3	0.0
Total 3	2	12	.143	62	15	4	0	0	184^{2}	196	144	126	10	6	157	47	1.912	6.14	77	5.88	.280	10	.169	-28	4	-2.8
• TURK, Lucas	Lucas Newton "Harlem,Chief" Turk b: 5/2/1898, Homer, GA d: 1/11/1994, Homer, GA BR/TR, 6', 165 lbs. Deb: 6/7/1922																									
1922 Was-A	0	0	....	5	0	0	0	0	11^{2}	16	10	9	0	0	5	1	1.800	6.94	56	5.63	.340	1	.250	-4	0	-0.4
• TURLEY, Bob	Robert Lee "Bullet Bob" Turley b: 9/19/1930, Troy, IL BR/TR, 6'2", 215 lbs. Deb: 9/29/1951 C																									
1951 StL-A	0	1	.000	1	1	0	0	0	7^{1}	11	6	6	0	0	3	5	1.909	7.36	60	6.37	.355	0	.000	-2	0	-0.3
1953 StL-A	2	6	.250	10	7	3	1	0	60^{1}	39	24	22	4	2	44	61	1.376	3.28	128	3.12	.184	5	.278	7	5	0.8
1954 Bal-A★	14	15	.483	35	35	14	0	0	247^{1}	178	106	95	7	7	181	**185**	1.451	3.46	104	3.16	**.203**	11	.136	5	16	0.3
1955* NY-A★	17	13	.567	36	34	13	6	1	246^{2}	168	92	84	16	7	177	210	1.399	3.06	122	3.35	**.193**	11	.134	8	16	0.8
1956* NY-A	8	4	.667	27	21	5	1	1	132	138	76	74	13	4	103	91	1.826	5.05	77	6.05	.273	8	.174	-20	4	-2.1
1957* NY-A	13	6	.684	32	23	9	4	3	176^{1}	120	59	53	17	9	85	152	1.163	2.71	133	2.88	**.194**	5	.088	15	13	1.4
1958* NY-A★	**21**	7	.750	33	31	**19**	6	1	245^{1}	178	82	81	24	8	128	168	1.247	2.97	119	3.22	**.206**	12	.136	11	18	1.0
1959 NY-A	8	11	.421	33	22	7	3	0	154^{1}	141	80	74	15	3	83	111	1.451	4.32	85	4.14	.245	4	.087	-12	4	-1.4
1960* NY-A	9	3	.750	34	24	4	1	5	173^{1}	138	67	63	14	5	87	87	1.298	3.27	109	3.35	.222	4	.073	1	12	-0.2
1961 NY-A	3	5	.375	15	12	1	0	0	72	74	47	46	11	4	51	48	1.736	5.75	65	6.21	.269	2	.095	-19	0	-2.0
1962 NY-A	3	3	.500	24	8	0	0	1	69	68	45	35	8	4	47	42	1.667	4.57	82	5.48	.263	0	.000	-7	1	-0.8
1963 LA-A	2	7	.222	19	12	3	2	0	87^{1}	71	41	32	5	2	51	70	1.397	3.30	104	3.39	.222	4	.160	1	3	0.2
Bos-A	1	4	.200	11	7	0	0	0	41^{1}	42	28	28	6	1	28	35	1.694	6.10	62	5.64	.256	3	.214	-10	0	-1.1
Yr.	3	11	.214	30	19	3	2	0	128^{2}	113	69	60	11	3	79	105	1.492	4.20	85	4.11	.233	7	.179	-9	3	-0.9
Total 12	101	85	.543	310	237	78	24	12	1712^{2}	1366	753	693	140	56	1068	1265	1.421	3.64	101	3.80	.220	69	.126	-22	92	-3.4
• TURNBOW, Derrick	Thomas Derrick Turnbow b: 1/25/1978, Union City, TN BR/TR, 6'3", 200 lbs. Deb: 4/17/2000																									
2000 Ana-A	0	0	....	24	1	0	0	0	38	36	21	20	7	2	36	25	1.895	4.74	107	7.05	.254	0	....	1	2	0.0
2003 Ana-A	2	0	1.000	11	0	0	0	0	15^{1}	7	1	1	0	0	3	15	.652	0.59	734	0.79	.140	0	....	6	2	0.6
Total 2	2	0	1.000	35	1	0	0	0	53^{1}	43	22	21	7	2	39	40	1.538	3.54	142	5.25	.224	0	....	7	4	0.6
• TURNER, Jim	James Riley "Milkman Jim" Turner b: 8/6/1903, Antioch, TN d: 11/29/1998, Nashville, TN BL/TR, 6', 185 lbs. Deb: 4/30/1937 C																									
1937 Bos-N	20	11	.645	33	30	**24**	**5**	1	256^{2}	228	80	68	13	0	52	69	1.091	**2.38**	**150**	2.40	.235	24	.250	28	**27**	**3.2**
1938 Bos-N★	14	18	.438	35	34	22	3	0	268	267	123	103	21	5	54	71	1.198	3.46	99	3.17	.259	22	.229	-2	15	0.2
1939 Bos-N	4	11	.267	25	22	9	0	0	157^{2}	181	83	75	10	4	51	50	1.471	4.28	86	4.36	.293	13	.236	-13	5	-1.1
1940* Cin-N	14	7	.667	24	23	11	0	0	187	187	70	60	9	0	32	53	1.171	2.89	131	2.90	.264	18	.240	12	18	1.5
1941 Cin-N	6	4	.600	23	10	3	0	0	113	120	49	39	5	1	24	34	1.274	3.11	116	3.37	.277	6	.146	6	8	0.6
1942 Cin-N	0	0	....	3	0	0	0	0	3^{1}	5	5	4	1	0	3	0	2.400	10.80	30	10.78	.333	0	.000	-3	0	-0.3
* NY-A	1	1	.500	5	0	0	0	1	7	4	1	1	0	0	1	2	.714	1.29	268	0.95	.167	0	.000	1	1	0.1
1943 NY-A	3	0	1.000	18	0	0	0	1	43^{1}	44	22	17	1	0	13	15	1.315	3.53	91	3.18	.260	1	.077	-2	2	-0.4
1944 NY-A	4	4	.500	35	0	0	0	7	41^{2}	42	23	16	3	0	22	13	1.536	3.46	101	4.17	.264	2	.200	-1	3	0.0
1945 NY-A	3	4	.429	30	0	0	0	**10**	54^{1}	45	26	22	4	0	31	22	1.399	3.64	95	3.39	.225	1	.091	-2	4	-0.4
Total 9	69	60	.535	231	119	69	8	20	1132	1123	482	405	67	10	283	329	1.242	3.22	111	3.19	.260	87	.218	25	83	3.5
• TURNER, Ken	Kenneth Charles Turner b: 8/17/1943, Framingham, MA BR/TL, 6'2", 190 lbs. Deb: 6/11/1967																									
1967 Cal-A	1	2	.333	13	1	0	0	0	17^{1}	16	9	8	4	1	4	6	1.154	4.15	76	4.05	.239	0	.000	-2	0	-0.2
• TURNER, Matt	William Matthew Turner b: 2/18/1967, Lexington, KY BR/TR, 6'5", 215 lbs. Deb: 4/23/1993																									
1993 Fla-N	4	5	.444	55	0	0	0	0	68	55	23	22	7	1	26	59	1.191	2.91	148	2.89	.227	0	.000	12	7	1.2
1994 Cle-A	1	0	1.000	9	0	0	0	1	12^{2}	13	6	3	0	3	7	5	1.579	2.13	221	4.50	.241	0	....	4	1	0.3
Total 2	5	5	.500	64	0	0	0	1	80^{2}	68	29	25	7	4	33	64	1.252	2.79	156	3.14	.230	0	.000	16	8	1.5
• TURNER, Ted	Theodore Holhot Turner b: 5/4/1892, Lawrenceburg, KY d: 2/4/1958, Lexington, KY BR/TR, 6', 180 lbs. Deb: 4/20/1920																									
1920 Chi-N	0	0	....	1	0	0	0	0	1^{1}	2	2	2	0	0	1	0	2.250	13.50	24	8.58	.400	0	.000	-2	0	-0.2
• TURNER, Tink	Thomas Lovatt Turner b: 2/20/1890, Swarthmore, PA d: 2/25/1962, Philadelphia, PA BR/TR, 6'1", 190 lbs. Deb: 9/24/1915																									
1915 Phi-A	0	1	.000	1	1	0	0	0	2	5	6	5	1	0	3	0	4.000	22.50	13	25.62	.500	0	....	-4	0	-0.5
• TUTWILER, Elmer	Elmer Strange Tutwiler b: 11/19/1905, Carbon Hill, AL d: 5/3/1976, Pensacola, FL BR/TR, 5'11", 158 lbs. Deb: 8/20/1928																									
1928 Pit-N	0	0	....	2	0	0	0	0	3^{2}	4	2	2	0	0	0	1	1.091	4.91	83	2.36	.267	0	.000	-0	0	0.0
• TWINING, Twink	Howard Earle "Doc" Twining b: 5/30/1894, Horsham, PA d: 6/14/1973, Lansdale, PA BR/TR, 6', 168 lbs. Deb: 7/9/1916																									
1916 Cin-N	0	0	....	1	0	0	0	0	2	4	3	3	1	1	1	0	2.500	13.50	19	18.73	.444	0	....	-2	0	-0.3
• TWITCHELL, Larry	Lawrence Grant Twitchell b: 2/18/1864, Cleveland, OH d: 4/23/1930, Cleveland, OH BR/TR, 6', 185 lbs. Deb: 4/30/1886 U ♦																									
1886 Det-N	0	2	.000	4	4	2	0	0	25	35	22	18	1	....	12	6	1.880	6.48	51	....	.319	1	.063	-9	0	-1.0
1887* Det-N	11	1	.917	15	12	11	0	**1**	112^{1}	156	74	54	3	10	36	24	1.389	4.33	93	....	.320	96	.353	-5	15	-0.4
1888 Det-N	0	0	....	2	0	0	0	1	4	6	3	3	1	0	0	3	1.500	6.75	41	....	.334	128	.244	-2	10	-1.8
1889 Cle-N	0	0	....	1	0	0	0	0	1	0	0	0	0	0	1	0	1.000	0.00	....	....	.000	151	.275	0	11	-1.6
1890 Buf-P	5	7	.417	13	12	12	0	0	104^{1}	112	77	53	3	15	72	29	1.764	4.57	90	....	.263	38	.221	-4	4	-0.6
1891 Col-a	1	1	.500	6	1	1	0	0	31	29	22	14	1	3	13	8	1.355	4.06	85	....	.239	62	.277	-3	8	-0.6
1894 Lou-N	0	0	....	1	0	0	0	0	3	5	2	2	1	0	1	0	2.000	6.00	85	9.90	.367	56	.267	-0	2	-0.5
Total 7	17	11	.607	42	29	26	0	2	280^{2}	343	200	144	10	28	135	70	1.575	4.62	83	0.11	.292	684	.265	-23	50	-6.6
• TWITCHELL, Wayne	Wayne Lee Twitchell b: 3/10/1948, Portland, OR BR/TR, 6'6", 220 lbs. Deb: 9/7/1970																									
1970 Mil-A	0	0	....	2	0	0	0	0	1^{2}	3	2	2	0	0	1	5	2.400	10.80	35	7.89	.333	0	....	-1	0	-0.1
1971 Phi-N	1	0	1.000	6	1	0	0	0	16	8	4	0	1	1	10	15	1.125	0.00	....	2.16	.145	0	.000	6	2	0.6
1972 Phi-N	5	9	.357	49	15	1	1	1	139^{2}	138	72	63	6	2	56	112	1.389	4.06	88	3.59	.259	2	.071	-9	4	-1.2
1973 Phi-N★	13	9	.591	34	28	10	5	0	223^{1}	172	71	62	16	10	99	169	1.213	2.50	152	2.97	.219	7	.097	30	21	2.7
1974 Phi-N	6	9	.400	25	18	2	0	0	112^{1}	122	71	65	11	7	65	72	1.665	5.21	73	5.34	.276	6	.171	-20	1	-2.2

YEAR	TM-L	W	L	PCT	G	GS	CG	SH	SV	IP	H	R	ER	HR	HB	BB	SO	RAT	ERA	ERA+	CERA	OAV	BH	AVG	PR+	WS	TPW
1975	Phi-N	5	10	.333	36	20	0	0	0	134^1	132	82	66	10	1	78	101	1.563	4.42	84	4.48	.261	3	.088	-14	3	-1.6
1976	Phi-N	3	1	.750	26	2	0	0	1	61^2	55	18	12	3	3	18	67	1.184	1.75	202	2.93	.241	1	.167	11	6	1.2
1977	Phi-N	0	5	.000	12	8	0	0	0	45^2	50	27	23	3	0	25	37	1.642	4.53	88	5.02	.287	1	.091	-3	0	-0.4
	Mon-N	6	5	.545	22	22	2	0	0	139	116	71	65	18	5	49	93	1.187	4.21	90	3.32	.230	8	.205	-7	7	-0.4
	Yr.	6	10	.375	34	30	2	0	0	184^2	166	98	88	21	5	74	130	1.300	4.29	90	3.74	.244	9	.180	-10	7	-0.8
1978	Mon-N	4	12	.250	33	15	0	0	0	112	121	68	67	16	5	71	69	1.714	5.38	65	6.08	.286	2	.083	-27	0	-2.9
1979	NY-N	5	3	.625	33	2	0	0	0	63^2	55	44	37	6	4	55	44	1.728	5.23	70	5.18	.243	3	.375	-12	1	-1.1
	Sea-A	0	2	.000	4	2	0	0	0	13^2	11	11	8	2	2	10	5	1.537	5.27	83	5.09	.220	0	....	-1	0	-0.1
Total	**10**	**48**	**65**	**.425**	**282**	**133**	**15**	**6**	**2**	**1063**	**983**	**541**	**470**	**92**	**40**	**537**	**789**	**1.430**	**3.98**	**93**	**4.11**	**.250**	**33**	**.127**	**-47**	**45**	**-5.6**

• TWITTY, Jeff Jeffrey Dean Twitty b: 11/10/1957, Lancaster, SC BL/TL, 6'2", 185 lbs. Deb: 7/5/1980

YEAR	TM-L	W	L	PCT	G	GS	CG	SH	SV	IP	H	R	ER	HR	HB	BB	SO	RAT	ERA	ERA+	CERA	OAV	BH	AVG	PR+	WS	TPW
1980	KC-A	2	1	.667	13	0	0	0	0	22^1	33	17	15	4	0	7	9	1.791	6.04	67	7.09	.351	0	....	-5	0	-0.5

• TWOMBLY, Cy Edwin Parker Twombly b: 6/15/1897, Groveland, MA d: 12/3/1974, Savannah, GA BL/TL, 5'10.5", 170 lbs. Deb: 6/25/1921

YEAR	TM-L	W	L	PCT	G	GS	CG	SH	SV	IP	H	R	ER	HR	HB	BB	SO	RAT	ERA	ERA+	CERA	OAV	BH	AVG	PR+	WS	TPW
1921	Chi-A	1	2	.333	7	4	0	0	0	27^2	26	21	18	1	2	25	7	1.843	5.86	72	5.46	.283	0	.000	-5	0	-0.6

• TYLER, Lefty George Albert Tyler b: 12/14/1889, Derry, NH d: 9/29/1953, Lowell, MA BL/TL, 6', 175 lbs. Deb: 9/20/1910

YEAR	TM-L	W	L	PCT	G	GS	CG	SH	SV	IP	H	R	ER	HR	HB	BB	SO	RAT	ERA	ERA+	CERA	OAV	BH	AVG	PR+	WS	TPW
1910	Bos-N	0	0	....	2	0	0	0	0	11^1	11	3	3	1	0	6	6	1.500	2.38	139	4.60	.275	2	.500	1	1	0.2
1911	Bos-N	7	10	.412	28	20	10	1	0	165^1	150	118	93	11	10	109	90	1.567	5.06	75	4.43	.243	10	.164	-20	3	-2.0
1912	Bos-N	12	22	.353	42	31	15	1	0	256^1	262	150	119	8	10	126	144	1.514	4.18	85	4.15	.276	19	.198	-14	11	-1.4
1913	Bos-N	16	17	.485	39	34	**28**	4	2	290^1	245	131	90	2	11	108	143	1.216	2.79	117	2.62	.235	21	.206	20	17	2.5
1914*	Bos-N	16	13	.552	38	34	21	5	2	271^1	247	113	81	7	14	101	140	1.283	2.69	102	3.14	.249	19	.202	-9	18	-0.8
1915	Bos-N	10	9	.526	32	24	15	1	0	204^2	182	87	65	6	5	84	89	1.300	2.86	94	3.05	.243	23	.261	-7	12	0.1
1916	Bos-N	17	9	.654	34	28	21	6	1	249^1	200	79	56	6	3	58	117	1.035	2.02	121	2.04	.226	19	.204	12	20	2.2
1917	Bos-N	14	12	.538	32	28	22	4	1	239	203	81	67	1	6	86	98	1.209	2.52	101	2.57	.240	31	.231	3	18	1.0
1918*	Chi-N	19	8	.704	33	30	22	6	1	269^1	218	72	60	1	5	67	102	1.058	2.00	139	1.99	.226	21	.210	30	24	3.5
1919	Chi-N	2	2	.500	6	5	3	0	0	30	20	8	7	0	0	13	9	1.100	2.10	137	1.81	.196	1	.143	3	3	0.4
1920	Chi-N	11	12	.478	27	27	18	2	0	193	193	83	71	6	3	57	57	1.295	3.31	97	3.24	.268	17	.262	0	12	0.5
1921	Chi-N	3	2	.600	10	6	4	0	0	50	59	22	18	2	0	14	8	1.460	3.24	118	4.15	.294	6	.231	3	4	0.4
Total	**12**	**127**	**116**	**.523**	**323**	**267**	**179**	**30**	**7**	**2230**	**1990**	**947**	**730**	**51**	**67**	**829**	**1003**	**1.264**	**2.95**	**103**	**2.97**	**.245**	**189**	**.217**	**24**	**143**	**6.6**

• TYNG, Jim James Alexander Tyng b: 5/27/1856, Philadelphia, PA d: 10/30/1931, New York, NY, 5'9", 155 lbs. Deb: 9/23/1879

YEAR	TM-L	W	L	PCT	G	GS	CG	SH	SV	IP	H	R	ER	HR	HB	BB	SO	RAT	ERA	ERA+	CERA	OAV	BH	AVG	PR+	WS	TPW
1879	Bos-N	1	2	.333	3	3	3	0	0	27	35	25	15	0	....	6	7	1.519	5.00	50	....	.295	5	.357	-9	1	-0.7
1888	Phi-N	0	0	....	1	0	0	0	1	4	8	4	2	0	1	2	2	2.500	4.50	66	....	.401	0	.000	-1	0	-0.1
Total	**2**	**1**	**2**	**.333**	**4**	**3**	**3**	**0**	**1**	**31**	**43**	**29**	**17**	**0**	**1**	**8**	**9**	**1.645**	**4.94**	**51**	**....**	**.310**	**5**	**.333**	**-9**	**1**	**-0.8**

• TYRIVER, Dave David Burton Tyriver b: 10/31/1937, Oshkosh, WI d: 10/28/1988, Oshkosh, WI BR/TR, 6', 175 lbs. Deb: 8/21/1962

YEAR	TM-L	W	L	PCT	G	GS	CG	SH	SV	IP	H	R	ER	HR	HB	BB	SO	RAT	ERA	ERA+	CERA	OAV	BH	AVG	PR+	WS	TPW
1962	Cle-A	0	0	....	4	0	0	0	0	10^2	10	6	5	2	1	7	7	1.594	4.22	92	5.63	.250	0	.000	-0	0	-0.1

• UCHRINSCKO, Jimmy James Emerson Uchrinscko b: 10/20/1900, West Newton, PA d: 3/17/1995, Mount Pleasant, PA BL/TR, 6', 180 lbs. Deb: 7/20/1926

YEAR	TM-L	W	L	PCT	G	GS	CG	SH	SV	IP	H	R	ER	HR	HB	BB	SO	RAT	ERA	ERA+	CERA	OAV	BH	AVG	PR+	WS	TPW
1926	Was-A	0	0	....	3	0	0	0	0	8	13	9	9	0	0	8	0	2.625	10.13	38	10.54	.433	0	.000	-6	0	-0.6

• UHL, Bob Robert Ellwood "Lefty" Uhl b: 9/17/1913, San Francisco, CA d: 8/21/1990, Santa Rosa, CA BB/TL, 5'11", 175 lbs. Deb: 5/8/1938

YEAR	TM-L	W	L	PCT	G	GS	CG	SH	SV	IP	H	R	ER	HR	HB	BB	SO	RAT	ERA	ERA+	CERA	OAV	BH	AVG	PR+	WS	TPW
1938	Chi-A	0	0	....	1	0	0	0	0	2	1	0	0	0	0	0	0	.500	0.00	....	0.55	.167	0	....	1	0	0.1
1940	Det-A	0	0	....	1	0	0	0	0	0	4	5	0	0	0	2	0	....	....	....	∞	1.000	0	....	0	0	0.0
Total	**2**	**0**	**0**	**....**	**2**	**0**	**0**	**0**	**0**	**2**	**5**	**5**	**0**	**0**	**0**	**2**	**0**	**3.500**	**0.00**	**....**	**0.55**	**.500**	**0**	**....**	**1**	**0**	**0.1**

• UHLE, George George Ernest "The Bull" Uhle b: 9/18/1898, Cleveland, OH d: 2/26/1985, Lakewood, OH BR/TR, 6', 190 lbs. Deb: 4/30/1919 C

YEAR	TM-L	W	L	PCT	G	GS	CG	SH	SV	IP	H	R	ER	HR	HB	BB	SO	RAT	ERA	ERA+	CERA	OAV	BH	AVG	PR+	WS	TPW
1919	Cle-A	10	5	.667	26	12	7	1	0	127	129	52	41	1	7	43	50	1.354	2.91	115	3.34	.261	13	.302	7	10	1.0
1920*	Cle-A	4	5	.444	27	6	2	0	1	84^2	98	52	49	3	8	29	27	1.500	5.21	73	4.50	.296	11	.344	-15	4	-1.2
1921	Cle-A	16	13	.552	41	28	13	2	2	238	288	132	106	9	4	63	63	1.475	4.01	106	4.29	.306	23	.245	7	16	0.9
1922	Cle-A	22	16	.579	50	**40**	23	**5**	3	287^1	328	147	130	6	13	89	82	1.451	4.07	98	4.02	.290	29	.266	5	22	1.2
1923	Cle-A	**26**	16	.619	54	**44**	**29**	1	5	**357^2**	378	167	150	8	12	102	109	1.342	3.77	105	3.41	.271	52	.361	11	**29**	2.7
1924	Cle-A	9	15	.375	28	25	15	0	1	196^1	238	134	104	6	13	75	57	1.594	4.77	90	4.79	.306	33	.308	-8	8	-0.2
1925	Cle-A	13	11	.542	29	26	17	1	0	210^2	218	118	96	5	8	78	68	1.405	4.10	108	3.60	.268	29	.287	8	15	1.3
1926	Cle-A	**27**	11	.711	39	**36**	**32**	3	1	**318^1**	300	114	100	7	13	118	159	1.313	2.83	143	3.13	.253	30	.227	36	**32**	3.9
1927	Cle-A	8	9	.471	25	22	10	1	1	153^1	187	88	74	3	9	59	69	1.604	4.34	97	4.73	.310	21	.266	-2	9	0.2
1928	Cle-A	12	17	.414	31	28	18	2	1	214^1	252	121	97	8	8	48	74	1.400	4.07	102	3.92	.300	28	.286	3	14	1.0
1929	Det-A	15	11	.577	32	30	23	1	0	249	283	141	113	9	2	58	100	1.369	4.08	105	3.63	.287	37	.343	14	16	2.1
1930	Det-A	12	12	.500	33	29	18	1	3	239	239	110	97	18	5	75	117	1.314	3.65	131	3.61	.264	36	.308	30	23	3.5
1931	Det-A	11	12	.478	29	18	15	2	2	193	190	88	75	10	4	49	63	1.238	3.50	131	3.11	.255	22	.244	23	19	2.6
1932	Det-A	6	6	.500	33	15	6	1	5	146^2	152	84	73	15	4	42	51	1.323	4.48	105	3.84	.266	10	.182	1	9	0.2
1933	Det-A	0	0	....	1	0	0	0	0	0^2	2	2	2	1	0	0	1	3.000	27.00	16	31.01	.500	0	....	-2	0	-0.2
	NY-N	1	1	.500	6	1	0	0	0	13^2	16	12	12	1	0	6	4	1.610	7.90	41	4.94	.302	0	.000	-7	0	-0.8
	NY-A	6	1	.857	12	6	4	0	0	61	63	42	35	4	3	20	26	1.361	5.16	75	3.75	.257	8	.400	-8	3	-0.4
	Yr.	6	1	.857	13	6	4	0	0	61^2	65	44	37	5	3	20	27	1.378	5.40	72	4.05	.261	8	.400	-10	3	-0.5
1934	NY-A	2	4	.333	10	2	0	0	0	16^1	30	19	18	3	0	7	10	2.265	9.92	41	10.16	.400	3	.600	-11	1	-0.8
1936	Cle-A	0	1	.000	7	0	0	0	0	12^2	26	12	12	2	0	5	5	2.447	8.53	59	11.37	.419	8	.381	-5	1	-0.1
Total	**17**	**200**	**166**	**.546**	**513**	**368**	**232**	**21**	**25**	**3119^2**	**3417**	**1635**	**1384**	**119**	**113**	**966**	**1135**	**1.405**	**3.99**	**105**	**3.85**	**.281**	**393**	**.289**	**87**	**231**	**16.9**

• UJDUR, Jerry Gerald Raymond Ujdur b: 3/5/1957, Duluth, MN BR/TR, 6'1", 195 lbs. Deb: 8/17/1980

YEAR	TM-L	W	L	PCT	G	GS	CG	SH	SV	IP	H	R	ER	HR	HB	BB	SO	RAT	ERA	ERA+	CERA	OAV	BH	AVG	PR+	WS	TPW
1980	Det-A	1	0	1.000	9	2	0	0	0	21^1	36	20	18	5	1	10	8	2.156	7.59	54	10.09	.383	0	....	-8	0	-0.8
1981	Det-A	0	0	....	4	4	0	0	0	14	19	12	10	2	0	5	5	1.714	6.43	59	6.30	.322	0	....	-4	0	-0.5
1982	Det-A	10	10	.500	25	25	7	0	0	178	150	76	73	29	3	69	86	1.230	3.69	110	3.68	.230	0	....	3	11	0.3
1983	Det-A	0	4	.000	11	6	0	0	0	34	41	33	27	6	1	20	13	1.794	7.15	55	6.74	.293	0	....	-13	0	-1.3
1984	Cle-A	1	2	.333	4	3	0	0	0	14^1	22	14	11	1	2	6	6	1.953	6.91	59	7.68	.355	0	....	-5	0	-0.5
Total	**5**	**12**	**16**	**.429**	**53**	**40**	**7**	**0**	**0**	**261^2**	**268**	**155**	**139**	**43**	**7**	**110**	**118**	**1.445**	**4.78**	**84**	**4.96**	**.266**	**0**	**....**	**-26**	**11**	**-2.7**

• ULLRICH, Sandy Carlos Santiago (Castello) Ullrich b: 7/25/1921, Havana, Cuba d: 4/21/2001, Miami, FL BR/TR, 6'1", 180 lbs. Deb: 5/3/1944

YEAR	TM-L	W	L	PCT	G	GS	CG	SH	SV	IP	H	R	ER	HR	HB	BB	SO	RAT	ERA	ERA+	CERA	OAV	BH	AVG	PR+	WS	TPW
1944	Was-A	0	0	....	3	0	0	0	0	9^2	17	10	10	2	1	4	2	2.172	9.31	35	10.41	.386	1	.333	-6	0	-0.7
1945	Was-A	3	3	.500	28	6	0	0	1	81^1	91	45	41	3	0	34	26	1.537	4.54	68	4.10	.276	6	.273	-13	2	-1.2
Total	**2**	**3**	**3**	**.500**	**31**	**6**	**0**	**0**	**1**	**91**	**108**	**55**	**51**	**5**	**1**	**38**	**28**	**1.604**	**5.04**	**62**	**4.77**	**.289**	**7**	**.280**	**-19**	**2**	**-1.9**

• ULRICH, Dutch Frank W. Ulrich b: 11/18/1899, Baltimore, MD d: 2/11/1929, Baltimore, MD BR/TR, 6'2", 195 lbs. Deb: 4/18/1925

YEAR	TM-L	W	L	PCT	G	GS	CG	SH	SV	IP	H	R	ER	HR	HB	BB	SO	RAT	ERA	ERA+	CERA	OAV	BH	AVG	PR+	WS	TPW
1925	Phi-N	3	3	.500	21	4	2	1	0	65	73	30	22	6	1	12	29	1.308	3.05	156	3.82	.285	2	.125	15	6	1.4
1926	Phi-N	8	13	.381	45	16	8	1	1	147^2	178	85	67	9	1	37	52	1.456	4.08	101	4.38	.304	12	.245	6	9	0.7
1927	Phi-N	8	11	.421	32	18	14	1	1	193^1	201	82	68	6	0	40	42	1.247	3.17	130	3.04	.271	9	.123	24	14	1.9
Total	**3**	**19**	**27**	**.413**	**98**	**38**	**24**	**3**	**2**	**406**	**452**	**197**	**157**	**21**	**2**	**89**	**123**	**1.333**	**3.48**	**121**	**3.65**	**.285**	**23**	**.167**	**45**	**29**	**4.0**

• UMBACH, Arnold Arnold William Umbach b: 12/6/1942, Williamsburg, VA BR/TR, 6'1", 180 lbs. Deb: 10/3/1964

YEAR	TM-L	W	L	PCT	G	GS	CG	SH	SV	IP	H	R	ER	HR	HB	BB	SO	RAT	ERA	ERA+	CERA	OAV	BH	AVG	PR+	WS	TPW
1964	Mil-N	1	0	1.000	1	1	0	0	0	8^1	11	5	3	0	0	4	7	1.800	3.24	109	5.63	.333	0	.000	0	0	0.0
1966	Atl-N	0	2	.000	22	3	0	0	0	40^2	40	15	14	1	2	18	23	1.426	3.10	117	3.64	.256	1	.200	2	2	0.3
Total	**2**	**1**	**2**	**.333**	**23**	**4**	**0**	**0**	**0**	**49**	**51**	**20**	**17**	**1**	**2**	**22**	**30**	**1.490**	**3.12**	**116**	**3.98**	**.270**	**1**	**.125**	**3**	**2**	**0.3**

• UMBARGER, Jim James Harold Umbarger b: 2/17/1953, Burbank, CA BL/TL, 6'6", 200 lbs. Deb: 4/8/1975

YEAR	TM-L	W	L	PCT	G	GS	CG	SH	SV	IP	H	R	ER	HR	HB	BB	SO	RAT	ERA	ERA+	CERA	OAV	BH	AVG	PR+	WS	TPW
1975	Tex-A	8	7	.533	56	12	3	2	2	131	134	63	60	11	2	59	50	1.473	4.12	91	4.35	.276	0	....	-5	7	-0.5
1976	Tex-A	10	12	.455	30	30	10	3	0	197^1	208	86	69	12	2	54	105	1.328	3.15	114	3.62	.274	0	....	9	12	0.9
1977	Oak-A	1	5	.167	12	8	1	0	0	44	62	40	32	3	4	28	24	2.045	6.55	61	7.87	.354	0	....	-12	0	-1.2
	Tex-A	1	1	.500	3	2	0	0	0	13	14	8	8	2	0	4	5	1.385	5.54	74	4.51	.275	0	....	-2	0	-0.2
	Yr.	2	6	.250	15	10	1	0	0	57	76	48	40	5	4	32	29	1.895	6.32	64	7.10	.336	0	....	-14	0	-1.4

YEAR TM-L	W	L	PCT	G	GS	CG	SH	SV	IP	H	R	ER	HR	HB	BB	SO	RAT	ERA	ERA+	CERA	OAV	BH	AVG	PR+	WS	TPW
1978 Tex-A	5	8	.385	32	9	1	0	1	97^{2}	116	58	53	9	2	36	60	1.556	4.88	77	5.03	.299	0	....	-12	2	-1.2
Total 4	25	33	.431	133	61	15	5	3	483	534	255	222	37	10	181	244	1.480	4.14	90	4.51	.287	0	....	-22	21	-2.2
• UMBRICHT, Jim	James Umbricht b: 9/17/1930, Chicago, IL d: 4/8/1964, Houston, TX BR/TR, 6'4", 215 lbs. Deb: 9/26/1959																									
1959 Pit-N	0	0	....	1	1	0	0	0	7	7	5	5	3	0	4	3	1.571	6.43	60	7.37	.259	0	.000	-2	0	-0.2
1960 Pit-N	1	2	.333	17	3	0	0	1	40^{2}	40	23	23	5	0	27	26	1.648	5.09	74	5.33	.270	2	.333	-7	1	-0.6
1961 Pit-N	0	0	....	1	0	0	0	0	3^{1}	5	2	1	0	0	2	1	2.100	2.70	148	6.27	.333	1	1.000	0	0	0.1
1962 Hou-N	4	0	1.000	34	0	0	0	2	67	51	19	15	3	2	17	55	1.015	2.01	185	2.10	.213	1	.111	14	8	1.3
1963 Hou-N	4	3	.571	35	3	0	0	0	76	52	23	22	6	1	21	48	.961	2.61	121	1.92	.195	1	.111	6	7	0.7
Total 5	9	5	.643	88	7	0	0	3	194	155	72	66	17	3	71	133	1.165	3.06	116	2.97	.222	5	.179	12	16	1.2
• UNDERHILL, Willie	Willie Vern Underhill b: 9/6/1904, Yowell, TX d: 10/26/1970, Bay City, TX BR/TR, 6'2", 185 lbs. Deb: 9/8/1927																									
1927 Cle-A	0	2	.000	4	1	0	0	0	8^{1}	12	11	9	0	0	11	4	2.760	9.72	43	9.72	.375	0	.000	-5	0	-0.5
1928 Cle-A	1	2	.333	11	3	1	0	0	28	33	23	14	0	1	20	16	1.893	4.50	92	5.42	.306	4	.364	-1	1	0.1
Total 2	1	4	.200	15	4	1	0	0	36^{1}	45	34	23	0	1	31	20	2.092	5.70	73	6.40	.322	4	.333	-6	1	-0.4
• UNDERWOOD, Fred	Frederick Theodore Underwood b: 10/14/1868, St. Louis County, MO d: 1/26/1906, Kansas City, MO, 5'7", 170 lbs. Deb: 7/18/1894																									
1894 Bro-N	2	4	.333	7	6	5	0	0	47	80	62	41	1	2	30	10	2.340	7.85	63	8.74	.372	7	.389	-15	1	-0.9
• UNDERWOOD, Pat	Patrick John Underwood b: 2/9/1957, Kokomo, IN BL/TL, 6', 175 lbs. Deb: 5/31/1979																									
1979 Det-A	6	4	.600	27	15	1	0	0	121^{2}	126	64	62	17	2	29	83	1.274	4.59	94	3.99	.269	0	....	-5	6	-0.5
1980 Det-A	3	6	.333	49	7	0	0	5	112^{2}	121	51	45	12	2	35	60	1.385	3.59	114	4.20	.277	0	....	8	8	0.8
1982 Det-A	4	8	.333	33	12	2	0	3	99	108	66	52	17	0	22	43	1.313	4.73	86	4.23	.269	0	....	-10	2	-1.0
1983 Det-A	0	0	....	4	0	0	0	0	10^{1}	11	10	10	1	0	6	2	1.645	8.71	45	5.53	.289	0	....	-6	0	-0.6
Total 4	13	18	.419	113	34	3	0	8	343^{2}	366	191	169	47	4	92	188	1.333	4.43	94	4.17	.272	0	....	-12	16	-1.2
• UNDERWOOD, Tom	Thomas Gerald Underwood b: 12/22/1953, Kokomo, IN BR/TL, 5'11", 170 lbs. Deb: 8/19/1974																									
1974 Phi-N	1	0	1.000	7	0	0	0	0	13	15	8	7	1	0	5	8	1.538	4.85	78	4.84	.313	0	.000	-2	0	-0.2
1975 Phi-N	14	13	.519	35	35	7	2	0	219^{1}	221	110	101	12	6	84	123	1.391	4.14	90	3.79	.262	9	.122	-16	9	-1.9
1976* Phi-N	10	5	.667	33	25	3	0	2	155^{2}	154	63	61	9	1	63	94	1.394	3.53	101	3.79	.260	5	.109	-2	9	-0.4
1977 Phi-N	3	2	.600	14	0	0	0	1	33^{1}	44	21	19	2	0	18	20	1.860	5.13	78	6.11	.328	0	.000	-5	1	-0.5
StL-N	6	9	.400	19	17	1	0	0	100	104	61	55	7	1	57	66	1.610	4.95	78	4.82	.278	4	.133	-14	1	-1.4
Yr.	9	11	.450	33	17	1	0	1	133^{1}	148	82	74	9	1	75	86	1.673	5.00	78	5.14	.291	4	.121	-19	2	-1.9
1978 Tor-A	6	14	.300	31	30	7	1	0	197^{2}	201	105	90	23	2	87	139	1.457	4.10	96	4.46	.263	0	....	-3	8	-0.3
1979 Tor-A	9	16	.360	33	32	12	1	0	227	213	113	93	23	9	95	127	1.357	3.69	118	4.02	.253	0	....	15	15	1.5
1980* NY-A	13	9	.591	38	27	2	2	2	187	163	85	76	15	4	66	116	1.225	3.66	107	3.16	.237	0	....	7	12	0.7
1981 NY-A	1	4	.200	9	6	0	0	0	32^{2}	32	17	16	2	0	13	29	1.378	4.41	81	3.69	.262	0	....	-3	1	-0.3
* Oak-A	3	2	.600	16	5	1	0	1	51	37	21	18	4	2	25	46	1.216	3.18	110	2.92	.202	0	....	1	3	0.1
Yr.	4	6	.400	25	11	1	0	1	83^{2}	69	38	34	6	2	38	75	1.279	3.66	96	3.22	.226	0	....	-2	4	-0.2
1982 Oak-A	10	6	.625	56	10	2	0	7	153	136	66	56	11	1	68	79	1.333	3.29	119	3.43	.241	0	....	10	12	1.0
1983 Oak-A	9	7	.563	51	15	0	0	4	144^{2}	156	69	65	13	2	50	62	1.424	4.04	95	4.25	.277	0	....	-4	8	-0.4
1984 Bal-A	1	0	1.000	37	1	0	0	1	71^{2}	78	33	28	8	0	31	39	1.521	3.52	110	4.69	.282	0	....	1	4	0.1
Total 11	86	87	.497	379	203	35	6	18	1586	1554	772	685	130	28	662	948	1.397	3.89	100	3.97	.259	18	.117	-14	83	-2.0
• UPCHURCH, Woody	Jefferson Woodrow Upchurch b: 4/13/1911, Buies Creek, NC d: 10/23/1971, Buies Creek, NC BR/TL, 6', 180 lbs. Deb: 9/14/1935																									
1935 Phi-A	0	2	.000	3	3	1	0	0	21^{1}	23	13	12	3	0	12	2	1.641	5.06	90	5.27	.271	2	.286	-1	1	0.0
1936 Phi-A	0	2	.000	7	2	1	0	0	22^{1}	36	27	24	7	0	14	6	2.239	9.67	53	10.55	.353	1	.143	-11	0	-1.0
Total 2	0	4	.000	10	5	2	0	0	43^{2}	59	40	36	10	0	26	8	1.947	7.42	66	7.97	.316	3	.214	-12	1	-1.1
• UPHAM, Bill	William Lawrence Upham b: 4/4/1888, Akron, OH d: 9/14/1959, Newark, NJ BB/TR, 6', 178 lbs. Deb: 4/10/1915																									
1915 Bro-F	7	8	.467	33	11	4	2	4	121	129	61	45	0	0	40	46	1.397	3.35	98	3.46	.274	4	.111	-2	6	-0.4
1918 Bos-N	1	1	.500	3	2	2	0	0	20^{2}	28	14	12	2	0	1	8	1.403	5.23	51	4.58	.326	2	.222	-5	0	-0.6
Total 2	8	9	.471	36	13	6	2	4	141^{2}	157	75	57	2	0	41	54	1.398	3.62	86	3.62	.282	6	.133	-7	6	-1.0
• UPHAM, John	John Leslie Upham b: 12/29/1941, Windsor, Canada BL/TL, 6', 180 lbs. Deb: 4/16/1967																									
1967 Chi-N	0	1	.000	5	0	0	0	0	1^{1}	4	5	5	1	0	2	2	4.500	33.75	11	29.70	.571	2	.667	-4	0	-0.4
1968 Chi-N	0	0	....	2	0	0	0	0	7	2	0	0	0	1	3	2	.714	0.00	....	0.96	.087	2	.200	2	1	0.2
Total 2	0	1	.000	7	0	0	0	0	8^{1}	6	5	5	1	1	5	4	1.320	5.40	66	5.56	.200	4	.308	-2	1	-0.2
• UPP, Jerry	George Henry Upp b: 12/10/1883, Sandusky, OH d: 6/30/1937, Sandusky, OH TL Deb: 9/2/1909																									
1909 Cle-A	2	1	.667	7	4	2	0	0	26^{2}	26	10	5	0	0	12	13	1.425	1.69	151	3.42	.260	2	.222	2	2	0.3
• UPSHAW, Cecil	Cecil Lee Upshaw b: 10/22/1942, Spearsville, LA d: 2/7/1995, Lawrenceville, GA BR/TR, 6'6", 205 lbs. Deb: 10/1/1966																									
1966 Atl-N	0	0	....	1	0	0	0	0	3	0	0	0	0	0	3	2	1.000	0.00	....	1.03	.000	1	1.000	1	1	0.2
1967 Atl-N	2	3	.400	30	0	0	0	8	45^{1}	42	14	13	4	4	8	31	1.103	2.58	129	2.98	.247	1	.167	3	6	0.4
1968 Atl-N	8	7	.533	52	0	0	0	13	116^{2}	98	41	32	6	4	24	74	1.046	2.47	121	2.27	.229	4	.174	6	12	0.8
1969* Atl-N	6	4	.600	62	0	0	0	27	105^{1}	102	36	34	7	1	29	57	1.244	2.91	124	3.17	.259	5	.238	9	16	1.1
1971 Atl-N	11	6	.647	49	0	0	0	17	82	95	33	32	5	2	28	56	1.500	3.51	106	4.28	.292	0	.000	2	11	0.1
1972 Atl-N	3	5	.375	42	0	0	0	13	53^{2}	50	22	22	5	1	19	23	1.286	3.69	103	3.28	.249	1	.143	1	7	0.1
1973 Atl-N	0	1	.000	5	0	0	0	0	3^{2}	8	5	4	0	0	2	3	2.727	9.82	40	10.54	.444	0	....	-2	0	-0.2
Hou-N	2	3	.400	35	0	0	0	1	38^{1}	38	21	19	3	1	15	21	1.383	4.46	81	3.75	.259	0	.000	-3	1	-0.4
Yr.	2	4	.333	40	0	0	0	1	42	46	26	23	3	1	17	24	1.500	4.93	75	4.35	.279	0	.000	-6	1	-0.6
1974 Cle-A	0	1	.000	7	0	0	0	0	8	10	4	3	1	0	4	7	1.750	3.38	107	6.13	.345	0	....	0	0	0.0
NY-A	1	5	.167	36	0	0	0	6	59^{2}	53	25	20	1	3	24	27	1.291	3.02	116	3.22	.254	0	....	2	4	0.2
Yr.	1	6	.143	43	0	0	0	6	67^{2}	63	29	23	2	3	28	34	1.345	3.06	114	3.56	.265	0	....	2	4	0.2
1975 Chi-A	1	1	.500	29	0	0	0	1	47^{1}	49	19	17	5	4	21	22	1.479	3.23	120	4.80	.271	0	....	4	3	0.4
Total 9	34	36	.486	348	0	0	0	86	563	545	220	196	37	20	177	323	1.282	3.13	112	3.40	.259	12	.160	24	61	2.6
• UPTON, Bill	William Ray Upton b: 6/18/1929, Esther, MO d: 1/2/1987, San Diego, CA BR/TR, 6', 167 lbs. Deb: 4/13/1954																									
1954 Phi-A	0	0	....	2	0	0	0	1	5	6	1	1	1	0	1	2	1.400	1.80	217	4.95	.300	0	....	1	1	0.1
• URBAN, Jack	Jack Elmer Urban b: 12/5/1928, Omaha, NE BR/TR, 5'8", 155 lbs. Deb: 6/13/1957																									
1957 KC-A	7	4	.636	31	13	3	0	0	129^{1}	111	55	48	7	1	45	55	1.206	3.34	118	2.84	.237	11	.282	10	10	1.2
1958 KC-A	8	11	.421	30	24	5	1	1	132	150	92	87	17	2	51	54	1.523	5.93	66	5.04	.286	7	.152	-29	0	-3.2
1959 StL-N	0	0	....	8	0	0	0	0	10^{2}	18	11	11	1	0	7	4	2.344	9.28	46	9.08	.409	0	.000	-6	0	-0.6
Total 3	15	15	.500	69	37	8	1	1	272	279	158	146	25	3	103	113	1.404	4.83	82	4.15	.269	18	.209	-26	10	-2.6
• URBANI, Tom	Thomas James Urbani b: 1/21/1968, Santa Cruz, CA BL/TL, 6'1", 190 lbs. Deb: 4/21/1993																									
1993 StL-N	1	3	.250	18	9	0	0	0	62	73	44	32	4	0	26	33	1.597	4.65	85	4.76	.296	3	.188	-5	0	-0.4
1994 StL-N	3	7	.300	20	10	0	0	0	80^{1}	98	48	46	12	3	21	43	1.481	5.15	81	5.32	.302	6	.250	-9	2	-0.7
1995 StL-N	3	5	.375	24	13	0	0	0	82^{2}	99	40	34	11	2	21	52	1.452	3.70	113	5.00	.305	6	.316	3	6	0.7
1996 StL-N	1	0	1.000	3	2	0	0	0	11^{2}	15	10	10	3	0	4	1	1.629	7.71	54	6.72	.319	1	.167	-5	0	-0.5
Det-A	2	2	.500	16	2	0	0	0	23^{2}	31	22	22	8	2	14	20	1.901	8.37	60	9.08	.310	0	....	-8	0	-0.7
Total 4	10	17	.370	81	36	0	0	0	260^{1}	316	164	144	38	7	86	149	1.544	4.98	85	5.49	.303	16	.246	-23	8	-1.7
• URBINA, Ugueth	Ugueth Urtain (Villarreal) Urbina b: 2/15/1974, Caracas, Venezuela BR/TR, 6'2", 185 lbs. Deb: 5/9/1995																									
1995 Mon-N	2	2	.500	7	4	0	0	0	23^{1}	26	17	16	6	0	14	15	1.714	6.17	70	6.66	.280	2	.333	-5	0	-0.4
1996 Mon-N	10	5	.667	33	17	0	0	0	114	102	54	47	18	1	44	108	1.281	3.71	117	3.78	.234	3	.103	8	8	0.7
1997 Mon-N	5	8	.385	63	0	0	0	27	64^{1}	52	29	27	9	1	29	84	1.259	3.78	111	3.42	.214	0	.000	3	10	0.2
1998 Mon-N★	6	3	.667	64	0	0	0	34	69^{1}	37	11	10	2	0	33	94	1.010	1.30	324	1.59	.157	0	.000	23	17	2.2
1999 Mon-N	6	6	.500	71	0	0	0	**41**	75^{2}	59	35	31	6	0	36	100	1.256	3.69	122	2.85	.208	0	.000	8	14	0.7

YEAR	TM-L	W	L	PCT	G	GS	CG	SH	SV	IP	H	R	ER	HR	HB	BB	SO	RAT	ERA	ERA+	CERA	OAV	BH	AVG	PR+	WS	TPW
2000	Mon-N	0	1	.000	13	0	0	0	8	13^{1}	11	6	6	1	0	5	22	1.200	4.05	118	2.95	.224	0	.000	1	2	0.1
2001	Mon-N	2	1	.667	45	0	0	0	15	46^{2}	42	24	22	8	0	21	57	1.350	4.24	105	4.13	.236	0	.000	2	6	0.2
	Bos-A	0	1	.000	19	0	0	0	9	20	16	5	5	1	0	3	32	.950	2.25	199	1.88	.219	0	....	5	5	0.5
2002	Bos-A★	1	6	.143	61	0	0	0	40	60	44	21	20	8	0	20	71	1.067	3.00	150	2.50	.202	0	....	9	11	0.9
2003	Tex-A	0	4	.000	39	0	0	0	26	38^{2}	33	19	18	6	0	18	41	1.319	4.19	118	3.74	.232	0	....	4	6	0.4
	*Fla-N	3	0	1.000	33	0	0	0	6	38^{1}	23	6	6	2	0	13	37	.939	1.41	291	1.61	.174	0	....	11	8	1.1
Total	9	35	37	.486	448	21	0	0	206	563^{2}	445	227	208	67	2	236	661	1.208	3.32	133	3.12	.214	5	.094	71	87	6.7

• URREA, John John Goody Urrea b: 2/9/1955, Los Angeles, CA BR/TR, 6'3", 205 lbs. Deb: 4/10/1977

YEAR	TM-L	W	L	PCT	G	GS	CG	SH	SV	IP	H	R	ER	HR	HB	BB	SO	RAT	ERA	ERA+	CERA	OAV	BH	AVG	PR+	WS	TPW
1977	StL-N	7	6	.538	41	12	2	1	4	139^{2}	126	56	49	13	0	35	81	1.153	3.16	122	2.97	.244	4	.138	8	10	1.0
1978	StL-N	4	9	.308	27	12	1	0	0	98^{2}	108	75	59	4	7	47	61	1.571	5.38	65	4.70	.284	3	.125	-21	0	-2.3
1979	StL-N	0	0	....	3	2	0	0	0	11^{1}	13	7	5	0	0	9	5	1.941	3.97	95	6.14	.310	1	.250	-1	0	0.0
1980	StL-N	4	1	.800	30	1	0	0	3	64^{2}	57	28	25	2	2	41	36	1.515	3.48	106	3.69	.239	3	.231	1	4	0.1
1981	SD-N	2	2	.500	38	0	0	0	2	49	43	14	13	1	3	28	19	1.449	2.39	136	3.73	.239	1	.250	5	4	0.5
Total	5	17	18	.486	139	27	3	1	9	363^{1}	347	180	151	20	12	160	202	1.395	3.74	97	3.77	.256	12	.162	-9	18	-0.8

• VAIL, Bob Robert Garfield "Doc" Vail b: 9/24/1881, Linneus, ME d: 5/28/1948, Pittsburgh, PA BR/TR, 5'10", 165 lbs. Deb: 8/27/1908

YEAR	TM-L	W	L	PCT	G	GS	CG	SH	SV	IP	H	R	ER	HR	HB	BB	SO	RAT	ERA	ERA+	CERA	OAV	BH	AVG	PR+	WS	TPW
1908	Pit-N	1	2	.333	4	1	0	0	0	15	15	10	10	0	1	7	9	1.467	6.00	38	3.87	.268	1	.333	-6	0	-0.7

• VALDES, Ismael Ismael (Alvarez) Valdes b: 8/21/1973, Victoria, Mexico BR/TR, 6'3", 185 lbs. Deb: 6/15/1994

YEAR	TM-L	W	L	PCT	G	GS	CG	SH	SV	IP	H	R	ER	HR	HB	BB	SO	RAT	ERA	ERA+	CERA	OAV	BH	AVG	PR+	WS	TPW
1994	LA-N	3	1	.750	21	1	0	0	0	28^{1}	21	10	10	2	0	10	28	1.094	3.18	124	2.25	.206	0	.000	2	3	0.2
1995*	LA-N	13	11	.542	33	27	6	2	1	197^{2}	168	76	67	17	1	51	150	1.108	3.05	124	2.62	.228	6	.097	16	15	1.3
1996*	LA-N	15	7	.682	33	33	0	0	0	225	219	94	83	20	3	54	173	1.213	3.32	116	3.18	.251	10	.143	16	16	1.4
1997	LA-N	10	11	.476	30	30	0	0	0	196^{2}	171	68	58	16	3	47	140	1.108	2.65	145	2.72	.234	5	.088	29	15	2.7
1998	LA-N	11	10	.524	27	27	2	2	0	174	171	82	77	17	2	66	122	1.362	3.98	100	3.89	.256	8	.167	0	9	0.1
1999	LA-N	9	14	.391	32	32	2	1	0	203^{1}	213	97	90	32	6	58	143	1.333	3.98	108	4.38	.270	5	.086	8	10	0.5
2000	Chi-N	2	4	.333	12	12	0	0	0	67	71	40	40	17	2	27	45	1.463	5.37	84	5.72	.273	4	.286	-6	2	-0.4
	LA-N	0	3	.000	9	8	0	0	0	40	53	29	27	5	1	13	29	1.650	6.08	71	6.15	.327	1	.091	-8	0	-0.7
	Yr.	2	7	.222	21	20	0	0	0	107	124	69	67	22	3	40	74	1.533	5.64	79	5.88	.294	5	.200	-13	2	-1.1
2001	Ana-A	9	13	.409	27	27	1	0	0	163^{2}	177	82	81	20	8	50	100	1.387	4.45	102	4.57	.277	1	.200	1	10	0.1
2002	Tex-A	6	9	.400	23	23	0	0	0	146^{2}	135	65	64	19	9	36	75	1.166	3.93	120	3.47	.242	0	.000	15	10	1.4
	Sea-A	2	3	.400	8	8	1	0	0	49^{1}	59	29	27	7	0	11	27	1.419	4.93	86	4.86	.299	0	....	-3	1	-0.3
	Yr.	8	12	.400	31	31	1	0	0	196	194	94	91	26	9	47	102	1.230	4.18	109	3.82	.257	0	.000	11	11	1.0
2003	Tex-A	8	8	.500	22	22	0	0	0	115	148	83	78	23	5	29	47	1.539	6.10	81	6.14	.318	0	.000	-13	3	-1.3
Total	10	88	94	.484	277	250	12	5	1	1606^{2}	1606	755	702	195	40	452	1079	1.281	3.93	108	3.88	.260	40	.120	57	94	4.9

• VALDES, Marc Marc Christopher Valdes b: 12/20/1971, Dayton, OH BR/TR, 6', 170 lbs. Deb: 8/28/1995

YEAR	TM-L	W	L	PCT	G	GS	CG	SH	SV	IP	H	R	ER	HR	HB	BB	SO	RAT	ERA	ERA+	CERA	OAV	BH	AVG	PR+	WS	TPW
1995	Fla-N	0	0	....	3	3	0	0	0	7	17	13	11	1	1	9	2	3.714	14.14	30	18.59	.459	0	.000	-8	0	-0.8
1996	Fla-N	1	3	.250	11	8	0	0	0	48^{2}	63	32	26	5	1	23	13	1.767	4.81	85	6.22	.315	0	.000	-5	1	-0.6
1997	Mon-N	4	4	.500	48	7	0	0	2	95	84	36	33	2	8	39	54	1.295	3.13	134	3.17	.240	2	.105	11	8	1.0
1998	Mon-N	1	3	.250	20	4	0	0	0	36^{1}	41	34	30	6	1	21	28	1.706	7.43	57	6.06	.285	2	.400	-12	0	-1.1
2000	Hou-N	5	5	.500	53	0	0	0	2	56^{2}	69	41	32	3	5	25	35	1.659	5.08	95	5.43	.301	0	.000	-0	3	-0.1
2001	Atl-N	1	0	1.000	9	0	0	0	0	7	7	6	6	4	0	1	3	1.143	7.71	57	5.90	.259	0	....	-3	0	-0.3
Total	6	12	15	.444	144	22	0	0	4	250^{2}	281	162	138	21	16	118	135	1.592	4.95	87	5.20	.285	4	.093	-17	12	-1.8

• VALDEZ, Carlos Carlos Luis (Lorenzo) Valdez b: 12/26/1971, Nizao Bani, Dominican Republic BR/TR, 5'11", 165 lbs. Deb: 7/18/1995

YEAR	TM-L	W	L	PCT	G	GS	CG	SH	SV	IP	H	R	ER	HR	HB	BB	SO	RAT	ERA	ERA+	CERA	OAV	BH	AVG	PR+	WS	TPW
1995	SF-N	0	1	.000	11	0	0	0	0	14^{2}	19	10	10	1	1	8	7	1.841	6.14	67	6.45	.322	0	.000	-3	0	-0.4
1998	Bos-A	1	0	1.000	4	0	0	0	0	3^{1}	1	0	0	0	0	5	4	1.800	0.00	....	3.41	.100	0	....	2	1	0.2
Total	2	1	1	.500	15	0	0	0	0	18	20	10	10	1	1	13	11	1.833	5.00	82	5.89	.290	0	.000	-2	1	-0.2

• VALDEZ, Efrain Efrain Antonio Valdez b: 7/11/1966, Nizao Bani, Dominican Republic BL/TL, 5'11", 180 lbs. Deb: 8/13/1990

YEAR	TM-L	W	L	PCT	G	GS	CG	SH	SV	IP	H	R	ER	HR	HB	BB	SO	RAT	ERA	ERA+	CERA	OAV	BH	AVG	PR+	WS	TPW
1990	Cle-A	1	1	.500	13	0	0	0	0	23^{2}	20	10	8	2	0	14	13	1.437	3.04	129	3.59	.233	0	....	3	1	0.3
1991	Cle-A	0	0	....	7	0	0	0	0	6	5	1	1	0	1	3	1	1.333	1.50	277	3.07	.238	0	....	2	1	0.2
1998	Ari-N	0	0	....	6	0	0	0	0	4^{1}	7	2	2	2	0	1	2	1.846	4.15	101	10.46	.368	0	....	0	0	0.0
Total	3	1	1	.500	26	0	0	0	0	34	32	13	11	4	1	18	16	1.471	2.91	137	4.37	.254	0	....	5	2	0.5

• VALDEZ, Rafael Rafael Emilio (Diaz) Valdez b: 12/17/1967, Nizao Bani, Dominican Republic BR/TR, 5'11", 165 lbs. Deb: 4/18/1990

YEAR	TM-L	W	L	PCT	G	GS	CG	SH	SV	IP	H	R	ER	HR	HB	BB	SO	RAT	ERA	ERA+	CERA	OAV	BH	AVG	PR+	WS	TPW
1990	SD-N	0	1	.000	3	0	0	0	0	5^{2}	11	7	7	4	0	2	3	2.294	11.12	34	15.39	.393	0	.000	-5	0	-0.5

• VALDEZ, Rene Rene (Gutierrez) Valdez b: 6/2/1929, Guanabacoa, Cuba BR/TR, 6'3", 175 lbs. Deb: 4/21/1957

YEAR	TM-L	W	L	PCT	G	GS	CG	SH	SV	IP	H	R	ER	HR	HB	BB	SO	RAT	ERA	ERA+	CERA	OAV	BH	AVG	PR+	WS	TPW
1957	Bro-N	1	1	.500	5	1	0	0	0	13	13	8	8	1	0	7	10	1.538	5.54	75	4.21	.265	0	.000	-2	0	-0.2

• VALDEZ, Sergio Sergio Sanchez Valdez b: 9/7/1964, Elias Pina, Dominican Republic BR/TR, 6', 190 lbs. Deb: 9/10/1986

YEAR	TM-L	W	L	PCT	G	GS	CG	SH	SV	IP	H	R	ER	HR	HB	BB	SO	RAT	ERA	ERA+	CERA	OAV	BH	AVG	PR+	WS	TPW
1986	Mon-N	0	4	.000	5	5	0	0	0	25	39	20	19	2	1	11	20	2.000	6.84	54	7.88	.361	1	.125	-9	0	-0.9
1989	Atl-N	1	2	.333	19	1	0	0	0	32^{2}	31	24	22	5	0	17	26	1.469	6.06	60	4.43	.246	1	1.000	-8	0	-0.8
1990	Atl-N	0	0	....	6	0	0	0	0	5^{1}	6	4	4	0	0	3	3	1.688	6.75	60	4.34	.273	0	....	-1	0	-0.2
	Cle-A	6	6	.500	24	13	0	0	0	102^{1}	109	62	54	17	1	35	63	1.407	4.75	82	4.72	.276	0	....	-8	3	-0.8
1991	Cle-A	1	0	1.000	6	0	0	0	0	16^{1}	15	11	10	3	0	5	11	1.224	5.51	75	3.58	.238	0	....	-2	0	-0.2
1992	Mon-N	0	2	.000	27	0	0	0	0	37^{1}	25	12	10	2	0	12	32	.991	2.41	144	1.79	.185	0	.000	4	2	0.4
1993	Mon-N	0	0	....	4	0	0	0	0	3	4	4	3	1	0	1	2	1.667	9.00	46	7.44	.308	0	....	-2	0	-0.2
1994	Bos-A	0	1	.000	12	1	0	0	0	14^{1}	25	14	13	4	0	8	4	2.302	8.16	62	11.42	.391	0	....	-5	0	-0.5
1995	SF-N	4	5	.444	13	11	1	0	0	66^{1}	78	43	35	12	3	17	29	1.432	4.75	86	5.22	.298	2	.095	-5	2	-0.7
Total	8	12	20	.375	116	31	1	0	0	302^{2}	332	194	170	46	5	109	190	1.457	5.06	78	4.97	.279	4	.121	-36	7	-3.8

• VALENTINE, Corky Harold Lewis Valentine b: 1/4/1929, Troy, OH BR/TR, 6'1", 203 lbs. Deb: 4/17/1954

YEAR	TM-L	W	L	PCT	G	GS	CG	SH	SV	IP	H	R	ER	HR	HB	BB	SO	RAT	ERA	ERA+	CERA	OAV	BH	AVG	PR+	WS	TPW
1954	Cin-N	12	11	.522	36	28	7	3	1	194^{1}	211	98	96	24	4	60	73	1.395	4.45	94	4.46	.282	9	.138	-8	10	-0.9
1955	Cin-N	2	1	.667	10	5	0	0	0	26^{2}	29	23	22	5	1	16	14	1.688	7.43	57	5.92	.276	0	.000	-9	0	-1.0
Total	2	14	12	.538	46	33	7	3	1	221	240	121	118	29	5	76	87	1.430	4.81	87	4.64	.282	9	.125	-17	10	-2.0

• VALENTINE, Joe Joseph John Valentine b: 12/24/1979, Las Vegas, NV BR/TR, 6'2", 195 lbs. Deb: 8/24/2003

YEAR	TM-L	W	L	PCT	G	GS	CG	SH	SV	IP	H	R	ER	HR	HB	BB	SO	RAT	ERA	ERA+	CERA	OAV	BH	AVG	PR+	WS	TPW
2003	Cin-N	0	0	....	2	0	0	0	0	2	5	4	4	1	0	1	1	3.000	18.00	24	18.76	.455	0	....	-3	0	-0.3

• VALENTINE, John John Gill Valentine b: 11/21/1855, Brooklyn, NY d: 10/10/1903, Central Islip, NY Deb: 5/3/1883 U

YEAR	TM-L	W	L	PCT	G	GS	CG	SH	SV	IP	H	R	ER	HR	HB	BB	SO	RAT	ERA	ERA+	CERA	OAV	BH	AVG	PR+	WS	TPW
1883	Col-a	2	10	.167	13	12	11	0	0	102	130	80	40	0	....	17	13	1.441	3.53	87	....	.291	17	.283	-5	4	-0.2

• VALENTINETTI, Vito Vito John Valentinetti b: 9/16/1928, West New York, NJ BR/TR, 6', 195 lbs. Deb: 6/20/1954

YEAR	TM-L	W	L	PCT	G	GS	CG	SH	SV	IP	H	R	ER	HR	HB	BB	SO	RAT	ERA	ERA+	CERA	OAV	BH	AVG	PR+	WS	TPW
1954	Chi-A	0	0	....	1	0	0	0	0	1	4	6	6	1	0	2	1	6.000	54.00	7	46.61	.571	0	....	-6	0	-0.6
1956	Chi-N	6	4	.600	42	2	0	0	1	95^{1}	84	47	40	10	1	36	26	1.259	3.78	100	3.33	.243	2	.100	-2	5	-0.3
1957	Chi-N	0	0	....	9	0	0	0	0	12	12	5	3	1	0	7	8	1.583	2.25	172	4.42	.255	0	.000	2	1	0.2
	Cle-A	2	2	.500	11	2	1	0	0	23^{2}	26	14	13	3	1	13	9	1.648	4.94	75	5.61	.289	1	.200	-3	1	-0.3
1958	Det-A	1	0	1.000	15	0	0	0	2	18^{2}	18	7	7	4	1	5	10	1.232	3.38	120	4.43	.257	0	....	1	2	0.1
	Was-A	4	6	.400	23	10	2	0	0	95^{2}	106	54	54	16	2	49	33	1.620	5.08	75	5.74	.286	9	.321	-11	3	-0.9
	Yr.	5	6	.455	38	10	2	0	2	114^{1}	124	61	61	20	3	54	43	1.557	4.80	80	5.53	.282	9	.321	-10	5	-0.8
1959	Was-A	0	2	.000	7	1	0	0	0	10^{2}	16	12	12	0	1	10	7	2.438	10.13	39	8.88	.356	0	....	-7	0	-0.7
Total	5	13	14	.481	108	15	3	0	3	257	266	145	135	35	6	122	94	1.510	4.73	81	4.97	.273	12	.218	-25	12	-2.4

• VALENZUELA, Fernando Fernando (Anguamea) Valenzuela b: 11/1/1960, Navojoa, Mexico BL/TL, 5'11", 195 lbs. Deb: 9/15/1980

YEAR	TM-L	W	L	PCT	G	GS	CG	SH	SV	IP	H	R	ER	HR	HB	BB	SO	RAT	ERA	ERA+	CERA	OAV	BH	AVG	PR+	WS	TPW
1980	LA-N	2	0	1.000	10	0	0	0	1	17^{2}	8	2	0	0	0	5	16	.736	0.00	....	0.88	.136	0	.000	7	3	0.7
1981*	LA-N★	13	7	.650	25	**25**	**11**	**8**	0	**192^{1}**	140	55	53	11	1	61	**180**	1.045	2.48	134	2.13	.205	16	.250	18	**17**	2.3
1982	LA-N★	19	13	.594	37	37	18	4	0	285	247	105	91	13	2	83	199	1.158	2.87	121	2.60	.236	16	.168	21	20	2.2
1983*	LA-N★	15	10	.600	35	35	9	4	0	257	245	122	107	16	3	99	189	1.339	3.75	96	3.49	.255	17	.187	1	12	0.3

YEAR TM-L	W	L	PCT	G	GS	CG	SH	SV	IP	H	R	ER	HR	HB	BB	SO	RAT	ERA	ERA+	CERA	OAV	BH	AVG	PR+	WS	TPW
1984 LA-N★	12	17	.414	34	34	12	2	0	261	218	109	88	14	2	106	240	1.241	3.03	116	2.94	.229	15	.190	17	18	2.2
1985* LA-N★	17	10	.630	35	35	14	5	0	272^1	211	92	74	14	1	101	208	1.146	2.45	142	2.46	.214	21	.216	30	21	3.5
1986 LA-N★	**21**	11	.656	34	34	**20**	3	0	269^1	226	104	94	18	1	85	242	1.155	3.14	110	2.67	.226	24	.220	15	21	2.0
1987 LA-N	14	14	.500	34	34	**12**	1	0	251	254	120	111	25	4	124	190	1.506	3.98	100	4.52	.262	13	.141	1	12	0.1
1988 LA-N	5	8	.385	23	22	3	0	1	142^1	142	71	67	11	0	76	64	1.532	4.24	79	4.41	.268	8	.182	-13	3	-1.3
1989 LA-N	10	13	.435	31	31	3	0	0	196^2	185	89	75	11	2	98	116	1.439	3.43	99	3.82	.251	12	.182	-2	8	-0.2
1990 LA-N	13	13	.500	33	33	5	2	0	204	223	112	104	19	0	77	115	1.471	4.59	80	4.39	.276	21	.304	-22	8	-1.5
1991 Cal-A	0	2	.000	2	2	0	0	0	6^2	14	10	9	3	0	3	5	2.550	12.15	34	15.15	.452	0	....	-6	0	-0.6
1993 Bal-A	8	10	.444	32	31	5	2	0	178^2	179	104	98	18	4	79	78	1.444	4.94	91	4.41	.266	0	....	-12	7	-1.1
1994 Phi-N	1	2	.333	8	7	0	0	0	45	42	16	15	8	0	7	19	1.089	3.00	143	3.20	.247	3	.250	7	3	0.7
1995 SD-N	8	3	.727	29	15	0	0	0	90^1	101	53	50	16	0	34	57	1.494	4.98	80	5.22	.289	8	.250	-11	4	-0.8
1996* SD-N	13	8	.619	33	31	0	0	0	171^2	177	78	69	17	0	67	95	1.421	3.62	109	4.20	.269	9	.143	7	10	0.6
1997 SD-N	2	8	.200	13	13	1	0	0	66^1	84	42	35	10	4	32	51	1.749	4.75	81	6.64	.309	3	.176	-6	1	-0.6
StL-N	0	4	.000	5	5	0	0	0	22^2	22	19	14	2	1	14	10	1.588	5.56	75	4.69	.253	1	.200	-4	0	-0.4
Yr.	2	12	.143	18	18	1	0	0	89	106	61	49	12	5	46	61	1.708	4.96	79	6.14	.295	4	.182	-9	1	-0.9
Total 17	173	153	.531	453	424	113	31	2	2930	2718	1303	1154	226	25	1151	2074	1.320	3.54	104	3.55	.248	187	.200	50	168	8.3

• VALERA, Julio Julio Enrique (Torres) Valera b: 10/13/1968, Aguadilla, Puerto Rico BR/TR, 6'2", 215 lbs. Deb: 9/1/1990

YEAR TM-L	W	L	PCT	G	GS	CG	SH	SV	IP	H	R	ER	HR	HB	BB	SO	RAT	ERA	ERA+	CERA	OAV	BH	AVG	PR+	WS	TPW
1990 NY-N	1	1	.500	3	3	0	0	0	13	20	11	10	1	0	7	4	2.077	6.92	54	7.82	.351	1	.200	-4	0	-0.5
1991 NY-N	0	0	....	2	0	0	0	0	2	1	0	0	0	0	4	3	2.500	0.00	....	5.16	.143	0	....	1	0	0.1
1992 Cal-A	8	11	.421	30	28	4	2	0	188	188	82	78	15	2	64	113	1.340	3.73	107	3.75	.262	0	....	4	12	0.4
1993 Cal-A	3	6	.333	19	5	0	0	4	53	77	44	39	8	2	15	28	1.736	6.62	68	6.83	.344	0	....	-13	0	-1.3
1996 KC-A	3	2	.600	31	2	0	0	1	61^1	75	44	44	7	2	27	31	1.663	6.46	78	5.75	.307	0	....	-10	2	-0.9
Total 5	15	20	.429	85	38	4	2	5	317^1	361	181	171	31	6	117	179	1.506	4.85	89	4.83	.289	1	.200	-22	14	-2.1

• VALVERDE, Jose Jose Rafael Valverde b: 7/24/1979, San Pedro de Macoris, Dominican Republic BR/TR, 6'4", 254 lbs. Deb: 6/1/2003

YEAR TM-L	W	L	PCT	G	GS	CG	SH	SV	IP	H	R	ER	HR	HB	BB	SO	RAT	ERA	ERA+	CERA	OAV	BH	AVG	PR+	WS	TPW
2003 Ari-N	2	1	.667	54	0	0	0	10	50^1	24	16	12	4	2	26	71	.993	2.15	217	1.77	.137	1	1.000	15	11	1.5

• VAN ALSTYNE, Clay Clayton Emory "Spike" Van Alstyne b: 5/24/1900, Stuyvesant, NY d: 1/5/1960, Hudson, NY BR/TR, 5'11", 180 lbs. Deb: 8/20/1927

YEAR TM-L	W	L	PCT	G	GS	CG	SH	SV	IP	H	R	ER	HR	HB	BB	SO	RAT	ERA	ERA+	CERA	OAV	BH	AVG	PR+	WS	TPW
1927 Was-A	0	0	....	2	0	0	0	0	3	3	1	1	0	0	0	0	1.000	3.00	135	1.95	.250	0	....	0	0	0.0
1928 Was-A	0	0	....	4	0	0	0	0	21^1	26	14	13	0	1	13	5	1.828	5.48	73	5.59	.329	2	.250	-4	1	-0.2
Total 2	0	0	....	6	0	0	0	0	24^1	29	15	14	0	1	13	5	1.726	5.18	77	5.14	.319	2	.250	-3	1	-0.2

• VAN ATTA, Russ Russell "Sheriff" Van Atta b: 6/21/1906, Augusta, NJ d: 10/10/1986, Andover, NJ BL/TL, 6', 184 lbs. Deb: 4/25/1933

YEAR TM-L	W	L	PCT	G	GS	CG	SH	SV	IP	H	R	ER	HR	HB	BB	SO	RAT	ERA	ERA+	CERA	OAV	BH	AVG	PR+	WS	TPW
1933 NY-A	12	4	.750	26	22	10	2	1	157	160	81	73	8	1	63	76	1.420	4.18	93	3.71	.262	17	.283	-3	10	0.0
1934 NY-A	3	5	.375	28	9	0	0	0	88	107	69	62	3	2	46	39	1.739	6.34	64	5.33	.307	6	.207	-24	0	-2.1
1935 NY-A	0	0	....	5	0	0	0	0	4^2	5	5	2	0	0	4	3	1.929	3.86	105	5.09	.263	0	.000	0	0	0.0
StL-A	9	16	.360	53	17	1	0	3	170^1	201	116	101	10	3	87	87	1.691	5.34	90	5.13	.292	9	.214	-9	9	-0.9
Yr.	9	16	.360	**58**	17	1	0	3	175	206	121	103	10	3	91	90	1.697	5.30	90	5.13	.291	9	.209	-9	9	-0.9
1936 StL-A	4	7	.364	**52**	9	2	0	2	122^2	164	101	90	9	2	68	59	1.891	6.60	81	6.37	.320	5	.172	-14	4	-1.3
1937 StL-A	1	2	.333	16	6	1	0	0	58^2	74	41	36	2	0	32	34	1.807	5.52	87	5.41	.307	6	.462	-4	3	-0.1
1938 StL-A	4	7	.364	25	12	3	1	0	104	118	75	70	7	1	61	35	1.721	6.06	82	5.22	.289	4	.133	-12	3	-1.2
1939 StL-A	0	0	....	2	1	0	0	0	7	9	10	9	0	1	7	6	2.286	11.57	42	7.41	.310	0	.000	-5	0	-0.5
Total 7	33	41	.446	207	76	17	3	6	712^1	838	498	443	39	10	368	339	1.693	5.60	83	5.11	.293	47	.228	-72	29	-6.1

• VAN BRABANT, Ozzie Camille Oscar Van Brabant b: 9/28/1926, Kingsville, Canada BR/TR, 6'1", 165 lbs. Deb: 4/13/1954

YEAR TM-L	W	L	PCT	G	GS	CG	SH	SV	IP	H	R	ER	HR	HB	BB	SO	RAT	ERA	ERA+	CERA	OAV	BH	AVG	PR+	WS	TPW
1954 Phi-A	0	2	.000	9	2	0	0	0	26^2	35	23	21	3	1	18	10	1.988	7.09	55	7.59	.347	1	.200	-9	0	-0.9
1955 KC-A	0	0	....	2	0	0	0	0	2	4	4	4	1	0	2	1	3.000	18.00	23	14.96	.400	0	....	-3	0	-0.3
Total 2	0	2	.000	11	2	0	0	0	28^2	39	27	25	4	1	20	11	2.058	7.85	50	8.10	.351	1	.200	-12	0	-1.2

• VAN CUYK, Chris Christian Gerald Van Cuyk b: 1/3/1927, Kimberly, WI d: 11/3/1992, Hudson, FL BL/TL, 6'6", 215 lbs. Deb: 7/16/1950

YEAR TM-L	W	L	PCT	G	GS	CG	SH	SV	IP	H	R	ER	HR	HB	BB	SO	RAT	ERA	ERA+	CERA	OAV	BH	AVG	PR+	WS	TPW
1950 Bro-N	1	3	.250	12	4	1	0	0	33^1	33	19	18	3	1	12	21	1.350	4.86	84	3.91	.266	1	.100	-4	1	-0.4
1951 Bro-N	1	2	.333	9	6	0	0	0	29^1	33	22	18	4	4	11	16	1.500	5.52	71	5.58	.295	2	.250	-6	0	-0.5
1952 Bro-N	5	6	.455	23	16	4	0	1	97^2	104	58	56	12	5	40	66	1.474	5.16	70	4.71	.271	8	.242	-17	2	-1.6
Total 3	7	11	.389	44	26	5	0	1	160^1	170	99	92	19	10	63	103	1.453	5.16	73	4.70	.274	11	.216	-27	3	-2.6

• VAN CUYK, Johnny John Henry Van Cuyk b: 7/7/1921, Little Chute, WI BL/TL, 6'1", 190 lbs. Deb: 9/18/1947

YEAR TM-L	W	L	PCT	G	GS	CG	SH	SV	IP	H	R	ER	HR	HB	BB	SO	RAT	ERA	ERA+	CERA	OAV	BH	AVG	PR+	WS	TPW
1947 Bro-N	0	0	....	2	0	0	0	0	3^1	5	2	2	0	0	1	2	1.800	5.40	77	5.58	.357	0	....	-1	0	-0.1
1948 Bro-N	0	0	....	3	0	0	0	0	5	4	3	2	1	0	1	1	1.000	3.60	111	2.61	.200	0	....	0	0	0.0
1949 Bro-N	0	0	....	2	0	0	0	0	2	3	2	2	0	0	1	0	2.000	9.00	46	7.09	.429	0	....	-1	0	-0.1
Total 3	0	0	....	7	0	0	0	0	10^1	12	7	6	1	0	3	3	1.452	5.23	78	4.43	.293	0	....	-2	0	-0.2

• VAN DYKE, Ben Benjamin Harrison Van Dyke b: 8/15/1888, Clintonville, PA d: 10/22/1973, Sarasota, FL BR/TL, 6'1", 150 lbs. Deb: 5/11/1909

YEAR TM-L	W	L	PCT	G	GS	CG	SH	SV	IP	H	R	ER	HR	HB	BB	SO	RAT	ERA	ERA+	CERA	OAV	BH	AVG	PR+	WS	TPW
1909 Phi-N	0	0	....	2	0	0	0	0	7^1	7	3	3	0	0	4	5	1.500	3.68	70	3.81	.269	0	.000	-1	0	-0.2
1912 Bos-A	0	0	....	3	1	0	0	0	14^1	13	10	5	0	1	7	8	1.395	3.14	109	3.40	.245	1	.250	0	0	0.0
Total 2	0	0	....	5	1	0	0	0	21^2	20	13	8	0	1	11	13	1.431	3.32	92	3.54	.253	1	.143	-1	0	-0.1

• VAN EGMOND, Tim Timothy Layne Van Egmond b: 5/31/1969, Shreveport, LA BR/TR, 6'2", 185 lbs. Deb: 6/26/1994

YEAR TM-L	W	L	PCT	G	GS	CG	SH	SV	IP	H	R	ER	HR	HB	BB	SO	RAT	ERA	ERA+	CERA	OAV	BH	AVG	PR+	WS	TPW
1994 Bos-A	2	3	.400	7	7	1	0	0	38^1	38	27	27	7	0	21	22	1.539	6.34	79	5.01	.255	0	....	-6	1	-0.6
1995 Bos-A	0	1	.000	4	1	0	0	0	6^2	9	7	7	2	0	6	5	2.250	9.45	51	10.03	.310	0	....	-3	0	-0.3
1996 Mil-A	3	5	.375	12	9	0	0	0	54^2	58	35	32	6	1	23	33	1.482	5.27	99	4.56	.274	0	....	-2	2	-0.1
Total 3	5	9	.357	23	17	1	0	0	99^2	105	69	66	15	1	50	60	1.555	5.96	85	5.10	.269	0	....	-11	3	-1.0

• VAN HALTREN, George George Edward Martin "Rip" Van Haltren b: 3/30/1866, St. Louis, MO d: 9/29/1945, Oakland, CA BL/TL, 5'11", 170 lbs. Deb: 6/27/1887 M ♦

YEAR TM-L	W	L	PCT	G	GS	CG	SH	SV	IP	H	R	ER	HR	HB	BB	SO	RAT	ERA	ERA+	CERA	OAV	BH	AVG	PR+	WS	TPW
1887 Chi-N	11	7	.611	20	18	18	1	**1**	161	243	113	69	7	16	66	76	1.509	3.86	115	....	.338	50	.267	11	13	0.0
1888 Chi-N	13	13	.500	30	24	24	4	1	245^2	263	149	96	15	13	60	139	1.315	3.52	86	....	.264	90	.283	-20	24	-0.4
1890 Bro-P	15	10	.600	28	25	23	0	2	223	272	190	106	8	21	89	48	1.619	4.28	104	....	.288	126	.335	2	30	1.5
1891 Bal-a	0	1	.000	6	1	0	0	0	23	38	34	13	1	4	10	7	2.087	5.09	73	....	.357	180	.318	-3	26	1.4
1892 Bal-N	0	0	....	4	0	0	0	0	14^2	28	17	15	1	0	7	5	2.386	9.20	37	9.77	.389	168	.302	-9	19	0.5
1895 NY-N	0	0	....	1	0	0	0	0	5	13	12	7	0	2	2	1	3.000	12.60	37	15.54	.473	177	.340	-4	22	1.4
1896 NY-N	1	0	1.000	2	0	0	0	0	8	5	2	2	1	0	1	3	.750	2.25	187	1.47	.179	197	.351	2	23	2.4
1900 NY-N	0	0	....	1	0	0	0	0	3	1	0	0	0	0	3	0	1.333	0.00	....	1.85	.105	180	.315	1	21	1.7
1901 NY-N	0	0	....	1	0	0	0	0	6	12	10	2	0	1	6	2	3.000	3.00	110	12.66	.411	182	.335	0	23	2.9
Total 9	40	31	.563	93	68	65	5	4	689^1	875	527	310	33	57	244	281	1.528	4.05	94	0.46	.299	2552	.317	-20	201	11.5

• VAN HEKKEN, Andy Andrew William Van Hekken b: 7/31/1979, Holland, MI BR/TL, 6'3", 175 lbs. Deb: 9/3/2002

YEAR TM-L	W	L	PCT	G	GS	CG	SH	SV	IP	H	R	ER	HR	HB	BB	SO	RAT	ERA	ERA+	CERA	OAV	BH	AVG	PR+	WS	TPW
2002 Det-A	1	3	.250	5	5	1	1	0	30	38	13	10	2	0	6	5	1.467	3.00	143	4.55	.311	0	....	5	2	0.4

• VAN LANDINGHAM, William William Joseph Van Landingham b: 7/16/1970, Columbia, TN BR/TR, 6'2", 210 lbs. Deb: 5/21/1994

YEAR TM-L	W	L	PCT	G	GS	CG	SH	SV	IP	H	R	ER	HR	HB	BB	SO	RAT	ERA	ERA+	CERA	OAV	BH	AVG	PR+	WS	TPW
1994 SF-N	8	2	.800	16	14	0	0	0	84	70	37	33	4	2	43	56	1.345	3.54	113	3.20	.223	2	.065	1	6	-0.1
1995 SF-N	6	3	.667	18	18	1	0	0	122^2	124	58	50	14	2	40	95	1.337	3.67	111	3.98	.264	7	.152	5	6	0.5
1996 SF-N	9	14	.391	32	32	0	0	0	181^2	196	123	109	17	9	78	97	1.508	5.40	76	4.73	.276	8	.131	-28	2	-2.8
1997 SF-N	4	7	.364	18	17	0	0	0	89	80	56	49	11	0	59	52	1.562	4.96	82	4.59	.237	3	.115	-9	2	-0.9
Total 4	27	26	.509	84	81	1	0	0	477^1	470	274	241	46	13	220	300	1.446	4.54	90	4.24	.257	20	.122	-30	16	-3.3

• VAN POPPEL, Todd Todd Matthew Van Poppel b: 12/9/1971, Hinsdale, IL BR/TR, 6'5", 210 lbs. Deb: 9/11/1991

YEAR TM-L	W	L	PCT	G	GS	CG	SH	SV	IP	H	R	ER	HR	HB	BB	SO	RAT	ERA	ERA+	CERA	OAV	BH	AVG	PR+	WS	TPW
1991 Oak-A	0	0	....	1	1	0	0	0	4^2	7	5	5	1	0	2	6	1.929	9.64	40	8.85	.368	0	....	-3	0	-0.3
1993 Oak-A	6	6	.500	16	16	0	0	0	84	76	50	47	10	2	62	47	1.643	5.04	81	5.17	.243	0	....	-9	3	-0.8
1994 Oak-A	7	10	.412	23	23	0	0	0	116^2	108	80	79	20	3	89	83	1.689	6.09	73	5.82	.250	0	....	-23	2	-2.1
1995 Oak-A	4	8	.333	36	14	1	0	0	138^1	125	77	75	16	4	56	122	1.308	4.88	91	3.82	.244	0	....	-6	5	-0.6

YEAR	TM-L	W	L	PCT	G	GS	CG	SH	SV	IP	H	R	ER	HR	HB	BB	SO	RAT	ERA	ERA+	CERA	OAV	BH	AVG	PR+	WS	TPW
1996	Oak-A	1	5	.167	28	6	0	0	1	63	86	56	54	13	2	33	37	1.889	7.71	64	7.81	.333	0	....	-21	0	-1.9
	Det-A	2	4	.333	9	9	1	1	0	36^1	53	51	46	11	1	29	16	2.257	11.39	44	10.57	.338	0	....	-25	0	-2.3
	Yr.	3	9	.250	37	15	1	1	1	99^1	139	107	100	24	3	62	53	2.023	9.06	55	8.82	.335	0	....	-45	0	-4.1
1998	Tex-A	1	2	.333	4	4	0	0	0	19^1	26	20	19	5	1	10	10	1.862	8.84	55	8.04	.313	0	.000	-8	0	-0.8
	Pit-N	1	2	.333	18	7	0	0	0	47	53	32	28	4	0	18	32	1.511	5.36	80	4.50	.286	3	.250	-6	1	-0.5
2000	Chi-N	4	5	.444	51	2	0	0	2	86^1	80	38	36	10	2	48	77	1.483	3.75	121	4.48	.249	0	.000	8	6	0.6
2001	Chi-N	4	1	.800	59	0	0	0	0	75	63	22	21	9	0	38	90	1.347	2.52	164	3.61	.223	2	.286	15	8	1.5
2002	Tex-A	3	2	.600	50	0	0	0	1	72^2	80	44	44	14	3	29	85	1.500	5.45	87	5.45	.275	0	.000	-5	3	-0.5
2003	Tex-A	1	0	1.000	7	1	0	0	0	12^2	20	14	12	1	0	9	9	2.289	8.53	58	8.27	.345	0	....	-5	0	-0.5
	Cin-N	2	1	.667	9	4	0	0	0	35^2	31	18	18	7	1	6	25	1.037	4.54	94	3.15	.228	1	.111	-1	2	-0.1
Total	10	36	46	.439	311	87	2	1	4	791^2	808	507	484	121	19	429	639	1.563	5.50	82	5.30	.265	6	.150	-89	30	-8.2
• VAN RYN, Ben		Benjamin Ashley Van Ryn	b: 8/9/1971, Fort Wayne, IN	BL/TL, 6'5", 185 lbs.	Deb: 5/9/1996																						
1996	Cal-A	0	0	....	1	0	0	0	0	1	1	0	0	0	0	1	0	2.000	0.00	....	5.48	.250	0	....	1	0	0.0
1998	Chi-N	0	0	....	9	0	0	0	0	8	9	3	3	0	1	6	6	1.875	3.38	131	5.89	.290	0	.000	1	1	0.1
	SD-N	0	1	.000	6	0	0	0	0	2^2	3	3	3	0	1	4	1	2.625	10.13	39	9.82	.273	0	....	-2	0	-0.2
	Yr.	0	1	.000	15	0	0	0	0	10^2	12	6	6	0	2	10	7	2.063	5.06	82	6.87	.286	0	.000	-1	1	-0.1
	Tor-A	0	1	.000	10	0	0	0	0	4	6	4	4	0	0	2	3	2.000	9.00	52	7.72	.400	0	....	-2	0	-0.2
Total	2	0	2	.000	26	0	0	0	0	15^2	19	10	10	0	2	13	10	2.043	5.74	76	7.00	.311	0	.000	-2	1	-0.2
• VAN ZANDT, Ike		Charles Isaac Van Zandt	b: 2/1876, Brooklyn, NY	d: 9/14/1908, Nashua, NH	BL/TL	Deb: 8/5/1901 ♦																					
1901	NY-N	0	0	....	2	0	0	0	0	12^2	16	15	10	0	1	8	2	1.895	7.11	47	5.84	.306	1	.167	-5	0	-0.6
1905	StL-A	0	0	....	1	0	0	0	0	6^2	2	0	0	0	1	2	3	.600	0.00	....	0.76	.096	75	.233	2	4	-2.0
Total	2	0	0	....	3	0	0	0	0	19^1	18	15	10	0	2	10	5	1.448	4.66	71	4.09	.247	76	.224	-3	4	-2.6
• VANCE, Cory		Cory Wade Vance	b: 6/20/1979, Dayton, OH	BL/TL, 6'1", 195 lbs.	Deb: 9/21/2002																						
2002	Col-N	0	0	....	2	1	0	0	0	4	4	3	3	2	1	4	1	2.000	6.75	71	11.75	.267	0	.000	-1	0	-0.1
2003	Col-N	1	3	.250	9	3	0	0	0	27^1	31	19	17	6	1	10	12	1.500	5.60	88	5.78	.287	2	.286	-2	1	-0.1
Total	2	1	3	.250	11	4	0	0	0	31^1	35	22	20	8	2	14	13	1.564	5.74	85	6.54	.285	2	.250	-2	1	-0.2
• VANCE, Dazzy		Clarence Arthur Vance	b: 3/4/1891, Orient, IA	d: 2/16/1961, Homosassa Springs, FL	BR/TR, 6'2", 200 lbs.	Deb: 4/16/1915	HOF: 1955																				
1915	Pit-N	0	1	.000	1	1	0	0	0	2^2	3	3	3	0	1	5	0	3.000	10.13	27	12.89	.375	0	.000	-2	0	-0.3
	NY-A	0	3	.000	8	3	1	0	0	28	23	14	11	1	2	16	18	1.393	3.54	83	3.47	.232	2	.667	-2	2	0.0
1918	NY-A	0	0	....	2	0	0	0	0	2^1	9	5	4	0	0	2	0	4.714	15.43	18	30.56	.692	0	....	-3	0	-0.4
1922	Bro-N	18	12	.600	36	31	16	**5**	0	245^2	259	122	101	9	8	94	**134**	1.437	3.70	110	3.89	.276	20	.225	12	16	1.3
1923	Bro-N	18	15	.545	37	35	21	3	0	280^1	263	127	109	10	11	100	**197**	1.295	3.50	111	3.19	.250	7	.084	12	18	1.0
1924	Bro-N	**28**	6	.824	35	34	**30**	3	0	308^1	238	89	74	11	9	77	**262**	1.022	**2.16**	**173**	**2.02**	**.213**	16	.151	**63**	**36**	**6.0**
1925	Bro-N	**22**	9	.710	31	31	26	**4**	0	265^1	247	115	104	8	10	66	**221**	1.180	3.53	118	2.78	.250	14	.143	28	20	2.6
1926	Bro-N	9	10	.474	24	22	12	0	1	169	172	80	73	7	1	58	**140**	1.361	3.89	98	3.53	.271	10	.182	2	11	0.1
1927	Bro-N	16	15	.516	34	32	**25**	2	1	273^1	242	98	82	12	6	69	**184**	1.138	2.70	147	2.56	**.239**	15	.167	38	25	3.6
1928	Bro-N	22	10	.688	38	32	24	**4**	2	280^1	226	79	65	11	7	72	**200**	1.063	**2.09**	**190**	**2.20**	**.221**	17	.177	**60**	**32**	**6.1**
1929	Bro-N	14	13	.519	31	27	17	1	0	231^1	244	110	100	15	9	47	126	1.258	3.89	119	3.45	.274	10	.135	24	19	2.0
1930	Bro-N	17	15	.531	35	31	20	**4**	0	258^2	241	97	75	15	5	55	173	1.144	**2.61**	**188**	**2.74**	**.246**	12	.135	**60**	**26**	**4.9**
1931	Bro-N	11	13	.458	30	29	12	2	0	218^2	221	99	82	12	0	53	150	1.253	3.38	113	3.14	.261	9	.134	13	15	1.1
1932	Bro-N	12	11	.522	27	24	9	1	1	175^2	171	90	82	10	1	57	103	1.298	4.20	91	3.28	.256	5	.089	-8	9	-1.1
1933	StL-N	6	2	.750	28	11	2	0	3	99	105	42	39	3	1	28	67	1.343	3.55	98	3.39	.267	5	.179	-1	6	-0.1
1934	Cin-N	0	2	.000	6	2	0	0	0	18	28	21	15	1	1	11	9	2.167	7.50	54	7.92	.350	1	.250	-6	0	-0.6
	* StL-N	1	1	.500	19	4	1	0	1	59	62	26	24	4	2	14	33	1.288	3.66	115	3.60	.271	2	.133	3	4	0.3
	Yr.	1	3	.250	25	6	1	0	1	77	90	47	39	5	3	25	42	1.494	4.56	91	4.61	.291	3	.158	-3	4	-0.3
1935	Bro-N	3	2	.600	20	0	0	0	2	51	55	29	25	3	3	16	28	1.392	4.41	90	3.95	.268	1	.059	-3	2	-0.5
Total	16	197	140	.585	442	349	216	29	11	2966^2	2809	1246	1068	132	77	840	2045	1.230	3.24	123	3.03	.251	146	.150	288	241	25.8
• VANCE, Joe		Joseph Albert "Sandy" Vance	b: 9/16/1905, Devine, TX	d: 7/4/1978, San Antonio, TX	BR/TR, 6'1.5", 190 lbs.	Deb: 4/18/1935																					
1935	Chi-A	2	2	.500	10	0	0	0	0	31	36	26	23	1	0	21	12	1.839	6.68	69	5.36	.295	2	.182	-7	0	-0.7
1937	NY-A	1	0	1.000	2	2	0	0	0	15	11	5	5	2	0	9	3	1.333	3.00	148	3.53	.204	0	.000	2	1	0.1
1938	NY-A	0	0	....	3	1	0	0	0	11^1	20	9	9	2	0	4	2	2.118	7.15	63	9.72	.408	3	.750	-3	1	-0.1
Total	3	3	2	.600	15	3	0	0	0	57^1	67	40	37	5	0	34	17	1.762	5.81	79	5.74	.298	5	.250	-9	2	-0.8
• VANCE, Sandy		Gene Covington Vance	b: 1/5/1947, Lamar, CO	BR/TR, 6'2", 180 lbs.	Deb: 4/26/1970																						
1970	LA-N	7	7	.500	20	18	2	0	0	115	109	47	40	9	1	37	45	1.270	3.13	122	3.34	.248	7	.189	7	7	0.7
1971	LA-N	2	1	.667	10	3	0	0	0	26	38	21	20	1	0	9	11	1.808	6.92	47	6.15	.355	0	.000	-11	0	-1.2
Total	2	9	8	.529	30	21	2	0	0	141	147	68	60	10	1	46	56	1.369	3.83	94	3.86	.269	7	.167	-4	7	-0.5
• VANDE BERG, Ed		Edward John Vande Berg	b: 10/26/1958, Redlands, CA	BR/TL, 6'2"	Deb: 4/7/1982																						
1982	Sea-A	9	4	.692	**78**	0	0	0	5	76	54	21	20	5	2	32	60	1.132	2.37	179	2.45	.207	0	....	16	11	1.6
1983	Sea-A	2	4	.333	68	0	0	0	5	64^1	59	32	24	6	1	22	49	1.259	3.36	127	3.27	.246	0	....	7	5	0.6
1984	Sea-A	8	12	.400	50	17	2	0	7	130^1	165	76	69	18	0	50	71	1.650	4.76	84	5.85	.313	0	....	-8	6	-0.8
1985	Sea-A	2	1	.667	76	0	0	0	3	67^2	71	30	28	4	1	31	34	1.507	3.72	113	4.26	.274	0	....	4	5	0.4
1986	LA-N	1	5	.167	60	0	0	0	0	71^1	83	32	27	8	1	33	42	1.626	3.41	101	5.23	.290	0	.000	2	3	0.2
1987	Cle-A	1	0	1.000	55	0	0	0	0	72^1	96	42	41	9	0	21	40	1.618	5.10	89	5.78	.325	0	....	-4	3	-0.3
1988	Tex-A	2	2	.500	26	0	0	0	2	37	44	19	17	2	0	11	18	1.486	4.14	99	4.32	.308	0	....	-0	2	0.0
Total	7	25	28	.472	413	17	2	0	22	519	572	252	226	52	5	200	314	1.487	3.92	104	4.62	.284	0	.000	16	35	1.6
• VANDENBERG, Hy		Harold Harris Vandenberg	b: 3/17/1907, Abilene, KS	d: 7/31/1994, Bloomington, MN	BR/TR, 6'4", 220 lbs.	Deb: 6/8/1935																					
1935	Bos-A	0	0	....	3	0	0	0	0	5^1	15	12	12	1	0	4	2	3.563	20.25	23	19.34	.500	1	1.000	-9	0	-0.8
1937	NY-N	0	1	.000	1	1	1	0	0	8	10	7	7	0	0	6	2	2.000	7.88	49	5.91	.313	0	.000	-4	0	-0.4
1938	NY-N	0	1	.000	6	1	0	0	0	18	28	16	15	2	0	12	7	2.222	7.50	50	8.85	.368	0	.000	-7	0	-0.8
1939	NY-N	0	0	....	2	1	0	0	0	6^1	10	5	4	0	0	6	3	2.526	5.68	69	8.55	.345	0	.000	-1	0	-0.2
1940	NY-N	1	1	.500	13	3	1	0	1	32^1	27	15	14	2	1	16	17	1.330	3.90	100	3.24	.227	1	.125	0	2	0.0
1944	Chi-N	7	4	.636	35	9	2	0	2	126^1	123	67	51	8	1	51	54	1.377	3.63	97	3.59	.255	9	.237	0	6	0.1
1945*	Chi-N	7	3	.700	30	7	3	1	2	95^1	91	44	37	4	4	33	35	1.301	3.49	105	3.38	.259	4	.125	0	6	-0.1
Total	7	15	10	.600	90	22	7	1	5	291^2	304	166	140	17	6	128	120	1.481	4.32	86	4.27	.271	15	.169	-21	14	-2.2
• VANDER MEER, Johnny		John Samuel "The Dutch Master,Double No-Hit" Vander Meer	b: 11/2/1914, Prospect Park, NJ	d: 10/6/1997, Tampa, FL	BB/TL, 6'1"	Deb: 4/22/1937																					
1937	Cin-N	3	5	.375	19	10	4	0	0	84^1	63	41	36	0	2	69	52	1.565	3.84	97	3.36	.209	5	.217	-1	4	0.1
1938	Cin-N★	15	10	.600	32	29	16	3	0	225^1	177	89	78	12	3	103	125	1.243	3.12	117	**2.75**	**.213**	15	.181	10	16	0.8
1939	Cin-N★	5	9	.357	30	21	8	0	0	129	128	76	67	7	2	95	102	1.729	4.67	82	4.90	.264	4	.111	-15	3	-1.7
1940*	Cin-N	3	1	.750	10	7	2	0	1	48	38	24	20	3	1	41	41	1.646	3.75	101	4.11	.211	6	.300	-2	4	0.0
1941	Cin-N	16	13	.552	33	32	18	6	0	226^1	172	83	71	8	1	126	**202**	1.317	2.82	127	2.86	.214	10	.132	20	19	1.7
1942	Cin-N★	18	12	.600	33	33	21	4	0	244	188	78	66	6	1	102	**186**	1.189	2.43	135	2.33	.208	11	.147	22	21	2.3
1943	Cin-N★	15	16	.484	36	**36**	21	3	0	289	228	102	92	5	3	162	**174**	1.349	2.87	116	2.95	.224	13	.137	7	19	0.5
1946	Cin-N	10	12	.455	29	25	11	4	0	204^1	175	77	72	11	0	78	94	1.238	3.17	106	2.85	.233	18	.247	-2	13	0.1
1947	Cin-N	9	14	.391	30	29	9	3	0	186	186	104	91	11	3	87	79	1.468	4.40	93	3.98	.261	5	.088	-4	7	-0.7
1948	Cin-N	17	14	.548	33	33	14	3	0	232	204	97	88	15	1	124	120	1.414	3.41	114	3.60	.239	11	.141	16	20	1.7
1949	Cin-N	5	10	.333	28	24	7	3	0	159^2	172	92	87	12	2	85	76	**1.610**	4.90	85	4.83	.281	4	.077	-13	4	-1.5
1950	Chi-N	3	4	.429	32	6	0	0	1	73^2	60	46	31	10	2	59	41	1.615	3.79	111	4.71	.221	2	.125	5	4	0.5
1951	Cle-A	0	1	.000	1	1	0	0	0	3	8	6	6	0	0	1	2	3.000	18.00	21	14.39	.500	0	.000	-5	0	-0.5
Total	13	119	121	.496	346	286	131	29	2	2104^2	1799	915	805	100	21	1132	1294	1.393	3.44	108	3.38	.232	104	.152	40	134	3.4

YEAR TM-L	W	L	PCT	G	GS	CG	SH	SV	IP	H	R	ER	HR	HB	BB	SO	RAT	ERA	ERA+	CERA	OAV	BH	AVG	PR+	WS	TPW
• VANGILDER, Elam	Elam Russell Vangilder b: 4/23/1896, Cape Girardeau, MO d: 4/30/1977, Cape Girardeau, MO BR/TR, 6'1", 192 lbs. Deb: 9/18/1919																									
1919 StL-A	1	0	1.000	3	1	1	0	0	13	15	4	3	0	0	3	6	1.385	2.08	160	3.80	.306	2	.667	2	2	0.3
1920 StL-A	3	8	.273	24	13	4	0	0	104^{2}	131	83	64	7	3	40	25	1.634	5.50	71	5.34	.310	4	.133	-19	1	-2.0
1921 StL-A	11	12	.478	31	21	10	1	0	180^{1}	196	98	79	10	2	67	48	1.458	3.94	114	4.02	.278	13	.200	12	12	0.9
1922 StL-A	19	13	.594	43	30	19	3	4	245	248	109	93	13	6	48	63	1.208	3.42	121	3.16	.270	32	.344	13	22	2.6
1923 StL-A	16	17	.485	41	35	20	4	1	282^{1}	276	129	96	11	6	120	74	1.403	3.06	136	3.62	.266	24	.218	32	23	3.0
1924 StL-A	5	10	.333	43	18	5	0	1	145^{1}	183	114	91	10	9	55	49	1.638	5.64	80	5.25	.317	13	.295	-19	4	-1.5
1925 StL-A	14	8	.636	52	16	4	1	6	193^{1}	225	127	101	11	6	92	61	1.640	4.70	99	5.01	.303	13	.183	-3	12	-0.5
1926 StL-A	9	11	.450	42	19	8	1	1	181	196	121	104	12	2	98	40	1.624	5.17	83	4.74	.285	11	.190	-19	7	-1.8
1927 StL-A	10	12	.455	44	23	12	3	1	203	245	136	108	13	5	102	62	1.709	4.79	91	4.83	.310	19	.279	-11	10	-0.8
1928 Det-A	11	10	.524	38	11	7	0	5	156^{1}	163	82	68	4	3	68	43	1.478	3.91	105	3.75	.272	15	.259	3	11	0.5
1929 Det-A	0	1	.000	6	0	0	0	0	11^{1}	16	11	8	1	0	7	3	2.029	6.35	67	7.29	.348	0	.000	-2	0	-0.2
Total 11	99	102	.493	367	187	90	13	19	1715^{2}	1894	1014	815	92	42	700	474	1.512	4.28	100	4.30	.288	146	.243	-12	104	0.5
• VARGA, Andy	Andrew William Varga b: 12/11/1930, Chicago, IL d: 11/4/1992, Orlando, FL BR/TL, 6'4", 187 lbs. Deb: 9/9/1950																									
1950 Chi-N	0	0	....	1	0	0	0	0	1	0	0	0	0	0	1	0	1.000	0.00	....	0.82	.000	0	....	0	0	0.0
1951 Chi-N	0	0	....	2	0	0	0	0	3	2	1	1	0	0	6	1	2.667	3.00	137	6.62	.200	0	....	0	0	0.0
Total 2	0	0	....	3	0	0	0	0	4	2	1	1	0	0	7	1	2.250	2.25	182	5.17	.200	0	....	1	0	0.1
• VARGAS, Claudio	Claudio (Almonte) Vargas b: 5/19/1979, Valverde Mao, Dominican Republic BR/TR, 6'3", 225 lbs. Deb: 4/26/2003																									
2003 Mon-N	6	8	.429	23	20	0	0	0	114	111	59	55	16	7	41	62	1.333	4.34	116	4.21	.255	0	.000	9	7	0.6
• VARGAS, Roberto	Roberto Enrique (Velez) Vargas b: 5/29/1929, Santurce, Puerto Rico BL/TL, 5'11", 170 lbs. Deb: 4/17/1955																									
1955 Mil-N	0	0	....	25	0	0	0	2	24^{2}	39	25	24	4	1	14	13	2.149	8.76	43	8.77	.355	1	.500	-14	0	-1.3
• VARGUS, Bill	William Fay Vargus b: 11/11/1899, North Scituate, MA d: 2/12/1979, Hyannis, MA BL/TL, 6', 165 lbs. Deb: 6/23/1925																									
1925 Bos-N	1	1	.500	11	2	1	0	0	36^{1}	45	24	16	1	2	13	5	1.596	3.96	101	4.70	.302	3	.250	-0	2	0.0
1926 Bos-N	0	0	....	4	0	0	0	0	3	4	1	1	0	0	1	0	1.667	3.00	118	4.74	.333	0	....	0	0	0.0
Total 2	1	1	.500	15	2	1	0	0	39^{1}	49	25	17	1	2	14	5	1.602	3.89	102	4.70	.304	3	.250	-0	2	0.0
• VARNEY, Dike	Lawrence Delano Varney b: 8/9/1880, Dover, NH d: 4/23/1950, Long Island City, NY BL/TL, 6', 165 lbs. Deb: 7/3/1902																									
1902 Cle-A	1	1	.500	3	3	0	0	0	14^{2}	14	15	10	0	5	12	7	1.773	6.14	56	5.61	.252	1	.167	-4	0	-0.4
• VASBINDER, Cal	Moses Calhoun Vasbinder b: 7/19/1880, Scio, OH d: 12/22/1950, Cadiz, OH BR/TR, 6'2" Deb: 4/27/1902																									
1902 Cle-A	0	0	....	2	0	0	0	0	5	5	5	5	1	0	8	2	2.600	9.00	38	9.58	.261	1	.500	-3	0	-0.3
• VASQUEZ, Rafael	Rafael Vasquez b: 6/28/1958, La Romana, Dominican Republic BR/TR, 6', 160 lbs. Deb: 4/6/1979																									
1979 Sea-A	1	0	1.000	9	0	0	0	0	16	23	9	9	4	1	6	9	1.813	5.06	86	8.41	.354	0	....	-1	1	-0.1
• VAUGHAN, Charlie	Charles Wayne Vaughan b: 10/6/1947, Mercedes, TX BR/TL, 6'1.5", 185 lbs. Deb: 9/3/1966																									
1966 Atl-N	1	0	1.000	1	1	0	0	0	7	8	2	2	0	0	3	6	1.571	2.57	141	4.28	.296	1	.250	1	1	0.1
1969 Atl-N	0	0	....	1	0	0	0	0	1	1	2	2	0	0	3	1	4.000	18.00	20	13.82	.250	0	....	-2	0	-0.2
Total 2	1	0	1.000	2	1	0	0	0	8	9	4	4	0	0	6	7	1.875	4.50	80	5.48	.290	1	.250	-1	1	-0.1
• VAUGHAN, Porter	Cecil Porter "Lefty" Vaughan b: 5/11/1919, Stevensville, VA BR/TL, 6'1", 178 lbs. Deb: 6/16/1940																									
1940 Phi-A	2	9	.182	18	15	5	0	2	99^{1}	104	74	59	9	3	61	46	1.661	5.35	83	4.97	.264	8	.235	-8	2	-0.8
1941 Phi-A	0	2	.000	5	3	1	0	0	22^{2}	32	25	20	3	0	12	6	1.941	7.94	53	7.05	.327	1	.143	-10	0	-1.0
1946 Phi-A	0	0	....	1	0	0	0	0	0	1	0	0	0	0	1	0	....	....	....	∞	1.000	0	....	0	0	0.0
Total 3	2	11	.154	24	18	6	0	2	122	137	99	79	12	3	74	52	1.730	5.83	75	5.36	.278	9	.220	-18	2	-1.7
• VAUGHN, De Wayne	De Wayne Mathew Vaughn b: 7/22/1959, Oklahoma City, OK BR/TR, 5'11", 180 lbs. Deb: 4/17/1988																									
1988 Tex-A	0	0	....	8	0	0	0	0	15^{1}	24	15	13	4	0	4	8	1.826	7.63	53	7.95	.348	0	....	-6	0	-0.6
• VAUGHN, Hippo	James Leslie Vaughn b: 4/9/1888, Weatherford, TX d: 5/29/1966, Chicago, IL BB/TL, 6'4", 215 lbs. Deb: 6/19/1908																									
1908 NY-A	0	0	....	2	0	0	0	0	2^{1}	1	1	1	0	0	4	2	2.143	3.86	64	5.26	.167	0	.000	-0	0	0.0
1910 NY-A	13	11	.542	30	25	18	5	1	221^{2}	190	76	45	1	10	58	107	1.119	1.83	145	2.42	.237	10	.133	26	18	2.7
1911 NY-A	8	10	.444	26	19	10	0	0	145^{2}	158	92	71	2	7	54	74	1.455	4.39	82	4.05	.284	7	.143	-10	7	-1.0
1912 NY-A	2	8	.200	15	10	5	1	0	63	66	48	36	1	1	37	46	1.635	5.14	70	4.30	.264	2	.095	-7	1	-0.9
Was-A	4	3	.571	12	8	4	0	0	81	75	33	26	0	4	43	49	1.457	2.89	116	3.63	.253	6	.200	1	5	0.1
Yr.	6	11	.353	27	18	9	1	0	144	141	81	62	1	5	80	95	1.535	3.88	90	3.92	.258	8	.157	-6	6	-0.8
1913 Chi-N	5	1	.833	7	6	5	2	0	56	37	13	9	0	2	27	36	1.143	1.45	219	1.93	.182	4	.190	10	6	1.0
1914 Chi-N	21	13	.618	42	35	23	4	1	293^{2}	236	119	67	1	8	109	165	1.175	2.05	135	2.32	.222	14	.144	29	21	3.1
1915 Chi-N	20	12	.625	41	34	18	4	1	269^{2}	240	105	86	4	11	77	148	1.176	2.87	97	2.56	.238	14	.163	1	19	0.2
1916 Chi-N	17	15	.531	44	35	21	4	1	294	269	94	72	4	7	67	144	1.143	2.20	132	2.48	.250	14	.135	27	24	2.7
1917 Chi-N	23	13	.639	41	38	27	5	0	295^{2}	255	97	66	3	9	91	195	1.170	2.01	144	2.46	.235	16	.160	34	24	3.8
1918★ Chi-N	**22**	10	.688	35	**33**	27	**8**	0	**290^{1}**	216	75	56	4	7	76	**148**	1.006	**1.74**	**160**	**1.79**	**.208**	23	.240	**41**	**28**	**5.0**
1919 Chi-N	21	14	.600	38	**37**	25	4	1	**306^{2}**	264	83	61	3	6	62	**141**	1.063	1.79	161	2.10	.234	17	.173	**40**	**30**	**4.4**
1920 Chi-N	19	16	.543	40	38	24	4	0	301	301	113	85	8	8	81	131	1.269	2.54	126	3.14	.264	22	.216	26	22	3.2
1921 Chi-N	3	11	.214	17	14	7	0	0	109^{1}	153	90	73	8	5	31	30	1.683	6.01	64	5.90	.341	10	.244	-27	0	-2.4
Total 13	178	137	.565	390	332	214	41	5	2730	2461	1039	754	39	85	817	1416	1.201	2.49	123	2.71	.244	159	.173	190	205	21.8
• VAUGHN, Roy	Clarence Leroy Vaughn b: 9/4/1911, Sedalia, MO d: 3/1/1937, Martinsville, VA BB/TR, 6'.5", 178 lbs. Deb: 7/1/1934																									
1934 Phi-A	0	0	....	2	0	0	0	0	4^{1}	3	2	1	1	0	3	1	1.385	2.08	211	3.94	.176	0	.000	1	0	0.1
• VAZQUEZ, Javier	Javier Carlos Vazquez b: 6/25/1976, Ponce, Puerto Rico BR/TR, 6'2", 195 lbs. Deb: 4/3/1998																									
1998 Mon-N	5	15	.250	33	32	0	0	0	172^{1}	196	121	116	31	11	68	139	1.532	6.06	69	5.79	.292	9	.173	-33	0	-3.1
1999 Mon-N	9	8	.529	26	26	3	1	0	154^{2}	154	98	86	20	4	52	113	1.332	5.00	90	4.02	.255	12	.286	-6	8	-0.2
2000 Mon-N	11	9	.550	33	33	2	1	0	217^{2}	247	104	98	24	5	61	196	1.415	4.05	118	4.45	.286	15	.231	20	14	2.1
2001 Mon-N	16	11	.593	32	32	5	**3**	0	223^{2}	197	92	85	24	3	44	208	1.077	3.42	130	2.75	.235	16	.258	30	21	3.3
2002 Mon-N	10	13	.435	34	34	2	0	0	230^{1}	243	111	100	28	4	49	179	1.268	3.91	109	3.80	.271	13	.178	9	12	0.9
2003 Mon-N	13	12	.520	34	34	4	1	0	230^{2}	198	93	83	28	4	57	241	1.105	3.24	156	2.90	.229	10	.154	47	22	4.5
Total 6	64	68	.485	192	191	16	6	0	1229^{1}	1235	619	568	155	31	331	1076	1.274	4.16	108	3.86	.260	75	.209	67	77	7.5
• VEACH, Al	Alvis Lindel Veach b: 8/6/1909, Maylene, AL d: 9/6/1990, Charlotte, NC BR/TR, 5'11", 178 lbs. Deb: 9/22/1935																									
1935 Phi-A	0	2	.000	2	2	1	0	0	10	20	15	13	1	0	9	3	2.900	11.70	39	12.52	.417	0	.000	-8	0	-0.8
• VEACH, Peek-A-Boo	William Walter Veach b: 6/15/1862, Indianapolis, IN d: 11/12/1937, Indianapolis, IN, 6', 175 lbs. Deb: 8/24/1884 ♦																									
1884 KC-U	3	9	.250	12	12	12	0	0	104	95	57	28	1	....	10	62	1.010	2.42	115	....	.227	11	.134	4	2	0.1
1887 Lou-a	0	1	.000	1	1	1	0	0	9	13	6	4	1	0	8	2	1.444	4.00	110	....	.326	1	.250	0	1	0.0
Total 2	3	10	.231	13	13	13	0	0	113	108	63	32	2	0	18	64	1.044	2.55	115	....	.236	77	.218	4	3	0.1
• VEALE, Bob	Robert Andrew Veale b: 10/28/1935, Birmingham, AL BB/TL, 6'6", 212 lbs. Deb: 4/16/1962																									
1962 Pit-N	2	2	.500	11	6	2	0	1	45^{2}	39	25	19	2	0	25	42	1.401	3.74	105	3.44	.235	4	.250	1	3	0.1
1963 Pit-N	5	2	.714	34	7	3	2	3	77^{2}	59	15	9	1	1	40	68	1.275	1.04	316	2.70	.215	2	.087	19	10	2.0
1964 Pit-N	18	12	.600	40	38	14	1	0	279^{2}	222	100	85	8	3	124	**250**	1.237	2.74	128	2.67	.217	15	.156	28	21	2.9
1965 Pit-N★	17	12	.586	39	37	14	7	0	266	221	98	84	5	7	119	276	1.278	2.84	124	2.84	.225	8	.086	14	18	1.1
1966 Pit-N★	16	12	.571	38	37	12	3	0	268^{1}	228	99	90	18	5	102	229	1.230	3.02	118	3.03	.232	13	.138	12	17	1.0
1967 Pit-N	16	8	.667	33	31	6	1	0	203	184	90	82	12	5	119	179	1.493	3.64	93	4.02	.245	3	.043	-9	9	-1.5
1968 Pit-N	13	14	.481	36	33	13	4	0	245^{1}	187	67	56	13	2	94	171	1.145	2.05	142	2.48	.211	9	.110	21	17	2.1
1969 Pit-N	13	14	.481	34	34	9	1	0	225^{2}	232	93	81	8	3	91	213	1.431	3.23	108	3.81	.267	4	.051	8	12	0.2
1970 Pit-N	10	15	.400	34	32	5	1	0	202	189	99	88	15	3	94	178	1.401	3.92	99	3.72	.246	11	.164	-6	9	-0.4
1971★ Pit-N	6	0	1.000	37	0	0	0	2	46^{1}	59	38	36	5	0	24	40	1.791	6.99	49	6.13	.314	3	.333	-19	0	-2.0

YEAR	TM-L	W	L	PCT	G	GS	CG	SH	SV	IP	H	R	ER	HR	HB	BB	SO	RAT	ERA	ERA+	CERA	OAV	BH	AVG	PR+	WS	TPW
1972	Pit-N	0	0	....	5	0	0	0	0	9	10	7	6	0	0	7	6	1.889	6.00	55	5.09	.313	0	.000	-3	0	-0.3
	Bos-A	2	0	1.000	6	0	0	0	2	8	2	0	0	0	0	3	10	.625	0.00	....	0.61	.083	0	.000	3	3	0.3
1973	Bos-A	2	3	.400	32	0	0	0	11	36^1	37	16	14	2	0	12	25	1.349	3.47	116	3.52	.268	0	....	2	5	0.2
1974	Bos-A	0	1	.000	18	0	0	0	2	13	15	8	8	2	0	4	16	1.462	5.54	69	4.73	.283	0	....	-2	0	-0.2
Total	13	120	95	.558	397	255	78	20	21	1926	1684	755	658	91	29	858	1703	1.320	3.07	114	3.24	.236	72	.114	68	124	5.5
• VEDDER, Lou	Louis Edward Vedder b: 4/20/1897, Oakville, MI d: 3/9/1990, Lake Placid, FL BR/TR, 5'10.5", 175 lbs. Deb: 9/18/1920																										
1920	Det-A	0	0	....	1	0	0	0	0	2	0	0	0	0	0	0	1	.000	0.00	....	0.00	.000	0	....	1	0	0.1
• VEIGEL, Al	Allen Francis Veigel b: 1/30/1917, Dover, OH BR/TR, 6'1", 180 lbs. Deb: 9/21/1939																										
1939	Bos-N	0	1	.000	2	2	0	0	0	2^2	3	6	2	0	0	5	1	3.000	6.75	55	8.03	.250	0	.000	-1	0	-0.1
• VEIL, Bucky	Frederick William Veil b: 8/2/1881, Tyrone, PA d: 4/16/1931, Altoona, PA BR/TR, 5'10", 165 lbs. Deb: 4/19/1903																										
1903*	Pit-N	5	3	.625	12	6	4	0	0	70^2	70	35	30	1	2	36	20	1.500	3.82	84	3.99	.269	6	.207	-7	4	-0.8
1904	Pit-N	0	0	....	1	1	0	0	0	4^2	4	3	3	0	1	4	1	1.714	5.79	47	5.10	.250	1	1.000	-2	0	-0.1
Total	2	5	3	.625	13	7	4	0	0	75^1	74	38	33	1	3	40	21	1.513	3.94	81	4.06	.268	7	.233	-9	4	-0.9
• VELAZQUEZ, Carlos	Carlos (Quinones) Velazquez b: 3/22/1948, Loiza, Puerto Rico BR/TR, 5'11", 180 lbs. Deb: 7/20/1973																										
1973	Mil-A	2	2	.500	18	0	0	0	2	38^1	46	15	11	5	0	10	12	1.461	2.58	146	4.81	.297	0	....	5	3	0.5
• VENAFRO, Mike	Michael Robert Venafro b: 8/2/1973, Takoma Park, MD BL/TL, 5'10", 180 lbs. Deb: 4/24/1999																										
1999*	Tex-A	3	2	.600	65	0	0	0	0	68^1	63	29	25	4	3	22	37	1.244	3.29	154	3.30	.251	0	....	14	7	1.3
2000	Tex-A	3	1	.750	77	0	0	0	1	56^1	64	27	24	2	4	21	32	1.509	3.83	130	4.49	.295	0	....	8	6	0.8
2001	Tex-A	5	5	.500	70	0	0	0	4	60	54	35	32	2	7	28	29	1.367	4.80	97	3.58	.240	0	....	-0	4	0.0
2002	Oak-A	2	2	.500	47	0	0	0	0	37	45	22	19	5	2	14	16	1.595	4.62	95	5.65	.308	0	....	-1	2	-0.1
2003	TB-A	1	0	1.000	24	0	0	0	0	19	24	10	10	1	3	3	9	1.421	4.74	96	4.89	.308	0	....	-1	1	-0.1
Total	5	14	10	.583	283	0	0	0	5	240^2	250	123	110	14	19	88	123	1.404	4.11	116	4.14	.273	0	....	21	20	1.9
• VERAS, Dario	Dario Antonio Veras b: 3/13/1973, Santiago, Dominican Republic BR/TR, 6'2", 165 lbs. Deb: 7/31/1996																										
1996*	SD-N	3	1	.750	23	0	0	0	0	29	24	10	9	3	1	10	23	1.172	2.79	142	2.97	.231	0	....	4	3	0.4
1997	SD-N	2	1	.667	23	0	0	0	0	24^2	28	18	14	5	2	12	21	1.622	5.11	75	6.11	.280	0	....	-3	0	-0.3
1998	Bos-A	0	1	.000	7	0	0	0	0	8	12	9	9	0	1	7	2	2.375	10.13	47	8.80	.343	0	....	-5	0	-0.5
Total	3	5	3	.625	53	0	0	0	0	61^2	64	37	32	8	4	29	46	1.508	4.67	87	4.99	.268	0	....	-4	3	-0.4
• VERBANIC, Joe	Joseph Michael Verbanic b: 4/24/1943, Washington, PA BR/TR, 6', 155 lbs. Deb: 7/22/1966																										
1966	Phi-N	1	1	.500	17	0	0	0	0	14	12	9	8	2	0	10	7	1.571	5.14	70	4.35	.226	0	....	-2	0	-0.3
1967	NY-A	4	3	.571	28	6	1	1	2	80^1	74	27	25	6	2	21	39	1.183	2.80	112	3.04	.249	2	.111	4	6	0.4
1968	NY-A	6	7	.462	40	11	2	1	4	97	104	36	34	6	6	41	40	1.495	3.15	92	4.47	.284	2	.080	-2	5	-0.3
1970	NY-A	1	0	1.000	7	0	0	0	0	15^2	20	9	8	1	1	12	8	2.043	4.60	76	7.23	.323	1	.333	-2	0	-0.2
Total	4	12	11	.522	92	17	3	2	6	207	210	81	75	15	9	84	94	1.420	3.26	95	4.12	.270	5	.109	-2	11	-0.4
• VERDEL, Al	Albert Alfred "Stumpy" Verdel b: 6/10/1921, Punxsutawney, PA d: 4/16/1991, Sarasota, FL BR/TR, 5'9.5", 186 lbs. Deb: 4/20/1944																										
1944	Phi-N	0	0	....	1	0	0	0	0	1	0	0	0	0	0	0	0	.000	0.00	....	0.00	.000	0	....	0	0	0.0
• VEREKER, Tommy	John James Vereker b: 12/2/1893, Baltimore, MD d: 4/2/1974, Baltimore, MD, 5'10", 185 lbs. Deb: 6/17/1915																										
1915	Bal-F	0	0	....	2	0	0	0	0	3	3	5	5	1	1	2	1	1.667	15.00	23	8.32	.273	0	....	-4	0	-0.4
• VERES, Dave	David Scott Veres b: 10/19/1966, Montgomery, AL BR/TR, 6'2", 195 lbs. Deb: 5/10/1994																										
1994	Hou-N	3	3	.500	32	0	0	0	1	41	39	13	11	4	1	7	28	1.122	2.41	164	2.89	.247	1	.500	7	4	0.7
1995	Hou-N	5	1	.833	72	0	0	0	1	103^1	89	29	26	5	4	30	94	1.152	2.26	171	2.70	.241	0	.000	21	10	2.0
1996	Mon-N	6	3	.667	68	0	0	0	4	77^2	85	39	36	10	6	32	81	1.506	4.17	104	5.11	.277	3	.375	2	6	0.3
1997	Mon-N	2	3	.400	53	0	0	0	1	62	68	28	24	5	2	27	47	1.532	3.48	121	4.59	.278	1	1.000	5	5	0.5
1998	Col-N	3	1	.750	63	0	0	0	8	76^1	67	26	24	6	2	27	74	1.231	2.83	183	3.15	.233	1	.333	20	11	2.0
1999	Col-N	4	8	.333	73	0	0	0	31	77	88	46	44	14	2	37	71	1.623	5.14	113	5.84	.290	0	.000	6	11	0.6
2000*	StL-N	3	5	.375	71	0	0	0	29	75^2	65	26	24	6	6	25	67	1.189	2.85	161	3.25	.239	0	.000	14	14	1.3
2001*	StL-N	3	2	.600	71	0	0	0	15	65^2	57	29	27	12	2	28	61	1.294	3.70	115	4.11	.232	0	.000	3	7	0.2
2002*	StL-N	5	8	.385	71	0	0	0	4	82^2	67	34	32	12	2	39	68	1.282	3.48	113	3.68	.224	1	.333	3	6	0.3
2003*	Chi-N	2	1	.667	31	0	0	0	1	32^2	36	17	17	4	1	5	26	1.255	4.68	90	3.98	.290	0	....	-2	2	-0.2
Total	10	36	35	.507	605	0	0	0	95	694	661	287	265	78	28	257	617	1.323	3.44	130	3.92	.253	7	.259	77	76	7.7
• VERES, Randy	Randolph Ruhland Veres b: 11/25/1965, San Francisco, CA BR/TR, 6'3", 210 lbs. Deb: 7/1/1989																										
1989	Mil-A	0	1	.000	3	1	0	0	0	8^1	9	5	4	0	0	4	8	1.560	4.32	89	4.23	.290	0	....	-0	0	0.0
1990	Mil-A	0	3	.000	26	0	0	0	1	41^2	38	17	17	5	1	16	16	1.296	3.67	105	3.68	.247	0	....	1	2	0.1
1994	Chi-N	1	1	.500	10	0	0	0	0	9^2	12	6	6	3	1	2	5	1.448	5.59	74	6.72	.308	0	.000	-2	0	-0.2
1995	Fla-N	4	4	.500	47	0	0	0	1	48^2	46	25	21	6	1	22	31	1.397	3.88	108	3.89	.251	0	.000	2	3	0.1
1996	Det-A	0	4	.000	25	0	0	0	0	30^1	38	29	28	6	2	23	28	2.011	8.31	61	7.85	.306	0	....	-10	0	-0.9
1997	KC-A	4	0	1.000	24	0	0	0	1	35^1	36	17	13	4	3	7	28	1.217	3.31	142	3.68	.273	0	....	5	3	0.5
Total	6	9	13	.409	135	1	0	0	3	174	179	99	89	24	8	74	116	1.454	4.60	96	4.66	.270	0	.000	-4	8	-0.4
• VERHOEVEN, John	John C. Verhoeven b: 7/3/1952, Long Beach, CA BR/TR, 6'5", 200 lbs. Deb: 7/6/1976																										
1976	Cal-A	0	2	.000	21	0	0	0	4	37^1	35	15	14	2	0	14	23	1.313	3.38	98	3.02	.252	0	....	-0	3	0.0
1977	Cal-A	0	2	.000	3	0	0	0	0	4^2	4	3	2	0	1	4	3	1.714	3.86	101	4.50	.222	0	....	0	0	0.0
	Chi-A	0	0	....	6	0	0	0	0	10^1	9	3	3	0	0	2	6	1.065	2.61	156	1.99	.231	0	....	2	1	0.2
	Yr.	0	2	.000	9	0	0	0	0	15	13	6	5	0	1	6	9	1.267	3.00	134	2.77	.228	0	....	2	1	0.2
1980	Min-A	3	4	.429	44	0	0	0	0	99^2	109	53	44	10	3	29	42	1.385	3.97	110	4.27	.289	0	....	4	5	0.4
1981	Min-A	0	0	....	25	0	0	0	0	52	57	27	23	4	2	14	16	1.365	3.98	99	3.98	.288	0	....	0	2	0.0
Total	4	3	8	.273	99	0	0	0	4	204	214	101	86	16	6	63	90	1.358	3.79	106	3.86	.278	0	....	6	11	0.6
• VERNON, Joe	Joseph Henry Vernon b: 11/25/1889, Mansfield, MA d: 3/13/1955, Philadelphia, PA BR/TR, 5'11", 160 lbs. Deb: 7/20/1912																										
1912	Chi-N	0	0	....	1	0	0	0	0	4	4	6	5	0	1	6	1	2.500	11.25	29	8.62	.286	0	.000	-4	0	-0.4
1914	Bro-F	0	0	....	1	1	0	0	0	3^1	4	4	4	0	0	5	0	2.700	10.80	30	8.42	.308	0	.000	-3	0	-0.3
Total	2	0	0	....	2	1	0	0	0	7^1	8	10	9	0	1	11	1	2.591	11.05	30	8.53	.297	0	.000	-6	0	-0.7
• VESELIC, Bob	Robert Michael Veselic b: 9/27/1955, Pittsburgh, PA d: 12/26/1995, Los Angeles, CA BR/TR, 6', 175 lbs. Deb: 9/18/1980																										
1980	Min-A	0	0	....	1	0	0	0	0	4	3	2	2	1	0	1	2	1.000	4.50	97	3.25	.214	0	....	-0	0	0.0
1981	Min-A	1	1	.500	5	0	0	0	0	22^2	22	8	8	1	0	12	13	1.500	3.18	124	3.76	.250	0	....	2	2	0.2
Total	2	1	1	.500	6	0	0	0	0	26^2	25	10	10	2	0	13	15	1.425	3.38	119	3.68	.245	0	....	2	2	0.2
• VIAU, Lee	Leon A. Viau b: 7/5/1866, Corinth, VT d: 12/17/1947, Hopewell, NJ BR/TR, 5'4", 160 lbs. Deb: 4/22/1888 U																										
1888	Cin-a	27	14	.659	42	42	42	1	0	387^2	331	192	114	7	20	110	164	1.138	2.65	120	....	.223	13	.087	13	30	0.2
1889	Cin-a	22	20	.524	47	42	38	1	1	373	379	224	157	8	10	136	152	1.381	3.79	103	....	.255	21	.143	1	24	-0.6
1890	Cin-N	7	5	.583	13	10	7	1	0	90	97	69	45	8	1	39	41	1.511	4.50	79	....	.267	5	.139	-11	4	-1.2
	Cle-N	4	9	.308	13	13	13	1	0	107	101	65	40	4	5	42	30	1.336	3.36	106	....	.242	7	.163	2	5	0.1
	Yr.	11	14	.440	26	23	20	2	0	197	198	134	85	12	6	81	71	1.416	3.88	92	....	.254	12	.152	-9	9	-1.1
1891	Cle-N	18	17	.514	45	38	31	0	0	343^2	367	239	115	3	15	138	130	1.469	3.01	115	....	.263	23	.160	21	19	1.7
1892	Cle-N	0	1	.000	1	1	0	0	0	1	5	5	4	0	0	1	0	6.000	36.00	9	36.73	.625	0	....	-4	0	-0.3
	Lou-N	4	11	.267	16	15	14	1	0	130^2	156	86	58	7	0	56	36	1.622	3.99	77	4.84	.285	13	.197	-15	5	-1.2
	Bos-N	1	0	1.000	1	1	1	0	0	9	5	1	0	0	0	4	1	1.000	0.00	....	1.44	.156	0	.000	3	2	0.3
	Yr.	5	12	.294	18	17	15	1	0	140^2	166	92	62	7	0	61	37	1.614	3.97	78	4.85	.283	13	.188	-15	7	-1.3
Total	5	83	77	.519	178	162	146	5	1	1442	1441	881	533	37	51	526	554	1.364	3.33	104	0.47	.251	82	.139	11	89	-1.1

• VICKERS, Rube Harry Porter Vickers b: 5/17/1878, St. Mary's, Canada d: 12/9/1958, Belleville, MI BL/TR, 6'2", 225 lbs. Deb: 9/21/1902

YEAR	TM-L	W	L	PCT	G	GS	CG	SH	SV	IP	H	R	ER	HR	HB	BB	SO	RAT	ERA	ERA+	CERA	OAV	BH	AVG	PR+	WS	TPW
1902	Cin-N	0	3	.000	3	3	3	0	0	21	31	20	14	0	1	8	6	1.857	6.00	50	5.98	.342	4	.364	-7	0	-0.8
1903	Bro-N	0	1	.000	4	1	1	0	0	14	27	23	17	0	1	9	5	2.571	10.93	29	10.22	.415	1	.100	-10	0	-1.1
1907	Phi-A	2	2	.500	10	4	3	1	0	50^1	44	27	19	1	1	12	21	1.113	3.40	77	2.27	.238	3	.150	-5	1	-0.6
1908	Phi-A	18	19	.486	53	34	21	6	1	317	264	114	78	0	11	71	156	1.057	2.21	115	2.01	.231	17	.160	19	22	2.2
1909	Phi-A	2	2	.500	18	3	1	0	1	55^2	60	32	21	0	2	19	25	1.419	3.40	71	3.54	.274	1	.063	-7	0	-0.9
Total	5	22	27	.449	88	45	29	7	2	458	426	216	149	1	16	119	213	1.190	2.93	90	2.66	.250	26	.160	-10	23	-1.2

• VICKERY, Tom Thomas Gill "Vinegar Tom" Vickery b: 5/5/1867, Milford, MA d: 3/21/1921, Burlington, NJ TR, 6', 170 lbs. Deb: 4/21/1890 U

YEAR	TM-L	W	L	PCT	G	GS	CG	SH	SV	IP	H	R	ER	HR	HB	BB	SO	RAT	ERA	ERA+	CERA	OAV	BH	AVG	PR+	WS	TPW
1890	Phi-N	24	22	.522	46	46	41	2	0	382	405	250	146	8	29	184	162	1.542	3.44	106	....	.264	33	.208	4	25	0.0
1891	Chi-N	6	5	.545	14	12	7	0	0	79^2	72	55	36	4	5	44	39	1.456	4.07	82	....	.232	7	.179	-8	4	-0.9
1892	Bal-N	8	10	.444	24	21	17	0	0	176	189	134	69	3	10	87	49	1.568	3.53	97	4.31	.264	18	.243	6	5	0.7
1893	Phi-N	4	5	.444	13	11	7	0	0	80	100	65	48	1	6	37	15	1.713	5.40	85	5.24	.297	11	.314	-9	4	-0.6
Total	4	42	42	.500	97	90	72	2	0	717^2	766	504	299	16	50	352	265	1.558	3.75	98	1.64	.264	69	.225	-7	38	-0.7

• VILLAFUERTE, Brandon Brandon Paul Villafuerte b: 12/17/1975, Hilo, HI BR/TR, 5'11", 180 lbs. Deb: 5/23/2000

YEAR	TM-L	W	L	PCT	G	GS	CG	SH	SV	IP	H	R	ER	HR	HB	BB	SO	RAT	ERA	ERA+	CERA	OAV	BH	AVG	PR+	WS	TPW
2000	Det-A	0	0	....	3	0	0	0	0	4^1	4	5	5	0	0	4	1	1.846	10.38	46	5.01	.250	0	....	-3	0	-0.2
2001	Tex-A	0	0	....	6	0	0	0	0	5^2	12	9	9	3	1	4	4	2.824	14.29	33	17.59	.414	0	....	-6	0	-0.6
2002	SD-N	1	2	.333	31	0	0	0	1	32	29	5	5	2	2	12	25	1.281	1.41	268	3.44	.248	0	....	9	3	0.9
2003	SD-N	0	2	.000	31	0	0	0	2	40^2	39	20	19	7	3	26	34	1.598	4.20	94	5.54	.252	0	.000	-1	1	-0.1
Total	4	1	4	.200	71	0	0	0	3	82^2	84	39	38	12	6	46	64	1.573	4.14	101	5.53	.265	0	.000	-1	4	-0.1

• VILLARREAL, Oscar Oscar Eduardo Villarreal b: 11/22/1981, Monterrey, Mexico BL/TR, 6', 177 lbs. Deb: 3/31/2003

YEAR	TM-L	W	L	PCT	G	GS	CG	SH	SV	IP	H	R	ER	HR	HB	BB	SO	RAT	ERA	ERA+	CERA	OAV	BH	AVG	PR+	WS	TPW
2003	Ari-N	10	7	.588	86	1	0	0	0	98	80	40	28	6	3	46	80	1.286	2.57	181	2.97	.222	0	.000	24	11	2.3

• VILLEGAS, Ismael Ismael (Diaz) Villegas b: 8/12/1976, Rio Piedras, Puerto Rico BR/TR, 6'1", 188 lbs. Deb: 7/3/2000

YEAR	TM-L	W	L	PCT	G	GS	CG	SH	SV	IP	H	R	ER	HR	HB	BB	SO	RAT	ERA	ERA+	CERA	OAV	BH	AVG	PR+	WS	TPW
2000	Atl-N	0	0	....	1	0	0	0	0	2^2	4	4	4	2	1	2	2	2.250	13.50	34	16.82	.333	0	.000	-3	0	-0.3

• VILLONE, Ron Ronald Thomas Villone b: 1/16/1970, Englewood, NJ BL/TL, 6'3", 230 lbs. Deb: 4/28/1995

YEAR	TM-L	W	L	PCT	G	GS	CG	SH	SV	IP	H	R	ER	HR	HB	BB	SO	RAT	ERA	ERA+	CERA	OAV	BH	AVG	PR+	WS	TPW
1995	Sea-A	0	2	.000	19	0	0	0	0	19^1	20	19	17	6	1	23	26	2.224	7.91	60	9.67	.270	0	....	-6	0	-0.6
	SD-N	2	1	.667	19	0	0	0	1	25^2	24	12	12	5	0	11	37	1.364	4.21	95	4.44	.242	0	.000	-1	2	-0.1
1996	SD-N	1	1	.500	21	0	0	0	0	18^1	17	6	6	2	1	7	19	1.309	2.95	134	3.90	.243	0	....	2	2	0.2
	Mil-A	0	0	....	23	0	0	0	2	24^2	14	9	9	4	4	18	19	1.297	3.28	158	4.21	.175	0	....	5	3	0.4
1997	Mil-A	1	0	1.000	50	0	0	0	0	52^2	54	23	20	4	1	36	40	1.709	3.42	135	5.30	.271	0	.000	5	4	0.5
1998	Cle-A	0	0	....	25	0	0	0	0	27	30	18	18	3	2	22	15	1.926	6.00	80	7.01	.297	0	....	-4	1	-0.3
1999	Cin-N	9	7	.563	29	22	0	0	2	142^2	114	70	67	8	5	73	97	1.311	4.23	110	3.20	.219	3	.070	3	8	0.0
2000	Cin-N	10	10	.500	35	23	2	0	0	141	154	95	85	22	9	78	77	1.645	5.43	87	5.97	.286	7	.163	-13	5	-1.3
2001	Col-N	1	3	.250	22	6	0	0	0	46^2	56	35	33	6	1	29	48	1.821	6.36	84	6.30	.295	0	.000	-6	1	-0.6
	*Hou-N	5	7	.417	31	6	0	0	0	68	77	46	42	12	4	24	65	1.485	5.56	82	5.46	.282	1	.077	-8	2	-0.8
	Yr.	6	10	.375	53	12	0	0	0	114^2	133	81	75	18	5	53	113	1.622	5.89	83	5.80	.287	1	.045	-13	3	-1.4
2002	Pit-N	4	6	.400	45	7	0	0	0	93	95	63	60	8	5	34	55	1.387	5.81	72	4.18	.270	4	.250	-18	1	-1.6
2003	Hou-N	6	6	.500	19	19	0	0	0	106^2	91	51	49	16	5	48	91	1.303	4.13	107	4.04	.233	7	.167	1	5	0.2
Total	9	39	43	.476	338	83	2	0	5	765^2	746	447	418	96	38	403	589	1.501	4.91	93	4.87	.258	22	.131	-39	34	-4.1

• VINES, Bob Robert Earl Vines b: 2/25/1897, Waxahachie, TX d: 10/18/1982, Orlando, FL BR/TR, 6'4", 184 lbs. Deb: 9/3/1924

YEAR	TM-L	W	L	PCT	G	GS	CG	SH	SV	IP	H	R	ER	HR	HB	BB	SO	RAT	ERA	ERA+	CERA	OAV	BH	AVG	PR+	WS	TPW
1924	StL-N	0	0	....	2	0	0	0	0	10^2	23	13	11	1	0	0	0	2.156	9.28	41	9.37	.426	0	.000	-7	0	-0.7
1925	Phi-N	0	0	....	3	0	0	0	0	4	9	10	5	0	0	3	0	3.000	11.25	42	11.84	.450	0	....	-3	0	-0.3
Total	2	0	0	....	5	0	0	0	0	14^2	32	23	16	1	0	3	0	2.386	9.82	41	10.04	.432	0	.000	-9	0	-1.0

• VINEYARD, Dave David Kent Vineyard b: 2/25/1941, Clay, WV BR/TR, 6'3", 195 lbs. Deb: 7/18/1964

YEAR	TM-L	W	L	PCT	G	GS	CG	SH	SV	IP	H	R	ER	HR	HB	BB	SO	RAT	ERA	ERA+	CERA	OAV	BH	AVG	PR+	WS	TPW
1964	Bal-A	2	5	.286	19	6	1	0	0	54	57	34	25	5	0	27	50	1.556	4.17	86	4.71	.274	2	.167	-5	0	-0.5

• VINING, Ken Kenneth Edward Vining b: 12/5/1974, Decatur, GA BL/TL, 6', 180 lbs. Deb: 5/23/2001

YEAR	TM-L	W	L	PCT	G	GS	CG	SH	SV	IP	H	R	ER	HR	HB	BB	SO	RAT	ERA	ERA+	CERA	OAV	BH	AVG	PR+	WS	TPW
2001	Chi-A	0	0	....	8	0	0	0	0	6^2	15	14	13	3	1	7	3	3.300	17.55	26	20.56	.441	0	....	-10	0	-0.9

• VINTON, Bill William Miller Vinton b: 4/27/1865, Winthrop, MA d: 9/3/1893, Pawtucket, RI BR/TR, 6'1", 160 lbs. Deb: 7/3/1884

YEAR	TM-L	W	L	PCT	G	GS	CG	SH	SV	IP	H	R	ER	HR	HB	BB	SO	RAT	ERA	ERA+	CERA	OAV	BH	AVG	PR+	WS	TPW
1884	Phi-N	10	10	.500	21	21	20	0	0	182	166	131	45	6	....	35	105	1.104	2.23	134	....	.230	9	.115	23	5	1.5
1885	Phi-N	3	6	.333	9	9	8	0	0	77	90	59	26	0	....	23	21	1.468	3.04	92	....	.279	2	.067	-3	2	-0.6
	Phi-a	4	3	.571	7	7	6	2	0	55	46	41	15	1	4	15	34	1.109	2.45	140	....	.218	4	.154	6	3	0.6
Total	2	17	19	.472	37	37	34	2	0	314	302	231	86	7	4	73	160	1.194	2.46	121	....	.240	15	.112	27	10	1.5

• VIOLA, Frank Frank John Viola b: 4/19/1960, Hempstead, NY BL/TL, 6'4", 209 lbs. Deb: 6/6/1982

YEAR	TM-L	W	L	PCT	G	GS	CG	SH	SV	IP	H	R	ER	HR	HB	BB	SO	RAT	ERA	ERA+	CERA	OAV	BH	AVG	PR+	WS	TPW
1982	Min-A	4	10	.286	22	22	3	1	0	126	152	77	73	22	0	38	84	1.508	5.21	81	5.53	.302	0	....	-15	3	-1.5
1983	Min-A	7	15	.318	35	34	4	0	0	210	242	141	128	34	8	92	127	**1.590**	5.49	77	5.70	.287	0	....	-31	4	-3.1
1984	Min-A	18	12	.600	35	35	10	4	0	257^2	225	101	92	28	4	73	149	1.157	3.21	131	3.09	.233	0	....	22	22	2.2
1985	Min-A	18	14	.563	36	36	9	0	0	250^2	262	136	114	26	2	68	135	1.316	4.09	108	3.87	.268	0	....	9	16	0.9
1986	Min-A	16	13	.552	37	**37**	7	1	0	245^2	257	136	123	37	3	83	191	1.384	4.51	96	4.52	.268	0	....	-3	13	-0.3
1987*	Min-A	17	10	.630	36	36	7	1	0	251^2	230	91	81	29	6	66	197	1.176	2.90	159	3.27	.241	0	....	47	24	4.5
1988	Min-A★	**24**	7	.774	35	35	7	2	0	255^1	236	80	75	20	3	54	193	1.136	2.64	154	2.88	.245	0	....	40	**25**	4.1
1989	Min-A	8	12	.400	24	24	7	1	0	175^2	171	80	74	17	3	47	138	1.241	3.79	109	3.47	.256	0	....	8	10	0.8
	NY-N	5	5	.500	12	12	2	1	0	85^1	75	35	32	5	1	27	73	1.195	3.38	97	2.84	.236	3	.130	-0	4	-0.1
1990	NY-N★	20	12	.625	35	**35**	7	3	0	**249^2**	227	83	74	15	2	60	182	1.150	2.67	140	2.76	.242	13	.153	**33**	**20**	**3.3**
1991	NY-N★	13	15	.464	35	35	3	0	0	231^1	259	112	102	25	1	54	132	1.353	3.97	92	4.16	.286	9	.127	-3	10	-0.5
1992	Bos-A	13	12	.520	35	35	6	1	0	238	214	99	91	13	7	89	121	1.273	3.44	122	3.22	.242	0	....	20	18	2.0
1993	Bos-A	11	8	.579	29	29	2	1	0	183^2	180	76	64	12	6	72	91	1.372	3.14	147	3.80	.259	0	....	29	16	2.8
1994	Bos-A	1	1	.500	6	6	0	0	0	31	34	17	16	2	0	17	9	1.645	4.65	108	5.14	.296	0	....	1	2	0.1
1995	Cin-N	0	1	.000	3	3	0	0	0	14^1	20	11	10	3	0	3	4	1.605	6.28	66	6.39	.333	1	.167	-4	0	-0.4
1996	Tor-A	1	3	.250	6	6	0	0	0	30^1	43	28	26	6	2	21	18	2.110	7.71	65	9.09	.350	0	....	-10	0	-0.9
Total	15	176	150	.540	421	420	74	16	0	2836^1	2827	1303	1175	294	48	864	1844	1.301	3.73	112	3.82	.260	26	.141	142	187	13.9

• VITELLI, Joe Antonio Joseph Vitelli b: 4/12/1908, McKees Rocks, PA d: 2/7/1967, Pittsburgh, PA BR/TR, 6'1", 195 lbs. Deb: 5/30/1944

YEAR	TM-L	W	L	PCT	G	GS	CG	SH	SV	IP	H	R	ER	HR	HB	BB	SO	RAT	ERA	ERA+	CERA	OAV	BH	AVG	PR+	WS	TPW
1944	Pit-N	0	0	....	4	0	0	0	0	7	5	6	2	1	1	7	2	1.714	2.57	144	4.93	.185	0	.000	1	0	0.1

• VITKO, Joe Joseph John Vitko b: 2/1/1970, Somerville, NJ BR/TR, 6'8", 210 lbs. Deb: 9/18/1992

YEAR	TM-L	W	L	PCT	G	GS	CG	SH	SV	IP	H	R	ER	HR	HB	BB	SO	RAT	ERA	ERA+	CERA	OAV	BH	AVG	PR+	WS	TPW
1992	NY-N	0	1	.000	3	1	0	0	0	4^2	12	11	7	1	0	1	6	2.786	13.50	26	13.62	.444	0	....	-5	0	-0.6

• VIZCAINO, Luis Luis (Arias) Vizcaino b: 6/1/1975, Bani, Dominican Republic BR/TR, 6'1", 169 lbs. Deb: 7/23/1999

YEAR	TM-L	W	L	PCT	G	GS	CG	SH	SV	IP	H	R	ER	HR	HB	BB	SO	RAT	ERA	ERA+	CERA	OAV	BH	AVG	PR+	WS	TPW
1999	Oak-A	0	0	....	1	0	0	0	0	3^1	3	2	2	1	0	3	2	1.800	5.40	86	7.01	.231	0	....	-0	0	0.0
2000	Oak-A	0	1	.000	12	0	0	0	0	19^1	25	17	16	2	2	11	18	1.862	7.45	64	6.83	.305	0	....	-6	0	-0.5
2001	Oak-A	2	1	.667	36	0	0	0	1	36^2	38	19	19	8	0	12	31	1.364	4.66	95	4.80	.266	0	....	-1	2	-0.1
2002	Mil-N	5	3	.625	76	0	0	0	5	81^1	55	27	27	6	3	30	79	1.045	2.99	137	2.20	.192	0	.000	10	8	1.0
2003	Mil-N	4	3	.571	75	0	0	0	0	62	64	45	44	16	1	25	61	1.435	6.39	66	5.37	.263	0	....	-14	1	-1.3
Total	5	11	8	.579	200	0	0	0	6	202^2	185	110	108	33	6	81	191	1.313	4.80	90	4.16	.241	0	.000	-10	11	-1.0

• VOGELSONG, Ryan Ryan Andrew Vogelsong b: 7/22/1977, Charlotte, NC BR/TR, 6'3", 195 lbs. Deb: 9/2/2000

YEAR	TM-L	W	L	PCT	G	GS	CG	SH	SV	IP	H	R	ER	HR	HB	BB	SO	RAT	ERA	ERA+	CERA	OAV	BH	AVG	PR+	WS	TPW
2000	SF-N	0	0	....	4	0	0	0	0	6	4	0	0	0	0	2	6	1.000	0.00	....	1.57	.182	0	....	3	1	0.3
2001	SF-N	0	3	.000	13	0	0	0	0	28^2	29	21	18	5	2	14	17	1.500	5.65	70	5.26	.257	1	.125	-5	0	-0.5
	Pit-N	0	2	.000	2	2	0	0	0	6	10	10	8	1	0	6	7	2.667	12.00	37	11.03	.357	0	.000	-5	0	-0.5
	Yr.	0	5	.000	15	2	0	0	0	34^2	39	31	26	6	2	20	24	1.702	6.75	61	6.26	.277	1	.100	-10	0	-1.0
2003	Pit-N	2	2	.500	6	5	0	0	0	22	30	19	16	1	2	9	15	1.773	6.55	67	5.72	.323	1	.167	-5	0	-0.5
Total	3	2	7	.222	25	7	0	0	0	62^2	73	50	42	7	4	31	45	1.660	6.03	70	5.62	.285	2	.125	-13	1	-1.3

YEAR TM-L	W	L	PCT	G	GS	CG	SH	SV	IP	H	R	ER	HR	HB	BB	SO	RAT	ERA	ERA+	CERA	OAV	BH	AVG	PR+	WS	TPW
• VOIGT, Ollie				Olen Edward "Ode" Voigt b: 1/29/1900, Wheaton, IL d: 4/7/1970, Scottsdale, AZ BL/TR, 6'1", 170 lbs. Deb: 4/19/1924																						
1924 StL-A	1	0	1.000	8	1	0	0	0	16^1	21	13	10	1	0	13	4	2.082	5.51	82	7.35	.356	1	.250	-2	1	-0.1
• VOISELLE, Bill				William Symmes "Ninety-Six,Big Bill" Voiselle b: 1/29/1919, Greenwood, SC BR/TR, 6'4", 200 lbs. Deb: 9/1/1942																						
1942 NY-N	0	1	.000	2	1	0	0	0	9	6	4	2	1	0	4	5	1.111	2.00	168	2.35	.176	0	.000	1	0	0.1
1943 NY-N	1	2	.333	4	4	3	0	0	31	18	10	7	1	0	14	19	1.032	2.03	169	1.52	.154	1	.111	5	2	0.5
1944 NY-N★	21	16	.568	43	**41**	25	1	0	**312**^{2}	276	138	105	31	4	118	**161**	1.260	3.02	121	3.26	.232	22	.210	20	24	2.3
1945 NY-N	14	14	.500	41	**35**	14	4	0	232^1	249	128	116	15	4	97	115	1.489	4.49	87	4.20	.273	10	.127	-15	10	-1.8
1946 NY-N	9	15	.375	36	25	10	2	0	178	171	88	74	14	0	85	89	1.438	3.74	92	3.82	.248	9	.164	-4	7	-0.5
1947 NY-N	1	4	.200	11	5	1	0	0	42^2	44	26	22	4	1	22	20	1.547	4.64	88	4.89	.284	2	.133	-3	1	-0.4
Bos-N	8	7	.533	22	20	7	0	0	131^1	146	66	63	10	1	51	59	1.500	4.32	90	4.44	.280	9	.170	-5	6	-0.6
Yr.	9	11	.450	33	25	8	0	0	174	190	92	85	14	2	73	79	1.511	4.40	90	4.55	.281	11	.162	-8	7	-0.9
1948* Bos-N	13	13	.500	37	30	9	2	2	215^2	226	93	87	18	3	90	89	1.465	3.63	106	4.26	.272	7	.097	3	12	0.0
1949 Bos-N	7	8	.467	30	22	5	4	1	169^1	170	84	76	14	1	78	63	1.465	4.04	94	4.14	.263	7	.115	-4	8	-0.6
1950 Chi-N	0	4	.000	19	7	0	0	0	51^1	64	39	33	7	1	29	25	1.812	5.79	73	6.41	.303	1	.077	-8	0	-0.9
Total 9	**74**	**84**	**.468**	**245**	**190**	**74**	**13**	**3**	**1373^1**	**1370**	**676**	**585**	**115**	**15**	**588**	**645**	**1.426**	**3.83**	**99**	**3.99**	**.258**	**68**	**.147**	**-9**	**70**	**-1.7**
• VOLZ, Jake				Jacob Phillip "Silent Jake" Volz b: 4/4/1878, San Antonio, TX d: 8/11/1962, San Antonio, TX BR/TR, 5'10", 175 lbs. Deb: 9/28/1901																						
1901 Bos-A	1	0	1.000	1	1	1	0	0	7	6	9	7	2	0	9	5	2.143	9.00	39	7.28	.229	0	.000	-5	0	-0.5
1905 Bos-N	0	2	.000	3	2	0	0	0	8^2	12	11	10	0	1	8	1	2.308	10.38	30	8.62	.364	0	.000	-7	0	-0.7
1908 Cin-N	1	2	.333	7	4	1	0	0	22^2	16	9	9	1	2	12	6	1.235	3.57	64	2.79	.195	1	.250	-3	1	-0.3
Total 3	**2**	**4**	**.333**	**11**	**7**	**2**	**0**	**0**	**38^1**	**34**	**29**	**26**	**3**	**3**	**29**	**12**	**1.643**	**6.10**	**46**	**4.93**	**.241**	**1**	**.100**	**-14**	**1**	**-1.5**
• VON FRICKEN, Tony				Anthony Von Fricken b: 5/30/1869, Brooklyn, NY d: 3/22/1947, Troy, NY BB/TR, 5'11.5", 160 lbs. Deb: 5/9/1890																						
1890 Bos-N	0	1	.000	1	1	1	0	0	8	23	16	9	0	0	8	2	3.875	10.13	37	....	.493	0	.000	-6	0	-0.5
• VON HOFF, Bruce				Bruce Frederick Von Hoff b: 11/17/1943, Oakland, CA BR/TR, 6', 187 lbs. Deb: 9/28/1965																						
1965 Hou-N	0	0	....	3	0	0	0	0	3	3	3	3	0	0	2	1	1.667	9.00	37	4.23	.250	0	....	-2	0	-0.2
1967 Hou-N	0	3	.000	10	10	0	0	0	50^1	52	29	27	3	0	28	22	1.589	4.83	69	4.47	.268	1	.067	-7	0	-0.9
Total 2	**0**	**3**	**.000**	**13**	**10**	**0**	**0**	**0**	**53^1**	**55**	**32**	**30**	**3**	**0**	**30**	**23**	**1.594**	**5.06**	**65**	**4.46**	**.267**	**1**	**.067**	**-9**	**0**	**-1.1**
• VON OHLEN, Dave				David Von Ohlen b: 10/25/1958, Flushing, NY BL/TL, 6'2", 200 lbs. Deb: 5/13/1983																						
1983 StL-N	3	2	.600	46	0	0	0	2	68^1	71	27	25	3	3	25	21	1.405	3.29	110	3.84	.280	1	.143	3	5	0.3
1984 StL-N	1	0	1.000	27	0	0	0	1	34^2	39	13	12	0	0	8	19	1.356	3.12	111	3.45	.300	1	1.000	1	3	0.1
1985 Cle-A	3	2	.600	26	0	0	0	0	43^1	47	20	14	3	0	20	12	1.546	2.91	142	4.24	.288	0	....	6	3	0.6
1986 Oak-A	0	3	.000	24	0	0	0	1	15^1	18	7	6	0	0	7	4	1.630	3.52	110	4.38	.300	0	....	1	1	0.1
1987 Oak-A	0	0	....	4	0	0	0	0	6	10	5	5	1	0	1	3	1.833	7.50	55	8.10	.400	0	....	-2	0	-0.2
Total 5	**7**	**7**	**.500**	**127**	**0**	**0**	**0**	**4**	**167^2**	**185**	**72**	**62**	**7**	**3**	**61**	**59**	**1.467**	**3.33**	**113**	**4.07**	**.293**	**2**	**.250**	**8**	**12**	**0.9**
• VORHEES, Cy				Henry Bert Vorhees b: 9/30/1874, Lodi, OH d: 2/8/1910, Perry, OH TR, 6'3", 200 lbs. Deb: 4/17/1902																						
1902 Phi-N	3	3	.500	10	5	3	1	0	53^2	63	33	23	1	1	20	24	1.547	3.86	73	4.32	.292	7	.350	-5	3	-0.3
Was-A	0	1	.000	1	1	1	0	0	8	10	6	4	0	0	2	1	1.500	4.50	82	4.11	.306	2	.667	-1	0	0.1
• VOSBERG, Ed				Edward John Vosberg b: 9/28/1961, Tucson, AZ BL/TL, 6'1", 190 lbs. Deb: 9/17/1986																						
1986 SD-N	0	1	.000	5	3	0	0	0	13^2	17	11	10	1	0	9	8	1.902	6.59	55	6.27	.304	0	.000	-4	0	-0.5
1990 SF-N	1	1	.500	18	0	0	0	0	24^1	21	16	15	3	0	12	12	1.356	5.55	66	3.71	.233	0	....	-5	0	-0.5
1994 Oak-A	0	2	.000	16	0	0	0	0	13^2	16	7	6	2	0	5	12	1.537	3.95	112	5.75	.320	0	....	1	1	0.1
1995 Tex-A	5	5	.500	44	0	0	0	4	36	32	15	12	3	0	16	36	1.333	3.00	161	3.45	.241	0	....	7	5	0.7
1996* Tex-A	1	1	.500	52	0	0	0	8	44	51	17	16	4	0	21	32	1.636	3.27	160	5.20	.298	0	....	10	6	0.9
1997 Tex-A	1	2	.333	42	0	0	0	0	41	44	23	21	3	2	15	29	1.439	4.61	104	4.10	.277	0	....	1	2	0.1
*Fla-N	1	1	.500	17	0	0	0	1	12	15	7	5	0	3	6	8	1.750	3.75	108	6.09	.313	0	....	0	1	0.0
1999 SD-N	0	0	....	15	0	0	0	0	8^1	16	11	9	1	2	3	6	2.280	9.72	43	10.59	.421	0	....	-5	0	-0.5
Ari-N	0	1	.000	4	0	0	0	0	2^2	6	1	1	0	0	0	2	2.250	3.38	135	9.88	.462	0	....	0	0	0.0
Yr.	0	1	.000	19	0	0	0	0	11	22	12	10	1	2	3	8	2.273	8.18	52	10.42	.431	0	....	-5	0	-0.5
2000 Phi-N	1	1	.500	31	0	0	0	0	24	21	11	11	4	0	18	23	1.625	4.13	113	5.42	.241	0	....	1	2	0.1
2001 Phi-N	0	0	....	18	0	0	0	0	12^2	8	4	4	0	0	3	11	.868	2.84	149	1.35	.186	0	....	2	1	0.2
2002 Mon-N	0	0	....	4	0	0	0	0	1	3	3	2	1	0	1	0	4.000	18.00	24	28.03	.429	0	....	-2	0	-0.2
Total 10	**10**	**15**	**.400**	**266**	**3**	**0**	**0**	**13**	**233^1**	**250**	**126**	**112**	**22**	**7**	**109**	**179**	**1.539**	**4.32**	**102**	**4.88**	**.279**	**0**	**.000**	**6**	**18**	**0.5**
• VOSS, Alex				Alexander Voss b: 5/16/1858, Roswell, GA d: 8/31/1906, Cincinnati, OH BR/TR, 6'1", 180 lbs. Deb: 4/17/1884 ♦																						
1884 Was-U	5	14	.263	27	20	18	0	0	186^1	206	136	74	2	....	32	112	1.277	3.57	84	....	.262	47	.192	-7	10	-1.4
KC-U	0	6	.000	7	6	6	0	0	53	74	45	25	2	....	7	17	1.528	4.25	66	....	.310	4	.089	-9	0	-1.2
Yr.	5	20	.200	34	26	24	0	0	239^1	280	181	99	4	....	39	129	1.333	3.72	79	....	.273	51	.176	-15	10	-2.6
• VOWINKEL, Rip				John Henry Vowinkel b: 11/18/1884, Oswego, NY d: 7/13/1966, Oswego, NY BR/TR, 5'10", 195 lbs. Deb: 9/5/1905																						
1905 Cin-N	3	3	.500	6	6	4	0	0	45^1	52	31	21	2	1	10	7	1.368	4.17	79	4.10	.302	1	.071	-5	1	-0.6
• VOYLES, Brad				Bradley Roy Voyles b: 12/30/1976, Green Bay, WI BR/TR, 6'1", 195 lbs. Deb: 9/8/2001																						
2001 KC-A	0	0	....	7	0	0	0	0	9^1	5	4	4	1	1	8	6	1.393	3.86	127	3.85	.161	0	....	1	1	0.1
2002 KC-A	0	2	.000	22	0	0	0	1	27^2	31	21	20	5	2	18	26	1.771	6.51	77	6.72	.284	0	....	-4	0	-0.4
2003 KC-A	0	2	.000	11	3	0	0	0	31^1	47	29	26	6	1	18	24	2.074	7.47	69	8.71	.348	0	.000	-8	0	-0.8
Total 3	**0**	**4**	**.000**	**40**	**3**	**0**	**0**	**1**	**68^1**	**83**	**54**	**50**	**12**	**4**	**44**	**56**	**1.859**	**6.59**	**77**	**7.24**	**.302**	**0**	**.000**	**-12**	**1**	**-1.1**
• VUCKOVICH, Pete				Peter Dennis Vuckovich b: 10/27/1952, Johnstown, PA BR/TR, 6'4", 220 lbs. Deb: 8/3/1975 C																						
1975 Chi-A	0	1	.000	4	2	0	0	0	10^1	17	15	15	0	0	7	5	2.323	13.06	30	8.42	.386	0	....	-10	0	-1.1
1976 Chi-A	7	4	.636	33	7	1	0	0	110^1	122	59	57	3	4	60	62	1.650	4.65	77	4.82	.287	0	....	-12	4	-1.3
1977 Tor-A	7	7	.500	53	8	3	1	8	148	143	64	57	13	5	59	123	1.365	3.47	121	3.90	.257	0	....	16	13	1.6
1978 StL-N	12	12	.500	45	23	6	2	1	198^1	187	65	56	9	2	59	149	1.240	2.54	138	3.04	.253	8	.138	20	14	2.0
1979 StL-N	15	10	.600	34	32	9	0	0	233	229	108	93	22	3	64	145	1.258	3.59	105	3.51	.260	12	.152	-1	14	-0.3
1980 StL-N	12	9	.571	32	30	7	3	1	222^1	203	96	84	18	2	68	132	1.219	3.40	109	3.18	.247	13	.183	4	12	0.6
1981* Mil-A	**14**	4	.778	24	23	2	1	0	149^2	137	61	59	9	4	57	84	1.296	3.55	97	3.45	.249	0	....	-4	9	-0.4
1982* Mil-A	18	6	.750	30	30	9	1	0	223^2	234	96	83	14	5	102	105	1.502	3.34	113	4.46	.275	0	....	8	13	0.8
1983 Mil-A	0	2	.000	3	3	0	0	0	14^2	15	9	8	0	1	10	10	1.705	4.91	76	4.61	.259	0	....	-2	0	-0.2
1985 Mil-A	6	10	.375	22	22	1	0	0	112^2	134	74	69	16	7	48	55	1.615	5.51	76	5.89	.298	0	....	-17	2	-1.7
1986 Mil-A	2	4	.333	6	6	0	0	0	32^1	33	18	11	3	2	11	12	1.361	3.06	141	4.18	.273	0	....	5	2	0.5
Total 11	**93**	**69**	**.574**	**286**	**186**	**38**	**8**	**10**	**1455^1**	**1454**	**665**	**592**	**107**	**35**	**545**	**882**	**1.374**	**3.66**	**103**	**3.92**	**.264**	**33**	**.159**	**7**	**83**	**0.5**
• WACHTEL, Paul				Paul Horine Wachtel b: 4/30/1888, Myersville, MD d: 12/15/1964, San Antonio, TX BR/TR, 5'11", 175 lbs. Deb: 9/18/1917																						
1917 Bro-N	0	0	....	2	0	0	0	0	6	9	7	7	0	0	4	3	2.167	10.50	27	7.21	.375	1	.333	-5	0	-0.6
• WACKER, Charlie				Charles James Wacker b: 12/8/1883, Jeffersonville, IN d: 8/7/1948, Evansville, IN BL/TL, 5'9" Deb: 4/28/1909																						
1909 Pit-N	0	0	....	1	0	0	0	0	2	2	2	0	0	0	1	0	1.500	0.00	....	3.61	.400	0	....	1	0	0.1
• WADDELL, Rube				George Edward Waddell b: 10/13/1876, Bradford, PA d: 4/1/1914, San Antonio, TX BR/TL, 6'1.5", 196 lbs. Deb: 9/8/1897 HOF: 1946																						
1897 Lou-N	0	1	.000	2	1	1	0	0	14	17	6	5	0	1	6	5	1.643	3.21	132	4.82	.298	0	.000	2	1	0.0
1899 Lou-N	7	2	.778	10	9	9	1	1	79	69	38	27	4	8	14	44	1.051	3.08	125	2.55	.235	8	.235	8	7	0.7
1900* Pit-N	8	13	.381	29	22	16	2	0	208^2	176	96	55	3	13	55	130	1.107	**2.37**	**153**	**2.31**	**.229**	14	.173	28	16	2.4
1901 Pit-N	0	2	.000	2	2	0	0	0	7^2	10	12	8	0	1	9	4	2.478	9.39	35	7.75	.313	0	.000	-5	0	-0.6
Chi-N	14	14	.500	29	28	26	0	0	243^2	239	123	76	5	9	66	168	1.252	2.81	115	2.89	.255	25	.255	14	17	2.0
Yr.	14	16	.467	31	30	26	0	0	251^1	249	135	84	5	10	75	172	1.289	3.01	108	3.04	.257	25	.248	9	17	1.4
1902 Phi-A	24	7	.774	33	27	26	3	0	276^1	224	90	63	7	10	64	**210**	1.042	2.05	179	2.11	.223	32	.286	**50**	33	**5.5**

YEAR	TM-L	W	L	PCT	G	GS	CG	SH	SV	IP	H	R	ER	HR	HB	BB	SO	RAT	ERA	ERA+	CERA	OAV	BH	AVG	PR+	WS	TPW
1903	Phi-A	21	16	.568	39	38	**34**	4	0	324	274	109	88	3	8	85	**302**	1.108	2.44	125	2.23	.229	14	.122	25	27	1.9
1904	Phi-A	25	19	.568	46	46	39	8	0	383	307	109	69	5	14	91	**349**	1.039	1.62	**165**	1.97	.221	17	.122	**54**	32	**5.3**
1905	Phi-A	**27**	10	.730	**46**	34	27	7	0	328^2	231	86	54	5	10	90	**287**	.977	**1.48**	**179**	1.66	**.200**	20	.172	**53**	**35**	**5.7**
1906	Phi-A	15	17	.469	43	34	22	8	0	272^2	221	89	67	1	10	92	**196**	1.148	2.21	123	2.26	.225	14	.163	16	18	1.8
1907	Phi-A	19	13	.594	44	33	20	7	0	284^2	234	115	68	2	15	73	**232**	1.078	2.15	121	2.14	.227	12	.119	13	20	0.9
1908	StL-A	19	14	.576	43	36	25	5	3	285^2	223	93	60	0	8	90	232	1.096	1.89	126	1.98	.213	10	.110	3	21	0.2
1909	StL-A	11	14	.440	31	28	16	5	0	220^1	204	78	58	1	7	57	141	1.185	2.37	102	2.68	.267	5	.067	0	12	-0.5
1910	StL-A	3	1	.750	10	2	0	0	1	33	31	19	13	1	1	11	16	1.273	3.55	70	2.95	.242	1	.111	-4	1	-0.4
Total	13	193	143	.574	407	340	261	50	5	2961^1	2460	1063	711	37	115	803	2316	1.102	2.16	133	2.23	.228	172	.161	257	240	24.9

• WADDELL, Tom Thomas David Waddell b: 9/17/1958, Dundee, Scotland BR/TR, 6'1", 185 lbs. Deb: 4/15/1984

YEAR	TM-L	W	L	PCT	G	GS	CG	SH	SV	IP	H	R	ER	HR	HB	BB	SO	RAT	ERA	ERA+	CERA	OAV	BH	AVG	PR+	WS	TPW
1984	Cle-A	7	4	.636	58	0	0	0	6	97	68	35	33	12	1	37	59	1.082	3.06	134	2.57	.202	0	....	10	9	1.0
1985	Cle-A	8	6	.571	49	9	1	0	9	112^2	104	61	61	20	1	39	53	1.269	4.87	85	3.91	.246	0	....	-9	6	-0.9
1987	Cle-A	0	1	.000	6	0	0	0	0	5^2	7	10	9	1	1	7	6	2.471	14.29	32	10.42	.292	0	....	-6	0	-0.6
Total	3	15	11	.577	113	9	1	0	15	215^1	179	106	103	33	3	83	118	1.217	4.30	96	3.48	.229	0	....	-5	15	-0.4

• WADE, Ben Benjamin Styron Wade b: 11/26/1922, Morehead City, NC d: 12/2/2002, Los Angeles, CA BR/TR, 6'3", 205 lbs. Deb: 4/30/1948

YEAR	TM-L	W	L	PCT	G	GS	CG	SH	SV	IP	H	R	ER	HR	HB	BB	SO	RAT	ERA	ERA+	CERA	OAV	BH	AVG	PR+	WS	TPW
1948	Chi-N	0	1	.000	2	0	0	0	0	5	4	4	4	0	0	4	1	1.600	7.20	54	3.43	.211	0	.000	-2	0	-0.2
1952	Bro-N	11	9	.550	37	24	5	1	3	180	166	81	72	19	2	94	118	1.444	3.60	101	4.11	.246	7	.117	-1	10	0.0
1953*	Bro-N	7	5	.583	32	0	0	0	3	90^1	79	40	38	15	4	33	65	1.240	3.79	113	3.81	.232	4	.167	3	7	0.3
1954	Bro-N	1	1	.500	23	0	0	0	3	45	62	46	41	9	0	21	25	1.844	8.20	50	7.29	.339	0	.000	-21	0	-2.1
	StL-N	0	0	....	13	0	0	0	0	23	27	15	14	3	2	15	19	1.826	5.48	75	6.64	.303	0	.000	-3	0	-0.4
	Yr.	1	1	.500	36	0	0	0	3	68	89	61	55	12	2	36	44	1.838	7.28	56	7.07	.327	0	.000	-24	0	-2.5
1955	Pit-N	0	1	.000	11	1	0	0	1	28	26	12	10	3	1	14	7	1.429	3.21	128	4.00	.252	0	.000	3	2	0.3
Total	5	19	17	.528	118	25	5	1	10	371^1	364	198	179	49	9	181	235	1.468	4.34	90	4.56	.259	11	.112	-20	19	-2.1

• WADE, Jake Jacob Fields "Whistling Jake" Wade b: 4/1/1912, Morehead City, NC BL/TL, 6'2", 175 lbs. Deb: 4/22/1936

YEAR	TM-L	W	L	PCT	G	GS	CG	SH	SV	IP	H	R	ER	HR	HB	BB	SO	RAT	ERA	ERA+	CERA	OAV	BH	AVG	PR+	WS	TPW
1936	Det-A	4	5	.444	13	11	4	1	0	78^1	93	60	46	7	1	52	30	1.851	5.29	94	6.05	.296	5	.172	-2	3	-0.2
1937	Det-A	7	10	.412	33	25	7	1	0	165^1	160	106	99	13	3	107	69	1.615	5.39	87	4.63	.257	11	.186	-11	7	-1.1
1938	Det-A	3	2	.600	27	2	0	0	0	70	73	56	51	9	0	48	23	1.729	6.56	76	5.49	.268	1	.048	-13	1	-1.3
1939	Bos-A	1	4	.200	20	6	1	0	0	47^2	68	34	33	1	0	37	21	2.203	6.23	76	7.57	.358	0	.000	-8	1	-0.9
	StL-A	0	2	.000	4	2	1	0	0	16^1	26	25	20	1	0	19	9	2.755	11.02	44	10.24	.356	0	.000	-11	0	-1.1
	Yr.	1	6	.143	24	8	2	0	0	64	94	59	53	2	0	56	30	2.344	7.45	64	8.25	.357	0	.000	-19	1	-2.0
1942	Chi-A	5	5	.500	15	10	3	0	0	85^2	84	45	39	2	0	56	32	1.634	4.10	88	4.18	.255	7	.241	-5	4	-0.5
1943	Chi-A	3	7	.300	21	9	3	1	0	83^2	66	34	28	3	4	54	41	1.434	3.01	111	3.42	.222	4	.148	3	5	0.3
1944	Chi-A	2	4	.333	19	5	1	0	2	74^2	75	46	40	3	0	41	35	1.554	4.82	71	4.07	.261	7	.292	-12	2	-1.1
1946	NY-A	2	1	.667	13	1	0	0	1	35^1	33	9	9	2	1	14	22	1.330	2.29	151	3.48	.250	1	.111	4	3	0.3
	Was-A	0	0	....	6	0	0	0	0	11^1	12	6	6	1	0	12	9	2.118	4.76	70	6.91	.279	0	.000	-2	0	-0.2
	Yr.	2	1	.667	19	1	0	0	1	46^2	45	15	15	3	1	26	31	1.521	2.89	118	4.31	.257	1	.100	2	3	0.2
Total	8	27	40	.403	171	71	20	3	3	668^1	690	421	371	42	9	440	291	1.691	5.00	85	4.94	.269	36	.167	-57	26	-5.7

• WADE, Terrell Hawatha Terrell Wade b: 1/25/1973, Rembert, SC BL/TL, 6'3", 205 lbs. Deb: 9/12/1995

YEAR	TM-L	W	L	PCT	G	GS	CG	SH	SV	IP	H	R	ER	HR	HB	BB	SO	RAT	ERA	ERA+	CERA	OAV	BH	AVG	PR+	WS	TPW
1995	Atl-N	0	1	.000	3	0	0	0	0	4	3	2	2	1	0	4	3	1.750	4.50	95	6.47	.214	0	....	-0	0	0.0
1996*	Atl-N	5	0	1.000	44	8	0	0	1	69^2	57	28	23	9	1	47	79	1.493	2.97	148	4.30	.227	2	.154	12	7	1.2
1997	Atl-N	2	3	.400	12	9	0	0	0	42	60	31	25	6	2	16	35	1.810	5.36	79	7.18	.349	3	.250	-6	0	-0.5
1998	TB-A	1	1	.500	2	2	0	0	0	10^2	14	6	6	3	0	2	8	1.500	5.06	95	6.51	.318	0	....	-1	1	-0.1
Total	4	8	5	.615	61	19	0	0	1	126^1	134	67	56	19	3	69	125	1.607	3.99	109	5.51	.279	5	.200	6	8	0.7

• WADSWORTH, Jack John L. Wadsworth b: 12/17/1867, Wellington, OH d: 7/8/1941, Elyria, OH BL/TR, 180 lbs. Deb: 5/1/1890

YEAR	TM-L	W	L	PCT	G	GS	CG	SH	SV	IP	H	R	ER	HR	HB	BB	SO	RAT	ERA	ERA+	CERA	OAV	BH	AVG	PR+	WS	TPW
1890	Cle-N	2	16	.111	20	19	19	0	0	169^2	202	139	98	6	6	81	26	**1.668**	5.20	69	....	.287	12	.176	-31	3	-2.9
1893	Bal-N	0	3	.000	3	3	0	0	0	16	37	30	20	0	0	8	2	2.813	11.25	42	12.04	.439	3	.429	-11	0	-0.8
1894	Lou-N	4	18	.182	22	22	20	0	0	173	261	204	146	10	4	103	57	2.104	7.60	67	7.56	.344	19	.257	-48	1	-3.6
1895	Lou-N	0	1	.000	2	0	0	0	0	9	24	20	16	0	0	7	2	3.444	16.00	29	15.96	.479	1	.250	-11	0	-0.9
Total	4	6	38	.136	47	44	39	0	0	367^2	524	393	280	16	10	199	87	1.966	6.85	64	4.47	.328	35	.229	-101	4	-8.3

• WAECHTER, Doug Douglas Michael Waechter b: 1/28/1981, St. Petersburg, FL BR/TR, 6'4", 209 lbs. Deb: 8/27/2003

YEAR	TM-L	W	L	PCT	G	GS	CG	SH	SV	IP	H	R	ER	HR	HB	BB	SO	RAT	ERA	ERA+	CERA	OAV	BH	AVG	PR+	WS	TPW
2003	TB-A	3	2	.600	6	5	1	1	0	35^1	29	13	13	4	1	15	29	1.245	3.31	137	3.48	.225	0	....	4	3	0.4

• WAGNER, Billy William Edward Wagner b: 7/25/1971, Tannersville, VA BL/TL, 5'10", 180 lbs. Deb: 9/13/1995

YEAR	TM-L	W	L	PCT	G	GS	CG	SH	SV	IP	H	R	ER	HR	HB	BB	SO	RAT	ERA	ERA+	CERA	OAV	BH	AVG	PR+	WS	TPW
1995	Hou-N	0	0	....	1	0	0	0	0	0^1	0	0	0	0	0	0	0	.000	0.00	....	0.00	.000	0	....	0	0	0.0
1996	Hou-N	2	2	.500	37	0	0	0	9	51^2	28	16	14	6	3	30	67	1.123	2.44	159	2.61	.165	0	.000	9	8	0.8
1997*	Hou-N	7	8	.467	62	0	0	0	23	66^1	49	23	21	5	3	30	106	1.191	2.85	140	2.85	.204	0	.000	8	11	0.7
1998*	Hou-N	4	3	.571	58	0	0	0	30	60	46	19	18	6	0	25	97	1.183	2.70	150	2.87	.211	1	.333	9	11	0.9
1999*	Hou-N★	4	1	.800	66	0	0	0	39	74^2	35	14	13	5	1	23	124	.777	1.57	281	1.20	.135	0	....	23	20	2.2
2000	Hou-N	2	4	.333	28	0	0	0	6	27^2	28	19	19	6	1	18	28	1.663	6.18	79	6.15	.255	0	.000	-4	1	-0.4
2001*	Hou-N★	2	5	.286	64	0	0	0	39	62^2	44	19	19	5	5	20	79	1.021	2.73	167	2.42	.198	0	....	13	13	1.2
2002	Hou-N	4	2	.667	70	0	0	0	35	75	51	21	21	7	2	22	88	.973	2.52	169	2.08	.196	0	.000	15	16	1.5
2003	Hou-N★	1	4	.200	78	0	0	0	44	86	52	18	17	8	3	23	105	.872	1.78	249	1.63	.169	0	.000	23	19	2.3
Total	9	26	29	.473	464	0	0	0	225	504^1	333	149	142	48	18	191	694	1.039	2.53	169	2.39	.186	1	.067	96	99	9.3

• WAGNER, Bull William George Wagner b: 12/25/1887, Lilley, MI d: 10/2/1967, Muskegon, MI BR/TR, 6'.5", 225 lbs. Deb: 6/2/1913

YEAR	TM-L	W	L	PCT	G	GS	CG	SH	SV	IP	H	R	ER	HR	HB	BB	SO	RAT	ERA	ERA+	CERA	OAV	BH	AVG	PR+	WS	TPW
1913	Bro-N	4	2	.667	18	1	0	0	0	70^2	77	49	43	5	3	30	11	1.514	5.48	60	4.57	.285	6	.231	-18	0	-1.8
1914	Bro-N	0	1	.000	6	0	0	0	0	12^1	14	11	9	0	1	12	4	2.108	6.57	43	6.60	.311	0	.000	-5	0	-0.6
Total	2	4	3	.571	24	1	0	0	0	83	91	60	52	5	4	42	15	1.602	5.64	57	4.87	.289	6	.222	-23	0	-2.4

• WAGNER, Charlie Charles Thomas "Broadway" Wagner b: 12/3/1912, Reading, PA BR/TR, 5'11", 170 lbs. Deb: 4/19/1938 C

YEAR	TM-L	W	L	PCT	G	GS	CG	SH	SV	IP	H	R	ER	HR	HB	BB	SO	RAT	ERA	ERA+	CERA	OAV	BH	AVG	PR+	WS	TPW
1938	Bos-A	1	3	.250	13	6	1	0	0	36^2	47	36	34	5	1	24	14	1.936	8.35	59	7.00	.309	2	.167	-14	0	-1.3
1939	Bos-A	3	1	.750	9	5	0	0	0	38^1	49	19	18	3	0	14	13	1.643	4.23	112	5.42	.320	1	.071	2	3	0.1
1940	Bos-A	1	0	1.000	12	1	0	0	0	29^1	45	22	18	5	0	8	13	1.807	5.52	81	7.14	.344	1	.200	-3	1	-0.3
1941	Bos-A	12	8	.600	29	25	12	3	0	187^1	175	76	64	14	1	85	51	1.388	3.07	136	3.63	.245	10	.159	25	15	2.3
1942	Bos-A	14	11	.560	29	26	17	2	0	205^1	184	87	75	5	5	95	52	1.359	3.29	113	3.24	.247	5	.077	5	13	0.1
1946	Bos-A	1	0	1.000	8	4	0	0	0	30^2	32	21	20	6	0	19	14	1.663	5.87	62	5.93	.276	1	.091	-8	0	-0.9
Total	6	32	23	.582	100	67	30	5	0	527^2	532	261	229	38	7	245	157	1.473	3.91	105	4.17	.264	20	.118	7	32	-0.1

• WAGNER, Gary Gary Edward Wagner b: 6/28/1940, Bridgeport, IL BR/TR, 6'4", 191 lbs. Deb: 4/18/1965

YEAR	TM-L	W	L	PCT	G	GS	CG	SH	SV	IP	H	R	ER	HR	HB	BB	SO	RAT	ERA	ERA+	CERA	OAV	BH	AVG	PR+	WS	TPW
1965	Phi-N	7	7	.500	59	0	0	0	7	105	87	43	35	6	2	49	91	1.295	3.00	115	3.13	.233	1	.077	5	9	0.5
1966	Phi-N	0	1	.000	5	1	0	0	0	6^1	8	6	6	1	0	5	2	2.053	8.53	42	8.17	.333	0	....	-3	0	-0.4
1967	Phi-N	0	0	....	1	0	0	0	0	2	1	0	0	0	0	0	1	.500	0.00	....	0.55	.167	0	....	1	0	0.1
1968	Phi-N	4	4	.500	44	0	0	0	8	78	69	27	26	0	5	31	43	1.282	3.00	100	2.91	.243	1	.083	1	7	0.0
1969	Phi-N	0	3	.000	9	2	0	0	0	19^1	31	22	17	3	0	7	8	1.966	7.91	45	7.62	.365	0	.000	-9	0	-1.0
	Bos-A	1	3	.250	6	1	0	0	0	16^1	18	11	11	1	0	15	9	2.020	6.06	63	6.94	.300	0	.000	-4	0	-0.4
1970	Bos-A	3	1	.750	38	0	0	0	7	40^1	36	21	15	3	2	19	20	1.364	3.35	118	3.59	.232	1	.167	4	4	0.4
Total	6	15	19	.441	162	4	0	0	22	267^1	250	130	110	14	9	126	174	1.406	3.70	93	3.79	.253	3	.081	-6	20	-0.8

• WAGNER, Hector Hector Raul Guerrero Wagner b: 11/26/1968, San Juan, Dominican Republic BR/TR, 6'3", 185 lbs. Deb: 9/10/1990

YEAR	TM-L	W	L	PCT	G	GS	CG	SH	SV	IP	H	R	ER	HR	HB	BB	SO	RAT	ERA	ERA+	CERA	OAV	BH	AVG	PR+	WS	TPW
1990	KC-A	0	2	.000	5	5	0	0	0	23^1	32	24	21	4	0	11	14	1.843	8.10	47	7.01	.323	0	....	-10	0	-1.1
1991	KC-A	1	1	.500	2	2	0	0	0	10	16	10	8	2	0	3	5	1.900	7.20	57	7.97	.348	0	....	-3	0	-0.3
Total	2	1	3	.250	7	7	0	0	0	33^1	48	34	29	6	0	14	19	1.860	7.83	50	7.30	.331	0	....	-14	0	-1.4

• WAGNER, Matt — Matthew William Wagner b: 4/4/1972, Cedar Falls, IA BR/TR, 6'5", 215 lbs. Deb: 6/5/1996

YEAR	TM-L	W	L	PCT	G	GS	CG	SH	SV	IP	H	R	ER	HR	HB	BB	SO	RAT	ERA	ERA+	CERA	OAV	BH	AVG	PR+	WS	TPW
1996	Sea-A	3	5	.375	15	14	1	0	0	80	91	62	61	15	3	38	41	1.613	6.86	72	5.97	.285	0	....	-17	1	-1.6

• WAGNER, Paul — Paul Alan Wagner b: 11/14/1967, Milwaukee, WI BR/TR, 6'3", 202 lbs. Deb: 7/26/1992

YEAR	TM-L	W	L	PCT	G	GS	CG	SH	SV	IP	H	R	ER	HR	HB	BB	SO	RAT	ERA	ERA+	CERA	OAV	BH	AVG	PR+	WS	TPW
1992	Pit-N	2	0	1.000	6	1	0	0	0	13	9	1	1	0	0	5	5	1.077	0.69	497	1.84	.191	1	.333	4	2	0.4
1993	Pit-N	8	8	.500	44	17	1	1	2	141^1	143	72	67	15	1	42	114	1.309	4.27	95	3.78	.263	8	.190	-5	8	-0.4
1994	Pit-N	7	8	.467	29	17	1	0	0	119^2	136	69	61	7	8	50	86	1.554	4.59	94	4.88	.293	6	.162	-5	6	-0.5
1995	Pit-N	5	16	.238	33	25	3	1	1	165	174	96	88	18	7	72	120	1.491	4.80	90	4.74	.273	9	.214	-7	7	-0.5
1996	Pit-N	4	8	.333	16	15	1	0	0	81^2	86	49	49	10	3	39	81	1.531	5.40	81	5.02	.275	1	.040	-8	2	-1.0
1997	Pit-N	0	0	....	14	0	0	0	0	16	17	7	7	3	0	13	9	1.875	3.94	109	6.26	.274	0	.000	1	1	0.1
	Mil-A	1	0	1.000	2	0	0	0	0	2	3	2	2	1	0	0	0	1.500	9.00	51	9.22	.375	0	....	-1	0	-0.1
1998	Mil-N	1	5	.167	13	9	0	0	0	55^2	67	49	44	10	1	31	37	1.760	7.11	60	6.59	.302	3	.158	-18	0	-1.8
1999	Cle-A	1	0	1.000	3	0	0	0	0	4^1	5	4	2	0	2	3	0	1.846	4.15	121	6.70	.263	0	....	0	0	0.0
Total	8	29	45	.392	160	84	6	2	3	598^2	640	349	321	64	22	255	452	1.495	4.83	88	4.76	.276	28	.166	-39	26	-3.8

• WAGNER, Ryan — Ryan Scott Wagner b: 7/15/1982, Yoakum, TX BR/TR, 6'4", 210 lbs. Deb: 7/19/2003

YEAR	TM-L	W	L	PCT	G	GS	CG	SH	SV	IP	H	R	ER	HR	HB	BB	SO	RAT	ERA	ERA+	CERA	OAV	BH	AVG	PR+	WS	TPW
2003	Cin-N	2	0	1.000	17	0	0	0	0	21^2	13	4	4	2	0	12	25	1.154	1.66	257	2.46	.173	0	....	6	3	0.6

• WAINHOUSE, Dave — David Paul Wainhouse b: 11/7/1967, Toronto, Canada BL/TR, 6'2", 190 lbs. Deb: 8/3/1991

YEAR	TM-L	W	L	PCT	G	GS	CG	SH	SV	IP	H	R	ER	HR	HB	BB	SO	RAT	ERA	ERA+	CERA	OAV	BH	AVG	PR+	WS	TPW
1991	Mon-N	0	1	.000	2	0	0	0	0	2^2	2	2	2	0	0	4	1	2.250	6.75	54	5.91	.222	0	....	-1	0	-0.1
1993	Sea-A	0	0	....	3	0	0	0	0	2^1	7	7	7	1	1	5	2	5.143	27.00	16	33.59	.500	0	....	-6	0	-0.6
1996	Pit-N	1	0	1.000	17	0	0	0	0	23^2	22	16	15	3	0	10	16	1.352	5.70	77	3.89	.250	0	.000	-3	1	-0.3
1997	Pit-N	0	1	.000	25	0	0	0	0	28	34	28	25	2	3	17	21	1.821	8.04	53	6.29	.301	0	.000	-11	0	-1.1
1998	Col-N	1	0	1.000	10	0	0	0	0	11	15	6	6	1	2	5	3	1.818	4.91	105	7.60	.341	0	.000	0	1	0.0
1999	Col-N	0	0	....	19	0	0	0	0	28^2	37	22	22	6	0	16	18	1.849	6.91	84	7.69	.330	0	.000	-3	1	-0.3
2000	StL-N	0	1	.000	9	0	0	0	0	8^2	13	10	9	2	2	4	5	1.962	9.35	49	9.40	.351	0	....	-5	0	-0.4
Total	7	2	3	.400	85	0	0	0	0	105	130	91	86	15	8	61	66	1.819	7.37	64	7.12	.312	0	.000	-29	3	-2.9

• WAITS, Rick — Michael Richard Waits b: 5/15/1952, Atlanta, GA BL/TL, 6'3", 195 lbs. Deb: 9/17/1973 C

YEAR	TM-L	W	L	PCT	G	GS	CG	SH	SV	IP	H	R	ER	HR	HB	BB	SO	RAT	ERA	ERA+	CERA	OAV	BH	AVG	PR+	WS	TPW
1973	Tex-A	0	0	....	1	0	0	0	1	1	1	1	1	0	0	1	0	2.000	9.00	41	6.99	.333	0	....	-1	0	-0.1
1975	Cle-A	6	2	.750	16	7	3	0	1	70^1	57	25	23	3	1	25	34	1.166	2.94	129	2.52	.221	0	....	6	6	0.6
1976	Cle-A	7	9	.438	26	22	4	2	0	123^2	143	60	55	7	0	54	65	1.593	4.00	87	4.93	.297	0	....	-7	4	-0.8
1977	Cle-A	9	7	.563	37	16	1	0	2	135^1	132	67	60	8	1	64	62	1.448	3.99	99	3.94	.262	0	....	-1	8	-0.1
1978	Cle-A	13	15	.464	34	33	15	2	0	230^1	206	97	82	16	2	86	97	1.268	3.20	117	3.26	.240	0	....	15	14	1.6
1979	Cle-A	16	13	.552	34	34	8	3	0	231	230	123	114	26	4	91	91	1.390	4.44	96	4.25	.264	0	....	0	14	0.0
1980	Cle-A	13	14	.481	33	33	9	2	0	224^1	231	118	111	18	1	82	109	1.395	4.45	91	3.99	.270	0	....	-8	12	-0.8
1981	Cle-A	8	10	.444	22	21	5	1	0	126^1	173	74	69	7	1	44	51	**1.718**	4.92	74	5.75	.330	0	....	-14	3	-1.4
1982	Cle-A	2	13	.133	25	21	2	0	0	115	128	74	69	13	1	57	44	1.609	5.40	75	5.32	.290	0	....	-16	1	-1.6
1983	Cle-A	0	1	.000	8	0	0	0	0	19^2	23	13	10	1	0	9	13	1.627	4.58	92	4.60	.307	0	....	-1	1	-0.1
	Mil-A	0	2	.000	10	2	0	0	0	30	39	20	17	1	0	11	20	1.667	5.10	73	5.22	.320	0	....	-5	0	-0.5
	Yr.	0	3	.000	18	2	0	0	0	49^2	62	33	27	2	0	20	33	1.651	4.89	80	4.97	.315	0	....	-5	1	-0.5
1984	Mil-A	2	4	.333	47	1	0	0	3	73	84	32	29	7	0	24	49	1.479	3.58	108	4.61	.297	0	....	3	4	0.3
1985	Mil-A	3	2	.600	24	0	0	0	1	47	67	37	34	3	0	20	24	1.851	6.51	64	6.30	.340	0	.000	-12	0	-1.2
Total	12	79	92	.462	317	190	47	10	8	1427	1514	741	674	110	11	568	659	1.459	4.25	92	4.33	.277	0	.000	-39	67	-4.0

• WAKEFIELD, Bill — William Sumner Wakefield b: 5/24/1941, Kansas City, MO BR/TR, 6', 175 lbs. Deb: 4/18/1964

YEAR	TM-L	W	L	PCT	G	GS	CG	SH	SV	IP	H	R	ER	HR	HB	BB	SO	RAT	ERA	ERA+	CERA	OAV	BH	AVG	PR+	WS	TPW
1964	NY-N	3	5	.375	62	4	0	0	2	119^2	103	57	48	10	9	61	61	1.370	3.61	99	3.82	.235	4	.167	-1	5	-0.2

• WAKEFIELD, Tim — Timothy Stephen Wakefield b: 8/2/1966, Melbourne, FL BR/TR, 6'2", 204 lbs. Deb: 7/31/1992

YEAR	TM-L	W	L	PCT	G	GS	CG	SH	SV	IP	H	R	ER	HR	HB	BB	SO	RAT	ERA	ERA+	CERA	OAV	BH	AVG	PR+	WS	TPW
1992*	Pit-N	8	1	.889	13	13	4	1	0	92	76	26	22	3	1	35	51	1.207	2.15	160	2.72	.232	2	.071	12	9	1.2
1993	Pit-N	6	11	.353	24	20	3	2	0	128^1	145	83	80	14	9	75	59	1.714	5.61	72	5.97	.291	7	.163	-23	2	-2.2
1995*	Bos-A	16	8	.667	27	27	6	1	0	195^1	163	76	64	22	9	68	119	1.183	2.95	165	3.28	.227	0	....	41	18	3.8
1996	Bos-A	14	13	.519	32	32	6	0	0	211^2	238	151	121	38	12	90	140	1.550	5.14	99	5.68	.280	0	....	3	10	0.3
1997	Bos-A	12	15	.444	35	29	4	2	0	201^1	193	109	95	24	16	87	151	1.391	4.25	109	4.47	.256	0	.000	9	12	0.8
1998*	Bos-A	17	8	.680	36	33	2	0	0	216	211	123	110	30	14	79	146	1.343	4.58	103	4.30	.252	0	.000	1	11	0.1
1999*	Bos-A	6	11	.353	49	17	0	0	15	140	146	93	79	19	5	72	104	1.557	5.08	98	5.12	.266	0	.000	-2	8	-0.2
2000	Bos-A	6	10	.375	51	17	0	0	0	159^1	170	107	97	31	4	65	102	1.475	5.48	92	5.23	.272	0	.000	-8	5	-0.7
2001	Bos-A	9	12	.429	45	17	0	0	3	168^2	156	84	73	13	18	73	148	1.358	3.90	115	4.02	.248	1	.333	14	11	1.4
2002	Bos-A	11	5	.688	45	15	0	0	3	163^1	121	57	51	15	9	51	134	1.053	2.81	160	2.54	.204	0	....	28	15	2.7
2003*	Bos-A	11	7	.611	35	33	0	0	1	202^1	193	106	92	23	12	71	169	1.305	4.09	111	3.92	.246	0	....	15	12	1.4
Total	11	116	101	.535	392	253	25	6	22	1878^1	1812	1015	884	232	109	766	1323	1.372	4.24	110	4.32	.253	10	.122	91	113	8.6

• WALBERG, Rube — George Elvin Walberg b: 7/27/1896, Pine City, MN d: 10/27/1978, Tempe, AZ BL/TL, 6'1.5", 190 lbs. Deb: 4/29/1923

YEAR	TM-L	W	L	PCT	G	GS	CG	SH	SV	IP	H	R	ER	HR	HB	BB	SO	RAT	ERA	ERA+	CERA	OAV	BH	AVG	PR+	WS	TPW
1923	NY-N	0	0	....	2	0	0	0	0	5	4	2	1	0	0	1	1	1.000	1.80	212	1.67	.211	0	.000	1	0	0.1
	Phi-A	4	8	.333	26	10	4	0	0	115	122	77	68	10	2	60	38	1.583	5.32	77	4.77	.280	13	.317	-13	4	-0.9
1924	Phi-A	0	0	....	6	2	0	0	0	7	10	10	10	0	0	10	3	2.857	12.86	33	9.67	.345	1	.500	-7	0	-0.6
1925	Phi-A	8	14	.364	53	20	7	0	7	191^2	197	99	85	11	2	77	82	1.430	3.99	116	3.89	.269	10	.156	16	13	1.1
1926	Phi-A	12	10	.545	40	19	5	2	2	151	168	67	47	4	6	60	72	1.510	2.80	149	4.33	.292	7	.152	23	13	2.0
1927	Phi-A	16	12	.571	46	33	14	0	4	249^1	257	139	109	18	4	91	136	1.396	3.93	108	3.87	.271	18	.207	12	17	1.4
1928	Phi-A	17	12	.586	38	30	15	3	1	235^2	236	111	93	19	3	64	112	1.273	3.55	113	3.42	.265	18	.209	13	17	1.3
1929*	Phi-A	18	11	.621	40	33	20	3	4	267^2	256	115	107	22	0	99	94	1.326	3.60	118	3.49	.254	23	.223	18	22	1.7
1930*	Phi-A	13	12	.520	38	30	12	2	1	205^1	207	121	107	6	2	85	100	1.422	4.69	99	3.56	.262	12	.164	-1	12	-0.3
1931*	Phi-A	20	12	.625	44	35	19	1	3	**291**	298	133	121	16	0	109	106	1.399	3.74	120	3.71	.266	13	.124	16	24	0.9
1932	Phi-A	17	10	.630	41	34	19	3	1	272	305	159	143	16	0	103	96	1.500	4.73	96	4.25	.282	16	.170	-7	15	-0.9
1933	Phi-A	9	13	.409	40	20	10	1	4	201	224	132	109	12	1	95	68	1.587	4.88	88	4.50	.278	9	.132	-7	7	-0.9
1934	Bos-A	6	7	.462	30	10	2	0	1	104^2	118	62	47	5	1	41	38	1.519	4.04	119	4.26	.284	6	.188	10	7	0.9
1935	Bos-A	5	9	.357	44	10	4	0	3	142^2	152	71	62	10	2	54	44	1.444	3.91	121	4.10	.273	6	.162	13	11	1.1
1936	Bos-A	5	4	.556	24	9	5	0	0	100^1	98	53	49	7	1	36	49	1.336	4.40	121	3.56	.257	5	.156	10	7	0.8
1937	Bos-A	5	7	.417	32	11	3	0	1	104^2	143	72	65	7	3	46	46	1.806	5.59	85	6.21	.332	5	.147	-8	4	-0.8
Total	15	155	141	.524	544	306	139	15	32	2644	2795	1423	1223	163	27	1031	1085	1.447	4.16	107	4.02	.274	162	.179	89	173	6.7

• WALDBAUER, Doc — Albert Charles Waldbauer b: 2/22/1892, Richmond, VA d: 7/16/1969, Yakima, WA BR/TR, 6', 172 lbs. Deb: 9/24/1917

YEAR	TM-L	W	L	PCT	G	GS	CG	SH	SV	IP	H	R	ER	HR	HB	BB	SO	RAT	ERA	ERA+	CERA	OAV	BH	AVG	PR+	WS	TPW
1917	Was-A	0	0	....	2	0	0	0	1	5	10	4	4	0	0	2	2	2.400	7.20	36	10.82	.476	0	.000	-3	0	-0.3

• WALK, Bob — Robert Vernon Walk b: 11/26/1956, Van Nuys, CA BR/TR, 6'3", 208 lbs. Deb: 5/26/1980

YEAR	TM-L	W	L	PCT	G	GS	CG	SH	SV	IP	H	R	ER	HR	HB	BB	SO	RAT	ERA	ERA+	CERA	OAV	BH	AVG	PR+	WS	TPW
1980*	Phi-N	11	7	.611	27	27	2	0	0	151^2	163	82	77	8	2	71	94	1.543	4.57	83	4.46	.276	7	.140	-13	5	-1.4
1981	Atl-N	1	4	.200	12	8	0	0	0	43^1	41	25	22	6	0	23	16	1.477	4.57	78	4.60	.250	1	.143	-5	0	-0.5
1982*	Atl-N	11	9	.550	32	27	3	1	0	164^1	179	101	89	19	6	59	84	1.448	4.87	77	4.69	.280	10	.196	-21	4	-2.1
1983	Atl-N	0	0	....	1	1	0	0	0	3^2	7	3	3	0	0	2	4	2.455	7.36	53	9.31	.412	0	.000	-1	0	-0.2
1984	Pit-N	1	1	.500	2	2	0	0	0	10^1	8	5	3	1	0	4	10	1.161	2.61	138	2.54	.200	0	.000	1	1	0.1
1985	Pit-N	2	3	.400	9	9	1	1	0	58^2	60	27	24	3	0	18	40	1.330	3.68	97	3.46	.265	0	.000	0	3	-0.1
1986	Pit-N	7	8	.467	44	15	1	1	2	141^2	129	66	59	14	3	64	78	1.362	3.75	102	3.90	.251	6	.154	1	6	0.1
1987	Pit-N	8	2	.800	39	12	1	1	0	117	107	52	43	11	3	51	78	1.350	3.31	124	3.80	.245	6	.231	8	9	0.9
1988	Pit-N★	12	10	.545	32	32	1	1	0	212^2	183	75	64	6	2	65	81	1.166	2.71	126	2.49	.230	6	.087	15	14	1.4
1989	Pit-N	13	10	.565	33	31	2	0	0	196	208	106	96	15	4	65	83	1.393	4.41	76	4.07	.271	13	.186	-23	4	-2.2
1990*	Pit-N	7	5	.583	26	24	1	1	1	129^2	136	59	54	17	4	36	73	1.326	3.75	96	4.22	.270	6	.162	-4	6	-0.3
1991*	Pit-N	9	2	.818	25	20	0	0	0	115	104	53	46	10	5	35	67	1.209	3.60	99	3.21	.240	8	.205	-1	6	0.1
1992*	Pit-N	10	6	.625	36	19	1	0	2	135	132	54	48	10	6	43	60	1.296	3.20	108	3.62	.258	4	.093	3	9	0.1
1993	Pit-N	13	14	.481	32	32	3	0	0	187	214	121	118	23	5	70	80	1.519	5.68	71	5.10	.294	7	.121	-35	3	-3.7
Total	14	105	81	.565	350	259	16	6	5	1666	1671	829	746	143	40	606	848	1.367	4.03	91	3.96	.263	74	.145	-75	70	-7.8

YEAR	TM-L	W	L	PCT	G	GS	CG	SH	SV	IP	H	R	ER	HR	HB	BB	SO	RAT	ERA	ERA+	CERA	OAV	BH	AVG	PR+	WS	TPW
• WALKER, Bill					William Henry Walker b: 10/7/1903, East St. Louis, IL d: 6/14/1966, East St. Louis, IL BR/TL, 6', 175 lbs. Deb: 9/13/1927																						
1927	NY-N	0	0	....	3	0	0	0	0	4	6	6	4	0	0	5	4	2.750	9.00	43	9.21	.429	0	....	-2	0	-0.2
1928	NY-N	3	6	.333	22	8	1	0	0	76^{1}	79	43	40	9	1	31	39	1.441	4.72	83	4.41	.275	2	.091	-8	2	-0.9
1929	NY-N	14	7	.667	29	23	13	1	0	177^{2}	188	71	61	11	4	57	65	1.379	**3.09**	148	3.81	.274	7	.115	27	15	2.1
1930	NY-N	17	15	.531	39	34	13	2	1	245^{1}	258	133	107	19	7	88	105	1.410	3.93	121	4.01	.268	16	.186	20	18	1.6
1931	NY-N	16	9	.640	37	28	19	**6**	3	239^{1}	212	78	60	6	3	64	121	1.153	**2.26**	**164**	**2.44**	.231	5	.065	**36**	21	2.9
1932	NY-N	8	12	.400	31	22	9	0	2	163	177	95	75	23	3	55	74	1.423	4.14	90	4.57	.274	7	.135	-5	5	-0.6
1933	StL-N	9	10	.474	29	20	6	2	0	158	168	71	60	8	1	67	41	**1.487**	3.42	102	4.08	.273	7	.132	1	8	-0.1
1934*	StL-N	12	4	.750	24	19	10	1	0	153	160	59	53	11	2	66	76	1.477	3.12	135	4.20	.270	5	.093	17	14	1.2
1935	StL-N★	13	8	.619	37	25	8	2	1	193^{1}	222	93	82	7	5	78	79	1.552	3.82	107	4.43	.288	6	.102	3	12	0.0
1936	StL-N	5	6	.455	21	13	4	1	1	79^{2}	106	62	52	5	2	27	22	1.669	5.87	67	5.31	.318	7	.280	-17	1	-1.5
Total	10	97	77	.557	272	192	83	15	8	1489^{2}	1576	711	594	99	28	538	626	1.419	3.59	113	3.98	.270	62	.127	72	96	4.5
• WALKER, Dixie					Ewart Gladstone Walker b: 6/1/1887, Brownsville, PA d: 11/14/1965, Leeds, AL BL/TR, 6', 192 lbs. Deb: 9/17/1909 C																						
1909	Was-A	3	1	.750	4	4	4	0	0	36	31	12	10	0	0	6	25	1.028	2.50	97	1.77	.217	2	.154	0	2	0.0
1910	Was-A	11	11	.500	29	26	16	3	0	199^{1}	177	83	73	2	8	68	84	1.229	3.30	75	2.85	.245	9	.130	-22	8	-2.7
1911	Was-A	8	13	.381	32	24	15	2	0	185^{2}	205	103	70	2	8	50	65	1.373	3.39	97	3.74	.286	20	.303	-3	11	0.1
1912	Was-A	3	6	.333	9	8	5	0	0	60	72	40	35	2	4	18	29	1.500	5.25	64	4.59	.300	2	.125	-15	1	-1.4
Total	4	25	31	.446	74	62	40	5	0	481	485	238	188	6	20	142	203	1.304	3.52	82	3.33	.266	33	.201	-40	22	-4.0
• WALKER, Ed					Edward Harrison Walker b: 8/11/1874, Cambois, England d: 9/29/1947, Akron, OH BL/TL, 6'5", 242 lbs. Deb: 9/26/1902																						
1902	Cle-A	0	1	.000	1	1	1	0	0	8	11	4	3	0	0	3	1	1.750	3.38	102	4.98	.327	1	.333	0	0	0.0
1903	Cle-A	0	1	.000	3	3	0	0	0	12	13	12	7	0	0	10	4	1.917	5.25	54	5.17	.275	0	.000	-3	0	-0.4
Total	2	0	2	.000	4	4	1	0	0	20	24	16	10	0	0	13	5	1.850	4.50	67	5.09	.297	1	.167	-3	0	-0.3
• WALKER, George					George A. Walker b: 1863, Hamilton, Canada TR, 5'9", 184 lbs. Deb: 8/1/1888																						
1888	Bal-a	1	3	.250	4	4	4	1	0	35	36	31	23	2	0	14	18	1.429	5.91	50	....	.257	1	.077	-11	0	-1.1
• WALKER, Jamie					James Ross Walker b: 7/1/1971, McMinnville, TN BL/TL, 6'2", 190 lbs. Deb: 4/2/1997																						
1997	KC-A	3	3	.500	50	0	0	0	0	43	46	28	26	6	3	20	24	1.535	5.44	87	5.10	.271	0	....	-4	2	-0.4
1998	KC-A	0	1	.000	6	2	0	0	0	17^{1}	30	20	19	5	2	3	15	1.904	9.87	49	9.69	.380	0	....	-10	0	-0.9
2002	Det-A	1	1	.500	57	0	0	0	1	43^{2}	32	19	18	9	4	9	40	.939	3.71	116	2.86	.199	0	....	3	4	0.3
2003	Det-A	4	3	.571	78	0	0	0	3	65	61	30	24	9	2	17	45	1.200	3.32	130	3.51	.247	0	....	7	6	0.7
Total	4	8	8	.500	191	2	0	0	4	169	169	97	87	29	11	49	124	1.290	4.63	98	4.38	.257	0	....	-3	12	-0.3
• WALKER, Jerry					Jerry Allen Walker b: 2/12/1939, Ada, OK BB/TR, 6'1", 195 lbs. Deb: 7/6/1957 C																						
1957	Bal-A	1	0	1.000	13	3	1	1	1	27^{2}	24	9	9	1	0	14	13	1.373	2.93	123	3.40	.245	0	.000	2	2	0.1
1958	Bal-A	0	0	....	6	0	0	0	0	10^{1}	16	8	8	2	0	5	6	2.032	6.97	52	8.43	.340	0	.000	-4	0	-0.4
1959	Bal-A★	11	10	.524	30	22	7	2	4	182	160	68	59	13	3	52	100	1.165	2.92	130	2.85	.240	11	.169	16	16	1.6
1960	Bal-A	3	4	.429	29	18	1	0	5	118	107	53	49	15	3	56	48	1.381	3.74	102	4.21	.247	14	.368	-1	9	0.3
1961	KC-A	8	14	.364	36	24	4	0	2	168	161	100	90	23	10	96	56	1.530	4.82	85	4.99	.253	16	.250	-11	7	-0.8
1962	KC-A	8	9	.471	31	21	3	1	0	143^{1}	165	101	94	27	7	78	57	1.695	5.90	70	6.37	.288	15	.263	-27	4	-2.2
1963	Cle-A	6	6	.500	39	2	0	0	1	88	92	53	48	15	2	36	41	1.455	4.91	74	4.78	.265	2	.105	-12	2	-1.3
1964	Cle-A	0	1	.000	6	0	0	0	0	9^{2}	9	5	5	1	0	4	5	1.345	4.66	77	4.01	.257	0	.000	-1	0	-0.1
Total	8	37	44	.457	190	90	16	4	13	747	734	397	362	97	25	341	326	1.439	4.36	90	4.56	.259	58	.230	-39	40	-2.9
• WALKER, Kevin					Kevin Michael Walker b: 9/20/1976, Irving, TX BL/TL, 6'4", 190 lbs. Deb: 4/14/2000																						
2000	SD-N	7	1	.875	70	0	0	0	0	66^{2}	49	35	31	5	5	38	56	1.305	4.19	103	3.23	.206	1	.250	0	5	0.0
2001	SD-N	0	0	....	16	0	0	0	0	12	5	4	4	0	0	8	17	1.083	3.00	133	1.33	.122	0	....	2	1	0.1
2002	SD-N	0	1	.000	11	0	0	0	0	8	12	6	5	2	0	5	11	2.125	5.63	67	8.79	.333	0	....	-2	0	-0.2
2003	SD-N	0	0	....	11	0	0	0	0	6^{2}	5	4	4	1	0	5	5	1.500	5.40	73	4.31	.200	0	....	-1	0	-0.1
Total	4	7	2	.778	108	0	0	0	0	93^{1}	71	49	44	8	5	56	89	1.361	4.24	98	3.54	.209	1	.250	-1	6	-0.1
• WALKER, Luke					James Luke Walker b: 9/2/1943, DeKalb, TX BL/TL, 6'2", 192 lbs. Deb: 9/7/1965																						
1965	Pit-N	0	0	....	2	0	0	0	0	5	2	0	0	0	0	1	5	.600	0.00	....	0.63	.118	0	....	2	1	0.2
1966	Pit-N	0	1	.000	10	1	0	0	0	10	8	9	5	0	1	15	7	2.300	4.50	79	6.03	.205	0	.000	-1	0	-0.2
1968	Pit-N	0	3	.000	39	2	0	0	3	61^{2}	42	18	14	1	1	39	66	1.314	2.04	143	2.69	.190	0	.000	5	4	0.5
1969	Pit-N	4	6	.400	31	15	3	1	0	118^{2}	98	51	48	5	2	57	96	1.306	3.64	96	3.08	.226	0	.000	-1	5	-0.4
1970*	Pit-N	15	6	.714	42	19	5	3	3	163	129	56	55	6	1	89	124	1.337	3.04	128	3.06	.219	6	.130	11	15	1.1
1971*	Pit-N	10	8	.556	28	24	4	2	0	159^{2}	157	69	63	9	2	53	86	1.315	3.55	96	3.51	.262	1	.022	-4	7	-0.7
1972*	Pit-N	4	6	.400	26	12	2	0	2	92^{2}	98	41	35	4	0	34	48	1.424	3.40	98	3.81	.278	2	.083	-2	4	-0.4
1973	Pit-N	7	12	.368	37	18	2	1	1	122	129	75	63	9	1	66	74	1.598	4.65	76	4.65	.270	2	.067	-15	1	-1.8
1974	Det-A	5	5	.500	28	9	0	0	0	92	100	56	51	9	2	54	52	1.674	4.99	76	5.42	.278	0	....	-12	3	-1.2
Total	9	45	47	.489	243	100	16	7	9	824^{2}	763	375	334	43	10	408	558	1.420	3.65	97	3.73	.247	11	.059	-17	40	-3.0
• WALKER, Marty					Martin Van Buren "Buddy" Walker b: 3/27/1899, Philadelphia, PA d: 4/24/1978, Philadelphia, PA BL/TL, 6', 170 lbs. Deb: 9/30/1928																						
1928	Phi-N	0	1	.000	1	1	0	0	0	0	2	0	0	0	3	0	0	....	....	....	∞	1.000	0	....	0	0	0.0
• WALKER, Mike					Michael Charles Walker b: 10/4/1966, Chicago, IL BR/TR, 6'2", 195 lbs. Deb: 9/9/1988																						
1988	Cle-A	0	1	.000	3	1	0	0	0	8^{2}	8	7	7	0	0	10	7	2.077	7.27	57	5.91	.258	0	....	-3	0	-0.3
1990	Cle-A	2	6	.250	18	11	0	0	0	75^{2}	82	49	41	6	6	42	34	1.639	4.88	80	5.22	.277	0	....	-7	1	-0.7
1991	Cle-A	0	1	.000	5	0	0	0	0	4^{1}	6	1	1	0	1	2	2	1.846	2.08	200	6.09	.316	0	....	1	0	0.1
1995	Chi-N	1	3	.250	42	0	0	0	1	44^{2}	45	22	16	2	0	24	20	1.545	3.22	127	3.96	.259	0	.000	4	3	0.4
1996	Det-A	0	0	....	20	0	0	0	1	27^{2}	40	26	26	10	1	17	13	2.060	8.46	60	10.43	.351	0	....	-10	0	-0.9
Total	5	3	11	.214	88	12	0	0	2	161	181	105	91	18	8	95	76	1.714	5.09	83	5.83	.285	0	.000	-14	4	-1.4
• WALKER, Mike					Michael Aaron Walker b: 6/23/1965, Houston, TX BR/TR, 6'3", 205 lbs. Deb: 6/16/1992																						
1992	Sea-A	0	3	.000	5	3	0	0	0	14^{2}	21	14	12	4	0	9	5	2.045	7.36	54	8.54	.333	0	....	-5	0	-0.6
• WALKER, Mysterious					Frederick Mitchell Walker b: 3/21/1884, Utica, NE d: 2/1/1958, Oak Park, IL BR/TR, 5'10.5", 185 lbs. Deb: 6/28/1910																						
1910	Cin-N	0	0	....	1	0	0	0	0	3	4	2	1	0	0	4	1	2.667	3.00	97	8.99	.333	0	.000	-0	0	0.0
1912	Cle-A	0	0	....	1	0	0	0	0	1	0	0	0	0	0	1	0	1.000	0.00	....	0.64	.000	0	....	0	0	0.0
1913	Bro-N	1	3	.250	11	8	3	0	0	58^{1}	44	26	23	3	5	35	35	1.354	3.55	93	3.62	.233	3	.167	-2	3	-0.3
1914	Pit-F	4	16	.200	35	21	12	0	0	169^{1}	197	108	81	3	3	74	79	**1.600**	4.31	71	4.59	.294	6	.113	-23	2	-2.5
1915	Bro-F	2	4	.333	13	7	2	0	1	65^{2}	61	37	27	3	0	22	28	1.264	3.70	80	3.01	.242	6	.222	-6	2	-0.5
Total	5	7	23	.233	61	36	17	0	1	297^{1}	306	173	132	9	8	136	143	1.487	4.00	77	4.08	.272	15	.152	-30	7	-3.3
• WALKER, Pete					Peter Brian Walker b: 4/8/1969, Beverly, MA BR/TR, 6'2", 195 lbs. Deb: 6/7/1995																						
1995	NY-N	1	0	1.000	13	0	0	0	0	17^{2}	24	9	9	3	0	5	5	1.642	4.58	88	6.35	.329	0	....	-1	1	-0.1
1996	SD-N	0	0	....	1	0	0	0	0	0^{2}	0	0	0	0	0	3	1	4.500	0.00	....	13.05	.000	0	....	0	0	0.0
2000	Col-N	0	0	....	3	0	0	0	0	4^{2}	10	9	9	1	0	4	2	3.000	17.36	33	15.29	.435	0	....	-6	0	-0.6
2001	NY-N	0	0	....	2	0	0	0	0	6^{2}	6	2	2	0	0	0	4	.900	2.70	153	1.63	.240	0	.000	1	1	0.1
2002	NY-N	0	0	....	1	0	0	0	0	1	2	1	1	0	0	0	0	2.000	9.00	44	7.48	.400	0	....	-1	0	-0.1
	Tor-A	10	5	.667	37	20	0	0	1	139^{1}	143	72	67	18	3	51	80	1.392	4.33	107	4.39	.270	0	....	6	9	0.5
2003	Tor-A	2	2	.500	23	7	0	0	0	55^{1}	59	31	30	11	2	24	29	1.500	4.88	94	5.51	.277	0	....	-1	3	-0.1
Total	6	13	7	.650	80	27	0	0	1	225^{1}	244	124	118	33	5	87	121	1.469	4.71	98	5.00	.281	0	.000	-2	14	-0.2
• WALKER, Roy					James Roy "Dixie" Walker b: 4/13/1893, Lawrenceburg, TN d: 2/10/1962, New Orleans, LA BR/TR, 6'1.5", 180 lbs. Deb: 9/16/1912																						
1912	Cle-A	0	0	....	1	0	0	0	0	2	0	0	0	0	0	2	1	1.000	0.00	....	0.80	.000	0	....	1	0	0.1
1915	Cle-A	4	9	.308	25	15	4	0	1	131	122	73	58	1	7	65	57	1.427	3.98	76	3.72	.261	5	.132	-13	4	-1.6

YEAR TM-L	W	L	PCT	G	GS	CG	SH	SV	IP	H	R	ER	HR	HB	BB	SO	RAT	ERA	ERA+	CERA	OAV	BH	AVG	PR+	WS	TPW
1917 Chi-N	0	1	.000	2	1	0	0	0	7	8	5	3	0	0	5	4	1.857	3.86	75	5.00	.286	0	.000	-1	0	-0.1
1918 Chi-N	1	3	.250	13	7	2	0	1	43^1	50	27	13	1	1	15	20	1.500	2.70	103	4.19	.298	0	.000	1	0	0.0
1921 StL-N	11	12	.478	38	23	11	0	3	170^2	194	93	80	10	1	53	52	1.447	4.22	86	4.21	.293	11	.204	-11	7	-1.1
1922 StL-N	1	2	.333	12	2	0	0	0	32	34	20	17	1	0	15	14	1.531	4.78	81	4.15	.293	1	.143	-3	1	-0.3
Total 6	17	27	.386	91	48	17	0	5	386	408	218	171	13	9	155	148	1.459	3.99	84	4.03	.283	17	.153	-25	12	-3.0

• WALKER, Tom Thomas William Walker b: 8/1/1881, Philadelphia, PA d: 7/10/1944, Woodbury Heights, NJ BR/TR, 5'11", 170 lbs. Deb: 9/27/1902 U

YEAR TM-L	W	L	PCT	G	GS	CG	SH	SV	IP	H	R	ER	HR	HB	BB	SO	RAT	ERA	ERA+	CERA	OAV	BH	AVG	PR+	WS	TPW
1902 Phi-A	0	1	.000	1	1	1	0	0	8	10	7	5	0	1	0	2	1.250	5.63	65	3.44	.306	1	.250	-2	0	-0.2
1904 Cin-N	15	8	.652	24	24	22	2	0	217	196	76	54	2	18	53	64	1.147	2.24	130	2.63	.238	9	.117	11	17	0.7
1905 Cin-N	9	7	.563	23	19	12	1	0	144^2	171	68	52	3	6	44	28	1.486	3.24	102	4.45	.305	7	.137	-2	7	-0.3
Total 3	24	16	.600	48	44	35	3	0	369^2	377	151	111	5	25	97	94	1.282	2.70	115	3.36	.266	17	.129	7	24	0.3

• WALKER, Tom Robert Thomas Walker b: 11/7/1948, Tampa, FL BR/TR, 6'1", 188 lbs. Deb: 4/23/1972

YEAR TM-L	W	L	PCT	G	GS	CG	SH	SV	IP	H	R	ER	HR	HB	BB	SO	RAT	ERA	ERA+	CERA	OAV	BH	AVG	PR+	WS	TPW
1972 Mon-N	2	2	.500	46	0	0	0	2	74^2	71	27	24	4	1	22	42	1.246	2.89	123	3.13	.248	0	.000	6	7	0.6
1973 Mon-N	7	5	.583	54	0	0	0	4	91^2	95	52	37	7	3	42	68	1.495	3.63	105	4.14	.274	0	.000	2	5	0.1
1974 Mon-N	4	5	.444	33	8	1	0	2	91^2	96	45	39	7	2	28	70	1.353	3.83	100	3.76	.266	3	.188	0	5	0.1
1975 Det-A	3	8	.273	36	9	1	0	0	115^1	116	69	57	16	5	40	60	1.353	4.45	90	4.22	.261	0	....	-3	4	-0.3
1976 StL-N	1	2	.333	10	0	0	0	3	19^2	22	10	9	2	0	3	11	1.271	4.12	86	3.46	.265	2	.400	-1	2	-0.1
1977 Mon-N	1	1	.500	11	0	0	0	0	19	15	10	10	2	0	7	10	1.158	4.74	80	2.99	.221	0	.000	-2	1	-0.2
Cal-A	0	0	....	1	0	0	0	0	2	3	2	2	2	0	0	1	1.500	9.00	43	13.34	.375	0	....	-1	0	-0.1
Total 6	18	23	.439	191	17	2	0	11	414	418	215	178	40	11	142	262	1.353	3.87	99	3.86	.262	5	.152	0	24	0.0

• WALKER, Tyler Tyler Lanier Walker b: 5/15/1976, San Francisco, CA BR/TR, 6'3", 255 lbs. Deb: 7/2/2002

YEAR TM-L	W	L	PCT	G	GS	CG	SH	SV	IP	H	R	ER	HR	HB	BB	SO	RAT	ERA	ERA+	CERA	OAV	BH	AVG	PR+	WS	TPW
2002 NY-N	1	0	1.000	5	1	0	0	0	10^2	11	7	7	3	0	5	7	1.500	5.91	67	5.46	.250	0	.000	-2	0	-0.2

• WALKUP, Jim James Huey Walkup b: 11/3/1895, Havana, AR d: 6/12/1990, Duncan, OK BR/TL, 5'8", 150 lbs. Deb: 4/30/1927

YEAR TM-L	W	L	PCT	G	GS	CG	SH	SV	IP	H	R	ER	HR	HB	BB	SO	RAT	ERA	ERA+	CERA	OAV	BH	AVG	PR+	WS	TPW
1927 Det-A	0	0	....	2	0	0	0	0	1^2	3	1	1	0	0	0	0	1.800	5.40	78	6.23	.429	0	.000	-0	0	0.0

• WALKUP, Jim James Elton Walkup b: 12/14/1909, Havana, AR d: 2/7/1997, Danville, AR BR/TR, 6'1", 170 lbs. Deb: 9/22/1934

YEAR TM-L	W	L	PCT	G	GS	CG	SH	SV	IP	H	R	ER	HR	HB	BB	SO	RAT	ERA	ERA+	CERA	OAV	BH	AVG	PR+	WS	TPW
1934 StL-A	0	0	....	3	0	0	0	0	8^1	6	4	2	0	0	5	6	1.320	2.16	231	2.52	.200	1	.333	3	1	0.2
1935 StL-A	6	9	.400	55	20	4	1	0	181^1	226	139	126	17	2	104	44	1.820	6.25	77	6.05	.305	6	.128	-28	4	-2.9
1936 StL-A	0	3	.000	5	2	0	0	0	15^2	20	17	14	0	0	6	5	1.660	8.04	67	4.67	.308	0	.000	-4	0	-0.4
1937 StL-A	9	12	.429	27	18	6	0	0	150^1	218	127	123	16	0	83	46	2.002	7.36	66	7.50	.347	14	.241	-41	2	-3.8
1938 StL-A	1	12	.077	18	13	1	0	0	94	127	83	71	13	3	53	28	1.915	6.80	73	7.31	.329	4	.138	-19	0	-1.9
1939 StL-A	0	1	.000	1	0	0	0	0	0^2	2	1	0	0	0	1	0	4.500	0.00	....	21.38	.500	0	....	0	0	0.0
Det-A	0	1	.000	7	0	0	0	0	12	15	10	10	3	0	8	5	1.917	7.50	65	7.59	.319	1	.500	-4	0	-0.3
Yr.	0	2	.000	8	0	0	0	0	12^2	17	11	10	3	0	9	5	2.053	7.11	69	8.32	.333	1	.500	-3	0	-0.3
Total 6	16	38	.296	116	53	11	1	0	462^1	614	381	346	49	5	260	134	1.890	6.74	72	6.73	.323	26	.182	-93	7	-9.0

• WALL, Donne Donnell Lee Wall b: 7/11/1967, Potosi, MO BR/TR, 6'1", 180 lbs. Deb: 9/2/1995

YEAR TM-L	W	L	PCT	G	GS	CG	SH	SV	IP	H	R	ER	HR	HB	BB	SO	RAT	ERA	ERA+	CERA	OAV	BH	AVG	PR+	WS	TPW
1995 Hou-N	3	1	.750	6	5	0	0	0	24^1	33	19	15	5	0	5	16	1.562	5.55	70	6.07	.320	0	.000	-4	0	-0.5
1996 Hou-N	9	8	.529	26	23	2	1	0	150	170	84	76	17	6	34	99	1.360	4.56	85	4.38	.286	9	.205	-9	6	-0.7
1997 Hou-N	2	5	.286	8	8	0	0	0	41^2	53	31	29	8	2	16	25	1.656	6.26	64	6.76	.315	1	.100	-11	0	-1.1
1998* SD-N	5	4	.556	46	1	0	0	1	70^1	50	20	19	6	1	32	56	1.166	2.43	162	2.69	.202	2	.286	11	8	1.2
1999 SD-N	7	4	.636	55	0	0	0	0	70^1	58	31	24	11	0	23	53	1.152	3.07	137	3.12	.219	0	.000	8	7	0.8
2000 SD-N	5	2	.714	44	0	0	0	1	53^2	36	20	20	4	0	21	29	1.062	3.35	129	2.21	.193	0	.000	5	6	0.5
2001 NY-N	0	4	.000	32	0	0	0	0	42^2	51	24	23	8	1	17	31	1.594	4.85	85	5.72	.300	0	....	-4	1	-0.4
2002 Ana-A	0	0	....	17	0	0	0	0	21	17	15	15	3	1	7	13	1.143	6.43	69	3.21	.221	0	....	-5	0	-0.5
Total 8	31	28	.525	234	37	2	1	2	474	468	244	221	62	11	155	322	1.314	4.20	96	4.06	.258	12	.176	-8	28	-0.7

• WALL, Murray Murray Wesley Wall b: 9/19/1926, Dallas, TX d: 10/8/1971, Lone Oak, TX BR/TR, 6'3", 185 lbs. Deb: 7/4/1950

YEAR TM-L	W	L	PCT	G	GS	CG	SH	SV	IP	H	R	ER	HR	HB	BB	SO	RAT	ERA	ERA+	CERA	OAV	BH	AVG	PR+	WS	TPW
1950 Bos-N	0	0	....	1	0	0	0	0	4	6	5	4	0	0	2	2	2.000	9.00	43	6.33	.333	0	.000	-2	0	-0.2
1957 Bos-A	3	0	1.000	11	0	0	0	1	24^1	21	11	9	3	0	2	13	.945	3.33	120	2.27	.233	2	.333	2	3	0.3
1958 Bos-A	8	9	.471	52	1	0	0	10	114^1	109	51	46	14	5	33	53	1.242	3.62	111	3.64	.255	3	.107	7	10	0.5
1959 Bos-A	1	4	.200	15	0	0	0	3	31^2	31	21	19	5	1	15	8	1.453	5.40	75	4.74	.272	0	.000	-5	0	-0.6
Was-A	0	0	....	1	0	0	0	0	1^1	3	1	1	1	0	0	0	2.250	6.75	58	22.91	.600	0	.000	-0	0	-0.1
Bos-A	1	1	.500	11	0	0	0	0	17^1	26	11	11	2	0	11	6	2.135	5.71	71	8.14	.366	0	.000	-3	1	-0.4
Yr.	2	5	.286	27	0	0	0	3	50^1	60	33	31	8	1	26	14	1.709	5.54	73	6.39	.316	0	.000	-8	1	-1.0
Total 4	13	14	.481	91	1	0	0	14	193	196	100	90	25	6	63	82	1.342	4.20	96	4.24	.270	5	.109	-2	14	-0.5

• WALL, Stan Stanley Arthur Wall b: 6/16/1951, Butler, MO BL/TL, 6'1", 175 lbs. Deb: 7/19/1975

YEAR TM-L	W	L	PCT	G	GS	CG	SH	SV	IP	H	R	ER	HR	HB	BB	SO	RAT	ERA	ERA+	CERA	OAV	BH	AVG	PR+	WS	TPW
1975 LA-N	0	1	.000	10	0	0	0	0	16	12	6	3	0	1	7	6	1.188	1.69	201	2.49	.222	0	....	3	1	0.3
1976 LA-N	2	2	.500	31	0	0	0	1	50	50	21	20	5	2	15	27	1.300	3.60	94	3.81	.269	0	.000	-2	3	-0.3
1977 LA-N	2	3	.400	25	0	0	0	0	32	36	20	19	3	1	13	22	1.531	5.34	72	4.70	.279	0	.000	-6	0	-0.6
Total 3	4	6	.400	66	0	0	0	1	98	98	47	42	8	4	35	55	1.357	3.86	93	3.89	.266	0	.000	-5	4	-0.6

• WALLACE, Bobby Rhoderick John Wallace b: 11/4/1873, Pittsburgh, PA d: 11/3/1960, Torrance, CA BR/TR, 5'8", 170 lbs. Deb: 9/15/1894 M/C/U HOF: 1953 ♦

YEAR TM-L	W	L	PCT	G	GS	CG	SH	SV	IP	H	R	ER	HR	HB	BB	SO	RAT	ERA	ERA+	CERA	OAV	BH	AVG	PR+	WS	TPW
1894 Cle-N	2	1	.667	4	3	2	0	0	26	28	25	15	1	0	20	10	1.846	5.19	105	5.29	.272	2	.154	1	2	0.0
1895 Cle-N	12	14	.462	30	28	22	1	1	228^2	271	166	104	3	0	87	63	1.566	4.09	122	4.30	.290	21	.214	23	14	1.6
1896* Cle-N	10	7	.588	22	16	13	2	0	145^1	167	75	54	2	0	49	46	1.486	3.34	135	3.96	.286	35	.235	19	15	1.1
1902 StL-A	0	0	....	1	1	0	0	0	2	3	2	0	0	0	0	1	1.500	0.00	....	4.60	.346	141	.285	1	22	2.4
Total 4	24	22	.522	57	48	37	3	1	402	469	268	173	6	0	156	120	1.555	3.87	126	4.24	.288	2309	.268	43	53	5.1

• WALLACE, Dave David William Wallace b: 9/7/1947, Waterbury, CT BR/TR, 5'10", 185 lbs. Deb: 7/18/1973 C

YEAR TM-L	W	L	PCT	G	GS	CG	SH	SV	IP	H	R	ER	HR	HB	BB	SO	RAT	ERA	ERA+	CERA	OAV	BH	AVG	PR+	WS	TPW
1973 Phi-N	0	0	....	4	0	0	0	0	3^2	13	9	9	1	0	2	2	4.091	22.09	17	26.07	.591	0	....	-7	0	-0.8
1974 Phi-N	0	1	.000	3	0	0	0	0	3	4	4	3	2	0	3	3	2.333	9.00	42	12.38	.308	0	....	-2	0	-0.2
1978 Tor-A	0	0	....	6	0	0	0	0	14	12	6	6	1	0	11	7	1.643	3.86	102	4.69	.245	0	....	0	1	0.0
Total 3	0	1	.000	13	0	0	0	0	20^2	29	19	18	4	0	16	12	2.177	7.84	49	9.60	.345	0	....	-9	1	-0.9

• WALLACE, Derek Derek Robert Wallace b: 9/1/1971, Van Nuys, CA BR/TR, 6'3", 200 lbs. Deb: 8/13/1996

YEAR TM-L	W	L	PCT	G	GS	CG	SH	SV	IP	H	R	ER	HR	HB	BB	SO	RAT	ERA	ERA+	CERA	OAV	BH	AVG	PR+	WS	TPW
1996 NY-N	2	3	.400	19	0	0	0	3	24^2	29	12	11	2	0	14	15	1.743	4.01	100	5.44	.290	0	....	-0	2	0.0
1999 KC-A	0	1	.000	8	0	0	0	0	8^1	7	4	3	2	0	5	5	1.440	3.24	154	5.35	.259	0	....	1	1	0.1
Total 2	2	4	.333	27	0	0	0	3	33	36	16	14	4	0	19	20	1.667	3.82	110	5.42	.283	0	....	1	3	0.1

• WALLACE, Huck Harry Clinton "Lefty" Wallace b: 7/27/1882, Richmond, IN d: 7/6/1951, Cleveland, OH BL/TL, 5'6", 160 lbs. Deb: 6/5/1912

YEAR TM-L	W	L	PCT	G	GS	CG	SH	SV	IP	H	R	ER	HR	HB	BB	SO	RAT	ERA	ERA+	CERA	OAV	BH	AVG	PR+	WS	TPW
1912 Phi-N	0	0	....	4	0	0	0	0	4^2	7	5	0	0	0	4	4	2.357	0.00	....	8.03	.350	0	....	2	0	0.2

• WALLACE, Jeff Jeffrey Allen Wallace b: 4/12/1976, Wheeling, WV BL/TL, 6'2", 240 lbs. Deb: 8/21/1997

YEAR TM-L	W	L	PCT	G	GS	CG	SH	SV	IP	H	R	ER	HR	HB	BB	SO	RAT	ERA	ERA+	CERA	OAV	BH	AVG	PR+	WS	TPW
1997 Pit-N	0	0	....	11	0	0	0	0	12	8	2	1	0	0	8	14	1.333	0.75	572	2.53	.200	0	....	5	2	0.5
1999 Pit-N	1	0	1.000	41	0	0	0	0	39	26	17	16	2	0	38	41	1.641	3.69	124	4.03	.195	0	....	4	3	0.4
2000 Pit-N	2	0	1.000	38	0	0	0	0	35^2	42	32	28	5	4	34	27	2.131	7.07	65	8.15	.290	0	.000	-9	0	-0.9
2001 TB-A	0	3	.000	29	1	0	0	0	50^1	43	26	19	4	1	37	38	1.589	3.40	132	4.53	.232	0	....	6	3	0.6
Total 4	3	3	.500	119	1	0	0	0	137	119	77	64	11	5	117	120	1.723	4.20	108	5.15	.237	0	.000	5	8	0.5

• WALLACE, Lefty James Harold Wallace b: 8/12/1921, Evansville, IN d: 7/28/1982, Evansville, IN BL/TL, 5'11", 160 lbs. Deb: 5/5/1942

YEAR TM-L	W	L	PCT	G	GS	CG	SH	SV	IP	H	R	ER	HR	HB	BB	SO	RAT	ERA	ERA+	CERA	OAV	BH	AVG	PR+	WS	TPW
1942 Bos-N	1	3	.250	19	3	1	0	0	49^1	39	21	21	3	2	24	20	1.277	3.83	87	3.03	.217	2	.143	-2	2	-0.3
1945 Bos-N	1	0	1.000	5	3	1	0	0	20	18	11	10	1	1	9	4	1.350	4.50	85	3.44	.240	0	.000	-2	1	-0.2
1946 Bos-N	3	3	.500	27	8	2	0	0	75^1	76	41	35	5	1	31	27	1.420	4.18	82	3.74	.253	1	.056	-6	1	-0.7
Total 3	5	6	.455	51	14	4	0	0	144^2	133	73	66	9	4	64	51	1.362	4.11	84	3.46	.240	3	.079	-10	4	-1.2

• WALLACE, Mike
Michael Sherman Wallace b: 2/3/1951, Gastonia, NC BL/TL, 6'2", 204 lbs. Deb: 6/27/1973

YEAR	TM-L	W	L	PCT	G	GS	CG	SH	SV	IP	H	R	ER	HR	HB	BB	SO	RAT	ERA	ERA+	CERA	OAV	BH	AVG	PR+	WS	TPW
1973	Phi-N	1	1	.500	20	3	1	0	1	33^1	38	16	14	1	0	15	20	1.590	3.78	100	4.44	.304	0	.000	-0	2	0.0
1974	Phi-N	1	0	1.000	8	0	0	0	0	8^1	12	6	5	0	0	2	1	1.680	5.40	70	5.07	.324	0	....	-2	0	-0.2
	NY-A	6	0	1.000	23	1	0	0	0	52^1	42	18	14	3	0	35	34	1.471	2.41	145	3.65	.222	0	....	5	5	0.6
1975	NY-A	0	0	....	3	0	0	0	0	4^1	11	7	7	1	0	1	2	2.769	14.54	25	14.68	.458	0	....	-5	0	-0.5
	StL-N	0	0	....	9	0	0	0	0	8^2	9	2	2	0	0	5	6	1.615	2.08	181	3.81	.281	0	....	2	1	0.2
1976	StL-N	3	2	.600	49	0	0	0	2	66^1	66	34	30	3	0	39	40	1.583	4.07	87	4.35	.264	1	.333	-4	3	-0.4
1977	Tex-A	0	0	....	5	0	0	0	0	8^1	10	7	7	1	0	10	2	2.400	7.56	54	9.09	.323	0	....	-3	0	-0.3
Total	5	11	3	.786	117	4	1	0	3	181^2	188	90	79	9	0	107	105	1.624	3.91	93	4.64	.273	1	.143	-8	11	-0.8

• WALLER, Red
John Francis Waller b: 6/16/1883, Washington, DC d: 2/9/1915, Secaucus, NJ BR/TR, 6' Deb: 4/27/1909

YEAR	TM-L	W	L	PCT	G	GS	CG	SH	SV	IP	H	R	ER	HR	HB	BB	SO	RAT	ERA	ERA+	CERA	OAV	BH	AVG	PR+	WS	TPW
1909	NY-N	0	0	....	1	0	0	0	0	1	3	2	0	0	1	0	1	3.000	0.00	....	19.12	.429	0	....	0	0	0.0

• WALROND, Les
Leslie Dale Walrond b: 11/7/1976, Muskogee, OK BL/TL, 6', 210 lbs. Deb: 6/8/2003

YEAR	TM-L	W	L	PCT	G	GS	CG	SH	SV	IP	H	R	ER	HR	HB	BB	SO	RAT	ERA	ERA+	CERA	OAV	BH	AVG	PR+	WS	TPW
2003	KC-A	0	2	.000	7	0	0	0	0	8	11	9	9	2	0	7	6	2.250	10.13	51	9.58	.324	0	....	-4	0	-0.4

• WALSH, Augie
August Sothley Walsh b: 8/17/1904, Wilmington, DE d: 11/12/1985, San Rafael, CA BR/TR, 6', 175 lbs. Deb: 10/2/1927

YEAR	TM-L	W	L	PCT	G	GS	CG	SH	SV	IP	H	R	ER	HR	HB	BB	SO	RAT	ERA	ERA+	CERA	OAV	BH	AVG	PR+	WS	TPW
1927	Phi-N	0	1	.000	1	1	1	0	0	10	12	5	5	3	0	5	0	1.700	4.50	92	7.86	.333	1	.250	-0	0	0.0
1928	Phi-N	4	9	.308	38	11	2	0	2	122^1	160	92	84	13	5	40	38	1.635	6.18	69	5.68	.321	10	.256	-24	3	-2.2
Total	2	4	10	.286	39	12	3	0	2	132^1	172	97	89	16	5	45	38	1.640	6.05	70	5.85	.322	11	.256	-24	3	-2.2

• WALSH, Connie
Cornelius R. Walsh b: 4/23/1882, St. Louis, MO d: 4/5/1953, St. Louis, MO TR Deb: 9/16/1907

YEAR	TM-L	W	L	PCT	G	GS	CG	SH	SV	IP	H	R	ER	HR	HB	BB	SO	RAT	ERA	ERA+	CERA	OAV	BH	AVG	PR+	WS	TPW
1907	Pit-N	0	0	....	1	0	0	0	0	1	1	1	1	0	0	1	0	2.000	9.00	27	5.17	.250	0	....	-1	0	-0.1

• WALSH, Dave
David Peter Walsh b: 9/25/1960, Arlington, MA BL/TL, 6'1", 185 lbs. Deb: 8/13/1990

YEAR	TM-L	W	L	PCT	G	GS	CG	SH	SV	IP	H	R	ER	HR	HB	BB	SO	RAT	ERA	ERA+	CERA	OAV	BH	AVG	PR+	WS	TPW
1990	LA-N	1	0	1.000	20	0	0	0	1	16^1	15	12	7	1	0	6	15	1.286	3.86	95	3.08	.242	0	....	-0	1	0.0

• WALSH, Ed
Edward Augustine "Big Ed" Walsh b: 5/14/1881, Plains, PA d: 5/26/1959, Pompano Beach, FL BR/TR, 6'1", 193 lbs. Deb: 5/7/1904 M/C/U HOF: 1946

YEAR	TM-L	W	L	PCT	G	GS	CG	SH	SV	IP	H	R	ER	HR	HB	BB	SO	RAT	ERA	ERA+	CERA	OAV	BH	AVG	PR+	WS	TPW
1904	Chi-A	6	3	.667	18	8	6	1	1	110^2	90	45	32	1	3	32	57	1.102	2.60	94	2.12	.223	9	.220	-4	7	-0.2
1905	Chi-A	8	3	.727	22	13	9	1	0	136^2	121	53	33	0	3	29	71	1.098	2.17	113	2.16	.240	9	.155	0	8	-0.1
1906*	Chi-A	17	13	.567	41	31	24	**10**	1	278^1	215	83	58	1	7	58	171	.981	1.88	135	1.69	.216	14	.141	17	22	1.7
1907	Chi-A	24	18	.571	**56**	**46**	**37**	5	**4**	**422^1**	341	120	75	3	8	87	206	1.013	**1.60**	**150**	1.86	.224	25	.162	**41**	**37**	4.4
1908	Chi-A	**40**	15	.727	**66**	**49**	**42**	**11**	**6**	**464**	343	111	73	2	9	56	**269**	.860	1.42	163	1.38	.203	27	.172	**51**	**47**	**6.1**
1909	Chi-A	15	11	.577	31	28	20	**8**	2	230^1	166	52	36	0	4	50	127	.938	1.41	166	1.52	.203	18	.214	**24**	23	**3.2**
1910	Chi-A	18	20	.474	**45**	36	33	7	**5**	369^2	242	87	52	5	4	61	258	.820	**1.27**	**189**	**1.27**	**.187**	30	.217	**48**	36	**5.8**
1911	Chi-A	27	18	.600	**56**	37	33	5	**4**	**368^2**	327	125	91	4	7	72	**255**	1.082	2.22	146	2.20	.239	34	.215	42	**31**	3.9
1912	Chi-A	27	17	.614	**62**	**41**	32	6	**10**	**393**	332	125	94	6	1	94	254	1.084	2.15	150	2.13	.231	33	.243	54	40	6.0
1913	Chi-A	8	3	.727	16	14	7	1	1	97^2	91	37	28	1	4	39	34	1.331	2.58	113	3.05	.243	5	.156	4	8	0.3
1914	Chi-A	2	3	.400	8	5	3	1	0	44^2	33	19	14	0	1	20	15	1.187	2.82	95	2.22	.212	1	.063	-1	2	-0.1
1915	Chi-A	3	0	1.000	3	3	3	1	0	27	19	4	4	0	0	7	12	.963	1.33	223	1.49	.202	4	.364	5	4	0.6
1916	Chi-A	0	1	.000	2	1	0	0	0	3^1	4	3	1	0	0	3	3	2.100	2.70	102	5.99	.286	0	....	-0	0	0.0
1917	Bos-N	0	1	.000	4	3	1	0	0	18	22	9	7	0	1	9	4	1.722	3.50	73	5.16	.314	1	.250	-2	0	-0.1
Total	14	195	126	.607	430	315	250	57	34	2964^1	2346	873	598	23	52	617	1736	1.000	1.82	146	1.84	.218	210	.193	280	265	31.5

• WALSH, Ed
Edward Arthur Walsh b: 2/11/1905, Meriden, CT d: 10/31/1937, Meriden, CT BR/TR, 6'1", 180 lbs. Deb: 7/4/1928

YEAR	TM-L	W	L	PCT	G	GS	CG	SH	SV	IP	H	R	ER	HR	HB	BB	SO	RAT	ERA	ERA+	CERA	OAV	BH	AVG	PR+	WS	TPW
1928	Chi-A	4	7	.364	14	10	3	0	0	78	86	45	43	2	5	42	32	1.641	4.96	82	4.19	.290	3	.111	-8	2	-1.0
1929	Chi-A	6	11	.353	24	20	7	0	0	129	156	94	81	9	4	64	31	1.705	5.65	76	5.46	.312	10	.233	-22	3	-1.9
1930	Chi-A	1	4	.200	37	4	0	0	0	103^2	131	67	62	8	4	30	37	1.553	5.38	86	5.02	.316	9	.265	-6	4	-0.5
1932	Chi-A	0	2	.000	4	4	1	0	0	20^1	26	22	19	3	0	13	7	1.918	8.41	51	6.78	.299	2	.286	-9	0	-0.8
Total	4	11	24	.314	79	38	11	0	0	331	399	228	205	22	13	149	107	1.656	5.57	78	5.11	.307	24	.216	-45	9	-4.1

• WALSH, Jim
James Thomas Walsh b: 7/10/1894, Roxbury, MA d: 5/13/1967, Boston, MA BL/TL, 5'11", 175 lbs. Deb: 8/25/1921

YEAR	TM-L	W	L	PCT	G	GS	CG	SH	SV	IP	H	R	ER	HR	HB	BB	SO	RAT	ERA	ERA+	CERA	OAV	BH	AVG	PR+	WS	TPW
1921	Det-A	0	0	....	3	0	0	0	0	4	2	1	1	0	0	1	3	.750	2.25	189	0.81	.125	0	....	1	0	0.1

• WALSH, Junior
James Gerald Walsh b: 3/7/1919, Newark, NJ d: 11/12/1990, Olyphant, PA BR/TR, 5'11", 185 lbs. Deb: 9/14/1946

YEAR	TM-L	W	L	PCT	G	GS	CG	SH	SV	IP	H	R	ER	HR	HB	BB	SO	RAT	ERA	ERA+	CERA	OAV	BH	AVG	PR+	WS	TPW
1946	Pit-N	0	1	.000	4	2	0	0	0	10^1	9	6	6	0	1	10	2	1.839	5.23	68	4.87	.237	0	.000	-2	0	-0.2
1948	Pit-N	1	0	1.000	2	0	0	0	0	4^1	4	5	5	1	0	5	0	2.077	10.38	39	7.33	.235	0	.000	-3	0	-0.3
1949	Pit-N	1	4	.200	9	7	1	1	0	42^2	40	27	24	5	0	16	24	1.313	5.06	83	3.67	.244	0	.000	-4	1	-0.5
1950	Pit-N	1	1	.500	38	2	0	0	2	62^1	56	36	35	6	1	34	33	1.444	5.05	87	4.02	.246	1	.167	-4	3	-0.3
1951	Pit-N	1	4	.200	36	1	0	0	0	73^1	92	66	56	9	1	46	32	1.882	6.87	61	6.49	.304	1	.143	-21	0	-2.0
Total	5	4	10	.286	89	12	1	1	2	193	201	140	126	21	3	111	91	1.617	5.88	72	5.00	.268	2	.065	-34	4	-3.4

• WALTER, Bernie
James Bernard Walter b: 8/15/1908, Dover, TN d: 10/30/1988, Nashville, TN BR/TR, 6'1", 175 lbs. Deb: 8/16/1930

YEAR	TM-L	W	L	PCT	G	GS	CG	SH	SV	IP	H	R	ER	HR	HB	BB	SO	RAT	ERA	ERA+	CERA	OAV	BH	AVG	PR+	WS	TPW
1930	Pit-N	0	0	....	1	0	0	0	0	1	0	0	0	0	0	0	1	.000	0.00	....	0.00	.000	0	....	1	0	0.0

• WALTER, Gene
Gene Winston Walter b: 11/22/1960, Chicago, IL BL/TL, 6'4", 200 lbs. Deb: 8/9/1985

YEAR	TM-L	W	L	PCT	G	GS	CG	SH	SV	IP	H	R	ER	HR	HB	BB	SO	RAT	ERA	ERA+	CERA	OAV	BH	AVG	PR+	WS	TPW
1985	SD-N	0	2	.000	15	0	0	0	3	22	12	6	5	0	0	8	18	.909	2.05	173	1.24	.158	0	.000	3	3	0.4
1986	SD-N	2	2	.500	57	0	0	0	1	98	89	47	42	7	4	49	84	1.408	3.86	95	3.84	.247	2	.200	-2	4	-0.1
1987	NY-N	1	2	.333	21	0	0	0	0	19^2	18	10	7	1	1	13	11	1.576	3.20	118	4.16	.243	0	.000	1	1	0.2
1988	NY-N	0	1	.000	19	0	0	0	0	16^2	21	9	7	0	0	11	14	1.920	3.78	85	5.72	.309	0	....	-1	0	-0.1
	Sea-A	1	0	1.000	16	0	0	0	0	26^1	21	16	15	0	2	15	13	1.367	5.13	81	2.91	.216	0	....	-3	1	-0.3
Total	4	4	7	.364	128	0	0	0	4	182^2	161	88	76	8	7	96	140	1.407	3.74	99	3.60	.238	2	.167	-1	9	0.0

• WALTERS, Bucky
William Henry Walters b: 4/19/1909, Philadelphia, PA d: 4/20/1991, Abington, PA BR/TR, 6'1", 180 lbs. Deb: 9/18/1931 M/C/U ♦

YEAR	TM-L	W	L	PCT	G	GS	CG	SH	SV	IP	H	R	ER	HR	HB	BB	SO	RAT	ERA	ERA+	CERA	OAV	BH	AVG	PR+	WS	TPW
1934	Phi-N	0	0	....	2	1	0	0	0	7	8	3	1	1	1	2	7	1.429	1.29	367	5.48	.296	78	.260	3	5	-1.2
1935	Phi-N	9	9	.500	24	22	8	2	0	151	168	86	70	9	7	68	40	1.563	4.17	109	4.77	.289	24	.250	8	11	1.0
1936	Phi-N	11	21	.344	40	33	15	**4**	0	258	284	146	122	11	5	115	66	1.547	4.26	106	4.32	.277	29	.240	16	14	2.1
1937	Phi-N★	14	15	.483	37	**34**	15	3	0	246^1	292	148	130	14	3	86	87	1.535	4.75	91	4.56	.295	38	.277	-7	14	-0.2
1938	Phi-N	4	8	.333	12	12	9	1	0	82^2	91	53	48	8	3	42	28	1.609	5.23	77	5.05	.276	10	.286	-9	3	-0.6
	Cin-N	11	6	.647	27	22	11	2	1	168^1	168	81	69	5	2	66	65	1.390	3.69	99	3.43	.255	9	.141	-3	9	-0.4
	Yr.	15	14	.517	39	34	20	3	1	251	259	134	117	13	5	108	93	1.462	4.20	90	3.96	.262	19	.192	-12	12	-0.9
1939*	Cin-N★	**27**	11	.711	39	**36**	**31**	2	0	**319**	250	98	81	15	6	109	**137**	1.125	**2.29**	**168**	**2.41**	**.220**	39	.325	**46**	**38**	**5.9**
1940*	Cin-N★	**22**	10	.688	36	36	**29**	3	0	**305**	241	95	84	19	5	92	115	1.092	**2.48**	**153**	2.43	**.220**	24	.205	33	**32**	3.6
1941	Cin-N★	19	15	.559	37	35	**27**	5	2	**302**	292	108	95	10	2	88	129	1.258	2.83	127	3.02	.255	20	.189	27	27	2.9
1942	Cin-N★	15	14	.517	34	32	21	2	0	253^2	223	101	75	8	5	73	109	1.167	2.66	123	2.54	.231	24	.242	16	20	2.5
1943	Cin-N	15	15	.500	34	34	21	5	0	246^1	244	105	97	8	1	109	80	1.433	3.54	94	3.67	.264	24	.267	-13	15	-0.5
1944	Cin-N★	**23**	8	.742	34	32	27	6	1	285	233	92	76	10	4	87	77	1.123	2.40	145	2.33	**.219**	30	.280	**28**	**32**	**3.7**
1945	Cin-N	10	10	.500	22	22	12	3	0	168	166	62	50	6	2	51	45	1.292	2.68	140	3.18	.259	14	.230	20	16	2.6
1946	Cin-N	10	7	.588	22	22	10	2	0	151^1	146	55	43	9	2	64	60	1.388	2.56	131	3.73	.258	7	.127	9	11	0.8
1947	Cin-N	8	8	.500	20	20	5	2	0	122	137	83	78	15	3	49	43	1.525	5.75	71	4.87	.278	12	.267	-21	3	-1.8
1948	Cin-N	0	3	.000	7	5	1	0	0	35	42	25	18	6	0	18	19	1.714	4.63	84	6.33	.316	4	.267	-2	1	-0.2
1950	Bos-N	0	0	....	1	0	0	0	0	4	5	2	2	0	0	2	0	1.750	4.50	86	4.86	.313	0	.000	-0	0	-0.1
Total	16	198	160	.553	428	398	242	42	4	3104^2	2990	1343	1139	154	51	1121	1107	1.324	3.30	116	3.40	.253	477	.243	151	251	20.2

• WALTERS, Charlie
Charles Leonard Walters b: 2/21/1947, Minneapolis, MN BR/TR, 6'4", 190 lbs. Deb: 4/11/1969

YEAR	TM-L	W	L	PCT	G	GS	CG	SH	SV	IP	H	R	ER	HR	HB	BB	SO	RAT	ERA	ERA+	CERA	OAV	BH	AVG	PR+	WS	TPW
1969	Min-A	0	0	....	6	0	0	0	0	6^2	6	4	4	1	1	3	2	1.350	5.40	68	4.56	.240	0	....	-1	0	-0.1

• WALTERS, Mike
Michael Charles Walters b: 10/18/1957, St. Louis, MO BR/TR, 6'5", 203 lbs. Deb: 7/8/1983

YEAR	TM-L	W	L	PCT	G	GS	CG	SH	SV	IP	H	R	ER	HR	HB	BB	SO	RAT	ERA	ERA+	CERA	OAV	BH	AVG	PR+	WS	TPW
1983	Min-A	1	1	.500	23	0	0	0	2	59	52	31	27	4	2	20	21	1.220	4.12	103	3.06	.243	0	....	0	3	0.0
1984	Min-A	0	3	.000	23	0	0	0	2	29	31	14	12	1	1	14	10	1.552	3.72	113	4.34	.287	0	....	1	2	0.1
Total	2	1	4	.200	46	0	0	0	4	88	83	45	39	5	3	34	31	1.330	3.99	106	3.48	.258	0	....	1	5	0.1

YEAR TM-L	W	L	PCT	G	GS	CG	SH	SV	IP	H	R	ER	HR	HB	BB	SO	RAT	ERA	ERA+	CERA	OAV	BH	AVG	PR+	WS	TPW
• WALTON, Bruce	Bruce Kenneth Walton b: 12/25/1962, Bakersfield, CA BR/TR, 6'2", 195 lbs. Deb: 5/11/1991																									
1991 Oak-A	1	0	1.000	12	0	0	0	0	13	11	9	9	3	1	6	10	1.308	6.23	62	4.68	.229	0	....	-3	0	-0.3
1992 Oak-A	0	0	....	7	0	0	0	0	10	17	11	11	1	0	3	7	2.000	9.90	38	7.93	.378	0	....	-7	0	-0.7
1993 Mon-N	0	0	....	4	0	0	0	0	5^{2}	11	6	6	1	0	3	0	2.471	9.53	44	10.84	.407	0	.000	-3	0	-0.3
1994 Col-N	1	0	1.000	4	0	0	0	0	5^{1}	6	5	5	1	0	3	1	1.688	8.44	59	5.44	.273	0	....	-2	0	-0.2
Total 4	**2**	**0**	**1.000**	**27**	**0**	**0**	**0**	**0**	**34**	**45**	**31**	**31**	**6**	**1**	**15**	**18**	**1.765**	**8.21**	**49**	**6.78**	**.317**	**0**	**.000**	**-16**	**0**	**-1.6**
• WANTZ, Dick	Richard Carter Wantz b: 4/11/1940, South Gate, CA d: 5/13/1965, Inglewood, CA BR/TR, 6'5", 175 lbs. Deb: 4/13/1965																									
1965 Cal-A	0	0	....	1	0	0	0	0	1	3	2	2	0	0	0	2	3.000	18.00	19	14.52	.500	0	....	-2	0	-0.2
• WAPNICK, Steve	Steven Lee Wapnick b: 9/25/1965, Panorama City, CA BR/TR, 6'2", 200 lbs. Deb: 4/14/1990																									
1990 Det-A	0	0	....	4	0	0	0	0	7	8	5	5	0	0	10	6	2.571	6.43	62	8.53	.296	0	....	-2	0	-0.2
1991 Chi-A	0	1	.000	6	0	0	0	0	5	2	1	1	0	0	4	1	1.200	1.80	221	1.65	.111	0	....	1	0	0.1
Total 2	**0**	**1**	**.000**	**10**	**0**	**0**	**0**	**0**	**12**	**10**	**6**	**6**	**0**	**0**	**14**	**7**	**2.000**	**4.50**	**88**	**5.66**	**.222**	**0**	**....**	**-1**	**0**	**-0.1**
• WARD, Bryan	Bryan Matthew Ward b: 1/25/1972, Bristol, PA BL/TL, 6'2", 205 lbs. Deb: 7/3/1998																									
1998 Chi-A	1	2	.333	28	0	0	0	1	27	30	13	10	4	0	7	17	1.370	3.33	137	4.46	.278	0	....	4	2	0.3
1999 Chi-A	0	1	.000	40	0	0	0	0	39^{1}	63	36	33	10	0	11	35	1.881	7.55	65	8.73	.368	0	....	-11	0	-1.0
2000 Phi-N	0	0	....	20	0	0	0	0	19^{1}	14	5	5	2	0	8	11	1.138	2.33	200	2.68	.206	0	....	5	2	0.5
Ana-A	0	0	....	7	0	0	0	0	8	8	6	5	1	0	2	3	1.250	5.63	90	3.35	.235	0	....	-1	0	-0.1
Total 3	**1**	**3**	**.250**	**95**	**0**	**0**	**0**	**1**	**93^{2}**	**115**	**60**	**53**	**17**	**0**	**28**	**66**	**1.527**	**5.09**	**94**	**5.79**	**.302**	**0**	**....**	**-4**	**4**	**-0.3**
• WARD, Colby	Robert Colby Ward b: 1/2/1964, Lansing, MI BR/TR, 6'2", 185 lbs. Deb: 7/27/1990																									
1990 Cle-A	1	3	.250	22	0	0	0	1	36	31	17	17	3	1	21	23	1.444	4.25	92	3.80	.238	0	....	-1	2	-0.1
• WARD, Colin	Colin Norval Ward b: 11/22/1960, Los Angeles, CA BL/TL, 6'3", 190 lbs. Deb: 9/21/1985																									
1985 SF-N	0	0	....	6	2	0	0	0	12^{1}	10	6	6	0	0	7	8	1.378	4.38	78	3.04	.233	0	.000	-1	0	-0.1
• WARD, Dick	Richard Ole Ward b: 5/21/1909, Herrick, SD d: 5/30/1966, Freeland, WA BR/TR, 6'1", 198 lbs. Deb: 5/3/1934																									
1934 Chi-N	0	0	....	3	0	0	0	0	6	9	6	2	0	0	2	1	1.833	3.00	129	5.92	.375	0	.000	1	0	0.0
1935 StL-N	0	0	....	1	0	0	0	0	0	0	1	0	0	0	1	0	....	....	....	∞	1.000	0	....	0	0	0.0
Total 2	**0**	**0**	**....**	**4**	**0**	**0**	**0**	**0**	**6**	**9**	**7**	**2**	**0**	**0**	**3**	**1**	**2.000**	**3.00**	**129**	**5.92**	**.375**	**0**	**.000**	**1**	**0**	**0.0**
• WARD, Duane	Roy Duane Ward b: 5/28/1964, Park View, NM BR/TR, 6'4", 210 lbs. Deb: 4/12/1986																									
1986 Atl-N	0	1	.000	10	0	0	0	0	16	22	13	13	2	0	8	8	1.875	7.31	54	7.29	.349	0	.000	-6	0	-0.6
Tor-A	0	1	.000	2	1	0	0	0	2	3	4	3	0	1	4	1	3.500	13.50	31	14.20	.300	0	....	-2	0	-0.2
1987 Tor-A	1	0	1.000	12	1	0	0	0	11^{2}	14	9	9	0	0	12	10	2.229	6.94	65	6.91	.326	0	....	-3	0	-0.3
1988 Tor-A	9	3	.750	64	0	0	0	15	111^{2}	101	46	41	5	5	60	91	1.442	3.30	119	3.75	.245	0	....	7	11	0.7
1989* Tor-A	4	10	.286	66	0	0	0	15	114^{2}	94	55	48	4	5	58	122	1.326	3.77	96	3.03	.230	0	....	-2	8	-0.2
1990 Tor-A	2	8	.200	73	0	0	0	11	127^{2}	101	51	49	9	1	42	112	1.120	3.45	118	2.50	.221	0	....	9	11	1.0
1991* Tor-A	7	6	.538	**81**	0	0	0	23	107^{1}	80	36	33	3	2	33	132	1.053	2.77	152	2.02	.207	0	....	18	19	1.8
1992* Tor-A	7	4	.636	79	0	0	0	12	101^{1}	76	27	22	5	1	39	103	1.135	1.95	209	2.37	.207	0	....	24	16	2.5
1993* Tor-A★	2	3	.400	71	0	0	0	**45**	71^{2}	49	17	17	4	1	25	97	1.033	2.13	202	2.04	.193	0	....	18	17	1.7
1995 Tor-A	0	1	.000	4	0	0	0	0	2^{2}	11	10	8	0	1	5	3	6.000	27.00	17	35.35	.579	0	....	-7	0	-0.6
Total 9	**32**	**37**	**.464**	**462**	**2**	**0**	**0**	**121**	**666^{2}**	**551**	**268**	**243**	**32**	**17**	**286**	**679**	**1.256**	**3.28**	**122**	**3.01**	**.228**	**0**	**.000**	**56**	**82**	**5.7**
• WARD, John	John Montgomery "Monte" Ward b: 3/3/1860, Bellefonte, PA d: 3/4/1925, Augusta, GA BL/TR, 5'9", 165 lbs. Deb: 7/15/1878 M/U HOF: 1964 ♦																									
1878 Pro-N	22	13	.629	37	37	37	6	0	334	308	151	56	3	....	34	116	1.024	**1.51**	**146**	....	.233	27	.196	21	24	2.2
1879 Pro-N	**47**	19	.712	70	60	58	2	**1**	587	571	270	140	5	....	36	**239**	1.034	2.15	110	....	.239	104	.286	8	51	**2.2**
1880 Pro-N	39	24	.619	70	67	59	**8**	1	595	501	230	115	5	....	45	230	.918	1.74	127	....	.217	81	.228	17	51	2.6
1881 Pro-N	18	18	.500	39	35	32	3	0	330	326	183	78	2	....	53	119	1.148	2.13	125	....	.247	87	.244	30	27	2.7
1882 Pro-N	19	13	.594	34	33	30	4	**1**	286	268	143	80	6	....	36	72	1.063	2.52	111	....	.234	87	.245	3	31	0.5
1883 NY-N	16	13	.552	34	25	24	1	0	277	278	165	83	3	....	31	121	1.116	2.70	115	....	.246	97	.255	11	28	2.3
1884 NY-N	3	3	.500	9	5	5	0	0	60^{2}	72	43	23	2	....	18	23	1.484	3.41	87	....	.279	122	.253	-3	16	0.0
Total 7	**164**	**103**	**.614**	**293**	**262**	**245**	**24**	**3**	**2469^{2}**	**2324**	**1185**	**575**	**26**	**....**	**253**	**920**	**1.043**	**2.10**	**120**	**....**	**.235**	**2136**	**.278**	**88**	**228**	**12.5**
• WARD, Johnny	John Ward b: East St. Louis, IL Deb: 9/19/1885																									
1885 Pro-N	0	1	.000	1	1	1	0	0	8	10	7	4	0	....	1	3	1.375	4.50	59	....	.292	0	.000	-2	0	-0.2
• WARDEN, Jon	Jonathan Edgar "Warbler" Warden b: 10/1/1946, Columbus, OH BB/TL, 6', 205 lbs. Deb: 4/11/1968																									
1968 Det-A	4	1	.800	28	0	0	0	3	37^{1}	30	15	15	5	0	15	25	1.205	3.62	83	3.15	.217	0	.000	-3	3	-0.3
• WARDLE, Curt	Curtis Ray Wardle b: 11/16/1960, Downey, CA BL/TL, 6'5", 220 lbs. Deb: 8/30/1984																									
1984 Min-A	0	0	....	2	0	0	0	0	4	3	2	2	2	0	0	5	.750	4.50	93	3.15	.200	0	....	-0	0	0.0
1985 Min-A	1	3	.250	35	0	0	0	1	49	49	32	30	9	1	28	47	1.571	5.51	80	5.55	.266	0	....	-6	1	-0.6
Cle-A	7	6	.538	15	12	0	0	0	66	78	51	49	11	1	34	37	1.697	6.68	62	6.19	.297	0	....	-19	0	-1.8
Yr.	8	9	.471	50	12	0	0	1	115	127	83	79	20	2	62	84	1.643	6.18	68	5.92	.284	0	....	-25	1	-2.4
Total 2	**8**	**9**	**.471**	**52**	**12**	**0**	**0**	**1**	**119**	**130**	**85**	**81**	**22**	**2**	**62**	**89**	**1.613**	**6.13**	**69**	**5.82**	**.281**	**0**	**....**	**-25**	**1**	**-2.4**
• WARE, Jeff	Jeffrey Allan Ware b: 11/11/1970, Norfolk, VA BR/TR, 6'3", 190 lbs. Deb: 9/2/1995																									
1995 Tor-A	2	1	.667	5	5	0	0	0	26^{1}	28	18	16	2	1	21	18	1.861	5.47	86	6.12	.277	0	....	-2	1	-0.2
1996 Tor-A	1	5	.167	13	4	0	0	0	32^{2}	35	34	33	6	2	31	11	2.020	9.09	55	7.68	.271	0	....	-16	0	-1.4
Total 2	**3**	**6**	**.333**	**18**	**9**	**0**	**0**	**0**	**59**	**63**	**52**	**49**	**8**	**3**	**52**	**29**	**1.949**	**7.47**	**66**	**6.98**	**.274**	**0**	**....**	**-18**	**1**	**-1.6**
• WARHOP, Jack	John Milton "Chief,Crab" Warhop b: 7/4/1884, Hinton, WV d: 10/4/1960, Freeport, IL BR/TR, 5'9.5", 168 lbs. Deb: 9/19/1908																									
1908 NY-A	1	2	.333	5	4	3	0	0	36^{1}	40	19	18	0	4	8	11	1.321	4.46	55	3.80	.292	1	.063	-7	0	-1.0
1909 NY-A	13	15	.464	36	23	21	3	2	243^{1}	197	84	65	2	26	81	95	1.142	2.40	105	2.69	.233	11	.128	10	13	0.9
1910 NY-A	14	14	.500	37	27	20	0	2	243	219	108	81	1	18	79	75	1.226	3.00	88	2.92	.246	14	.177	-3	14	-0.3
1911 NY-A	12	13	.480	31	25	17	1	0	209^{2}	239	118	97	6	15	44	71	1.350	4.16	86	3.86	.286	12	.156	-9	11	-1.3
1912 NY-A	10	19	.345	39	22	16	0	3	258	256	121	82	3	16	59	110	1.221	2.86	126	3.10	.266	19	.207	36	16	3.5
1913 NY-A	4	6	.400	15	7	1	0	0	62^{1}	69	42	26	1	12	33	11	1.636	3.75	79	5.35	.292	3	.130	-5	1	-0.6
1914 NY-A	8	15	.348	37	23	15	0	0	216^{2}	182	75	57	8	11	44	56	1.043	2.37	116	2.40	.235	10	.141	7	14	0.6
1915 NY-A	7	9	.438	21	19	12	0	0	143^{1}	164	74	63	7	12	52	34	1.507	3.96	74	5.00	.309	7	.137	-18	4	-2.1
Total 8	**69**	**93**	**.426**	**221**	**150**	**105**	**4**	**7**	**1412^{2}**	**1366**	**641**	**489**	**28**	**114**	**400**	**463**	**1.250**	**3.12**	**96**	**3.31**	**.262**	**77**	**.156**	**10**	**73**	**-0.3**
• WARMOTH, Cy	Wallace Walter Warmoth b: 2/2/1893, Bone Gap, IL d: 6/20/1957, Mount Carmel, IL BL/TL, 5'11", 158 lbs. Deb: 8/31/1916																									
1916 StL-N	0	0	....	3	0	0	0	0	5	12	10	8	0	1	4	1	3.200	14.40	18	15.53	.500	0	.000	-7	0	-0.8
1922 Was-A	1	0	1.000	5	1	1	0	0	19	15	6	3	0	0	9	8	1.263	1.42	271	2.36	.205	1	.143	5	2	0.4
1923 Was-A	7	5	.583	21	13	3	0	0	105	103	64	50	4	1	76	45	1.705	4.29	88	4.62	.261	8	.222	-10	4	-0.7
Total 3	**8**	**5**	**.615**	**29**	**14**	**4**	**0**	**0**	**129**	**130**	**80**	**61**	**4**	**2**	**89**	**54**	**1.698**	**4.26**	**84**	**4.71**	**.264**	**9**	**.200**	**-12**	**6**	**-1.1**
• WARNEKE, Lon	Lonnie "The Arkansas Hummingbird" Warneke b: 3/28/1909, Mount Ida, AR d: 6/23/1976, Hot Springs, AR BR/TR, 6'2", 185 lbs. Deb: 4/18/1930 U																									
1930 Chi-N	0	0	....	1	0	0	0	0	1^{1}	2	5	5	0	0	5	0	5.250	33.75	14	19.24	.400	0	....	-4	0	-0.4
1931 Chi-N	2	4	.333	20	7	3	0	0	64^{1}	67	33	23	1	3	37	27	1.617	3.22	120	4.26	.269	5	.263	5	4	0.6
1932* Chi-N	**22**	6	.786	35	32	25	**4**	0	277	247	84	73	12	2	64	106	1.123	**2.37**	**159**	2.50	.237	19	.192	38	**31**	3.7
1933 Chi-N★	18	13	.581	36	34	**26**	4	1	287^{1}	262	83	64	8	3	75	133	1.173	2.00	163	2.61	.244	30	.300	34	29	4.7
1934 Chi-N★	22	10	.688	43	35	23	3	3	291^{1}	273	116	104	16	2	66	143	1.164	3.21	121	2.75	.244	22	.195	19	26	1.8
1935* Chi-N	20	13	.606	42	30	20	1	4	261^{2}	257	102	89	19	3	50	120	1.173	3.06	128	3.03	.257	20	.220	16	22	1.6
1936 Chi-N★	16	13	.552	40	29	13	**4**	1	240^{1}	246	108	92	10	4	76	113	1.340	3.45	115	3.46	.264	17	.202	9	17	0.9
1937 StL-N	18	11	.621	36	33	18	2	0	238^{2}	280	139	120	32	0	69	87	1.462	4.53	88	4.75	.287	21	.263	-13	12	-0.8
1938 StL-N	13	8	.619	31	26	12	4	0	197	199	102	87	14	2	64	89	1.335	3.97	99	3.52	.256	23	.324	0	12	0.5

YEAR TM-L	W	L	PCT	G	GS	CG	SH	SV	IP	H	R	ER	HR	HB	BB	SO	RAT	ERA	ERA+	CERA	OAV	BH	AVG	PR+	WS	TPW
1939 StL-N★	13	7	.650	34	21	6	2	2	162	160	73	68	14	2	49	59	1.290	3.78	109	3.56	.259	10	.192	4	12	0.5
1940 StL-N	16	10	.615	33	31	17	1	0	232	235	103	81	17	3	47	85	1.216	3.14	127	3.18	.257	18	.209	26	18	2.8
1941 StL-N★	17	9	.654	37	30	12	4	0	246	227	100	86	19	3	82	83	1.256	3.15	120	3.27	.249	9	.117	13	19	1.2
1942 StL-N	6	4	.600	12	12	5	0	0	82	76	34	30	8	0	15	31	1.110	3.29	104	2.76	.238	10	.333	0	6	0.3
Chi-N	5	7	.417	15	12	8	1	2	99	97	33	25	2	0	21	28	1.192	2.27	141	2.72	.259	6	.188	12	8	1.2
Yr.	11	11	.500	27	24	13	1	2	181	173	67	55	10	0	36	59	1.155	2.73	121	2.74	.249	16	.258	12	14	1.6
1943 Chi-N	4	5	.444	21	10	4	0	0	88^1	82	40	31	3	0	18	30	1.132	3.16	106	2.53	.246	5	.192	3	4	0.5
1945 Chi-N	0	1	.000	9	1	0	0	0	14	16	9	6	0	0	1	6	1.214	3.86	95	2.73	.267	0	.000	-1	0	0.0
Total 15	192	121	.613	445	343	192	30	13	2782^1	2726	1164	984	175	27	739	1140	1.245	3.18	120	3.19	.255	215	.223	163	220	19.3
• WARNER, Ed	Edward Emory Warner b: 6/20/1889, Fitchburg, MA d: 2/5/1954, New York, NY BR/TL, 5'10.5", 165 lbs. Deb: 7/2/1912																									
1912 Pit-N	1	1	.500	11	3	1	1	0	45	40	20	18	0	3	18	13	1.289	3.60	90	2.97	.242	2	.133	-2	2	-0.3
• WARNER, Jack	Jack Dyer Warner b: 7/12/1940, Brandywine, WV BR/TR, 5'11", 190 lbs. Deb: 4/10/1962																									
1962 Chi-N	0	0	....	7	0	0	0	0	7	9	7	6	3	0	0	3	1.286	7.71	54	6.38	.321	0	....	-3	0	-0.3
1963 Chi-N	0	1	.000	8	0	0	0	0	22^2	21	7	7	1	0	8	7	1.279	2.78	126	3.14	.256	1	.250	1	2	0.2
1964 Chi-N	0	0	....	7	0	0	0	0	9^1	12	3	3	0	0	4	6	1.714	2.89	128	5.33	.333	0	....	1	1	0.1
1965 Chi-N	0	1	.000	11	0	0	0	0	15^2	22	16	15	1	0	9	7	1.979	8.62	43	7.02	.355	0	.000	-8	0	-0.9
Total 4	0	2	.000	33	0	0	0	0	54^2	64	33	31	5	0	21	23	1.555	5.10	73	5.04	.308	1	.200	-9	3	-0.9
• WARREN, Mike	Michael Bruce Warren b: 3/26/1961, Inglewood, CA BR/TR, 6'1", 175 lbs. Deb: 6/12/1983																									
1983 Oak-A	5	3	.625	12	9	3	1	0	65^2	51	33	30	4	1	18	30	1.051	4.11	94	2.25	.215	0	....	-2	3	-0.2
1984 Oak-A	3	6	.333	24	12	0	0	0	90	104	52	49	11	3	44	61	1.644	4.90	76	5.64	.291	0	....	-12	2	-1.2
1985 Oak-A	1	4	.200	16	6	0	0	0	49	52	42	36	13	4	38	48	1.837	6.61	58	7.49	.261	0	....	-15	0	-1.4
Total 3	9	13	.409	52	27	3	1	0	204^2	207	127	115	28	8	100	139	1.500	5.06	75	5.00	.261	0	....	-29	5	-2.9
• WARREN, Tommy	Thomas Gentry Warren b: 7/5/1917, Tulsa, OK d: 1/2/1968, Tulsa, OK BB/TL, 6'1", 190 lbs. Deb: 4/18/1944																									
1944 Bro-N	1	4	.200	22	4	2	0	0	68^2	74	52	38	4	0	40	18	1.660	4.98	71	4.61	.270	11	.256	-9	1	-0.7
• WARTHEN, Dan	Daniel Dean Warthen b: 12/1/1952, Omaha, NE BB/TL, 6', 200 lbs. Deb: 5/18/1975 C																									
1975 Mon-N	8	6	.571	40	18	2	0	3	167^2	130	62	58	8	1	87	128	1.294	3.11	123	2.98	.217	6	.118	13	14	1.1
1976 Mon-N	2	10	.167	23	16	2	1	0	90	76	59	53	8	2	66	67	1.578	5.30	70	4.47	.232	0	.000	-16	0	-2.0
1977 Mon-N	2	3	.400	12	6	1	0	0	35	33	34	31	7	0	38	26	2.029	7.97	48	7.37	.262	1	.111	-16	0	-1.7
Phi-N	0	1	.000	3	0	0	0	0	3^2	4	3	0	0	0	5	1	2.455	0.00	....	7.09	.267	0	....	2	0	0.2
Yr.	2	4	.333	15	6	1	0	0	38^2	37	37	31	7	0	43	27	2.069	7.22	53	7.34	.262	1	.111	-15	0	-1.5
1978 Hou-N	0	1	.000	5	1	0	0	0	10^2	10	5	5	3	0	2	2	1.125	4.22	78	4.06	.250	0	.000	-1	0	-0.1
Total 4	12	21	.364	83	41	5	1	3	307	253	163	147	26	3	198	224	1.469	4.31	87	4.00	.228	7	.079	-18	14	-2.5
• WASDIN, John	John Truman Wasdin b: 8/5/1972, Fort Belvoir, VA BR/TR, 6'2", 190 lbs. Deb: 8/24/1995																									
1995 Oak-A	1	1	.500	5	2	0	0	0	17^1	14	9	9	4	1	3	6	.981	4.67	95	3.19	.215	0	....	-0	1	0.0
1996 Oak-A	8	7	.533	25	21	1	0	0	131^1	145	96	87	24	4	50	75	1.485	5.96	82	5.32	.283	0	....	-17	4	-1.6
1997 Bos-A	4	6	.400	53	7	0	0	0	124^2	121	68	61	18	3	38	84	1.275	4.40	105	3.82	.251	0	....	3	7	0.3
1998* Bos-A	6	4	.600	47	8	0	0	0	96	111	57	56	14	2	27	59	1.438	5.25	90	4.70	.288	0	....	-6	4	-0.6
1999* Bos-A	8	3	.727	45	0	0	0	2	74^1	66	38	34	14	0	18	57	1.130	4.12	121	3.41	.236	0	....	7	7	0.7
2000 Bos-A	1	3	.250	25	1	0	0	1	44^2	48	25	25	8	2	15	36	1.410	5.04	100	4.87	.273	0	....	0	2	0.0
Col-N	0	3	.000	14	3	1	0	0	35^2	42	23	23	6	3	9	35	1.430	5.80	100	5.38	.302	2	.250	-0	1	0.0
2001 Col-N	2	1	.667	18	0	0	0	0	24^1	32	19	19	7	1	8	17	1.644	7.03	76	7.27	.320	1	.333	-5	1	-0.4
Bal-A	1	1	.500	26	0	0	0	0	49^2	54	25	23	4	5	16	47	1.409	4.17	103	4.36	.277	0	....	0	2	0.0
2003 Tor-A	0	1	.000	3	2	0	0	0	5	16	13	13	2	0	4	5	4.000	23.40	20	25.15	.533	0	....	-10	0	-1.0
Total 8	31	30	.508	261	44	2	0	3	603	649	373	350	101	21	188	421	1.388	5.22	93	4.75	.274	3	.273	-29	29	-2.6
• WASHBURN, George	George Edward Washburn b: 10/6/1914, Solon, ME d: 1/5/1979, Baton Rouge, LA BL/TR, 6'1", 175 lbs. Deb: 5/4/1941																									
1941 NY-A	0	1	.000	1	1	0	0	0	2	2	4	3	0	0	5	1	3.500	13.50	29	11.54	.286	0	.000	-2	0	-0.2
• WASHBURN, Greg	Gregory James Washburn b: 12/3/1946, Coal City, IL BR/TR, 6', 190 lbs. Deb: 6/7/1969																									
1969 Cal-A	0	2	.000	8	2	0	0	0	11^1	21	11	10	0	1	5	4	2.294	7.94	44	9.02	.404	0	....	-6	0	-0.6
• WASHBURN, Jarrod	Jarrod Michael Washburn b: 8/13/1974, La Crosse, WI BL/TL, 6'1", 187 lbs. Deb: 6/2/1998																									
1998 Ana-A	6	3	.667	15	11	0	0	0	74	70	40	38	11	3	27	48	1.311	4.62	102	4.09	.248	0	.000	1	4	0.1
1999 Ana-A	4	5	.444	16	10	0	0	0	61^2	61	36	36	6	1	26	39	1.411	5.25	92	4.20	.261	0	....	-3	3	-0.3
2000 Ana-A	7	2	.778	14	14	0	0	0	84^1	64	38	35	16	1	37	49	1.198	3.74	136	3.66	.215	1	.333	10	7	1.0
2001 Ana-A	11	10	.524	30	30	1	0	0	193^1	196	89	81	25	7	54	126	1.293	3.77	121	4.03	.263	3	.600	16	15	1.7
2002* Ana-A	18	6	.750	32	32	1	0	0	206	183	75	72	19	3	59	139	1.175	3.15	141	3.02	.235	1	.200	23	18	2.2
2003 Ana-A	10	15	.400	32	32	2	0	0	207^1	205	106	102	34	11	54	118	1.249	4.43	97	4.07	.256	1	.200	-6	9	-0.5
Total 6	56	41	.577	139	129	4	0	0	826^2	779	384	364	111	26	257	519	1.253	3.96	115	3.77	.248	6	.316	41	56	4.1
• WASHBURN, Libe	Libeus Washburn b: 6/16/1874, Lynn, NH d: 3/22/1940, Malone, NY BB/TL, 5'10", 180 lbs. Deb: 5/30/1902 ♦																									
1903 Phi-N	0	4	.000	4	4	4	0	0	35	44	23	17	0	0	11	9	1.571	4.37	75	4.71	.326	3	.167	-5	0	-0.6
• WASHBURN, Ray	Ray Clark Washburn b: 5/31/1938, Pasco, WA BR/TR, 6'1", 205 lbs. Deb: 9/20/1961																									
1961 StL-N	1	1	.500	3	2	1	0	0	20^1	10	4	4	1	1	7	12	.836	1.77	248	1.44	.152	1	.125	6	2	0.5
1962 StL-N	12	9	.571	34	25	2	1	0	175^2	187	90	80	25	3	58	109	1.395	4.10	104	4.52	.273	10	.179	2	10	0.3
1963 StL-N	5	3	.625	11	11	4	2	0	64^1	50	25	22	5	1	14	47	.995	3.08	115	2.20	.212	1	.053	3	4	0.2
1964 StL-N	3	4	.429	15	10	0	0	2	60	60	29	27	7	5	17	28	1.283	4.05	94	4.04	.264	2	.133	-2	3	-0.2
1965 StL-N	9	11	.450	28	16	1	1	2	119^1	114	57	48	15	1	28	67	1.190	3.62	106	3.32	.254	5	.152	2	7	0.3
1966 StL-N	11	9	.550	27	26	4	1	0	170	183	75	71	15	1	44	98	1.335	3.76	96	3.91	.280	5	.093	-5	8	-0.6
1967* StL-N	10	7	.588	27	27	3	1	0	186^1	190	78	73	14	4	42	98	1.245	3.53	92	3.38	.265	6	.091	-6	9	-0.9
1968* StL-N	14	8	.636	31	30	8	4	0	215	191	67	54	9	1	47	124	1.107	2.26	128	2.44	.239	5	.083	13	15	1.5
1969 StL-N	3	8	.273	28	16	2	0	1	132^1	133	59	45	9	1	49	80	1.375	3.06	117	3.67	.261	3	.081	6	6	0.5
1970* Cin-N	4	4	.500	35	3	0	0	0	66^1	90	61	51	7	0	48	37	2.080	6.92	60	7.33	.324	0	.000	-20	0	-2.2
Total 10	72	64	.529	239	166	25	10	5	1209^2	1208	545	475	107	18	354	700	1.291	3.53	102	3.63	.261	38	.105	0	64	-0.5
• WASHER, Buck	William Washer b: 10/11/1882, Akron, OH d: 12/8/1955, Akron, OH BR/TR, 5'10", 175 lbs. Deb: 4/25/1905																									
1905 Phi-N	0	0	....	1	0	0	0	0	3	4	2	2	0	0	5	0	3.000	6.00	48	10.31	.000	0	.000	-1	0	-0.1
• WASLEWSKI, Gary	Gary Lee Waslewski b: 7/21/1941, Meriden, CT BR/TR, 6'4", 195 lbs. Deb: 6/11/1967																									
1967* Bos-A	2	2	.500	12	8	0	0	0	42	34	18	15	3	1	20	20	1.286	3.21	108	3.17	.225	1	.091	1	2	0.1
1968 Bos-A	4	7	.364	34	11	2	0	2	105^1	108	50	43	9	6	40	59	1.405	3.67	86	4.15	.269	1	.038	-5	3	-0.8
1969 StL-N	0	2	.000	12	0	0	0	1	20^2	19	9	9	3	1	8	16	1.306	3.92	91	3.74	.244	0	.000	-1	1	-0.1
Mon-N	3	7	.300	30	14	3	1	1	109^1	102	53	40	5	8	63	63	1.509	3.29	112	4.23	.252	1	.033	5	5	0.3
Yr.	3	9	.250	42	14	3	1	2	130	121	62	49	8	9	71	79	1.477	3.39	108	4.15	.251	1	.032	4	6	0.2
1970 Mon-N	0	2	.000	6	4	0	0	0	24^2	23	14	14	3	0	15	19	1.541	5.11	80	4.42	.247	0	.000	-3	0	-0.3
NY-A	2	2	.500	26	5	0	0	0	55	42	20	19	4	4	27	27	1.255	3.11	113	3.19	.219	1	.100	2	3	0.2
1971 NY-A	0	1	.000	24	0	0	0	1	35^2	28	15	13	2	1	16	17	1.234	3.28	98	2.79	.214	0	.000	0	2	0.0
1972 Oak-A	0	3	.000	8	0	0	0	0	17^2	12	5	4	3	0	8	8	1.132	2.04	140	2.98	.190	0	.000	1	1	0.1
Total 6	11	26	.297	152	42	5	1	5	410^1	368	184	157	32	21	197	229	1.377	3.44	100	3.77	.243	4	.045	1	17	-0.5
• WATERBURY, Steve	Steven Craig Waterbury b: 4/6/1952, Carbondale, IL BR/TR, 6'5", 190 lbs. Deb: 9/14/1976																									
1976 StL-N	0	0	....	5	0	0	0	0	6	7	4	4	0	0	3	4	1.667	6.00	59	4.92	.304	0	....	-2	0	-0.2
• WATERS, Fred	Fred Warren Waters b: 2/2/1927, Benton, MS d: 8/28/1989, Pensacola, FL BL/TL, 5'11", 185 lbs. Deb: 9/20/1955																									
1955 Pit-N	0	0	....	2	0	0	0	0	5	7	2	2	1	0	2	0	1.800	3.60	114	7.12	.318	0	.000	0	0	0.0

YEAR TM-L	W	L	PCT	G	GS	CG	SH	SV	IP	H	R	ER	HR	HB	BB	SO	RAT	ERA	ERA+	CERA	OAV	BH	AVG	PR+	WS	TPW
1956 Pit-N	2	2	.500	23	5	1	0	0	51	48	18	16	3	1	30	14	1.529	2.82	134	4.28	.258	1	.050	6	4	0.5
Total 2	2	2	.500	25	5	1	0	0	56	55	20	18	4	1	32	14	1.554	2.89	132	4.53	.264	1	.048	6	4	0.5
• WATKINS, Bob																										
Robert Cecil Watkins b: 3/12/1948, San Francisco, CA BR/TR, 6'1", 170 lbs. Deb: 9/6/1969																										
1969 Hou-N	0	0	....	5	0	0	0	0	15^2	13	9	9	1	0	13	11	1.660	5.17	68	4.77	.241	0	.000	-3	0	-0.3
• WATKINS, Scott																										
Scott Allen Watkins b: 5/15/1970, Tulsa, OK BL/TL, 6'3", 180 lbs. Deb: 8/1/1995																										
1995 Min-A	0	0	....	27	0	0	0	0	21^2	22	14	13	2	0	11	11	1.523	5.40	88	4.55	.278	0	....	-1	1	-0.1
• WATSON, Allen																										
Allen Kenneth Watson b: 11/18/1970, Jamaica, NY BL/TL, 6'3", 190 lbs. Deb: 7/8/1993																										
1993 StL-N	6	7	.462	16	15	0	0	0	86	90	53	44	11	3	28	49	1.372	4.60	86	4.32	.271	6	.231	-6	3	-0.4
1994 StL-N	6	5	.545	22	22	0	0	0	115^2	130	73	71	15	8	53	74	1.582	5.52	75	5.58	.286	6	.158	-18	3	-1.7
1995 StL-N	7	9	.438	21	19	0	0	0	114^1	126	68	63	17	5	41	49	1.461	4.96	84	5.18	.285	15	.417	-11	5	-0.5
1996 SF-N	8	12	.400	29	29	2	0	0	185^2	189	105	95	28	5	69	128	1.390	4.61	89	4.58	.273	15	.231	-12	7	-0.7
1997 Ana-A	12	12	.500	35	34	0	0	0	199	220	121	109	37	8	73	141	1.472	4.93	94	5.34	.279	0	....	-8	9	-0.8
1998 Ana-A	6	7	.462	28	14	1	0	0	92^1	122	67	62	12	3	34	64	1.690	6.04	78	6.30	.323	0	....	-13	2	-1.2
1999 NY-N	2	2	.500	14	4	0	0	1	39^2	36	18	18	5	1	22	32	1.462	4.08	107	4.36	.252	3	.300	1	3	0.2
Sea-A	0	1	.000	3	0	0	0	0	3	6	9	4	5	0	3	2	3.000	12.00	42	28.71	.400	0	....	-2	0	-0.2
*NY-A	4	0	1.000	21	0	0	0	0	34^1	30	8	8	3	0	10	30	1.165	2.10	225	2.99	.236	0	....	10	4	1.0
Yr.	4	1	.800	24	0	0	0	0	37^1	36	17	12	8	0	13	32	1.313	2.89	166	5.06	.254	0	....	8	4	0.7
2000 NY-A	0	0	....	17	0	0	0	0	22	30	25	25	6	2	18	20	2.182	10.23	47	10.00	.330	0	....	-13	0	-1.2
Total 8	51	55	.481	206	137	3	0	1	892	979	547	499	139	35	351	589	1.491	5.03	86	5.25	.283	45	.257	-72	36	-5.6
• WATSON, Doc																										
Charles John Watson b: 1/30/1885, Carroll County, OH d: 12/30/1949, San Diego, CA BR/TL, 6', 170 lbs. Deb: 9/3/1913																										
1913 Chi-N	1	0	1.000	1	1	1	0	0	9	8	2	1	0	1	6	1	1.556	1.00	317	4.04	.242	0	.000	2	1	0.2
1914 Chi-F	9	8	.529	26	18	10	3	1	172	145	50	39	2	4	49	69	1.128	2.04	144	2.30	.236	5	.093	13	13	1.0
StL-F	3	4	.429	9	7	4	2	0	56	41	18	12	1	3	24	18	1.161	1.93	180	2.34	.211	2	.125	11	6	1.0
Yr.	12	12	.500	35	25	14	5	1	228	186	68	51	3	7	73	87	1.136	2.01	152	2.31	.230	7	.100	24	19	2.0
1915 StL-F	9	9	.500	33	20	6	0	0	135^2	132	66	60	1	4	58	45	1.400	3.98	78	3.67	.273	5	.125	-15	5	-1.9
Total 3	22	21	.512	69	46	21	5	1	372^2	326	136	112	4	12	137	133	1.242	2.70	114	2.84	.246	12	.107	10	25	0.3
• WATSON, Mark																										
Mark Bradford Watson b: 1/23/1974, Atlanta, GA BR/TL, 6'4", 215 lbs. Deb: 5/19/2000																										
2000 Cle-A	0	1	.000	6	0	0	0	0	6^1	12	7	6	0	1	2	4	2.211	8.53	58	9.18	.400	0	....	-2	0	-0.2
2002 Sea-A	1	0	1.000	3	0	0	0	0	4	8	8	8	1	0	4	1	3.000	18.00	23	14.76	.421	0	....	-6	0	-0.6
2003 Cin-N	0	0	....	2	0	0	0	0	2	2	1	1	0	0	1	2	1.500	4.50	95	3.63	.250	0	....	-0	0	0.0
Total 3	1	1	.500	11	0	0	0	0	12^1	22	16	15	1	1	7	7	2.351	10.95	41	10.09	.386	0	....	-9	0	-0.8
• WATSON, Milt																										
Milton Wilson "Mule" Watson b: 1/10/1890, Flovilla, GA d: 4/10/1962, Pine Bluff, AR BR/TR, 6'1", 180 lbs. Deb: 7/26/1916																										
1916 StL-N	4	6	.400	18	13	5	2	0	103	109	51	35	3	4	33	27	1.379	3.06	86	3.73	.283	7	.219	-5	4	-0.5
1917 StL-N	10	13	.435	41	20	5	3	0	161^1	149	74	63	3	9	51	45	1.240	3.51	76	2.98	.252	5	.098	-17	6	-2.3
1918 Phi-N	5	7	.417	23	11	6	0	0	112^2	126	51	43	1	2	36	29	1.438	3.43	87	3.75	.293	3	.075	-5	5	-1.0
1919 Phi-N	2	4	.333	8	4	3	0	0	47	51	30	27	3	2	19	12	1.489	5.17	62	4.32	.282	1	.063	-10	0	-1.3
Total 4	21	30	.412	90	48	19	5	0	424	435	206	168	10	17	139	113	1.354	3.57	79	3.51	.274	16	.115	-37	15	-5.1
• WATSON, Mother																										
Walter L. Watson b: 1/27/1865, Middleport, OH d: 11/23/1898, Middleport, OH, 5'9", 145 lbs. Deb: 5/19/1887 ♦																										
1887 Cin-a	0	1	.000	2	2	1	0	0	14	28	18	9	0	0	6	1	2.000	5.79	75	....	.401	2	.222	-3	0	-0.3
• WATSON, Mule																										
John Reeves Watson b: 10/15/1896, Homer, LA d: 8/25/1949, Shreveport, LA BR/TR, 6'1.5", 185 lbs. Deb: 7/4/1918																										
1918 Phi-A	7	10	.412	21	19	11	3	0	141^2	139	74	53	0	2	44	30	1.292	3.37	87	3.10	.288	6	.128	-11	5	-1.6
1919 Phi-A	0	1	.000	4	2	0	0	0	14^1	17	11	11	2	0	7	6	1.674	6.91	50	6.05	.309	0	.000	-5	0	-0.6
1920 Bos-N	0	0	....	1	0	0	0	0	3	0	0	0	0	0	0	0	.000	0.00	....	0.00	.000	0	.000	1	0	0.1
Pit-N	0	0	....	5	0	0	0	0	11^1	15	11	11	2	0	7	1	1.941	8.74	37	7.37	.326	0	.000	-7	0	-0.8
Bos-N	5	4	.556	12	10	4	2	0	71^2	79	33	30	0	1	17	16	1.340	3.77	81	3.42	.298	3	.130	-7	4	-0.8
Yr.	5	4	.556	18	10	4	2	0	86	94	44	41	2	1	24	17	1.372	4.29	72	3.82	.302	3	.111	-12	4	-1.6
1921 Bos-N	14	13	.519	44	31	15	1	2	259^1	269	128	111	11	7	57	48	1.257	3.85	95	3.22	.270	12	.138	-8	12	-1.2
1922 Bos-N	8	14	.364	41	27	8	1	1	201	262	140	105	9	5	59	53	1.597	4.70	85	4.95	.317	13	.197	-13	6	-1.3
1923 Bos-N	1	2	.333	11	4	1	0	1	31^1	42	26	18	2	0	20	10	1.979	5.17	77	6.72	.339	2	.250	-4	0	-0.4
*NY-N	8	5	.615	17	15	8	0	0	108^1	117	43	41	11	1	21	26	1.274	3.41	112	3.78	.280	8	.174	4	8	0.2
Yr.	9	7	.563	28	19	9	0	1	139^2	159	69	59	13	1	41	36	1.432	3.80	102	4.44	.293	10	.185	-0	8	-0.1
1924*NY-N	7	4	.636	22	16	6	1	0	99^2	122	54	42	7	1	24	18	1.465	3.79	97	4.49	.303	9	.257	-2	6	0.2
Total 7	50	53	.485	178	124	53	8	4	941^2	1062	520	422	44	17	256	208	1.400	4.03	89	3.98	.294	53	.165	-52	41	-6.2
• WATT, Eddie																										
Eddie Dean Watt b: 4/4/1941, Lamoni, IA BR/TR, 5'10", 197 lbs. Deb: 4/12/1966																										
1966 Bal-A	9	7	.563	43	13	1	0	4	145^2	123	67	62	11	5	44	102	1.146	3.83	87	2.85	.230	14	.304	-9	8	-0.3
1967 Bal-A	3	5	.375	49	0	0	0	8	103^2	67	26	26	5	3	37	93	1.003	2.26	140	1.83	.183	4	.182	8	10	1.1
1968 Bal-A	5	5	.500	59	0	0	0	11	83^1	63	32	21	1	2	35	72	1.176	2.27	129	2.24	.209	0	.000	5	8	0.5
1969*Bal-A	5	2	.714	56	0	0	0	16	71	49	18	13	3	2	26	46	1.056	1.65	216	1.97	.194	0	.000	12	13	1.3
1970*Bal-A	7	7	.500	53	0	0	0	12	55^1	44	20	20	3	5	29	33	1.319	3.25	112	3.49	.239	1	.125	1	7	0.1
1971*Bal-A	3	1	.750	35	0	0	0	11	39^2	39	12	8	1	0	8	26	1.185	1.82	184	2.73	.260	0	.000	6	7	0.7
1972 Bal-A	2	3	.400	38	0	0	0	7	45^2	30	12	11	2	2	20	23	1.095	2.17	142	2.04	.191	0	.000	4	5	0.4
1973*Bal-A	3	4	.429	30	0	0	0	5	71	62	26	26	8	2	21	38	1.169	3.30	113	3.11	.235	0	....	0	5	0.0
1974 Phi-N	1	1	.500	42	0	0	0	6	38^1	39	20	17	3	2	26	23	1.696	3.99	95	4.96	.275	0	.000	-2	2	-0.2
1975 Chi-N	0	1	.000	6	0	0	0	0	6	14	11	9	0	1	8	6	3.667	13.50	28	14.95	.452	0	....	-6	0	-0.7
Total 10	38	36	.514	411	13	1	0	80	659^2	530	244	213	37	24	254	462	1.188	2.91	116	2.77	.222	19	.190	20	65	2.8
• WATT, Frank																										
Frank Marion "Kilowatt" Watt b: 12/15/1902, Washington, DC d: 8/31/1956, Washington, DC BR/TR, 6'1", 205 lbs. Deb: 4/14/1931																										
1931 Phi-N	5	5	.500	38	12	5	0	2	122^2	147	81	66	5	3	49	25	1.598	4.84	88	4.70	.296	8	.205	-7	5	-0.6
• WAUGH, Jim																										
James Elden Waugh b: 11/25/1933, Lancaster, OH BR/TR, 6'3", 185 lbs. Deb: 4/19/1952																										
1952 Pit-N	1	6	.143	17	7	1	0	0	52^1	61	43	37	4	2	32	18	1.777	6.36	63	5.54	.285	1	.100	-13	0	-1.4
1953 Pit-N	4	5	.444	29	11	1	0	0	90^1	108	70	65	21	0	56	23	1.815	6.48	69	7.07	.295	5	.227	-20	1	-1.8
Total 2	5	11	.313	46	18	2	0	0	142^2	169	113	102	25	2	88	41	1.801	6.43	67	6.51	.291	6	.188	-33	1	-3.2
• WAYENBERG, Frank																										
Frank Wayenberg b: 8/27/1898, Franklin, KS d: 4/16/1975, Zanesville, OH BR/TR, 6'.5", 172 lbs. Deb: 8/25/1924																										
1924 Cle-A	0	0	....	2	1	0	0	0	6^2	7	4	4	0	1	5	3	1.800	5.40	79	4.79	.259	1	.500	-1	0	0.0
• WAYNE, Gary																										
Gary Anthony Wayne b: 11/30/1962, Dearborn, MI BL/TL, 6'3", 192 lbs. Deb: 4/7/1989																										
1989 Min-A	3	4	.429	60	0	0	0	1	71	55	28	26	4	1	36	41	1.282	3.30	126	2.90	.212	0	....	7	6	0.7
1990 Min-A	1	1	.500	38	0	0	0	1	38^2	38	19	18	5	1	13	28	1.319	4.19	99	4.00	.255	0	....	-0	2	0.0
1991 Min-A	1	0	1.000	8	0	0	0	1	12^1	11	7	7	1	1	4	7	1.216	5.11	83	3.38	.244	0	....	-1	1	-0.1
1992 Min-A	3	3	.500	41	0	0	0	0	48	46	18	14	2	3	19	29	1.354	2.63	154	3.43	.260	0	....	7	4	0.7
1993 Col-N	5	3	.625	65	0	0	0	1	62^1	68	40	35	8	1	26	49	1.508	5.05	94	4.58	.276	1	1.000	0	4	0.0
1994 LA-N	1	3	.250	19	0	0	0	0	17^1	19	13	9	2	3	6	10	1.442	4.67	84	4.97	.279	0	.000	-1	0	-0.1
Total 6	14	14	.500	231	0	0	0	4	249^2	237	125	109	22	10	104	164	1.366	3.93	109	3.76	.251	1	.500	12	17	1.2
• WAYNE, Justin																										
Justin Morgan Wayne b: 4/16/1979, Honolulu, HI BR/TR, 6'3", 200 lbs. Deb: 9/3/2002																										
2002 Fla-N	2	3	.400	5	5	0	0	0	23^2	22	16	14	3	0	13	16	1.479	5.32	74	4.41	.244	0	.000	-4	0	-0.5
2003 Fla-N	0	2	.000	2	2	0	0	0	5^1	9	7	7	1	1	5	1	2.625	11.81	35	12.39	.375	0	.000	-5	0	-0.5
Total 2	2	5	.286	7	7	0	0	0	29	31	23	21	4	1	18	17	1.690	6.52	61	5.87	.272	0	.000	-8	0	-0.9

YEAR TM-L	W	L	PCT	G	GS	CG	SH	SV	IP	H	R	ER	HR	HB	BB	SO	RAT	ERA	ERA+	CERA	OAV	BH	AVG	PR+	WS	TPW
• WEAFER, Ken				Kenneth Albert "Al" Weafer b: 2/6/1914, Woburn, MA BR/TR, 6'.5", 183 lbs. Deb: 5/29/1936																						
1936 Bos-N	0	0	....	1	0	0	0	0	3	6	4	4	1	0	3	0	3.000	12.00	32	14.46	.375	0	.000	-3	0	-0.3
• WEATHERS, Dave				John David Weathers b: 9/25/1969, Lawrenceburg, TN BR/TR, 6'3", 205 lbs. Deb: 8/2/1991																						
1991 Tor-A	1	0	1.000	15	0	0	0	0	14^2	15	9	8	1	2	17	13	2.182	4.91	86	6.88	.263	0	....	-1	1	-0.1
1992 Tor-A	0	0	....	2	0	0	0	0	3^1	5	3	3	1	0	2	3	2.100	8.10	50	10.97	.385	0	....	-1	0	-0.2
1993 Fla-N	2	3	.400	14	6	0	0	0	45^2	57	26	26	3	1	13	34	1.533	5.12	84	4.86	.306	1	.100	-3	1	-0.4
1994 Fla-N	8	12	.400	24	24	0	0	0	135	166	87	79	13	4	59	72	**1.667**	5.27	83	5.52	.306	3	.068	-15	3	-1.7
1995 Fla-N	4	5	.444	28	15	0	0	0	90^1	104	68	60	8	5	52	60	1.727	5.98	70	5.79	.295	4	.154	-18	0	-1.8
1996 Fla-N	2	2	.500	31	8	0	0	0	71^1	85	41	36	7	4	28	40	1.584	4.54	90	5.35	.302	3	.158	-5	3	-0.4
*NY-A	0	2	.000	11	4	0	0	0	17^1	23	19	18	1	2	14	13	2.135	9.35	53	7.66	.315	0	....	-8	0	-0.7
1997 NY-A	0	1	.000	10	0	0	0	0	9	15	10	10	1	0	7	4	2.444	10.00	45	10.26	.375	0	....	-5	0	-0.5
Cle-A	1	2	.333	9	1	0	0	0	16^2	23	14	14	2	1	8	14	1.860	7.56	62	7.23	.343	0	....	-5	0	-0.5
Yr.	1	3	.250	19	1	0	0	0	25^2	38	24	24	3	1	15	18	2.065	8.42	55	8.29	.355	0	....	-11	0	-1.0
1998 Cin-N	2	4	.333	16	9	0	0	0	62^1	86	47	43	3	1	27	51	1.813	6.21	69	6.04	.330	1	.067	-13	0	-1.3
Mil-N	4	1	.800	28	0	0	0	0	47^2	44	22	17	3	2	14	43	1.217	3.21	133	3.15	.246	1	.125	5	4	0.5
Yr.	6	5	.545	44	9	0	0	0	110	130	69	60	6	3	41	94	1.555	4.91	87	4.79	.295	2	.087	-8	4	-0.8
1999 Mil-N	7	4	.636	63	0	0	0	2	93	102	49	48	14	2	38	74	1.505	4.65	98	5.04	.279	1	.143	-0	6	0.0
2000 Mil-N	3	5	.375	69	0	0	0	1	76^1	73	29	26	7	2	32	50	1.376	3.07	148	3.90	.260	0	.000	11	7	1.1
2001 Mil-N	3	4	.429	52	0	0	0	4	57^2	37	14	13	3	2	25	46	1.075	2.03	211	2.01	.188	0	.000	14	8	1.4
Chi-N	1	1	.500	28	0	0	0	0	28^1	28	10	10	3	1	9	20	1.306	3.18	130	3.90	.269	0	....	4	2	0.3
Yr.	4	5	.444	80	0	0	0	4	86	65	24	23	6	3	34	66	1.151	2.41	176	2.63	.216	0	.000	18	10	1.8
2002 NY-N	6	3	.667	71	0	0	0	0	77^1	69	30	25	6	3	36	61	1.358	2.91	136	3.60	.245	0	.000	10	7	1.0
2003 NY-N	1	6	.143	77	0	0	0	7	87^2	87	33	30	6	6	40	75	1.449	3.08	135	4.21	.264	0	.000	11	8	1.0
Total 13	**45**	**55**	**.450**	**548**	**67**	**0**	**0**	**14**	**933^2**	**1019**	**511**	**466**	**82**	**38**	**421**	**673**	**1.542**	**4.49**	**96**	**4.85**	**.282**	**14**	**.104**	**-21**	**50**	**-2.3**
• WEAVER, Eric				James Eric Weaver b: 8/4/1973, Springfield, IL BR/TR, 6'5", 230 lbs. Deb: 5/30/1998																						
1998 LA-N	2	0	1.000	7	0	0	0	0	9^2	5	1	1	1	0	6	5	1.138	0.93	426	2.77	.179	0	.000	3	2	0.3
1999 Sea-A	0	1	.000	8	0	0	0	0	9^1	14	12	11	2	0	8	14	2.357	10.61	47	9.41	.318	0	....	-6	0	-0.5
2000 Ana-A	0	2	.000	17	0	0	0	0	18^1	20	16	14	5	0	16	8	1.964	6.87	74	7.69	.267	0	....	-4	0	-0.4
Total 3	**2**	**3**	**.400**	**32**	**0**	**0**	**0**	**0**	**37^1**	**39**	**29**	**26**	**8**	**0**	**30**	**27**	**1.848**	**6.27**	**79**	**6.85**	**.265**	**0**	**.000**	**-7**	**2**	**-0.6**
• WEAVER, Floyd				David Floyd Weaver b: 5/12/1941, Ben Franklin, TX BR/TR, 6'4", 195 lbs. Deb: 9/30/1962																						
1962 Cle-A	1	0	1.000	1	1	0	0	0	5	3	1	1	1	0	0	8	.600	1.80	215	1.30	.167	1	.500	1	1	0.1
1965 Cle-A	2	2	.500	32	1	0	0	1	61^1	61	40	37	10	5	24	37	1.386	5.43	64	4.72	.265	1	.091	-13	0	-1.4
1970 Chi-A	1	2	.333	31	3	0	0	0	61^2	52	33	30	7	2	31	51	1.346	4.38	89	3.74	.233	0	.000	-2	2	-0.3
1971 Mil-A	0	1	.000	21	0	0	0	0	27^1	33	22	22	3	1	18	12	1.866	7.24	48	6.32	.320	0	....	-12	0	-1.3
Total 4	**4**	**5**	**.444**	**85**	**5**	**0**	**0**	**1**	**155^1**	**149**	**96**	**90**	**21**	**8**	**73**	**108**	**1.429**	**5.21**	**69**	**4.50**	**.260**	**2**	**.100**	**-26**	**3**	**-2.8**
• WEAVER, Harry				Harry Abraham Weaver b: 2/26/1892, Clarendon, PA d: 5/30/1983, Rochester, NY BR/TR, 5'11", 160 lbs. Deb: 9/18/1915																						
1915 Phi-A	0	2	.000	2	2	2	0	0	18	18	10	6	1	1	10	1	1.556	3.00	97	4.96	.290	1	.167	-0	0	0.0
1916 Phi-A	0	0	....	3	0	0	0	0	8	14	10	9	0	0	5	2	2.375	10.13	28	9.57	.424	1	.500	-6	0	-0.7
1917 Chi-N	1	1	.500	4	2	1	1	0	19^2	17	10	6	0	0	7	8	1.220	2.75	105	2.43	.230	1	.200	1	1	0.1
1918 Chi-N	2	2	.500	8	3	1	1	1	32^2	27	13	8	1	0	7	9	1.041	2.20	126	2.03	.227	2	.250	3	2	0.3
1919 Chi-N	0	1	.000	2	1	0	0	0	3^1	6	7	4	0	1	2	1	2.400	10.80	27	9.83	.375	0	.000	-3	0	-0.3
Total 5	**3**	**6**	**.333**	**19**	**8**	**4**	**2**	**1**	**81^2**	**82**	**50**	**33**	**2**	**2**	**31**	**21**	**1.384**	**3.64**	**79**	**3.83**	**.270**	**5**	**.227**	**-6**	**3**	**-0.6**
• WEAVER, Jeff				Jeffrey Charles Weaver b: 8/22/1976, Northridge, CA BR/TR, 6'5", 200 lbs. Deb: 4/14/1999																						
1999 Det-A	9	12	.429	30	29	0	0	0	163^2	176	104	101	27	17	56	114	1.418	5.55	89	5.21	.278	2	.500	-11	7	-0.9
2000 Det-A	11	15	.423	31	30	2	0	0	200	205	102	96	26	15	52	136	1.285	4.32	112	4.18	.266	0	.000	12	12	1.1
2001 Det-A	13	16	.448	33	33	5	0	0	229^1	235	116	104	19	14	68	152	1.321	4.08	106	3.89	.266	0	.000	10	13	0.9
2002 Det-A	6	8	.429	17	17	3	3	0	121^2	112	50	43	4	8	33	75	1.192	3.18	135	2.94	.243	2	.286	16	9	1.6
*NY-A	5	3	.625	15	8	0	0	2	78	81	38	35	12	3	15	57	1.231	4.04	108	3.86	.260	0	....	5	5	0.5
Yr.	11	11	.500	32	25	3	**3**	2	199^2	193	88	78	16	11	48	132	1.207	3.52	123	3.30	.250	2	.286	21	14	2.1
2003*NY-A	7	9	.438	32	24	0	0	0	159^1	211	113	106	16	11	47	93	1.619	5.99	73	5.77	.320	0	....	-25	2	-2.4
Total 5	**51**	**63**	**.447**	**158**	**141**	**10**	**3**	**2**	**952**	**1020**	**523**	**485**	**104**	**68**	**271**	**627**	**1.356**	**4.59**	**99**	**4.37**	**.274**	**4**	**.211**	**7**	**48**	**0.8**
• WEAVER, Jim				James Brian "Fluff" Weaver b: 2/19/1939, Lancaster, PA BL/TL, 6', 178 lbs. Deb: 8/13/1967																						
1967 Cal-A	3	0	1.000	13	2	0	0	1	30^1	26	11	9	2	1	9	20	1.154	2.67	118	2.78	.232	0	.000	1	3	0.1
1968 Cal-A	0	1	.000	14	0	0	0	0	22^2	22	7	6	4	0	10	8	1.412	2.38	122	4.53	.259	0	.000	1	1	0.1
Total 2	**3**	**1**	**.750**	**27**	**2**	**0**	**0**	**1**	**53**	**48**	**18**	**15**	**6**	**1**	**19**	**28**	**1.264**	**2.55**	**119**	**3.52**	**.244**	**0**	**.000**	**2**	**4**	**0.2**
• WEAVER, Jim				James Dement "Big Jim" Weaver b: 11/25/1903, Obion County, TN d: 12/12/1983, Lakeland, FL BR/TR, 6'6", 230 lbs. Deb: 8/27/1928																						
1928 Was-A	0	0	....	3	0	0	0	0	6	2	2	1	0	1	6	2	1.333	1.50	267	2.70	.143	0	.000	2	1	0.1
1931 NY-A	2	1	.667	17	5	2	0	0	57^2	66	37	34	1	1	29	28	1.647	5.31	75	4.49	.280	1	.050	-9	1	-1.1
1934 StL-A	2	0	1.000	5	5	2	0	0	19^2	17	14	14	3	0	20	11	1.881	6.41	78	5.89	.236	1	.143	-3	1	-0.3
Chi-N	11	9	.550	27	20	8	1	0	159	163	77	69	5	4	54	98	1.365	3.91	99	3.47	.263	3	.058	-2	9	-0.7
1935 Pit-N	14	8	.636	33	22	11	**4**	0	176^1	177	85	67	9	2	58	87	1.333	3.42	120	3.37	.254	4	.071	15	12	1.1
1936 Pit-N	14	8	.636	38	31	11	1	0	225^2	239	125	108	12	1	74	108	1.387	4.31	94	3.72	.272	8	.101	-5	10	-1.0
1937 Pit-N	8	5	.615	32	9	2	1	0	109^2	106	49	39	2	0	31	44	1.249	3.20	121	2.84	.255	4	.148	7	8	0.7
1938 StL-A	0	1	.000	1	1	0	0	0	7	9	7	7	0	0	9	4	2.571	9.00	55	7.94	.321	0	.000	-3	0	-0.3
Cin-N	6	4	.600	30	15	2	0	3	129^1	109	58	45	6	1	54	64	1.260	3.13	116	2.80	.227	9	.205	5	9	0.6
1939 Cin-N	0	0	....	3	0	0	0	0	3	3	1	1	0	0	1	3	1.333	3.00	128	2.97	.250	0	.000	0	0	0.0
Total 8	**57**	**36**	**.613**	**189**	**108**	**38**	**7**	**3**	**893^1**	**891**	**455**	**385**	**38**	**10**	**336**	**449**	**1.374**	**3.88**	**103**	**3.48**	**.258**	**30**	**.104**	**8**	**51**	**-0.8**
• WEAVER, Monte				Montgomery Morton "Prof" Weaver b: 6/15/1906, Helton, NC d: 6/14/1994, Orlando, FL BL/TR, 6', 170 lbs. Deb: 9/20/1931																						
1931 Was-A	1	0	1.000	3	1	1	0	0	10	11	6	5	0	0	6	6	1.700	4.50	95	4.26	.268	0	.000	-0	1	-0.1
1932 Was-A	22	10	.688	43	30	13	1	2	234	236	126	106	9	0	112	83	1.487	4.08	106	3.86	.261	27	.287	0	19	0.5
1933*Was-A	10	5	.667	23	21	12	1	0	152^1	147	57	55	3	1	53	45	1.313	3.25	129	3.16	.257	7	.125	12	12	0.9
1934 Was-A	11	15	.423	31	31	11	0	0	204^2	255	127	109	16	0	63	51	1.554	4.79	90	4.84	.306	13	.163	-10	8	-1.1
1935 Was-A	1	1	.500	5	2	0	0	0	12	16	8	7	1	0	6	4	1.833	5.25	82	6.15	.320	1	.333	-1	0	-0.1
1936 Was-A	6	4	.600	26	5	3	0	1	91	92	57	44	3	0	38	15	1.429	4.35	110	3.58	.262	5	.200	3	6	0.3
1937 Was-A	12	9	.571	30	26	9	0	0	188^2	197	102	88	21	0	70	44	1.415	4.20	105	4.22	.266	14	.206	2	11	0.3
1938 Was-A	7	6	.538	31	18	7	0	0	139	157	93	81	9	3	74	43	1.662	5.24	86	4.93	.282	12	.267	-12	6	-0.7
1939 Bos-A	1	0	1.000	9	1	1	0	1	20^1	26	15	15	0	1	13	6	1.918	6.64	71	5.82	.321	0	.000	-4	1	-0.5
Total 9	**71**	**50**	**.587**	**201**	**135**	**57**	**2**	**4**	**1052**	**1137**	**591**	**510**	**62**	**5**	**435**	**297**	**1.494**	**4.36**	**101**	**4.20**	**.275**	**79**	**.209**	**-9**	**64**	**-0.4**
• WEAVER, Orlie				Orville Forest Weaver b: 6/4/1886, Newport, KY d: 11/28/1970, New Orleans, LA BR/TR, 6', 180 lbs. Deb: 9/14/1910																						
1910 Chi-N	1	1	.500	7	2	2	0	0	32	34	17	13	2	1	15	22	1.531	3.66	79	4.44	.270	2	.154	-3	1	-0.4
1911 Chi-N	2	2	.500	6	3	1	1	0	43^2	29	12	10	0	4	17	20	1.053	2.06	160	2.02	.196	1	.059	5	4	0.4
Bos-N	3	12	.200	27	17	4	0	0	121	140	102	87	9	7	84	50	1.851	6.47	59	6.32	.303	5	.122	-33	0	-3.5
Yr.	5	14	.263	33	20	5	1	0	164^2	169	114	97	9	11	101	70	**1.640**	5.30	71	5.18	.277	6	.103	-28	4	-3.1
Total 2	**6**	**15**	**.286**	**40**	**22**	**7**	**1**	**0**	**196^2**	**203**	**131**	**110**	**11**	**12**	**116**	**92**	**1.622**	**5.03**	**72**	**5.06**	**.276**	**8**	**.113**	**-31**	**5**	**-3.5**
• WEAVER, Roger				Roger Edward Weaver b: 10/6/1954, Amsterdam, NY BR/TR, 6'3", 190 lbs. Deb: 6/6/1980																						
1980 Det-A	3	4	.429	19	6	0	0	0	63^2	56	32	29	5	1	34	42	1.414	4.10	100	3.89	.247	0	....	1	3	0.1
• WEAVER, Sam				Samuel H. Weaver b: 7/10/1855, Philadelphia, PA d: 2/1/1914, Philadelphia, PA BR/TR, 5'10", 175 lbs. Deb: 10/25/1875																						
1875 Phi-n	1	0	1.000	1	1	1	0	0	6	6	....	1	0	....	2	2	1.333	1.50	168	....	.237	1	.250	1	....	0.1
1878 Mil-N	12	31	.279	45	43	39	1	0	383	371	214	83	2	....	21	95	1.023	1.95	134	....	.242	34	.200	**49**	18	**4.5**

YEAR TM-L	W	L	PCT	G	GS	CG	SH	SV	IP	H	R	ER	HR	HB	BB	SO	RAT	ERA	ERA+	CERA	OAV	BH	AVG	PR+	WS	TPW
1882 Phi-a	26	15	.634	42	41	41	2	0	371	374	182	113	6	....	35	104	1.102	2.74	109	....	.245	36	.232	3	33	0.6
1883 Lou-a	24	22	.522	46	46	45	4	0	400^{2}	451	261	165	3	....	35	105	1.213	3.71	77	....	.266	37	.192	-32	24	-2.9
1884 Phi-U	5	10	.333	17	17	14	0	0	136	206	146	87	3	....	11	40	**1.596**	5.76	50	....	.328	18	.214	-37	2	-3.4
1886 Phi-a	0	2	.000	2	2	1	0	0	11	30	29	18	0	1	2	2	2.909	14.73	24	....	.474	1	.143	-13	0	-1.2
Total 5	67	80	.456	152	149	140	7	0	1301^{2}	1432	832	466	14	1	104	346	1.180	3.22	89	....	.263	126	.207	-29	77	-2.5
• WEBB, Bill	Willie Fred Webb b: 12/12/1913, Atlanta, GA d: 6/1/1994, Austell, GA BR/TR, 6'2", 180 lbs. Deb: 5/15/1943																									
1943 Phi-N	0	0	....	1	0	0	0	0	1	1	1	1	1	0	1	0	2.000	9.00	37	17.60	.333	0	....	-1	0	-0.1
• WEBB, Brandon	Brandon Tyler Webb b: 5/9/1979, Ashland, KY BR/TR, 6'3", 228 lbs. Deb: 4/22/2003																									
2003 Ari-N	10	9	.526	29	28	1	1	0	180^{2}	140	65	57	12	13	68	172	1.151	2.84	164	2.80	.212	5	.100	38	17	3.6
• WEBB, Hank	Henry Gaylon Matthew Webb b: 5/21/1950, Copiague, NY BR/TR, 6'3", 175 lbs. Deb: 9/5/1972																									
1972 NY-N	0	0	....	6	2	0	0	0	18^{1}	18	9	9	1	0	9	15	1.473	4.42	76	3.97	.261	0	.000	-2	0	-0.3
1973 NY-N	0	0	....	2	0	0	0	0	1^{2}	2	2	2	1	0	2	1	2.400	10.80	33	13.35	.286	0	....	-1	0	-0.1
1974 NY-N	0	2	.000	3	2	0	0	0	10	15	9	8	1	1	10	8	2.500	7.20	49	10.23	.341	0	.000	-4	0	-0.5
1975 NY-N	7	6	.538	29	15	3	1	0	115	102	58	52	12	1	62	38	1.426	4.07	85	3.97	.236	8	.258	-9	5	-0.8
1976 NY-N	0	1	.000	8	0	0	0	0	16	17	9	8	2	2	7	7	1.500	4.50	73	5.15	.274	0	.000	-2	0	-0.2
1977 LA-N	0	0	....	5	0	0	0	0	8	5	2	2	1	1	1	2	.750	2.25	170	1.92	.192	0	....	1	1	0.1
Total 6	7	9	.438	53	19	3	1	0	169	159	89	81	18	5	91	71	1.479	4.31	80	4.45	.248	8	.200	-18	6	-1.7
• WEBB, Lefty	Cleon Earl Webb b: 3/1/1885, Mount Gilead, OH d: 1/12/1958, Circleville, OH BB/TL, 5'11", 165 lbs. Deb: 5/23/1910																									
1910 Pit-N	2	1	.667	7	3	2	0	0	27	29	17	17	0	2	9	6	1.407	5.67	55	3.62	.266	2	.200	-8	0	-0.8
• WEBB, Red	Samuel Henry Webb b: 9/25/1924, Washington, DC d: 2/7/1996, Hyattsville, MD BL/TR, 6', 175 lbs. Deb: 9/15/1948																									
1948 NY-N	2	1	.667	5	3	2	0	0	28	27	12	10	2	1	10	9	1.321	3.21	122	3.41	.248	2	.222	2	2	0.2
1949 NY-N	1	1	.500	20	0	0	0	0	44^{2}	41	23	20	3	0	21	9	1.388	4.03	99	3.59	.248	4	.400	-0	2	0.2
Total 2	3	2	.600	25	3	2	0	0	72^{2}	68	35	30	5	1	31	18	1.362	3.72	107	3.52	.248	6	.316	2	4	0.4
• WEBBER, Les	Lester Elmer Webber b: 5/6/1915, Kelseyville, CA d: 11/13/1986, Santa Maria, CA BR/TR, 6'.5", 185 lbs. Deb: 5/17/1942																									
1942 Bro-N	3	2	.600	19	3	1	0	1	51^{2}	46	17	17	2	0	22	23	1.316	2.96	110	3.00	.235	1	.071	1	4	0.0
1943 Bro-N	2	2	.500	54	0	0	0	**10**	115^{2}	112	54	49	6	5	69	24	1.565	3.81	88	4.35	.264	3	.120	-4	5	-0.5
1944 Bro-N	7	8	.467	48	9	1	0	3	140^{1}	157	85	77	9	1	64	42	1.575	4.94	72	4.53	.282	8	.205	-17	3	-1.6
1945 Bro-N	7	3	.700	17	7	5	0	0	75^{1}	69	37	30	3	1	25	30	1.248	3.58	105	2.88	.237	2	.091	2	5	0.1
1946 Bro-N	3	3	.500	11	4	0	0	0	43	34	11	11	5	0	15	16	1.140	2.30	147	2.88	.225	1	.100	5	4	0.4
Cle-A	1	1	.500	4	2	0	0	0	5^{1}	13	14	14	0	0	5	5	3.375	23.63	14	14.53	.464	0	.000	-12	0	-1.2
1948 Cle-A	0	0	....	1	0	0	0	0	0^{2}	3	3	3	0	0	1	1	6.000	40.50	10	33.87	.750	0	....	-3	0	-0.3
Total 6	23	19	.548	154	25	7	0	14	432	434	221	201	25	7	201	141	1.470	4.19	83	4.01	.263	15	.135	-28	21	-3.1
• WEBER, Ben	Benjamin Edward Weber b: 11/17/1969, Port Arthur, TX BR/TR, 6'4", 212 lbs. Deb: 4/3/2000																									
2000 SF-N	0	1	.000	9	0	0	0	0	8	16	13	13	0	0	4	6	2.500	14.63	29	9.72	.400	0	....	-9	0	-0.9
Ana-A	1	0	1.000	10	0	0	0	0	14^{2}	12	6	3	0	0	2	8	.955	1.84	275	1.52	.214	0	....	5	2	0.5
2001 Ana-A	6	2	.750	56	0	0	0	0	68^{1}	66	28	26	4	5	31	40	1.420	3.42	133	3.90	.251	0	....	8	7	0.8
2002* Ana-A	7	2	.778	63	0	0	0	7	78	70	25	22	4	3	22	43	1.179	2.54	174	2.96	.249	0	....	14	11	1.3
2003 Ana-A	5	1	.833	62	0	0	0	0	80^{1}	84	26	24	7	0	22	46	1.320	2.69	160	3.71	.275	0	....	13	8	1.3
Total 4	19	6	.760	200	0	0	0	7	249^{1}	248	98	88	15	8	81	143	1.320	3.18	139	3.59	.262	0	....	31	28	3.0
• WEBER, Charlie	Charles P. "Count" Weber b: 10/22/1868, Cincinnati, OH d: 6/13/1914, Beaumont, TX TR Deb: 7/30/1898																									
1898 Was-N	0	1	.000	1	1	0	0	0	4	9	9	7	0	2	1	0	2.500	15.75	23	12.68	.440	0	.000	-5	0	-0.5
• WEBER, Neil	Neil Aaron Weber b: 12/6/1972, Newport Beach, CA BL/TL, 6'5" Deb: 9/11/1998																									
1998 Ari-N	0	0	....	4	0	0	0	0	2^{1}	5	3	3	0	0	3	4	3.429	11.57	36	14.38	.417	0	....	-2	0	-0.2
• WEGENER, Mike	Michael Denis Wegener b: 10/8/1946, Denver, CO BR/TR, 6'4", 215 lbs. Deb: 4/9/1969																									
1969 Mon-N	5	14	.263	32	26	4	1	0	165^{2}	150	92	81	10	4	96	124	1.485	4.40	84	3.98	.243	13	.241	-13	5	-1.1
1970 Mon-N	3	6	.333	25	16	1	0	0	104^{1}	100	70	61	16	4	56	35	1.495	5.26	78	4.91	.252	4	.118	-14	1	-1.6
Total 2	8	20	.286	57	42	5	1	0	270	250	162	142	26	8	152	159	1.489	4.73	81	4.34	.247	17	.193	-27	6	-2.6
• WEGMAN, Bill	William Edward Wegman b: 12/19/1962, Cincinnati, OH BR/TR, 6'5", 220 lbs. Deb: 9/14/1985																									
1985 Mil-A	2	0	1.000	3	3	0	0	0	17^{2}	17	8	7	3	0	3	6	1.132	3.57	117	3.35	.246	0	....	1	2	0.1
1986 Mil-A	5	12	.294	35	32	2	0	0	198^{1}	217	120	113	32	7	43	82	1.311	5.13	84	4.48	.279	0	....	-16	6	-1.6
1987 Mil-A	12	11	.522	34	33	7	0	0	225	229	113	106	31	6	53	102	1.253	4.24	108	3.92	.265	0	....	10	14	1.0
1988 Mil-A	13	13	.500	32	31	4	1	0	199	207	104	91	24	4	50	84	1.291	4.12	97	3.86	.265	0	....	-5	9	-0.5
1989 Mil-A	2	6	.250	11	8	0	0	0	51	69	44	38	6	0	21	27	1.765	6.71	57	6.21	.321	0	....	-16	0	-1.7
1990 Mil-A	2	2	.500	8	5	1	1	0	29^{2}	37	21	16	6	0	6	20	1.449	4.85	80	5.25	.298	0	....	-3	0	-0.3
1991 Mil-A	15	7	.682	28	28	7	2	0	193^{1}	176	76	61	16	7	40	89	1.117	2.84	140	2.90	.242	0	....	24	15	2.4
1992 Mil-A	13	14	.481	35	35	7	0	0	261^{2}	251	104	93	28	9	55	127	1.169	3.20	120	3.28	.250	0	....	13	16	1.3
1993 Mil-A	4	14	.222	20	18	5	0	0	120^{2}	135	70	60	13	2	34	50	1.401	4.48	95	4.40	.291	0	....	-2	4	-0.2
1994 Mil-A	8	4	.667	19	19	0	0	0	115^{2}	140	64	58	14	2	26	59	1.435	4.51	111	4.83	.303	0	....	3	7	0.3
1995 Mil-A	5	7	.417	37	4	0	0	2	70^{2}	89	45	42	14	3	21	50	1.557	5.35	93	6.13	.312	0	....	-4	3	-0.4
Total 11	81	90	.474	262	216	33	4	2	1482^{2}	1567	769	685	187	40	352	696	1.294	4.16	102	4.06	.271	0	....	5	76	0.5
• WEHDE, Biggs	Wilbur Wehde b: 11/23/1906, Holstein, IA d: 9/21/1970, Sioux Falls, SD BR/TR, 5'10.5", 180 lbs. Deb: 9/15/1930																									
1930 Chi-A	0	0	....	4	0	0	0	0	6^{1}	7	8	7	1	1	7	3	2.211	9.95	46	6.93	.304	0	.000	-4	0	-0.3
1931 Chi-A	1	0	1.000	8	0	0	0	0	16	19	12	12	0	2	10	3	1.813	6.75	63	6.15	.333	0	.000	-4	0	-0.4
Total 2	1	0	1.000	12	0	0	0	0	22^{1}	26	20	19	1	3	17	6	1.925	7.66	57	6.37	.325	0	.000	-8	0	-0.8
• WEHMEIER, Herm	Herman Ralph Wehmeier b: 2/18/1927, Cincinnati, OH d: 5/21/1973, Dallas, TX BR/TR, 6'2", 200 lbs. Deb: 9/7/1945																									
1945 Cin-N	0	1	.000	2	2	0	0	0	5	10	7	7	0	0	4	0	2.800	12.60	30	11.64	.435	0	.000	-5	0	-0.5
1947 Cin-N	0	0	....	1	0	0	0	0	1	0	0	0	0	0	0	0	.000	0.00	....	0.00	.000	0	....	0	0	0.0
1948 Cin-N	11	8	.579	33	24	6	0	0	147^{1}	179	105	96	21	2	75	56	1.724	5.86	67	6.06	.299	5	.091	-30	2	-3.3
1949 Cin-N	11	12	.478	33	29	11	1	0	213^{1}	202	119	111	20	7	117	80	1.495	4.68	89	4.33	.253	20	.256	-12	9	-0.9
1950 Cin-N	10	18	.357	41	32	12	0	4	230	255	157	145	27	4	135	121	**1.696**	5.67	75	5.51	.281	14	.152	-34	4	-3.6
1951 Cin-N	7	10	.412	39	22	10	2	2	184^{2}	167	82	76	15	4	89	93	1.386	3.70	110	3.70	.241	17	.288	9	13	1.2
1952 Cin-N	9	11	.450	33	26	6	1	0	190^{1}	197	115	109	23	7	103	83	1.576	5.15	73	5.05	.269	12	.188	-30	3	-2.9
1953 Cin-N	1	6	.143	28	10	2	0	0	81^{2}	100	71	65	20	0	47	32	1.800	7.16	61	7.06	.299	4	.200	-27	0	-2.6
1954 Cin-N	0	3	.000	12	3	0	0	2	33^{2}	36	29	25	6	1	21	13	1.693	6.68	63	5.89	.271	0	.000	-10	0	-1.1
Phi-N	10	8	.556	25	17	10	2	0	138	117	61	59	10	1	51	49	1.217	3.85	105	2.90	.231	6	.120	2	9	0.1
Yr.	10	11	.476	37	20	10	2	2	171^{2}	153	90	84	16	2	72	62	1.311	4.40	93	3.49	.239	6	.102	-7	9	-1.0
1955 Phi-N	10	12	.455	31	29	10	1	0	193^{2}	176	101	95	21	2	67	85	1.255	4.41	90	3.40	.241	20	.278	-12	10	-0.8
1956 Phi-N	0	2	.000	3	3	0	0	0	20	18	9	9	2	0	11	8	1.450	4.05	92	4.06	.240	0	.000	-0	1	-0.1
StL-N	12	9	.571	34	19	7	2	1	170^{2}	150	80	70	16	1	71	68	1.295	3.69	103	3.41	.240	13	.224	2	11	0.6
Yr.	12	11	.522	37	22	7	2	1	190^{2}	168	89	79	18	1	82	76	1.311	3.73	101	3.48	.240	13	.197	2	12	0.5
1957 StL-N	10	7	.588	36	18	5	0	0	165	165	91	79	25	2	54	91	1.327	4.31	92	4.03	.253	12	.203	-6	7	-0.6
1958 StL-N	0	1	.000	3	3	0	0	0	6	13	9	9	2	0	2	4	2.500	13.50	31	14.34	.448	1	.500	-6	0	-0.6
Det-A	1	0	1.000	7	3	0	0	0	22^{2}	21	8	6	2	0	5	11	1.147	2.38	169	2.90	.241	0	.000	4	2	0.4
Total 13	92	108	.460	361	240	79	9	9	1803	1806	1044	961	210	31	852	794	1.474	4.80	84	4.49	.261	124	.196	-154	71	-14.7
• WEHRMEISTER, Dave	David Thomas Wehrmeister b: 11/9/1952, Berwyn, IL BR/TR, 6'4", 195 lbs. Deb: 4/16/1976																									
1976 SD-N	0	4	.000	7	4	0	0	0	19^{1}	27	17	16	0	0	11	10	1.966	7.45	44	6.17	.333	0	.000	-9	0	-1.0
1977 SD-N	1	3	.250	30	6	0	0	0	69^{2}	81	53	47	8	3	44	32	1.794	6.07	58	6.18	.293	2	.167	-19	0	-1.9

YEAR TM-L	W	L	PCT	G	GS	CG	SH	SV	IP	H	R	ER	HR	HB	BB	SO	RAT	ERA	ERA+	CERA	OAV	BH	AVG	PR+	WS	TPW
1978 SD-N	1	0	1.000	4	0	0	0	0	7^1	8	5	5	1	0	5	2	1.773	6.14	54	5.65	.276	0	....	-2	0	-0.2
1981 NY-A	0	0	....	5	0	0	0	0	7	6	4	4	0	0	7	7	1.857	5.14	70	4.25	.240	0	....	-1	0	-0.1
1984 Phi-N	0	0	....	7	0	0	0	0	15	18	12	12	1	1	7	13	1.667	7.20	50	5.13	.300	0	.000	-6	0	-0.6
1985 Chi-A	2	2	.500	23	0	0	0	2	39^1	35	15	15	4	3	10	32	1.144	3.43	126	3.32	.241	0	....	4	3	0.4
Total 6	4	9	.308	76	10	0	0	2	157^2	175	106	99	14	7	84	96	1.643	5.65	64	5.25	.284	2	.100	-34	3	-3.6

• WEIK, Dick Richard Henry "Legs" Weik b: 11/17/1927, Waterloo, IA d: 4/21/1991, Harvey, IL BR/TR, 6'3.5", 184 lbs. Deb: 9/8/1948

YEAR TM-L	W	L	PCT	G	GS	CG	SH	SV	IP	H	R	ER	HR	HB	BB	SO	RAT	ERA	ERA+	CERA	OAV	BH	AVG	PR+	WS	TPW
1948 Was-A	1	2	.333	3	3	0	0	0	12^2	14	8	8	1	0	22	8	2.842	5.68	76	10.17	.311	3	.750	-2	1	0.0
1949 Was-A	3	12	.200	27	14	2	2	1	95^1	78	61	57	5	0	103	58	1.899	5.38	79	5.09	.230	5	.179	-8	2	-0.9
1950 Was-A	1	3	.250	14	5	1	0	0	44	38	27	21	2	0	47	26	1.932	4.30	105	5.15	.236	2	.154	1	2	0.0
Cle-A	1	3	.250	11	2	0	0	0	26	18	17	11	1	1	26	16	1.692	3.81	114	4.11	.205	1	.200	1	1	0.1
Yr.	2	6	.250	25	7	1	0	0	70	56	44	32	3	1	73	42	1.843	4.11	108	4.77	.225	3	.167	2	3	0.2
1953 Det-A	0	1	.000	12	1	0	0	0	19^1	32	30	30	3	0	23	6	2.845	13.97	29	12.12	.386	1	.500	-21	0	-2.0
1954 Det-A	0	1	.000	9	1	0	0	0	16^1	23	14	13	3	1	16	9	2.388	7.16	52	10.10	.348	0	.000	-6	0	-0.7
Total 5	6	22	.214	76	26	3	2	1	213^2	203	157	140	15	2	237	123	2.059	5.90	71	6.31	.260	12	.226	-35	6	-3.4

• WEILAND, Bob Robert George "Lefty" Weiland b: 12/14/1905, Chicago, IL d: 11/9/1988, Chicago, IL BL/TL, 6'4", 215 lbs. Deb: 9/30/1928

YEAR TM-L	W	L	PCT	G	GS	CG	SH	SV	IP	H	R	ER	HR	HB	BB	SO	RAT	ERA	ERA+	CERA	OAV	BH	AVG	PR+	WS	TPW
1928 Chi-A	1	0	1.000	1	1	1	1	0	9	7	0	0	0	1	5	9	1.333	0.00	....	3.00	.212	1	.333	4	2	0.4
1929 Chi-A	2	4	.333	15	9	1	0	1	62	62	42	40	3	3	43	25	1.694	5.81	74	4.87	.268	2	.111	-11	1	-1.2
1930 Chi-A	0	4	.000	14	3	0	0	0	32^2	38	31	24	1	2	21	15	1.806	6.61	70	5.45	.297	0	.000	-6	0	-0.7
1931 Chi-A	2	7	.222	15	8	3	0	0	75	75	55	43	3	4	46	38	1.613	5.16	82	4.35	.259	4	.182	-6	2	-0.4
1932 Bos-A	6	16	.273	43	27	7	0	1	195^2	231	125	98	11	6	97	63	1.676	4.51	100	5.14	.295	9	.148	3	9	0.2
1933 Bos-A	8	14	.364	39	27	12	0	3	216^1	197	107	93	19	5	100	97	1.373	3.87	113	3.70	.244	7	.108	12	12	0.8
1934 Bos-A	1	5	.167	11	7	2	0	0	55^2	63	41	34	4	0	27	29	1.617	5.50	87	4.79	.293	2	.105	-4	1	-0.4
Cle-A	1	5	.167	16	7	2	0	0	70	71	41	32	5	0	30	42	1.443	4.11	111	3.94	.262	3	.125	4	3	0.3
Yr.	2	10	.167	27	14	4	0	0	125^2	134	82	66	9	0	57	71	1.520	4.73	99	4.32	.276	5	.116	-0	4	-0.1
1935 StL-A	0	2	.000	14	4	0	0	0	32	39	35	34	6	1	31	11	2.188	9.56	50	8.43	.298	0	.000	-17	0	-1.7
1937 StL-N	15	14	.517	41	**34**	21	2	0	264^1	283	127	104	14	5	94	105	1.426	3.54	112	3.95	.276	15	.169	15	16	1.5
1938 StL-N	16	11	.593	35	29	11	1	1	228^1	248	118	91	14	4	67	117	1.380	3.59	110	3.82	.272	11	.138	10	13	0.7
1939 StL-N	10	12	.455	32	23	6	3	1	146^1	146	69	58	4	6	50	63	1.339	3.57	115	3.40	.264	3	.065	7	9	0.3
1940 StL-N	0	0	....	1	0	0	0	0	1	3	3	3	1	0	0	0	3.000	27.00	15	30.73	.600	0	....	-3	0	-0.3
Total 12	62	94	.397	277	179	66	7	7	1388^1	1463	794	654	85	37	611	614	1.494	4.24	101	4.25	.272	57	.129	8	68	-0.5

• WEILAND, Ed Edwin Nicholas Weiland b: 11/26/1914, Evanston, IL d: 7/12/1971, Chicago, IL BL/TR, 5'11", 180 lbs. Deb: 5/1/1940

YEAR TM-L	W	L	PCT	G	GS	CG	SH	SV	IP	H	R	ER	HR	HB	BB	SO	RAT	ERA	ERA+	CERA	OAV	BH	AVG	PR+	WS	TPW
1940 Chi-A	0	0	....	5	0	0	0	0	14^1	15	15	14	5	0	7	3	1.535	8.79	50	6.30	.263	1	.200	-7	0	-0.7
1942 Chi-A	0	0	....	5	0	0	0	0	9^2	18	11	8	0	0	3	4	2.172	7.45	48	7.69	.383	0	.000	-4	0	-0.5
Total 2	0	0	....	10	0	0	0	0	24	33	26	22	5	0	10	7	1.792	8.25	49	6.86	.317	1	.143	-11	0	-1.2

• WEILMAN, Carl Carl Woolworth "Zeke" Weilman b: 11/29/1889, Hamilton, OH d: 5/25/1924, Hamilton, OH BL/TL, 6'5.5", 187 lbs. Deb: 8/24/1912

YEAR TM-L	W	L	PCT	G	GS	CG	SH	SV	IP	H	R	ER	HR	HB	BB	SO	RAT	ERA	ERA+	CERA	OAV	BH	AVG	PR+	WS	TPW
1912 StL-A	2	4	.333	8	6	5	2	1	48^1	42	19	15	0	0	3	24	.931	2.79	119	1.62	.227	2	.118	2	4	0.2
1913 StL-A	10	19	.345	39	28	17	2	0	251^2	262	122	95	2	4	60	79	1.279	3.40	86	3.28	.281	12	.146	-17	9	-2.1
1914 StL-A	17	12	.586	44	36	20	3	1	299	260	96	69	1	11	84	119	1.151	2.08	130	2.47	.237	15	.149	24	24	2.5
1915 StL-A	18	19	.486	47	31	19	3	4	295^2	240	110	77	6	3	83	125	1.092	2.34	122	2.27	.229	23	.230	13	21	1.6
1916 StL-A	17	18	.486	46	31	19	1	2	276	237	90	66	3	8	76	91	1.134	2.15	127	2.51	.242	14	.154	12	19	1.2
1917 StL-A	1	2	.333	5	3	0	0	0	19	19	9	4	1	0	6	9	1.316	1.89	137	3.52	.268	0	.000	2	1	0.1
1919 StL-A	10	6	.625	20	20	12	3	0	148	133	51	34	3	3	45	44	1.203	2.07	160	2.76	.244	9	.191	19	14	2.0
1920 StL-A	9	13	.409	30	24	13	1	2	183^1	201	103	91	6	3	61	45	1.429	4.47	88	3.98	.291	11	.175	-12	9	-1.3
Total 8	84	93	.475	239	179	105	15	10	1521	1394	600	451	22	32	418	536	1.191	2.67	114	2.77	.251	86	.170	43	101	4.2

• WEIMER, Jake Jacob "Tornado Jake" Weimer b: 11/29/1873, Ottumwa, IA d: 6/19/1928, Chicago, IL BR/TL, 5'11", 175 lbs. Deb: 4/17/1903 U

YEAR TM-L	W	L	PCT	G	GS	CG	SH	SV	IP	H	R	ER	HR	HB	BB	SO	RAT	ERA	ERA+	CERA	OAV	BH	AVG	PR+	WS	TPW
1903 Chi-N	20	8	.714	35	33	27	3	0	282	241	111	72	4	11	104	128	1.223	2.30	136	2.65	**.225**	21	.196	22	23	2.3
1904 Chi-N	20	14	.588	37	37	31	5	0	307	229	96	65	1	7	97	177	1.062	1.91	139	1.89	.204	21	.183	20	28	2.0
1905 Chi-N	18	12	.600	33	30	26	2	1	250^1	212	84	63	1	12	80	107	1.166	2.26	131	2.48	.229	19	.207	11	21	1.3
1906 Cin-N	20	14	.588	41	39	31	6	1	304^2	263	105	75	0	13	99	141	1.188	2.22	124	2.58	.236	29	.269	15	27	2.4
1907 Cin-N	11	14	.440	29	26	19	3	0	209	165	73	56	6	23	63	67	1.091	2.41	107	2.62	.226	14	.194	2	11	0.4
1908 Cin-N	8	7	.533	15	15	9	2	0	116^2	110	38	31	2	6	50	36	1.371	2.39	96	3.50	.255	11	.244	0	9	0.3
1909 NY-N	0	0	....	1	0	0	0	0	3	7	4	3	0	1	0	1	2.333	9.00	28	11.88	.467	0	.000	-2	0	-0.2
Total 7	97	69	.584	191	180	143	21	2	1472^2	1227	511	365	14	73	493	657	1.168	2.23	124	2.53	.227	115	.213	68	119	8.4

• WEINERT, Lefty Phillip Walter Weinert b: 4/21/1902, Philadelphia, PA d: 4/17/1973, Rockledge, FL BL/TL, 6'1", 195 lbs. Deb: 9/24/1919

YEAR TM-L	W	L	PCT	G	GS	CG	SH	SV	IP	H	R	ER	HR	HB	BB	SO	RAT	ERA	ERA+	CERA	OAV	BH	AVG	PR+	WS	TPW
1919 Phi-N	0	0	....	1	0	0	0	0	4	11	9	8	0	0	2	0	3.250	18.00	18	14.93	.478	2	1.000	-7	1	-0.6
1920 Phi-N	1	1	.500	10	2	0	0	0	22	27	17	15	1	1	19	10	2.091	6.14	56	7.08	.333	0	.000	-7	0	-0.8
1921 Phi-N	1	0	1.000	8	0	0	0	0	12^1	8	6	2	1	1	5	2	1.054	1.46	289	2.60	.216	1	1.000	4	2	0.4
1922 Phi-N	8	11	.421	34	22	10	0	1	166^2	189	103	63	10	5	70	58	1.554	3.40	137	4.54	.289	14	.241	24	12	2.3
1923 Phi-N	4	17	.190	38	20	8	0	1	156	207	131	94	10	8	81	46	**1.846**	5.42	85	6.33	.327	19	.322	-10	4	-0.7
1924 Phi-N	0	1	.000	8	1	0	0	0	14^2	10	7	4	0	0	11	7	1.432	2.45	182	2.74	.204	0	.000	4	1	0.3
1927 Chi-N	1	1	.500	5	3	1	0	0	19^2	21	13	10	2	0	6	5	1.373	4.58	84	3.72	.259	1	.200	-2	0	-0.2
1928 Chi-N	1	0	1.000	10	1	0	0	0	17	24	10	10	0	1	9	8	1.941	5.29	73	7.12	.393	0	.000	-3	1	-0.4
1931 NY-A	2	2	.500	17	0	0	0	0	24^2	31	19	17	2	5	19	24	2.027	6.20	64	7.42	.316	0	.000	-6	0	-0.6
Total 9	18	33	.353	131	49	19	0	2	437	528	315	223	26	21	222	160	1.716	4.59	94	5.51	.307	37	.261	-3	21	-0.1

• WEIR, Roy William Franklin "Bill" Weir b: 2/25/1911, Portland, ME d: 9/30/1989, Anaheim, CA BL/TL, 5'8.5", 170 lbs. Deb: 6/25/1936

YEAR TM-L	W	L	PCT	G	GS	CG	SH	SV	IP	H	R	ER	HR	HB	BB	SO	RAT	ERA	ERA+	CERA	OAV	BH	AVG	PR+	WS	TPW
1936 Bos-N	4	3	.571	12	7	3	2	0	57^1	53	23	18	0	0	24	29	1.343	2.83	136	2.92	.241	5	.278	6	6	0.8
1937 Bos-N	1	1	.500	10	4	1	0	0	33	27	18	14	0	0	19	8	1.394	3.82	94	2.95	.227	0	.000	-2	1	-0.3
1938 Bos-N	1	0	1.000	5	0	0	0	0	13^1	14	10	10	4	0	6	3	1.500	6.75	51	5.91	.269	1	.333	-5	0	-0.5
1939 Bos-N	0	0	....	2	0	0	0	0	2^2	1	0	0	0	0	1	2	.750	0.00	....	0.81	.125	0	.000	1	0	0.1
Total 4	6	4	.600	29	11	4	2	0	106^1	95	51	42	4	0	50	42	1.364	3.55	103	3.25	.238	6	.188	0	7	0.1

• WELCH, Bob Robert Lynn Welch b: 11/3/1956, Detroit, MI BR/TR, 6'3", 190 lbs. Deb: 6/20/1978 C

YEAR TM-L	W	L	PCT	G	GS	CG	SH	SV	IP	H	R	ER	HR	HB	BB	SO	RAT	ERA	ERA+	CERA	OAV	BH	AVG	PR+	WS	TPW
1978* LA-N	7	4	.636	23	13	4	3	3	111^1	92	28	25	6	1	26	66	1.060	2.02	173	2.32	.229	5	.172	18	12	1.9
1979 LA-N	5	6	.455	25	12	1	0	5	81^1	82	42	36	7	3	32	64	1.402	3.98	91	4.12	.265	3	.158	-2	4	-0.2
1980 LA-N★	14	9	.609	32	32	3	2	0	213^2	190	85	78	15	3	79	141	1.259	3.29	106	3.20	.242	17	.243	2	14	0.6
1981* LA-N	9	5	.643	23	23	2	1	0	141^1	141	56	54	11	3	41	88	1.288	3.44	97	3.54	.259	10	.222	-2	8	0.0
1982 LA-N	16	11	.593	36	36	9	3	0	235^2	199	94	88	19	5	81	176	1.188	3.36	103	2.98	.229	12	.141	5	13	0.3
1983* LA-N	15	12	.556	31	31	4	3	0	204	164	73	60	13	3	72	156	1.157	2.65	136	2.68	.222	7	.096	26	16	2.4
1984 LA-N	13	13	.500	31	29	3	1	0	178^2	191	86	75	11	2	58	126	1.394	3.78	93	3.87	.273	4	.078	-3	9	-0.6
1985* LA-N	14	4	.778	23	23	8	3	0	167^1	141	49	43	16	6	35	96	1.052	2.31	150	2.61	.225	9	.180	21	15	2.4
1986 LA-N	7	13	.350	33	33	7	3	0	235^2	227	95	86	14	7	55	183	1.197	3.28	105	3.03	.251	8	.105	9	13	0.9
1987 LA-N	15	9	.625	35	35	6	**4**	0	251^2	204	94	90	21	4	86	196	1.152	3.22	123	2.78	.221	13	.157	23	19	2.4
1988* Oak-A	17	9	.654	36	36	4	2	0	244^2	237	107	99	22	10	81	158	1.300	3.64	104	3.74	.257	0	....	1	13	0.1
1989* Oak-A	17	8	.680	33	33	1	0	0	209^2	191	82	70	13	6	78	137	1.283	3.00	122	3.32	.241	0	....	13	14	1.3
1990* Oak-A★	**27**	6	.818	35	35	2	2	0	238	214	90	78	26	5	77	127	1.223	2.95	126	3.40	.242	0	....	15	18	1.5
1991 Oak-A	12	13	.480	35	**35**	7	1	0	220	220	124	112	25	11	91	101	1.414	4.58	84	4.46	.263	0	....	-18	7	-1.8
1992* Oak-A	11	7	.611	20	20	0	0	0	123^2	114	47	45	13	2	43	47	1.270	3.27	114	3.60	.247	0	....	5	9	0.6
1993 Oak-A	9	11	.450	30	28	0	0	0	166^2	208	102	98	25	7	56	63	1.584	5.29	77	5.83	.310	0	....	-22	4	-2.1
1994 Oak-A	3	6	.333	25	8	0	0	0	68^2	79	56	54	10	1	43	44	1.777	7.08	63	6.20	.290	0	.000	-21	0	-1.9
Total 17	211	146	.591	506	462	61	28	8	3092	2894	1310	1191	267	79	1034	1969	1.270	3.47	106	3.50	.249	88	.151	69	188	7.6

• WELCH, Johnny John Vernon Welch b: 12/2/1906, Washington, DC d: 9/2/1940, St. Louis, MO BL/TR, 6'3", 184 lbs. Deb: 5/22/1926

YEAR TM-L	W	L	PCT	G	GS	CG	SH	SV	IP	H	R	ER	HR	HB	BB	SO	RAT	ERA	ERA+	CERA	OAV	BH	AVG	PR+	WS	TPW
1926 Chi-N	0	0	....	3	0	0	0	0	4^1	5	2	1	0	0	1	0	1.385	2.08	185	4.16	.357	1	1.000	1	1	0.1

YEAR TM-L	W	L	PCT	G	GS	CG	SH	SV	IP	H	R	ER	HR	HB	BB	SO	RAT	ERA	ERA+	CERA	OAV	BH	AVG	PR+	WS	TPW
1927 Chi-N	0	0	....	1	0	0	0	0	1	0	1	1	0	0	3	1	3.000	9.00	43	4.94	.000	0	....	-1	0	-0.1
1928 Chi-N	0	0	....	3	0	0	0	0	4	13	7	7	0	0	0	2	3.250	15.75	24	17.91	.591	0	....	-5	0	-0.5
1931 Chi-N	2	1	.667	8	3	1	0	0	33^{2}	39	16	14	2	1	10	7	1.455	3.74	103	4.29	.291	5	.417	1	3	0.3
1932 Bos-A	4	6	.400	20	8	3	1	0	72^{1}	93	46	42	3	3	38	26	1.811	5.23	86	5.79	.312	9	.250	-5	3	-0.3
1933 Bos-A	4	9	.308	47	7	1	0	3	129	142	81	66	6	2	67	68	1.620	4.60	95	4.62	.283	6	.162	-3	5	-0.4
1934 Bos-A	13	15	.464	41	22	8	1	0	206^{1}	223	112	103	14	8	76	91	1.449	4.49	107	4.18	.274	15	.203	9	13	0.7
1935 Bos-A	10	9	.526	31	19	10	1	2	143	155	82	71	4	4	53	48	1.455	4.47	106	3.90	.273	9	.180	4	10	0.4
1936 Bos-A	2	1	.667	9	3	1	0	0	32^{2}	43	24	20	4	0	8	9	1.561	5.51	96	5.17	.305	3	.273	-1	2	0.0
Pit-N	0	0	....	9	1	0	0	1	22	22	12	11	3	0	6	5	1.273	4.50	90	3.77	.265	2	.286	-1	1	0.0
Total 9	35	41	.461	172	63	24	3	6	648^{1}	735	383	336	36	18	262	257	1.538	4.66	98	4.51	.285	50	.219	-1	38	0.2
• WELCH, Mickey	Michael Francis "Smiling Mickey" Welch b: 7/4/1859, Brooklyn, NY d: 7/30/1941, Concord, NH BR/TR, 5'8", 160 lbs. Deb: 5/1/1880 U HOF: 1973																									
1880 Tro-N	34	30	.531	65	64	64	4	0	574	575	321	162	7	....	80	123	1.141	2.54	99	....	.248	72	.287	-5	42	0.6
1881 Tro-N	21	18	.538	40	40	40	4	0	368	371	186	109	7	....	78	104	1.220	2.67	111	....	.251	30	.203	-6	25	-0.8
1882 Tro-N	14	16	.467	33	33	30	5	0	281	334	221	108	7	....	62	53	1.409	3.46	81	....	.279	37	.245	-19	12	-1.7
1883 NY-N	25	23	.521	54	52	46	4	0	426	431	271	129	11	....	66	144	1.167	2.73	114	....	.247	75	.234	16	31	1.0
1884 NY-N	39	21	.650	65	65	62	4	0	557^{1}	528	275	155	12	....	146	345	1.209	2.50	119	....	.236	60	.241	28	46	3.3
1885 NY-N	44	11	.800	56	55	55	7	1	492	372	170	91	4	....	131	258	1.022	1.66	160	....	.200	41	.206	31	57	3.4
1886 NY-N	33	22	.600	59	59	56	1	0	500	514	279	166	13	....	163	272	1.354	2.99	107	....	.256	46	.216	11	29	1.0
1887 NY-N	22	15	.595	41	40	39	2	0	346	430	191	129	7	5	91	115	1.243	3.36	111	....	.296	42	.273	8	27	1.0
1888* NY-N	26	19	.578	47	47	47	5	0	425^{1}	328	156	91	12	14	108	167	1.025	1.93	141	....	.205	32	.189	25	32	2.7
1889* NY-N	27	12	.692	45	41	39	3	**2**	375	340	196	126	14	10	149	125	1.304	3.02	131	....	.234	30	.192	36	31	3.0
1890 NY-N	17	14	.548	37	37	33	2	0	292^{1}	268	145	97	5	12	122	97	1.334	2.99	117	....	.237	22	.179	15	19	1.1
1891 NY-N	5	9	.357	22	15	14	0	1	160	177	136	76	7	11	97	46	**1.713**	4.28	75	....	.269	10	.141	-21	3	-2.2
1892 NY-N	0	0	....	1	1	0	0	0	5	11	9	8	0	0	4	1	3.000	14.40	22	12.54	.423	1	.333	-6	0	-0.6
Total 13	307	210	.594	565	549	525	41	4	4802	4679	2556	1447	106	52	1297	1850	1.226	2.71	113	0.01	.244	498	.226	112	354	11.9
• WELCH, Mike	Michael Paul Welch b: 8/25/1972, Haverhill, MA BL/TR, 6'2" Deb: 7/17/1998																									
1998 Phi-N	0	2	.000	10	2	0	0	0	20^{2}	26	19	19	7	2	7	15	1.597	8.27	52	7.74	.310	0	.000	-9	0	-0.9
• WELCH, Ted	Floyd John Welch b: 10/17/1892, Coyville, KS d: 1/7/1943, Great Bend, KS BL/TR, 5'9.5", 160 lbs. Deb: 5/15/1914																									
1914 StL-F	0	0	....	3	0	0	0	0	6	6	4	4	0	3	3	2	1.500	6.00	58	5.32	.273	0	.000	-2	0	-0.2
• WELCHEL, Don	Donald Ray Welchel b: 2/3/1957, Atlanta, TX BR/TR, 6'4", 205 lbs. Deb: 9/15/1982																									
1982 Bal-A	1	0	1.000	2	0	0	0	0	4^{1}	6	6	4	0	0	2	3	1.846	8.31	49	5.35	.300	0	....	-2	0	-0.2
1983 Bal-A	0	2	.000	11	0	0	0	0	26^{2}	33	18	16	1	0	10	16	1.613	5.40	73	4.63	.297	0	....	-4	0	-0.4
Total 2	1	2	.333	13	0	0	0	0	31	39	24	20	1	0	12	19	1.645	5.81	68	4.73	.298	0	....	-6	0	-0.6
• WELLEMEYER, Todd	Todd Allen Wellemeyer b: 8/30/1978, Louisville, KY BR/TR, 6'3", 195 lbs. Deb: 5/15/2003																									
2003 Chi-N	1	1	.500	15	0	0	0	1	27^{2}	25	22	20	5	0	19	30	1.590	6.51	65	5.33	.245	0	.000	-7	0	-0.7
• WELLS, Bob	Robert Lee Wells b: 11/1/1966, Yakima, WA BR/TR, 6', 180 lbs. Deb: 5/16/1994																									
1994 Phi-N	1	0	1.000	6	0	0	0	0	5	4	1	1	0	1	3	3	1.400	1.80	239	4.04	.235	0	....	1	1	0.1
Sea-A	1	0	1.000	1	0	0	0	0	4	4	1	1	0	0	1	3	1.250	2.25	217	2.77	.250	0	....	1	1	0.1
1995* Sea-A	4	3	.571	30	4	0	0	0	76^{2}	88	51	49	11	3	39	38	1.657	5.75	82	5.71	.284	0	....	-7	2	-0.6
1996 Sea-A	12	7	.632	36	16	1	1	0	130^{2}	141	78	77	25	6	46	94	1.431	5.30	93	5.11	.274	0	....	-6	6	-0.5
1997* Sea-A	2	0	1.000	46	1	0	0	2	67^{1}	88	49	43	11	3	18	51	1.574	5.75	78	5.98	.314	0	....	-9	1	-0.8
1998 Sea-A	2	2	.500	30	0	0	0	0	51^{2}	54	38	35	12	2	16	29	1.355	6.10	76	4.89	.261	0	....	-8	1	-0.7
1999 Min-A	8	3	.727	**76**	0	0	0	1	87^{1}	79	41	37	8	5	28	44	1.225	3.81	133	3.37	.245	0	....	13	9	1.2
2000 Min-A	0	7	.000	76	0	0	0	10	86^{1}	80	39	35	14	4	15	76	1.100	3.65	141	3.35	.247	0	....	16	10	1.4
2001 Min-A	8	5	.615	65	0	0	0	2	68^{2}	72	39	39	12	10	18	49	1.311	5.11	90	4.89	.273	0	....	-4	5	-0.3
2002* Min-A	2	1	.667	48	0	0	0	0	58	78	41	38	8	1	16	30	1.621	5.90	76	5.97	.325	0	....	-9	1	-0.9
Total 9	40	28	.588	414	21	1	1	15	635^{2}	688	378	355	101	35	200	417	1.397	5.03	95	4.81	.276	0	....	-10	37	-1.0
• WELLS, David	David Lee "Boomer" Wells b: 5/20/1963, Torrance, CA BL/TL, 6'3", 225 lbs. Deb: 6/30/1987																									
1987 Tor-A	4	3	.571	18	2	0	0	1	29^{1}	37	14	13	0	0	12	32	1.670	3.99	113	4.91	.311	0	....	1	2	0.1
1988 Tor-A	3	5	.375	41	0	0	0	4	64^{1}	65	36	33	12	2	31	56	1.492	4.62	85	5.11	.269	0	....	-5	2	-0.5
1989* Tor-A	7	4	.636	54	0	0	0	2	86^{1}	66	25	23	5	0	28	78	1.089	2.40	151	2.16	.207	0	....	12	9	1.2
1990 Tor-A	11	6	.647	43	25	0	0	3	189	165	72	66	14	2	45	115	1.111	3.14	130	2.67	.235	0	....	20	15	2.1
1991* Tor-A	15	10	.600	40	28	2	0	1	198^{1}	188	88	82	24	2	49	106	1.195	3.72	113	3.41	.251	0	....	11	14	1.1
1992* Tor-A	7	9	.438	41	14	0	0	2	120	138	84	72	16	8	36	62	1.450	5.40	76	4.98	.289	0	....	-17	1	-1.7
1993 Det-A	11	9	.550	32	30	0	0	0	187	183	93	87	26	7	42	139	1.203	4.19	102	3.64	.254	0	....	2	10	0.2
1994 Det-A	5	7	.417	16	16	5	1	0	111^{1}	113	54	49	13	2	24	71	1.231	3.96	122	3.54	.260	0	....	13	7	1.2
1995 Det-A★	10	3	.769	18	18	3	0	0	130^{1}	120	54	44	17	2	37	83	1.205	3.04	157	3.40	.242	0	....	27	13	2.5
* Cin-N	6	5	.545	11	11	3	0	0	72^{2}	74	34	29	6	0	16	50	1.239	3.59	115	3.31	.265	4	.143	3	4	0.2
1996* Bal-A	11	14	.440	34	34	3	0	0	224^{1}	247	132	128	32	7	51	130	1.328	5.14	96	4.39	.285	0	....	-5	10	-0.5
1997* NY-A	16	10	.615	32	32	5	2	0	218	239	109	102	24	6	45	156	1.303	4.21	106	4.04	.278	0	....	8	12	0.8
1998* NY-A★	18	4	.818	30	30	8	**5**	0	214^{1}	195	86	83	29	1	29	163	1.045	3.49	126	2.83	.239	1	.250	18	18	1.7
1999 Tor-A	17	10	.630	34	34	**7**	1	0	**231^{2}**	246	132	124	32	6	62	169	1.329	4.82	102	4.26	.271	0	.000	2	13	0.1
2000 Tor-A★	**20**	8	.714	35	**35**	**9**	1	0	229^{2}	266	115	105	23	8	31	166	1.293	4.11	123	4.05	.289	1	.167	24	18	2.2
2001 Chi-A	5	7	.417	16	16	1	0	0	100^{2}	120	55	50	12	3	21	59	1.401	4.47	103	4.69	.297	0	.000	1	5	0.1
2002* NY-A	19	7	.731	31	31	2	1	0	206^{1}	210	100	86	21	5	45	137	1.236	3.75	116	3.50	.259	0	.000	20	15	1.9
2003* NY-A	15	7	.682	31	30	4	1	0	213	242	101	98	24	8	20	101	1.230	4.14	105	3.87	.286	1	.167	10	14	1.0
Total 17	200	128	.610	557	386	52	12	13	2826^{2}	2914	1384	1274	330	69	624	1873	1.252	4.06	110	3.75	.266	7	.125	145	182	13.6
• WELLS, Ed	Edwin Lee "Satchelfoot" Wells b: 6/7/1900, Ashland, OH d: 5/1/1986, Montgomery, AL BL/TL, 6'1.5", 183 lbs. Deb: 6/16/1923																									
1923 Det-A	0	0	....	7	0	0	0	0	10	11	6	6	0	0	6	6	1.700	5.40	72	4.70	.306	0	.000	-2	0	-0.2
1924 Det-A	6	8	.429	29	15	5	0	4	102	117	58	46	2	1	42	33	1.559	4.06	101	4.07	.291	7	.212	1	6	0.0
1925 Det-A	6	9	.400	35	14	5	0	2	134^{1}	190	106	93	8	2	62	45	1.876	6.23	69	6.43	.345	12	.279	-29	2	-2.5
1926 Det-A	12	10	.545	36	26	9	**4**	0	178	201	101	82	7	2	76	58	1.556	4.15	98	4.49	.297	15	.205	0	9	0.0
1927 Det-A	0	1	.000	8	1	0	0	1	20	28	16	15	3	0	5	5	1.650	6.75	62	6.13	.333	2	.286	-5	0	-0.5
1929 NY-A	13	9	.591	31	23	10	3	0	193^{1}	179	102	93	19	1	81	78	1.345	4.33	89	3.62	.248	17	.230	-12	10	-1.0
1930 NY-A	12	3	.800	27	21	7	0	0	150^{2}	185	101	87	11	4	49	46	1.553	5.20	83	4.86	.302	15	.259	-13	6	-1.2
1931 NY-A	9	5	.643	27	10	6	0	2	116^{2}	130	68	56	7	1	37	34	1.431	4.32	92	4.13	.286	10	.222	-5	6	-0.4
1932 NY-A	3	3	.500	22	0	0	0	2	31^{2}	38	19	15	1	0	12	13	1.579	4.26	96	4.43	.302	0	.000	-1	2	-0.1
1933 StL-A	6	14	.300	36	22	10	0	1	203^{2}	230	113	95	13	1	63	58	1.439	4.20	111	4.01	.278	14	.197	6	12	0.5
1934 StL-A	1	7	.125	33	8	2	0	1	92	108	60	49	7	0	35	27	1.554	4.79	104	4.67	.292	1	.045	1	4	-0.1
Total 11	68	69	.496	291	140	54	7	13	1232^{1}	1417	750	637	78	12	468	403	1.530	4.65	91	4.50	.291	93	.215	-60	57	-5.5
• WELLS, John	John Frederick Wells b: 11/25/1922, Junction City, KS d: 10/23/1993, Olean, NY BR/TR, 5'11.5", 180 lbs. Deb: 9/14/1944																									
1944 Bro-N	0	2	.000	4	2	0	0	0	15	18	9	9	1	0	11	7	1.933	5.40	66	6.44	.316	1	.250	-3	0	-0.3
• WELLS, Kip	Robert Kip Wells b: 4/21/1977, Houston, TX BR/TR, 6'3", 195 lbs. Deb: 8/2/1999																									
1999 Chi-A	4	1	.800	7	7	0	0	0	35^{2}	33	17	16	2	3	15	29	1.346	4.04	121	3.80	.248	0	....	4	3	0.3
2000 Chi-A	6	9	.400	20	20	0	0	0	98^{2}	126	76	66	15	2	58	71	1.865	6.02	83	7.01	.312	0	.000	-13	2	-1.2
2001 Chi-A	10	11	.476	40	20	0	0	0	133^{1}	145	80	71	14	12	61	99	1.545	4.79	96	5.16	.281	1	.167	-3	6	-0.3
2002 Pit-N	12	14	.462	33	33	1	1	0	198^{1}	197	92	79	21	7	71	134	1.351	3.58	116	4.00	.261	12	.190	12	13	1.3
2003 Pit-N	10	9	.526	31	31	1	0	0	197^{1}	171	77	72	24	7	76	147	1.252	3.28	133	3.49	.233	13	.191	24	15	2.6
Total 5	42	44	.488	131	111	2	1	0	663^{1}	672	342	304	76	31	281	480	1.437	4.12	109	4.52	.264	26	.187	23	39	2.7

YEAR	TM-L	W	L	PCT	G	GS	CG	SH	SV	IP	H	R	ER	HR	HB	BB	SO	RAT	ERA	ERA+	CERA	OAV	BH	AVG	PR+	WS	TPW
• WELLS, Terry	Terry Wells b: 9/10/1963, Kankakee, IL BL/TL, 6'3", 205 lbs. Deb: 7/3/1990																										
1990	LA-N	1	2	.333	5	5	0	0	0	20^2	25	23	18	4	0	14	18	1.887	7.84	47	7.02	.287	0	.000	-10	0	-1.1
• WELSH, Chris	Christopher Charles Welsh b: 4/14/1955, Wilmington, DE BL/TL, 6'2", 185 lbs. Deb: 4/12/1981																										
1981	SD-N	6	7	.462	22	19	4	2	0	123^2	122	55	52	9	1	41	51	1.318	3.78	86	3.63	.264	6	.146	-8	4	-0.8
1982	SD-N	8	8	.500	28	20	3	1	0	139^1	146	88	76	16	3	63	48	1.500	4.91	70	4.71	.268	11	.262	-24	1	-2.2
1983	SD-N	0	1	.000	7	1	0	0	0	14^1	13	5	4	2	0	2	5	1.047	2.51	139	2.72	.236	0	.000	1	1	0.1
	Mon-N	0	1	.000	16	5	0	0	0	44^2	46	30	25	5	4	18	17	1.433	5.04	71	4.73	.267	4	.286	-8	0	-0.7
	Yr.	0	2	.000	23	6	0	0	0	59	59	35	29	7	4	20	22	1.339	4.42	81	4.24	.260	4	.222	-7	1	-0.6
1985	Tex-A	2	5	.286	25	6	0	0	0	76^1	101	40	35	11	4	25	31	1.651	4.13	103	6.18	.316	0	....	2	4	0.2
1986	Cin-N	6	9	.400	24	24	1	0	0	139^1	163	79	74	9	3	40	40	1.457	4.78	81	4.47	.301	5	.119	-13	4	-1.3
Total	**5**	**22**	**31**	**.415**	**122**	**75**	**8**	**3**	**0**	**537^2**	**591**	**297**	**266**	**52**	**15**	**189**	**192**	**1.451**	**4.45**	**81**	**4.56**	**.282**	**26**	**.182**	**-49**	**14**	**-4.7**
• WELTEROTH, Dick	Richard John Welteroth b: 8/3/1927, Williamsport, PA BR/TR, 5'11", 165 lbs. Deb: 5/16/1948																										
1948	Was-A	2	1	.667	33	2	0	0	1	65^1	73	43	40	6	1	50	16	1.883	5.51	79	6.05	.286	1	.100	-7	2	-0.8
1949	Was-A	2	5	.286	52	2	0	0	2	95^1	107	83	78	6	1	89	37	2.056	7.36	58	6.53	.296	1	.059	-29	0	-2.9
1950	Was-A	0	0	....	5	0	0	0	0	6	5	5	2	0	0	6	2	1.833	3.00	150	4.24	.217	0	....	1	0	0.1
Total	**3**	**4**	**6**	**.400**	**90**	**4**	**0**	**0**	**3**	**166^2**	**185**	**131**	**120**	**12**	**2**	**145**	**55**	**1.980**	**6.48**	**66**	**6.26**	**.290**	**2**	**.074**	**-36**	**2**	**-3.6**
• WELZER, Tony	Anton Frank Welzer b: 4/5/1899, Germany d: 3/18/1971, Milwaukee, WI BR/TR, 5'11", 160 lbs. Deb: 4/13/1926																										
1926	Bos-A	4	3	.571	39	5	1	1	0	139	167	88	75	5	3	53	29	1.583	4.86	84	4.56	.308	8	.211	-10	6	-0.7
1927	Bos-A	6	11	.353	37	19	8	0	1	171^2	214	109	90	10	4	71	56	1.660	4.72	89	5.27	.318	4	.095	-8	7	-0.9
Total	**2**	**10**	**14**	**.417**	**76**	**24**	**9**	**1**	**1**	**310^2**	**381**	**197**	**165**	**15**	**7**	**124**	**85**	**1.626**	**4.78**	**87**	**4.95**	**.314**	**12**	**.150**	**-17**	**13**	**-1.6**
• WENDELL, Turk	Steven John Wendell b: 5/19/1967, Pittsfield, MA BB/TR, 6'2", 190 lbs. Deb: 6/17/1993																										
1993	Chi-N	1	2	.333	7	4	0	0	0	22^2	24	13	11	0	0	8	15	1.412	4.37	91	3.42	.273	1	.143	-1	1	-0.1
1994	Chi-N	0	1	.000	6	2	0	0	0	14^1	22	20	19	3	0	10	9	2.233	11.93	35	9.21	.349	0	.000	-12	0	-1.2
1995	Chi-N	3	1	.750	43	0	0	0	0	60^1	71	35	33	11	2	24	50	1.575	4.92	83	5.79	.298	0	.000	-6	2	-0.6
1996	Chi-N	4	5	.444	70	0	0	0	18	79^1	58	26	25	8	3	44	75	1.286	2.84	153	3.25	.201	1	.500	12	12	1.3
1997	Chi-N	3	5	.375	52	0	0	0	4	60	53	32	28	4	1	39	54	1.533	4.20	103	4.03	.238	0	.000	1	4	0.1
	NY-N	0	0	....	13	0	0	0	1	16^1	15	10	9	3	1	14	10	1.776	4.96	81	6.38	.250	0	.000	-2	0	-0.2
	Yr.	3	5	.375	65	0	0	0	5	76^1	68	42	37	7	2	53	64	1.585	4.36	97	4.54	.240	0	.000	-1	4	-0.1
1998	NY-N	5	1	.833	66	0	0	0	4	76^2	62	25	25	4	2	33	58	1.239	2.93	141	2.78	.221	0	.000	10	10	0.9
1999*	NY-N	5	4	.556	80	0	0	0	3	85^2	80	31	29	9	2	37	77	1.366	3.05	144	3.80	.245	0	.000	12	9	1.1
2000*	NY-N	8	6	.571	77	0	0	0	1	82^2	60	36	33	9	5	41	73	1.222	3.59	123	3.14	.206	1	.250	8	8	0.8
2001	NY-N	4	3	.571	49	0	0	0	1	51^1	42	23	20	8	3	22	41	1.247	3.51	118	3.59	.223	0	.000	3	5	0.3
	Phi-N	0	2	.000	21	0	0	0	0	15^2	21	13	13	4	1	12	15	2.106	7.47	57	9.04	.323	0	....	-6	0	-0.6
	Yr.	4	5	.444	70	0	0	0	1	67	63	36	33	12	4	34	56	1.448	4.43	94	4.87	.249	0	.000	-3	5	-0.3
2003	Phi-N	3	3	.500	56	0	0	0	1	64	54	24	24	6	6	28	27	1.281	3.38	118	3.57	.235	0	.000	4	6	0.4
Total	**10**	**36**	**33**	**.522**	**540**	**6**	**0**	**0**	**33**	**629**	**562**	**288**	**269**	**69**	**26**	**312**	**504**	**1.390**	**3.85**	**109**	**4.00**	**.240**	**3**	**.073**	**24**	**57**	**2.1**
• WENGERT, Don	Donald Paul Wengert b: 11/6/1969, Sioux City, IA BR/TR, 6'2", 205 lbs. Deb: 4/30/1995																										
1995	Oak-A	1	1	.500	19	0	0	0	0	29^2	30	14	11	3	1	12	16	1.416	3.34	133	4.19	.263	0	....	4	2	0.4
1996	Oak-A	7	11	.389	36	25	1	1	0	161^1	200	102	100	29	6	60	75	1.612	5.58	88	6.16	.307	0	....	-14	6	-1.3
1997	Oak-A	5	11	.313	49	12	1	0	2	134	177	96	90	21	8	41	68	1.627	6.04	74	6.24	.321	0	....	-20	3	-1.9
1998	SD-N	0	0	....	10	0	0	0	1	13^2	21	9	9	2	0	5	5	1.902	5.93	66	7.77	.356	0	.000	-3	0	-0.3
	Chi-N	1	5	.167	21	6	0	0	0	49^2	55	29	28	8	3	23	41	1.570	5.07	87	5.70	.279	0	.000	-3	1	-0.4
	Yr.	1	5	.167	31	6	0	0	1	63^1	76	38	37	10	3	28	46	1.642	5.26	81	6.15	.297	0	.000	-6	1	-0.7
1999	KC-A	0	1	.000	11	1	0	0	0	24^1	41	26	25	6	0	5	10	1.890	9.25	54	8.72	.376	0	....	-12	0	-1.1
2000	Atl-N	0	1	.000	10	0	0	0	0	10	12	9	8	2	0	5	7	1.700	7.20	64	6.31	.286	0	....	-3	0	-0.3
2001	Pit-N	0	2	.000	4	4	0	0	0	16	33	22	22	2	0	6	4	2.438	12.38	36	10.93	.429	0	.000	-14	0	-1.4
Total	**7**	**14**	**32**	**.304**	**160**	**48**	**2**	**1**	**3**	**438^2**	**569**	**307**	**293**	**73**	**18**	**157**	**226**	**1.655**	**6.01**	**77**	**6.37**	**.316**	**0**	**.000**	**-65**	**12**	**-6.3**
• WENSLOFF, Butch	Charles William Wensloff b: 12/3/1915, Sausalito, CA d: 2/18/2001, San Rafael, CA BR/TR, 5'11", 185 lbs. Deb: 5/2/1943																										
1943	NY-A	13	11	.542	29	27	18	1	1	223^1	179	80	63	7	1	70	105	1.115	2.54	127	2.23	.219	14	.177	13	16	1.4
1947*	NY-A	3	1	.750	11	5	1	0	0	51^2	41	17	15	3	0	22	18	1.219	2.61	135	2.72	.217	5	.263	5	4	0.6
1948	Cle-A	0	1	.000	1	0	0	0	0	1^2	2	2	2	1	0	3	2	3.000	10.80	38	15.92	.286	0	....	-1	0	-0.1
Total	**3**	**16**	**13**	**.552**	**41**	**32**	**19**	**1**	**1**	**276^2**	**222**	**99**	**80**	**11**	**1**	**95**	**125**	**1.146**	**2.60**	**126**	**2.40**	**.219**	**19**	**.194**	**17**	**20**	**1.8**
• WENZ, Fred	Frederick Charles "Fireball" Wenz b: 8/26/1941, Bound Brook, NJ BR/TR, 6'3", 214 lbs. Deb: 6/4/1968																										
1968	Bos-A	0	0	....	1	0	0	0	0	1	0	0	0	0	0	2	3	2.000	0.00	....	3.47	.000	0	....	0	0	0.0
1969	Bos-A	1	0	1.000	8	0	0	0	0	11	9	7	7	7	0	10	11	1.727	5.73	66	9.10	.225	0	....	-2	0	-0.2
1970	Phi-N	2	0	1.000	22	0	0	0	1	30^1	27	16	15	2	1	13	24	1.319	4.45	90	3.36	.237	0	.000	-1	2	-0.2
Total	**3**	**3**	**0**	**1.000**	**31**	**0**	**0**	**0**	**1**	**42^1**	**36**	**23**	**22**	**9**	**1**	**25**	**38**	**1.441**	**4.68**	**84**	**4.86**	**.234**	**0**	**.000**	**-3**	**2**	**-0.3**
• WERDEN, Perry	Percival Wheritt "Moose" Werden b: 7/21/1865, St. Louis, MO d: 1/9/1934, Minneapolis, MN BR/TR, 6'2", 220 lbs. Deb: 4/24/1884 ♦																										
1884	StL-U	12	1	.923	16	16	12	1	0	141^1	113	61	31	1	....	22	51	.955	1.97	151	....	.205	18	.237	9	15	0.7
• WERLE, Bill	William George "Bugs" Werle b: 12/21/1920, Oakland, CA BL/TL, 6'2.5", 182 lbs. Deb: 4/22/1949 C																										
1949	Pit-N	12	13	.480	35	29	10	2	0	221	243	117	104	22	8	51	106	1.330	4.24	99	4.04	.278	9	.117	1	12	-0.2
1950	Pit-N	8	16	.333	48	22	6	0	8	215^1	249	127	110	25	6	65	78	1.458	4.60	95	4.75	.290	13	.194	-4	11	-0.2
1951	Pit-N	8	6	.571	59	9	2	0	6	149^2	181	102	94	20	6	51	57	1.550	5.65	75	5.43	.304	12	.300	-22	5	-1.8
1952	Pit-N	0	0	....	5	0	0	0	0	4	9	5	4	1	0	1	1	2.500	9.00	44	12.71	.429	0	....	-2	0	-0.2
	StL-N	1	2	.333	19	0	0	0	1	39	40	23	21	6	1	15	23	1.410	4.85	77	4.62	.268	1	.111	-5	1	-0.6
	Yr.	1	2	.333	24	0	0	0	1	43	49	28	25	7	1	16	24	1.512	5.23	72	5.37	.288	1	.111	-7	1	-0.8
1953	Bos-A	0	1	.000	5	0	0	0	0	11^2	7	3	2	1	0	1	4	.686	1.54	273	1.18	.179	0	.000	3	1	0.3
1954	Bos-A	0	1	.000	14	0	0	0	0	24^2	41	13	12	5	2	10	14	2.068	4.38	94	9.30	.376	0	.000	-0	1	-0.1
Total	**6**	**29**	**39**	**.426**	**185**	**60**	**18**	**2**	**15**	**665^1**	**770**	**390**	**347**	**80**	**23**	**194**	**283**	**1.449**	**4.69**	**90**	**4.81**	**.291**	**35**	**.176**	**-29**	**31**	**-2.8**
• WERLEY, George	George William Werley b: 9/8/1938, St. Louis, MO BR/TR, 6'2", 196 lbs. Deb: 9/29/1956																										
1956	Bal-A	0	0	....	1	0	0	0	0	1	1	1	1	0	0	2	0	3.000	9.00	44	9.51	.250	0	....	-1	0	-0.1
• WERTS, Johnny	Henry Levi Werts b: 4/20/1898, Pomaria, SC d: 9/24/1990, Newberry, SC BR/TR, 5'10", 180 lbs. Deb: 4/14/1926																										
1926	Bos-N	11	9	.550	32	23	7	1	0	189^1	212	85	69	6	10	47	65	1.368	3.28	108	3.78	.287	17	.266	8	14	1.2
1927	Bos-N	4	10	.286	42	15	4	0	1	164^1	204	95	83	5	4	52	39	1.558	4.55	82	4.64	.315	7	.163	-12	5	-1.2
1928	Bos-N	0	2	.000	10	2	0	0	0	18^1	31	22	21	2	0	8	5	2.127	10.31	38	8.36	.369	1	.333	-12	0	-1.2
1929	Bos-N	0	0	....	4	0	0	0	1	6	13	8	7	1	0	4	2	2.833	10.50	45	13.59	.433	1	1.000	-4	0	-0.3
Total	**4**	**15**	**21**	**.417**	**88**	**40**	**11**	**1**	**2**	**378**	**460**	**210**	**180**	**14**	**14**	**111**	**111**	**1.511**	**4.29**	**86**	**4.53**	**.307**	**26**	**.234**	**-20**	**19**	**-1.5**
• WERTZ, Bill	William Charles Wertz b: 1/15/1967, Cleveland, OH BR/TR, 6'6", 220 lbs. Deb: 5/22/1993																										
1993	Cle-A	2	3	.400	34	0	0	0	0	59^2	54	28	24	5	1	32	53	1.441	3.62	119	3.94	.238	0	....	5	3	0.4
1994	Cle-A	0	0	....	1	0	0	0	0	4^1	9	5	5	0	0	1	1	2.308	10.38	45	9.02	.409	0	....	-3	0	-0.3
Total	**2**	**2**	**3**	**.400**	**35**	**0**	**0**	**0**	**0**	**64**	**63**	**33**	**29**	**5**	**1**	**33**	**54**	**1.500**	**4.08**	**108**	**4.29**	**.253**	**0**	**....**	**2**	**3**	**0.2**
• WEST, David	David Lee West b: 9/1/1964, Memphis, TN BL/TL, 6'6", 230 lbs. Deb: 9/24/1988																										
1988	NY-N	1	0	1.000	2	1	0	0	0	6	6	2	2	0	0	3	3	1.500	3.00	107	3.97	.273	2	1.000	0	1	0.2
1989	NY-N	0	2	.000	11	2	0	0	0	24^1	25	20	20	4	1	14	19	1.603	7.40	44	5.38	.260	1	.200	-11	0	-1.2
	Min-A	3	2	.600	10	5	0	0	0	39^1	48	29	28	5	2	19	31	1.703	6.41	65	6.12	.306	0	....	-10	0	-1.0
1990	Min-A	7	9	.438	29	27	2	0	0	146^1	142	88	83	21	4	78	92	1.503	5.10	81	4.88	.256	0	....	-16	4	-1.6
1991*	Min-A	4	4	.500	15	12	0	0	0	71^1	66	37	36	13	1	28	52	1.318	4.54	94	4.22	.244	0	....	-3	3	-0.3

YEAR TM-L	W	L	PCT	G	GS	CG	SH	SV	IP	H	R	ER	HR	HB	BB	SO	RAT	ERA	ERA+	CERA	OAV	BH	AVG	PR+	WS	TPW
1992 Min-A	1	3	.250	9	3	0	0	0	28^1	32	24	22	3	1	20	19	1.835	6.99	58	6.08	.276	0	....	-9	0	-1.0
1993* Phi-N	6	4	.600	76	0	0	0	3	86^1	60	37	28	6	5	51	87	1.286	2.92	136	3.01	.194	2	.400	11	9	1.2
1994 Phi-N	4	10	.286	31	14	0	0	0	99	74	44	39	7	1	61	83	1.364	3.55	121	3.28	.205	2	.071	9	5	0.7
1995 Phi-N	3	2	.600	8	8	0	0	0	38	34	17	16	5	1	19	25	1.395	3.79	112	4.26	.241	1	.125	2	3	0.2
1996 Phi-N	2	2	.500	7	6	0	0	0	28^1	31	17	15	0	0	11	22	1.482	4.76	91	3.76	.272	2	.286	-2	1	-0.1
1998 Bos-A	0	0	....	6	0	0	0	0	2	7	6	6	1	0	7	4	7.000	27.00	17	44.11	.538	0	....	-5	0	-0.5
Total 10	**31**	**38**	**.449**	**204**	**78**	**2**	**0**	**3**	**569^1**	**525**	**321**	**295**	**65**	**16**	**311**	**437**	**1.468**	**4.66**	**88**	**4.44**	**.244**	**10**	**.182**	**-34**	**26**	**-3.3**
• WEST, Frank	J. Franklin West b: 1/1874, Johnstown, PA d: 9/6/1932, Wilmerding, PA, 180 lbs. Deb: 7/11/1894																									
1894 Bos-N	0	0	....	1	0	0	0	0	3	5	5	3	0	0	2	1	2.333	9.00	66	8.24	.367	0	.000	-1	0	-0.1
• WEST, Hi	James Hiram West b: 8/8/1884, Roseville, IL d: 5/24/1963, Los Angeles, CA BR/TR, 6', 185 lbs. Deb: 9/8/1905																									
1905 Cle-A	2	2	.500	6	4	4	1	0	33	43	23	15	0	3	10	15	1.606	4.09	64	4.92	.317	1	.077	-5	0	-0.7
1911 Cle-A	3	4	.429	13	8	3	0	1	64^2	84	35	27	1	3	18	17	1.577	3.76	91	5.28	.343	3	.130	-3	3	-0.5
Total 2	**5**	**6**	**.455**	**19**	**12**	**7**	**1**	**1**	**97^2**	**127**	**58**	**42**	**1**	**6**	**28**	**32**	**1.587**	**3.87**	**80**	**5.16**	**.334**	**4**	**.111**	**-9**	**3**	**-1.2**
• WEST, Lefty	Weldon Edison West b: 9/3/1915, Gibsonville, NC d: 7/23/1979, Hendersonville, NC BR/TL, 6', 165 lbs. Deb: 4/30/1944																									
1944 StL-A	0	0	....	11	0	0	0	0	24^1	34	18	17	1	1	19	11	2.178	6.29	57	7.75	.366	1	.143	-7	0	-0.8
1945 StL-A	3	4	.429	24	8	1	0	0	74^1	71	37	30	2	0	31	38	1.372	3.63	97	3.21	.245	2	.074	-1	3	-0.4
Total 2	**3**	**4**	**.429**	**35**	**8**	**1**	**0**	**0**	**98^2**	**105**	**55**	**47**	**3**	**1**	**50**	**49**	**1.571**	**4.29**	**83**	**4.33**	**.274**	**3**	**.088**	**-8**	**3**	**-1.1**
• WESTBROOK, Jake	Jacob Cauthen Westbrook b: 9/29/1977, Athens, GA BR/TR, 6'3", 200 lbs. Deb: 6/17/2000																									
2000 NY-A	0	2	.000	3	2	0	0	0	6^2	15	10	10	1	0	4	1	2.850	13.50	36	13.53	.469	0	....	-6	0	-0.6
2001 Cle-A	4	4	.500	23	6	0	0	0	64^2	79	43	42	6	4	22	48	1.562	5.85	77	5.25	.306	0	.000	-8	2	-0.8
2002 Cle-A	1	3	.250	11	4	0	0	0	41^2	50	30	27	6	1	12	20	1.488	5.83	75	5.12	.296	0	....	-6	1	-0.6
2003 Cle-A	7	10	.412	34	22	1	0	0	133	142	70	64	9	12	56	58	1.489	4.33	102	4.78	.281	0	....	-1	6	-0.1
Total 4	**12**	**19**	**.387**	**71**	**34**	**1**	**0**	**0**	**246**	**286**	**153**	**143**	**22**	**17**	**94**	**127**	**1.545**	**5.23**	**85**	**5.20**	**.297**	**0**	**.000**	**-22**	**9**	**-2.1**
• WESTERVELT, Huyler	Huyler Westervelt b: 10/1/1869, Tenafly, NJ d: 10/14/1949, Pelham Manor, NY TR, 5'9", 170 lbs. Deb: 4/21/1894																									
1894 NY-N	7	10	.412	23	18	11	1	0	141	170	118	79	4	5	76	35	1.745	5.04	104	5.25	.295	8	.143	2	9	-0.2
• WESTON, Mickey	Michael Lee Weston b: 3/26/1961, Flint, MI BR/TR, 6'1", 187 lbs. Deb: 6/18/1989																									
1989 Bal-A	1	0	1.000	7	0	0	0	1	13	18	8	8	1	1	2	7	1.538	5.54	68	5.84	.346	0	....	-3	0	-0.3
1990 Bal-A	0	1	.000	9	2	0	0	0	21	28	20	18	6	0	6	9	1.619	7.71	49	6.99	.322	0	....	-9	0	-1.0
1991 Tor-A	0	0	....	2	0	0	0	0	2	1	0	0	0	0	1	1	1.000	0.00	....	0.94	.143	0	....	1	0	0.1
1992 Phi-N	0	1	.000	1	1	0	0	0	3^2	7	5	5	1	1	1	0	2.182	12.27	28	12.67	.412	0	.000	-4	0	-0.4
1993 NY-N	0	0	....	4	0	0	0	0	5^2	11	5	5	0	1	1	2	2.118	7.94	50	8.67	.393	0	....	-3	0	-0.2
Total 5	**1**	**2**	**.333**	**23**	**3**	**0**	**0**	**1**	**45^1**	**65**	**38**	**36**	**8**	**3**	**11**	**19**	**1.676**	**7.15**	**53**	**7.07**	**.340**	**0**	**.000**	**-17**	**0**	**-1.8**
• WETTELAND, John	John Karl Wetteland b: 8/21/1966, San Mateo, CA BR/TR, 6'2", 195 lbs. Deb: 5/31/1989																									
1989 LA-N	5	8	.385	31	12	0	0	1	102^2	81	46	43	8	0	34	96	1.120	3.77	91	2.55	.218	3	.143	-5	3	-0.5
1990 LA-N	2	4	.333	22	5	0	0	0	43	44	28	23	6	4	17	36	1.419	4.81	76	4.73	.263	1	.143	-6	1	-0.5
1991 LA-N	1	0	1.000	6	0	0	0	0	9	5	2	0	0	1	3	9	.889	0.00	....	1.47	.161	0	....	4	1	0.4
1992 Mon-N	4	4	.500	67	0	0	0	37	83^1	64	27	27	6	4	36	99	1.200	2.92	119	2.90	.213	1	.200	5	12	0.6
1993 Mon-N	9	3	.750	70	0	0	0	43	85^1	58	17	13	3	2	28	113	1.008	1.37	304	1.79	.188	0	.000	26	21	2.6
1994 Mon-N	4	6	.400	52	0	0	0	25	63^2	46	22	20	5	3	21	68	1.052	2.83	149	2.28	.202	1	.250	10	12	1.0
1995* NY-A	1	5	.167	60	0	0	0	31	61^1	40	22	20	6	0	14	66	.880	2.93	157	1.69	.185	0	....	11	13	1.0
1996* NY-A★	2	3	.400	62	0	0	0	**43**	63^2	54	23	20	9	0	21	69	1.178	2.83	175	3.11	.224	0	....	16	13	1.5
1997 Tex-A	7	2	.778	61	0	0	0	31	65	43	18	14	5	0	21	63	.985	1.94	247	1.85	.182	1	1.000	22	16	2.1
1998* Tex-A★	3	1	.750	63	0	0	0	42	62	47	17	14	6	0	14	72	.984	2.03	237	2.09	.203	0	....	20	15	1.9
1999* Tex-A★	4	4	.500	62	0	0	0	43	66	67	30	27	9	0	19	60	1.303	3.68	138	3.90	.262	0	....	11	12	1.0
2000 Tex-A	6	5	.545	62	0	0	0	34	60	67	35	28	10	2	24	53	1.517	4.20	119	5.28	.285	0	....	7	8	0.6
Total 12	**48**	**45**	**.516**	**618**	**17**	**0**	**0**	**330**	**765**	**616**	**287**	**249**	**73**	**16**	**252**	**804**	**1.135**	**2.93**	**142**	**2.80**	**.218**	**7**	**.167**	**121**	**127**	**11.6**
• WETZEL, Buzz	Charles Edward Wetzel b: 8/25/1894, Jay, OK d: 3/7/1941, Globe, AZ BR/TR, 6'1", 162 lbs. Deb: 7/25/1927																									
1927 Phi-A	0	0	....	2	1	0	0	0	4^2	8	5	4	0	0	5	0	2.786	7.71	55	10.78	.400	1	1.000	-2	0	-0.1
• WETZEL, Shorty	George William Wetzel b: 1868, Philadelphia, PA d: 2/25/1899, Dayton, OH Deb: 8/26/1885																									
1885 Bal-a	0	2	.000	2	2	1	0	0	17	27	26	16	0	3	9	6	2.118	8.47	38	....	.346	0	.000	-9	0	-0.9
• WEVER, Stefan	Stefan Matthew Wever b: 4/22/1958, Marburg, West Germany BR/TR, 6'8", 245 lbs. Deb: 9/17/1982																									
1982 NY-A	0	1	.000	1	1	0	0	0	2^2	6	9	8	1	0	3	2	3.375	27.00	15	17.71	.429	0	....	-7	0	-0.7
• WEYHING, Gus	August "Cannonball" Weyhing b: 9/29/1866, Louisville, KY d: 9/4/1955, Louisville, KY BR/TR, 5'10", 145 lbs. Deb: 5/2/1887 U																									
1887 Phi-a	26	28	.481	55	55	53	2	0	466^1	632	342	221	12	37	167	193	1.355	4.27	100	....	.312	48	.223	-3	27	-1.0
1888 Phi-a	28	18	.609	47	47	45	3	0	404	314	198	101	4	42	111	204	1.052	2.25	133	....	.207	40	.217	31	31	3.3
1889 Phi-a	30	21	.588	54	53	50	4	0	449	382	271	147	15	34	212	213	1.323	2.95	128	....	.223	25	.131	26	30	1.0
1890 Bro-P	30	16	.652	49	46	38	3	0	390	419	250	156	10	17	179	177	1.533	3.60	124	....	.263	27	.164	33	32	2.2
1891 Phi-a	31	20	.608	52	51	51	3	0	450	428	231	159	12	31	161	219	1.309	3.18	120	....	.242	22	.111	32	37	1.3
1892 Phi-N	32	21	.604	59	49	46	6	**3**	469^2	411	213	139	9	18	168	202	1.233	2.66	122	2.77	.226	29	.136	23	36	0.9
1893 Phi-N	23	16	.590	42	40	33	2	0	345^1	399	235	182	10	20	145	101	1.575	4.74	96	4.61	.281	22	.150	-12	19	-1.7
1894 Phi-N	16	14	.533	40	36	26	2	1	279^1	379	224	172	12	16	120	83	1.786	5.54	92	5.95	.321	20	.174	-10	12	-1.4
1895 Phi-N	0	2	.000	2	2	0	0	0	9	23	22	20	0	0	13	5	4.000	20.00	24	18.12	.469	0	.000	-15	0	-1.3
Pit-N	1	0	1.000	1	1	1	0	0	9	10	7	1	0	0	5	3	1.667	1.00	451	4.40	.277	1	.250	3	1	0.3
Lou-N	7	19	.269	28	25	22	1	0	213	285	205	128	9	8	66	53	1.648	5.41	86	5.29	.316	20	.225	-9	5	-0.7
Yr.	8	21	.276	31	28	23	1	0	231	318	234	149	9	8	84	61	1.740	5.81	80	5.76	.322	21	.216	-21	6	-1.7
1896 Lou-N	2	3	.400	5	5	4	0	0	42	62	46	31	6	2	15	9	1.833	6.64	65	7.23	.340	2	.133	-10	0	-0.9
1898 Was-N	15	26	.366	45	42	39	0	0	361	428	232	181	10	16	84	92	1.418	4.51	81	4.05	.293	25	.177	-27	13	-3.0
1899 Was-N	17	21	.447	43	38	34	2	0	334^2	414	223	169	8	28	76	96	1.464	4.54	86	4.43	.303	26	.206	-11	12	-1.0
1900 StL-N	3	2	.600	7	5	3	0	0	46^2	60	44	24	2	1	21	6	1.736	4.63	78	5.46	.311	2	.095	-4	0	-0.6
Bro-N	3	4	.429	8	8	3	0	0	48	66	33	23	1	2	20	8	1.792	4.31	89	5.76	.326	4	.222	-3	3	-0.3
Yr.	6	6	.500	15	13	6	0	0	94^2	126	77	47	3	3	41	14	1.764	4.47	83	5.61	.319	6	.154	-7	3	-0.9
1901 Cle-A	0	0	....	2	1	0	0	0	11^1	20	11	10	0	4	5	0	2.206	7.94	45	9.42	.380	0	.000	-5	0	-0.6
Cin-N	0	1	.000	1	1	1	0	0	9	11	9	3	0	2	2	3	1.444	3.00	107	4.63	.299	0	.000	0	0	0.0
Total 14	**264**	**232**	**.532**	**540**	**505**	**449**	**28**	**4**	**4337^1**	**4743**	**2796**	**1867**	**120**	**278**	**1570**	**1667**	**1.417**	**3.87**	**103**	**2.26**	**.271**	**313**	**.169**	**40**	**258**	**-3.5**
• WEYHING, John	John Weyhing b: 6/24/1869, Louisville, KY d: 6/20/1890, Louisville, KY BL/TL, 6'2", 185 lbs. Deb: 7/13/1888																									
1888 Cin-a	3	4	.429	8	8	7	0	0	65^2	52	26	9	0	0	17	30	1.051	1.23	257	....	.210	3	.130	12	6	1.0
1889 Col-a	0	0	....	1	0	0	0	0	1	1	3	3	0	0	4	0	5.000	27.00	13	....	.252	0	....	-3	0	-0.2
Total 2	**3**	**4**	**.429**	**9**	**8**	**7**	**0**	**0**	**66^2**	**53**	**29**	**12**	**0**	**0**	**21**	**30**	**1.110**	**1.62**	**202**	**....**	**.211**	**3**	**.130**	**10**	**6**	**0.8**
• WHEAT, Lee	Leroy William Wheat b: 9/15/1929, Edwardsville, IL BR/TR, 6'4", 200 lbs. Deb: 4/21/1954																									
1954 Phi-A	0	2	.000	8	1	0	0	0	28^1	38	18	18	1	1	9	7	1.659	5.72	68	4.96	.304	1	.125	-5	0	-0.6
1955 KC-A	0	0	....	3	0	0	0	0	2	8	7	5	1	0	3	1	5.500	22.50	19	32.27	.533	0	....	-4	0	-0.4
Total 2	**0**	**2**	**.000**	**11**	**1**	**0**	**0**	**0**	**30^1**	**46**	**25**	**23**	**2**	**1**	**12**	**8**	**1.912**	**6.82**	**58**	**6.76**	**.329**	**1**	**.125**	**-9**	**0**	**-1.0**
• WHEATLEY, Charlie	Charles Wheatley b: 6/27/1893, Rosedale, KS d: 12/10/1982, Tulsa, OK BR/TR, 5'11", 174 lbs. Deb: 9/6/1912																									
1912 Det-A	1	4	.200	5	5	2	0	0	35	45	27	24	1	2	17	14	1.771	6.17	53	5.99	.331	0	.000	-11	0	-1.3
• WHEATON, Woody	Elwood Pierce Wheaton b: 10/3/1914, Philadelphia, PA d: 12/11/1995, Lancaster, PA BL/TL, 5'8.5", 160 lbs. Deb: 9/28/1943 ♦																									
1944 Phi-A	0	1	.000	11	1	1	0	0	38	36	17	15	1	1	20	15	1.474	3.55	98	3.72	.255	11	.186	-0	2	-0.2

YEAR	TM-L	W	L	PCT	G	GS	CG	SH	SV	IP	H	R	ER	HR	HB	BB	SO	RAT	ERA	ERA+	CERA	OAV	BH	AVG	PR+	WS	TPW
• WHEELER, Daniel	Daniel Michael Wheeler b: 12/10/1977, Providence, RI BR/TR, 6'3", 222 lbs. Deb: 9/1/1999																										
1999	TB-A	0	4	.000	6	6	0	0	0	30^2	35	20	20	7	0	13	32	1.565	5.87	85	5.96	.287	0	....	-3	1	-0.3
2000	TB-A	1	1	.500	11	2	0	0	0	23	29	14	14	2	2	11	17	1.739	5.48	90	5.87	.302	0	....	-2	1	-0.2
2001	TB-A	1	0	1.000	13	0	0	0	0	17^2	30	17	17	3	0	5	12	1.981	8.66	52	8.38	.375	0	....	-8	0	-0.8
2003	NY-N	1	3	.250	35	0	0	0	2	51	49	23	21	6	1	17	35	1.294	3.71	112	3.69	.253	0	.000	3	3	0.3
Total	4	3	8	.273	65	8	0	0	2	122^1	143	74	72	18	3	46	96	1.545	5.30	87	5.34	.291	0	.000	-10	5	-1.0
• WHEELER, George	George L. Wheeler b: 7/30/1869, Methuen, MA d: 3/21/1946, Santa Ana, CA BB/TR, 5'9", 180 lbs. Deb: 9/18/1896																										
1896	Phi-N	1	1	.500	3	2	2	0	0	16^1	18	11	7	0	2	5	2	1.408	3.86	112	3.91	.278	1	.111	1	1	0.0
1897	Phi-N	11	10	.524	26	19	17	0	0	191	229	114	84	3	3	62	35	1.524	3.96	106	4.26	.295	16	.203	9	12	0.7
1898	Phi-N	6	8	.429	15	13	10	0	0	112^1	155	94	52	1	6	36	20	1.700	4.17	82	5.37	.325	8	.186	-8	2	-0.8
1899	Phi-N	3	1	.750	6	5	3	0	0	39	44	30	26	1	3	13	3	1.462	6.00	61	4.19	.284	4	.235	-11	1	-0.8
Total	4	21	20	.512	50	39	32	0	0	358^2	446	249	169	5	14	116	60	1.567	4.24	91	4.58	.303	29	.196	-9	16	-1.0
• WHEELER, Harry	Harry Eugene Wheeler b: 3/3/1858, Versailles, IN d: 10/9/1900, Cincinnati, OH BR/TR, 5'11", 165 lbs. Deb: 6/19/1878 M/U ♦																										
1878	Pro-N	6	1	.857	7	6	6	0	0	62	70	40	24	1	....	25	25	1.532	3.48	63	....	.271	4	.148	-10	3	-1.0
1879	Cin-N	0	1	.000	1	1	0	0	0	1	6	10	9	0	....	4	0	10.00	81.00	3	....	.659	0	.000	-9	0	-0.9
1882	Cin-a	1	2	.333	4	1	1	0	0	21^2	21	17	13	0	....	12	10	1.523	5.40	49	....	.238	86	.250	-7	9	-1.6
1883	Col-a	0	1	.000	1	1	0	0	0	5	13	7	4	0	....	2	0	3.000	7.20	43	....	.456	84	.226	-2	4	-1.5
1884	KC-U	0	1	.000	1	1	1	0	0	8	7	6	1	0	....	0	6	.875	1.13	248	....	.220	16	.258	1	2	0.2
Total	5	7	6	.538	14	10	8	0	0	97^2	117	80	51	1	....	43	41	1.638	4.70	51	....	.281	256	.228	-26	18	-4.7
• WHEELER, Rip	Floyd Clark Wheeler b: 3/2/1898, Marion, KY d: 9/18/1968, Marion, KY BR/TR, 6', 180 lbs. Deb: 9/30/1921																										
1921	Pit-N	0	0	....	1	0	0	0	0	3	6	4	3	0	1	1	0	2.333	9.00	43	11.68	.500	0	.000	-2	0	-0.2
1922	Pit-N	0	0	....	1	0	0	0	0	1	1	0	0	0	0	2	0	3.000	0.00	....	10.60	.333	0	....	0	0	0.0
1923	Chi-N	1	2	.333	3	3	1	0	0	24	28	14	13	2	3	5	5	1.375	4.88	82	4.58	.298	1	.111	-3	1	-0.4
1924	Chi-N	3	6	.333	29	4	0	0	0	101^1	103	53	44	8	0	21	16	1.224	3.91	100	3.23	.265	7	.219	-2	5	-0.2
Total	4	4	8	.333	34	7	1	0	0	129^1	138	71	60	10	4	29	21	1.291	4.18	94	3.73	.277	8	.190	-6	6	-0.7
• WHEELOCK, Gary	Gary Richard Wheelock b: 11/29/1951, Bakersfield, CA BR/TR, 6'3", 205 lbs. Deb: 9/17/1976																										
1976	Cal-A	0	0	....	2	0	0	0	0	2	6	6	6	0	1	1	2	3.500	27.00	12	19.55	.500	0	....	-5	0	-0.6
1977	Sea-A	6	9	.400	17	17	2	0	0	88^1	94	58	48	16	2	26	47	1.358	4.89	84	4.64	.268	0	....	-9	3	-0.9
1980	Sea-A	0	0	....	1	1	0	0	0	3	4	2	2	0	0	1	1	1.667	6.00	69	5.24	.333	0	....	-1	0	-0.1
Total	3	6	9	.400	20	18	2	0	0	93^1	104	66	56	16	3	28	50	1.414	5.40	74	4.98	.277	0	....	-15	3	-1.5
• WHILLOCK, Jack	Jack Franklin Whillock b: 11/4/1942, Clinton, AR BR/TR, 6'3", 195 lbs. Deb: 8/29/1971																										
1971	Det-A	0	2	.000	7	0	0	0	1	8	10	5	5	0	0	2	6	1.500	5.63	64	4.18	.323	0	.000	-2	0	-0.2
• WHISENANT, Matt	Matthew Michael Whisenant b: 6/8/1971, Los Angeles, CA BR/TL, 6'3", 215 lbs. Deb: 7/4/1997																										
1997	Fla-N	0	0	....	4	0	0	0	0	2^2	4	6	5	0	0	6	4	3.750	16.88	24	13.34	.333	0	....	-4	0	-0.4
	KC-A	1	0	1.000	24	0	0	0	0	19	15	7	6	0	3	12	16	1.421	2.84	166	3.60	.211	0	....	4	2	0.4
1998	KC-A	2	1	.667	70	0	0	0	2	60^2	61	37	33	3	3	33	45	1.549	4.90	99	4.53	.271	0	....	0	5	0.0
1999	KC-A	4	4	.500	48	0	0	0	1	39^2	40	28	28	4	7	26	27	1.664	6.35	79	5.95	.267	0	....	-7	1	-0.6
	SD-N	0	1	.000	19	0	0	0	0	14^2	10	6	6	0	0	10	10	1.364	3.68	114	2.76	.200	0	....	1	1	0.1
2000	SD-N	2	2	.500	24	0	0	0	0	21^1	16	12	9	1	0	17	12	1.547	3.80	114	3.73	.213	0	....	1	1	0.1
Total	4	9	8	.529	189	0	0	0	3	158	146	96	87	8	13	104	114	1.582	4.96	95	4.65	.250	0	....	-5	10	-0.5
• WHITAKER, Pat	William H. Whitaker b: 1865, St. Louis, MO d: 7/15/1902, St. Louis, MO TR Deb: 10/11/1888																										
1888	Bal-a	1	1	.500	2	2	2	0	0	14	13	12	8	0	2	6	5	1.357	5.14	58	....	.237	0	.000	-3	0	-0.4
1889	Bal-a	1	0	1.000	1	1	1	0	0	9	10	4	2	0	0	4	1	1.556	2.00	190	....	.273	1	.250	2	1	0.2
Total	2	2	1	.667	3	3	3	0	0	23	23	16	10	0	2	10	6	1.435	3.91	79	....	.252	1	.100	-1	1	-0.2
• WHITBY, Bill	William Edward Whitby b: 7/29/1943, Crewe, VA BR/TR, 6'1", 190 lbs. Deb: 6/17/1964																										
1964	Min-A	0	0	....	4	0	0	0	0	6^1	8	6	6	3	0	1	2	1.421	8.53	42	7.41	.308	0	.000	-3	0	-0.4
• WHITCHER, Bob	Robert Arthur Whitcher b: 4/29/1917, Berlin, NH d: 5/8/1997, Akron, OH BL/TL, 5'8", 165 lbs. Deb: 8/20/1945																										
1945	Bos-N	0	2	.000	6	3	0	0	0	15^2	12	6	5	1	0	12	6	1.532	2.87	133	4.01	.235	1	.333	2	1	0.2
• WHITE, Abe	Adel White b: 5/16/1904, Winder, GA d: 10/1/1978, Atlanta, GA BR/TL, 6', 185 lbs. Deb: 7/10/1937																										
1937	StL-N	0	1	.000	5	0	0	0	0	9^1	14	7	7	1	0	3	2	1.821	6.75	59	6.71	.341	1	1.000	-3	0	-0.2
• WHITE, Deke	George Frederick White b: 9/8/1872, Albany, NY d: 11/27/1957, Albany, NY BB/TL Deb: 9/14/1895																										
1895	Phi-N	1	0	1.000	3	1	1	0	1	17^1	17	23	19	1	2	13	6	1.731	9.87	48	5.23	.253	1	.125	-10	0	-0.9
• WHITE, Doc	Guy Harris White b: 4/9/1879, Washington, DC d: 2/19/1969, Silver Spring, MD BL/TL, 6'1", 150 lbs. Deb: 4/22/1901 U ♦																										
1901	Phi-N	14	13	.519	31	27	22	0	0	236^2	241	122	84	2	14	56	132	1.255	3.19	106	3.09	.262	27	.276	5	16	1.0
1902	Phi-N	16	20	.444	36	35	34	3	1	306	277	126	86	3	13	72	185	1.141	2.53	111	2.47	.242	47	.263	18	27	2.0
1903	Chi-A	17	16	.515	37	36	29	3	0	300	258	119	71	4	14	69	114	1.090	2.13	132	2.26	.232	20	.202	28	23	3.5
1904	Chi-A	16	12	.571	30	30	23	7	0	228	201	82	45	6	9	68	115	1.180	1.78	138	2.50	.238	12	.158	12	17	1.4
1905	Chi-A	17	13	.567	36	33	25	4	0	260^1	204	67	51	2	9	58	120	1.006	1.76	140	1.86	.218	15	.167	13	22	1.5
1906*	Chi-A	18	6	.750	28	24	20	7	0	219^1	160	47	37	2	5	38	95	.903	**1.52**	**167**	**1.52**	.207	12	.185	22	25	2.8
1907	Chi-A	**27**	13	.675	46	35	24	6	1	291	270	93	73	3	6	38	141	1.058	2.26	106	2.18	.249	20	.222	7	25	1.1
1908	Chi-A	18	13	.581	41	37	24	5	0	296	262	94	84	3	9	69	126	1.118	2.55	90	2.42	.244	25	.229	-5	20	0.0
1909	Chi-A	11	9	.550	24	21	14	3	0	177^2	149	56	34	1	7	31	77	1.013	1.72	136	2.10	.226	45	.234	12	20	1.9
1910	Chi-A	15	13	.536	33	29	20	2	1	236^2	219	84	70	2	12	50	111	1.137	2.66	90	2.53	.243	25	.198	-6	15	-0.4
1911	Chi-A	10	14	.417	34	29	16	4	2	214^1	219	91	71	2	9	35	72	1.185	2.98	109	2.94	.271	20	.256	6	14	0.9
1912	Chi-A	8	10	.444	32	19	9	1	0	172	172	81	62	1	8	47	57	1.273	3.24	99	3.20	.267	7	.125	3	9	0.1
1913	Chi-A	2	4	.333	19	8	2	0	0	103	106	56	40	2	5	39	39	1.408	3.50	84	3.90	.278	3	.120	-7	2	-0.8
Total	13	189	156	.548	427	363	262	45	5	3041	2738	1118	808	33	120	670	1384	1.121	2.39	113	2.45	.243	278	.217	109	235	15.0
• WHITE, Ernie	Ernest Daniel White b: 9/5/1916, Pacolet Mills, SC d: 5/22/1974, Augusta, GA BR/TL, 5'11.5", 175 lbs. Deb: 5/9/1940 C																										
1940	StL-N	1	1	.500	8	1	0	0	0	21^2	29	13	10	0	1	14	15	1.985	4.15	96	6.01	.315	3	.429	-0	1	0.1
1941	StL-N	17	7	.708	32	25	12	3	2	210	169	72	56	12	6	70	117	1.138	2.40	157	2.52	.217	15	.190	28	22	3.0
1942*	StL-N	7	5	.583	26	19	7	1	2	128^1	113	57	36	11	2	41	67	1.200	2.52	136	2.97	.232	8	.195	11	9	1.2
1943*	StL-N	5	5	.500	14	10	5	1	0	78^2	78	38	33	4	1	33	28	1.411	3.78	89	3.66	.257	6	.214	-6	3	-0.6
1946	Bos-N	0	1	.000	12	1	0	0	0	23^2	22	11	11	1	0	12	8	1.437	4.18	82	3.71	.256	1	.250	-2	1	-0.2
1947	Bos-N	0	0	....	1	1	0	0	0	4	1	0	0	0	0	1	1	.500	0.00	....	0.41	.083	1	1.000	2	1	0.2
1948	Bos-N	0	2	.000	15	0	0	0	2	23	13	7	5	0	0	17	8	1.304	1.96	196	2.15	.167	0	.000	5	3	0.4
Total	7	30	21	.588	108	57	24	5	6	489^1	425	198	151	28	10	188	244	1.253	2.78	129	3.00	.231	34	.209	39	40	4.2
• WHITE, Gabe	Gabriel Allen White b: 11/20/1971, Sebring, FL BL/TL, 6'2", 200 lbs. Deb: 5/27/1994																										
1994	Mon-N	1	1	.500	7	5	0	0	1	23^2	24	16	16	4	1	11	17	1.479	6.08	69	5.03	.261	0	.000	-5	0	-0.5
1995	Mon-N	1	2	.333	19	1	0	0	0	25^2	26	21	20	7	1	9	25	1.364	7.01	61	5.12	.260	0	.000	-8	0	-0.8
1997	Cin-N	2	2	.500	12	6	0	0	1	41	39	20	20	6	1	8	25	1.146	4.39	98	3.37	.253	1	.111	-1	3	-0.1
1998	Cin-N	5	5	.500	69	3	0	0	9	98^2	86	46	44	17	1	27	83	1.145	4.01	107	3.30	.231	1	.167	3	8	0.3
1999	Cin-N	1	2	.333	50	0	0	0	0	61	68	31	30	13	2	14	61	1.344	4.43	105	4.95	.281	0	....	-0	3	0.0
2000	Cin-N	0	0	....	1	0	0	0	0	1	2	2	2	1	0	1	2	3.000	18.00	26	23.01	.400	0	....	-1	0	-0.1
	Col-N	11	2	.846	67	0	0	0	5	83	62	21	20	5	3	14	82	.916	2.17	267	1.82	.208	2	.222	33	15	3.2
	Yr.	11	2	.846	68	0	0	0	5	84	64	23	22	6	3	15	84	.940	2.36	241	2.08	.211	2	.222	32	15	3.0
2001	Col-N	1	7	.125	69	0	0	0	0	67^2	70	47	47	18	1	26	47	1.419	6.25	85	5.42	.270	0	.000	-7	2	-0.7
2002	Cin-N	6	1	.857	62	0	0	0	0	54^1	49	19	18	3	2	10	41	1.086	2.98	142	2.56	.238	0	.000	8	7	0.7

YEAR	TM-L	W	L	PCT	G	GS	CG	SH	SV	IP	H	R	ER	HR	HB	BB	SO	RAT	ERA	ERA+	CERA	OAV	BH	AVG	PR+	WS	TPW
2003	Cin-N	3	0	1.000	34	0	0	0	0	34^1	36	15	15	5	1	6	23	1.223	3.93	108	3.81	.275	0	.000	1	3	0.1
	*NY-A	2	1	.667	12	0	0	0	0	12^1	8	7	6	2	1	2	6	.811	4.38	100	1.89	.182	0	....	0	1	0.0
Total	9	33	23	.589	402	15	0	0	16	502^2	470	245	238	81	14	128	412	1.190	4.26	108	3.68	.247	4	.105	23	42	2.1
• WHITE, Hal	Harold George White b: 3/18/1919, Utica, NY d: 4/21/2001, Venice, FL BR/TR, 5'10", 170 lbs. Deb: 4/22/1941																										
1941	Det-A	0	0	....	4	0	0	0	0	9	11	6	6	0	0	6	2	1.889	6.00	76	5.16	.306	0	.000	-1	0	-0.1
1942	Det-A	12	12	.500	34	25	12	4	1	216^2	212	80	70	6	5	82	93	1.357	2.91	136	3.34	.252	13	.169	28	18	2.7
1943	Det-A	7	12	.368	32	24	7	2	2	177^2	150	84	67	6	1	71	58	1.244	3.39	104	2.74	.228	8	.140	3	8	0.3
1946	Det-A	1	1	.500	11	1	1	0	0	27^1	34	20	17	5	0	15	12	1.793	5.60	65	6.84	.312	0	.000	-6	0	-0.7
1947	Det-A	4	5	.444	35	5	0	0	2	84^2	91	43	34	5	2	47	33	1.630	3.61	104	4.81	.279	3	.167	3	5	0.4
1948	Det-A	2	1	.667	27	0	0	0	1	42^2	46	31	29	2	1	26	17	1.688	6.12	71	4.81	.272	2	.154	-7	1	-0.7
1949	Det-A	1	0	1.000	9	0	0	0	2	12	5	0	0	0	0	4	4	.750	0.00	....	0.86	.125	1	.333	6	3	0.6
1950	Det-A	9	6	.600	42	8	3	1	1	111	96	59	56	7	1	65	53	1.450	4.54	103	3.68	.239	4	.121	1	7	-0.1
1951	Det-A	3	4	.429	38	4	0	0	4	76	74	45	40	7	2	49	23	1.618	4.74	88	4.87	.264	4	.250	-4	4	-0.4
1952	Det-A	1	8	.111	41	0	0	0	5	63^1	53	29	26	1	0	39	18	1.453	3.69	103	3.32	.237	2	.182	2	4	0.2
1953	StL-A	0	0	....	10	0	0	0	0	10^1	8	3	3	1	1	3	2	1.065	2.61	161	2.52	.205	0	.000	2	1	0.2
	StL-N	6	5	.545	49	0	0	0	7	84^2	84	32	28	5	0	39	32	1.453	2.98	143	3.99	.272	0	.000	13	9	1.1
1954	StL-N	0	0	....	4	0	0	0	0	5	11	11	11	2	1	4	2	3.000	19.80	21	18.21	.440	0	.000	-9	0	-0.9
Total	12	46	54	.460	336	67	23	7	25	920^1	875	443	387	47	14	450	349	1.440	3.78	106	3.81	.253	37	.145	32	60	2.6
• WHITE, Kirby	Oliver Kirby "Red,Buck" White b: 1/3/1884, Hillsboro, OH d: 4/22/1943, Hillsboro, OH BL/TR, 6', 190 lbs. Deb: 5/4/1909																										
1909	Bos-N	6	13	.316	23	19	11	1	0	148^1	134	73	53	5	1	80	53	1.443	3.22	87	3.61	.245	8	.160	-7	6	-0.8
1910	Bos-N	1	2	.333	3	3	3	0	0	26	15	7	4	2	3	12	6	1.038	1.38	239	2.58	.188	2	.333	5	3	0.6
	Pit-N	10	9	.526	30	21	7	3	2	153^1	142	73	59	2	5	75	42	1.415	3.46	91	3.60	.258	12	.261	-7	10	-0.3
	Yr.	11	11	.500	33	24	10	3	2	179^1	157	80	63	4	8	87	48	1.361	3.16	100	3.45	.249	14	.269	-2	13	0.3
1911	Pit-N	0	1	.000	2	1	0	0	0	3	3	4	3	1	0	1	1	1.333	9.00	38	5.23	.250	0	.000	-2	0	-0.2
Total	3	17	25	.405	58	44	21	4	2	330^2	294	157	119	10	9	168	102	1.397	3.24	92	3.54	.247	22	.214	-10	19	-0.7
• WHITE, Larry	Larry David White b: 9/24/1958, San Fernando, CA BR/TR, 6'5", 190 lbs. Deb: 9/20/1983																										
1983	LA-N	0	0	....	4	0	0	0	0	7	4	1	1	0	0	3	5	1.000	1.29	279	1.60	.174	0	....	2	1	0.2
1984	LA-N	0	1	.000	7	1	0	0	0	12	9	5	4	2	0	6	10	1.250	3.00	118	3.31	.209	0	.000	1	1	0.1
Total	2	0	1	.000	11	1	0	0	0	19	13	6	5	2	0	9	15	1.158	2.37	150	2.68	.197	0	.000	3	2	0.3
• WHITE, Matt	Matthew J. White b: 8/19/1977, Pittsfield, MA BR/TL, 6'1", 180 lbs. Deb: 5/27/2003																										
2003	Bos-A	0	1	.000	3	0	0	0	0	3^2	10	11	11	1	0	3	0	3.545	27.00	17	20.66	.526	0	....	-9	0	-0.9
	Sea-A	0	0	....	3	0	0	0	0	2	3	3	3	2	0	2	0	2.500	13.50	32	20.49	.375	0	....	-2	0	-0.2
	Yr.	0	1	.000	6	0	0	0	0	5^2	13	14	14	3	0	5	0	3.176	22.24	20	20.60	.481	0	....	-11	0	-1.1
• WHITE, Rick	Richard Allen White b: 12/23/1968, Springfield, OH BR/TR, 6'4", 215 lbs. Deb: 4/6/1994																										
1994	Pit-N	4	5	.444	43	5	0	0	6	75^1	79	35	32	9	6	17	38	1.274	3.82	113	4.11	.280	1	.077	3	7	0.3
1995	Pit-N	2	3	.400	15	9	0	0	0	55	66	33	29	3	2	18	29	1.527	4.75	91	4.70	.299	1	.067	-2	2	-0.3
1998	TB-A	2	6	.250	38	3	0	0	0	68^2	66	32	29	8	2	23	39	1.296	3.80	126	3.82	.253	1	.333	5	5	0.5
1999	TB-A	5	3	.625	63	1	0	0	0	108	132	56	49	8	1	38	81	1.574	4.08	122	4.96	.304	0	....	11	7	1.0
2000	TB-A	3	6	.333	44	0	0	0	2	71^1	57	30	27	7	5	26	47	1.164	3.41	145	3.09	.220	0	....	11	7	1.0
	*NY-N	2	3	.400	22	0	0	0	1	28^1	26	14	12	2	2	12	20	1.341	3.81	116	3.51	.232	1	.200	2	2	0.2
2001	NY-N	4	5	.444	55	0	0	0	2	69^2	71	38	30	7	2	17	51	1.263	3.88	107	3.52	.257	0	.000	2	5	0.1
2002	Col-N	2	6	.250	41	0	0	0	0	40^2	49	30	28	4	1	18	27	1.648	6.20	77	5.47	.310	0	....	-6	1	-0.6
	*StL-N	3	1	.750	20	0	0	0	0	22	13	3	2	0	0	3	14	.727	0.82	483	0.94	.169	0	.000	7	4	0.7
	Yr.	5	7	.417	61	0	0	0	0	62^2	62	33	30	4	1	21	41	1.324	4.31	109	3.88	.264	0	.000	1	5	0.1
2003	Chi-A	1	2	.333	34	0	0	0	1	47^2	56	39	35	11	1	13	37	1.448	6.61	68	5.58	.295	0	....	-12	0	-1.1
	Hou-N	0	0	....	15	0	0	0	0	19^1	18	9	8	2	3	8	17	1.345	3.72	119	4.33	.243	0	....	1	1	0.1
Total	8	28	40	.412	390	18	0	0	12	606	633	319	281	61	25	193	400	1.363	4.17	109	4.16	.270	4	.100	23	41	1.9
• WHITE, Steve	Stephen Vincent White b: 12/21/1884, Dorchester, MA d: 1/29/1975, Braintree, MA BR/TR, 5'10", 160 lbs. Deb: 5/29/1912																										
1912	Was-A	0	0	....	1	0	0	0	0	0^2	2	2	0	1	0	0	1	3.000	0.00	....	41.53	.667	0	....	0	0	0.0
	Bos-N	0	0	....	3	0	0	0	0	6	9	5	4	0	1	5	2	2.333	6.00	59	9.45	.429	0	.000	-2	0	-0.2
• WHITE, Will	William Henry "Whoop-La" White b: 10/11/1854, Caton, NY d: 8/31/1911, Port Carling, Canada BB/TR, 5'9.5", 175 lbs. Deb: 7/20/1877 M																										
1877	Bos-N	2	1	.667	3	3	3	1	0	27	27	15	9	0	....	2	7	1.074	3.00	94	....	.245	3	.200	-1	2	-0.1
1878	Cin-N	30	21	.588	52	52	52	5	0	468	477	249	93	1	....	45	169	1.115	1.79	119	....	.251	28	.142	12	30	0.5
1879	Cin-N	43	31	.581	**76**	**75**	**75**	4	0	**680**	676	404	150	10	....	68	232	1.094	1.99	117	....	.243	40	.136	22	33	0.7
1880	Cin-N	18	42	.300	62	62	58	3	0	517^1	550	323	123	9	....	56	161	1.171	2.14	116	....	.259	35	.169	**30**	17	2.3
1881	Det-N	0	2	.000	2	2	2	0	0	18	24	18	10	0	....	2	5	1.444	5.00	58	....	.307	0	.000	-4	0	-0.5
1882	Cin-a	**40**	12	.769	54	54	**52**	**8**	0	**480**	411	164	82	3	....	71	122	1.004	1.54	171	....	.216	55	.266	**50**	**54**	**5.1**
1883	Cin-a	**43**	22	.662	65	64	64	**6**	0	577	473	255	134	16	....	104	141	1.000	**2.09**	155	....	.209	54	.225	53	51	4.9
1884	Cin-a	34	18	.654	52	52	52	**7**	0	456	479	224	168	16	35	74	118	1.213	3.32	100	....	.256	35	.190	-8	33	-0.8
1885	Cin-a	18	15	.545	34	34	33	2	0	293^1	295	169	115	9	27	64	80	1.224	3.53	92	....	.251	20	.169	-12	18	-1.3
1886	Cin-a	1	2	.333	3	3	3	0	0	26	28	23	12	1	6	10	6	1.462	4.15	85	....	.263	1	.111	-2	1	-0.2
Total	10	229	166	.580	403	401	394	36	0	3542^2	3440	1844	896	65	68	496	1041	1.111	2.28	121	....	.240	271	.183	142	239	10.5
• WHITEHEAD, John	John Henderson "Silent John" Whitehead b: 4/27/1909, Coleman, TX d: 10/20/1964, Bonham, TX BR/TR, 6'2", 195 lbs. Deb: 4/19/1935																										
1935	Chi-A	13	13	.500	28	27	18	1	0	222^1	209	101	92	17	2	101	72	1.394	3.72	124	3.75	.250	12	.146	20	17	1.4
1936	Chi-A	13	13	.500	34	32	15	1	1	230^2	254	137	119	9	5	98	70	1.526	4.64	112	4.21	.276	21	.241	12	16	1.1
1937	Chi-A	11	8	.579	26	24	8	4	0	165^2	191	84	75	14	5	56	45	1.491	4.07	113	4.71	.294	13	.224	6	12	0.6
1938	Chi-A	10	11	.476	32	24	10	2	2	183^1	218	108	97	12	3	80	38	1.625	4.76	103	5.00	.299	6	.100	3	9	-0.1
1939	Chi-A	0	3	.000	7	4	0	0	0	32	60	30	29	4	0	5	9	2.031	8.16	58	8.60	.408	0	.000	-13	0	-1.3
	StL-A	1	3	.250	26	4	0	0	1	66	88	49	43	10	2	17	9	1.591	5.86	83	5.81	.321	1	.059	-6	2	-0.7
	Yr.	1	6	.143	33	8	0	0	1	98	148	79	72	14	2	22	18	1.735	6.61	73	6.72	.352	1	.038	-18	2	-1.9
1940	StL-A	1	3	.250	15	4	1	1	0	40	46	25	24	3	0	14	11	1.500	5.40	85	4.43	.286	2	.167	-3	1	-0.4
1942	StL-A	0	0	....	4	0	0	0	0	4	8	3	3	0	1	1	0	2.250	6.75	55	10.03	.421	0	....	-1	0	-0.1
Total	7	49	54	.476	172	119	52	9	4	944	1074	537	482	69	18	372	254	1.532	4.60	105	4.64	.287	55	.169	18	57	0.7
• WHITEHILL, Earl	Earl Oliver Whitehill b: 2/7/1900, Cedar Rapids, IA d: 10/22/1954, Omaha, NE BL/TL, 5'9.5", 174 lbs. Deb: 9/15/1923 C																										
1923	Det-A	2	0	1.000	8	3	1	0	0	33	22	14	10	2	3	15	19	1.121	2.73	142	2.42	.188	4	.364	4	3	0.6
1924	Det-A	17	9	.654	35	32	16	2	0	233	260	125	100	8	13	79	65	1.455	3.86	106	4.11	.288	19	.213	7	16	0.7
1925	Det-A	11	11	.500	35	**33**	15	1	2	239^1	267	135	124	13	10	88	83	1.483	4.66	92	4.40	.293	19	.218	-10	13	-0.9
1926	Det-A	16	13	.552	36	34	13	0	0	252^1	271	136	112	7	8	79	109	1.387	3.99	101	3.64	.277	23	.253	4	15	0.8
1927	Det-A	16	14	.533	41	31	17	3	3	236	238	110	88	4	9	105	95	1.453	3.36	125	3.71	.267	16	.205	25	19	2.3
1928	Det-A	11	16	.407	31	30	12	1	0	196^1	214	131	94	8	1	78	93	1.487	4.31	95	3.91	.277	13	.194	-4	7	-0.5
1929	Det-A	14	15	.483	38	28	18	1	1	245^1	267	147	126	16	3	96	103	1.480	4.62	93	4.24	.280	23	.256	-1	12	0.4
1930	Det-A	17	13	.567	34	31	16	0	1	220^2	248	139	104	8	8	80	109	1.486	4.24	113	4.16	.285	16	.193	14	14	0.9
1931	Det-A	13	16	.448	34	34	22	0	0	271^1	287	152	123	22	5	118	81	1.493	4.08	112	4.36	.274	15	.155	15	18	1.0
1932	Det-A	16	12	.571	33	31	17	3	0	244	255	136	123	17	5	93	81	1.426	4.54	104	4.00	.269	22	.244	1	14	0.2
1933*	Was-A	22	8	.733	39	**37**	19	2	1	270	271	112	100	9	4	100	96	1.374	3.33	125	3.51	.262	24	.222	20	23	2.0
1934	Was-A	14	11	.560	32	31	15	0	0	235	269	129	118	10	3	94	96	1.545	4.52	96	4.40	.290	17	.200	-5	14	-0.1
1935	Was-A	14	13	.519	34	34	19	1	0	279^1	318	149	133	16	7	104	102	1.511	4.29	101	4.43	.289	19	.183	2	13	0.1
1936	Was-A	14	11	.560	28	28	14	0	0	212^1	252	124	115	17	2	89	63	1.606	4.87	98	5.02	.294	13	.169	-5	12	-0.5
1937	Cle-A	8	8	.500	33	22	6	1	2	147	189	111	106	9	6	80	53	1.830	6.49	71	6.18	.322	11	.224	-29	3	-2.6
1938	Cle-A	9	8	.529	26	23	4	0	0	160^1	187	109	99	18	9	83	60	1.684	5.56	83	5.67	.289	7	.125	-17	6	-1.7

YEAR	TM-L	W	L	PCT	G	GS	CG	SH	SV	IP	H	R	ER	HR	HB	BB	SO	RAT	ERA	ERA+	CERA	OAV	BH	AVG	PR+	WS	TPW
1939	Chi-N	4	7	.364	24	11	2	1	1	89^1	102	59	51	8	5	50	42	1.701	5.14	77	5.51	.292	3	.103	-10	1	-1.1
Total	17	218	185	.541	541	473	226	16	11	3564^2	3917	2018	1726	192	101	1431	1350	1.500	4.36	100	4.31	.282	264	.204	10	203	1.6
• WHITEHOUSE, Charlie	Charles Evis "Lefty" Whitehouse b: 1/25/1894, Charleston, IL d: 7/19/1960, Indianapolis, IN BB/TL, 6', 152 lbs. Deb: 8/29/1914																										
1914	Ind-F	2	0	1.000	8	2	2	0	0	26	34	14	14	1	0	5	10	1.500	4.85	72	4.50	.324	0	.000	-4	1	-0.6
1915	New-F	2	2	.500	11	3	1	0	0	39^2	46	29	19	0	5	17	18	1.588	4.31	66	4.67	.299	0	.000	-7	0	-0.8
1919	Was-A	0	1	.000	6	1	0	0	0	12	13	7	6	1	0	6	5	1.583	4.50	71	4.87	.283	0	.000	-2	0	-0.2
Total	3	4	3	.571	25	6	3	0	0	77^2	93	50	39	2	5	28	33	1.558	4.52	68	4.65	.305	0	.000	-12	1	-1.5
• WHITEHOUSE, Len	Leonard Joseph Whitehouse b: 9/10/1957, Burlington, VT BL/TL, 5'11", 175 lbs. Deb: 9/1/1981																										
1981	Tex-A	0	1	.000	2	1	0	0	0	3^1	8	7	6	1	0	2	2	3.000	16.20	21	16.31	.500	0	....	-5	0	-0.5
1983	Min-A	7	1	.875	60	0	0	0	2	73^2	70	34	34	6	2	44	44	1.548	4.15	102	4.36	.261	0	....	-0	5	0.0
1984	Min-A	2	2	.500	30	0	0	0	1	31^1	29	11	11	3	2	17	18	1.468	3.16	133	4.38	.254	0	....	3	3	0.3
1985	Min-A	0	0	....	5	0	0	0	1	7^1	12	9	9	4	0	2	4	1.909	11.05	40	11.04	.353	0	....	-5	0	-0.5
Total	4	9	4	.692	97	1	0	0	4	115^2	119	61	60	14	4	65	68	1.591	4.67	89	5.13	.275	0	....	-7	8	-0.8
• WHITEHURST, Wally	Walter Richard Whitehurst b: 4/11/1964, Shreveport, LA BR/TR, 6'3", 195 lbs. Deb: 7/17/1989																										
1989	NY-N	0	1	.000	9	1	0	0	0	14	17	7	7	2	0	5	9	1.571	4.50	72	5.33	.293	0	.000	-2	0	-0.2
1990	NY-N	1	0	1.000	38	0	0	0	2	65^2	63	27	24	5	0	9	46	1.096	3.29	114	2.69	.251	2	.250	4	5	0.5
1991	NY-N	7	12	.368	36	20	0	0	1	133^1	142	67	62	12	4	25	87	1.253	4.19	87	3.64	.274	6	.182	-5	5	-0.4
1992	NY-N	3	9	.250	44	11	0	0	0	97	99	45	39	4	4	33	70	1.361	3.62	96	3.58	.264	4	.182	-0	4	0.0
1993	SD-N	4	7	.364	21	19	0	0	0	105^2	109	47	45	11	3	30	57	1.315	3.83	108	3.95	.276	2	.083	4	5	0.2
1994	SD-N	4	7	.364	13	13	0	0	0	64	84	37	35	8	1	26	43	1.719	4.92	84	6.14	.319	2	.105	-4	2	-0.4
1996	NY-A	1	1	.500	2	2	0	0	0	8	11	6	6	1	0	2	1	1.625	6.75	73	5.88	.324	0	....	-1	0	-0.1
Total	7	20	37	.351	163	66	0	0	3	487^2	525	236	218	43	12	130	313	1.343	4.02	94	3.98	.277	16	.150	-5	21	-0.4
• WHITESIDE, Matt	Matthew Christopher Whiteside b: 8/8/1967, Charleston, MO BR/TR, 6', 205 lbs. Deb: 8/5/1992																										
1992	Tex-A	1	1	.500	20	0	0	0	4	28	26	8	6	1	0	11	13	1.321	1.93	197	3.12	.245	0	....	6	4	0.6
1993	Tex-A	2	1	.667	60	0	0	0	1	73	78	37	35	7	1	23	39	1.384	4.32	96	4.15	.281	0	....	0	4	0.0
1994	Tex-A	2	2	.500	47	0	0	0	1	61	68	40	34	6	1	28	37	1.574	5.02	96	4.97	.286	0	....	0	3	0.0
1995	Tex-A	5	4	.556	40	0	0	0	3	53	48	24	24	5	1	19	46	1.264	4.08	118	3.37	.242	0	....	5	6	0.4
1996	Tex-A	0	1	.000	14	0	0	0	0	32^1	43	24	24	8	0	11	15	1.670	6.68	79	6.87	.321	0	....	-5	1	-0.5
1997	Tex-A	4	1	.800	42	1	0	0	0	72^2	85	45	41	4	3	26	44	1.528	5.08	94	4.65	.296	0	....	-1	3	-0.1
1998	Phi-N	1	1	.500	10	0	0	0	0	18	27	18	17	6	0	5	14	1.778	8.50	51	8.40	.338	0	.000	-8	0	-0.8
1999	SD-N	1	0	1.000	10	0	0	0	0	11	19	17	17	1	0	5	9	2.182	13.91	30	8.89	.396	0	....	-12	0	-1.1
2000	SD-N	2	3	.400	28	0	0	0	0	37	32	21	17	6	1	17	27	1.324	4.14	104	3.94	.232	0	....	0	2	0.0
2001	Atl-N	0	1	.000	13	0	0	0	0	16^1	23	14	13	5	1	7	10	1.837	7.16	61	8.26	.319	0	....	-5	0	-0.5
Total	10	18	15	.545	284	1	0	0	9	402^1	449	248	228	49	8	152	254	1.494	5.10	89	4.88	.284	0	.000	-20	23	-1.9
• WHITESIDE, Sean	David Sean Whiteside b: 4/19/1971, Lakeland, FL BL/TL, 6'4", 190 lbs. Deb: 4/29/1995																										
1995	Det-A	0	0	....	2	0	0	0	0	3^2	7	6	6	1	0	4	2	3.000	14.73	32	14.10	.438	0	....	-4	0	-0.4
• WHITING, Jesse	Jesse W. Whiting b: 5/30/1879, Philadelphia, PA d: 10/28/1937, Philadelphia, PA TR, 5'10" Deb: 9/27/1902																										
1902	Phi-N	0	1	.000	1	1	1	0	0	9	13	8	5	0	0	6	0	2.111	5.00	56	7.12	.337	1	.333	-2	0	-0.2
1906	Bro-N	1	1	.500	3	2	2	1	0	24^2	26	10	8	0	1	6	7	1.297	2.92	86	3.42	.286	3	.300	-1	1	0.0
1907	Bro-N	0	0	....	1	0	0	0	0	3	3	4	4	0	0	3	2	2.000	12.00	19	5.58	.273	0	.000	-3	0	-0.4
Total	3	1	2	.333	5	3	3	1	0	36^2	42	22	17	0	1	15	9	1.555	4.17	61	4.50	.299	4	.267	-6	1	-0.6
• WHITNEY, Jim	James Evans "Grasshopper Jim" Whitney b: 11/10/1857, Conklin, NY d: 5/21/1891, Binghamton, NY BL/TR, 6'2", 172 lbs. Deb: 5/2/1881 U ♦																										
1881	Bos-N	**31**	33	.484	**66**	**63**	**57**	6	0	**552^1**	548	284	152	6	....	90	162	1.155	2.48	107	....	.248	72	.255	12	**42**	2.2
1882	Bos-N	24	21	.533	49	48	46	3	0	420	404	229	123	3	....	41	180	1.060	2.64	108	....	.239	81	.323	17	40	**3.8**
1883	Bos-N	37	21	.638	62	56	54	1	**2**	514	492	258	128	7	....	35	**345**	1.025	2.24	138	....	.237	115	.281	**54**	57	**6.4**
1884	Bos-N	23	14	.622	38	37	35	6	0	336	272	140	78	12	....	27	270	.890	2.09	138	....	.209	70	.259	24	37	2.9
1885	Bos-N	18	32	.360	51	50	50	2	0	441^1	503	286	146	14	....	37	200	1.224	2.98	90	....	.274	68	.234	3	24	0.7
1886	KC-N	12	32	.273	46	44	42	3	0	393	465	292	196	9	....	55	167	1.323	4.49	83	....	.284	59	.239	-22	21	-1.0
1887	Was-N	24	21	.533	47	47	46	3	0	404^2	472	253	145	16	16	42	146	1.166	3.22	125	....	.283	71	.324	44	34	4.8
1888	Was-N	18	21	.462	39	39	37	2	0	325	317	184	110	7	9	54	79	1.142	3.05	91	....	.246	24	.170	-8	17	-0.9
1889	Ind-N	2	7	.222	9	8	7	0	0	70	106	73	53	4	2	19	16	1.786	6.81	61	....	.338	12	.375	-21	2	-1.3
1890	Phi-a	2	2	.500	6	4	3	0	0	40	61	27	23	1	1	11	6	1.800	5.18	74	....	.340	5	.238	-4	1	-0.3
Total	10	191	204	.484	413	396	377	26	2	3496^1	3640	2026	1154	79	28	411	1571	1.147	2.97	105	....	.256	577	.267	99	275	17.3
• WHITROCK, Bill	William Franklin Whitrock b: 3/4/1870, Cincinnati, OH d: 7/26/1935, Derby, CT TR, 5'7.5", 170 lbs. Deb: 5/3/1890																										
1890	StL-a	5	6	.455	16	11	10	0	1	105	104	62	41	2	7	40	39	1.371	3.51	123	....	.251	7	.146	9	8	0.5
1893	Lou-N	2	5	.286	8	8	5	0	0	46^2	64	44	42	3	4	18	8	1.757	8.10	54	6.16	.317	7	.280	-19	1	-1.4
1894	Lou-N	0	1	.000	1	1	0	0	0	4	8	8	4	0	0	2	0	2.500	9.00	57	9.81	.410	0	.000	-2	0	-0.2
	Cin-N	2	6	.250	11	9	8	0	0	79^1	121	88	52	7	9	39	9	2.017	5.90	94	7.90	.347	13	.217	-3	2	-0.7
	Yr.	2	7	.222	12	10	8	0	0	83^1	129	96	56	7	9	41	9	2.040	6.05	91	7.99	.350	13	.210	-5	2	-0.9
1896	Phi-N	0	1	.000	2	1	1	0	0	9	10	5	3	0	0	3	1	1.444	3.00	143	3.64	.279	0	.000	1	1	0.1
Total	4	9	19	.321	38	30	24	0	1	244	307	207	142	12	20	102	57	1.676	5.24	91	4.04	.301	27	.196	-13	12	-1.7
• WHITSON, Ed	Eddie Lee Whitson b: 5/19/1955, Johnson City, TN BR/TR, 6'3", 195 lbs. Deb: 9/4/1977																										
1977	Pit-N	1	0	1.000	5	2	0	0	0	15^2	11	6	6	0	0	9	10	1.277	3.45	116	2.36	.204	0	.000	1	1	0.0
1978	Pit-N	5	6	.455	43	0	0	0	4	74^1	66	31	27	5	2	37	64	1.386	3.27	113	3.64	.243	2	.182	5	5	0.5
1979	Pit-N	2	3	.400	19	7	0	0	1	57^2	53	36	28	6	1	36	31	1.543	4.37	89	4.40	.238	0	.000	-4	1	-0.5
	SF-N	5	8	.385	18	17	2	0	0	100^1	98	47	44	5	4	39	62	1.365	3.95	88	3.54	.254	5	.156	-4	4	-0.5
	Yr.	7	11	.389	37	24	2	0	1	158	151	83	72	11	5	75	93	1.430	4.10	89	3.86	.248	5	.111	-8	5	-1.0
1980	SF-N★	11	13	.458	34	34	6	2	0	211^2	222	88	73	7	4	56	90	1.313	3.10	114	3.38	.271	6	.091	14	12	1.1
1981	SF-N	6	9	.400	22	22	2	1	0	123	130	61	55	10	2	47	65	1.439	4.02	85	4.21	.273	3	.091	-7	3	-0.9
1982	Cle-A	4	2	.667	40	9	1	1	2	107^2	91	43	39	6	0	58	61	1.384	3.26	125	3.36	.231	0	....	11	9	1.1
1983	SD-N	5	7	.417	31	21	2	0	1	144^1	143	73	69	23	1	50	81	1.337	4.30	81	4.22	.256	8	.182	-15	4	-1.5
1984*	SD-N	14	8	.636	31	31	1	0	0	189	181	72	68	16	3	42	103	1.180	3.24	110	3.14	.255	3	.049	3	11	-0.2
1985	NY-A	10	8	.556	30	30	2	2	0	158^2	201	100	86	19	2	43	89	1.538	4.88	82	5.30	.309	0	....	-18	4	-1.7
1986	NY-A	5	2	.714	14	4	0	0	0	37	54	37	31	5	0	23	27	2.081	7.54	54	7.85	.335	0	....	-14	0	-1.4
	SD-N	1	7	.125	17	12	0	0	0	75^2	85	48	47	8	0	37	46	1.612	5.59	65	5.26	.287	3	.167	-16	0	-1.7
1987	SD-N	10	13	.435	36	34	3	1	0	205^2	197	113	108	36	3	64	135	1.269	4.73	84	4.07	.251	8	.123	-19	6	-2.1
1988	SD-N	13	11	.542	34	33	3	1	0	205^1	202	93	86	17	1	45	118	1.203	3.77	90	3.20	.259	11	.167	-12	9	-1.1
1989	SD-N	16	11	.593	33	33	5	1	0	227	198	77	67	22	5	48	117	1.084	2.66	132	2.72	.235	10	.139	19	18	2.1
1990	SD-N	14	9	.609	32	32	6	3	0	228^2	215	73	66	13	1	47	127	1.146	2.60	147	2.76	.251	10	.149	30	19	3.2
1991	SD-N	4	6	.400	13	12	2	0	0	78^2	93	47	44	13	0	17	40	1.398	5.03	75	4.80	.299	3	.125	-11	1	-1.2
Total	15	126	123	.506	452	333	35	12	8	2240^1	2240	1045	944	211	29	698	1266	1.311	3.79	97	3.73	.261	72	.125	-38	107	-4.9
• WHITTAKER, Walt	Walter Elton "Doc" Whittaker b: 6/11/1894, Chelsea, MA d: 8/7/1965, Pembroke, MA BL/TR, 5'9.5", 165 lbs. Deb: 7/6/1916																										
1916	Phi-A	0	0	....	1	0	0	0	0	2	3	1	1	0	0	2	0	2.500	4.50	63	9.12	.375	0	....	-0	0	0.0
• WICKANDER, Kevin	Kevin Dean Wickander b: 1/4/1965, Fort Dodge, IA BL/TL, 6'2", 202 lbs. Deb: 8/10/1989																										
1989	Cle-A	0	0	....	2	0	0	0	0	2^2	6	1	1	0	0	2	0	3.000	3.38	117	12.51	.462	0	....	0	0	0.0
1990	Cle-A	0	1	.000	10	0	0	0	0	12^1	14	6	5	0	1	4	10	1.459	3.65	107	4.26	.304	0	....	1	1	0.1
1992	Cle-A	2	0	1.000	44	0	0	0	1	41	39	14	14	1	4	28	38	1.634	3.07	127	4.63	.258	0	....	4	4	0.4
1993	Cle-A	0	0	....	11	0	0	0	0	8^2	15	7	4	3	0	3	3	2.077	4.15	104	10.38	.366	0	....	0	0	0.0
	Cin-N	1	0	1.000	33	0	0	0	0	25^1	32	20	19	5	2	19	20	2.013	6.75	60	8.28	.308	0	.000	-7	0	-0.8

YEAR TM-L	W	L	PCT	G	GS	CG	SH	SV	IP	H	R	ER	HR	HB	BB	SO	RAT	ERA	ERA+	CERA	OAV	BH	AVG	PR+	WS	TPW
1995 Det-A	0	0	....	21	0	0	0	1	17^1	18	6	5	1	1	9	9	1.558	2.60	183	4.33	.273	0	....	4	2	0.4
Mil-A	0	0	....	8	0	0	0	0	6	1	0	0	0	0	3	2	.667	0.00	....	0.46	.059	0	....	3	1	0.3
Yr.	0	0	....	29	0	0	0	1	23^1	19	6	5	1	1	12	11	1.329	1.93	247	3.34	.229	0	....	8	3	0.7
1996 Mil-A	2	0	1.000	21	0	0	0	0	25^1	26	16	14	2	0	17	19	1.697	4.97	104	4.92	.265	0	....	0	2	0.0
Total 6	5	1	.833	150	0	0	0	2	138^2	151	70	62	12	8	85	101	1.702	4.02	106	5.61	.282	0	.000	5	10	0.5
• WICKER, Bob	Robert Kitridge Wicker b: 5/24/1878, Bedford, IN d: 1/22/1955, Evanston, IL BR/TR, 6'2", 210 lbs. Deb: 8/11/1901																									
1901 StL-N	0	0	....	1	0	0	0	0	3	4	3	0	0	0	1	2	1.667	0.00	....	4.87	.318	1	.333	1	0	0.1
1902 StL-N	5	12	.294	22	16	14	1	0	152^1	159	82	54	1	2	45	78	1.339	3.19	86	3.25	.269	18	.234	-5	5	-0.5
1903 StL-N	0	0	....	1	0	0	0	0	5	4	1	0	0	0	3	3	1.400	0.00	....	2.30	.174	0	.000	2	1	0.1
Chi-N	20	9	.690	32	27	24	1	1	247	236	114	83	3	3	74	110	1.255	3.02	103	2.92	.253	24	.245	-1	19	0.5
Yr.	20	9	.690	33	27	24	1	1	252	240	115	83	3	3	77	113	1.258	2.96	105	2.91	.251	24	.240	1	20	0.6
1904 Chi-N	17	9	.654	30	27	23	4	0	229	201	92	68	6	3	58	99	1.131	2.67	99	2.41	.232	34	.219	-4	17	-1.3
1905 Chi-N	13	6	.684	22	22	17	4	0	178	139	46	40	3	1	47	86	1.045	2.02	147	2.03	.221	10	.139	12	17	1.0
1906 Chi-N	3	5	.375	10	8	5	0	0	72^1	70	36	24	0	0	19	25	1.230	2.99	88	2.76	.257	2	.100	-5	2	-0.6
Cin-N	6	11	.353	20	17	14	0	0	150	150	69	45	3	1	46	69	1.307	2.70	102	3.22	.263	9	.180	-0	8	0.2
Yr.	9	16	.360	30	25	19	0	0	222^1	220	105	69	3	1	65	94	1.282	2.79	97	3.07	.261	11	.157	-5	10	-0.4
Total 6	64	52	.552	138	117	97	10	1	1036^2	963	443	314	16	10	293	472	1.212	2.73	104	2.74	.247	98	.205	-0	69	-0.5
• WICKER, Kemp	Kemp Caswell Wicker b: 8/13/1906, Kernersville, NC d: 6/11/1973, Kernersville, NC BR/TL, 5'11", 182 lbs. Deb: 8/14/1936																									
1936 NY-A	1	2	.333	7	0	0	0	0	20	31	18	17	2	0	11	5	2.100	7.65	61	7.90	.356	1	.143	-7	0	-0.6
1937* NY-A	7	3	.700	16	10	6	1	0	88	107	52	43	8	0	26	14	1.511	4.40	101	4.68	.296	4	.114	-1	4	-0.3
1938 NY-A	1	0	1.000	1	0	0	0	0	1	0	0	0	0	0	1	0	1.000	0.00	....	0.80	.000	0	....	0	0	0.0
1941 Bro-N	1	2	.333	16	2	0	0	1	32	30	14	13	3	0	14	8	1.375	3.66	100	3.73	.252	1	.250	-0	2	0.0
Total 4	10	7	.588	40	12	6	1	1	141	168	84	73	13	0	52	27	1.560	4.66	93	4.89	.296	6	.130	-8	6	-0.9
• WICKERSHAM, Dave	David Clifford Wickersham b: 9/27/1935, Erie, PA BR/TR, 6'3", 190 lbs. Deb: 9/18/1960																									
1960 KC-A	0	0	....	5	0	0	0	2	8^1	4	1	1	0	0	1	3	.600	1.08	369	0.73	.148	0	.000	3	2	0.3
1961 KC-A	2	1	.667	17	0	0	0	2	21	25	12	12	0	2	5	10	1.429	5.14	80	4.21	.309	2	.667	-2	2	-0.1
1962 KC-A	11	4	.733	30	9	3	0	1	110	105	53	51	13	8	43	61	1.345	4.17	100	4.28	.257	2	.057	1	8	-0.2
1963 KC-A	12	15	.444	38	34	4	1	1	237^2	244	116	108	21	9	79	118	1.359	4.09	94	4.03	.268	11	.138	-5	12	-0.8
1964 Det-A	19	12	.613	40	36	11	1	1	254	224	108	97	28	12	81	164	1.201	3.44	107	3.34	.232	6	.073	5	16	0.0
1965 Det-A	9	14	.391	34	27	8	3	0	195^1	179	91	82	12	11	61	109	1.229	3.78	92	3.18	.241	4	.069	-5	8	-1.0
1966 Det-A	8	3	.727	38	14	3	0	1	140^2	139	64	50	14	8	54	93	1.372	3.20	109	4.17	.261	2	.044	4	8	0.1
1967 Det-A	4	5	.444	36	4	0	0	4	85^1	72	30	26	6	4	33	44	1.230	2.74	119	3.19	.235	0	.000	4	6	0.3
1968 Pit-N	1	0	1.000	11	0	0	0	1	20^2	21	12	8	0	0	13	9	1.645	3.48	84	3.97	.276	1	.333	-2	0	-0.1
1969 KC-A	2	3	.400	34	0	0	0	5	50	58	27	22	6	2	14	27	1.440	3.96	93	4.80	.294	0	.000	-1	3	-0.1
Total 10	68	57	.544	283	124	29	5	18	1123	1071	514	457	100	56	384	638	1.296	3.66	100	3.71	.252	28	.086	2	65	-1.6
• WICKMAN, Bob	Robert Joe Wickman b: 2/6/1969, Green Bay, WI BR/TR, 6'1", 212 lbs. Deb: 8/24/1992																									
1992 NY-A	6	1	.857	8	8	0	0	0	50^1	51	25	23	2	2	20	21	1.411	4.11	95	3.99	.273	0	....	-1	3	-0.1
1993 NY-A	14	4	.778	41	19	1	1	4	140	156	82	72	13	5	69	70	1.607	4.63	90	5.16	.284	0	....	-7	7	-0.7
1994 NY-A	5	4	.556	**53**	0	0	0	6	70	54	26	24	3	1	27	56	1.157	3.09	148	2.45	.213	0	....	10	9	1.0
1995* NY-A	2	4	.333	63	1	0	0	1	80	77	38	36	6	5	33	51	1.375	4.05	114	3.92	.253	0	....	5	6	0.4
1996 NY-A	4	1	.800	58	0	0	0	0	79	94	41	41	7	5	34	61	1.620	4.67	106	5.51	.299	0	....	4	5	0.3
Mil-A	3	0	1.000	12	0	0	0	0	16^2	12	9	6	3	0	10	14	1.320	3.24	160	3.66	.200	0	....	3	2	0.3
Yr.	7	1	.875	70	0	0	0	0	95^2	106	50	47	10	5	44	75	1.568	4.42	113	5.19	.283	0	....	7	7	0.6
1997 Mil-A	7	6	.538	74	0	0	0	1	95^2	89	32	29	8	3	41	78	1.359	2.73	169	3.76	.252	0	....	17	11	1.6
1998 Mil-N	6	9	.400	72	0	0	0	25	82^1	79	38	34	5	4	39	71	1.433	3.72	115	4.05	.262	0	.000	4	11	0.4
1999 Mil-N	3	8	.273	71	0	0	0	37	74^1	75	31	28	6	2	38	60	1.520	3.39	134	4.38	.262	0	.000	10	11	1.0
2000 Mil-N★	2	2	.500	43	0	0	0	16	46	37	18	15	1	1	20	44	1.239	2.93	155	2.62	.215	0	....	8	8	0.7
Cle-A	1	3	.250	26	0	0	0	14	26^2	27	12	10	0	0	12	11	1.463	3.38	147	3.47	.270	0	....	5	4	0.5
2001* Cle-A	5	0	1.000	70	0	0	0	32	67^2	61	18	18	4	2	14	66	1.108	2.39	189	2.69	.240	0	....	17	14	1.7
2002 Cle-A	1	3	.250	36	0	0	0	20	34^1	42	22	17	3	1	10	36	1.515	4.46	99	4.72	.284	0	....	0	4	0.0
Total 11	59	45	.567	627	28	1	1	156	863	854	392	353	61	31	367	639	1.415	3.68	121	4.03	.260	0	.000	75	95	7.0
• WIDMAR, Al	Albert Joseph Widmar b: 3/20/1925, Cleveland, OH BR/TR, 6'3", 185 lbs. Deb: 4/25/1947 C																									
1947 Bos-A	0	0	....	2	0	0	0	0	1^1	1	2	2	1	0	2	1	2.250	13.50	29	12.49	.200	0	....	-1	0	-0.1
1948 StL-A	2	6	.250	49	0	0	0	1	82^2	88	42	41	4	0	48	34	1.645	4.46	102	4.65	.275	3	.300	2	5	0.3
1950 StL-A	7	15	.318	36	26	8	1	4	194^2	211	115	103	16	3	74	78	1.464	4.76	104	4.24	.271	10	.149	10	12	0.7
1951 StL-A	4	9	.308	26	16	4	0	0	107^2	157	84	78	19	2	52	28	1.941	6.52	67	7.85	.344	5	.167	-23	0	-2.3
1952 Chi-A	0	0	....	1	0	0	0	0	2	4	1	1	1	0	0	2	2.000	4.50	81	13.26	.444	0	....	-0	0	0.0
Total 5	13	30	.302	114	42	12	1	5	388^1	461	244	225	41	5	176	143	1.640	5.21	89	5.40	.294	18	.168	-12	17	-1.5
• WIDNER, Wild Bill	William Waterfield Widner b: 6/3/1867, Cincinnati, OH d: 12/10/1908, Cincinnati, OH BR/TR, 6', 180 lbs. Deb: 6/8/1887																									
1887 Cin-a	1	0	1.000	1	1	1	0	0	9	13	8	5	2	1	2	0	1.444	5.00	87	....	.326	1	.250	-1	1	-0.1
1888 Was-N	5	7	.417	13	13	13	0	0	115	111	69	36	7	6	22	33	1.157	2.82	99	....	.244	12	.200	0	6	-0.2
1889 Col-a	12	20	.375	41	34	25	2	1	294	368	241	170	11	18	85	63	1.541	5.20	69	....	.297	28	.211	-52	9	-4.5
1890 Col-a	4	8	.333	13	10	8	1	0	96	103	52	35	3	3	24	14	1.323	3.28	109	....	.266	8	.195	-1	6	-0.1
1891 Cin-a	0	1	.000	1	1	1	0	0	8	13	7	7	0	2	4	0	2.125	7.88	52	....	.354	1	.250	-3	0	-0.3
Total 5	22	36	.379	69	59	48	3	1	522	608	377	253	23	30	137	110	1.423	4.36	80	....	.282	50	.207	-56	22	-5.2
• WIEAND, Ted	Franklin Delano Roosevelt Wieand b: 4/4/1933, Walnutport, PA BR/TR, 6'2", 195 lbs. Deb: 9/27/1958																									
1958 Cin-N	0	0	....	1	0	0	0	0	2	4	2	2	1	0	0	2	2.000	9.00	46	11.88	.400	0	....	-1	0	-0.1
1960 Cin-N	0	1	.000	5	0	0	0	0	4^1	4	5	5	2	0	5	3	2.077	10.38	37	9.76	.250	0	....	-3	0	-0.3
Total 2	0	1	.000	6	0	0	0	0	6^1	8	7	7	3	0	5	5	2.053	9.95	39	10.43	.308	0	....	-4	0	-0.4
• WIEDEMEYER, Charlie	Charles John "Chick" Wiedemeyer b: 1/31/1914, Chicago, IL d: 10/27/1979, Lake Geneva, FL BL/TL, 6'3", 180 lbs. Deb: 9/9/1934																									
1934 Chi-N	0	0	....	4	1	0	0	0	8^1	16	10	9	0	1	4	2	2.400	9.72	40	10.12	.432	0	.000	-5	0	-0.5
• WIEDMAN, Stump	George Edward Wiedman b: 2/17/1861, Rochester, NY d: 3/3/1905, New York, NY BR/TR, 5'7.5", 165 lbs. Deb: 8/26/1880 U ♦																									
1880 Buf-N	0	9	.000	17	13	9	0	0	113^2	141	77	43	1	....	9	25	1.320	3.40	72	....	.289	8	.103	-6	2	-1.4
1881 Det-N	8	5	.615	13	13	13	1	0	115	108	48	23	1	....	12	26	1.043	**1.80**	**162**	....	.238	12	.255	14	10	1.3
1882 Det-N	25	20	.556	46	45	43	4	0	411	391	204	120	10	....	39	161	1.046	2.63	111	....	.237	42	.218	22	35	1.5
1883 Det-N	20	24	.455	52	47	41	3	**2**	402^1	435	265	158	8	....	72	183	1.260	3.53	88	....	.260	58	.185	-12	17	-2.9
1884 Det-N	4	21	.160	26	26	24	0	0	212^2	257	179	88	9	....	57	96	1.476	3.72	78	....	.283	49	.163	-12	5	-3.5
1885 Det-N	14	24	.368	38	38	37	3	0	330	343	198	115	7	....	63	149	1.230	3.14	90	....	.256	24	.157	-6	14	-1.2
1886 KC-N	12	36	.250	51	51	48	1	0	427^2	549	323	214	11	....	112	168	1.546	4.50	83	....	.300	30	.168	-25	17	-2.9
1887 Det-N	13	7	.650	21	21	20	0	0	183	281	132	109	9	9	60	56	1.536	5.36	75	....	.342	20	.235	-29	8	-2.7
NY-a	4	8	.333	12	12	11	1	0	97	147	84	50	3	0	25	37	1.515	4.64	91	....	.337	11	.220	-1	3	-0.2
NY-N	0	1	.000	1	1	1	0	0	8	12	6	1	0	9	2	4	1.500	1.13	332	....	.337	1	.333	2	1	0.2
Yr.	13	8	.619	22	22	21	0	0	191	293	138	110	9	18	62	60	1.534	5.18	77	....	.342	21	.239	-26	9	-2.5
1888 NY-N	1	1	.500	2	2	2	0	0	18	17	20	7	2	2	8	5	1.389	3.50	78	....	.240	0	.000	-2	0	-0.2
Total 9	101	156	.393	279	269	249	13	2	2318^1	2681	1536	928	61	20	459	910	1.317	3.60	90	....	.276	255	.181	-56	112	-12.0
• WIENEKE, Jack	John Wieneke b: 3/10/1894, Saltsburg, PA d: 3/16/1933, Pleasant Ridge, MI BR/TL, 6', 182 lbs. Deb: 7/4/1921																									
1921 Chi-A	0	1	.000	10	3	0	0	0	25^1	39	24	23	4	1	17	10	2.211	8.17	52	8.86	.351	1	.111	-11	0	-1.1

YEAR TM-L	W	L	PCT	G	GS	CG	SH	SV	IP	H	R	ER	HR	HB	BB	SO	RAT	ERA	ERA+	CERA	OAV	BH	AVG	PR+	WS	TPW
• WIESLER, Bob	Robert George Wiesler b: 8/13/1930, St. Louis, MO BB/TL, 6'3", 195 lbs. Deb: 8/3/1951																									
1951 NY-A	0	2	.000	4	3	0	0	0	9^1	13	15	14	0	0	11	3	2.571	13.50	28	8.96	.361	0	.000	-10	0	-1.1
1954 NY-A	3	2	.600	6	5	0	0	0	30^1	28	15	14	0	0	30	25	1.912	4.15	83	5.12	.259	3	.273	-3	2	-0.3
1955 NY-A	0	2	.000	16	7	0	0	0	53	39	27	23	1	1	49	22	1.660	3.91	96	4.18	.212	2	.143	-3	1	-0.4
1956 Was-A	3	12	.200	37	21	3	0	0	123	141	98	88	11	3	112	49	2.057	6.44	67	7.21	.300	3	.091	-25	0	-2.7
1957 Was-A	1	1	.500	3	2	1	0	0	16^1	15	8	8	2	1	11	9	1.592	4.41	88	5.30	.250	1	.167	-1	1	0.0
1958 Was-A	0	0	....	4	0	0	0	0	9^1	14	8	7	2	1	5	5	2.036	6.75	57	9.45	.359	0	.000	-3	0	-0.3
Total 6	**7**	**19**	**.269**	**70**	**38**	**4**	**0**	**0**	**241^1**	**250**	**171**	**154**	**16**	**6**	**218**	**113**	**1.939**	**5.74**	**70**	**6.31**	**.279**	**9**	**.130**	**-45**	**4**	**-4.8**
• WIGGINS, Scott	Scott Joseph Wiggins b: 3/24/1976, Fort Thomas, KY BL/TL, 6'3", 205 lbs. Deb: 9/11/2002																									
2002 Tor-A	0	0	....	3	0	0	0	0	2^2	5	1	1	1	0	1	3	2.250	3.38	137	12.82	.417	0	....	0	0	0.0
• WIGGS, Jimmy	James Alvin "Big Jim" Wiggs b: 9/1/1876, Trondheim, Norway d: 1/20/1963, Xenia, OH BB/TR, 6'4", 200 lbs. Deb: 4/23/1903																									
1903 Cin-N	0	1	.000	2	1	0	0	0	5	12	7	3	0	1	2	2	2.800	5.40	66	14.27	.500	0	.000	-1	0	-0.1
1905 Det-A	3	3	.500	7	7	4	0	0	41^1	30	25	15	0	1	29	37	1.427	3.27	83	2.92	.205	2	.133	-3	1	-0.4
1906 Det-A	0	0	....	4	1	0	0	0	10^1	11	9	6	1	2	7	7	1.742	5.23	53	6.10	.276	1	.333	-3	0	-0.3
Total 3	**3**	**4**	**.429**	**13**	**9**	**4**	**0**	**0**	**56^2**	**53**	**41**	**24**	**1**	**4**	**38**	**46**	**1.606**	**3.81**	**74**	**4.50**	**.252**	**3**	**.158**	**-7**	**1**	**-0.8**
• WIGHT, Bill	William Robert "Lefty" Wight b: 4/12/1922, Rio Vista, CA BL/TL, 6'1", 180 lbs. Deb: 4/17/1946																									
1946 NY-A	2	2	.500	14	4	1	0	0	40^1	44	22	20	1	1	30	11	1.835	4.46	77	5.31	.289	0	.000	-6	1	-0.7
1947 NY-A	1	0	1.000	1	1	1	0	0	9	8	3	1	0	0	2	3	1.111	1.00	354	2.26	.242	0	.000	2	1	0.3
1948 Chi-A	9	20	.310	34	32	7	1	1	223^1	238	132	119	9	1	135	68	1.670	4.80	89	4.70	.278	6	.082	-16	9	-2.2
1949 Chi-A	15	13	.536	35	33	14	3	1	245	254	106	90	9	0	96	78	1.429	3.31	126	3.80	.275	14	.165	22	18	2.0
1950 Chi-A	10	16	.385	30	28	13	3	0	206	213	89	82	10	0	79	62	1.417	3.58	125	3.76	.270	0	.000	16	15	0.7
1951 Bos-A	7	7	.500	34	17	4	2	0	118^1	128	77	67	5	0	63	38	1.614	5.10	88	4.56	.282	3	.073	-8	4	-1.2
1952 Bos-A	2	1	.667	10	2	0	0	0	24^1	14	11	8	3	1	14	5	1.151	2.96	133	2.70	.169	1	.143	3	2	0.3
Det-A	5	9	.357	23	19	8	3	0	143^2	167	71	62	7	0	55	65	1.545	3.88	98	4.46	.291	11	.220	2	7	0.2
Yr.	7	10	.412	33	21	8	3	0	168	181	82	70	10	1	69	70	1.488	3.75	102	4.20	.276	12	.211	4	9	0.5
1953 Det-A	0	3	.000	13	4	0	0	0	25^1	35	33	25	4	0	14	10	1.934	8.88	46	7.17	.333	3	.429	-13	0	-1.2
Cle-A	2	1	.667	20	0	0	0	1	26^2	29	12	11	1	0	16	14	1.688	3.71	101	4.81	.282	0	.000	0	2	-0.1
Yr.	2	4	.333	33	4	0	0	1	52	64	45	36	5	0	30	24	1.808	6.23	64	5.96	.308	3	.250	-13	2	-1.3
1955 Cle-A	0	0	....	17	0	0	0	1	24	24	8	7	0	0	9	9	1.375	2.63	152	3.24	.261	0	....	4	2	0.4
Bal-A	6	8	.429	19	14	8	2	2	117^1	111	43	32	6	1	39	54	1.278	2.45	155	3.19	.252	3	.083	19	9	1.7
Yr.	6	8	.429	36	14	8	2	3	141^1	135	51	39	6	1	48	63	1.295	2.48	155	3.20	.254	3	.083	23	11	2.0
1956 Bal-A	9	12	.429	35	26	7	1	0	174^2	198	92	78	7	6	72	84	**1.546**	4.02	98	4.56	.289	12	.200	-1	10	-0.1
1957 Bal-A	6	6	.500	27	17	2	0	0	121	122	53	49	4	4	54	50	1.455	3.64	99	4.00	.271	1	.029	-3	6	-0.6
1958 Cin-N	0	1	.000	7	0	0	0	0	6^2	7	4	3	1	0	4	5	1.650	4.05	102	6.07	.292	0	....	0	0	0.0
StL-N	3	0	1.000	28	1	1	0	2	57^1	64	35	32	7	0	32	18	1.674	5.02	82	5.51	.290	1	.100	-6	2	-0.6
Yr.	3	1	.750	35	1	1	0	2	64	71	39	35	8	0	36	23	1.672	4.92	84	5.57	.290	1	.100	-6	2	-0.6
Total 12	**77**	**99**	**.438**	**347**	**198**	**66**	**15**	**8**	**1563**	**1656**	**791**	**686**	**74**	**14**	**714**	**574**	**1.516**	**3.95**	**103**	**4.24**	**.277**	**55**	**.115**	**16**	**88**	**-1.2**
• WIGINGTON, Fred	Fred Thomas Wigington b: 12/16/1897, Rogers, NE d: 5/8/1980, Mesa, AZ BR/TR, 5'10", 168 lbs. Deb: 4/20/1923																									
1923 StL-N	0	0	....	4	0	0	0	0	8^1	11	4	3	0	0	5	2	1.920	3.24	120	5.94	.367	0	.000	1	1	0.1
• WIHTOL, Sandy	Alexander Ames Wihtol b: 6/1/1955, Palo Alto, CA BR/TR, 6'1", 195 lbs. Deb: 9/7/1979																									
1979 Cle-A	0	0	....	5	0	0	0	0	10^2	10	4	4	0	0	3	6	1.219	3.38	126	2.57	.238	0	....	1	1	0.1
1980 Cle-A	1	0	1.000	17	0	0	0	1	35^1	35	18	14	2	2	14	20	1.387	3.57	114	3.76	.257	0	....	2	2	0.2
1982 Cle-A	0	0	....	6	0	0	0	0	11^2	9	6	6	1	1	7	8	1.371	4.63	88	3.89	.220	0	....	-1	1	-0.1
Total 3	**1**	**0**	**1.000**	**28**	**0**	**0**	**0**	**1**	**57^2**	**54**	**28**	**24**	**3**	**3**	**24**	**34**	**1.353**	**3.75**	**109**	**3.56**	**.247**	**0**	**....**	**3**	**4**	**0.3**
• WILCOX, Milt	Milton Edward Wilcox b: 4/20/1950, Honolulu, HI BR/TR, 6'2", 185 lbs. Deb: 9/5/1970																									
1970* Cin-N	3	1	.750	5	2	1	1	1	22^1	19	6	6	2	1	7	13	1.164	2.42	173	3.06	.229	1	.200	4	3	0.4
1971 Cin-N	2	2	.500	18	3	0	0	1	43^1	43	22	16	2	2	17	21	1.385	3.32	98	3.74	.269	0	.000	-1	2	-0.3
1972 Cle-A	7	14	.333	32	27	4	2	0	156	145	67	59	18	5	72	90	1.391	3.40	94	4.09	.251	9	.200	-5	7	-0.4
1973 Cle-A	8	10	.444	26	19	4	0	0	134^1	143	90	87	14	8	68	82	1.571	5.83	67	5.10	.275	0	....	-28	2	-2.9
1974 Cle-A	2	2	.500	41	2	1	0	4	71^1	74	42	37	10	5	24	33	1.374	4.67	77	4.53	.271	0	....	-9	2	-0.9
1975 Chi-N	0	1	.000	25	0	0	0	0	38^1	50	27	24	4	1	17	21	1.748	5.63	68	6.13	.323	1	.333	-6	0	-0.6
1977 Det-A	6	2	.750	20	13	1	0	0	106^1	96	46	43	13	1	37	82	1.251	3.64	118	3.55	.241	0	....	8	8	0.8
1978 Det-A	13	12	.520	29	27	16	2	0	215^1	208	94	90	22	8	68	132	1.282	3.76	103	3.73	.255	0	....	-1	13	-0.1
1979 Det-A	12	10	.545	33	29	7	0	0	196^1	201	105	95	18	11	73	109	1.396	4.35	99	4.20	.267	0	....	-3	10	-0.3
1980 Det-A	13	11	.542	32	31	13	1	0	198^2	201	112	99	24	6	68	97	1.354	4.48	92	4.13	.262	0	....	-6	9	-0.6
1981 Det-A	12	9	.571	24	24	8	1	0	166^1	152	61	56	10	6	52	79	1.226	3.03	125	3.17	.247	0	....	10	13	1.1
1982 Det-A	12	10	.545	29	29	9	1	0	193^2	187	91	78	18	7	85	112	1.404	3.62	112	4.13	.257	0	....	5	12	0.5
1983 Det-A	11	10	.524	26	26	9	2	0	186	164	89	82	19	4	74	101	1.280	3.97	98	3.52	.237	0	....	-4	9	-0.4
1984* Det-A	17	8	.680	33	33	0	0	0	193^2	183	99	86	13	8	66	119	1.286	4.00	98	3.47	.252	0	....	-3	9	-0.3
1985 Det-A	1	3	.250	8	8	0	0	0	39	51	24	21	6	0	14	20	1.667	4.85	84	6.08	.315	0	....	-3	1	-0.3
1986 Sea-A	0	8	.000	13	10	0	0	0	55^2	74	38	34	11	1	28	26	1.832	5.50	77	7.49	.327	0	....	-8	1	-0.7
Total 16	**119**	**113**	**.513**	**394**	**283**	**73**	**10**	**6**	**2016^2**	**1991**	**1013**	**913**	**204**	**74**	**770**	**1137**	**1.369**	**4.07**	**96**	**4.09**	**.260**	**11**	**.177**	**-49**	**101**	**-5.0**
• WILES, Randy	Randall E. Wiles b: 9/10/1951, Fort Belvoir, VA BL/TL, 6'1", 185 lbs. Deb: 8/7/1977																									
1977 Chi-A	1	1	.500	5	0	0	0	0	2^2	5	3	3	1	0	3	0	3.000	10.13	40	14.88	.417	0		-2	0	-0.2
• WILEY, Mark	Mark Eugene Wiley b: 2/28/1948, National City, CA BR/TR, 6'1", 200 lbs. Deb: 6/17/1975 C																									
1975 Min-A	1	3	.250	15	3	1	0	2	38^2	50	30	26	4	1	13	15	1.629	6.05	64	5.75	.325	0	....	-9	0	-0.9
1978 SD-N	1	0	1.000	4	1	0	0	0	7^2	11	6	5	1	0	1	1	1.565	5.87	57	5.59	.324	0	.000	-2	0	-0.3
Tor-A	0	0	....	2	0	0	0	0	2^2	3	2	2	0	0	1	2	1.500	6.75	58	3.84	.273	0	....	-1	0	-0.1
Total 2	**2**	**3**	**.400**	**21**	**4**	**1**	**0**	**2**	**49**	**64**	**38**	**33**	**5**	**1**	**15**	**18**	**1.612**	**6.06**	**62**	**5.62**	**.322**	**0**	**.000**	**-12**	**0**	**-1.3**
• WILHELM, Harry	Harry Lester Wilhelm b: 4/7/1874, Uniontown, PA d: 2/20/1944, Republic, PA BR/TR, 5'7", 155 lbs. Deb: 8/12/1899																									
1899 Lou-N	1	0	1.000	5	3	2	0	0	25	36	22	17	1	1	3	6	1.560	6.12	63	5.16	.336	3	.250	-6	1	-0.4
• WILHELM, Hoyt	James Hoyt Wilhelm b: 7/26/1922, Huntersville, NC d: 8/23/2002, Sarasota, FL BR/TR, 6', 195 lbs. Deb: 4/18/1952 HOF: 1985																									
1952 NY-N	15	3	.833	**71**	0	0	0	11	159^1	127	60	43	12	5	57	108	1.155	**2.43**	**152**	2.76	.220	6	.158	23	18	2.4
1953 NY-N★	7	8	.467	**68**	0	0	0	15	145	127	61	49	13	4	77	71	1.407	3.04	141	3.80	.238	5	.152	20	14	2.0
1954* NY-N	12	4	.750	57	0	0	0	7	111^1	77	32	26	5	5	52	64	1.159	2.10	192	2.42	.198	1	.048	23	15	2.0
1955 NY-N	4	1	.800	59	0	0	0	0	103	104	53	45	10	2	40	71	1.398	3.93	102	4.02	.266	3	.158	1	6	0.0
1956 NY-N	4	9	.308	64	0	0	0	8	89^1	97	45	38	7	2	43	71	1.567	3.83	99	4.59	.280	2	.222	-0	6	0.0
1957 StL-N	1	4	.200	40	0	0	0	11	55	52	28	26	7	3	21	29	1.327	4.25	93	4.18	.254	0	.000	-2	4	-0.2
Cle-A	1	0	1.000	2	0	0	0	1	3^2	2	1	1	1	1	1	0	.818	2.45	151	3.23	.154	0	....	1	1	0.1
1958 Cle-A	2	7	.222	30	6	1	0	5	90^1	70	32	25	4	1	35	57	1.162	2.49	146	2.49	.215	2	.095	11	7	1.0
Bal-A	1	3	.250	9	4	3	1	0	40^2	25	9	9	2	1	10	35	.861	1.99	181	1.46	.179	1	.091	7	4	0.7
Yr.	3	10	.231	39	10	4	1	5	131	95	41	34	6	2	45	92	1.069	2.34	156	2.17	.204	3	.094	19	11	1.7
1959 Bal-A★	15	11	.577	32	27	13	3	0	226	178	64	55	13	10	77	139	1.128	**2.19**	**173**	2.69	.224	4	.053	38	23	3.2
1960 Bal-A	11	8	.579	41	11	3	1	7	147	125	69	54	13	1	39	107	1.116	3.31	115	2.71	.228	3	.071	5	11	0.2
1961 Bal-A★	9	7	.563	51	1	0	0	18	109^2	89	35	28	5	4	41	87	1.185	2.30	170	2.66	.219	1	.050	18	16	1.7
1962 Bal-A★	7	10	.412	52	0	0	0	15	93	64	28	20	5	3	34	90	1.054	1.94	194	2.16	.197	2	.125	18	14	1.8
1963 Chi-A	5	8	.385	55	3	0	0	21	136^1	106	47	40	8	4	30	111	.998	2.64	133	2.09	.215	2	.069	12	15	1.2
1964 Chi-A	12	9	.571	73	0	0	0	27	131^1	94	35	29	7	2	30	95	.944	1.99	174	1.80	.202	3	.143	18	21	1.8

YEAR	TM-L	W	L	PCT	G	GS	CG	SH	SV	IP	H	R	ER	HR	HB	BB	SO	RAT	ERA	ERA+	CERA	OAV	BH	AVG	PR+	WS	TPW
1965	Chi-A	7	7	.500	66	0	0	0	20	144	88	34	29	11	2	32	106	.833	1.81	176	1.47	.177	0	.000	20	19	2.0
1966	Chi-A	5	2	.714	46	0	0	0	6	81^{1}	50	21	15	6	1	17	61	.824	1.66	191	1.46	.178	1	.125	13	10	1.4
1967	Chi-A	8	3	.727	49	0	0	0	12	89	58	21	13	2	4	34	76	1.034	1.31	236	1.83	.183	1	.077	17	13	1.8
1968	Chi-A	4	4	.500	72	0	0	0	12	93^{2}	69	20	18	4	2	24	72	.993	1.73	175	1.89	.205	0	.000	14	12	1.6
1969	Cal-A	5	7	.417	44	0	0	0	10	65^{2}	45	21	18	4	3	18	53	.959	2.47	141	1.90	.194	0	.000	6	9	0.6
	Atl-N	2	0	1.000	8	0	0	0	4	12^{1}	5	1	1	0	1	4	14	.730	0.73	494	0.98	.119	0	.000	4	4	0.4
1970	Atl-N★	6	4	.600	50	0	0	0	13	78^{1}	69	29	27	7	1	39	67	1.379	3.10	138	3.60	.234	1	.091	12	11	1.2
	Chi-N	0	1	.000	3	0	0	0	0	3^{2}	4	4	4	1	0	3	1	1.909	9.82	46	7.64	.286	0	....	-2	0	-0.2
	Yr.	6	5	.545	53	0	0	0	13	82	73	33	31	8	1	42	68	1.402	3.40	127	3.78	.236	1	.091	10	11	1.0
1971	Atl-N	0	0	....	3	0	0	0	0	2^{1}	6	5	4	2	0	1	1	3.000	15.43	24	24.67	.500	0	....	-3	0	-0.3
	LA-N	0	1	.000	9	0	0	0	3	17^{2}	6	2	2	1	0	4	15	.566	1.02	317	0.74	.111	0	.000	4	3	0.4
	Yr.	0	1	.000	12	0	0	0	3	20	12	7	6	3	0	5	16	.850	2.70	131	3.53	.182	0	.000	1	3	0.1
1972	LA-N	0	1	.000	16	0	0	0	1	25^{1}	20	16	13	0	0	15	9	1.382	4.62	72	2.85	.217	0	.000	-4	0	-0.4
Total	21	143	122	.540	1070	52	20	5	227	2254^{1}	1757	773	632	150	62	778	1610	1.125	2.52	147	2.61	.216	38	.088	277	256	26.4

• WILHELM, Kaiser Irvin Key Wilhelm b: 1/26/1874, Wooster, OH d: 5/22/1936, Rochester, NY BR/TR, 6', 162 lbs. Deb: 4/18/1903 M/C/U

YEAR	TM-L	W	L	PCT	G	GS	CG	SH	SV	IP	H	R	ER	HR	HB	BB	SO	RAT	ERA	ERA+	CERA	OAV	BH	AVG	PR+	WS	TPW
1903	Pit-N	5	3	.625	12	9	7	1	0	86	88	61	31	0	3	25	20	1.314	3.24	99	3.19	.264	3	.088	-4	5	-0.5
1904	Bos-N	14	20	.412	39	36	30	3	0	288	316	150	118	8	7	74	73	1.354	3.69	74	3.72	.285	7	.070	-22	11	-3.2
1905	Bos-N	3	23	.115	34	28	23	0	0	242^{1}	287	166	122	7	5	75	76	**1.494**	4.53	68	4.31	.295	16	.160	-33	0	-3.9
1908	Bro-N	16	22	.421	42	36	33	6	0	332	266	110	69	3	6	83	99	1.051	1.87	124	1.89	.217	12	.108	15	23	1.2
1909	Bro-N	3	13	.188	22	17	14	1	0	163	176	92	59	3	2	59	45	**1.442**	3.26	79	3.98	.289	13	.228	-11	4	-0.9
1910	Bro-N	3	7	.300	15	5	0	0	0	68^{1}	88	45	36	3	1	18	17	1.551	4.74	64	4.84	.314	6	.316	-14	1	-1.2
1914	Bal-F	12	17	.414	47	27	11	1	5	243^{2}	263	141	109	10	0	81	113	1.412	4.03	79	4.04	.291	21	.250	-18	9	-1.5
1915	Bal-F	0	0	....	1	0	0	0	0	1	0	0	0	0	0	0	0	.000	0.00	....	0.00	.000	0	....	0	0	0.0
1921	Phi-N	0	0	....	4	0	0	0	0	8	11	3	3	0	0	3	1	1.750	3.38	125	5.61	.393	0	.000	1	1	0.1
Total	9	56	105	.348	216	158	118	12	5	1432^{1}	1495	768	547	34	24	418	444	1.336	3.44	83	3.51	.274	78	.154	-85	54	-9.8

• WILKIE, Lefty Aldon Jay Wilkie b: 10/30/1914, Zealandia, Canada d: 8/5/1992, Tualatin, OR BL/TL, 5'11.5", 175 lbs. Deb: 4/22/1941

YEAR	TM-L	W	L	PCT	G	GS	CG	SH	SV	IP	H	R	ER	HR	HB	BB	SO	RAT	ERA	ERA+	CERA	OAV	BH	AVG	PR+	WS	TPW
1941	Pit-N	2	4	.333	26	6	2	1	2	79	90	42	40	1	1	40	16	1.646	4.56	79	4.49	.289	7	.292	-7	3	-0.7
1942	Pit-N	6	7	.462	35	6	3	0	1	107^{1}	112	53	50	4	1	37	18	1.388	4.19	81	3.55	.269	10	.263	-8	5	-0.7
1946	Pit-N	0	0	....	7	0	0	0	0	7^{2}	13	9	9	0	0	3	3	2.087	10.57	33	7.53	.382	0	....	-6	0	-0.6
Total	3	8	11	.421	68	12	5	1	3	194	215	104	99	5	2	80	37	1.521	4.59	76	4.09	.283	17	.274	-22	8	-2.0

• WILKINS, Dean Dean Allan Wilkins b: 8/24/1966, Blue Island, IL BR/TR, 6'1", 170 lbs. Deb: 8/21/1989

YEAR	TM-L	W	L	PCT	G	GS	CG	SH	SV	IP	H	R	ER	HR	HB	BB	SO	RAT	ERA	ERA+	CERA	OAV	BH	AVG	PR+	WS	TPW
1989	Chi-N	1	0	1.000	11	0	0	0	0	15^{2}	13	9	8	2	0	9	14	1.404	4.60	82	3.84	.228	0	.000	-1	0	-0.2
1990	Chi-N	0	0	....	7	0	0	0	1	7^{1}	11	8	8	1	1	7	3	2.455	9.82	42	10.37	.333	0	....	-4	0	-0.5
1991	Hou-N	2	1	.667	7	0	0	0	1	8	16	14	10	0	0	10	4	3.250	11.25	31	12.26	.410	0	.000	-7	0	-0.7
Total	3	3	1	.750	25	0	0	0	2	31	40	31	26	3	1	26	21	2.129	7.55	50	7.56	.310	0	.000	-13	0	-1.4

• WILKINS, Eric Eric Lamoine Wilkins b: 12/9/1956, St. Louis, MO BR/TR, 6'1", 190 lbs. Deb: 4/11/1979

YEAR	TM-L	W	L	PCT	G	GS	CG	SH	SV	IP	H	R	ER	HR	HB	BB	SO	RAT	ERA	ERA+	CERA	OAV	BH	AVG	PR+	WS	TPW
1979	Cle-A	2	4	.333	16	14	0	0	0	69^{2}	77	41	34	4	4	38	52	1.651	4.39	97	5.22	.289	0	....	0	3	0.0

• WILKINS, Marc Marc Allen Wilkins b: 10/21/1970, Mansfield, OH BR/TR, 5'11", 200 lbs. Deb: 5/11/1996

YEAR	TM-L	W	L	PCT	G	GS	CG	SH	SV	IP	H	R	ER	HR	HB	BB	SO	RAT	ERA	ERA+	CERA	OAV	BH	AVG	PR+	WS	TPW
1996	Pit-N	4	3	.571	47	2	0	0	1	75	75	36	32	6	6	36	62	1.480	3.84	114	4.47	.266	2	.222	5	5	0.6
1997	Pit-N	9	5	.643	70	0	0	0	2	75^{2}	65	33	31	7	4	33	47	1.295	3.69	116	3.72	.242	0	.000	6	8	0.6
1998	Pit-N	0	0	....	16	0	0	0	0	15^{1}	13	6	6	1	2	9	17	1.435	3.52	122	4.07	.236	0	....	1	1	0.1
1999	Pit-N	2	3	.400	46	0	0	0	0	51	49	28	24	3	4	26	44	1.471	4.24	108	4.25	.257	0	.000	2	3	0.2
2000	Pit-N	4	2	.667	52	0	0	0	0	60^{1}	54	34	34	4	6	43	37	1.608	5.07	91	4.76	.248	1	.167	-2	3	-0.2
2001	Pit-N	0	1	.000	14	0	0	0	0	17^{1}	22	13	13	2	1	8	11	1.731	6.75	66	6.27	.319	0	....	-4	0	-0.4
Total	6	19	14	.576	245	2	0	0	3	294^{2}	278	150	140	23	23	155	218	1.469	4.28	104	4.38	.256	3	.150	8	20	0.8

• WILKINSON, Bill William Carl Wilkinson b: 8/10/1964, Greybull, WY BR/TL, 5'10", 160 lbs. Deb: 6/13/1985

YEAR	TM-L	W	L	PCT	G	GS	CG	SH	SV	IP	H	R	ER	HR	HB	BB	SO	RAT	ERA	ERA+	CERA	OAV	BH	AVG	PR+	WS	TPW
1985	Sea-A	0	2	.000	2	2	0	0	0	6	8	9	9	2	0	6	5	2.333	13.50	31	11.08	.333	0	....	-6	0	-0.6
1987	Sea-A	3	4	.429	56	0	0	0	10	76^{1}	61	33	31	8	0	21	73	1.074	3.66	129	2.60	.223	0	....	9	10	0.8
1988	Sea-A	2	2	.500	30	0	0	0	2	31	28	14	12	3	0	15	25	1.387	3.48	119	3.75	.233	0	....	2	3	0.2
Total	3	5	8	.385	88	2	0	0	12	113^{1}	97	56	52	13	0	42	103	1.226	4.13	109	3.36	.232	0	....	5	13	0.5

• WILKINSON, Roy Roy Hamilton Wilkinson b: 5/8/1894, Canandaigua, NY d: 7/2/1956, Louisville, KY BR/TR, 6'1", 170 lbs. Deb: 4/29/1918

YEAR	TM-L	W	L	PCT	G	GS	CG	SH	SV	IP	H	R	ER	HR	HB	BB	SO	RAT	ERA	ERA+	CERA	OAV	BH	AVG	PR+	WS	TPW
1918	Cle-A	0	0	....	1	0	0	0	0	1	0	0	0	0	0	0	0	.000	0.00	....	0.00	.000	0	....	0	0	0.0
1919*	Chi-A	1	1	.500	4	1	1	1	0	22	21	9	5	0	0	10	5	1.409	2.05	155	3.46	.266	3	.375	2	2	0.4
1920	Chi-A	7	9	.438	34	12	8	0	2	145	162	75	65	6	2	48	30	1.448	4.03	93	4.27	.297	7	.146	-6	7	-0.9
1921	Chi-A	4	20	.167	36	23	11	0	3	198^{1}	259	135	113	4	4	78	50	1.699	5.13	83	5.19	.334	8	.123	-20	6	-2.2
1922	Chi-A	0	1	.000	4	1	0	0	1	14^{1}	24	15	14	1	1	6	3	2.093	8.79	46	8.63	.393	0	.000	-8	0	-0.8
Total	5	12	31	.279	79	37	20	1	6	380^{2}	466	234	197	11	7	142	88	1.597	4.66	86	4.86	.319	18	.145	-31	15	-3.4

• WILKS, Ted Theodore "Cork" Wilks b: 11/13/1915, Fulton, NY d: 8/21/1989, Houston, TX BR/TR, 5'9.5", 178 lbs. Deb: 4/25/1944 C

YEAR	TM-L	W	L	PCT	G	GS	CG	SH	SV	IP	H	R	ER	HR	HB	BB	SO	RAT	ERA	ERA+	CERA	OAV	BH	AVG	PR+	WS	TPW
1944*	StL-N	17	4	.810	36	21	16	4	0	207^{2}	173	61	61	12	1	49	70	1.069	2.64	133	2.34	.227	9	.141	15	18	1.5
1945	StL-N	4	7	.364	18	16	4	1	0	98^{1}	103	39	32	9	1	29	28	1.342	2.93	128	3.86	.270	4	.133	7	6	0.6
1946*	StL-N	8	0	1.000	40	4	0	0	1	95	88	41	36	13	2	38	40	1.326	3.41	101	3.91	.248	5	.208	-1	7	-0.1
1947	StL-N	4	0	1.000	37	0	0	0	5	50^{1}	57	33	28	10	2	11	28	1.351	5.01	83	4.78	.279	1	.167	-5	3	-0.5
1948	StL-N	6	6	.500	57	2	1	0	13	130^{2}	113	40	38	5	0	39	71	1.163	2.62	156	2.55	.235	5	.167	22	17	2.2
1949	StL-N	10	3	.769	**59**	0	0	0	**9**	118^{1}	105	52	49	7	0	38	71	1.208	3.73	112	2.87	.240	1	.037	5	12	0.2
1950	StL-N	2	0	1.000	18	0	0	0	0	24^{1}	27	18	18	4	1	9	15	1.479	6.66	65	5.21	.287	0	.000	-6	0	-0.7
1951	StL-N	0	0	....	17	0	0	0	1	18	19	7	6	1	0	5	5	1.333	3.00	132	3.66	.279	0	.000	2	2	0.2
	Pit-N	3	5	.375	48	1	1	0	12	82^{2}	69	31	26	6	2	24	43	1.125	2.83	149	2.68	.231	1	.083	14	10	1.3
	Yr.	3	5	.375	**65**	1	1	0	**13**	100^{2}	88	38	32	7	2	29	48	1.162	2.86	146	2.86	.240	1	.077	16	12	1.5
1952	Pit-N	5	5	.500	44	0	0	0	4	72^{1}	65	32	29	9	2	31	24	1.327	3.61	111	3.85	.245	1	.125	4	6	0.3
	Cle-A	0	0	....	7	0	0	0	1	11^{2}	8	6	5	0	0	7	6	1.286	3.86	87	2.17	.186	0	....	-1	1	-0.1
1953	Cle-A	0	0	....	4	0	0	0	0	3^{2}	5	4	3	0	0	3	2	2.182	7.36	51	5.99	.278	0	....	-1	0	-0.1
Total	10	59	30	.663	385	44	22	5	46	913	832	364	331	76	11	283	403	1.221	3.26	119	3.17	.244	27	.131	54	82	4.9

• WILLETT, Ed Robert Edgar Willett b: 3/7/1884, Norfolk, VA d: 5/10/1934, Wellington, KS BR/TR, 6', 183 lbs. Deb: 9/5/1906

YEAR	TM-L	W	L	PCT	G	GS	CG	SH	SV	IP	H	R	ER	HR	HB	BB	SO	RAT	ERA	ERA+	CERA	OAV	BH	AVG	PR+	WS	TPW
1906	Det-A	0	3	.000	3	3	3	0	0	25	24	12	11	0	2	8	16	1.280	3.96	70	3.19	.256	0	.000	-3	0	-0.5
1907	Det-A	1	5	.167	10	6	1	0	0	48^{2}	47	31	20	0	2	20	27	1.377	3.70	70	3.18	.256	1	.077	-6	0	-0.7
1908	Det-A	15	8	.652	30	23	18	2	1	197^{1}	186	67	50	2	14	60	77	1.247	2.28	106	3.18	.261	11	.164	6	13	0.5
1909*	Det-A	21	10	.677	41	34	25	3	1	292^{2}	239	112	76	5	15	76	89	1.076	2.34	107	2.23	.221	22	.196	6	21	1.0
1910	Det-A	16	11	.593	37	25	18	4	0	224^{1}	175	85	59	2	17	74	65	1.110	2.37	111	2.33	.217	11	.133	7	15	0.5
1911	Det-A	13	14	.481	38	27	15	2	1	231^{1}	261	136	94	5	14	80	86	1.474	3.66	95	4.36	.295	22	.268	-2	16	0.4
1912	Det-A	17	15	.531	37	31	28	1	0	284^{1}	281	144	104	3	17	84	89	1.284	3.29	100	3.25	.262	19	.165	1	14	0.0
1913	Det-A	13	14	.481	34	30	19	0	0	242	237	117	83	0	11	89	59	1.347	3.09	94	3.87	.260	26	.283	2	13	1.1
1914	StL-F	4	17	.190	27	22	14	0	0	175	208	102	82	5	10	56	73	1.509	4.22	82	4.48	.295	15	.234	-11	6	-0.9
1915	StL-F	2	3	.400	17	2	1	0	2	52^{2}	61	36	27	2	3	18	19	1.500	4.61	67	4.54	.295	3	.200	-10	0	-1.0
Total	10	102	100	.505	274	203	142	12	5	1773^{1}	1719	842	606	24	105	565	600	1.288	3.08	96	3.34	.258	130	.199	-10	98	0.4

• WILLEY, Carl Carlton Francis Willey b: 6/6/1931, Cherryfield, ME BR/TR, 6', 175 lbs. Deb: 4/30/1958

YEAR	TM-L	W	L	PCT	G	GS	CG	SH	SV	IP	H	R	ER	HR	HB	BB	SO	RAT	ERA	ERA+	CERA	OAV	BH	AVG	PR+	WS	TPW
1958*	Mil-N	9	7	.563	23	19	9	**4**	0	140	110	44	42	14	2	53	74	1.164	2.70	130	2.88	.215	5	.104	11	11	0.9
1959	Mil-N	5	9	.357	26	15	5	2	0	117	126	60	54	12	2	31	51	1.342	4.15	85	3.97	.273	4	.103	-7	4	-0.9
1960	Mil-N	6	7	.462	28	21	2	1	0	144^{2}	136	78	70	19	7	65	109	1.389	4.35	79	4.25	.248	7	.146	-13	4	-1.2
1961	Mil-N	6	12	.333	35	22	4	0	0	159^{2}	147	71	68	20	2	65	91	1.328	3.83	97	3.82	.247	1	.019	-1	7	-0.8
1962	Mil-N	2	5	.286	30	6	0	0	1	73^{1}	95	49	44	9	1	20	40	1.568	5.40	70	5.49	.319	3	.273	-13	1	-1.2

YEAR	TM-L	W	L	PCT	G	GS	CG	SH	SV	IP	H	R	ER	HR	HB	BB	SO	RAT	ERA	ERA+	CERA	OAV	BH	AVG	PR+	WS	TPW
1963	NY-N	9	14	.391	30	28	7	4	0	183	149	74	63	24	4	69	101	1.191	3.10	113	3.27	.220	6	.111	10	12	1.0
1964	NY-N	0	2	.000	14	3	0	0	0	30	37	19	12	5	1	8	14	1.500	3.60	99	5.27	.301	0	.000	-0	1	-0.1
1965	NY-N	1	2	.333	13	3	1	0	0	28	30	13	13	2	2	15	13	1.607	4.18	84	4.99	.270	0	.000	-2	1	-0.3
Total	**8**	38	58	.396	199	117	28	11	1	875^{2}	830	408	366	105	21	326	493	1.320	3.76	95	3.87	.250	26	.099	-16	41	-2.5

• WILLHITE, Nick

Jon Nicholas Willhite b: 1/27/1941, Tulsa, OK BL/TL, 6'2", 195 lbs. Deb: 6/16/1963

YEAR	TM-L	W	L	PCT	G	GS	CG	SH	SV	IP	H	R	ER	HR	HB	BB	SO	RAT	ERA	ERA+	CERA	OAV	BH	AVG	PR+	WS	TPW
1963	LA-N	2	3	.400	8	8	1	1	0	38	44	19	16	5	0	10	28	1.421	3.79	80	4.54	.286	3	.300	-3	1	-0.2
1964	LA-N	2	4	.333	10	7	2	0	0	43^{2}	43	19	18	4	0	13	24	1.282	3.71	87	3.52	.264	0	.000	-2	1	-0.3
1965	Was-A	0	0	....	5	0	0	0	0	6^{1}	10	11	5	2	0	4	3	2.211	7.11	49	10.47	.345	0	....	-3	0	-0.3
	LA-N	2	2	.500	15	6	0	0	1	42	47	26	25	7	2	22	28	1.643	5.36	61	6.08	.288	4	.400	-10	1	-0.8
1966	LA-N	0	0	....	6	0	0	0	0	4^{1}	3	1	1	0	0	5	4	1.846	2.08	159	4.82	.214	0	....	1	0	0.1
1967	Cal-A	0	2	.000	10	7	0	0	0	39^{1}	39	20	19	8	0	16	22	1.398	4.35	72	4.84	.258	0	.000	-6	0	-0.7
	NY-N	0	1	.000	4	1	0	0	0	8^{1}	9	8	8	1	0	5	9	1.680	8.64	39	5.22	.257	0	.000	-5	0	-0.6
Total	**5**	6	12	.333	58	29	3	1	1	182	195	104	92	27	2	75	118	1.484	4.55	71	4.96	.275	7	.163	-28	3	-2.8

• WILLIAMS, Ace

Robert Fulton Williams b: 3/18/1917, Montclair, NJ d: 9/16/1999, Fort Myers, FL BR/TL, 6'2", 174 lbs. Deb: 7/15/1940

YEAR	TM-L	W	L	PCT	G	GS	CG	SH	SV	IP	H	R	ER	HR	HB	BB	SO	RAT	ERA	ERA+	CERA	OAV	BH	AVG	PR+	WS	TPW
1940	Bos-N	0	0	....	5	0	0	0	0	9	21	17	16	0	1	12	5	3.667	16.00	23	16.52	.457	0	.000	-12	0	-1.3
1946	Bos-N	0	0	....	1	0	0	0	0	0	1	0	0	0	0	1	0	....	....	....	∞	1.000	0	....	0	0	0.0
Total	**2**	0	0	....	6	0	0	0	0	9	22	17	16	0	1	13	5	3.889	16.00	23	16.52	.468	0	.000	-12	0	-1.3

• WILLIAMS, Al

Almon Edward Williams b: 5/11/1914, Valhermosa Springs, AL d: 7/19/1969, Groves, TX BR/TR, 6'3", 200 lbs. Deb: 4/19/1937

YEAR	TM-L	W	L	PCT	G	GS	CG	SH	SV	IP	H	R	ER	HR	HB	BB	SO	RAT	ERA	ERA+	CERA	OAV	BH	AVG	PR+	WS	TPW
1937	Phi-A	4	1	.800	16	8	2	0	1	75^{1}	88	51	45	0	1	49	27	1.819	5.38	88	5.21	.300	2	.083	-6	3	-0.7
1938	Phi-A	0	7	.000	30	8	1	0	0	93^{1}	128	93	72	6	1	54	25	1.950	6.94	70	6.55	.324	1	.040	-19	0	-2.0
Total	**2**	4	8	.333	46	16	3	0	1	168^{2}	216	144	117	6	2	103	52	1.891	6.24	77	5.95	.314	3	.061	-25	3	-2.7

• WILLIAMS, Albert

Albert Hamilton Williams b: 5/6/1954, Laguna De Perlas, Nicaragua BR/TR, 6'4", 190 lbs. Deb: 5/7/1980

YEAR	TM-L	W	L	PCT	G	GS	CG	SH	SV	IP	H	R	ER	HR	HB	BB	SO	RAT	ERA	ERA+	CERA	OAV	BH	AVG	PR+	WS	TPW
1980	Min-A	6	2	.750	18	9	3	0	1	77	73	33	30	9	0	30	35	1.338	3.51	124	3.93	.253	0	....	7	7	0.7
1981	Min-A	6	10	.375	23	22	4	0	0	150	160	72	68	11	1	52	76	1.413	4.08	97	4.09	.276	0	....	-1	7	-0.1
1982	Min-A	9	7	.563	26	26	3	0	0	153^{2}	166	74	72	18	0	55	61	1.438	4.22	100	4.44	.276	0	....	-1	8	-0.1
1983	Min-A	11	14	.440	36	29	4	1	1	193^{1}	196	105	89	21	4	68	68	1.366	4.14	102	4.07	.262	0	....	-0	10	0.0
1984	Min-A	3	5	.375	17	11	1	0	0	68^{2}	75	46	44	9	7	22	22	1.413	5.77	73	5.01	.284	0	....	-14	1	-1.4
Total	**5**	35	38	.479	120	97	15	1	2	642^{2}	670	330	303	68	12	227	262	1.396	4.24	98	4.25	.270	0	....	-9	33	-0.9

• WILLIAMS, Brian

Brian O'Neal Williams b: 2/15/1969, Lancaster, SC BR/TR, 6'3", 195 lbs. Deb: 9/16/1991

YEAR	TM-L	W	L	PCT	G	GS	CG	SH	SV	IP	H	R	ER	HR	HB	BB	SO	RAT	ERA	ERA+	CERA	OAV	BH	AVG	PR+	WS	TPW
1991	Hou-N	0	1	.000	2	2	0	0	0	12	11	5	5	2	1	4	4	1.250	3.75	93	4.33	.250	0	.000	-0	0	-0.1
1992	Hou-N	7	6	.538	16	16	0	0	0	96^{1}	92	44	42	10	0	42	54	1.391	3.92	86	3.99	.255	4	.133	-6	3	-0.7
1993	Hou-N	4	4	.500	42	5	0	0	3	82	76	48	44	7	4	38	56	1.390	4.83	80	3.91	.248	2	.200	-9	3	-0.9
1994	Hou-N	6	5	.545	20	13	0	0	0	78^{1}	112	64	50	9	4	41	49	1.953	5.74	69	7.43	.343	6	.261	-16	0	-1.5
1995	SD-N	3	10	.231	44	6	0	0	0	72	79	54	48	3	8	38	75	1.625	6.00	67	4.96	.279	1	.071	-17	0	-1.8
1996	Det-A	3	10	.231	40	17	2	1	2	121	145	107	91	21	6	85	72	1.901	6.77	75	7.42	.304	0	....	-20	1	-1.9
1997	Bal-A	0	0	....	13	0	0	0	0	24	20	8	8	0	0	18	14	1.583	3.00	147	3.64	.220	0	....	4	2	0.3
1999	Hou-N	2	1	.667	50	0	0	0	0	67^{1}	69	35	33	4	5	35	53	1.545	4.41	100	4.64	.272	1	.333	-1	4	0.0
2000	Chi-N	1	1	.500	22	0	0	0	1	24^{1}	28	27	26	4	3	23	14	2.096	9.62	47	8.36	.304	1	.500	-14	0	-1.2
	Cle-A	0	0	....	7	0	0	0	0	18	23	9	8	2	1	8	6	1.722	4.00	124	6.36	.324	0	....	2	1	0.2
Total	**9**	26	38	.406	256	59	2	1	6	595^{1}	655	401	355	62	32	332	397	1.658	5.37	78	5.56	.284	15	.176	-77	14	-7.4

• WILLIAMS, Charlie

Charles Prosek Williams b: 10/11/1947, Flushing, NY BR/TR, 6'2", 200 lbs. Deb: 4/23/1971

YEAR	TM-L	W	L	PCT	G	GS	CG	SH	SV	IP	H	R	ER	HR	HB	BB	SO	RAT	ERA	ERA+	CERA	OAV	BH	AVG	PR+	WS	TPW
1971	NY-N	5	6	.455	31	9	1	0	0	90^{1}	92	53	48	7	2	41	53	1.472	4.78	71	4.15	.267	2	.087	-15	0	-1.7
1972	SF-N	0	2	.000	3	2	0	0	0	9^{1}	14	10	9	3	0	3	3	1.821	8.68	40	8.22	.333	0	.000	-5	0	-0.6
1973	SF-N	3	0	1.000	12	2	0	0	0	23	32	19	17	2	0	7	11	1.696	6.65	57	5.52	.330	1	.333	-7	0	-0.7
1974	SF-N	1	3	.250	39	7	0	0	0	100^{1}	93	38	31	6	2	31	48	1.236	2.78	137	3.09	.250	3	.136	12	7	1.1
1975	SF-N	5	3	.625	55	2	0	0	3	98	94	41	38	2	4	66	45	1.633	3.49	109	4.30	.261	2	.125	3	7	0.4
1976	SF-N	2	0	1.000	48	2	0	0	1	85	80	33	28	4	2	39	34	1.400	2.96	122	3.69	.256	1	.125	8	7	0.8
1977	SF-N	6	5	.545	55	8	1	0	0	119^{1}	116	62	53	9	3	60	41	1.475	4.00	98	4.13	.262	4	.222	1	7	0.1
1978	SF-N	1	3	.250	25	1	0	0	0	48	60	31	29	5	1	28	22	1.833	5.44	63	6.27	.314	0	.000	-11	0	-1.2
Total	**8**	23	22	.511	268	33	2	0	4	573^{1}	581	287	253	38	14	275	257	1.493	3.97	92	4.22	.269	13	.134	-14	28	-1.8

• WILLIAMS, Dale

Elisha Alphonso Williams b: 10/6/1855, Ludlow, KY d: 10/22/1939, Covington, KY BR/TR, 5'9", 175 lbs. Deb: 8/12/1876 U

YEAR	TM-L	W	L	PCT	G	GS	CG	SH	SV	IP	H	R	ER	HR	HB	BB	SO	RAT	ERA	ERA+	CERA	OAV	BH	AVG	PR+	WS	TPW
1876	Cin-N	1	8	.111	9	9	9	0	0	83	123	75	39	1	....	4	9	1.530	4.23	52	....	.319	7	.200	-14	1	-1.3

• WILLIAMS, Dave

David Owen Williams b: 2/7/1881, Scranton, PA d: 4/25/1918, Hot Springs, AR BR/TL, 5'11.5", 167 lbs. Deb: 7/2/1902

YEAR	TM-L	W	L	PCT	G	GS	CG	SH	SV	IP	H	R	ER	HR	HB	BB	SO	RAT	ERA	ERA+	CERA	OAV	BH	AVG	PR+	WS	TPW
1902	Bos-A	0	0	....	3	0	0	0	0	18^{2}	22	18	11	0	1	11	7	1.768	5.30	67	5.10	.294	3	.333	-4	0	-0.3

• WILLIAMS, Dave

David Aaron Williams b: 3/12/1979, Anchorage, AK BL/TL, 6'2", 205 lbs. Deb: 6/6/2001

YEAR	TM-L	W	L	PCT	G	GS	CG	SH	SV	IP	H	R	ER	HR	HB	BB	SO	RAT	ERA	ERA+	CERA	OAV	BH	AVG	PR+	WS	TPW
2001	Pit-N	3	7	.300	22	18	0	0	0	114	100	53	47	15	7	45	57	1.272	3.71	121	3.89	.244	4	.118	10	7	0.9
2002	Pit-N	2	5	.286	9	9	0	0	0	43^{1}	38	26	24	9	4	24	33	1.431	4.98	84	4.99	.232	2	.125	-4	1	-0.4
Total	**2**	5	12	.294	31	27	0	0	0	157^{1}	138	79	71	24	11	69	90	1.316	4.06	108	4.20	.241	6	.120	6	8	0.5

• WILLIAMS, Don

Donald Reid "Dino" Williams b: 9/2/1935, Los Angeles, CA d: 12/20/1991, La Jolla, CA BR/TR, 6'5", 218 lbs. Deb: 8/4/1963 C

YEAR	TM-L	W	L	PCT	G	GS	CG	SH	SV	IP	H	R	ER	HR	HB	BB	SO	RAT	ERA	ERA+	CERA	OAV	BH	AVG	PR+	WS	TPW
1963	Min-A	0	0	....	3	0	0	0	0	4^{1}	8	5	5	1	0	6	2	3.231	10.38	35	15.31	.381	0	....	-3	0	-0.3

• WILLIAMS, Don

Donald Fred Williams b: 9/14/1931, Floyd, VA BR/TR, 6'2", 180 lbs. Deb: 9/12/1958

YEAR	TM-L	W	L	PCT	G	GS	CG	SH	SV	IP	H	R	ER	HR	HB	BB	SO	RAT	ERA	ERA+	CERA	OAV	BH	AVG	PR+	WS	TPW
1958	Pit-N	0	0	....	2	0	0	0	0	4	6	3	3	1	0	1	3	1.750	6.75	57	8.43	.375	0	....	-1	0	-0.1
1959	Pit-N	0	0	....	6	0	0	0	0	12	17	9	9	1	0	3	3	1.667	6.75	57	5.82	.362	1	.333	-4	0	-0.3
1962	KC-A	0	0	....	3	0	0	0	0	4	6	4	4	0	1	0	1	1.500	9.00	46	5.46	.353	0	.000	-2	0	-0.2
Total	**3**	0	0	....	11	0	0	0	0	20	29	16	16	2	1	4	7	1.650	7.20	55	6.27	.363	1	.250	-7	0	-0.7

• WILLIAMS, Frank

Frank Lee Williams b: 2/13/1958, Seattle, WA BR/TR, 6'1", 190 lbs. Deb: 4/5/1984

YEAR	TM-L	W	L	PCT	G	GS	CG	SH	SV	IP	H	R	ER	HR	HB	BB	SO	RAT	ERA	ERA+	CERA	OAV	BH	AVG	PR+	WS	TPW
1984	SF-N	9	4	.692	61	1	1	1	3	106^{1}	88	49	42	2	3	51	91	1.307	3.55	99	2.88	.226	4	.222	2	6	0.4
1985	SF-N	2	4	.333	49	0	0	0	0	73	65	39	34	5	6	35	54	1.370	4.19	82	3.71	.242	0	.000	-5	2	-0.6
1986	SF-N	3	1	.750	36	0	0	0	1	52^{1}	35	8	7	0	4	21	33	1.070	1.20	292	2.14	.212	1	.500	13	7	1.4
1987	Cin-N	4	0	1.000	85	0	0	0	2	105^{2}	101	37	27	5	2	39	60	1.325	2.30	184	3.32	.254	0	.000	22	11	2.2
1988	Cin-N	3	2	.600	60	0	0	0	1	62^{2}	59	24	18	6	2	35	43	1.500	2.59	139	4.39	.252	0	.000	6	5	0.6
1989	Det-A	3	3	.500	42	0	0	0	1	71^{2}	70	37	29	5	3	46	33	1.619	3.64	105	4.52	.254	0	....	2	4	0.2
Total	**6**	24	14	.632	333	1	1	1	8	471^{2}	418	194	157	23	20	227	314	1.367	3.00	122	3.47	.242	5	.172	40	35	4.2

• WILLIAMS, Gus

Augustine H. Williams b: 1870, New York, NY d: 10/14/1890, New York, NY, 5'11", 170 lbs. Deb: 4/18/1890

YEAR	TM-L	W	L	PCT	G	GS	CG	SH	SV	IP	H	R	ER	HR	HB	BB	SO	RAT	ERA	ERA+	CERA	OAV	BH	AVG	PR+	WS	TPW
1890	Bro-a	0	1	.000	2	2	1	0	0	12	13	15	10	0	0	12	2	2.083	7.50	52	....	.268	2	.500	-5	0	-0.4

• WILLIAMS, Jeff

Jeffrey F. Williams b: 6/6/1972, Canberra, Australia BR/TL, 6', 185 lbs. Deb: 9/12/1999

YEAR	TM-L	W	L	PCT	G	GS	CG	SH	SV	IP	H	R	ER	HR	HB	BB	SO	RAT	ERA	ERA+	CERA	OAV	BH	AVG	PR+	WS	TPW
1999	LA-N	2	0	1.000	5	3	0	0	0	17^{2}	12	10	8	2	0	9	7	1.189	4.08	105	2.86	.190	1	.200	1	1	0.1
2000	LA-N	0	0	....	7	0	0	0	0	5^{2}	12	11	10	1	0	8	3	3.529	15.88	27	17.89	.462	0	....	-7	0	-0.7
2001	LA-N	2	1	.667	15	1	0	0	0	24^{1}	26	18	17	5	1	17	9	1.767	6.29	64	7.02	.295	0	.000	-6	0	-0.6
2002	LA-N	0	0	....	10	0	0	0	0	10	15	13	13	2	1	7	11	2.200	11.70	33	9.45	.333	1	.500	-9	0	-0.8
Total	**4**	4	1	.800	37	4	0	0	0	57^{2}	65	52	48	10	2	41	30	1.838	7.49	54	7.24	.293	2	.182	-22	1	-2.1

• WILLIAMS, Jerome

Jerome Lee Williams b: 12/4/1981, Honolulu, HI BR/TR, 6'3", 180 lbs. Deb: 4/26/2003

YEAR	TM-L	W	L	PCT	G	GS	CG	SH	SV	IP	H	R	ER	HR	HB	BB	SO	RAT	ERA	ERA+	CERA	OAV	BH	AVG	PR+	WS	TPW
2003*	SF-N	7	5	.583	21	21	2	1	0	131	116	54	48	10	7	49	88	1.260	3.30	124	3.42	.242	4	.108	9	9	0.7

YEAR TM-L	W	L	PCT	G	GS	CG	SH	SV	IP	H	R	ER	HR	HB	BB	SO	RAT	ERA	ERA+	CERA	OAV	BH	AVG	PR+	WS	TPW
• WILLIAMS, Johnnie	John Brodie "Honolulu Johnny" Williams b: 7/16/1889, Honolulu, HI d: 9/8/1963, Long Beach, CA BR/TR, 6', 180 lbs. Deb: 4/21/1914																									
1914 Det-A	0	2	.000	4	3	1	0	0	11^1	17	12	8	0	0	5	4	1.941	6.35	44	6.90	.378	0	.000	-4	0	-0.5
• WILLIAMS, Lefty	Claude Preston Williams b: 3/9/1893, Aurora, MO d: 11/4/1959, Laguna Beach, CA BR/TL, 5'9", 160 lbs. Deb: 9/17/1913																									
1913 Det-A	1	3	.250	5	4	3	0	1	29	34	18	16	0	1	4	9	1.310	4.97	59	3.38	.286	1	.100	-6	0	-0.7
1914 Det-A	0	1	.000	1	1	0	0	0	1	3	5	0	0	0	2	0	5.000	0.00	....	20.94	.429	0	....	0	0	0.0
1916 Chi-A	13	7	.650	43	26	10	2	1	224^1	220	99	72	5	8	65	138	1.270	2.89	95	3.27	.267	10	.135	-6	11	-0.7
1917* Chi-A	17	8	.680	45	29	8	1	1	230	221	94	76	3	9	81	85	1.313	2.97	89	3.17	.252	6	.090	-7	11	-1.0
1918 Chi-A	6	4	.600	15	14	7	2	1	105^2	76	32	32	0	5	47	30	1.164	2.73	100	2.26	.209	5	.132	1	7	-0.1
1919* Chi-A	23	11	.676	41	**40**	27	5	1	297	265	104	87	7	11	58	125	1.088	2.64	120	2.47	.244	17	.181	11	23	1.3
1920 Chi-A	22	14	.611	39	38	25	0	0	299	302	145	130	15	12	90	128	1.311	3.91	96	3.65	.271	22	.218	-9	19	-0.8
Total 7	82	48	.631	189	152	80	10	5	1186	1121	497	413	30	46	347	515	1.238	3.13	98	3.07	.255	61	.159	-14	71	-2.0
• WILLIAMS, Leon	Leon Theo Williams b: 12/2/1905, Macon, GA d: 11/20/1984, Atlanta, GA BL/TL, 5'10.5", 154 lbs. Deb: 6/2/1926																									
1926 Bro-N	0	0	....	8	0	0	0	0	8^1	16	6	5	0	0	2	3	2.160	5.40	71	8.36	.421	1	.200	-1	0	-0.1
• WILLIAMS, Marsh	Marshall McDiarmid "Cap" Williams b: 2/21/1893, Faison, NC d: 2/22/1935, Tucson, AZ BR/TR, 6', 180 lbs. Deb: 7/7/1916																									
1916 Phi-A	0	6	.000	10	4	3	0	0	51^1	71	53	45	4	0	31	17	1.987	7.89	36	7.37	.350	2	.105	-28	0	-3.2
• WILLIAMS, Matt	Matthew Evan Williams b: 7/25/1959, Houston, TX BR/TR, 6'1", 200 lbs. Deb: 8/2/1983																									
1983 Tor-A	1	1	.500	4	3	0	0	0	8	13	13	13	5	1	7	5	2.500	14.63	29	15.83	.361	0	....	-9	0	-0.9
1985 Tex-A	2	1	.667	6	3	0	0	0	26	20	7	7	3	0	10	22	1.154	2.42	175	2.90	.211	0	....	6	3	0.6
Total 2	3	2	.600	10	6	0	0	0	34	33	20	20	8	1	17	27	1.471	5.29	81	5.94	.252	0	....	-4	3	-0.4
• WILLIAMS, Matt	Matthew Taylor Williams b: 4/12/1971, Virginia Beach, VA BB/TL, 6', 190 lbs. Deb: 4/5/2000																									
2000 Mil-N	0	0	....	11	0	0	0	0	9	7	7	7	2	1	13	7	2.222	7.00	65	8.82	.219	0	.000	-3	0	-0.3
• WILLIAMS, Mike	Michael Darren Williams b: 7/29/1968, Radford, VA BR/TR, 6'2", 199 lbs. Deb: 6/30/1992																									
1992 Phi-N	1	1	.500	5	5	1	0	0	28^2	29	20	17	3	0	7	5	1.256	5.34	65	3.52	.259	4	.400	-6	1	-0.5
1993 Phi-N	1	3	.250	17	4	0	0	0	51	50	32	30	5	0	22	33	1.412	5.29	75	4.00	.253	1	.083	-7	1	-0.8
1994 Phi-N	2	4	.333	12	8	0	0	0	50^1	61	31	28	7	0	20	29	1.609	5.01	86	5.62	.310	2	.167	-4	1	-0.3
1995 Phi-N	3	3	.500	33	8	0	0	0	87^2	78	37	32	10	3	29	57	1.221	3.29	129	3.39	.239	2	.125	8	6	0.8
1996 Phi-N	6	14	.300	32	29	0	0	0	167	188	107	101	25	6	67	103	1.527	5.44	79	5.37	.290	8	.157	-22	3	-2.2
1997 KC-A	0	2	.000	10	0	0	0	1	14	20	11	10	1	1	8	10	2.000	6.43	73	7.23	.333	0	....	-3	0	-0.3
1998 Pit-N	4	2	.667	37	1	0	0	0	51	39	12	11	1	0	16	59	1.078	1.94	222	1.95	.211	0	.000	13	7	1.3
1999 Pit-N	3	4	.429	58	0	0	0	23	58^1	63	36	33	9	1	37	76	1.714	5.09	90	5.80	.276	0	.000	-3	5	-0.3
2000 Pit-N	3	4	.429	72	0	0	0	24	72	56	34	28	8	4	40	71	1.333	3.50	131	3.72	.218	0	.000	10	11	0.9
2001 Pit-N	2	4	.333	40	0	0	0	22	41^2	39	18	17	6	0	21	43	1.440	3.67	122	4.32	.244	0	....	4	6	0.4
* Hou-N	4	0	1.000	25	0	0	0	0	22^1	21	10	10	3	0	14	16	1.567	4.03	113	4.70	.244	0	....	1	2	0.1
Yr.	6	4	.600	65	0	0	0	22	64	60	28	27	9	0	35	59	1.484	3.80	119	4.45	.244	0	....	5	8	0.5
2002 Pit-N	2	6	.250	59	0	0	0	46	61^1	54	24	20	6	1	21	43	1.223	2.93	142	3.14	.233	0	.000	8	12	0.8
2003 Pit-N★	1	3	.250	40	0	0	0	25	37^1	42	26	26	5	1	22	20	1.714	6.27	70	5.84	.282	0	....	-8	2	-0.8
Phi-N	0	4	.000	28	0	0	0	3	25^2	24	18	17	0	3	19	19	1.675	5.96	67	4.17	.247	0	....	-6	0	-0.5
Yr.	1	7	.125	68	0	0	0	28	63	66	44	43	5	4	41	39	1.698	6.14	69	5.16	.268	0	....	-13	2	-1.3
Total 12	32	54	.372	468	55	1	0	144	768^1	764	416	380	89	20	343	584	1.441	4.45	96	4.41	.260	17	.157	-14	57	-1.4
• WILLIAMS, Mitch	Mitchell Steven "Wild Thing" Williams b: 11/17/1964, Santa Ana, CA BL/TL, 6'3", 205 lbs. Deb: 4/9/1986																									
1986 Tex-A	8	6	.571	**80**	0	0	0	8	98	69	39	39	8	11	79	90	1.510	3.58	120	4.22	.202	0	....	8	9	0.8
1987 Tex-A	8	6	.571	85	1	0	0	6	108^2	63	47	39	9	7	94	129	1.445	3.23	139	3.64	.175	0	....	16	10	1.5
1988 Tex-A	2	7	.222	67	0	0	0	18	68	48	38	35	4	6	47	61	1.397	4.63	88	3.57	.203	0	....	-5	6	-0.5
1989* Chi-N★	4	4	.500	**76**	0	0	0	36	81^2	71	27	25	6	8	52	67	1.506	2.76	136	4.40	.238	1	.200	9	12	1.1
1990 Chi-N	1	8	.111	59	2	0	0	16	66^1	60	38	29	4	1	50	55	1.658	3.93	104	4.39	.239	0	.000	3	5	0.3
1991 Phi-N	12	5	.706	69	0	0	0	30	88^1	56	24	23	4	8	62	84	1.336	2.34	156	3.06	.182	0	.000	13	18	1.4
1992 Phi-N	5	8	.385	66	0	0	0	29	81	69	39	34	4	6	64	74	1.642	3.78	92	4.68	.240	1	.250	-2	6	-0.2
1993* Phi-N	3	7	.300	65	0	0	0	43	62	56	30	23	3	2	44	60	1.613	3.34	119	4.45	.245	1	1.000	5	9	0.5
1994 Hou-N	1	4	.200	25	0	0	0	6	20	21	17	17	4	1	24	21	2.250	7.65	52	8.44	.269	0	....	-8	0	-0.8
1995 Cal-A	1	2	.333	20	0	0	0	0	10^2	13	10	8	1	2	21	9	3.188	6.75	70	13.39	.317	0	....	-3	0	-0.2
1997 KC-A	0	1	.000	7	0	0	0	0	6^2	11	8	8	2	0	7	10	2.700	10.80	44	12.57	.367	0	....	-5	0	-0.4
Total 11	45	58	.437	619	3	0	0	192	691^1	537	317	280	49	52	544	660	1.564	3.65	110	4.37	.218	3	.188	33	75	3.5
• WILLIAMS, Mutt	David Carter Williams b: 7/31/1891, Ozark, AR d: 3/30/1962, Fayetteville, AR BR/TR, 6'3.5", 195 lbs. Deb: 10/4/1913																									
1913 Was-A	1	0	1.000	1	1	0	0	0	4	4	3	2	1	0	2	1	1.500	4.50	66	6.07	.286	1	.500	-1	0	0.0
1914 Was-A	0	0	....	5	0	0	0	1	7	5	5	4	0	0	4	3	1.286	5.14	55	2.77	.227	0	....	-2	0	-0.2
Total 2	1	0	1.000	6	1	0	0	1	11	9	8	6	1	0	6	4	1.364	4.91	58	3.97	.250	1	.500	-3	0	-0.3
• WILLIAMS, Pop	Walter Merrill Williams b: 5/19/1874, Bowdoinham, ME d: 8/4/1959, Topsham, ME BL/TR, 5'11", 190 lbs. Deb: 9/14/1898																									
1898 Was-N	0	2	.000	2	2	2	0	0	17	32	18	16	0	0	7	3	2.294	8.47	43	8.61	.396	3	.375	-9	0	-0.7
1902 Chi-N	11	16	.407	32	32	27	1	0	263^1	267	112	71	1	10	63	99	1.253	2.43	111	2.98	.263	23	.198	7	14	0.9
1903 Chi-N	0	1	.000	1	1	1	0	0	5	9	3	3	0	0	0	2	1.800	5.40	58	6.84	.409	0	.000	-1	0	-0.1
Phi-N	1	1	.500	2	2	2	0	0	18	21	11	6	0	1	6	8	1.500	3.00	109	4.37	.304	2	.286	0	1	0.0
Bos-N	4	5	.444	10	10	9	1	0	83	97	59	38	3	9	37	20	1.614	4.12	78	5.13	.295	10	.238	-10	3	-1.0
Yr.	5	7	.417	13	13	12	1	0	106	127	73	47	3	10	43	30	1.604	3.99	80	5.08	.302	12	.235	-11	4	-1.1
Total 3	16	25	.390	47	47	41	2	0	386^1	426	203	134	4	20	113	132	1.395	3.12	95	3.80	.281	38	.217	-13	18	-0.8
• WILLIAMS, Rick	Richard Allen Williams b: 11/9/1952, Merced, CA BR/TR, 6'1", 180 lbs. Deb: 6/12/1978 C																									
1978 Hou-N	1	2	.333	17	1	0	0	0	34^2	43	19	18	2	0	10	17	1.529	4.67	71	4.41	.301	0	.000	-5	0	-0.5
1979 Hou-N	4	7	.364	31	16	2	2	0	121^1	122	45	44	6	2	30	37	1.253	3.26	108	3.22	.261	8	.258	4	8	0.7
Total 2	5	9	.357	48	17	2	2	0	156	165	64	62	8	2	40	54	1.314	3.58	96	3.49	.270	8	.222	-1	8	0.1
• WILLIAMS, Shad	Shad Clayton Williams b: 3/10/1971, Fresno, CA BR/TR, 6', 198 lbs. Deb: 5/18/1996																									
1996 Cal-A	0	2	.000	13	2	0	0	0	28^1	42	34	28	7	2	21	26	2.224	8.89	55	9.72	.341	0	....	-13	0	-1.1
1997 Ana-A	0	0	....	1	0	0	0	0	1	1	0	0	0	0	1	0	2.000	0.00	....	5.48	.250	0	....	1	0	0.0
Total 2	0	2	.000	14	2	0	0	0	29^1	43	34	28	7	2	22	26	2.216	8.59	57	9.57	.339	0	....	-12	0	-1.1
• WILLIAMS, Stan	Stanley Wilson "Big Daddy" Williams b: 9/14/1936, Enfield, NH BR/TR, 6'5", 230 lbs. Deb: 5/17/1958 C																									
1958 LA-N	9	7	.563	27	21	3	2	0	119	99	58	53	10	7	65	80	1.378	4.01	102	3.82	.228	2	.050	1	7	-0.2
1959* LA-N	5	5	.500	35	15	2	0	0	124^2	102	64	55	12	9	86	89	1.508	3.97	106	4.35	.228	7	.194	3	7	0.4
1960 LA-N★	14	10	.583	38	30	9	2	1	207^1	162	84	69	26	5	72	175	1.129	3.00	132	2.91	.210	9	.141	20	17	2.1
1961 LA-N	15	12	.556	41	35	6	2	0	235^1	213	114	102	21	6	108	205	1.364	3.90	111	3.76	.242	13	.167	10	16	1.0
1962 LA-N	14	12	.538	40	28	4	1	1	185^2	184	104	92	16	0	98	108	1.519	4.46	81	4.22	.253	5	.076	-17	5	-1.9
1963* NY-A	9	8	.529	29	21	6	1	0	146	137	59	52	7	6	57	98	1.329	3.21	110	3.49	.249	5	.102	2	9	0.1
1964 NY-A	1	5	.167	21	10	1	0	0	82	76	39	35	7	0	38	54	1.390	3.84	94	3.79	.248	3	.143	-3	2	-0.3
1965 Cle-A	0	0	....	3	0	0	0	0	4^1	6	4	3	1	0	3	1	2.077	6.23	56	8.58	.353	0	....	-1	0	-0.1
1967 Cle-A	6	4	.600	16	8	2	1	1	79	64	26	23	6	1	24	75	1.114	2.62	125	2.53	.218	2	.091	6	6	0.6
1968 Cle-A	13	11	.542	44	24	6	2	9	194^1	163	64	54	14	10	51	147	1.101	2.50	118	2.65	.225	9	.161	8	16	1.0
1969 Cle-A	6	14	.300	61	15	3	0	12	178^1	155	86	78	25	12	67	139	1.245	3.94	96	3.75	.235	4	.100	-2	8	-0.3
1970* Min-A	10	1	.909	68	0	0	0	15	113^1	85	34	25	8	5	32	76	1.032	1.99	187	2.25	.208	0	.000	21	16	2.0

YEAR	TM-L	W	L	PCT	G	GS	CG	SH	SV	IP	H	R	ER	HR	HB	BB	SO	RAT	ERA	ERA+	CERA	OAV	BH	AVG	PR+	WS	TPW
1971	Min-A	4	5	.444	46	1	0	0	4	78	63	44	36	7	8	44	47	1.372	4.15	85	3.79	.220	0	.000	-4	3	-0.5
	StL-N	3	0	1.000	10	0	0	0	0	12^2	13	2	2	0	2	2	8	1.184	1.42	253	3.00	.265	0	.000	3	2	0.3
1972	Bos-A	0	0	....	3	0	0	0	0	4^1	5	3	3	0	0	1	3	1.385	6.23	52	3.69	.294	0	....	-1	0	-0.2
Total	**14**	**109**	**94**	**.537**	**482**	**208**	**42**	**11**	**43**	**1764^1**	**1527**	**785**	**682**	**160**	**71**	**748**	**1305**	**1.289**	**3.48**	**108**	**3.47**	**.232**	**59**	**.118**	**47**	**114**	**4.1**

• WILLIAMS, Steamboat

Rees Gephardt Williams b: 1/31/1892, Cascade, MT d: 6/29/1979, Deer River, MN BL/TR, 5'11", 170 lbs. Deb: 7/12/1914

YEAR	TM-L	W	L	PCT	G	GS	CG	SH	SV	IP	H	R	ER	HR	HB	BB	SO	RAT	ERA	ERA+	CERA	OAV	BH	AVG	PR+	WS	TPW
1914	StL-N	0	1	.000	5	1	0	0	0	11	13	8	8	1	0	6	2	1.727	6.55	43	4.75	.295	0	.000	-5	0	-0.5
1916	StL-N	6	7	.462	36	8	5	0	1	105	121	63	49	6	1	27	25	1.410	4.20	63	3.99	.291	5	.208	-18	2	-1.9
Total	**2**	**6**	**8**	**.429**	**41**	**9**	**5**	**0**	**1**	**116**	**134**	**71**	**57**	**7**	**1**	**33**	**27**	**1.440**	**4.42**	**60**	**4.06**	**.291**	**5**	**.200**	**-23**	**2**	**-2.4**

• WILLIAMS, Todd

Todd Michael Williams b: 2/13/1971, Syracuse, NY BR/TR, 6'3", 185 lbs. Deb: 4/29/1995

YEAR	TM-L	W	L	PCT	G	GS	CG	SH	SV	IP	H	R	ER	HR	HB	BB	SO	RAT	ERA	ERA+	CERA	OAV	BH	AVG	PR+	WS	TPW
1995	LA-N	2	2	.500	16	0	0	0	0	19^1	19	11	11	3	0	7	8	1.345	5.12	74	4.01	.264	1	.500	-3	1	-0.2
1998	Cin-N	0	1	.000	6	0	0	0	0	9^1	15	8	8	1	0	6	4	2.250	7.71	56	8.58	.341	0	.000	-4	0	-0.4
1999	Sea-A	0	0	....	13	0	0	0	0	9^2	11	5	5	1	1	7	7	1.862	4.66	107	6.67	.289	0	....	0	1	0.0
2001	NY-A	1	0	1.000	15	0	0	0	0	15^1	22	9	8	1	2	9	13	2.022	4.70	96	7.01	.324	0	....	-0	1	0.0
Total	**4**	**3**	**3**	**.500**	**50**	**0**	**0**	**0**	**0**	**53^2**	**67**	**33**	**32**	**6**	**3**	**29**	**32**	**1.789**	**5.37**	**79**	**6.14**	**.302**	**1**	**.250**	**-6**	**3**	**-0.6**

• WILLIAMS, Tom

Thomas C. Williams b: 8/19/1870, Minersville, OH d: 7/27/1940, Columbus, OH Deb: 5/1/1892

YEAR	TM-L	W	L	PCT	G	GS	CG	SH	SV	IP	H	R	ER	HR	HB	BB	SO	RAT	ERA	ERA+	CERA	OAV	BH	AVG	PR+	WS	TPW
1892	Cle-N	1	0	1.000	2	1	1	0	0	9	9	4	3	1	0	1	3	1.111	3.00	113	3.04	.250	1	.100	0	1	-0.1
1893	Cle-N	1	1	.500	5	2	2	0	0	24	33	18	13	1	0	10	6	1.792	4.88	100	5.78	.317	5	.278	0	2	-0.1
Total	**2**	**2**	**1**	**.667**	**7**	**3**	**3**	**0**	**0**	**33**	**42**	**22**	**16**	**2**	**0**	**11**	**9**	**1.606**	**4.36**	**103**	**5.03**	**.300**	**6**	**.214**	**1**	**3**	**-0.2**

• WILLIAMS, Woody

Gregory Scott Williams b: 8/19/1966, Houston, TX BR/TR, 6', 190 lbs. Deb: 5/14/1993

YEAR	TM-L	W	L	PCT	G	GS	CG	SH	SV	IP	H	R	ER	HR	HB	BB	SO	RAT	ERA	ERA+	CERA	OAV	BH	AVG	PR+	WS	TPW
1993	Tor-A	3	1	.750	30	0	0	0	0	37	40	18	18	2	1	22	24	1.676	4.38	99	4.85	.274	0	....	0	2	0.0
1994	Tor-A	1	3	.250	38	0	0	0	0	59^1	44	24	24	5	2	33	56	1.298	3.64	132	3.25	.205	0	....	8	5	0.8
1995	Tor-A	1	2	.333	23	3	0	0	0	53^2	44	23	22	6	2	28	41	1.342	3.69	128	3.72	.220	0	....	6	4	0.6
1996	Tor-A	4	5	.444	12	10	1	0	0	59	64	33	31	8	1	21	43	1.441	4.73	106	4.73	.278	0	....	1	3	0.0
1997	Tor-A	9	14	.391	31	31	0	0	0	194^2	201	98	94	31	5	66	124	1.372	4.35	106	4.55	.269	1	.500	2	11	0.2
1998	Tor-A	10	9	.526	32	32	1	1	0	209^2	196	112	104	36	2	81	151	1.321	4.46	105	4.15	.245	2	.333	4	12	0.5
1999	SD-N	12	12	.500	33	33	0	0	0	208^1	213	106	102	33	2	73	137	1.373	4.41	95	4.46	.268	13	.178	-6	10	-0.5
2000	SD-N	10	8	.556	23	23	4	0	0	168	152	74	70	23	3	54	111	1.226	3.75	115	3.55	.239	15	.259	8	12	1.4
2001	SD-N	8	8	.500	23	23	0	0	0	145	170	88	80	28	5	37	102	1.428	4.97	80	5.26	.296	9	.164	-13	3	-1.1
	*StL-N	7	1	.875	11	11	3	1	0	75	54	22	19	7	3	19	52	.973	2.28	187	2.24	.205	7	.259	15	8	1.7
	Yr.	15	9	.625	34	34	3	1	0	220	224	110	99	35	8	56	154	1.273	4.05	100	4.23	.268	16	.195	2	11	0.5
2002*	StL-N	9	4	.692	17	17	1	0	0	103^1	84	30	29	10	4	25	76	1.055	2.53	157	2.63	.222	6	.207	15	10	1.7
2003	StL-N★	18	9	.667	34	33	0	0	0	220^2	220	101	95	20	11	55	153	1.246	3.87	105	3.52	.256	17	.243	4	13	1.1
Total	**11**	**92**	**76**	**.548**	**307**	**216**	**10**	**2**	**0**	**1533^2**	**1482**	**729**	**688**	**209**	**41**	**514**	**1070**	**1.301**	**4.04**	**108**	**3.98**	**.254**	**70**	**.219**	**44**	**93**	**6.4**

• WILLIAMSON, Al

Silas Albert Williamson b: 2/20/1900, Buckville, AR d: 11/29/1978, Hot Springs, AR BR/TR, 5'11", 160 lbs. Deb: 4/27/1928

YEAR	TM-L	W	L	PCT	G	GS	CG	SH	SV	IP	H	R	ER	HR	HB	BB	SO	RAT	ERA	ERA+	CERA	OAV	BH	AVG	PR+	WS	TPW
1928	Chi-A	0	0	....	1	0	0	0	0	2	1	0	0	0	0	0	0	.500	0.00	....	0.54	.167	0	....	1	0	0.1

• WILLIAMSON, Mark

Mark Alan Williamson b: 7/21/1959, Corpus Christi, TX BR/TR, 6', 172 lbs. Deb: 4/8/1987

YEAR	TM-L	W	L	PCT	G	GS	CG	SH	SV	IP	H	R	ER	HR	HB	BB	SO	RAT	ERA	ERA+	CERA	OAV	BH	AVG	PR+	WS	TPW
1987	Bal-A	8	9	.471	61	2	0	0	3	125	122	59	56	12	3	41	73	1.304	4.03	109	3.62	.261	0	....	5	10	0.5
1988	Bal-A	5	8	.385	37	10	2	0	2	117^2	125	70	64	14	2	40	69	1.402	4.90	80	4.30	.272	0	....	-14	4	-1.4
1989	Bal-A	10	5	.667	65	0	0	0	9	107^1	105	35	35	4	2	30	55	1.258	2.93	129	3.05	.261	0	....	10	12	1.0
1990	Bal-A	8	2	.800	49	0	0	0	1	85^1	65	25	21	8	0	28	60	1.090	2.21	171	2.49	.215	0	....	14	9	1.4
1991	Bal-A	5	5	.500	65	0	0	0	4	80^1	87	42	40	9	0	35	53	1.519	4.48	88	4.60	.275	0	....	-5	4	-0.5
1992	Bal-A	0	0	....	12	0	0	0	1	18^2	16	3	2	1	0	10	14	1.393	0.96	417	3.51	.239	0	....	6	2	0.6
1993	Bal-A	7	5	.583	48	1	0	0	0	88	106	54	48	5	0	25	45	1.489	4.91	91	4.30	.304	0	....	-6	4	-0.5
1994	Bal-A	3	1	.750	28	2	0	0	1	67^1	75	33	30	9	2	17	28	1.366	4.01	125	4.44	.278	0	....	7	5	0.6
Total	**8**	**46**	**35**	**.568**	**365**	**15**	**2**	**0**	**21**	**689^2**	**701**	**321**	**296**	**62**	**9**	**226**	**397**	**1.344**	**3.86**	**108**	**3.79**	**.266**	**0**	**....**	**17**	**50**	**1.7**

• WILLIAMSON, Ned

Edward Nagle Williamson b: 10/24/1857, Philadelphia, PA d: 3/3/1894, Mountain Valley Springs, AR BR/TR, 5'11", 210 lbs. Deb: 5/1/1878 U ♦

YEAR	TM-L	W	L	PCT	G	GS	CG	SH	SV	IP	H	R	ER	HR	HB	BB	SO	RAT	ERA	ERA+	CERA	OAV	BH	AVG	PR+	WS	TPW
1881	Chi-N	1	1	.500	3	1	1	0	0	18	14	9	4	0	....	0	2	.778	2.00	140	....	.205	92	.268	1	14	2.1
1882	Chi-N	0	0	....	1	0	0	0	0	3	9	8	2	1	....	1	0	3.333	6.00	45	....	.494	98	.282	-1	16	3.1
1883	Chi-N	0	0	....	1	0	0	0	0	1	1	2	1	0	....	1	1	2.000	9.00	37	....	.245	111	.276	-1	16	1.8
1884	Chi-N	0	0	....	2	0	0	0	0	2	8	8	4	0	....	2	0	5.000	18.00	17	....	.567	116	.278	-3	19	4.0
1885*	Chi-N	0	0	....	2	0	0	0	**2**	6	2	0	0	0	....	0	3	.333	0.00	....	....	.099	97	.238	2	21	1.5
1886*	Chi-N	0	0	....	2	0	0	0	1	3	2	2	0	0	....	0	1	.667	0.00	....	....	.182	93	.216	1	14	-0.4
1887	Chi-N	0	0	....	1	0	0	0	0	2	3	2	2	0	0	1	0	1.500	9.00	49	....	.337	190	.371	-1	13	-2.6
Total	**7**	**1**	**1**	**.500**	**12**	**1**	**1**	**0**	**3**	**35**	**39**	**31**	**13**	**1**	**0**	**5**	**7**	**1.229**	**3.34**	**93**	**....**	**.270**	**1232**	**.266**	**-2**	**113**	**9.4**

• WILLIAMSON, Scott

Scott Ryan Williamson b: 2/17/1976, Fort Polk, LA BR/TR, 6', 185 lbs. Deb: 4/5/1999

YEAR	TM-L	W	L	PCT	G	GS	CG	SH	SV	IP	H	R	ER	HR	HB	BB	SO	RAT	ERA	ERA+	CERA	OAV	BH	AVG	PR+	WS	TPW
1999	Cin-N★	12	7	.632	62	0	0	0	19	93^1	54	29	25	8	1	43	107	1.039	2.41	193	2.05	.171	0	.000	21	17	1.9
2000	Cin-N	5	8	.385	48	10	0	0	6	112	92	45	41	7	3	75	136	1.491	3.29	143	3.85	.224	1	.063	16	11	1.5
2001	Cin-N	0	0	....	2	0	0	0	0	0^2	1	0	0	0	1	2	0	4.500	0.00	....	24.61	.333	0	....	0	0	0.0
2002	Cin-N	3	4	.429	63	0	0	0	8	74	46	27	24	5	2	36	84	1.108	2.92	145	2.24	.181	0	....	11	10	1.1
2003	Cin-N	5	3	.625	42	0	0	0	21	42^1	34	15	15	6	1	25	53	1.394	3.19	134	3.87	.214	0	....	5	7	0.5
	*Bos-A	0	1	.000	24	0	0	0	0	20^1	20	15	14	1	0	9	21	1.426	6.20	74	3.58	.253	0	....	-3	0	-0.3
Total	**5**	**25**	**23**	**.521**	**241**	**10**	**0**	**0**	**54**	**342^2**	**247**	**131**	**119**	**27**	**8**	**190**	**401**	**1.275**	**3.13**	**145**	**3.04**	**.202**	**1**	**.043**	**50**	**45**	**4.7**

• WILLIS, Carl

Carl Blake Willis b: 12/28/1960, Danville, VA BL/TR, 6'4", 213 lbs. Deb: 6/9/1984

YEAR	TM-L	W	L	PCT	G	GS	CG	SH	SV	IP	H	R	ER	HR	HB	BB	SO	RAT	ERA	ERA+	CERA	OAV	BH	AVG	PR+	WS	TPW
1984	Det-A	0	2	.000	10	2	0	0	0	16	25	13	13	1	0	5	4	1.875	7.31	54	6.75	.362	0	....	-6	0	-0.6
	Cin-N	0	1	.000	7	0	0	0	1	9^2	8	4	4	1	0	2	3	1.034	3.72	101	2.42	.222	0	....	0	1	0.0
1985	Cin-N	1	0	1.000	11	0	0	0	1	13^2	21	18	14	3	0	5	6	1.902	9.22	41	7.77	.344	0	.000	-8	0	-0.9
1986	Cin-N	1	3	.250	29	0	0	0	0	52^1	54	29	26	4	1	32	24	1.643	4.47	86	4.80	.278	1	.333	-3	2	-0.3
1988	Chi-A	0	0	....	6	0	0	0	0	12	17	12	11	3	0	7	6	2.000	8.25	48	9.15	.362	0	....	-6	0	-0.6
1991*	Min-A	8	3	.727	40	0	0	0	2	89	76	31	26	4	1	19	53	1.067	2.63	162	2.30	.232	0	....	15	10	1.5
1992	Min-A	7	3	.700	59	0	0	0	1	79^1	73	25	24	4	0	11	45	1.059	2.72	149	2.39	.246	0	....	11	8	1.1
1993	Min-A	3	0	1.000	53	0	0	0	5	58	56	23	20	2	0	17	44	1.259	3.10	140	3.00	.259	0	....	9	8	0.8
1994	Min-A	2	4	.333	49	0	0	0	3	59^1	89	48	39	6	0	12	37	1.702	5.92	82	5.85	.335	0	....	-6	2	-0.5
1995	Min-A	0	0	....	3	0	0	0	0	0^2	5	7	7	0	0	5	0	15.00	94.50	5	93.77	.833	0	....	-7	0	-0.6
Total	**9**	**22**	**16**	**.579**	**267**	**2**	**0**	**0**	**13**	**390**	**424**	**210**	**184**	**28**	**2**	**115**	**222**	**1.382**	**4.25**	**99**	**4.04**	**.279**	**1**	**.250**	**-1**	**31**	**0.0**

• WILLIS, Dale

Dale Jerome Willis b: 5/29/1938, Calhoun, GA BR/TR, 5'11", 165 lbs. Deb: 4/14/1963

YEAR	TM-L	W	L	PCT	G	GS	CG	SH	SV	IP	H	R	ER	HR	HB	BB	SO	RAT	ERA	ERA+	CERA	OAV	BH	AVG	PR+	WS	TPW
1963	KC-A	0	2	.000	25	0	0	0	1	44^2	46	28	25	3	4	25	47	1.590	5.04	76	4.79	.266	1	.167	-6	1	-0.6

• WILLIS, Dontrelle

Dontrelle Wayne Willis b: 1/12/1982, Oakland, CA BL/TL, 6'4", 195 lbs. Deb: 5/9/2003

YEAR	TM-L	W	L	PCT	G	GS	CG	SH	SV	IP	H	R	ER	HR	HB	BB	SO	RAT	ERA	ERA+	CERA	OAV	BH	AVG	PR+	WS	TPW
2003*	Fla-N★	14	6	.700	27	27	2	2	0	160^2	148	61	59	13	3	58	142	1.282	3.30	124	3.49	.245	14	.241	13	14	1.7

• WILLIS, Jim

James Gladden Willis b: 3/20/1927, Doyline, LA BL/TR, 6'3", 175 lbs. Deb: 4/22/1953

YEAR	TM-L	W	L	PCT	G	GS	CG	SH	SV	IP	H	R	ER	HR	HB	BB	SO	RAT	ERA	ERA+	CERA	OAV	BH	AVG	PR+	WS	TPW
1953	Chi-N	2	1	.667	13	3	2	0	0	43^1	37	15	15	1	3	17	15	1.246	3.12	143	2.89	.228	0	.000	8	4	0.7
1954	Chi-N	0	1	.000	14	1	0	0	0	23	22	10	10	1	3	18	5	1.739	3.91	107	5.15	.256	0	.000	1	1	0.0
Total	**2**	**2**	**2**	**.500**	**27**	**4**	**2**	**0**	**0**	**66^1**	**59**	**25**	**25**	**2**	**6**	**35**	**20**	**1.417**	**3.39**	**128**	**3.67**	**.238**	**0**	**.000**	**9**	**5**	**0.7**

• WILLIS, Joe

Joseph Denk Willis b: 4/9/1890, Coal Grove, OH d: 12/4/1966, Ironton, OH BR/TL, 6'1", 185 lbs. Deb: 5/3/1911

YEAR	TM-L	W	L	PCT	G	GS	CG	SH	SV	IP	H	R	ER	HR	HB	BB	SO	RAT	ERA	ERA+	CERA	OAV	BH	AVG	PR+	WS	TPW
1911	StL-A	0	1	.000	1	1	0	0	0	7	8	5	4	0	0	3	0	1.571	5.14	66	4.49	.308	0	.000	-1	0	-0.1
	StL-N	0	1	.000	2	2	1	0	0	15	13	9	7	0	0	4	5	1.133	4.20	80	2.23	.232	0	.000	-1	0	-0.2

YEAR TM-L	W	L	PCT	G	GS	CG	SH	SV	IP	H	R	ER	HR	HB	BB	SO	RAT	ERA	ERA+	CERA	OAV	BH	AVG	PR+	WS	TPW
1912 StL-N	4	9	.308	31	17	4	0	2	129^{2}	143	83	64	3	5	62	55	1.581	4.44	77	4.43	.288	6	.158	-15	4	-1.7
1913 StL-N	0	0	....	7	0	0	0	1	9^{2}	9	9	8	0	0	11	6	2.069	7.45	43	5.25	.257	0	.000	-5	0	-0.5
Total 3	4	11	.267	41	20	5	0	3	161^{1}	173	106	83	3	5	80	66	1.568	4.63	73	4.28	.282	6	.125	-23	4	-2.5

• WILLIS, Lefty Charles William Willis b: 11/4/1905, Leetown, WV d: 5/10/1962, Bethesda, MD BL/TL, 6'1", 175 lbs. Deb: 10/3/1925

YEAR TM-L	W	L	PCT	G	GS	CG	SH	SV	IP	H	R	ER	HR	HB	BB	SO	RAT	ERA	ERA+	CERA	OAV	BH	AVG	PR+	WS	TPW
1925 Phi-A	0	0	....	1	1	0	0	0	5	9	7	6	2	0	2	3	2.200	10.80	43	12.02	.409	0	.000	-3	0	-0.4
1926 Phi-A	0	0	....	13	1	0	0	1	32^{1}	31	9	5	0	1	12	13	1.330	1.39	299	3.20	.270	2	.222	10	4	1.0
1927 Phi-A	3	1	.750	15	2	1	0	0	27	32	18	17	2	0	11	7	1.593	5.67	75	4.83	.308	0	.000	-4	1	-0.4
Total 3	3	1	.750	29	4	1	0	1	64^{1}	72	34	28	4	1	25	23	1.508	3.92	110	4.57	.299	2	.111	3	5	0.2

• WILLIS, Les Lester Evans "Wimpy,Lefty" Willis b: 1/17/1908, Nacogdoches, TX d: 1/22/1982, Jasper, TX BL/TL, 5'9.5", 195 lbs. Deb: 4/28/1947

YEAR TM-L	W	L	PCT	G	GS	CG	SH	SV	IP	H	R	ER	HR	HB	BB	SO	RAT	ERA	ERA+	CERA	OAV	BH	AVG	PR+	WS	TPW
1947 Cle-A	0	2	.000	22	2	0	0	1	44	58	26	17	3	0	24	10	1.864	3.48	100	6.21	.324	1	.091	-1	1	-0.2

• WILLIS, Mike Michael Henry Willis b: 12/26/1950, Oklahoma City, OK BL/TL, 6'2", 210 lbs. Deb: 4/13/1977

YEAR TM-L	W	L	PCT	G	GS	CG	SH	SV	IP	H	R	ER	HR	HB	BB	SO	RAT	ERA	ERA+	CERA	OAV	BH	AVG	PR+	WS	TPW
1977 Tor-A	2	6	.250	43	3	0	0	5	107^{1}	105	48	47	15	0	38	59	1.332	3.94	106	4.01	.260	0	....	6	7	0.6
1978 Tor-A	3	7	.300	44	2	1	0	7	100^{2}	104	55	51	11	0	39	52	1.421	4.56	86	4.26	.271	0	....	-6	5	-0.7
1979 Tor-A	0	3	.000	17	1	0	0	0	26^{2}	35	27	25	1	1	16	8	1.913	8.44	51	6.29	.333	0	....	-12	0	-1.2
1980 Tor-A	2	1	.667	20	0	0	0	3	26^{1}	25	6	5	3	1	11	14	1.367	1.71	252	3.85	.248	0	....	7	4	0.7
1981 Tor-A	0	4	.000	20	0	0	0	0	35	43	25	23	6	1	20	16	1.800	5.91	67	6.68	.301	0	....	-7	0	-0.8
Total 5	7	21	.250	144	6	1	0	15	296	312	161	151	36	3	124	149	1.473	4.59	89	4.60	.274	0	....	-13	16	-1.4

• WILLIS, Ron Ronald Earl Willis b: 7/12/1943, Willisville, TN d: 11/21/1977, Memphis, TN BR/TR, 6'2", 195 lbs. Deb: 9/20/1966

YEAR TM-L	W	L	PCT	G	GS	CG	SH	SV	IP	H	R	ER	HR	HB	BB	SO	RAT	ERA	ERA+	CERA	OAV	BH	AVG	PR+	WS	TPW
1966 StL-N	0	0	....	4	0	0	0	1	3	1	0	0	0	0	1	2	.667	0.00	....	0.46	.100	0	....	1	1	0.1
1967* StL-N	6	5	.545	65	0	0	0	10	81	76	27	24	3	3	43	42	1.469	2.67	122	3.58	.257	3	.375	5	8	0.7
1968* StL-N	2	3	.400	48	0	0	0	4	63^{2}	50	25	24	4	1	28	39	1.225	3.39	85	2.57	.213	0	.000	-4	3	-0.6
1969 StL-N	1	2	.333	26	0	0	0	0	32^{1}	26	16	15	4	1	19	23	1.392	4.18	86	3.83	.224	1	1.000	-2	1	-0.2
Hou-N	0	0	....	3	0	0	0	0	2^{1}	3	0	0	0	0	0	2	1.286	0.00	....	2.96	.300	0	....	1	0	0.1
Yr.	1	2	.333	29	0	0	0	0	34^{2}	29	16	15	4	1	19	25	1.385	3.89	92	3.77	.230	1	1.000	-1	1	-0.1
1970 SD-N	2	2	.500	42	0	0	0	4	56	53	33	25	4	4	28	20	1.446	4.02	99	3.96	.247	0	.000	-0	3	-0.1
Total 5	11	12	.478	188	0	0	0	19	238^{1}	209	101	88	15	9	119	128	1.376	3.32	101	3.39	.237	4	.160	0	16	0.1

• WILLIS, Vic Victor Gazaway Willis b: 4/12/1876, Cecil County, MD d: 8/3/1947, Elkton, MD BR/TR, 6'2", 185 lbs. Deb: 4/20/1898 U HOF: 1995

YEAR TM-L	W	L	PCT	G	GS	CG	SH	SV	IP	H	R	ER	HR	HB	BB	SO	RAT	ERA	ERA+	CERA	OAV	BH	AVG	PR+	WS	TPW
1898 Bos-N	25	13	.658	41	38	29	1	0	311	264	143	98	5	29	148	160	1.325	2.84	130	3.17	.229	17	.145	21	25	1.5
1899 Bos-N	27	8	.771	41	38	35	**5**	2	342^{2}	277	126	95	6	30	117	120	1.150	2.50	**167**	2.54	**.222**	29	.216	50	**39**	4.3
1900 Bos-N	10	17	.370	32	29	22	2	0	236	258	157	110	11	12	106	53	1.542	4.19	98	4.47	.278	12	.136	-7	12	-1.1
1901 Bos-N	20	17	.541	38	35	33	**6**	0	305^{1}	262	111	80	6	11	78	133	1.114	2.36	**153**	2.32	.230	20	.187	38	**33**	3.7
1902 Bos-N	27	20	.574	**51**	**46**	**45**	4	**3**	**410**	372	142	100	6	14	101	**225**	1.154	2.20	128	2.52	.242	23	.153	26	29	2.2
1903 Bos-N	12	18	.400	33	32	29	2	0	278	256	121	92	3	10	88	125	1.237	2.98	107	2.96	.251	24	.188	1	19	-0.2
1904 Bos-N	18	25	.419	43	43	**39**	2	0	350	357	182	111	7	14	109	196	1.331	2.85	96	3.43	.266	27	.182	5	19	0.6
1905 Bos-N	12	29	.293	41	41	36	4	0	342	340	174	122	7	13	107	149	1.307	3.21	96	3.36	.265	20	.153	3	17	0.1
1906 Pit-N	23	13	.639	41	36	32	6	1	322	295	84	62	0	5	76	124	1.152	1.73	154	2.50	.250	20	.174	32	29	3.5
1907 Pit-N	21	11	.656	39	37	27	6	1	292^{2}	234	96	76	4	7	69	107	1.035	2.34	104	2.00	.219	14	.136	8	20	0.6
1908 Pit-N	23	11	.676	41	38	25	7	0	304^{2}	239	95	70	2	6	69	97	1.011	2.07	110	1.82	.213	17	.165	8	20	0.8
1909* Pit-N	22	11	.667	39	**35**	24	4	1	289^{2}	243	84	72	3	4	83	95	1.125	2.24	115	2.32	.231	14	.136	7	24	0.5
1910 StL-N	9	12	.429	33	23	12	1	3	212	224	113	79	6	1	61	67	1.344	3.35	89	3.52	.275	11	.167	-3	7	-0.5
Total 13	249	205	.548	513	471	388	50	11	3996	3621	1628	1167	66	156	1212	1651	1.209	2.63	116	2.80	.243	248	.166	189	293	16.1

• WILLOUGHBY, Claude Claude William "Flunky,Weeping Willie" Willoughby b: 11/14/1898, Buffalo, KS d: 8/14/1973, McPherson, KS BR/TR, 5'9.5", 165 lbs. Deb: 9/18/1925

YEAR TM-L	W	L	PCT	G	GS	CG	SH	SV	IP	H	R	ER	HR	HB	BB	SO	RAT	ERA	ERA+	CERA	OAV	BH	AVG	PR+	WS	TPW
1925 Phi-N	2	1	.667	3	3	1	0	0	23	26	7	5	0	1	11	6	1.609	1.96	244	4.50	.295	0	.000	8	3	0.6
1926 Phi-N	8	12	.400	47	19	6	0	1	168	218	125	111	7	5	71	37	**1.720**	5.95	70	5.53	.327	11	.212	-28	3	-2.8
1927 Phi-N	3	7	.300	35	6	1	1	2	97^{2}	126	83	71	7	2	53	14	1.833	6.54	63	6.08	.321	2	.077	-24	0	-2.6
1928 Phi-N	6	5	.545	35	13	5	1	1	130^{2}	180	92	77	6	3	83	26	2.013	5.30	80	6.87	.340	6	.150	-13	4	-1.3
1929 Phi-N	15	14	.517	49	35	14	1	4	243^{1}	288	156	135	15	5	108	50	1.627	4.99	104	4.94	.296	13	.143	10	15	0.5
1930 Phi-N	4	17	.190	41	24	5	1	1	153	241	147	129	17	2	68	38	2.020	7.59	72	7.90	.369	5	.104	-32	1	-3.2
1931 Pit-N	0	2	.000	9	2	1	0	0	25^{2}	32	21	18	4	0	12	4	1.714	6.31	61	6.02	.305	2	.286	-7	0	-0.7
Total 7	38	58	.396	219	102	33	4	9	841^{1}	1111	631	546	56	18	406	175	1.803	5.84	80	6.05	.326	39	.143	-87	26	-9.5

• WILLOUGHBY, Jim James Arthur Willoughby b: 1/31/1949, Salinas, CA BR/TR, 6'2", 185 lbs. Deb: 9/5/1971

YEAR TM-L	W	L	PCT	G	GS	CG	SH	SV	IP	H	R	ER	HR	HB	BB	SO	RAT	ERA	ERA+	CERA	OAV	BH	AVG	PR+	WS	TPW
1971 SF-N	0	1	.000	2	1	0	0	0	4	8	4	4	0	0	1	3	2.250	9.00	38	8.60	.400	0	.000	-2	0	-0.3
1972 SF-N	6	4	.600	11	11	7	0	0	87^{2}	72	25	23	8	2	14	40	.981	2.36	148	2.20	.222	5	.185	11	7	1.2
1973 SF-N	4	5	.444	39	12	1	1	1	123	138	74	64	21	3	37	60	1.423	4.68	81	5.11	.295	4	.143	-11	3	-1.0
1974 SF-N	1	4	.200	18	4	0	0	0	40^{2}	51	27	21	7	0	9	12	1.475	4.65	82	5.20	.304	1	.100	-4	0	-0.4
1975* Bos-A	5	2	.714	24	0	0	0	8	48^{1}	46	25	19	6	2	16	29	1.283	3.54	115	3.70	.247	0	....	3	6	0.3
1976 Bos-A	3	12	.200	54	0	0	0	10	99	94	38	31	4	8	31	37	1.263	2.82	139	3.19	.256	0	.000	13	9	1.4
1977 Bos-A	6	2	.750	31	0	0	0	2	54^{2}	54	32	30	5	2	18	33	1.317	4.94	91	3.71	.258	0	....	-2	4	-0.2
1978 Chi-A	1	6	.143	59	0	0	0	13	93^{1}	95	41	40	6	4	19	36	1.221	3.86	99	3.45	.275	0	....	0	7	0.0
Total 8	26	36	.419	238	28	8	1	34	550^{2}	558	266	232	57	21	145	250	1.277	3.79	102	3.79	.267	10	.149	9	36	1.0

• WILLS, Frank Frank Lee Wills b: 10/26/1958, New Orleans, LA BR/TR, 6'2", 202 lbs. Deb: 7/31/1983

YEAR TM-L	W	L	PCT	G	GS	CG	SH	SV	IP	H	R	ER	HR	HB	BB	SO	RAT	ERA	ERA+	CERA	OAV	BH	AVG	PR+	WS	TPW
1983 KC-A	2	1	.667	6	4	0	0	0	34^{2}	35	17	16	2	0	15	23	1.442	4.15	98	3.91	.259	0	....	-0	2	0.0
1984 KC-A	2	3	.400	10	5	0	0	0	37	39	21	21	3	0	13	21	1.405	5.11	79	4.01	.271	0	....	-5	1	-0.5
1985 Sea-A	5	11	.313	24	18	1	0	1	123	122	85	82	18	3	68	67	1.545	6.00	70	5.14	.266	0	....	-24	1	-2.4
1986 Cle-A	4	4	.500	26	0	0	0	4	40^{1}	43	23	22	6	0	16	32	1.463	4.91	84	4.46	.272	0	....	-3	3	-0.3
1987 Cle-A	0	1	.000	6	0	0	0	1	5^{1}	3	3	3	0	0	7	4	1.875	5.06	89	4.16	.176	0	....	-0	0	0.0
1988 Tor-A	0	0	....	10	0	0	0	0	20^{2}	22	12	12	2	0	6	19	1.355	5.23	75	3.78	.272	0	....	-3	0	-0.3
1989 Tor-A	3	1	.750	24	4	0	0	0	71^{1}	65	31	29	4	1	30	41	1.332	3.66	99	3.40	.242	0	....	-0	4	0.0
1990 Tor-A	6	4	.600	44	4	0	0	0	99	101	54	52	13	1	38	72	1.404	4.73	87	4.34	.266	0	....	-7	4	-0.7
1991 Tor-A	0	1	.000	4	0	0	0	0	4^{1}	8	8	8	2	1	5	2	3.000	16.62	25	17.94	.421	0	....	-6	0	-0.6
Total 9	22	26	.458	154	35	1	0	6	435^{2}	438	254	245	50	6	198	281	1.460	5.06	80	4.47	.264	0	....	-48	15	-4.8

• WILLS, Ted Theodore Carl Wills b: 2/9/1934, Fresno, CA BL/TL, 6'2", 200 lbs. Deb: 5/24/1959

YEAR TM-L	W	L	PCT	G	GS	CG	SH	SV	IP	H	R	ER	HR	HB	BB	SO	RAT	ERA	ERA+	CERA	OAV	BH	AVG	PR+	WS	TPW
1959 Bos-A	2	6	.250	9	8	2	0	0	56^{1}	68	35	33	9	1	24	24	1.633	5.27	77	5.92	.302	4	.250	-8	1	-0.7
1960 Bos-A	1	1	.500	15	0	0	0	1	30^{1}	38	26	25	4	3	16	28	1.780	7.42	55	6.81	.317	2	.250	-11	0	-1.0
1961 Bos-A	3	2	.600	17	0	0	0	0	19^{2}	24	17	13	2	0	19	11	2.186	5.95	70	7.69	.304	0	.000	-4	0	-0.4
1962 Bos-A	0	0	....	1	0	0	0	0	0	2	1	0	0	0	1	0	....	....	....	∞	1.000	0	....	0	0	0.0
Cin-N	0	2	.000	26	5	0	0	3	61	61	36	36	12	5	23	58	1.377	5.31	76	5.11	.266	5	.313	-9	2	-0.8
1965 Chi-A	2	0	1.000	15	0	0	0	1	19	17	8	6	2	1	14	12	1.632	2.84	112	5.06	.258	0	.000	1	1	0.1
Total 5	8	11	.421	83	13	2	0	5	186^{1}	210	123	113	29	10	97	133	1.648	5.46	73	5.90	.291	11	.250	-31	4	-2.8

• WILMET, Paul Paul Richard Wilmet b: 11/8/1958, Green Bay, WI BR/TR, 5'11", 170 lbs. Deb: 7/25/1989

YEAR TM-L	W	L	PCT	G	GS	CG	SH	SV	IP	H	R	ER	HR	HB	BB	SO	RAT	ERA	ERA+	CERA	OAV	BH	AVG	PR+	WS	TPW
1989 Tex-A	0	0	....	3	0	0	0	0	2^{1}	5	4	4	0	0	2	1	3.000	15.43	26	11.29	.417	0	....	-3	0	-0.3

• WILSHERE, Whitey Vernon Sprague Wilshere b: 8/3/1912, Poplar Ridge, NY d: 5/23/1985, Cooperstown, NY BL/TL, 6', 180 lbs. Deb: 6/24/1934

YEAR TM-L	W	L	PCT	G	GS	CG	SH	SV	IP	H	R	ER	HR	HB	BB	SO	RAT	ERA	ERA+	CERA	OAV	BH	AVG	PR+	WS	TPW
1934 Phi-A	0	1	.000	9	2	0	0	0	21^{2}	39	30	29	0	1	15	19	2.492	12.05	36	9.43	.394	0	.000	-19	0	-1.8
1935 Phi-A	9	9	.500	27	18	7	3	1	142^{1}	136	69	64	8	10	78	80	1.504	4.05	112	4.17	.253	4	.093	10	9	0.6
1936 Phi-A	1	2	.333	5	3	0	0	0	18^{1}	21	17	14	1	0	19	4	2.182	6.87	74	6.74	.288	0	.000	-4	0	-0.3
Total 3	10	12	.455	41	23	7	3	1	182^{1}	196	116	107	9	11	112	103	1.689	5.28	86	5.06	.276	4	.080	-12	9	-1.5

• WILSHUSEN, Terry Terry Wayne Wilshusen b: 3/22/1949, Atascadero, CA d: 12/1/2000, Lomita, CA BR/TR, 6'2", 210 lbs. Deb: 4/7/1973

YEAR TM-L	W	L	PCT	G	GS	CG	SH	SV	IP	H	R	ER	HR	HB	BB	SO	RAT	ERA	ERA+	CERA	OAV	BH	AVG	PR+	WS	TPW
1973 Cal-A	0	0	....	1	0	0	0	0	0^{1}	0	3	3	0	1	2	0	6.000	81.00	4	33.46	.000	0	....	-3	0	-0.3

• WILSON, Bill

William Harlan Wilson b: 9/21/1942, Pomeroy, OH d: 8/11/1993, Broken Arrow, OK BR/TR, 6'2", 200 lbs. Deb: 4/8/1969

YEAR	TM-L	W	L	PCT	G	GS	CG	SH	SV	IP	H	R	ER	HR	HB	BB	SO	RAT	ERA	ERA+	CERA	OAV	BH	AVG	PR+	WS	TPW
1969	Phi-N	2	5	.286	37	0	0	0	6	62^1	53	26	23	6	1	36	48	1.428	3.32	107	3.76	.231	0	.000	2	4	0.1
1970	Phi-N	1	0	1.000	37	0	0	0	0	58^1	57	35	31	5	0	33	41	1.543	4.78	83	4.52	.263	1	.250	-5	2	-0.4
1971	Phi-N	4	6	.400	38	0	0	0	7	58^2	39	20	20	4	1	22	40	1.040	3.07	115	2.01	.188	1	.100	2	7	0.1
1972	Phi-N	1	1	.500	23	0	0	0	0	30	26	13	11	1	0	11	18	1.233	3.30	109	2.63	.234	0	....	1	2	0.1
1973	Phi-N	1	3	.250	44	0	0	0	4	48^2	54	39	36	7	0	29	24	1.705	6.66	57	5.76	.293	0	.000	-16	0	-1.7
Total	**5**	**9**	**15**	**.375**	**179**	**0**	**0**	**0**	**17**	**258**	**229**	**133**	**121**	**23**	**2**	**131**	**171**	**1.395**	**4.22**	**88**	**3.78**	**.241**	**2**	**.083**	**-16**	**15**	**-1.8**

• WILSON, Don

Donald Edward Wilson b: 2/12/1945, Monroe, LA d: 1/5/1975, Houston, TX BR/TR, 6'2.5", 205 lbs. Deb: 9/29/1966

YEAR	TM-L	W	L	PCT	G	GS	CG	SH	SV	IP	H	R	ER	HR	HB	BB	SO	RAT	ERA	ERA+	CERA	OAV	BH	AVG	PR+	WS	TPW
1966	Hou-N	1	0	1.000	1	0	0	0	0	6	5	2	2	1	0	1	7	1.000	3.00	114	2.95	.238	1	.500	0	1	0.1
1967	Hou-N	10	9	.526	31	28	7	3	0	184	141	67	57	10	7	69	159	1.141	2.79	119	2.57	.209	6	.091	15	10	1.4
1968	Hou-N	13	16	.448	33	30	9	3	0	208^2	187	85	76	9	4	70	175	1.232	3.28	90	2.87	.236	15	.214	-3	11	0.1
1969	Hou-N	16	12	.571	34	34	13	1	0	225	210	119	100	16	9	97	235	1.364	4.00	89	3.68	.245	8	.099	-9	8	-1.1
1970	Hou-N	11	6	.647	29	27	3	0	0	184^1	188	92	80	15	7	66	94	1.378	3.91	99	3.95	.259	8	.116	-0	9	-0.3
1971	Hou-N★	16	10	.615	35	34	18	3	0	268	195	80	73	15	7	79	180	1.022	2.45	137	2.10	**.202**	14	.154	25	22	2.6
1972	Hou-N	15	10	.600	33	33	13	3	0	228^1	196	79	68	16	2	66	172	1.147	2.68	125	2.75	.233	8	.105	18	17	1.6
1973	Hou-N	11	16	.407	37	32	10	3	2	239^1	187	94	85	21	7	92	149	1.166	3.20	114	2.84	.213	14	.177	12	17	1.3
1974	Hou-N	11	13	.458	33	27	5	4	0	204^2	170	80	70	16	4	100	112	1.319	3.08	112	3.38	.227	13	.206	6	13	0.8
Total	**9**	**104**	**92**	**.531**	**266**	**245**	**78**	**20**	**2**	**1748^1**	**1479**	**698**	**611**	**119**	**47**	**640**	**1283**	**1.212**	**3.15**	**109**	**2.98**	**.228**	**87**	**.146**	**63**	**108**	**6.6**

• WILSON, Duane

Duane Lewis Wilson b: 6/29/1934, Wichita, KS BL/TL, 6'1", 185 lbs. Deb: 7/3/1958

YEAR	TM-L	W	L	PCT	G	GS	CG	SH	SV	IP	H	R	ER	HR	HB	BB	SO	RAT	ERA	ERA+	CERA	OAV	BH	AVG	PR+	WS	TPW
1958	Bos-A	0	0	....	2	2	0	0	0	6^1	10	5	4	0	0	7	3	2.684	5.68	71	9.76	.400	0	.000	-1	0	-0.1

• WILSON, Earl

Robert Earl Wilson b: 10/2/1934, Ponchatoula, LA BR/TR, 6'3", 216 lbs. Deb: 7/28/1959

YEAR	TM-L	W	L	PCT	G	GS	CG	SH	SV	IP	H	R	ER	HR	HB	BB	SO	RAT	ERA	ERA+	CERA	OAV	BH	AVG	PR+	WS	TPW
1959	Bos-A	1	1	.500	9	4	0	0	0	23^2	21	17	16	2	0	31	17	2.197	6.08	67	6.85	.241	4	.500	-5	1	-0.4
1960	Bos-A	3	2	.600	13	9	2	0	0	65	61	36	34	4	0	48	40	1.677	4.71	86	4.67	.247	4	.174	-3	3	-0.3
1962	Bos-A	12	8	.600	31	28	4	1	0	191^1	163	86	83	21	6	111	137	1.432	3.90	106	4.13	.231	12	.174	4	13	0.7
1963	Bos-A	11	16	.407	37	34	6	3	0	210^2	184	99	88	18	1	105	123	1.372	3.76	101	3.62	.234	15	.208	2	12	0.7
1964	Bos-A	11	12	.478	33	31	5	0	0	202^1	213	121	101	37	2	73	166	1.414	4.49	86	4.79	.269	15	.205	-10	8	-0.1
1965	Bos-A	13	14	.481	36	36	8	1	0	230^2	221	119	102	27	4	77	164	1.292	3.98	94	3.73	.250	14	.177	-3	12	0.7
1966	Bos-A	5	5	.500	15	14	5	1	0	100^2	88	45	43	14	2	36	67	1.232	3.84	99	3.55	.235	8	.250	0	7	0.4
	Det-A	13	6	.684	23	23	8	2	0	163^1	126	49	47	16	4	38	133	1.004	2.59	134	2.37	.213	15	.234	16	17	2.6
	Yr.	18	11	.621	38	37	13	3	0	264	214	94	90	30	6	74	200	1.091	3.07	118	2.82	.222	23	.240	16	24	3.0
1967	Det-A	**22**	11	.667	39	38	12	0	0	264	216	103	96	34	3	92	184	1.167	3.27	100	3.10	.224	20	.185	-3	18	0.5
1968★	Det-A	13	12	.520	34	33	10	3	0	224^1	192	77	71	20	0	65	168	1.146	2.85	106	2.81	.231	20	.227	3	17	1.5
1969	Det-A	12	10	.545	35	35	5	1	0	214^2	209	93	79	23	4	69	150	1.295	3.31	113	3.74	.256	10	.132	9	13	1.0
1970	Det-A	4	6	.400	18	16	4	1	0	96	87	53	47	15	2	32	74	1.240	4.41	85	3.72	.238	6	.194	-4	4	-0.3
	SD-N	1	6	.143	15	9	0	0	0	65	82	36	35	5	2	19	29	1.554	4.85	82	5.07	.309	1	.059	-6	1	-0.6
Total	**11**	**121**	**109**	**.526**	**338**	**310**	**69**	**13**	**0**	**2051^2**	**1863**	**934**	**842**	**236**	**30**	**796**	**1452**	**1.296**	**3.69**	**99**	**3.67**	**.242**	**144**	**.195**	**-0**	**126**	**6.5**

• WILSON, Fin

Finis Elbert Wilson b: 12/9/1889, East Fork, KY d: 3/9/1959, Coral Gables, FL BL/TL, 6'1", 194 lbs. Deb: 9/26/1914

YEAR	TM-L	W	L	PCT	G	GS	CG	SH	SV	IP	H	R	ER	HR	HB	BB	SO	RAT	ERA	ERA+	CERA	OAV	BH	AVG	PR+	WS	TPW
1914	Bro-F	0	1	.000	2	1	1	0	0	7	7	7	6	0	0	11	4	2.571	7.71	42	7.38	.269	1	.500	-3	0	-0.3
1915	Bro-F	1	8	.111	18	11	5	0	0	102^1	85	56	43	2	4	53	47	1.349	3.78	79	3.41	.249	11	.314	-10	3	-0.7
Total	**2**	**1**	**9**	**.100**	**20**	**12**	**6**	**0**	**0**	**109^1**	**92**	**63**	**49**	**2**	**4**	**64**	**51**	**1.427**	**4.03**	**74**	**3.67**	**.250**	**12**	**.324**	**-13**	**3**	**-1.0**

• WILSON, Gary

Gary Steven Wilson b: 11/21/1954, Camden, AR BR/TR, 6'2", 185 lbs. Deb: 4/13/1979

YEAR	TM-L	W	L	PCT	G	GS	CG	SH	SV	IP	H	R	ER	HR	HB	BB	SO	RAT	ERA	ERA+	CERA	OAV	BH	AVG	PR+	WS	TPW
1979	Hou-N	0	0	....	6	0	0	0	0	7^1	15	11	10	2	0	6	6	2.864	12.27	29	14.78	.441	0	....	-7	0	-0.7

• WILSON, Gary

Gary Morris Wilson b: 1/1/1970, Arcata, CA BR/TR, 6'3", 190 lbs. Deb: 4/28/1995

YEAR	TM-L	W	L	PCT	G	GS	CG	SH	SV	IP	H	R	ER	HR	HB	BB	SO	RAT	ERA	ERA+	CERA	OAV	BH	AVG	PR+	WS	TPW
1995	Pit-N	0	1	.000	10	0	0	0	0	14^1	13	8	8	2	2	5	8	1.256	5.02	86	4.24	.241	0	....	-1	0	-0.1

• WILSON, Highball

Howard Paul Wilson b: 8/9/1878, Philadelphia, PA d: 10/16/1934, Havre de Grace, MD TR, 5'9" Deb: 9/13/1899

YEAR	TM-L	W	L	PCT	G	GS	CG	SH	SV	IP	H	R	ER	HR	HB	BB	SO	RAT	ERA	ERA+	CERA	OAV	BH	AVG	PR+	WS	TPW
1899	Cle-N	0	1	.000	1	1	1	0	0	8	12	8	8	0	0	5	1	2.125	9.00	41	6.99	.346	1	.333	-4	0	-0.3
1902	Phi-A	7	4	.636	13	10	8	0	0	96^1	103	44	26	1	9	19	18	1.266	2.43	151	3.35	.274	6	.171	14	8	1.2
1903	Was-A	7	18	.280	30	28	25	1	0	242^1	269	123	89	7	10	43	56	1.287	3.31	95	3.39	.280	17	.200	-2	15	0.1
1904	Was-A	0	3	.000	3	3	3	0	0	25	33	17	13	0	2	4	11	1.480	4.68	57	4.55	.318	2	.222	-5	0	-0.5
Total	**4**	**14**	**26**	**.350**	**47**	**42**	**37**	**1**	**0**	**371^2**	**417**	**192**	**136**	**8**	**21**	**71**	**86**	**1.313**	**3.29**	**97**	**3.54**	**.283**	**26**	**.197**	**2**	**23**	**0.5**

• WILSON, Jack

John Francis "Black Jack" Wilson b: 4/12/1912, Portland, OR d: 4/19/1995, Edmonds, WA BR/TR, 5'11", 210 lbs. Deb: 9/9/1934

YEAR	TM-L	W	L	PCT	G	GS	CG	SH	SV	IP	H	R	ER	HR	HB	BB	SO	RAT	ERA	ERA+	CERA	OAV	BH	AVG	PR+	WS	TPW
1934	Phi-A	0	1	.000	2	2	1	0	0	9	15	12	12	1	0	9	2	2.667	12.00	37	11.43	.405	0	.000	-8	0	-0.8
1935	Bos-A	3	4	.429	23	6	2	0	1	64	72	35	30	0	2	36	19	1.688	4.22	112	4.66	.290	5	.313	4	5	0.5
1936	Bos-A	6	8	.429	43	9	2	0	3	136^1	152	83	67	4	1	86	74	1.746	4.42	120	4.97	.284	11	.220	13	9	1.1
1937	Bos-A	16	10	.615	51	21	14	1	7	221^1	209	111	91	13	3	119	137	1.482	3.70	128	3.88	.248	14	.165	30	20	2.5
1938	Bos-A	15	15	.500	37	27	11	3	1	194^2	200	108	93	16	2	91	96	1.495	4.30	115	4.22	.262	15	.221	12	14	1.0
1939	Bos-A	11	11	.500	36	22	6	0	2	177^1	198	109	92	10	1	75	80	1.539	4.67	101	4.35	.281	10	.159	2	11	-0.2
1940	Bos-A	12	6	.667	41	16	9	0	5	157^2	170	104	89	17	3	87	102	1.630	5.08	88	5.07	.270	18	.273	-9	9	-0.4
1941	Bos-A	4	13	.235	27	12	4	1	1	116^1	140	82	65	7	5	70	55	1.805	5.03	83	5.75	.302	7	.159	-10	2	-1.1
1942	Was-A	1	4	.200	12	6	1	0	0	42	57	34	31	2	1	23	18	1.905	6.64	55	6.24	.322	2	.118	-12	0	-1.3
	Det-A	0	0	....	9	0	0	0	0	13	20	8	7	3	0	5	7	1.923	4.85	81	8.24	.351	0	.000	-1	0	-0.1
	Yr.	1	4	.200	21	6	1	0	0	55	77	42	38	5	1	28	25	1.909	6.22	60	6.72	.329	2	.111	-13	0	-1.5
Total	**9**	**68**	**72**	**.486**	**281**	**121**	**50**	**5**	**20**	**1131^2**	**1233**	**686**	**577**	**73**	**18**	**601**	**590**	**1.621**	**4.59**	**101**	**4.74**	**.277**	**82**	**.199**	**20**	**70**	**1.3**

• WILSON, Jim

James Alger Wilson b: 2/20/1922, San Diego, CA d: 9/2/1986, Newport Beach, CA BR/TR, 6'1.5", 200 lbs. Deb: 4/18/1945

YEAR	TM-L	W	L	PCT	G	GS	CG	SH	SV	IP	H	R	ER	HR	HB	BB	SO	RAT	ERA	ERA+	CERA	OAV	BH	AVG	PR+	WS	TPW
1945	Bos-A	6	8	.429	23	21	8	2	0	144^1	121	61	53	7	1	88	50	1.448	3.30	103	3.46	.228	13	.245	0	9	0.2
1946	Bos-A	0	0	....	1	0	0	0	0	0^2	2	2	2	1	0	0	0	3.000	27.00	14	31.01	.500	0	....	-2	0	-0.2
1948	StL-A	0	0	....	4	0	0	0	0	2^2	5	4	4	0	0	5	1	3.750	13.50	34	14.36	.417	0	....	-3	0	-0.3
1949	Phi-A	0	0	....	2	0	0	0	0	5	7	8	8	2	0	5	2	2.400	14.40	29	12.47	.350	0	.000	-6	0	-0.6
1951	Bos-N	7	7	.500	20	15	5	0	1	110	131	67	66	14	4	40	33	1.555	5.40	68	5.31	.294	7	.179	-20	2	-2.0
1952	Bos-N	12	14	.462	33	33	14	0	0	234	234	114	110	19	4	90	104	1.385	4.23	85	3.90	.262	14	.163	-12	9	-1.3
1953	Mil-N	4	9	.308	20	18	5	0	0	114	107	59	55	16	3	43	71	1.316	4.34	90	3.88	.243	6	.167	-6	4	-0.6
1954	Mil-N★	8	2	.800	27	19	6	4	0	127^2	129	55	50	12	5	36	52	1.292	3.52	106	3.77	.266	7	.159	1	8	0.1
1955	Bal-A★	12	18	.400	34	31	14	4	0	235^1	200	104	90	17	4	87	96	1.220	3.44	111	2.96	.228	15	.169	13	13	1.1
1956	Bal-A	4	2	.667	7	7	1	0	0	48^1	49	27	27	5	2	16	31	1.345	5.03	78	4.09	.268	4	.267	-6	3	-0.3
	Chi-A★	9	12	.429	28	21	6	3	0	159^2	149	82	72	15	2	70	82	1.372	4.06	101	3.85	.248	19	.306	-0	9	0.4
	Yr.	13	14	.481	35	28	7	3	0	208	198	109	99	20	4	86	113	1.365	4.28	95	3.90	.253	23	.299	-6	12	0.0
1957	Chi-A	15	8	.652	30	29	12	**5**	0	201^2	189	85	78	22	3	65	100	1.260	3.48	107	3.51	.249	10	.147	2	12	0.1
1958	Chi-A	9	9	.500	28	23	4	1	1	155^2	156	75	71	21	1	63	70	1.407	4.10	89	4.38	.268	4	.078	-10	6	-1.3
Total	**12**	**86**	**89**	**.491**	**257**	**217**	**75**	**19**	**2**	**1539**	**1479**	**743**	**686**	**151**	**29**	**608**	**692**	**1.356**	**4.01**	**93**	**3.86**	**.254**	**99**	**.181**	**-48**	**75**	**-4.5**

• WILSON, John

John Nicodemus Wilson b: 6/15/1890, Boonsboro, MD d: 9/23/1954, Annapolis, MD BR/TL, 6'1", 185 lbs. Deb: 6/11/1913

YEAR	TM-L	W	L	PCT	G	GS	CG	SH	SV	IP	H	R	ER	HR	HB	BB	SO	RAT	ERA	ERA+	CERA	OAV	BH	AVG	PR+	WS	TPW
1913	Was-A	0	0	....	3	0	0	0	0	4	4	2	2	0	0	3	1	1.750	4.50	66	4.60	.267	0	....	-1	0	-0.1

• WILSON, John

John Samuel Wilson b: 4/25/1905, Coal City, AL d: 8/27/1980, Chattanooga, TN BR/TR, 6'2", 164 lbs. Deb: 5/9/1927

YEAR	TM-L	W	L	PCT	G	GS	CG	SH	SV	IP	H	R	ER	HR	HB	BB	SO	RAT	ERA	ERA+	CERA	OAV	BH	AVG	PR+	WS	TPW
1927	Bos-A	0	2	.000	5	2	2	0	0	25^1	31	19	10	1	0	13	8	1.737	3.55	119	5.42	.326	1	.111	2	1	0.1
1928	Bos-A	0	0	....	2	0	0	0	0	5	6	5	5	0	0	6	1	2.400	9.00	46	7.69	.333	0	.000	-3	0	-0.3
Total	**2**	**0**	**2**	**.000**	**7**	**2**	**2**	**0**	**0**	**30^1**	**37**	**24**	**15**	**1**	**0**	**19**	**9**	**1.846**	**4.45**	**94**	**5.80**	**.327**	**1**	**.100**	**-1**	**1**	**-0.2**

YEAR TM-L	W	L	PCT	G	GS	CG	SH	SV	IP	H	R	ER	HR	HB	BB	SO	RAT	ERA	ERA+	CERA	OAV	BH	AVG	PR+	WS	TPW
• WILSON, Kris	Kristopher Kyle Wilson b: 8/6/1976, Washington, DC BR/TR, 6'4", 225 lbs. Deb: 7/28/2000																									
2000 KC-A	0	1	.000	20	0	0	0	0	34^1	38	16	16	3	0	11	17	1.427	4.19	122	4.25	.288	0	....	3	2	0.3
2001 KC-A	6	5	.545	29	15	0	0	1	109^1	132	78	63	26	7	32	67	1.500	5.19	95	6.17	.297	1	.333	-6	4	-0.6
2002 KC-A	2	0	1.000	12	0	0	0	0	18^2	29	18	17	7	2	5	10	1.821	8.20	61	9.63	.354	0	....	-7	0	-0.6
2003 KC-A	6	3	.667	29	4	0	0	0	72^2	92	49	43	13	6	16	42	1.486	5.33	97	5.69	.305	0	....	-1	4	-0.1
Total 4	14	9	.609	90	19	0	0	1	235	291	161	139	49	15	64	136	1.511	5.32	94	6.01	.303	1	.333	-11	10	-1.1
• WILSON, Max	Max Wilson b: 6/3/1916, Haw River, NC d: 1/2/1977, Greensboro, NC BL/TL, 5'7", 160 lbs. Deb: 9/10/1940																									
1940 Phi-N	0	0	....	3	0	0	0	0	7	16	13	10	1	0	2	3	2.571	12.86	30	12.06	.444	0	.000	-7	0	-0.7
1946 Was-A	0	1	.000	9	0	0	0	0	12^2	16	12	10	1	0	9	8	1.974	7.11	47	6.60	.320	0	.000	-5	0	-0.5
Total 2	0	1	.000	12	0	0	0	0	19^2	32	25	20	2	0	11	11	2.186	9.15	39	8.54	.372	0	.000	-12	0	-1.3
• WILSON, Mutt	William Clarence "Mutt,Lank" Wilson b: 7/20/1896, Keyser, NC d: 8/31/1962, Leesburg, FL BR/TR, 6'3", 167 lbs. Deb: 9/11/1920																									
1920 Det-A	1	1	.500	3	2	1	0	0	13	12	10	5	0	0	5	4	1.308	3.46	107	2.82	.240	1	.250	1	0	0.1
• WILSON, Paul	Paul Anthony Wilson b: 3/28/1973, Orlando, FL BR/TR, 6'5", 235 lbs. Deb: 4/4/1996																									
1996 NY-N	5	12	.294	26	26	1	0	0	149	157	102	89	15	10	71	109	1.530	5.38	75	4.77	.268	4	.080	-24	1	-2.5
2000 TB-A	1	4	.200	11	7	0	0	0	51	38	20	19	1	4	16	40	1.059	3.35	147	2.17	.209	0	....	8	4	0.8
2001 TB-A	8	9	.471	37	24	0	0	0	151^1	165	94	82	21	13	52	119	1.434	4.88	92	4.94	.278	0	....	-7	6	-0.7
2002 TB-A	6	12	.333	30	30	1	0	0	193^2	219	113	104	29	13	67	111	1.477	4.83	92	5.30	.287	0	.000	-11	7	-1.1
2003 Cin-N	8	10	.444	28	28	0	0	0	166^2	190	97	86	24	7	50	93	1.440	4.64	92	4.92	.285	6	.115	-7	6	-0.8
Total 5	28	47	.373	132	115	2	0	0	711^2	769	426	380	90	47	256	472	1.440	4.81	90	4.80	.276	10	.093	-40	24	-4.3
• WILSON, Pete	Peter Alex Wilson b: 10/9/1885, Springfield, MA d: 6/5/1957, St. Petersburg, FL TL Deb: 9/15/1908																									
1908 NY-A	3	3	.500	6	6	4	1	0	39	27	16	15	0	1	33	28	1.538	3.46	71	3.12	.191	1	.071	-3	1	-0.4
1909 NY-A	6	5	.545	14	13	7	1	0	93^2	82	55	33	2	4	43	44	1.335	3.17	80	3.09	.230	4	.118	-4	2	-0.6
Total 2	9	8	.529	20	19	11	2	0	132^2	109	71	48	2	5	76	72	1.394	3.26	77	3.10	.219	5	.104	-8	3	-1.0
• WILSON, Roy	Roy Edward "Lefty" Wilson b: 9/13/1896, Foster, IA d: 12/3/1969, Clarion, IA BL/TL, 6', 175 lbs. Deb: 4/18/1928																									
1928 Chi-A	0	0	....	1	0	0	0	0	3^1	2	0	0	0	0	3	2	1.500	0.00	....	2.73	.167	0	.000	1	1	0.1
• WILSON, Steve	Stephen Douglas Wilson b: 12/13/1964, Victoria, Canada BL/TL, 6'4", 195 lbs. Deb: 9/16/1988																									
1988 Tex-A	0	0	....	3	0	0	0	0	7^2	7	5	5	1	0	4	1	1.435	5.87	69	4.41	.259	0	....	-2	0	-0.2
1989* Chi-N	6	4	.600	53	8	0	0	2	85^2	83	43	40	6	1	31	65	1.331	4.20	89	3.51	.257	1	.063	-4	5	-0.5
1990 Chi-N	4	9	.308	45	15	1	0	1	139	140	77	74	17	2	43	95	1.317	4.79	85	3.85	.259	6	.162	-7	5	-0.7
1991 Chi-N	0	0	....	8	0	0	0	0	12^1	13	7	6	1	0	5	9	1.459	4.38	89	4.20	.277	0	.000	-0	0	-0.1
LA-N	0	0	....	11	0	0	0	2	8^1	1	0	0	0	0	4	5	.600	0.00	....	0.49	.042	0	.000	3	3	0.3
Yr.	0	0	....	19	0	0	0	2	20^2	14	7	6	1	0	9	14	1.113	2.61	149	2.70	.197	0	.000	3	3	0.3
1992 LA-N	2	5	.286	60	0	0	0	0	66^2	74	37	31	6	1	29	54	1.545	4.19	82	4.58	.282	1	.333	-4	1	-0.4
1993 LA-N	1	0	1.000	25	0	0	0	1	25^2	30	13	13	2	1	14	23	1.714	4.56	84	5.30	.288	0	.000	-2	1	-0.2
Total 6	13	18	.419	205	23	1	0	6	345^1	348	182	169	33	5	130	252	1.384	4.40	87	3.96	.262	8	.133	-16	15	-1.7
• WILSON, Tex	Gomer Russell Wilson b: 7/8/1901, Trenton, TX d: 9/15/1946, Sulphur Springs, TX BR/TL, 5'10", 170 lbs. Deb: 9/2/1924																									
1924 Bro-N	0	0	....	2	0	0	0	0	3^2	7	6	6	0	0	1	1	2.182	14.73	25	7.58	.412	0	.000	-4	0	-0.5
• WILSON, Trevor	Trevor Kirk Wilson b: 6/7/1966, Torrance, CA BL/TL, 6', 195 lbs. Deb: 9/5/1988																									
1988 SF-N	0	2	.000	4	4	0	0	0	22	25	14	10	1	0	8	15	1.500	4.09	80	4.34	.298	2	.286	-2	0	-0.2
1989 SF-N	2	3	.400	14	4	0	0	0	39^1	28	20	19	2	4	24	22	1.322	4.35	78	3.42	.207	2	.250	-5	1	-0.4
1990 SF-N	8	7	.533	27	17	3	2	0	110^1	87	52	49	11	1	49	66	1.233	4.00	91	3.12	.218	4	.138	-5	5	-0.5
1991 SF-N	13	11	.542	44	29	2	1	0	202	173	87	80	13	5	77	139	1.238	3.56	100	3.07	.234	12	.235	-2	11	0.3
1992 SF-N	8	14	.364	26	26	1	1	0	154	152	82	72	18	6	64	88	1.403	4.21	78	4.35	.265	3	.077	-19	3	-2.1
1993 SF-N	7	5	.583	22	18	1	0	0	110	110	45	44	8	6	40	57	1.364	3.60	108	4.11	.275	4	.138	1	6	0.2
1995 SF-N	3	4	.429	17	17	0	0	0	82^2	82	42	36	8	4	38	38	1.452	3.92	104	4.55	.269	7	.233	1	5	0.2
1998 Ana-A	0	0	....	15	0	0	0	0	7^2	8	4	3	0	1	5	6	1.696	3.52	133	4.40	.267	0	....	1	1	0.1
Total 8	41	46	.471	169	115	7	4	0	728	665	346	313	61	27	305	431	1.332	3.87	93	3.74	.249	34	.176	-30	32	-2.4
• WILSON, Walter	Walter Wood Wilson b: 11/24/1913, Glenn, GA d: 4/17/1994, Bremen, GA BL/TR, 6'4", 190 lbs. Deb: 4/17/1945																									
1945 Det-A	1	3	.250	25	4	1	0	0	70^1	76	40	36	4	3	35	28	1.578	4.61	76	4.74	.284	1	.053	-9	1	-1.2
• WILSON, Willy	William Wilson b: 1/7/1884, Columbus, OH d: 10/28/1925, Seattle, WA BR/TR Deb: 10/3/1906																									
1906 Was-A	0	1	.000	1	1	1	0	0	7	3	2	2	0	1	2	1	.714	2.57	102	1.02	.133	0	.000	0	0	0.0
• WILSON, Zeke	Frank Ealton Wilson b: 12/24/1869, Benton, AL d: 4/26/1928, Montgomery, AL BR/TR, 5'10", 165 lbs. Deb: 4/23/1895 U																									
1895 Bos-N	2	4	.333	6	6	4	0	0	45	54	48	26	1	0	27	5	1.800	5.20	96	5.25	.293	6	.316	-1	2	0.0
Cle-N	3	1	.750	9	8	4	0	0	52^2	75	38	21	4	4	24	20	1.880	3.59	139	6.83	.330	2	.111	8	3	0.5
Yr.	5	5	.500	15	14	8	0	0	97^2	129	86	47	5	4	51	25	1.843	4.33	115	6.10	.313	8	.216	7	5	0.4
1896 Cle-N	17	9	.654	33	29	20	1	1	240	265	150	107	9	8	81	56	1.442	4.01	113	4.01	.278	27	.270	14	20	1.4
1897 Cle-N	16	11	.593	34	30	26	1	0	263^2	323	171	122	9	9	83	69	1.540	4.16	108	4.58	.299	26	.224	-5	19	-0.7
1898 Cle-N	13	18	.419	33	31	28	1	0	254^2	307	141	102	4	7	51	45	1.406	3.60	100	3.90	.296	21	.178	-2	13	-0.5
1899 StL-N	1	1	.500	5	2	2	0	0	26	30	18	13	0	2	4	3	1.308	4.50	88	3.52	.289	0	.000	-2	1	-0.3
Total 5	52	44	.542	120	106	84	3	1	882	1054	566	391	27	30	270	198	1.501	3.99	107	4.36	.294	82	.215	12	58	0.3
• WILTSE, Hal	Harold James "Whitey" Wiltse b: 8/6/1903, Clay City, IL d: 11/2/1983, Bunkie, LA BL/TL, 5'9", 168 lbs. Deb: 4/13/1926																									
1926 Bos-A	8	15	.348	37	29	9	1	0	196^1	201	112	92	6	6	99	59	1.528	4.22	96	4.06	.273	5	.085	0	10	-0.4
1927 Bos-A	10	18	.357	36	29	13	1	1	219	276	146	124	5	4	76	47	1.607	5.10	83	4.79	.321	16	.208	-19	7	-1.9
1928 Bos-A	0	2	.000	2	2	1	0	0	12	16	12	12	1	3	1	5	1.417	9.00	46	5.50	.314	0	.000	-7	0	-0.7
StL-A	2	5	.286	26	5	0	0	0	72	93	49	42	4	3	35	23	1.778	5.25	80	5.62	.316	5	.227	-8	2	-0.8
Yr.	2	7	.222	28	7	1	0	0	84	109	61	54	5	6	36	28	1.726	5.79	72	5.60	.316	5	.192	-15	2	-1.5
1931 Phi-N	0	0	....	1	0	0	0	0	1	3	1	1	0	0	0	0	3.000	9.00	47	17.53	.600	0	....	-1	0	-0.1
Total 4	20	40	.333	102	65	23	2	1	500^1	589	320	271	16	16	211	134	1.599	4.87	85	4.67	.303	26	.160	-34	19	-3.9
• WILTSE, Hooks	George Leroy Wiltse b: 9/7/1880, Hamilton, NY d: 1/21/1959, Long Beach, NY BR/TL, 6', 185 lbs. Deb: 4/21/1904 C																									
1904 NY-N	13	3	.813	24	16	14	2	3	164^2	150	66	52	8	5	61	105	1.281	2.84	96	3.18	.240	15	.224	-5	13	-0.3
1905 NY-N	15	6	.714	32	19	18	1	3	197	158	71	54	5	4	61	120	1.112	2.47	118	2.29	.219	20	.278	11	19	1.8
1906 NY-N	16	11	.593	38	26	21	4	6	249^1	227	92	63	3	3	58	125	1.143	2.27	114	2.45	.241	18	.191	8	19	1.1
1907 NY-N	13	12	.520	33	21	14	3	2	190^1	171	63	46	3	5	48	79	1.151	2.18	114	2.55	.241	9	.134	13	15	1.4
1908 NY-N	23	14	.622	44	38	30	7	2	330	266	95	82	4	9	73	118	1.027	2.24	107	2.03	.224	26	.236	10	25	1.9
1909 NY-N	20	11	.645	37	30	22	4	3	269^1	228	91	60	9	6	51	119	1.036	2.00	127	2.23	.233	19	.200	19	22	2.3
1910 NY-N	14	12	.538	36	30	18	2	2	235^1	232	96	71	4	2	52	88	1.207	2.72	109	2.86	.261	13	.176	10	15	1.0
1911* NY-N	12	9	.571	30	24	11	4	0	187^1	177	83	68	7	2	39	92	1.153	3.27	102	2.73	.251	13	.188	5	12	0.3
1912 NY-N	9	6	.600	28	17	5	0	3	134	140	63	47	7	1	28	58	1.254	3.16	107	3.26	.273	15	.326	3	11	0.6
1913* NY-N	0	0	....	17	2	0	0	3	57^2	53	24	10	1	1	8	25	1.058	1.56	200	2.15	.237	5	.208	10	5	0.9
1914 NY-N	1	1	.500	20	0	0	0	1	38	41	21	12	2	0	12	19	1.395	2.84	93	3.84	.289	2	.667	-1	2	0.1
1915 Bro-F	3	5	.375	18	3	1	0	5	59^1	49	22	15	1	2	7	17	.944	2.28	131	1.83	.226	1	.045	4	5	0.2
Total 12	139	90	.607	357	226	154	27	33	2112^1	1892	787	580	54	40	498	965	1.131	2.47	112	2.53	.241	156	.210	86	163	11.5

YEAR	TM-L	W	L	PCT	G	GS	CG	SH	SV	IP	H	R	ER	HR	HB	BB	SO	RAT	ERA	ERA+	CERA	OAV	BH	AVG	PR+	WS	TPW
• WILTSE, Snake	Lewis De Witt Wiltse b: 12/5/1871, Bouckville, NY d: 8/25/1928, Harrisburg, PA BR/TL Deb: 5/5/1901																										
1901	Pit-N	1	4	.200	7	5	3	0	0	44^{1}	57	28	21	2	5	13	10	1.579	4.26	76	5.23	.310	3	.158	-5	1	-0.6
	Phi-A	13	5	.722	19	19	18	2	0	166	185	91	66	1	7	35	40	1.325	3.58	105	3.43	.279	25	.373	3	15	1.1
1902	Phi-A	8	8	.500	19	17	13	0	1	138	182	99	79	7	5	41	28	1.616	5.15	71	5.19	.318	10	.175	-22	4	-2.2
	Bal-A	7	11	.389	19	18	18	0	0	164	215	127	93	4	8	51	37	1.622	5.10	74	4.90	.316	39	.295	-16	7	-1.1
	Yr.	15	19	.441	38	35	31	0	1	302	397	226	172	11	13	92	65	1.619	5.13	73	5.03	.317	49	.259	-38	11	-3.2
1903	NY-A	0	3	.000	4	3	2	0	1	25	35	17	15	1	1	6	6	1.640	5.40	58	5.34	.329	2	.222	-6	0	-0.6
Total	**3**	**29**	**31**	**.483**	**68**	**62**	**54**	**2**	**2**	**537^{1}**	**674**	**362**	**274**	**15**	**26**	**146**	**121**	**1.526**	**4.59**	**80**	**4.57**	**.306**	**79**	**.278**	**-46**	**27**	**-3.4**
• WINCHELL, Fred	Frederick Russell Winchell b: 1/23/1882, Arlington, MA d: 8/8/1958, Toronto, Canada TR, 5'8" Deb: 9/16/1909																										
1909	Cle-A	0	3	.000	4	3	0	0	1	14^{1}	16	11	10	0	0	2	7	1.256	6.28	41	3.24	.296	1	.200	-6	0	-0.7
• WINCHESTER, Scott	Scott Joseph Winchester b: 4/20/1973, Midland, MI BR/TR, 6'2", 210 lbs. Deb: 9/8/1997																										
1997	Cin-N	0	0	....	5	0	0	0	0	6	9	5	4	1	1	2	3	1.833	6.00	72	7.95	.360	0	....	-1	0	-0.1
1998	Cin-N	3	6	.333	16	16	1	0	0	79	101	56	51	12	4	27	40	1.620	5.81	74	6.07	.312	3	.130	-13	0	-1.4
2000	Cin-N	0	0	....	5	0	0	0	0	7^{1}	10	4	3	1	0	2	3	1.636	3.68	128	5.64	.313	0	....	1	0	0.1
2001	Cin-N	0	2	.000	12	1	0	0	0	24	29	19	12	7	3	4	9	1.375	4.50	101	6.09	.315	0	.000	1	0	0.0
Total	**4**	**3**	**8**	**.273**	**38**	**17**	**1**	**0**	**0**	**116^{1}**	**149**	**84**	**70**	**21**	**8**	**35**	**55**	**1.582**	**5.42**	**80**	**6.15**	**.315**	**3**	**.115**	**-13**	**0**	**-1.4**
• WINEAPPLE, Ed	Edward "Lefty" Wineapple b: 8/10/1905, Boston, MA d: 7/23/1996, Delray Beach, FL BL/TL, 6', 210 lbs. Deb: 9/15/1929																										
1929	Was-A	0	0	....	1	0	0	0	0	4	7	4	2	0	0	3	1	2.500	4.50	94	10.99	.467	0	.000	-0	0	0.0
• WINEGARNER, Ralph	Ralph Lee Winegarner b: 10/29/1909, Benton, KS d: 4/14/1988, Wichita, KS BR/TR, 6', 182 lbs. Deb: 9/20/1930 C ♦																										
1932	Cle-A	1	0	1.000	5	1	1	0	0	17^{1}	7	4	2	0	0	13	5	1.154	1.04	457	1.56	.123	1	.143	7	2	0.6
1934	Cle-A	5	4	.556	22	6	4	0	0	78^{1}	91	55	48	1	2	39	32	1.660	5.51	82	4.59	.289	10	.196	-8	3	-0.6
1935	Cle-A	2	2	.500	25	4	2	0	0	67^{1}	89	51	43	10	1	29	41	1.752	5.75	78	6.35	.313	26	.310	-8	4	0.0
1936	Cle-A	0	0	....	9	0	0	0	0	14^{2}	18	9	8	0	0	6	3	1.636	4.91	103	4.41	.295	2	.125	0	1	-0.1
1949	StL-A	0	0	....	9	0	0	0	0	16^{2}	24	16	14	2	0	2	8	1.560	7.56	60	5.55	.329	2	.400	-5	0	-0.3
Total	**5**	**8**	**6**	**.571**	**70**	**11**	**7**	**0**	**0**	**194^{1}**	**229**	**135**	**115**	**13**	**3**	**89**	**89**	**1.636**	**5.33**	**86**	**5.00**	**.290**	**51**	**.276**	**-14**	**10**	**-0.4**
• WINFORD, Jim	James Head "Cowboy" Winford b: 10/9/1909, Shelbyville, TN d: 12/16/1970, Miami, OK BR/TR, 6'1", 180 lbs. Deb: 9/10/1932																										
1932	StL-N	1	1	.500	4	1	0	0	0	8^{1}	9	7	6	0	0	5	4	1.680	6.48	61	4.38	.273	2	.667	-2	0	-0.1
1934	StL-N	0	2	.000	5	1	0	0	0	12^{2}	17	13	11	0	2	6	3	1.816	7.82	54	6.08	.327	0	.000	-5	0	-0.5
1935	StL-N	0	0	....	2	1	0	0	0	11^{1}	13	5	5	1	0	5	7	1.588	3.97	103	4.86	.283	0	.000	0	1	0.0
1936	StL-N	11	10	.524	39	23	10	1	3	192	203	90	81	10	5	68	72	1.411	3.80	104	3.83	.269	5	.085	3	13	-0.1
1937	StL-N	2	4	.333	16	4	0	0	0	46^{1}	56	31	30	2	0	27	17	1.791	5.83	68	5.46	.311	1	.125	-9	0	-1.0
1938	Bro-N	0	1	.000	2	1	0	0	0	5^{2}	9	10	7	1	0	4	4	2.294	11.12	35	9.03	.346	0	.000	-4	0	-0.4
Total	**6**	**14**	**18**	**.438**	**68**	**31**	**10**	**1**	**3**	**276^{1}**	**307**	**156**	**140**	**14**	**7**	**115**	**107**	**1.527**	**4.56**	**87**	**4.37**	**.281**	**8**	**.108**	**-18**	**14**	**-2.1**
• WINGARD, Ernie	Ernest James "Jim" Wingard b: 10/17/1900, Prattville, AL d: 1/17/1977, Prattville, AL BL/TL, 6'2", 176 lbs. Deb: 5/1/1924																										
1924	StL-A	13	12	.520	36	26	14	0	1	218	215	103	85	6	3	85	23	1.376	3.51	129	3.36	.262	18	.234	22	19	2.3
1925	StL-A	9	10	.474	32	18	8	0	0	145	183	111	89	10	3	77	20	1.793	5.52	85	5.96	.319	15	.288	-15	6	-1.1
1926	StL-A	5	8	.385	39	16	7	0	3	169	188	86	67	9	5	76	30	1.562	3.57	120	4.54	.290	14	.230	12	12	1.2
1927	StL-A	2	13	.133	38	17	7	0	0	156^{1}	213	132	114	7	2	79	28	**1.868**	6.56	66	6.17	.340	10	.179	-39	1	-3.6
Total	**4**	**29**	**43**	**.403**	**145**	**77**	**36**	**0**	**4**	**688^{1}**	**799**	**432**	**355**	**32**	**13**	**317**	**101**	**1.621**	**4.64**	**96**	**4.83**	**.299**	**57**	**.232**	**-20**	**38**	**-1.1**
• WINGFIELD, Ted	Frederick Davis Wingfield b: 8/7/1899, Bedford, VA d: 7/18/1975, Johnson City, TN BR/TR, 5'11", 168 lbs. Deb: 9/23/1923																										
1923	Was-A	0	0	....	1	0	0	0	0	1	0	0	0	0	0	0	1	.000	0.00	....	0.00	.000	0	....	0	0	0.0
1924	Was-A	0	0	....	4	0	0	0	0	7	9	2	2	0	0	4	2	1.857	2.57	157	5.15	.300	0	.000	1	1	0.1
	Bos-A	0	2	.000	4	3	2	0	0	25^{2}	23	12	7	0	0	8	4	1.208	2.45	178	2.46	.240	3	.333	6	2	0.6
	Yr.	0	2	.000	8	3	2	0	0	32^{2}	32	14	9	0	0	12	6	1.347	2.48	173	3.04	.254	3	.273	7	3	0.7
1925	Bos-A	12	19	.387	41	27	18	2	2	254^{1}	267	149	112	11	8	92	30	1.412	3.96	115	3.82	.278	23	.245	24	15	2.3
1926	Bos-A	11	16	.407	43	20	9	1	3	190^{2}	220	119	94	11	2	50	30	1.416	4.44	92	4.03	.298	15	.217	-4	10	-0.4
1927	Bos-A	1	7	.125	20	8	2	0	0	74^{2}	105	60	42	2	3	27	1	1.768	5.06	83	5.86	.357	4	.222	-6	1	-0.6
Total	**5**	**24**	**44**	**.353**	**113**	**58**	**31**	**3**	**5**	**553^{1}**	**624**	**342**	**257**	**24**	**13**	**181**	**68**	**1.455**	**4.18**	**103**	**4.11**	**.295**	**45**	**.234**	**20**	**29**	**2.0**
• WINHAM, Lave	Lafayette Sharkey "Lefty" Winham b: 10/23/1881, Brooklyn, NY d: 9/12/1951, Brooklyn, NY BL/TL, 5'11", 200 lbs. Deb: 4/21/1902																										
1902	Bro-N	0	0	....	1	0	0	0	0	3	4	2	0	0	0	2	1	2.000	0.00	....	6.11	.319	0	.000	1	0	0.1
1903	Pit-N	3	1	.750	5	4	3	1	0	36	33	20	9	0	0	21	22	1.500	2.25	143	3.30	.231	1	.071	2	3	0.1
Total	**2**	**3**	**1**	**.750**	**6**	**4**	**3**	**1**	**0**	**39**	**37**	**22**	**9**	**0**	**0**	**23**	**23**	**1.538**	**2.08**	**155**	**3.51**	**.238**	**1**	**.063**	**3**	**3**	**0.2**
• WINKELSAS, Joe	Joseph Winkelsas b: 9/14/1973, Buffalo, NY BR/TR, 6'3", 188 lbs. Deb: 4/10/1999																										
1999	Atl-N	0	0	....	1	0	0	0	0	0^{1}	4	2	2	0	0	1	0	15.00	54.00	8	99.97	1.000	0	....	-2	0	-0.2
• WINN, George	George Benjamin "Breezy,Lefty" Winn b: 10/26/1897, Perry, GA d: 11/1/1969, Roberta, GA BL/TL, 5'11", 170 lbs. Deb: 4/29/1919																										
1919	Bos-A	0	0	....	3	0	0	0	0	4^{2}	6	4	4	0	0	1	0	1.500	7.71	39	4.82	.353	0	.000	-2	0	-0.3
1922	Cle-A	1	2	.333	8	3	1	0	0	33^{2}	44	20	17	2	0	5	7	1.455	4.54	88	4.47	.317	3	.333	-1	2	0.0
1923	Cle-A	0	0	....	1	0	0	0	0	2	0	0	0	0	0	1	0	.500	0.00	....	0.23	.000	0	....	1	0	0.1
Total	**3**	**1**	**2**	**.333**	**12**	**3**	**1**	**0**	**0**	**40^{1}**	**50**	**24**	**21**	**2**	**0**	**7**	**7**	**1.413**	**4.69**	**80**	**4.30**	**.321**	**3**	**.300**	**-3**	**2**	**-0.2**
• WINN, Jim	James Francis Winn b: 9/23/1959, Stockton, CA BR/TR, 6'3", 210 lbs. Deb: 4/10/1983																										
1983	Pit-N	0	0	....	7	0	0	0	0	11	12	9	9	2	0	6	3	1.636	7.36	50	5.69	.267	0	....	-4	0	-0.5
1984	Pit-N	1	0	1.000	9	0	0	0	1	18^{2}	19	8	8	2	0	9	11	1.500	3.86	93	4.54	.264	0	.000	-1	1	-0.1
1985	Pit-N	3	6	.333	30	7	0	0	0	75^{2}	77	45	44	4	2	31	22	1.427	5.23	68	3.98	.266	2	.111	-13	1	-1.4
1986	Pit-N	3	5	.375	50	3	0	0	3	88	85	44	35	9	2	38	70	1.398	3.58	107	4.03	.258	1	.063	3	4	0.2
1987	Chi-A	4	6	.400	56	0	0	0	6	94	95	54	50	10	6	62	44	1.670	4.79	96	5.57	.271	0	....	-5	4	-0.5
1988	Min-A	1	0	1.000	9	0	0	0	0	21	33	15	14	4	0	10	9	2.048	6.00	68	8.60	.355	0	....	-5	0	-0.5
Total	**6**	**12**	**17**	**.414**	**161**	**10**	**0**	**0**	**10**	**308^{1}**	**321**	**175**	**160**	**31**	**10**	**156**	**159**	**1.547**	**4.67**	**85**	**4.89**	**.272**	**3**	**.086**	**-25**	**10**	**-2.6**
• WINSTON, Darrin	Darrin Alexander Winston b: 7/6/1966, Passaic, NJ BR/TL, 6', 195 lbs. Deb: 9/10/1997																										
1997	Phi-N	2	0	1.000	7	1	0	0	0	12	8	8	7	4	2	3	8	.917	5.25	81	3.52	.178	1	.500	-1	1	-0.1
1998	Phi-N	2	2	.500	27	0	0	0	1	25	31	18	17	7	2	6	11	1.480	6.12	71	6.36	.298	0	.000	-5	0	-0.5
Total	**2**	**4**	**2**	**.667**	**34**	**1**	**0**	**0**	**1**	**37**	**39**	**26**	**24**	**11**	**4**	**9**	**19**	**1.297**	**5.84**	**74**	**5.44**	**.262**	**1**	**.333**	**-6**	**1**	**-0.6**
• WINSTON, Hank	Henry Rudolph Winston b: 6/15/1904, Youngsville, NC d: 2/4/1974, Jacksonville, FL BL/TR, 6'3.5", 226 lbs. Deb: 9/30/1933																										
1933	Phi-A	0	0	....	1	0	0	0	0	6^{2}	7	5	5	0	0	6	2	1.950	6.75	64	5.29	.280	0	.000	-2	0	-0.2
1936	Bro-N	1	3	.250	14	0	0	0	0	32^{1}	40	27	22	2	1	16	8	1.732	6.12	67	5.38	.301	1	.091	-7	0	-0.7
Total	**2**	**1**	**3**	**.250**	**15**	**0**	**0**	**0**	**0**	**39**	**47**	**32**	**27**	**2**	**1**	**22**	**10**	**1.769**	**6.23**	**67**	**5.36**	**.297**	**1**	**.071**	**-8**	**0**	**-0.9**
• WINTER, George	George Lovington "Sassafrass" Winter b: 4/27/1878, New Providence, PA d: 5/26/1951, Ramsey, NJ TR, 5'8", 155 lbs. Deb: 6/15/1901 U																										
1901	Bos-A	16	12	.571	28	28	26	1	0	241	234	127	75	4	4	66	63	1.245	2.80	126	2.81	.252	19	.190	10	16	0.5
1902	Bos-A	11	9	.550	20	20	18	0	0	168^{1}	149	77	56	2	7	53	51	1.200	2.99	119	2.65	.238	10	.164	6	12	0.4
1903	Bos-A	9	8	.529	24	19	14	0	0	178^{1}	182	92	61	4	7	37	64	1.228	3.08	99	3.05	.264	7	.106	-6	9	-1.1
1904	Bos-A	8	4	.667	20	16	12	1	0	135^{2}	126	47	35	4	6	27	31	1.128	2.32	115	2.60	.247	5	.116	5	9	0.4
1905	Bos-A	16	17	.485	35	27	24	2	0	264^{1}	249	118	87	5	5	54	119	1.146	2.96	91	2.55	.251	24	.261	-7	17	-0.3
1906	Bos-A	6	18	.250	29	22	18	1	2	207^{2}	215	118	95	8	5	38	72	1.218	4.12	67	3.09	.270	17	.246	-29	5	-3.0
1907	Bos-A	12	15	.444	35	27	21	4	1	256^{2}	198	91	59	2	3	61	88	1.009	2.07	124	**1.75**	.216	21	.223	3	17	0.5

YEAR	TM-L	W	L	PCT	G	GS	CG	SH	SV	IP	H	R	ER	HR	HB	BB	SO	RAT	ERA	ERA+	CERA	OAV	BH	AVG	PR+	WS	TPW
1908	Bos-A	4	14	.222	22	17	8	0	0	147^{2}	150	71	50	3	4	34	55	1.246	3.05	81	3.21	.274	9	.184	-13	3	-1.6
	*Det-A	1	5	.167	7	6	5	0	1	56^{1}	49	19	10	0	3	7	25	.994	1.60	151	2.06	.240	2	.111	6	4	0.6
	Yr.	5	19	.208	29	23	13	0	1	204	199	90	60	3	7	41	80	1.176	2.65	92	2.89	.265	11	.164	-7	7	-1.0
Total	**8**	**83**	**102**	**.449**	**220**	**182**	**146**	**9**	**4**	**1656**	**1552**	**760**	**528**	**32**	**44**	**377**	**568**	**1.165**	**2.87**	**100**	**2.64**	**.250**	**114**	**.193**	**-25**	**92**	**-3.6**
• WINTERS, Clarence		Clarence John Winters b: 9/7/1898, Detroit, MI d: 6/29/1945, Detroit, MI TR Deb: 8/28/1924																									
1924	Bos-A	0	1	.000	4	2	0	0	0	7	22	16	16	0	0	4	3	3.714	20.57	21	17.88	.512	1	.333	-13	0	-1.2
• WINTERS, Jesse		Jesse Franklin "Buck,T-Bone" Winters b: 12/22/1893, Stephenville, TX d: 6/5/1986, Abilene, TX BR/TR, 6'1", 165 lbs. Deb: 5/3/1919																									
1919	NY-N	1	2	.333	16	2	0	0	3	28	39	18	17	1	3	13	6	1.857	5.46	51	6.51	.339	0	.000	-9	0	-1.0
1920	NY-N	0	0	....	21	0	0	0	0	46^{1}	37	19	18	1	4	28	14	1.403	3.50	86	3.49	.233	0	.000	-3	2	-0.5
1921	Phi-N	5	10	.333	18	14	10	0	0	114	142	73	46	4	4	28	22	1.491	3.63	116	4.39	.310	5	.128	10	6	0.7
1922	Phi-N	6	6	.500	34	9	4	0	2	138^{1}	176	100	82	8	4	56	29	1.677	5.33	87	5.35	.319	11	.256	-10	6	-0.9
1923	Phi-N	1	6	.143	21	6	1	0	1	78^{1}	116	76	64	7	4	39	23	1.979	7.35	62	7.33	.348	4	.160	-22	0	-2.1
Total	**5**	**13**	**24**	**.351**	**110**	**31**	**15**	**0**	**6**	**405**	**510**	**286**	**227**	**21**	**19**	**164**	**94**	**1.664**	**5.04**	**83**	**5.33**	**.315**	**20**	**.171**	**-34**	**14**	**-3.8**
• WIRTH, Alan		Alan Lee Wirth b: 12/8/1956, Mesa, AZ BR/TR, 6'4", 190 lbs. Deb: 4/9/1978																									
1978	Oak-A	5	6	.455	16	14	2	1	0	81^{1}	72	39	31	6	3	34	31	1.303	3.43	106	3.65	.252	0	....	3	5	0.3
1979	Oak-A	1	0	1.000	5	1	0	0	0	12	14	8	8	2	1	8	7	1.833	6.00	67	7.04	.298	0	....	-2	0	-0.2
1980	Oak-A	0	0	....	2	0	0	0	0	2	3	1	1	0	0	0	1	1.500	4.50	84	4.47	.333	0	....	-0	0	0.0
Total	**3**	**6**	**6**	**.500**	**23**	**15**	**2**	**1**	**0**	**95^{1}**	**89**	**48**	**40**	**8**	**4**	**42**	**39**	**1.374**	**3.78**	**98**	**4.09**	**.260**	**0**	**....**	**1**	**5**	**0.1**
• WISE, Archie		Archibald Edwin Wise b: 7/31/1912, Waxahachie, TX d: 2/2/1978, Dallas, TX BR/TR, 6', 165 lbs. Deb: 7/24/1932																									
1932	Chi-A	0	0	....	2	0	0	0	0	7^{1}	8	5	4	1	1	5	2	1.773	4.91	88	6.05	.258	0	.000	-0	0	-0.1
• WISE, Bill		William E. Wise b: 3/15/1861, Washington, DC d: 5/5/1940, Washington, DC Deb: 5/2/1882 ♦																									
1882	Bal-a	1	2	.333	3	3	3	0	0	26	30	14	8	1	....	4	9	1.308	2.77	99	....	.271	2	.100	0	1	-0.1
1884	Was-U	23	18	.561	50	41	34	4	0	364^{1}	383	219	123	5	....	60	268	1.216	3.04	99	....	.253	79	.233	9	30	1.6
1886	Was-N	0	1	.000	1	1	0	0	0	3	6	6	3	0	....	2	0	2.667	9.00	36	....	.401	0	.000	-2	0	-0.2
Total	**3**	**24**	**21**	**.533**	**54**	**45**	**37**	**4**	**0**	**393^{1}**	**419**	**239**	**134**	**6**	**....**	**66**	**277**	**1.233**	**3.07**	**97**	**....**	**.255**	**81**	**.224**	**7**	**31**	**1.3**
• WISE, Matt		Matthew John Wise b: 11/18/1975, Montclair, CA BR/TR, 6'4", 197 lbs. Deb: 8/2/2000																									
2000	Ana-A	3	3	.500	8	6	0	0	0	37^{1}	40	23	23	7	1	13	20	1.420	5.54	91	4.96	.272	0	....	-3	2	-0.3
2001	Ana-A	1	4	.200	11	9	0	0	0	49^{1}	47	27	24	11	2	18	50	1.318	4.38	104	4.65	.250	0	....	1	2	0.1
2002	Ana-A	0	0	....	7	0	0	0	0	8^{1}	7	3	3	0	1	1	6	.960	3.24	137	2.07	.233	0	....	1	1	0.1
Total	**3**	**4**	**7**	**.364**	**26**	**15**	**0**	**0**	**0**	**95**	**94**	**53**	**50**	**18**	**4**	**32**	**76**	**1.326**	**4.74**	**101**	**4.55**	**.258**	**0**	**....**	**-1**	**5**	**-0.1**
• WISE, Rick		Richard Charles Wise b: 9/13/1945, Jackson, MI BR/TR, 6'1", 195 lbs. Deb: 4/18/1964																									
1964	Phi-N	5	3	.625	25	8	0	0	0	69	78	41	31	7	3	25	39	1.493	4.04	86	4.69	.277	5	.294	-5	2	-0.3
1966	Phi-N	5	6	.455	22	13	3	0	0	99^{1}	100	50	41	5	3	24	58	1.248	3.71	97	3.24	.262	0	.000	-2	4	-0.5
1967	Phi-N	11	11	.500	36	25	6	3	0	181^{1}	177	69	66	8	4	45	111	1.224	3.28	104	3.08	.259	11	.208	3	11	0.6
1968	Phi-N	9	15	.375	30	30	7	1	0	182	210	100	92	12	6	37	97	1.357	4.55	66	4.06	.292	14	.241	-29	3	-2.6
1969	Phi-N	15	13	.536	33	31	14	4	0	220	215	100	79	17	2	61	144	1.255	3.23	110	3.35	.257	20	.270	8	15	1.6
1970	Phi-N	13	14	.481	35	34	5	1	0	220^{1}	253	115	102	15	3	65	113	1.443	4.17	96	4.26	.287	15	.200	-2	13	0.3
1971	Phi-N★	17	14	.548	38	37	17	4	0	272^{1}	261	110	87	20	4	70	155	1.215	2.88	122	3.18	.254	23	.237	16	23	2.8
1972	StL-N	16	16	.500	35	35	20	2	0	269	250	98	93	16	1	71	142	1.193	3.11	109	2.92	.251	16	.172	9	20	1.0
1973	StL-N★	16	12	.571	35	34	14	5	0	259	259	113	97	18	3	59	144	1.228	3.37	108	3.16	.257	17	.193	8	13	1.5
1974	Bos-A	3	4	.429	9	9	1	0	0	49	47	23	21	2	1	16	25	1.286	3.86	100	3.19	.251	0	....	0	3	0.0
1975*	Bos-A	19	12	.613	35	35	17	1	0	255^{1}	262	126	112	34	4	72	141	1.308	3.95	103	4.00	.263	0	....	4	17	0.4
1976	Bos-A	14	11	.560	34	34	11	4	0	224^{1}	218	100	88	18	2	48	93	1.186	3.53	111	3.12	.255	0	....	12	14	1.2
1977	Bos-A	11	5	.688	26	20	4	2	0	128^{1}	151	68	68	19	4	28	85	1.395	4.77	94	4.81	.291	0	....	-2	8	-0.2
1978	Cle-A	9	19	.321	33	31	9	1	0	211^{2}	226	116	102	22	3	59	106	1.346	4.34	86	4.04	.275	0	....	-12	6	-1.3
1979	Cle-A	15	10	.600	34	34	9	2	0	231^{2}	229	111	96	24	1	68	108	1.282	3.73	114	3.56	.256	0	....	18	17	1.8
1980	SD-N	6	8	.429	27	27	1	0	0	154^{1}	172	69	63	14	0	37	59	1.354	3.67	93	3.96	.285	8	.138	-6	6	-0.7
1981	SD-N	4	8	.333	18	18	0	0	0	98	116	44	41	10	0	19	27	1.378	3.77	87	4.25	.296	1	.040	-6	3	-0.8
1982	SD-N	0	0	....	1	0	0	0	0	2	3	2	2	0	0	0	0	1.500	9.00	38	4.47	.333	0	....	-1	0	-0.1
Total	**18**	**188**	**181**	**.509**	**506**	**455**	**138**	**30**	**0**	**3127**	**3227**	**1455**	**1281**	**261**	**44**	**804**	**1647**	**1.289**	**3.69**	**100**	**3.61**	**.267**	**130**	**.195**	**12**	**178**	**4.6**
• WISE, Roy		Roy Ogden Wise b: 11/18/1925, Springfield, IL BB/TR, 6'2", 170 lbs. Deb: 5/12/1944																									
1944	Pit-N	0	0	....	2	0	0	0	0	3	4	3	3	0	0	3	1	2.333	9.00	41	7.69	.333	0	....	-2	0	-0.2
• WISNER, Jack		John Henry Wisner b: 11/5/1899, Grand Rapids, MI d: 12/15/1981, Jackson, MI BR/TR, 6'3", 195 lbs. Deb: 9/12/1919																									
1919	Pit-N	1	0	1.000	4	1	1	0	0	18^{2}	12	3	2	0	1	7	4	1.018	0.96	313	1.68	.185	0	.000	4	2	0.4
1920	Pit-N	1	3	.250	17	2	1	0	0	44^{2}	46	19	17	1	1	10	13	1.254	3.43	94	3.11	.274	0	.000	-1	2	-0.2
1925	NY-N	0	0	....	25	0	0	0	0	40^{1}	33	19	17	4	2	14	13	1.165	3.79	106	2.99	.228	0	.000	1	3	0.0
1926	NY-N	2	2	.500	5	3	2	0	0	28	21	12	11	4	0	10	5	1.107	3.54	106	2.79	.208	2	.200	0	2	0.0
Total	**4**	**4**	**5**	**.444**	**51**	**6**	**4**	**0**	**0**	**131^{2}**	**112**	**53**	**47**	**9**	**4**	**41**	**35**	**1.162**	**3.21**	**112**	**2.80**	**.234**	**2**	**.065**	**5**	**9**	**0.2**
• WISTERT, Whitey		Francis Michael Wistert b: 2/20/1912, Chicago, IL d: 4/23/1985, Painesville, OH BR/TR, 6'4", 210 lbs. Deb: 9/11/1934																									
1934	Cin-N	0	1	.000	2	1	0	0	0	8	5	1	1	1	0	5	1	1.250	1.13	363	2.99	.185	0	.000	3	1	0.2
• WITASICK, Jay		Gerald Alphonse Witasick b: 8/28/1972, Baltimore, MD BR/TR, 6'4", 205 lbs. Deb: 7/7/1996																									
1996	Oak-A	1	1	.500	12	0	0	0	0	13	12	9	9	5	0	5	12	1.308	6.23	79	5.52	.245	0	....	-2	0	-0.2
1997	Oak-A	0	0	....	8	0	0	0	0	11	14	7	7	2	0	6	8	1.818	5.73	79	6.81	.304	0	....	-1	0	-0.1
1998	Oak-A	1	3	.250	7	3	0	0	0	27	36	24	19	9	0	15	29	1.889	6.33	72	8.53	.310	0	....	-5	0	-0.5
1999	KC-A	9	12	.429	32	28	1	1	0	158^{1}	191	108	98	23	8	83	102	1.731	5.57	90	6.45	.304	0	.000	-13	5	-1.3
2000	KC-A	3	8	.273	22	14	2	0	0	89^{1}	109	65	59	15	4	38	67	1.646	5.94	86	6.19	.301	0	.000	-10	2	-1.0
	SD-N	3	2	.600	11	11	0	0	0	60^{2}	69	42	38	9	3	35	54	1.714	5.64	77	5.94	.284	3	.136	-10	1	-1.0
2001	SD-N	5	2	.714	31	0	0	0	1	38^{2}	31	14	8	3	4	15	53	1.190	1.86	215	3.05	.218	0	.000	10	4	0.9
	*NY-A	3	0	1.000	32	0	0	0	0	40^{1}	47	27	21	5	2	18	53	1.612	4.69	96	5.43	.283	0	....	-0	2	0.0
2002*	SF-N	1	0	1.000	44	0	0	0	0	68^{1}	58	19	18	3	4	21	54	1.156	2.37	163	2.78	.234	0	.000	11	6	1.0
2003	SD-N	3	7	.300	46	0	0	0	2	45^{2}	42	24	23	6	1	25	42	1.467	4.53	87	4.34	.244	0	....	-3	2	-0.3
Total	**8**	**29**	**35**	**.453**	**245**	**56**	**3**	**1**	**3**	**552^{1}**	**609**	**339**	**300**	**80**	**26**	**261**	**474**	**1.575**	**4.89**	**95**	**5.50**	**.280**	**3**	**.081**	**-24**	**22**	**-2.3**
• WITHEM, Shannon		Shannon Bolt Withem b: 9/21/1972, Ann Arbor, MI BR/TR, 6'3" Deb: 9/18/1998																									
1998	Tor-A	0	0	....	1	0	0	0	0	3	3	1	1	0	0	2	2	1.667	3.00	156	4.23	.250	0	....	1	0	0.1
• WITHEROW, Charles		Charles Lafayette Witherow b: 4/1852, Washington, DC d: 7/3/1948, Washington, DC Deb: 7/1/1875																									
1875	Was-n	0	1	.000	1	1	0	0	0	1	4	5	2	0	....	0	0	4.000	18.00	15	....	.554	0	.000	-2	....	-0.2
• WITHERUP, Roy		Foster Leroy Witherup b: 7/26/1886, North Washington, PA d: 12/23/1941, New Bethlehem, PA BR/TR, 6', 185 lbs. Deb: 5/14/1906																									
1906	Bos-N	0	3	.000	8	3	3	0	0	46	59	37	32	2	1	19	14	1.696	6.26	43	5.55	.322	2	.133	-18	0	-2.1
1908	Was-A	2	4	.333	6	6	4	0	0	48^{1}	51	21	16	0	1	8	31	1.221	2.98	77	2.83	.264	3	.167	-4	1	-0.5
1909	Was-A	1	5	.167	12	8	5	0	0	68	79	41	32	1	0	20	26	1.456	4.24	57	4.16	.306	1	.053	-13	0	-1.7
Total	**3**	**3**	**12**	**.200**	**26**	**17**	**12**	**0**	**0**	**162^{1}**	**189**	**99**	**80**	**3**	**2**	**47**	**71**	**1.454**	**4.44**	**56**	**4.16**	**.298**	**6**	**.115**	**-35**	**1**	**-4.2**
• WITT, Bobby		Robert Andrew Witt b: 5/11/1964, Arlington, VA BR/TR, 6'2", 205 lbs. Deb: 4/10/1986																									
1986	Tex-A	11	9	.550	31	31	0	0	0	157^{2}	130	104	96	18	3	143	174	1.732	5.48	78	5.18	.223	0	....	-20	3	-2.0
1987	Tex-A	8	10	.444	26	25	1	0	0	143	114	82	78	10	3	140	160	1.776	4.91	91	5.00	.219	0	.000	-5	6	-0.5
1988	Tex-A	8	10	.444	22	22	13	2	0	174^{1}	134	83	76	13	1	101	148	1.348	3.92	104	3.37	.216	0	....	2	10	0.2
1989	Tex-A	12	13	.480	31	31	5	1	0	194^{1}	182	123	111	14	2	114	166	**1.523**	5.14	77	4.22	.248	0	....	-24	5	-2.5

YEAR	TM-L	W	L	PCT	G	GS	CG	SH	SV	IP	H	R	ER	HR	HB	BB	SO	RAT	ERA	ERA+	CERA	OAV	BH	AVG	PR+	WS	TPW
1990	Tex-A	17	10	.630	33	32	7	1	0	222	197	98	83	12	4	110	221	1.383	3.36	116	3.56	.238	0	....	13	17	1.3
1991	Tex-A	3	7	.300	17	16	1	1	0	88^{2}	84	66	60	4	1	74	82	1.782	6.09	66	5.11	.254	0	....	-19	0	-1.9
1992	Tex-A	9	13	.409	25	25	0	0	0	161^{1}	152	87	80	14	2	95	100	1.531	4.46	85	4.50	.254	0	....	-9	6	-0.9
	* Oak-A	1	1	.500	6	6	0	0	0	31^{2}	31	12	12	2	0	19	25	1.579	3.41	110	4.47	.265	0	....	1	2	0.1
	Yr.	10	14	.417	31	31	0	0	0	193	183	99	92	16	2	114	125	**1.539**	4.29	88	4.49	.256	0	....	-8	8	-0.8
1993	Oak-A	14	13	.519	35	33	5	1	0	220	226	112	103	16	3	91	131	1.441	4.21	97	4.14	.269	0	....	-2	11	-0.2
1994	Oak-A	8	10	.444	24	24	5	3	0	135^{2}	151	88	76	22	5	70	111	1.629	5.04	88	5.80	.283	0	....	-11	4	-1.0
1995	Fla-N	2	7	.222	19	19	1	0	0	110^{2}	104	52	48	8	2	47	95	1.364	3.90	108	3.73	.251	2	.063	4	5	0.2
	Tex-A	3	4	.429	10	10	1	0	0	61^{1}	81	35	31	4	1	21	46	1.663	4.55	106	5.57	.324	0	....	2	4	0.2
1996*	Tex-A	16	12	.571	33	32	2	0	0	199^{2}	235	129	120	28	2	96	157	1.658	5.41	97	5.82	.295	0	....	-4	10	-0.4
1997	Tex-A	12	12	.500	34	32	3	0	0	209	245	118	112	33	2	74	121	1.526	4.82	99	5.38	.294	2	.333	2	11	0.4
1998	Tex-A	5	4	.556	14	13	0	0	0	69^{1}	95	62	59	14	0	33	30	1.846	7.66	63	7.43	.328	0	.000	-21	0	-2.0
	StL-N	2	5	.286	17	5	0	0	0	47^{1}	55	32	26	7	2	20	28	1.585	4.94	85	5.53	.289	2	.200	-4	1	-0.3
1999	TB-A	7	15	.318	32	32	3	2	0	180^{1}	213	130	117	23	3	96	123	**1.713**	5.84	85	6.11	.304	0	.000	-17	5	-1.6
2000	Cle-A	0	1	.000	7	2	0	0	0	15^{1}	28	13	13	4	0	6	6	2.217	7.63	65	10.80	.394	0	....	-4	0	-0.4
2001*	Ari-N	4	1	.800	14	7	0	0	0	43^{1}	36	23	23	6	3	25	31	1.408	4.78	96	4.26	.222	3	.250	-2	2	-0.1
Total	**16**	**142**	**157**	**.475**	**430**	**397**	**47**	**11**	**0**	**2465**	**2493**	**1449**	**1324**	**252**	**39**	**1375**	**1955**	**1.569**	**4.83**	**90**	**4.87**	**.265**	**9**	**.141**	**-119**	**102**	**-11.5**

• WITT, George

George Adrian "Red" Witt b: 11/9/1933, Long Beach, CA BR/TR, 6'3", 200 lbs. Deb: 9/21/1957

YEAR	TM-L	W	L	PCT	G	GS	CG	SH	SV	IP	H	R	ER	HR	HB	BB	SO	RAT	ERA	ERA+	CERA	OAV	BH	AVG	PR+	WS	TPW
1957	Pit-N	0	1	.000	1	1	0	0	0	1^{1}	4	6	6	1	0	5	1	6.750	40.50	9	44.82	.500	0	....	-5	0	-0.6
1958	Pit-N	9	2	.818	18	15	5	3	0	106	78	22	19	2	2	59	81	1.292	1.61	240	2.76	.209	6	.154	24	13	2.3
1959	Pit-N	0	7	.000	15	11	0	0	0	50^{2}	58	43	39	7	1	32	30	1.776	6.93	56	6.30	.293	0	.000	-18	0	-1.9
1960*	Pit-N	1	2	.333	10	6	0	0	0	30	33	18	14	3	0	12	15	1.500	4.20	89	4.81	.300	0	.000	-2	1	-0.3
1961	Pit-N	0	1	.000	9	1	0	0	0	15^{2}	17	12	11	5	0	5	9	1.404	6.32	63	5.85	.274	1	.500	-4	0	-0.3
1962	LA-A	1	1	.500	5	2	0	0	0	10	15	12	9	4	0	5	10	2.000	8.10	48	10.21	.349	1	.333	-5	0	-0.4
	Hou-N	0	2	.000	8	2	0	0	0	15^{1}	20	14	12	2	1	9	10	1.891	7.04	53	7.36	.339	1	.250	-5	0	-0.5
Total	**6**	**11**	**16**	**.407**	**66**	**38**	**5**	**3**	**0**	**229**	**225**	**127**	**110**	**24**	**4**	**127**	**156**	**1.537**	**4.32**	**89**	**4.90**	**.263**	**9**	**.130**	**-15**	**14**	**-1.7**

• WITT, Mike

Michael Atwater Witt b: 7/20/1960, Fullerton, CA BR/TR, 6'7", 192 lbs. Deb: 4/11/1981

YEAR	TM-L	W	L	PCT	G	GS	CG	SH	SV	IP	H	R	ER	HR	HB	BB	SO	RAT	ERA	ERA+	CERA	OAV	BH	AVG	PR+	WS	TPW
1981	Cal-A	8	9	.471	22	21	7	1	0	129	123	60	47	9	11	47	75	1.318	3.28	111	3.75	.251	0	....	5	6	0.5
1982*	Cal-A	8	6	.571	33	26	5	1	0	179^{2}	177	77	70	8	7	47	85	1.247	3.51	116	3.25	.260	0	....	8	12	0.8
1983	Cal-A	7	14	.333	43	19	2	0	5	154	173	90	84	14	6	75	77	1.610	4.91	82	5.28	.293	0	....	-15	5	-1.5
1984	Cal-A	15	11	.577	34	34	9	2	0	246^{2}	227	103	95	17	5	84	196	1.261	3.47	114	3.27	.244	0	....	13	17	1.3
1985	Cal-A	15	9	.625	35	35	6	1	0	250	228	115	99	22	4	98	180	1.304	3.56	115	3.54	.243	0	....	7	16	0.7
1986*	Cal-A★	18	10	.643	34	34	14	3	0	269	218	95	85	22	3	73	208	1.082	2.84	145	2.55	.221	0	....	32	23	3.2
1987	Cal-A★	16	14	.533	36	36	10	0	0	247	252	128	110	34	4	84	192	1.360	4.01	107	4.23	.261	0	....	7	14	0.7
1988	Cal-A	13	16	.448	34	34	12	2	0	249^{2}	263	130	115	14	5	87	133	1.402	4.15	93	3.89	.272	0	....	-7	11	-0.7
1989	Cal-A	9	15	.375	33	33	5	0	0	220	252	119	111	26	2	48	123	1.364	4.54	84	4.35	.292	0	....	-21	6	-2.2
1990	Cal-A	0	3	.000	10	0	0	0	1	20^{1}	19	9	4	1	1	13	14	1.574	1.77	215	4.26	.250	0	....	5	2	0.5
	NY-A	5	6	.455	16	16	2	1	0	96^{2}	87	53	48	8	4	34	60	1.252	4.47	89	3.36	.240	0	....	-5	4	-0.5
	Yr.	5	9	.357	26	16	2	1	1	117	106	62	52	9	5	47	74	1.308	4.00	99	3.52	.241	0	....	-1	6	-0.1
1991	NY-A	0	1	.000	2	2	0	0	0	5^{1}	8	7	6	1	0	1	0	1.688	10.13	41	6.41	.320	0	....	-4	0	-0.4
1993	NY-A	3	2	.600	9	9	0	0	0	41	39	26	24	7	3	22	30	1.488	5.27	79	5.17	.248	0	....	-5	1	-0.5
Total	**12**	**117**	**116**	**.502**	**341**	**299**	**72**	**11**	**6**	**2108^{1}**	**2066**	**1012**	**898**	**183**	**55**	**713**	**1373**	**1.318**	**3.83**	**104**	**3.74**	**.257**	**0**	**....**	**19**	**117**	**1.8**

• WITTIG, Johnnie

John Carl "Hans" Wittig b: 6/16/1914, Baltimore, MD d: 2/24/1999, Nassawadox, VA BR/TR, 6', 180 lbs. Deb: 8/4/1938

YEAR	TM-L	W	L	PCT	G	GS	CG	SH	SV	IP	H	R	ER	HR	HB	BB	SO	RAT	ERA	ERA+	CERA	OAV	BH	AVG	PR+	WS	TPW
1938	NY-N	2	3	.400	13	6	2	0	0	39^{1}	41	22	21	4	0	26	14	1.703	4.81	78	5.13	.263	0	.000	-5	1	-0.6
1939	NY-N	0	2	.000	5	2	1	0	0	16^{2}	18	15	14	0	1	14	4	1.920	7.56	52	5.36	.281	0	.000	-7	0	-0.7
1941	NY-N	3	5	.375	25	9	0	0	0	85^{1}	111	57	53	5	1	45	47	1.828	5.59	66	5.98	.319	5	.200	-18	1	-1.9
1943	NY-N	5	15	.250	40	22	4	1	4	164	172	85	77	14	0	76	56	1.512	4.23	81	4.44	.273	5	.098	-12	5	-1.7
1949	Bos-A	0	0	....	1	0	0	0	0	2	2	2	2	0	0	2	0	2.000	9.00	48	5.81	.286	0	....	-1	0	-0.1
Total	**5**	**10**	**25**	**.286**	**84**	**39**	**7**	**1**	**4**	**307^{1}**	**344**	**181**	**167**	**23**	**2**	**163**	**121**	**1.650**	**4.89**	**74**	**5.02**	**.286**	**10**	**.110**	**-43**	**7**	**-5.0**

• WOHLERS, Mark

Mark Edward Wohlers b: 1/23/1970, Holyoke, MA BR/TR, 6'4", 207 lbs. Deb: 8/17/1991

YEAR	TM-L	W	L	PCT	G	GS	CG	SH	SV	IP	H	R	ER	HR	HB	BB	SO	RAT	ERA	ERA+	CERA	OAV	BH	AVG	PR+	WS	TPW
1991*	Atl-N	3	1	.750	17	0	0	0	2	19^{2}	17	7	7	1	2	13	13	1.525	3.20	121	4.07	.239	0	.000	2	2	0.1
1992*	Atl-N	1	2	.333	32	0	0	0	4	35^{1}	28	11	10	0	1	14	17	1.189	2.55	144	2.37	.235	0	.000	4	4	0.4
1993*	Atl-N	6	2	.750	46	0	0	0	0	48	37	25	24	2	1	22	45	1.229	4.50	89	2.69	.218	0	....	-3	4	-0.3
1994	Atl-N	7	2	.778	51	0	0	0	1	51	51	35	26	1	0	33	58	1.647	4.59	93	4.02	.264	1	1.000	-1	3	-0.1
1995*	Atl-N	7	3	.700	65	0	0	0	25	64^{2}	51	16	15	2	1	24	90	1.160	2.09	204	2.36	.211	0	.000	16	16	1.6
1996*	Atl-N★	2	4	.333	77	0	0	0	39	77^{1}	71	30	26	8	2	21	100	1.190	3.03	146	3.17	.240	0	.000	13	14	1.2
1997*	Atl-N	5	7	.417	71	0	0	0	33	69^{1}	57	29	27	4	0	38	92	1.370	3.50	120	3.33	.224	0	.000	5	11	0.5
1998	Atl-N	0	1	.000	27	0	0	0	8	20^{1}	18	23	23	2	1	33	22	2.508	10.18	41	8.41	.231	0	....	-14	0	-1.4
1999	Atl-N	0	0	....	2	0	0	0	0	0^{2}	1	2	2	0	0	6	0	10.50	27.00	17	41.75	.333	0	....	-2	0	-0.2
2000	Cin-N	1	2	.333	20	0	0	0	0	28	19	14	14	3	0	17	20	1.286	4.50	104	3.14	.192	0	....	0	2	0.0
2001	Cin-N	3	1	.750	30	0	0	0	0	32	36	20	14	5	1	7	21	1.344	3.94	116	4.41	.286	0	....	3	2	0.3
	* NY-A	1	0	1.000	31	0	0	0	0	35^{2}	33	20	18	3	1	18	33	1.430	4.54	99	3.96	.241	0	....	1	2	0.0
2002	Cle-A	3	4	.429	64	0	0	0	7	71^{1}	71	41	38	6	3	26	46	1.360	4.79	92	3.94	.261	0	....	-2	5	-0.2
Total	**12**	**39**	**29**	**.574**	**533**	**0**	**0**	**0**	**119**	**553^{1}**	**490**	**273**	**244**	**37**	**13**	**272**	**557**	**1.377**	**3.97**	**108**	**3.57**	**.238**	**1**	**.083**	**21**	**65**	**2.1**

• WOJCIECHOWSKI, Steve

Steven Joseph Wojciechowski b: 7/29/1970, Blue Island, IL BL/TL, 6'2", 185 lbs. Deb: 7/18/1995

YEAR	TM-L	W	L	PCT	G	GS	CG	SH	SV	IP	H	R	ER	HR	HB	BB	SO	RAT	ERA	ERA+	CERA	OAV	BH	AVG	PR+	WS	TPW
1995	Oak-A	2	3	.400	14	7	0	0	0	48^{2}	51	28	28	7	1	28	13	1.623	5.18	86	5.50	.273	0	....	-4	2	-0.4
1996	Oak-A	5	5	.500	16	15	0	0	0	79^{2}	97	57	50	10	2	28	30	1.569	5.65	87	5.47	.300	0	....	-8	3	-0.7
1997	Oak-A	0	2	.000	2	2	0	0	0	10^{1}	17	9	9	2	0	1	5	1.742	7.84	57	7.77	.386	0	....	-4	0	-0.3
Total	**3**	**7**	**10**	**.412**	**32**	**24**	**0**	**0**	**0**	**138^{2}**	**165**	**94**	**87**	**19**	**3**	**57**	**48**	**1.601**	**5.65**	**83**	**5.65**	**.298**	**0**	**....**	**-15**	**5**	**-1.4**

• WOJEY, Pete

Peter Paul Wojey b: 12/1/1919, Stowe, PA d: 4/23/1991, Mobile, AL BR/TR, 5'11", 185 lbs. Deb: 7/2/1954

YEAR	TM-L	W	L	PCT	G	GS	CG	SH	SV	IP	H	R	ER	HR	HB	BB	SO	RAT	ERA	ERA+	CERA	OAV	BH	AVG	PR+	WS	TPW
1954	Bro-N	1	1	.500	14	1	0	0	1	27^{2}	24	13	10	3	2	14	21	1.373	3.25	126	4.00	.242	0	.000	3	2	0.2
1956	Det-A	0	0	....	2	0	0	0	0	4	2	1	1	0	0	1	1	.750	2.25	183	1.01	.167	0	....	1	0	0.1
1957	Det-A	0	0	....	2	0	0	0	0	1^{1}	1	0	0	0	0	0	0	.750	0.00	....	0.94	.200	0	....	1	0	0.1
Total	**3**	**1**	**1**	**.500**	**18**	**1**	**0**	**0**	**1**	**33**	**27**	**14**	**11**	**3**	**2**	**15**	**22**	**1.273**	**3.00**	**136**	**3.52**	**.233**	**0**	**.000**	**4**	**2**	**0.4**

• WOJNA, Ed

Edward David Wojna b: 8/20/1960, Bridgeport, CT BR/TR, 6'1", 185 lbs. Deb: 6/16/1985

YEAR	TM-L	W	L	PCT	G	GS	CG	SH	SV	IP	H	R	ER	HR	HB	BB	SO	RAT	ERA	ERA+	CERA	OAV	BH	AVG	PR+	WS	TPW
1985	SD-N	2	4	.333	15	7	0	0	0	42	53	35	27	6	3	19	18	1.714	5.79	61	6.43	.312	2	.167	-11	0	-1.2
1986	SD-N	2	2	.500	7	7	1	0	0	39	42	19	14	2	1	16	19	1.487	3.23	113	4.05	.268	2	.143	2	2	0.2
1987	SD-N	0	3	.000	5	3	0	0	0	18^{1}	25	12	12	2	1	6	13	1.691	5.89	67	6.31	.333	0	.000	-4	0	-0.5
1989	Cle-A	0	1	.000	9	3	0	0	0	33	31	17	15	0	0	14	10	1.364	4.09	97	3.14	.254	0	....	-0	1	0.0
Total	**4**	**4**	**10**	**.286**	**36**	**20**	**1**	**0**	**0**	**132^{1}**	**151**	**83**	**68**	**10**	**5**	**55**	**60**	**1.557**	**4.62**	**80**	**4.89**	**.288**	**4**	**.129**	**-14**	**3**	**-1.5**

• WOLCOTT, Bob

Robert William Wolcott b: 9/8/1973, Huntington Beach, CA BR/TR, 6', 190 lbs. Deb: 8/18/1995

YEAR	TM-L	W	L	PCT	G	GS	CG	SH	SV	IP	H	R	ER	HR	HB	BB	SO	RAT	ERA	ERA+	CERA	OAV	BH	AVG	PR+	WS	TPW
1995*	Sea-A	3	2	.600	7	6	0	0	0	36^{2}	43	18	18	6	2	14	19	1.555	4.42	107	5.77	.297	0	....	2	2	0.2
1996	Sea-A	7	10	.412	30	28	1	0	0	149^{1}	179	101	95	26	7	54	78	1.560	5.73	87	5.79	.297	0	....	-13	5	-1.2
1997	Sea-A	5	6	.455	19	18	0	0	0	100	129	71	67	22	5	29	58	1.580	6.03	75	6.46	.314	0	.000	-16	2	-1.5
1998	Ari-N	1	3	.250	6	6	0	0	0	33	32	27	26	7	0	13	21	1.364	7.09	59	4.62	.252	2	.222	-11	0	-1.0
1999	Bos-A	0	0	....	4	0	0	0	0	6^{2}	8	6	6	1	1	3	2	1.650	8.10	61	7.05	.333	0	....	-2	0	-0.2
Total	**5**	**16**	**21**	**.432**	**66**	**58**	**1**	**0**	**0**	**325^{2}**	**391**	**223**	**212**	**62**	**15**	**113**	**178**	**1.548**	**5.86**	**80**	**5.90**	**.298**	**2**	**.200**	**-40**	**9**	**-3.8**

YEAR	TM-L	W	L	PCT	G	GS	CG	SH	SV	IP	H	R	ER	HR	HB	BB	SO	RAT	ERA	ERA+	CERA	OAV	BH	AVG	PR+	WS	TPW
• WOLF, Ernie					Ernest Adolph Wolf b: 2/2/1889, Newark, NJ d: 5/23/1964, Atlantic Highlands, NJ BR/TR, 5'11", 174 lbs. Deb: 9/10/1912																						
1912	Cle-A	0	0	....	1	0	0	0	0	5^{2}	8	6	4	0	0	4	1	2.118	6.35	54	7.09	.348	0	.000	-2	0	-0.2
• WOLF, Lefty					Walter Francis Wolf b: 6/10/1900, Hartford, CT d: 9/25/1971, New Orleans, LA BR/TL, 5'10", 163 lbs. Deb: 7/4/1921																						
1921	Phi-A	0	0	....	8	0	0	0	0	15	15	15	12	0	2	16	11	2.067	7.20	62	6.12	.273	1	.250	-4	0	-0.4
• WOLF, Randy					Randall Christopher Wolf b: 8/22/1976, Canoga Park, CA BL/TL, 6', 194 lbs. Deb: 6/11/1999																						
1999	Phi-N	6	9	.400	22	21	0	0	0	121^{2}	126	78	75	20	5	67	116	1.586	5.55	85	5.54	.266	7	.233	-13	4	-1.1
2000	Phi-N	11	9	.550	32	32	1	0	0	206^{1}	210	107	100	25	8	83	160	1.420	4.36	107	4.54	.269	11	.193	6	13	0.7
2001	Phi-N	10	11	.476	28	25	4	2	0	163	150	74	67	15	10	51	152	1.233	3.70	115	3.46	.248	8	.178	8	11	0.9
2002	Phi-N	11	9	.550	31	31	3	2	0	210^{2}	172	77	75	23	7	63	172	1.116	3.20	122	2.88	.223	8	.136	15	15	1.7
2003	Phi-N★	16	10	.615	33	33	2	2	0	200	176	101	94	27	6	78	177	1.270	4.23	94	3.67	.233	14	.200	-5	12	-0.1
Total	5	54	48	.529	146	142	10	6	0	901^{2}	834	437	411	110	36	342	777	1.304	4.10	104	3.90	.246	48	.184	12	55	2.1
• WOLF, Wally					Walter Beck Wolf b: 1/5/1942, South Gate, CA BR/TR, 6'.5", 191 lbs. Deb: 9/27/1969																						
1969	Cal-A	0	0	....	2	0	0	0	0	2^{1}	3	3	3	1	0	3	2	2.571	11.57	30	13.85	.333	0	....	-2	0	-0.2
1970	Cal-A	0	0	....	4	0	0	0	0	5^{1}	3	3	3	1	0	4	5	1.313	5.06	71	3.96	.176	0	....	-1	0	-0.1
Total	2	0	0	....	6	0	0	0	0	7^{2}	6	6	6	2	0	7	7	1.696	7.04	50	6.97	.231	0	....	-3	0	-0.3
• WOLFE, Barney					Wilbert Otto Wolfe b: 6/7/1876, Independence, PA d: 2/27/1953, Gibsontown, PA BR/TR, 6'1" Deb: 4/24/1903																						
1903	NY-A	6	9	.400	20	16	12	1	0	148^{1}	143	66	49	1	6	26	48	1.139	2.97	105	2.51	.253	4	.075	3	8	-0.1
1904	NY-A	0	3	.000	7	3	2	0	0	33^{2}	31	18	12	1	2	4	8	1.040	3.21	84	2.36	.246	0	.000	-3	1	-0.4
	Was-A	6	10	.375	17	16	13	2	0	126^{2}	131	64	46	0	11	22	44	1.208	3.27	81	2.96	.268	5	.119	-5	3	-0.7
	Yr.	6	13	.316	24	19	15	2	0	160^{1}	162	82	58	1	13	26	52	1.173	3.26	82	2.83	.263	5	.096	-8	4	-1.1
1905	Was-A	9	14	.391	28	23	17	1	1	182	162	76	52	1	8	37	52	1.093	2.57	103	2.29	.241	8	.127	-4	11	-0.5
1906	Was-A	0	3	.000	4	3	2	0	0	20	17	11	9	0	2	10	8	1.350	4.05	65	3.15	.233	2	.286	-3	0	-0.3
Total	4	21	39	.350	76	61	46	4	1	510^{2}	484	235	168	3	29	99	160	1.142	2.96	94	2.56	.251	19	.109	-11	23	-2.1
• WOLFE, Bill					William F. Wolfe b: Jersey City, NJ Deb: 9/10/1902																						
1902	Phi-N	0	1	.000	1	1	1	0	0	9	11	5	4	0	1	4	3	1.667	4.00	70	6.14	.301	1	.333	-1	0	-0.1
• WOLFE, Chuck					Charles Hunt Wolfe b: 2/15/1897, Wolfsburg, PA d: 11/27/1957, Schellsburg, PA BL/TR, 5'7", 175 lbs. Deb: 8/2/1923																						
1923	Phi-A	0	0	....	3	0	0	0	0	9^{2}	6	4	4	1	0	8	1	1.448	3.72	110	3.66	.194	1	.333	1	1	0.1
• WOLFE, Ed					Edward Anthony Wolfe b: 1/2/1928, Los Angeles, CA BR/TR, 6'3", 185 lbs. Deb: 4/19/1952																						
1952	Pit-N	0	0	....	3	0	0	0	0	3^{2}	7	3	3	1	1	5	1	3.273	7.36	54	19.36	.467	0	....	-1	0	-0.1
• WOLFF, Roger					Roger Francis Wolff b: 4/10/1911, Evansville, IL d: 3/23/1994, Chester, IL BR/TR, 6'.5", 208 lbs. Deb: 9/20/1941																						
1941	Phi-A	0	2	.000	2	2	2	0	0	17	15	6	6	0	0	4	2	1.118	3.18	132	2.16	.231	1	.200	2	1	0.2
1942	Phi-A	12	15	.444	32	25	15	2	3	214^{1}	206	99	79	16	3	69	94	1.283	3.32	114	3.32	.249	6	.088	16	14	1.3
1943	Phi-A	10	15	.400	41	26	13	2	6	221	232	97	87	11	4	72	91	1.376	3.54	96	3.75	.274	9	.122	2	12	-0.1
1944	Was-A	4	15	.211	33	21	5	0	2	155	186	107	86	9	6	60	73	**1.587**	4.99	65	4.78	.295	12	.218	-28	0	-2.9
1945	Was-A	20	10	.667	33	29	21	4	2	250	200	68	59	7	1	53	108	1.012	2.12	146	**1.87**	.215	9	.107	29	24	2.5
1946	Was-A	5	8	.385	21	17	6	0	0	122	115	51	35	8	5	30	50	1.189	2.58	130	3.04	.249	4	.103	13	7	1.2
1947	Cle-A	0	0	....	7	2	0	0	0	16	15	7	7	1	2	10	5	1.563	3.94	89	4.69	.259	0	.000	-1	0	-0.2
	Pit-N	1	4	.200	13	6	1	0	0	30	49	33	29	4	1	18	7	2.233	8.70	49	9.12	.368	0	.000	-15	0	-1.5
Total	7	52	69	.430	182	128	63	8	13	1025^{1}	1018	468	388	56	22	316	430	1.301	3.41	101	3.42	.258	41	.122	17	58	0.6
• WOLFGANG, Mellie					Meldon John "Red" Wolfgang b: 3/20/1890, Albany, NY d: 6/30/1947, Albany, NY BR/TR, 5'9", 160 lbs. Deb: 4/18/1914																						
1914	Chi-A	9	5	.643	24	11	9	2	0	119^{1}	96	42	25	0	0	32	50	1.073	1.89	142	1.95	.219	7	.175	11	11	1.2
1915	Chi-A	2	2	.500	17	2	0	0	0	53^{2}	39	18	11	0	1	12	21	.950	1.84	161	1.64	.211	2	.118	7	4	0.6
1916	Chi-A	4	6	.400	27	14	6	1	0	127	103	39	28	2	2	42	36	1.142	1.98	139	2.40	.228	9	.225	9	10	1.0
1917	Chi-A	0	0	....	5	0	0	0	0	17^{2}	18	10	10	1	1	6	3	1.358	5.09	52	4.43	.305	0	.000	-5	0	-0.6
1918	Chi-A	0	1	.000	4	0	0	0	0	8^{1}	12	6	5	0	0	3	1	1.800	5.40	51	5.60	.333	1	.500	-2	0	-0.3
Total	5	15	14	.517	77	27	15	3	0	326	268	115	79	3	4	95	111	1.113	2.18	126	2.30	.229	19	.184	20	25	2.0
• WOLTER, Harry					Harry Meigs Wolter b: 7/11/1884, Monterey, CA d: 7/6/1970, Palo Alto, CA BL/TL, 5'10", 175 lbs. Deb: 5/14/1907 ♦																						
1907	Pit-N	0	0	....	1	0	0	0	0	2	3	2	1	0	0	2	0	2.500	4.50	54	8.24	.333	0	.000	-0	0	-0.1
	StL-N	0	2	.000	3	3	1	0	0	23	27	13	11	1	2	18	8	1.957	4.30	58	6.81	.318	16	.340	-5	2	0.0
	Yr.	0	2	.000	4	3	1	0	0	25	30	15	12	1	2	20	8	2.000	4.32	58	6.93	.319	16	.333	-5	2	-0.1
1909	Bos-A	4	4	.500	11	6	0	0	0	59	66	25	23	0	4	30	21	1.627	3.51	71	5.62	.303	29	.240	-8	4	-0.7
Total	2	4	6	.400	15	9	1	0	0	84	96	40	35	1	6	50	29	1.738	3.75	66	6.01	.308	514	.270	-13	6	-0.7
• WOLTERS, Rynie					Reinder Albertus Wolters b: 12/18/1842, Schantz, Holland d: 1/3/1917, Newark, NJ TR, 6', 165 lbs. Deb: 5/18/1871																						
1871	Mut-n	16	16	.500	**32**	**32**	**31**	**1**	0	**283**	345	283	108	7	....	39	22	1.357	3.43	110	....	**.262**	51	.370	10	....	1.9
1872	Cle-n	3	6	.333	12	8	5	0	0	75^{1}	115	106	51	3	....	7	4	1.619	6.09	69	....	.309	16	.232	-11	....	-0.8
1873	Res-n	0	1	.000	1	1	1	0	0	9	13	23	0	0	....	1	1	1.556	0.00	....	....	.300	0	.000	4	....	0.3
Total	3 n	19	23	.452	45	41	37	1	0	367^{1}	473	412	159	10	....	47	27	1.416	3.90	101	....	.273	67	.318	3	....	1.4
• WOMACK, Dooley					Horace Guy Womack b: 8/25/1939, Columbia, SC BL/TR, 6', 170 lbs. Deb: 4/14/1966																						
1966	NY-A	7	3	.700	42	1	0	0	4	75	52	25	22	6	3	23	50	1.000	2.64	126	2.17	.198	1	.200	6	7	0.6
1967	NY-A	5	6	.455	65	0	0	0	18	97	80	33	26	6	3	35	57	1.186	2.41	130	2.66	.230	4	.286	9	13	1.1
1968	NY-A	3	7	.300	45	0	0	0	2	61^{2}	53	23	22	6	1	29	27	1.330	3.21	90	3.52	.244	1	.200	-1	3	-0.1
1969	Hou-N	2	1	.667	30	0	0	0	0	51^{1}	49	21	20	1	3	20	32	1.344	3.51	101	3.35	.259	1	.167	1	3	0.1
	Sea-A	2	1	.667	9	0	0	0	0	14^{1}	15	4	4	0	0	3	8	1.256	2.51	145	2.76	.273	0	.000	2	1	0.2
1970	Oak-A	0	0	....	2	0	0	0	0	3	4	5	5	2	0	1	3	1.667	15.00	24	10.06	.308	0	....	-4	0	-0.4
Total	5	19	18	.514	193	1	0	0	24	302^{1}	253	111	99	21	10	111	177	1.204	2.95	109	2.91	.233	7	.226	13	27	1.5
• WOOD, Joe					Joe "Smokey Joe" Wood b: 10/25/1889, Kansas City, MO d: 7/27/1985, West Haven, CT BR/TR, 5'11", 180 lbs. Deb: 8/24/1908 ♦																						
1908	Bos-A	1	1	.500	6	2	1	1	0	22^{2}	14	12	6	0	1	16	11	1.324	2.38	103	2.55	.161	0	.000	-0	1	-0.1
1909	Bos-A	11	7	.611	24	19	13	4	0	160^{2}	121	51	39	1	6	43	88	1.021	2.18	114	1.88	.209	9	.164	3	13	0.3
1910	Bos-A	12	13	.480	35	17	14	3	0	198^{2}	155	81	37	3	10	56	145	1.062	1.68	152	2.19	.220	18	.261	20	14	2.8
1911	Bos-A	23	17	.575	44	33	25	5	3	275^{2}	226	113	62	2	11	76	231	1.096	2.02	162	2.21	.223	23	.261	38	26	4.6
1912*	Bos-A	**34**	5	.872	43	38	**35**	**10**	1	344	267	104	73	2	12	82	258	1.015	1.91	179	1.85	.216	36	.290	58	44	6.9
1913	Bos-A	11	5	.688	23	18	12	1	2	145^{2}	120	54	37	0	8	61	123	1.243	2.29	128	2.70	.229	15	.268	13	13	1.8
1914	Bos-A	9	3	.750	18	14	11	1	1	113^{1}	94	38	33	1	0	34	67	1.129	2.62	102	2.27	.229	6	.140	-1	8	-0.2
1915	Bos-A	15	5	.750	25	16	10	3	2	157^{1}	120	32	26	1	1	44	63	1.042	**1.49**	187	1.92	.216	14	.259	21	20	2.7
1917	Cle-A	0	1	.000	5	1	0	0	1	15^{2}	17	7	6	0	0	7	2	1.532	3.45	82	4.40	.309	0	.000	-1	1	-0.3
1919	Cle-A	0	0	....	1	0	0	0	1	0^{2}	0	0	0	0	0	0	0	.000	0.00	....	0.00	.000	49	.255	0	6	-0.6
1920*	Cle-A	0	0	....	1	0	0	0	0	2	4	5	5	0	0	2	1	3.000	22.50	17	12.74	.444	37	.270	-4	5	-0.4
Total	11	116	57	.671	225	158	121	28	11	1436^{1}	1138	497	324	10	49	421	989	1.085	2.03	144	2.15	.220	553	.283	147	151	17.6
• WOOD, Joe					Joe Frank Wood b: 5/20/1916, Shohola, PA d: 10/10/2002, Old Saybrook, CT BR/TR, 6', 190 lbs. Deb: 5/1/1944																						
1944	Bos-A	0	1	.000	3	1	0	0	0	9^{2}	13	9	7	0	0	3	5	1.655	6.52	52	4.72	.317	0	.000	-3	0	-0.4
• WOOD, John					John B. Wood b: 1871, Philadelphia, PA d: 1/30/1929, Philadelphia, PA, 5'7", 142 lbs. Deb: 5/9/1896																						
1896	StL-N	0	0	....	1	0	0	0	0	0	1	0	0	0	2	2	0	....	....	....	∞	1.000	0	....	0	0	0.0

YEAR	TM-L	W	L	PCT	G	GS	CG	SH	SV	IP	H	R	ER	HR	HB	BB	SO	RAT	ERA	ERA+	CERA	OAV	BH	AVG	PR+	WS	TPW

• WOOD, Kerry　　Kerry Lee Wood　b: 6/16/1977, Irving, TX　BR/TR, 6'5", 220 lbs.　Deb: 4/12/1998

YEAR	TM-L	W	L	PCT	G	GS	CG	SH	SV	IP	H	R	ER	HR	HB	BB	SO	RAT	ERA	ERA+	CERA	OAV	BH	AVG	PR+	WS	TPW
1998*	Chi-N	13	6	.684	26	26	1	0	0	166²	117	69	63	14	11	85	233	1.212	3.40	130	3.03	.196	7	.130	22	14	2.1
2000	Chi-N	8	7	.533	23	23	1	0	0	137	112	77	73	17	9	87	132	1.453	4.80	95	4.43	.226	10	.250	-3	7	0.0
2001	Chi-N	12	6	.667	28	28	1	1	0	174¹	127	70	65	16	10	92	217	1.256	3.36	124	3.22	.202	9	.188	18	13	1.9
2002	Chi-N	12	11	.522	33	33	4	1	0	213²	169	92	87	22	16	97	217	1.245	3.66	110	3.46	.221	12	.167	10	12	1.1
2003*	Chi-N★	14	11	.560	32	32	4	2	0	211	152	77	75	24	21	100	**266**	1.194	3.20	131	3.31	.203	10	.164	24	18	2.5
Total 5		59	41	.590	142	142	11	5	0	902²	677	385	363	93	67	461	1065	1.261	3.62	117	3.45	.209	48	.175	70	64	7.5

• WOOD, Mike　　Michael Burton Wood　b: 4/26/1980, West Palm Beach, FL　BR/TR, 6'3", 180 lbs.　Deb: 8/21/2003

| 2003 | Oak-A | 2 | 1 | .667 | 7 | 1 | 0 | 0 | 0 | 13² | 24 | 17 | 16 | 1 | 2 | 7 | 15 | 2.268 | 10.54 | 43 | 9.45 | .387 | 0 | .... | -9 | 0 | -0.9 |

• WOOD, Pete　　Peter Burke Wood　b: 2/1/1857, Hamilton, Canada　d: 3/15/1923, Chicago, IL　TR, 5'7", 185 lbs.　Deb: 7/15/1885

1885	Buf-N	8	15	.348	24	22	21	0	0	198²	235	170	98	8	....	66	38	1.515	4.44	67	....	.281	23	.221	-20	4	-2.1
1889	Phi-N	1	1	.500	3	2	2	0	0	19	28	15	11	0	0	3	8	1.632	5.21	84	....	.332	0	.000	-1	1	-0.2
Total 2		9	16	.360	27	24	23	0	0	217²	263	185	109	8	0	69	46	1.525	4.51	68	....	.286	23	.205	-21	5	-2.3

• WOOD, Spades　　Charles Asher Wood　b: 1/13/1909, Spartanburg, SC　d: 5/18/1986, Wichita, KS　BL/TL, 5'10.5", 150 lbs.　Deb: 8/16/1930

1930	Pit-N	4	3	.571	9	7	4	2	0	58	61	34	33	4	0	32	23	1.603	5.12	97	4.59	.270	5	.250	-1	4	0.0
1931	Pit-N	2	6	.250	15	10	2	0	0	64	69	45	43	2	1	46	33	1.797	6.05	84	5.09	.273	5	.227	-17	0	-1.6
Total 2		6	9	.400	24	17	6	2	0	122	130	79	76	6	1	78	56	1.705	5.61	76	4.85	.272	10	.238	-18	4	-1.6

• WOOD, Wilbur　　Wilbur Forrester "Wilbah" Wood　b: 10/22/1941, Cambridge, MA　BR/TL, 6', 180 lbs.　Deb: 6/30/1961

1961	Bos-A	0	0	....	6	1	0	0	0	13	14	8	8	2	0	7	7	1.615	5.54	75	5.27	.269	0	.000	-2	0	-0.2
1962	Bos-A	0	0	....	1	1	0	0	0	7²	6	3	3	0	0	3	3	1.174	3.52	117	2.30	.214	0	.000	0	0	0.0
1963	Bos-A	0	5	.000	25	6	0	0	0	64²	67	35	27	10	3	13	28	1.237	3.76	101	4.03	.270	0	.000	1	2	-0.1
1964	Bos-A	0	0	....	4	0	0	0	0	5²	13	11	11	1	0	3	5	2.824	17.47	22	12.54	.433	0	.000	-8	0	-0.9
	Pit-N	0	2	.000	3	2	1	0	0	17¹	16	8	7	0	2	11	9	1.558	3.63	97	3.91	.246	0	.000	-0	1	-0.1
1965	Pit-N	1	1	.500	34	1	0	0	0	51¹	44	21	18	3	1	16	29	1.169	3.16	111	2.78	.237	0	.000	1	3	0.0
1967	Chi-A	4	2	.667	51	8	0	0	4	95¹	95	34	26	2	1	28	47	1.290	2.45	127	3.06	.260	1	.063	7	7	0.7
1968	Chi-A	13	12	.520	**88**	2	0	0	16	159	127	39	33	8	3	33	74	1.006	1.87	162	2.02	.222	2	.091	21	19	2.4
1969	Chi-A	10	11	.476	**76**	0	0	0	15	119²	113	48	40	13	3	40	73	1.279	3.01	128	3.43	.248	0	.000	13	14	1.2
1970	Chi-A	9	13	.409	**77**	0	0	0	21	121²	118	50	38	7	2	36	85	1.266	2.81	139	3.22	.258	2	.111	17	14	1.7
1971	Chi-A★	22	13	.629	44	42	22	7	1	334	272	95	71	21	7	62	210	1.000	1.91	**188**	2.18	.222	5	.052	**68**	33	**6.9**
1972	Chi-A★	**24**	17	.585	49	**49**	20	8	0	**376²**	325	119	105	28	7	74	193	1.093	2.51	124	2.53	.235	17	.136	34	29	3.6
1973	Chi-A	**24**	20	.545	49	48	21	4	0	**359¹**	381	166	138	25	7	91	199	1.314	3.46	114	3.67	.270	0	....	25	23	2.6
1974	Chi-A★	20	19	.513	42	**42**	22	1	0	320¹	305	143	128	27	9	80	169	1.202	3.60	104	3.24	.254	0	....	8	19	0.9
1975	Chi-A	16	20	.444	43	**43**	14	2	0	291¹	309	148	133	26	5	92	140	1.376	4.11	94	4.08	.272	0	....	-3	13	-0.3
1976	Chi-A	4	3	.571	7	7	5	1	0	56¹	51	24	14	3	0	11	31	1.101	2.24	159	2.54	.242	0	....	9	5	1.0
1977	Chi-A	7	8	.467	24	18	5	1	0	122²	139	75	68	10	10	50	42	1.541	4.99	82	5.12	.293	0	....	-9	4	-0.9
1978	Chi-A	10	10	.500	28	27	4	0	0	166	187	103	96	13	3	74	69	**1.554**	5.20	73	5.22	.285	0	....	-25	4	-2.5
Total 17		164	156	.513	651	297	114	24	57	2684	2582	1130	965	209	63	724	1411	1.232	3.24	114	3.32	.254	27	.084	157	190	15.8

• WOODALL, Brad　　David Bradley Woodall　b: 6/25/1969, Atlanta, GA　BB/TL, 6', 175 lbs.　Deb: 7/22/1994

1994	Atl-N	0	1	.000	1	1	0	0	0	6	5	3	3	2	0	2	1	1.167	4.50	94	4.51	.227	1	.500	-0	0	0.0
1995	Atl-N	1	1	.500	9	0	0	0	0	10¹	13	10	7	1	0	8	5	2.032	6.10	70	6.79	.310	1	1.000	-2	0	-0.1
1996	Atl-N	2	2	.500	8	3	0	0	0	19²	28	19	16	4	0	4	20	1.627	7.32	60	6.41	.333	1	.200	-6	0	-0.6
1998	Mil-N	7	9	.438	31	20	0	0	0	138	145	81	76	25	6	47	85	1.391	4.96	86	4.89	.273	9	.237	-12	5	-0.8
1999	Chi-N	0	1	.000	6	3	0	0	0	16	17	12	10	5	1	6	7	1.438	5.63	80	6.12	.270	1	.500	-2	1	-0.1
Total 5		10	14	.417	55	27	0	0	0	190	208	125	112	37	7	67	119	1.447	5.31	81	5.24	.280	13	.271	-22	6	-1.6

• WOODARD, Steve　　Steve Larry Woodard　b: 5/15/1975, Hartselle, AL　BL/TR, 6'4", 225 lbs.　Deb: 7/28/1997

1997	Mil-A	3	3	.500	7	7	0	0	0	36²	39	25	21	5	2	6	32	1.227	5.15	90	3.98	.269	0	....	-3	1	-0.3
1998	Mil-N	10	12	.455	34	26	0	0	0	165²	170	83	77	19	9	33	135	1.225	4.18	102	3.73	.264	7	.140	-0	9	-0.1
1999	Mil-N	11	8	.579	31	29	2	0	0	185	219	101	93	23	6	36	119	1.378	4.52	100	4.52	.294	7	.132	2	9	0.2
2000	Mil-N	1	7	.125	27	11	1	0	0	93²	125	70	62	16	4	33	65	1.687	5.96	76	6.55	.325	1	.045	-16	0	-1.6
	Cle-A	3	3	.500	13	11	0	0	0	54	57	35	34	10	2	11	35	1.259	5.67	88	4.31	.269	0	....	-4	2	-0.3
2001	Cle-A	3	3	.500	29	10	0	0	0	97	129	59	56	10	5	17	52	1.505	5.20	87	5.33	.325	0	.000	-5	4	-0.5
2002	Tex-A	0	0	....	14	0	0	0	0	17²	20	13	13	4	2	8	12	1.585	6.62	71	6.28	.274	0	....	-4	0	-0.3
2003	Bos-A	1	0	1.000	7	0	0	0	0	17²	23	10	10	3	1	5	12	1.585	5.09	90	5.87	.311	0	....	-1	1	-0.1
Total 7		32	36	.471	162	94	3	0	0	667¹	782	396	366	90	31	149	464	1.395	4.94	92	4.76	.292	15	.119	-31	26	-3.1

• WOODBURN, Gene　　Eugene Stewart Woodburn　b: 8/20/1886, Bellaire, OH　d: 1/18/1961, Sandusky, OH　BR/TR, 6', 175 lbs.　Deb: 7/27/1911

1911	StL-N	1	5	.167	11	6	1	0	0	38¹	22	32	23	0	6	40	23	1.617	5.40	62	3.60	.167	1	.167	-9	1	-0.7
1912	StL-N	1	4	.200	20	5	1	0	0	48¹	60	48	30	0	4	42	25	2.110	5.59	61	6.66	.306	0	.000	-12	0	-1.3
Total 2		2	9	.182	31	11	2	0	0	86²	82	80	53	0	10	82	48	1.892	5.50	62	5.31	.250	1	.053	-21	1	-2.1

• WOODCOCK, Fred　　Fred Wayland Woodcock　b: 5/17/1868, Winchendon, MA　d: 8/11/1943, Ashburnham, MA　BL/TL, 6'2", 190 lbs.　Deb: 5/17/1892

| 1892 | Pit-N | 1 | 2 | .333 | 5 | 4 | 3 | 0 | 0 | 33 | 42 | 28 | 13 | 1 | 2 | 17 | 8 | 1.788 | 3.55 | 93 | 5.67 | .298 | 3 | .200 | -2 | 1 | -0.1 |

• WOODEND, George　　George Anthony "Dandy" Woodend　b: 12/9/1917, Hartford, CT　d: 5/1/1980, Hartford, CT　BR/TR, 6', 200 lbs.　Deb: 4/22/1944

| 1944 | Bos-N | 0 | 0 | .... | 3 | 0 | 0 | 0 | 0 | 2 | 5 | 4 | 3 | 0 | 0 | 5 | 0 | 5.000 | 13.50 | 28 | 23.32 | .556 | 0 | .... | -2 | 0 | -0.2 |

• WOODESHICK, Hal　　Harold Joseph Woodeshick　b: 8/24/1932, Wilkes-Barre, PA　BR/TL, 6'3", 200 lbs.　Deb: 9/14/1956

1956	Det-A	0	2	.000	2	2	0	0	0	5¹	12	8	8	1	0	3	1	2.813	13.50	14.23		.444	0	....	-6	0	-0.5
1958	Cle-A	6	6	.500	14	9	3	0	0	71²	71	32	29	4	6	25	27	1.340	3.64	100	3.94	.265	4	.167	-0	4	-0.1
1959	Was-A	2	4	.333	31	3	0	0	0	61	58	39	25	2	1	36	30	1.541	3.69	106	3.79	.253	0	.000	4	2	0.3
1960	Was-A	4	5	.444	41	14	1	0	4	115	131	67	60	7	3	60	46	1.661	4.70	84	5.12	.289	2	.069	-8	4	-1.0
1961	Was-A	3	2	.600	7	6	1	0	0	40¹	38	19	18	3	3	24	24	1.537	4.02	97	4.64	.257	2	.125	-1	2	-0.1
	Det-A	1	1	.500	12	2	0	0	0	18¹	25	17	16	3	0	17	13	2.291	7.85	52	8.74	.316	0	.000	-8	0	-0.8
	Yr.	4	3	.571	19	8	1	0	0	58²	63	36	34	6	3	41	37	1.773	5.22	77	5.92	.278	2	.100	-8	2	-0.9
1962	Hou-N	5	16	.238	31	26	2	1	0	139¹	161	84	68	3	3	54	82	1.543	4.39	85	4.32	.290	3	.081	-8	3	-0.9
1963	Hou-N★	11	9	.550	55	0	0	0	10	114	75	29	25	6	6	42	94	1.026	1.97	160	1.83	.186	3	.130	17	17	1.9
1964	Hou-N	2	9	.182	61	0	0	0	**23**	78¹	73	32	24	3	7	32	58	1.340	2.76	124	3.40	.249	0	.000	7	10	0.7
1965	Hou-N	3	4	.429	27	0	0	0	3	32¹	27	13	11	3	0	18	22	1.392	3.06	110	3.45	.227	1	.167	2	3	0.2
	StL-N	3	2	.600	51	0	0	0	15	59²	47	14	12	1	2	27	37	1.240	1.81	212	2.49	.221	0	.000	13	11	1.3
	Yr.	6	6	.500	78	0	0	0	18	92	74	27	23	4	2	45	59	1.293	2.25	160	2.83	.223	1	.071	15	14	1.5
1966	StL-N	2	1	.667	59	0	0	0	4	70¹	57	17	15	2	0	23	30	1.137	1.92	188	2.60	.224	1	.200	13	8	1.3
1967*	StL-N	2	1	.667	36	0	0	0	0	41²	41	29	24	2	3	28	20	1.656	5.18	63	4.36	.252	0	.000	-9	0	-1.0
Total 11		44	62	.415	427	62	7	1	61	847¹	816	400	335	40	35	389	484	1.422	3.56	103	3.81	.254	16	.092	16	64	1.2

• WOODMAN, Dan　　Daniel Courtenay "Cocoa" Woodman　b: 7/8/1893, Danvers, MA　d: 12/14/1962, Danvers, MA　BR/TR, 5'8", 160 lbs.　Deb: 7/10/1914

1914	Buf-F	0	0	....	13	0	0	0	1	33²	30	16	9	0	1	11	13	1.218	2.41	139	2.60	.246	1	.143	3	2	0.3
1915	Buf-F	0	0	....	5	1	0	0	0	15¹	14	9	7	0	0	9	1	1.500	4.11	75	3.44	.246	1	.250	-2	0	-0.2
Total 2		0	0	....	18	1	0	0	1	49	44	25	16	0	1	20	14	1.306	2.94	109	2.86	.246	2	.182	1	2	0.1

• WOODS, Clarence　　Clarence Cofield Woods　b: 6/11/1892, Woods Ridge, IN　d: 7/2/1969, Rising Sun, IN　BR/TR, 6'5", 230 lbs.　Deb: 8/8/1914

| 1914 | Ind-F | 0 | 0 | .... | 2 | 0 | 0 | 0 | 1 | 2 | 1 | 1 | 1 | 0 | 0 | 2 | 1 | 1.500 | 4.50 | 77 | 2.62 | .167 | 0 | .... | -0 | 0 | 0.0 |

YEAR TM-L	W	L	PCT	G	GS	CG	SH	SV	IP	H	R	ER	HR	HB	BB	SO	RAT	ERA	ERA+	CERA	OAV	BH	AVG	PR+	WS	TPW
• WOODS, John	John Fulton "Abe" Woods b: 1/18/1898, Princeton, WV d: 10/4/1946, Norfolk, VA BR/TR, 6', 175 lbs. Deb: 9/16/1924																									
1924 Bos-A	0	0	....	1	0	0	0	0	1	0	0	0	0	0	3	0	3.000	0.00	....	5.85	.000	0	....	0	0	0.0
• WOODS, Pinky	George Rowland Woods b: 5/22/1915, Waterbury, CT d: 10/29/1982, Los Angeles, CA BR/TR, 6'5", 225 lbs. Deb: 6/20/1943																									
1943 Bos-A	5	6	.455	23	12	2	0	1	100^2	109	61	55	6	1	55	32	1.629	4.92	67	4.81	.284	8	.222	-18	0	-2.1
1944 Bos-A	4	8	.333	38	20	5	1	0	170^2	171	73	62	4	6	88	56	1.518	3.27	104	4.02	.266	7	.146	2	8	0.1
1945 Bos-A	4	7	.364	24	12	3	0	2	107^1	108	56	50	3	1	63	36	1.593	4.19	81	4.22	.268	9	.214	-10	3	-1.0
Total 3	13	21	.382	85	44	10	1	3	378^2	388	190	167	13	8	206	124	1.569	3.97	85	4.29	.272	24	.190	-27	11	-3.0
• WOODS, Walt	Walter Sydney Woods b: 4/28/1875, Rye, NH d: 10/30/1951, Portsmouth, NH BR/TR, 5'9.5", 165 lbs. Deb: 4/20/1898																									
1898 Chi-N	9	13	.409	27	22	18	3	0	215	224	128	75	7	10	59	26	1.316	3.14	114	3.46	.267	27	.175	9	11	-0.3
1899 Lou-N	9	13	.409	26	21	17	0	0	186^1	216	100	68	9	7	37	21	1.358	3.28	117	3.91	.290	19	.151	15	12	0.5
1900 Pit-N	0	0	....	1	0	0	0	0	3	9	7	7	0	0	1	1	3.333	21.00	17	16.49	.513	0	.000	-6	0	-0.5
Total 3	18	26	.409	54	43	35	3	0	404^1	449	235	150	16	17	97	48	1.350	3.34	111	3.77	.280	46	.164	18	23	-0.4
• WOODSON, Dick	Richard Lee Woodson b: 3/30/1945, Oelwein, IA BR/TR, 6'5", 207 lbs. Deb: 4/8/1969																									
1969* Min-A	7	5	.583	44	10	2	0	1	110^1	99	49	45	11	3	49	66	1.341	3.67	99	3.73	.237	2	.074	-2	6	-0.3
1970* Min-A	1	2	.333	21	0	0	0	1	30^2	29	18	13	2	0	19	22	1.565	3.82	98	4.23	.244	0	.000	-0	1	-0.1
1972 Min-A	14	14	.500	36	36	9	3	0	251^2	193	93	76	19	2	101	150	1.168	2.72	118	2.69	.211	7	.080	12	15	0.7
1973 Min-A	10	8	.556	23	23	4	2	0	141^1	137	68	62	12	2	68	53	1.450	3.95	100	4.19	.254	0	....	1	8	0.1
1974 Min-A	1	1	.500	5	4	0	0	0	27	30	16	13	5	1	4	12	1.259	4.33	87	4.36	.273	0	....	-2	1	-0.2
NY-A	1	2	.333	8	3	0	0	0	28	34	19	18	6	1	12	12	1.643	5.79	60	6.38	.301	0	....	-8	0	-0.8
Yr.	2	3	.400	13	7	0	0	0	55	64	35	31	11	2	16	24	1.455	5.07	71	5.39	.287	0	....	-9	1	-1.0
Total 5	34	32	.515	137	76	15	5	2	589	522	263	227	55	9	253	315	1.316	3.47	103	3.58	.236	9	.077	1	31	-0.5
• WOODSON, Kerry	Walter Browne Woodson b: 5/18/1969, Jacksonville, FL BR/TR, 6'2", 190 lbs. Deb: 7/19/1992																									
1992 Sea-A	0	1	.000	8	1	0	0	0	13^2	12	7	5	0	2	11	6	1.683	3.29	121	4.93	.245	0	....	1	1	0.1
• WOODWARD, Frank	Frank Russell Woodward b: 5/17/1894, New Haven, CT d: 6/11/1961, New Haven, CT BR/TR, 5'10", 175 lbs. Deb: 4/17/1918																									
1918 Phi-N	0	0	....	2	0	0	0	0	6	6	4	4	0	0	4	4	1.667	6.00	50	4.05	.250	1	.333	-2	0	-0.2
1919 Phi-N	6	9	.400	17	12	6	0	0	100^2	109	63	53	5	5	35	27	1.430	4.74	68	4.14	.291	6	.207	-16	2	-1.7
StL-N	3	5	.375	17	7	2	0	1	72	65	27	21	1	1	28	18	1.292	2.63	106	2.90	.248	1	.048	0	4	-0.2
Yr.	9	14	.391	34	19	8	0	1	172^2	174	90	74	6	6	63	45	1.373	3.86	80	3.62	.273	7	.140	-16	6	-1.9
1921 Was-A	0	0	....	3	1	0	0	0	10^2	11	7	7	0	0	3	4	1.313	5.91	70	3.04	.282	1	.333	-2	0	-0.2
1922 Was-A	0	0	....	1	0	0	0	0	2^1	3	3	3	0	0	3	2	2.571	11.57	33	8.65	.375	0	.000	-2	0	-0.2
1923 Chi-A	0	1	.000	2	1	0	0	0	2	5	3	3	0	0	1	0	3.000	13.50	29	13.07	.500	0	....	-2	0	-0.2
Total 5	9	15	.375	42	21	8	0	1	193^2	199	107	91	6	6	74	55	1.410	4.23	75	3.76	.277	9	.158	-24	6	-2.7
• WOODWARD, Rob	Robert John Woodward b: 9/28/1962, Hanover, NH BR/TR, 6'3", 185 lbs. Deb: 9/5/1985																									
1985 Bos-A	1	0	1.000	5	2	0	0	0	26^2	17	8	5	0	2	9	16	.975	1.69	254	1.58	.168	0	....	8	3	0.8
1986 Bos-A	2	3	.400	9	6	0	0	0	35^2	46	26	21	4	1	11	14	1.598	5.30	79	5.61	.313	0	....	-4	1	-0.4
1987 Bos-A	1	1	.500	9	6	0	0	0	37	53	33	29	6	1	15	15	1.838	7.05	64	7.29	.338	0	....	-10	0	-1.0
1988 Bos-A	0	0	....	1	0	0	0	0	0^2	2	1	1	0	0	1	0	4.500	13.50	30	22.07	.500	0	....	-1	0	-0.1
Total 4	4	4	.500	24	14	0	0	0	100	118	68	56	10	4	36	45	1.540	5.04	87	5.27	.289	0	....	-7	4	-0.6
• WOOLDRIDGE, Floyd	Floyd Lewis Wooldridge b: 8/25/1928, Jerico Springs, MO BR/TR, 6'1", 185 lbs. Deb: 5/1/1955																									
1955 StL-N	2	4	.333	18	8	2	0	0	57^2	64	36	31	9	1	27	14	1.578	4.84	84	5.34	.281	4	.222	-4	2	-0.4
• WORDEN, Fred	Frederick Bamford Worden b: 9/4/1894, St. Louis, MO d: 11/9/1941, St. Louis, MO BR/TR Deb: 9/28/1914																									
1914 Phi-A	0	0	....	1	0	0	0	0	2	8	5	4	0	0	0	1	4.000	18.00	14	24.18	.615	0	.000	-3	0	-0.4
• WORKMAN, Hoge	Harry Hall Workman b: 9/25/1899, Huntington, WV d: 5/20/1972, Fort Myers, FL BR/TR, 5'11", 170 lbs. Deb: 6/27/1924																									
1924 Bos-A	0	0	....	11	0	0	0	0	18	25	19	17	2	2	11	7	2.000	8.50	51	7.08	.325	0	.000	-8	0	-0.8
• WORKS, Ralph	Ralph Talmadge "Judge" Works b: 3/16/1888, Payson, IL d: 8/8/1941, Pasadena, CA BL/TR, 6'2.5", 185 lbs. Deb: 5/1/1909																									
1909* Det-A	4	1	.800	16	4	4	0	2	64	62	19	14	0	1	17	31	1.234	1.97	128	2.85	.261	1	.059	4	6	0.3
1910 Det-A	3	6	.333	18	10	5	0	1	85^2	73	47	34	1	4	39	36	1.307	3.57	74	3.03	.235	8	.267	-9	3	-0.9
1911 Det-A	11	5	.688	30	15	9	3	0	167^1	173	93	72	3	6	67	68	1.434	3.87	89	3.77	.268	9	.148	-6	10	-0.9
1912 Det-A	5	10	.333	27	16	9	1	1	157	185	101	74	1	7	66	64	**1.599**	4.24	77	4.73	.308	8	.143	-16	3	-1.9
Cin-N	1	1	.500	3	1	1	0	0	9^2	4	5	3	0	1	5	5	.931	2.79	120	1.42	.133	1	.200	1	1	0.1
1913 Cin-N	0	1	.000	5	2	0	0	0	15	15	14	13	0	3	8	4	1.533	7.80	42	3.95	.242	1	.167	-8	0	-0.8
Total 5	24	24	.500	99	48	28	4	4	498^2	512	279	210	5	22	202	208	1.432	3.79	83	3.79	.271	28	.160	-33	23	-4.2
• WORRELL, Tim	Timothy Howard Worrell b: 7/5/1967, Pasadena, CA BR/TR, 6'4", 220 lbs. Deb: 6/25/1993																									
1993 SD-N	2	7	.222	21	16	0	0	0	100^2	104	63	55	11	0	43	52	1.460	4.92	84	4.31	.269	1	.032	-8	2	-1.1
1994 SD-N	0	1	.000	3	3	0	0	0	14^2	9	7	6	0	0	5	14	.955	3.68	112	1.40	.170	1	.500	1	1	0.2
1995 SD-N	1	0	1.000	9	0	0	0	0	13^1	16	7	7	2	1	6	13	1.650	4.73	85	6.01	.291	0	.000	-1	1	-0.1
1996* SD-N	9	7	.563	50	11	0	0	1	121	109	45	41	9	6	39	99	1.223	3.05	130	3.22	.236	3	.150	13	10	1.2
1997 SD-N	4	8	.333	60	10	0	0	3	106^1	116	67	61	14	7	50	81	1.561	5.16	74	5.34	.280	3	.200	-14	3	-1.3
1998 Det-A	2	6	.250	15	9	0	0	0	61^2	66	42	41	11	1	19	47	1.378	5.98	79	4.68	.270	0	....	-10	1	-0.9
Cle-A	0	0	....	3	0	0	0	0	5^1	6	3	3	0	0	2	2	1.500	5.06	94	3.84	.300	0	....	-0	0	0.0
Oak-A	0	1	.000	25	0	0	0	0	36	34	17	16	5	0	8	33	1.167	4.00	114	3.20	.241	0	....	3	2	0.3
Yr.	2	7	.222	43	9	0	0	0	103	106	62	60	16	1	29	82	1.311	5.24	89	4.12	.262	0	....	-7	3	-0.7
1999 Oak-A	2	2	.500	53	0	0	0	0	69^1	69	38	32	6	3	34	62	1.486	4.15	112	4.42	.256	0	....	4	4	0.4
2000 Bal-A	2	2	.500	5	0	0	0	0	7^1	12	6	6	3	0	5	5	2.318	7.36	64	11.13	.353	0	....	-2	0	-0.2
Chi-N	3	4	.429	54	0	0	0	3	62	60	20	17	7	1	24	52	1.355	2.47	184	3.75	.252	0	.000	15	7	1.3
2001 SF-N	2	5	.286	73	0	0	0	0	78^1	71	33	30	4	3	33	63	1.328	3.45	116	3.32	.240	0	.000	5	5	0.4
2002* SF-N	8	2	.800	80	0	0	0	0	72	55	21	18	3	0	30	55	1.181	2.25	172	2.47	.212	0	.000	12	9	1.2
2003* SF-N	4	4	.500	76	0	0	0	38	78^1	74	35	25	5	0	28	65	1.302	2.87	143	3.19	.246	0	.000	9	13	0.9
Total 11	39	49	.443	527	49	0	0	45	826^1	801	404	358	80	22	326	643	1.364	3.90	107	3.90	.252	8	.101	25	58	2.2
• WORRELL, Todd	Todd Roland Worrell b: 9/28/1959, Arcadia, CA BR/TR, 6'5", 222 lbs. Deb: 8/28/1985																									
1985* StL-N	3	0	1.000	17	0	0	0	5	21^2	17	7	7	2	0	7	17	1.108	2.91	121	2.46	.215	0	.000	1	3	0.1
1986 StL-N	9	10	.474	74	0	0	0	**36**	103^2	86	29	24	9	1	41	73	1.225	2.08	175	2.87	.229	1	.143	14	19	1.5
1987* StL-N	8	6	.571	75	0	0	0	33	94^2	86	29	28	8	0	34	92	1.268	2.66	156	3.15	.242	1	.100	15	17	1.4
1988 StL-N★	5	9	.357	68	0	0	0	32	90	69	32	30	7	1	34	78	1.144	3.00	116	2.45	.214	0	.000	4	15	0.4
1989 StL-N	3	5	.375	47	0	0	0	20	51^2	42	21	17	4	0	26	41	1.316	2.96	122	2.90	.222	0	.000	3	7	0.3
1992 StL-N	5	3	.625	67	0	0	0	3	64	45	15	15	4	1	25	64	1.094	2.11	161	2.24	.198	0	....	8	9	0.9
1993 LA-N	1	1	.500	35	0	0	0	5	38^2	46	28	26	6	0	11	31	1.474	6.05	63	5.13	.313	0	....	-10	0	-0.9
1994 LA-N	6	5	.545	38	0	0	0	11	42	37	21	20	4	1	12	44	1.167	4.29	92	3.02	.236	0	....	-1	6	-0.1
1995 LA-N★	4	1	.800	59	0	0	0	32	62^1	50	15	14	4	1	19	61	1.107	2.02	188	2.51	.221	0	.000	12	14	1.2
1996* LA-N★	4	6	.400	72	0	0	0	**44**	65^1	70	29	22	5	2	15	66	1.301	3.03	128	3.62	.265	0	....	7	11	0.6
1997 LA-N	2	6	.250	65	0	0	0	35	59^2	60	38	35	12	0	23	61	1.391	5.28	73	4.57	.250	0	....	-9	4	-0.9
Total 11	50	52	.490	617	0	0	0	256	693^2	608	264	238	65	7	247	628	1.233	3.09	121	3.10	.235	2	.074	45	105	4.5
• WORTHAM, Rich	Richard Cooper Wortham b: 10/22/1953, Odessa, TX BR/TL, 6', 185 lbs. Deb: 5/3/1978																									
1978 Chi-A	3	2	.600	8	8	2	0	0	59	59	24	20	1	0	23	25	1.390	3.05	125	3.54	.267	0	....	5	4	0.6
1979 Chi-A	14	14	.500	34	33	5	0	0	204	195	126	111	21	3	100	119	1.446	4.90	87	4.25	.255	0	....	-15	7	-1.5

YEAR TM-L	W	L	PCT	G	GS	CG	SH	SV	IP	H	R	ER	HR	HB	BB	SO	RAT	ERA	ERA+	CERA	OAV	BH	AVG	PR+	WS	TPW
1980 Chi-A	4	7	.364	41	10	0	0	1	92	102	73	61	4	3	58	45	1.739	5.97	67	5.19	.285	0	....	-19	0	-1.9
1983 Oak-A	0	0	....	1	0	0	0	0	0	3	1	0	0	0	1	0	....	....	....	∞	1.000	0	....	0	0	0.0
Total 4	21	23	.477	84	51	7	0	1	355	359	224	192	26	6	182	189	1.524	4.87	85	4.37	.266	0	....	-29	11	-2.8

• WORTHINGTON, Al

Allan Fulton "Red" Worthington b: 2/5/1929, Birmingham, AL BR/TR, 6'2", 205 lbs. Deb: 7/6/1953 C

YEAR TM-L	W	L	PCT	G	GS	CG	SH	SV	IP	H	R	ER	HR	HB	BB	SO	RAT	ERA	ERA+	CERA	OAV	BH	AVG	PR+	WS	TPW
1953 NY-N	4	8	.333	20	17	5	2	0	102	103	55	39	6	2	54	52	1.539	3.44	125	4.20	.258	2	.065	10	5	0.7
1954 NY-N	0	2	.000	10	1	0	0	0	18	21	7	7	0	0	15	8	2.000	3.50	115	6.15	.333	0	.000	1	1	0.0
1956 NY-N	7	14	.333	28	24	4	0	0	165^2	158	82	73	20	4	74	95	1.400	3.97	95	4.22	.254	12	.235	-3	8	-0.1
1957 NY-N	8	11	.421	55	12	1	1	4	157^2	140	75	74	19	5	56	90	1.243	4.22	93	3.48	.237	4	.100	-5	8	-0.7
1958 SF-N	11	7	.611	54	12	1	0	6	151^1	152	72	61	17	2	57	76	1.381	3.63	105	3.98	.255	8	.182	5	10	0.5
1959 SF-N	2	3	.400	42	3	0	0	2	73^1	68	34	30	8	5	37	45	1.432	3.68	103	4.32	.253	1	.077	1	4	0.0
1960 Bos-A	0	1	.000	6	0	0	0	0	11^2	17	12	10	1	0	11	7	2.400	7.71	52	8.47	.340	0	.000	-4	0	-0.5
Chi-A	1	1	.500	4	0	0	0	0	5^1	3	2	2	0	0	4	1	1.313	3.38	112	2.19	.176	2	1.000	0	1	0.1
Yr.	1	2	.333	10	0	0	0	0	17	20	14	12	1	0	15	8	2.059	6.35	63	6.50	.299	2	.667	-4	1	-0.4
1963 Cin-N	4	4	.500	50	0	0	0	10	81^1	75	34	27	6	3	31	55	1.303	2.99	112	3.49	.248	1	.083	3	7	0.3
1964 Cin-N	1	0	1.000	6	0	0	0	0	7	14	11	8	0	1	2	6	2.286	10.29	35	8.90	.400	0	....	-5	0	-0.6
Min-A	5	6	.455	41	0	0	0	14	72^1	47	18	11	4	0	28	59	1.037	1.37	262	1.82	.183	1	.063	19	11	1.8
1965* Min-A	10	7	.588	62	0	0	0	21	80^1	57	25	19	4	3	41	59	1.220	2.13	167	2.73	.207	1	.100	12	12	1.3
1966 Min-A	6	3	.667	65	0	0	0	16	91^1	66	26	25	6	1	27	93	1.018	2.46	146	2.05	.199	3	.273	12	15	1.4
1967 Min-A	8	9	.471	59	0	0	0	16	92	77	36	29	6	1	38	80	1.250	2.84	122	2.90	.229	0	.000	8	11	0.8
1968 Min-A	4	5	.444	54	0	0	0	**18**	76^1	67	26	23	1	0	32	57	1.297	2.71	114	2.70	.238	0	.000	4	10	0.4
1969* Min-A	4	1	.800	46	0	0	0	3	61	65	31	31	7	0	20	51	1.393	4.57	80	4.31	.278	0	.000	-7	3	-0.8
Total 14	75	82	.478	602	69	11	3	110	1246^2	1130	546	469	105	27	527	834	1.329	3.39	110	3.56	.243	35	.137	50	106	4.9

• WRIGHT, Bob

Robert Cassius Wright b: 12/13/1891, Decatur County, IN d: 7/30/1993, Carmichael, CA BR/TR, 6'1.5", 175 lbs. Deb: 9/21/1915

YEAR TM-L	W	L	PCT	G	GS	CG	SH	SV	IP	H	R	ER	HR	HB	BB	SO	RAT	ERA	ERA+	CERA	OAV	BH	AVG	PR+	WS	TPW
1915 Chi-N	0	0	....	2	0	0	0	0	4	6	4	1	0	0	0	3	1.500	2.25	123	4.76	.353	0	....	0	0	0.0

• WRIGHT, Clyde

Clyde Wright b: 2/20/1941, Jefferson City, TN BR/TL, 6'1", 185 lbs. Deb: 6/15/1966

YEAR TM-L	W	L	PCT	G	GS	CG	SH	SV	IP	H	R	ER	HR	HB	BB	SO	RAT	ERA	ERA+	CERA	OAV	BH	AVG	PR+	WS	TPW
1966 Cal-A	4	7	.364	20	13	3	1	0	91^1	92	39	38	11	1	25	37	1.281	3.74	90	3.78	.265	3	.103	-5	4	-0.7
1967 Cal-A	5	5	.500	20	11	1	0	0	77^1	76	33	28	5	1	24	35	1.293	3.26	96	3.44	.260	6	.273	-2	4	0.0
1968 Cal-A	10	6	.625	41	13	2	1	3	125^2	123	58	55	13	2	44	71	1.329	3.94	74	3.78	.256	8	.216	-16	5	-1.6
1969 Cal-A	1	8	.111	37	5	0	0	0	63^2	66	33	29	4	1	30	31	1.508	4.10	85	4.38	.278	2	.182	-5	1	-0.5
1970 Cal-A★	22	12	.647	39	39	7	2	0	260^2	226	97	82	24	7	88	110	1.205	2.83	128	3.13	.232	18	.171	16	20	1.9
1971 Cal-A	16	17	.485	37	37	10	2	0	276^2	225	105	92	17	3	82	135	1.110	2.99	108	2.49	.226	14	.154	4	18	0.6
1972 Cal-A	18	11	.621	35	35	15	2	0	251	229	101	83	14	4	80	87	1.231	2.98	98	3.08	.246	18	.217	-4	16	0.3
1973 Cal-A	11	19	.367	37	36	13	1	0	257	273	120	105	26	3	76	65	1.358	3.68	96	4.06	.273	0	....	-1	13	-0.1
1974 Mil-A	9	20	.310	38	32	15	0	0	232	264	122	114	22	0	54	64	1.371	4.42	82	4.10	.284	0	....	-22	7	-2.3
1975 Tex-A	4	6	.400	25	14	1	0	0	93^1	105	56	46	7	1	47	32	1.629	4.44	85	5.01	.294	0	....	-7	3	-0.7
Total 10	100	111	.474	329	235	67	9	3	1728^2	1679	764	672	143	23	550	667	1.289	3.50	96	3.53	.256	69	.183	-41	91	-3.0

• WRIGHT, Dan

Jonathan Daniel Wright b: 12/14/1977, Longview, TX BR/TR, 6'5", 225 lbs. Deb: 7/27/2001

YEAR TM-L	W	L	PCT	G	GS	CG	SH	SV	IP	H	R	ER	HR	HB	BB	SO	RAT	ERA	ERA+	CERA	OAV	BH	AVG	PR+	WS	TPW
2001 Chi-A	5	3	.625	13	12	0	0	0	66^1	78	45	42	12	2	39	36	1.764	5.70	81	6.74	.300	0	....	-8	2	-0.8
2002 Chi-A	14	12	.538	33	33	1	1	0	196^1	200	124	113	32	6	71	136	1.380	5.18	88	4.55	.263	0	.000	-15	7	-1.5
2003 Chi-A	1	7	.125	20	15	0	0	1	86^1	91	63	59	16	3	46	47	1.587	6.15	73	5.72	.277	0	.000	-17	0	-1.7
Total 3	20	22	.476	66	60	1	1	1	349	369	232	214	60	11	156	219	1.504	5.52	82	5.26	.273	0	.000	-41	9	-4.0

• WRIGHT, Dave

David William Wright b: 8/27/1875, Dennison, OH d: 1/18/1946, Dennison, OH BR/TR, 6', 185 lbs. Deb: 7/22/1895

YEAR TM-L	W	L	PCT	G	GS	CG	SH	SV	IP	H	R	ER	HR	HB	BB	SO	RAT	ERA	ERA+	CERA	OAV	BH	AVG	PR+	WS	TPW
1895 Pit-N	0	0	....	1	0	0	0	0	2	6	6	6	0	0	1	0	3.500	27.00	17	17.28	.509	0	.000	-5	0	-0.4
1897 Chi-N	1	0	1.000	1	1	1	0	0	7	17	14	12	1	2	2	4	2.714	15.43	29	14.82	.459	1	.333	-8	0	-0.7
Total 2	1	0	1.000	2	1	1	0	0	9	23	20	18	1	2	3	4	2.889	18.00	25	15.37	.471	1	.250	-13	0	-1.1

• WRIGHT, Ed

Henderson Edward Wright b: 5/15/1919, Dyersburg, TN d: 11/19/1995, Dyersburg, TN BR/TR, 6'1", 180 lbs. Deb: 7/29/1945

YEAR TM-L	W	L	PCT	G	GS	CG	SH	SV	IP	H	R	ER	HR	HB	BB	SO	RAT	ERA	ERA+	CERA	OAV	BH	AVG	PR+	WS	TPW
1945 Bos-N	8	3	.727	15	12	7	1	0	111^1	104	35	31	7	0	33	24	1.231	2.51	153	3.11	.254	5	.128	16	10	1.4
1946 Bos-N	12	9	.571	36	21	9	2	0	176^1	164	82	69	8	2	71	44	1.333	3.52	97	3.30	.250	18	.305	-1	11	0.5
1947 Bos-N	3	3	.500	23	6	1	0	0	64^2	80	52	46	9	2	35	14	1.778	6.40	61	6.32	.305	3	.130	-17	0	-1.7
1948 Bos-N	0	0	....	3	0	0	0	0	4^2	9	3	1	0	0	2	2	2.357	1.93	199	10.05	.474	0	....	1	0	0.1
1952 Phi-A	2	1	.667	24	0	0	0	1	41^1	55	36	30	6	3	20	9	1.815	6.53	61	6.87	.320	1	.143	-11	0	-1.2
Total 5	25	16	.610	101	39	17	3	1	398^1	412	208	177	30	7	161	93	1.438	4.00	92	4.19	.271	27	.211	-12	21	-0.8

• WRIGHT, Gene

Clarence Eugene "Big Gene" Wright b: 12/11/1878, Cleveland, OH d: 10/29/1930, Barberton, OH BR/TR, 6'2", 185 lbs. Deb: 10/5/1901

YEAR TM-L	W	L	PCT	G	GS	CG	SH	SV	IP	H	R	ER	HR	HB	BB	SO	RAT	ERA	ERA+	CERA	OAV	BH	AVG	PR+	WS	TPW
1901 Bro-N	1	0	1.000	1	1	1	0	0	9	6	2	1	0	0	1	6	.778	1.00	335	1.11	.189	1	.333	2	1	0.2
1902 Cle-A	7	11	.389	21	18	15	1	1	148	150	94	65	6	8	75	52	1.520	3.95	87	4.20	.264	10	.143	-9	5	-1.1
1903 Cle-A	3	9	.250	15	12	8	0	0	101^2	122	94	65	1	4	58	42	1.770	5.75	50	5.01	.296	9	.209	-34	1	-3.3
StL-A	3	5	.375	8	8	7	1	0	61	73	29	25	2	4	16	37	1.459	3.69	79	4.41	.296	3	.143	-5	2	-0.6
Yr.	6	14	.300	23	20	15	1	0	162^2	195	123	90	3	8	74	79	**1.654**	4.98	58	4.78	.296	12	.188	-39	3	-3.9
1904 StL-A	0	1	.000	1	1	0	0	0	4	10	6	6	0	0	2	3	3.000	13.50	18	13.67	.469	0	.000	-5	0	-0.6
Total 4	14	26	.350	46	40	31	2	1	323^2	361	225	162	9	16	152	140	1.585	4.50	68	4.52	.282	23	.167	-51	9	-5.3

• WRIGHT, Harry

William Henry Wright b: 1/10/1835, Sheffield, England d: 10/3/1895, Atlantic City, NJ BR/TR, 5'9.5", 157 lbs. Deb: 5/5/1871 M/U HOF: 1953 ♦

YEAR TM-L	W	L	PCT	G	GS	CG	SH	SV	IP	H	R	ER	HR	HB	BB	SO	RAT	ERA	ERA+	CERA	OAV	BH	AVG	PR+	WS	TPW
1871 Bos-n	1	0	1.000	9	0	0	0	**3**	18^2	34	31	13	0	....	4	0	2.036	6.27	66	....	.347	44	.299	-5	....	-0.2
1872 Bos-n	1	0	1.000	7	0	0	0	**4**	25^2	26	12	6	0	....	0	1	1.013	2.10	177	....	.228	52	.250	2	....	-0.4
1873 Bos-n	2	2	.500	13	5	0	0	**4**	38^1	65	46	18	0	....	7	0	1.878	4.23	78	....	.335	67	.252	-4	....	-1.0
1874 Bos-n	0	2	.000	6	2	0	0	**3**	16^2	24	13	4	0	....	4	0	1.680	2.16	110	....	.303	58	.315	0	....	0.2
Total 4 n	4	4	.500	35	7	0	0	14	99^1	149	102	41	0	....	15	1	1.651	3.71	93	....	.307	222	.274	-6	....	-1.4

• WRIGHT, Jamey

Jamey Alan Wright b: 12/24/1974, Oklahoma City, OK BR/TR, 6'6", 205 lbs. Deb: 7/3/1996

YEAR TM-L	W	L	PCT	G	GS	CG	SH	SV	IP	H	R	ER	HR	HB	BB	SO	RAT	ERA	ERA+	CERA	OAV	BH	AVG	PR+	WS	TPW
1996 Col-N	4	4	.500	16	15	0	0	0	91^1	105	60	50	8	7	41	45	1.599	4.93	106	5.50	.298	2	.077	5	5	0.4
1997 Col-N	8	12	.400	26	26	1	0	0	149^2	198	113	104	19	11	71	59	1.797	6.25	83	6.96	.327	6	.125	-16	3	-1.7
1998 Col-N	9	14	.391	34	34	1	0	0	206^1	235	143	130	24	11	95	86	**1.599**	5.67	91	5.57	.294	10	.175	-12	8	-1.0
1999 Col-N	4	3	.571	16	16	0	0	0	94^1	110	52	51	10	4	54	49	1.739	4.87	119	6.19	.307	4	.125	10	7	0.8
2000 Mil-N	7	9	.438	26	25	0	0	0	164^2	157	81	75	12	18	88	96	1.488	4.10	111	4.67	.261	3	.065	6	9	0.2
2001 Mil-N	11	12	.478	33	33	1	1	0	194^2	201	115	106	26	20	98	129	1.536	4.90	88	5.36	.272	13	.194	-14	7	-1.2
2002 Mil-N	5	13	.278	19	19	1	1	0	114^1	115	72	68	15	11	63	69	1.557	5.35	76	5.28	.270	5	.152	-16	1	-1.5
StL-N	2	0	1.000	4	3	0	0	0	15	15	8	8	2	0	12	8	1.800	4.80	82	5.87	.259	0	.000	-2	1	-0.2
Yr.	7	13	.350	23	22	1	1	0	129^1	130	80	76	17	11	75	77	1.585	5.29	77	5.35	.269	5	.132	-17	2	-1.8
2003 KC-A	1	2	.333	4	4	2	1	0	25^1	23	14	12	1	1	11	19	1.342	4.26	121	3.53	.245	0	....	3	2	0.2
Total 8	51	69	.425	178	175	6	3	0	1055^2	1159	658	604	117	83	533	560	1.603	5.15	93	5.56	.287	43	.137	-36	43	-3.9

• WRIGHT, Jaret

Jaret Samuel Wright b: 12/29/1975, Anaheim, CA BR/TR, 6'2", 220 lbs. Deb: 6/24/1997

YEAR TM-L	W	L	PCT	G	GS	CG	SH	SV	IP	H	R	ER	HR	HB	BB	SO	RAT	ERA	ERA+	CERA	OAV	BH	AVG	PR+	WS	TPW
1997* Cle-A	8	3	.727	16	16	0	0	0	90^1	81	45	44	9	5	35	63	1.284	4.38	107	3.63	.238	0	.000	4	6	0.3
1998* Cle-A	12	10	.545	32	32	1	1	0	192^2	207	109	101	22	11	87	140	1.526	4.72	101	5.07	.277	3	.429	2	11	0.3
1999* Cle-A	8	10	.444	26	26	0	0	0	133^2	144	99	90	18	7	77	91	1.653	6.06	83	5.77	.277	0	.000	-14	3	-1.3
2000 Cle-A	3	4	.429	9	9	1	1	0	51^2	44	27	27	6	1	28	36	1.394	4.70	106	4.13	.235	0	.000	2	3	0.2
2001 Cle-A	2	2	.500	7	7	0	0	0	29	36	23	21	2	0	22	18	2.000	6.52	69	6.82	.313	1	.500	-6	0	-0.5
2002 Cle-A	2	3	.400	8	6	0	0	0	18^1	40	34	32	3	2	19	12	3.218	15.71	28	15.90	.435	0	....	-23	0	-2.2

YEAR TM-L	W	L	PCT	G	GS	CG	SH	SV	IP	H	R	ER	HR	HB	BB	SO	RAT	ERA	ERA+	CERA	OAV	BH	AVG	PR+	WS	TPW
2003 SD-N	1	5	.167	39	0	0	0	2	47^1	69	44	44	9	2	28	41	2.049	8.37	47	8.71	.348	1	.250	-23	0	-2.2
*Atl-N	1	0	1.000	11	0	0	0	0	9	7	2	2	0	1	3	9	1.111	2.00	211	2.51	.226	0	....	2	1	0.2
Yr.	2	5	.286	50	0	0	0	2	56^1	76	46	46	9	3	31	50	1.899	7.35	54	7.72	.332	1	.250	-21	1	-2.0
Total 7	37	37	.500	148	96	2	2	2	572	628	383	361	69	29	299	410	1.621	5.68	82	5.62	.282	5	.278	-56	24	-5.3

• WRIGHT, Jim
James "Jiggs" Wright b: 9/19/1900, Hyde, England d: 4/11/1963, Oakland, CA BR/TR, 6'2.5", 195 lbs. Deb: 9/14/1927

YEAR TM-L	W	L	PCT	G	GS	CG	SH	SV	IP	H	R	ER	HR	HB	BB	SO	RAT	ERA	ERA+	CERA	OAV	BH	AVG	PR+	WS	TPW
1927 StL-A	1	0	1.000	2	1	1	0	0	12	8	6	6	0	0	4	4	1.000	4.50	97	1.49	.182	0	.000	-0	1	-0.1
1928 StL-A	0	0	....	2	0	0	0	0	2	3	3	3	0	0	2	2	2.500	13.50	31	8.24	.375	0	....	-2	0	-0.2
Total 2	1	0	1.000	4	1	1	0	0	14	11	9	9	0	0	6	6	1.214	5.79	74	2.46	.212	0	.000	-2	1	-0.3

• WRIGHT, Jim
James Clifton Wright b: 12/21/1950, Reed City, MI BR/TR, 6'1", 165 lbs. Deb: 4/15/1978

YEAR TM-L	W	L	PCT	G	GS	CG	SH	SV	IP	H	R	ER	HR	HB	BB	SO	RAT	ERA	ERA+	CERA	OAV	BH	AVG	PR+	WS	TPW
1978 Bos-A	8	4	.667	24	16	5	3	0	116	122	51	46	8	7	24	56	1.259	3.57	115	3.69	.276	0	....	6	8	0.6
1979 Bos-A	1	0	1.000	11	1	0	0	0	23	19	13	13	5	3	7	15	1.130	5.09	87	3.99	.226	0	....	-2	1	-0.2
Total 2	9	4	.692	35	17	5	3	0	139	141	64	59	13	10	31	71	1.237	3.82	109	3.74	.268	0	....	5	9	0.5

• WRIGHT, Jim
James Leon Wright b: 3/3/1955, St. Joseph, MO BR/TR, 6'5", 205 lbs. Deb: 4/22/1981 C

YEAR TM-L	W	L	PCT	G	GS	CG	SH	SV	IP	H	R	ER	HR	HB	BB	SO	RAT	ERA	ERA+	CERA	OAV	BH	AVG	PR+	WS	TPW
1981 KC-A	2	3	.400	17	4	0	0	0	52	57	21	20	5	2	21	27	1.500	3.46	104	4.55	.277	0	....	1	3	0.1
1982 KC-A	0	0	....	7	0	0	0	0	23^2	32	18	14	3	0	6	9	1.606	5.32	77	5.65	.320	0	....	-3	0	-0.3
Total 2	2	3	.400	24	4	0	0	0	75^2	89	39	34	8	2	27	36	1.533	4.04	94	4.89	.291	0	....	-2	3	-0.2

• WRIGHT, Ken
Kenneth Warren Wright b: 9/4/1946, Pensacola, FL BR/TR, 6'2", 210 lbs. Deb: 4/10/1970

YEAR TM-L	W	L	PCT	G	GS	CG	SH	SV	IP	H	R	ER	HR	HB	BB	SO	RAT	ERA	ERA+	CERA	OAV	BH	AVG	PR+	WS	TPW
1970 KC-A	1	2	.333	47	0	0	0	3	53^1	49	33	31	2	7	29	30	1.463	5.23	71	4.39	.261	0	.000	-9	1	-1.0
1971 KC-A	3	6	.333	21	12	1	1	1	78	66	34	32	6	3	47	56	1.449	3.69	93	3.97	.230	2	.091	-2	3	-0.3
1972 KC-A	1	2	.333	17	0	0	0	4	18^1	15	10	10	0	1	15	18	1.636	4.91	62	4.00	.231	0	.000	-4	0	-0.4
1973 KC-A	6	5	.545	25	12	1	0	0	80^2	60	48	44	6	0	82	75	1.760	4.91	84	4.87	.210	0	....	-6	3	-0.6
1974 NY-A	0	0	....	3	0	0	0	0	5^2	5	2	2	0	0	7	2	2.118	3.18	110	5.69	.227	0	....	0	0	0.0
Total 5	11	15	.423	113	24	2	1	8	236	195	127	119	14	11	180	181	1.589	4.54	81	4.42	.230	2	.071	-21	7	-2.4

• WRIGHT, Lucky
William Simmons "William The Red,Deacon" Wright b: 2/21/1880, Waterville, OH d: 7/7/1941, Tontogany, OH BR/TR, 6', 178 lbs. Deb: 4/18/1909

YEAR TM-L	W	L	PCT	G	GS	CG	SH	SV	IP	H	R	ER	HR	HB	BB	SO	RAT	ERA	ERA+	CERA	OAV	BH	AVG	PR+	WS	TPW
1909 Cle-A	0	4	.000	5	4	3	0	0	28	21	16	10	0	0	7	5	1.000	3.21	79	1.80	.223	0	.000	-2	0	-0.4

• WRIGHT, Mel
Melvin James Wright b: 5/11/1928, Manila, AR d: 5/16/1983, Houston, TX BR/TR, 6'3", 210 lbs. Deb: 4/17/1954 C

YEAR TM-L	W	L	PCT	G	GS	CG	SH	SV	IP	H	R	ER	HR	HB	BB	SO	RAT	ERA	ERA+	CERA	OAV	BH	AVG	PR+	WS	TPW
1954 StL-N	0	0	....	9	0	0	0	0	10^1	16	15	12	2	2	11	4	2.613	10.45	39	11.83	.348	0	.000	-7	0	-0.7
1955 StL-N	2	2	.500	29	0	0	0	1	36^1	44	26	25	4	1	9	18	1.459	6.19	66	4.74	.308	0	.000	-8	0	-0.9
1960 Chi-N	0	1	.000	9	0	0	0	2	16^1	17	9	9	1	0	3	8	1.224	4.96	76	3.15	.279	0	.000	-2	1	-0.2
1961 Chi-N	0	1	.000	11	0	0	0	0	21	42	26	25	3	0	4	6	2.190	10.71	39	9.85	.416	0	.000	-15	0	-1.5
Total 4	2	4	.333	58	0	0	0	3	84	119	76	71	10	3	27	36	1.738	7.61	53	6.58	.339	0	.000	-32	1	-3.4

• WRIGHT, Rasty
Wayne Bromley Wright b: 11/5/1895, Ceredo, WV d: 6/12/1948, Columbus, OH BR/TR, 5'11", 160 lbs. Deb: 6/22/1917

YEAR TM-L	W	L	PCT	G	GS	CG	SH	SV	IP	H	R	ER	HR	HB	BB	SO	RAT	ERA	ERA+	CERA	OAV	BH	AVG	PR+	WS	TPW
1917 StL-A	0	1	.000	16	1	0	0	0	39^2	48	31	24	0	1	10	5	1.462	5.45	48	3.99	.300	2	.200	-13	0	-1.3
1918 StL-A	8	2	.800	18	13	6	1	0	111^1	99	39	31	1	5	18	25	1.051	2.51	109	2.19	.244	10	.294	2	9	0.6
1919 StL-A	0	5	.000	24	5	2	0	0	63^1	79	44	39	1	1	20	14	1.563	5.54	60	4.70	.315	1	.083	-16	0	-1.8
1922 StL-A	9	7	.563	31	16	5	0	5	154	148	64	50	7	8	50	44	1.286	2.92	141	3.37	.262	7	.140	17	13	1.5
1923 StL-A	7	4	.636	20	8	4	0	0	82^2	107	64	59	6	5	34	26	1.706	6.42	65	5.73	.317	6	.222	-22	1	-2.1
Total 5	24	19	.558	109	43	17	1	5	451	481	242	203	15	20	132	114	1.359	4.05	86	3.75	.280	26	.195	-31	23	-3.1

• WRIGHT, Ricky
James Richard Wright b: 11/22/1958, Paris, TX BL/TL, 6'3", 175 lbs. Deb: 7/28/1982

YEAR TM-L	W	L	PCT	G	GS	CG	SH	SV	IP	H	R	ER	HR	HB	BB	SO	RAT	ERA	ERA+	CERA	OAV	BH	AVG	PR+	WS	TPW
1982 LA-N	2	1	.667	14	5	0	0	0	32^2	28	12	11	1	0	20	24	1.469	3.03	114	3.23	.233	1	.125	2	2	0.2
1983 LA-N	0	0	....	6	0	0	0	0	6^1	5	2	2	0	0	2	5	1.105	2.84	126	1.79	.227	0	....	1	0	0.1
Tex-A	0	0	....	1	0	0	0	0	2	0	0	0	0	0	1	2	.500	0.00	....	0.24	.000	0	....	1	0	0.1
1984 Tex-A	0	2	.000	8	1	0	0	0	14^2	20	10	10	3	0	11	6	2.114	6.14	68	9.32	.357	0	....	-3	0	-0.3
1985 Tex-A	0	0	....	5	0	0	0	0	7^2	5	4	4	0	0	5	7	1.304	4.70	90	2.31	.185	0	....	-0	0	0.0
1986 Tex-A	1	0	1.000	21	1	0	0	0	39^1	44	22	22	1	0	21	23	1.653	5.03	85	4.76	.284	0	....	-3	1	-0.3
Total 5	3	3	.500	55	7	0	0	0	102^2	102	50	49	5	0	60	67	1.578	4.30	93	4.47	.268	1	.125	-3	3	-0.3

• WRIGHT, Roy
Roy Earl Wright b: 9/26/1933, Buchtel, OH BR/TR, 6'2", 170 lbs. Deb: 9/30/1956

YEAR TM-L	W	L	PCT	G	GS	CG	SH	SV	IP	H	R	ER	HR	HB	BB	SO	RAT	ERA	ERA+	CERA	OAV	BH	AVG	PR+	WS	TPW
1956 NY-N	0	1	.000	1	1	0	0	0	2^2	8	5	5	1	0	2	0	3.750	16.88	22	24.25	.533	0	.000	-4	0	-0.4

• WUNSCH, Kelly
Kelly Douglas Wunsch b: 7/12/1972, Houston, TX BL/TL, 6'5", 225 lbs. Deb: 4/3/2000

YEAR TM-L	W	L	PCT	G	GS	CG	SH	SV	IP	H	R	ER	HR	HB	BB	SO	RAT	ERA	ERA+	CERA	OAV	BH	AVG	PR+	WS	TPW
2000* Chi-A	6	3	.667	**83**	0	0	0	1	61^1	50	22	20	4	2	29	51	1.288	2.93	170	3.22	.221	0	....	13	8	1.2
2001 Chi-A	2	1	.667	33	0	0	0	0	22^1	21	19	19	4	6	9	16	1.343	7.66	60	5.11	.247	0	....	-8	0	-0.7
2002 Chi-A	2	1	.667	50	0	0	0	0	31^2	26	12	12	3	5	19	22	1.421	3.41	134	4.51	.230	0	....	4	3	0.4
2003 Chi-A	0	0	....	43	0	0	0	0	36	17	13	11	1	7	25	33	1.167	2.75	163	2.28	.139	0	....	6	3	0.6
Total 4	10	5	.667	209	0	0	0	1	151^1	114	66	62	12	20	82	122	1.295	3.69	127	3.55	.209	0	....	16	14	1.4

• WURM, Frank
Frank James Wurm b: 4/27/1924, Cambridge, NY d: 9/19/1993, Glens Falls, NY BB/TL, 6'1", 175 lbs. Deb: 9/4/1944

YEAR TM-L	W	L	PCT	G	GS	CG	SH	SV	IP	H	R	ER	HR	HB	BB	SO	RAT	ERA	ERA+	CERA	OAV	BH	AVG	PR+	WS	TPW
1944 Bro-N	0	0	....	1	1	0	0	0	0^1	1	4	4	0	0	5	1	18.00	108.00	3	80.25	.500	0	....	-4	0	-0.4

• WYATT, John
John Thomas Wyatt b: 4/19/1935, Chicago, IL d: 4/6/1998, Omaha, NE BR/TR, 5'11.5", 200 lbs. Deb: 9/8/1961

YEAR TM-L	W	L	PCT	G	GS	CG	SH	SV	IP	H	R	ER	HR	HB	BB	SO	RAT	ERA	ERA+	CERA	OAV	BH	AVG	PR+	WS	TPW
1961 KC-A	0	0	....	5	0	0	0	1	7^1	8	3	2	0	1	4	6	1.636	2.45	168	4.79	.296	0	....	1	1	0.1
1962 KC-A	10	7	.588	59	9	0	0	11	125	121	66	62	12	5	80	106	1.608	4.46	93	4.88	.253	3	.103	-3	9	-0.5
1963 KC-A	6	4	.600	63	0	0	0	21	92	83	37	32	12	0	43	81	1.370	3.13	123	3.90	.239	0	.000	8	12	0.7
1964 KC-A★	9	8	.529	**81**	0	0	0	20	128	111	53	51	23	1	52	74	1.273	3.59	107	3.87	.236	0	.000	5	12	0.4
1965 KC-A	2	6	.250	65	0	0	0	18	88^2	78	36	32	8	4	53	70	1.477	3.25	107	3.99	.241	0	.000	3	7	0.3
1966 KC-A	0	3	.000	19	0	0	0	2	23^2	19	14	14	3	2	16	25	1.479	5.32	64	4.18	.213	0	....	-5	0	-0.6
Bos-A	3	4	.429	42	0	0	0	8	71^2	59	27	25	3	4	27	63	1.200	3.14	121	2.82	.229	0	.000	6	7	0.5
Yr.	3	7	.300	61	0	0	0	10	95^1	78	41	39	6	6	43	88	1.269	3.68	99	3.16	.225	0	.000	1	7	-0.1
1967* Bos-A	10	7	.588	60	0	0	0	20	93^1	71	30	27	6	2	39	68	1.179	2.60	134	2.69	.217	1	.083	10	14	1.0
1968 Bos-A	1	2	.333	8	0	0	0	0	10^2	9	7	5	2	1	6	11	1.406	4.22	75	4.86	.231	0	....	-1	0	-0.1
NY-A	0	2	.000	7	0	0	0	0	8^1	7	3	2	1	0	9	6	1.920	2.16	134	5.74	.219	0	.000	1	0	0.1
Det-A	1	0	1.000	22	0	0	0	2	30^1	26	9	8	2	1	11	25	1.220	2.37	127	3.01	.236	0	.000	2	3	0.2
Yr.	2	4	.333	37	0	0	0	2	49^1	42	19	15	5	2	26	42	1.378	2.74	111	3.87	.232	0	.000	2	3	0.2
1969 Oak-A	0	1	.000	4	0	0	0	0	8^1	8	5	5	0	2	6	5	1.680	5.40	64	4.99	.250	0	.000	-2	0	-0.2
Total 9	42	44	.488	435	9	0	0	103	687^1	600	290	265	72	23	346	540	1.376	3.47	107	3.84	.237	4	.048	24	65	2.0

• WYATT, Whit
John Whitlow Wyatt b: 9/27/1907, Kensington, GA d: 7/16/1999, Carrollton, GA BR/TR, 6'1", 185 lbs. Deb: 9/16/1929 C

YEAR TM-L	W	L	PCT	G	GS	CG	SH	SV	IP	H	R	ER	HR	HB	BB	SO	RAT	ERA	ERA+	CERA	OAV	BH	AVG	PR+	WS	TPW
1929 Det-A	0	1	.000	4	4	1	0	0	25^1	30	22	19	1	1	18	14	1.895	6.75	63	5.91	.309	1	.100	-6	0	-0.7
1930 Det-A	4	5	.444	21	7	2	0	2	85^2	76	41	34	6	3	35	68	1.296	3.57	134	3.32	.239	12	.353	12	9	1.3
1931 Det-A	0	2	.000	4	1	1	0	0	20^1	30	23	20	2	1	12	8	2.066	8.85	52	8.10	.361	2	.286	-10	0	-0.9
1932 Det-A	9	13	.409	43	22	10	0	1	205^2	228	136	115	12	3	102	82	1.605	5.03	93	4.70	.286	15	.192	-11	8	-1.0
1933 Det-A	0	1	.000	10	0	0	0	0	17	20	9	8	1	2	9	9	1.706	4.24	102	5.52	.299	0	.000	-0	1	0.0
Chi-A	3	4	.429	26	7	2	0	1	87^2	91	51	45	7	2	45	31	1.551	4.62	92	4.47	.266	6	.214	-3	4	-0.2
Yr.	3	5	.375	36	7	2	0	1	104^2	111	60	53	8	4	54	40	1.576	4.56	93	4.64	.271	6	.200	-3	5	-0.3
1934 Chi-A	4	11	.267	23	6	2	0	2	67^2	83	59	54	10	1	37	36	1.773	7.18	66	6.30	.303	6	.231	-17	0	-1.5
1935 Chi-A	4	3	.571	30	1	0	0	5	52	65	41	39	6	2	25	22	1.731	6.75	68	5.97	.308	3	.231	-13	2	-1.1
1936 Chi-A	0	0	....	3	0	0	0	1	3	3	0	0	0	0	0	0	1.000	0.00	....	2.18	.273	0	....	2	1	0.1
1937 Cle-A	2	3	.400	29	4	2	0	0	73	67	38	36	3	0	40	52	1.466	4.44	104	3.58	.244	7	.389	2	6	0.5
1939 Bro-N★	8	3	.727	16	14	6	2	0	109	88	34	28	3	2	39	52	1.165	2.31	174	2.39	.224	6	.167	21	12	2.1

YEAR TM-L	W	L	PCT	G	GS	CG	SH	SV	IP	H	R	ER	HR	HB	BB	SO	RAT	ERA	ERA+	CERA	OAV	BH	AVG	PR+	WS	TPW
1940 Bro-N★	15	14	.517	37	34	16	**5**	0	239^1	233	105	92	19	5	62	124	1.233	3.46	116	3.26	.254	14	.175	15	16	1.5
1941* Bro-N★	**22**	10	.688	38	35	23	**7**	1	288^1	223	89	75	10	2	82	176	1.058	2.34	157	**2.06**	**.212**	26	.239	**38**	**28**	**4.5**
1942 Bro-N★	19	7	.731	31	30	16	0	0	217^1	185	82	66	9	7	63	104	1.141	2.73	119	2.51	.225	14	.182	10	16	1.2
1943 Bro-N	14	5	.737	26	26	13	3	0	180^2	139	55	50	5	0	43	80	1.007	2.49	135	**1.81**	**.207**	17	.283	20	16	2.6
1944 Bro-N	2	6	.250	9	9	1	0	0	37^2	51	37	30	1	2	16	4	1.779	7.17	50	5.46	.311	2	.154	-14	0	-1.5
1945 Phi-N	0	7	.000	10	10	2	0	0	51^1	72	38	30	3	0	14	10	1.675	5.26	73	5.40	.330	2	.125	-7	0	-0.6
Total 16	106	95	.527	360	210	97	17	13	1761	1684	860	741	98	33	642	872	1.321	3.79	107	3.43	.251	133	.219	40	119	6.4

• WYCKOFF, Weldon John Weldon Wyckoff b: 2/19/1892, Williamsport, PA d: 5/8/1961, Sheboygan Falls, WI BR/TR, 6'1", 175 lbs. Deb: 4/19/1913

YEAR TM-L	W	L	PCT	G	GS	CG	SH	SV	IP	H	R	ER	HR	HB	BB	SO	RAT	ERA	ERA+	CERA	OAV	BH	AVG	PR+	WS	TPW
1913 Phi-A	2	4	.333	17	7	4	0	0	61^2	56	44	30	1	3	46	31	1.654	4.38	63	4.09	.233	4	.190	-11	0	-1.2
1914* Phi-A	11	7	.611	32	20	11	0	2	185	153	82	62	2	4	103	86	1.384	3.02	86	3.12	.228	11	.147	-9	8	-1.1
1915 Phi-A	10	22	.313	43	34	20	1	0	276	238	139	108	1	5	165	157	1.460	3.52	83	3.52	.246	12	.125	-16	5	-2.1
1916 Phi-A	0	1	.000	7	2	1	0	0	21^1	20	16	13	1	1	20	4	1.875	5.48	52	5.33	.247	3	.375	-6	0	-0.6
Bos-A	0	0	....	8	0	0	0	1	22^2	19	13	12	0	0	18	18	1.632	4.76	58	3.81	.232	1	.167	-5	0	-0.5
Yr.	0	1	.000	15	2	1	0	1	44	39	29	25	1	1	38	22	1.750	5.11	55	4.55	.239	4	.286	-11	0	-1.1
1917 Bos-A	0	0	....	1	0	0	0	0	5	4	3	1	0	1	4	1	1.600	1.80	143	4.26	.222	0	.000	0	0	0.0
1918 Bos-A	0	0	....	1	0	0	0	0	2	4	1	0	0	0	1	2	2.500	0.00	....	9.55	.400	0	.000	1	0	0.0
Total 6	23	34	.404	109	63	36	1	3	573^2	494	298	226	5	14	357	299	1.483	3.55	79	3.56	.239	31	.149	-46	13	-5.4

• WYNN, Early Early "Gus" Wynn b: 1/6/1920, Hartford, AL d: 4/4/1999, Venice, FL BB/TR, 6', 200 lbs. Deb: 9/13/1939 C HOF: 1972

YEAR TM-L	W	L	PCT	G	GS	CG	SH	SV	IP	H	R	ER	HR	HB	BB	SO	RAT	ERA	ERA+	CERA	OAV	BH	AVG	PR+	WS	TPW
1939 Was-A	0	2	.000	3	3	1	0	0	20^1	26	15	13	0	0	10	1	1.770	5.75	76	4.99	.313	1	.167	-3	0	-0.3
1941 Was-A	3	1	.750	5	5	4	0	0	40	35	14	7	1	0	10	15	1.125	1.58	257	2.25	.226	2	.133	11	4	1.1
1942 Was-A	10	16	.385	30	28	10	1	0	190	246	129	108	6	3	73	58	**1.679**	5.12	71	5.15	.314	15	.217	-23	3	-2.2
1943 Was-A	18	12	.600	37	**33**	12	3	0	256^2	232	97	83	15	1	83	89	1.227	2.91	110	2.93	.240	29	.296	9	19	1.7
1944 Was-A	8	17	.320	33	25	19	2	2	207^2	221	97	78	3	2	67	65	1.387	3.38	96	3.52	.277	19	.207	-1	8	0.1
1946 Was-A	8	5	.615	17	12	9	0	0	107	112	45	37	8	3	33	36	1.355	3.11	107	3.82	.267	15	.319	5	9	1.2
1947 Was-A	17	15	.531	33	31	22	2	0	247	251	114	100	13	5	90	73	1.381	3.64	102	3.70	.262	33	.275	6	20	1.4
1948 Was-A	8	19	.296	33	31	15	1	0	198	236	144	128	18	1	94	49	1.667	5.82	75	5.26	.295	23	.217	-29	3	-2.4
1949 Cle-A	11	7	.611	26	23	6	0	0	164^2	186	84	76	8	1	57	62	1.476	4.15	96	4.13	.282	10	.143	-5	8	-0.6
1950 Cle-A	18	8	.692	32	28	14	2	0	213^2	166	88	76	20	4	101	143	1.250	**3.20**	135	**3.03**	**.212**	18	.234	26	21	3.0
1951 Cle-A	20	13	.606	37	**34**	21	3	1	**274**^{1}	227	102	92	18	3	107	133	1.217	3.02	126	2.84	.225	20	.185	24	**24**	2.4
1952 Cle-A	23	12	.657	42	33	19	4	3	285^2	239	103	92	23	1	132	153	1.299	2.90	115	3.24	.231	22	.222	16	21	2.2
1953 Cle-A	17	12	.586	36	34	16	1	0	251^2	234	121	110	19	4	107	138	1.355	3.93	95	3.57	.245	25	.275	-5	16	0.3
1954* Cle-A	**23**	11	.676	40	**36**	20	3	2	**270**^{2}	225	93	82	21	0	83	155	1.138	2.73	135	2.62	.225	17	.183	24	**24**	2.6
1955 Cle-A★	17	11	.607	32	31	16	6	0	230	207	86	72	19	3	80	122	1.248	2.82	142	3.24	.240	15	.179	30	21	3.1
1956 Cle-A★	20	9	.690	38	35	18	4	2	277^2	233	93	84	19	5	91	158	1.167	2.72	154	2.76	.228	23	.228	47	**28**	**4.9**
1957 Cle-A★	14	17	.452	40	**37**	13	1	1	263	270	139	126	32	5	104	**184**	1.422	4.31	86	4.38	.265	10	.116	-14	10	-1.6
1958 Chi-A★	14	16	.467	40	34	11	4	2	239^2	214	115	110	27	6	104	**179**	1.327	4.13	88	3.81	.242	15	.200	-16	11	-1.4
1959* Chi-A★	**22**	10	.688	37	**37**	14	5	0	**255**^{2}	202	106	90	20	9	119	179	1.256	3.17	118	3.15	.216	22	.244	12	23	2.1
1960 Chi-A★	13	12	.520	36	35	13	**4**	1	237^1	220	105	92	20	4	112	158	1.399	3.49	108	3.90	.247	15	.200	4	16	1.1
1961 Chi-A	8	2	.800	17	16	5	0	0	110^1	88	43	43	11	1	47	64	1.224	3.51	112	3.13	.220	6	.162	6	9	0.6
1962 Chi-A	7	15	.318	27	26	11	3	0	167^2	171	90	83	15	3	56	91	1.354	4.46	88	3.91	.264	7	.130	-9	5	-0.9
1963 Cle-A	1	2	.333	20	5	1	0	1	55^1	50	14	14	2	0	15	29	1.175	2.28	159	2.64	.250	3	.273	9	6	1.0
Total 23	300	244	.551	691	612	290	49	15	4564	4291	2037	1796	338	64	1775	2334	1.329	3.54	106	3.53	.248	365	.214	123	309	19.4

• WYNNE, Bill William Andrew Wynne b: 3/27/1869, Neuse, NC d: 8/7/1951, Raleigh, NC BR/TR, 5'11.5", 161 lbs. Deb: 8/31/1894

YEAR TM-L	W	L	PCT	G	GS	CG	SH	SV	IP	H	R	ER	HR	HB	BB	SO	RAT	ERA	ERA+	CERA	OAV	BH	AVG	PR+	WS	TPW
1894 Was-N	0	1	.000	1	1	1	0	0	8	10	11	6	0	2	8	2	2.250	6.75	78	7.77	.303	0	.000	-1	0	-0.1

• WYNNE, Billy Billy Vernon Wynne b: 7/31/1943, Williamston, NC BL/TR, 6'3", 206 lbs. Deb: 8/6/1967

YEAR TM-L	W	L	PCT	G	GS	CG	SH	SV	IP	H	R	ER	HR	HB	BB	SO	RAT	ERA	ERA+	CERA	OAV	BH	AVG	PR+	WS	TPW
1967 NY-N	0	0	....	6	1	0	0	0	8^2	12	4	3	0	0	2	4	1.615	3.12	109	4.59	.324	0	.000	0	0	0.0
1968 Chi-A	0	0	....	1	0	0	0	0	2	2	2	1	0	0	2	1	2.000	4.50	67	5.48	.250	0	....	-0	0	0.0
1969 Chi-A	7	7	.500	20	20	6	1	0	128^2	143	63	58	14	3	50	67	1.500	4.06	95	4.77	.283	5	.122	-1	7	-0.1
1970 Chi-A	1	4	.200	12	9	0	0	0	44	54	30	26	8	1	22	19	1.727	5.32	73	6.28	.298	1	.077	-6	0	-0.7
1971 Cal-A	0	0	....	3	0	0	0	0	3^2	6	2	2	0	0	2	6	2.182	4.91	66	7.97	.375	0	....	-1	0	-0.1
Total 5	8	11	.421	42	30	6	1	0	187	217	101	90	22	4	78	97	1.578	4.33	88	5.18	.290	6	.109	-8	7	-1.0

• WYSE, Hank Henry Washington "Hooks" Wyse b: 3/1/1918, Lunsford, AR d: 10/22/2000, Pryor, OK BR/TR, 5'11.5", 185 lbs. Deb: 9/7/1942

YEAR TM-L	W	L	PCT	G	GS	CG	SH	SV	IP	H	R	ER	HR	HB	BB	SO	RAT	ERA	ERA+	CERA	OAV	BH	AVG	PR+	WS	TPW
1942 Chi-N	2	1	.667	4	4	1	1	0	28	33	10	6	1	0	6	8	1.393	1.93	166	3.77	.287	1	.125	4	2	0.5
1943 Chi-N	9	7	.563	38	15	8	2	5	156	159	57	51	4	2	34	45	1.237	2.94	113	3.00	.264	4	.080	10	10	0.7
1944 Chi-N	16	15	.516	41	34	14	3	1	257^1	277	113	90	9	2	57	86	1.298	3.15	112	3.39	.278	16	.178	15	16	1.4
1945* Chi-N★	22	10	.688	38	34	23	2	0	278^1	272	95	83	17	5	55	77	1.175	2.68	136	2.96	.256	17	.168	26	**24**	2.3
1946 Chi-N	14	12	.538	40	27	12	2	1	201^1	206	73	60	7	3	52	52	1.281	2.68	124	3.22	.265	18	.243	18	16	2.0
1947 Chi-N	6	9	.400	37	19	5	1	1	142	158	84	68	12	3	64	53	1.563	4.31	92	4.79	.286	5	.111	-5	6	-0.7
1950 Phi-A	9	14	.391	41	23	4	0	0	170^2	192	121	111	16	8	87	33	1.635	5.85	78	5.30	.287	9	.153	-24	3	-2.5
1951 Phi-A	1	2	.333	9	1	0	0	0	14^2	24	14	13	0	0	8	5	2.182	7.98	54	7.79	.381	1	.250	-6	0	-0.6
Was-A	0	0	....	3	2	0	0	0	9^1	17	14	10	0	1	10	3	2.893	9.64	42	10.91	.378	0	.000	-6	0	-0.6
Yr.	1	2	.333	12	3	0	0	0	24	41	28	23	0	1	18	8	2.458	8.63	49	9.00	.380	1	.125	-12	0	-1.2
Total 8	79	70	.530	251	159	67	11	8	1257^2	1338	581	492	66	24	373	362	1.360	3.52	107	3.75	.274	71	.163	31	77	2.4

• WYSONG, Biff Harlan Wysong b: 4/13/1905, Clarkville, OH d: 8/8/1951, Xenia, OH BL/TL, 6'3", 195 lbs. Deb: 8/10/1930

YEAR TM-L	W	L	PCT	G	GS	CG	SH	SV	IP	H	R	ER	HR	HB	BB	SO	RAT	ERA	ERA+	CERA	OAV	BH	AVG	PR+	WS	TPW
1930 Cin-N	0	1	.000	1	1	0	0	0	2^1	6	5	5	0	0	3	1	3.857	19.29	25	17.07	.545	0	....	-4	0	-0.3
1931 Cin-N	0	2	.000	12	2	0	0	0	21^2	25	22	19	2	0	23	5	2.215	7.89	47	7.30	.298	1	.250	-10	0	-1.0
1932 Cin-N	1	0	1.000	7	0	0	0	0	12^1	13	7	5	0	0	8	5	1.703	3.65	106	4.28	.277	0	.000	0	1	0.0
Total 3	1	3	.250	20	3	0	0	0	36^1	44	34	29	2	0	34	11	2.147	7.18	54	6.90	.310	1	.167	-14	1	-1.3

• YAN, Esteban Esteban Luis Yan b: 6/22/1975, Campina Del Seibo, Dominican Republic BR/TR, 6'4", 230 lbs. Deb: 5/20/1996

YEAR TM-L	W	L	PCT	G	GS	CG	SH	SV	IP	H	R	ER	HR	HB	BB	SO	RAT	ERA	ERA+	CERA	OAV	BH	AVG	PR+	WS	TPW
1996 Bal-A	0	0	....	4	0	0	0	0	9^1	13	7	6	3	0	3	7	1.714	5.79	85	7.88	.333	0	....	-1	0	-0.1
1997 Bal-A	0	1	.000	3	2	0	0	0	9^2	20	18	17	3	2	7	4	2.793	15.83	28	15.60	.417	0	....	-12	0	-1.2
1998 TB-A	5	4	.556	64	0	0	0	1	88^2	78	41	38	11	5	41	77	1.342	3.86	124	4.02	.236	0	....	6	7	0.5
1999 TB-A	3	4	.429	50	1	0	0	0	61	77	41	40	8	9	32	46	1.787	5.90	84	7.13	.326	0	....	-6	2	-0.6
2000 TB-A	7	8	.467	43	20	0	0	0	137^2	158	98	95	26	11	42	111	1.453	6.21	79	5.46	.285	1	1.000	-22	4	-1.8
2001 TB-A	4	6	.400	54	0	0	0	22	62^1	64	34	27	7	5	11	64	1.203	3.90	115	3.68	.262	0	....	4	8	0.4
2002 TB-A	7	8	.467	55	0	0	0	19	69	70	35	33	10	3	29	53	1.435	4.30	104	4.67	.259	0	....	0	7	0.0
2003 Tex-A	0	1	.000	15	0	0	0	0	23^1	31	19	18	5	2	7	25	1.629	6.94	71	6.64	.307	0	....	-5	0	-0.5
StL-N	2	0	1.000	39	0	0	0	1	43^1	53	29	29	8	5	16	28	1.592	6.02	67	6.26	.308	1	1.000	-9	1	-0.9
Total 8	28	32	.467	327	23	0	0	43	504^1	564	322	303	81	42	188	415	1.491	5.41	87	5.44	.283	2	1.000	-45	29	-4.1

• YARNALL, Ed Harvey Edward Yarnall b: 12/4/1975, Lima, PA BL/TL, 6'3", 235 lbs. Deb: 7/15/1999

YEAR TM-L	W	L	PCT	G	GS	CG	SH	SV	IP	H	R	ER	HR	HB	BB	SO	RAT	ERA	ERA+	CERA	OAV	BH	AVG	PR+	WS	TPW
1999 NY-A	1	0	1.000	5	2	0	0	0	17	17	8	7	1	0	10	13	1.588	3.71	128	4.46	.254	0	....	2	1	0.2
2000 NY-A	0	0	....	2	1	0	0	0	3	5	5	5	1	1	3	1	2.667	15.00	32	16.77	.417	0	....	-3	0	-0.3
Total 2	1	0	1.000	7	3	0	0	0	20	22	13	12	2	1	13	14	1.750	5.40	88	6.30	.278	0	....	-1	1	-0.1

• YARNALL, Rusty Waldo Ward Yarnall b: 10/22/1902, Chicago, IL d: 10/9/1985, Lowell, MA BR/TR, 6', 175 lbs. Deb: 6/30/1926

YEAR TM-L	W	L	PCT	G	GS	CG	SH	SV	IP	H	R	ER	HR	HB	BB	SO	RAT	ERA	ERA+	CERA	OAV	BH	AVG	PR+	WS	TPW
1926 Phi-N	0	1	.000	1	0	0	0	0	1	3	2	2	0	0	1	0	4.000	18.00	23	16.66	.500	0	.000	-2	0	-0.2

• YARRISON, Rube Byron Wardsworth Yarrison b: 3/9/1896, Montgomery, PA d: 4/22/1977, Williamsport, PA BR/TR, 5'11", 165 lbs. Deb: 4/13/1922

YEAR	TM-L	W	L	PCT	G	GS	CG	SH	SV	IP	H	R	ER	HR	HB	BB	SO	RAT	ERA	ERA+	CERA	OAV	BH	AVG	PR+	WS	TPW
1922	Phi-A	1	2	.333	18	1	0	0	0	33^2	50	32	31	4	2	12	10	1.842	8.29	51	7.32	.362	1	.167	-15	0	-1.4
1924	Bro-N	0	2	.000	3	2	0	0	0	11	12	10	8	0	1	3	2	1.364	6.55	57	3.37	.267	0	.000	-3	0	-0.3
Total	2	1	4	.200	21	3	0	0	0	44^2	62	42	39	4	3	15	12	1.724	7.86	53	6.34	.339	1	.125	-18	0	-1.8

• YDE, Emil Emil Ogden Yde b: 1/28/1900, Great Lakes, IL d: 12/4/1968, Leesburg, FL BB/TL, 5'11", 165 lbs. Deb: 4/21/1924

YEAR	TM-L	W	L	PCT	G	GS	CG	SH	SV	IP	H	R	ER	HR	HB	BB	SO	RAT	ERA	ERA+	CERA	OAV	BH	AVG	PR+	WS	TPW
1924	Pit-N	16	3	.842	33	22	14	**4**	0	194	171	70	61	3	6	62	53	1.201	2.83	136	2.69	.244	21	.239	14	19	1.6
1925*	Pit-N	17	9	.654	33	28	13	0	0	207	254	125	95	11	2	75	41	1.589	4.13	108	4.91	.309	17	.191	3	12	0.1
1926	Pit-N	8	7	.533	37	22	12	1	0	187^1	181	97	76	3	2	81	34	1.399	3.65	108	3.33	.260	17	.230	3	11	0.5
1927*	Pit-N	1	3	.250	9	2	0	0	0	29^2	45	35	32	1	2	15	9	2.022	9.71	42	7.27	.375	3	.167	-19	0	-1.9
1929	Det-A	7	3	.700	29	6	4	1	0	86^2	100	60	51	8	0	63	23	1.881	5.30	81	6.06	.296	16	.333	-7	4	-0.3
Total	5	49	25	.662	141	80	43	6	0	704^2	751	387	315	26	12	296	160	1.486	4.02	103	4.12	.281	74	.233	-6	46	0.0

• YEAGER, Joe Joseph F. "Little Joe" Yeager b: 8/28/1875, Philadelphia, PA d: 7/2/1937, Detroit, MI BR/TR, 5'10", 160 lbs. Deb: 4/22/1898 ♦

YEAR	TM-L	W	L	PCT	G	GS	CG	SH	SV	IP	H	R	ER	HR	HB	BB	SO	RAT	ERA	ERA+	CERA	OAV	BH	AVG	PR+	WS	TPW
1898	Bro-N	12	22	.353	36	33	32	0	0	291^1	333	177	118	4	6	80	70	1.418	3.65	98	3.78	.285	23	.172	1	13	-0.3
1899	Bro-N	2	2	.500	10	4	2	1	1	47^2	56	29	25	1	2	16	6	1.510	4.72	83	4.30	.293	9	.191	-5	3	-0.5
1900	Bro-N	1	1	.500	2	2	2	0	0	17	21	13	13	1	0	5	2	1.529	6.88	56	4.62	.303	3	.333	-6	0	-0.6
1901	Det-A	12	11	.522	26	25	22	2	1	199^2	209	105	58	4	8	46	38	1.277	2.61	147	3.23	.266	37	.296	25	21	3.1
1902	Det-A	6	12	.333	19	15	14	0	0	140	171	90	75	5	5	41	28	1.514	4.82	76	4.50	.301	39	.242	-20	6	-2.0
1903	Det-A	0	1	.000	1	1	1	0	0	9	15	7	4	0	0	0	1	1.667	4.00	73	5.72	.369	103	.256	-1	9	-1.4
Total	6	33	49	.402	94	80	73	3	2	704^2	805	421	293	15	21	188	145	1.409	3.74	98	3.85	.285	467	.252	-6	52	-1.6

• YEARGIN, Al James Almond Yeargin b: 10/16/1901, Mauldin, SC d: 5/8/1937, Greenville, SC BR/TR, 5'11", 170 lbs. Deb: 10/1/1922

YEAR	TM-L	W	L	PCT	G	GS	CG	SH	SV	IP	H	R	ER	HR	HB	BB	SO	RAT	ERA	ERA+	CERA	OAV	BH	AVG	PR+	WS	TPW
1922	Bos-N	0	1	.000	1	1	1	0	0	7	5	3	1	1	0	2	1	1.000	1.29	311	2.33	.192	0	.000	2	1	0.2
1924	Bos-N	1	11	.083	32	12	6	0	0	141^1	162	90	80	7	3	42	34	1.443	5.09	75	4.12	.293	6	.143	-19	2	-2.0
Total	2	1	12	.077	33	13	7	0	0	148^1	167	93	81	8	3	44	35	1.422	4.91	78	4.04	.288	6	.133	-17	3	-1.9

• YELLEN, Larry Lawrence Alan Yellen b: 1/4/1943, Brooklyn, NY BR/TR, 5'11", 190 lbs. Deb: 9/26/1963

YEAR	TM-L	W	L	PCT	G	GS	CG	SH	SV	IP	H	R	ER	HR	HB	BB	SO	RAT	ERA	ERA+	CERA	OAV	BH	AVG	PR+	WS	TPW
1963	Hou-N	0	0	....	1	1	0	0	0	5	7	4	2	0	0	1	3	1.600	3.60	88	3.91	.280	0	.000	-0	0	0.0
1964	Hou-N	0	0	....	13	1	0	0	0	21	27	19	16	4	0	10	9	1.762	6.86	50	6.36	.297	0	.000	-8	0	-0.9
Total	2	0	0	....	14	2	0	0	0	26	34	23	18	4	0	11	12	1.731	6.23	54	5.89	.293	0	.000	-8	0	-0.9

• YELLOWHORSE, Chief Moses J. Yellowhorse b: 1/28/1898, Pawnee, OK d: 4/10/1964, Pawnee, OK BR/TR, 5'10", 180 lbs. Deb: 4/15/1921

YEAR	TM-L	W	L	PCT	G	GS	CG	SH	SV	IP	H	R	ER	HR	HB	BB	SO	RAT	ERA	ERA+	CERA	OAV	BH	AVG	PR+	WS	TPW
1921	Pit-N	5	3	.625	10	4	1	0	1	48^1	45	17	16	1	0	13	19	1.200	2.98	129	2.70	.254	0	.000	4	5	0.2
1922	Pit-N	3	1	.750	28	4	2	0	0	77^2	92	48	39	0	2	20	24	1.442	4.52	90	3.88	.305	6	.316	-3	4	-0.2
Total	2	8	4	.667	38	8	3	0	1	126	137	65	55	1	2	33	43	1.349	3.93	102	3.43	.286	6	.167	2	9	0.0

• YERKES, Carroll Charles Carroll "Lefty" Yerkes b: 6/13/1903, McSherrystown, PA d: 12/20/1950, Oakland, CA BR/TL, 5'11", 180 lbs. Deb: 5/31/1927

YEAR	TM-L	W	L	PCT	G	GS	CG	SH	SV	IP	H	R	ER	HR	HB	BB	SO	RAT	ERA	ERA+	CERA	OAV	BH	AVG	PR+	WS	TPW
1927	Phi-A	0	0	....	1	0	0	0	0	1	0	0	0	0	0	1	0	1.000	0.00	....	0.80	.000	0	....	0	0	0.0
1928	Phi-A	0	1	.000	2	1	1	0	0	8^2	7	2	2	0	0	2	1	1.038	2.08	193	1.72	.233	0	.000	2	1	0.1
1929	Phi-A	1	0	1.000	19	2	0	0	1	37^1	47	20	19	0	1	13	11	1.607	4.58	92	4.78	.329	0	.000	-2	2	-0.3
1932	Chi-N	0	0	....	2	0	0	0	0	9	5	3	3	2	0	3	4	.889	3.00	126	2.32	.167	1	.333	1	1	0.1
1933	Chi-N	0	0	....	1	0	0	0	0	2	2	1	1	0	0	1	0	1.500	4.50	73	3.50	.286	0	....	-0	0	0.0
Total	5	1	1	.500	25	3	1	0	1	58	61	26	25	2	1	20	16	1.397	3.88	106	3.83	.291	1	.063	1	4	-0.1

• YERKES, Stan Stanley Lewis "Yank" Yerkes b: 11/28/1874, Cheltenham, PA d: 7/28/1940, Boston, MA BR/TR, 5'10", 165 lbs. Deb: 5/3/1901

YEAR	TM-L	W	L	PCT	G	GS	CG	SH	SV	IP	H	R	ER	HR	HB	BB	SO	RAT	ERA	ERA+	CERA	OAV	BH	AVG	PR+	WS	TPW
1901	Bal-A	0	1	.000	1	1	1	0	0	8	12	9	6	0	0	2	4	1.750	6.75	57	5.55	.342	1	.333	-2	0	-0.2
	StL-N	3	1	.750	4	4	4	0	0	34	35	14	12	2	1	6	15	1.206	3.18	100	3.14	.264	1	.083	-1	2	-0.2
1902	StL-N	12	21	.364	39	37	27	1	0	272^2	341	160	111	1	2	79	81	**1.540**	3.66	75	4.30	.306	12	.132	-23	7	-2.7
1903	StL-N	0	1	.000	1	1	0	0	0	5	8	6	1	0	0	0	3	1.600	1.80	181	4.80	.333	0	.000	1	0	0.0
Total	3	15	24	.385	45	43	32	1	0	319^2	396	189	130	3	3	87	103	1.511	3.66	77	4.22	.303	14	.130	-25	9	-3.0

• YETT, Rich Richard Martin Yett b: 10/6/1962, Pomona, CA BR/TR, 6'2", 187 lbs. Deb: 4/13/1985

YEAR	TM-L	W	L	PCT	G	GS	CG	SH	SV	IP	H	R	ER	HR	HB	BB	SO	RAT	ERA	ERA+	CERA	OAV	BH	AVG	PR+	WS	TPW
1985	Min-A	0	0	....	1	1	0	0	0	0^1	1	1	1	0	0	2	0	9.000	27.00	16	35.68	.333	0	....	-1	0	-0.1
1986	Cle-A	5	3	.625	39	3	1	1	1	78^2	84	48	45	10	1	37	50	1.538	5.15	80	4.92	.275	0	....	-8	3	-0.8
1987	Cle-A	3	9	.250	37	11	2	0	1	97^2	96	63	57	21	3	49	59	1.485	5.25	86	5.31	.257	0	....	-6	3	-0.6
1988	Cle-A	9	6	.600	23	22	0	0	0	134^1	146	72	69	11	1	55	71	1.496	4.62	89	4.50	.275	0	....	-5	6	-0.5
1989	Cle-A	5	6	.455	32	12	1	0	0	99	111	56	55	10	2	47	47	1.596	5.00	79	5.16	.283	0	....	-11	3	-1.1
1990	Min-A	0	0	....	4	0	0	0	0	4^1	6	2	1	1	0	1	2	1.615	2.08	200	6.44	.353	0	....	1	0	0.1
Total	6	22	24	.478	136	49	4	1	2	414^1	444	242	228	53	7	191	229	1.533	4.95	84	4.97	.274	0	....	-31	15	-3.0

• YINGLING, Earl Earl Hershey "Chink" Yingling b: 10/29/1888, Chillicothe, OH d: 10/2/1962, Columbus, OH BL/TL, 5'11.5", 180 lbs. Deb: 4/12/1911

YEAR	TM-L	W	L	PCT	G	GS	CG	SH	SV	IP	H	R	ER	HR	HB	BB	SO	RAT	ERA	ERA+	CERA	OAV	BH	AVG	PR+	WS	TPW
1911	Cle-A	1	0	1.000	4	3	1	0	0	22^1	30	17	11	1	1	9	6	1.746	4.43	77	5.87	.326	3	.273	-3	1	-0.3
1912	Bro-N	6	11	.353	25	16	12	0	0	163	186	90	65	10	1	56	51	1.485	3.59	93	4.33	.293	16	.250	-2	7	0.1
1913	Bro-N	8	8	.500	26	13	8	2	0	146^2	158	56	42	2	2	10	40	1.145	2.58	127	2.76	.280	23	.383	10	13	1.9
1914	Cin-N	9	13	.409	34	27	8	3	0	198	207	102	76	6	6	54	80	1.318	3.45	85	3.39	.274	23	.192	-11	8	-1.4
1918	Was-A	1	2	.333	5	2	2	0	0	38	30	15	9	0	1	12	15	1.105	2.13	128	2.21	.238	7	.467	1	3	0.5
Total	5	25	34	.424	94	61	31	5	0	568	611	280	203	19	11	141	192	1.324	3.22	97	3.52	.281	72	.267	-5	32	0.8

• YINGLING, Joe Joseph Granville Yingling b: 7/23/1866, Westminster, MD d: 10/24/1946, Manchester, MD BR/TL, 5'7.5", 145 lbs. Deb: 5/28/1886 ♦

YEAR	TM-L	W	L	PCT	G	GS	CG	SH	SV	IP	H	R	ER	HR	HB	BB	SO	RAT	ERA	ERA+	CERA	OAV	BH	AVG	PR+	WS	TPW
1886	Was-N	0	0	....	1	0	0	0	0	3	7	6	4	0	....	....	1	....	12.00	27	....	.438	0	.000	-3	0	-0.3

• YOCHIM, Len Leonard Joseph Yochim b: 10/16/1928, New Orleans, LA BL/TL, 6'2", 200 lbs. Deb: 9/18/1951

YEAR	TM-L	W	L	PCT	G	GS	CG	SH	SV	IP	H	R	ER	HR	HB	BB	SO	RAT	ERA	ERA+	CERA	OAV	BH	AVG	PR+	WS	TPW
1951	Pit-N	1	1	.500	2	2	0	0	0	8^2	10	9	8	0	1	11	5	2.423	8.31	51	7.47	.278	0	.000	-4	0	-0.4
1954	Pit-N	0	1	.000	10	1	0	0	0	19^2	30	17	16	2	0	8	7	1.932	7.32	57	7.16	.361	1	.500	-6	0	-0.6
Total	2	1	2	.333	12	3	0	0	0	28^1	40	26	24	2	1	19	12	2.082	7.62	55	7.26	.336	1	.200	-10	0	-1.0

• YOCHIM, Ray Raymond Austin Aloysius Yochim b: 7/19/1922, New Orleans, LA d: 1/26/2002, New Orleans, LA BR/TR, 6'1", 170 lbs. Deb: 5/2/1948

YEAR	TM-L	W	L	PCT	G	GS	CG	SH	SV	IP	H	R	ER	HR	HB	BB	SO	RAT	ERA	ERA+	CERA	OAV	BH	AVG	PR+	WS	TPW
1948	StL-N	0	0	....	1	0	0	0	0	1	0	0	0	0	0	3	1	3.000	0.00	....	5.85	.000	0	....	0	0	0.0
1949	StL-N	0	0	....	3	0	0	0	0	2^1	3	4	4	1	0	4	3	3.000	15.43	27	13.29	.273	0	....	-3	0	-0.3
Total	2	0	0	....	4	0	0	0	0	3^1	3	4	4	1	0	7	4	3.000	10.80	39	11.06	.273	0	....	-2	0	-0.2

• YORK, Jim James Harlan York b: 8/27/1947, Maywood, CA BR/TR, 6'3", 200 lbs. Deb: 9/21/1970

YEAR	TM-L	W	L	PCT	G	GS	CG	SH	SV	IP	H	R	ER	HR	HB	BB	SO	RAT	ERA	ERA+	CERA	OAV	BH	AVG	PR+	WS	TPW
1970	KC-A	1	1	.500	4	0	0	0	0	8	5	3	3	2	0	2	6	.875	3.38	111	2.38	.179	0	.000	0	1	0.0
1971	KC-A	5	5	.500	53	0	0	0	3	93^1	70	32	30	7	3	44	103	1.221	2.89	119	2.77	.203	2	.118	6	8	0.7
1972	Hou-N	0	1	.000	26	0	0	0	0	36	45	21	21	3	1	18	25	1.750	5.25	64	5.93	.321	0	.000	-7	0	-0.8
1973	Hou-N	3	4	.429	41	0	0	0	6	53	65	26	26	4	1	20	22	1.604	4.42	82	5.00	.305	0	.000	-5	3	-0.5
1974	Hou-N	2	2	.500	28	0	0	0	1	38^1	48	20	14	1	1	19	15	1.748	3.29	105	5.01	.298	0	.000	0	2	0.0
1975	Hou-N	4	4	.500	19	4	0	0	0	46^2	43	22	20	1	5	25	17	1.457	3.86	87	3.86	.251	1	.091	-3	2	-0.3
1976	NY-A	1	0	1.000	3	0	0	0	0	9^2	14	7	6	1	1	4	6	1.862	5.59	61	7.30	.333	0	....	-3	0	-0.3
Total	7	16	17	.485	174	4	0	0	10	285	290	131	120	19	12	132	194	1.481	3.79	91	4.21	.264	3	.075	-11	16	-1.2

• YORK, Lefty James Edward York b: 11/1/1892, West Fork, AR d: 4/9/1961, York, PA BL/TL, 5'10", 185 lbs. Deb: 9/12/1919

YEAR	TM-L	W	L	PCT	G	GS	CG	SH	SV	IP	H	R	ER	HR	HB	BB	SO	RAT	ERA	ERA+	CERA	OAV	BH	AVG	PR+	WS	TPW
1919	Phi-A	0	2	.000	2	2	0	0	0	4^1	13	13	12	0	0	5	2	4.154	24.92	14	19.82	.500	0	.000	-10	0	-1.1
1921	Chi-N	5	9	.357	40	11	4	1	1	139	170	82	73	5	5	63	57	1.676	4.73	81	5.09	.308	5	.128	-14	5	-1.6
Total	2	5	11	.313	42	13	4	1	1	143^1	183	95	85	5	5	68	59	1.751	5.34	70	5.54	.317	5	.125	-24	5	-2.7

• YORK, Mike Michael David York b: 9/6/1964, Oak Park, IL BR/TR, 6'1", 187 lbs. Deb: 8/17/1990

YEAR	TM-L	W	L	PCT	G	GS	CG	SH	SV	IP	H	R	ER	HR	HB	BB	SO	RAT	ERA	ERA+	CERA	OAV	BH	AVG	PR+	WS	TPW
1990	Pit-N	1	1	.500	4	1	0	0	0	12^2	13	5	4	0	1	5	4	1.421	2.84	127	3.75	.277	1	.333	1	1	0.1
1991	Cle-A	1	4	.200	14	4	0	0	0	34^2	45	29	26	2	2	19	19	1.846	6.75	62	6.30	.333	0	....	-9	0	-0.9
Total	2	2	5	.286	18	5	0	0	0	47^1	58	34	30	2	3	24	23	1.732	5.70	71	5.62	.319	1	.333	-9	1	-0.8

• YOSHII, Masato Masato Yoshii b: 4/20/1965, Osaka, Japan BR/TR, 6'2", 210 lbs. Deb: 4/5/1998

YEAR	TM-L	W	L	PCT	G	GS	CG	SH	SV	IP	H	R	ER	HR	HB	BB	SO	RAT	ERA	ERA+	CERA	OAV	BH	AVG	PR+	WS	TPW
1998	NY-N	6	8	.429	29	29	1	0	0	171^2	166	79	75	22	6	53	117	1.276	3.93	105	3.83	.255	3	.063	3	9	0.1
1999*	NY-N	12	8	.600	31	29	1	0	0	174	168	86	85	25	6	58	105	1.299	4.40	100	4.14	.260	9	.164	-2	9	-0.3
2000	Col-N	6	15	.286	29	29	0	0	0	167^1	201	112	109	32	2	53	88	1.518	5.86	99	5.71	.306	9	.180	-2	7	-0.1
2001	Mon-N	4	7	.364	42	11	0	0	0	113	127	65	60	18	5	26	63	1.354	4.78	93	4.60	.279	2	.125	-2	5	-0.2
2002	Mon-N	4	9	.308	31	20	1	0	0	131^1	143	66	60	15	4	32	74	1.332	4.11	104	4.22	.281	2	.057	2	6	0.1
Total	5	32	47	.405	162	118	3	0	0	757^1	805	408	389	112	23	222	447	1.356	4.62	100	4.50	.276	25	.123	0	36	-0.4

• YOST, Gus August Yost, 6'5" Deb: 6/12/1893

YEAR	TM-L	W	L	PCT	G	GS	CG	SH	SV	IP	H	R	ER	HR	HB	BB	SO	RAT	ERA	ERA+	CERA	OAV	BH	AVG	PR+	WS	TPW
1893	Chi-N	0	1	.000	1	1	0	0	0	2^2	3	4	4	0	0	8	1	4.125	13.50	34	15.06	.276	0	.000	-3	0	-0.2

• YOUMANS, Floyd Floyd Everett Youmans b: 5/11/1964, Tampa, FL BR/TR, 6'2", 190 lbs. Deb: 7/1/1985

YEAR	TM-L	W	L	PCT	G	GS	CG	SH	SV	IP	H	R	ER	HR	HB	BB	SO	RAT	ERA	ERA+	CERA	OAV	BH	AVG	PR+	WS	TPW
1985	Mon-N	4	3	.571	14	12	0	0	0	77	57	27	21	3	1	49	54	1.377	2.45	138	3.16	.206	1	.053	7	5	0.7
1986	Mon-N	13	12	.520	33	32	6	2	0	219	145	93	86	14	4	118	202	1.201	3.53	104	2.62	.188	12	.160	3	13	0.5
1987	Mon-N	9	8	.529	23	23	3	3	0	116^1	112	63	60	13	1	47	94	1.367	4.64	91	3.92	.251	6	.150	-4	5	-0.3
1988	Mon-N	3	6	.333	14	13	1	1	0	84	64	35	30	8	2	41	54	1.250	3.21	112	3.18	.213	4	.154	2	4	0.2
1989	Phi-N	1	5	.167	10	10	0	0	0	42^2	50	31	27	7	2	25	20	1.758	5.70	62	6.46	.299	1	.077	-10	0	-1.2
Total	5	30	34	.469	94	90	10	6	0	539	428	249	224	45	10	280	424	1.314	3.74	100	3.37	.218	24	.139	-1	27	0.0

• YOUNG, Anthony Anthony Wayne Young b: 1/19/1966, Houston, TX BR/TR, 6'2", 210 lbs. Deb: 8/5/1991

YEAR	TM-L	W	L	PCT	G	GS	CG	SH	SV	IP	H	R	ER	HR	HB	BB	SO	RAT	ERA	ERA+	CERA	OAV	BH	AVG	PR+	WS	TPW
1991	NY-N	2	5	.286	10	8	0	0	0	49^1	48	20	17	4	1	12	20	1.216	3.10	117	3.30	.257	2	.143	4	3	0.4
1992	NY-N	2	14	.125	52	13	1	0	15	121	134	66	56	8	1	31	64	1.364	4.17	83	3.84	.285	3	.111	-8	4	-0.9
1993	NY-N	1	16	.059	39	10	1	0	3	100^1	103	62	42	8	1	42	62	1.445	3.77	106	3.96	.265	2	.143	2	3	0.2
1994	Chi-N	4	6	.400	20	19	0	0	0	114^2	103	57	50	12	0	46	65	1.299	3.92	106	3.61	.246	6	.176	2	6	0.2
1995	Chi-N	3	4	.429	32	1	0	0	2	41^1	47	20	17	5	3	14	15	1.476	3.70	111	5.07	.288	2	.667	2	3	0.2
1996	Hou-N	3	3	.500	28	0	0	0	0	33^1	36	18	17	4	4	22	19	1.740	4.59	84	6.04	.279	0	.000	-2	2	-0.2
Total	6	15	48	.238	181	51	2	0	20	460	471	243	199	41	10	167	245	1.387	3.89	99	4.02	.268	15	.160	0	21	0.0

• YOUNG, Charlie Charles "Cy" Young b: 1/12/1893, Philadelphia, PA d: 5/12/1952, Riverside, NJ BB/TR, 5'10.5", 155 lbs. Deb: 9/5/1915

YEAR	TM-L	W	L	PCT	G	GS	CG	SH	SV	IP	H	R	ER	HR	HB	BB	SO	RAT	ERA	ERA+	CERA	OAV	BH	AVG	PR+	WS	TPW
1915	Bal-F	2	3	.400	9	5	1	0	0	35	39	32	23	0	4	21	13	1.714	5.91	57	4.98	.289	2	.222	-9	0	-1.0

• YOUNG, Cliff Clifford Raphael Young b: 8/2/1964, Willis, TX d: 11/4/1993, Montgomery County, TX BL/TL, 6'4", 200 lbs. Deb: 7/14/1990

YEAR	TM-L	W	L	PCT	G	GS	CG	SH	SV	IP	H	R	ER	HR	HB	BB	SO	RAT	ERA	ERA+	CERA	OAV	BH	AVG	PR+	WS	TPW
1990	Cal-A	1	1	.500	17	0	0	0	0	30^2	40	14	12	2	1	7	19	1.533	3.52	108	4.94	.325	0	....	1	2	0.1
1991	Cal-A	1	0	1.000	11	0	0	0	0	12^2	12	6	6	3	0	3	6	1.184	4.26	96	4.19	.261	0	....	-0	1	0.0
1993	Cle-A	3	3	.500	21	7	0	0	1	60^1	74	35	31	9	3	18	31	1.525	4.62	93	5.50	.298	0	....	-2	2	-0.2
Total	3	5	4	.556	49	7	0	0	1	103^2	126	55	49	14	4	28	56	1.486	4.25	98	5.17	.302	0	....	-1	5	-0.1

• YOUNG, Curt Curtis Allen Young b: 4/16/1960, Saginaw, MI BR/TL, 6'1", 180 lbs. Deb: 6/24/1983

YEAR	TM-L	W	L	PCT	G	GS	CG	SH	SV	IP	H	R	ER	HR	HB	BB	SO	RAT	ERA	ERA+	CERA	OAV	BH	AVG	PR+	WS	TPW
1983	Oak-A	0	1	.000	8	2	0	0	0	9	17	17	16	1	1	5	5	2.444	16.00	24	10.84	.386	0	....	-12	0	-1.2
1984	Oak-A	9	4	.692	20	17	2	1	0	108^2	118	53	49	9	8	31	41	1.371	4.06	92	4.25	.274	0	....	-4	5	-0.4
1985	Oak-A	0	4	.000	19	7	0	0	0	46	57	38	37	15	1	22	19	1.717	7.24	53	7.72	.300	0	....	-17	0	-1.7
1986	Oak-A	13	9	.591	29	27	5	2	0	198	176	88	76	19	7	57	116	1.177	3.45	112	3.12	.236	0	....	9	12	0.9
1987	Oak-A	13	7	.650	31	31	6	0	0	203	194	102	92	38	3	44	124	1.172	4.08	101	3.77	.252	0	.000	3	11	0.3
1988*	Oak-A	11	8	.579	26	26	1	0	0	156^1	162	77	72	23	4	50	69	1.356	4.14	91	4.52	.275	0	....	-8	6	-0.9
1989	Oak-A	5	9	.357	25	20	1	0	0	111	117	56	46	10	3	47	55	1.477	3.73	99	4.42	.264	0	....	-2	4	-0.2
1990*	Oak-A	9	6	.600	26	21	0	0	0	124^1	124	70	67	17	2	53	56	1.424	4.85	77	4.61	.266	0	....	-18	3	-1.9
1991	Oak-A	4	2	.667	41	1	0	0	0	68^1	74	38	38	8	2	34	27	1.580	5.00	77	5.18	.278	0	....	-9	2	-0.9
1992	KC-A	1	2	.333	10	2	0	0	0	24^1	29	14	14	1	0	7	7	1.479	5.18	78	4.19	.293	0	....	-3	1	-0.3
	NY-A	3	0	1.000	13	5	0	0	0	43^1	51	21	16	1	2	10	13	1.408	3.32	118	4.00	.298	0	....	3	2	0.3
	Yr.	4	2	.667	23	7	0	0	0	67^2	80	35	30	2	2	17	20	1.433	3.99	100	4.07	.296	0	....	0	3	0.0
1993	Oak-A	1	1	.500	3	3	0	0	0	14^2	14	7	7	5	0	6	4	1.364	4.30	95	5.43	.241	0	....	-0	1	0.0
Total	11	69	53	.566	251	162	15	3	0	1107	1133	581	530	147	33	366	536	1.354	4.31	89	4.31	.265	0	.000	-59	47	-6.0

• YOUNG, Cy Denton True Young b: 3/29/1867, Gilmore, OH d: 11/4/1955, Newcomerstown, OH BR/TR, 6'2", 210 lbs. Deb: 8/6/1890 M/U HOF: 1937

YEAR	TM-L	W	L	PCT	G	GS	CG	SH	SV	IP	H	R	ER	HR	HB	BB	SO	RAT	ERA	ERA+	CERA	OAV	BH	AVG	PR+	WS	TPW
1890	Cle-N	9	7	.563	17	16	16	0	0	147^2	145	87	57	6	5	30	39	1.185	3.47	103	....	.249	8	.123	1	8	-0.4
1891	Cle-N	27	22	.551	55	46	43	0	2	423^2	431	244	134	4	11	140	147	1.348	2.85	121	....	.254	29	.167	34	28	2.8
1892*	Cle-N	**36**	12	.750	53	49	48	**9**	0	453	363	158	97	8	8	118	168	1.062	**1.93**	**176**	**2.02**	.211	31	.158	**75**	44	**6.3**
1893	Cle-N	34	16	.680	53	46	42	1	1	422^2	442	230	158	10	10	103	102	1.289	3.36	145	3.25	.261	44	.235	**73**	35	5.6
1894	Cle-N	26	21	.553	52	47	44	2	1	408^2	488	265	179	19	6	106	108	1.454	3.94	138	4.11	.293	40	.215	69	39	4.7
1895*	Cle-N	**35**	10	.778	47	40	36	**4**	0	369^2	363	177	134	10	8	75	121	1.185	3.26	153	**2.70**	.253	30	.214	**71**	37	5.4
1896*	Cle-N	28	15	.651	51	46	42	**5**	**3**	414^1	477	214	149	7	10	62	**140**	1.301	3.24	140	3.35	.287	52	.289	60	**43**	**5.7**
1897	Cle-N	21	19	.525	46	38	35	2	0	335^2	391	189	141	7	9	49	88	1.311	3.78	119	3.51	.289	34	.222	8	28	0.3
1898	Cle-N	25	13	.658	46	41	40	1	0	377^2	387	167	106	6	9	41	101	1.133	2.53	143	2.59	.263	39	.253	43	34	4.5
1899	StL-N	26	16	.619	44	42	**40**	4	1	369^1	368	173	106	10	6	44	111	1.116	2.58	154	2.48	.260	32	.216	**54**	35	**4.9**
1900	StL-N	19	19	.500	41	35	32	**4**	0	321^1	337	144	107	7	4	36	115	1.161	3.00	121	2.73	.269	22	.177	28	22	2.4
1901	Bos-A	**33**	10	.767	43	41	38	**5**	0	371^1	324	112	67	6	8	37	**158**	.972	**1.62**	**217**	**1.87**	**.232**	32	.209	**63**	**41**	**5.7**
1902	Bos-A	**32**	11	.744	**45**	**43**	**41**	3	0	**384^2**	350	136	92	6	13	53	160	1.048	2.15	166	2.23	.243	34	.230	50	**38**	5.0
1903*	Bos-A	**28**	9	.757	40	35	**34**	**7**	**2**	**341^2**	294	115	79	6	9	37	176	.969	2.08	146	1.89	.232	44	.321	26	**38**	**4.0**
1904	Bos-A	26	16	.619	43	41	40	**10**	1	380	327	104	83	6	4	29	200	.937	1.97	136	1.73	.233	33	.223	29	35	3.4
1905	Bos-A	18	19	.486	38	33	31	4	0	320^2	248	99	65	3	10	30	210	.867	1.82	148	**1.49**	.216	18	.150	32	28	3.4
1906	Bos-A	13	21	.382	39	34	28	0	2	287^2	288	137	102	3	8	25	140	1.088	3.19	86	2.45	.264	16	.154	-11	13	-1.4
1907	Bos-A	21	15	.583	43	37	33	6	2	343^1	286	101	76	3	7	51	147	.982	1.99	129	1.85	.229	27	.216	7	27	0.9
1908	Bos-A	21	11	.656	36	33	30	3	2	299	230	68	42	1	2	37	150	.893	1.26	194	1.48	.213	26	.226	33	27	3.9
1909	Cle-A	19	15	.559	35	34	30	3	0	294^1	267	110	74	4	8	59	109	1.108	2.26	113	2.39	.250	21	.196	7	20	0.9
1910	Cle-A	7	10	.412	21	20	14	1	0	163^1	149	62	46	0	4	27	58	1.078	2.53	102	2.26	.252	8	.145	-0	10	0.0
1911	Cle-A	3	4	.429	7	7	4	0	0	46^1	54	28	20	2	1	13	20	1.446	3.88	88	4.19	.298	1	.063	-3	2	-0.5
	Bos-N	4	5	.444	11	11	8	2	0	80	83	47	33	4	3	15	35	1.225	3.71	103	3.18	.268	2	.080	2	2	0.0
Total	22	511	316	.618	906	815	749	76	17	7356	7092	3167	2147	138	163	1217	2803	1.130	2.63	137	2.30	.252	623	.210	753	634	67.6

• YOUNG, Danny Daniel Bracy Young b: 11/3/1971, Smyrna, TN BR/TL, 6'4", 210 lbs. Deb: 3/30/2000

YEAR	TM-L	W	L	PCT	G	GS	CG	SH	SV	IP	H	R	ER	HR	HB	BB	SO	RAT	ERA	ERA+	CERA	OAV	BH	AVG	PR+	WS	TPW
2000	Chi-N	0	1	.000	4	0	0	0	0	3	5	7	7	1	0	6	0	3.667	21.00	22	18.23	.357	0	....	-5	0	-0.5

• YOUNG, Harley Harlan Edward "Cy The Third" Young b: 9/28/1883, Portland, IN d: 3/26/1975, Jacksonville, FL BR/TR, 6'2" Deb: 4/21/1908

YEAR	TM-L	W	L	PCT	G	GS	CG	SH	SV	IP	H	R	ER	HR	HB	BB	SO	RAT	ERA	ERA+	CERA	OAV	BH	AVG	PR+	WS	TPW
1908	Pit-N	0	2	.000	8	3	0	0	0	48^1	40	21	12	0	5	10	17	1.034	2.23	102	2.29	.234	1	.083	0	1	0.0
	Bos-N	0	1	.000	6	2	1	0	0	27^1	29	19	10	0	3	4	12	1.207	3.29	73	3.12	.269	2	.200	-3	0	-0.4
	Yr.	0	3	.000	14	5	1	0	0	75^2	69	40	22	0	8	14	29	1.097	2.62	89	2.59	.248	3	.136	-3	1	-0.4

• YOUNG, Irv Irving Melrose "Young Cy,Cy The Second" Young b: 7/21/1877, Columbia Falls, ME d: 1/14/1935, Brewer, ME BL/TL, 5'10", 170 lbs. Deb: 4/14/1905 U

YEAR	TM-L	W	L	PCT	G	GS	CG	SH	SV	IP	H	R	ER	HR	HB	BB	SO	RAT	ERA	ERA+	CERA	OAV	BH	AVG	PR+	WS	TPW
1905	Bos-N	20	21	.488	43	**42**	**41**	7	0	**378**	337	146	122	6	8	71	156	1.079	2.90	106	2.32	.241	14	.103	17	29	1.0
1906	Bos-N	16	25	.390	43	**41**	**37**	4	0	**358^1**	349	157	116	7	6	83	151	1.206	2.91	92	2.93	.263	12	.096	-6	20	-1.4
1907	Bos-N	10	23	.303	40	32	22	3	1	245^1	287	131	108	5	13	58	86	1.406	3.96	64	4.29	.306	13	.163	-41	4	-4.7

YEAR	TM-L	W	L	PCT	G	GS	CG	SH	SV	IP	H	R	ER	HR	HB	BB	SO	RAT	ERA	ERA+	CERA	OAV	BH	AVG	PR+	WS	TPW
1908	Bos-N	4	9	.308	16	11	7	1	0	85	94	49	27	2	2	19	32	1.329	2.86	84	3.66	.289	5	.156	-6	2	-0.8
	Pit-N	4	3	.571	16	7	3	1	1	89^2	73	31	20	1	5	21	31	1.048	2.01	114	2.17	.225	6	.200	3	5	0.5
	Yr.	8	12	.400	32	18	10	2	1	174^2	167	80	47	3	7	40	63	1.185	2.42	97	2.90	.257	11	.177	-4	7	-0.4
1910	Chi-A	4	8	.333	27	17	7	4	0	135^2	122	54	41	0	3	39	64	1.187	2.72	88	2.61	.247	5	.114	-4	5	-0.7
1911	Chi-A	5	6	.455	24	11	3	1	2	92^2	99	61	45	2	0	25	40	1.338	4.37	74	2.80	.229	5	.179	-12	2	-1.2
Total	**6**	**63**	**95**	**.399**	**209**	**161**	**120**	**21**	**4**	**1384^2**	**1361**	**629**	**479**	**23**	**37**	**316**	**560**	**1.211**	**3.11**	**87**	**2.96**	**.260**	**60**	**.126**	**-50**	**67**	**-7.4**
• YOUNG, J.B.	Joseph B. Young b: 6/1857, Mount Carmel, PA Deb: 6/10/1892																										
1892	StL-N	0	0	....	1	0	0	0	0	2	9	13	5	0	0	2	1	5.500	22.50	14	32.30	.600	0	.000	-4	0	-0.4
• YOUNG, Jason	Jason Kariya Young b: 9/28/1979, Oakland, CA BR/TR, 6'5", 210 lbs. Deb: 5/12/2003																										
2003	Col-N	0	2	.000	8	3	0	0	0	21^1	34	22	20	8	1	9	18	2.016	8.44	58	10.29	.354	2	.286	-8	0	-0.7
• YOUNG, Kip	Kip Lane Young b: 10/29/1954, Georgetown, OH BR/TR, 5'11", 175 lbs. Deb: 7/21/1978																										
1978	Det-A	6	7	.462	14	13	7	0	0	105^2	94	34	33	9	2	30	49	1.174	2.81	137	3.12	.246	0	....	11	9	1.1
1979	Det-A	2	2	.500	13	7	0	0	0	43^2	60	32	31	11	1	11	22	1.626	6.39	68	6.91	.323	0	....	-10	0	-1.0
Total	**2**	**8**	**9**	**.471**	**27**	**20**	**7**	**0**	**0**	**149^1**	**154**	**66**	**64**	**20**	**3**	**41**	**71**	**1.306**	**3.86**	**106**	**4.23**	**.271**	**0**	**....**	**0**	**9**	**0.1**
• YOUNG, Matt	Matthew John Young b: 8/9/1958, Pasadena, CA BL/TL, 6'3", 205 lbs. Deb: 4/6/1983																										
1983	Sea-A★	11	15	.423	33	32	5	2	0	203^2	178	86	74	17	7	79	130	1.262	3.27	130	3.38	.236	0	....	23	16	2.3
1984	Sea-A	6	8	.429	22	22	1	0	0	113^1	141	81	72	11	1	57	73	1.747	5.72	70	5.93	.307	0	....	-19	1	-1.9
1985	Sea-A	12	19	.387	37	35	5	2	1	218^1	242	135	119	23	7	76	136	1.456	4.91	86	4.67	.282	0	....	-16	7	-1.6
1986	Sea-A	8	6	.571	65	5	1	0	13	103^2	108	50	44	9	8	46	82	1.486	3.82	111	4.71	.272	0	....	5	10	0.5
1987	LA-N	5	8	.385	47	0	0	0	11	54^1	62	30	27	3	0	17	42	1.454	4.47	89	4.10	.288	0	.000	-3	4	-0.3
1989*	Oak-A	1	4	.200	26	4	0	0	0	37^1	42	31	28	2	0	31	27	1.955	6.75	55	5.98	.286	0	....	-13	0	-1.4
1990	Sea-A	8	18	.308	34	33	7	1	0	225^1	198	106	88	15	6	107	176	1.354	3.51	113	3.53	.237	0	....	11	12	1.2
1991	Bos-A	3	7	.300	19	16	0	0	0	88^2	92	55	51	4	2	53	69	1.635	5.18	83	4.69	.266	0	....	-9	2	-0.9
1992	Bos-A	0	4	.000	28	8	1	0	0	70^2	69	42	36	7	3	42	57	1.571	4.58	92	4.79	.257	0	....	-3	2	-0.3
1993	Cle-A	1	6	.143	22	8	0	0	0	74^1	75	45	43	8	3	57	65	1.776	5.21	83	5.89	.266	0	....	-7	1	-0.7
Total	**10**	**55**	**95**	**.367**	**333**	**163**	**20**	**5**	**25**	**1189^2**	**1207**	**661**	**582**	**99**	**37**	**565**	**857**	**1.489**	**4.40**	**94**	**4.46**	**.265**	**0**	**.000**	**-31**	**55**	**-3.1**
• YOUNG, Pete	Bryan Owen Young b: 3/19/1968, Meadville, MS BR/TR, 6', 225 lbs. Deb: 6/5/1992																										
1992	Mon-N	0	0	....	13	0	0	0	0	20^1	18	9	9	0	1	9	11	1.328	3.98	87	3.02	.247	0	....	-1	1	-0.1
1993	Mon-N	1	0	1.000	4	0	0	0	0	5^1	4	2	2	1	0	0	3	.750	3.38	123	1.77	.211	0	.000	0	1	0.0
Total	**2**	**1**	**0**	**1.000**	**17**	**0**	**0**	**0**	**0**	**25^2**	**22**	**11**	**11**	**1**	**1**	**9**	**14**	**1.208**	**3.86**	**93**	**2.76**	**.239**	**0**	**.000**	**-1**	**2**	**-0.1**
• YOUNG, Tim	Timothy R. Young b: 10/15/1973, Gulfport, MS BL/TL, 5'9", 170 lbs. Deb: 9/5/1998																										
1998	Mon-N	0	0	....	10	0	0	0	0	6	6	4	4	0	0	4	7	1.667	6.00	70	4.07	.250	0	....	-1	0	-0.1
2000	Bos-A	0	0	....	8	0	0	0	0	7	7	5	5	3	1	2	6	1.286	6.43	78	6.90	.269	0	....	-1	0	-0.1
Total	**2**	**0**	**0**	**....**	**18**	**0**	**0**	**0**	**0**	**13**	**13**	**9**	**9**	**3**	**1**	**6**	**13**	**1.462**	**6.23**	**74**	**5.59**	**.260**	**0**	**....**	**-2**	**0**	**-0.2**
• YOUNGBLOOD, Chief	Albert Clyde Youngblood b: 6/13/1900, Hillsboro, TX d: 7/6/1968, Amarillo, TX BL/TR, 6'3", 202 lbs. Deb: 7/16/1922																										
1922	Was-A	0	0	....	2	0	0	0	0	4^1	9	9	7	0	2	7	0	3.692	14.54	27	16.18	.429	0	.000	-5	0	-0.5
• YOUNT, Ducky	Herbert Macon "Hub" Yount b: 12/7/1885, Iredell County, NC d: 5/9/1970, Winston-Salem, NC BR/TR, 6'2", 178 lbs. Deb: 5/20/1914																										
1914	Bal-F	1	1	.500	13	1	1	0	0	41^1	44	28	19	2	2	19	19	1.524	4.14	77	4.36	.280	1	.083	-3	1	-0.5
• YOUNT, Larry	Lawrence King Yount b: 2/15/1950, Houston, TX BR/TR, 6'2", 185 lbs. Deb: 9/15/1971																										
1971	Hou-N	0	0	....	1	0	0	0	0	0	0	0	0	0	0	0	0	....	....	....	....	1.000	0	....	0	0	0.0
• YOWELL, Carl	Carl Columbus "Sundown" Yowell b: 12/20/1902, Madison, VA d: 7/27/1985, Jacksonville, TX BL/TL, 6'4", 180 lbs. Deb: 9/5/1924																										
1924	Cle-A	1	1	.500	4	2	2	0	0	27	37	21	20	1	0	13	8	1.852	6.67	64	6.10	.343	2	.182	-7	0	-0.7
1925	Cle-A	2	3	.400	12	4	1	0	0	36^1	40	21	18	1	1	17	12	1.569	4.46	99	4.74	.310	1	.125	-0	2	-0.1
Total	**2**	**3**	**4**	**.429**	**16**	**6**	**3**	**0**	**0**	**63^1**	**77**	**42**	**38**	**2**	**1**	**30**	**20**	**1.689**	**5.40**	**80**	**5.32**	**.325**	**3**	**.158**	**-7**	**2**	**-0.8**
• YUHAS, Eddie	John Edward Yuhas b: 8/5/1924, Youngstown, OH d: 7/6/1986, Winston-Salem, NC BR/TR, 6'1", 180 lbs. Deb: 4/17/1952																										
1952	StL-N	12	2	.857	54	2	0	0	6	99^1	90	35	30	5	2	35	39	1.258	2.72	136	3.08	.243	4	.190	11	11	1.2
1953	StL-N	0	0	....	2	0	0	0	0	1	3	2	2	0	0	0	0	3.000	18.00	24	14.52	.500	0	....	-2	0	-0.1
Total	**2**	**12**	**2**	**.857**	**56**	**2**	**0**	**0**	**6**	**100^1**	**93**	**37**	**32**	**5**	**2**	**35**	**39**	**1.276**	**2.87**	**130**	**3.19**	**.247**	**4**	**.190**	**9**	**11**	**1.1**
• ZABALA, Adrian	Adrian (Rodriguez) Zabala b: 8/26/1916, San Antonio de los Banos, Cuba d: 1/4/2002, Jacksonville, FL BL/TL, 5'11", 165 lbs. Deb: 8/11/1945																										
1945	NY-N	2	4	.333	11	5	1	0	0	43^1	46	25	23	2	0	20	14	1.523	4.78	82	4.29	.284	3	.231	-4	2	-0.4
1949	NY-N	2	3	.400	15	4	2	1	1	41	44	28	24	5	1	10	13	1.317	5.27	76	4.09	.278	1	.077	-6	1	-0.6
Total	**2**	**4**	**7**	**.364**	**26**	**9**	**3**	**1**	**1**	**84^1**	**90**	**53**	**47**	**7**	**1**	**30**	**27**	**1.423**	**5.02**	**79**	**4.19**	**.281**	**4**	**.154**	**-10**	**3**	**-1.0**
• ZABEL, Zip	George Washington Zabel b: 2/18/1891, Wetmore, KS d: 5/31/1970, Beloit, WI BR/TR, 6'1.5", 185 lbs. Deb: 10/5/1913																										
1913	Chi-N	1	0	1.000	1	1	0	0	0	5	3	0	0	0	0	1	0	.800	0.00	....	1.09	.167	0	.000	2	1	0.2
1914	Chi-N	4	4	.500	29	7	2	0	3	128	104	45	31	5	2	45	50	1.164	2.18	127	2.60	.235	7	.184	11	9	1.1
1915	Chi-N	7	10	.412	36	17	8	3	0	163	124	80	58	3	4	84	60	1.276	3.20	87	2.63	.218	4	.074	-5	6	-1.0
Total	**3**	**12**	**14**	**.462**	**66**	**25**	**10**	**3**	**3**	**296**	**231**	**125**	**89**	**8**	**6**	**130**	**110**	**1.220**	**2.71**	**102**	**2.59**	**.224**	**11**	**.117**	**7**	**16**	**0.3**
• ZACHARY, Chink	Albert Myron Zachary b: 10/19/1917, Brooklyn, NY BR/TR, 5'11", 182 lbs. Deb: 4/30/1944																										
1944	Bro-N	0	2	.000	4	2	0	0	0	10^1	10	11	11	2	1	7	3	1.645	9.58	37	5.67	.238	0	.000	-7	0	-0.7
• ZACHARY, Chris	William Christopher Zachary b: 2/19/1944, Knoxville, TN d: 4/19/2003, Knoxville, TN BL/TR, 6'2", 200 lbs. Deb: 4/11/1963																										
1963	Hou-N	2	2	.500	22	7	0	0	0	57	62	38	31	5	3	22	42	1.474	4.89	64	4.52	.272	0	.000	-10	0	-1.2
1964	Hou-N	0	1	.000	1	1	0	0	0	4	6	5	4	1	0	1	2	1.750	9.00	38	7.08	.333	0	.000	-2	0	-0.3
1965	Hou-N	0	2	.000	4	2	0	0	0	10^2	12	6	5	0	0	6	4	1.688	4.22	80	4.36	.273	0	.000	-1	0	-0.1
1966	Hou-N	3	5	.375	10	8	0	0	0	55	44	22	21	1	1	32	37	1.382	3.44	100	3.12	.221	4	.222	0	3	0.2
1967	Hou-N	1	6	.143	9	7	0	0	0	36^1	42	27	23	5	2	12	18	1.486	5.70	58	5.09	.290	1	.100	-9	0	-1.0
1969	KC-A	0	1	.000	8	2	0	0	0	18^1	27	17	16	4	0	7	6	1.855	7.85	47	7.85	.346	1	.500	-8	0	-0.8
1971	StL-N	3	10	.231	23	12	1	1	0	89^2	114	58	53	3	4	26	48	1.561	5.32	68	4.78	.316	8	.242	-15	0	-1.5
1972*	Det-A	1	1	.500	25	1	0	0	1	38^1	27	6	6	2	1	15	21	1.096	1.41	223	2.25	.201	1	.500	7	5	0.9
1973	Pit-N	0	1	.000	6	0	0	0	1	12	10	4	4	1	0	1	6	.917	3.00	117	1.88	.222	0	.000	1	1	0.0
Total	**9**	**10**	**29**	**.256**	**108**	**40**	**1**	**1**	**2**	**321^1**	**344**	**183**	**163**	**22**	**11**	**122**	**184**	**1.450**	**4.57**	**75**	**4.27**	**.275**	**15**	**.181**	**-37**	**9**	**-3.8**
• ZACHARY, Tom	Jonathan Thompson Walton Zachary b: 5/7/1896, Graham, NC d: 1/24/1969, Burlington, NC BL/TL, 6'1", 187 lbs. Deb: 7/11/1918																										
1918	Phi-A	2	0	1.000	2	2	0	0	0	8	9	5	5	0	0	7	1	2.000	5.63	52	6.13	.320	2	.500	-3	1	-0.2
1919	Was-A	1	5	.167	17	7	0	0	0	61^2	68	29	20	0	1	20	9	1.427	2.92	110	3.68	.290	5	.333	3	3	0.5
1920	Was-A	15	16	.484	44	31	19	3	2	262^2	289	141	110	7	4	78	53	1.397	3.77	99	3.66	.280	29	.261	1	14	0.6
1921	Was-A	18	16	.529	39	31	17	2	1	250	314	130	110	10	6	59	53	1.492	3.96	104	4.55	.310	23	.256	0	19	0.3
1922	Was-A	15	10	.600	32	25	13	1	1	184^2	190	74	64	6	3	43	37	1.262	3.12	124	3.20	.270	21	.296	10	16	1.5
1923	Was-A	10	16	.385	35	29	10	0	0	204^1	270	117	102	9	4	63	40	**1.630**	4.49	84	5.07	.320	15	.192	-23	6	-2.3
1924*	Was-A	15	9	.625	33	27	13	1	2	202^2	198	74	62	5	3	53	45	1.238	2.75	147	2.98	.260	22	.306	24	21	2.6
1925*	Was-A	12	15	.444	38	**33**	11	1	2	217^2	247	112	93	10	2	74	58	1.475	3.85	110	4.21	.290	12	.174	3	13	0.1
1926	StL-A	14	15	.483	34	31	18	3	0	247^1	264	126	99	14	6	97	53	1.460	3.60	119	4.14	.280	23	.267	17	19	2.1

YEAR	TM-L	W	L	PCT	G	GS	CG	SH	SV	IP	H	R	ER	HR	HB	BB	SO	RAT	ERA	ERA+	CERA	OAV	BH	AVG	PR+	WS	TPW
1927	StL-A	4	6	.400	13	12	6	0	0	78^{1}	110	48	38	4	0	27	13	1.749	4.37	100	5.80	.340	3	.107	-1	4	-0.3
	Was-A	4	7	.364	15	14	5	1	0	102^{2}	116	54	45	2	2	30	13	1.422	3.94	103	3.80	.290	5	.139	0	5	-0.2
	Yr.	8	13	.381	28	26	11	1	0	181	226	102	83	6	2	57	26	1.564	4.13	101	4.67	.312	8	.125	-0	9	-0.4
1928	Was-A	6	9	.400	20	14	5	1	0	102^{2}	130	72	62	5	1	40	19	1.656	5.44	74	5.20	.320	10	.303	-18	2	-1.6
	*NY-A	3	3	.500	7	6	3	0	1	45^{2}	54	26	20	1	0	15	7	1.511	3.94	95	3.82	.320	2	.133	-0	2	0.0
	Yr.	9	12	.429	27	20	8	1	1	148^{1}	184	98	82	6	1	55	26	1.611	4.98	79	4.78	.320	12	.250	-18	4	-1.6
1929	NY-A	12	0	1.000	26	11	7	2	2	119^{2}	131	43	33	5	2	30	35	1.345	2.48	155	3.60	.270	10	.238	17	12	1.6
1930	NY-A	1	1	.500	3	3	0	0	0	16^{2}	18	16	12	0	0	9	1	1.620	6.48	66	3.83	.260	2	.250	-4	0	-0.3
	Bos-N	11	5	.688	24	22	10	1	0	151^{1}	192	90	77	9	0	50	57	1.599	4.58	108	4.99	.310	13	.241	6	11	0.7
1931	Bos-N	11	15	.423	33	28	16	3	2	229	243	87	79	8	1	53	64	1.293	3.10	122	3.28	.270	14	.167	19	20	1.7
1932	Bos-N	12	11	.522	32	24	12	1	0	212	231	83	73	5	2	55	67	1.349	3.10	121	3.47	.280	21	.273	15	17	2.0
1933	Bos-N	7	9	.438	26	20	6	2	2	125	134	64	49	1	0	35	22	1.352	3.53	87	3.29	.270	5	.119	-6	4	-0.8
1934	Bos-N	1	2	.333	5	4	2	1	0	24	27	9	9	1	0	8	4	1.458	3.38	113	3.99	.278	0	.000	1	2	0.0
	Bro-N	5	6	.455	22	12	4	0	2	101^{2}	122	53	50	5	2	21	28	1.407	4.43	88	4.15	.301	7	.184	-5	5	-0.4
	Yr.	6	8	.429	27	16	6	1	2	125^{2}	149	62	59	6	2	29	32	1.416	4.23	92	4.12	.297	7	.152	-4	7	-0.4
1935	Bro-N	7	12	.368	25	21	9	1	4	158	193	76	63	10	2	35	33	1.443	3.59	111	4.29	.297	7	.135	5	9	0.4
1936	Bro-N	0	0	....	1	0	0	0	0	0^{1}	2	2	2	0	0	1	0	9.000	54.00	8	54.30	1.000	0	....	-2	0	-0.2
	Phi-N	0	3	.000	7	2	0	0	1	20^{1}	28	20	18	2	0	11	8	1.918	7.97	57	6.58	.329	3	.333	-7	0	-0.6
	Yr.	0	3	.000	8	2	0	0	1	20^{2}	30	22	20	2	0	12	8	2.032	8.71	52	7.35	.345	3	.333	-9	0	-0.7
Total	19	186	191	.493	533	409	186	24	22	3126^{1}	3580	1551	1295	119	41	914	720	1.437	3.73	106	4.03	.290	254	.226	52	205	7.3

• ZACHRY, Pat Patrick Paul Zachry b: 4/24/1952, Richmond, TX BR/TR, 6'5", 180 lbs. Deb: 4/11/1976

YEAR	TM-L	W	L	PCT	G	GS	CG	SH	SV	IP	H	R	ER	HR	HB	BB	SO	RAT	ERA	ERA+	CERA	OAV	BH	AVG	PR+	WS	TPW
1976*	Cin-N	14	7	.667	38	28	6	1	0	204	170	70	62	8	2	83	143	1.240	2.74	128	2.84	.228	7	.113	16	14	1.4
1977	Cin-N	3	7	.300	12	12	3	0	0	75	78	45	42	7	1	29	36	1.427	5.04	78	4.30	.273	3	.136	-10	1	-1.1
	NY-N	7	6	.538	19	19	2	1	0	119^{2}	129	59	50	14	3	48	63	1.479	3.76	99	4.73	.278	6	.143	-1	6	-0.2
	Yr.	10	13	.435	31	31	5	1	0	194^{2}	207	104	92	21	4	77	99	1.459	4.25	90	4.56	.276	9	.141	-10	7	-1.3
1978	NY-N★	10	6	.625	21	21	5	2	0	138	120	57	51	9	1	60	78	1.304	3.33	105	3.27	.236	3	.070	1	8	0.0
1979	NY-N	5	1	.833	7	7	1	0	0	42^{2}	44	19	17	3	2	21	17	1.523	3.59	101	4.41	.267	2	.125	-0	3	-0.1
1980	NY-N	6	10	.375	28	26	7	3	0	164^{2}	145	65	55	16	5	58	88	1.233	3.01	118	3.34	.240	2	.043	10	9	0.6
1981	NY-N	7	14	.333	24	24	3	0	0	139	151	78	64	13	4	56	76	**1.489**	4.14	84	4.62	.282	6	.158	-9	3	-0.9
1982	NY-N	6	9	.400	36	16	2	0	1	137^{2}	149	69	62	10	0	57	69	1.496	4.05	90	4.38	.279	3	.079	-5	5	-0.7
1983*	LA-N	6	1	.857	40	1	0	0	0	61^{1}	63	22	17	4	1	21	36	1.370	2.49	144	3.76	.278	2	.500	9	6	1.0
1984	LA-N	5	6	.455	58	0	0	0	2	82^{2}	84	38	35	3	2	51	55	1.633	3.81	93	4.34	.267	2	.333	-2	5	-0.1
1985	Phi-N	0	0	....	10	0	0	0	0	12^{2}	14	7	6	1	0	11	8	1.974	4.26	86	6.34	.280	0	.000	-1	0	-0.1
Total	10	69	67	.507	293	154	29	7	3	1177^{1}	1147	529	461	88	21	495	669	1.395	3.52	102	3.88	.259	36	.113	9	60	-0.2

• ZACKERT, George George Carl "Zeke" Zackert b: 12/24/1884, Horton, VT d: 2/18/1977, Burlington, IA BL/TL, 6', 177 lbs. Deb: 9/22/1911

YEAR	TM-L	W	L	PCT	G	GS	CG	SH	SV	IP	H	R	ER	HR	HB	BB	SO	RAT	ERA	ERA+	CERA	OAV	BH	AVG	PR+	WS	TPW
1911	StL-N	0	2	.000	4	1	0	0	0	7^{1}	17	13	9	0	0	6	6	3.136	11.05	30	14.47	.486	0	.000	-6	0	-0.6
1912	StL-N	0	0	....	1	0	0	0	0	1	2	2	2	0	1	1	0	3.000	18.00	19	18.54	.667	0	....	-2	0	-0.2
Total	2	0	2	.000	5	1	0	0	0	8^{1}	19	15	11	0	1	7	6	3.120	11.88	28	14.96	.500	0	.000	-8	0	-0.8

• ZAHN, Geoff Geoffrey Clayton Zahn b: 12/19/1945, Baltimore, MD BL/TL, 6'1", 180 lbs. Deb: 9/2/1973

YEAR	TM-L	W	L	PCT	G	GS	CG	SH	SV	IP	H	R	ER	HR	HB	BB	SO	RAT	ERA	ERA+	CERA	OAV	BH	AVG	PR+	WS	TPW
1973	LA-N	1	0	1.000	6	1	0	0	0	13^{1}	5	2	2	2	0	2	9	.525	1.35	254	0.86	.116	0	.000	3	2	0.3
1974	LA-N	3	5	.375	21	10	1	0	0	79^{2}	78	28	18	3	2	16	33	1.180	2.03	167	2.86	.254	4	.174	13	5	1.3
1975	LA-N	0	1	.000	2	0	0	0	0	3	2	3	3	0	0	5	1	2.333	9.00	38	6.15	.222	0	....	-2	0	-0.2
	Chi-N	2	7	.222	16	10	0	0	1	62^{2}	67	37	31	2	0	26	21	1.484	4.45	86	3.99	.282	2	.133	-2	2	-0.3
	Yr.	2	8	.200	18	10	0	0	1	65^{2}	69	40	34	2	0	31	22	1.523	4.66	81	4.09	.279	2	.133	-4	2	-0.5
1976	Chi-N	0	1	.000	3	2	0	0	0	8^{1}	16	10	10	0	1	2	4	2.160	10.80	36	8.77	.410	0	.000	-6	0	-0.7
1977	Min-A	12	14	.462	34	32	7	1	0	198	234	116	103	20	5	66	88	**1.515**	4.68	85	4.98	.299	0	....	-15	8	-1.5
1978	Min-A	14	14	.500	35	35	12	1	0	252^{1}	260	101	85	18	4	81	106	1.351	3.03	126	3.88	.274	0	....	21	17	2.2
1979	Min-A	13	7	.650	26	24	4	0	0	169	181	74	67	13	0	41	58	1.314	3.57	123	3.76	.279	0	....	15	14	1.5
1980	Min-A	14	18	.438	38	35	13	5	0	232^{2}	273	138	114	17	2	66	96	1.457	4.41	99	4.53	.302	0	....	-3	11	-0.3
1981	Cal-A	10	11	.476	25	25	9	0	0	161^{1}	181	93	79	18	0	43	52	1.388	4.41	83	4.32	.285	0	....	-14	4	-1.5
1982*	Cal-A	18	8	.692	34	34	12	4	0	229^{1}	225	100	95	18	4	65	81	1.265	3.73	109	3.49	.259	0	....	4	16	0.4
1983	Cal-A	9	11	.450	29	28	11	3	0	203	212	90	75	22	0	51	81	1.296	3.33	121	3.79	.269	0	....	16	14	1.6
1984	Cal-A	13	10	.565	28	27	9	**5**	0	199^{1}	200	78	69	11	1	48	61	1.244	3.12	127	3.21	.263	0	....	18	16	1.8
1985	Cal-A	2	2	.500	7	7	1	1	0	37	44	19	18	5	0	14	14	1.568	4.38	94	5.39	.299	0	....	-2	2	-0.2
Total	13	111	109	.505	304	270	79	20	1	1849	1978	889	769	149	19	526	705	1.354	3.74	107	3.97	.278	6	.140	46	111	4.4

• ZAHNISER, Paul Paul Vernon Zahniser b: 9/6/1896, Sac City, IA d: 9/26/1964, Klamath Falls, OR BR/TR, 5'10.5", 170 lbs. Deb: 5/18/1923

YEAR	TM-L	W	L	PCT	G	GS	CG	SH	SV	IP	H	R	ER	HR	HB	BB	SO	RAT	ERA	ERA+	CERA	OAV	BH	AVG	PR+	WS	TPW
1923	Was-A	9	10	.474	33	21	10	1	0	177	201	103	76	7	3	76	52	1.565	3.86	97	4.46	.291	5	.096	-8	7	-0.9
1924	Was-A	5	7	.417	24	14	5	1	0	92	98	52	45	2	4	49	28	1.598	4.40	92	4.41	.283	4	.129	-6	3	-0.7
1925	Bos-A	5	12	.294	37	21	7	1	1	176^{2}	232	124	101	6	1	89	30	**1.817**	5.15	88	5.70	.327	8	.138	-7	5	-1.0
1926	Bos-A	6	18	.250	30	24	7	1	0	172	213	106	95	5	3	69	35	1.640	4.97	82	4.87	.321	8	.163	-14	6	-1.4
1929	Cin-N	0	0	....	1	0	0	0	0	1	2	3	3	1	0	1	0	3.000	27.00	17	22.62	.400	0	....	-2	0	-0.2
Total	5	25	47	.347	125	80	29	4	1	618^{2}	746	388	320	21	11	284	145	1.665	4.66	89	4.95	.309	25	.132	-37	21	-4.3

• ZAMBRANO, Carlos Carlos Alberto Zambrano b: 6/1/1981, Carabobo, Venezuela BB/TR, 6'4", 220 lbs. Deb: 8/20/2001

YEAR	TM-L	W	L	PCT	G	GS	CG	SH	SV	IP	H	R	ER	HR	HB	BB	SO	RAT	ERA	ERA+	CERA	OAV	BH	AVG	PR+	WS	TPW
2001	Chi-N	1	2	.333	6	1	0	0	0	7^{2}	11	13	13	2	1	8	4	2.478	15.26	27	11.86	.355	0	.000	-9	0	-0.9
2002	Chi-N	4	8	.333	32	16	0	0	0	108^{1}	94	53	44	9	4	63	93	1.449	3.66	110	4.02	.235	1	.033	5	5	0.3
2003*	Chi-N	13	11	.542	32	32	3	1	0	214	188	88	74	9	10	94	168	1.318	3.11	135	3.28	.239	18	.240	26	18	3.2
Total	3	18	21	.462	70	49	3	1	0	330	293	154	131	20	15	165	265	1.388	3.57	116	3.72	.241	19	.178	22	23	2.5

• ZAMBRANO, Victor Victor Manuel Zambrano b: 8/6/1974, Los Teques, Venezuela BR/TR, 6', 190 lbs. Deb: 6/21/2001

YEAR	TM-L	W	L	PCT	G	GS	CG	SH	SV	IP	H	R	ER	HR	HB	BB	SO	RAT	ERA	ERA+	CERA	OAV	BH	AVG	PR+	WS	TPW
2001	TB-A	6	2	.750	36	0	0	0	2	51^{1}	38	21	18	6	3	18	58	1.091	3.16	142	2.80	.201	0	....	7	6	0.7
2002	TB-A	8	8	.500	42	11	0	0	1	114	120	77	70	15	4	68	73	1.649	5.53	81	5.52	.278	0	.000	-15	4	-1.5
2003	TB-A	12	10	.545	34	28	1	0	0	188^{1}	165	97	88	21	20	106	132	1.439	4.21	108	4.51	.237	0	.000	2	10	0.2
Total	3	26	20	.565	112	39	1	0	3	353^{2}	323	195	176	42	27	192	263	1.456	4.48	100	4.59	.245	0	.000	-6	20	-0.6

• ZAMLOCH, Carl Carl Eugene Zamloch b: 10/6/1889, Oakland, CA d: 8/19/1963, Santa Barbara, CA BR/TR, 6'1", 176 lbs. Deb: 5/7/1913

YEAR	TM-L	W	L	PCT	G	GS	CG	SH	SV	IP	H	R	ER	HR	HB	BB	SO	RAT	ERA	ERA+	CERA	OAV	BH	AVG	PR+	WS	TPW
1913	Det-A	1	6	.143	17	5	3	0	1	69^{2}	66	31	19	1	3	23	28	1.278	2.45	119	3.02	.257	4	.182	6	3	0.5

• ZAMORA, Oscar Oscar Jose (Sosa) Zamora b: 9/23/1944, Camaguey, Cuba BR/TR, 5'10", 178 lbs. Deb: 6/18/1974

YEAR	TM-L	W	L	PCT	G	GS	CG	SH	SV	IP	H	R	ER	HR	HB	BB	SO	RAT	ERA	ERA+	CERA	OAV	BH	AVG	PR+	WS	TPW
1974	Chi-N	3	9	.250	56	0	0	0	10	83^{2}	82	33	29	6	0	19	38	1.207	3.12	122	3.00	.264	2	.182	11	9	1.1
1975	Chi-N	5	2	.714	52	0	0	0	10	71	84	42	40	17	0	15	28	1.394	5.07	76	5.22	.298	1	.167	-7	4	-0.8
1976	Chi-N	5	3	.625	40	2	0	0	3	55	70	34	32	8	1	17	27	1.582	5.24	74	5.50	.317	0	.000	-8	2	-0.9
1978	Hou-N	0	0	....	10	0	0	0	0	15	20	12	12	2	0	7	6	1.800	7.20	46	6.36	.328	0	.000	-6	0	-0.7
Total	4	13	14	.481	158	2	0	0	23	224^{2}	256	121	113	33	1	58	99	1.398	4.53	83	4.54	.293	3	.107	-10	15	-1.3

• ZANNI, Dom Dominick Thomas Zanni b: 3/1/1932, Bronx, NY BR/TR, 5'11", 180 lbs. Deb: 9/28/1958

YEAR	TM-L	W	L	PCT	G	GS	CG	SH	SV	IP	H	R	ER	HR	HB	BB	SO	RAT	ERA	ERA+	CERA	OAV	BH	AVG	PR+	WS	TPW
1958	SF-N	1	0	1.000	1	0	0	0	0	4	7	1	1	1	0	1	3	2.000	2.25	170	10.26	.412	0	.000	1	1	0.0
1959	SF-N	0	0	....	9	0	0	0	0	11	12	10	8	2	1	8	11	1.818	6.55	58	6.86	.273	0	....	-3	0	-0.3
1961	SF-N	1	0	1.000	8	0	0	0	0	13^{2}	13	7	6	1	0	12	11	1.829	3.95	96	5.34	.277	0	....	-0	1	0.0
1962	Chi-A	6	5	.545	44	2	0	0	5	86^{1}	67	42	36	12	1	31	66	1.135	3.75	104	2.96	.214	5	.278	2	7	0.4
1963	Chi-A	0	0	....	5	0	0	0	0	4^{1}	5	4	4	1	0	4	2	2.077	8.31	42	8.58	.294	0	....	-2	0	-0.2
	Cin-N	1	1	.500	31	1	0	0	5	43	39	22	20	2	4	21	40	1.395	4.19	80	3.75	.247	1	.333	-4	2	-0.4
1965	Cin-N	0	0	....	8	0	0	0	0	13^{1}	7	2	2	1	0	5	10	.900	1.35	278	1.59	.159	0	.000	4	1	0.4

YEAR TM-L	W	L	PCT	G	GS	CG	SH	SV	IP	H	R	ER	HR	HB	BB	SO	RAT	ERA	ERA+	CERA	OAV	BH	AVG	PR+	WS	TPW
1966 Cin-N	0	0	....	5	0	0	0	0	7^1	5	1	0	0	1	3	5	1.091	0.00	....	2.11	.192	1	1.000	3	1	0.4
Total 7	9	6	.600	111	3	0	0	10	183	155	89	77	20	7	85	148	1.311	3.79	98	3.72	.233	7	.280	-0	13	0.2
• ZASKE, Jeff	Lloyd Jeffrey Zaske b: 10/6/1960, Seattle, WA BR/TR, 6'5", 180 lbs. Deb: 7/21/1984																									
1984 Pit-N	0	0	....	3	0	0	0	0	5	4	0	0	0	0	1	2	1.000	0.00	....	1.70	.211	0	....	2	1	0.2
• ZAVARAS, Clint	Clinton Wayne Zavaras b: 1/4/1967, Denver, CO BR/TR, 6'1", 175 lbs. Deb: 6/3/1989																									
1989 Sea-A	1	6	.143	10	10	0	0	0	52	49	33	30	4	2	30	31	1.519	5.19	78	4.41	.253	0	....	-7	1	-0.7
• ZEISER, Matt	Matthew J. Zeiser b: 9/25/1888, Chicago, IL d: 6/10/1942, Chicago, IL BR/TR, 5'10", 170 lbs. Deb: 4/27/1914																									
1914 Bos-A	0	0	....	2	0	0	0	0	10	9	4	2	0	1	8	0	1.700	1.80	149	5.10	.281	0	.000	1	1	0.0
• ZEPP, Bill	William Clinton Zepp b: 7/22/1946, Detroit, MI BR/TR, 6'2", 185 lbs. Deb: 8/12/1969																									
1969 Min-A	0	0	....	4	0	0	0	0	5^1	6	7	4	1	0	4	2	1.875	6.75	54	6.21	.286	0	.000	-2	0	-0.2
1970* Min-A	9	4	.692	43	20	1	1	2	151	154	63	54	9	9	51	64	1.358	3.22	116	3.88	.266	6	.136	8	9	0.7
1971 Det-A	1	1	.500	16	4	0	0	2	31^2	41	20	18	2	3	17	15	1.832	5.12	70	6.40	.328	0	.000	-5	0	-0.6
Total 3	10	5	.667	63	24	1	1	4	188	201	90	76	12	12	72	81	1.452	3.64	101	4.37	.278	6	.122	0	9	-0.2
• ZERBE, Chad	William Chad Zerbe b: 4/27/1972, Findlay, OH BL/TL, 6', 190 lbs. Deb: 9/18/2000																									
2000 SF-N	0	0	....	4	0	0	0	0	6	6	3	3	1	0	1	5	1.167	4.50	94	3.69	.273	0	....	-0	0	0.0
2001 SF-N	3	0	1.000	27	1	0	0	0	39	41	21	17	3	1	10	22	1.308	3.92	102	3.83	.281	2	.222	0	2	0.0
2002* SF-N	2	0	1.000	50	0	0	0	0	56^1	52	22	19	3	4	21	26	1.296	3.04	128	3.45	.248	1	.167	5	4	0.5
2003 SF-N	1	1	.500	33	1	0	0	0	49^2	60	26	26	3	1	14	17	1.490	4.71	87	4.53	.311	0	.000	-4	2	-0.5
Total 4	6	1	.857	114	2	0	0	0	151	159	72	65	10	6	46	70	1.358	3.87	103	3.91	.278	3	.150	0	8	0.0
• ZETTLEIN, George	George "Charmer" Zettlein b: 7/18/1844, Brooklyn, NY d: 5/23/1905, Patchogue, NY BR/TR, 5'9", 162 lbs. Deb: 5/8/1871																									
1871 Chi-n	18	9	.667	28	28	25	0	0	240^2	298	233	73	6	....	25	22	1.342	**2.73**	**168**	....	.265	32	.250	**38**	....	**2.0**
1872 Tro-n	14	8	.636	25	22	17	2	1	187^2	209	132	45	2	....	8	17	1.156	2.16	146	....	.246	29	.257	18	....	1.2
Eck-n	1	8	.111	9	9	8	0	0	75^1	105	62	23	1	....	6	8	1.473	2.75	116	....	.289	3	.088	12	....	0.6
Yr.	15	16	.484	34	31	25	2	1	263	314	194	68	3	....	14	25	1.247	2.33	136	....	.259	32	.218	30	....	1.8
1873 Phi-n	36	15	.706	51	51	49	0	0	460	593	368	138	3	....	41	28	1.378	2.70	122	....	.277	50	.207	16	....	0.6
1874 Chi-n	27	30	.474	57	57	57	3	0	515^2	653	439	139	3	....	43	26	1.350	2.43	99	....	.276	47	.193	-13	....	-1.6
1875 Chi-n	17	14	.548	31	31	29	6	0	282	269	142	57	0	....	6	18	.975	1.82	138	....	.228	29	.218	18	....	1.2
Phi-n	12	8	.600	21	21	20	1	0	181^1	209	121	48	0	....	10	13	1.208	2.38	106	....	.263	15	.181	1	....	-0.2
Yr.	29	22	.569	52	52	49	**7**	0	463^1	478	263	105	0	....	16	31	1.066	2.04	123	....	.242	44	.204	19	....	1.0
1876 Phi-N	4	20	.167	28	25	23	1	2	234	358	212	101	2	....	6	10	1.556	3.88	62	....	.327	27	.211	-23	2	-2.4
Total 5 n	125	92	.576	222	219	205	12	1	1942^2	2336	1497	523	15	....	139	132	1.274	2.42	121	....	.265	205	.210	90	....	4.0
• ZICK, Bob	Robert George Zick b: 4/26/1927, Chicago, IL BL/TR, 6', 168 lbs. Deb: 5/2/1954																									
1954 Chi-N	0	0	....	8	0	0	0	0	16^1	23	15	15	1	0	7	9	1.837	8.27	51	6.37	.343	1	.250	-7	0	-0.7
• ZIEGLER, George	George J. Ziegler b: 1872, Chicago, IL d: 7/22/1916, Kankakee, IL, 5'8" Deb: 6/19/1890																									
1890 Pit-N	0	1	.000	1	1	0	0	0	6	12	7	7	0	0	0	1	2.000	10.50	31	....	.404	0	.000	-4	0	-0.4
• ZIEM, Steve	Stephen Graeling Ziem b: 10/24/1961, Milwaukee, WI BR/TR, 6'2", 210 lbs. Deb: 4/30/1987																									
1987 Atl-N	0	1	.000	2	0	0	0	0	2^1	4	3	2	0	0	1	0	2.143	7.71	56	7.52	.364	0	....	-1	0	-0.1
• ZIMMERMAN, Jeff	Jeffrey Ross Zimmerman b: 8/9/1972, Kelowna, Canada BR/TR, 6'1", 200 lbs. Deb: 4/13/1999																									
1999* Tex-A★	9	3	.750	65	0	0	0	3	87^2	50	24	23	9	2	23	67	.833	2.36	215	1.57	.166	0	....	28	14	2.6
2000 Tex-A	4	5	.444	65	0	0	0	1	69^2	80	45	41	10	2	34	74	1.636	5.30	94	5.58	.286	0	....	-1	4	-0.1
2001 Tex-A	4	4	.500	66	0	0	0	28	71^1	48	19	19	10	4	16	72	.897	2.40	195	2.23	.192	0	....	19	12	1.8
Total 3	17	12	.586	196	0	0	0	32	228^2	178	88	83	29	8	73	213	1.098	3.27	151	3.00	.214	0	....	45	30	4.2
• ZIMMERMAN, Jordan	Jordan William Zimmerman b: 4/28/1975, Kelowna, Canada BR/TL, 6', 200 lbs. Deb: 5/17/1999																									
1999 Sea-A	0	0	....	12	0	0	0	0	8	14	8	7	0	1	4	3	2.250	7.88	63	9.05	.389	0	....	-3	0	-0.2
• ZINK, Walter	Walter Noble Zink b: 11/21/1898, Pittsfield, MA d: 6/12/1964, Quincy, MA BR/TR, 6', 165 lbs. Deb: 7/6/1921																									
1921 NY-N	0	0	....	2	0	0	0	0	4	4	3	1	0	0	3	1	1.750	2.25	163	3.86	.235	0	.000	1	0	0.0
• ZINN, Jimmy	James Edward Zinn b: 1/21/1895, Benton, AR d: 2/26/1991, Memphis, TN BL/TR, 6'.5", 195 lbs. Deb: 9/4/1919																									
1919 Phi-A	1	3	.250	5	3	2	0	0	25^2	38	20	18	1	1	10	9	1.870	6.31	54	6.93	.365	4	.308	-7	0	-0.6
1920 Pit-N	1	1	.500	6	3	2	0	0	31	32	14	12	2	1	5	18	1.194	3.48	92	3.13	.260	3	.200	-1	2	-0.1
1921 Pit-N	7	6	.538	32	9	5	1	4	127^1	159	63	52	3	2	30	49	1.484	3.68	104	4.27	.318	11	.224	2	9	0.1
1922 Pit-N	0	0	....	5	0	0	0	1	9^2	11	4	2	1	0	2	3	1.345	1.86	219	4.18	.297	0	.000	3	1	0.2
1929 Cle-A	4	6	.400	18	11	6	1	2	105^1	150	75	59	8	3	33	29	1.737	5.04	88	6.09	.340	16	.381	-6	6	0.1
Total 5	13	16	.448	66	26	15	2	7	299	390	176	143	15	7	80	108	1.572	4.30	91	5.02	.324	34	.283	-10	18	-0.2
• ZINSER, Bill	William Francis Zinser b: 1/6/1918, Astoria, NY d: 2/16/1993, Englewood, FL BR/TR, 6'1", 185 lbs. Deb: 8/19/1944																									
1944 Was-A	0	0	....	2	0	0	0	0	0^2	1	2	2	0	0	5	1	9.000	27.00	12	34.80	.333	0	....	-2	0	-0.2
• ZITO, Barry	Barry William Zito b: 5/13/1978, Las Vegas, NV BL/TL, 6'4", 205 lbs. Deb: 7/22/2000																									
2000* Oak-A	7	4	.636	14	14	1	1	0	92^2	64	30	28	6	2	45	78	1.176	2.72	174	2.63	.195	0	....	22	9	2.0
2001* Oak-A	17	8	.680	35	**35**	3	2	0	214^1	184	92	83	18	13	80	205	1.232	3.49	127	3.33	.230	0	.000	22	15	2.0
2002* Oak-A★	**23**	5	.821	35	**35**	1	0	0	229^1	182	79	70	24	9	78	182	1.134	2.75	160	2.92	.218	0	.000	43	**25**	4.1
2003* Oak-A★	14	12	.538	35	35	4	1	0	231^2	186	98	85	19	6	88	146	1.183	3.30	137	2.91	.219	0	.000	31	18	2.9
Total 4	61	29	.678	119	119	9	4	0	768	616	299	266	67	30	291	611	1.181	3.12	144	3.00	.219	0	.000	118	67	11.1
• ZMICH, Ed	Edward Albert Zmich b: 10/1/1884, Cleveland, OH d: 8/20/1950, Cleveland, OH BL/TL, 6', 180 lbs. Deb: 7/23/1910																									
1910 StL-N	0	5	.000	9	6	2	0	0	36	38	27	25	0	3	29	19	1.861	6.25	48	5.87	.304	1	.077	-12	0	-1.4
1911 StL-N	1	0	1.000	4	0	0	0	0	12^2	8	5	3	0	1	8	4	1.263	2.13	158	2.45	.182	0	.000	2	1	0.1
Total 2	1	5	.167	13	6	2	0	0	48^2	46	32	28	0	4	37	23	1.705	5.18	58	4.98	.272	1	.059	-10	1	-1.3
• ZOLDAK, Sam	Samuel Walter "Sad Sam" Zoldak b: 12/8/1918, Brooklyn, NY d: 8/25/1966, New Hyde Park, NY BL/TL, 5'11.5", 185 lbs. Deb: 5/13/1944																									
1944 StL-A	0	0	....	18	0	0	0	0	38^2	49	22	16	1	0	19	15	1.759	3.72	97	5.23	.310	2	.333	0	1	0.1
1945 StL-A	3	2	.600	26	1	1	0	0	69^2	74	32	26	3	0	18	19	1.321	3.36	105	3.38	.267	1	.050	1	4	-0.1
1946 StL-A	9	11	.450	35	21	9	2	2	170^1	166	71	65	11	1	57	51	1.309	3.43	109	3.39	.256	9	.173	6	11	0.6
1947 StL-A	9	10	.474	35	19	6	1	1	171	162	76	66	7	0	76	36	1.392	3.47	112	3.49	.254	10	.172	10	13	0.9
1948 StL-A	2	4	.333	11	9	0	0	0	54	64	30	28	4	1	19	13	1.537	4.67	98	4.78	.296	6	.273	0	3	0.1
Cle-A	9	6	.600	23	12	4	1	0	105^2	104	37	33	6	0	24	17	1.211	2.81	144	3.06	.261	5	.139	12	8	1.0
Yr.	11	10	.524	34	21	4	1	0	159^2	168	67	61	10	1	43	30	1.322	3.44	124	3.64	.274	11	.190	13	11	1.1
1949 Cle-A	1	2	.333	27	0	0	0	0	53	60	30	25	4	0	18	11	1.472	4.25	94	4.25	.291	3	.375	-2	2	-0.1
1950 Cle-A	4	2	.667	33	3	0	0	4	63^2	64	33	28	6	1	21	15	1.335	3.96	109	3.73	.259	3	.188	2	5	0.3
1951 Phi-A	6	10	.375	26	18	8	1	0	128	127	51	45	9	0	24	18	1.180	3.16	135	2.98	.257	7	.156	14	9	1.1
1952 Phi-A	0	6	.000	16	10	2	0	1	75^1	86	41	34	3	0	25	12	1.473	4.06	97	4.14	.290	4	.174	0	3	0.0
Total 9	43	53	.448	250	93	30	5	8	929^1	956	423	366	54	3	301	207	1.353	3.54	112	3.60	.267	50	.175	45	59	3.8
• ZUBER, Bill	William Henry "Goober" Zuber b: 3/26/1913, Middle Amana, IA d: 11/2/1982, Cedar Rapids, IA BR/TR, 6'2", 195 lbs. Deb: 9/16/1936																									
1936 Cle-A	1	1	.500	2	2	1	0	0	13^2	14	11	10	0	0	15	5	2.122	6.59	77	5.93	.269	1	.200	-2	0	-0.2
1938 Cle-A	0	3	.000	15	0	0	0	1	28^2	33	18	16	0	0	20	14	1.849	5.02	92	5.20	.295	0	.000	-1	1	-0.2
1939 Cle-A	2	0	1.000	16	1	0	0	0	31^2	41	24	21	2	1	19	16	1.895	5.97	74	6.30	.323	1	.200	-5	1	-0.5
1940 Cle-A	1	1	.500	17	0	0	0	0	24	25	17	15	3	0	14	12	1.625	5.63	75	4.91	.260	1	.333	-4	0	-0.4
1941 Was-A	6	4	.600	36	7	1	0	2	96^1	110	63	58	5	2	61	51	1.775	5.42	75	5.42	.291	0	.000	-14	3	-1.6

YEAR	TM-L	W	L	PCT	G	GS	CG	SH	SV	IP	H	R	ER	HR	HB	BB	SO	RAT	ERA	ERA+	CERA	OAV	BH	AVG	PR+	WS	TPW
1942	Was-A	9	9	.500	37	7	3	1	1	126²	115	66	54	5	0	82	64	1.555	3.84	95	3.87	.243	6	.154	3	5	0.3
1943	NY-A	8	4	.667	20	13	7	0	1	118	100	54	51	3	0	74	57	1.475	3.89	83	3.44	.234	7	.184	-11	5	-1.0
1944	NY-A	5	7	.417	22	13	2	1	0	107	101	54	50	5	1	54	59	1.449	4.21	83	3.77	.255	4	.129	-11	3	-1.3
1945	NY-A	5	11	.313	21	14	7	0	1	127	121	50	45	2	0	56	50	1.394	3.19	108	3.39	.259	7	.167	1	7	0.0
1946	NY-A	0	1	.000	3	0	0	0	0	5²	10	9	8	2	0	3	3	2.294	12.71	27	11.89	.385	0	.000	-6	0	-0.7
	*Bos-A	5	1	.833	15	7	2	1	0	56²	37	20	16	4	0	39	29	1.341	2.54	144	2.96	.187	2	.111	7	5	0.6
	Yr.	5	2	.714	18	7	2	1	0	62¹	47	29	24	6	0	42	32	1.428	3.47	104	3.77	.210	2	.100	1	5	0.0
1947	Bos-A	1	0	1.000	20	1	0	0	0	50²	60	32	30	4	0	31	23	1.796	5.33	73	5.87	.311	2	.154	-8	1	-0.9
Total 11		43	42	.506	224	65	23	3	6	786	767	418	374	35	4	468	383	1.571	4.28	87	4.24	.260	31	.135	-52	31	-5.8

• ZUVERINK, George

George Zuverink b: 8/20/1924, Holland, MI BR/TR, 6'4", 200 lbs. Deb: 4/21/1951

YEAR	TM-L	W	L	PCT	G	GS	CG	SH	SV	IP	H	R	ER	HR	HB	BB	SO	RAT	ERA	ERA+	CERA	OAV	BH	AVG	PR+	WS	TPW
1951	Cle-A	0	0	....	16	0	0	0	0	25¹	24	17	15	2	1	13	14	1.461	5.33	71	3.98	.253	0	....	-4	0	-0.4
1952	Cle-A	0	0	....	1	0	0	0	0	1¹	1	0	0	0	0	0	1	.750	0.00	....	1.13	.200	0	....	1	0	0.1
1954	Cin-N	0	0	....	2	0	0	0	0	6	10	6	6	1	0	1	2	1.833	9.00	47	7.74	.385	1	.500	-3	0	-0.3
	Det-A	9	13	.409	35	25	9	2	4	203	201	93	81	22	8	62	70	1.296	3.59	103	3.75	.257	8	.125	2	11	-0.2
1955	Det-A	0	5	.000	14	1	0	0	0	28¹	38	27	22	6	1	14	13	1.835	6.99	55	7.06	.309	0	.000	-10	0	-1.0
	Bal-A	4	3	.571	28	5	0	0	4	86¹	80	28	21	5	4	17	31	1.124	2.19	174	3.01	.264	5	.217	17	8	1.8
	Yr.	4	8	.333	42	6	0	0	4	114²	118	55	43	11	5	31	44	1.299	3.38	113	4.01	.277	5	.185	7	8	0.7
1956	Bal-A	7	6	.538	62	0	0	0	16	97¹	112	52	45	6	3	34	33	1.500	4.16	94	4.40	.294	2	.118	-2	9	-0.3
1957	Bal-A	10	6	.625	56	0	0	0	9	112²	105	37	31	9	4	39	36	1.278	2.48	145	3.32	.257	3	.130	12	12	1.2
1958	Bal-A	2	2	.500	45	0	0	0	7	69	74	29	26	4	6	17	22	1.319	3.39	106	3.90	.286	2	.222	2	6	0.3
1959	Bal-A	0	1	.000	6	0	0	0	0	13	15	7	6	1	0	6	1	1.615	4.15	91	5.40	.306	0	....	-1	1	0.0
Total 8		32	36	.471	265	31	9	2	40	642¹	660	296	253	56	27	203	223	1.344	3.54	106	3.91	.271	21	.148	13	47	1.1

Chapter 62

The Postseason Register

Carl Furillo

In Game 2 of the 1953 World Series, Furillo scored past Yankee catcher Yogi Berra, but the Dodgers lost the game, 4-2, and the Series in six.

Major league postseason competition goes back to the dawn of professional league play, in 1871. The first such contest to determine the "champions of the world" was held in 1884, and it is from that date that we present the annual and cumulative batting and pitching records of every individual to have appeared in a World Series.

In 1969 the American and National Leagues each expanded to 12 teams and realigned into Eastern and Western divisions. This produced a new layer of competition: the League Championship Series (LCS). Through 1984 it was a best-of-five match, but in the years since, it has been expanded to the best-of-seven format that has marked the World Series since 1922.

In 1995 the first Division Series was held. The major leagues' 28 teams—which expanded to 30 in 1998—were arranged into three divisions in each league. The second-place team with the best record in each league, known as the Wild Card, reached the post-season along with the three division winners.

What follows are the annual and career records for every player and pitcher in postseason history. Records are broken down by series and postseason level. For example, each Division Series performance is listed and marked with a "D"; a total for that round is given if the player made multiple Division Series appearances. (The 1981 Divisional Playoffs caused by the strike-interrupted schedule are included in Division Series totals.) All LCS performances are marked with an "L." World Series statistics, for both National League vs. American Association from 1884–90 and American League vs. National League from 1903 to present, are marked with a "W."

For more detail about a particular year's postseason competition, see the Postseason Play chapter. For an overview of that year's regular-season play, see the Annual Record. And for further details about a particular individual, refer to the Player and Pitcher Registers.

SER-YEAR	TM-L	AVG	G	AB	R	H	2B	3B	HR	RBI	BB	SO	SB	POS
• AARON, Hank														
L 1969	Atl-N	.357	3	14	3	5	2	0	3	7	0	1	0	O-3
W 1957	Mil-N	.393	7	28	5	11	0	1	3	7	1	6	0	O-7
W 1958	Mil-N	.333	7	27	3	9	2	0	0	2	4	6	0	O-7
W Total	2	.364	14	55	8	20	2	1	3	9	5	12	0	....
• AARON, Tommie														
L 1969	Atl-N	.000	1	1	0	0	0	0	0	0	0	0	0	....
• ABBATICCHIO, Ed														
W 1909	Pit-N	.000	1	1	0	0	0	0	0	0	0	1	0	....
• ABBOTT, Glenn														
L 1975	Oak-A	....	1	0	0	0	0	0	0	0	0	0	0	....
• ABBOTT, Jeff														
D 2000	Chi-A	.000	1	1	0	0	0	0	0	0	0	0	0	O-1
• ABBOTT, Kurt														
D 1997	Fla-N	.250	3	8	0	2	0	0	0	0	0	0	0	2-2
D 2000	NY-N	.000	1	2	0	0	0	0	0	0	0	1	0	S-1
D Total	2	.200	4	10	0	2	0	0	0	0	0	1	0	....
L 1997	Fla-N	.375	2	8	0	3	1	0	0	0	0	2	0	2-2
L 2000	NY-N	.000	2	3	0	0	0	0	0	0	0	2	0	S-2
L Total	2	.273	4	11	0	3	1	0	0	0	0	4	0	....
W 1997	Fla-N	.000	3	3	0	0	0	0	0	0	0	1	0	D-1
W 2000	NY-N	.250	5	8	0	2	1	0	0	0	1	3	0	S-5
W Total	2	.182	8	11	0	2	1	0	0	0	1	4	0	....
• ABREU, Bobby														
D 1997	Hou-N	.333	3	3	0	1	0	0	0	0	0	2	1	....
• ABSTEIN, Bill														
W 1909	Pit-N	.231	7	26	3	6	2	0	0	2	3	9	1	1-7
• ADAIR, Jerry														
W 1967	Bos-A	.125	5	16	0	2	0	0	0	1	0	3	1	2-4
• ADAMS, Sparky														
W 1930	StL-N	.143	6	21	0	3	0	0	0	1	0	4	0	3-6
W 1931	StL-N	.250	2	4	0	1	0	0	0	0	0	1	0	3-2
W Total	2	.160	8	25	0	4	0	0	0	1	0	5	0	....
• ADAMS, Spencer														
W 1925	Was-A	.000	2	1	0	0	0	0	0	0	0	0	0	2-1
W 1926	NY-A	....	2	0	0	0	0	0	0	0	0	0	0	....
W Total	2	.000	4	1	0	0	0	0	0	0	0	0	0	....
• ADCOCK, Joe														
W 1957	Mil-N	.200	5	15	1	3	0	0	0	2	0	2	0	1-5
W 1958	Mil-N	.308	4	13	1	4	0	0	0	0	1	3	0	1-3
W Total	2	.250	9	28	2	7	0	0	0	2	1	5	0	....
• AGBAYANI, Benny														
D 1999	NY-N	.300	4	10	1	3	1	0	0	1	0	3	0	O-4
D 2000	NY-N	.333	4	15	1	5	1	0	1	1	3	3	0	O-4
D Total	2	.320	8	25	2	8	2	0	1	2	3	6	0	....
L 1999	NY-N	.143	4	7	2	1	0	0	0	0	4	2	1	O-3
L 2000	NY-N	.353	5	17	0	6	2	0	0	3	4	0	0	O-5
L Total	2	.292	9	24	2	7	2	0	0	3	8	2	1	....
W 2000	NY-N	.278	5	18	2	5	2	0	0	2	3	6	0	O-5
• AGEE, Tommie														
L 1969	NY-N	.357	3	14	4	5	1	0	2	4	2	5	2	O-3
W 1969	NY-N	.167	5	18	1	3	0	0	1	1	2	5	1	O-5
• AGNEW, Sam														
W 1918	Bos-A	.000	4	9	0	0	0	0	0	0	0	0	0	C-4
• AGUAYO, Luis														
D 1981	Phi-N	....	2	0	1	0	0	0	0	0	0	0	0	....
• AIKENS, Willie														
D 1981	KC-A	.333	3	9	0	3	0	0	0	0	3	2	0	1-3
L 1980	KC-A	.364	3	11	0	4	0	0	0	2	0	1	0	1-3
W 1980	KC-A	.400	6	20	5	8	0	1	4	8	6	8	0	1-6
• ALDRETE, Mike														
L 1987	SF-N	.100	5	10	0	1	0	0	0	1	0	2	0	O-3
L 1996	NY-A	....	1	0	0	0	0	0	0	0	0	0	0	....
L Total	2	.100	6	10	0	1	0	0	0	1	0	2	0	....
W 1996	NY-A	.000	2	1	0	0	0	0	0	0	0	0	0	O-1
• ALEXANDER, Doyle														
L 1973	Bal-A	....	1	0	0	0	0	0	0	0	0	0	0	....
L 1985	Tor-A	....	2	0	0	0	0	0	0	0	0	0	0	....
L 1987	Det-A	....	2	0	0	0	0	0	0	0	0	0	0	....
L Total	3	....	5	0	0	0	0	0	0	0	0	0	0	....
W 1976	NY-A	....	1	0	0	0	0	0	0	0	0	0	0	....
• ALEXANDER, Manny														
D 1996	Bal-A	....	3	0	2	0	0	0	0	0	0	0	0	D-1
D 1998	Chi-N	.000	2	5	0	0	0	0	0	0	0	1	0	S-1
D Total	2	.000	5	5	2	0	0	0	0	0	0	1	0	....
• ALEXANDER, Matt														
L 1979	Pit-N	....	1	0	1	0	0	0	0	0	0	0	0	....
W 1979	Pit-N	....	1	0	0	0	0	0	0	0	0	0	0	O-1
• ALFONZO, Edgardo														
D 1999	NY-N	.250	4	16	6	4	1	0	3	6	3	2	0	2-4
D 2000	NY-N	.278	4	18	1	5	2	0	1	5	1	2	0	2-4
D 2003	SF-N	.529	4	17	3	9	4	0	0	5	1	1	0	3-4
D Total	3	.353	12	51	10	18	7	0	4	16	5	5	0	....
L 1999	NY-N	.222	6	27	2	6	4	0	0	1	1	9	0	2-6

SER-YEAR	TM-L	AVG	G	AB	R	H	2B	3B	HR	RBI	BB	SO	SB	POS
L 2000	NY-N	.444	5	18	5	8	1	1	0	4	4	1	0	2-5
L Total	2	.311	11	45	7	14	5	1	0	5	5	10	0	....
W 2000	NY-N	.143	5	21	1	3	0	0	0	1	1	5	0	2-5
• ALICEA, Luis														
D 1995	Bos-A	.600	3	10	1	6	1	0	1	1	2	2	1	2-3
D 1996	StL-N	.182	3	11	1	2	2	0	0	0	1	4	0	2-3
D 1998	Tex-A	.000	1	1	0	0	0	0	0	0	0	0	0	D-1
D Total	3	.364	7	22	2	8	3	0	1	1	3	6	1	....
L 1996	StL-N	.000	5	8	0	0	0	0	0	0	2	1	0	2-4
• ALLEN, Dick														
L 1976	Phi-N	.222	3	9	1	2	0	0	0	0	3	2	0	1-3
• ALLEY, Gene														
L 1970	Pit-N	.000	2	7	0	0	0	0	0	0	1	2	0	S-2
L 1971	Pit-N	.500	1	2	1	1	0	0	0	0	0	0	0	S-1
L 1972	Pit-N	.000	5	16	1	0	0	0	0	0	0	3	0	S-5
L Total	3	.040	8	25	2	1	0	0	0	0	1	5	0	....
W 1971	Pit-N	.000	2	2	0	0	0	0	0	0	1	0	0	S-2
• ALLISON, Bob														
L 1969	Min-A	.000	2	8	0	0	0	0	0	1	0	0	0	O-2
L 1970	Min-A	.000	3	2	0	0	0	0	0	0	1	1	0	....
L Total	2	.000	5	10	0	0	0	0	0	1	1	1	0	....
W 1965	Min-A	.125	5	16	3	2	1	0	1	2	2	9	1	O-5
• ALOMAR, Roberto														
D 1996	Bal-A	.294	4	17	2	5	0	0	1	4	2	3	0	2-4
D 1997	Bal-A	.300	4	10	1	3	2	0	0	2	1	1	0	2-4
D 1999	Cle-A	.368	5	19	4	7	4	0	0	3	2	3	2	2-5
D 2001	Cle-A	.190	5	21	3	4	3	0	0	3	2	5	0	2-5
D Total	4	.284	18	67	10	19	9	0	1	12	7	12	2	....
L 1991	Tor-A	.474	5	19	3	9	0	0	0	4	2	3	2	2-5
L 1992	Tor-A	.423	6	26	4	11	1	0	2	4	2	1	5	2-6
L 1993	Tor-A	.292	6	24	3	7	2	0	0	4	4	3	4	2-6
L 1996	Bal-A	.217	5	23	2	5	2	0	0	1	0	4	0	2-5
L 1997	Bal-A	.182	6	22	2	4	0	0	1	2	7	3	0	2-6
L Total	5	.316	28	114	14	36	5	0	3	15	15	14	11	....
W 1992	Tor-A	.208	6	24	3	5	1	0	0	0	3	3	3	2-6
W 1993	Tor-A	.480	6	25	5	12	2	1	0	6	2	3	4	2-6
W Total	2	.347	12	49	8	17	3	1	0	6	5	6	7	....
• ALOMAR JR., Sandy														
D 1995	Cle-A	.182	3	11	1	2	1	0	0	1	0	1	0	C-3
D 1996	Cle-A	.125	4	16	0	2	0	0	0	3	0	2	0	C-4
D 1997	Cle-A	.316	5	19	4	6	1	0	2	5	0	2	0	C-5
D 1998	Cle-A	.231	4	13	2	3	3	0	0	2	1	4	0	C-4
D 1999	Cle-A	.143	5	14	1	2	0	0	0	1	2	6	0	C-5
D Total	5	.205	21	73	8	15	5	0	2	12	3	15	0	....
L 1995	Cle-A	.267	5	15	0	4	1	1	0	1	1	1	0	C-5
L 1997	Cle-A	.125	6	24	3	3	0	0	1	4	1	3	0	C-6
L 1998	Cle-A	.063	5	16	1	1	0	0	0	0	0	2	0	C-5
L Total	3	.145	16	55	4	8	1	1	1	5	2	6	0	....
W 1995	Cle-A	.200	5	15	0	3	2	0	0	1	0	2	0	C-5
W 1997	Cle-A	.367	7	30	5	11	1	0	2	10	2	3	0	C-7
W Total	2	.311	12	45	5	14	3	0	2	11	2	5	0	....
• ALOMAR SR., Sandy														
L 1976	NY-A	.000	2	1	0	0	0	0	0	0	0	0	0	D-1
• ALOU, Felipe														
L 1969	Atl-N	.000	1	1	0	0	0	0	0	0	0	0	0	....
W 1962	SF-N	.269	7	26	2	7	1	1	0	1	1	4	0	O-7
• ALOU, Jesus														
L 1973	Oak-A	.333	4	6	0	2	0	0	0	1	0	1	0	D-1
L 1974	Oak-A	1.000	1	1	0	1	0	0	0	0	0	0	0	....
L Total	2	.429	5	7	0	3	0	0	0	1	0	1	0	....
W 1973	Oak-A	.158	7	19	0	3	1	0	0	3	0	0	0	O-6
W 1974	Oak-A	.000	1	1	0	0	0	0	0	0	0	1	0	....
W Total	2	.150	8	20	0	3	1	0	0	3	0	1	0	....
• ALOU, Matty														
L 1970	Pit-N	.250	3	12	1	3	1	0	0	0	2	1	0	O-3
L 1972	Oak-A	.381	5	21	2	8	4	0	0	2	0	2	1	O-5
L Total	2	.333	8	33	3	11	5	0	0	2	2	3	1	....
W 1962	SF-N	.333	6	12	2	4	1	0	0	1	0	1	0	O-4
W 1972	Oak-A	.042	7	24	0	1	0	0	0	0	3	0	1	O-7
W Total	2	.139	13	36	2	5	1	0	0	1	3	1	1	....
• ALOU, Moises														
D 1997	Fla-N	.214	3	14	1	3	1	0	0	1	0	3	0	O-3
D 1998	Hou-N	.188	4	16	0	3	0	0	0	0	0	2	0	O-4
D 2001	Hou-N	.167	3	12	0	2	1	0	0	1	0	1	0	O-3
D 2003	Chi-N	.500	5	20	3	10	1	0	0	3	1	4	1	O-5
D Total	4	.290	15	62	4	18	3	0	0	5	1	10	1	....
L 1997	Fla-N	.067	5	15	0	1	1	0	0	5	1	3	0	O-4
L 2003	Chi-N	.310	7	29	4	9	1	0	2	5	2	1	0	O-7
L Total	2	.227	12	44	4	10	2	0	2	10	3	4	0	....
W 1997	Fla-N	.321	7	28	6	9	2	0	3	9	3	6	1	O-7
• ALVAREZ, Wilson														
D 1997	SF-N	.000	1	2	0	0	0	0	0	0	0	0	0	....
L 1993	Chi-A	....	1	0	0	0	0	0	0	0	0	0	0	....
• ALYEA, Brant														
L 1970	Min-A	.000	3	7	1	0	0	0	0	0	2	3	0	O-2
• AMARAL, Rich														
D 1997	Sea-A	.500	2	4	2	2	0	0	0	0	0	1	0	1-2
L 1995	Sea-A	.000	2	2	0	0	0	0	0	0	0	1	0	....

YEAR	TM-L	AVG	G	AB	R	H	2B	3B	HR	RBI	BB	SO	SB	POS
• AMARO, Ruben														
L 1995	Cle-A	.000	3	1	1	0	0	0	0	0	0	0	0	D-1
W 1995	Cle-A	.000	2	2	0	0	0	0	0	0	0	1	0	O-1
• AMOROS, Sandy														
W 1952	Bro-N	....	1	0	0	0	0	0	0	0	0	0	0	....
W 1955	Bro-N	.333	5	12	3	4	0	0	1	3	4	4	0	O-5
W 1956	Bro-N	.053	6	19	1	1	0	0	0	1	2	4	0	O-6
W Total	3	.161	12	31	4	5	0	0	1	4	6	8	0	....
• ANDERSON, Brady														
D 1996	Bal-A	.294	4	17	3	5	0	0	2	4	2	3	0	O-4
D 1997	Bal-A	.353	4	17	3	6	1	0	1	4	1	4	1	O-4
D Total	2	.324	8	34	6	11	1	0	3	8	3	7	1	....
L 1996	Bal-A	.190	5	21	5	4	1	0	1	1	3	5	0	O-5
L 1997	Bal-A	.360	6	25	5	9	2	0	2	3	4	4	2	O-6
L Total	2	.283	11	46	10	13	3	0	3	4	7	9	2	....
• ANDERSON, Dave														
L 1985	LA-N	.000	4	5	1	0	0	0	0	0	3	1	0	3-1,S-3
W 1988	LA-N	.000	1	1	0	0	0	0	0	0	0	1	0	D-1
• ANDERSON, Garret														
D 2002	Ana-A	.389	4	18	5	7	2	0	1	4	1	3	0	O-4
L 2002	Ana-A	.250	5	20	3	5	1	0	1	3	1	0	0	O-5
W 2002	Ana-A	.281	7	32	3	9	1	0	0	6	0	3	0	O-7
• ANDERSON, Jim														
L 1979	Cal-A	.091	4	11	0	1	0	0	0	0	0	1	0	S-4
• ANDREWS, Mike														
L 1973	Oak-A	.000	2	1	0	0	0	0	0	0	0	0	0	1-1,D-1
W 1967	Bos-A	.308	5	13	2	4	0	0	0	1	0	1	0	2-3
W 1973	Oak-A	.000	2	3	0	0	0	0	0	0	1	1	0	2-1
W Total	2	.250	7	16	2	4	0	0	0	1	1	2	0	....
• ANSON, Cap														
W 1885	Chi-N	.423	7	26	8	11	1	1	0	7	2	0	0	1-7
W 1886	Chi-N	.238	6	21	3	5	1	0	0	1	4	0	1	1-6,C-2
W Total	2	.340	13	47	11	16	2	1	0	8	6	0	1	....
• ANTHONY, Eric														
L 1995	Cin-N	.000	2	1	0	0	0	0	0	0	1	1	0	....
• ANTONELLI, Johnny														
W 1954	NY-N	.000	2	3	0	0	0	0	0	1	0	0	0	....
• APARICIO, Luis														
W 1959	Chi-A	.308	6	26	1	8	1	0	0	0	2	3	1	S-6
W 1966	Bal-A	.250	4	16	0	4	1	0	0	2	0	0	0	S-4
W Total	2	.286	10	42	1	12	2	0	0	2	2	3	1	....
• ARCHER, Jimmy														
W 1907	Det-A	.000	1	3	0	0	0	0	0	0	0	1	0	C-1
W 1910	Chi-N	.182	3	11	1	2	1	0	0	0	0	4	0	1-1,C-2
W Total	2	.143	4	14	1	2	1	0	0	0	0	5	0	....
• ARIAS, Alex														
D 1997	Fla-N	1.000	1	1	0	1	0	0	0	1	0	0	0	....
L 1997	Fla-N	1.000	3	1	0	1	0	0	0	0	0	0	0	3-2
W 1997	Fla-N	.000	2	1	1	0	0	0	0	0	0	0	0	3-1,D-1
• ARIAS, George														
D 1998	SD-N	.000	1	1	0	0	0	0	0	0	0	1	0	....
• ARMAS, Tony														
D 1981	Oak-A	.545	3	11	1	6	2	0	0	3	1	1	0	O-3
L 1981	Oak-A	.167	3	12	0	2	0	0	0	0	0	5	0	O-3
L 1986	Bos-A	.125	5	16	1	2	1	0	0	0	0	2	0	O-5
L Total	2	.143	8	28	1	4	1	0	0	0	0	7	0	....
W 1986	Bos-A	.000	1	1	0	0	0	0	0	0	0	1	0	....
• ARMBRISTER, Ed														
L 1973	Cin-N	.167	3	6	0	1	0	0	0	0	0	5	0	O-1
L 1975	Cin-N	....	2	0	0	0	0	0	0	1	0	0	0	....
L 1976	Cin-N	....	1	0	0	0	0	0	0	0	0	0	0	....
L Total	3	.167	6	6	0	1	0	0	0	1	0	5	0	....
W 1975	Cin-N	.000	4	1	1	0	0	0	0	0	2	0	0	....
• ARMSTRONG, Jack														
W 1990	Cin-N	....	1	0	0	0	0	0	0	0	0	0	0	....
• ARNOVICH, Morrie														
W 1940	Cin-N	.000	1	1	0	0	0	0	0	0	0	0	0	O-1
• ASHBURN, Richie														
W 1950	Phi-N	.176	4	17	0	3	1	0	0	1	0	4	0	O-4
• ASHBY, Alan														
D 1981	Hou-N	.111	3	9	1	1	0	0	1	2	2	0	0	C-3
L 1980	Hou-N	.125	2	8	0	1	0	0	0	1	0	0	0	C-2
L 1986	Hou-N	.130	6	23	2	3	1	0	1	2	2	1	0	C-6
L Total	2	.129	8	31	2	4	1	0	1	3	2	1	0	....
• ASHLEY, Billy														
D 1995	LA-N	....	1	0	0	0	0	0	0	0	1	0	0	....
D 1996	LA-N	.000	2	2	0	0	0	0	0	0	0	2	0	....
D Total	2	.000	3	2	0	0	0	0	0	0	1	2	0	....
• ASPROMONTE, Bob														
L 1969	Atl-N	.000	3	3	0	0	0	0	0	0	0	0	0	....
• AUERBACH, Rick														
L 1974	LA-N	1.000	1	1	0	1	1	0	0	0	0	0	0	....
L 1979	Cin-N	.000	2	2	0	0	0	0	0	0	0	1	0	....
L Total	2	.333	3	3	0	1	1	0	0	0	0	1	0	....
W 1974	LA-N	....	1	0	0	0	0	0	0	0	0	0	0	....

YEAR	TM-L	AVG	G	AB	R	H	2B	3B	HR	RBI	BB	SO	SB	POS
• AURILIA, Rich														
D 2000	SF-N	.133	4	15	0	2	1	0	0	0	0	3	0	S-4
D 2002	SF-N	.238	5	21	4	5	1	0	2	7	1	5	0	S-5
D 2003	SF-N	.133	4	15	4	2	1	0	0	1	3	3	0	S-4
D Total	3	.176	13	51	8	9	3	0	2	8	4	11	0	....
L 2002	SF-N	.333	5	15	4	5	1	0	2	5	2	2	0	S-5
W 2002	SF-N	.250	7	32	5	8	2	0	2	5	1	9	0	S-7
• AUSMUS, Brad														
D 1997	Hou-N	.400	2	5	1	2	1	0	0	2	0	1	0	C-2
D 1998	Hou-N	.222	4	9	0	2	0	0	0	0	0	4	0	C-4
D 2001	Hou-N	.250	3	8	1	2	0	0	1	2	0	0	0	C-2
D Total	3	.273	9	22	2	6	1	0	1	4	0	5	0	....
• AVERILL, Earl														
W 1940	Det-A	.000	3	3	0	0	0	0	0	0	0	0	0	....
• AVILA, Bobby														
W 1954	Cle-A	.133	4	15	1	2	0	0	0	0	2	1	0	2-4
• AVILES, Ramon														
D 1981	Phi-N	....	1	0	0	0	0	0	0	0	1	0	0	....
L 1980	Phi-N	....	1	0	1	0	0	0	0	0	0	0	0	....
• AYALA, Benny														
L 1983	Bal-A	....	1	0	0	0	0	0	0	1	0	0	0	D-1
W 1979	Bal-A	.333	4	6	1	2	0	0	1	2	1	0	0	O-3
W 1983	Bal-A	1.000	1	1	1	1	0	0	0	1	0	0	0	....
W Total	2	.429	5	7	2	3	0	0	1	3	1	0	0	....
• AYALA, Bobby														
D 1995	Sea-A	....	2	0	0	0	0	0	0	0	0	0	0	....
• AYBAR, Manuel														
D 2002	SF-N	....	2	0	0	0	0	0	0	0	0	0	0	....
• BACKMAN, Wally														
L 1986	NY-N	.238	6	21	5	5	0	0	0	2	2	4	1	2-6
L 1988	NY-N	.273	7	22	2	6	1	0	0	2	2	5	1	2-7
L 1990	Pit-N	.143	3	7	1	1	1	0	0	0	1	3	1	3-2
L Total	3	.240	16	50	8	12	2	0	0	4	5	12	3	....
W 1986	NY-N	.333	6	18	4	6	0	0	0	1	3	2	1	2-6
• BAERGA, Carlos														
D 1995	Cle-A	.286	3	14	2	4	1	0	0	1	0	1	0	2-3
L 1995	Cle-A	.400	6	25	3	10	0	0	1	4	2	3	0	2-6
W 1995	Cle-A	.192	6	26	1	5	2	0	0	4	1	1	0	2-6
• BAGWELL, Jeff														
D 1997	Hou-N	.083	3	12	0	1	0	0	0	0	1	5	0	1-3
D 1998	Hou-N	.143	4	14	0	2	0	0	0	4	1	6	0	1-4
D 1999	Hou-N	.154	4	13	3	2	0	0	0	0	5	4	0	1-4
D 2001	Hou-N	.429	3	7	0	3	0	0	0	0	5	1	0	1-3
D Total	4	.174	14	46	3	8	0	0	0	4	12	16	0	....
• BAILEY, Ed														
W 1962	SF-N	.071	6	14	1	1	0	0	1	2	0	3	0	C-3
• BAILOR, Bob														
L 1985	LA-N	.000	2	1	0	0	0	0	0	0	0	0	0	3-2
• BAINES, Harold														
D 1997	Bal-A	.400	2	5	2	2	0	0	1	1	1	0	0	D-1
D 1999	Cle-A	.357	4	14	1	5	0	0	1	4	2	1	0	D-4
D 2000	Chi-A	.250	2	4	1	1	0	0	0	0	0	1	0	D-1
D Total	3	.348	8	23	4	8	1	0	2	5	3	2	0	....
L 1983	Chi-A	.125	4	16	0	2	0	0	0	0	1	3	0	O-4
L 1990	Oak-A	.357	4	14	2	5	1	0	0	3	2	1	1	D-4
L 1992	Oak-A	.440	6	25	6	11	2	0	1	4	0	3	0	D-6
L 1997	Bal-A	.353	6	17	1	6	0	0	1	2	2	1	0	D-6
L Total	4	.333	20	72	9	24	3	0	2	9	5	8	1	....
W 1990	Oak-A	.143	3	7	1	1	0	0	1	2	1	2	0	D-2
• BAKER, Bill														
W 1940	Cin-N	.250	3	4	1	1	0	0	0	0	0	1	0	C-3
• BAKER, Doug														
L 1984	Det-A	....	1	0	0	0	0	0	0	0	0	0	0	S-1
• BAKER, Dusty														
D 1981	LA-N	.167	5	18	2	3	1	0	0	1	2	0	0	O-5
L 1977	LA-N	.357	4	14	4	5	1	0	2	8	2	3	0	O-4
L 1978	LA-N	.467	4	15	1	7	2	0	0	1	3	0	0	O-4
L 1981	LA-N	.316	5	19	3	6	1	0	0	3	1	0	0	O-5
L 1983	LA-N	.357	4	14	4	5	1	0	1	1	2	0	0	O-4
L Total	4	.371	17	62	12	23	5	0	3	13	8	3	0	....
W 1977	LA-N	.292	6	24	4	7	0	0	1	5	0	2	0	O-6
W 1978	LA-N	.238	6	21	2	5	0	0	1	1	1	3	0	O-6
W 1981	LA-N	.167	6	24	3	4	0	0	0	1	1	6	0	O-6
W Total	3	.232	18	69	9	16	0	0	2	7	2	11	0	....
• BAKER, Floyd														
W 1944	StL-A	.000	2	2	0	0	0	0	0	0	0	2	0	2-2
• BAKER, Frank														
W 1910	Phi-A	.409	5	22	6	9	3	0	0	4	2	1	0	3-5
W 1911	Phi-A	.375	6	24	7	9	2	0	2	5	1	5	0	3-6
W 1913	Phi-A	.450	5	20	2	9	0	0	1	7	0	2	1	3-5
W 1914	Phi-A	.250	4	16	0	4	2	0	0	2	1	3	0	3-4
W 1921	NY-A	.250	4	8	0	2	0	0	0	0	1	0	0	3-2
W 1922	NY-A	.000	1	1	0	0	0	0	0	0	0	0	0	....
W Total	6	.363	25	91	15	33	7	0	3	18	5	11	1	....
• BAKER, Frank														
L 1973	Bal-A	....	2	0	0	0	0	0	0	0	0	0	0	S-2

SER-YEAR	TM-L	AVG	G	AB	R	H	2B	3B	HR	RBI	BB	SO	SB	POS
L 1974	Bal-A	....	2	0	0	0	0	0	0	0	0	0	0	S-2
L Total	**2**	**....**	**4**	**0**	**0**	**0**	**0**	**0**	**0**	**0**	**0**	**0**	**0**	**....**
• BAKER, Gene														
W 1960	Pit-N	.000	3	3	0	0	0	0	0	0	0	1	0	....
• BAKO, Paul														
D 2000	Atl-N	.000	2	1	0	0	0	0	0	0	0	1	0	C-2
D 2001	Atl-N	.286	3	7	1	2	1	0	1	3	1	0	0	C-3
D 2003	Chi-N	.000	3	4	0	0	0	0	0	1	2	2	0	C-3
D Total	**3**	**.167**	**8**	**12**	**1**	**2**	**1**	**0**	**1**	**4**	**3**	**3**	**0**	**....**
L 2001	Atl-N	.000	3	3	0	0	0	0	0	0	0	0	0	C-3
L 2003	Chi-N	.250	6	16	4	4	1	0	0	1	1	7	0	C-6
L Total	**2**	**.211**	**9**	**19**	**4**	**4**	**1**	**0**	**0**	**1**	**1**	**7**	**0**	**....**
• BALBONI, Steve														
L 1984	KC-A	.091	3	11	0	1	0	0	0	0	1	4	0	1-3
L 1985	KC-A	.120	7	25	1	3	0	0	0	1	2	8	0	1-7
L Total	**2**	**.111**	**10**	**36**	**1**	**4**	**0**	**0**	**0**	**1**	**3**	**12**	**0**	**....**
W 1985	KC-A	.320	7	25	2	8	0	0	0	3	5	4	0	1-7
• BALDWIN, Harry														
W 1924	NY-N	....	1	0	0	0	0	0	0	0	0	0	0	....
• BALDWIN, Lady														
W 1887	Det-N	.235	5	17	1	4	1	0	0	1	2	2	1	P-5
• BALL, Neal														
W 1912	Bos-A	.000	1	1	0	0	0	0	0	0	0	1	0	....
• BALLOU, Win														
W 1925	Was-A	....	2	0	0	0	0	0	0	0	0	0	0	....
• BANCROFT, Dave														
W 1915	Phi-N	.294	5	17	2	5	0	0	0	1	2	2	0	S-5
W 1921	NY-N	.152	8	33	3	5	1	0	0	3	1	5	0	S-8
W 1922	NY-N	.211	5	19	4	4	0	0	0	2	2	1	0	S-5
W 1923	NY-N	.083	6	24	1	2	0	0	0	1	1	2	1	S-6
W Total	**4**	**.172**	**24**	**93**	**10**	**16**	**1**	**0**	**0**	**7**	**6**	**10**	**1**	**....**
• BANDO, Sal														
D 1981	Mil-A	.294	5	17	1	5	3	0	0	1	2	3	0	3-5
L 1971	Oak-A	.364	3	11	3	4	2	0	1	1	1	0	0	3-3
L 1972	Oak-A	.200	5	20	0	4	0	0	0	0	0	3	0	3-5
L 1973	Oak-A	.167	5	18	2	3	0	0	2	3	3	6	0	3-5
L 1974	Oak-A	.231	4	13	4	3	0	0	2	2	4	0	0	3-4
L 1975	Oak-A	.500	3	12	1	6	2	0	0	2	0	3	0	3-3
L Total	**5**	**.270**	**20**	**74**	**10**	**20**	**4**	**0**	**5**	**8**	**8**	**12**	**0**	**....**
W 1972	Oak-A	.269	7	26	2	7	1	0	0	1	2	5	0	3-7
W 1973	Oak-A	.231	7	26	5	6	1	1	0	1	4	7	0	3-7
W 1974	Oak-A	.063	5	16	3	1	0	0	0	2	2	5	0	3-5
W Total	**3**	**.206**	**19**	**68**	**10**	**14**	**2**	**1**	**0**	**4**	**8**	**17**	**0**	**....**
• BANKHEAD, Dan														
W 1947	Bro-N	....	1	0	1	0	0	0	0	0	0	0	0	....
• BANKS, Brian														
D 2003	Fla-N	.000	2	2	0	0	0	0	0	0	0	0	0	....
L 2003	Fla-N	.000	2	1	1	0	0	0	0	0	1	0	0	....
• BARAJAS, Rod														
D 2001	Ari-N	....	1	0	0	0	0	0	0	0	0	0	0	C-1
D 2002	Ari-N	.250	2	4	1	1	0	0	1	1	0	1	0	C-2
D Total	**2**	**.250**	**3**	**4**	**1**	**1**	**0**	**0**	**1**	**1**	**0**	**1**	**0**	**....**
W 2001	Ari-N	.400	2	5	1	2	0	0	1	1	0	0	0	C-2
• BARBER, Turner														
W 1918	Chi-N	.000	3	2	0	0	0	0	0	0	0	0	0	....
• BARBIERI, Jim														
W 1966	LA-N	.000	1	1	0	0	0	0	0	0	0	1	0	....
• BARFIELD, Jesse														
L 1985	Tor-A	.280	7	25	3	7	1	0	1	4	3	7	1	O-7
• BARKER, Glen														
D 1999	Hou-N	.000	2	3	1	0	0	0	0	0	0	2	1	O-2
• BARKLEY, Sam														
W 1885	StL-A	.087	7	23	3	2	0	0	0	0	2	0	0	2-7
• BARNEY, Rex														
W 1947	Bro-N	.000	3	1	0	0	0	0	0	0	0	0	0	....
W 1949	Bro-N	....	1	0	0	0	0	0	0	0	0	0	0	....
W Total	**2**	**.000**	**4**	**1**	**0**	**0**	**0**	**0**	**0**	**0**	**0**	**0**	**0**	**....**
• BARNHART, Clyde														
W 1925	Pit-N	.250	7	28	1	7	1	0	0	5	3	5	1	O-7
W 1927	Pit-N	.313	4	16	0	5	1	0	0	4	0	0	0	O-4
W Total	**2**	**.273**	**11**	**44**	**1**	**12**	**2**	**0**	**0**	**9**	**3**	**5**	**1**	**....**
• BARRETT, Marty														
L 1986	Bos-A	.367	7	30	4	11	2	0	0	5	2	2	0	2-7
L 1988	Bos-A	.067	4	15	2	1	0	0	0	0	1	0	0	2-4
L 1990	Bos-A	....	3	0	0	0	0	0	0	0	0	0	0	2-3
L Total	**3**	**.267**	**14**	**45**	**6**	**12**	**2**	**0**	**0**	**5**	**3**	**2**	**0**	**....**
W 1986	Bos-A	.433	7	30	1	13	2	0	0	4	5	2	0	2-7
• BARRETT, Red														
W 1948	Bos-N	....	2	0	0	0	0	0	0	0	0	0	0	....
• BARRY, Jack														
W 1910	Phi-A	.235	5	17	3	4	2	0	0	3	1	3	0	S-5
W 1911	Phi-A	.368	6	19	2	7	4	0	0	2	0	2	2	S-6
W 1913	Phi-A	.300	5	20	3	6	3	0	0	1	0	0	0	S-5
W 1914	Phi-A	.071	4	14	1	1	0	0	0	0	1	3	1	S-4
W 1915	Bos-A	.176	5	17	1	3	0	0	0	1	1	2	0	2-5
W Total	**5**	**.241**	**25**	**87**	**10**	**21**	**9**	**0**	**0**	**7**	**3**	**10**	**3**	**....**
• BARTELL, Dick														
W 1936	NY-N	.381	6	21	5	8	3	0	1	3	4	4	0	S-6
W 1937	NY-N	.238	5	21	3	5	1	0	0	1	0	3	0	S-5
W 1940	Det-A	.269	7	26	2	7	2	0	0	3	3	3	0	S-7
W Total	**3**	**.294**	**18**	**68**	**10**	**20**	**6**	**0**	**1**	**7**	**7**	**10**	**0**	**....**
• BASS, Kevin														
L 1986	Hou-N	.292	6	24	0	7	2	0	0	0	4	4	2	O-6
• BATES, Billy														
L 1990	Cin-N	....	2	0	1	0	0	0	0	0	0	0	0	....
W 1990	Cin-N	1.000	1	1	1	1	0	0	0	0	0	0	0	....
• BATES, Jason														
D 1995	Col-N	.250	4	4	0	1	0	0	0	0	0	0	0	2-1,3-1
• BATHE, Bill														
L 1989	SF-N	.000	2	1	0	0	0	0	0	0	0	1	0	....
W 1989	SF-N	.500	2	2	1	1	0	0	1	3	0	0	0	....
• BATISTE, Kim														
L 1993	Phi-N	1.000	4	1	0	1	1	0	0	1	0	0	0	3-4
W 1993	Phi-N	....	3	0	0	0	0	0	0	0	0	0	0	3-3
• BATTEY, Earl														
W 1965	Min-A	.120	7	25	1	3	0	1	0	2	0	5	0	C-7
• BATTLE, Howard														
D 1999	Atl-N	.000	1	1	0	0	0	0	0	0	0	0	0	....
L 1999	Atl-N	.000	3	2	0	0	0	0	0	0	0	2	1	1-1
W 1999	Atl-N	....	1	0	0	0	0	0	0	0	0	0	0	....
• BAUER, Hank														
W 1949	NY-A	.167	3	6	0	1	0	0	0	0	0	0	0	O-3
W 1950	NY-A	.133	4	15	0	2	0	0	0	1	0	0	0	O-4
W 1951	NY-A	.167	6	18	0	3	0	1	0	3	1	1	0	O-6
W 1952	NY-A	.056	7	18	2	1	0	0	0	1	4	3	0	O-7
W 1953	NY-A	.261	6	23	6	6	0	1	0	1	2	4	0	O-6
W 1955	NY-A	.429	6	14	1	6	0	0	0	1	0	1	0	O-5
W 1956	NY-A	.281	7	32	3	9	0	0	1	3	0	5	1	O-7
W 1957	NY-A	.258	7	31	3	8	2	1	2	6	1	6	0	O-7
W 1958	NY-A	.323	7	31	6	10	0	0	4	8	0	5	0	O-7
W Total	**9**	**.245**	**53**	**188**	**21**	**46**	**2**	**3**	**7**	**24**	**8**	**25**	**1**	**....**
• BAUTISTA, Danny														
D 1997	Atl-N	.333	3	3	0	1	0	0	0	2	0	1	0	O-3
D 1998	Atl-N	.500	2	2	0	1	1	0	0	0	0	0	0	O-2
D 2001	Ari-N	.000	3	6	1	0	0	0	0	1	0	1	0	O-2
D Total	**3**	**.182**	**8**	**11**	**1**	**2**	**1**	**0**	**0**	**3**	**0**	**2**	**0**	**....**
L 1997	Atl-N	.250	2	4	0	1	0	0	0	0	0	0	0	O-2
L 1998	Atl-N	.000	5	5	0	0	0	0	0	0	0	1	0	O-4
L 2001	Ari-N	.250	2	4	1	1	0	0	0	1	1	1	0	O-2
L Total	**3**	**.154**	**9**	**13**	**1**	**2**	**0**	**0**	**0**	**1**	**1**	**2**	**0**	**....**
W 2001	Ari-N	.583	5	12	1	7	2	0	0	7	1	1	0	O-4,D-1
• BAYLOR, Don														
L 1973	Bal-A	.273	4	11	3	3	0	0	0	1	3	5	0	O-3
L 1974	Bal-A	.267	4	15	0	4	0	0	0	0	0	2	0	O-4
L 1979	Cal-A	.188	4	16	2	3	0	0	1	2	1	2	0	O-1,D-3
L 1982	Cal-A	.294	5	17	2	5	1	1	1	10	2	0	0	D-5
L 1986	Bos-A	.346	7	26	6	9	3	0	1	2	4	5	0	D-7
L 1987	Min-A	.400	2	5	0	2	0	0	0	1	0	0	0	D-2
L 1988	Oak-A	.000	2	6	0	0	0	0	0	1	1	2	0	D-2
L Total	**7**	**.271**	**28**	**96**	**13**	**26**	**4**	**1**	**3**	**17**	**11**	**16**	**0**	**....**
W 1986	Bos-A	.182	4	11	1	2	1	0	0	1	1	3	0	D-3
W 1987	Min-A	.385	5	13	3	5	0	0	1	3	1	1	0	D-3
W 1988	Oak-A	.000	1	1	0	0	0	0	0	0	0	1	0	....
W Total	**3**	**.280**	**10**	**25**	**4**	**7**	**1**	**0**	**1**	**4**	**2**	**5**	**0**	**....**
• BEARD, Dave														
D 1981	Oak-A	....	1	0	0	0	0	0	0	0	0	0	0	....
L 1981	Oak-A	....	1	0	0	0	0	0	0	0	0	0	0	....
• BEARDEN, Gene														
W 1948	Cle-A	.500	2	4	1	2	1	0	0	0	0	1	0	....
• BEAUCHAMP, Jim														
W 1973	NY-N	.000	4	4	0	0	0	0	0	0	0	1	0	....
• BEAUMONT, Ginger														
T 1900	Pit-N	.267	4	15	2	4	0	0	0	1	1	0	1	O-4
W 1903	Pit-N	.265	8	34	6	9	0	1	0	1	2	4	2	O-8
W 1910	Chi-N	.000	3	2	1	0	0	0	0	0	1	1	0	....
W Total	**2**	**.250**	**11**	**36**	**7**	**9**	**0**	**1**	**0**	**1**	**3**	**5**	**2**	**....**
• BECKER, Beals														
W 1911	NY-N	.000	3	3	0	0	0	0	0	0	0	0	0	....
W 1912	NY-N	.000	2	4	1	0	0	0	0	0	2	0	0	O-1
W 1915	Phi-N	....	2	0	0	0	0	0	0	0	0	0	0	O-2
W Total	**3**	**.000**	**7**	**7**	**1**	**0**	**0**	**0**	**0**	**0**	**2**	**0**	**0**	**....**
• BECKER, Heinz														
W 1945	Chi-N	.500	3	2	0	1	0	0	0	0	1	1	0	....
• BECKWITH, Joe														
L 1983	LA-N	....	2	0	0	0	0	0	0	0	0	0	0	....
W 1985	KC-A	....	1	0	0	0	0	0	0	0	0	0	0	....
• BELANGER, Mark														
L 1969	Bal-A	.267	3	15	4	4	0	1	1	1	0	0	0	S-3
L 1970	Bal-A	.333	3	12	5	4	0	0	0	1	1	0	0	S-3
L 1971	Bal-A	.250	3	8	1	2	0	0	0	1	3	2	0	S-3
L 1973	Bal-A	.125	5	16	0	2	0	0	0	1	1	1	0	S-5
L 1974	Bal-A	.000	4	9	0	0	0	0	0	0	1	3	0	S-4

YEAR	TM-L	AVG	G	AB	R	H	2B	3B	HR	RBI	BB	SO	SB	POS
L 1979	Bal-A	.200	3	5	0	1	0	0	0	1	0	2	0	S-3
L Total	6	.200	21	65	10	13	0	1	1	5	6	8	0	....
W 1969	Bal-A	.200	5	15	2	3	0	0	0	1	2	1	0	S-5
W 1970	Bal-A	.105	5	19	0	2	0	0	0	1	1	2	0	S-5
W 1971	Bal-A	.238	7	21	4	5	0	1	0	0	5	2	1	S-7
W 1979	Bal-A	.000	5	6	1	0	0	0	0	0	1	1	0	S-5
W Total	4	.164	22	61	7	10	0	1	0	2	9	6	1	....
• BELARDI, Wayne														
W 1953	Bro-N	.000	2	2	0	0	0	0	0	0	0	1	0	....
• BELL, David														
D 2000	Sea-A	.364	3	11	0	4	1	0	0	1	2	2	0	3-3
D 2001	Sea-A	.313	5	16	2	5	1	0	1	2	1	6	0	3-5
D 2002	SF-N	.188	5	16	3	3	0	0	0	1	3	4	0	3-5
D Total	3	.279	13	43	5	12	2	0	1	4	6	12	0	....
L 2000	Sea-A	.222	5	18	0	4	0	0	0	0	0	0	0	2-1,3-4
L 2001	Sea-A	.188	5	16	1	3	0	0	0	4	0	3	0	3-5
L 2002	SF-N	.412	5	17	4	7	1	0	1	1	2	3	0	3-5
L Total	3	.275	15	51	5	14	1	0	1	5	2	6	0	....
W 2002	SF-N	.304	7	23	4	7	0	0	1	4	5	4	0	3-7
• BELL, Derek														
D 1997	Hou-N	.000	3	13	0	0	0	0	0	0	0	3	0	O-3
D 1998	Hou-N	.125	4	16	1	2	0	0	1	1	0	7	0	O-4
D 1999	Hou-N	.333	2	3	0	1	0	0	0	0	0	0	0	O-1
D 2000	NY-N	.000	1	1	0	0	0	0	0	0	0	0	0	O-1
D Total	4	.091	10	33	1	3	0	0	1	1	0	10	0	....
L 1992	Tor-A	....	2	0	1	0	0	0	0	0	1	0	0	O-2
W 1992	Tor-A	.000	2	1	1	0	0	0	0	0	1	0	0	....
• BELL, Gary														
W 1967	Bos-A	....	3	0	0	0	0	0	0	0	0	0	0	....
• BELL, George														
L 1985	Tor-A	.321	7	28	4	9	3	0	0	1	0	4	0	O-7
L 1989	Tor-A	.200	5	20	2	4	0	0	1	2	0	3	0	O-2,D-3
L Total	2	.271	12	48	6	13	3	0	1	3	0	7	0	....
• BELL, Gus														
W 1961	Cin-N	.000	3	3	0	0	0	0	0	0	0	0	0	....
• BELL, Jay														
D 1999	Ari-N	.286	4	14	3	4	1	0	0	3	1	0	0	2-4
D 2001	Ari-N	.250	2	4	0	1	0	0	0	0	0	1	0	2-1
D Total	2	.278	6	18	3	5	1	0	0	3	1	1	0	....
L 1990	Pit-N	.250	6	20	3	5	1	0	1	1	4	3	0	S-6
L 1991	Pit-N	.414	7	29	2	12	2	0	1	1	0	10	0	S-7
L 1992	Pit-N	.172	7	29	3	5	2	0	1	4	3	4	0	S-7
L 2001	Ari-N	.000	1	4	0	0	0	0	0	0	0	0	0	2-1
L Total	4	.268	21	82	8	22	5	0	3	6	7	17	0	....
W 2001	Ari-N	.143	3	7	3	1	0	0	0	1	0	2	0	2-1
• BELL, Les														
W 1926	StL-N	.259	7	27	4	7	1	0	1	6	2	5	0	3-7
• BELLE, Albert														
D 1995	Cle-A	.273	3	11	3	3	1	0	1	3	4	3	0	O-3
D 1996	Cle-A	.200	4	15	2	3	0	0	2	6	3	2	1	O-4
D Total	2	.231	7	26	5	6	1	0	3	9	7	5	1	....
L 1995	Cle-A	.222	5	18	1	4	1	0	1	1	3	5	0	O-5
W 1995	Cle-A	.235	6	17	4	4	0	0	2	4	7	5	0	O-6
• BELLIARD, Rafael														
D 1995	Atl-N	.000	4	5	1	0	0	0	0	0	0	1	0	S-4
D 1996	Atl-N	....	3	0	0	0	0	0	0	0	0	0	0	S-3
D Total	2	.000	7	5	1	0	0	0	0	0	0	1	0	....
L 1991	Atl-N	.211	7	19	0	4	0	0	0	1	3	3	0	S-7
L 1992	Atl-N	.000	4	2	1	0	0	0	0	0	1	0	0	2-1,S-2
L 1993	Atl-N	.000	2	1	1	0	0	0	0	0	0	1	0	2-1,S-1
L 1995	Atl-N	.273	4	11	1	3	0	0	0	0	0	3	0	S-4
L 1996	Atl-N	.667	4	6	0	4	0	0	0	2	0	0	0	2-1,S-3
L Total	5	.282	21	39	3	11	0	0	0	3	4	7	0	....
W 1991	Atl-N	.375	7	16	0	6	1	0	0	4	1	2	0	S-7
W 1992	Atl-N	....	4	0	0	0	0	0	0	0	0	0	0	2-1,S-3
W 1995	Atl-N	.000	6	16	0	0	0	0	0	1	0	4	0	S-6
W 1996	Atl-N	....	4	0	0	0	0	0	0	0	0	0	0	S-3,D-1
W Total	4	.188	21	32	0	6	1	0	0	5	1	6	0	....
• BELLINGER, Clay														
D 1999	NY-A	....	1	0	0	0	0	0	0	0	0	0	0	D-1
D 2000	NY-A	1.000	2	1	0	1	1	0	0	1	0	0	0	O-2
D 2001	NY-A	....	1	0	0	0	0	0	0	0	0	0	0	....
D Total	3	1.000	4	1	0	1	1	0	0	1	0	0	0	....
L 1999	NY-A	.000	3	1	0	0	0	0	0	0	0	1	0	S-1,D-2
L 2000	NY-A	....	5	0	0	0	0	0	0	0	0	0	0	O-5
L 2001	NY-A	.000	1	1	0	0	0	0	0	0	0	0	0	O-1
L Total	3	.000	9	2	0	0	0	0	0	0	0	1	0	....
W 2000	NY-A	....	4	0	0	0	0	0	0	0	0	0	0	O-4
W 2001	NY-A	.000	2	2	0	0	0	0	0	0	0	2	0	O-2
W Total	2	.000	6	2	0	0	0	0	0	0	0	2	0	....
• BENARD, Marvin														
D 1997	SF-N	.000	2	2	0	0	0	0	0	0	0	1	0	....
D 2000	SF-N	.071	4	14	0	1	0	0	0	1	1	7	0	O-3
D Total	2	.063	6	16	0	1	0	0	0	1	1	8	0	....
• BENCH, Johnny														
L 1970	Cin-N	.222	3	9	2	2	0	0	1	1	3	1	0	C-3
L 1972	Cin-N	.333	5	18	3	6	1	1	1	2	1	3	2	C-5
L 1973	Cin-N	.263	5	19	1	5	2	0	1	1	2	3	0	C-5
L 1975	Cin-N	.077	3	13	1	1	0	0	0	0	1	6	1	C-3
L 1976	Cin-N	.333	3	12	3	4	1	0	1	1	1	2	1	C-3
L 1979	Cin-N	.250	3	12	1	3	0	1	1	1	2	2	0	C-3
L Total	6	.253	22	83	11	21	4	2	5	6	10	17	4	....
W 1970	Cin-N	.211	5	19	3	4	0	0	1	3	1	2	0	C-5
W 1972	Cin-N	.261	7	23	4	6	1	0	1	1	5	5	2	C-7
W 1975	Cin-N	.207	7	29	5	6	2	0	1	4	2	4	0	C-7
W 1976	Cin-N	.533	4	15	4	8	1	1	2	6	0	1	0	C-4
W Total	4	.279	23	86	16	24	4	1	5	14	8	12	2	....
• BENEDICT, Bruce														
L 1982	Atl-N	.250	3	8	1	2	1	0	0	0	2	1	0	C-3
• BENES, Alan														
L 1996	StL-N	.000	2	1	0	0	0	0	0	0	0	1	0	....
• BENES, Andy														
D 1995	Sea-A	....	2	0	0	0	0	0	0	0	0	0	0	....
D 1996	StL-N	.500	1	2	1	1	0	0	0	0	0	1	0	....
D 2002	StL-N	.000	1	1	0	0	0	0	0	1	0	0	0	....
D Total	3	.333	4	3	1	1	0	0	0	1	0	1	0	....
L 1996	StL-N	.250	3	4	0	1	1	0	0	0	1	2	0	....
L 2000	StL-N	.333	1	3	1	1	0	0	0	0	0	2	0	....
L 2002	StL-N	.000	1	2	0	0	0	0	0	0	0	0	0	....
L Total	3	.222	5	9	1	2	1	0	0	0	1	4	0	....
• BENGOUGH, Benny														
W 1927	NY-A	.000	2	4	1	0	0	0	0	0	1	0	0	C-2
W 1928	NY-A	.231	4	13	1	3	0	0	0	1	1	1	0	C-4
W Total	2	.176	6	17	2	3	0	0	0	1	2	1	0	....
• BENIQUEZ, Juan														
L 1975	Bos-A	.250	3	12	2	3	1	0	0	1	0	1	2	D-3
L 1982	Cal-A	....	2	0	0	0	0	0	0	0	0	0	0	O-2
L Total	2	.250	5	12	2	3	1	0	0	1	0	1	2	....
W 1975	Bos-A	.125	3	8	0	1	0	0	0	1	1	1	0	O-2
• BENJAMIN, Mike														
D 1998	Bos-A	.091	4	11	1	1	0	0	0	0	1	3	0	1-1,2-4
• BENNETT, Charlie														
T 1892	Bos-N	.286	2	7	2	2	0	0	1	1	0	2	1	C-2
W 1887	Det-N	.311	11	45	6	14	2	1	0	9	3	5	5	C-10,1-3
• BENTON, Rube														
W 1917	NY-N	.000	2	4	0	0	0	0	0	0	0	3	0	....
• BENZINGER, Todd														
L 1988	Bos-A	.091	4	11	0	1	0	0	0	0	1	3	0	1-3
L 1990	Cin-N	.333	5	9	0	3	0	0	0	0	2	0	0	1-2
L Total	2	.200	9	20	0	4	0	0	0	0	3	3	0	....
W 1990	Cin-N	.182	4	11	1	2	0	0	0	0	0	0	0	1-3
• BERENGUER, Juan														
L 1987	Min-A	....	4	0	0	0	0	0	0	0	0	0	0	....
W 1987	Min-A	....	3	0	0	0	0	0	0	0	0	0	0	....
• BERGAMO, Augie														
W 1944	StL-N	.000	3	6	0	0	0	0	0	1	2	3	0	O-2
• BERGEN, Marty														
T 1897	Bos-N	.500	1	4	0	2	0	0	0	1	0	1	1	C-1
• BERGER, Wally														
W 1937	NY-N	.000	3	3	0	0	0	0	0	0	0	1	0	....
W 1939	Cin-N	.000	4	15	0	0	0	0	0	1	0	4	0	O-4
W Total	2	.000	7	18	0	0	0	0	0	1	0	5	0	....
• BERGMAN, Dave														
L 1980	Hou-N	.333	4	3	0	1	0	1	0	2	0	0	0	1-3
L 1984	Det-A	1.000	2	1	1	1	0	0	0	0	0	0	1	1-2
L 1987	Det-A	.250	4	4	0	1	0	0	0	2	0	1	0	1-1,D-1
L Total	3	.375	10	8	1	3	0	1	0	4	0	1	1	....
W 1984	Det-A	.000	5	5	0	0	0	0	0	0	0	1	0	1-5
• BERKMAN, Lance														
D 2001	Hou-N	.167	3	12	0	2	0	0	0	0	0	4	0	O-3
• BERRA, Yogi														
W 1947	NY-A	.158	6	19	2	3	0	0	1	2	1	2	0	O-2,C-4
W 1949	NY-A	.063	4	16	2	1	0	0	0	1	1	3	0	C-4
W 1950	NY-A	.200	4	15	2	3	0	0	1	2	2	1	0	C-4
W 1951	NY-A	.261	6	23	4	6	1	0	0	0	2	1	0	C-6
W 1952	NY-A	.214	7	28	2	6	1	0	2	3	2	4	0	C-7
W 1953	NY-A	.429	6	21	3	9	1	0	1	4	3	3	0	C-6
W 1955	NY-A	.417	7	24	5	10	1	0	1	2	3	1	0	C-7
W 1956	NY-A	.360	7	25	5	9	2	0	3	10	4	1	0	C-7
W 1957	NY-A	.320	7	25	5	8	1	0	1	2	4	0	0	C-7
W 1958	NY-A	.222	7	27	3	6	3	0	0	2	1	0	0	C-7
W 1960	NY-A	.318	7	22	6	7	0	0	1	8	2	0	0	O-4,C-3
W 1961	NY-A	.273	4	11	2	3	0	0	1	3	5	1	0	O-4
W 1962	NY-A	.000	2	2	0	0	0	0	0	0	2	0	0	C-1
W 1963	NY-A	.000	1	1	0	0	0	0	0	0	0	0	0	....
W Total	14	.274	75	259	41	71	10	0	12	39	32	17	0	....
• BERROA, Geronimo														
D 1997	Bal-A	.385	4	13	4	5	1	0	2	2	2	2	0	O-1,D-3
L 1997	Bal-A	.286	6	21	1	6	2	0	0	3	0	3	0	O-4,D-2
• BERRY, Sean														
D 1997	Hou-N	.000	1	1	0	0	0	0	0	0	0	0	0	....
D 1998	Hou-N	.000	1	2	0	0	0	0	0	0	0	1	0	3-1
D Total	2	.000	2	3	0	0	0	0	0	0	0	1	0	....
• BERRYHILL, Damon														
D 1997	SF-N	.000	1	1	0	0	0	0	0	0	0	0	0	....

SER-YEAR	TM-L	AVG	G	AB	R	H	2B	3B	HR	RBI	BB	SO	SB	POS
L 1992	Atl-N	.167	7	24	1	4	1	0	0	1	3	2	0	C-7
L 1993	Atl-N	.211	6	19	2	4	0	0	1	3	1	5	0	C-6
L Total	**2**	**.186**	**13**	**43**	**3**	**8**	**1**	**0**	**1**	**4**	**4**	**7**	**0**	**....**
W 1992	Atl-N	.091	6	22	1	2	0	0	1	3	1	11	0	C-6
• BEVACQUA, Kurt														
L 1984	SD-N	.000	2	2	0	0	0	0	0	0	0	0	0	....
W 1984	SD-N	.412	5	17	4	7	2	0	2	4	1	2	0	D-5
• BEVENS, Bill														
W 1947	NY-A	.000	2	4	0	0	0	0	0	0	0	2	0	....
• BIANCALANA, Buddy														
L 1984	KC-A	.000	2	1	0	0	0	0	0	0	0	1	0	S-2
L 1985	KC-A	.222	7	18	2	4	1	0	0	1	1	6	0	S-7
L Total	**2**	**.211**	**9**	**19**	**2**	**4**	**1**	**0**	**0**	**1**	**1**	**7**	**0**	**....**
W 1985	KC-A	.278	7	18	2	5	0	0	0	2	5	4	0	S-7
• BICHETTE, Dante														
D 1995	Col-N	.588	4	17	6	10	3	0	1	3	1	3	0	O-4
• BIGBEE, Carson														
W 1925	Pit-N	.333	4	3	1	1	1	0	0	1	0	0	1	O-1
• BIGGIO, Craig														
D 1997	Hou-N	.083	3	12	0	1	0	0	0	0	1	0	0	2-3
D 1998	Hou-N	.182	4	11	3	2	1	0	0	1	4	4	0	2-4
D 1999	Hou-N	.105	4	19	1	2	0	0	0	0	1	5	0	2-4
D 2001	Hou-N	.167	3	12	0	2	0	0	0	0	0	1	0	2-3
D Total	**4**	**.130**	**14**	**54**	**4**	**7**	**1**	**0**	**0**	**1**	**6**	**10**	**0**	**....**
• BISHOP, Max														
W 1929	Phi-A	.190	5	21	2	4	0	0	0	1	2	3	0	2-5
W 1930	Phi-A	.222	6	18	5	4	0	0	0	0	7	3	0	2-6
W 1931	Phi-A	.148	7	27	4	4	0	0	0	0	3	5	0	2-7
W Total	**3**	**.182**	**18**	**66**	**11**	**12**	**0**	**0**	**0**	**1**	**12**	**11**	**0**	**....**
• BLADES, Ray														
W 1928	StL-N	.000	1	1	0	0	0	0	0	0	0	1	0	....
W 1930	StL-N	.111	5	9	2	1	0	0	0	0	2	2	0	O-3
W 1931	StL-N	.000	2	2	0	0	0	0	0	0	0	2	0	....
W Total	**3**	**.083**	**8**	**12**	**2**	**1**	**0**	**0**	**0**	**0**	**2**	**5**	**0**	**....**
• BLAIR, Footsie														
W 1929	Chi-N	.000	1	1	0	0	0	0	0	0	0	0	0	....
• BLAIR, Paul														
L 1969	Bal-A	.400	3	15	1	6	2	0	1	6	2	2	0	O-3
L 1970	Bal-A	.077	3	13	0	1	0	0	0	0	1	4	0	O-3
L 1971	Bal-A	.333	3	9	1	3	1	0	0	2	0	3	0	O-2
L 1973	Bal-A	.167	5	18	2	3	0	0	0	0	1	5	0	O-5
L 1974	Bal-A	.286	4	14	3	4	0	0	1	2	2	2	0	O-4
L 1977	NY-A	.400	3	5	1	2	0	0	0	0	0	0	0	O-3
L 1978	NY-A	.000	4	6	1	0	0	0	0	0	0	1	0	O-3,2-1
L Total	**7**	**.238**	**25**	**80**	**9**	**19**	**3**	**0**	**2**	**10**	**6**	**17**	**0**	**....**
W 1966	Bal-A	.167	4	6	2	1	0	0	1	1	1	0	0	O-4
W 1969	Bal-A	.100	5	20	1	2	0	0	0	0	2	5	1	O-5
W 1970	Bal-A	.474	5	19	5	9	1	0	0	3	2	4	0	O-5
W 1971	Bal-A	.333	4	9	2	3	1	0	0	0	0	1	0	O-4
W 1977	NY-A	.250	4	4	0	1	0	0	0	1	0	0	0	O-3
W 1978	NY-A	.375	6	8	2	3	1	0	0	0	1	4	0	O-6
W Total	**6**	**.288**	**28**	**66**	**12**	**19**	**3**	**0**	**1**	**5**	**6**	**14**	**1**	**....**
• BLAKE, Harry														
T 1895	Cle-N	.250	5	20	1	5	3	0	0	2	0	2	0	O-5
T 1896	Cle-N	.071	4	14	1	1	0	0	0	0	1	1	1	O-4
T Total	**2**	**.176**	**9**	**34**	**2**	**6**	**3**	**0**	**0**	**2**	**1**	**3**	**1**	**....**
• BLANCHARD, Johnny														
W 1960	NY-A	.455	5	11	2	5	2	0	0	2	0	0	0	C-2
W 1961	NY-A	.400	4	10	4	4	1	0	2	3	2	0	0	O-2
W 1962	NY-A	.000	1	1	0	0	0	0	0	0	0	1	0	....
W 1963	NY-A	.000	1	3	0	0	0	0	0	0	0	0	0	O-1
W 1964	NY-A	.250	4	4	0	1	1	0	0	0	0	1	0	....
W Total	**5**	**.345**	**15**	**29**	**6**	**10**	**4**	**0**	**2**	**5**	**2**	**2**	**0**	**....**
• BLANCO, Henry														
D 2002	Atl-N	.167	2	6	0	1	0	0	0	0	0	2	0	C-2
• BLANKENSHIP, Lance														
L 1989	Oak-A	....	1	0	0	0	0	0	0	0	0	0	0	2-1
L 1990	Oak-A	....	3	0	1	0	0	0	0	0	0	0	1	D-3
L 1992	Oak-A	.231	5	13	2	3	0	0	0	0	3	4	1	2-5
L Total	**3**	**.231**	**9**	**13**	**3**	**3**	**0**	**0**	**0**	**0**	**3**	**4**	**2**	**....**
W 1989	Oak-A	.500	1	2	1	1	0	0	0	0	0	0	0	2-1
W 1990	Oak-A	.000	1	1	0	0	0	0	0	0	0	1	0	....
W Total	**2**	**.333**	**2**	**3**	**1**	**1**	**0**	**0**	**0**	**0**	**0**	**1**	**0**	**....**
• BLASINGAME, Don														
W 1961	Cin-N	.143	3	7	1	1	0	0	0	0	0	3	0	2-3
• BLAUSER, Jeff														
D 1995	Atl-N	.000	3	6	0	0	0	0	0	0	1	3	0	S-3
D 1996	Atl-N	.111	3	9	0	1	0	0	0	0	1	3	0	S-3
D 1997	Atl-N	.300	3	10	2	3	0	0	1	4	2	2	0	S-3
D 1998	Chi-N	.000	2	2	0	0	0	0	0	0	0	1	0	....
D Total	**4**	**.148**	**11**	**27**	**2**	**4**	**0**	**0**	**1**	**4**	**4**	**9**	**0**	**....**
L 1991	Atl-N	.000	2	2	0	0	0	0	0	0	0	0	0	S-2
L 1992	Atl-N	.208	7	24	3	5	0	1	1	4	4	2	0	S-7
L 1993	Atl-N	.280	6	25	5	7	1	0	2	4	4	7	0	S-6
L 1995	Atl-N	.000	1	4	0	0	0	0	0	0	1	2	0	S-1
L 1996	Atl-N	.176	7	17	5	3	0	1	0	2	4	6	0	S-7
L 1997	Atl-N	.300	6	20	5	6	0	0	1	1	3	6	0	S-6
L Total	**6**	**.228**	**29**	**92**	**18**	**21**	**1**	**2**	**4**	**11**	**16**	**23**	**0**	**....**
W 1991	Atl-N	.167	5	6	0	1	0	0	0	0	1	1	0	S-5
W 1992	Atl-N	.250	6	24	2	6	0	0	0	0	1	9	2	S-6
W 1996	Atl-N	.167	6	18	2	3	1	0	0	1	1	4	0	S-6
W Total	**3**	**.208**	**17**	**48**	**4**	**10**	**1**	**0**	**0**	**1**	**3**	**14**	**2**	**....**
• BLEFARY, Curt														
L 1971	Oak-A	.000	1	1	0	0	0	0	0	0	0	1	0	....
W 1966	Bal-A	.077	4	13	0	1	0	0	0	0	2	3	0	O-4
• BLIGH, Ned														
W 1890	Lou-A	.000	2	3	0	0	0	0	0	0	0	1	0	C-2
• BLOCK, Cy														
W 1945	Chi-N	....	1	0	0	0	0	0	0	0	0	0	0	....
• BLOODWORTH, Jimmy														
W 1950	Phi-N	....	1	0	0	0	0	0	0	0	0	0	0	2-1
• BLOWERS, Mike														
D 1995	Sea-A	.167	5	18	0	3	0	0	0	1	3	7	0	1-1,3-5
D 1997	Sea-A	.200	3	5	0	1	0	0	0	0	0	3	0	3-3
D Total	**2**	**.174**	**8**	**23**	**0**	**4**	**0**	**0**	**0**	**1**	**3**	**10**	**0**	**....**
L 1995	Sea-A	.222	6	18	1	4	0	0	1	2	0	4	0	3-6
• BLUEGE, Ossie														
W 1924	Was-A	.192	7	26	2	5	0	0	0	3	3	4	1	3-4,S-5
W 1925	Was-A	.278	5	18	2	5	1	0	0	2	0	4	0	3-5
W 1933	Was-A	.125	5	16	1	2	1	0	0	0	1	6	0	3-5
W Total	**3**	**.200**	**17**	**60**	**5**	**12**	**2**	**0**	**0**	**5**	**4**	**14**	**1**	**....**
• BOCHY, Bruce														
L 1980	Hou-N	.000	1	1	0	0	0	0	0	0	0	0	0	C-1
W 1984	SD-N	1.000	1	1	0	1	0	0	0	0	0	0	0	....
• BOGAR, Tim														
D 1999	Hou-N	.750	2	4	0	3	1	0	0	1	1	0	0	S-1
• BOGGS, Wade														
D 1995	NY-A	.263	4	19	4	5	2	0	1	3	3	5	0	3-4
D 1996	NY-A	.083	3	12	0	1	1	0	0	0	0	2	0	3-3
D 1997	NY-A	.429	3	7	1	3	0	0	0	2	0	0	0	3-2
D Total	**3**	**.237**	**10**	**38**	**5**	**9**	**3**	**0**	**1**	**5**	**3**	**7**	**0**	**....**
L 1986	Bos-A	.233	7	30	3	7	1	1	0	2	4	1	0	3-7
L 1988	Bos-A	.385	4	13	2	5	0	0	0	3	3	4	0	3-4
L 1990	Bos-A	.438	4	16	1	7	1	0	1	1	0	3	0	3-4
L 1996	NY-A	.133	3	15	1	2	0	0	0	0	1	3	0	3-3
L Total	**4**	**.284**	**18**	**74**	**7**	**21**	**2**	**1**	**1**	**6**	**8**	**11**	**0**	**....**
W 1986	Bos-A	.290	7	31	3	9	3	0	0	3	4	2	0	3-7
W 1996	NY-A	.273	4	11	0	3	1	0	0	2	1	0	0	3-4
W Total	**2**	**.286**	**11**	**42**	**3**	**12**	**4**	**0**	**0**	**5**	**5**	**2**	**0**	**....**
• BOLEY, Joe														
W 1929	Phi-A	.235	5	17	1	4	0	0	0	1	0	3	0	S-5
W 1930	Phi-A	.095	6	21	1	2	0	0	0	1	0	1	0	S-6
W 1931	Phi-A	.000	1	1	0	0	0	0	0	0	0	1	0	....
W Total	**3**	**.154**	**12**	**39**	**2**	**6**	**0**	**0**	**0**	**2**	**0**	**5**	**0**	**....**
• BOLLWEG, Don														
W 1953	NY-A	.000	3	2	0	0	0	0	0	0	0	2	0	1-1
• BOLTON, Cliff														
W 1933	Was-A	.000	2	2	0	0	0	0	0	0	0	0	0	....
• BONDS, Barry														
D 1997	SF-N	.250	3	12	0	3	2	0	0	2	0	3	1	O-3
D 2000	SF-N	.176	4	17	2	3	1	1	0	1	3	4	1	O-4
D 2002	SF-N	.294	5	17	5	5	0	0	3	4	4	1	0	O-5
D 2003	SF-N	.222	4	9	3	2	1	0	0	2	8	0	1	O-4
D Total	**4**	**.236**	**16**	**55**	**10**	**13**	**4**	**1**	**3**	**9**	**15**	**8**	**3**	**....**
L 1990	Pit-N	.167	6	18	4	3	0	0	0	1	6	5	2	O-6
L 1991	Pit-N	.148	7	27	1	4	1	0	0	0	2	4	3	O-7
L 1992	Pit-N	.261	7	23	5	6	1	0	1	2	6	4	1	O-7
L 2002	SF-N	.273	5	11	5	3	0	1	1	6	10	2	0	O-5
L Total	**4**	**.203**	**25**	**79**	**15**	**16**	**2**	**1**	**2**	**9**	**24**	**15**	**6**	**....**
W 2002	SF-N	.471	7	17	8	8	2	0	4	6	13	3	0	O-7
• BONDS, Bobby														
L 1971	SF-N	.250	3	8	0	2	0	0	0	0	2	4	0	O-3
• BONGIOVANNI, Nino														
W 1939	Cin-N	.000	1	1	0	0	0	0	0	0	0	0	0	....
• BONILLA, Bobby														
D 1996	Bal-A	.200	4	15	4	3	0	0	2	5	4	6	0	O-4
D 1997	Fla-N	.333	3	12	1	4	0	0	1	3	2	1	0	3-3
D 1999	NY-N	.000	2	1	1	0	0	0	0	0	1	0	0	....
D 2000	Atl-N	.000	3	2	0	0	0	0	0	0	2	0	0	O-1
D Total	**4**	**.233**	**12**	**30**	**6**	**7**	**0**	**0**	**3**	**8**	**9**	**7**	**0**	**....**
L 1990	Pit-N	.190	6	21	0	4	1	0	0	1	3	1	0	O-5,3-3
L 1991	Pit-N	.304	7	23	2	7	2	0	0	1	6	2	0	O-7
L 1996	Bal-A	.050	5	20	1	1	0	0	1	2	1	4	0	O-5
L 1997	Fla-N	.261	6	23	3	6	1	0	0	4	1	6	0	3-6
L 1999	NY-N	.333	3	3	0	1	0	0	0	0	0	2	0	....
L Total	**5**	**.211**	**27**	**90**	**6**	**19**	**4**	**0**	**1**	**8**	**11**	**15**	**0**	**....**
W 1997	Fla-N	.207	7	29	5	6	1	0	1	3	3	5	0	3-7
• BONNER, Frank														
T 1894	Bal-N	.000	2	5	0	0	0	0	0	0	0	2	0	S-1,O-1
• BOONE, Aaron														
D 2003	NY-A	.200	4	15	1	3	1	0	0	0	0	3	1	3-4
L 2003	NY-A	.176	7	17	2	3	0	0	1	2	1	6	1	3-7
W 2003	NY-A	.143	6	21	1	3	0	0	1	2	0	6	0	3-6
• BOONE, Bob														
D 1981	Phi-N	.000	3	5	0	0	0	0	0	0	0	0	0	C-3

YEAR	TM-L	AVG	G	AB	R	H	2B	3B	HR	RBI	BB	SO	SB	POS
L 1976	Phi-N	.286	3	7	0	2	0	0	0	1	1	0	0	C-3
L 1977	Phi-N	.400	4	10	1	4	0	0	0	0	0	0	0	C-4
L 1978	Phi-N	.182	3	11	0	2	0	0	0	0	0	1	0	C-3
L 1980	Phi-N	.222	5	18	1	4	0	0	0	2	1	2	0	C-5
L 1982	Cal-A	.250	5	16	3	4	0	0	1	4	0	2	0	C-5
L 1986	Cal-A	.455	7	22	4	10	0	0	1	2	1	3	0	C-7
L Total	**6**	**.310**	**27**	**84**	**9**	**26**	**0**	**0**	**2**	**9**	**3**	**8**	**0**	**....**
W 1980	Phi-N	.412	6	17	3	7	2	0	0	4	4	0	0	C-6
• BOONE, Bret														
D 1995	Cin-N	.300	3	10	4	3	1	0	1	1	1	3	1	2-3
D 1999	Atl-N	.474	4	19	3	9	1	0	0	1	0	4	1	2-4
D 2001	Sea-A	.095	5	21	1	2	0	0	0	0	1	11	1	2-5
D Total	**3**	**.280**	**12**	**50**	**8**	**14**	**2**	**0**	**1**	**2**	**2**	**18**	**3**	**....**
L 1995	Cin-N	.214	4	14	1	3	0	0	0	0	1	2	0	2-4
L 1999	Atl-N	.182	6	22	2	4	1	0	0	1	1	7	2	2-6
L 2001	Sea-A	.316	5	19	2	6	0	0	2	6	2	2	0	2-5
L Total	**3**	**.236**	**15**	**55**	**5**	**13**	**1**	**0**	**2**	**7**	**4**	**11**	**2**	**....**
W 1999	Atl-N	.538	4	13	1	7	4	0	0	3	1	3	0	2-3
• BOONE, Ray														
W 1948	Cle-A	.000	1	1	0	0	0	0	0	0	0	1	0	....
• BORDAGARAY, Frenchy														
W 1939	Cin-N	....	2	0	0	0	0	0	0	0	0	0	0	....
W 1941	NY-A	....	1	0	0	0	0	0	0	0	0	0	0	....
W Total	**2**	**....**	**3**	**0**	**0**	**0**	**0**	**0**	**0**	**0**	**0**	**0**	**0**	**....**
• BORDERS, Pat														
L 1989	Tor-A	1.000	1	1	0	1	0	0	0	1	0	0	0	C-1
L 1991	Tor-A	.263	5	19	0	5	1	0	0	2	0	0	0	C-5
L 1992	Tor-A	.318	6	22	3	7	0	0	1	3	1	1	0	C-6
L 1993	Tor-A	.250	6	24	1	6	1	0	0	3	0	6	1	C-6
L Total	**4**	**.288**	**18**	**66**	**4**	**19**	**2**	**0**	**1**	**9**	**1**	**7**	**1**	**....**
W 1992	Tor-A	.450	6	20	2	9	3	0	1	3	2	1	0	C-6
W 1993	Tor-A	.304	6	23	2	7	0	0	0	1	2	1	0	C-6
W Total	**2**	**.372**	**12**	**43**	**4**	**16**	**3**	**0**	**1**	**4**	**4**	**2**	**0**	**....**
• BORDICK, Mike														
D 1997	Bal-A	.400	4	10	4	4	1	0	0	4	4	2	0	S-4
D 2000	NY-N	.167	4	12	3	2	0	0	0	0	3	4	0	S-4
D Total	**2**	**.273**	**8**	**22**	**7**	**6**	**1**	**0**	**0**	**4**	**7**	**6**	**0**	**....**
L 1992	Oak-A	.053	6	19	1	1	0	0	0	0	1	2	1	2-2,S-4
L 1997	Bal-A	.158	6	19	0	3	1	0	0	2	0	6	0	S-6
L 2000	NY-N	.077	5	13	2	1	0	0	0	0	3	1	0	S-5
L Total	**3**	**.098**	**17**	**51**	**3**	**5**	**1**	**0**	**0**	**2**	**4**	**9**	**1**	**....**
W 1990	Oak-A	....	3	0	0	0	0	0	0	0	0	0	0	S-3
W 2000	NY-N	.125	4	8	0	1	0	0	0	0	0	3	0	S-4
W Total	**2**	**.125**	**7**	**8**	**0**	**1**	**0**	**0**	**0**	**0**	**0**	**3**	**0**	**....**
• BOROM, Red														
W 1945	Det-A	.000	2	1	0	0	0	0	0	0	0	0	0	....
• BOSETTI, Rick														
D 1981	Oak-A	....	1	0	0	0	0	0	0	0	0	0	0	0-1
L 1981	Oak-A	.250	2	4	1	1	1	0	0	0	0	1	0	0-1,D-1
• BOSIO, Chris														
D 1995	Sea-A	....	2	0	0	0	0	0	0	0	0	0	0	....
• BOSLEY, Thad														
D 1981	Mil-A	....	1	0	0	0	0	0	0	0	0	0	0	D-1
L 1984	Chi-N	.000	2	2	0	0	0	0	0	0	0	2	0	....
• BOSMAN, Dick														
L 1975	Oak-A	....	1	0	0	0	0	0	0	0	0	0	0	....
• BOSWELL, Dave														
L 1969	Min-A	.000	1	4	0	0	0	0	0	0	0	4	0	....
W 1965	Min-A	....	1	0	0	0	0	0	0	0	0	0	0	....
• BOSWELL, Ken														
L 1969	NY-N	.333	3	12	4	4	0	0	2	5	1	2	0	2-3
L 1973	NY-N	.000	1	1	0	0	0	0	0	0	0	0	0	....
L Total	**2**	**.308**	**4**	**13**	**4**	**4**	**0**	**0**	**2**	**5**	**1**	**2**	**0**	**....**
W 1969	NY-N	.333	1	3	1	1	0	0	0	0	0	0	0	2-1
W 1973	NY-N	1.000	3	3	1	3	0	0	0	0	0	0	0	....
W Total	**2**	**.667**	**4**	**6**	**2**	**4**	**0**	**0**	**0**	**0**	**0**	**0**	**0**	**....**
• BOTTOMLEY, Jim														
W 1926	StL-N	.345	7	29	4	10	3	0	0	5	1	2	0	1-7
W 1928	StL-N	.214	4	14	1	3	0	1	1	3	2	6	0	1-4
W 1930	StL-N	.045	6	22	1	1	1	0	0	0	2	9	0	1-6
W 1931	StL-N	.160	7	25	2	4	1	0	0	2	2	5	0	1-7
W Total	**4**	**.200**	**24**	**90**	**8**	**18**	**5**	**1**	**1**	**10**	**7**	**22**	**0**	**....**
• BOUDREAU, Lou														
W 1948	Cle-A	.273	6	22	1	6	4	0	0	3	1	1	0	S-6
• BOURQUE, Pat														
L 1973	Oak-A	.000	2	1	0	0	0	0	0	0	2	1	0	D-2
W 1973	Oak-A	.500	2	2	0	1	0	0	0	0	0	0	0	1-2
• BOWA, Larry														
D 1981	Phi-N	.176	5	17	0	3	1	0	0	1	0	0	0	S-5
L 1976	Phi-N	.125	3	8	1	1	1	0	0	1	3	0	0	S-3
L 1977	Phi-N	.118	4	17	2	2	0	0	0	1	1	0	0	S-4
L 1978	Phi-N	.333	4	18	2	6	0	0	0	0	1	2	0	S-4
L 1980	Phi-N	.316	5	19	2	6	0	0	0	0	3	3	1	S-5
L 1984	Chi-N	.200	5	15	1	3	1	0	0	1	1	0	0	S-5
L Total	**5**	**.234**	**21**	**77**	**8**	**18**	**2**	**0**	**0**	**3**	**9**	**5**	**1**	**....**
W 1980	Phi-N	.375	6	24	3	9	1	0	0	2	0	0	3	S-6

YEAR	TM-L	AVG	G	AB	R	H	2B	3B	HR	RBI	BB	SO	SB	POS
• BOWERMAN, Frank														
T 1897	Bal-N	.500	2	8	2	4	0	1	0	4	0	0	0	C-1,1-1
• BOWMAN, Ernie														
W 1962	SF-N	.000	2	1	1	0	0	0	0	0	0	0	0	S-2
• BOYER, Clete														
L 1969	Atl-N	.111	3	9	0	1	0	0	0	3	2	3	0	3-3
W 1960	NY-A	.250	4	12	1	3	2	1	0	1	0	1	0	3-4,S-1
W 1961	NY-A	.267	5	15	0	4	2	0	0	3	4	0	0	3-5
W 1962	NY-A	.318	7	22	2	7	1	0	1	4	1	3	0	3-7
W 1963	NY-A	.077	4	13	0	1	0	0	0	0	1	6	0	3-4
W 1964	NY-A	.208	7	24	2	5	1	0	1	3	1	5	1	3-7
W Total	**5**	**.233**	**27**	**86**	**5**	**20**	**6**	**1**	**2**	**11**	**7**	**15**	**1**	**....**
• BOYER, Ken														
W 1964	StL-N	.222	7	27	5	6	1	0	2	6	1	5	0	3-7
• BOYLE, Jack														
W 1887	StL-A	.208	6	24	1	5	0	0	0	2	0	4	0	C-6
W 1888	StL-A	.438	4	16	4	7	0	1	0	4	2	2	3	C-4,0-1
W Total	**2**	**.300**	**10**	**40**	**5**	**12**	**0**	**1**	**0**	**6**	**2**	**6**	**3**	**....**
• BRADY, Steve														
W 1884	NY-A	.000	3	10	1	0	0	0	0	0	0	1	0	0-3
• BRAGAN, Bobby														
W 1947	Bro-N	1.000	1	1	0	1	1	0	0	1	0	0	0	....
• BRAGG, Darren														
D 1998	Bos-A	.083	3	12	0	1	0	0	0	0	0	5	0	0-3
D 2002	Atl-N	.000	4	3	0	0	0	0	0	0	0	0	0	0-1
D 2003	Atl-N	.000	2	5	0	0	0	0	0	1	0	1	0	0-1
D Total	**3**	**.050**	**9**	**20**	**0**	**1**	**0**	**0**	**0**	**1**	**0**	**6**	**0**	**....**
• BRAGGS, Glenn														
L 1990	Cin-N	.200	2	5	0	1	0	0	0	0	0	1	0	0-2
W 1990	Cin-N	.000	2	4	0	0	0	0	0	2	1	0	0	0-1
• BRANSFIELD, Kitty														
W 1903	Pit-N	.207	8	29	3	6	0	2	0	1	1	6	1	1-8
• BRANSON, Jeff														
D 1995	Cin-N	.286	3	7	0	2	1	0	0	2	2	0	0	3-3
L 1995	Cin-N	.111	4	9	2	1	1	0	0	0	0	2	1	3-4
L 1997	Cle-A	.000	1	2	0	0	0	0	0	0	0	2	0	D-1
L 1998	Cle-A	.000	1	1	0	0	0	0	0	0	0	0	0	....
L Total	**3**	**.083**	**6**	**12**	**2**	**1**	**1**	**0**	**0**	**0**	**0**	**4**	**1**	**....**
W 1997	Cle-A	.000	1	1	0	0	0	0	0	0	0	1	0	....
• BRANYAN, Russ														
D 2001	Cle-A	.333	2	3	1	1	0	0	0	0	0	1	0	0-1
• BRAUN, Steve														
L 1978	KC-A	.000	2	5	0	0	0	0	0	0	1	1	0	0-1
L 1982	StL-N	.000	1	1	0	0	0	0	0	0	0	0	0	....
L 1985	StL-N	.000	2	2	0	0	0	0	0	0	0	0	0	....
L Total	**3**	**.000**	**5**	**8**	**0**	**0**	**0**	**0**	**0**	**0**	**1**	**1**	**0**	**....**
W 1982	StL-N	.500	2	2	0	1	0	0	0	2	1	0	0	D-2
W 1985	StL-N	.000	1	1	0	0	0	0	0	0	0	0	0	....
W Total	**2**	**.333**	**3**	**3**	**0**	**1**	**0**	**0**	**0**	**2**	**1**	**0**	**0**	**....**
• BRAVO, Angel														
L 1970	Cin-N	.000	1	1	0	0	0	0	0	0	0	0	0	....
W 1970	Cin-N	.000	4	2	0	0	0	0	0	0	1	1	0	....
• BREAM, Sid														
L 1990	Pit-N	.500	4	8	1	4	1	0	1	3	2	3	0	1-4
L 1991	Atl-N	.300	4	10	1	3	0	0	1	3	0	1	0	1-4
L 1992	Atl-N	.273	7	22	5	6	3	0	1	2	3	0	0	1-7
L 1993	Atl-N	1.000	1	1	1	1	0	0	0	0	0	0	0	1-1
L Total	**4**	**.341**	**16**	**41**	**8**	**14**	**4**	**0**	**3**	**8**	**5**	**4**	**0**	**....**
W 1991	Atl-N	.125	7	24	0	3	2	0	0	0	3	4	0	1-7
W 1992	Atl-N	.200	5	15	1	3	0	0	0	0	4	0	0	1-5
W Total	**2**	**.154**	**12**	**39**	**1**	**6**	**2**	**0**	**0**	**0**	**7**	**4**	**0**	**....**
• BRENLY, Bob														
L 1987	SF-N	.235	6	17	3	4	1	0	1	2	3	7	0	C-6
• BRENNAN, Don														
W 1937	NY-N	....	2	0	0	0	0	0	0	0	0	0	0	....
• BRESNAHAN, Roger														
W 1905	NY-N	.313	5	16	3	5	2	0	0	1	4	0	1	C-5
• BRESSOUD, Eddie														
W 1967	StL-N	....	2	0	0	0	0	0	0	0	0	0	0	S-2
• BRETT, George														
D 1981	KC-A	.167	3	12	0	2	0	0	0	0	0	0	0	3-3
L 1976	KC-A	.444	5	18	4	8	1	1	1	5	2	1	0	3-5
L 1977	KC-A	.300	5	20	2	6	0	2	0	2	1	0	0	3-5
L 1978	KC-A	.389	4	18	7	7	1	1	3	3	0	1	0	3-4
L 1980	KC-A	.273	3	11	3	3	1	0	2	4	1	0	0	3-3
L 1984	KC-A	.231	3	13	0	3	0	0	0	0	0	2	0	3-3
L 1985	KC-A	.348	7	23	6	8	2	0	3	5	7	5	0	3-7
L Total	**6**	**.340**	**27**	**103**	**22**	**35**	**5**	**4**	**9**	**19**	**11**	**9**	**0**	**....**
W 1980	KC-A	.375	6	24	3	9	2	1	1	3	2	4	1	3-6
W 1985	KC-A	.370	7	27	5	10	1	0	0	1	4	7	1	3-7
W Total	**2**	**.373**	**13**	**51**	**8**	**19**	**3**	**1**	**1**	**4**	**6**	**11**	**2**	**....**
• BRICKELL, Fred														
W 1927	Pit-N	.000	2	2	1	0	0	0	0	0	0	0	0	....
• BRIGHT, Harry														
W 1963	NY-A	.000	2	2	0	0	0	0	0	0	0	2	0	....

SER-YEAR	TM-L	AVG	G	AB	R	H	2B	3B	HR	RBI	BB	SO	SB	POS
• BRINKMAN, Ed														
L 1972	Det-A	.250	1	4	0	1	1	0	0	0	0	0	0	S-1
• BROCK, Greg														
L 1983	LA-N	.000	3	9	1	0	0	0	0	0	0	3	0	1-3
L 1985	LA-N	.083	5	12	2	1	0	0	1	2	2	2	0	1-4
L **Total**	2	.048	8	21	3	1	0	0	1	2	2	5	0	....
• BROCK, Lou														
W 1964	StL-N	.300	7	30	2	9	2	0	1	5	0	3	0	0-7
W 1967	StL-N	.414	7	29	8	12	2	1	1	3	2	3	7	0-7
W 1968	StL-N	.464	7	28	6	13	3	1	2	5	3	4	7	0-7
W **Total**	3	.391	21	87	16	34	7	2	4	13	5	10	14	....
• BRODIE, Steve														
T 1894	Bal-N	.000	4	15	2	0	0	0	0	0	2	1	1	0-4
T 1895	Bal-N	.200	5	20	1	4	0	0	0	2	0	0	0	0-5
T 1896	Bal-N	.067	4	15	1	1	0	0	0	3	0	0	1	0-4
T **Total**	3	.100	13	50	4	5	0	0	0	5	2	1	2	....
• BROOKENS, Tom														
L 1984	Det-A	.000	2	2	0	0	0	0	0	0	0	1	0	2-1,3-1
L 1987	Det-A	.000	5	13	0	0	0	0	0	0	0	3	0	3-5
L **Total**	2	.000	7	15	0	0	0	0	0	0	0	4	0	....
W 1984	Det-A	.000	3	3	0	0	0	0	0	0	0	1	0	3-3
• BROSIUS, Scott														
D 1998	NY-A	.400	3	10	1	4	0	0	1	3	0	3	0	3-3
D 1999	NY-A	.100	3	10	0	1	1	0	0	1	0	0	0	3-3
D 2000	NY-A	.176	5	17	0	3	1	0	0	1	1	4	0	3-5
D 2001	NY-A	.059	5	17	0	1	0	0	0	1	0	3	0	3-5
D **Total**	4	.167	16	54	1	9	2	0	1	6	1	10	0	....
L 1998	NY-A	.300	6	20	2	6	1	0	1	6	2	4	0	3-6
L 1999	NY-A	.222	5	18	3	4	0	1	2	3	1	4	0	3-5
L 2000	NY-A	.222	6	18	2	4	0	0	0	0	2	3	0	3-6
L 2001	NY-A	.188	5	16	3	3	2	0	0	2	0	6	0	3-5
L **Total**	4	.236	22	72	10	17	3	1	3	11	5	17	0	....
W 1998	NY-A	.471	4	17	3	8	0	0	2	6	0	4	0	3-4
W 1999	NY-A	.375	4	16	2	6	1	0	0	1	0	5	0	3-4
W 2000	NY-A	.308	5	13	2	4	0	0	1	3	2	2	0	3-5
W 2001	NY-A	.167	7	24	1	4	2	0	1	3	0	8	0	3-7
W **Total**	4	.314	20	70	8	22	3	0	4	13	2	19	0	....
• BROSNAN, Jim														
W 1961	Cin-N	....	3	0	0	0	0	0	0	0	0	0	0	....
• BROUHARD, Mark														
L 1982	Mil-A	.750	1	4	4	3	1	0	1	3	0	0	0	0-1
• BROUTHERS, Dan														
T 1894	Bal-N	.188	4	16	2	3	0	0	0	0	1	0	3	1-4
W 1887	Det-N	.667	1	3	0	2	0	0	0	0	0	0	0	1-1
• BROWER, Jim														
D 2003	SF-N	....	2	0	0	0	0	0	0	0	0	0	0	....
• BROWN, Adrian														
D 2003	Bos-A	.000	4	2	0	0	0	0	0	0	0	1	0	0-2
• BROWN, Bobby														
D 1981	NY-A	....	1	0	0	0	0	0	0	0	0	0	0	....
L 1980	NY-A	.000	3	10	1	0	0	0	0	0	1	2	0	0-3
L 1981	NY-A	1.000	3	1	2	1	0	0	0	0	0	0	0	0-2
L 1984	SD-N	.000	3	4	1	0	0	0	0	0	1	2	1	0-1
L **Total**	3	.067	9	15	4	1	0	0	0	0	2	4	1	....
W 1981	NY-A	.000	4	1	1	0	0	0	0	0	0	1	0	0-2
W 1984	SD-N	.067	5	15	1	1	0	0	0	2	0	4	0	0-5
W **Total**	2	.063	9	16	2	1	0	0	0	2	0	5	0	....
• BROWN, Bobby														
W 1947	NY-A	1.000	4	3	2	3	2	0	0	3	1	0	0	....
W 1949	NY-A	.500	4	12	4	6	1	2	0	5	2	2	0	3-3
W 1950	NY-A	.333	4	12	2	4	1	1	0	1	0	0	0	3-3
W 1951	NY-A	.357	5	14	1	5	1	0	0	0	2	1	0	3-4
W **Total**	4	.439	17	41	9	18	5	3	0	9	5	3	0	....
• BROWN, Brant														
D 1998	Chi-N	.000	1	1	0	0	0	0	0	0	0	0	0	....
• BROWN, Gates														
L 1972	Det-A	.000	3	2	1	0	0	0	0	0	1	0	0	....
W 1968	Det-A	.000	1	1	0	0	0	0	0	0	0	0	0	....
• BROWN, Ike														
L 1972	Det-A	.500	1	2	0	1	0	0	0	2	0	1	0	1-1
• BROWN, Jarvis														
L 1991	Min-A	....	1	0	1	0	0	0	0	0	0	0	0	D-1
W 1991	Min-A	.000	3	2	0	0	0	0	0	0	0	0	0	0-2,D-1
• BROWN, Jimmy														
W 1942	StL-N	.300	5	20	2	6	0	0	0	1	3	0	0	2-5
• BROWN, Larry														
L 1973	Bal-A	....	1	0	0	0	0	0	0	0	0	0	0	3-1
• BROWN, Mordecai														
W 1906	Chi-N	.333	3	6	0	2	0	0	0	0	0	4	0	....
W 1907	Chi-N	.000	1	3	0	0	0	0	0	0	1	0	0	....
W 1908	Chi-N	.000	2	4	0	0	0	0	0	0	0	2	0	....
W 1910	Chi-N	.000	3	7	0	0	0	0	0	0	0	1	0	....
W **Total**	4	.100	9	20	0	2	0	0	0	0	1	7	0	....
• BROWN, Ollie														
L 1976	Phi-N	.000	1	2	0	0	0	0	0	0	1	1	0	0-1

SER-YEAR	TM-L	AVG	G	AB	R	H	2B	3B	HR	RBI	BB	SO	SB	POS
L 1977	Phi-N	.000	2	2	0	0	0	0	0	0	0	1	0	....
L **Total**	2	.000	3	4	0	0	0	0	0	0	1	2	0	....
• BROWN, Tommy														
W 1949	Bro-N	.000	2	2	0	0	0	0	0	0	0	1	0	....
• BROWN, Willard														
W 1888	NY-N	.375	2	8	1	3	1	0	0	0	0	0	0	C-2
W 1889	NY-N	.600	1	5	3	3	0	0	1	2	0	0	0	C-1
W **Total**	2	.462	3	13	4	6	1	0	1	2	0	0	0	....
• BROWNE, George														
W 1905	NY-N	.182	5	22	2	4	0	0	0	1	0	2	2	0-5
• BROWNE, Jerry														
L 1992	Oak-A	.400	4	10	3	4	0	0	0	2	2	0	0	0-1,3-2
• BRUMMER, Glenn														
W 1982	StL-N	....	1	0	0	0	0	0	0	0	0	0	0	C-1
• BRUNANSKY, Tom														
L 1987	Min-A	.412	5	17	5	7	4	0	2	9	4	3	0	0-5
L 1990	Bos-A	.083	4	12	0	1	0	0	0	1	1	3	0	0-4
L **Total**	2	.276	9	29	5	8	4	0	2	10	5	6	0	....
W 1987	Min-A	.200	7	25	5	5	0	0	0	2	4	4	1	0-7
• BRUTON, Bill														
W 1958	Mil-N	.412	7	17	2	7	0	0	1	2	5	5	0	0-7
• BUCHEK, Jerry														
W 1964	StL-N	1.000	4	1	1	1	0	0	0	0	0	0	0	2-4
• BUCKNER, Bill														
L 1974	LA-N	.167	4	18	0	3	1	0	0	0	0	2	0	0-4
L 1986	Bos-A	.214	7	28	3	6	1	0	0	3	0	2	0	1-7
L **Total**	2	.196	11	46	3	9	2	0	0	3	0	4	0	....
W 1974	LA-N	.250	5	20	1	5	1	0	1	1	0	1	0	0-5
W 1986	Bos-A	.188	7	32	2	6	0	0	0	1	0	3	0	1-7
W **Total**	2	.212	12	52	3	11	1	0	1	2	0	4	0	....
• BUECHELE, Steve														
L 1991	Pit-N	.304	7	23	2	7	2	0	0	0	4	6	0	3-7
• BUFORD, Damon														
D 1996	Tex-A	....	2	0	0	0	0	0	0	0	0	0	0	D-1
D 1998	Bos-A	.000	3	1	2	0	0	0	0	0	0	0	0	0-1,D-1
D 1999	Bos-A	.000	1	3	0	0	0	0	0	0	0	1	0	0-1
D **Total**	3	.000	6	4	2	0	0	0	0	0	0	1	0	....
L 1999	Bos-A	.400	4	5	1	2	0	0	0	0	0	2	1	0-4
• BUFORD, Don														
L 1969	Bal-A	.286	3	14	3	4	1	0	0	1	3	0	0	0-3
L 1970	Bal-A	.429	2	7	2	3	1	0	1	3	2	0	0	0-2
L 1971	Bal-A	.429	2	7	1	3	0	1	0	0	2	1	0	0-2
L **Total**	3	.357	7	28	6	10	2	1	1	4	7	1	0	....
W 1969	Bal-A	.100	5	20	1	2	1	0	1	2	2	4	0	0-5
W 1970	Bal-A	.267	4	15	3	4	0	0	1	1	3	2	0	0-4
W 1971	Bal-A	.261	6	23	3	6	1	0	2	4	3	3	0	0-6
W **Total**	3	.207	15	58	7	12	2	0	4	7	8	9	0	....
• BUHNER, Jay														
D 1995	Sea-A	.458	5	24	2	11	1	0	1	3	2	4	0	0-5
D 1997	Sea-A	.231	4	13	2	3	0	0	2	2	3	6	0	0-4
D 2000	Sea-A	.200	2	5	1	1	0	0	1	1	2	0	0	0-2
D 2001	Sea-A	.000	2	3	0	0	0	0	0	0	2	1	0	0-2
D **Total**	4	.333	13	45	5	15	1	0	4	6	9	11	0	....
L 1995	Sea-A	.304	6	23	5	7	2	0	3	5	2	8	0	0-6
L 2000	Sea-A	.182	4	11	0	2	0	0	0	0	1	6	0	0-3
L 2001	Sea-A	.333	3	6	2	2	0	0	1	1	1	3	0	0-3
L **Total**	3	.275	13	40	7	11	2	0	4	6	4	17	0	....
• BUMBRY, Al														
L 1973	Bal-A	.000	2	7	1	0	0	0	0	0	2	2	1	0-2
L 1974	Bal-A	.000	2	1	0	0	0	0	0	0	0	1	0	....
L 1979	Bal-A	.250	4	16	5	4	0	1	0	0	4	3	2	0-4
L 1983	Bal-A	.125	3	8	0	1	1	0	0	1	0	2	0	0-2,D-1
L **Total**	4	.156	11	32	6	5	1	1	0	1	6	8	3	....
W 1979	Bal-A	.143	7	21	3	3	0	0	0	1	2	1	0	0-7
W 1983	Bal-A	.091	4	11	0	1	1	0	0	1	0	1	0	0-4
W **Total**	2	.125	11	32	3	4	1	0	0	2	2	2	0	....
• BURGESS, Smoky														
W 1960	Pit-N	.333	5	18	2	6	1	0	0	0	2	1	0	C-5
• BURKE, Eddie														
T 1894	NY-N	.389	4	18	3	7	1	0	0	2	1	0	1	0-4
• BURKE, Glenn														
L 1977	LA-N	.000	4	7	0	0	0	0	0	0	0	3	0	0-4
W 1977	LA-N	.200	3	5	0	1	0	0	0	0	0	1	0	0-3
• BURKETT, Jesse														
T 1892	Cle-N	.320	6	25	3	8	1	0	0	1	0	2	4	0-6
T 1895	Cle-N	.450	5	20	3	9	2	0	0	2	0	0	1	0-5
T 1896	Cle-N	.333	4	15	1	5	0	0	0	0	2	3	0	0-4
T **Total**	3	.367	15	60	7	22	3	0	0	3	2	5	5	....
• BURKS, Ellis														
D 1995	Col-N	.333	2	6	1	2	1	0	0	2	0	1	0	0-2
D 2000	SF-N	.231	4	13	2	3	1	0	1	4	4	2	0	0-4
D 2001	Cle-A	.316	5	19	4	6	1	0	1	1	1	3	0	D-5
D **Total**	3	.289	11	38	7	11	3	0	2	7	5	6	0	....
L 1988	Bos-A	.235	4	17	2	4	1	0	0	1	0	3	0	0-4
L 1990	Bos-A	.267	4	15	1	4	2	0	0	0	1	1	1	0-4

YEAR	TM-L	AVG	G	AB	R	H	2B	3B	HR	RBI	BB	SO	SB	POS
L 1993	Chi-A	.304	6	23	4	7	1	0	1	3	4	5	0	O-6
L Total	**3**	**.273**	**14**	**55**	**7**	**15**	**4**	**0**	**1**	**4**	**5**	**9**	**1**	**....**
• BURLESON, Rick														
L 1975	Bos-A	.444	3	9	2	4	2	0	0	1	1	0	0	S-3
L 1986	Cal-A	.273	4	11	0	3	0	0	0	0	0	0	0	2-2,D-1
L Total	**2**	**.350**	**7**	**20**	**2**	**7**	**2**	**0**	**0**	**1**	**1**	**0**	**0**	**....**
W 1975	Bos-A	.292	7	24	1	7	1	0	0	2	4	2	0	S-7
• BURNS, Ed														
W 1915	Phi-N	.188	5	16	1	3	0	0	0	0	1	2	0	C-5
• BURNS, George														
W 1913	NY-N	.158	5	19	2	3	2	0	0	2	1	5	1	O-5
W 1917	NY-N	.227	6	22	3	5	0	0	0	2	3	6	1	O-6
W 1921	NY-N	.333	8	33	2	11	4	1	0	2	3	5	1	O-8
W Total	**3**	**.257**	**19**	**74**	**7**	**19**	**6**	**1**	**0**	**6**	**7**	**16**	**3**	**....**
• BURNS, George														
W 1920	Cle-A	.300	5	10	1	3	1	0	0	3	3	3	0	1-4
W 1929	Phi-A	.000	1	2	0	0	0	0	0	0	0	1	0	....
W Total	**2**	**.250**	**6**	**12**	**1**	**3**	**1**	**0**	**0**	**3**	**3**	**4**	**0**	**....**
• BURNS, Oyster														
W 1889	Bro-A	.229	9	35	8	8	3	0	2	11	5	6	0	O-9
W 1890	Bro-N	.222	7	27	6	6	2	0	1	5	3	4	0	O-4,3-3
W Total	**2**	**.226**	**16**	**62**	**14**	**14**	**5**	**0**	**3**	**16**	**8**	**10**	**0**	**....**
• BURNS, Tom														
W 1885	Chi-N	.080	7	25	3	2	0	1	0	0	0	0	0	S-4,3-3
W 1886	Chi-N	.286	6	21	2	6	2	1	0	1	0	2	0	3-6,O-1
W Total	**2**	**.174**	**13**	**46**	**5**	**8**	**2**	**2**	**0**	**1**	**0**	**2**	**0**	**....**
• BURROUGHS, Jeff														
L 1985	Tor-A	.000	1	1	0	0	0	0	0	0	0	0	0	....
• BUSH, Donie														
W 1909	Det-A	.304	7	23	5	7	1	0	0	3	5	3	1	S-7
• BUSH, Homer														
D 1998	NY-A	....	1	0	0	0	0	0	0	0	0	0	1	D-1
L 1998	NY-A	....	2	0	1	0	0	0	0	0	0	0	1	D-1
W 1998	NY-A	....	2	0	0	0	0	0	0	0	0	0	0	D-1
• BUSH, Randy														
L 1987	Min-A	.250	4	12	4	3	0	1	0	2	3	2	3	D-4
W 1987	Min-A	.167	4	6	1	1	1	0	0	2	0	1	0	D-2
W 1991	Min-A	.250	3	4	0	1	0	0	0	0	0	1	0	O-2
W Total	**2**	**.200**	**7**	**10**	**1**	**2**	**1**	**0**	**0**	**2**	**0**	**2**	**0**	**....**
• BUSHONG, Doc														
W 1885	StL-A	.154	4	13	1	2	0	0	0	2	0	0	0	C-4
W 1886	StL-A	.188	6	16	4	3	1	0	0	2	4	5	0	C-6
W 1887	StL-A	.333	9	33	3	11	0	0	0	1	4	1	0	C-9
W 1889	Bro-A	.000	3	8	0	0	0	0	0	0	1	0	0	C-3
W 1890	Bro-N	.000	2	6	0	0	0	0	0	0	0	1	0	C-2
W Total	**5**	**.211**	**24**	**76**	**8**	**16**	**1**	**0**	**0**	**5**	**9**	**7**	**0**	**....**
• BUTERA, Sal														
L 1987	Min-A	.667	1	3	0	2	0	0	0	0	0	0	0	C-1
W 1987	Min-A	....	1	0	0	0	0	0	0	0	0	0	0	C-1
• BUTLER, Brett														
D 1995	LA-N	.267	3	15	1	4	0	0	0	1	0	3	0	O-3
L 1982	Atl-N	.000	2	1	0	0	0	0	0	0	0	0	0	O-1
L 1989	SF-N	.211	5	19	6	4	0	0	0	0	3	3	0	O-5
L Total	**2**	**.200**	**7**	**20**	**6**	**4**	**0**	**0**	**0**	**0**	**3**	**3**	**0**	**....**
W 1989	SF-N	.286	4	14	1	4	1	0	0	1	2	1	2	O-4
• BUTLER, Rob														
W 1993	Tor-A	.500	2	2	1	1	0	0	0	0	0	0	0	....
• BYRD, Sammy														
W 1932	NY-A	....	1	0	0	0	0	0	0	0	0	0	0	O-1
• BYRNE, Bobby														
W 1909	Pit-N	.250	7	24	5	6	1	0	0	0	1	4	1	3-7
W 1915	Phi-N	.000	1	1	0	0	0	0	0	0	0	0	0	....
W Total	**2**	**.240**	**8**	**25**	**5**	**6**	**1**	**0**	**0**	**0**	**1**	**4**	**1**	**....**
• BYRNES, Eric														
D 2001	Oak-A	.000	2	2	0	0	0	0	0	0	0	1	0	D-1
D 2002	Oak-A	.000	2	1	0	0	0	0	0	0	0	1	0	O-1
D 2003	Oak-A	.462	5	13	2	6	1	0	0	2	0	5	1	O-4
D Total	**3**	**.375**	**9**	**16**	**2**	**6**	**1**	**0**	**0**	**2**	**0**	**7**	**1**	**....**
• BYRNES, Milt														
W 1944	StL-A	.000	3	2	0	0	0	0	0	0	1	2	0	....
• CABALLERO, Putsy														
W 1950	Phi-N	.000	3	1	0	0	0	0	0	0	0	1	0	....
• CABELL, Enos														
L 1974	Bal-A	.250	3	4	0	1	0	0	0	0	0	2	0	O-1,D-1
L 1980	Hou-N	.238	5	21	1	5	1	0	0	0	1	3	0	3-5
L 1985	LA-N	.077	5	13	1	1	0	0	0	0	0	3	0	1-3
L Total	**3**	**.184**	**13**	**38**	**2**	**7**	**1**	**0**	**0**	**0**	**1**	**8**	**0**	**....**
• CABRERA, Francisco														
L 1992	Atl-N	.500	2	2	0	1	0	0	0	2	0	0	0	....
L 1993	Atl-N	.667	3	3	0	2	0	0	0	1	0	1	0	C-1
L Total	**2**	**.600**	**5**	**5**	**0**	**3**	**0**	**0**	**0**	**3**	**0**	**1**	**0**	**....**
W 1991	Atl-N	.000	3	1	0	0	0	0	0	0	0	0	0	C-1
W 1992	Atl-N	.000	1	1	0	0	0	0	0	0	0	0	0	....
W Total	**2**	**.000**	**4**	**2**	**0**	**0**	**0**	**0**	**0**	**0**	**0**	**0**	**0**	**....**

YEAR	TM-L	AVG	G	AB	R	H	2B	3B	HR	RBI	BB	SO	SB	POS
• CABRERA, Jolbert														
D 2001	Cle-A	1.000	2	1	1	1	0	0	0	1	0	0	0	O-2
• CABRERA, Miguel														
D 2003	Fla-N	.286	4	14	1	4	2	0	0	3	1	6	0	3-4
L 2003	Fla-N	.333	7	30	9	10	0	0	3	6	2	6	0	O-5,3-3,S-1
W 2003	Fla-N	.167	6	24	1	4	0	0	1	3	1	7	0	O-6
• CADY, Hick														
W 1912	Bos-A	.136	7	22	1	3	0	0	0	1	0	3	0	C-7
W 1915	Bos-A	.333	4	6	0	2	0	0	0	0	1	2	0	C-4
W 1916	Bos-A	.250	2	4	1	1	0	0	0	0	3	0	0	C-2
W Total	**3**	**.188**	**13**	**32**	**2**	**6**	**0**	**0**	**0**	**1**	**4**	**5**	**0**	**....**
• CAIRO, Miguel														
D 2001	StL-N	.200	3	5	0	1	0	0	0	0	0	1	1	O-2
D 2002	StL-N	1.000	2	4	2	4	1	0	0	3	0	0	0	3-2
D Total	**2**	**.556**	**5**	**9**	**2**	**5**	**1**	**0**	**0**	**3**	**0**	**1**	**1**	**....**
L 2002	StL-N	.385	3	13	2	5	0	0	1	2	0	2	0	3-3
• CAMERON, Mike														
D 2000	Sea-A	.250	3	12	2	3	0	0	0	2	0	0	1	O-3
D 2001	Sea-A	.222	5	18	2	4	3	0	1	3	2	7	0	O-5
D Total	**2**	**.233**	**8**	**30**	**4**	**7**	**3**	**0**	**1**	**5**	**2**	**7**	**1**	**....**
L 2000	Sea-A	.111	6	18	3	2	0	0	0	1	2	7	1	O-6
L 2001	Sea-A	.176	5	17	3	3	2	0	0	0	4	4	0	O-5
L Total	**2**	**.143**	**11**	**35**	**6**	**5**	**2**	**0**	**0**	**1**	**6**	**11**	**1**	**....**
• CAMILLI, Dolph														
W 1941	Bro-N	.167	5	18	1	3	1	0	0	1	1	6	0	1-5
• CAMINITI, Ken														
D 1996	SD-N	.300	3	10	3	3	0	0	3	3	2	5	0	3-3
D 1998	SD-N	.143	4	14	2	2	0	0	0	0	1	3	0	3-4
D 1999	Hou-N	.471	4	17	3	8	0	0	3	8	2	1	0	3-4
D 2001	Atl-N	.000	2	2	0	0	0	0	0	0	0	1	0	....
D Total	**4**	**.302**	**13**	**43**	**8**	**13**	**0**	**0**	**6**	**11**	**5**	**10**	**0**	**....**
L 1998	SD-N	.273	6	22	3	6	0	0	2	4	5	4	0	3-6
W 1998	SD-N	.143	4	14	1	2	1	0	0	1	2	7	0	3-4
• CAMP, Rick														
L 1982	Atl-N	....	1	0	0	0	0	0	0	0	0	0	0	....
• CAMPANELLA, Roy														
W 1949	Bro-N	.267	5	15	2	4	1	0	1	2	3	1	0	C-5
W 1952	Bro-N	.214	7	28	0	6	0	0	0	1	1	6	0	C-7
W 1953	Bro-N	.273	6	22	6	6	0	0	1	2	2	3	0	C-6
W 1955	Bro-N	.259	7	27	4	7	3	0	2	4	3	3	0	C-7
W 1956	Bro-N	.182	7	22	2	4	1	0	0	3	3	7	0	C-7
W Total	**5**	**.237**	**32**	**114**	**14**	**27**	**5**	**0**	**4**	**12**	**12**	**20**	**0**	**....**
• CAMPANERIS, Bert														
L 1971	Oak-A	.167	3	12	0	2	1	0	0	0	0	1	0	S-3
L 1972	Oak-A	.429	2	7	3	3	0	0	0	0	1	0	2	S-2
L 1973	Oak-A	.333	5	21	3	7	1	0	2	3	2	2	0	S-5
L 1974	Oak-A	.176	4	17	0	3	0	0	0	3	0	3	0	S-4
L 1975	Oak-A	.000	3	11	1	0	0	0	0	0	1	1	0	S-3
L 1979	Cal-A	....	1	0	0	0	0	0	0	0	0	0	0	S-1
L Total	**6**	**.221**	**18**	**68**	**7**	**15**	**2**	**0**	**2**	**6**	**4**	**7**	**2**	**....**
W 1972	Oak-A	.179	7	28	1	5	0	0	0	0	1	4	0	S-7
W 1973	Oak-A	.290	7	31	6	9	0	1	1	3	1	7	3	S-7
W 1974	Oak-A	.353	5	17	1	6	2	0	0	2	0	2	1	S-5
W Total	**3**	**.263**	**19**	**76**	**8**	**20**	**2**	**1**	**1**	**5**	**2**	**13**	**4**	**....**
• CAMPBELL, Bruce														
W 1940	Det-A	.360	7	25	4	9	1	0	1	5	4	4	0	O-7
• CAMPBELL, Paul														
W 1946	Bos-A	....	1	0	0	0	0	0	0	0	0	0	0	....
• CANATE, Willie														
W 1993	Tor-A	....	1	0	0	0	0	0	0	0	0	0	0	....
• CANDAELE, Casey														
D 1996	Cle-A	....	2	0	1	0	0	0	0	0	1	0	0	D-1
• CANGELOSI, John														
D 1997	Fla-N	.000	1	1	0	0	0	0	0	0	0	0	0	....
L 1997	Fla-N	.200	3	5	0	1	0	0	0	0	1	0	0	O-1
W 1997	Fla-N	.333	3	3	0	1	0	0	0	0	0	2	0	....
• CANSECO, Jose														
D 1995	Bos-A	.000	3	13	0	0	0	0	0	0	2	2	0	O-1,D-2
L 1988	Oak-A	.313	4	16	4	5	1	0	3	4	1	2	1	O-4
L 1989	Oak-A	.294	5	17	1	5	0	0	1	3	3	7	0	O-5
L 1990	Oak-A	.182	4	11	3	2	0	0	0	1	5	5	2	O-4
L Total	**3**	**.273**	**13**	**44**	**8**	**12**	**1**	**0**	**4**	**8**	**9**	**14**	**3**	**....**
W 1988	Oak-A	.053	5	19	1	1	0	0	1	5	2	5	1	O-5
W 1989	Oak-A	.357	4	14	5	5	0	0	1	3	4	3	1	O-4
W 1990	Oak-A	.083	4	12	1	1	0	0	1	2	2	3	0	O-3,D-1
W 2000	NY-A	.000	1	1	0	0	0	0	0	0	0	1	0	....
W Total	**4**	**.152**	**14**	**46**	**7**	**7**	**0**	**0**	**3**	**10**	**8**	**12**	**2**	**....**
• CARBO, Bernie														
L 1970	Cin-N	.000	2	6	0	0	0	0	0	0	1	2	0	O-2
W 1970	Cin-N	.000	4	8	0	0	0	0	0	0	2	3	0	O-2
W 1975	Bos-A	.429	4	7	3	3	1	0	2	4	1	1	0	O-2
W Total	**2**	**.200**	**8**	**15**	**3**	**3**	**1**	**0**	**2**	**4**	**3**	**4**	**0**	**....**
• CARDENAL, Jose														
L 1978	Phi-N	.167	2	6	0	1	0	0	0	0	1	1	0	1-2
W 1980	KC-A	.200	4	10	0	2	0	0	0	0	0	3	0	O-4
• CARDENAS, Leo														
L 1969	Min-A	.154	3	13	0	2	0	1	0	0	0	7	0	S-3

SER-YEAR	TM-L	AVG	G	AB	R	H	2B	3B	HR	RBI	BB	SO	SB	POS
L 1970	Min-A	.182	3	11	1	2	0	0	0	1	1	1	0	S-3
L Total	2	.167	6	24	1	4	0	1	0	1	1	8	0	....
W 1961	Cin-N	.333	3	3	0	1	1	0	0	0	0	1	0	....
• CAREW, Rod														
L 1969	Min-A	.071	3	14	0	1	0	0	0	0	1	4	0	2-3
L 1970	Min-A	.000	2	2	0	0	0	0	0	0	0	1	0	....
L 1979	Cal-A	.412	4	17	4	7	3	0	0	1	0	0	1	1-4
L 1982	Cal-A	.176	5	17	2	3	1	0	0	0	4	4	1	1-5
L Total	4	.220	14	50	6	11	4	0	0	1	5	9	2	....
• CAREY, Andy														
W 1955	NY-A	.500	2	2	0	1	0	1	0	1	0	0	0	....
W 1956	NY-A	.158	7	19	2	3	0	0	0	0	1	6	0	3-7
W 1957	NY-A	.286	2	7	0	2	1	0	0	1	1	0	0	3-2
W 1958	NY-A	.083	5	12	1	1	0	0	0	0	0	3	0	3-5
W Total	4	.175	16	40	3	7	1	1	0	2	2	9	0	....
• CAREY, Max														
W 1925	Pit-N	.458	7	24	6	11	4	0	0	2	2	3	3	O-7
• CAREY, Scoops														
T 1895	Bal-N	.263	5	19	0	5	1	0	0	1	0	0	0	1-5
• CARR, Chuck														
D 1997	Hou-N	.250	2	4	1	1	0	0	1	1	1	3	0	O-2
• CARRIGAN, Bill														
W 1912	Bos-A	.000	2	7	0	0	0	0	0	0	0	0	0	C-2
W 1915	Bos-A	.000	1	2	0	0	0	0	0	0	1	1	0	C-1
W 1916	Bos-A	.667	1	3	0	2	0	0	0	1	0	1	0	C-1
W Total	3	.167	4	12	0	2	0	0	0	1	1	2	0	....
• CARROLL, Cliff														
W 1884	Pro-N	.100	3	10	2	1	0	0	0	1	1	1	0	O-3
• CARROLL, Tom														
W 1955	NY-A	....	2	0	0	0	0	0	0	0	0	0	0	....
• CARTER, Gary														
D 1981	Mon-N	.421	5	19	3	8	3	0	2	6	1	1	0	C-5
L 1981	Mon-N	.438	5	16	3	7	1	0	0	0	4	2	0	C-5
L 1986	NY-N	.148	6	27	1	4	1	0	0	2	2	5	0	C-6
L 1988	NY-N	.222	7	27	0	6	1	1	0	4	1	3	0	C-7
L Total	3	.243	18	70	4	17	3	1	0	6	7	10	0	....
W 1986	NY-N	.276	7	29	4	8	2	0	2	9	0	4	0	C-7
• CARTER, Joe														
L 1991	Tor-A	.263	5	19	3	5	2	0	1	4	1	5	0	O-3,D-2
L 1992	Tor-A	.192	6	26	2	5	0	0	1	3	2	4	2	O-6,1-2
L 1993	Tor-A	.259	6	27	2	7	0	0	0	2	1	5	0	O-6
L Total	3	.236	17	72	7	17	2	0	2	9	4	14	2	....
W 1992	Tor-A	.273	6	22	2	6	2	0	2	3	3	2	1	O-4,1-2
W 1993	Tor-A	.280	6	25	6	7	1	0	2	8	0	4	0	O-6
W Total	2	.277	12	47	8	13	3	0	4	11	3	6	1	....
• CARTY, Rico														
L 1969	Atl-N	.300	3	10	4	3	2	0	0	0	3	1	0	O-3
• CARUTHERS, Bob														
W 1885	StL-A	.200	5	15	1	3	0	1	0	0	1	0	0	P-3,O-2
W 1886	StL-A	.250	6	24	6	6	1	2	0	5	1	4	1	P-3,O-3
W 1887	StL-A	.255	10	47	2	12	0	0	0	3	1	1	3	P-8,O-3
W 1889	Bro-A	.250	4	8	1	2	0	0	0	1	3	3	0	P-4
W 1890	Bro-N	.000	2	6	0	0	0	0	0	0	2	0	0	O-2
W Total	5	.230	27	100	10	23	1	3	0	9	8	8	4	....
• CASH, Dave														
L 1970	Pit-N	.125	2	8	1	1	1	0	0	0	1	1	0	2-2
L 1971	Pit-N	.421	4	19	5	8	2	0	0	1	0	1	1	2-4
L 1972	Pit-N	.211	5	19	0	4	0	0	0	3	0	0	0	2-5
L 1976	Phi-N	.308	3	13	1	4	1	0	0	1	0	0	0	2-3
L Total	4	.288	14	59	7	17	4	0	0	5	1	2	1	....
W 1971	Pit-N	.133	7	30	2	4	1	0	0	1	3	1	1	2-7
• CASH, Norm														
L 1972	Det-A	.250	5	16	1	4	0	0	1	2	2	3	0	1-5
W 1959	Chi-A	.000	4	4	0	0	0	0	0	0	0	2	0	....
W 1968	Det-A	.385	7	26	5	10	0	0	1	5	3	5	0	1-7
W Total	2	.333	11	30	5	10	0	0	1	5	3	7	0	....
• CASTILLA, Vinny														
D 1995	Col-N	.467	4	15	3	7	1	0	3	6	0	1	0	3-4
D 2001	Hou-N	.273	3	11	1	3	0	0	1	1	0	3	0	3-3
D 2002	Atl-N	.389	5	18	5	7	0	0	1	4	2	2	0	3-5
D 2003	Atl-N	.250	5	16	0	4	0	0	0	1	3	6	0	3-5
D Total	4	.350	17	60	9	21	1	0	5	12	5	12	0	....
• CASTILLO, Luis														
D 2003	Fla-N	.294	4	17	2	5	3	0	0	1	3	3	0	2-4
L 2003	Fla-N	.214	7	28	3	6	1	0	0	2	5	2	2	2-7
W 2003	Fla-N	.154	6	26	1	4	0	0	0	1	0	7	1	2-6
• CASTILLO, Marty														
L 1984	Det-A	.250	3	8	0	2	0	0	0	2	0	3	1	3-3
W 1984	Det-A	.333	3	9	2	3	0	0	1	2	2	1	0	3-3
• CASTRO, Juan														
D 1996	LA-N	.200	2	5	0	1	1	0	0	1	1	1	0	2-2
• CATHER, Ted														
W 1914	Bos-N	.000	1	5	0	0	0	0	0	0	0	1	0	O-1
• CAVARRETTA, Phil														
W 1935	Chi-N	.125	6	24	1	3	0	0	0	0	0	5	0	1-6
W 1938	Chi-N	.462	4	13	1	6	1	0	0	0	0	1	0	O-3

SER-YEAR	TM-L	AVG	G	AB	R	H	2B	3B	HR	RBI	BB	SO	SB	POS
W 1945	Chi-N	.423	7	26	7	11	2	0	1	5	4	3	0	1-7
W Total	3	.317	17	63	9	20	3	0	1	5	4	9	0	....
• CEDENO, Cesar														
D 1981	Hou-N	.214	4	14	0	3	1	0	0	0	2	2	2	1-4
L 1980	Hou-N	.182	3	11	1	2	0	0	0	1	1	0	0	O-3
L 1985	StL-N	.167	5	12	2	2	1	0	0	0	2	3	0	O-4
L Total	2	.174	8	23	3	4	1	0	0	1	3	3	0	....
W 1985	StL-N	.133	5	15	1	2	1	0	0	1	2	2	0	O-5
• CEDENO, Roger														
D 1999	NY-N	.286	4	7	1	2	0	0	0	2	1	1	1	O-4
L 1999	NY-N	.500	5	12	2	6	1	0	0	1	0	1	2	O-4
• CEPEDA, Orlando														
L 1969	Atl-N	.455	3	11	2	5	2	0	1	3	1	2	1	1-3
W 1962	SF-N	.158	5	19	1	3	1	0	0	2	0	4	0	1-5
W 1967	StL-N	.103	7	29	1	3	2	0	0	1	0	4	0	1-7
W 1968	StL-N	.250	7	28	2	7	0	0	2	6	2	3	0	1-7
W Total	3	.171	19	76	4	13	3	0	2	9	2	11	0	....
• CERONE, Rick														
D 1981	NY-A	.333	5	18	1	6	2	0	1	5	0	2	0	C-5
L 1980	NY-A	.333	3	12	1	4	0	0	1	2	0	1	0	C-3
L 1981	NY-A	.100	3	10	1	1	0	0	0	0	0	0	0	C-3
L Total	2	.227	6	22	2	5	0	0	1	2	0	1	0	....
W 1981	NY-A	.190	6	21	2	4	1	0	1	3	4	2	0	C-6
• CERV, Bob														
W 1955	NY-A	.125	5	16	1	2	0	0	1	1	0	4	0	O-4
W 1956	NY-A	1.000	1	1	0	1	0	0	0	0	0	0	0	....
W 1960	NY-A	.357	4	14	1	5	0	0	0	0	0	3	0	O-3
W Total	3	.258	10	31	2	8	0	0	1	1	0	7	0	....
• CEY, Ron														
L 1974	LA-N	.313	4	16	2	5	3	0	1	1	3	2	0	3-4
L 1977	LA-N	.308	4	13	4	4	1	0	1	4	2	4	1	3-4
L 1978	LA-N	.313	4	16	4	5	1	0	1	3	2	4	0	3-4
L 1981	LA-N	.278	5	18	1	5	1	0	0	3	3	2	0	3-5
L 1984	Chi-N	.158	5	19	3	3	1	0	1	3	3	3	0	3-5
L Total	5	.268	22	82	14	22	7	0	4	14	13	15	1	....
W 1974	LA-N	.176	5	17	1	3	0	0	0	0	3	3	0	3-5
W 1977	LA-N	.190	6	21	2	4	1	0	1	3	3	5	0	3-6
W 1978	LA-N	.286	6	21	2	6	0	0	1	4	3	3	0	3-6
W 1981	LA-N	.350	6	20	3	7	0	0	1	6	3	3	0	3-6
W Total	4	.253	23	79	8	20	1	0	3	13	12	14	0	....
• CHACON, Elio														
W 1961	Cin-N	.250	4	12	2	3	0	0	0	0	1	2	0	2-3
• CHALK, Dave														
W 1980	KC-A	....	1	0	1	0	0	0	0	0	1	0	1	3-1
• CHAMBERLAIN, Wes														
L 1993	Phi-N	.364	4	11	1	4	3	0	0	1	1	3	0	O-3
W 1993	Phi-N	.000	2	2	0	0	0	0	0	0	0	1	0	....
• CHAMBLISS, Chris														
L 1976	NY-A	.524	5	21	5	11	1	1	2	8	0	1	2	1-5
L 1977	NY-A	.059	5	17	0	1	0	0	0	0	3	4	0	1-5
L 1978	NY-A	.400	4	15	1	6	0	0	0	2	0	4	0	1-4
L 1982	Atl-N	.000	3	10	0	0	0	0	0	0	1	0	0	1-3
L Total	4	.286	17	63	6	18	1	1	2	10	4	9	2	....
W 1976	NY-A	.313	4	16	1	5	1	0	0	1	0	2	0	1-4
W 1977	NY-A	.292	6	24	4	7	2	0	1	4	0	2	0	1-6
W 1978	NY-A	.182	3	11	1	2	0	0	0	0	1	1	0	1-3
W Total	3	.275	13	51	6	14	3	0	1	5	1	5	0	....
• CHANCE, Frank														
W 1906	Chi-N	.238	6	21	3	5	1	0	0	0	2	1	2	1-6
W 1907	Chi-N	.214	4	14	3	3	1	0	0	0	3	2	3	1-4
W 1908	Chi-N	.421	5	19	4	8	0	0	0	2	3	1	5	1-5
W 1910	Chi-N	.353	5	17	1	6	1	1	0	4	0	2	0	1-5
W Total	4	.310	20	71	11	22	3	1	0	6	8	6	10	....
• CHANEY, Darrel														
L 1972	Cin-N	.188	5	16	3	3	0	0	0	1	1	1	1	S-5
L 1973	Cin-N	.000	5	9	0	0	0	0	0	0	3	4	0	S-5
L Total	2	.120	10	25	3	3	0	0	0	1	4	5	1	....
W 1970	Cin-N	.000	3	1	0	0	0	0	0	0	0	1	0	S-3
W 1972	Cin-N	.000	4	7	0	0	0	0	0	0	2	2	0	S-3
W 1975	Cin-N	.000	2	2	0	0	0	0	0	0	0	1	0	....
W Total	3	.000	9	10	0	0	0	0	0	0	2	4	0	....
• CHAPMAN, Ben														
W 1932	NY-A	.294	4	17	1	5	2	0	0	6	2	4	0	O-4
• CHARLES, Ed														
W 1969	NY-N	.133	4	15	1	2	1	0	0	0	0	2	0	3-4
• CHARTAK, Mike														
W 1944	StL-A	.000	2	2	0	0	0	0	0	0	0	2	0	....
• CHAVEZ, Eric														
D 2000	Oak-A	.333	5	21	4	7	3	0	0	4	0	5	0	3-5
D 2001	Oak-A	.143	5	21	0	3	1	0	0	0	0	5	0	3-5
D 2002	Oak-A	.381	5	21	3	8	0	0	1	5	2	1	0	3-5
D 2003	Oak-A	.045	5	22	1	1	1	0	0	0	1	3	1	3-5
D Total	4	.224	20	85	8	19	5	0	1	9	3	14	1	....
• CHILDS, Cupid														
T 1892	Cle-N	.409	6	22	3	9	0	2	0	0	5	1	0	2-6
T 1895	Cle-N	.190	5	21	4	4	1	0	0	2	1	0	1	2-5

YEAR	TM-L	AVG	G	AB	R	H	2B	3B	HR	RBI	BB	SO	SB	POS
T 1896	Cle-N	.231	4	13	2	3	0	0	0	0	4	0	1	2-4
T Total	3	.286	15	56	9	16	1	2	0	2	10	1	2	....
• CHIOZZA, Lou														
W 1937	NY-N	.286	2	7	0	2	0	0	0	0	1	1	0	0-2
• CHRISTENSEN, McKay														
D 2000	Chi-A	....	1	0	0	0	0	0	0	0	0	0	0	0-1
• CHRISTENSON, Ryan														
D 2000	Oak-A	.500	2	2	0	1	0	0	0	1	0	1	0	0-2
• CHRISTMAN, Mark														
W 1944	StL-A	.091	6	22	0	2	0	0	0	1	0	6	0	3-6
• CHRISTOPHER, Joe														
W 1960	Pit-N	....	3	0	2	0	0	0	0	0	0	0	0	....
• CHURN, Chuck														
W 1959	LA-N	....	1	0	0	0	0	0	0	0	0	0	0	....
• CIANFROCCO, Archi														
D 1996	SD-N	.333	3	3	1	1	0	0	0	0	0	1	0	1-3
• CICOTTE, Eddie														
W 1917	Chi-A	.143	3	7	0	1	0	0	0	0	1	2	0	....
W 1919	Chi-A	.000	3	8	0	0	0	0	0	0	0	3	0	....
W Total	2	.067	6	15	0	1	0	0	0	0	1	5	0	....
• CIMOLI, Gino														
W 1956	Bro-N	....	1	0	0	0	0	0	0	0	0	0	0	0-1
W 1960	Pit-N	.250	7	20	4	5	0	0	0	1	2	4	0	0-6
W Total	2	.250	8	20	4	5	0	0	0	1	2	4	0	....
• CINTRON, Alex														
D 2002	Ari-N	....	2	0	0	0	0	0	0	0	0	0	0	3-1
• CLARK, Allie														
W 1947	NY-A	.500	3	2	1	1	0	0	0	1	1	0	0	0-1
W 1948	Cle-A	.000	1	3	0	0	0	0	0	0	0	1	0	0-1
W Total	2	.200	4	5	1	1	0	0	0	1	1	1	0	....
• CLARK, Bob														
W 1889	Bro-A	.417	4	12	3	5	2	0	0	3	2	2	0	C-4
W 1890	Bro-N	.667	1	3	2	2	0	1	0	1	0	0	0	C-1
W Total	2	.467	5	15	5	7	2	1	0	4	2	2	0	....
• CLARK, Bobby														
L 1979	Cal-A	.000	1	3	0	0	0	0	0	0	0	2	0	0-1
L 1982	Cal-A	....	2	0	0	0	0	0	0	0	0	0	0	0-2
L Total	2	.000	3	3	0	0	0	0	0	0	0	2	0	....
• CLARK, Dave														
D 1996	LA-N	.000	2	2	0	0	0	0	0	0	0	2	0	....
D 1998	Hou-N	....	2	0	0	0	0	0	0	0	2	0	0	....
D Total	2	.000	4	2	0	0	0	0	0	0	2	2	0	....
• CLARK, Jack														
L 1985	StL-N	.381	6	21	4	8	0	0	1	4	5	5	0	1-6
L 1987	StL-N	.000	1	1	0	0	0	0	0	0	0	1	0	....
L Total	2	.364	7	22	4	8	0	0	1	4	5	6	0	....
W 1985	StL-N	.240	7	25	1	6	2	0	0	4	3	9	0	1-7
• CLARK, Will														
D 1996	Tex-A	.125	4	16	1	2	0	0	0	0	3	2	0	1-4
D 1998	Tex-A	.091	3	11	0	1	0	0	0	0	1	2	0	1-3
D 2000	StL-N	.250	3	12	3	3	0	0	1	4	1	3	0	1-3
D Total	3	.154	10	39	4	6	0	0	1	4	5	7	0	....
L 1987	SF-N	.360	7	25	3	9	2	0	1	3	3	6	1	1-7
L 1989	SF-N	.650	5	20	8	13	3	1	2	8	2	2	0	1-5
L 2000	StL-N	.412	5	17	3	7	2	0	1	1	2	1	0	1-5
L Total	3	.468	17	62	14	29	7	1	4	12	7	9	1	....
W 1989	SF-N	.250	4	16	2	4	1	0	0	0	1	3	0	1-4
• CLARKE, Boileryard														
T 1895	Bal-N	.286	2	7	1	2	0	0	0	0	0	0	2	C-2
T 1897	Bal-N	.563	4	16	5	9	1	1	1	4	1	0	0	C-4
T Total	2	.478	6	23	6	11	1	1	1	4	1	0	2	....
• CLARKE, Fred														
W 1903	Pit-N	.265	8	34	3	9	2	1	0	2	1	5	1	0-8
W 1909	Pit-N	.211	7	19	7	4	0	0	2	7	5	3	3	0-7
W Total	2	.245	15	53	10	13	2	1	2	9	6	8	4	....
• CLARKSON, John														
T 1892	Cle-N	.250	2	8	1	2	0	0	1	3	0	1	0	P-2
W 1885	Chi-N	.154	4	13	1	2	1	0	0	0	0	0	0	P-3,0-2
W 1886	Chi-N	.067	4	15	0	1	0	0	0	1	0	2	1	P-4,0-1
W Total	2	.107	8	28	1	3	1	0	0	1	0	2	1	....
• CLARY, Ellis														
W 1944	StL-A	.000	1	1	0	0	0	0	0	0	0	0	0	....
• CLAYTON, Royce														
D 1996	StL-N	.333	2	6	1	2	0	0	0	0	3	1	0	S-2
D 1998	Tex-A	.222	3	9	0	2	0	0	0	0	0	4	0	S-3
D 1999	Tex-A	.000	3	10	0	0	0	0	0	0	0	1	0	S-3
D Total	3	.160	8	25	1	4	0	0	0	0	3	6	0	....
L 1996	StL-N	.350	5	20	4	7	0	0	0	1	1	4	1	S-5
• CLEMENTE, Roberto														
L 1970	Pit-N	.214	3	14	1	3	0	0	0	1	0	4	0	0-3
L 1971	Pit-N	.333	4	18	2	6	0	0	0	4	1	6	0	0-4
L 1972	Pit-N	.235	5	17	1	4	1	0	1	2	3	5	0	0-5
L Total	3	.265	12	49	4	13	1	0	1	7	4	15	0	....
W 1960	Pit-N	.310	7	29	1	9	0	0	0	3	0	4	0	0-7
W 1971	Pit-N	.414	7	29	3	12	2	1	2	4	2	2	0	0-7
W Total	2	.362	14	58	4	21	2	1	2	7	2	6	0	....
• CLENDENON, Donn														
W 1969	NY-N	.357	4	14	4	5	1	0	3	4	2	6	0	1-4
• CLIFTON, Flea														
W 1935	Det-A	.000	4	16	1	0	0	0	0	0	2	4	0	3-4
• CLINE, Ty														
L 1970	Cin-N	1.000	2	1	2	1	0	1	0	0	1	0	0	0-1
W 1970	Cin-N	.333	3	3	0	1	0	0	0	0	0	0	0	....
• CLINES, Gene														
L 1971	Pit-N	.333	1	3	1	1	0	0	1	1	0	1	0	0-1
L 1972	Pit-N	.000	3	2	1	0	0	0	0	0	0	1	0	....
L 1974	Pit-N	.000	2	1	1	0	0	0	0	0	0	0	0	0-2
L Total	3	.167	6	6	3	1	0	0	1	1	0	2	0	....
W 1971	Pit-N	.091	3	11	2	1	0	1	0	0	1	1	1	0-3
• COBB, Ty														
W 1907	Det-A	.200	5	20	1	4	0	1	0	0	0	3	0	0-5
W 1908	Det-A	.368	5	19	3	7	1	0	0	4	1	2	2	0-5
W 1909	Det-A	.231	7	26	3	6	3	0	0	5	2	2	2	0-7
W Total	3	.262	17	65	7	17	4	1	0	9	3	7	4	....
• COCHRANE, Mickey														
W 1929	Phi-A	.400	5	15	5	6	1	0	0	0	7	0	0	C-5
W 1930	Phi-A	.222	6	18	5	4	1	0	2	4	5	2	0	C-6
W 1931	Phi-A	.160	7	25	2	4	0	0	0	1	5	2	0	C-7
W 1934	Det-A	.214	7	28	2	6	1	0	0	1	4	3	0	C-7
W 1935	Det-A	.292	6	24	3	7	1	0	0	1	4	1	0	C-6
W Total	5	.245	31	110	17	27	4	0	2	7	25	8	0	....
• COFFMAN, Dick														
W 1936	NY-N	....	2	0	0	0	0	0	0	0	0	0	0	....
W 1937	NY-N	.000	2	1	0	0	0	0	0	0	0	1	0	....
W Total	2	.000	4	1	0	0	0	0	0	0	0	1	0	....
• COGGINS, Rich														
L 1973	Bal-A	.444	2	9	1	4	1	0	0	0	0	0	0	0-2
L 1974	Bal-A	.000	3	11	0	0	0	0	0	0	0	3	0	0-3
L Total	2	.200	5	20	1	4	1	0	0	0	0	3	0	....
• COLBRUNN, Greg														
D 1997	Atl-N	1.000	1	1	0	1	0	0	0	2	0	0	0	....
D 1998	Atl-N	.000	2	2	0	0	0	0	0	0	0	0	0	....
D 1999	Ari-N	.400	2	5	1	2	1	0	1	2	2	2	0	1-2
D 2001	Ari-N	.333	4	6	0	2	0	0	0	1	1	0	0	1-1
D 2002	Ari-N	.000	1	3	1	0	0	0	0	0	1	1	0	1-1
D Total	5	.294	10	17	2	5	1	0	1	5	4	3	0	....
L 1997	Atl-N	.667	3	3	0	2	0	0	0	0	0	0	0	....
L 1998	Atl-N	.333	6	6	0	2	0	0	0	0	0	2	0	....
L 2001	Ari-N	.000	1	1	0	0	0	0	0	0	0	0	0	....
L Total	3	.400	10	10	0	4	0	0	0	0	0	2	0	....
W 2001	Ari-N	.400	1	5	2	2	0	0	0	1	1	1	0	1-1
• COLE, Alex														
L 1992	Pit-N	.200	4	10	2	2	0	0	0	1	3	2	0	0-4
• COLEMAN, Gordy														
W 1961	Cin-N	.250	5	20	2	5	0	0	1	2	0	1	0	1-5
• COLEMAN, Jerry														
W 1949	NY-A	.250	5	20	0	5	3	0	0	4	0	4	0	2-5
W 1950	NY-A	.286	4	14	2	4	1	0	0	3	2	0	0	2-4
W 1951	NY-A	.250	5	8	2	2	0	0	0	0	1	2	0	2-5
W 1955	NY-A	.000	3	3	0	0	0	0	0	0	0	1	0	S-3
W 1956	NY-A	.000	2	2	0	0	0	0	0	0	0	0	0	2-2
W 1957	NY-A	.364	7	22	2	8	2	0	0	2	3	1	0	2-7
W Total	6	.275	26	69	6	19	6	0	0	9	6	8	0	....
• COLEMAN, Vince														
D 1995	Sea-A	.217	5	23	6	5	0	1	1	1	2	4	1	0-5
L 1985	StL-N	.286	3	14	2	4	0	0	0	1	0	2	1	0-3
L 1987	StL-N	.269	7	26	3	7	1	0	0	4	4	6	1	0-7
L 1995	Sea-A	.100	6	20	0	2	0	0	0	0	2	6	4	0-5
L Total	3	.217	16	60	5	13	1	0	0	5	6	14	6	....
W 1987	StL-N	.143	7	28	5	4	2	0	0	2	2	10	6	0-7
• COLLINS, Dave														
L 1979	Cin-N	.357	3	14	0	5	1	0	0	1	0	2	2	0-3
• COLLINS, Eddie														
W 1910	Phi-A	.429	5	21	5	9	4	0	0	3	2	0	4	2-5
W 1911	Phi-A	.286	6	21	4	6	1	0	0	1	2	3	2	2-6
W 1913	Phi-A	.421	5	19	5	8	0	2	0	3	1	2	3	2-5
W 1914	Phi-A	.214	4	14	0	3	0	0	0	1	2	1	1	2-4
W 1917	Chi-A	.409	6	22	4	9	1	0	0	2	2	3	3	2-6
W 1919	Chi-A	.226	8	31	2	7	1	0	0	1	1	2	1	2-8
W Total	6	.328	34	128	20	42	7	2	0	11	10	11	14	....
• COLLINS, Hub														
W 1889	Bro-A	.371	9	35	13	13	3	0	1	2	7	5	6	2-9
W 1890	Bro-N	.310	7	29	7	9	0	1	0	1	3	0	2	2-7
W Total	2	.344	16	64	20	22	3	1	1	3	10	5	8	....
• COLLINS, Jimmy														
T 1897	Bos-N	.182	5	22	2	4	0	0	0	4	1	0	0	3-5
W 1903	Bos-A	.250	8	36	5	9	1	2	0	1	1	1	3	3-8
• COLLINS, Joe														
W 1950	NY-A	....	1	0	0	0	0	0	0	0	0	0	0	1-1
W 1951	NY-A	.222	6	18	2	4	0	0	1	3	2	1	0	0-1,1-6
W 1952	NY-A	.000	6	12	1	0	0	0	0	0	1	3	0	1-6

SER-YEAR	TM-L	AVG	G	AB	R	H	2B	3B	HR	RBI	BB	SO	SB	POS
W 1953	NY-A	.167	6	24	4	4	1	0	1	2	3	8	0	1-6
W 1955	NY-A	.167	5	12	6	2	0	0	2	3	6	4	1	0-1,1-5
W 1956	NY-A	.238	6	21	2	5	2	0	0	2	2	3	0	1-5
W 1957	NY-A	.000	6	5	0	0	0	0	0	0	0	3	0	1-5
W Total	7	.163	36	92	15	15	3	0	4	10	14	22	1	....
• COLLINS, Pat														
W 1926	NY-A	.000	3	2	0	0	0	0	0	0	0	1	0	C-3
W 1927	NY-A	.600	2	5	0	3	1	0	0	0	3	0	0	C-2
W 1928	NY-A	1.000	1	1	0	1	1	0	0	0	0	0	0	C-1
W Total	3	.500	6	8	0	4	2	0	0	0	3	1	0	....
• COLLINS, Ray														
W 1912	Bos-A	.000	2	5	0	0	0	0	0	0	0	2	0	....
• COLLINS, Rip														
W 1921	NY-A	....	1	0	0	0	0	0	0	0	0	0	0	....
• COLLINS, Ripper														
W 1931	StL-N	.000	2	2	0	0	0	0	0	0	0	1	0	....
W 1934	StL-N	.367	7	30	4	11	1	0	0	3	1	2	0	1-7
W 1938	Chi-N	.133	4	15	1	2	0	0	0	0	0	3	0	1-4
W Total	3	.277	13	47	5	13	1	0	0	3	1	6	0	....
• COLLINS, Shano														
W 1917	Chi-A	.286	6	21	2	6	1	0	0	0	0	2	0	0-6
W 1919	Chi-A	.250	4	16	2	4	1	0	0	0	0	0	0	0-4
W Total	2	.270	10	37	4	10	2	0	0	0	0	2	0	....
• COMBS, Earle														
W 1926	NY-A	.357	7	28	3	10	2	0	0	2	5	2	0	0-7
W 1927	NY-A	.313	4	16	6	5	0	0	0	2	1	2	0	0-4
W 1928	NY-A	....	1	0	0	0	0	0	0	1	0	0	0	....
W 1932	NY-A	.375	4	16	8	6	1	0	1	4	4	3	0	0-4
W Total	4	.350	16	60	17	21	3	0	1	9	10	7	0	....
• COMER, Wayne														
W 1968	Det-A	1.000	1	1	0	1	0	0	0	0	0	0	0	....
• COMISKEY, Charlie														
W 1885	StL-A	.292	7	24	6	7	0	0	0	1	0	0	0	1-7
W 1886	StL-A	.292	6	24	2	7	1	0	0	2	0	4	0	1-6
W 1887	StL-A	.317	15	63	8	20	2	0	0	5	1	1	4	1-14,0-1
W 1888	StL-A	.268	10	41	6	11	1	1	0	3	1	1	4	1-10,0-1
W Total	4	.296	38	152	22	45	4	1	0	11	2	6	8	....
• CONATSER, Clint														
W 1948	Bos-N	.000	2	4	0	0	0	0	0	1	0	0	0	0-2
• CONCEPCION, Dave														
L 1970	Cin-N	....	5	0	0	0	0	0	0	0	0	0	0	S-2
L 1972	Cin-N	.000	3	2	0	0	0	0	0	0	0	0	0	S-1
L 1975	Cin-N	.455	3	11	2	5	0	0	1	1	1	2	2	S-3
L 1976	Cin-N	.200	3	10	4	2	1	0	0	0	2	1	0	S-3
L 1979	Cin-N	.429	3	14	1	6	1	0	0	0	0	3	0	S-3
L Total	5	.351	17	37	7	13	2	0	1	1	3	6	2	....
W 1970	Cin-N	.333	3	9	0	3	0	1	0	3	0	0	0	S-3
W 1972	Cin-N	.308	6	13	2	4	0	1	0	2	2	2	1	S-5
W 1975	Cin-N	.179	7	28	3	5	1	0	1	4	0	1	3	S-7
W 1976	Cin-N	.357	4	14	1	5	1	1	0	3	1	3	1	S-4
W Total	4	.266	20	64	6	17	2	3	1	12	3	6	5	....
• CONCEPCION, Onix														
L 1984	KC-A	.000	3	7	0	0	0	0	0	0	0	0	0	S-3
L 1985	KC-A	.000	4	1	0	0	0	0	0	0	0	0	0	S-3
L Total	2	.000	7	8	0	0	0	0	0	0	0	0	0	....
W 1980	KC-A	....	3	0	0	0	0	0	0	0	0	0	0	....
W 1985	KC-A	....	3	0	1	0	0	0	0	0	0	0	0	S-2
W Total	2	....	6	0	1	0	0	0	0	0	0	0	0	....
• CONIGLIARO, Billy														
L 1973	Oak-A	.000	1	4	0	0	0	0	0	0	0	2	0	0-1
W 1973	Oak-A	.000	3	3	0	0	0	0	0	0	0	1	0	....
• CONINE, Jeff														
D 1997	Fla-N	.364	3	11	3	4	1	0	0	0	1	0	0	1-3
D 2003	Fla-N	.267	4	15	2	4	0	0	0	2	2	1	0	0-4
D Total	2	.308	7	26	5	8	1	0	0	2	3	1	0	....
L 1997	Fla-N	.111	6	18	1	2	0	0	0	1	1	4	0	1-6
L 2003	Fla-N	.458	7	24	4	11	1	1	1	3	4	2	0	0-7
L Total	2	.310	13	42	5	13	1	1	1	4	5	6	0	....
W 1997	Fla-N	.231	6	13	1	3	0	0	0	2	0	0	0	1-6
W 2003	Fla-N	.333	6	21	4	7	1	0	0	0	3	2	0	0-3
W Total	2	.294	12	34	5	10	1	0	0	2	3	2	0	....
• CONNOLLY, Joe														
W 1914	Bos-N	.111	3	9	1	1	0	0	0	1	1	1	0	0-3
• CONNOR, Roger														
W 1888	NY-N	.304	7	23	7	7	1	2	0	3	4	0	4	1-7
W 1889	NY-N	.343	9	35	9	12	2	2	0	12	3	2	8	1-9
W Total	2	.328	16	58	16	19	3	4	0	15	7	2	12	....
• COOK, Dennis														
D 1997	Fla-N	....	2	0	0	0	0	0	0	0	0	0	0	....
D 1999	NY-N	....	1	0	0	0	0	0	0	0	0	0	0	....
D 2000	NY-N	....	2	0	0	0	0	0	0	0	0	0	0	....
D Total	3	....	5	0	0	0	0	0	0	0	0	0	0	....
L 1999	NY-N	....	3	0	0	0	0	0	0	0	0	0	0	....
L 2000	NY-N	....	1	0	0	0	0	0	0	0	0	0	0	....
L Total	2	....	4	0	0	0	0	0	0	0	0	0	0	....
W 2000	NY-N	....	3	0	0	0	0	0	0	0	0	0	0	....
• COOMER, Ron														
D 2002	NY-A	.500	1	2	0	1	0	0	0	0	0	0	0	D-1
• COOPER, Cecil														
D 1981	Mil-A	.222	5	18	1	4	0	0	0	3	1	3	0	1-5
L 1975	Bos-A	.400	3	10	0	4	2	0	0	1	0	2	0	1-3
L 1982	Mil-A	.150	5	20	1	3	2	0	0	4	0	6	0	1-5
L Total	2	.233	8	30	1	7	4	0	0	5	0	8	0	....
W 1975	Bos-A	.053	5	19	0	1	1	0	0	1	0	3	0	1-4
W 1982	Mil-A	.286	7	28	3	8	1	0	1	6	1	1	0	1-7
W Total	2	.191	12	47	3	9	2	0	1	7	1	4	0	....
• COOPER, Claude														
W 1913	NY-N	....	2	0	0	0	0	0	0	0	0	0	1	....
• COOPER, Walker														
W 1942	StL-N	.286	5	21	3	6	1	0	0	4	0	1	0	C-5
W 1943	StL-N	.294	5	17	1	5	0	0	0	0	0	1	0	C-5
W 1944	StL-N	.318	6	22	1	7	2	1	0	2	3	2	0	C-6
W Total	3	.300	16	60	5	18	3	1	0	6	3	4	0	....
• CORA, Joey														
D 1995	Sea-A	.316	5	19	7	6	1	0	1	1	3	0	1	2-5
D 1997	Sea-A	.176	4	17	1	3	0	0	0	0	0	4	0	2-4
D 1998	Cle-A	.000	4	10	2	0	0	0	0	0	3	2	0	2-4
D Total	3	.196	13	46	10	9	1	0	1	1	6	6	1	....
L 1993	Chi-A	.136	6	22	1	3	0	0	0	1	3	6	0	2-6
L 1995	Sea-A	.174	6	23	3	4	1	0	0	0	1	0	2	2-6
L 1998	Cle-A	.143	2	7	1	1	0	0	0	0	2	1	0	2-2
L Total	3	.154	14	52	5	8	1	0	0	1	6	7	2	....
• CORBETT, Joe														
T 1896	Bal-N	.500	2	6	1	3	1	0	0	0	1	1	0	P-2
T 1897	Bal-N	.667	2	6	2	4	1	0	1	2	0	1	0	P-2
T Total	2	.583	4	12	3	7	2	0	1	2	1	2	0	....
• CORDERO, Wil														
D 1999	Cle-A	.556	3	9	3	5	0	0	1	2	1	2	0	0-1,D-2
D 2001	Cle-A	.000	1	1	0	0	0	0	0	0	0	0	0	0-1
D Total	2	.500	4	10	3	5	0	0	1	2	1	2	0	....
• CORDOVA, Marty														
D 2001	Cle-A	.250	4	12	0	3	0	0	0	1	0	5	0	0-4
• CORKHILL, Pop														
W 1889	Bro-A	.208	9	24	4	5	1	0	1	5	6	2	1	0-9
• CORRALES, Pat														
W 1970	Cin-N	.000	1	1	0	0	0	0	0	0	0	0	0	....
• CORWIN, Al														
W 1951	NY-N	....	1	0	0	0	0	0	0	0	0	0	0	....
• COSCARART, Pete														
W 1941	Bro-N	.000	3	7	1	0	0	0	0	0	1	2	0	2-3
• COTTO, Henry														
L 1984	Chi-N	1.000	3	1	1	1	0	0	0	0	0	0	0	0-3
• COUGHLIN, Bill														
W 1907	Det-A	.250	5	20	0	5	0	0	0	0	1	4	1	3-5
W 1908	Det-A	.125	3	8	0	1	0	0	0	1	0	1	0	3-3
W Total	2	.214	8	28	0	6	0	0	0	1	1	5	1	....
• COUNSELL, Craig														
D 1997	Fla-N	.400	3	5	0	2	1	0	0	1	1	0	0	2-3
D 2001	Ari-N	.188	5	16	2	3	0	0	1	3	2	2	0	2-5
D Total	2	.238	8	21	2	5	1	0	1	4	3	2	0	....
L 1997	Fla-N	.429	5	14	0	6	0	0	0	2	3	3	0	2-4
L 2001	Ari-N	.381	5	21	5	8	3	0	0	4	0	3	1	2-4,S-1
L Total	2	.400	10	35	5	14	3	0	0	6	3	6	1	....
W 1997	Fla-N	.182	7	22	4	4	1	0	0	2	6	5	1	2-7
W 2001	Ari-N	.083	6	24	1	2	0	0	1	1	0	7	0	2-6
W Total	2	.130	13	46	5	6	1	0	1	3	6	12	1	....
• COVINGTON, Wes														
W 1957	Mil-N	.208	7	24	1	5	1	0	0	1	2	6	1	0-7
W 1958	Mil-N	.269	7	26	2	7	0	0	0	4	2	4	0	0-7
W 1966	LA-N	.000	1	1	0	0	0	0	0	0	0	1	0	....
W Total	3	.235	15	51	3	12	1	0	0	5	4	11	1	....
• COWENS, Al														
L 1976	KC-A	.190	5	21	3	4	0	1	0	0	1	1	2	0-5
L 1977	KC-A	.263	5	19	2	5	0	0	1	5	1	3	0	0-5
L 1978	KC-A	.133	4	15	2	2	0	0	0	1	0	2	0	0-4
L Total	3	.200	14	55	7	11	0	1	1	6	2	6	2	....
• COX, Billy														
W 1949	Bro-N	.333	2	3	0	1	0	0	0	0	0	1	0	3-1
W 1952	Bro-N	.296	7	27	4	8	2	0	0	0	3	4	0	3-7
W 1953	Bro-N	.304	6	23	3	7	3	0	1	6	1	4	0	3-6
W Total	3	.302	15	53	7	16	5	0	1	6	4	9	0	....
• CRAFT, Harry														
W 1939	Cin-N	.091	4	11	0	1	0	0	0	0	0	6	0	0-4
W 1940	Cin-N	.000	1	1	0	0	0	0	0	0	0	0	0	....
W Total	2	.083	5	12	0	1	0	0	0	0	0	6	0	....
• CRAMER, Doc														
W 1931	Phi-A	.500	2	2	0	1	0	0	0	2	0	0	0	....
W 1945	Det-A	.379	7	29	7	11	0	0	0	4	1	0	1	0-7
W Total	2	.387	9	31	7	12	0	0	0	6	1	0	1	....
• CRANDALL, Del														
W 1957	Mil-N	.211	6	19	1	4	0	0	1	1	1	1	0	C-6

YEAR	TM-L	AVG	G	AB	R	H	2B	3B	HR	RBI	BB	SO	SB	POS
W 1958	Mil-N	.240	7	25	4	6	0	0	1	3	3	10	0	C-7
W Total	2	.227	13	44	5	10	0	0	2	4	4	11	0	....
• CRAVATH, Gavvy														
W 1915	Phi-N	.125	5	16	2	2	1	1	0	1	2	6	0	0-5
• CRAWFORD, Pat														
W 1934	StL-N	.000	2	2	0	0	0	0	0	0	0	0	0	....
• CRAWFORD, Sam														
W 1907	Det-A	.238	5	21	1	5	1	0	0	3	0	3	0	0-5
W 1908	Det-A	.238	5	21	2	5	1	0	0	1	1	2	0	0-5
W 1909	Det-A	.250	7	28	4	7	3	0	1	4	1	1	1	0-7,1-1
W Total	3	.243	17	70	7	17	5	0	1	8	2	6	1	....
• CRAWFORD, Willie														
L 1974	LA-N	.250	2	4	1	1	0	0	0	1	1	1	0	0-2
L 1965	LA-N	.500	2	2	1	1	0	0	0	0	0	1	0	....
W 1974	LA-N	.333	3	6	1	2	0	0	1	1	0	0	0	0-2
W Total	2	.375	5	8	1	3	0	0	1	1	0	1	0	....
• CRESPI, Creepy														
W 1942	StL-N	....	1	0	1	0	0	0	0	0	0	0	0	....
• CRESPO, Felipe														
D 2000	SF-N	.250	4	4	0	1	0	0	0	0	0	0	0	....
• CRIGER, Lou														
W 1903	Bos-A	.231	8	26	1	6	0	0	0	4	2	3	0	C-8
• CRITZ, Hughie														
W 1933	NY-N	.136	5	22	2	3	0	0	0	1	0	0	0	2-5
• CROMARTIE, Warren														
D 1981	Mon-N	.227	5	22	1	5	0	0	0	1	0	9	0	1-5
L 1981	Mon-N	.167	5	18	0	3	1	0	0	2	0	2	0	1-5
• CRONIN, Joe														
W 1933	Was-A	.318	5	22	1	7	0	0	0	2	0	2	0	S-5
• CROSBY, Ed														
L 1973	Cin-N	.500	3	2	0	1	0	0	0	0	1	0	0	S-2
• CROSETTI, Frankie														
W 1932	NY-A	.133	4	15	2	2	1	0	0	0	2	3	0	S-4
W 1936	NY-A	.269	6	26	5	7	2	0	0	3	3	5	0	S-6
W 1937	NY-A	.048	5	21	2	1	0	0	0	0	3	2	0	S-5
W 1938	NY-A	.250	4	16	1	4	2	1	1	6	2	4	0	S-4
W 1939	NY-A	.063	4	16	2	1	0	0	0	1	2	2	0	S-4
W 1942	NY-A	.000	1	3	0	0	0	0	0	0	0	1	0	3-1
W 1943	NY-A	.278	5	18	4	5	0	0	0	1	2	3	1	S-5
W Total	7	.174	29	115	16	20	5	1	1	11	14	20	1	....
• CROSS, Lave														
T 1900	Bro-N	.278	4	18	2	5	0	1	0	1	0	0	1	3-4
W 1905	Phi-A	.105	5	19	0	2	0	0	0	0	1	1	0	3-5
• CROSS, Monte														
W 1905	Phi-A	.176	5	17	0	3	0	0	0	0	0	7	0	S-5
• CROUCHER, Frank														
W 1940	Det-A	....	1	0	0	0	0	0	0	0	0	0	0	S-1
• CROWLEY, Terry														
L 1973	Bal-A	.000	2	2	0	0	0	0	0	0	0	0	0	0-1
L 1975	Cin-N	....	1	0	0	0	0	0	0	0	0	0	0	....
L 1979	Bal-A	.500	2	2	0	1	0	0	0	1	0	0	0	....
L Total	3	.250	5	4	0	1	0	0	0	1	0	0	0	....
W 1970	Bal-A	.000	1	1	0	0	0	0	0	0	0	0	0	....
W 1975	Cin-N	.500	2	2	0	1	0	0	0	0	1	0	0	....
W 1979	Bal-A	.250	5	4	0	1	1	0	0	2	1	0	0	....
W Total	3	.286	8	7	0	2	1	0	0	2	1	1	0	....
• CRUZ, Hector														
L 1979	Cin-N	.200	2	5	1	1	0	0	0	0	1	0	0	0-1
• CRUZ, Jose														
D 1981	Hou-N	.300	5	20	0	6	1	0	0	0	1	3	1	0-5
L 1980	Hou-N	.400	5	15	3	6	1	1	0	4	8	1	0	0-5
L 1986	Hou-N	.192	6	26	0	5	0	0	0	2	1	8	0	0-6
L Total	2	.268	11	41	3	11	1	1	0	6	9	9	0	....
• CRUZ, Julio														
L 1983	Chi-A	.333	4	12	0	4	0	0	0	0	3	4	2	2-4
• CRUZ, Todd														
L 1983	Bal-A	.133	4	15	0	2	0	0	0	0	1	0	5	3-4
W 1983	Bal-A	.125	5	16	1	2	0	0	0	0	1	3	0	3-5
• CRUZ JR., Jose														
D 2003	SF-N	.000	4	11	0	0	0	0	0	0	1	2	4	0-4
• CUDDYER, Mike														
D 2002	Min-A	.385	5	13	1	5	1	0	0	1	3	3	0	0-5
D 2003	Min-A	.250	3	5	0	1	0	0	0	1	0	3	0	....
D Total	2	.353	6	17	1	6	1	0	0	2	3	6	0	....
L 2002	Min-A	.200	3	5	0	1	0	0	0	0	1	1	0	0-3
• CULBERSON, Leon														
W 1946	Bos-A	.222	5	9	1	2	0	0	1	1	1	2	1	0-3
• CULLEN, Tim														
L 1972	Oak-A	.000	2	1	0	0	0	0	0	0	0	0	0	S-2
• CULLENBINE, Roy														
W 1942	NY-A	.263	5	19	3	5	1	0	0	2	1	2	1	0-5
W 1945	Det-A	.227	7	22	5	5	2	0	0	4	8	2	1	0-7
W Total	2	.244	12	41	8	10	3	0	0	6	9	4	2	....
• CUMMINGS, Midre														
D 1998	Bos-A	.000	3	3	0	0	0	0	0	0	0	0	0	....
D 2001	Ari-N	.000	2	0	1	0	0	0	0	0	0	0	0	....
D Total	2	.000	5	3	1	0	0	0	0	0	0	0	0	....
L 2001	Ari-N	.000	1	1	0	0	0	0	0	0	0	0	0	....
W 2001	Ari-N	....	2	0	2	0	0	0	0	0	0	0	0	D-1
• CUNNANE, Will														
D 2003	Atl-N	....	2	0	0	0	0	0	0	0	0	0	0	....
• CUNNINGHAM, Bill														
W 1922	NY-N	.200	4	10	0	2	0	0	0	2	2	1	0	0-4
W 1923	NY-N	.143	4	7	0	1	0	0	0	1	0	1	0	0-3
W Total	2	.176	8	17	0	3	0	0	0	3	2	2	0	....
• CURTIS, Chad														
D 1996	LA-N	.000	1	2	0	0	0	0	0	0	1	1	0	0-1
D 1997	NY-A	.167	4	6	0	1	0	0	0	0	3	1	0	0-4
D 1998	NY-A	.667	3	3	1	2	1	0	0	0	1	1	1	0-3
D 1999	NY-A	.000	3	3	1	0	0	0	0	0	0	0	0	0-3
D Total	4	.214	11	14	2	3	1	0	0	0	5	3	1	....
L 1998	NY-A	.000	2	4	0	0	0	0	0	0	1	2	0	0-2
L 1999	NY-A	.000	3	6	1	0	0	0	0	0	0	2	1	0-2,D-1
L Total	2	.000	5	10	1	0	0	0	0	0	1	4	1	....
W 1999	NY-A	.333	3	6	3	2	0	0	2	2	0	0	0	0-3
• CUTSHAW, George														
W 1916	Bro-N	.105	5	19	2	2	1	0	0	2	1	1	0	2-5
• CUYLER, Kiki														
W 1925	Pit-N	.269	7	26	3	7	3	0	1	6	1	4	0	0-7
W 1929	Chi-N	.300	5	20	4	6	1	0	0	4	1	7	0	0-5
W 1932	Chi-N	.278	4	18	2	5	1	1	1	2	0	3	1	0-4
W Total	3	.281	16	64	9	18	5	1	2	12	2	14	1	....
• DAHLEN, Bill														
T 1900	Bro-N	.176	4	17	3	3	0	1	0	2	0	3	1	S-4
W 1905	NY-N	.000	5	15	1	0	0	0	0	0	3	2	2	S-5
• DAHLGREN, Babe														
W 1939	NY-A	.214	4	14	2	3	2	0	1	2	0	4	0	1-4
• DAILY, Ed														
W 1890	Lou-A	.136	6	22	1	3	1	1	0	3	1	2	2	0-4,P-2
• DALRYMPLE, Abner														
W 1885	Chi-N	.269	7	26	4	7	2	0	1	0	2	0	0	0-7
W 1886	Chi-N	.190	6	21	2	4	1	1	0	2	0	5	1	0-6
W Total	2	.234	13	47	6	11	3	1	1	2	2	5	1	....
• DALRYMPLE, Clay														
W 1969	Bal-A	1.000	2	2	0	2	0	0	0	0	0	0	0	....
• DALY, Tom														
T 1900	Bro-N	.154	4	13	2	2	1	0	0	1	3	1	0	2-4
W 1890	Bro-N	.182	6	22	1	4	2	0	0	3	0	4	2	C-6,1-1
• DAMON, Johnny														
D 2001	Oak-A	.409	5	22	3	9	2	1	0	1	1	2	0	0-5
D 2003	Bos-A	.316	5	19	2	6	2	0	1	3	2	1	2	0-5
D Total	2	.366	10	41	5	15	4	1	1	3	3	2	4	....
L 2003	Bos-A	.200	5	20	1	4	1	0	0	1	3	3	1	0-5
• DANFORTH, Dave														
W 1917	Chi-A	....	1	0	0	0	0	0	0	0	0	0	0	....
• DANNING, Harry														
W 1936	NY-N	.000	2	2	0	0	0	0	0	0	0	0	0	C-1
W 1937	NY-N	.250	3	12	0	3	1	0	0	2	0	2	0	C-3
W Total	2	.214	5	14	0	3	1	0	0	2	0	3	0	....
• DARK, Alvin														
W 1948	Bos-N	.167	6	24	2	4	1	0	0	0	0	2	0	S-6
W 1951	NY-N	.417	6	24	5	10	3	0	1	4	2	3	0	S-6
W 1954	NY-N	.412	4	17	2	7	0	0	0	0	1	1	0	S-4
W Total	3	.323	16	65	9	21	4	0	1	4	3	6	0	....
• DAUBACH, Brian														
D 1999	Bos-A	.250	4	16	3	4	2	0	1	3	0	7	0	1-1,D-4
L 1999	Bos-A	.176	5	17	2	3	1	0	1	3	1	4	0	1-1,D-5
• DAUBERT, Jake														
W 1916	Bro-N	.176	4	17	1	3	0	1	0	0	2	3	0	1-4
W 1919	Cin-N	.241	8	29	4	7	0	1	0	1	1	2	1	1-8
W Total	2	.217	12	46	5	10	0	2	0	1	3	5	1	....
• DAUER, Rich														
L 1979	Bal-A	.182	4	11	0	2	0	0	0	0	0	1	0	2-4
L 1983	Bal-A	.000	4	14	0	0	0	0	0	0	1	0	0	2-4
L Total	2	.080	8	25	0	2	0	0	0	0	1	1	0	....
W 1979	Bal-A	.294	6	17	2	5	1	0	1	1	0	1	0	2-6
W 1983	Bal-A	.211	5	19	2	4	0	0	0	3	0	3	0	2-5,3-1
W Total	2	.250	11	36	4	9	2	0	1	4	0	4	0	....
• DAULTON, Darren														
L 1993	Phi-N	.263	6	19	2	5	1	0	1	3	6	3	0	C-6
L 1997	Fla-N	.250	3	4	1	1	0	0	0	1	1	2	0	1-2
L Total	2	.261	9	23	3	6	1	0	1	4	7	5	0	....
W 1993	Phi-N	.217	6	23	4	5	0	1	0	4	4	5	0	C-6
W 1997	Fla-N	.389	7	18	7	7	2	0	1	2	3	0	1	1-5,D-1
W Total	2	.293	13	41	11	12	2	1	1	6	7	5	1	....
• DAVALILLO, Vic														
L 1971	Pit-N	.000	2	2	0	0	0	0	0	0	0	1	0	....
L 1972	Pit-N	....	1	1	0	0	0	0	0	0	0	1	0	....
L 1973	Oak-A	.625	4	8	2	5	1	1	0	1	1	0	0	0-2,1-2

SER-YEAR	TM-L	AVG	G	AB	R	H	2B	3B	HR	RBI	BB	SO	SB	POS
L 1977	LA-N	1.000	1	1	1	1	0	0	0	0	0	0	0	....
L Total	4	.545	8	11	3	6	1	1	0	1	2	1	0	....
W 1971	Pit-N	.333	3	3	1	1	0	0	0	0	0	0	0	0-2
W 1973	Oak-A	.091	6	11	0	1	0	0	0	0	2	1	0	0-4,1-1
W 1977	LA-N	.333	3	3	0	1	0	0	0	1	0	0	0	....
W 1978	LA-N	.333	2	3	0	1	0	0	0	0	0	0	0	D-1
W Total	4	.200	14	20	1	4	0	0	0	1	2	1	0	....
• DAVENPORT, Jim														
W 1962	SF-N	.136	7	22	1	3	1	0	0	1	4	7	0	3-7
• DAVIDSON, Mark														
L 1987	Min-A	....	1	0	0	0	0	0	0	0	0	0	0	....
W 1987	Min-A	.000	2	1	0	0	0	0	0	0	0	0	0	0-1
• DAVIS, Chili														
D 1998	NY-A	.167	2	6	0	1	0	0	0	0	0	2	0	D-2
D 1999	NY-A	.333	1	3	0	1	0	0	0	0	0	2	0	D-1
D Total	2	.222	3	9	0	2	0	0	0	0	0	4	0	....
L 1987	SF-N	.150	6	20	2	3	1	0	0	0	1	4	0	0-6
L 1991	Min-A	.294	5	17	3	5	2	0	0	2	5	8	1	D-5
L 1998	NY-A	.286	5	14	2	4	1	0	1	5	2	3	0	D-5
L 1999	NY-A	.091	5	11	0	1	0	0	0	1	3	4	0	D-5
L Total	4	.210	21	62	7	13	4	0	1	8	11	19	1	....
W 1991	Min-A	.222	6	18	4	4	0	0	2	4	2	3	0	0-1,D-4
W 1998	NY-A	.286	3	7	3	2	0	0	0	2	3	2	0	D-2
W 1999	NY-A	.000	1	4	0	0	0	0	0	0	0	2	0	D-1
W Total	3	.207	10	29	7	6	0	0	2	6	5	7	0	....
• DAVIS, Dick														
D 1981	Phi-N	.000	1	2	0	0	0	0	0	0	0	1	0	0-1
• DAVIS, Eric														
D 1997	Bal-A	.222	3	9	0	2	0	0	0	2	0	5	0	0-3
D 2000	StL-N	.000	2	4	0	0	0	0	0	0	0	2	0	0-1
D Total	2	.154	5	13	0	2	0	0	0	2	0	7	0	....
L 1990	Cin-N	.174	6	23	2	4	1	0	0	2	1	9	0	0-6
L 1997	Bal-A	.154	6	13	1	2	0	0	1	1	1	3	0	0-3,D-3
L 2000	StL-N	.200	4	10	1	2	1	0	0	1	0	2	0	0-2
L Total	3	.174	16	46	4	8	2	0	1	4	2	14	0	....
W 1990	Cin-N	.286	4	14	3	4	0	0	1	5	0	0	0	0-4
• DAVIS, George														
T 1892	Cle-N	.167	3	6	0	1	0	0	0	0	0	1	0	3-2
T 1894	NY-N	.313	4	16	5	5	2	2	0	5	2	0	2	3-4
T Total	2	.273	7	22	5	6	2	2	0	5	2	1	2	....
W 1906	Chi-A	.308	3	13	4	4	3	0	0	6	0	1	1	S-3
• DAVIS, Glenn														
L 1986	Hou-N	.269	6	26	3	7	1	0	1	3	1	3	0	1-6
• DAVIS, Harry														
W 1905	Phi-A	.200	5	20	0	4	1	0	0	0	0	1	0	1-5
W 1910	Phi-A	.353	5	17	5	6	3	0	0	2	3	4	0	1-5
W 1911	Phi-A	.208	6	24	3	5	1	0	0	5	0	3	0	1-6
W Total	3	.246	16	61	8	15	5	0	0	7	3	8	0	....
• DAVIS, Jody														
L 1984	Chi-N	.389	5	18	3	7	2	0	2	6	0	3	0	C-5
• DAVIS, Jumbo														
W 1889	Bro-A	.000	1	4	0	0	0	0	0	0	0	0	0	S-1
• DAVIS, Kiddo														
W 1933	NY-N	.368	5	19	1	7	1	0	0	0	0	3	0	0-5
W 1936	NY-N	.500	4	2	2	1	0	0	0	0	0	0	0	....
W Total	2	.381	9	21	3	8	1	0	0	0	0	3	0	....
• DAVIS, Mike														
L 1981	Oak-A	1.000	1	1	0	1	0	0	0	0	0	0	0	....
L 1988	LA-N	.000	4	2	0	0	0	0	0	0	1	0	0	....
L Total	2	.333	5	3	0	1	0	0	0	0	1	0	0	....
W 1988	LA-N	.143	4	7	3	1	0	0	1	2	4	0	2	0-1,D-2
• DAVIS, Ron														
W 1968	StL-N	.000	2	7	0	0	0	0	0	0	0	2	0	0-2
• DAVIS, Russ														
D 1995	NY-A	.200	2	5	0	1	0	0	0	0	0	2	0	3-2
D 2000	SF-N	.000	2	2	0	0	0	0	0	0	0	1	0	....
D Total	2	.143	4	7	0	1	0	0	0	0	0	3	0	....
• DAVIS, Spud														
W 1934	StL-N	1.000	2	2	0	2	0	0	0	1	0	0	0	....
• DAVIS, Tommy														
L 1971	Oak-A	.375	3	8	1	3	1	0	0	0	0	0	0	1-2
L 1973	Bal-A	.286	5	21	1	6	1	0	0	2	1	0	0	D-5
L 1974	Bal-A	.267	4	15	0	4	0	0	0	1	0	1	0	D-4
L Total	3	.295	12	44	2	13	2	0	0	3	1	1	0	....
W 1963	LA-N	.400	4	15	0	6	0	2	0	2	0	2	1	0-4
W 1966	LA-N	.250	4	8	0	2	0	0	0	0	1	1	0	0-3
W Total	2	.348	8	23	0	8	0	2	0	2	1	3	1	....
• DAVIS, Willie														
L 1979	Cal-A	.500	2	2	1	1	1	0	0	0	0	0	0	....
W 1963	LA-N	.167	4	12	2	2	2	0	0	3	0	6	0	0-4
W 1965	LA-N	.231	7	26	3	6	0	0	0	0	0	2	3	0-7
W 1966	LA-N	.063	4	16	0	1	0	0	0	0	0	4	0	0-4
W Total	3	.167	15	54	5	9	2	0	0	3	0	12	3	....
• DAWSON, Andre														
D 1981	Mon-N	.300	5	20	1	6	0	1	0	0	1	6	2	0-5
L 1981	Mon-N	.150	5	20	2	3	0	0	0	0	0	4	0	0-5

SER-YEAR	TM-L	AVG	G	AB	R	H	2B	3B	HR	RBI	BB	SO	SB	POS
L 1989	Chi-N	.105	5	19	0	2	1	0	0	3	2	6	0	0-5
L Total	2	.128	10	39	2	5	1	0	0	3	2	10	0	....
• DEAL, Charlie														
W 1914	Bos-N	.125	4	16	1	2	2	0	0	0	0	0	2	3-4
W 1918	Chi-N	.176	6	17	0	3	0	0	0	0	0	1	0	3-6
W Total	2	.152	10	33	1	5	2	0	0	0	0	1	2	....
• DEAN, Paul														
W 1934	StL-N	.167	2	6	0	1	0	0	0	2	0	1	0	....
• DECINCES, Doug														
L 1979	Bal-A	.308	4	13	4	4	1	0	0	3	1	1	0	3-4
L 1982	Cal-A	.316	5	19	5	6	2	0	0	0	1	5	0	3-5
L 1986	Cal-A	.281	7	32	2	9	3	0	1	3	0	2	0	3-7
L Total	3	.297	16	64	11	19	6	0	1	6	2	8	0	....
W 1979	Bal-A	.200	7	25	2	5	0	0	1	3	5	5	1	3-7
• DEJESUS, Ivan														
L 1983	Phi-N	.250	4	12	0	3	0	0	0	1	3	3	0	S-4
W 1983	Phi-N	.125	5	16	0	2	0	0	0	0	1	2	0	S-5
W 1985	StL-N	.000	1	1	0	0	0	0	0	0	0	0	0	....
W Total	2	.118	6	17	0	2	0	0	0	0	1	2	0	....
• DEL TORO, Miguel														
D 2000	SF-N	....	1	0	0	0	0	0	0	0	0	0	0	....
• DELAHANTY, Jim														
W 1909	Det-A	.346	7	26	2	9	4	0	0	4	2	5	0	2-7
• DELANCEY, Bill														
W 1934	StL-N	.172	7	29	3	5	3	0	1	4	2	8	0	C-7
• DELLUCCI, David														
D 2001	Ari-N	....	2	0	0	0	0	0	0	0	0	0	0	....
D 2002	Ari-N	.286	3	7	1	2	0	0	1	2	0	1	0	0-3
D 2003	NY-A	....	1	0	0	0	0	0	0	0	0	0	0	....
D Total	3	.286	6	7	1	2	0	0	1	2	0	1	0	....
L 2001	Ari-N	.500	2	2	1	1	0	0	0	0	0	0	0	....
L 2003	NY-A	.333	3	3	2	1	0	0	0	0	0	1	1	0-1
L Total	2	.400	5	5	3	2	0	0	0	0	0	1	1	....
W 2001	Ari-N	.500	2	2	0	1	0	0	0	0	0	0	0	0-1
W 2003	NY-A	.000	4	2	1	0	0	0	0	0	0	0	0	0-2
W Total	2	.250	6	4	1	1	0	0	0	0	0	0	0	....
• DEMAESTRI, Joe														
W 1960	NY-A	.500	4	2	1	1	0	0	0	0	0	1	0	S-3
• DEMAREE, Frank														
W 1932	Chi-N	.286	2	7	1	2	0	0	1	4	1	0	0	0-2
W 1935	Chi-N	.250	6	24	2	6	1	0	2	2	1	4	0	0-6
W 1938	Chi-N	.100	3	10	1	1	0	0	0	0	1	2	0	0-3
W 1943	StL-N	.000	1	1	0	0	0	0	0	0	0	0	0	....
W Total	4	.214	12	42	4	9	1	0	3	6	3	6	0	....
• DEMERIT, John														
W 1957	Mil-N	....	1	0	0	0	0	0	0	0	0	0	0	....
• DEMETER, Don														
W 1959	LA-N	.250	6	12	2	3	0	0	0	0	1	3	0	0-6
• DEMPSEY, Rick														
L 1979	Bal-A	.400	3	10	3	4	2	0	0	2	1	0	1	C-3
L 1983	Bal-A	.167	4	12	1	2	0	0	0	0	1	1	0	C-4
L 1988	LA-N	.400	4	5	1	2	2	0	0	2	1	0	0	C-3
L Total	3	.296	11	27	5	8	4	0	0	4	3	1	1	....
W 1979	Bal-A	.286	7	21	3	6	2	0	0	0	1	3	0	C-7
W 1983	Bal-A	.385	5	13	3	5	4	0	1	2	2	2	0	C-5
W 1988	LA-N	.200	2	5	0	1	1	0	0	1	1	2	0	C-2
W Total	3	.308	14	39	6	12	7	0	1	3	4	7	0	....
• DENNY, Jerry														
W 1884	Pro-N	.444	3	9	3	4	0	1	1	2	0	3	0	3-3
• DENT, Bucky														
L 1977	NY-A	.214	5	14	1	3	1	0	0	2	1	0	0	S-5
L 1978	NY-A	.200	4	15	0	3	0	0	0	4	0	0	0	S-4
L 1980	NY-A	.182	3	11	0	2	0	0	0	0	0	1	0	S-3
L Total	3	.200	12	40	1	8	1	0	0	6	1	1	0	....
W 1977	NY-A	.263	6	19	0	5	0	0	0	2	2	1	0	S-6
W 1978	NY-A	.417	6	24	3	10	1	0	0	7	1	2	0	S-6
W Total	2	.349	12	43	3	15	1	0	0	9	3	3	0	....
• DENTE, Sam														
W 1954	Cle-A	.000	3	3	1	0	0	0	0	0	1	0	0	S-3
• DERNIER, Bob														
L 1983	Phi-N	....	1	0	0	0	0	0	0	0	0	0	0	0-1
L 1984	Chi-N	.235	5	17	5	4	2	0	1	1	5	4	2	0-5
L Total	2	.235	6	17	5	4	2	0	1	1	5	4	2	....
W 1983	Phi-N	....	1	0	1	0	0	0	0	0	0	0	0	....
• DEROSA, Mark														
D 2001	Atl-N	1.000	1	1	0	1	0	0	0	0	0	0	0	S-1
D 2002	Atl-N	.429	4	7	2	3	1	1	0	3	1	1	0	2-3
D 2003	Atl-N	.429	4	7	1	3	2	0	0	2	1	2	0	2-2,3-1
D Total	3	.467	9	15	3	7	3	1	0	5	2	3	0	....
L 2001	Atl-N	.000	4	4	0	0	0	0	0	0	0	0	0	S-1
• DESHIELDS, Delino														
D 1995	LA-N	.250	3	12	1	3	0	0	0	0	1	3	0	2-3
D 1996	LA-N	.000	2	4	0	0	0	0	0	0	0	1	0	2-2
D Total	2	.188	5	16	1	3	0	0	0	0	1	4	0	....
• DEVEREAUX, Mike														
D 1995	Atl-N	.200	4	5	1	1	0	0	0	0	0	0	0	0-3

YEAR	TM-L	AVG	G	AB	R	H	2B	3B	HR	RBI	BB	SO	SB	POS
D 1996	Bal-A	.000	4	1	0	0	0	0	0	0	0	0	0	O-3
D Total	2	.167	8	6	1	1	0	0	0	0	0	0	0	....
L 1995	Atl-N	.308	4	13	2	4	1	0	1	5	1	2	0	O-4
L 1996	Bal-A	.000	3	2	0	0	0	0	0	0	0	1	0	O-3
L Total	2	.267	7	15	2	4	1	0	1	5	1	3	0	....
W 1995	Atl-N	.250	5	4	0	1	0	0	0	1	2	1	0	O-4,D-1
• DEVLIN, Art														
W 1905	NY-N	.250	5	16	0	4	1	0	0	1	1	3	3	3-5
• DEVLIN, Jim														
W 1888	StL-A	.000	1	3	0	0	0	0	0	0	0	0	0	P-1
• DEVORE, Josh														
W 1911	NY-N	.167	6	24	1	4	1	0	0	3	1	8	0	O-6
W 1912	NY-N	.250	7	24	4	6	0	0	0	0	7	5	4	O-6
W 1914	Bos-N	.000	1	1	0	0	0	0	0	0	0	1	0	....
W Total	3	.204	14	49	5	10	1	0	0	3	8	14	4	....
• DEVORMER, Al														
W 1921	NY-A	.000	2	1	0	0	0	0	0	0	0	0	0	C-1
• DIAZ, Alex														
D 1995	Sea-A	.333	2	3	0	1	0	0	0	0	1	1	0	O-1
L 1995	Sea-A	.429	4	7	0	3	1	0	0	0	1	1	0	O-3
• DIAZ, Bo														
L 1983	Phi-N	.154	4	13	0	2	1	0	0	0	2	1	0	C-4
W 1983	Phi-N	.333	5	15	1	5	1	0	0	0	1	2	0	C-5
• DIAZ, Einar														
D 1999	Cle-A	.000	2	1	0	0	0	0	0	0	0	0	0	C-2
D 2001	Cle-A	.313	5	16	3	5	0	0	0	2	2	1	0	C-5
D Total	2	.294	7	17	3	5	0	0	0	2	2	1	0	....
L 1998	Cle-A	.000	4	4	0	0	0	0	0	0	0	1	0	C-4
• DICKEY, Bill														
W 1932	NY-A	.438	4	16	2	7	0	0	0	4	2	1	0	C-4
W 1936	NY-A	.120	6	25	5	3	0	0	1	5	3	4	0	C-6
W 1937	NY-A	.211	5	19	3	4	0	1	0	3	2	2	0	C-5
W 1938	NY-A	.400	4	15	2	6	0	0	1	2	1	0	1	C-4
W 1939	NY-A	.267	4	15	2	4	0	0	2	5	1	2	0	C-4
W 1941	NY-A	.167	5	18	3	3	1	0	0	1	3	1	0	C-5
W 1942	NY-A	.263	5	19	1	5	0	0	0	0	1	0	0	C-5
W 1943	NY-A	.278	5	18	1	5	0	0	1	4	2	2	0	C-5
W Total	8	.255	38	145	19	37	1	1	5	24	15	12	1	....
• DIDIER, Bob														
L 1969	Atl-N	.000	3	11	0	0	0	0	0	0	0	2	0	C-3
• DIETZ, Dick														
L 1971	SF-N	.067	4	15	0	1	0	0	0	0	2	5	0	C-4
• DIFELICE, Mike														
L 2002	StL-N	.000	1	1	0	0	0	0	0	0	0	0	0	....
• DIMAGGIO, Dom														
W 1946	Bos-A	.259	7	27	2	7	3	0	0	3	2	2	0	O-7
• DIMAGGIO, Joe														
W 1936	NY-A	.346	6	26	3	9	3	0	0	3	1	3	0	O-6
W 1937	NY-A	.273	5	22	2	6	0	0	1	4	0	3	0	O-5
W 1938	NY-A	.267	4	15	4	4	0	0	1	2	1	1	0	O-4
W 1939	NY-A	.313	4	16	3	5	0	0	1	3	1	1	0	O-4
W 1941	NY-A	.263	5	19	1	5	0	0	0	1	2	2	0	O-5
W 1942	NY-A	.333	5	21	3	7	0	0	0	3	0	1	0	O-5
W 1947	NY-A	.231	7	26	4	6	0	0	2	5	6	2	0	O-7
W 1949	NY-A	.111	5	18	2	2	0	0	1	2	3	5	0	O-5
W 1950	NY-A	.308	4	13	2	4	1	0	1	2	3	1	0	O-4
W 1951	NY-A	.261	6	23	3	6	2	0	1	5	2	4	0	O-6
W Total	10	.271	51	199	27	54	6	0	8	30	19	23	0	....
• DOBY, Larry														
W 1948	Cle-A	.318	6	22	1	7	1	0	1	2	2	4	0	O-6
W 1954	Cle-A	.125	4	16	0	2	0	0	0	0	2	4	0	O-4
W Total	2	.237	10	38	1	9	1	0	1	2	4	8	0	....
• DOERR, Bobby														
W 1946	Bos-A	.409	6	22	1	9	1	0	1	3	2	2	0	2-6
• DOLJACK, Frank														
W 1934	Det-A	.000	2	2	0	0	0	0	0	0	0	0	0	O-1
• DONAHUE, Jiggs														
W 1906	Chi-A	.333	6	18	0	6	2	1	0	4	3	4	0	1-6
• DONLIN, Mike														
W 1905	NY-N	.263	5	19	4	5	1	0	0	1	2	1	1	O-5
• DONNELS, Chris														
D 2002	Ari-N	.000	3	2	0	0	0	0	0	0	1	0	0	....
• DONOVAN, Patsy														
W 1890	Bro-N	.471	5	17	5	8	1	0	0	3	2	1	3	O-5
• DORAN, Bill														
L 1986	Hou-N	.222	6	27	3	6	0	0	1	3	2	2	2	2-6
• DOUGHERTY, Patsy														
W 1903	Bos-A	.235	8	34	3	8	0	2	2	5	2	6	0	O-8
W 1906	Chi-A	.100	6	20	1	2	0	0	0	1	3	3	2	O-6
W Total	2	.185	14	54	4	10	0	2	2	6	5	9	2	....
• DOUTHIT, Taylor														
W 1926	StL-N	.267	4	15	3	4	2	0	0	1	3	2	0	O-4
W 1928	StL-N	.091	3	11	1	1	0	0	0	1	1	1	0	O-3
W 1930	StL-N	.083	6	24	1	2	0	0	1	2	0	2	0	O-6
W Total	3	.140	13	50	5	7	2	0	1	4	4	5	0	....

YEAR	TM-L	AVG	G	AB	R	H	2B	3B	HR	RBI	BB	SO	SB	POS
• DOWNING, Brian														
L 1979	Cal-A	.200	4	15	1	3	0	0	0	1	1	1	0	C-4
L 1982	Cal-A	.158	5	19	4	3	1	0	0	0	3	2	0	O-5
L 1986	Cal-A	.222	7	27	2	6	0	0	1	7	4	5	0	O-7
L Total	3	.197	16	61	7	12	1	0	1	8	8	8	0	....
• DOWNS, Kelly														
L 1987	SF-N	....	1	0	0	0	0	0	0	0	0	0	0	....
L 1989	SF-N	.000	2	3	0	0	0	0	0	0	0	1	0	....
L 1992	Oak-A	....	2	0	0	0	0	0	0	0	0	0	0	....
L Total	3	.000	5	3	0	0	0	0	0	0	0	1	0	....
W 1989	SF-N	....	3	0	0	0	0	0	0	0	0	0	0	....
• DOWNS, Red														
W 1908	Det-A	.167	2	6	1	1	1	0	0	1	1	2	0	2-2
• DOYLE, Brian														
L 1978	NY-A	.286	3	7	0	2	0	0	0	1	1	1	0	2-3
W 1978	NY-A	.438	6	16	4	7	1	0	0	2	0	0	0	2-6
• DOYLE, Denny														
L 1975	Bos-A	.273	3	11	3	3	0	0	0	2	0	1	0	2-3
W 1975	Bos-A	.267	7	30	3	8	1	1	0	0	2	1	0	2-7
• DOYLE, Jack														
T 1894	NY-N	.588	4	17	4	10	1	1	0	6	1	1	6	1-4
T 1896	Bal-N	.294	4	17	3	5	1	0	0	4	0	0	2	1-4
T 1897	Bal-N	.526	5	19	7	10	2	0	0	9	0	1	2	1-5
T Total	3	.472	13	53	14	25	4	1	0	19	1	2	10	....
• DOYLE, Larry														
W 1911	NY-N	.304	6	23	3	7	3	1	0	1	2	1	2	2-6
W 1912	NY-N	.242	8	33	5	8	0	0	1	2	3	2	2	2-8
W 1913	NY-N	.150	5	20	1	3	0	0	0	2	0	1	0	2-5
W Total	3	.237	19	76	9	18	3	1	1	5	5	4	4	....
• DREISEWERD, Clem														
W 1946	Bos-A	....	1	0	0	0	0	0	0	0	0	0	0	....
• DREW, J.D.														
D 2000	StL-N	.167	2	6	1	1	0	0	0	0	2	1	2	O-2
D 2001	StL-N	.154	5	13	1	2	0	0	1	2	3	1	0	O-5
D 2002	StL-N	.222	2	9	1	2	0	0	1	1	1	2	0	O-2
D Total	3	.179	9	28	3	5	0	0	2	3	6	4	2	....
L 2000	StL-N	.333	5	12	2	4	1	0	0	1	0	3	0	O-5
L 2002	StL-N	.385	5	13	1	5	0	0	1	1	1	2	0	O-4
L Total	2	.360	10	25	3	9	1	0	1	2	1	5	0	....
• DRIESSEN, Dan														
L 1973	Cin-N	.167	4	12	0	2	1	0	0	1	0	2	0	3-4
L 1976	Cin-N	.000	1	1	0	0	0	0	0	0	0	0	0	....
L 1979	Cin-N	.083	3	12	1	1	0	0	0	0	1	3	0	1-3
L 1987	StL-N	.250	5	12	1	3	2	0	0	1	1	1	0	1-4
L Total	4	.162	13	37	2	6	3	0	0	2	2	6	0	....
W 1975	Cin-N	.000	2	2	0	0	0	0	0	0	0	0	0	....
W 1976	Cin-N	.357	4	14	4	5	2	0	1	1	2	0	1	D-4
W 1987	StL-N	.231	4	13	3	3	2	0	0	1	1	1	0	1-4
W Total	3	.276	10	29	7	8	4	0	1	2	3	1	1	....
• DRUMRIGHT, Keith														
D 1981	Oak-A	.250	1	4	0	1	0	0	0	0	0	0	0	D-1
L 1981	Oak-A	.000	3	4	0	0	0	0	0	0	1	0	0	D-1
• DUBUC, Jean														
W 1918	Bos-A	.000	1	1	0	0	0	0	0	0	0	1	0	....
• DUCEY, Rob														
D 1997	Sea-A	.500	2	4	0	2	0	0	0	1	0	0	0	O-1
L 1991	Tor-A	.000	1	1	0	0	0	0	0	0	0	0	0	O-1
• DUFFY, Frank														
L 1971	SF-N	.000	1	1	0	0	0	0	0	0	0	1	0	....
• DUFFY, Hugh														
T 1892	Bos-N	.462	6	26	3	12	3	2	1	9	1	0	3	O-6
T 1897	Bos-N	.524	5	21	6	11	2	0	0	7	1	0	0	O-5
T Total	2	.489	11	47	9	23	5	2	1	16	2	0	3	....
• DUGAN, Joe														
W 1922	NY-A	.250	5	20	4	5	1	0	0	0	0	1	0	3-5
W 1923	NY-A	.280	6	25	5	7	2	1	1	5	3	0	0	3-6
W 1926	NY-A	.333	7	24	2	8	1	0	0	2	1	1	0	3-7
W 1927	NY-A	.200	4	15	2	3	0	0	0	0	0	0	0	3-4
W 1928	NY-A	.167	3	6	0	1	0	0	0	1	0	0	0	3-3
W Total	5	.267	25	90	13	24	4	1	1	8	4	2	0	....
• DUGEY, Oscar														
W 1915	Phi-N	....	2	0	0	0	0	0	0	0	0	0	1	....
• DUNCAN, Dave														
L 1971	Oak-A	.500	2	6	0	3	1	0	0	2	0	0	0	C-2
L 1972	Oak-A	.000	2	2	0	0	0	0	0	0	1	1	0	C-2
L Total	2	.375	4	8	0	3	1	0	0	2	1	1	0	....
W 1972	Oak-A	.200	3	5	0	1	0	0	0	0	1	3	0	C-1
• DUNCAN, Mariano														
D 1995	Cin-N	.667	2	3	1	2	0	0	0	1	0	0	1	2-1
D 1996	NY-A	.313	4	16	0	5	0	0	0	3	0	4	0	2-4
D Total	2	.368	6	19	1	7	0	0	0	4	0	4	1	....
L 1985	LA-N	.222	5	18	2	4	2	1	0	1	1	3	1	S-5
L 1990	Cin-N	.300	6	20	1	6	0	0	1	4	0	8	0	2-6
L 1993	Phi-N	.267	3	15	3	4	0	2	0	0	0	5	0	2-3
L 1995	Cin-N	.000	3	3	0	0	0	0	0	0	1	1	0	1-1
L 1996	NY-A	.200	4	15	0	3	2	0	0	0	0	3	0	2-4
L Total	5	.239	21	71	6	17	4	3	1	5	2	20	1	....

SER-YEAR	TM-L	AVG	G	AB	R	H	2B	3B	HR	RBI	BB	SO	SB	POS
W 1990	Cin-N	.143	4	14	1	2	0	0	0	1	2	2	1	2-4
W 1993	Phi-N	.345	6	29	5	10	0	1	0	2	1	7	3	2-5,D-1
W 1996	NY-A	.053	6	19	1	1	0	0	0	0	0	4	1	2-6
W Total	**3**	**.210**	**16**	**62**	**7**	**13**	**0**	**1**	**0**	**3**	**3**	**13**	**5**	**....**
• DUNCAN, Pat														
W 1919	Cin-N	.269	8	26	3	7	2	0	0	8	2	2	0	0-8
• DUNLAP, Fred														
W 1887	Det-N	.150	11	40	5	6	0	1	0	1	0	4	4	2-11
• DUNSTON, Shawon														
D 1999	NY-N	.167	4	6	0	1	0	0	0	0	0	1	0	0-2
D 2000	StL-N	1.000	1	1	0	1	0	0	0	0	0	0	0	....
D 2002	SF-N	.000	2	1	0	0	0	0	0	0	0	1	0	....
D Total	**3**	**.250**	**7**	**8**	**0**	**2**	**0**	**0**	**0**	**0**	**0**	**2**	**0**	**....**
L 1989	Chi-N	.316	5	19	2	6	0	0	0	0	1	1	1	S-5
L 1999	NY-N	.143	5	7	2	1	0	0	0	0	0	2	1	0-1
L 2000	StL-N	.333	4	6	1	2	1	0	0	0	0	0	0	0-2
L 2002	SF-N	.500	2	2	0	1	0	0	0	0	0	1	0	0-1
L Total	**4**	**.294**	**16**	**34**	**5**	**10**	**1**	**0**	**0**	**0**	**1**	**4**	**2**	**....**
W 2002	SF-N	.222	4	9	1	2	0	0	1	3	0	1	0	D-2
• DURAZO, Erubiel														
D 1999	Ari-N	.143	2	7	1	1	0	0	1	1	1	0	0	1-2
D 2001	Ari-N	.000	1	1	0	0	0	0	0	0	0	0	0	....
D 2002	Ari-N	.000	2	4	0	0	0	0	0	0	1	1	0	1-1
D 2003	Oak-A	.238	5	21	3	5	2	0	0	3	3	4	0	....
D Total	**4**	**.182**	**10**	**33**	**4**	**6**	**2**	**0**	**1**	**4**	**5**	**5**	**0**	**....**
L 2001	Ari-N	.333	2	3	1	1	0	0	1	2	0	1	0	1-1
W 2001	Ari-N	.364	4	11	0	4	1	0	0	1	3	4	0	D-3
• DURHAM, Leon														
L 1984	Chi-N	.150	5	20	2	3	0	0	2	4	1	4	0	1-5
• DURHAM, Ray														
D 2000	Chi-A	.200	3	10	2	2	1	0	1	1	3	3	0	2-3
D 2002	Oak-A	.333	5	21	7	7	3	0	2	2	2	4	1	D-5
D 2003	SF-N	.235	4	17	2	4	0	0	0	0	1	5	0	2-4
D Total	**3**	**.271**	**12**	**48**	**11**	**13**	**4**	**0**	**3**	**3**	**6**	**12**	**1**	**....**
• DUROCHER, Leo														
W 1928	NY-A	.000	4	2	0	0	0	0	0	0	0	1	0	2-4
W 1934	StL-N	.259	7	27	4	7	1	1	0	0	0	0	0	S-7
W Total	**2**	**.241**	**11**	**29**	**4**	**7**	**1**	**1**	**0**	**0**	**0**	**1**	**0**	**....**
• DURST, Cedric														
W 1927	NY-A	.000	1	1	0	0	0	0	0	0	0	0	0	....
W 1928	NY-A	.375	4	8	3	3	0	0	1	2	0	1	0	0-4
W Total	**2**	**.333**	**5**	**9**	**3**	**3**	**0**	**0**	**1**	**2**	**0**	**1**	**0**	**....**
• DUSAK, Erv														
W 1946	StL-N	.250	4	4	0	1	1	0	0	0	2	2	0	0-4
• DWYER, Jim														
L 1983	Bal-A	.250	2	4	1	1	1	0	0	0	1	0	0	0-1
W 1983	Bal-A	.375	2	8	3	3	1	0	1	1	0	0	0	0-2
• DYBZINSKI, Jerry														
L 1983	Chi-A	.250	2	4	0	1	0	0	0	0	0	0	0	S-2
• DYE, Jermaine														
D 1996	Atl-N	.182	3	11	1	2	0	0	1	1	0	6	1	0-3
D 2001	Oak-A	.231	4	13	0	3	2	0	0	0	2	2	0	0-4
D 2002	Oak-A	.400	5	20	3	8	2	0	1	1	1	5	0	0-5
D 2003	Oak-A	.231	4	13	2	3	0	0	1	3	0	2	0	0-4
D Total	**4**	**.281**	**16**	**57**	**6**	**16**	**4**	**0**	**3**	**5**	**3**	**15**	**1**	**....**
L 1996	Atl-N	.214	7	28	2	6	1	0	0	4	1	7	0	0-7
W 1996	Atl-N	.118	5	17	0	2	0	0	0	1	1	1	0	0-5
• DYER, Duffy														
L 1975	Pit-N	....	1	0	0	0	0	0	0	1	1	0	0	....
W 1969	NY-N	.000	1	1	0	0	0	0	0	0	0	0	0	....
• DYKES, Jimmie														
W 1929	Phi-A	.421	5	19	2	8	1	0	0	4	1	1	0	3-5
W 1930	Phi-A	.222	6	18	2	4	3	0	1	5	5	3	0	3-6
W 1931	Phi-A	.227	7	22	2	5	0	0	0	2	5	1	0	3-7
W Total	**3**	**.288**	**18**	**59**	**6**	**17**	**4**	**0**	**1**	**11**	**11**	**5**	**0**	**....**
• DYKSTRA, Lenny														
L 1986	NY-N	.304	6	23	3	7	1	1	1	3	2	4	1	0-6
L 1988	NY-N	.429	7	14	6	6	3	0	1	3	4	0	0	0-7
L 1993	Phi-N	.280	6	25	5	7	1	0	2	2	5	8	0	0-6
L Total	**3**	**.323**	**19**	**62**	**14**	**20**	**5**	**1**	**4**	**8**	**11**	**12**	**1**	**....**
W 1986	NY-N	.296	7	27	4	8	0	0	2	3	2	7	0	0-7
W 1993	Phi-N	.348	6	23	9	8	1	0	4	8	7	4	4	0-6
W Total	**2**	**.320**	**13**	**50**	**13**	**16**	**1**	**0**	**6**	**11**	**9**	**11**	**4**	**....**
• EARNSHAW, George														
W 1929	Phi-A	.000	2	5	1	0	0	0	0	0	0	4	0	....
W 1930	Phi-A	.000	3	9	0	0	0	0	0	0	0	5	0	....
W 1931	Phi-A	.000	3	8	0	0	0	0	0	0	0	2	0	....
W Total	**3**	**.000**	**8**	**22**	**1**	**0**	**0**	**0**	**0**	**0**	**0**	**11**	**0**	**....**
• EASLER, Mike														
L 1979	Pit-N	.000	1	1	0	0	0	0	0	0	0	0	0	....
W 1979	Pit-N	.000	2	1	0	0	0	0	0	0	1	0	0	....
• EASTWICK, Rawly														
L 1975	Cin-N	....	2	0	0	0	0	0	0	0	0	0	0	....
L 1976	Cin-N	....	2	0	0	0	0	0	0	0	0	0	0	....
L 1978	Phi-N	....	1	0	0	0	0	0	0	0	0	0	0	....
L Total	**3**	**....**	**5**	**0**	**0**	**0**	**0**	**0**	**0**	**0**	**0**	**0**	**0**	**....**
W 1975	Cin-N	.000	5	1	0	0	0	0	0	0	0	0	0	....
• EATON, Zeb														
W 1945	Det-A	.000	1	1	0	0	0	0	0	0	0	1	0	....
• ECKSTEIN, David														
D 2002	Ana-A	.278	4	18	2	5	0	0	0	1	0	0	1	S-4
L 2002	Ana-A	.286	5	21	1	6	0	0	0	2	0	2	0	S-5
W 2002	Ana-A	.310	7	29	6	9	0	0	0	3	3	2	1	S-7
• EDMONDS, Jim														
D 2000	StL-N	.571	3	14	5	8	4	0	2	7	1	2	1	0-3
D 2001	StL-N	.235	5	17	3	4	1	0	2	3	3	6	0	0-5
D 2002	StL-N	.273	3	11	1	3	0	0	1	2	2	4	0	0-3
D Total	**3**	**.357**	**11**	**42**	**9**	**15**	**5**	**0**	**5**	**12**	**6**	**12**	**1**	**....**
L 2000	StL-N	.227	5	22	1	5	1	0	1	6	1	9	0	0-5
L 2002	StL-N	.400	5	20	2	8	2	0	1	4	2	5	0	0-5
L Total	**2**	**.310**	**10**	**42**	**3**	**13**	**3**	**0**	**2**	**10**	**3**	**14**	**0**	**....**
• EDWARDS, Bruce														
W 1947	Bro-N	.222	7	27	3	6	1	0	0	2	2	7	0	C-7
W 1949	Bro-N	.500	2	2	0	1	0	0	0	0	0	1	0	....
W Total	**2**	**.241**	**9**	**29**	**3**	**7**	**1**	**0**	**0**	**2**	**2**	**8**	**0**	**....**
• EDWARDS, Johnny														
W 1961	Cin-N	.364	3	11	1	4	2	0	0	2	0	0	0	C-3
W 1968	StL-N	.000	1	1	0	0	0	0	0	0	0	1	0	....
W Total	**2**	**.333**	**4**	**12**	**1**	**4**	**2**	**0**	**0**	**2**	**0**	**1**	**0**	**....**
• EDWARDS, Marshall														
D 1981	Mil-A	.000	2	1	0	0	0	0	0	0	0	1	0	0-2
L 1982	Mil-A	.000	3	1	2	0	0	0	0	0	0	0	1	0-1,D-2
W 1982	Mil-A	....	1	0	0	0	0	0	0	0	0	0	0	0-1
• EISENREICH, Jim														
D 1997	Fla-N	....	2	0	0	0	0	0	0	0	2	0	0	....
L 1993	Phi-N	.133	6	15	0	2	1	0	0	1	0	2	0	0-5
L 1997	Fla-N	.000	1	3	0	0	0	0	0	0	0	0	0	0-1
L Total	**2**	**.111**	**7**	**18**	**0**	**2**	**1**	**0**	**0**	**1**	**0**	**2**	**0**	**....**
W 1993	Phi-N	.231	6	26	3	6	0	0	1	7	2	4	0	0-6
W 1997	Fla-N	.500	5	8	1	4	0	0	1	3	3	1	0	1-2,D-2
W Total	**2**	**.294**	**11**	**34**	**4**	**10**	**0**	**0**	**2**	**10**	**5**	**5**	**0**	**....**
• ELLIOTT, Bob														
W 1948	Bos-N	.333	6	21	4	7	0	0	2	5	2	2	0	3-6
• ELLIS, Mark														
D 2002	Oak-A	.368	5	19	1	7	2	0	1	4	1	2	0	2-5
D 2003	Oak-A	.118	5	17	2	2	0	0	0	0	4	7	0	2-5
D Total	**2**	**.250**	**10**	**36**	**3**	**9**	**2**	**0**	**1**	**4**	**5**	**9**	**0**	**....**
• ELSTER, Kevin														
D 1996	Tex-A	.333	4	12	2	4	2	0	0	0	3	2	1	S-4
L 1986	NY-N	.000	4	3	0	0	0	0	0	0	0	1	0	S-4
L 1988	NY-N	.250	5	8	1	2	1	0	0	1	3	0	0	S-5
L Total	**2**	**.182**	**9**	**11**	**1**	**2**	**1**	**0**	**0**	**1**	**3**	**1**	**0**	**....**
W 1986	NY-N	.000	1	1	0	0	0	0	0	0	0	0	0	S-1
• ELY, Bones														
T 1900	Pit-N	.286	4	14	1	4	1	0	0	0	1	1	2	S-4
• ENCARNACION, Juan														
D 2003	Fla-N	.133	4	15	1	2	0	0	1	1	2	3	0	0-4
L 2003	Fla-N	.250	5	12	1	3	1	0	1	1	0	4	0	0-5
W 2003	Fla-N	.182	6	11	1	2	0	0	0	1	1	5	0	0-5
• ENGLE, Clyde														
W 1912	Bos-A	.333	3	3	1	1	1	0	0	2	0	0	0	....
• ENGLISH, Woody														
W 1929	Chi-N	.190	5	21	1	4	2	0	0	0	1	6	0	S-5
W 1932	Chi-N	.176	4	17	2	3	0	0	0	1	2	2	0	3-4
W Total	**2**	**.184**	**9**	**38**	**3**	**7**	**2**	**0**	**0**	**1**	**3**	**8**	**0**	**....**
• ENNIS, Del														
W 1950	Phi-N	.143	4	14	1	2	1	0	0	0	0	1	0	0-4
• EPSTEIN, Mike														
L 1971	Oak-A	.200	2	5	0	1	0	0	0	0	0	3	0	1-1
L 1972	Oak-A	.188	5	16	1	3	0	0	1	1	4	5	1	1-5
L Total	**2**	**.190**	**7**	**21**	**1**	**4**	**0**	**0**	**1**	**1**	**4**	**8**	**1**	**....**
W 1972	Oak-A	.000	6	16	1	0	0	0	0	0	5	3	0	1-6
• ERSTAD, Darin														
D 2002	Ana-A	.421	4	19	4	8	2	0	0	2	0	1	1	0-4
L 2002	Ana-A	.364	5	22	4	8	0	0	1	2	0	3	1	0-5
W 2002	Ana-A	.300	7	30	6	9	3	0	1	3	1	4	1	0-7
• ESPER, Duke														
T 1894	Bal-N	.000	1	2	0	0	0	0	0	0	1	1	0	P-1
T 1895	Bal-N	.000	1	3	0	0	0	0	0	0	1	2	0	P-1
T Total	**2**	**.000**	**2**	**5**	**0**	**0**	**0**	**0**	**0**	**0**	**2**	**3**	**0**	**....**
• ESPINOZA, Alvaro														
D 1995	Cle-A	.000	1	1	0	0	0	0	0	0	0	0	0	3-1
L 1995	Cle-A	.125	4	8	1	1	0	0	0	0	0	3	0	3-4
W 1995	Cle-A	.500	2	2	1	1	0	0	0	0	0	0	0	3-1
• ESPOSITO, Sammy														
W 1959	Chi-A	.000	2	2	0	0	0	0	0	0	0	1	0	3-2
• ESPY, Cecil														
L 1991	Pit-N	.000	2	2	0	0	0	0	0	0	0	2	0	....
L 1992	Pit-N	.667	4	3	0	2	0	0	0	0	0	1	0	0-2
L Total	**2**	**.400**	**6**	**5**	**0**	**2**	**0**	**0**	**0**	**0**	**0**	**3**	**0**	**....**
• ESSEGIAN, Chuck														
W 1959	LA-N	.667	4	3	2	2	0	0	2	2	1	1	0	....

YEAR	TM-L	AVG	G	AB	R	H	2B	3B	HR	RBI	BB	SO	SB	POS
• ESTALELLA, Bobby														
D 2000	SF-N	.083	4	12	1	1	0	0	0	1	0	2	0	C-4
• ESTERBROOK, Dude														
W 1884	NY-A	.300	3	10	0	3	1	0	0	0	0	3	1	3-3
• ETCHEBARREN, Andy														
L 1969	Bal-A	.000	2	4	0	0	0	0	0	0	0	0	0	C-2
L 1970	Bal-A	.111	2	9	1	1	0	0	0	0	0	3	0	C-2
L 1971	Bal-A	.000	2	5	0	0	0	0	0	0	0	0	0	C-2
L 1973	Bal-A	.357	4	14	1	5	1	0	1	4	0	1	0	C-4
L 1974	Bal-A	.333	2	6	0	2	0	0	0	0	0	0	0	C-2
L Total	**5**	**.211**	**12**	**38**	**2**	**8**	**1**	**0**	**1**	**4**	**0**	**4**	**0**	....
W 1966	Bal-A	.083	4	12	2	1	0	0	0	0	2	4	0	C-4
W 1969	Bal-A	.000	2	6	0	0	0	0	0	0	0	1	0	C-2
W 1970	Bal-A	.143	2	7	1	1	0	0	0	0	2	3	0	C-2
W 1971	Bal-A	.000	1	2	0	0	0	0	0	0	0	0	0	C-1
W Total	**4**	**.074**	**9**	**27**	**3**	**2**	**0**	**0**	**0**	**0**	**4**	**8**	**0**	....
• ETTEN, Nick														
W 1943	NY-A	.105	5	19	0	2	0	0	0	2	1	2	0	1-5
• EUSEBIO, Tony														
D 1997	Hou-N	.667	1	3	1	2	0	0	0	0	0	1	1	C-1
D 1998	Hou-N	.333	1	3	0	1	1	0	0	0	0	2	0	C-1
D 1999	Hou-N	.267	4	15	2	4	0	0	1	3	1	2	0	C-4
D 2001	Hou-N	.667	1	3	1	2	1	0	0	0	0	0	0	C-1
D Total	**4**	**.375**	**7**	**24**	**4**	**9**	**2**	**0**	**1**	**3**	**1**	**5**	**1**	....
• EVANS, Darrell														
L 1984	Det-A	.300	3	10	1	3	1	0	0	1	1	0	1	1-3,3-1
L 1987	Det-A	.294	5	17	0	5	0	0	0	0	4	2	0	1-5,3-1
L Total	**2**	**.296**	**8**	**27**	**1**	**8**	**1**	**0**	**0**	**1**	**5**	**2**	**1**	....
W 1984	Det-A	.067	5	15	1	1	0	0	0	1	4	4	0	1-4,3-2
• EVANS, Dwight														
L 1975	Bos-A	.100	3	10	1	1	1	0	0	0	1	2	0	O-3
L 1986	Bos-A	.214	7	28	2	6	1	0	1	4	3	3	0	O-7
L 1988	Bos-A	.167	4	12	1	2	1	0	0	1	3	5	0	O-4
L 1990	Bos-A	.231	4	13	0	3	1	0	0	0	1	3	0	D-4
L Total	**4**	**.190**	**18**	**63**	**4**	**12**	**4**	**0**	**1**	**5**	**8**	**13**	**0**	....
W 1975	Bos-A	.292	7	24	3	7	1	1	1	5	3	4	0	O-7
W 1986	Bos-A	.308	7	26	4	8	2	0	2	9	4	3	0	O-7
W Total	**2**	**.300**	**14**	**50**	**7**	**15**	**3**	**1**	**3**	**14**	**7**	**7**	**0**	....
• EVANS, Joe														
W 1920	Cle-A	.308	4	13	0	4	0	0	0	0	1	0	0	O-4
• EVERETT, Carl														
D 1998	Hou-N	.154	4	13	1	2	0	0	0	0	0	4	0	O-3
D 1999	Hou-N	.133	4	15	2	2	0	0	0	1	2	8	1	O-4
D Total	**2**	**.143**	**8**	**28**	**3**	**4**	**0**	**0**	**0**	**1**	**2**	**12**	**1**	....
• EVERS, Johnny														
W 1906	Chi-N	.150	6	20	2	3	1	0	0	1	1	3	2	2-6
W 1907	Chi-N	.350	5	20	2	7	2	0	0	1	0	1	3	2-5,S-1
W 1908	Chi-N	.350	5	20	5	7	1	0	0	2	1	2	2	2-5
W 1914	Bos-N	.438	4	16	2	7	0	0	0	2	2	2	1	2-4
W Total	**4**	**.316**	**20**	**76**	**11**	**24**	**4**	**0**	**0**	**6**	**4**	**8**	**8**	....
• EWING, Buck														
W 1888	NY-N	.346	7	26	5	9	0	2	1	6	1	3	5	C-6,1-1
W 1889	NY-N	.250	8	36	5	9	4	0	0	7	2	5	1	C-8
W Total	**2**	**.290**	**15**	**62**	**10**	**18**	**4**	**2**	**1**	**13**	**3**	**8**	**6**	....
• FABREGAS, Jorge														
L 1999	Atl-N	.000	2	2	0	0	0	0	0	0	0	1	0	....
W 1999	Atl-N	.000	1	1	0	0	0	0	0	0	0	1	0	....
• FAIRLY, Ron														
W 1959	LA-N	.000	6	3	0	0	0	0	0	0	0	1	0	O-4
W 1963	LA-N	.000	4	1	0	0	0	0	0	0	3	0	0	O-4
W 1965	LA-N	.379	7	29	7	11	3	0	2	6	0	1	0	O-7
W 1966	LA-N	.143	3	7	0	1	0	0	0	0	2	4	0	O-2,1-1
W Total	**4**	**.300**	**20**	**40**	**7**	**12**	**3**	**0**	**2**	**6**	**5**	**6**	**0**	....
• FALLON, George														
W 1944	StL-N	.000	2	2	0	0	0	0	0	0	0	1	0	2-2
• FARRELL, Duke														
T 1894	NY-N	.400	4	15	5	6	0	0	0	2	1	1	1	C-4
T 1900	Bro-N	.375	2	8	0	3	0	0	0	1	0	0	1	C-2
T Total	**2**	**.391**	**6**	**23**	**5**	**9**	**0**	**0**	**0**	**3**	**1**	**1**	**2**	....
W 1903	Bos-A	.000	2	2	0	0	0	0	0	1	0	0	0	....
• FARRELL, Jack														
W 1884	Pro-N	.444	3	9	3	4	2	0	0	0	0	0	1	2-3
• FASANO, Sal														
D 2000	Oak-A	....	1	0	0	0	0	0	0	0	0	0	0	C-1
• FELIX, Junior														
L 1989	Tor-A	.273	3	11	0	3	1	0	0	3	0	2	0	O-3
• FELIZ, Pedro														
D 2002	SF-N	.000	1	1	0	0	0	0	0	0	0	1	0	....
D 2003	SF-N	.667	3	3	1	2	0	1	0	1	0	1	0	....
D Total	**2**	**.500**	**4**	**4**	**1**	**2**	**0**	**1**	**0**	**1**	**0**	**2**	**0**	....
L 2002	SF-N	.000	1	1	0	0	0	0	0	0	0	0	0	....
W 2002	SF-N	.000	3	5	0	0	0	0	0	0	0	2	0	D-1
• FELSCH, Happy														
W 1917	Chi-A	.273	6	22	4	6	1	0	1	3	1	5	0	O-6
W 1919	Chi-A	.192	8	26	2	5	1	0	0	3	1	4	0	O-8
W Total	**2**	**.229**	**14**	**48**	**6**	**11**	**2**	**0**	**1**	**6**	**2**	**9**	**0**	....

YEAR	TM-L	AVG	G	AB	R	H	2B	3B	HR	RBI	BB	SO	SB	POS
• FERGUSON, Joe														
L 1974	LA-N	.231	4	13	3	3	0	0	0	2	5	1	0	O-3,C-2
L 1978	LA-N	.000	2	2	0	0	0	0	0	0	0	1	0	....
L Total	**2**	**.200**	**6**	**15**	**3**	**3**	**0**	**0**	**0**	**2**	**5**	**2**	**0**	....
W 1974	LA-N	.125	5	16	2	2	0	0	1	2	4	6	1	O-4,C-2
W 1978	LA-N	.500	2	4	1	2	2	0	0	0	0	1	0	C-2
W Total	**2**	**.200**	**7**	**20**	**3**	**4**	**2**	**0**	**1**	**2**	**4**	**7**	**1**	....
• FERMIN, Felix														
D 1995	Sea-A	.000	3	1	0	0	0	0	0	0	0	1	0	2-1,S-1
L 1995	Sea-A	....	2	0	0	0	0	0	0	0	0	0	0	2-1,S-1
• FERNANDEZ, Tony														
D 1995	NY-A	.238	5	21	0	5	2	0	0	0	2	2	0	S-5
D 1997	Cle-A	.182	4	11	0	2	1	0	0	4	0	0	0	2-4
D Total	**2**	**.219**	**9**	**32**	**0**	**7**	**3**	**0**	**0**	**4**	**2**	**2**	**0**	....
L 1985	Tor-A	.333	7	24	2	8	2	0	0	2	1	2	0	S-7
L 1989	Tor-A	.350	5	20	6	7	3	0	0	1	1	2	5	S-5
L 1993	Tor-A	.318	6	22	1	7	0	0	0	1	2	4	0	S-6
L 1997	Cle-A	.357	5	14	1	5	1	0	1	2	1	2	0	2-5
L Total	**4**	**.338**	**23**	**80**	**10**	**27**	**6**	**0**	**1**	**6**	**5**	**10**	**5**	....
W 1993	Tor-A	.333	6	21	2	7	1	0	0	9	3	3	0	S-6
W 1997	Cle-A	.471	5	17	1	8	1	0	0	4	0	1	0	2-5
W Total	**2**	**.395**	**11**	**38**	**3**	**15**	**2**	**0**	**0**	**13**	**3**	**4**	**0**	....
• FERRARA, Al														
W 1966	LA-N	1.000	1	1	0	1	0	0	0	0	0	0	0	....
• FERRIS, Hobe														
W 1903	Bos-A	.290	8	31	3	9	0	1	0	5	0	6	0	2-8
• FEWSTER, Chick														
W 1921	NY-A	.200	4	10	3	2	0	0	1	2	3	3	0	O-4
• FICK, Robert														
D 2003	Atl-N	.000	4	11	0	0	0	0	0	0	1	2	0	1-3
• FIELDER, Cecil														
D 1996	NY-A	.364	3	11	2	4	0	0	1	4	1	2	0	D-3
D 1997	NY-A	.125	2	8	0	1	0	0	0	1	0	3	0	D-2
D Total	**2**	**.263**	**5**	**19**	**2**	**5**	**0**	**0**	**1**	**5**	**1**	**5**	**0**	....
L 1985	Tor-A	.333	3	3	0	1	1	0	0	0	0	1	0	....
L 1996	NY-A	.167	5	18	3	3	0	0	2	8	4	5	0	D-5
L Total	**2**	**.190**	**8**	**21**	**3**	**4**	**1**	**0**	**2**	**8**	**4**	**6**	**0**	....
W 1996	NY-A	.391	6	23	1	9	2	0	0	2	2	2	0	1-3,D-3
• FIGGINS, Chone														
D 2002	Ana-A	....	1	0	1	0	0	0	0	0	0	0	1	D-1
L 2002	Ana-A	1.000	3	1	2	1	0	0	0	0	0	0	0	....
W 2002	Ana-A	....	2	0	1	0	0	0	0	0	0	0	0	....
• FIMPLE, Jack														
L 1983	LA-N	.143	3	7	0	1	0	0	0	1	0	3	0	C-3
• FINLEY, Steve														
D 1996	SD-N	.083	3	12	0	1	0	0	0	1	0	4	1	O-3
D 1998	SD-N	.100	4	10	2	1	1	0	0	1	1	4	0	O-4
D 1999	Ari-N	.385	4	13	0	5	1	0	0	5	3	1	0	O-4
D 2001	Ari-N	.421	5	19	1	8	1	0	0	2	0	2	0	O-5
D 2002	Ari-N	.222	3	9	1	2	0	0	0	1	2	2	1	O-3
D Total	**5**	**.270**	**19**	**63**	**4**	**17**	**3**	**0**	**0**	**10**	**6**	**13**	**2**	....
L 1998	SD-N	.333	6	21	3	7	1	0	0	2	6	2	1	O-6
L 2001	Ari-N	.286	5	14	1	4	1	0	0	5	3	1	1	O-5
L Total	**2**	**.314**	**11**	**35**	**4**	**11**	**2**	**0**	**0**	**7**	**9**	**3**	**2**	....
W 1998	SD-N	.083	3	12	0	1	1	0	0	0	0	2	1	O-3
W 2001	Ari-N	.368	6	19	5	7	0	0	1	2	4	5	0	O-6
W Total	**2**	**.258**	**9**	**31**	**5**	**8**	**1**	**0**	**1**	**2**	**4**	**7**	**1**	....
• FISHER, Showboat														
W 1930	StL-N	.500	2	2	0	1	1	0	0	0	0	1	0	....
• FISK, Carlton														
L 1975	Bos-A	.417	3	12	4	5	1	0	0	2	0	2	1	C-3
L 1983	Chi-A	.176	4	17	0	3	1	0	0	0	1	3	0	C-4
L Total	**2**	**.276**	**7**	**29**	**4**	**8**	**2**	**0**	**0**	**2**	**1**	**5**	**1**	....
W 1975	Bos-A	.240	7	25	5	6	0	0	2	4	7	7	0	C-7
• FLACK, Max														
W 1918	Chi-N	.263	6	19	2	5	0	0	0	0	4	1	1	O-6
• FLAHERTY, John														
D 1996	SD-N	.000	2	4	0	0	0	0	0	0	0	1	0	C-2
W 2003	NY-A	.000	1	2	0	0	0	0	0	0	0	0	0	C-1
• FLANNERY, Tim														
L 1984	SD-N	.500	3	2	2	1	0	0	0	0	0	0	0	....
W 1984	SD-N	1.000	1	1	0	1	0	0	0	0	0	0	0	2-1
• FLETCHER, Art														
W 1911	NY-N	.130	6	23	1	3	1	0	0	1	0	4	0	S-6
W 1912	NY-N	.179	8	28	1	5	1	0	0	3	1	4	1	S-8
W 1913	NY-N	.278	5	18	1	5	0	0	0	3	1	1	1	S-5
W 1917	NY-N	.200	6	25	2	5	1	0	0	0	0	2	0	S-6
W Total	**4**	**.191**	**25**	**94**	**5**	**18**	**3**	**0**	**0**	**7**	**2**	**11**	**2**	....
• FLETCHER, Scott														
L 1983	Chi-A	.000	3	7	0	0	0	0	0	0	1	0	0	S-3
• FLINT, Silver														
W 1885	Chi-N	.143	4	14	0	2	0	0	0	0	0	0	0	C-4
W 1886	Chi-N	.000	1	3	0	0	0	0	0	1	0	1	0	C-1
W Total	**2**	**.118**	**5**	**17**	**0**	**2**	**0**	**0**	**0**	**1**	**0**	**1**	**0**	....
• FLOOD, Curt														
W 1964	StL-N	.200	7	30	5	6	0	1	0	3	3	1	0	O-7

SER-YEAR	TM-L	AVG	G	AB	R	H	2B	3B	HR	RBI	BB	SO	SB	POS
W 1967	StL-N	.179	7	28	2	5	1	0	0	3	3	3	0	0-7
W 1968	StL-N	.286	7	28	4	8	1	0	0	2	2	2	3	0-7
W Total	**3**	**.221**	**21**	**86**	**11**	**19**	**2**	**1**	**0**	**8**	**8**	**6**	**3**	....
• FLOWERS, Jake														
W 1926	StL-N	.000	3	3	0	0	0	0	0	0	0	1	0	....
W 1931	StL-N	.091	5	11	1	1	1	0	0	0	1	0	0	3-4
W Total	**2**	**.071**	**8**	**14**	**1**	**1**	**1**	**0**	**0**	**0**	**1**	**1**	**0**	....
• FLOYD, Cliff														
W 1997	Fla-N	.000	4	2	1	0	0	0	0	0	1	1	0	D-1
• FLYNN, Doug														
L 1976	Cin-N	....	1	0	0	0	0	0	0	0	0	0	0	2-1
• FOLI, Tim														
L 1979	Pit-N	.333	3	12	1	4	1	0	0	3	0	0	0	S-3
L 1982	Cal-A	.125	5	16	0	2	0	0	0	1	0	3	0	S-5
L Total	**2**	**.214**	**8**	**28**	**1**	**6**	**1**	**0**	**0**	**4**	**0**	**3**	**0**	....
W 1979	Pit-N	.333	7	30	6	10	1	1	0	3	2	0	0	S-7
• FONVILLE, Chad														
D 1995	LA-N	.500	3	12	1	6	0	0	0	0	0	1	0	S-3
• FOOTE, Barry														
D 1981	NY-A	....	1	0	0	0	0	0	0	0	0	0	0	....
L 1978	Phi-N	.000	1	1	0	0	0	0	0	0	0	1	0	....
L 1981	NY-A	1.000	2	1	0	1	0	0	0	0	0	0	0	C-1
L Total	**2**	**.500**	**3**	**2**	**0**	**1**	**0**	**0**	**0**	**0**	**0**	**1**	**0**	....
W 1981	NY-A	.000	1	1	0	0	0	0	0	0	0	1	0	....
• FORD, Curt														
L 1987	StL-N	.333	4	9	2	3	0	0	0	0	1	1	0	0-4
W 1987	StL-N	.308	5	13	1	4	0	0	0	2	1	1	0	0-4
• FORD, Dan														
L 1979	Cal-A	.294	4	17	2	5	1	0	2	4	0	0	0	0-4
L 1983	Bal-A	.200	2	5	0	1	1	0	0	0	0	1	0	0-1,D-1
L Total	**2**	**.273**	**6**	**22**	**2**	**6**	**2**	**0**	**2**	**4**	**0**	**1**	**0**	....
W 1983	Bal-A	.167	5	12	1	2	0	0	1	1	1	5	0	0-4
• FORD, Lew														
D 2003	Min-A	.000	1	1	0	0	0	0	0	0	0	1	0	....
• FORSTER, Tom														
W 1884	NY-A	.000	1	3	0	0	0	0	0	0	0	1	0	2-1
• FOSSE, Ray														
L 1973	Oak-A	.091	5	11	2	1	1	0	0	3	2	2	0	C-5
L 1974	Oak-A	.333	4	12	1	4	1	0	1	3	1	2	0	C-4
L 1975	Oak-A	.000	1	2	0	0	0	0	0	0	0	1	0	C-1
L Total	**3**	**.200**	**10**	**25**	**3**	**5**	**2**	**0**	**1**	**6**	**3**	**5**	**0**	....
W 1973	Oak-A	.158	7	19	0	3	1	0	0	0	1	4	0	C-7
W 1974	Oak-A	.143	5	14	1	2	0	0	1	1	1	5	0	C-5
W Total	**2**	**.152**	**12**	**33**	**1**	**5**	**1**	**0**	**1**	**1**	**2**	**9**	**0**	....
• FOSTER, George														
L 1972	Cin-N	....	1	0	1	0	0	0	0	0	0	0	0	....
L 1975	Cin-N	.364	3	11	3	4	0	0	0	0	1	2	1	0-3
L 1976	Cin-N	.167	3	12	2	2	0	0	2	4	0	4	0	0-3
L 1979	Cin-N	.200	3	10	1	2	0	0	1	2	4	3	0	0-3
L Total	**4**	**.242**	**10**	**33**	**7**	**8**	**0**	**0**	**3**	**6**	**5**	**9**	**1**	....
W 1972	Cin-N	....	2	0	0	0	0	0	0	0	0	0	0	0-1
W 1975	Cin-N	.276	7	29	1	8	1	0	0	2	1	1	1	0-7
W 1976	Cin-N	.429	4	14	3	6	1	0	0	4	2	3	0	0-4
W Total	**3**	**.326**	**13**	**43**	**4**	**14**	**2**	**0**	**0**	**6**	**3**	**4**	**1**	....
• FOUTZ, Dave														
W 1885	StL-A	.167	4	12	1	2	0	0	0	0	0	0	0	P-4
W 1886	StL-A	.200	4	15	2	3	1	1	0	3	0	3	0	P-2,0-2
W 1887	StL-A	.197	15	61	4	12	2	1	0	3	2	3	0	0-11,P-3,1-1
W 1889	Bro-A	.286	9	35	7	10	2	0	1	9	4	2	3	1-9,P-1
W 1890	Bro-N	.300	7	30	6	9	2	1	0	4	0	1	1	1-7,0-1
W Total	**5**	**.235**	**39**	**153**	**20**	**36**	**7**	**3**	**1**	**19**	**6**	**9**	**4**	....
• FOX, Andy														
D 1996	NY-A	....	2	0	0	0	0	0	0	0	0	0	0	D-2
D 1997	NY-A	....	2	0	0	0	0	0	0	0	0	0	0	2-2
D 1999	Ari-N	.000	1	3	0	0	0	0	0	0	0	1	0	S-1
D Total	**3**	**.000**	**5**	**3**	**0**	**0**	**0**	**0**	**0**	**0**	**0**	**1**	**0**	....
L 1996	NY-A	....	2	0	0	0	0	0	0	0	0	0	0	D-2
W 1996	NY-A	....	4	0	1	0	0	0	0	0	0	0	0	2-1,3-1,D-1
• FOX, Chad														
D 2003	Fla-N	....	3	0	0	0	0	0	0	0	0	0	0	....
L 2003	Fla-N	....	3	0	0	0	0	0	0	0	0	0	0	....
W 2003	Fla-N	....	2	0	0	0	0	0	0	0	0	0	0	....
• FOX, Eric														
L 1992	Oak-A	.000	4	1	0	0	0	0	0	0	1	0	2	0-1,D-2
• FOX, Nellie														
W 1959	Chi-A	.375	6	24	4	9	3	0	0	0	4	1	0	2-6
• FOX, Pete														
W 1934	Det-A	.286	7	28	1	8	6	0	0	2	1	4	0	0-7
W 1935	Det-A	.385	6	26	1	10	3	1	0	4	0	1	0	0-6
W 1940	Det-A	.000	1	1	0	0	0	0	0	0	0	0	0	....
W Total	**3**	**.327**	**14**	**55**	**2**	**18**	**9**	**1**	**0**	**6**	**1**	**5**	**0**	....
• FOXX, Jimmie														
W 1929	Phi-A	.350	5	20	5	7	1	0	2	5	1	1	0	1-5
W 1930	Phi-A	.333	6	21	3	7	2	1	1	3	2	4	0	1-6
W 1931	Phi-A	.348	7	23	3	8	0	0	1	3	6	5	0	1-7
W Total	**3**	**.344**	**18**	**64**	**11**	**22**	**3**	**1**	**4**	**11**	**9**	**10**	**0**	....

SER-YEAR	TM-L	AVG	G	AB	R	H	2B	3B	HR	RBI	BB	SO	SB	POS
• FOY, Joe														
W 1967	Bos-A	.133	6	15	2	2	1	0	0	1	1	5	0	3-3
• FRANCO, Julio														
D 1996	Cle-A	.133	4	15	1	2	0	0	0	1	1	6	0	1-3,D-1
D 2001	Atl-N	.308	3	13	3	4	0	0	1	1	0	1	0	1-3
D 2002	Atl-N	.182	5	22	2	4	0	0	0	1	2	3	1	1-5
D 2003	Atl-N	.500	4	8	1	4	1	0	0	0	2	2	0	1-3
D Total	**4**	**.241**	**16**	**58**	**7**	**14**	**1**	**0**	**1**	**3**	**5**	**12**	**1**	....
L 2001	Atl-N	.261	5	23	2	6	0	0	1	2	0	2	0	1-5
• FRANCO, Matt														
D 1999	NY-N	....	1	0	0	0	0	0	0	0	1	0	0	....
D 2002	Atl-N	.000	4	2	0	0	0	0	0	0	0	0	0	....
D 2003	Atl-N	.000	2	2	1	0	0	0	0	0	0	1	0	....
D Total	**3**	**.000**	**7**	**4**	**1**	**0**	**0**	**0**	**0**	**0**	**1**	**1**	**0**	....
L 1999	NY-N	.500	5	2	1	1	1	0	0	0	1	0	0	....
L 2000	NY-N	.000	2	3	0	0	0	0	0	0	0	1	0	1-1
L Total	**2**	**.200**	**7**	**5**	**1**	**1**	**1**	**0**	**0**	**0**	**1**	**1**	**0**	....
W 2000	NY-N	.000	1	1	0	0	0	0	0	0	0	1	0	1-1
• FRANCONA, Terry														
D 1981	Mon-N	.333	5	12	0	4	0	0	0	0	2	2	2	0-5
L 1981	Mon-N	.000	2	1	0	0	0	0	0	0	0	1	0	0-1
• FRANKS, Herman														
W 1941	Bro-N	.000	1	1	0	0	0	0	0	0	0	0	0	C-1
• FREEHAN, Bill														
L 1972	Det-A	.250	3	12	2	3	1	0	1	3	0	1	0	C-3
W 1968	Det-A	.083	7	24	0	2	1	0	0	2	4	8	0	C-7
• FREEMAN, Buck														
W 1903	Bos-A	.281	8	32	6	9	0	3	0	4	2	2	0	0-8
• FREESE, Gene														
W 1961	Cin-N	.063	5	16	0	1	1	0	0	0	3	4	0	3-5
• FRENCH, Walter														
W 1929	Phi-A	.000	1	1	0	0	0	0	0	0	0	1	0	....
• FREY, Lonny														
W 1939	Cin-N	.000	4	17	0	0	0	0	0	0	1	4	0	2-4
W 1940	Cin-N	.000	3	2	0	0	0	0	0	0	0	0	0	2-1
W 1947	NY-A	.000	1	1	0	0	0	0	0	1	0	0	0	....
W Total	**3**	**.000**	**8**	**20**	**0**	**0**	**0**	**0**	**0**	**1**	**1**	**4**	**0**	....
• FRIAS, Hanley														
D 1999	Ari-N	.000	4	7	0	0	0	0	0	0	0	3	0	S-4
• FRISCH, Frankie														
W 1921	NY-N	.300	8	30	5	9	0	1	0	1	4	3	3	3-8
W 1922	NY-N	.471	5	17	3	8	1	0	0	2	1	0	1	2-5
W 1923	NY-N	.400	6	25	2	10	0	1	0	1	0	0	0	2-6
W 1924	NY-N	.333	7	30	1	10	4	1	0	0	4	1	1	2-7,3-1
W 1928	StL-N	.231	4	13	1	3	0	0	0	1	2	2	2	2-4
W 1930	StL-N	.208	6	24	0	5	2	0	0	0	0	0	1	2-6
W 1931	StL-N	.259	7	27	2	7	2	0	0	1	1	2	1	2-7
W 1934	StL-N	.194	7	31	2	6	1	0	0	4	0	1	0	2-7
W Total	**8**	**.294**	**50**	**197**	**16**	**58**	**10**	**3**	**0**	**10**	**12**	**9**	**9**	....
• FRYMAN, Travis														
D 1998	Cle-A	.154	4	13	1	2	1	0	0	0	3	4	1	3-4
D 1999	Cle-A	.267	5	15	2	4	0	0	1	4	3	2	1	3-5
D 2001	Cle-A	.176	5	17	4	3	1	0	0	2	2	7	0	3-5
D Total	**3**	**.200**	**14**	**45**	**7**	**9**	**2**	**0**	**1**	**6**	**8**	**13**	**2**	....
L 1998	Cle-A	.174	6	23	2	4	0	0	0	0	1	5	1	3-6
• FUENTES, Tito														
L 1971	SF-N	.313	4	16	4	5	1	0	1	2	1	3	0	2-4
• FULLER, Shorty														
T 1894	NY-N	.286	4	14	4	4	0	0	0	2	2	0	1	S-4
• FULLIS, Chick														
W 1934	StL-N	.400	3	5	0	2	0	0	0	0	0	0	0	0-3
• FULLMER, Brad														
D 2002	Ana-A	.286	3	7	1	2	1	0	0	0	1	1	0	D-3
L 2002	Ana-A	.333	4	12	2	4	2	0	1	4	0	2	0	D-4
W 2002	Ana-A	.267	5	15	3	4	0	0	0	1	2	2	2	D-4
• FURCAL, Rafael														
D 2000	Atl-N	.091	3	11	2	1	0	0	0	0	3	0	1	2-1,S-3
D 2002	Atl-N	.250	5	24	2	6	1	1	0	2	0	5	1	S-5
D 2003	Atl-N	.211	5	19	3	4	0	0	0	0	3	5	1	S-5
D Total	**3**	**.204**	**13**	**54**	**7**	**11**	**1**	**1**	**0**	**2**	**6**	**10**	**3**	....
• FURILLO, Carl														
W 1947	Bro-N	.353	6	17	2	6	2	0	0	3	3	0	0	0-6
W 1949	Bro-N	.125	3	8	0	1	0	0	0	0	1	0	0	0-2
W 1952	Bro-N	.174	7	23	1	4	2	0	0	0	3	3	0	0-7
W 1953	Bro-N	.333	6	24	4	8	2	0	1	4	1	3	0	0-6
W 1955	Bro-N	.296	7	27	4	8	1	0	1	3	3	5	0	0-7
W 1956	Bro-N	.240	7	25	2	6	2	0	0	1	2	3	0	0-7
W 1959	LA-N	.250	4	4	0	1	0	0	0	2	0	1	0	0-1
W Total	**7**	**.266**	**40**	**128**	**13**	**34**	**9**	**0**	**2**	**13**	**13**	**15**	**0**	....
• GABLER, Frank														
W 1936	NY-N	....	2	0	0	0	0	0	0	0	1	0	0	....
• GAETTI, Gary														
D 1996	StL-N	.091	3	11	1	1	0	0	1	3	0	3	0	3-3
D 1998	Chi-N	.091	3	11	0	1	0	0	0	0	0	4	0	3-3
D Total	**2**	**.091**	**6**	**22**	**1**	**2**	**0**	**0**	**1**	**3**	**0**	**7**	**0**	....
L 1987	Min-A	.300	5	20	5	6	1	0	2	5	1	3	0	3-5

YEAR	TM-L	AVG	G	AB	R	H	2B	3B	HR	RBI	BB	SO	SB	POS
L 1996	StL-N	.292	7	24	1	7	0	0	1	4	1	5	0	3-7
L **Total**	2	.295	12	44	6	13	1	0	3	9	2	8	0	....
W 1987	Min-A	.259	7	27	4	7	2	1	1	4	2	5	2	3-7
• GAGLIANO, Phil														
L 1973	Cin-N	.000	3	3	0	0	0	0	0	0	0	1	0	....
W 1967	StL-N	.000	1	1	0	0	0	0	0	0	0	0	0	....
W 1968	StL-N	.000	3	3	0	0	0	0	0	0	0	0	0	....
W **Total**	2	.000	4	4	0	0	0	0	0	0	0	0	0	....
• GAGNE, Greg														
D 1996	LA-N	.273	3	11	2	3	1	0	0	0	0	5	0	S-3
L 1987	Min-A	.278	5	18	5	5	3	0	2	3	3	4	0	S-5
L 1991	Min-A	.235	5	17	1	4	0	0	0	1	1	5	0	S-5
L **Total**	2	.257	10	35	6	9	3	0	2	4	4	9	0	....
W 1987	Min-A	.200	7	30	5	6	1	0	1	3	1	6	0	S-7
W 1991	Min-A	.167	7	24	1	4	1	0	1	3	0	7	0	S-7
W **Total**	2	.185	14	54	6	10	2	0	2	6	1	13	0	....
• GAINER, Del														
W 1915	Bos-A	.333	1	3	1	1	0	0	0	0	0	0	0	1-1
W 1916	Bos-A	1.000	1	1	0	1	0	0	0	1	0	0	0	....
W **Total**	2	.500	2	4	1	2	0	0	0	1	0	0	0	....
• GALAN, Augie														
W 1935	Chi-N	.160	6	25	2	4	1	0	0	2	2	2	0	0-6
W 1938	Chi-N	.000	2	2	0	0	0	0	0	0	0	1	0	....
W 1941	Bro-N	.000	2	2	0	0	0	0	0	0	0	1	0	....
W **Total**	3	.138	10	29	2	4	1	0	0	2	2	4	0	....
• GALARRAGA, Andres														
D 1995	Col-N	.278	4	18	1	5	1	0	0	2	0	6	0	1-4
D 1998	Atl-N	.250	3	12	1	3	0	0	0	0	1	3	0	1-3
D 2000	Atl-N	.200	3	10	1	2	1	0	0	1	2	4	0	1-3
D 2003	SF-N	.000	2	5	0	0	0	0	0	0	0	1	0	1-1
D **Total**	4	.222	12	45	3	10	2	0	0	3	3	14	0	....
L 1998	Atl-N	.095	6	21	1	2	0	0	1	4	6	6	0	1-6
• GALLAGHER, Al														
L 1971	SF-N	.100	4	10	0	1	0	0	0	0	0	2	0	3-4
• GALLEGO, Mike														
D 1996	StL-N	.000	2	1	0	0	0	0	0	0	0	1	0	2-1,3-1
L 1988	Oak-A	.083	4	12	1	1	0	0	0	0	0	3	0	2-4
L 1989	Oak-A	.273	4	11	3	3	1	0	0	1	0	2	0	2-2,S-2
L 1990	Oak-A	.400	4	10	1	4	1	0	0	2	1	1	0	2-2,S-3
L 1996	StL-N	.143	7	14	1	2	0	0	0	0	1	3	0	2-5,3-2
L **Total**	4	.213	19	47	6	10	2	0	0	3	2	9	0	....
W 1988	Oak-A	....	1	0	0	0	0	0	0	0	0	0	0	2-1
W 1989	Oak-A	.000	2	1	0	0	0	0	0	0	0	0	0	2-1,3-1
W 1990	Oak-A	.091	4	11	0	1	0	0	0	1	1	3	1	S-4
W **Total**	3	.083	7	12	0	1	0	0	0	1	1	3	1	....
• GAMBLE, Lee														
W 1939	Cin-N	.000	1	1	0	0	0	0	0	0	0	1	0	....
• GAMBLE, Oscar														
D 1981	NY-A	.667	4	9	2	6	2	0	2	3	1	2	0	D-4
L 1976	NY-A	.250	3	8	1	2	1	0	0	1	1	1	0	0-3
L 1980	NY-A	.200	2	5	1	1	0	0	0	0	1	1	0	0-1,D-1
L 1981	NY-A	.167	3	6	2	1	0	0	0	1	5	3	0	0-1,D-2
L **Total**	3	.211	8	19	4	4	1	0	0	2	7	5	0	....
W 1976	NY-A	.125	3	8	0	1	0	0	0	1	0	0	0	0-2
W 1981	NY-A	.333	3	6	1	2	0	0	0	1	1	0	0	0-2
W **Total**	2	.214	6	14	1	3	0	0	0	2	1	0	0	....
• GANDIL, Chick														
W 1917	Chi-A	.261	6	23	1	6	1	0	0	5	0	2	1	1-6
W 1919	Chi-A	.233	8	30	1	7	0	1	0	5	1	3	1	1-8
W **Total**	2	.245	14	53	2	13	1	1	0	10	1	5	2	....
• GANT, Ron														
D 1995	Cin-N	.231	3	13	3	3	0	0	1	2	0	3	0	0-3
D 1996	StL-N	.400	3	10	3	4	1	0	1	4	2	0	2	0-3
D 2001	Oak-A	.182	4	11	1	2	0	0	1	1	0	3	0	0-2,D-2
D **Total**	3	.265	10	34	7	9	1	0	3	7	2	6	2	....
L 1991	Atl-N	.259	7	27	4	7	1	0	1	3	2	4	7	0-7
L 1992	Atl-N	.182	7	22	5	4	0	0	2	6	4	4	1	0-7
L 1993	Atl-N	.185	6	27	4	5	3	0	0	3	2	9	0	0-6
L 1995	Cin-N	.188	4	16	1	3	0	0	0	1	0	3	0	0-4
L 1996	StL-N	.240	7	25	3	6	1	0	2	4	2	6	0	0-7
L **Total**	5	.214	31	117	17	25	5	0	5	17	10	26	8	....
W 1991	Atl-N	.267	7	30	3	8	0	1	0	4	2	3	1	0-7
W 1992	Atl-N	.125	4	8	2	1	1	0	0	0	1	2	2	0-3
W **Total**	2	.237	11	38	5	9	1	1	0	4	3	5	3	....
• GANTNER, Jim														
D 1981	Mil-A	.143	4	14	1	2	1	0	0	0	0	2	0	2-4
L 1982	Mil-A	.188	5	16	1	3	0	0	0	2	1	1	0	2-5
W 1982	Mil-A	.333	7	24	5	8	4	1	0	4	1	1	0	2-7
• GANZEL, Charlie														
T 1892	Bos-N	.500	2	8	1	4	0	0	0	2	1	0	0	C-2
W 1887	Det-N	.237	14	59	5	14	1	0	0	2	3	2	3	1-10,C-7
• GARAGIOLA, Joe														
W 1946	StL-N	.316	5	19	2	6	2	0	0	4	0	3	0	C-5
• GARBEY, Barbaro														
L 1984	Det-A	.333	3	9	1	3	0	0	0	0	0	1	0	D-2
W 1984	Det-A	.000	4	12	0	0	0	0	0	0	0	2	0	D-4
• GARCIA, Carlos														
L 1992	Pit-N	.000	1	1	0	0	0	0	0	0	0	0	0	2-1

YEAR	TM-L	AVG	G	AB	R	H	2B	3B	HR	RBI	BB	SO	SB	POS
• GARCIA, Damaso														
L 1985	Tor-A	.233	7	30	4	7	4	0	0	1	3	3	0	2-7
• GARCIA, Jesse														
D 2003	Atl-N	....	2	0	1	0	0	0	0	0	0	0	0	2-2
• GARCIA, Karim														
L 2003	NY-A	.250	5	16	1	4	0	0	0	3	2	4	0	0-5
W 2003	NY-A	.286	5	14	1	4	0	0	0	0	0	3	0	0-5
• GARCIA, Kiko														
D 1981	Hou-N	.000	2	4	0	0	0	0	0	0	0	1	0	S-1
L 1979	Bal-A	.273	3	11	1	3	0	0	0	2	2	4	0	S-3
W 1979	Bal-A	.400	6	20	4	8	2	1	0	6	1	3	0	S-6
• GARCIAPARRA, Nomar														
D 1998	Bos-A	.333	4	15	4	5	1	0	3	11	1	0	0	S-4
D 1999	Bos-A	.417	4	12	6	5	2	0	2	4	3	3	0	S-4
D 2003	Bos-A	.300	5	20	2	6	1	0	0	0	3	2	1	S-5
D **Total**	3	.340	13	47	12	16	4	0	5	15	7	5	1	....
L 1999	Bos-A	.400	5	20	2	8	2	0	2	5	2	2	1	S-5
L 2003	Bos-A	.241	7	29	2	7	0	1	0	1	2	8	0	S-7
L **Total**	2	.306	12	49	4	15	2	1	2	6	4	10	1	....
• GARDNER, Billy														
W 1961	NY-A	.000	1	1	0	0	0	0	0	0	0	0	0	....
• GARDNER, Larry														
W 1912	Bos-A	.179	8	28	4	5	2	1	1	5	2	5	0	3-8
W 1915	Bos-A	.235	5	17	2	4	0	1	0	0	1	0	0	3-5
W 1916	Bos-A	.176	5	17	2	3	0	0	2	6	0	2	0	3-5
W 1920	Cle-A	.208	7	24	1	5	1	0	0	2	1	1	0	3-7
W **Total**	4	.198	25	86	9	17	3	2	3	13	4	8	0	....
• GARMS, Debs														
W 1943	StL-N	.000	2	5	0	0	0	0	0	0	0	2	0	0-1
W 1944	StL-N	.000	2	2	0	0	0	0	0	0	0	0	0	....
W **Total**	2	.000	4	7	0	0	0	0	0	0	0	2	0	....
• GARNER, Phil														
D 1981	Hou-N	.111	5	18	1	2	0	0	0	0	3	3	0	2-5
L 1975	Oak-A	.000	3	5	0	0	0	0	0	0	0	1	0	2-3
L 1979	Pit-N	.417	3	12	4	5	0	1	1	1	1	0	0	2-3,S-1
L 1986	Hou-N	.222	3	9	1	2	1	0	0	2	1	2	0	3-3
L **Total**	3	.269	9	26	5	7	1	1	1	3	2	3	0	....
W 1979	Pit-N	.500	7	24	4	12	4	0	0	5	3	1	0	2-7
• GARRETT, Wayne														
L 1969	NY-N	.385	3	13	3	5	2	0	1	3	2	2	1	3-3
L 1973	NY-N	.087	5	23	1	2	1	0	0	1	0	5	0	3-5
L **Total**	2	.194	8	36	4	7	3	0	1	4	2	7	1	....
W 1969	NY-N	.000	2	1	0	0	0	0	0	0	2	1	0	3-2
W 1973	NY-N	.167	7	30	4	5	0	0	2	2	5	11	0	3-7
W **Total**	2	.161	9	31	4	5	0	0	2	2	7	12	0	....
• GARRIDO, Gil														
L 1969	Atl-N	.200	3	10	0	2	0	0	0	0	1	1	0	S-3
• GARVEY, Steve														
D 1981	LA-N	.368	5	19	4	7	0	1	2	4	0	2	0	1-5
L 1974	LA-N	.389	4	18	4	7	1	0	2	5	1	1	0	1-4
L 1977	LA-N	.308	4	13	2	4	0	0	0	0	2	1	1	1-4
L 1978	LA-N	.389	4	18	6	7	1	1	4	7	0	1	0	1-4
L 1981	LA-N	.286	5	21	2	6	0	0	1	2	0	4	0	1-5
L 1984	SD-N	.400	5	20	1	8	1	0	1	7	1	2	0	1-5
L **Total**	5	.356	22	90	15	32	3	1	8	21	4	9	1	....
W 1974	LA-N	.381	5	21	2	8	0	0	0	1	0	3	0	1-5
W 1977	LA-N	.375	6	24	5	9	1	1	1	3	1	4	0	1-6
W 1978	LA-N	.208	6	24	1	5	1	0	0	0	1	7	1	1-6
W 1981	LA-N	.417	6	24	3	10	1	0	0	0	2	5	0	1-6
W 1984	SD-N	.200	5	20	2	4	2	0	0	2	0	2	0	1-5
W **Total**	5	.319	28	113	13	36	5	1	1	6	4	21	1	....
• GASPAR, Rod														
L 1969	NY-N	....	3	0	0	0	0	0	0	0	0	0	0	0-3
W 1969	NY-N	.000	3	2	1	0	0	0	0	0	0	0	0	0-1
• GATES, Brent														
D 1997	Sea-A	.000	2	4	0	0	0	0	0	0	0	0	0	3-2
• GAZELLA, Mike														
W 1926	NY-A	....	1	0	0	0	0	0	0	0	0	0	0	3-1
• GEARIN, Dinty														
W 1923	NY-N	....	1	0	0	0	0	0	0	0	0	0	0	....
• GEDMAN, Rich														
L 1986	Bos-A	.357	7	28	4	10	1	0	1	6	0	4	0	C-7
L 1988	Bos-A	.357	4	14	1	5	0	0	1	1	2	1	0	C-4
L **Total**	2	.357	11	42	5	15	1	0	2	7	2	5	0	....
W 1986	Bos-A	.200	7	30	1	6	1	0	1	1	0	10	0	C-7
• GEHRIG, Lou														
W 1926	NY-A	.348	7	23	1	8	2	0	0	4	5	4	0	1-7
W 1927	NY-A	.308	4	13	2	4	2	2	0	4	3	3	0	1-4
W 1928	NY-A	.545	4	11	5	6	1	0	4	9	6	0	0	1-4
W 1932	NY-A	.529	4	17	9	9	1	0	3	8	2	1	0	1-4
W 1936	NY-A	.292	6	24	5	7	1	0	2	7	3	2	0	1-6
W 1937	NY-A	.294	5	17	4	5	1	1	1	3	5	4	0	1-5
W 1938	NY-A	.286	4	14	4	4	0	0	0	0	2	3	0	1-4
W **Total**	7	.361	34	119	30	43	8	3	10	35	26	17	0	....
• GEHRINGER, Charlie														
W 1934	Det-A	.379	7	29	5	11	1	0	1	2	3	0	1	2-7
W 1935	Det-A	.375	6	24	4	9	3	0	0	4	2	1	1	2-6

SER-YEAR	TM-L	AVG	G	AB	R	H	2B	3B	HR	RBI	BB	SO	SB	POS
W 1940	Det-A	.214	7	28	3	6	0	0	0	1	2	0	0	2-7
W Total	3	.321	20	81	12	26	4	0	1	7	7	1	2	....
• GELBERT, Charlie														
W 1930	StL-N	.353	6	17	2	6	0	1	0	2	3	3	0	S-6
W 1931	StL-N	.261	7	23	0	6	1	0	0	3	0	4	0	S-7
W Total	2	.300	13	40	2	12	1	1	0	5	3	7	0	....
• GERNERT, Dick														
W 1961	Cin-N	.000	4	4	0	0	0	0	0	0	0	1	0	....
• GERONIMO, Cesar														
D 1981	KC-A	....	1	0	0	0	0	0	0	0	0	0	0	....
L 1972	Cin-N	.100	5	20	2	2	0	0	1	1	0	2	0	O-5
L 1973	Cin-N	.067	4	15	0	1	0	0	0	0	0	7	0	O-4
L 1975	Cin-N	.000	3	10	0	0	0	0	0	1	1	6	0	O-3
L 1976	Cin-N	.182	3	11	0	2	0	1	0	2	1	3	0	O-3
L 1979	Cin-N	.143	2	7	0	1	0	0	0	0	0	5	0	O-2
L Total	5	.095	17	63	2	6	0	1	1	4	2	23	0	....
W 1972	Cin-N	.158	7	19	1	3	0	0	0	3	1	4	1	O-7
W 1975	Cin-N	.280	7	25	3	7	0	1	2	3	3	5	0	O-7
W 1976	Cin-N	.308	4	13	3	4	2	0	0	1	2	2	2	O-4
W Total	3	.246	18	57	7	14	2	1	2	7	6	11	3	....
• GESSLER, Doc														
W 1906	Chi-N	.000	2	1	0	0	0	0	0	0	1	0	0	....
• GETZ, Gus														
W 1916	Bro-N	.000	1	1	0	0	0	0	0	0	0	0	0	....
• GIAMBI, Jason														
D 2000	Oak-A	.286	5	14	2	4	0	0	0	1	7	2	0	1-5
D 2001	Oak-A	.353	5	17	2	6	0	0	1	4	4	2	0	1-5
D 2002	NY-A	.357	4	14	5	5	0	0	1	3	4	1	0	1-3,D-1
D 2003	NY-A	.250	4	16	1	4	2	0	0	2	2	5	0	....
D Total	4	.311	18	61	10	19	2	0	2	10	17	10	0	....
L 2003	NY-A	.231	7	26	4	6	0	0	3	3	4	7	0	....
W 2003	NY-A	.235	6	17	2	4	1	0	1	1	4	3	0	1-2
• GIAMBI, Jeremy														
D 2000	Oak-A	.333	4	9	1	3	0	0	0	1	2	2	0	O-2,D-2
D 2001	Oak-A	.308	5	13	0	4	1	0	0	2	1	0	1	D-5
D Total	2	.318	9	22	1	7	1	0	0	3	3	2	1	....
• GIBSON, Bob														
W 1964	StL-N	.222	3	9	1	2	0	0	0	0	0	3	0	....
W 1967	StL-N	.091	3	11	1	1	0	0	1	1	1	2	0	....
W 1968	StL-N	.125	3	8	2	1	0	0	1	2	1	2	0	....
W Total	3	.143	9	28	4	4	0	0	2	3	2	7	0	....
• GIBSON, George														
W 1909	Pit-N	.240	7	25	2	6	2	0	0	2	1	1	2	C-7
• GIBSON, Kirk														
L 1984	Det-A	.417	3	12	2	5	1	0	1	2	2	1	1	O-3
L 1987	Det-A	.286	5	21	4	6	1	0	1	4	3	8	3	O-5
L 1988	LA-N	.154	7	26	2	4	0	0	2	6	3	6	2	O-7
L Total	3	.254	15	59	8	15	2	0	4	12	8	15	6	....
W 1984	Det-A	.333	5	18	4	6	0	0	2	7	4	4	3	O-5
W 1988	LA-N	1.000	1	1	1	1	0	0	1	2	0	0	0	....
W Total	2	.368	6	19	5	7	0	0	3	9	4	4	3	....
• GIBSON, Russ														
W 1967	Bos-A	.000	2	2	0	0	0	0	0	0	0	2	0	C-2
• GIL, Benji														
D 2002	Ana-A	.800	2	5	1	4	0	0	0	1	0	0	0	2-2
L 2002	Ana-A	.000	1	2	0	0	0	0	0	0	0	1	0	2-1
W 2002	Ana-A	.800	3	5	1	4	1	0	0	0	0	1	0	2-1
• GILBERT, Billy														
W 1905	NY-N	.235	5	17	1	4	0	0	0	2	0	2	1	2-5
• GILBERT, Larry														
W 1914	Bos-N	....	1	0	0	0	0	0	0	0	1	0	0	....
• GILES, Brian														
D 1996	Cle-A	.000	1	1	0	0	0	0	0	0	0	1	0	....
D 1997	Cle-A	.143	3	7	0	1	0	0	0	0	0	1	0	O-3
D 1998	Cle-A	.200	3	10	1	2	1	0	0	0	1	4	0	O-2,D-1
D Total	3	.167	7	18	1	3	1	0	0	0	1	6	0	....
L 1997	Cle-A	.188	6	16	1	3	3	0	0	0	2	6	0	O-6
L 1998	Cle-A	.083	4	12	0	1	0	0	0	0	1	3	0	O-3
L Total	2	.143	10	28	1	4	3	0	0	0	3	9	0	....
W 1997	Cle-A	.500	5	4	1	2	1	0	0	2	4	1	0	O-2
• GILES, Marcus														
D 2001	Atl-N	.250	3	12	2	3	1	0	0	1	0	3	0	2-3
D 2002	Atl-N	.500	3	2	0	1	0	0	0	0	0	0	0	....
D 2003	Atl-N	.357	5	14	3	5	0	0	1	3	2	2	0	2-4
D Total	3	.321	11	28	5	9	1	0	1	4	2	5	0	....
L 2001	Atl-N	.200	5	20	4	4	1	0	1	1	3	4	0	2-5
• GILKEY, Bernard														
D 1999	Ari-N	.000	2	6	0	0	0	0	0	0	0	0	0	O-2
L 2001	Atl-N	.200	3	5	0	1	0	0	0	0	2	1	0	O-2
• GILLESPIE, Paul														
W 1945	Chi-N	.000	3	6	0	0	0	0	0	0	0	0	0	C-1
• GILLIAM, Jim														
W 1953	Bro-N	.296	6	27	4	8	3	0	2	4	0	2	0	2-6
W 1955	Bro-N	.292	7	24	2	7	1	0	0	3	8	1	1	O-4,2-5
W 1956	Bro-N	.083	7	24	2	2	0	0	0	2	7	3	1	O-1,2-6
W 1959	LA-N	.240	6	25	2	6	0	0	0	0	2	2	2	3-6
W 1963	LA-N	.154	4	13	3	2	0	0	0	0	3	1	0	3-4

SER-YEAR	TM-L	AVG	G	AB	R	H	2B	3B	HR	RBI	BB	SO	SB	POS
W 1965	LA-N	.214	7	28	2	6	1	0	0	2	1	0	0	3-7
W 1966	LA-N	.000	2	6	0	0	0	0	0	1	2	0	0	3-2
W Total	7	.211	39	147	15	31	5	0	2	12	23	9	4	....
• GILLIGAN, Barney														
W 1884	Pro-N	.444	3	9	3	4	2	0	0	2	0	1	0	C-3
• GIONFRIDDO, Al														
W 1947	Bro-N	.000	4	3	2	0	0	0	0	0	1	0	1	O-1
• GIPSON, Charles														
D 2001	Sea-A	.000	1	1	0	0	0	0	0	0	0	0	0	....
L 2000	Sea-A	....	2	0	0	0	0	0	0	0	0	0	0	O-2
L 2001	Sea-A	.000	2	1	1	0	0	0	0	0	0	0	0	O-1,D-1
L Total	2	.000	4	1	1	0	0	0	0	0	0	0	0	....
• GIRARDI, Joe														
D 1995	Col-N	.125	4	16	0	2	0	0	0	0	0	2	0	C-4
D 1996	NY-A	.222	4	9	1	2	0	0	0	0	4	1	0	C-4
D 1997	NY-A	.133	5	15	2	2	0	0	0	0	1	3	0	C-5
D 1998	NY-A	.429	2	7	0	3	0	0	0	0	0	1	0	C-2
D 1999	NY-A	.000	2	6	0	0	0	0	0	0	0	1	0	C-2
D Total	5	.170	17	53	3	9	0	0	0	0	5	8	0	....
L 1989	Chi-N	.100	4	10	1	1	0	0	0	0	1	2	0	C-4
L 1996	NY-A	.250	4	12	1	3	0	1	0	0	1	3	0	C-4
L 1998	NY-A	.250	3	8	2	2	0	0	0	0	1	0	0	C-3
L 1999	NY-A	.250	3	8	0	2	0	0	0	0	0	2	0	C-3
L Total	4	.211	14	38	4	8	0	1	0	0	3	7	0	....
W 1996	NY-A	.200	4	10	1	2	0	1	0	1	1	2	0	C-4
W 1998	NY-A	.000	2	6	0	0	0	0	0	0	0	2	0	C-2
W 1999	NY-A	.286	2	7	1	2	0	0	0	0	0	1	0	C-2
W Total	3	.174	8	23	2	4	0	1	0	1	1	5	0	....
• GLADDEN, Dan														
L 1987	Min-A	.350	5	20	5	7	2	0	0	5	2	1	0	O-5
L 1991	Min-A	.261	5	23	4	6	0	0	0	3	1	3	3	O-5
L Total	2	.302	10	43	9	13	2	0	0	8	3	4	3	....
W 1987	Min-A	.290	7	31	3	9	2	1	1	7	3	4	2	O-7
W 1991	Min-A	.233	7	30	5	7	2	2	0	0	3	4	2	O-7
W Total	2	.262	14	61	8	16	4	3	1	7	6	8	4	....
• GLANVILLE, Doug														
D 2003	Chi-N	.000	2	1	1	0	0	0	0	0	0	0	0	....
L 2003	Chi-N	1.000	1	1	0	1	0	1	0	1	0	0	0	O-1
• GLAUS, Troy														
D 2002	Ana-A	.313	4	16	4	5	0	0	3	3	1	3	0	3-4
L 2002	Ana-A	.316	5	19	4	6	0	1	1	2	2	5	0	3-5
W 2002	Ana-A	.385	7	26	7	10	3	0	3	8	4	6	0	3-7
• GLEASON, Bill														
W 1885	StL-A	.231	7	26	5	6	2	0	0	0	1	0	0	S-7
W 1886	StL-A	.208	6	24	3	5	0	0	0	5	1	3	1	S-6
W 1887	StL-A	.212	13	52	3	11	0	0	0	1	3	2	1	S-13
W Total	3	.216	26	102	11	22	2	0	0	6	5	5	2	....
• GLEASON, Kid														
T 1894	Bal-N	.200	2	5	0	1	0	1	0	1	0	1	0	P-2
T 1895	Bal-N	.105	5	19	0	2	0	0	0	0	0	1	0	2-5
T Total	2	.125	7	24	0	3	0	1	0	1	0	2	0	....
• GLYNN, Bill														
W 1954	Cle-A	.500	2	2	1	1	1	0	0	0	0	1	0	1-1
• GOLIAT, Mike														
W 1950	Phi-N	.214	4	14	1	3	0	0	0	1	1	2	0	2-4
• GOLTZ, Dave														
L 1982	Cal-A	....	1	0	0	0	0	0	0	0	0	0	0	....
W 1981	LA-N	....	2	0	0	0	0	0	0	0	0	0	0	....
• GOMEZ, Chris														
D 1996	SD-N	.167	3	12	0	2	0	0	0	1	0	4	0	S-3
D 1998	SD-N	.273	4	11	1	3	0	0	0	0	4	1	0	S-4
D 2003	Min-A	....	1	0	0	0	0	0	0	0	0	0	0	2-1
D Total	3	.217	8	23	1	5	0	0	0	1	4	5	0	....
L 1998	SD-N	.150	6	20	2	3	1	0	0	0	2	5	0	S-6
W 1998	SD-N	.364	4	11	2	4	0	1	0	0	1	1	0	S-4
• GONZALES, Rene														
D 1996	Tex-A	....	1	0	0	0	0	0	0	0	0	0	0	S-1
L 1991	Tor-A	....	2	0	0	0	0	0	0	0	0	0	0	1-1,S-1
• GONZALEZ, Alex														
D 2003	Fla-N	.063	4	16	2	1	0	0	0	0	1	3	0	S-4
L 2003	Fla-N	.125	7	24	1	3	2	0	0	4	0	6	0	S-7
W 2003	Fla-N	.273	6	22	3	6	2	0	1	2	0	7	0	S-6
• GONZALEZ, Alex														
D 2003	Chi-N	.250	5	12	1	3	0	0	1	1	2	3	0	S-5
L 2003	Chi-N	.286	7	28	5	8	2	0	3	7	2	7	0	S-7
• GONZALEZ, Jose														
L 1988	LA-N	....	5	0	2	0	0	0	0	0	0	0	0	O-4
W 1988	LA-N	.000	4	2	0	0	0	0	0	0	0	2	0	O-3
• GONZALEZ, Juan														
D 1996	Tex-A	.438	4	16	5	7	0	0	5	9	3	2	0	O-4
D 1998	Tex-A	.083	3	12	1	1	1	0	0	0	0	3	0	O-3
D 1999	Tex-A	.182	3	11	1	2	0	0	1	1	1	3	0	O-3
D 2001	Cle-A	.348	5	23	4	8	3	0	2	5	0	7	0	O-5
D Total	4	.290	15	62	11	18	4	0	8	15	4	15	0	....
• GONZALEZ, Luis														
D 1997	Hou-N	.333	3	12	0	4	0	0	0	0	0	1	0	O-3
D 1999	Ari-N	.200	4	10	3	2	1	0	1	2	5	1	0	O-4

YEAR	TM-L	AVG	G	AB	R	H	2B	3B	HR	RBI	BB	SO	SB	POS
D 2001	Ari-N	.263	5	19	1	5	0	0	1	1	2	4	0	0-5
D Total	3	.268	12	41	4	11	1	0	2	3	7	6	0	....
L 2001	Ari-N	.211	5	19	4	4	0	0	1	4	3	3	0	0-5
W 2001	Ari-N	.259	7	27	4	7	2	0	1	5	1	11	0	0-7
• GONZALEZ, Mike														
W 1929	Chi-N	.000	2	1	0	0	0	0	0	0	0	1	0	C-1
• GONZALEZ, Orlando														
L 1978	Phi-N	.000	1	1	0	0	0	0	0	0	0	1	0	....
• GONZALEZ, Pedro														
W 1964	NY-A	.000	1	1	0	0	0	0	0	0	0	0	0	3-1
• GONZALEZ, Tony														
L 1969	Atl-N	.357	3	14	4	5	1	0	1	2	1	4	0	0-3
• GOOCH, Johnny														
W 1925	Pit-N	.000	3	3	0	0	0	0	0	0	0	0	0	C-3
W 1927	Pit-N	.000	3	5	0	0	0	0	0	0	1	1	0	C-3
W Total	2	.000	6	8	0	0	0	0	0	0	1	1	0	....
• GOODMAN, Billy														
W 1959	Chi-A	.231	5	13	1	3	0	0	0	1	0	5	0	3-5
• GOODMAN, Ival														
W 1939	Cin-N	.333	4	15	3	5	1	0	0	1	1	2	1	0-4
W 1940	Cin-N	.276	7	29	5	8	2	0	0	5	0	3	0	0-7
W Total	2	.295	11	44	8	13	3	0	0	6	1	5	1	....
• GOODSON, Ed														
L 1977	LA-N	.000	1	1	0	0	0	0	0	0	0	0	0	....
W 1977	LA-N	.000	1	1	0	0	0	0	0	0	0	1	0	....
• GOODWIN, Tom														
D 1998	Tex-A	.250	2	4	0	1	0	0	0	0	0	1	0	0-2
D 1999	Tex-A	.143	3	7	0	1	0	0	0	0	0	1	0	0-3
D 2002	SF-N	.000	2	2	0	0	0	0	0	0	0	2	0	....
D 2003	Chi-N	1.000	2	1	0	1	1	0	0	2	0	0	0	....
D Total	4	.214	9	14	0	3	1	0	0	2	0	4	0	....
L 2002	SF-N	.000	2	3	0	0	0	0	0	0	0	2	0	0-2
L 2003	Chi-N	.250	5	4	1	1	0	1	0	0	0	3	0	0-1
L Total	2	.143	7	7	1	1	0	1	0	0	0	5	0	....
W 2002	SF-N	.000	5	4	0	0	0	0	0	0	1	2	1	0-2,D-2
• GORDON, Joe														
W 1938	NY-A	.400	4	15	3	6	2	0	1	6	1	3	1	2-4
W 1939	NY-A	.143	4	14	1	2	0	0	1	1	0	2	0	2-4
W 1941	NY-A	.500	5	14	2	7	1	1	1	5	7	0	0	2-5
W 1942	NY-A	.095	5	21	1	2	1	0	0	0	0	7	0	2-5
W 1943	NY-A	.235	5	17	2	4	1	0	1	2	3	3	0	2-5
W 1948	Cle-A	.182	6	22	3	4	0	0	1	2	1	2	1	2-6
W Total	6	.243	29	103	12	25	5	1	4	16	12	17	2	....
• GORE, George														
W 1885	Chi-N	.000	1	3	1	0	0	0	0	0	1	0	0	0-1
W 1886	Chi-N	.174	6	23	4	4	0	0	1	2	3	3	0	0-6
W 1888	NY-N	.455	3	11	5	5	1	0	0	0	2	2	2	0-2,3-1
W 1889	NY-N	.333	5	21	5	7	1	1	0	1	3	0	2	0-5
W Total	4	.276	15	58	15	16	2	1	1	3	9	5	4	....
• GORMAN, Tom														
W 1952	NY-A	....	1	0	0	0	0	0	0	0	0	0	0	....
W 1953	NY-A	.000	1	1	0	0	0	0	0	0	0	1	0	....
W Total	2	.000	2	1	0	0	0	0	0	0	0	1	0	....
• GOSLIN, Goose														
W 1924	Was-A	.344	7	32	4	11	1	0	3	7	0	7	0	0-7
W 1925	Was-A	.308	7	26	6	8	1	0	3	6	3	3	0	0-7
W 1933	Was-A	.250	5	20	2	5	1	0	1	1	1	3	0	0-5
W 1934	Det-A	.241	7	29	2	7	1	0	0	2	3	1	0	0-7
W 1935	Det-A	.273	6	22	2	6	1	0	0	3	5	0	0	0-6
W Total	5	.287	32	129	16	37	5	0	7	19	12	14	0	....
• GOWDY, Hank														
W 1914	Bos-N	.545	4	11	3	6	3	1	1	3	5	1	1	C-4
W 1923	NY-N	.000	3	4	0	0	0	0	0	0	1	0	0	C-2
W 1924	NY-N	.259	7	27	4	7	0	0	0	1	2	2	0	C-7
W Total	3	.310	14	42	7	13	3	1	1	4	8	3	1	....
• GRABOWSKI, Johnny														
W 1927	NY-A	.000	1	2	0	0	0	0	0	0	0	0	0	C-1
• GRACE, Mark														
D 1998	Chi-N	.083	3	12	0	1	0	0	0	1	0	2	0	1-3
D 2001	Ari-N	.214	4	14	0	3	1	0	0	0	2	3	0	1-4
D 2002	Ari-N	.250	2	4	0	1	0	0	0	0	1	0	0	1-2
D Total	3	.167	9	30	0	5	1	0	0	1	3	5	0	....
L 1989	Chi-N	.647	5	17	3	11	3	1	1	8	4	1	1	1-5
L 2001	Ari-N	.375	5	16	1	6	0	0	0	1	2	1	0	1-5
L Total	2	.515	10	33	4	17	3	1	1	9	6	2	1	....
W 2001	Ari-N	.263	6	19	1	5	1	0	1	3	4	1	0	1-6
• GRAFFANINO, Tony														
D 1997	Atl-N	.000	3	3	0	0	0	0	0	0	2	1	0	2-3
D 1998	Atl-N	....	1	0	0	0	0	0	0	0	0	0	0	....
D 2000	Chi-A	....	1	0	0	0	0	0	0	0	0	0	0	3-1
D Total	3	.000	5	3	0	0	0	0	0	0	2	1	0	....
L 1997	Atl-N	.250	3	8	1	2	1	0	0	0	0	3	0	2-3
L 1998	Atl-N	.333	4	3	2	1	1	0	0	1	2	1	0	2-3
L Total	2	.273	7	11	3	3	2	0	0	1	2	4	0	....
• GRANEY, Jack														
W 1920	Cle-A	.000	3	3	0	0	0	0	0	0	0	2	0	0-2
• GRANT, Eddie														
W 1913	NY-N	.000	2	1	1	0	0	0	0	0	0	0	0	....
• GRANTHAM, George														
W 1925	Pit-N	.133	5	15	0	2	0	0	0	0	0	3	1	1-4
W 1927	Pit-N	.364	3	11	0	4	1	0	0	0	1	1	0	2-3
W Total	2	.231	8	26	0	6	1	0	0	0	1	4	1	....
• GRASSO, Mickey														
W 1954	Cle-A	....	1	0	0	0	0	0	0	0	0	0	0	C-1
• GRBA, Eli														
W 1960	NY-A	....	1	0	0	0	0	0	0	0	0	0	0	....
• GREBECK, Craig														
L 1993	Chi-A	1.000	1	1	0	1	0	0	0	0	0	0	0	3-1
• GREEN, David														
L 1982	StL-N	1.000	2	1	1	1	0	0	0	0	0	0	0	0-2
W 1982	StL-N	.200	7	10	3	2	1	1	0	0	1	3	0	0-4,D-3
• GREEN, Dick														
L 1971	Oak-A	.286	3	7	0	2	0	0	0	0	1	1	0	2-3
L 1972	Oak-A	.125	5	8	0	1	1	0	0	0	0	0	0	2-5
L 1973	Oak-A	.077	5	13	0	1	1	0	0	1	0	4	0	2-5
L 1974	Oak-A	.222	4	9	0	2	0	0	0	0	2	1	0	2-4
L Total	4	.162	17	37	0	6	2	0	0	1	3	6	0	....
W 1972	Oak-A	.333	7	18	0	6	2	0	0	1	0	4	0	2-7
W 1973	Oak-A	.063	7	16	0	1	0	0	0	0	1	6	0	2-7
W 1974	Oak-A	.000	5	13	1	0	0	0	0	1	1	4	0	2-5
W Total	3	.149	19	47	1	7	2	0	0	2	2	14	0	....
• GREENBERG, Hank														
W 1934	Det-A	.321	7	28	4	9	2	1	1	7	4	9	1	1-7
W 1935	Det-A	.167	2	6	1	1	0	0	1	2	1	0	0	1-2
W 1940	Det-A	.357	7	28	5	10	2	1	1	6	2	5	0	0-7
W 1945	Det-A	.304	7	23	7	7	3	0	2	7	6	5	0	0-7
W Total	4	.318	23	85	17	27	7	2	5	22	13	19	1	....
• GREENE, Todd														
L 2001	NY-A	.000	1	1	0	0	0	0	0	0	0	0	0	C-1
W 2001	NY-A	.500	1	2	1	1	1	0	0	0	0	0	0	C-1
• GREENWELL, Mike														
D 1995	Bos-A	.200	3	15	0	3	0	0	0	0	0	1	0	0-3
L 1986	Bos-A	.500	2	2	0	1	0	0	0	0	0	0	0	....
L 1988	Bos-A	.214	4	14	2	3	1	0	1	3	3	0	0	0-4
L 1990	Bos-A	.000	4	14	1	0	0	0	0	0	2	2	0	0-4
L Total	3	.133	10	30	3	4	1	0	1	3	5	2	0	....
W 1986	Bos-A	.000	4	3	0	0	0	0	0	0	1	2	0	....
• GREER, Rusty														
D 1996	Tex-A	.125	4	16	2	2	0	0	0	0	3	3	0	0-4
D 1998	Tex-A	.091	3	11	0	1	0	0	0	0	1	2	0	0-3
D 1999	Tex-A	.111	3	9	0	1	0	0	0	0	3	1	0	0-3
D Total	3	.111	10	36	2	4	0	0	0	0	7	6	0	....
• GREGG, Tommy														
L 1991	Atl-N	.250	4	4	0	1	0	0	0	0	0	2	0	....
L 1997	Atl-N	.000	4	4	0	0	0	0	0	0	0	1	0	....
L Total	2	.125	8	8	0	1	0	0	0	0	0	3	0	....
W 1991	Atl-N	.000	4	3	0	0	0	0	0	0	0	1	0	....
• GRICH, Bobby														
L 1973	Bal-A	.100	5	20	1	2	0	0	1	1	2	5	0	2-5
L 1974	Bal-A	.250	4	16	2	4	1	0	1	2	0	1	0	2-4
L 1979	Cal-A	.154	4	13	0	2	1	0	0	2	1	1	0	2-4
L 1982	Cal-A	.200	5	15	1	3	1	0	0	1	2	7	0	2-5
L 1986	Cal-A	.208	6	24	1	5	0	0	1	3	0	8	0	1-3,2-3
L Total	5	.182	24	88	5	16	3	0	3	9	5	22	0	....
• GRIEVE, Ben														
D 2000	Oak-A	.118	5	17	1	2	0	0	0	2	3	7	0	0-5
• GRIFFEY JR., Ken														
D 1995	Sea-A	.391	5	23	9	9	0	0	5	7	2	4	1	0-5
D 1997	Sea-A	.133	4	15	0	2	0	0	0	2	1	3	2	0-4
D Total	2	.289	9	38	9	11	0	0	5	9	3	7	3	....
L 1995	Sea-A	.333	6	21	2	7	2	0	1	2	4	4	2	0-6
• GRIFFEY SR., Ken														
L 1973	Cin-N	.143	3	7	0	1	1	0	0	0	0	1	0	0-2
L 1975	Cin-N	.333	3	12	3	4	1	0	0	4	0	3	0	0-3
L 1976	Cin-N	.385	3	13	2	5	0	1	0	2	2	1	2	0-3
L Total	3	.313	9	32	5	10	2	1	0	6	2	5	5	....
W 1975	Cin-N	.269	7	26	4	7	3	1	0	4	4	2	2	0-7
W 1976	Cin-N	.059	4	17	2	1	0	0	0	1	0	1	1	0-4
W Total	2	.186	11	43	6	8	3	1	0	5	4	3	3	....
• GRIFFIN, Alfredo														
L 1988	LA-N	.160	7	25	1	4	1	0	0	3	0	5	0	S-7
L 1992	Tor-A	.000	2	2	0	0	0	0	0	0	0	0	0	S-1
L Total	2	.148	9	27	1	4	1	0	0	3	0	5	0	....
W 1988	LA-N	.188	5	16	2	3	0	0	0	0	2	4	0	S-5
W 1992	Tor-A	....	2	0	0	0	0	0	0	0	0	0	0	S-2
W 1993	Tor-A	....	3	0	0	0	0	0	0	0	0	0	0	3-2
W Total	3	.188	10	16	2	3	0	0	0	0	2	4	0	....
• GRIFFIN, Doug														
W 1975	Bos-A	.000	1	1	0	0	0	0	0	0	0	0	0	....
• GRIFFITH, Tommy														
W 1920	Bro-N	.190	7	21	1	4	2	0	0	3	0	2	0	0-7

SER-YEAR	TM-L	AVG	G	AB	R	H	2B	3B	HR	RBI	BB	SO	SB	POS
• GRIMM, Charlie														
W 1929	Chi-N	.389	5	18	2	7	0	0	1	4	1	2	0	1-5
W 1932	Chi-N	.333	4	15	2	5	2	0	0	1	2	2	0	1-4
W Total	**2**	**.364**	**9**	**33**	**4**	**12**	**2**	**0**	**1**	**5**	**3**	**4**	**0**	....
• GRISSOM, Marquis														
D 1995	Atl-N	.524	4	21	5	11	2	0	3	4	0	3	2	0-4
D 1996	Atl-N	.083	3	12	2	1	0	0	0	0	1	2	1	0-3
D 1997	Cle-A	.235	5	17	3	4	0	1	0	0	1	2	0	0-5
D 2003	SF-N	.143	4	14	1	2	0	0	0	1	2	5	0	0-4
D Total	**4**	**.281**	**16**	**64**	**11**	**18**	**2**	**1**	**3**	**5**	**4**	**12**	**3**	....
L 1995	Atl-N	.263	4	19	2	5	0	1	0	0	1	4	0	0-4
L 1996	Atl-N	.286	7	35	7	10	1	0	1	3	0	8	2	0-7
L 1997	Cle-A	.261	6	23	2	6	0	0	1	4	1	9	3	0-6
L Total	**3**	**.273**	**17**	**77**	**11**	**21**	**1**	**1**	**2**	**7**	**2**	**21**	**5**	....
W 1995	Atl-N	.360	6	25	3	9	1	0	0	1	1	3	3	0-6
W 1996	Atl-N	.444	6	27	4	12	2	1	0	5	1	2	1	0-6
W 1997	Cle-A	.360	7	25	5	9	1	0	0	2	4	4	0	0-7
W Total	**3**	**.390**	**19**	**77**	**12**	**30**	**4**	**1**	**0**	**8**	**6**	**9**	**4**	....
• GROAT, Dick														
W 1960	Pit-N	.214	7	28	3	6	2	0	0	2	0	1	0	S-7
W 1964	StL-N	.192	7	26	3	5	1	1	0	1	4	3	0	S-7
W Total	**2**	**.204**	**14**	**54**	**6**	**11**	**3**	**1**	**0**	**3**	**4**	**4**	**0**	....
• GROH, Heinie														
W 1919	Cin-N	.172	8	29	6	5	2	0	0	2	6	4	0	3-8
W 1922	NY-N	.474	5	19	4	9	0	1	0	0	2	1	0	3-5
W 1923	NY-N	.182	6	22	3	4	0	1	0	2	3	1	0	3-6
W 1924	NY-N	1.000	1	1	0	1	0	0	0	0	0	0	0	....
W 1927	Pit-N	.000	1	1	0	0	0	0	0	0	0	0	0	....
W Total	**5**	**.264**	**21**	**72**	**13**	**19**	**2**	**2**	**0**	**4**	**11**	**6**	**0**	....
• GROSS, Greg														
D 1981	Phi-N	.000	4	4	0	0	0	0	0	0	0	0	0	0-2
L 1980	Phi-N	.750	4	4	2	3	0	0	0	1	0	0	0	0-1
L 1983	Phi-N	.000	4	5	1	0	0	0	0	0	2	2	0	0-3
L Total	**2**	**.333**	**8**	**9**	**3**	**3**	**0**	**0**	**0**	**1**	**2**	**2**	**0**	....
W 1980	Phi-N	.000	4	2	0	0	0	0	0	0	0	0	0	0-3
W 1983	Phi-N	.000	2	6	0	0	0	0	0	0	0	0	0	0-2
W Total	**2**	**.000**	**6**	**8**	**0**	**0**	**0**	**0**	**0**	**0**	**0**	**0**	**0**	....
• GROSS, Wayne														
D 1981	Oak-A	.400	2	5	1	2	0	0	1	3	0	0	0	3-1
L 1981	Oak-A	.000	3	5	0	0	0	0	0	0	0	0	0	3-3
• GROTE, Jerry														
L 1969	NY-N	.167	3	12	3	2	1	0	0	1	1	4	0	C-3
L 1973	NY-N	.211	5	19	2	4	0	0	0	2	1	3	0	C-5
L 1977	LA-N	....	2	0	0	0	0	0	0	0	1	0	0	C-1
L 1978	LA-N	....	1	0	0	0	0	0	0	0	0	0	0	C-1
L Total	**4**	**.194**	**11**	**31**	**5**	**6**	**1**	**0**	**0**	**3**	**3**	**7**	**0**	....
W 1969	NY-N	.211	5	19	1	4	2	0	0	1	1	3	0	C-5
W 1973	NY-N	.267	7	30	2	8	0	0	0	0	0	1	0	C-7
W 1977	LA-N	.000	1	1	0	0	0	0	0	0	0	0	0	C-1
W 1978	LA-N	....	2	0	0	0	0	0	0	0	0	0	0	C-2
W Total	**4**	**.240**	**15**	**50**	**3**	**12**	**2**	**0**	**0**	**1**	**1**	**4**	**0**	....
• GRUBB, Johnny														
L 1984	Det-A	.250	1	4	0	1	1	0	0	2	0	0	0	D-1
L 1987	Det-A	.571	4	7	0	4	0	0	0	0	0	1	0	D-1
L Total	**2**	**.455**	**5**	**11**	**0**	**5**	**1**	**0**	**0**	**2**	**0**	**1**	**0**	....
W 1984	Det-A	.333	4	3	0	1	0	0	0	0	0	0	0	D-3
• GRUBER, Kelly														
L 1989	Tor-A	.294	5	17	2	5	1	0	0	1	3	2	1	3-5
L 1991	Tor-A	.286	5	21	1	6	1	0	0	4	0	4	1	3-5
L 1992	Tor-A	.091	6	22	3	2	1	0	1	2	2	3	0	3-6
L Total	**3**	**.217**	**16**	**60**	**6**	**13**	**3**	**0**	**1**	**7**	**5**	**9**	**2**	....
W 1992	Tor-A	.105	6	19	2	2	0	0	1	1	2	5	1	3-6
• GRUDZIELANEK, Mark														
D 2003	Chi-N	.150	5	20	2	3	0	0	0	0	3	4	0	2-5
L 2003	Chi-N	.200	7	30	2	6	1	1	0	3	0	5	0	2-7
• GRYBOSKI, Kevin														
D 2002	Atl-N	....	3	0	0	0	0	0	0	0	0	0	0	....
D 2003	Atl-N	....	5	0	0	0	0	0	0	0	0	0	0	....
D Total	**2**	....	**8**	**0**	**0**	**0**	**0**	**0**	**0**	**0**	**0**	**0**	**0**	....
• GUDAT, Marv														
W 1932	Chi-N	.000	2	2	0	0	0	0	0	0	0	1	0	....
• GUERRERO, Pedro														
D 1981	LA-N	.176	5	17	1	3	1	0	1	1	2	4	1	3-5
L 1981	LA-N	.105	5	19	1	2	0	0	1	2	1	4	0	0-5
L 1983	LA-N	.250	4	12	1	3	1	1	0	2	3	3	0	3-4
L 1985	LA-N	.250	6	20	2	5	1	0	0	4	5	2	2	0-6
L Total	**3**	**.196**	**15**	**51**	**4**	**10**	**2**	**1**	**1**	**8**	**9**	**9**	**2**	....
W 1981	LA-N	.333	6	21	2	7	1	1	2	7	2	6	0	0-6
• GUILLEN, Carlos														
D 2000	Sea-A	1.000	1	1	0	1	0	0	0	1	0	0	0	....
L 2000	Sea-A	.200	2	5	1	1	0	0	1	2	2	2	0	3-2
L 2001	Sea-A	.250	3	8	1	2	0	0	0	0	0	1	0	S-3
L Total	**2**	**.231**	**5**	**13**	**2**	**3**	**0**	**0**	**1**	**2**	**2**	**3**	**0**	....
• GUILLEN, Jose														
D 2003	Oak-A	.455	4	11	1	5	1	0	0	1	3	2	0	0-4
• GUILLEN, Ozzie														
D 1998	Atl-N	.000	1	1	0	0	0	0	0	0	0	0	0	....
D 1999	Atl-N	.000	1	1	0	0	0	0	0	0	0	0	0	....
D Total	**2**	**.000**	**2**	**2**	**0**	**0**	**0**	**0**	**0**	**0**	**0**	**0**	**0**	....
L 1993	Chi-A	.273	6	22	4	6	1	0	0	2	0	2	1	S-6
L 1998	Atl-N	.417	4	12	1	5	0	0	0	1	0	1	0	S-3
L 1999	Atl-N	.333	3	3	0	1	0	0	0	1	0	0	0	S-2
L Total	**3**	**.324**	**13**	**37**	**5**	**12**	**1**	**0**	**0**	**4**	**0**	**3**	**1**	....
W 1999	Atl-N	.000	3	5	0	0	0	0	0	0	0	1	0	S-1,D-1
• GUMBERT, Harry														
W 1936	NY-N	....	2	0	0	0	0	0	0	0	0	0	0	....
W 1937	NY-N	....	2	0	0	0	0	0	0	0	0	0	0	....
W 1942	StL-N	....	2	0	0	0	0	0	0	0	0	0	0	....
W Total	**3**	....	**6**	**0**	**0**	**0**	**0**	**0**	**0**	**0**	**0**	**0**	**0**	....
• GUTIERREZ, Ricky														
D 1997	Hou-N	.125	3	8	0	1	0	0	0	0	2	1	0	S-3
D 1998	Hou-N	.300	4	10	1	3	0	0	0	0	3	7	1	S-4
D 1999	Hou-N	.000	3	10	0	0	0	0	0	0	2	5	0	S-3
D Total	**3**	**.143**	**10**	**28**	**1**	**4**	**0**	**0**	**0**	**0**	**7**	**13**	**1**	....
• GUTTERIDGE, Don														
W 1944	StL-A	.143	6	21	1	3	1	0	0	0	3	5	0	2-6
W 1946	Bos-A	.400	3	5	1	2	0	0	0	1	0	0	0	2-2
W Total	**2**	**.192**	**9**	**26**	**2**	**5**	**1**	**0**	**0**	**1**	**3**	**5**	**0**	....
• GUZMAN, Cristian														
D 2002	Min-A	.286	5	21	5	6	2	0	1	2	2	4	2	S-5
D 2003	Min-A	.154	4	13	1	2	0	0	0	0	1	2	0	S-4
D Total	**2**	**.235**	**9**	**34**	**6**	**8**	**2**	**0**	**1**	**2**	**3**	**6**	**2**	....
L 2002	Min-A	.167	5	18	1	3	1	0	0	0	0	3	0	S-5
• GWYNN, Chris														
D 1995	LA-N	.000	1	1	0	0	0	0	0	0	0	1	0	....
D 1996	SD-N	1.000	2	2	1	2	0	0	0	0	0	0	0	....
D Total	**2**	**.667**	**3**	**3**	**1**	**2**	**0**	**0**	**0**	**0**	**0**	**1**	**0**	....
• GWYNN, Tony														
D 1996	SD-N	.308	3	13	0	4	1	0	0	1	0	2	1	0-3
D 1998	SD-N	.200	4	15	1	3	2	0	0	2	0	2	0	0-4
D Total	**2**	**.250**	**7**	**28**	**1**	**7**	**3**	**0**	**0**	**3**	**0**	**4**	**1**	....
L 1984	SD-N	.368	5	19	6	7	3	0	0	3	1	2	0	0-5
L 1998	SD-N	.231	6	26	1	6	1	0	0	2	1	2	0	0-6
L Total	**2**	**.289**	**11**	**45**	**7**	**13**	**4**	**0**	**0**	**5**	**2**	**4**	**0**	....
W 1984	SD-N	.263	5	19	1	5	0	0	0	0	3	2	1	0-5
W 1998	SD-N	.500	4	16	2	8	0	0	1	3	1	0	0	0-4
W Total	**2**	**.371**	**9**	**35**	**3**	**13**	**0**	**0**	**1**	**3**	**4**	**2**	**1**	....
• HAAS, Mule														
W 1929	Phi-A	.238	5	21	3	5	0	0	2	6	1	3	0	0-5
W 1930	Phi-A	.111	6	18	1	2	0	1	0	1	1	3	0	0-6
W 1931	Phi-A	.130	7	23	1	3	1	0	0	2	3	5	0	0-7
W Total	**3**	**.161**	**18**	**62**	**5**	**10**	**1**	**1**	**2**	**9**	**5**	**11**	**0**	....
• HACK, Stan														
W 1932	Chi-N	....	1	0	0	0	0	0	0	0	0	0	0	....
W 1935	Chi-N	.227	6	22	2	5	1	1	0	0	2	2	1	3-6,S-1
W 1938	Chi-N	.471	4	17	3	8	1	0	0	1	1	2	0	3-4
W 1945	Chi-N	.367	7	30	1	11	3	0	0	4	4	2	0	3-7
W Total	**4**	**.348**	**18**	**69**	**6**	**24**	**5**	**1**	**0**	**5**	**7**	**6**	**1**	....
• HAFEY, Chick														
W 1926	StL-N	.185	7	27	2	5	2	0	0	0	0	7	0	0-7
W 1928	StL-N	.200	4	15	0	3	0	0	0	0	1	4	0	0-4
W 1930	StL-N	.273	6	22	2	6	5	0	0	2	1	3	0	0-6
W 1931	StL-N	.167	6	24	1	4	0	0	0	0	0	5	1	0-6
W Total	**4**	**.205**	**23**	**88**	**5**	**18**	**7**	**0**	**0**	**2**	**2**	**19**	**1**	....
• HAGUE, Joe														
L 1972	Cin-N	....	2	0	0	0	0	0	0	0	2	0	0	....
W 1972	Cin-N	.000	3	3	0	0	0	0	0	0	0	0	0	0-1
• HAHN, Don														
L 1973	NY-N	.235	5	17	2	4	0	0	0	1	2	4	0	0-5
W 1973	NY-N	.241	7	29	2	7	1	1	0	2	1	6	0	0-7
• HAHN, Ed														
W 1906	Chi-A	.273	6	22	4	6	0	0	0	0	1	1	0	0-6
• HAINES, Hinkey														
W 1923	NY-A	.000	2	1	1	0	0	0	0	0	0	0	0	0-2
• HAIRSTON, Jerry														
L 1983	Chi-A	.000	2	3	0	0	0	0	0	0	1	1	0	0-2
• HALL, Jimmie														
W 1965	Min-A	.143	2	7	0	1	0	0	0	0	1	5	0	0-2
• HALLER, Tom														
L 1972	Det-A	.000	1	1	0	0	0	0	0	0	0	0	0	....
W 1962	SF-N	.286	4	14	1	4	1	0	1	3	0	2	0	C-4
• HAMBURG, Charlie														
W 1890	Lou-A	.269	7	26	3	7	1	0	0	2	0	3	0	0-7
• HAMILTON, Billy														
T 1897	Bos-N	.500	4	16	6	8	1	0	0	2	5	3	2	0-4
• HAMILTON, Darryl														
D 1996	Tex-A	.158	4	19	0	3	0	0	0	0	0	2	0	0-4
D 1997	SF-N	.000	2	5	1	0	0	0	0	0	0	1	0	0-2
D 1999	NY-N	.125	4	8	0	1	0	0	0	2	2	0	0	0-4
D 2000	NY-N	.500	3	4	1	2	1	0	0	0	1	1	0	0-3
D Total	**4**	**.167**	**13**	**36**	**2**	**6**	**1**	**0**	**0**	**2**	**3**	**4**	**0**	....
L 1999	NY-N	.353	5	17	0	6	1	0	0	2	0	4	0	0-5

YEAR	TM-L	AVG	G	AB	R	H	2B	3B	HR	RBI	BB	SO	SB	POS
L 2000	NY-N	.000	3	2	0	0	0	0	0	0	0	0	0	....
L Total	2	.316	8	19	0	6	1	0	0	2	0	4	0	....
W 2000	NY-N	.000	4	3	0	0	0	0	0	0	0	2	0	....
• HAMILTON, Jeff														
L 1988	LA-N	.217	7	23	2	5	0	0	0	1	3	4	0	3-7
W 1988	LA-N	.105	5	19	1	2	0	0	0	0	1	4	0	3-5
• HAMMONDS, Jeffrey														
D 1997	Bal-A	.100	4	10	3	1	1	0	0	2	2	2	1	0-4
D 2003	SF-N	.400	3	5	1	2	0	0	0	0	1	0	0	0-1
D Total	2	.200	7	15	4	3	1	0	0	2	3	2	1	....
L 1997	Bal-A	.000	5	3	0	0	0	0	0	0	1	2	1	0-4
• HAMNER, Granny														
W 1950	Phi-N	.429	4	14	1	6	2	1	0	0	1	2	1	S-4
• HANEBRINK, Harry														
W 1958	Mil-N	.000	2	2	0	0	0	0	0	0	0	0	0	....
• HANEY, Larry														
W 1974	Oak-A	....	2	0	0	0	0	0	0	0	0	0	0	C-2
• HANLON, Ned														
W 1887	Det-N	.291	15	55	5	16	1	1	0	4	5	1	7	0-15
• HANSEN, Dave														
D 1995	LA-N	.667	3	3	0	2	0	0	0	0	0	0	0	....
D 1996	LA-N	.000	2	2	0	0	0	0	0	0	0	0	0	3-1
D Total	2	.400	5	5	0	2	0	0	0	0	0	0	0	....
• HARLOW, Larry														
L 1979	Cal-A	.125	3	8	0	1	0	0	0	1	1	2	0	0-2
• HARMON, Terry														
L 1976	Phi-N	....	1	0	1	0	0	0	0	0	0	0	0	....
• HARPER, Brian														
L 1985	StL-N	.000	1	1	0	0	0	0	0	0	0	0	0	....
L 1991	Min-A	.278	5	18	1	5	2	0	0	1	0	2	0	C-5
L Total	2	.263	6	19	1	5	2	0	0	1	0	2	0	....
W 1985	StL-N	.250	4	4	0	1	0	0	0	1	0	1	0	....
W 1991	Min-A	.381	7	21	2	8	2	0	0	1	2	2	0	C-7
W Total	2	.360	11	25	2	9	2	0	0	2	2	3	0	....
• HARPER, George														
W 1928	StL-N	.111	3	9	1	1	0	0	0	0	2	2	0	0-3
• HARPER, Terry														
L 1982	Atl-N	.000	1	1	1	0	0	0	0	0	0	0	0	0-1
• HARPER, Tommy														
L 1975	Oak-A	....	1	0	0	0	0	0	0	0	1	0	0	....
• HARRELSON, Bud														
L 1969	NY-N	.182	3	11	2	2	1	1	0	3	1	2	0	S-3
L 1973	NY-N	.167	5	18	1	3	0	0	0	2	1	1	0	S-5
L Total	2	.172	8	29	3	5	1	1	0	5	2	3	0	....
W 1969	NY-N	.176	5	17	1	3	0	0	0	3	4	0		S-5
W 1973	NY-N	.250	7	24	2	6	1	0	0	1	5	3	0	S-7
W Total	2	.220	12	41	3	9	1	0	0	1	8	7	0	....
• HARRELSON, Ken														
W 1967	Bos-A	.077	4	13	0	1	0	0	0	1	1	3	0	0-4
• HARRIS, Bucky														
W 1924	Was-A	.333	7	33	5	11	0	0	2	7	1	4	0	2-7
W 1925	Was-A	.087	7	23	2	2	0	0	0	0	1	3	0	2-7
W Total	2	.232	14	56	7	13	0	0	2	7	2	7	0	....
• HARRIS, Dave														
W 1933	Was-A	.000	3	2	0	0	0	0	0	0	2	0	0	0-1
• HARRIS, Joe														
W 1925	Was-A	.440	7	25	5	11	2	0	3	6	3	4	0	0-7
W 1927	Pit-N	.200	5	15	0	3	0	0	0	1	0	0	0	1-4
W Total	2	.350	11	40	5	14	2	0	3	7	3	4	0	....
• HARRIS, Lenny														
D 1999	Ari-N	.000	2	2	0	0	0	0	0	0	0	0	0	3-1
D 2000	NY-N	.000	2	2	0	0	0	0	0	0	0	0	1	....
D 2003	Fla-N	.500	2	2	0	1	0	0	0	0	0	0	0	....
D Total	3	.167	6	6	1	1	0	0	0	0	0	0	1	....
L 1995	Cin-N	1.000	3	2	0	2	0	0	0	1	0	0	1	....
L 2000	NY-N	.000	2	1	0	0	0	0	0	0	0	1	0	....
L 2003	Fla-N	.000	3	2	0	0	0	0	0	0	0	1	0	....
L Total	3	.400	8	5	0	2	0	0	0	1	1	1	1	....
W 2000	NY-N	.000	3	4	1	0	0	0	0	0	1	1	0	D-1
• HART, Jim Ray														
L 1971	SF-N	.000	3	5	0	0	0	0	0	0	0	2	0	3-1
• HARTNETT, Gabby														
W 1929	Chi-N	.000	3	3	0	0	0	0	0	0	0	3	0	....
W 1932	Chi-N	.313	4	16	2	5	2	0	1	1	1	3	0	C-4
W 1935	Chi-N	.292	6	24	1	7	0	0	1	2	0	3	0	C-6
W 1938	Chi-N	.091	3	11	0	1	0	1	0	0	0	2	0	C-3
W Total	4	.241	16	54	3	13	2	1	2	3	1	11	0	....
• HARTSEL, Topsy														
W 1905	Phi-A	.294	5	17	1	5	1	0	0	0	2	1	2	0-5
W 1910	Phi-A	.200	1	5	2	1	0	0	0	0	0	1	2	0-1
W Total	2	.273	6	22	3	6	1	0	0	0	2	2	4	....
• HARTUNG, Clint														
W 1951	NY-N	.000	2	4	0	0	0	0	0	0	0	0	0	0-2
• HASELMAN, Bill														
D 1995	Bos-A	.000	1	2	0	0	0	0	0	0	0	0	0	C-1
• HASSETT, Buddy														
W 1942	NY-A	.333	3	9	1	3	1	0	0	2	0	1	0	1-3
• HASSEY, Ron														
L 1988	Oak-A	.500	4	8	2	4	1	0	1	3	1	1	0	C-4
L 1989	Oak-A	.167	2	6	0	1	0	0	0	1	1	2	0	C-2
L 1990	Oak-A	.333	2	3	0	1	0	0	0	0	2	0	0	C-1,D-1
L Total	3	.353	8	17	2	6	1	0	1	4	4	3	0	....
W 1988	Oak-A	.250	5	8	0	2	0	0	0	1	3	3	0	C-4
W 1990	Oak-A	.333	3	6	0	2	0	0	0	1	0	0	0	C-1
W Total	2	.286	8	14	0	4	0	0	0	2	3	3	0	....
• HATCHER, Billy														
L 1986	Hou-N	.280	6	25	4	7	0	0	1	2	3	2	3	0-6
L 1990	Cin-N	.333	4	15	2	5	1	0	1	2	0	2	0	0-4
L Total	2	.300	10	40	6	12	1	0	2	4	3	4	3	....
W 1990	Cin-N	.750	4	12	6	9	4	1	0	2	2	0	0	0-4
• HATCHER, Mickey														
L 1988	LA-N	.238	6	21	4	5	2	0	0	3	3	0	0	0-1,1-6
W 1988	LA-N	.368	5	19	5	7	1	0	2	5	1	3	0	0-5
• HATTEBERG, Scott														
D 1998	Bos-A	.111	3	9	1	1	0	0	0	0	3	1	0	C-3
D 1999	Bos-A	1.000	1	1	1	1	0	0	0	1	0	0	0	C-1
D 2002	Oak-A	.500	5	14	5	7	2	0	1	3	3	0	0	1-5
D 2003	Oak-A	.176	5	17	3	3	0	0	0	0	5	3	0	1-5
D Total	4	.293	14	41	9	12	2	0	1	4	11	4	0	....
L 1999	Bos-A	.000	3	1	0	0	0	0	0	0	0	1	0	C-1
• HAWKE, Bill														
T 1894	Bal-N	.000	1	2	0	0	0	0	0	0	0	1	0	P-1
• HAYES, Charlie														
D 1996	NY-A	.200	3	5	1	0	0	0	0	1	0	0	0	3-2
D 1997	NY-A	.333	5	15	0	5	0	0	0	1	0	2	0	2-1,3-5
D Total	2	.300	8	20	0	6	0	0	0	2	0	2	0	....
L 1996	NY-A	.143	4	7	0	1	0	0	0	0	2	2	0	3-2,D-1
W 1996	NY-A	.188	5	16	2	3	0	0	0	1	1	5	0	1-1,3-4
• HAYES, Von														
L 1983	Phi-N	.000	2	2	0	0	0	0	0	0	0	0	0	0-1
W 1983	Phi-N	.000	4	3	0	0	0	0	0	0	0	1	0	0-2
• HAYWORTH, Ray														
W 1934	Det-A	....	1	0	0	0	0	0	0	0	0	0	0	C-1
• HAYWORTH, Red														
W 1944	StL-A	.118	6	17	1	2	1	0	0	1	3	1	0	C-6
• HAZLE, Bob														
W 1957	Mil-N	.154	4	13	2	2	0	0	0	0	1	2	0	0-4
• HEARN, Jim														
W 1951	NY-N	.000	2	3	0	0	0	0	0	0	0	1	0	....
• HEARRON, Jeff														
L 1985	Tor-A	....	2	0	0	0	0	0	0	0	0	0	0	C-2
• HEATH, Mike														
D 1981	Oak-A	.000	2	8	0	0	0	0	0	0	0	1	0	C-2
L 1981	Oak-A	.333	3	6	1	2	0	0	0	0	1	0	0	0-1,C-2
L 1987	Det-A	.286	3	7	1	2	0	0	1	2	0	0	0	C-3
L Total	2	.308	6	13	2	4	0	0	1	2	1	0	0	....
W 1978	NY-A	....	1	0	0	0	0	0	0	0	0	0	0	C-1
• HEATHCOTE, Cliff														
W 1929	Chi-N	.000	2	1	0	0	0	0	0	0	0	0	0	....
• HEBNER, Richie														
L 1970	Pit-N	.667	2	6	0	4	2	0	0	0	2	1	0	3-2
L 1971	Pit-N	.294	4	17	3	5	1	0	2	4	0	4	0	3-4
L 1972	Pit-N	.188	5	16	2	3	1	0	0	1	1	3	0	3-5
L 1974	Pit-N	.231	4	13	1	3	0	0	1	4	1	4	0	3-4
L 1975	Pit-N	.333	3	12	2	4	1	0	2	1	1	3	0	3-3
L 1977	Phi-N	.357	4	14	2	5	2	0	0	0	1	0	0	1-3
L 1978	Phi-N	.111	3	9	0	1	0	0	0	1	0	0	0	1-2
L 1984	Chi-N	.000	2	1	0	0	0	0	0	0	0	0	0	....
L Total	8	.284	27	88	10	25	7	0	3	12	5	14	0	....
W 1971	Pit-N	.167	3	12	2	2	0	0	1	3	3	3	0	3-3
• HEEP, Danny														
L 1980	Hou-N	.000	1	1	0	0	0	0	0	0	0	0	0	....
L 1986	NY-N	.250	5	4	0	1	0	0	0	1	0	2	0	0-1
L 1988	LA-N	.000	3	1	0	0	0	0	0	0	1	0	0	....
L 1990	Bos-A	.000	2	2	0	0	0	0	0	0	0	0	0	....
L Total	4	.125	11	8	0	1	0	0	0	1	1	3	0	....
W 1986	NY-N	.091	5	11	0	1	0	0	0	2	1	1	0	0-1,D-2
W 1988	LA-N	.250	3	8	0	2	1	0	0	0	0	2	0	0-1,D-1
W Total	2	.158	8	19	0	3	1	0	0	2	1	3	0	....
• HEGAN, Jim														
W 1948	Cle-A	.211	6	19	2	4	0	0	1	5	1	4	1	C-6
W 1954	Cle-A	.154	4	13	1	2	0	0	0	0	1	1	0	C-4
W Total	2	.188	10	32	3	6	1	0	1	5	2	5	1	....
• HEGAN, Mike														
L 1971	Oak-A	.000	1	1	0	0	0	0	0	0	1	0	0	....
L 1972	Oak-A	.000	3	1	1	0	0	0	0	0	0	0	0	1-1
L Total	2	.000	4	2	1	0	0	0	0	0	1	0	0	....
W 1964	NY-A	.000	3	1	1	0	0	0	0	0	1	1	0	....

SER-YEAR	TM-L	AVG	G	AB	R	H	2B	3B	HR	RBI	BB	SO	SB	POS
W 1972	Oak-A	.200	6	5	0	1	0	0	0	0	0	2	0	1-5
W Total	**2**	**.167**	**9**	**6**	**1**	**1**	**0**	**0**	**0**	**0**	**1**	**3**	**0**	**....**
• HELMS, Tommy														
L 1970	Cin-N	.273	3	11	0	3	0	0	0	0	0	1	0	2-3
W 1970	Cin-N	.222	5	18	1	4	0	0	0	0	1	1	0	2-5
• HELMS, Wes														
D 2002	Atl-N	....	1	0	0	0	0	0	0	0	0	0	0	1-1
• HEMMING, George														
T 1894	Bal-N	.000	1	3	0	0	0	0	0	0	1	1	0	P-1
• HEMSLEY, Rollie														
W 1932	Chi-N	.000	3	3	0	0	0	0	0	0	0	3	0	C-1
• HENDERSON, Dave														
L 1986	Bos-A	.111	5	9	3	1	0	0	1	4	2	2	0	O-5
L 1988	Oak-A	.375	4	16	2	6	1	0	1	4	1	7	0	O-4
L 1989	Oak-A	.263	5	19	4	5	3	0	1	1	2	5	0	O-5
L 1990	Oak-A	.167	2	6	0	1	0	0	0	1	0	2	1	O-2
L Total	**4**	**.260**	**16**	**50**	**9**	**13**	**4**	**0**	**3**	**10**	**5**	**16**	**1**	**....**
W 1986	Bos-A	.400	7	25	6	10	1	1	2	5	2	6	0	O-7
W 1988	Oak-A	.300	5	20	1	6	2	0	0	1	2	7	0	O-5
W 1989	Oak-A	.308	4	13	6	4	2	0	2	4	4	3	0	O-4
W 1990	Oak-A	.231	4	13	2	3	1	0	0	0	1	3	0	O-3
W Total	**4**	**.324**	**20**	**71**	**15**	**23**	**6**	**1**	**4**	**10**	**9**	**19**	**0**	**....**
• HENDERSON, Ken														
L 1971	SF-N	.313	4	16	3	5	1	0	0	2	2	1	1	O-4
• HENDERSON, Rickey														
D 1981	Oak-A	.182	3	11	3	2	0	0	0	0	2	0	2	O-3
D 1996	SD-N	.333	3	12	2	4	0	0	1	1	2	3	0	O-3
D 1999	NY-N	.400	4	15	5	6	0	0	0	1	3	1	6	O-4
D 2000	Sea-A	.400	3	5	3	2	0	0	0	0	1	0	1	O-2
D Total	**4**	**.326**	**13**	**43**	**13**	**14**	**0**	**0**	**1**	**2**	**8**	**4**	**9**	**....**
L 1981	Oak-A	.364	3	11	0	4	2	1	0	1	1	2	2	O-3
L 1989	Oak-A	.400	5	15	8	6	1	1	2	5	7	0	8	O-5
L 1990	Oak-A	.294	4	17	1	5	0	0	0	3	1	2	2	O-4
L 1992	Oak-A	.261	6	23	5	6	0	0	0	1	4	4	2	O-6
L 1993	Tor-A	.120	6	25	4	3	2	0	0	0	4	5	2	O-6
L 1999	NY-N	.174	6	23	2	4	1	0	0	1	0	5	1	O-6
L 2000	Sea-A	.222	3	9	2	2	1	0	0	1	2	2	0	O-3
L Total	**7**	**.244**	**33**	**123**	**22**	**30**	**7**	**2**	**2**	**12**	**19**	**20**	**17**	**....**
W 1989	Oak-A	.474	4	19	4	9	1	2	1	3	2	2	3	O-4
W 1990	Oak-A	.333	4	15	2	5	2	0	1	1	3	4	3	O-4
W 1993	Tor-A	.227	6	22	6	5	2	0	0	2	5	2	1	O-6
W Total	**3**	**.339**	**14**	**56**	**12**	**19**	**5**	**2**	**2**	**6**	**10**	**8**	**7**	**....**
• HENDRICK, George														
L 1972	Oak-A	.143	5	7	2	1	0	0	0	0	0	1	0	O-1
L 1982	StL-N	.308	3	13	2	4	0	0	0	2	1	2	0	O-3
L 1986	Cal-A	.083	3	12	0	1	0	0	0	0	0	2	0	O-2,1-1
L Total	**3**	**.188**	**11**	**32**	**4**	**6**	**0**	**0**	**0**	**2**	**1**	**5**	**0**	**....**
W 1972	Oak-A	.133	5	15	3	2	0	0	0	0	1	2	0	O-5
W 1982	StL-N	.321	7	28	5	9	0	0	0	5	2	2	0	O-7
W Total	**2**	**.256**	**12**	**43**	**8**	**11**	**0**	**0**	**0**	**5**	**3**	**4**	**0**	**....**
• HENDRICK, Harvey														
W 1923	NY-A	.000	1	1	0	0	0	0	0	0	0	0	0	....
• HENDRICKS, Ellie														
L 1969	Bal-A	.250	3	8	2	2	2	0	0	3	1	2	0	C-3
L 1970	Bal-A	.400	1	5	2	2	0	0	0	0	0	1	0	C-1
L 1971	Bal-A	.500	2	4	1	2	0	0	1	2	1	1	0	C-2
L 1974	Bal-A	.167	3	6	1	1	0	0	0	0	1	3	0	C-3
L 1976	NY-A	1.000	1	1	0	1	0	0	0	0	0	0	0	....
L Total	**5**	**.333**	**10**	**24**	**6**	**8**	**2**	**0**	**1**	**5**	**3**	**7**	**0**	**....**
W 1969	Bal-A	.100	3	10	1	1	0	0	0	0	1	0	0	C-3
W 1970	Bal-A	.364	3	11	1	4	1	0	1	4	1	2	0	C-3
W 1971	Bal-A	.263	6	19	3	5	1	0	0	1	3	3	0	C-6
W 1976	NY-A	.000	2	2	0	0	0	0	0	0	0	0	0	....
W Total	**4**	**.238**	**14**	**42**	**5**	**10**	**2**	**0**	**1**	**5**	**5**	**5**	**0**	**....**
• HENNEMAN, Mike														
L 1987	Det-A	....	3	0	0	0	0	0	0	0	0	0	0	....
• HENRICH, Tommy														
W 1938	NY-A	.250	4	16	3	4	1	0	1	1	0	1	0	O-4
W 1941	NY-A	.167	5	18	4	3	1	0	1	1	3	3	0	O-5
W 1947	NY-A	.323	7	31	2	10	2	0	1	5	2	3	0	O-7
W 1949	NY-A	.263	5	19	4	5	0	0	1	1	3	0	0	1-5
W Total	**4**	**.262**	**21**	**84**	**13**	**22**	**4**	**0**	**4**	**8**	**8**	**7**	**0**	**....**
• HENRIKSEN, Olaf														
W 1912	Bos-A	1.000	2	1	0	1	1	0	0	1	0	0	0	....
W 1915	Bos-A	.000	2	2	0	0	0	0	0	0	0	0	0	....
W 1916	Bos-A	....	1	0	1	0	0	0	0	0	1	0	0	....
W Total	**3**	**.333**	**5**	**3**	**1**	**1**	**1**	**0**	**0**	**1**	**1**	**0**	**0**	**....**
• HERMAN, Billy														
W 1932	Chi-N	.222	4	18	5	4	1	0	0	1	1	3	0	2-4
W 1935	Chi-N	.333	6	24	3	8	2	1	1	6	0	2	0	2-6
W 1938	Chi-N	.188	4	16	1	3	0	0	0	0	1	4	0	2-4
W 1941	Bro-N	.125	4	8	0	1	0	0	0	0	2	0	0	2-4
W Total	**4**	**.242**	**18**	**66**	**9**	**16**	**3**	**1**	**1**	**7**	**4**	**9**	**0**	**....**
• HERMANSKI, Gene														
W 1947	Bro-N	.158	7	19	4	3	0	1	0	1	3	3	0	O-7
W 1949	Bro-N	.308	4	13	1	4	0	1	0	2	3	3	0	O-4
W Total	**2**	**.219**	**11**	**32**	**5**	**7**	**0**	**2**	**0**	**3**	**6**	**6**	**0**	**....**

SER-YEAR	TM-L	AVG	G	AB	R	H	2B	3B	HR	RBI	BB	SO	SB	POS
• HERNANDEZ, Carlos														
D 1998	SD-N	.417	4	12	0	5	0	0	0	0	0	0	0	C-4
D 2000	StL-N	.273	3	11	3	3	0	0	1	1	1	2	0	C-3
D Total	**2**	**.348**	**7**	**23**	**3**	**8**	**0**	**0**	**1**	**1**	**1**	**2**	**0**	**....**
L 1998	SD-N	.333	6	18	2	6	1	0	0	0	1	5	0	C-6
L 2000	StL-N	.250	5	16	3	4	0	0	0	1	1	1	0	C-5
L Total	**2**	**.294**	**11**	**34**	**5**	**10**	**1**	**0**	**0**	**1**	**2**	**6**	**0**	**....**
W 1998	SD-N	.200	4	10	0	2	0	0	0	0	0	3	0	C-4
• HERNANDEZ, Jackie														
L 1971	Pit-N	.231	4	13	2	3	0	0	0	1	0	4	0	S-4
W 1971	Pit-N	.222	7	18	2	4	0	0	0	1	2	5	1	S-7
• HERNANDEZ, Jose														
D 1998	Chi-N	.286	2	7	1	2	0	0	0	0	0	2	0	S-2
D 1999	Atl-N	.091	4	11	1	1	0	0	0	0	1	3	1	S-4
D Total	**2**	**.167**	**6**	**18**	**2**	**3**	**0**	**0**	**0**	**0**	**1**	**5**	**1**	**....**
L 1999	Atl-N	.500	2	2	0	1	0	0	0	2	0	1	0	....
W 1999	Atl-N	.200	2	5	0	1	1	0	0	2	0	2	1	S-1,D-1
• HERNANDEZ, Keith														
L 1982	StL-N	.333	3	12	3	4	0	0	0	1	2	3	0	1-3
L 1986	NY-N	.269	6	26	3	7	1	1	0	3	3	6	0	1-6
L 1988	NY-N	.269	7	26	2	7	0	0	1	5	6	7	1	1-7
L Total	**3**	**.281**	**16**	**64**	**8**	**18**	**1**	**1**	**1**	**9**	**11**	**16**	**1**	**....**
W 1982	StL-N	.259	7	27	4	7	2	0	1	8	4	2	0	1-7
W 1986	NY-N	.231	7	26	1	6	0	0	0	4	5	1	0	1-7
W Total	**2**	**.245**	**14**	**53**	**5**	**13**	**2**	**0**	**1**	**12**	**9**	**3**	**0**	**....**
• HERNANDEZ, Ramon														
D 2000	Oak-A	.375	5	16	3	6	2	0	0	3	0	3	0	C-5
D 2001	Oak-A	.000	5	10	0	0	0	0	0	0	1	4	0	C-5
D 2002	Oak-A	.059	5	17	0	1	0	0	0	0	0	4	0	C-5
D 2003	Oak-A	.200	4	15	1	3	0	0	0	2	2	1	0	C-4
D Total	**4**	**.172**	**19**	**58**	**4**	**10**	**2**	**0**	**0**	**5**	**3**	**12**	**0**	**....**
• HERNDON, Larry														
L 1984	Det-A	.200	2	5	1	1	0	0	1	1	1	2	0	O-2
L 1987	Det-A	.333	3	9	1	3	1	0	0	2	1	1	0	O-2,D-1
L Total	**2**	**.286**	**5**	**14**	**2**	**4**	**1**	**0**	**1**	**3**	**2**	**3**	**0**	**....**
W 1984	Det-A	.333	5	15	1	5	0	0	1	3	3	2	0	O-5
• HERR, Ed														
W 1888	StL-A	.091	3	11	2	1	0	0	0	0	0	5	1	O-3
• HERR, Tom														
L 1982	StL-N	.231	3	13	1	3	1	0	0	0	1	2	0	2-3
L 1985	StL-N	.333	6	21	2	7	4	0	1	6	5	2	1	2-6
L 1987	StL-N	.222	7	27	0	6	0	0	0	3	0	1	1	2-7
L Total	**3**	**.262**	**16**	**61**	**3**	**16**	**5**	**0**	**1**	**9**	**6**	**5**	**2**	**....**
W 1982	StL-N	.160	7	25	2	4	2	0	0	5	3	3	0	2-7
W 1985	StL-N	.154	7	26	2	4	2	0	0	0	2	2	0	2-7
W 1987	StL-N	.250	7	28	2	7	0	0	1	1	2	2	0	2-7
W Total	**3**	**.190**	**21**	**79**	**6**	**15**	**4**	**0**	**1**	**6**	**7**	**7**	**0**	**....**
• HERSHBERGER, Willard														
W 1939	Cin-N	.500	3	2	0	1	0	0	0	1	0	0	0	C-2
• HERZOG, Buck														
W 1911	NY-N	.190	6	21	3	4	2	0	0	0	2	3	2	3-6
W 1912	NY-N	.400	8	30	6	12	4	1	0	5	1	3	2	3-8
W 1913	NY-N	.053	5	19	1	1	0	0	0	0	0	1	0	3-5
W 1917	NY-N	.250	6	24	1	6	0	1	0	2	0	4	0	2-6
W Total	**4**	**.245**	**25**	**94**	**11**	**23**	**6**	**2**	**0**	**7**	**3**	**11**	**4**	**....**
• HEVING, Johnnie														
W 1931	Phi-A	.000	1	1	0	0	0	0	0	0	0	0	0	....
• HICKMAN, Charlie														
T 1897	Bos-N	.250	1	4	0	1	1	0	0	1	0	0	0	P-1,O-1
• HIDALGO, Richard														
D 1997	Hou-N	.000	2	5	1	0	0	0	0	0	1	2	0	O-2
D 1998	Hou-N	.250	1	4	0	1	0	0	0	0	0	1	0	O-1
D 2001	Hou-N	.125	3	8	1	1	0	0	0	0	3	2	0	O-3
D Total	**3**	**.118**	**6**	**17**	**2**	**2**	**0**	**0**	**0**	**0**	**4**	**5**	**0**	**....**
• HIGGINS, Pinky														
W 1940	Det-A	.333	7	24	2	8	3	1	1	6	3	3	0	3-7
W 1946	Bos-A	.208	7	24	1	5	1	0	0	2	2	0	0	3-7
W Total	**2**	**.271**	**14**	**48**	**3**	**13**	**4**	**1**	**1**	**8**	**5**	**3**	**0**	**....**
• HIGH, Andy														
W 1928	StL-N	.294	4	17	1	5	2	0	0	1	1	3	0	3-4
W 1930	StL-N	.500	1	2	1	1	0	0	0	0	0	0	0	3-1
W 1931	StL-N	.267	4	15	3	4	0	0	0	0	0	2	0	3-4
W Total	**3**	**.294**	**9**	**34**	**5**	**10**	**2**	**0**	**0**	**1**	**1**	**5**	**0**	**....**
• HILL, Glenallen														
D 1997	SF-N	.000	3	7	0	0	0	0	0	0	2	2	0	O-2
D 1998	Chi-N	.333	1	3	0	1	0	0	0	0	1	2	1	O-1
D 2000	NY-A	.083	4	12	1	1	0	0	0	2	1	5	0	D-3
D Total	**3**	**.091**	**8**	**22**	**1**	**2**	**0**	**0**	**0**	**2**	**4**	**9**	**1**	**....**
L 2000	NY-A	.000	2	2	0	0	0	0	0	0	0	2	0	....
W 2000	NY-A	.000	3	3	0	0	0	0	0	0	0	0	0	O-1
• HILLER, Chuck														
W 1962	SF-N	.269	7	26	4	7	3	0	1	5	3	4	0	2-7
• HINES, Paul														
W 1884	Pro-N	.250	3	8	5	2	0	0	0	1	3	0	2	O-3
• HOAG, Myril														
W 1932	NY-A	....	1	0	1	0	0	0	0	0	0	0	0	....
W 1937	NY-A	.300	5	20	4	6	1	0	1	2	0	1	0	O-5

YEAR	TM-L	AVG	G	AB	R	H	2B	3B	HR	RBI	BB	SO	SB	POS
W 1938	NY-A	.400	2	5	3	2	1	0	0	1	0	0	0	0-1
W Total	3	.320	8	25	8	8	2	0	1	3	0	1	0	....
• HOAK, Don														
W 1955	Bro-N	.333	3	3	0	1	0	0	0	0	2	0	0	3-1
W 1960	Pit-N	.217	7	23	3	5	2	0	0	3	4	1	0	3-7
W Total	2	.231	10	26	3	6	2	0	0	3	6	1	0	....
• HOBLITZEL, Dick														
W 1915	Bos-A	.313	5	16	1	5	0	0	0	1	0	1	1	1-5
W 1916	Bos-A	.235	5	17	3	4	1	1	0	2	6	0	0	1-5
W Total	2	.273	10	33	4	9	1	1	0	3	6	1	1	....
• HOCKING, Dennis														
D 2002	Min-A	.500	3	6	0	3	1	0	0	1	0	1	0	0-1,2-1
D 2003	Min-A	....	1	0	0	0	0	0	0	0	0	0	0	2-1
D Total	2	.500	4	6	0	3	1	0	0	1	0	1	0	....
• HODGES, Gil														
W 1947	Bro-N	.000	1	1	0	0	0	0	0	0	0	1	0	....
W 1949	Bro-N	.235	5	17	2	4	0	0	1	4	1	4	0	1-5
W 1952	Bro-N	.000	7	21	1	0	0	0	0	1	5	6	0	1-7
W 1953	Bro-N	.364	6	22	3	8	0	0	1	1	3	3	1	1-6
W 1955	Bro-N	.292	7	24	2	7	0	0	1	5	3	2	0	1-7
W 1956	Bro-N	.304	7	23	5	7	2	0	1	8	4	4	0	1-7
W 1959	LA-N	.391	6	23	2	9	0	1	1	2	1	2	0	1-6
W Total	7	.267	39	131	15	35	2	1	5	21	17	22	1	....
• HODGES, Ron														
W 1973	NY-N	....	1	0	0	0	0	0	0	0	1	0	0	....
• HOFFER, Bill														
T 1895	Bal-N	.000	2	7	0	0	0	0	0	0	0	2	0	P-2
T 1896	Bal-N	.286	2	7	1	2	0	2	0	0	0	1	0	P-2
T 1897	Bal-N	.250	2	8	2	2	1	0	0	0	0	0	0	P-2
T Total	3	.182	6	22	3	4	1	2	0	0	0	3	0	....
• HOFFMAN, Danny														
W 1905	Phi-A	.000	1	1	0	0	0	0	0	0	0	1	0	....
• HOFMAN, Solly														
W 1906	Chi-N	.304	6	23	3	7	1	0	0	2	3	5	1	0-6
W 1908	Chi-N	.316	5	19	2	6	0	1	0	4	1	4	2	0-5
W 1910	Chi-N	.267	5	15	2	4	0	0	0	2	4	3	0	0-5
W Total	3	.298	16	57	7	17	1	1	0	8	8	12	3	....
• HOFMANN, Fred														
W 1923	NY-A	.000	2	1	0	0	0	0	0	0	1	0	0	....
• HOILES, Chris														
D 1996	Bal-A	.143	4	7	1	1	0	0	0	0	3	3	0	C-4
D 1997	Bal-A	.143	3	7	1	1	0	0	1	1	2	1	0	C-3
D Total	2	.143	7	14	2	2	0	0	1	1	5	4	0	....
L 1996	Bal-A	.167	4	12	1	2	0	0	1	2	1	3	0	C-4
L 1997	Bal-A	.143	4	14	1	2	0	0	0	0	2	5	0	C-4
L Total	2	.154	8	26	2	4	0	0	1	2	3	8	0	....
• HOLBERT, Bill														
W 1884	NY-A	.000	1	2	0	0	0	0	0	0	0	1	0	C-1
• HOLKE, Walter														
W 1917	NY-N	.286	6	21	2	6	2	0	0	1	0	6	0	1-6
• HOLLANDSWORTH, Todd														
D 1995	LA-N	.000	2	2	0	0	0	0	0	0	0	0	0	0-2
D 1996	LA-N	.333	3	12	1	4	3	0	0	1	0	3	0	0-3
D 2003	Fla-N	.333	3	3	1	1	0	0	0	0	0	2	0	....
D Total	3	.294	8	17	2	5	3	0	0	1	0	5	0	....
L 2003	Fla-N	1.000	4	3	2	3	1	0	0	2	1	0	0	....
W 2003	Fla-N	.000	2	2	0	0	0	0	0	0	0	1	0	....
• HOLLIDAY, Bug														
W 1885	Chi-N	.000	1	4	0	0	0	0	0	0	0	0	0	0-1
• HOLLINS, Dave														
L 1993	Phi-N	.200	6	20	2	4	1	0	2	4	5	4	1	3-6
W 1993	Phi-N	.261	6	23	5	6	1	0	0	2	6	5	0	3-6
• HOLLOCHER, Charlie														
W 1918	Chi-N	.190	6	21	2	4	0	1	0	1	1	1	1	S-6
• HOLM, Wattie														
W 1926	StL-N	.125	5	16	1	2	0	0	0	1	1	2	0	0-4
W 1928	StL-N	.167	3	6	0	1	0	0	0	1	0	1	0	0-1
W Total	2	.136	8	22	1	3	0	0	0	2	1	3	0	....
• HOLMES, Darren														
D 1995	Col-N	....	3	0	0	0	0	0	0	0	0	0	0	....
D 1999	Ari-N	....	1	0	0	0	0	0	0	0	0	0	0	....
D 2002	Atl-N	....	3	0	0	0	0	0	0	0	0	0	0	....
D Total	3	....	7	0	0	0	0	0	0	0	0	0	0	....
• HOLMES, Tommy														
W 1948	Bos-N	.192	6	26	3	5	0	0	0	1	0	0	0	0-6
W 1952	Bro-N	.000	3	1	0	0	0	0	0	0	0	0	0	0-3
W Total	2	.185	9	27	3	5	0	0	0	1	0	0	0	....
• HOLT, Chris														
D 1999	Hou-N	....	1	0	0	0	0	0	0	0	0	0	0	....
• HOLT, Jim														
L 1970	Min-A	.000	3	5	0	0	0	0	0	0	0	2	0	0-3
L 1974	Oak-A	....	2	0	0	0	0	0	0	0	1	0	0	1-1
L 1975	Oak-A	.333	3	3	0	1	1	0	0	0	0	0	0	1-1
L Total	3	.125	8	8	0	1	1	0	0	0	1	2	0	....
W 1974	Oak-A	.667	4	3	0	2	0	0	0	2	0	0	0	1-1

YEAR	TM-L	AVG	G	AB	R	H	2B	3B	HR	RBI	BB	SO	SB	POS
• HOOPER, Harry														
W 1912	Bos-A	.290	8	31	3	9	2	1	0	2	4	4	1	0-8
W 1915	Bos-A	.350	5	20	4	7	0	0	2	3	2	4	0	0-5
W 1916	Bos-A	.333	5	21	6	7	1	1	0	1	3	1	1	0-5
W 1918	Bos-A	.200	6	20	0	4	0	0	0	0	2	2	0	0-6
W Total	4	.293	24	92	13	27	3	2	2	6	11	11	2	....
• HOOVER, Joe														
W 1945	Det-A	.333	1	3	1	1	0	0	0	1	0	0	0	S-1
• HOPKINS, Don														
L 1975	Oak-A	.000	1	1	0	0	0	0	0	0	0	0	0	D-1
• HOPP, Johnny														
W 1942	StL-N	.176	5	17	3	3	0	0	0	0	1	1	0	1-5
W 1943	StL-N	.000	1	4	0	0	0	0	0	0	0	1	0	0-1
W 1944	StL-N	.185	6	27	2	5	0	0	0	0	0	8	0	0-6
W 1950	NY-A	.000	3	2	0	0	0	0	0	0	0	0	0	1-3
W 1951	NY-A	....	1	0	0	0	0	0	0	0	1	0	0	....
W Total	5	.160	16	50	5	8	0	0	0	0	2	10	0	....
• HORNER, Bob														
L 1982	Atl-N	.091	3	11	0	1	0	0	0	0	0	2	0	3-3
• HORNSBY, Rogers														
W 1926	StL-N	.250	7	28	2	7	1	0	0	4	2	2	1	2-7
W 1929	Chi-N	.238	5	21	4	5	1	1	0	1	1	8	0	2-5
W Total	2	.245	12	49	6	12	2	1	0	5	3	10	1	....
• HORTON, Willie														
L 1972	Det-A	.100	5	10	0	1	0	0	0	0	1	3	0	0-3
W 1968	Det-A	.304	7	23	6	7	1	1	1	3	5	6	0	0-7
• HOSEY, Dwayne														
D 1995	Bos-A	.000	3	12	1	0	0	0	0	0	2	3	1	0-3
• HOSTETLER, Chuck														
W 1945	Det-A	.000	3	3	0	0	0	0	0	0	0	0	0	....
• HOUK, Ralph														
W 1947	NY-A	1.000	1	1	0	1	0	0	0	0	0	0	0	....
W 1952	NY-A	.000	1	1	0	0	0	0	0	0	0	0	0	....
W Total	2	.500	2	2	0	1	0	0	0	0	0	0	0	....
• HOUSTON, Tyler														
D 1998	Chi-N	.167	3	6	1	1	0	0	1	1	0	3	0	C-3
• HOWARD, Del														
W 1907	Chi-N	.200	2	5	0	1	0	0	0	0	0	2	1	1-1
W 1908	Chi-N	.000	1	1	0	0	0	0	0	0	0	0	0	....
W Total	2	.167	3	6	0	1	0	0	0	0	0	2	1	....
• HOWARD, Elston														
W 1955	NY-A	.192	7	26	3	5	0	0	1	3	1	8	0	0-7
W 1956	NY-A	.400	1	5	1	2	1	0	1	1	0	0	0	0-1
W 1957	NY-A	.273	6	11	2	3	0	0	1	3	1	3	0	1-3
W 1958	NY-A	.222	6	18	4	4	0	0	0	2	1	4	1	0-5
W 1960	NY-A	.462	5	13	4	6	1	1	1	4	1	4	0	C-4
W 1961	NY-A	.250	5	20	5	5	3	0	1	1	2	3	0	C-5
W 1962	NY-A	.143	6	21	1	3	1	0	0	1	1	4	0	C-6
W 1963	NY-A	.333	4	15	0	5	0	0	0	1	0	3	0	C-4
W 1964	NY-A	.292	7	24	5	7	1	0	0	2	4	6	0	C-7
W 1967	Bos-A	.111	7	18	0	2	0	0	0	1	1	2	0	C-7
W Total	10	.246	54	171	25	42	7	1	5	19	12	37	1	....
• HOWARD, Frank														
W 1963	LA-N	.300	3	10	2	3	1	0	1	1	0	2	0	0-3
• HOWARD, Thomas														
D 1995	Cin-N	.100	3	10	0	1	1	0	0	0	0	2	0	0-3
D 1997	Hou-N	.000	2	1	0	0	0	0	0	0	1	1	0	....
D Total	2	.091	5	11	0	1	1	0	0	0	1	3	0	....
L 1995	Cin-N	.250	4	8	0	2	1	0	0	1	2	0	0	0-3
• HOWE, Art														
D 1981	Hou-N	.188	5	16	1	3	0	0	1	1	2	1	0	3-5
L 1974	Pit-N	.000	1	1	0	0	0	0	0	0	0	0	0	....
L 1980	Hou-N	.200	5	15	0	3	1	1	0	2	2	2	0	1-4
L Total	2	.188	6	16	0	3	1	1	0	2	2	2	0	....
• HOWELL, Harry														
T 1900	Bro-N	.000	1	3	0	0	0	0	0	0	0	2	0	P-1
• HOWELL, Jack														
L 1986	Cal-A	.000	2	1	0	0	0	0	0	0	1	1	0	....
• HOWELL, Roy														
D 1981	Mil-A	.400	4	5	0	2	0	0	0	0	2	2	0	D-3
L 1982	Mil-A	.000	1	3	0	0	0	0	0	0	0	1	0	D-1
W 1982	Mil-A	.000	4	11	1	0	0	0	0	0	0	3	0	D-4
• HRBEK, Kent														
L 1987	Min-A	.150	5	20	4	3	0	0	1	1	3	0	0	1-5
L 1991	Min-A	.143	5	21	0	3	0	0	0	3	1	3	0	1-5
L Total	2	.146	10	41	4	6	0	0	1	4	4	3	0	....
W 1987	Min-A	.208	7	24	4	5	0	0	1	6	5	3	0	1-7
W 1991	Min-A	.115	7	26	2	3	1	0	1	2	2	6	0	1-7
W Total	2	.160	14	50	6	8	1	0	2	8	7	9	0	....
• HUBBARD, Glenn														
L 1982	Atl-N	.222	3	9	1	2	0	0	0	1	0	3	0	2-3
W 1988	Oak-A	.250	4	12	2	3	0	0	0	0	1	2	1	2-4
• HUBBARD, Trenidad														
D 1995	Col-N	.000	3	2	0	0	0	0	0	0	0	0	0	....
• HUGHES, Jim														
W 1953	Bro-N	.000	1	1	0	0	0	0	0	0	0	1	0	....

SER-YEAR	TM-L	AVG	G	AB	R	H	2B	3B	HR	RBI	BB	SO	SB	POS
• HUGHES, Roy														
W 1945	Chi-N	.294	6	17	1	5	1	0	0	3	4	5	0	S-6
• HUNTER, Brian														
D 1999	Atl-N	.000	3	4	0	0	0	0	0	0	1	3	0	1-3
L 1991	Atl-N	.333	5	18	2	6	2	0	1	4	0	2	0	1-5
L 1992	Atl-N	.200	3	5	1	1	0	0	0	0	0	1	0	1-2
L 1999	Atl-N	.100	6	10	1	1	0	0	0	2	5	2	1	1-6
L Total	3	.242	14	33	4	8	2	0	1	6	5	5	1	....
W 1991	Atl-N	.190	7	21	2	4	1	0	1	3	0	2	0	0-4,1-4
W 1992	Atl-N	.200	4	5	0	1	0	0	0	2	0	1	0	1-3
W 1999	Atl-N	.250	2	4	0	1	0	0	0	0	0	1	0	1-2
W Total	3	.200	13	30	2	6	1	0	1	5	0	4	0	....
• HUNTER, Torii														
D 2002	Min-A	.300	5	20	4	6	4	0	0	2	1	4	0	0-5
D 2003	Min-A	.429	4	14	3	6	0	1	1	2	2	2	0	0-4
D Total	2	.353	9	34	7	12	4	1	1	4	3	6	0	....
L 2002	Min-A	.167	5	18	2	3	2	0	0	0	1	3	0	0-5
• HURDLE, Clint														
D 1981	KC-A	.273	3	11	0	3	0	0	0	0	1	1	0	0-3
L 1978	KC-A	.375	4	8	1	3	0	1	0	1	2	3	0	0-2
L 1980	KC-A	.000	3	2	0	0	0	0	0	0	0	1	0	0-3
L Total	2	.300	7	10	1	3	0	1	0	1	2	4	0	....
W 1980	KC-A	.417	4	12	1	5	1	0	0	0	2	1	1	0-4
• HUSKEY, Butch														
D 1999	Bos-A	.200	2	5	0	1	0	0	0	0	0	1	0	D-2
L 1999	Bos-A	.200	4	5	1	1	1	0	0	0	1	1	0	D-3
• HUTCHINGS, Johnny														
W 1940	Cin-N	....	1	0	0	0	0	0	0	0	0	0	0	....
• HUTTON, Tom														
L 1976	Phi-N	.000	1	1	0	0	0	0	0	0	0	0	0	....
L 1977	Phi-N	.000	3	3	0	0	0	0	0	0	0	0	0	1-1
L Total	2	.000	4	4	0	0	0	0	0	0	0	0	0	....
• HYATT, Ham														
W 1909	Pit-N	.000	2	4	1	0	0	0	0	1	1	0	0	0-1
• IBANEZ, Raul														
D 2000	Sea-A	.375	3	8	2	3	0	0	0	0	0	0	0	0-3
L 2000	Sea-A	.000	6	9	0	0	0	0	0	0	0	2	0	0-3
• INCAVIGLIA, Pete														
D 1996	Bal-A	.200	2	5	1	1	0	0	0	0	0	4	0	0-2
D 1998	Hou-N	.000	1	1	0	0	0	0	0	0	0	1	0	....
D Total	2	.167	3	6	1	1	0	0	0	0	0	5	0	....
L 1993	Phi-N	.167	3	12	2	2	0	0	1	1	0	3	0	0-3
L 1996	Bal-A	.500	1	2	1	1	0	0	0	0	0	0	0	D-1
L Total	2	.214	4	14	3	3	0	0	1	1	0	3	0	....
W 1993	Phi-N	.143	3	7	0	1	0	0	0	1	0	4	0	0-3
• IORG, Dane														
L 1984	KC-A	.500	2	2	0	1	0	0	0	1	0	0	0	....
L 1985	KC-A	.500	4	2	0	1	1	0	0	0	2	0	0	....
L Total	2	.500	6	4	0	2	1	0	0	1	2	0	0	....
W 1982	StL-N	.529	5	17	4	9	4	1	0	1	0	0	0	D-5
W 1985	KC-A	.500	2	2	0	1	0	0	0	2	0	0	0	....
W Total	2	.526	7	19	4	10	4	1	0	3	0	0	0	....
• IORG, Garth														
L 1985	Tor-A	.133	6	15	1	2	0	0	0	0	1	3	0	3-6
• IRVIN, Monte														
W 1951	NY-N	.458	6	24	3	11	0	1	0	2	2	1	2	0-6
W 1954	NY-N	.222	4	9	1	2	1	0	0	2	0	3	0	0-4
W Total	2	.394	10	33	4	13	1	1	0	4	2	4	2	....
• IRWIN, Arthur														
W 1884	Pro-N	.222	3	9	3	2	0	1	0	2	0	2	0	S-3
• ISBELL, Frank														
W 1906	Chi-A	.308	6	26	4	8	4	0	0	4	0	6	1	2-6
• JACKSON, Bo														
L 1993	Chi-A	.000	3	10	1	0	0	0	0	0	3	6	0	D-3
• JACKSON, Damian														
D 2003	Bos-A	.000	4	5	0	0	0	0	0	0	0	2	0	2-4
L 2003	Bos-A	.333	5	3	0	1	0	0	0	1	0	1	0	2-4
• JACKSON, Danny														
L 1985	KC-A	....	2	0	0	0	0	0	0	0	0	0	0	....
L 1990	Cin-N	.000	2	3	0	0	0	0	0	0	0	2	0	....
L 1992	Pit-N	....	1	0	0	0	0	0	0	0	0	0	0	....
L 1993	Phi-N	.250	1	4	0	1	0	0	0	1	0	3	0	....
L 1996	StL-N	.000	1	1	0	0	0	0	0	0	0	1	0	....
L Total	5	.125	7	8	0	1	0	0	0	1	0	6	0	....
W 1985	KC-A	.000	2	6	0	0	0	0	0	0	0	5	0	....
W 1990	Cin-N	.000	1	1	0	0	0	0	0	0	0	1	0	....
W 1993	Phi-N	.000	1	1	0	0	0	0	0	0	0	1	0	....
W Total	3	.000	4	8	0	0	0	0	0	0	0	7	0	....
• JACKSON, Joe														
W 1917	Chi-A	.304	6	23	4	7	0	0	0	2	1	0	1	0-6
W 1919	Chi-A	.375	8	32	5	12	3	0	1	6	1	2	0	0-8
W Total	2	.345	14	55	9	19	3	0	1	8	2	2	1	....
• JACKSON, Randy														
W 1956	Bro-N	.000	3	3	0	0	0	0	0	0	0	2	0	....
• JACKSON, Reggie														
D 1981	NY-A	.300	5	20	4	6	0	0	2	4	1	5	0	0-5
L 1971	Oak-A	.333	3	12	2	4	1	0	2	2	0	1	0	0-3
L 1972	Oak-A	.278	5	18	1	5	1	0	0	2	1	6	2	0-5
L 1973	Oak-A	.143	5	21	0	3	0	0	0	0	0	6	0	0-5
L 1974	Oak-A	.167	4	12	0	2	1	0	0	1	5	2	0	0-1,D-3
L 1975	Oak-A	.417	3	12	1	5	0	0	1	3	0	2	0	0-3
L 1977	NY-A	.125	5	16	1	2	0	0	0	1	2	2	1	0-4,D-1
L 1978	NY-A	.462	4	13	5	6	1	0	2	6	3	4	0	0-1,D-3
L 1980	NY-A	.273	3	11	1	3	1	0	0	0	1	4	0	0-3
L 1981	NY-A	.000	2	4	1	0	0	0	0	1	1	0	1	0-2
L 1982	Cal-A	.111	5	18	2	2	0	0	1	2	2	7	0	0-5
L 1986	Cal-A	.192	6	26	2	5	2	0	0	2	2	7	0	D-6
L Total	11	.227	45	163	16	37	7	0	6	20	17	41	4	....
W 1973	Oak-A	.310	7	29	3	9	3	1	1	6	2	7	0	0-7
W 1974	Oak-A	.286	5	14	3	4	1	0	1	1	5	3	1	0-5
W 1977	NY-A	.450	6	20	10	9	1	0	5	8	3	4	0	0-6
W 1978	NY-A	.391	6	23	2	9	1	0	2	8	3	7	0	D-6
W 1981	NY-A	.333	3	12	3	4	1	0	1	1	2	3	0	0-3
W Total	5	.357	27	98	21	35	7	1	10	24	15	24	1	....
• JACKSON, Ron														
L 1982	Cal-A	1.000	1	1	0	1	0	0	0	0	0	0	0	....
• JACKSON, Sonny														
L 1969	Atl-N	....	1	0	0	0	0	0	0	0	0	0	0	S-1
• JACKSON, Travis														
W 1923	NY-N	.000	1	1	0	0	0	0	0	0	0	0	0	....
W 1924	NY-N	.074	7	27	3	2	0	0	0	1	1	4	1	S-7
W 1933	NY-N	.222	5	18	3	4	1	0	0	2	1	3	0	3-5
W 1936	NY-N	.190	6	21	1	4	0	0	0	1	1	3	0	3-6
W Total	4	.149	19	67	7	10	1	0	0	4	3	10	1	....
• JAMES, Charlie														
W 1964	StL-N	.000	3	3	0	0	0	0	0	0	0	1	0	....
• JAMES, Dion														
D 1995	NY-A	.083	4	12	0	1	0	0	0	0	1	1	0	0-4
• JAMIESON, Charlie														
W 1920	Cle-A	.333	6	15	2	5	1	0	0	1	1	0	1	0-5
• JANVRIN, Hal														
W 1915	Bos-A	.000	1	1	0	0	0	0	0	0	0	0	0	S-1
W 1916	Bos-A	.217	5	23	2	5	3	0	0	1	0	6	0	2-5
W Total	2	.208	6	24	2	5	3	0	0	1	0	6	0	....
• JAVIER, Julian														
W 1964	StL-N	....	1	0	1	0	0	0	0	0	0	0	0	2-1
W 1967	StL-N	.360	7	25	2	9	3	0	1	4	0	6	0	2-7
W 1968	StL-N	.333	7	27	1	9	1	0	0	3	3	4	1	2-7
W 1972	Cin-N	.000	4	2	0	0	0	0	0	0	0	0	0	....
W Total	4	.333	19	54	4	18	4	0	1	7	3	10	1	....
• JAVIER, Stan														
D 1997	SF-N	.417	3	12	2	5	1	0	0	1	0	2	1	0-3
D 1999	Hou-N	.273	4	11	1	3	0	0	0	0	1	1	0	0-4
D 2000	Sea-A	.167	3	6	0	1	0	0	0	1	0	3	0	0-3
D 2001	Sea-A	.250	4	8	2	2	1	0	0	0	2	1	0	0-4
D Total	4	.297	14	37	5	11	2	0	0	2	3	7	1	....
L 1988	Oak-A	.500	2	4	0	2	0	0	0	1	1	0	0	0-2
L 1989	Oak-A	.000	1	2	0	0	0	0	0	0	0	1	0	0-1
L 2000	Sea-A	.071	4	14	0	1	0	0	0	1	0	4	0	0-4
L 2001	Sea-A	.214	5	14	2	3	0	0	1	2	1	3	1	0-4
L Total	4	.176	12	34	2	6	0	0	1	4	2	8	1	....
W 1988	Oak-A	.500	3	4	0	2	0	0	0	2	0	1	0	0-2
W 1989	Oak-A	....	1	0	0	0	0	0	0	0	0	0	0	0-1
W Total	2	.500	4	4	0	2	0	0	0	2	0	1	0	....
• JEFFERIES, Gregg														
L 1988	NY-N	.333	7	27	2	9	2	0	0	1	4	0	0	3-7
• JEFFERSON, Reggie														
D 1995	Bos-A	.250	1	4	1	1	0	0	0	0	0	1	0	D-1
• JENNINGS, Doug														
L 1990	Oak-A	.000	1	1	0	0	0	0	0	0	0	0	0	0-1
W 1990	Oak-A	1.000	1	1	0	1	0	0	0	0	0	0	0	....
• JENNINGS, Hughie														
T 1894	Bal-N	.143	4	14	0	2	0	0	0	1	0	2	0	S-4
T 1895	Bal-N	.368	5	19	3	7	2	0	0	2	1	0	1	S-5
T 1896	Bal-N	.333	4	15	5	5	2	0	0	3	1	2	1	S-4
T 1897	Bal-N	.318	5	22	5	7	2	0	0	3	4	0	0	S-5
T 1900	Bro-N	.167	4	18	1	3	1	0	0	2	1	1	0	1-4
T Total	5	.273	22	88	14	24	7	0	0	11	7	5	2	....
• JENSEN, Jackie														
W 1950	NY-A	....	1	0	0	0	0	0	0	0	0	0	0	....
• JETER, Derek														
D 1996	NY-A	.412	4	17	2	7	1	0	0	1	0	2	0	S-4
D 1997	NY-A	.333	5	21	6	7	1	0	2	2	3	5	1	S-5
D 1998	NY-A	.111	3	9	0	1	0	0	0	0	2	2	0	S-3
D 1999	NY-A	.455	3	11	3	5	1	1	0	0	2	3	0	S-3
D 2000	NY-A	.211	5	19	1	4	0	0	0	2	2	3	0	S-5
D 2001	NY-A	.444	5	18	2	8	1	0	0	1	1	0	0	S-5
D 2002	NY-A	.500	4	16	6	8	0	0	2	3	2	3	0	S-4
D 2003	NY-A	.429	4	14	2	6	0	0	1	1	4	2	1	S-4
D Total	8	.368	33	125	22	46	4	1	5	10	16	20	2	....
L 1996	NY-A	.417	5	24	5	10	2	0	1	1	0	5	2	S-5
L 1998	NY-A	.200	6	25	3	5	1	1	0	2	2	5	3	S-6
L 1999	NY-A	.350	5	20	3	7	1	0	1	3	2	3	0	S-5
L 2000	NY-A	.318	6	22	6	7	0	0	2	5	6	7	1	S-6
L 2001	NY-A	.118	5	17	0	2	0	0	0	2	2	2	0	S-5

YEAR	TM-L	AVG	G	AB	R	H	2B	3B	HR	RBI	BB	SO	SB	POS
L 2003	NY-A	.233	7	30	3	7	2	0	1	2	2	4	1	S-7
L Total	6	.275	34	138	20	38	6	1	5	15	14	26	7	....
W 1996	NY-A	.250	6	20	5	5	0	0	0	1	4	6	1	S-6
W 1998	NY-A	.353	4	17	4	6	0	0	0	1	3	3	0	S-4
W 1999	NY-A	.353	4	17	4	6	1	0	0	1	1	3	3	S-4
W 2000	NY-A	.409	5	22	6	9	2	1	2	2	3	8	0	S-5
W 2001	NY-A	.148	7	27	3	4	0	0	1	1	0	6	0	S-7
W 2003	NY-A	.346	6	26	5	9	3	0	0	2	1	7	0	S-6
W Total	6	.302	32	129	27	39	6	1	3	8	12	33	4	....
• JETER, Johnny														
L 1970	Pit-N	.000	3	2	0	0	0	0	0	0	0	2	0	0-1
• JOHNSON, Billy														
W 1943	NY-A	.300	5	20	3	6	1	1	0	3	0	3	0	3-5
W 1947	NY-A	.269	7	26	8	7	0	3	0	2	3	4	0	3-7
W 1949	NY-A	.143	2	7	0	1	0	0	0	0	0	2	1	3-2
W 1950	NY-A	.000	4	6	0	0	0	0	0	0	0	3	0	3-4
W Total	4	.237	18	59	11	14	1	4	0	5	3	12	1	....
• JOHNSON, Brian														
D 1996	SD-N	.375	2	8	2	3	1	0	0	0	0	1	0	C-2
D 1997	SF-N	.100	3	10	2	1	0	0	1	1	1	4	0	C-3
D Total	2	.222	5	18	4	4	1	0	1	1	1	5	0	....
• JOHNSON, Charles														
D 1997	Fla-N	.250	3	8	5	2	1	0	1	2	3	2	0	C-3
D 2000	Chi-A	.333	3	9	0	3	0	0	0	0	1	1	0	C-3
D Total	2	.294	6	17	5	5	1	0	1	2	4	3	0	....
L 1997	Fla-N	.118	6	17	1	2	2	0	0	5	3	8	0	C-6
W 1997	Fla-N	.357	7	28	4	10	0	0	1	3	1	6	0	C-7
• JOHNSON, Cliff														
D 1981	Oak-A	.286	2	7	0	2	1	0	0	0	0	1	0	D-2
L 1977	NY-A	.400	5	15	2	6	2	0	1	2	1	2	0	D-4
L 1978	NY-A	.000	1	1	0	0	0	0	0	0	0	0	0	....
L 1981	Oak-A	.000	2	6	0	0	0	0	0	0	2	2	0	D-2
L 1985	Tor-A	.368	7	19	1	7	2	0	0	2	1	4	0	D-7
L Total	4	.317	15	41	3	13	4	0	1	4	4	8	0	....
W 1977	NY-A	.000	2	1	0	0	0	0	0	0	0	0	0	C-1
W 1978	NY-A	.000	2	2	0	0	0	0	0	0	0	0	0	....
W Total	2	.000	4	3	0	0	0	0	0	0	0	0	0	....
• JOHNSON, Darrell														
W 1961	Cin-N	.500	2	4	0	2	0	0	0	0	0	0	0	C-2
• JOHNSON, Davey														
L 1969	Bal-A	.231	3	13	2	3	0	0	0	0	2	1	0	2-3
L 1970	Bal-A	.364	3	11	4	4	0	0	2	4	1	1	0	2-3
L 1971	Bal-A	.300	3	10	2	3	2	0	0	0	3	1	0	2-3
L 1977	Phi-N	.250	1	4	0	1	0	0	0	2	0	1	0	1-1
L Total	4	.289	10	38	8	11	2	0	2	6	6	4	0	....
W 1966	Bal-A	.286	4	14	1	4	1	0	0	1	0	1	0	2-4
W 1969	Bal-A	.063	5	16	1	1	0	0	0	0	2	1	0	2-5
W 1970	Bal-A	.313	5	16	2	5	2	0	0	2	5	2	0	2-5
W 1971	Bal-A	.148	7	27	1	4	0	0	0	3	0	1	0	2-7
W Total	4	.192	21	73	5	14	3	0	0	6	7	5	0	....
• JOHNSON, Deron														
L 1973	Oak-A	.100	4	10	0	1	0	0	0	0	2	6	0	D-4
W 1973	Oak-A	.300	6	10	0	3	1	0	0	0	1	4	0	1-2
• JOHNSON, Don														
W 1945	Chi-N	.172	7	29	4	5	2	1	0	0	0	8	1	2-7
• JOHNSON, Ernie														
W 1923	NY-A	....	2	0	1	0	0	0	0	0	0	0	0	S-1
• JOHNSON, Howard														
L 1986	NY-N	.000	2	2	0	0	0	0	0	0	0	0	0	....
L 1988	NY-N	.056	6	18	3	1	0	0	0	0	1	6	1	3-1,S-5
L Total	2	.050	8	20	3	1	0	0	0	0	1	6	1	....
W 1984	Det-A	.000	1	1	0	0	0	0	0	0	0	0	0	D-1
W 1986	NY-N	.000	2	5	0	0	0	0	0	0	0	2	0	3-1,S-1
W Total	2	.000	3	6	0	0	0	0	0	0	0	2	0	....
• JOHNSON, Ken														
W 1950	Phi-N	....	1	0	1	0	0	0	0	0	0	0	0	....
• JOHNSON, Lance														
D 1998	Chi-N	.167	3	12	0	2	0	0	0	1	0	1	0	0-3
L 1987	StL-N	....	1	0	1	0	0	0	0	0	0	0	1	....
L 1993	Chi-A	.217	6	23	2	5	1	1	1	6	2	1	1	0-6
L Total	2	.217	7	23	3	5	1	1	1	6	2	1	2	....
W 1987	StL-N	....	1	0	0	0	0	0	0	0	0	0	1	....
• JOHNSON, Lou														
W 1965	LA-N	.296	7	27	3	8	2	0	2	4	1	3	0	0-7
W 1966	LA-N	.267	4	15	1	4	1	0	0	0	1	1	0	0-4
W Total	2	.286	11	42	4	12	3	0	2	4	2	4	0	....
• JOHNSON, Nick														
D 2002	NY-A	.182	3	11	1	2	0	0	0	1	1	5	0	1-1,D-2
D 2003	NY-A	.077	4	13	2	1	1	0	0	2	3	2	0	1-4
D Total	2	.125	7	24	3	3	1	0	0	3	4	7	0	....
L 2003	NY-A	.231	7	26	4	6	1	0	1	3	2	4	0	1-7
W 2003	NY-A	.294	6	17	3	5	1	0	0	0	2	3	0	1-5
• JOHNSON, Roy														
W 1936	NY-A	.000	2	1	0	0	0	0	0	0	0	1	0	....
• JOHNSON, Russ														
D 1997	Hou-N	.000	1	1	0	0	0	0	0	0	0	1	0	....
D 1999	Hou-N	1.000	2	1	0	1	1	0	0	0	1	0	0	....
D Total	2	.500	3	2	0	1	1	0	0	0	1	1	0	....
• JOHNSON, Wallace														
D 1981	Mon-N	.500	2	2	0	1	0	0	0	1	0	0	0	....
• JOHNSTON, Doc														
W 1920	Cle-A	.273	5	11	1	3	0	0	0	0	2	1	1	1-5
• JOHNSTON, Jimmy														
W 1916	Bro-N	.300	3	10	1	3	0	1	0	0	1	0	0	0-2
W 1920	Bro-N	.214	4	14	2	3	0	0	0	0	0	2	1	3-4
W Total	2	.250	7	24	3	6	0	1	0	0	1	2	1	....
• JOHNSTONE, Jay														
D 1981	LA-N	.000	1	1	0	0	0	0	0	0	0	0	0	....
L 1976	Phi-N	.778	3	9	1	7	1	1	0	2	1	0	0	0-2
L 1977	Phi-N	.200	2	5	0	1	0	0	0	0	0	2	0	0-2
L 1981	LA-N	.000	2	2	0	0	0	0	0	0	0	0	0	....
L 1985	LA-N	.000	1	1	0	0	0	0	0	0	0	0	0	....
L Total	4	.471	8	17	1	8	1	1	0	2	1	2	0	....
W 1978	NY-A	....	2	0	0	0	0	0	0	0	0	1	0	0-2
W 1981	LA-N	.667	3	3	1	2	0	0	1	3	0	0	0	....
W Total	2	.667	5	3	1	2	0	0	1	3	0	1	0	....
• JONES, Andruw														
D 1996	Atl-N	....	3	0	0	0	0	0	0	0	1	0	0	0-3
D 1997	Atl-N	.000	3	5	1	0	0	0	0	1	1	1	0	0-3
D 1998	Atl-N	.000	3	9	2	0	0	0	0	1	3	2	2	0-3
D 1999	Atl-N	.222	4	18	1	4	1	0	0	2	1	3	0	0-4
D 2000	Atl-N	.111	3	9	3	1	0	0	1	1	4	1	0	0-3
D 2001	Atl-N	.500	3	12	2	6	0	0	1	1	0	3	0	0-3
D 2002	Atl-N	.316	5	19	4	6	1	0	0	2	2	3	0	0-5
D 2003	Atl-N	.059	5	17	1	1	0	0	0	1	4	7	0	0-5
D Total	8	.202	29	89	14	18	2	0	2	9	16	20	2	....
L 1996	Atl-N	.222	5	9	3	2	0	0	1	3	3	2	0	0-5
L 1997	Atl-N	.444	5	9	0	4	0	0	0	1	1	1	0	0-5
L 1998	Atl-N	.273	6	22	3	6	0	0	1	2	1	4	1	0-6
L 1999	Atl-N	.217	6	23	5	5	0	0	0	1	4	3	0	0-6
L 2001	Atl-N	.176	5	17	4	3	0	0	1	1	1	5	0	0-5
L Total	5	.250	27	80	15	20	0	0	3	8	10	15	1	....
W 1996	Atl-N	.400	6	20	4	8	1	0	2	6	3	6	1	0-6
W 1999	Atl-N	.077	4	13	1	1	0	0	0	0	1	3	0	0-4
W Total	2	.273	10	33	5	9	1	0	2	6	4	9	1	....
• JONES, Chipper														
D 1995	Atl-N	.389	4	18	4	7	2	0	2	4	2	2	0	3-4
D 1996	Atl-N	.222	3	9	2	2	0	0	1	2	3	4	1	3-3
D 1997	Atl-N	.500	3	8	3	4	0	0	1	2	3	2	1	3-3
D 1998	Atl-N	.200	3	10	2	2	0	0	0	1	4	3	0	3-3
D 1999	Atl-N	.231	4	13	2	3	0	0	0	1	5	2	0	3-4
D 2000	Atl-N	.333	3	12	2	4	1	0	0	1	1	4	0	3-3
D 2001	Atl-N	.444	3	9	2	4	0	0	2	5	3	1	0	3-3
D 2002	Atl-N	.294	5	17	3	5	0	0	0	2	5	2	0	0-5
D 2003	Atl-N	.167	5	18	3	3	0	0	2	6	3	4	0	0-5
D Total	9	.298	33	114	23	34	3	0	8	24	29	24	2	....
L 1995	Atl-N	.438	4	16	3	7	0	0	1	3	3	1	1	3-4
L 1996	Atl-N	.440	7	25	6	11	2	0	0	4	3	1	1	3-7
L 1997	Atl-N	.292	6	24	5	7	1	0	2	4	2	3	0	3-6
L 1998	Atl-N	.208	6	24	2	5	1	0	0	1	4	5	0	3-6
L 1999	Atl-N	.263	6	19	3	5	2	0	0	1	9	7	3	3-6
L 2001	Atl-N	.263	5	19	1	5	1	0	0	2	3	6	0	3-5
L Total	6	.315	34	127	20	40	7	0	3	15	24	23	5	....
W 1995	Atl-N	.286	6	21	3	6	3	0	0	1	4	3	0	3-6
W 1996	Atl-N	.286	6	21	3	6	3	0	0	3	4	2	1	3-6,S-1
W 1999	Atl-N	.231	4	13	2	3	0	0	1	2	4	2	0	3-4
W Total	3	.273	16	55	8	15	6	0	1	6	12	7	1	....
• JONES, Cleon														
L 1969	NY-N	.429	3	14	4	6	2	0	1	4	1	2	2	0-3
L 1973	NY-N	.300	5	20	3	6	2	0	0	3	2	4	0	0-5
L Total	2	.353	8	34	7	12	4	0	1	7	3	6	2	....
W 1969	NY-N	.158	5	19	2	3	1	0	0	0	0	1	0	0-5
W 1973	NY-N	.286	7	28	5	8	2	0	1	1	4	2	0	0-7
W Total	2	.234	12	47	7	11	3	0	1	1	4	3	0	....
• JONES, Dalton														
W 1967	Bos-A	.389	6	18	2	7	0	0	0	1	1	3	0	3-5
• JONES, Davy														
W 1907	Det-A	.353	5	17	1	6	0	0	0	0	4	0	3	0-5
W 1908	Det-A	.000	3	2	1	0	0	0	0	0	1	1	0	....
W 1909	Det-A	.233	7	30	6	7	0	0	1	1	2	1	1	0-7
W Total	3	.265	15	49	8	13	0	0	1	1	7	2	4	....
• JONES, Fielder														
T 1900	Bro-N	.278	4	18	3	5	0	0	0	4	1	1	1	0-4
W 1906	Chi-A	.143	6	21	4	3	0	0	0	0	3	3	0	0-6
• JONES, Jacque														
D 2002	Min-A	.250	5	20	3	5	3	0	0	1	1	8	0	0-5
D 2003	Min-A	.125	4	16	0	2	0	0	0	0	0	5	0	0-4
D Total	2	.194	9	36	3	7	3	0	0	1	1	13	0	....
L 2002	Min-A	.100	5	20	0	2	1	0	0	2	0	4	0	0-5
• JONES, Lynn														
L 1984	KC-A	.200	3	5	1	1	0	0	0	0	0	0	0	0-2
L 1985	KC-A	....	5	0	0	0	0	0	0	0	0	0	0	0-5
L Total	2	.200	8	5	1	1	0	0	0	0	0	0	0	....
W 1985	KC-A	.667	6	3	0	2	1	1	0	0	0	0	0	0-4

SER-YEAR	TM-L	AVG	G	AB	R	H	2B	3B	HR	RBI	BB	SO	SB	POS
• JONES, Nippy														
W 1946	StL-N	.000	1	1	0	0	0	0	0	0	0	1	0	....
W 1957	Mil-N	.000	3	2	0	0	0	0	0	0	0	0	0	....
W Total	**2**	**.000**	**4**	**3**	**0**	**0**	**0**	**0**	**0**	**0**	**0**	**1**	**0**	**....**
• JONES, Ruppert														
L 1984	Det-A	.000	2	5	1	0	0	0	0	0	1	1	0	O-2
L 1986	Cal-A	.176	6	17	4	3	1	0	0	2	5	2	0	O-5
L Total	**2**	**.136**	**8**	**22**	**5**	**3**	**1**	**0**	**0**	**2**	**6**	**3**	**0**	**....**
W 1984	Det-A	.000	2	3	0	0	0	0	0	0	0	1	0	O-2
• JONES, Tom														
W 1909	Det-A	.250	7	24	3	6	1	0	0	2	2	0	1	1-7
• JONES, Willie														
W 1950	Phi-N	.286	4	14	1	4	1	0	0	0	0	3	0	3-4
• JOOST, Eddie														
W 1940	Cin-N	.200	7	25	0	5	0	0	0	2	1	2	0	2-7
• JORDAN, Brian														
D 1996	StL-N	.333	3	12	4	4	0	0	1	3	1	3	1	O-3
D 1999	Atl-N	.471	4	17	2	8	1	0	1	7	1	2	0	O-4
D 2000	Atl-N	.364	3	11	1	4	1	0	0	4	1	1	0	O-3
D 2001	Atl-N	.182	3	11	1	2	0	0	1	2	0	5	0	O-3
D Total	**4**	**.353**	**13**	**51**	**8**	**18**	**2**	**0**	**3**	**16**	**3**	**11**	**1**	**....**
L 1996	StL-N	.240	7	25	3	6	1	1	1	2	1	3	0	O-7
L 1999	Atl-N	.200	6	25	3	5	0	0	2	5	3	5	0	O-6
L 2001	Atl-N	.190	5	21	1	4	2	0	0	3	0	6	0	O-5
L Total	**3**	**.211**	**18**	**71**	**7**	**15**	**3**	**1**	**3**	**10**	**4**	**14**	**0**	**....**
W 1999	Atl-N	.077	4	13	1	1	0	0	0	1	4	2	0	O-4
• JORDAN, Ricky														
L 1993	Phi-N	.000	2	1	0	0	0	0	0	0	1	0	0	....
W 1993	Phi-N	.200	3	10	0	2	0	0	0	0	0	2	0	D-2
• JORGENSEN, Mike														
L 1985	StL-N	.000	2	2	0	0	0	0	0	0	0	1	0	....
W 1985	StL-N	.000	2	3	0	0	0	0	0	0	0	0	0	O-1
• JORGENSEN, Spider														
W 1947	Bro-N	.200	7	20	1	4	2	0	0	3	2	4	0	3-7
W 1949	Bro-N	.182	4	11	1	2	2	0	0	0	2	2	0	3-3
W Total	**2**	**.194**	**11**	**31**	**2**	**6**	**4**	**0**	**0**	**3**	**4**	**6**	**0**	**....**
• JOSHUA, Von														
L 1974	LA-N	....	1	0	0	0	0	0	0	0	1	0	0	....
W 1974	LA-N	.000	4	4	0	0	0	0	0	0	0	0	0	....
• JOYNER, Wally														
D 1996	SD-N	.111	3	9	0	1	0	0	0	0	0	2	0	1-3
D 1998	SD-N	.167	4	6	1	1	0	0	1	2	1	2	0	1-4
D 2000	Atl-N	.333	3	3	0	1	1	0	0	0	0	0	0	....
D Total	**3**	**.167**	**10**	**18**	**1**	**3**	**1**	**0**	**1**	**2**	**1**	**4**	**0**	**....**
L 1986	Cal-A	.455	3	11	3	5	2	0	1	2	2	0	0	1-3
L 1998	SD-N	.313	6	16	3	5	0	0	0	2	4	3	0	1-6
L Total	**2**	**.370**	**9**	**27**	**6**	**10**	**2**	**0**	**1**	**4**	**6**	**3**	**0**	**....**
W 1998	SD-N	.000	3	8	0	0	0	0	0	0	3	1	0	1-3
• JUDGE, Joe														
W 1924	Was-A	.385	7	26	4	10	1	0	0	0	5	2	0	1-7
W 1925	Was-A	.174	7	23	2	4	1	0	1	4	3	2	0	1-7
W Total	**2**	**.286**	**14**	**49**	**6**	**14**	**2**	**0**	**1**	**4**	**8**	**4**	**0**	**....**
• JUDNICH, Wally														
W 1948	Cle-A	.077	4	13	1	1	0	0	0	1	1	4	0	O-4
• JURGES, Billy														
W 1932	Chi-N	.364	3	11	1	4	1	0	0	1	0	1	2	S-3
W 1935	Chi-N	.250	6	16	3	4	0	0	0	1	4	4	0	S-6
W 1938	Chi-N	.231	4	13	0	3	1	0	0	0	1	3	0	S-4
W Total	**3**	**.275**	**13**	**40**	**4**	**11**	**2**	**0**	**0**	**2**	**5**	**8**	**2**	**....**
• JURISICH, Al														
W 1944	StL-N	....	1	0	0	0	0	0	0	0	0	0	0	....
• JUSTICE, David														
D 1995	Atl-N	.231	4	13	2	3	0	0	0	0	5	2	0	O-4
D 1997	Cle-A	.263	5	19	3	5	2	0	1	2	2	3	0	D-5
D 1998	Cle-A	.313	4	16	2	5	4	0	1	6	0	1	0	O-2,D-2
D 1999	Cle-A	.000	3	8	0	0	0	0	0	1	2	2	0	O-3
D 2000	NY-A	.222	5	18	2	4	0	0	1	1	3	4	0	O-5
D 2001	NY-A	.231	4	13	3	3	0	1	1	1	2	5	0	O-2,D-2
D 2002	Oak-A	.238	5	21	2	5	1	1	0	4	0	4	0	O-5
D Total	**7**	**.231**	**30**	**108**	**14**	**25**	**7**	**2**	**4**	**15**	**14**	**21**	**0**	**....**
L 1991	Atl-N	.200	7	25	4	5	1	0	1	2	3	7	0	O-7
L 1992	Atl-N	.280	7	25	5	7	1	0	2	6	6	2	0	O-7
L 1993	Atl-N	.143	6	21	2	3	1	0	0	4	3	3	0	O-6
L 1995	Atl-N	.273	3	11	1	3	0	0	0	1	2	1	0	O-3
L 1997	Cle-A	.333	6	21	3	7	1	0	0	0	2	4	0	D-6
L 1998	Cle-A	.158	6	19	2	3	0	0	1	2	3	3	0	O-1,D-4
L 2000	NY-A	.231	6	26	4	6	2	0	2	8	2	7	0	O-6
L 2001	NY-A	.278	5	18	3	5	1	0	0	4	3	1	0	D-5
L Total	**8**	**.235**	**46**	**166**	**24**	**39**	**7**	**0**	**6**	**27**	**24**	**28**	**0**	**....**
W 1991	Atl-N	.259	7	27	5	7	0	0	2	6	5	5	2	O-7
W 1992	Atl-N	.158	6	19	4	3	0	0	1	3	6	5	1	O-6
W 1995	Atl-N	.250	6	20	3	5	1	0	1	5	5	1	0	O-6
W 1997	Cle-A	.185	7	27	4	5	0	0	0	4	6	8	0	O-4,D-3
W 2000	NY-A	.158	5	19	1	3	2	0	0	3	3	2	0	O-5
W 2001	NY-A	.167	5	12	0	2	0	0	0	0	1	9	0	O-2,D-2
W Total	**6**	**.202**	**36**	**124**	**17**	**25**	**3**	**0**	**4**	**21**	**26**	**30**	**3**	**....**
• KALINE, Al														
L 1972	Det-A	.263	5	19	3	5	0	0	1	1	2	2	0	O-5
W 1968	Det-A	.379	7	29	6	11	2	0	2	8	0	7	0	O-7
• KANE, John														
W 1910	Chi-N	....	1	0	0	0	0	0	0	0	0	0	0	....
• KAPLER, Gabe														
D 2003	Bos-A	.000	4	9	0	0	0	0	0	0	0	3	0	O-5
L 2003	Bos-A	.125	3	8	0	1	0	0	0	0	0	3	0	....
• KARKOVICE, Ron														
L 1993	Chi-A	.000	6	15	0	0	0	0	0	0	1	7	0	C-6
• KARROS, Eric														
D 1995	LA-N	.500	3	12	3	6	1	0	2	4	1	0	0	1-3
D 1996	LA-N	.000	3	9	0	0	0	0	0	0	2	3	0	1-3
D 2003	Chi-N	.375	4	16	4	6	0	0	2	2	0	3	0	1-4
D Total	**3**	**.324**	**10**	**37**	**7**	**12**	**1**	**0**	**4**	**6**	**3**	**6**	**0**	**....**
L 2003	Chi-N	.231	5	13	2	3	0	0	0	0	2	3	0	1-5
• KASKO, Eddie														
W 1961	Cin-N	.318	5	22	1	7	0	0	0	1	0	2	0	S-5
• KAUFF, Benny														
W 1917	NY-N	.160	6	25	2	4	1	0	2	5	0	2	1	O-6
• KEELER, Willie														
T 1894	Bal-N	.250	3	12	1	3	0	0	0	1	1	0	0	O-3
T 1895	Bal-N	.235	5	17	3	4	0	0	0	1	3	1	0	O-5
T 1896	Bal-N	.471	4	17	4	8	1	2	0	4	0	0	1	O-4
T 1897	Bal-N	.391	5	23	5	9	2	0	0	2	4	0	0	O-5
T 1900	Bro-N	.353	4	17	0	6	0	0	0	0	1	0	0	O-4
T Total	**5**	**.349**	**21**	**86**	**13**	**30**	**3**	**2**	**0**	**8**	**9**	**1**	**1**	**....**
• KELLER, Charlie														
W 1939	NY-A	.438	4	16	8	7	1	1	3	6	1	2	0	O-4
W 1941	NY-A	.389	5	18	5	7	2	0	0	5	3	1	0	O-5
W 1942	NY-A	.200	5	20	2	4	0	0	2	5	1	3	0	O-5
W 1943	NY-A	.222	5	18	3	4	0	1	0	2	2	5	1	O-5
W Total	**4**	**.306**	**19**	**72**	**18**	**22**	**3**	**2**	**5**	**18**	**7**	**11**	**1**	**....**
• KELLERT, Frank														
W 1955	Bro-N	.333	3	3	0	1	0	0	0	0	0	0	0	....
• KELLEY, Joe														
T 1894	Bal-N	.333	4	15	2	5	1	1	0	0	3	2	1	O-4
T 1895	Bal-N	.368	5	19	1	7	0	0	0	5	1	1	1	O-5
T 1896	Bal-N	.471	4	17	3	8	1	0	0	4	0	1	2	O-4
T 1897	Bal-N	.313	4	16	7	5	3	0	0	5	5	0	0	O-4
T 1900	Bro-N	.176	4	17	2	3	0	0	0	1	2	3	0	O-4
T Total	**5**	**.333**	**21**	**84**	**15**	**28**	**5**	**1**	**0**	**15**	**11**	**7**	**4**	**....**
• KELLY, George														
W 1921	NY-N	.233	8	30	3	7	1	0	0	4	3	10	0	1-8
W 1922	NY-N	.278	5	18	0	5	0	0	0	2	0	3	0	1-5
W 1923	NY-N	.182	6	22	1	4	0	0	0	1	1	2	0	1-6
W 1924	NY-N	.290	7	31	7	9	1	0	1	4	1	8	0	O-4,1-4,2-1
W Total	**4**	**.248**	**26**	**101**	**11**	**25**	**2**	**0**	**1**	**11**	**5**	**23**	**0**	**....**
• KELLY, King														
T 1892	Bos-N	.000	2	8	0	0	0	0	0	0	0	2	1	C-2
W 1885	Chi-N	.346	7	26	9	9	3	1	0	0	2	0	0	O-4,C-3
W 1886	Chi-N	.208	6	24	4	5	0	0	1	1	2	2	1	C-5,S-2,1-1,3-1
W Total	**2**	**.280**	**13**	**50**	**13**	**14**	**3**	**1**	**1**	**1**	**4**	**2**	**1**	**....**
• KELLY, Pat														
L 1979	Bal-A	.364	3	11	3	4	0	0	1	4	1	3	2	O-1,D-2
W 1979	Bal-A	.250	5	4	0	1	0	0	0	0	1	1	0	....
• KELLY, Pat														
D 1995	NY-A	.000	5	3	3	0	0	0	0	1	1	3	0	2-4
• KELLY, Roberto														
D 1995	LA-N	.364	3	11	0	4	0	0	0	0	1	0	0	O-3
D 1997	Sea-A	.308	4	13	1	4	3	0	0	1	0	3	0	O-3
D 1998	Tex-A	.143	2	7	0	1	1	0	0	0	0	2	0	O-2
D 1999	Tex-A	.333	1	3	0	1	0	0	0	0	0	2	0	O-1
D Total	**4**	**.294**	**10**	**34**	**1**	**10**	**4**	**0**	**0**	**1**	**1**	**7**	**0**	**....**
• KELTNER, Ken														
W 1948	Cle-A	.095	6	21	3	2	0	0	0	0	2	3	0	3-6
• KENNEDY, Adam														
D 2002	Ana-A	.500	4	8	4	4	1	0	1	3	1	2	1	2-4
L 2002	Ana-A	.357	4	14	5	5	0	0	3	5	0	2	1	2-4
W 2002	Ana-A	.280	7	25	1	7	2	0	0	2	0	7	0	2-6
• KENNEDY, Bob														
W 1948	Cle-A	.500	3	2	0	1	0	0	0	1	0	1	0	O-3
• KENNEDY, Brickyard														
W 1903	Pit-N	.500	1	2	0	1	1	0	0	0	0	0	0	....
• KENNEDY, Ed														
W 1884	NY-A	.000	3	7	0	0	0	0	0	0	0	2	0	O-3
• KENNEDY, John														
W 1965	LA-N	.000	4	1	0	0	0	0	0	0	0	0	0	3-4
W 1966	LA-N	.200	2	5	0	1	0	0	0	0	0	0	0	3-2
W Total	**2**	**.167**	**6**	**6**	**0**	**1**	**0**	**0**	**0**	**0**	**0**	**0**	**0**	**....**
• KENNEDY, Monte														
W 1951	NY-N	....	2	0	0	0	0	0	0	0	0	0	0	....
• KENNEDY, Terry														
L 1984	SD-N	.222	5	18	2	4	0	0	0	1	1	3	0	C-5
L 1989	SF-N	.188	5	16	0	3	1	0	0	0	1	4	0	C-5
L Total	**2**	**.206**	**10**	**34**	**2**	**7**	**1**	**0**	**0**	**1**	**2**	**7**	**0**	**....**
W 1984	SD-N	.211	5	19	2	4	1	0	1	3	1	1	0	C-5

YEAR	TM-L	AVG	G	AB	R	H	2B	3B	HR	RBI	BB	SO	SB	POS
W 1989	SF-N	.167	4	12	1	2	0	0	0	2	1	3	0	C-4
W Total	2	.194	9	31	3	6	1	0	1	5	2	4	0	....
• KENT, Jeff														
D 1996	Cle-A	.125	4	8	2	1	1	0	0	0	0	0	0	1-1,2-1,3-2
D 1997	SF-N	.300	3	10	2	3	0	0	2	2	2	1	0	1-1,2-3
D 2000	SF-N	.375	4	16	3	6	1	0	0	1	1	3	1	1-1,2-4
D 2002	SF-N	.263	5	19	1	5	2	0	0	1	2	7	0	2-5
D Total	4	.283	16	53	8	15	4	0	2	4	5	11	1	....
L 2002	SF-N	.263	5	19	3	5	0	0	0	0	2	4	0	2-5
W 2002	SF-N	.276	7	29	6	8	1	0	3	7	1	7	0	2-7
• KERR, John														
W 1933	Was-A	....	1	0	0	0	0	0	0	0	0	0	0	....
• KIELTY, Bobby														
D 2002	Min-A	.000	3	4	0	0	0	0	0	0	0	1	0	0-2,D-1
L 2002	Min-A	.000	4	3	0	0	0	0	0	1	1	2	0	0-1,D-1
• KILDUFF, Pete														
W 1920	Bro-N	.095	7	21	0	2	0	0	0	0	1	4	0	2-7
• KILLEBREW, Harmon														
L 1969	Min-A	.125	3	8	2	1	1	0	0	0	6	2	0	3-3
L 1970	Min-A	.273	3	11	2	3	0	0	2	4	2	4	0	1-1,3-2
L Total	2	.211	6	19	4	4	1	0	2	4	8	6	0	....
W 1965	Min-A	.286	7	21	2	6	0	0	1	2	6	4	0	3-7
• KILLEFER, Bill														
W 1915	Phi-N	.000	1	1	0	0	0	0	0	0	0	0	0	....
W 1918	Chi-N	.118	6	17	2	2	1	0	0	2	2	0	0	C-6
W Total	2	.111	7	18	2	2	1	0	0	2	2	0	0	....
• KING, Hal														
L 1973	Cin-N	.500	3	2	0	1	0	0	0	0	1	1	0	....
• KING, Jeff														
L 1990	Pit-N	.100	5	10	0	1	0	0	0	0	1	5	0	3-4
L 1992	Pit-N	.241	7	29	4	7	4	0	0	2	0	1	0	3-7
L Total	2	.205	12	39	4	8	4	0	0	2	1	6	0	....
• KING, Lee														
W 1922	NY-N	1.000	2	1	0	1	0	0	0	1	0	0	0	0-2
• KINGERY, Mike														
D 1995	Col-N	.200	4	10	1	2	0	0	0	0	0	1	0	0-4
• KINGMAN, Dave														
L 1971	SF-N	.111	4	9	0	1	0	0	0	0	1	3	0	0-2
• KIRBY, Wayne														
D 1995	Cle-A	1.000	3	1	0	1	0	0	0	0	0	0	0	0-2
D 1996	LA-N	.125	3	8	1	1	0	0	0	0	2	1	0	0-3
D Total	2	.222	6	9	1	2	0	0	0	0	2	1	0	....
L 1995	Cle-A	.200	5	5	2	1	0	0	0	0	0	0	1	0-2
W 1995	Cle-A	.000	3	1	0	0	0	0	0	0	0	1	0	0-1
• KIRKPATRICK, Ed														
L 1974	Pit-N	.000	3	9	0	0	0	0	0	0	2	0	0	1-3
L 1975	Pit-N	.000	2	2	0	0	0	0	0	0	0	0	0	....
L Total	2	.000	5	11	0	0	0	0	0	0	2	0	0	....
• KITSON, Frank														
T 1900	Bro-N	.000	1	3	0	0	0	0	0	0	1	2	0	P-1
• KITTLE, Ron														
L 1983	Chi-A	.286	3	7	1	2	1	0	0	0	1	2	0	0-3
• KLEIN, Chuck														
W 1935	Chi-N	.333	5	12	2	4	0	0	1	2	0	2	0	0-3
• KLEIN, Lou														
W 1943	StL-N	.136	5	22	0	3	0	0	0	0	1	2	0	2-5
• KLESKO, Ryan														
D 1995	Atl-N	.467	4	15	5	7	1	0	0	1	0	3	0	0-4
D 1996	Atl-N	.125	3	8	1	1	0	0	1	1	3	4	1	0-3
D 1997	Atl-N	.250	3	8	2	2	1	0	1	1	0	2	0	0-3
D 1998	Atl-N	.273	3	11	1	3	0	0	1	4	0	3	0	0-3
D 1999	Atl-N	.333	4	12	3	4	0	0	0	1	1	4	0	1-4
D Total	5	.315	17	54	12	17	2	0	3	8	4	16	1	....
L 1995	Atl-N	.000	4	7	0	0	0	0	0	0	3	4	0	0-3
L 1996	Atl-N	.250	6	16	1	4	0	0	1	3	2	6	0	0-6
L 1997	Atl-N	.235	5	17	2	4	0	0	2	4	2	3	0	0-5
L 1998	Atl-N	.083	5	12	2	1	0	0	0	1	6	3	0	0-5
L 1999	Atl-N	.125	4	8	1	1	0	0	1	1	2	1	0	1-4
L Total	5	.167	24	60	6	10	0	0	4	9	15	17	0	....
W 1995	Atl-N	.313	6	16	4	5	0	0	3	4	3	4	0	0-3,D-3
W 1996	Atl-N	.100	5	10	2	1	0	0	0	1	2	4	0	0-2,1-1,D-1
W 1999	Atl-N	.167	4	12	0	2	0	0	0	0	0	1	0	1-4
W Total	3	.211	15	38	6	8	0	0	3	5	5	9	0	....
• KLINE, Steve														
D 2001	StL-N	....	4	0	0	0	0	0	0	0	0	0	0	....
D 2002	StL-N	....	2	0	0	0	0	0	0	0	0	0	0	....
D Total	2	....	6	0	0	0	0	0	0	0	0	0	0	....
L 2002	StL-N	....	4	0	0	0	0	0	0	0	0	0	0	....
• KLING, Johnny														
W 1906	Chi-N	.176	6	17	2	3	1	0	0	0	4	3	0	C-6
W 1907	Chi-N	.211	5	19	2	4	0	0	0	1	1	4	0	C-5
W 1908	Chi-N	.250	5	16	2	4	1	0	0	2	2	2	0	C-5
W 1910	Chi-N	.077	5	13	0	1	0	0	0	1	1	2	0	C-3
W Total	4	.185	21	65	6	12	2	0	0	4	8	11	0	....
• KLOBEDANZ, Fred														
T 1897	Bos-N	1.000	2	5	3	5	0	0	0	0	0	0	0	P-2
• KLUSZEWSKI, Ted														
W 1959	Chi-A	.391	6	23	5	9	1	0	3	10	2	0	0	1-6
• KLUTTS, Mickey														
D 1981	Oak-A	.143	2	7	0	1	0	0	0	0	0	1	0	3-2
L 1981	Oak-A	.429	3	7	1	3	0	0	0	0	0	1	0	3-3
• KNIGHT, Ray														
L 1979	Cin-N	.286	3	14	0	4	1	0	0	0	0	2	1	3-3
L 1986	NY-N	.167	6	24	1	4	0	0	0	2	1	5	0	3-6
L Total	2	.211	9	38	1	8	1	0	0	2	1	7	1	....
W 1986	NY-N	.391	6	23	4	9	1	0	1	5	2	2	0	3-6
• KNOBLAUCH, Chuck														
D 1998	NY-A	.091	3	11	0	1	0	0	0	0	0	4	0	2-3
D 1999	NY-A	.167	3	12	1	2	0	0	0	0	1	3	0	2-3
D 2000	NY-A	.333	3	9	1	3	0	0	0	1	0	2	1	D-3
D 2001	NY-A	.273	5	22	1	6	1	0	0	1	0	0	1	0-5
D Total	4	.222	14	54	3	12	1	0	0	2	1	9	2	....
L 1991	Min-A	.350	5	20	5	7	2	0	0	3	3	3	2	2-5
L 1998	NY-A	.200	6	25	4	5	1	0	0	0	4	2	0	2-6
L 1999	NY-A	.333	5	18	3	6	1	0	0	1	3	0	1	2-5
L 2000	NY-A	.261	6	23	3	6	2	0	0	2	3	4	0	D-6
L 2001	NY-A	.333	5	18	0	6	1	0	0	3	2	3	0	0-5
L Total	5	.288	27	104	15	30	7	0	0	9	15	12	3	....
W 1991	Min-A	.308	7	26	3	8	1	0	0	2	4	2	4	2-7
W 1998	NY-A	.375	4	16	3	6	0	0	1	3	3	2	1	2-4
W 1999	NY-A	.313	4	16	5	5	1	0	1	3	1	3	1	2-4
W 2000	NY-A	.100	4	10	1	1	0	0	0	1	2	1	0	D-2
W 2001	NY-A	.056	6	18	1	1	0	0	0	0	1	2	0	0-4,D-2
W Total	5	.244	25	86	13	21	2	0	2	9	11	10	6	....
• KNORR, Randy														
W 1993	Tor-A	....	1	0	0	0	0	0	0	0	0	0	0	C-1
• KNOX, John														
L 1972	Det-A	....	1	0	0	0	0	0	0	0	0	0	0	....
• KOENIG, Mark														
W 1926	NY-A	.125	7	32	2	4	1	0	0	2	0	6	0	S-7
W 1927	NY-A	.500	4	18	5	9	2	0	0	2	0	2	0	S-4
W 1928	NY-A	.158	4	19	1	3	0	0	0	0	0	1	0	S-4
W 1932	Chi-N	.250	2	4	1	1	0	1	0	1	1	0	0	S-1
W 1936	NY-N	.333	3	3	0	1	0	0	0	0	0	1	0	2-1
W Total	5	.237	20	76	9	18	3	1	0	5	1	10	0	....
• KONERKO, Paul														
D 2000	Chi-A	.000	3	9	1	0	0	0	0	0	1	1	0	1-2
• KONETCHY, Ed														
W 1920	Bro-N	.174	7	23	0	4	0	1	0	2	3	2	0	1-7
• KOPF, Larry														
W 1919	Cin-N	.222	8	27	3	6	0	2	0	2	3	2	0	S-8
• KOSCO, Andy														
L 1973	Cin-N	.300	3	10	0	3	0	0	0	0	2	3	0	0-3
• KOSKIE, Corey														
D 2002	Min-A	.143	5	21	3	3	0	1	1	5	2	6	0	3-5
D 2003	Min-A	.200	4	15	0	3	1	0	0	0	0	5	0	3-4
D Total	2	.167	9	36	3	6	1	1	1	5	2	11	0	....
L 2002	Min-A	.278	5	18	3	5	2	0	0	2	2	8	0	3-5
• KRANEPOOL, Ed														
L 1969	NY-N	.250	3	12	2	3	1	0	0	1	1	2	0	1-3
L 1973	NY-N	.500	1	2	0	1	0	0	0	2	0	0	0	0-1
L Total	2	.286	4	14	2	4	1	0	0	3	1	2	0	....
W 1969	NY-N	.250	1	4	1	1	0	0	1	1	0	0	0	1-1
W 1973	NY-N	.000	4	3	0	0	0	0	0	0	0	0	0	....
W Total	2	.143	5	7	1	1	0	0	1	1	0	0	0	....
• KREEVICH, Mike														
W 1944	StL-A	.231	6	26	0	6	3	0	0	0	0	5	0	0-6
• KRUEGER, Ernie														
W 1920	Bro-N	.167	4	6	0	1	0	0	0	0	0	0	0	C-3
• KRUK, John														
L 1993	Phi-N	.250	6	24	4	6	2	1	1	5	4	5	0	1-6
W 1993	Phi-N	.348	6	23	4	8	1	0	0	4	7	7	0	1-6
• KRUKOW, Mike														
L 1987	SF-N	.000	1	2	0	0	0	0	0	0	1	0	0	....
• KUBEK, Tony														
W 1957	NY-A	.286	7	28	4	8	0	0	2	4	0	4	0	0-5,3-2
W 1958	NY-A	.048	7	21	0	1	0	0	0	1	1	7	0	S-7
W 1960	NY-A	.333	7	30	6	10	1	0	0	3	2	2	0	0-2,S-7
W 1961	NY-A	.227	5	22	3	5	0	0	0	1	1	4	0	S-5
W 1962	NY-A	.276	7	29	2	8	1	0	0	1	1	3	0	S-7
W 1963	NY-A	.188	4	16	1	3	0	0	0	0	0	3	0	S-4
W Total	6	.240	37	146	16	35	2	0	2	10	5	23	0	....
• KUBIAK, Ted														
L 1972	Oak-A	.500	4	4	0	2	0	0	0	1	0	0	0	2-3,S-1
L 1973	Oak-A	.000	3	2	0	0	0	0	0	0	0	1	0	2-3
L Total	2	.333	7	6	0	2	0	0	0	1	0	1	0	....
W 1972	Oak-A	.333	4	3	0	1	0	0	0	0	0	0	0	2-4
W 1973	Oak-A	.000	4	3	1	0	0	0	0	0	1	1	0	2-4
W Total	2	.167	8	6	1	1	0	0	0	0	1	1	0	....
• KUCKS, Johnny														
W 1955	NY-A	....	2	0	0	0	0	0	0	0	0	0	0	....
W 1956	NY-A	.000	3	3	0	0	0	0	0	0	0	1	0	....
W 1957	NY-A	....	1	0	0	0	0	0	0	0	0	0	0	....

SER-YEAR	TM-L	AVG	G	AB	R	H	2B	3B	HR	RBI	BB	SO	SB	POS
W 1958	NY-A	1.000	2	1	0	1	0	0	0	0	0	0	0	....
W Total	**4**	**.250**	**8**	**4**	**0**	**1**	**0**	**0**	**0**	**0**	**0**	**1**	**0**	....
• KUENN, Harvey														
W 1962	SF-N	.083	3	12	1	1	0	0	0	0	1	1	0	O-3
• KUHEL, Joe														
W 1933	Was-A	.150	5	20	1	3	0	0	0	1	1	4	0	1-5
• KUNTZ, Rusty														
L 1984	Det-A	.000	1	1	0	0	0	0	0	0	0	0	0	O-1
W 1984	Det-A	.000	2	1	0	0	0	0	0	1	0	1	0	D-2
• KUROWSKI, Whitey														
W 1942	StL-N	.267	5	15	3	4	0	1	1	5	2	3	0	3-5
W 1943	StL-N	.222	5	18	2	4	1	0	0	1	0	3	0	3-5
W 1944	StL-N	.217	6	23	2	5	1	0	0	1	1	4	0	3-6
W 1946	StL-N	.296	7	27	5	8	3	0	0	2	0	3	0	3-7
W Total	**4**	**.253**	**23**	**83**	**12**	**21**	**5**	**1**	**1**	**9**	**3**	**13**	**0**	....
• KUTCHER, Randy														
L 1990	Bos-A	....	2	0	0	0	0	0	0	0	0	0	0	....
• LAABS, Chet														
W 1944	StL-A	.200	5	15	1	3	1	1	0	0	2	6	0	O-4
• LACHANCE, Candy														
W 1903	Bos-A	.240	8	25	5	6	2	1	0	4	3	2	0	1-8
• LACKEY, John														
W 2002	Ana-A	.500	3	2	0	1	0	0	0	0	0	0	0	....
• LACOCK, Pete														
L 1977	KC-A	.000	1	1	0	0	0	0	0	0	1	1	0	1-1
L 1978	KC-A	.364	4	11	1	4	2	1	0	1	3	1	1	1-3
L 1980	KC-A	....	1	0	0	0	0	0	0	0	0	0	0	1-1
L Total	**3**	**.333**	**6**	**12**	**1**	**4**	**2**	**1**	**0**	**1**	**4**	**2**	**1**	....
W 1980	KC-A	....	1	0	0	0	0	0	0	0	0	0	0	1-1
• LACY, Lee														
L 1974	LA-N	....	1	0	0	0	0	0	0	0	0	0	0	....
L 1977	LA-N	1.000	1	1	1	1	0	0	0	0	0	0	0	....
L 1978	LA-N	.000	2	2	0	0	0	0	0	0	0	0	0	....
L Total	**3**	**.333**	**4**	**3**	**1**	**1**	**0**	**0**	**0**	**0**	**0**	**0**	**0**	....
W 1974	LA-N	.000	1	1	0	0	0	0	0	0	0	1	0	....
W 1977	LA-N	.429	4	7	1	3	0	0	0	2	1	1	0	O-2
W 1978	LA-N	.143	4	14	0	2	0	0	0	1	1	3	0	D-4
W 1979	Pit-N	.250	4	4	0	1	0	0	0	0	0	1	0	....
W Total	**4**	**.231**	**13**	**26**	**1**	**6**	**0**	**0**	**0**	**3**	**2**	**6**	**0**	....
• LAHOUD, Joe														
L 1977	KC-A	.000	1	1	2	0	0	0	0	0	2	0	0	D-1
• LAKE, Fred														
T 1897	Bos-N	.000	1	3	0	0	0	0	0	0	0	1	0	C-1
• LAKE, Steve														
L 1984	Chi-N	1.000	1	1	0	1	1	0	0	0	0	0	0	C-1
W 1987	StL-N	.333	3	3	0	1	0	0	0	1	0	0	0	C-3
• LAMAR, Bill														
W 1920	Bro-N	.000	3	3	0	0	0	0	0	0	0	0	0	....
• LAMB, David														
L 2002	Min-A	....	2	0	0	0	0	0	0	0	0	0	0	2-2
• LAMPKIN, Tom														
D 2001	Sea-A	.000	2	2	0	0	0	0	0	0	0	2	0	C-2
L 2001	Sea-A	.250	2	4	0	1	0	0	0	0	1	2	0	C-2
• LANDESTOY, Rafael														
L 1980	Hou-N	.222	5	9	3	2	0	0	0	2	1	0	1	2-3,S-1
L 1983	LA-N	.000	2	2	0	0	0	0	0	0	0	1	0	....
L Total	**2**	**.182**	**7**	**11**	**3**	**2**	**0**	**0**	**0**	**2**	**1**	**1**	**1**	....
W 1977	LA-N	....	1	0	0	0	0	0	0	0	0	0	0	....
• LANDIS, Jim														
W 1959	Chi-A	.292	6	24	6	7	0	0	0	1	1	7	1	O-6
• LANDREAUX, Ken														
D 1981	LA-N	.200	5	20	1	4	1	0	0	1	0	1	0	O-5
L 1981	LA-N	.100	5	10	0	1	1	0	0	0	3	2	0	O-5
L 1983	LA-N	.143	4	14	0	2	0	0	0	1	1	3	0	O-4
L 1985	LA-N	.389	5	18	4	7	3	0	0	2	1	1	0	O-3
L Total	**3**	**.238**	**14**	**42**	**4**	**10**	**4**	**0**	**0**	**3**	**5**	**6**	**0**	....
W 1981	LA-N	.167	5	6	1	1	1	0	0	0	0	2	1	O-3
• LANDRUM, Tito														
L 1983	Bal-A	.200	4	10	2	2	0	0	1	1	0	2	0	O-3
L 1985	StL-N	.429	5	14	2	6	0	0	0	4	1	1	1	O-4
L Total	**2**	**.333**	**9**	**24**	**4**	**8**	**0**	**0**	**1**	**5**	**1**	**3**	**1**	....
W 1983	Bal-A	....	3	0	0	0	0	0	0	0	0	0	1	O-3
W 1985	StL-N	.360	7	25	3	9	2	0	1	1	0	2	0	O-7
W Total	**2**	**.360**	**10**	**25**	**3**	**9**	**2**	**0**	**1**	**1**	**0**	**2**	**1**	....
• LANIER, Hal														
L 1971	SF-N	.000	1	1	0	0	0	0	0	0	0	0	0	3-1
• LANKFORD, Ray														
D 1996	StL-N	.500	1	2	1	1	0	0	0	0	1	0	0	O-1
D 2000	StL-N	.200	3	10	2	2	1	0	0	3	2	5	0	O-3
D Total	**2**	**.250**	**4**	**12**	**3**	**3**	**1**	**0**	**0**	**3**	**3**	**5**	**0**	....
L 1996	StL-N	.000	5	13	1	0	0	0	0	1	1	4	0	O-3
L 2000	StL-N	.333	5	12	1	4	1	0	0	1	1	5	0	O-4
L Total	**2**	**.160**	**10**	**25**	**2**	**4**	**1**	**0**	**0**	**2**	**2**	**9**	**0**	....
• LANSFORD, Carney														
L 1979	Cal-A	.294	4	17	2	5	0	0	0	3	1	2	1	3-4
L 1988	Oak-A	.294	4	17	4	5	1	0	1	2	0	2	0	3-4
L 1989	Oak-A	.455	3	11	2	5	0	0	0	4	2	1	2	3-3
L 1990	Oak-A	.438	4	16	2	7	1	0	0	2	0	1	0	3-4
L 1992	Oak-A	.167	5	18	0	3	0	0	0	1	1	1	0	3-5
L Total	**5**	**.316**	**20**	**79**	**10**	**25**	**2**	**0**	**1**	**12**	**4**	**7**	**3**	....
W 1988	Oak-A	.167	5	18	2	3	0	0	0	1	2	2	0	3-5
W 1989	Oak-A	.438	4	16	5	7	1	0	1	4	3	1	0	3-4
W 1990	Oak-A	.267	4	15	0	4	0	0	0	1	1	0	1	3-4
W Total	**3**	**.286**	**13**	**49**	**7**	**14**	**1**	**0**	**1**	**6**	**6**	**3**	**1**	....
• LAPP, Jack														
W 1910	Phi-A	.250	1	4	0	1	0	0	0	1	0	2	0	C-1
W 1911	Phi-A	.250	2	8	1	2	0	0	0	0	0	1	0	C-2
W 1913	Phi-A	.250	1	4	0	1	0	0	0	0	0	1	0	C-1
W 1914	Phi-A	.000	1	1	0	0	0	0	0	0	0	0	0	C-1
W Total	**4**	**.235**	**5**	**17**	**1**	**4**	**0**	**0**	**0**	**1**	**0**	**4**	**0**	....
• LARKER, Norm														
W 1959	LA-N	.188	6	16	2	3	0	0	0	0	2	3	0	O-6
• LARKIN, Barry														
D 1995	Cin-N	.385	3	13	2	5	0	0	0	1	1	2	4	S-3
L 1990	Cin-N	.261	6	23	5	6	2	0	0	1	3	1	3	S-6
L 1995	Cin-N	.389	4	18	1	7	2	1	0	0	1	1	1	S-4
L Total	**2**	**.317**	**10**	**41**	**6**	**13**	**4**	**1**	**0**	**1**	**4**	**2**	**4**	....
W 1990	Cin-N	.353	4	17	3	6	1	1	0	1	2	0	0	S-4
• LARKIN, Gene														
L 1987	Min-A	1.000	1	1	0	1	1	0	0	1	0	0	0	....
L 1991	Min-A	.000	3	3	0	0	0	0	0	0	0	1	0	....
L Total	**2**	**.250**	**4**	**4**	**0**	**1**	**1**	**0**	**0**	**1**	**0**	**1**	**0**	....
W 1987	Min-A	.000	5	3	1	0	0	0	0	0	1	0	0	1-1,D-1
W 1991	Min-A	.500	4	4	0	2	0	0	0	1	0	0	0	D-1
W Total	**2**	**.286**	**9**	**7**	**1**	**2**	**0**	**0**	**0**	**1**	**1**	**0**	**0**	....
• LASHER, Fred														
W 1968	Det-A	....	1	0	0	0	0	0	0	0	0	0	0	....
• LATHAM, Arlie														
W 1885	StL-A	.318	7	22	5	7	3	0	0	5	2	0	0	3-7
W 1886	StL-A	.174	6	23	4	4	0	1	0	3	3	4	2	3-6,C-1
W 1887	StL-A	.388	15	67	12	26	1	0	1	2	9	2	15	3-15
W 1888	StL-A	.250	10	40	10	10	0	0	0	3	5	6	11	3-10
W Total	**4**	**.309**	**38**	**152**	**31**	**47**	**4**	**1**	**1**	**13**	**19**	**12**	**28**	....
• LAUDNER, Tim														
L 1987	Min-A	.071	5	14	1	1	1	0	0	2	2	5	0	C-5
W 1987	Min-A	.318	7	22	4	7	1	0	1	4	5	4	0	C-7
• LAVAGETTO, Cookie														
W 1941	Bro-N	.100	3	10	1	1	0	0	0	0	2	0	0	3-3
W 1947	Bro-N	.143	5	7	0	1	1	0	0	3	0	2	0	3-3
W Total	**2**	**.118**	**8**	**17**	**1**	**2**	**1**	**0**	**0**	**3**	**2**	**2**	**0**	....
• LAVALLIERE, Mike														
L 1990	Pit-N	.000	3	6	1	0	0	0	0	0	3	1	0	C-3
L 1991	Pit-N	.333	3	6	0	2	0	0	0	1	2	0	0	C-3
L 1992	Pit-N	.200	3	10	1	2	0	0	0	0	0	3	0	C-3
L 1993	Chi-A	.333	2	3	0	1	0	0	0	0	1	0	0	C-2
L Total	**4**	**.200**	**11**	**25**	**2**	**5**	**0**	**0**	**0**	**1**	**6**	**4**	**0**	....
• LAW, Rudy														
L 1983	Chi-A	.389	4	18	1	7	1	0	0	0	0	1	2	O-4
• LAW, Vance														
L 1983	Chi-A	.182	4	11	0	2	0	0	0	1	1	3	0	3-4
L 1989	Chi-N	.000	2	3	0	0	0	0	0	0	0	3	0	3-1
L Total	**2**	**.143**	**6**	**14**	**0**	**2**	**0**	**0**	**0**	**1**	**1**	**6**	**0**	....
• LAW, Vern														
W 1960	Pit-N	.333	3	6	1	2	1	0	0	1	0	1	0	....
• LAWLESS, Tom														
L 1987	StL-N	.333	3	6	0	2	0	0	0	0	1	1	0	O-1,3-2
W 1985	StL-N	....	1	0	0	0	0	0	0	0	0	0	0	....
W 1987	StL-N	.100	3	10	1	1	0	0	1	3	0	4	0	3-3
W Total	**2**	**.100**	**4**	**10**	**1**	**1**	**0**	**0**	**1**	**3**	**0**	**4**	**0**	....
• LAZZERI, Tony														
W 1926	NY-A	.192	7	26	2	5	1	0	0	3	1	6	0	2-7
W 1927	NY-A	.267	4	15	1	4	1	0	0	2	1	4	0	2-4
W 1928	NY-A	.250	4	12	2	3	1	0	0	0	1	0	2	2-4
W 1932	NY-A	.294	4	17	4	5	0	0	2	5	2	1	0	2-4
W 1936	NY-A	.250	6	20	4	5	0	0	1	7	4	4	0	2-6
W 1937	NY-A	.400	5	15	3	6	0	1	1	2	3	3	0	2-5
W 1938	Chi-N	.000	2	2	0	0	0	0	0	0	0	1	0	....
W Total	**7**	**.262**	**32**	**107**	**16**	**28**	**3**	**1**	**4**	**19**	**12**	**19**	**2**	....
• LEACH, Tommy														
T 1900	Pit-N	.176	4	17	4	3	0	0	0	1	1	2	0	O-4
W 1903	Pit-N	.273	8	33	3	9	0	4	0	7	1	4	1	3-8
W 1909	Pit-N	.360	7	25	8	9	4	0	0	2	2	1	1	O-7,3-1
W Total	**2**	**.310**	**15**	**58**	**11**	**18**	**4**	**4**	**0**	**9**	**3**	**5**	**2**	....
• LECROY, Matt														
D 2002	Min-A	.444	3	9	1	4	0	0	0	1	0	3	0	D-3
D 2003	Min-A	.091	3	11	1	1	0	0	0	0	1	4	0	....
D Total	**2**	**.250**	**6**	**20**	**2**	**5**	**0**	**0**	**0**	**1**	**1**	**7**	**0**	....
L 2002	Min-A	.333	1	3	0	1	0	0	0	0	0	1	0	D-1
• LEDEE, Ricky														
D 1999	NY-A	.273	3	11	1	3	2	0	0	2	1	5	0	O-3
L 1998	NY-A	.000	3	5	0	0	0	0	0	0	0	0	0	O-2,D-1

YEAR	TM-L	AVG	G	AB	R	H	2B	3B	HR	RBI	BB	SO	SB	POS
L 1999	NY-A	.250	3	8	2	2	0	0	1	4	1	4	0	0-2,D-1
L Total	2	.154	6	13	2	2	0	0	1	4	1	4	0	....
W 1998	NY-A	.600	4	10	1	6	3	0	0	4	2	1	0	0-4
W 1999	NY-A	.200	3	10	0	2	1	0	0	1	1	4	0	0-3
W Total	2	.400	7	20	1	8	4	0	0	5	3	5	0	....
• LEE, Carlos														
D 2000	Chi-A	.091	3	11	0	1	1	0	0	1	0	2	0	0-3
• LEE, Derrek														
D 2003	Fla-N	.250	4	16	2	4	1	0	0	2	1	2	1	1-4
L 2003	Fla-N	.188	7	32	2	6	2	0	1	4	1	8	1	1-7
W 2003	Fla-N	.208	6	24	2	5	0	0	0	2	1	7	0	1-6
• LEE, Manuel														
L 1985	Tor-A	....	1	0	0	0	0	0	0	0	0	0	0	2-1
L 1989	Tor-A	.250	2	8	2	2	0	0	0	0	0	1	0	2-2
L 1991	Tor-A	.125	5	16	3	2	0	0	0	0	1	5	0	S-5
L 1992	Tor-A	.278	6	18	2	5	1	1	0	3	1	2	0	S-6
L Total	4	.214	14	42	7	9	1	1	0	3	2	8	0	....
W 1992	Tor-A	.105	6	19	1	2	0	0	0	0	1	2	0	S-6
• LEFEBVRE, Jim														
W 1965	LA-N	.400	3	10	2	4	0	0	0	0	0	0	0	2-3
W 1966	LA-N	.167	4	12	1	2	0	0	1	1	3	4	0	2-4
W Total	2	.273	7	22	3	6	0	0	1	1	3	4	0	....
• LEFEBVRE, Joe														
L 1980	NY-A	....	1	0	0	0	0	0	0	0	0	0	0	0-1
L 1983	Phi-N	.000	2	2	0	0	0	0	0	1	0	1	0	0-1
L Total	2	.000	3	2	0	0	0	0	0	1	0	1	0	....
W 1983	Phi-N	.200	3	5	0	1	1	0	0	2	0	1	0	0-2
• LEIBER, Hank														
W 1936	NY-N	.000	2	6	0	0	0	0	0	0	2	2	0	0-2
W 1937	NY-N	.364	3	11	2	4	0	0	0	2	1	1	0	0-3
W Total	2	.235	5	17	2	4	0	0	0	2	3	3	0	....
• LEIBOLD, Nemo														
W 1917	Chi-A	.400	2	5	1	2	0	0	0	2	1	1	0	0-2
W 1919	Chi-A	.056	5	18	0	1	0	0	0	0	2	3	1	0-5
W 1924	Was-A	.167	3	6	1	1	1	0	0	0	1	0	0	0-1
W 1925	Was-A	.500	3	2	1	1	1	0	0	0	1	0	0	....
W Total	4	.161	13	31	3	5	2	0	0	2	5	4	1	....
• LEIUS, Scott														
L 1991	Min-A	.000	3	4	0	0	0	0	0	0	1	1	0	3-3
W 1991	Min-A	.357	7	14	2	5	0	0	1	2	1	2	0	3-6,S-1
• LEJOHN, Don														
W 1965	LA-N	.000	1	1	0	0	0	0	0	0	0	1	0	....
• LEMKE, Mark														
D 1995	Atl-N	.211	4	19	3	4	1	0	0	1	1	3	0	2-4
D 1996	Atl-N	.167	3	12	1	2	1	0	0	2	0	1	0	2-3
D Total	2	.194	7	31	4	6	2	0	0	3	1	4	0	....
L 1991	Atl-N	.200	7	20	1	4	1	0	0	1	4	0	0	2-7
L 1992	Atl-N	.333	7	21	2	7	1	0	0	2	5	3	0	2-7,3-1
L 1993	Atl-N	.208	6	24	2	5	2	0	0	4	1	6	0	2-6
L 1995	Atl-N	.167	4	18	2	3	0	0	0	1	1	0	0	2-4
L 1996	Atl-N	.444	7	27	4	12	2	0	1	5	4	2	0	2-7
L Total	5	.282	31	110	11	31	6	0	1	13	15	11	0	....
W 1991	Atl-N	.417	6	24	4	10	1	3	0	4	2	4	0	2-6
W 1992	Atl-N	.211	6	19	0	4	0	0	0	2	1	3	0	2-6
W 1995	Atl-N	.273	6	22	1	6	0	0	0	0	3	2	0	2-6
W 1996	Atl-N	.231	6	26	2	6	1	0	0	2	0	3	0	2-6
W Total	4	.286	24	91	7	26	2	3	0	8	6	12	0	....
• LEMON, Chet														
L 1984	Det-A	.000	3	13	1	0	0	0	0	0	0	1	0	0-3
L 1987	Det-A	.278	5	18	4	5	0	0	2	4	1	4	0	0-5
L Total	2	.161	8	31	5	5	0	0	2	4	1	5	0	....
W 1984	Det-A	.294	5	17	1	5	0	0	0	1	2	2	2	0-5
• LEONARD, Dutch														
W 1915	Bos-A	.000	1	3	0	0	0	0	0	0	0	2	0	....
W 1916	Bos-A	.000	1	3	0	0	0	0	0	0	1	3	0	....
W Total	2	.000	2	6	0	0	0	0	0	0	1	5	0	....
• LEONARD, Jeffrey														
L 1980	Hou-N	.000	3	3	0	0	0	0	0	0	0	2	0	0-1
L 1987	SF-N	.417	7	24	5	10	0	0	4	5	3	4	0	0-7
L Total	2	.370	10	27	5	10	0	0	4	5	3	6	0	....
• LESLIE, Sam														
W 1936	NY-N	.667	3	3	0	2	0	0	0	0	0	0	0	....
W 1937	NY-N	.000	2	1	0	0	0	0	0	0	1	0	0	....
W Total	2	.500	5	4	0	2	0	0	0	0	1	0	0	....
• LEWIS, Allan														
L 1973	Oak-A	....	2	0	1	0	0	0	0	0	0	0	0	....
W 1972	Oak-A	....	6	0	2	0	0	0	0	0	0	0	0	....
W 1973	Oak-A	....	3	0	1	0	0	0	0	0	0	0	0	....
W Total	2	....	9	0	3	0	0	0	0	0	0	0	0	....
• LEWIS, Darren														
D 1995	Cin-N	.000	3	3	0	0	0	0	0	0	0	1	0	0-3
D 1998	Bos-A	.357	4	14	4	5	2	0	0	0	1	3	1	0-4
D 1999	Bos-A	.375	4	16	5	6	1	0	0	2	0	2	1	0-4
D Total	3	.333	11	33	9	11	3	0	0	2	1	6	2	....
L 1995	Cin-N	.000	2	1	0	0	0	0	0	0	0	0	0	0-2
L 1999	Bos-A	.118	5	17	2	2	1	0	0	1	1	3	1	0-5
L Total	2	.111	7	18	2	2	1	0	0	1	1	3	1	....
• LEWIS, Duffy														
W 1912	Bos-A	.156	8	32	4	5	3	0	0	1	2	2	0	0-8
W 1915	Bos-A	.444	5	18	1	8	1	0	1	5	1	4	0	0-5
W 1916	Bos-A	.353	5	17	3	6	2	1	0	1	2	1	0	0-5
W Total	3	.284	18	67	8	19	6	1	1	7	5	7	0	....
• LEWIS, Mark														
D 1995	Cin-N	.500	2	2	2	1	0	0	1	5	1	0	0	3-2
D 1997	SF-N	.600	1	5	0	3	0	0	0	1	0	0	0	2-1
D Total	2	.571	3	7	2	4	0	0	1	6	1	0	0	....
L 1995	Cin-N	.250	2	4	0	1	0	0	0	0	1	1	0	3-2
• LEWIS, Ted														
T 1897	Bos-N	.500	3	6	1	3	1	0	0	1	1	0	0	P-3
• LEYRITZ, Jim														
D 1995	NY-A	.143	2	7	1	1	0	0	1	2	0	1	0	C-2
D 1996	NY-A	.000	2	3	0	0	0	0	0	1	0	1	0	C-1,D-1
D 1998	SD-N	.400	4	10	3	4	0	0	3	5	0	2	0	1-3,C-1
D 1999	NY-A	.000	2	2	0	0	0	0	0	1	1	0	0	D-2
D Total	4	.227	10	22	4	5	0	0	4	9	1	4	0	....
L 1996	NY-A	.250	3	8	1	2	0	0	1	2	1	4	0	0-1,C-2
L 1998	SD-N	.167	5	12	1	2	0	0	1	4	0	2	0	1-3,C-2
L Total	2	.200	8	20	2	4	0	0	2	6	1	6	0	....
W 1996	NY-A	.375	4	8	1	3	0	0	1	3	3	2	1	C-3
W 1998	SD-N	.000	4	10	0	0	0	0	0	0	1	4	0	1-2,C-1,D-1
W 1999	NY-A	1.000	2	1	1	1	0	0	1	2	1	0	0	D-1
W Total	3	.211	10	19	2	4	0	0	2	5	5	6	1	....
• LEZCANO, Sixto														
L 1983	Phi-N	.308	4	13	2	4	0	0	1	2	1	1	0	0-4
W 1983	Phi-N	.125	4	8	0	1	0	0	0	0	0	2	0	0-3
• LIND, Jose														
L 1990	Pit-N	.238	6	21	1	5	1	1	1	2	1	4	0	2-6
L 1991	Pit-N	.160	7	25	0	4	0	0	0	3	0	6	0	2-7
L 1992	Pit-N	.222	7	27	5	6	2	1	1	5	1	4	0	2-7
L Total	3	.205	20	73	6	15	3	2	2	10	2	14	0	....
• LINDELL, Johnny														
W 1943	NY-A	.111	4	9	1	1	0	0	0	0	1	4	0	0-4
W 1947	NY-A	.500	6	18	3	9	3	1	0	7	5	2	0	0-6
W 1949	NY-A	.143	2	7	0	1	0	0	0	0	0	2	0	0-2
W Total	3	.324	12	34	4	11	3	1	0	7	6	8	0	....
• LINDEMAN, Jim														
L 1987	StL-N	.308	5	13	1	4	0	0	1	3	0	3	0	1-5
W 1987	StL-N	.333	6	15	3	5	1	0	0	2	0	3	0	0-1,1-6
• LINDSTROM, Freddie														
W 1924	NY-N	.333	7	30	1	10	2	0	0	4	3	6	0	3-7
W 1935	Chi-N	.200	4	15	0	3	1	0	0	0	1	1	0	0-4,3-1
W Total	2	.289	11	45	1	13	3	0	0	4	4	7	0	....
• LINZ, Phil														
W 1963	NY-A	.333	3	3	0	1	0	0	0	0	0	1	0	....
W 1964	NY-A	.226	7	31	5	7	1	0	2	2	2	5	0	S-7
W Total	2	.235	10	34	5	8	1	0	2	2	2	6	0	....
• LIRIANO, Nelson														
L 1989	Tor-A	.429	3	7	1	3	0	0	0	1	2	0	3	2-3
• LITTLE, Mark														
D 2002	Ari-N	.000	2	4	0	0	0	0	0	0	0	2	0	0-2
• LITTON, Greg														
L 1989	SF-N	1.000	1	1	0	1	0	0	0	0	0	0	0	3-1
W 1989	SF-N	.500	2	6	1	3	1	0	1	3	0	0	0	2-2,3-1
• LITWHILER, Danny														
W 1943	StL-N	.267	5	15	0	4	1	0	0	2	2	4	0	0-4
W 1944	StL-N	.200	5	20	2	4	1	0	1	1	2	7	0	0-5
W Total	2	.229	10	35	2	8	2	0	1	3	4	11	0	....
• LIVINGSTON, Mickey														
W 1945	Chi-N	.364	6	22	3	8	3	0	0	4	1	1	0	C-6
• LIVINGSTONE, Scott														
D 1996	SD-N	.500	2	2	1	1	0	0	0	0	0	0	0	....
• LOCKHART, Keith														
D 1997	Atl-N	.000	2	6	0	0	0	0	0	0	0	1	0	2-2
D 1998	Atl-N	.333	3	12	2	4	0	0	0	0	1	0	0	2-3
D 1999	Atl-N	.000	3	1	0	0	0	0	0	0	0	1	0	2-1
D 2000	Atl-N	.125	3	8	0	1	0	0	0	0	0	1	0	2-3
D 2001	Atl-N	.500	1	2	1	1	1	0	0	0	0	0	0	2-1
D 2002	Atl-N	.333	5	12	1	4	0	0	1	4	2	4	0	2-5
D Total	6	.244	17	41	4	10	1	0	1	4	3	7	0	....
L 1997	Atl-N	.500	5	16	4	8	1	1	0	3	1	1	0	2-5
L 1998	Atl-N	.235	6	17	2	4	1	1	0	0	0	4	0	2-6
L 1999	Atl-N	.400	3	5	0	2	0	1	0	1	0	2	0	2-1
L 2001	Atl-N	.000	2	1	0	0	0	0	0	0	1	0	0	....
L Total	4	.359	16	39	6	14	2	3	0	4	2	7	0	....
W 1999	Atl-N	.143	4	7	1	1	0	0	0	0	2	0	0	2-2,D-1
• LOCKMAN, Whitey														
W 1951	NY-N	.240	6	25	1	6	2	0	1	4	1	2	0	1-6
W 1954	NY-N	.111	4	18	2	2	0	0	0	0	1	2	0	1-4
W Total	2	.186	10	43	3	8	2	0	1	4	2	4	0	....
• LOFTON, Kenny														
D 1995	Cle-A	.154	3	13	1	2	0	0	0	0	1	3	0	0-3
D 1996	Cle-A	.167	4	18	3	3	0	0	0	1	2	3	5	0-4
D 1997	Atl-N	.154	3	13	2	2	1	0	0	0	1	2	0	0-3
D 1998	Cle-A	.375	4	16	5	6	1	0	2	4	1	1	2	0-4

SER-YEAR	TM-L	AVG	G	AB	R	H	2B	3B	HR	RBI	BB	SO	SB	POS
D 1999	Cle-A	.125	5	16	5	2	1	0	0	1	5	6	2	0-5
D 2001	Cle-A	.105	5	19	2	2	0	0	1	3	3	5	0	0-5
D 2002	SF-N	.350	5	20	5	7	1	0	0	2	2	3	1	0-5
D 2003	Chi-N	.286	5	21	3	6	1	0	0	1	2	2	3	0-5
D Total	8	.221	34	136	26	30	5	0	3	12	17	25	13	....
L 1995	Cle-A	.458	6	24	4	11	0	2	0	3	4	6	5	0-6
L 1997	Atl-N	.185	6	27	3	5	0	1	0	1	1	7	1	0-6
L 1998	Cle-A	.185	6	27	2	5	1	0	1	3	1	7	1	0-6
L 2002	SF-N	.238	5	21	4	5	0	0	1	2	2	4	1	0-5
L 2003	Chi-N	.323	7	31	8	10	1	0	0	2	3	4	1	0-7
L Total	5	.277	30	130	21	36	2	3	2	11	11	28	9	....
W 1995	Cle-A	.200	6	25	6	5	1	0	0	0	3	1	6	0-6
W 2002	SF-N	.290	7	31	7	9	1	1	0	2	2	2	3	0-7
W Total	2	.250	13	56	13	14	2	1	0	2	5	3	9	....
• LOGAN, Johnny														
W 1957	Mil-N	.185	7	27	5	5	1	0	1	2	3	6	0	S-7
W 1958	Mil-N	.120	7	25	3	3	2	0	0	2	2	4	0	S-7
W Total	2	.154	14	52	8	8	3	0	1	4	5	10	0	....
• LOHRKE, Jack														
W 1951	NY-N	.000	2	2	0	0	0	0	0	0	0	1	0	....
• LOLLAR, Sherm														
W 1947	NY-A	.750	2	4	3	3	2	0	0	1	0	0	0	C-2
W 1959	Chi-A	.227	6	22	3	5	0	0	1	5	1	3	0	C-6
W Total	2	.308	8	26	6	8	2	0	1	6	1	3	0	....
• LOMBARDI, Ernie														
W 1939	Cin-N	.214	4	14	0	3	0	0	0	2	0	1	0	C-4
W 1940	Cin-N	.333	2	3	0	1	1	0	0	0	1	0	0	C-1
W Total	2	.235	6	17	0	4	1	0	0	2	1	1	0	....
• LOMBARDOZZI, Steve														
L 1987	Min-A	.267	5	15	2	4	0	0	0	1	2	2	0	2-5
W 1987	Min-A	.412	6	17	3	7	1	0	1	4	2	2	0	2-6
• LONBORG, Jim														
L 1976	Phi-N	.000	1	1	0	0	0	0	0	0	0	0	0	....
L 1977	Phi-N	.000	1	1	0	0	0	0	0	0	0	1	0	....
L Total	2	.000	2	2	0	0	0	0	0	0	0	1	0	....
W 1967	Bos-A	.000	3	9	0	0	0	0	0	0	0	7	0	....
• LONG, Dale														
W 1960	NY-A	.333	3	3	0	1	0	0	0	0	0	0	0	....
W 1962	NY-A	.200	2	5	0	1	0	0	0	1	0	1	0	1-2
W Total	2	.250	5	8	0	2	0	0	0	1	0	1	0	....
• LONG, Herman														
T 1892	Bos-N	.222	6	27	4	6	0	0	0	1	0	0	2	S-6
T 1897	Bos-N	.286	5	21	4	6	1	1	1	5	2	2	1	S-5
T Total	2	.250	11	48	8	12	1	1	1	6	2	2	3	....
• LONG, Terrence														
D 2000	Oak-A	.158	5	19	2	3	0	0	1	1	3	2	0	0-5
D 2001	Oak-A	.389	5	18	3	7	3	0	2	3	1	2	0	0-5
D 2002	Oak-A	.167	5	18	1	3	0	0	1	1	1	2	0	0-5
D 2003	Oak-A	.250	4	8	0	2	0	0	0	0	1	3	0	0-3
D Total	4	.238	19	63	6	15	3	0	4	5	6	9	0	....
• LONGMIRE, Tony														
L 1993	Phi-N	.000	1	1	0	0	0	0	0	0	0	1	0	....
• LOPATA, Stan														
W 1950	Phi-N	.000	2	1	0	0	0	0	0	0	0	1	0	C-1
• LOPES, Davey														
D 1981	LA-N	.200	5	20	1	4	1	0	0	0	3	7	1	2-5
L 1974	LA-N	.267	4	15	4	4	0	1	0	3	5	1	2	2-4
L 1977	LA-N	.235	4	17	2	4	0	0	0	3	2	0	0	2-4
L 1978	LA-N	.389	4	18	3	7	1	1	2	5	0	1	1	2-4
L 1981	LA-N	.278	5	18	0	5	0	0	0	0	1	3	5	2-5
L 1984	Chi-N	.000	2	1	0	0	0	0	0	0	0	0	0	0-1
L 1986	Hou-N	.000	3	2	1	0	0	0	0	0	1	0	0	....
L Total	6	.282	22	71	10	20	1	2	2	11	9	5	8	....
W 1974	LA-N	.111	5	18	2	2	0	0	0	0	3	4	2	2-5
W 1977	LA-N	.167	6	24	3	4	0	1	1	2	4	3	2	2-6
W 1978	LA-N	.308	6	26	7	8	0	0	3	7	2	1	2	2-6
W 1981	LA-N	.227	6	22	6	5	1	0	0	2	4	3	4	2-6
W Total	4	.211	23	90	18	19	1	1	4	11	13	11	10	....
• LOPEZ, Hector														
W 1960	NY-A	.429	3	7	0	3	0	0	0	0	0	0	0	0-1
W 1961	NY-A	.333	4	9	3	3	0	1	1	7	2	3	0	0-3
W 1962	NY-A	.000	2	2	0	0	0	0	0	0	0	0	0	....
W 1963	NY-A	.250	3	8	1	2	2	0	0	0	0	1	0	0-2
W 1964	NY-A	.000	3	2	0	0	0	0	0	0	0	2	0	0-1
W Total	5	.286	15	28	4	8	2	1	1	7	2	6	0	....
• LOPEZ, Javy														
D 1995	Atl-N	.444	3	9	0	4	0	0	0	3	0	3	0	C-3
D 1996	Atl-N	.286	2	7	1	2	0	0	1	1	1	0	1	C-2
D 1997	Atl-N	.286	2	7	3	2	2	0	0	1	2	1	0	C-2
D 1998	Atl-N	.286	2	7	1	2	0	0	1	1	1	1	0	C-2
D 2000	Atl-N	.091	3	11	0	1	0	0	0	0	0	1	0	C-3
D 2002	Atl-N	.333	4	15	4	5	1	0	2	4	1	3	0	C-4
D 2003	Atl-N	.333	5	21	1	7	2	0	0	0	0	6	0	C-5
D Total	7	.299	21	77	10	23	5	0	4	10	5	15	1	....
L 1992	Atl-N	.000	1	1	0	0	0	0	0	0	0	0	0	C-1
L 1995	Atl-N	.357	3	14	2	5	1	0	1	3	0	1	0	C-3
L 1996	Atl-N	.542	7	24	8	13	5	0	2	6	3	1	1	C-7
L 1997	Atl-N	.059	5	17	0	1	1	0	0	2	1	7	0	C-5
L 1998	Atl-N	.300	6	20	2	6	0	0	1	1	0	7	0	C-6
L 2001	Atl-N	.143	5	14	1	2	0	0	1	2	1	4	0	C-5
L Total	6	.300	27	90	13	27	7	0	5	14	5	20	1	....
W 1995	Atl-N	.176	6	17	1	3	2	0	1	3	1	1	0	C-6
W 1996	Atl-N	.190	6	21	3	4	0	0	0	1	3	4	0	C-6
W Total	2	.184	12	38	4	7	2	0	1	4	4	5	0	....
• LOPEZ, Luis														
D 1996	SD-N	....	1	0	0	0	0	0	0	0	0	0	0	....
• LORD, Bris														
W 1905	Phi-A	.100	5	20	0	2	0	0	0	2	0	5	0	0-5
W 1910	Phi-A	.182	5	22	3	4	2	0	0	1	1	3	0	0-5
W 1911	Phi-A	.185	6	27	2	5	2	0	0	1	0	5	0	0-6
W Total	3	.159	16	69	5	11	4	0	0	4	1	13	0	....
• LOWDERMILK, Grover														
W 1919	Chi-A	....	1	0	0	0	0	0	0	0	0	0	0	....
• LOWE, Bobby														
T 1892	Bos-N	.130	6	23	2	3	0	0	0	0	1	2	1	0-6
T 1897	Bos-N	.391	5	23	6	9	2	0	0	6	1	0	1	2-5
T Total	2	.261	11	46	8	12	2	0	0	6	2	2	2	....
• LOWELL, Mike														
D 2003	Fla-N	.000	2	3	0	0	0	0	0	0	0	1	0	3-2
L 2003	Fla-N	.200	7	20	5	4	0	0	2	3	3	4	0	3-7
W 2003	Fla-N	.217	6	23	1	5	1	0	0	2	2	3	0	3-6
• LOWENSTEIN, John														
L 1979	Bal-A	.167	4	6	2	1	0	0	1	3	2	2	0	0-3
L 1983	Bal-A	.167	3	6	0	1	1	0	0	2	1	2	0	0-2,D-1
L Total	2	.167	7	12	2	2	1	0	1	5	3	4	0	....
W 1979	Bal-A	.231	6	13	2	3	1	0	0	3	1	3	0	0-5
W 1983	Bal-A	.385	4	13	2	5	1	0	1	1	0	3	0	0-4
W Total	2	.308	10	26	4	8	2	0	1	4	1	6	0	....
• LOWREY, Peanuts														
W 1945	Chi-N	.310	7	29	4	9	1	0	0	0	1	2	0	0-7
• LUDERUS, Fred														
W 1915	Phi-N	.438	5	16	1	7	2	0	1	6	1	4	0	1-5
• LUGO, Julio														
D 2001	Hou-N	.000	3	8	1	0	0	0	0	0	0	2	0	S-2
• LUM, Mike														
L 1969	Atl-N	1.000	2	2	0	2	1	0	0	0	0	0	0	0-1
L 1976	Cin-N	.000	1	1	0	0	0	0	0	0	0	0	0	....
L Total	2	.667	3	3	0	2	1	0	0	0	0	0	0	....
• LUMPE, Jerry														
W 1957	NY-A	.286	6	14	0	4	0	0	0	2	1	1	0	3-3
W 1958	NY-A	.167	6	12	0	2	0	0	0	0	1	2	0	3-3,S-2
W Total	2	.231	12	26	0	6	0	0	0	2	2	3	0	....
• LUNTE, Harry														
W 1920	Cle-A	....	1	0	0	0	0	0	0	0	0	0	0	2-1
• LUQUE, Dolf														
W 1919	Cin-N	.000	2	1	0	0	0	0	0	0	0	1	0	....
W 1933	NY-N	1.000	1	1	0	1	0	0	0	0	0	0	0	....
W Total	2	.500	3	2	0	1	0	0	0	0	0	1	0	....
• LUZINSKI, Greg														
L 1976	Phi-N	.273	3	11	2	3	2	0	1	3	1	4	0	0-3
L 1977	Phi-N	.286	4	14	2	4	1	0	1	2	3	3	1	0-4
L 1978	Phi-N	.375	4	16	3	6	0	1	2	3	1	2	0	0-4
L 1980	Phi-N	.294	5	17	3	5	2	0	1	4	0	6	0	0-4
L 1983	Chi-A	.133	4	15	0	2	1	0	0	0	1	5	0	D-4
L Total	5	.274	20	73	10	20	6	1	5	12	6	20	1	....
W 1980	Phi-N	.000	3	9	0	0	0	0	0	0	1	5	0	0-1,D-2
• LYNCH, Jerry														
W 1961	Cin-N	.000	4	3	0	0	0	0	0	0	1	1	0	....
• LYNN, Byrd														
W 1917	Chi-A	.000	1	1	0	0	0	0	0	0	0	1	0	....
W 1919	Chi-A	.000	1	1	0	0	0	0	0	0	0	0	0	C-1
W Total	2	.000	2	2	0	0	0	0	0	0	0	1	0	....
• LYNN, Fred														
L 1975	Bos-A	.364	3	11	1	4	1	0	0	2	0	0	0	0-3
L 1982	Cal-A	.611	5	18	4	11	2	0	1	5	2	3	0	0-5
L Total	2	.517	8	29	5	15	3	0	1	7	2	3	0	....
W 1975	Bos-A	.280	7	25	3	7	1	0	1	5	3	5	0	0-7
• LYONS, Harry														
W 1887	StL-A	.375	2	8	3	3	0	0	0	2	1	0	0	S-2
W 1888	StL-A	.118	5	17	0	2	0	0	0	1	1	5	0	0-5
W Total	2	.200	7	25	3	5	0	0	0	3	2	5	0	....
• MABRY, John														
D 1996	StL-N	.300	3	10	1	3	0	1	0	1	1	1	0	1-3
D 2002	Oak-A	.000	2	2	0	0	0	0	0	0	0	1	0	0-1,1-1
D Total	2	.250	5	12	1	3	0	1	0	1	1	2	0	....
L 1996	StL-N	.261	7	23	1	6	0	0	0	0	0	6	0	0-2,1-6
• MACFARLANE, Mike														
D 1995	Bos-A	.333	3	9	0	3	0	0	0	1	0	3	0	C-3
• MACK, Shane														
L 1991	Min-A	.333	5	18	4	6	1	1	0	3	2	4	2	0-5
W 1991	Min-A	.130	6	23	0	3	1	0	0	1	0	7	0	0-6
• MADDOX, Elliott														
L 1976	NY-A	.222	3	9	0	2	1	0	0	1	0	1	0	0-3
W 1976	NY-A	.200	2	5	0	1	0	1	0	0	1	2	0	0-1,D-1

YEAR	TM-L	AVG	G	AB	R	H	2B	3B	HR	RBI	BB	SO	SB	POS
• MADDOX, Garry														
D 1981	Phi-N	.333	2	3	0	1	1	0	0	0	0	0	0	O-2
L 1976	Phi-N	.231	3	13	2	3	1	0	0	1	1	0	0	O-3
L 1977	Phi-N	.429	2	7	1	3	0	0	0	2	0	1	0	O-2
L 1978	Phi-N	.263	4	19	1	5	0	0	0	2	0	3	0	O-4
L 1980	Phi-N	.300	5	20	2	6	2	0	0	3	2	2	2	O-5
L 1983	Phi-N	.273	3	11	0	3	1	0	0	1	0	1	0	O-3
L Total	**5**	**.286**	**17**	**70**	**6**	**20**	**4**	**0**	**0**	**9**	**3**	**7**	**2**	**....**
W 1980	Phi-N	.227	6	22	1	5	2	0	0	1	1	3	0	O-6
W 1983	Phi-N	.250	4	12	1	3	1	0	1	1	0	2	0	O-3
W Total	**2**	**.235**	**10**	**34**	**2**	**8**	**3**	**0**	**1**	**2**	**1**	**5**	**0**	**....**
• MADLOCK, Bill														
L 1979	Pit-N	.250	3	12	1	3	0	0	1	2	2	0	2	3-3
L 1985	LA-N	.333	6	24	5	8	1	0	3	7	0	2	1	3-6
L 1987	Det-A	.000	1	5	0	0	0	0	0	0	0	3	0	D-1
L Total	**3**	**.268**	**10**	**41**	**6**	**11**	**1**	**0**	**4**	**9**	**2**	**5**	**3**	**....**
W 1979	Pit-N	.375	7	24	2	9	1	0	0	3	5	1	0	3-7
• MAGADAN, Dave														
L 1988	NY-N	.000	3	3	0	0	0	0	0	0	0	2	0	....
• MAGEE, Sherry														
W 1919	Cin-N	.500	2	2	0	1	0	0	0	0	0	0	0	....
• MAGUIRE, Freddie														
W 1923	NY-N	....	2	0	1	0	0	0	0	0	0	0	0	....
• MAHOMES, Pat														
D 1999	NY-N	....	1	0	0	0	0	0	0	0	0	0	0	....
L 1999	NY-N	.000	3	2	0	0	0	0	0	0	0	2	0	....
• MAIER, Bob														
W 1945	Det-A	1.000	1	1	0	1	0	0	0	0	0	0	0	....
• MAJESKI, Hank														
W 1954	Cle-A	.167	4	6	1	1	0	0	1	3	0	1	0	3-1
• MALDONADO, Candy														
L 1983	LA-N	.000	2	2	0	0	0	0	0	0	0	1	0	....
L 1985	LA-N	.143	4	7	0	1	0	0	0	1	0	3	0	O-3
L 1987	SF-N	.211	5	19	2	4	1	0	0	2	0	3	0	O-5
L 1989	SF-N	.000	3	3	1	0	0	0	0	1	2	0	0	O-3
L 1991	Tor-A	.100	5	20	1	2	1	0	0	1	1	6	0	O-5
L 1992	Tor-A	.273	6	22	3	6	0	0	2	6	3	4	0	O-6
L Total	**6**	**.178**	**25**	**73**	**7**	**13**	**2**	**0**	**2**	**11**	**6**	**17**	**0**	**....**
W 1989	SF-N	.091	4	11	1	1	0	1	0	0	0	4	0	O-3
W 1992	Tor-A	.158	6	19	1	3	0	0	1	2	2	5	0	O-5
W Total	**2**	**.133**	**10**	**30**	**2**	**4**	**0**	**1**	**1**	**2**	**2**	**9**	**0**	**....**
• MALLOY, Marty														
L 1998	Atl-N	.000	4	1	1	0	0	0	0	0	0	1	0	2-1
• MANCUSO, Frank														
W 1944	StL-A	.667	2	3	0	2	0	0	0	1	0	0	0	C-1
• MANCUSO, Gus														
W 1930	StL-N	.286	2	7	1	2	0	0	0	0	1	2	0	C-2
W 1931	StL-N	.000	2	1	0	0	0	0	0	0	0	0	0	C-1
W 1933	NY-N	.118	5	17	2	2	1	0	0	2	3	0	0	C-5
W 1936	NY-N	.263	6	19	3	5	2	0	0	1	3	3	0	C-6
W 1937	NY-N	.000	3	8	0	0	0	0	0	1	0	1	0	C-2
W Total	**5**	**.173**	**18**	**52**	**6**	**9**	**3**	**0**	**0**	**4**	**7**	**6**	**0**	**....**
• MANGUAL, Angel														
L 1971	Oak-A	.167	3	12	1	2	1	1	0	2	0	1	0	O-3
L 1972	Oak-A	.000	3	3	0	0	0	0	0	0	0	1	0	....
L 1973	Oak-A	.111	3	9	1	1	0	0	0	0	0	3	0	O-3
L 1974	Oak-A	.250	1	4	0	1	0	0	0	0	0	0	0	D-1
L Total	**4**	**.143**	**10**	**28**	**2**	**4**	**1**	**1**	**0**	**2**	**0**	**5**	**0**	**....**
W 1972	Oak-A	.300	4	10	1	3	0	0	0	1	0	0	0	O-3
W 1973	Oak-A	.000	5	6	0	0	0	0	0	0	0	3	0	O-1
W 1974	Oak-A	.000	1	1	0	0	0	0	0	0	0	1	0	....
W Total	**3**	**.176**	**10**	**17**	**1**	**3**	**0**	**0**	**0**	**1**	**0**	**4**	**0**	**....**
• MANN, Les														
W 1914	Bos-N	.286	3	7	1	2	0	0	0	1	0	1	0	O-2
W 1918	Chi-N	.227	6	22	0	5	2	0	0	2	0	0	0	O-6
W Total	**2**	**.241**	**9**	**29**	**1**	**7**	**2**	**0**	**0**	**3**	**0**	**1**	**0**	**....**
• MANTILLA, Felix														
W 1957	Mil-N	.000	4	10	1	0	0	0	0	0	1	0	0	2-3
W 1958	Mil-N	....	4	0	1	0	0	0	0	0	0	0	0	S-1
W Total	**2**	**.000**	**8**	**10**	**2**	**0**	**0**	**0**	**0**	**0**	**1**	**0**	**0**	**....**
• MANTLE, Mickey														
W 1951	NY-A	.200	2	5	1	1	0	0	0	0	2	1	0	O-2
W 1952	NY-A	.345	7	29	5	10	1	1	2	3	3	4	0	O-7
W 1953	NY-A	.208	6	24	3	5	0	0	2	7	3	8	0	O-6
W 1955	NY-A	.200	3	10	1	2	0	0	1	1	0	2	0	O-2
W 1956	NY-A	.250	7	24	6	6	1	0	3	4	6	5	1	O-7
W 1957	NY-A	.263	6	19	3	5	0	0	1	2	3	1	0	O-5
W 1958	NY-A	.250	7	24	4	6	0	1	2	3	7	4	0	O-7
W 1960	NY-A	.400	7	25	8	10	1	0	3	11	8	9	0	O-7
W 1961	NY-A	.167	2	6	0	1	0	0	0	0	0	2	0	O-2
W 1962	NY-A	.120	7	25	2	3	1	0	0	0	4	5	2	O-7
W 1963	NY-A	.133	4	15	1	2	0	0	1	1	1	5	0	O-4
W 1964	NY-A	.333	7	24	8	8	2	0	3	8	6	8	0	O-7
W Total	**12**	**.257**	**65**	**230**	**42**	**59**	**6**	**2**	**18**	**40**	**43**	**54**	**3**	**....**
• MANUEL, Charlie														
L 1969	Min-A	....	1	0	0	0	0	0	0	0	1	0	0	....
L 1970	Min-A	.000	1	1	0	0	0	0	0	0	0	1	0	....
L Total	**2**	**.000**	**2**	**1**	**0**	**0**	**0**	**0**	**0**	**0**	**1**	**1**	**0**	**....**
• MANUEL, Jerry														
D 1981	Mon-N	.071	5	14	0	1	0	0	0	0	2	5	0	2-5
L 1981	Mon-N	....	1	0	0	0	0	0	0	0	0	0	0	....
• MANUSH, Heinie														
W 1933	Was-A	.111	5	18	2	2	0	0	0	0	2	1	0	O-5
• MANWARING, Kirt														
L 1989	SF-N	.000	3	2	0	0	0	0	0	0	0	0	0	C-3
W 1989	SF-N	1.000	1	1	1	1	1	0	0	0	0	0	0	C-1
• MAPES, Cliff														
W 1949	NY-A	.100	4	10	3	1	1	0	0	2	2	4	0	O-4
W 1950	NY-A	.000	1	4	0	0	0	0	0	0	0	1	0	O-1
W Total	**2**	**.071**	**5**	**14**	**3**	**1**	**1**	**0**	**0**	**2**	**2**	**5**	**0**	**....**
• MARANVILLE, Rabbit														
W 1914	Bos-N	.308	4	13	1	4	0	0	0	3	1	1	2	S-4
W 1928	StL-N	.308	4	13	2	4	1	0	0	0	1	1	1	S-4
W Total	**2**	**.308**	**8**	**26**	**3**	**8**	**1**	**0**	**0**	**3**	**2**	**2**	**3**	**....**
• MARION, Marty														
W 1942	StL-N	.111	5	18	2	2	0	1	0	3	1	2	0	S-5
W 1943	StL-N	.357	5	14	1	5	2	0	1	2	3	1	1	S-5
W 1944	StL-N	.227	6	22	1	5	3	0	0	2	2	3	0	S-6
W 1946	StL-N	.250	7	24	1	6	2	0	0	4	1	1	0	S-7
W Total	**4**	**.231**	**23**	**78**	**5**	**18**	**7**	**1**	**1**	**11**	**7**	**7**	**1**	**....**
• MARIS, Roger														
W 1960	NY-A	.267	7	30	6	8	1	0	2	2	2	4	0	O-7
W 1961	NY-A	.105	5	19	4	2	1	0	1	2	4	6	0	O-5
W 1962	NY-A	.174	7	23	4	4	1	0	1	5	5	2	0	O-7
W 1963	NY-A	.000	2	5	0	0	0	0	0	0	0	1	0	O-2
W 1964	NY-A	.200	7	30	4	6	0	0	1	1	1	4	0	O-7
W 1967	StL-N	.385	7	26	3	10	1	0	1	7	3	1	0	O-7
W 1968	StL-N	.158	6	19	5	3	1	0	0	1	3	3	0	O-5
W Total	**7**	**.217**	**41**	**152**	**26**	**33**	**5**	**0**	**6**	**18**	**18**	**21**	**0**	**....**
• MARQUARD, Rube														
W 1911	NY-N	.000	3	2	0	0	0	0	0	0	0	2	0	....
W 1912	NY-N	.000	2	4	0	0	0	0	0	0	1	0	0	....
W 1913	NY-N	.000	2	1	0	0	0	0	0	0	0	0	0	....
W 1916	Bro-N	.000	2	3	0	0	0	0	0	0	0	1	0	....
W 1920	Bro-N	.000	2	1	0	0	0	0	0	0	0	0	0	....
W Total	**5**	**.000**	**11**	**11**	**0**	**0**	**0**	**0**	**0**	**0**	**1**	**3**	**0**	**....**
• MARQUEZ, Gonzalo														
L 1972	Oak-A	.667	3	3	1	2	0	0	0	1	0	0	0	....
W 1972	Oak-A	.600	5	5	0	3	0	0	0	1	0	0	0	....
• MARQUIS, Jason														
L 2001	Atl-N	....	4	0	0	0	0	0	0	0	0	0	0	....
• MARRERO, Eli														
D 2001	StL-N	.000	3	7	0	0	0	0	0	0	0	0	0	C-3
D 2002	StL-N	.000	2	6	0	0	0	0	0	1	0	1	0	O-2
D Total	**2**	**.000**	**5**	**13**	**0**	**0**	**0**	**0**	**0**	**1**	**0**	**1**	**0**	**....**
L 2000	StL-N	.000	4	4	0	0	0	0	0	1	0	1	0	C-3
L 2002	StL-N	.188	4	16	1	3	1	0	1	1	1	1	0	O-4
L Total	**2**	**.150**	**8**	**20**	**1**	**3**	**1**	**0**	**1**	**2**	**1**	**2**	**0**	**....**
• MARSHALL, Mike														
D 1981	LA-N	.000	1	1	0	0	0	0	0	0	0	1	0	....
L 1983	LA-N	.133	4	15	1	2	1	0	1	2	1	6	0	O-2,1-3
L 1985	LA-N	.217	6	23	1	5	2	0	1	3	1	3	0	O-6
L 1988	LA-N	.233	7	30	3	7	1	1	0	5	2	9	0	O-7
L 1990	Bos-A	.333	3	3	0	1	0	0	0	0	0	0	0	....
L Total	**4**	**.211**	**20**	**71**	**5**	**15**	**4**	**1**	**2**	**10**	**4**	**18**	**0**	**....**
W 1988	LA-N	.231	5	13	2	3	0	1	1	3	0	5	0	O-5
• MARTIN, Al														
D 2000	Sea-A	.000	1	1	0	0	0	0	0	0	0	0	0	....
D 2001	Sea-A	.000	3	2	1	0	0	0	0	0	0	0	0	D-1
D Total	**2**	**.000**	**4**	**3**	**1**	**0**	**0**	**0**	**0**	**0**	**0**	**0**	**0**	**....**
L 2000	Sea-A	.182	4	11	1	2	2	0	0	0	2	3	0	O-3
L 2001	Sea-A	.500	2	2	1	1	0	1	0	0	0	0	0	D-1
L Total	**2**	**.231**	**6**	**13**	**2**	**3**	**2**	**1**	**0**	**0**	**2**	**3**	**0**	**....**
• MARTIN, Billy														
W 1951	NY-A	....	1	0	1	0	0	0	0	0	0	0	0	....
W 1952	NY-A	.217	7	23	2	5	0	0	1	4	2	2	0	2-7
W 1953	NY-A	.500	6	24	5	12	1	2	2	8	1	2	1	2-6
W 1955	NY-A	.320	7	25	2	8	1	1	0	4	1	5	0	2-7
W 1956	NY-A	.296	7	27	5	8	0	0	2	3	1	6	0	2-7,3-2
W Total	**5**	**.333**	**28**	**99**	**15**	**33**	**2**	**3**	**5**	**19**	**5**	**15**	**1**	**....**
• MARTIN, J.C.														
L 1969	NY-N	.500	2	2	0	1	0	0	0	2	0	0	0	....
W 1969	NY-N	....	1	0	0	0	0	0	0	0	0	0	0	....
• MARTIN, Jerry														
L 1976	Phi-N	.000	1	1	1	0	0	0	0	0	0	0	0	O-1
L 1977	Phi-N	.000	3	4	0	0	0	0	0	0	0	2	0	O-1
L 1978	Phi-N	.222	4	9	1	2	1	0	1	2	1	3	0	O-3
L Total	**3**	**.143**	**8**	**14**	**2**	**2**	**1**	**0**	**1**	**2**	**1**	**5**	**0**	**....**
• MARTIN, Pepper														
W 1928	StL-N	....	1	0	1	0	0	0	0	0	0	0	0	....
W 1931	StL-N	.500	7	24	5	12	4	0	1	5	2	3	5	O-7
W 1934	StL-N	.355	7	31	8	11	3	1	0	4	3	3	2	3-7
W Total	**3**	**.418**	**15**	**55**	**14**	**23**	**7**	**1**	**1**	**9**	**5**	**6**	**7**	**....**
• MARTINEZ, Buck														
L 1976	KC-A	.333	5	15	0	5	0	0	0	4	1	3	0	C-5

SER-YEAR	TM-L	AVG	G	AB	R	H	2B	3B	HR	RBI	BB	SO	SB	POS
• MARTINEZ, Carmelo														
L 1984	SD-N	.176	5	17	1	3	0	0	0	0	2	4	0	0-5
L 1990	Pit-N	.250	2	8	0	2	2	0	0	2	0	1	0	1-2
L Total	2	.200	7	25	1	5	2	0	0	2	2	5	0	....
W 1984	SD-N	.176	5	17	0	3	0	0	0	0	1	9	0	0-5
• MARTINEZ, Dave														
D 2001	Atl-N	.000	1	1	0	0	0	0	0	0	0	0	0	....
L 2001	Atl-N	.200	4	5	0	1	0	0	0	0	0	1	0	0-1
• MARTINEZ, Edgar														
D 1995	Sea-A	.571	5	21	6	12	3	0	2	10	6	2	0	D-5
D 1997	Sea-A	.188	4	16	2	3	0	0	2	3	0	3	0	D-4
D 2000	Sea-A	.364	3	11	2	4	1	0	1	2	2	1	0	D-3
D 2001	Sea-A	.313	5	16	3	5	1	0	2	5	5	2	1	D-5
D Total	4	.375	17	64	13	24	5	0	7	20	13	8	1	....
L 1995	Sea-A	.087	6	23	0	2	0	0	0	0	2	5	1	D-6
L 2000	Sea-A	.238	6	21	2	5	1	0	1	4	3	5	0	D-6
L 2001	Sea-A	.150	5	20	1	3	1	0	0	0	1	6	0	D-5
L Total	3	.156	17	64	3	10	2	0	1	4	6	16	1	....
• MARTINEZ, Pedro														
D 1998	Bos-A	....	1	0	0	0	0	0	0	0	0	0	0	....
• MARTINEZ, Ramon														
D 2000	SF-N	.333	2	6	0	2	0	0	0	0	0	2	0	2-1,S-1
D 2002	SF-N	....	1	0	0	0	0	0	0	0	1	0	0	....
D 2003	Chi-N	.000	2	4	0	0	0	0	0	0	0	2	0	....
D Total	3	.200	5	10	0	2	0	0	0	0	1	4	0	....
L 2002	SF-N	.000	2	1	0	0	0	0	0	1	0	0	0	S-1
L 2003	Chi-N	.000	4	4	0	0	0	0	0	0	0	1	0	2-1,S-3
L Total	2	.000	6	5	0	0	0	0	0	1	0	1	0	....
W 2002	SF-N	.000	2	2	0	0	0	0	0	0	0	2	0	....
• MARTINEZ, Sandy														
D 1998	Chi-N	1.000	1	1	1	1	0	0	0	0	0	0	0	C-1
• MARTINEZ, Ted														
L 1975	Oak-A	....	3	0	0	0	0	0	0	0	0	0	0	2-3
W 1973	NY-N	....	2	0	0	0	0	0	0	0	0	0	0	....
• MARTINEZ, Tino														
D 1995	Sea-A	.409	5	22	4	9	1	0	1	5	3	4	0	1-5
D 1996	NY-A	.267	4	15	3	4	2	0	0	0	3	1	0	1-4
D 1997	NY-A	.222	5	18	1	4	1	0	1	4	2	4	0	1-5
D 1998	NY-A	.273	3	11	1	3	2	0	0	0	0	2	0	1-3
D 1999	NY-A	.182	3	11	2	2	0	0	0	0	2	2	0	1-3
D 2000	NY-A	.421	5	19	2	8	2	0	0	4	1	3	0	1-5
D 2001	NY-A	.111	5	18	1	2	0	0	1	2	1	6	0	1-5
D 2002	StL-N	.000	3	11	2	0	0	0	0	0	2	1	0	1-3
D Total	8	.256	33	125	16	32	8	0	3	15	14	23	0	....
L 1995	Sea-A	.136	6	22	1	3	0	0	0	0	3	7	0	1-6
L 1996	NY-A	.182	5	22	3	4	1	0	0	0	0	2	0	1-5
L 1998	NY-A	.105	6	19	1	2	1	0	0	1	6	8	2	1-6
L 1999	NY-A	.263	5	19	3	5	1	0	1	3	2	4	0	1-5
L 2000	NY-A	.320	6	25	5	8	2	0	1	1	2	4	0	1-6
L 2001	NY-A	.250	5	20	3	5	1	0	1	3	0	4	0	1-5
L 2002	StL-N	.143	4	14	1	2	0	0	0	1	2	1	1	1-4
L Total	7	.206	37	141	17	29	6	0	3	9	15	30	3	....
W 1996	NY-A	.091	6	11	0	1	0	0	0	0	2	5	0	1-5
W 1998	NY-A	.385	4	13	4	5	0	0	1	4	4	2	0	1-4
W 1999	NY-A	.267	4	15	3	4	0	0	1	5	2	4	0	1-4
W 2000	NY-A	.364	5	22	3	8	1	0	0	2	1	4	0	1-5
W 2001	NY-A	.190	6	21	1	4	0	0	1	3	2	2	0	1-6
W Total	5	.268	25	82	11	22	1	0	3	14	11	17	0	....
• MARTY, Joe														
W 1938	Chi-N	.500	3	12	1	6	1	0	1	5	0	2	0	0-3
• MASI, Phil														
W 1948	Bos-N	.125	5	8	1	1	1	0	0	1	0	0	0	C-5
• MASON, Jim														
L 1976	NY-A	....	2	0	0	0	0	0	0	0	0	0	0	S-2
W 1976	NY-A	1.000	3	1	1	1	0	0	1	1	0	0	0	S-3
• MATCHICK, Tom														
W 1968	Det-A	.000	3	3	0	0	0	0	0	0	0	1	0	....
• MATHENY, Mike														
D 2001	StL-N	.200	4	10	0	2	0	0	0	0	0	3	0	C-4
D 2002	StL-N	.444	3	9	3	4	1	0	0	2	2	1	0	C-3
D Total	2	.316	7	19	3	6	1	0	0	2	2	4	0	....
L 2002	StL-N	.316	5	19	2	6	2	0	1	1	0	2	0	C-5
• MATHEWS, Eddie														
W 1957	Mil-N	.227	7	22	4	5	3	0	1	4	8	5	0	3-7
W 1958	Mil-N	.160	7	25	3	4	2	0	0	3	6	11	1	3-7
W 1968	Det-A	.333	2	3	0	1	0	0	0	0	1	1	0	3-1
W Total	3	.200	16	50	7	10	5	0	1	7	15	17	1	....
• MATSUI, Hideki														
D 2003	NY-A	.267	4	15	2	4	1	0	1	3	2	3	0	0-4
L 2003	NY-A	.308	7	26	3	8	3	0	0	4	1	3	0	0-7
W 2003	NY-A	.261	6	23	1	6	0	0	1	4	3	2	0	0-6
• MATTHEWS, Gary														
D 1981	Phi-N	.400	5	20	3	8	0	1	1	1	0	2	0	0-5
L 1983	Phi-N	.429	4	14	4	6	0	0	3	8	2	1	1	0-4
L 1984	Chi-N	.200	5	15	4	3	0	0	2	5	6	4	1	0-5
L Total	2	.310	9	29	8	9	0	0	5	13	8	5	2	....
W 1983	Phi-N	.250	5	16	1	4	0	0	1	1	2	2	0	0-5
• MATTINGLY, Don														
D 1995	NY-A	.417	5	24	3	10	4	0	1	6	1	5	0	1-5
• MATUSZEK, Len														
L 1985	LA-N	1.000	3	1	1	1	0	0	0	0	0	0	0	1-1
• MAXVILL, Dal														
L 1972	Oak-A	.125	5	8	0	1	0	0	0	0	1	2	1	2-1,S-4
L 1974	Oak-A	.000	1	1	0	0	0	0	0	0	0	1	0	2-1
L Total	2	.111	6	9	0	1	0	0	0	0	1	3	1	....
W 1964	StL-N	.200	7	20	0	4	1	0	0	1	1	4	0	2-7
W 1967	StL-N	.158	7	19	1	3	0	1	0	1	4	1	0	S-7
W 1968	StL-N	.000	7	22	1	0	0	0	0	0	3	5	0	S-7
W 1974	Oak-A	....	2	0	0	0	0	0	0	0	0	0	0	2-2
W Total	4	.115	23	61	2	7	1	1	0	2	8	10	0	....
• MAY, Carlos														
L 1976	NY-A	.200	3	10	1	2	1	0	0	0	1	4	0	D-3
W 1976	NY-A	.000	4	9	0	0	0	0	0	0	0	1	0	D-4
• MAY, Dave														
L 1969	Bal-A	.000	1	1	0	0	0	0	0	0	0	0	0	....
W 1969	Bal-A	.000	2	1	0	0	0	0	0	0	1	1	0	....
• MAY, Lee														
D 1981	KC-A	....	1	0	0	0	0	0	0	0	0	0	0	1-1
L 1970	Cin-N	.167	3	12	0	2	1	0	0	2	0	2	0	1-3
L 1979	Bal-A	.143	2	7	0	1	0	0	0	1	1	3	0	D-2
L Total	2	.158	5	19	0	3	1	0	0	3	1	5	0	....
W 1970	Cin-N	.389	5	18	6	7	2	0	2	8	2	2	0	1-5
W 1979	Bal-A	.000	2	1	0	0	0	0	0	0	1	1	0	....
W Total	2	.368	7	19	6	7	2	0	2	8	3	3	0	....
• MAY, Milt														
L 1971	Pit-N	.000	1	1	0	0	0	0	0	0	0	0	0	....
L 1972	Pit-N	.500	1	2	0	1	0	0	0	1	0	0	0	C-1
L Total	2	.333	2	3	0	1	0	0	0	1	0	0	0	....
W 1971	Pit-N	.500	2	2	0	1	0	0	0	1	0	0	0	....
• MAYBERRY, John														
L 1976	KC-A	.222	5	18	4	4	0	0	1	3	1	0	0	1-5
L 1977	KC-A	.167	4	12	1	2	1	0	1	3	1	2	0	1-4
L Total	2	.200	9	30	5	6	1	0	2	6	2	2	0	....
• MAYO, Eddie														
W 1936	NY-N	.000	1	1	0	0	0	0	0	0	0	0	0	3-1
W 1945	Det-A	.250	7	28	4	7	1	0	0	2	3	2	0	2-7
W Total	2	.241	8	29	4	7	1	0	0	2	3	2	0	....
• MAYO, Jackie														
W 1950	Phi-N	....	3	0	0	0	0	0	0	0	1	0	0	0-1
• MAYS, Willie														
L 1971	SF-N	.267	4	15	2	4	2	0	1	3	3	3	1	0-4
L 1973	NY-N	.333	1	3	1	1	0	0	0	1	0	0	0	0-1
L Total	2	.278	5	18	3	5	2	0	1	4	3	3	1	....
W 1951	NY-N	.182	6	22	1	4	0	0	0	1	2	2	0	0-6
W 1954	NY-N	.286	4	14	4	4	1	0	0	3	4	1	1	0-4
W 1962	SF-N	.250	7	28	3	7	2	0	0	1	1	5	1	0-7
W 1973	NY-N	.286	3	7	1	2	0	0	0	1	0	1	0	0-2
W Total	4	.239	20	71	9	17	3	0	0	6	7	9	2	....
• MAZEROSKI, Bill														
L 1970	Pit-N	.000	1	2	0	0	0	0	0	0	2	0	0	2-1
L 1971	Pit-N	1.000	1	1	1	1	0	0	0	0	0	0	0	....
L 1972	Pit-N	.500	2	2	0	1	0	0	0	0	0	1	0	....
L Total	3	.400	4	5	1	2	0	0	0	0	2	1	0	....
W 1960	Pit-N	.320	7	25	4	8	2	0	2	5	0	3	0	2-7
W 1971	Pit-N	.000	1	1	0	0	0	0	0	0	0	0	0	....
W Total	2	.308	8	26	4	8	2	0	2	5	0	3	0	....
• MAZZILLI, Lee														
L 1986	NY-N	.200	5	5	0	1	0	0	0	0	0	3	0	....
L 1988	NY-N	.500	3	2	0	1	0	0	0	0	0	0	1	....
L 1989	Tor-A	.000	3	8	0	0	0	0	0	0	0	2	0	D-2
L Total	3	.133	11	15	0	2	0	0	0	0	0	5	1	....
W 1986	NY-N	.400	4	5	2	2	0	0	0	0	0	0	0	0-1,D-1
• MCALEER, Jimmy														
T 1892	Cle-N	.182	6	22	0	4	0	0	0	1	2	2	1	0-6
T 1895	Cle-N	.286	5	21	2	6	0	0	0	2	0	0	1	0-5
T 1896	Cle-N	.133	4	15	0	2	0	0	0	1	1	2	1	0-4
T Total	3	.207	15	58	2	12	0	0	0	4	3	4	3	....
• MCANANY, Jim														
W 1959	Chi-A	.000	3	5	0	0	0	0	0	0	1	0	0	0-3
• MCAULIFFE, Dick														
L 1972	Det-A	.200	5	20	3	4	0	0	1	1	1	3	0	2-1,S-4
W 1968	Det-A	.222	7	27	5	6	0	0	1	3	4	6	0	2-7
• MCBRIDE, Bake														
D 1981	Phi-N	.200	4	15	1	3	1	0	0	0	0	5	0	0-4
L 1977	Phi-N	.222	4	18	2	4	0	0	1	2	1	2	0	0-4
L 1978	Phi-N	.222	3	9	2	2	0	0	1	1	0	2	0	0-2
L 1980	Phi-N	.238	5	21	0	5	0	0	0	0	1	5	2	0-5
L Total	3	.229	12	48	4	11	0	0	2	3	2	9	2	....
W 1980	Phi-N	.304	6	23	3	7	1	0	1	5	2	1	0	0-6
• MCBRIDE, Tom														
W 1946	Bos-A	.167	5	12	0	2	0	0	0	1	0	1	0	0-2
• MCCABE, Bill														
W 1918	Chi-N	.000	3	1	1	0	0	0	0	0	0	0	0	....

YEAR	TM-L	AVG	G	AB	R	H	2B	3B	HR	RBI	BB	SO	SB	POS
W 1920	Bro-N	....	1	0	0	0	0	0	0	0	0	0	0	....
W Total	2	.000	4	1	1	0	0	0	0	0	0	0	0	....
• MCCARTHY, Johnny														
W 1937	NY-N	.211	5	19	1	4	1	0	0	1	1	2	0	1-5
• MCCARTHY, Tommy														
T 1892	Bos-N	.381	6	21	8	8	2	0	0	2	6	1	3	O-6
W 1888	StL-A	.244	10	41	10	10	1	0	1	9	0	0	6	O-10
• MCCARTY, David														
D 2003	Bos-A	....	1	0	0	0	0	0	0	0	0	0	0	....
L 2003	Bos-A	.000	1	1	0	0	0	0	0	0	0	1	0	....
• MCCARTY, Lew														
W 1917	NY-N	.400	3	5	1	2	0	1	0	1	0	0	0	C-2
• MCCARVER, Tim														
L 1976	Phi-N	.000	2	4	0	0	0	0	0	0	0	1	0	C-1
L 1977	Phi-N	.167	3	6	1	1	0	0	0	0	1	3	0	C-2
L 1978	Phi-N	.000	2	4	2	0	0	0	0	1	2	0	0	C-1
L Total	3	.071	7	14	3	1	0	0	0	1	3	4	0	....
W 1964	StL-N	.478	7	23	4	11	1	1	1	5	5	1	1	C-7
W 1967	StL-N	.125	7	24	3	3	1	0	0	2	2	2	0	C-7
W 1968	StL-N	.333	7	27	3	9	0	2	1	4	3	2	0	C-7
W Total	3	.311	21	74	10	23	2	3	2	11	10	5	1	....
• MCCLENDON, Lloyd														
L 1989	Chi-N	.667	3	3	0	2	0	0	0	0	1	0	0	O-1,C-2
L 1991	Pit-N	.000	3	2	0	0	0	0	0	0	1	0	0	1-1
L 1992	Pit-N	.727	5	11	4	8	2	0	1	4	4	1	0	O-5
L Total	3	.625	11	16	4	10	2	0	1	4	6	1	0	....
• MCCLURE, Bob														
D 1981	Mil-A	....	3	0	0	0	0	0	0	0	0	0	0	....
L 1982	Mil-A	....	1	0	0	0	0	0	0	0	0	0	0	....
W 1982	Mil-A	....	5	0	0	0	0	0	0	0	0	0	0	....
• MCCORMICK, Frank														
W 1939	Cin-N	.400	4	15	1	6	1	0	0	1	0	1	0	1-4
W 1940	Cin-N	.214	7	28	2	6	1	0	0	0	1	1	0	1-7
W 1948	Bos-N	.200	3	5	0	1	0	0	0	0	0	2	0	1-1
W Total	3	.271	14	48	3	13	2	0	0	1	1	4	0	....
• MCCORMICK, Mike														
W 1940	Cin-N	.310	7	29	1	9	3	0	0	2	1	6	0	O-7
W 1948	Bos-N	.261	6	23	1	6	0	0	0	2	0	4	0	O-6
W 1949	Bro-N	....	1	0	0	0	0	0	0	0	0	0	0	O-1
W Total	3	.288	14	52	2	15	3	0	0	4	1	10	0	....
• MCCORMICK, Moose														
W 1912	NY-N	.250	5	4	0	1	0	0	0	1	0	0	0	....
W 1913	NY-N	.500	2	2	1	1	0	0	0	0	0	0	0	....
W Total	2	.333	7	6	1	2	0	0	0	1	0	0	0	....
• MCCOSKY, Barney														
W 1940	Det-A	.304	7	23	5	7	1	0	0	1	7	0	0	O-7
• MCCOVEY, Willie														
L 1971	SF-N	.429	4	14	2	6	0	0	2	6	4	2	0	1-4
W 1962	SF-N	.200	4	15	2	3	0	1	1	1	1	3	0	O-2,1-2
• MCCRACKEN, Quinton														
D 2002	Ari-N	.364	3	11	1	4	1	0	0	2	1	2	0	O-3
• MCCULLOUGH, Clyde														
W 1945	Chi-N	.000	1	1	0	0	0	0	0	0	0	1	0	....
• MCDOUGALD, Gil														
W 1951	NY-A	.261	6	23	2	6	1	0	1	7	2	2	0	2-4,3-5
W 1952	NY-A	.200	7	25	5	5	0	0	1	3	5	2	1	3-7
W 1953	NY-A	.167	6	24	2	4	0	1	2	4	1	3	0	3-6
W 1955	NY-A	.259	7	27	2	7	0	0	1	1	2	6	0	3-7
W 1956	NY-A	.143	7	21	0	3	0	0	0	1	3	6	0	S-7
W 1957	NY-A	.250	7	24	3	6	0	0	0	2	3	3	1	S-7
W 1958	NY-A	.321	7	28	5	9	2	0	2	4	2	4	0	2-7
W 1960	NY-A	.278	6	18	4	5	1	0	0	2	2	3	0	3-6
W Total	8	.237	53	190	23	45	4	1	7	24	20	29	2	....
• MCDOWELL, Jack														
D 1995	NY-A	....	2	0	0	0	0	0	0	0	0	0	0	....
L 1993	Chi-A	....	2	0	0	0	0	0	0	0	0	0	0	....
• MCEWING, Joe														
D 2000	NY-N	1.000	4	1	0	1	0	0	0	0	0	0	0	O-3,3-1
L 2000	NY-N	....	4	0	2	0	0	0	0	0	0	0	0	O-3,3-1
W 2000	NY-N	.000	3	1	1	0	0	0	0	0	0	0	0	O-2
• MCFARLAND, Ed														
W 1906	Chi-A	.000	1	1	0	0	0	0	0	0	0	0	0	....
• MCGANN, Dan														
W 1905	NY-N	.235	5	17	1	4	2	0	0	4	2	7	0	1-5
• MCGARR, Chippy														
T 1895	Cle-N	.368	5	19	3	7	2	0	0	1	1	1	2	3-5
T 1896	Cle-N	.063	4	16	0	1	0	0	0	0	0	3	2	3-4
T Total	2	.229	9	35	3	8	2	0	0	1	1	4	4	....
• MCGEE, Willie														
D 1995	Bos-A	.250	2	4	0	1	0	0	0	1	0	2	0	O-2
D 1996	StL-N	.100	3	10	1	1	0	0	0	1	1	3	0	O-3
D Total	2	.143	5	14	1	2	0	0	0	2	1	5	0	....
L 1982	StL-N	.308	3	13	4	4	0	2	1	5	0	5	0	O-3
L 1985	StL-N	.269	6	26	6	7	1	0	0	3	3	6	2	O-6
L 1987	StL-N	.308	7	26	2	8	1	1	0	2	0	5	0	O-7
L 1990	Oak-A	.222	3	9	3	2	1	0	0	0	1	2	2	O-2,D-1

YEAR	TM-L	AVG	G	AB	R	H	2B	3B	HR	RBI	BB	SO	SB	POS
L 1996	StL-N	.333	6	15	0	5	0	0	0	0	0	3	0	O-5
L Total	5	.292	25	89	15	26	3	3	1	10	4	21	4	....
W 1982	StL-N	.240	6	25	6	6	0	0	2	5	1	3	2	O-6
W 1985	StL-N	.259	7	27	2	7	2	0	1	2	1	3	1	O-7
W 1987	StL-N	.370	7	27	2	10	2	0	0	4	0	9	0	O-7
W 1990	Oak-A	.200	4	10	1	2	1	0	0	0	0	2	1	O-3
W Total	4	.281	24	89	11	25	5	0	3	11	2	17	4	....
• MCGRAW, John														
T 1894	Bal-N	.250	4	16	2	4	0	0	0	2	0	0	1	3-4
T 1895	Bal-N	.400	5	20	4	8	2	0	0	1	2	0	2	3-5
T 1896	Bal-N	.267	4	15	4	4	0	0	0	1	0	0	4	3-4
T 1897	Bal-N	.300	5	20	6	6	1	1	0	6	7	0	0	3-5
T Total	4	.310	18	71	16	22	3	1	0	10	9	0	7	....
• MCGRIFF, Fred														
D 1995	Atl-N	.333	4	18	4	6	0	0	2	6	2	3	0	1-4
D 1996	Atl-N	.333	3	9	1	3	1	0	1	3	2	1	0	1-3
D 1997	Atl-N	.222	3	9	4	2	0	0	0	1	3	2	0	1-3
D Total	3	.306	10	36	9	11	1	0	3	10	7	6	0	....
L 1989	Tor-A	.143	5	21	1	3	0	0	0	3	0	4	0	1-5
L 1993	Atl-N	.435	6	23	6	10	3	0	1	4	4	7	0	1-6
L 1995	Atl-N	.438	4	16	5	7	4	0	0	0	3	0	0	1-4
L 1996	Atl-N	.250	7	28	6	7	0	1	2	7	3	5	0	1-7
L 1997	Atl-N	.333	6	21	0	7	1	0	0	4	2	7	0	1-6
L Total	5	.312	28	109	18	34	8	1	3	18	12	23	0	....
W 1995	Atl-N	.261	6	23	5	6	2	0	2	3	3	7	1	1-6
W 1996	Atl-N	.300	6	20	4	6	0	0	2	6	5	4	0	1-6
W Total	2	.279	12	43	9	12	2	0	4	9	8	11	1	....
• MCGUIRE, Deacon														
T 1900	Bro-N	.375	2	8	1	3	1	0	0	0	0	1	0	C-2
• MCGWIRE, Mark														
D 2000	StL-N	.500	3	2	1	1	0	0	1	1	1	0	0	....
D 2001	StL-N	.091	4	11	0	1	0	0	0	0	0	6	0	1-3
D Total	2	.154	7	13	1	2	0	0	1	1	1	6	0	....
L 1988	Oak-A	.333	4	15	4	5	0	0	1	3	1	5	0	1-4
L 1989	Oak-A	.389	5	18	3	7	1	0	1	3	1	4	0	1-5
L 1990	Oak-A	.154	4	13	2	2	0	0	0	2	3	3	0	1-4
L 1992	Oak-A	.150	6	20	1	3	0	0	1	3	5	4	0	1-6
L 2000	StL-N	.000	3	2	0	0	0	0	0	0	1	0	0	....
L Total	5	.250	22	68	10	17	1	0	3	11	11	16	0	....
W 1988	Oak-A	.059	5	17	1	1	0	0	1	1	3	4	0	1-5
W 1989	Oak-A	.294	4	17	0	5	1	0	0	1	1	3	0	1-4
W 1990	Oak-A	.214	4	14	1	3	0	0	0	0	2	4	0	1-4
W Total	3	.188	13	48	2	9	1	0	1	2	6	11	0	....
• MCHALE, John														
W 1945	Det-A	.000	3	3	0	0	0	0	0	0	0	1	0	....
• MCINNIS, Stuffy														
W 1911	Phi-A	....	1	0	0	0	0	0	0	0	0	0	0	1-1
W 1913	Phi-A	.118	5	17	1	2	1	0	0	2	0	2	0	1-5
W 1914	Phi-A	.143	4	14	2	2	1	0	0	0	3	3	0	1-4
W 1918	Bos-A	.250	6	20	2	5	0	0	0	1	1	1	0	1-6
W 1925	Pit-N	.286	4	14	0	4	0	0	0	1	0	2	0	1-3
W Total	5	.200	20	65	5	13	2	0	0	4	4	8	0	....
• MCINTYRE, Matty														
W 1908	Det-A	.222	5	18	2	4	1	0	0	0	3	2	1	O-5
W 1909	Det-A	.000	4	3	0	0	0	0	0	0	0	1	0	O-1
W Total	2	.190	9	21	2	4	1	0	0	0	3	3	1	....
• MCKAY, Dave														
D 1981	Oak-A	.273	3	11	1	3	0	0	1	1	1	1	0	2-3
L 1981	Oak-A	.273	3	11	0	3	0	0	0	1	0	2	0	2-3
• MCKEAN, Ed														
T 1892	Cle-N	.440	6	25	2	11	0	0	0	6	1	3	0	S-6
T 1895	Cle-N	.300	5	20	2	6	1	1	0	4	3	0	1	S-5
T 1896	Cle-N	.313	4	16	0	5	1	1	0	1	1	2	1	S-4
T Total	3	.361	15	61	4	22	2	2	0	11	5	5	2	....
• MCLAIN, Denny														
W 1968	Det-A	.000	3	6	0	0	0	0	0	0	0	4	0	....
• MCLEAN, Larry														
W 1913	NY-N	.500	5	12	0	6	0	0	0	2	0	0	0	C-4
• MCLEMORE, Mark														
D 1996	Tex-A	.133	4	15	1	2	0	0	0	2	0	4	0	2-4
D 1998	Tex-A	.100	3	10	0	1	1	0	0	0	2	3	0	2-3
D 1999	Tex-A	.100	3	10	0	1	0	0	0	0	1	3	0	2-3
D 2000	Sea-A	.111	3	9	1	1	0	0	0	0	2	1	0	2-3
D 2001	Sea-A	.167	5	18	0	3	0	0	0	3	1	8	0	O-1,S-5
D Total	5	.129	18	62	2	8	1	0	0	5	6	19	0	....
L 2000	Sea-A	.250	5	16	2	4	3	0	0	2	2	1	0	2-5
L 2001	Sea-A	.143	5	14	1	2	0	1	0	3	2	2	0	O-1,2-1,S-3
L Total	2	.200	10	30	3	6	3	1	0	5	4	3	0	....
• MCMAHON, Sadie														
T 1895	Bal-N	.000	2	7	0	0	0	0	0	0	0	0	0	P-2
• MCMILLAN, Norm														
W 1922	NY-A	.000	1	2	0	0	0	0	0	0	0	0	0	O-1
W 1929	Chi-N	.100	5	20	0	2	0	0	0	0	2	6	1	3-5
W Total	2	.091	6	22	0	2	0	0	0	0	2	6	1	....
• MCMILLON, Billy														
D 2003	Oak-A	.167	3	6	0	1	0	0	0	1	1	1	0	O-1
• MCMULLEN, Ken														
L 1974	LA-N	.000	1	1	0	0	0	0	0	0	0	1	0	....

SER-YEAR	TM-L	AVG	G	AB	R	H	2B	3B	HR	RBI	BB	SO	SB	POS
• MCMULLIN, Fred														
W 1917	Chi-A	.125	6	24	1	3	1	0	0	2	1	6	0	3-6
W 1919	Chi-A	.500	2	2	0	1	0	0	0	0	0	0	0	....
W Total	2	.154	8	26	1	4	1	0	0	2	1	6	0	....
• MCNAIR, Eric														
W 1930	Phi-A	.000	1	1	0	0	0	0	0	0	0	0	0	....
W 1931	Phi-A	.000	2	2	1	0	0	0	0	0	0	1	0	2-1
W Total	2	.000	3	3	1	0	0	0	0	0	0	1	0	....
• MCNALLY, Mike														
W 1916	Bos-A	....	1	0	1	0	0	0	0	0	0	0	0	....
W 1921	NY-A	.200	7	20	3	4	1	0	0	1	1	3	2	3-7
W 1922	NY-A	....	1	0	0	0	0	0	0	0	0	0	0	2-1
W Total	3	.200	9	20	4	4	1	0	0	1	1	3	2	....
• MCNEELY, Earl														
W 1924	Was-A	.222	7	27	4	6	3	0	0	1	4	4	1	O-6
W 1925	Was-A	....	4	0	2	0	0	0	0	0	0	0	1	O-2
W Total	2	.222	11	27	6	6	3	0	0	1	4	4	2	....
• MCQUINN, George														
W 1944	StL-A	.438	6	16	2	7	2	0	1	5	7	2	0	1-6
W 1947	NY-A	.130	7	23	3	3	0	0	0	1	5	8	0	1-7
W Total	2	.256	13	39	5	10	2	0	1	6	12	10	0	....
• MCRAE, Hal														
D 1981	KC-A	.091	3	11	0	1	1	0	0	0	1	1	0	D-3
L 1970	Cin-N	.000	2	4	0	0	0	0	0	0	0	2	0	O-1
L 1972	Cin-N	....	1	0	0	0	0	0	0	0	0	0	0	....
L 1976	KC-A	.118	5	17	2	2	1	1	0	1	1	4	0	O-2,D-3
L 1977	KC-A	.444	5	18	6	8	3	0	1	2	3	1	0	O-2,D-3
L 1978	KC-A	.214	4	14	0	3	0	0	0	2	2	2	1	D-4
L 1980	KC-A	.200	3	10	0	2	0	0	0	0	1	3	0	D-3
L 1984	KC-A	1.000	2	2	0	2	1	0	0	1	0	0	0	D-2
L 1985	KC-A	.261	6	23	1	6	2	0	0	3	1	6	0	D-6
L Total	8	.261	28	88	9	23	7	1	1	9	8	18	1	....
W 1970	Cin-N	.455	3	11	1	5	2	0	0	3	0	1	0	O-3
W 1972	Cin-N	.444	5	9	1	4	1	0	0	2	0	1	0	O-2
W 1980	KC-A	.375	6	24	3	9	3	0	0	1	2	2	0	D-6
W 1985	KC-A	.000	3	1	0	0	0	0	0	0	1	0	0	....
W Total	4	.400	17	45	5	18	6	0	0	6	3	4	0	....
• MCREYNOLDS, Kevin														
L 1984	SD-N	.300	4	10	2	3	0	0	1	4	3	1	0	O-4
L 1988	NY-N	.250	7	28	4	7	2	0	2	4	3	5	2	O-7
L Total	2	.263	11	38	6	10	2	0	3	8	6	6	2	....
• MEDWICK, Joe														
W 1934	StL-N	.379	7	29	4	11	0	1	1	5	1	7	0	O-7
W 1941	Bro-N	.235	5	17	1	4	1	0	0	0	1	2	0	O-5
W Total	2	.326	12	46	5	15	1	1	1	5	2	9	0	....
• MEEKIN, Jouett														
T 1894	NY-N	.556	2	9	2	5	0	0	0	3	0	1	0	P-2
• MEJIA, Miguel														
D 1996	StL-N	....	1	0	0	0	0	0	0	0	0	0	0	....
L 1996	StL-N	.000	3	1	1	0	0	0	0	0	0	1	0	O-2
• MELHUSE, Adam														
D 2003	Oak-A	.600	2	5	1	3	0	1	0	1	0	1	0	C-1
• MELVIN, Bob														
L 1987	SF-N	.429	3	7	0	3	0	0	0	0	1	1	0	C-2
• MENDOZA, Mario														
L 1974	Pit-N	.200	3	5	0	1	0	0	0	1	1	0	0	S-3
• MENECHINO, Frank														
D 2000	Oak-A	....	1	0	0	0	0	0	0	0	0	0	0	2-1
D 2001	Oak-A	.083	4	12	2	1	0	0	0	0	1	4	0	2-4
D 2003	Oak-A	....	1	0	0	0	0	0	0	0	0	0	0	2-1
D Total	3	.083	6	12	2	1	0	0	0	0	1	4	0	....
• MENKE, Denis														
L 1972	Cin-N	.250	5	16	1	4	1	0	0	0	4	3	0	3-5
L 1973	Cin-N	.222	3	9	1	2	0	0	1	1	1	2	0	3-2,S-2
L Total	2	.240	8	25	2	6	1	0	1	1	5	5	0	....
W 1972	Cin-N	.083	7	24	1	2	0	0	1	2	2	6	0	3-7
• MERCED, Orlando														
D 2001	Hou-N	.000	1	1	0	0	0	0	0	0	0	0	0	....
L 1991	Pit-N	.222	3	9	1	2	0	0	1	1	0	1	0	1-2
L 1992	Pit-N	.100	4	10	0	1	1	0	0	2	2	4	0	1-4
L Total	2	.158	7	19	1	3	1	0	1	3	2	5	0	....
• MERKLE, Fred														
W 1911	NY-N	.150	6	20	1	3	1	0	0	1	2	6	0	1-6
W 1912	NY-N	.273	8	33	5	9	2	1	0	3	0	7	1	1-8
W 1913	NY-N	.231	4	13	3	3	0	0	1	3	1	2	0	1-4
W 1916	Bro-N	.250	3	4	0	1	0	0	0	1	2	0	0	1-1
W 1918	Chi-N	.278	6	18	1	5	0	0	0	1	4	3	0	1-6
W Total	5	.239	27	88	10	21	3	1	1	9	9	18	1	....
• MERLONI, Lou														
D 1999	Bos-A	.333	3	6	1	2	0	0	0	1	1	1	0	S-3
L 1999	Bos-A	....	1	0	0	0	0	0	0	0	1	0	0	....
• MERRITT, Jim														
L 1970	Cin-N	.000	1	2	0	0	0	0	0	0	0	2	0	....
W 1965	Min-A	....	2	0	0	0	0	0	0	0	0	0	0	....
W 1970	Cin-N	.000	1	1	0	0	0	0	0	0	0	1	0	....
W Total	2	.000	3	1	0	0	0	0	0	0	0	1	0	....

SER-YEAR	TM-L	AVG	G	AB	R	H	2B	3B	HR	RBI	BB	SO	SB	POS
• MERTES, Sam														
W 1905	NY-N	.176	5	17	2	3	1	0	0	2	2	5	0	O-5
• MERULLO, Lennie														
W 1945	Chi-N	.000	3	2	0	0	0	0	0	0	0	1	0	S-3
• METHENY, Bud														
W 1943	NY-A	.125	2	8	0	1	0	0	0	0	0	2	0	O-2
• METKOVICH, Catfish														
W 1946	Bos-A	.500	2	2	1	1	1	0	0	0	0	0	0	....
• MEUSEL, Bob														
W 1921	NY-A	.200	8	30	3	6	2	0	0	3	2	5	1	O-8
W 1922	NY-A	.300	5	20	2	6	1	0	0	2	1	3	1	O-5
W 1923	NY-A	.269	6	26	1	7	1	2	0	8	0	3	0	O-6
W 1926	NY-A	.238	7	21	3	5	1	1	0	0	6	1	0	O-7
W 1927	NY-A	.118	4	17	1	2	0	0	0	1	1	7	1	O-4
W 1928	NY-A	.200	4	15	5	3	1	0	1	3	2	5	2	O-4
W Total	6	.225	34	129	15	29	6	3	1	17	12	24	5	....
• MEUSEL, Irish														
W 1921	NY-N	.345	8	29	4	10	2	1	1	7	2	3	1	O-8
W 1922	NY-N	.250	5	20	3	5	0	0	1	7	0	1	0	O-5
W 1923	NY-N	.280	6	25	3	7	1	1	1	2	0	2	0	O-6
W 1924	NY-N	.154	4	13	0	2	0	0	0	1	2	0	0	O-5
W Total	4	.276	23	87	10	24	3	2	3	17	4	6	1	....
• MEYERS, Chief														
W 1911	NY-N	.300	6	20	2	6	2	0	0	2	0	3	0	C-6
W 1912	NY-N	.357	8	28	2	10	0	1	0	3	2	3	1	C-8
W 1913	NY-N	.000	1	4	0	0	0	0	0	0	0	0	0	C-1
W 1916	Bro-N	.200	3	10	0	2	0	1	0	0	1	0	0	C-3
W Total	4	.290	18	62	4	18	2	2	0	5	3	6	1	....
• MIENTKIEWICZ, Doug														
D 2002	Min-A	.250	5	20	3	5	0	0	2	4	1	1	0	1-5
D 2003	Min-A	.133	4	15	0	2	0	0	0	0	1	2	0	1-4
D Total	2	.200	9	35	3	7	0	0	2	4	2	3	0	....
L 2002	Min-A	.278	5	18	1	5	1	0	0	2	1	2	0	1-5
• MIERKOWICZ, Ed														
W 1945	Det-A	....	1	0	0	0	0	0	0	0	0	0	0	O-1
• MIESKE, Matt														
D 1999	Hou-N	.000	2	4	1	0	0	0	0	0	1	0	0	O-1
• MIKSIS, Eddie														
W 1947	Bro-N	.250	5	4	1	1	0	0	0	0	0	1	0	O-2,2-1
W 1949	Bro-N	.286	3	7	0	2	1	0	0	0	0	1	0	3-2
W Total	2	.273	8	11	1	3	1	0	0	0	0	2	0	....
• MILBOURNE, Larry														
D 1981	NY-A	.316	5	19	4	6	1	0	0	0	0	1	0	S-5
L 1981	NY-A	.462	3	13	4	6	0	0	0	1	0	0	0	S-3
W 1981	NY-A	.250	6	20	2	5	2	0	0	3	4	0	0	S-6
• MILLAN, Felix														
L 1969	Atl-N	.333	3	12	2	4	1	0	0	0	3	0	0	2-3
L 1973	NY-N	.316	5	19	5	6	0	0	0	2	2	1	0	2-5
L Total	2	.323	8	31	7	10	1	0	0	2	5	1	0	....
W 1973	NY-N	.188	7	32	3	6	1	1	0	1	1	1	0	2-7
• MILLAR, Kevin														
D 2003	Bos-A	.238	5	21	0	5	0	0	0	0	2	4	0	1-5
L 2003	Bos-A	.241	7	29	3	7	0	0	1	3	1	9	0	1-7
• MILLER, Bing														
W 1929	Phi-A	.368	5	19	1	7	1	0	0	4	0	2	0	O-5
W 1930	Phi-A	.143	6	21	0	3	2	0	0	3	0	4	0	O-6
W 1931	Phi-A	.269	7	26	3	7	1	0	0	1	0	4	0	O-7
W Total	3	.258	18	66	4	17	4	0	0	8	0	10	0	....
• MILLER, Damian														
D 2001	Ari-N	.267	5	15	1	4	0	0	0	0	1	3	0	C-5
D 2002	Ari-N	.500	1	2	0	1	1	0	0	0	2	0	0	C-1
D 2003	Chi-N	.091	4	11	0	1	1	0	0	1	2	5	0	C-4
D Total	3	.214	10	28	1	6	2	0	0	1	5	8	0	....
L 2001	Ari-N	.176	5	17	0	3	0	0	0	0	2	5	0	C-5
L 2003	Chi-N	.200	4	10	0	2	1	0	0	1	2	2	0	C-4
L Total	2	.185	9	27	0	5	1	0	0	1	4	7	0	....
W 2001	Ari-N	.190	6	21	3	4	2	0	0	2	1	11	0	C-6
• MILLER, Dots														
W 1909	Pit-N	.250	7	28	2	7	1	0	0	4	2	5	3	2-7
• MILLER, Elmer														
W 1921	NY-A	.161	8	31	3	5	1	0	0	2	2	5	0	O-8
• MILLER, Hack														
W 1918	Bos-A	.000	1	1	0	0	0	0	0	0	0	0	0	....
• MILLER, Otto														
W 1916	Bro-N	.125	2	8	0	1	0	0	0	0	0	1	0	C-2
W 1920	Bro-N	.143	6	14	0	2	0	0	0	0	1	2	0	C-6
W Total	2	.136	8	22	0	3	0	0	0	0	1	3	0	....
• MILLER, Ralph														
W 1924	Was-A	.182	4	11	0	2	0	0	0	2	1	0	0	3-4
• MILLER, Rick														
L 1979	Cal-A	.250	4	16	2	4	0	0	0	0	0	1	0	O-4
W 1975	Bos-A	.000	3	2	0	0	0	0	0	0	0	0	0	O-2
• MILLIGAN, Jocko														
W 1888	StL-A	.400	8	25	5	10	2	1	0	4	3	3	0	C-8,1-1

YEAR	TM-L	AVG	G	AB	R	H	2B	3B	HR	RBI	BB	SO	SB	POS
• MILLS, Brad														
D 1981	Mon-N	....	1	0	0	0	0	0	0	0	1	0	0	....
• MILNER, Eddie														
L 1987	SF-N	.143	6	7	0	1	0	0	0	0	0	3	0	O-4
• MILNER, John														
D 1981	Mon-N	.500	2	2	0	1	0	0	0	1	0	0	0	....
L 1973	NY-N	.176	5	17	2	3	0	0	0	1	5	3	0	1-5
L 1979	Pit-N	.000	3	9	0	0	0	0	0	0	2	0	0	O-3
L 1981	Mon-N	.000	1	1	0	0	0	0	0	0	0	1	0	....
L **Total**	3	.111	9	27	2	3	0	0	0	1	7	4	0	....
W 1973	NY-N	.296	7	27	2	8	0	0	0	2	5	1	0	1-7
W 1979	Pit-N	.333	3	9	2	3	1	0	0	1	2	0	0	O-3
W **Total**	2	.306	10	36	4	11	1	0	0	3	7	1	0	....
• MINCHER, Don														
L 1972	Oak-A	.000	1	1	0	0	0	0	0	0	0	1	0	....
W 1965	Min-A	.130	7	23	3	3	0	0	1	1	2	7	0	1-7
W 1972	Oak-A	1.000	3	1	0	1	0	0	0	1	0	0	0	....
W **Total**	2	.167	10	24	3	4	0	0	1	2	2	7	0	....
• MIRABELLI, Doug														
D 2000	SF-N	.000	2	2	0	0	0	0	0	0	1	1	0	C-2
D 2003	Bos-A	.500	2	4	2	2	1	0	0	0	0	2	0	C-2
D **Total**	2	.333	4	6	2	2	1	0	0	0	1	3	0	....
L 2003	Bos-A	.286	3	7	0	2	0	0	0	0	0	2	0	C-3
• MITCHELL, Dale														
W 1948	Cle-A	.174	6	23	4	4	1	0	1	1	2	0	0	O-6
W 1954	Cle-A	.000	3	2	0	0	0	0	0	0	1	0	0	....
W 1956	Bro-N	.000	4	4	0	0	0	0	0	0	0	1	0	....
W **Total**	3	.138	13	29	4	4	1	0	1	1	3	1	0	....
• MITCHELL, Keith														
L 1991	Atl-N	.000	5	4	0	0	0	0	0	0	0	1	0	O-5
W 1991	Atl-N	.000	3	2	0	0	0	0	0	0	0	1	0	O-3
• MITCHELL, Kevin														
L 1986	NY-N	.250	2	8	1	2	0	0	0	0	0	1	0	O-2
L 1987	SF-N	.267	7	30	2	8	1	0	1	2	0	3	1	3-7
L 1989	SF-N	.353	5	17	5	6	0	0	2	7	3	3	0	O-5
L **Total**	3	.291	14	55	8	16	1	0	3	9	3	7	1	....
W 1986	NY-N	.250	5	8	1	2	0	0	0	0	0	3	0	O-2,D-2
W 1989	SF-N	.294	4	17	2	5	0	0	1	2	0	3	0	O-4
W **Total**	2	.280	9	25	3	7	0	0	1	2	0	6	0	....
• MITTERWALD, George														
L 1969	Min-A	.143	2	7	0	1	0	0	0	0	1	3	0	C-2
L 1970	Min-A	.500	2	8	2	4	1	0	0	2	0	2	0	C-2
L **Total**	2	.333	4	15	2	5	1	0	0	2	1	5	0	....
• MIZE, Johnny														
W 1949	NY-A	1.000	2	2	0	2	0	0	0	2	0	0	0	....
W 1950	NY-A	.133	4	15	0	2	0	0	0	0	0	1	0	1-4
W 1951	NY-A	.286	4	7	2	2	1	0	0	1	2	0	0	1-2
W 1952	NY-A	.400	5	15	3	6	1	0	3	6	3	1	0	1-4
W 1953	NY-A	.000	3	3	0	0	0	0	0	0	0	1	0	....
W **Total**	5	.286	18	42	5	12	2	0	3	9	5	3	0	....
• MOELLER, Chad														
D 2002	Ari-N	.400	3	5	0	2	0	0	0	0	0	1	0	C-1
• MOHR, Dustan														
D 2002	Min-A	1.000	4	2	1	2	1	0	0	0	1	0	0	O-4
L 2002	Min-A	.417	5	12	3	5	1	0	0	0	0	4	1	O-5
• MOLINA, Ben														
D 2002	Ana-A	.267	4	15	0	4	2	0	0	2	0	1	0	C-4
L 2002	Ana-A	.214	5	14	0	3	0	1	0	2	1	2	0	C-5
W 2002	Ana-A	.286	7	21	2	6	2	0	0	2	3	1	0	C-7
• MOLINA, Jose														
L 2002	Ana-A	.000	3	1	0	0	0	0	0	0	0	0	0	C-3
W 2002	Ana-A	....	3	0	0	0	0	0	0	0	0	0	0	C-3
• MOLITOR, Paul														
D 1981	Mil-A	.250	5	20	2	5	0	0	1	1	2	5	0	O-5
L 1982	Mil-A	.316	5	19	4	6	1	0	2	5	2	3	1	3-5
L 1993	Tor-A	.391	6	23	7	9	2	1	1	5	3	3	0	D-6
L **Total**	2	.357	11	42	11	15	3	1	3	10	5	6	1	....
W 1982	Mil-A	.355	7	31	5	11	0	0	0	3	2	4	1	3-7
W 1993	Tor-A	.500	6	24	10	12	2	2	2	8	3	0	1	1-1,3-2,D-3
W **Total**	2	.418	13	55	15	23	2	2	2	11	5	4	2	....
• MONDAY, Rick														
D 1981	LA-N	.214	5	14	1	3	0	0	0	1	2	4	0	O-5
L 1971	Oak-A	.000	1	3	0	0	0	0	0	0	1	2	0	O-1
L 1977	LA-N	.286	3	7	1	2	1	0	0	0	2	1	0	O-3
L 1978	LA-N	.200	3	10	2	2	0	1	0	0	1	5	0	O-5
L 1981	LA-N	.333	3	9	2	3	0	0	1	1	0	4	0	O-2
L 1983	LA-N	....	1	0	0	0	0	0	0	0	0	0	0	....
L **Total**	5	.241	11	29	5	7	1	1	1	1	4	12	0	....
W 1977	LA-N	.167	4	12	0	2	0	0	0	0	0	3	0	O-4
W 1978	LA-N	.154	5	13	2	2	1	0	0	0	4	3	0	O-4,D-1
W 1981	LA-N	.231	5	13	1	3	1	0	0	0	3	6	0	O-4
W **Total**	3	.184	14	38	3	7	2	0	0	0	7	12	0	....
• MONDESI, Raul														
D 1995	LA-N	.222	3	9	0	2	0	0	0	1	0	2	0	O-3
D 1996	LA-N	.182	3	11	0	2	2	0	0	1	0	4	0	O-3
D 2002	NY-A	.250	4	12	1	3	0	0	0	1	3	1	0	O-4
D **Total**	3	.219	10	32	1	7	2	0	0	3	3	7	0	....

YEAR	TM-L	AVG	G	AB	R	H	2B	3B	HR	RBI	BB	SO	SB	POS
• MONEY, Don														
D 1981	Mil-A	.000	2	3	0	0	0	0	0	0	0	0	0	2-1,D-1
L 1982	Mil-A	.182	4	11	2	2	0	0	0	1	3	1	0	D-4
W 1982	Mil-A	.231	5	13	4	3	1	0	0	1	2	3	0	D-5
• MONTGOMERY, Bob														
W 1975	Bos-A	.000	1	1	0	0	0	0	0	0	0	0	0	....
• MOON, Wally														
W 1959	LA-N	.261	6	23	3	6	0	0	1	2	2	2	1	O-6
W 1965	LA-N	.000	2	2	0	0	0	0	0	0	0	0	0	....
W **Total**	2	.240	8	25	3	6	0	0	1	2	2	2	1	....
• MOORE, Charlie														
D 1981	Mil-A	.222	4	9	0	2	0	0	0	1	1	2	0	O-2,D-2
L 1982	Mil-A	.462	5	13	3	6	0	0	0	0	1	2	0	O-5
W 1982	Mil-A	.346	7	26	3	9	3	0	0	2	1	0	0	O-7
• MOORE, Donnie														
L 1982	Atl-N	....	2	0	0	0	0	0	0	0	0	0	0	....
L 1986	Cal-A	....	3	0	0	0	0	0	0	0	0	0	0	....
L **Total**	2	....	5	0	0	0	0	0	0	0	0	0	0	....
• MOORE, Eddie														
W 1925	Pit-N	.231	7	26	7	6	1	0	1	2	5	2	0	2-7
• MOORE, Gene														
W 1944	StL-A	.182	6	22	4	4	0	0	0	0	3	6	0	O-6
• MOORE, Jimmy														
W 1930	Phi-A	.333	3	3	0	1	0	0	0	0	1	1	0	O-1
W 1931	Phi-A	.333	2	3	0	1	0	0	0	0	0	1	0	O-1
W **Total**	2	.333	5	6	0	2	0	0	0	0	1	2	0	....
• MOORE, Johnny														
W 1932	Chi-N	.000	2	7	1	0	0	0	0	0	2	1	0	O-2
• MOORE, Jo-Jo														
W 1933	NY-N	.227	5	22	1	5	1	0	0	1	1	3	0	O-5
W 1936	NY-N	.214	6	28	4	6	2	0	1	1	1	4	0	O-6
W 1937	NY-N	.391	5	23	1	9	1	0	0	1	0	1	0	O-5
W **Total**	3	.274	16	73	6	20	4	0	1	3	2	8	0	....
• MOORE, Kelvin														
D 1981	Oak-A	.000	2	8	0	0	0	0	0	0	0	2	0	1-2
L 1981	Oak-A	.250	3	8	0	2	0	0	0	0	0	1	0	1-3
• MOORE, Terry														
W 1942	StL-N	.294	5	17	2	5	1	0	0	2	2	3	0	O-5
W 1946	StL-N	.148	7	27	1	4	0	0	0	2	2	6	0	O-7
W **Total**	2	.205	12	44	3	9	1	0	0	4	4	9	0	....
• MORA, Melvin														
D 1999	NY-N	.000	3	1	1	0	0	0	0	0	1	0	0	O-4
L 1999	NY-N	.429	6	14	3	6	0	0	1	2	2	2	2	O-5
• MORALES, Jose														
L 1983	LA-N	.000	2	2	0	0	0	0	0	0	0	1	0	....
• MORAN, Herbie														
W 1914	Bos-N	.077	3	13	2	1	1	0	0	0	1	1	1	O-3
• MORAN, Pat														
W 1906	Chi-N	.000	2	2	0	0	0	0	0	0	0	0	0	....
W 1907	Chi-N	....	1	0	0	0	0	0	0	0	0	0	0	....
W **Total**	2	.000	3	2	0	0	0	0	0	0	0	0	0	....
• MORANDINI, Mickey														
D 1998	Chi-N	.222	3	9	1	2	0	0	0	1	2	2	0	2-3
L 1993	Phi-N	.250	4	16	1	4	0	1	0	2	0	3	1	2-4
W 1993	Phi-N	.200	3	5	1	1	0	0	0	0	1	2	0	2-1
• MORDECAI, Mike														
D 1995	Atl-N	.667	2	3	1	2	1	0	0	2	0	0	0	S-1
L 1995	Atl-N	.000	2	2	0	0	0	0	0	0	0	1	0	S-1
L 1996	Atl-N	.250	4	4	1	1	0	0	0	0	0	1	0	2-2,3-1
L 2003	Fla-N	.200	3	5	1	1	1	0	0	3	0	0	0	2-1,S-2
L **Total**	3	.182	9	11	2	2	1	0	0	3	0	2	0	....
W 1995	Atl-N	.333	3	3	0	1	0	0	0	0	0	1	0	S-2,D-1
W 1996	Atl-N	.000	1	1	0	0	0	0	0	0	0	0	0	....
W **Total**	2	.250	4	4	0	1	0	0	0	0	0	1	0	....
• MORELAND, Keith														
D 1981	Phi-N	.462	4	13	2	6	0	0	1	3	1	1	0	C-4
L 1980	Phi-N	.000	2	1	0	0	0	0	0	1	0	0	0	C-1
L 1984	Chi-N	.333	5	18	3	6	2	0	0	2	1	1	0	O-5
L **Total**	2	.316	7	19	3	6	2	0	0	3	1	1	0	....
W 1980	Phi-N	.333	3	12	1	4	0	0	0	1	0	1	0	D-3
• MORENO, Omar														
L 1979	Pit-N	.250	3	12	3	3	0	1	0	0	2	2	1	O-3
W 1979	Pit-N	.333	7	33	4	11	2	0	0	3	1	7	0	O-7
• MORGAN, Bobby														
W 1952	Bro-N	.000	2	1	0	0	0	0	0	0	0	0	0	3-1
W 1953	Bro-N	.000	1	1	0	0	0	0	0	0	0	0	0	....
W **Total**	2	.000	3	2	0	0	0	0	0	0	0	0	0	....
• MORGAN, Joe														
L 1972	Cin-N	.263	5	19	5	5	0	0	2	3	1	2	1	2-5
L 1973	Cin-N	.100	5	20	1	2	1	0	0	1	2	2	0	2-5
L 1975	Cin-N	.273	3	11	2	3	3	0	0	1	3	2	4	2-3
L 1976	Cin-N	.000	3	7	2	0	0	0	0	0	6	1	2	2-3
L 1979	Cin-N	.000	3	11	0	0	0	0	0	0	3	1	1	2-3
L 1980	Hou-N	.154	4	13	1	2	1	1	0	0	6	1	0	2-4
L 1983	Phi-N	.067	4	15	1	1	0	0	0	0	2	1	0	2-4
L **Total**	7	.135	27	96	12	13	5	1	2	5	23	10	8	....

SER-YEAR	TM-L	AVG	G	AB	R	H	2B	3B	HR	RBI	BB	SO	SB	POS
W 1972	Cin-N	.125	7	24	4	3	2	0	0	1	6	3	2	2-7
W 1975	Cin-N	.259	7	27	4	7	1	0	0	3	5	1	2	2-7
W 1976	Cin-N	.333	4	15	3	5	1	1	1	2	2	2	2	2-4
W 1983	Phi-N	.263	5	19	3	5	0	1	2	2	2	3	1	2-5
W Total	**4**	**.235**	**23**	**85**	**14**	**20**	**4**	**2**	**3**	**8**	**15**	**9**	**7**	....
• MORIARTY, George														
W 1909	Det-A	.273	7	22	4	6	1	0	0	1	3	1	0	3-7
• MORRIS, Hal														
D 1995	Cin-N	.500	3	10	5	5	1	0	0	2	3	1	1	1-3
L 1990	Cin-N	.417	5	12	3	5	1	0	0	1	1	0	0	1-4
L 1995	Cin-N	.167	4	12	0	2	1	0	0	1	1	1	1	1-4
L Total	**2**	**.292**	**9**	**24**	**3**	**7**	**2**	**0**	**0**	**2**	**2**	**1**	**1**	....
W 1990	Cin-N	.071	4	14	0	1	0	0	0	2	1	1	0	1-2,D-2
• MORRIS, John														
L 1987	StL-N	.000	2	3	0	0	0	0	0	0	0	0	0	0-2
W 1987	StL-N	.000	1	2	0	0	0	0	0	0	0	0	0	0-1
• MORRISON, Jim														
L 1978	Phi-N	.000	1	1	0	0	0	0	0	0	0	1	0	....
L 1987	Det-A	.400	2	5	1	2	0	0	0	0	0	1	0	3-1,D-1
L Total	**2**	**.333**	**3**	**6**	**1**	**2**	**0**	**0**	**0**	**0**	**0**	**2**	**0**	....
• MOSEBY, Lloyd														
L 1985	Tor-A	.226	7	31	5	7	1	0	0	4	2	3	1	0-7
L 1989	Tor-A	.313	5	16	4	5	0	0	1	2	5	2	1	0-5
L Total	**2**	**.255**	**12**	**47**	**9**	**12**	**1**	**0**	**1**	**6**	**7**	**5**	**2**	....
• MOSES, Wally														
W 1946	Bos-A	.417	4	12	1	5	0	0	0	0	1	2	0	0-4
• MOSSI, Don														
W 1954	Cle-A	....	3	0	0	0	0	0	0	0	0	0	0	....
• MOTA, Manny														
L 1974	LA-N	.333	3	3	0	1	0	0	0	1	0	0	0	0-1
L 1977	LA-N	1.000	1	1	1	1	1	0	0	0	0	0	0	....
L 1978	LA-N	1.000	2	1	0	1	1	0	0	0	0	0	0	....
L Total	**3**	**.600**	**6**	**5**	**1**	**3**	**2**	**0**	**0**	**1**	**0**	**0**	**0**	....
W 1977	LA-N	.000	3	3	0	0	0	0	0	0	0	1	0	....
W 1978	LA-N	....	1	0	0	0	0	0	0	0	1	0	0	....
W Total	**2**	**.000**	**4**	**3**	**0**	**0**	**0**	**0**	**0**	**0**	**1**	**1**	**0**	....
• MOTLEY, Darryl														
L 1984	KC-A	.167	3	12	0	2	0	0	0	1	1	3	0	0-3
L 1985	KC-A	.333	2	3	1	1	0	0	0	1	1	2	0	0-2
L Total	**2**	**.200**	**5**	**15**	**1**	**3**	**0**	**0**	**0**	**2**	**2**	**5**	**0**	....
W 1985	KC-A	.364	5	11	1	4	0	0	1	3	0	1	0	0-4
• MOTTON, Curt														
L 1969	Bal-A	.500	2	2	0	1	0	0	0	1	0	0	0	....
L 1971	Bal-A	1.000	1	1	0	1	1	0	0	1	0	0	0	....
L 1974	Bal-A	.000	1	1	0	0	0	0	0	0	0	0	0	....
L Total	**3**	**.500**	**4**	**4**	**0**	**2**	**1**	**0**	**0**	**2**	**0**	**0**	**0**	....
W 1969	Bal-A	.000	1	1	0	0	0	0	0	0	0	0	0	....
• MOWREY, Mike														
W 1916	Bro-N	.176	5	17	2	3	0	0	0	1	3	2	0	3-5
• MUELLER, Bill														
D 1997	SF-N	.250	3	12	1	3	0	0	1	1	0	0	0	3-3
D 2000	SF-N	.250	4	20	2	5	2	0	0	0	0	4	0	3-4
D 2003	Bos-A	.105	5	19	0	2	1	0	0	0	3	4	0	3-5
D Total	**3**	**.196**	**12**	**51**	**3**	**10**	**3**	**0**	**1**	**1**	**3**	**8**	**0**	....
L 2003	Bos-A	.222	7	27	1	6	2	0	0	0	2	7	0	3-7
• MUELLER, Don														
W 1954	NY-N	.389	4	18	4	7	0	0	0	1	0	1	0	0-4
• MULLIN, George														
W 1907	Det-A	.000	2	6	0	0	0	0	0	0	0	1	0	....
W 1908	Det-A	.333	1	3	1	1	0	0	0	1	1	0	0	....
W 1909	Det-A	.188	6	16	1	3	1	0	0	0	1	3	0	....
W Total	**3**	**.160**	**9**	**25**	**2**	**4**	**1**	**0**	**0**	**1**	**2**	**4**	**0**	....
• MULLINIKS, Rance														
L 1985	Tor-A	.364	5	11	1	4	1	0	1	3	2	2	0	3-5
L 1989	Tor-A	.000	1	1	0	0	0	0	0	0	0	1	0	....
L 1991	Tor-A	.125	5	8	1	1	0	0	0	0	3	0	0	D-3
L Total	**3**	**.250**	**11**	**20**	**2**	**5**	**1**	**0**	**1**	**3**	**5**	**3**	**0**	....
• MUMPHREY, Jerry														
D 1981	NY-A	.095	5	21	2	2	0	0	0	0	0	1	1	0-5
L 1981	NY-A	.500	3	12	2	6	1	0	0	0	3	2	0	0-3
W 1981	NY-A	.200	5	15	2	3	0	0	0	0	3	2	1	0-5
• MUNOZ, Mike														
D 1995	Col-N	....	4	0	0	0	0	0	0	0	0	0	0	....
• MUNSON, Thurman														
L 1976	NY-A	.435	5	23	3	10	2	0	0	3	0	1	0	C-5
L 1977	NY-A	.286	5	21	3	6	1	0	1	5	0	2	0	C-5
L 1978	NY-A	.278	4	18	2	5	1	0	1	2	0	0	0	C-4
L Total	**3**	**.339**	**14**	**62**	**8**	**21**	**4**	**0**	**2**	**10**	**0**	**3**	**0**	....
W 1976	NY-A	.529	4	17	2	9	0	0	0	2	0	1	0	C-4
W 1977	NY-A	.320	6	25	4	8	2	0	1	3	2	8	0	C-6
W 1978	NY-A	.320	6	25	5	8	3	0	0	7	3	7	1	C-6
W Total	**3**	**.373**	**16**	**67**	**11**	**25**	**5**	**0**	**1**	**12**	**5**	**16**	**1**	....
• MURCER, Bobby														
D 1981	NY-A	.000	2	1	0	0	0	0	0	0	1	0	0	....
L 1980	NY-A	.000	1	4	0	0	0	0	0	0	0	2	0	D-1

SER-YEAR	TM-L	AVG	G	AB	R	H	2B	3B	HR	RBI	BB	SO	SB	POS
L 1981	NY-A	.333	1	3	0	1	0	0	0	0	1	1	0	D-1
L Total	**2**	**.143**	**2**	**7**	**0**	**1**	**0**	**0**	**0**	**0**	**1**	**3**	**0**	....
W 1981	NY-A	.000	4	3	0	0	0	0	0	0	0	0	0	....
• MURPHY, Dale														
L 1982	Atl-N	.273	3	11	1	3	0	0	0	0	0	2	1	0-4
• MURPHY, Danny														
W 1905	Phi-A	.188	5	16	0	3	1	0	0	0	0	2	0	2-5
W 1910	Phi-A	.350	5	20	6	7	3	0	1	9	1	0	1	0-5
W 1911	Phi-A	.304	6	23	4	7	3	0	0	3	0	3	0	0-6
W Total	**3**	**.288**	**16**	**59**	**10**	**17**	**7**	**0**	**1**	**12**	**1**	**5**	**1**	....
• MURPHY, Dwayne														
D 1981	Oak-A	.545	3	11	4	6	1	0	1	2	1	1	0	0-3
L 1981	Oak-A	.250	3	8	0	2	1	0	0	1	2	3	0	0-3
• MURPHY, Eddie														
W 1913	Phi-A	.227	5	22	2	5	0	0	0	0	2	0	0	0-5
W 1914	Phi-A	.188	4	16	2	3	2	0	0	0	2	2	0	0-4
W 1919	Chi-A	.000	3	2	0	0	0	0	0	0	0	1	0	....
W Total	**3**	**.200**	**12**	**40**	**4**	**8**	**2**	**0**	**0**	**0**	**4**	**3**	**0**	....
• MURPHY, Pat														
W 1888	NY-N	.100	3	10	1	1	0	0	0	1	0	0	0	C-3
• MURPHY, Yale														
T 1894	NY-N	.000	1	1	0	0	0	0	0	0	0	0	0	0-1
• MURRAY, Calvin														
D 2000	SF-N	.200	3	5	0	1	0	0	0	0	0	3	0	0-3
• MURRAY, Eddie														
D 1995	Cle-A	.385	3	13	3	5	0	1	1	3	2	1	0	D-3
D 1996	Bal-A	.400	4	15	1	6	1	0	0	1	3	4	1	D-4
D Total	**2**	**.393**	**7**	**28**	**4**	**11**	**1**	**1**	**1**	**4**	**5**	**5**	**1**	....
L 1979	Bal-A	.417	4	12	3	5	0	0	1	5	5	2	0	1-4
L 1983	Bal-A	.267	4	15	5	4	0	0	1	3	3	3	1	1-4
L 1995	Cle-A	.250	6	24	2	6	1	0	1	3	2	3	0	D-6
L 1996	Bal-A	.267	5	15	1	4	0	0	1	2	2	2	0	D-5
L Total	**4**	**.288**	**19**	**66**	**11**	**19**	**1**	**0**	**4**	**13**	**12**	**10**	**1**	....
W 1979	Bal-A	.154	7	26	3	4	1	0	1	2	4	4	1	1-7
W 1983	Bal-A	.250	5	20	2	5	0	0	2	3	1	4	0	1-5
W 1995	Cle-A	.105	6	19	1	2	0	0	1	3	5	4	0	1-3,D-3
W Total	**3**	**.169**	**18**	**65**	**6**	**11**	**1**	**0**	**4**	**8**	**10**	**12**	**1**	....
• MURRAY, Red														
W 1911	NY-N	.000	6	21	0	0	0	0	0	0	2	5	0	0-6
W 1912	NY-N	.323	8	31	5	10	4	1	0	4	2	2	0	0-8
W 1913	NY-N	.250	5	16	2	4	0	0	0	1	2	2	2	0-5
W Total	**3**	**.206**	**19**	**68**	**7**	**14**	**4**	**1**	**0**	**5**	**6**	**9**	**2**	....
• MUSIAL, Stan														
W 1942	StL-N	.222	5	18	2	4	1	0	0	2	4	0	0	0-5
W 1943	StL-N	.278	5	18	2	5	0	0	0	0	2	2	0	0-5
W 1944	StL-N	.304	6	23	2	7	2	0	1	2	2	0	0	0-6
W 1946	StL-N	.222	7	27	3	6	4	1	0	4	4	2	1	1-7
W Total	**4**	**.256**	**23**	**86**	**9**	**22**	**7**	**1**	**1**	**8**	**12**	**4**	**1**	....
• MYER, Buddy														
W 1925	Was-A	.250	3	8	0	2	0	0	0	0	1	2	0	3-3
W 1933	Was-A	.300	5	20	2	6	1	0	0	2	2	3	0	2-5
W Total	**2**	**.286**	**8**	**28**	**2**	**8**	**1**	**0**	**0**	**2**	**3**	**5**	**0**	....
• MYERS, Billy														
W 1939	Cin-N	.333	4	12	2	4	0	1	0	0	2	3	0	S-4
W 1940	Cin-N	.130	7	23	0	3	0	0	0	2	2	5	0	S-7
W Total	**2**	**.200**	**11**	**35**	**2**	**7**	**0**	**1**	**0**	**2**	**4**	**8**	**0**	....
• MYERS, Greg														
D 1998	SD-N	....	1	0	0	0	0	0	0	0	0	0	0	C-1
D 2001	Oak-A	.143	3	7	0	1	0	0	0	0	0	3	0	C-3
D 2002	Oak-A	.000	2	1	0	0	0	0	0	0	0	1	0	C-2
D Total	**3**	**.125**	**6**	**8**	**0**	**1**	**0**	**0**	**0**	**0**	**0**	**4**	**0**	....
L 1998	SD-N	1.000	2	1	1	1	0	0	1	2	1	0	0	....
L 1999	Atl-N	.000	2	2	0	0	0	0	0	0	1	1	0	C-2
L Total	**2**	**.333**	**4**	**3**	**1**	**1**	**0**	**0**	**1**	**2**	**2**	**1**	**0**	....
W 1998	SD-N	.000	2	4	0	0	0	0	0	0	0	2	0	C-1
W 1999	Atl-N	.333	4	6	0	2	0	0	0	1	1	0	0	C-3
W Total	**2**	**.200**	**6**	**10**	**0**	**2**	**0**	**0**	**0**	**1**	**1**	**2**	**0**	....
• MYERS, Hy														
W 1916	Bro-N	.182	5	22	2	4	0	0	1	3	0	3	0	0-5
W 1920	Bro-N	.231	7	26	0	6	0	0	0	1	0	1	0	0-7
W Total	**2**	**.208**	**12**	**48**	**2**	**10**	**0**	**0**	**1**	**4**	**0**	**4**	**0**	....
• NAEHRING, Tim														
D 1995	Bos-A	.308	3	13	2	4	0	0	1	1	0	1	0	3-3
• NARAGON, Hal														
W 1954	Cle-A	....	1	0	0	0	0	0	0	0	0	0	0	C-1
• NARRON, Jerry														
L 1986	Cal-A	.500	4	2	1	1	0	0	0	0	1	1	0	C-3
• NARRON, Sam														
W 1943	StL-N	.000	1	1	0	0	0	0	0	0	0	0	0	....
• NASH, Billy														
T 1892	Bos-N	.167	6	24	3	4	0	0	0	4	2	3	2	3-6
• NATHAN, Joe														
D 2003	SF-N	....	2	0	0	0	0	0	0	0	0	0	0	....
• NEAL, Charlie														
W 1956	Bro-N	.000	1	4	0	0	0	0	0	0	0	1	0	2-1

YEAR	TM-L	AVG	G	AB	R	H	2B	3B	HR	RBI	BB	SO	SB	POS
W 1959	LA-N	.370	6	27	4	10	2	0	2	6	0	1	1	2-6
W Total	2	.323	7	31	4	10	2	0	2	6	0	2	1	....
• NEALE, Greasy														
W 1919	Cin-N	.357	8	28	3	10	1	1	0	4	2	5	1	0-8
• NEEDHAM, Tom														
W 1910	Chi-N	.000	1	1	0	0	0	0	0	0	0	0	0	....
• NEIS, Bernie														
W 1920	Bro-N	.000	4	5	0	0	0	0	0	0	1	0	0	0-2
• NELSON, Candy														
W 1884	NY-A	.100	3	10	0	1	0	0	0	0	0	1	0	S-3
• NELSON, Dave														
L 1976	KC-A	.000	2	2	0	0	0	0	0	0	0	0	0	....
• NELSON, Rocky														
W 1952	Bro-N	.000	4	3	0	0	0	0	0	0	1	2	0	....
W 1960	Pit-N	.333	4	9	2	3	0	0	1	2	1	1	0	1-3
W Total	2	.250	8	12	2	3	0	0	1	2	2	3	0	....
• NETTLES, Graig														
D 1981	NY-A	.059	5	17	1	1	0	0	0	1	3	1	0	3-5
L 1969	Min-A	1.000	1	1	0	1	0	0	0	0	0	0	0	....
L 1976	NY-A	.235	5	17	2	4	1	0	2	4	3	3	0	3-5
L 1977	NY-A	.150	5	20	1	3	0	0	0	1	0	3	0	3-5
L 1978	NY-A	.333	4	15	3	5	0	1	1	2	0	1	0	3-4
L 1980	NY-A	.167	2	6	1	1	0	0	1	1	0	1	0	3-2
L 1981	NY-A	.500	3	12	2	6	2	0	1	9	1	0	0	3-3
L 1984	SD-N	.143	4	14	1	2	0	0	0	2	1	1	0	3-4
L Total	7	.259	24	85	10	22	3	1	5	19	5	9	0	....
W 1976	NY-A	.250	4	12	0	3	0	0	0	2	3	1	0	3-4
W 1977	NY-A	.190	6	21	1	4	1	0	0	2	2	3	0	3-6
W 1978	NY-A	.160	6	25	2	4	0	0	0	1	0	6	0	3-6
W 1981	NY-A	.400	3	10	1	4	1	0	0	0	1	1	0	3-3
W 1984	SD-N	.250	5	12	2	3	0	0	0	2	5	0	0	3-5
W Total	5	.225	24	80	6	18	2	0	0	7	11	11	0	....
• NEWMAN, Al														
L 1987	Min-A	.000	1	2	0	0	0	0	0	0	0	0	0	2-1
L 1991	Min-A	....	2	0	0	0	0	0	0	0	0	0	0	3-1,S-1
L Total	2	.000	3	2	0	0	0	0	0	0	0	0	0	....
W 1987	Min-A	.200	4	5	0	1	0	0	0	0	1	1	0	2-3
W 1991	Min-A	.500	4	2	0	1	0	1	0	1	0	0	0	2-1,3-2,S-1
W Total	2	.286	8	7	0	2	0	1	0	1	1	1	0	....
• NEWMAN, Jeff														
D 1981	Oak-A	.000	1	3	0	0	0	0	0	0	0	1	0	C-1
L 1981	Oak-A	.000	2	5	0	0	0	0	0	0	0	2	0	C-2
• NEWSON, Warren														
D 1995	Sea-A	.000	1	1	0	0	0	0	0	0	0	1	0	S-1
D 1996	Tex-A	.000	2	1	0	0	0	0	0	0	1	0	0	....
D Total	2	.000	3	2	0	0	0	0	0	0	1	1	0	....
L 1993	Chi-A	.200	2	5	1	1	0	0	1	1	0	1	0	D-1
• NIARHOS, Gus														
W 1949	NY-A	....	1	0	0	0	0	0	0	0	0	0	0	C-1
• NICHOLSON, Bill														
W 1945	Chi-N	.214	7	28	1	6	1	1	0	8	2	5	0	0-7
• NICOL, Hugh														
W 1885	StL-A	.000	1	2	0	0	0	0	0	0	0	0	0	0-1
• NICOSIA, Steve														
W 1979	Pit-N	.063	4	16	1	1	0	0	0	0	0	2	0	C-4
• NIEHOFF, Bert														
W 1915	Phi-N	.063	5	16	1	1	0	0	0	0	1	5	0	2-5
• NIEMAN, Bob														
W 1962	SF-N	....	1	0	0	0	0	0	0	0	1	0	0	....
• NIETO, Tom														
L 1985	StL-N	.000	1	3	1	0	0	0	0	0	1	2	0	C-1
W 1985	StL-N	.000	2	5	0	0	0	0	0	1	1	2	0	C-2
• NIXON, Donell														
L 1989	SF-N	.000	3	3	0	0	0	0	0	0	0	1	1	0-2
W 1989	SF-N	.200	2	5	1	1	0	0	0	0	1	1	0	0-2
• NIXON, Otis														
D 1999	Atl-N	1.000	1	1	1	1	0	0	0	0	0	0	1	0-1
L 1992	Atl-N	.286	7	28	5	8	2	0	0	2	4	4	3	0-7
L 1993	Atl-N	.348	6	23	3	8	2	0	0	4	5	6	0	0-6
L 1999	Atl-N	....	2	0	1	0	0	0	0	0	0	0	2	....
L Total	3	.314	15	51	9	16	4	0	0	6	9	10	5	....
W 1992	Atl-N	.296	6	27	3	8	1	0	0	1	1	3	5	0-6
W 1999	Atl-N	.500	2	2	0	1	0	0	0	0	0	0	0	0-1
W Total	2	.310	8	29	3	9	1	0	0	1	1	3	5	....
• NIXON, Trot														
D 1998	Bos-A	.333	2	3	0	1	0	0	0	0	1	0	0	0-2
D 1999	Bos-A	.214	5	14	5	3	3	0	0	6	4	5	0	0-5
D 2003	Bos-A	.200	4	10	1	2	0	0	1	2	1	3	0	0-3
D Total	3	.222	11	27	6	6	3	0	1	8	6	8	0	....
L 1999	Bos-A	.286	4	14	2	4	2	0	0	0	1	5	0	0-4
L 2003	Bos-A	.333	7	24	3	8	1	0	3	5	3	7	1	0-7
L Total	2	.316	11	38	5	12	3	0	3	5	4	12	1	....
• NOBLE, Ray														
W 1951	NY-N	.000	2	2	0	0	0	0	0	0	0	1	0	C-2
• NOKES, Matt														
L 1987	Det-A	.143	5	14	2	2	0	0	1	2	1	4	0	C-3,D-2
• NOLAN, Joe														
L 1983	Bal-A	....	1	0	0	0	0	0	0	1	0	0	0	D-1
W 1983	Bal-A	.000	2	2	0	0	0	0	0	0	1	0	0	C-2
• NOPS, Jerry														
T 1897	Bal-N	.286	2	7	0	2	0	0	0	1	1	5	0	P-2
• NOREN, Irv														
W 1952	NY-A	.300	4	10	0	3	0	0	0	1	1	3	0	0-3
W 1953	NY-A	.000	2	1	0	0	0	0	0	0	1	0	0	....
W 1955	NY-A	.063	5	16	0	1	0	0	0	1	1	1	0	0-5
W Total	3	.148	11	27	0	4	0	0	0	2	3	4	0	....
• NORTH, Billy														
L 1974	Oak-A	.063	4	16	3	1	1	0	0	0	2	1	0	0-4
L 1975	Oak-A	.000	3	10	0	0	0	0	0	1	2	0	0	0-3
L 1978	LA-N	.000	4	8	0	0	0	0	0	0	0	1	0	0-4
L Total	3	.029	11	34	3	1	1	0	0	1	4	2	0	....
W 1974	Oak-A	.059	5	17	3	1	0	0	0	0	2	5	1	0-5
W 1978	LA-N	.125	4	8	2	1	1	0	0	2	1	0	1	0-4
W Total	2	.080	9	25	5	2	1	0	0	2	3	5	2	....
• NORTHRUP, Jim														
L 1972	Det-A	.357	5	14	0	5	0	0	0	1	2	3	1	0-5
W 1968	Det-A	.250	7	28	4	7	0	1	2	8	1	5	0	0-7
• NOSSEK, Joe														
W 1965	Min-A	.200	6	20	0	4	0	0	0	0	0	1	0	0-5
• NUNAMAKER, Les														
W 1920	Cle-A	.500	2	2	0	1	0	0	0	0	0	0	0	C-1
• OATES, Johnny														
L 1976	Phi-N	.000	1	1	0	0	0	0	0	0	0	0	0	C-1
W 1977	LA-N	.000	1	1	0	0	0	0	0	0	0	0	0	C-1
W 1978	LA-N	1.000	1	1	0	1	0	0	0	0	1	0	0	C-1
W Total	2	.500	2	2	0	1	0	0	0	0	1	0	0	....
• OBERKFELL, Ken														
L 1982	StL-N	.200	3	15	1	3	0	0	0	2	0	0	0	3-3
L 1989	SF-N	.000	3	4	0	0	0	0	0	0	0	0	0	3-1
L Total	2	.158	6	19	1	3	0	0	0	2	0	0	0	....
W 1982	StL-N	.292	7	24	4	7	1	0	0	1	2	1	2	3-7
W 1989	SF-N	.333	4	6	1	2	0	0	0	0	3	0	0	3-4
W Total	2	.300	11	30	5	9	1	0	0	1	5	1	2	....
• O'BRIEN, Charlie														
D 1995	Atl-N	.200	2	5	0	1	0	0	0	0	1	1	0	C-2
L 1995	Atl-N	.400	2	5	1	2	0	0	1	3	0	1	0	C-1
W 1995	Atl-N	.000	2	3	0	0	0	0	0	0	0	1	0	C-2
• O'BRIEN, Darby														
W 1889	Bro-A	.161	9	31	8	5	0	1	0	4	12	6	6	0-9
W 1890	Bro-N	.125	6	24	3	3	0	1	0	3	1	5	3	0-6
W Total	2	.145	15	55	11	8	0	2	0	7	13	11	9	....
• O'BRIEN, Jack														
W 1903	Bos-A	.000	2	2	0	0	0	0	0	0	0	1	0	....
• O'BRIEN, Tom														
T 1897	Bal-N	.400	1	5	2	2	1	0	0	0	0	0	0	0-1
T 1900	Pit-N	.125	4	16	1	2	1	0	0	2	0	1	0	1-4
T Total	2	.190	5	21	3	4	2	0	0	2	0	1	0	....
• OCHOA, Alex														
D 2002	Ana-A	....	3	0	0	0	0	0	0	0	0	0	0	0-3
L 2002	Ana-A	.000	4	4	2	0	0	0	0	0	0	3	0	0-4
W 2002	Ana-A	.000	5	1	0	0	0	0	0	0	0	0	0	0-5
• O'CONNELL, Jimmy														
W 1923	NY-N	.000	2	1	0	0	0	0	0	0	0	1	0	....
• O'CONNOR, Jack														
T 1892	Cle-N	.136	6	22	1	3	0	0	0	0	2	3	0	0-6
T 1896	Cle-N	.286	4	14	1	4	0	0	0	1	1	2	0	1-4
T 1900	Pit-N	.250	2	4	0	1	0	0	0	1	1	0	0	C-2
T Total	3	.200	12	40	2	8	0	0	0	2	4	5	0	....
• O'CONNOR, Paddy														
W 1909	Pit-N	.000	1	1	0	0	0	0	0	0	0	1	0	....
• O'DEA, Ken														
W 1935	Chi-N	1.000	1	1	0	1	0	0	0	1	0	0	0	....
W 1938	Chi-N	.200	3	5	1	1	0	0	1	2	1	0	0	C-1
W 1942	StL-N	1.000	1	1	0	1	0	0	0	1	0	0	0	....
W 1943	StL-N	.667	2	3	0	2	0	0	0	0	0	0	0	C-1
W 1944	StL-N	.333	3	3	0	1	0	0	0	2	0	0	0	....
W Total	5	.462	10	13	1	6	0	0	1	6	1	0	0	....
• O'DOUL, Lefty														
W 1933	NY-N	1.000	1	1	1	1	0	0	0	2	0	0	0	....
• OESTER, Ron														
L 1990	Cin-N	.333	4	3	1	1	0	0	0	0	0	1	0	2-2
W 1990	Cin-N	1.000	1	1	0	1	0	0	0	1	0	0	0	....
• O'FARRELL, Bob														
W 1918	Chi-N	.000	3	3	0	0	0	0	0	0	0	0	0	C-1
W 1926	StL-N	.304	7	23	2	7	1	0	0	2	2	2	0	C-7
W Total	2	.269	10	26	2	7	1	0	0	2	2	2	0	....
• OFFERMAN, Jose														
D 1995	LA-N	....	1	0	0	0	0	0	0	0	0	0	0	....
D 1999	Bos-A	.389	5	18	4	7	1	0	1	6	7	0	0	2-5
D Total	2	.389	6	18	4	7	1	0	1	6	7	0	0	....
L 1999	Bos-A	.458	5	24	4	11	0	1	0	2	1	3	1	2-5

SER-YEAR	TM-L	AVG	G	AB	R	H	2B	3B	HR	RBI	BB	SO	SB	POS
• OGLIVIE, Ben														
D 1981	Mil-A	.167	5	18	0	3	1	0	0	1	0	7	0	O-5
L 1982	Mil-A	.133	4	15	1	2	0	0	1	1	0	3	0	O-4
W 1982	Mil-A	.222	7	27	4	6	0	1	1	1	2	4	0	O-7
• OLDIS, Bob														
W 1960	Pit-N	....	2	0	0	0	0	0	0	0	0	0	0	C-2
• OLDRING, Rube														
W 1911	Phi-A	.200	6	25	2	5	2	0	1	3	0	4	0	O-6
W 1913	Phi-A	.273	5	22	5	6	0	1	0	0	0	1	1	O-5
W 1914	Phi-A	.067	4	15	0	1	0	0	0	0	0	5	0	O-4
W Total	**3**	**.194**	**15**	**62**	**7**	**12**	**2**	**1**	**1**	**3**	**0**	**10**	**1**	....
• O'LEARY, Charley														
W 1907	Det-A	.059	5	17	0	1	0	0	0	0	1	3	0	S-5
W 1908	Det-A	.158	5	19	2	3	0	0	0	0	0	3	0	S-5
W 1909	Det-A	.000	1	3	0	0	0	0	0	0	0	0	0	3-1
W Total	**3**	**.103**	**11**	**39**	**2**	**4**	**0**	**0**	**0**	**0**	**1**	**6**	**0**	....
• O'LEARY, Troy														
D 1998	Bos-A	.063	4	16	0	1	0	0	0	0	1	4	0	O-4
D 1999	Bos-A	.200	5	20	4	4	0	0	2	7	2	3	0	O-5
D 2003	Chi-N	.000	1	1	0	0	0	0	0	0	0	0	0	....
D Total	**3**	**.135**	**10**	**37**	**4**	**5**	**0**	**0**	**2**	**7**	**3**	**7**	**0**	....
L 1999	Bos-A	.350	5	20	2	7	3	0	0	1	2	5	0	O-5
L 2003	Chi-N	.333	3	3	1	1	0	0	1	1	0	0	0	O-1
L Total	**2**	**.348**	**8**	**23**	**3**	**8**	**3**	**0**	**1**	**2**	**2**	**5**	**0**	....
• OLERUD, John														
D 1999	NY-N	.438	4	16	3	7	0	0	1	6	3	2	0	1-4
D 2000	Sea-A	.300	3	10	2	3	0	0	1	2	2	1	0	1-3
D 2001	Sea-A	.176	5	17	1	3	0	0	0	1	3	5	0	1-5
D Total	**3**	**.302**	**12**	**43**	**6**	**13**	**0**	**0**	**2**	**9**	**8**	**8**	**0**	....
L 1991	Tor-A	.158	5	19	1	3	0	0	0	3	3	1	0	1-5
L 1992	Tor-A	.348	6	23	4	8	2	0	1	4	2	5	0	1-6
L 1993	Tor-A	.348	6	23	5	8	1	0	0	3	4	1	0	1-6
L 1999	NY-N	.296	6	27	4	8	0	0	2	6	2	3	0	1-6
L 2000	Sea-A	.350	6	20	3	7	3	0	1	2	2	2	1	1-6
L 2001	Sea-A	.211	5	19	2	4	0	0	1	3	2	4	0	1-5
L Total	**6**	**.290**	**34**	**131**	**19**	**38**	**6**	**0**	**5**	**21**	**15**	**16**	**1**	....
W 1992	Tor-A	.308	4	13	2	4	0	0	0	0	0	4	0	1-4
W 1993	Tor-A	.235	5	17	5	4	1	0	1	2	4	1	0	1-5
W Total	**2**	**.267**	**9**	**30**	**7**	**8**	**1**	**0**	**1**	**2**	**4**	**5**	**0**	....
• OLIVA, Tony														
L 1969	Min-A	.385	3	13	3	5	2	0	1	2	1	3	1	O-3
L 1970	Min-A	.500	3	12	2	6	2	0	1	1	0	1	0	O-3
L Total	**2**	**.440**	**6**	**25**	**5**	**11**	**4**	**0**	**2**	**3**	**1**	**4**	**1**	....
W 1965	Min-A	.192	7	26	2	5	1	0	1	2	1	6	0	O-7
• OLIVER, Al														
L 1970	Pit-N	.250	2	8	0	2	0	0	0	1	1	0	0	1-2
L 1971	Pit-N	.250	4	12	2	3	0	0	1	5	1	3	0	O-4
L 1972	Pit-N	.250	5	20	3	5	2	1	1	3	0	4	0	O-5
L 1974	Pit-N	.143	4	14	1	2	0	0	0	1	2	2	0	O-4
L 1975	Pit-N	.182	3	11	1	2	0	0	1	2	2	0	0	O-3
L 1985	Tor-A	.375	5	8	0	3	1	0	0	3	0	0	0	D-5
L Total	**6**	**.233**	**23**	**73**	**7**	**17**	**3**	**1**	**3**	**15**	**6**	**9**	**0**	....
W 1971	Pit-N	.211	5	19	1	4	2	0	0	2	2	5	0	O-4
• OLIVER, Joe														
D 2000	Sea-A	.250	3	4	1	1	0	0	1	1	0	1	0	C-3
L 1990	Cin-N	.143	5	14	1	2	0	0	0	0	0	2	0	C-5
L 2000	Sea-A	.167	4	6	0	1	0	0	0	0	1	1	0	C-4
L Total	**2**	**.150**	**9**	**20**	**1**	**3**	**0**	**0**	**0**	**0**	**1**	**3**	**0**	....
W 1990	Cin-N	.333	4	18	2	6	3	0	0	2	0	1	0	C-4
• OLIVER, Nate														
W 1966	LA-N	....	1	0	0	0	0	0	0	0	0	0	0	....
• OLMO, Luis														
W 1949	Bro-N	.273	4	11	2	3	0	0	1	2	0	2	0	O-4
• OLSON, Greg														
L 1991	Atl-N	.333	7	24	3	8	1	0	1	4	4	3	1	C-7
L 1993	Atl-N	.333	2	3	0	1	1	0	0	0	0	1	0	C-2
L Total	**2**	**.333**	**9**	**27**	**3**	**9**	**2**	**0**	**1**	**4**	**4**	**4**	**1**	....
W 1991	Atl-N	.222	7	27	3	6	2	0	0	1	5	4	1	C-7
• OLSON, Ivy														
W 1916	Bro-N	.250	5	16	1	4	0	1	0	2	2	2	0	S-5
W 1920	Bro-N	.320	7	25	2	8	1	0	0	0	3	1	0	S-7
W Total	**2**	**.293**	**12**	**41**	**3**	**12**	**1**	**1**	**0**	**2**	**5**	**3**	**0**	....
• O'MARA, Ollie														
W 1916	Bro-N	.000	1	1	0	0	0	0	0	0	0	1	0	....
• O'NEILL, Bill														
W 1906	Chi-A	.000	1	1	1	0	0	0	0	0	0	0	0	O-1
• O'NEILL, Paul														
D 1995	NY-A	.333	5	18	5	6	0	0	3	6	5	5	0	O-5
D 1996	NY-A	.133	4	15	0	2	0	0	0	0	0	2	0	O-4
D 1997	NY-A	.421	5	19	5	8	2	0	2	7	3	0	0	O-5
D 1998	NY-A	.364	3	11	1	4	2	0	1	1	1	1	0	O-3
D 1999	NY-A	.250	2	8	2	2	0	0	0	0	1	1	0	O-2
D 2000	NY-A	.211	5	19	4	4	1	0	0	0	2	4	0	O-5
D 2001	NY-A	.091	3	11	1	1	1	0	0	0	0	0	0	O-1,D-2
D Total	**7**	**.267**	**27**	**101**	**18**	**27**	**6**	**0**	**6**	**14**	**12**	**13**	**0**	....
L 1990	Cin-N	.471	5	17	1	8	3	0	1	4	1	1	1	O-5
L 1996	NY-A	.273	4	11	1	3	0	0	1	2	3	2	0	O-4
L 1998	NY-A	.280	6	25	6	7	2	0	1	3	3	4	2	O-6
L 1999	NY-A	.286	5	21	2	6	0	0	0	1	1	5	0	O-5
L 2000	NY-A	.250	6	20	0	5	0	0	0	5	1	2	0	O-6
L 2001	NY-A	.417	5	12	2	5	0	0	2	3	1	0	0	O-5
L Total	**6**	**.321**	**31**	**106**	**12**	**34**	**5**	**0**	**5**	**18**	**10**	**14**	**3**	....
W 1990	Cin-N	.083	4	12	2	1	0	0	0	1	5	2	1	O-4
W 1996	NY-A	.167	5	12	1	2	2	0	0	0	3	2	0	O-4
W 1998	NY-A	.211	4	19	3	4	1	0	0	0	1	2	0	O-4
W 1999	NY-A	.200	4	15	0	3	0	0	0	4	2	2	0	O-4
W 2000	NY-A	.474	5	19	2	9	2	2	0	2	3	4	0	O-5
W 2001	NY-A	.333	5	15	1	5	1	0	0	0	2	2	1	O-5
W Total	**6**	**.261**	**27**	**92**	**9**	**24**	**6**	**2**	**0**	**7**	**16**	**14**	**2**	....
• O'NEILL, Steve														
W 1920	Cle-A	.333	7	21	1	7	3	0	0	2	4	3	0	C-7
• O'NEILL, Tip														
W 1885	StL-A	.208	7	24	4	5	0	0	0	0	0	0	0	O-7
W 1886	StL-A	.400	6	20	4	8	0	2	2	5	4	5	2	O-6
W 1887	StL-A	.200	15	65	7	13	2	1	1	9	0	2	0	O-15
W 1888	StL-A	.243	10	37	8	9	1	0	2	11	6	3	0	O-10
W Total	**4**	**.240**	**38**	**146**	**23**	**35**	**3**	**3**	**5**	**25**	**10**	**10**	**2**	....
• OQUENDO, Jose														
L 1987	StL-N	.167	5	12	3	2	0	0	1	4	3	2	0	O-5,3-1
W 1987	StL-N	.250	7	24	2	6	0	0	0	2	1	4	0	O-3,3-4
• ORDONEZ, Magglio														
D 2000	Chi-A	.182	3	11	0	2	0	1	0	1	2	2	1	O-3
• ORDONEZ, Rey														
D 1999	NY-N	.286	4	14	1	4	1	0	0	2	0	5	1	S-4
L 1999	NY-N	.042	6	24	0	1	0	0	0	0	0	2	0	S-6
• O'ROURKE, Jim														
W 1888	NY-N	.222	10	36	4	8	0	0	0	1	4	2	3	O-7,1-2
W 1889	NY-N	.389	9	36	7	14	2	2	2	7	2	2	3	S-1,O-9
W Total	**2**	**.306**	**19**	**72**	**11**	**22**	**2**	**2**	**2**	**8**	**6**	**4**	**6**	....
• ORR, Dave														
W 1884	NY-A	.111	3	9	0	1	0	0	0	0	0	0	0	1-3
• ORSATTI, Ernie														
W 1928	StL-N	.286	4	7	1	2	1	0	0	0	1	3	0	O-1
W 1930	StL-N	.000	1	1	0	0	0	0	0	0	0	0	0	....
W 1931	StL-N	.000	1	3	0	0	0	0	0	0	0	3	0	O-1
W 1934	StL-N	.318	7	22	3	7	0	1	0	2	3	1	0	O-6
W Total	**4**	**.273**	**13**	**33**	**4**	**9**	**1**	**1**	**0**	**2**	**4**	**7**	**0**	....
• ORSINO, John														
W 1962	SF-N	.000	1	1	0	0	0	0	0	0	0	0	0	C-1
• ORTA, Jorge														
L 1984	KC-A	.100	3	10	1	1	0	1	0	1	0	2	0	D-3
L 1985	KC-A	.000	2	5	0	0	0	0	0	0	0	1	0	D-1
L Total	**2**	**.067**	**5**	**15**	**1**	**1**	**0**	**1**	**0**	**1**	**0**	**3**	**0**	....
W 1985	KC-A	.333	3	3	0	1	0	0	0	0	0	0	0	....
• ORTIZ, David														
D 2002	Min-A	.231	4	13	0	3	2	0	0	2	0	5	0	D-4
D 2003	Bos-A	.095	5	21	0	2	1	0	0	2	2	7	0	....
D Total	**2**	**.147**	**9**	**34**	**0**	**5**	**3**	**0**	**0**	**4**	**2**	**12**	**0**	....
L 2002	Min-A	.313	5	16	0	5	1	0	0	2	0	5	0	D-5
L 2003	Bos-A	.269	7	26	4	7	1	0	2	6	3	8	0	....
L Total	**2**	**.286**	**12**	**42**	**4**	**12**	**2**	**0**	**2**	**8**	**3**	**13**	**0**	....
• ORTIZ, Junior														
L 1991	Min-A	.000	3	3	0	0	0	0	0	0	0	0	0	C-3
W 1991	Min-A	.200	3	5	0	1	0	0	0	1	0	1	0	C-3
• ORTIZ, Ramon														
W 2002	Ana-A	.000	1	3	0	0	0	0	0	0	0	2	0	....
• OSTROWSKI, Joe														
W 1951	NY-A	....	1	0	0	0	0	0	0	0	0	0	0	....
• OTIS, Amos														
D 1981	KC-A	.000	3	12	0	0	0	0	0	1	0	4	0	O-3
L 1976	KC-A	.000	1	1	0	0	0	0	0	0	0	0	0	O-1
L 1977	KC-A	.125	5	16	1	2	1	0	0	2	2	3	2	O-5
L 1978	KC-A	.429	4	14	2	6	2	0	0	1	3	5	4	O-4
L 1980	KC-A	.333	3	12	2	4	1	0	0	0	0	3	2	O-3
L Total	**4**	**.279**	**13**	**43**	**5**	**12**	**4**	**0**	**0**	**3**	**5**	**11**	**8**	....
W 1980	KC-A	.478	6	23	4	11	2	0	3	7	3	3	0	O-6
• OTT, Ed														
L 1979	Pit-N	.231	3	13	0	3	0	0	0	0	0	2	0	C-3
W 1979	Pit-N	.333	3	12	2	4	1	0	0	3	0	2	0	C-3
• OTT, Mel														
W 1933	NY-N	.389	5	18	3	7	0	0	2	4	4	4	0	O-5
W 1936	NY-N	.304	6	23	4	7	2	0	1	3	3	1	0	O-6
W 1937	NY-N	.200	5	20	1	4	0	0	1	3	1	4	0	3-5
W Total	**3**	**.295**	**16**	**61**	**8**	**18**	**2**	**0**	**4**	**10**	**8**	**9**	**0**	....
• OUTLAW, Jimmy														
W 1945	Det-A	.179	7	28	1	5	0	0	0	3	2	1	1	3-7
• OWEN, Marv														
W 1934	Det-A	.069	7	29	0	2	0	0	0	1	0	5	1	3-7
W 1935	Det-A	.050	6	20	2	1	0	0	0	1	2	3	0	1-4,3-2
W Total	**2**	**.061**	**13**	**49**	**2**	**3**	**0**	**0**	**0**	**2**	**2**	**8**	**1**	....
• OWEN, Mickey														
W 1941	Bro-N	.167	5	12	1	2	0	1	0	2	3	0	0	C-5
• OWEN, Spike														
L 1986	Bos-A	.429	7	21	5	9	0	1	0	3	2	2	1	S-7

YEAR	TM-L	AVG	G	AB	R	H	2B	3B	HR	RBI	BB	SO	SB	POS
L 1988	Bos-A	....	1	0	0	0	0	0	0	0	1	0	0	D-1
L Total	2	.429	8	21	5	9	0	1	0	3	3	2	1	....
W 1986	Bos-A	.300	7	20	2	6	0	0	0	2	5	6	0	S-7
• OWENS, Jayhawk														
D 1995	Col-N	.000	1	1	0	0	0	0	0	0	0	1	0	C-1
• OYLER, Ray														
W 1968	Det-A	....	4	0	0	0	0	0	0	0	0	0	0	S-4
• PACIOREK, Tom														
L 1974	LA-N	1.000	1	1	0	1	0	0	0	0	0	0	0	O-1
L 1983	Chi-A	.250	4	16	1	4	0	0	0	1	1	2	0	O-2,1-3
L Total	2	.294	5	17	1	5	0	0	0	1	1	2	0	....
W 1974	LA-N	.500	3	2	1	1	1	0	0	0	0	0	0	....
• PAFKO, Andy														
W 1945	Chi-N	.214	7	28	5	6	2	1	0	2	2	5	1	O-7
W 1952	Bro-N	.190	7	21	0	4	0	0	0	2	0	4	0	O-5
W 1957	Mil-N	.214	6	14	1	3	0	0	0	0	0	1	0	O-5
W 1958	Mil-N	.333	4	9	0	3	1	0	0	1	0	0	0	O-4
W Total	4	.222	24	72	6	16	3	1	0	5	2	10	1	....
• PAGAN, Jose														
L 1970	Pit-N	.333	1	3	0	1	0	0	0	0	1	1	0	3-1
L 1971	Pit-N	.000	1	1	0	0	0	0	0	0	0	0	0	3-1
L Total	2	.250	2	4	0	1	0	0	0	0	1	1	0	....
W 1962	SF-N	.368	7	19	2	7	0	0	1	2	0	1	0	S-7
W 1971	Pit-N	.267	4	15	0	4	2	0	0	2	0	1	0	3-4
W Total	2	.324	11	34	2	11	2	0	1	4	0	2	0	....
• PAGLIARULO, Mike														
L 1991	Min-A	.333	5	15	4	5	1	0	1	3	0	2	0	3-5
W 1991	Min-A	.273	6	11	1	3	0	0	1	2	1	2	0	3-6
• PAGNOZZI, Tom														
D 1996	StL-N	.273	3	11	0	3	0	0	0	2	1	3	0	C-3
L 1987	StL-N	.000	1	1	0	0	0	0	0	0	0	0	0	....
L 1996	StL-N	.158	7	19	1	3	1	0	0	1	1	4	0	C-7
L Total	2	.150	8	20	1	3	1	0	0	1	1	4	0	....
W 1987	StL-N	.250	2	4	0	1	0	0	0	0	0	0	0	D-1
• PALMEIRO, Orlando														
L 2002	Ana-A	.000	2	2	0	0	0	0	0	0	0	1	0	O-1
W 2002	Ana-A	.250	4	4	1	1	1	0	0	0	0	2	0	....
• PALMEIRO, Rafael														
D 1996	Bal-A	.176	4	17	4	3	1	0	1	2	1	6	0	1-4
D 1997	Bal-A	.250	4	12	2	3	2	0	0	0	0	2	0	1-4
D 1999	Tex-A	.273	3	11	0	3	0	0	0	0	1	1	0	D-3
D Total	3	.225	11	40	6	9	3	0	1	2	2	9	0	....
L 1996	Bal-A	.235	5	17	4	4	0	0	2	4	4	4	0	1-5
L 1997	Bal-A	.280	6	25	3	7	2	0	1	2	0	10	0	1-6
L Total	2	.262	11	42	7	11	2	0	3	6	4	14	0	....
• PALMER, Dean														
D 1996	Tex-A	.211	4	19	3	4	1	0	1	2	0	5	0	3-4
• PANKOVITS, Jim														
L 1986	Hou-N	.000	2	2	0	0	0	0	0	0	0	1	0	....
• PAQUETTE, Craig														
D 2000	StL-N	.000	2	2	0	0	0	0	0	0	0	0	0	O-1,3-1
D 2001	StL-N	.143	2	7	0	1	0	0	0	0	0	5	0	O-2,3-1
D Total	2	.111	4	9	0	1	0	0	0	0	0	5	0	....
L 2000	StL-N	.167	4	6	0	1	0	0	0	0	0	2	0	O-2,3-1
• PARENT, Freddy														
W 1903	Bos-A	.281	8	32	8	9	0	3	0	4	1	1	0	S-8
• PARENT, Mark														
D 1996	Bal-A	.200	4	5	0	1	0	0	0	0	0	2	0	C-4
L 1996	Bal-A	.167	2	6	0	1	0	0	0	0	0	2	0	C-2
• PARKER, Dave														
L 1974	Pit-N	.125	3	8	0	1	0	0	0	0	0	1	0	O-2
L 1975	Pit-N	.000	3	10	2	0	0	0	0	0	1	3	0	O-3
L 1979	Pit-N	.333	3	12	2	4	0	0	0	2	2	3	1	O-3
L 1988	Oak-A	.250	3	12	1	3	1	0	0	0	0	4	0	O-1,D-2
L 1989	Oak-A	.188	4	16	2	3	0	0	2	3	0	0	0	D-4
L Total	5	.190	16	58	7	11	1	0	2	5	3	11	1	....
W 1979	Pit-N	.345	7	29	2	10	3	0	0	4	2	7	0	O-7
W 1988	Oak-A	.200	4	15	0	3	0	0	0	0	2	4	0	O-2,D-2
W 1989	Oak-A	.222	3	9	2	2	1	0	1	2	0	2	0	D-2
W Total	3	.283	14	53	4	15	4	0	1	6	4	13	0	....
• PARKER, Wes														
W 1965	LA-N	.304	7	23	3	7	0	1	1	2	3	3	2	1-7
W 1966	LA-N	.231	4	13	0	3	2	0	0	0	1	3	0	1-4
W Total	2	.278	11	36	3	10	2	1	1	2	4	6	2	....
• PARRISH, Lance														
L 1984	Det-A	.250	3	12	1	3	1	0	1	3	0	3	0	C-3
W 1984	Det-A	.278	5	18	3	5	1	0	1	2	3	2	1	C-5
• PARRISH, Larry														
D 1981	Mon-N	.150	5	20	3	3	1	0	0	1	1	3	0	3-5
L 1981	Mon-N	.263	5	19	2	5	2	0	0	2	1	1	0	3-5
L 1988	Bos-A	.000	4	6	0	0	0	0	0	0	0	2	0	1-2,D-1
L Total	2	.200	9	25	2	5	2	0	0	2	1	3	0	....
• PARTEE, Roy														
W 1946	Bos-A	.100	5	10	1	1	0	0	0	1	1	2	0	C-5
• PASCHAL, Ben														
W 1926	NY-A	.250	5	4	0	1	0	0	0	1	1	2	0	....
W 1928	NY-A	.200	3	10	0	2	0	0	0	1	1	0	0	O-3
W Total	2	.214	8	14	0	3	0	0	0	2	2	2	0	....
• PASKERT, Dode														
W 1915	Phi-N	.158	5	19	2	3	0	0	0	0	1	2	0	O-5
W 1918	Chi-N	.190	6	21	0	4	1	0	0	2	2	2	0	O-6
W Total	2	.175	11	40	2	7	1	0	0	2	3	4	0	....
• PASQUA, Dan														
L 1993	Chi-A	.000	2	6	1	0	0	0	0	0	1	2	0	1-2
• PATEK, Freddie														
L 1970	Pit-N	.000	1	3	0	0	0	0	0	0	1	2	0	S-1
L 1976	KC-A	.389	5	18	2	7	2	0	0	4	0	1	0	S-5
L 1977	KC-A	.389	5	18	4	7	3	1	0	5	1	2	0	S-5
L 1978	KC-A	.077	4	13	2	1	0	0	1	2	1	4	0	S-4
L Total	4	.288	15	52	8	15	5	1	1	11	3	9	0	....
• PAUL, Josh														
D 2000	Chi-A	....	1	0	0	0	0	0	0	0	0	0	0	C-1
• PAVANO, Carl														
D 2003	Fla-N	....	3	0	0	0	0	0	0	0	0	0	0	....
L 2003	Fla-N	.000	3	2	0	0	0	0	0	0	0	1	0	....
W 2003	Fla-N	.000	1	2	0	0	0	0	0	0	0	1	0	....
• PAYNE, Fred														
W 1907	Det-A	.250	2	4	0	1	0	0	0	1	0	0	1	C-1
• PAYTON, Jay														
D 2000	NY-N	.176	4	17	1	3	0	0	0	2	0	4	1	O-4
L 2000	NY-N	.158	5	19	1	3	0	0	1	3	2	5	0	O-5
W 2000	NY-N	.333	5	21	3	7	0	0	1	3	0	5	0	O-5
• PECK, Hal														
W 1948	Cle-A	....	1	0	0	0	0	0	0	0	0	0	0	O-1
• PECKINPAUGH, Roger														
W 1921	NY-A	.179	8	28	2	5	1	0	0	0	4	3	0	S-8
W 1924	Was-A	.417	4	12	1	5	2	0	0	2	1	0	1	S-4
W 1925	Was-A	.250	7	24	1	6	1	0	1	3	1	2	1	S-7
W Total	3	.250	19	64	4	16	4	0	1	5	6	5	2	....
• PECOTA, Bill														
L 1993	Atl-N	.333	4	3	1	1	0	0	0	0	1	1	0	....
• PEEL, Homer														
W 1933	NY-N	.500	2	2	0	1	0	0	0	0	0	0	0	O-1
• PENA, Tony														
D 1995	Cle-A	.500	2	2	1	1	0	0	1	1	0	0	0	C-2
D 1996	Cle-A	....	1	0	0	0	0	0	0	0	0	0	0	C-1
D 1997	Hou-N	....	2	0	0	0	0	0	0	0	0	0	0	C-2
D Total	3	.500	5	2	1	1	0	0	1	1	0	0	0	....
L 1987	StL-N	.381	7	21	5	8	0	1	0	0	3	4	1	C-7
L 1990	Bos-A	.214	4	14	0	3	0	0	0	0	0	0	0	C-4
L 1995	Cle-A	.333	4	6	1	2	1	0	0	0	1	0	0	C-4
L Total	3	.317	15	41	6	13	1	1	0	0	4	4	1	....
W 1987	StL-N	.409	7	22	2	9	1	0	0	4	3	2	1	C-6,D-1
W 1995	Cle-A	.167	2	6	0	1	0	0	0	0	0	0	0	C-2
W Total	2	.357	9	28	2	10	1	0	0	4	3	2	1	....
• PENDLETON, Terry														
D 1996	Atl-N	.000	1	1	0	0	0	0	0	0	0	1	0	....
L 1985	StL-N	.208	6	24	2	5	1	0	0	4	1	3	0	3-6
L 1987	StL-N	.211	6	19	3	4	0	1	0	1	0	6	0	3-6
L 1991	Atl-N	.167	7	30	1	5	1	1	0	1	1	3	0	3-7
L 1992	Atl-N	.233	7	30	2	7	2	0	0	3	0	2	0	3-7
L 1993	Atl-N	.346	6	26	4	9	1	0	1	5	0	2	0	3-6
L 1996	Atl-N	.000	6	6	0	0	0	0	0	0	1	3	0	3-2
L Total	6	.222	38	135	12	30	5	2	1	14	3	19	0	....
W 1985	StL-N	.261	7	23	3	6	1	1	0	3	3	2	0	3-7
W 1987	StL-N	.429	3	7	2	3	0	0	0	1	1	1	2	D-2
W 1991	Atl-N	.367	7	30	6	11	3	0	2	3	3	1	0	3-7
W 1992	Atl-N	.240	6	25	2	6	2	0	0	2	1	5	0	3-6
W 1996	Atl-N	.222	4	9	1	2	1	0	0	0	1	1	0	3-1,D-2
W Total	5	.298	27	94	14	28	7	1	2	9	9	10	2	....
• PENNOCK, Herb														
W 1914	Phi-A	.000	1	1	0	0	0	0	0	0	0	0	0	....
W 1923	NY-A	.000	3	6	0	0	0	0	0	0	0	2	0	....
W 1926	NY-A	.143	3	7	1	1	1	0	0	0	0	0	0	....
W 1927	NY-A	.000	1	4	1	0	0	0	0	1	0	1	0	....
W 1932	NY-A	.000	2	1	0	0	0	0	0	0	0	0	0	....
W Total	5	.053	10	19	2	1	1	0	0	1	0	3	0	....
• PENNY, Brad														
D 2003	Fla-N	1.000	2	1	0	1	0	0	0	0	0	0	0	....
L 2003	Fla-N	.000	3	1	0	0	0	0	0	0	0	1	0	....
W 2003	Fla-N	.500	1	2	0	1	0	0	0	2	0	0	0	....
• PEPITONE, Joe														
W 1963	NY-A	.154	4	13	0	2	0	0	0	0	1	3	0	1-4
W 1964	NY-A	.154	7	26	1	4	1	0	1	5	2	3	0	1-7
W Total	2	.154	11	39	1	6	1	0	1	5	3	6	0	....
• PEREZ, Eddie														
D 1996	Atl-N	.333	1	3	0	1	0	0	0	0	0	0	0	C-1
D 1997	Atl-N	.000	1	3	0	0	0	0	0	0	0	1	0	C-1
D 1998	Atl-N	.200	1	5	1	1	0	0	1	4	0	2	0	C-1
D 1999	Atl-N	.250	4	16	1	4	0	0	0	3	0	3	0	C-4
D Total	4	.222	7	27	2	6	0	0	1	7	0	6	0	....
L 1996	Atl-N	.000	4	1	0	0	0	0	0	0	1	0	0	1-1,C-3
L 1997	Atl-N	.000	2	3	0	0	0	0	0	0	0	0	0	C-2
L 1998	Atl-N	.750	3	4	0	3	0	0	0	0	0	0	0	C-3

SER-YEAR	TM-L	AVG	G	AB	R	H	2B	3B	HR	RBI	BB	SO	SB	POS
L 1999	Atl-N	.500	6	20	2	10	2	0	2	5	1	3	0	C-6
L Total	**4**	**.464**	**15**	**28**	**2**	**13**	**2**	**0**	**2**	**5**	**2**	**3**	**0**	....
W 1996	Atl-N	.000	2	1	0	0	0	0	0	0	0	0	0	C-2
W 1999	Atl-N	.125	3	8	0	1	0	0	0	0	1	3	0	C-3
W Total	**2**	**.111**	**5**	**9**	**0**	**1**	**0**	**0**	**0**	**0**	**1**	**3**	**0**	....
• PEREZ, Eduardo														
D 2002	StL-N	.000	1	1	0	0	0	0	0	0	0	0	0	....
L 2002	StL-N	.250	3	4	1	1	0	0	1	1	1	0	0	0-1
• PEREZ, Neifi														
D 2003	SF-N	.333	3	3	1	1	1	0	0	0	1	0	0	2-1
• PEREZ, Timo														
D 2000	NY-N	.294	4	17	2	5	1	0	0	3	0	2	1	0-4
L 2000	NY-N	.304	5	23	8	7	2	0	0	0	1	3	2	0-4
W 2000	NY-N	.125	5	16	1	2	0	0	0	0	1	4	0	0-5
• PEREZ, Tony														
L 1970	Cin-N	.333	3	12	1	4	2	0	1	2	1	1	0	3-3
L 1972	Cin-N	.200	5	20	0	4	1	0	0	2	0	7	0	1-5
L 1973	Cin-N	.091	5	22	1	2	0	0	1	2	0	4	0	1-5
L 1975	Cin-N	.417	3	12	3	5	0	0	1	3	1	2	0	1-3
L 1976	Cin-N	.200	3	10	1	2	0	0	0	4	1	2	0	1-3
L 1983	Phi-N	1.000	1	1	0	1	0	0	0	0	0	0	0	....
L Total	**6**	**.234**	**20**	**77**	**6**	**18**	**3**	**0**	**3**	**13**	**3**	**16**	**0**	....
W 1970	Cin-N	.056	5	18	2	1	0	0	0	0	3	4	0	3-5
W 1972	Cin-N	.435	7	23	3	10	2	0	0	2	4	4	0	1-7
W 1975	Cin-N	.179	7	28	4	5	0	0	3	7	3	9	1	1-7
W 1976	Cin-N	.313	4	16	1	5	1	0	0	2	1	2	0	1-4
W 1983	Phi-N	.200	4	10	0	2	0	0	0	0	0	2	0	1-2
W Total	**5**	**.242**	**27**	**95**	**10**	**23**	**3**	**0**	**3**	**11**	**11**	**21**	**1**	....
• PERRY, Herb														
D 1995	Cle-A	.000	1	1	0	0	0	0	0	0	0	0	0	....
D 2000	Chi-A	.444	3	9	0	4	1	0	0	1	2	2	0	3-3
D Total	**2**	**.400**	**4**	**10**	**0**	**4**	**1**	**0**	**0**	**1**	**2**	**2**	**0**	....
L 1995	Cle-A	.000	3	8	0	0	0	0	0	0	1	3	0	1-3
W 1995	Cle-A	.000	3	5	0	0	0	0	0	0	0	2	0	1-3
• PESKY, Johnny														
W 1946	Bos-A	.233	7	30	2	7	0	0	0	0	1	3	1	S-7
• PETROCELLI, Rico														
L 1975	Bos-A	.167	3	12	1	2	0	0	1	2	0	3	0	3-3
W 1967	Bos-A	.200	7	20	3	4	1	0	2	3	3	8	0	S-7
W 1975	Bos-A	.308	7	26	3	8	1	0	0	4	3	6	0	3-7
W Total	**2**	**.261**	**14**	**46**	**6**	**12**	**2**	**0**	**2**	**7**	**6**	**14**	**0**	....
• PETTIS, Gary														
L 1986	Cal-A	.346	7	26	4	9	1	0	1	4	3	5	0	0-7
• PFEFFER, Fred														
W 1885	Chi-N	.407	7	27	5	11	2	0	1	7	0	0	0	2-7
W 1886	Chi-N	.286	6	21	7	6	0	0	1	4	2	1	2	2-6
W Total	**2**	**.354**	**13**	**48**	**12**	**17**	**2**	**0**	**2**	**11**	**2**	**1**	**2**	....
• PHELPS, Ed														
W 1903	Pit-N	.231	8	26	1	6	2	0	0	1	1	6	0	C-7
• PHELPS, Ken														
L 1989	Oak-A	1.000	1	1	0	1	1	0	0	0	0	0	0	....
W 1989	Oak-A	.000	1	1	0	0	0	0	0	0	0	0	0	....
• PHILLEY, Dave														
W 1954	Cle-A	.125	4	8	0	1	0	0	0	0	1	3	0	0-2
• PHILLIPS, Bubba														
W 1959	Chi-A	.300	3	10	0	3	1	0	0	0	0	0	0	0-1,3-3
• PHILLIPS, Jack														
W 1947	NY-A	.000	2	2	0	0	0	0	0	0	0	0	0	1-1
• PHILLIPS, Mike														
D 1981	Mon-N	.000	1	1	0	0	0	0	0	0	0	0	0	2-1
• PHILLIPS, Tony														
L 1988	Oak-A	.286	2	7	0	2	1	0	0	0	1	3	0	0-2,2-1
L 1989	Oak-A	.167	5	18	1	3	1	0	0	1	2	4	2	2-3,3-3
L Total	**2**	**.200**	**7**	**25**	**1**	**5**	**2**	**0**	**0**	**1**	**3**	**7**	**2**	....
W 1988	Oak-A	.250	2	4	1	1	0	0	0	0	1	2	0	0-1,2-1
W 1989	Oak-A	.235	4	17	2	4	1	0	1	3	0	3	0	0-1,2-4,3-2
W Total	**2**	**.238**	**6**	**21**	**3**	**5**	**1**	**0**	**1**	**3**	**1**	**5**	**0**	....
• PIATT, Adam														
D 2000	Oak-A	.167	3	6	2	1	0	0	0	0	0	1	0	0-2,D-1
D 2002	Oak-A	.333	3	3	0	1	1	0	0	0	0	1	0	0-1
D Total	**2**	**.222**	**6**	**9**	**2**	**2**	**1**	**0**	**0**	**0**	**0**	**2**	**0**	....
• PIAZZA, Mike														
D 1995	LA-N	.214	3	14	1	3	1	0	1	1	0	2	0	C-3
D 1996	LA-N	.300	3	10	1	3	0	0	0	2	1	2	0	C-3
D 1999	NY-N	.222	2	9	0	2	0	0	0	0	0	4	0	C-2
D 2000	NY-N	.214	4	14	1	3	1	0	0	0	4	3	0	C-4
D Total	**4**	**.234**	**12**	**47**	**3**	**11**	**2**	**0**	**1**	**3**	**5**	**11**	**0**	....
L 1999	NY-N	.167	6	24	1	4	0	0	1	4	1	6	0	C-6
L 2000	NY-N	.412	5	17	7	7	3	0	2	4	5	0	0	C-5
L Total	**2**	**.268**	**11**	**41**	**8**	**11**	**3**	**0**	**3**	**8**	**6**	**6**	**0**	....
W 2000	NY-N	.273	5	22	3	6	2	0	2	4	0	4	0	C-4,D-1
• PICCIOLO, Rob														
D 1981	Oak-A	.333	1	3	0	1	0	0	0	0	0	0	0	S-1
L 1981	Oak-A	.200	2	5	1	1	0	0	0	0	0	2	0	S-2
• PICK, Charlie														
W 1918	Chi-N	.389	6	18	2	7	1	0	0	0	1	1	1	2-6
• PIERRE, Juan														
D 2003	Fla-N	.263	4	19	5	5	1	0	0	3	1	1	1	0-4
L 2003	Fla-N	.303	7	33	5	10	1	2	0	1	2	1	1	0-7
W 2003	Fla-N	.333	6	21	2	7	2	0	0	3	5	2	1	0-6
• PIERZYNSKI, A.J.														
D 2002	Min-A	.438	5	16	4	7	0	1	1	4	2	2	0	C-5
D 2003	Min-A	.231	4	13	1	3	0	0	1	1	2	0	0	C-4
D Total	**2**	**.345**	**9**	**29**	**5**	**10**	**0**	**1**	**2**	**5**	**4**	**2**	**0**	....
L 2002	Min-A	.250	5	16	1	4	0	0	0	2	0	2	0	C-5
• PIGNATANO, Joe														
W 1959	LA-N	....	1	0	0	0	0	0	0	0	0	0	0	C-1
• PINIELLA, Lou														
D 1981	NY-A	.200	4	10	1	2	0	0	1	3	0	0	0	D-3
L 1976	NY-A	.273	4	11	1	3	1	0	0	0	0	1	0	D-3
L 1977	NY-A	.333	5	21	1	7	3	0	0	2	0	1	0	0-4,D-1
L 1978	NY-A	.235	4	17	2	4	0	0	0	0	0	3	0	0-4
L 1980	NY-A	.200	2	5	1	1	0	0	1	1	2	1	0	0-2
L 1981	NY-A	.600	3	5	2	3	0	0	1	3	0	0	0	0-1,D-2
L Total	**5**	**.305**	**18**	**59**	**7**	**18**	**4**	**0**	**2**	**6**	**2**	**6**	**0**	....
W 1976	NY-A	.333	4	9	1	3	1	0	0	0	0	0	0	0-2,D-2
W 1977	NY-A	.273	6	22	1	6	0	0	0	3	0	3	0	0-6
W 1978	NY-A	.280	6	25	3	7	0	0	0	4	0	0	1	0-6
W 1981	NY-A	.438	6	16	2	7	1	0	0	3	0	1	1	0-3
W Total	**4**	**.319**	**22**	**72**	**7**	**23**	**2**	**0**	**0**	**10**	**0**	**4**	**2**	....
• PINKNEY, George														
W 1889	Bro-A	.258	9	31	2	8	2	0	0	3	4	2	2	3-9
W 1890	Bro-N	.357	4	14	4	5	0	2	0	3	2	1	1	3-4
W Total	**2**	**.289**	**13**	**45**	**6**	**13**	**2**	**2**	**0**	**6**	**6**	**3**	**3**	....
• PINSON, Vada														
W 1961	Cin-N	.091	5	22	0	2	1	0	0	0	0	1	0	0-5
• PIPP, Wally														
W 1921	NY-A	.154	8	26	1	4	1	0	0	2	2	3	1	1-8
W 1922	NY-A	.286	5	21	0	6	1	0	0	3	0	2	1	1-5
W 1923	NY-A	.250	6	20	2	5	0	0	0	2	4	1	0	1-6
W Total	**3**	**.224**	**19**	**67**	**3**	**15**	**2**	**0**	**0**	**7**	**6**	**6**	**2**	....
• PITTMAN, Joe														
D 1981	Hou-N	.000	2	2	0	0	0	0	0	0	0	0	0	....
• POCOROBA, Biff														
L 1982	Atl-N	.000	1	1	0	0	0	0	0	0	0	0	0	....
• POLANCO, Placido														
D 2000	StL-N	.300	3	10	1	3	0	0	0	3	1	0	1	3-3
D 2001	StL-N	.267	5	15	1	4	0	0	0	1	1	1	1	3-5
D Total	**2**	**.280**	**8**	**25**	**2**	**7**	**0**	**0**	**0**	**4**	**2**	**1**	**2**	....
L 2000	StL-N	.200	4	5	0	1	0	0	0	0	2	1	0	3-2
• POLONIA, Luis														
D 1995	Atl-N	.333	3	3	0	1	0	0	0	2	0	1	1	....
D 1996	Atl-N	.000	2	2	0	0	0	0	0	0	0	1	0	....
D 2000	NY-A	1.000	1	1	0	1	0	0	0	0	0	0	0	....
D Total	**3**	**.333**	**6**	**6**	**0**	**2**	**0**	**0**	**0**	**2**	**0**	**2**	**1**	....
L 1988	Oak-A	.400	3	5	0	2	0	0	0	0	1	2	0	0-1,D-1
L 1995	Atl-N	.500	3	2	0	1	0	0	0	1	0	0	0	0-1
L 1996	Atl-N	.000	3	3	0	0	0	0	0	0	0	0	0	....
L 2000	NY-A	.000	1	1	0	0	0	0	0	0	0	1	0	....
L Total	**4**	**.273**	**10**	**11**	**0**	**3**	**0**	**0**	**0**	**1**	**1**	**3**	**0**	....
W 1988	Oak-A	.111	3	9	1	1	0	0	0	0	0	2	0	0-2
W 1995	Atl-N	.286	6	14	3	4	1	0	1	4	1	3	1	0-4
W 1996	Atl-N	.000	6	5	0	0	0	0	0	0	1	3	0	....
W 2000	NY-A	.500	2	2	0	1	0	0	0	0	0	0	0	....
W Total	**4**	**.200**	**17**	**30**	**4**	**6**	**1**	**0**	**1**	**4**	**2**	**8**	**1**	....
• PONSON, Sidney														
D 2003	SF-N	.000	1	1	0	0	0	0	0	0	0	0	0	....
• POPE, Dave														
W 1954	Cle-A	.000	3	3	0	0	0	0	0	0	1	1	0	0-2
• POPOVICH, Paul														
L 1974	Pit-N	.600	3	5	1	3	0	0	0	0	0	0	0	S-3
• POQUETTE, Tom														
L 1976	KC-A	.188	5	16	1	3	2	0	0	4	2	3	0	0-5
L 1977	KC-A	.167	2	6	0	1	0	0	0	0	0	0	0	0-2
L 1978	KC-A	.000	1	1	0	0	0	0	0	0	0	0	0	....
L Total	**3**	**.174**	**8**	**23**	**1**	**4**	**2**	**0**	**0**	**4**	**2**	**3**	**0**	....
• PORTER, Bo														
D 2000	Oak-A	1.000	2	1	0	1	0	0	0	1	0	0	0	0-2
• PORTER, Darrell														
L 1977	KC-A	.333	5	15	3	5	0	0	0	0	3	0	0	C-5
L 1978	KC-A	.357	4	14	1	5	1	0	0	3	2	0	0	C-4
L 1980	KC-A	.100	3	10	2	1	0	0	0	0	1	0	0	C-3
L 1982	StL-N	.556	3	9	3	5	3	0	0	1	5	2	0	C-3
L 1985	StL-N	.267	5	15	1	4	1	0	0	0	5	4	0	C-5
L Total	**5**	**.317**	**20**	**63**	**10**	**20**	**5**	**0**	**0**	**4**	**16**	**6**	**0**	....
W 1980	KC-A	.143	5	14	1	2	0	0	0	0	3	4	0	C-4
W 1982	StL-N	.286	7	28	1	8	2	0	1	5	1	4	0	C-7
W 1985	StL-N	.133	5	15	0	2	0	0	0	0	2	5	0	C-5
W Total	**3**	**.211**	**17**	**57**	**2**	**12**	**2**	**0**	**1**	**5**	**6**	**13**	**0**	....
• POSADA, Jorge														
D 1995	NY-A	....	1	0	1	0	0	0	0	0	0	0	0	....
D 1997	NY-A	.000	2	2	0	0	0	0	0	0	0	1	0	C-2
D 1998	NY-A	.000	1	2	1	0	0	0	0	0	1	2	0	C-1
D 1999	NY-A	.250	1	4	0	1	1	0	0	0	0	0	0	C-1

YEAR	TM-L	AVG	G	AB	R	H	2B	3B	HR	RBI	BB	SO	SB	POS
D 2000	NY-A	.235	5	17	2	4	2	0	0	1	3	5	0	C-5
D 2001	NY-A	.444	5	18	3	8	1	0	1	2	2	2	1	C-5
D 2002	NY-A	.235	4	17	2	4	0	0	1	3	0	3	0	C-4
D 2003	NY-A	.176	4	17	1	3	1	0	0	0	0	6	0	C-4
D Total	**8**	**.260**	**23**	**77**	**10**	**20**	**5**	**0**	**2**	**6**	**6**	**19**	**1**	**....**
L 1998	NY-A	.182	5	11	1	2	0	0	1	2	4	2	0	C-5
L 1999	NY-A	.100	3	10	1	1	0	0	1	2	1	2	0	C-3
L 2000	NY-A	.158	6	19	2	3	1	0	0	3	5	5	0	C-6
L 2001	NY-A	.214	5	14	4	3	1	0	0	0	6	7	0	C-5
L 2003	NY-A	.296	7	27	5	8	4	0	1	6	3	4	0	C-7
L Total	**5**	**.210**	**26**	**81**	**13**	**17**	**6**	**0**	**3**	**13**	**19**	**20**	**0**	**....**
W 1998	NY-A	.333	3	9	2	3	0	0	1	2	2	2	0	C-3
W 1999	NY-A	.250	2	8	0	2	1	0	0	1	0	3	0	C-2
W 2000	NY-A	.222	5	18	2	4	1	0	0	1	5	4	0	C-5
W 2001	NY-A	.174	7	23	2	4	1	0	1	1	3	8	0	C-7
W 2003	NY-A	.158	6	19	0	3	1	0	0	1	5	7	1	C-6
W Total	**5**	**.208**	**23**	**77**	**6**	**16**	**4**	**0**	**2**	**6**	**15**	**24**	**1**	**....**
• POSE, Scott														
D 1997	NY-A	....	1	0	0	0	0	0	0	0	0	0	0	....
• POST, Wally														
W 1961	Cin-N	.333	5	18	3	6	1	0	1	2	0	1	0	0-5
• POWELL, Boog														
L 1969	Bal-A	.385	3	13	2	5	0	0	1	1	2	0	0	1-3
L 1970	Bal-A	.429	3	14	2	6	2	0	1	6	0	3	0	1-3
L 1971	Bal-A	.300	3	10	4	3	0	0	2	3	3	3	0	1-3
L 1973	Bal-A	.000	1	4	1	0	0	0	0	0	0	1	0	1-1
L 1974	Bal-A	.125	2	8	0	1	0	0	0	1	0	0	0	1-2
L Total	**5**	**.306**	**12**	**49**	**9**	**15**	**2**	**0**	**4**	**11**	**5**	**7**	**0**	**....**
W 1966	Bal-A	.357	4	14	1	5	1	0	0	1	0	1	0	1-4
W 1969	Bal-A	.263	5	19	0	5	0	0	0	0	1	4	0	1-5
W 1970	Bal-A	.294	5	17	6	5	1	0	2	5	5	2	0	1-5
W 1971	Bal-A	.111	7	27	1	3	0	0	0	1	1	3	0	1-7
W Total	**4**	**.234**	**21**	**77**	**8**	**18**	**2**	**0**	**2**	**7**	**7**	**10**	**0**	**....**
• POWELL, Dante														
D 1997	SF-N	....	1	0	0	0	0	0	0	0	0	0	0	0-1
• POWELL, Jake														
W 1936	NY-A	.455	6	22	8	10	1	0	1	5	4	4	1	0-6
W 1937	NY-A	.000	1	1	0	0	0	0	0	0	0	1	0	....
W 1938	NY-A	....	1	0	0	0	0	0	0	0	0	0	0	0-1
W Total	**3**	**.435**	**8**	**23**	**8**	**10**	**1**	**0**	**1**	**5**	**4**	**5**	**1**	**....**
• POWERS, Doc														
W 1905	Phi-A	.143	3	7	0	1	1	0	0	0	0	0	0	C-3
• PRATT, Todd														
D 1999	NY-N	.125	3	8	2	1	0	0	1	1	2	1	0	C-2
D 2000	NY-N	.000	1	1	0	0	0	0	0	0	0	0	0	C-1
D Total	**2**	**.111**	**4**	**9**	**2**	**1**	**0**	**0**	**1**	**1**	**2**	**1**	**0**	**....**
L 1993	Phi-N	.000	1	1	0	0	0	0	0	0	0	1	0	C-1
L 1999	NY-N	.500	4	2	0	1	0	0	0	3	1	1	0	C-2
L Total	**2**	**.333**	**5**	**3**	**0**	**1**	**0**	**0**	**0**	**3**	**1**	**2**	**0**	**....**
W 2000	NY-N	.000	1	2	1	0	0	0	0	0	1	2	0	C-1
• PRICE, Jim														
W 1968	Det-A	.000	2	2	0	0	0	0	0	0	0	1	0	....
• PRIDDY, Jerry														
W 1942	NY-A	.100	3	10	0	1	1	0	0	1	1	0	0	1-3,3-1
• PRINCE, Tom														
D 2002	Min-A	.000	1	2	0	0	0	0	0	0	0	2	0	C-1
L 2002	Min-A	.000	1	1	0	0	0	0	0	0	0	0	0	C-1
• PRIOR, Mark														
D 2003	Chi-N	.000	1	3	0	0	0	0	0	0	0	0	0	....
L 2003	Chi-N	.000	2	4	0	0	0	0	0	0	0	2	0	....
• PRYOR, Greg														
L 1984	KC-A	....	1	0	0	0	0	0	0	0	0	0	0	3-1
W 1985	KC-A	....	1	0	0	0	0	0	0	0	0	0	0	3-1
• PUCCINELLI, George														
W 1930	StL-N	.000	1	1	0	0	0	0	0	0	0	0	0	....
• PUCKETT, Kirby														
L 1987	Min-A	.208	5	24	3	5	1	0	1	3	0	5	1	0-5
L 1991	Min-A	.429	5	21	4	9	1	0	2	6	1	4	0	0-5
L Total	**2**	**.311**	**10**	**45**	**7**	**14**	**2**	**0**	**3**	**9**	**1**	**9**	**1**	**....**
W 1987	Min-A	.357	7	28	5	10	1	1	0	3	2	1	1	0-7
W 1991	Min-A	.250	7	24	4	6	0	1	2	4	5	7	1	0-7
W Total	**2**	**.308**	**14**	**52**	**9**	**16**	**1**	**2**	**2**	**7**	**7**	**8**	**2**	**....**
• PUHL, Terry														
D 1981	Hou-N	.190	5	21	2	4	1	0	0	0	0	1	1	0-5
L 1980	Hou-N	.526	5	19	4	10	2	0	0	3	3	2	2	0-4
L 1986	Hou-N	.667	3	3	0	2	0	0	0	0	0	0	1	....
L Total	**2**	**.545**	**8**	**22**	**4**	**12**	**2**	**0**	**0**	**3**	**3**	**2**	**3**	**....**
• PUJOLS, Albert														
D 2001	StL-N	.111	5	18	1	2	0	0	1	2	2	2	0	0-3,1-4
D 2002	StL-N	.300	3	10	3	3	0	1	0	3	3	1	0	0-3,1-1,3-1
D Total	**2**	**.179**	**8**	**28**	**4**	**5**	**0**	**1**	**1**	**5**	**5**	**3**	**0**	**....**
L 2002	StL-N	.263	5	19	2	5	1	0	1	2	2	5	0	0-2,1-1,3-2
• PUJOLS, Luis														
D 1981	Hou-N	.000	2	6	0	0	0	0	0	0	0	1	0	C-2
L 1980	Hou-N	.100	4	10	1	1	0	1	0	0	3	0	0	C-4
• QUILICI, Frank														
L 1970	Min-A	.000	3	2	0	0	0	0	0	0	0	1	0	2-2
W 1965	Min-A	.200	7	20	2	4	2	0	0	1	4	3	0	2-7
• QUINN, Joe														
T 1892	Bos-N	.286	6	21	2	6	1	1	0	4	1	2	0	2-6
T 1896	Bal-N	.000	1	3	1	0	0	0	0	0	0	0	0	3-1
T Total	**2**	**.250**	**7**	**24**	**3**	**6**	**1**	**1**	**0**	**4**	**1**	**2**	**0**	**....**
• QUINONES, Luis														
L 1990	Cin-N	.500	3	2	1	1	0	0	0	2	0	0	1	....
• QUINTANA, Carlos														
L 1990	Bos-A	.000	4	13	0	0	0	0	0	1	1	0	0	1-4
• QUIRK, Jamie														
L 1976	KC-A	.143	4	7	1	1	0	1	0	2	0	3	0	D-2
L 1985	KC-A	.000	1	1	0	0	0	0	0	0	0	0	0	....
L 1990	Oak-A	1.000	1	1	0	1	0	0	0	0	0	0	0	....
L 1992	Oak-A	.000	1	1	0	0	0	0	0	0	0	0	0	....
L Total	**4**	**.200**	**7**	**10**	**1**	**2**	**0**	**1**	**0**	**2**	**0**	**3**	**0**	**....**
W 1990	Oak-A	.000	1	3	0	0	0	0	0	0	0	2	0	C-1
• RACKLEY, Marv														
W 1949	Bro-N	.000	2	5	0	0	0	0	0	0	0	2	0	0-2
• RADFORD, Paul														
W 1884	Pro-N	.000	3	7	1	0	0	0	0	1	0	1	0	0-3
• RAINES, Tim														
D 1996	NY-A	.250	4	16	3	4	0	0	0	0	3	1	0	0-4
D 1997	NY-A	.211	5	19	4	4	0	0	1	3	3	1	2	0-3,D-2
D 1998	NY-A	.250	2	4	1	1	1	0	0	0	1	1	0	D-2
D Total	**3**	**.231**	**11**	**39**	**8**	**9**	**1**	**0**	**1**	**3**	**7**	**3**	**2**	**....**
L 1981	Mon-N	.238	5	21	1	5	2	0	0	1	0	3	0	0-5
L 1993	Chi-A	.444	6	27	5	12	3	0	0	1	2	2	1	0-6
L 1996	NY-A	.267	5	15	2	4	1	0	0	0	1	1	0	0-5
L 1998	NY-A	.100	3	10	0	1	0	0	0	1	2	5	0	0-1,D-2
L Total	**4**	**.301**	**19**	**73**	**8**	**22**	**6**	**0**	**0**	**3**	**5**	**11**	**1**	**....**
W 1996	NY-A	.214	4	14	2	3	0	0	0	0	2	1	0	0-4
• RAMIREZ, Aramis														
D 2003	Chi-N	.278	5	18	2	5	1	0	1	3	2	2	0	3-5
L 2003	Chi-N	.231	7	26	4	6	0	1	3	7	5	6	0	3-7
• RAMIREZ, Manny														
D 1995	Cle-A	.000	3	12	1	0	0	0	0	0	1	2	0	0-3
D 1996	Cle-A	.375	4	16	4	6	2	0	2	2	1	4	0	0-4
D 1997	Cle-A	.143	5	21	2	3	1	0	0	3	0	3	0	0-5
D 1998	Cle-A	.357	4	14	2	5	2	0	2	3	1	4	0	0-4
D 1999	Cle-A	.056	5	18	5	1	1	0	0	1	4	8	0	0-5
D 2003	Bos-A	.200	5	20	2	4	0	0	1	3	3	7	0	0-5
D Total	**6**	**.188**	**26**	**101**	**16**	**19**	**6**	**0**	**5**	**12**	**10**	**28**	**0**	**....**
L 1995	Cle-A	.286	6	21	2	6	0	0	2	2	2	5	0	0-6
L 1997	Cle-A	.286	6	21	3	6	1	0	2	3	5	5	0	0-6
L 1998	Cle-A	.333	6	21	2	7	1	0	2	4	4	9	0	0-6
L 2003	Bos-A	.310	7	29	6	9	1	0	2	4	1	4	0	0-7
L Total	**4**	**.304**	**25**	**92**	**13**	**28**	**3**	**0**	**8**	**13**	**12**	**23**	**0**	**....**
W 1995	Cle-A	.222	6	18	2	4	0	0	1	2	4	5	1	0-6
W 1997	Cle-A	.154	7	26	3	4	0	0	2	6	6	5	0	0-7
W Total	**2**	**.182**	**13**	**44**	**5**	**8**	**0**	**0**	**3**	**8**	**10**	**10**	**1**	**....**
• RAMIREZ, Mario														
L 1984	SD-N	.000	2	2	0	0	0	0	0	0	0	0	0	....
• RAMIREZ, Rafael														
L 1982	Atl-N	.182	3	11	1	2	0	0	0	1	1	1	0	S-3
• RAMOS, Domingo														
L 1989	Chi-N	.000	1	1	0	0	0	0	0	0	0	0	0	....
• RAMSEY, Mike														
W 1982	StL-N	.000	3	1	1	0	0	0	0	0	0	1	0	3-2
• RANDOLPH, Willie														
D 1981	NY-A	.200	5	20	0	4	0	0	0	1	1	4	0	2-5
L 1975	Pit-N	.000	2	2	1	0	0	0	0	0	0	1	0	2-1
L 1976	NY-A	.118	5	17	0	2	0	0	0	1	3	1	1	2-5
L 1977	NY-A	.278	5	18	4	5	1	0	0	2	1	0	0	2-5
L 1980	NY-A	.385	3	13	0	5	2	0	0	1	1	3	0	2-3
L 1981	NY-A	.333	3	12	2	4	0	0	1	2	0	1	0	2-3
L 1990	Oak-A	.375	4	8	1	3	0	0	0	3	1	0	0	2-4
L Total	**6**	**.271**	**22**	**70**	**8**	**19**	**3**	**0**	**1**	**9**	**6**	**6**	**1**	**....**
W 1976	NY-A	.071	4	14	1	1	0	0	0	0	1	3	0	2-4
W 1977	NY-A	.160	6	25	5	4	2	0	1	1	2	2	0	2-6
W 1981	NY-A	.222	6	18	5	4	1	1	2	3	9	0	1	2-6
W 1990	Oak-A	.267	4	15	0	4	0	0	0	0	1	0	1	2-4
W Total	**4**	**.181**	**20**	**72**	**11**	**13**	**3**	**1**	**3**	**4**	**13**	**5**	**2**	**....**
• RARIDEN, Bill														
W 1917	NY-N	.385	5	13	2	5	0	0	0	2	2	1	0	C-5
W 1919	Cin-N	.211	5	19	0	4	0	0	0	2	0	0	1	C-5
W Total	**2**	**.281**	**10**	**32**	**2**	**9**	**0**	**0**	**0**	**4**	**2**	**1**	**1**	**....**
• RATH, Morrie														
W 1919	Cin-N	.226	8	31	5	7	1	0	0	2	4	1	2	2-8
• RATLIFF, Paul														
L 1970	Min-A	.250	1	4	0	1	0	0	0	0	0	1	0	C-1
• RAWLINGS, Johnny														
W 1921	NY-N	.333	8	30	2	10	3	0	0	4	0	3	0	2-8
• RAYMOND, Harry														
W 1890	Lou-A	.148	7	27	5	4	1	1	0	1	2	5	1	S-5
• READY, Randy														
L 1992	Oak-A	.000	1	1	0	0	0	0	0	0	0	1	0	....

SER-YEAR	TM-L	AVG	G	AB	R	H	2B	3B	HR	RBI	BB	SO	SB	POS
• REBOULET, Jeff														
D 1997	Bal-A	.200	2	5	1	1	0	0	1	1	0	2	0	2-2
L 1997	Bal-A	.000	1	2	1	0	0	0	0	0	0	1	0	S-1
• REDMAN, Mark														
D 2003	Fla-N	.000	1	2	0	0	0	0	0	0	0	1	0	....
L 2003	Fla-N	.000	2	2	0	0	0	0	0	0	1	0	0	....
• REDMOND, Mike														
L 2003	Fla-N	....	1	0	1	0	0	0	0	0	1	0	0	C-1
W 2003	Fla-N	.000	1	1	0	0	0	0	0	0	0	0	0	C-1
• REDUS, Gary														
L 1990	Pit-N	.250	5	8	1	2	0	0	0	0	1	3	1	1-2
L 1991	Pit-N	.158	5	19	1	3	0	0	0	0	1	4	2	1-5
L 1992	Pit-N	.438	5	16	4	7	4	1	0	3	2	3	0	1-5
L Total	**3**	**.279**	**15**	**43**	**6**	**12**	**4**	**1**	**0**	**3**	**4**	**10**	**3**	....
• REED, Jack														
W 1961	NY-A	....	3	0	0	0	0	0	0	0	0	0	0	0-3
• REED, Jeff														
L 1990	Cin-N	.000	4	7	0	0	0	0	0	0	0	2	0	C-4
• REED, Jody														
D 1996	SD-N	.273	3	11	0	3	1	0	0	2	0	1	0	2-3
L 1988	Bos-A	.273	4	11	0	3	1	0	0	0	2	1	0	S-4
L 1990	Bos-A	.133	4	15	0	2	0	0	0	1	0	2	0	2-4,S-3
L Total	**2**	**.192**	**8**	**26**	**0**	**5**	**1**	**0**	**0**	**1**	**2**	**3**	**0**	....
• REED, Rick														
D 1999	NY-N	.000	1	1	0	0	0	0	0	0	0	1	0	....
D 2000	NY-N	.000	1	1	0	0	0	0	0	0	0	0	0	....
D Total	**2**	**.000**	**2**	**2**	**0**	**0**	**0**	**0**	**0**	**0**	**0**	**1**	**0**	....
L 1999	NY-N	.000	1	2	0	0	0	0	0	0	0	0	0	....
L 2000	NY-N	.000	1	1	0	0	0	0	0	0	0	0	0	....
L Total	**2**	**.000**	**2**	**3**	**0**	**0**	**0**	**0**	**0**	**0**	**0**	**0**	**0**	....
W 2000	NY-N	1.000	1	1	0	1	0	0	0	0	0	0	0	....
• REESE, Pee Wee														
W 1941	Bro-N	.200	5	20	1	4	0	0	0	2	0	0	0	S-5
W 1947	Bro-N	.304	7	23	5	7	1	0	0	4	6	3	3	S-7
W 1949	Bro-N	.316	5	19	2	6	1	0	1	2	1	0	1	S-5
W 1952	Bro-N	.345	7	29	4	10	0	0	1	4	2	2	1	S-7
W 1953	Bro-N	.208	6	24	0	5	0	1	0	0	4	1	0	S-6
W 1955	Bro-N	.296	7	27	5	8	1	0	0	2	3	5	0	S-7
W 1956	Bro-N	.222	7	27	3	6	0	1	0	2	2	6	0	S-7
W Total	**7**	**.272**	**44**	**169**	**20**	**46**	**3**	**2**	**2**	**16**	**18**	**17**	**5**	....
• REESE, Rich														
L 1969	Min-A	.167	3	12	0	2	0	0	0	2	1	1	0	1-3
L 1970	Min-A	.143	2	7	0	1	0	0	0	0	1	1	0	1-2
L Total	**2**	**.158**	**5**	**19**	**0**	**3**	**0**	**0**	**0**	**2**	**2**	**2**	**0**	....
• REGALADO, Rudy														
W 1954	Cle-A	.333	4	3	0	1	0	0	0	1	0	0	0	3-1
• REIPSCHLAGER, Charlie														
W 1884	NY-A	.000	2	5	1	0	0	0	0	0	0	1	0	C-2
• REISER, Pete														
W 1941	Bro-N	.200	5	20	1	4	1	1	1	3	1	6	0	0-5
W 1947	Bro-N	.250	5	8	1	2	0	0	0	0	3	1	0	0-3
W Total	**2**	**.214**	**10**	**28**	**2**	**6**	**1**	**1**	**1**	**3**	**4**	**7**	**0**	....
• REITZ, Heinie														
T 1894	Bal-N	.333	4	15	1	5	0	0	0	4	1	3	1	2-4
T 1896	Bal-N	.133	4	15	1	2	0	0	0	2	1	0	0	2-4
T 1897	Bal-N	.250	5	20	4	5	1	0	1	4	2	0	0	2-5
T Total	**3**	**.240**	**13**	**50**	**6**	**12**	**1**	**0**	**1**	**10**	**4**	**3**	**1**	....
• RENICK, Rick														
L 1969	Min-A	.000	1	1	0	0	0	0	0	0	0	0	0	....
L 1970	Min-A	.200	2	5	0	1	0	0	0	0	0	1	0	3-1
L Total	**2**	**.167**	**3**	**6**	**0**	**1**	**0**	**0**	**0**	**0**	**0**	**1**	**0**	....
• RENTERIA, Edgar														
D 1997	Fla-N	.154	3	13	1	2	0	0	0	1	2	4	0	S-3
D 2000	StL-N	.200	3	10	5	2	0	0	0	0	4	1	2	S-3
D 2001	StL-N	.235	5	17	2	4	1	0	1	1	2	4	0	S-5
D 2002	StL-N	.250	3	12	3	3	0	0	0	0	1	1	2	S-3
D Total	**4**	**.212**	**14**	**52**	**11**	**11**	**1**	**0**	**1**	**2**	**9**	**10**	**4**	....
L 1997	Fla-N	.227	6	22	4	5	1	0	0	0	3	6	1	S-6
L 2000	StL-N	.300	5	20	4	6	1	0	0	4	0	2	3	S-5
L 2002	StL-N	.158	5	19	0	3	0	0	0	1	0	2	0	S-5
L Total	**3**	**.230**	**16**	**61**	**8**	**14**	**2**	**0**	**0**	**5**	**3**	**10**	**4**	....
W 1997	Fla-N	.290	7	31	3	9	2	0	0	3	3	5	0	S-7
• REPULSKI, Rip														
W 1959	LA-N	....	1	0	0	0	0	0	0	0	1	0	0	0-1
• RETTENMUND, Merv														
L 1969	Bal-A	....	1	0	0	0	0	0	0	0	0	0	0	....
L 1970	Bal-A	.333	1	3	1	1	0	0	0	1	2	1	0	0-1
L 1971	Bal-A	.250	3	8	0	2	1	0	0	1	0	3	0	0-3
L 1973	Bal-A	.091	3	11	1	1	0	0	0	0	3	2	0	0-3
L 1975	Cin-N	.000	2	1	1	0	0	0	0	0	1	0	0	....
L 1979	Cal-A	.000	2	2	0	0	0	0	0	0	2	1	0	D-1
L Total	**6**	**.160**	**12**	**25**	**3**	**4**	**1**	**0**	**0**	**2**	**8**	**7**	**0**	....
W 1969	Bal-A	....	1	0	0	0	0	0	0	0	0	0	0	....
W 1970	Bal-A	.400	2	5	2	2	0	0	1	2	1	0	0	0-1
W 1971	Bal-A	.185	7	27	3	5	0	0	1	4	0	4	0	0-6
W 1975	Cin-N	.000	3	3	0	0	0	0	0	0	0	1	0	....
W Total	**4**	**.200**	**13**	**35**	**5**	**7**	**0**	**0**	**2**	**6**	**1**	**5**	**0**	....
• REVERING, Dave														
D 1981	NY-A	....	2	0	0	0	0	0	0	0	0	0	0	1-2
L 1981	NY-A	.500	2	2	0	1	0	0	0	0	0	0	0	1-2
• REYNOLDS, Carl														
W 1938	Chi-N	.000	4	12	0	0	0	0	0	0	1	3	0	0-3
• REYNOLDS, Craig														
D 1981	Hou-N	.333	2	3	1	1	0	0	0	0	0	1	0	S-1
L 1975	Pit-N	.000	2	1	0	0	0	0	0	0	0	0	0	S-1
L 1980	Hou-N	.154	4	13	2	2	1	0	0	0	3	1	0	S-4
L 1986	Hou-N	.333	4	12	1	4	0	0	0	0	1	3	0	S-4
L Total	**3**	**.231**	**10**	**26**	**3**	**6**	**1**	**0**	**0**	**0**	**4**	**4**	**0**	....
• REYNOLDS, R.J.														
L 1990	Pit-N	.200	6	10	0	2	0	0	0	0	2	2	1	0-3
• RHODES, Dusty														
W 1954	NY-N	.667	3	6	2	4	0	0	2	7	1	2	0	0-2
• RHYNE, Hal														
W 1927	Pit-N	.000	1	4	0	0	0	0	0	0	0	0	0	2-1
• RICE, Del														
W 1946	StL-N	.500	3	6	2	3	1	0	0	0	2	0	0	C-3
W 1957	Mil-N	.167	2	6	0	1	0	0	0	0	1	2	0	C-2
W Total	**2**	**.333**	**5**	**12**	**2**	**4**	**1**	**0**	**0**	**0**	**3**	**2**	**0**	....
• RICE, Jim														
L 1986	Bos-A	.161	7	31	8	5	1	0	2	6	1	8	0	0-7
L 1988	Bos-A	.154	4	13	0	2	0	0	0	1	2	4	0	D-4
L Total	**2**	**.159**	**11**	**44**	**8**	**7**	**1**	**0**	**2**	**7**	**3**	**12**	**0**	....
W 1986	Bos-A	.333	7	27	6	9	1	1	0	0	6	9	0	0-7
• RICE, Sam														
W 1924	Was-A	.207	7	29	2	6	0	0	0	1	3	2	2	0-7
W 1925	Was-A	.364	7	33	5	12	0	0	0	3	0	1	0	0-7
W 1933	Was-A	1.000	1	1	0	1	0	0	0	0	0	0	0	....
W Total	**3**	**.302**	**15**	**63**	**7**	**19**	**0**	**0**	**0**	**4**	**3**	**3**	**2**	....
• RICHARDS, Paul														
W 1945	Det-A	.211	7	19	0	4	2	0	0	6	4	3	0	C-7
• RICHARDSON, Bobby														
W 1957	NY-A	....	2	0	0	0	0	0	0	0	0	0	0	2-1
W 1958	NY-A	.000	4	5	0	0	0	0	0	0	0	0	0	3-4
W 1960	NY-A	.367	7	30	8	11	2	2	1	12	1	1	0	2-7
W 1961	NY-A	.391	5	23	2	9	1	0	0	0	0	0	1	2-5
W 1962	NY-A	.148	7	27	3	4	0	0	0	0	3	1	0	2-7
W 1963	NY-A	.214	4	14	0	3	1	0	0	0	1	3	0	2-4
W 1964	NY-A	.406	7	32	3	13	2	0	0	3	0	2	1	2-7
W Total	**7**	**.305**	**36**	**131**	**16**	**40**	**6**	**2**	**1**	**15**	**5**	**7**	**2**	....
• RICHARDSON, Danny														
W 1888	NY-N	.167	9	36	6	6	2	0	0	6	3	5	3	2-9
W 1889	NY-N	.314	9	35	8	11	1	1	3	8	3	5	3	2-9
W Total	**2**	**.239**	**18**	**71**	**14**	**17**	**3**	**1**	**3**	**14**	**6**	**10**	**6**	....
• RICHARDSON, Hardy														
W 1887	Det-N	.209	15	67	12	14	5	2	1	4	1	9	7	0-10,2-5,3-1
• RICKERT, Marv														
W 1948	Bos-N	.211	5	19	2	4	0	0	1	2	0	4	0	0-5
• RICKETTS, Dave														
W 1967	StL-N	.000	3	3	0	0	0	0	0	0	0	0	0	....
W 1968	StL-N	1.000	1	1	0	1	0	0	0	0	0	0	0	....
W Total	**2**	**.250**	**4**	**4**	**0**	**1**	**0**	**0**	**0**	**0**	**0**	**0**	**0**	....
• RIGGS, Lew														
W 1940	Cin-N	.000	3	3	1	0	0	0	0	0	0	2	0	....
W 1941	Bro-N	.250	3	8	0	2	0	0	0	1	1	1	0	3-2
W Total	**2**	**.182**	**6**	**11**	**1**	**2**	**0**	**0**	**0**	**1**	**1**	**3**	**0**	....
• RIGNEY, Bill														
W 1951	NY-N	.250	4	4	0	1	0	0	0	1	0	1	0	....
• RILES, Ernest														
L 1989	SF-N	.000	1	1	0	0	0	0	0	0	0	0	0	....
W 1989	SF-N	.000	4	8	0	0	0	0	0	0	0	1	0	D-2
• RIOS, Armando														
D 2000	SF-N	.500	2	2	0	1	0	0	0	0	0	0	0	....
• RIPKEN JR., Cal														
D 1996	Bal-A	.444	4	18	2	8	3	0	0	2	0	3	0	S-4
D 1997	Bal-A	.438	4	16	1	7	2	0	0	1	2	2	0	3-4
D Total	**2**	**.441**	**8**	**34**	**3**	**15**	**5**	**0**	**0**	**3**	**2**	**5**	**0**	....
L 1983	Bal-A	.400	4	15	5	6	2	0	0	1	2	3	0	S-4
L 1996	Bal-A	.250	5	20	1	5	1	0	0	0	1	4	0	S-5
L 1997	Bal-A	.348	6	23	3	8	2	0	1	3	4	6	0	3-6
L Total	**3**	**.328**	**15**	**58**	**9**	**19**	**5**	**0**	**1**	**4**	**7**	**13**	**0**	....
W 1983	Bal-A	.167	5	18	2	3	0	0	0	1	3	4	0	S-5
• RIPPLE, Jimmy														
W 1936	NY-N	.333	5	12	2	4	0	0	1	3	3	3	0	0-5
W 1937	NY-N	.294	5	17	2	5	0	0	0	0	3	1	0	0-5
W 1940	Cin-N	.333	7	21	3	7	2	0	1	6	4	2	0	0-7
W Total	**3**	**.320**	**17**	**50**	**7**	**16**	**2**	**0**	**2**	**9**	**10**	**6**	**0**	....
• RISBERG, Swede														
W 1917	Chi-A	.500	2	2	0	1	0	0	0	1	0	0	0	....
W 1919	Chi-A	.080	8	25	3	2	0	1	0	0	5	3	1	S-8
W Total	**2**	**.111**	**10**	**27**	**3**	**3**	**0**	**1**	**0**	**1**	**5**	**3**	**1**	....
• RITCHEY, Claude														
T 1900	Pit-N	.333	4	15	3	5	1	0	0	1	1	0	0	2-4

YEAR	TM-L	AVG	G	AB	R	H	2B	3B	HR	RBI	BB	SO	SB	POS
W 1903	Pit-N	.111	8	27	2	3	1	0	0	2	4	7	1	2-8
• RIVAS, Luis														
D 2002	Min-A	.250	4	12	2	3	1	0	0	0	1	2	0	2-4
D 2003	Min-A	.000	4	13	0	0	0	0	0	1	0	4	0	2-4
D Total	2	.120	8	25	2	3	1	0	0	1	1	6	0	....
L 2002	Min-A	.250	5	12	1	3	0	0	0	0	1	3	0	2-5
• RIVERA, Jim														
W 1959	Chi-A	.000	5	11	1	0	0	0	0	0	3	1	0	0-5
• RIVERA, Juan														
D 2002	NY-A	.250	4	12	2	3	0	0	0	3	1	3	0	0-4
D 2003	NY-A	.333	4	12	2	4	0	0	0	0	1	0	0	0-4
D Total	2	.292	8	24	4	7	0	0	0	3	2	3	0	....
L 2003	NY-A	.000	2	2	0	0	0	0	0	0	0	1	0	0-2
W 2003	NY-A	.167	4	6	0	1	1	0	0	1	1	1	0	0-2
• RIVERA, Luis														
L 1990	Bos-A	.222	4	9	1	2	1	0	0	0	0	2	0	S-4
• RIVERA, Ruben														
D 1996	NY-A	.000	2	1	0	0	0	0	0	0	0	1	0	0-2
D 1998	SD-N	.000	3	6	0	0	0	0	0	0	0	3	0	0-3
D Total	2	.000	5	7	0	0	0	0	0	0	0	4	0	....
L 1998	SD-N	.231	6	13	1	3	2	0	0	0	0	7	1	0-6
W 1998	SD-N	.800	3	5	1	4	2	0	0	1	0	0	0	0-3
• RIVERS, Mickey														
L 1976	NY-A	.348	5	23	5	8	0	1	0	0	1	1	0	0-5
L 1977	NY-A	.391	5	23	5	9	2	0	0	2	0	2	1	0-5
L 1978	NY-A	.455	4	11	0	5	0	0	0	0	2	0	0	0-4
L Total	3	.386	14	57	10	22	2	1	0	2	3	3	1	....
W 1976	NY-A	.167	4	18	1	3	0	0	0	0	1	2	1	0-4
W 1977	NY-A	.222	6	27	1	6	2	0	0	1	0	2	1	0-6
W 1978	NY-A	.333	5	18	2	6	0	0	0	1	0	2	1	0-4
W Total	3	.238	15	63	4	15	2	0	0	2	1	6	3	....
• RIZZUTO, Phil														
W 1941	NY-A	.111	5	18	0	2	0	0	0	0	3	1	1	S-5
W 1942	NY-A	.381	5	21	2	8	0	0	1	1	2	1	2	S-5
W 1947	NY-A	.308	7	26	3	8	1	0	0	2	4	0	2	S-7
W 1949	NY-A	.167	5	18	2	3	0	0	0	1	3	1	1	S-5
W 1950	NY-A	.143	4	14	1	2	0	0	0	0	3	0	1	S-4
W 1951	NY-A	.320	6	25	5	8	0	0	1	3	2	3	0	S-6
W 1952	NY-A	.148	7	27	2	4	1	0	0	0	5	2	0	S-7
W 1953	NY-A	.316	6	19	4	6	1	0	0	0	3	2	1	S-6
W 1955	NY-A	.267	7	15	2	4	0	0	0	1	5	1	2	S-7
W Total	9	.246	52	183	21	45	3	0	2	8	30	11	10	....
• ROBERTS, Bip														
D 1997	Cle-A	.316	5	19	1	6	0	0	0	1	2	2	2	0-4,2-2
L 1997	Cle-A	.150	5	20	0	3	1	0	0	0	0	8	1	0-2,2-4
W 1997	Cle-A	.273	6	22	3	6	4	0	0	4	3	5	0	0-2,2-4
• ROBERTS, Dave														
D 1981	Hou-N	.000	1	1	0	0	0	0	0	0	0	1	0	....
• ROBERTS, Dave														
D 1999	Cle-A	.000	2	3	0	0	0	0	0	0	0	2	0	0-2
• ROBERTSON, Andre														
L 1981	NY-A	.000	1	1	0	0	0	0	0	0	0	0	0	S-1
W 1981	NY-A	....	1	0	0	0	0	0	0	0	0	0	0	....
• ROBERTSON, Bob														
L 1970	Pit-N	.200	2	5	0	1	1	0	0	0	0	0	0	1-1
L 1971	Pit-N	.438	4	16	5	7	1	0	4	6	0	2	0	1-4
L 1972	Pit-N	....	4	0	0	0	0	0	0	0	1	0	0	1-4
L 1974	Pit-N	.000	1	5	1	0	0	0	0	0	0	0	0	1-1
L 1975	Pit-N	.500	3	2	0	1	0	0	0	1	1	0	0	1-1
L Total	5	.321	14	28	6	9	2	0	4	7	2	2	0	....
W 1971	Pit-N	.240	7	25	4	6	0	0	2	5	4	8	0	1-7
• ROBERTSON, Dave														
W 1917	NY-N	.500	6	22	3	11	1	1	0	1	0	0	2	0-6
• ROBERTSON, Gene														
W 1928	NY-A	.125	3	8	1	1	0	0	0	2	1	0	0	3-3
• ROBINSON, Aaron														
W 1947	NY-A	.200	3	10	2	2	0	0	0	1	2	1	0	C-3
• ROBINSON, Bill														
L 1975	Pit-N	.000	2	2	0	0	0	0	0	0	0	1	0	....
L 1979	Pit-N	.000	3	3	0	0	0	0	0	0	0	0	0	0-3
L Total	2	.000	5	5	0	0	0	0	0	0	0	1	0	....
W 1979	Pit-N	.263	7	19	2	5	1	0	0	2	0	4	0	0-6
• ROBINSON, Brooks														
L 1969	Bal-A	.500	3	14	1	7	1	0	0	0	0	0	0	3-3
L 1970	Bal-A	.583	3	12	3	7	2	0	0	1	0	1	0	3-3
L 1971	Bal-A	.364	3	11	2	4	1	0	1	3	0	1	0	3-3
L 1973	Bal-A	.250	5	20	1	5	2	0	0	2	1	1	0	3-5
L 1974	Bal-A	.083	4	12	1	1	0	0	1	1	1	0	0	3-4
L Total	5	.348	18	69	8	24	6	0	2	7	2	3	0	....
W 1966	Bal-A	.214	4	14	2	3	0	0	1	1	1	0	0	3-4
W 1969	Bal-A	.053	5	19	0	1	0	0	0	2	0	3	0	3-5
W 1970	Bal-A	.429	5	21	5	9	2	0	2	6	0	2	0	3-5
W 1971	Bal-A	.318	7	22	2	7	0	0	0	5	3	1	0	3-7
W Total	4	.263	21	76	9	20	2	0	3	14	4	6	0	....
• ROBINSON, Eddie														
W 1948	Cle-A	.300	6	20	0	6	0	0	0	1	1	0	0	1-6
W 1955	NY-A	.667	4	3	0	2	0	0	0	1	2	1	0	1-1
W Total	2	.348	10	23	0	8	0	0	0	2	3	1	0	....
• ROBINSON, Frank														
L 1969	Bal-A	.333	3	12	1	4	2	0	1	2	3	3	0	0-3
L 1970	Bal-A	.200	3	10	3	2	0	0	1	2	5	2	0	0-3
L 1971	Bal-A	.083	3	12	2	1	1	0	0	1	1	4	0	0-3
L Total	3	.206	9	34	6	7	3	0	2	5	9	9	0	....
W 1961	Cin-N	.200	5	15	3	3	2	0	1	4	3	4	0	0-5
W 1966	Bal-A	.286	4	14	4	4	0	1	2	3	2	3	0	0-4
W 1969	Bal-A	.188	5	16	2	3	0	0	1	1	4	3	0	0-5
W 1970	Bal-A	.273	5	22	5	6	0	0	2	4	0	5	0	0-5
W 1971	Bal-A	.280	7	25	5	7	0	0	2	2	2	8	0	0-7
W Total	5	.250	26	92	19	23	2	1	8	14	11	23	0	....
• ROBINSON, Jackie														
W 1947	Bro-N	.259	7	27	3	7	2	0	0	3	2	4	2	1-7
W 1949	Bro-N	.188	5	16	2	3	1	0	0	2	4	2	0	2-5
W 1952	Bro-N	.174	7	23	4	4	0	0	1	2	7	5	2	2-7
W 1953	Bro-N	.320	6	25	3	8	2	0	0	2	1	0	1	0-6
W 1955	Bro-N	.182	6	22	5	4	1	1	0	1	2	1	1	3-6
W 1956	Bro-N	.250	7	24	5	6	1	0	1	2	5	2	0	3-7
W Total	6	.234	38	137	22	32	7	1	2	12	21	14	6	....
• ROBINSON, Kerry														
D 2001	StL-N	.500	4	2	0	1	0	0	0	1	0	0	0	0-3
D 2002	StL-N	.500	2	2	0	1	0	0	0	1	0	0	0	....
D Total	2	.500	6	4	0	2	0	0	0	2	0	0	0	....
L 2002	StL-N	.000	3	2	1	0	0	0	0	0	1	1	0	0-1
• ROBINSON, Wilbert														
T 1894	Bal-N	.267	4	15	1	4	0	0	0	1	1	1	1	C-4
T 1895	Bal-N	.250	3	12	1	3	1	0	0	0	0	1	0	C-3
T 1896	Bal-N	.267	4	15	1	4	1	0	0	2	0	3	0	C-4
T Total	3	.262	11	42	3	11	2	0	0	3	1	5	1	....
• ROBINSON, Yank														
W 1885	StL-A	.174	7	23	5	4	0	1	0	0	1	0	0	0-4,C-3
W 1886	StL-A	.316	6	19	5	6	1	1	0	3	2	3	2	2-6
W 1887	StL-A	.446	15	56	5	25	5	1	0	4	10	6	4	2-15
W 1888	StL-A	.250	10	36	7	9	2	1	0	7	6	12	2	2-10
W Total	4	.328	38	134	22	44	8	4	0	14	19	21	8	....
• RODRIGUEZ, Alex														
D 1995	Sea-A	.000	1	1	1	0	0	0	0	0	0	0	0	S-1
D 1997	Sea-A	.313	4	16	1	5	1	0	1	1	0	5	0	S-4
D 2000	Sea-A	.308	3	13	0	4	0	0	0	2	0	2	0	S-3
D Total	3	.300	8	30	2	9	1	0	1	3	0	7	0	....
L 1995	Sea-A	.000	1	1	0	0	0	0	0	0	0	1	0	....
L 2000	Sea-A	.409	6	22	4	9	2	0	2	5	3	8	1	S-6
L Total	2	.391	7	23	4	9	2	0	2	5	3	9	1	....
• RODRIGUEZ, Aurelio														
L 1972	Det-A	.000	5	16	0	0	0	0	0	0	2	2	0	3-5
L 1980	NY-A	.333	2	6	0	2	1	0	0	0	0	0	0	3-2
L 1981	NY-A	....	1	0	0	0	0	0	0	0	0	0	0	3-1
L 1983	Chi-A	....	2	0	0	0	0	0	0	0	0	0	0	3-2
L Total	4	.091	10	22	0	2	1	0	0	0	2	2	0	....
W 1981	NY-A	.417	4	12	1	5	0	0	0	0	1	2	0	3-4
• RODRIGUEZ, Francisco														
W 2002	Ana-A	....	4	0	0	0	0	0	0	0	0	0	0	....
• RODRIGUEZ, Henry														
D 1998	Chi-N	.143	3	7	0	1	1	0	0	0	1	2	0	0-2
• RODRIGUEZ, Ivan														
D 1996	Tex-A	.375	4	16	1	6	1	0	0	2	2	3	0	C-4
D 1998	Tex-A	.100	3	10	0	1	0	0	0	1	0	5	0	C-3
D 1999	Tex-A	.250	3	12	0	3	1	0	0	0	0	2	1	C-3
D 2003	Fla-N	.353	4	17	3	6	1	0	1	6	3	1	0	C-4
D Total	4	.291	14	55	4	16	3	0	1	9	5	11	1	....
L 2003	Fla-N	.321	7	28	5	9	2	0	2	10	5	7	0	C-7
W 2003	Fla-N	.273	6	22	2	6	2	0	0	1	1	4	0	C-6
• ROENICKE, Gary														
L 1979	Bal-A	.200	2	5	1	1	0	0	0	1	0	0	0	0-2
L 1983	Bal-A	.750	3	4	4	3	1	0	1	4	5	0	0	0-3
L Total	2	.444	5	9	5	4	1	0	1	5	5	0	0	....
W 1979	Bal-A	.125	6	16	1	2	1	0	0	0	0	6	0	0-5
W 1983	Bal-A	.000	3	7	0	0	0	0	0	0	0	2	0	0-2
W Total	2	.087	9	23	1	2	1	0	0	0	0	8	0	....
• ROENICKE, Ron														
W 1984	SD-N	....	2	0	0	0	0	0	0	0	0	0	0	0-1
• ROETTGER, Wally														
W 1931	StL-N	.286	3	14	1	4	1	0	0	0	0	3	0	0-3
• ROGELL, Billy														
W 1934	Det-A	.276	7	29	3	8	1	0	0	4	1	4	1	S-7
W 1935	Det-A	.292	6	24	1	7	2	0	0	1	2	5	0	S-6
W Total	2	.283	13	53	4	15	3	0	0	5	3	9	1	....
• ROHE, George														
W 1906	Chi-A	.333	6	21	2	7	1	2	0	4	3	1	2	3-6
• ROJAS, Cookie														
L 1976	KC-A	.333	4	9	2	3	0	0	0	1	0	0	1	2-4
L 1977	KC-A	.250	1	4	0	1	0	0	0	0	0	1	1	D-1
L Total	2	.308	5	13	2	4	0	0	0	1	0	1	2	....
• ROLEN, Scott														
D 2002	StL-N	.429	2	7	1	3	0	0	1	2	0	2	0	3-2

SER-YEAR	TM-L	AVG	G	AB	R	H	2B	3B	HR	RBI	BB	SO	SB	POS
• ROLFE, Red														
W 1936	NY-A	.400	6	25	5	10	0	0	0	4	3	1	0	3-6
W 1937	NY-A	.300	5	20	3	6	2	1	0	1	3	2	0	3-5
W 1938	NY-A	.167	4	18	0	3	0	0	0	1	0	3	1	3-4
W 1939	NY-A	.125	4	16	2	2	0	0	0	0	0	0	0	3-4
W 1941	NY-A	.300	5	20	2	6	0	0	0	0	2	1	0	3-5
W 1942	NY-A	.353	4	17	5	6	2	0	0	0	1	2	0	3-4
W Total	**6**	**.284**	**28**	**116**	**17**	**33**	**4**	**1**	**0**	**6**	**9**	**9**	**1**	**....**
• ROLLINS, Rich														
W 1965	Min-A	.000	3	2	0	0	0	0	0	0	1	0	0	....
• ROMANO, Johnny														
W 1959	Chi-A	.000	1	1	0	0	0	0	0	0	0	0	0	....
• ROMERO, Ed														
D 1981	Mil-A	.500	1	2	1	1	0	0	0	0	0	1	0	2-1
L 1986	Bos-A	.000	1	2	0	0	0	0	0	0	0	0	0	S-1
L 1988	Bos-A	....	1	0	0	0	0	0	0	0	0	0	0	....
L Total	**2**	**.000**	**2**	**2**	**0**	**0**	**0**	**0**	**0**	**0**	**0**	**0**	**0**	**....**
W 1986	Bos-A	.000	3	1	0	0	0	0	0	0	0	0	0	S-3
• ROMINE, Kevin														
L 1988	Bos-A	....	2	0	1	0	0	0	0	0	0	0	0	D-2
• ROSAR, Buddy														
W 1941	NY-A	....	1	0	0	0	0	0	0	0	0	0	0	C-1
W 1942	NY-A	1.000	1	1	0	1	0	0	0	0	0	0	0	....
W Total	**2**	**1.000**	**2**	**1**	**0**	**1**	**0**	**0**	**0**	**0**	**0**	**0**	**0**	**....**
• ROSARIO, Jimmy														
L 1971	SF-N	....	1	0	0	0	0	0	0	0	0	0	0	....
• ROSE, Pete														
D 1981	Phi-N	.300	5	20	1	6	1	0	0	2	2	0	0	1-5
L 1970	Cin-N	.231	3	13	1	3	0	0	0	1	0	0	0	0-3
L 1972	Cin-N	.450	5	20	1	9	4	0	0	2	1	2	0	0-5
L 1973	Cin-N	.381	5	21	3	8	1	0	2	2	2	2	0	0-5
L 1975	Cin-N	.357	3	14	3	5	0	0	1	2	0	2	0	3-3
L 1976	Cin-N	.429	3	14	3	6	2	1	0	2	1	0	0	3-3
L 1980	Phi-N	.400	5	20	3	8	0	0	0	2	5	3	0	1-5
L 1983	Phi-N	.375	4	16	3	6	0	0	0	0	1	1	1	1-4
L Total	**7**	**.381**	**28**	**118**	**17**	**45**	**7**	**1**	**3**	**11**	**10**	**10**	**1**	**....**
W 1970	Cin-N	.250	5	20	2	5	1	0	1	2	2	0	0	0-5
W 1972	Cin-N	.214	7	28	3	6	0	0	1	2	4	4	1	0-7
W 1975	Cin-N	.370	7	27	3	10	1	1	0	2	5	1	0	3-7
W 1976	Cin-N	.188	4	16	1	3	1	0	0	1	2	2	0	3-4
W 1980	Phi-N	.261	6	23	2	6	1	0	0	1	2	2	0	1-6
W 1983	Phi-N	.313	5	16	1	5	1	0	0	1	1	3	0	0-1,1-3
W Total	**6**	**.269**	**34**	**130**	**12**	**35**	**5**	**1**	**2**	**9**	**16**	**12**	**1**	**....**
• ROSEBORO, Johnny														
L 1969	Min-A	.200	2	5	0	1	0	0	0	0	0	0	0	C-2
W 1959	LA-N	.095	6	21	0	2	0	0	0	1	0	2	0	C-6
W 1963	LA-N	.143	4	14	1	2	0	0	1	3	0	4	0	C-4
W 1965	LA-N	.286	7	21	1	6	1	0	0	3	5	3	1	C-7
W 1966	LA-N	.071	4	14	0	1	0	0	0	0	0	3	0	C-4
W Total	**4**	**.157**	**21**	**70**	**2**	**11**	**1**	**0**	**1**	**7**	**5**	**12**	**1**	**....**
• ROSEMAN, Chief														
W 1884	NY-A	.333	3	9	1	3	0	0	0	1	0	1	0	0-3
• ROSEN, Al														
W 1948	Cle-A	.000	1	1	0	0	0	0	0	0	0	0	0	....
W 1954	Cle-A	.250	3	12	0	3	0	0	0	0	1	0	0	3-3
W Total	**2**	**.231**	**4**	**13**	**0**	**3**	**0**	**0**	**0**	**0**	**1**	**0**	**0**	**....**
• ROSSMAN, Claude														
W 1907	Det-A	.400	5	20	1	8	0	1	0	2	1	0	1	1-5
W 1908	Det-A	.211	5	19	3	4	0	0	0	3	1	4	0	1-5
W Total	**2**	**.308**	**10**	**39**	**4**	**12**	**0**	**1**	**0**	**5**	**2**	**4**	**1**	**....**
• ROTHROCK, Jack														
W 1934	StL-N	.233	7	30	3	7	3	1	0	6	1	2	0	0-7
• ROUSH, Edd														
W 1919	Cin-N	.214	8	28	6	6	2	1	0	7	3	0	2	0-8
• ROWE, Jack														
W 1887	Det-N	.354	15	65	12	23	1	1	0	7	2	1	5	S-15
• ROYSTER, Jerry														
L 1982	Atl-N	.182	3	11	0	2	0	0	0	0	0	2	0	0-3,3-1
• RUDI, Joe														
L 1971	Oak-A	.143	2	7	0	1	1	0	0	0	1	0	0	0-2
L 1972	Oak-A	.240	7	25	1	6	1	0	1	1	2	3	0	0-5
L 1973	Oak-A	.222	5	18	1	4	0	0	1	3	3	1	0	0-5
L 1974	Oak-A	.154	4	13	0	2	0	1	0	1	3	2	0	0-4
L 1975	Oak-A	.250	3	12	1	3	2	0	0	0	0	1	0	0-1,1-2
L Total	**5**	**.213**	**21**	**75**	**3**	**16**	**4**	**1**	**2**	**5**	**9**	**7**	**0**	**....**
W 1972	Oak-A	.240	7	25	1	6	0	0	1	1	2	5	0	0-7
W 1973	Oak-A	.333	7	27	3	9	2	0	0	4	3	4	0	0-7
W 1974	Oak-A	.333	5	18	1	6	0	0	1	4	0	3	0	0-5,1-2
W Total	**3**	**.300**	**19**	**70**	**5**	**21**	**2**	**0**	**2**	**9**	**5**	**12**	**0**	**....**
• RUEL, Muddy														
W 1924	Was-A	.095	7	21	2	2	1	0	0	0	6	1	0	C-7
W 1925	Was-A	.316	7	19	0	6	1	0	0	1	3	2	0	C-7
W Total	**2**	**.200**	**14**	**40**	**2**	**8**	**2**	**0**	**0**	**1**	**9**	**3**	**0**	**....**
• RUSIE, Amos														
T 1894	NY-N	.429	2	7	1	3	1	0	0	1	0	1	0	P-2
• RUSSELL, Bill														
D 1981	LA-N	.250	5	16	1	4	1	0	0	2	3	1	0	S-5
L 1974	LA-N	.389	4	18	1	7	0	0	0	3	1	0	0	S-4
L 1977	LA-N	.278	4	18	3	5	1	0	0	2	0	0	0	S-4
L 1978	LA-N	.412	4	17	1	7	1	0	0	2	1	1	0	S-4
L 1981	LA-N	.313	5	16	2	5	0	1	0	1	1	1	0	S-5
L 1983	LA-N	.286	4	14	1	4	0	0	0	0	2	4	1	S-4
L Total	**5**	**.337**	**21**	**83**	**8**	**28**	**2**	**1**	**0**	**8**	**5**	**6**	**1**	**....**
W 1974	LA-N	.222	5	18	0	4	0	1	0	2	0	2	0	S-5
W 1977	LA-N	.154	6	26	3	4	0	1	0	2	1	3	0	S-6
W 1978	LA-N	.423	6	26	1	11	2	0	0	2	2	2	1	S-6
W 1981	LA-N	.240	6	25	1	6	0	0	0	2	0	1	1	S-6
W Total	**4**	**.263**	**23**	**95**	**5**	**25**	**2**	**2**	**0**	**8**	**3**	**8**	**2**	**....**
• RUSSELL, Rip														
W 1946	Bos-A	1.000	2	2	1	2	0	0	0	0	0	0	0	3-1
• RUTH, Babe														
W 1915	Bos-A	.000	1	1	0	0	0	0	0	0	0	0	0	....
W 1916	Bos-A	.000	1	5	0	0	0	0	0	1	0	2	0	....
W 1918	Bos-A	.200	3	5	0	1	0	1	0	2	0	2	0	P-2,0-2
W 1921	NY-A	.313	6	16	3	5	0	0	1	4	5	8	2	0-5
W 1922	NY-A	.118	5	17	1	2	1	0	0	1	2	3	0	0-5
W 1923	NY-A	.368	6	19	8	7	1	1	3	3	8	6	0	0-6,1-1
W 1926	NY-A	.300	7	20	6	6	0	0	4	5	11	2	1	0-7
W 1927	NY-A	.400	4	15	4	6	0	0	2	7	2	2	1	0-4
W 1928	NY-A	.625	4	16	9	10	3	0	3	4	1	2	0	0-4
W 1932	NY-A	.333	4	15	6	5	0	0	2	6	4	3	0	0-4
W Total	**10**	**.326**	**41**	**129**	**37**	**42**	**5**	**2**	**15**	**33**	**33**	**30**	**4**	**....**
• RYAN, Blondy														
W 1933	NY-N	.278	5	18	0	5	0	0	0	1	1	5	0	S-5
W 1937	NY-N	.000	1	1	0	0	0	0	0	0	0	1	0	....
W Total	**2**	**.263**	**6**	**19**	**0**	**5**	**0**	**0**	**0**	**1**	**1**	**6**	**0**	**....**
• RYAN, Connie														
W 1948	Bos-N	.000	2	1	0	0	0	0	0	0	0	1	0	....
• RYAN, Jack														
W 1890	Lou-A	.053	6	19	0	1	0	0	0	2	0	1	1	C-6
• RYAN, Michael														
D 2003	Min-A	.000	1	1	0	0	0	0	0	0	0	1	0	....
• RYAN, Mike														
W 1967	Bos-A	.000	1	2	0	0	0	0	0	0	0	1	0	C-1
• RYBA, Mike														
W 1946	Bos-A	....	1	0	0	0	0	0	0	0	0	0	0	....
• SABO, Chris														
L 1990	Cin-N	.227	6	22	1	5	0	0	1	3	1	4	0	3-6
W 1990	Cin-N	.563	4	16	2	9	1	0	2	5	2	2	0	3-4
• SADLER, Donnie														
D 1998	Bos-A	....	3	0	0	0	0	0	0	0	0	0	0	2-3
D 1999	Bos-A	.500	2	2	1	1	1	0	0	0	0	1	0	3-1,D-1
D Total	**2**	**.500**	**5**	**2**	**1**	**1**	**1**	**0**	**0**	**0**	**0**	**1**	**0**	**....**
L 1999	Bos-A	....	2	0	0	0	0	0	0	0	0	0	0	0-1,D-1
• SAENZ, Olmedo														
D 2000	Oak-A	.231	4	13	1	3	0	0	1	4	0	2	0	D-4
D 2001	Oak-A	.000	3	4	0	0	0	0	0	0	0	1	0	D-1
D 2002	Oak-A	....	1	0	0	0	0	0	0	0	1	0	0	1-1
D Total	**3**	**.176**	**8**	**17**	**1**	**3**	**0**	**0**	**1**	**4**	**1**	**3**	**0**	**....**
• SAKATA, Lenn														
W 1983	Bal-A	.000	1	1	0	0	0	0	0	0	0	0	0	2-1
• SALAZAR, Luis														
L 1984	SD-N	.200	3	5	0	1	0	1	0	0	0	1	0	0-2,3-1
L 1989	Chi-N	.368	5	19	2	7	0	1	1	2	0	0	0	3-5
L Total	**2**	**.333**	**8**	**24**	**2**	**8**	**0**	**2**	**1**	**2**	**0**	**1**	**0**	**....**
W 1984	SD-N	.333	4	3	0	1	0	0	0	0	0	0	0	0-2,3-1
• SALKELD, Bill														
W 1948	Bos-N	.222	5	9	2	2	0	0	1	1	5	1	0	C-4
• SALMON, Chico														
L 1969	Bal-A	.000	1	1	0	0	0	0	0	0	0	0	0	....
W 1969	Bal-A	....	2	0	0	0	0	0	0	0	0	0	0	....
W 1970	Bal-A	1.000	1	1	1	1	0	0	0	0	0	0	0	....
W Total	**2**	**1.000**	**3**	**1**	**1**	**1**	**0**	**0**	**0**	**0**	**0**	**0**	**0**	**....**
• SALMON, Tim														
D 2002	Ana-A	.263	4	19	3	5	1	0	2	7	1	5	0	0-4
L 2002	Ana-A	.214	5	14	0	3	0	0	0	0	3	1	0	0-5
W 2002	Ana-A	.346	7	26	7	9	1	0	2	5	4	7	1	0-7
• SAMUEL, Juan														
L 1983	Phi-N	....	1	0	0	0	0	0	0	0	0	0	0	....
W 1983	Phi-N	.000	3	1	0	0	0	0	0	0	0	0	0	....
• SANCHEZ, Rey														
D 1997	NY-A	.200	5	15	1	3	1	0	0	1	1	2	0	2-5
D 2001	Atl-N	.222	3	9	1	2	1	0	0	0	0	2	0	S-3
D Total	**2**	**.208**	**8**	**24**	**2**	**5**	**2**	**0**	**0**	**1**	**1**	**4**	**0**	**....**
L 2001	Atl-N	.294	5	17	1	5	1	0	0	1	0	4	0	S-5
• SANDBERG, Ryne														
L 1984	Chi-N	.368	5	19	3	7	2	0	0	2	3	2	3	2-5
L 1989	Chi-N	.400	5	20	6	8	3	1	1	4	3	4	0	2-5
L Total	**2**	**.385**	**10**	**39**	**9**	**15**	**5**	**1**	**1**	**6**	**6**	**6**	**3**	**....**
• SANDERS, Deion														
L 1992	Atl-N	.000	4	5	0	0	0	0	0	0	0	3	0	0-3
L 1993	Atl-N	.000	5	3	0	0	0	0	0	0	0	1	0	0-1
L Total	**2**	**.000**	**9**	**8**	**0**	**0**	**0**	**0**	**0**	**0**	**0**	**4**	**0**	**....**
W 1992	Atl-N	.533	4	15	4	8	2	0	0	1	2	1	5	0-4

YEAR	TM-L	AVG	G	AB	R	H	2B	3B	HR	RBI	BB	SO	SB	POS
• SANDERS, Ray														
W 1942	StL-N	.000	2	1	1	0	0	0	0	0	1	0	0	....
W 1943	StL-N	.294	5	17	3	5	0	0	1	2	3	4	0	1-5
W 1944	StL-N	.286	6	21	5	6	0	0	1	1	5	8	0	1-6
W 1948	Bos-N	.000	1	1	0	0	0	0	0	0	0	0	0	....
W Total	**4**	**.275**	**14**	**40**	**9**	**11**	**0**	**0**	**2**	**3**	**9**	**12**	**0**	**....**
• SANDERS, Reggie														
D 1995	Cin-N	.154	3	13	3	2	1	0	1	2	1	9	2	0-3
D 2000	Atl-N	.000	3	9	0	0	0	0	0	0	2	5	0	0-3
D 2001	Ari-N	.357	5	14	2	5	1	0	1	1	3	3	1	0-5
D 2002	SF-N	.222	5	18	1	4	1	0	0	1	3	5	0	0-5
D Total	**4**	**.204**	**16**	**54**	**6**	**11**	**3**	**0**	**2**	**4**	**9**	**22**	**3**	**....**
L 1995	Cin-N	.125	4	16	0	2	0	0	0	0	2	10	0	0-4
L 2001	Ari-N	.118	5	17	2	2	0	0	0	1	5	5	1	0-5
L 2002	SF-N	.063	4	16	0	1	0	0	0	0	0	4	0	0-4
L Total	**3**	**.102**	**13**	**49**	**2**	**5**	**0**	**0**	**0**	**1**	**7**	**19**	**1**	**....**
W 2001	Ari-N	.304	6	23	6	7	1	0	0	1	1	7	1	0-6
W 2002	SF-N	.238	7	21	3	5	0	0	2	6	2	9	1	0-7
W Total	**2**	**.273**	**13**	**44**	**9**	**12**	**1**	**0**	**2**	**7**	**3**	**16**	**2**	**....**
• SANDS, Charlie														
W 1971	Pit-N	.000	1	1	0	0	0	0	0	0	0	1	0	....
• SANGUILLEN, Manny														
L 1970	Pit-N	.167	3	12	0	2	0	0	0	0	0	1	0	C-3
L 1971	Pit-N	.267	4	15	1	4	0	0	0	1	1	1	1	C-4
L 1972	Pit-N	.313	5	16	4	5	1	0	1	2	0	0	0	C-5
L 1974	Pit-N	.250	4	16	0	4	1	0	0	0	0	0	0	C-4
L 1975	Pit-N	.167	3	12	0	2	0	0	0	0	0	0	0	C-3
L Total	**5**	**.239**	**19**	**71**	**5**	**17**	**2**	**0**	**1**	**3**	**1**	**2**	**1**	**....**
W 1971	Pit-N	.379	7	29	3	11	1	0	0	0	0	3	2	C-7
W 1979	Pit-N	.333	3	3	0	1	0	0	0	1	0	0	0	....
W Total	**2**	**.375**	**10**	**32**	**3**	**12**	**1**	**0**	**0**	**1**	**0**	**3**	**2**	**....**
• SANTANA, Rafael														
L 1986	NY-N	.176	6	17	0	3	0	0	0	0	0	3	0	S-6
W 1986	NY-N	.250	7	20	3	5	0	0	0	2	2	5	0	S-7
• SANTANGELO, F.P.														
D 2001	Oak-A	.333	2	3	0	1	1	0	0	0	0	0	0	2-2
• SANTIAGO, Benito														
D 1995	Cin-N	.333	3	9	2	3	0	0	1	3	3	3	0	C-3
D 2002	SF-N	.238	5	21	1	5	2	0	0	5	1	5	0	C-5
D 2003	SF-N	.182	4	11	0	2	0	0	0	0	1	2	0	C-3
D Total	**3**	**.244**	**12**	**41**	**3**	**10**	**2**	**0**	**1**	**8**	**5**	**10**	**0**	**....**
L 1995	Cin-N	.231	4	13	0	3	0	0	0	0	2	3	0	C-4
L 2002	SF-N	.300	5	20	2	6	0	0	2	6	2	4	0	C-5
L Total	**2**	**.273**	**9**	**33**	**2**	**9**	**0**	**0**	**2**	**6**	**4**	**7**	**0**	**....**
W 2002	SF-N	.231	7	26	2	6	0	0	0	5	3	4	0	C-7
• SANTIAGO, Jose														
W 1967	Bos-A	.500	3	2	1	1	0	0	1	1	0	1	0	....
• SASSER, Mackey														
L 1988	NY-N	.200	4	5	0	1	0	0	0	0	0	1	0	C-2
• SAUER, Ed														
W 1945	Chi-N	.000	2	2	0	0	0	0	0	0	0	2	0	....
• SAUNDERS, Tony														
L 1997	Fla-N	.000	1	2	0	0	0	0	0	0	0	2	0	....
• SAWATSKI, Carl														
W 1957	Mil-N	.000	2	2	0	0	0	0	0	0	0	2	0	....
• SAX, Steve														
D 1981	LA-N	....	1	0	0	0	0	0	0	0	0	0	0	2-1
L 1981	LA-N	....	1	0	0	0	0	0	0	0	0	0	0	2-1
L 1983	LA-N	.250	4	16	0	4	0	0	0	0	1	0	1	2-4
L 1985	LA-N	.300	6	20	1	6	3	0	0	1	1	5	0	2-6
L 1988	LA-N	.267	7	30	7	8	0	0	0	3	3	3	5	2-7
L Total	**4**	**.273**	**18**	**66**	**8**	**18**	**3**	**0**	**0**	**4**	**5**	**8**	**6**	**....**
W 1981	LA-N	.000	2	1	0	0	0	0	0	0	0	0	0	2-1
W 1988	LA-N	.300	5	20	3	6	0	0	0	0	1	1	1	2-5
W Total	**2**	**.286**	**7**	**21**	**3**	**6**	**0**	**0**	**0**	**0**	**1**	**1**	**1**	**....**
• SCHAEFER, Germany														
W 1907	Det-A	.143	5	21	1	3	0	0	0	0	0	3	0	2-5
W 1908	Det-A	.125	5	16	0	2	0	0	0	0	1	4	1	2-3,3-2
W Total	**2**	**.135**	**10**	**37**	**1**	**5**	**0**	**0**	**0**	**0**	**1**	**7**	**1**	**....**
• SCHALK, Ray														
W 1917	Chi-A	.263	6	19	1	5	0	0	0	0	2	1	1	C-6
W 1919	Chi-A	.304	8	23	1	7	0	0	0	2	4	2	1	C-8
W Total	**2**	**.286**	**14**	**42**	**2**	**12**	**0**	**0**	**0**	**2**	**6**	**3**	**2**	**....**
• SCHANG, Wally														
W 1913	Phi-A	.357	4	14	2	5	0	1	1	7	2	4	0	C-4
W 1914	Phi-A	.167	4	12	1	2	1	0	0	0	1	4	0	C-4
W 1918	Bos-A	.444	5	9	1	4	0	0	0	1	2	3	1	C-5
W 1921	NY-A	.286	8	21	1	6	1	1	0	1	5	4	0	C-8
W 1922	NY-A	.188	5	16	0	3	1	0	0	0	0	3	0	C-5
W 1923	NY-A	.318	6	22	3	7	1	0	0	0	1	2	0	C-6
W Total	**6**	**.287**	**32**	**94**	**8**	**27**	**4**	**2**	**1**	**9**	**11**	**20**	**1**	**....**
• SCHENZ, Hank														
W 1951	NY-N	....	1	0	0	0	0	0	0	0	0	0	0	....
• SCHMANDT, Ray														
W 1920	Bro-N	.000	1	1	0	0	0	0	0	0	0	0	0	....
• SCHMIDT, Boss														
W 1907	Det-A	.167	4	12	0	2	0	0	0	0	2	1	0	C-3
W 1908	Det-A	.071	4	14	0	1	0	0	0	1	0	2	0	C-4
W 1909	Det-A	.222	6	18	0	4	2	0	0	4	2	0	0	C-6
W Total	**3**	**.159**	**14**	**44**	**0**	**7**	**2**	**0**	**0**	**5**	**4**	**3**	**0**	**....**
• SCHMIDT, Butch														
W 1914	Bos-N	.294	4	17	2	5	0	0	0	2	0	2	1	1-4
• SCHMIDT, Jason														
D 2002	SF-N	.000	1	2	0	0	0	0	0	0	0	1	0	....
D 2003	SF-N	.000	1	3	0	0	0	0	0	0	0	2	0	....
D Total	**2**	**.000**	**2**	**5**	**0**	**0**	**0**	**0**	**0**	**0**	**0**	**3**	**0**	**....**
L 2002	SF-N	.000	1	2	0	0	0	0	0	0	0	2	0	....
W 2002	SF-N	.000	2	1	0	0	0	0	0	0	0	1	0	....
• SCHMIDT, Mike														
D 1981	Phi-N	.250	5	16	3	4	1	0	1	2	4	2	0	3-5
L 1976	Phi-N	.308	3	13	1	4	2	0	0	2	0	2	0	3-3
L 1977	Phi-N	.063	4	16	2	1	0	0	0	1	2	3	0	3-4
L 1978	Phi-N	.200	4	15	1	3	2	0	0	1	2	2	0	3-4
L 1980	Phi-N	.208	5	24	1	5	1	0	0	1	1	6	1	3-5
L 1983	Phi-N	.467	4	15	5	7	2	0	1	2	2	3	0	3-4
L Total	**5**	**.241**	**20**	**83**	**10**	**20**	**7**	**0**	**1**	**7**	**7**	**16**	**1**	**....**
W 1980	Phi-N	.381	6	21	6	8	1	0	2	7	4	3	0	3-6
W 1983	Phi-N	.050	5	20	0	1	0	0	0	0	0	6	0	3-5
W Total	**2**	**.220**	**11**	**41**	**6**	**9**	**1**	**0**	**2**	**7**	**4**	**9**	**0**	**....**
• SCHOENDIENST, Red														
W 1946	StL-N	.233	7	30	3	7	1	0	0	1	0	2	1	2-7
W 1957	Mil-N	.278	5	18	0	5	1	0	0	2	0	1	0	2-5
W 1958	Mil-N	.300	7	30	5	9	3	1	0	0	2	1	0	2-7
W Total	**3**	**.269**	**19**	**78**	**8**	**21**	**5**	**1**	**0**	**3**	**2**	**4**	**1**	**....**
• SCHOENEWEIS, Scott														
W 2002	Ana-A	....	2	0	0	0	0	0	0	0	0	0	0	....
• SCHOFIELD, Dick														
W 1960	Pit-N	.333	3	3	0	1	0	0	0	0	1	0	0	S-2
W 1968	StL-N	....	2	0	0	0	0	0	0	0	0	0	0	S-1
W Total	**2**	**.333**	**5**	**3**	**0**	**1**	**0**	**0**	**0**	**0**	**1**	**0**	**0**	**....**
• SCHOFIELD, Dick														
L 1986	Cal-A	.300	7	30	4	9	1	0	1	2	1	5	1	S-7
• SCHRECKENGOST, Ossee														
W 1905	Phi-A	.222	3	9	2	2	1	0	0	0	0	0	0	C-3
• SCHRIVER, Pop														
T 1900	Pit-N	.000	1	1	0	0	0	0	0	0	0	0	0	
• SCHULTE, Frank														
W 1906	Chi-N	.269	6	26	1	7	3	0	0	3	1	3	0	0-6
W 1907	Chi-N	.250	5	20	3	5	0	0	0	2	1	2	0	0-5
W 1908	Chi-N	.389	5	18	4	7	0	1	0	2	2	1	2	0-5
W 1910	Chi-N	.412	5	17	3	7	3	0	0	2	2	3	0	0-5
W Total	**4**	**.321**	**21**	**81**	**11**	**26**	**6**	**1**	**0**	**9**	**6**	**9**	**2**	**....**
• SCHULTE, Fred														
W 1933	Was-A	.333	5	21	1	7	1	0	1	4	1	1	0	0-5
• SCHUSTER, Bill														
W 1945	Chi-N	.000	2	1	1	0	0	0	0	0	0	0	0	S-1
• SCIOSCIA, Mike														
D 1981	LA-N	.154	4	13	0	2	0	0	0	1	1	2	0	C-4
L 1981	LA-N	.133	5	15	1	2	0	0	1	1	2	1	0	C-5
L 1985	LA-N	.250	6	16	2	4	0	0	0	1	4	0	0	C-6
L 1988	LA-N	.364	7	22	3	8	1	0	1	2	1	2	0	C-7
L Total	**3**	**.264**	**18**	**53**	**6**	**14**	**1**	**0**	**2**	**4**	**7**	**3**	**0**	**....**
W 1981	LA-N	.250	3	4	1	1	0	0	0	0	1	0	0	C-3
W 1988	LA-N	.214	4	14	0	3	0	0	0	1	0	2	0	C-4
W Total	**2**	**.222**	**7**	**18**	**1**	**4**	**0**	**0**	**0**	**1**	**1**	**2**	**0**	**....**
• SCOTT, Everett														
W 1915	Bos-A	.056	5	18	0	1	0	0	0	0	0	3	0	S-5
W 1916	Bos-A	.125	5	16	1	2	0	1	0	1	1	1	0	S-5
W 1918	Bos-A	.100	6	20	0	2	0	0	0	1	1	1	0	S-6
W 1922	NY-A	.143	5	14	0	2	0	0	0	1	1	0	0	S-5
W 1923	NY-A	.318	6	22	2	7	0	0	0	3	0	1	0	S-6
W Total	**5**	**.156**	**27**	**90**	**3**	**14**	**0**	**1**	**0**	**6**	**3**	**6**	**0**	**....**
• SCOTT, George														
W 1967	Bos-A	.231	7	26	3	6	1	1	0	0	3	6	0	1-7
• SCOTT, Rodney														
L 1981	Mon-N	.167	5	18	0	3	0	0	0	0	1	3	1	2-5
• SCOTT, Tony														
D 1981	Hou-N	.150	5	20	0	3	0	0	0	2	1	6	0	0-5
• SEANEZ, Rudy														
D 1998	Atl-N	....	1	0	0	0	0	0	0	0	0	0	0	....
D 2001	Atl-N	....	1	0	0	0	0	0	0	0	0	0	0	....
D Total	**2**	**....**	**2**	**0**	**0**	**0**	**0**	**0**	**0**	**0**	**0**	**0**	**0**	**....**
L 1998	Atl-N	....	4	0	0	0	0	0	0	0	0	0	0	....
L 2001	Atl-N	....	2	0	0	0	0	0	0	0	0	0	0	....
L Total	**2**	**....**	**6**	**0**	**0**	**0**	**0**	**0**	**0**	**0**	**0**	**0**	**0**	**....**
• SEBRING, Jimmy														
W 1903	Pit-N	.367	8	30	3	11	0	1	1	3	1	4	0	0-8
• SECORY, Frank														
W 1945	Chi-N	.400	5	5	0	2	0	0	0	0	0	2	0	....
• SEEDS, Bob														
W 1936	NY-A	....	1	0	0	0	0	0	0	0	0	0	0	....

SER-YEAR	TM-L	AVG	G	AB	R	H	2B	3B	HR	RBI	BB	SO	SB	POS
• SEITZER, Kevin														
D 1996	Cle-A	.294	4	17	1	5	1	0	0	4	2	4	1	1-1,D-3
D 1997	Cle-A	.000	1	4	0	0	0	0	0	0	0	0	0	1-1
D Total	**2**	**.238**	**5**	**21**	**1**	**5**	**1**	**0**	**0**	**4**	**2**	**4**	**1**	....
L 1997	Cle-A	.000	4	4	0	0	0	0	0	0	1	2	0	1-3
W 1997	Cle-A	.000	1	1	0	0	0	0	0	0	0	0	0	....
• SELKIRK, George														
W 1936	NY-A	.333	6	24	6	8	0	1	2	3	4	4	0	O-6
W 1937	NY-A	.263	5	19	5	5	1	0	0	6	2	0	0	O-5
W 1938	NY-A	.200	3	10	0	2	0	0	0	1	2	1	0	O-3
W 1939	NY-A	.167	4	12	0	2	1	0	0	0	3	2	0	O-4
W 1941	NY-A	.500	2	2	0	1	0	0	0	0	0	0	0	....
W 1942	NY-A	.000	1	1	0	0	0	0	0	0	0	0	0	....
W Total	**6**	**.265**	**21**	**68**	**11**	**18**	**2**	**1**	**2**	**10**	**11**	**7**	**0**	....
• SEMINICK, Andy														
W 1950	Phi-N	.182	4	11	0	2	0	0	0	0	1	3	0	C-4
• SERVAIS, Scott														
D 1998	Chi-N	.667	1	3	0	2	0	0	0	0	0	0	0	C-1
• SEVEREID, Hank														
W 1925	Was-A	.333	1	3	0	1	0	0	0	0	0	0	0	C-1
W 1926	NY-A	.273	7	22	1	6	1	0	0	1	1	2	0	C-7
W Total	**2**	**.280**	**8**	**25**	**1**	**7**	**1**	**0**	**0**	**1**	**1**	**2**	**0**	....
• SEWELL, Joe														
W 1920	Cle-A	.174	7	23	0	4	0	0	0	0	2	1	0	S-7
W 1932	NY-A	.333	4	15	4	5	1	0	0	3	4	0	0	3-4
W Total	**2**	**.237**	**11**	**38**	**4**	**9**	**1**	**0**	**0**	**3**	**6**	**1**	**0**	....
• SEWELL, Luke														
W 1933	Was-A	.176	5	17	1	3	0	0	0	1	2	0	1	C-5
• SEXSON, Richie														
D 1998	Cle-A	.000	3	2	0	0	0	0	0	0	2	1	0	1-3
D 1999	Cle-A	.167	3	6	1	1	0	0	0	1	1	3	0	O-1,1-1
D Total	**2**	**.125**	**6**	**8**	**1**	**1**	**0**	**0**	**0**	**1**	**3**	**4**	**0**	....
L 1998	Cle-A	.000	3	6	0	0	0	0	0	0	0	3	0	1-3
• SEYBOLD, Socks														
W 1905	Phi-A	.125	5	16	0	2	0	0	0	0	2	3	0	O-5
• SHAFER, Tillie														
W 1912	NY-N	....	3	0	0	0	0	0	0	0	0	0	0	S-3
W 1913	NY-N	.158	5	19	2	3	1	1	0	1	2	3	0	O-5,3-1
W Total	**2**	**.158**	**8**	**19**	**2**	**3**	**1**	**1**	**0**	**1**	**2**	**3**	**0**	....
• SHAMSKY, Art														
L 1969	NY-N	.538	3	13	3	7	0	0	0	1	0	3	0	O-3
W 1969	NY-N	.000	3	6	0	0	0	0	0	0	0	0	0	O-1
• SHANNON, Mike														
W 1964	StL-N	.214	7	28	6	6	0	0	1	2	0	9	1	O-7
W 1967	StL-N	.208	7	24	3	5	1	0	1	2	1	4	0	3-7
W 1968	StL-N	.276	7	29	3	8	1	0	1	4	1	5	0	3-7
W Total	**3**	**.235**	**21**	**81**	**12**	**19**	**2**	**0**	**3**	**8**	**2**	**18**	**1**	....
• SHARPERSON, Mike														
L 1988	LA-N	.000	2	1	0	0	0	0	0	1	1	0	0	3-1,S-1
• SHEAFFER, Danny														
L 1996	StL-N	.000	2	3	0	0	0	0	0	0	0	1	0	C-2
• SHEAN, Dave														
W 1918	Bos-A	.211	6	19	2	4	1	0	0	0	4	3	1	2-6
• SHECKARD, Jimmy														
W 1906	Chi-N	.000	6	21	0	0	0	0	0	1	2	4	1	O-6
W 1907	Chi-N	.238	5	21	0	5	2	0	0	2	0	4	1	O-5
W 1908	Chi-N	.238	5	21	2	5	2	0	0	1	2	3	1	O-5
W 1910	Chi-N	.286	5	14	5	4	2	0	0	1	7	2	1	O-5
W Total	**4**	**.182**	**21**	**77**	**7**	**14**	**6**	**0**	**0**	**5**	**11**	**13**	**4**	....
• SHEEHAN, Jack														
W 1920	Bro-N	.182	3	11	0	2	0	0	0	0	0	1	0	3-3
• SHEETS, Andy														
D 1997	Sea-A	.333	2	3	0	1	0	0	0	0	0	2	0	3-2
D 1998	SD-N	....	2	0	0	0	0	0	0	0	0	0	0	2-1
D Total	**2**	**.333**	**4**	**3**	**0**	**1**	**0**	**0**	**0**	**0**	**0**	**2**	**0**	....
L 1998	SD-N	.000	3	3	0	0	0	0	0	0	0	1	0	S-2
W 1998	SD-N	.000	2	2	0	0	0	0	0	0	0	1	0	S-2
• SHEFFIELD, Gary														
D 1997	Fla-N	.556	3	9	3	5	1	0	1	1	5	0	1	O-3
D 2002	Atl-N	.063	5	16	3	1	0	0	1	1	7	3	0	O-5
D 2003	Atl-N	.143	4	14	0	2	0	0	0	1	2	0	0	O-4
D Total	**3**	**.205**	**12**	**39**	**6**	**8**	**1**	**0**	**2**	**3**	**14**	**3**	**1**	....
L 1997	Fla-N	.235	6	17	6	4	0	0	1	1	7	3	0	O-6
W 1997	Fla-N	.292	7	24	4	7	1	0	1	5	8	5	0	O-7
• SHELBY, John														
L 1983	Bal-A	.222	3	9	1	2	0	0	0	0	1	3	1	O-3
L 1988	LA-N	.167	7	24	3	4	0	0	0	3	5	12	2	O-7
L Total	**2**	**.182**	**10**	**33**	**4**	**6**	**0**	**0**	**0**	**3**	**6**	**15**	**3**	....
W 1983	Bal-A	.444	5	9	1	4	0	0	0	1	0	4	0	O-5
W 1988	LA-N	.222	5	18	0	4	1	0	0	1	2	7	1	O-5
W Total	**2**	**.296**	**10**	**27**	**1**	**8**	**1**	**0**	**0**	**2**	**2**	**11**	**1**	....
• SHERIDAN, Pat														
L 1984	KC-A	.000	3	6	1	0	0	0	0	0	3	3	0	O-3
L 1985	KC-A	.150	7	20	4	3	0	0	2	3	2	3	0	O-7
L 1987	Det-A	.300	5	10	2	3	1	0	1	2	0	2	1	O-4

SER-YEAR	TM-L	AVG	G	AB	R	H	2B	3B	HR	RBI	BB	SO	SB	POS
L 1989	SF-N	.154	5	13	1	2	0	1	0	0	0	4	0	O-5
L Total	**4**	**.163**	**20**	**49**	**8**	**8**	**1**	**1**	**3**	**5**	**5**	**12**	**1**	....
W 1985	KC-A	.222	5	18	0	4	2	0	0	1	0	7	0	O-4
W 1989	SF-N	.000	1	2	0	0	0	0	0	0	0	0	0	O-1
W Total	**2**	**.200**	**6**	**20**	**0**	**4**	**2**	**0**	**0**	**1**	**0**	**7**	**0**	....
• SHIELDS, Scot														
W 2002	Ana-A	....	1	0	0	0	0	0	0	0	0	0	0	....
• SHINJO, Tsuyoshi														
L 2002	SF-N	.000	1	1	0	0	0	0	0	0	0	0	0	O-1
W 2002	SF-N	.167	3	6	1	1	0	0	0	0	0	3	0	O-1,D-2
• SHINNICK, Tim														
W 1890	Lou-A	.292	7	24	3	7	1	1	0	3	2	2	2	2-7
• SHIRLEY, Mule														
W 1924	Was-A	.500	3	2	1	1	0	0	0	1	0	0	0	....
• SHOPAY, Tom														
W 1971	Bal-A	.000	5	4	0	0	0	0	0	0	0	0	0	....
• SHORTEN, Chick														
W 1916	Bos-A	.571	2	7	0	4	0	0	0	2	0	1	0	O-2
• SHUBA, George														
W 1952	Bro-N	.300	4	10	0	3	1	0	0	0	0	4	0	O-3
W 1953	Bro-N	1.000	2	1	1	1	0	0	1	2	0	0	0	....
W 1955	Bro-N	.000	1	1	0	0	0	0	0	0	0	0	0	....
W Total	**3**	**.333**	**7**	**12**	**1**	**4**	**1**	**0**	**1**	**2**	**0**	**4**	**0**	....
• SIEBERN, Norm														
W 1956	NY-A	.000	1	1	0	0	0	0	0	0	0	0	0	....
W 1958	NY-A	.125	3	8	1	1	0	0	0	0	3	2	0	O-3
W 1967	Bos-A	.333	3	3	0	1	0	0	0	1	0	0	0	O-1
W Total	**3**	**.167**	**7**	**12**	**1**	**2**	**0**	**0**	**0**	**1**	**3**	**2**	**0**	....
• SIERRA, Ruben														
D 1995	NY-A	.174	5	23	2	4	2	0	2	5	2	7	0	D-5
D 2003	NY-A	.000	1	2	0	0	0	0	0	0	0	0	0	O-1
D Total	**2**	**.160**	**6**	**25**	**2**	**4**	**2**	**0**	**2**	**5**	**2**	**7**	**0**	....
L 1992	Oak-A	.333	6	24	4	8	2	1	1	7	2	1	1	O-6
L 2003	NY-A	.500	3	2	1	1	0	0	1	1	1	0	0	O-1
L Total	**2**	**.346**	**9**	**26**	**5**	**9**	**2**	**1**	**2**	**8**	**3**	**1**	**1**	....
W 2003	NY-A	.250	5	4	0	1	0	1	0	2	1	3	0	O-1
• SILVERA, Charlie														
W 1949	NY-A	.000	1	2	0	0	0	0	0	0	0	0	0	C-1
• SILVESTRI, Ken														
W 1950	Phi-N	....	1	0	0	0	0	0	0	0	0	0	0	C-1
• SIMMONS, Al														
W 1929	Phi-A	.300	5	20	6	6	1	0	2	5	1	4	0	O-5
W 1930	Phi-A	.364	6	22	4	8	2	0	2	4	2	2	0	O-7
W 1931	Phi-A	.333	7	27	4	9	2	0	2	8	3	3	0	O-7
W 1939	Cin-N	.250	1	4	1	1	1	0	0	0	0	0	0	O-1
W Total	**4**	**.329**	**19**	**73**	**15**	**24**	**6**	**0**	**6**	**17**	**6**	**9**	**0**	....
• SIMMONS, Ted														
D 1981	Mil-A	.222	5	18	1	4	1	0	1	4	2	2	0	C-5
L 1982	Mil-A	.167	5	18	3	3	0	0	0	1	1	4	0	C-5
W 1982	Mil-A	.174	7	23	2	4	0	0	2	3	5	3	0	C-7
• SIMMS, Mike														
D 1998	Tex-A	.200	2	5	0	1	0	0	0	0	0	2	0	D-2
• SIMON, Randall														
D 2003	Chi-N	.429	4	7	1	3	1	0	0	2	0	2	0	1-3
L 2003	Chi-N	.294	6	17	3	5	2	0	1	4	0	3	0	1-5
• SIMPSON, Harry														
W 1957	NY-A	.083	5	12	0	1	0	0	0	1	0	4	0	1-4
• SIMS, Duke														
L 1972	Det-A	.214	4	14	0	3	2	1	0	0	1	2	0	O-2,C-2
• SINGLETON, Chris														
D 2000	Chi-A	.111	3	9	1	1	0	1	0	1	0	2	0	O-3
D 2003	Oak-A	.286	2	7	2	2	2	0	0	0	1	1	1	O-2
D Total	**2**	**.188**	**5**	**16**	**3**	**3**	**2**	**1**	**0**	**1**	**1**	**3**	**1**	....
• SINGLETON, Ken														
L 1979	Bal-A	.375	4	16	4	6	2	0	0	2	1	2	0	O-4
L 1983	Bal-A	.250	4	12	0	3	2	0	0	1	2	2	0	D-4
L Total	**2**	**.321**	**8**	**28**	**4**	**9**	**4**	**0**	**0**	**3**	**3**	**4**	**0**	....
W 1979	Bal-A	.357	7	28	1	10	1	0	0	2	2	5	0	O-7
W 1983	Bal-A	.000	2	1	0	0	0	0	0	1	1	1	0	....
W Total	**2**	**.345**	**9**	**29**	**1**	**10**	**1**	**0**	**0**	**3**	**3**	**6**	**0**	....
• SISLER, Dick														
W 1946	StL-N	.000	2	2	0	0	0	0	0	0	0	0	0	....
W 1950	Phi-N	.059	4	17	0	1	0	0	0	1	0	5	0	O-4
W Total	**2**	**.053**	**6**	**19**	**0**	**1**	**0**	**0**	**0**	**1**	**0**	**5**	**0**	....
• SISTI, Sibby														
W 1948	Bos-N	.000	2	1	0	0	0	0	0	0	0	0	0	2-1
• SIZEMORE, Ted														
L 1977	Phi-N	.231	4	13	1	3	0	0	0	0	2	0	0	2-4
L 1978	Phi-N	.385	4	13	3	5	0	1	0	1	1	0	0	2-4
L Total	**2**	**.308**	**8**	**26**	**4**	**8**	**0**	**1**	**0**	**1**	**3**	**0**	**0**	....
• SKAGGS, Dave														
L 1979	Bal-A	.000	1	4	0	0	0	0	0	0	0	0	0	C-1
W 1979	Bal-A	.333	1	3	1	1	0	0	0	0	0	0	0	C-1

YEAR	TM-L	AVG	G	AB	R	H	2B	3B	HR	RBI	BB	SO	SB	POS
• SKINNER, Bob														
W 1960	Pit-N	.200	2	5	2	1	0	0	0	1	1	0	1	0-2
W 1964	StL-N	.667	4	3	0	2	1	0	0	1	1	0	0	....
W Total	**2**	**.375**	**6**	**8**	**2**	**3**	**1**	**0**	**0**	**2**	**2**	**0**	**1**	....
• SKOWRON, Bill														
W 1955	NY-A	.333	5	12	2	4	2	0	1	3	0	1	0	1-3
W 1956	NY-A	.100	3	10	1	1	0	0	1	4	0	3	0	1-2
W 1957	NY-A	.000	2	4	0	0	0	0	0	0	0	0	0	1-2
W 1958	NY-A	.259	7	27	3	7	0	0	2	7	1	4	0	1-7
W 1960	NY-A	.375	7	32	7	12	2	0	2	6	0	6	0	1-7
W 1961	NY-A	.353	5	17	3	6	0	0	1	5	3	4	0	1-5
W 1962	NY-A	.222	6	18	1	4	0	1	0	1	1	5	0	1-6
W 1963	LA-N	.385	4	13	2	5	0	0	1	3	1	3	0	1-4
W Total	**8**	**.293**	**39**	**133**	**19**	**39**	**4**	**1**	**8**	**29**	**6**	**26**	**0**	....
• SLAGLE, Jimmy														
W 1907	Chi-N	.273	5	22	3	6	0	0	0	3	2	3	5	0-5
• SLATTERY, Mike														
W 1888	NY-N	.205	10	39	6	8	2	0	0	5	0	5	6	0-10,2-1
W 1889	NY-N	.188	4	16	6	3	0	0	0	1	3	1	1	0-4
W Total	**2**	**.200**	**14**	**55**	**12**	**11**	**2**	**0**	**0**	**6**	**3**	**6**	**7**	....
• SLAUGHT, Don														
L 1984	KC-A	.364	3	11	0	4	0	0	0	0	0	0	0	C-3
L 1990	Pit-N	.091	4	11	0	1	1	0	0	1	2	3	0	C-4
L 1991	Pit-N	.235	6	17	0	4	0	0	0	1	1	4	0	C-6
L 1992	Pit-N	.333	5	12	5	4	1	0	1	5	6	3	0	C-5
L Total	**4**	**.255**	**18**	**51**	**5**	**13**	**2**	**0**	**1**	**7**	**9**	**10**	**0**	....
• SLAUGHTER, Enos														
W 1942	StL-N	.263	5	19	3	5	1	0	1	2	3	2	0	0-5
W 1946	StL-N	.320	7	25	5	8	1	1	1	2	4	3	1	0-7
W 1956	NY-A	.350	6	20	6	7	0	0	1	4	4	0	0	0-6
W 1957	NY-A	.250	5	12	2	3	1	0	0	0	3	2	0	0-5
W 1958	NY-A	.000	4	3	1	0	0	0	0	0	1	1	0	....
W Total	**5**	**.291**	**27**	**79**	**17**	**23**	**3**	**1**	**3**	**8**	**15**	**8**	**1**	....
• SMALLEY, Roy														
W 1987	Min-A	.500	4	2	0	1	1	0	0	0	2	0	0	....
• SMITH, Al														
W 1954	Cle-A	.214	4	14	2	3	0	0	1	2	2	2	0	0-4
W 1959	Chi-A	.250	6	20	1	5	3	0	0	1	4	4	0	0-6
W Total	**2**	**.235**	**10**	**34**	**3**	**8**	**3**	**0**	**1**	**3**	**6**	**6**	**0**	....
• SMITH, Billy														
L 1979	Bal-A	.000	1	4	0	0	0	0	0	0	0	1	0	2-1
W 1979	Bal-A	.286	4	7	1	2	0	0	0	0	2	0	0	2-4
• SMITH, Dwight														
D 1995	Atl-N	.667	4	3	0	2	1	0	0	1	0	0	0	....
L 1989	Chi-N	.200	4	15	2	3	1	0	0	0	2	2	1	0-4
L 1995	Atl-N	.000	2	2	0	0	0	0	0	0	0	0	0	....
L Total	**2**	**.176**	**6**	**17**	**2**	**3**	**1**	**0**	**0**	**0**	**2**	**2**	**1**	....
W 1995	Atl-N	.500	3	2	0	1	0	0	0	0	1	0	0	....
• SMITH, Earl														
W 1921	NY-N	.000	3	7	0	0	0	0	0	0	1	0	0	C-2
W 1922	NY-N	.143	4	7	0	1	0	0	0	0	0	2	0	C-1
W 1925	Pit-N	.350	6	20	0	7	1	0	0	0	1	2	0	C-6
W 1927	Pit-N	.000	3	8	0	0	0	0	0	0	0	0	0	C-2
W 1928	StL-N	.750	1	4	0	3	0	0	0	0	0	0	0	C-1
W Total	**5**	**.239**	**17**	**46**	**0**	**11**	**1**	**0**	**0**	**0**	**2**	**4**	**0**	....
• SMITH, Elmer														
W 1920	Cle-A	.308	5	13	1	4	0	1	1	5	1	1	0	0-5
W 1922	NY-A	.000	2	2	0	0	0	0	0	0	0	2	0	....
W Total	**2**	**.267**	**7**	**15**	**1**	**4**	**0**	**1**	**1**	**5**	**1**	**3**	**0**	....
• SMITH, Germany														
W 1889	Bro-A	.172	8	29	2	5	2	1	0	2	3	2	2	S-8
W 1890	Bro-N	.276	7	29	3	8	0	2	0	7	0	3	1	S-7
W Total	**2**	**.224**	**15**	**58**	**5**	**13**	**2**	**3**	**0**	**9**	**3**	**5**	**3**	....
• SMITH, Hal														
W 1960	Pit-N	.375	3	8	1	3	0	0	1	3	0	0	0	C-3
• SMITH, Harry														
W 1903	Pit-N	.000	1	3	0	0	0	0	0	0	0	0	0	C-1
• SMITH, Jimmy														
W 1919	Cin-N	....	1	0	0	0	0	0	0	0	0	0	0	....
• SMITH, Lonnie														
D 1981	Phi-N	.263	5	19	1	5	1	0	0	0	0	4	0	0-5
L 1980	Phi-N	.600	3	5	2	3	0	0	0	0	0	0	1	0-2
L 1982	StL-N	.273	3	11	1	3	0	0	0	1	0	1	0	0-3
L 1985	KC-A	.250	7	28	2	7	2	0	0	1	3	6	1	0-7
L 1991	Atl-N	.250	7	24	3	6	3	0	0	0	4	5	1	0-7
L 1992	Atl-N	.333	6	6	1	2	0	1	0	1	0	0	0	....
L Total	**5**	**.284**	**26**	**74**	**9**	**21**	**5**	**1**	**0**	**3**	**7**	**12**	**3**	....
W 1980	Phi-N	.263	6	19	2	5	1	0	0	1	1	1	0	0-5,D-1
W 1982	StL-N	.321	7	28	6	9	4	1	0	1	1	5	2	0-6,D-1
W 1985	KC-A	.333	7	27	4	9	3	0	0	4	3	8	2	0-7
W 1991	Atl-N	.231	7	26	5	6	0	0	3	3	3	4	1	0-3,D-4
W 1992	Atl-N	.167	5	12	1	2	0	0	1	5	1	4	0	D-3
W Total	**5**	**.277**	**32**	**112**	**18**	**31**	**8**	**1**	**4**	**14**	**9**	**22**	**5**	....
• SMITH, Ozzie														
D 1996	StL-N	.333	2	3	1	1	0	0	0	0	2	0	0	S-1
L 1982	StL-N	.556	3	9	0	5	0	0	0	3	3	0	1	S-3
L 1985	StL-N	.435	6	23	4	10	1	1	1	3	3	1	1	S-6
L 1987	StL-N	.200	7	25	2	5	0	1	0	1	3	4	0	S-7
L 1996	StL-N	.000	3	9	0	0	0	0	0	0	0	1	0	S-2
L Total	**4**	**.303**	**19**	**66**	**6**	**20**	**1**	**2**	**1**	**7**	**9**	**6**	**2**	....
W 1982	StL-N	.208	7	24	3	5	0	0	0	1	3	0	1	S-7
W 1985	StL-N	.087	7	23	1	2	0	0	0	0	4	0	1	S-7
W 1987	StL-N	.214	7	28	3	6	0	0	0	2	2	3	2	S-7
W Total	**3**	**.173**	**21**	**75**	**7**	**13**	**0**	**0**	**0**	**3**	**9**	**3**	**4**	....
• SMITH, Reggie														
D 1981	LA-N	.000	2	1	0	0	0	0	0	1	0	1	0	....
L 1977	LA-N	.188	4	16	2	3	0	1	0	1	2	5	1	0-4
L 1978	LA-N	.188	4	16	2	3	1	0	0	1	0	2	0	0-4
L 1981	LA-N	1.000	1	1	0	1	0	0	0	1	0	0	0	....
L Total	**3**	**.212**	**9**	**33**	**4**	**7**	**1**	**1**	**0**	**3**	**2**	**7**	**1**	....
W 1967	Bos-A	.250	7	24	3	6	1	0	2	3	2	2	0	0-7
W 1977	LA-N	.273	6	22	7	6	1	0	3	5	4	3	0	0-6
W 1978	LA-N	.200	6	25	3	5	0	0	1	5	2	6	0	0-6
W 1981	LA-N	.500	2	2	0	1	0	0	0	0	0	1	0	....
W Total	**4**	**.247**	**21**	**73**	**13**	**18**	**2**	**0**	**6**	**13**	**8**	**12**	**0**	....
• SNIDER, Duke														
W 1949	Bro-N	.143	5	21	2	3	1	0	0	0	0	8	0	0-5
W 1952	Bro-N	.345	7	29	5	10	2	0	4	8	1	5	1	0-7
W 1953	Bro-N	.320	6	25	3	8	3	0	1	5	2	6	0	0-6
W 1955	Bro-N	.320	7	25	5	8	1	0	4	7	2	6	0	0-7
W 1956	Bro-N	.304	7	23	5	7	1	0	1	4	6	8	0	0-7
W 1959	LA-N	.200	4	10	1	2	0	0	1	2	2	0	0	0-3
W Total	**6**	**.286**	**36**	**133**	**21**	**38**	**8**	**0**	**11**	**26**	**13**	**33**	**1**	....
• SNODGRASS, Fred														
W 1911	NY-N	.105	6	19	1	2	0	0	0	1	2	7	0	0-6
W 1912	NY-N	.212	8	33	2	7	2	0	0	2	2	5	0	0-8
W 1913	NY-N	.333	2	3	0	1	0	0	0	0	0	0	0	0-1,1-1
W Total	**3**	**.182**	**16**	**55**	**3**	**10**	**2**	**0**	**0**	**3**	**4**	**12**	**0**	....
• SNOW, J.T.														
D 1997	SF-N	.167	3	6	0	1	0	0	0	0	1	1	0	1-3
D 2000	SF-N	.400	4	10	1	4	0	0	1	3	4	1	0	1-4
D 2002	SF-N	.316	5	19	3	6	2	0	1	3	1	5	0	1-5
D 2003	SF-N	.313	4	16	0	5	0	0	0	3	0	3	0	1-4
D Total	**4**	**.314**	**16**	**51**	**4**	**16**	**2**	**0**	**2**	**9**	**6**	**10**	**0**	....
L 2002	SF-N	.250	5	20	1	5	1	1	0	2	1	4	0	1-5
W 2002	SF-N	.407	7	27	6	11	1	0	1	4	2	1	0	1-7
• SNYDER, Frank														
W 1921	NY-N	.364	7	22	4	8	1	0	1	3	0	2	0	C-6
W 1922	NY-N	.333	4	15	1	5	0	0	0	0	0	1	0	C-4
W 1923	NY-N	.118	5	17	1	2	0	0	1	2	0	2	0	C-5
W 1924	NY-N	.000	1	1	0	0	0	0	0	0	0	0	0	....
W Total	**4**	**.273**	**17**	**55**	**6**	**15**	**1**	**0**	**2**	**5**	**0**	**5**	**0**	....
• SNYDER, Russ														
W 1966	Bal-A	.167	3	6	1	1	0	0	0	1	2	0	0	0-3
• SODERHOLM, Eric														
L 1980	NY-A	.167	2	6	0	1	0	0	0	0	0	0	0	D-2
• SOJO, Luis														
D 1995	Sea-A	.250	5	20	0	5	0	0	0	3	0	3	0	S-5
D 1996	NY-A	....	2	0	0	0	0	0	0	0	0	0	0	2-2
D 2000	NY-A	.188	5	16	2	3	2	0	0	5	2	1	0	2-5
D Total	**3**	**.222**	**12**	**36**	**2**	**8**	**2**	**0**	**0**	**8**	**2**	**4**	**0**	....
L 1995	Sea-A	.250	6	20	0	5	2	0	0	1	0	2	0	S-6
L 1996	NY-A	.200	3	5	0	1	0	0	0	0	0	1	0	2-3
L 1998	NY-A	....	1	0	0	0	0	0	0	0	0	0	0	1-1
L 1999	NY-A	.000	2	1	0	0	0	0	0	0	0	0	0	2-2
L 2000	NY-A	.261	6	23	1	6	1	0	0	2	2	3	0	2-6,3-1
L 2001	NY-A	.000	1	1	0	0	0	0	0	0	0	0	0	1-1
L Total	**6**	**.240**	**19**	**50**	**1**	**12**	**3**	**0**	**0**	**3**	**2**	**6**	**0**	....
W 1996	NY-A	.600	5	5	0	3	1	0	0	1	0	0	0	2-3
W 1999	NY-A	....	1	0	0	0	0	0	0	0	0	0	0	2-1
W 2000	NY-A	.286	4	7	0	2	0	0	0	2	1	0	1	2-2,3-2
W 2001	NY-A	.333	2	3	0	1	0	0	0	1	0	0	0	1-1
W Total	**4**	**.400**	**12**	**15**	**0**	**6**	**1**	**0**	**0**	**4**	**1**	**0**	**1**	....
• SORIANO, Alfonso														
D 2001	NY-A	.222	5	18	2	4	0	0	0	3	1	5	2	2-5
D 2002	NY-A	.118	4	17	2	2	1	0	1	2	1	4	1	2-4
D 2003	NY-A	.368	4	19	2	7	1	0	0	4	0	6	2	2-4
D Total	**3**	**.241**	**13**	**54**	**6**	**13**	**2**	**0**	**1**	**9**	**2**	**15**	**5**	....
L 2001	NY-A	.400	5	15	5	6	0	0	1	2	3	3	2	2-5
L 2003	NY-A	.133	7	30	0	4	1	0	0	3	1	11	2	2-7
L Total	**2**	**.222**	**12**	**45**	**5**	**10**	**1**	**0**	**1**	**5**	**4**	**14**	**4**	....
W 2001	NY-A	.240	7	25	1	6	0	0	1	2	0	7	0	2-7
W 2003	NY-A	.227	6	22	2	5	0	0	1	2	2	9	1	0-1,2-5
W Total	**2**	**.234**	**13**	**47**	**3**	**11**	**0**	**0**	**2**	**4**	**2**	**16**	**1**	....
• SORRENTO, Paul														
D 1995	Cle-A	.300	3	10	2	3	0	0	0	1	2	3	0	1-3
D 1997	Sea-A	.300	4	10	2	3	1	0	1	1	2	3	0	1-4
D Total	**2**	**.300**	**7**	**20**	**4**	**6**	**1**	**0**	**1**	**2**	**4**	**6**	**0**	....
L 1991	Min-A	.000	1	1	0	0	0	0	0	0	0	1	0	....
L 1995	Cle-A	.154	4	13	2	2	1	0	0	0	2	3	0	1-4
L Total	**2**	**.143**	**5**	**14**	**2**	**2**	**1**	**0**	**0**	**0**	**2**	**4**	**0**	....
W 1991	Min-A	.000	3	2	0	0	0	0	0	0	1	2	0	1-1
W 1995	Cle-A	.182	6	11	0	2	1	0	0	0	0	4	0	1-3
W Total	**2**	**.154**	**9**	**13**	**0**	**2**	**1**	**0**	**0**	**0**	**1**	**6**	**0**	....
• SOSA, Sammy														
D 1998	Chi-N	.182	3	11	0	2	1	0	0	0	1	4	0	0-3

SER-YEAR	TM-L	AVG	G	AB	R	H	2B	3B	HR	RBI	BB	SO	SB	POS
D 2003	Chi-N	.188	5	16	1	3	1	0	0	1	6	4	1	O-5
D Total	2	.185	8	27	1	5	2	0	0	1	7	8	1	....
L 2003	Chi-N	.308	7	26	7	8	1	0	2	6	6	9	0	O-7
• SOUTHWORTH, Billy														
W 1924	NY-N	.000	5	1	1	0	0	0	0	0	0	0	0	O-2
W 1926	StL-N	.345	7	29	6	10	1	1	1	4	0	0	1	O-7
W Total	2	.333	12	30	7	10	1	1	1	4	0	0	1	....
• SPEAKER, Tris														
W 1912	Bos-A	.300	8	30	4	9	1	2	0	2	4	2	1	O-8
W 1915	Bos-A	.294	5	17	2	5	0	1	0	0	4	1	0	O-5
W 1920	Cle-A	.320	7	25	6	8	2	1	0	1	3	1	0	O-7
W Total	3	.306	20	72	12	22	3	4	0	3	11	4	1	....
• SPEIER, Chris														
D 1981	Mon-N	.400	5	15	4	6	2	0	0	3	4	2	0	S-5
L 1971	SF-N	.357	4	14	4	5	1	0	1	1	1	1	0	S-4
L 1981	Mon-N	.188	5	16	0	3	0	0	0	0	2	0	0	S-5
L 1987	SF-N	.000	3	5	0	0	0	0	0	0	0	2	0	2-1
L Total	3	.229	12	35	4	8	1	0	1	1	3	3	0	....
• SPENCER, Jim														
D 1981	Oak-A	.250	1	4	0	1	1	0	0	0	0	0	0	1-1
L 1980	NY-A	.000	1	1	0	0	0	0	0	0	0	0	0	....
L 1981	Oak-A	.000	2	3	0	0	0	0	0	0	0	0	0	1-2
L Total	2	.000	3	4	0	0	0	0	0	0	0	0	0	....
W 1978	NY-A	.167	4	12	3	2	0	0	0	0	2	4	0	1-3
• SPENCER, Roy														
W 1927	Pit-N	.000	1	1	0	0	0	0	0	0	0	0	0	C-1
• SPENCER, Shane														
D 1998	NY-A	.500	2	6	3	3	0	0	2	4	0	1	0	O-2
D 2001	NY-A	.250	3	8	1	2	1	0	0	0	1	4	0	O-3
D 2002	NY-A	....	1	0	0	0	0	0	0	0	0	0	0	O-1
D Total	3	.357	6	14	4	5	1	0	2	4	1	5	0	....
L 1998	NY-A	.100	3	10	1	1	0	0	0	0	1	3	0	O-3
L 1999	NY-A	.111	3	9	1	1	0	0	0	0	1	6	0	O-3
L 2001	NY-A	.286	5	7	1	2	1	0	0	0	1	1	1	O-5
L Total	3	.154	11	26	3	4	1	0	0	0	3	10	1	....
W 1998	NY-A	.333	1	3	1	1	1	0	0	0	0	2	0	O-1
W 2001	NY-A	.200	7	20	1	4	0	0	1	2	2	6	0	O-5
W Total	2	.217	8	23	2	5	1	0	1	2	2	8	0	....
• SPIERS, Bill														
D 1997	Hou-N	.000	3	11	1	0	0	0	0	0	1	2	0	3-3
D 1998	Hou-N	.286	4	14	2	4	3	0	0	1	1	3	0	3-4
D 1999	Hou-N	.273	4	11	0	3	0	0	0	1	0	1	1	O-3
D Total	3	.194	11	36	3	7	3	0	0	2	2	6	1	....
• SPIEZIO, Ed														
W 1967	StL-N	.000	1	1	0	0	0	0	0	0	0	0	0	....
W 1968	StL-N	1.000	1	1	0	1	0	0	0	0	0	0	0	....
W Total	2	.500	2	2	0	1	0	0	0	0	0	0	0	....
• SPIEZIO, Scott														
D 2002	Ana-A	.400	4	15	2	6	1	0	1	6	2	1	0	1-4
L 2002	Ana-A	.353	5	17	5	6	2	0	1	5	2	1	1	1-5
W 2002	Ana-A	.261	7	23	3	6	1	1	1	8	6	1	1	1-7
• SPILMAN, Harry														
D 1981	Hou-N	.000	1	1	0	0	0	0	0	0	0	0	0	....
L 1979	Cin-N	.000	2	2	0	0	0	0	0	0	0	0	0	....
L 1987	SF-N	.500	3	2	1	1	0	0	1	1	0	0	0	....
L Total	2	.250	5	4	1	1	0	0	1	1	0	0	0	....
• SPIVEY, Junior														
D 2002	Ari-N	.154	3	13	0	2	0	0	0	0	1	3	0	2-3
• SPRAGUE, Ed														
D 2001	Sea-A	.000	1	1	0	0	0	0	0	0	0	0	0	....
L 1992	Tor-A	.500	2	2	0	1	0	0	0	0	0	1	0	....
L 1993	Tor-A	.286	6	21	0	6	0	1	0	4	2	4	0	3-6
L Total	2	.304	8	23	0	7	0	1	0	4	2	5	0	....
W 1992	Tor-A	.500	3	2	1	1	0	0	1	2	1	0	0	1-1
W 1993	Tor-A	.067	5	15	0	1	0	0	0	2	1	6	0	1-1,3-4
W Total	2	.118	8	17	1	2	0	0	1	4	2	6	0	....
• SQUIRES, Mike														
L 1983	Chi-A	.000	4	4	0	0	0	0	0	0	0	0	0	1-2
• ST.CLAIRE, Randy														
W 1991	Atl-N	....	1	0	0	0	0	0	0	0	0	0	0	....
• STAHL, Chick														
T 1897	Bos-N	.381	5	21	6	8	1	0	0	6	3	2	2	O-5
W 1903	Bos-A	.303	8	33	6	10	1	3	0	3	1	2	2	O-8
• STAHL, Jake														
W 1912	Bos-A	.281	8	32	3	9	2	0	0	2	0	6	2	1-8
• STAHL, Larry														
L 1973	Cin-N	.500	4	4	1	2	0	0	0	0	0	1	0	....
• STAINBACK, Tuck														
W 1942	NY-A	....	2	0	0	0	0	0	0	0	0	0	0	....
W 1943	NY-A	.176	5	17	0	3	0	0	0	0	0	2	0	O-5
W Total	2	.176	7	17	0	3	0	0	0	0	0	2	0	....
• STAIRS, Matt														
D 1995	Bos-A	.000	1	1	0	0	0	0	0	0	0	1	0	....
D 2000	Oak-A	.111	3	9	0	1	1	0	0	0	0	1	0	O-2
D Total	2	.100	4	10	0	1	1	0	0	0	0	2	0	....

SER-YEAR	TM-L	AVG	G	AB	R	H	2B	3B	HR	RBI	BB	SO	SB	POS
• STANAGE, Oscar														
W 1909	Det-A	.200	2	5	0	1	0	0	0	2	0	2	0	C-2
• STANKY, Eddie														
W 1947	Bro-N	.240	7	25	4	6	1	0	0	2	3	2	0	2-7
W 1948	Bos-N	.286	6	14	0	4	1	0	0	1	7	0	0	2-6
W 1951	NY-N	.136	6	22	3	3	0	0	0	1	3	2	0	2-6
W Total	3	.213	19	61	7	13	2	0	0	4	13	4	0	....
• STANLEY, Fred														
D 1981	Oak-A	.000	3	6	0	0	0	0	0	0	1	1	0	S-3
L 1976	NY-A	.333	5	15	1	5	2	0	0	0	2	0	0	S-5
L 1977	NY-A	....	2	0	0	0	0	0	0	0	0	0	0	S-2
L 1978	NY-A	.200	2	5	0	1	0	0	0	0	0	2	0	2-2
L 1981	Oak-A	.333	2	3	0	1	0	0	0	1	0	1	0	S-2
L Total	4	.304	11	23	1	7	2	0	0	1	2	3	0	....
W 1976	NY-A	.167	4	6	1	1	1	0	0	1	3	1	0	S-4
W 1977	NY-A	....	1	0	0	0	0	0	0	0	0	0	0	S-1
W 1978	NY-A	.200	3	5	0	1	1	0	0	0	1	0	0	2-3
W Total	3	.182	8	11	1	2	2	0	0	1	4	1	0	....
• STANLEY, Mickey														
L 1972	Det-A	.250	3	4	0	1	0	0	0	0	0	0	0	O-3
W 1968	Det-A	.214	7	28	4	6	0	1	0	0	2	4	0	O-4,S-7
• STANLEY, Mike														
D 1995	NY-A	.313	4	16	2	5	0	0	1	3	2	1	0	C-4
D 1997	NY-A	.750	2	4	1	3	1	0	0	1	0	1	0	D-1
D 1998	Bos-A	.267	4	15	1	4	0	0	0	0	2	5	0	D-4
D 1999	Bos-A	.500	5	20	4	10	2	1	0	2	2	3	0	1-5
D Total	4	.400	15	55	8	22	3	1	1	6	6	10	0	....
L 1999	Bos-A	.222	5	18	1	4	0	0	0	1	2	4	0	1-5
• STANTON, Mike														
D 1995	Bos-A	....	1	0	0	0	0	0	0	0	0	0	0	....
D 2000	NY-A	....	3	0	0	0	0	0	0	0	0	0	0	....
D Total	2	....	4	0	0	0	0	0	0	0	0	0	0	....
L 1991	Atl-N	.000	3	1	0	0	0	0	0	0	0	0	0	....
L 1992	Atl-N	1.000	5	1	1	1	1	0	0	1	0	0	0	....
L 1993	Atl-N	....	1	0	0	0	0	0	0	0	0	0	0	....
L 1998	NY-A	....	3	0	0	0	0	0	0	0	0	0	0	....
L Total	4	.500	12	2	1	1	1	0	0	1	0	0	0	....
W 1991	Atl-N	....	5	0	0	0	0	0	0	0	0	0	0	....
W 1992	Atl-N	....	4	0	0	0	0	0	0	0	0	0	0	....
W 2000	NY-A	....	4	0	0	0	0	0	0	0	0	0	0	....
W 2001	NY-A	....	5	0	0	0	0	0	0	0	0	0	0	....
W Total	4	....	18	0	0	0	0	0	0	0	0	0	0	....
• STAPLETON, Dave														
L 1986	Bos-A	.667	4	3	2	2	0	0	0	0	1	0	0	1-4
W 1986	Bos-A	.000	3	1	0	0	0	0	0	0	0	0	0	1-3
• STARGELL, Willie														
L 1970	Pit-N	.500	3	12	0	6	1	0	0	1	1	1	0	O-3
L 1971	Pit-N	.000	4	14	1	0	0	0	0	0	2	6	0	O-4
L 1972	Pit-N	.063	5	16	1	1	1	0	0	1	2	5	0	O-1,1-5
L 1974	Pit-N	.400	4	15	3	6	0	0	2	4	1	2	0	O-4
L 1975	Pit-N	.182	3	11	1	2	1	0	0	0	1	3	0	1-3
L 1979	Pit-N	.455	3	11	2	5	2	0	2	6	3	2	0	1-3
L Total	6	.253	22	79	8	20	5	0	4	12	10	19	0	....
W 1971	Pit-N	.208	7	24	3	5	1	0	0	1	7	9	0	O-7
W 1979	Pit-N	.400	7	30	7	12	4	0	3	7	0	6	0	1-7
W Total	2	.315	14	54	10	17	5	0	3	8	7	15	0	....
• START, Joe														
W 1884	Pro-N	.100	3	10	0	1	0	0	0	1	0	2	0	1-3
• STAUB, Rusty														
L 1973	NY-N	.200	4	15	4	3	0	0	3	5	3	2	0	O-4
W 1973	NY-N	.423	7	26	1	11	2	0	1	6	2	2	0	O-6
• STECHSCHULTE, Gene														
D 2001	StL-N	....	2	0	0	0	0	0	0	0	0	0	0	....
• STEINBACH, Terry														
L 1988	Oak-A	.250	2	4	0	1	0	0	0	0	2	0	0	C-2
L 1989	Oak-A	.200	4	15	0	3	0	0	0	1	1	5	0	C-3,D-1
L 1990	Oak-A	.455	3	11	2	5	0	0	0	1	1	2	0	C-3
L 1992	Oak-A	.292	6	24	1	7	0	0	1	5	2	7	0	C-6
L Total	4	.296	15	54	3	16	0	0	1	7	6	14	0	....
W 1988	Oak-A	.364	3	11	0	4	1	0	0	0	0	2	0	C-2,D-1
W 1989	Oak-A	.250	4	16	3	4	0	1	1	7	2	1	0	C-4
W 1990	Oak-A	.125	3	8	0	1	0	0	0	0	0	1	0	C-3
W Total	3	.257	10	35	3	9	1	1	1	7	2	4	0	....
• STEINFELDT, Harry														
W 1906	Chi-N	.250	6	20	2	5	1	0	0	2	1	0	0	3-6
W 1907	Chi-N	.471	5	17	2	8	1	1	0	2	1	2	1	3-5
W 1908	Chi-N	.250	5	16	3	4	0	0	0	3	2	5	1	3-5
W 1910	Chi-N	.100	5	20	0	2	1	0	0	1	0	4	0	3-5
W Total	4	.260	21	73	7	19	3	1	0	8	4	11	2	....
• STENGEL, Casey														
W 1916	Bro-N	.364	4	11	2	4	0	0	0	0	0	1	0	O-3
W 1922	NY-N	.400	2	5	0	2	0	0	0	0	0	1	0	O-2
W 1923	NY-N	.417	6	12	3	5	0	0	2	4	4	0	0	O-6
W Total	3	.393	12	28	5	11	0	0	2	4	4	2	0	....
• STENNETT, Rennie														
L 1972	Pit-N	.286	5	21	2	6	0	0	0	1	1	0	0	O-5,2-1
L 1974	Pit-N	.063	4	16	1	1	0	0	0	0	1	1	0	2-4
L 1975	Pit-N	.214	3	14	0	3	0	0	0	0	0	1	0	2-3,S-1

YEAR	TM-L	AVG	G	AB	R	H	2B	3B	HR	RBI	BB	SO	SB	POS
L 1979	Pit-N	....	1	0	0	0	0	0	0	0	0	0	0	2-1
L Total	4	.196	13	51	3	10	0	0	0	1	2	2	0	....
W 1979	Pit-N	1.000	1	1	0	1	0	0	0	0	0	0	0	....
• STENZEL, Jake														
T 1897	Bal-N	.381	5	21	7	8	1	1	0	3	2	0	2	0-5
• STEPHENS, Vern														
W 1944	StL-A	.227	6	22	2	5	1	0	0	0	3	3	0	S-6
• STEPHENSON, Riggs														
W 1929	Chi-N	.316	5	19	3	6	1	0	0	3	2	2	0	0-5
W 1932	Chi-N	.444	4	18	2	8	1	0	0	4	0	0	0	0-4
W Total	2	.378	9	37	5	14	2	0	0	7	2	2	0	....
• STEPHENSON, Walter														
W 1935	Chi-N	.000	1	1	0	0	0	0	0	0	0	1	0	....
• STEVENS, Lee														
D 1998	Tex-A	.000	1	3	0	0	0	0	0	0	0	1	0	D-1
D 1999	Tex-A	.111	3	9	0	1	1	0	0	0	1	2	0	1-3
D Total	2	.083	4	12	0	1	1	0	0	0	1	3	0	....
• STEWART, Jimmy														
L 1970	Cin-N	.000	1	2	0	0	0	0	0	0	0	0	0	0-1
W 1970	Cin-N	.000	2	2	0	0	0	0	0	0	0	1	0	....
• STEWART, Shannon														
D 2003	Min-A	.400	4	15	0	6	2	0	0	0	2	4	1	0-4
• STINNETT, Kelly														
D 1999	Ari-N	.143	4	14	1	2	1	0	0	0	1	4	0	C-4
• STINSON, Bob														
L 1976	KC-A	.000	2	1	0	0	0	0	0	0	0	0	0	C-1
• STIRNWEISS, Snuffy														
W 1943	NY-A	.000	1	1	1	0	0	0	0	0	0	0	0	....
W 1947	NY-A	.259	7	27	3	7	0	1	0	3	8	8	0	2-7
W 1949	NY-A	....	1	0	0	0	0	0	0	0	0	0	0	....
W Total	3	.250	9	28	4	7	0	1	0	3	8	8	0	....
• STOCK, Milt														
W 1915	Phi-N	.118	5	17	1	2	1	0	0	0	1	0	0	3-5
• STOCKER, Kevin														
L 1993	Phi-N	.182	6	22	0	4	1	0	0	1	2	5	0	S-6
W 1993	Phi-N	.211	6	19	1	4	1	0	0	1	5	5	0	S-6
• STRANG, Sammy														
W 1905	NY-N	.000	1	1	0	0	0	0	0	0	0	1	0	....
• STRANGE, Doug														
D 1995	Sea-A	.000	2	4	0	0	0	0	0	1	1	1	0	3-2
L 1995	Sea-A	.000	4	4	0	0	0	0	0	0	0	2	0	3-2
• STRAWBERRY, Darryl														
D 1995	NY-A	.000	2	2	0	0	0	0	0	0	0	1	0	....
D 1996	NY-A	.000	2	5	0	0	0	0	0	0	0	2	0	D-2
D 1999	NY-A	.333	2	6	2	2	0	0	1	3	1	0	0	D-2
D Total	3	.154	6	13	2	2	0	0	1	3	1	3	0	....
L 1986	NY-N	.227	6	22	4	5	1	0	2	5	3	12	1	0-6
L 1988	NY-N	.300	7	30	5	9	2	0	1	6	2	5	0	0-7
L 1996	NY-A	.417	4	12	4	5	0	0	3	5	2	2	0	0-4
L 1999	NY-A	.333	3	6	1	2	0	0	1	1	1	2	0	D-3
L Total	4	.300	20	70	14	21	3	0	7	17	8	21	1	....
W 1986	NY-N	.208	7	24	4	5	1	0	1	1	4	6	3	0-7
W 1996	NY-A	.188	5	16	0	3	0	0	0	1	4	6	0	0-5
W 1999	NY-A	.333	2	3	0	1	0	0	0	0	1	2	0	D-1
W Total	3	.209	14	43	4	9	1	0	1	2	9	14	3	....
• STRICKLAND, George														
W 1954	Cle-A	.000	3	9	0	0	0	0	0	0	0	2	0	S-3
• STRUNK, Amos														
W 1910	Phi-A	.278	4	18	2	5	1	1	0	2	2	5	0	0-4
W 1911	Phi-A	....	1	0	0	0	0	0	0	0	0	0	0	....
W 1913	Phi-A	.118	5	17	3	2	0	0	0	0	2	2	0	0-5
W 1914	Phi-A	.286	2	7	0	2	0	0	0	0	0	2	0	0-2
W 1918	Bos-A	.174	6	23	1	4	1	1	0	0	0	5	0	0-6
W Total	5	.200	18	65	6	13	2	2	0	2	4	14	0	....
• STUART, Dick														
W 1960	Pit-N	.150	5	20	0	3	0	0	0	0	0	3	0	1-5
W 1966	LA-N	.000	2	2	0	0	0	0	0	0	0	1	0	....
W Total	2	.136	7	22	0	3	0	0	0	0	0	4	0	....
• STUBBS, Franklin														
L 1988	LA-N	.250	4	8	0	2	0	0	0	0	0	4	0	1-3
W 1988	LA-N	.294	5	17	3	5	2	0	0	2	1	3	0	1-5
• STUPER, John														
L 1982	StL-N	.000	1	1	0	0	0	0	0	0	0	0	0	....
W 1982	StL-N	....	2	0	0	0	0	0	0	0	0	0	0	....
• STURM, Johnny														
W 1941	NY-A	.286	5	21	0	6	0	0	0	2	0	2	1	1-5
• SULLIVAN, Billy														
W 1906	Chi-A	.000	6	21	0	0	0	0	0	0	0	9	0	C-6
• SULLIVAN, Billy														
W 1940	Det-A	.154	5	13	3	2	0	0	0	0	5	2	0	C-4
• SULLIVAN, Jim														
T 1897	Bos-N	.000	1	1	0	0	0	0	0	0	0	0	0	P-1
• SUMMA, Homer														
W 1929	Phi-A	.000	1	1	0	0	0	0	0	0	0	1	0	....

YEAR	TM-L	AVG	G	AB	R	H	2B	3B	HR	RBI	BB	SO	SB	POS
• SUMMERS, Champ														
L 1984	SD-N	.000	2	2	0	0	0	0	0	0	0	1	0	....
W 1984	SD-N	.000	1	1	0	0	0	0	0	0	0	1	0	....
• SUNDAY, Billy														
W 1885	Chi-N	.273	6	22	5	6	2	0	0	1	2	0	0	0-6
• SUNDBERG, Jim														
L 1985	KC-A	.167	7	24	3	4	1	1	1	6	1	7	0	C-7
W 1985	KC-A	.250	7	24	6	6	2	0	0	1	6	4	0	C-7
• SURHOFF, B.J.														
D 1996	Bal-A	.385	4	13	3	5	0	0	3	5	0	1	0	0-3
D 1997	Bal-A	.273	3	11	0	3	1	0	0	2	0	2	0	0-3
D 2000	Atl-N	.500	2	2	0	1	0	0	0	0	0	0	0	....
D 2001	Atl-N	.273	3	11	1	3	1	0	0	0	0	0	1	0-3
D Total	4	.324	12	37	4	12	2	0	3	7	0	3	1	....
L 1996	Bal-A	.267	5	15	0	4	0	0	0	2	1	2	0	0-5
L 1997	Bal-A	.200	6	25	1	5	2	0	0	1	2	2	0	0-6,1-1
L 2001	Atl-N	.231	4	13	1	3	0	0	1	2	0	1	0	0-3
L Total	3	.226	15	53	2	12	2	0	1	5	3	5	0	....
• SUTCLIFFE, Sy														
W 1887	Det-N	.167	4	12	1	2	0	0	0	0	1	1	1	1-3,C-1
• SUZUKI, Ichiro														
D 2001	Sea-A	.600	5	20	4	12	1	0	0	2	1	0	1	0-5
L 2001	Sea-A	.222	5	18	3	4	1	0	0	1	4	4	2	0-5
• SWEENEY, Mark														
D 1996	StL-N	1.000	1	1	0	1	0	0	0	0	0	0	0	....
D 1998	SD-N	.000	2	1	0	0	0	0	0	0	1	0	0	....
D Total	2	.500	3	2	0	1	0	0	0	0	1	0	0	....
L 1996	StL-N	.000	5	4	1	0	0	0	0	0	0	2	0	0-2
L 1998	SD-N	.000	3	2	1	0	0	0	0	0	1	1	0	....
L Total	2	.000	8	6	2	0	0	0	0	0	1	3	0	....
W 1998	SD-N	.667	3	3	0	2	0	0	0	1	0	0	0	....
• SWIFT, Bob														
W 1945	Det-A	.250	3	4	1	1	0	0	0	0	2	0	0	C-3
• SWOBODA, Ron														
W 1969	NY-N	.400	4	15	1	6	1	0	0	1	1	3	0	0-4
• TABLER, Pat														
L 1991	Tor-A	.000	2	1	0	0	0	0	0	0	1	0	0	D-2
W 1992	Tor-A	.000	2	2	0	0	0	0	0	0	0	0	0	....
• TANNEHILL, Lee														
W 1906	Chi-A	.111	3	9	1	1	0	0	0	0	0	2	0	S-3
• TARASCO, Tony														
L 1993	Atl-N	.000	2	1	0	0	0	0	0	0	0	1	0	0-2
L 1996	Bal-A	.000	2	1	0	0	0	0	0	0	0	1	0	0-2
L Total	2	.000	4	2	0	0	0	0	0	0	0	2	0	....
• TARTABULL, Jose														
W 1967	Bos-A	.154	7	13	1	2	0	0	0	0	1	2	0	0-6
• TATE, Bennie														
W 1924	Was-A	....	3	0	0	0	0	0	0	1	3	0	0	....
• TATIS, Fernando														
L 2000	StL-N	.231	5	13	1	3	2	0	0	2	1	5	0	3-4
• TAUBENSEE, Eddie														
L 1995	Cin-N	.500	2	2	0	1	0	0	0	0	0	0	0	C-1
• TAVERAS, Frank														
L 1974	Pit-N	.000	2	2	0	0	0	0	0	0	0	0	0	S-2
L 1975	Pit-N	.143	3	7	0	1	0	0	0	1	1	2	0	S-3
L Total	2	.111	5	9	0	1	0	0	0	1	1	2	0	....
• TAYLOR, Harry														
W 1890	Lou-A	.300	7	30	6	9	1	0	0	2	2	3	3	1-7
• TAYLOR, Tommy														
W 1924	Was-A	.000	3	2	0	0	0	0	0	0	0	2	0	3-2
• TAYLOR, Tony														
L 1972	Det-A	.133	4	15	0	2	2	0	0	0	0	2	0	2-4
• TAYLOR, Zack														
W 1929	Chi-N	.176	5	17	0	3	0	0	0	3	0	3	0	C-5
• TEBBETTS, Birdie														
W 1940	Det-A	.000	4	11	0	0	0	0	0	0	0	0	0	C-3
• TEBEAU, Patsy														
T 1892	Cle-N	.000	5	18	1	0	0	0	0	0	0	2	1	3-5
T 1895	Cle-N	.286	5	21	3	6	1	0	0	3	1	0	0	1-5
T 1896	Cle-N	.000	1	1	0	0	0	0	0	0	0	0	0	1-1
T Total	3	.150	11	40	4	6	1	0	0	3	1	2	1	....
• TEJADA, Miguel														
D 2000	Oak-A	.350	5	20	5	7	2	0	0	1	2	2	1	S-5
D 2001	Oak-A	.286	5	21	1	6	3	0	0	1	0	3	0	S-5
D 2002	Oak-A	.143	5	21	3	3	1	0	1	4	1	7	0	S-5
D 2003	Oak-A	.087	5	23	0	2	1	0	0	2	0	4	0	S-5
D Total	4	.212	20	85	9	18	7	0	1	8	3	16	1	....
• TEJERA, Michael														
L 2003	Fla-N	....	2	0	0	0	0	0	0	0	0	0	0	....
• TEMPLETON, Garry														
L 1984	SD-N	.333	5	15	2	5	1	0	0	2	2	0	1	S-5
W 1984	SD-N	.316	5	19	1	6	1	0	0	0	0	3	0	S-5
• TENACE, Gene														
L 1971	Oak-A	.000	1	3	0	0	0	0	0	0	1	1	0	C-1

SER-YEAR	TM-L	AVG	G	AB	R	H	2B	3B	HR	RBI	BB	SO	SB	POS
L 1972	Oak-A	.059	5	17	1	1	0	0	0	1	3	5	0	2-2,C-5
L 1973	Oak-A	.235	5	17	3	4	1	0	0	0	2	4	0	1-5,C-3
L 1974	Oak-A	.000	4	11	1	0	0	0	0	1	4	4	1	1-4
L 1975	Oak-A	.000	3	9	0	0	0	0	0	0	3	2	0	1-1,C-3
L Total	5	.088	18	57	5	5	1	0	0	2	13	16	1	....
W 1972	Oak-A	.348	7	23	5	8	1	0	4	9	2	4	0	1-1,C-6
W 1973	Oak-A	.158	7	19	0	3	1	0	0	3	11	7	0	1-7,C-3
W 1974	Oak-A	.222	5	9	0	2	0	0	0	0	3	4	0	1-5
W 1982	StL-N	.000	5	6	0	0	0	0	0	0	1	2	0	D-1
W Total	4	.228	24	57	5	13	2	0	4	12	17	17	0	....
• TENNEY, Fred														
T 1897	Bos-N	.286	5	21	4	6	0	0	0	2	4	1	2	1-5
• TERRY, Bill														
W 1924	NY-N	.429	5	14	3	6	0	1	1	1	3	1	0	1-4
W 1933	NY-N	.273	5	22	3	6	1	0	1	1	0	0	0	1-5
W 1936	NY-N	.240	6	25	1	6	0	0	0	5	1	4	0	1-6
W Total	3	.295	16	61	7	18	1	1	2	7	4	5	0	....
• TETTLETON, Mickey														
D 1996	Tex-A	.083	4	12	1	1	0	0	0	1	5	7	0	D-4
• TEUFEL, Tim														
L 1986	NY-N	.167	2	6	0	1	0	0	0	0	0	0	0	2-2
L 1988	NY-N	.000	1	3	0	0	0	0	0	0	0	1	0	2-1
L Total	2	.111	3	9	0	1	0	0	0	0	0	1	0	....
W 1986	NY-N	.444	3	9	1	4	1	0	1	1	1	2	0	2-3
• THEODORE, George														
W 1973	NY-N	.000	2	2	0	0	0	0	0	0	0	0	0	0-1
• THEVENOW, Tommy														
W 1926	StL-N	.417	7	24	5	10	1	0	1	4	0	1	0	S-7
W 1928	StL-N	....	1	0	0	0	0	0	0	0	0	0	0	S-1
W Total	2	.417	8	24	5	10	1	0	1	4	0	1	0	....
• THOMAS, Derrel														
D 1981	LA-N	.000	4	2	1	0	0	0	0	0	0	1	0	0-4
L 1981	LA-N	1.000	2	1	2	1	0	0	0	0	0	0	0	0-1,3-1
L 1983	LA-N	.444	4	9	0	4	1	0	0	0	0	3	1	0-3
L Total	2	.500	6	10	2	5	1	0	0	0	0	3	1	....
W 1981	LA-N	.000	5	7	2	0	0	0	0	1	1	2	0	0-3,3-2,S-1
• THOMAS, Frank														
D 2000	Chi-A	.000	3	9	0	0	0	0	0	0	4	0	0	1-1,D-2
L 1993	Chi-A	.353	6	17	2	6	0	0	1	3	10	5	0	1-4,D-2
• THOMAS, Fred														
W 1918	Bos-A	.118	6	17	0	2	0	0	0	0	1	2	0	3-6
• THOMAS, George														
W 1967	Bos-A	.000	2	2	0	0	0	0	0	0	0	1	0	0-1
• THOMAS, Gorman														
D 1981	Mil-A	.111	5	18	2	2	0	0	1	1	1	9	0	0-3,D-2
L 1982	Mil-A	.067	5	15	1	1	0	0	1	3	2	7	0	0-5
W 1982	Mil-A	.115	7	26	0	3	0	0	0	3	2	7	0	0-7
• THOMAS, Ira														
W 1908	Det-A	.500	2	4	0	2	1	0	0	1	1	0	0	C-1
W 1910	Phi-A	.250	4	12	2	3	0	0	0	1	4	1	0	C-4
W 1911	Phi-A	.083	4	12	1	1	0	0	0	1	1	2	0	C-4
W Total	3	.214	10	28	3	6	1	0	0	3	6	3	0	....
• THOMAS, Pinch														
W 1915	Bos-A	.200	2	5	0	1	0	0	0	0	0	0	0	C-2
W 1916	Bos-A	.143	3	7	0	1	0	1	0	0	0	1	0	C-2
W 1920	Cle-A	....	1	0	0	0	0	0	0	0	0	0	0	C-1
W Total	3	.167	6	12	0	2	0	1	0	0	0	1	0	....
• THOMASSON, Gary														
L 1978	NY-A	.000	3	1	0	0	0	0	0	0	0	0	0	0-3
W 1978	NY-A	.250	3	4	0	1	0	0	0	0	0	1	0	0-3
• THOME, Jim														
D 1995	Cle-A	.154	3	13	1	2	0	0	1	3	1	6	0	3-3
D 1996	Cle-A	.300	4	10	1	3	0	0	0	0	1	5	0	3-4
D 1997	Cle-A	.200	4	15	1	3	0	0	0	1	0	5	0	1-4
D 1998	Cle-A	.133	4	15	2	2	0	0	2	2	2	5	0	1-3,D-1
D 1999	Cle-A	.353	5	17	7	6	0	0	4	10	4	5	0	1-5
D 2001	Cle-A	.158	5	19	2	3	0	0	1	1	2	8	0	1-5
D Total	6	.213	25	89	14	19	0	0	8	17	10	34	0	....
L 1995	Cle-A	.267	5	15	2	4	0	0	2	5	2	3	0	3-5
L 1997	Cle-A	.071	6	14	3	1	0	0	0	0	5	4	0	1-6
L 1998	Cle-A	.304	6	23	4	7	0	0	4	8	1	8	0	1-4,D-2
L Total	3	.231	17	52	9	12	0	0	6	13	8	15	0	....
W 1995	Cle-A	.211	6	19	1	4	1	0	1	2	2	5	0	3-6
W 1997	Cle-A	.286	7	28	8	8	0	1	2	4	5	7	0	1-7
W Total	2	.255	13	47	9	12	1	1	3	6	7	12	0	....
• THOMPSON, Danny														
L 1970	Min-A	.125	3	8	0	1	1	0	0	0	1	0	0	2-3
• THOMPSON, Don														
W 1953	Bro-N	....	2	0	0	0	0	0	0	0	0	0	0	0-2
• THOMPSON, Hank														
W 1951	NY-N	.143	5	14	3	2	0	0	0	0	5	2	0	0-5
W 1954	NY-N	.364	4	11	6	4	1	0	0	2	7	1	0	3-4
W Total	2	.240	9	25	9	6	1	0	0	2	12	3	0	....
• THOMPSON, Milt														
L 1993	Phi-N	.231	6	13	2	3	1	0	0	0	1	2	0	0-5
W 1993	Phi-N	.313	6	16	3	5	1	1	1	6	1	2	0	0-6

SER-YEAR	TM-L	AVG	G	AB	R	H	2B	3B	HR	RBI	BB	SO	SB	POS
• THOMPSON, Robby														
L 1987	SF-N	.100	7	20	4	2	0	1	1	2	5	7	2	2-6
L 1989	SF-N	.278	5	18	5	5	0	0	2	3	3	2	0	2-5
L Total	2	.184	12	38	9	7	0	1	3	5	8	9	2	....
W 1989	SF-N	.091	4	11	0	1	0	0	0	2	0	4	0	2-4
• THOMPSON, Sam														
W 1887	Det-N	.393	15	61	8	24	2	0	2	8	3	3	5	0-15
• THOMSON, Bobby														
W 1951	NY-N	.238	6	21	1	5	1	0	0	2	5	0	0	3-6
• THON, Dickie														
D 1981	Hou-N	.182	4	11	0	2	0	0	0	0	1	0	0	S-4
L 1979	Cal-A	....	1	0	1	0	0	0	0	0	0	0	0	S-1
L 1986	Hou-N	.250	6	12	1	3	0	0	1	1	0	1	0	S-6
L Total	2	.250	7	12	2	3	0	0	1	1	0	1	0	....
• THORNTON, Lou														
L 1985	Tor-A	....	2	0	1	0	0	0	0	0	0	0	0	D-1
• THORPE, Jim														
W 1917	NY-N	....	1	0	0	0	0	0	0	0	0	0	0	0-1
• THRONEBERRY, Marv														
W 1958	NY-A	.000	1	1	0	0	0	0	0	0	0	1	0	....
• TIERNAN, Mike														
T 1894	NY-N	.294	4	17	5	5	0	1	0	3	2	2	0	0-4
W 1888	NY-N	.342	10	38	8	13	0	0	1	6	8	2	5	0-10
W 1889	NY-N	.289	9	38	12	11	1	1	1	5	5	3	3	0-9
W Total	2	.316	19	76	20	24	1	1	2	11	13	5	8	....
• TILLMAN, Bob														
L 1969	Atl-N	....	1	0	0	0	0	0	0	0	0	0	0	C-1
• TINKER, Joe														
W 1906	Chi-N	.167	6	18	4	3	0	0	0	1	2	2	3	S-6
W 1907	Chi-N	.154	5	13	4	2	0	0	0	1	3	3	1	S-5
W 1908	Chi-N	.263	5	19	2	5	0	0	1	4	0	2	2	S-5
W 1910	Chi-N	.333	5	18	2	6	2	0	0	0	2	2	1	S-5
W Total	4	.235	21	68	12	16	2	0	1	6	7	9	7	....
• TINSLEY, Lee														
D 1995	Bos-A	.000	1	5	0	0	0	0	0	0	1	2	0	0-1
• TIPTON, Joe														
W 1948	Cle-A	.000	1	1	0	0	0	0	0	0	0	1	0	....
• TODT, Phil														
W 1931	Phi-A	....	1	0	0	0	0	0	0	0	1	0	0	....
• TOLAN, Bobby														
L 1970	Cin-N	.417	3	12	3	5	0	0	1	2	1	1	1	0-3
L 1972	Cin-N	.238	5	21	3	5	1	1	0	4	0	4	0	0-5
L 1976	Phi-N	.000	3	2	0	0	0	0	0	0	1	0	0	0-1,1-1
L Total	3	.286	11	35	6	10	1	1	1	6	2	5	1	....
W 1967	StL-N	.000	3	2	1	0	0	0	0	0	1	1	0	....
W 1968	StL-N	.000	1	1	0	0	0	0	0	0	0	1	0	....
W 1970	Cin-N	.211	5	19	5	4	1	0	1	1	3	2	1	0-5
W 1972	Cin-N	.269	7	26	2	7	1	0	0	6	1	4	5	0-7
W Total	4	.229	16	48	8	11	2	0	1	7	5	8	6	....
• TOLSON, Chick														
W 1929	Chi-N	.000	1	1	0	0	0	0	0	0	0	1	0	....
• TOMNEY, Phil														
W 1890	Lou-A	.200	3	5	1	1	0	0	0	0	3	1	0	S-3
• TOPORCER, Specs														
W 1926	StL-N	....	1	0	0	0	0	0	0	1	0	0	0	....
• TORGESON, Earl														
W 1948	Bos-N	.389	5	18	2	7	3	0	0	1	2	1	1	1-5
W 1959	Chi-A	.000	3	1	1	0	0	0	0	0	1	0	0	1-1
W Total	2	.368	8	19	3	7	3	0	0	1	3	1	1	....
• TORRE, Frank														
W 1957	Mil-N	.300	7	10	2	3	0	0	2	3	2	0	0	1-7
W 1958	Mil-N	.176	7	17	0	3	0	0	0	1	2	0	0	1-5
W Total	2	.222	14	27	2	6	0	0	2	4	4	0	0	....
• TORREALBA, Steve														
D 2001	Atl-N	1.000	1	1	0	1	1	0	0	0	0	0	0	C-1
• TORREALBA, Yorvit														
D 2003	SF-N	.000	2	3	0	0	0	0	0	1	0	0	0	C-2
• TOVAR, Cesar														
L 1969	Min-A	.077	3	13	0	1	0	0	0	0	1	2	1	0-3
L 1970	Min-A	.385	3	13	2	5	0	1	0	1	0	0	0	0-4,2-1
L 1975	Oak-A	.500	2	2	2	1	0	0	0	0	1	0	0	2-1
L Total	3	.250	8	28	4	7	0	1	0	1	2	2	1	....
• TOWNE, Babe														
W 1906	Chi-A	.000	1	1	0	0	0	0	0	0	0	0	0	....
• TRACEWSKI, Dick														
W 1963	LA-N	.154	4	13	1	2	0	0	0	0	1	2	0	2-4
W 1965	LA-N	.118	6	17	0	2	0	0	0	0	1	5	0	2-5
W 1968	Det-A	....	2	0	1	0	0	0	0	0	0	0	0	3-1
W Total	3	.133	12	30	2	4	0	0	0	0	2	7	0	....
• TRAMMELL, Alan														
L 1984	Det-A	.364	3	11	2	4	0	1	1	3	3	1	0	S-3
L 1987	Det-A	.200	5	20	3	4	1	0	0	2	1	2	0	S-5
L Total	2	.258	8	31	5	8	1	1	1	5	4	3	0	....
W 1984	Det-A	.450	5	20	5	9	1	0	2	6	2	2	1	S-5

YEAR	TM-L	AVG	G	AB	R	H	2B	3B	HR	RBI	BB	SO	SB	POS
• TRAMMELL, Bubba														
L 2000	NY-N	.000	3	3	0	0	0	0	0	0	0	2	0	....
W 2000	NY-N	.400	4	5	1	2	0	0	0	3	1	1	0	0-2
• TRAYNOR, Pie														
W 1925	Pit-N	.346	7	26	2	9	0	2	1	4	3	1	1	3-7
W 1927	Pit-N	.200	4	15	1	3	1	0	0	0	0	1	0	3-4
W Total	2	.293	11	41	3	12	1	2	1	4	3	2	1	....
• TREADWAY, Jeff														
L 1991	Atl-N	.333	1	3	0	1	0	0	0	0	0	0	0	2-1
L 1992	Atl-N	.667	3	3	1	2	0	0	0	0	0	1	0	2-1
L Total	2	.500	4	6	1	3	0	0	0	0	0	1	0	....
W 1991	Atl-N	.250	3	4	1	1	0	0	0	0	1	2	0	2-1
W 1992	Atl-N	.000	1	1	0	0	0	0	0	0	0	0	0	....
W Total	2	.200	4	5	1	1	0	0	0	0	1	2	0	....
• TRESH, Tom														
W 1962	NY-A	.321	7	28	5	9	1	0	1	4	1	4	2	0-7
W 1963	NY-A	.200	4	15	1	3	0	0	1	2	1	6	0	0-4
W 1964	NY-A	.273	7	22	4	6	2	0	2	7	6	7	0	0-7
W Total	3	.277	18	65	10	18	3	0	4	13	8	17	2	....
• TRILLO, Manny														
D 1981	Phi-N	.188	5	16	1	3	0	0	0	1	4	0	0	2-5
L 1974	Oak-A	....	1	0	1	0	0	0	0	0	0	0	0	....
L 1980	Phi-N	.381	5	21	1	8	2	1	0	4	0	2	0	2-5
L Total	2	.381	6	21	2	8	2	1	0	4	0	2	0	....
W 1980	Phi-N	.217	6	23	4	5	2	0	0	2	0	0	0	2-6
• TROWBRIDGE, Bob														
W 1957	Mil-N	....	1	0	0	0	0	0	0	0	0	0	0	....
• TROY, Dasher														
W 1884	NY-A	.200	2	5	0	1	0	0	0	1	0	1	0	2-2
• TRUBY, Chris														
D 2001	Hou-N	.000	1	1	0	0	0	0	0	0	0	1	0	....
• TUCKER, Michael														
D 1997	Atl-N	.167	2	6	0	1	0	0	0	1	0	1	0	0-2
D 1998	Atl-N	.250	3	8	1	2	0	0	1	2	2	0	1	0-3
D Total	2	.214	5	14	1	3	0	0	1	3	2	1	1	....
L 1997	Atl-N	.100	5	10	1	1	0	0	1	1	3	4	0	0-4
L 1998	Atl-N	.385	6	13	1	5	1	0	1	5	2	5	0	0-5
L Total	2	.261	11	23	2	6	1	0	2	6	5	9	0	....
• TUCKER, Thurman														
W 1948	Cle-A	.333	1	3	1	1	0	0	0	0	1	0	0	0-1
• TUCKER, Tommy														
T 1892	Bos-N	.261	6	23	2	6	0	0	1	2	0	1	0	1-6
• TURNER, Tom														
W 1944	StL-A	.000	1	1	0	0	0	0	0	0	0	0	0	....
• TWITCHELL, Larry														
W 1887	Det-N	.250	6	20	5	5	1	0	1	3	0	1	1	0-6
• UHLAENDER, Ted														
L 1969	Min-A	.167	2	6	0	1	0	0	0	0	0	0	0	0-2
L 1972	Cin-N	.500	2	2	0	1	0	0	0	0	0	0	0	....
L Total	2	.250	4	8	0	2	0	0	0	0	0	0	0	....
W 1972	Cin-N	.250	4	4	0	1	1	0	0	0	0	1	0	....
• UNSER, Del														
L 1980	Phi-N	.400	5	5	2	2	1	0	0	1	0	2	0	0-2
W 1980	Phi-N	.500	3	6	2	3	2	0	0	2	0	1	0	0-3
• UPSHAW, Willie														
L 1985	Tor-A	.231	7	26	2	6	2	0	0	1	1	4	0	1-7
• URBINA, Ugueth														
D 2003	Fla-N	....	3	0	0	0	0	0	0	0	0	0	0	....
L 2003	Fla-N	....	4	0	0	0	0	0	0	0	0	0	0	....
W 2003	Fla-N	....	2	0	0	0	0	0	0	0	0	0	0	....
• URIBE, Jose														
L 1987	SF-N	.269	7	26	1	7	1	0	0	2	0	4	1	S-7
L 1989	SF-N	.235	5	17	2	4	1	0	0	1	1	5	1	S-5
L Total	2	.256	12	43	3	11	2	0	0	3	1	9	2	....
W 1989	SF-N	.200	3	5	1	1	0	0	0	0	0	0	0	S-3
• VALDESPINO, Sandy														
W 1965	Min-A	.273	5	11	1	3	1	0	0	0	0	1	0	0-2
• VALENTIN, John														
D 1995	Bos-A	.250	3	12	1	3	1	0	1	2	3	1	0	S-3
D 1998	Bos-A	.467	4	15	5	7	1	0	0	0	3	1	0	3-4
D 1999	Bos-A	.318	5	22	6	7	2	0	3	12	0	4	0	3-5
D Total	3	.347	12	49	12	17	4	0	4	14	6	6	0	....
L 1999	Bos-A	.348	5	23	3	8	2	0	1	5	2	4	0	3-5
• VALENTIN, Jose														
D 2000	Chi-A	.300	3	10	2	3	2	0	0	1	2	2	3	S-3
• VAN HALTREN, George														
T 1894	NY-N	.500	4	14	3	7	1	1	0	0	2	2	2	0-4
• VAN SLYKE, Andy														
L 1985	StL-N	.091	5	11	1	1	0	0	0	1	2	1	0	0-5
L 1990	Pit-N	.208	6	24	3	5	1	1	0	3	1	7	1	0-6
L 1991	Pit-N	.160	7	25	3	4	2	0	1	2	5	5	1	0-7
L 1992	Pit-N	.276	7	29	1	8	3	1	0	4	1	5	0	0-7
L Total	4	.202	25	89	8	18	6	2	1	10	9	18	2	....
W 1985	StL-N	.091	6	11	0	1	0	0	0	0	0	5	0	0-6

YEAR	TM-L	AVG	G	AB	R	H	2B	3B	HR	RBI	BB	SO	SB	POS
• VANDER WAL, John														
D 1995	Col-N	.000	4	4	0	0	0	0	0	0	0	2	0	....
D 1998	SD-N	.333	3	3	1	1	0	1	0	2	0	1	0	....
D 2002	NY-A	.000	2	2	0	0	0	0	0	0	0	1	0	0-1
D Total	3	.111	9	9	1	1	0	1	0	2	0	4	0	....
L 1998	SD-N	.429	3	7	1	3	0	0	1	2	0	2	0	0-2
W 1998	SD-N	.400	4	5	0	2	1	0	0	0	0	2	0	0-1
• VARITEK, Jason														
D 1998	Bos-A	.250	1	4	0	1	0	0	0	1	0	1	0	C-1
D 1999	Bos-A	.238	5	21	7	5	3	0	1	3	0	4	0	C-5
D 2003	Bos-A	.286	5	14	4	4	0	0	2	2	2	2	0	C-4
D Total	3	.256	11	39	11	10	3	0	3	6	2	7	0	....
L 1999	Bos-A	.200	5	20	1	4	1	1	1	1	1	4	0	C-5
L 2003	Bos-A	.300	6	20	4	6	2	0	2	3	1	5	0	C-6
L Total	2	.250	11	40	5	10	3	1	3	4	2	9	0	....
• VARSHO, Gary														
L 1991	Pit-N	.500	2	2	0	1	0	0	0	0	0	1	0	....
L 1992	Pit-N	.500	2	2	0	1	0	0	0	0	0	0	0	0-1
L Total	2	.500	4	4	0	2	0	0	0	0	0	1	0	....
• VAUGHAN, Arky														
W 1947	Bro-N	.500	3	2	0	1	1	0	0	0	1	0	0	....
• VAUGHN, Greg														
D 1996	SD-N	.000	3	3	0	0	0	0	0	0	0	1	0	....
D 1998	SD-N	.333	4	15	2	5	1	0	1	1	0	4	0	0-4
D Total	2	.278	7	18	2	5	1	0	1	1	0	5	0	....
L 1998	SD-N	.250	3	8	1	2	0	0	0	0	1	1	0	0-2
W 1998	SD-N	.133	4	15	3	2	0	0	2	4	1	2	0	0-3,D-1
• VAUGHN, Mo														
D 1995	Bos-A	.000	3	14	0	0	0	0	0	0	1	7	0	1-3
D 1998	Bos-A	.412	4	17	3	7	2	0	2	7	1	5	0	1-4
D Total	2	.226	7	31	3	7	2	0	2	7	2	12	0	....
• VAZQUEZ, Ramon														
D 2001	Sea-A	....	1	0	0	0	0	0	0	0	0	0	0	S-1
• VEACH, Bobby														
W 1925	Was-A	.000	2	1	0	0	0	0	0	1	0	0	0	....
• VELARDE, Randy														
D 1995	NY-A	.176	5	17	3	3	0	0	0	1	6	4	0	0-2,2-4,3-2
D 2000	Oak-A	.250	5	20	2	5	1	0	0	3	2	3	1	2-5
D 2001	NY-A	.200	2	5	0	1	0	0	0	0	0	1	0	D-2
D 2002	Oak-A	.600	4	5	1	3	1	0	0	1	0	1	0	1-3,2-1
D Total	4	.255	16	47	6	12	2	0	0	5	8	9	1	....
L 2001	NY-A	.000	1	1	0	0	0	0	0	0	0	0	0	3-1
W 2001	NY-A	.000	1	3	0	0	0	0	0	0	1	1	0	1-1
• VELEZ, Otto														
L 1976	NY-A	.000	1	1	0	0	0	0	0	0	0	0	0	....
W 1976	NY-A	.000	3	3	0	0	0	0	0	0	0	3	0	....
• VENTURA, Robin														
D 1999	NY-N	.214	4	14	1	3	2	0	0	1	4	2	0	3-4
D 2000	NY-N	.143	4	14	1	2	0	0	1	2	4	1	0	1-1,3-4
D 2002	NY-A	.286	4	14	1	4	2	0	0	4	1	2	0	3-4
D Total	3	.214	12	42	3	9	4	0	1	7	9	5	0	....
L 1993	Chi-A	.200	6	20	2	4	0	0	1	5	6	6	0	1-1,3-6
L 1999	NY-N	.120	6	25	2	3	1	0	0	1	2	5	0	3-6
L 2000	NY-N	.214	5	14	4	3	1	0	0	5	6	0	0	3-5
L Total	3	.169	17	59	8	10	2	0	1	11	14	11	0	....
W 2000	NY-N	.150	5	20	1	3	1	0	1	1	1	5	0	3-5
• VERAS, Quilvio														
D 1998	SD-N	.133	4	15	1	2	0	0	0	0	1	6	0	2-4
L 1998	SD-N	.250	6	24	2	6	1	0	0	2	5	7	0	2-6
W 1998	SD-N	.200	4	15	3	3	2	0	0	1	3	4	0	2-4
• VERBAN, Emil														
W 1944	StL-N	.412	6	17	1	7	0	0	0	2	2	0	0	2-6
• VERES, Dave														
D 2000	StL-N	....	2	0	0	0	0	0	0	0	0	0	0	....
D 2001	StL-N	....	2	0	0	0	0	0	0	0	0	0	0	....
D 2003	Chi-N	....	2	0	0	0	0	0	0	0	0	0	0	....
D Total	3	....	6	0	0	0	0	0	0	0	0	0	0	....
L 2000	StL-N	....	3	0	0	0	0	0	0	0	0	0	0	....
L 2002	StL-N	....	2	0	0	0	0	0	0	0	0	0	0	....
L 2003	Chi-N	....	3	0	0	0	0	0	0	0	0	0	0	....
L Total	3	....	8	0	0	0	0	0	0	0	0	0	0	....
• VERSALLES, Zoilo														
W 1965	Min-A	.286	7	28	3	8	1	1	1	4	2	7	1	S-7
• VERYZER, Tom														
L 1984	Chi-N	.000	3	1	0	0	0	0	0	0	0	0	0	3-1,S-2
• VILLONE, Ron														
D 2001	Hou-N	....	1	0	0	0	0	0	0	0	0	0	0	....
• VINA, Fernando														
D 2000	StL-N	.308	3	13	3	4	0	0	1	3	1	1	0	2-3
D 2001	StL-N	.316	5	19	2	6	0	0	1	2	0	1	1	2-5
D 2002	StL-N	.600	3	15	3	9	0	0	0	1	1	0	0	2-3
D Total	3	.404	11	47	8	19	0	0	2	6	2	2	1	....
L 2000	StL-N	.261	5	23	3	6	1	0	0	1	1	4	0	2-5
L 2002	StL-N	.261	5	23	2	6	2	0	0	2	0	0	0	2-5
L Total	2	.261	10	46	5	12	3	0	0	3	1	4	0	....
• VIRDON, Bill														
W 1960	Pit-N	.241	7	29	2	7	3	0	0	5	1	3	1	0-7

SER-YEAR	TM-L	AVG	G	AB	R	H	2B	3B	HR	RBI	BB	SO	SB	POS
• VIRGIL, Ozzie														
L 1983	Phi-N	.000	1	1	0	0	0	0	0	0	0	1	0	....
W 1983	Phi-N	.500	3	2	0	1	0	0	0	1	0	0	0	C-1
• VIRTUE, Jake														
T 1892	Cle-N	.125	6	24	1	3	0	0	0	0	2	5	1	1-6
• VISNER, Joe														
W 1889	Bro-A	.125	5	16	2	2	1	0	0	0	2	3	0	C-3,O-2
• VIZCAINO, Jose														
D 1996	Cle-A	.333	3	12	1	4	2	0	0	1	1	1	0	2-3
D 1997	SF-N	.182	3	11	1	2	1	0	0	0	0	5	0	S-3
D 2000	NY-A	....	1	0	1	0	0	0	0	0	0	0	0	2-1
D 2001	Hou-N	.167	3	6	0	1	0	0	0	0	0	1	0	S-2
D Total	**4**	**.241**	**10**	**29**	**3**	**7**	**3**	**0**	**0**	**1**	**1**	**7**	**0**	**....**
L 2000	NY-A	1.000	4	2	3	2	1	0	0	2	0	0	2	2-2,3-1
W 2000	NY-A	.235	4	17	0	4	0	0	0	1	0	5	0	2-4
• VIZQUEL, Omar														
D 1995	Cle-A	.167	3	12	2	2	1	0	0	4	2	2	1	S-3
D 1996	Cle-A	.429	4	14	4	6	1	0	0	2	3	4	4	S-4
D 1997	Cle-A	.500	5	18	3	9	0	0	0	1	2	1	4	S-5
D 1998	Cle-A	.067	4	15	1	1	0	0	0	0	1	0	0	S-4
D 1999	Cle-A	.238	5	21	3	5	1	1	0	3	2	3	0	S-5
D 2001	Cle-A	.409	5	22	2	9	1	1	0	6	1	1	1	S-5
D Total	**6**	**.314**	**26**	**102**	**15**	**32**	**4**	**2**	**0**	**16**	**11**	**11**	**10**	**....**
L 1995	Cle-A	.087	6	23	2	2	1	0	0	2	5	2	3	S-6
L 1997	Cle-A	.040	6	25	1	1	0	0	0	0	2	10	0	S-6
L 1998	Cle-A	.440	6	25	2	11	0	1	0	0	1	3	4	S-6
L Total	**3**	**.192**	**18**	**73**	**5**	**14**	**1**	**1**	**0**	**2**	**8**	**15**	**7**	**....**
W 1995	Cle-A	.174	6	23	3	4	0	1	0	1	3	5	1	S-6
W 1997	Cle-A	.233	7	30	5	7	2	0	0	1	3	5	5	S-7
W Total	**2**	**.208**	**13**	**53**	**8**	**11**	**2**	**1**	**0**	**2**	**6**	**10**	**6**	**....**
• VUKOVICH, George														
D 1981	Phi-N	.444	5	9	1	4	0	0	1	2	0	3	0	O-3
L 1980	Phi-N	.000	4	3	0	0	0	0	0	0	0	0	0	O-1
• WADDELL, Rube														
T 1900	Pit-N	.200	2	5	0	1	0	0	0	0	0	1	0	P-2
• WAGNER, Hal														
W 1946	Bos-A	.000	5	13	0	0	0	0	0	0	0	1	0	C-5
• WAGNER, Heinie														
W 1912	Bos-A	.167	8	30	1	5	1	0	0	0	3	6	1	S-8
• WAGNER, Honus														
T 1900	Pit-N	.400	4	15	2	6	1	0	0	3	0	1	2	O-4
W 1903	Pit-N	.222	8	27	2	6	1	0	0	3	3	4	3	S-8
W 1909	Pit-N	.333	7	24	4	8	2	1	0	6	4	2	6	S-7
W Total	**2**	**.275**	**15**	**51**	**6**	**14**	**3**	**1**	**0**	**9**	**7**	**6**	**9**	**....**
• WAITKUS, Eddie														
W 1950	Phi-N	.267	4	15	0	4	1	0	0	0	2	0	0	1-4
• WALKER, Dixie														
W 1941	Bro-N	.222	5	18	3	4	2	0	0	0	2	1	0	O-5
W 1947	Bro-N	.222	7	27	1	6	1	0	1	4	3	1	1	O-7
W Total	**2**	**.222**	**12**	**45**	**4**	**10**	**3**	**0**	**1**	**4**	**5**	**2**	**1**	**....**
• WALKER, Gee														
W 1934	Det-A	.333	3	3	0	1	0	0	0	1	0	1	0	....
W 1935	Det-A	.250	3	4	1	1	0	0	0	0	1	0	0	O-1
W Total	**2**	**.286**	**6**	**7**	**1**	**2**	**0**	**0**	**0**	**1**	**1**	**1**	**0**	**....**
• WALKER, Greg														
L 1983	Chi-A	.333	2	3	0	1	0	0	0	0	1	2	0	1-1
• WALKER, Harry														
W 1942	StL-N	.000	1	1	0	0	0	0	0	0	0	1	0	....
W 1943	StL-N	.167	5	18	0	3	1	0	0	0	0	2	0	O-4
W 1946	StL-N	.412	7	17	3	7	2	0	0	6	4	2	0	O-7
W Total	**3**	**.278**	**13**	**36**	**3**	**10**	**3**	**0**	**0**	**6**	**4**	**5**	**0**	**....**
• WALKER, Hub														
W 1945	Det-A	.500	2	2	1	1	1	0	0	0	0	0	0	....
• WALKER, Larry														
D 1995	Col-N	.214	4	14	3	3	0	0	1	3	3	4	1	O-4
• WALKER, Rube														
W 1956	Bro-N	.000	2	2	0	0	0	0	0	0	0	0	0	....
• WALKER, Tilly														
W 1916	Bos-A	.273	3	11	1	3	0	1	0	1	1	2	0	O-3
• WALKER, Todd														
D 2003	Bos-A	.313	5	16	4	5	0	0	3	4	0	1	0	2-5
L 2003	Bos-A	.370	7	27	5	10	1	1	2	2	1	2	0	2-6
• WALLACE, Bobby														
T 1896	Cle-N	.200	3	5	0	1	0	0	0	0	0	0	0	P-1
• WALLACH, Tim														
D 1981	Mon-N	.250	4	4	1	1	1	0	0	0	4	0	0	O-3
D 1995	LA-N	.083	3	12	0	1	0	0	0	0	1	3	0	3-3
D 1996	LA-N	.000	3	11	0	0	0	0	0	0	0	1	0	3-3
D Total	**3**	**.074**	**10**	**27**	**1**	**2**	**1**	**0**	**0**	**0**	**5**	**4**	**0**	**....**
L 1981	Mon-N	.000	1	1	0	0	0	0	0	0	0	0	0	....
• WALLING, Denny														
D 1981	Hou-N	.500	3	6	0	3	0	0	0	1	0	1	0	1-1,3-1
L 1980	Hou-N	.111	3	9	2	1	0	0	0	2	1	0	0	O-2,1-1
L 1986	Hou-N	.158	5	19	1	3	1	0	0	2	0	4	0	3-5
L Total	**2**	**.143**	**8**	**28**	**3**	**4**	**1**	**0**	**0**	**4**	**1**	**4**	**0**	**....**

SER-YEAR	TM-L	AVG	G	AB	R	H	2B	3B	HR	RBI	BB	SO	SB	POS
• WALSH, Jimmy														
W 1914	Phi-A	.333	3	6	0	2	1	0	0	1	3	1	0	O-2
W 1916	Bos-A	.000	1	3	0	0	0	0	0	0	0	0	0	O-1
W Total	**2**	**.222**	**4**	**9**	**0**	**2**	**1**	**0**	**0**	**1**	**3**	**1**	**0**	**....**
• WALTON, Jerome														
D 1995	Cin-N	.000	3	3	0	0	0	0	0	0	1	1	0	O-3
D 1997	Bal-A	.000	2	4	0	0	0	0	0	0	0	2	0	1-2
D Total	**2**	**.000**	**5**	**7**	**0**	**0**	**0**	**0**	**0**	**0**	**1**	**3**	**0**	**....**
L 1989	Chi-N	.364	5	22	4	8	0	0	0	2	2	2	0	O-5
L 1995	Cin-N	.000	2	7	0	0	0	0	0	0	0	2	0	O-2
L 1997	Bal-A	....	1	0	0	0	0	0	0	0	0	0	0	O-1
L Total	**3**	**.276**	**8**	**29**	**4**	**8**	**0**	**0**	**0**	**2**	**2**	**4**	**0**	**....**
• WAMBSGANSS, Bill														
W 1920	Cle-A	.154	7	26	3	4	0	0	0	1	2	1	0	2-7
• WANER, Lloyd														
W 1927	Pit-N	.400	4	15	5	6	1	1	0	0	1	0	0	O-4
• WANER, Paul														
W 1927	Pit-N	.333	4	15	0	5	1	0	0	3	0	1	0	O-4
• WARD, Aaron														
W 1921	NY-A	.231	8	26	1	6	0	0	0	4	2	6	0	2-8
W 1922	NY-A	.154	5	13	3	2	0	0	2	3	3	3	0	2-5
W 1923	NY-A	.417	6	24	4	10	0	0	1	2	1	3	1	2-6
W Total	**3**	**.286**	**19**	**63**	**8**	**18**	**0**	**0**	**3**	**9**	**6**	**12**	**1**	**....**
• WARD, Daryle														
D 1999	Hou-N	.143	3	7	1	1	0	0	1	1	0	2	0	O-2
D 2001	Hou-N	.500	2	2	1	1	0	0	1	2	0	0	0	....
D Total	**2**	**.222**	**5**	**9**	**2**	**2**	**0**	**0**	**2**	**3**	**0**	**2**	**0**	**....**
• WARD, John														
T 1894	NY-N	.294	4	17	1	5	0	0	0	6	0	0	0	2-4
W 1888	NY-N	.379	8	29	4	11	1	0	0	6	1	0	6	S-8
W 1889	NY-N	.417	9	36	10	15	0	1	0	7	5	2	10	S-9
W Total	**2**	**.400**	**17**	**65**	**14**	**26**	**1**	**1**	**0**	**13**	**6**	**2**	**16**	**....**
• WARD, Turner														
D 1999	Ari-N	.500	3	2	2	1	0	0	1	3	1	0	0	....
• WARWICK, Carl														
W 1964	StL-N	.750	5	4	2	3	0	0	0	1	1	0	0	....
• WASDELL, Jimmy														
W 1941	Bro-N	.200	3	5	0	1	1	0	0	2	0	0	0	O-1
• WASHBURN, Jarrod														
W 2002	Ana-A	.000	2	1	0	0	0	0	0	0	0	0	0	....
• WASHINGTON, Claudell														
L 1974	Oak-A	.273	4	11	1	3	1	0	0	0	0	0	0	O-3
L 1975	Oak-A	.250	3	12	1	3	1	0	0	1	0	2	0	O-2,D-1
L 1982	Atl-N	.333	3	9	0	3	0	0	0	0	2	2	0	O-3
L Total	**3**	**.281**	**10**	**32**	**2**	**9**	**2**	**0**	**0**	**1**	**2**	**4**	**0**	**....**
W 1974	Oak-A	.571	5	7	1	4	0	0	0	0	1	1	0	O-5
• WASHINGTON, Herb														
L 1974	Oak-A	....	2	0	0	0	0	0	0	0	0	0	0	D-1
W 1974	Oak-A	....	3	0	0	0	0	0	0	0	0	0	0	....
• WASHINGTON, U L														
D 1981	KC-A	.222	3	9	0	2	0	0	0	0	0	1	0	S-3
L 1980	KC-A	.364	3	11	1	4	1	0	0	1	2	3	0	S-3
L 1984	KC-A	.000	2	1	0	0	0	0	0	0	0	1	0	D-1
L Total	**2**	**.333**	**5**	**12**	**1**	**4**	**1**	**0**	**0**	**1**	**2**	**4**	**0**	**....**
W 1980	KC-A	.273	6	22	1	6	0	0	0	2	0	6	0	S-6
• WATHAN, John														
D 1981	KC-A	.300	3	10	1	3	0	0	0	0	1	1	0	C-3
L 1976	KC-A	....	1	0	0	0	0	0	0	0	0	0	0	C-1
L 1977	KC-A	.000	4	6	0	0	0	0	0	0	0	3	0	1-2,C-1,D-1
L 1978	KC-A	.000	1	3	0	0	0	0	0	0	0	0	0	1-1
L 1980	KC-A	.000	3	6	1	0	0	0	0	0	3	1	0	O-3
L 1984	KC-A	.000	1	1	0	0	0	0	0	0	0	0	0	D-1
L Total	**5**	**.000**	**10**	**16**	**1**	**0**	**0**	**0**	**0**	**0**	**3**	**4**	**0**	**....**
W 1980	KC-A	.286	3	7	1	2	0	0	0	1	2	1	0	O-1,C-2
W 1985	KC-A	.000	2	1	0	0	0	0	0	0	0	1	0	....
W Total	**2**	**.250**	**5**	**8**	**1**	**2**	**0**	**0**	**0**	**1**	**2**	**2**	**0**	**....**
• WATKINS, George														
W 1930	StL-N	.167	4	12	2	2	0	0	1	1	1	3	0	O-4
W 1931	StL-N	.286	5	14	4	4	1	0	1	2	2	1	1	O-5
W Total	**2**	**.231**	**9**	**26**	**6**	**6**	**1**	**0**	**2**	**3**	**3**	**4**	**1**	**....**
• WATSON, Bob														
D 1981	NY-A	.438	5	16	2	7	0	0	0	1	1	1	0	1-5
L 1980	NY-A	.500	3	12	0	6	3	1	0	0	0	0	0	1-3
L 1981	NY-A	.250	3	12	0	3	0	0	0	1	0	1	0	1-3
L Total	**2**	**.375**	**6**	**24**	**0**	**9**	**3**	**1**	**0**	**1**	**0**	**1**	**0**	**....**
W 1981	NY-A	.318	6	22	2	7	1	0	2	7	3	0	0	1-6
• WEATHERLY, Roy														
W 1943	NY-A	.000	1	1	0	0	0	0	0	0	0	0	0	....
• WEAVER, Buck														
W 1917	Chi-A	.333	6	21	3	7	1	0	0	1	0	2	0	S-6
W 1919	Chi-A	.324	8	34	4	11	4	1	0	0	0	2	0	3-8
W Total	**2**	**.327**	**14**	**55**	**7**	**18**	**5**	**1**	**0**	**1**	**0**	**4**	**0**	**....**
• WEAVER, Farmer														
W 1890	Lou-A	.259	7	27	4	7	1	0	0	4	1	2	5	O-7
• WEBB, Skeeter														
W 1945	Det-A	.185	7	27	4	5	0	0	0	1	2	1	0	S-7

YEAR	TM-L	AVG	G	AB	R	H	2B	3B	HR	RBI	BB	SO	SB	POS
• WEBER, Ben														
W 2002	Ana-A	....	4	0	0	0	0	0	0	0	0	0	0	....
• WEBSTER, Lenny														
D 1997	Bal-A	.167	3	6	1	1	0	0	0	1	1	0	0	C-3
L 1997	Bal-A	.222	4	9	0	2	0	0	0	0	0	1	0	C-3
• WEBSTER, Mitch														
D 1995	LA-N	.000	2	2	0	0	0	0	0	0	0	0	0	....
L 1989	Chi-N	.333	3	3	0	1	0	0	0	0	0	0	0	0-2
• WECKBECKER, Pete														
W 1890	Lou-A	.000	1	4	0	0	0	0	0	0	0	1	0	C-1
• WEHNER, John														
D 1997	Fla-N	....	1	0	0	0	0	0	0	0	0	0	0	0-1
L 1992	Pit-N	.000	2	2	0	0	0	0	0	0	0	2	0	....
• WEIS, Al														
L 1969	NY-N	.000	3	1	1	0	0	0	0	0	0	0	0	2-3
W 1969	NY-N	.455	5	11	1	5	0	0	1	3	4	2	0	2-5
• WEISS, Walt														
D 1995	Col-N	.167	4	12	1	2	0	0	0	0	3	3	1	S-4
D 1998	Atl-N	.154	3	13	2	2	0	0	0	0	1	3	0	S-3
D 1999	Atl-N	.167	3	6	1	1	0	0	0	0	0	2	0	S-3
D 2000	Atl-N	.667	1	3	0	2	1	0	0	2	0	0	0	S-1
D Total	4	.206	11	34	4	7	1	0	0	2	4	8	1	....
L 1988	Oak-A	.333	4	15	2	5	2	0	0	2	0	4	0	S-4
L 1989	Oak-A	.111	4	9	2	1	1	0	0	0	1	1	1	S-4
L 1990	Oak-A	.000	2	7	2	0	0	0	0	0	2	2	0	S-2
L 1992	Oak-A	.167	3	6	1	1	0	0	0	0	2	1	2	S-3
L 1998	Atl-N	.200	4	15	0	3	0	0	0	1	2	5	1	S-4
L 1999	Atl-N	.286	6	21	2	6	2	0	0	1	2	4	2	S-6
L Total	6	.219	23	73	9	16	5	0	0	4	9	17	6	....
W 1988	Oak-A	.063	5	16	1	1	0	0	0	0	0	2	1	S-5
W 1989	Oak-A	.133	4	15	3	2	0	0	1	1	2	2	0	S-4
W 1999	Atl-N	.222	3	9	1	2	0	0	0	0	0	1	0	S-3
W Total	3	.125	12	40	5	5	0	0	1	1	2	5	1	....
• WELCH, Curt														
W 1885	StL-A	.148	7	27	5	4	1	1	0	2	0	0	0	0-7
W 1886	StL-A	.350	6	20	7	7	2	0	0	1	3	4	2	0-6
W 1887	StL-A	.207	15	58	6	12	3	1	1	8	0	2	1	0-15
W Total	3	.219	28	105	18	23	6	2	1	11	3	6	3	....
• WERBER, Billy														
W 1939	Cin-N	.250	4	16	1	4	0	0	0	2	2	0	0	3-4
W 1940	Cin-N	.370	7	27	5	10	4	0	0	2	4	2	0	3-7
W Total	2	.326	11	43	6	14	4	0	0	4	6	2	0	....
• WERT, Don														
W 1968	Det-A	.118	6	17	1	2	0	0	0	2	6	5	0	3-6
• WERTZ, Vic														
W 1954	Cle-A	.500	4	16	2	8	2	1	1	3	2	2	0	1-4
• WESTLAKE, Wally														
W 1954	Cle-A	.143	2	7	0	1	0	0	0	0	1	3	0	0-2
• WESTRUM, Wes														
W 1951	NY-N	.235	6	17	1	4	1	0	0	0	5	3	0	C-6
W 1954	NY-N	.273	4	11	0	3	0	0	0	3	1	3	0	C-4
W Total	2	.250	10	28	1	7	1	0	0	3	6	6	0	....
• WHEAT, Zack														
W 1916	Bro-N	.211	5	19	2	4	0	1	0	1	2	2	1	0-5
W 1920	Bro-N	.333	7	27	2	9	2	0	0	2	1	2	0	0-7
W Total	2	.283	12	46	4	13	2	1	0	3	3	4	1	....
• WHISENTON, Larry														
L 1982	Atl-N	.000	2	2	0	0	0	0	0	0	0	1	0	....
• WHITAKER, Lou														
L 1984	Det-A	.143	3	14	3	2	0	0	0	0	0	3	0	2-3
L 1987	Det-A	.176	5	17	4	3	0	0	1	1	7	3	1	2-5
L Total	2	.161	8	31	7	5	0	0	1	1	7	6	1	....
W 1984	Det-A	.278	5	18	6	5	2	0	0	0	4	4	0	2-5
• WHITE, Bill														
W 1888	StL-A	.143	10	35	4	5	1	0	0	4	3	6	1	S-10
• WHITE, Bill														
W 1964	StL-N	.111	7	27	2	3	1	0	0	2	2	6	1	1-7
• WHITE, Deacon														
W 1887	Det-N	.233	15	60	8	14	1	1	0	5	2	0	2	3-14,1-1
• WHITE, Devon														
D 1997	Fla-N	.182	3	11	1	2	0	0	1	4	2	3	0	0-3
L 1986	Cal-A	.500	4	2	2	1	0	0	0	0	0	1	0	0-3
L 1991	Tor-A	.364	5	22	5	8	1	0	0	0	2	3	3	0-5
L 1992	Tor-A	.348	6	23	2	8	2	0	0	2	5	6	0	0-6
L 1993	Tor-A	.444	6	27	3	12	1	1	1	2	1	5	0	0-6
L 1997	Fla-N	.190	6	21	4	4	1	0	0	1	2	7	1	0-6
L Total	5	.347	27	95	16	33	5	1	1	5	10	22	4	....
W 1992	Tor-A	.231	6	26	2	6	1	0	0	2	0	6	1	0-6
W 1993	Tor-A	.292	6	24	8	7	3	2	1	7	4	7	1	0-6
W 1997	Fla-N	.242	7	33	0	8	3	1	0	2	3	10	1	0-7
W Total	3	.253	19	83	10	21	7	3	1	11	7	23	3	....
• WHITE, Frank														
D 1981	KC-A	.182	3	11	1	2	0	0	0	0	1	1	0	2-3
L 1976	KC-A	.125	4	8	2	1	0	0	0	0	0	1	0	2-4
L 1977	KC-A	.278	5	18	1	5	1	0	0	2	0	4	1	2-5
L 1978	KC-A	.231	4	13	1	3	0	0	0	2	0	0	0	2-4
L 1980	KC-A	.545	3	11	3	6	1	0	1	3	0	1	1	2-3
L 1984	KC-A	.091	3	11	1	1	0	0	0	0	0	3	0	2-3
L 1985	KC-A	.200	7	25	1	5	0	0	0	3	1	2	0	2-7
L Total	6	.244	26	86	9	21	2	0	1	10	1	11	2	....
W 1980	KC-A	.080	6	25	0	2	0	0	0	0	1	5	1	2-6
W 1985	KC-A	.250	7	28	4	7	3	0	1	6	3	4	1	2-7
W Total	2	.170	13	53	4	9	3	0	1	6	4	9	2	....
• WHITE, Jerry														
D 1981	Mon-N	.167	5	18	3	3	1	0	0	1	2	2	3	0-5
L 1981	Mon-N	.313	5	16	2	5	1	0	1	3	3	1	1	0-5
• WHITE, Jo-Jo														
W 1934	Det-A	.130	7	23	6	3	0	0	0	0	8	4	1	0-7
W 1935	Det-A	.263	5	19	3	5	0	0	0	1	5	7	0	0-5
W Total	2	.190	12	42	9	8	0	0	0	1	13	11	1	....
• WHITE, Rondell														
D 2002	NY-A	.333	1	3	1	1	0	0	1	1	0	0	0	D-1
• WHITE, Roy														
L 1976	NY-A	.294	5	17	4	5	3	0	0	3	5	1	1	0-5
L 1977	NY-A	.400	4	5	2	2	2	0	0	0	1	0	0	0-1,D-1
L 1978	NY-A	.313	4	16	5	5	1	0	1	1	1	2	0	0-3,D-1
L Total	3	.316	13	38	11	12	6	0	1	4	7	3	1	....
W 1976	NY-A	.133	4	15	0	2	0	0	0	0	3	0	0	0-4
W 1977	NY-A	.000	2	2	0	0	0	0	0	0	0	0	0	....
W 1978	NY-A	.333	6	24	9	8	0	0	1	4	4	5	2	0-6
W Total	3	.244	12	41	9	10	0	0	1	4	7	5	2	....
• WHITEHEAD, Burgess														
W 1934	StL-N	....	1	0	0	0	0	0	0	0	0	0	0	S-1
W 1936	NY-N	.048	6	21	1	1	0	0	0	2	1	3	0	2-6
W 1937	NY-N	.250	5	16	1	4	2	0	0	0	2	0	1	2-5
W Total	3	.135	12	37	2	5	2	0	0	2	3	3	1	....
• WHITEMAN, George														
W 1918	Bos-A	.250	6	20	2	5	0	1	0	1	2	1	1	0-6
• WHITEN, Mark														
L 1998	Cle-A	.286	2	7	2	2	1	0	1	1	1	3	0	0-2
• WHITFIELD, Terry														
L 1985	LA-N	....	1	0	0	0	0	0	0	0	0	0	0	....
• WHITMAN, Dick														
W 1949	Bro-N	.000	1	1	0	0	0	0	0	0	0	1	0	....
W 1950	Phi-N	.000	3	2	0	0	0	0	0	0	1	0	0	....
W Total	2	.000	4	3	0	0	0	0	0	0	1	1	0	....
• WHITNEY, Art														
W 1888	NY-N	.324	10	37	7	12	0	1	0	12	1	4	2	3-9,0-1
W 1889	NY-N	.229	9	35	4	8	2	1	0	3	1	0	0	3-9
W Total	2	.278	19	72	11	20	2	2	0	15	2	4	2	....
• WHITT, Ernie														
L 1985	Tor-A	.190	7	21	1	4	1	0	0	2	2	4	0	C-7
L 1989	Tor-A	.125	5	16	1	2	0	0	1	3	2	3	0	C-5
L Total	2	.162	12	37	2	6	1	0	1	5	4	7	0	....
• WHITTED, Possum														
W 1914	Bos-N	.214	4	14	2	3	0	1	0	2	3	1	1	0-4
W 1915	Phi-N	.067	5	15	0	1	0	0	0	1	1	0	1	0-5,1-1
W Total	2	.138	9	29	2	4	0	1	0	3	4	1	2	....
• WIDGER, Chris														
D 1995	Sea-A	.000	2	3	0	0	0	0	0	0	0	3	0	C-2
L 1995	Sea-A	.000	3	1	0	0	0	0	0	0	0	1	0	C-3
• WIGGINS, Alan														
L 1984	SD-N	.316	5	19	4	6	0	0	0	1	2	2	0	2-5
W 1984	SD-N	.364	5	22	2	8	1	0	0	1	0	2	1	2-5
• WILFONG, Rob														
L 1982	Cal-A	.000	2	1	0	0	0	0	0	0	0	1	0	....
L 1986	Cal-A	.308	4	13	1	4	1	0	0	2	0	2	0	2-4
L Total	2	.286	6	14	1	4	1	0	0	2	0	3	0	....
• WILHOIT, Joe														
W 1917	NY-N	.000	2	1	0	0	0	0	0	0	1	0	0	....
• WILKERSON, Curtis														
L 1989	Chi-N	.500	3	2	1	1	0	0	0	0	0	0	0	3-1
L 1991	Pit-N	.000	4	4	0	0	0	0	0	0	0	3	0	....
L Total	2	.167	7	6	1	1	0	0	0	0	0	3	0	....
• WILKINS, Rick														
D 1997	Sea-A	....	1	0	0	0	0	0	0	0	1	0	0	C-1
L 2000	StL-N	.000	2	2	0	0	0	0	0	0	0	0	0	....
• WILLARD, Jerry														
L 1991	Atl-N	.000	2	2	0	0	0	0	0	0	0	1	0	....
W 1991	Atl-N	....	1	0	0	0	0	0	0	1	0	0	0	....
• WILLIAMS, Bernie														
D 1995	NY-A	.429	5	21	8	9	2	0	2	5	7	3	1	0-5
D 1996	NY-A	.467	4	15	5	7	0	0	3	5	2	1	1	0-4
D 1997	NY-A	.118	5	17	3	2	1	0	0	1	4	3	0	0-5
D 1998	NY-A	.000	3	11	0	0	0	0	0	0	1	4	0	0-3
D 1999	NY-A	.364	3	11	2	4	1	0	1	6	1	2	0	0-3
D 2000	NY-A	.250	5	20	3	5	3	0	0	1	1	4	0	0-5
D 2001	NY-A	.222	5	18	4	4	3	0	0	5	3	3	0	0-5
D 2002	NY-A	.333	4	15	4	5	1	0	1	3	3	2	0	0-4
D 2003	NY-A	.400	4	15	3	6	2	0	0	3	2	2	0	0-4
D Total	9	.294	38	143	32	42	13	0	7	29	24	24	2	....
L 1996	NY-A	.474	5	19	6	9	3	0	2	6	5	4	1	0-5
L 1998	NY-A	.381	6	21	4	8	1	0	0	5	7	4	1	0-6

SER-YEAR	TM-L	AVG	G	AB	R	H	2B	3B	HR	RBI	BB	SO	SB	POS
L 1999	NY-A	.250	5	20	3	5	1	0	1	2	2	5	1	0-5
L 2000	NY-A	.435	6	23	5	10	1	0	1	3	2	3	1	0-6
L 2001	NY-A	.235	5	17	4	4	0	0	3	5	5	4	0	0-5
L 2003	NY-A	.192	7	26	5	5	1	0	0	2	4	3	0	0-7
L Total	6	.325	34	126	27	41	7	0	7	23	25	23	4	....
W 1996	NY-A	.167	6	24	3	4	0	0	1	4	3	6	1	0-6
W 1998	NY-A	.063	4	16	2	1	0	0	1	3	2	5	0	0-4
W 1999	NY-A	.231	4	13	2	3	0	0	0	0	4	2	1	0-4
W 2000	NY-A	.111	5	18	2	2	0	0	1	1	5	5	0	0-5
W 2001	NY-A	.208	7	24	2	5	1	0	0	1	4	6	0	0-7
W 2003	NY-A	.400	6	25	5	10	2	0	2	5	2	2	0	0-6
W Total	6	.208	32	120	16	25	3	0	5	14	20	26	2	....
• WILLIAMS, Billy														
L 1975	Oak-A	.000	3	8	0	0	0	0	0	0	0	1	1	0 D-2
• WILLIAMS, Davey														
W 1951	NY-N	.000	2	1	0	0	0	0	0	0	0	0	0	....
W 1954	NY-N	.000	4	11	0	0	0	0	0	1	2	2	0	2-4
W Total	2	.000	6	12	0	0	0	0	0	1	2	2	0	....
• WILLIAMS, Dewey														
W 1945	Chi-N	.000	2	2	0	0	0	0	0	0	0	1	0	C-1
• WILLIAMS, Dib														
W 1931	Phi-A	.320	7	25	2	8	1	0	0	1	2	9	0	S-7
• WILLIAMS, Dick														
W 1953	Bro-N	.500	3	2	0	1	0	0	0	0	1	1	0	....
• WILLIAMS, Earl														
L 1973	Bal-A	.278	5	18	2	5	2	0	1	4	2	2	0	1-4,C-1
L 1974	Bal-A	.000	2	6	0	0	0	0	0	0	0	2	0	1-2
L Total	2	.208	7	24	2	5	2	0	1	4	2	4	0	....
• WILLIAMS, Gerald														
D 1995	NY-A	.000	5	5	1	0	0	0	0	0	2	3	0	0-5
D 1998	Atl-N	.500	2	2	1	1	0	0	0	1	0	1	0	0-2
D 1999	Atl-N	.389	4	18	2	7	1	0	0	3	0	3	1	0-4
D Total	3	.320	11	25	4	8	1	0	0	4	2	7	1	....
L 1998	Atl-N	.154	5	13	0	2	0	0	0	0	1	6	1	0-5
L 1999	Atl-N	.179	6	28	4	5	2	0	0	1	2	2	3	0-6
L Total	2	.171	11	41	4	7	2	0	0	1	3	8	4	....
W 1999	Atl-N	.176	4	17	2	3	0	1	0	0	0	4	0	0-4
• WILLIAMS, Jerome														
D 2003	SF-N	.000	1	1	0	0	0	0	0	0	0	1	0	....
• WILLIAMS, Jimmy														
T 1900	Pit-N	.214	4	14	0	3	0	0	0	0	1	0	0	3-4
• WILLIAMS, Matt														
D 1997	Cle-A	.235	5	17	4	4	1	0	1	3	3	3	0	3-5
D 1999	Ari-N	.375	4	16	3	6	1	0	0	0	0	1	0	3-4
D 2001	Ari-N	.063	5	16	0	1	1	0	0	0	4	4	0	3-5
D 2002	Ari-N	.083	3	12	0	1	0	0	0	0	0	3	0	3-3
D Total	4	.197	17	61	7	12	3	0	1	3	7	11	0	....
L 1989	SF-N	.300	5	20	2	6	1	0	2	9	0	2	0	3-5,S-1
L 1997	Cle-A	.217	6	23	1	5	1	0	0	2	3	7	1	3-6
L 2001	Ari-N	.278	5	18	1	5	1	0	0	3	2	3	0	3-5
L Total	3	.262	16	61	4	16	3	0	2	14	5	12	1	....
W 1989	SF-N	.125	4	16	1	2	0	0	1	1	0	6	0	3-3,S-4
W 1997	Cle-A	.385	7	26	8	10	1	0	1	3	7	6	0	3-7
W 2001	Ari-N	.269	7	26	3	7	2	0	1	7	0	6	0	3-7
W Total	3	.279	18	68	12	19	3	0	3	11	7	18	0	....
• WILLIAMS, Mike														
D 2001	Hou-N	....	1	0	0	0	0	0	0	0	0	0	0	....
• WILLIAMS, Ted														
W 1946	Bos-A	.200	7	25	2	5	0	0	0	1	5	5	0	0-7
• WILLIAMSON, Ned														
W 1885	Chi-N	.087	7	23	1	2	0	0	0	3	4	0	0	3-4,S-3
W 1886	Chi-N	.056	6	18	2	1	0	1	0	3	4	5	1	S-6,P-2,C-1,0-1
W Total	2	.073	13	41	3	3	0	1	0	6	8	5	1	....
• WILLIS, Dontrelle														
D 2003	Fla-N	1.000	2	3	1	3	0	1	0	0	0	0	0	....
L 2003	Fla-N	....	2	0	0	0	0	0	0	0	0	0	0	....
W 2003	Fla-N	....	2	0	0	0	0	0	0	0	0	0	0	....
• WILLS, Maury														
W 1959	LA-N	.250	6	20	2	5	0	0	0	1	0	3	1	S-6
W 1963	LA-N	.133	4	15	1	2	0	0	0	0	1	3	1	S-4
W 1965	LA-N	.367	7	30	3	11	3	0	0	3	1	3	3	S-7
W 1966	LA-N	.077	4	13	0	1	0	0	0	0	3	3	1	S-4
W Total	4	.244	21	78	6	19	3	0	0	4	5	12	6	....
• WILSON, Art														
W 1911	NY-N	.000	1	1	0	0	0	0	0	0	0	0	0	C-1
W 1912	NY-N	1.000	2	1	0	1	0	0	0	0	0	0	0	C-2
W 1913	NY-N	.000	3	3	0	0	0	0	0	0	0	2	0	C-3
W Total	3	.200	6	5	0	1	0	0	0	0	0	2	0	....
• WILSON, Chief														
W 1909	Pit-N	.154	7	26	2	4	1	0	0	1	0	2	1	0-7
• WILSON, Dan														
D 1995	Sea-A	.118	5	17	0	2	0	0	0	1	2	6	0	C-5
D 1997	Sea-A	.000	4	13	0	0	0	0	0	0	0	9	0	C-4
D 2000	Sea-A	.000	2	3	0	0	0	0	0	1	1	2	0	C-2
D 2001	Sea-A	.200	5	15	0	3	1	0	0	0	0	5	0	C-5
D Total	4	.104	16	48	0	5	1	0	0	2	3	22	0	....
L 1995	Sea-A	.000	6	16	0	0	0	0	0	0	0	4	0	C-6
L 2000	Sea-A	.091	4	11	0	1	0	0	0	0	1	5	0	C-4
L 2001	Sea-A	.154	4	13	2	2	0	0	0	0	0	1	0	C-4
L Total	3	.075	14	40	2	3	0	0	0	0	1	10	0	....
• WILSON, Enrique														
D 1998	Cle-A	.000	1	2	0	0	0	0	0	0	0	0	0	2-1
D 1999	Cle-A	.000	3	2	0	0	0	0	0	0	0	0	0	2-2
D 2002	NY-A	....	1	0	0	0	0	0	0	0	0	0	0	....
D Total	3	.000	5	4	0	0	0	0	0	0	0	0	0	....
L 1998	Cle-A	.214	5	14	2	3	0	0	0	1	1	3	0	2-5
L 2001	NY-A	1.000	1	1	0	1	0	0	0	0	0	0	0	S-1
L 2003	NY-A	.143	2	7	0	1	0	0	0	0	0	1	0	3-2
L Total	3	.227	8	22	2	5	0	0	0	1	1	4	0	....
W 2001	NY-A	.000	2	3	0	0	0	0	0	0	0	0	0	S-1
W 2003	NY-A	.500	2	4	0	2	1	0	0	1	1	0	0	2-1,3-1
W Total	2	.286	4	7	0	2	1	0	0	1	1	0	0	....
• WILSON, George														
W 1956	NY-A	.000	1	1	0	0	0	0	0	0	0	1	0	....
• WILSON, Hack														
W 1924	NY-N	.233	7	30	1	7	1	0	0	3	1	9	0	0-7
W 1929	Chi-N	.471	5	17	2	8	0	1	0	0	4	3	0	0-5
W Total	2	.319	12	47	3	15	1	1	0	3	5	12	0	....
• WILSON, Jimmie														
W 1928	StL-N	.091	3	11	1	1	1	0	0	1	0	3	0	C-3
W 1930	StL-N	.267	4	15	0	4	1	0	0	2	0	1	0	C-4
W 1931	StL-N	.217	7	23	0	5	0	0	0	2	1	1	0	C-7
W 1940	Cin-N	.353	6	17	2	6	0	0	0	0	1	2	1	C-6
W Total	4	.242	20	66	3	16	2	0	0	5	2	7	1	....
• WILSON, Mookie														
L 1986	NY-N	.115	6	26	2	3	0	0	0	1	1	7	1	0-7
L 1988	NY-N	.154	4	13	2	2	0	0	0	1	2	2	0	0-3
L 1989	Tor-A	.263	5	19	2	5	0	0	0	2	2	2	1	0-5
L 1991	Tor-A	.250	3	8	1	2	0	0	0	0	1	3	1	0-2,D-1
L Total	4	.182	18	66	7	12	0	0	0	4	6	14	3	....
W 1986	NY-N	.269	7	26	3	7	1	0	0	0	1	6	3	0-6
• WILSON, Nigel														
D 1996	Cle-A	.000	1	1	0	0	0	0	0	0	0	0	0	....
• WILSON, Willie														
D 1981	KC-A	.308	3	13	0	4	0	0	0	1	0	0	0	0-3
L 1978	KC-A	.250	3	4	0	1	0	0	0	0	0	2	0	0-3
L 1980	KC-A	.308	3	13	2	4	2	1	0	4	1	2	0	0-3
L 1984	KC-A	.154	3	13	0	2	0	0	0	0	1	2	0	0-3
L 1985	KC-A	.310	7	29	5	9	0	0	1	2	1	5	1	0-7
L 1992	Oak-A	.227	6	22	0	5	1	0	0	0	1	5	7	0-6
L Total	5	.259	22	81	7	21	3	1	1	6	4	16	8	....
W 1980	KC-A	.154	6	26	3	4	1	0	0	0	4	12	2	0-6
W 1985	KC-A	.367	7	30	2	11	0	1	0	3	1	4	3	0-7
W Total	2	.268	13	56	5	15	1	1	0	3	5	16	5	....
• WINFIELD, Dave														
D 1981	NY-A	.350	5	20	2	7	2	1	0	0	1	5	0	0-5
L 1981	NY-A	.154	3	13	2	2	1	0	0	2	2	2	1	0-3
L 1992	Tor-A	.250	6	24	7	6	1	0	2	3	4	2	0	D-6
L Total	2	.216	9	37	9	8	2	0	2	5	6	4	1	....
W 1981	NY-A	.045	6	22	0	1	0	0	0	1	5	4	1	0-6
W 1992	Tor-A	.227	6	22	0	5	1	0	0	3	2	3	0	0-3,D-3
W Total	2	.136	12	44	0	6	1	0	0	4	7	7	1	....
• WINGO, Ivey														
W 1919	Cin-N	.571	3	7	1	4	0	0	0	1	3	1	0	C-3
• WINNINGHAM, Herm														
L 1990	Cin-N	.286	3	7	1	2	1	0	0	1	1	1	1	0-2
W 1990	Cin-N	.500	2	4	1	2	0	0	0	0	0	0	0	0-1
• WISE, Casey														
W 1958	Mil-N	.000	2	1	0	0	0	0	0	0	0	1	0	....
• WITASICK, Jay														
D 2002	SF-N	....	2	0	0	0	0	0	0	0	0	0	0	....
L 2002	SF-N	....	1	0	0	0	0	0	0	0	0	0	0	....
W 2001	NY-A	....	1	0	0	0	0	0	0	0	0	0	0	....
W 2002	SF-N	....	2	0	0	0	0	0	0	0	0	0	0	....
W Total	2	....	3	0	0	0	0	0	0	0	0	0	0	....
• WITT, Whitey														
W 1922	NY-A	.222	5	18	1	4	1	1	0	0	1	2	0	0-5
W 1923	NY-A	.240	6	25	1	6	2	0	0	4	1	1	0	0-6
W Total	2	.233	11	43	2	10	3	1	0	4	2	3	0	....
• WOHLFORD, Jim														
L 1976	KC-A	.182	5	11	3	2	0	0	0	0	3	1	2	0-5
• WOLF, Jimmy														
W 1890	Lou-A	.360	7	25	4	9	3	1	0	8	3	0	2	3-5,0-3
• WOMACK, Tony														
D 1999	Ari-N	.111	4	18	2	2	0	1	0	0	0	6	0	0-4,S-2
D 2001	Ari-N	.294	5	17	1	5	1	0	0	1	3	2	0	S-5
D 2002	Ari-N	.154	3	13	1	2	0	0	0	0	1	1	0	S-3
D Total	3	.188	12	48	4	9	1	1	0	1	4	9	0	....
L 2001	Ari-N	.200	4	20	4	4	1	0	0	0	0	2	0	S-4
W 2001	Ari-N	.250	7	32	3	8	3	0	0	3	1	7	1	S-7
• WOOD, Joe														
W 1912	Bos-A	.286	4	7	1	2	0	0	0	1	1	0	0	....
W 1920	Cle-A	.200	4	10	2	2	1	0	0	0	1	2	0	0-4
W Total	2	.235	8	17	3	4	1	0	0	1	2	2	0	....

YEAR	TM-L	AVG	G	AB	R	H	2B	3B	HR	RBI	BB	SO	SB	POS
• WOODLING, Gene														
W 1949	NY-A	.400	3	10	4	4	3	0	0	0	3	0	0	O-3
W 1950	NY-A	.429	4	14	2	6	0	0	0	1	2	0	0	O-4
W 1951	NY-A	.167	6	18	6	3	1	1	1	1	5	3	0	O-5
W 1952	NY-A	.348	7	23	4	8	1	1	1	1	3	3	0	O-6
W 1953	NY-A	.300	6	20	5	6	0	0	1	3	6	2	0	O-6
W Total	5	.318	26	85	21	27	5	2	3	6	19	8	0	....
• WOODS, Gary														
D 1981	Hou-N	.000	2	2	0	0	0	0	0	0	0	1	0	....
L 1980	Hou-N	.250	4	8	0	2	0	0	0	1	1	3	1	O-3
L 1984	Chi-N	.000	1	1	0	0	0	0	0	0	0	1	0	O-1
L Total	2	.222	5	9	0	2	0	0	0	1	1	4	1	....
• WOODSON, Tracy														
L 1988	LA-N	.250	3	4	0	1	0	0	0	0	0	1	0	1-3
W 1988	LA-N	.000	4	4	0	0	0	0	0	1	0	0	0	1-3
• WOODWARD, Woody														
L 1970	Cin-N	.100	3	10	0	1	0	0	0	0	1	0	0	3-2,S-3
W 1970	Cin-N	.200	4	5	0	1	0	0	0	0	0	0	0	S-3
• WOOTEN, Shawn														
D 2002	Ana-A	.667	3	9	4	6	0	0	1	2	0	1	0	D-3
L 2002	Ana-A	.250	3	8	1	2	0	0	0	1	0	3	0	D-3
W 2002	Ana-A	.500	3	2	0	1	0	0	0	0	0	0	0	1-2
• WORTMAN, Chuck														
W 1918	Chi-N	.000	1	1	0	0	0	0	0	0	0	0	0	2-1
• WRIGHT, Glenn														
W 1925	Pit-N	.185	7	27	3	5	1	0	1	3	1	4	0	S-7
W 1927	Pit-N	.154	4	13	1	2	0	0	0	2	0	0	0	S-4
W Total	2	.175	11	40	4	7	1	0	1	5	1	4	0	....
• WRONA, Rick														
L 1989	Chi-N	.000	2	5	0	0	0	0	0	0	0	3	0	C-2
• WYNN, Jimmy														
L 1974	LA-N	.200	4	10	4	2	2	0	0	2	9	1	0	O-4
W 1974	LA-N	.188	5	16	1	3	1	0	1	2	4	4	0	O-5
• WYNNE, Marvell														
L 1989	Chi-N	.167	4	6	0	1	0	0	0	0	0	0	0	O-2
• YASTRZEMSKI, Carl														
L 1975	Bos-A	.455	3	11	4	5	1	0	1	2	1	1	0	O-3
W 1967	Bos-A	.400	7	25	4	10	2	0	3	5	4	1	0	O-7
W 1975	Bos-A	.310	7	29	7	9	0	0	0	4	4	1	0	O-4,1-4
W Total	2	.352	14	54	11	19	2	0	3	9	8	2	0	....
• YEAGER, George														
T 1897	Bos-N	.500	3	12	2	6	1	1	0	2	2	0	0	C-3
• YEAGER, Steve														
D 1981	LA-N	.400	2	5	1	2	1	0	0	0	0	1	0	C-2
L 1974	LA-N	.000	3	9	1	0	0	0	0	0	3	3	0	C-3
L 1977	LA-N	.231	4	13	1	3	0	0	0	2	1	3	0	C-4
L 1978	LA-N	.231	4	13	2	3	0	0	1	2	2	2	1	C-4
L 1981	LA-N	.500	1	2	1	1	0	0	0	0	0	0	0	C-1
L 1983	LA-N	.167	2	6	0	1	1	0	0	0	0	0	0	C-2
L 1985	LA-N	.000	1	2	0	0	0	0	0	0	1	1	0	C-1
L Total	6	.178	15	45	5	8	1	0	1	4	7	9	1	....
W 1974	LA-N	.364	4	11	0	4	1	0	0	1	1	4	0	C-4
W 1977	LA-N	.316	6	19	2	6	1	0	2	5	1	1	0	C-6
W 1978	LA-N	.231	5	13	2	3	1	0	0	0	1	2	0	C-5
W 1981	LA-N	.286	6	14	2	4	1	0	2	4	0	2	0	C-6
W Total	4	.298	21	57	6	17	4	0	4	10	3	9	0	....
• YERKES, Steve														
W 1912	Bos-A	.250	8	32	3	8	0	2	0	4	2	3	0	2-8
• YORK, Rudy														
W 1940	Det-A	.231	7	26	3	6	0	1	1	2	4	7	0	1-7
W 1945	Det-A	.179	7	28	1	5	1	0	0	3	3	4	0	1-7
W 1946	Bos-A	.261	7	23	6	6	1	1	2	5	6	4	0	1-7
W Total	3	.221	21	77	10	17	2	2	3	10	13	15	0	....
• YOST, Ned														
W 1982	Mil-A	....	1	0	0	0	0	0	0	0	1	0	0	C-1
• YOUNG, Dmitri														
L 1996	StL-N	.286	4	7	1	2	0	1	0	2	0	2	0	1-2
• YOUNG, Eric														
D 1995	Col-N	.438	4	16	3	7	1	0	1	2	2	2	1	2-4
• YOUNGS, Ross														
W 1921	NY-N	.280	8	25	3	7	1	1	0	4	7	2	2	O-8
W 1922	NY-N	.375	5	16	2	6	0	0	0	2	3	1	0	O-5
W 1923	NY-N	.348	6	23	2	8	0	0	1	3	2	0	0	O-6
W 1924	NY-N	.185	7	27	3	5	1	0	0	1	5	6	1	O-8
W Total	4	.286	26	91	10	26	2	1	1	10	17	9	3	....
• YOUNT, Robin														
D 1981	Mil-A	.316	5	19	4	6	0	1	0	1	2	2	1	S-5
L 1982	Mil-A	.250	5	16	1	4	0	0	0	0	5	0	0	S-5
W 1982	Mil-A	.414	7	29	6	12	3	0	1	6	2	2	0	S-7
• YVARS, Sal														
W 1951	NY-N	.000	1	1	0	0	0	0	0	0	0	0	0	....
• ZAMBRANO, Carlos														
D 2003	Chi-N	.000	1	3	0	0	0	0	0	0	0	2	0	....
L 2003	Chi-N	.000	2	3	0	0	0	0	0	0	0	3	0	....
• ZARILLA, Al														
W 1944	StL-A	.100	4	10	1	1	0	0	0	1	0	4	0	O-3
• ZAUN, Gregg														
L 1997	Fla-N	....	1	0	0	0	0	0	0	0	0	0	0	C-1
W 1997	Fla-N	.000	2	2	0	0	0	0	0	0	0	0	0	C-1
• ZDEB, Joe														
L 1977	KC-A	.000	4	9	0	0	0	0	0	0	0	2	1	O-4
• ZEBER, George														
W 1977	NY-A	.000	2	2	0	0	0	0	0	0	0	2	0	....
• ZEIDER, Rollie														
W 1918	Chi-N	....	2	0	0	0	0	0	0	0	2	0	0	3-2
• ZEILE, Todd														
D 1996	Bal-A	.263	4	19	2	5	1	0	0	0	2	5	0	3-4
D 1998	Tex-A	.333	3	9	0	3	0	0	0	0	0	2	0	3-3
D 1999	Tex-A	.100	3	10	0	1	0	0	0	0	2	1	0	3-3
D 2000	NY-N	.071	4	14	0	1	1	0	0	0	4	3	0	1-4
D Total	4	.192	14	52	2	10	2	0	0	0	8	11	0	....
L 1996	Bal-A	.364	5	22	3	8	0	0	3	5	2	1	0	3-5
L 2000	NY-N	.368	5	19	1	7	3	0	1	8	2	4	0	1-5
L Total	2	.366	10	41	4	15	3	0	4	13	4	5	0	....
W 2000	NY-N	.400	5	20	1	8	2	0	0	1	1	5	0	1-5
• ZERBE, Chad														
W 2002	SF-N	....	3	0	0	0	0	0	0	0	0	0	0	....
• ZIMMER, Chief														
T 1892	Cle-N	.261	6	23	2	6	1	1	0	2	0	3	0	C-6
T 1895	Cle-N	.333	4	18	2	6	2	0	0	3	3	5	0	C-4
T 1896	Cle-N	.214	4	14	0	3	1	0	0	1	2	6	0	C-4
T 1900	Pit-N	.111	3	9	1	1	0	0	0	1	0	2	1	C-3
T Total	4	.250	17	64	5	16	4	1	0	7	5	16	1	....
• ZIMMER, Don														
W 1955	Bro-N	.222	4	9	0	2	0	0	0	2	2	5	0	2-4
W 1959	LA-N	.000	1	1	0	0	0	0	0	0	0	0	0	S-1
W Total	2	.200	5	10	0	2	0	0	0	2	2	5	0	....
• ZIMMERMAN, Heinie														
W 1907	Chi-N	.000	1	1	0	0	0	0	0	0	0	1	0	2-1
W 1910	Chi-N	.235	5	17	0	4	1	0	0	2	1	3	1	2-5
W 1917	NY-N	.120	6	25	1	3	0	1	0	0	0	0	0	3-6
W Total	3	.163	12	43	1	7	1	1	0	2	1	4	1	....
• ZIMMERMAN, Jerry														
W 1961	Cin-N	....	2	0	0	0	0	0	0	0	0	0	0	C-2
W 1965	Min-A	.000	2	1	0	0	0	0	0	0	0	0	0	C-2
W Total	2	.000	4	1	0	0	0	0	0	0	0	0	0	....
• ZISK, Richie														
L 1974	Pit-N	.300	3	10	1	3	0	0	0	0	0	3	0	O-2
L 1975	Pit-N	.500	3	10	0	5	1	0	0	0	2	2	0	O-3
L Total	2	.400	6	20	1	8	1	0	0	0	2	5	0	....

YEAR	TM-L	W	L	ERA	G	GS	CG	SV	SHO	IP	H	ER	BB	SO
• AASE, Don														
L 1979	Cal-A	1	0	1.80	2	0	0	0	0	5	4	1	2	6
• ABBOTT, Glenn														
L 1975	Oak-A	0	0	0.00	1	0	0	0	0	1	0	0	0	0
• ABBOTT, Paul														
D 2000	Sea-A	1	0	1.59	1	1	0	0	0	5^2	5	1	3	1
D 2001	Sea-A	0	0	24.00	1	0	0	0	0	3	9	8	5	3
D Total	**2**	**1**	**0**	**9.35**	**2**	**1**	**0**	**0**	**0**	8^2	**14**	**9**	**8**	**4**
L 2000	Sea-A	0	1	5.40	1	1	0	0	0	5	3	3	3	3
L 2001	Sea-A	0	0	0.00	1	1	0	0	0	5	0	0	8	2
L Total	**2**	**0**	**1**	**2.70**	**2**	**2**	**0**	**0**	**0**	**10**	**3**	**3**	**11**	**5**
• ACKER, Jim														
L 1985	Tor-A	0	0	0.00	2	0	0	0	0	6	2	0	0	5
L 1989	Tor-A	0	0	1.42	5	0	0	0	0	6^1	4	1	1	4
L 1991	Tor-A	0	0	0.00	1	0	0	0	0	0^2	1	0	0	1
L Total	**3**	**0**	**0**	**0.69**	**8**	**0**	**0**	**0**	**0**	**13**	**7**	**1**	**1**	**10**
• ADAMS, Babe														
W 1909	Pit-N	3	0	1.33	3	3	3	0	1	27	18	4	6	11
W 1925	Pit-N	0	0	0.00	1	0	0	0	0	1	2	0	0	0
W Total	**2**	**3**	**0**	**1.29**	**4**	**3**	**3**	**0**	**1**	**28**	**20**	**4**	**6**	**11**
• AGOSTO, Juan														
L 1983	Chi-A	0	0	0.00	1	0	0	0	0	0^1	0	0	0	0
• AGUILERA, Rick														
D 1995	Bos-A	0	0	13.50	1	0	0	0	0	0^2	3	1	0	1
L 1986	NY-N	0	0	0.00	2	0	0	0	0	5	2	0	2	2
L 1988	NY-N	0	0	1.29	3	0	0	0	0	7	3	1	2	4
L 1991	Min-A	0	0	0.00	3	0	0	3	0	3^1	1	0	0	3
L Total	**3**	**0**	**0**	**0.59**	**8**	**0**	**0**	**3**	**0**	15^1	**6**	**1**	**4**	**9**
W 1986	NY-N	1	0	12.00	2	0	0	0	0	3	8	4	1	4
W 1991	Min-A	1	1	1.80	4	0	0	2	0	5	6	1	1	3
W Total	**2**	**2**	**1**	**5.63**	**6**	**0**	**0**	**2**	**0**	**8**	**14**	**5**	**2**	**7**
• ALDRIDGE, Vic														
W 1925	Pit-N	2	0	4.42	3	3	2	0	0	18^1	18	9	9	9
W 1927	Pit-N	0	1	7.36	1	1	0	0	0	7^1	10	6	4	4
W Total	**2**	**2**	**1**	**5.26**	**4**	**4**	**2**	**0**	**0**	25^2	**28**	**15**	**13**	**13**
• ALEXANDER, Doyle														
L 1973	Bal-A	0	1	4.91	1	1	0	0	0	3^2	5	2	0	1
L 1985	Tor-A	0	1	8.71	2	2	0	0	0	10^1	14	10	3	9
L 1987	Det-A	0	2	10.00	2	2	0	0	0	9	14	10	1	5
L Total	**3**	**0**	**4**	**8.61**	**5**	**5**	**0**	**0**	**0**	**23**	**33**	**22**	**4**	**15**
W 1976	NY-A	0	1	7.50	1	1	0	0	0	6	9	5	2	1
• ALEXANDER, Pete														
W 1915	Phi-N	1	1	1.53	2	2	2	0	0	17^2	14	3	4	10
W 1926	StL-N	2	0	1.33	3	2	2	1	0	20^1	12	3	4	17
W 1928	StL-N	0	1	19.80	2	1	0	0	0	5	10	11	4	2
W Total	**3**	**3**	**2**	**3.56**	**7**	**5**	**4**	**1**	**0**	**43**	**36**	**17**	**12**	**29**
• ALFONSECA, Antonio														
D 2003	Chi-N	0	0	0.00	1	0	0	0	0	1	1	0	0	0
L 2003	Chi-N	0	0	0.00	3	0	0	0	0	2^1	2	0	2	0
W 1997	Fla-N	0	0	0.00	3	0	0	0	0	6^1	6	0	1	5
• ALLEN, Johnny														
W 1932	NY-A	0	0	40.50	1	1	0	0	0	0^2	5	3	0	0
W 1941	Bro-N	0	0	0.00	3	0	0	0	0	3^2	1	0	3	0
W Total	**2**	**0**	**0**	**6.23**	**4**	**1**	**0**	**0**	**0**	4^1	**6**	**3**	**3**	**0**
• ALTROCK, Nick														
W 1906	Chi-A	1	1	1.00	2	2	2	0	0	18	11	2	2	5
• ALVAREZ, Wilson														
D 1997	SF-N	0	1	6.00	1	1	0	0	0	6	6	4	4	4
L 1993	Chi-A	1	0	1.00	1	1	1	0	0	9	7	1	2	6
• AMES, Red														
W 1905	NY-N	0	0	0.00	1	0	0	0	0	1	1	0	1	1
W 1911	NY-N	0	1	2.25	2	1	0	0	0	8	6	2	1	6
W 1912	NY-N	0	0	4.50	1	0	0	0	0	2	3	1	1	0
W Total	**3**	**0**	**1**	**2.45**	**4**	**1**	**0**	**0**	**0**	**11**	**10**	**3**	**3**	**7**
• ANDERSEN, Larry														
L 1986	Hou-N	0	0	0.00	2	0	0	0	0	5	1	0	2	3
L 1990	Bos-A	0	1	6.00	3	0	0	0	0	3	3	2	3	3
L 1993	Phi-N	0	0	15.43	3	0	0	1	0	2^1	4	4	1	3
L Total	**3**	**0**	**1**	**5.23**	**8**	**0**	**0**	**1**	**0**	10^1	**8**	**6**	**6**	**9**
W 1983	Phi-N	0	0	2.25	2	0	0	0	0	4	4	1	0	1
W 1993	Phi-N	0	0	12.27	4	0	0	0	0	3^2	5	5	3	3
W Total	**2**	**0**	**0**	**7.04**	**6**	**0**	**0**	**0**	**0**	7^2	**9**	**6**	**3**	**4**
• ANDERSON, Brian														
D 1999	Ari-N	0	0	2.57	1	1	0	0	0	7	7	2	0	4
D 2001	Ari-N	0	0	2.25	2	0	0	0	0	4	3	1	0	3
D Total	**2**	**0**	**0**	**2.45**	**3**	**1**	**0**	**0**	**0**	**11**	**10**	**3**	**0**	**7**
L 1997	Cle-A	1	0	1.42	3	0	0	0	0	6^1	1	1	3	7
L 2001	Ari-N	1	0	2.70	1	0	0	0	0	3^1	4	1	1	0
L Total	**2**	**2**	**0**	**1.86**	**4**	**0**	**0**	**0**	**0**	9^2	**5**	**2**	**4**	**7**
W 1997	Cle-A	0	0	2.45	3	0	0	1	0	3^2	2	1	0	2
W 2001	Ari-N	0	1	3.38	1	1	0	0	0	5^1	5	2	3	1
W Total	**2**	**0**	**1**	**3.00**	**4**	**1**	**0**	**1**	**0**	**9**	**7**	**3**	**3**	**3**
• ANDERSON, Fred														
W 1917	NY-N	0	1	18.00	1	0	0	0	0	2	5	4	0	3
• ANDREWS, Ivy														
W 1937	NY-A	0	0	3.18	1	0	0	0	0	5^2	6	2	4	1
• ANDUJAR, Joaquin														
L 1980	Hou-N	0	0	0.00	1	0	0	1	0	1	0	0	1	0
L 1982	StL-N	1	0	2.70	1	1	0	0	0	6^2	6	2	2	4
L 1985	StL-N	0	1	6.97	2	2	0	0	0	10^1	14	8	4	9
L Total	**3**	**1**	**1**	**5.00**	**4**	**3**	**0**	**1**	**0**	**18**	**20**	**10**	**7**	**13**
W 1982	StL-N	2	0	1.35	2	2	0	0	0	13^1	10	2	1	4
W 1985	StL-N	0	1	9.82	2	1	0	0	0	3^2	10	4	4	3
W Total	**2**	**2**	**1**	**3.18**	**4**	**3**	**0**	**0**	**0**	**17**	**20**	**6**	**5**	**7**
• ANKIEL, Rick														
D 2000	StL-N	0	0	13.50	1	1	0	0	0	2^2	4	4	6	3
L 2000	StL-N	0	0	20.25	2	1	0	0	0	1^1	1	3	5	2
• ANTONELLI, Johnny														
W 1954	NY-N	1	0	0.84	2	1	1	1	0	10^2	8	1	7	12
• APPIER, Kevin														
D 2000	Oak-A	0	1	3.48	2	1	0	0	0	10^1	10	4	6	13
D 2002	Ana-A	0	0	5.40	1	1	0	0	0	5	5	3	3	3
D Total	**2**	**0**	**1**	**4.11**	**3**	**2**	**0**	**0**	**0**	15^1	**15**	**7**	**9**	**16**
L 2002	Ana-A	0	1	3.48	2	2	0	0	0	10^1	10	4	4	3
W 2002	Ana-A	0	0	11.37	2	2	0	0	0	6^1	9	8	5	4
• ARMSTRONG, Jack														
W 1990	Cin-N	0	0	0.00	1	0	0	0	0	3	1	0	0	3
• ARROYO, Bronson														
L 2003	Bos-A	0	0	2.70	3	0	0	0	0	3^1	2	1	2	5
• ARROYO, Luis														
W 1960	NY-A	0	0	13.50	1	0	0	0	0	0^2	2	1	0	1
W 1961	NY-A	1	0	2.25	2	0	0	0	0	4	4	1	2	3
W Total	**2**	**1**	**0**	**3.86**	**3**	**0**	**0**	**0**	**0**	4^2	**6**	**2**	**2**	**4**
• ASHBY, Andy														
D 1996	SD-N	0	0	6.75	1	1	0	0	0	5^1	7	4	1	5
D 1998	SD-N	0	0	6.75	1	1	0	0	0	4	6	3	1	4
D 2000	Atl-N	0	0	2.45	2	0	0	0	0	3^2	1	1	3	5
D Total	**3**	**0**	**0**	**5.54**	**4**	**2**	**0**	**0**	**0**	**13**	**14**	**8**	**5**	**14**
L 1998	SD-N	0	0	2.08	2	2	0	0	0	13	14	3	2	5
W 1998	SD-N	0	1	13.50	1	1	0	0	0	2^2	10	4	1	1
• ASSENMACHER, Paul														
D 1995	Cle-A	0	0	0.00	3	0	0	0	0	1^2	0	0	0	3
D 1996	Cle-A	1	0	0.00	3	0	0	0	0	1^2	0	0	1	2
D 1997	Cle-A	0	0	5.40	4	0	0	0	0	3^1	2	2	2	2
D 1998	Cle-A	0	0	0.00	3	0	0	0	0	1	2	0	0	2
D 1999	Cle-A	0	0	27.00	1	0	0	0	0	1	5	3	0	0
D Total	**5**	**1**	**0**	**5.19**	**14**	**0**	**0**	**0**	**0**	8^2	**9**	**5**	**3**	**9**
L 1989	Chi-N	0	0	13.50	2	0	0	0	0	0^2	3	1	0	0
L 1995	Cle-A	0	0	0.00	3	0	0	0	0	1^1	0	0	1	2
L 1997	Cle-A	1	0	9.00	5	0	0	0	0	2	5	2	1	3
L 1998	Cle-A	0	0	0.00	3	0	0	0	0	2	0	0	0	3
L Total	**4**	**1**	**0**	**4.50**	**13**	**0**	**0**	**0**	**0**	**6**	**8**	**3**	**2**	**8**
W 1995	Cle-A	0	0	6.75	4	0	0	0	0	1^1	1	1	3	3
W 1997	Cle-A	0	0	0.00	5	0	0	0	0	4	5	0	0	6
W Total	**2**	**0**	**0**	**1.69**	**9**	**0**	**0**	**0**	**0**	5^1	**6**	**1**	**3**	**9**
• ASTACIO, Pedro														
D 1995	LA-N	0	0	0.00	3	0	0	0	0	3^1	1	0	0	5
D 1996	LA-N	0	0	0.00	1	0	0	0	0	1^2	0	0	0	1
D Total	**2**	**0**	**0**	**0.00**	**4**	**0**	**0**	**0**	**0**	**5**	**1**	**0**	**0**	**6**
• ATHERTON, Keith														
L 1987	Min-A	0	0	0.00	1	0	0	0	0	0^1	1	0	0	0
W 1987	Min-A	0	0	6.75	2	0	0	0	0	1^1	0	1	1	0
• AUKER, Elden														
W 1934	Det-A	1	1	5.56	2	2	1	0	0	11^1	16	7	5	2
W 1935	Det-A	0	0	3.00	1	1	0	0	0	6	6	2	2	1
W Total	**2**	**1**	**1**	**4.67**	**3**	**3**	**1**	**0**	**0**	17^1	**22**	**9**	**7**	**3**
• AVERY, Steve														
D 1995	Atl-N	0	0	13.50	1	0	0	0	0	0^2	1	1	0	1
L 1991	Atl-N	2	0	0.00	2	2	0	0	0	16^1	9	0	4	17
L 1992	Atl-N	1	1	9.00	3	2	0	0	0	8	13	8	2	3
L 1993	Atl-N	0	0	2.77	2	2	0	0	0	13	9	4	6	10
L 1995	Atl-N	1	0	0.00	2	1	0	0	0	6	2	0	4	6
L 1996	Atl-N	0	0	0.00	2	0	0	0	0	2	2	0	1	1
L Total	**5**	**4**	**1**	**2.38**	**11**	**7**	**0**	**0**	**0**	45^1	**35**	**12**	**17**	**37**
W 1991	Atl-N	0	0	3.46	2	2	0	0	0	13	10	5	1	8
W 1992	Atl-N	0	1	3.75	2	2	0	0	0	12	11	5	3	11
W 1995	Atl-N	1	0	1.50	1	1	0	0	0	6	3	1	5	3
W 1996	Atl-N	0	1	13.50	1	0	0	0	0	0^2	1	1	3	0
W Total	**4**	**1**	**2**	**3.41**	**6**	**5**	**0**	**0**	**0**	31^2	**25**	**12**	**12**	**22**
• AYALA, Bobby														
D 1995	Sea-A	0	0	54.00	2	0	0	0	0	0^2	6	4	1	0
D 1997	Sea-A	0	0	40.50	1	0	0	0	0	1^1	4	6	3	2
D Total	**2**	**0**	**0**	**45.00**	**3**	**0**	**0**	**0**	**0**	**2**	**10**	**10**	**4**	**2**
L 1995	Sea-A	0	0	2.45	2	0	0	0	0	3^2	3	1	3	3
• AYBAR, Manuel														
D 2002	SF-N	0	0	6.75	2	0	0	0	0	2^2	2	2	1	3
• BAEZ, Danys														
D 2001	Cle-A	0	0	2.45	3	0	0	0	0	3^2	4	1	0	6
• BAGBY, Jim														
W 1920	Cle-A	1	1	1.80	2	2	1	0	0	15	20	3	1	3
• BAGBY, Jim														
W 1946	Bos-A	0	0	3.00	1	0	0	0	0	3	6	1	1	1

YEAR	TM-L	W	L	ERA	G	GS	CG	SV	SHO	IP	H	ER	BB	SO
• BAHNSEN, Stan														
D 1981	Mon-N	0	0	0.00	1	0	0	0	0	1^1	1	0	1	1
• BAIR, Doug														
L 1979	Cin-N	0	1	9.00	1	0	0	0	0	1	2	1	1	0
L 1982	StL-N	0	0	0.00	1	0	0	0	0	1	2	0	3	0
L Total	2	0	1	4.50	2	0	0	0	0	2	4	1	4	0
W 1982	StL-N	0	1	9.00	3	0	0	0	0	2	2	2	2	3
W 1984	Det-N	0	0	0.00	1	0	0	0	0	0^2	0	0	0	1
W Total	2	0	1	6.75	4	0	0	0	0	2^2	2	2	2	4
• BALDWIN, Harry														
W 1924	NY-N	0	0	0.00	1	0	0	0	0	2	1	0	0	1
• BALDWIN, James														
D 2000	Chi-A	0	0	1.50	1	1	0	0	0	6	3	1	3	2
• BALDWIN, Lady														
W 1887	Det-N	4	1	1.50	5	5	5	0	1	42	28	7	10	4
• BALLOU, Win														
W 1925	Was-A	0	0	0.00	2	0	0	0	0	1^2	0	0	1	1
• BANNISTER, Floyd														
L 1983	Chi-A	0	1	4.50	1	1	0	0	0	6	5	3	1	5
• BANTA, Jack														
W 1949	Bro-N	0	0	3.18	3	0	0	0	0	5^2	5	2	1	4
• BARCELO, Lorenzo														
D 2000	Chi-A	0	0	0.00	1	0	0	0	0	1^2	0	0	1	0
• BARLOW, Mike														
L 1979	Cal-A	0	0	0.00	1	0	0	0	0	1	0	0	0	0
• BARNES, Jesse														
W 1921	NY-N	2	0	1.65	3	0	0	0	0	16^1	10	3	6	18
W 1922	NY-N	0	0	1.80	1	1	1	0	0	10	8	2	2	6
W Total	2	2	0	1.71	4	1	1	0	0	26^1	18	5	8	24
• BARNES, Virgil														
W 1923	NY-N	0	0	0.00	2	0	0	0	0	4^2	4	0	0	4
W 1924	NY-N	0	1	5.68	2	2	0	0	0	12^2	15	8	1	9
W Total	2	0	1	4.15	4	2	0	0	0	17^1	19	8	1	13
• BARNEY, Rex														
W 1947	Bro-N	0	1	2.70	3	1	0	0	0	6^2	4	2	10	3
W 1949	Bro-N	0	1	16.88	1	1	0	0	0	2^2	3	5	6	2
W Total	2	0	2	6.75	4	2	0	0	0	9^1	7	7	16	5
• BAROJAS, Salome														
L 1983	Chi-A	0	0	18.00	2	0	0	0	0	1	4	2	0	0
• BARR, Jim														
L 1971	SF-N	0	0	9.00	1	0	0	0	0	1	3	1	0	2
• BARRETT, Red														
W 1948	Bos-N	0	0	0.00	2	0	0	0	0	3^2	1	0	0	1
• BATISTA, Miguel														
D 2001	Ari-N	1	0	2.70	2	1	0	0	0	6^2	3	2	1	4
D 2002	Ari-N	0	1	9.82	1	1	0	0	0	3^2	5	4	3	1
D Total	2	1	1	5.23	3	2	0	0	0	10^1	8	6	4	5
L 2001	Ari-N	0	1	5.14	2	1	0	0	0	7	5	4	2	3
W 2001	Ari-N	0	0	0.00	2	1	0	0	0	8	5	0	5	6
• BEARD, Dave														
D 1981	Oak-A	0	0	0.00	1	0	0	1	0	3^2	1	0	0	2
L 1981	Oak-A	0	0	40.50	1	0	0	0	0	0^2	5	3	0	0
• BEARDEN, Gene														
W 1948	Cle-A	1	0	0.00	2	1	1	1	1	10^2	6	0	1	4
• BEATTIE, Jim														
L 1978	NY-A	1	0	1.69	1	1	0	0	0	5^1	2	1	5	3
W 1978	NY-A	1	0	2.00	1	1	1	0	0	9	9	2	4	8
• BEAZLEY, Johnny														
W 1942	StL-N	2	0	2.50	2	2	2	0	0	18	17	5	3	6
W 1946	StL-N	0	0	0.00	1	0	0	0	0	1	1	0	0	1
W Total	2	2	0	2.37	3	2	2	0	0	19	18	5	3	7
• BECANNON, Buck														
W 1884	NY-A	0	1	10.50	1	1	1	0	0	6	9	7	2	1
• BECK, Rod														
D 1997	SF-N	0	0	0.00	1	0	0	0	0	1^1	1	0	0	1
D 1998	Chi-N	0	0	16.20	1	0	0	0	0	1^2	5	3	2	1
D 1999	Bos-A	0	0	0.00	2	0	0	0	0	2	2	0	0	2
D Total	3	0	0	5.40	4	0	0	0	0	5	8	3	2	4
L 1999	Bos-A	0	1	27.00	1	0	0	0	0	0^2	2	2	0	1
• BECKETT, Josh														
D 2003	Fla-N	0	1	1.29	1	1	0	0	0	7	2	1	5	9
L 2003	Fla-N	1	0	3.26	3	2	1	0	1	19^1	11	7	2	19
W 2003	Fla-N	1	1	1.10	2	2	1	0	1	16^1	8	2	5	19
• BECKWITH, Joe														
L 1983	LA-N	0	0	0.00	2	0	0	0	0	2^1	1	0	2	3
W 1985	KC-A	0	0	0.00	1	0	0	0	0	2	1	0	0	3
• BEDIENT, Hugh														
W 1912	Bos-A	1	0	0.50	4	2	1	0	0	18	10	1	7	7
• BEDROSIAN, Steve														
L 1982	Atl-N	0	0	18.00	2	0	0	0	0	1	3	2	1	2
L 1989	SF-N	0	0	2.70	4	0	0	3	0	3^1	4	1	2	2
L 1991	Min-A	0	0	0.00	2	0	0	0	0	1^1	3	0	2	2
L Total	3	0	0	4.76	8	0	0	3	0	5^2	10	3	5	6
W 1989	SF-N	0	0	0.00	2	0	0	0	0	2^2	0	0	2	2
W 1991	Min-A	0	0	5.40	3	0	0	0	0	3^1	3	2	0	2
W Total	2	0	0	3.00	5	0	0	0	0	6	3	2	2	4
• BEGGS, Joe														
W 1940	Cin-N	0	0	9.00	1	0	0	0	0	1	3	1	0	1
• BEHRMAN, Hank														
W 1947	Bro-N	0	0	7.11	5	0	0	0	0	6^1	9	5	5	3
• BELCHER, Tim														
D 1995	Sea-A	0	1	6.23	2	0	0	0	0	4^1	4	3	5	0
L 1988	LA-N	2	0	4.11	2	2	0	0	0	15^1	12	7	4	16
L 1993	Chi-N	0	0	2.45	1	0	0	0	0	3^2	3	1	3	1
L 1995	Sea-A	0	1	6.35	1	1	0	0	0	5^2	9	4	2	1
L Total	3	2	1	4.38	4	3	0	0	0	24^2	24	12	9	18
W 1988	LA-N	1	0	6.23	2	2	0	0	0	8^2	10	6	6	10
• BELINDA, Stan														
D 1995	Bos-A	0	0	0.00	1	0	0	0	0	0^1	0	0	0	0
L 1990	Pit-N	0	0	2.45	3	0	0	0	0	3^2	3	1	0	4
L 1991	Pit-N	0	0	0.00	3	0	0	0	0	5	0	0	3	4
L 1992	Pit-N	0	0	0.00	2	0	0	0	0	1^2	2	0	1	2
L Total	3	1	0	0.87	8	0	0	0	0	10^1	5	1	4	10
• BELL, Gary														
W 1967	Bos-A	0	1	5.06	3	1	0	1	0	5^1	8	3	1	1
• BELL, Hi														
W 1926	StL-N	0	0	9.00	2	0	0	0	0	2	4	2	1	1
W 1930	StL-N	0	0	0.00	1	0	0	0	0	1	0	0	0	0
W 1933	NY-N	0	0	0.00	1	0	0	0	0	1	0	0	0	0
W Total	3	0	0	4.50	3	0	0	0	0	4	4	2	1	1
• BENDER, Chief														
W 1905	Phi-A	1	1	1.06	2	2	2	0	1	17	9	2	6	13
W 1910	Phi-A	1	1	1.93	2	2	2	0	0	18^2	13	4	4	14
W 1911	Phi-A	2	1	1.04	3	3	3	0	0	26	16	3	8	20
W 1913	Phi-A	2	0	4.00	2	2	2	0	0	18	19	8	1	9
W 1914	Phi-A	0	0	10.13	1	1	0	0	0	5^1	8	6	2	3
W Total	5	6	4	2.44	10	10	9	0	1	85	65	23	21	59
• BENES, Alan														
L 1996	StL-N	0	0	2.84	2	2	0	0	0	6^1	3	2	2	5
L 2000	StL-N	1	0	2.25	1	1	0	0	0	8	6	2	3	5
L Total	2	1	1	2.51	3	2	0	0	0	14^1	9	4	5	10
• BENES, Andy														
D 1995	Sea-A	0	0	5.40	2	2	0	0	0	11^2	10	7	9	8
D 1996	StL-N	0	0	5.14	1	1	0	0	0	7	6	4	1	9
D 2002	StL-N	0	0	5.79	1	1	0	0	0	4^2	2	3	4	5
D Total	3	0	0	5.40	4	4	0	0	0	23^1	18	14	14	22
L 1995	Sea-A	0	1	23.14	1	1	0	0	0	2^1	6	6	2	3
L 1996	StL-N	0	0	5.28	3	2	0	0	0	15^1	19	9	3	9
L 2002	StL-N	0	0	3.38	1	1	0	0	0	5^1	2	2	4	5
L Total	3	0	1	6.65	5	4	0	0	0	23	27	17	9	17
• BENITEZ, Armando														
D 1996	Bal-A	2	0	2.25	3	0	0	0	0	4	1	1	2	6
D 1997	Bal-A	0	0	3.00	3	0	0	0	0	3	3	1	2	4
D 1999	NY-N	0	0	0.00	2	0	0	0	0	2^1	2	0	1	2
D 2000	NY-N	1	0	6.00	2	0	0	0	0	3	4	2	1	3
D Total	4	3	0	2.92	10	0	0	0	0	12^1	10	4	6	15
L 1996	Bal-A	0	0	7.71	3	0	0	1	0	2^1	3	2	3	2
L 1997	Bal-A	0	2	12.00	4	0	0	0	0	3	3	4	4	6
L 1999	NY-N	0	0	1.35	5	0	0	1	0	6^2	3	1	2	9
L 2000	NY-N	0	0	0.00	3	0	0	1	0	3	3	0	2	2
L Total	4	0	2	4.20	15	0	0	3	0	15	12	7	11	19
W 2000	NY-N	0	0	3.00	3	0	0	1	0	3	3	1	2	2
• BENTLEY, Jack														
W 1923	NY-N	0	1	9.45	2	1	0	0	0	6^2	10	7	4	1
W 1924	NY-N	1	2	3.18	3	2	1	0	0	17	18	6	8	10
W Total	2	1	3	4.94	5	3	1	0	0	23^2	28	13	12	11
• BENTON, Al														
W 1945	Det-A	0	0	1.93	3	0	0	0	0	4^2	6	1	0	5
• BENTON, Rube														
W 1917	NY-N	1	1	0.00	2	2	1	0	1	14	9	0	1	8
• BERE, Jason														
L 1993	Chi-A	1	0	11.57	1	1	0	0	0	2^1	5	3	2	3
• BERENGUER, Juan														
L 1987	Min-A	0	0	1.50	4	0	0	1	0	6	1	1	3	6
W 1987	Min-A	0	1	10.38	3	0	0	0	0	4^1	10	5	0	1
• BERNARD, Dwight														
D 1981	Mil-A	0	0	0.00	2	0	0	0	0	2^1	1	0	0	0
L 1982	Mil-A	0	0	0.00	1	0	0	0	0	1	0	0	0	0
W 1982	Mil-A	0	0	0.00	1	0	0	0	0	1	0	0	0	1
• BESSENT, Don														
W 1955	Bro-N	0	0	0.00	3	0	0	0	0	3^1	3	0	1	1
W 1956	Bro-N	1	0	1.80	2	0	0	0	0	10	8	2	3	5
W Total	2	1	0	1.35	5	0	0	0	0	13^1	11	2	4	6
• BEVENS, Bill														
W 1947	NY-A	0	1	2.38	2	1	1	0	0	11^1	3	3	11	7
• BIBBY, Jim														
L 1979	Pit-N	0	0	1.29	1	1	0	0	0	7	4	1	4	5
W 1979	Pit-N	0	0	2.61	2	2	0	0	0	10^1	10	3	2	10
• BICKFORD, Vern														
W 1948	Bos-N	0	1	2.70	1	1	0	0	0	3^1	4	1	5	1

YEAR	TM-L	W	L	ERA	G	GS	CG	SV	SHO	IP	H	ER	BB	SO
• BIELECKI, Mike														
D 1996	Atl-N	0	0	0.00	1	0	0	0	0	0^2	0	0	1	1
L 1989	Chi-N	0	1	3.65	2	2	0	0	0	12^1	7	5	6	11
L 1996	Atl-N	0	0	0.00	3	0	0	0	0	3	0	0	1	5
L Total	**2**	**0**	**1**	**2.93**	**5**	**2**	**0**	**0**	**0**	**15^1**	**7**	**5**	**7**	**16**
W 1996	Atl-N	0	0	0.00	2	0	0	0	0	3	0	0	3	6
• BILLINGHAM, Jack														
L 1972	Cin-N	0	0	3.86	1	1	0	0	0	4^2	5	2	2	4
L 1973	Cin-N	0	1	4.50	2	2	0	0	0	12	9	6	4	9
L Total	**2**	**0**	**1**	**4.32**	**3**	**3**	**0**	**0**	**0**	**16^2**	**14**	**8**	**6**	**13**
W 1972	Cin-N	1	0	0.00	3	2	0	1	0	13^2	6	0	4	11
W 1975	Cin-N	0	0	1.00	3	1	0	0	0	9	8	1	5	7
W 1976	Cin-N	1	0	0.00	1	0	0	0	0	2^2	0	0	0	1
W Total	**3**	**2**	**0**	**0.36**	**7**	**3**	**0**	**1**	**0**	**25^1**	**14**	**1**	**9**	**19**
• BIRD, Doug														
L 1976	KC-A	1	0	1.93	1	0	0	0	0	4^2	4	1	0	1
L 1977	KC-A	0	0	0.00	3	0	0	0	0	2	4	0	0	1
L 1978	KC-A	0	1	9.00	2	0	0	0	0	1	2	1	0	1
L Total	**3**	**1**	**1**	**2.35**	**6**	**0**	**0**	**0**	**0**	**7^2**	**10**	**2**	**0**	**3**
• BLACK, Bud														
L 1984	KC-A	0	1	7.20	1	1	0	0	0	5	7	4	1	3
L 1985	KC-A	0	0	1.69	3	1	0	0	0	10^2	11	2	4	8
L Total	**2**	**0**	**1**	**3.45**	**4**	**2**	**0**	**0**	**0**	**15^2**	**18**	**6**	**5**	**11**
W 1985	KC-A	0	1	5.06	2	1	0	0	0	5^1	4	3	5	4
• BLACK, Joe														
W 1952	Bro-N	1	2	2.53	3	3	1	0	0	21^1	15	6	8	9
W 1953	Bro-N	0	0	9.00	1	0	0	0	0	1	1	1	0	2
W Total	**2**	**1**	**2**	**2.82**	**4**	**3**	**1**	**0**	**0**	**22^1**	**16**	**7**	**8**	**11**
• BLACKWELL, Ewell														
W 1952	NY-A	0	0	7.20	1	1	0	0	0	5	4	4	3	4
• BLAIR, Willie														
D 1996	SD-N	0	0	0.00	1	0	0	0	0	2	1	0	2	3
• BLAKE, Sheriff														
W 1929	Chi-N	0	1	13.50	2	0	0	0	0	1^1	4	2	0	1
• BLASS, Steve														
L 1971	Pit-N	0	1	11.57	2	2	0	0	0	7	14	9	2	11
L 1972	Pit-N	1	0	1.72	2	2	0	0	0	15^2	12	3	6	5
L Total	**2**	**1**	**1**	**4.76**	**4**	**4**	**0**	**0**	**0**	**22^2**	**26**	**12**	**8**	**16**
W 1971	Pit-N	2	0	1.00	2	2	2	0	0	18	7	2	4	13
• BLUE, Vida														
L 1971	Oak-A	0	1	6.43	1	1	0	0	0	7	7	5	2	8
L 1972	Oak-A	0	0	0.00	4	0	0	1	0	5^1	4	0	1	5
L 1973	Oak-A	0	1	10.29	2	2	0	0	0	7	8	8	5	3
L 1974	Oak-A	1	0	0.00	1	1	1	0	1	9	2	0	0	7
L 1975	Oak-A	0	0	9.00	1	1	0	0	0	3	6	3	0	2
L Total	**5**	**1**	**2**	**4.60**	**9**	**5**	**1**	**1**	**1**	**31^1**	**27**	**16**	**8**	**25**
W 1972	Oak-A	0	1	4.15	4	1	0	1	0	8^2	8	4	5	5
W 1973	Oak-A	0	1	4.91	2	2	0	0	0	11	10	6	3	8
W 1974	Oak-A	0	1	3.29	2	2	0	0	0	13^2	10	5	7	9
W Total	**3**	**0**	**3**	**4.05**	**8**	**5**	**0**	**1**	**0**	**33^1**	**28**	**15**	**15**	**22**
• BLYLEVEN, Bert														
L 1970	Min-A	0	0	0.00	1	0	0	0	0	2	2	0	0	2
L 1979	Pit-N	1	0	1.00	1	1	1	0	0	9	8	1	0	9
L 1987	Min-A	2	0	4.05	2	2	0	0	0	13^1	12	6	3	9
L Total	**3**	**3**	**0**	**2.59**	**4**	**3**	**1**	**0**	**0**	**24^1**	**22**	**7**	**3**	**20**
W 1979	Pit-N	1	0	1.80	2	1	0	0	0	10	8	2	3	4
W 1987	Min-A	1	1	2.77	2	2	0	0	0	13	13	4	2	12
W Total	**2**	**2**	**1**	**2.35**	**4**	**3**	**0**	**0**	**0**	**23**	**21**	**6**	**5**	**16**
• BOCHTLER, Doug														
D 1996	SD-N	0	1	27.00	1	0	0	0	0	0^1	0	1	2	0
• BODDICKER, Mike														
L 1983	Bal-A	1	0	0.00	1	1	1	0	1	9	5	0	3	14
L 1988	Bos-A	0	1	20.25	1	1	0	0	0	2^2	8	6	1	2
L 1990	Bos-A	0	1	2.25	1	1	1	0	0	8	6	2	3	7
L Total	**3**	**1**	**2**	**3.66**	**3**	**3**	**2**	**0**	**1**	**19^2**	**19**	**8**	**7**	**23**
W 1983	Bal-A	1	0	0.00	1	1	1	0	0	9	3	0	0	6
• BOEHRINGER, Brian														
D 1996	NY-A	1	0	6.75	2	0	0	0	0	1^1	3	1	2	0
D 1997	NY-A	0	0	0.00	1	0	0	0	0	1^2	1	0	1	2
D Total	**2**	**1**	**0**	**3.00**	**3**	**0**	**0**	**0**	**0**	**3**	**4**	**1**	**3**	**2**
L 1998	SD-N	0	0	0.00	3	0	0	0	0	3	3	0	1	1
W 1996	NY-A	0	0	5.40	2	0	0	0	0	5	5	3	0	5
W 1998	SD-N	0	0	9.00	2	0	0	0	0	2	4	2	2	3
W Total	**2**	**0**	**0**	**6.43**	**4**	**0**	**0**	**0**	**0**	**7**	**9**	**5**	**2**	**8**
• BOLIN, Bobby														
W 1962	SF-N	0	0	6.75	2	0	0	0	0	2^2	4	2	2	2
• BOLTON, Tom														
L 1990	Bos-A	0	0	0.00	2	0	0	0	0	3	2	0	2	3
• BONHAM, Tiny														
W 1941	NY-A	1	0	1.00	1	1	1	0	0	9	4	1	2	2
W 1942	NY-A	0	1	4.09	2	1	1	0	0	11	9	5	3	3
W 1943	NY-A	0	1	4.50	1	1	0	0	0	8	6	4	3	9
W Total	**3**	**1**	**2**	**3.21**	**4**	**3**	**2**	**0**	**0**	**28**	**19**	**10**	**8**	**14**
• BOOKER, Greg														
L 1984	SD-N	0	0	0.00	1	0	0	0	0	2	2	0	1	2
W 1984	SD-N	0	0	9.00	1	0	0	0	0	1	0	1	4	0

YEAR	TM-L	W	L	ERA	G	GS	CG	SV	SHO	IP	H	ER	BB	SO
• BORBON, Pedro														
L 1972	Cin-N	0	0	2.08	3	0	0	0	0	4^1	2	1	0	1
L 1973	Cin-N	1	0	0.00	4	0	0	1	0	4^2	3	0	0	3
L 1975	Cin-N	0	0	0.00	1	0	0	1	0	1	0	0	0	1
L 1976	Cin-N	0	0	0.00	2	0	0	1	0	4^1	4	0	1	1
L Total	**4**	**1**	**0**	**0.63**	**10**	**0**	**0**	**3**	**0**	**14^1**	**9**	**1**	**1**	**6**
W 1972	Cin-N	0	1	3.86	6	0	0	0	0	7	7	3	2	4
W 1975	Cin-N	0	0	6.00	3	0	0	0	0	3	3	2	2	1
W 1976	Cin-N	0	0	0.00	1	0	0	0	0	1^2	0	0	0	0
W Total	**3**	**0**	**1**	**3.86**	**10**	**0**	**0**	**0**	**0**	**11^2**	**10**	**5**	**4**	**5**
• BORBON, Pedro														
D 1995	Atl-N	0	0	0.00	1	0	0	0	0	1	1	0	0	3
W 1995	Atl-N	0	0	0.00	1	0	0	1	0	1	0	0	0	2
• BOROWSKI, Joe														
D 2003	Chi-N	0	0	0.00	2	0	0	1	0	2	1	0	0	5
L 2003	Chi-N	1	0	1.59	3	0	0	0	0	5^2	5	1	3	1
• BOROWY, Hank														
W 1942	NY-A	0	0	18.00	1	1	0	0	0	3	6	6	3	1
W 1943	NY-A	1	0	2.25	1	1	0	0	0	8	6	2	3	4
W 1945	Chi-N	2	2	4.00	4	3	1	0	1	18	21	8	6	8
W Total	**3**	**3**	**2**	**4.97**	**6**	**5**	**1**	**0**	**1**	**29**	**33**	**16**	**12**	**13**
• BOSIO, Chris														
D 1995	Sea-A	0	0	10.57	2	2	0	0	0	7^2	10	9	4	2
L 1995	Sea-A	0	1	3.38	1	1	0	0	0	5^1	7	2	2	3
• BOSMAN, Dick														
L 1975	Oak-A	0	0	0.00	1	0	0	0	0	0^1	0	0	0	0
• BOSWELL, Dave														
L 1969	Min-A	0	1	0.84	1	1	0	0	0	10^2	7	1	7	4
W 1965	Min-A	0	0	3.38	1	0	0	0	0	2^2	3	1	2	3
• BOUTON, Jim														
W 1963	NY-A	0	1	1.29	1	1	0	0	0	7	4	1	5	4
W 1964	NY-A	2	0	1.56	2	2	1	0	0	17^1	15	3	5	7
W Total	**2**	**2**	**1**	**1.48**	**3**	**3**	**1**	**0**	**0**	**24^1**	**19**	**4**	**10**	**11**
• BOWIE, Micah														
D 2002	Oak-A	0	0	0.00	1	0	0	0	0	1^1	0	0	0	3
• BOYD, Oil Can														
L 1986	Bos-A	1	1	4.61	2	2	0	0	0	13^2	17	7	3	8
W 1986	Bos-A	0	1	7.71	1	1	0	0	0	7	9	6	1	3
• BRADFORD, Chad														
D 2000	Chi-A	0	0	0.00	1	0	0	0	0	0^2	2	0	0	0
D 2001	Oak-A	0	0	0.00	1	0	0	0	0	1	0	0	0	1
D 2002	Oak-A	0	0	0.00	2	0	0	0	0	3	1	0	0	1
D 2003	Oak-A	0	0	0.00	4	0	0	0	0	3^2	4	0	2	5
D Total	**4**	**0**	**0**	**0.00**	**8**	**0**	**0**	**0**	**0**	**8^1**	**7**	**0**	**2**	**7**
• BRANCA, Ralph														
W 1947	Bro-N	1	1	8.64	3	1	0	0	0	8^1	12	8	5	8
W 1949	Bro-N	0	1	4.15	1	1	0	0	0	8^2	4	4	4	6
W Total	**2**	**1**	**2**	**6.35**	**4**	**2**	**0**	**0**	**0**	**17**	**16**	**12**	**9**	**14**
• BRANTLEY, Jeff														
D 1995	Cin-N	0	0	6.00	3	0	0	1	0	3	5	2	0	2
L 1989	SF-N	0	0	0.00	3	0	0	0	0	5	1	0	2	3
L 1995	Cin-N	0	0	0.00	2	0	0	0	0	2^2	0	0	2	1
L Total	**2**	**0**	**0**	**0.00**	**5**	**0**	**0**	**0**	**0**	**7^2**	**1**	**0**	**4**	**4**
W 1989	SF-N	0	0	4.15	3	0	0	0	0	4^1	5	2	3	1
• BRAZLE, Al														
W 1943	StL-N	0	1	3.68	1	1	0	0	0	7^1	5	3	2	4
W 1946	StL-N	0	1	5.40	1	0	0	0	0	6^2	7	4	6	4
W Total	**2**	**0**	**2**	**4.50**	**2**	**1**	**0**	**0**	**0**	**14**	**12**	**7**	**8**	**8**
• BRECHEEN, Harry														
W 1943	StL-N	0	1	2.45	3	0	0	0	0	3^2	5	1	3	3
W 1944	StL-N	1	0	1.00	1	1	1	0	0	9	9	1	4	4
W 1946	StL-N	3	0	0.45	3	2	2	0	1	20	14	1	5	11
W Total	**3**	**4**	**1**	**0.83**	**7**	**3**	**3**	**0**	**1**	**32^2**	**28**	**3**	**12**	**18**
• BRENNAN, Don														
W 1937	NY-N	0	0	0.00	2	0	0	0	0	3	1	0	1	1
• BRETT, Ken														
L 1974	Pit-N	0	0	7.71	1	0	0	0	0	2^1	3	2	2	1
L 1975	Pit-N	0	0	0.00	2	0	0	0	0	2^1	1	0	0	1
L Total	**2**	**0**	**0**	**3.86**	**3**	**0**	**0**	**0**	**0**	**4^2**	**4**	**2**	**2**	**2**
W 1967	Bos-A	0	0	0.00	2	0	0	0	0	1^1	0	0	1	1
• BREUER, Marv														
W 1941	NY-A	0	0	0.00	1	0	0	0	0	3	3	0	1	2
W 1942	NY-A	0	0	....	1	0	0	0	0	0	2	0	0	0
W Total	**2**	**0**	**0**	**0.00**	**2**	**0**	**0**	**0**	**0**	**3**	**5**	**0**	**1**	**2**
• BREWER, Jim														
W 1965	LA-N	0	0	4.50	1	0	0	0	0	2	3	1	0	1
W 1966	LA-N	0	0	0.00	1	0	0	0	0	1	0	0	0	1
W 1974	LA-N	0	0	0.00	1	0	0	0	0	0^1	0	0	0	1
W Total	**3**	**0**	**0**	**2.70**	**3**	**0**	**0**	**0**	**0**	**3^1**	**3**	**1**	**0**	**3**
• BRIDGES, Marshall														
W 1962	NY-A	0	0	4.91	2	0	0	0	0	3^2	4	2	2	3
• BRIDGES, Tommy														
W 1934	Det-A	1	1	3.63	3	2	1	0	0	17^1	21	7	1	12
W 1935	Det-A	2	0	2.50	2	2	2	0	0	18	18	5	4	9
W 1940	Det-A	1	0	3.00	1	1	1	0	0	9	10	3	1	5

YEAR	TM-L	W	L	ERA	G	GS	CG	SV	SHO	IP	H	ER	BB	SO
W 1945	Det-A	0	0	16.20	1	0	0	0	0	1^2	3	3	3	1
W Total	4	4	1	3.52	7	5	4	0	0	46	52	18	9	27
• **BRILES, Nelson**														
L 1972	Pit-N	0	0	3.00	1	1	0	0	0	6	6	2	1	3
W 1967	StL-N	1	0	1.64	2	1	1	0	0	11	7	2	1	4
W 1968	StL-N	0	1	5.56	2	2	0	0	0	11^1	13	7	4	7
W 1971	Pit-N	1	0	0.00	1	1	1	0	1	9	2	0	2	2
W Total	3	2	1	2.59	5	4	2	0	1	31^1	22	9	7	13
• **BRITTON, Jim**														
L 1969	Atl-N	0	0	0.00	1	0	0	0	0	0^1	0	0	1	0
• **BROHAWN, Troy**														
W 2001	Ari-N	0	0	0.00	1	0	0	0	0	1	1	0	0	1
• **BROSNAN, Jim**														
W 1961	Cin-N	0	0	7.50	3	0	0	0	0	6	9	5	4	5
• **BROWER, Jim**														
D 2003	SF-N	0	0	6.00	2	0	0	0	0	3	5	2	3	3
• **BROWN, Kevin**														
D 1997	Fla-N	0	0	1.29	1	1	0	0	0	7	4	1	0	5
D 1998	SD-N	1	0	0.61	2	2	0	0	0	14^2	5	1	7	21
D Total	2	1	0	0.83	3	3	0	0	0	21^2	9	2	7	26
L 1997	Fla-N	2	0	4.20	2	2	1	0	0	15	16	7	5	11
L 1998	SD-N	1	1	2.61	2	1	1	0	1	10^1	5	3	4	12
L Total	2	3	1	3.55	4	3	2	0	1	25^1	21	10	9	23
W 1997	Fla-N	0	2	8.18	2	2	0	0	0	11	15	10	5	6
W 1998	SD-N	0	1	4.40	2	2	0	0	0	14^1	14	7	6	13
W Total	2	0	3	6.04	4	4	0	0	0	25^1	29	17	11	19
• **BROWN, Mace**														
W 1946	Bos-A	0	0	27.00	1	0	0	0	0	1	4	3	1	0
• **BROWN, Mordecai**														
W 1906	Chi-N	1	2	3.20	3	3	2	0	1	19^2	14	7	4	12
W 1907	Chi-N	1	0	0.00	1	1	1	0	1	9	7	0	1	4
W 1908	Chi-N	2	0	0.00	2	1	1	0	1	11	6	0	1	5
W 1910	Chi-N	1	2	5.50	3	2	1	0	0	18	23	11	7	14
W Total	4	5	4	2.81	9	7	5	0	3	57^2	50	18	13	35
• **BROWNING, Tom**														
L 1990	Cin-N	1	1	3.27	2	2	0	0	0	11	9	4	6	5
W 1990	Cin-N	1	0	4.50	1	1	0	0	0	6	6	3	2	2
• **BRUSSTAR, Warren**														
D 1981	Phi-N	0	0	4.91	2	0	0	0	0	3^2	5	2	1	3
L 1977	Phi-N	0	0	3.38	2	0	0	0	0	2^2	2	1	1	2
L 1978	Phi-N	0	0	0.00	3	0	0	0	0	2^2	2	0	1	0
L 1980	Phi-N	1	0	3.38	2	0	0	0	0	2^2	1	1	1	0
L 1984	Chi-N	0	0	0.00	3	0	0	0	0	4^1	6	0	0	1
L Total	4	1	0	1.46	10	0	0	0	0	12^1	11	2	3	3
W 1980	Phi-N	0	0	0.00	1	0	0	0	0	2^1	0	0	1	0
• **BRYANT, Clay**														
W 1938	Chi-N	0	1	6.75	1	1	0	0	0	5^1	6	4	5	3
• **BRYANT, Ron**														
L 1971	SF-N	0	0	4.50	1	0	0	0	0	2	1	1	1	2
• **BUEHRLE, Mark**														
D 2000	Chi-A	0	0	0.00	1	0	0	0	0	0^1	2	0	0	1
• **BUHL, Bob**														
W 1957	Mil-N	0	1	10.80	2	2	0	0	0	3^1	6	4	6	4
• **BUMP, Nate**														
L 2003	Fla-N	0	0	6.00	2	0	0	0	0	3	3	2	0	3
• **BUNKER, Wally**														
W 1966	Bal-A	1	0	0.00	1	1	1	0	1	9	6	0	1	6
• **BURBA, Dave**														
D 1995	Cin-N	1	0	0.00	1	0	0	0	0	1	2	0	1	0
D 1998	Cle-A	1	0	5.06	1	0	0	0	0	5^1	4	3	2	4
D 1999	Cle-A	0	0	0.00	1	1	0	0	0	4	1	0	1	0
D 2001	Cle-A	0	0	0.00	1	0	0	0	0	1	0	0	0	1
D Total	4	2	0	2.38	4	1	0	0	0	11^1	7	3	4	5
L 1995	Cin-N	0	0	0.00	2	0	0	0	0	3^2	3	0	4	0
L 1998	Cle-A	1	0	3.00	3	0	0	0	0	6	3	2	5	8
L Total	2	1	0	1.86	5	0	0	0	0	9^2	6	2	9	8
• **BURDETTE, Lew**														
W 1957	Mil-N	3	0	0.67	3	3	3	0	2	27	21	2	4	13
W 1958	Mil-N	1	2	5.64	3	3	1	0	0	22^1	22	14	4	12
W Total	2	4	2	2.92	6	6	4	0	2	49^1	43	16	8	25
• **BURKETT, John**														
D 1996	Tex-A	1	0	2.00	1	1	1	0	0	9	10	2	1	7
D 2000	Atl-N	0	0	6.75	1	0	0	0	0	1^1	1	1	0	0
D 2001	Atl-N	1	0	2.84	1	1	0	0	0	6^1	6	2	2	4
D 2003	Bos-A	0	0	6.75	1	1	0	0	0	5^1	9	4	2	1
D Total	4	2	0	3.68	4	3	1	0	0	22	26	9	5	12
L 2001	Atl-N	0	1	8.31	1	1	0	0	0	4^1	7	4	2	2
L 2003	Bos-A	0	0	7.36	1	1	0	0	0	3^2	7	3	0	1
L Total	2	0	1	7.88	2	2	0	0	0	8	14	7	2	3
• **BURNS, Britt**														
L 1983	Chi-A	0	1	0.96	1	1	0	0	0	9^1	6	1	5	8
• **BURNS, Todd**														
W 1988	Oak-A	0	0	0.00	1	0	0	0	0	0^1	0	0	0	0
W 1989	Oak-A	0	0	0.00	2	0	0	0	0	1^2	1	0	1	0

YEAR	TM-L	W	L	ERA	G	GS	CG	SV	SHO	IP	H	ER	BB	SO
W 1990	Oak-A	0	0	16.20	2	0	0	0	0	1^2	5	3	2	0
W Total	3	0	0	7.36	5	0	0	0	0	3^2	6	3	3	0
• **BURRIS, Ray**														
D 1981	Mon-N	0	1	5.06	1	1	0	0	0	5^1	7	3	4	4
L 1981	Mon-N	1	0	0.53	2	2	1	0	1	17	10	1	3	4
• **BURTON, Jim**														
W 1975	Bos-A	0	1	9.00	2	0	0	0	0	1	1	1	3	0
• **BUSH, Guy**														
W 1929	Chi-N	1	0	0.82	2	1	1	0	0	11	12	1	2	4
W 1932	Chi-N	0	1	14.29	2	2	0	0	0	5^2	5	9	6	2
W Total	2	1	1	5.40	4	3	1	0	0	16^2	17	10	8	6
• **BUSH, Joe**														
W 1913	Phi-A	1	0	1.00	1	1	1	0	0	9	5	1	4	3
W 1914	Phi-A	0	1	3.27	1	1	1	0	0	11	9	4	4	4
W 1918	Bos-A	0	1	3.00	2	1	1	1	0	9	7	3	3	0
W 1922	NY-A	0	2	4.80	2	2	1	0	0	15	21	8	5	6
W 1923	NY-A	1	1	1.08	3	1	1	0	0	16^2	7	2	4	5
W Total	5	2	5	2.67	9	6	5	1	0	60^2	49	18	20	18
• **BYERLY, Bud**														
W 1944	StL-N	0	0	0.00	1	0	0	0	0	1^1	0	0	0	1
• **BYRNE, Tommy**														
W 1949	NY-A	0	0	2.70	1	1	0	0	0	3^1	2	1	2	1
W 1955	NY-A	1	1	1.88	2	2	1	0	0	14^1	8	3	8	8
W 1956	NY-A	0	0	0.00	1	0	0	0	0	0^1	1	0	0	1
W 1957	NY-A	0	0	5.40	2	0	0	0	0	3^1	1	2	2	1
W Total	4	1	1	2.53	6	3	1	0	0	21^1	12	6	12	11
• **BYSTROM, Marty**														
L 1980	Phi-N	0	0	1.69	1	1	0	0	0	5^1	7	1	2	1
W 1980	Phi-N	0	0	5.40	1	1	0	0	0	5	10	3	1	4
W 1983	Phi-N	0	0	0.00	1	0	0	0	0	1	0	0	0	1
W Total	2	0	0	4.50	2	1	0	0	0	6	10	3	1	5
• **CABRERA, Jose**														
D 1999	Hou-N	0	0	0.00	1	0	0	0	0	2	2	0	0	6
• **CADARET, Greg**														
L 1988	Oak-A	0	0	27.00	1	0	0	0	0	0^1	1	1	0	0
W 1988	Oak-A	0	0	0.00	3	0	0	0	0	2	2	0	0	3
• **CADORE, Leon**														
W 1920	Bro-N	0	1	9.00	2	1	0	0	0	2	4	2	1	1
• **CALDWELL, Mike**														
D 1981	Mil-A	0	1	4.32	2	1	0	0	0	8^1	9	4	0	4
L 1982	Mil-A	0	1	15.00	1	1	0	0	0	3	7	5	1	2
W 1982	Mil-A	2	0	2.04	3	2	1	0	1	17^2	19	4	3	6
• **CALDWELL, Ray**														
W 1920	Cle-A	0	1	27.00	1	1	0	0	0	0^1	2	1	1	0
• **CALHOUN, Jeff**														
L 1986	Hou-N	0	0	9.00	1	0	0	0	0	1	1	1	1	0
• **CAMNITZ, Howie**														
W 1909	Pit-N	0	1	9.82	2	1	0	0	0	3^2	8	4	2	2
• **CAMP, Rick**														
L 1982	Atl-N	0	1	36.00	1	1	0	0	0	1	4	4	1	0
• **CAMPBELL, Bill**														
L 1985	StL-N	0	0	0.00	3	0	0	0	0	2^1	3	0	0	2
W 1985	StL-N	0	0	2.25	3	0	0	0	0	4	4	1	2	5
• **CANDELARIA, John**														
L 1975	Pit-N	0	0	3.52	1	1	0	0	0	7^2	3	3	2	14
L 1979	Pit-N	0	0	2.57	1	1	0	0	0	7	5	2	1	4
L 1986	Cal-A	1	1	0.84	2	2	0	0	0	10^2	11	1	6	7
L Total	3	1	1	2.13	4	4	0	0	0	25^1	19	6	9	25
W 1979	Pit-N	1	1	5.00	2	2	0	0	0	9	14	5	2	4
• **CANDIOTTI, Tom**														
D 1996	LA-N	0	0	0.00	1	0	0	0	0	2	0	0	0	1
L 1991	Tor-A	0	1	8.22	2	2	0	0	0	7^2	17	7	2	5
• **CARDWELL, Don**														
W 1969	NY-N	0	0	0.00	1	0	0	0	0	1	0	0	0	0
• **CARLETON, Tex**														
W 1934	StL-N	0	0	7.36	2	1	0	0	0	3^2	5	3	2	2
W 1935	Chi-N	0	1	1.29	1	1	0	0	0	7	6	1	7	4
W 1938	Chi-N	0	0	....	1	0	0	0	0	0	1	2	2	0
W Total	3	0	1	5.06	4	2	0	0	0	10^2	12	6	11	6
• **CARLSON, Hal**														
W 1929	Chi-N	0	0	6.75	2	0	0	0	0	4	7	3	1	3
• **CARLTON, Steve**														
D 1981	Phi-N	0	2	3.86	2	2	0	0	0	14	14	6	8	13
L 1976	Phi-N	0	1	5.14	1	1	0	0	0	7	8	4	5	6
L 1977	Phi-N	0	1	6.94	2	2	0	0	0	11^2	13	9	8	6
L 1978	Phi-N	1	0	4.00	1	1	1	0	0	9	8	4	2	8
L 1980	Phi-N	1	0	2.19	2	2	0	0	0	12^1	11	3	8	6
L 1983	Phi-N	2	0	0.66	2	2	0	0	0	13^2	13	1	5	13
L Total	5	4	2	3.52	8	8	1	0	0	53^2	53	21	28	39
W 1967	StL-N	0	1	0.00	1	1	0	0	0	6	3	0	2	5
W 1968	StL-N	0	0	6.75	2	0	0	0	0	4	7	3	1	3
W 1980	Phi-N	2	0	2.40	2	2	0	0	0	15	14	4	9	17
W 1983	Phi-N	0	1	2.70	1	1	0	0	0	6^2	5	2	3	7
W Total	4	2	2	2.56	6	4	0	0	0	31^2	29	9	15	32
• **CARRASCO, Hector**														
L 1995	Cin-N	0	0	0.00	1	0	0	0	0	1^1	1	0	0	3

YEAR	TM-L	W	L	ERA	G	GS	CG	SV	SHO	IP	H	ER	BB	SO
• CARRITHERS, Don														
L 1971	SF-N	0	0	....	1	0	0	0	0	0	3	3	0	0
• CARROLL, Clay														
L 1970	Cin-N	0	0	0.00	2	0	0	1	0	1^1	2	0	0	2
L 1972	Cin-N	1	1	3.38	2	0	0	0	0	2^2	2	1	3	0
L 1973	Cin-N	1	0	1.29	3	0	0	0	0	7	5	1	1	2
L 1975	Cin-N	0	0	0.00	1	0	0	0	0	1	0	0	1	1
L Total	**4**	**2**	**1**	**1.50**	**8**	**0**	**0**	**1**	**0**	**12**	**9**	**2**	**5**	**5**
W 1970	Cin-N	1	0	0.00	4	0	0	0	0	9	5	0	2	11
W 1972	Cin-N	0	1	1.59	5	0	0	1	0	5^2	6	1	4	3
W 1975	Cin-N	1	0	3.18	5	0	0	0	0	5^2	4	2	2	3
W Total	**3**	**2**	**1**	**1.33**	**14**	**0**	**0**	**1**	**0**	**20^1**	**15**	**3**	**8**	**17**
• CARUTHERS, Bob														
W 1885	StL-A	1	1	2.42	3	3	3	0	0	26	25	7	4	16
W 1886	StL-A	2	1	2.42	3	3	3	0	1	26	18	7	6	12
W 1887	StL-A	4	4	2.15	8	8	8	0	0	71	76	17	12	19
W 1889	Bro-A	0	2	3.75	4	2	2	1	0	24	28	10	6	6
W Total	**4**	**7**	**8**	**2.51**	**18**	**16**	**16**	**1**	**1**	**147**	**147**	**41**	**28**	**53**
• CASEY, Hugh														
W 1941	Bro-N	0	2	3.38	3	0	0	0	0	5^1	9	2	2	1
W 1947	Bro-N	2	0	0.87	6	0	0	1	0	10^1	5	1	1	3
W Total	**2**	**2**	**2**	**1.72**	**9**	**0**	**0**	**1**	**0**	**15^2**	**14**	**3**	**3**	**4**
• CASTER, George														
W 1945	Det-A	0	0	0.00	1	0	0	0	0	0^2	0	0	0	1
• CASTILLO, Bobby														
L 1981	LA-N	0	0	0.00	1	0	0	0	0	1	0	0	0	1
L 1985	LA-N	0	0	3.38	1	0	0	0	0	5^1	4	2	2	4
L Total	**2**	**0**	**0**	**2.84**	**2**	**0**	**0**	**0**	**0**	**6^1**	**4**	**2**	**2**	**5**
W 1981	LA-N	0	0	9.00	1	0	0	0	0	1	0	1	5	0
• CASTILLO, Tony														
L 1993	Tor-A	0	0	0.00	2	0	0	0	0	2	0	0	1	1
W 1993	Tor-A	1	0	8.10	2	0	0	0	0	3^1	6	3	3	1
• CASTLEMAN, Slick														
W 1936	NY-N	0	0	2.08	1	0	0	0	0	4^1	3	1	2	5
• CATHER, Mike														
D 1997	Atl-N	0	0	0.00	1	0	0	0	0	2	0	0	1	2
L 1997	Atl-N	0	0	0.00	4	0	0	0	0	2^2	3	0	0	3
• CERUTTI, John														
L 1989	Tor-A	0	0	0.00	2	0	0	0	0	2^2	0	0	3	1
• CHALMERS, George														
W 1915	Phi-N	0	1	2.25	1	1	1	0	0	8	8	2	3	6
• CHAMBERLAIN, Elton														
W 1888	StL-A	2	3	5.32	5	5	5	0	1	44	52	26	16	13
• CHANCE, Dean														
L 1969	Min-A	0	0	13.50	1	0	0	0	0	2	4	3	0	2
• CHANDLER, Spud														
W 1941	NY-A	0	1	3.60	1	1	0	0	0	5	4	2	2	2
W 1942	NY-A	0	1	1.08	2	1	0	1	0	8^1	5	1	1	3
W 1943	NY-A	2	0	0.50	2	2	2	0	1	18	17	1	3	10
W 1947	NY-A	0	0	9.00	1	0	0	0	0	2	2	2	3	1
W Total	**4**	**2**	**2**	**1.62**	**6**	**4**	**2**	**1**	**1**	**33^1**	**28**	**6**	**9**	**16**
• CHARLTON, Norm														
D 1995	Sea-A	1	0	2.45	4	0	0	1	0	7^1	4	2	3	9
D 1997	Sea-A	0	0	0.00	2	0	0	0	0	2^1	2	0	0	1
D 2001	Sea-A	0	0	0.00	1	0	0	0	0	1^2	0	0	0	2
D Total	**3**	**1**	**0**	**1.59**	**7**	**0**	**0**	**1**	**0**	**11^1**	**6**	**2**	**3**	**12**
L 1990	Cin-N	1	1	1.80	4	0	0	0	0	5	4	1	3	3
L 1995	Sea-A	1	0	0.00	3	0	0	1	0	6	1	0	1	5
L 2001	Sea-A	0	0	0.00	2	0	0	0	0	1^2	1	0	2	2
L Total	**3**	**2**	**1**	**0.71**	**9**	**0**	**0**	**1**	**0**	**12^2**	**6**	**1**	**6**	**10**
W 1990	Cin-N	0	0	0.00	1	0	0	0	0	1	1	0	0	0
• CHENEY, Larry														
W 1916	Bro-N	0	0	3.00	1	0	0	0	0	3	4	1	1	5
• CHENEY, Tom														
W 1960	Pit-N	0	0	4.50	3	0	0	0	0	4	4	2	1	6
• CHIPMAN, Bob														
W 1945	Chi-N	0	0	0.00	1	0	0	0	0	0^1	0	0	1	0
• CHOATE, Randy														
D 2000	NY-A	0	0	6.75	1	0	0	0	0	1^1	0	1	1	1
L 2000	NY-A	0	0	0.00	1	0	0	0	0	0^1	0	0	0	1
W 2001	NY-A	0	0	2.45	2	0	0	0	0	3^2	7	1	1	2
• CHOUINARD, Bobby														
D 1999	Ari-N	0	0	4.50	2	0	0	0	0	2	3	1	0	1
• CHRISTENSON, Larry														
D 1981	Phi-N	1	0	1.50	1	1	0	0	0	6	4	1	1	8
L 1977	Phi-N	0	0	8.10	1	1	0	0	0	3^1	7	3	0	2
L 1978	Phi-N	0	1	12.46	1	1	0	0	0	4^1	7	6	1	3
L 1980	Phi-N	0	0	4.05	2	1	0	0	0	6^2	5	3	5	2
L Total	**3**	**0**	**1**	**7.53**	**4**	**3**	**0**	**0**	**0**	**14^1**	**19**	**12**	**6**	**7**
W 1980	Phi-N	0	1	108.00	1	1	0	0	0	0^1	5	4	0	0
• CHRISTIANSEN, Jason														
D 2000	StL-N	0	0	0.00	1	0	0	0	0	0^1	0	0	0	0
D 2003	SF-N	0	0	....	1	0	0	0	0	0	1	0	0	0
D Total	**2**	**0**	**0**	**0.00**	**2**	**0**	**0**	**0**	**0**	**0^1**	**1**	**0**	**0**	**0**
L 2000	StL-N	0	0	0.00	2	0	0	0	0	2	0	0	0	1
• CHRISTOPHER, Russ														
W 1948	Cle-A	0	0	....	1	0	0	0	0	0	2	1	0	0
• CHURN, Chuck														
W 1959	LA-N	0	0	27.00	1	0	0	0	0	0^2	5	2	0	0
• CICOTTE, Eddie														
W 1917	Chi-A	1	1	1.96	3	2	2	0	0	23	23	5	2	13
W 1919	Chi-A	1	2	2.91	3	3	2	0	0	21^2	19	7	5	7
W Total	**2**	**2**	**3**	**2.42**	**6**	**5**	**4**	**0**	**0**	**44^2**	**42**	**12**	**7**	**20**
• CLANCY, Jim														
L 1985	Tor-A	0	1	9.00	1	0	0	0	0	1	2	1	1	0
L 1991	Atl-N	0	0	0.00	1	0	0	0	0	0^1	0	0	0	0
L Total	**2**	**0**	**1**	**6.75**	**2**	**0**	**0**	**0**	**0**	**1^1**	**2**	**1**	**1**	**0**
W 1991	Atl-N	1	0	4.15	3	0	0	0	0	4^1	3	2	4	2
• CLARK, Mark														
D 1998	Chi-N	0	1	3.00	1	1	0	0	0	6	7	2	1	4
• CLARKSON, John														
T 1892	Cle-N	0	2	5.29	2	2	2	0	0	17	24	10	5	9
W 1885	Chi-N	1	1	0.78	3	3	3	0	0	23	19	2	3	19
W 1886	Chi-N	2	2	2.01	4	4	3	0	1	31^1	25	7	12	28
W Total	**2**	**3**	**3**	**1.49**	**7**	**7**	**6**	**0**	**1**	**54^1**	**44**	**9**	**15**	**47**
• CLAY, Ken														
L 1978	NY-A	0	0	0.00	1	0	0	1	0	3^2	0	0	3	2
W 1977	NY-A	0	0	2.45	2	0	0	0	0	3^2	2	1	1	0
W 1978	NY-A	0	0	11.57	1	0	0	0	0	2^1	4	3	2	2
W Total	**2**	**0**	**0**	**6.00**	**3**	**0**	**0**	**0**	**0**	**6**	**6**	**4**	**3**	**2**
• CLEAR, Mark														
L 1979	Cal-A	0	0	4.76	1	0	0	0	0	5^2	4	3	2	3
• CLEMENS, Roger														
D 1995	Bos-A	0	0	3.86	1	1	0	0	0	7	5	3	1	5
D 1999	NY-A	1	0	0.00	1	1	0	0	0	7	3	0	2	2
D 2000	NY-A	0	2	8.18	2	2	0	0	0	11	13	10	8	10
D 2001	NY-A	0	1	5.40	2	2	0	0	0	8^1	9	5	4	6
D 2002	NY-A	0	0	6.35	1	1	0	0	0	5^2	8	4	3	5
D 2003	NY-A	1	0	1.29	1	1	0	0	0	7	5	1	1	6
D Total	**6**	**2**	**3**	**4.50**	**8**	**8**	**0**	**0**	**0**	**46**	**43**	**23**	**19**	**34**
L 1986	Bos-A	1	1	4.37	3	3	0	0	0	22^2	22	11	7	17
L 1988	Bos-A	0	0	3.86	1	1	0	0	0	7	6	3	0	8
L 1990	Bos-A	0	1	3.52	2	2	0	0	0	7^2	7	3	5	4
L 1999	NY-A	0	1	22.50	1	1	0	0	0	2	6	5	2	2
L 2000	NY-A	1	0	0.00	1	1	1	0	1	9	1	0	2	15
L 2001	NY-A	0	0	0.00	1	1	0	0	0	5	1	0	4	7
L 2003	NY-A	1	0	5.00	2	2	0	0	0	9	11	5	2	8
L Total	**7**	**3**	**3**	**3.90**	**11**	**11**	**1**	**0**	**1**	**62^1**	**54**	**27**	**22**	**61**
W 1986	Bos-A	0	0	3.18	2	2	0	0	0	11^1	9	4	6	11
W 1999	NY-A	1	0	1.17	1	1	0	0	0	7^2	4	1	2	4
W 2000	NY-A	1	0	0.00	1	1	0	0	0	8	2	0	0	9
W 2001	NY-A	1	0	1.35	2	2	0	0	0	13^1	10	2	4	19
W 2003	NY-A	0	0	3.86	1	1	0	0	0	7	8	3	0	5
W Total	**5**	**3**	**0**	**1.90**	**7**	**7**	**0**	**0**	**0**	**47^1**	**33**	**10**	**12**	**48**
• CLEMENT, Matt														
D 2003	Chi-N	0	1	7.71	1	1	0	0	0	4^2	8	4	4	3
L 2003	Chi-N	1	0	3.52	1	1	0	0	0	7^2	5	3	2	3
• CLEVELAND, Reggie														
L 1975	Bos-A	0	0	5.40	1	1	0	0	0	5	7	3	1	2
W 1975	Bos-A	0	1	6.75	3	1	0	0	0	6^2	7	5	3	5
• CLONINGER, Tony														
L 1970	Cin-N	0	0	3.60	1	1	0	0	0	5	7	2	4	1
W 1970	Cin-N	0	1	7.36	2	1	0	0	0	7^1	10	6	5	4
• CLONTZ, Brad														
D 1995	Atl-N	0	0	0.00	1	0	0	0	0	1^1	0	0	0	2
L 1995	Atl-N	0	0	0.00	1	0	0	0	0	0^1	1	0	0	0
L 1996	Atl-N	0	0	0.00	1	0	0	0	0	0^2	0	0	0	0
L Total	**2**	**0**	**0**	**0.00**	**2**	**0**	**0**	**0**	**0**	**1**	**1**	**0**	**0**	**0**
W 1995	Atl-N	0	0	2.70	2	0	0	0	0	3^1	2	1	0	2
W 1996	Atl-N	0	0	0.00	3	0	0	0	0	1^2	1	0	1	2
W Total	**2**	**0**	**0**	**1.80**	**5**	**0**	**0**	**0**	**0**	**5**	**3**	**1**	**1**	**4**
• COAKLEY, Andy														
W 1905	Phi-A	0	1	2.00	1	1	1	0	0	9	8	2	5	2
• COATES, Jim														
W 1960	NY-A	0	0	5.68	3	0	0	0	0	6^1	6	4	1	3
W 1961	NY-A	0	0	0.00	1	0	0	1	0	4	1	0	1	2
W 1962	NY-A	0	1	6.75	2	0	0	0	0	2^2	1	2	1	3
W Total	**3**	**0**	**1**	**4.15**	**6**	**0**	**0**	**1**	**0**	**13**	**8**	**6**	**3**	**8**
• COFFMAN, Dick														
W 1936	NY-N	0	0	32.40	2	0	0	0	0	1^2	5	6	1	1
W 1937	NY-N	0	0	4.15	2	0	0	0	0	4^1	2	2	5	1
W Total	**2**	**0**	**0**	**12.00**	**4**	**0**	**0**	**0**	**0**	**6**	**7**	**8**	**6**	**2**
• COLE, King														
W 1910	Chi-N	0	0	3.38	1	1	0	0	0	8	10	3	3	5
• COLEMAN, Joe														
L 1972	Det-A	1	0	0.00	1	1	1	0	1	9	7	0	3	14
• COLEMAN, Rip														
W 1955	NY-A	0	0	9.00	1	0	0	0	0	1	5	1	0	1
• COLLINS, Ray														
W 1912	Bos-A	0	0	1.26	2	1	0	0	0	14^1	14	2	0	6
• COLLINS, Rip														
W 1921	NY-A	0	0	54.00	1	0	0	0	0	0^2	4	4	1	0

YEAR	TM-L	W	L	ERA	G	GS	CG	SV	SHO	IP	H	ER	BB	SO
• COLON, Bartolo														
D 1998	Cle-A	0	0	1.59	1	1	0	0	0	5^2	5	1	3	3
D 1999	Cle-A	0	1	9.00	2	2	0	0	0	9	11	9	4	12
D 2001	Cle-A	1	1	1.84	2	2	0	0	0	14^2	12	3	6	13
D Total	3	1	2	3.99	5	5	0	0	0	29^1	28	13	13	28
L 1998	Cle-A	1	0	1.00	1	1	1	0	0	9	4	1	4	3
• CONE, David														
D 1995	NY-A	1	0	4.60	2	2	0	0	0	15^2	15	8	9	14
D 1996	NY-A	0	1	9.00	1	1	0	0	0	6	8	6	2	8
D 1997	NY-A	0	0	16.20	1	1	0	0	0	3^1	7	6	2	2
D 1998	NY-A	1	0	0.00	1	1	0	0	0	5^2	2	0	1	6
D Total	4	2	1	5.87	5	5	0	0	0	30^2	32	20	14	30
L 1988	NY-N	1	1	4.50	3	2	1	0	0	12	10	6	5	9
L 1992	Tor-A	1	1	3.00	2	2	0	0	0	12	11	4	5	9
L 1996	NY-A	0	0	3.00	1	1	0	0	0	6	5	2	5	5
L 1998	NY-A	1	0	4.15	2	2	0	0	0	13	12	6	6	13
L 1999	NY-A	1	0	2.57	1	1	0	0	0	7	7	2	3	9
L 2000	NY-A	0	0	0.00	1	0	0	0	0	1	0	0	0	0
L Total	6	4	2	3.53	10	8	1	0	0	51	45	20	24	45
W 1992	Tor-A	0	0	3.48	2	2	0	0	0	10^1	9	4	8	8
W 1996	NY-A	1	0	1.50	1	1	0	0	0	6	4	1	4	3
W 1998	NY-A	0	0	3.00	1	1	0	0	0	6	2	2	3	4
W 1999	NY-A	1	0	0.00	1	1	0	0	0	7	1	0	5	4
W 2000	NY-A	0	0	0.00	1	0	0	0	0	0^1	0	0	0	0
W Total	5	2	0	2.12	6	5	0	0	0	29^2	16	7	20	19
• CONLEY, Gene														
W 1957	Mil-N	0	0	10.80	1	0	0	0	0	1^2	2	2	1	0
• CONTRERAS, Jose														
L 2003	NY-A	0	1	5.79	4	0	0	0	0	4^2	6	3	2	7
W 2003	NY-A	0	1	5.68	4	0	0	0	0	6^1	5	4	5	10
• CONWAY, Pete														
W 1887	Det-N	2	2	3.00	4	4	4	0	0	33	31	11	6	10
• COOK, Dennis														
D 1996	Tex-A	0	0	0.00	2	0	0	0	0	1^1	0	0	1	0
D 1997	Fla-N	1	0	0.00	2	0	0	0	0	3	0	0	1	3
D 1999	NY-N	0	0	0.00	1	0	0	0	0	1^2	1	0	1	1
D 2000	NY-N	0	0	0.00	2	0	0	0	0	1^1	0	0	2	1
D Total	4	1	0	0.00	7	0	0	0	0	7^1	1	0	5	5
L 1997	Fla-N	0	0	0.00	2	0	0	0	0	2^1	0	0	0	2
L 1999	NY-N	0	0	0.00	3	0	0	0	0	1^1	1	0	2	1
L 2000	NY-N	0	0	0.00	1	0	0	0	0	1	1	0	0	2
L Total	3	0	0	0.00	6	0	0	0	0	4^2	2	0	2	5
W 1997	Fla-N	1	0	0.00	3	0	0	0	0	3^2	1	0	1	5
W 2000	NY-N	0	0	0.00	3	0	0	0	0	0^2	1	0	3	1
W Total	2	1	0	0.00	6	0	0	0	0	4^1	2	0	4	6
• COOMBS, Jack														
W 1910	Phi-A	3	0	3.33	3	3	3	0	0	27	24	10	14	17
W 1911	Phi-A	1	0	1.35	2	2	1	0	0	20	11	3	6	16
W 1916	Bro-N	1	0	4.26	1	1	0	0	0	6^1	7	3	1	1
W Total	3	5	0	2.70	6	6	4	0	0	53^1	42	16	21	34
• COOPER, Mort														
W 1942	StL-N	0	1	5.54	2	2	0	0	0	13	17	8	4	9
W 1943	StL-N	1	1	2.81	2	2	1	0	0	16	11	5	3	10
W 1944	StL-N	1	1	1.13	2	2	1	0	1	16	9	2	5	16
W Total	3	2	3	3.00	6	6	2	0	1	45	37	15	12	35
• COPPINGER, Rocky														
L 1996	Bal-A	0	1	8.44	1	1	0	0	0	5^1	6	5	1	3
• CORBETT, Doug														
L 1986	Cal-A	1	0	5.40	3	0	0	0	0	6^2	9	4	2	2
• CORBETT, Joe														
T 1896	Bal-N	2	0	0.53	2	2	2	0	1	17	11	1	7	10
T 1897	Bal-N	1	0	9.00	2	1	1	0	0	12	21	12	8	5
T Total	2	3	0	4.03	4	3	3	0	1	29	32	13	15	15
• CORMIER, Rheal														
D 1995	Bos-A	0	0	13.50	2	0	0	0	0	0^2	2	1	1	2
D 1999	Bos-A	0	0	0.00	2	0	0	0	0	4	2	0	1	4
D Total	2	0	0	1.93	4	0	0	0	0	4^2	4	1	2	6
L 1999	Bos-A	0	0	0.00	4	0	0	0	0	3^2	3	0	3	4
• CORSI, Jim														
D 1998	Bos-A	0	0	0.00	2	0	0	0	0	3	1	0	1	2
L 1992	Oak-A	0	0	0.00	3	0	0	0	0	2	2	0	3	0
• CORWIN, Al														
W 1951	NY-N	0	0	0.00	1	0	0	0	0	1^2	1	0	0	1
• COVELESKI, Stan														
W 1920	Cle-A	3	0	0.67	3	3	3	0	1	27	15	2	2	8
W 1925	Was-A	0	2	3.77	2	2	1	0	0	14^1	16	6	5	3
W Total	2	3	2	1.74	5	5	4	0	1	41^1	31	8	7	11
• COX, Danny														
L 1985	StL-N	1	0	3.00	1	1	0	0	0	6	4	2	5	4
L 1987	StL-N	1	1	2.12	2	2	2	0	1	17	17	4	3	11
L 1992	Pit-N	0	0	0.00	2	0	0	0	0	1^1	1	0	1	1
L 1993	Tor-A	0	0	0.00	2	0	0	0	0	5	3	0	2	5
L Total	4	2	1	1.84	7	3	2	0	1	29^1	25	6	11	21
W 1985	StL-N	0	0	1.29	2	2	0	0	0	14	14	2	4	13
W 1987	StL-N	1	2	7.71	3	2	0	0	0	11^2	13	10	8	9
W 1993	Tor-A	0	0	8.10	3	0	0	0	0	3^1	6	3	5	6
W Total	3	1	2	4.66	8	4	0	0	0	29	33	15	17	28
• CRABTREE, Tim														
D 1998	Tex-A	0	0	0.00	2	0	0	0	0	4	1	0	0	2
D 1999	Tex-A	0	0	5.40	2	0	0	0	0	1^2	1	1	1	1
D Total	2	0	0	1.59	4	0	0	0	0	5^2	2	1	1	3
• CRAIG, Roger														
W 1955	Bro-N	1	0	3.00	1	1	0	0	0	6	4	2	5	4
W 1956	Bro-N	0	1	12.00	2	1	0	0	0	6	10	8	3	4
W 1959	LA-N	0	1	8.68	2	2	0	0	0	9^1	15	9	5	8
W 1964	StL-N	1	0	0.00	2	0	0	0	0	5	2	0	3	9
W Total	4	2	2	6.49	7	4	0	0	0	26^1	31	19	16	25
• CRANDALL, Doc														
W 1911	NY-N	1	0	0.00	2	0	0	0	0	4	2	0	0	2
W 1912	NY-N	0	0	0.00	1	0	0	0	0	2	1	0	0	2
W 1913	NY-N	0	0	3.86	2	0	0	0	0	4^2	4	2	0	2
W Total	3	1	0	1.69	5	0	0	0	0	10^2	7	2	0	6
• CRANE, Ed														
W 1888	NY-N	1	1	2.12	2	2	2	0	0	17	15	4	6	12
W 1889	NY-N	4	1	3.72	5	5	4	0	0	38^2	29	16	32	19
W Total	2	5	2	3.23	7	7	6	0	0	55^2	44	20	38	31
• CRAWFORD, Steve														
L 1986	Bos-A	1	0	0.00	1	0	0	0	0	1^2	1	0	2	1
W 1986	Bos-A	1	0	6.23	3	0	0	0	0	4^1	5	3	0	4
• CROWDER, Alvin														
W 1933	Was-A	0	1	7.36	2	2	0	0	0	11	16	9	5	7
W 1934	Det-A	0	1	1.50	2	1	0	0	0	6	6	1	1	2
W 1935	Det-A	1	0	1.00	1	1	1	0	0	9	5	1	3	5
W Total	3	1	2	3.81	5	4	1	0	0	26	27	11	9	14
• CRUDALE, Mike														
D 2002	StL-N	0	0	0.00	1	0	0	0	0	1	0	0	1	2
L 2002	StL-N	0	0	10.80	1	0	0	0	0	1^2	1	2	1	2
• CRUZ, Juan														
D 2003	Chi-N	0	0	0.00	1	0	0	0	0	1	0	0	1	2
• CRUZ, Nelson														
D 2001	Hou-N	0	0	0.00	2	0	0	0	0	2^2	1	0	1	1
• CUELLAR, Mike														
L 1969	Bal-A	0	0	2.25	1	1	0	0	0	8	3	2	1	7
L 1970	Bal-A	0	0	12.46	1	1	0	0	0	4^1	10	6	1	2
L 1971	Bal-A	1	0	1.00	1	1	1	0	0	9	6	1	1	2
L 1973	Bal-A	0	1	1.80	1	1	1	0	0	10	4	2	3	11
L 1974	Bal-A	1	1	2.84	2	2	0	0	0	12^2	9	4	13	6
L Total	5	2	2	3.07	6	6	2	0	0	44	32	15	19	28
W 1969	Bal-A	1	0	1.13	2	2	1	0	0	16	13	2	4	13
W 1970	Bal-A	1	0	3.18	2	2	1	0	0	11^1	10	4	2	5
W 1971	Bal-A	0	2	3.86	2	2	0	0	0	14	11	6	6	10
W Total	3	2	2	2.61	6	6	2	0	0	41^1	34	12	12	28
• CUMBERLAND, John														
L 1971	SF-N	0	1	9.00	1	1	0	0	0	3	7	3	0	4
• CUMMINGS, John														
D 1995	LA-N	0	0	20.25	2	0	0	0	0	1^1	3	3	2	3
• CUNNANE, Will														
D 2003	Atl-N	0	0	5.40	2	0	0	0	0	1^2	3	1	0	2
• CUPPY, Nig														
T 1892	Cle-N	0	1	1.13	1	1	1	0	0	8	6	1	4	1
T 1895	Cle-N	1	1	3.18	2	2	2	0	0	17	14	6	4	6
T 1896	Cle-N	0	2	4.76	2	2	2	0	0	17	19	9	0	4
T Total	3	1	4	3.43	5	5	5	0	0	42	39	16	8	11
• CVENGROS, Mike														
W 1927	Pit-N	0	0	3.86	2	0	0	0	0	2^1	3	1	0	2
• DAAL, Omar														
D 1999	Ari-N	0	1	6.75	1	1	0	0	0	4	6	3	3	4
• DAILY, Ed														
W 1890	Lou-A	0	2	2.65	2	2	2	0	0	17	12	5	8	5
• DALEY, Bud														
W 1961	NY-A	1	0	0.00	2	0	0	0	0	7	5	0	0	3
W 1962	NY-A	0	0	0.00	1	0	0	0	0	1	1	0	1	0
W Total	2	1	0	0.00	3	0	0	0	0	8	6	0	1	3
• DANFORTH, Dave														
W 1917	Chi-A	0	0	18.00	1	0	0	0	0	1	3	2	0	2
• DARCY, Pat														
W 1975	Cin-N	0	1	4.50	2	0	0	0	0	4	3	2	2	1
• DARLING, Ron														
L 1986	NY-N	0	0	7.20	1	1	0	0	0	5	6	4	2	5
L 1988	NY-N	0	1	7.71	2	2	0	0	0	7	11	6	4	7
L 1992	Oak-A	0	1	6.00	1	1	0	0	0	6	4	4	2	3
L Total	3	0	2	7.00	4	4	0	0	0	18	21	14	8	15
W 1986	NY-N	1	1	1.53	3	3	0	0	0	17^2	13	3	10	12
• DAVIS, Curt														
W 1941	Bro-N	0	1	5.06	1	1	0	0	0	5^1	6	3	3	1
• DAVIS, Ron														
D 1981	NY-A	1	0	0.00	3	0	0	0	0	6	1	0	2	6
L 1980	NY-A	0	0	2.25	1	0	0	0	0	4	3	1	1	3
L 1981	NY-A	0	0	0.00	2	0	0	0	0	3^1	0	0	2	4
L Total	2	0	0	1.23	3	0	0	0	0	7^1	3	1	3	7
W 1981	NY-A	0	0	23.14	4	0	0	0	0	2^1	4	6	5	4

YEAR	TM-L	W	L	ERA	G	GS	CG	SV	SHO	IP	H	ER	BB	SO
DAVIS, Storm														
L 1983	Bal-A	0	0	0.00	1	1	0	0	0	6	5	0	2	2
L 1988	Oak-A	0	0	0.00	1	1	0	0	0	6¹	2	0	5	4
L 1989	Oak-A	0	1	7.11	1	1	0	0	0	6¹	5	5	2	3
L Total	3	0	1	2.41	3	3	0	0	0	18²	12	5	9	9
W 1983	Bal-A	0	0	5.40	1	1	0	0	0	5	6	3	1	3
W 1988	Oak-A	0	2	11.25	2	2	0	0	0	8	14	10	1	7
W Total	2	1	2	9.00	3	3	0	0	0	13	20	13	2	10
DAWSON, Joe														
W 1927	Pit-N	0	0	0.00	1	0	0	0	0	1	0	0	0	0
DAYLEY, Ken														
L 1985	StL-N	0	0	0.00	5	0	0	2	0	6	2	0	1	3
L 1987	StL-N	0	0	0.00	3	0	0	2	0	4	1	0	2	4
L Total	2	0	0	0.00	8	0	0	4	0	10	3	0	3	7
W 1985	StL-N	1	0	0.00	4	0	0	0	0	6	1	0	3	5
W 1987	StL-N	0	0	1.93	4	0	0	1	0	4²	2	1	0	3
W Total	2	1	0	0.84	8	0	0	1	0	10²	3	1	3	8
DEAN, Dizzy														
W 1934	StL-N	2	1	1.73	3	3	2	0	1	26	20	5	5	17
W 1938	Chi-N	0	1	6.48	2	1	0	0	0	8¹	8	6	1	2
W Total	2	2	2	2.88	5	4	2	0	1	34¹	28	11	6	19
DEAN, Paul														
W 1934	StL-N	2	0	1.00	2	2	2	0	0	18	15	2	7	11
DEAN, Wayland														
W 1924	NY-N	0	0	4.50	2	0	0	0	0	2	3	1	0	2
DEL TORO, Miguel														
D 2000	SF-N	0	0	0.00	1	0	0	0	0	1	1	0	0	2
DELEON, Jose														
L 1993	Chi-A	0	0	1.93	2	0	0	0	0	4²	7	1	1	6
DELL, Wheezer														
W 1916	Bro-N	0	0	0.00	1	0	0	0	0	1	0	0	0	0
DEMAREE, Al														
W 1913	NY-N	0	1	4.50	1	1	0	0	0	4	7	2	1	0
DEMERY, Larry														
L 1974	Pit-N	0	0	36.00	2	0	0	0	0	1	3	4	2	0
L 1975	Pit-N	0	0	18.00	1	0	0	0	0	2	4	4	1	1
L Total	2	0	0	24.00	3	0	0	0	0	3	7	8	3	1
DENNY, John														
L 1983	Phi-N	0	1	0.00	1	1	0	0	0	6	5	0	3	3
W 1983	Phi-N	1	1	3.46	2	2	0	0	0	13	12	5	3	9
DEPAULA, Sean														
D 1999	Cle-A	0	0	1.80	3	0	0	0	0	5	2	1	3	5
DERRINGER, Paul														
W 1931	StL-N	0	2	4.26	3	2	0	0	0	12²	14	6	7	14
W 1939	Cin-N	0	1	2.35	2	2	1	0	0	15¹	9	4	3	9
W 1940	Cin-N	2	1	2.79	3	3	2	0	0	19¹	17	6	10	6
W 1945	Chi-N	0	0	6.75	3	0	0	0	0	5¹	5	4	7	1
W Total	4	2	4	3.42	11	7	3	0	0	52²	45	20	27	30
DEVLIN, Jim														
W 1888	StL-N	1	0	2.57	2	0	0	0	0	7	5	2	2	5
DIAZ, Carlos														
L 1985	LA-N	0	0	3.00	2	0	0	0	0	3	5	1	1	2
DIBBLE, Rob														
L 1990	Cin-N	0	0	0.00	4	0	0	1	0	5	0	0	1	10
W 1990	Cin-N	1	0	0.00	2	0	0	0	0	4²	3	0	1	4
DICKSON, Murry														
W 1943	StL-N	0	0	0.00	1	0	0	0	0	0²	0	0	1	0
W 1946	StL-N	0	1	3.86	2	2	0	0	0	14	11	6	4	7
W 1958	NY-A	0	0	4.50	2	0	0	0	0	4	4	2	0	1
W Total	3	0	1	3.86	5	2	0	0	0	18²	15	8	5	8
DINEEN, Bill														
W 1903	Bos-A	3	1	2.06	4	4	4	0	2	35	29	8	8	28
DITMAR, Art														
W 1957	NY-A	0	0	0.00	2	0	0	0	0	6	2	0	0	2
W 1958	NY-A	0	0	0.00	1	0	0	0	0	3²	2	0	0	2
W 1960	NY-A	0	2	21.60	2	2	0	0	0	1²	6	4	1	0
W Total	3	0	2	3.18	5	2	0	0	0	11¹	10	4	1	4
DOBSON, Joe														
W 1946	Bos-A	1	0	0.00	3	1	1	0	0	12²	4	0	3	10
DOBSON, Pat														
W 1968	Det-A	0	0	3.86	3	0	0	0	0	4²	5	2	1	0
W 1971	Bal-A	0	0	4.05	3	1	0	0	0	6²	13	3	4	6
W Total	2	0	0	3.97	6	1	0	0	0	11¹	18	5	5	6
DONALD, Atley														
W 1941	NY-A	0	0	9.00	1	1	0	0	0	4	6	4	3	2
W 1942	NY-A	0	1	6.00	1	0	0	0	0	3	3	2	2	1
W Total	2	0	1	7.71	2	1	0	0	0	7	9	6	5	3
DONNELLY, Blix														
W 1944	StL-N	1	0	0.00	2	0	0	0	0	6	2	0	1	9
DONNELLY, Brendan														
D 2002	Ana-A	0	0	13.50	3	0	0	0	0	2	3	3	1	2
L 2002	Ana-A	0	0	8.10	3	0	0	0	0	3¹	3	3	0	5
W 2002	Ana-A	1	0	0.00	5	0	0	0	0	7²	0	0	4	6
DONOVAN, Bill														
W 1907	Det-A	0	1	1.71	2	2	2	0	0	21	17	4	5	16
W 1908	Det-A	0	2	4.24	2	2	2	0	0	17	17	8	4	10
W 1909	Det-A	1	1	3.00	2	2	1	0	0	12	7	4	8	7
W Total	3	1	4	2.88	6	6	5	0	0	50	41	16	17	33
DONOVAN, Dick														
W 1959	Chi-A	0	1	5.40	3	1	0	1	0	8¹	4	5	3	5
DOTEL, Octavio														
D 1999	NY-N	0	0	54.00	1	0	0	0	0	0¹	1	2	2	0
D 2001	Hou-N	0	0	5.40	2	0	0	0	0	3¹	5	2	0	5
D Total	2	0	0	9.82	3	0	0	0	0	3²	6	4	2	5
L 1999	NY-N	1	0	3.00	2	0	0	0	0	3	4	1	2	5
DOTSON, Richard														
L 1983	Chi-A	0	1	10.80	1	1	0	0	0	5	6	6	3	3
DOUGLAS, Phil														
W 1918	Chi-N	0	1	0.00	1	0	0	0	0	1	1	0	0	0
W 1921	NY-N	2	1	2.08	3	3	2	0	0	26	20	6	5	17
W Total	2	2	2	2.00	4	3	2	0	0	27	21	6	5	17
DOWNING, Al														
L 1974	LA-N	0	0	0.00	1	0	0	0	0	4	1	0	1	0
W 1963	NY-A	0	1	5.40	1	1	0	0	0	5	7	3	1	6
W 1964	NY-A	0	1	8.22	3	1	0	0	0	7²	9	7	2	5
W 1974	LA-N	0	1	2.45	1	1	0	0	0	3²	4	1	4	3
W Total	3	0	3	6.06	5	3	0	0	0	16¹	20	11	7	14
DOWNS, Kelly														
L 1987	SF-N	0	0	0.00	1	0	0	0	0	1¹	1	0	0	0
L 1989	SF-N	1	0	3.12	2	0	0	0	0	8²	8	3	6	6
L 1992	Oak-A	0	1	3.86	2	0	0	0	0	2¹	3	1	1	0
L Total	3	1	1	2.92	5	0	0	0	0	12¹	12	4	7	6
W 1989	SF-N	0	0	7.71	3	0	0	0	0	4²	3	4	2	4
DOYLE, Paul														
L 1969	Atl-N	0	0	0.00	1	0	0	0	0	1	2	0	1	3
DRABEK, Doug														
L 1990	Pit-N	1	1	1.65	2	2	1	0	0	16¹	12	3	3	13
L 1991	Pit-N	1	1	0.60	2	2	1	0	0	15	10	1	5	10
L 1992	Pit-N	0	3	3.71	3	3	0	0	0	17	18	7	6	10
L Total	3	2	5	2.05	7	7	2	0	0	48¹	40	11	14	33
DRABOWSKY, Moe														
W 1966	Bal-A	1	0	0.00	1	0	0	0	0	6²	1	0	2	11
W 1970	Bal-A	0	0	2.70	2	0	0	0	0	3¹	2	1	1	1
W Total	2	1	0	0.90	3	0	0	0	0	10	3	1	3	12
DRAGO, Dick														
L 1975	Bos-A	0	0	0.00	2	0	0	0	0	4²	2	0	1	2
W 1975	Bos-A	0	1	2.25	2	0	0	0	0	4	3	1	1	1
DRAVECKY, Dave														
L 1984	SD-N	0	0	0.00	3	0	0	0	0	6	2	0	0	5
L 1987	SF-N	1	1	0.60	2	2	1	0	1	15	7	1	4	14
L Total	2	1	1	0.43	5	2	1	0	1	21	9	1	4	19
W 1984	SD-N	0	0	0.00	2	0	0	0	0	4²	3	0	1	5
DREIFORT, Darren														
D 1996	LA-N	0	0	0.00	1	0	0	0	0	0²	0	0	0	0
DREISEWERD, Clem														
W 1946	Bos-A	0	0	0.00	1	0	0	0	0	0¹	0	0	0	0
DREWS, Karl														
W 1947	NY-A	0	0	3.00	2	0	0	0	0	3	2	1	1	0
DRYSDALE, Don														
W 1956	Bro-N	0	0	9.00	1	0	0	0	0	2	2	2	1	1
W 1959	LA-N	1	0	1.29	1	1	0	0	0	7	11	1	4	5
W 1963	LA-N	1	0	0.00	1	1	1	0	1	9	3	0	1	9
W 1965	LA-N	1	1	3.86	2	2	1	0	0	11²	12	5	3	15
W 1966	LA-N	0	2	4.50	2	2	1	0	0	10	8	5	3	6
W Total	5	3	3	2.95	7	6	3	0	1	39²	36	13	12	36
DUKES, Tom														
W 1971	Bal-A	0	0	0.00	2	0	0	0	0	4	2	0	0	1
DUREN, Ryne														
W 1958	NY-A	1	1	1.93	3	0	0	1	0	9¹	7	2	6	14
W 1960	NY-A	0	0	2.25	2	0	0	0	0	4	2	1	1	5
W Total	2	1	1	2.03	5	0	0	1	0	13¹	9	3	7	19
EARNSHAW, George														
W 1929	Phi-A	1	1	2.63	2	2	0	0	0	13²	14	4	6	17
W 1930	Phi-A	2	0	0.72	3	3	2	0	0	25	13	2	7	19
W 1931	Phi-A	1	2	1.88	3	3	2	0	1	24	12	5	4	20
W Total	3	4	3	1.58	8	8	5	0	1	62²	39	11	17	56
EASTERLY, Jamie														
D 1981	Mil-A	0	0	6.75	2	0	0	0	0	1¹	2	1	0	1
EASTWICK, Rawly														
L 1975	Cin-N	1	0	0.00	2	0	0	0	0	3²	2	0	2	1
L 1976	Cin-N	1	0	12.00	2	0	0	0	0	3	7	4	2	1
L 1978	Phi-N	0	0	9.00	1	0	0	0	0	1	3	1	0	1
L Total	3	2	0	5.87	5	0	0	0	0	7²	12	5	4	3
W 1975	Cin-N	2	0	2.25	5	0	0	1	0	8	6	2	3	4
ECKERSLEY, Dennis														
D 1995	StL-N	0	0	0.00	3	0	0	3	0	3²	1	0	0	1
D 1998	Bos-A	0	0	9.00	1	0	0	0	0	1	1	1	0	1
D Total	2	0	0	1.93	4	0	0	3	0	4²	4	1	0	3
L 1984	Chi-N	0	1	8.44	1	1	0	0	0	5¹	9	5	0	0

YEAR	TM-L	W	L	ERA	G	GS	CG	SV	SHO	IP	H	ER	BB	SO
L 1988	Oak-A	0	0	0.00	4	0	0	4	0	6	1	0	2	5
L 1989	Oak-A	0	0	1.59	4	0	0	3	0	5^2	4	1	0	2
L 1990	Oak-A	0	0	0.00	3	0	0	2	0	3^1	2	0	0	3
L 1992	Oak-A	0	0	6.00	3	0	0	1	0	3	8	2	0	2
L 1996	StL-N	1	0	0.00	3	0	0	1	0	3^1	2	0	0	4
L Total	6	1	1	2.70	18	1	0	11	0	26^2	26	8	2	16
W 1988	Oak-A	0	1	10.80	2	0	0	0	0	1^2	2	2	1	2
W 1989	Oak-A	0	0	0.00	2	0	0	1	0	1^2	0	0	0	0
W 1990	Oak-A	0	1	6.75	2	0	0	0	0	1^1	3	1	0	1
W Total	3	0	2	5.79	6	0	0	1	0	4^2	5	3	1	3
• EHMKE, Howard														
W 1929	Phi-A	1	0	1.42	2	2	1	0	0	12^2	14	2	3	13
• EHRET, Red														
W 1890	Lou-A	2	0	1.35	3	2	2	1	0	20	12	3	6	13
• EICHHORN, Mark														
L 1992	Tor-A	0	0	0.00	1	0	0	0	0	1	0	0	0	0
L 1993	Tor-A	0	0	0.00	1	0	0	0	0	2	1	0	1	1
L Total	2	0	0	0.00	2	0	0	0	0	3	1	0	1	1
W 1992	Tor-A	0	0	0.00	1	0	0	0	0	1	0	0	0	1
W 1993	Tor-A	0	0	0.00	1	0	0	0	0	0^1	1	0	1	0
W Total	2	0	0	0.00	2	0	0	0	0	1^1	1	0	1	1
• ELARTON, Scott														
D 1998	Hou-N	0	1	4.50	1	0	0	0	0	2	1	1	1	3
D 1999	Hou-N	0	0	3.86	2	0	0	0	0	2^1	4	1	1	3
D Total	2	0	1	4.15	3	0	0	0	0	4^1	5	2	2	6
• ELLER, Hod														
W 1919	Cin-N	2	0	2.00	2	2	2	0	1	18	13	4	2	15
• ELLIS, Dock														
L 1970	Pit-N	0	1	2.79	1	1	0	0	0	9^2	9	3	4	1
L 1971	Pit-N	1	0	3.60	1	1	0	0	0	5	6	2	4	1
L 1972	Pit-N	0	1	0.00	1	1	0	0	0	5	5	0	1	3
L 1975	Pit-N	0	0	0.00	1	0	0	0	0	2	2	0	0	2
L 1976	NY-A	1	0	3.38	1	1	0	0	0	8	6	3	2	5
L Total	5	2	2	2.43	5	4	0	0	0	29^2	28	8	11	12
W 1971	Pit-N	0	1	15.43	1	1	0	0	0	2^1	4	4	1	1
W 1976	NY-A	0	1	10.80	1	1	0	0	0	3^1	7	4	0	1
W Total	2	0	2	12.71	2	2	0	0	0	5^2	11	8	1	2
• EMBREE, Alan														
D 1996	Cle-A	0	0	9.00	3	0	0	0	0	1	0	1	0	1
D 2000	SF-N	0	0	0.00	2	0	0	0	0	1^2	0	0	0	0
D 2003	Bos-A	0	0	0.00	3	0	0	0	0	2	1	0	0	0
D Total	3	0	0	1.93	8	0	0	0	0	4^2	1	1	0	1
L 1995	Cle-A	0	0	0.00	1	0	0	0	0	0^1	0	0	0	1
L 1997	Atl-N	0	0	0.00	1	0	0	0	0	1	0	0	1	1
L 2003	Bos-A	1	0	0.00	5	0	0	0	0	4^2	3	0	0	1
L Total	3	1	0	0.00	7	0	0	0	0	6	3	0	1	3
W 1995	Cle-A	0	0	2.70	4	0	0	0	0	3^1	2	1	2	2
• ERICKSON, Paul														
W 1945	Chi-N	0	0	3.86	4	0	0	0	0	7	8	3	3	5
• ERICKSON, Scott														
D 1996	Bal-A	0	0	4.05	1	1	0	0	0	6^2	6	3	2	6
D 1997	Bal-A	1	0	4.05	1	1	0	0	0	6^2	7	3	2	6
D Total	2	1	0	4.05	2	2	0	0	0	13^1	13	6	4	12
L 1991	Min-A	0	0	4.50	1	1	0	0	0	4	3	2	5	2
L 1996	Bal-A	0	1	2.38	2	2	0	0	0	11^1	14	3	4	8
L 1997	Bal-A	1	0	4.26	2	2	0	0	0	12^2	15	6	1	6
L Total	3	1	1	3.54	5	5	0	0	0	28	32	11	10	16
W 1991	Min-A	0	0	5.06	2	2	0	0	0	10^2	10	6	4	5
• ERSKINE, Carl														
W 1949	Bro-N	0	0	16.20	2	0	0	0	0	1^2	3	3	1	0
W 1952	Bro-N	1	1	4.50	3	2	1	0	0	18	12	9	10	10
W 1953	Bro-N	1	0	5.79	3	3	1	0	0	14	14	9	9	16
W 1955	Bro-N	0	0	9.00	1	1	0	0	0	3	3	3	2	3
W 1956	Bro-N	0	1	5.40	2	1	0	0	0	5	4	3	2	2
W Total	5	2	2	5.83	11	7	2	0	0	41^2	36	27	24	31
• ESPER, Duke														
T 1894	Bal-N	0	1	4.00	1	1	1	0	0	9	13	4	1	3
T 1895	Bal-N	1	0	0.00	1	1	1	0	1	9	5	0	0	3
T Total	2	1	1	2.00	2	2	2	0	1	18	18	4	1	6
• ESTES, Shawn														
D 1997	SF-N	0	0	15.00	1	1	0	0	0	3	5	5	4	3
D 2000	SF-N	0	0	6.00	1	1	0	0	0	3	3	2	3	3
D Total	2	0	0	10.50	2	2	0	0	0	6	8	7	7	6
• EYRE, Scott														
D 2002	SF-N	0	0	0.00	3	0	0	0	0	1^1	1	0	0	0
D 2003	SF-N	0	0	0.00	1	0	0	0	0	0^1	0	0	0	0
D Total	2	0	0	0.00	4	0	0	0	0	1^2	1	0	0	0
L 2002	SF-N	0	0	0.00	4	0	0	0	0	1^2	2	0	0	0
W 2002	SF-N	0	0	0.00	3	0	0	0	0	3	5	0	1	2
• FABER, Red														
W 1917	Chi-A	3	1	2.33	4	3	2	0	0	27	21	7	3	9
• FACE, Roy														
W 1960	Pit-N	0	0	5.23	4	0	0	3	0	10^1	9	6	2	4
• FARNSWORTH, Kyle														
D 2003	Chi-N	0	0	0.00	3	0	0	0	0	2^2	1	0	1	2
L 2003	Chi-N	0	0	10.13	5	0	0	0	0	5^1	6	6	2	7

YEAR	TM-L	W	L	ERA	G	GS	CG	SV	SHO	IP	H	ER	BB	SO
• FARR, Steve														
L 1985	KC-A	1	0	1.42	2	0	0	0	0	6^1	4	1	1	3
• FASSERO, Jeff														
D 1997	Sea-A	1	0	1.13	1	1	0	0	0	8	3	1	4	3
D 1999	Tex-A	0	0	9.00	1	0	0	0	0	1	2	1	1	1
D 2002	StL-N	2	0	0.00	3	0	0	0	0	2^2	3	0	0	2
D Total	3	3	0	1.54	5	1	0	0	0	11^2	8	2	5	6
L 2002	StL-N	0	0	0.00	1	0	0	0	0	0^2	0	0	0	1
• FELLER, Bob														
W 1948	Cle-A	0	2	5.02	2	2	1	0	0	14^1	10	8	5	7
• FERGUSON, Alex														
W 1925	Was-A	1	1	3.21	2	2	0	0	0	14	13	5	6	11
• FERNANDEZ, Alex														
D 1997	Fla-N	1	0	2.57	1	1	0	0	0	7	7	2	0	5
L 1993	Chi-A	0	2	1.80	2	2	0	0	0	15	15	3	6	10
L 1997	Fla-N	0	1	16.88	1	1	0	0	0	2^2	6	5	1	3
L Total	2	0	3	4.08	3	3	0	0	0	17^2	21	8	7	13
• FERNANDEZ, Sid														
L 1986	NY-N	0	1	4.50	1	1	0	0	0	6	3	3	1	5
L 1988	NY-N	0	1	13.50	1	1	0	0	0	4	7	6	1	5
L Total	2	0	2	8.10	2	2	0	0	0	10	10	9	2	10
W 1986	NY-N	0	0	1.35	3	0	0	0	0	6^2	6	1	1	10
• FERRICK, Tom														
W 1950	NY-A	1	0	0.00	1	0	0	0	0	1	1	0	1	0
• FERRISS, Dave														
W 1946	Bos-A	1	0	2.03	2	2	1	0	1	13^1	13	3	2	4
• FETTERS, Mike														
D 2002	Ari-N	0	0	0.00	1	0	0	0	0	0^2	1	0	1	1
• FIGUEROA, Ed														
L 1976	NY-A	0	1	5.84	2	2	0	0	0	12^1	14	8	2	5
L 1977	NY-A	0	0	10.80	1	1	0	0	0	3^1	5	4	2	3
L 1978	NY-A	0	1	27.00	1	1	0	0	0	1	5	3	0	0
L Total	3	0	2	8.10	4	4	0	0	0	16^2	24	15	4	8
W 1976	NY-A	0	1	5.63	1	1	0	0	0	8	6	5	5	2
W 1978	NY-A	0	1	8.10	2	2	0	0	0	6^2	9	6	5	2
W Total	2	0	2	6.75	3	3	0	0	0	14^2	15	11	10	4
• FINGERS, Rollie														
D 1981	Mil-A	0	0	3.86	3	0	0	2	0	4^2	7	2	1	5
L 1971	Oak-A	0	0	7.71	2	0	0	0	0	2^1	2	2	1	2
L 1972	Oak-A	1	0	1.69	3	0	0	0	0	5^1	4	1	1	2
L 1973	Oak-A	0	1	1.93	3	0	0	1	0	4^2	4	1	2	4
L 1974	Oak-A	0	0	3.00	2	0	0	1	0	3	3	1	1	3
L 1975	Oak-A	0	1	6.75	1	0	0	0	0	4	5	3	1	3
L Total	5	1	2	3.72	11	0	0	2	0	19^1	18	8	6	14
W 1972	Oak-A	1	1	1.74	6	0	0	2	0	10^1	4	2	4	11
W 1973	Oak-A	0	1	0.66	6	0	0	2	0	13^2	13	1	4	8
W 1974	Oak-A	1	0	1.93	4	0	0	2	0	9^1	8	2	2	6
W Total	3	2	2	1.35	16	0	0	6	0	33^1	25	5	10	25
• FINLEY, Chuck														
D 2001	Cle-A	0	2	7.27	2	2	0	0	0	8^2	9	7	6	10
D 2002	StL-N	0	0	0.00	1	1	0	0	0	6^1	4	0	2	7
D Total	2	0	2	4.20	3	3	0	0	0	15	13	7	8	17
L 1986	Cal-A	0	0	0.00	3	0	0	0	0	2	1	0	0	1
L 2002	StL-N	1	0	7.20	1	1	0	0	0	5	7	4	3	1
L Total	2	1	0	5.14	4	1	0	0	0	7	8	4	3	2
• FIORE, Tony														
D 2002	Min-A	0	0	20.25	1	0	0	0	0	1^1	4	3	2	0
• FISHER, Ray														
W 1919	Cin-N	0	1	2.35	2	1	0	0	0	7^2	7	2	2	2
• FITZSIMMONS, Freddie														
W 1933	NY-N	0	1	5.14	1	1	0	0	0	7	9	4	0	2
W 1936	NY-N	0	2	5.40	2	2	1	0	0	11^2	13	7	2	6
W 1941	Bro-N	0	0	0.00	1	1	0	0	0	7	4	0	3	1
W Total	3	0	3	3.86	4	4	1	0	0	25^2	26	11	5	9
• FLANAGAN, Mike														
L 1979	Bal-A	1	0	5.14	1	1	0	0	0	7	6	4	1	2
L 1983	Bal-A	1	0	1.80	1	1	0	0	0	5	5	1	0	1
L 1989	Tor-A	0	1	10.38	1	1	0	0	0	4^1	7	5	1	3
L Total	3	2	1	5.51	3	3	0	0	0	16^1	18	10	2	6
W 1979	Bal-A	1	1	3.00	3	2	1	0	0	15	18	5	2	13
W 1983	Bal-A	0	0	4.50	1	1	0	0	0	4	6	2	1	1
W Total	2	1	1	3.32	4	3	1	0	0	19	24	7	3	14
• FORD, Whitey														
W 1950	NY-A	1	0	0.00	1	1	0	0	0	8^2	7	0	1	7
W 1953	NY-A	0	1	4.50	2	2	0	0	0	8	9	4	2	7
W 1955	NY-A	2	0	2.12	2	2	1	0	0	17	13	4	8	10
W 1956	NY-A	1	1	5.25	2	2	1	0	0	12	14	7	2	8
W 1957	NY-A	1	1	1.13	2	2	1	0	0	16	11	2	5	7
W 1958	NY-A	0	1	4.11	3	3	0	0	0	15^1	19	7	5	16
W 1960	NY-A	2	0	0.00	2	2	2	0	2	18	11	0	2	8
W 1961	NY-A	2	0	0.00	2	2	1	0	1	14	6	0	1	7
W 1962	NY-A	1	1	4.12	3	3	1	0	0	19^2	24	9	4	12
W 1963	NY-A	0	2	4.50	2	2	0	0	0	12	10	6	3	8
W 1964	NY-A	0	1	8.44	1	1	0	0	0	5^1	8	5	1	4
W Total	11	10	8	2.71	22	22	7	0	3	146	132	44	34	94
• FORSCH, Bob														
L 1982	StL-N	1	0	0.00	1	1	1	0	1	9	3	0	0	6

YEAR	TM-L	W	L	ERA	G	GS	CG	SV	SHO	IP	H	ER	BB	SO
L 1985	StL-N	0	0	5.40	1	1	0	0	0	3^{1}	3	2	2	0
L 1987	StL-N	1	1	12.00	3	0	0	0	0	3	4	4	1	3
L Total	3	2	1	3.52	5	2	1	0	1	15^{1}	10	6	3	9
W 1982	StL-N	0	2	4.97	2	2	0	0	0	12^{2}	18	7	3	4
W 1985	StL-N	0	1	12.00	2	1	0	0	0	3	6	4	1	3
W 1987	StL-N	1	0	9.95	3	0	0	0	0	6^{1}	8	7	5	3
W Total	3	1	3	7.36	7	3	0	0	0	22	32	18	9	10
• FORSCH, Ken														
L 1980	Hou-N	0	1	4.15	2	1	1	0	0	8^{2}	10	4	1	6
• FORSTER, Terry														
D 1981	LA-N	0	0	0.00	1	0	0	0	0	0^{1}	0	0	0	0
L 1978	LA-N	1	0	0.00	1	0	0	0	0	1	1	0	0	2
L 1981	LA-N	0	0	0.00	1	0	0	0	0	0^{1}	0	0	0	1
L Total	2	1	0	0.00	2	0	0	0	0	1^{1}	1	0	0	3
W 1978	LA-N	0	0	0.00	3	0	0	0	0	4	5	0	1	6
W 1981	LA-N	0	0	0.00	2	0	0	0	0	2	1	0	3	0
W Total	2	0	0	0.00	5	0	0	0	0	6	6	0	4	6
• FOSSAS, Tony														
L 1996	StL-N	0	0	2.08	5	0	0	0	0	4^{1}	1	1	3	1
• FOSTER, Rube														
W 1915	Bos-A	2	0	2.00	2	2	2	0	0	18	12	4	2	13
W 1916	Bos-A	0	0	0.00	1	0	0	0	0	3	3	0	0	1
W Total	2	2	0	1.71	3	2	2	0	0	21	15	4	2	14
• FOULKE, Keith														
D 2000	Chi-A	0	1	11.57	2	0	0	0	0	2^{1}	4	3	2	2
D 2003	Oak-A	0	1	3.60	3	0	0	0	0	5	4	2	2	3
D Total	2	0	2	6.14	5	0	0	0	0	7^{1}	8	5	4	5
• FOUTZ, Dave														
W 1885	StL-A	2	2	0.61	4	4	4	0	0	29^{1}	30	2	9	14
W 1886	StL-A	1	1	3.60	2	2	2	0	0	15	16	6	6	7
W 1887	StL-A	0	3	3.46	3	3	3	0	0	26	45	10	9	6
W 1889	Bro-A	0	0	7.20	1	0	0	0	0	5	5	4	2	2
W Total	4	3	6	2.63	10	9	9	0	0	75^{1}	96	22	26	29
• FOX, Chad														
D 2003	Fla-N	0	0	1.80	3	0	0	0	0	5	3	1	3	3
L 2003	Fla-N	1	0	5.40	3	0	0	0	0	3^{1}	5	2	2	2
W 2003	Fla-N	0	0	6.00	3	0	0	0	0	3	4	2	4	4
• FRANCO, John														
D 1999	NY-N	1	0	0.00	3	0	0	0	0	3^{2}	1	0	0	2
D 2000	NY-N	0	0	0.00	2	0	0	1	0	2	1	0	0	2
D Total	2	1	0	0.00	5	0	0	1	0	5^{2}	2	0	0	4
L 1999	NY-N	0	0	3.38	3	0	0	0	0	2^{2}	3	1	1	3
L 2000	NY-N	0	0	6.75	3	0	0	0	0	2^{2}	3	2	2	2
L Total	2	0	0	5.06	6	0	0	0	0	5^{1}	6	3	3	5
W 2000	NY-N	1	0	0.00	4	0	0	0	0	3^{1}	3	0	0	1
• FRAZIER, George														
L 1981	NY-A	1	0	0.00	1	0	0	0	0	5^{2}	5	0	1	5
L 1984	Chi-N	0	0	10.80	1	0	0	0	0	1^{2}	2	2	0	1
L Total	2	1	0	2.45	2	0	0	0	0	7^{1}	7	2	1	6
W 1981	NY-A	0	3	17.18	3	0	0	0	0	3^{2}	9	7	3	2
W 1987	Min-A	0	0	0.00	1	0	0	0	0	2	1	0	0	2
W Total	2	0	3	11.12	4	0	0	0	0	5^{2}	10	7	3	4
• FREEMAN, Marvin														
L 1992	Atl-N	0	0	14.73	3	0	0	0	0	3^{2}	8	6	2	1
• FRENCH, Larry														
W 1935	Chi-N	0	2	3.38	2	1	1	0	0	10^{2}	15	4	2	8
W 1938	Chi-N	0	0	2.70	3	0	0	0	0	3^{1}	1	1	1	2
W 1941	Bro-N	0	0	0.00	2	0	0	0	0	1	0	0	0	0
W Total	3	0	2	3.00	7	1	1	0	0	15	16	5	3	10
• FRIEND, Bob														
W 1960	Pit-N	0	2	13.50	3	2	0	0	0	6	13	9	3	7
• FROST, Dave														
L 1979	Cal-A	0	1	18.69	2	1	0	0	0	4^{1}	8	9	5	1
• FRYMAN, Woodie														
D 1981	Mon-N	0	0	6.75	1	0	0	0	0	1^{1}	3	1	1	0
L 1972	Det-A	0	2	3.65	2	2	0	0	0	12^{1}	11	5	2	8
L 1981	Mon-N	0	0	36.00	1	0	0	0	0	1	3	4	1	1
L Total	2	0	2	6.08	3	2	0	0	0	13^{1}	14	9	3	9
• FULTZ, Aaron														
D 2000	SF-N	0	1	6.75	1	0	0	0	0	1^{1}	3	1	0	0
D 2002	SF-N	0	0	....	2	0	0	0	0	0	2	1	0	0
D Total	2	0	1	13.50	3	0	0	0	0	1^{1}	5	2	0	0
L 2002	SF-N	0	0	0.00	1	0	0	0	0	0^{1}	0	0	0	0
W 2002	SF-N	0	0	3.86	2	0	0	0	0	2^{1}	4	1	1	0
• GABLER, Frank														
W 1936	NY-N	0	0	7.20	2	0	0	0	0	5	7	4	4	0
• GALE, Rich														
W 1980	KC-A	0	1	4.26	2	2	0	0	0	6^{1}	11	3	4	4
• GALEHOUSE, Denny														
W 1944	StL-A	1	1	1.50	2	2	2	0	0	18	13	3	5	15
• GARBER, Gene														
L 1976	Phi-N	0	1	13.50	2	0	0	0	0	0^{2}	2	1	1	0
L 1977	Phi-N	1	1	3.38	3	0	0	0	0	5^{1}	4	2	0	3
L 1982	Atl-N	0	1	8.10	2	0	0	0	0	3^{1}	4	3	1	3
L Total	3	1	3	5.79	7	0	0	0	0	9^{1}	10	6	2	6

YEAR	TM-L	W	L	ERA	G	GS	CG	SV	SHO	IP	H	ER	BB	SO
• GARCES, Rich														
D 1999	Bos-A	1	0	3.86	2	0	0	0	0	2^{1}	2	1	3	2
L 1999	Bos-A	0	0	12.00	2	0	0	0	0	3	3	4	1	2
• GARCIA, Freddy														
D 2000	Sea-A	0	0	10.80	1	1	0	0	0	3^{1}	6	4	3	2
D 2001	Sea-A	1	1	3.86	2	2	0	0	0	11^{2}	13	5	3	13
D Total	2	1	1	5.40	3	3	0	0	0	15	19	9	6	15
L 2000	Sea-A	2	0	1.54	2	2	0	0	0	11^{2}	10	2	4	11
L 2001	Sea-A	0	1	3.68	1	1	0	0	0	7^{1}	7	3	4	6
L Total	2	2	1	2.37	3	3	0	0	0	19	17	5	8	17
• GARCIA, Mike														
W 1954	Cle-A	0	1	5.40	2	1	0	0	0	5	6	3	4	4
• GARCIA, Ramon														
D 1997	Hou-N	0	0	0.00	2	0	0	0	0	1	1	0	1	1
• GARDNER, Mark														
D 2000	SF-N	0	1	8.31	1	1	0	0	0	4^{1}	4	4	2	5
• GARDNER, Wes														
L 1988	Bos-A	0	0	5.79	1	0	0	0	0	4^{2}	6	3	2	8
• GARLAND, Wayne														
L 1974	Bal-A	0	0	0.00	1	0	0	0	0	0^{2}	1	0	1	0
• GARMAN, Mike														
L 1977	LA-N	0	0	0.00	2	0	0	1	0	1^{1}	0	0	0	1
W 1977	LA-N	0	0	0.00	2	0	0	0	0	4	2	0	1	3
• GARRELTS, Scott														
L 1987	SF-N	0	0	6.75	2	0	0	0	0	2^{2}	2	2	4	4
L 1989	SF-N	1	0	5.40	2	2	0	0	0	11^{2}	16	7	2	8
L Total	2	1	0	5.65	4	2	0	0	0	14^{1}	18	9	6	12
W 1989	SF-N	0	2	9.82	2	2	0	0	0	7^{1}	13	8	1	8
• GENTRY, Gary														
L 1969	NY-N	0	0	9.00	1	1	0	0	0	2	5	2	1	1
W 1969	NY-N	1	0	0.00	1	1	0	0	0	6^{2}	3	0	5	4
• GEORGE, Bill														
W 1888	NY-N	0	1	7.20	1	1	1	0	0	10	15	8	3	4
• GETZEIN, Charlie														
W 1887	Det-N	4	2	2.48	6	6	6	0	1	58	76	16	15	17
• GIBBON, Joe														
L 1970	Pit-N	0	0	0.00	2	0	0	0	0	0^{1}	1	0	0	1
W 1960	Pit-N	0	0	9.00	2	0	0	0	0	3	4	3	1	2
• GIBSON, Bob														
W 1964	StL-N	2	1	3.00	3	3	2	0	0	27	23	9	8	31
W 1967	StL-N	3	0	1.00	3	3	3	0	1	27	14	3	5	26
W 1968	StL-N	2	1	1.67	3	3	3	0	1	27	18	5	4	35
W Total	3	7	2	1.89	9	9	8	0	2	81	55	17	17	92
• GIUSTI, Dave														
L 1970	Pit-N	0	0	3.86	2	0	0	0	0	2^{1}	3	1	1	1
L 1971	Pit-N	0	0	0.00	4	0	0	0	0	5^{1}	1	0	2	3
L 1972	Pit-N	0	1	6.75	3	0	0	1	0	2^{2}	5	2	0	3
L 1974	Pit-N	0	1	21.60	3	0	0	0	0	3^{1}	13	8	5	1
L 1975	Pit-N	0	0	0.00	1	0	0	0	0	1^{1}	0	0	0	1
L Total	5	0	2	6.60	13	0	0	1	0	15	22	11	8	9
W 1971	Pit-N	0	0	0.00	3	0	0	1	0	5^{1}	3	0	2	4
• GLAVINE, Tom														
D 1995	Atl-N	0	0	2.57	1	1	0	0	0	7	5	2	1	3
D 1996	Atl-N	1	0	1.35	1	1	0	0	0	6^{2}	5	1	3	7
D 1997	Atl-N	1	0	4.50	1	1	0	0	0	6	5	3	5	4
D 1998	Atl-N	0	0	1.29	1	1	0	0	0	7	3	1	1	8
D 1999	Atl-N	0	0	3.00	1	1	0	0	0	6	5	2	3	6
D 2000	Atl-N	0	1	27.00	1	1	0	0	0	2^{1}	6	7	1	2
D 2001	Atl-N	1	0	0.00	1	1	0	0	0	8	6	0	2	3
D 2002	Atl-N	0	2	15.26	2	2	0	0	0	7^{2}	17	13	7	4
D Total	8	3	3	5.15	9	9	0	0	0	50^{2}	52	29	23	37
L 1991	Atl-N	0	2	3.29	2	2	0	0	0	13^{2}	12	5	6	11
L 1992	Atl-N	0	2	12.27	2	2	0	0	0	7^{1}	13	10	3	2
L 1993	Atl-N	1	0	2.57	1	1	0	0	0	7	6	2	0	5
L 1995	Atl-N	0	0	1.29	1	1	0	0	0	7	7	1	2	5
L 1996	Atl-N	1	1	2.08	2	2	0	0	0	13	10	3	0	9
L 1997	Atl-N	1	1	5.40	2	2	0	0	0	13^{1}	13	8	11	9
L 1998	Atl-N	0	2	2.31	2	2	0	0	0	11^{2}	13	3	9	8
L 1999	Atl-N	1	0	0.00	1	1	0	0	0	7	7	0	1	8
L 2001	Atl-N	1	1	1.50	2	2	0	0	0	12	10	2	5	5
L Total	9	5	9	3.33	15	15	0	0	0	92	91	34	37	62
W 1991	Atl-N	1	1	2.70	2	2	1	0	0	13^{1}	8	4	7	8
W 1992	Atl-N	1	1	1.59	2	2	2	0	0	17	10	3	4	8
W 1995	Atl-N	2	0	1.29	2	2	0	0	0	14	4	2	6	11
W 1996	Atl-N	0	1	1.29	1	1	0	0	0	7	4	1	3	8
W 1999	Atl-N	0	0	5.14	1	1	0	0	0	7	7	4	0	3
W Total	5	4	3	2.16	8	8	3	0	0	58^{1}	33	14	20	38
• GLEASON, Kid														
T 1894	Bal-N	0	1	9.69	2	1	1	0	0	13	25	14	6	3
• GOLTZ, Dave														
L 1982	Cal-A	0	0	7.36	1	0	0	0	0	3^{2}	4	3	2	2
W 1981	LA-N	0	0	5.40	2	0	0	0	0	3^{1}	4	2	1	2
• GOMEZ, Lefty														
W 1932	NY-A	1	0	1.00	1	1	1	0	0	9	9	1	1	8
W 1936	NY-A	2	0	4.70	2	2	1	0	0	15^{1}	14	8	11	9
W 1937	NY-A	2	0	1.50	2	2	2	0	0	18	16	3	2	8
W 1938	NY-A	1	0	3.86	1	1	0	0	0	7	9	3	1	5

YEAR	TM-L	W	L	ERA	G	GS	CG	SV	SHO	IP	H	ER	BB	SO
W 1939	NY-A	0	0	9.00	1	1	0	0	0	1	3	1	0	1
W Total	5	6	0	2.86	7	7	4	0	0	50^1	51	16	15	31
• GOMEZ, Ruben														
W 1954	NY-N	1	0	2.45	1	1	0	0	0	7^1	4	2	3	2
• GOODEN, Dwight														
D 1997	NY-A	0	0	1.59	1	1	0	0	0	5^2	5	1	3	5
D 1998	Cle-A	0	0	54.00	1	1	0	0	0	0^1	1	2	2	1
D 2000	NY-A	0	0	21.60	1	0	0	0	0	1^2	4	4	1	1
D Total	3	0	0	8.22	3	2	0	0	0	7^2	10	7	6	7
L 1986	NY-N	0	1	1.06	2	2	0	0	0	17	16	2	5	9
L 1988	NY-N	0	0	2.95	3	2	0	0	0	18^1	10	6	8	20
L 1998	Cle-A	0	1	5.79	1	1	0	0	0	4^2	3	3	3	3
L 2000	NY-A	0	0	0.00	1	0	0	0	0	2^1	1	0	0	1
L Total	4	0	2	2.34	7	5	0	0	0	42^1	30	11	16	33
W 1986	NY-N	0	2	8.00	2	2	0	0	0	9	17	8	4	9
• GORDON, Tom														
D 1998	Bos-A	0	1	9.00	2	0	0	0	0	3	4	3	4	1
D 1999	Bos-A	0	0	4.50	2	0	0	0	0	2	1	1	1	3
D Total	2	0	1	7.20	4	0	0	0	0	5	5	4	5	4
L 1999	Bos-A	0	0	13.50	3	0	0	0	0	2	3	3	1	3
• GORMAN, Tom														
W 1952	NY-A	0	0	0.00	1	0	0	0	0	0^2	1	0	0	0
W 1953	NY-A	0	0	3.00	1	0	0	0	0	3	4	1	0	1
W Total	2	0	0	2.45	2	0	0	0	0	3^2	5	1	0	1
• GORSICA, Johnny														
W 1940	Det-A	0	0	0.79	2	0	0	0	0	11^1	6	1	4	4
• GOSSAGE, Rich														
D 1981	NY-A	0	0	0.00	3	0	0	3	0	6^2	3	0	2	8
L 1978	NY-A	1	0	4.50	2	0	0	1	0	4	3	2	0	3
L 1980	NY-A	0	1	54.00	1	0	0	0	0	0^1	3	2	0	0
L 1981	NY-A	0	0	0.00	2	0	0	1	0	2^2	1	0	0	2
L 1984	SD-N	0	0	4.50	3	0	0	1	0	4	5	2	1	5
L Total	4	1	1	4.91	8	0	0	3	0	11	12	6	1	10
W 1978	NY-A	1	0	0.00	3	0	0	0	0	6	1	0	1	4
W 1981	NY-A	0	0	0.00	3	0	0	2	0	5	2	0	2	5
W 1984	SD-N	0	0	13.50	2	0	0	0	0	2^2	3	4	1	2
W Total	3	1	0	2.63	8	0	0	2	0	13^2	6	4	4	11
• GRANGER, Wayne														
L 1970	Cin-N	0	0	0.00	1	0	0	0	0	0^2	1	0	0	0
W 1968	StL-N	0	0	0.00	1	0	0	0	0	2	0	0	1	1
W 1970	Cin-N	0	0	33.75	2	0	0	0	0	1^1	7	5	1	1
W Total	2	0	0	13.50	3	0	0	0	0	3^1	7	5	2	2
• GRANT, Mudcat														
L 1971	Oak-A	0	0	0.00	1	0	0	0	0	2	3	0	0	2
W 1965	Min-A	2	1	2.74	3	3	2	0	0	23	22	7	2	12
• GRAY, Jeff														
L 1990	Bos-A	0	0	2.70	2	0	0	0	0	3^1	4	1	1	2
• GREEN, Fred														
W 1960	Pit-N	0	0	22.50	3	0	0	0	0	4	11	10	1	3
• GREENE, Tommy														
L 1993	Phi-N	1	1	9.64	2	2	0	0	0	9^1	12	10	7	7
W 1993	Phi-N	0	0	27.00	1	1	0	0	0	2^1	7	7	4	1
• GREGG, Hal														
W 1947	Bro-N	0	1	3.55	3	1	0	0	0	12^2	9	5	8	10
• GRIM, Bob														
W 1955	NY-A	0	1	4.15	3	1	0	1	0	8^2	8	4	5	8
W 1957	NY-A	0	1	7.71	2	0	0	0	0	2^1	3	2	0	2
W Total	2	0	2	4.91	5	1	0	1	0	11	11	6	5	10
• GRIMES, Burleigh														
W 1920	Bro-N	1	2	4.19	3	3	1	0	1	19^1	23	9	9	4
W 1930	StL-N	0	2	3.71	2	2	2	0	0	17	10	7	6	13
W 1931	StL-N	2	0	2.04	2	2	1	0	0	17^2	9	4	9	11
W 1932	Chi-N	0	0	23.63	2	0	0	0	0	2^2	7	7	2	0
W Total	4	3	4	4.29	9	7	4	0	1	56^2	49	27	26	28
• GRIMSLEY, Jason														
L 2000	NY-A	0	0	0.00	2	0	0	0	0	1	2	0	3	1
W 1999	NY-A	0	0	0.00	1	0	0	0	0	2^1	2	0	2	0
• GRIMSLEY, Ross														
L 1972	Cin-N	1	0	1.00	1	1	1	0	0	9	2	1	0	5
L 1973	Cin-N	0	1	12.27	2	1	0	0	0	3^2	7	5	2	3
L 1974	Bal-A	0	0	1.69	2	0	0	0	0	5^1	1	1	2	2
L Total	3	1	1	3.50	5	2	1	0	0	18	10	7	4	10
W 1972	Cin-N	2	1	2.57	4	1	0	0	0	7	7	2	3	2
• GRISSOM, Lee														
W 1939	Cin-N	0	0	0.00	1	0	0	0	0	1^1	0	0	1	0
• GRISSOM, Marv														
W 1954	NY-N	1	0	0.00	1	0	0	0	0	2^2	1	0	3	2
• GROMEK, Steve														
W 1948	Cle-A	1	0	1.00	1	1	1	0	0	9	7	1	1	2
• GROVE, Lefty														
W 1929	Phi-A	0	0	0.00	2	0	0	2	0	6^1	3	0	1	10
W 1930	Phi-A	2	1	1.42	3	2	2	0	0	19	15	3	3	10
W 1931	Phi-A	2	1	2.42	3	3	2	0	0	26	28	7	2	16
W Total	3	4	2	1.75	8	5	4	2	0	51^1	46	10	6	36
• GRYBOSKI, Kevin														
D 2002	Atl-N	0	0	0.00	3	0	0	0	0	3^2	2	0	2	3

YEAR	TM-L	W	L	ERA	G	GS	CG	SV	SHO	IP	H	ER	BB	SO
D 2003	Atl-N	0	0	3.00	5	0	0	0	0	3	2	1	2	4
D Total	2	0	0	1.35	8	0	0	0	0	6^2	4	1	4	7
• GRZENDA, Joe														
L 1969	Min-A	0	0	0.00	1	0	0	0	0	0^2	0	0	0	0
• GUARDADO, Eddie														
D 2002	Min-A	0	0	13.50	2	0	0	1	0	2	5	3	1	1
D 2003	Min-A	0	0	9.00	2	0	0	1	0	2	5	2	0	2
D Total	2	0	0	11.25	4	0	0	2	0	4	10	5	1	3
L 2002	Min-A	0	0	0.00	1	0	0	1	0	1	0	0	1	2
• GUBICZA, Mark														
L 1985	KC-A	1	0	3.24	2	1	0	0	0	8^1	4	3	4	4
• GUIDRY, Ron														
D 1981	NY-A	0	0	5.40	2	2	0	0	0	8^1	11	5	3	8
L 1977	NY-A	1	0	3.97	2	2	1	0	0	11^1	9	5	3	8
L 1978	NY-A	1	0	1.13	1	1	0	0	0	8	7	1	1	7
L 1980	NY-A	0	1	12.00	1	1	0	0	0	3	5	4	4	2
L Total	3	2	1	4.03	4	4	1	0	0	22^1	21	10	8	17
W 1977	NY-A	1	0	2.00	1	1	1	0	0	9	4	2	3	7
W 1978	NY-A	1	0	1.00	1	1	1	0	0	9	8	1	7	4
W 1981	NY-A	1	1	1.93	2	2	0	0	0	14	8	3	4	15
W Total	3	3	1	1.69	4	4	2	0	0	32	20	6	14	26
• GULLETT, Don														
L 1970	Cin-N	0	0	0.00	2	0	0	1	0	3^2	1	0	2	3
L 1972	Cin-N	0	1	8.00	2	2	0	0	0	9	12	8	0	5
L 1973	Cin-N	0	1	2.00	3	1	0	0	0	9	4	2	3	6
L 1975	Cin-N	1	0	3.00	1	1	1	0	0	9	8	3	2	5
L 1976	Cin-N	1	0	1.13	1	1	0	0	0	8	2	1	3	4
L 1977	NY-A	0	1	18.00	1	1	0	0	0	2	4	4	2	0
L Total	6	2	3	3.98	10	6	1	1	0	40^2	31	18	12	23
W 1970	Cin-N	0	0	1.35	3	0	0	0	0	6^2	5	1	4	4
W 1972	Cin-N	0	0	1.08	1	1	0	0	0	8^1	5	1	2	4
W 1975	Cin-N	1	1	4.34	3	3	0	0	0	18^2	19	9	10	15
W 1976	Cin-N	1	0	1.23	1	1	0	0	0	7^1	5	1	3	4
W 1977	NY-A	0	1	6.39	2	2	0	0	0	12^2	13	9	7	10
W Total	5	2	2	3.52	10	7	0	0	0	53^2	47	21	26	37
• GULLICKSON, Bill														
D 1981	Mon-N	1	0	1.17	1	1	0	0	0	7^2	6	1	1	3
L 1981	Mon-N	0	2	2.51	2	2	0	0	0	14^1	12	4	6	12
• GUMBERT, Harry														
W 1936	NY-N	0	0	36.00	2	0	0	0	0	2	7	8	4	2
W 1937	NY-N	0	0	27.00	2	0	0	0	0	1^1	4	4	1	1
W 1942	StL-N	0	0	0.00	2	0	0	0	0	0^2	1	0	0	0
W Total	3	0	0	27.00	6	0	0	0	0	4	12	12	5	3
• GURA, Larry														
D 1981	KC-A	0	1	20.25	1	1	0	0	0	1^1	7	3	3	3
L 1976	KC-A	0	1	4.22	2	2	0	0	0	10^2	18	5	1	4
L 1977	KC-A	0	1	18.00	2	1	0	0	0	2	7	4	1	2
L 1978	KC-A	1	0	2.84	1	1	0	0	0	6^1	8	2	2	2
L 1980	KC-A	1	0	2.00	1	1	1	0	0	9	10	2	1	4
L Total	4	2	2	4.18	6	5	1	0	0	28	43	13	5	12
W 1980	KC-A	0	0	2.19	2	2	0	0	0	12^1	8	3	3	4
• GUTHRIE, Mark														
D 1995	LA-N	0	0	6.75	3	0	0	0	0	1^1	2	1	1	1
D 1996	LA-N	0	0	0.00	1	0	0	0	0	0^1	0	0	1	1
D 2001	Oak-A	0	0	0.00	2	0	0	0	0	3	0	0	0	2
D 2003	Chi-N	0	0	27.00	1	0	0	0	0	0^2	2	2	1	0
D Total	4	0	0	5.06	7	0	0	0	0	5^1	4	3	3	4
L 1991	Min-A	1	0	0.00	2	0	0	0	0	2^2	0	0	0	0
L 2003	Chi-N	0	1	9.00	2	0	0	0	0	1	1	1	0	0
L Total	2	1	1	2.45	4	0	0	0	0	3^2	1	1	0	0
W 1991	Min-A	0	1	2.25	4	0	0	0	0	4	3	1	4	3
• GUZMAN, Juan														
L 1991	Tor-A	1	0	3.18	1	1	0	0	0	5^2	4	2	4	2
L 1992	Tor-A	2	0	2.08	2	2	0	0	0	13	12	3	5	11
L 1993	Tor-A	2	0	2.08	2	2	0	0	0	13	8	3	9	9
L Total	3	5	0	2.27	5	5	0	0	0	31^2	24	8	18	22
W 1992	Tor-A	0	0	1.13	1	1	0	0	0	8	8	1	1	7
W 1993	Tor-A	0	1	3.75	2	2	0	0	0	12	10	5	8	12
W Total	2	0	1	2.70	3	3	0	0	0	20	18	6	9	19
• HAAS, Moose														
D 1981	Mil-A	0	2	9.45	2	2	0	0	0	6^2	13	7	1	1
L 1982	Mil-A	1	0	4.91	1	1	0	0	0	7^1	5	4	5	7
W 1982	Mil-A	0	0	7.36	2	1	0	0	0	7^1	8	6	3	4
• HADDIX, Harvey														
W 1960	Pit-N	2	0	2.45	2	1	0	0	0	7^1	6	2	2	6
• HADLEY, Bump														
W 1936	NY-A	1	0	1.13	1	1	0	0	0	8	10	1	1	2
W 1937	NY-A	0	1	33.75	1	1	0	0	0	1^1	6	5	0	0
W 1939	NY-A	1	0	2.25	1	0	0	0	0	8	7	2	3	2
W Total	3	2	1	4.15	3	2	0	0	0	17^1	23	8	4	4
• HAINES, Jesse														
W 1926	StL-N	2	0	1.08	3	2	1	0	1	16^2	13	2	9	5
W 1928	StL-N	0	1	4.50	1	1	0	0	0	6	6	3	3	3
W 1930	StL-N	1	0	1.00	1	1	1	0	0	9	4	1	4	2
W 1934	StL-N	0	0	0.00	1	0	0	0	0	0^2	1	0	0	2
W Total	4	3	1	1.67	6	4	2	0	1	32^1	24	6	16	12
• HALAMA, John														
D 2001	Sea-A	0	0	0.00	2	0	0	0	0	3	3	0	0	3

YEAR	TM-L	W	L	ERA	G	GS	CG	SV	SHO	IP	H	ER	BB	SO
L 2000	Sea-A	0	0	2.89	2	2	0	0	0	9^1	10	3	5	3
L 2001	Sea-A	0	0	13.50	2	0	0	0	0	2	3	3	0	0
L Total	**2**	**0**	**0**	**4.76**	**4**	**2**	**0**	**0**	**0**	**11^1**	**13**	**6**	**5**	**3**
• HALL, Charley														
W 1912	Bos-A	0	0	3.38	2	0	0	0	0	10^2	11	4	9	1
• HALL, Dick														
L 1969	Bal-A	1	0	0.00	1	0	0	0	0	0^2	0	0	0	1
L 1970	Bal-A	1	0	0.00	1	0	0	0	0	4^2	1	0	0	3
L Total	**2**	**2**	**0**	**0.00**	**2**	**0**	**0**	**0**	**0**	**5^1**	**1**	**0**	**0**	**4**
W 1969	Bal-A	0	1	....	1	0	0	0	0	0	1	0	1	0
W 1970	Bal-A	0	0	0.00	1	0	0	1	0	2^1	0	0	0	0
W 1971	Bal-A	0	0	0.00	1	0	0	1	0	1	1	0	0	0
W Total	**3**	**0**	**1**	**0.00**	**3**	**0**	**0**	**2**	**0**	**3^1**	**2**	**0**	**1**	**0**
• HALL, Tom														
L 1969	Min-A	0	0	0.00	1	0	0	0	0	0^2	0	0	0	0
L 1970	Min-A	0	1	6.75	2	1	0	0	0	5^1	6	4	4	6
L 1972	Cin-N	1	0	1.23	2	0	0	0	0	7^1	3	1	3	8
L 1973	Cin-N	0	0	67.50	3	0	0	0	0	0^2	3	5	3	1
L 1976	KC-A	0	0	0.00	1	0	0	0	0	0^1	1	0	0	0
L Total	**5**	**1**	**1**	**6.28**	**9**	**1**	**0**	**0**	**0**	**14^1**	**13**	**10**	**10**	**15**
W 1972	Cin-N	0	0	0.00	4	0	0	1	0	8^1	6	0	2	7
• HALLAHAN, Bill														
W 1926	StL-N	0	0	4.50	1	0	0	0	0	2	2	1	3	1
W 1930	StL-N	1	1	1.64	2	2	1	0	1	11	9	2	8	8
W 1931	StL-N	2	0	0.49	3	2	2	1	1	18^1	12	1	8	12
W 1934	StL-N	0	0	2.16	1	1	0	0	0	8^1	6	2	4	6
W Total	**4**	**3**	**1**	**1.36**	**7**	**5**	**3**	**1**	**2**	**39^2**	**29**	**6**	**23**	**27**
• HAMILTON, Dave														
L 1972	Oak-A	0	0	....	1	0	0	0	0	0	1	0	1	0
W 1972	Oak-A	0	0	27.00	2	0	0	0	0	1^1	3	4	1	1
• HAMILTON, Joey														
D 1996	SD-N	0	1	4.50	1	1	0	0	0	6	5	3	0	6
D 1998	SD-N	0	0	0.00	2	0	0	0	0	3^1	1	0	2	3
D Total	**2**	**0**	**1**	**2.89**	**3**	**1**	**0**	**0**	**0**	**9^1**	**6**	**3**	**2**	**9**
L 1998	SD-N	0	1	4.91	2	1	0	0	0	7^1	7	4	3	6
W 1998	SD-N	0	0	0.00	1	0	0	0	0	1	0	0	1	1
• HAMILTON, Steve														
L 1971	SF-N	0	0	9.00	1	0	0	0	0	1	1	1	0	3
W 1963	NY-A	0	0	0.00	1	0	0	0	0	1	0	0	0	1
W 1964	NY-A	0	0	4.50	2	0	0	1	0	2	3	1	0	2
W Total	**2**	**0**	**0**	**3.00**	**3**	**0**	**0**	**1**	**0**	**3**	**3**	**1**	**0**	**3**
• HAMMAKER, Atlee														
L 1987	SF-N	0	1	7.88	2	2	0	0	0	8	12	7	0	7
L 1989	SF-N	0	0	0.00	1	0	0	0	0	1	1	0	0	0
L Total	**2**	**0**	**1**	**7.00**	**3**	**2**	**0**	**0**	**0**	**9**	**13**	**7**	**0**	**7**
W 1989	SF-N	0	0	15.43	2	0	0	0	0	2^1	8	4	0	2
• HAMMOND, Chris														
D 2002	Atl-N	0	0	6.75	3	0	0	0	0	2^2	2	2	3	2
W 2003	NY-A	0	0	0.00	1	0	0	0	0	2	2	0	0	0
• HAMPTON, Mike														
D 1997	Hou-N	0	1	11.57	1	1	0	0	0	4^2	2	6	8	2
D 1998	Hou-N	0	0	1.50	1	1	0	0	0	6	2	1	1	2
D 1999	Hou-N	0	0	3.86	1	1	0	0	0	7	6	3	1	9
D 2000	NY-N	0	1	8.44	1	1	0	0	0	5^1	6	5	3	2
D 2003	Atl-N	0	0	4.26	2	2	0	0	0	12^2	11	6	6	16
D Total	**5**	**0**	**2**	**5.30**	**6**	**6**	**0**	**0**	**0**	**35^2**	**27**	**21**	**19**	**31**
L 2000	NY-N	2	0	0.00	2	2	1	0	1	16	9	0	4	12
W 2000	NY-N	0	1	6.00	1	1	0	0	0	6	8	4	5	4
• HANSON, Erik														
D 1995	Bos-A	0	1	4.50	1	1	1	0	0	8	4	4	4	5
• HARDEN, Rich														
D 2003	Oak-A	1	1	13.50	2	0	0	0	0	1^1	2	2	2	1
• HARPER, Harry														
W 1921	NY-A	0	0	20.25	1	1	0	0	0	1^1	3	3	2	1
• HARRIS, Greg														
L 1984	SD-N	0	0	31.50	1	0	0	0	0	2	9	7	3	2
L 1990	Bos-A	0	1	27.00	1	0	0	0	0	0^1	3	1	0	0
L Total	**2**	**0**	**1**	**30.86**	**2**	**0**	**0**	**0**	**0**	**2^1**	**12**	**8**	**3**	**2**
W 1984	SD-N	0	0	0.00	1	0	0	0	0	5^1	3	0	3	5
• HARRIS, Mickey														
W 1946	Bos-A	0	2	3.72	2	2	0	0	0	9^2	11	4	4	5
• HASSLER, Andy														
L 1976	KC-A	0	1	6.14	2	1	0	0	0	7^1	8	5	6	4
L 1977	KC-A	0	1	4.76	1	1	0	0	0	5^2	5	3	0	3
L 1982	Cal-A	0	0	0.00	2	0	0	0	0	2^2	0	0	0	2
L Total	**3**	**0**	**2**	**4.60**	**5**	**2**	**0**	**0**	**0**	**15^2**	**13**	**8**	**6**	**9**
• HATFIELD, Gil														
W 1888	NY-N	0	0	12.60	1	0	0	0	0	5	12	7	3	2
• HATTEN, Joe														
W 1947	Bro-N	0	0	7.00	4	1	0	0	0	9	12	7	7	5
W 1949	Bro-N	0	0	16.20	2	0	0	0	0	1^2	4	3	2	0
W Total	**2**	**0**	**0**	**8.44**	**6**	**1**	**0**	**0**	**0**	**10^2**	**16**	**10**	**9**	**5**
• HAWKE, Bill														
T 1894	Bal-N	0	1	9.00	1	1	0	0	0	4	9	4	1	0
• HAWKINS, Andy														
L 1984	SD-N	0	0	0.00	3	0	0	0	0	3^2	0	0	2	1
W 1984	SD-N	1	1	0.75	3	0	0	0	0	12	4	1	6	4
• HAWKINS, La Troy														
D 2002	Min-A	0	0	0.00	3	0	0	0	0	2^1	0	0	0	5
D 2003	Min-A	1	0	6.00	3	0	0	0	0	3	5	2	0	5
D Total	**2**	**1**	**0**	**3.38**	**6**	**0**	**0**	**0**	**0**	**5^1**	**5**	**2**	**0**	**10**
L 2002	Min-A	0	0	20.25	4	0	0	0	0	1^1	4	3	1	1
• HEARN, Jim														
W 1951	NY-N	1	0	1.04	2	1	0	0	0	8^2	5	1	8	1
• HEINTZELMAN, Ken														
W 1950	Phi-N	0	0	1.17	1	1	0	0	0	7^2	4	1	6	3
• HELLING, Rick														
D 1998	Tex-A	0	1	4.50	1	1	0	0	0	6	8	3	1	9
D 1999	Tex-A	0	1	2.84	1	1	0	0	0	6^1	5	2	1	8
D 2002	Ari-N	0	0	0.00	2	0	0	0	0	4	1	0	0	2
D 2003	Fla-N	0	0	27.00	1	0	0	0	0	0^1	2	1	2	0
D Total	**4**	**0**	**2**	**3.24**	**5**	**2**	**0**	**0**	**0**	**16^2**	**16**	**6**	**4**	**19**
L 2003	Fla-N	0	0	6.35	2	0	0	0	0	5^2	7	4	4	5
W 2003	Fla-N	0	0	6.75	1	0	0	0	0	2^2	2	2	0	2
• HEMMING, George														
T 1894	Bal-N	0	1	1.13	1	1	1	0	0	8	10	1	3	2
• HENDRIX, Claude														
W 1918	Chi-N	0	0	0.00	1	0	0	0	0	1	0	0	0	0
• HENKE, Tom														
L 1985	Tor-A	2	0	4.26	3	0	0	0	0	6^1	5	3	4	4
L 1989	Tor-A	0	0	0.00	3	0	0	0	0	2^2	0	0	0	3
L 1991	Tor-A	0	0	0.00	2	0	0	0	0	2^2	0	0	1	5
L 1992	Tor-A	0	0	0.00	4	0	0	3	0	4^2	3	0	2	2
L Total	**4**	**2**	**0**	**1.65**	**12**	**0**	**0**	**3**	**0**	**16^1**	**8**	**3**	**7**	**14**
W 1992	Tor-A	0	0	2.70	3	0	0	2	0	3^1	2	1	2	1
• HENNEMAN, Mike														
D 1996	Tex-A	0	0	0.00	3	0	0	0	0	1	1	0	1	1
L 1987	Det-A	1	0	10.80	3	0	0	0	0	5	6	6	6	3
• HENRY, Bill														
W 1961	Cin-N	0	0	19.29	2	0	0	0	0	2^1	4	5	2	3
• HENRY, Doug														
D 1997	SF-N	0	0	0.00	1	0	0	0	0	2	1	0	3	2
D 1998	Hou-N	0	0	5.40	2	0	0	0	0	1^2	2	1	0	1
D 1999	Hou-N	0	0	0.00	2	0	0	0	0	3^2	1	0	3	2
D 2000	SF-N	0	0	2.25	3	0	0	0	0	4	1	1	3	1
D Total	**4**	**0**	**0**	**1.59**	**8**	**0**	**0**	**0**	**0**	**11^1**	**5**	**2**	**9**	**6**
• HENSHAW, Roy														
W 1935	Chi-N	0	0	7.36	1	0	0	0	0	3^2	2	3	5	2
• HENTGEN, Pat														
L 1993	Tor-A	0	1	18.00	1	1	0	0	0	3	9	6	2	3
L 2000	StL-N	0	1	14.73	1	1	0	0	0	3^2	7	6	5	2
L Total	**2**	**0**	**2**	**16.20**	**2**	**2**	**0**	**0**	**0**	**6^2**	**16**	**12**	**7**	**5**
W 1993	Tor-A	1	0	1.50	1	1	0	0	0	6	5	1	3	6
• HEREDIA, Felix														
D 1998	Chi-N	0	0	54.00	1	0	0	0	0	0^1	0	2	2	0
D 2003	NY-A	0	0	0.00	1	0	0	0	0	2	1	0	1	1
D Total	**2**	**0**	**0**	**7.71**	**2**	**0**	**0**	**0**	**0**	**2^1**	**1**	**2**	**3**	**1**
L 1997	Fla-N	0	0	5.40	2	0	0	0	0	3^1	3	2	2	4
L 2003	NY-A	0	0	3.38	5	0	0	0	0	2^2	0	1	3	3
L Total	**2**	**0**	**0**	**4.50**	**7**	**0**	**0**	**0**	**0**	**6**	**3**	**3**	**5**	**7**
W 1997	Fla-N	0	0	0.00	4	0	0	0	0	5^1	2	0	1	5
• HEREDIA, Gil														
D 2000	Oak-A	1	1	12.79	2	2	0	0	0	6^1	11	9	3	3
• HERGES, Matt														
D 2003	SF-N	0	0	0.00	3	0	0	0	0	4^1	1	0	2	5
• HERMANSON, Dustin														
D 2001	StL-N	0	0	0.00	1	0	0	0	0	3	0	0	0	0
D 2003	SF-N	0	0	0.00	1	0	0	0	0	1	1	0	1	0
D Total	**2**	**0**	**0**	**0.00**	**2**	**0**	**0**	**0**	**0**	**4**	**1**	**0**	**1**	**0**
• HERNANDEZ, Livan														
D 1997	Fla-N	0	0	2.25	1	0	0	0	0	4	3	1	0	3
D 2000	SF-N	1	0	1.17	1	1	0	0	0	7^2	5	1	5	5
D 2002	SF-N	1	0	3.24	1	1	0	0	0	8^1	8	3	2	6
D Total	**3**	**2**	**0**	**2.25**	**3**	**2**	**0**	**0**	**0**	**20**	**16**	**5**	**7**	**14**
L 1997	Fla-N	2	0	0.84	2	1	1	0	0	10^2	5	1	2	16
L 2002	SF-N	0	0	2.84	1	1	0	0	0	6^1	9	2	1	0
L Total	**2**	**2**	**0**	**1.59**	**3**	**2**	**1**	**0**	**0**	**17**	**14**	**3**	**3**	**16**
W 1997	Fla-N	2	0	5.27	2	2	0	0	0	13^2	15	8	10	7
W 2002	SF-N	0	2	14.29	2	2	0	0	0	5^2	9	9	9	4
W Total	**2**	**2**	**2**	**7.91**	**4**	**4**	**0**	**0**	**0**	**19^1**	**24**	**17**	**19**	**11**
• HERNANDEZ, Orlando														
D 1999	NY-A	1	0	0.00	1	1	0	0	0	8	2	0	6	4
D 2000	NY-A	1	0	2.45	2	1	0	0	0	7^1	5	2	5	5
D 2001	NY-A	1	0	3.18	1	1	0	0	0	5^2	8	2	2	5
D 2002	NY-A	0	1	2.84	2	0	0	0	0	6^1	5	2	0	7
D Total	**4**	**3**	**1**	**1.98**	**6**	**3**	**0**	**0**	**0**	**27^1**	**20**	**6**	**13**	**21**
L 1998	NY-A	1	0	0.00	1	1	0	0	0	7	3	0	2	6
L 1999	NY-A	1	0	1.80	2	2	0	0	0	15	12	3	6	13
L 2000	NY-A	2	0	4.20	2	2	0	0	0	15	13	7	8	14
L 2001	NY-A	0	1	7.20	1	1	0	0	0	5	5	4	5	7
L Total	**4**	**4**	**1**	**3.00**	**6**	**6**	**0**	**0**	**0**	**42**	**33**	**14**	**21**	**40**
W 1998	NY-A	1	0	1.29	1	1	0	0	0	7	6	1	3	7

YEAR	TM-L	W	L	ERA	G	GS	CG	SV	SHO	IP	H	ER	BB	SO
W 1999	NY-A	1	0	1.29	1	1	0	0	0	7	1	1	2	10
W 2000	NY-A	0	1	4.91	1	1	0	0	0	7^1	9	4	3	12
W 2001	NY-A	0	0	1.42	1	1	0	0	0	6^1	4	1	4	5
W Total	**4**	**2**	**1**	**2.28**	**4**	**4**	**0**	**0**	**0**	**27^2**	**20**	**7**	**12**	**34**
• HERNANDEZ, Ramon														
L 1972	Pit-N	0	0	2.70	3	0	0	0	0	3^1	1	1	0	3
L 1974	Pit-N	0	0	0.00	2	0	0	0	0	4^1	3	0	1	2
L 1975	Pit-N	0	1	27.00	1	0	0	0	0	0^2	3	2	0	0
L Total	**3**	**0**	**1**	**3.24**	**6**	**0**	**0**	**0**	**0**	**8^1**	**7**	**3**	**1**	**5**
• HERNANDEZ, Roberto														
D 1997	SF-N	0	1	20.25	3	0	0	0	0	1^1	5	3	3	1
D 2003	Atl-N	0	0	0.00	1	0	0	0	0	1	1	0	0	0
D Total	**2**	**0**	**1**	**11.57**	**4**	**0**	**0**	**0**	**0**	**2^1**	**6**	**3**	**3**	**1**
L 1993	Chi-A	0	0	0.00	4	0	0	1	0	4	4	0	0	1
• HERNANDEZ, Willie														
L 1984	Det-A	0	0	2.25	3	0	0	1	0	4	3	1	1	3
L 1987	Det-A	0	0	0.00	1	0	0	0	0	0^1	2	0	0	0
L Total	**2**	**0**	**0**	**2.08**	**4**	**0**	**0**	**1**	**0**	**4^1**	**5**	**1**	**1**	**3**
W 1983	Phi-N	0	0	0.00	3	0	0	0	0	4	0	0	1	4
W 1984	Det-A	0	0	1.69	3	0	0	2	0	5^1	4	1	0	0
W Total	**2**	**0**	**0**	**0.96**	**6**	**0**	**0**	**2**	**0**	**9^1**	**4**	**1**	**1**	**4**
• HERNANDEZ, Xavier														
L 1995	Cin-N	0	0	27.00	1	0	0	0	0	0^2	3	2	0	0
• HERSHISER, Orel														
D 1995	Cle-A	1	0	0.00	1	1	0	0	0	7^1	3	0	2	7
D 1996	Cle-A	0	0	5.40	1	1	0	0	0	5	7	3	3	3
D 1997	Cle-A	0	0	3.97	2	2	0	0	0	11^1	14	5	2	4
D 1999	NY-N	0	0	0.00	1	0	0	0	0	1	0	0	0	1
D Total	**4**	**1**	**0**	**2.92**	**5**	**4**	**0**	**0**	**0**	**24^2**	**24**	**8**	**7**	**15**
L 1985	LA-N	1	0	3.52	2	2	1	0	0	15^1	17	6	6	5
L 1988	LA-N	1	0	1.09	4	3	1	1	1	24^2	18	3	7	15
L 1995	Cle-A	2	0	1.29	2	2	0	0	0	14	9	2	3	15
L 1997	Cle-A	0	0	0.00	1	1	0	0	0	7	4	0	1	7
L 1999	NY-N	0	0	0.00	2	0	0	0	0	4^1	1	0	3	5
L Total	**5**	**4**	**0**	**1.52**	**11**	**8**	**2**	**1**	**1**	**65^1**	**49**	**11**	**20**	**47**
W 1988	LA-N	2	0	1.00	2	2	2	0	1	18	7	2	6	17
W 1995	Cle-A	1	1	2.57	2	2	0	0	0	14	8	4	4	13
W 1997	Cle-A	0	2	11.70	2	2	0	0	0	10	15	13	6	5
W Total	**3**	**3**	**3**	**4.07**	**6**	**6**	**2**	**0**	**1**	**42**	**30**	**19**	**16**	**35**
• HICKMAN, Charlie														
T 1897	Bos-N	0	1	3.60	1	1	0	0	0	5	7	2	2	0
• HIGBE, Kirby														
W 1941	Bro-N	0	0	7.36	1	1	0	0	0	3^2	6	3	2	1
• HILDEBRAND, Oral														
W 1939	NY-A	0	0	0.00	1	1	0	0	0	4	2	0	0	3
• HILJUS, Erik														
D 2001	Oak-A	0	0	27.00	1	0	0	0	0	0^1	0	1	2	0
• HILL, Carmen														
W 1927	Pit-N	0	0	4.50	1	1	0	0	0	6	9	3	1	6
• HILL, Ken														
D 1995	Cle-A	1	0	0.00	1	0	0	0	0	1^1	1	0	0	2
D 1996	Tex-A	0	0	4.50	1	1	0	0	0	6	5	3	3	1
D Total	**2**	**1**	**0**	**3.68**	**2**	**1**	**0**	**0**	**0**	**7^1**	**6**	**3**	**3**	**3**
L 1995	Cle-A	1	0	0.00	1	1	0	0	0	7	5	0	3	6
W 1995	Cle-A	0	1	4.26	2	1	0	0	0	6^1	7	3	4	1
• HILLER, John														
L 1972	Det-A	1	0	0.00	3	0	0	0	0	3^1	1	0	1	1
W 1968	Det-A	0	0	13.50	2	0	0	0	0	2	6	3	3	1
• HITCHCOCK, Sterling														
D 1995	NY-A	0	0	5.40	2	0	0	0	0	1^2	2	1	2	1
D 1998	SD-N	1	0	1.50	1	1	0	0	0	6	3	1	0	11
D 2001	NY-A	0	0	6.00	1	0	0	0	0	3	5	2	0	2
D Total	**3**	**1**	**0**	**3.38**	**4**	**1**	**0**	**0**	**0**	**10^2**	**10**	**4**	**2**	**14**
L 1998	SD-N	2	0	0.90	2	2	0	0	0	10	5	1	8	14
W 1998	SD-N	0	0	1.50	1	1	0	0	0	6	7	1	1	7
W 2001	NY-A	1	0	0.00	2	0	0	0	0	4	1	0	0	6
W Total	**2**	**1**	**0**	**0.90**	**3**	**1**	**0**	**0**	**0**	**10**	**8**	**1**	**1**	**13**
• HOERNER, Joe														
W 1967	StL-N	0	0	40.50	2	0	0	0	0	0^2	4	3	1	0
W 1968	StL-N	0	1	3.86	3	0	0	1	0	4^2	5	2	5	3
W Total	**2**	**0**	**1**	**8.44**	**5**	**0**	**0**	**1**	**0**	**5^1**	**9**	**5**	**6**	**3**
• HOFFER, Bill														
T 1895	Bal-N	0	2	4.24	2	2	2	0	0	17	21	8	6	4
T 1896	Bal-N	2	0	1.50	2	2	2	0	0	18	15	3	5	10
T 1897	Bal-N	2	0	3.38	2	2	2	0	0	16	25	6	4	2
T Total	**3**	**4**	**2**	**3.00**	**6**	**6**	**6**	**0**	**0**	**51**	**61**	**17**	**15**	**16**
• HOFFMAN, Trevor														
D 1996	SD-N	0	1	10.80	2	0	0	0	0	1^2	3	2	1	2
D 1998	SD-N	0	0	0.00	4	0	0	2	0	3	3	0	1	4
D Total	**2**	**0**	**1**	**3.86**	**6**	**0**	**0**	**2**	**0**	**4^2**	**6**	**2**	**2**	**6**
L 1998	SD-N	1	0	2.08	3	0	0	1	0	4^1	2	1	2	7
W 1998	SD-N	0	1	9.00	1	0	0	0	0	2	2	2	1	0
• HOGSETT, Chief														
W 1934	Det-A	0	0	1.23	3	0	0	0	0	7^1	6	1	3	3
W 1935	Det-A	0	0	0.00	1	0	0	0	0	1	0	0	1	0
W Total	**2**	**0**	**0**	**1.08**	**4**	**0**	**0**	**0**	**0**	**8^1**	**6**	**1**	**4**	**3**
• HOGUE, Bobby														
W 1951	NY-A	0	0	0.00	2	0	0	0	0	2^2	1	0	0	0
• HOLLAND, Al														
L 1983	Phi-N	0	0	0.00	2	0	0	1	0	3	1	0	0	3
W 1983	Phi-N	0	0	0.00	2	0	0	1	0	3^2	1	0	0	5
• HOLLINGSWORTH, Al														
W 1944	StL-A	0	0	2.25	1	0	0	0	0	4	5	1	2	1
• HOLMES, Darren														
D 1995	Col-N	1	0	0.00	3	0	0	0	0	1^2	6	0	0	2
D 1999	Ari-N	0	0	27.00	1	0	0	0	0	1^1	1	4	3	0
D 2002	Atl-N	0	0	0.00	3	0	0	0	0	2^2	1	0	0	5
D Total	**3**	**1**	**0**	**6.35**	**7**	**0**	**0**	**0**	**0**	**5^2**	**8**	**4**	**3**	**7**
• HOLT, Chris														
D 1999	Hou-N	0	0	....	1	0	0	0	0	0	3	3	0	0
• HOLTON, Brian														
L 1988	LA-N	0	0	2.25	3	0	0	1	0	4	2	1	1	2
W 1988	LA-N	0	0	0.00	1	0	0	0	0	2	0	0	1	0
• HOLTZMAN, Ken														
L 1972	Oak-A	0	1	4.50	1	1	0	0	0	4	4	2	2	2
L 1973	Oak-A	1	0	0.82	1	1	1	0	0	11	3	1	1	7
L 1974	Oak-A	1	0	0.00	1	1	1	0	1	9	5	0	2	3
L 1975	Oak-A	0	2	4.09	2	2	0	0	0	11	12	5	1	7
L Total	**4**	**2**	**3**	**2.06**	**5**	**5**	**2**	**0**	**1**	**35**	**24**	**8**	**6**	**19**
W 1972	Oak-A	1	0	2.13	3	2	0	0	0	12^2	11	3	3	4
W 1973	Oak-A	2	1	4.22	3	3	0	0	0	10^2	13	5	5	6
W 1974	Oak-A	1	0	1.50	2	2	0	0	0	12	13	2	4	10
W Total	**3**	**4**	**1**	**2.55**	**8**	**7**	**0**	**0**	**0**	**35^1**	**37**	**10**	**12**	**20**
• HONEYCUTT, Rick														
D 1996	StL-N	1	0	3.38	3	0	0	0	0	2^2	3	1	1	2
L 1983	LA-N	0	0	21.60	2	0	0	0	0	1^2	4	4	0	2
L 1985	LA-N	0	0	13.50	2	0	0	0	0	1^1	4	2	2	1
L 1988	Oak-A	1	0	0.00	3	0	0	0	0	2	0	0	2	0
L 1989	Oak-A	0	0	32.40	3	0	0	0	0	1^2	6	6	5	1
L 1990	Oak-A	0	0	0.00	3	0	0	1	0	1^2	0	0	0	0
L 1992	Oak-A	0	0	0.00	2	0	0	0	0	2	0	0	0	1
L 1996	StL-N	0	0	9.00	5	0	0	0	0	4	5	4	3	3
L Total	**7**	**1**	**0**	**10.05**	**20**	**0**	**0**	**1**	**0**	**14^1**	**19**	**16**	**12**	**8**
W 1988	Oak-A	1	0	0.00	3	0	0	0	0	3^1	0	0	0	5
W 1989	Oak-A	0	0	6.75	3	0	0	0	0	2^2	4	2	0	2
W 1990	Oak-A	0	0	0.00	1	0	0	0	0	1^2	2	0	1	0
W Total	**3**	**1**	**0**	**2.35**	**7**	**0**	**0**	**0**	**0**	**7^2**	**6**	**2**	**1**	**7**
• HOOTON, Burt														
D 1981	LA-N	1	0	1.29	1	1	0	0	0	7	3	1	3	2
L 1977	LA-N	0	0	16.20	1	1	0	0	0	1^2	2	3	4	1
L 1978	LA-N	0	0	7.71	1	1	0	0	0	4^2	10	4	0	5
L 1981	LA-N	2	0	0.00	2	2	0	0	0	14^2	11	0	6	7
L Total	**3**	**2**	**0**	**3.00**	**4**	**4**	**0**	**0**	**0**	**21**	**23**	**7**	**10**	**13**
W 1977	LA-N	1	1	3.75	2	2	1	0	0	12	8	5	2	9
W 1978	LA-N	1	1	6.48	2	2	0	0	0	8^1	13	6	3	6
W 1981	LA-N	1	1	1.59	2	2	0	0	0	11^1	8	2	9	3
W Total	**3**	**3**	**3**	**3.69**	**6**	**6**	**1**	**0**	**0**	**31^2**	**29**	**13**	**14**	**18**
• HORLEN, Joe														
L 1972	Oak-A	0	0	....	1	0	0	0	0	0	0	0	1	0
W 1972	Oak-A	0	0	6.75	1	0	0	0	0	1^1	2	1	2	1
• HORTON, Ricky														
L 1985	StL-N	0	0	9.00	3	0	0	0	0	3	4	3	2	1
L 1987	StL-N	0	0	0.00	1	0	0	0	0	3	2	0	0	2
L 1988	LA-N	0	0	0.00	4	0	0	0	0	4^1	4	0	2	3
L Total	**3**	**0**	**0**	**2.61**	**8**	**0**	**0**	**0**	**0**	**10^1**	**10**	**3**	**4**	**6**
W 1985	StL-N	0	0	6.75	3	0	0	0	0	4	4	3	5	5
W 1987	StL-N	0	0	6.00	2	0	0	0	0	3	5	2	0	1
W Total	**2**	**0**	**0**	**6.43**	**5**	**0**	**0**	**0**	**0**	**7**	**9**	**5**	**5**	**6**
• HOUGH, Charlie														
L 1974	LA-N	0	0	7.71	1	0	0	0	0	2^1	4	2	0	2
L 1977	LA-N	0	0	4.50	1	0	0	0	0	2	2	1	0	3
L 1978	LA-N	0	0	4.50	1	0	0	0	0	2	1	1	0	1
L Total	**3**	**0**	**0**	**5.68**	**3**	**0**	**0**	**0**	**0**	**6^1**	**7**	**4**	**0**	**6**
W 1974	LA-N	0	0	0.00	1	0	0	0	0	2	0	0	1	4
W 1977	LA-N	0	0	1.80	2	0	0	0	0	5	3	1	0	5
W 1978	LA-N	0	0	8.44	2	0	0	0	0	5^1	10	5	2	5
W Total	**3**	**0**	**0**	**4.38**	**5**	**0**	**0**	**0**	**0**	**12^1**	**13**	**6**	**3**	**14**
• HOUTTEMAN, Art														
W 1954	Cle-A	0	0	4.50	1	0	0	0	0	2	2	1	1	1
• HOWE, Steve														
D 1981	LA-N	0	0	0.00	2	0	0	0	0	2	1	0	0	2
D 1995	NY-A	0	0	18.00	2	0	0	0	0	1	4	2	0	0
D Total	**2**	**0**	**0**	**6.00**	**4**	**0**	**0**	**0**	**0**	**3**	**5**	**2**	**0**	**2**
L 1981	LA-N	0	0	0.00	2	0	0	0	0	2	1	0	0	2
W 1981	LA-N	1	0	3.86	3	0	0	1	0	7	7	3	1	4
• HOWELL, Harry														
T 1900	Bro-N	0	1	3.38	1	1	1	0	0	8	13	3	2	3
• HOWELL, Jay														
L 1988	LA-N	0	1	27.00	2	0	0	0	0	0^2	1	2	2	1
W 1988	LA-N	0	1	3.38	2	0	0	1	0	2^2	3	1	1	2
• HOWELL, Ken														
L 1985	LA-N	0	0	0.00	1	0	0	0	0	2	0	0	0	2
• HOWRY, Bobby														
D 2000	Chi-A	0	0	3.38	2	0	0	0	0	2^2	2	1	2	4

YEAR	TM-L	W	L	ERA	G	GS	CG	SV	SHO	IP	H	ER	BB	SO
• HOYT, La Marr														
L 1983	Chi-A	1	0	1.00	1	1	1	0	0	9	5	1	0	4
• HOYT, Waite														
W 1921	NY-A	2	1	0.00	3	3	3	0	1	27	18	0	11	18
W 1922	NY-A	0	1	1.13	2	1	0	0	0	8	11	1	2	4
W 1923	NY-A	0	0	15.43	1	1	0	0	0	2^{1}	4	4	1	0
W 1926	NY-A	1	1	1.20	2	2	1	0	0	15	19	2	1	10
W 1927	NY-A	1	0	4.91	1	1	0	0	0	7^{1}	8	4	1	2
W 1928	NY-A	2	0	1.50	2	2	2	0	0	18	14	3	6	14
W 1931	Phi-A	0	1	4.50	1	1	0	0	0	6	7	3	0	1
W Total	7	6	4	1.83	12	11	6	0	1	83^{2}	81	17	22	49
• HRABOSKY, Al														
L 1978	KC-A	0	0	3.00	3	0	0	0	0	3	3	1	0	2
• HUBBELL, Carl														
W 1933	NY-N	2	0	0.00	2	2	2	0	0	20	13	0	6	15
W 1936	NY-N	1	1	2.25	2	2	1	0	0	16	15	4	2	10
W 1937	NY-N	1	1	3.77	2	2	1	0	0	14^{1}	12	6	4	7
W Total	3	4	2	1.79	6	6	4	0	0	50^{1}	40	10	12	32
• HUDSON, Charles														
L 1983	Phi-N	1	0	2.00	1	1	1	0	0	9	4	2	2	9
W 1983	Phi-N	0	2	8.64	2	2	0	0	0	8^{1}	9	8	1	6
• HUDSON, Joe														
D 1995	Bos-A	0	0	0.00	1	0	0	0	0	1	2	0	1	0
• HUDSON, Nat														
W 1886	StL-A	1	0	2.57	1	1	1	0	0	7	3	2	3	3
• HUDSON, Tim														
D 2000	Oak-A	0	1	3.38	1	1	1	0	0	8	6	3	4	5
D 2001	Oak-A	1	0	0.93	2	1	0	0	0	9^{2}	8	1	1	5
D 2002	Oak-A	0	1	6.23	2	2	0	0	0	8^{2}	13	6	4	8
D 2003	Oak-A	0	0	3.52	2	2	0	0	0	7^{2}	10	3	1	6
D Total	4	1	2	3.44	7	6	1	0	0	34	37	13	10	24
• HUGHES, Dick														
W 1967	StL-N	0	1	5.00	2	2	0	0	0	9	9	5	3	7
W 1968	StL-N	0	0	0.00	1	0	0	0	0	0^{1}	2	0	0	0
W Total	2	0	1	4.82	3	2	0	0	0	9^{1}	11	5	3	7
• HUGHES, Jim														
W 1953	Bro-N	0	0	2.25	1	0	0	0	0	4	3	1	1	3
• HUGHES, Mickey														
W 1889	Bro-A	1	0	7.71	1	1	0	0	0	7	14	6	3	3
• HUGHES, Tom														
W 1903	Bos-A	0	1	9.00	1	1	0	0	0	2	4	2	2	0
• HUGHSON, Tex														
W 1946	Bos-A	0	1	3.14	3	2	0	0	0	14^{1}	14	5	3	8
• HUISMANN, Mark														
L 1984	KC-A	0	0	6.75	1	0	0	0	0	2^{2}	6	2	1	2
• HUME, Tom														
L 1979	Cin-N	0	1	6.75	3	0	0	0	0	4	6	3	0	2
• HUMPHREYS, Bob														
W 1964	StL-N	0	0	0.00	1	0	0	0	0	1	0	0	0	1
• HUNT, Ken														
W 1961	Cin-N	0	0	0.00	1	0	0	0	0	1	0	0	1	1
• HUNTER, Catfish														
L 1971	Oak-A	0	1	5.63	1	1	1	0	0	8	7	5	2	6
L 1972	Oak-A	0	0	1.17	2	2	0	0	0	15^{1}	10	2	5	9
L 1973	Oak-A	2	0	1.65	2	2	1	0	1	16^{1}	12	3	5	6
L 1974	Oak-A	1	1	4.63	2	2	0	0	0	11^{2}	11	6	2	6
L 1976	NY-A	1	1	4.50	2	2	1	0	0	12	10	6	1	5
L 1978	NY-A	0	0	4.50	1	1	0	0	0	6	7	3	3	5
L Total	6	4	3	3.25	10	10	3	0	1	69^{1}	57	25	18	37
W 1972	Oak-A	2	0	2.81	3	2	0	0	0	16	12	5	6	11
W 1973	Oak-A	1	0	2.03	2	2	0	0	0	13^{1}	11	3	4	6
W 1974	Oak-A	1	0	1.17	2	1	0	1	0	7^{2}	5	1	2	5
W 1976	NY-A	0	1	3.12	1	1	1	0	0	8^{2}	10	3	4	5
W 1977	NY-A	0	1	10.38	2	1	0	0	0	4^{1}	6	5	0	1
W 1978	NY-A	1	1	4.15	2	2	0	0	0	13	13	6	1	5
W Total	6	5	3	3.29	12	9	1	1	0	63	57	23	17	33
• HURST, Bruce														
L 1986	Bos-A	1	0	2.40	2	2	1	0	0	15	18	4	1	8
L 1988	Bos-A	0	2	2.77	2	2	1	0	0	13	10	4	5	12
L Total	2	1	2	2.57	4	4	2	0	0	28	28	8	6	20
W 1986	Bos-A	2	0	1.96	3	3	1	0	0	23	18	5	6	17
• HUTCHINGS, Johnny														
W 1940	Cin-N	0	0	9.00	1	0	0	0	0	1	2	1	1	0
• HUTCHINSON, Fred														
W 1940	Det-A	0	0	9.00	1	0	0	0	0	1	1	1	1	1
• IRABU, Hideki														
L 1999	NY-A	0	0	13.50	1	0	0	0	0	4^{2}	13	7	0	3
• ISRINGHAUSEN, Jason														
D 2000	Oak-A	0	0	0.00	2	0	0	1	0	2	1	0	0	3
D 2001	Oak-A	0	0	0.00	2	0	0	2	0	2	1	0	1	3
D 2002	StL-N	0	0	0.00	2	0	0	2	0	2	0	0	0	1
D Total	3	0	0	0.00	6	0	0	5	0	6	2	0	1	7
L 2002	StL-N	0	0	4.50	2	0	0	1	0	2	1	1	3	3
• JACKSON, Danny														
L 1985	KC-A	1	0	0.00	2	1	1	0	1	10	10	0	1	7
L 1990	Cin-N	1	0	2.38	2	2	0	0	0	11^{1}	8	3	7	8
L 1992	Pit-N	0	1	21.60	1	1	0	0	0	1^{2}	4	4	2	0
L 1993	Phi-N	1	0	1.17	1	1	0	0	0	7^{2}	9	1	2	6
L 1996	StL-N	0	0	9.00	1	0	0	0	0	3	7	3	3	3
L Total	5	3	1	2.94	7	5	1	0	1	33^{2}	38	11	15	24
W 1985	KC-A	1	1	1.69	2	2	1	0	0	16	9	3	5	12
W 1990	Cin-N	0	0	10.13	1	1	0	0	0	2^{2}	6	3	2	0
W 1993	Phi-N	0	1	7.20	1	1	0	0	0	5	6	4	1	1
W Total	3	1	2	3.80	4	4	1	0	0	23^{2}	21	10	8	13
• JACKSON, Grant														
L 1973	Bal-A	1	0	0.00	2	0	0	0	0	3	0	0	1	0
L 1974	Bal-A	0	0	0.00	1	0	0	0	0	0^{1}	1	0	0	1
L 1976	NY-A	0	0	8.10	2	0	0	0	0	3^{1}	4	3	1	3
L 1979	Pit-N	1	0	0.00	2	0	0	0	0	2	1	0	1	2
L Total	4	2	0	3.12	7	0	0	0	0	8^{2}	6	3	3	6
W 1971	Bal-A	0	0	0.00	1	0	0	0	0	0^{2}	0	0	1	0
W 1976	NY-A	0	0	4.91	1	0	0	0	0	3^{2}	4	2	0	3
W 1979	Pit-N	1	0	0.00	4	0	0	0	0	4^{2}	1	0	2	2
W Total	3	1	0	2.00	6	0	0	0	0	9	5	2	3	5
• JACKSON, Mike														
D 1995	Cin-N	0	0	0.00	3	0	0	0	0	3^{2}	4	0	0	1
D 1997	Cle-A	1	0	0.00	4	0	0	0	0	4^{1}	3	0	1	5
D 1998	Cle-A	0	0	4.50	3	0	0	3	0	4	3	2	1	1
D 1999	Cle-A	0	0	4.50	2	0	0	0	0	2	2	1	1	1
D 2001	Hou-N	0	1	27.00	2	0	0	0	0	0^{2}	3	2	0	1
D 2002	Min-A	0	0	0.00	1	0	0	0	0	0^{2}	1	0	0	0
D Total	6	1	1	2.93	15	0	0	3	0	15^{1}	16	5	3	9
L 1995	Cin-N	0	1	23.14	3	0	0	0	0	2^{1}	5	6	4	1
L 1997	Cle-A	0	0	0.00	5	0	0	0	0	4^{1}	1	0	1	7
L 1998	Cle-A	0	0	0.00	1	0	0	1	0	1	0	0	0	2
L 2002	Min-A	0	0	27.00	3	0	0	0	0	1	5	3	2	2
L Total	4	0	1	9.35	12	0	0	1	0	8^{2}	11	9	7	12
W 1997	Cle-A	0	0	1.93	4	0	0	0	0	4^{2}	5	1	3	4
• JAKUCKI, Sig														
W 1944	StL-A	0	1	9.00	1	1	0	0	0	3	5	3	0	4
• JAMES, Bill														
W 1914	Bos-N	2	0	0.00	2	1	1	0	1	11	2	0	6	9
• JAMES, Bill														
W 1919	Chi-A	0	0	5.79	1	0	0	0	0	4^{2}	8	3	3	2
• JAMES, Mike														
D 2000	StL-N	1	0	0.00	2	0	0	0	0	4^{1}	1	0	1	1
L 2000	StL-N	0	0	15.43	4	0	0	0	0	2^{1}	5	4	1	0
• JANSEN, Larry														
W 1951	NY-N	0	2	6.30	3	2	0	0	0	10	8	7	4	6
• JARVIS, Pat														
L 1969	Atl-N	0	1	12.46	1	1	0	0	0	4^{1}	10	6	0	6
• JASTER, Larry														
W 1967	StL-N	0	0	0.00	1	0	0	0	0	0^{1}	2	0	0	0
W 1968	StL-N	0	0	....	1	0	0	0	0	0	2	3	1	0
W Total	2	0	0	81.00	2	0	0	0	0	0^{1}	4	3	1	0
• JAY, Joey														
W 1961	Cin-N	1	1	5.59	2	2	1	0	0	9^{2}	8	6	6	6
• JOHN, Tommy														
D 1981	NY-A	0	1	6.43	1	1	0	0	0	7	8	5	2	0
L 1977	LA-N	1	0	0.66	2	2	1	0	0	13^{2}	11	1	5	11
L 1978	LA-N	1	0	0.00	1	1	1	0	1	9	4	0	2	4
L 1980	NY-A	0	0	2.70	1	1	0	0	0	6^{2}	8	2	1	3
L 1981	NY-A	1	0	1.50	1	1	0	0	0	6	6	1	1	3
L 1982	Cal-A	1	1	5.11	2	2	1	0	0	12^{1}	11	7	6	6
L Total	5	4	1	2.08	7	7	3	0	1	47^{2}	40	11	15	27
W 1977	LA-N	0	1	6.00	1	1	0	0	0	6	9	4	3	7
W 1978	LA-N	1	0	3.07	2	2	0	0	0	14^{2}	14	5	4	6
W 1981	NY-A	1	0	0.69	3	2	0	0	0	13	11	1	0	8
W Total	3	2	1	2.67	6	5	0	0	0	33^{2}	34	10	7	21
• JOHNSON, Bob														
L 1971	Pit-N	1	0	0.00	1	1	0	0	0	8	5	0	3	7
L 1972	Pit-N	0	0	3.00	2	0	0	0	0	6	4	2	2	7
L Total	2	1	0	1.29	3	1	0	0	0	14	9	2	5	14
W 1971	Pit-N	0	1	9.00	2	1	0	0	0	5	5	5	3	3
• JOHNSON, Earl														
W 1946	Bos-A	1	0	2.70	3	0	0	0	0	3^{1}	1	1	2	1
• JOHNSON, Ernie														
W 1957	Mil-N	0	1	1.29	3	0	0	0	0	7	2	1	1	8
• JOHNSON, Jerry														
L 1971	SF-N	0	0	13.50	1	0	0	0	0	1^{1}	1	2	1	2
• JOHNSON, Ken														
W 1961	Cin-N	0	0	0.00	1	0	0	0	0	0^{2}	0	0	0	0
• JOHNSON, Randy														
D 1995	Sea-A	2	0	2.70	2	1	0	0	0	10	5	3	6	16
D 1997	Sea-A	0	2	5.54	2	2	1	0	0	13	14	8	6	16
D 1998	Hou-N	0	2	1.93	2	2	0	0	0	14	12	3	2	17
D 1999	Ari-N	0	1	7.56	1	1	0	0	0	8^{1}	8	7	3	11
D 2001	Ari-N	0	1	3.38	1	1	0	0	0	8	6	3	2	9
D 2002	Ari-N	0	1	7.50	1	1	0	0	0	6	10	5	2	4
D Total	6	2	7	4.40	9	8	1	0	0	59^{1}	55	29	21	73
L 1995	Sea-A	0	1	2.35	2	2	0	0	0	15^{1}	12	4	2	13
L 2001	Ari-N	2	0	1.13	2	2	1	0	1	16	10	2	3	19
L Total	2	2	1	1.72	4	4	1	0	1	31^{1}	22	6	5	32

YEAR	TM-L	W	L	ERA	G	GS	CG	SV	SHO	IP	H	ER	BB	SO
W 2001	Ari-N	3	0	1.04	3	2	1	0	1	17¹	9	2	3	19
JOHNSON, Syl														
W 1928	StL-N	0	0	4.50	2	0	0	0	0	2	4	1	1	1
W 1930	StL-N	0	0	7.20	2	0	0	0	0	5	4	4	3	4
W 1931	StL-N	0	1	3.00	3	1	0	0	0	9	10	3	1	6
W Total	3	0	1	4.50	7	1	0	0	0	16	18	8	5	11
JOHNSON, Walter														
W 1924	Was-A	1	2	2.25	3	2	2	0	0	24	30	6	11	20
W 1925	Was-A	2	1	2.08	3	3	3	0	1	26	26	6	4	15
W Total	2	3	3	2.16	6	5	5	0	1	50	56	12	15	35
JONES, Bobby														
D 2000	NY-N	1	0	0.00	1	1	1	0	1	9	1	0	2	5
L 2000	NY-N	0	0	13.50	1	1	0	0	0	4	6	6	0	2
W 2000	NY-N	0	1	5.40	1	1	0	0	0	5	4	3	3	3
JONES, Doug														
D 1998	Cle-A	0	0	6.75	1	0	0	0	0	2²	3	2	1	1
D 2000	Oak-A	0	0	0.00	2	0	0	0	0	1¹	1	0	0	1
D Total	2	0	0	4.50	3	0	0	0	0	4	4	2	1	2
JONES, Jeff														
L 1981	Oak-A	0	0	4.50	1	0	0	0	0	2	2	1	1	0
JONES, Mike														
D 1981	KC-A	0	1	2.25	1	1	0	0	0	8	9	2	0	2
L 1984	KC-A	0	0	6.75	1	0	0	0	0	1¹	1	1	0	0
JONES, Sam														
W 1918	Bos-A	0	1	3.00	1	1	1	0	0	9	7	3	5	5
W 1922	NY-A	0	0	0.00	2	0	0	0	0	2	1	0	1	0
W 1923	NY-A	0	1	0.90	2	1	0	1	0	10	5	1	2	3
W 1926	NY-A	0	0	9.00	1	0	0	0	0	1	2	1	2	1
W Total	4	0	2	2.05	6	2	1	1	0	22	15	5	10	9
JONES, Sheldon														
W 1951	NY-N	0	0	2.08	2	0	0	1	0	4¹	5	1	1	4
JONES, Sherman														
W 1961	Cin-N	0	0	0.00	1	0	0	0	0	0²	0	0	0	0
JONES, Todd														
L 2003	Bos-A	0	0	0.00	1	0	0	0	0	0¹	1	0	1	1
JONNARD, Claude														
W 1923	NY-N	0	0	0.00	2	0	0	0	0	2	1	0	1	1
W 1924	NY-N	0	0	.....	1	0	0	0	0	0	0	0	1	0
W Total	2	0	0	0.00	3	0	0	0	0	2	1	0	2	1
JUDEN, Jeff														
L 1997	Cle-A	0	0	0.00	3	0	0	0	0	1	2	0	2	2
W 1997	Cle-A	0	0	4.50	2	0	0	0	0	2	2	1	2	0
JURISICH, Al														
W 1944	StL-N	0	0	27.00	1	0	0	0	0	0²	2	2	1	0
KAAT, Jim														
L 1970	Min-A	0	1	9.00	1	1	0	0	0	2	6	2	2	1
L 1976	Phi-N	0	0	3.00	1	1	0	0	0	6	3	2	1	1
L Total	2	0	1	4.50	2	2	0	0	0	8	9	4	3	2
W 1965	Min-A	1	2	3.77	3	3	1	0	0	14¹	18	6	2	6
W 1982	StL-N	0	0	3.86	4	0	0	0	0	2¹	4	1	2	2
W Total	2	1	2	3.78	7	3	1	0	0	16²	22	7	4	8
KAMIENIECKI, Scott														
D 1995	NY-A	0	0	7.20	1	1	0	0	0	5	9	4	4	4
L 1997	Bal-A	1	0	0.00	2	1	0	0	0	8	4	0	2	5
KARCHNER, Matt														
D 1998	Chi-N	0	0	13.50	1	0	0	0	0	0²	1	1	0	1
KARSAY, Steve														
D 1999	Cle-A	0	0	9.00	1	0	0	0	0	3	5	3	1	3
D 2001	Atl-N	0	0	0.00	1	0	0	0	0	1	0	0	0	1
D 2002	NY-A	1	0	6.75	4	0	0	0	0	2²	3	2	0	1
D Total	3	1	0	6.75	7	0	0	0	0	6²	8	5	1	5
L 2001	Atl-N	0	0	2.08	4	0	0	0	0	4¹	3	1	1	6
KEEFE, Tim														
W 1884	NY-A	0	2	3.60	2	2	2	0	0	15	10	6	3	12
W 1888	NY-N	4	0	0.51	4	4	4	0	0	35	18	2	9	30
W 1889	NY-N	0	1	8.18	2	1	1	1	0	11	17	10	2	4
W Total	3	4	3	2.66	8	7	7	1	0	61	45	18	14	46
KEEN, Vic														
W 1926	StL-N	0	0	0.00	1	0	0	0	0	1	0	0	0	0
KENNEDY, Brickyard														
W 1903	Pit-N	0	1	5.14	1	1	0	0	0	7	10	4	3	3
KENNEDY, Monte														
W 1951	NY-N	0	0	6.00	2	0	0	0	0	3	3	2	1	4
KEOUGH, Matt														
L 1981	Oak-A	0	1	1.08	1	1	0	0	0	8¹	7	1	6	4
KERFELD, Charlie														
L 1986	Hou-N	0	1	2.25	3	0	0	0	0	4	2	1	1	4
KERR, Dickie														
W 1919	Chi-A	2	0	1.42	2	2	2	0	1	19	14	3	3	6
KEY, Jimmy														
D 1996	NY-A	0	0	3.60	1	1	0	0	0	5	5	2	1	3
D 1997	Bal-A	0	1	3.86	1	1	0	0	0	4²	8	2	0	4
D Total	2	0	1	3.72	2	2	0	0	0	9²	13	4	1	7
L 1985	Tor-A	0	1	5.19	2	2	0	0	0	8²	15	5	2	5
L 1989	Tor-A	1	0	4.50	1	1	0	0	0	6	7	3	2	2
L 1991	Tor-A	0	0	3.00	1	1	0	0	0	6	5	2	1	1
L 1992	Tor-A	0	0	0.00	1	1	0	0	0	3	2	0	2	1
L 1996	NY-A	1	0	2.25	1	1	0	0	0	8	3	2	1	5
L 1997	Bal-A	0	0	2.57	2	1	0	0	0	7	5	2	3	7
L Total	6	2	1	3.26	8	6	0	0	0	38²	37	14	11	21
W 1992	Tor-A	2	0	1.00	2	1	0	0	0	9	6	1	0	6
W 1996	NY-A	1	1	3.97	2	2	0	0	0	11¹	15	5	5	1
W Total	2	3	1	2.66	4	3	0	0	0	20¹	21	6	5	7
KIECKER, Dana														
L 1990	Bos-A	0	0	1.59	1	1	0	0	0	5²	6	1	1	2
KILE, Darryl														
D 1997	Hou-N	0	1	2.57	1	1	0	0	0	7	2	2	2	4
D 2000	StL-N	1	0	2.57	1	1	0	0	0	7	4	2	2	6
D 2001	StL-N	0	0	3.00	1	0	0	0	0	6	3	2	5	5
D Total	3	1	1	2.70	3	3	0	0	0	20	9	6	9	15
L 2000	StL-N	0	2	9.00	2	2	0	0	0	10	13	10	5	3
KILGUS, Paul														
L 1989	Chi-N	0	0	0.00	1	0	0	0	0	3	4	0	1	1
KILLIAN, Ed														
W 1907	Det-A	0	0	2.25	1	0	0	0	0	4	3	1	1	1
W 1908	Det-A	0	0	11.57	1	1	0	0	0	2¹	5	3	3	1
W Total	2	0	0	5.68	2	1	0	0	0	6¹	8	4	4	2
KIM, Byung-Hyun														
D 2001	Ari-N	0	0	0.00	1	0	0	1	0	1¹	1	0	2	1
D 2002	Ari-N	0	0	18.00	1	0	0	0	0	1	2	2	3	0
D 2003	Bos-A	0	0	13.50	1	0	0	0	0	0²	0	1	1	1
D Total	3	0	0	9.00	3	0	0	1	0	3	3	3	6	2
L 2001	Ari-N	0	0	0.00	3	0	0	2	0	5	0	0	1	3
W 2001	Ari-N	0	1	13.50	2	0	0	0	0	3¹	6	5	1	6
KING, Eric														
L 1987	Det-A	0	0	1.69	2	0	0	0	0	5¹	3	1	2	4
KING, Ray														
D 2003	Atl-N	0	0	0.00	4	0	0	0	0	1	1	0	1	0
KING, Silver														
W 1887	StL-A	1	3	2.03	4	4	4	0	0	31	26	7	2	21
W 1888	StL-A	1	3	2.31	5	5	4	0	0	35	37	9	9	12
W Total	2	2	6	2.18	9	9	8	0	0	66	63	16	11	33
KINGMAN, Brian														
L 1981	Oak-A	0	0	81.00	1	0	0	0	0	0¹	3	3	0	0
KIPPER, Bob														
L 1991	Pit-N	0	0	4.50	1	0	0	0	0	2	2	1	0	1
KISON, Bruce														
L 1971	Pit-N	1	0	0.00	2	0	0	0	0	4²	2	0	2	3
L 1972	Pit-N	1	0	0.00	2	0	0	0	0	2¹	1	0	0	3
L 1974	Pit-N	1	0	0.00	1	1	0	0	0	6²	2	0	6	5
L 1975	Pit-N	0	0	4.50	1	0	0	0	0	2	2	1	0	1
L 1982	Cal-A	1	0	1.93	2	2	1	0	0	14	8	3	3	12
L Total	5	4	0	1.21	7	3	1	0	0	29²	15	4	11	24
W 1971	Pit-N	1	0	0.00	1	0	0	0	0	6¹	1	0	2	3
W 1979	Pit-N	0	1	108.00	1	0	0	0	0	0¹	3	4	2	0
W Total	2	1	1	5.40	3	1	0	0	0	6²	4	4	4	3
KITSON, Frank														
T 1900	Bro-N	1	0	1.00	1	1	0	0	0	9	4	1	1	2
KLIEMAN, Ed														
W 1948	Cle-A	0	0	.....	1	0	0	0	0	1	3	2	0	
KLINE, Steve														
D 2001	StL-N	0	1	2.08	4	0	0	2	0	4¹	4	1	2	0
D 2002	StL-N	0	0	0.00	2	0	0	0	0	1¹	1	0	1	0
D Total	2	0	1	1.59	6	0	0	2	0	5²	5	1	3	0
L 2002	StL-N	0	0	0.00	2	0	0	0	0	2¹	2	0	0	1
KLINGER, Bob														
W 1946	Bos-A	0	1	13.50	1	0	0	0	0	0²	2	1	1	0
KLINK, Joe														
W 1990	Oak-A	0	0	.....	1	0	0	0	0	0	0	0	1	0
KLIPPSTEIN, Johnny														
W 1959	LA-N	0	0	0.00	1	0	0	0	0	2	1	0	0	2
W 1965	Min-A	0	0	0.00	2	0	0	0	0	2²	2	0	2	3
W Total	2	0	0	0.00	3	0	0	0	0	4²	3	0	2	5
KLOBEDANZ, Fred														
T 1897	Bos-N	0	1	9.35	2	1	0	0	0	8²	12	9	8	0
KNAPP, Chris														
L 1979	Cal-A	0	1	7.71	1	1	0	0	0	2¹	5	2	1	0
KNEPPER, Bob														
D 1981	Hou-N	0	1	5.40	1	1	0	0	0	5	6	3	2	4
L 1986	Hou-N	0	0	3.52	2	2	0	0	0	15¹	13	6	1	9
KNOWLES, Darold														
L 1971	Oak-A	0	0	0.00	1	0	0	0	0	0¹	1	0	0	0
W 1973	Oak-A	0	0	0.00	7	0	0	2	0	6¹	4	0	5	5
KOCH, Billy														
D 2002	Oak-A	0	0	9.00	3	0	0	1	0	3	5	3	2	3
KONIKOWSKI, Alex														
W 1951	NY-N	0	0	0.00	1	0	0	0	0	1	0	0	0	0
KONSTANTY, Jim														
W 1950	Phi-N	0	1	2.40	3	1	0	0	0	15	9	4	4	3

YEAR	TM-L	W	L	ERA	G	GS	CG	SV	SHO	IP	H	ER	BB	SO
• KOOSMAN, Jerry														
L 1969	NY-N	0	0	11.57	1	1	0	0	0	4^{2}	7	6	4	5
L 1973	NY-N	1	0	2.00	1	1	1	0	0	9	8	2	0	9
L 1983	Chi-A	0	0	54.00	1	0	0	0	0	0^{1}	1	2	2	0
L Total	3	1	0	6.43	3	2	1	0	0	14	16	10	6	14
W 1969	NY-N	2	0	2.04	2	2	1	0	0	17^{2}	7	4	4	9
W 1973	NY-N	1	0	3.12	2	2	0	0	0	8^{2}	9	3	7	8
W Total	2	3	0	2.39	4	4	1	0	0	26^{1}	16	7	11	17
• KOPLOVE, Mike														
D 2002	Ari-N	0	1	6.75	1	0	0	0	0	1^{1}	2	1	0	1
• KOSLO, Dave														
W 1951	NY-N	1	1	3.00	2	2	1	0	0	15	12	5	7	6
• KOUFAX, Sandy														
W 1959	LA-N	0	1	1.00	2	1	0	0	0	9	5	1	1	7
W 1963	LA-N	2	0	1.50	2	2	2	0	0	18	12	3	3	23
W 1965	LA-N	2	1	0.38	3	3	2	0	2	24	13	1	5	29
W 1966	LA-N	0	1	1.50	1	1	0	0	0	6	6	1	2	2
W Total	4	4	3	0.95	8	7	4	0	2	57	36	6	11	61
• KOWALIK, Fabian														
W 1935	Chi-N	0	0	2.08	1	0	0	0	0	4^{1}	3	1	1	1
• KRAMER, Jack														
W 1944	StL-A	1	0	0.00	2	1	1	0	0	11	9	0	4	12
• KREMER, Ray														
W 1925	Pit-N	2	1	3.00	3	2	2	0	0	21	17	7	4	9
W 1927	Pit-N	0	1	3.60	1	1	0	0	0	5	5	2	3	1
W Total	2	2	2	3.12	4	3	2	0	0	26	22	9	7	10
• KRIST, Howie														
W 1943	StL-N	0	0	....	1	0	0	0	0	0	1	0	0	0
• KRUKOW, Mike														
L 1987	SF-N	1	0	2.00	1	1	1	0	0	9	9	2	1	3
• KUCKS, Johnny														
W 1955	NY-A	0	0	6.00	2	0	0	0	0	3	4	2	1	1
W 1956	NY-A	1	0	0.82	3	1	1	0	1	11	6	1	3	2
W 1957	NY-A	0	0	0.00	1	0	0	0	0	0^{2}	1	0	1	1
W 1958	NY-A	0	0	2.08	2	0	0	0	0	4^{1}	4	1	1	0
W Total	4	1	0	1.89	8	1	1	0	1	19	15	4	6	4
• KUZAVA, Bob														
W 1951	NY-A	0	0	0.00	1	0	0	1	0	1	0	0	0	0
W 1952	NY-A	0	0	0.00	1	0	0	1	0	2^{2}	0	0	0	2
W 1953	NY-A	0	0	13.50	1	0	0	0	0	0^{2}	2	1	0	1
W Total	3	0	0	2.08	3	0	0	2	0	4^{1}	2	1	0	3
• LABINE, Clem														
W 1953	Bro-N	0	2	3.60	3	0	0	1	0	5	10	2	1	3
W 1955	Bro-N	1	0	2.89	4	0	0	1	0	9^{1}	6	3	2	2
W 1956	Bro-N	1	0	0.00	2	1	1	0	1	12	8	0	3	7
W 1959	LA-N	0	0	0.00	1	0	0	0	0	1	0	0	0	1
W 1960	Pit-N	0	0	13.50	3	0	0	0	0	4	13	6	1	2
W Total	5	2	2	3.16	13	1	1	2	1	31^{1}	37	11	7	15
• LACKEY, John														
D 2002	Ana-A	0	0	0.00	1	0	0	0	0	3	3	0	1	3
L 2002	Ana-A	1	0	0.00	1	1	0	0	0	7	3	0	0	7
W 2002	Ana-A	1	0	4.38	3	2	0	0	0	12^{1}	15	6	5	7
• LACORTE, Frank														
D 1981	Hou-N	0	0	0.00	2	0	0	0	0	3^{2}	2	0	1	5
L 1980	Hou-N	1	1	3.00	2	0	0	0	0	3	7	1	2	2
• LACOSS, Mike														
L 1979	Cin-N	0	1	10.80	1	1	0	0	0	1^{2}	1	2	4	0
L 1987	SF-N	0	0	0.00	2	0	0	0	0	3^{1}	1	0	3	2
L 1989	SF-N	0	0	9.00	1	1	0	0	0	3	7	3	0	2
L Total	3	0	1	5.63	4	2	0	0	0	8	9	5	7	4
W 1989	SF-N	0	0	6.23	2	0	0	0	0	4^{1}	4	3	3	2
• LADD, Pete														
L 1982	Mil-A	0	0	0.00	3	0	0	1	0	3^{1}	0	0	0	5
W 1982	Mil-A	0	0	0.00	1	0	0	0	0	0^{2}	1	0	2	0
• LAGROW, Lerrin														
L 1972	Det-A	0	0	0.00	1	0	0	0	0	1	0	0	0	1
• LAHTI, Jeff														
L 1985	StL-N	1	0	0.00	2	0	0	0	0	2	2	0	0	1
W 1982	StL-N	0	0	10.80	2	0	0	0	0	1^{2}	4	2	1	1
W 1985	StL-N	0	0	12.27	3	0	0	1	0	3^{2}	10	5	0	2
W Total	2	0	0	11.81	5	0	0	1	0	5^{1}	14	7	1	3
• LAMABE, Jack														
W 1967	StL-N	0	1	6.75	3	0	0	0	0	2^{2}	5	2	0	4
• LAMP, Dennis														
L 1983	Chi-A	0	0	0.00	3	0	0	0	0	2	0	0	2	1
L 1985	Tor-A	0	0	0.00	3	0	0	0	0	9^{1}	2	0	1	10
L 1990	Bos-A	0	0	108.00	1	0	0	0	0	0^{1}	2	4	2	0
L Total	3	0	0	3.09	7	0	0	0	0	11^{2}	4	4	5	11
• LANCASTER, Les														
L 1989	Chi-N	1	1	6.00	3	0	0	0	0	6	6	4	1	3
• LANDRUM, Bill														
L 1990	Pit-N	0	0	0.00	2	0	0	0	0	2	0	0	0	1
L 1991	Pit-N	0	0	9.00	1	0	0	0	0	1	2	1	2	2
L Total	2	0	0	3.00	3	0	0	0	0	3	2	1	2	3
• LANGFORD, Rick														
D 1981	Oak-A	1	0	1.23	1	1	0	0	0	7^{1}	10	1	0	3

YEAR	TM-L	W	L	ERA	G	GS	CG	SV	SHO	IP	H	ER	BB	SO
• LANGSTON, Mark														
L 1998	SD-N	0	0	0.00	3	0	0	0	0	1^{1}	1	0	0	1
W 1998	SD-N	0	0	40.50	1	0	0	0	0	0^{2}	1	3	2	0
• LANIER, Max														
W 1942	StL-N	1	0	0.00	2	0	0	0	0	4	3	0	1	1
W 1943	StL-N	0	1	1.76	3	2	0	0	0	15^{1}	13	3	3	13
W 1944	StL-N	1	0	2.19	2	2	0	0	0	12^{1}	8	3	8	11
W Total	3	2	1	1.71	7	4	0	0	0	31^{2}	24	6	12	25
• LAPOINT, Dave														
W 1982	StL-N	0	0	3.24	2	1	0	0	0	8^{1}	10	3	2	3
• LAROCHE, Dave														
L 1979	Cal-A	0	0	6.75	1	0	0	0	0	1^{1}	2	1	1	1
W 1981	NY-A	0	0	0.00	1	0	0	0	0	1	0	0	0	2
• LARSEN, Don														
W 1955	NY-A	0	1	11.25	1	1	0	0	0	4	5	5	2	2
W 1956	NY-A	1	0	0.00	2	2	1	0	1	10^{2}	1	0	4	7
W 1957	NY-A	1	1	3.72	2	1	0	0	0	9^{2}	8	4	5	6
W 1958	NY-A	1	0	0.96	2	2	0	0	0	9^{1}	9	1	6	9
W 1962	SF-N	1	0	3.86	3	0	0	0	0	2^{1}	1	1	2	0
W Total	5	4	2	2.75	10	6	1	0	1	36	24	11	19	24
• LASHER, Fred														
W 1968	Det-A	0	0	0.00	1	0	0	0	0	2	1	0	0	1
• LAVELLE, Gary														
L 1985	Tor-A	0	0	....	1	0	0	0	0	0	0	0	1	0
• LAW, Vern														
W 1960	Pit-N	2	0	3.44	3	3	0	0	0	18^{1}	22	7	3	8
• LEACH, Terry														
L 1988	NY-N	0	0	0.00	3	0	0	0	0	5	4	0	1	4
W 1991	Min-A	0	0	3.86	2	0	0	0	0	2^{1}	2	1	0	2
• LEARY, Tim														
L 1988	LA-N	0	1	6.23	2	1	0	0	0	4^{1}	8	3	3	3
W 1988	LA-N	0	0	1.35	2	0	0	0	0	6^{2}	6	1	2	4
• LEE, Bill														
W 1935	Chi-N	0	0	4.35	2	1	0	1	0	10^{1}	11	5	5	5
W 1938	Chi-N	0	2	2.45	2	2	0	0	0	11	15	3	1	8
W Total	2	0	2	3.38	4	3	0	1	0	21^{1}	26	8	6	13
• LEE, Bill														
D 1981	Mon-N	0	0	0.00	1	0	0	0	0	0^{2}	2	0	0	1
L 1981	Mon-N	0	0	0.00	1	0	0	0	0	0^{1}	1	0	0	0
W 1975	Bos-A	0	0	3.14	2	2	0	0	0	14^{1}	12	5	3	7
• LEEVER, Sam														
T 1900	Pit-N	0	2	1.38	2	2	1	0	0	13	13	2	4	4
W 1903	Pit-N	0	2	5.40	2	2	1	0	0	10	13	6	3	2
• LEFFERTS, Craig														
L 1984	SD-N	2	0	0.00	3	0	0	0	0	4	1	0	1	1
L 1987	SF-N	0	0	0.00	3	0	0	0	0	2	3	0	1	0
L 1989	SF-N	0	0	9.00	2	0	0	0	0	1	1	1	2	1
L Total	3	2	0	1.29	8	0	0	0	0	7	5	1	4	2
W 1984	SD-N	0	0	0.00	3	0	0	1	0	6	2	0	1	7
W 1989	SF-N	0	0	3.38	3	0	0	0	0	2^{2}	2	1	2	1
W Total	2	0	0	1.04	6	0	0	1	0	8^{2}	4	1	3	8
• LEHMAN, Ken														
W 1952	Bro-N	0	0	0.00	1	0	0	0	0	2	2	0	1	0
• LEIBRANDT, Charlie														
L 1979	Cin-N	0	0	0.00	1	0	0	0	0	0^{1}	0	0	0	0
L 1984	KC-A	0	1	1.13	1	1	1	0	0	8	3	1	4	6
L 1985	KC-A	1	2	5.28	3	2	0	0	0	15^{1}	17	9	4	6
L 1991	Atl-N	0	0	1.35	1	1	0	0	0	6^{2}	8	1	3	6
L 1992	Atl-N	0	0	1.93	2	0	0	0	0	4^{2}	4	1	3	3
L Total	5	1	3	3.09	8	4	1	0	0	35	32	12	14	21
W 1985	KC-A	0	1	2.76	2	2	0	0	0	16^{1}	10	5	4	10
W 1991	Atl-N	0	2	11.25	2	1	0	0	0	4	8	5	1	3
W 1992	Atl-N	0	1	9.00	1	0	0	0	0	2	3	2	0	0
W Total	3	0	4	4.84	5	3	0	0	0	22^{1}	21	12	5	13
• LEIFIELD, Lefty														
W 1909	Pit-N	0	1	11.25	1	1	0	0	0	4	7	5	1	0
• LEITER, Al														
D 1997	Fla-N	0	0	9.00	1	1	0	0	0	4	7	4	3	3
D 1999	NY-N	0	0	3.52	1	1	0	0	0	7^{2}	3	3	3	4
D 2000	NY-N	0	0	2.25	1	1	0	0	0	8	5	2	3	6
D Total	3	0	0	4.12	3	3	0	0	0	19^{2}	15	9	9	13
L 1993	Tor-A	0	0	3.38	2	0	0	0	0	2^{2}	4	1	2	2
L 1997	Fla-N	0	1	4.32	2	1	0	0	0	8^{1}	13	4	2	6
L 1999	NY-N	0	1	6.43	2	2	0	0	0	7	5	5	4	5
L 2000	NY-N	0	0	3.86	1	1	0	0	0	7	8	3	0	9
L Total	4	0	2	4.68	7	4	0	0	0	25	30	13	8	22
W 1993	Tor-A	1	0	7.71	3	0	0	0	0	7	12	6	2	5
W 1997	Fla-N	0	0	5.06	2	2	0	0	0	10^{2}	10	6	10	10
W 2000	NY-N	0	1	2.87	2	2	0	0	0	15^{2}	12	5	6	16
W Total	3	1	1	4.59	7	4	0	0	0	33^{1}	34	17	18	31
• LEMON, Bob														
W 1948	Cle-A	2	0	1.65	2	2	1	0	0	16^{1}	16	3	7	6
W 1954	Cle-A	0	2	6.75	2	2	1	0	0	13^{1}	16	10	8	11
W Total	2	2	2	3.94	4	4	2	0	0	29^{2}	32	13	15	17
• LEONARD, Dennis														
D 1981	KC-A	0	1	1.13	1	1	0	0	0	8	7	1	1	3
L 1976	KC-A	0	0	19.29	2	2	0	0	0	2^{1}	9	5	2	0

YEAR	TM-L	W	L	ERA	G	GS	CG	SV	SHO	IP	H	ER	BB	SO
L 1977	KC-A	1	1	3.00	2	1	1	0	0	9	5	3	2	4
L 1978	KC-A	0	2	3.75	2	2	1	0	0	12	13	5	2	11
L 1980	KC-A	1	0	2.25	1	1	0	0	0	8	7	2	1	8
L Total	**4**	**2**	**3**	**4.31**	**7**	**6**	**2**	**0**	**0**	**31^1**	**34**	**15**	**7**	**23**
W 1980	KC-A	1	1	6.75	2	2	0	0	0	10^2	15	8	2	5
• LEONARD, Dutch														
W 1915	Bos-A	1	0	1.00	1	1	1	0	0	9	3	1	0	6
W 1916	Bos-A	1	0	1.00	1	1	1	0	0	9	5	1	4	3
W Total	**2**	**2**	**0**	**1.00**	**2**	**2**	**2**	**0**	**0**	**18**	**8**	**2**	**4**	**9**
• LEONHARD, Dave														
W 1969	Bal-A	0	0	4.50	1	0	0	0	0	2	1	1	1	1
W 1971	Bal-A	0	0	0.00	1	0	0	0	0	1	0	0	1	0
W Total	**2**	**0**	**0**	**3.00**	**2**	**0**	**0**	**0**	**0**	**3**	**1**	**1**	**2**	**1**
• LERCH, Randy														
D 1981	Mil-A	1	0	1.50	1	1	0	0	0	6	3	1	4	3
L 1978	Phi-N	0	0	5.06	1	1	0	0	0	5^1	7	3	0	0
• LESKANIC, Curt														
D 1995	Col-N	0	1	6.00	3	0	0	0	0	3	3	2	0	4
• LEWIS, Ted														
T 1897	Bos-N	1	1	6.00	3	1	0	0	0	12	18	8	9	4
• LIDDLE, Don														
W 1954	NY-N	1	0	1.29	2	1	0	0	0	7	5	1	1	2
• LIDLE, Cory														
D 2001	Oak-A	0	1	10.80	1	1	0	0	0	3^1	5	4	3	0
D 2002	Oak-A	0	0	9.00	1	0	0	0	0	1	2	1	0	0
D Total	**2**	**0**	**1**	**10.38**	**2**	**1**	**0**	**0**	**0**	**4^1**	**7**	**5**	**3**	**0**
• LIGTENBERG, Kerry														
D 1998	Atl-N	0	0	0.00	3	0	0	0	0	3^1	1	0	4	3
D 2000	Atl-N	0	0	5.40	3	0	0	0	0	1^2	0	1	1	3
D 2002	Atl-N	0	0	0.00	1	0	0	0	0	2	0	0	0	1
D Total	**3**	**0**	**0**	**1.29**	**7**	**0**	**0**	**0**	**0**	**7**	**1**	**1**	**5**	**7**
L 1997	Atl-N	0	0	0.00	2	0	0	0	0	3	1	0	0	4
L 1998	Atl-N	0	1	7.36	4	0	0	0	0	3^2	3	3	2	5
L 2001	Atl-N	0	0	0.00	2	0	0	0	0	3	0	0	1	2
L Total	**3**	**0**	**1**	**2.79**	**8**	**0**	**0**	**0**	**0**	**9^2**	**4**	**3**	**3**	**11**
• LILLY, Ted														
D 2002	Oak-A	0	1	13.50	2	0	0	0	0	4	10	6	1	3
D 2003	Oak-A	0	0	0.00	2	1	0	0	0	9	2	0	2	7
D Total	**2**	**0**	**1**	**4.15**	**4**	**1**	**0**	**0**	**0**	**13**	**12**	**6**	**3**	**10**
• LIMA, Jose														
D 1997	Hou-N	0	0	0.00	1	0	0	0	0	1	0	0	1	1
D 1999	Hou-N	0	1	5.40	1	1	0	0	0	6^2	9	4	2	4
D Total	**2**	**0**	**1**	**4.70**	**2**	**1**	**0**	**0**	**0**	**7^2**	**9**	**4**	**3**	**5**
• LINDBLAD, Paul														
L 1975	Oak-A	0	0	1.93	2	0	0	0	0	4^2	5	1	1	0
W 1973	Oak-A	1	0	0.00	3	0	0	0	0	3^1	4	0	1	1
W 1978	NY-A	0	0	11.57	1	0	0	0	0	2^1	4	3	0	1
W Total	**2**	**1**	**0**	**4.76**	**4**	**0**	**0**	**0**	**0**	**5^2**	**8**	**3**	**1**	**2**
• LINDSEY, Jim														
W 1930	StL-N	0	0	1.93	2	0	0	0	0	4^2	1	1	1	2
W 1931	StL-N	0	0	5.40	2	0	0	0	0	3^1	4	2	3	2
W Total	**2**	**0**	**0**	**3.38**	**4**	**0**	**0**	**0**	**0**	**8**	**5**	**3**	**4**	**4**
• LITTELL, Mark														
L 1976	KC-A	0	1	1.93	3	0	0	0	0	4^2	4	1	1	3
L 1977	KC-A	0	0	3.00	2	0	0	0	0	3	5	1	3	1
L Total	**2**	**0**	**1**	**2.35**	**5**	**0**	**0**	**0**	**0**	**7^2**	**9**	**2**	**4**	**4**
• LLOYD, Graeme														
D 1996	NY-A	0	0	0.00	2	0	0	0	0	1	1	0	0	0
D 1997	NY-A	0	0	0.00	2	0	0	0	0	1^1	0	0	0	1
D 1998	NY-A	0	0	0.00	1	0	0	0	0	0^1	0	0	0	0
D Total	**3**	**0**	**0**	**0.00**	**5**	**0**	**0**	**0**	**0**	**2^2**	**1**	**0**	**0**	**1**
L 1996	NY-A	0	0	0.00	2	0	0	0	0	1^2	0	0	0	1
L 1998	NY-A	0	0	0.00	1	0	0	0	0	0^2	1	0	0	0
L Total	**2**	**0**	**0**	**0.00**	**3**	**0**	**0**	**0**	**0**	**2^1**	**1**	**0**	**0**	**1**
W 1996	NY-A	1	0	0.00	4	0	0	0	0	2^2	0	0	0	4
W 1998	NY-A	0	0	0.00	1	0	0	0	0	0^1	0	0	0	0
W Total	**2**	**1**	**0**	**0.00**	**5**	**0**	**0**	**0**	**0**	**3**	**0**	**0**	**0**	**4**
• LOAIZA, Esteban														
D 1999	Tex-A	0	1	3.86	1	1	0	0	0	7	5	3	1	4
• LOCKER, Bob														
L 1971	Oak-A	0	0	0.00	1	0	0	0	0	0^2	0	0	2	0
L 1972	Oak-A	0	1	13.50	2	0	0	0	0	2	4	3	0	1
L Total	**2**	**0**	**1**	**10.13**	**3**	**0**	**0**	**0**	**0**	**2^2**	**4**	**3**	**2**	**1**
W 1972	Oak-A	0	0	0.00	1	0	0	0	0	0^1	1	0	0	0
• LOES, Billy														
W 1952	Bro-N	0	1	4.35	2	1	0	0	0	10^1	11	5	5	5
W 1953	Bro-N	1	0	3.38	1	1	0	0	0	8	8	3	2	8
W 1955	Bro-N	0	1	9.82	1	1	0	0	0	3^2	7	4	1	5
W Total	**3**	**1**	**2**	**4.91**	**4**	**3**	**0**	**0**	**0**	**22**	**26**	**12**	**8**	**18**
• LOHSE, Kyle														
D 2002	Min-A	0	0	0.00	2	0	0	0	0	4	2	0	0	5
D 2003	Min-A	0	1	5.40	1	1	0	0	0	5	6	3	2	5
D Total	**2**	**0**	**1**	**3.00**	**3**	**1**	**0**	**0**	**0**	**9**	**8**	**3**	**2**	**10**
L 2002	Min-A	0	0	0.00	1	0	0	0	0	1	0	0	0	1
• LOLICH, Mickey														
L 1972	Det-A	0	1	1.42	2	2	0	0	0	19	15	3	5	9
W 1968	Det-A	3	0	1.67	3	3	3	0	0	27	20	5	6	21
• LOLLAR, Tim														
L 1984	SD-N	0	0	6.23	1	1	0	0	0	4^1	3	3	4	3
W 1984	SD-N	0	1	21.60	1	1	0	0	0	1^2	4	4	4	0
• LOMBARDI, Vic														
W 1947	Bro-N	0	1	12.15	2	2	0	0	0	6^2	14	9	1	5
• LONBORG, Jim														
L 1976	Phi-N	0	1	1.69	1	1	0	0	0	5^1	2	1	2	2
L 1977	Phi-N	0	1	11.25	1	1	0	0	0	4	5	5	1	1
L Total	**2**	**0**	**2**	**5.79**	**2**	**2**	**0**	**0**	**0**	**9^1**	**7**	**6**	**3**	**3**
W 1967	Bos-A	2	1	2.63	3	3	2	0	1	24	14	7	2	11
• LOOPER, Braden														
D 2003	Fla-N	1	0	0.00	2	0	0	0	0	1^2	1	0	2	0
L 2003	Fla-N	0	0	0.00	2	0	0	1	0	1^2	1	0	1	1
W 2003	Fla-N	1	0	9.82	4	0	0	0	0	3^2	6	4	0	4
• LOPAT, Ed														
W 1949	NY-A	1	0	6.35	1	1	0	0	0	5^2	9	4	1	4
W 1950	NY-A	0	0	2.25	1	1	0	0	0	8	9	2	0	5
W 1951	NY-A	2	0	0.50	2	2	2	0	0	18	10	1	3	4
W 1952	NY-A	0	1	4.76	2	2	0	0	0	11^1	14	6	4	3
W 1953	NY-A	1	0	2.00	1	1	1	0	0	9	9	2	4	3
W Total	**5**	**4**	**1**	**2.60**	**7**	**7**	**3**	**0**	**0**	**52**	**51**	**15**	**12**	**19**
• LOPEZ, Albie														
D 2001	Ari-N	0	1	12.00	1	1	0	0	0	3	4	4	3	0
L 2001	Ari-N	0	0	6.00	1	1	0	0	0	3	5	2	1	1
W 2001	Ari-N	0	1	27.00	1	0	0	0	0	0^1	2	1	0	0
• LOPEZ, Aurelio														
L 1984	Det-A	1	0	0.00	1	0	0	0	0	3	4	0	1	2
L 1986	Hou-N	0	1	8.10	2	0	0	0	0	3^1	7	3	4	3
L Total	**2**	**1**	**1**	**4.26**	**3**	**0**	**0**	**0**	**0**	**6^1**	**11**	**3**	**5**	**5**
W 1984	Det-A	1	0	0.00	2	0	0	0	0	3	1	0	1	4
• LOPEZ, Marcelino														
L 1969	Bal-A	0	0	0.00	1	0	0	0	0	0^1	1	0	2	0
W 1970	Bal-A	0	0	0.00	1	0	0	0	0	0^1	0	0	0	0
• LOVETT, Tom														
W 1889	Bro-A	0	1	24.00	1	1	0	0	0	3	8	8	2	1
W 1890	Bro-N	2	2	2.83	4	4	4	0	0	35	29	11	6	14
W Total	**2**	**2**	**3**	**4.50**	**5**	**5**	**4**	**0**	**0**	**38**	**37**	**19**	**8**	**15**
• LOWDERMILK, Grover														
W 1919	Chi-A	0	0	9.00	1	0	0	0	0	1	2	1	1	0
• LOWE, Derek														
D 1998	Bos-A	0	0	2.08	2	0	0	0	0	4^1	3	1	1	2
D 1999	Bos-A	1	1	4.32	3	0	0	0	0	8^1	6	4	1	7
D 2003	Bos-A	0	1	0.93	3	1	0	1	0	9^2	7	1	7	6
D Total	**3**	**1**	**2**	**2.42**	**8**	**1**	**0**	**1**	**0**	**22^1**	**16**	**6**	**9**	**15**
L 1999	Bos-A	0	0	1.42	3	0	0	0	0	6^1	6	1	2	7
L 2003	Bos-A	0	2	6.43	2	2	0	0	0	14	14	10	7	5
L Total	**2**	**0**	**2**	**4.87**	**5**	**2**	**0**	**0**	**0**	**20^1**	**20**	**11**	**9**	**12**
• LOWN, Turk														
W 1959	Chi-A	0	0	0.00	3	0	0	0	0	3^1	2	0	1	3
• LUCAS, Gary														
L 1986	Cal-A	0	0	11.57	4	0	0	0	0	2^1	3	3	1	2
• LUQUE, Dolf														
W 1919	Cin-N	0	0	0.00	2	0	0	0	0	5	1	0	0	6
W 1933	NY-N	1	0	0.00	1	0	0	0	0	4^1	2	0	2	5
W Total	**2**	**1**	**0**	**0.00**	**3**	**0**	**0**	**0**	**0**	**9^1**	**3**	**0**	**2**	**11**
• LYLE, Sparky														
D 1981	Phi-N	0	0	0.00	3	0	0	0	0	2^1	4	0	2	1
L 1976	NY-A	0	0	0.00	1	0	0	1	0	1	0	0	1	0
L 1977	NY-A	2	0	0.96	4	0	0	0	0	9^1	7	1	0	3
L 1978	NY-A	0	0	13.50	1	0	0	0	0	1^1	3	2	0	0
L Total	**3**	**2**	**0**	**2.31**	**6**	**0**	**0**	**1**	**0**	**11^2**	**10**	**3**	**1**	**3**
W 1976	NY-A	0	0	0.00	2	0	0	0	0	2^2	1	0	0	3
W 1977	NY-A	1	0	1.93	2	0	0	0	0	4^2	2	1	0	2
W Total	**2**	**1**	**0**	**1.23**	**4**	**0**	**0**	**0**	**0**	**7^1**	**3**	**1**	**0**	**5**
• MAAS, Duke														
W 1958	NY-A	0	0	81.00	1	0	0	0	0	0^1	2	3	1	0
W 1960	NY-A	0	0	4.50	1	0	0	0	0	2	2	1	0	1
W Total	**2**	**0**	**0**	**15.43**	**2**	**0**	**0**	**0**	**0**	**2^1**	**4**	**4**	**1**	**1**
• MACDONALD, Bob														
L 1991	Tor-A	0	0	9.00	1	0	0	0	0	1	1	1	1	0
• MADDOX, Nick														
W 1909	Pit-N	1	0	1.00	1	1	1	0	0	9	11	1	2	4
• MADDUX, Greg														
D 1995	Atl-N	1	0	4.50	2	2	0	0	0	14	19	7	2	7
D 1996	Atl-N	1	0	0.00	1	1	0	0	0	7	3	0	0	7
D 1997	Atl-N	1	0	1.00	1	1	1	0	0	9	7	1	1	6
D 1998	Atl-N	1	0	2.57	1	1	0	0	0	7	7	2	0	4
D 1999	Atl-N	0	1	2.57	2	1	0	0	0	7	10	2	5	5
D 2000	Atl-N	0	1	11.25	1	1	0	0	0	4	9	5	3	2
D 2001	Atl-N	0	0	3.00	1	1	0	0	0	6	4	2	3	5
D 2002	Atl-N	1	0	3.00	1	1	0	0	0	6	5	2	1	3
D 2003	Atl-N	0	0	3.00	1	1	0	0	0	6	6	2	1	1
D Total	**9**	**5**	**2**	**3.14**	**11**	**10**	**1**	**0**	**0**	**66**	**70**	**23**	**16**	**40**
L 1989	Chi-N	0	1	13.50	2	2	0	0	0	7^1	13	11	4	5
L 1993	Atl-N	1	1	4.97	2	2	0	0	0	12^2	11	7	7	11
L 1995	Atl-N	1	0	1.13	1	1	0	0	0	8	7	1	2	4

YEAR	TM-L	W	L	ERA	G	GS	CG	SV	SHO	IP	H	ER	BB	SO
L 1996	Atl-N	1	1	2.51	2	2	0	0	0	14^1	15	4	2	10
L 1997	Atl-N	0	2	1.38	2	2	0	0	0	13	9	2	4	16
L 1998	Atl-N	0	1	3.00	2	1	0	1	0	6	5	2	3	4
L 1999	Atl-N	1	0	1.93	2	2	0	0	0	14	12	3	1	7
L 2001	Atl-N	0	2	5.40	2	2	0	0	0	10	14	6	2	7
L Total	**8**	**4**	**8**	**3.80**	**15**	**14**	**0**	**1**	**0**	**85^1**	**86**	**36**	**25**	**64**
W 1995	Atl-N	1	1	2.25	2	2	1	0	0	16	9	4	3	8
W 1996	Atl-N	1	1	1.72	2	2	0	0	0	15^2	14	3	1	5
W 1999	Atl-N	0	1	2.57	1	1	0	0	0	7	5	2	3	5
W Total	**3**	**2**	**3**	**2.09**	**5**	**5**	**1**	**0**	**0**	**38^2**	**28**	**9**	**7**	**18**
• MADDUX, Mike														
D 1995	Bos-A	0	0	0.00	2	0	0	0	0	3	2	0	1	1
• MAGLIE, Sal														
W 1951	NY-N	0	1	7.20	1	1	0	0	0	5	8	4	2	3
W 1954	NY-N	0	0	2.57	1	1	0	0	0	7	7	2	2	2
W 1956	Bro-N	1	1	2.65	2	2	2	0	0	17	14	5	6	15
W Total	**3**	**1**	**2**	**3.41**	**4**	**4**	**2**	**0**	**0**	**29**	**29**	**11**	**10**	**20**
• MAGNANTE, Mike														
D 1997	Hou-N	0	0	4.50	2	0	0	0	0	2	4	1	0	2
D 2000	Oak-A	0	0	0.00	2	0	0	0	0	3	1	0	0	2
D 2001	Oak-A	0	0	0.00	1	0	0	0	0	1^1	3	0	1	1
D Total	**3**	**0**	**0**	**1.42**	**5**	**0**	**0**	**0**	**0**	**6^1**	**8**	**1**	**1**	**5**
• MAGRANE, Joe														
L 1987	StL-N	0	0	9.00	1	1	0	0	0	4	4	4	2	3
W 1987	StL-N	0	1	8.59	2	2	0	0	0	7^1	9	7	5	5
• MAHAFFEY, Roy														
W 1931	Phi-A	0	0	9.00	1	0	0	0	0	1	1	1	1	0
• MAHLER, Rick														
L 1982	Atl-N	0	0	0.00	1	0	0	0	0	1^2	3	0	2	0
L 1990	Cin-N	0	0	0.00	1	0	0	0	0	1^2	2	0	0	0
L Total	**2**	**0**	**0**	**0.00**	**2**	**0**	**0**	**0**	**0**	**3^1**	**5**	**0**	**2**	**0**
• MAHOMES, Pat														
D 1999	NY-N	0	0	5.40	1	0	0	0	0	1^2	3	1	0	1
L 1999	NY-N	0	0	1.42	3	0	0	0	0	6^1	4	1	3	3
• MAILS, Duster														
W 1920	Cle-A	1	0	0.00	2	1	1	0	1	15^2	6	0	6	6
• MALONE, Pat														
W 1929	Chi-N	0	2	4.15	3	2	1	0	0	13	12	6	7	11
W 1932	Chi-N	0	0	0.00	1	0	0	0	0	2^2	1	0	4	4
W 1936	NY-A	0	1	1.80	2	0	0	1	0	5	2	1	1	2
W Total	**3**	**0**	**3**	**3.05**	**6**	**2**	**1**	**1**	**0**	**20^2**	**15**	**7**	**12**	**17**
• MALONEY, Jim														
W 1961	Cin-N	0	0	27.00	1	0	0	0	0	0^2	4	2	1	1
• MAMAUX, Al														
W 1920	Bro-N	0	0	4.50	3	0	0	0	0	4	2	2	0	5
• MANTEI, Matt														
D 1999	Ari-N	0	1	4.50	1	0	0	0	0	2	1	1	3	1
D 2002	Ari-N	0	0	54.00	1	0	0	0	0	0^1	1	2	1	0
D Total	**2**	**0**	**1**	**11.57**	**2**	**0**	**0**	**0**	**0**	**2^1**	**2**	**3**	**4**	**1**
• MARBERRY, Firpo														
W 1924	Was-A	0	1	1.13	4	1	0	2	0	8	9	1	4	10
W 1925	Was-A	0	0	0.00	2	0	0	1	0	2^1	3	0	0	2
W 1934	Det-A	0	0	21.60	2	0	0	0	0	1^2	5	4	1	0
W Total	**3**	**0**	**1**	**3.75**	**8**	**1**	**0**	**3**	**0**	**12**	**17**	**5**	**5**	**12**
• MARICHAL, Juan														
L 1971	SF-N	0	1	2.25	1	1	1	0	0	8	4	2	0	6
W 1962	SF-N	0	0	0.00	1	1	0	0	0	4	2	0	2	4
• MARQUARD, Rube														
W 1911	NY-N	0	1	1.54	3	2	0	0	0	11^2	9	2	1	8
W 1912	NY-N	2	0	0.50	2	2	2	0	0	18	14	1	2	9
W 1913	NY-N	0	1	7.00	2	1	0	0	0	9	10	7	3	3
W 1916	Bro-N	0	2	5.73	2	2	0	0	0	11	12	7	6	9
W 1920	Bro-N	0	1	1.00	2	1	0	0	0	9	7	1	3	6
W Total	**5**	**2**	**5**	**2.76**	**11**	**8**	**2**	**0**	**0**	**58^2**	**52**	**18**	**15**	**35**
• MARQUIS, Jason														
L 2001	Atl-N	0	0	0.00	2	0	0	0	0	2	2	0	2	3
• MARSHALL, Mike														
L 1974	LA-N	0	0	0.00	2	0	0	0	0	3	0	0	0	1
W 1974	LA-N	0	1	1.00	5	0	0	1	0	9	6	1	1	10
• MARTIN, Renie														
D 1981	KC-A	0	0	0.00	2	0	0	0	0	5	1	0	2	2
W 1980	KC-A	0	0	2.79	3	0	0	0	0	9^2	11	3	3	2
• MARTIN, Tom														
D 1997	Hou-N	0	0	0.00	2	0	0	0	0	0^2	1	0	1	0
• MARTINA, Joe														
W 1924	Was-A	0	0	0.00	1	0	0	0	0	1	0	0	0	1
• MARTINEZ, Dennis														
D 1995	Cle-A	0	0	3.00	1	1	0	0	0	6	5	2	0	2
L 1979	Bal-A	0	0	3.24	1	1	0	0	0	8^1	8	3	0	4
L 1995	Cle-A	1	1	2.03	2	2	0	0	0	13^1	10	3	3	7
L 1998	Atl-N	1	0	0.00	4	0	0	0	0	3^1	1	0	1	0
L Total	**3**	**2**	**1**	**2.16**	**7**	**3**	**0**	**0**	**0**	**25**	**19**	**6**	**4**	**11**
W 1979	Bal-A	0	0	18.00	2	1	0	0	0	2	6	4	0	0
W 1995	Cle-A	0	1	3.48	2	2	0	0	0	10^1	12	4	8	5
W Total	**2**	**0**	**1**	**5.84**	**4**	**3**	**0**	**0**	**0**	**12^1**	**18**	**8**	**8**	**5**

YEAR	TM-L	W	L	ERA	G	GS	CG	SV	SHO	IP	H	ER	BB	SO
• MARTINEZ, Pedro														
D 1998	Bos-A	1	0	3.86	1	1	0	0	0	7	6	3	0	8
D 1999	Bos-A	0	0	0.00	2	1	0	0	0	10	6	0	4	11
D 2003	Bos-A	1	0	3.86	2	2	0	0	0	14	13	6	5	9
D Total	**3**	**2**	**0**	**2.61**	**5**	**4**	**0**	**0**	**0**	**31**	**25**	**9**	**9**	**28**
L 1999	Bos-A	1	0	0.00	1	1	0	0	0	7	2	0	2	12
L 2003	Bos-A	0	1	5.65	2	2	0	0	0	14^1	16	9	2	14
L Total	**2**	**1**	**1**	**3.80**	**3**	**3**	**0**	**0**	**0**	**21^1**	**18**	**9**	**4**	**26**
• MARTINEZ, Ramon														
D 1995	LA-N	0	1	14.54	1	1	0	0	0	4^1	10	7	2	3
D 1996	LA-N	0	0	1.13	1	1	0	0	0	8	3	1	3	6
D 1999	Bos-A	0	0	3.18	1	1	0	0	0	5^2	5	2	3	6
D Total	**3**	**0**	**1**	**5.00**	**3**	**3**	**0**	**0**	**0**	**18**	**18**	**10**	**8**	**15**
L 1999	Bos-A	0	1	4.05	1	1	0	0	0	6^2	6	3	3	5
• MARTINEZ, Tippy														
L 1983	Bal-A	1	0	0.00	2	0	0	0	0	6	5	0	3	5
W 1979	Bal-A	0	0	6.75	3	0	0	0	0	1^1	3	1	0	1
W 1983	Bal-A	0	0	3.00	3	0	0	2	0	3	3	1	0	0
W Total	**2**	**0**	**0**	**4.15**	**6**	**0**	**0**	**2**	**0**	**4^1**	**6**	**2**	**0**	**1**
• MASON, Roger														
L 1991	Pit-N	0	0	0.00	3	0	0	1	0	4^1	3	0	1	2
L 1992	Pit-N	0	0	0.00	2	0	0	0	0	3^1	0	0	2	1
L 1993	Phi-N	0	0	0.00	2	0	0	0	0	3	1	0	0	2
L Total	**3**	**0**	**0**	**0.00**	**7**	**0**	**0**	**1**	**0**	**10^2**	**4**	**0**	**3**	**5**
W 1993	Phi-N	0	0	1.17	4	0	0	0	0	7^2	4	1	1	7
• MATHEWS, Greg														
L 1987	StL-N	1	0	3.48	2	2	0	0	0	10^1	6	4	3	10
W 1987	StL-N	0	0	2.45	1	1	0	0	0	3^2	2	1	2	3
• MATHEWS, T.J.														
D 1996	StL-N	1	0	0.00	1	0	0	0	0	1	1	0	0	2
L 1996	StL-N	0	0	0.00	2	0	0	0	0	0^2	2	0	1	2
• MATHEWS, Terry														
D 1996	Bal-A	0	0	0.00	3	0	0	0	0	2^2	3	0	1	2
D 1997	Bal-A	0	0	18.00	1	0	0	0	0	1	2	2	0	1
D Total	**2**	**0**	**0**	**4.91**	**4**	**0**	**0**	**0**	**0**	**3^2**	**5**	**2**	**1**	**3**
L 1996	Bal-A	0	0	0.00	3	0	0	0	0	2^1	0	0	2	3
• MATHEWSON, Christy														
W 1905	NY-N	3	0	0.00	3	3	3	0	3	27	13	0	1	18
W 1911	NY-N	1	2	2.00	3	3	2	0	0	27	25	6	2	13
W 1912	NY-N	0	2	1.26	3	3	3	0	0	28^2	23	4	5	10
W 1913	NY-N	1	1	0.95	2	2	2	0	1	19	14	2	2	7
W Total	**4**	**5**	**5**	**1.06**	**11**	**11**	**10**	**0**	**4**	**101^2**	**75**	**12**	**10**	**48**
• MATLACK, Jon														
L 1973	NY-N	1	0	0.00	1	1	1	0	1	9	2	0	3	9
W 1973	NY-N	1	2	2.16	3	3	0	0	0	16^2	10	4	5	11
• MATTHEWS, Mike														
D 2001	StL-N	0	1	40.50	1	0	0	0	0	0^2	4	3	0	0
• MAY, Jakie														
W 1932	Chi-N	0	1	11.57	2	0	0	0	0	4^2	9	6	3	4
• MAY, Rudy														
D 1981	NY-A	0	0	0.00	1	0	0	0	0	2	1	0	0	1
L 1980	NY-A	0	1	3.38	1	1	1	0	0	8	6	3	3	4
L 1981	NY-A	0	0	8.10	1	1	0	0	0	3^1	6	3	0	5
L Total	**2**	**0**	**1**	**4.76**	**2**	**2**	**1**	**0**	**0**	**11^1**	**12**	**6**	**3**	**9**
W 1981	NY-A	0	0	2.84	3	0	0	0	0	6^1	5	2	1	5
• MAYER, Erskine														
W 1915	Phi-N	0	1	2.38	2	2	1	0	0	11^1	16	3	2	7
W 1919	Chi-A	0	0	0.00	1	0	0	0	0	1	0	0	1	0
W Total	**2**	**0**	**1**	**2.19**	**3**	**2**	**1**	**0**	**0**	**12^1**	**16**	**3**	**3**	**7**
• MAYS, Carl														
W 1916	Bos-A	0	1	5.06	2	1	0	1	0	5^1	8	3	3	2
W 1918	Bos-A	2	0	1.00	2	2	2	0	0	18	10	2	3	5
W 1921	NY-A	1	2	1.73	3	3	3	0	1	26	20	5	0	9
W 1922	NY-A	0	1	4.50	1	1	0	0	0	8	9	4	2	1
W Total	**4**	**3**	**4**	**2.20**	**8**	**7**	**5**	**1**	**1**	**57^1**	**47**	**14**	**8**	**17**
• MAYS, Joe														
D 2002	Min-A	0	1	14.73	1	1	0	0	0	3^2	9	6	2	1
L 2002	Min-A	1	0	2.03	2	2	0	0	0	13^1	12	3	0	3
• MCCASKILL, Kirk														
L 1986	Cal-A	0	2	7.71	2	2	0	0	0	9^1	16	8	5	7
L 1993	Chi-A	0	0	0.00	3	0	0	0	0	3^2	3	0	1	3
L Total	**2**	**0**	**2**	**5.54**	**5**	**2**	**0**	**0**	**0**	**13**	**19**	**8**	**6**	**10**
• MCCATTY, Steve														
D 1981	Oak-A	1	0	1.00	1	1	1	0	0	9	6	1	4	3
L 1981	Oak-A	0	1	13.50	1	1	0	0	0	3^1	6	5	2	2
• MCCLURE, Bob														
D 1981	Mil-A	0	0	0.00	3	0	0	0	0	3^1	4	0	0	2
L 1982	Mil-A	1	0	0.00	1	0	0	0	0	1^2	2	0	0	0
W 1982	Mil-A	0	2	4.15	5	0	0	2	0	4^1	5	2	3	5
• MCCOLL, Alex														
W 1933	Was-A	0	0	0.00	1	0	0	0	0	2	0	0	0	0
• MCCORMICK, Jim														
W 1885	Chi-N	3	2	2.00	5	5	5	0	0	36	29	8	4	15
W 1886	Chi-N	0	1	6.75	1	1	1	0	0	8	13	6	2	4
W Total	**2**	**3**	**3**	**2.86**	**6**	**6**	**6**	**0**	**0**	**44**	**42**	**14**	**6**	**19**

YEAR	TM-L	W	L	ERA	G	GS	CG	SV	SHO	IP	H	ER	BB	SO
• MCDERMOTT, Mickey														
W 1956	NY-A	0	0	3.00	1	0	0	0	0	3	2	1	3	3
• MCDONALD, Jim														
W 1953	NY-A	1	0	5.87	1	1	0	0	0	7^2	12	5	0	3
• MCDOWELL, Jack														
D 1995	NY-A	0	2	9.00	2	1	0	0	0	7	8	7	4	6
D 1996	Cle-A	0	0	6.35	1	1	0	0	0	5^2	6	4	1	5
D Total	**2**	**0**	**2**	**7.82**	**3**	**2**	**0**	**0**	**0**	**12^2**	**14**	**11**	**5**	**11**
L 1993	Chi-A	0	2	10.00	2	2	0	0	0	9	18	10	5	5
• MCDOWELL, Roger														
L 1986	NY-N	0	0	0.00	2	0	0	0	0	7	1	0	0	3
L 1988	NY-N	0	1	4.50	4	0	0	0	0	6	6	3	2	5
L Total	**2**	**0**	**1**	**2.08**	**6**	**0**	**0**	**0**	**0**	**13**	**7**	**3**	**2**	**8**
W 1986	NY-N	1	0	4.91	5	0	0	0	0	7^1	10	4	6	2
• MCENANEY, Will														
L 1975	Cin-N	0	0	6.75	1	0	0	0	0	1^1	1	1	0	1
W 1975	Cin-N	0	0	2.70	5	0	0	1	0	6^2	3	2	2	5
W 1976	Cin-N	0	0	0.00	2	0	0	2	0	4^2	2	0	1	2
W Total	**2**	**0**	**0**	**1.59**	**7**	**0**	**0**	**3**	**0**	**11^1**	**5**	**2**	**3**	**7**
• MCGINNITY, Joe														
T 1900	Bro-N	2	0	0.00	2	2	2	0	0	18	14	0	3	5
W 1905	NY-N	1	1	0.00	2	2	1	0	1	17	10	0	3	6
• MCGLINCHY, Kevin														
D 1999	Atl-N	0	0	0.00	1	0	0	0	0	0^1	0	0	0	0
L 1999	Atl-N	0	1	18.00	1	0	0	0	0	1	2	2	4	1
W 1999	Atl-N	0	0	0.00	1	0	0	0	0	2	2	0	1	2
• MCGLOTHLIN, Jim														
L 1972	Cin-N	0	0	0.00	1	0	0	0	0	1	0	0	0	0
W 1970	Cin-N	0	0	8.31	1	1	0	0	0	4^1	6	4	2	2
W 1972	Cin-N	0	0	12.00	1	1	0	0	0	3	2	4	2	3
W Total	**2**	**0**	**0**	**9.82**	**2**	**2**	**0**	**0**	**0**	**7^1**	**8**	**8**	**4**	**5**
• MCGRAW, Tug														
D 1981	Phi-N	1	0	0.00	2	0	0	0	0	4	2	0	0	2
L 1969	NY-N	0	0	0.00	1	0	0	0	0	3	1	0	1	1
L 1973	NY-N	0	0	0.00	2	0	0	0	0	5	4	0	3	3
L 1976	Phi-N	0	0	11.57	2	0	0	0	0	2^1	4	3	1	5
L 1977	Phi-N	0	0	0.00	2	0	0	1	0	3	1	0	2	3
L 1978	Phi-N	0	1	1.59	3	0	0	0	0	5^2	3	1	5	5
L 1980	Phi-N	0	1	4.50	5	0	0	2	0	8	8	4	4	5
L Total	**6**	**0**	**2**	**2.67**	**15**	**0**	**0**	**3**	**0**	**27**	**21**	**8**	**16**	**22**
W 1973	NY-N	1	0	2.63	5	0	0	1	0	13^2	8	4	9	14
W 1980	Phi-N	1	1	1.17	4	0	0	2	0	7^2	7	1	8	10
W Total	**2**	**2**	**1**	**2.11**	**9**	**0**	**0**	**3**	**0**	**21^1**	**15**	**5**	**17**	**24**
• MCGREGOR, Scott														
L 1979	Bal-A	1	0	0.00	1	1	1	0	1	9	6	0	1	4
L 1983	Bal-A	0	1	1.35	1	1	0	0	0	6^2	6	1	3	2
L Total	**2**	**1**	**1**	**0.57**	**2**	**2**	**1**	**0**	**1**	**15^2**	**12**	**1**	**4**	**6**
W 1979	Bal-A	1	1	3.18	2	2	1	0	0	17	16	6	2	8
W 1983	Bal-A	1	1	1.06	2	2	1	0	1	17	9	2	2	12
W Total	**2**	**2**	**2**	**2.12**	**4**	**4**	**2**	**0**	**1**	**34**	**25**	**8**	**4**	**20**
• MCINTIRE, Harry														
W 1910	Chi-N	0	1	6.75	2	0	0	0	0	5^1	4	4	3	3
• MCKAIN, Archie														
W 1940	Det-A	0	0	3.00	1	0	0	0	0	3	4	1	0	0
• MCLAIN, Denny														
W 1968	Det-A	1	2	3.24	3	3	1	0	0	16^2	18	6	4	13
• MCMAHON, Don														
L 1971	SF-N	0	0	0.00	2	0	0	0	0	3	0	0	0	3
W 1957	Mil-N	0	0	0.00	3	0	0	0	0	5	3	0	3	5
W 1958	Mil-N	0	0	5.40	3	0	0	0	0	3^1	3	2	3	5
W 1968	Det-A	0	0	13.50	2	0	0	0	0	2	4	3	0	1
W Total	**3**	**0**	**0**	**4.35**	**8**	**0**	**0**	**0**	**0**	**10^1**	**10**	**5**	**6**	**11**
• MCMAHON, Sadie														
T 1895	Bal-N	0	2	5.94	2	2	2	0	0	16^2	27	11	3	2
• MCMICHAEL, Greg														
D 1995	Atl-N	0	0	6.75	2	0	0	0	0	1^1	1	1	2	1
D 1996	Atl-N	0	0	6.75	2	0	0	0	0	1^1	1	1	1	3
D Total	**2**	**0**	**0**	**6.75**	**4**	**0**	**0**	**0**	**0**	**2^2**	**2**	**2**	**3**	**4**
L 1993	Atl-N	0	1	6.75	4	0	0	0	0	4	7	3	2	1
L 1995	Atl-N	1	0	0.00	3	0	0	1	0	2^2	0	0	1	2
L 1996	Atl-N	0	1	9.00	3	0	0	0	0	2	4	2	1	3
L Total	**3**	**1**	**2**	**5.19**	**10**	**0**	**0**	**1**	**0**	**8^2**	**11**	**5**	**4**	**6**
W 1995	Atl-N	0	0	2.70	3	0	0	0	0	3^1	3	1	2	2
W 1996	Atl-N	0	0	27.00	2	0	0	0	0	1	5	3	0	1
W Total	**2**	**0**	**0**	**8.31**	**5**	**0**	**0**	**0**	**0**	**4^1**	**8**	**4**	**2**	**3**
• MCNALLY, Dave														
L 1969	Bal-A	1	0	0.00	1	1	1	0	1	11	3	0	5	11
L 1970	Bal-A	1	0	3.00	1	1	1	0	0	9	6	3	5	5
L 1971	Bal-A	1	0	3.86	1	1	0	0	0	7	7	3	1	5
L 1973	Bal-A	0	1	5.87	1	1	0	0	0	7^2	7	5	2	7
L 1974	Bal-A	0	1	1.59	1	1	0	0	0	5^2	6	1	2	2
L Total	**5**	**3**	**2**	**2.68**	**5**	**5**	**2**	**0**	**1**	**40^1**	**29**	**12**	**15**	**30**
W 1966	Bal-A	1	0	1.59	2	2	1	0	1	11^1	6	2	7	5
W 1969	Bal-A	0	1	2.81	2	2	1	0	0	16	11	5	5	13
W 1970	Bal-A	1	0	3.00	1	1	1	0	0	9	9	3	2	5
W 1971	Bal-A	2	1	1.98	4	2	1	0	0	13^2	10	3	5	12
W Total	**4**	**4**	**2**	**2.34**	**9**	**7**	**4**	**0**	**1**	**50**	**36**	**13**	**19**	**35**

YEAR	TM-L	W	L	ERA	G	GS	CG	SV	SHO	IP	H	ER	BB	SO
• MCQUILLAN, Hugh														
W 1922	NY-N	1	0	3.00	1	1	1	0	0	9	8	3	2	4
W 1923	NY-N	0	1	5.00	2	1	0	0	0	9	11	5	4	3
W 1924	NY-N	1	0	2.57	3	1	0	1	0	7	2	2	6	2
W Total	**3**	**2**	**1**	**3.60**	**6**	**3**	**1**	**1**	**0**	**25**	**21**	**10**	**12**	**9**
• MEADOWS, Lee														
W 1925	Pit-N	0	1	3.38	1	1	0	0	0	8	6	3	0	4
W 1927	Pit-N	0	1	9.95	1	1	0	0	0	6^1	7	7	1	6
W Total	**2**	**0**	**2**	**6.28**	**2**	**2**	**0**	**0**	**0**	**14^1**	**13**	**10**	**1**	**10**
• MEAKIM, George														
W 1890	Lou-A	0	0	0.00	1	0	0	0	0	4	6	0	1	1
• MECIR, Jim														
D 2000	Oak-A	0	0	0.00	3	0	0	0	0	5^1	1	0	0	2
D 2001	Oak-A	0	0	5.40	2	0	0	0	0	3^1	4	2	0	4
D 2002	Oak-A	0	0	0.00	1	0	0	0	0	1	0	0	0	2
D 2003	Oak-A	0	0	0.00	1	0	0	0	0	0^2	1	0	1	0
D Total	**4**	**0**	**0**	**1.74**	**7**	**0**	**0**	**0**	**0**	**10^1**	**6**	**2**	**1**	**8**
• MEDICH, Doc														
W 1982	Mil-A	0	0	18.00	1	0	0	0	0	2	5	4	1	0
• MEEKIN, Jouett														
T 1894	NY-N	2	0	1.59	2	2	2	0	0	17	13	3	8	6
• MELTON, Cliff														
W 1937	NY-N	0	2	4.91	3	2	0	0	0	11	12	6	6	7
• MENDOZA, Ramiro														
D 1997	NY-A	1	1	2.45	2	0	0	0	0	3^2	3	1	0	2
D 2001	NY-A	0	0	0.00	3	0	0	0	0	4^1	2	0	1	5
D 2002	NY-A	0	0	13.50	2	0	0	0	0	1^1	5	2	0	0
D Total	**3**	**1**	**1**	**2.89**	**7**	**0**	**0**	**0**	**0**	**9^1**	**10**	**3**	**1**	**7**
L 1998	NY-A	0	0	0.00	2	0	0	0	0	4^1	4	0	0	1
L 1999	NY-A	0	0	0.00	2	0	0	1	0	2^1	0	0	0	2
L 2001	NY-A	0	0	1.69	3	0	0	0	0	5^1	3	1	2	4
L Total	**3**	**0**	**0**	**0.75**	**7**	**0**	**0**	**1**	**0**	**12**	**7**	**1**	**2**	**7**
W 1998	NY-A	1	0	9.00	1	0	0	0	0	1	2	1	0	1
W 1999	NY-A	0	0	10.80	1	0	0	0	0	1^2	3	2	1	0
W 2001	NY-A	0	0	0.00	2	0	0	0	0	2^2	1	0	0	1
W Total	**3**	**1**	**0**	**5.06**	**4**	**0**	**0**	**0**	**0**	**5^1**	**6**	**3**	**1**	**2**
• MERCKER, Kent														
D 1995	Atl-N	0	0	0.00	1	0	0	0	0	0^1	0	0	0	0
D 1999	Bos-A	0	0	10.80	1	1	0	0	0	1^2	3	2	3	1
D 2003	Atl-N	0	0	0.00	1	0	0	0	0	1	0	0	1	1
D Total	**3**	**0**	**0**	**6.00**	**3**	**1**	**0**	**0**	**0**	**3**	**3**	**2**	**4**	**2**
L 1991	Atl-N	0	1	13.50	1	0	0	0	0	0^2	0	1	2	0
L 1992	Atl-N	0	0	0.00	2	0	0	0	0	3	1	0	1	1
L 1993	Atl-N	0	0	1.80	5	0	0	0	0	5	3	1	2	4
L 1999	Bos-A	0	1	4.70	2	2	0	0	0	7^2	12	4	4	5
L Total	**4**	**0**	**2**	**3.31**	**10**	**2**	**0**	**0**	**0**	**16^1**	**16**	**6**	**9**	**10**
W 1991	Atl-N	0	0	0.00	2	0	0	0	0	1	0	0	0	1
W 1995	Atl-N	0	0	4.50	1	0	0	0	0	2	1	1	2	2
W Total	**2**	**0**	**0**	**3.00**	**3**	**0**	**0**	**0**	**0**	**3**	**1**	**1**	**2**	**3**
• MERRITT, Jim														
L 1970	Cin-N	1	0	1.69	1	1	0	0	0	5^1	3	1	0	2
W 1965	Min-A	0	0	2.70	2	0	0	0	0	3^1	2	1	0	1
W 1970	Cin-N	0	1	21.60	1	1	0	0	0	1^2	3	4	1	0
W Total	**2**	**0**	**1**	**9.00**	**3**	**1**	**0**	**0**	**0**	**5**	**5**	**5**	**1**	**1**
• MESA, Jose														
D 1995	Cle-A	0	0	0.00	2	0	0	0	0	2	0	0	2	0
D 1996	Cle-A	0	1	3.86	2	0	0	0	0	4^2	8	2	0	7
D 1997	Cle-A	0	0	2.70	2	0	0	1	0	3^1	5	1	1	2
D 2000	Sea-A	1	0	0.00	2	0	0	0	0	2	0	0	1	2
D Total	**4**	**1**	**1**	**2.25**	**8**	**0**	**0**	**1**	**0**	**12**	**13**	**3**	**4**	**11**
L 1995	Cle-A	0	0	2.25	4	0	0	1	0	4	3	1	1	1
L 1997	Cle-A	1	0	3.38	4	0	0	2	0	5^1	5	2	3	5
L 2000	Sea-A	0	0	12.46	3	0	0	0	0	4^1	5	6	3	3
L Total	**3**	**1**	**0**	**5.93**	**11**	**0**	**0**	**3**	**0**	**13^2**	**13**	**9**	**7**	**9**
W 1995	Cle-A	1	0	4.50	2	0	0	1	0	4	5	2	1	4
W 1997	Cle-A	0	0	5.40	5	0	0	1	0	5	10	3	1	5
W Total	**2**	**1**	**0**	**5.00**	**7**	**0**	**0**	**2**	**0**	**9**	**15**	**5**	**2**	**9**
• MESSERSMITH, Andy														
L 1974	LA-N	1	0	2.57	1	1	0	0	0	7	8	2	3	0
W 1974	LA-N	0	2	4.50	2	2	0	0	0	14	11	7	7	12
• MEYER, Russ														
W 1950	Phi-N	0	1	5.40	2	0	0	0	0	1^2	4	1	0	1
W 1953	Bro-N	0	0	6.23	1	0	0	0	0	4^1	8	3	4	5
W 1955	Bro-N	0	0	0.00	1	0	0	0	0	5^2	4	0	2	4
W Total	**3**	**0**	**1**	**3.09**	**4**	**0**	**0**	**0**	**0**	**11^2**	**16**	**4**	**6**	**10**
• MICELI, Dan														
D 1998	SD-N	1	1	2.70	3	0	0	0	0	3^1	2	1	0	4
L 1998	SD-N	0	0	13.50	3	0	0	0	0	0^2	4	1	0	1
W 1998	SD-N	0	0	0.00	2	0	0	0	0	1^2	2	0	2	1
• MIKKELSEN, Pete														
W 1964	NY-A	0	1	5.79	4	0	0	0	0	4^2	4	3	2	4
• MILJUS, Johnny														
W 1927	Pit-N	0	1	1.35	2	0	0	0	0	6^2	4	1	4	6
• MILLER, Bob														
W 1950	Phi-N	0	1	27.00	1	1	0	0	0	0^1	2	1	0	0
• MILLER, Bob														
L 1969	Min-A	0	1	5.40	1	1	0	0	0	1^2	5	1	0	0

YEAR	TM-L	W	L	ERA	G	GS	CG	SV	SHO	IP	H	ER	BB	SO
L 1971	Pit-N	0	0	6.00	1	0	0	0	0	3	3	2	3	3
L 1972	Pit-N	0	0	0.00	1	0	0	0	0	1	0	0	0	1
L Total	**3**	**0**	**1**	**4.76**	**3**	**1**	**0**	**0**	**0**	**5^2**	**8**	**3**	**3**	**4**
W 1965	LA-N	0	0	0.00	2	0	0	0	0	1^1	0	0	0	0
W 1966	LA-N	0	0	0.00	1	0	0	0	0	3	2	0	2	1
W 1971	Pit-N	0	1	3.86	3	0	0	0	0	4^2	7	2	1	2
W Total	**3**	**0**	**1**	**2.00**	**6**	**0**	**0**	**0**	**0**	**9**	**9**	**2**	**3**	**3**
• MILLER, Stu														
W 1962	SF-N	0	0	0.00	2	0	0	0	0	1^1	1	0	2	0
• MILLER, Trever														
D 1998	Hou-N	0	0	....	1	0	0	0	0	0	0	0	1	0
D 1999	Hou-N	0	0	0.00	2	0	0	0	0	1^1	1	0	0	2
D Total	**2**	**0**	**0**	**0.00**	**3**	**0**	**0**	**0**	**0**	**1^1**	**1**	**0**	**1**	**2**
• MILLER, Wade														
D 2001	Hou-N	0	0	2.57	1	1	0	0	0	7	7	2	0	6
• MILLIKEN, Bob														
W 1953	Bro-N	0	0	0.00	1	0	0	0	0	2	2	0	1	0
• MILLS, Alan														
D 1997	Bal-A	0	0	0.00	1	0	0	0	0	1	1	0	0	1
L 1996	Bal-A	0	0	3.86	3	0	0	0	0	2^1	3	1	1	3
L 1997	Bal-A	0	1	2.70	3	0	0	0	0	3^1	1	1	2	3
L Total	**2**	**0**	**1**	**3.18**	**6**	**0**	**0**	**0**	**0**	**5^2**	**4**	**2**	**3**	**6**
• MILLWOOD, Kevin														
D 1999	Atl-N	1	0	0.90	2	1	1	1	0	10	1	1	0	9
D 2000	Atl-N	0	1	7.71	1	1	0	0	0	4^2	4	4	3	3
D 2002	Atl-N	1	1	3.27	2	2	0	0	0	11	7	4	0	14
D Total	**3**	**2**	**2**	**3.16**	**5**	**4**	**1**	**1**	**0**	**25^2**	**12**	**9**	**3**	**26**
L 1999	Atl-N	1	0	3.55	2	2	0	0	0	12^2	13	5	1	9
L 2001	Atl-N	0	0	0.00	1	0	0	0	0	1	0	0	0	1
L Total	**2**	**1**	**0**	**3.29**	**3**	**2**	**0**	**0**	**0**	**13^2**	**13**	**5**	**1**	**10**
W 1999	Atl-N	0	1	18.00	1	1	0	0	0	2	8	4	2	2
• MILTON, Eric														
D 2002	Min-A	1	0	2.57	1	1	0	0	0	7	6	2	1	3
D 2003	Min-A	0	0	0.00	1	0	0	0	0	3^1	2	0	0	2
D Total	**2**	**1**	**0**	**1.74**	**2**	**1**	**0**	**0**	**0**	**10^1**	**8**	**2**	**1**	**5**
L 2002	Min-A	0	0	1.50	1	1	0	0	0	6	5	1	2	4
• MINGORI, Steve														
L 1976	KC-A	0	0	2.70	3	0	0	1	0	3^1	4	1	0	1
L 1977	KC-A	0	0	0.00	3	0	0	0	0	1^1	0	0	0	1
L 1978	KC-A	0	0	7.36	1	0	0	0	0	3^2	5	3	3	0
L Total	**3**	**0**	**0**	**4.32**	**7**	**0**	**0**	**1**	**0**	**8^1**	**9**	**4**	**3**	**2**
• MINNER, Paul														
W 1949	Bro-N	0	0	0.00	1	0	0	0	0	1	1	0	0	0
• MITCHELL, Clarence														
W 1920	Bro-N	0	0	0.00	1	0	0	0	0	4^2	3	0	3	1
W 1928	StL-N	0	0	1.59	1	0	0	0	0	5^2	2	1	2	3
W Total	**2**	**0**	**0**	**0.87**	**2**	**0**	**0**	**0**	**0**	**10^1**	**5**	**1**	**5**	**4**
• MIZELL, Vinegar Bend														
W 1960	Pit-N	0	1	15.43	2	1	0	0	0	2^1	4	4	2	1
• MLICKI, Dave														
D 2001	Hou-N	0	1	0.00	1	1	0	0	0	5	4	0	2	0
• MOELLER, Joe														
W 1966	LA-N	0	0	4.50	1	0	0	0	0	2	1	1	1	0
• MOGRIDGE, George														
W 1924	Was-A	1	0	2.25	2	1	0	0	0	12	7	3	6	5
• MONROE, Zach														
W 1958	NY-A	0	0	27.00	1	0	0	0	0	1	3	3	1	1
• MONTAGUE, John														
L 1979	Cal-A	0	1	9.00	2	0	0	0	0	4	4	4	2	2
• MOONEY, Jim														
W 1934	StL-N	0	0	0.00	1	0	0	0	0	1	1	0	0	0
• MOORE, Donnie														
L 1982	Atl-N	0	0	0.00	2	0	0	0	0	2^2	2	0	0	1
L 1986	Cal-A	0	1	7.20	3	0	0	1	0	5	8	4	2	0
L Total	**2**	**0**	**1**	**4.70**	**5**	**0**	**0**	**1**	**0**	**7^2**	**10**	**4**	**2**	**1**
• MOORE, Mike														
L 1989	Oak-A	1	0	0.00	1	1	0	0	0	7	3	0	2	3
L 1990	Oak-A	1	0	1.50	1	1	0	0	0	6	4	1	1	5
L 1992	Oak-A	0	2	7.45	2	2	0	0	0	9^2	11	8	5	7
L Total	**3**	**2**	**2**	**3.57**	**4**	**4**	**0**	**0**	**0**	**22^2**	**18**	**9**	**8**	**15**
W 1989	Oak-A	2	0	2.08	2	2	0	0	0	13	9	3	3	10
W 1990	Oak-A	0	1	6.75	1	1	0	0	0	2^2	8	2	0	1
W Total	**2**	**2**	**1**	**2.87**	**3**	**3**	**0**	**0**	**0**	**15^2**	**17**	**5**	**3**	**11**
• MOORE, Ray														
W 1959	Chi-A	0	0	9.00	1	0	0	0	0	1	1	1	0	1
• MOORE, Whitey														
W 1939	Cin-N	0	0	0.00	1	0	0	0	0	3	0	0	0	2
W 1940	Cin-N	0	0	3.24	3	0	0	0	0	8^1	8	3	6	7
W Total	**2**	**0**	**0**	**2.38**	**4**	**0**	**0**	**0**	**0**	**11^1**	**8**	**3**	**6**	**9**
• MOORE, Wilcy														
W 1927	NY-A	1	0	0.84	2	1	1	1	0	10^2	11	1	2	2
W 1932	NY-A	1	0	0.00	1	0	0	0	0	5^1	2	0	0	1
W Total	**2**	**2**	**0**	**0.56**	**3**	**1**	**1**	**1**	**0**	**16**	**13**	**1**	**2**	**3**
• MOOSE, Bob														
L 1970	Pit-N	0	1	3.52	1	1	0	0	0	7^2	4	3	2	4
L 1971	Pit-N	0	0	0.00	1	0	0	0	0	2	0	0	0	0
L 1972	Pit-N	0	1	54.00	2	1	0	0	0	0^2	5	4	0	0
L Total	**3**	**0**	**2**	**6.10**	**4**	**2**	**0**	**0**	**0**	**10^1**	**9**	**7**	**2**	**4**
W 1971	Pit-N	0	0	6.52	3	1	0	0	0	9^2	12	7	2	7
• MOREHEAD, Dave														
W 1967	Bos-A	0	0	0.00	2	0	0	0	0	3^1	0	0	4	3
• MORET, Roger														
L 1975	Bos-A	1	0	0.00	1	0	0	0	0	1	1	0	1	0
W 1975	Bos-A	0	0	0.00	3	0	0	0	0	1^2	2	0	3	1
• MORGAN, Mike														
D 1998	Chi-N	0	0	0.00	2	0	0	0	0	1^1	0	0	0	1
D 2001	Ari-N	0	0	4.50	3	0	0	0	0	2	2	1	2	1
D Total	**2**	**0**	**0**	**2.70**	**5**	**0**	**0**	**0**	**0**	**3^1**	**2**	**1**	**2**	**2**
L 2001	Ari-N	0	0	27.00	2	0	0	0	0	1	3	3	1	1
W 2001	Ari-N	0	0	0.00	3	0	0	0	0	4^2	1	0	0	1
• MORGAN, Tom														
W 1951	NY-A	0	0	0.00	1	0	0	0	0	2	2	0	1	3
W 1955	NY-A	0	0	4.91	2	0	0	0	0	3^2	3	2	3	1
W 1956	NY-A	0	1	9.00	2	0	0	0	0	4	6	4	4	3
W Total	**3**	**0**	**1**	**5.59**	**5**	**0**	**0**	**0**	**0**	**9^2**	**11**	**6**	**8**	**7**
• MORMAN, Alvin														
D 1997	Cle-A	0	0	....	1	0	0	0	0	0	0	0	1	0
L 1997	Cle-A	0	0	0.00	2	0	0	0	0	1^1	0	0	0	1
W 1997	Cle-A	0	0	0.00	2	0	0	0	0	0^1	0	0	2	1
• MORRIS, Jack														
L 1984	Det-A	1	0	1.29	1	1	0	0	0	7	5	1	1	4
L 1987	Det-A	0	1	6.75	1	1	1	0	0	8	6	6	3	7
L 1991	Min-A	2	0	4.05	2	2	0	0	0	13^1	17	6	1	7
L 1992	Tor-A	0	1	6.57	2	2	1	0	0	12^1	11	9	9	6
L Total	**4**	**3**	**2**	**4.87**	**6**	**6**	**2**	**0**	**0**	**40^2**	**39**	**22**	**14**	**24**
W 1984	Det-A	2	0	2.00	2	2	2	0	0	18	13	4	3	13
W 1991	Min-A	2	0	1.17	3	3	1	0	1	23	18	3	9	15
W 1992	Tor-A	0	2	8.44	2	2	0	0	0	10^2	13	10	6	12
W Total	**3**	**4**	**2**	**2.96**	**7**	**7**	**3**	**0**	**1**	**51^2**	**44**	**17**	**18**	**40**
• MORRIS, Matt														
D 2000	StL-N	0	0	0.00	2	0	0	0	0	2	0	0	1	0
D 2001	StL-N	0	1	1.20	2	2	0	0	0	15	13	2	5	12
D 2002	StL-N	1	0	1.29	1	1	0	0	0	7	7	1	2	3
D Total	**3**	**1**	**1**	**1.13**	**5**	**3**	**0**	**0**	**0**	**24**	**20**	**3**	**8**	**15**
L 2000	StL-N	0	0	4.91	2	0	0	0	0	3^2	3	2	2	2
L 2002	StL-N	0	2	6.23	2	2	0	0	0	13	16	9	6	6
L Total	**2**	**0**	**2**	**5.94**	**4**	**2**	**0**	**0**	**0**	**16^2**	**19**	**11**	**8**	**8**
• MORRISON, Johnny														
W 1925	Pit-N	0	0	2.89	3	0	0	0	0	9^1	11	3	1	7
• MOSS, Damian														
D 2002	Atl-N	0	0	3.00	2	0	0	0	0	3	2	1	1	3
• MOSSI, Don														
W 1954	Cle-A	0	0	0.00	3	0	0	0	0	4	3	0	0	1
• MOYER, Jamie														
D 1997	Sea-A	0	1	5.79	1	1	0	0	0	4^2	5	3	1	2
D 2001	Sea-A	2	0	1.50	2	2	0	0	0	12	8	2	2	10
D Total	**2**	**2**	**1**	**2.70**	**3**	**3**	**0**	**0**	**0**	**16^2**	**13**	**5**	**3**	**12**
L 2001	Sea-A	1	0	2.57	1	1	0	0	0	7	4	2	1	5
• MUELLER, Les														
W 1945	Det-A	0	0	0.00	1	0	0	0	0	2	0	0	1	1
• MULDER, Mark														
D 2001	Oak-A	1	1	2.45	2	2	0	0	0	11	14	3	2	7
D 2002	Oak-A	1	1	2.08	2	2	0	0	0	13	14	3	3	12
D Total	**2**	**2**	**2**	**2.25**	**4**	**4**	**0**	**0**	**0**	**24**	**28**	**6**	**5**	**19**
• MULHOLLAND, Terry														
D 1998	Chi-N	0	1	11.57	2	0	0	0	0	2^1	2	3	2	2
D 1999	Atl-N	0	0	27.00	2	0	0	0	0	0^2	3	2	0	0
D 2000	Atl-N	0	0	5.40	3	0	0	0	0	3^1	1	2	2	1
D Total	**3**	**0**	**1**	**9.95**	**7**	**0**	**0**	**0**	**0**	**6^1**	**6**	**7**	**4**	**3**
L 1993	Phi-N	0	1	7.20	1	1	0	0	0	5	9	4	1	2
L 1999	Atl-N	0	0	0.00	2	0	0	0	0	2^2	1	0	1	2
L Total	**2**	**0**	**1**	**4.70**	**3**	**1**	**0**	**0**	**0**	**7^2**	**10**	**4**	**2**	**4**
W 1993	Phi-N	1	0	6.75	2	2	0	0	0	10^2	14	8	3	5
W 1999	Atl-N	0	0	7.36	2	0	0	0	0	3^2	5	3	1	3
W Total	**2**	**1**	**0**	**6.91**	**4**	**2**	**0**	**0**	**0**	**14^1**	**19**	**11**	**4**	**8**
• MULLIN, George														
W 1907	Det-A	0	2	2.12	2	2	2	0	0	17	15	4	7	8
W 1908	Det-A	1	0	0.00	1	1	1	0	0	9	7	0	1	8
W 1909	Det-A	2	1	2.25	4	3	3	0	1	32	23	8	8	20
W Total	**3**	**3**	**3**	**1.86**	**7**	**6**	**6**	**0**	**1**	**58**	**45**	**12**	**16**	**36**
• MUNCRIEF, Bob														
W 1944	StL-A	0	1	1.35	2	0	0	0	0	6^2	5	1	4	4
W 1948	Cle-A	0	0	0.00	1	0	0	0	0	2	1	0	0	0
W Total	**2**	**0**	**1**	**1.04**	**3**	**0**	**0**	**0**	**0**	**8^2**	**6**	**1**	**4**	**4**
• MUNGER, Red														
W 1946	StL-N	1	0	1.00	1	1	1	0	0	9	9	1	3	2
• MUNOZ, Mike														
D 1995	Col-N	0	1	13.50	4	0	0	0	0	1^1	4	2	1	1

YEAR	TM-L	W	L	ERA	G	GS	CG	SV	SHO	IP	H	ER	BB	SO
• MURPHY, Johnny														
W 1936	NY-A	0	0	3.38	1	0	0	1	0	2^{2}	1	1	1	1
W 1937	NY-A	0	0	0.00	1	0	0	1	0	0^{1}	0	0	0	0
W 1938	NY-A	0	0	0.00	1	0	0	1	0	2	2	0	1	1
W 1939	NY-A	1	0	2.70	1	0	0	0	0	3^{1}	5	1	0	2
W 1941	NY-A	1	0	0.00	2	0	0	0	0	6	2	0	1	3
W 1943	NY-A	0	0	0.00	2	0	0	1	0	2	1	0	1	1
W Total	**6**	**2**	**0**	**1.10**	**8**	**0**	**0**	**4**	**0**	16^{1}	**11**	**2**	**4**	**8**
• MURPHY, Rob														
L 1990	Bos-A	0	0	13.50	1	0	0	0	0	0^{2}	2	1	1	0
• MUSSINA, Mike														
D 1996	Bal-A	0	0	4.50	1	1	0	0	0	6	7	3	2	6
D 1997	Bal-A	2	0	1.93	2	2	0	0	0	14	7	3	3	16
D 2001	NY-A	1	0	0.00	1	1	0	0	0	7	4	0	1	4
D 2002	NY-A	0	0	9.00	1	1	0	0	0	4	6	4	0	2
D 2003	NY-A	0	1	3.86	1	1	0	0	0	7	7	3	3	6
D Total	**5**	**3**	**1**	**3.08**	**6**	**6**	**0**	**0**	**0**	**38**	**31**	**13**	**9**	**34**
L 1996	Bal-A	0	1	5.87	1	1	0	0	0	7^{2}	8	5	2	6
L 1997	Bal-A	0	0	0.60	2	2	0	0	0	15	4	1	4	25
L 2001	NY-A	1	0	3.00	1	1	0	0	0	6	4	2	1	3
L 2003	NY-A	0	2	4.11	3	2	0	0	0	15^{1}	16	7	4	17
L Total	**4**	**1**	**3**	**3.07**	**7**	**6**	**0**	**0**	**0**	**44**	**32**	**15**	**11**	**51**
W 2001	NY-A	0	1	4.09	2	2	0	0	0	11	11	5	4	14
W 2003	NY-A	1	0	1.29	1	1	0	0	0	7	7	1	1	9
W Total	**2**	**1**	**1**	**3.00**	**3**	**3**	**0**	**0**	**0**	**18**	**18**	**6**	**5**	**23**
• MYERS, Mike														
D 2002	Ari-N	0	0	0.00	2	0	0	0	0	1^{2}	2	0	0	1
• MYERS, Randy														
D 1996	Bal-A	0	0	0.00	3	0	0	2	0	3	0	0	0	3
D 1997	Bal-A	0	0	0.00	2	0	0	1	0	2	0	0	0	5
D Total	**2**	**0**	**0**	**0.00**	**5**	**0**	**0**	**3**	**0**	**5**	**0**	**0**	**0**	**8**
L 1988	NY-N	2	0	0.00	3	0	0	0	0	4^{2}	1	0	2	0
L 1990	Cin-N	0	0	0.00	4	0	0	3	0	5^{2}	2	0	3	7
L 1996	Bal-A	0	1	2.25	3	0	0	0	0	4	4	1	3	2
L 1997	Bal-A	0	1	5.06	4	0	0	1	0	5^{1}	6	3	3	7
L 1998	SD-N	0	0	13.50	4	0	0	0	0	2	3	3	2	3
L Total	**5**	**2**	**2**	**2.91**	**18**	**0**	**0**	**4**	**0**	21^{2}	**16**	**7**	**13**	**19**
W 1990	Cin-N	0	0	0.00	3	0	0	1	0	3	2	0	0	3
W 1998	SD-N	0	0	9.00	3	0	0	0	0	1	0	1	1	2
W Total	**2**	**0**	**0**	**2.25**	**6**	**0**	**0**	**1**	**0**	**4**	**2**	**1**	**1**	**5**
• NAGY, Charles														
D 1995	Cle-A	1	0	1.29	1	1	0	0	0	7	4	1	5	6
D 1996	Cle-A	0	1	7.15	2	2	0	0	0	11^{1}	15	9	5	13
D 1997	Cle-A	0	1	9.82	1	1	0	0	0	3^{2}	2	4	6	1
D 1998	Cle-A	1	0	1.13	1	1	0	0	0	8	4	1	0	3
D 1999	Cle-A	1	0	7.20	2	2	0	0	0	10	11	8	2	6
D Total	**5**	**3**	**2**	**5.18**	**7**	**7**	**0**	**0**	**0**	**40**	**36**	**23**	**18**	**29**
L 1995	Cle-A	0	0	1.13	1	1	0	0	0	8	5	1	0	6
L 1997	Cle-A	0	0	2.77	2	2	0	0	0	13	17	4	5	5
L 1998	Cle-A	0	1	3.72	2	2	0	0	0	9^{2}	13	4	1	6
L Total	**3**	**0**	**1**	**2.64**	**5**	**5**	**0**	**0**	**0**	30^{2}	**35**	**9**	**6**	**17**
W 1995	Cle-A	0	0	6.43	1	1	0	0	0	7	8	5	1	4
W 1997	Cle-A	0	1	6.43	2	1	0	0	0	7	8	5	5	5
W Total	**2**	**0**	**1**	**6.43**	**3**	**2**	**0**	**0**	**0**	**14**	**16**	**10**	**6**	**9**
• NARLESKI, Ray														
W 1954	Cle-A	0	0	2.25	2	0	0	0	0	4	1	1	1	2
• NATHAN, Joe														
D 2003	SF-N	0	1	81.00	2	0	0	0	0	0^{1}	4	3	1	1
• NEAGLE, Denny														
L 1992	Pit-N	0	0	27.00	2	0	0	0	0	1^{2}	4	5	3	0
L 1996	Atl-N	0	0	2.35	2	1	0	0	0	7^{2}	2	2	3	8
L 1997	Atl-N	1	0	0.00	2	1	1	0	1	12	5	0	1	9
L 1998	Atl-N	0	0	3.52	2	1	0	0	0	7^{2}	8	3	2	9
L 2000	NY-A	0	2	4.50	2	2	0	0	0	10	6	5	7	7
L Total	**5**	**1**	**2**	**3.46**	**10**	**5**	**1**	**0**	**1**	**39**	**25**	**15**	**16**	**33**
W 1996	Atl-N	0	0	3.00	2	1	0	0	0	6	5	2	4	3
W 2000	NY-A	0	0	3.86	1	1	0	0	0	4^{2}	4	2	2	3
W Total	**2**	**0**	**0**	**3.38**	**3**	**2**	**0**	**0**	**0**	10^{2}	**9**	**4**	**6**	**6**
• NEHF, Art														
W 1921	NY-N	1	2	1.38	3	3	3	0	1	26	13	4	13	8
W 1922	NY-N	1	0	2.25	2	2	1	0	0	16	11	4	3	6
W 1923	NY-N	1	1	2.76	2	2	1	0	1	16^{1}	10	5	6	7
W 1924	NY-N	1	1	1.83	3	2	1	0	0	19^{2}	15	4	9	7
W 1929	Chi-N	0	0	18.00	2	0	0	0	0	1	1	2	1	0
W Total	**5**	**4**	**4**	**2.16**	**12**	**9**	**6**	**0**	**2**	**79**	**50**	**19**	**32**	**28**
• NEIBAUER, Gary														
L 1969	Atl-N	0	0	0.00	1	0	0	0	0	1	0	0	0	1
• NELSON, Gene														
L 1988	Oak-A	2	0	0.00	2	0	0	0	0	4^{2}	5	0	1	0
L 1989	Oak-A	0	0	0.00	1	0	0	0	0	1^{1}	1	0	0	2
L 1990	Oak-A	0	0	0.00	1	0	0	0	0	1^{2}	3	0	0	0
L Total	**3**	**2**	**0**	**0.00**	**4**	**0**	**0**	**0**	**0**	7^{2}	**9**	**0**	**1**	**2**
W 1988	Oak-A	0	0	1.42	3	0	0	0	0	6^{1}	4	1	3	3
W 1989	Oak-A	0	0	54.00	2	0	0	0	0	1	4	6	2	1
W 1990	Oak-A	0	0	0.00	2	0	0	0	0	5	3	0	2	0
W Total	**3**	**0**	**0**	**5.11**	**7**	**0**	**0**	**0**	**0**	12^{1}	**11**	**7**	**7**	**4**
• NELSON, Jeff														
D 1995	Sea-A	0	1	3.18	3	0	0	0	0	5^{2}	7	2	3	7
D 1996	NY-A	1	0	0.00	2	0	0	0	0	3^{2}	2	0	2	5
D 1997	NY-A	0	0	0.00	4	0	0	0	0	4	4	0	2	0
D 1998	NY-A	0	0	0.00	2	0	0	0	0	2^{2}	2	0	1	2
D 1999	NY-A	0	0	0.00	3	0	0	0	0	1^{2}	1	0	1	3
D 2000	NY-A	0	0	0.00	2	0	0	0	0	2	0	0	0	2
D 2001	Sea-A	0	0	0.00	3	0	0	0	0	3	1	0	1	5
D 2003	NY-A	0	0	....	1	0	0	0	0	0	0	0	1	0
D Total	**8**	**1**	**1**	**0.79**	**20**	**0**	**0**	**0**	**0**	22^{2}	**17**	**2**	**11**	**24**
L 1995	Sea-A	0	0	0.00	3	0	0	0	0	3	3	0	5	3
L 1996	NY-A	0	1	11.57	2	0	0	0	0	2^{1}	5	3	0	2
L 1998	NY-A	0	1	20.25	3	0	0	0	0	1^{1}	3	3	1	3
L 1999	NY-A	0	0	0.00	2	0	0	0	0	0^{2}	0	0	0	0
L 2000	NY-A	0	0	9.00	3	0	0	0	0	3	5	3	0	6
L 2001	Sea-A	0	0	0.00	2	0	0	0	0	2^{1}	1	0	1	3
L 2003	NY-A	0	0	6.00	4	0	0	0	0	3	4	2	0	3
L Total	**7**	**0**	**2**	**6.32**	**19**	**0**	**0**	**0**	**0**	15^{2}	**21**	**11**	**7**	**20**
W 1996	NY-A	0	0	0.00	3	0	0	0	0	4^{1}	1	0	1	5
W 1998	NY-A	0	0	0.00	3	0	0	0	0	2^{1}	2	0	1	4
W 1999	NY-A	0	0	0.00	4	0	0	0	0	2^{2}	2	0	1	3
W 2000	NY-A	1	0	10.13	3	0	0	0	0	2^{2}	5	3	1	1
W 2003	NY-A	0	0	0.00	3	0	0	0	0	4	4	0	2	5
W Total	**5**	**1**	**0**	**1.69**	**16**	**0**	**0**	**0**	**0**	**16**	**14**	**3**	**6**	**18**
• NELSON, Mel														
W 1968	StL-N	0	0	0.00	1	0	0	0	0	1	0	0	0	1
• NELSON, Roger														
L 1973	Cin-N	0	0	0.00	1	0	0	0	0	2^{1}	0	0	1	0
• NEN, Robb														
D 1997	Fla-N	1	0	0.00	2	0	0	0	0	2	1	0	2	2
D 2000	SF-N	0	0	0.00	2	0	0	0	0	2^{1}	2	0	1	3
D 2002	SF-N	0	0	0.00	4	0	0	2	0	2^{2}	4	0	1	1
D Total	**3**	**1**	**0**	**0.00**	**8**	**0**	**0**	**2**	**0**	**7**	**7**	**0**	**4**	**6**
L 1997	Fla-N	0	0	0.00	2	0	0	2	0	2	0	0	0	0
L 2002	SF-N	0	0	2.70	3	0	0	3	0	3^{1}	3	1	1	4
L Total	**2**	**0**	**0**	**1.69**	**5**	**0**	**0**	**5**	**0**	5^{1}	**3**	**1**	**1**	**4**
W 1997	Fla-N	0	0	7.71	4	0	0	2	0	4^{2}	8	4	2	7
W 2002	SF-N	0	0	0.00	3	0	0	2	0	3	2	0	1	3
W Total	**2**	**0**	**0**	**4.70**	**7**	**0**	**0**	**4**	**0**	7^{2}	**10**	**4**	**3**	**10**
• NEWCOMBE, Don														
W 1949	Bro-N	0	2	3.09	2	2	1	0	0	11^{2}	10	4	3	11
W 1955	Bro-N	0	1	9.53	1	1	0	0	0	5^{2}	8	6	2	4
W 1956	Bro-N	0	1	21.21	2	2	0	0	0	4^{2}	11	11	3	4
W Total	**3**	**0**	**4**	**8.59**	**5**	**5**	**1**	**0**	**0**	**22**	**29**	**21**	**8**	**19**
• NEWHOUSER, Hal														
W 1945	Det-A	2	1	6.10	3	3	2	0	0	20^{2}	25	14	4	22
W 1954	Cle-A	0	0	....	1	0	0	0	0	0	1	1	1	0
W Total	**2**	**2**	**1**	**6.53**	**4**	**3**	**2**	**0**	**0**	20^{2}	**26**	**15**	**5**	**22**
• NEWSOM, Bobo														
W 1940	Det-A	2	1	1.38	3	3	3	0	1	26	18	4	4	17
W 1947	NY-A	0	1	19.29	2	1	0	0	0	2^{1}	6	5	2	0
W Total	**2**	**2**	**2**	**2.86**	**5**	**4**	**3**	**0**	**1**	28^{1}	**24**	**9**	**6**	**17**
• NICHOLS, Kid														
T 1892	Bos-N	2	0	1.00	2	2	2	0	1	18	17	2	4	13
T 1897	Bos-N	0	0	12.00	1	1	0	0	0	6	14	8	0	3
T Total	**2**	**2**	**0**	**3.75**	**3**	**3**	**2**	**0**	**1**	**24**	**31**	**10**	**4**	**16**
• NIEDENFUER, Tom														
D 1981	LA-N	0	0	0.00	1	0	0	0	0	0^{1}	1	0	1	1
L 1981	LA-N	0	0	0.00	1	0	0	0	0	0^{1}	2	0	0	0
L 1983	LA-N	0	0	0.00	2	0	0	1	0	2	0	0	1	3
L 1985	LA-N	0	2	6.35	3	0	0	1	0	5^{2}	5	4	2	5
L Total	**3**	**0**	**2**	**4.50**	**6**	**0**	**0**	**2**	**0**	**8**	**7**	**4**	**3**	**8**
W 1981	LA-N	0	0	0.00	2	0	0	0	0	5	3	0	1	0
• NIEKRO, Joe														
D 1981	Hou-N	0	0	0.00	1	1	0	0	0	8	7	0	3	4
L 1980	Hou-N	0	0	0.00	1	1	0	0	0	10	6	0	1	2
W 1987	Min-A	0	0	0.00	1	0	0	0	0	2	1	0	1	1
• NIEKRO, Phil														
L 1969	Atl-N	0	1	4.50	1	1	0	0	0	8	9	4	4	4
L 1982	Atl-N	0	0	3.00	1	1	0	0	0	6	6	2	4	5
L Total	**2**	**0**	**1**	**3.86**	**2**	**2**	**0**	**0**	**0**	**14**	**15**	**6**	**8**	**9**
• NIPPER, Al														
W 1986	Bos-A	0	1	7.11	2	1	0	0	0	6^{1}	10	5	2	2
• NOLAN, Gary														
L 1970	Cin-N	1	0	0.00	1	1	0	0	0	9	8	0	4	6
L 1972	Cin-N	0	0	1.50	1	1	0	0	0	6	4	1	1	4
L 1975	Cin-N	0	0	3.00	1	1	0	0	0	6	5	2	0	5
L 1976	Cin-N	0	0	1.59	1	1	0	0	0	5^{2}	6	1	2	1
L Total	**4**	**1**	**0**	**1.35**	**4**	**4**	**0**	**0**	**0**	26^{2}	**23**	**4**	**7**	**16**
W 1970	Cin-N	0	1	7.71	2	2	0	0	0	9^{1}	9	8	3	9
W 1972	Cin-N	0	1	3.38	2	2	0	0	0	10^{2}	7	4	2	3
W 1975	Cin-N	0	0	6.00	2	2	0	0	0	6	6	4	1	2
W 1976	Cin-N	1	0	2.70	1	1	0	0	0	6^{2}	8	2	1	1
W Total	**4**	**1**	**2**	**4.96**	**7**	**7**	**0**	**0**	**0**	32^{2}	**30**	**18**	**7**	**15**
• NOLES, Dickie														
D 1981	Phi-N	0	0	4.50	1	1	0	0	0	4	4	2	2	5
L 1980	Phi-N	0	0	0.00	2	0	0	0	0	2^{2}	1	0	3	0
W 1980	Phi-N	0	0	1.93	1	0	0	0	0	4^{2}	5	1	2	6
• NOMO, Hideo														
D 1995	LA-N	0	1	9.00	1	1	0	0	0	5	7	5	2	6

YEAR	TM-L	W	L	ERA	G	GS	CG	SV	SHO	IP	H	ER	BB	SO
D 1996	LA-N	0	1	12.27	1	1	0	0	0	3^2	5	5	5	3
D Total 2		0	2	10.38	2	2	0	0	0	8^2	12	10	7	9
• NOPS, Jerry														
T 1897	Bal-N	1	1	12.86	2	2	1	0	0	14	23	20	9	3
• NORMAN, Fred														
L 1973	Cin-N	0	0	1.80	1	1	0	0	0	5	1	1	3	3
L 1975	Cin-N	1	0	1.50	1	1	0	0	0	6	4	1	5	4
L 1979	Cin-N	0	0	18.00	1	0	0	0	0	2	4	4	1	1
L Total 3		1	0	4.15	3	2	0	0	0	13	9	6	9	8
W 1975	Cin-N	0	1	9.00	2	1	0	0	0	4	8	4	3	2
W 1976	Cin-N	0	0	4.26	1	0	0	0	0	6^1	9	3	2	2
W Total 2		0	1	6.10	3	2	0	0	0	10^1	17	7	5	4
• NORRIS, Mike														
D 1981	Oak-A	1	0	0.00	1	1	1	0	1	5^1	4	0	3	2
L 1981	Oak-A	0	1	3.68	1	1	0	0	0	7^1	6	3	2	4
• O'BRIEN, Buck														
W 1912	Bos-A	0	2	5.00	2	2	0	0	0	9	12	5	3	4
• O'DAY, Hank														
W 1889	NY-N	2	0	1.17	3	2	2	0	0	23	10	3	14	12
• O'DELL, Billy														
W 1962	SF-N	0	1	4.38	3	1	0	1	0	12^1	12	6	3	9
• ODOM, Blue Moon														
L 1972	Oak-A	2	0	0.00	2	2	1	0	1	14	5	0	2	5
L 1973	Oak-A	0	0	1.80	1	0	0	0	0	5	6	1	2	4
L 1974	Oak-A	0	0	0.00	1	0	0	0	0	3^1	1	0	0	1
L Total 3		2	0	0.40	4	2	1	0	1	22^1	12	1	4	10
W 1972	Oak-A	0	1	1.59	2	2	0	0	0	11^1	5	2	6	13
W 1973	Oak-A	0	0	3.86	2	0	0	0	0	4^2	5	2	2	2
W 1974	Oak-A	1	0	0.00	2	0	0	0	0	1^1	0	0	1	2
W Total 3		1	1	2.08	6	2	0	0	0	17^1	10	4	9	17
• OGDEN, Curly														
W 1924	Was-A	0	0	0.00	1	1	0	0	0	0^1	0	0	1	1
• OGEA, Chad														
D 1996	Cle-A	0	0	0.00	1	0	0	0	0	0^1	0	0	1	0
D 1997	Cle-A	0	0	1.69	1	0	0	0	0	5^1	2	1	0	1
D Total 2		0	0	1.59	2	0	0	0	0	5^2	2	1	1	1
L 1995	Cle-A	0	0	0.00	1	0	0	0	0	0^2	1	0	0	2
L 1997	Cle-A	0	2	3.21	2	2	0	0	0	14	12	5	5	7
L 1998	Cle-A	0	1	8.10	2	1	0	0	0	6^2	9	6	5	4
L Total 3		0	3	4.64	5	3	0	0	0	21^1	22	11	10	13
W 1997	Cle-A	2	0	1.54	2	2	0	0	0	11^2	11	2	3	5
• OJEDA, Bob														
L 1986	NY-N	1	0	2.57	2	2	0	0	0	14	15	4	4	6
W 1986	NY-N	1	0	2.08	2	2	0	0	0	13	13	3	5	9
• OLDHAM, Red														
W 1925	Pit-N	0	0	0.00	1	0	0	1	0	1	0	0	0	2
• OLIVER, Darren														
D 1996	Tex-A	0	1	3.38	1	1	0	0	0	8	6	3	2	3
• OLSON, Gregg														
D 1999	Ari-N	0	0	0.00	2	0	0	0	0	0^1	0	0	1	0
• OROSCO, Jesse														
D 1996	Bal-A	0	1	36.00	4	0	0	0	0	1	2	4	3	2
D 1997	Bal-A	0	0	0.00	2	0	0	0	0	1^1	1	0	0	1
D Total 2		0	1	15.43	6	0	0	0	0	2^1	3	4	3	3
L 1986	NY-N	3	0	3.38	4	0	0	0	0	8	5	3	2	10
L 1988	LA-N	0	0	7.71	4	0	0	0	0	2^1	4	2	3	0
L 1996	Bal-A	0	0	4.50	4	0	0	0	0	2	2	1	1	2
L 1997	Bal-A	0	0	0.00	2	0	0	0	0	1^1	0	0	1	1
L Total 4		3	0	3.95	14	0	0	0	0	13^2	11	6	7	13
W 1986	NY-N	0	0	0.00	4	0	0	2	0	5^2	2	0	0	6
• ORTIZ, Ramon														
D 2002	Ana-A	0	0	20.25	1	1	0	0	0	2^2	3	6	4	1
L 2002	Ana-A	1	0	5.06	1	1	0	0	0	5^1	10	3	1	3
W 2002	Ana-A	0	1	7.20	1	1	0	0	0	5	5	4	4	3
• ORTIZ, Russ														
D 2000	SF-N	0	0	1.69	1	1	0	0	0	5^1	2	1	4	4
D 2002	SF-N	2	0	2.19	2	2	0	0	0	12^1	9	3	8	8
D 2003	Atl-N	0	0	5.06	2	2	0	0	0	10^2	15	6	7	9
D Total 3		2	0	3.18	5	5	0	0	0	28^1	26	10	19	21
L 2002	SF-N	0	0	7.71	2	2	0	0	0	4^2	4	4	3	3
W 2002	SF-N	0	0	10.13	2	2	0	0	0	8	13	9	2	2
• OSBORNE, Donovan														
D 1996	StL-N	0	0	9.00	1	1	0	0	0	4	7	4	0	5
L 1996	StL-N	1	1	9.39	2	2	0	0	0	7^2	12	8	4	6
• OSINSKI, Dan														
W 1967	Bos-A	0	0	6.75	2	0	0	0	0	1^1	2	1	0	0
• OSTEEN, Claude														
W 1965	LA-N	1	1	0.64	2	2	1	0	0	14	9	1	5	4
W 1966	LA-N	0	1	1.29	1	1	0	0	0	7	3	1	1	3
W Total 2		1	2	0.86	3	3	1	0	1	21	12	2	6	7
• OSTROWSKI, Joe														
W 1951	NY-A	0	0	0.00	1	0	0	0	0	2	1	0	0	1
• OSUNA, Antonio														
D 1995	LA-N	0	0	2.70	3	0	0	0	0	3^1	3	1	1	3
D 1996	LA-N	0	1	4.50	2	0	0	0	0	2	3	1	1	4
D Total 2		0	2	3.38	5	0	0	0	0	5^1	6	2	2	7
• O'TOOLE, Jim														
W 1961	Cin-N	0	2	3.00	2	2	1	0	0	12	11	4	7	4
• OVERALL, Orval														
W 1906	Chi-N	0	0	2.25	2	0	0	0	0	12	10	3	3	8
W 1907	Chi-N	1	0	1.00	2	2	1	0	0	18	14	2	4	11
W 1908	Chi-N	2	0	0.98	3	2	2	0	1	18^1	7	2	7	15
W 1910	Chi-N	0	1	9.00	1	1	0	0	0	3	6	3	1	1
W Total 4		3	1	1.75	8	5	3	0	1	51^1	37	10	15	35
• OVERMIRE, Stubby														
W 1945	Det-A	0	1	3.00	1	1	0	0	0	6	4	2	2	2
• OWCHINKO, Bob														
L 1981	Oak-A	0	0	5.40	1	0	0	0	0	1^2	3	1	0	0
• OWEN, Frank														
W 1906	Chi-A	0	0	3.00	1	0	0	0	0	6	6	2	3	2
• PAGE, Joe														
W 1947	NY-A	1	1	4.15	4	0	0	1	0	13	12	6	2	7
W 1949	NY-A	1	0	2.00	3	0	0	1	0	9	6	2	3	8
W Total 2		2	1	3.27	7	0	0	2	0	22	18	8	5	15
• PAGE, Vance														
W 1938	Chi-N	0	0	13.50	1	0	0	0	0	1^1	2	2	0	0
• PAIGE, Satchel														
W 1948	Cle-A	0	0	0.00	1	0	0	0	0	0^2	0	0	0	0
• PAINTER, Lance														
D 1995	Col-N	0	0	5.40	1	1	0	0	0	5	5	3	2	4
• PALICA, Erv														
W 1949	Bro-N	0	0	0.00	1	0	0	0	0	2	1	0	1	4
• PALMER, Jim														
L 1969	Bal-A	1	0	2.00	1	1	1	0	0	9	10	2	2	4
L 1970	Bal-A	1	0	1.00	1	1	1	0	0	9	7	1	3	12
L 1971	Bal-A	1	0	3.00	1	1	1	0	0	9	7	3	3	8
L 1973	Bal-A	1	0	1.84	3	2	1	0	1	14^2	11	3	8	15
L 1974	Bal-A	0	1	1.00	1	1	1	0	0	9	4	1	1	4
L 1979	Bal-A	0	0	3.00	1	1	1	0	0	9	7	3	2	3
L Total 6		4	1	1.96	8	7	5	0	1	59^2	46	13	19	46
W 1966	Bal-A	1	0	0.00	1	1	1	0	0	9	4	0	3	6
W 1969	Bal-A	0	1	6.00	1	1	0	0	0	6	5	4	4	5
W 1970	Bal-A	1	0	4.60	2	2	0	0	0	15^2	11	8	9	9
W 1971	Bal-A	1	0	2.65	2	2	0	0	0	17	15	5	9	15
W 1979	Bal-A	0	1	3.60	2	2	0	0	0	15	18	6	5	8
W 1983	Bal-A	1	0	0.00	1	0	0	0	0	2	2	0	1	1
W Total 6		4	2	3.20	9	8	1	0	1	64^2	55	23	31	44
• PANIAGUA, Jose														
D 2000	Sea-A	1	0	0.00	2	0	0	0	0	2^1	1	0	2	3
D 2001	Sea-A	0	0	27.00	2	0	0	0	0	2	4	6	2	1
D Total 2		1	0	12.46	4	0	0	0	0	4^1	5	6	4	4
L 2000	Sea-A	0	1	4.15	5	0	0	0	0	4^1	4	2	1	4
L 2001	Sea-A	0	0	12.27	3	0	0	0	0	3^2	7	5	1	1
L Total 2		0	1	7.88	8	0	0	0	0	8	11	7	2	5
• PAPPAS, Milt														
L 1969	Atl-N	0	0	11.57	1	0	0	0	0	2^1	4	3	0	4
• PARKER, Harry														
L 1973	NY-N	0	1	9.00	1	0	0	0	0	1	1	1	0	0
W 1973	NY-N	0	1	0.00	3	0	0	0	0	3^1	2	0	2	2
• PARQUE, Jim														
D 2000	Chi-A	0	0	4.50	1	1	0	0	0	6	6	3	1	2
• PARRETT, Jeff														
L 1992	Oak-A	0	0	11.57	3	0	0	0	0	2^1	6	3	0	1
• PASCUAL, Camilo														
W 1965	Min-A	0	1	5.40	1	1	0	0	0	5	8	3	2	2
• PASSEAU, Claude														
W 1945	Chi-N	1	0	2.70	3	2	1	0	1	16^2	7	5	8	3
• PASTORE, Frank														
L 1979	Cin-N	0	0	2.57	1	1	0	0	0	7	7	2	3	1
• PATTERSON, Bob														
L 1990	Pit-N	0	0	0.00	2	0	0	1	0	1	1	0	2	0
L 1991	Pit-N	0	0	0.00	1	0	0	0	0	2	1	0	0	3
L 1992	Pit-N	0	0	5.40	2	0	0	0	0	1^2	3	1	1	1
L Total 3		0	0	1.93	5	0	0	1	0	4^2	5	1	3	4
• PATTERSON, Danny														
D 1996	Tex-A	0	0	0.00	1	0	0	0	0	0^1	1	0	0	0
D 1999	Tex-A	0	0	0.00	1	0	0	0	0	1	1	0	0	0
D Total 2		0	0	0.00	2	0	0	0	0	1^1	2	0	0	0
• PATTERSON, Daryl														
W 1968	Det-A	0	0	3.60	3	0	0	0	0	5	5	2	1	4
• PATTIN, Marty														
L 1976	KC-A	0	0	27.00	2	0	0	0	0	0^1	1	1	0	1
L 1977	KC-A	0	0	1.50	1	0	0	0	0	6	6	1	0	0
L 1978	KC-A	0	0	27.00	1	0	0	0	0	0^2	2	2	0	0
L Total 3		0	0	5.14	4	0	0	0	0	7	8	4	1	0
W 1980	KC-A	0	0	0.00	1	0	0	0	0	0^2	0	0	0	2
• PAVANO, Carl														
D 2003	Fla-N	2	0	0.00	3	0	0	0	0	2^2	1	0	1	1
L 2003	Fla-N	0	0	2.35	3	1	0	0	0	7^2	8	2	1	8

YEAR	TM-L	W	L	ERA	G	GS	CG	SV	SHO	IP	H	ER	BB	SO
W 2003	Fla-N	0	0	1.00	2	1	0	0	0	9	8	1	1	6
• PAVLIK, Roger														
D 1996	Tex-A	0	1	6.75	1	0	0	0	0	2^2	4	2	0	1
• PEARSON, Monte														
W 1936	NY-A	1	0	2.00	1	1	1	0	0	9	7	2	2	7
W 1937	NY-A	1	0	1.04	1	1	0	0	0	8^2	5	1	2	4
W 1938	NY-A	1	0	1.00	1	1	1	0	0	9	5	1	2	9
W 1939	NY-A	1	0	0.00	1	1	1	0	1	9	2	0	1	8
W Total	4	4	0	1.01	4	4	3	0	1	35^2	19	4	7	28
• PENA, Alejandro														
D 1995	Atl-N	2	0	0.00	3	0	0	0	0	3	3	0	1	2
L 1981	LA-N	0	0	0.00	2	0	0	0	0	2^1	1	0	0	0
L 1983	LA-N	0	0	6.75	1	0	0	0	0	2^2	4	2	1	3
L 1988	LA-N	1	1	4.15	3	0	0	1	0	4^1	1	2	5	1
L 1991	Atl-N	0	0	0.00	4	0	0	3	0	4^1	1	0	0	4
L 1995	Atl-N	0	0	0.00	3	0	0	0	0	3	2	0	1	4
L Total	5	1	1	2.16	13	0	0	4	0	16^2	9	4	7	12
W 1988	LA-N	1	0	0.00	2	0	0	0	0	5	2	0	1	7
W 1991	Atl-N	0	1	3.38	3	0	0	0	0	5^1	6	2	3	7
W 1995	Atl-N	0	1	9.00	2	0	0	0	0	1	3	1	2	0
W Total	3	1	2	2.38	7	0	0	0	0	11^1	11	3	6	14
• PENNOCK, Herb														
W 1914	Phi-A	0	0	0.00	1	0	0	0	0	3	2	0	2	3
W 1923	NY-A	2	0	3.63	3	2	1	1	0	17^1	19	7	1	8
W 1926	NY-A	2	0	1.23	3	2	2	0	0	22	13	3	4	8
W 1927	NY-A	1	0	1.00	1	1	1	0	0	9	3	1	0	1
W 1932	NY-A	0	0	2.25	2	0	0	2	0	4	2	1	1	4
W Total	5	5	0	1.95	10	5	4	3	0	55^1	39	12	8	24
• PENNY, Brad														
D 2003	Fla-N	0	0	6.35	2	1	0	0	0	5^2	5	4	1	6
L 2003	Fla-N	1	1	15.75	3	1	0	0	0	4	9	7	3	0
W 2003	Fla-N	2	0	2.19	2	2	0	0	0	12^1	15	3	5	7
• PERCIVAL, Troy														
D 2002	Ana-A	0	0	5.40	3	0	0	2	0	3^1	6	2	0	4
L 2002	Ana-A	0	0	0.00	3	0	0	2	0	3^1	0	0	0	3
W 2002	Ana-A	0	0	3.00	3	0	0	3	0	3	2	1	1	3
• PEREZ, Odalis														
D 1998	Atl-N	1	0	0.00	1	0	0	0	0	0^2	0	0	0	1
L 1998	Atl-N	0	0	54.00	2	0	0	0	0	0^1	5	2	2	0
• PEREZ, Pascual														
L 1982	Atl-N	0	1	5.19	2	1	0	0	0	8^2	10	5	2	4
• PERRANOSKI, Ron														
L 1969	Min-A	0	1	5.79	3	0	0	0	0	4^2	8	3	0	2
L 1970	Min-A	0	0	19.29	2	0	0	0	0	2^1	5	5	1	3
L Total	2	0	1	10.29	5	0	0	0	0	7	13	8	1	5
W 1963	LA-N	0	0	0.00	1	0	0	1	0	0^2	1	0	0	1
W 1965	LA-N	0	0	7.36	2	0	0	0	0	3^2	3	3	4	1
W 1966	LA-N	0	0	5.40	2	0	0	0	0	3^1	4	2	1	2
W Total	3	0	0	5.87	5	0	0	1	0	7^2	8	5	5	4
• PERRITT, Pol														
W 1917	NY-N	0	0	1.08	3	0	0	0	0	8^1	9	1	3	3
• PERRY, Gaylord														
L 1971	SF-N	1	1	6.14	2	2	1	0	0	14^2	19	10	3	11
• PERRY, Jim														
L 1969	Min-A	0	0	3.38	1	1	0	0	0	8	6	3	3	3
L 1970	Min-A	0	1	13.50	2	1	0	0	0	5^1	10	8	1	3
L Total	2	0	1	7.43	3	2	0	0	0	13^1	16	11	4	6
W 1965	Min-A	0	0	4.50	2	0	0	0	0	4	5	2	2	4
• PETKOVSEK, Mark														
D 1996	StL-N	0	0	0.00	1	0	0	0	0	2	0	0	0	1
L 1996	StL-N	0	1	7.36	6	0	0	0	0	7^1	11	6	3	7
• PETRY, Dan														
L 1984	Det-A	0	0	2.57	1	1	0	0	0	7	4	2	1	4
L 1987	Det-A	0	0	0.00	1	0	0	0	0	3^1	1	0	0	1
L Total	2	0	0	1.74	2	1	0	0	0	10^1	5	2	1	5
W 1984	Det-A	0	1	9.00	2	2	0	0	0	8	14	8	5	4
• PETTITTE, Andy														
D 1995	NY-A	0	0	5.14	1	1	0	0	0	7	9	4	3	0
D 1996	NY-A	0	0	5.68	1	1	0	0	0	6^1	4	4	6	3
D 1997	NY-A	0	2	8.49	2	2	0	0	0	11^2	15	11	1	5
D 1998	NY-A	1	0	1.29	1	1	0	0	0	7	3	1	0	8
D 1999	NY-A	1	0	1.23	1	1	0	0	0	7^1	7	1	0	5
D 2000	NY-A	1	0	3.97	2	2	0	0	0	11^1	15	5	3	7
D 2001	NY-A	0	1	1.42	1	1	0	0	0	6^1	7	1	2	4
D 2002	NY-A	0	0	12.00	1	1	0	0	0	3	8	4	0	1
D 2003	NY-A	1	0	1.29	1	1	0	0	0	7	4	1	3	10
D Total	9	4	3	4.30	11	11	0	0	0	67	72	32	18	43
L 1996	NY-A	1	0	3.60	2	2	0	0	0	15	10	6	5	7
L 1998	NY-A	0	1	11.57	1	1	0	0	0	4^2	8	6	3	1
L 1999	NY-A	1	0	2.45	1	1	0	0	0	7^1	8	2	1	5
L 2000	NY-A	1	0	2.70	1	1	0	0	0	6^2	9	2	1	2
L 2001	NY-A	2	0	2.51	2	2	0	0	0	14^1	11	4	2	8
L 2003	NY-A	1	0	4.63	2	2	0	0	0	11^2	17	6	4	10
L Total	6	6	1	3.92	9	9	0	0	0	59^2	63	26	16	33
W 1996	NY-A	1	1	5.91	2	2	0	0	0	10^2	11	7	4	5
W 1998	NY-A	1	0	0.00	1	1	0	0	0	7^1	5	0	3	4
W 1999	NY-A	0	0	12.27	1	1	0	0	0	3^2	10	5	1	1
W 2000	NY-A	0	0	1.98	2	2	0	0	0	13^2	16	3	4	9
W 2001	NY-A	0	2	10.00	2	2	0	0	0	9	12	10	2	9
W 2003	NY-A	1	1	0.57	2	2	0	0	0	15^2	12	1	4	14
W Total	6	3	4	3.90	10	10	0	0	0	60	66	26	18	42
• PFEFFER, Jeff														
W 1916	Bro-N	0	1	1.69	3	1	0	1	0	10^2	7	2	4	5
W 1920	Bro-N	0	0	3.00	1	0	0	0	0	3	4	1	2	1
W Total	2	0	1	1.98	4	1	0	1	0	13^2	11	3	6	6
• PFIESTER, Jack														
W 1906	Chi-N	0	2	6.10	2	1	1	0	0	10^1	7	7	3	11
W 1907	Chi-N	1	0	1.00	1	1	1	0	0	9	10	1	1	3
W 1908	Chi-N	0	1	7.88	1	1	0	0	0	8	11	7	3	1
W 1910	Chi-N	0	0	0.00	1	0	0	0	0	6^2	10	0	1	1
W Total	4	1	3	3.97	5	3	2	0	0	34	38	15	8	16
• PHILLIPPE, Deacon														
T 1900	Pit-N	1	0	0.00	1	1	1	0	1	9	6	0	2	5
W 1903	Pit-N	3	2	2.86	5	5	5	0	0	44	38	14	3	22
W 1909	Pit-N	0	0	0.00	2	0	0	0	0	6	2	0	1	2
W Total	2	3	2	2.52	7	5	5	0	0	50	40	14	4	24
• PHOEBUS, Tom														
W 1970	Bal-A	1	0	0.00	1	0	0	0	0	1^2	1	0	0	0
• PIERCE, Billy														
W 1959	Chi-A	0	0	0.00	3	0	0	0	0	4	2	0	2	3
W 1962	SF-N	1	1	2.40	2	2	1	0	0	15	8	4	2	5
W Total	2	1	1	1.89	5	2	1	0	0	19	10	4	4	8
• PIERCY, Bill														
W 1921	NY-A	0	0	0.00	1	0	0	0	0	1	2	0	0	2
• PINA, Horacio														
L 1973	Oak-A	0	0	0.00	1	0	0	0	0	2	3	0	1	1
W 1973	Oak-A	0	0	0.00	2	0	0	0	0	3	6	0	2	0
• PINEIRO, Joel														
L 2001	Sea-A	0	0	4.50	1	0	0	0	0	2	4	1	2	5
• PIPGRAS, George														
W 1927	NY-A	1	0	2.00	1	1	1	0	0	9	7	2	1	2
W 1928	NY-A	1	0	2.00	1	1	1	0	0	9	4	2	4	8
W 1932	NY-A	1	0	4.50	1	1	0	0	0	8	9	4	3	1
W Total	3	3	0	2.77	3	3	2	0	0	26	20	8	8	11
• PIZARRO, Juan														
L 1974	Pit-N	0	0	0.00	1	0	0	0	0	0^2	0	0	1	0
W 1957	Mil-N	0	0	10.80	1	0	0	0	0	1^2	3	2	2	1
W 1958	Mil-N	0	0	5.40	1	0	0	0	0	1^2	2	1	1	3
W Total	2	0	0	8.10	2	0	0	0	0	3^1	5	3	3	4
• PLANK, Eddie														
W 1905	Phi-A	0	2	1.59	2	2	2	0	0	17	15	3	4	11
W 1911	Phi-A	1	1	1.86	2	1	1	0	0	9^2	6	2	0	8
W 1913	Phi-A	1	1	0.95	2	2	2	0	0	19	9	2	3	7
W 1914	Phi-A	0	1	1.00	1	1	1	0	0	9	7	1	4	6
W Total	4	2	5	1.32	7	6	6	0	0	54^2	37	8	11	32
• PLEIS, Bill														
W 1965	Min-A	0	0	9.00	1	0	0	0	0	1	2	1	0	0
• PLESAC, Dan														
D 1999	Ari-N	0	0	54.00	1	0	0	0	0	0^1	3	2	0	0
• PLUNK, Eric														
D 1995	Cle-A	0	0	0.00	1	0	0	0	0	1^1	1	0	1	1
D 1996	Cle-A	0	1	6.75	3	0	0	0	0	4	1	3	2	6
D 1997	Cle-A	0	1	27.00	1	0	0	0	0	1^1	4	4	0	1
D Total	3	0	2	9.45	5	0	0	0	0	6^2	6	7	3	8
L 1988	Oak-A	0	0	0.00	1	0	0	0	0	0^1	1	0	0	1
L 1995	Cle-A	0	0	9.00	3	0	0	0	0	2	1	2	3	2
L 1997	Cle-A	1	0	0.00	1	0	0	0	0	0^2	1	0	0	0
L Total	3	1	0	6.00	5	0	0	0	0	3	3	2	3	3
W 1988	Oak-A	0	0	0.00	2	0	0	0	0	1^2	0	0	0	3
W 1997	Cle-A	0	1	9.00	3	0	0	0	0	3	3	3	4	3
W Total	2	0	1	5.79	5	0	0	0	0	4^2	3	3	4	6
• PODRES, Johnny														
W 1953	Bro-N	0	1	3.38	1	1	0	0	0	2^2	1	1	2	0
W 1955	Bro-N	2	0	1.00	2	2	2	0	1	18	15	2	4	10
W 1959	LA-N	1	0	4.82	2	2	0	0	0	9^1	7	5	6	4
W 1963	LA-N	1	0	1.08	1	1	0	0	0	8^1	6	1	1	4
W Total	4	4	1	2.11	6	6	2	0	1	38^1	29	9	13	18
• POLE, Dick														
W 1975	Bos-A	0	0	....	1	0	0	0	0	0	0	1	2	0
• POLLET, Howie														
W 1942	StL-N	0	0	0.00	1	0	0	0	0	0^1	0	0	0	0
W 1946	StL-N	0	1	3.48	2	2	1	0	0	10^1	12	4	4	3
W Total	2	0	1	3.38	3	2	1	0	0	10^2	12	4	4	3
• PONSON, Sidney														
D 2003	SF-N	0	0	7.20	1	1	0	0	0	5	7	4	0	3
• POOLE, Jim														
D 1995	Cle-A	0	0	5.40	1	0	0	0	0	1^2	2	1	1	2
D 1998	Cle-A	0	0	0.00	2	0	0	0	0	1	1	0	1	2
D Total	2	0	0	3.38	3	0	0	0	0	2^2	3	1	2	4
L 1995	Cle-A	0	0	0.00	1	0	0	0	0	1	0	0	0	2
L 1998	Cle-A	0	0	0.00	4	0	0	0	0	1^1	0	0	1	2
L Total	2	0	0	0.00	5	0	0	0	0	2^1	0	0	1	4
W 1995	Cle-A	0	1	3.86	2	0	0	0	0	2^1	1	1	0	1
• PORTUGAL, Mark														
L 1995	Cin-N	0	1	36.00	1	0	0	0	0	1	3	4	1	0

YEAR	TM-L	W	L	ERA	G	GS	CG	SV	SHO	IP	H	ER	BB	SO
• POTTER, Nels														
W 1944	StL-A	0	1	0.93	2	2	0	0	0	9^2	10	1	3	6
W 1948	Bos-N	0	0	8.44	2	1	0	0	0	5^1	6	5	2	1
W Total	2	0	1	3.60	4	3	0	0	0	15	16	6	5	7
• POWELL, Jay														
D 1998	Hou-N	0	0	11.57	3	0	0	0	0	2^1	2	3	3	3
D 1999	Hou-N	0	1	6.00	3	0	0	0	0	3	3	2	1	3
D Total	2	0	1	8.44	6	0	0	0	0	5^1	5	5	4	6
L 1997	Fla-N	0	0	0.00	1	0	0	0	0	0^2	0	0	0	1
W 1997	Fla-N	1	0	7.36	4	0	0	0	0	3^2	5	3	4	2
• POWER, Ted														
L 1990	Pit-N	0	0	3.60	3	1	0	1	0	5	6	2	2	3
• PRICE, Joe														
L 1987	SF-N	1	0	0.00	2	0	0	0	0	5^2	3	0	1	7
• PRIM, Ray														
W 1945	Chi-N	0	1	9.00	2	1	0	0	0	4	4	4	1	1
• PRIOR, Mark														
D 2003	Chi-N	1	0	1.00	1	1	1	0	0	9	2	1	4	7
L 2003	Chi-N	1	1	3.14	2	2	0	0	0	14^1	14	5	5	11
• PURKEY, Bob														
W 1961	Cin-N	0	1	1.64	2	1	1	0	0	11	6	2	3	5
• QUINN, Jack														
W 1921	NY-A	0	1	9.82	1	0	0	0	0	3^2	8	4	2	2
W 1929	Phi-A	0	0	9.00	1	1	0	0	0	5	7	5	2	2
W 1930	Phi-A	0	0	4.50	1	0	0	0	0	2	3	1	0	1
W Total	3	0	1	8.44	3	1	0	0	0	10^2	18	10	4	5
• QUISENBERRY, Dan														
D 1981	KC-A	0	0	0.00	1	0	0	0	0	0^1	1	0	0	0
L 1980	KC-A	1	0	0.00	2	0	0	1	0	4^2	4	0	2	1
L 1984	KC-A	0	1	3.00	1	0	0	0	0	3	2	1	1	1
L 1985	KC-A	0	1	3.86	4	0	0	1	0	4^2	7	2	0	3
L Total	3	1	2	2.19	7	0	0	2	0	12^1	13	3	3	5
W 1980	KC-A	1	2	5.23	6	0	0	1	0	10^1	10	6	3	0
W 1985	KC-A	1	0	2.08	4	0	0	0	0	4^1	5	1	3	3
W Total	2	2	2	4.30	10	0	0	1	0	14^2	15	7	6	3
• RADBOURN, Charley														
W 1884	Pro-N	3	0	0.00	3	3	3	0	1	22	11	0	0	17
• RADINSKY, Scott														
D 1996	LA-N	0	0	0.00	2	0	0	0	0	1^1	0	0	1	2
L 1993	Chi-A	0	0	10.80	4	0	0	0	0	1^2	3	2	1	1
• RADKE, Brad														
D 2002	Min-A	2	0	1.54	2	2	0	0	0	11^2	14	2	1	7
D 2003	Min-A	0	1	2.84	1	1	0	0	0	6^1	5	2	2	4
D Total	2	2	1	2.00	3	3	0	0	0	18	19	4	3	11
L 2002	Min-A	0	1	2.70	1	1	0	0	0	6^2	5	2	1	4
• RAMSAY, Robert														
L 2000	Sea-A	0	0	0.00	2	0	0	0	0	1^2	2	0	0	1
• RAPP, Pat														
L 1999	Bos-A	0	0	0.00	1	0	0	0	0	1	0	0	1	0
• RASCHI, Vic														
W 1947	NY-A	0	0	6.75	2	0	0	0	0	1^1	2	1	0	1
W 1949	NY-A	1	1	4.30	2	2	0	0	0	14^2	15	7	5	11
W 1950	NY-A	1	0	0.00	1	1	1	0	1	9	2	0	1	5
W 1951	NY-A	1	1	0.87	2	2	0	0	0	10^1	12	1	8	4
W 1952	NY-A	2	0	1.59	3	2	1	0	0	17	12	3	8	18
W 1953	NY-A	0	1	3.38	1	1	1	0	0	8	9	3	3	4
W Total	6	5	3	2.24	11	8	3	0	1	60^1	52	15	25	43
• RAU, Doug														
L 1974	LA-N	0	1	40.50	1	1	0	0	0	0^2	3	3	1	0
L 1977	LA-N	0	0	0.00	1	0	0	0	0	1	0	0	0	1
L 1978	LA-N	0	0	3.60	1	1	0	0	0	5	5	2	2	1
L Total	3	0	1	6.75	3	2	0	0	0	6^2	8	5	3	2
W 1977	LA-N	0	1	11.57	2	1	0	0	0	2^1	4	3	0	1
W 1978	LA-N	0	0	0.00	1	0	0	0	0	2	1	0	0	3
W Total	2	0	1	6.23	3	1	0	0	0	4^1	5	3	0	4
• RAUTZHAN, Lance														
L 1977	LA-N	1	0	0.00	1	0	0	0	0	0^1	0	0	0	0
L 1978	LA-N	0	0	6.75	1	0	0	0	0	1^1	3	1	2	0
L Total	2	1	0	5.40	2	0	0	0	0	1^2	3	1	2	0
W 1977	LA-N	0	0	0.00	1	0	0	0	0	0^1	0	0	2	0
W 1978	LA-N	0	0	13.50	2	0	0	0	0	2	4	3	0	0
W Total	2	0	0	11.57	3	0	0	0	0	2^1	4	3	2	0
• REAMES, Britt														
D 2000	StL-N	1	0	0.00	2	0	0	0	0	3^1	0	0	3	2
L 2000	StL-N	0	0	1.42	2	0	0	0	0	6^1	5	1	4	6
• REARDON, Jeff														
D 1981	Mon-N	0	1	2.08	3	0	0	2	0	4^1	1	1	1	2
L 1981	Mon-N	0	0	27.00	1	0	0	0	0	1	3	3	0	0
L 1987	Min-A	1	1	5.06	4	0	0	2	0	5^1	7	3	3	5
L 1990	Bos-A	0	0	9.00	1	0	0	0	0	2	3	2	1	0
L 1992	Atl-N	1	0	0.00	3	0	0	1	0	3	0	0	2	3
L Total	4	2	1	6.35	9	0	0	3	0	11^1	13	8	6	8
W 1987	Min-A	0	0	0.00	4	0	0	1	0	4^2	5	0	0	3
W 1992	Atl-N	0	1	13.50	2	0	0	0	0	1^1	2	2	1	1
W Total	2	0	1	3.00	6	0	0	1	0	6	7	2	1	4

YEAR	TM-L	W	L	ERA	G	GS	CG	SV	SHO	IP	H	ER	BB	SO
• REDMAN, Mark														
D 2003	Fla-N	0	0	3.00	1	1	0	0	0	6	7	2	3	4
L 2003	Fla-N	0	0	6.52	2	2	0	0	0	9^2	13	7	4	4
W 2003	Fla-N	0	1	15.43	1	1	0	0	0	2^1	5	4	2	2
• REED, Howie														
W 1965	LA-N	0	0	8.10	2	0	0	0	0	3^1	2	3	2	4
• REED, Rick														
D 1999	NY-N	1	0	3.00	1	1	0	0	0	6	4	2	3	2
D 2000	NY-N	0	0	3.00	1	1	0	0	0	6	7	2	2	6
D 2002	Min-A	0	1	7.20	1	1	0	0	0	5	6	4	2	8
D 2003	Min-A	0	0	0.00	1	0	0	0	0	0^2	1	0	0	0
D Total	4	1	1	4.08	4	3	0	0	0	17^2	18	8	7	16
L 1999	NY-N	0	0	2.57	1	1	0	0	0	7	3	2	0	5
L 2000	NY-N	0	1	10.80	1	1	0	0	0	3^1	8	4	1	4
L 2002	Min-A	0	1	10.13	1	1	0	0	0	5^1	8	6	0	0
L Total	3	0	2	6.89	3	3	0	0	0	15^2	19	12	1	9
W 2000	NY-N	0	0	3.00	1	1	0	0	0	6	6	2	1	8
• REED, Ron														
D 1981	Phi-N	0	0	3.00	4	0	0	0	0	6	5	2	3	4
L 1969	Atl-N	0	1	21.60	1	1	0	0	0	1^2	5	4	3	3
L 1976	Phi-N	0	0	7.71	2	0	0	0	0	4^2	6	4	2	2
L 1977	Phi-N	0	0	1.80	3	0	0	0	0	5	3	1	2	5
L 1978	Phi-N	0	0	2.25	2	0	0	0	0	4	6	1	0	2
L 1980	Phi-N	0	1	18.00	3	0	0	0	0	2	3	4	1	1
L 1983	Phi-N	0	0	2.70	2	0	0	0	0	3^1	4	1	1	3
L Total	6	0	2	6.53	13	1	0	0	0	20^2	27	15	9	16
W 1980	Phi-N	0	0	0.00	2	0	0	1	0	2	2	0	0	2
W 1983	Phi-N	0	0	2.70	3	0	0	0	0	3^1	4	1	2	4
W Total	2	0	0	1.69	5	0	0	1	0	5^1	6	1	2	6
• REED, Steve														
D 1995	Col-N	0	0	0.00	3	0	0	0	0	2^2	2	0	1	3
D 1998	Cle-A	1	0	40.50	2	0	0	0	0	0^2	1	3	1	1
D 1999	Cle-A	0	0	30.86	2	0	0	0	0	2^1	9	8	1	1
D 2001	Atl-N	0	0	0.00	1	0	0	0	0	0^1	0	0	0	0
D Total	4	1	0	16.50	8	0	0	0	0	6	12	11	3	5
L 1998	Cle-A	0	0	0.00	3	0	0	0	0	1^2	0	0	1	0
L 2001	Atl-N	0	0	....	1	0	0	0	0	0	0	0	0	0
L Total	2	0	0	0.00	4	0	0	0	0	1^2	0	0	1	0
• REGAN, Phil														
W 1966	LA-N	0	0	0.00	2	0	0	0	0	1^2	0	0	1	2
• REINHART, Art														
W 1926	StL-N	0	1	....	1	0	0	0	0	0	1	4	4	0
• REMLINGER, Mike														
D 1999	Atl-N	0	0	9.82	2	0	0	0	0	3^2	4	4	3	4
D 2000	Atl-N	0	0	2.70	3	0	0	0	0	3^1	6	1	0	3
D 2001	Atl-N	0	0	0.00	1	0	0	0	0	0^1	0	0	0	0
D 2002	Atl-N	0	0	4.50	3	0	0	0	0	2	3	1	2	3
D 2003	Chi-N	0	0	0.00	2	0	0	0	0	0^2	0	0	1	1
D Total	5	0	0	5.40	11	0	0	0	0	10	13	6	6	11
L 1999	Atl-N	0	1	3.18	5	0	0	0	0	5^2	3	2	3	4
L 2001	Atl-N	0	0	0.00	3	0	0	0	0	2^1	3	0	2	2
L 2003	Chi-N	0	0	2.70	5	0	0	1	0	3^1	3	1	1	2
L Total	3	0	1	2.38	13	0	0	1	0	11^1	9	3	6	8
W 1999	Atl-N	0	1	9.00	2	0	0	0	0	1	1	1	1	0
• RENIFF, Hal														
W 1963	NY-A	0	0	0.00	3	0	0	0	0	3	0	0	1	1
W 1964	NY-A	0	0	0.00	1	0	0	0	0	0^1	2	0	0	0
W Total	2	0	0	0.00	4	0	0	0	0	3^1	2	0	1	1
• REULBACH, Ed														
W 1906	Chi-N	1	0	2.45	2	2	1	0	0	11	6	3	8	4
W 1907	Chi-N	1	0	0.75	2	1	1	0	0	12	6	1	3	4
W 1908	Chi-N	0	0	4.70	2	1	0	0	0	7^2	9	4	1	5
W 1910	Chi-N	0	0	9.00	1	1	0	0	0	2	3	2	2	0
W Total	4	2	0	2.76	7	5	2	0	0	32^2	24	10	14	13
• REUSCHEL, Rick														
D 1981	NY-A	0	1	3.00	1	1	0	0	0	6	4	2	1	3
L 1987	SF-N	0	1	6.30	2	2	0	0	0	10	15	7	2	2
L 1989	SF-N	1	1	5.19	2	2	0	0	0	8^2	12	5	2	5
L Total	2	1	2	5.79	4	4	0	0	0	18^2	27	12	4	7
W 1981	NY-A	0	0	4.91	2	1	0	0	0	3^2	7	2	3	2
W 1989	SF-N	0	1	11.25	1	1	0	0	0	4	5	5	4	2
W Total	2	0	1	8.22	3	2	0	0	0	7^2	12	7	7	4
• REUSS, Jerry														
D 1981	LA-N	1	0	0.00	2	2	1	0	1	18	10	0	5	7
L 1974	Pit-N	0	2	3.72	2	2	0	0	0	9^2	7	4	8	3
L 1975	Pit-N	0	1	13.50	1	1	0	0	0	2^2	4	4	4	1
L 1981	LA-N	0	1	5.14	1	1	0	0	0	7	7	4	1	2
L 1983	LA-N	0	2	4.50	2	2	0	0	0	12	14	6	3	4
L 1985	LA-N	0	1	10.80	1	1	0	0	0	1^2	5	2	1	0
L Total	5	0	7	5.45	7	7	0	0	0	33	37	20	17	10
W 1981	LA-N	1	1	3.86	2	2	1	0	0	11^2	10	5	3	8
• REYNOLDS, Allie														
W 1947	NY-A	1	0	4.76	2	2	1	0	0	11^1	15	6	3	6
W 1949	NY-A	1	0	0.00	2	1	1	1	1	12^1	2	0	4	14
W 1950	NY-A	1	0	0.87	2	1	1	1	0	10^1	7	1	4	7
W 1951	NY-A	1	1	4.20	2	2	1	0	0	15	16	7	11	8
W 1952	NY-A	2	1	1.77	4	2	1	1	1	20^1	12	4	6	18
W 1953	NY-A	1	0	6.75	3	1	0	1	0	8	9	6	4	9
W Total	6	7	2	2.79	15	9	5	4	2	77^1	61	24	32	62

YEAR	TM-L	W	L	ERA	G	GS	CG	SV	SHO	IP	H	ER	BB	SO
• REYNOLDS, Bob														
L 1973	Bal-A	0	0	3.18	2	0	0	0	0	5^{2}	5	2	3	5
L 1974	Bal-A	0	0	0.00	1	0	0	0	0	1^{1}	0	0	3	1
L Total	**2**	**0**	**0**	**2.57**	**3**	**0**	**0**	**0**	**0**	**7**	**5**	**2**	**6**	**6**
• REYNOLDS, Shane														
D 1997	Hou-N	0	1	3.00	1	1	0	0	0	6	5	2	1	5
D 1998	Hou-N	0	0	2.57	1	1	0	0	0	7	4	2	1	5
D 1999	Hou-N	1	1	4.09	2	2	0	0	0	11	16	5	3	5
D 2001	Hou-N	0	1	9.00	1	1	0	0	0	4	6	4	1	1
D Total	**4**	**1**	**3**	**4.18**	**5**	**5**	**0**	**0**	**0**	**28**	**31**	**13**	**6**	**16**
• REYNOSO, Armando														
D 1995	Col-N	0	0	0.00	1	0	0	0	0	1	2	0	0	0
• RHEM, Flint														
W 1926	StL-N	0	0	6.75	1	1	0	0	0	4	7	3	2	4
W 1928	StL-N	0	0	0.00	1	0	0	0	0	2	0	0	0	1
W 1930	StL-N	0	1	10.80	1	1	0	0	0	3^{1}	7	4	2	3
W 1931	StL-N	0	0	0.00	1	0	0	0	0	1	1	0	0	1
W Total	**4**	**0**	**1**	**6.10**	**4**	**2**	**0**	**0**	**0**	**10^{1}**	**15**	**7**	**4**	**9**
• RHODEN, Rick														
L 1977	LA-N	0	0	0.00	1	0	0	0	0	4^{1}	2	0	2	0
L 1978	LA-N	0	0	2.25	1	0	0	0	0	4	2	1	1	3
L Total	**2**	**0**	**0**	**1.08**	**2**	**0**	**0**	**0**	**0**	**8^{1}**	**4**	**1**	**3**	**3**
W 1977	LA-N	0	1	2.57	2	0	0	0	0	7	4	2	1	5
• RHODES, Arthur														
D 1996	Bal-A	0	0	9.00	2	0	0	0	0	1	1	1	1	1
D 1997	Bal-A	0	0	0.00	1	0	0	0	0	2^{1}	0	0	0	4
D 2000	Sea-A	0	0	0.00	3	0	0	0	0	2^{2}	0	0	2	2
D 2001	Sea-A	0	0	0.00	3	0	0	0	0	2^{2}	1	0	0	1
D Total	**4**	**0**	**0**	**1.04**	**9**	**0**	**0**	**0**	**0**	**8^{2}**	**2**	**1**	**3**	**8**
L 1996	Bal-A	0	0	0.00	3	0	0	0	0	2	2	0	0	2
L 1997	Bal-A	0	0	0.00	2	0	0	0	0	2^{1}	2	0	3	2
L 2000	Sea-A	0	1	31.50	4	0	0	0	0	2	8	7	4	5
L 2001	Sea-A	0	0	4.50	2	0	0	0	0	2	2	1	0	2
L Total	**4**	**0**	**1**	**8.64**	**11**	**0**	**0**	**0**	**0**	**8^{1}**	**14**	**8**	**7**	**11**
• RICHARDSON, Gordie														
W 1964	StL-N	0	0	40.50	2	0	0	0	0	0^{2}	3	3	2	0
• RICHERT, Pete														
L 1969	Bal-A	0	0	0.00	1	0	0	0	0	1	0	0	2	2
W 1969	Bal-A	0	0	....	1	0	0	0	0	0	0	0	0	0
W 1970	Bal-A	0	0	0.00	1	0	0	1	0	0^{1}	0	0	0	0
W 1971	Bal-A	0	0	0.00	1	0	0	0	0	0^{2}	0	0	0	1
W Total	**3**	**0**	**0**	**0.00**	**3**	**0**	**0**	**1**	**0**	**1**	**0**	**0**	**0**	**1**
• RICHIE, Lew														
W 1910	Chi-N	0	0	0.00	1	0	0	0	0	1	1	0	0	0
• RIDDLE, Elmer														
W 1940	Cin-N	0	0	0.00	1	0	0	0	0	1	0	0	0	2
• RIGHETTI, Dave														
D 1981	NY-A	2	0	1.00	2	1	0	0	0	9	8	1	3	13
L 1981	NY-A	1	0	0.00	1	1	0	0	0	6	4	0	2	4
W 1981	NY-A	0	0	13.50	1	1	0	0	0	2	5	3	2	1
• RIJO, Jose														
L 1990	Cin-N	1	0	4.38	2	2	0	0	0	12^{1}	10	6	7	15
W 1990	Cin-N	2	0	0.59	2	2	0	0	0	15^{1}	9	1	5	14
• RINCON, Juan														
D 2003	Min-A	0	0	0.00	3	0	0	0	0	2^{1}	1	0	4	1
• RINCON, Ricardo														
D 1999	Cle-A	0	0	40.50	1	0	0	0	0	0^{2}	2	3	1	1
D 2001	Cle-A	0	0	9.00	3	0	0	0	0	2	2	2	0	3
D 2002	Oak-A	0	0	0.00	2	0	0	0	0	3	2	0	0	2
D 2003	Oak-A	0	0	4.50	4	0	0	0	0	4	4	2	1	3
D Total	**4**	**0**	**0**	**6.52**	**10**	**0**	**0**	**0**	**0**	**9^{2}**	**10**	**7**	**2**	**9**
• RING, Jimmy														
W 1919	Cin-N	1	1	0.64	2	1	1	0	1	14	7	1	6	4
• RISKE, David														
D 2001	Cle-A	0	0	0.00	3	0	0	0	0	3^{2}	2	0	1	5
• RISLEY, Bill														
D 1995	Sea-A	0	0	6.00	4	0	0	1	0	3	2	2	0	1
L 1995	Sea-A	0	0	0.00	3	0	0	0	0	2^{2}	2	0	1	2
• RITZ, Kevin														
D 1995	Col-N	0	0	7.71	2	1	0	0	0	7	12	6	3	5
• RIVERA, Ben														
L 1993	Phi-N	0	0	4.50	1	0	0	0	0	2	1	1	1	2
W 1993	Phi-N	0	0	27.00	1	0	0	0	0	1^{1}	4	4	2	3
• RIVERA, Mariano														
D 1995	NY-A	1	0	0.00	3	0	0	0	0	5^{1}	3	0	1	8
D 1996	NY-A	0	0	0.00	2	0	0	0	0	4^{2}	0	0	1	1
D 1997	NY-A	0	0	4.50	2	0	0	1	0	2	2	1	0	1
D 1998	NY-A	0	0	0.00	3	0	0	2	0	3^{1}	1	0	1	2
D 1999	NY-A	0	0	0.00	2	0	0	2	0	3	1	0	0	3
D 2000	NY-A	0	0	0.00	3	0	0	3	0	5	2	0	0	2
D 2001	NY-A	0	0	0.00	3	0	0	2	0	5	4	0	0	4
D 2002	NY-A	0	0	0.00	1	0	0	1	0	1	1	0	0	0
D 2003	NY-A	0	0	0.00	2	0	0	2	0	4	0	0	0	4
D Total	**9**	**1**	**0**	**0.27**	**21**	**0**	**0**	**13**	**0**	**33^{1}**	**14**	**1**	**3**	**25**
L 1996	NY-A	1	0	0.00	2	0	0	0	0	4	6	0	1	5
L 1998	NY-A	0	0	0.00	4	0	0	1	0	5^{2}	0	0	1	5
L 1999	NY-A	1	0	0.00	3	0	0	2	0	4^{2}	5	0	0	3
L 2000	NY-A	0	0	1.93	3	0	0	1	0	4^{2}	4	1	0	1
L 2001	NY-A	1	0	1.93	4	0	0	2	0	4^{2}	2	1	1	3
L 2003	NY-A	1	0	1.13	4	0	0	2	0	8	5	1	0	6
L Total	**6**	**4**	**0**	**0.85**	**20**	**0**	**0**	**8**	**0**	**31^{2}**	**22**	**3**	**3**	**23**
W 1996	NY-A	0	0	1.59	4	0	0	0	0	5^{2}	4	1	3	4
W 1998	NY-A	0	0	0.00	3	0	0	3	0	4^{1}	5	0	0	4
W 1999	NY-A	1	0	0.00	3	0	0	2	0	4^{2}	3	0	1	3
W 2000	NY-A	0	0	3.00	4	0	0	2	0	6	4	2	1	7
W 2001	NY-A	1	1	1.42	4	0	0	1	0	6^{1}	6	1	1	7
W 2003	NY-A	0	0	0.00	2	0	0	1	0	4	2	0	0	4
W Total	**6**	**2**	**1**	**1.16**	**20**	**0**	**0**	**9**	**0**	**31**	**24**	**4**	**6**	**29**
• RIXEY, Eppa														
W 1915	Phi-N	0	1	4.05	1	0	0	0	0	6^{2}	4	3	2	2
• ROBERTS, Dave														
L 1979	Pit-N	0	0	....	1	0	0	0	0	0	0	0	1	0
• ROBERTS, Robin														
W 1950	Phi-N	0	1	1.64	2	1	1	0	0	11	11	2	3	5
• ROBINSON, Don														
L 1979	Pit-N	1	0	0.00	2	0	0	1	0	2	0	0	1	3
L 1987	SF-N	0	1	9.00	3	0	0	0	0	3	3	3	0	3
L 1989	SF-N	1	0	0.00	1	0	0	0	0	1^{2}	3	0	0	0
L Total	**3**	**2**	**1**	**4.05**	**6**	**0**	**0**	**1**	**0**	**6^{2}**	**6**	**3**	**1**	**6**
W 1979	Pit-N	1	0	5.40	4	0	0	0	0	5	4	3	6	3
W 1989	SF-N	0	1	21.60	1	1	0	0	0	1^{2}	4	4	1	0
W Total	**2**	**1**	**1**	**9.45**	**5**	**1**	**0**	**0**	**0**	**6^{2}**	**8**	**7**	**7**	**3**
• ROBINSON, Jeff														
L 1987	Det-A	0	0	0.00	1	0	0	0	0	0^{1}	1	0	0	0
• ROCKER, John														
D 1998	Atl-N	0	0	0.00	2	0	0	0	0	1^{1}	1	0	0	2
D 1999	Atl-N	1	0	0.00	2	0	0	1	0	3^{1}	0	0	2	5
D 2000	Atl-N	0	0	0.00	1	0	0	0	0	0^{2}	0	0	1	0
D 2001	Cle-A	0	0	0.00	1	0	0	0	0	1	1	0	0	1
D Total	**4**	**1**	**0**	**0.00**	**6**	**0**	**0**	**1**	**0**	**6^{1}**	**2**	**0**	**3**	**8**
L 1998	Atl-N	1	0	0.00	6	0	0	0	0	4^{2}	3	0	1	5
L 1999	Atl-N	0	0	0.00	6	0	0	2	0	6^{2}	3	0	2	9
L Total	**2**	**1**	**0**	**0.00**	**12**	**0**	**0**	**2**	**0**	**11^{1}**	**6**	**0**	**3**	**14**
W 1999	Atl-N	0	0	0.00	2	0	0	0	0	3	2	0	2	4
• RODRIGUEZ, Felix														
D 2000	SF-N	0	1	6.23	3	0	0	0	0	4^{1}	6	3	1	6
D 2002	SF-N	0	0	0.00	3	0	0	0	0	3	1	0	2	2
D 2003	SF-N	0	1	2.25	3	0	0	0	0	4	4	1	1	5
D Total	**3**	**0**	**2**	**3.18**	**9**	**0**	**0**	**0**	**0**	**11^{1}**	**11**	**4**	**4**	**13**
L 2002	SF-N	0	0	1.93	4	0	0	0	0	4^{2}	3	1	2	2
W 2002	SF-N	0	1	4.76	6	0	0	0	0	5^{2}	4	3	1	3
• RODRIGUEZ, Francisco														
D 2002	Ana-A	2	0	3.18	3	0	0	0	0	5^{2}	2	2	2	8
L 2002	Ana-A	2	0	0.00	4	0	0	0	0	4^{1}	2	0	2	7
W 2002	Ana-A	1	1	2.08	4	0	0	0	0	8^{2}	6	2	1	13
• RODRIGUEZ, Rich														
D 1997	SF-N	0	0	0.00	2	0	0	0	0	1	1	0	0	0
• RODRIGUEZ, Rosario														
L 1991	Pit-N	0	0	27.00	1	0	0	0	0	1	1	3	2	1
• ROE, Preacher														
W 1949	Bro-N	1	0	0.00	1	1	1	0	1	9	6	0	0	3
W 1952	Bro-N	1	0	3.18	3	1	1	0	0	11^{1}	9	4	6	7
W 1953	Bro-N	0	1	4.50	1	1	1	0	0	8	5	4	4	4
W Total	**3**	**2**	**1**	**2.54**	**5**	**3**	**3**	**0**	**1**	**28^{1}**	**20**	**8**	**10**	**14**
• ROEBUCK, Ed														
W 1955	Bro-N	0	0	0.00	1	0	0	0	0	2	1	0	0	0
W 1956	Bro-N	0	0	2.08	3	0	0	0	0	4^{1}	1	1	0	5
W Total	**2**	**0**	**0**	**1.42**	**4**	**0**	**0**	**0**	**0**	**6^{1}**	**2**	**1**	**0**	**5**
• ROGERS, Kenny														
D 1996	NY-A	0	0	9.00	2	1	0	0	0	2	5	2	2	1
D 1999	NY-N	0	1	8.31	1	1	0	0	0	4^{1}	5	4	2	6
D 2003	Min-A	0	0	0.00	1	0	0	0	0	1^{1}	1	0	1	3
D Total	**3**	**0**	**1**	**7.04**	**4**	**2**	**0**	**0**	**0**	**7^{2}**	**11**	**6**	**5**	**10**
L 1996	NY-A	0	0	12.00	1	1	0	0	0	3	5	4	2	3
L 1999	NY-N	0	2	5.87	3	1	0	0	0	7^{2}	11	5	7	2
L Total	**2**	**0**	**2**	**7.59**	**4**	**2**	**0**	**0**	**0**	**10^{2}**	**16**	**9**	**9**	**5**
W 1996	NY-A	0	0	22.50	1	1	0	0	0	2	5	5	2	0
• ROGERS, Steve														
D 1981	Mon-N	2	0	0.51	2	2	1	0	1	17^{2}	16	1	3	5
L 1981	Mon-N	1	1	1.80	2	1	1	0	0	10	8	2	1	6
• ROGERS, Tom														
W 1921	NY-A	0	0	6.75	1	0	0	0	0	1^{1}	3	1	0	1
• ROMERO, J.C.														
D 2002	Min-A	0	0	0.00	3	0	0	0	0	3^{1}	3	0	1	2
D 2003	Min-A	0	0	0.00	3	0	0	0	0	3^{1}	3	0	2	1
D Total	**2**	**0**	**0**	**0.00**	**6**	**0**	**0**	**0**	**0**	**6^{2}**	**6**	**0**	**3**	**3**
L 2002	Min-A	0	1	22.50	4	0	0	0	0	2	4	5	2	3
• ROMMEL, Eddie														
W 1929	Phi-A	1	0	9.00	1	0	0	0	0	1	2	1	1	0
W 1931	Phi-A	0	0	9.00	1	0	0	0	0	1	3	1	0	0
W Total	**2**	**1**	**0**	**9.00**	**2**	**0**	**0**	**0**	**0**	**2**	**5**	**2**	**1**	**0**
• ROMO, Enrique														
L 1979	Pit-N	0	0	0.00	2	0	0	0	0	0^{1}	3	0	1	1
W 1979	Pit-N	0	0	3.86	2	0	0	0	0	4^{2}	5	2	3	4

YEAR	TM-L	W	L	ERA	G	GS	CG	SV	SHO	IP	H	ER	BB	SO
• ROOKER, Jim														
L 1974	Pit-N	0	0	2.57	1	1	0	0	0	7	6	2	5	4
L 1975	Pit-N	0	1	9.00	1	1	0	0	0	4	7	4	0	4
L Total	2	0	1	4.91	2	2	0	0	0	11	13	6	5	8
W 1979	Pit-N	0	0	1.04	2	1	0	0	0	8²	5	1	3	4
• ROOT, Charley														
W 1929	Chi-N	0	1	4.73	2	2	0	0	0	13¹	12	7	2	8
W 1932	Chi-N	0	1	10.38	1	1	0	0	0	4¹	6	5	3	4
W 1935	Chi-N	0	1	18.00	2	1	0	0	0	2	5	4	1	2
W 1938	Chi-N	0	0	3.00	1	0	0	0	0	3	3	1	0	1
W Total	4	0	3	6.75	6	4	0	0	0	22²	26	17	6	15
• ROWE, Schoolboy														
W 1934	Det-A	1	1	2.95	3	2	2	0	0	21¹	19	7	0	12
W 1935	Det-A	1	2	2.57	3	2	2	0	0	21	19	6	1	14
W 1940	Det-A	0	2	17.18	2	2	0	0	0	3²	12	7	1	1
W Total	3	2	5	3.91	8	6	4	0	0	46	50	20	2	27
• RUCKER, Nap														
W 1916	Bro-N	0	0	0.00	1	0	0	0	0	2	1	0	0	3
• RUDOLPH, Dick														
W 1914	Bos-N	2	0	0.50	2	2	2	0	0	18	12	1	4	15
• RUETER, Kirk														
D 1997	SF-N	0	0	1.29	1	1	0	0	0	7	4	1	3	5
D 2000	SF-N	0	0	0.00	1	0	0	0	0	4¹	3	0	1	1
D 2002	SF-N	0	1	18.00	1	1	0	0	0	3	7	6	2	1
D 2003	SF-N	0	0	3.60	1	1	0	0	0	5	3	2	2	2
D Total	4	0	1	4.19	4	3	0	0	0	19¹	17	9	8	9
L 2002	SF-N	1	0	4.09	2	2	0	0	0	11	15	5	2	3
W 2002	SF-N	0	0	2.70	2	1	0	0	0	10	10	3	1	5
• RUETHER, Dutch														
W 1919	Cin-N	1	0	2.57	2	2	1	0	0	14	12	4	4	1
W 1926	NY-A	0	1	8.31	1	1	0	0	0	4¹	7	4	2	1
W Total	2	1	1	3.93	3	3	1	0	0	18¹	19	8	6	2
• RUFFIN, Bruce														
D 1995	Col-N	0	0	2.70	4	0	0	0	0	3¹	3	1	2	2
• RUFFING, Red														
W 1932	NY-A	1	0	3.00	1	1	1	0	0	9	10	3	6	10
W 1936	NY-A	0	1	5.14	2	2	1	0	0	14	16	8	5	12
W 1937	NY-A	1	0	1.00	1	1	1	0	0	9	7	1	3	8
W 1938	NY-A	2	0	1.50	2	2	2	0	0	18	17	3	2	11
W 1939	NY-A	1	0	1.00	1	1	1	0	0	9	4	1	1	4
W 1941	NY-A	1	0	1.00	1	1	1	0	0	9	6	1	3	5
W 1942	NY-A	1	1	4.08	2	2	1	0	0	17²	14	8	7	11
W Total	7	7	2	2.63	10	10	8	0	0	85²	74	25	27	61
• RUHLE, Vern														
D 1981	Hou-N	0	1	2.25	1	1	1	0	0	8	4	2	2	1
L 1980	Hou-N	0	0	3.86	1	1	0	0	0	7	8	3	1	3
L 1986	Cal-A	0	0	13.50	1	0	0	0	0	0²	2	1	0	0
L Total	2	0	0	4.70	2	1	0	0	0	7²	10	4	1	3
• RUSCH, Glendon														
D 2000	NY-N	0	0	0.00	1	0	0	0	0	0²	0	0	0	2
L 2000	NY-N	1	0	0.00	2	0	0	0	0	3²	3	0	0	3
W 2000	NY-N	0	0	2.25	3	0	0	0	0	4	6	1	2	2
• RUSH, Bob														
W 1958	Mil-N	0	1	3.00	1	1	0	0	0	6	3	2	5	2
• RUSIE, Amos														
T 1894	NY-N	2	0	0.50	2	2	2	0	0	18	14	1	3	9
• RUSSELL, Allan														
W 1924	Was-A	0	0	3.00	1	0	0	0	0	3	4	1	0	0
• RUSSELL, Jack														
W 1933	Was-A	0	1	0.87	3	0	0	0	0	10¹	8	1	0	7
W 1938	Chi-N	0	0	0.00	2	0	0	0	0	1²	1	0	1	0
W Total	2	0	1	0.75	5	0	0	0	0	12	9	1	1	7
• RUSSELL, Jeff														
D 1996	Tex-A	0	0	3.00	2	0	0	0	0	3	3	1	0	1
L 1992	Oak-A	1	0	9.00	3	0	0	0	0	2	2	2	4	0
• RUSSELL, Reb														
W 1917	Chi-A	0	0	....	1	0	0	0	0	0	2	2	1	0
• RUSSO, Marius														
W 1941	NY-A	1	0	1.00	1	1	1	0	0	9	4	1	2	5
W 1943	NY-A	1	0	0.00	1	1	1	0	0	9	7	0	1	2
W Total	2	2	0	0.50	2	2	2	0	0	18	11	1	3	7
• RUTH, Babe														
W 1916	Bos-A	1	0	0.64	1	1	1	0	0	14	6	1	3	4
W 1918	Bos-A	2	0	1.06	2	2	1	0	1	17	13	2	7	4
W Total	2	3	0	0.87	3	3	2	0	1	31	19	3	10	8
• RUTHERFORD, Johnny														
W 1952	Bro-N	0	0	9.00	1	0	0	0	0	1	1	1	1	1
• RUTHVEN, Dick														
D 1981	Phi-N	0	1	4.50	1	1	0	0	0	4	3	2	1	0
L 1978	Phi-N	0	1	5.79	1	1	0	0	0	4²	6	3	0	3
L 1980	Phi-N	1	0	2.00	1	1	0	0	0	9	3	2	5	4
L Total	2	1	1	3.29	3	2	0	0	0	13²	9	5	5	7
W 1980	Phi-N	0	0	3.00	1	1	0	0	0	9	9	3	0	7
• RYAN, Jimmy														
W 1886	Chi-N	0	0	9.00	1	1	0	0	0	5	8	5	4	4
• RYAN, Nolan														
D 1981	Hou-N	1	1	1.80	2	2	1	0	0	15	6	3	3	14
D 1969	NY-N	1	0	2.57	1	0	0	0	0	7	3	2	2	7
L 1979	Cal-A	0	0	1.29	1	1	0	0	0	7	4	1	3	8
L 1980	Hou-N	0	0	5.40	2	2	0	0	0	13¹	16	8	3	14
L 1986	Hou-N	0	1	3.86	2	2	0	0	0	14	9	6	1	17
L Total	4	1	1	3.70	6	5	0	0	0	41¹	32	17	9	46
W 1969	NY-N	0	0	0.00	1	0	0	1	0	2¹	1	0	2	3
• RYAN, Rosy														
W 1922	NY-N	1	0	0.00	1	0	0	0	0	2	1	0	0	2
W 1923	NY-N	1	0	0.96	3	0	0	0	0	9¹	11	1	3	3
W 1924	NY-N	0	0	3.18	2	0	0	0	0	5²	7	2	4	3
W Total	3	2	0	1.59	6	0	0	0	0	17	19	3	7	8
• RYBA, Mike														
W 1946	Bos-A	0	0	13.50	1	0	0	0	0	0²	2	1	1	0
• SABATHIA, C.C.														
D 2001	Cle-A	1	0	3.00	1	1	0	0	0	6	6	2	5	5
• SABERHAGEN, Bret														
D 1995	Col-N	0	1	11.25	1	1	0	0	0	4	7	5	1	3
D 1998	Bos-A	0	1	3.86	1	1	0	0	0	7	4	3	1	7
D 1999	Bos-A	0	1	27.00	2	2	0	0	0	3²	9	11	4	2
D Total	3	0	3	11.66	4	4	0	0	0	14²	20	19	6	12
L 1985	KC-A	0	0	2.25	1	1	0	0	0	8	6	2	1	5
L 1985	KC-A	0	0	6.14	2	2	0	0	0	7¹	12	5	2	6
L 1999	Bos-A	0	1	1.50	1	1	0	0	0	6	5	1	1	5
L Total	3	0	1	3.38	4	4	0	0	0	21¹	23	8	4	16
W 1985	KC-A	2	0	0.50	2	2	2	0	0	18	11	1	1	10
• SADECKI, Ray														
W 1964	StL-N	1	0	8.53	2	2	0	0	0	6¹	12	6	5	2
W 1973	NY-N	0	0	1.93	4	0	0	0	0	4²	5	1	1	6
W Total	2	1	0	5.73	6	2	0	1	0	11	17	7	6	8
• SAIN, Johnny														
W 1948	Bos-N	1	1	1.06	2	2	2	0	1	17	9	2	0	9
W 1951	NY-A	0	0	9.00	1	0	0	0	0	2	4	2	2	2
W 1952	NY-A	0	1	3.00	1	0	0	0	0	6	6	2	3	3
W 1953	NY-A	1	0	4.76	2	0	0	0	0	5²	8	3	1	1
W Total	4	2	2	2.64	6	2	2	0	1	30²	27	9	6	15
• SALLEE, Slim														
W 1917	NY-N	0	2	5.28	2	2	1	0	0	15¹	20	9	4	4
W 1919	Cin-N	1	1	1.35	2	2	1	0	0	13¹	19	2	1	2
W Total	2	1	3	3.45	4	4	2	0	0	28²	39	11	5	6
• SAMBITO, Joe														
D 1981	Hou-N	0	0	16.20	2	0	0	0	0	1²	5	3	2	2
L 1980	Hou-N	0	1	4.91	3	0	0	0	0	3²	4	2	2	6
L 1986	Bos-A	0	0	0.00	3	0	0	0	0	0²	1	0	1	0
L Total	2	0	1	4.15	6	0	0	0	0	4¹	5	2	3	6
W 1986	Bos-A	0	0	27.00	2	0	0	0	0	0¹	2	1	2	0
• SANCHEZ, Luis														
L 1982	Cal-A	0	1	6.75	2	0	0	0	0	2²	4	2	1	1
• SANDERS, Scott														
D 1996	SD-N	0	0	8.31	1	1	0	0	0	4¹	3	4	4	4
• SANDERSON, Scott														
D 1981	Mon-N	0	0	6.75	1	1	0	0	0	2²	4	2	2	2
L 1984	Chi-N	0	0	5.79	1	1	0	0	0	4²	6	3	1	2
L 1989	Chi-N	0	0	0.00	1	0	0	0	0	2	2	0	0	1
L Total	2	0	0	4.05	2	1	0	0	0	6²	8	3	1	3
W 1990	Oak-A	0	0	10.80	2	0	0	0	0	1²	4	2	1	0
• SANFORD, Jack														
W 1962	SF-N	1	2	1.93	3	3	1	0	1	23¹	16	5	8	19
• SANTANA, Johan														
D 2002	Min-A	0	0	6.00	2	0	0	0	0	3	3	2	2	2
D 2003	Min-A	0	1	7.04	2	0	0	0	0	7²	9	6	3	6
D Total	2	0	1	6.75	4	2	0	0	0	10²	12	8	5	8
L 2002	Min-A	0	1	10.80	4	0	0	0	0	3¹	4	4	0	4
• SANTIAGO, Jose														
W 1967	Bos-A	0	2	5.59	3	2	0	0	0	9²	16	6	3	6
• SARMIENTO, Manny														
L 1976	Cin-N	0	0	18.00	1	0	0	0	0	1	2	2	1	0
• SASAKI, Kazuhiro														
D 2000	Sea-A	0	0	0.00	2	0	0	2	0	2	1	0	0	5
D 2001	Sea-A	0	0	0.00	3	0	0	1	0	3	1	0	0	5
D Total	2	0	0	0.00	5	0	0	3	0	5	2	0	0	10
L 2000	Sea-A	0	0	0.00	2	0	0	1	0	2²	3	0	1	3
L 2001	Sea-A	0	1	54.00	1	0	0	0	0	0¹	2	2	0	0
L Total	2	0	1	6.00	3	0	0	1	0	3	5	2	1	3
• SAUCIER, Kevin														
L 1980	Phi-N	0	0	0.00	2	0	0	0	0	0²	1	0	2	0
W 1980	Phi-N	0	0	0.00	1	0	0	0	0	0²	0	0	2	0
• SAUERBECK, Scott														
L 2003	Bos-A	0	0	0.00	2	0	0	0	0	0¹	1	0	1	0
• SAUNDERS, Tony														
L 1997	Fla-N	0	0	3.38	2	1	0	0	0	5¹	4	2	3	3
W 1997	Fla-N	0	1	27.00	1	1	0	0	0	2	7	6	3	2
• SCARBOROUGH, Ray														
W 1952	NY-A	0	0	9.00	1	0	0	0	0	1	1	1	0	1

YEAR	TM-L	W	L	ERA	G	GS	CG	SV	SHO	IP	H	ER	BB	SO
• SCHALLOCK, Art														
W 1953	NY-A	0	0	4.50	1	0	0	0	0	2	2	1	1	1
• SCHATZEDER, Dan														
L 1987	Min-A	0	0	0.00	2	0	0	0	0	4¹	2	0	0	5
W 1987	Min-A	1	0	6.23	3	0	0	0	0	4¹	4	3	3	3
• SCHERMAN, Fred														
L 1972	Det-A	0	0	0.00	1	0	0	0	0	0²	1	0	0	1
• SCHERRER, Bill														
W 1984	Det-A	0	0	3.00	3	0	0	0	0	3	5	1	0	0
• SCHILLING, Curt														
D 2001	Ari-N	2	0	0.50	2	2	2	0	1	18	9	1	2	18
D 2002	Ari-N	0	0	1.29	1	1	0	0	0	7	7	1	1	7
D Total	2	2	0	0.72	3	3	2	0	1	25	16	2	3	25
L 1993	Phi-N	0	0	1.69	2	2	0	0	0	16	11	3	5	19
L 2001	Ari-N	1	0	1.00	1	1	1	0	0	9	4	1	2	12
L Total	2	1	0	1.44	3	3	1	0	0	25	15	4	7	31
W 1993	Phi-N	1	1	3.52	2	2	1	0	1	15¹	13	6	5	9
W 2001	Ari-N	1	0	1.69	3	3	0	0	0	21¹	12	4	2	26
W Total	2	2	1	2.45	5	5	1	0	1	36²	25	10	7	35
• SCHIRALDI, Calvin														
L 1986	Bos-A	0	1	1.50	4	0	0	1	0	6	5	1	3	9
W 1986	Bos-A	0	2	13.50	3	0	0	1	0	4	7	6	3	2
• SCHMIDT, Freddy														
W 1944	StL-N	0	0	0.00	1	0	0	0	0	3¹	1	0	1	1
• SCHMIDT, Jason														
D 2002	SF-N	0	1	6.75	1	1	0	0	0	5¹	3	4	4	5
D 2003	SF-N	1	0	0.00	1	1	1	0	1	9	3	0	0	5
D Total	2	1	1	2.51	2	2	1	0	1	14¹	6	4	4	10
L 2002	SF-N	1	0	1.17	1	1	0	0	0	7²	4	1	1	8
W 2002	SF-N	1	0	5.23	2	2	0	0	0	10¹	16	6	4	14
• SCHOENEWEIS, Scott														
D 2002	Ana-A	0	0	27.00	3	0	0	0	0	0¹	2	1	0	0
L 2002	Ana-A	0	0	0.00	1	0	0	0	0	0²	0	0	0	0
W 2002	Ana-A	0	0	0.00	2	0	0	0	0	2	1	0	1	2
• SCHOUREK, Pete														
D 1995	Cin-N	1	0	2.57	1	1	0	0	0	7	5	2	3	5
D 1998	Bos-A	0	0	0.00	1	1	0	0	0	5¹	2	0	4	1
D Total	2	1	0	1.46	2	2	0	0	0	12¹	7	2	7	6
L 1995	Cin-N	0	0	1.26	1	1	0	0	0	14¹	14	2	3	13
• SCHULTZ, Barney														
W 1964	StL-N	0	1	18.00	4	0	0	1	0	4	9	8	3	1
• SCHUMACHER, Hal														
W 1933	NY-N	1	0	2.45	2	2	1	0	0	14²	13	4	5	3
W 1936	NY-N	1	1	5.25	2	2	1	0	0	12	13	7	10	11
W 1937	NY-N	0	1	6.00	1	1	0	0	0	6	9	4	4	3
W Total	3	2	2	4.13	5	5	2	0	0	32²	35	15	19	17
• SCHUPP, Ferdie														
W 1917	NY-N	1	0	1.74	2	2	1	0	1	10¹	11	2	2	9
• SCOTT, Jack														
W 1922	NY-N	1	0	0.00	1	1	1	0	1	9	4	0	1	2
W 1923	NY-N	0	1	12.00	2	1	0	0	0	3	9	4	1	2
W Total	2	1	1	3.00	3	2	1	0	1	12	13	4	2	4
• SCOTT, Mike														
L 1986	Hou-N	2	0	0.50	2	2	2	0	1	18	8	1	1	19
• SCUDDER, Scott														
L 1990	Cin-N	0	0	0.00	1	0	0	0	0	1	1	0	0	1
W 1990	Cin-N	0	0	0.00	1	0	0	0	0	1¹	0	0	2	2
• SEANEZ, Rudy														
D 1998	Atl-N	0	0	0.00	1	0	0	0	0	0	0	0	0	0
D 2001	Atl-N	1	0	0.00	1	0	0	0	0	1	0	0	1	0
D Total	2	1	0	0.00	2	0	0	0	0	1	0	0	1	0
L 1998	Atl-N	0	0	6.00	4	0	0	0	0	3	2	2	1	4
L 2001	Atl-N	0	0	0.00	2	0	0	0	0	2	1	0	3	3
L Total	2	0	0	3.60	6	0	0	0	0	5	3	2	4	7
• SEAVER, Tom														
L 1969	NY-N	1	0	6.43	1	1	0	0	0	7	8	5	3	2
L 1973	NY-N	1	1	1.62	2	2	1	0	0	16²	13	3	5	17
L 1979	Cin-N	0	0	2.25	1	1	0	0	0	8	5	2	2	5
L Total	3	2	1	2.84	4	4	1	0	0	31²	26	10	10	24
W 1969	NY-N	1	1	3.00	2	2	0	0	0	15	12	5	3	9
W 1973	NY-N	0	1	2.40	2	2	0	0	0	15	13	4	3	18
W Total	2	1	2	2.70	4	4	1	0	0	30	25	9	6	27
• SEELBACH, Chuck														
L 1972	Det-A	0	0	18.00	2	0	0	0	0	1	4	2	0	0
• SEGUI, Diego														
L 1971	Oak-A	0	1	5.79	1	1	0	0	0	4²	6	3	6	4
W 1975	Bos-A	0	0	0.00	1	0	0	0	0	1	0	0	0	0
• SELE, Aaron														
D 1998	Tex-A	0	1	6.00	1	1	0	0	0	6	8	4	1	4
D 1999	Tex-A	0	1	5.40	1	1	0	0	0	5	6	3	5	3
D 2000	Sea-A	0	0	1.23	1	1	0	0	0	7¹	3	1	3	1
D 2001	Sea-A	0	1	9.00	1	1	0	0	0	4	5	4	0	0
D Total	4	0	3	4.43	4	4	0	0	0	20¹	22	10	9	8
L 2000	Sea-A	0	0	6.00	1	1	0	0	0	6	9	4	0	4
L 2001	Sea-A	0	2	3.60	2	2	0	0	0	10	11	4	4	5
L Total	2	0	3	4.50	3	3	0	0	0	16	20	8	4	9
• SHANTZ, Bobby														
W 1957	NY-A	0	1	4.05	3	1	0	0	0	6²	8	3	2	7
W 1960	NY-A	0	0	4.26	3	0	0	1	0	6¹	4	3	1	1
W Total	2	0	1	4.15	6	1	0	1	0	13	12	6	3	8
• SHAW, Bob														
W 1959	Chi-A	1	1	2.57	2	2	0	0	0	14	17	4	2	2
• SHAWKEY, Bob														
W 1914	Phi-A	0	1	3.60	1	1	0	0	0	5	4	2	2	0
W 1921	NY-A	0	1	7.00	2	1	0	0	0	9	13	7	6	5
W 1922	NY-A	0	0	2.70	1	1	1	0	0	10	8	3	2	4
W 1923	NY-A	1	0	3.52	1	1	0	0	0	7²	12	3	4	2
W 1926	NY-A	0	1	5.40	3	1	0	0	0	10	8	6	2	7
W Total	5	1	3	4.54	8	5	1	0	0	41²	45	21	16	18
• SHEA, Spec														
W 1947	NY-A	2	0	2.35	3	3	1	0	0	15¹	10	4	8	10
• SHELDON, Rollie														
W 1964	NY-A	0	0	0.00	1	0	0	0	0	2²	2	0	0	0
• SHERDEL, Bill														
W 1926	StL-N	0	2	2.12	2	2	1	0	0	17	15	4	8	3
W 1928	StL-N	0	2	4.73	2	2	0	0	0	13¹	15	7	3	3
W Total	2	0	4	3.26	4	4	1	0	0	30¹	30	11	11	6
• SHERRY, Larry														
W 1959	LA-N	2	0	0.71	4	0	0	2	0	12²	8	1	2	5
• SHIELDS, Scot														
W 2002	Ana-A	0	0	5.40	1	0	0	0	0	1²	5	1	0	1
• SHIRLEY, Tex														
W 1944	StL-A	0	0	0.00	1	0	0	0	0	2	2	0	1	1
• SHOCKER, Urban														
W 1926	NY-A	0	1	5.87	2	1	0	0	0	7²	13	5	0	3
• SHORE, Ernie														
W 1915	Bos-A	1	1	2.12	2	2	2	0	0	17	12	4	8	6
W 1916	Bos-A	2	0	1.53	2	2	1	0	0	17²	12	3	4	9
W Total	2	3	1	1.82	4	4	3	0	0	34²	24	7	12	15
• SHORES, Bill														
W 1930	Phi-A	0	0	13.50	1	0	0	0	0	1¹	3	2	0	0
• SHOW, Eric														
L 1984	SD-N	0	1	13.50	1	0	0	0	0	5¹	8	8	4	2
W 1984	SD-N	0	1	10.13	1	1	0	0	0	2²	4	3	1	2
• SHUEY, Paul														
D 1996	Cle-A	0	0	9.00	3	0	0	0	0	2	5	2	2	2
D 1998	Cle-A	0	0	0.00	3	0	0	0	0	3	3	0	1	4
D 1999	Cle-A	1	1	11.25	3	0	0	0	0	4	4	5	4	5
D 2001	Cle-A	0	0	6.75	2	0	0	0	0	1¹	3	1	0	2
D Total	4	1	1	6.97	11	0	0	0	0	10¹	15	8	7	13
L 1998	Cle-A	0	0	0.00	5	0	0	0	0	6¹	4	0	7	7
• SIEVER, Ed														
W 1907	Det-A	0	1	4.50	1	1	0	0	0	4	7	2	0	1
• SIMAS, Bill														
D 2000	Chi-A	0	0	6.75	2	0	0	0	0	1¹	0	1	1	2
• SIMMONS, Curt														
W 1964	StL-N	0	1	2.51	1	1	0	0	0	14¹	11	4	3	8
• SIROTKA, Mike														
D 2000	Chi-A	0	1	4.76	1	1	0	0	0	5²	7	3	2	0
• SISK, Doug														
L 1986	NY-N	0	0	0.00	1	0	0	0	0	1	1	0	1	0
W 1986	NY-N	0	0	0.00	1	0	0	0	0	0²	0	0	1	1
• SLATON, Jim														
D 1981	Mil-A	0	0	3.00	4	0	0	0	0	6	6	2	0	2
L 1982	Mil-A	0	0	1.93	2	0	0	1	0	4²	3	1	1	3
W 1982	Mil-A	0	0	0.00	2	0	0	0	0	2²	1	0	2	1
• SLOCUMB, Heathcliff														
D 1997	Sea-A	0	0	4.50	2	0	0	0	0	2	3	1	1	0
• SMILEY, John														
D 1995	Cin-N	0	0	3.00	1	1	0	0	0	6	9	2	0	1
L 1990	Pit-N	0	0	0.00	1	1	0	0	0	2	2	0	0	0
L 1991	Pit-N	0	2	23.63	2	2	0	0	0	2²	8	7	1	3
L 1995	Cin-N	0	0	3.60	1	1	0	0	0	5	5	2	0	1
L Total	3	0	2	8.38	4	3	0	0	0	9²	15	9	1	4
• SMITH, Al														
W 1936	NY-N	0	0	81.00	1	0	0	0	0	0¹	2	3	1	0
W 1937	NY-N	0	0	3.00	2	0	0	0	0	3	2	1	0	1
W Total	2	0	0	10.80	3	0	0	0	0	3¹	4	4	1	1
• SMITH, Billy														
D 1981	Hou-N	0	0	0.00	1	0	0	0	0	0¹	0	0	0	0
• SMITH, Bob														
W 1932	Chi-N	0	0	9.00	1	0	0	0	0	1	2	1	0	1
• SMITH, Bud														
D 2001	StL-N	1	0	1.80	1	1	0	0	0	5	4	1	4	2
• SMITH, Clay														
W 1940	Det-A	0	0	2.25	1	0	0	0	0	4	1	1	3	1
• SMITH, Dave														
D 1981	Hou-N	0	0	3.86	2	0	0	0	0	2¹	2	1	0	4
L 1980	Hou-N	1	0	3.86	3	0	0	0	0	2¹	4	1	2	4

YEAR	TM-L	W	L	ERA	G	GS	CG	SV	SHO	IP	H	ER	BB	SO
L 1986	Hou-N	0	1	9.00	2	0	0	0	0	2	2	2	3	2
L Total	**2**	**1**	**1**	**6.23**	**5**	**0**	**0**	**0**	**0**	**4^{1}**	**6**	**3**	**5**	**6**
• SMITH, Lee														
L 1984	Chi-N	0	1	9.00	2	0	0	1	0	2	3	2	0	3
L 1988	Bos-A	0	1	8.10	2	0	0	0	0	3^{1}	6	3	1	4
L Total	**2**	**0**	**2**	**8.44**	**4**	**0**	**0**	**1**	**0**	**5^{1}**	**9**	**5**	**1**	**7**
• SMITH, Pete														
L 1992	Atl-N	0	0	2.45	2	0	0	0	0	3^{2}	2	1	3	3
W 1992	Atl-N	0	0	0.00	1	0	0	0	0	3	3	0	0	0
• SMITH, Sherry														
W 1916	Bro-N	0	1	1.35	1	1	1	0	0	13^{1}	7	2	6	2
W 1920	Bro-N	1	1	0.53	2	2	2	0	0	17	10	1	3	3
W Total	**2**	**1**	**2**	**0.89**	**3**	**3**	**3**	**0**	**0**	**30^{1}**	**17**	**3**	**9**	**5**
• SMITH, Zane														
D 1995	Bos-A	0	1	6.75	1	0	0	0	0	1^{1}	1	1	0	0
L 1990	Pit-N	0	2	6.00	2	1	0	0	0	9	14	6	1	8
L 1991	Pit-N	1	1	0.61	2	2	0	0	0	14^{2}	15	1	3	10
L Total	**2**	**1**	**3**	**2.66**	**4**	**3**	**0**	**0**	**0**	**23^{2}**	**29**	**7**	**4**	**18**
• SMITHSON, Mike														
L 1988	Bos-A	0	0	0.00	1	0	0	0	0	2^{1}	3	0	0	1
• SMOLTZ, John														
D 1995	Atl-N	0	0	7.94	1	1	0	0	0	5^{2}	5	5	1	6
D 1996	Atl-N	1	0	1.00	1	1	0	0	0	9	4	1	2	7
D 1997	Atl-N	1	0	1.00	1	1	1	0	0	9	3	1	1	11
D 1998	Atl-N	1	0	1.17	1	1	0	0	0	7^{2}	5	1	0	6
D 1999	Atl-N	1	0	5.14	1	1	0	0	0	7	6	4	3	3
D 2001	Atl-N	0	0	2.25	3	0	0	2	0	4	3	1	0	3
D 2002	Atl-N	0	0	2.70	2	0	0	0	0	3^{1}	2	1	2	7
D 2003	Atl-N	0	0	6.00	2	0	0	1	0	3	4	2	0	1
D Total	**8**	**4**	**0**	**2.96**	**12**	**5**	**1**	**3**	**0**	**48^{2}**	**32**	**16**	**9**	**44**
L 1991	Atl-N	2	0	1.76	2	2	1	0	1	15^{1}	14	3	3	15
L 1992	Atl-N	2	0	2.66	3	3	0	0	0	20^{1}	14	6	10	19
L 1993	Atl-N	0	1	0.00	1	1	0	0	0	6^{1}	8	0	5	10
L 1995	Atl-N	0	0	2.57	1	1	0	0	0	7	7	2	2	2
L 1996	Atl-N	2	0	1.20	2	2	0	0	0	15	12	2	3	12
L 1997	Atl-N	0	1	7.50	1	1	0	0	0	6	5	5	5	9
L 1998	Atl-N	0	0	3.95	2	2	0	0	0	13^{2}	13	6	6	13
L 1999	Atl-N	0	0	6.23	3	1	0	1	0	8^{2}	8	6	0	8
L 2001	Atl-N	0	0	0.00	2	0	0	0	0	3	0	0	0	1
L Total	**9**	**6**	**2**	**2.83**	**17**	**13**	**1**	**1**	**1**	**95^{1}**	**81**	**30**	**34**	**89**
W 1991	Atl-N	0	0	1.26	2	2	0	0	0	14^{1}	13	2	1	11
W 1992	Atl-N	1	0	2.70	2	2	0	0	0	13^{1}	13	4	7	12
W 1995	Atl-N	0	0	15.43	1	1	0	0	0	2^{1}	6	4	2	4
W 1996	Atl-N	1	1	0.64	2	2	0	0	0	14	6	1	8	14
W 1999	Atl-N	0	1	3.86	1	1	0	0	0	7	6	3	3	11
W Total	**5**	**2**	**2**	**2.47**	**8**	**8**	**0**	**0**	**0**	**51**	**44**	**14**	**21**	**52**
• SOLOMON, Eddie														
L 1974	LA-N	0	0	0.00	1	0	0	0	0	2	2	0	1	1
• SOSA, Elias														
D 1981	Mon-N	0	0	3.00	2	0	0	0	0	3	4	1	0	1
L 1977	LA-N	0	1	10.13	2	0	0	0	0	2^{2}	5	3	0	0
L 1981	Mon-N	0	0	0.00	1	0	0	0	0	0^{1}	1	0	1	0
L Total	**2**	**0**	**1**	**9.00**	**3**	**0**	**0**	**0**	**0**	**3**	**6**	**3**	**1**	**0**
W 1977	LA-N	0	0	11.57	2	0	0	0	0	2^{1}	3	3	1	1
• SOTO, Mario														
L 1979	Cin-N	0	0	0.00	1	0	0	0	0	2	0	0	0	1
• SPAHN, Warren														
W 1948	Bos-N	1	1	3.00	3	1	0	0	0	12	10	4	3	12
W 1957	Mil-N	1	1	4.70	2	2	1	0	0	15^{1}	18	8	2	2
W 1958	Mil-N	2	1	2.20	3	3	2	0	1	28^{2}	19	7	8	18
W Total	**3**	**4**	**3**	**3.05**	**8**	**6**	**3**	**0**	**1**	**56**	**47**	**19**	**13**	**32**
• SPARKS, Steve														
D 2003	Oak-A	0	0	4.50	1	0	0	0	0	4	2	2	3	1
• SPARMA, Joe														
W 1968	Det-A	0	0	54.00	1	0	0	0	0	0^{1}	2	2	0	0
• SPEECE, By														
W 1924	Was-A	0	0	9.00	1	0	0	0	0	1	3	1	0	0
• SPENCER, George														
W 1951	NY-N	0	0	18.90	2	0	0	0	0	3^{1}	6	7	3	0
• SPLITTORFF, Paul														
L 1976	KC-A	1	0	1.93	2	0	0	0	0	9^{1}	7	2	5	2
L 1977	KC-A	1	0	2.40	2	2	0	0	0	15	14	4	3	4
L 1978	KC-A	0	0	4.91	1	1	0	0	0	7^{1}	9	4	0	2
L 1980	KC-A	0	0	1.69	1	1	0	0	0	5^{1}	5	1	2	3
L Total	**4**	**2**	**0**	**2.68**	**6**	**4**	**0**	**0**	**0**	**37**	**35**	**11**	**10**	**11**
W 1980	KC-A	0	0	5.40	1	0	0	0	0	1^{2}	4	1	0	0
• SPOLJARIC, Paul														
D 1997	Sea-A	0	0	0.00	2	0	0	0	0	1^{2}	4	0	0	1
• SPOONER, Karl														
W 1955	Bro-N	0	1	13.50	2	1	0	0	0	3^{1}	4	5	3	6
• SPRINGER, Russ														
D 1997	Hou-N	0	0	5.40	2	0	0	0	0	1^{2}	2	1	1	3
D 1999	Atl-N	0	0	0.00	1	0	0	0	0	1	2	0	1	1
D Total	**2**	**0**	**0**	**3.38**	**3**	**0**	**0**	**0**	**0**	**2^{2}**	**4**	**1**	**2**	**4**
L 1999	Atl-N	1	0	0.00	2	0	0	0	0	2	0	0	1	1
W 1999	Atl-N	0	0	0.00	2	0	0	0	0	2^{1}	1	0	0	1

YEAR	TM-L	W	L	ERA	G	GS	CG	SV	SHO	IP	H	ER	BB	SO
• ST.CLAIRE, Randy														
W 1991	Atl-N	0	0	9.00	1	0	0	0	0	1	1	1	0	0
• STAFFORD, Bill														
W 1960	NY-A	0	0	1.50	2	0	0	0	0	6	5	1	1	2
W 1961	NY-A	0	0	2.70	1	1	0	0	0	6^{2}	7	2	2	5
W 1962	NY-A	1	0	2.00	1	1	1	0	0	9	4	2	2	5
W Total	**3**	**1**	**0**	**2.08**	**4**	**2**	**1**	**0**	**0**	**21^{2}**	**16**	**5**	**5**	**12**
• STALEY, Gerry														
W 1959	Chi-A	0	1	2.16	4	0	0	1	0	8^{1}	8	2	0	3
• STALEY, Harry														
T 1892	Bos-N	1	0	3.00	1	1	1	0	0	9	10	3	1	0
• STANGE, Lee														
W 1967	Bos-A	0	0	0.00	1	0	0	0	0	2	3	0	0	0
• STANHOUSE, Don														
L 1979	Bal-A	1	1	6.00	3	0	0	0	0	3	5	2	3	0
W 1979	Bal-A	0	1	13.50	3	0	0	0	0	2	6	3	3	0
• STANLEY, Bob														
L 1986	Bos-A	0	0	4.76	3	0	0	0	0	5^{2}	7	3	3	1
L 1988	Bos-A	0	0	9.00	2	0	0	0	0	1	2	1	1	0
L Total	**2**	**0**	**0**	**5.40**	**5**	**0**	**0**	**0**	**0**	**6^{2}**	**9**	**4**	**4**	**1**
W 1986	Bos-A	0	0	0.00	5	0	0	1	0	6^{1}	5	0	1	4
• STANTON, Mike														
D 1995	Bos-A	0	0	0.00	1	0	0	0	0	2^{1}	1	0	0	4
D 1996	Tex-A	0	1	2.70	3	0	0	0	0	3^{1}	2	1	3	3
D 1997	NY-A	0	0	0.00	3	0	0	0	0	1	1	0	1	3
D 2000	NY-A	1	0	2.08	3	0	0	0	0	4^{1}	5	1	1	3
D 2001	NY-A	1	0	0.00	3	0	0	0	0	4^{2}	3	0	0	1
D 2002	NY-A	0	1	10.13	3	0	0	0	0	2^{2}	6	3	1	1
D Total	**6**	**2**	**2**	**2.45**	**16**	**0**	**0**	**0**	**0**	**18^{1}**	**18**	**5**	**6**	**15**
L 1991	Atl-N	0	0	2.45	3	0	0	0	0	3^{2}	4	1	3	3
L 1992	Atl-N	0	0	0.00	5	0	0	0	0	4^{1}	2	0	2	5
L 1993	Atl-N	0	0	0.00	1	0	0	0	0	1	1	0	1	0
L 1998	NY-A	0	0	0.00	3	0	0	0	0	3^{2}	2	0	1	4
L 1999	NY-A	0	0	0.00	3	0	0	0	0	0^{1}	1	0	1	0
L 2001	NY-A	0	0	27.00	2	0	0	0	0	1	1	3	2	0
L Total	**6**	**0**	**0**	**2.57**	**17**	**0**	**0**	**0**	**0**	**14**	**11**	**4**	**10**	**12**
W 1991	Atl-N	1	0	0.00	5	0	0	0	0	7^{1}	5	0	2	7
W 1992	Atl-N	0	0	0.00	4	0	0	1	0	5	3	0	2	1
W 1998	NY-A	0	0	27.00	1	0	0	0	0	0^{2}	3	2	0	1
W 1999	NY-A	0	0	0.00	1	0	0	0	0	0^{1}	0	0	0	1
W 2000	NY-A	2	0	0.00	4	0	0	0	0	4^{1}	0	0	0	7
W 2001	NY-A	0	0	3.18	5	0	0	0	0	5^{2}	3	2	1	3
W Total	**6**	**3**	**0**	**1.54**	**20**	**0**	**0**	**1**	**0**	**23^{1}**	**14**	**4**	**5**	**20**
• STECHSCHULTE, Gene														
D 2001	StL-N	0	0	0.00	2	0	0	0	0	0^{1}	3	0	0	0
• STEPHENSON, Garrett														
D 2000	StL-N	0	0	2.45	1	1	0	0	0	3^{2}	3	1	2	2
• STEPHENSON, Jerry														
W 1967	Bos-A	0	0	9.00	1	0	0	0	0	2	3	2	1	0
• STEWART, Dave														
D 1981	LA-N	0	2	40.50	2	0	0	0	0	0^{2}	4	3	0	1
L 1988	Oak-A	1	0	1.35	2	2	0	0	0	13^{1}	9	2	6	11
L 1989	Oak-A	2	0	2.81	2	2	0	0	0	16	13	5	3	9
L 1990	Oak-A	2	0	1.13	2	2	0	0	0	16	8	2	2	4
L 1992	Oak-A	1	0	2.70	2	2	1	0	0	16^{2}	14	5	6	7
L 1993	Tor-A	2	0	2.03	2	2	0	0	0	13^{1}	8	3	8	8
L Total	**5**	**8**	**0**	**2.03**	**10**	**10**	**1**	**0**	**0**	**75^{1}**	**52**	**17**	**25**	**39**
W 1981	LA-N	0	0	0.00	2	0	0	0	0	1^{2}	1	0	2	1
W 1988	Oak-A	0	1	3.14	2	2	0	0	0	14^{1}	12	5	5	5
W 1989	Oak-A	2	0	1.69	2	2	1	0	1	16	10	3	2	14
W 1990	Oak-A	0	2	3.46	2	2	1	0	0	13	10	5	6	5
W 1993	Tor-A	0	1	6.75	2	2	0	0	0	12	10	9	8	8
W Total	**5**	**2**	**4**	**3.47**	**10**	**8**	**2**	**0**	**1**	**57**	**43**	**22**	**23**	**33**
• STEWART, Lefty														
W 1933	Was-A	0	1	9.00	1	1	0	0	0	2	6	2	0	0
• STEWART, Sammy														
L 1983	Bal-A	0	0	0.00	2	0	0	1	0	4^{1}	2	0	1	2
W 1979	Bal-A	0	0	0.00	1	0	0	0	0	2^{2}	4	0	1	0
W 1983	Bal-A	0	0	0.00	3	0	0	0	0	5	2	0	2	6
W Total	**2**	**0**	**0**	**0.00**	**4**	**0**	**0**	**0**	**0**	**7^{2}**	**6**	**0**	**3**	**6**
• STIEB, Dave														
L 1985	Tor-A	1	1	3.10	3	3	0	0	0	20^{1}	11	7	10	18
L 1989	Tor-A	0	2	6.35	2	2	0	0	0	11^{1}	12	8	6	10
L Total	**2**	**1**	**3**	**4.26**	**5**	**5**	**0**	**0**	**0**	**31^{2}**	**23**	**15**	**16**	**28**
• STIVETTS, Jack														
T 1892	Bos-N	2	0	0.93	3	3	3	0	1	29	21	3	7	17
T 1897	Bos-N	0	1	18.47	2	1	0	0	0	6^{1}	16	13	7	0
T Total	**2**	**2**	**1**	**4.08**	**5**	**4**	**3**	**0**	**1**	**35^{1}**	**37**	**16**	**14**	**17**
• STODDARD, Tim														
L 1984	Chi-N	0	0	4.50	2	0	0	0	0	2	1	1	2	2
W 1979	Bal-A	1	0	5.40	4	0	0	0	0	5	6	3	1	3
• STONE, George														
L 1969	Atl-N	0	0	9.00	1	0	0	0	0	1	2	1	0	0
L 1973	NY-N	0	0	1.35	1	1	0	0	0	6^{2}	3	1	2	4
L Total	**2**	**0**	**0**	**2.35**	**2**	**1**	**0**	**0**	**0**	**7^{2}**	**5**	**2**	**2**	**4**
W 1973	NY-N	0	0	0.00	2	0	0	1	0	3	4	0	1	3

YEAR	TM-L	W	L	ERA	G	GS	CG	SV	SHO	IP	H	ER	BB	SO
• STONE, Steve														
W 1979	Bal-A	0	0	9.00	1	0	0	0	0	2	4	2	2	2
• STOTTLEMYRE, Mel														
W 1964	NY-A	1	1	3.15	3	3	1	0	0	20	18	7	6	12
• STOTTLEMYRE, Todd														
D 1996	StL-N	1	0	1.35	1	1	0	0	0	6^2	5	1	2	7
D 1998	Tex-A	0	1	2.25	1	1	1	0	0	8	6	2	4	8
D 1999	Ari-N	1	0	1.35	1	1	0	0	0	6^2	4	1	5	6
D Total	3	2	1	1.69	3	3	1	0	0	21^1	15	4	11	21
L 1989	Tor-A	0	1	7.20	1	1	0	0	0	5	7	4	2	3
L 1991	Tor-A	0	1	9.82	1	1	0	0	0	3^2	7	4	1	3
L 1992	Tor-A	0	0	2.45	1	0	0	0	0	3^2	3	1	0	1
L 1993	Tor-A	0	1	7.50	1	1	0	0	0	6	6	5	4	4
L 1996	StL-N	1	1	12.38	3	2	0	0	0	8	15	11	3	11
L Total	5	1	4	8.54	7	5	0	0	0	26^1	38	25	10	22
W 1992	Tor-A	0	0	0.00	4	0	0	0	0	3^2	4	0	0	4
W 1993	Tor-A	0	0	27.00	1	1	0	0	0	2	3	6	4	1
W Total	2	0	0	9.53	5	1	0	0	0	5^2	7	6	4	5
• STRAKER, Les														
L 1987	Min-A	0	0	16.88	1	1	0	0	0	2^2	3	5	4	1
W 1987	Min-A	0	0	4.00	2	2	0	0	0	9	9	4	3	6
• STRATTON, Scott														
W 1890	Lou-A	1	1	2.37	3	3	1	0	0	19	26	5	4	8
• STUPER, John														
L 1982	StL-N	0	0	3.00	1	1	0	0	0	6	4	2	1	4
W 1982	StL-N	1	0	3.46	2	2	1	0	0	13	10	5	5	5
• STURDIVANT, Tom														
W 1955	NY-A	0	0	6.00	2	0	0	0	0	3	5	2	2	0
W 1956	NY-A	1	0	2.79	2	1	1	0	0	9^2	8	3	8	9
W 1957	NY-A	0	0	6.00	2	1	0	0	0	6	6	4	1	2
W Total	3	1	0	4.34	6	2	1	0	0	18^2	19	9	11	11
• SULLIVAN, Jim														
T 1897	Bos-N	0	0	3.00	1	0	0	0	0	3	6	1	0	0
• SUMMERS, Ed														
W 1908	Det-A	0	2	4.30	2	1	0	0	0	14^2	18	7	4	7
W 1909	Det-A	0	2	8.59	2	2	0	0	0	7^1	13	7	4	4
W Total	2	0	4	5.73	4	3	0	0	0	22	31	14	8	11
• SUNDRA, Steve														
W 1939	NY-A	0	0	0.00	1	0	0	0	0	2^2	4	0	1	2
• SUTCLIFFE, Rick														
L 1984	Chi-N	1	1	3.38	2	2	0	0	0	13^1	9	5	8	10
L 1989	Chi-N	0	0	4.50	1	1	0	0	0	6	5	3	4	2
L Total	2	1	1	3.72	3	3	0	0	0	19^1	14	8	12	12
• SUTTER, Bruce														
L 1982	StL-N	1	0	0.00	2	0	0	1	0	4^1	0	0	0	1
W 1982	StL-N	1	0	4.70	4	0	0	2	0	7^2	6	4	3	6
• SUTTON, Don														
L 1974	LA-N	2	0	0.53	2	2	1	0	1	17	7	1	2	13
L 1977	LA-N	1	0	1.00	1	1	1	0	0	9	9	1	0	4
L 1978	LA-N	0	1	6.35	1	1	0	0	0	5^2	7	4	2	0
L 1982	Mil-A	1	0	3.52	1	1	0	0	0	7^2	8	3	2	9
L 1986	Cal-A	0	0	1.86	2	1	0	0	0	9^2	6	2	1	4
L Total	5	4	1	2.02	7	6	2	0	1	49	37	11	7	30
W 1974	LA-N	1	0	2.77	2	2	0	0	0	13	9	4	3	12
W 1977	LA-N	1	0	3.94	2	2	1	0	0	16	17	7	1	6
W 1978	LA-N	0	2	7.50	2	2	0	0	0	12	17	10	4	8
W 1982	Mil-A	0	1	7.84	2	2	0	0	0	10^1	12	9	1	5
W Total	4	2	3	5.26	8	8	1	0	0	51^1	55	30	9	31
• SWIFT, Bill														
D 1995	Col-N	0	0	6.00	1	1	0	0	0	6	7	4	2	3
• SWINDELL, Greg														
D 1998	Bos-A	0	0	0.00	1	0	0	0	0	1^1	0	0	1	1
D 1999	Ari-N	0	0	0.00	3	0	0	0	0	3^1	1	0	3	1
D 2001	Ari-N	0	0	0.00	2	0	0	0	0	1^2	1	0	0	2
D 2002	Ari-N	0	0	27.00	2	0	0	0	0	0^1	2	1	1	0
D Total	4	0	0	1.35	8	0	0	0	0	6^2	4	1	5	4
L 2001	Ari-N	0	0	27.00	2	0	0	0	0	0^1	1	1	0	0
W 2001	Ari-N	0	0	0.00	3	0	0	0	0	2^2	1	0	1	2
• TAM, Jeff														
D 2000	Oak-A	0	0	0.00	3	0	0	0	0	2	3	0	1	1
D 2001	Oak-A	0	0	18.00	1	0	0	0	0	1	3	2	0	0
D Total	2	0	0	6.00	4	0	0	0	0	3	6	2	1	1
• TANANA, Frank														
L 1979	Cal-A	0	0	3.60	1	1	0	0	0	5	6	2	2	3
L 1987	Det-A	0	1	5.06	1	1	0	0	0	5^1	6	3	4	1
L Total	2	0	1	4.35	2	2	0	0	0	10^1	12	5	6	4
• TAPANI, Kevin														
D 1995	LA-N	0	0	81.00	2	0	0	0	0	0^1	0	3	4	1
D 1998	Chi-N	0	0	1.00	1	1	0	0	0	9	5	1	3	6
D Total	2	0	0	3.86	3	1	0	0	0	9^1	5	4	7	7
L 1991	Min-A	0	1	7.84	2	2	0	0	0	10^1	16	9	3	9
W 1991	Min-A	1	1	4.50	2	2	0	0	0	12	13	6	2	7
• TAVAREZ, Julian														
D 1995	Cle-A	0	0	6.75	3	0	0	0	0	2^2	5	2	0	3
D 1996	Cle-A	0	0	0.00	2	0	0	0	0	1^1	1	0	2	1
D 1997	SF-N	0	1	4.50	3	0	0	0	0	4	4	2	2	0
D Total	3	0	1	4.50	8	0	0	0	0	8	10	4	4	4
L 1995	Cle-A	0	1	2.70	4	0	0	0	0	3^1	3	1	1	2
W 1995	Cle-A	0	0	0.00	5	0	0	0	0	4^1	3	0	2	1
• TAYLOR, Harry														
W 1947	Bro-N	0	0	....	1	1	0	0	0	0	2	0	1	0
• TAYLOR, Ron														
L 1969	NY-N	1	0	0.00	2	0	0	0	0	3^1	3	0	0	4
W 1964	StL-N	0	0	0.00	2	0	0	1	0	4^2	0	0	1	2
W 1969	NY-N	0	0	0.00	2	0	0	1	0	2^1	0	0	1	3
W Total	2	0	0	0.00	4	0	0	2	0	7	0	0	2	5
• TEJERA, Michael														
L 2003	Fla-N	0	1	6.75	2	0	0	0	0	1^1	2	1	0	1
• TEKULVE, Kent														
L 1975	Pit-N	0	0	6.75	2	0	0	0	0	1^1	3	1	1	2
L 1979	Pit-N	0	0	3.38	2	0	0	0	0	2^2	2	1	2	2
L Total	2	0	0	4.50	4	0	0	0	0	4	5	2	3	4
W 1979	Pit-N	0	1	2.89	5	0	0	3	0	9^1	4	3	3	10
• TERRELL, Walt														
L 1987	Det-A	0	0	9.00	1	1	0	0	0	6	7	6	4	4
• TERRY, Adonis														
W 1889	Bro-A	2	3	6.14	5	5	4	0	0	36^2	47	25	18	14
W 1890	Bro-N	1	1	3.60	3	3	3	0	1	25	25	10	10	8
W Total	2	3	4	5.11	8	8	7	0	1	61^2	72	35	28	22
• TERRY, Ralph														
W 1960	NY-A	0	2	5.40	2	1	0	0	0	6^2	7	4	1	5
W 1961	NY-A	0	1	4.82	2	2	0	0	0	9^1	12	5	2	7
W 1962	NY-A	2	1	1.80	3	3	2	0	1	25	17	5	2	16
W 1963	NY-A	0	0	3.00	1	0	0	0	0	3	3	1	1	0
W 1964	NY-A	0	0	0.00	1	0	0	0	0	2	2	0	0	3
W Total	5	2	4	2.93	9	6	2	0	1	46	41	15	6	31
• TESREAU, Jeff														
W 1912	NY-N	1	2	3.13	3	3	1	0	0	23	19	8	11	15
W 1913	NY-N	0	1	6.48	2	1	0	0	0	8^1	11	6	1	4
W 1917	NY-N	0	0	0.00	1	0	0	0	0	1	0	0	1	1
W Total	3	1	3	3.90	6	4	1	0	0	32^1	30	14	13	20
• THIGPEN, Bobby														
L 1993	Phi-N	0	0	5.40	2	0	0	0	0	1^2	1	1	1	3
W 1993	Phi-N	0	0	0.00	2	0	0	0	0	2^2	1	0	1	0
• THOMAS, Myles														
W 1926	NY-A	0	0	3.00	2	0	0	0	0	3	3	1	0	0
• THOMAS, Tommy														
W 1933	Was-A	0	0	0.00	2	0	0	0	0	1^1	1	0	0	2
• THOMPSON, Gus														
W 1903	Pit-N	0	0	4.50	1	0	0	0	0	2	3	1	0	1
• THOMPSON, Junior														
W 1939	Cin-N	0	1	13.50	1	1	0	0	0	4^2	5	7	4	3
W 1940	Cin-N	0	1	16.20	1	1	0	0	0	3^1	8	6	4	2
W Total	2	0	2	14.63	2	2	0	0	0	8	13	13	8	5
• THOMPSON, Mark														
D 1995	Col-N	0	0	0.00	1	0	0	1	0	1	0	0	0	0
• THURMOND, Mark														
L 1984	SD-N	0	1	9.82	1	1	0	0	0	3^2	7	4	2	1
L 1987	Det-A	0	0	0.00	1	0	0	0	0	0^1	0	0	0	0
L Total	2	0	1	9.00	2	1	0	0	0	4	7	4	2	1
W 1984	SD-N	0	1	10.13	2	2	0	0	0	5^1	12	6	3	2
• TIANT, Luis														
L 1970	Min-A	0	0	13.50	1	0	0	0	0	0^2	1	1	0	0
L 1975	Bos-A	1	0	0.00	1	1	1	0	0	9	3	0	3	8
L Total	2	1	0	0.93	2	1	1	0	0	9^2	4	1	3	8
W 1975	Bos-A	2	0	3.60	3	3	2	0	1	25	25	10	8	12
• TIDROW, Dick														
L 1976	NY-A	1	0	3.68	3	0	0	0	0	7^1	6	3	4	0
L 1977	NY-A	0	0	3.86	2	0	0	0	0	7	6	3	3	3
L 1978	NY-A	0	0	4.76	1	0	0	0	0	5^2	8	3	2	1
L 1983	Chi-A	0	0	3.00	1	0	0	0	0	3	1	1	3	3
L Total	4	1	0	3.91	7	0	0	0	0	23	21	10	12	7
W 1976	NY-A	0	0	7.71	2	0	0	0	0	2^1	5	2	1	1
W 1977	NY-A	0	0	4.91	2	0	0	0	0	3^2	5	2	0	1
W 1978	NY-A	0	0	1.93	2	0	0	0	0	4^2	4	1	0	5
W Total	3	0	0	4.22	6	0	0	0	0	10^2	14	5	1	7
• TIMLIN, Mike														
D 1997	Sea-A	0	0	54.00	1	0	0	0	0	0^2	3	4	1	1
D 2000	StL-N	0	0	10.80	2	0	0	0	0	1^2	5	2	1	2
D 2001	StL-N	0	0	0.00	1	0	0	0	0	1^1	1	0	0	0
D 2003	Bos-A	0	0	0.00	3	0	0	0	0	4^1	0	0	0	5
D Total	4	0	0	6.75	7	0	0	0	0	8	9	6	2	8
L 1991	Tor-A	0	1	3.18	4	0	0	0	0	5^2	5	2	2	5
L 1992	Tor-A	0	0	6.75	2	0	0	0	0	1^1	4	1	0	1
L 1993	Tor-A	0	0	3.86	1	0	0	0	0	2^1	3	1	0	2
L 2000	StL-N	0	1	0.00	3	0	0	0	0	3^1	1	0	2	0
L 2003	Bos-A	0	0	0.00	5	0	0	0	0	5^1	1	0	2	6
L Total	5	0	2	2.00	15	0	0	0	0	18	14	4	6	14
W 1992	Tor-A	0	0	0.00	2	0	0	1	0	1^1	0	0	0	0
W 1993	Tor-A	0	0	0.00	2	0	0	0	0	2^1	2	0	0	4
W Total	2	0	0	0.00	4	0	0	1	0	3^2	2	0	0	4
• TINNING, Bud														
W 1932	Chi-N	0	0	0.00	2	0	0	0	0	2^1	0	0	0	3

YEAR	TM-L	W	L	ERA	G	GS	CG	SV	SHO	IP	H	ER	BB	SO
• TITCOMB, Cannonball														
W 1888	NY-N	0	1	6.75	1	1	0	0	0	4	5	3	2	2
• TOBIN, Jim														
W 1945	Det-A	0	0	6.00	1	0	0	0	0	3	4	2	1	0
• TODD, Jim														
L 1975	Oak-A	0	0	9.00	3	0	0	0	0	3	1	0	0	0
• TOMKO, Brett														
D 2000	Sea-A	0	0	0.00	1	0	0	0	0	2²	1	0	1	0
L 2000	Sea-A	0	0	7.20	2	0	0	0	0	5	3	4	4	4
• TOMLIN, Dave														
L 1973	Cin-N	0	0	16.20	1	0	0	0	0	1²	5	3	1	1
L 1979	Cin-N	0	0	0.00	3	0	0	0	0	3	3	0	2	3
L Total 2		0	0	5.79	4	0	0	0	0	4²	8	3	3	4
• TOMLIN, Randy														
L 1991	Pit-N	0	0	3.00	1	1	0	0	0	6	6	2	2	1
L 1992	Pit-N	0	0	6.75	2	0	0	0	0	2²	5	2	1	0
L Total 2		0	0	4.15	3	1	0	0	0	8²	11	4	3	1
• TONEY, Fred														
W 1921	NY-N	0	0	23.63	2	2	0	0	0	2²	7	7	3	1
• TORREZ, Mike														
L 1977	NY-A	0	1	4.09	2	1	0	0	0	11	11	5	5	5
W 1977	NY-A	2	0	2.50	2	2	2	0	0	18	16	5	5	15
• TROUT, Dizzy														
W 1940	Det-A	0	1	9.00	1	1	0	0	0	2	6	2	1	1
W 1945	Det-A	1	1	0.66	2	1	1	0	0	13²	9	1	3	9
W Total 2		1	2	1.72	3	2	1	0	0	15²	15	3	4	10
• TROUT, Steve														
L 1984	Chi-N	1	0	2.00	2	1	0	0	0	9	5	2	3	3
• TROWBRIDGE, Bob														
W 1957	Mil-N	0	0	45.00	1	0	0	0	0	1	2	5	3	1
• TRUCKS, Virgil														
W 1945	Det-A	1	0	3.38	2	2	1	0	0	13¹	14	5	5	7
• TUDOR, John														
L 1985	StL-N	1	1	2.84	2	2	0	0	0	12²	10	4	3	8
L 1987	StL-N	1	1	1.76	2	2	0	0	0	15¹	16	3	5	12
L 1988	LA-N	0	0	7.20	1	1	0	0	0	5	8	4	1	1
L Total 3		2	2	3.00	5	5	0	0	0	33	34	11	9	21
W 1985	StL-N	2	1	3.00	3	3	1	0	1	18	15	6	7	14
W 1987	StL-N	1	1	5.73	2	2	0	0	0	11	15	7	3	8
W 1988	LA-N	0	0	0.00	1	1	0	0	0	1¹	0	0	0	1
W Total 3		3	2	3.86	6	6	1	0	1	30¹	30	13	10	23
• TUNNELL, Lee														
W 1987	StL-N	0	0	2.08	2	0	0	0	0	4¹	4	1	2	1
• TURLEY, Bob														
W 1955	NY-A	0	1	8.44	3	1	0	0	0	5¹	7	5	4	7
W 1956	NY-A	0	1	0.82	3	1	1	0	0	11	4	1	8	14
W 1957	NY-A	1	0	2.31	3	2	1	0	0	11²	7	3	6	12
W 1958	NY-A	2	1	2.76	4	2	1	1	1	16¹	10	5	7	13
W 1960	NY-A	1	0	4.82	2	2	0	0	0	9¹	15	5	4	0
W Total 5		4	3	3.19	15	8	3	1	1	53²	43	19	29	46
• TURNER, Jim														
W 1940	Cin-N	0	1	7.50	1	1	0	0	0	6	8	5	0	4
W 1942	NY-A	0	0	0.00	1	0	0	0	0	1	0	0	1	0
W Total 2		0	1	6.43	2	1	0	0	0	7	8	5	1	4
• TYLER, Lefty														
W 1914	Bos-N	0	0	3.60	1	1	0	0	0	10	8	4	3	4
W 1918	Chi-N	1	1	1.17	3	3	1	0	0	23	14	3	11	4
W Total 2		1	1	1.91	4	4	1	0	0	33	22	7	14	8
• UHLE, George														
W 1920	Cle-A	0	0	0.00	2	0	0	0	0	3	1	0	0	3
• UNDERWOOD, Tom														
D 1981	Oak-A	0	0	0.00	1	0	0	0	0	0¹	0	0	0	1
L 1976	Phi-N	0	0	0.00	1	0	0	0	0	0¹	1	0	2	0
L 1980	NY-A	0	0	0.00	2	0	0	0	0	3	3	0	0	3
L 1981	Oak-A	0	0	13.50	2	0	0	0	0	1¹	4	2	2	0
L Total 3		0	0	3.86	5	0	0	0	0	4²	8	2	4	3
• UPSHAW, Cecil														
L 1969	Atl-N	0	0	2.84	3	0	0	0	0	6¹	5	2	1	4
• URBINA, Ugueth														
D 2003	Fla-N	0	0	3.00	3	0	0	1	0	3	4	1	1	2
L 2003	Fla-N	1	0	2.57	4	0	0	1	0	7	2	2	0	10
W 2003	Fla-N	0	0	6.00	3	0	0	2	0	3	2	2	3	2
• VALDES, Ismael														
D 1995	LA-N	0	0	0.00	1	1	0	0	0	7	3	0	1	6
D 1996	LA-N	0	1	4.26	1	1	0	0	0	6¹	5	3	0	5
D Total 2		0	1	2.03	2	2	0	0	0	13¹	8	3	1	11
• VALENZUELA, Fernando														
D 1981	LA-N	1	0	1.06	2	2	1	0	0	17	10	2	3	10
D 1996	SD-N	0	0	0.00	1	0	0	0	0	0²	0	0	2	0
D Total 2		1	0	1.02	3	2	1	0	0	17²	10	2	5	10
L 1981	LA-N	1	1	2.45	2	2	0	0	0	14²	10	4	5	10
L 1983	LA-N	1	0	1.13	1	1	0	0	0	8	7	1	4	5
L 1985	LA-N	1	0	1.88	2	2	0	0	0	14¹	11	3	10	13
L Total 3		3	1	1.95	5	5	0	0	0	37	28	8	19	28
W 1981	LA-N	1	0	4.00	1	1	1	0	0	9	9	4	7	6
• VANCE, Dazzy														
W 1934	StL-N	0	0	0.00	1	0	0	0	0	1¹	2	0	1	3
• VANDENBERG, Hy														
W 1945	Chi-N	0	0	0.00	3	0	0	0	0	6	1	0	3	3
• VANDER MEER, Johnny														
W 1940	Cin-N	0	0	0.00	1	0	0	0	0	3	2	0	3	2
• VAUGHN, Hippo														
W 1918	Chi-N	1	2	1.00	3	3	3	0	1	27	17	3	5	17
• VEALE, Bob														
W 1971	Pit-N	0	0	13.50	1	0	0	0	0	0²	1	1	2	0
• VEIL, Bucky														
W 1903	Pit-N	0	0	1.29	1	0	0	0	0	7	5	1	5	1
• VENAFRO, Mike														
D 1999	Tex-A	0	0	0.00	2	0	0	0	0	1	2	0	1	0
• VERAS, Dario														
D 1996	SD-N	0	0	0.00	2	0	0	0	1	1	1	0	0	1
• VERES, Dave														
D 2000	StL-N	0	0	0.00	2	0	0	1	0	2	1	0	0	4
D 2001	StL-N	0	0	0.00	2	0	0	0	0	1	1	0	1	1
D 2003	Chi-N	0	1	13.50	2	0	0	0	0	1¹	2	2	2	0
D Total 3		0	1	4.15	6	0	0	1	0	4¹	4	2	3	5
L 2000	StL-N	0	0	0.00	3	0	0	0	0	2¹	2	0	0	3
L 2002	StL-N	0	0	0.00	3	0	0	0	0	3²	2	0	1	5
L 2003	Chi-N	0	0	3.00	3	0	0	0	0	3	4	1	1	0
L Total 3		0	0	1.00	8	0	0	0	0	9	8	1	2	8
• VILLONE, Ron														
D 2001	Hou-N	0	0	0.00	1	0	0	0	0	0²	0	0	0	0
• VIOLA, Frank														
L 1987	Min-A	1	0	5.25	2	2	0	0	0	12	14	7	5	9
W 1987	Min-A	2	1	3.72	3	3	0	0	0	19¹	17	8	3	16
• VOISELLE, Bill														
W 1948	Bos-N	0	0	2.53	2	1	0	0	0	10²	8	3	2	2
• VOSBERG, Ed														
D 1996	Tex-A	0	0	....	1	0	0	0	0	0	1	0	0	0
L 1997	Fla-N	0	0	0.00	2	0	0	0	0	2²	2	0	1	3
W 1997	Fla-N	0	0	6.00	2	0	0	0	0	3	3	2	3	2
• VUCKOVICH, Pete														
D 1981	Mil-A	1	0	0.00	2	1	0	0	0	5¹	2	0	3	4
L 1982	Mil-A	0	1	4.40	2	2	1	0	0	14¹	15	7	7	8
W 1982	Mil-A	0	0	4.50	2	2	0	0	0	14	16	7	5	4
• WADDELL, Rube														
T 1900	Pit-N	0	1	1.93	2	1	0	0	0	14	15	3	3	7
• WADE, Ben														
W 1953	Bro-N	0	0	15.43	2	0	0	0	0	2¹	4	4	1	2
• WADE, Terrell														
L 1996	Atl-N	0	0	0.00	1	0	0	0	0	0¹	0	0	0	1
W 1996	Atl-N	0	0	0.00	2	0	0	0	0	0²	0	0	1	0
• WAGNER, Billy														
D 1997	Hou-N	0	0	18.00	1	0	0	0	0	1	3	2	0	2
D 1998	Hou-N	1	0	18.00	1	0	0	0	0	1	4	2	0	1
D 1999	Hou-N	0	0	0.00	1	0	0	0	0	1	0	0	0	1
D 2001	Hou-N	0	0	5.40	2	0	0	0	0	1²	1	1	0	3
D Total 4		1	0	9.64	5	0	0	0	0	4²	8	5	0	7
• WAKEFIELD, Tim														
D 1995	Bos-A	0	1	11.81	1	1	0	0	0	5¹	5	7	5	4
D 1998	Bos-A	0	1	33.75	1	1	0	0	0	1¹	3	5	2	1
D 1999	Bos-A	0	0	13.50	2	0	0	0	0	2	3	3	4	4
D 2003	Bos-A	0	1	3.52	2	1	0	0	0	7²	6	3	3	7
D Total 4		0	3	9.92	6	3	0	0	0	16¹	17	18	14	16
L 1992	Pit-N	2	0	3.00	2	2	2	0	0	18	14	6	5	7
L 2003	Bos-A	2	1	2.57	3	2	0	0	0	14	8	4	6	10
L Total 2		4	1	2.81	5	4	2	0	0	32	22	10	11	17
• WALBERG, Rube														
W 1929	Phi-A	1	0	0.00	2	0	0	0	0	6¹	3	0	0	8
W 1930	Phi-A	0	1	3.86	1	1	0	0	0	4²	4	2	1	3
W 1931	Phi-A	0	0	3.00	2	0	0	0	0	3	3	1	2	4
W Total 3		1	1	1.93	5	1	0	0	0	14	10	3	3	15
• WALK, Bob														
L 1982	Atl-N	0	0	9.00	1	0	0	0	0	1	2	1	1	1
L 1990	Pit-N	1	1	4.85	2	2	0	0	0	13	11	7	2	8
L 1991	Pit-N	0	0	1.93	3	0	0	1	0	9¹	5	2	3	5
L 1992	Pit-N	1	0	3.86	2	1	1	0	0	11²	6	5	7	6
L Total 4		2	1	3.86	8	3	1	1	0	35	24	15	13	20
W 1980	Phi-N	1	0	7.71	1	1	0	0	0	7	8	6	3	3
• WALKER, Bill														
W 1934	StL-N	0	2	7.11	2	0	0	0	0	6¹	6	5	6	2
• WALKER, Luke														
L 1970	Pit-N	0	1	1.29	1	1	0	0	0	7	5	1	1	5
L 1971	Pit-N	0	0	18.00	1	0	0	0	0	1	3	2	0	0
L Total 2		0	1	3.38	2	1	0	0	0	8	8	3	1	5
W 1971	Pit-N	0	1	40.50	1	1	0	0	0	0²	3	3	1	0
• WALL, Donne														
D 1998	SD-N	0	0	9.00	1	0	0	0	0	2	2	2	0	2
D 1998	SD-N	0	0	3.00	3	0	0	1	0	3	3	1	4	4
W 1998	SD-N	0	1	6.75	2	0	0	0	0	2²	3	2	3	1

YEAR	TM-L	W	L	ERA	G	GS	CG	SV	SHO	IP	H	ER	BB	SO
• WALLACE, Bobby														
T 1896	Cle-N	0	1	4.50	1	1	1	0	0	8	10	4	2	4
• WALSH, Ed														
W 1906	Chi-A	2	0	1.20	2	2	1	0	1	15	7	2	6	17
• WALTERS, Bucky														
W 1939	Cin-N	0	2	4.91	2	1	1	0	0	11	13	6	1	6
W 1940	Cin-N	2	0	1.50	2	2	2	0	1	18	8	3	6	6
W Total	**2**	**2**	**2**	**2.79**	**4**	**3**	**3**	**0**	**1**	**29**	**21**	**9**	**7**	**12**
• WARD, Duane														
L 1989	Tor-A	0	0	7.36	2	0	0	0	0	3^2	6	3	3	5
L 1991	Tor-A	0	1	6.23	2	0	0	1	0	4^1	4	3	1	6
L 1992	Tor-A	1	0	6.75	3	0	0	0	0	4	6	3	1	2
L 1993	Tor-A	0	0	5.79	4	0	0	2	0	4^2	4	3	4	8
L Total	**4**	**1**	**1**	**6.48**	**11**	**0**	**0**	**3**	**0**	16^2	**20**	**12**	**9**	**21**
W 1992	Tor-A	2	0	0.00	4	0	0	0	0	3^1	1	0	1	6
W 1993	Tor-A	1	0	1.93	4	0	0	1	0	4^2	3	1	0	7
W Total	**2**	**3**	**0**	**1.13**	**8**	**0**	**0**	**1**	**0**	**8**	**4**	**1**	**1**	**13**
• WARNEKE, Lon														
W 1932	Chi-N	0	1	5.91	2	1	1	0	0	10^2	15	7	5	8
W 1935	Chi-N	2	0	0.54	3	2	1	0	1	16^2	9	1	4	5
W Total	**2**	**2**	**1**	**2.63**	**5**	**3**	**2**	**0**	**1**	27^1	**24**	**8**	**9**	**13**
• WASDIN, John														
D 1998	Bos-A	0	0	10.80	1	0	0	0	0	1^2	2	2	1	2
D 1999	Bos-A	0	0	27.00	2	0	0	0	0	1^2	2	5	4	1
D Total	**2**	**0**	**0**	**18.90**	**3**	**0**	**0**	**0**	**0**	3^1	**4**	**7**	**5**	**3**
• WASHBURN, Jarrod														
D 2002	Ana-A	1	0	3.75	2	2	0	0	0	12	12	5	3	4
L 2002	Ana-A	0	0	1.29	1	1	0	0	0	7	6	1	0	7
W 2002	Ana-A	0	2	9.31	2	2	0	0	0	9^2	12	10	7	6
• WASHBURN, Ray														
W 1967	StL-N	0	0	0.00	2	0	0	0	0	2^1	1	0	1	2
W 1968	StL-N	1	1	9.82	2	2	0	0	0	7^1	7	8	7	6
W 1970	Cin-N	0	0	13.50	1	0	0	0	0	1^1	2	2	2	0
W Total	**3**	**1**	**1**	**8.18**	**5**	**2**	**0**	**0**	**0**	**11**	**10**	**10**	**10**	**8**
• WASLEWSKI, Gary														
W 1967	Bos-A	0	0	2.16	2	1	0	0	0	8^1	4	2	2	7
• WATSON, Allen														
L 1999	NY-A	0	0	0.00	3	0	0	0	0	1	2	0	2	1
• WATSON, Mule														
W 1923	NY-N	0	0	13.50	1	1	0	0	0	2	4	3	1	1
W 1924	NY-N	0	0	0.00	1	0	0	1	0	0^2	0	0	0	0
W Total	**2**	**0**	**0**	**10.13**	**2**	**1**	**0**	**1**	**0**	2^2	**4**	**3**	**1**	**1**
• WATT, Eddie														
L 1969	Bal-A	0	0	0.00	1	0	0	0	0	2	0	0	0	2
L 1971	Bal-A	0	0	0.00	1	0	0	1	0	2	2	0	0	1
L 1973	Bal-A	0	0	0.00	1	0	0	0	0	0^1	0	0	0	0
L Total	**3**	**0**	**0**	**0.00**	**3**	**0**	**0**	**1**	**0**	4^1	**2**	**0**	**0**	**3**
W 1969	Bal-A	0	1	3.00	2	0	0	0	0	3	4	1	0	3
W 1970	Bal-A	0	1	9.00	1	0	0	0	0	1	2	1	1	3
W 1971	Bal-A	0	1	3.86	2	0	0	0	0	2^1	4	1	0	2
W Total	**3**	**0**	**3**	**4.26**	**5**	**0**	**0**	**0**	**0**	6^1	**10**	**3**	**1**	**8**
• WEATHERS, Dave														
D 1996	NY-A	1	0	0.00	2	0	0	0	0	5	1	0	0	5
L 1996	NY-A	1	0	0.00	2	0	0	0	0	3	3	0	0	0
W 1996	NY-A	0	0	3.00	3	0	0	0	0	3	2	1	3	3
• WEAVER, Jeff														
D 2002	NY-A	0	0	6.75	2	0	0	0	0	2^2	4	2	3	1
W 2003	NY-A	0	1	9.00	1	0	0	0	0	1	1	1	0	0
• WEAVER, Monte														
W 1933	Was-A	0	1	1.74	1	1	0	0	0	10^1	11	2	4	3
• WEBER, Ben														
D 2002	Ana-A	0	1	18.00	2	0	0	0	0	1	2	2	2	0
L 2002	Ana-A	0	0	3.38	3	0	0	0	0	2^2	3	1	0	3
W 2002	Ana-A	0	0	13.50	4	0	0	0	0	4^2	10	7	2	5
• WELCH, Bob														
D 1981	LA-N	0	0	0.00	1	0	0	0	0	1	0	0	1	1
L 1978	LA-N	1	0	2.08	1	0	0	0	0	4^1	2	1	0	5
L 1981	LA-N	0	0	5.40	3	0	0	1	0	1^2	2	1	0	2
L 1983	LA-N	0	1	6.75	1	1	0	0	0	1^1	0	1	2	0
L 1985	LA-N	0	1	6.75	1	1	0	0	0	2^2	5	2	6	2
L 1988	Oak-A	0	0	27.00	1	1	0	0	0	1^2	6	5	2	0
L 1989	Oak-A	1	0	3.18	1	1	0	0	0	5^2	8	2	1	4
L 1990	Oak-A	1	0	1.23	1	1	0	0	0	7^1	6	1	3	4
L 1992	Oak-A	0	0	2.57	1	1	0	0	0	7	7	2	1	7
L Total	**8**	**3**	**2**	**4.26**	**10**	**6**	**0**	**1**	**0**	31^2	**36**	**15**	**15**	**24**
W 1978	LA-N	0	1	6.23	3	0	0	1	0	4^1	4	3	2	6
W 1981	LA-N	0	0	....	1	1	0	0	0	0	3	2	1	0
W 1988	Oak-A	0	0	1.80	1	1	0	0	0	5	6	1	3	8
W 1990	Oak-A	0	0	4.91	1	1	0	0	0	7^1	9	4	2	2
W Total	**4**	**0**	**1**	**5.40**	**6**	**3**	**0**	**1**	**0**	16^2	**22**	**10**	**8**	**16**
• WELCH, Mickey														
W 1888	NY-N	1	1	2.65	2	2	2	0	0	17	10	5	9	2
W 1889	NY-N	0	1	9.00	1	1	0	0	0	5	11	5	3	1
W Total	**2**	**1**	**2**	**4.09**	**3**	**3**	**2**	**0**	**0**	**22**	**21**	**10**	**12**	**3**
• WELLS, Bob														
D 1995	Sea-A	0	0	9.00	1	0	0	0	0	1	2	1	1	0
D 1997	Sea-A	0	0	0.00	1	0	0	0	0	1^1	1	0	0	1
D Total	**2**	**0**	**0**	**3.86**	**2**	**0**	**0**	**0**	**0**	2^1	**3**	**1**	**1**	**1**
L 1995	Sea-A	0	0	3.00	1	0	0	0	0	3	2	1	2	2
L 2002	Min-A	0	0	9.00	2	0	0	0	0	1	2	1	0	2
L Total	**2**	**0**	**0**	**4.50**	**3**	**0**	**0**	**0**	**0**	**4**	**4**	**2**	**2**	**4**
• WELLS, David														
D 1995	Cin-N	1	0	0.00	1	1	0	0	0	6^1	6	0	1	8
D 1996	Bal-A	1	0	4.61	2	2	0	0	0	13^2	15	7	4	6
D 1997	NY-A	1	0	1.00	1	1	1	0	0	9	5	1	0	1
D 1998	NY-A	1	0	0.00	1	1	0	0	0	8	5	0	1	9
D 2002	NY-A	0	1	15.43	1	1	0	0	0	4^2	10	8	0	0
D 2003	NY-A	1	0	1.17	1	1	0	0	0	7^2	8	1	0	5
D Total	**6**	**5**	**1**	**3.10**	**7**	**7**	**1**	**0**	**0**	49^1	**49**	**17**	**6**	**29**
L 1989	Tor-A	0	0	0.00	1	0	0	0	0	1	0	0	2	1
L 1991	Tor-A	0	0	2.35	4	0	0	0	0	7^2	6	2	2	9
L 1995	Cin-N	0	1	4.50	1	1	0	0	0	6	8	3	2	3
L 1996	Bal-A	1	0	4.05	1	1	0	0	0	6^2	8	3	3	6
L 1998	NY-A	2	0	2.87	2	2	0	0	0	15^2	12	5	2	18
L 2003	NY-A	1	0	2.35	2	1	0	0	0	7^2	5	2	2	5
L Total	**6**	**4**	**1**	**3.02**	**11**	**5**	**0**	**0**	**0**	44^2	**39**	**15**	**13**	**42**
W 1992	Tor-A	0	0	0.00	4	0	0	0	0	4^1	1	0	2	3
W 1998	NY-A	1	0	6.43	1	1	0	0	0	7	7	5	2	4
W 2003	NY-A	0	1	3.38	2	2	0	0	0	8	6	3	2	1
W Total	**3**	**1**	**1**	**3.72**	**7**	**3**	**0**	**0**	**0**	19^1	**14**	**8**	**6**	**8**
• WENDELL, Turk														
D 1999	NY-N	1	0	0.00	2	0	0	0	0	2	0	0	2	0
D 2000	NY-N	0	0	0.00	2	0	0	0	0	2	0	0	1	5
D Total	**2**	**1**	**0**	**0.00**	**4**	**0**	**0**	**0**	**0**	**4**	**0**	**0**	**3**	**5**
L 1999	NY-N	1	0	4.76	5	0	0	0	0	5^2	2	3	4	5
L 2000	NY-N	1	0	0.00	2	0	0	0	0	1^1	1	0	1	2
L Total	**2**	**2**	**0**	**3.86**	**7**	**0**	**0**	**0**	**0**	**7**	**3**	**3**	**5**	**7**
W 2000	NY-N	0	1	5.40	2	0	0	0	0	1^2	3	1	2	2
• WENSLOFF, Butch														
W 1947	NY-A	0	0	0.00	1	0	0	0	0	2	0	0	0	0
• WEST, David														
L 1991	Min-A	1	0	0.00	2	0	0	0	0	5^2	1	0	4	4
L 1993	Phi-N	0	0	13.50	3	0	0	0	0	2^2	5	4	2	5
L Total	**2**	**1**	**0**	**4.32**	**5**	**0**	**0**	**0**	**0**	8^1	**6**	**4**	**6**	**9**
W 1991	Min-A	0	0	....	2	0	0	0	0	0	2	4	4	0
W 1993	Phi-N	0	0	27.00	3	0	0	0	0	1	5	3	1	0
W Total	**2**	**0**	**0**	**63.00**	**5**	**0**	**0**	**0**	**0**	**1**	**7**	**7**	**5**	**0**
• WETTELAND, John														
D 1995	NY-A	0	1	14.54	3	0	0	0	0	4^1	8	7	2	5
D 1996	NY-A	0	0	0.00	3	0	0	2	0	4	2	0	4	4
D 1998	Tex-A	0	0	0.00	1	0	0	0	0	1	0	0	1	1
D 1999	Tex-A	0	0	0.00	1	0	0	0	0	1	0	0	0	1
D Total	**4**	**0**	**1**	**6.10**	**8**	**0**	**0**	**2**	**0**	10^1	**10**	**7**	**7**	**11**
L 1996	NY-A	0	0	4.50	4	0	0	1	0	4	2	2	1	5
W 1996	NY-A	0	0	2.08	5	0	0	4	0	4^1	4	1	1	6
• WHITE, Doc														
W 1906	Chi-A	1	1	1.80	3	2	1	1	0	15	12	3	7	4
• WHITE, Ernie														
W 1942	StL-N	1	0	0.00	1	1	1	0	1	9	6	0	0	6
• WHITE, Gabe														
D 2003	NY-A	0	0	0.00	1	0	0	0	0	1^1	1	0	0	1
L 2003	NY-A	0	0	4.50	2	0	0	0	0	2	4	1	0	1
• WHITE, Rick														
D 2000	NY-N	1	0	0.00	2	0	0	0	0	2^2	6	0	2	4
D 2002	StL-N	0	0	0.00	2	0	0	0	0	2	1	0	1	1
D Total	**2**	**1**	**0**	**0.00**	**4**	**0**	**0**	**0**	**0**	4^2	**7**	**0**	**3**	**5**
L 2000	NY-N	0	0	9.00	1	0	0	0	0	3	5	3	1	1
L 2002	StL-N	0	1	4.50	3	0	0	0	0	4	2	2	2	5
L Total	**2**	**0**	**1**	**6.43**	**4**	**0**	**0**	**0**	**0**	**7**	**7**	**5**	**3**	**6**
W 2000	NY-N	0	0	6.75	1	0	0	0	0	1^1	1	1	1	1
• WHITEHILL, Earl														
W 1933	Was-A	1	0	0.00	1	1	1	0	1	9	5	0	2	2
• WHITSON, Ed														
L 1984	SD-N	1	0	1.13	1	1	0	0	0	8	5	1	2	6
W 1984	SD-N	0	0	40.50	1	1	0	0	0	0^2	5	3	0	0
• WICKER, Kemp														
W 1937	NY-A	0	0	0.00	1	0	0	0	0	1	0	0	0	0
• WICKMAN, Bob														
D 1995	NY-A	0	0	0.00	3	0	0	0	0	3	5	0	0	3
D 2001	Cle-A	0	0	0.00	1	0	0	0	0	1	0	0	0	2
D Total	**2**	**0**	**0**	**0.00**	**4**	**0**	**0**	**0**	**0**	**4**	**5**	**0**	**0**	**5**
• WILCOX, Milt														
L 1970	Cin-N	1	0	0.00	1	0	0	0	0	3	1	0	2	5
L 1984	Det-A	1	0	0.00	1	1	0	0	0	8	2	0	2	8
L Total	**2**	**2**	**0**	**0.00**	**2**	**1**	**0**	**0**	**0**	**11**	**3**	**0**	**4**	**13**
W 1970	Cin-N	0	1	9.00	2	0	0	0	0	2	3	2	0	2
W 1984	Det-A	1	0	1.50	1	1	0	0	0	6	7	1	2	4
W Total	**2**	**1**	**1**	**3.38**	**3**	**1**	**0**	**0**	**0**	**8**	**10**	**3**	**2**	**6**
• WILHELM, Hoyt														
W 1954	NY-N	0	0	0.00	2	0	0	1	0	2^1	1	0	0	3
• WILKINSON, Roy														
W 1919	Chi-A	0	0	1.23	2	0	0	0	0	7^1	9	1	4	3

YEAR	TM-L	W	L	ERA	G	GS	CG	SV	SHO	IP	H	ER	BB	SO
• WILKS, Ted														
W 1944	StL-N	0	1	5.68	2	1	0	1	0	6^1	5	4	3	7
W 1946	StL-N	0	0	0.00	1	0	0	0	0	1	2	0	0	0
W Total	2	0	1	4.91	3	1	0	1	0	7^1	7	4	3	7
• WILLETT, Ed														
W 1909	Det-A	0	0	0.00	2	0	0	0	0	7^2	3	0	0	1
• WILLEY, Carl														
W 1958	Mil-N	0	0	0.00	1	0	0	0	0	1	0	0	0	2
• WILLIAMS, Jerome														
D 2003	SF-N	0	0	13.50	1	1	0	0	0	2	5	3	1	1
• WILLIAMS, Lefty														
W 1917	Chi-A	0	0	9.00	1	0	0	0	0	1	2	1	0	3
W 1919	Chi-A	0	3	6.61	3	3	1	0	0	16^1	12	12	8	4
W Total	2	0	3	6.75	4	3	1	0	0	17^1	14	13	8	7
• WILLIAMS, Mike														
D 2001	Hou-N	0	0	9.00	1	0	0	0	0	1	3	1	0	1
• WILLIAMS, Mitch														
L 1989	Chi-N	0	0	0.00	2	0	0	0	0	1	1	0	0	2
L 1993	Phi-N	2	0	1.69	4	0	0	2	0	5^1	6	1	2	5
L Total	2	2	0	1.42	6	0	0	2	0	6^1	7	1	2	7
W 1993	Phi-N	0	2	20.25	3	0	0	1	0	2^2	5	6	4	1
• WILLIAMS, Stan														
L 1970	Min-A	0	0	0.00	2	0	0	0	0	6	2	0	1	2
W 1959	LA-N	0	0	0.00	1	0	0	0	0	2	0	0	2	1
W 1963	NY-A	0	0	0.00	1	0	0	0	0	3	1	0	0	5
W Total	2	0	0	0.00	2	0	0	0	0	5	1	0	2	6
• WILLIAMS, Woody														
D 2001	StL-N	1	0	1.29	1	1	0	0	0	7	4	1	1	9
L 2002	StL-N	0	1	4.50	1	1	0	0	0	6	6	3	1	7
• WILLIAMSON, Ned														
W 1886	Chi-N	0	1	4.50	2	0	0	0	0	2	4	1	1	2
• WILLIAMSON, Scott														
D 2003	Bos-A	2	0	0.00	5	0	0	0	0	5	2	0	3	8
L 2003	Bos-A	0	0	3.00	3	0	0	3	0	3	1	1	0	6
• WILLIS, Carl														
L 1991	Min-A	0	0	0.00	3	0	0	0	0	5^1	2	0	0	3
W 1991	Min-A	0	0	5.14	4	0	0	0	0	7	6	4	2	2
• WILLIS, Dontrelle														
D 2003	Fla-N	0	0	7.94	2	1	0	0	0	5^2	7	5	2	3
L 2003	Fla-N	0	1	18.90	2	1	0	0	0	3^1	4	7	6	4
W 2003	Fla-N	0	0	0.00	3	0	0	0	0	3^2	4	0	2	3
• WILLIS, Ron														
W 1967	StL-N	0	0	27.00	3	0	0	0	0	1	2	3	4	1
W 1968	StL-N	0	0	8.31	3	0	0	0	0	4^1	2	4	4	3
W Total	2	0	0	11.81	6	0	0	0	0	5^1	4	7	8	4
• WILLIS, Vic														
W 1909	Pit-N	0	1	3.97	1	0	0	0	0	11^1	10	5	8	3
• WILLOUGHBY, Jim														
W 1975	Bos-A	0	1	0.00	3	0	0	0	0	6^1	3	0	0	2
• WILSON, Earl														
W 1968	Det-A	0	1	6.23	1	1	0	0	0	4^1	4	3	6	3
• WILSON, Steve														
L 1989	Chi-N	0	1	4.91	2	0	0	0	0	3^2	3	2	1	4
• WILTSE, Hooks														
W 1911	NY-N	0	0	18.90	2	0	0	0	0	3^1	8	7	0	2
• WINTER, George														
W 1908	Det-A	0	0	0.00	1	0	0	0	0	1	1	0	1	0
• WISE, Rick														
L 1975	Bos-A	1	0	2.45	1	1	0	0	0	7^1	6	2	3	2
W 1975	Bos-A	1	0	8.44	2	1	0	0	0	5^1	6	5	2	2
• WITASICK, Jay														
D 2001	NY-A	0	0	13.50	1	0	0	0	0	0^2	1	1	1	0
D 2002	SF-N	0	0	0.00	2	0	0	0	0	2^1	0	0	0	1
D Total	2	0	0	3.00	3	0	0	0	0	3	1	1	1	1
L 2001	NY-A	0	0	9.00	1	0	0	0	0	3	6	3	0	2
L 2002	SF-N	0	1	9.00	1	0	0	0	0	1	1	1	0	0
L Total	2	0	1	9.00	2	0	0	0	0	4	7	4	0	2
W 2001	NY-A	0	0	54.00	1	0	0	0	0	1^1	10	8	0	4
W 2002	SF-N	0	0	54.00	2	0	0	0	0	0^1	3	2	2	1
W Total	2	0	0	54.00	3	0	0	0	0	1^2	13	10	2	5
• WITT, Bobby														
D 1996	Tex-A	0	0	8.10	1	1	0	0	0	3^1	4	3	2	3
L 1992	Oak-A	0	0	18.00	1	0	0	0	0	1	2	2	1	1
L 2001	Ari-N	0	0	27.00	1	0	0	0	0	0^1	3	1	0	0
L Total	2	0	0	20.25	2	0	0	0	0	1^1	5	3	1	1
W 2001	Ari-N	0	0	0.00	1	0	0	0	0	1	0	0	1	1
• WITT, George														
W 1960	Pit-N	0	0	0.00	3	0	0	0	0	2^2	5	0	2	1
• WITT, Mike														
L 1982	Cal-A	0	0	6.00	1	0	0	0	0	3	2	2	2	3
L 1986	Cal-A	1	0	2.55	2	2	1	0	0	17^2	13	5	2	8
L Total	2	1	0	3.05	3	2	1	0	0	20^2	15	7	4	11
• WOHLERS, Mark														
D 1995	Atl-N	0	1	6.75	3	0	0	2	0	2^2	6	2	2	4
D 1996	Atl-N	0	0	0.00	3	0	0	3	0	3^1	1	0	0	4
D 1997	Atl-N	0	0	0.00	1	0	0	0	0	1	1	0	0	1
D Total	3	0	1	2.57	7	0	0	5	0	7	8	2	2	9
L 1991	Atl-N	0	0	0.00	3	0	0	0	0	1^2	2	0	1	1
L 1992	Atl-N	0	0	0.00	3	0	0	0	0	3	2	0	1	2
L 1993	Atl-N	0	1	3.38	4	0	0	0	0	5^1	2	2	3	10
L 1995	Atl-N	1	0	1.80	4	0	0	1	0	5	2	1	0	8
L 1996	Atl-N	0	0	0.00	3	0	0	2	0	3	0	0	0	4
L 1997	Atl-N	0	0	0.00	1	0	0	0	0	1	0	0	1	1
L 2001	NY-A	0	0	13.50	1	0	0	0	0	0^2	3	1	1	1
L Total	7	1	1	1.83	19	0	0	3	0	19^2	12	4	7	27
W 1991	Atl-N	0	0	0.00	3	0	0	0	0	1^2	2	0	2	1
W 1992	Atl-N	0	0	0.00	2	0	0	0	0	0^2	0	0	1	0
W 1995	Atl-N	0	0	1.80	4	0	0	2	0	5	4	1	3	3
W 1996	Atl-N	0	0	6.23	4	0	0	0	0	4^1	7	3	2	4
W Total	4	0	0	3.09	13	0	0	2	0	11^2	13	4	8	8
• WOLCOTT, Bob														
L 1995	Sea-A	1	0	2.57	1	1	0	0	0	7	8	2	5	2
• WOOD, Joe														
W 1912	Bos-A	3	1	3.68	4	3	2	0	0	22	27	9	3	21
• WOOD, Kerry														
D 1998	Chi-N	0	1	1.80	1	1	0	0	0	5	3	1	4	5
D 2003	Chi-N	2	0	1.76	2	2	0	0	0	15^1	7	3	7	18
D Total	2	2	1	1.77	3	3	0	0	0	20^1	10	4	11	23
L 2003	Chi-N	0	1	7.30	2	2	0	0	0	12^1	14	10	7	13
• WOODESHICK, Hal														
W 1967	StL-N	0	0	0.00	1	0	0	0	0	1	0	0	0	0
• WOODSON, Dick														
L 1969	Min-A	0	0	10.80	1	0	0	0	0	1^2	3	2	3	2
L 1970	Min-A	0	0	9.00	1	0	0	0	0	1	2	1	1	0
L Total	2	0	0	10.13	2	0	0	0	0	2^2	5	3	4	2
• WORKS, Ralph														
W 1909	Det-A	0	0	9.00	1	0	0	0	0	2	4	2	1	2
• WORRELL, Tim														
D 1996	SD-N	0	0	2.45	2	0	0	0	0	3^2	4	1	1	2
D 2002	SF-N	0	0	12.00	3	0	0	0	0	3	7	4	2	3
D 2003	SF-N	0	1	0.00	2	0	0	0	0	2^2	3	0	3	0
D Total	3	0	1	4.82	7	0	0	0	0	9^1	14	5	6	5
L 2002	SF-N	2	0	2.08	4	0	0	0	0	4^1	2	1	0	4
W 2002	SF-N	1	1	3.18	6	0	0	0	0	5^2	4	2	1	4
• WORRELL, Todd														
D 1996	LA-N	0	0	0.00	1	0	0	0	0	1	0	0	1	1
L 1985	StL-N	1	0	1.42	4	0	0	0	0	6^1	4	1	2	3
L 1987	StL-N	0	0	2.08	3	0	0	1	0	4^1	4	1	1	6
L Total	2	1	0	1.69	7	0	0	1	0	10^2	8	2	3	9
W 1985	StL-N	0	1	3.86	3	0	0	1	0	4^2	4	2	2	6
W 1987	StL-N	0	0	1.29	4	0	0	2	0	7	6	1	4	3
W Total	2	0	1	2.31	7	0	0	3	0	11^2	10	3	6	9
• WORTHINGTON, Al														
L 1969	Min-A	0	0	6.75	1	0	0	0	0	1^1	3	1	0	1
W 1965	Min-A	0	0	0.00	2	0	0	0	0	4	2	0	2	2
• WRIGHT, Jaret														
D 1997	Cle-A	2	0	3.97	2	2	0	0	0	11^1	11	5	7	10
D 1998	Cle-A	0	1	12.46	1	1	0	0	0	4^1	7	6	2	6
D 1999	Cle-A	0	1	22.50	1	0	0	0	0	2	4	5	1	1
D 2003	Atl-N	0	0	0.00	4	0	0	0	0	4	0	0	2	4
D Total	4	2	2	6.65	8	3	0	0	0	21^2	22	16	12	21
L 1997	Cle-A	0	0	15.00	1	1	0	0	0	3	6	5	2	3
L 1998	Cle-A	0	1	8.10	2	1	0	0	0	6^2	7	6	8	4
L Total	2	0	1	10.24	3	2	0	0	0	9^2	13	11	10	7
W 1997	Cle-A	1	0	2.92	2	2	0	0	0	12^1	7	4	10	12
• WUNSCH, Kelly														
D 2000	Chi-A	0	1	0.00	3	0	0	0	0	0^2	2	0	0	0
• WYATT, John														
W 1967	Bos-A	1	0	4.91	2	0	0	0	0	3^2	1	2	3	1
• WYATT, Whit														
W 1941	Bro-N	1	1	2.50	2	2	2	0	0	18	15	5	10	14
• WYCKOFF, Weldon														
W 1914	Phi-A	0	0	2.45	1	0	0	0	0	3^2	3	1	1	2
• WYNN, Early														
W 1954	Cle-A	0	0	3.86	1	1	0	0	0	7	4	3	2	5
W 1959	Chi-A	1	1	5.54	3	3	0	0	0	13	19	8	4	10
W Total	2	1	2	4.95	4	4	0	0	0	20	23	11	6	15
• WYSE, Hank														
W 1945	Chi-N	0	1	7.04	3	1	0	0	0	7^2	8	6	4	1
• YDE, Emil														
W 1925	Pit-N	0	1	11.57	1	0	0	0	0	2^1	5	3	3	1
• YOSHII, Masato														
D 1999	NY-N	0	0	6.75	1	1	0	0	0	5^1	6	4	0	3
L 1999	NY-N	0	1	4.70	2	2	0	0	0	7^2	9	4	3	4
• YOUNG, Curt														
L 1988	Oak-A	0	0	6.00	1	0	0	0	0	1^1	1	0	0	2
W 1988	Oak-A	0	0	0.00	1	0	0	0	0	1	1	0	0	1
W 1990	Oak-A	0	0	0.00	1	0	0	0	0	1	0	0	0	0
W Total	2	0	0	0.00	2	0	0	0	0	2	2	0	0	0

• YOUNG, Cy

YEAR	TM-L	W	L	ERA	G	GS	CG	SV	SHO	IP	H	ER	BB	SO
T 1892	Cle-N	0	2	3.00	3	3	3	0	1	27	26	9	3	9
T 1895	Cle-N	3	0	2.33	3	3	3	0	0	27	28	7	4	2
T 1896	Cle-N	0	1	6.00	1	1	1	0	0	9	13	6	1	0
T Total 3		**3**	**3**	**3.14**	**7**	**7**	**7**	**0**	**1**	**63**	**67**	**22**	**8**	**11**
W 1903	Bos-A	2	1	1.85	4	3	3	0	0	34	31	7	4	17

• YOUNG, Matt

YEAR	TM-L	W	L	ERA	G	GS	CG	SV	SHO	IP	H	ER	BB	SO
L 1989	Oak-A	0	0	0.00	1	0	0	0	0	0¹	0	0	2	0

• ZACHARY, Chris

YEAR	TM-L	W	L	ERA	G	GS	CG	SV	SHO	IP	H	ER	BB	SO
L 1972	Det-A	0	0	....	1	0	0	0	0	0	0	1	1	0

• ZACHARY, Tom

YEAR	TM-L	W	L	ERA	G	GS	CG	SV	SHO	IP	H	ER	BB	SO
W 1924	Was-A	2	0	2.04	2	2	1	0	0	17²	13	4	3	3
W 1925	Was-A	0	0	10.80	1	0	0	0	0	1²	3	2	1	0
W 1928	NY-A	1	0	3.00	1	1	1	0	0	9	9	3	1	7
W Total 3		**3**	**0**	**2.86**	**4**	**3**	**2**	**0**	**0**	**28¹**	**25**	**9**	**5**	**10**

• ZACHRY, Pat

YEAR	TM-L	W	L	ERA	G	GS	CG	SV	SHO	IP	H	ER	BB	SO
L 1976	Cin-N	1	0	3.60	1	1	0	0	0	5	6	2	3	3
L 1983	LA-N	0	0	2.25	2	0	0	0	0	4	4	1	2	2
L Total 2		**1**	**0**	**3.00**	**3**	**1**	**0**	**0**	**0**	**9**	**10**	**3**	**5**	**5**
W 1976	Cin-N	1	0	2.70	1	1	0	0	0	6²	6	2	5	6

• ZAHN, Geoff

YEAR	TM-L	W	L	ERA	G	GS	CG	SV	SHO	IP	H	ER	BB	SO
L 1982	Cal-A	0	1	7.36	1	1	0	0	0	3²	4	3	1	2

• ZAMBRANO, Carlos

YEAR	TM-L	W	L	ERA	G	GS	CG	SV	SHO	IP	H	ER	BB	SO
D 2003	Chi-N	0	0	4.76	1	1	0	0	0	5²	11	3	0	4
L 2003	Chi-N	0	1	5.73	2	2	0	0	0	11	14	7	5	8

• ZEPP, Bill

YEAR	TM-L	W	L	ERA	G	GS	CG	SV	SHO	IP	H	ER	BB	SO
L 1970	Min-A	0	0	6.75	2	0	0	0	0	1¹	2	1	2	2

• ZERBE, Chad

YEAR	TM-L	W	L	ERA	G	GS	CG	SV	SHO	IP	H	ER	BB	SO
W 2002	SF-N	1	0	3.00	3	0	0	0	0	6	6	2	0	0

• ZIMMERMAN, Jeff

YEAR	TM-L	W	L	ERA	G	GS	CG	SV	SHO	IP	H	ER	BB	SO
D 1999	Tex-A	0	0	0.00	1	0	0	0	0	1	1	0	0	1

• ZITO, Barry

YEAR	TM-L	W	L	ERA	G	GS	CG	SV	SHO	IP	H	ER	BB	SO
D 2000	Oak-A	1	0	1.59	1	1	0	0	0	5²	7	1	2	5
D 2001	Oak-A	0	1	1.13	1	1	0	0	0	8	2	1	1	6
D 2002	Oak-A	1	0	4.50	1	1	0	0	0	6	5	3	4	8
D 2003	Oak-A	1	1	3.46	2	2	0	0	0	13	9	5	4	13
D Total 4		**3**	**2**	**2.76**	**5**	**5**	**0**	**0**	**0**	**32²**	**23**	**10**	**11**	**32**

• ZUBER, Bill

YEAR	TM-L	W	L	ERA	G	GS	CG	SV	SHO	IP	H	ER	BB	SO
W 1946	Bos-N	0	0	4.50	1	0	0	0	0	2	3	1	1	1

Appendix

Al Kaline
Winner of an AL batting crown at age 20, Kaline played 22 years for the Tigers, collecting 3,007 hits and 399 home runs.

FAMOUS FIRSTS

1922: The 30-30 club is born when Ken Williams becomes the first player to hit 30 home runs with 30 stolen bases in a season.

1938: Johnny Vander Meer no-hits Brooklyn to become the first pitcher to toss back-to-back no hitters.

1946: Lou Boudreau becomes the first major leaguer to record five extra-base hits in a single game.

1947: Johnny Mize becomes the first player to hit 50 home runs with fewer than 50 strikeouts in a season.

1965: Rick Monday is the first player selected as Major League Baseball conducts its first amateur draft.

1993: Selected in the 43rd round by the Chicago White Sox, Carey Schueler, 18, becomes the first woman chosen in the amateur free agent draft.

1999: Sammy Sosa becomes the first major leaguer to record back-to-back 60 home run seasons.

Appendix A

Major League Attendance

By Robert L. Tiemann

Today's box scores contain all manner of statistics, including one that has nothing to do with the outcome of the specific game on the field but everything to do with the popularity of The Game, the paid attendance. Although home gate revenues now account for less than 40 percent of major league teams' total income, home attendance still stands as the most visible measure of a club's financial health and its standing in the community.

From modest beginnings, major league attendance has shown generally steady growth, albeit with some slack periods and some spectacular jumps. The first-ever pennant race in 1871 brought out good crowds averaging nearly 2,100 per championship game. While the number of official games increased in the subsequent NA years, the average dropped steadily. The founding of the National League in 1876 helped bring out the first big league crowds exceeding 10,000 paying customers. But the League's 50-cent-minimum admission price, coupled with a poor national economy, caused attendance to suffer in the late 1870s, with the average dropping below 800 in both 1879 and 1880. The founding of the American Association (with a 25-cent pricing policy) helped revive public interest in the early 1880s. In 1882 the St. Louis and Chicago clubs became the first to top the 100,000 mark in regular-season attendance. By the end of the decade a couple of games had drawn over 20,000 customers, and a couple of clubs had topped 300,000 in a season. The Players League war of 1890 hurt all clubs, but with the merger of four AA clubs into the NL in 1892, steady growth returned. The Phillies soared to 474,000 when they unveiled a state-of-the-art ballpark in 1895, and the overall league attendance reached 2.9 million the following year.

Following another slump in the late 1890s, the new century saw a new spurt in interest, stimulated by the founding of the American League. Two red-hot pennant races in 1908 brought the aggregate gate over 7 million for the first time and spawned a stadium-building boom that began in 1909. Alas, in the next decade attendance slumped, with sharp drop-offs during the Federal League war and in the World War I year of 1918. But the national "Return to Normalcy" in the 1920s helped the major leagues draw over 8.5 million every year. Nearly every ballpark underwent some expansion during the decade, and nearly every club established new single-game and season-total attendance records. The 1920 Yankees, with newly acquired Babe Ruth, became the first to top a million in a season. Using the new medium of radio to expand their fan base, the Cubs became the first NL team to reach that milestone in 1927. In 1930 major league attendance passed 10 million for the first time.

The Depression decade of the 1930s was accompanied by a downturn in big league revenues. The Cubs still topped the million mark in 1930 and 1931 before declining, while the sad-sack St. Louis Browns drew under 100,000 in 1933 and 1935. Beginning with the Cincinnati Reds in 1935, clubs began to stage

Wrigley Field
Chicago's legendary ballfield, opened in 1914, mixes bleacher bums with the neighboring fans in baseball's most intimate setting.

night games on a limited basis, helping to combat the slide.

World War II brought large numbers of night games, and the end of the war saw a spectacular boost in attendance. In 1946 the Yankees broke the old single-season record by July 17 on their way to becoming the first club to top 2 million. That same season no fewer than 11 of the 16 major league clubs established new franchise attendance marks and the overall total was 70 perecent higher than the previous record. The postwar peak came in 1948, when the total nearly reached 21 million and the pennant-winning Indians set a record with 2.6 million, including eleven paying crowds of more than 70,000 fans.

By 1952, however, big league gate totals had dropped below 15 million as television and other entertainment cut into baseball's prominence. The major leagues suffered less than the minors from this trend, to be sure, as they were able to profit from TV contracts. But the ancient arrangement of 16 franchises in just 11 cities needed to be changed. The first franchise move, the Braves to Milwaukee, was a tremendous success, and they set a new National League single-season record in 1953. Four other teams had moved by 1958, and by the end of the decade overall patronage was nearly 20 million again.

As other cities clamored for franchises, expanding the number of clubs was the next logical step, and eight clubs were added by the end of the 1960s. Total attendance topped 27 million, although the per-team average was down from ten years before. The Los Angeles Dodgers set the pace for much of the era, opening their new stadium in 1962 to a new single-season record of 2,755,000 and leading the majors for five years in a row. Other new parks spurred interest, either as attractions in themselves, like Houston's Astrodome, or when accompanied by winning teams, like the Cardinals in new Busch Stadium.

The dawn of free agency and two new American League expansion teams led to a new surge in ticket sales in the late 1970s, sending totals over 40 million by 1978. The Dodgers once again took the lead and topped 3 million for the first time that season. The eight-week-long players' strike in 1981 checked attendance growth temporarily. But by 1986 a milestone was achieved when all 26 big league clubs drew more than a million paying customers. In 1987 the 50-million plateau was reached for the first time. In the late 1980s and early 1990s, another round of new parks, notably SkyDome (where the Blue Jays topped 4 million in 1991 and 1992) and Oriole Park at Camden Yards, attracted sellout after sellout. And the spectacular success of the expansion Colorado Rockies (who set the record that still stands with 4,483,350) and Florida Marlins leapfrogged total attendance to over 70 million in 1993. The strike that ended the 1994 season, however, had a more lasting effect on the fans, and it took two new expansion teams and a dramatic home-run race in 1998 to restore the 70-million fan totals.

If you have the patience to sift through them, the figures on the following pages, dating from 1871 through 2003, tell a remarkable story. Season attendance has approached 4.5 million in Colorado in 1993, and it has been as little as 6,088 in Cleveland in 1899, when the awful Spiders went 20-134. The first club to pass the million mark was the New York Yankees of 1920, featuring a new-comer named Ruth and a ballpark borrowed from the Giants (who did not reach the mark themselves until 1945). In the depths of the Depression, the St. Louis Browns posted annual attendance figures (88,113 in 1933; 80,922 in 1935) below what a weekend set produces in many major league venues today.

Why did attendance stagnate in the 1890s? How much did the entry of the American League into National League strongholds New York, Chicago, Philadelphia, and St. Louis hurt the senior franchises? Were the Dodgers justified in leaving Brooklyn? How did baseball survive in Washington as long as it did, surpassing the million mark only once from 1892 to 1971? Did anyone notice that Atlanta's attendance of 1990 doubled, and then tripled, over the next two years? Or that while major league attendance increased by 25.8 percent from 1992 to 1993, almost all of that gain came from the senior circuit? (The American League rose a modest 5 percent while the National League posted a whopping gain of 53 percent. That season the league not only added two teams, Colorado and Florida, but the NL also started to count tickets sold, which followed the long-standing practice in the AL.)

You get the picture. There's stuff here that permits you to chart trends in baseball that you already know about, and if you are eagle-eyed you may pick up a figure that prompts you to rethink what you thought you knew. Should Major League Baseball contract two teams … or expand to 32?

A researcher's goldmine, the tables that follow tell an interesting story for the average fan as well. Does winning a pennant correlate with higher attendance? Are first-division teams more profitable than those in the second division? What is the impact on attendance of a new stadium? What's the story in Milwaukee, anyway?

By the time the next edition rolls around we may be able to gather figures going back to the dawn of professional baseball. Here are some scattered tidbits:

● In their first year of existence, 1871, the Boston Red Stockings counted 36,500 fans in 18 home games. The NA's debut game of May 4, in which the Forest City of Rockford played against the Kekionga in Fort Wayne, drew an estimated paid crowd of 200.

● In 1882, the last year of its existence as an NL franchise, the Troy Haymakers drew a whopping 26,488 attendees for its 42 home games, with one late season date posting a recorded crowd of 12 (that's not a typo). On the road they were no more appealing, attracting a paid admission of 6 to a game played in Worcester on September 28 of that year.

● The 1891 American Association, in its final year of operation, counted 1,173,000 fans, or an average of 146,625 per team, a figure very comparable to the 169,060 of the National League. In 1892, with the AA gone and the NL a 12-team circuit, the average team attendance was less than 152,000. Is there a lesson to be drawn from this?

Yes, and the lesson is plain for magnates no less than for fans and students of the game.

MILESTONE REGULAR SEASON CROWDS

Date	Paid Attendance	Clubs	Milestone
May 4, 1871	*200	Forest City at Kekionga NA (Ft. Wayne)	First NA Game
May 6, 1876	3,171	Cincinnati at Chicago NL	Largest NL Opener
May 30, 1876	10,094	Boston at Chicago NL	First over 10,000 paid
September 28, 1882	6	Troy at Worcester NL	Smallest NL crowd
May 30, 1886	20,632	Detroit at New York NL (holiday p.m.)	First over 20,000 paid
May 16, 1903	*31,500	Pittsburgh at New York NL	First over 30,000
April 18, 1923	47,586	Boston at New York AL (season opener)	First over 40,000 paid
August 23, 1923	52,809	Pittsburgh at New York NL	First over 50,000 paid
July 4, 1927	66,202	Washington at New York AL	First over 60,000 paid
September 9, 1928	76,285	Philadelphia at New York AL (doubleheader)	First over 70,000 paid
May 24, 1935	20,422	Philadelphia at Cincinnati	First big league night game
May 30, 1938	81,891	Boston at New York AL	First over 80,000 paid
September 12, 1954	84,587	New York at Cleveland AL (doubleheader)	All-Time Regular Season Record
April 18, 1958	78,672	San Francisco at Los Angeles NL (home opener)	NL record until 1993
April 9, 1993	80,227	Montreal at Colorado NL (home opener)	NL record *estimated

NATIONAL ASSOCIATION AND LEAGUE 1871-1880

	1871	1872	1873	1874	1875	1876	1877	1878	1879	1880
ATH	51,000	61,000	36,000	33,000	45,500	—	—	—	—	—
ATL	—	10,000	20,000	21,000	11,000	—	—	—	—	—
BAL	—	—	40,500	25,000	12,000	—	—	—	—	—
BOS	36,500	38,500	52,000	46,500	50,000	51,000	55,240	48,915	36,501	34,000
BUF	—	—	—	—	—	—	—	—	26,000	20,000
CEN	—	—	—	—	4,500	—	—	—	—	—
CHI	69,000	—	—	66,000	60,323	65,441	46,454	58,691	67,687	66,708
CIN	—	—	—	—	—	24,000	28,000	41,000	28,000	21,000
CLE	16,000	7,500	—	—	—	—	—	—	—	—
ECK	—	4,000	—	—	—	—	—	—	—	—
HAR	—	—	—	30,500	41,000	18,000	22,000	—	—	—
IND	—	—	—	—	—	—	—	12,000	—	—
KEK	3,500	—	—	—	—	—	—	—	—	—
LOU	—	—	—	—	—	25,000	24,000	—	—	—
MAN	—	5,500	—	—	—	—	—	—	—	—
MAR	—	—	1,500	—	—	—	—	—	—	—
MIL	—	—	—	—	—	—	—	17,000	—	—
MUT	40,500	48,500	29,000	37,000	32,000	—	—	—	—	—
NAT	—	1,500	—	—	—	—	—	—	—	—
NH	—	—	—	—	17,500	—	—	—	—	—
NY	—	—	—	—	—	23,000	—	—	—	—
OLY	26,000	3,000	—	—	—	—	—	—	—	—
PHI	—	—	50,000	23,000	29,500	24,000	—	—	—	—
PRO	—	—	—	—	—	—	—	46,000	47,595	37,220
RES	—	—	3,000	—	—	—	—	—	—	—
RS	—	—	—	—	6,500	—	—	—	—	—
ROK	6,500	—	—	—	—	—	—	—	—	—
STL	—	—	—	—	78,500	36,000	29,000	—	—	—
SYR	—	—	—	—	—	—	—	—	9,000	—
TRO	17,500	17,000	—	—	—	—	—	—	12,000	18,500
WAS	—	—	8,000	—	7,500	—	—	—	—	—
WES	—	—	—	—	4,000	—	—	—	—	—
WOR	—	—	—	—	—	—	—	—	—	24,000
TOTAL	266,500	237,000	224,500	269,000	387,823	266,441	204,694	223,606	251,783	256,428

NATIONAL LEAGUE 1881-1890

	1881	1882	1883	1884	1885	1886	1887	1888	1889	1890
BOS	34,343	50,971	128,968	146,777	110,290	133,683	261,000	265,015	283,257	147,539
BRO	—	—	—	—	—	—	—	—	—	121,412
BUF	32,173	28,000	32,000	42,000	35,000	—	—	—	—	—
CHI	82,000	125,452	124,880	87,667	117,519	142,438	217,070	228,906	149,175	102,536
CIN	—	—	—	—	—	—	—	—	—	131,980
CLE	34,000	30,000	63,000	38,000	—	—	—	—	144,425	47,478
DET	53,720	75,000	70,000	32,000	43,000	105,000	95,000	75,000	—	—
IND	—	—	—	—	—	—	84,000	78,000	105,850	—
KC	—	—	—	—	—	55,000	—	—	—	—
NY	—	—	75,000	105,000	185,000	189,000	270,945	305,455	201,989	60,667
PHI	—	—	55,992	100,475	150,698	175,623	253,671	151,804	281,869	148,366
PIT	—	—	—	—	—	—	140,000	112,000	117,338	16,064
PRO	30,000	57,477	61,314	64,409	49,000	—	—	—	—	—
STL	—	—	—	—	62,000	99,000	—	—	—	—
TRO	18,000	26,488	—	—	—	—	—	—	—	—
WAS	—	—	—	—	—	60,000	80,000	57,000	68,652	—
WOR	17,000	11,000	—	—	—	—	—	—	—	—
TOTAL	301,236	404,388	611,154	616,328	752,507	959,744	1,401,686	1,273,180	1,352,555	776,042

AMERICAN ASSOCATION 1882-1891

	1882	1883	1884	1885	1886	1887	1888	1889	1890	1891
BAL	36,000	110,000	—	—	—	—	—	—	—	—
BOS	—	—	—	—	—	—	—	—	—	170,000
BRO	—	—	65,000	85,000	185,000	273,000	245,000	353,690	37,000	—
CIN	65,000	86,000	110,000	120,000	138,563	185,397	132,606	131,000	—	63,000
CLE	—	—	—	—	—	72,000	60,000	—	—	—
COL	—	48,000	66,000	—	—	—	—	90,000	85,000	105,000
IND	—	—	56,000	—	—	—	—	—	—	—
KC	—	—	—	—	—	—	50,000	85,000	—	—
LOU	50,000	78,000	111,000	108,000	123,000	128,000	76,000	60,000	206,200	140,000
MIL	—	—	—	—	—	—	—	—	—	45,000
NY	—	50,000	68,000	64,000	67,000	105,000	—	—	—	—
PHI	72,000	305,000	116,000	169,000	179,000	163,000	201,000	220,000	134,000	168,000
PIT	42,000	85,000	60,000	82,000	195,000	—	—	—	—	—
RIC	—	—	16,000	—	—	—	—	—	—	—
ROC	—	—	—	—	—	—	—	—	82,000	—
STL	135,000	243,000	212,000	129,000	205,000	244,000	166,000	175,000	105,000	220,000
SYR	—	—	—	—	—	—	—	—	50,000	—
TOL	—	—	55,000	—	—	—	—	—	70,000	—
WAS	—	—	25,000	—	—	—	—	—	—	112,000
TOTAL	400,000	1,005,000	1,080,000	817,000	1,162,563	1,312,397	968,606	1,229,690	803,200	1,173,000
ML TOTAL	804,388	1,616,154	1,696,328	1,569,507	2,122,307	2,714,083	2,241,786	2,582,245	1,579,242	2,525,487

NATIONAL LEAGUE 1891–1900

	1891	1892	1893	1894	1895	1896	1897	1898	1899	1900
BAL	93,589	143,000	328,000	293,000	249,448	273,046	123,416	121,935		
BOS	184,472	146,421	193,300	152,800	242,000	240,000	334,800	229,275	200,384	190,000
BRO	181,477	183,727	235,000	214,000	230,000	201,000	220,831	122,514	269,641	170,000
CHI	201,188	109,067	223,500	239,000	382,300	317,500	327,160	424,352	352,130	248,577
CIN	97,500	196,473	194,250	158,000	281,000	373,000	336,800	336,378	259,536	155,000
CLE	132,000	139,928	130,000	82,000	143,000	152,000	115,250	70,496	6,088	—
LOU	—	131,159	53,683	75,000	92,000	133,000	145,210	128,980	109,319	—
NY	210,568	130,566	290,000	387,000	240,000	274,000	390,340	206,700	121,384	175,000
PHI	217,282	193,731	293,019	352,773	474,971	357,025	288,816	265,414	388,933	301,913
PIT	128,000	177,205	184,000	159,000	188,000	197,000	165,950	150,900	251,834	250,000
STL	—	192,442	195,000	155,000	170,000	184,000	136,400	151,700	373,909	255,000
WAS	—	128,279	90,000	125,000	153,000	223,000	151,028	103,250	86,392	—
TOTAL	1,352,487	1,822,587	2,224,752	2,427,573	2,889,271	2,900,973	2,885,631	2,313,375	2,541,485	1,745,490
ML TOTAL	2,525,487	1,822,587	2,224,752	2,427,573	2,889,271	2,900,973	2,885,631	2,313,375	2,541,485	1,745,490

MAJOR LEAGUE BASEBALL 1901–1910

	1901	1902	1903	1904	1905	1906	1907	1908	1909	1910
NATIONAL LEAGUE										
BOS	146,502	116,960	143,155	140,694	150,003	143,280	203,221	253,750	195,188	149,027
BRO	198,200	199,868	224,670	214,600	227,924	277,400	312,500	275,600	321,300	279,321
CHI	205,071	263,700	386,205	439,100	509,900	654,300	422,550	665,325	633,480	526,152
CIN	205,728	217,300	351,680	391,915	313,927	330,056	317,500	399,200	424,643	380,622
NY	297,650	302,875	579,530	609,826	552,700	402,850	538,350	910,000	783,700	511,785
PHI	234,937	112,066	151,729	140,771	317,932	294,680	341,216	420,660	303,177	296,597
PIT	251,955	243,826	326,855	340,615	369,124	394,877	319,506	382,444	534,950	436,586
STL	379,988	226,417	226,538	386,750	292,800	283,770	185,377	205,129	299,982	355,668
TOTAL	1,920,031	1,683,012	2,390,362	2,664,271	2,734,310	2,781,213	2,640,220	3,512,108	3,496,420	2,935,758
AMERICAN LEAGUE										
BAL	141,952	174,606	—	—	—	—	—	—	—	—
BOS	289,448	348,567	379,338	623,295	468,828	410,209	436,777	473,048	668,965	584,619
CHI	354,350	337,898	286,183	557,123	687,419	585,202	666,307	636,096	478,400	552,084
CLE	131,380	275,395	311,280	264,749	316,306	325,733	382,046	422,262	354,627	293,456
DET	259,430	189,469	224,523	177,796	193,384	174,043	297,079	436,199	490,490	391,288
MIL	139,034									
NY	—	—	211,808	438,919	309,100	434,700	350,020	305,500	501,700	355,857
PHI	206,329	420,078	422,473	512,294	554,576	489,129	625,581	455,062	674,915	588,905
STL	—	272,283	380,405	318,108	339,112	389,157	419,025	618,947	366,274	249,889
WAS	161,661	188,158	128,878	131,744	252,027	129,903	221,929	264,252	205,199	254,591
TOTAL	1,683,584	2,206,454	2,344,888	3,024,028	3,120,752	2,938,076	3,398,764	3,611,366	3,740,570	3,270,689
ML TOTAL	3,603,615	3,889,466	4,735,250	5,688,299	5,855,062	5,719,289	6,038,984	7,123,474	7,236,990	6,206,447

MAJOR LEAGUE BASEBALL 1911–1920

	1911	1912	1913	1914	1915	1916	1917	1918	1919	1920
NATIONAL LEAGUE										
BOS	116,000	121,000	208,000	382,913	376,283	313,495	174,253	84,938	167,401	162,483
BRO	269,000	243,000	347,000	122,671	297,766	447,747	221,619	83,831	360,721	808,722
CHI	576,000	514,000	419,000	202,516	217,058	453,685	360,218	337,256	424,430	480,783
CIN	300,000	344,000	258,000	100,791	218,878	255,846	269,056	163,009	532,501	568,107
NY	675,000	638,000	630,000	364,313	391,850	552,056	500,264	256,618	708,857	929,609
PHI	416,000	250,000	470,000	138,474	449,898	515,365	354,428	122,266	240,424	330,998
PIT	432,000	384,000	296,000	139,620	225,743	289,132	192,807	213,610	276,810	429,037
STL	447,768	241,759	203,531	256,099	252,666	224,308	288,491	110,599	167,059	326,836
TOTAL	3,231,768	2,735,759	2,831,531	1,707,397	2,430,142	3,051,634	2,361,136	1,372,127	2,878,203	4,036,575
AMERICAN LEAGUE										
BOS	503,961	597,096	437,194	481,359	539,885	496,397	387,856	249,513	417,291	402,445
CHI	583,208	602,241	644,501	469,290	539,461	679,923	684,521	195,081	627,186	833,492
CLE	406,296	336,844	541,000	185,997	159,285	492,106	477,298	295,515	538,135	912,832
DET	484,988	402,870	398,502	416,225	476,105	616,772	457,289	203,719	643,805	579,650
NY	302,444	242,194	357,551	359,477	256,035	469,211	330,294	282,047	619,164	1,289,422
PHI	605,749	517,653	571,896	346,641	146,223	184,471	221,432	177,926	225,209	287,888
STL	207,984	214,070	250,330	244,714	150,358	335,740	210,486	122,076	349,350	419,311
WAS	244,884	350,663	325,831	243,888	167,332	177,265	89,682	182,122	234,096	359,260
TOTAL	3,339,514	3,263,631	3,526,805	2,747,591	2,434,684	3,451,885	2,858,858	1,707,999	3,654,236	5,084,300
ML TOTAL	6,571,282	5,999,390	6,358,336	4,454,988	4,864,826	6,503,519	5,219,994	3,080,126	6,532,439	9,120,875

MAJOR LEAGUE BASEBALL 1921–1930

	1921	1922	1923	1924	1925	1926	1927	1928	1929	1930
NATIONAL LEAGUE										
BOS	318,627	167,965	227,802	177,478	313,528	303,598	288,685	227,001	372,351	464,835
BRO	613,245	498,865	564,666	818,883	659,435	650,819	637,230	664,863	731,886	1,097,329
CHI	410,107	542,283	703,705	716,922	622,610	885,063	1,159,168	1,143,740	1,485,166	1,463,624
CIN	311,227	493,754	575,063	473,707	464,920	672,987	442,164	490,490	295,040	386,727
NY	973,477	945,809	820,780	844,068	778,993	700,362	858,190	916,191	868,806	868,714
PHI	273,961	232,471	228,168	299,818	304,905	240,600	305,420	182,168	281,200	299,007
PIT	701,567	523,675	611,082	736,883	804,354	798,542	869,720	495,070	491,377	357,795
STL	384,773	536,998	338,551	272,885	404,959	668,428	749,340	761,574	399,887	508,501
TOTAL	3,986,984	3,941,820	4,069,817	4,340,644	4,353,704	4,920,399	5,309,917	4,881,097	4,925,713	5,446,532
AMERICAN LEAGUE										
BOS	279,273	259,184	229,688	448,556	267,782	285,155	305,275	396,920	394,620	444,045
CHI	543,650	602,860	573,778	606,658	832,231	710,339	614,423	494,152	426,795	406,123
CLE	748,705	528,145	558,856	481,905	419,005	627,426	373,138	375,907	536,210	528,657
DET	661,527	861,206	911,377	1,015,136	820,766	711,914	773,716	474,323	869,318	649,450
NY	1,230,696	1,026,134	1,007,066	1,053,533	697,267	1,027,675	1,164,015	1,072,132	960,148	1,169,230
PHI	344,430	425,356	534,122	531,992	869,703	714,508	605,529	689,756	839,176	721,663
STL	355,978	712,918	430,296	533,349	462,898	283,986	247,879	339,497	280,697	152,088
WAS	456,069	458,552	357,406	584,310	817,199	551,580	528,976	378,501	355,506	614,474
TOTAL	4,620,328	4,874,355	4,602,589	5,255,439	5,186,851	4,912,583	4,612,951	4,221,188	4,662,470	4,685,730
ML TOTAL	8,607,312	8,816,175	8,672,406	9,596,083	9,540,555	9,832,982	9,922,868	9,102,285	9,588,183	10,132,262

MAJOR LEAGUE BASEBALL 1931–1940

	1931	1932	1933	1934	1935	1936	1937	1938	1939	1940
NATIONAL LEAGUE										
BOS	515,005	507,606	517,803	303,205	232,754	340,585	385,339	341,149	285,994	241,616
BRO	753,133	681,827	526,815	434,188	470,517	489,618	482,481	663,087	955,668	975,978
CHI	1,086,422	974,688	594,112	707,525	692,604	699,370	895,020	951,640	726,663	534,878
CIN	263,316	356,950	218,281	206,773	448,247	466,345	411,221	706,756	981,443	850,180
NY	812,163	484,868	604,471	730,851	748,748	837,952	926,887	799,633	702,457	747,852
PHI	284,849	268,914	156,421	169,885	205,470	249,219	212,790	166,111	277,973	207,177
PIT	260,392	287,262	288,747	322,622	352,885	372,524	459,679	641,033	376,734	507,934
STL	608,535	279,219	256,171	325,056	506,084	448,078	430,811	291,418	400,245	324,078
TOTAL	4,583,815	3,841,334	3,162,821	3,200,105	3,657,309	3,903,691	4,204,228	4,560,827	4,707,177	4,389,693
AMERICAN LEAGUE										
BOS	350,975	182,150	268,715	610,640	558,568	626,895	559,659	646,459	573,070	716,234
CHI	403,550	233,198	397,789	236,559	470,281	440,810	589,245	338,278	594,104	660,336
CLE	483,027	468,953	387,936	391,338	397,615	500,391	564,849	652,006	563,926	902,576
DET	434,056	397,157	320,972	919,161	1,034,929	875,948	1,072,276	799,557	836,279	1,112,693
NY	912,437	962,320	728,014	854,682	657,508	976,913	998,148	970,916	859,785	988,975
PHI	627,464	405,500	297,138	305,847	233,173	285,173	430,738	385,357	395,022	432,145
STL	179,126	112,558	88,113	115,305	80,922	93,267	123,121	130,417	109,159	239,591
WAS	492,657	371,396	437,533	330,074	255,011	379,525	397,799	522,694	339,257	381,241
TOTAL	3,883,292	3,133,232	2,926,210	3,763,606	3,688,007	4,178,922	4,735,835	4,445,684	4,270,602	5,433,791
ML TOTAL	8,467,107	6,974,566	6,089,031	6,963,711	7,345,316	8,082,613	8,940,063	9,006,511	8,977,779	9,823,484

MAJOR LEAGUE BASEBALL 1941–1950

	1941	1942	1943	1944	1945	1946	1947	1948	1949	1950
NATIONAL LEAGUE										
BOS	263,680	285,332	271,289	208,691	374,178	969,673	1,277,361	1,455,439	1,081,795	944,391
BRO	1,214,910	1,037,765	661,739	605,905	1,059,220	1,796,824	1,807,526	1,398,967	1,633,747	1,185,896
CHI	545,159	590,972	508,247	640,110	1,036,386	1,342,970	1,364,039	1,237,792	1,143,139	1,165,944
CIN	643,513	427,031	379,122	409,567	290,070	715,751	899,975	823,386	707,782	538,794
NY	763,098	779,621	466,095	674,483	1,016,468	1,219,873	1,600,793	1,459,269	1,218,446	1,008,878
PHI	231,401	230,183	466,975	369,586	285,057	1,045,247	907,332	767,429	819,698	1,217,035
PIT	482,241	448,897	498,740	604,278	604,694	749,962	1,283,531	1,517,021	1,449,435	1,166,267
STL	633,645	553,552	517,135	461,968	594,630	1,061,807	1,247,913	1,111,440	1,430,676	1,093,411
TOTAL	4,777,647	4,353,353	3,769,342	3,974,588	5,260,703	8,902,107	10,388,470	9,770,743	9,484,718	8,320,616
AMERICAN LEAGUE										
BOS	718,497	730,340	358,275	506,975	603,794	1,416,944	1,427,315	1,558,798	1,596,650	1,344,080
CHI	677,077	425,734	508,962	563,539	657,981	983,403	876,948	777,844	937,151	781,330
CLE	745,948	459,447	438,894	475,272	558,182	1,057,289	1,521,978	2,620,627	2,233,771	1,727,464
DET	684,915	580,087	606,287	923,176	1,280,341	1,722,590	1,398,093	1,743,035	1,821,204	1,951,474
NY	964,722	922,011	618,330	789,995	881,845	2,265,512	2,178,937	2,373,901	2,283,676	2,081,380
PHI	528,894	423,487	376,735	505,322	462,631	621,793	911,566	945,076	816,514	309,805
STL	176,240	255,617	214,392	508,644	482,986	526,435	320,474	335,564	270,936	247,131
WAS	415,663	403,493	574,694	525,235	652,660	1,027,216	850,758	795,254	770,745	699,697
TOTAL	4,911,956	4,200,216	3,696,569	4,798,158	5,580,420	9,621,182	9,486,069	11,150,099	10,730,647	9,142,361
ML TOTAL	9,689,603	8,553,569	7,465,911	8,772,746	10,841,123	18,523,288	19,874,540	20,920,842	20,215,364	17,462,976

2422   Total Baseball

MAJOR LEAGUE BASEBALL 1951–1960

	1951	1952	1953	1954	1955	1956	1957	1958	1959	1960
NATIONAL LEAGUE										
BOS	487,475	281,278	—	—	—	—	—	—	—	—
BRO	1,282,628	1,088,704	1,163,419	1,020,531	1,033,589	1,213,562	1,028,258	—	—	—
CHI	894,415	1,024,826	763,658	748,183	875,800	720,118	670,629	979,904	858,255	809,770
CIN	588,268	604,197	548,086	704,167	693,662	1,125,928	1,070,850	788,582	801,298	663,486
LA	—	—	—	—	—	—	—	1,845,556	2,071,045	2,253,887
MIL			1,826,397	2,131,388	2,005,836	2,046,331	2,215,404	1,971,101	1,749,112	1,497,799
NY	1,059,539	984,940	811,518	1,155,067	824,112	629,179	653,923	—	—	—
PHI	937,658	755,417	853,644	738,991	922,886	934,798	1,146,230	931,110	802,815	862,205
PIT	980,590	686,673	572,757	475,494	469,397	949,878	850,732	1,311,988	1,359,917	1,705,828
STL	1,013,429	913,113	880,242	1,039,698	849,130	1,029,773	1,183,575	1,063,730	929,953	1,096,632
SF	—	—	—	—	—	—	—	1,272,625	1,422,130	1,795,356
TOTAL	7,244,002	6,339,148	7,419,721	8,013,519	7,674,412	8,649,567	8,819,601	10,164,596	9,994,525	10,684,963
AMERICAN LEAGUE										
BAL	—	—	—	1,060,910	852,039	901,201	1,029,581	829,991	891,926	1,187,849
BOS	1,312,282	1,115,750	1,026,133	931,127	1,203,200	1,137,158	1,181,087	1,077,047	984,102	1,129,866
CHI	1,328,234	1,231,675	1,191,353	1,231,629	1,175,684	1,000,090	1,135,668	797,451	1,423,144	1,644,460
CLE	1,704,984	1,444,607	1,069,176	1,335,472	1,221,780	865,467	722,256	663,805	1,497,976	950,985
DET	1,132,641	1,026,846	884,658	1,079,847	1,181,838	1,051,182	1,272,346	1,098,924	1,221,221	1,167,669
KC	—	—	—	—	1,393,054	1,015,154	901,067	925,090	963,683	774,944
NY	1,950,107	1,629,665	1,537,811	1,475,171	1,490,138	1,491,784	1,497,134	1,428,438	1,552,030	1,627,349
PHI	465,469	627,100	362,113	304,666	—	—	—	—	—	—
STL	293,790	518,796	297,238	—	—	—	—	—	—	—
WAS	695,167	699,457	595,594	503,542	425,238	431,647	457,079	475,288	615,372	743,404
TOTAL	8,882,674	8,293,896	6,964,076	7,922,364	8,942,971	7,893,683	8,196,218	7,296,034	9,149,454	9,226,526
ML TOTAL	16,126,676	14,633,044	14,383,797	15,935,883	16,617,383	16,543,250	17,015,820	17,460,630	19,143,980	19,911,488

MAJOR LEAGUE BASEBALL 1961–1970

	1961	1962	1963	1964	1965	1966	1967	1968	1969	1970
NATIONAL LEAGUE										
ATL	—	—	—	—	1,539,801	1,389,222	1,126,540	1,458,320	1,078,848	—
CHI	673,057	609,802	979,551	751,647	641,361	635,891	977,226	1,043,409	1,674,993	1,642,705
CIN	1,117,603	982,095	858,805	862,466	1,047,824	742,958	958,300	733,354	987,991	1,803,568
HOU	—	924,456	719,502	725,773	2,151,470	1,872,108	1,348,303	1,312,887	1,442,995	1,253,444
LA	1,804,250	2,755,184	2,538,602	2,228,751	2,553,577	2,617,029	1,664,362	1,581,093	1,784,527	1,697,142
MIL	1,101,441	766,921	773,018	910,911	555,584		—	—	—	—
MON	—	—	—	—	—	—	—	—	1,212,608	1,424,683
NY	—	922,530	1,080,108	1,732,597	1,768,389	1,932,693	1,565,492	1,781,657	2,175,373	2,697,479
PHI	590,039	762,034	907,141	1,425,891	1,166,376	1,108,201	828,888	664,546	519,414	708,247
PIT	1,199,128	1,090,648	783,648	759,496	909,279	1,196,618	907,012	693,485	769,369	1,341,947
STL	855,305	953,895	1,170,546	1,143,294	1,241,201	1,712,980	2,090,145	2,011,167	1,682,783	1,629,736
SD	—	—	—	—	—	—	—	—	512,970	643,679
SF	1,390,679	1,592,594	1,571,306	1,504,364	1,546,075	1,657,192	1,242,480	837,220	873,603	740,720
TOTAL	8,731,502	11,360,159	11,382,227	12,045,190	13,581,136	15,015,471	12,971,430	11,785,358	15,094,946	16,662,198
AMERICAN LEAGUE										
BAL	951,089	—	—	—	—	—	—	—	—	—
BOS	850,589	733,080	942,642	883,276	652,201	811,172	1,727,832	1,940,788	1,833,246	1,595,278
CAL	—	—	—	—	566,727	1,400,321	1,317,713	1,025,956	758,388	1,077,741
CHI	1,146,019	1,131,562	1,158,848	1,250,053	1,130,519	990,016	985,634	803,775	589,546	495,355
CLE	725,547	716,076	562,507	653,293	934,786	903,359	662,980	857,994	619,970	729,752
DET	1,600,710	1,207,881	821,952	816,139	1,029,645	1,124,293	1,447,143	2,031,847	1,577,481	1,501,293
KC	683,817	635,675	762,364	642,478	528,344	773,929	726,639	—	902,414	693,047
LA	603,510	1,144,063	821,015	760,439	—	—	—	—	—	—
MIL	—	—	—	—	—	—	—	—	—	933,690
MIN	1,256,723	1,433,116	1,406,652	1,207,514	1,463,258	1,259,374	1,483,547	1,143,257	1,349,328	1,261,887
NY	1,747,725	1,493,574	1,308,920	1,305,638	1,213,552	1,124,648	1,259,514	1,185,666	1,067,996	1,136,879
OAK	—	—	—	—	—	—	—	837,466	778,232	778,355
SEA	—	—	—	—	—	—	—	—	677,944	—
WAS	597,287	729,775	535,604	600,106	560,083	576,260	770,868	546,661	918,106	824,789
TOTAL	10,163,016	10,015,056	9,094,847	9,235,151	8,860,764	10,166,738	11,336,923	11,317,387	12,134,745	12,085,135
ML TOTAL	18,894,518	21,375,216	20,477,074	21,280,340	22,441,900	25,182,208	24,308,352	23,102,744	27,229,692	28,747,332

MAJOR LEAGUE BASEBALL 1971–1980

	1971	1972	1973	1974	1975	1976	1977	1978	1979	1980
NATIONAL LEAGUE										
ATL	1,006,320	752,973	800,655	981,085	534,672	818,179	872,464	904,494	769,465	1,048,411
CHI	1,653,007	1,299,163	1,351,705	1,015,378	1,034,819	1,026,217	1,439,834	1,525,311	1,648,587	1,206,776
CIN	1,501,122	1,611,459	2,017,601	2,164,307	2,315,603	2,629,708	2,519,670	2,532,497	2,356,933	2,022,450
HOU	1,261,589	1,469,247	1,394,004	1,090,728	858,002	886,146	1,109,560	1,126,145	1,900,312	2,278,217
LA	2,064,594	1,860,858	2,136,192	2,632,474	2,539,349	2,386,301	2,955,087	3,347,845	2,860,954	3,249,287
MON	1,290,963	1,142,145	1,246,863	1,019,134	908,292	646,704	1,433,757	1,427,007	2,102,173	2,208,175
NY	2,266,680	2,134,185	1,912,390	1,722,209	1,730,566	1,468,754	1,066,825	1,007,328	788,905	1,192,073
PHI	1,511,223	1,343,329	1,475,934	1,808,648	1,909,233	2,480,150	2,700,070	2,583,389	2,775,011	2,651,650
PIT	1,501,132	1,427,460	1,319,913	1,110,552	1,270,018	1,025,945	1,237,349	964,106	1,435,454	1,646,757
STL	1,604,671	1,196,894	1,574,046	1,838,413	1,695,270	1,207,079	1,659,287	1,278,215	1,627,256	1,385,147
SD	557,513	644,273	611,826	1,075,399	1,281,747	1,458,478	1,376,269	1,670,107	1,456,967	1,139,026
SF	1,106,043	647,744	834,193	519,987	522,919	626,868	700,056	1,740,477	1,456,402	1,096,115
TOTAL	17,324,856	15,529,730	16,675,322	16,978,314	16,600,490	16,660,529	19,070,228	20,106,922	21,178,416	21,124,086
AMERICAN LEAGUE										
BAL	1,023,037	899,950	958,667	962,572	1,002,157	1,058,609	1,195,769	1,051,724	1,681,009	1,797,438
BOS	1,678,732	1,441,718	1,481,002	1,556,411	1,748,587	1,895,846	2,074,549	2,320,643	2,353,114	1,956,092
CAL	926,373	744,190	1,058,206	917,269	1,058,163	1,006,774	1,432,633	1,755,386	2,523,575	2,297,327
CHI	833,891	1,177,318	1,302,527	1,149,596	750,802	914,945	1,657,135	1,491,100	1,280,702	1,200,365
CLE	591,361	626,354	615,107	1,114,262	977,039	948,776	900,365	800,584	1,011,644	1,033,827
DET	1,591,073	1,892,386	1,724,146	1,243,080	1,058,836	1,467,020	1,359,856	1,714,893	1,630,929	1,785,293
KC	910,784	707,656	1,345,341	1,173,292	1,151,836	1,680,265	1,852,603	2,255,493	2,261,845	2,288,714
MIL	731,531	600,440	1,092,158	955,741	1,213,357	1,012,164	1,114,938	1,601,406	1,918,343	1,857,408
MIN	940,858	797,901	907,499	662,401	737,156	715,394	1,162,727	787,878	1,070,521	769,206
NY	1,070,771	966,328	1,262,103	1,273,075	1,288,048	2,012,434	2,103,092	2,335,871	2,537,765	2,627,417
OAK	914,993	921,323	1,000,763	845,693	1,075,518	780,593	495,599	526,999	306,763	842,259
SEA	—	—	—	—	—	—	1,338,511	877,440	844,447	836,204
TEX	—	662,974	686,085	1,193,902	1,127,924	1,164,982	1,250,722	1,447,963	1,519,671	1,198,175
TOR	—	—	—	—	—	—	1,701,052	1,562,585	1,431,651	1,400,327
WAS	655,156	—	—	—	—	—	—	—	—	—
TOTAL	11,868,560	11,438,538	13,433,604	13,047,294	13,189,423	14,657,802	19,639,552	20,529,964	22,371,980	21,890,052
ML TOTAL	29,193,416	26,968,268	30,108,926	30,025,608	29,789,912	31,318,332	38,709,780	40,636,888	43,550,396	43,014,136

MAJOR LEAGUE BASEBALL 1981–1990

	1981	1982	1983	1984	1985	1986	1987	1988	1989	1990
NATIONAL LEAGUE										
ATL	535,418	1,801,985	2,119,935	1,724,892	1,350,137	1,387,181	1,217,402	848,089	984,930	980,129
CHI	565,637	1,249,278	1,479,717	2,107,655	2,161,534	1,859,102	2,035,130	2,089,034	2,491,942	2,243,791
CIN	1,093,730	1,326,528	1,190,419	1,275,887	1,834,619	1,692,432	2,185,205	2,072,528	1,979,320	2,400,892
HOU	1,321,282	1,558,555	1,351,962	1,229,862	1,184,314	1,734,276	1,909,902	1,933,505	1,834,908	1,310,927
LA	2,381,292	3,608,881	3,510,313	3,134,824	3,264,593	3,023,208	2,797,409	2,980,262	2,944,653	3,002,396
MON	1,534,564	2,318,292	2,320,651	1,606,531	1,502,494	1,128,981	1,850,324	1,478,659	1,783,533	1,373,087
NY	704,244	1,323,036	1,112,774	1,842,695	2,761,601	2,767,601	3,034,129	3,055,445	2,918,710	2,732,745
PHI	1,638,752	2,376,394	2,128,339	2,062,693	1,830,350	1,933,335	2,100,110	1,990,041	1,861,985	1,992,484
PIT	541,789	1,024,106	1,225,916	773,500	735,900	1,000,917	1,161,193	1,866,713	1,374,141	2,049,908
STL	1,010,247	2,111,906	2,317,914	2,037,448	2,637,563	2,471,974	3,072,122	2,892,799	3,080,980	2,573,225
SD	519,161	1,607,516	1,539,815	1,983,904	2,210,352	1,805,716	1,454,061	1,506,896	2,009,031	1,856,396
SF	632,274	1,200,948	1,251,530	1,001,545	818,697	1,528,748	1,917,168	1,785,297	2,059,701	1,975,528
TOTAL	12,478,390	21,507,424	21,549,284	20,781,436	22,292,156	22,333,472	24,734,156	24,499,268	25,323,834	24,491,508
AMERICAN LEAGUE										
BAL	1,024,247	1,613,031	2,042,071	2,045,784	2,132,387	1,973,176	1,835,692	1,660,738	2,535,208	2,415,189
BOS	1,060,379	1,950,124	1,782,285	1,661,618	1,786,633	2,147,641	2,231,551	2,464,851	2,510,012	2,528,986
CAL	1,441,545	2,807,360	2,555,016	2,402,997	2,567,427	2,655,872	2,696,299	2,340,925	2,647,291	2,555,688
CHI	946,651	1,567,787	2,132,821	2,136,988	1,669,888	1,424,313	1,208,060	1,115,749	1,045,651	2,002,357
CLE	661,395	1,044,021	768,941	734,079	655,181	1,471,805	1,077,898	1,411,610	1,285,542	1,225,240
DET	1,149,144	1,636,058	1,829,636	2,704,794	2,286,609	1,899,437	2,061,830	2,081,162	1,543,656	1,495,785
KC	1,279,403	2,284,464	1,963,875	1,810,018	2,162,717	2,320,794	2,392,471	2,350,181	2,477,700	2,244,956
MIL	874,292	1,978,896	2,397,131	1,608,509	1,360,265	1,265,041	1,909,244	1,923,238	1,970,735	1,752,900
MIN	469,090	921,186	858,939	1,598,692	1,651,814	1,255,453	2,081,976	3,030,672	2,277,438	1,751,584
NY	1,614,353	2,041,219	2,257,976	1,821,815	2,214,587	2,268,030	2,427,672	2,633,701	2,170,485	2,006,436
OAK	1,304,052	1,735,489	1,294,941	1,353,281	1,334,599	1,314,646	1,678,921	2,287,335	2,667,225	2,900,217
SEA	636,276	1,070,404	813,537	870,372	1,128,696	1,029,045	1,134,255	1,022,398	1,298,443	1,509,727
TEX	850,076	1,154,432	1,363,469	1,102,471	1,112,497	1,692,002	1,763,053	1,581,901	2,043,993	2,057,911
TOR	755,083	1,275,978	1,930,415	2,110,009	2,468,925	2,455,477	2,778,429	2,595,175	3,375,883	3,885,284
TOTAL	14,065,986	23,080,448	23,991,052	23,961,428	24,532,220	25,172,732	27,277,350	28,499,636	29,849,264	30,332,260
ML TOTAL	26,544,376	44,587,872	45,540,336	44,742,864	46,824,376	47,506,204	52,011,504	52,998,904	55,173,096	54,823,768

MAJOR LEAGUE BASEBALL 1991–2000

	1991	1992	1993	1994	1995	1996	1997	1998	1999	2000
NATIONAL LEAGUE										
ARI	—	—	—	—	—	—	3,600,412	3,019,654	2,942,516	2,819,539
ATL	2,140,217	3,077,400	3,884,725	2,539,240	2,561,831	2,901,242	3,464,488	3,361,350	3,284,897	3,234,301
CHI	2,314,250	2,126,720	2,653,763	1,845,208	1,918,265	2,219,110	2,190,308	2,623,000	2,813,854	2,789,511
CIN	2,372,377	2,315,946	2,453,232	1,897,681	1,837,649	1,861,428	1,785,788	1,793,679	2,061,222	2,577,351
COL	—	—	4,483,350	3,281,511	3,390,037	3,891,014	3,888,453	3,789,347	3,481,065	3,285,710
FLA	—	—	3,064,847	1,937,467	1,700,466	1,746,767	2,364,387	1,750,395	1,369,421	1,218,326
HOU	1,196,152	1,211,412	2,084,546	1,561,136	1,363,801	1,975,888	2,046,781	2,450,451	2,706,017	3,056,139
LA	3,348,170	2,473,266	3,170,392	2,279,355	2,766,251	3,188,454	3,319,504	3,089,201	3,095,346	3,010,819
MIL	—	—	—	—	—	—	—	1,811,548	1,701,796	1,573,621
MON	934,742	1,669,077	1,641,437	1,276,250	1,309,618	1,616,709	1,497,609	914,717	773,277	926,263
NY	2,284,484	1,779,534	1,873,183	1,151,471	1,273,183	1,588,323	1,766,174	2,287,942	2,725,668	2,800,221
PHI	2,050,012	1,927,448	3,137,674	2,290,971	2,043,598	1,801,677	1,490,638	1,715,702	1,825,337	1,612,769
PIT	2,065,302	1,829,395	1,650,593	1,222,520	905,517	1,332,150	1,657,022	1,560,950	1,638,023	1,748,908
STL	2,448,699	2,418,483	2,844,328	1,866,544	1,756,727	2,654,718	2,634,014	3,194,092	3,225,334	3,336,493
SD	1,804,289	1,722,102	1,375,432	953,857	1,041,805	2,187,886	2,089,333	2,555,901	2,523,538	2,423,149
SF	1,737,478	1,561,987	2,606,354	1,704,608	1,241,500	1,413,922	1,690,869	1,925,634	2,078,399	3,315,330
TOTAL	24,696,174	24,112,770	36,923,856	25,807,820	25,110,248	30,379,288	31,885,364	38,424,324	38,322,848	39,851,424
AMERICAN LEAGUE										
ANA	—	—	—	—	—	—	1,767,330	2,519,107	2,253,123	2,066,977
BAL	2,552,753	3,567,819	3,644,965	2,535,359	3,098,475	3,646,950	3,711,132	3,685,194	3,433,150	3,295,128
BOS	2,562,435	2,468,574	2,422,021	1,775,818	2,164,410	2,315,231	2,226,136	2,343,947	2,446,162	2,586,032
CAL	2,416,236	2,065,444	2,057,460	1,512,622	1,748,680	1,820,521	—	—	—	—
CHI	2,934,154	2,681,156	2,581,091	1,697,398	1,609,773	1,676,403	1,864,782	1,391,146	1,338,851	1,947,799
CLE	1,051,863	1,224,274	2,177,908	1,995,174	2,842,745	3,318,174	3,404,750	3,467,299	3,468,456	3,456,278
DET	1,641,661	1,423,963	1,971,421	1,184,783	1,180,979	1,168,610	1,365,157	1,409,391	2,026,441	2,533,752
KC	2,161,537	1,867,689	1,934,578	1,400,494	1,233,530	1,435,997	1,517,638	1,494,875	1,506,068	1,677,915
MIL	1,478,729	1,857,314	1,688,080	1,268,399	1,087,560	1,327,155	1,444,027	—	—	—
MIN	2,293,842	2,482,428	2,048,673	1,398,565	1,057,667	1,437,352	1,411,064	1,165,980	1,202,829	1,059,715
NY	1,863,733	1,748,733	2,416,965	1,675,556	1,705,263	2,250,877	2,580,325	2,919,046	3,292,736	3,227,657
OAK	2,713,493	2,494,160	2,035,025	1,242,692	1,174,310	1,148,380	1,264,218	1,232,339	1,434,610	1,728,888
SEA	2,147,905	1,651,398	2,051,853	1,104,206	1,643,203	2,723,850	3,192,237	2,644,305	2,916,346	3,148,317
TB	—	—	—	—	—	—	—	2,261,158	1,562,827	1,549,052
TEX	2,297,720	2,198,231	2,244,616	2,503,198	1,985,910	2,889,020	2,945,228	2,927,409	2,771,469	2,800,147
TOR	4,001,527	4,028,318	4,057,947	2,907,933	2,826,483	2,559,573	2,589,297	2,454,283	2,163,464	1,819,886
TOTAL	32,117,584	31,759,506	33,332,598	24,202,196	25,358,990	29,718,094	31,283,320	31,915,480	31,816,532	32,897,544
ML TOTAL	56,813,760	55,872,276	70,256,456	50,010,016	50,469,240	60,097,384	63,168,684	70,339,808	70,139,376	72,748,968

MAJOR LEAGUE BASEBALL 2001–2003

	2001	2002	2003
NATIONAL LEAGUE			
ARI	2,740,554	3,200,725	2,805,542
ATL	2,823,494	2,603,482	2,401,084
CHI	2,779,456	2,693,071	2,962,630
CIN	1,882,732	1,855,973	2,355,259
COL	3,159,385	2,737,918	2,334,085
FLA	1,261,220	813,111	1,303,215
HOU	2,904,280	2,517,407	2,454,241
LA	3,017,502	3,131,077	3,138,626
MIL	2,811,041	1,969,693	1,700,354
MON	609,473	732,901	1,025,639
NY	2,658,279	2,804,838	2,140,599
PHI	1,782,460	1,618,141	2,259,948
PIT	2,436,126	1,784,993	1,636,751
STL	3,113,091	3,011,756	2,910,386
SD	2,377,969	2,220,416	2,030,084
SF	3,277,244	3,253,205	3,264,898
TOTAL	39,634,306	36,948,707	36,723,341
AMERICAN LEAGUE			
ANA	2,000,917	2,305,565	3,061,094
BAL	3,094,841	2,682,917	2,454,523
BOS	2,625,333	2,650,063	2,724,165
CHI	1,766,172	1,676,804	1,939,524
CLE	3,175,523	2,616,940	1,730,002
DET	1,921,305	1,503,623	1,368,245
KC	1,536,371	1,323,034	1,779,895
MIN	1,782,926	1,924,473	1,946,011
NY	3,264,777	3,461,644	3,465,600
OAK	2,133,277	2,169,811	2,216,596
SEA	3,507,975	3,540,482	3,268,509
TB	1,227,673	1,065,762	1,058,695
TEX	2,831,111	2,352,447	2,094,394
TOR	1,915,438	1,636,904	1,799,458
TOTAL	32,783,639	30,910,469	30,906,711
ML TOTAL	72,417,945	67,859,176	67,630,052

1884 UNION ASSOCIATION

ALT	11,000
BAL	45,000
BOS	28,000
CIN	41,000
CP	28,000
KC	54,000
MIL	10,000
PHI	19,000
STL	116,000
STP	0
WAS	56,000
WIL	3,000
TOT	411,000

1890 PLAYERS LEAGUE

BOS	197,346
BRO	79,272
BUF	61,244
CHI	148,876
CLE	58,430
NY	148,197
PHI	170,399
PIT	117,123
TOT	980,887

Appendix B

The Amateur Free Agent Draft

The 39 years of the Amateur Draft has resulted in literally thousands of picks by major league baseball teams. This section lists the 1,015 players taken in the first round, from Rick Monday—the first player taken in the inaugural draft of 1965—to Mitch Maier—the final first-round selection of 2003.

The selections below are listed in the order in which they were drafted in the first round of each year's primary June draft. The first pick of the first round is awarded to the worst team in the American or National League. Each season the leagues alternate the first pick and proceed through the first round in reverse order of finish from the previous season's standings. The American League picks first in odd-numbered years.

From 1965 to 1985 two amateur drafts were held each year. The first phase was held in June, followed in January of the next year by the secondary phase for previously drafted players who did not sign with the team that had selected them. The January draft was eliminated in 1986. Teams that fail to sign their first-round picks now receive a supplemental pick in the following draft.

Residents of the United States, Canada and Puerto Rico, or any other U.S. territory, are eligible for the draft if they are graduating high-school seniors, are players in junior-college or have completed their third year of college, plus players who turn 21 within 45 days of the draft. Players under 21 not in college can apply for draft eligibility. Although there have been discussions to expand the draft, foreign-born players (with the exception of those from Canada, Puerto Rico and U.S. territories) are not eligible.

For various reasons—most often the desire of a high school player to go on to college—some players do not sign when they are first drafted. Often these players are drafted again and do sign. Ron Cey is included below as an example of a player who was originally drafted by the Mets in 1966, did not sign, and then went on to be drafted again two years later and signed with the Dodgers.

Bob Horner and Hubie Brooks
The 1978 amateur draft featured two Arizona State stars. Horner, left, was picked No. 1 overall, by Atlanta; Brooks went No. 3 to the Mets.

After selecting a player, a club has the exclusive right to sign him until a week prior to the next draft or until he enrolls in a four-year college. Clubs are barred from drafting the same player in two consecutive years without written consent from the player. Teams are not allowed to trade future draft picks or trade drafted players during the year after the draft. Teams can, however, lose draft picks as compensation for off-season signings of another team's free agents. In such cases the compensation pick is based on a free-agent rating system, with players being rated Type A, Type B or Type C, and with the cost of a Type A free agent being a first round or second round draft pick, plus a supplemental pick.

MAJOR LEAGUE BASEBALL FIRST ROUND DRAFT PICKS

1965

Pick	Team	Player	Position	School/Hometown
1	Athletics	Rick Monday	OF	Arizona State U
2	Mets	Les Rohr	LHP	Billings, MT
3	Senators	Joe Coleman	RHP	Natick, MA
4	Astros	Alex Barrett	SS	Winton, CA
5	Red Sox	Billy Conigliaro	OF	Swampscott, MA
6	Cubs	Rick James	RHP	Florence, AL
7	Indians	Ray Fosse	C	Marion, IL
8	Dodgers	John Wyatt	SS	Bakersfield, CA
9	Twins	*Eddie Leon	SS	U of Arizona
10	Pirates	Doug Dickerson	OF	Birmingham, AL
11	Angels	Jim Spencer	1B	Glen Burnie, MD
12	Braves	Dick Grant	1B	Watertown, MA
13	Tigers	Gene Lamont	C	Kirkland, IL
14	Giants	Al Gallagher	3B	Santa Clara U
15	Orioles	Scott McDonald	RHP	Yakima, WA
16	Reds	Bernie Carbo	3B	Garden City, MI
17	White Sox	Ken Plesha	C	Notre Dame U
18	Phillies	*Mike Adamson	RHP	San Diego, CA
19	Yankees	Bill Burbach	RHP	Dickeyville, WI
20	Cardinals	Joe DiFabio	RHP	Delta State U

1966

Pick	Team	Player	Position	School/Hometown
1	Mets	Steve Chilcott	C	Lancaster, CA
2	Athletics	Reggie Jackson	OF	Arizona State U
3	Astros	Wayne Twitchell	RHP	Portland, OR
4	Red Sox	Ken Brett	LHP	El Segundo, CA
5	Cubs	Dean Burk	RHP	Highland, IL
6	Senators	Tom Grieve	OF	Pittsfield, MA
7	Cardinals	Leron Lee	OF	Sacramento, CA
8	Angels	Jim DeNeff	SS	Indiana U
9	Phillies	Mike Biko	RHP	Dallas, TX
10	Yankees	Jim Lyttle	OF	Florida State U
11	Braves	Al Santorini	RHP	Union, NJ
12	Indians	*John Curtis	LHP	Smithtown, NY
13	Reds	Gary Nolan	RHP	Oroville, CA
14	Tigers	*Rick Konik	1B	Detroit, MI
15	Pirates	Richie Hebner	SS	Norwood, MA
16	Orioles	Ted Parks	SS	U of California
17	Giants	Bob Reynolds	RHP	Seattle, WA
18	White Sox	Carlos May	OF	Birmingham, AL
19	Dodgers	Larry Hutton	RHP	Greenfield, IN
20	Twins	Bob Jones	3B	Dawson, GA

* Did not sign

1967

Pick	Team	Player	Position	School/Hometown
1	Yankees	Ron Blomberg	1B	Atlanta, GA
2	Cubs	Terry Hughes	SS	Spartanburg, SC
3	Red Sox	Mike Garman	RHP	Caldwell, ID
4	Mets	Jon Matlack	LHP	West Chester, PA
5	Senators	John Jones	C	St. Joseph, TN
6	Astros	John Mayberry	1B	Detroit, MI
7	Athletics	Brian Bickerton	LHP	Santee, CA
8	Reds	Wayne Simpson	RHP	Los Angeles, CA
9	Angels	Mike Nunn	C	Greensboro, NC
10	Cardinals	Ted Simmons	C	Southfield, MI
11	Indians	Jack Heidemann	SS	Brenham, TX
12	Braves	Andrew Finlay	OF	Sacramento, CA
13	White Sox	Dan Haynes	3B	East Point, GA
14	Phillies	Phil Meyer	LHP	Downey, CA
15	Tigers	Jim Foor	LHP	Ferguson, MO
16	Pirates	Joe Grigas	OF	Brockton, MA
17	Twins	Steve Brye	3B-OF	Oakland, CA
18	Giants	Dave Rader	C	Bakersfield, CA
19	Orioles	Bobby Grich	SS	Long Beach, CA
20	Dodgers	Don Denbow	3B	Southern Methodist U

1968

Pick	Team	Player	Position	School/Hometown
1	Mets	Tim Foli	SS	Canoga Park, CA
2	Athletics	*Peter Broberg	RHP	Palm Beach, FL
3	Astros	Marty Cott	C	Buffalo, NY
4	Yankees	Thurman Munson	C	Kent State U
5	Dodgers	Bobby Valentine	OF	Stamford, CT
6	Indians	Robert Weaver	SS	Jacksonville, FL
7	Braves	Curtis Moore	OF	Denison, TX
8	Senators	Donnie Castle	LHP-OF	Coldwater, MS
9	Pirates	Dick Sharon	OF	Redwood City, CA
10	Orioles	Junior Kennedy	SS	Arvin, CA
11	Phillies	Greg Luzinski	1B	Prospect Heights, IL
12	Angels	Lloyd Allen	RHP	Selma, CA
13	Reds	Tim Grant	RHP	Boykins, VA
14	White Sox	Rich McKinney	SS	Ohio U
15	Cubs	Ralph Rickey	OF	U of Oklahoma
16	Twins	Alex Rowell	OF	Luther College
17	Giants	Gary Matthews	OF	Pacoima, CA
18	Tigers	Robert Robinson	OF	Chester, VA
19	Cardinals	James Hairston	OF	Dayton, OH
20	Red Sox	Tom Maggard	OF-C	Norwalk, CA

1969

Pick	Team	Player	Position	School/Hometown
1	Senators	Jeff Burroughs	OF	Long Beach, CA
2	Astros	J.R. Richard	RHP	Ruston, LA
3	White Sox	Ted Nicholson	3B	Laurel, MS
4	Mets	Randy Sterling	RHP	Key West, FL
5	Angels	*Alan Bannister	SS	Buena Park, CA
6	Phillies	Mike Anderson	1B	Timmonsville, SC
7	Twins	Paul Ray Powell	OF	Arizona State U
8	Dodgers	Terry McDermott	C	West Hempstead, NY
9	Athletics	Don Stanhouse	RHP-SS	DuQuoin, IL
10	Pirates	Bob May	RHP	Merritt Island, FL
11	Yankees	Charlie Spikes	3B-OF	Bogalusa, LA
12	Braves	Gene Holbert	C	Campbelltown, PA
13	Red Sox	Noel Jenke	OF	U of Minnesota
14	Reds	Don Gullett	LHP	Lynn, KY
15	Indians	Alvin McGrew	OF	Fairfield, AL
16	Cubs	Roger Metzger	SS	St. Edward's U
17	Orioles	Don Hood	LHP	Florence, SC
18	Giants	Mike Phillips	SS	Irving, TX
19	Tigers	Lenny Baxley	1B	Redding, CA
20	Cardinals	Charles Minott	LHP	Covina, CA
21	Pilots	Gorman Thomas	SS	Charleston, SC
22	Expos	Balor Moore	LHP	Deer Park, TX
23	Royals	*John Simmons	SS	Childersburg, AL
24	Padres	Randy Elliott	1B	Camarillo, CA

1970

Pick	Team	Player	Position	School/Hometown
1	Padres	Mike Ivie	C	Decatur, GA
2	Indians	Steve Dunning	RHP	Stanford U
3	Expos	Barry Foote	C	Smithfield, NC
4	Brewers	Darrell Porter	C	Oklahoma City, OK
5	Phillies	Mike Martin	LHP	Columbia, SC
6	White Sox	Lee Richard	SS	Southern U
7	Astros	*Randy Scarbery	RHP	Fresno, CA
8	Royals	Rex Goodson	C	Longview, TX
9	Dodgers	Jim Haller	RHP	Omaha, NE
10	Angels	Paul Dade	3B-OF	Seattle, WA
11	Cardinals	Jim Browning	RHP	Gadsden, AL
12	Yankees	Dave Cheadle	LHP	Asheville, NC
13	Pirates	John Bedard	RHP	Springfield, MA
14	Senators	Charles Maxwell	3B-SS	Kingston, OH
15	Reds	Gary Polczynski	SS	West Allis, WI
16	Red Sox	*Jimmy Hacker	SS	Temple, TX
17	Giants	John D'Acquisto	RHP	San Diego, CA
18	Athletics	Dan Ford	OF	Los Angeles, CA
19	Cubs	Gene Hiser	OF	U of Maryland
20	Tigers	Terry Mappin	C	Louisville, KY
21	Braves	Ron Broaddus	RHP	Freeport, TX
22	Twins	Bob Gorinski	SS	Calumet, PA
23	Mets	*George Ambrow	SS	Long Beach, CA
24	Orioles	James West	C	St. Louis, MO

1971

Pick	Team	Player	Position	School/Hometown
1	White Sox	*Danny Goodwin	C	Peoria, IL
2	Padres	Jay Franklin	RHP	Vienna, VA
3	Brewers	Tom Bianco	SS	Elmont, NY
4	Expos	*C. Holloway	SS	Huntsville, AL
5	Royals	Roy Branch	RHP	St. Louis, MO
6	Phillies	Roy Thomas	RHP	Lompoc, CA
7	Senators	Roger Quiroga	RHP	Galveston, TX
8	Cardinals	Ed Kurpiel	1B-LHP	Hollis, NY
9	Indians	David Sloan	RHP	Santa Clara, CA
10	Braves	Taylor Duncan	SS	Sacramento, CA
11	Tigers	Tom Veryzer	SS	Islip, NY
12	Astros	Neil Rasmussen	SS	Arcadia, CA
13	Angels	Frank Tanana	LHP	Detroit, MI
14	Mets	Rich Puig	2B	Tampa, FL
15	Red Sox	Jim Rice	OF	Anderson, SC
16	Cubs	Jeff Wehmeier	RHP	Indianapolis, IN
17	Athletics	Sugar Bear Daniels	RHP	Detroit, MI
18	Giants	Frank Riccelli	LHP	Syracuse, NY
19	Yankees	Terry Whitfield	OF	Blythe, CA
20	Dodgers	Rick Rhoden	RHP	Boynton Beach, FL
21	Twins	Dale Soderholm	SS	Miami, FL
22	Pirates	Craig Reynolds	SS	Houston, TX
23	Orioles	Randy Stein	RHP	Pomona, CA
24	Reds	*Mike Miley	SS	New Orleans, LA

1972

Pick	Team	Player	Position	School/Hometown
1	Padres	Dave Roberts	3B	U of Oregon
2	Indians	Rick Manning	SS	Niagara Falls, NY
3	Phillies	Larry Christenson	RHP	Marysville, WA
4	Rangers	Roy Howell	3B	Lompoc, CA
5	Expos	Bob Goodman	C	Memphis, TN
6	Brewers	Danny Thomas	1B	Southern Illinois U
7	Reds	Larry Payne	RHP	Bedias, TX
8	Twins	*Dick Ruthven	RHP	Fresno State U
9	Astros	Steve Englishbey	OF	Houston, TX
10	Angels	Dave Chalk	3B	U of Texas
11	Braves	Preston Hanna	RHP	Pensacola, FL
12	White Sox	Mike Ondina	OF	Rancho Cordova, CA
13	Mets	Richard Bengston	C	Peoria, IL
14	Yankees	Scott McGregor	LHP	El Segundo, CA
15	Cubs	Brian Vernoy	LHP	Westminster, CA
16	Red Sox	Joel Bishop	SS	Sacramento, CA
17	Dodgers	John Harbin	SS	Newberry College
18	Royals	Jamie Quirk	SS	Whittier, CA
19	Giants	Rob Dressler	RHP	Portland, OR
20	Tigers	Jerry Manuel	SS	Rancho Cordova, CA
21	Cardinals	Dan Larson	RHP	Alhambra, CA
22	Athletics	Chet Lemon	SS	Los Angeles, CA
23	Pirates	Dwayne Peltier	SS	Anaheim, CA
24	Orioles	Ken Thomas	C	Bellville, OH

1973

Pick	Team	Player	Position	School/Hometown
1	Rangers	David Clyde	LHP	Houston, TX
2	Phillies	John Stearns	C	U of Colorado
3	Brewers	Robin Yount	SS	Woodland Hills, CA
4	Padres	Dave Winfield	OF	U of Minnesota
5	Indians	Glenn Tufts	1B	Bridgewater, MA
6	Giants	Johnnie LeMaster	SS	Paintsville, KY
7	Angels	Billy Taylor	OF	Savannah, Ga
8	Expos	Gary Roenicke	SS	West Covina, CA

9	Royals	Lew Olsen	RHP	Alamo, CA
10	Braves	Pat Rockett	SS	San Antonio, TX
11	Twins	Eddie Bane	LHP	Arizona State U
12	Cardinals	Joe Edelen	3B-RHP	Gracemont, OK
13	Yankees	Doug Heinhold	RHP	Victoria, TX
14	Mets	Lee Mazzilli	OF	Brooklyn, NY
15	Orioles	Mike Parrott	RHP	Camarillo, CA
16	Cubs	Jerry Tabb	1B	U of Tulsa
17	Red Sox	Ted Cox	SS	Midwest City, OK
18	Dodgers	Ted Farr	C	Spokane, WA
19	Tigers	Charles Bates	1B	Cal State Los Angeles
20	Astros	Calvin Portley	SS	Longview, TX
21	White Sox	Steve Swisher	C	Ohio U
22	Reds	Charles Kessler	OF	Claremont, CA
23	Athletics	Randy Scarbery	RHP	U of S. California
24	Pirates	Steve Nicosia	C	N. Miami Beach, FL

1974

Pick	Team	Player	Position	School/Hometown
1	Padres	Bill Almon	SS	Brown U
2	Rangers	Tommy Boggs	RHP	Austin, TX
3	Phillies	Lonnie Smith	OF	Compton, CA
4	Indians	Tom Brennan	RHP	Lewis U
5	Braves	Dale Murphy	C	Portland, OR
6	Brewers	Butch Edge	RHP	Sacramento, CA
7	Cubs	Scot Thompson	OF	Renfrew, PA
8	White Sox	Larry Monroe	RHP	Mt. Prospect, IL
9	Expos	Ron Sorey	3B	Dayton, OH
10	Angels	Mike Miley	SS	Louisiana State U
11	Pirates	Rod Scurry	LHP	Sparks, NV
12	Yankees	Dennis Sherrill	SS	Miami, FL
13	Cardinals	Garry Templeton	SS	Santa Ana, CA
14	Twins	Ted Shipley	SS	Vanderbilt U
15	Astros	Kevin Drake	OF	Lompoc, CA
16	Tigers	Lance Parrish	3B	Diamond Bar, CA
17	Mets	Cliff Speck	RHP	Beaverton, OR
18	Royals	Willie Wilson	OF	Summit, NJ
19	Giants	Terry Lee	2B	San Luis Obispo, CA
20	Red Sox	Eddie Ford	SS	U of South Carolina
21	Dodgers	Rick Sutcliffe	RHP	Kansas City, MO
22	Athletics	*Jerry Johnson	C	Austin, TX
23	Reds	Steve Reed	RHP	Fort Wayne, IN
24	Orioles	Rich Dauer	3B	U of Southern California

1975

Pick	Team	Player	Position	School/Hometown
1	Angels	Danny Goodwin	C	Southern U
2	Padres	Mike Lentz	LHP	Kirkland, WA
3	Tigers	Les Filkins	OF	Chicago, IL
4	Cubs	Brian Rosinski	OF	Evanston, IL
5	Brewers	Rich O'Keefe	LHP	Yorktown Hts., NY
6	Mets	Butch Benton	C	Tallahassee, FL
7	Indians	Rick Cerone	C	Seton Hall U
8	Giants	Ted Barnicle	LHP	Jacksonville State U
9	Royals	Clint Hurdle	OF	Merritt Island, FL
10	Expos	Art Miles	SS	Austin, TX
11	White Sox	Chris Knapp	RHP	Central Michigan U
12	Phillies	Sam Welborn	RHP	Wichita Falls, TX
13	Twins	Rick Sofield	SS	Morristown, NJ
14	Astros	Bo McLaughlin	RHP	David Lipscomb Col.
15	Red Sox	Otis Foster	1B	High Point College
16	Cardinals	David Johnson	LHP	Gaylord, MI
17	Rangers	Jim Gideon	RHP	U of Texas
18	Braves	Donald Young	C	Goleta, CA
19	Yankees	Jim McDonald	1B	Los Angeles, CA
20	Pirates	Dale Berra	SS	Montclair, NJ
21	Athletics	Bruce Robinson	C	Stanford U
22	Reds	Tony Moretto	OF	Evansville, IN
23	Orioles	Dave Ford	RHP	Cleveland, OH
24	Dodgers	Mark Bradley	SS	Elizabethtown, KY

1976

Pick	Team	Player	Position	School/Hometown
1	Astros	Floyd Bannister	LHP	Arizona State U
2	Tigers	Pat Underwood	LHP	Kokomo, IN
3	Braves	Ken Smith	3B	Youngstown, OH
4	Brewers	*Bill Bordley	LHP	Rolling Hills Estates, CA
5	Padres	Bob Owchinko	LHP	Eastern Michigan U
6	Angels	Ken Landreaux	OF	Arizona State U
7	Cubs	Herm Segelke	RHP	South Sacramento, CA
8	White Sox	Steve Trout	LHP	South Holland, IL
9	Expos	Bob James	RHP	Sunland, CA
10	Twins	*Jamie Allen	3B-RHP	Yakima, WA

11	Giants	Mark Kuecker	SS	Brenham, TX
12	Rangers	Billy Simpson	OF	Lakewood, CA
13	Mets	Tom Thurberg	OF-RHP	South Weymouth, MA
14	Indians	Tim Glass	C	Springfield, OH
15	Cardinals	Leon Durham	1B	Cincinnati, OH
16	Yankees	Pat Tabler	OF	Cincinnati, OH
17	Phillies	Jeff Kraus	SS	Cincinnati, OH
18	Royals	Ben Grzybek	RHP	Hialeah, FL
19	Dodgers	Mike Scioscia	C	Morton, PA
20	Orioles	Dallas Williams	OF	Brooklyn, NY
21	Pirates	Jim Parke	RHP	Sterling Heights, MI
22	Red Sox	Bruce Hurst	LHP	St. George, UT
23	Reds	Mark King	RHP	Owensboro, KY
24	Athletics	*Mike Sullivan	RHP	Woodbridge, VA

1977

Pick	Team	Player	Position	School/Hometown
1	White Sox	Harold Baines	OF	St. Michaels, MD
2	Expos	Bill Gullickson	RHP	Orland Park, IL
3	Brewers	Paul Molitor	SS	U of Minnesota
4	Braves	Tim Cole	LHP	Saugerties, NY
5	Tigers	Kevin Richards	RHP	Wyandotte, MI
6	Cardinals	Terry Kennedy	C	Florida State U
7	Angels	Richard Dotson	RHP	Cincinnati, OH
8	Padres	Brian Greer	OF	Brea, CA
9	Rangers	David Hibner	SS	Howell, MI
10	Giants	Craig Landis	SS	Napa, CA
11	Indians	Bruce Compton	OF	Norman, OK
12	Cubs	Randy Martz	RHP	U of South Carolina
13	Red Sox	Andrew Madden	RHP	New Hartford, NY
14	Astros	Ricky Adams	SS	Montclair, CA
15	Twins	Paul Croft	OF	Morristown, NJ
16	Mets	Wally Backman	SS	Beaverton, OR
17	Athletics	Craig Harris	RHP	Sierra Vista, AZ
18	Pirates	Anthony Nicely	OF	Dayton, OH
19	Orioles	Drungo Hazewood	OF	Sacramento, CA
20	Dodgers	Bob Welch	RHP	E. Michigan U
21	Royals	Mike Jones	LHP	Pittsford, NY
22	Phillies	Scott Munninghoff	RHP	Cincinnati, OH
23	Yankees	Steve Taylor	RHP	U of Delaware
24	Reds	Tad Venger	3B	Newhall, CA
25	Blue Jays	Tom Goffena	SS	Sidney, OH
26	Mariners	Dave Henderson	OF	Dos Palos, CA

1978

Pick	Team	Player	Position	School/Hometown
1	Braves	Bob Horner	3B	Arizona State U
2	Blue Jays	Lloyd Moseby	1B	Oakland, CA
3	Mets	Hubie Brooks	SS	Arizona State U
4	Athletics	Mike Morgan	RHP	Las Vegas, NV
5	Padres	Andy Hawkins	RHP	Waco, TX
6	Mariners	Tito Nanni	OF	Philadelphia, PA
7	Giants	Bob Cummings	C	Chicago, IL
8	Brewers	Nick Hernandez	C	Hialeah, FL
9	Expos	Glenn Franklin	SS	Chipola (FL) JC
10	Indians	Phil Lansford	SS	Santa Clara, CA
11	Astros	Rod Boxberger	RHP	U of Southern California
12	Tigers	Kirk Gibson	OF	Michigan State U
13	Cubs	Bill Hayes	C	Indiana State U
14	Angels	Tom Brunansky	OF	West Covina, CA
15	Cardinals	Robert Hicks	1B	Pensacola, FL
16	Twins	Lenny Faedo	SS	Tampa, FL
17	Reds	Nick Esasky	SS	Carol City, FL
18	Yankees	Rex Hudler	SS	Fresno, CA
19	Pirates	Brad Garnett	1B	DeSoto, TX
20	Athletics	Tim Conroy	LHP	Monroeville, PA
21	Pirates	Gerry Aubin	OF	Albany, GA
22	Orioles	Robert Boyce	3B	Cincinnati, OH
23	Phillies	Rip Rollins	1B-RHP	Sparta, NC
24	Yankees	Matt Winters	OF	Williamsville, NY
25	Royals	Buddy Biancalana	SS	Greenbrae, CA
26	Yankees	Brian Ryder	RHP	Shrewsbury, MA

1979

Pick	Team	Player	Position	School/Hometown
1	Mariners	Al Chambers	OF	Harrisburg, PA
2	Mets	Tim Leary	RHP	UCLA
3	Blue Jays	Jay Schroeder	C	Pacific Palisades, CA
4	Braves	Brad Komminsk	OF	Lima, OH
5	Athletics	*Juan Bustabad	SS	Hialeah, FL
6	Cardinals	Andy Van Slyke	OF	New Hartford, NY
7	Indians	Jon Bohnet	LHP	Vallejo, CA
8	Astros	John Mizerock	C	Punxsutawney, PA

9	White Sox	*Steve Buechele	SS	Fullerton, CA
10	Expos	Tim Wallach	1B	Cal State Fullerton
11	Twins	Kevin Brandt	OF	Nekoosa, WI
12	Cubs	Jon Perlman	RHP	Baylor U
13	Tigers	Rick Leach	OF	U of Michigan
14	Padres	Joe Lansford	1B	San Jose, CA
15	Giants	Scott Garrelts	RHP	Buckley, IL
16	Dodgers	Steve Howe	LHP	U of Michigan
17	Rangers	Jerry Don Gleaton	LHP	U of Texas
18	Giants	*Rick Luecken	RHP	Houston, TX
19	White Sox	Rick Seilheimer	C	Brenham, TX
20	Reds	Dan Lamar	OF	Houston, TX
21	Royals	Atlee Hammaker	LHP	E. Tennessee State U
22	Reds	Mike Sullivan	RHP	Clemson U
23	Tigers	Chris Baker	OF	Dearborn Heights, MI
24	Padres	Bob Geren	C	San Diego, CA
25	Dodgers	Steve Perry	RHP	U of Michigan
26	Athletics	*Mike Stenhouse	OF	Harvard U

1980

Pick	Team	Player	Position	School/Hometown
1	Mets	Darryl Strawberry	OF	Los Angeles, CA
2	Blue Jays	Garry Harris	SS	San Diego, CA
3	Braves	Ken Dayley	LHP	U of Portland
4	Athletics	Mike King	LHP	Morningside College
5	Padres	Jeff Pyburn	OF	U of Georgia
6	Mariners	Darnell Coles	SS	Rialto, CA
7	Giants	Jay Reid	1B	Lynwood, CA
8	White Sox	Cecil Espy	OF	San Diego, CA
9	Dodgers	Ross Jones	SS	U of Miami
10	Indians	Kelly Gruber	SS	Austin, TX
11	Cubs	Don Schulze	RHP	Roselle, IL
12	Twins	Jeff Reed	C	Joliet, IL
13	Phillies	Lebo Powell	C	Pensacola, FL
14	Rangers	Tim Maki	RHP	Humtertown, IN
15	Cardinals	Don Collins	RHP	Newport News, VA
16	Royals	Frank Wills	RHP	Tulane U
17	Angels	Dennis Rasmussen	LHP	Creighton U
18	Tigers	Glenn Wilson	3B	Sam Houston State U
19	Reds	Ron Robinson	RHP-SS	Woodlake, CA
20	Pirates	Rich Renteria	SS	South Gate, CA
21	Braves	Jim Acker	RHP	U of Texas
22	Expos	Terry Francona	OF	U of Arizona
23	Mets	Billy Beane	OF	Rancho Bernardo, CA
24	Mets	John Gibbons	C	San Antonio, TX
25	Brewers	Dion James	OF	Sacramento, CA
26	Orioles	Jeff Williams	OF	Cincinnati, OH

1981

Pick	Team	Player	Position	School/Hometown
1	Mariners	Mike Moore	RHP	Oral Roberts U
2	Cubs	Joe Carter	OF	Wichita State U
3	Angels	Dick Schofield	SS	Springfield, IL
4	Mets	Terry Blocker	OF	Tennessee State U
5	Blue Jays	Matt Williams	RHP	Rice U
6	Padres	Kevin McReynolds	OF	U of Arkansas
7	White Sox	Daryl Boston	OF	Cincinnati, OH
8	Cardinals	Bobby Meacham	SS	San Diego State U
9	Rangers	Ron Darling	RHP	Yale U
10	Giants	Mark Grant	RHP	Joliet, IL
11	Twins	Mike Sodders	3B	Arizona State U
12	Braves	Jay Roberts	OF	Centralia, WA
13	Indians	George Alpert	OF	Livingston, NJ
14	Pirates	Jim Winn	RHP	John Brown U
15	Athletics	Tim Pyznarski	3B-OF	Eastern Illinois U
16	Cubs	Vance Lovelace	LHP	Tampa, FL
17	Tigers	Ricky Barlow	RHP	Woodville, TX
18	Expos	Darren Dilks	LHP	Oklahoma State U
19	Red Sox	Steve Lyons	OF-SS	Oregon State U
20	Phillies	Johnny Abrego	RHP	San Jose, CA
21	Blue Jays	John Cerutti	LHP	Amherst College
22	Dodgers	Dave Anderson	SS	Memphis State U
23	Royals	Dave Leeper	OF	U of Southern California
24	Rangers	Al Lachowicz	RHP	U of Pittsburgh
25	Red Sox	Kevin Burrell	C	Poway, CA
26	Padres	Frank Castro	C	U of Miami

1982

Pick	Team	Player	Position	School/Hometown
1	Cubs	Shawon Dunston	SS	Brooklyn, NY
2	Blue Jays	Augie Schmidt	SS	U of New Orleans
3	Padres	Jimmy Jones	RHP	Dallas, TX
4	Twins	Bryan Oelkers	LHP	Wichita State U

5	Mets	Dwight Gooden	RHP	Tampa, FL
6	Mariners	Spike Owen	SS	U of Texas
7	Pirates	Sam Khalifa	SS	Tucson, AZ
8	Angels	Bob Kipper	LHP	Aurora, IL
9	Braves	Duane Ward	RHP	Farmington, NM
10	Royals	John Morris	OF	Seton Hall U
11	Giants	Steve Stanicek	1B	U of Nebraksa
12	Indians	Mark Snyder	RHP	Knoxville, TN
13	Phillies	John Russell	C-OF	U of Oklahoma
14	White Sox	Ron Karkovice	C	Orlando, FL
15	Astros	Steve Swain	OF	El Cajon, CA
16	Red Sox	Sam Horn	1B	San Diego, CA
17	Cubs	Tony Woods	SS	Whittier College
18	Red Sox	Rob Parkins	RHP	Cerritos, CA
19	Dodgers	Franklin Stubbs	1B	Virginia Tech
20	Tigers	Rich Monteleone	RHP	Tampa, FL
21	Cardinals	Todd Worrell	RHP	Biola College
22	Reds	Scott Jones	LHP	Hinsdale, IL
23	Reds	Bill Hawley	RHP	West Columbia, SC
24	Orioles	Joe Kucharski	RHP	U of South Carolina
25	Brewers	Dale Sveum	SS	Pinole, CA
26	Red Sox	Jeff Ledbetter	1B-OF	Florida State U

1983

Pick	Team	Player	Position	School/Hometown
1	Twins	*Tim Belcher	RHP	Mt. Vernon Nazarene Col
2	Reds	Kurt Stillwell	SS	Thousand Oaks, CA
3	Rangers	Jeff Kunkel	SS	Rider College
4	Mets	Eddie Williams	3B	San Diego, CA
5	Athletics	Stan Hilton	RHP	Baylor U
6	Cubs	Jackie Davidson	RHP	Everman, TX
7	Mariners	Darrel Akerfelds	RHP	Mesa College
8	Astros	Robbie Wine	C	Oklahoma State U
9	Blue Jays	Matt Stark	C	Hacienda Heights, CA
10	Padres	Ray Hayward	LHP	Oklahoma U
11	Indians	Dave Clark	OF	Jackson State U
12	Pirates	Ron DeLucchi	OF	Moraga, CA
13	White Sox	Joel Davis	RHP	Jacksonville, FL
14	Expos	Rich Stoll	RHP	U of Michigan
15	Tigers	Wayne Dotson	RHP	Lubbock, TX
16	Expos	Brian Holman	RHP	Wichita, KA
17	Mariners	Terry Bell	C	Old Dominion U
18	Dodgers	Erik Sonberg	LHP	Wichita State U
19	Red Sox	Roger Clemens	RHP	U of Texas
20	Mets	Stan Jefferson	OF	Bethune-Cookman College
21	Royals	Gary Thurman	OF	Indianapolis, IN
22	Phillies	Ricky Jordan	1B	Sacramento, CA
23	Angels	Mark Doran	OF	U of Wisconsin
24	Cardinals	Jim Lindeman	3B	Bradley U
25	Orioles	Wayne Wilson	RHP	Redondo Beach, CA
26	Brewers	Dan Plesac	LHP	North Carolina St. U

1984

Pick	Team	Player	Position	School/Hometown
1	Mets	Shawn Abner	OF	Mechanicsburg, PA
2	Mariners	Billy Swift	RHP	U of Maine
3	Cubs	Drew Hall	LHP	Morehead State U
4	Indians	Cory Snyder	SS	Brigham Young U
5	Reds	Pat Pacillo	RHP	Seton Hall U
6	Angels	Erik Pappas	C	Chicago, IL
7	Cardinals	Mike Dunne	RHP	Bradley U
8	Twins	Jay Bell	SS	Pensacola, FL
9	Giants	Alan Cockrell	OF	U of Tennessee
10	Athletics	Mark McGwire	1B	U of Southern California
11	Padres	Shane Mack	OF	UCLA
12	Rangers	Oddibe McDowell	OF	Arizona State U
13	Expos	Bob Caffrey	C	Cal State Fullerton
14	Red Sox	John Marzano	C	Temple U
15	Pirates	Kevin Andersh	LHP	U of New Mexico
16	Royals	Scott Bankhead	RHP	U of North Carolina
17	Astros	Don August	RHP	Chapman College
18	Brewers	Isaiah Clark	SS	Crockett, TX
19	Braves	Drew Denson	1B-OF	Cincinnati, OH
20	White Sox	Tony Menendez	RHP	Carol City, FL
21	Phillies	Pete Smith	RHP	Burlington, MA
22	Yankees	Jeff Pries	RHP	UCLA
23	Dodgers	Dennis Livingston	LHP	Oklahoma State U
24	Giants	Terry Mulholland	LHP	Marietta College
25	Orioles	John Hoover	RHP	Fresno State U
26	White Sox	Tom Hartley	OF	Vancouver, WA

1985

Pick	Team	Player	Position	School/Hometown
1	Brewers	B.J. Surhoff	C	U of North Carolina
2	Giants	Will Clark	1B	Mississippi State U
3	Rangers	Bobby Witt	RHP	U of Oklahoma
4	Reds	Barry Larkin	SS	U of Michigan
5	White Sox	Kurt Brown	C	Glendora, CA
6	Pirates	Barry Bonds	OF	Arizona State U
7	Mariners	Mike Campbell	RHP	U of Hawaii
8	Expos	Pete Incaviglia	OF	Oklahoma State U
9	Indians	Mike Poehl	RHP	U of Texas
10	Dodgers	Chris Gwynn	OF	San Diego State U
11	Athletics	Walt Weiss	SS	U of North Carolina
12	Astros	Cameron Drew	OF	U of New Haven
13	Twins	Jeff Bumgarner	RHP	Richland, WA
14	Braves	Tommy Greene	RHP	Whiteville, NC
15	Angels	Willie Fraser	RHP	Concordia College
16	Phillies	Trey McCall	C	Abingdon, VA
17	Royals	Brian McRae	SS	Blue Springs, FL
18	Cardinals	Joe Magrane	LHP	U of Arizona
19	Angels	Mike Cook	RHP	U of South Carolina
20	Mets	Gregg Jefferies	SS	Millbrae, CA
21	Red Sox	Dan Gabriele	RHP	Walled Lake, MI
22	Cubs	Rafael Palmeiro	OF	Mississippi State U
23	Padres	Joey Cora	SS	Vanderbilt U
24	Cubs	Dave Masters	RHP	U of California
25	Blue Jays	Greg David	OF	Naples, FL
26	Tigers	Randy Nosek	RHP	Chillicothe, MO

1986

Pick	Team	Player	Position	School/Hometown
1	Pirates	Jeff King	3B	U of Arkansas
2	Indians	Greg Swindell	LHP	U of Texas
3	Giants	Matt Williams	SS	U of Nevada-Las Vegas
4	Rangers	Kevin Brown	RHP	Georgia Tech
5	Braves	Kent Mercker	LHP	Dublin, OH
6	Brewers	Gary Sheffield	SS	Tampa, FL
7	Phillies	Brad Brink	RHP	U of Southern California
8	Mariners	Patrick Lennon	SS	Whiteville, NC
9	Cubs	Derrick May	OF	Newark, DE
10	Twins	Derek Parks	C	Upland, CA
11	Padres	Thomas Howard	OF	Ball State U
12	Athletics	Scott Hemond	C	U of South Florida
13	Astros	Ryan Bowen	RHP	Hanford, CA
14	Red Sox	*Greg McMurtry	OF	Brockton, MA
15	Expos	Kevin Dean	OF	Vallejo, CA
16	Angels	Roberto Hernandez	RHP	U of South Carolina
17	Reds	Scott Scudder	RHP	Blossom, TX
18	Tigers	Phil Clark	C	Crockett, TX
19	Dodgers	Mike White	OF	Loudon, TN
20	White Sox	Grady Hall	LHP	Northwestern U
21	Mets	Lee May	OF	Cincinnati, OH
22	Angels	Lee Stevens	OF	Lawrence, KS
23	Cardinals	Luis Alicea	2B	Florida State U
24	Royals	Tony Clements	SS	Chino, CA
25	Angels	Terry Carr	OF	Salisbury, MD
26	Blue Jays	Earl Sanders	RHP	Jackson State U

1987

Pick	Team	Player	Position	School/Hometown
1	Mariners	Ken Griffey, Jr.	OF	Cincinnati, OH
2	Pirates	Mark Merchant	OF	Oviedo, FL
3	Twins	Willie Banks	RHP	Jersey City, NJ
4	Cubs	Mike Harkey	RHP	Cal State Fullerton
5	White Sox	Jack McDowell	RHP	Stanford U
6	Braves	Derek Lilliquist	LHP	U of Georgia
7	Orioles	Chris Myers	LHP	Tampa, FL
8	Dodgers	Dan Opperman	RHP	Las Vegas, NV
9	Royals	Kevin Appier	RHP	Antelope Valley JC
10	Padres	Kevin Garner	RHP-OF	U of Texas
11	Athletics	Lee Tinsley	OF	Shelbyville, KY
12	Expos	Delino DeShields	SS-2B	Seaford, DE
13	Brewers	Bill Spiers	SS	Clemson U
14	Cardinals	Cris Carpenter	RHP	U of Georgia
15	Orioles	*Brad DuVall	RHP	Virginia Tech
16	Giants	Mike Remlinger	LHP	Dartmouth College
17	Blue Jays	Alex Sanchez	RHP	UCLA
18	Reds	Jack Armstrong	RHP	U of Oklahoma
19	Rangers	Brian Bohanon	LHP	Houston, TX
20	Tigers	Bill Henderson	C	Miami, FL
21	Tigers	Steve Pegues	OF	Pontotoc, MS
22	Astros	Craig Biggio	C	Seton Hall U

23	Rangers	Bill Haselman	C	UCLA
24	Mets	Chris Donnels	3B	Loyola Marymount U
25	Angels	John Orton	C	Cal Poly San Luis Obispo
26	Red Sox	Reggie Harris	RHP	Waynesboro, VA

1988

Pick	Team	Player	Position	School/Hometown
1	Padres	Andy Benes	RHP	U of Evansville
2	Indians	Mark Lewis	SS	Hamilton, OH
3	Braves	Steve Avery	LHP	Taylor, MI
4	Orioles	Gregg Olson	RHP	Auburn U
5	Dodgers	Bill Bene	RHP	Cal State - LA
6	Rangers	Monty Fariss	SS	Oklahoma State U
7	Astros	Willie Ansley	OF	Plainview, TX
8	Angels	Jim Abbott	LHP	U of Michigan
9	Cubs	Ty Griffin	2B	Georgia Tech
10	White Sox	Robin Ventura	3B	Oklahoma State U
11	Phillies	Pat Combs	LHP	Baylor U
12	Red Sox	Tom Fischer	LHP	U of Wisconsin
13	Pirates	Austin Manahan	SS	Phoenix, AZ
14	Mariners	Tino Martinez	1B	U of Tampa
15	Giants	Royce Clayton	SS	Playa del Rey, CA
16	Athletics	Stan Royer	3B	Eastern Illinois U
17	Indians	Charles Nagy	RHP	U of Connecticut
18	Royals	Hugh Walker	OF	Jacksonville, AR
19	Expos	David Wainhouse	RHP	Washington State U
20	Twins	Johnny Ard	RHP	Manatee JC
21	Mets	Dave Proctor	RHP	Allen County CC
22	Cardinals	John Ericks	RHP	U of Illinois
23	Cardinals	Brad DuVall	RHP	Virginia Tech
24	Brewers	*Alex Fernandez	RHP	Miami, FL
25	Blue Jays	Ed Sprague	3B	Stanford U
26	Tigers	Rico Brogna	1B	Watertown, CT

1989

Pick	Team	Player	Position	School/Hometown
1	Orioles	Ben McDonald	RHP	Louisiana State U
2	Braves	Tyler Houston	C	Las Vegas, NV
3	Mariners	Roger Salkeld	RHP	Saugus, CA
4	Phillies	Jeff Jackson	OF	Chicago, IL
5	Rangers	Donald Harris	OF	Texas Tech
6	Cardinals	Paul Coleman	OF	Frankston, TX
7	White Sox	Frank Thomas	1B	Auburn U
8	Cubs	Earl Cunningham	OF	Lancaster, SC
9	Angels	Kyle Abbot	LHP	Long Beach State U
10	Expos	*Charles Johnson	C	Fort Pierce, FL
11	Indians	*Calvin Murray	3B	Dallas, TX
12	Astros	Jeff Juden	RHP	Salem, MA
13	Royals	Brent Mayne	C	Cal State Fullerton
14	Giants	Steve Hosey	OF	Fresno State U
15	Dodgers	Kiki Jones	RHP	Tampa, FL
16	Red Sox	Greg Blosser	OF	Sarasota, FL
17	Brewers	Cal Eldred	RHP	U of Iowa
18	Pirates	Willie Greene	SS	Gray, GA
19	Blue Jays	Eddie Zosky	SS	Fresno State U
20	Reds	Scott Bryant	OF-RHP	U of Texas
21	Tigers	Greg Gohr	RHP	Santa Clara U
22	Dodgers	Tom Goodwin	OF	Frenso State U
23	Red Sox	Maurice Vaughn	1B	Seton Hall U
24	Mets	Alan Zinter	C	U of Arizona
25	Twins	Chuck Knoblauch	SS	Texas A&M
26	Mariners	*Scott Burrell	RHP	Hamden, CT

1990

Pick	Team	Player	Position	School/Hometown
1	Braves	Chipper Jones	SS	Pierson, FL
2	Tigers	Tony Clark	OF	El Cajon, CA
3	Phillies	Mike Lieberthal	C	Westlake, CA
4	White Sox	Alex Fernandez	RHP	Miami-Dade South CC
5	Pirates	Kurt Miller	RHP	Bakersfield, CA
6	Mariners	Marc Newfield	1B	Huntington Beach, CA
7	Reds	Daniel Wilson	C	U of Minnesota
8	Indians	Timothy Costo	SS	U of Iowa
9	Dodgers	Ronnie Walden	LHP	Blanchard, OK
10	Yankees	Carl Everett	OF	Tampa, FL
11	Expos	Darrell Andrews	SS-RHP	Carlsbad, NM
12	Twins	Todd Ritchie	RHP	Duncanville, TX
13	Cardinals	Donovan Osborne	LHP	U of Nevada
14	Athletics	Todd Van Poppel	RHP	Arlington, TX
15	Giants	Adam Hyzdu	OF	Cincinnati, OH
16	Rangers	Daniel Smith	LHP	Creighton U
17	Mets	Jeromy Burnitz	OF	Oklahoma State U
18	Cardinals	Aaron Holbert	SS	Long Beach, CA

19	Giants	Eric Christopherson	C	San Diego State U
20	Orioles	Michael Mussina	RHP	Stanford U
21	Astros	Thomas Nevers	SS	Edina, MN
22	Blue Jays	Steve Karsay	RHP	College Point, NY
23	Cubs	Lance Dickson	LHP	U of Arizona
24	Expos	Rondell White	OF	Gray, GA
25	Padres	Robert Beckett	LHP	Austin, TX
26	Athletics	Donald Peters	RHP	College of St. Francis

1991

Pick	Team	Player	Position	School/Hometown
1	Yankees	Brien Taylor	LHP	Beaufort, NC
2	Braves	Mike Kelly	OF	Arizona State U
3	Twins	David McCarty	OF	Stanford U
4	Cardinals	Dmitri Young	SS	Camarillo, CA
5	Brewers	James Henderson	RHP	Ringgold, GA
6	Astros	John Burke	RHP	U of Florida
7	Royals	Joseph Vitiello	OF	U of Alabama
8	Padres	Johns Hamilton	RHP	Georgia Southern U
9	Orioles	Mark Smith	OF	U of Southern California
10	Phillies	Tyler Green	RHP	Wichita State U
11	Mariners	Aaron Estes	LHP	Gardnerville, NV
12	Cubs	Douglas Glanville	OF	U of Pennsylvania
13	Indians	Manuel Ramirez	OF	New York, NY
14	Expos	Cornelius Floyd	1B	Markham, IL
15	Brewers	Tyrone Hill	LHP	Yucaipa, CA
16	Blue Jays	Shawn Green	OF	Santa Ana, CA
17	Angels	Eduardo Perez	1B	Florida State U
18	Mets	Alfred Shirley	OF	George Washington U
19	Rangers	Benjamin Gil	SS	San Diego, CA
20	Reds	Calvin Reese	SS	Columbia, SC
21	Cardinals	Allen Watson	LHP	New York Institute
22	Cardinals	Brian Barber	RHP	Orlando, FL
23	Red Sox	Aaron Sele	RHP	Washington State U
24	Pirates	Jonathan Farrell	OF	Florida CC
25	White Sox	Scott Ruffcorn	RHP	Baylor U
26	Athletics	Brent Gates	SS	U of Minnesota

1992

Pick	Team	Player	Position	School/Hometown
1	Astros	Phil Nevin	3B	Cal State Fullerton
2	Indians	Paul Shuey	RHP	U of North Carolina
3	Expos	Billy Wallace	LHP	Mississippi State U
4	Orioles	Jeffrey Hammonds	OF	Stanford U
5	Reds	Chad Mottola	OF	Central Florida U
6	Yankees	Derek Jeter	SS	Kalamazoo, MI
7	Giants	Calvin Murray	OF-3B	U of Texas
8	Angels	Pete Janicki	RHP	U of California
9	Mets	Preston Wilson	SS-OF	Bamberg, SC
10	Royals	Michael Tucker	SS-2B	Longwood College
11	Cubs	Derek Wallace	RHP	Pepperdine U
12	Brewers	Kenneth Felder	OF	Florida State U
13	Phillies	Chad McConnell	OF	Creighton U
14	Mariners	Ronald Villone	LHP	U of Massachusetts
15	Cardinals	Jonathan Lowe	RHP	Arizona State U
16	Tigers	Richard Greene	RHP	Louisiana State U
17	Royals	James Pittsley	RHP	Dubois, PA
18	Mets	Christopher Roberts	OF-LHP	Florida State U
19	Blue Jays	Shannon Stewart	OF	Miami, FL
20	Athletics	Michael Grigsby	RHP	San Diego State U
21	Braves	James Arnold	RHP	Kissimmee, FL
22	Rangers	Ricky Helling	RHP	Stanford U
23	Pirates	Jason Kendall	C	Torrance, CA
24	White Sox	Eddie Pearson	3B	Bishop St JC
25	Blue Jays	Todd Steverson	OF	Arizona State U
26	Twins	Daniel Serafini	LHP	San Bruno, CA
27	Rockies	John Burke	RHP	U of Florida
28	Marlins	Charles Johnson	C	U of Miami

1993

Pick	Team	Player	Position	School/Hometown
1	Mariners	Alex Rodriguez	SS	Miami, FL
2	Dodgers	Darren Dreifort	RHP	Wichita State U
3	Angels	Brian Anderson	LHP	Wright State U
4	Phillies	Wayne Gomes	RHP	Old Dominion U
5	Royals	Jeff Granger	LHP	Texas A&M U
6	Giants	Steve Soderstrom	RHP	Fresno State U
7	Red Sox	Trot Nixon	OF	Wilmington, NC
8	Mets	Kirk Presley	RHP	Tupelo, MS
9	Tigers	Matt Brunson	SS	Englewood, CO
10	Cubs	Brooks Kieschnick	OF-RHP	U of Texas
11	Indians	Daron Kirkreit	RHP	U of Cal-Riverside
12	Astros	Billy Wagner	LHP	Ferrum College

13	Yankees	Matt Drews	RHP	Sarasota, FL
14	Padres	Derrek Lee	1B	Granite Bay, CA
15	Blue Jays	Chris Carpenter	RHP	Manchester, NH
16	Cardinals	Alan Benes	RHP	Creighton U
17	White Sox	Scott Christman	LHP	Oregon State U
18	Expos	Chris Schwab	OF	Eagan, MN
19	Orioles	Jay Powell	RHP	Mississippi State U
20	Twins	Torii Hunter	OF	Pine Bluff, AR
21	Twins	*Jason Varitek	C	Georgia Tech
22	Pirates	Charles Peterson	OF	Laurens, SC
23	Brewers	Jeff D'Amico	RHP	Pinellas Park, FL
24	Cubs	Jon Ratliff	RHP	LeMoyne College
25	Athletics	John Wasdin	RHP	Florida State U
26	Brewers	Kelly Wunsch	LHP	Texas A&M
27	Marlins	Marc Valdes	RHP	U of Florida
28	Rockies	Jamey Wright	RHP	Oklahoma City, OK

1994

Pick	Team	Player	Position	School/Hometown
1	Mets	Paul Wilson	RHP	Florida State U
2	Athletics	Ben Grieve	OF	Arlington, TX
3	Padres	Dustin Hermanson	RHP	Kent State U
4	Brewers	Tony Williamson	3B	Arizona State U
5	Marlins	Josh Booty	SS	Shreveport, LA
6	Angels	McKay Christensen	OF	Clovis, CA
7	Rockies	Doug Million	LHP	Sarasota, FL
8	Twins	Todd Walker	2B	Louisiana State U
9	Reds	C.J. Nitkowski	LHP	St. John's U
10	Indians	Jaret Wright	RHP	Anaheim, CA
11	Pirates	Mark Farris	OF	Angleton, TX
12	Red Sox	Nomar Garciaparra	SS	Georgia Tech
13	Dodgers	Paul Konerko	C	Scottsdale, AZ
14	Mariners	Jason Varitek	C	Georgia Tech
15	Cubs	Jayson Peterson	RHP	Denver, CO
16	Royals	Matt Smith	1B	Grants Pass, OR
17	Astros	Ramon Castro	C	Vega Baja, PR
18	Tigers	Cade Gaspar	RHP	Pepperdine U
19	Cardinals	Bret Wagner	LHP	Wake Forest U
20	Mets	Terrence Long	1B	Millbrook, AL
21	Expos	Hiram Bocachica	SS	Bayamon, PR
22	Giants	Dante Powell	OF	Cal State Fullerton
23	Phillies	Carlton Loewer	RHP	Mississippi State U
24	Yankees	Brian Buchanan	1B	U of Virginia
25	Astros	Scott Elarton	RHP	Lamar, CO
26	White Sox	Mark Johnson	C	Warner Robbins, GA
27	Braves	Jacob Shumate	RHP	Hartville, SC
28	Blue Jays	Kevin Witt	SS	Jacksonville, FL

1995

Pick	Team	Player	Position	School/Hometown
1	Angels	Darin Erstad	OF	U of Nebraska
2	Padres	Mark Davis	C	Malvern, PA
3	Mariners	Jose Cruz, Jr.	OF	Rice U
4	Cubs	Kerry Wood	RHP	Grand Prairie, TX
5	Athletics	Ariel Prieto	RHP	Palm Springs, CA
6	Marlins	Jamie Jones	OF	San Diego, CA
7	Rangers	Jonathan Johnson	RHP	Florida State U
8	Rockies	Todd Helton	1B	U of Tennessee
9	Brewers	Geoff Jenkins	OF	U of South California
10	Pirates	Chad Hermansen	SS	Henderson, NV
11	Tigers	Mike Drumright	RHP	Wichita State U
12	Cardinals	Matt Morris	RHP	Seton Hall U
13	Twins	Mark Redman	LHP	U of Oklahoma
14	Phillies	Reggie Taylor	OF	Newberry, SC
15	Red Sox	Andy Yount	RHP	Kingwood, TX
16	Giants	Joe Fontenot	RHP	Lafayette, LA
17	Blue Jays	Roy Halladay	RHP	Golden, CO
18	Mets	Ryan Jaroncyk	SS	Escondido, CA
19	Royals	Juan Lebron	OF	Arroyo, PR
20	Dodgers	David Yocum	LHP	Florida State U
21	Orioles	Alvie Shepherd	RHP	U of Nebraska
22	Astros	Tony McKnight	RHP	Texarkana, AR
23	Indians	David Miller	1B	Clemson U
24	Red Sox	Corey Jenkins	OF	Columbia, SC
25	White Sox	Jeff Liefer	3B	Long Beach State U
26	Braves	*Chad Hutchinson	RHP	Encinitas, CA
27	Yankees	Shea Morenz	OF	U of Texas
28	Expos	Michael Barrett	SS	Pace Academy

1996

Pick	Team	Player	Position	School/Hometown
1	Pirates	Kris Benson	RHP	Clemson U
2	Twins	Travis Lee	1B	San Diego State U

3	Cardinals	Braden Looper	RHP	Wichita State U
4	Blue Jays	Billy Koch	RHP	Clemson U
5	Expos	John Patterson	RHP	Orange, TX
6	Tigers	Seth Greisinger	RHP	U of Virginia
7	Giants	Matt White	RHP	Waynesboro, PA
8	Brewers	Chad Green	OF	U of Kentucky
9	Marlins	Mark Kotsay	OF	Cal State Fullerton
10	Athletics	Eric Chavez	3B	San Diego, CA
11	Phillies	Adam Eaton	RHP	Snohomish, WA
12	White Sox	Bobby Seay	LHP	Sarasota, FL
13	Mets	Robert Stratton	OF	Santa Barbara, CA
14	Royals	Dermal Brown	OF	Marlboro, NY
15	Padres	Matt Halloran	SS	Fredericksburg, VA
16	Blue Jays	Joe Lawrence	SS	Lake Charles, LA
17	Cubs	Todd Noel	RHP	Maurice, LA
18	Rangers	R.A. Dickey	RHP	U of Tennessee
19	Astros	Mark Johnson	RHP	U of Hawaii
20	Yankees	Eric Milton	LHP	U of Maryland
21	Rockies	Jake Westbrook	RHP	Danielsville, GA
22	Mariners	Gilbert Meche	RHP	Lafayette, LA
23	Dodgers	Damian Rolls	3B	Kansas City, KS
24	Rangers	Sam Marsonek	RHP	Tampa, FL
25	Reds	John Oliver	OF	Lehman, PA
26	Red Sox	Josh Garrett	RHP	Richland, IN
27	Braves	A.J. Zapp	1B	Greenwood, IN
28	Indians	Danny Peoples	1B	U of Texas
29	Devil Rays	Paul Wilder	OF	Raleigh, NC
30	D'backs	Nick Bierbrodt	LHP	Long Beach, CA

1997

Pick	Team	Player	Position	School/Hometown
1	Tigers	Matt Anderson	RHP	Rice U
2	Phillies	*J.D. Drew	OF	Florida State U
3	Angels	Troy Glaus	3B	UCLA
4	Giants	Jason Grilli	RHP	Seton Hall U
5	Blue Jays	Vernon Wells	OF	Arlington, TX
6	Mets	Geoff Goetz	LHP	Tampa, FL
7	Royals	Dan Reichert	RHP	U of the Pacific
8	Pirates	J.J. Davis	1B	Pomona, CA
9	Twins	Michael Cuddyer	SS	Chesapeake, VA
10	Cubs	Jon Garland	RHP	Granada Hills, CA
11	Athletics	Chris Enochs	RHP	West Virginia U
12	Marlins	Aaron Akin	RHP	Cowley County CC
13	Brewers	Kyle Peterson	RHP	Stanford U
14	Reds	Brandon Larson	SS	Louisiana State U
15	White Sox	Jason Dellaero	SS	U of South Florida
16	Astros	Lance Berkman	1B	Rice U
17	Red Sox	John Curtice	LHP	Chesapeake, VA
18	Rockies	Mark Mangum	RHP	Kingwood, TX
19	Mariners	Ryan Anderson	LHP	Westland, MI
20	Cardinals	Adam Kennedy	SS	Cal State Northridge
21	Athletics	Eric DuBose	LHP	Mississippi State U
22	Orioles	Jayson Werth	C	Chatham, IL
23	Expos	Donnie Bridges	RHP	Hattiesburg, MS
24	Yankees	*Tyrell Godwin	OF	Elizabethtown, NC
25	Dodgers	Glenn Davis	1B	Vanderbilt U
26	Orioles	Darnell McDonald	OF	Englewood, CO
27	Padres	Kevin Nicholson	SS	Stetson U
28	Indians	Tim Drew	RHP	Hahira, GA
29	Braves	Troy Cameron	SS	Ft. Lauderdale, FL
30	D'backs	Jack Cust	1B	Flemington, NJ
31	Devil Rays	Jason Standridge	RHP	Trussville, AL

1998

Pick	Team	Player	Position	School/Hometown
1	Phillies	Pat Burrell	1B	U of Miami (FL)
2	Athletics	Mark Mulder	LHP	Michigan State U
3	Cubs	Corey Patterson	OF	Kennesaw, GA
4	Royals	Jeff Austin	RHP	Stanford U
5	Cardinals	J.D. Drew	OF	No School
6	Twins	Ryan Mills	LHP	Arizona State U
7	Reds	Austin Kearns	RF	Lexington, KY
8	Blue Jays	Felipe Lopez	SS	Altamonta Springs, FL
9	Padres	Sean Burroughs	3B	Long Beach, CA
10	Rangers	Carlos Pena	1B	Northeastern U
11	Expos	Josh McKinley	SS	Dowingtown, PA
12	Red Sox	Jeffrey Everett	SS	U of South Carolina
13	Brewers	J.M. Gold	RHP	Toms River, NJ
14	Tigers	Jeff Weaver	RHP	Fresno State U
15	Pirates	Clinton Johnston	LHP	Vanderbilt U
16	White Sox	Robert Wells	RHP	Baylor U
17	Astros	Brad Lidge	RHP	U of Notre Dame
18	Angels	Seth Etherton	RHP	U of Southern Cal.
19	Giants	Anthony Torcato	3B	Woodland, CA

20	Indians	Carsten Sabathia	LHP	Vallejo, CA
21	Mets	Jason Tyner	CF	Texas A&M U
22	Mariners	Matthew Thornton	LHP	Centreville, MI
23	Dodgers	Bubba Crosby	CF	Rice U
24	Yankees	Andrew Brown	OF	Richmond, IN
25	Giants	Nathan Bump	RHP	Penn State U
26	Orioles	Rick Elder	OF	Marietta, GA
27	Marlins	Chip Ambres	OF	Beaumont, TX
28	Rockies	Matt Roney	RHP	Edmond, OK
29	Giants	Arturo McDowell	OF	Jackson, MS
30	Royals	Matt Burch	RHP	Va. Commonwealth U

1999

Pick	Team	Player	Position	School/Hometown
1	Devil Rays	Josh Hamilton	OF	Raleigh, NC
2	Marlins	Josh Beckett	RHP	Spring, Texas
3	Tigers	Eric Munson	C	U of Southern California
4	D'backs	Corey Myers	SS	Scottsdale, AZ
5	Twins	B.J. Garbe	OF	Moses Lake, WA
6	Expos	Josh Girdley	LHP	Jasper, Texas
7	Royals	Kyle Snyder	RHP	U of North Carolina
8	Pirates	Bobby Bradley	RHP	W. Palm Beach, FL
9	Athletics	Barry Zito	LHP	U of Southern California
10	Brewers	Ben Sheets	RHP	NE Louisiana U
11	Mariners	Ryan Christianson	C	Riverside, CA
12	Phillies	Brett Myers	RHP	Jacksonville, FL
13	Orioles	Mike Paradis	RHP	Clemson U
14	Reds	Ty Howington	LHP	Vancouver, WA
15	White Sox	Jason Stumm	RHP	Centralia, WA
16	Rockies	Jason Jennings	RHP	Baylor U
17	Red Sox	Rick Asadoorian	OF	Whitinsville, MA
18	Orioles	Richard Stahl	LHP	Covington, GA
19	Blue Jays	Alex Rios	3B/OF	Guaynabo, PR
20	Padres	Vince Faison	OF	Lyons, GA
21	Orioles	Larry Bigbie	OF	Ball State U
22	White Sox	Matt Ginter	RHP	Mississippi State U
23	Orioles	Keith Reed	OF	Providence College
24	Giants	Kurt Ainsworth	RHP	Louisiana State U
25	Royals	Mike Macdougal	RHP	Wake Forest U
26	Cubs	Ben Christiansen	RHP	Wichita State U
27	Yankees	David Walling	RHP	U of Arkansas
28	Padres	Gerik Baxter	RHP	Edmonds, WA
29	Padres	Omar Ortiz	RHP	Texas-Pan Am U
30	Cardinals	Chance Caple	RHP	Texas A&M U

2000

Pick	Team	Player	Position	School/Hometown
1	Marlins	Adrian Gonzalez	1B	Chula Vista, CA
2	Twins	Adam Johnson	RHP	San Diego, CA
3	Cubs	Luis Montanez	SS	Miami, FL
4	Royals	Mike Stodolka	LHP	Corona, CA
5	Expos	Justin Wayne	RHP	Honolulu, HI
6	Devil Rays	Rocco Baldelli	OF	Warwick, RI
7	Rockies	Matt Harrington	RHP	Palmdale, CA
8	Tigers	Matt Wheatland	RHP	San Diego, CA
9	Padres	Mark Phillips	LHP	Hanover, PA
10	Angels	Joe Torres	LHP	Kissimmee, FL
11	Brewers	Dave Krynzel	OF	Henderson, NV
12	White Sox	Joe Borchard	OF	Camarillo, CA
13	Cardinals	Shaun Boyd	2B	Oceanside, CA
14	Orioles	Beau Hale	RHP	Mauriceville, TX
15	Phillies	Chase Utley	2B	Long Beach, CA
16	Mets	Billy Traber	LHP	El Segundo, CA
17	Dodgers	Ben Diggins	RHP	Phoenix, AZ
18	Blue Jays	Miguel Negron	OF	Caguas, PR
19	Pirates	Sean Burnett	LHP	Wellington, FL
20	Angels	Chris Bootcheck	RHP	LaPorte, IN
21	Giants	John Bonser	RHP	Pinellas Park, FL
22	Red Sox	Phil Dumatrait	LHP	Bakersfield, CA
23	Reds	David Espinosa	SS	Miami, FL
24	Cardinals	Blake Williams	RHP	San Marcos, TX
25	Rangers	Scott Heard	C	San Diego, CA
26	Indians	Corey Smith	SS	Piscataway, NJ
27	Astros	Robert Stiehl	C	Torrance, CA
28	Yankees	David Parrish	C	Yorba Linda, CA
29	Braves	Adam Wainwright	RHP	St. Simons Island, GA
30	Braves	Scott Thorman	3B	Cambridge, Ontario

2001

Pick	Team	Player	Position	School/Hometown
1	Twins	Joe Mauer	C	Cretin-Derham Hall HS, St. Paul
2	Cubs	Mark Prior	RHP	U of Southern California
3	Devil Rays	Dewon Brazelton	RHP	Middle Tennessee State U

4	Phillies	Gavin Floyd	RHP	Mt. St. Joseph HS, Baltimore
5	Rangers	Mark Teixeira	3B	Georgia Tech
6	Expos	Josh Karp	RHP	UCLA
7	Orioles	Chris Smith	LHP	Cumberland (Tenn.) U
8	Pirates	John Van Benschoten	1B-OF	Kent State U
9	Royals	Colt Griffin	RHP	Marshall (Texas) HS
10	Astros	Chris Burke	SS	U of Tennessee
11	Tigers	Kenny Baugh	RHP	Rice U
12	Brewers	Mike Jones	RHP	Thunderbird HS, Phoenix
13	Angels	Casey Kotchman	1B	Seminole (Fla.) HS
14	Padres	Jake Gautreau	3B	Tulane U
15	Blue Jays	Gabe Gross	OF	Auburn U
16	White Sox	Kris Honel	RHP	Providence HS, New Lenox, Ill
17	Indians	Dan Denham	RHP	Deer Valley HS, Antioch, CA
18	Mets	Aaron Heilman	RHP	U of Notre Dame
19	Orioles	Mike Fontenot	2B	Louisiana State U
20	Reds	Jeremy Sowers	LHP	Ballard HS, Louisville
21	Giants	Brad Hennessey	RHP	Youngstown State U
22	D'backs	Jason Bulger	RHP	Valdosta State U
23	Yankees	John-Ford Griffin	OF	Florida State U
24	Braves	Macay McBride	LHP	Screven County HS, Sylvania, Ga
25	Athletics	Bobby Crosby	SS	Long Beach State U
26	Athletics	Jeremy Bonderman	RHP	Pasco (Wash.) HS
27	Indians	Alan Horne	RHP	Marianna (Fla.) HS
28	Cardinals	Justin Pope	RHP	U of Central Florida
29	Braves	Josh Burrus	SS	Wheeler HS, Marietta, Ga
30	Giants	Noah Lowry	LHP	Pepperdine U

2002

Pick	Team	Player	Position	School/Hometown
1	Pirates	Bryan Bullington	RHP	Ball State U
2	Devil Rays	B.J. Upton	SS	Greenbriar Christian, Chesapeake, VA
3	Reds	Chris Gruler	RHP	Liberty HS, Brentwood, CA
4	Orioles	Adam Loewen	LHP	Fraser Valley Christian, Surrey, BC
5	Expos	Clint Everts	RHP	Cypress Falls HS, Houston
6	Royals	Zack Greinke	RHP	Apoka HS, Orlando
7	Brewers	Prince Fielder	1B	Eau Gaillie HS, Melbourne, Fla.
8	Tigers	Scott Moore	SS	Cypress (Calif.) HS
9	Rockies	Jeff Francis	LHP	U of British Columbia
10	Rangers	Drew Meyer	SS	U of South Carolina
11	Marlins	Jeremy Hermida	OF	Wheeler HS, Marietta, Ga.
12	Angels	Joe Saunders	LHP	Virginia Tech
13	Padres	Khalil Greene	SS	Clemson U
14	Blue Jays	Russ Adams	SS-2B	U of North Carolina
15	Mets	Scott Kazmir	LHP	Cypress Falls HS, Houston
16	Athletics	Nick Swisher	1B-OF	Ohio State U
17	Phillies	Cole Hamels	RHP	Rancho Bernardo HS, San Diego
18	White Sox	Royce Ring	LHP	San Diego State U
19	Dodgers	James Loney	1B-LHP	Elkins HS, Missouri City, TX
20	Twins	Denard Span	OF	Tampa Catholic HS
21	Cubs	Bobby Brownlie	RHP	Rutgers U
22	Indians	Jeremy Guthrie	RHP	Stanford U
23	Braves	Jeff Francoeur	OF	Parkview HS, Lilburn, Ga.
24	Athletics	Joseph Blanton	RHP	University of Kentucky
25	Giants	Matt Cain	RHP	Houston HS, Germantown, TN
26	Athletics	John McCurdy	SS	U of Maryland
27	D'backs	Sergio Santos	SS	Mater Dei HS, Hacienda Heights, CA
28	Mariners	John Mayberry Jr.	1B	Rockhurst HS, Kansas City, MO
29	Astros	Derick Grigsby	RHP	Northeast Texas, CC
30	Athletics	Ben Fritz	RHP	Fresno State U

2003

Pick	Team	Player	Position	School/Hometown
1	Devils	Delmon Young	OF	Camarillo HS, CA
2	Brewers	Rickie Weeks	2B	Southern U. LA
3	Tigers	Kyle Sleeth	RHP	Wake Forest U.
4	Padres	Tim Stauffer	RHP	U of Richmond, VA
5	Royals	Chris Lubanski	OF	Kennedy-Kenrick HS, Schwenksville, PA
6	Cubs	Ryan Harvey	OF	Dunedin (Fla) HS, FL
7	Orioles	Nick Markakis	OF	Young Harris (Ga) JC, GA
8	Pirates	Paul Maholm	LHP	Mississippi State U
9	Rangers	John Danks	LHP	Round Rock (Texas) HS, TX
10	Rockies	Ian Stewart	3B	La Quinta HS, Garden Grove, CA
11	Indians	Michael Aubrey	1B	Tulane U
12	Mets	Lastings Milledge	OF	Lakewood Ranch HS, Palmetto, FL
13	Blue Jays	Aaron Hill	SS	Louisiana State U.
14	Reds	Ryan Wagner	RHP	U of Houston
15	White Sox	Brian Anderson	OF	U of Arizona
16	Marlins	Jeff Allison	RHP	Veterans Memorial HS, Peabody, MA
17	Red Sox	David Murphy	OF	Baylor U
18	Indians	Brad Snyder	OF	Ball State U
19	D'backs	Conor Jackson	3B	U of California
20	Expos	Chad Cordero	RHP	Cal State Fullerton
21	Twins	Matt Moses	3B	Mills Godwin HS, Richmond, VA
22	Giants	David Aardsma	RHP	Rice U
23	Angels	Brandon Wood	SS	Horizon HS, Scottsdale, AZ
24	Dodgers	Chad Billingsley	RHP	Defiance HS, OH
25	Athletics	Brad Sullivan	RHP	U of Houston
26	Athletics	Brian Snyder	3B	Stetson U
27	Yankees	Eric Duncan	3B	Seton Hall Prep, Florham Park, NJ
28	Cardinals	Daric Barton	C	Marina HS, Huntington Beach, CA
29	D'backs	Carlos Quentin	OF	Stanford U
30	Royals	Mitch Maier	C	U of Toledo

Appendix E Evolution of Baseball Records

Maury Wills
Ty Cobb's single-season stolen base record of 96 was broken in 1962 by Wills, here completing his 104th steal to set a record that stood for 12 years.

By Marty Appel and Tom Ruane

Throughout baseball history if a player was a league leader his record would forever show an asterisk or boldface so we could readily remember the achievement. But if the player set an *all-time* record that was later broken his name would pass from the record books forever. Thus Roger Connor, who was baseball's all-time home-run champion before Babe Ruth, is a forgotten man as far as statistical compilations go.

The following is a chronology of major batting, baserunning and pitching records for a career and for a season. It is an attempt to honor those who set the standards of their times. After the player's name appears, we show the total he concluded with—before the mark was broken—followed by the years in which the record belonged to him. Records at the end of the season are the basis for establishing new leaders to avoid the daily leap-frogging

that may have occurred in some cases. This does create the possibility of someone holding a record briefly within a season yet not being included here.

Changes in rules and scoring practices are worth mentioning. An asterisk marks the sections for single-season batting average, hits, at bats, and hitting streaks because of a change in scoring practice in 1887 that counted walks as hits. An asterisk marks the first post-1887 record holder on those lists; a similar note is made following a change in the definition of a stolen base after 1897 to exclude extra bases taken on teammates' hits. Likewise, single-season pitching records are given both before and after 1893, when the pitching distance was established at the current 60 feet, 6 inches. In records for strikeouts and hits per game, a game is defined as nine innings.

The authors extend special thanks to Pete Palmer for his assistance in compiling this section.

CAREER BATTING AND BASERUNNING

GAMES PLAYED

Players	Record	Years Held
Jack Manning, Jim O'Rourke, Harry Schafer, George Wright	70	1876
Jim O'Rourke, George Wright	131	1877
Jim O'Rourke	191	1878
George Wright	275	1879
Jim O'Rourke	619	1880-84
Paul Hines	731	1884-85
John Morrill	1219	1885-89
Paul Hines	1327	1889-90
Cap Anson	2277	1890-1906
Jake Beckley	2389	1906-09
Bill Dahlen	2444	1909-15
Honus Wagner	2792	1915-26
Ty Cobb	3035	1926-74
Hank Aaron	3298	1974-83
Carl Yastrzemski	3308	1983-84
Pete Rose	3562	1984-present

CONSECUTIVE GAMES
(incomplete for 19th century)

George Pinkney	577	1889-1920
Everett Scott	1307	1920-33
Lou Gehrig	2130	1933-95
Cal Ripken Jr.	2632	1995-present

AT BATS

George Wright	1288	1876-80
Paul Hines	6096	1880-91

Cap Anson	9176	1891-1906
Jake Beckley	9538	1906-15
Honus Wagner	10439	1915-26
Ty Cobb	11434	1926-74
Hank Aaron	12364	1974-82
Pete Rose	14053	1982-present

RUNS

Ross Barnes	142	1876-78
Jim O'Rourke	173	1878-79
George Wright	244	1879-80
Jim O'Rourke	965	1880-88
King Kelly	1160	1888-90
Harry Stovey	1492	1890-94
Cap Anson	1722	1894-1916

Honus Wagner	1739	1916-23
Ty Cobb	2246	1923-2001
Rickey Henderson	2295	2001-present

HITS

Ross Barnes	138	1876-77
Deacon White	207	1877-78
Deacon White, Cal McVey	288	1878-79
Paul Hines	1027	1879-85
Cap Anson	3056	1885-1914
Honus Wagner	3420	1914-23
Ty Cobb	4189	1923-85
Pete Rose	4256	1985-present

DOUBLES

Ross Barnes, Dick Higham, Paul Hines	21	1876-77
George Wright	33	1877-78
Jim O'Rourke	48	1878-79
Tom York	72	1879-80
Paul Hines	213	1880-85
Cap Anson	529	1885-1911
Nap Lajoie	657	1911-25
Tris Speaker	792	1925-present

TRIPLES

Ross Barnes	14	1876-77
George Hall	21	1877-78
Tom York	24	1878-79
Charley Jones	31	1879-80
Charley Jones, Jim O'Rourke	34	1880-81
Jim O'Rourke	55	1881-84
Charley Jones	90	1884-87
Roger Connor	233	1887-1905
Jake Beckley	244	1905-13
Sam Crawford	309	1913-present

HOME RUNS

George Hall	5	1876-77
Charley Jones	40	1877-85
Harry Stovey	57	1885-87
Dan Brouthers	74	1887-89
Harry Stovey	122	1889-95
Roger Connor	138	1895-1921
Babe Ruth	714	1921-74
Hank Aaron	755	1974-present

RBIs

Deacon White	190	1876-80
Cap Anson	1880	1880-1927
Ty Cobb	1938	1927-32
Babe Ruth	2213	1932-75
Hank Aaron	2297	1975-present

STRIKEOUTS

Johnny Ryan	23	1876-77
Lew Brown	120	1877-80
Will White	127	1880-81
Pud Galvin	418	1881-86
John Morrill	656	1886-95
Tom Brown	709	1895-1926
Babe Ruth	1330	1926-64
Mickey Mantle	1710	1964-78
Willie Stargell	1912	1978-82
Reggie Jackson	2597	1982-present

WALKS

Ross Barnes	20	1876-77
Jim O'Rourke	40	1877-79
Charley Jones	55	1879-80
Jim O'Rourke	114	1880-83
Tom York	133	1883-84
George Gore	385	1884-88
Ned Williamson	447	1888-89
George Gore	650	1889-92
Roger Connor	1002	1892-99
Billy Hamilton	1189	1899-1923
Eddie Collins	1499	1923-30
Babe Ruth	2062	1930-2001
Rickey Henderson	2190	2001-present

HIT BY PITCH

Ed Swartwood	15	1884-85
Bill Gleason	34	1885-87
Fred Mann	43	1887-88
Curt Welch	171	1888-93
Tommy Tucker	272	1893-1901
Hughie Jennings	287	1901-present

INTENTIONAL WALKS (since 1955)

Ted Kluszewski	47	1955-57
Ted Williams	61	1957-58
Stan Musial	97	1958-61
Ernie Banks	183	1961-68
Hank Aaron	293	1968-99
Barry Bonds	483	1999-present

STOLEN BASES

Harry Stovey	68	1886-87
Arlie Latham	739	1887-97
Billy Hamilton	789	1897-98
*Ed Delahanty	58	1898-99
John McGraw	169	1899-1902
Sam Mertes	294	1902-05
Honus Wagner	723	1905-18
Ty Cobb	892	1918-77
Lou Brock	938	1977-91
Rickey Henderson	1406	1991-present

BATTING AVERAGE
(3,000 at bat minimum)

Jim O'Rourke	.316	1884-85
Cap Anson	.342	1885-87
Dan Brouthers	.362	1887-88
Pete Browning	.366	1888-89
Dan Brouthers	.356	1889-90
Pete Browning	.354	1890-92
Dan Brouthers	.349	1892-96
Billy Hamilton	.351	1896-97
Jesse Burkett	.352	1897-99
Willie Keeler	.364	1899-1905
Nap Lajoie	.350	1905-11
Ty Cobb	.366	1911-present

ON-BASE PERCENTAGE
(3,000 at bat minimum)

Jim O'Rourke	.351	1884-85
Cap Anson	.380	1885-87
Dan Brouthers	.423	1887-94
Billy Hamilton	.460	1894-99
John McGraw	.466	1899-1923
Babe Ruth	.474	1923-47
Ted Williams	.483	1947-present

SLUGGING PCT. (3,000 at bat minimum)

Paul Hines	.434	1884-85
Cap Anson	.471	1885-87
Dan Brouthers	.520	1887-1903
Nap Lajoie	.529	1903-07
Dan Brouthers	.519	1907-16
Joe Jackson	.522	1916-17
Dan Brouthers	.519	1917-22
Rogers Hornsby	.536	1922-23
Babe Ruth	.690	1923-present

AT BATS PER HOME RUN
(3,000 at bat minimum)

Paul Hines	136.62	1884-85
Abner Dalrymple	84.35	1885-86
Charley Jones	64.10	1886-87
Dan Brouthers	50.59	1887-90
Harry Stovey	47.56	1890-92
Jimmy Ryan	47.25	1892-93
Mike Tiernan	47.09	1893-95
Sam Thompson	47.13	1895-1904
Buck Freeman	43.49	1904-05
Sam Thompson	47.13	1905-06
Bill Joyce	47.20	1906-17
Gavvy Cravath	33.20	1917-23
Babe Ruth	11.76	1923-98
Mark McGwire	10.61	1998-present

CAREER PITCHING RECORDS

GAMES PITCHED

Jim Devlin	129	1876-78
Tommy Bond	294	1878-83
Jim McCormick	386	1883-85
Pud Galvin	697	1885-1905
Cy Young	906	1905-68
Hoyt Wilhelm	1070	1968-1998
Dennis Eckersley	1071	1998-99
Jesse Orosco	1252	1999-present

WINS

Al Spalding	47	1876-77
Tommy Bond	180	1877-84
Will White	228	1884-86
Jim McCormick	252	1886-87
Pud Galvin	360	1887-1903
Cy Young	511	1903-present

LOSSES

Jim Devlin	60	1876-79
George Bradley	82	1879-80
Tommy Bond	97	1880-81
Jim McCormick	173	1881-85
Pud Galvin	308	1885-1911
Cy Young	316	1911-present

INNINGS PITCHED

Jim Devlin	1181	1876-78
Tommy Bond	2547.2	1878-83
Jim McCormick	3353.2	1883-85
Pud Galvin	5941.1	1885-1906
Cy Young	7356	1906-present

GAMES STARTED

Jim Devlin	129	1876-78
Tommy Bond	288	1878-83
Jim McCormick	379	1883-85
Pud Galvin	682	1885-1907
Cy Young	815	1907-present

COMPLETE GAMES

Jim Devlin	127	1876-78
Tommy Bond	270	1878-83
Will White	306	1883-84
Jim McCormick	392	1884-86
Pud Galvin	639	1886-1907
Cy Young	749	1907-present

STRIKEOUTS

Jim Devlin	263	1876-78
Tommy Bond	715	1878-82
Jim McCormick	1704	1882-88
Tim Keefe	2545	1888-1908
Cy Young	2803	1908-21
Walter Johnson	3509	1921-83
Steve Carlton	3709	1983-84
Nolan Ryan	5714	1984-present

WALKS

Joe Borden	51	1876-77
Jim Devlin	78	1877-78
Terry Larkin	84	1878-79
Will White	171	1879-81
Jim McCormick	565	1881-86
Mickey Welch	1297	1886-93
Tony Mullane	1408	1893-95
Amos Rusie	1707	1895-1952
Bobo Newsom	1732	1952-55
Bob Feller	1764	1955-63
Early Wynn	1775	1963-81
Nolan Ryan	2795	1981-present

HITS ALLOWED

Bobby Mathews	693	1876-77
Jim Devlin	1183	1877-78
Tommy Bond	2610	1878-83
Pud Galvin	6419	1883-1908
Cy Young	7092	1908-present

HOME RUNS ALLOWED

Bobby Mathews	8	1876-78
Tommy Bond	20	1878-80

Tommy Bond, George Bradley	21	1880-81
Tommy Bond	24	1881-82
George Bradley	28	1882-83
Will White	39	1883-84
Larry Corcoran	66	1884-86
Jim McCormick	84	1886-88
John Clarkson	88	1888-89
Pud Galvin	105	1889-90
John Clarkson	161	1890-1930
Grover Cleveland Alexander	164	1930-36
George Blaeholder	173	1936-38
Earl Whitehill	184	1938-39
Red Ruffing	254	1939-56
Murry Dickson	269	1956-57
Robin Roberts	505	1957-present

SHUTOUTS

George Bradley	18	1876-78
Tommy Bond	35	1878-84
Pud Galvin	56	1884-1904
Cy Young	76	1904-14
Christy Mathewson	77	1914-18
Christy Mathewson, Walter Johnson	79	1918-19
Walter Johnson	110	1919-present

SAVES

Jack Manning	6	1876-89
Tony Mullane	15	1889-98
Tony Millane, Kid Nichols	15	1898-99
Kid Nichols	17	1899-1907
Joe McGinnity	24	1907-10
Mordecai Brown	49	1910-26
Firpo Marberry	101	1926-46
Johnny Murphy	107	1946-62
Roy Face	136	1962-64
Hoyt Wilhelm	227	1964-80
Rollie Fingers	341	1980-92
Jeff Reardon	357	1992-93
Lee Smith	478	1993-present

RUNS ALLOWED

Bobby Mathews	395	1876-77
Jim Devlin	597	1877-78
Tommy Bond	634	1878-79
Terry Larkin	857	1879-80
Tommy Bond	1155	1880-82
Will White	1173	1882-83
Pud Galvin	3318	1883-present

EARNED RUNS ALLOWED

Bobby Mathews	164	1876-77
Jim Devlin	248	1877-78
Tommy Bond	605	1878-83
Pud Galvin	1895	1883-1907
Cy Young	2146	1907-present

EARNED RUN AVERAGE
(1,500 innings pitched minimum)

Tommy Bond	1.97	1879-80
John Ward	1.90	1880-82
Will White	1.95	1882-84
Old Hoss Radbourn	1.95	1884-86
John Ward	2.10	1886-1905
Christy Mathewson	2.08	1905-06
John Ward	2.10	1906-07
Addie Joss	1.89	1907-09
Mordecai Brown	1.63	1909-10
Ed Walsh	1.70	1910-12
Walter Johnson	1.80	1912-22
Ed Walsh	1.82	1922-present

WINNING PCT.
(1,500 innings pitched minimum)

Tommy Bond	.694	1879-80
John Ward	.659	1880-81
Tommy Bond	.641	1881-83
Larry Corcoran.	.692	1883-84
Old Hoss Radbourn	.684	1884-86
Larry Corcoran	.670	1886-87
John Clarkson	.701	1887-88
Bob Caruthers	.708	1888-92
Dave Foutz	.690	1892-1911
Ed Ruelbach	.691	1911-12
Dave Foutz	.690	1912-31
Lefty Grove	.693	1931-36
Dave Foutz	.690	1936-39
Lefty Grove	.691	1939-40
Dave Foutz	.690	1940-53
Vic Raschi	.706	1953-54
Dave Foutz	.690	1954-59
Whitey Ford	.696	1959-67
Dave Foutz	.690	1967-83
Ron Guidry	.705	1983-84
Dave Foutz	.690	1984-85
Ron Guidry	.694	1984-86
Dave Foutz	.690	1986-90
Dwight Gooden	.714	1990-92
Dave Foutz	.690	1992-2000
Pedro Martinez	.712	2000-present

STRIKEOUTS PER GAME
(1,500 innings pitched minimum)

Tommy Bond	2.65	1879-80
John Ward	3.29	1880-83
Larry Corcoran	4.11	1883-84
Jim Whitney	4.60	1884-86
Ed Morris	5.32	1886-87
Charlie Buffinton	5.13	1887-88
Toad Ramsey	6.49	1888-1904
Rube Waddell	7.04	1904-45
Bob Feller	7.07	1945-50
Rube Waddell	7.04	1950-61
Sam Jones	7.55	1961-64
Sandy Koufax	9.28	1964-69
Sam McDowell	9.34	1969-71
Sandy Koufax	9.28	1971-75
Nolan Ryan	9.55	1975-96
Randy Johnson	11.16	1996-present

INTENTIONAL WALKS (since 1955)

Hal Jeffcoat	12	1955-56
Bob Friend	115	1956-68
Don Drysdale	123	1968-73
Lindy McDaniel	136	1973-78
Gaylord Perry	164	1978-88
Kent Tekulve	179	1988-present

FEWEST HITS PER GAME
(1,500 innings pitched minimum)

Tommy Bond	8.92	1879-80
John Ward	8.33	1880-83
Larry Corcoran	7.91	1883-84
Tony Mullane	7.79	1884-85
Tim Keefe	7.72	1885-86
Ed Morris	8.10	1886-88
Tim Keefe	8.06	1888-92
Amos Rusie	8.08	1892-1902
Vic Willis	8.07	1902-04
Rube Waddell	7.44	1904-07
Addie Joss	7.26	1907-09
Ed Walsh	6.79	1909-11
Ed Reulbach	6.99	1911-13
Walter Johnson	7.09	1913-22
Ed Walsh	7.12	1922-45
Bob Feller	7.01	1945-48
Ed Walsh	7.12	1948-61
Bob Turley	7.12	1961-63
Ed Walsh	7.12	1963-64
Sandy Koufax	6.79	1964-74
Andy Messersmith	6.71	1974-75
Nolan Ryan	6.56	1975-present

HIT BY PITCH

Will White	68	1884-87
Tony Mullane	82	1887-92
Tim Keefe	98	1892-99
Kid Nichols	118	1899-1902
Chick Fraser	168	1902-07
Joe McGinnity	182	1907-14
Eddie Plank	196	1914-26
Eddie Plank, Walter Johnson	196	1926-27
Walter Johnson	203	1927-present

BALKS

Fred Goldsmith, Jack Lynch, Lee Richmond, Jim Whitney	1	1881-82
Fred Goldsmith, Jack Lynch, Lee Richmond, Jim Whitney, Pud Galvin	1	1882-83
Fred Goldsmith	2	1883-84
Fred Goldsmith, John Henry	2	1884-85
Charlie Ferguson	3	1885-93
Charlie Ferguson, Al Maul	3	1893-97
Charlie Ferguson, Al Maul, Cy Seymour	3	1897-98
Cy Seymour	8	1898-1911
Cy Seymour, Ed Walsh	8	1911-12
Ed Walsh	14	1912-31
Ed Walsh, Tom Zachary	14	1931-35
Tom Zachary	15	1935-63
Jack Sanford	21	1963-77
Steve Carlton	90	1977-present

WILD PITCHES

George Bradley	116	1876-80
Will White	141	1880-84
John Ward	144	1884-85
Will White	166	1885-86
Mickey Welch	274	1886-1992
Mickey Welch, Nolan Ryan	274	1992-93
Nolan Ryan	277	1993-present

SINGLE-SEASON BATTING AND BASERUNNING RECORDS

GAMES

Jack Manning, Jim O'Rourke, Harry Schafer, George Wright	70	1876-79
Paul Hines, Mike McGeary, George Wright	85	1879-80
Emil Gross	87	1880-83
Joe Farrell, Sadie Houck, Martin Powell	101	1883-84
Roger Connor, Billy Geer, Alex McKinnon	116	1884-86
Bill McClellan, Bill Phillips, George Pinkney	141	1886-88
George Pinkney	143	1888-92
Roger Connor	155	1892-98
George Van Haltren	156	1898-1904
Jimmy Barrett	162	1904-61
Rocky Colavito, Brooks Robinson	163	1961-62
Maury Wills	165	1962-present

AT BATS

George Wright	343	1876-79
Paul Hines	409	1879-83
Jud Birchall	449	1883-84
Abner Dalrymple	521	1884-86
George Pinkney	597	1886-87
Arlie Latham	672	1887-92
*Tom Brown	660	1892-1921
Jack Tobin	671	1921-22
Rabbit Maranville	672	1922-31
Lloyd Waner	681	1931-35
Lloyd Waner, JoJo Moore	681	1935-36
Woody Jensen	696	1936-69
Matty Alou	698	1969-75
Dave Cash	699	1975-80
Willie Wilson	705	1980-present

RUNS

Ross Barnes	126	1876-84
Fred Dunlap	160	1884-87
Tip O'Neill	167	1887-91
Tom Brown	177	1891-94
Billy Hamilton	198	1894-present

HITS

Ross Barnes	138	1876-79
Paul Hines	146	1879-83
Dan Brouthers	159	1883-84
Fred Dunlap	185	1884-86
Dave Orr	193	1886-87
Tip O'Neill, Pete Browning	275	1887-94

*Hugh Duffy	237	1894-96
Jesse Burkett	240	1896-1911
Ty Cobb	248	1911-20
George Sisler	257	1920-present

DOUBLES

Ross Barnes, Dick Higham,		
Paul Hines	21	1876-78
Dick Higham	22	1878-79
Charlie Eden	31	1879-82
King Kelly	37	1882-83
Ned Williamson	49	1883-87
Tip O'Neill	52	1887-99
Ed Delahanty	55	1899-1923
Tris Speaker	59	1923-26
George Burns	64	1926-31
Earl Webb	67	1931-present

TRIPLES

Ross Barnes	14	1876-79
Ross Barnes, Buttercup Dickerson	14	1879-80
Ross Barnes, Buttercup Dickerson,		
Harry Stovey	14	1880-82
Roger Connor	18	1882-84
Harry Stovey	23	1884-86
Dave Orr	31	1886-94
Dave Orr, Heinie Reitz	31	1894-1912
Chief Wilson	36	1912-present

HOME RUNS

George Hall	5	1876-79
Charley Jones	9	1879-83
Harry Stovey	14	1883-84
Ned Williamson	27	1884-1919
Babe Ruth	29	1919-20
Babe Ruth	54	1920-21
Babe Ruth	59	1921-27
Babe Ruth	60	1927-61
Roger Maris	61	1961-98
Mark McGwire	70	1998-2001
Barry Bonds	73	2001-present

RBIs

Deacon White	60	1876-79
Charley Jones, John O'Rourke	62	1879-80
Cap Anson	74	1880-82
Cap Anson	83	1882-83
Dan Brouthers	97	1883-84
Cap Anson	102	1884-86
Cap Anson	147	1886-87
Sam Thompson	166	1887-1921
Babe Ruth	171	1921-27
Lou Gehrig	175	1927-30
Hack Wilson	191	1930-present

STRIKEOUTS

Johnny Ryan	23	1876-77
Lew Brown	33	1877-78
Will White	41	1878-79
Will White, Pud Galvin	41	1879-80
Pud Galvin	57	1880-81
Pud Galvin	70	1881-83
Pud Galvin	79	1883-84
Sam Wise	104	1884-1914
Gus Williams	120	1914-38
Vince DiMaggio	134	1938-56
Jim Lemon	138	1956-61
Jake Wood	141	1961-62
Harmon Killebrew	142	1962-63
Dave Nicholson	175	1963-69
Bobby Bonds	187	1969-70
Bobby Bonds	189	1970-present

WALKS

Ross Barnes	20	1876-77
Ross Barnes, Jim O'Rourke	20	1877-79
Charley Jones	29	1879-81
John Clapp	35	1881-83
Tom York	37	1883-84
Candy Nelson	74	1884-85
Ned Williamson	75	1885-86
George Gore	102	1886-87
Paul Radford	106	1887-88
Yank Robinson	116	1888-89
Yank Robinson	118	1889-90
Bill Joyce	123	1890-92
Jack Crooks	136	1892-1911
Jimmy Sheckard	147	1911-20
Babe Ruth	150	1920-23
Babe Ruth	170	1923-2001
Barry Bonds	177	2001-2002
Barry Bonds	198	2002-present

HIT BY PITCH

Ed Swartwood	15	1884-85
Bill Gleason, Ed Swartwood	15	1885-86
Frank Fennelly	18	1886-87
Tommy Tucker	29	1887-88
Tommy Tucker, Curt Welch	29	1888-89
Tommy Tucker	33	1889-90
Curt Welch	34	1890-91
Curt Welch	36	1891-96
Hughie Jennings	51	1896-present

STOLEN BASES

Harry Stovey	68	1886-87
Hugh Nicol	138	1887-98
*Ed Delahanty	58	1898-99
Jimmy Sheckard	77	1899-1910

Eddie Collins	81	1910-11
Ty Cobb	83	1911-12
Clyde Milan	88	1912-15
Ty Cobb	96	1915-62
Maury Wills	104	1962-74
Lou Brock	118	1974-82
Rickey Henderson	130	1982-present

BATTING AVERAGE

Ross Barnes	.404	1876-84
Fred Dunlap	.412	1884-7
Tip O'Neill	.485	1887-94
*Hugh Duffy	.440	1894-present

SLUGGING PERCENTAGE

Ross Barnes	.590	1876-84
Fred Dunlap	.621	1884-87
Tip O'Neill	.691	1887-94
Hugh Duffy	.694	1894-1921
Babe Ruth	.847	1921-2001
Barry Bonds	.863	2001-present

ON-BASE PERCENTAGE

Ross Barnes	.462	1876-86
King Kelly	.483	1886-87
Tip O'Neill	.4895	1887-93
Billy Hamilton	.4896	1893-94
Billy Hamilton	.522	1894-99
John McGraw	.547	1899-1941
Ted Williams	.551	1941-2002
Barry Bonds	.582	2002-present

BATTING STREAKS

Denny Lyons	52	1887-93
*George Davis	33	1893-94
Billy Hamilton	36	1894
Bill Dahlen	42	1894-97
Willie Keeler	44	1897-1941
Joe DiMaggio	56	1941-present

AT BATS PER HOME RUN

George Hall	53.60	1876-79
Charley Jones	39.44	1879-81
Dan Brouthers	33.75	1881-83
Harry Stovey	30.07	1883-84
Ned Williamson	15.44	1884-1919
Babe Ruth	14.90	1919-20
Babe Ruth	8.48	1920-96
Mark McGwire	8.13	1996-98
Mark McGwire	7.27	1998-2001
Barry Bonds	6.52	2001-present

SINGLE-SEASON PITCHING RECORDS

(acknowledging 1893 change in pitching distance)

GAMES PITCHED

Jim Devlin	68	1876-79
Will White	76	1879-83
Will White, Pud Galvin,		
Old Hoss Radbourn	76	1883-93
Amos Rusie	56	1893-94
Amos Rusie, Ted Breitenstein	56	1894-95
Amos Rusie, Ted Breitenstein,		
Pink Hawley	56	1895-1907
Amos Rusie, Ted Breitenstein,		
Pink Hawley, Ed Walsh	56	1907-08
Ed Walsh	66	1908-43
Ace Adams	70	1943-50
Jim Konstanty	74	1950-64
John Wyatt	81	1964-65
Ted Abernathy	84	1965-68
Wilbur Wood	88	1968-69
Wayne Granger	90	1969-73
Mike Marshall	92	1973-74
Mike Marshall	106	1974-present

WINS

Al Spalding	47	1876-79
Al Spalding, John Ward	47	1879-83
Old Hoss Radbourn	48	1883-84
Old Hoss Radbourn	59	1884-93

Frank Killen	36	1893-94
Frank Killen, Amos Rusie	36	1894-1904
Jack Chesbro	41	1904-present

LOSSES

Jim Devlin	35	1876-79
George Bradley, Jim McCormick	40	1879-80
Will White	42	1880-83
John Coleman	48	1883-93
Duke Esper	28	1893-95
Ted Breitenstein	30	1895-97
Red Donahue	35	1897-present

INNINGS PITCHED

Jim Devlin	622	1876-79
Will White	680	1879-93
Amos Rusie	482	1893-present

GAMES STARTED

Jim Devlin	68	1876-79
Will White	75	1879-83
Will White, Pud Galvin	75	1883-93
Amos Rusie	52	1893-present

COMPLETE GAMES

Jim Devlin	66	1876-79
Will White	75	1879-93
Amos Rusie	50	1893-present

STRIKEOUTS

Jim Devlin	122	1876-77
Tommy Bond	170	1877-78
Tommy Bond	182	1878-79
Monte Ward	239	1879-80
Larry Corcoran	268	1880-83
Tim Keefe	361	1883-84
Hugh Daily	483	1884-86
Matt Kilroy	513	1886-93
Amos Rusie	208	1893-98
Cy Seymour	239	1898-1901
Cy Seymour, Noodles Hahn	239	1901-03
Rube Waddell	302	1903-04
Rube Waddell	349	1904-65
Sandy Koufax	382	1965-73
Nolan Ryan	383	1973-present

STRIKEOUTS PER GAME

Tommy Bond	1.94	1876-77
Bobby Mitchell	3.69	1877-78
Bobby Mitchell	5.74	1878-83
Jim Whitney	6.04	1883-84
Hugh Daily	8.68	1884-93
Amos Rusie	3.88	1893-94
Amos Rusie	3.95	1894-95
Amos Rusie	4.60	1895-97
Cy Seymour	4.83	1897-98
Cy Seymour	6.03	1898-1901

Tom Hughes	6.57	1901-02
Rube Waddell	6.84	1902-03
Rube Waddell	8.39	1903-46
Hal Newhouser	8.46	1946-55
Herb Score	9.70	1955-60
Sandy Koufax	10.13	1960-62
Sandy Koufax	10.55	1962-65
Sam McDowell	10.71	1965-84
Dwight Gooden	11.39	1984-87
Nolan Ryan	11.48	1987-95
Randy Johnson	12.35	1995-98
Kerry Wood	12.58	1998-99
Pedro Martinez	13.20	1999-2001
Randy Johnson	13.41	2001-present

WALKS

Joe Borden	51	1876-77
Terry Larkin, Tricky Nichols	53	1877-78
The Only Nolan	56	1878-79
Jim McCormick	74	1879-80
Larry Corcoran	99	1880-82
Jim McCormick	103	1882-83
Frank Mountain	123	1883-84
Mickey Welch	146	1884-86
Toad Ramsey	207	1886-89
Mark Baldwin	274	1889-90
Amos Rusie	289	1890-93
Amos Rusie	218	1893-present

INTENTIONAL WALKS (since 1955)

Hal Jeffcoat	12	1955-56
Bob Friend	18	1956-64
Ron Perranoski	19	1964-65
Lindy McDaniel	20	1965-67
Lindy McDaniel, Jim Bunning, Ron Willis	20	1967-75
Mike Garman	23	1975-82
Mike Garman, Kent Tekulve	23	1982-present

HITS ALLOWED

Bobby Mathews	693	1876-83
John Coleman	772	1883-93
Amos Rusie	451	1893-94
Ted Breitenstein	497	1894-present

FEWEST HITS PER GAME

George Bradley	7.38	1876-80
Tim Keefe	6.09	1880-93
Amos Rusie	8.42	1893-96
Billy Rhines	8.06	1896-98
Kid Nichols	7.33	1898-99
Vic Willis	7.28	1899-1902
Bill Bernhard	7.01	1902-04
Mordecai Brown	6.57	1904-05
Rube Waddell	6.33	1905-06
Ed Reulbach	5.33	1906-68
Luis Tiant	5.30	1968-72
Nolan Ryan	5.26	1972-present

HOME RUNS ALLOWED

Bobby Mathews	8	876-79
George Bradley	12	1879-82
Jim McCormick	14	1882-83
John Coleman	17	1883-84
Larry Corcoran	35	1884-93
Harry Staley	22	1893-94
Frank Dwyer, Jack Stivetts	27	1894-1930
Ray Kremer	29	1930-34
Phil Collins	30	1934-37
Lon Warneke	32	1937-48
Murry Dickson	39	1948-55
Robin Roberts	41	1955-56
Robin Roberts	46	1956-86
Bert Blyleven	50	1986-present

SHUTOUTS

George Bradley	16	1876-93
Red Ehret, Amos Rusie	4	1893-95
Red Ehret, Amos Rusie, Pink Hawley, Bill Hoffer, Sadie McMahon, Cy Young	4	1895-96
Frank Killen, Cy Young	5	1896-98
Jack Powell, Wiley Piatt	6	1898-1901
Jack Powell, Wiley Piatt, Jack Chesbro, Al Orth, Vic Willis	6	1901-02
Jack Chesbro, Christy Mathewson	8	1902-04
Cy Young	10	1904-06
Cy Young, Ed Walsh	10	1906-08
Christy Mathewson, Ed Walsh	11	1908-10
Jack Coombs	13	1910-16
Grover Cleveland Alexander	16	1916-present

SAVES

Jack Manning	5	1876-89
Jack Manning, Tony Mullane	5	1889-93
Mark Baldwin, Tom Colcolough, Frank Donnelly, Frank Dwyer, Tony Mullane	2	1893-94
Tony Mullane	4	1894-98
Tony Mullane, Kid Nichols	4	1898-1900
Tony Mullane, Kid Nichols, Frank Kitson	4	1900-04
Joe McGinnity	5	1904-05
Claud Elliott	6	1905-06
George Ferguson	7	1906-09
Frank Arellanes	8	1909-11
Mordecai Brown	13	1911-13
Mordecai Brown, Chief Bender	13	1913-24
Firpo Marberry	15	1924-26
Firpo Marberry	22	1926-49
Joe Page	27	1949-53
Joe Page, Ellis Kinder	27	1953-61
Luis Arroyo	29	1961-64
Luis Arroyo, Dick Radatz	29	1964-65
Ted Abernathy	31	1965-66
Jack Aker	32	1966-70
Wayne Granger	35	1970-72
Clay Carroll	37	1972-73
John Hiller	38	1973-83
Dan Quisenberry	45	1983-84
Dan Quisenberry, Bruce Sutter	45	1984-86
Dave Righetti	46	1986-90
Bobby Thigpen	57	1990-present

RUNS ALLOWED

Bobby Mathews	395	1876-79
Will White	404	1879-83
John Coleman	510	1883-93
Duke Esper	277	1893-94
Ted Breitenstein	320	1894-present

EARNED RUNS ALLOWED

Bobby Mathews	164	1876-81
Lee Richmond	174	1881-83
John Coleman	291	1883-93
Scott Stratton	196	1893-94
Ted Breitenstein	238	1894-present

EARNED RUN AVERAGE

George Bradley	1.23	1876-80
Tim Keefe	0.86	1880-93
Ted Breitenstein	3.18	1893-94
Amos Rusie	2.78	1894-95
Al Maul	2.45	1895-96
Billy Rhines	2.45	1896-98
Clark Griffith	1.88	1898-1901
Cy Young	1.62	1901-02
Jack Taylor	1.29	1902-05
Christy Mathewson	1.28	1905-06
Mordecai Brown	1.04	1906-14
Dutch Leonard	0.96	1914-present

WINNING PERCENTAGE

Al Spalding	.797	1876-80
Fred Goldsmith	.875	1880-84
Perry Werden	.923	1884-93
Hank Gastright	.750	1893-94
Jouett Meekin	.786	1894-95
Bill Hoffer	.838	1895-1907
Bill Donovan	.862	1907-12
Joe Wood	.872	1912-31
Lefty Grove	886	1931-17
Johnny Allen	..938	1937-59
Roy Face	.947	1959-present

HIT BY PITCH

Will White	35	1884-87
Gus Weyhing	37	1887-93
Kid Nichols	15	1893-97
Win Mercer, Jack Taylor	28	1897-98
Cy Seymour	32	1898-99
Ed Doheny	37	1899-1900
Joe McGinnity	40	1900-present

BALKS

Fred Goldsmith, Jack Lynch, Lee Richmond, Jim Whitney	1	1881-82
Fred Goldsmith, Jack Lynch, Lee Richmond, Jim Whitney, Pud Galvin	1	1882-84
John Henry	2	1884-85
Charlie Ferguson	3	1885-99
Bert Cunningham, Cy Seymour	4	1899-1909
Bert Cunningham, Cy Seymour, Al Mattern	4	1909-12
Ed Walsh	5	1912-15
Joe Boehling	6	1915-16
Joe Boehling, Al Mamaux	6	1916-50
Joe Boehling, Al Mamaux, Vic Raschi	6	1950-63
Bob Shaw	8	1963-74
Bob Shaw, Bill Bonham	8	1974-78
Bob Shaw, Bill Bonham, Frank Tanana	8	1978-79
Steve Carlton	11	1979-88
Dave Stewart	16	1988-present

WILD PITCHES

George Bradley	34	1876-77
George Bradley	39	1877-78
Will White	40	1878-79
Will White	49	1879-85
Hardie Henderson	55	1885-86
Bill Stemmeyer	63	1886-93
Amos Rusie	26	1893-96
Chick Fraser	27	1896-1905
Red Ames	30	1905-present

Appendix D

An Important Change to the Official Record of Major League Baseball

By Jerome Holtzman,
Major League Baseball's Official Historian

Major League Baseball was pleased to announce that, beginning with the seventh edition of *Total Baseball* (2001), all batting averages were to be recorded as they were at the time they were reported, and not in accordance with the decision of a 1968 Special Baseball Records Committee. For the sake of conformity, the committee ruled that the 1887 batting averages be recalculated and that walks not be counted as base hits (as they were that year) or as outs (as they were in 1876).

John Thorn, the eminent editor of *Total Baseball*, has described it as an attempt to normalize baseball's "gloriously messy" statistical history and bring the abnormal 1887 season in line with modern statistics. It was the only season when walks were considered hits and hence skewed the averages upwards.

For example, there were eleven .400 hitters, all properly listed in the 1888 Spalding and Reach guides, the official statistical compendiums of the time. (An arithmetic check has revealed that Paul Radford, the 11th and final such batsman, in fact batted "only" .397.) The acknowledged batting champions were Tip O'Neill, at .492, for the St. Louis Browns of the old American Association, and Cap Anson, .421, for the Chicago National League entry. (As with Radford, an arithmetic correction reduces O'Neill's average to .485, still the all-time record.)

The special committee, in deciding walks were not hits, took 50 hits away from O'Neill, dropping his average to .435. Anson, stripped of 60 hits, fell to .347 and lost his batting title, fairly won. Worse, he no longer qualified for the 3,000 Hit Club of which he was the first member.

Revisionist history is admirable when new and undisputed evidence is brought forth. But this was an abomination, an absolute falsehood and twisting of the known facts for the singular purpose of regulating history to conform to previous and subsequent standards. It was a grievous corruption. If a walk was a hit in 1887 it should stand as a hit forevermore.

The committee was formed by General William Eckert, baseball's fourth commissioner. Eckert always had good intentions but was ill-equipped and didn't have a schoolboy's knowledge of the game. The day after he took office in 1965, during his first press unveiling, it was painfully apparent he was unaware the Los Angeles Dodgers had been transplanted from Brooklyn.

The committee was co-chaired by Dave Grote, public relations director of the National League and Robert Holbrook, his American League counterpart. Neither was qualified to rule on such matters. The other members were Jack Lang, secretary-treasurer of the Baseball Writers Association of America; Joseph Reichler, director of public relations of the Commissioner's Office, and Lee Allen, the historian of the Baseball Hall of Fame.

Why the committee was formed remains a puzzle. The general belief is that it was at the request of the Macmillan Company, which was preparing a new encyclopedia, trumpeted as better and more complete than any of its predecessors. It went on sale the next year.

To heighten the launch, the committee mostly reviewed statistics accumulated in the period before 1920, "a time that was somewhat chaotic for record-keeping procedures." Perhaps the encyclopedia's editors were eager to find previously published errors; adjustments would strengthen the authenticity and value of the new enterprise.

The only established historians on the committee were Joe Reichler, who had been the national baseball writer for the Associated Press, subsequently honored with the prestigious J. G. Taylor Spink Award; and the distinguished Lee Allen, widely respected, the author of a half dozen noteworthy books, including delightful histories of the American and National Leagues.

Reichler knew his stuff. A stickler for accuracy at any cost, he had edited an earlier encyclopedia, published in 1962 by Ronald Press. Allen was a compulsive researcher and known for his fascinating player anecdotes of the late 19th and early 20th centuries. He also wrote a wonderful weekly column, "Cooperstown Corner," for *The Sporting News* and was not concerned with current events. They agreed to the changes. However, a year before he died, Allen admitted to historian David Voigt that "past records ought not to be tampered with."

The change in record-keeping procedure that commenced with publication of the seventh edition of *Total Baseball* should not be interpreted as a blanket damning of Macmillan's *The Baseball Encyclopedia*. In mid-life, it became known, fondly, as the "Big Mac," and was the final statistical authority, an enormous aid to sportswriters, book authors, researchers, and super-fans. There were 10 editions. Sales may have approached a million copies.

Nor is this a total condemnation of Eckert's Special Baseball Records Committee. The committee voted on 17 thorny issues and responded with good reason, with two exceptions: the 1876 scoring of walks as an at-bat (if a player drew four walks he was 0 for 4), a practice that has also been restored in this edition; and the 1887 statistical butchery. A listing of the significant 1887 batting averages restored to their proper dimension follows.

Batter (1968–2000)	Team	Restored Avg.	Previous Avg.
Tip O'Neill	St. Louis (AA)	.485	.435
Pete Browning	Louisville (AA)	.457	.402
Bob Caruthers	St. Louis (AA)	.456	.357
Yank Robinson	St. Louis (AA)	.427	.305
Cap Anson	Chicago (NL)	.421	.347
Dan Brouthers	Detroit (NL)	.420	.338
Denny Lyons	Philadelphia (AA)	.415	.367
Reddy Mack	Louisville (AA)	.410	.308
Oyster Burns	Baltimore (AA)	.409	.341
Sam Thompson	Detroit (NL)	.407	.372

Appendix E

All-Time Leaders

This section is divided into two parts: lifetime leaders and single-season leaders. Both groups command our attention and convey the pleasures of the game, which lie as much in contemplation of the past as in experiencing the present: Henry Aaron, 755; Babe Ruth, 714; Barry Bonds, 660+—this is no mere aggregation of names and numbers, as in a telephone directory. It comprises the romance and lore of the home run, and of baseball itself. Jack Chesbro, 41, 1904; Bob Gibson, 1.12, 1968; Nolan Ryan, 383, 1973 ... you can fill in the blanks that tell the story of pitching's most glorious seasons.

What follows are baseball's all-time great achievements, both the traditional statistics and the new. For most of these we will give the top 50. And for many stats we will offer a second kind of ranking, broken down into six distinct eras of baseball, with the top 5 or 10 leaders in each.

To be eligible for a lifetime pitching category that is stated as an average, a man must have pitched 1,500 or more innings, or 750 or more innings if he is a relief pitcher, in the major leagues; for a counting statistic, he must simply have attained the necessary quantity to crack the list. For a single-season category expressed as an average, he must have pitched one inning per league-scheduled game or have attained the necessary quantity (wins, strikeouts, saves) to head a counted list.

To be eligible for a lifetime batting category that is stated as an average, a man must have played in 1,000 or more games; for counting stats he must simply have attained the necessary quantity to crack the list. For Pitcher Batting Average, the criterion is 1,500 innings pitched or 100 hits. And to reach the single-season batting lists, a man must have 3.1 plate appearances per scheduled game.

We provide tables of the top fielding performances, too, sorted by position, including only games played at the position, rather than combining data from secondary positions under the dominant position. As we establish a 1,000-game minimum for inclusion in all but a few batting and baserunning categories, we likewise establish for these positional rankings a minimum of 1,000 games played at the position.

Ties are calculated to as many decimal places as needed to break them, but averages are shown to only three places. When two or

Carlton Fisk
The Hall of Fame catcher ended a splendid career as the all-time leader in games played at his position with 2,226.

more players are tied in an averaged category with a narrow base of data, such as a season's won-lost percentage, the reader can presume a numerical dead heat (and obviously this goes for counting stats, too—one man's 39 doubles are as good as another's). But where there is a tie for batting average, earned run average, or any of the Sabermetric measures, the reader may assume that the man listed above the other(s) has the minutely higher average.

Games

1	Rose, Pete (1963-1986)	3562
2	Yastrzemski, Carl (1961-1983)	3308
3	Aaron, Hank (1954-1976)	3298
4	Henderson, Rickey (1979-2003)	3081
5	Cobb, Ty (1905-1928)	3035
6	Murray, Eddie (1977-1997)	3026
	Musial, Stan (1941-1963)	3026
8	Ripken, Cal (1981-2001)	3001
9	Mays, Willie (1951-1973)	2992
10	Winfield, Dave (1973-1995)	2973
11	Staub, Rusty (1963-1985)	2951
12	Robinson, Brooks (1955-1977)	2896
13	Yount, Robin (1974-1993)	2856
14	Kaline, Al (1953-1974)	2834
15	Baines, Harold (1980-2001)	2830
16	Collins, Eddie (1906-1930)	2826
17	Jackson, Reggie (1967-1987)	2820
18	Robinson, Frank (1956-1976)	2808
19	Wagner, Honus (1897-1917)	2794
20	Speaker, Tris (1907-1928)	2789
21	Perez, Tony (1964-1986)	2777
22	Ott, Mel (1926-1947)	2730
23	Brett, George (1973-1993)	2707
24	Nettles, Graig (1967-1988)	2700
25	Evans, Darrell (1969-1989)	2687
26	Molitor, Paul (1978-1998)	2683
27	Maranville, Rabbit (1912-1935)	2670
28	Morgan, Joe (1963-1984)	2649
29	Dawson, Andre (1976-1996)	2627
30	Brock, Lou (1961-1979)	2616
31	Evans, Dwight (1972-1991)	2606
32	Aparicio, Luis (1956-1973)	2601
33	McCovey, Willie (1959-1980)	2588
34	Smith, Ozzie (1978-1996)	2573
35	Bonds, Barry (1986-2003)	2569
36	Palmeiro, Rafael (1986-2003)	2567
37	Waner, Paul (1926-1945)	2549
38	Banks, Ernie (1953-1971)	2528
39	Buckner, Bill (1969-1990)	2517
	Crawford, Sam (1899-1917)	2517
41	Gaetti, Gary (1981-2000)	2507
42	Ruth, Babe (1914-1935)	2503
43	Raines, Tim (1979-2002)	2502
44	Fisk, Carlton (1969-1993)	2499
45	Concepcion, Dave (1970-1988)	2488
	Williams, Billy (1959-1976)	2488
47	Lajoie, Nap (1896-1916)	2480
48	Carey, Max (1910-1929)	2476
49	Carew, Rod (1967-1985)	2469
	Pinson, Vada (1958-1975)	2469
51	Parker, Dave (1973-1991)	2466
52	Simmons, Ted (1968-1988)	2456
53	Dahlen, Bill (1891-1911)	2444
54	Fairly, Ron (1958-1978)	2442
55	Boggs, Wade (1982-1999)	2440
	Gwynn, Tony (1982-2001)	2440
57	Davis, Chili (1981-1999)	2436
58	Killebrew, Harmon (1954-1975)	2435
59	Clemente, Roberto (1955-1972)	2433
	McGriff, Fred (1986-2003)	2433
61	Davis, Willie (1960-1979)	2429
62	Appling, Luke (1930-1950)	2422
63	Wheat, Zack (1909-1927)	2410
64	Vernon, Mickey (1939-1960)	2409
65	Bell, Buddy (1972-1989)	2405
66	Rice, Sam (1915-1934)	2404
	Schmidt, Mike (1972-1989)	2404
68	Mantle, Mickey (1951-1968)	2401
69	Mathews, Eddie (1952-1968)	2391
70	Whitaker, Lou (1977-1995)	2390
71	Beckley, Jake (1888-1907)	2389
72	Wallace, Bobby (1894-1918)	2383
73	Slaughter, Enos (1938-1959)	2380
74	Davis, George (1890-1909)	2372
75	Oliver, Al (1968-1985)	2368
76	Fox, Nellie (1947-1965)	2367
77	Stargell, Willie (1962-1982)	2360
78	Cruz, Jose (1970-1988)	2353
79	Downing, Brian (1973-1992)	2344
80	Garvey, Steve (1969-1987)	2332
81	Campaneris, Bert (1964-1983)	2328
82	White, Frank (1973-1990)	2324
83	Alomar, Roberto (1988-2003)	2323
	Gehringer, Charlie (1924-1942)	2323
85	Foxx, Jimmie (1925-1945)	2317
86	Frisch, Frankie (1919-1937)	2311
87	Hooper, Harry (1909-1925)	2309
88	Carter, Gary (1974-1992)	2296
89	Trammell, Alan (1977-1996)	2293
90	Baylor, Don (1970-1988)	2292
	Williams, Ted (1939-1960)	2292
92	Goslin, Goose (1921-1938)	2287
93	Dykes, Jimmie (1918-1939)	2282
94	Cross, Lave (1887-1907)	2278
95	Anson, Cap (1871-1897)	2277
96	Boone, Bob (1972-1990)	2264
97	Speier, Chris (1971-1989)	2260
98	Hornsby, Rogers (1915-1937)	2259
99	Biggio, Craig (1988-2003)	2253
100	Galarraga, Andres (1985-2003)	2250

At Bats

1	Rose, Pete (1963-1986)	14053
2	Aaron, Hank (1954-1976)	12364
3	Yastrzemski, Carl (1961-1983)	11988
4	Ripken, Cal (1981-2001)	11551
5	Cobb, Ty (1905-1928)	11434
6	Murray, Eddie (1977-1997)	11336
7	Yount, Robin (1974-1993)	11008
8	Winfield, Dave (1973-1995)	11003
9	Musial, Stan (1941-1963)	10972
10	Henderson, Rickey (1979-2003)	10961
11	Mays, Willie (1951-1973)	10881
12	Molitor, Paul (1978-1998)	10835
13	Robinson, Brooks (1955-1977)	10654
14	Wagner, Honus (1897-1917)	10439
15	Brett, George (1973-1993)	10349
16	Brock, Lou (1961-1979)	10332
17	Aparicio, Luis (1956-1973)	10230
18	Speaker, Tris (1907-1928)	10195
19	Kaline, Al (1953-1974)	10116
20	Maranville, Rabbit (1912-1935)	10078
21	Robinson, Frank (1956-1976)	10006
22	Collins, Eddie (1906-1930)	9949
23	Dawson, Andre (1976-1996)	9927
24	Baines, Harold (1980-2001)	9908
25	Jackson, Reggie (1967-1987)	9864
26	Perez, Tony (1964-1986)	9778
27	Staub, Rusty (1963-1985)	9720
28	Pinson, Vada (1958-1975)	9645
29	Lajoie, Nap (1896-1916)	9589
30	Crawford, Sam (1899-1917)	9570
31	Palmeiro, Rafael (1986-2003)	9553
32	Beckley, Jake (1888-1907)	9538
33	Waner, Paul (1926-1945)	9459
34	Ott, Mel (1926-1947)	9456
35	Clemente, Roberto (1955-1972)	9454
36	Banks, Ernie (1953-1971)	9421
37	Buckner, Bill (1969-1990)	9397
38	Smith, Ozzie (1978-1996)	9396
39	Carey, Max (1910-1929)	9363
40	Parker, Dave (1973-1991)	9358
41	Williams, Billy (1959-1976)	9350
42	Carew, Rod (1967-1985)	9315
43	Gwynn, Tony (1982-2001)	9288
44	Morgan, Joe (1963-1984)	9277
45	Rice, Sam (1915-1934)	9269
46	Fox, Nellie (1947-1965)	9232
47	Boggs, Wade (1982-1999)	9180
48	Anson, Cap (1871-1897)	9176
49	Davis, Willie (1960-1979)	9174
50	Cramer, Doc (1929-1948)	9140
51	Frisch, Frankie (1919-1937)	9112
52	Wheat, Zack (1909-1927)	9106
53	Cross, Lave (1887-1907)	9100
54	Oliver, Al (1968-1985)	9049
55	Davis, George (1890-1909)	9045
56	Dahlen, Bill (1891-1911)	9036
57	Evans, Dwight (1972-1991)	8996
58	Bell, Buddy (1972-1989)	8995
59	Nettles, Graig (1967-1988)	8986
60	Evans, Darrell (1969-1989)	8973
61	Gaetti, Gary (1981-2000)	8951
62	Alomar, Roberto (1988-2003)	8902
63	Raines, Tim (1979-2002)	8872
64	Gehringer, Charlie (1924-1942)	8860
65	Appling, Luke (1930-1950)	8856
66	Garvey, Steve (1969-1987)	8835
67	Corcoran, Tommy (1890-1907)	8812
68	Hooper, Harry (1909-1925)	8785
69	Simmons, Al (1924-1944)	8759
70	Fisk, Carlton (1969-1993)	8756
71	Vernon, Mickey (1939-1960)	8731
72	Bonds, Barry (1986-2003)	8725
73	Concepcion, Dave (1970-1988)	8723
74	McGriff, Fred (1986-2003)	8685
75	Campaneris, Bert (1964-1983)	8684
76	Simmons, Ted (1968-1988)	8680
77	Davis, Chili (1981-1999)	8673
78	Goslin, Goose (1921-1938)	8656
79	Wallace, Bobby (1894-1918)	8618
80	Keeler, Willie (1892-1910)	8591
81	Biggio, Craig (1988-2003)	8588
82	Clarke, Fred (1894-1915)	8584
83	Whitaker, Lou (1977-1995)	8570
84	Mathews, Eddie (1952-1968)	8537
85	Schoendienst, Red (1945-1963)	8479
86	Burkett, Jesse (1890-1905)	8426
87	Carter, Joe (1983-1998)	8422
88	Bowa, Larry (1970-1985)	8418
89	Ruth, Babe (1914-1935)	8399
90	Sandberg, Ryne (1981-1997)	8385
91	Ashburn, Richie (1948-1962)	8365
92	McPhee, Bid (1882-1899)	8358
93	Schmidt, Mike (1972-1989)	8352
94	Trammell, Alan (1977-1996)	8288
95	Sisler, George (1915-1930)	8267
96	Rice, Jim (1974-1989)	8225
	Ryan, Jimmy (1885-1903)	8225
98	Baylor, Don (1970-1988)	8198
99	McCovey, Willie (1959-1980)	8197
100	Butler, Brett (1981-1997)	8180

Runs

1	Henderson, Rickey (1979-2003)	2295
2	Cobb, Ty (1905-1928)	2246
3	Aaron, Hank (1954-1976)	2174
	Ruth, Babe (1914-1935)	2174
5	Rose, Pete (1963-1986)	2165
6	Mays, Willie (1951-1973)	2062
7	Musial, Stan (1941-1963)	1949
8	Bonds, Barry (1986-2003)	1941
9	Gehrig, Lou (1923-1939)	1888
10	Speaker, Tris (1907-1928)	1882
11	Ott, Mel (1926-1947)	1859
12	Robinson, Frank (1956-1976)	1829
13	Collins, Eddie (1906-1930)	1821
14	Yastrzemski, Carl (1961-1983)	1816
15	Williams, Ted (1939-1960)	1798
16	Molitor, Paul (1978-1998)	1782
17	Gehringer, Charlie (1924-1942)	1774
18	Foxx, Jimmie (1925-1945)	1751
19	Wagner, Honus (1897-1917)	1739
20	Anson, Cap (1871-1897)	1722
21	Burkett, Jesse (1890-1905)	1720
22	Keeler, Willie (1892-1910)	1719
23	Hamilton, Billy (1888-1901)	1697
24	McPhee, Bid (1882-1899)	1684
25	Mantle, Mickey (1951-1968)	1677
26	Winfield, Dave (1973-1995)	1669
27	Morgan, Joe (1963-1984)	1650
28	Ripken, Cal (1981-2001)	1647
29	Ryan, Jimmy (1885-1903)	1643
30	Van Haltren, George (1887-1903)	1642
31	Yount, Robin (1974-1993)	1632
32	Murray, Eddie (1977-1997)	1627
	Waner, Paul (1926-1945)	1627
34	Clarke, Fred (1894-1915)	1622
	Kaline, Al (1953-1974)	1622
36	Connor, Roger (1880-1897)	1620
37	Brock, Lou (1961-1979)	1610
38	Beckley, Jake (1888-1907)	1602
39	Delahanty, Ed (1888-1903)	1600
40	Dahlen, Bill (1891-1911)	1590
41	Brett, George (1973-1993)	1583
42	Hornsby, Rogers (1915-1937)	1579
43	Raines, Tim (1979-2002)	1571
44	Duffy, Hugh (1888-1906)	1554
45	Jackson, Reggie (1967-1987)	1551
46	Palmeiro, Rafael (1986-2003)	1548
47	Carey, Max (1910-1929)	1545
	Davis, George (1890-1909)	1545
49	Frisch, Frankie (1919-1937)	1532
50	Brouthers, Dan (1879-1904)	1523
	Brown, Tom (1882-1898)	1523
52	Rice, Sam (1915-1934)	1514
53	Boggs, Wade (1982-1999)	1513
54	Mathews, Eddie (1952-1968)	1509
55	Simmons, Al (1924-1944)	1507
56	Schmidt, Mike (1972-1989)	1506
57	Lajoie, Nap (1896-1916)	1504
58	Biggio, Craig (1988-2003)	1503
59	Stovey, Harry (1880-1893)	1492
60	Alomar, Roberto (1988-2003)	1490
61	Goslin, Goose (1921-1938)	1483
62	Latham, Arlie (1880-1909)	1481
63	Evans, Dwight (1972-1991)	1470
64	Long, Herman (1889-1904)	1456
65	O'Rourke, Jim (1872-1904)	1446
66	Hooper, Harry (1909-1925)	1429
	Hoy, Dummy (1888-1902)	1429
68	Carew, Rod (1967-1985)	1424
69	Kelley, Joe (1891-1908)	1421
70	Clemente, Roberto (1955-1972)	1416
71	Ward, John (1878-1894)	1410
	Williams, Billy (1959-1976)	1410
73	Griffin, Mike (1887-1898)	1406
74	Bagwell, Jeff (1991-2003)	1402
75	Crawford, Sam (1899-1917)	1391
76	DiMaggio, Joe (1936-1951)	1390
77	Whitaker, Lou (1977-1995)	1386
78	Gwynn, Tony (1982-2001)	1383
79	Dawson, Andre (1976-1996)	1373
80	Pinson, Vada (1958-1975)	1366
81	Butler, Brett (1981-1997)	1359
82	Cramer, Doc (1929-1948)	1357
	Kelly, King (1878-1893)	1357
84	Leach, Tommy (1898-1918)	1355
85	Evans, Darrell (1969-1989)	1344
86	McGriff, Fred (1986-2003)	1342
87	Cross, Lave (1887-1907)	1338
	Reese, Pee Wee (1940-1958)	1338
89	Aparicio, Luis (1956-1973)	1335
90	Gore, George (1879-1892)	1327
91	Ashburn, Richie (1948-1962)	1322
92	Donovan, Patsy (1890-1907)	1321
93	Appling, Luke (1930-1950)	1319
94	Sandberg, Ryne (1981-1997)	1318
95	Tiernan, Mike (1887-1899)	1316
96	Sosa, Sammy (1989-2003)	1314
97	Banks, Ernie (1953-1971)	1305
	Cuyler, Kiki (1921-1938)	1305
99	Phillips, Tony (1982-1999)	1300
100	Baines, Harold (1980-2001)	1299

Hits

1	Rose, Pete (1963-1986)	4256
2	Cobb, Ty (1905-1928)	4189
3	Aaron, Hank (1954-1976)	3771
4	Musial, Stan (1941-1963)	3630
5	Speaker, Tris (1907-1928)	3514
6	Wagner, Honus (1897-1917)	3420
7	Yastrzemski, Carl (1961-1983)	3419
8	Molitor, Paul (1978-1998)	3319
9	Collins, Eddie (1906-1930)	3315
10	Mays, Willie (1951-1973)	3283
11	Murray, Eddie (1977-1997)	3255
12	Lajoie, Nap (1896-1916)	3242
13	Ripken, Cal (1981-2001)	3184
14	Brett, George (1973-1993)	3154
15	Waner, Paul (1926-1945)	3152
16	Yount, Robin (1974-1993)	3142
17	Gwynn, Tony (1982-2001)	3141
18	Winfield, Dave (1973-1995)	3110
19	Anson, Cap (1871-1897)	3056
20	Henderson, Rickey (1979-2003)	3055
21	Carew, Rod (1967-1985)	3053
22	Brock, Lou (1961-1979)	3023
23	Boggs, Wade (1982-1999)	3010
24	Kaline, Al (1953-1974)	3007
25	Clemente, Roberto (1955-1972)	3000
26	Rice, Sam (1915-1934)	2987
27	Crawford, Sam (1899-1917)	2961
28	Robinson, Frank (1956-1976)	2943
29	Beckley, Jake (1888-1907)	2934
30	Keeler, Willie (1892-1910)	2932
31	Hornsby, Rogers (1915-1937)	2930
32	Simmons, Al (1924-1944)	2927
33	Wheat, Zack (1909-1927)	2884
34	Frisch, Frankie (1919-1937)	2880
35	Ott, Mel (1926-1947)	2876
36	Ruth, Babe (1914-1935)	2873
37	Baines, Harold (1980-2001)	2866
38	Burkett, Jesse (1890-1905)	2850
39	Robinson, Brooks (1955-1977)	2848
40	Gehringer, Charlie (1924-1942)	2839
41	Sisler, George (1915-1930)	2812
42	Palmeiro, Rafael (1986-2003)	2780
43	Dawson, Andre (1976-1996)	2774
44	Pinson, Vada (1958-1975)	2757
45	Appling, Luke (1930-1950)	2749
46	Oliver, Al (1968-1985)	2743
47	Goslin, Goose (1921-1938)	2735
48	Perez, Tony (1964-1986)	2732
49	Gehrig, Lou (1923-1939)	2721
50	Staub, Rusty (1963-1985)	2716
51	Buckner, Bill (1969-1990)	2715
52	Parker, Dave (1973-1991)	2712
53	Williams, Billy (1959-1976)	2711
54	Cramer, Doc (1929-1948)	2705
55	Alomar, Roberto (1988-2003)	2679
56	Clarke, Fred (1894-1915)	2678
57	Aparicio, Luis (1956-1973)	2677
58	Cross, Lave (1887-1907)	2666
59	Carey, Max (1910-1929)	2665
	Davis, George (1890-1909)	2665
61	Fox, Nellie (1947-1965)	2663
62	Heilmann, Harry (1914-1932)	2660
63	Williams, Ted (1939-1960)	2654
64	Foxx, Jimmie (1925-1945)	2646
65	Maranville, Rabbit (1912-1935)	2605
	Raines, Tim (1979-2002)	2605
67	Garvey, Steve (1969-1987)	2599
68	Delahanty, Ed (1888-1903)	2597
69	Bonds, Barry (1986-2003)	2595
70	Jackson, Reggie (1967-1987)	2584
71	Banks, Ernie (1953-1971)	2583
72	Ashburn, Richie (1948-1962)	2574
73	Davis, Willie (1960-1979)	2561
74	Ryan, Jimmy (1885-1903)	2556
75	Van Haltren, George (1887-1903)	2552
76	Connor, Roger (1880-1897)	2542
77	Manush, Heinie (1923-1939)	2524
78	Morgan, Joe (1963-1984)	2517
79	Bell, Buddy (1972-1989)	2514
80	Vernon, Mickey (1939-1960)	2495
81	McGriff, Fred (1986-2003)	2477
82	Simmons, Ted (1968-1988)	2472
83	Medwick, Joe (1932-1948)	2471
84	Hooper, Harry (1909-1925)	2466
85	Biggio, Craig (1988-2003)	2461
86	Dahlen, Bill (1891-1911)	2460
	Smith, Ozzie (1978-1996)	2460
88	Waner, Lloyd (1927-1945)	2459
89	Rice, Jim (1974-1989)	2452
90	Schoendienst, Red (1945-1963)	2449
91	Evans, Dwight (1972-1991)	2446
92	Grace, Mark (1988-2003)	2445
93	Traynor, Pie (1920-1937)	2416
94	Mantle, Mickey (1951-1968)	2415
95	McInnis, Stuffy (1909-1927)	2405
96	Sandberg, Ryne (1981-1997)	2386
97	Slaughter, Enos (1938-1959)	2383
98	Davis, Chili (1981-1999)	2380
99	Roush, Edd (1913-1931)	2376
100	Butler, Brett (1981-1997)	2375

Doubles

1	Speaker, Tris (1907-1928)	792
2	Rose, Pete (1963-1986)	746
3	Musial, Stan (1941-1963)	725
4	Cobb, Ty (1905-1928)	724
5	Brett, George (1973-1993)	665
6	Lajoie, Nap (1896-1916)	657
7	Yastrzemski, Carl (1961-1983)	646
8	Wagner, Honus (1897-1917)	643
9	Aaron, Hank (1954-1976)	624
10	Molitor, Paul (1978-1998)	605
	Waner, Paul (1926-1945)	605
12	Ripken, Cal (1981-2001)	603
13	Yount, Robin (1974-1993)	583
14	Boggs, Wade (1982-1999)	578
15	Gehringer, Charlie (1924-1942)	574
16	Murray, Eddie (1977-1997)	560
17	Gwynn, Tony (1982-2001)	543
	Palmeiro, Rafael (1986-2003)	543
19	Heilmann, Harry (1914-1932)	542
20	Hornsby, Rogers (1915-1937)	541
21	Medwick, Joe (1932-1948)	540
	Winfield, Dave (1973-1995)	540
23	Simmons, Al (1924-1944)	539
24	Bonds, Barry (1986-2003)	536
25	Gehrig, Lou (1923-1939)	534
26	Anson, Cap (1871-1897)	529
	Oliver, Al (1968-1985)	529
28	Robinson, Frank (1956-1976)	528
29	Parker, Dave (1973-1991)	526
30	Williams, Ted (1939-1960)	525
31	Mays, Willie (1951-1973)	523
32	Delahanty, Ed (1888-1903)	522
33	Biggio, Craig (1988-2003)	517
34	Cronin, Joe (1926-1945)	515
35	Grace, Mark (1988-2003)	511
36	Henderson, Rickey (1979-2003)	510
37	Ruth, Babe (1914-1935)	506
38	Perez, Tony (1964-1986)	505
39	Dawson, Andre (1976-1996)	503
40	Goslin, Goose (1921-1938)	500
41	Staub, Rusty (1963-1985)	499
42	Alomar, Roberto (1988-2003)	498
	Buckner, Bill (1969-1990)	498
	Kaline, Al (1953-1974)	498
	Rice, Sam (1915-1934)	498
46	Manush, Heinie (1923-1939)	491
	Martinez, Edgar (1987-2003)	491
48	Vernon, Mickey (1939-1960)	490
49	Baines, Harold (1980-2001)	488
	Ott, Mel (1926-1947)	488
51	Brock, Lou (1961-1979)	486
	Herman, Billy (1931-1947)	486
53	Pinson, Vada (1958-1975)	485
54	McRae, Hal (1968-1987)	484
55	Evans, Dwight (1972-1991)	483
	Simmons, Ted (1968-1988)	483
57	Robinson, Brooks (1955-1977)	482
58	Wheat, Zack (1909-1927)	476
59	Beckley, Jake (1888-1907)	473
	Olerud, John (1989-2003)	473
61	Frisch, Frankie (1919-1937)	466
62	Bottomley, Jim (1922-1937)	465
63	Jackson, Reggie (1967-1987)	463
64	Brouthers, Dan (1879-1904)	460
65	Crawford, Sam (1899-1917)	458
	Foxx, Jimmie (1925-1945)	458
67	Bagwell, Jeff (1991-2003)	455
68	Davis, George (1890-1909)	453
	Dykes, Jimmie (1918-1939)	453
70	O'Neill, Paul (1985-2001)	451
	Ryan, Jimmy (1885-1903)	451
72	Morgan, Joe (1963-1984)	449
73	Carew, Rod (1967-1985)	445
74	Burns, George (1914-1929)	444
	Galarraga, Andres (1985-2003)	444
76	Gaetti, Gary (1981-2000)	443
77	Bartell, Dick (1927-1946)	442
	Mattingly, Don (1982-1995)	442
79	Connor, Roger (1880-1897)	441
80	Appling, Luke (1930-1950)	440
	Clark, Will (1986-2000)	440
	Clemente, Roberto (1955-1972)	440
	Garvey, Steve (1969-1987)	440
84	Collins, Eddie (1906-1930)	438
	McGriff, Fred (1986-2003)	438
86	Cedeno, Cesar (1970-1986)	436
	Sewell, Joe (1920-1933)	436
88	Moses, Wally (1935-1951)	435
	Walker, Larry (1989-2003)	435
90	Williams, Billy (1959-1976)	434
91	Judge, Joe (1915-1934)	433
92	Carter, Joe (1983-1998)	432
	Wallach, Tim (1980-1996)	432
94	Gonzalez, Luis (1990-2003)	430
	Raines, Tim (1979-2002)	430
96	Thomas, Frank (1990-2003)	428
97	Schoendienst, Red (1945-1963)	427
98	Hernandez, Keith (1974-1990)	426
	Larkin, Barry (1986-2003)	426
100	3 players tied	425

Triples

1	Crawford, Sam (1899-1917)	309
2	Cobb, Ty (1905-1928)	295
3	Wagner, Honus (1897-1917)	252
4	Beckley, Jake (1888-1907)	244
5	Connor, Roger (1880-1897)	233
6	Speaker, Tris (1907-1928)	222
7	Clarke, Fred (1894-1915)	220
8	Brouthers, Dan (1879-1904)	205
9	Kelley, Joe (1891-1908)	194
10	Waner, Paul (1926-1945)	191
11	McPhee, Bid (1882-1899)	189
12	Collins, Eddie (1906-1930)	187
13	Delahanty, Ed (1888-1903)	186
14	Rice, Sam (1915-1934)	184
15	Burkett, Jesse (1890-1905)	182
	Konetchy, Ed (1907-1921)	182
	Roush, Edd (1913-1931)	182
18	Ewing, Buck (1880-1897)	178
19	Maranville, Rabbit (1912-1935)	177
	Musial, Stan (1941-1963)	177
21	Stovey, Harry (1880-1893)	174
22	Goslin, Goose (1921-1938)	173
23	Leach, Tommy (1898-1918)	172
	Wheat, Zack (1909-1927)	172
25	Hornsby, Rogers (1915-1937)	169
26	Jackson, Joe (1908-1920)	168
27	Clemente, Roberto (1955-1972)	166
	Magee, Sherry (1904-1919)	166
29	Daubert, Jake (1910-1924)	165
30	Flick, Elmer (1898-1910)	164
	Sisler, George (1915-1930)	164
	Traynor, Pie (1920-1937)	164
33	Dahlen, Bill (1891-1911)	163
	Davis, George (1890-1909)	163
	Gehrig, Lou (1923-1939)	163
	Lajoie, Nap (1896-1916)	163
37	Tiernan, Mike (1887-1899)	162
38	Thompson, Sam (1885-1906)	161
	Van Haltren, George (1887-1903)	161
40	Hooper, Harry (1909-1925)	160
	Manush, Heinie (1923-1939)	160
42	Carey, Max (1910-1929)	159
	Judge, Joe (1915-1934)	159
44	McKean, Ed (1887-1899)	158
45	Cuyler, Kiki (1921-1938)	157
	Ryan, Jimmy (1885-1903)	157
47	Corcoran, Tommy (1890-1907)	155
48	Combs, Earle (1924-1935)	154
49	Bottomley, Jim (1922-1937)	151
	Heilmann, Harry (1914-1932)	151
51	Selbach, Kip (1894-1906)	149
	Simmons, Al (1924-1944)	149
53	Pipp, Wally (1913-1928)	148
	Slaughter, Enos (1938-1959)	148
55	Veach, Bobby (1912-1925)	147
	Wilson, Willie (1976-1994)	147
57	Gehringer, Charlie (1924-1942)	146
58	Davis, Harry (1895-1917)	145
	Keeler, Willie (1892-1910)	145
60	Wallace, Bobby (1894-1918)	143
61	Brock, Lou (1961-1979)	141
62	Mays, Willie (1951-1973)	140
63	Reilly, John (1880-1891)	139
64	Brown, Tom (1882-1898)	138
	Davis, Willie (1960-1979)	138
	Frisch, Frankie (1919-1937)	138
	Williams, Jimmy (1899-1909)	138
68	Brett, George (1973-1993)	137
69	Cross, Lave (1887-1907)	136
	Ruth, Babe (1914-1935)	136
	Sheckard, Jimmy (1897-1913)	136
	Smith, Elmer (1886-1901)	136
73	Rose, Pete (1963-1986)	135
74	Collins, Shano (1910-1925)	133
75	O'Rourke, Jim (1872-1904)	132
	Wood, George (1880-1892)	132
77	Butler, Brett (1981-1997)	131
	DiMaggio, Joe (1936-1951)	131
	Freeman, Buck (1891-1907)	131
80	Myer, Buddy (1925-1941)	130
81	Burns, Oyster (1884-1895)	129
	Gardner, Larry (1908-1924)	129
83	Averill, Earl (1929-1941)	128
	Vaughan, Arky (1932-1948)	128
85	Pinson, Vada (1958-1975)	127
86	Richardson, Hardy (1879-1892)	126
	Yount, Robin (1974-1993)	126
88	Foxx, Jimmie (1925-1945)	125
89	Anderson, John (1894-1908)	124
	Anson, Cap (1871-1897)	124
	Chase, Hal (1905-1919)	124
	Schulte, Frank (1904-1918)	124
93	Doyle, Larry (1907-1920)	123
	Farrell, Duke (1888-1905)	123
95	Hoy, Dummy (1888-1902)	121
96	Pfeffer, Fred (1882-1897)	120
	Vernon, Mickey (1939-1960)	120
98	Duffy, Hugh (1888-1906)	119
99	3 players tied	118

Home Runs

1	Aaron, Hank (1954-1976)	755
2	Ruth, Babe (1914-1935)	714
3	Mays, Willie (1951-1973)	660
4	Bonds, Barry (1986-2003)	658
5	Robinson, Frank (1956-1976)	586
6	McGwire, Mark (1986-2001)	583
7	Killebrew, Harmon (1954-1975)	573
8	Jackson, Reggie (1967-1987)	563
9	Schmidt, Mike (1972-1989)	548
10	Sosa, Sammy (1989-2003)	539
11	Mantle, Mickey (1951-1968)	536
12	Foxx, Jimmie (1925-1945)	534
13	Palmeiro, Rafael (1986-2003)	528
14	McCovey, Willie (1959-1980)	521
	Williams, Ted (1939-1960)	521
16	Banks, Ernie (1953-1971)	512
	Mathews, Eddie (1952-1968)	512
18	Ott, Mel (1926-1947)	511
19	Murray, Eddie (1977-1997)	504
20	Gehrig, Lou (1923-1939)	493
21	McGriff, Fred (1986-2003)	491
22	Griffey, Ken (1989-2003)	481
23	Musial, Stan (1941-1963)	475
	Stargell, Willie (1962-1982)	475
25	Winfield, Dave (1973-1995)	465
26	Canseco, Jose (1985-2001)	462
27	Yastrzemski, Carl (1961-1983)	452
28	Kingman, Dave (1971-1986)	442
29	Dawson, Andre (1976-1996)	438
30	Ripken, Cal (1981-2001)	431
31	Gonzalez, Juan (1989-2003)	429
32	Williams, Billy (1959-1976)	426
33	Bagwell, Jeff (1991-2003)	419
34	Thomas, Frank (1990-2003)	418
35	Evans, Darrell (1969-1989)	414
36	Snider, Duke (1947-1964)	407
37	Kaline, Al (1953-1974)	399
38	Galarraga, Andres (1985-2003)	398
	Murphy, Dale (1976-1993)	398
40	Carter, Joe (1983-1998)	396
41	Nettles, Graig (1967-1988)	390
42	Bench, Johnny (1967-1983)	389
43	Evans, Dwight (1972-1991)	385
44	Baines, Harold (1980-2001)	384
45	Howard, Frank (1958-1973)	382
	Rice, Jim (1974-1989)	382
47	Belle, Albert (1989-2000)	381
	Thome, Jim (1991-2003)	381
49	Cepeda, Orlando (1958-1974)	379
	Perez, Tony (1964-1986)	379
	Sheffield, Gary (1988-2003)	379
52	Williams, Matt (1987-2003)	378
53	Cash, Norm (1958-1974)	377
54	Fisk, Carlton (1969-1993)	376
55	Colavito, Rocky (1955-1968)	374
56	Hodges, Gil (1943-1963)	370
57	Kiner, Ralph (1946-1955)	369
58	DiMaggio, Joe (1936-1951)	361
59	Gaetti, Gary (1981-2000)	360
60	Mize, Johnny (1936-1953)	359
61	Berra, Yogi (1946-1965)	358
	Piazza, Mike (1992-2003)	358
63	Vaughn, Greg (1989-2003)	355
64	May, Lee (1965-1982)	354
65	Allen, Dick (1963-1977)	351
	Burks, Ellis (1987-2003)	351
	Walker, Larry (1989-2003)	351
68	Davis, Chili (1981-1999)	350
69	Foster, George (1969-1986)	348
70	Ramirez, Manny (1993-2003)	347
71	Rodriguez, Alex (1994-2003)	345
72	Santo, Ron (1960-1974)	342
73	Clark, Jack (1975-1992)	340
74	Parker, Dave (1973-1991)	339
	Powell, Boog (1961-1977)	339
76	Baylor, Don (1970-1988)	338
77	Adcock, Joe (1950-1966)	336
78	Strawberry, Darryl (1983-1999)	335
79	Bonds, Bobby (1968-1981)	332
80	Greenberg, Hank (1930-1947)	331
81	Vaughn, Mo (1991-2003)	328
82	Horton, Willie (1963-1980)	325
83	Carter, Gary (1974-1992)	324
	Parrish, Lance (1977-1995)	324
85	Gant, Ron (1987-2003)	321
86	Fielder, Cecil (1985-1998)	319
87	Sievers, Roy (1949-1965)	318
88	Brett, George (1973-1993)	317
89	Cey, Ron (1971-1987)	316
90	Smith, Reggie (1966-1982)	314
91	Buhner, Jay (1987-2001)	310
92	Luzinski, Greg (1970-1984)	307
	Simmons, Al (1924-1944)	307
94	Lynn, Fred (1974-1990)	306
95	Justice, David (1989-2002)	305
96	Delgado, Carlos (1993-2003)	304
97	Hornsby, Rogers (1915-1937)	301
98	Klein, Chuck (1928-1944)	300
99	Martinez, Tino (1990-2003)	299
100	2 players tied	297

Home Run Percentage

1	McGwire, Mark (1986-2001)	9.42
2	Ruth, Babe (1914-1935)	8.50
3	Bonds, Barry (1986-2003)	7.54
4	Thome, Jim (1991-2003)	7.30
5	Sosa, Sammy (1989-2003)	7.15
6	Kiner, Ralph (1946-1955)	7.09
7	Killebrew, Harmon (1954-1975)	7.03
8	Ramirez, Manny (1993-2003)	6.93
9	Rodriguez, Alex (1994-2003)	6.92
10	Griffey, Ken (1989-2003)	6.79
11	Williams, Ted (1939-1960)	6.76
12	Piazza, Mike (1992-2003)	6.69
13	Delgado, Carlos (1993-2003)	6.68
14	Gonzalez, Juan (1989-2003)	6.67
15	Kingman, Dave (1971-1986)	6.62
16	Mantle, Mickey (1951-1968)	6.62
17	Foxx, Jimmie (1925-1945)	6.57
18	Schmidt, Mike (1972-1989)	6.56
19	Canseco, Jose (1985-2001)	6.55
20	Belle, Albert (1989-2000)	6.51
21	Greenberg, Hank (1930-1947)	6.37
22	McCovey, Willie (1959-1980)	6.36
23	Thomas, Frank (1990-2003)	6.32
24	Guerrero, Vladimir (1996-2003)	6.22
25	Fielder, Cecil (1985-1998)	6.19
26	Buhner, Jay (1987-2001)	6.18
27	Strawberry, Darryl (1983-1999)	6.18
28	Gehrig, Lou (1923-1939)	6.16
29	Aaron, Hank (1954-1976)	6.11
30	Mays, Willie (1951-1973)	6.07
31	Sauer, Hank (1941-1959)	6.01
32	Mathews, Eddie (1952-1968)	6.00
33	Stargell, Willie (1962-1982)	5.99
34	Giambi, Jason (1995-2003)	5.99
35	Giles, Brian (1995-2003)	5.94
36	Vaughn, Mo (1991-2003)	5.93
37	Deer, Rob (1984-1996)	5.93
38	Howard, Frank (1958-1973)	5.89
39	Bagwell, Jeff (1991-2003)	5.88
40	Robinson, Frank (1956-1976)	5.86
41	Vaughn, Greg (1989-2003)	5.82
42	Horner, Bob (1978-1988)	5.77
43	Campanella, Roy (1948-1957)	5.76
44	Stairs, Matt (1992-2003)	5.75
45	Colavito, Rocky (1955-1968)	5.75
46	Zernial, Gus (1949-1959)	5.74
47	Thomas, Gorman (1973-1986)	5.73
48	Jackson, Reggie (1967-1987)	5.71
49	Stuart, Dick (1958-1969)	5.70
50	Snider, Duke (1947-1964)	5.68
51	Edmonds, Jim (1993-2003)	5.66
52	Mitchell, Kevin (1984-1998)	5.66
53	McGriff, Fred (1986-2003)	5.65
54	Sheffield, Gary (1988-2003)	5.63
55	Cash, Norm (1958-1974)	5.62
56	Palmer, Dean (1989-2003)	5.61
57	Burnitz, Jeromy (1993-2003)	5.60
58	Mize, Johnny (1936-1953)	5.57
59	Klesko, Ryan (1992-2003)	5.57
60	Allen, Dick (1963-1977)	5.54
61	Walker, Larry (1989-2003)	5.54
62	Palmeiro, Rafael (1986-2003)	5.53
63	Jones, Chipper (1993-2003)	5.44
64	Banks, Ernie (1953-1971)	5.43
65	Justice, David (1989-2002)	5.42
66	Ott, Mel (1926-1947)	5.40
67	Williams, Matt (1987-2003)	5.40
68	Maris, Roger (1957-1968)	5.39
69	Jones, Andruw (1996-2003)	5.37
70	Hundley, Todd (1990-2003)	5.36
71	Lopez, Javy (1992-2003)	5.35
72	Davis, Eric (1984-2001)	5.30
73	DiMaggio, Joe (1936-1951)	5.29
74	Hodges, Gil (1943-1963)	5.26
75	Post, Wally (1949-1964)	5.24
76	Tartabull, Danny (1984-1997)	5.23
77	Tettleton, Mickey (1984-1997)	5.21
78	Salmon, Tim (1992-2003)	5.20
79	Rosen, Al (1947-1956)	5.15
80	Green, Shawn (1993-2003)	5.13
81	Wilson, Hack (1923-1934)	5.13
82	Davis, Glenn (1984-1993)	5.11
83	Allison, Bob (1958-1970)	5.09
84	Adcock, Joe (1950-1966)	5.09
85	Bench, Johnny (1967-1983)	5.08
86	Powell, Boog (1961-1977)	5.07
87	Barfield, Jesse (1981-1992)	5.06
88	Colbert, Nate (1966-1976)	5.06
89	Hill, Glenallen (1989-2001)	5.01
90	Murphy, Dale (1976-1993)	5.00
91	Keller, Charlie (1939-1952)	4.99
92	Sievers, Roy (1949-1965)	4.98
93	Gant, Ron (1987-2003)	4.98
94	Johnson, Cliff (1972-1986)	4.97
95	Mincher, Don (1960-1972)	4.97
96	Clark, Jack (1975-1992)	4.97
97	Foster, George (1969-1986)	4.96
98	Batista, Tony (1996-2003)	4.94
99	Rolen, Scott (1996-2003)	4.94
100	Galarraga, Andres (1985-2003)	4.92

Total Bases

1	Aaron, Hank (1954-1976)	6856
2	Musial, Stan (1941-1963)	6134
3	Mays, Willie (1951-1973)	6066
4	Cobb, Ty (1905-1928)	5854
5	Ruth, Babe (1914-1935)	5793
6	Rose, Pete (1963-1986)	5752
7	Yastrzemski, Carl (1961-1983)	5539
8	Murray, Eddie (1977-1997)	5397
9	Robinson, Frank (1956-1976)	5373
10	Bonds, Barry (1986-2003)	5253
11	Winfield, Dave (1973-1995)	5221
12	Ripken, Cal (1981-2001)	5168
13	Speaker, Tris (1907-1928)	5101
14	Gehrig, Lou (1923-1939)	5060
15	Brett, George (1973-1993)	5044
16	Ott, Mel (1926-1947)	5041
17	Palmeiro, Rafael (1986-2003)	4983
18	Foxx, Jimmie (1925-1945)	4956
19	Williams, Ted (1939-1960)	4884
20	Wagner, Honus (1897-1917)	4870
21	Molitor, Paul (1978-1998)	4854
22	Kaline, Al (1953-1974)	4852
23	Jackson, Reggie (1967-1987)	4834
24	Dawson, Andre (1976-1996)	4787
25	Yount, Robin (1974-1993)	4730
26	Hornsby, Rogers (1915-1937)	4712
27	Banks, Ernie (1953-1971)	4706
28	Simmons, Al (1924-1944)	4685
29	Baines, Harold (1980-2001)	4604
30	Williams, Billy (1959-1976)	4599
31	Henderson, Rickey (1979-2003)	4588
32	Perez, Tony (1964-1986)	4532
33	Mantle, Mickey (1951-1968)	4511
34	Clemente, Roberto (1955-1972)	4492
35	Waner, Paul (1926-1945)	4478
36	Lajoie, Nap (1896-1916)	4474
37	McGriff, Fred (1986-2003)	4436
38	Parker, Dave (1973-1991)	4405
39	Schmidt, Mike (1972-1989)	4404
40	Mathews, Eddie (1952-1968)	4349
41	Crawford, Sam (1899-1917)	4328
42	Goslin, Goose (1921-1938)	4325
43	Robinson, Brooks (1955-1977)	4270
44	Collins, Eddie (1906-1930)	4268
45	Pinson, Vada (1958-1975)	4264
46	Gwynn, Tony (1982-2001)	4259
47	Gehringer, Charlie (1924-1942)	4257
48	Brock, Lou (1961-1979)	4238
49	Evans, Dwight (1972-1991)	4230
50	McCovey, Willie (1959-1980)	4219
51	Stargell, Willie (1962-1982)	4190
52	Staub, Rusty (1963-1985)	4185
53	Beckley, Jake (1888-1907)	4156
54	Killebrew, Harmon (1954-1975)	4143
55	Rice, Jim (1974-1989)	4129
56	Anson, Cap (1871-1897)	4124
57	Sosa, Sammy (1989-2003)	4121
58	Wheat, Zack (1909-1927)	4100
59	Oliver, Al (1968-1985)	4083
60	Boggs, Wade (1982-1999)	4064
61	Heilmann, Harry (1914-1932)	4053
62	Galarraga, Andres (1985-2003)	4032
63	Fisk, Carlton (1969-1993)	3999
64	Carew, Rod (1967-1985)	3998
65	Griffey, Ken (1989-2003)	3977
66	Morgan, Joe (1963-1984)	3962
67	Cepeda, Orlando (1958-1974)	3959
68	Rice, Sam (1915-1934)	3955
69	Alomar, Roberto (1988-2003)	3951
70	DiMaggio, Joe (1936-1951)	3948
71	Garvey, Steve (1969-1987)	3941
72	Frisch, Frankie (1919-1937)	3937
73	Davis, Chili (1981-1999)	3914
74	Carter, Joe (1983-1998)	3910
75	Bagwell, Jeff (1991-2003)	3909
76	Gaetti, Gary (1981-2000)	3881
77	Sisler, George (1915-1930)	3871
78	Evans, Darrell (1969-1989)	3866
79	Snider, Duke (1947-1964)	3865
80	Connor, Roger (1880-1897)	3863
81	Medwick, Joe (1932-1948)	3852
82	Buckner, Bill (1969-1990)	3833
83	Delahanty, Ed (1888-1903)	3794
84	Simmons, Ted (1968-1988)	3793
85	Sandberg, Ryne (1981-1997)	3787
86	Nettles, Graig (1967-1988)	3779
	Santo, Ron (1960-1974)	3779
88	Davis, Willie (1960-1979)	3778
89	Raines, Tim (1979-2002)	3771
90	Burkett, Jesse (1890-1905)	3759
91	Thomas, Frank (1990-2003)	3752
92	Vernon, Mickey (1939-1960)	3741
93	Bottomley, Jim (1922-1937)	3737
94	Murphy, Dale (1976-1993)	3733
95	Biggio, Craig (1988-2003)	3710
96	Burks, Ellis (1987-2003)	3682
97	Clarke, Fred (1894-1915)	3680
98	Ryan, Jimmy (1885-1903)	3675
99	Manush, Heinie (1923-1939)	3665
100	Davis, George (1890-1909)	3663

Runs Batted In

1	Aaron, Hank (1954-1976)	2297
2	Ruth, Babe (1914-1935)	2213
3	Gehrig, Lou (1923-1939)	1995
4	Musial, Stan (1941-1963)	1951
5	Cobb, Ty (1905-1928)	1938
6	Foxx, Jimmie (1925-1945)	1922
7	Murray, Eddie (1977-1997)	1917
8	Mays, Willie (1951-1973)	1903
9	Anson, Cap (1871-1897)	1880
10	Ott, Mel (1926-1947)	1860
11	Yastrzemski, Carl (1961-1983)	1844
12	Williams, Ted (1939-1960)	1839
13	Winfield, Dave (1973-1995)	1833
14	Simmons, Al (1924-1944)	1827
15	Robinson, Frank (1956-1976)	1812
16	Bonds, Barry (1986-2003)	1742
17	Wagner, Honus (1897-1917)	1733
18	Jackson, Reggie (1967-1987)	1702
19	Ripken, Cal (1981-2001)	1695
20	Palmeiro, Rafael (1986-2003)	1687
21	Perez, Tony (1964-1986)	1652
22	Banks, Ernie (1953-1971)	1636
23	Baines, Harold (1980-2001)	1628
24	Goslin, Goose (1921-1938)	1609
25	Lajoie, Nap (1896-1916)	1599
26	Brett, George (1973-1993)	1595
	Schmidt, Mike (1972-1989)	1595
28	Dawson, Andre (1976-1996)	1591
29	Hornsby, Rogers (1915-1937)	1584
	Killebrew, Harmon (1954-1975)	1584
31	Kaline, Al (1953-1974)	1583
32	Beckley, Jake (1888-1907)	1577
33	McCovey, Willie (1959-1980)	1555
34	McGriff, Fred (1986-2003)	1543
35	Stargell, Willie (1962-1982)	1540
36	Heilmann, Harry (1914-1932)	1539
37	DiMaggio, Joe (1936-1951)	1537
38	Speaker, Tris (1907-1928)	1529
39	Crawford, Sam (1899-1917)	1525
40	Mantle, Mickey (1951-1968)	1509
41	Parker, Dave (1973-1991)	1493
42	Williams, Billy (1959-1976)	1475
43	Delahanty, Ed (1888-1903)	1466
	Staub, Rusty (1963-1985)	1466
45	Mathews, Eddie (1952-1968)	1453
46	Rice, Jim (1974-1989)	1451
47	Sosa, Sammy (1989-2003)	1450
48	Carter, Joe (1983-1998)	1445
49	Davis, George (1890-1909)	1439
50	Berra, Yogi (1946-1965)	1430
51	Gehringer, Charlie (1924-1942)	1427
52	Cronin, Joe (1926-1945)	1424
53	Galarraga, Andres (1985-2003)	1423
54	Bottomley, Jim (1922-1937)	1422
55	Bagwell, Jeff (1991-2003)	1421
56	McGwire, Mark (1986-2001)	1414
57	Canseco, Jose (1985-2001)	1407
58	Yount, Robin (1974-1993)	1406
59	Thomas, Frank (1990-2003)	1390
60	Simmons, Ted (1968-1988)	1389
61	Gonzalez, Juan (1989-2003)	1387
62	Evans, Dwight (1972-1991)	1384
	Griffey, Ken (1989-2003)	1384
64	Medwick, Joe (1932-1948)	1383
65	Cross, Lave (1887-1907)	1378
66	Bench, Johnny (1967-1983)	1376
67	Davis, Chili (1981-1999)	1372
68	Cepeda, Orlando (1958-1974)	1365
69	Robinson, Brooks (1955-1977)	1357
70	Evans, Darrell (1969-1989)	1354
71	Gaetti, Gary (1981-2000)	1341
72	Mize, Johnny (1936-1953)	1337
73	Snider, Duke (1947-1964)	1333
74	Santo, Ron (1960-1974)	1331
75	Fisk, Carlton (1969-1993)	1330
76	Oliver, Al (1968-1985)	1326
77	Connor, Roger (1880-1897)	1323
78	Nettles, Graig (1967-1988)	1314
	Rose, Pete (1963-1986)	1314
80	Vernon, Mickey (1939-1960)	1311
81	Waner, Paul (1926-1945)	1309
82	Garvey, Steve (1969-1987)	1308
83	Molitor, Paul (1978-1998)	1307
84	Clemente, Roberto (1955-1972)	1305
	Thompson, Sam (1885-1906)	1305
86	Slaughter, Enos (1938-1959)	1304
87	Duffy, Hugh (1888-1906)	1302
88	Collins, Eddie (1906-1930)	1300
89	Brouthers, Dan (1879-1904)	1296
90	Ennis, Del (1946-1959)	1284
91	Johnson, Bob (1933-1945)	1283
92	Baylor, Don (1970-1988)	1276
	Greenberg, Hank (1930-1947)	1276
94	Hodges, Gil (1943-1963)	1274
95	Traynor, Pie (1920-1937)	1273
96	O'Neill, Paul (1985-2001)	1269
97	Murphy, Dale (1976-1993)	1266
98	Wheat, Zack (1909-1927)	1248
99	Doerr, Bobby (1937-1951)	1247
100	2 players tied	1244

Runs Batted In per Game

1	Thompson, Sam (1885-1906)	.926
2	Gehrig, Lou (1923-1939)	.922
3	Greenberg, Hank (1930-1947)	.915
4	DiMaggio, Joe (1936-1951)	.885
5	Ruth, Babe (1914-1935)	.884
6	Gonzalez, Juan (1989-2003)	.838
7	Foxx, Jimmie (1925-1945)	.830
8	Anson, Cap (1871-1897)	.826
9	Simmons, Al (1924-1944)	.825
10	Ramirez, Manny (1993-2003)	.824
11	Belle, Albert (1989-2000)	.805
12	Williams, Ted (1939-1960)	.802
13	Delahanty, Ed (1888-1903)	.798
14	Wilson, Hack (1923-1934)	.789
15	Rodriguez, Alex (1994-2003)	.776
16	Brouthers, Dan (1879-1904)	.775
17	Meusel, Bob (1920-1930)	.758
18	Piazza, Mike (1992-2003)	.758
19	McGwire, Mark (1986-2001)	.755
20	Trosky, Hal (1933-1946)	.751
21	Thomas, Frank (1990-2003)	.751
22	Duffy, Hugh (1888-1906)	.749
23	Canseco, Jose (1985-2001)	.746
24	Delgado, Carlos (1993-2003)	.741
25	Bagwell, Jeff (1991-2003)	.727
26	Griffey, Ken (1989-2003)	.723
27	Sosa, Sammy (1989-2003)	.721
28	O'Neill, Tip (1883-1892)	.720
29	York, Rudy (1934-1948)	.719
30	Heilmann, Harry (1914-1932)	.717
31	Giambi, Jason (1995-2003)	.715
32	Bottomley, Jim (1922-1937)	.714
33	Mize, Johnny (1936-1953)	.710
34	Larkin, Henry (1884-1893)	.706
35	Campanella, Roy (1948-1957)	.705
36	Vaughn, Mo (1991-2003)	.704
37	Goslin, Goose (1921-1938)	.704
38	Hornsby, Rogers (1915-1937)	.701
39	Burns, Oyster (1884-1895)	.700
40	Guerrero, Vladimir (1996-2003)	.699
41	Averill, Earl (1929-1941)	.698
42	Medwick, Joe (1932-1948)	.697
43	Aaron, Hank (1954-1976)	.696
44	Rice, Jim (1974-1989)	.695
45	Kiner, Ralph (1946-1955)	.690
46	Thome, Jim (1991-2003)	.689
47	Johnson, Bob (1933-1945)	.689
48	Rosen, Al (1947-1956)	.687
49	Fielder, Cecil (1985-1998)	.686
50	Klein, Chuck (1928-1944)	.685
51	Lazzeri, Tony (1926-1939)	.684
52	Stephens, Vern (1941-1955)	.683
53	Ott, Mel (1926-1947)	.681
54	McKean, Ed (1887-1899)	.679
55	Bonds, Barry (1986-2003)	.678
56	Dickey, Bill (1928-1946)	.676
57	Ennis, Del (1946-1959)	.675
58	Berra, Yogi (1946-1965)	.675
59	Kent, Jeff (1992-2003)	.674
60	Alou, Moises (1990-2003)	.673
61	Lyons, Denny (1885-1897)	.673
62	Horner, Bob (1978-1988)	.672
63	Ewing, Buck (1880-1897)	.671
64	Rolen, Scott (1996-2003)	.671
65	Jones, Chipper (1993-2003)	.671
66	Walker, Larry (1989-2003)	.671
67	Cronin, Joe (1926-1945)	.670
68	Bichette, Dante (1988-2001)	.670
69	Doerr, Bobby (1937-1951)	.669
70	Stuart, Dick (1958-1969)	.668
71	Berger, Wally (1930-1940)	.665
72	Schmidt, Mike (1972-1989)	.663
73	Connor, Roger (1880-1897)	.662
74	Foutz, Dave (1884-1896)	.660
75	Carter, Joe (1983-1998)	.660
76	Beckley, Jake (1888-1907)	.660
77	Tartabull, Danny (1984-1997)	.658
78	Palmeiro, Rafael (1986-2003)	.657
79	Traynor, Pie (1920-1937)	.656
80	Buhner, Jay (1987-2001)	.656
81	Jennings, Hughie (1891-1918)	.655
82	Sheffield, Gary (1988-2003)	.655
83	Williams, Ken (1915-1929)	.654
84	Martinez, Tino (1990-2003)	.653
85	Giles, Brian (1995-2003)	.653
86	Kelly, King (1878-1893)	.653
87	Williams, Matt (1987-2003)	.653
88	Stargell, Willie (1962-1982)	.653
89	Killebrew, Harmon (1954-1975)	.651
90	Keller, Charlie (1939-1952)	.650
91	Hafey, Chick (1924-1937)	.649
92	Reilly, John (1880-1891)	.648
93	Banks, Ernie (1953-1971)	.647
94	Wright, Glenn (1924-1935)	.646
95	Jensen, Jackie (1950-1961)	.646
96	Robinson, Frank (1956-1976)	.645
97	Lajoie, Nap (1896-1916)	.645
98	Musial, Stan (1941-1963)	.645
99	Kelley, Joe (1891-1908)	.644
100	Cepeda, Orlando (1958-1974)	.643

Walks

1	Henderson, Rickey (1979-2003)	2190
2	Bonds, Barry (1986-2003)	2070
3	Ruth, Babe (1914-1935)	2062
4	Williams, Ted (1939-1960)	2021
5	Morgan, Joe (1963-1984)	1865
6	Yastrzemski, Carl (1961-1983)	1845
7	Mantle, Mickey (1951-1968)	1733
8	Ott, Mel (1926-1947)	1708
9	Yost, Eddie (1944-1962)	1614
10	Evans, Darrell (1969-1989)	1605
11	Musial, Stan (1941-1963)	1599
12	Rose, Pete (1963-1986)	1566
13	Killebrew, Harmon (1954-1975)	1559
14	Gehrig, Lou (1923-1939)	1508
15	Schmidt, Mike (1972-1989)	1507
16	Collins, Eddie (1906-1930)	1499
17	Mays, Willie (1951-1973)	1464
18	Foxx, Jimmie (1925-1945)	1452
19	Mathews, Eddie (1952-1968)	1444
20	Robinson, Frank (1956-1976)	1420
21	Boggs, Wade (1982-1999)	1412
22	Aaron, Hank (1954-1976)	1402
23	Evans, Dwight (1972-1991)	1391
24	Thomas, Frank (1990-2003)	1386
25	Speaker, Tris (1907-1928)	1381
26	Jackson, Reggie (1967-1987)	1375
27	McCovey, Willie (1959-1980)	1345
28	Murray, Eddie (1977-1997)	1333
29	Raines, Tim (1979-2002)	1330
30	Phillips, Tony (1982-1999)	1319
31	McGwire, Mark (1986-2001)	1317
32	Appling, Luke (1930-1950)	1302
33	McGriff, Fred (1986-2003)	1296
34	Bagwell, Jeff (1991-2003)	1287
35	Kaline, Al (1953-1974)	1277
36	Singleton, Ken (1970-1984)	1263
37	Clark, Jack (1975-1992)	1262
38	Staub, Rusty (1963-1985)	1255
39	Cobb, Ty (1905-1928)	1249
40	Randolph, Willie (1975-1992)	1243
41	Martinez, Edgar (1987-2003)	1225
42	Palmeiro, Rafael (1986-2003)	1224
	Wynn, Jimmy (1963-1977)	1224
44	Winfield, Dave (1973-1995)	1216
45	Reese, Pee Wee (1940-1958)	1210
46	Ashburn, Richie (1948-1962)	1198
	Olerud, John (1989-2003)	1198
48	Downing, Brian (1973-1992)	1197
	Whitaker, Lou (1977-1995)	1197
50	Davis, Chili (1981-1999)	1194
51	Hamilton, Billy (1888-1901)	1189
52	Gehringer, Charlie (1924-1942)	1186
53	Bush, Donie (1908-1923)	1158
54	Bishop, Max (1924-1935)	1153
	Harrah, Toby (1969-1986)	1153
56	Hooper, Harry (1909-1925)	1136
57	Sheckard, Jimmy (1897-1913)	1135
58	Butler, Brett (1981-1997)	1129
	Ripken, Cal (1981-2001)	1129
60	Sheffield, Gary (1988-2003)	1110
61	Santo, Ron (1960-1974)	1108
	Thome, Jim (1991-2003)	1108
63	Brett, George (1973-1993)	1096
64	Molitor, Paul (1978-1998)	1094
65	Blue, Lu (1921-1933)	1092
	Hack, Stan (1932-1947)	1092
67	Waner, Paul (1926-1945)	1091
68	Nettles, Graig (1967-1988)	1088
69	Grich, Bobby (1970-1986)	1087
70	Grace, Mark (1988-2003)	1075
	Johnson, Bob (1933-1945)	1075
72	Smith, Ozzie (1978-1996)	1072
73	Clift, Harlond (1934-1945)	1070
	Hernandez, Keith (1974-1990)	1070
75	Dahlen, Bill (1891-1911)	1064
76	Baines, Harold (1980-2001)	1062
77	Cronin, Joe (1926-1945)	1059
78	Ventura, Robin (1989-2003)	1053
79	Fairly, Ron (1958-1978)	1052
80	Williams, Billy (1959-1976)	1045
81	Cash, Norm (1958-1974)	1043
	Joost, Eddie (1936-1955)	1043
83	Thomas, Roy (1899-1911)	1042
84	Carey, Max (1910-1929)	1040
85	Hornsby, Rogers (1915-1937)	1038
86	Gilliam, Jim (1953-1966)	1036
87	Bando, Sal (1966-1981)	1031
88	Burkett, Jesse (1890-1905)	1029
89	Biggio, Craig (1988-2003)	1020
90	Alomar, Roberto (1988-2003)	1018
	Carew, Rod (1967-1985)	1018
	Slaughter, Enos (1938-1959)	1018
93	Cey, Ron (1971-1987)	1012
94	Kiner, Ralph (1946-1955)	1011
95	Hoy, Dummy (1888-1902)	1006
96	Huggins, Miller (1904-1916)	1003
97	Connor, Roger (1880-1897)	1002
98	Powell, Boog (1961-1977)	1001
99	Stanky, Eddie (1943-1953)	996
100	Childs, Cupid (1888-1901)	991

Walk Percentage

1	Williams, Ted (1939-1960)	.206
2	Bishop, Max (1924-1935)	.200
3	Ruth, Babe (1914-1935)	.194
4	Bonds, Barry (1986-2003)	.189
5	Fain, Ferris (1947-1955)	.184
6	Stanky, Eddie (1943-1953)	.183
7	Cullenbine, Roy (1938-1947)	.178
8	Tenace, Gene (1969-1983)	.178
9	Yost, Eddie (1944-1962)	.176
10	Mantle, Mickey (1951-1968)	.175
11	Thome, Jim (1991-2003)	.173
12	McGwire, Mark (1986-2001)	.172
13	Keller, Charlie (1939-1952)	.170
14	McGraw, John (1891-1906)	.170
15	Thomas, Frank (1990-2003)	.170
16	Tettleton, Mickey (1984-1997)	.165
17	Morgan, Joe (1963-1984)	.165
18	Henderson, Rickey (1979-2003)	.164
19	Giles, Brian (1995-2003)	.162
20	Torgeson, Earl (1947-1961)	.162
21	Carbo, Bernie (1969-1980)	.162
22	Kiner, Ralph (1946-1955)	.162
23	Killebrew, Harmon (1954-1975)	.159
24	Thomas, Roy (1899-1911)	.158
25	Hamilton, Billy (1888-1901)	.156
26	Gehrig, Lou (1923-1939)	.156
27	Clift, Harlond (1934-1945)	.155
28	Ferguson, Joe (1970-1983)	.155
29	Valo, Elmer (1940-1961)	.155
30	Joost, Eddie (1936-1955)	.154
31	Clark, Jack (1975-1992)	.153
32	Wynn, Jimmy (1963-1977)	.153
33	Blue, Lu (1921-1933)	.152
34	Giambi, Jason (1995-2003)	.151
35	Martinez, Edgar (1987-2003)	.151
36	Ott, Mel (1926-1947)	.151
37	Foxx, Jimmie (1925-1945)	.150
38	Schmidt, Mike (1972-1989)	.150
39	Evans, Darrell (1969-1989)	.149
40	Abreu, Bobby (1996-2003)	.149
41	Bagwell, Jeff (1991-2003)	.149
42	Camilli, Dolph (1933-1945)	.149
43	Singleton, Ken (1970-1984)	.148
44	Cunningham, Joe (1954-1966)	.148
45	Huggins, Miller (1904-1916)	.148
46	Cangelosi, John (1985-1999)	.147
47	Childs, Cupid (1888-1901)	.147
48	Fletcher, Elbie (1934-1949)	.146
49	Daulton, Darren (1983-1997)	.145
50	Phillips, Tony (1982-1999)	.145
51	Rettenmund, Merv (1968-1980)	.145
52	Magadan, Dave (1986-2001)	.145
53	Hartsel, Topsy (1898-1911)	.144
54	Hargrove, Mike (1974-1985)	.144
55	Thompson, Jason (1976-1986)	.144
56	Garrett, Wayne (1969-1978)	.143
57	Olerud, John (1989-2003)	.143
58	Mathews, Eddie (1952-1968)	.143
59	Murphy, Dwayne (1978-1989)	.143
60	Kruk, John (1986-1995)	.141
61	Salmon, Tim (1992-2003)	.141
62	Jones, Chipper (1993-2003)	.141
63	Galan, Augie (1934-1949)	.140
64	Greenberg, Hank (1930-1947)	.140
65	Woodling, Gene (1943-1962)	.139
66	Thornton, Andre (1973-1987)	.139
67	McCovey, Willie (1959-1980)	.139
68	Delgado, Carlos (1993-2003)	.139
69	Doby, Larry (1947-1959)	.138
70	Sheffield, Gary (1988-2003)	.138
71	Cochrane, Mickey (1925-1937)	.138
72	Porter, Darrell (1971-1987)	.138
73	Briggs, Johnny (1964-1975)	.137
74	Justice, David (1989-2002)	.137
75	Davis, Alvin (1984-1992)	.137
76	Mayberry, John (1968-1982)	.137
77	Radford, Paul (1883-1894)	.136
78	North, Billy (1971-1981)	.136
79	Braun, Steve (1971-1985)	.135
80	Siebern, Norm (1956-1968)	.134
81	Hansen, Dave (1990-2003)	.134
82	Allison, Bob (1958-1970)	.134
83	Rosen, Al (1947-1956)	.134
84	Ramirez, Manny (1993-2003)	.134
85	Buhner, Jay (1987-2001)	.134
86	Johnson, Bob (1933-1945)	.134
87	Mazzilli, Lee (1976-1989)	.133
88	Bresnahan, Roger (1897-1915)	.133
89	Bush, Donie (1908-1923)	.133
90	Grich, Bobby (1970-1986)	.132
91	Schang, Wally (1913-1931)	.132
92	Jorgensen, Mike (1968-1985)	.132
93	Yastrzemski, Carl (1961-1983)	.132
94	Cash, Norm (1958-1974)	.132
95	Ferrell, Rick (1929-1947)	.132
96	Henrich, Tommy (1937-1950)	.132
97	Evans, Dwight (1972-1991)	.132
98	Harrah, Toby (1969-1986)	.132
99	Hatton, Grady (1946-1960)	.132
100	Boggs, Wade (1982-1999)	.131

Strikeouts

1	Jackson, Reggie (1967-1987)	2597
2	Galarraga, Andres (1985-2003)	2000
3	Sosa, Sammy (1989-2003)	1977
4	Canseco, Jose (1985-2001)	1942
5	Stargell, Willie (1962-1982)	1936
6	Schmidt, Mike (1972-1989)	1883
7	Perez, Tony (1964-1986)	1867
8	McGriff, Fred (1986-2003)	1863
9	Kingman, Dave (1971-1986)	1816
10	Bonds, Bobby (1968-1981)	1757
11	Murphy, Dale (1976-1993)	1748
12	Brock, Lou (1961-1979)	1730
13	Mantle, Mickey (1951-1968)	1710
14	Killebrew, Harmon (1954-1975)	1699
15	Davis, Chili (1981-1999)	1698
16	Evans, Dwight (1972-1991)	1697
17	Henderson, Rickey (1979-2003)	1694
18	Winfield, Dave (1973-1995)	1686
19	Gaetti, Gary (1981-2000)	1602
20	McGwire, Mark (1986-2001)	1596
21	May, Lee (1965-1982)	1570
22	Thome, Jim (1991-2003)	1559
23	Allen, Dick (1963-1977)	1556
24	McCovey, Willie (1959-1980)	1550
25	Parker, Dave (1973-1991)	1537
26	Robinson, Frank (1956-1976)	1532
27	Parrish, Lance (1977-1995)	1527
28	Mays, Willie (1951-1973)	1526
	White, Devon (1985-2001)	1526
30	Murray, Eddie (1977-1997)	1516
31	Monday, Rick (1966-1984)	1513
	Vaughn, Greg (1989-2003)	1513
33	Dawson, Andre (1976-1996)	1509
34	Phillips, Tony (1982-1999)	1499
35	Lankford, Ray (1990-2002)	1495
	Luzinski, Greg (1970-1984)	1495
37	Mathews, Eddie (1952-1968)	1487
38	Howard, Frank (1958-1973)	1460
39	Bell, Jay (1986-2003)	1443
40	Samuel, Juan (1983-1998)	1442
41	Baines, Harold (1980-2001)	1441
	Clark, Jack (1975-1992)	1441
43	Vaughn, Mo (1991-2003)	1429
44	Wynn, Jimmy (1963-1977)	1427
45	Rice, Jim (1974-1989)	1423
46	Foster, George (1969-1986)	1419
47	Scott, George (1966-1979)	1418
48	Gant, Ron (1987-2003)	1411
49	Evans, Darrell (1969-1989)	1410
50	Deer, Rob (1984-1996)	1409
51	Bagwell, Jeff (1991-2003)	1406
	Buhner, Jay (1987-2001)	1406
53	Davis, Eric (1984-2001)	1398
54	Yastrzemski, Carl (1961-1983)	1393
55	Bonds, Barry (1986-2003)	1387
	Carter, Joe (1983-1998)	1387
57	Fisk, Carlton (1969-1993)	1386
58	Aaron, Hank (1954-1976)	1383
59	Biggio, Craig (1988-2003)	1373
60	Fryman, Travis (1990-2002)	1369
61	Williams, Matt (1987-2003)	1363
62	Tartabull, Danny (1984-1997)	1362
63	Parrish, Larry (1974-1988)	1359
64	Strawberry, Darryl (1983-1999)	1352
65	Yount, Robin (1974-1993)	1350
66	Santo, Ron (1960-1974)	1343
67	Thomas, Gorman (1973-1986)	1339
68	Burks, Ellis (1987-2003)	1332
	Palmer, Dean (1989-2003)	1332
70	Ruth, Babe (1914-1935)	1330
71	Sanders, Reggie (1991-2003)	1320
72	Johnson, Deron (1960-1976)	1318
73	Fielder, Cecil (1985-1998)	1316
74	Horton, Willie (1963-1980)	1313
75	Foxx, Jimmie (1925-1945)	1311
76	Tettleton, Mickey (1984-1997)	1307
	Wallach, Tim (1980-1996)	1307
78	Ripken, Cal (1981-2001)	1305
79	Gibson, Kirk (1979-1995)	1285
80	Bench, Johnny (1967-1983)	1278
	Grich, Bobby (1970-1986)	1278
82	Incaviglia, Pete (1986-1998)	1277
83	Salmon, Tim (1992-2003)	1275
84	Washington, Claudell (1974-1990)	1266
85	Sandberg, Ryne (1981-1997)	1260
86	Griffey, Ken (1989-2003)	1256
87	Gonzalez, Juan (1989-2003)	1254
88	Singleton, Ken (1970-1984)	1246
89	Molitor, Paul (1978-1998)	1244
	Palmeiro, Rafael (1986-2003)	1244
91	McGee, Willie (1982-1999)	1238
92	Snider, Duke (1947-1964)	1237
93	Banks, Ernie (1953-1971)	1236
94	Cey, Ron (1971-1987)	1235
	Santiago, Benito (1986-2003)	1235
96	Barfield, Jesse (1981-1992)	1234
97	Clemente, Roberto (1955-1972)	1230
	Hernandez, Jose (1991-2003)	1230
99	Powell, Boog (1961-1977)	1226
100	Nettles, Graig (1967-1988)	1209

At Bats per Strikeout

1	Sewell, Joe (1920-1933)	62.6
2	Waner, Lloyd (1927-1945)	44.9
3	Fox, Nellie (1947-1965)	42.7
4	Holmes, Tommy (1942-1952)	40.9
5	High, Andy (1922-1934)	33.8
6	Rice, Sam (1915-1934)	33.7
7	Frisch, Frankie (1919-1937)	33.5
8	Mitchell, Dale (1946-1956)	33.5
9	Cooney, Johnny (1921-1944)	31.5
10	McCormick, Frank (1934-1948)	30.3
11	Mueller, Don (1948-1959)	29.9
12	Southworth, Billy (1913-1929)	29.5
13	Radcliff, Rip (1934-1943)	28.9
14	Roush, Edd (1913-1931)	28.3
15	Traynor, Pie (1920-1937)	27.2
16	Cramer, Doc (1929-1948)	26.5
17	Bigbee, Carson (1916-1926)	26.0
18	Severeid, Hank (1911-1926)	25.5
19	Sisler, George (1915-1930)	25.3
20	Waner, Paul (1926-1945)	25.2
21	Rowe, Jack (1879-1890)	25.0
22	White, Deacon (1871-1890)	25.0
23	Adams, Sparky (1922-1934)	24.9
24	Finney, Lou (1931-1947)	24.9
25	Sutton, Ezra (1871-1888)	24.7
26	Meusel, Irish (1914-1927)	24.6
27	Schoendienst, Red (1945-1963)	24.5
28	Power, Vic (1954-1965)	24.5
29	Vaughan, Arky (1932-1948)	24.0
30	Millan, Felix (1966-1977)	23.9
31	Cochrane, Mickey (1925-1937)	23.8
32	Gehringer, Charlie (1924-1942)	23.8
33	Ward, John (1878-1894)	23.6
34	Kell, George (1943-1957)	23.4
35	Cutshaw, George (1912-1923)	23.2
36	Tobin, Jack (1914-1927)	23.1
37	Wright, Taffy (1938-1949)	23.1
38	Critz, Hughie (1924-1935)	23.1
39	Koenig, Mark (1925-1936)	22.5
40	Lombardi, Ernie (1931-1947)	22.3
41	Manush, Heinie (1923-1939)	22.2
42	Richardson, Bobby (1955-1966)	22.2
43	Moore, Jo-Jo (1930-1941)	22.0
44	Sheely, Earl (1921-1931)	21.8
45	Dickey, Bill (1928-1946)	21.8
46	Pesky, Johnny (1942-1954)	21.8
47	Ferrell, Rick (1929-1947)	21.8
48	Beckert, Glenn (1965-1975)	21.4
49	Gwynn, Tony (1982-2001)	21.4
50	Siebert, Dick (1932-1945)	21.2
51	Waitkus, Eddie (1941-1955)	20.9
52	Flack, Max (1914-1925)	20.8
53	Buckner, Bill (1969-1990)	20.7
54	Walker, Dixie (1931-1949)	20.7
55	Hines, Paul (1872-1891)	20.7
56	Scott, Everett (1914-1926)	20.7
57	Combs, Earle (1924-1935)	20.7
58	Lindstrom, Freddie (1924-1936)	20.3
59	Owen, Mickey (1937-1954)	20.2
60	Vosmik, Joe (1930-1944)	20.1
61	Boudreau, Lou (1938-1952)	19.5
62	Stock, Milt (1913-1926)	19.5
63	Marshall, Willard (1942-1955)	19.3
64	Garms, Debs (1932-1945)	19.3
65	Grimm, Charlie (1916-1936)	19.3
66	Rice, Harry (1923-1933)	19.3
67	Newsome, Skeeter (1935-1947)	19.2
68	Walker, Curt (1919-1930)	19.1
69	Lowrey, Peanuts (1942-1955)	19.1
70	Jamieson, Charlie (1915-1932)	19.0
71	Ruel, Muddy (1915-1934)	19.0
72	Griffith, Tommy (1913-1925)	18.9
73	Thevenow, Tommy (1924-1938)	18.8
74	Stripp, Joe (1928-1938)	18.6
75	DiMaggio, Joe (1936-1951)	18.5
76	Fothergill, Bob (1922-1933)	18.5
77	Miller, Bing (1921-1936)	18.3
78	Stephenson, Riggs (1921-1934)	18.3
79	Berra, Yogi (1946-1965)	18.2
80	Herman, Billy (1931-1947)	18.0
81	Magee, Lee (1911-1919)	18.0
82	Cash, Dave (1969-1980)	18.0
83	Valo, Elmer (1940-1961)	17.7
84	Groh, Heinie (1912-1927)	17.6
85	Sewell, Luke (1921-1942)	17.5
86	Dauer, Rich (1976-1985)	17.5
87	Lewis, Buddy (1935-1949)	17.4
88	Goodman, Billy (1947-1962)	17.2
89	Gilliam, Jim (1953-1966)	17.1
90	Kuenn, Harvey (1952-1966)	17.1
91	Mancuso, Gus (1928-1945)	17.1
92	Wilson, Jimmie (1923-1940)	17.1
93	Cox, Billy (1941-1955)	17.0
94	Williams, Ken (1915-1929)	16.9
95	Case, George (1937-1947)	16.9
96	Travis, Cecil (1933-1947)	16.9
97	Appling, Luke (1930-1950)	16.8
98	Hayes, Jackie (1927-1940)	16.8
99	Harper, Brian (1979-1995)	16.8
100	Robinson, Jackie (1947-1956)	16.8

Batting Average

1	Cobb, Ty (1905-1928)	.366
2	Hornsby, Rogers (1915-1937)	.358
3	Jackson, Joe (1908-1920)	.356
4	Brouthers, Dan (1879-1904)	.349
5	Browning, Pete (1882-1894)	.349
6	Delahanty, Ed (1888-1903)	.346
7	Speaker, Tris (1907-1928)	.345
8	Hamilton, Billy (1888-1901)	.344
9	Williams, Ted (1939-1960)	.344
10	Ruth, Babe (1914-1935)	.342
11	Heilmann, Harry (1914-1932)	.342
12	Keeler, Willie (1892-1910)	.341
13	Terry, Bill (1923-1936)	.341
14	Sisler, George (1915-1930)	.340
15	Gehrig, Lou (1923-1939)	.340
16	Burkett, Jesse (1890-1905)	.338
17	Gwynn, Tony (1982-2001)	.338
18	Lajoie, Nap (1896-1916)	.338
19	Stephenson, Riggs (1921-1934)	.336
20	Thompson, Sam (1885-1906)	.335
21	Simmons, Al (1924-1944)	.334
22	O'Neill, Tip (1883-1892)	.334
23	McGraw, John (1891-1906)	.334
24	Waner, Paul (1926-1945)	.333
25	Collins, Eddie (1906-1930)	.333
26	Anson, Cap (1871-1897)	.333
27	Donlin, Mike (1899-1914)	.333
28	Musial, Stan (1941-1963)	.331
29	Manush, Heinie (1923-1939)	.330
30	Boggs, Wade (1982-1999)	.328
31	Carew, Rod (1967-1985)	.328
32	Wagner, Honus (1897-1917)	.328
33	Fothergill, Bob (1922-1933)	.325
34	Foxx, Jimmie (1925-1945)	.325
35	Combs, Earle (1924-1935)	.325
36	DiMaggio, Joe (1936-1951)	.325
37	Herman, Babe (1926-1945)	.324
38	Duffy, Hugh (1888-1906)	.324
39	Medwick, Joe (1932-1948)	.324
40	Connor, Roger (1880-1897)	.323
41	Guerrero, Vladimir (1996-2003)	.323
42	Roush, Edd (1913-1931)	.323
43	Rice, Sam (1915-1934)	.322
44	Youngs, Ross (1917-1926)	.322
45	Cuyler, Kiki (1921-1938)	.321
46	Gehringer, Charlie (1924-1942)	.320
47	Klein, Chuck (1928-1944)	.320
48	Traynor, Pie (1920-1937)	.320
49	Cochrane, Mickey (1925-1937)	.320
50	Piazza, Mike (1992-2003)	.319
51	Williams, Ken (1915-1929)	.319
52	Puckett, Kirby (1984-1995)	.318
53	Averill, Earl (1929-1941)	.318
54	Lyons, Denny (1885-1897)	.318
55	Vaughan, Arky (1932-1948)	.318
56	Jeter, Derek (1995-2003)	.317
57	Clemente, Roberto (1955-1972)	.317
58	Hafey, Chick (1924-1937)	.317
59	Kelley, Joe (1891-1908)	.317
60	Ramirez, Manny (1993-2003)	.317
61	Wheat, Zack (1909-1927)	.317
62	Van Haltren, George (1887-1903)	.317
63	Waner, Lloyd (1927-1945)	.316
64	Frisch, Frankie (1919-1937)	.316
65	Goslin, Goose (1921-1938)	.316
66	Martinez, Edgar (1987-2003)	.315
67	Walker, Larry (1989-2003)	.314
68	Falk, Bibb (1920-1931)	.314
69	Tiernan, Mike (1887-1899)	.314
70	Travis, Cecil (1933-1947)	.314
71	Kelly, King (1878-1893)	.314
72	Greenberg, Hank (1930-1947)	.313
73	Fournier, Jack (1912-1927)	.313
74	Flick, Elmer (1898-1910)	.313
75	O'Rourke, Jim (1872-1904)	.313
76	Dickey, Bill (1928-1946)	.313
77	Mitchell, Dale (1946-1956)	.312
78	Mize, Johnny (1936-1953)	.312
79	Sewell, Joe (1920-1933)	.312
80	Clarke, Fred (1894-1915)	.312
81	Smith, Elmer (1886-1901)	.312
82	McCosky, Barney (1939-1953)	.312
83	Jennings, Hughie (1891-1918)	.312
84	Lindstrom, Freddie (1924-1936)	.311
85	Miller, Bing (1921-1936)	.311
86	Robinson, Jackie (1947-1956)	.311
87	Jacobson, Baby Doll (1915-1927)	.311
88	Wright, Taffy (1938-1949)	.311
89	Radcliff, Rip (1934-1943)	.311
90	Beaumont, Ginger (1899-1910)	.311
91	Ryan, Jimmy (1885-1903)	.311
92	Appling, Luke (1930-1950)	.310
93	Meusel, Irish (1914-1927)	.310
94	Veach, Bobby (1912-1925)	.310
95	Larkin, Henry (1884-1893)	.310
96	Thomas, Frank (1990-2003)	.310
97	Bottomley, Jim (1922-1937)	.310
98	Stone, John (1928-1938)	.310
99	Crawford, Sam (1899-1917)	.309
100	Meusel, Bob (1920-1930)	.309

On-Base Percentage

1	Williams, Ted (1939-1960)	.483
2	Ruth, Babe (1914-1935)	.474
3	McGraw, John (1891-1906)	.466
4	Hamilton, Billy (1888-1901)	.455
5	Gehrig, Lou (1923-1939)	.447
6	Bonds, Barry (1986-2003)	.437
7	Thomas, Frank (1990-2003)	.434
8	Hornsby, Rogers (1915-1937)	.434
9	Cobb, Ty (1905-1928)	.433
10	Foxx, Jimmie (1925-1945)	.428
11	Speaker, Tris (1907-1928)	.428
12	Martinez, Edgar (1987-2003)	.427
13	Fain, Ferris (1947-1955)	.425
14	Collins, Eddie (1906-1930)	.424
15	Brouthers, Dan (1879-1904)	.423
16	Jackson, Joe (1908-1920)	.423
17	Bishop, Max (1924-1935)	.423
18	Mantle, Mickey (1951-1968)	.423
19	Giles, Brian (1995-2003)	.422
20	Giambi, Jason (1995-2003)	.420
21	Cochrane, Mickey (1925-1937)	.419
22	Boggs, Wade (1982-1999)	.419
23	Musial, Stan (1941-1963)	.418
24	Ramirez, Manny (1993-2003)	.416
25	Childs, Cupid (1888-1901)	.416
26	Bagwell, Jeff (1991-2003)	.415
27	Burkett, Jesse (1890-1905)	.415
28	Thome, Jim (1991-2003)	.414
29	Ott, Mel (1926-1947)	.414
30	Thomas, Roy (1899-1911)	.413
31	Abreu, Bobby (1996-2003)	.412
32	Greenberg, Hank (1930-1947)	.412
33	Delahanty, Ed (1888-1903)	.411
34	Keller, Charlie (1939-1952)	.410
35	Stanky, Eddie (1943-1953)	.410
36	Robinson, Jackie (1947-1956)	.410
37	Heilmann, Harry (1914-1932)	.410
38	Cullenbine, Roy (1938-1947)	.408
39	Jones, Chipper (1993-2003)	.408
40	Lyons, Denny (1885-1897)	.407
41	Stephenson, Riggs (1921-1934)	.407
42	Cunningham, Joe (1954-1966)	.406
43	Olerud, John (1989-2003)	.406
44	Vaughan, Arky (1932-1948)	.406
45	Sheffield, Gary (1988-2003)	.405
46	Waner, Paul (1926-1945)	.404
47	Gehringer, Charlie (1924-1942)	.404
48	Walker, Larry (1989-2003)	.403
49	Henderson, Rickey (1979-2003)	.403
50	Browning, Pete (1882-1894)	.403
51	Blue, Lu (1921-1933)	.402
52	Kelley, Joe (1891-1908)	.402
53	Kruk, John (1986-1995)	.400
54	Hargrove, Mike (1974-1985)	.400
55	Appling, Luke (1930-1950)	.399
56	Valo, Elmer (1940-1961)	.399
57	Youngs, Ross (1917-1926)	.399
58	Kiner, Ralph (1946-1955)	.398
59	DiMaggio, Joe (1936-1951)	.398
60	McGwire, Mark (1986-2001)	.398
61	Delgado, Carlos (1993-2003)	.398
62	Smith, Elmer (1886-1901)	.398
63	Ashburn, Richie (1948-1962)	.397
64	Mize, Johnny (1936-1953)	.397
65	Combs, Earle (1924-1935)	.397
66	Connor, Roger (1880-1897)	.397
67	Morgan, Joe (1963-1984)	.395
68	Carew, Rod (1967-1985)	.395
69	Wilson, Hack (1923-1934)	.395
70	Yost, Eddie (1944-1962)	.395
71	Averill, Earl (1929-1941)	.395
72	Anson, Cap (1871-1897)	.395
73	Pesky, Johnny (1942-1954)	.394
74	Magadan, Dave (1986-2001)	.394
75	Chance, Frank (1898-1914)	.394
76	Hack, Stan (1932-1947)	.394
77	Williams, Ken (1915-1929)	.393
78	Schang, Wally (1913-1931)	.393
79	Williams, Bernie (1991-2003)	.393
80	Johnson, Bob (1933-1945)	.393
81	Terry, Bill (1923-1936)	.393
82	Guerrero, Vladimir (1996-2003)	.392
83	O'Neill, Tip (1883-1892)	.392
84	Grantham, George (1922-1934)	.392
85	Robinson, Frank (1956-1976)	.392
86	Salmon, Tim (1992-2003)	.392
87	Fournier, Jack (1912-1927)	.392
88	Tiernan, Mike (1887-1899)	.392
89	Gwynn, Tony (1982-2001)	.392
90	Minoso, Minnie (1949-1980)	.391
91	Jeter, Derek (1995-2003)	.391
92	Wagner, Honus (1897-1917)	.391
93	Sewell, Joe (1920-1933)	.391
94	Singleton, Ken (1970-1984)	.391
95	Tenace, Gene (1969-1983)	.391
96	Jennings, Hughie (1891-1918)	.391
97	Greer, Rusty (1994-2002)	.391
98	Galan, Augie (1934-1949)	.390
99	Clift, Harlond (1934-1945)	.390
100	Piazza, Mike (1992-2003)	.390

Slugging Average

1	Ruth, Babe (1914-1935)	.690
2	Williams, Ted (1939-1960)	.634
3	Gehrig, Lou (1923-1939)	.632
4	Foxx, Jimmie (1925-1945)	.609
5	Greenberg, Hank (1930-1947)	.605
6	Bonds, Barry (1986-2003)	.602
7	Ramirez, Manny (1993-2003)	.598
8	McGwire, Mark (1986-2001)	.588
9	Guerrero, Vladimir (1996-2003)	.588
10	Rodriguez, Alex (1994-2003)	.581
11	DiMaggio, Joe (1936-1951)	.579
12	Hornsby, Rogers (1915-1937)	.577
13	Piazza, Mike (1992-2003)	.572
14	Thome, Jim (1991-2003)	.568
15	Thomas, Frank (1990-2003)	.568
16	Walker, Larry (1989-2003)	.567
17	Belle, Albert (1989-2000)	.564
18	Gonzalez, Juan (1989-2003)	.563
19	Giles, Brian (1995-2003)	.563
20	Mize, Johnny (1936-1953)	.562
21	Griffey, Ken (1989-2003)	.562
22	Musial, Stan (1941-1963)	.559
23	Delgado, Carlos (1993-2003)	.558
24	Mays, Willie (1951-1973)	.557
25	Mantle, Mickey (1951-1968)	.557
26	Aaron, Hank (1954-1976)	.555
27	Giambi, Jason (1995-2003)	.549
28	Bagwell, Jeff (1991-2003)	.549
29	Kiner, Ralph (1946-1955)	.548
30	Sosa, Sammy (1989-2003)	.546
31	Wilson, Hack (1923-1934)	.545
32	Klein, Chuck (1928-1944)	.543
33	Jones, Chipper (1993-2003)	.541
34	Snider, Duke (1947-1964)	.540
35	Robinson, Frank (1956-1976)	.537
36	Simmons, Al (1924-1944)	.535
37	Allen, Dick (1963-1977)	.534
38	Averill, Earl (1929-1941)	.534
39	Ott, Mel (1926-1947)	.533
40	Edmonds, Jim (1993-2003)	.533
41	Herman, Babe (1926-1945)	.532
42	Williams, Ken (1915-1929)	.530
43	Stargell, Willie (1962-1982)	.529
44	Schmidt, Mike (1972-1989)	.527
45	Sheffield, Gary (1988-2003)	.527
46	Hafey, Chick (1924-1937)	.526
47	Martinez, Edgar (1987-2003)	.525
48	Vaughn, Mo (1991-2003)	.523
49	Palmeiro, Rafael (1986-2003)	.522
50	Trosky, Hal (1933-1946)	.522
51	Berger, Wally (1930-1940)	.522
52	Klesko, Ryan (1992-2003)	.521
53	Heilmann, Harry (1914-1932)	.520
54	Mitchell, Kevin (1984-1998)	.520
55	Brouthers, Dan (1879-1904)	.519
56	Keller, Charlie (1939-1952)	.518
57	Jackson, Joe (1908-1920)	.517
58	McCovey, Willie (1959-1980)	.515
59	Canseco, Jose (1985-2001)	.515
60	Green, Shawn (1993-2003)	.513
61	Abreu, Bobby (1996-2003)	.513
62	Cobb, Ty (1905-1928)	.512
63	Burks, Ellis (1987-2003)	.511
64	McGriff, Fred (1986-2003)	.511
65	Rolen, Scott (1996-2003)	.510
66	Mathews, Eddie (1952-1968)	.509
67	Heath, Jeff (1936-1949)	.509
68	Killebrew, Harmon (1954-1975)	.509
69	Alou, Moises (1990-2003)	.508
70	Salmon, Tim (1992-2003)	.506
71	Johnson, Bob (1933-1945)	.506
72	Terry, Bill (1923-1936)	.506
73	Thompson, Sam (1885-1906)	.506
74	Strawberry, Darryl (1983-1999)	.505
75	Delahanty, Ed (1888-1903)	.505
76	Medwick, Joe (1932-1948)	.505
77	Kent, Jeff (1992-2003)	.503
78	Rice, Jim (1974-1989)	.502
79	Lopez, Javy (1992-2003)	.502
80	Speaker, Tris (1907-1928)	.500
81	Justice, David (1989-2002)	.500
82	Bottomley, Jim (1922-1937)	.500
83	Stairs, Matt (1992-2003)	.500
84	Goslin, Goose (1921-1938)	.500
85	Campanella, Roy (1948-1957)	.500
86	Banks, Ernie (1953-1971)	.500
87	Cepeda, Orlando (1958-1974)	.499
88	Horner, Bob (1978-1988)	.499
89	Bichette, Dante (1988-2001)	.499
90	Galarraga, Andres (1985-2003)	.499
91	Howard, Frank (1958-1973)	.499
92	Kluszewski, Ted (1947-1961)	.498
93	Meusel, Bob (1920-1930)	.497
94	Clark, Will (1986-2000)	.497
95	Sauer, Hank (1941-1959)	.496
96	Floyd, Cliff (1993-2003)	.496
97	Tartabull, Danny (1984-1997)	.496
98	Rosen, Al (1947-1956)	.495
99	Jones, Andruw (1996-2003)	.494
100	Buhner, Jay (1987-2001)	.494

On-Base Plus Slugging

1	Ruth, Babe (1914-1935)	1164
2	Williams, Ted (1939-1960)	1116
3	Gehrig, Lou (1923-1939)	1080
4	Bonds, Barry (1986-2003)	1039
5	Foxx, Jimmie (1925-1945)	1038
6	Greenberg, Hank (1930-1947)	1017
7	Ramirez, Manny (1993-2003)	1014
8	Hornsby, Rogers (1915-1937)	1010
9	Thomas, Frank (1990-2003)	1002
10	McGwire, Mark (1986-2001)	986
11	Giles, Brian (1995-2003)	984
12	Thome, Jim (1991-2003)	982
13	Guerrero, Vladimir (1996-2003)	980
14	Mantle, Mickey (1951-1968)	979
15	Musial, Stan (1941-1963)	977
16	DiMaggio, Joe (1936-1951)	977
17	Walker, Larry (1989-2003)	971
18	Giambi, Jason (1995-2003)	969
19	Rodriguez, Alex (1994-2003)	966
20	Bagwell, Jeff (1991-2003)	964
21	Piazza, Mike (1992-2003)	962
22	Mize, Johnny (1936-1953)	959
23	Delgado, Carlos (1993-2003)	957
24	Martinez, Edgar (1987-2003)	952
25	Jones, Chipper (1993-2003)	949
26	Ott, Mel (1926-1947)	947
27	Kiner, Ralph (1946-1955)	946
28	Cobb, Ty (1905-1928)	945
29	Mays, Willie (1951-1973)	944
30	Griffey, Ken (1989-2003)	944
31	Brouthers, Dan (1879-1904)	942
32	Jackson, Joe (1908-1920)	940
33	Wilson, Hack (1923-1934)	940
34	Belle, Albert (1989-2000)	938
35	Sheffield, Gary (1988-2003)	933
36	Aaron, Hank (1954-1976)	932
37	Heilmann, Harry (1914-1932)	930
38	Robinson, Frank (1956-1976)	929
39	Averill, Earl (1929-1941)	928
40	Speaker, Tris (1907-1928)	928
41	Keller, Charlie (1939-1952)	928
42	Abreu, Bobby (1996-2003)	925
43	Williams, Ken (1915-1929)	924
44	Klein, Chuck (1928-1944)	922
45	Snider, Duke (1947-1964)	921
46	Delahanty, Ed (1888-1903)	916
47	Edmonds, Jim (1993-2003)	916
48	Herman, Babe (1926-1945)	915
49	Simmons, Al (1924-1944)	915
50	Allen, Dick (1963-1977)	914
51	Schmidt, Mike (1972-1989)	912
52	Gonzalez, Juan (1989-2003)	911
53	Vaughn, Mo (1991-2003)	909
54	Johnson, Bob (1933-1945)	899
55	Terry, Bill (1923-1936)	899
56	Salmon, Tim (1992-2003)	899
57	Hafey, Chick (1924-1937)	898
58	Sosa, Sammy (1989-2003)	898
59	Palmeiro, Rafael (1986-2003)	898
60	Cochrane, Mickey (1925-1937)	897
61	Klesko, Ryan (1992-2003)	895
62	Trosky, Hal (1933-1946)	892
63	McCovey, Willie (1959-1980)	892
64	Stargell, Willie (1962-1982)	892
65	McGriff, Fred (1986-2003)	891
66	Thompson, Sam (1885-1906)	890
67	Rolen, Scott (1996-2003)	888
68	Mathews, Eddie (1952-1968)	888
69	Hamilton, Billy (1888-1901)	888
70	Killebrew, Harmon (1954-1975)	887
71	Goslin, Goose (1921-1938)	887
72	Williams, Bernie (1991-2003)	885
73	Clark, Will (1986-2000)	885
74	Gehringer, Charlie (1924-1942)	884
75	Mitchell, Kevin (1984-1998)	883
76	Robinson, Jackie (1947-1956)	883
77	Connor, Roger (1880-1897)	883
78	Rosen, Al (1947-1956)	882
79	Justice, David (1989-2002)	881
80	Berger, Wally (1930-1940)	881
81	Camilli, Dolph (1933-1945)	880
82	Stephenson, Riggs (1921-1934)	880
83	Alou, Moises (1990-2003)	879
84	Heath, Jeff (1936-1949)	879
85	Burks, Ellis (1987-2003)	878
86	Waner, Paul (1926-1945)	878
87	Doby, Larry (1947-1959)	877
88	Olerud, John (1989-2003)	877
89	McGraw, John (1891-1906)	876
90	Fournier, Jack (1912-1927)	875
91	Henrich, Tommy (1937-1950)	873
92	Green, Shawn (1993-2003)	873
93	Canseco, Jose (1985-2001)	871
94	Bottomley, Jim (1922-1937)	869
95	Browning, Pete (1882-1894)	869
96	Greer, Rusty (1994-2002)	869
97	Dickey, Bill (1928-1946)	868
98	Tartabull, Danny (1984-1997)	867
99	Medwick, Joe (1932-1948)	867
100	Cash, Norm (1958-1974)	865

On-Base Plus Slugging Adjusted

1	Ruth, Babe (1914-1935)	209
2	Williams, Ted (1939-1960)	187
3	Bonds, Barry (1986-2003)	183
4	Gehrig, Lou (1923-1939)	182
5	Hornsby, Rogers (1915-1937)	175
6	Mantle, Mickey (1951-1968)	173
7	Brouthers, Dan (1879-1904)	170
8	Cobb, Ty (1905-1928)	168
9	Jackson, Joe (1908-1920)	168
10	Thomas, Frank (1990-2003)	165
11	McGwire, Mark (1986-2001)	164
12	Browning, Pete (1882-1894)	164
13	Foxx, Jimmie (1925-1945)	161
14	Musial, Stan (1941-1963)	157
15	Speaker, Tris (1907-1928)	157
16	Allen, Dick (1963-1977)	157
17	Mize, Johnny (1936-1953)	157
18	Greenberg, Hank (1930-1947)	156
19	Mays, Willie (1951-1973)	156
20	DiMaggio, Joe (1936-1951)	156
21	Aaron, Hank (1954-1976)	156
22	Ramirez, Manny (1993-2003)	156
23	Piazza, Mike (1992-2003)	156
24	Ott, Mel (1926-1947)	155
25	Connor, Roger (1880-1897)	155
26	Bagwell, Jeff (1991-2003)	154
27	Robinson, Frank (1956-1976)	154
28	Keller, Charlie (1939-1952)	153
29	Giambi, Jason (1995-2003)	153
30	Delahanty, Ed (1888-1903)	152
31	Thome, Jim (1991-2003)	151
32	Martinez, Edgar (1987-2003)	151
33	Wagner, Honus (1897-1917)	151
34	Giles, Brian (1995-2003)	150
35	Lajoie, Nap (1896-1916)	150
36	Flick, Elmer (1898-1910)	149
37	Cravath, Gavvy (1908-1920)	149
38	McCovey, Willie (1959-1980)	148
39	Sheffield, Gary (1988-2003)	148
40	Kiner, Ralph (1946-1955)	148
41	Stargell, Willie (1962-1982)	148
42	Heilmann, Harry (1914-1932)	148
43	Schmidt, Mike (1972-1989)	147
44	Thompson, Sam (1885-1906)	146
45	Guerrero, Vladimir (1996-2003)	145
46	Mathews, Eddie (1952-1968)	145
47	Belle, Albert (1989-2000)	144
48	Griffey, Ken (1989-2003)	144
49	Wilson, Hack (1923-1934)	144
50	Rodriguez, Alex (1994-2003)	144
51	Howard, Frank (1958-1973)	144
52	Mitchell, Kevin (1984-1998)	144
53	Crawford, Sam (1899-1917)	143
54	Collins, Eddie (1906-1930)	143
55	Donlin, Mike (1899-1914)	143
56	Delgado, Carlos (1993-2003)	142
57	Fournier, Jack (1912-1927)	142
58	Killebrew, Harmon (1954-1975)	142
59	Jones, Chipper (1993-2003)	142
60	Stovey, Harry (1880-1893)	142
61	Larkin, Henry (1884-1893)	141
62	Heath, Jeff (1936-1949)	141
63	Herman, Babe (1926-1945)	141
64	Jackson, Reggie (1967-1987)	140
65	Berger, Wally (1930-1940)	140
66	Abreu, Bobby (1996-2003)	140
67	Strawberry, Darryl (1983-1999)	140
68	Hamilton, Billy (1888-1901)	139
69	Tiernan, Mike (1887-1899)	139
70	Burkett, Jesse (1890-1905)	139
71	Clark, Will (1986-2000)	139
72	O'Neill, Tip (1883-1892)	139
73	Lyons, Denny (1885-1897)	139
74	Johnson, Bob (1933-1945)	139
75	Guerrero, Pedro (1978-1992)	139
76	Rosen, Al (1947-1956)	139
77	Anson, Cap (1871-1897)	138
78	Snider, Duke (1947-1964)	138
79	Clark, Jack (1975-1992)	138
80	Cash, Norm (1958-1974)	137
81	Tenace, Gene (1969-1983)	137
82	Doby, Larry (1947-1959)	137
83	Smith, Reggie (1966-1982)	137
84	Kelly, King (1878-1893)	137
85	Baker, Frank (1908-1922)	136
86	Terry, Bill (1923-1936)	136
87	Magee, Sherry (1904-1919)	136
88	Burns, Oyster (1884-1895)	136
89	Vaughan, Arky (1932-1948)	135
90	Edmonds, Jim (1993-2003)	135
91	Brett, George (1973-1993)	135
92	Williams, Ken (1915-1929)	135
93	Chance, Frank (1898-1914)	135
94	McGriff, Fred (1986-2003)	135
95	McGraw, John (1891-1906)	135
96	Palmeiro, Rafael (1986-2003)	134
97	Camilli, Dolph (1933-1945)	134
98	O'Rourke, Jim (1872-1904)	134
99	Walker, Larry (1989-2003)	134
100	Gore, George (1879-1892)	134

The All-Time Leaders: Batters – Lifetime 2445

Batting Runs

1	Ruth, Babe (1914-1935)	1370
2	Williams, Ted (1939-1960)	1196
3	Bonds, Barry (1986-2003)	1073
4	Cobb, Ty (1905-1928)	1039
5	Musial, Stan (1941-1963)	991
6	Gehrig, Lou (1923-1939)	921
7	Aaron, Hank (1954-1976)	910
8	Mays, Willie (1951-1973)	871
9	Hornsby, Rogers (1915-1937)	845
10	Mantle, Mickey (1951-1968)	843
11	Speaker, Tris (1907-1928)	840
12	Foxx, Jimmie (1925-1945)	813
13	Robinson, Frank (1956-1976)	803
14	Ott, Mel (1926-1947)	785
15	Wagner, Honus (1897-1917)	667
16	Thomas, Frank (1990-2003)	651
17	Brouthers, Dan (1879-1904)	644
18	Collins, Eddie (1906-1930)	623
19	Yastrzemski, Carl (1961-1983)	623
20	Henderson, Rickey (1979-2003)	621
21	Schmidt, Mike (1972-1989)	601
22	Bagwell, Jeff (1991-2003)	589
23	McGwire, Mark (1986-2001)	557
24	Connor, Roger (1880-1897)	555
25	Anson, Cap (1871-1897)	554
26	Lajoie, Nap (1896-1916)	549
27	Killebrew, Harmon (1954-1975)	547
28	Martinez, Edgar (1987-2003)	541
29	Morgan, Joe (1963-1984)	538
30	McCovey, Willie (1959-1980)	535
31	Delahanty, Ed (1888-1903)	527
32	Kaline, Al (1953-1974)	526
33	Mize, Johnny (1936-1953)	526
34	Walker, Larry (1989-2003)	519
35	Brett, George (1973-1993)	518
36	Heilmann, Harry (1914-1932)	518
37	DiMaggio, Joe (1936-1951)	517
38	Burkett, Jesse (1890-1905)	512
39	Palmeiro, Rafael (1986-2003)	499
40	Waner, Paul (1926-1945)	497
41	Mathews, Eddie (1952-1968)	496
42	Boggs, Wade (1982-1999)	491
43	Crawford, Sam (1899-1917)	489
44	Stargell, Willie (1962-1982)	487
45	Allen, Dick (1963-1977)	486
46	Hamilton, Billy (1888-1901)	485
47	Jackson, Reggie (1967-1987)	480
48	Greenberg, Hank (1930-1947)	480
49	Sheffield, Gary (1988-2003)	475
50	Griffey, Ken (1989-2003)	474
51	Williams, Billy (1959-1976)	470
52	McGriff, Fred (1986-2003)	453
53	Ramirez, Manny (1993-2003)	450
54	Jackson, Joe (1908-1920)	444
55	Snider, Duke (1947-1964)	442
56	Thome, Jim (1991-2003)	437
57	Carew, Rod (1967-1985)	434
58	Murray, Eddie (1977-1997)	431
59	Raines, Tim (1979-2002)	430
60	Evans, Dwight (1972-1991)	423
61	Gwynn, Tony (1982-2001)	407
62	Kiner, Ralph (1946-1955)	403
63	Rose, Pete (1963-1986)	403
64	Cash, Norm (1958-1974)	398
65	Simmons, Al (1924-1944)	397
66	Gehringer, Charlie (1924-1942)	393
67	Winfield, Dave (1973-1995)	392
68	Molitor, Paul (1978-1998)	385
69	Kelley, Joe (1891-1908)	382
70	Clarke, Fred (1894-1915)	381
71	Smith, Reggie (1966-1982)	377
72	Klein, Chuck (1928-1944)	376
73	Johnson, Bob (1933-1945)	372
74	Clark, Will (1986-2000)	372
75	Vaughan, Arky (1932-1948)	369
76	Rice, Jim (1974-1989)	367
77	Clark, Jack (1975-1992)	367
78	Thompson, Sam (1885-1906)	363
79	Jones, Chipper (1993-2003)	363
80	Browning, Pete (1882-1894)	358
81	Goslin, Goose (1921-1938)	357
82	Giambi, Jason (1995-2003)	357
83	Piazza, Mike (1992-2003)	354
84	Olerud, John (1989-2003)	354
85	Rodriguez, Alex (1994-2003)	354
86	Clemente, Roberto (1955-1972)	353
87	Stovey, Harry (1880-1893)	350
88	Belle, Albert (1989-2000)	350
89	Medwick, Joe (1932-1948)	349
90	Flick, Elmer (1898-1910)	347
91	Santo, Ron (1960-1974)	347
92	Keeler, Willie (1892-1910)	340
93	Cepeda, Orlando (1958-1974)	336
94	Singleton, Ken (1970-1984)	335
95	Averill, Earl (1929-1941)	335
96	Wheat, Zack (1909-1927)	334
97	Magee, Sherry (1904-1919)	332
98	Sosa, Sammy (1989-2003)	330
99	Howard, Frank (1958-1973)	329
100	Camilli, Dolph (1933-1945)	329

Adjusted Batting Runs

1	Ruth, Babe (1914-1935)	1429
2	Bonds, Barry (1986-2003)	1163
3	Williams, Ted (1939-1960)	1069
4	Cobb, Ty (1905-1928)	1015
5	Gehrig, Lou (1923-1939)	1006
6	Aaron, Hank (1954-1976)	951
7	Musial, Stan (1941-1963)	913
8	Mantle, Mickey (1951-1968)	903
9	Mays, Willie (1951-1973)	889
10	Hornsby, Rogers (1915-1937)	873
11	Speaker, Tris (1907-1928)	796
12	Ott, Mel (1926-1947)	794
13	Robinson, Frank (1956-1976)	775
14	Foxx, Jimmie (1925-1945)	761
15	Henderson, Rickey (1979-2003)	721
16	Thomas, Frank (1990-2003)	680
17	Wagner, Honus (1897-1917)	642
18	Collins, Eddie (1906-1930)	637
19	Brouthers, Dan (1879-1904)	621
20	Bagwell, Jeff (1991-2003)	617
21	McGwire, Mark (1986-2001)	604
22	Morgan, Joe (1963-1984)	582
23	Mathews, Eddie (1952-1968)	576
24	Connor, Roger (1880-1897)	558
25	Schmidt, Mike (1972-1989)	554
26	Martinez, Edgar (1987-2003)	554
27	McCovey, Willie (1959-1980)	554
28	Lajoie, Nap (1896-1916)	552
29	Delahanty, Ed (1888-1903)	546
30	DiMaggio, Joe (1936-1951)	539
31	Jackson, Reggie (1967-1987)	534
32	Heilmann, Harry (1914-1932)	533
33	Sheffield, Gary (1988-2003)	509
34	Killebrew, Harmon (1954-1975)	498
35	Mize, Johnny (1936-1953)	498
36	Brett, George (1973-1993)	496
37	Stargell, Willie (1962-1982)	492
38	Yastrzemski, Carl (1961-1983)	492
39	Burkett, Jesse (1890-1905)	488
40	Allen, Dick (1963-1977)	485
41	Kaline, Al (1953-1974)	480
42	Palmeiro, Rafael (1986-2003)	476
43	Waner, Paul (1926-1945)	473
44	Murray, Eddie (1977-1997)	472
45	Crawford, Sam (1899-1917)	465
46	Griffey, Ken (1989-2003)	460
47	Winfield, Dave (1973-1995)	453
48	Gwynn, Tony (1982-2001)	451
49	Raines, Tim (1979-2002)	451
50	Boggs, Wade (1982-1999)	447
51	McGriff, Fred (1986-2003)	440
52	Anson, Cap (1871-1897)	439
53	Greenberg, Hank (1930-1947)	437
54	Hamilton, Billy (1888-1901)	435
55	Thome, Jim (1991-2003)	431
56	Ramirez, Manny (1993-2003)	426
57	Jackson, Joe (1908-1920)	426
58	Piazza, Mike (1992-2003)	417
59	Carew, Rod (1967-1985)	413
60	Molitor, Paul (1978-1998)	402
61	Clark, Will (1986-2000)	394
62	Johnson, Bob (1933-1945)	394
63	Snider, Duke (1947-1964)	393
64	Browning, Pete (1882-1894)	386
65	Williams, Billy (1959-1976)	385
66	Giambi, Jason (1995-2003)	377
67	Clark, Jack (1975-1992)	377
68	Clarke, Fred (1894-1915)	377
69	Kiner, Ralph (1946-1955)	376
70	Olerud, John (1989-2003)	374
71	Belle, Albert (1989-2000)	368
72	Goslin, Goose (1921-1938)	365
73	Howard, Frank (1958-1973)	365
74	Simmons, Al (1924-1944)	364
75	Clemente, Roberto (1955-1972)	363
76	Singleton, Ken (1970-1984)	362
77	Cash, Norm (1958-1974)	361
78	Vaughan, Arky (1932-1948)	361
79	Rose, Pete (1963-1986)	357
80	Flick, Elmer (1898-1910)	357
81	Gehringer, Charlie (1924-1942)	352
82	Walker, Larry (1989-2003)	349
83	Jones, Chipper (1993-2003)	349
84	Thompson, Sam (1885-1906)	348
85	Sosa, Sammy (1989-2003)	346
86	Staub, Rusty (1963-1985)	345
87	Evans, Dwight (1972-1991)	343
88	Smith, Reggie (1966-1982)	342
89	Cepeda, Orlando (1958-1974)	340
90	Rodriguez, Alex (1994-2003)	338
91	Terry, Bill (1923-1936)	337
92	Wheat, Zack (1909-1927)	336
93	Kelley, Joe (1891-1908)	333
94	Magee, Sherry (1904-1919)	325
95	Herman, Babe (1926-1945)	325
96	Canseco, Jose (1985-2001)	324
97	Hernandez, Keith (1974-1990)	319
98	Tiernan, Mike (1887-1899)	318
99	Wilson, Hack (1923-1934)	318
100	Powell, Boog (1961-1977)	314

Runs Created

1	Ruth, Babe (1914-1935)	2849
2	Cobb, Ty (1905-1928)	2810
3	Musial, Stan (1941-1963)	2625
4	Aaron, Hank (1954-1976)	2550
5	Williams, Ted (1939-1960)	2539
6	Bonds, Barry (1986-2003)	2480
7	Mays, Willie (1951-1973)	2372
8	Speaker, Tris (1907-1928)	2325
9	Gehrig, Lou (1923-1939)	2321
10	Wagner, Honus (1897-1917)	2239
11	Ott, Mel (1926-1947)	2235
12	Rose, Pete (1963-1986)	2220
13	Foxx, Jimmie (1925-1945)	2191
14	Henderson, Rickey (1979-2003)	2167
15	Yastrzemski, Carl (1961-1983)	2147
16	Robinson, Frank (1956-1976)	2127
17	Hornsby, Rogers (1915-1937)	2074
18	Mantle, Mickey (1951-1968)	2069
19	Collins, Eddie (1906-1930)	2062
20	Murray, Eddie (1977-1997)	1939
21	Lajoie, Nap (1896-1916)	1907
22	Palmeiro, Rafael (1986-2003)	1896
23	Brett, George (1973-1993)	1878
24	Molitor, Paul (1978-1998)	1872
25	Waner, Paul (1926-1945)	1853
26	Kaline, Al (1953-1974)	1846
27	Delahanty, Ed (1888-1903)	1832
28	Winfield, Dave (1973-1995)	1813
29	Morgan, Joe (1963-1984)	1804
30	Burkett, Jesse (1890-1905)	1801
31	Gehringer, Charlie (1924-1942)	1787
32	Simmons, Al (1924-1944)	1777
33	Jackson, Reggie (1967-1987)	1772
34	Schmidt, Mike (1972-1989)	1757
35	Anson, Cap (1871-1897)	1756
36	Boggs, Wade (1982-1999)	1751
37	Mathews, Eddie (1952-1968)	1738
38	Ripken, Cal (1981-2001)	1728
39	Crawford, Sam (1899-1917)	1716
40	Hamilton, Billy (1888-1901)	1708
41	Goslin, Goose (1921-1938)	1707
42	McGriff, Fred (1986-2003)	1698
43	Heilmann, Harry (1914-1932)	1698
44	Thomas, Frank (1990-2003)	1687
45	Keeler, Willie (1892-1910)	1686
46	Beckley, Jake (1888-1907)	1686
47	Clarke, Fred (1894-1915)	1679
48	Williams, Billy (1959-1976)	1671
49	Bagwell, Jeff (1991-2003)	1668
50	Yount, Robin (1974-1993)	1655
51	Connor, Roger (1880-1897)	1647
52	McCovey, Willie (1959-1980)	1638
53	Davis, George (1890-1909)	1637
54	Raines, Tim (1979-2002)	1636
55	Gwynn, Tony (1982-2001)	1634
56	Brouthers, Dan (1879-1904)	1622
57	Evans, Dwight (1972-1991)	1611
58	Killebrew, Harmon (1954-1975)	1609
59	Baines, Harold (1980-2001)	1608
60	DiMaggio, Joe (1936-1951)	1606
61	Carew, Rod (1967-1985)	1595
62	Van Haltren, George (1887-1903)	1568
63	Martinez, Edgar (1987-2003)	1567
64	Ryan, Jimmy (1885-1903)	1560
65	Clemente, Roberto (1955-1972)	1557
66	Alomar, Roberto (1988-2003)	1557
67	Wheat, Zack (1909-1927)	1540
68	Griffey, Ken (1989-2003)	1535
69	Staub, Rusty (1963-1985)	1534
70	Kelley, Joe (1891-1908)	1533
71	Stargell, Willie (1962-1982)	1531
72	McGwire, Mark (1986-2001)	1530
73	Perez, Tony (1964-1986)	1523
74	Dawson, Andre (1976-1996)	1519
75	Biggio, Craig (1988-2003)	1513
76	Banks, Ernie (1953-1971)	1513
77	Brock, Lou (1961-1979)	1512
78	Duffy, Hugh (1888-1906)	1509
79	Dahlen, Bill (1891-1911)	1509
80	Mize, Johnny (1936-1953)	1502
81	Rice, Sam (1915-1934)	1501
82	Evans, Darrell (1969-1989)	1499
83	Sisler, George (1915-1930)	1498
84	Appling, Luke (1930-1950)	1493
85	Sheffield, Gary (1988-2003)	1491
86	Walker, Larry (1989-2003)	1489
87	Snider, Duke (1947-1964)	1487
88	Carey, Max (1910-1929)	1472
89	Frisch, Frankie (1919-1937)	1464
90	Parker, Dave (1973-1991)	1452
91	Sosa, Sammy (1989-2003)	1443
92	Slaughter, Enos (1938-1959)	1432
93	Cronin, Joe (1926-1945)	1426
94	Johnson, Bob (1933-1945)	1418
95	Clark, Will (1986-2000)	1417
96	Davis, Chili (1981-1999)	1416
97	Grace, Mark (1988-2003)	1404
98	Whitaker, Lou (1977-1995)	1396
99	Pinson, Vada (1958-1975)	1394
100	Manush, Heinie (1923-1939)	1389

Runs Created per Game

1	Ruth, Babe (1914-1935)	13.09
2	Williams, Ted (1939-1960)	12.96
3	Gehrig, Lou (1923-1939)	11.21
4	Hamilton, Billy (1888-1901)	10.91
5	Bonds, Barry (1986-2003)	10.31
6	Foxx, Jimmie (1925-1945)	10.22
7	McGraw, John (1891-1906)	9.88
8	Brouthers, Dan (1879-1904)	9.86
9	Hornsby, Rogers (1915-1937)	9.86
10	Delahanty, Ed (1888-1903)	9.81
11	Greenberg, Hank (1930-1947)	9.63
12	Cobb, Ty (1905-1928)	9.54
13	Mantle, Mickey (1951-1968)	9.47
14	Thomas, Frank (1990-2003)	9.34
15	Ramirez, Manny (1993-2003)	9.25
16	Musial, Stan (1941-1963)	9.20
17	DiMaggio, Joe (1936-1951)	9.06
18	Thome, Jim (1991-2003)	9.03
19	Giles, Brian (1995-2003)	8.97
20	Browning, Pete (1882-1894)	8.93
21	Mize, Johnny (1936-1953)	8.91
22	Giambi, Jason (1995-2003)	8.81
23	Ott, Mel (1926-1947)	8.81
24	Jackson, Joe (1908-1920)	8.79
25	Walker, Larry (1989-2003)	8.70
26	Thompson, Sam (1885-1906)	8.67
27	Martinez, Edgar (1987-2003)	8.64
28	McGwire, Mark (1986-2001)	8.61
29	Speaker, Tris (1907-1928)	8.56
30	Keller, Charlie (1939-1952)	8.52
31	Burkett, Jesse (1890-1905)	8.45
32	Delgado, Carlos (1993-2003)	8.40
33	Bagwell, Jeff (1991-2003)	8.39
34	Kiner, Ralph (1946-1955)	8.32
35	Tiernan, Mike (1887-1899)	8.31
36	Rodriguez, Alex (1994-2003)	8.30
37	Connor, Roger (1880-1897)	8.30
38	Kelley, Joe (1891-1908)	8.26
39	Duffy, Hugh (1888-1906)	8.26
40	Jones, Chipper (1993-2003)	8.26
41	Heilmann, Harry (1914-1932)	8.19
42	O'Neill, Tip (1883-1892)	8.16
43	Averill, Earl (1929-1941)	8.09
44	Wagner, Honus (1897-1917)	8.07
45	Abreu, Bobby (1996-2003)	8.07
46	Klein, Chuck (1928-1944)	8.05
47	Lyons, Denny (1885-1897)	8.02
48	Guerrero, Vladimir (1996-2003)	7.98
49	Wilson, Hack (1923-1934)	7.96
50	Mays, Willie (1951-1973)	7.95
51	Sheffield, Gary (1988-2003)	7.94
52	Piazza, Mike (1992-2003)	7.93
53	Griffey, Ken (1989-2003)	7.85
54	Donlin, Mike (1899-1914)	7.85
55	Simmons, Al (1924-1944)	7.82
56	Cochrane, Mickey (1925-1937)	7.74
57	Stovey, Harry (1880-1893)	7.73
58	Anson, Cap (1871-1897)	7.71
59	Herman, Babe (1926-1945)	7.66
60	Smith, Elmer (1886-1901)	7.64
61	Robinson, Frank (1956-1976)	7.63
62	Flick, Elmer (1898-1910)	7.63
63	Lajoie, Nap (1896-1916)	7.62
64	Terry, Bill (1923-1936)	7.60
65	Vaughan, Arky (1932-1948)	7.57
66	Gehringer, Charlie (1924-1942)	7.57
67	Williams, Ken (1915-1929)	7.56
68	Camilli, Dolph (1933-1945)	7.55
69	Edmonds, Jim (1993-2003)	7.54
70	Aaron, Hank (1954-1976)	7.54
71	Kelly, King (1878-1893)	7.52
72	Van Haltren, George (1887-1903)	7.52
73	Snider, Duke (1947-1964)	7.51
74	Jennings, Hughie (1891-1918)	7.50
75	Johnson, Bob (1933-1945)	7.49
76	Robinson, Jackie (1947-1956)	7.49
77	Salmon, Tim (1992-2003)	7.49
78	Waner, Paul (1926-1945)	7.43
79	Keeler, Willie (1892-1910)	7.43
80	Vaughn, Mo (1991-2003)	7.40
81	Stephenson, Riggs (1921-1934)	7.39
82	Collins, Eddie (1906-1930)	7.38
83	Trosky, Hal (1933-1946)	7.36
84	Griffin, Mike (1887-1898)	7.35
85	Ewing, Buck (1880-1897)	7.34
86	Belle, Albert (1989-2000)	7.33
87	Goslin, Goose (1921-1938)	7.33
88	Burns, Oyster (1884-1895)	7.32
89	Schmidt, Mike (1972-1989)	7.31
90	Allen, Dick (1963-1977)	7.30
91	Clark, Will (1986-2000)	7.27
92	Ryan, Jimmy (1885-1903)	7.26
93	Mathews, Eddie (1952-1968)	7.24
94	Hafey, Chick (1924-1937)	7.24
95	Doby, Larry (1947-1959)	7.23
96	Clarke, Fred (1894-1915)	7.21
97	Boggs, Wade (1982-1999)	7.20
98	Henrich, Tommy (1937-1950)	7.20
99	Heath, Jeff (1936-1949)	7.18
100	Palmeiro, Rafael (1986-2003)	7.17

Adjusted Batting Wins

1	Ruth, Babe (1914-1935)	123.5
2	Bonds, Barry (1986-2003)	106.0
3	Hornsby, Rogers (1915-1937)	94.3
4	Williams, Ted (1939-1960)	93.5
5	Cobb, Ty (1905-1928)	89.7
6	Mantle, Mickey (1951-1968)	82.7
7	Aaron, Hank (1954-1976)	81.5
8	Mays, Willie (1951-1973)	80.4
9	Musial, Stan (1941-1963)	78.2
10	Morgan, Joe (1963-1984)	78.1
11	Gehrig, Lou (1923-1939)	77.3
12	Wagner, Honus (1897-1917)	74.7
13	Collins, Eddie (1906-1930)	71.2
14	Speaker, Tris (1907-1928)	66.4
15	Ott, Mel (1926-1947)	64.9
16	Robinson, Frank (1956-1976)	64.7
17	Henderson, Rickey (1979-2003)	60.4
18	Lajoie, Nap (1896-1916)	59.3
19	Mathews, Eddie (1952-1968)	56.8
20	Foxx, Jimmie (1925-1945)	56.0
21	Schmidt, Mike (1972-1989)	55.3
22	Thomas, Frank (1990-2003)	52.2
23	Piazza, Mike (1992-2003)	50.0
24	DiMaggio, Joe (1936-1951)	47.2
25	Vaughan, Arky (1932-1948)	47.2
26	Brouthers, Dan (1879-1904)	45.7
27	Martinez, Edgar (1987-2003)	45.1
28	Sheffield, Gary (1988-2003)	45.0
29	McGwire, Mark (1986-2001)	44.9
30	Allen, Dick (1963-1977)	44.0
31	Bagwell, Jeff (1991-2003)	44.0
32	Griffey, Ken (1989-2003)	43.8
33	Boggs, Wade (1982-1999)	43.5
34	Killebrew, Harmon (1954-1975)	43.3
35	Gehringer, Charlie (1924-1942)	43.1
36	McCovey, Willie (1959-1980)	43.0
37	Jackson, Reggie (1967-1987)	42.9
38	Carew, Rod (1967-1985)	42.8
39	Brett, George (1973-1993)	42.6
40	Rodriguez, Alex (1994-2003)	41.4
41	Connor, Roger (1880-1897)	41.3
42	Larkin, Barry (1986-2003)	40.3
43	Ripken, Cal (1981-2001)	39.7
44	Delahanty, Ed (1888-1903)	39.2
45	Mize, Johnny (1936-1953)	38.9
46	Grich, Bobby (1970-1986)	38.8
47	Heilmann, Harry (1914-1932)	38.6
48	Stargell, Willie (1962-1982)	38.5
49	Biggio, Craig (1988-2003)	38.1
50	Yount, Robin (1974-1993)	37.9
51	Jackson, Joe (1908-1920)	37.7
52	Raines, Tim (1979-2002)	37.2
53	Appling, Luke (1930-1950)	37.0
54	Crawford, Sam (1899-1917)	36.9
55	Kaline, Al (1953-1974)	36.0
56	Alomar, Roberto (1988-2003)	36.0
57	Gwynn, Tony (1982-2001)	35.5
58	Cronin, Joe (1926-1945)	35.0
59	Bench, Johnny (1967-1983)	34.5
60	Jones, Chipper (1993-2003)	34.3
61	Dickey, Bill (1928-1946)	34.0
62	Hartnett, Gabby (1922-1941)	33.9
63	Winfield, Dave (1973-1995)	33.3
64	Yastrzemski, Carl (1961-1983)	33.2
65	Trammell, Alan (1977-1996)	33.2
66	Ramirez, Manny (1993-2003)	33.2
67	Molitor, Paul (1978-1998)	33.1
68	Thome, Jim (1991-2003)	32.9
69	Whitaker, Lou (1977-1995)	32.8
70	Berra, Yogi (1946-1965)	32.2
71	Snider, Duke (1947-1964)	31.7
72	Cochrane, Mickey (1925-1937)	31.6
73	Greenberg, Hank (1930-1947)	31.6
74	Baker, Frank (1908-1922)	31.2
75	Waner, Paul (1926-1945)	31.0
76	Fisk, Carlton (1969-1993)	30.3
77	Torre, Joe (1960-1977)	30.3
78	Hack, Stan (1932-1947)	30.3
79	Burkett, Jesse (1890-1905)	30.2
80	Boudreau, Lou (1938-1952)	30.2
81	Browning, Pete (1882-1894)	30.1
82	Williams, Bernie (1991-2003)	29.9
83	Rose, Pete (1963-1986)	29.5
84	Hamilton, Billy (1888-1901)	29.4
85	Lazzeri, Tony (1926-1939)	29.4
86	Anson, Cap (1871-1897)	29.3
87	Harrah, Toby (1969-1986)	29.2
88	Flick, Elmer (1898-1910)	29.1
89	Howard, Frank (1958-1973)	29.0
90	Clark, Jack (1975-1992)	28.9
91	Santo, Ron (1960-1974)	28.8
92	Lombardi, Ernie (1931-1947)	28.5
93	Johnson, Bob (1933-1945)	28.4
94	Robinson, Jackie (1947-1956)	28.3
95	Murray, Eddie (1977-1997)	28.3
96	Davis, George (1890-1909)	28.1
97	Belle, Albert (1989-2000)	28.1
98	Kiner, Ralph (1946-1955)	28.0
99	Smith, Reggie (1966-1982)	27.8
100	Singleton, Ken (1970-1984)	27.7

Extra Base Hits

1	Aaron, Hank (1954-1976)	1477
2	Musial, Stan (1941-1963)	1377
3	Ruth, Babe (1914-1935)	1356
4	Mays, Willie (1951-1973)	1323
5	Bonds, Barry (1986-2003)	1268
6	Gehrig, Lou (1923-1939)	1190
7	Robinson, Frank (1956-1976)	1186
8	Yastrzemski, Carl (1961-1983)	1157
9	Cobb, Ty (1905-1928)	1136
10	Speaker, Tris (1907-1928)	1131
11	Brett, George (1973-1993)	1119
12	Foxx, Jimmie (1925-1945)	1117
	Williams, Ted (1939-1960)	1117
14	Palmeiro, Rafael (1986-2003)	1109
15	Murray, Eddie (1977-1997)	1099
16	Winfield, Dave (1973-1995)	1093
17	Ripken, Cal (1981-2001)	1078
18	Jackson, Reggie (1967-1987)	1075
19	Ott, Mel (1926-1947)	1071
20	Rose, Pete (1963-1986)	1041
21	Dawson, Andre (1976-1996)	1039
22	Schmidt, Mike (1972-1989)	1015
23	Hornsby, Rogers (1915-1937)	1011
24	Banks, Ernie (1953-1971)	1009
25	Wagner, Honus (1897-1917)	996
26	Simmons, Al (1924-1944)	995
27	Kaline, Al (1953-1974)	972
28	Perez, Tony (1964-1986)	963
29	Yount, Robin (1974-1993)	960
30	McGriff, Fred (1986-2003)	953
	Molitor, Paul (1978-1998)	953
	Stargell, Willie (1962-1982)	953
33	Mantle, Mickey (1951-1968)	952
34	Williams, Billy (1959-1976)	948
35	Evans, Dwight (1972-1991)	941
36	Parker, Dave (1973-1991)	940
37	Mathews, Eddie (1952-1968)	938
38	Baines, Harold (1980-2001)	921
	Goslin, Goose (1921-1938)	921
40	McCovey, Willie (1959-1980)	920
41	Waner, Paul (1926-1945)	909
42	Bagwell, Jeff (1991-2003)	904
	Gehringer, Charlie (1924-1942)	904
44	Lajoie, Nap (1896-1916)	903
45	Sosa, Sammy (1989-2003)	901
46	Griffey, Ken (1989-2003)	899
47	Killebrew, Harmon (1954-1975)	887
48	Carter, Joe (1983-1998)	881
	DiMaggio, Joe (1936-1951)	881
50	Heilmann, Harry (1914-1932)	876
51	Galarraga, Andres (1985-2003)	874
52	Henderson, Rickey (1979-2003)	873
53	Pinson, Vada (1958-1975)	868
54	Crawford, Sam (1899-1917)	864
55	Medwick, Joe (1932-1948)	858
56	Thomas, Frank (1990-2003)	857
57	Snider, Duke (1947-1964)	850
58	Clemente, Roberto (1955-1972)	846
59	Fisk, Carlton (1969-1993)	844
60	Walker, Larry (1989-2003)	843
61	Gaetti, Gary (1981-2000)	842
62	McGwire, Mark (1986-2001)	841
63	Staub, Rusty (1963-1985)	838
64	Gonzalez, Juan (1989-2003)	837
65	Bottomley, Jim (1922-1937)	835
66	Rice, Jim (1974-1989)	834
67	Oliver, Al (1968-1985)	825
68	Cepeda, Orlando (1958-1974)	823
69	Robinson, Brooks (1955-1977)	818
70	Burks, Ellis (1987-2003)	816
	Canseco, Jose (1985-2001)	816
72	Morgan, Joe (1963-1984)	813
73	Connor, Roger (1880-1897)	812
74	Delahanty, Ed (1888-1903)	809
	Mize, Johnny (1936-1953)	809
76	Beckley, Jake (1888-1907)	804
	Davis, Chili (1981-1999)	804
78	Cronin, Joe (1926-1945)	803
	Martinez, Edgar (1987-2003)	803
80	Bench, Johnny (1967-1983)	794
81	Belle, Albert (1989-2000)	791
82	Murphy, Dale (1976-1993)	787
83	Alomar, Roberto (1988-2003)	782
	Vernon, Mickey (1939-1960)	782
85	Greenberg, Hank (1930-1947)	781
86	Wheat, Zack (1909-1927)	780
87	Evans, Darrell (1969-1989)	779
	Johnson, Bob (1933-1945)	779
89	Biggio, Craig (1988-2003)	778
	Simmons, Ted (1968-1988)	778
91	Brock, Lou (1961-1979)	776
92	Santo, Ron (1960-1974)	774
93	Klein, Chuck (1928-1944)	772
94	Brouthers, Dan (1879-1904)	771
	Clark, Will (1986-2000)	771
96	Averill, Earl (1929-1941)	767
97	Gonzalez, Luis (1990-2003)	763
	Gwynn, Tony (1982-2001)	763
99	Manush, Heinie (1923-1939)	761
	Sandberg, Ryne (1981-1997)	761

Total Player Wins/150G

1	Ruth, Babe (1914-1935)	8.01
2	Bonds, Barry (1986-2003)	6.49
3	Williams, Ted (1939-1960)	6.12
4	Hornsby, Rogers (1915-1937)	5.72
5	Lajoie, Nap (1896-1916)	5.66
6	Wagner, Honus (1897-1917)	5.51
7	Gehrig, Lou (1923-1939)	5.17
8	Schmidt, Mike (1972-1989)	5.14
9	Mantle, Mickey (1951-1968)	5.10
10	Piazza, Mike (1992-2003)	5.02
11	Rodriguez, Alex (1994-2003)	5.01
12	Collins, Eddie (1906-1930)	4.74
13	Mays, Willie (1951-1973)	4.49
14	Cobb, Ty (1905-1928)	4.48
15	Morgan, Joe (1963-1984)	4.42
16	Speaker, Tris (1907-1928)	4.41
17	Boudreau, Lou (1938-1952)	4.38
18	Robinson, Jackie (1947-1956)	4.37
19	Grich, Bobby (1970-1986)	4.35
20	Vaughan, Arky (1932-1948)	4.19
21	Jackson, Joe (1908-1920)	4.09
22	DiMaggio, Joe (1936-1951)	4.09
23	Rolen, Scott (1996-2003)	4.04
24	Musial, Stan (1941-1963)	3.94
25	Brouthers, Dan (1879-1904)	3.90
26	Aaron, Hank (1954-1976)	3.89
27	Foxx, Jimmie (1925-1945)	3.88
28	Thomas, Frank (1990-2003)	3.84
29	Baker, Frank (1908-1922)	3.84
30	Bagwell, Jeff (1991-2003)	3.81
31	Ott, Mel (1926-1947)	3.81
32	Greenberg, Hank (1930-1947)	3.78
33	Giles, Brian (1995-2003)	3.74
34	Larkin, Barry (1986-2003)	3.74
35	Browning, Pete (1882-1894)	3.57
36	Ewing, Buck (1880-1897)	3.56
37	Mathews, Eddie (1952-1968)	3.56
38	Martinez, Edgar (1987-2003)	3.56
39	Ramirez, Manny (1993-2003)	3.53
40	Griffey, Ken (1989-2003)	3.51
41	Kelly, King (1878-1893)	3.45
42	Jennings, Hughie (1891-1918)	3.40
43	Allen, Dick (1963-1977)	3.39
44	Robinson, Frank (1956-1976)	3.38
45	Connor, Roger (1880-1897)	3.38
46	Gordon, Joe (1938-1950)	3.35
47	Sheffield, Gary (1988-2003)	3.29
48	McGwire, Mark (1986-2001)	3.28
49	Childs, Cupid (1888-1901)	3.27
50	Stanky, Eddie (1943-1953)	3.26
51	Delahanty, Ed (1888-1903)	3.20
52	McGraw, John (1891-1906)	3.16
53	Frisch, Frankie (1919-1937)	3.14
54	Flick, Elmer (1898-1910)	3.13
55	Keller, Charlie (1939-1952)	3.12
56	Edmonds, Jim (1993-2003)	3.12
57	Mize, Johnny (1936-1953)	3.10
58	Bancroft, Dave (1915-1930)	3.09
59	McPhee, Bid (1882-1899)	3.09
60	Gehringer, Charlie (1924-1942)	3.07
61	Richardson, Hardy (1879-1892)	3.03
62	Cronin, Joe (1926-1945)	3.01
63	Cochrane, Mickey (1925-1937)	2.98
64	Giambi, Jason (1995-2003)	2.97
65	Henderson, Rickey (1979-2003)	2.97
66	Herman, Billy (1931-1947)	2.96
67	McDougald, Gil (1951-1960)	2.95
68	Glasscock, Jack (1879-1895)	2.93
69	Guerrero, Vladimir (1996-2003)	2.92
70	Thompson, Sam (1885-1906)	2.91
71	Boggs, Wade (1982-1999)	2.86
72	Thome, Jim (1991-2003)	2.86
73	Hartnett, Gabby (1922-1941)	2.84
74	Dickey, Bill (1928-1946)	2.84
75	Belle, Albert (1989-2000)	2.80
76	Chance, Frank (1898-1914)	2.80
77	Groh, Heinie (1912-1927)	2.80
78	Whitaker, Lou (1977-1995)	2.78
79	Stirnweiss, Snuffy (1943-1952)	2.77
80	Lyons, Denny (1885-1897)	2.74
81	Brett, George (1973-1993)	2.72
82	Doerr, Bobby (1937-1951)	2.71
83	Lazzeri, Tony (1926-1939)	2.68
84	Sewell, Joe (1920-1933)	2.67
85	Johnson, Bob (1933-1945)	2.67
86	Tinker, Joe (1902-1916)	2.62
87	Collins, Jimmy (1895-1908)	2.60
88	Ventura, Robin (1989-2003)	2.58
89	Randolph, Willie (1975-1992)	2.58
90	Cullenbine, Roy (1938-1947)	2.58
91	Mitchell, Kevin (1984-1998)	2.56
92	Jones, Chipper (1993-2003)	2.55
93	Kent, Jeff (1992-2003)	2.54
94	Berra, Yogi (1946-1965)	2.53
95	Bresnahan, Roger (1897-1915)	2.53
96	Hamilton, Billy (1888-1901)	2.52
97	Abreu, Bobby (1996-2003)	2.50
98	Bench, Johnny (1967-1983)	2.50
99	Appling, Luke (1930-1950)	2.50
100	Tenace, Gene (1969-1983)	2.48

Pinch Hits

1	Harris, Lenny	181
2	Mota, Manny	150
3	Burgess, Smoky	145
4	Gross, Greg	143
5	Hansen, Dave	129
6	Vander Wal, John	125
7	Morales, Jose	123
8	Lynch, Jerry	116
9	Lucas, Red	114
10	Braun, Steve	113
11	Crowley, Terry	108
	Walling, Denny	108
13	Brown, Gates	107
14	Lum, Mike	103
15	Dwyer, Jim	102
16	Staub, Rusty	100
17	Sweeney, Mark	97
18	Clark , Dave	96
19	Biitner, Larry	95
	Davalillo, Vic	95
	Perry, Gerald	95
22	Hairston, Jerry	94
23	Philey, Dave	93
	Youngblood, Joel	93
25	Johnstone, Jay	92
	Magadan, Dave	92

Pinch Hit Average (min. 150 AB)

1	Colbrunn, Greg	.322
2	Arias, Alex	.320
3	Davis, Tommy	.320
4	Bordagaray, Frenchy	.312
5	Baines, Harold	.311
6	Baumholtz, Frankie	.307
7	Bream, Sid	.306
	Carreon, Mark	.306
9	Schoendienst, Red	.303
10	Fothergill, Bob	.300
11	Philley, Dave	.299
12	Stairs, Matt	.298
13	Mota, Manny	.297
14	Easterly, Ted	.296
15	Hendrick, Harvey	.295
16	Herndon, Larry	.294
17	Mulliniks, Rance	.292
18	Puhl, Terry	.289
19	Hale, Chip	.289
20	Palmeiro, Orlando	.288
21	Sanguillen, Manny	.288
22	Hill, Glenallen	.287
23	Burgess, Smoky	.286
24	Miller, Rick	.286
25	Mize, Johnny	.283

Pinch Hit Home Runs

1	Johnson, Cliff	20
2	Lynch, Jerry	18
	Vander Wal, John	18
4	Brown, Gates	16
	Burgess, Smoky	16
	McCovey, Willie	16
7	Crowe, George	14
	Hansen, Dave	14
9	Hill, Glenallen	13
10	Adcock, Joe	12
	Cerv, Bob	12
	Morales, Jose	12
	Nettles, Graig	12
14	Burroughs, Jeff	11
	Johnstone, Jay	11
	Merced, Orlando	11
	Maldonado, Candy	11
	Whitfield, Fred	11
	Williams, Cy	11
20	Carreon, Mark	10
	Clark, Dave	10
	Dwyer, Jim	10
	Lum, Mike	10
	McMullen, Ken	10
	Mincher, Don	10
	Post, Wally	10
	Summers, Champ	10
	Turner, Jerry	10
	Zernial, Gus	10

Stolen Bases

1	Henderson, Rickey (1979-2003)	1406
2	Brock, Lou (1961-1979)	938
3	Hamilton, Billy (1888-1901)	914
4	Cobb, Ty (1905-1928)	892
5	Raines, Tim (1979-2002)	808
6	Coleman, Vince (1985-1997)	752
7	Latham, Arlie (1880-1909)	742
8	Collins, Eddie (1906-1930)	741
9	Carey, Max (1910-1929)	738
10	Wagner, Honus (1897-1917)	723
11	Morgan, Joe (1963-1984)	689
12	Wilson, Willie (1976-1994)	668
13	Brown, Tom (1882-1898)	657
14	Campaneris, Bert (1964-1983)	649
15	Nixon, Otis (1983-1999)	620
16	Davis, George (1890-1909)	616
17	Hoy, Dummy (1888-1902)	596
18	Wills, Maury (1959-1972)	586
19	Van Haltren, George (1887-1903)	583
20	Smith, Ozzie (1978-1996)	580
21	Duffy, Hugh (1888-1906)	574
22	McPhee, Bid (1882-1899)	568
23	Butler, Brett (1981-1997)	558
24	Lopes, Davey (1972-1987)	557
25	Cedeno, Cesar (1970-1986)	550
26	Dahlen, Bill (1891-1911)	547
27	Ward, John (1878-1894)	540
28	Lofton, Kenny (1991-2003)	538
29	Long, Herman (1889-1904)	537
30	Donovan, Patsy (1890-1907)	518
31	Doyle, Jack (1889-1905)	517
32	Clarke, Fred (1894-1915)	509
	Stovey, Harry (1880-1893)	509
34	Aparicio, Luis (1956-1973)	506
35	Molitor, Paul (1978-1998)	504
36	Bonds, Barry (1986-2003)	500
37	Keeler, Willie (1892-1910)	495
	Milan, Clyde (1907-1922)	495
39	Moreno, Omar (1975-1986)	487
40	Alomar, Roberto (1988-2003)	474
41	Griffin, Mike (1887-1898)	473
42	McCarthy, Tommy (1884-1896)	468
43	Sheckard, Jimmy (1897-1913)	465
44	DeShields, Delino (1990-2002)	463
45	Bonds, Bobby (1968-1981)	461
46	Delahanty, Ed (1888-1903)	455
	LeFlore, Ron (1974-1982)	455
48	Welch, Curt (1884-1893)	453
49	Sax, Steve (1981-1994)	444
50	Kelley, Joe (1891-1908)	443
51	Magee, Sherry (1904-1919)	441
52	McGraw, John (1891-1906)	436
	Young, Eric (1992-2003)	436
54	Speaker, Tris (1907-1928)	432
55	Bescher, Bob (1908-1918)	428
	Tiernan, Mike (1887-1899)	428
57	Grissom, Marquis (1989-2003)	425
58	Comiskey, Charlie (1882-1894)	419
	Frisch, Frankie (1919-1937)	419
60	Ryan, Jimmy (1885-1903)	418
61	Harper, Tommy (1962-1976)	408
62	Knoblauch, Chuck (1991-2002)	407
63	Bush, Donie (1908-1923)	404
64	Chance, Frank (1898-1914)	403
65	Lange, Bill (1893-1899)	399
66	Davis, Willie (1960-1979)	398
67	Mertes, Sam (1896-1906)	396
	Samuel, Juan (1983-1998)	396
69	Collins, Dave (1975-1990)	395
	North, Billy (1971-1981)	395
71	Biggio, Craig (1988-2003)	389
	Burkett, Jesse (1890-1905)	389
73	Corcoran, Tommy (1890-1907)	387
74	Daly, Tom (1887-1903)	385
	Patek, Freddie (1968-1981)	385
76	Burns, George (1911-1925)	383
	Nicol, Hugh (1881-1890)	383
	Wilmot, Walt (1888-1898)	383
79	Pfeffer, Fred (1882-1897)	382
80	Lajoie, Nap (1896-1916)	380
81	Larkin, Barry (1986-2003)	377
82	Hooper, Harry (1909-1925)	375
	Sisler, George (1915-1930)	375
84	Glasscock, Jack (1879-1895)	372
85	Smith, Lonnie (1978-1994)	370
86	Dowd, Tommy (1891-1901)	368
	Kelly, King (1878-1893)	368
88	Crawford, Sam (1899-1917)	366
89	Goodwin, Tom (1991-2003)	364
90	Chase, Hal (1905-1919)	363
91	Leach, Tommy (1898-1918)	361
92	Jennings, Hughie (1891-1918)	359
	Jones, Fielder (1896-1915)	359
94	Ewing, Buck (1880-1897)	354
	Pettis, Gary (1982-1992)	354
96	Carew, Rod (1967-1985)	353
97	McGee, Willie (1982-1999)	352
	Tucker, Tommy (1887-1899)	352
99	Rice, Sam (1915-1934)	351
100	Case, George (1937-1947)	349

Stolen Base Average

1	Raines, Tim (1979-2002)	84.70
2	Davis, Eric (1984-2001)	84.10
3	Wilson, Willie (1976-1994)	83.29
4	Womack, Tony (1993-2003)	83.06
5	Larkin, Barry (1986-2003)	83.04
6	Lopes, Davey (1972-1987)	83.01
7	Javier, Stan (1984-2001)	82.83
8	Glanville, Doug (1996-2003)	81.63
9	Cruz, Julio (1977-1986)	81.47
10	Hunter, Brian (1994-2003)	81.00
11	Morgan, Joe (1963-1984)	80.96
12	Coleman, Vince (1985-1997)	80.95
13	Alomar, Roberto (1988-2003)	80.89
14	Henderson, Rickey (1979-2003)	80.76
15	Van Slyke, Andy (1983-1995)	80.59
16	Mantle, Mickey (1951-1968)	80.10
17	Dykstra, Lenny (1985-1996)	79.83
18	Smith, Ozzie (1978-1996)	79.67
19	Redus, Gary (1982-1994)	79.51
20	Rodriguez, Alex (1994-2003)	79.37
21	Molitor, Paul (1978-1998)	79.37
22	Lofton, Kenny (1991-2003)	79.12
23	Grissom, Marquis (1989-2003)	78.85
24	Aparicio, Luis (1956-1973)	78.82
25	Jeter, Derek (1995-2003)	78.76
26	Damon, Johnny (1995-2003)	78.71
27	Otis, Amos (1967-1984)	78.57
28	Cameron, Mike (1995-2003)	78.54
29	Gibson, Kirk (1979-1995)	78.45
30	Bonds, Barry (1986-2003)	78.13
31	White, Devon (1985-2001)	77.93
32	Harper, Tommy (1962-1976)	77.86
33	Carter, Joe (1983-1998)	77.78
34	Knoblauch, Chuck (1991-2002)	77.67
35	Pettis, Gary (1982-1992)	77.29
36	Biggio, Craig (1988-2003)	77.03
37	Wilson, Mookie (1980-1991)	76.94
38	Bell, Derek (1991-2001)	76.92
	Nixon, Otis (1983-1999)	76.92
40	Aaron, Hank (1954-1976)	76.68
41	Mays, Willie (1951-1973)	76.64
42	Green, Shawn (1993-2003)	76.57
43	Campaneris, Bert (1964-1983)	76.53
44	Thompson, Milt (1984-1996)	76.43
45	Sandberg, Ryne (1981-1997)	76.27
46	LeFlore, Ron (1974-1982)	76.21
47	Case, George (1937-1947)	76.20
48	Floyd, Cliff (1993-2003)	76.13
49	Anderson, Brady (1988-2002)	75.90
50	DeShields, Delino (1990-2002)	75.90
51	Lansing, Mike (1993-2001)	75.80
52	Johnson, Lance (1987-2000)	75.69
53	Jefferies, Gregg (1987-2000)	75.68
54	Erstad, Darin (1996-2003)	75.66
55	Goodwin, Tom (1991-2003)	75.52
56	Cedeno, Cesar (1970-1986)	75.45
57	Brock, Lou (1961-1979)	75.34
58	Duncan, Mariano (1985-1997)	75.32
59	Moseby, Lloyd (1980-1991)	75.27
60	Davis, Willie (1960-1979)	75.24
61	Bowa, Larry (1970-1985)	75.18
62	Johnson, Howard (1982-1995)	75.00
63	Rivers, Mickey (1970-1984)	74.79
64	Walker, Larry (1989-2003)	74.75
65	Concepcion, Dave (1970-1988)	74.65
66	Patek, Freddie (1968-1981)	74.61
67	Herr, Tom (1979-1991)	74.60
68	Schofield, Dick (1983-1996)	74.53
69	Temple, Johnny (1952-1964)	74.47
70	McGee, Willie (1982-1999)	74.42
71	McBride, Bake (1973-1983)	74.39
72	Grudzielanek, Mark (1995-2003)	74.36
	Jones, Chipper (1993-2003)	74.36
74	Young, Eric (1992-2003)	74.28
75	Randolph, Willie (1975-1992)	74.25
76	Dawson, Andre (1976-1996)	74.23
77	Collins, Dave (1975-1990)	73.97
78	Alomar, Sandy (1964-1978)	73.94
79	Taveras, Frank (1971-1982)	73.89
80	Durham, Ray (1995-2003)	73.89
81	Renteria, Edgar (1996-2003)	73.83
82	Wills, Maury (1959-1972)	73.80
83	Kelly, Roberto (1987-2000)	73.67
84	Roberts, Bip (1986-1998)	73.54
85	Richards, Gene (1977-1984)	73.51
86	Samuel, Juan (1983-1998)	73.47
87	Finley, Steve (1989-2003)	73.45
88	Eisenreich, Jim (1982-1998)	73.43
89	Bumbry, Al (1972-1985)	73.41
90	Jones, Andruw (1996-2003)	73.29
91	Morandini, Mickey (1990-2000)	73.21
92	Bonds, Bobby (1968-1981)	73.17
93	Landis, Jim (1957-1967)	73.16
94	Sierra, Ruben (1986-2003)	73.06
95	Maddox, Garry (1972-1986)	72.94
96	Griffey, Ken (1989-2003)	72.84
97	Moreno, Omar (1975-1986)	72.80
98	Leonard, Jeffrey (1977-1990)	72.77
99	Martin, Al (1992-2003)	72.69
100	Abreu, Bobby (1996-2003)	72.65

Stolen Base Runs

1	Henderson, Rickey (1979-2003)	159
2	Raines, Tim (1979-2002)	112
3	Wilson, Willie (1976-1994)	87
4	Coleman, Vince (1985-1997)	86
5	Morgan, Joe (1963-1984)	79
6	Lopes, Davey (1972-1987)	71
7	Brock, Lou (1961-1979)	68
8	Smith, Ozzie (1978-1996)	61
9	Lofton, Kenny (1991-2003)	54
10	Alomar, Roberto (1988-2003)	54
11	Campaneris, Bert (1964-1983)	53
12	Nixon, Otis (1983-1999)	53
13	Molitor, Paul (1978-1998)	52
14	Aparicio, Luis (1956-1973)	50
15	Larkin, Barry (1986-2003)	48
16	Davis, Eric (1984-2001)	47
17	Bonds, Barry (1986-2003)	47
18	Grissom, Marquis (1989-2003)	42
19	Cedeno, Cesar (1970-1986)	40
20	Cruz, Julio (1977-1986)	40
21	Womack, Tony (1993-2003)	40
22	Harper, Tommy (1962-1976)	38
23	Knoblauch, Chuck (1991-2002)	37
24	LeFlore, Ron (1974-1982)	36
25	DeShields, Delino (1990-2002)	36
26	Wills, Maury (1959-1972)	35
27	Redus, Gary (1982-1994)	33
28	Biggio, Craig (1988-2003)	33
29	Otis, Amos (1967-1984)	33
30	White, Devon (1985-2001)	32
31	Javier, Stan (1984-2001)	31
32	Pettis, Gary (1982-1992)	31
33	Dykstra, Lenny (1985-1996)	30
34	Hunter, Brian (1994-2003)	30
35	Davis, Willie (1960-1979)	29
36	Mays, Willie (1951-1973)	28
37	Young, Eric (1992-2003)	28
38	Wilson, Mookie (1980-1991)	28
39	Sandberg, Ryne (1981-1997)	28
40	Gibson, Kirk (1979-1995)	27
41	Van Slyke, Andy (1983-1995)	27
42	Goodwin, Tom (1991-2003)	27
43	Patek, Freddie (1968-1981)	26
44	Bonds, Bobby (1968-1981)	25
45	Moreno, Omar (1975-1986)	25
46	Johnson, Lance (1987-2000)	25
47	Collins, Dave (1975-1990)	24
48	Anderson, Brady (1988-2002)	24
49	Damon, Johnny (1995-2003)	24
50	McGee, Willie (1982-1999)	23
51	Samuel, Juan (1983-1998)	23
52	Bowa, Larry (1970-1985)	23
53	Concepcion, Dave (1970-1988)	22
54	Carter, Joe (1983-1998)	21
55	Hartzell, Roy (1906-1916)	20
56	Moseby, Lloyd (1980-1991)	20
57	Dawson, Andre (1976-1996)	20
58	Aaron, Hank (1954-1976)	20
59	Glanville, Doug (1996-2003)	19
60	Cameron, Mike (1995-2003)	19
61	Smith, Lonnie (1978-1994)	18
62	Taveras, Frank (1971-1982)	18
63	Rodriguez, Alex (1994-2003)	18
	Rivers, Mickey (1970-1984)	18
65	Sax, Steve (1981-1994)	18
66	Jeter, Derek (1995-2003)	18
67	Thompson, Milt (1984-1996)	17
68	Randolph, Willie (1975-1992)	17
69	Finley, Steve (1989-2003)	17
70	Mantle, Mickey (1951-1968)	17
71	Johnson, Howard (1982-1995)	16
72	Roberts, Bip (1986-1998)	15
73	Walker, Larry (1989-2003)	15
74	Jefferies, Gregg (1987-2000)	15
75	Bumbry, Al (1972-1985)	14
76	Bell, Derek (1991-2001)	14
77	Richards, Gene (1977-1984)	14
78	Durham, Ray (1995-2003)	14
79	North, Billy (1971-1981)	14
80	Alomar, Sandy (1964-1978)	14
81	Gwynn, Tony (1982-2001)	14
82	Kelly, Roberto (1987-2000)	14
83	Renteria, Edgar (1996-2003)	13
84	Maddox, Garry (1972-1986)	13
85	Duncan, Mariano (1985-1997)	13
86	Herr, Tom (1979-1991)	13
87	Yount, Robin (1974-1993)	12
88	Pinson, Vada (1958-1975)	12
89	Sanders, Reggie (1991-2003)	12
90	Hayes, Von (1981-1992)	12
91	Franco, Julio (1982-2003)	12
92	McBride, Bake (1973-1983)	12
93	Green, Shawn (1993-2003)	11
94	Mondesi, Raul (1993-2003)	11
95	Erstad, Darin (1996-2003)	11
96	Vizquel, Omar (1989-2003)	10
97	Robinson, Frank (1956-1976)	10
98	Harrah, Toby (1969-1986)	10
99	Cardenal, Jose (1963-1980)	10
100	Bagwell, Jeff (1991-2003)	10

Fielding Wins

1	Lajoie, Nap (1896-1916)	34.3
2	McPhee, Bid (1882-1899)	29.6
3	Tinker, Joe (1902-1916)	29.1
4	Wagner, Honus (1897-1917)	27.7
5	Schmidt, Mike (1972-1989)	27.1
6	Mazeroski, Bill (1956-1972)	25.2
7	Smith, Ozzie (1978-1996)	24.7
8	Frisch, Frankie (1919-1937)	23.4
9	Robinson, Brooks (1955-1977)	22.5
10	Maranville, Rabbit (1912-1935)	21.3
11	Bancroft, Dave (1915-1930)	21.2
12	Dahlen, Bill (1891-1911)	20.3
13	Pendleton, Terry (1984-1998)	19.8
14	Rizzuto, Phil (1941-1956)	19.7
15	Concepcion, Dave (1970-1988)	19.6
16	Belanger, Mark (1965-1982)	19.6
17	Nettles, Graig (1967-1988)	19.5
18	Grich, Bobby (1970-1986)	19.4
19	Boyer, Clete (1955-1971)	18.9
20	Evans, Darrell (1969-1989)	18.9
21	Doolan, Mickey (1905-1918)	18.3
22	Collins, Eddie (1906-1930)	18.2
23	Glasscock, Jack (1879-1895)	18.1
24	Boudreau, Lou (1938-1952)	17.9
25	Bell, Buddy (1972-1989)	17.8
26	Collins, Jimmy (1895-1908)	17.7
27	Wallace, Bobby (1894-1918)	17.7
28	Ventura, Robin (1989-2003)	16.3
29	Long, Herman (1889-1904)	16.3
30	McBride, George (1901-1920)	16.2
31	Cutshaw, George (1912-1923)	16.1
32	Marion, Marty (1940-1953)	15.9
33	Fletcher, Art (1909-1922)	15.8
34	Speaker, Tris (1907-1928)	15.7
35	McMillan, Roy (1951-1966)	15.6
36	Scott, Everett (1914-1926)	15.1
37	Ferris, Hobe (1901-1909)	14.6
38	Lowe, Bobby (1890-1907)	14.5
39	Dunlap, Fred (1880-1891)	14.4
40	Gaetti, Gary (1981-2000)	14.4
41	Clemente, Roberto (1955-1972)	14.3
42	Randolph, Willie (1975-1992)	14.2
43	Jennings, Hughie (1891-1918)	14.2
44	Evers, Johnny (1902-1929)	14.1
45	Tannehill, Lee (1903-1912)	13.7
46	Gerhardt, Joe (1873-1891)	13.6
47	Peckinpaugh, Roger (1910-1927)	13.3
48	Corcoran, Tommy (1890-1907)	13.1
49	Bartell, Dick (1927-1946)	13.0
50	Maxvill, Dal (1962-1975)	12.8

Fielding Runs

1	McPhee, Bid (1882-1899)	341
2	Lajoie, Nap (1896-1916)	326
3	Tinker, Joe (1902-1916)	274
4	Wagner, Honus (1897-1917)	266
5	Schmidt, Mike (1972-1989)	259
6	Mazeroski, Bill (1956-1972)	242
7	Frisch, Frankie (1919-1937)	240
8	Smith, Ozzie (1978-1996)	236
9	Dahlen, Bill (1891-1911)	219
10	Robinson, Brooks (1955-1977)	211
11	Bancroft, Dave (1915-1930)	204
12	Maranville, Rabbit (1912-1935)	204
13	Glasscock, Jack (1879-1895)	202
14	Rizzuto, Phil (1941-1956)	197
15	Collins, Jimmy (1895-1908)	193
16	Grich, Bobby (1970-1986)	190
17	Pendleton, Terry (1984-1998)	190
18	Belanger, Mark (1965-1982)	188
19	Concepcion, Dave (1970-1988)	188
20	Nettles, Graig (1967-1988)	186
21	Boyer, Clete (1955-1971)	183
22	Evans, Darrell (1969-1989)	182
23	Long, Herman (1889-1904)	182
24	Wallace, Bobby (1894-1918)	180
25	Boudreau, Lou (1938-1952)	176
26	Bell, Buddy (1972-1989)	176
27	Doolan, Mickey (1905-1918)	170
28	Collins, Eddie (1906-1930)	170
29	Jennings, Hughie (1891-1918)	170
30	Ventura, Robin (1989-2003)	169
31	Ward, John (1878-1894)	161
32	Dunlap, Fred (1880-1891)	159
33	Lowe, Bobby (1890-1907)	156
34	McMillan, Roy (1951-1966)	155
35	Marion, Marty (1940-1953)	154
36	Corcoran, Tommy (1890-1907)	154
37	Gerhardt, Joe (1873-1891)	150
38	McBride, George (1901-1920)	150
39	Scott, Everett (1914-1926)	150
40	Cutshaw, George (1912-1923)	148
41	Speaker, Tris (1907-1928)	147
42	Smith, Germany (1884-1898)	146
43	Bierbauer, Lou (1886-1898)	144
44	Gaetti, Gary (1981-2000)	143
45	Fletcher, Art (1909-1922)	141
46	Randolph, Willie (1975-1992)	140
47	Ferris, Hobe (1901-1909)	139
48	Clemente, Roberto (1955-1972)	138
49	Bartell, Dick (1927-1946)	134
50	Evers, Johnny (1902-1929)	132

Win Shares – Batters

1	Ruth, Babe (1914-1935)	756
2	Cobb, Ty (1905-1928)	722
3	Wagner, Honus (1897-1917)	655
4	Aaron, Hank (1954-1976)	643
5	Mays, Willie (1951-1973)	642
6	Speaker, Tris (1907-1928)	630
7	Bonds, Barry (1986-2003)	611
8	Musial, Stan (1941-1963)	604
9	Collins, Eddie (1906-1930)	574
10	Mantle, Mickey (1951-1968)	565
11	Williams, Ted (1939-1960)	555
12	Rose, Pete (1963-1986)	547
13	Henderson, Rickey (1979-2003)	535
14	Ott, Mel (1926-1947)	528
15	Robinson, Frank (1956-1976)	519
16	Morgan, Joe (1963-1984)	512
17	Hornsby, Rogers (1915-1937)	502
18	Lajoie, Nap (1896-1916)	496
19	Gehrig, Lou (1923-1939)	489
20	Yastrzemski, Carl (1961-1983)	488
21	Schmidt, Mike (1972-1989)	467
22	Mathews, Eddie (1952-1968)	450
23	Crawford, Sam (1899-1917)	446
24	Jackson, Reggie (1967-1987)	444
25	Kaline, Al (1953-1974)	443
26	Murray, Eddie (1977-1997)	437
27	Foxx, Jimmie (1925-1945)	435
28	Brett, George (1973-1993)	432
29	Ripken, Cal (1981-2001)	427
30	Waner, Paul (1926-1945)	423
	Yount, Robin (1974-1993)	423
32	Winfield, Dave (1973-1995)	415
33	Molitor, Paul (1978-1998)	414
34	Ward, John (1878-1894)	409
35	McCovey, Willie (1959-1980)	408
36	Clarke, Fred (1894-1915)	400
37	Mullane, Tony (1881-1894)	399
38	Davis, George (1890-1909)	398
	Gwynn, Tony (1982-2001)	398
40	Boggs, Wade (1982-1999)	394
	Dahlen, Bill (1891-1911)	394
42	Radbourn, Charley (1880-1891)	391
43	Raines, Tim (1979-2002)	390
44	Burkett, Jesse (1890-1905)	389
45	DiMaggio, Joe (1936-1951)	387
46	Carew, Rod (1967-1985)	384
47	Gehringer, Charlie (1924-1942)	383
48	Anson, Cap (1871-1897)	381
49	Wheat, Zack (1909-1927)	380
50	Appling, Luke (1930-1950)	378
51	Biggio, Craig (1988-2003)	377
	Clemente, Roberto (1955-1972)	377
53	Berra, Yogi (1946-1965)	375
	Simmons, Al (1924-1944)	375
55	Williams, Billy (1959-1976)	374
56	Alomar, Roberto (1988-2003)	373
57	Palmeiro, Rafael (1986-2003)	372
58	Killebrew, Harmon (1954-1975)	371
59	Stargell, Willie (1962-1982)	370
60	Fisk, Carlton (1969-1993)	368
61	Frisch, Frankie (1919-1937)	366
62	Connor, Roger (1880-1897)	363
	Evans, Darrell (1969-1989)	363
64	Bagwell, Jeff (1991-2003)	362
65	Staub, Rusty (1963-1985)	358
66	Bench, Johnny (1967-1983)	356
	Heilmann, Harry (1914-1932)	356
	Robinson, Brooks (1955-1977)	356
	Vaughan, Arky (1932-1948)	356
70	Brouthers, Dan (1879-1904)	355
	Delahanty, Ed (1888-1903)	355
	Goslin, Goose (1921-1938)	355
73	Magee, Sherry (1904-1919)	354
74	Snider, Duke (1947-1964)	352
75	Carey, Max (1910-1929)	351
	Whitaker, Lou (1977-1995)	351
77	Perez, Tony (1964-1986)	349
78	Brock, Lou (1961-1979)	348
79	Evans, Dwight (1972-1991)	347
	Thomas, Frank (1990-2003)	347
81	Sandberg, Ryne (1981-1997)	346
82	Wallace, Bobby (1894-1918)	345
83	Van Haltren, George (1887-1903)	344
84	Allen, Dick (1963-1977)	342
	McGwire, Mark (1986-2001)	342
86	McGriff, Fred (1986-2003)	341
87	Dawson, Andre (1976-1996)	340
88	Sheckard, Jimmy (1897-1913)	339
89	Mize, Johnny (1936-1953)	338
90	Carter, Gary (1974-1992)	337
	Caruthers, Bob (1884-1893)	337
	Hamilton, Billy (1888-1901)	337
	Sheffield, Gary (1988-2003)	337
94	Larkin, Barry (1986-2003)	336
95	Cronin, Joe (1926-1945)	333
	Keeler, Willie (1892-1910)	333
97	Banks, Ernie (1953-1971)	332
98	Clark, Will (1986-2000)	331
99	Ashburn, Richie (1948-1962)	329
	Grich, Bobby (1970-1986)	329

Total Player Wins – Batters

1	Ruth, Babe (1914-1935)	133.6
2	Bonds, Barry (1986-2003)	111.1
3	Wagner, Honus (1897-1917)	102.7
4	Lajoie, Nap (1896-1916)	93.6
5	Williams, Ted (1939-1960)	93.5
6	Cobb, Ty (1905-1928)	90.6
7	Mays, Willie (1951-1973)	89.6
8	Collins, Eddie (1906-1930)	89.4
9	Hornsby, Rogers (1915-1937)	86.1
10	Aaron, Hank (1954-1976)	85.4
11	Schmidt, Mike (1972-1989)	82.3
12	Speaker, Tris (1907-1928)	82.0
13	Mantle, Mickey (1951-1968)	81.7
14	Musial, Stan (1941-1963)	79.5
15	Morgan, Joe (1963-1984)	78.1
16	Gehrig, Lou (1923-1939)	74.6
17	Ott, Mel (1926-1947)	69.3
18	Robinson, Frank (1956-1976)	63.3
19	Henderson, Rickey (1979-2003)	61.0
20	Foxx, Jimmie (1925-1945)	59.9
21	Grich, Bobby (1970-1986)	58.2
22	Mathews, Eddie (1952-1968)	56.7
23	Larkin, Barry (1986-2003)	51.6
24	Vaughan, Arky (1932-1948)	50.7
25	Bagwell, Jeff (1991-2003)	49.7
26	Brett, George (1973-1993)	49.1
27	Piazza, Mike (1992-2003)	48.9
28	Frisch, Frankie (1919-1937)	48.4
29	Ripken, Cal (1981-2001)	48.1
30	Boudreau, Lou (1938-1952)	48.1
31	Gehringer, Charlie (1924-1942)	47.6
32	Thomas, Frank (1990-2003)	47.4
33	DiMaggio, Joe (1936-1951)	47.3
34	Boggs, Wade (1982-1999)	46.5
35	Martinez, Edgar (1987-2003)	45.4
36	Connor, Roger (1880-1897)	45.1
37	Griffey, Ken (1989-2003)	44.8
38	Whitaker, Lou (1977-1995)	44.3
39	McPhee, Bid (1882-1899)	44.0
40	Brouthers, Dan (1879-1904)	43.5
41	McCovey, Willie (1959-1980)	42.7
42	Rodriguez, Alex (1994-2003)	42.6
43	Cronin, Joe (1926-1945)	42.6
44	Jackson, Reggie (1967-1987)	42.3
45	Smith, Ozzie (1978-1996)	41.3
46	Sheffield, Gary (1988-2003)	41.3
47	McGwire, Mark (1986-2001)	41.0
48	Yastrzemski, Carl (1961-1983)	40.3
49	Baker, Frank (1908-1922)	40.3
50	Appling, Luke (1930-1950)	40.3
51	Robinson, Jackie (1947-1956)	40.2
52	Yount, Robin (1974-1993)	40.0
53	Dahlen, Bill (1891-1911)	39.8
54	Carew, Rod (1967-1985)	39.6
55	Allen, Dick (1963-1977)	39.5
56	Bancroft, Dave (1915-1930)	39.4
57	Evans, Darrell (1969-1989)	39.4
58	Delahanty, Ed (1888-1903)	39.2
59	Mize, Johnny (1936-1953)	39.0
60	Kaline, Al (1953-1974)	38.8
61	Clemente, Roberto (1955-1972)	38.8
62	Killebrew, Harmon (1954-1975)	38.7
63	Randolph, Willie (1975-1992)	37.9
64	Herman, Billy (1931-1947)	37.9
65	Hartnett, Gabby (1922-1941)	37.7
66	Alomar, Roberto (1988-2003)	37.1
67	Davis, George (1890-1909)	37.0
68	Wallace, Bobby (1894-1918)	36.7
69	Jackson, Joe (1908-1920)	36.3
70	Bench, Johnny (1967-1983)	35.9
71	Gwynn, Tony (1982-2001)	35.8
72	Berra, Yogi (1946-1965)	35.8
73	Raines, Tim (1979-2002)	35.7
74	Molitor, Paul (1978-1998)	35.2
75	Greenberg, Hank (1930-1947)	35.2
76	Gordon, Joe (1938-1950)	35.0
77	Winfield, Dave (1973-1995)	34.4
78	Fisk, Carlton (1969-1993)	34.3
79	Carter, Gary (1974-1992)	34.2
80	Ventura, Robin (1989-2003)	34.1
81	Glasscock, Jack (1879-1895)	33.9
82	Sewell, Joe (1920-1933)	33.9
83	Dickey, Bill (1928-1946)	33.8
84	Heilmann, Harry (1914-1932)	33.8
85	Doerr, Bobby (1937-1951)	33.7
86	Trammell, Alan (1977-1996)	33.7
87	Kelly, King (1878-1893)	33.4
88	Stargell, Willie (1962-1982)	33.3
89	Johnson, Bob (1933-1945)	33.2
90	Biggio, Craig (1988-2003)	33.0
91	Murray, Eddie (1977-1997)	32.8
92	Ramirez, Manny (1993-2003)	32.6
93	Santo, Ron (1960-1974)	32.5
94	Anson, Cap (1871-1897)	32.3
95	Concepcion, Dave (1970-1988)	32.1
96	Childs, Cupid (1888-1901)	31.7
97	Hernandez, Keith (1974-1990)	31.7
98	Tinker, Joe (1902-1916)	31.5
99	Groh, Heinie (1912-1927)	31.2
100	Ewing, Buck (1880-1897)	31.2
101	Lazzeri, Tony (1926-1939)	31.1
102	Flick, Elmer (1898-1910)	31.0
103	Palmeiro, Rafael (1986-2003)	30.2
104	Collins, Jimmy (1895-1908)	29.9
105	Crawford, Sam (1899-1917)	29.8
106	Walker, Larry (1989-2003)	29.7
107	Cash, Norm (1958-1974)	29.7
108	Nettles, Graig (1967-1988)	29.6
109	Sandberg, Ryne (1981-1997)	29.5
110	Waner, Paul (1926-1945)	29.5
111	Cochrane, Mickey (1925-1937)	29.4
112	Thome, Jim (1991-2003)	29.2
113	Jennings, Hughie (1891-1918)	29.1
114	Howard, Frank (1958-1973)	29.0
115	Belle, Albert (1989-2000)	28.8
116	Reese, Pee Wee (1940-1958)	28.5
117	Rolen, Scott (1996-2003)	28.3
118	Williams, Billy (1959-1976)	28.2
119	Olerud, John (1989-2003)	28.2
120	Browning, Pete (1882-1894)	28.2
121	Traynor, Pie (1920-1937)	28.2
122	Smith, Reggie (1966-1982)	28.1
123	Clark, Jack (1975-1992)	27.8
124	Wynn, Jimmy (1963-1977)	27.8
125	Rose, Pete (1963-1986)	27.8
126	Kent, Jeff (1992-2003)	27.7
127	Snider, Duke (1947-1964)	27.5
128	Burkett, Jesse (1890-1905)	27.5
129	Stanky, Eddie (1943-1953)	27.4
130	Cey, Ron (1971-1987)	27.4
131	Thompson, Sam (1885-1906)	27.3
132	Rizzuto, Phil (1941-1956)	27.3
133	Robinson, Brooks (1955-1977)	27.3
134	Williams, Bernie (1991-2003)	27.0
135	Hack, Stan (1932-1947)	27.0
136	Edmonds, Jim (1993-2003)	26.9
137	Terry, Bill (1923-1936)	26.9
138	Campaneris, Bert (1964-1983)	26.9
139	Richardson, Hardy (1879-1892)	26.9
140	Hamilton, Billy (1888-1901)	26.8
141	Konetchy, Ed (1907-1921)	26.7
142	Fernandez, Tony (1983-2001)	26.5
143	Torre, Joe (1960-1977)	26.5
144	Singleton, Ken (1970-1984)	26.3
145	McDougald, Gil (1951-1960)	26.3
146	Clark, Will (1986-2000)	26.2
147	Banks, Ernie (1953-1971)	26.1
148	Giles, Brian (1995-2003)	26.0
149	Simmons, Ted (1968-1988)	25.8
150	Tenace, Gene (1969-1983)	25.7
151	Bonds, Bobby (1968-1981)	25.7
152	Clarke, Fred (1894-1915)	25.6
153	Simmons, Al (1924-1944)	25.3
154	Fletcher, Art (1909-1922)	25.1
155	Goslin, Goose (1921-1938)	25.1
156	Downing, Brian (1973-1992)	25.1
157	Giambi, Jason (1995-2003)	25.1
158	Beckley, Jake (1888-1907)	25.0
159	Sosa, Sammy (1989-2003)	25.0
160	Evans, Dwight (1972-1991)	24.9
161	Lombardi, Ernie (1931-1947)	24.9
162	Rodriguez, Ivan (1991-2003)	24.7
163	Schang, Wally (1913-1931)	24.6
164	Elliott, Bob (1939-1953)	24.5
165	Mazeroski, Bill (1956-1972)	24.4
166	Keller, Charlie (1939-1952)	24.4
167	Bresnahan, Roger (1897-1915)	24.3
168	Bartell, Dick (1927-1946)	24.3
169	Evers, Johnny (1902-1929)	24.3
170	Clift, Harlond (1934-1945)	24.1
171	Chance, Frank (1898-1914)	24.0
172	Kiner, Ralph (1946-1955)	24.0
173	Wheat, Zack (1909-1927)	24.0
174	Jones, Chipper (1993-2003)	23.9
175	Bell, Buddy (1972-1989)	23.8
176	Fournier, Jack (1912-1927)	23.7
177	Fregosi, Jim (1961-1978)	23.2
178	McGraw, John (1891-1906)	23.1
179	Huggins, Miller (1904-1916)	23.0
180	Staub, Rusty (1963-1985)	22.8
181	Cepeda, Orlando (1958-1974)	22.5
182	Phillips, Tony (1982-1999)	22.4
183	Berger, Wally (1930-1940)	22.2
184	Strawberry, Darryl (1983-1999)	22.1
185	Williams, Matt (1987-2003)	22.1
186	Caminiti, Ken (1987-2001)	22.1
187	Magee, Sherry (1904-1919)	22.0
188	Guerrero, Pedro (1978-1992)	21.9
189	Johnson, Davey (1965-1978)	21.9
190	Cedeno, Cesar (1970-1986)	21.8
191	Stovey, Harry (1880-1893)	21.7
192	Minoso, Minnie (1949-1980)	21.7
193	Lopes, Davey (1972-1987)	21.5
194	Canseco, Jose (1985-2001)	21.5
195	Wilson, Hack (1923-1934)	21.4
196	Ward, John (1878-1894)	21.3
197	Stephens, Vern (1941-1955)	21.2
198	Doby, Larry (1947-1959)	21.2
199	Pratt, Del (1912-1924)	21.1
200	Averill, Earl (1929-1941)	20.9
201	Mitchell, Kevin (1984-1998)	20.8
202	Salmon, Tim (1992-2003)	20.7
203	Sheckard, Jimmy (1897-1913)	20.7
204	Medwick, Joe (1932-1948)	20.6
205	Lyons, Denny (1885-1897)	20.5
206	Puckett, Kirby (1984-1995)	20.4
207	Klein, Chuck (1928-1944)	20.4
208	Cullenbine, Roy (1938-1947)	20.3
209	Cravath, Gavvy (1908-1920)	20.2
210	Boyer, Ken (1955-1969)	20.1
211	Lynn, Fred (1974-1990)	20.0
212	Colavito, Rocky (1955-1968)	19.9
213	Dykstra, Lenny (1985-1996)	19.9
214	McGriff, Fred (1986-2003)	19.9
215	Maranville, Rabbit (1912-1935)	19.6
216	Tenney, Fred (1894-1911)	19.6
217	Guerrero, Vladimir (1996-2003)	19.6
218	Davis, Eric (1984-2001)	19.5
219	Oliva, Tony (1962-1976)	19.5
220	Bonilla, Bobby (1986-2001)	19.4
221	Rice, Jim (1974-1989)	19.2
222	Veach, Bobby (1912-1925)	19.2
223	Munson, Thurman (1969-1979)	19.2
224	Van Slyke, Andy (1983-1995)	19.2
225	Frey, Lonny (1933-1948)	19.0
226	Davis, Chili (1981-1999)	19.0
227	Stirnweiss, Snuffy (1943-1952)	19.0
228	Bando, Sal (1966-1981)	19.0
229	Gore, George (1879-1892)	18.9
230	Campanella, Roy (1948-1957)	18.9
231	Bishop, Max (1924-1935)	18.8
232	Kelley, Joe (1891-1908)	18.8
233	Nicholson, Bill (1936-1953)	18.8
234	Peckinpaugh, Roger (1910-1927)	18.7
235	Williams, Jimmy (1899-1909)	18.6
236	Carty, Rico (1963-1979)	18.5
237	Lofton, Kenny (1991-2003)	18.4
238	Thomas, Roy (1899-1911)	18.4
239	Myer, Buddy (1925-1941)	18.3
240	Freehan, Bill (1961-1976)	18.1
241	Gonzalez, Juan (1989-2003)	18.1
242	Jackson, Travis (1922-1936)	18.1
243	Dawson, Andre (1976-1996)	18.1
244	McAuliffe, Dick (1960-1975)	18.0
245	Fox, Nellie (1947-1965)	17.9
246	Slaughter, Enos (1938-1959)	17.9
247	Lemon, Chet (1975-1990)	17.9
248	Porter, Darrell (1971-1987)	17.8
249	Sisler, George (1915-1930)	17.8
250	O'Rourke, Jim (1872-1904)	17.7
251	Avila, Bobby (1949-1959)	17.7
252	Jones, Andruw (1996-2003)	17.7
253	Herman, Babe (1926-1945)	17.6
254	Gonzalez, Luis (1990-2003)	17.6
255	Heath, Jeff (1936-1949)	17.6
256	Ashburn, Richie (1948-1962)	17.5
257	Butler, Brett (1981-1997)	17.5
258	Lankford, Ray (1990-2002)	17.5
259	Speier, Chris (1971-1989)	17.4
260	Leach, Tommy (1898-1918)	17.3
261	Camilli, Dolph (1933-1945)	17.2
262	Henrich, Tommy (1937-1950)	17.2
263	Petrocelli, Rico (1963-1976)	17.2
264	Devlin, Art (1904-1913)	17.1
265	Cruz, Jose (1970-1988)	17.0
266	Justice, David (1989-2002)	16.9
267	Belanger, Mark (1965-1982)	16.9
268	Abreu, Bobby (1996-2003)	16.8
269	Tiernan, Mike (1887-1899)	16.8
270	Tettleton, Mickey (1984-1997)	16.8
271	Rosen, Al (1947-1956)	16.7
272	Fain, Ferris (1947-1955)	16.7
273	Logan, Johnny (1951-1963)	16.6
274	Powell, Boog (1961-1977)	16.6
275	Murcer, Bobby (1965-1983)	16.6
276	Cuyler, Kiki (1921-1938)	16.5
277	Luzinski, Greg (1970-1984)	16.4
278	Williams, Ken (1915-1929)	16.4
279	Parrish, Lance (1977-1995)	16.4
280	Franco, Julio (1982-2003)	16.4
281	Galan, Augie (1934-1949)	16.0
282	Smalley, Roy (1975-1987)	15.9
283	Griffin, Mike (1887-1898)	15.9
284	Burks, Ellis (1987-2003)	15.8
285	Burleson, Rick (1974-1987)	15.8
286	Harrah, Toby (1969-1986)	15.8
287	Delgado, Carlos (1993-2003)	15.6
288	Bell, Jay (1986-2003)	15.6
289	White, Roy (1965-1979)	15.6
290	Keeler, Willie (1892-1910)	15.3
291	Gordon, Sid (1941-1955)	15.3
292	Van Haltren, George (1887-1903)	15.3
293	Youngs, Ross (1917-1926)	15.2
294	Keltner, Ken (1937-1950)	15.1
295	Baines, Harold (1980-2001)	15.1
296	Ryan, Jimmy (1885-1903)	15.0
297	Bennett, Charlie (1878-1893)	15.0
298	Murphy, Dale (1976-1993)	15.0
299	Perez, Tony (1964-1986)	14.9
300	Grantham, George (1922-1934)	14.9

Wins

1	Young, Cy (1890-1911)	511
2	Johnson, Walter (1907-1927)	417
3	Alexander, Grover (1911-1930)	373
	Mathewson, Christy (1900-1916)	373
5	Spahn, Warren (1942-1965)	363
6	Galvin, Pud (1875-1892)	361
	Nichols, Kid (1890-1906)	361
8	Keefe, Tim (1880-1893)	342
9	Carlton, Steve (1965-1988)	329
10	Clarkson, John (1882-1894)	328
11	Plank, Eddie (1901-1917)	326
12	Ryan, Nolan (1966-1993)	324
	Sutton, Don (1966-1988)	324
14	Niekro, Phil (1964-1987)	318
15	Perry, Gaylord (1962-1983)	314
16	Seaver, Tom (1967-1986)	311
17	Clemens, Roger (1984-2003)	310
18	Radbourn, Charley (1881-1891)	309
19	Welch, Mickey (1880-1892)	307
20	Grove, Lefty (1925-1941)	300
	Wynn, Early (1939-1963)	300
22	Maddux, Greg (1986-2003)	289
23	John, Tommy (1963-1989)	288
24	Blyleven, Bert (1970-1992)	287
25	Roberts, Robin (1948-1966)	286
26	Jenkins, Fergie (1965-1983)	284
	Mullane, Tony (1881-1894)	284
28	Kaat, Jim (1959-1983)	283
29	Ruffing, Red (1924-1947)	273
30	Grimes, Burleigh (1916-1934)	270
31	Palmer, Jim (1965-1984)	268
32	Feller, Bob (1936-1956)	266
	Rixey, Eppa (1912-1933)	266
34	McCormick, Jim (1878-1887)	265
35	Weyhing, Gus (1887-1901)	264
36	Lyons, Ted (1923-1946)	260
37	Faber, Red (1914-1933)	254
	Morris, Jack (1977-1994)	254
39	Hubbell, Carl (1928-1943)	253
40	Gibson, Bob (1959-1975)	251
	Glavine, Tom (1987-2003)	251
42	Willis, Vic (1898-1910)	249
43	Quinn, Jack (1909-1933)	247
44	McGinnity, Joe (1899-1908)	246
	Rusie, Amos (1889-1901)	246
46	Martinez, Dennis (1976-1998)	245
	Powell, Jack (1897-1912)	245
48	Marichal, Juan (1960-1975)	243
49	Pennock, Herb (1912-1934)	241
50	Tanana, Frank (1973-1993)	240
51	Brown, Mordecai (1903-1916)	239
52	Griffith, Clark (1891-1914)	237
	Hoyt, Waite (1918-1938)	237
54	Ford, Whitey (1950-1967)	236
55	Buffinton, Charlie (1882-1892)	233
56	Johnson, Randy (1988-2003)	230
57	Jones, Sam (1914-1935)	229
	Tiant, Luis (1964-1982)	229
	White, Will (1877-1886)	229
60	Mullin, George (1902-1915)	228
61	Bunning, Jim (1955-1971)	224
	Hunter, Catfish (1965-1979)	224
63	Derringer, Paul (1931-1945)	223
	Harder, Mel (1928-1947)	223
65	Dauss, Hooks (1912-1926)	222
	Koosman, Jerry (1967-1985)	222
67	Niekro, Joe (1967-1988)	221
68	Reuss, Jerry (1969-1990)	220
69	Caruthers, Bob (1884-1892)	218
	Whitehill, Earl (1923-1939)	218
71	Fitzsimmons, Freddie (1925-1943)	217
	Lolich, Mickey (1963-1979)	217
73	Cooper, Wilbur (1912-1926)	216
	Hough, Charlie (1970-1994)	216
75	Coveleski, Stan (1912-1928)	215
	Perry, Jim (1959-1975)	215
77	Reuschel, Rick (1972-1991)	214
78	Bender, Chief (1903-1925)	212
79	Newsom, Bobo (1929-1953)	211
	Pierce, Billy (1945-1964)	211
	Welch, Bob (1978-1994)	211
82	Haines, Jesse (1918-1937)	210
83	Blue, Vida (1969-1986)	209
	Cicotte, Eddie (1905-1920)	209
	Drysdale, Don (1956-1969)	209
	Pappas, Milt (1957-1973)	209
87	Mays, Carl (1915-1929)	208
88	Lemon, Bob (1946-1958)	207
	Newhouser, Hal (1939-1955)	207
90	Hershiser, Orel (1983-2000)	204
	Orth, Al (1895-1909)	204
92	Burdette, Lew (1950-1967)	203
	King, Silver (1886-1897)	203
	Stivetts, Jack (1889-1899)	203
95	Marquard, Rube (1908-1925)	201
	Root, Charley (1923-1941)	201
97	Finley, Chuck (1986-2002)	200
	Uhle, George (1919-1936)	200
	Wells, David (1987-2003)	200
100	Mussina, Mike (1991-2003)	199

Losses

1	Young, Cy (1890-1911)	316
2	Galvin, Pud (1875-1892)	308
3	Ryan, Nolan (1966-1993)	292
4	Johnson, Walter (1907-1927)	279
5	Niekro, Phil (1964-1987)	274
6	Perry, Gaylord (1962-1983)	265
7	Sutton, Don (1966-1988)	256
8	Powell, Jack (1897-1912)	254
9	Rixey, Eppa (1912-1933)	251
10	Blyleven, Bert (1970-1992)	250
11	Roberts, Robin (1948-1966)	245
	Spahn, Warren (1942-1965)	245
13	Carlton, Steve (1965-1988)	244
	Wynn, Early (1939-1963)	244
15	Kaat, Jim (1959-1983)	237
16	Tanana, Frank (1973-1993)	236
17	Weyhing, Gus (1887-1901)	232
18	John, Tommy (1963-1989)	231
19	Friend, Bob (1951-1966)	230
	Lyons, Ted (1923-1946)	230
21	Jenkins, Fergie (1965-1983)	226
22	Keefe, Tim (1880-1893)	225
	Ruffing, Red (1924-1947)	225
24	Newsom, Bobo (1929-1953)	222
25	Mullane, Tony (1881-1894)	220
26	Quinn, Jack (1909-1933)	218
27	Jones, Sam (1914-1935)	217
28	Hough, Charlie (1970-1994)	216
29	McCormick, Jim (1878-1887)	214
30	Faber, Red (1914-1933)	213
31	Derringer, Paul (1931-1945)	212
	Fraser, Chick (1896-1909)	212
	Grimes, Burleigh (1916-1934)	212
34	Welch, Mickey (1880-1892)	210
35	Koosman, Jerry (1967-1985)	209
36	Alexander, Grover (1911-1930)	208
	Nichols, Kid (1890-1906)	208
38	Seaver, Tom (1967-1986)	205
	Willis, Vic (1898-1910)	205
40	Niekro, Joe (1967-1988)	204
	Whitney, Jim (1881-1890)	204
42	Mullin, George (1902-1915)	196
	Terry, Adonis (1884-1897)	196
44	Osteen, Claude (1957-1975)	195
	Radbourn, Charley (1881-1891)	195
46	Plank, Eddie (1901-1917)	194
47	Martinez, Dennis (1976-1998)	193
48	Lolich, Mickey (1963-1979)	191
	Reuschel, Rick (1972-1991)	191
	Reuss, Jerry (1969-1990)	191
	Zachary, Tom (1918-1936)	191
52	Orth, Al (1895-1909)	189
53	Mathewson, Christy (1900-1916)	188
54	Harder, Mel (1928-1947)	186
	Morgan, Mike (1978-2002)	186
	Morris, Jack (1977-1994)	186
57	Whitehill, Earl (1923-1939)	185
58	Bunning, Jim (1955-1971)	184
	Bush, Joe (1912-1928)	184
60	Jackson, Larry (1955-1968)	183
	Simmons, Curt (1947-1967)	183
62	Darwin, Danny (1978-1998)	182
	Dauss, Hooks (1912-1926)	182
	Hoyt, Waite (1918-1938)	182
65	Dickson, Murry (1939-1959)	181
	Leonard, Dutch (1933-1953)	181
	Wise, Rick (1964-1982)	181
68	Meadows, Lee (1915-1929)	180
69	Hawley, Pink (1892-1901)	179
	Luque, Dolf (1914-1935)	179
71	Clarkson, John (1882-1894)	178
	Cooper, Wilbur (1912-1926)	178
73	Dineen, Bill (1898-1909)	177
	Marquard, Rube (1908-1925)	177
75	Moore, Mike (1982-1995)	176
76	Donahue, Red (1893-1906)	175
77	Alexander, Doyle (1971-1989)	174
	Gibson, Bob (1959-1975)	174
	Hughes, Tom (1900-1913)	174
	Perry, Jim (1959-1975)	174
	Rusie, Amos (1889-1901)	174
82	Finley, Chuck (1986-2002)	173
83	Tiant, Luis (1964-1982)	172
84	Eckersley, Dennis (1975-1998)	171
	French, Larry (1929-1942)	171
86	Breitenstein, Ted (1891-1901)	170
	Pascual, Camilo (1954-1971)	170
88	Pierce, Billy (1945-1964)	169
89	Ames, Red (1903-1919)	167
	Clancy, Jim (1977-1991)	167
	Cunningham, Bert (1887-1901)	167
	Ehret, Red (1888-1898)	167
93	Drysdale, Don (1956-1969)	166
	Ehmke, Howard (1915-1930)	166
	Hunter, Catfish (1965-1979)	166
	Uhle, George (1919-1936)	166
	White, Will (1877-1886)	166
98	Hadley, Bump (1926-1941)	165
	Johnson, Si (1928-1947)	165
100	4 players tied	164

Winning Percentage – Starters

1	Martinez, Pedro (1992-2003)	.712
2	Foutz, Dave (1884-1894)	.690
3	Ford, Whitey (1950-1967)	.690
4	Caruthers, Bob (1884-1892)	.688
5	Grove, Lefty (1925-1941)	.680
6	Johnson, Randy (1988-2003)	.669
7	Raschi, Vic (1946-1955)	.667
8	Corcoran, Larry (1880-1887)	.665
9	Mathewson, Christy (1900-1916)	.665
10	Leever, Sam (1898-1910)	.660
11	Clemens, Roger (1984-2003)	.660
12	Maglie, Sal (1945-1958)	.657
13	Pettitte, Andy (1995-2003)	.656
14	Koufax, Sandy (1955-1966)	.655
15	Allen, Johnny (1932-1944)	.654
16	Guidry, Ron (1975-1988)	.651
17	Gomez, Lefty (1930-1943)	.649
18	Clarkson, John (1882-1894)	.648
19	Brown, Mordecai (1903-1916)	.648
20	Mussina, Mike (1991-2003)	.644
21	Dean, Dizzy (1930-1947)	.644
22	Alexander, Grover (1911-1930)	.642
23	Maddux, Greg (1986-2003)	.639
24	Palmer, Jim (1965-1984)	.638
25	Nichols, Kid (1890-1906)	.634
26	Phillippe, Deacon (1899-1911)	.634
27	McGinnity, Joe (1899-1908)	.634
28	Gooden, Dwight (1984-2000)	.634
29	Reulbach, Ed (1905-1917)	.632
30	Marichal, Juan (1960-1975)	.631
31	Cooper, Mort (1938-1949)	.631
32	Reynolds, Allie (1942-1954)	.630
33	Tannehill, Jesse (1894-1911)	.627
34	Kremer, Ray (1924-1933)	.627
35	Marberry, Firpo (1923-1936)	.627
36	Plank, Eddie (1901-1917)	.627
37	Bond, Tommy (1874-1884)	.627
38	Bender, Chief (1903-1925)	.625
39	Newcombe, Don (1949-1960)	.623
40	Cuppy, Nig (1892-1901)	.623
41	Mays, Carl (1915-1929)	.623
42	Joss, Addie (1902-1910)	.623
43	Goldsmith, Fred (1879-1884)	.622
44	Crandall, Doc (1908-1918)	.622
45	Hubbell, Carl (1928-1943)	.622
46	Feller, Bob (1936-1956)	.621
47	Parnell, Mel (1947-1956)	.621
48	Rueter, Kirk (1993-2003)	.620
49	Tudor, John (1979-1990)	.619
50	Griffith, Clark (1891-1914)	.619
51	Lemon, Bob (1946-1958)	.618
52	Young, Cy (1890-1911)	.618
53	Glavine, Tom (1987-2003)	.615
54	Shocker, Urban (1916-1928)	.615
55	Tesreau, Jeff (1912-1918)	.615
56	Maloney, Jim (1960-1971)	.615
57	Ward, John (1878-1884)	.614
58	Key, Jimmy (1984-1998)	.614
59	Warneke, Lon (1930-1945)	.613
60	Radbourn, Charley (1881-1891)	.613
61	Nolan, Gary (1967-1977)	.611
62	Rowe, Schoolboy (1933-1949)	.610
63	Erskine, Carl (1948-1959)	.610
64	Wells, David (1987-2003)	.610
65	Walsh, Ed (1904-1917)	.607
66	Ferguson, Charlie (1884-1887)	.607
67	McNally, Dave (1962-1975)	.607
68	Wiltse, Hooks (1904-1915)	.607
69	Cone, David (1986-2003)	.606
70	Stivetts, Jack (1889-1899)	.606
71	Martinez, Ramon (1988-2001)	.605
72	Nehf, Art (1915-1929)	.605
73	Buffinton, Charlie (1882-1892)	.605
74	Overall, Orval (1905-1913)	.603
75	Keefe, Tim (1880-1893)	.603
76	Seaver, Tom (1967-1986)	.603
77	Coveleski, Stan (1912-1928)	.602
78	Roe, Preacher (1938-1954)	.602
79	Ferrell, Wes (1927-1941)	.601
80	Richard, J.R. (1971-1980)	.601
81	Brown, Kevin (1986-2003)	.601
82	Chesbro, Jack (1899-1909)	.600
83	Johnson, Walter (1907-1927)	.599
84	Pennock, Herb (1912-1934)	.598
85	Fitzsimmons, Freddie (1925-1943)	.598
86	Lopat, Ed (1944-1955)	.597
87	Spahn, Warren (1942-1965)	.597
88	Sewell, Rip (1932-1949)	.596
89	Garcia, Mike (1948-1961)	.594
90	Welch, Mickey (1880-1892)	.594
91	McDowell, Jack (1987-1999)	.593
92	Malone, Pat (1928-1937)	.593
93	Bagby, Jim (1912-1923)	.593
94	Crowder, Alvin (1926-1936)	.592
95	Candelaria, John (1975-1993)	.592
96	Brecheen, Harry (1940-1953)	.591
97	Welch, Bob (1978-1994)	.591
98	Gibson, Bob (1959-1975)	.591
99	Ruether, Dutch (1917-1927)	.591
100	McLain, Denny (1963-1972)	.590

Games

1	Orosco, Jesse (1979-2003)	1252
2	Eckersley, Dennis (1975-1998)	1071
3	Wilhelm, Hoyt (1952-1972)	1070
4	Plesac, Dan (1986-2003)	1064
5	Tekulve, Kent (1974-1989)	1050
6	Franco, John (1984-2003)	1036
7	Smith, Lee (1980-1997)	1022
8	Gossage, Rich (1972-1994)	1002
9	McDaniel, Lindy (1955-1975)	987
10	Jackson, Mike (1986-2002)	960
11	Fingers, Rollie (1968-1985)	944
12	Garber, Gene (1969-1988)	931
13	Young, Cy (1890-1911)	906
14	Lyle, Sparky (1967-1982)	899
15	Kaat, Jim (1959-1983)	898
16	Stanton, Mike (1989-2003)	885
17	Assenmacher, Paul (1986-1999)	884
18	Reardon, Jeff (1979-1994)	880
19	McMahon, Don (1957-1974)	874
20	Niekro, Phil (1964-1987)	864
21	Hough, Charlie (1970-1994)	858
22	Face, Roy (1953-1969)	848
23	Jones, Doug (1982-2000)	846
24	McGraw, Tug (1965-1984)	824
25	Ryan, Nolan (1966-1993)	807
26	Johnson, Walter (1907-1927)	802
27	Honeycutt, Rick (1977-1997)	797
28	Perry, Gaylord (1962-1983)	777
29	Sutton, Don (1966-1988)	774
30	Guthrie, Mark (1989-2003)	765
	Knowles, Darold (1965-1980)	765
32	Hernandez, Roberto (1991-2003)	762
	Mesa, Jose (1987-2003)	762
34	John, Tommy (1963-1989)	760
35	Quinn, Jack (1909-1933)	756
36	Reed, Ron (1966-1984)	751
37	Spahn, Warren (1942-1965)	750
38	Burgmeier, Tom (1968-1984)	745
	Lavelle, Gary (1974-1987)	745
40	Hernandez, Willie (1977-1989)	744
41	Carlton, Steve (1965-1988)	741
42	Reed, Steve (1992-2003)	738
43	Perranoski, Ron (1961-1973)	737
44	Kline, Ron (1952-1970)	736
	Timlin, Mike (1991-2003)	736
46	Aguilera, Rick (1985-2000)	732
	Bedrosian, Steve (1981-1995)	732
48	Carroll, Clay (1964-1978)	731
49	Myers, Randy (1985-1998)	728
50	Marshall, Mike (1967-1981)	723
	McDowell, Roger (1985-1996)	723
52	Righetti, Dave (1979-1995)	718
53	Darwin, Danny (1978-1998)	716
54	Nelson, Jeff (1992-2003)	714
	Plunk, Eric (1986-1999)	714
56	Klippstein, Johnny (1950-1967)	711
57	Minton, Greg (1975-1990)	710
58	Quantrill, Paul (1992-2003)	705
59	Miller, Stu (1952-1968)	704
60	Harris, Greg (1981-1995)	703
61	Niekro, Joe (1967-1988)	702
62	Campbell, Bill (1973-1987)	700
	Montgomery, Jeff (1987-1999)	700
64	Andersen, Larry (1975-1994)	699
65	McClure, Bob (1975-1993)	698
66	Galvin, Pud (1875-1892)	697
67	Alexander, Grover (1911-1930)	696
	Lefferts, Craig (1983-1994)	696
69	Miller, Bob (1957-1974)	694
70	Blyleven, Bert (1970-1992)	692
	Jackson, Grant (1965-1982)	692
	Martinez, Dennis (1976-1998)	692
	Rixey, Eppa (1912-1933)	692
74	Wynn, Early (1939-1963)	691
75	Fisher, Eddie (1959-1973)	690
76	Abernathy, Ted (1955-1972)	681
77	Groom, Buddy (1992-2003)	679
78	Beck, Rod (1991-2003)	678
79	Roberts, Robin (1948-1966)	676
80	Hoyt, Waite (1918-1938)	674
	Quisenberry, Dan (1979-1990)	674
82	Faber, Red (1914-1933)	669
83	Giusti, Dave (1962-1977)	668
84	Jones, Todd (1993-2003)	666
85	Cook, Dennis (1988-2002)	665
86	Jenkins, Fergie (1965-1983)	664
	Swindell, Greg (1986-2002)	664
88	Sutter, Bruce (1976-1988)	661
89	Seaver, Tom (1967-1986)	656
90	Lindblad, Paul (1965-1978)	655
91	McElroy, Chuck (1989-2001)	654
92	Wood, Wilbur (1961-1978)	651
93	Jones, Sam (1914-1935)	647
	LaRoche, Dave (1970-1983)	647
95	Nen, Robb (1993-2002)	643
96	Henke, Tom (1982-1995)	642
97	Hoffman, Trevor (1993-2003)	641
98	Leonard, Dutch (1933-1953)	640
	Staley, Gerry (1947-1961)	640
100	3 players tied	639

Games Started

1	Young, Cy (1890-1911)	815
2	Ryan, Nolan (1966-1993)	773
3	Sutton, Don (1966-1988)	756
4	Niekro, Phil (1964-1987)	716
5	Carlton, Steve (1965-1988)	709
6	John, Tommy (1963-1989)	700
7	Perry, Gaylord (1962-1983)	690
8	Blyleven, Bert (1970-1992)	685
9	Galvin, Pud (1875-1892)	681
10	Johnson, Walter (1907-1927)	666
11	Spahn, Warren (1942-1965)	665
12	Seaver, Tom (1967-1986)	647
13	Kaat, Jim (1959-1983)	625
14	Tanana, Frank (1973-1993)	616
15	Wynn, Early (1939-1963)	612
16	Roberts, Robin (1948-1966)	609
17	Clemens, Roger (1984-2003)	606
18	Alexander, Grover (1911-1930)	600
19	Jenkins, Fergie (1965-1983)	594
	Keefe, Tim (1880-1893)	594
21	Maddux, Greg (1986-2003)	571
22	Martinez, Dennis (1976-1998)	562
	Nichols, Kid (1890-1906)	562
24	Rixey, Eppa (1912-1933)	554
25	Mathewson, Christy (1900-1916)	552
26	Welch, Mickey (1880-1892)	549
27	Reuss, Jerry (1969-1990)	547
28	Ruffing, Red (1924-1947)	538
29	Glavine, Tom (1987-2003)	537
30	Plank, Eddie (1901-1917)	529
	Reuschel, Rick (1972-1991)	529
32	Koosman, Jerry (1967-1985)	527
	Morris, Jack (1977-1994)	527
34	Palmer, Jim (1965-1984)	521
35	Bunning, Jim (1955-1971)	519
36	Clarkson, John (1882-1894)	518
37	Powell, Jack (1897-1912)	516
38	Weyhing, Gus (1887-1901)	505
39	Mullane, Tony (1881-1894)	504
40	Radbourn, Charley (1881-1891)	502
41	Niekro, Joe (1967-1988)	500
42	Friend, Bob (1951-1966)	497
	Grimes, Burleigh (1916-1934)	497
44	Lolich, Mickey (1963-1979)	496
45	Osteen, Claude (1957-1975)	488
46	Jones, Sam (1914-1935)	487
47	McCormick, Jim (1878-1887)	485
48	Feller, Bob (1936-1956)	484
	Lyons, Ted (1923-1946)	484
	Tiant, Luis (1964-1982)	484
51	Faber, Red (1914-1933)	483
	Newsom, Bobo (1929-1953)	483
53	Gibson, Bob (1959-1975)	482
54	Hunter, Catfish (1965-1979)	476
55	Blue, Vida (1969-1986)	473
	Whitehill, Earl (1923-1939)	473
57	Willis, Vic (1898-1910)	471
58	Finley, Chuck (1986-2002)	467
59	Hershiser, Orel (1983-2000)	466
60	Drysdale, Don (1956-1969)	465
	Pappas, Milt (1957-1973)	465
62	Alexander, Doyle (1971-1989)	464
63	Welch, Bob (1978-1994)	462
64	Simmons, Curt (1947-1967)	461
65	Torrez, Mike (1967-1984)	458
66	Grove, Lefty (1925-1941)	457
	Marichal, Juan (1960-1975)	457
68	Wise, Rick (1964-1982)	455
69	Perry, Jim (1959-1975)	447
70	Derringer, Paul (1931-1945)	445
71	Johnson, Randy (1988-2003)	444
	Quinn, Jack (1909-1933)	444
73	Brown, Kevin (1986-2003)	441
74	Hough, Charlie (1970-1994)	440
	Moore, Mike (1982-1995)	440
76	Ford, Whitey (1950-1967)	438
77	Harder, Mel (1928-1947)	433
	Hubbell, Carl (1928-1943)	433
79	Pierce, Billy (1945-1964)	432
80	Jackson, Larry (1955-1968)	429
81	Langston, Mark (1984-1999)	428
	Mullin, George (1902-1915)	428
83	Rusie, Amos (1889-1901)	427
84	Fitzsimmons, Freddie (1925-1943)	426
85	Hoyt, Waite (1918-1938)	425
86	Valenzuela, Fernando (1980-1997)	424
87	Burkett, John (1987-2003)	423
88	Forsch, Bob (1974-1989)	422
89	Moyer, Jamie (1986-2003)	420
	Viola, Frank (1982-1996)	420
91	Cone, David (1986-2003)	419
	Pennock, Herb (1912-1934)	419
93	Knepper, Bob (1976-1990)	413
94	Stieb, Dave (1979-1998)	412
95	Morgan, Mike (1978-2002)	411
96	Candiotti, Tom (1983-1999)	410
	Gooden, Dwight (1984-2000)	410
	Holtzman, Ken (1965-1979)	410
99	Zachary, Tom (1918-1936)	409
100	2 players tied	407

Complete Games

1	Young, Cy (1890-1911)	749
2	Galvin, Pud (1875-1892)	639
3	Keefe, Tim (1880-1893)	554
4	Nichols, Kid (1890-1906)	532
5	Johnson, Walter (1907-1927)	531
6	Welch, Mickey (1880-1892)	525
7	Radbourn, Charley (1881-1891)	488
8	Clarkson, John (1882-1894)	485
9	Mullane, Tony (1881-1894)	468
10	McCormick, Jim (1878-1887)	466
11	Weyhing, Gus (1887-1901)	449
12	Alexander, Grover (1911-1930)	437
13	Mathewson, Christy (1900-1916)	435
14	Powell, Jack (1897-1912)	422
15	Plank, Eddie (1901-1917)	410
16	White, Will (1877-1886)	394
17	Rusie, Amos (1889-1901)	393
18	Willis, Vic (1898-1910)	388
19	Spahn, Warren (1942-1965)	382
20	Whitney, Jim (1881-1890)	377
21	Terry, Adonis (1884-1897)	367
22	Lyons, Ted (1923-1946)	356
23	Mullin, George (1902-1915)	353
24	Buffinton, Charlie (1882-1892)	351
25	Fraser, Chick (1896-1909)	342
26	Griffith, Clark (1891-1914)	337
27	Ruffing, Red (1924-1947)	335
28	King, Silver (1886-1897)	328
29	Orth, Al (1895-1909)	324
30	Hutchison, Bill (1884-1897)	321
31	Grimes, Burleigh (1916-1934)	314
	McGinnity, Joe (1899-1908)	314
33	Donahue, Red (1893-1906)	312
	Hecker, Guy (1882-1890)	312
35	Dineen, Bill (1898-1909)	306
36	Roberts, Robin (1948-1966)	305
37	Perry, Gaylord (1962-1983)	303
38	Breitenstein, Ted (1891-1901)	301
39	Caruthers, Bob (1884-1892)	298
	Grove, Lefty (1925-1941)	298
41	Hawley, Pink (1892-1901)	297
	Morris, Ed (1884-1890)	297
43	Baldwin, Mark (1887-1893)	295
44	Bond, Tommy (1874-1884)	294
	Kennedy, Brickyard (1892-1903)	294
46	Rixey, Eppa (1912-1933)	290
	Wynn, Early (1939-1963)	290
48	Donovan, Bill (1898-1918)	289
	Mathews, Bobby (1871-1887)	289
50	Cunningham, Bert (1887-1901)	287
51	Cooper, Wilbur (1912-1926)	279
	Feller, Bob (1936-1956)	279
	McMahon, Sadie (1889-1897)	279
54	Stivetts, Jack (1889-1899)	278
	Taylor, Jack (1898-1907)	278
56	Getzein, Charlie (1884-1892)	277
57	Faber, Red (1914-1933)	273
58	Brown, Mordecai (1903-1916)	271
	Dwyer, Frank (1888-1899)	271
60	Meekin, Jouett (1891-1900)	270
61	Jenkins, Fergie (1965-1983)	267
62	Chamberlain, Elton (1886-1896)	264
	Kilroy, Matt (1886-1898)	264
	Tannehill, Jesse (1894-1911)	264
65	White, Doc (1901-1913)	262
66	Waddell, Rube (1897-1910)	261
67	Chesbro, Jack (1899-1909)	260
	Ehret, Red (1888-1898)	260
	Hubbell, Carl (1928-1943)	260
70	Corcoran, Larry (1880-1887)	256
71	Bender, Chief (1903-1925)	255
	Gibson, Bob (1959-1975)	255
73	Carlton, Steve (1965-1988)	254
74	Killen, Frank (1891-1900)	253
	Mercer, Win (1894-1902)	253
76	Derringer, Paul (1931-1945)	251
77	Jones, Sam (1914-1935)	250
	Walsh, Ed (1904-1917)	250
79	Cicotte, Eddie (1905-1920)	249
	Wiedman, Stump (1880-1888)	249
81	Pennock, Herb (1912-1934)	247
82	Newsom, Bobo (1929-1953)	246
83	Bradley, George (1875-1884)	245
	Dauss, Hooks (1912-1926)	245
	Niekro, Phil (1964-1987)	245
	Ward, John (1878-1884)	245
87	Howell, Harry (1898-1910)	244
	Marichal, Juan (1960-1975)	244
89	Quinn, Jack (1909-1933)	243
90	Blyleven, Bert (1970-1992)	242
	Phillippe, Deacon (1899-1911)	242
	Walters, Bucky (1934-1950)	242
93	Leever, Sam (1898-1910)	241
94	Gleason, Kid (1888-1895)	240
95	Joss, Addie (1902-1910)	234
96	Uhle, George (1919-1936)	232
97	Mays, Carl (1915-1929)	231
	Seaver, Tom (1967-1986)	231
	Staley, Harry (1888-1895)	231
100	Moore, Earl (1901-1914)	230

Shutouts

1	Johnson, Walter (1907-1927)	110
2	Alexander, Grover (1911-1930)	90
3	Mathewson, Christy (1900-1916)	79
4	Young, Cy (1890-1911)	76
5	Plank, Eddie (1901-1917)	69
6	Spahn, Warren (1942-1965)	63
7	Ryan, Nolan (1966-1993)	61
	Seaver, Tom (1967-1986)	61
9	Blyleven, Bert (1970-1992)	60
10	Sutton, Don (1966-1988)	58
11	Walsh, Ed (1904-1917)	57
12	Galvin, Pud (1875-1892)	56
	Gibson, Bob (1959-1975)	56
14	Brown, Mordecai (1903-1916)	55
	Carlton, Steve (1965-1988)	55
16	Palmer, Jim (1965-1984)	53
	Perry, Gaylord (1962-1983)	53
18	Marichal, Juan (1960-1975)	52
19	Waddell, Rube (1897-1910)	50
	Willis, Vic (1898-1910)	50
21	Drysdale, Don (1956-1969)	49
	Jenkins, Fergie (1965-1983)	49
	Tiant, Luis (1964-1982)	49
	Wynn, Early (1939-1963)	49
25	Nichols, Kid (1890-1906)	48
26	Clemens, Roger (1984-2003)	46
	John, Tommy (1963-1989)	46
	Powell, Jack (1897-1912)	46
29	Ford, Whitey (1950-1967)	45
	Joss, Addie (1902-1910)	45
	Niekro, Phil (1964-1987)	45
	Roberts, Robin (1948-1966)	45
	Ruffing, Red (1924-1947)	45
	White, Doc (1901-1913)	45
35	Adams, Babe (1906-1926)	44
	Feller, Bob (1936-1956)	44
37	Pappas, Milt (1957-1973)	43
38	Hunter, Catfish (1965-1979)	42
	Walters, Bucky (1934-1950)	42
40	Lolich, Mickey (1963-1979)	41
	Vaughn, Hippo (1908-1921)	41
	Welch, Mickey (1880-1892)	41
43	Bender, Chief (1903-1925)	40
	Bunning, Jim (1955-1971)	40
	French, Larry (1929-1942)	40
	Koufax, Sandy (1955-1966)	40
	Osteen, Claude (1957-1975)	40
	Reulbach, Ed (1905-1917)	40
	Stottlemyre, Mel (1964-1974)	40
50	Keefe, Tim (1880-1893)	39
	Leever, Sam (1898-1910)	39
	Reuss, Jerry (1969-1990)	39
53	Coveleski, Stan (1912-1928)	38
	Pierce, Billy (1945-1964)	38
	Rucker, Nap (1907-1916)	38
56	Blue, Vida (1969-1986)	37
	Clarkson, John (1882-1894)	37
	Jackson, Larry (1955-1968)	37
	Rixey, Eppa (1912-1933)	37
	Rogers, Steve (1973-1985)	37
61	Bush, Joe (1912-1928)	36
	Cuellar, Mike (1959-1977)	36
	Friend, Bob (1951-1966)	36
	Hubbell, Carl (1928-1943)	36
	Jones, Sam (1914-1935)	36
	Pascual, Camilo (1954-1971)	36
	Reynolds, Allie (1942-1954)	36
	Simmons, Curt (1947-1967)	36
	White, Will (1877-1886)	36
70	Bond, Tommy (1874-1884)	35
	Chesbro, Jack (1899-1909)	35
	Cicotte, Eddie (1905-1920)	35
	Coombs, Jack (1906-1920)	35
	Cooper, Wilbur (1912-1926)	35
	Donovan, Bill (1898-1918)	35
	Grimes, Burleigh (1916-1934)	35
	Grove, Lefty (1925-1941)	35
	Johnson, Randy (1988-2003)	35
	Mullin, George (1902-1915)	35
	Pennock, Herb (1912-1934)	35
	Radbourn, Charley (1881-1891)	35
82	Doak, Bill (1912-1929)	34
	Maddux, Greg (1986-2003)	34
	Moore, Earl (1901-1914)	34
	Tanana, Frank (1973-1993)	34
	Tannehill, Jesse (1894-1911)	34
87	Bridges, Tommy (1930-1946)	33
	Burdette, Lew (1950-1967)	33
	Chance, Dean (1961-1971)	33
	Cooper, Mort (1938-1949)	33
	Koosman, Jerry (1967-1985)	33
	Leifield, Lefty (1905-1920)	33
	Leonard, Dutch (1913-1925)	33
	McCormick, Jim (1878-1887)	33
	McNally, Dave (1962-1975)	33
	Newhouser, Hal (1939-1955)	33
	Shawkey, Bob (1913-1927)	33
	Trucks, Virgil (1941-1958)	33
99	3 players tied	32

Saves

1	Smith, Lee (1980-1997)	478
2	Franco, John (1984-2003)	424
3	Eckersley, Dennis (1975-1998)	390
4	Reardon, Jeff (1979-1994)	367
5	Hoffman, Trevor (1993-2003)	352
6	Myers, Randy (1985-1998)	347
7	Fingers, Rollie (1968-1985)	341
8	Wetteland, John (1989-2000)	330
9	Hernandez, Roberto (1991-2003)	320
10	Aguilera, Rick (1985-2000)	318
11	Nen, Robb (1993-2002)	314
12	Henke, Tom (1982-1995)	311
13	Gossage, Rich (1972-1994)	310
14	Montgomery, Jeff (1987-1999)	304
15	Jones, Doug (1982-2000)	303
16	Sutter, Bruce (1976-1988)	300
17	Beck, Rod (1991-2003)	286
18	Percival, Troy (1995-2003)	283
	Rivera, Mariano (1995-2003)	283
20	Worrell, Todd (1985-1997)	256
21	Righetti, Dave (1979-1995)	252
22	Mesa, Jose (1987-2003)	249
23	Quisenberry, Dan (1979-1990)	244
24	Lyle, Sparky (1967-1982)	238
25	Wilhelm, Hoyt (1952-1972)	227
26	Wagner, Billy (1995-2003)	225
27	Garber, Gene (1969-1988)	218
28	Olson, Gregg (1988-2001)	217
29	Smith, Dave (1980-1992)	216
30	Urbina, Ugueth (1995-2003)	206
31	Shaw, Jeff (1990-2001)	203
32	Thigpen, Bobby (1986-1994)	201
33	Benitez, Armando (1994-2003)	197
34	Face, Roy (1953-1969)	193
	Henneman, Mike (1987-1996)	193
36	Williams, Mitch (1986-1997)	192
37	Marshall, Mike (1967-1981)	188
38	Russell, Jeff (1983-1996)	186
39	Bedrosian, Steve (1981-1995)	184
	Jones, Todd (1993-2003)	184
	Tekulve, Kent (1974-1989)	184
42	McGraw, Tug (1965-1984)	180
43	Perranoski, Ron (1961-1973)	179
44	Harvey, Bryan (1987-1995)	177
45	Brantley, Jeff (1988-2001)	172
	McDaniel, Lindy (1955-1975)	172
47	McDowell, Roger (1985-1996)	159
48	Plesac, Dan (1986-2003)	158
49	Wickman, Bob (1992-2002)	156
50	Howell, Jay (1980-1994)	155
	Koch, Billy (1999-2003)	155
52	Miller, Stu (1952-1968)	154
53	McMahon, Don (1957-1974)	153
54	Minton, Greg (1975-1990)	150
55	Abernathy, Ted (1955-1972)	148
56	Hernandez, Willie (1977-1989)	147
57	Giusti, Dave (1962-1977)	145
58	Orosco, Jesse (1979-2003)	144
	Williams, Mike (1992-2003)	144
60	Carroll, Clay (1964-1978)	143
	Foulke, Keith (1997-2003)	143
	Knowles, Darold (1965-1980)	143
63	Jackson, Mike (1986-2002)	142
64	Lavelle, Gary (1974-1987)	136
65	Brewer, Jim (1960-1976)	132
	Farr, Steve (1984-1994)	132
	Stanley, Bob (1977-1989)	132
68	Graves, Danny (1996-2003)	131
69	Davis, Ron (1978-1988)	130
	Isringhausen, Jason (1995-2003)	130
71	Sasaki, Kazuhiro (2000-2003)	129
72	Forster, Terry (1971-1986)	127
73	Campbell, Bill (1973-1987)	126
	LaRoche, Dave (1970-1983)	126
	Rojas, Mel (1990-1999)	126
76	Hiller, John (1965-1980)	125
77	Aker, Jack (1964-1974)	123
78	Radatz, Dick (1962-1969)	122
79	Alfonseca, Antonio (1997-2003)	121
	Ward, Duane (1986-1995)	121
81	Wohlers, Mark (1991-2002)	119
82	Guardado, Eddie (1993-2003)	116
	Timlin, Mike (1991-2003)	116
84	Martinez, Tippy (1974-1988)	115
85	Bottalico, Ricky (1994-2003)	114
86	Linzy, Frank (1963-1974)	111
87	Gordon, Tom (1988-2003)	110
	Smoltz, John (1988-2003)	110
	Worthington, Al (1953-1969)	110
90	Gladding, Fred (1961-1973)	109
91	Granger, Wayne (1968-1976)	108
	Kline, Ron (1952-1970)	108
93	Gagne, Eric (1999-2003)	107
	Murphy, Johnny (1932-1947)	107
95	Caudill, Bill (1979-1987)	106
96	Reed, Ron (1966-1984)	103
	Wyatt, John (1961-1969)	103
98	4 players tied	102

Relief Games

1	Orosco, Jesse	1248
2	Plesac, Dan	1050
	Tekulve, Kent	1050
4	Franco, John	1036
5	Wilhelm, Hoyt	1018
6	Smith, Lee	1016
7	Gossage, Rich	965
8	Jackson, Mike	953
9	Garber, Gene	922
10	McDaniel, Lindy	913
11	Fingers, Rollie	907
12	Lyle, Sparky	899
13	Stanton, Mike	884
14	Assenmacher, Paul	883
15	Reardon, Jeff	880
16	McMahon, Don	872
17	Jones, Doug	842
18	Face, Roy	821
19	McGraw, Tug	785
20	Hernandez, Roberto	759
21	Knowles, Darold	757
22	Burgmeier, Tom	742
	Lavelle, Gary	742
24	Reed, Steve	738
25	Perranoski, Ron	736

Relief Innings

1	Wilhelm, Hoyt	1871.0
2	McDaniel, Lindy	1694.0
3	Gossage, Goose	1556.2
4	Fingers, Rollie	1500.1
5	Garber, Gene	1452.2
6	Tekulve, Kent	1436.2
7	Lyle, Sparky	1390.1
8	McGraw, Tug	1301.1
9	McMahon, Don	1297.0
10	Orosco, Jesse	1277.0
11	Marshall, Mike	1259.1
12	Smith, Lee	1252.1
13	Burgmeier, Tom	1248.2
14	Face, Roy	1212.1
15	Carroll, Clay	1204.2
16	Fisher, Eddie	1186.0
17	Franco, John	1184.2
18	Campbell, Bill	1177.1
19	Perronoski, Ron	1170.2
20	Stanley, Bob	1157.0
21	Reardon, Jeff	1132.1
22	Jackson, Mike	1108.0
23	Jones, Doug	1097.1
24	Miller, Stu	1094.2
25	Minton, Greg	1087.1

Relief Wins

1	Wilhelm, Hoyt	124
2	McDaniel, Lindy	119
3	Gossage, Rich	115
4	Fingers, Rollie	107
5	Lyle, Sparky	99
6	Face, Roy	96
7	Garber, Gene	94
	Tekulve, Kent	94
9	Marshall, Mike	92
10	McMahon, Don	90
11	McGraw, Tug	89
12	Carroll, Clay	88
	Franco, John	88
14	Orosco, Jesse	87
15	Stanley, Bob	85

Relief Losses

1	Garber, Gene	108
2	Wilhelm, Hoyt	103
3	Fingers, Rollie	101
4	Marshall, Mike	98
5	Tekulve, Kent	90
6	McDaniel, Lindy	88
7	Smith, Lee	87
8	Gossage, Rich	85
9	Face, Roy	82
10	Franco, John	79
11	Jones, Doug	78
	Orosco, Jesse	78
13	Reardon, Jeff	77
14	Lyle, Sparky	76
15	Lavelle, Gary	75

Relief Percentage

1	Gagne, Eric	96.40
2	Smotz, John	92.44
3	Hoffman, Trevor	88.89
4	Rivera, Mariano	86.54
5	Percival, Troy	86.28
6	Foulke, Keith	85.63
7	Wagner, Billy	85.55
8	Sasaki, Kazuhiro	85.43
9	Nen, Robb	85.33
10	Mesa, Jose	85.27
11	Myers, Randy	85.26
12	Williams, Mike	85.21
13	Koch, Billy	85.16
14	Henke, Tom	84.97
15	Benitez, Armando	84.91

Innings Pitched

1	Young, Cy (1890-1911)	7356.0
2	Galvin, Pud (1875-1892)	5941.1
3	Johnson, Walter (1907-1927)	5914.2
4	Niekro, Phil (1964-1987)	5404.1
5	Ryan, Nolan (1966-1993)	5386.0
6	Perry, Gaylord (1962-1983)	5350.1
7	Sutton, Don (1966-1988)	5282.1
8	Spahn, Warren (1942-1965)	5243.2
9	Carlton, Steve (1965-1988)	5217.1
10	Alexander, Grover (1911-1930)	5190.0
11	Nichols, Kid (1890-1906)	5066.1
12	Keefe, Tim (1880-1893)	5049.2
13	Blyleven, Bert (1970-1992)	4970.0
14	Welch, Mickey (1880-1892)	4802.0
15	Mathewson, Christy (1900-1916)	4788.2
16	Seaver, Tom (1967-1986)	4782.2
17	John, Tommy (1963-1989)	4710.1
18	Roberts, Robin (1948-1966)	4688.2
19	Wynn, Early (1939-1963)	4564.0
20	Clarkson, John (1882-1894)	4536.1
21	Mullane, Tony (1881-1894)	4531.1
22	Kaat, Jim (1959-1983)	4530.1
23	Radbourn, Charley (1881-1891)	4527.1
24	Jenkins, Fergie (1965-1983)	4500.2
25	Plank, Eddie (1901-1917)	4495.2
26	Rixey, Eppa (1912-1933)	4494.2
27	Powell, Jack (1897-1912)	4389.0
28	Ruffing, Red (1924-1947)	4344.0
29	Weyhing, Gus (1887-1901)	4337.1
30	Clemens, Roger (1984-2003)	4278.2
31	McCormick, Jim (1878-1887)	4275.2
32	Tanana, Frank (1973-1993)	4188.1
33	Grimes, Burleigh (1916-1934)	4179.2
34	Lyons, Ted (1923-1946)	4161.0
35	Faber, Red (1914-1933)	4086.2
36	Martinez, Dennis (1976-1998)	3999.2
37	Willis, Vic (1898-1910)	3996.0
38	Maddux, Greg (1986-2003)	3968.2
39	Palmer, Jim (1965-1984)	3948.0
40	Grove, Lefty (1925-1941)	3940.2
41	Quinn, Jack (1909-1933)	3920.1
42	Gibson, Bob (1959-1975)	3884.1
43	Jones, Sam (1914-1935)	3883.0
44	Koosman, Jerry (1967-1985)	3839.1
45	Feller, Bob (1936-1956)	3827.0
46	Morris, Jack (1977-1994)	3824.0
47	Hough, Charlie (1970-1994)	3801.1
48	Rusie, Amos (1889-1901)	3778.2
49	Hoyt, Waite (1918-1938)	3762.1
50	Bunning, Jim (1955-1971)	3760.1
51	Newsom, Bobo (1929-1953)	3759.1
52	Mullin, George (1902-1915)	3686.2
53	Reuss, Jerry (1969-1990)	3669.2
54	Derringer, Paul (1931-1945)	3645.0
55	Lolich, Mickey (1963-1979)	3638.1
56	Friend, Bob (1951-1966)	3611.0
57	Hubbell, Carl (1928-1943)	3590.1
58	Niekro, Joe (1967-1988)	3584.0
59	Pennock, Herb (1912-1934)	3571.2
60	Whitehill, Earl (1923-1939)	3564.2
61	Reuschel, Rick (1972-1991)	3548.1
62	White, Will (1877-1886)	3542.2
63	Glavine, Tom (1987-2003)	3528.0
64	Terry, Adonis (1884-1897)	3514.1
65	Marichal, Juan (1960-1975)	3507.1
66	Whitney, Jim (1881-1890)	3496.1
67	Tiant, Luis (1964-1982)	3486.1
68	Cooper, Wilbur (1912-1926)	3480.0
69	Osteen, Claude (1957-1975)	3460.1
70	Hunter, Catfish (1965-1979)	3449.1
71	McGinnity, Joe (1899-1908)	3441.1
72	Drysdale, Don (1956-1969)	3432.0
73	Harder, Mel (1928-1947)	3426.1
74	Buffinton, Charlie (1882-1892)	3404.0
75	Dauss, Hooks (1912-1926)	3390.2
76	Griffith, Clark (1891-1914)	3385.2
77	Alexander, Doyle (1971-1989)	3367.2
78	Fraser, Chick (1896-1909)	3364.0
79	Orth, Al (1895-1909)	3354.2
80	Simmons, Curt (1947-1967)	3348.1
81	Blue, Vida (1969-1986)	3343.1
82	Marquard, Rube (1908-1925)	3306.2
	Pierce, Billy (1945-1964)	3306.2
84	Eckersley, Dennis (1975-1998)	3285.2
	Perry, Jim (1959-1975)	3285.2
86	Jackson, Larry (1955-1968)	3262.2
87	Fitzsimmons, Freddie (1925-1943)	3223.2
88	Cicotte, Eddie (1905-1920)	3223.1
89	Luque, Dolf (1914-1935)	3220.1
90	Leonard, Dutch (1933-1953)	3218.1
91	Haines, Jesse (1918-1937)	3208.2
92	Ames, Red (1903-1919)	3198.0
93	Finley, Chuck (1986-2002)	3197.1
	Root, Charley (1923-1941)	3197.1
95	Pappas, Milt (1957-1973)	3186.0
96	King, Silver (1886-1897)	3180.1
97	Brown, Mordecai (1903-1916)	3172.1
98	Ford, Whitey (1950-1967)	3170.1
99	Meadows, Lee (1915-1929)	3160.2
100	French, Larry (1929-1942)	3152.0

Hits per Game

1	Ryan, Nolan (1966-1993)	6.56
2	Martinez, Pedro (1992-2003)	6.72
3	Koufax, Sandy (1955-1966)	6.79
4	Fernandez, Sid (1983-1997)	6.85
5	Richard, J.R. (1971-1980)	6.88
6	Messersmith, Andy (1968-1979)	6.94
7	Wilhelm, Hoyt (1952-1972)	7.01
8	Johnson, Randy (1988-2003)	7.02
9	McDowell, Sam (1961-1975)	7.03
10	Walsh, Ed (1904-1917)	7.12
11	Turley, Bob (1951-1963)	7.18
12	Overall, Orval (1905-1913)	7.22
13	Tesreau, Jeff (1912-1918)	7.24
14	Reulbach, Ed (1905-1917)	7.24
15	Soto, Mario (1977-1988)	7.26
16	Joss, Addie (1902-1910)	7.30
17	DeLeon, Jose (1983-1995)	7.38
18	Maloney, Jim (1960-1971)	7.39
19	Gossage, Rich (1972-1994)	7.45
20	Seaver, Tom (1967-1986)	7.47
21	Johnson, Walter (1907-1927)	7.48
22	Waddell, Rube (1897-1910)	7.48
23	Gibson, Bob (1959-1975)	7.60
24	Wilson, Don (1966-1974)	7.61
25	Palmer, Jim (1965-1984)	7.63
26	Cheney, Larry (1911-1919)	7.68
27	Brown, Mordecai (1903-1916)	7.68
28	Jones, Sam (1951-1964)	7.68
29	Nomo, Hideo (1995-2003)	7.68
30	Feller, Bob (1936-1956)	7.69
31	Vander Meer, Johnny (1937-1951)	7.69
32	Hunter, Catfish (1965-1979)	7.72
33	Downing, Al (1961-1977)	7.72
34	Scott, Jim (1909-1917)	7.73
35	Clemens, Roger (1984-2003)	7.73
36	Smoltz, John (1988-2003)	7.74
37	Hough, Charlie (1970-1994)	7.77
38	Cone, David (1986-2003)	7.77
39	Bolin, Bobby (1961-1973)	7.79
40	Williams, Stan (1958-1972)	7.79
41	Fingers, Rollie (1968-1985)	7.80
42	Chance, Dean (1961-1971)	7.81
43	Smith, Frank (1904-1915)	7.82
44	McGraw, Tug (1965-1984)	7.83
45	Pelty, Barney (1903-1912)	7.84
46	Ford, Whitey (1950-1967)	7.85
47	McLain, Denny (1963-1972)	7.85
48	Veale, Bob (1962-1974)	7.87
49	Bender, Chief (1903-1925)	7.89
50	McQuillan, George (1907-1918)	7.89
51	Coombs, Jack (1906-1920)	7.89
52	Drabowsky, Moe (1956-1972)	7.90
53	Blue, Vida (1969-1986)	7.91
54	Rucker, Nap (1907-1916)	7.92
55	Reynolds, Allie (1942-1954)	7.92
56	Plank, Eddie (1901-1917)	7.92
57	Mathewson, Christy (1900-1916)	7.94
58	Tiant, Luis (1964-1982)	7.94
59	May, Rudy (1965-1983)	7.94
60	Culp, Ray (1963-1973)	7.95
61	Schilling, Curt (1988-2003)	7.96
62	Donovan, Bill (1898-1918)	7.99
63	Camnitz, Howie (1904-1915)	7.99
64	Sutton, Don (1966-1988)	7.99
65	Pizarro, Juan (1957-1974)	7.99
66	Stieb, Dave (1979-1998)	7.99
67	Bell, Gary (1958-1969)	8.01
68	Moore, Earl (1901-1914)	8.02
69	Siebert, Sonny (1964-1975)	8.03
70	Martinez, Ramon (1988-2001)	8.03
71	Tyler, Lefty (1910-1921)	8.03
72	Newhouser, Hal (1939-1955)	8.04
73	Hendrix, Claude (1911-1920)	8.06
74	Carlton, Steve (1965-1988)	8.06
75	Wiltse, Hooks (1904-1915)	8.06
76	Leiter, Al (1987-2003)	8.07
77	Rusie, Amos (1889-1901)	8.07
78	Mitchell, Willie (1909-1919)	8.07
79	Singer, Bill (1964-1977)	8.08
80	Lemon, Bob (1946-1958)	8.08
81	Scott, Mike (1979-1991)	8.08
82	Miller, Stu (1952-1968)	8.09
83	Drysdale, Don (1956-1969)	8.09
84	Nolan, Gary (1967-1977)	8.09
85	Cicotte, Eddie (1905-1920)	8.09
86	Marichal, Juan (1960-1975)	8.09
87	Keefe, Tim (1880-1893)	8.10
88	White, Doc (1901-1913)	8.10
89	Trucks, Virgil (1941-1958)	8.11
90	Vaughn, Hippo (1908-1921)	8.11
91	Odom, Blue Moon (1964-1976)	8.12
92	Higbe, Kirby (1937-1950)	8.13
93	Shaw, Jim (1913-1921)	8.13
94	Cuellar, Mike (1959-1977)	8.13
95	Pierce, Billy (1945-1964)	8.14
96	Cooper, Mort (1938-1949)	8.15
97	Corcoran, Larry (1880-1887)	8.15
98	Ames, Red (1903-1919)	8.15
99	Willis, Vic (1898-1910)	8.16
100	Brecheen, Harry (1940-1953)	8.17

Home Runs Allowed

1	Roberts, Robin (1948-1966)	505
2	Jenkins, Fergie (1965-1983)	484
3	Niekro, Phil (1964-1987)	482
4	Sutton, Don (1966-1988)	472
5	Tanana, Frank (1973-1993)	448
6	Spahn, Warren (1942-1965)	434
7	Blyleven, Bert (1970-1992)	430
8	Carlton, Steve (1965-1988)	414
9	Perry, Gaylord (1962-1983)	399
10	Kaat, Jim (1959-1983)	395
11	Morris, Jack (1977-1994)	389
12	Hough, Charlie (1970-1994)	383
13	Seaver, Tom (1967-1986)	380
14	Hunter, Catfish (1965-1979)	374
15	Bunning, Jim (1955-1971)	372
	Martinez, Dennis (1976-1998)	372
17	Eckersley, Dennis (1975-1998)	347
	Lolich, Mickey (1963-1979)	347
19	Tiant, Luis (1964-1982)	346
20	Wynn, Early (1939-1963)	338
21	Wells, David (1987-2003)	330
22	Alexander, Doyle (1971-1989)	324
23	Clemens, Roger (1984-2003)	321
	Darwin, Danny (1978-1998)	321
	Ryan, Nolan (1966-1993)	321
26	Marichal, Juan (1960-1975)	320
27	Ramos, Pedro (1955-1970)	316
28	Moyer, Jamie (1986-2003)	314
29	Langston, Mark (1984-1999)	311
30	Perry, Jim (1959-1975)	308
31	Finley, Chuck (1986-2002)	304
32	Palmer, Jim (1965-1984)	303
33	Dickson, Murry (1939-1959)	302
	John, Tommy (1963-1989)	302
35	Pappas, Milt (1957-1973)	298
36	Sanderson, Scott (1978-1996)	297
37	Viola, Frank (1982-1996)	294
38	Grant, Mudcat (1958-1971)	292
39	Bannister, Floyd (1977-1992)	291
	Moore, Mike (1982-1995)	291
41	Koosman, Jerry (1967-1985)	290
42	Benes, Andy (1989-2002)	289
	Burdette, Lew (1950-1967)	289
44	Friend, Bob (1951-1966)	286
45	Pierce, Billy (1945-1964)	284
46	Johnson, Randy (1988-2003)	283
47	Gullickson, Bill (1979-1994)	282
48	Drysdale, Don (1956-1969)	280
49	Mussina, Mike (1991-2003)	278
50	Slaton, Jim (1971-1986)	277
51	Niekro, Joe (1967-1988)	276
52	Morgan, Mike (1978-2002)	270
53	Mulholland, Terry (1986-2003)	269
54	Glavine, Tom (1987-2003)	268
	Law, Vern (1950-1967)	268
56	Welch, Bob (1978-1994)	267
57	Trachsel, Steve (1993-2003)	265
58	Belcher, Tim (1987-2000)	264
	Stewart, Dave (1978-1995)	264
60	Blue, Vida (1969-1986)	263
	Schilling, Curt (1988-2003)	263
62	Swindell, Greg (1986-2002)	262
63	Wise, Rick (1964-1982)	261
64	Tapani, Kevin (1989-2001)	260
65	Jackson, Larry (1955-1968)	259
66	Astacio, Pedro (1992-2003)	258
	Cone, David (1986-2003)	258
	Hurst, Bruce (1980-1994)	258
69	Burkett, John (1987-2003)	257
	Gibson, Bob (1959-1975)	257
71	McCormick, Mike (1956-1971)	256
	Pascual, Camilo (1954-1971)	256
73	Simmons, Curt (1947-1967)	255
74	Key, Jimmy (1984-1998)	254
	Ruffing, Red (1924-1947)	254
76	Hentgen, Pat (1991-2003)	253
77	Newcombe, Don (1949-1960)	252
	Witt, Bobby (1986-2001)	252
79	Flanagan, Mike (1975-1992)	251
80	Candiotti, Tom (1983-1999)	250
	Neagle, Denny (1991-2003)	250
82	Holtzman, Ken (1965-1979)	249
	Osteen, Claude (1957-1975)	249
84	Renko, Steve (1969-1983)	248
85	Rogers, Kenny (1989-2003)	247
86	Drabek, Doug (1986-1998)	246
	Radke, Brad (1995-2003)	246
	Stottlemyre, Todd (1988-2002)	246
89	Candelaria, John (1975-1993)	245
	Reuss, Jerry (1969-1990)	245
91	Clancy, Jim (1977-1991)	244
92	McLain, Denny (1963-1972)	242
	Podres, Johnny (1953-1969)	242
94	Haddix, Harvey (1952-1965)	240
	Sadecki, Ray (1960-1977)	240
96	Darling, Ron (1983-1995)	239
	Helling, Rick (1994-2003)	239
98	Buhl, Bob (1953-1967)	238
99	Gardner, Mark (1989-2001)	237
100	3 players tied	236

Walks

1	Ryan, Nolan (1966-1993)	2795
2	Carlton, Steve (1965-1988)	1833
3	Niekro, Phil (1964-1987)	1809
4	Wynn, Early (1939-1963)	1775
5	Feller, Bob (1936-1956)	1764
6	Newsom, Bobo (1929-1953)	1732
7	Rusie, Amos (1889-1901)	1707
8	Hough, Charlie (1970-1994)	1665
9	Weyhing, Gus (1887-1901)	1570
10	Ruffing, Red (1924-1947)	1541
11	Hadley, Bump (1926-1941)	1442
12	Spahn, Warren (1942-1965)	1434
13	Whitehill, Earl (1923-1939)	1431
14	Mullane, Tony (1881-1894)	1408
15	Jones, Sam (1914-1935)	1396
16	Morris, Jack (1977-1994)	1390
	Seaver, Tom (1967-1986)	1390
18	Clemens, Roger (1984-2003)	1379
	Perry, Gaylord (1962-1983)	1379
20	Witt, Bobby (1986-2001)	1375
21	Torrez, Mike (1967-1984)	1371
22	Johnson, Walter (1907-1927)	1363
23	Sutton, Don (1966-1988)	1343
24	Fraser, Chick (1896-1909)	1338
25	Gibson, Bob (1959-1975)	1336
26	Finley, Chuck (1986-2002)	1332
27	Blyleven, Bert (1970-1992)	1322
28	McDowell, Sam (1961-1975)	1312
29	Palmer, Jim (1965-1984)	1311
30	Baldwin, Mark (1887-1893)	1307
31	Terry, Adonis (1884-1897)	1298
32	Welch, Mickey (1880-1892)	1297
33	Grimes, Burleigh (1916-1934)	1295
34	Langston, Mark (1984-1999)	1289
35	Nichols, Kid (1890-1906)	1272
36	Bush, Joe (1912-1928)	1263
37	Niekro, Joe (1967-1988)	1262
38	Reynolds, Allie (1942-1954)	1261
39	John, Tommy (1963-1989)	1259
40	Johnson, Randy (1988-2003)	1258
41	Tanana, Frank (1973-1993)	1255
42	Lemon, Bob (1946-1958)	1251
43	Newhouser, Hal (1939-1955)	1249
44	Mullin, George (1902-1915)	1238
45	Keefe, Tim (1880-1893)	1233
46	Young, Cy (1890-1911)	1217
47	Faber, Red (1914-1933)	1213
48	Willis, Vic (1898-1910)	1212
49	Breitenstein, Ted (1891-1901)	1207
50	Glavine, Tom (1987-2003)	1206
51	Kennedy, Brickyard (1892-1903)	1201
52	Koosman, Jerry (1967-1985)	1198
53	Bridges, Tommy (1930-1946)	1192
54	Clarkson, John (1882-1894)	1191
55	Grove, Lefty (1925-1941)	1187
56	Blue, Vida (1969-1986)	1185
57	Pierce, Billy (1945-1964)	1178
58	Martinez, Dennis (1976-1998)	1165
59	Moore, Mike (1982-1995)	1156
60	Stivetts, Jack (1889-1899)	1155
61	Valenzuela, Fernando (1980-1997)	1151
62	Cone, David (1986-2003)	1137
63	Hutchison, Bill (1884-1897)	1132
	Vander Meer, Johnny (1937-1951)	1132
65	Reuss, Jerry (1969-1990)	1127
66	Lyons, Ted (1923-1946)	1121
	Walters, Bucky (1934-1950)	1121
68	Harder, Mel (1928-1947)	1118
69	Moore, Earl (1901-1914)	1108
70	Buhl, Bob (1953-1967)	1105
71	Tiant, Luis (1964-1982)	1104
72	Lolich, Mickey (1963-1979)	1099
73	Gomez, Lefty (1930-1943)	1095
74	Trucks, Virgil (1941-1958)	1088
75	Ford, Whitey (1950-1967)	1086
76	Kaat, Jim (1959-1983)	1083
77	Rixey, Eppa (1912-1933)	1082
78	Sutcliffe, Rick (1976-1994)	1081
79	Plank, Eddie (1901-1917)	1072
80	Pascual, Camilo (1954-1971)	1069
81	Turley, Bob (1951-1963)	1068
82	Dauss, Hooks (1912-1926)	1067
83	Chamberlain, Elton (1886-1896)	1065
84	Cunningham, Bert (1887-1901)	1064
85	Simmons, Curt (1947-1967)	1063
86	Donovan, Bill (1898-1918)	1059
87	Dickson, Murry (1939-1959)	1058
88	Meekin, Jouett (1891-1900)	1056
89	Kennedy, Vern (1934-1945)	1049
90	Trout, Dizzy (1939-1957)	1046
91	Ehmke, Howard (1915-1930)	1042
92	Ferrell, Wes (1927-1941)	1040
93	Byrne, Tommy (1943-1957)	1037
94	Ames, Red (1903-1919)	1034
	Stewart, Dave (1978-1995)	1034
	Stieb, Dave (1979-1998)	1034
	Welch, Bob (1978-1994)	1034
98	Walberg, Rube (1923-1937)	1031
99	Powell, Jack (1897-1912)	1021
100	Shawkey, Bob (1913-1927)	1018

Strikeouts

1	Ryan, Nolan (1966-1993)	5714
2	Carlton, Steve (1965-1988)	4136
3	Clemens, Roger (1984-2003)	4099
4	Johnson, Randy (1988-2003)	3871
5	Blyleven, Bert (1970-1992)	3701
6	Seaver, Tom (1967-1986)	3640
7	Sutton, Don (1966-1988)	3574
8	Perry, Gaylord (1962-1983)	3534
9	Johnson, Walter (1907-1927)	3509
10	Niekro, Phil (1964-1987)	3342
11	Jenkins, Fergie (1965-1983)	3192
12	Gibson, Bob (1959-1975)	3117
13	Bunning, Jim (1955-1971)	2855
14	Lolich, Mickey (1963-1979)	2832
15	Young, Cy (1890-1911)	2803
16	Tanana, Frank (1973-1993)	2773
17	Maddux, Greg (1986-2003)	2765
18	Cone, David (1986-2003)	2668
19	Finley, Chuck (1986-2002)	2610
20	Spahn, Warren (1942-1965)	2583
21	Feller, Bob (1936-1956)	2581
22	Keefe, Tim (1880-1893)	2564
23	Koosman, Jerry (1967-1985)	2556
24	Schilling, Curt (1988-2003)	2542
25	Mathewson, Christy (1900-1916)	2507
26	Drysdale, Don (1956-1969)	2486
27	Morris, Jack (1977-1994)	2478
28	Langston, Mark (1984-1999)	2464
29	Kaat, Jim (1959-1983)	2461
30	McDowell, Sam (1961-1975)	2453
31	Martinez, Pedro (1992-2003)	2426
32	Tiant, Luis (1964-1982)	2416
33	Eckersley, Dennis (1975-1998)	2401
34	Koufax, Sandy (1955-1966)	2396
35	Hough, Charlie (1970-1994)	2362
36	Roberts, Robin (1948-1966)	2357
37	Wynn, Early (1939-1963)	2334
38	Waddell, Rube (1897-1910)	2316
39	Smoltz, John (1988-2003)	2313
40	Marichal, Juan (1960-1975)	2303
41	Gooden, Dwight (1984-2000)	2293
42	Grove, Lefty (1925-1941)	2266
43	Brown, Kevin (1986-2003)	2264
44	Plank, Eddie (1901-1917)	2246
45	John, Tommy (1963-1989)	2245
46	Palmer, Jim (1965-1984)	2212
47	Alexander, Grover (1911-1930)	2198
48	Blue, Vida (1969-1986)	2175
49	Pascual, Camilo (1954-1971)	2167
50	Martinez, Dennis (1976-1998)	2149
51	Glavine, Tom (1987-2003)	2136
52	Mussina, Mike (1991-2003)	2126
53	Newsom, Bobo (1929-1953)	2082
54	Valenzuela, Fernando (1980-1997)	2074
55	Vance, Dazzy (1915-1935)	2045
56	Reuschel, Rick (1972-1991)	2015
57	Hershiser, Orel (1983-2000)	2014
58	Hunter, Catfish (1965-1979)	2012
59	Benes, Andy (1989-2002)	2000
60	Pierce, Billy (1945-1964)	1999
61	Appier, Kevin (1989-2003)	1992
62	Ruffing, Red (1924-1947)	1987
63	Clarkson, John (1882-1894)	1978
64	Welch, Bob (1978-1994)	1969
65	Ford, Whitey (1950-1967)	1956
66	Witt, Bobby (1986-2001)	1955
67	Rusie, Amos (1889-1901)	1950
68	Darwin, Danny (1978-1998)	1942
69	Reuss, Jerry (1969-1990)	1907
70	Nichols, Kid (1890-1906)	1880
71	Wells, David (1987-2003)	1873
72	Welch, Mickey (1880-1892)	1850
73	Viola, Frank (1982-1996)	1844
74	Radbourn, Charley (1881-1891)	1830
75	Mullane, Tony (1881-1894)	1803
76	Nomo, Hideo (1995-2003)	1802
77	Galvin, Pud (1875-1892)	1799
78	Newhouser, Hal (1939-1955)	1796
79	Guidry, Ron (1975-1988)	1778
80	Burkett, John (1987-2003)	1766
81	Leiter, Al (1987-2003)	1760
	May, Rudy (1965-1983)	1760
83	Niekro, Joe (1967-1988)	1747
84	Fernandez, Sid (1983-1997)	1743
85	Stewart, Dave (1978-1995)	1741
86	Walsh, Ed (1904-1917)	1736
87	Candiotti, Tom (1983-1999)	1735
88	Friend, Bob (1951-1966)	1734
89	Coleman, Joe (1965-1979)	1728
	Pappas, Milt (1957-1973)	1728
91	Gross, Kevin (1983-1997)	1727
92	Bannister, Floyd (1977-1992)	1723
93	Saberhagen, Bret (1984-2001)	1715
94	Bender, Chief (1903-1925)	1711
95	Jackson, Larry (1955-1968)	1709
96	McCormick, Jim (1878-1887)	1704
97	Veale, Bob (1962-1974)	1703
98	Ames, Red (1903-1919)	1702
99	Buffinton, Charlie (1882-1892)	1700
100	Simmons, Curt (1947-1967)	1697

Strikeouts per Game

1	Johnson, Randy (1988-2003)	11.16
2	Martinez, Pedro (1992-2003)	10.50
3	Ryan, Nolan (1966-1993)	9.55
4	Koufax, Sandy (1955-1966)	9.28
5	Nomo, Hideo (1995-2003)	9.07
6	McDowell, Sam (1961-1975)	8.86
7	Schilling, Curt (1988-2003)	8.85
8	Clemens, Roger (1984-2003)	8.62
9	Fernandez, Sid (1983-1997)	8.40
10	Richard, J.R. (1971-1980)	8.37
11	Cone, David (1986-2003)	8.28
12	Gordon, Tom (1988-2003)	8.15
13	Veale, Bob (1962-1974)	7.96
14	Smoltz, John (1988-2003)	7.95
15	Maloney, Jim (1960-1971)	7.81
16	Rijo, Jose (1984-2002)	7.69
17	Leiter, Al (1987-2003)	7.63
18	DeLeon, Jose (1983-1995)	7.56
19	Soto, Mario (1977-1988)	7.54
20	Jones, Sam (1951-1964)	7.54
21	Fassero, Jeff (1991-2003)	7.51
22	Langston, Mark (1984-1999)	7.49
23	Gossage, Rich (1972-1994)	7.47
24	Gooden, Dwight (1984-2000)	7.37
25	Finley, Chuck (1986-2002)	7.35
26	Gibson, Bob (1959-1975)	7.22
27	Benes, Andy (1989-2002)	7.18
28	Mussina, Mike (1991-2003)	7.17
29	Witt, Bobby (1986-2001)	7.14
30	Carlton, Steve (1965-1988)	7.13
31	Burba, Dave (1990-2003)	7.13
32	Reynolds, Shane (1992-2003)	7.06
33	Waddell, Rube (1897-1910)	7.04
34	Astacio, Pedro (1992-2003)	7.02
35	Lolich, Mickey (1963-1979)	7.01
36	Kile, Darryl (1991-2002)	6.93
37	Appier, Kevin (1989-2003)	6.92
38	Fingers, Rollie (1968-1985)	6.87
39	Seaver, Tom (1967-1986)	6.85
40	Bunning, Jim (1955-1971)	6.83
41	Alvarez, Wilson (1989-2003)	6.80
42	Hanson, Erik (1988-1998)	6.80
43	Martinez, Ramon (1988-2001)	6.77
44	Neagle, Denny (1991-2003)	6.74
45	Pizarro, Juan (1957-1974)	6.73
46	Bolin, Bobby (1961-1973)	6.71
47	Blyleven, Bert (1970-1992)	6.70
48	Guidry, Ron (1975-1988)	6.69
49	Culp, Ray (1963-1973)	6.69
50	Lieber, Jon (1994-2002)	6.68
51	Brown, Kevin (1986-2003)	6.68
52	Williams, Stan (1958-1972)	6.66
53	Pascual, Camilo (1954-1971)	6.65
54	Turley, Bob (1951-1963)	6.65
55	Wilson, Don (1966-1974)	6.60
56	McGraw, Tug (1965-1984)	6.59
57	Eckersley, Dennis (1975-1998)	6.58
58	Lemaster, Denny (1962-1972)	6.57
59	Messersmith, Andy (1968-1979)	6.56
60	Drysdale, Don (1956-1969)	6.52
61	Stottlemyre, Todd (1988-2002)	6.52
62	Downing, Al (1961-1977)	6.50
63	Bannister, Floyd (1977-1992)	6.49
64	Ramsey, Toad (1885-1890)	6.49
65	Segui, Diego (1962-1977)	6.46
66	Chance, Dean (1961-1971)	6.43
67	Wilhelm, Hoyt (1952-1972)	6.43
68	Gardner, Mark (1989-2001)	6.41
69	Pettitte, Andy (1995-2003)	6.40
70	Fernandez, Alex (1990-2000)	6.40
71	Scott, Mike (1979-1991)	6.39
72	Jenkins, Fergie (1965-1983)	6.38
73	Drabowsky, Moe (1956-1972)	6.37
74	Valenzuela, Fernando (1980-1997)	6.37
75	Wilson, Earl (1959-1970)	6.37
76	Haddix, Harvey (1952-1965)	6.34
77	Wakefield, Tim (1992-2003)	6.34
78	Siebert, Sonny (1964-1975)	6.32
79	Short, Chris (1959-1973)	6.31
80	Hurst, Bruce (1980-1994)	6.29
81	Harnisch, Pete (1988-2001)	6.28
82	Williams, Woody (1993-2003)	6.28
83	Singer, Bill (1964-1977)	6.27
84	Maddux, Greg (1986-2003)	6.27
85	Sele, Aaron (1993-2003)	6.27
86	Gross, Kevin (1983-1997)	6.25
87	McDowell, Jack (1987-1999)	6.25
88	Tiant, Luis (1964-1982)	6.24
89	Swindell, Greg (1986-2002)	6.21
90	Farrell, Turk (1956-1969)	6.21
91	Castillo, Frank (1991-2002)	6.21
92	Vance, Dazzy (1915-1935)	6.20
93	Miller, Stu (1952-1968)	6.18
94	Kirby, Clay (1969-1976)	6.17
95	Trachsel, Steve (1993-2003)	6.16
96	Bell, Gary (1958-1969)	6.15
97	Peters, Gary (1959-1972)	6.14
98	McLain, Denny (1963-1972)	6.12
99	Sutton, Don (1966-1988)	6.09
100	Krukow, Mike (1976-1989)	6.07

Ratio

1	Joss, Addie (1902-1910)	.968
2	Walsh, Ed (1904-1917)	1.000
3	Martinez, Pedro (1992-2003)	1.013
4	Ward, John (1878-1884)	1.043
5	Mathewson, Christy (1900-1916)	1.059
6	Johnson, Walter (1907-1927)	1.061
7	Brown, Mordecai (1903-1916)	1.066
8	Bond, Tommy (1874-1884)	1.092
9	Adams, Babe (1906-1926)	1.092
10	Marichal, Juan (1960-1975)	1.101
11	Bradley, George (1875-1884)	1.101
12	Waddell, Rube (1897-1910)	1.102
13	Corcoran, Larry (1880-1887)	1.105
14	Phillippe, Deacon (1899-1911)	1.105
15	Koufax, Sandy (1955-1966)	1.106
16	Morris, Ed (1884-1890)	1.108
17	White, Will (1877-1886)	1.111
18	Bender, Chief (1903-1925)	1.113
19	Ferguson, Charlie (1884-1887)	1.117
20	Schilling, Curt (1988-2003)	1.117
21	Larkin, Terry (1876-1880)	1.117
22	Plank, Eddie (1901-1917)	1.119
23	White, Doc (1901-1913)	1.121
24	Seaver, Tom (1967-1986)	1.121
25	Alexander, Grover (1911-1930)	1.121
26	Keefe, Tim (1880-1893)	1.123
27	Wilhelm, Hoyt (1952-1972)	1.125
28	Maddux, Greg (1986-2003)	1.125
29	Young, Cy (1890-1911)	1.130
30	McQuillan, George (1907-1918)	1.131
31	Wiltse, Hooks (1904-1915)	1.131
32	Hahn, Noodles (1899-1906)	1.132
33	McCormick, Jim (1878-1887)	1.132
34	Hunter, Catfish (1965-1979)	1.134
35	Saberhagen, Bret (1984-2001)	1.141
36	Altrock, Nick (1898-1924)	1.141
37	Leever, Sam (1898-1910)	1.141
38	Jenkins, Fergie (1965-1983)	1.142
39	Sutton, Don (1966-1988)	1.142
40	Reulbach, Ed (1905-1917)	1.143
41	Messersmith, Andy (1968-1979)	1.143
42	Fernandez, Sid (1983-1997)	1.144
43	Tesreau, Jeff (1912-1918)	1.145
44	Nolan, Gary (1967-1977)	1.145
45	Whitney, Jim (1881-1890)	1.147
46	Drysdale, Don (1956-1969)	1.148
47	Radbourn, Charley (1881-1891)	1.149
48	Pelty, Barney (1903-1912)	1.150
49	Chesbro, Jack (1899-1909)	1.152
50	Bonham, Tiny (1940-1949)	1.153
51	Goldsmith, Fred (1879-1884)	1.153
52	Cicotte, Eddie (1905-1920)	1.155
53	Fingers, Rollie (1968-1985)	1.156
54	Caruthers, Bob (1884-1892)	1.158
55	Rudolph, Dick (1910-1927)	1.158
56	Mussina, Mike (1991-2003)	1.159
57	Eckersley, Dennis (1975-1998)	1.161
58	Overall, Orval (1905-1913)	1.161
59	McLain, Denny (1963-1972)	1.163
60	McGinnis, Jumbo (1882-1887)	1.164
61	Winter, George (1901-1908)	1.165
62	Hubbell, Carl (1928-1943)	1.166
63	Smith, Frank (1904-1915)	1.166
64	Hecker, Guy (1882-1890)	1.168
65	Roberts, Robin (1948-1966)	1.170
66	Sallee, Slim (1908-1921)	1.170
67	Smoltz, John (1988-2003)	1.172
68	Rucker, Nap (1907-1916)	1.175
69	Foutz, Dave (1884-1894)	1.178
70	Ewing, Bob (1902-1912)	1.178
71	Taylor, Jack (1898-1907)	1.178
72	Bunning, Jim (1955-1971)	1.179
73	Scott, Jim (1909-1917)	1.180
74	Palmer, Jim (1965-1984)	1.180
75	Perry, Gaylord (1962-1983)	1.181
76	Clemens, Roger (1984-2003)	1.182
77	Johnson, Randy (1988-2003)	1.183
78	Guidry, Ron (1975-1988)	1.184
79	Candelaria, John (1975-1993)	1.184
80	Tannehill, Jesse (1894-1911)	1.186
81	Soto, Mario (1977-1988)	1.186
82	Terry, Ralph (1956-1967)	1.186
83	Toney, Fred (1911-1923)	1.188
84	McGinnity, Joe (1899-1908)	1.188
85	Gibson, Bob (1959-1975)	1.188
86	Brecheen, Harry (1940-1953)	1.188
87	Hendrix, Claude (1911-1920)	1.189
88	Horlen, Joe (1961-1972)	1.190
89	Weilman, Carl (1912-1920)	1.191
90	Peterson, Fritz (1966-1976)	1.191
91	Douglas, Phil (1912-1922)	1.192
92	Fisher, Eddie (1959-1973)	1.193
93	Galvin, Pud (1875-1892)	1.194
94	Spahn, Warren (1942-1965)	1.195
95	Shaw, Dupee (1883-1888)	1.195
96	Cuellar, Mike (1959-1977)	1.197
97	Tudor, John (1979-1990)	1.198
98	Blyleven, Bert (1970-1992)	1.198
99	Tiant, Luis (1964-1982)	1.199
100	Johnson, Ken (1958-1970)	1.199

Earned Run Average

1	Walsh, Ed (1904-1917)	1.82
2	Joss, Addie (1902-1910)	1.89
3	Brown, Mordecai (1903-1916)	2.06
4	Ward, John (1878-1884)	2.10
5	Mathewson, Christy (1900-1916)	2.13
6	Waddell, Rube (1897-1910)	2.16
7	Johnson, Walter (1907-1927)	2.17
8	Overall, Orval (1905-1913)	2.23
9	Bond, Tommy (1874-1884)	2.25
10	White, Will (1877-1886)	2.28
11	Reulbach, Ed (1905-1917)	2.28
12	Scott, Jim (1909-1917)	2.30
13	Plank, Eddie (1901-1917)	2.35
14	Corcoran, Larry (1880-1887)	2.36
15	McQuillan, George (1907-1918)	2.38
16	Cicotte, Eddie (1905-1920)	2.38
17	Killian, Ed (1903-1910)	2.38
18	White, Doc (1901-1913)	2.39
19	Rucker, Nap (1907-1916)	2.42
20	Tesreau, Jeff (1912-1918)	2.43
21	McCormick, Jim (1878-1887)	2.43
22	Larkin, Terry (1876-1880)	2.43
23	Bender, Chief (1903-1925)	2.46
24	Wiltse, Hooks (1904-1915)	2.47
25	Leever, Sam (1898-1910)	2.47
26	Leifield, Lefty (1905-1920)	2.47
27	Vaughn, Hippo (1908-1921)	2.49
28	Ewing, Bob (1902-1912)	2.49
29	Bradley, George (1875-1884)	2.50
30	Wilhelm, Hoyt (1952-1972)	2.52
31	Hahn, Noodles (1899-1906)	2.55
32	Alexander, Grover (1911-1930)	2.56
33	Sallee, Slim (1908-1921)	2.56
34	Martinez, Pedro (1992-2003)	2.58
35	Phillippe, Deacon (1899-1911)	2.59
36	Smith, Frank (1904-1915)	2.59
37	Siever, Ed (1901-1908)	2.60
38	Rhoads, Bob (1902-1909)	2.61
39	Keefe, Tim (1880-1893)	2.62
40	Young, Cy (1890-1911)	2.63
41	Willis, Vic (1898-1910)	2.63
42	Ames, Red (1903-1919)	2.63
43	Pelty, Barney (1903-1912)	2.63
44	Altrock, Nick (1898-1924)	2.65
45	Hendrix, Claude (1911-1920)	2.65
46	McGinnity, Joe (1899-1908)	2.66
47	Rudolph, Dick (1910-1927)	2.66
48	Taylor, Jack (1898-1907)	2.66
49	Weilman, Carl (1912-1920)	2.67
50	Ferguson, Charlie (1884-1887)	2.67
51	Radbourn, Charley (1881-1891)	2.68
52	Falkenberg, Cy (1903-1917)	2.68
53	Chesbro, Jack (1899-1909)	2.68
54	Toney, Fred (1911-1923)	2.69
55	Donovan, Bill (1898-1918)	2.69
56	Cheney, Larry (1911-1919)	2.70
57	Welch, Mickey (1880-1892)	2.71
58	Goldsmith, Fred (1879-1884)	2.73
59	Howell, Harry (1898-1910)	2.74
60	Ford, Whitey (1950-1967)	2.75
61	Taylor, Dummy (1900-1908)	2.75
62	Camnitz, Howie (1904-1915)	2.75
63	Adams, Babe (1906-1926)	2.76
64	Leonard, Dutch (1913-1925)	2.76
65	Koufax, Sandy (1955-1966)	2.76
66	Pfeffer, Jeff (1911-1924)	2.77
67	Moore, Earl (1901-1914)	2.78
68	Tannehill, Jesse (1894-1911)	2.78
69	Coombs, Jack (1906-1920)	2.78
70	Sparks, Tully (1897-1910)	2.78
71	Douglas, Phil (1912-1922)	2.80
72	Clarkson, John (1882-1894)	2.81
73	Morris, Ed (1884-1890)	2.82
74	Fisher, Ray (1910-1920)	2.82
75	Mullin, George (1902-1915)	2.82
76	Caruthers, Bob (1884-1892)	2.83
77	Foutz, Dave (1884-1894)	2.84
78	Palmer, Jim (1965-1984)	2.86
79	Messersmith, Andy (1968-1979)	2.86
80	Seaver, Tom (1967-1986)	2.86
81	Winter, George (1901-1908)	2.87
82	Galvin, Pud (1875-1892)	2.87
83	Mitchell, Willie (1909-1919)	2.88
84	Marichal, Juan (1960-1975)	2.89
85	Coveleski, Stan (1912-1928)	2.89
86	Maddux, Greg (1986-2003)	2.89
87	Cooper, Wilbur (1912-1926)	2.89
88	Fingers, Rollie (1968-1985)	2.90
89	Hecker, Guy (1882-1890)	2.91
90	Gibson, Bob (1959-1975)	2.91
91	Brecheen, Harry (1940-1953)	2.92
92	Mays, Carl (1915-1929)	2.92
93	Crandall, Doc (1908-1918)	2.92
94	Chance, Dean (1961-1971)	2.92
95	Davenport, Dave (1914-1919)	2.93
96	Tyler, Lefty (1910-1921)	2.95
97	McGinnis, Jumbo (1882-1887)	2.95
98	Drysdale, Don (1956-1969)	2.95
99	Nichols, Kid (1890-1906)	2.95
100	Buffinton, Charlie (1882-1892)	2.96

Adjusted Earned Run Average

1	Martinez, Pedro (1992-2003)	172
2	Johnson, Walter (1907-1927)	149
3	Grove, Lefty (1925-1941)	148
4	Wilhelm, Hoyt (1952-1972)	147
5	Walsh, Ed (1904-1917)	146
6	Joss, Addie (1902-1910)	143
7	Maddux, Greg (1986-2003)	142
8	Brown, Mordecai (1903-1916)	142
9	Johnson, Randy (1988-2003)	141
10	Clemens, Roger (1984-2003)	140
11	Nichols, Kid (1890-1906)	139
12	Alexander, Grover (1911-1930)	138
13	Young, Cy (1890-1911)	137
14	Koufax, Sandy (1955-1966)	135
15	Mathewson, Christy (1900-1916)	134
16	Clarkson, John (1882-1894)	134
17	Brecheen, Harry (1940-1953)	133
18	Waddell, Rube (1897-1910)	133
19	Ford, Whitey (1950-1967)	132
20	Newhouser, Hal (1939-1955)	132
21	Hahn, Noodles (1899-1906)	132
22	Brown, Kevin (1986-2003)	131
23	Hubbell, Carl (1928-1943)	130
24	Dean, Dizzy (1930-1947)	129
25	Mussina, Mike (1991-2003)	129
26	Schilling, Curt (1988-2003)	128
27	Gibson, Bob (1959-1975)	128
28	Seaver, Tom (1967-1986)	127
29	Rusie, Amos (1889-1901)	127
30	Coveleski, Stan (1912-1928)	127
31	Cuppy, Nig (1892-1901)	127
32	Maglie, Sal (1945-1958)	127
33	Keefe, Tim (1880-1893)	126
34	Lanier, Max (1938-1953)	126
35	Bridges, Tommy (1930-1946)	126
36	Saberhagen, Bret (1984-2001)	125
37	Cooper, Mort (1938-1949)	125
38	Palmer, Jim (1965-1984)	125
39	Tudor, John (1979-1990)	125
40	Foutz, Dave (1884-1894)	124
41	Gossage, Rich (1972-1994)	124
42	Trout, Dizzy (1939-1957)	124
43	Overall, Orval (1905-1913)	124
44	Gomez, Lefty (1930-1943)	124
45	Parnell, Mel (1947-1956)	124
46	Shocker, Urban (1916-1928)	124
47	Corcoran, Larry (1880-1887)	124
48	Vance, Dazzy (1915-1935)	123
49	Reulbach, Ed (1905-1917)	123
50	Smoltz, John (1988-2003)	123
51	King, Silver (1886-1897)	123
52	Vaughn, Hippo (1908-1921)	123
53	Cicotte, Eddie (1905-1920)	123
54	Caruthers, Bob (1884-1892)	122
55	Marichal, Juan (1960-1975)	122
56	Leever, Sam (1898-1910)	122
57	Plank, Eddie (1901-1917)	122
58	Rommel, Eddie (1920-1932)	122
59	Stieb, Dave (1979-1998)	122
60	Appier, Kevin (1989-2003)	121
61	Radbourn, Charley (1881-1891)	121
62	Feller, Bob (1936-1956)	121
63	Stivetts, Jack (1889-1899)	121
64	White, Will (1877-1886)	121
65	Messersmith, Andy (1968-1979)	121
66	Key, Jimmy (1984-1998)	121
67	Griffith, Clark (1891-1914)	121
68	Drysdale, Don (1956-1969)	121
69	Rijo, Jose (1984-2002)	120
70	Bonham, Tiny (1940-1949)	120
71	Mays, Carl (1915-1929)	120
72	Glavine, Tom (1987-2003)	120
73	Warneke, Lon (1930-1945)	120
74	Shantz, Bobby (1949-1964)	120
75	Ward, John (1878-1884)	120
76	Guidry, Ron (1975-1988)	119
77	Cone, David (1986-2003)	119
78	Ferguson, Charlie (1884-1887)	119
79	Chance, Dean (1961-1971)	119
80	Fingers, Rollie (1968-1985)	119
81	Faber, Red (1914-1933)	119
82	Pierce, Billy (1945-1964)	119
83	McGinnity, Joe (1899-1908)	119
84	Leonard, Dutch (1933-1953)	119
85	Lemon, Bob (1946-1958)	119
86	Mullane, Tony (1881-1894)	119
87	McCormick, Jim (1878-1887)	119
88	Scott, Jim (1909-1917)	119
89	Lee, Thornton (1933-1948)	118
90	Lyons, Ted (1923-1946)	118
91	Spahn, Warren (1942-1965)	118
92	Rucker, Nap (1907-1916)	118
93	Morris, Ed (1884-1890)	118
94	Stanley, Bob (1977-1989)	118
95	Blyleven, Bert (1970-1992)	117
96	Phillippe, Deacon (1899-1911)	117
97	Garcia, Mike (1948-1961)	117
98	Perry, Gaylord (1962-1983)	117
99	McMahon, Sadie (1889-1897)	117
100	Adams, Babe (1906-1926)	117

Pitching Runs

1	Young, Cy (1890-1911)	749
2	Johnson, Walter (1907-1927)	704
3	Grove, Lefty (1925-1941)	594
4	Clemens, Roger (1984-2003)	565
5	Nichols, Kid (1890-1906)	532
6	Maddux, Greg (1986-2003)	509
7	Alexander, Grover (1911-1930)	481
8	Spahn, Warren (1942-1965)	470
9	Martinez, Pedro (1992-2003)	432
10	Johnson, Randy (1988-2003)	430
11	Seaver, Tom (1967-1986)	419
12	Mathewson, Christy (1900-1916)	417
13	Rusie, Amos (1889-1901)	417
14	Keefe, Tim (1880-1893)	399
15	Hubbell, Carl (1928-1943)	393
16	Ford, Whitey (1950-1967)	386
17	Feller, Bob (1936-1956)	385
18	Brown, Kevin (1986-2003)	379
19	Palmer, Jim (1965-1984)	374
20	Clarkson, John (1882-1894)	365
21	Gomez, Lefty (1930-1943)	322
22	Mussina, Mike (1991-2003)	313
23	Lyons, Ted (1923-1946)	313
24	Perry, Gaylord (1962-1983)	311
25	Wilhelm, Hoyt (1952-1972)	310
26	Walsh, Ed (1904-1917)	310
27	Ryan, Nolan (1966-1993)	309
28	Radbourn, Charley (1881-1891)	294
29	Faber, Red (1914-1933)	292
30	Brown, Mordecai (1903-1916)	292
31	Gibson, Bob (1959-1975)	289
32	Vance, Dazzy (1915-1935)	280
33	Blyleven, Bert (1970-1992)	271
34	Ruffing, Red (1924-1947)	271
35	Leonard, Dutch (1933-1953)	267
36	Drysdale, Don (1956-1969)	266
37	Plank, Eddie (1901-1917)	265
38	Roberts, Robin (1948-1966)	264
39	Marichal, Juan (1960-1975)	261
40	Sutton, Don (1966-1988)	259
41	Coveleski, Stan (1912-1928)	257
42	Newhouser, Hal (1939-1955)	256
43	Bridges, Tommy (1930-1946)	256
44	Glavine, Tom (1987-2003)	251
45	Lemon, Bob (1946-1958)	250
46	Pierce, Billy (1945-1964)	250
47	Rixey, Eppa (1912-1933)	248
48	Luque, Dolf (1914-1935)	244
49	Schilling, Curt (1988-2003)	244
50	Cone, David (1986-2003)	243
51	Koufax, Sandy (1955-1966)	243
52	Mullane, Tony (1881-1894)	242
53	Waddell, Rube (1897-1910)	239
54	Carlton, Steve (1965-1988)	236
55	Saberhagen, Bret (1984-2001)	232
56	Griffith, Clark (1891-1914)	231
57	Key, Jimmy (1984-1998)	223
58	Appier, Kevin (1989-2003)	220
59	Mays, Carl (1915-1929)	216
60	Joss, Addie (1902-1910)	215
61	John, Tommy (1963-1989)	214
62	McCormick, Jim (1878-1887)	213
63	Caruthers, Bob (1884-1892)	212
64	Welch, Mickey (1880-1892)	211
65	Shocker, Urban (1916-1928)	209
66	Hoyt, Waite (1918-1938)	208
67	Smoltz, John (1988-2003)	206
68	Finley, Chuck (1986-2002)	205
69	King, Silver (1886-1897)	201
70	Guidry, Ron (1975-1988)	201
71	Cuppy, Nig (1892-1901)	199
72	Cicotte, Eddie (1905-1920)	199
73	Stieb, Dave (1979-1998)	198
74	White, Will (1877-1886)	197
75	Brecheen, Harry (1940-1953)	194
76	Niekro, Phil (1964-1987)	192
77	Harder, Mel (1928-1947)	190
78	Warneke, Lon (1930-1945)	187
79	Dean, Dizzy (1930-1947)	187
80	Lopat, Ed (1944-1955)	186
81	McGinnity, Joe (1899-1908)	183
82	Hershiser, Orel (1983-2000)	179
83	Bunning, Jim (1955-1971)	179
84	Rommel, Eddie (1920-1932)	178
85	Trout, Dizzy (1939-1957)	177
86	French, Larry (1929-1942)	177
87	Morris, Ed (1884-1890)	176
88	Chandler, Spud (1937-1947)	176
89	Garcia, Mike (1948-1961)	174
90	Fitzsimmons, Freddie (1925-1943)	173
91	Leever, Sam (1898-1910)	172
92	Messersmith, Andy (1968-1979)	172
93	McMahon, Sadie (1889-1897)	171
94	Wynn, Early (1939-1963)	170
95	Lee, Thornton (1933-1948)	169
96	Willis, Vic (1898-1910)	168
97	Cooper, Wilbur (1912-1926)	166
98	Reulbach, Ed (1905-1917)	165
99	Eckersley, Dennis (1975-1998)	164
100	Rivera, Mariano (1995-2003)	160

Adjusted Pitching Runs

1	Young, Cy (1890-1911)	753
2	Grove, Lefty (1925-1941)	654
3	Clemens, Roger (1984-2003)	644
4	Nichols, Kid (1890-1906)	588
5	Johnson, Walter (1907-1927)	587
6	Maddux, Greg (1986-2003)	564
7	Alexander, Grover (1911-1930)	508
8	Johnson, Randy (1988-2003)	466
9	Martinez, Pedro (1992-2003)	447
10	Clarkson, John (1882-1894)	436
11	Mathewson, Christy (1900-1916)	424
12	Seaver, Tom (1967-1986)	384
13	Rusie, Amos (1889-1901)	366
14	Niekro, Phil (1964-1987)	343
15	Newhouser, Hal (1939-1955)	336
16	Brown, Kevin (1986-2003)	335
17	Gibson, Bob (1959-1975)	332
18	Spahn, Warren (1942-1965)	326
19	Blyleven, Bert (1970-1992)	324
20	Hubbell, Carl (1928-1943)	323
21	Perry, Gaylord (1962-1983)	314
22	Mussina, Mike (1991-2003)	303
23	Lyons, Ted (1923-1946)	294
24	Bridges, Tommy (1930-1946)	293
25	Vance, Dazzy (1915-1935)	288
26	Glavine, Tom (1987-2003)	286
27	Feller, Bob (1936-1956)	281
28	Walsh, Ed (1904-1917)	280
29	Wilhelm, Hoyt (1952-1972)	277
30	Schilling, Curt (1988-2003)	273
31	Marichal, Juan (1960-1975)	271
32	Jenkins, Fergie (1965-1983)	271
33	Keefe, Tim (1880-1893)	271
34	Saberhagen, Bret (1984-2001)	267
35	Griffith, Clark (1891-1914)	266
36	Coveleski, Stan (1912-1928)	265
37	Faber, Red (1914-1933)	264
38	Plank, Eddie (1901-1917)	261
39	Ford, Whitey (1950-1967)	259
40	Waddell, Rube (1897-1910)	257
41	Trout, Dizzy (1939-1957)	254
42	Carlton, Steve (1965-1988)	252
43	Leonard, Dutch (1933-1953)	245
44	Cone, David (1986-2003)	241
45	Brown, Mordecai (1903-1916)	241
46	Smoltz, John (1988-2003)	240
47	Palmer, Jim (1965-1984)	239
48	Rommel, Eddie (1920-1932)	237
49	Quinn, Jack (1909-1933)	237
50	Stieb, Dave (1979-1998)	231
51	Roberts, Robin (1948-1966)	231
52	Rixey, Eppa (1912-1933)	230
53	Appier, Kevin (1989-2003)	228
54	Drysdale, Don (1956-1969)	228
55	Cuppy, Nig (1892-1901)	225
56	Reuschel, Rick (1972-1991)	223
57	McGinnity, Joe (1899-1908)	223
58	Galvin, Pud (1875-1892)	223
59	Ryan, Nolan (1966-1993)	222
60	King, Silver (1886-1897)	220
61	Radbourn, Charley (1881-1891)	216
62	Koufax, Sandy (1955-1966)	216
63	Shocker, Urban (1916-1928)	213
64	McMahon, Sadie (1889-1897)	212
65	Ferrell, Wes (1927-1941)	212
66	Eckersley, Dennis (1975-1998)	209
67	Key, Jimmy (1984-1998)	208
68	Buffinton, Charlie (1882-1892)	200
69	Stivetts, Jack (1889-1899)	199
70	Gomez, Lefty (1930-1943)	199
71	Pierce, Billy (1945-1964)	198
72	Dean, Dizzy (1930-1947)	197
73	Bunning, Jim (1955-1971)	194
74	Harder, Mel (1928-1947)	193
75	Finley, Chuck (1986-2002)	193
76	Vaughn, Hippo (1908-1921)	190
77	Brecheen, Harry (1940-1953)	190
78	Caruthers, Bob (1884-1892)	189
79	Willis, Vic (1898-1910)	189
80	Tiant, Luis (1964-1982)	186
81	Mullane, Tony (1881-1894)	186
82	Luque, Dolf (1914-1935)	185
83	Cicotte, Eddie (1905-1920)	185
84	Trucks, Virgil (1941-1958)	183
85	Joss, Addie (1902-1910)	182
86	Lemon, Bob (1946-1958)	180
87	Passeau, Claude (1935-1947)	177
88	John, Tommy (1963-1989)	177
89	Hahn, Noodles (1899-1906)	175
90	Mays, Carl (1915-1929)	172
91	Hoyt, Waite (1918-1938)	172
92	Lee, Thornton (1933-1948)	164
93	Parnell, Mel (1947-1956)	163
94	Warneke, Lon (1930-1945)	163
95	Jackson, Larry (1955-1968)	162
96	Cooper, Wilbur (1912-1926)	162
97	McCormick, Jim (1878-1887)	162
98	Rivera, Mariano (1995-2003)	160
99	Garver, Ned (1948-1961)	159
100	Wood, Wilbur (1961-1978)	157

Adjusted Pitching Wins

1	Young, Cy (1890-1911)	68.4
2	Clemens, Roger (1984-2003)	62.4
3	Johnson, Walter (1907-1927)	61.4
4	Grove, Lefty (1925-1941)	60.7
5	Maddux, Greg (1986-2003)	56.2
6	Alexander, Grover (1911-1930)	53.4
7	Nichols, Kid (1890-1906)	51.2
8	Johnson, Randy (1988-2003)	44.6
9	Mathewson, Christy (1900-1916)	44.2
10	Martinez, Pedro (1992-2003)	42.5
11	Seaver, Tom (1967-1986)	40.1
12	Clarkson, John (1882-1894)	38.5
13	Niekro, Phil (1964-1987)	36.3
14	Gibson, Bob (1959-1975)	35.0
15	Newhouser, Hal (1939-1955)	34.6
16	Blyleven, Bert (1970-1992)	33.3
17	Perry, Gaylord (1962-1983)	33.3
18	Brown, Kevin (1986-2003)	32.6
19	Spahn, Warren (1942-1965)	32.3
20	Hubbell, Carl (1928-1943)	31.6
21	Rusie, Amos (1889-1901)	30.3
22	Walsh, Ed (1904-1917)	30.1
23	Mussina, Mike (1991-2003)	28.9
24	Marichal, Juan (1960-1975)	28.8
25	Wilhelm, Hoyt (1952-1972)	28.6
26	Jenkins, Fergie (1965-1983)	28.5
27	Glavine, Tom (1987-2003)	28.3
28	Bridges, Tommy (1930-1946)	27.7
29	Lyons, Ted (1923-1946)	27.7
30	Plank, Eddie (1901-1917)	27.6
31	Vance, Dazzy (1915-1935)	27.3
32	Schilling, Curt (1988-2003)	27.0
33	Feller, Bob (1936-1956)	27.0
34	Carlton, Steve (1965-1988)	26.7
35	Waddell, Rube (1897-1910)	26.7
36	Coveleski, Stan (1912-1928)	26.5
37	Ford, Whitey (1950-1967)	26.4
38	Saberhagen, Bret (1984-2001)	26.3
39	Brown, Mordecai (1903-1916)	26.1
40	Faber, Red (1914-1933)	25.9
41	Trout, Dizzy (1939-1957)	25.8
42	Palmer, Jim (1965-1984)	24.9
43	Keefe, Tim (1880-1893)	24.3
44	Leonard, Dutch (1933-1953)	24.0
45	Smoltz, John (1988-2003)	23.8
46	Drysdale, Don (1956-1969)	23.6
47	Cone, David (1986-2003)	23.6
48	Quinn, Jack (1909-1933)	23.5
49	Griffith, Clark (1891-1914)	23.3
50	Stieb, Dave (1979-1998)	23.2
51	Reuschel, Rick (1972-1991)	23.2
52	Roberts, Robin (1948-1966)	22.9
53	Rixey, Eppa (1912-1933)	22.8
54	Rommel, Eddie (1920-1932)	22.7
55	Ryan, Nolan (1966-1993)	22.7
56	Koufax, Sandy (1955-1966)	22.6
57	Appier, Kevin (1989-2003)	22.1
58	Vaughn, Hippo (1908-1921)	21.6
59	McGinnity, Joe (1899-1908)	21.4
60	Eckersley, Dennis (1975-1998)	21.1
61	Shocker, Urban (1916-1928)	20.6
62	Tiant, Luis (1964-1982)	20.3
63	Key, Jimmy (1984-1998)	20.2
64	Galvin, Pud (1875-1892)	19.9
65	Joss, Addie (1902-1910)	19.9
66	Pierce, Billy (1945-1964)	19.9
67	Bunning, Jim (1955-1971)	19.8
68	Cicotte, Eddie (1905-1920)	19.8
69	Ferrell, Wes (1927-1941)	19.5
70	Dean, Dizzy (1930-1947)	19.4
71	Radbourn, Charley (1881-1891)	19.2
72	Brecheen, Harry (1940-1953)	19.2
73	Willis, Vic (1898-1910)	19.1
74	Cuppy, Nig (1892-1901)	19.0
75	King, Silver (1886-1897)	18.9
76	John, Tommy (1963-1989)	18.6
77	Finley, Chuck (1986-2002)	18.6
78	Trucks, Virgil (1941-1958)	18.5
79	Gomez, Lefty (1930-1943)	18.3
80	Passeau, Claude (1935-1947)	18.1
81	McMahon, Sadie (1889-1897)	18.1
82	Lemon, Bob (1946-1958)	17.9
83	Buffinton, Charlie (1882-1892)	17.8
84	Luque, Dolf (1914-1935)	17.7
85	Mays, Carl (1915-1929)	17.5
86	Harder, Mel (1928-1947)	17.5
87	Wood, Wilbur (1961-1978)	17.2
88	Cooper, Wilbur (1912-1926)	17.2
89	Hahn, Noodles (1899-1906)	17.1
90	Jackson, Larry (1955-1968)	16.9
91	Stivetts, Jack (1889-1899)	16.8
92	Hoyt, Waite (1918-1938)	16.6
93	Mullane, Tony (1881-1894)	16.6
94	Warneke, Lon (1930-1945)	16.5
95	Caruthers, Bob (1884-1892)	16.4
96	Franco, John (1984-2003)	15.9
97	Hershiser, Orel (1983-2000)	15.9
98	Parnell, Mel (1947-1956)	15.8
99	Guidry, Ron (1975-1988)	15.7
100	Gossage, Rich (1972-1994)	15.6

Opponents Batting Average

1	Ryan, Nolan (1966-1993)	.204
2	Koufax, Sandy (1955-1966)	.205
3	Martinez, Pedro (1992-2003)	.206
4	Fernandez, Sid (1983-1997)	.209
5	Richard, J.R. (1971-1980)	.212
6	Messersmith, Andy (1968-1979)	.212
7	Johnson, Randy (1988-2003)	.215
8	McDowell, Sam (1961-1975)	.215
9	Wilhelm, Hoyt (1952-1972)	.216
10	Walsh, Ed (1904-1917)	.218
11	Soto, Mario (1977-1988)	.220
12	Turley, Bob (1951-1963)	.220
13	Overall, Orval (1905-1913)	.223
14	Joss, Addie (1902-1910)	.223
15	Tesreau, Jeff (1912-1918)	.223
16	Maloney, Jim (1960-1971)	.224
17	DeLeon, Jose (1983-1995)	.224
18	Reulbach, Ed (1905-1917)	.224
19	Seaver, Tom (1967-1986)	.226
20	Johnson, Walter (1907-1927)	.227
21	Wilson, Don (1966-1974)	.228
22	Waddell, Rube (1897-1910)	.228
23	Gibson, Bob (1959-1975)	.228
24	Gossage, Rich (1972-1994)	.228
25	Corcoran, Larry (1880-1887)	.229
26	Keefe, Tim (1880-1893)	.230
27	Palmer, Jim (1965-1984)	.230
28	Jones, Sam (1951-1964)	.230
29	Clemens, Roger (1984-2003)	.231
30	Nomo, Hideo (1995-2003)	.231
31	Hunter, Catfish (1965-1979)	.231
32	Bolin, Bobby (1961-1973)	.231
33	Feller, Bob (1936-1956)	.231
34	Downing, Al (1961-1977)	.232
35	Smoltz, John (1988-2003)	.232
36	Cone, David (1986-2003)	.232
37	Williams, Stan (1958-1972)	.232
38	Vander Meer, Johnny (1937-1951)	.232
39	Brown, Mordecai (1903-1916)	.233
40	Hough, Charlie (1970-1994)	.233
41	Cheney, Larry (1911-1919)	.234
42	Rusie, Amos (1889-1901)	.234
43	McLain, Denny (1963-1972)	.234
44	Chance, Dean (1961-1971)	.234
45	Ward, John (1878-1884)	.235
46	Ford, Whitey (1950-1967)	.235
47	Fingers, Rollie (1968-1985)	.235
48	Culp, Ray (1963-1973)	.235
49	Drabowsky, Moe (1956-1972)	.236
50	Veale, Bob (1962-1974)	.236
51	Sutton, Don (1966-1988)	.236
52	Mathewson, Christy (1900-1916)	.236
53	Schilling, Curt (1988-2003)	.236
54	Tiant, Luis (1964-1982)	.236
55	Smith, Frank (1904-1915)	.237
56	McGraw, Tug (1965-1984)	.237
57	Marichal, Juan (1960-1975)	.237
58	Blue, Vida (1969-1986)	.237
59	Pizarro, Juan (1957-1974)	.237
60	Scott, Jim (1909-1917)	.238
61	Reynolds, Allie (1942-1954)	.238
62	Siebert, Sonny (1964-1975)	.238
63	May, Rudy (1965-1983)	.238
64	Nolan, Gary (1967-1977)	.239
65	Martinez, Ramon (1988-2001)	.239
66	Newhouser, Hal (1939-1955)	.239
67	Donovan, Bill (1898-1918)	.239
68	Bender, Chief (1903-1925)	.239
69	Plank, Eddie (1901-1917)	.239
70	Pelty, Barney (1903-1912)	.239
71	Bell, Gary (1958-1969)	.239
72	Drysdale, Don (1956-1969)	.239
73	Stieb, Dave (1979-1998)	.239
74	Singer, Bill (1964-1977)	.240
75	Morris, Ed (1884-1890)	.240
76	Scott, Mike (1979-1991)	.240
77	Cooper, Mort (1938-1949)	.240
78	Trucks, Virgil (1941-1958)	.240
79	Mullane, Tony (1881-1894)	.240
80	White, Will (1877-1886)	.240
81	Pierce, Billy (1945-1964)	.240
82	Carlton, Steve (1965-1988)	.240
83	Lemon, Bob (1946-1958)	.241
84	Wiltse, Hooks (1904-1915)	.241
85	Higbe, Kirby (1937-1950)	.241
86	Coombs, Jack (1906-1920)	.241
87	McQuillan, George (1907-1918)	.241
88	Ferguson, Charlie (1884-1887)	.241
89	Moore, Earl (1901-1914)	.241
90	Leiter, Al (1987-2003)	.241
91	Gomez, Lefty (1930-1943)	.242
92	Wilson, Earl (1959-1970)	.242
93	Bunning, Jim (1955-1971)	.242
94	Gordon, Tom (1988-2003)	.242
95	Brecheen, Harry (1940-1953)	.242
96	Camnitz, Howie (1904-1915)	.242
97	Miller, Stu (1952-1968)	.242
98	Rijo, Jose (1984-2002)	.243
99	White, Doc (1901-1913)	.243
100	Cuellar, Mike (1959-1977)	.243

Pitcher Fielding Runs

1	Maddux, Greg (1986-2003)	98
2	Walsh, Ed (1904-1917)	87
3	Mays, Carl (1915-1929)	78
4	Mathewson, Christy (1900-1916)	68
5	Fitzsimmons, Freddie (1925-1943)	63
6	Lemon, Bob (1946-1958)	62
7	Grimes, Burleigh (1916-1934)	58
8	John, Tommy (1963-1989)	54
9	Gumbert, Harry (1935-1950)	51
10	Howell, Harry (1898-1910)	49
11	Rogers, Kenny (1989-2003)	47
12	Brown, Kevin (1986-2003)	46
13	Clarkson, John (1882-1894)	45
14	Martinez, Dennis (1976-1998)	44
15	Rommel, Eddie (1920-1932)	44
16	Doak, Bill (1912-1929)	43
17	Hudlin, Willis (1926-1944)	39
18	Shantz, Bobby (1949-1964)	39
19	Trout, Dizzy (1939-1957)	38
20	Dauss, Hooks (1912-1926)	37
21	Hershiser, Orel (1983-2000)	37
22	Reuschel, Rick (1972-1991)	36
23	Valenzuela, Fernando (1980-1997)	36
24	Stottlemyre, Mel (1964-1974)	36
25	Quinn, Jack (1909-1933)	36
26	Glavine, Tom (1987-2003)	36
27	Alexander, Grover (1911-1930)	34
28	Joss, Addie (1902-1910)	34
29	Altrock, Nick (1898-1924)	34
30	Schmitz, Johnny (1941-1956)	34
31	Russell, Jack (1926-1940)	33
32	Galvin, Pud (1875-1892)	33
33	Sudhoff, Willie (1897-1906)	33
34	Mullane, Tony (1881-1894)	33
35	Ehmke, Howard (1915-1930)	32
36	Jones, Randy (1973-1982)	32
37	Schumacher, Hal (1931-1946)	32
38	Stieb, Dave (1979-1998)	32
39	Dickson, Murry (1939-1959)	31
40	Buffinton, Charlie (1882-1892)	31
41	Denny, John (1974-1986)	31
42	Christopher, Russ (1942-1948)	31
43	Davis, Curt (1934-1946)	30
44	Bond, Tommy (1874-1884)	30
45	Walters, Bucky (1934-1950)	29
46	Cantwell, Ben (1927-1937)	29
47	Ames, Red (1903-1919)	28
48	Chandler, Spud (1937-1947)	28
49	Niekro, Phil (1964-1987)	28
50	Staley, Gerry (1947-1961)	28
51	Willett, Ed (1906-1915)	28
52	Boddicker, Mike (1980-1993)	27
53	Willis, Vic (1898-1910)	27
54	Smith, Frank (1904-1915)	27
55	Ford, Whitey (1950-1967)	27
56	Burgmeier, Tom (1968-1984)	27
57	Abernathy, Ted (1955-1972)	27
58	Reulbach, Ed (1905-1917)	27
59	Drysdale, Don (1956-1969)	27
60	Rusie, Amos (1889-1901)	26
61	Ward, John (1878-1884)	26
62	Hampton, Mike (1993-2003)	26
63	Smith, Sherry (1911-1927)	25
64	White, Doc (1901-1913)	25
65	Kilroy, Matt (1886-1898)	25
66	Mullin, George (1902-1915)	25
67	Quisenberry, Dan (1979-1990)	25
68	Hudson, Sid (1940-1954)	25
69	McCormick, Jim (1878-1887)	24
70	Rueter, Kirk (1993-2003)	24
71	Hubbell, Carl (1928-1943)	24
72	Dubuc, Jean (1908-1919)	24
73	Petry, Dan (1979-1991)	24
74	Jackson, Larry (1955-1968)	24
75	Callahan, Nixey (1894-1903)	24
76	Leibrandt, Charlie (1979-1993)	24
77	Fraser, Chick (1896-1909)	23
78	Hecker, Guy (1882-1890)	23
79	Stricklett, Elmer (1904-1907)	23
80	Caldwell, Mike (1971-1984)	23
81	McDowell, Roger (1985-1996)	23
82	Young, Cy (1890-1911)	23
83	Tekulve, Kent (1974-1989)	23
84	Leonard, Dutch (1933-1953)	23
85	Horlen, Joe (1961-1972)	23
86	Corridon, Frank (1904-1910)	23
87	Tyler, Lefty (1910-1921)	23
88	Key, Jimmy (1984-1998)	23
89	Perry, Gaylord (1962-1983)	22
90	Swift, Bill (1985-1998)	22
91	Newhouser, Hal (1939-1955)	22
92	Owen, Frank (1901-1909)	22
93	Miller, Stu (1952-1968)	22
94	Brewer, Tom (1954-1961)	22
95	Seymour, Cy (1896-1902)	21
96	Moore, Mike (1982-1995)	21
97	Purkey, Bob (1954-1966)	21
98	Nagy, Charles (1990-2003)	21
99	McDaniel, Lindy (1955-1975)	21
100	Erickson, Scott (1990-2002)	21

Pitcher Fielding Wins

1	Maddux, Greg (1986-2003)	10
2	Walsh, Ed (1904-1917)	9
3	Mays, Carl (1915-1929)	8
4	Mathewson, Christy (1900-1916)	7
5	Lemon, Bob (1946-1958)	6
6	Fitzsimmons, Freddie (1925-1943)	6
7	Grimes, Burleigh (1916-1934)	6
8	John, Tommy (1963-1989)	6
9	Howell, Harry (1898-1910)	5
10	Gumbert, Harry (1935-1950)	5
11	Doak, Bill (1912-1929)	5
12	Rogers, Kenny (1989-2003)	5
13	Martinez, Dennis (1976-1998)	4
14	Brown, Kevin (1986-2003)	4
15	Rommel, Eddie (1920-1932)	4
16	Shantz, Bobby (1949-1964)	4
17	Clarkson, John (1882-1894)	4
18	Stottlemyre, Mel (1964-1974)	4
19	Trout, Dizzy (1939-1957)	4
20	Dauss, Hooks (1912-1926)	4
21	Reuschel, Rick (1972-1991)	4
22	Hershiser, Orel (1983-2000)	4
23	Valenzuela, Fernando (1980-1997)	4
24	Altrock, Nick (1898-1924)	4
25	Quinn, Jack (1909-1933)	4
26	Hudlin, Willis (1926-1944)	4
27	Alexander, Grover (1911-1930)	4
28	Joss, Addie (1902-1910)	4
29	Glavine, Tom (1987-2003)	4
30	Schmitz, Johnny (1941-1956)	3
31	Jones, Randy (1973-1982)	3
32	Sudhoff, Willie (1897-1906)	3
33	Christopher, Russ (1942-1948)	3
34	Denny, John (1974-1986)	3
35	Schumacher, Hal (1931-1946)	3
36	Stieb, Dave (1979-1998)	3
37	Dickson, Murry (1939-1959)	3
38	Ehmke, Howard (1915-1930)	3
39	Russell, Jack (1926-1940)	3
40	Davis, Curt (1934-1946)	3
41	Ames, Red (1903-1919)	3
42	Niekro, Phil (1964-1987)	3
43	Smith, Frank (1904-1915)	3
44	Mullane, Tony (1881-1894)	3
45	Galvin, Pud (1875-1892)	3
46	Walters, Bucky (1934-1950)	3
47	Willett, Ed (1906-1915)	3
48	Willis, Vic (1898-1910)	3
49	Reulbach, Ed (1905-1917)	3
50	Abernathy, Ted (1955-1972)	3
51	Buffinton, Charlie (1882-1892)	3
52	Cantwell, Ben (1927-1937)	3
53	Burgmeier, Tom (1968-1984)	3
54	Chandler, Spud (1937-1947)	3
55	Staley, Gerry (1947-1961)	3
56	White, Doc (1901-1913)	3
57	Drysdale, Don (1956-1969)	3
58	Ford, Whitey (1950-1967)	3
59	Bond, Tommy (1874-1884)	3
60	Boddicker, Mike (1980-1993)	3
61	Mullin, George (1902-1915)	3
62	Smith, Sherry (1911-1927)	3
63	Dubuc, Jean (1908-1919)	3
64	Hampton, Mike (1993-2003)	3
65	Stricklett, Elmer (1904-1907)	3
66	Jackson, Larry (1955-1968)	3
67	Corridon, Frank (1904-1910)	2
68	Quisenberry, Dan (1979-1990)	2
69	Hudson, Sid (1940-1954)	2
70	Horlen, Joe (1961-1972)	2
71	Ward, John (1878-1884)	2
72	Petry, Dan (1979-1991)	2
73	Tyler, Lefty (1910-1921)	2
74	Perry, Gaylord (1962-1983)	2
75	Owen, Frank (1901-1909)	2
76	Hubbell, Carl (1928-1943)	2
77	Leibrandt, Charlie (1979-1993)	2
78	Rueter, Kirk (1993-2003)	2
79	Tekulve, Kent (1974-1989)	2
80	Caldwell, Mike (1971-1984)	2
81	McDowell, Roger (1985-1996)	2
82	Newhouser, Hal (1939-1955)	2
83	Leonard, Dutch (1933-1953)	2
84	Coveleski, Harry (1907-1918)	2
85	Swift, Bill (1985-1998)	2
86	Miller, Stu (1952-1968)	2
87	Fraser, Chick (1896-1909)	2
88	Brewer, Tom (1954-1961)	2
89	Barnes, Jesse (1915-1927)	2
90	McDaniel, Lindy (1955-1975)	2
91	Rusie, Amos (1889-1901)	2
92	Callahan, Nixey (1894-1903)	2
93	Key, Jimmy (1984-1998)	2
94	McCormick, Jim (1878-1887)	2
95	Linzy, Frank (1963-1974)	2
96	Purkey, Bob (1954-1966)	2
97	Kilroy, Matt (1886-1898)	2
98	Benz, Joe (1911-1919)	2
99	Knowles, Darold (1965-1980)	2
100	Krapp, Gene (1911-1915)	2

Win Shares – Pitchers

1	Young, Cy (1890-1911)	634
2	Johnson, Walter (1907-1927)	560
3	Nichols, Kid (1890-1906)	478
4	Alexander, Grover (1911-1930)	476
5	Mathewson, Christy (1900-1916)	426
6	Keefe, Tim (1880-1893)	413
7	Spahn, Warren (1942-1965)	412
8	Galvin, Pud (1875-1892)	403
9	Mullane, Tony (1881-1894)	399
10	Clarkson, John (1882-1894)	396
11	Grove, Lefty (1925-1941)	391
	Radbourn, Charley (1881-1891)	391
13	Seaver, Tom (1967-1986)	388
14	Clemens, Roger (1984-2003)	378
15	Niekro, Phil (1964-1987)	374
16	Perry, Gaylord (1962-1983)	369
17	Carlton, Steve (1965-1988)	366
18	Plank, Eddie (1901-1917)	361
19	Welch, Mickey (1880-1892)	354
20	Ruth, Babe (1914-1933)	351
21	Maddux, Greg (1986-2003)	347
22	Blyleven, Bert (1970-1992)	339
	Roberts, Robin (1948-1966)	339
24	Caruthers, Bob (1884-1892)	335
25	McCormick, Jim (1878-1887)	334
	Ryan, Nolan (1966-1993)	334
27	Jenkins, Fergie (1965-1983)	323
28	Ruffing, Red (1924-1947)	322
29	Sutton, Don (1966-1988)	319
30	Gibson, Bob (1959-1975)	317
31	Rixey, Eppa (1912-1933)	315
32	Lyons, Ted (1923-1946)	312
	Palmer, Jim (1965-1984)	312
34	Wynn, Early (1939-1963)	309
35	Hubbell, Carl (1928-1943)	305
36	Eckersley, Dennis (1975-1998)	301
37	Brown, Mordecai (1903-1916)	296
38	Rusie, Amos (1889-1901)	293
	Willis, Vic (1898-1910)	293
40	Faber, Red (1914-1933)	292
	Feller, Bob (1936-1956)	292
42	Foutz, Dave (1884-1894)	290
43	John, Tommy (1963-1989)	289
44	Powell, Jack (1897-1912)	287
	Quinn, Jack (1909-1933)	287
46	Grimes, Burleigh (1916-1934)	286
47	Stivetts, Jack (1889-1899)	285
48	Buffinton, Charlie (1882-1892)	283
49	Whitney, Jim (1881-1890)	275
50	Griffith, Clark (1891-1914)	273
	Terry, Adonis (1884-1897)	273
52	McGinnity, Joe (1899-1908)	269
53	Kaat, Jim (1959-1983)	268
54	Cooper, Wilbur (1912-1926)	266
55	Walsh, Ed (1904-1917)	265
56	Newhouser, Hal (1939-1955)	264
57	King, Silver (1886-1897)	263
	Marichal, Juan (1960-1975)	263
59	Hoyt, Waite (1918-1938)	262
60	Ford, Whitey (1950-1967)	261
	Glavine, Tom (1987-2003)	261
	Johnson, Randy (1988-2003)	261
63	Hecker, Guy (1882-1890)	259
64	Drysdale, Don (1956-1969)	258
	Weyhing, Gus (1887-1901)	258
66	Bunning, Jim (1955-1971)	257
67	Mays, Carl (1915-1929)	256
	Tiant, Luis (1964-1982)	256
	Wilhelm, Hoyt (1952-1972)	256
70	Mullin, George (1902-1915)	255
71	Walters, Bucky (1934-1950)	251
72	Pierce, Billy (1945-1964)	248
73	Cicotte, Eddie (1905-1920)	247
74	Coveleski, Stan (1912-1928)	245
	Jones, Sam (1914-1935)	245
76	Adams, Babe (1906-1926)	243
	Bond, Tommy (1874-1884)	243
	Orth, Al (1895-1909)	243
79	Luque, Dolf (1914-1935)	241
	Tanana, Frank (1973-1993)	241
	Vance, Dazzy (1915-1935)	241
82	Koosman, Jerry (1967-1985)	240
	Pennock, Herb (1912-1934)	240
	Reuschel, Rick (1972-1991)	240
	Waddell, Rube (1897-1910)	240
86	White, Will (1877-1886)	239
87	Newsom, Bobo (1929-1953)	237
88	White, Doc (1901-1913)	235
89	Harder, Mel (1928-1947)	234
90	Ferrell, Wes (1927-1941)	233
	Hough, Charlie (1970-1994)	233
	Leonard, Dutch (1933-1953)	233
	Martinez, Dennis (1976-1998)	233
	Tannehill, Jesse (1894-1911)	233
95	Brown, Kevin (1986-2003)	232
	Lemon, Bob (1946-1958)	232
97	Bender, Chief (1903-1925)	231
	Derringer, Paul (1931-1945)	231
	Uhle, George (1919-1936)	231
100	2 players tied	228

Total Player Wins – Pitchers

1	Johnson, Walter (1907-1927)	72.1
2	Young, Cy (1890-1911)	67.6
3	Clemens, Roger (1984-2003)	62.6
4	Maddux, Greg (1986-2003)	57.8
5	Grove, Lefty (1925-1941)	57.3
6	Alexander, Grover (1911-1930)	56.1
7	Nichols, Kid (1890-1906)	51.7
8	Mathewson, Christy (1900-1916)	50.3
9	Johnson, Randy (1988-2003)	43.6
10	Seaver, Tom (1967-1986)	43.2
11	Gibson, Bob (1959-1975)	41.9
12	Martinez, Pedro (1992-2003)	41.7
13	Spahn, Warren (1942-1965)	40.2
14	Clarkson, John (1882-1894)	39.7
15	Niekro, Phil (1964-1987)	36.2
16	Newhouser, Hal (1939-1955)	36.0
17	Brown, Kevin (1986-2003)	32.2
18	Carlton, Steve (1965-1988)	32.0
19	Blyleven, Bert (1970-1992)	32.0
20	Walsh, Ed (1904-1917)	31.5
21	Perry, Gaylord (1962-1983)	31.5
22	Rusie, Amos (1889-1901)	31.3
23	Glavine, Tom (1987-2003)	31.1
24	Hubbell, Carl (1928-1943)	30.9
25	Lyons, Ted (1923-1946)	30.9
26	Jenkins, Fergie (1965-1983)	30.3
27	Plank, Eddie (1901-1917)	29.7
28	Marichal, Juan (1960-1975)	29.6
29	Drysdale, Don (1956-1969)	29.6
30	Ferrell, Wes (1927-1941)	29.6
31	Trout, Dizzy (1939-1957)	29.2
32	Mussina, Mike (1991-2003)	29.0
33	Caruthers, Bob (1884-1892)	28.7
34	Ford, Whitey (1950-1967)	28.7
35	Brown, Mordecai (1903-1916)	27.7
36	Bridges, Tommy (1930-1946)	27.3
37	Griffith, Clark (1891-1914)	26.6
38	Keefe, Tim (1880-1893)	26.6
39	Roberts, Robin (1948-1966)	26.5
40	Smoltz, John (1988-2003)	26.4
41	Wilhelm, Hoyt (1952-1972)	26.4
42	Schilling, Curt (1988-2003)	26.3
43	Saberhagen, Bret (1984-2001)	26.1
44	Lemon, Bob (1946-1958)	26.0
45	Feller, Bob (1936-1956)	25.9
46	Vance, Dazzy (1915-1935)	25.8
47	Palmer, Jim (1965-1984)	25.5
48	Ruffing, Red (1924-1947)	25.5
49	Waddell, Rube (1897-1910)	24.9
50	Reuschel, Rick (1972-1991)	24.3
51	Cone, David (1986-2003)	24.0
52	Mays, Carl (1915-1929)	23.8
53	Shocker, Urban (1916-1928)	23.6
54	Faber, Red (1914-1933)	23.3
55	Stieb, Dave (1979-1998)	23.2
56	Coveleski, Stan (1912-1928)	23.2
57	Quinn, Jack (1909-1933)	22.9
58	Stivetts, Jack (1889-1899)	21.9
59	Rommel, Eddie (1920-1932)	21.9
60	Leonard, Dutch (1933-1953)	21.9
61	Vaughn, Hippo (1908-1921)	21.8
62	Appier, Kevin (1989-2003)	21.7
63	Radbourn, Charley (1881-1891)	21.6
64	Rixey, Eppa (1912-1933)	21.5
65	Eckersley, Dennis (1975-1998)	21.1
66	Luque, Dolf (1914-1935)	21.1
67	Mullane, Tony (1881-1894)	20.9
68	Dean, Dizzy (1930-1947)	20.9
69	Cooper, Wilbur (1912-1926)	20.8
70	Tiant, Luis (1964-1982)	20.8
71	Ryan, Nolan (1966-1993)	20.6
72	Cicotte, Eddie (1905-1920)	20.5
73	Brecheen, Harry (1940-1953)	20.3
74	Walters, Bucky (1934-1950)	20.2
75	Key, Jimmy (1984-1998)	20.1
76	Koufax, Sandy (1955-1966)	20.0
77	McGinnity, Joe (1899-1908)	19.8
78	Pierce, Billy (1945-1964)	19.7
79	Cuppy, Nig (1892-1901)	19.7
80	Bunning, Jim (1955-1971)	19.6
81	Passeau, Claude (1935-1947)	19.5
82	King, Silver (1886-1897)	19.4
83	Wynn, Early (1939-1963)	19.4
84	Warneke, Lon (1930-1945)	19.3
85	Grimes, Burleigh (1916-1934)	19.2
86	Hershiser, Orel (1983-2000)	19.1
87	John, Tommy (1963-1989)	18.6
88	Garver, Ned (1948-1961)	18.5
89	Joss, Addie (1902-1910)	18.4
90	Lucas, Red (1923-1938)	18.3
91	Finley, Chuck (1986-2002)	18.2
92	Hecker, Guy (1882-1890)	18.0
93	Kaat, Jim (1959-1983)	18.0
94	Adams, Babe (1906-1926)	17.8
95	Whitney, Jim (1881-1890)	17.3
96	Rowe, Schoolboy (1933-1949)	17.1
97	Newcombe, Don (1949-1960)	17.0
98	Ferguson, Charlie (1884-1887)	17.0
99	Uhle, George (1919-1936)	16.9
100	Hahn, Noodles (1899-1906)	16.9
101	Jackson, Larry (1955-1968)	16.6
102	Trucks, Virgil (1941-1958)	16.5
103	Galvin, Pud (1875-1892)	16.4
104	Gooden, Dwight (1984-2000)	16.3
105	Messersmith, Andy (1968-1979)	16.3
106	Tannehill, Jesse (1894-1911)	16.2
107	Willis, Vic (1898-1910)	16.1
108	Buffinton, Charlie (1882-1892)	16.0
109	McMahon, Sadie (1889-1897)	15.9
110	Taylor, Jack (1898-1907)	15.9
111	Wood, Wilbur (1961-1978)	15.8
112	Guidry, Ron (1975-1988)	15.6
113	Lee, Thornton (1933-1948)	15.5
114	Hendrix, Claude (1911-1920)	15.5
115	Bender, Chief (1903-1925)	15.4
116	French, Larry (1929-1942)	15.3
117	Gossage, Rich (1972-1994)	15.3
118	Parnell, Mel (1947-1956)	15.2
119	Davis, Curt (1934-1946)	15.1
120	Gomez, Lefty (1930-1943)	15.0
121	McCormick, Jim (1878-1887)	15.0
122	White, Doc (1901-1913)	15.0
123	Harder, Mel (1928-1947)	14.9
124	Dickson, Murry (1939-1959)	14.9
125	Rijo, Jose (1984-2002)	14.8
126	Hoyt, Waite (1918-1938)	14.6
127	Tudor, John (1979-1990)	14.4
128	Shantz, Bobby (1949-1964)	14.3
129	Leever, Sam (1898-1910)	14.1
130	Simmons, Curt (1947-1967)	14.0
131	Fitzsimmons, Freddie (1925-1943)	14.0
132	Viola, Frank (1982-1996)	13.9
133	Pettitte, Andy (1995-2003)	13.8
134	Candelaria, John (1975-1993)	13.8
135	Stanley, Bob (1977-1989)	13.8
136	Cooper, Mort (1938-1949)	13.8
137	Wells, David (1987-2003)	13.6
138	Rogers, Steve (1973-1985)	13.6
139	Maloney, Jim (1960-1971)	13.4
140	Antonelli, Johnny (1948-1961)	13.4
141	Lopat, Ed (1944-1955)	13.2
142	Stottlemyre, Mel (1964-1974)	13.1
143	Maglie, Sal (1945-1958)	13.0
144	Garcia, Mike (1948-1961)	12.9
145	Rucker, Nap (1907-1916)	12.7
146	Dwyer, Frank (1888-1899)	12.7
147	Dauss, Hooks (1912-1926)	12.6
148	Ward, John (1878-1884)	12.5
149	Siebert, Sonny (1964-1975)	12.4
150	Pollet, Howie (1941-1956)	12.2
151	Matlack, Jon (1971-1983)	12.0
152	Hampton, Mike (1993-2003)	12.0
153	Lanier, Max (1938-1953)	12.0
154	Welch, Mickey (1880-1892)	11.9
155	Sutton, Don (1966-1988)	11.8
156	Lary, Frank (1954-1965)	11.7
157	Phillippe, Deacon (1899-1911)	11.7
158	Mullin, George (1902-1915)	11.6
159	Hutchison, Bill (1884-1897)	11.6
160	Wiltse, Hooks (1904-1915)	11.5
161	Leonard, Dutch (1913-1925)	11.5
162	Reulbach, Ed (1905-1917)	11.5
163	Shawkey, Bob (1913-1927)	11.5
164	Candiotti, Tom (1983-1999)	11.4
165	Rogers, Kenny (1989-2003)	11.4
166	Killen, Frank (1891-1900)	11.3
167	Mungo, Van (1931-1945)	11.3
168	McDowell, Sam (1961-1975)	11.3
169	Pfeffer, Jeff (1911-1924)	11.2
170	Pascual, Camilo (1954-1971)	11.2
171	Kilroy, Matt (1886-1898)	11.2
172	Haddix, Harvey (1952-1965)	11.1
173	Ostermueller, Fritz (1934-1948)	11.1
174	Rush, Bob (1948-1960)	11.1
175	Breitenstein, Ted (1891-1901)	11.0
176	Tanana, Frank (1973-1993)	11.0
177	Koosman, Jerry (1967-1985)	10.9
178	Sullivan, Frank (1953-1963)	10.9
179	Peters, Gary (1959-1972)	10.8
180	Leiter, Al (1987-2003)	10.8
181	Radke, Brad (1995-2003)	10.6
182	Pappas, Milt (1957-1973)	10.6
183	Newsom, Bobo (1929-1953)	10.6
184	White, Will (1877-1886)	10.5
185	Sallee, Slim (1908-1921)	10.4
186	Chance, Dean (1961-1971)	10.4
187	Sewell, Rip (1932-1949)	10.2
188	Perry, Jim (1959-1975)	10.2
189	Schumacher, Hal (1931-1946)	10.1
190	Moyer, Jamie (1986-2003)	10.1
191	Gubicza, Mark (1984-1997)	10.1
192	Foutz, Dave (1884-1894)	10.1
193	Fernandez, Alex (1990-2000)	10.0
194	Hough, Charlie (1970-1994)	10.0
195	Fingers, Rollie (1968-1985)	9.9
196	Hands, Bill (1965-1975)	9.8
197	Tobin, Jim (1937-1945)	9.8
198	Crandall, Doc (1908-1918)	9.7
199	Ewing, Bob (1902-1912)	9.7
200	Blue, Vida (1969-1986)	9.7
201	Garber, Gene (1969-1988)	9.7
202	Chesbro, Jack (1899-1909)	9.6
203	Fernandez, Sid (1983-1997)	9.6
204	Langston, Mark (1984-1999)	9.6
205	Howell, Harry (1898-1910)	9.4
206	Root, Charley (1923-1941)	9.4
207	Miller, Stu (1952-1968)	9.3
208	Mossi, Don (1954-1965)	9.3
209	Hawley, Pink (1892-1901)	9.2
210	Orth, Al (1895-1909)	9.2
211	Ramsey, Toad (1885-1890)	9.2
212	Leibrandt, Charlie (1979-1993)	9.1
213	Gordon, Tom (1988-2003)	8.9
214	Mercer, Win (1894-1902)	8.9
215	Morris, Ed (1884-1890)	8.8
216	Clark, Watty (1924-1937)	8.7
217	Marberry, Firpo (1923-1936)	8.7
218	Ruether, Dutch (1917-1927)	8.6
219	Swindell, Greg (1986-2002)	8.6
220	Wakefield, Tim (1992-2003)	8.6
221	Scott, Jim (1909-1917)	8.5
222	Hooton, Burt (1971-1985)	8.5
223	Alvarez, Wilson (1989-2003)	8.4
224	Nolan, Gary (1967-1977)	8.3
225	Valenzuela, Fernando (1980-1997)	8.3
226	Sain, Johnny (1942-1955)	8.3
227	Smith, Sherry (1911-1927)	8.2
228	McGraw, Tug (1965-1984)	8.2
229	Darwin, Danny (1978-1998)	8.1
230	Overall, Orval (1905-1913)	8.0
231	Ehmke, Howard (1915-1930)	8.0
232	Allen, Johnny (1932-1944)	8.0
233	Derringer, Paul (1931-1945)	8.0
234	Martinez, Dennis (1976-1998)	7.9
235	Leifield, Lefty (1905-1920)	7.8
236	McDaniel, Lindy (1955-1975)	7.8
237	Haines, Jesse (1918-1937)	7.7
238	Boddicker, Mike (1980-1993)	7.7
239	Fassero, Jeff (1991-2003)	7.7
240	Gromek, Steve (1941-1957)	7.7
241	Chamberlain, Elton (1886-1896)	7.7
242	Dobson, Joe (1939-1954)	7.6
243	Hentgen, Pat (1991-2003)	7.6
244	Welch, Bob (1978-1994)	7.6
245	Osteen, Claude (1957-1975)	7.5
246	Benton, Al (1934-1952)	7.4
247	Rhoden, Rick (1974-1989)	7.4
248	Tesreau, Jeff (1912-1918)	7.3
249	Casey, Dan (1884-1890)	7.3
250	Zachary, Tom (1918-1936)	7.3
251	Raffensberger, Ken (1939-1954)	7.3
252	Roe, Preacher (1938-1954)	7.1
253	Baldwin, Mark (1887-1893)	7.1
254	McDowell, Jack (1987-1999)	7.0
255	Reed, Ron (1966-1984)	7.0
256	Lee, Bill (1969-1982)	6.9
257	Lolich, Mickey (1963-1979)	6.9
258	Bagby, Jim (1912-1923)	6.9
259	Bonham, Tiny (1940-1949)	6.9
260	Walberg, Rube (1923-1937)	6.7
261	Pennock, Herb (1912-1934)	6.7
262	Ames, Red (1903-1919)	6.7
263	Jansen, Larry (1947-1956)	6.7
264	Swift, Bill (1932-1943)	6.6
265	Kremer, Ray (1924-1933)	6.6
266	Tyler, Lefty (1910-1921)	6.6
267	Wilson, Don (1966-1974)	6.6
268	Callahan, Nixey (1894-1903)	6.6
269	Wilson, Earl (1959-1970)	6.5
270	Williams, Woody (1993-2003)	6.4
271	Terry, Adonis (1884-1897)	6.4
272	Wyatt, Whit (1929-1945)	6.4
273	Barr, Jim (1971-1983)	6.2
274	Sherdel, Bill (1918-1932)	6.2
275	Schmitz, Johnny (1941-1956)	6.1
276	Jones, Sam (1914-1935)	6.0
277	Richard, J.R. (1971-1980)	5.9
278	Leonard, Dennis (1974-1986)	5.9
279	Horlen, Joe (1961-1972)	5.9
280	Friend, Bob (1951-1966)	5.8
281	Nehf, Art (1915-1929)	5.8
282	Taylor, Jack (1891-1899)	5.8
283	Brandt, Ed (1928-1938)	5.8
284	Nomo, Hideo (1995-2003)	5.6
285	Stewart, Lefty (1921-1935)	5.6
286	Gray, Dolly (1924-1933)	5.6
287	Lee, Bill (1934-1947)	5.6
288	Veale, Bob (1962-1974)	5.5
289	Hurst, Bruce (1980-1994)	5.5
290	Donovan, Bill (1898-1918)	5.4
291	Cheney, Larry (1911-1919)	5.4
292	Rhines, Billy (1890-1899)	5.3
293	Hudlin, Willis (1926-1944)	5.3
294	Stratton, Scott (1888-1895)	5.2
295	Law, Vern (1950-1967)	5.2
296	Pizarro, Juan (1957-1974)	5.2
297	Rooker, Jim (1968-1980)	5.1
298	Kennedy, Brickyard (1892-1903)	5.1
299	O'Dell, Billy (1954-1967)	5.1
300	Killian, Ed (1903-1910)	5.0

At Bats

1	Wilson, Willie (1980)	705
2	Samuel, Juan (1984)	701
3	Cash, Dave (1975)	699
4	Alou, Matty (1969)	698
5	Jensen, Woody (1936)	696
	Soriano, Alfonso (2002)	696
7	Moreno, Omar (1979)	695
	Wills, Maury (1962)	695
9	Richardson, Bobby (1962)	692
	Suzuki, Ichiro (2001)	692
11	Puckett, Kirby (1985)	691
12	Perez, Neifi (1999)	690
13	Alomar, Sandy (1971)	689
	Brock, Lou (1967)	689
15	Cash, Dave (1974)	687
	Fernandez, Tony (1986)	687
17	Clarke, Horace (1970)	686
	Rodriguez, Alex (1998)	686
19	Garciaparra, Nomar (1997)	684
20	Johnson, Lance (1996)	682
	Soriano, Alfonso (2003)	682
22	Moore, Jo-Jo (1935)	681
	Waner, Lloyd (1931)	681
24	Puckett, Kirby (1986)	680
	Rose, Pete (1973)	680
	Taveras, Frank (1979)	680
27	Flood, Curt (1964)	679
	Kuenn, Harvey (1953)	679
	Richardson, Bobby (1964)	679
	Suzuki, Ichiro (2003)	679
31	Glanville, Doug (1998)	678
	Groat, Dick (1962)	678
	Wells, Vernon (2003)	678
34	Alou, Matty (1970)	677
	Mattingly, Don (1986)	677
	Rice, Jim (1978)	677
37	Erstad, Darin (2000)	676
	Millan, Felix (1975)	676
	Moreno, Omar (1980)	676
40	Buckner, Bill (1985)	673
	Stennett, Rennie (1974)	673
	Surhoff, B.J. (1999)	673
43	Alomar, Sandy (1970)	672
	Anderson, Garret (2001)	672
	Latham, Arlie (1887)	672
	Maranville, Rabbit (1922)	672
	Oliva, Tony (1964)	672
	Templeton, Garry (1979)	672
49	Grissom, Marquis (1996)	671
	Tobin, Jack (1921)	671
51	Bell, Buddy (1979)	670
	Rose, Pete (1965)	670
	Simmons, Al (1932)	670
54	Bowa, Larry (1974)	669
	Pinson, Vada (1965)	669
56	Garr, Ralph (1973)	668
	Lewis, Buddy (1937)	668
	Pierre, Juan (2003)	668
	Robinson, Brooks (1961)	668
60	Furillo, Carl (1951)	667
61	Alou, Felipe (1966)	666
	Cash, Dave (1976)	666
	Herman, Billy (1935)	666
	LeFlore, Ron (1978)	666
	Molitor, Paul (1982)	666
	Versalles, Zoilo (1965)	666
	Young, Mike (2003)	666
68	Davis, Tommy (1962)	665
	Molitor, Paul (1991)	665
	Rose, Pete (1976)	665
71	Brock, Lou (1970)	664
	Douthit, Taylor (1930)	664
	Furcal, Rafael (2003)	664
	Kessinger, Don (1969)	664
	Richardson, Bobby (1965)	664
76	Beltran, Carlos (1999)	663
	Bonds, Bobby (1970)	663
	Burleson, Rick (1977)	663
	Carter, Joe (1986)	663
	Ripken, Cal (1983)	663
	Samuel, Juan (1985)	663
	Virdon, Bill (1962)	663
	Wood, Jake (1961)	663
84	Alou, Felipe (1968)	662
	Ashburn, Richie (1949)	662
	Bichette, Dante (1998)	662
	Critz, Hughie (1930)	662
	Flood, Curt (1963)	662
	Hamner, Granny (1949)	662
	Lofton, Kenny (1996)	662
	Richardson, Bobby (1961)	662
	Rose, Pete (1975)	662
	Tejada, Miguel (2002)	662
	Waner, Lloyd (1929)	662
95	Cooper, Cecil (1983)	661
	Cramer, Doc (1933)	661
	Cramer, Doc (1940)	661
	Hubbs, Ken (1962)	661
	Sierra, Ruben (1991)	661
100	5 players tied	660

Runs

1	Hamilton, Billy (1894)	198
2	Brown, Tom (1891)	177
	Ruth, Babe (1921)	177
4	Gehrig, Lou (1936)	167
	O'Neill, Tip (1887)	167
6	Hamilton, Billy (1895)	166
7	Keeler, Willie (1894)	165
	Kelley, Joe (1894)	165
9	Gehrig, Lou (1931)	163
	Latham, Arlie (1887)	163
	Ruth, Babe (1928)	163
12	Keeler, Willie (1895)	162
13	Duffy, Hugh (1890)	161
14	Burkett, Jesse (1896)	160
	Duffy, Hugh (1894)	160
	Dunlap, Fred (1884)	160
17	Jennings, Hughie (1895)	159
18	Klein, Chuck (1930)	158
	Lowe, Bobby (1894)	158
	Ruth, Babe (1920)	158
	Ruth, Babe (1927)	158
22	Hornsby, Rogers (1929)	156
	McGraw, John (1894)	156
24	Cuyler, Kiki (1930)	155
	Kelly, King (1886)	155
26	Brouthers, Dan (1887)	153
	Burkett, Jesse (1895)	153
	Hamilton, Billy (1896)	153
	Keeler, Willie (1896)	153
30	Bagwell, Jeff (2000)	152
	English, Woody (1930)	152
	Griffin, Mike (1889)	152
	Hamilton, Billy (1897)	152
	Klein, Chuck (1932)	152
	Latham, Arlie (1886)	152
	O'Doul, Lefty (1929)	152
	Simmons, Al (1930)	152
	Stovey, Harry (1889)	152
39	DiMaggio, Joe (1937)	151
	Foxx, Jimmie (1932)	151
	Ruth, Babe (1923)	151
42	Dahlen, Bill (1894)	150
	Gore, George (1886)	150
	Ruth, Babe (1930)	150
	Stenzel, Jake (1894)	150
	Williams, Ted (1949)	150
47	Delahanty, Ed (1895)	149
	Gehrig, Lou (1927)	149
	Long, Herman (1893)	149
	Ruth, Babe (1931)	149
51	Collins, Hub (1890)	148
	Delahanty, Ed (1894)	148
	Kelley, Joe (1896)	148
	Kelley, Joe (1895)	148
55	Cobb, Ty (1911)	147
	Donovan, Patsy (1894)	147
	Duffy, Hugh (1893)	147
	Tiernan, Mike (1889)	147
59	Biggio, Craig (1997)	146
	Brown, Tom (1890)	146
	Henderson, Rickey (1985)	146
	O'Brien, Darby (1889)	146
	Sosa, Sammy (2001)	146
	Wilson, Hack (1930)	146
65	Burkett, Jesse (1893)	145
	Childs, Cupid (1893)	145
	Clift, Harlond (1936)	145
	Delahanty, Ed (1893)	145
	Keeler, Willie (1897)	145
	Lajoie, Nap (1901)	145
71	Cobb, Ty (1915)	144
	Cuyler, Kiki (1925)	144
	Duffy, Hugh (1889)	144
	Gehringer, Charlie (1936)	144
	Gehringer, Charlie (1930)	144
	Greenberg, Hank (1938)	144
	Hamilton, Billy (1889)	144
	Simmons, Al (1932)	144
79	Bagwell, Jeff (1999)	143
	Childs, Cupid (1894)	143
	Combs, Earle (1932)	143
	Dykstra, Lenny (1993)	143
	Gehrig, Lou (1930)	143
	Herman, Babe (1930)	143
	McGraw, John (1898)	143
	Rolfe, Red (1937)	143
	Ruth, Babe (1924)	143
	Walker, Larry (1997)	143
89	Burkett, Jesse (1901)	142
	Burks, Ellis (1996)	142
	Griffin, Mike (1887)	142
	Stovey, Harry (1890)	142
	Waner, Paul (1928)	142
	Williams, Ted (1946)	142
95	Hamilton, Billy (1891)	141
	Hornsby, Rogers (1922)	141
	Rodriguez, Alex (1996)	141
	Williams, Ted (1942)	141
99	9 players tied	140

Hits

1	Browning, Pete (1887)	275
	O'Neill, Tip (1887)	275
3	Sisler, George (1920)	257
4	Lyons, Denny (1887)	256
5	O'Doul, Lefty (1929)	254
	Terry, Bill (1930)	254
7	Simmons, Al (1925)	253
8	Burns, Oyster (1887)	251
9	Hornsby, Rogers (1922)	250
	Klein, Chuck (1930)	250
11	Cobb, Ty (1911)	248
12	Sisler, George (1922)	246
13	Latham, Arlie (1887)	243
14	Suzuki, Ichiro (2001)	242
15	Herman, Babe (1930)	241
	Manush, Heinie (1928)	241
17	Boggs, Wade (1985)	240
	Brouthers, Dan (1887)	240
	Burkett, Jesse (1896)	240
	Erstad, Darin (2000)	240
21	Carew, Rod (1977)	239
	Keeler, Willie (1897)	239
23	Delahanty, Ed (1899)	238
	Mattingly, Don (1986)	238
25	Duffy, Hugh (1894)	237
	Heilmann, Harry (1921)	237
	Medwick, Joe (1937)	237
	Waner, Paul (1927)	237
29	Tobin, Jack (1921)	236
30	Hornsby, Rogers (1921)	235
	Radford, Paul (1887)	235
	Thompson, Sam (1887)	235
33	Puckett, Kirby (1988)	234
	Waner, Lloyd (1929)	234
35	Jackson, Joe (1911)	233
36	Averill, Earl (1936)	232
	Lajoie, Nap (1901)	232
38	Alou, Matty (1969)	231
	Combs, Earle (1927)	231
	Lindstrom, Freddie (1930)	231
	Lindstrom, Freddie (1928)	231
42	Davis, Tommy (1962)	230
	Mack, Reddy (1887)	230
	Musial, Stan (1948)	230
	Rose, Pete (1973)	230
	Torre, Joe (1971)	230
	Wilson, Willie (1980)	230
48	Hornsby, Rogers (1929)	229
49	Cuyler, Kiki (1930)	228
	Musial, Stan (1946)	228
51	Bottomley, Jim (1925)	227
	Gehringer, Charlie (1936)	227
	Herman, Billy (1935)	227
	Hornsby, Rogers (1924)	227
	Johnson, Lance (1996)	227
	Lajoie, Nap (1910)	227
	Rice, Sam (1925)	227
58	Burkett, Jesse (1901)	226
	Cobb, Ty (1912)	226
	Jackson, Joe (1912)	226
	Klein, Chuck (1932)	226
	Terry, Bill (1929)	226
63	Burkett, Jesse (1895)	225
	Cobb, Ty (1917)	225
	Hamilton, Billy (1894)	225
	Heilmann, Harry (1925)	225
	Hodapp, Johnny (1930)	225
	Molitor, Paul (1996)	225
	Terry, Bill (1932)	225
70	Anson, Cap (1887)	224
	Collins, Eddie (1920)	224
	Holmes, Tommy (1945)	224
	McClellan, Bill (1887)	224
	Medwick, Joe (1935)	224
	Sisler, George (1925)	224
76	Aaron, Hank (1959)	223
	Frisch, Frankie (1923)	223
	Klein, Chuck (1933)	223
	Medwick, Joe (1936)	223
	Puckett, Kirby (1986)	223
	Robinson, Yank (1887)	223
	Waner, Lloyd (1927)	223
	Waner, Paul (1928)	223
84	Fennelly, Frank (1887)	222
	Jamieson, Charlie (1923)	222
	Speaker, Tris (1912)	222
	Thompson, Sam (1893)	222
88	Ashburn, Richie (1951)	221
	Burkett, Jesse (1899)	221
	Manush, Heinie (1933)	221
	Waner, Lloyd (1928)	221
	Wheat, Zack (1925)	221
93	Cuyler, Kiki (1925)	220
	Gehrig, Lou (1930)	220
	Gwynn, Tony (1997)	220
	Musial, Stan (1943)	220
	Williams, Jimmy (1899)	220
98	10 players tied	219

Doubles

1	Webb, Earl (1931)	67
2	Burns, George (1926)	64
	Medwick, Joe (1936)	64
4	Greenberg, Hank (1934)	63
5	Waner, Paul (1932)	62
6	Gehringer, Charlie (1936)	60
7	Helton, Todd (2000)	59
	Klein, Chuck (1930)	59
	Speaker, Tris (1923)	59
10	Delgado, Carlos (2000)	57
	Herman, Billy (1935)	57
	Herman, Billy (1936)	57
13	Anderson, Garret (2002)	56
	Biggio, Craig (1999)	56
	Garciaparra, Nomar (2002)	56
	Kell, George (1950)	56
	Medwick, Joe (1937)	56
18	Berkman, Lance (2001)	55
	Delahanty, Ed (1899)	55
	Walker, Gee (1936)	55
21	Grudzielanek, Mark (1997)	54
	Helton, Todd (2001)	54
	McRae, Hal (1977)	54
	Olerud, John (1993)	54
	Rodriguez, Alex (1996)	54
26	Cirillo, Jeff (2000)	53
	Mattingly, Don (1986)	53
	Musial, Stan (1953)	53
	Simmons, Al (1926)	53
	Speaker, Tris (1912)	53
	Waner, Paul (1936)	53
32	Belle, Albert (1995)	52
	Frederick, Johnny (1929)	52
	Gehrig, Lou (1927)	52
	Martinez, Edgar (1996)	52
	Martinez, Edgar (1995)	52
	O'Neill, Tip (1887)	52
	Slaughter, Enos (1939)	52
	Speaker, Tris (1921)	52
	Speaker, Tris (1926)	52
41	Bell, Beau (1937)	51
	Biggio, Craig (1998)	51
	Boggs, Wade (1989)	51
	Burns, George (1927)	51
	Cronin, Joe (1938)	51
	Duffy, Hugh (1894)	51
	Garciaparra, Nomar (2000)	51
	Grace, Mark (1995)	51
	Hodapp, Johnny (1930)	51
	Jacobson, Baby Doll (1926)	51
	Lajoie, Nap (1910)	51
	Musial, Stan (1944)	51
	Pujols, Albert (2003)	51
	Robinson, Frank (1962)	51
	Rose, Pete (1978)	51
	Soriano, Alfonso (2002)	51
	Vernon, Mickey (1946)	51
	Vidro, Jose (2000)	51
59	Abreu, Bobby (2002)	50
	Chapman, Ben (1936)	50
	Cuyler, Kiki (1930)	50
	Gehringer, Charlie (1934)	50
	Gonzalez, Juan (1998)	50
	Greenberg, Hank (1940)	50
	Hale, Odell (1936)	50
	Heilmann, Harry (1927)	50
	Klein, Chuck (1932)	50
	Musial, Stan (1946)	50
	Speaker, Tris (1920)	50
	Spence, Stan (1946)	50
	Waner, Paul (1928)	50
72	Anderson, Garret (2003)	49
	Delahanty, Ed (1895)	49
	Giles, Marcus (2003)	49
	Green, Shawn (2003)	49
	Greenberg, Hank (1937)	49
	Gwynn, Tony (1997)	49
	Helton, Todd (2003)	49
	Kent, Jeff (2001)	49
	Lajoie, Nap (1904)	49
	Manush, Heinie (1930)	49
	Palmeiro, Rafael (1991)	49
	Rolen, Scott (2003)	49
	Sisler, George (1920)	49
	Stephenson, Riggs (1932)	49
	Wells, Vernon (2003)	49
	Williamson, Ned (1883)	49
	Yount, Robin (1980)	49
89	18 players tied	48

Triples

1	Wilson, Chief (1912)	36
2	Orr, Dave (1886)	31
	Reitz, Heinie (1894)	31
4	Werden, Perry (1893)	29
5	Davis, Harry (1897)	28
	Thompson, Sam (1894)	28
7	Davis, George (1893)	27
	Williams, Jimmy (1899)	27
9	Crawford, Sam (1914)	26
	Cuyler, Kiki (1925)	26
	Jackson, Joe (1912)	26
	Reilly, John (1890)	26
	Treadway, George (1894)	26
14	Connor, Roger (1894)	25
	Crawford, Sam (1903)	25
	Doyle, Larry (1911)	25
	Freeman, Buck (1899)	25
	Long, Tom (1915)	25
19	Cobb, Ty (1911)	24
	Cobb, Ty (1917)	24
	McKean, Ed (1893)	24
22	Brouthers, Dan (1894)	23
	Cobb, Ty (1912)	23
	Combs, Earle (1927)	23
	Comorosky, Adam (1930)	23
	Crawford, Sam (1913)	23
	Lajoie, Nap (1897)	23
	Mitchell, Dale (1949)	23
	Smith, Elmer (1893)	23
	Stovey, Harry (1884)	23
	Thompson, Sam (1887)	23
32	Anderson, John (1898)	22
	Beckley, Jake (1890)	22
	Bradley, Bill (1903)	22
	Combs, Earle (1930)	22
	Connor, Roger (1887)	22
	Crawford, Sam (1902)	22
	Cree, Birdie (1911)	22
	Daubert, Jake (1922)	22
	Flick, Elmer (1906)	22
	Keeler, Willie (1894)	22
	Leach, Tommy (1902)	22
	McPhee, Bid (1890)	22
	Mitchell, Mike (1911)	22
	Myers, Hy (1920)	22
	Selbach, Kip (1895)	22
	Speaker, Tris (1913)	22
	Stirnweiss, Snuffy (1945)	22
	Visner, Joe (1890)	22
	Wagner, Honus (1900)	22
	Waner, Paul (1926)	22
52	Baker, Frank (1912)	21
	Brown, Tom (1891)	21
	Combs, Earle (1928)	21
	Crawford, Sam (1912)	21
	Delahanty, Ed (1892)	21
	Jackson, Joe (1916)	21
	Johnson, Lance (1996)	21
	Keister, Bill (1901)	21
	McCreery, Tom (1896)	21
	Orr, Dave (1885)	21
	Roush, Edd (1924)	21
	Saier, Vic (1913)	21
	Schulte, Frank (1911)	21
	Seymour, Cy (1905)	21
	Shindle, Billy (1890)	21
	Thompson, Sam (1895)	21
	Tiernan, Mike (1890)	21
	Tiernan, Mike (1895)	21
	Van Haltren, George (1896)	21
	Wallace, Bobby (1897)	21
	Williams, Jimmy (1901)	21
	Williams, Jimmy (1902)	21
	Wilson, Willie (1985)	21
75	37 players tied	20

Home Runs

1	Bonds, Barry (2001)	73
2	McGwire, Mark (1998)	70
3	Sosa, Sammy (1998)	66
4	McGwire, Mark (1999)	65
5	Sosa, Sammy (2001)	64
6	Sosa, Sammy (1999)	63
7	Maris, Roger (1961)	61
8	Ruth, Babe (1927)	60
9	Ruth, Babe (1921)	59
10	Foxx, Jimmie (1932)	58
	Greenberg, Hank (1938)	58
	McGwire, Mark (1997)	58
13	Gonzalez, Luis (2001)	57
	Rodriguez, Alex (2002)	57
15	Griffey, Ken (1997)	56
	Griffey, Ken (1998)	56
	Wilson, Hack (1930)	56
18	Kiner, Ralph (1949)	54
	Mantle, Mickey (1961)	54
	Ruth, Babe (1928)	54
	Ruth, Babe (1920)	54
22	Foster, George (1977)	52
	Mantle, Mickey (1956)	52
	Mays, Willie (1965)	52
	McGwire, Mark (1996)	52
	Rodriguez, Alex (2001)	52
	Thome, Jim (2002)	52
28	Fielder, Cecil (1990)	51
	Kiner, Ralph (1947)	51
	Mays, Willie (1955)	51
	Mize, Johnny (1947)	51
32	Anderson, Brady (1996)	50
	Belle, Albert (1995)	50
	Foxx, Jimmie (1938)	50
	Sosa, Sammy (2000)	50
	Vaughn, Greg (1998)	50
37	Belle, Albert (1998)	49
	Bonds, Barry (2000)	49
	Dawson, Andre (1987)	49
	Gehrig, Lou (1936)	49
	Gehrig, Lou (1934)	49
	Green, Shawn (2001)	49
	Griffey, Ken (1996)	49
	Helton, Todd (2001)	49
	Killebrew, Harmon (1969)	49
	Killebrew, Harmon (1964)	49
	Kluszewski, Ted (1954)	49
	Mays, Willie (1962)	49
	McGwire, Mark (1987)	49
	Robinson, Frank (1966)	49
	Ruth, Babe (1930)	49
	Sosa, Sammy (2002)	49
	Thome, Jim (2001)	49
	Walker, Larry (1997)	49
55	Belle, Albert (1996)	48
	Foxx, Jimmie (1933)	48
	Griffey, Ken (1999)	48
	Howard, Frank (1969)	48
	Killebrew, Harmon (1962)	48
	Kingman, Dave (1979)	48
	Schmidt, Mike (1980)	48
	Stargell, Willie (1971)	48
63	Aaron, Hank (1971)	47
	Bagwell, Jeff (2000)	47
	Banks, Ernie (1958)	47
	Bell, George (1987)	47
	Galarraga, Andres (1996)	47
	Gehrig, Lou (1927)	47
	Glaus, Troy (2000)	47
	Gonzalez, Juan (1996)	47
	Jackson, Reggie (1969)	47
	Kiner, Ralph (1950)	47
	Kluszewski, Ted (1955)	47
	Mathews, Eddie (1953)	47
	Mays, Willie (1964)	47
	Mitchell, Kevin (1989)	47
	Palmeiro, Rafael (2001)	47
	Palmeiro, Rafael (1999)	47
	Rodriguez, Alex (2003)	47
	Ruth, Babe (1926)	47
	Thome, Jim (2003)	47
82	Bonds, Barry (1993)	46
	Bonds, Barry (2002)	46
	Canseco, Jose (1998)	46
	Castilla, Vinny (1998)	46
	Cepeda, Orlando (1961)	46
	DiMaggio, Joe (1937)	46
	Gehrig, Lou (1931)	46
	Gentile, Jim (1961)	46
	Gonzalez, Juan (1993)	46
	Killebrew, Harmon (1961)	46
	Mathews, Eddie (1959)	46
	Rice, Jim (1978)	46
	Ruth, Babe (1924)	46
	Ruth, Babe (1931)	46
	Ruth, Babe (1929)	46
97	16 players tied	45

Home Run Percentage

1	Bonds, Barry (2001)	15.34
2	McGwire, Mark (1998)	13.75
3	McGwire, Mark (1999)	12.48
4	McGwire, Mark (1996)	12.29
5	Ruth, Babe (1920)	11.79
6	Bonds, Barry (2003)	11.54
7	Bonds, Barry (2002)	11.41
8	Ruth, Babe (1927)	11.11
9	Sosa, Sammy (2001)	11.09
10	Ruth, Babe (1921)	10.93
11	Thome, Jim (2002)	10.83
12	McGwire, Mark (1997)	10.74
13	Mantle, Mickey (1961)	10.51
14	Greenberg, Hank (1938)	10.43
15	Maris, Roger (1961)	10.34
16	Sosa, Sammy (1998)	10.26
17	Bonds, Barry (2000)	10.21
18	Sosa, Sammy (1999)	10.08
19	Ruth, Babe (1928)	10.07
20	Foxx, Jimmie (1932)	9.91
21	Kiner, Ralph (1949)	9.84
22	Mantle, Mickey (1956)	9.76
23	Bagwell, Jeff (1994)	9.75
24	Mitchell, Kevin (1994)	9.68
25	Williams, Matt (1994)	9.66
26	Wilson, Hack (1930)	9.57
27	Thomas, Frank (1994)	9.52
28	Aaron, Hank (1971)	9.49
	Ruth, Babe (1926)	9.49
30	Gentile, Jim (1961)	9.47
31	Bonds, Barry (1994)	9.46
32	Ruth, Babe (1930)	9.46
33	Stargell, Willie (1971)	9.39
34	Gonzalez, Luis (2001)	9.36
35	Mays, Willie (1965)	9.32
36	Thome, Jim (2001)	9.32
37	Griffey, Ken (1994)	9.24
38	Ruth, Babe (1929)	9.22
39	Griffey, Ken (1997)	9.21
40	Powell, Boog (1964)	9.20
41	McCovey, Willie (1969)	9.16
42	Belle, Albert (1995)	9.16
43	Rodriguez, Alex (2002)	9.13
44	Williams, Ted (1957)	9.05
45	Kiner, Ralph (1947)	9.03
46	Kingman, Dave (1979)	9.02
47	McGwire, Mark (1992)	8.99
48	Griffey, Ken (1996)	8.99
49	Ruth, Babe (1932)	8.97
50	Fielder, Cecil (1990)	8.90
51	Foxx, Jimmie (1938)	8.85
52	Griffey, Ken (1998)	8.85
53	Killebrew, Harmon (1969)	8.83
54	Sosa, Sammy (2002)	8.81
55	McGwire, Mark (1987)	8.80
56	Mays, Willie (1955)	8.79
57	Schmidt, Mike (1980)	8.76
58	Schmidt, Mike (1981)	8.76
59	Belle, Albert (1994)	8.74
	Killebrew, Harmon (1963)	8.74
61	Vaughn, Greg (1998)	8.73
62	Edmonds, Jim (2003)	8.72
63	Mize, Johnny (1947)	8.70
64	Killebrew, Harmon (1962)	8.70
65	Ruth, Babe (1924)	8.70
66	Gonzalez, Juan (1996)	8.69
67	Ramirez, Manny (2000)	8.66
68	Mitchell, Kevin (1989)	8.66
69	Anderson, Brady (1996)	8.64
70	Walker, Larry (1997)	8.63
71	Ruth, Babe (1922)	8.62
72	Ruth, Babe (1931)	8.61
73	Kiner, Ralph (1950)	8.59
74	Sheffield, Gary (2000)	8.58
75	Gonzalez, Juan (1993)	8.58
76	Jackson, Reggie (1969)	8.56
77	Kluszewski, Ted (1954)	8.55
78	Bonds, Barry (1993)	8.53
79	Buhner, Jay (1995)	8.51
80	Robinson, Frank (1966)	8.51
81	Killebrew, Harmon (1961)	8.50
82	Killebrew, Harmon (1964)	8.49
83	Gehrig, Lou (1936)	8.46
	Gehrig, Lou (1934)	8.46
85	Foster, George (1977)	8.46
86	Walker, Larry (1999)	8.45
87	Giambi, Jason (2000)	8.43
88	Ramirez, Manny (1999)	8.43
	Stargell, Willie (1973)	8.43
90	Greenberg, Hank (1946)	8.41
91	Mathews, Eddie (1954)	8.40
92	Sheffield, Gary (1994)	8.39
93	Colavito, Rocky (1958)	8.38
94	Foxx, Jimmie (1933)	8.38
95	Adcock, Joe (1956)	8.37
96	Rodriguez, Alex (1999)	8.37
97	Clark, Jack (1987)	8.35
98	Glaus, Troy (2000)	8.35
99	Helton, Todd (2001)	8.35
100	Palmeiro, Rafael (1999)	8.32

Total Bases

1	Ruth, Babe (1921)	457
2	Hornsby, Rogers (1922)	450
3	Gehrig, Lou (1927)	447
4	Klein, Chuck (1930)	445
5	Foxx, Jimmie (1932)	438
6	Musial, Stan (1948)	429
7	Sosa, Sammy (2001)	425
8	Wilson, Hack (1930)	423
9	Klein, Chuck (1932)	420
10	Gehrig, Lou (1930)	419
	Gonzalez, Luis (2001)	419
12	DiMaggio, Joe (1937)	418
13	Ruth, Babe (1927)	417
14	Herman, Babe (1930)	416
	Sosa, Sammy (1998)	416
16	Bonds, Barry (2001)	411
17	Gehrig, Lou (1931)	410
18	Gehrig, Lou (1934)	409
	Hornsby, Rogers (1929)	409
	Walker, Larry (1997)	409
21	O'Neill, Tip (1887)	407
22	Medwick, Joe (1937)	406
	Rice, Jim (1978)	406
24	Helton, Todd (2000)	405
	Klein, Chuck (1929)	405
	Trosky, Hal (1936)	405
27	Foxx, Jimmie (1933)	403
	Gehrig, Lou (1936)	403
29	Helton, Todd (2001)	402
30	Aaron, Hank (1959)	400
31	Belle, Albert (1998)	399
	Ruth, Babe (1923)	399
	Sisler, George (1920)	399
34	Foxx, Jimmie (1938)	398
35	Greenberg, Hank (1937)	397
	O'Doul, Lefty (1929)	397
	Sosa, Sammy (1999)	397
38	Pujols, Albert (2003)	394
39	Griffey, Ken (1997)	393
	Rodriguez, Alex (2001)	393
41	Burks, Ellis (1996)	392
	Simmons, Al (1925)	392
	Simmons, Al (1930)	392
	Terry, Bill (1930)	392
45	Ruth, Babe (1924)	391
46	Greenberg, Hank (1935)	389
	Rodriguez, Alex (2002)	389
48	Foster, George (1977)	388
	Mattingly, Don (1986)	388
	Ruth, Babe (1920)	388
51	Griffey, Ken (1998)	387
52	Averill, Earl (1936)	385
53	Greenberg, Hank (1940)	384
	Rodriguez, Alex (1998)	384
55	McGwire, Mark (1998)	383
	Sosa, Sammy (2000)	383
57	Gonzalez, Juan (1998)	382
	Mays, Willie (1962)	382
	Mays, Willie (1955)	382
	Musial, Stan (1949)	382
	Rice, Jim (1977)	382
62	Hornsby, Rogers (1925)	381
	Soriano, Alfonso (2002)	381
64	Castilla, Vinny (1998)	380
	Greenberg, Hank (1938)	380
	Robinson, Frank (1962)	380
	Ruth, Babe (1928)	380
68	Banks, Ernie (1958)	379
	Guerrero, Vladimir (2000)	379
	Rodriguez, Alex (1996)	379
	Ruth, Babe (1930)	379
72	Delgado, Carlos (2000)	378
	Hornsby, Rogers (1921)	378
	Snider, Duke (1954)	378
75	Belle, Albert (1995)	377
	Mays, Willie (1954)	377
77	Galarraga, Andres (1996)	376
	Mantle, Mickey (1956)	376
79	Belle, Albert (1996)	375
80	Duffy, Hugh (1894)	374
	Oliva, Tony (1964)	374
	Ruth, Babe (1931)	374
	Trosky, Hal (1934)	374
84	Hornsby, Rogers (1924)	373
	Simmons, Al (1929)	373
	Terry, Bill (1932)	373
	Wells, Vernon (2003)	373
	Williams, Billy (1970)	373
89	McGwire, Mark (1997)	371
90	Aaron, Hank (1963)	370
	Gehrig, Lou (1932)	370
	Green, Shawn (2001)	370
	Mattingly, Don (1985)	370
	Snider, Duke (1953)	370
	Vaughn, Mo (1996)	370
96	7 players tied	369

Runs Batted In

1	Wilson, Hack (1930)	191
2	Gehrig, Lou (1931)	184
3	Greenberg, Hank (1937)	183
4	Foxx, Jimmie (1938)	175
	Gehrig, Lou (1927)	175
6	Gehrig, Lou (1930)	174
7	Ruth, Babe (1921)	171
8	Greenberg, Hank (1935)	170
	Klein, Chuck (1930)	170
10	Foxx, Jimmie (1932)	169
11	DiMaggio, Joe (1937)	167
12	Thompson, Sam (1887)	166
13	Gehrig, Lou (1934)	165
	Ramirez, Manny (1999)	165
	Simmons, Al (1930)	165
	Thompson, Sam (1895)	165
17	Ruth, Babe (1927)	164
18	Foxx, Jimmie (1933)	163
	Ruth, Babe (1931)	163
20	Trosky, Hal (1936)	162
21	Sosa, Sammy (2001)	160
22	Gehrig, Lou (1937)	159
	Stephens, Vern (1949)	159
	Williams, Ted (1949)	159
	Wilson, Hack (1929)	159
26	Sosa, Sammy (1998)	158
27	Gonzalez, Juan (1998)	157
	Simmons, Al (1929)	157
29	Foxx, Jimmie (1930)	156
30	DiMaggio, Joe (1948)	155
	Williams, Ken (1922)	155
32	Medwick, Joe (1937)	154
	Ruth, Babe (1929)	154
34	Davis, Tommy (1962)	153
	Ruth, Babe (1930)	153
36	Belle, Albert (1998)	152
	Gehrig, Lou (1936)	152
	Hornsby, Rogers (1922)	152
39	Gehrig, Lou (1932)	151
	Ott, Mel (1929)	151
	Simmons, Al (1932)	151
42	Galarraga, Andres (1996)	150
	Greenberg, Hank (1940)	150
44	Foster, George (1977)	149
	Hornsby, Rogers (1929)	149
46	Belle, Albert (1996)	148
	Bench, Johnny (1970)	148
	Palmeiro, Rafael (1999)	148
49	Anson, Cap (1886)	147
	Griffey, Ken (1997)	147
	Helton, Todd (2000)	147
	McGwire, Mark (1999)	147
	McGwire, Mark (1998)	147
	Thompson, Sam (1894)	147
55	Delahanty, Ed (1893)	146
	Greenberg, Hank (1938)	146
	Griffey, Ken (1998)	146
	Helton, Todd (2001)	146
	Richardson, Hardy (1890)	146
	Ruth, Babe (1926)	146
61	Delgado, Carlos (2003)	145
	Duffy, Hugh (1894)	145
	Klein, Chuck (1929)	145
	Martinez, Edgar (2000)	145
	Mattingly, Don (1985)	145
	Ramirez, Manny (1998)	145
	Rosen, Al (1953)	145
	Williams, Ted (1939)	145
69	Castilla, Vinny (1998)	144
	Dropo, Walt (1950)	144
	Gonzalez, Juan (1996)	144
	Stephens, Vern (1950)	144
	Sweeney, Mike (2000)	144
74	Averill, Earl (1931)	143
	Banks, Ernie (1959)	143
	Foxx, Jimmie (1936)	143
	Hornsby, Rogers (1925)	143
	Hurst, Don (1932)	143
	Thomas, Frank (2000)	143
	Vaughn, Mo (1996)	143
81	Campanella, Roy (1953)	142
	Cepeda, Orlando (1961)	142
	Gehrig, Lou (1928)	142
	Gonzalez, Luis (2001)	142
	Maris, Roger (1961)	142
	Palmeiro, Rafael (1996)	142
	Rodriguez, Alex (2002)	142
	Ruth, Babe (1928)	142
	Trosky, Hal (1934)	142
	Williams, Matt (1999)	142
91	Bichette, Dante (1996)	141
	Boone, Bret (2001)	141
	Gentile, Jim (1961)	141
	Kluszewski, Ted (1954)	141
	Martinez, Tino (1997)	141
	Mays, Willie (1962)	141
	Sosa, Sammy (1999)	141
	Wilson, Preston (2003)	141
99	6 players tied	140

Runs Batted In per Game

1	Meyerle, Levi (1871)	1.538
2	McVey, Cal (1871)	1.483
3	Thompson, Sam (1894)	1.441
4	Pike, Lip (1871)	1.393
5	Thompson, Sam (1895)	1.387
6	Wolters, Rynie (1871)	1.375
7	Treacey, Fred (1871)	1.320
8	Reach, Al (1871)	1.308
9	Thompson, Sam (1887)	1.307
10	Wilson, Hack (1930)	1.232
11	Malone, Fergy (1871)	1.222
12	Meyerle, Levi (1873)	1.208
13	Simmons, Al (1930)	1.196
14	Greenberg, Hank (1937)	1.188
15	Gehrig, Lou (1931)	1.187
16	Anson, Cap (1886)	1.176
17	Foxx, Jimmie (1938)	1.174
18	King, Steve (1871)	1.172
19	Duffy, Hugh (1894)	1.160
20	Orr, Dave (1890)	1.159
21	Delahanty, Ed (1894)	1.147
22	Ruth, Babe (1929)	1.141
23	Gehrig, Lou (1930)	1.130
24	Gehrig, Lou (1927)	1.129
25	Ruth, Babe (1921)	1.125
26	Ruth, Babe (1931)	1.124
27	Richardson, Hardy (1890)	1.123
28	Ramirez, Manny (1999)	1.122
29	Addy, Bob (1873)	1.122
30	Greenberg, Hank (1935)	1.118
31	Delahanty, Ed (1893)	1.106
32	DiMaggio, Joe (1937)	1.106
33	McMullin, John (1871)	1.103
34	White, Deacon (1873)	1.100
35	Simmons, Al (1929)	1.098
36	Foxx, Jimmie (1932)	1.097
37	Barnes, Ross (1871)	1.097
38	Foxx, Jimmie (1933)	1.094
39	Klein, Chuck (1930)	1.090
40	Pike, Lip (1872)	1.089
41	Anson, Cap (1872)	1.087
42	Ruth, Babe (1927)	1.086
43	Cross, Lave (1894)	1.082
44	Burns, Oyster (1890)	1.076
45	Gonzalez, Juan (1996)	1.075
46	Trosky, Hal (1936)	1.073
47	Cuthbert, Ned (1871)	1.071
	Gehrig, Lou (1934)	1.071
49	McKean, Ed (1893)	1.064
50	McVey, Cal (1875)	1.061
51	Wilson, Hack (1929)	1.060
52	Dropo, Walt (1950)	1.059
	Foutz, Dave (1887)	1.059
54	Mills, Everett (1873)	1.056
55	Ruth, Babe (1930)	1.055
56	Bagwell, Jeff (1994)	1.055
57	Ewing, Buck (1893)	1.052
	Leonard, Andy (1873)	1.052
59	Bechtel, George (1871)	1.050
	DiMaggio, Joe (1939)	1.050
61	Brouthers, Dan (1894)	1.041
62	Davis, George (1897)	1.038
63	Puckett, Kirby (1994)	1.037
64	Hornsby, Rogers (1925)	1.036
65	O'Rourke, Jim (1890)	1.036
66	Wood, Jimmy (1871)	1.036
67	Ramirez, Manny (2000)	1.034
68	Barnes, Ross (1873)	1.033
69	Gould, Charlie (1871)	1.032
70	Start, Joe (1871)	1.030
71	Ruth, Babe (1932)	1.030
72	Stephens, Vern (1949)	1.026
	Williams, Ted (1949)	1.026
74	Delahanty, Ed (1896)	1.024
75	Brodie, Steve (1895)	1.023
	Kelley, Joe (1895)	1.023
77	Fisler, Wes (1872)	1.021
78	Foxx, Jimmie (1930)	1.020
79	Gonzalez, Juan (1998)	1.019
80	Craver, Bill (1874)	1.018
	Orr, Dave (1884)	1.018
82	McVey, Cal (1874)	1.014
83	Greenberg, Hank (1940)	1.014
84	DiMaggio, Joe (1948)	1.013
	Williams, Ken (1922)	1.013
86	Gehrig, Lou (1937)	1.013
87	Anson, Cap (1882)	1.012
88	Brett, George (1980)	1.009
89	DiMaggio, Joe (1940)	1.008
90	Ott, Mel (1929)	1.007
91	11 players tied	1.000

Walks

1	Bonds, Barry (2002)	198
2	Bonds, Barry (2001)	177
3	Ruth, Babe (1923)	170
4	McGwire, Mark (1998)	162
	Williams, Ted (1947)	162
	Williams, Ted (1949)	162
7	Williams, Ted (1946)	156
8	Bonds, Barry (1996)	151
	Yost, Eddie (1956)	151
10	Ruth, Babe (1920)	150
11	Bagwell, Jeff (1999)	149
	Joost, Eddie (1949)	149
13	Bonds, Barry (2003)	148
	Stanky, Eddie (1945)	148
	Wynn, Jimmy (1969)	148
16	Sheckard, Jimmy (1911)	147
	Williams, Ted (1941)	147
18	Mantle, Mickey (1957)	146
19	Bonds, Barry (1997)	145
	Killebrew, Harmon (1969)	145
	Ruth, Babe (1921)	145
	Williams, Ted (1942)	145
23	Ruth, Babe (1926)	144
	Stanky, Eddie (1950)	144
	Williams, Ted (1951)	144
26	Ruth, Babe (1924)	142
	Sheffield, Gary (1996)	142
28	Yost, Eddie (1950)	141
29	Thomas, Frank (1991)	138
30	Cullenbine, Roy (1947)	137
	Giambi, Jason (2000)	137
	Kiner, Ralph (1951)	137
	McCovey, Willie (1970)	137
	Ruth, Babe (1927)	137
	Ruth, Babe (1928)	137
	Stanky, Eddie (1946)	137
37	Clark, Jack (1987)	136
	Crooks, Jack (1892)	136
	Fain, Ferris (1949)	136
	Ruth, Babe (1930)	136
	Thomas, Frank (1995)	136
	Williams, Ted (1954)	136
43	Bagwell, Jeff (1996)	135
	Giles, Brian (2002)	135
	Yost, Eddie (1959)	135
46	Fain, Ferris (1950)	133
	McGwire, Mark (1999)	133
48	Clark, Jack (1989)	132
	Gehrig, Lou (1935)	132
	Howard, Frank (1970)	132
	Morgan, Joe (1975)	132
	Phillips, Tony (1993)	132
53	Elliott, Bob (1948)	131
	Killebrew, Harmon (1967)	131
	Yost, Eddie (1954)	131
56	Bonds, Barry (1998)	130
	Gehrig, Lou (1936)	130
	Ruth, Babe (1932)	130
59	Dykstra, Lenny (1993)	129
	Giambi, Jason (2001)	129
	Giambi, Jason (2003)	129
	Mantle, Mickey (1958)	129
	Yost, Eddie (1952)	129
64	Bishop, Max (1930)	128
	Bishop, Max (1929)	128
	Dunn, Adam (2002)	128
	Hamilton, Billy (1894)	128
	Killebrew, Harmon (1970)	128
	Ruth, Babe (1931)	128
	Schmidt, Mike (1983)	128
	Yastrzemski, Carl (1970)	128
72	Bagwell, Jeff (1997)	127
	Blue, Lu (1931)	127
	Bonds, Barry (1992)	127
	Gehrig, Lou (1937)	127
	Stanky, Eddie (1951)	127
	Thome, Jim (1999)	127
	Wynn, Jimmy (1976)	127
79	Blue, Lu (1929)	126
	Bonds, Barry (1993)	126
	Evans, Darrell (1974)	126
	Henderson, Rickey (1989)	126
	Jones, Chipper (1999)	126
	Mantle, Mickey (1961)	126
	Williams, Ted (1948)	126
	Yost, Eddie (1951)	126
87	Ashburn, Richie (1954)	125
	Boggs, Wade (1988)	125
	Henderson, Rickey (1996)	125
	Olerud, John (1999)	125
	Phillips, Tony (1996)	125
	Tenace, Gene (1977)	125
	Yost, Eddie (1960)	125
94	Cash, Norm (1961)	124
	Evans, Darrell (1973)	124
	Mathews, Eddie (1963)	124
	McGraw, John (1899)	124
98	6 players tied	123

Strikeouts

1	Bonds, Bobby (1970)	189
2	Hernandez, Jose (2002)	188
3	Bonds, Bobby (1969)	187
	Wilson, Preston (2000)	187
5	Deer, Rob (1987)	186
6	Hernandez, Jose (2001)	185
	Incaviglia, Pete (1986)	185
	Thome, Jim (2001)	185
9	Fielder, Cecil (1990)	182
	Thome, Jim (2003)	182
11	Vaughn, Mo (2000)	181
12	Schmidt, Mike (1975)	180
13	Deer, Rob (1986)	179
14	Sexson, Richie (2001)	178
15	Hernandez, Jose (2003)	177
16	Cameron, Mike (2002)	176
17	Buhner, Jay (1997)	175
	Canseco, Jose (1986)	175
	Deer, Rob (1991)	175
	Nicholson, Dave (1963)	175
	Thomas, Gorman (1979)	175
22	Sosa, Sammy (1997)	174
23	Jackson, Bo (1989)	172
	Presley, Jim (1986)	172
25	Jackson, Reggie (1968)	171
	Sosa, Sammy (1999)	171
	Sosa, Sammy (1998)	171
	Thome, Jim (1999)	171
	Thome, Jim (2000)	171
30	Dunn, Adam (2002)	170
	Thomas, Gorman (1980)	170
32	Deer, Rob (1993)	169
	Galarraga, Andres (1990)	169
34	Incaviglia, Pete (1987)	168
	Samuel, Juan (1984)	168
	Sosa, Sammy (2000)	168
37	Edmonds, Jim (2000)	167
38	Alexander, Gary (1978)	166
	Balboni, Steve (1985)	166
	Snyder, Cory (1987)	166
41	Lee, Derrek (2002)	164
42	Clendenon, Donn (1968)	163
	Glaus, Troy (2000)	163
44	Burrell, Pat (2001)	162
	Gant, Ron (1997)	162
	Hobson, Butch (1977)	162
	Samuel, Juan (1987)	162
48	Allen, Dick (1968)	161
	Jackson, Reggie (1971)	161
	Wilkerson, Brad (2002)	161
51	Rodriguez, Henry (1996)	160
	Tettleton, Mickey (1990)	160
53	Buhner, Jay (1996)	159
	McGwire, Mark (1997)	159
	Canseco, Jose (1998)	159
	Grieve, Ben (2001)	159
57	Burnitz, Jeromy (1998)	158
	Canseco, Jose (1990)	158
	Deer, Rob (1989)	158
	Galarraga, Andres (1989)	158
	Glaus, Troy (2001)	158
	Jackson, Bo (1987)	158
	Nieves, Melvin (1996)	158
64	Canseco, Jose (1987)	157
	Galarraga, Andres (1996)	157
	Nieves, Melvin (1997)	157
	Presley, Jim (1987)	157
	Soriano, Alfonso (2002)	157
	Stevens, Lee (2001)	157
	Tartabull, Danny (1986)	157
71	Agee, Tommie (1970)	156
	Armas, Tony (1984)	156
	Jackson, Reggie (1982)	156
	Kingman, Dave (1982)	156
	Tartabull, Danny (1993)	156
	Wilson, Preston (1999)	156
77	Burroughs, Jeff (1975)	155
	Cameron, Mike (2001)	155
	Howard, Frank (1967)	155
	McGwire, Mark (1998)	155
	Wilkerson, Brad (2003)	155
82	Palmer, Dean (1992)	154
	Palmer, Dean (1993)	154
	Parrish, Larry (1987)	154
	Stargell, Willie (1971)	154
	Vaughn, Mo (1997)	154
	Vaughn, Mo (1996)	154
88	Burrell, Pat (2002)	153
	Deer, Rob (1988)	153
	Galarraga, Andres (1988)	153
	Incaviglia, Pete (1988)	153
	Kingman, Dave (1975)	153
	Palmer, Dean (1999)	153
	Sosa, Sammy (2001)	153
95	Canseco, Jose (1991)	152
	Hisle, Larry (1969)	152
	Scott, George (1966)	152
98	9 players tied	151

At Bats per Strikeout

1	Spalding, Al (1873)	322.0
2	McGeary, Mike (1875)	310.0
3	Eggler, Dave (1874)	299.0
4	Schafer, Harry (1873)	295.0
5	Force, Davy (1874)	294.0
6	O'Rourke, Jim (1873)	280.0
7	McGeary, Mike (1876)	278.0
8	McGeary, Mike (1873)	275.0
9	Mills, Everett (1873)	263.0
10	Anson, Cap (1878)	261.0
11	Anson, Cap (1874)	260.0
12	Bechtel, George (1873)	258.0
13	Pearce, Dickey (1874)	255.0
	Wright, George (1872)	255.0
15	Anson, Cap (1873)	254.0
16	Hall, George (1872)	250.0
17	York, Tom (1872)	248.0
18	Higham, Dick (1873)	245.0
19	McVey, Cal (1872)	237.0
	Spalding, Al (1872)	237.0
21	McGeary, Mike (1872)	225.0
22	Addy, Bob (1874)	213.0
23	Wood, Jimmy (1873)	209.0
24	Pearce, Dickey (1872)	206.0
25	White, Deacon (1875)	185.5
26	Hines, Paul (1873)	181.0
27	Booth, Eddie (1872)	179.0
28	Burdock, Jack (1872)	174.0
29	Leonard, Andy (1874)	169.5
30	Beals, Tommy (1873)	169.0
31	Sewell, Joe (1932)	167.7
32	Dehlman, Herman (1872)	165.0
33	Anson, Cap (1875)	163.0
	Pearce, Dickey (1871)	163.0
35	Wright, George (1873)	162.5
36	Barnes, Ross (1873)	161.0
37	White, Warren (1873)	160.0
38	Peters, John (1876)	159.5
39	Barnes, Ross (1871)	157.0
	Mills, Everett (1871)	157.0
41	Addy, Bob (1875)	155.0
	White, Deacon (1873)	155.0
43	Clapp, John (1876)	153.0
44	Sewell, Joe (1925)	152.0
45	Gould, Charlie (1871)	151.0
46	Schafer, Harry (1871)	149.0
47	Radcliffe, John (1872)	148.5
48	Leonard, Andy (1871)	148.0
49	White, Deacon (1871)	146.0
50	Carey, Tom (1873)	145.0
	Radcliffe, John (1871)	145.0
	York, Tom (1871)	145.0
53	Sewell, Joe (1929)	144.5
54	King, Steve (1871)	144.0
	Spalding, Al (1871)	144.0
56	Doyle, Jack (1894)	142.3
57	McGeary, Mike (1874)	135.5
	Start, Joe (1877)	135.5
59	Eggler, Dave (1873)	134.0
60	Mills, Everett (1872)	133.0
61	Craver, Bill (1874)	132.5
	Start, Joe (1876)	132.5
63	McBride, Dick (1871)	132.0
64	Barnes, Ross (1875)	131.0
	Pearce, Dickey (1873)	131.0
	Sewell, Joe (1933)	131.0
67	Meyerle, Levi (1871)	130.0
68	Barnes, Ross (1874)	129.5
	Meyerle, Levi (1876)	129.5
70	McBride, Dick (1872)	129.0
71	Hatfield, John (1873)	127.5
72	Carey, Tom (1875)	127.3
73	Sensenderfer, Count (1871)	127.0
74	Fisher, Cherokee (1871)	123.0
75	Radcliffe, John (1873)	122.5
76	Mills, Everett (1874)	121.5
	Sutton, Ezra (1874)	121.5
78	Holdsworth, Jim (1876)	121.0
	Knight, Lon (1876)	121.0
	Sutton, Ezra (1873)	121.0
81	Anson, Cap (1871)	120.0
	Glenn, John (1871)	120.0
	Leonard, Andy (1872)	120.0
84	Sutton, Ezra (1876)	119.5
85	Sutton, Ezra (1875)	119.3
86	Hollocher, Charlie (1922)	118.4
87	Ward, John (1893)	117.6
88	McVey, Cal (1874)	114.3
	Spalding, Al (1875)	114.3
90	Boyd, Bill (1873)	114.0
	Mills, Everett (1875)	114.0
92	Mathews, Bobby (1872)	111.5
93	Mathews, Bobby (1876)	110.5
94	Fisler, Wes (1873)	109.0
95	Holdsworth, Jim (1875)	108.0
96	McInnis, Stuffy (1922)	107.4
97	White, Warren (1874)	105.5
98	Wright, Harry (1872)	104.0
99	Remsen, Jack (1873)	103.5
100	White, Deacon (1876)	103.3

Batting Average

1	Meyerle, Levi (1871)	.492
2	O'Neill, Tip (1887)	.485
3	Browning, Pete (1887)	.457
4	Caruthers, Bob (1887)	.456
5	Duffy, Hugh (1894)	.440
6	Barnes, Ross (1872)	.432
7	McVey, Cal (1871)	.431
8	Robinson, Yank (1887)	.427
9	Lajoie, Nap (1901)	.426
10	Barnes, Ross (1873)	.425
11	Keeler, Willie (1897)	.424
12	Hornsby, Rogers (1924)	.424
13	Anson, Cap (1887)	.421
14	Brouthers, Dan (1887)	.420
15	Sisler, George (1922)	.420
16	Cobb, Ty (1911)	.420
17	Force, Davy (1872)	.418
18	Lyons, Denny (1887)	.415
19	Anson, Cap (1872)	.415
20	Thompson, Sam (1894)	.415
21	Dunlap, Fred (1884)	.412
22	Mack, Reddy (1887)	.410
23	Delahanty, Ed (1899)	.410
24	Burkett, Jesse (1896)	.410
25	Burns, Oyster (1887)	.409
26	Cobb, Ty (1912)	.409
27	Jackson, Joe (1911)	.408
28	Sisler, George (1920)	.407
29	Thompson, Sam (1887)	.407
30	Williams, Ted (1941)	.406
31	Burkett, Jesse (1895)	.405
32	Delahanty, Ed (1895)	.404
33	Delahanty, Ed (1894)	.404
34	Barnes, Ross (1876)	.404
35	Hamilton, Billy (1894)	.403
36	Hornsby, Rogers (1925)	.403
37	Heilmann, Harry (1923)	.403
38	Hornsby, Rogers (1922)	.401
39	Barnes, Ross (1871)	.401
40	Terry, Bill (1930)	.401
41	Jennings, Hughie (1896)	.401
42	Cobb, Ty (1922)	.401
43	Anson, Cap (1881)	.399
44	O'Doul, Lefty (1929)	.398
45	Heilmann, Harry (1927)	.398
46	Anson, Cap (1873)	.398
47	Hornsby, Rogers (1921)	.397
	Radford, Paul (1887)	.397
49	Delahanty, Ed (1896)	.397
50	Burkett, Jesse (1899)	.396
51	King, Steve (1871)	.396
52	Jackson, Joe (1912)	.395
53	Gwynn, Tony (1994)	.394
54	Meyerle, Levi (1874)	.394
55	Heilmann, Harry (1921)	.394
56	Ruth, Babe (1923)	.393
57	Heilmann, Harry (1925)	.393
58	Herman, Babe (1930)	.393
59	Kelley, Joe (1894)	.393
60	Thompson, Sam (1895)	.392
61	Kelly, King (1887)	.391
62	McGraw, John (1899)	.391
63	White, Deacon (1873)	.390
64	Cobb, Ty (1913)	.390
65	Foutz, Dave (1887)	.390
66	Simmons, Al (1931)	.390
67	Brett, George (1980)	.390
68	Clarke, Fred (1897)	.390
69	Schomberg, Otto (1887)	.389
70	Speaker, Tris (1925)	.389
71	Lange, Bill (1895)	.389
72	Hamilton, Billy (1895)	.389
73	Cobb, Ty (1921)	.389
74	Williams, Ted (1957)	.388
75	Kelly, King (1886)	.388
76	Carew, Rod (1977)	.388
77	Appling, Luke (1936)	.388
78	Wright, George (1873)	.388
79	Speaker, Tris (1920)	.388
80	Cross, Lave (1894)	.387
81	White, Deacon (1877)	.387
82	Simmons, Al (1925)	.387
83	Hornsby, Rogers (1928)	.387
84	Speaker, Tris (1916)	.386
85	Keeler, Willie (1896)	.386
86	Klein, Chuck (1930)	.386
87	Jennings, Hughie (1895)	.386
88	Keeler, Willie (1898)	.385
89	Vaughan, Arky (1935)	.385
90	Hornsby, Rogers (1923)	.384
91	Cobb, Ty (1919)	.384
92	Lajoie, Nap (1910)	.384
93	Cobb, Ty (1910)	.383
94	Burkett, Jesse (1897)	.383
95	Connor, Roger (1887)	.383
96	Speaker, Tris (1912)	.383
97	Cobb, Ty (1917)	.383
98	O'Doul, Lefty (1930)	.383
99	Jackson, Joe (1920)	.382
100	Wise, Sam (1887)	.382

On-Base Percentage

1	Bonds, Barry (2002)	.584
2	Williams, Ted (1941)	.553
3	McGraw, John (1899)	.547
4	Ruth, Babe (1923)	.545
5	Ruth, Babe (1920)	.532
6	Bonds, Barry (2003)	.531
7	Williams, Ted (1957)	.528
8	Hamilton, Billy (1894)	.521
9	Bonds, Barry (2001)	.517
10	Williams, Ted (1954)	.516
11	Ruth, Babe (1926)	.516
12	Mantle, Mickey (1957)	.515
13	Ruth, Babe (1924)	.513
14	Ruth, Babe (1921)	.512
15	Hornsby, Rogers (1924)	.507
16	McGraw, John (1900)	.505
17	Kelley, Joe (1894)	.502
18	Duffy, Hugh (1894)	.502
19	Delahanty, Ed (1895)	.500
	Meyerle, Levi (1871)	.500
21	Williams, Ted (1942)	.499
22	Williams, Ted (1947)	.499
23	Hornsby, Rogers (1928)	.498
24	Williams, Ted (1946)	.497
25	Williams, Ted (1948)	.497
26	Joyce, Bill (1894)	.496
27	Ruth, Babe (1931)	.495
28	Thomas, Frank (1994)	.494
29	Ruth, Babe (1930)	.493
30	Vaughan, Arky (1935)	.491
31	Williams, Ted (1949)	.490
32	Hamilton, Billy (1895)	.490
33	Hamilton, Billy (1893)	.490
34	O'Neill, Tip (1887)	.490
35	Hornsby, Rogers (1925)	.489
	Ruth, Babe (1932)	.489
37	Cash, Norm (1961)	.488
38	Mantle, Mickey (1962)	.488
39	Cobb, Ty (1915)	.486
40	Ruth, Babe (1927)	.486
41	Giambi, Jason (2001)	.483
42	Speaker, Tris (1920)	.483
43	Kelly, King (1886)	.483
44	Burkett, Jesse (1895)	.482
45	Martinez, Edgar (1995)	.482
46	Giambi, Jason (2000)	.482
47	Heilmann, Harry (1923)	.481
48	Boggs, Wade (1988)	.480
49	Hamilton, Billy (1898)	.480
50	Speaker, Tris (1925)	.479
	Williams, Ted (1956)	.479
52	Hamilton, Billy (1896)	.479
53	Olerud, John (1993)	.478
54	Gehrig, Lou (1936)	.478
55	Childs, Cupid (1894)	.475
56	McGraw, John (1898)	.475
57	Delahanty, Ed (1894)	.475
58	Heilmann, Harry (1927)	.475
59	Speaker, Tris (1922)	.474
60	Gehrig, Lou (1927)	.474
61	Appling, Luke (1936)	.474
62	Gehrig, Lou (1930)	.473
63	Gehrig, Lou (1937)	.473
64	McGwire, Mark (1998)	.473
65	Delgado, Carlos (2000)	.472
66	Jennings, Hughie (1896)	.472
67	Delahanty, Ed (1896)	.472
68	McGraw, John (1897)	.471
69	Morgan, Joe (1975)	.471
70	Brouthers, Dan (1891)	.471
71	Helton, Todd (2000)	.470
72	Speaker, Tris (1916)	.470
73	Joyce, Bill (1896)	.470
74	Kelley, Joe (1896)	.469
75	Sheffield, Gary (1996)	.469
	Speaker, Tris (1923)	.469
77	Foxx, Jimmie (1932)	.469
78	Burkett, Jesse (1897)	.468
79	Cobb, Ty (1925)	.468
80	McGwire, Mark (1996)	.468
81	Jackson, Joe (1911)	.468
82	Gehrig, Lou (1928)	.467
83	Cobb, Ty (1913)	.467
84	Sisler, George (1922)	.467
85	Childs, Cupid (1896)	.467
86	Mantle, Mickey (1956)	.467
87	Martinez, Edgar (1996)	.467
88	Boggs, Wade (1987)	.467
89	Cobb, Ty (1911)	.467
90	Brouthers, Dan (1890)	.466
91	Gehrig, Lou (1935)	.466
92	Gehrig, Lou (1934)	.465
93	O'Doul, Lefty (1929)	.465
94	Griffin, Mike (1894)	.465
95	Thomas, Frank (1996)	.465
96	Bonds, Barry (1996)	.465
97	Thompson, Sam (1894)	.465
98	Foxx, Jimmie (1939)	.464
99	Speaker, Tris (1912)	.464
100	Delahanty, Ed (1899)	.464

Slugging Average

1	Bonds, Barry (2001)	.863
2	Ruth, Babe (1920)	.847
3	Ruth, Babe (1921)	.846
4	Bonds, Barry (2002)	.799
5	Ruth, Babe (1927)	.772
6	Gehrig, Lou (1927)	.765
7	Ruth, Babe (1923)	.764
8	Hornsby, Rogers (1925)	.756
9	McGwire, Mark (1998)	.752
10	Bagwell, Jeff (1994)	.750
11	Bonds, Barry (2003)	.749
	Foxx, Jimmie (1932)	.749
13	Ruth, Babe (1924)	.739
14	Ruth, Babe (1926)	.737
15	Sosa, Sammy (2001)	.737
16	Williams, Ted (1941)	.735
17	Ruth, Babe (1930)	.732
18	Williams, Ted (1957)	.731
19	McGwire, Mark (1996)	.730
20	Thomas, Frank (1994)	.729
21	Wilson, Hack (1930)	.723
22	Hornsby, Rogers (1922)	.722
23	Gehrig, Lou (1930)	.721
24	Walker, Larry (1997)	.720
25	Belle, Albert (1994)	.714
26	Walker, Larry (1999)	.710
27	Ruth, Babe (1928)	.709
28	Simmons, Al (1930)	.708
29	Gehrig, Lou (1934)	.706
30	Mantle, Mickey (1956)	.705
31	Foxx, Jimmie (1938)	.704
32	Foxx, Jimmie (1933)	.703
33	Musial, Stan (1948)	.702
34	Ruth, Babe (1931)	.700
35	Meyerle, Levi (1871)	.700
36	Helton, Todd (2000)	.698
37	Ruth, Babe (1929)	.697
38	Ramirez, Manny (2000)	.697
39	McGwire, Mark (1999)	.697
40	Thompson, Sam (1894)	.696
41	Gehrig, Lou (1936)	.696
42	Hornsby, Rogers (1924)	.696
43	Duffy, Hugh (1894)	.694
44	Foxx, Jimmie (1939)	.694
45	O'Neill, Tip (1887)	.691
46	Belle, Albert (1995)	.690
47	Gonzalez, Luis (2001)	.688
48	Bonds, Barry (2000)	.688
49	Mantle, Mickey (1961)	.687
50	Klein, Chuck (1930)	.687
51	Helton, Todd (2001)	.685
52	Greenberg, Hank (1938)	.683
53	Mitchell, Kevin (1994)	.681
54	Hornsby, Rogers (1929)	.679
55	Herman, Babe (1930)	.678
56	Bonds, Barry (1993)	.677
57	Thome, Jim (2002)	.677
58	Griffey, Ken (1994)	.674
59	DiMaggio, Joe (1937)	.673
60	Ruth, Babe (1922)	.672
61	DiMaggio, Joe (1939)	.671
62	Greenberg, Hank (1940)	.670
63	Aaron, Hank (1971)	.669
64	Greenberg, Hank (1937)	.668
65	Williams, Ted (1946)	.667
66	Mays, Willie (1954)	.667
67	Pujols, Albert (2003)	.667
68	Mantle, Mickey (1957)	.665
69	Delgado, Carlos (2000)	.664
70	Guerrero, Vladimir (2000)	.664
71	Brett, George (1980)	.664
72	Ramirez, Manny (1999)	.663
73	Gehrig, Lou (1931)	.662
74	Walker, Larry (2001)	.662
75	Cash, Norm (1961)	.662
76	Ruth, Babe (1932)	.661
77	Giambi, Jason (2001)	.660
78	Mays, Willie (1955)	.659
79	Kiner, Ralph (1949)	.658
80	Klein, Chuck (1929)	.657
81	Ruth, Babe (1919)	.657
82	McCovey, Willie (1969)	.656
83	Belle, Albert (1998)	.655
84	Thompson, Sam (1895)	.654
85	Pike, Lip (1871)	.654
86	Foxx, Jimmie (1934)	.653
87	Hafey, Chick (1930)	.652
88	Williams, Ted (1949)	.650
89	Joyce, Bill (1894)	.648
90	Gehrig, Lou (1928)	.648
91	Williams, Ted (1942)	.648
92	Snider, Duke (1954)	.647
93	Bonds, Barry (1994)	.647
	Giambi, Jason (2000)	.647
95	Sosa, Sammy (1998)	.647
96	Ramirez, Manny (2002)	.647
97	Griffey, Ken (1997)	.646
	McGwire, Mark (1997)	.646
99	Klein, Chuck (1932)	.646
100	Gentile, Jim (1961)	.646

On-Base Plus Slugging

1	Bonds, Barry (2002)	1383
2	Bonds, Barry (2001)	1380
3	Ruth, Babe (1920)	1379
4	Ruth, Babe (1921)	1359
5	Ruth, Babe (1923)	1309
6	Williams, Ted (1941)	1287
7	Bonds, Barry (2003)	1280
8	Williams, Ted (1957)	1259
9	Ruth, Babe (1927)	1258
10	Ruth, Babe (1926)	1253
11	Ruth, Babe (1924)	1252
12	Hornsby, Rogers (1925)	1245
13	Gehrig, Lou (1927)	1240
14	McGwire, Mark (1998)	1225
15	Ruth, Babe (1930)	1225
16	Thomas, Frank (1994)	1223
17	Foxx, Jimmie (1932)	1218
18	Bagwell, Jeff (1994)	1211
19	Hornsby, Rogers (1924)	1203
20	Meyerle, Levi (1871)	1200
21	McGwire, Mark (1996)	1199
22	Duffy, Hugh (1894)	1196
23	Ruth, Babe (1931)	1195
24	Gehrig, Lou (1930)	1194
25	Sosa, Sammy (2001)	1181
26	Hornsby, Rogers (1922)	1181
27	O'Neill, Tip (1887)	1180
28	Mantle, Mickey (1957)	1179
29	Wilson, Hack (1930)	1177
30	Walker, Larry (1997)	1175
31	Gehrig, Lou (1936)	1174
32	Walker, Larry (1999)	1174
33	Mantle, Mickey (1956)	1172
34	Ruth, Babe (1928)	1172
35	Gehrig, Lou (1934)	1172
36	Helton, Todd (2000)	1168
37	Foxx, Jimmie (1938)	1166
38	Williams, Ted (1946)	1164
39	Thompson, Sam (1894)	1161
40	Foxx, Jimmie (1939)	1158
41	Ramirez, Manny (2000)	1157
42	Belle, Albert (1994)	1156
43	Foxx, Jimmie (1933)	1153
44	Musial, Stan (1948)	1152
45	Williams, Ted (1954)	1151
46	Ruth, Babe (1932)	1150
47	Cash, Norm (1961)	1150
48	Williams, Ted (1942)	1147
49	Joyce, Bill (1894)	1143
50	Giambi, Jason (2001)	1143
51	Williams, Ted (1949)	1141
52	Bonds, Barry (1993)	1140
53	Hornsby, Rogers (1929)	1139
54	Mantle, Mickey (1961)	1138
55	Delgado, Carlos (2000)	1137
56	Williams, Ted (1947)	1133
57	Bonds, Barry (2000)	1133
58	Herman, Babe (1930)	1132
59	Simmons, Al (1930)	1130
60	Hornsby, Rogers (1928)	1130
61	Giambi, Jason (2000)	1129
62	Ruth, Babe (1929)	1128
63	Thome, Jim (2002)	1127
64	Brett, George (1980)	1124
65	McGwire, Mark (1999)	1124
66	Klein, Chuck (1930)	1123
67	Greenberg, Hank (1938)	1122
68	Helton, Todd (2001)	1120
69	Gonzalez, Luis (2001)	1120
70	DiMaggio, Joe (1939)	1119
71	Mitchell, Kevin (1994)	1119
72	Walker, Larry (2001)	1117
73	Delahanty, Ed (1895)	1117
74	Gehrig, Lou (1937)	1116
75	Gehrig, Lou (1928)	1115
76	Ruth, Babe (1919)	1114
77	McCovey, Willie (1969)	1114
78	Heilmann, Harry (1923)	1113
79	Williams, Ted (1948)	1112
80	Ramirez, Manny (1999)	1111
81	Martinez, Edgar (1995)	1110
82	Pujols, Albert (2003)	1109
83	Gehrig, Lou (1931)	1108
84	Lajoie, Nap (1901)	1106
85	Ruth, Babe (1922)	1106
86	Greenberg, Hank (1937)	1105
87	Kelley, Joe (1894)	1104
88	Greenberg, Hank (1940)	1103
89	Delahanty, Ed (1896)	1103
90	Foxx, Jimmie (1934)	1102
91	Vaughan, Arky (1935)	1098
92	Ramirez, Manny (2002)	1097
93	Hornsby, Rogers (1921)	1097
94	Foxx, Jimmie (1935)	1096
95	Sheffield, Gary (1996)	1094
96	Belle, Albert (1995)	1094
97	Mantle, Mickey (1962)	1093
98	Helton, Todd (2003)	1092
99	Thomas, Frank (1996)	1091
100	Heilmann, Harry (1927)	1091

On-Base Plus Slugging Adjusted

1	Bonds, Barry (2002)	272
2	Bonds, Barry (2001)	267
3	Ruth, Babe (1920)	252
4	Dunlap, Fred (1884)	248
5	Meyerle, Levi (1871)	243
6	Ruth, Babe (1923)	238
7	Ruth, Babe (1921)	236
8	Bonds, Barry (2003)	236
9	Williams, Ted (1941)	232
10	Ruth, Babe (1927)	229
11	Browning, Pete (1882)	228
12	Ruth, Babe (1926)	228
13	Williams, Ted (1957)	227
14	Gehrig, Lou (1927)	224
15	Ruth, Babe (1919)	224
16	Ruth, Babe (1931)	223
17	Hornsby, Rogers (1924)	223
18	Mantle, Mickey (1957)	223
19	Barnes, Ross (1876)	222
20	Ruth, Babe (1924)	221
21	Bagwell, Jeff (1994)	220
22	McGwire, Mark (1998)	218
23	Ruth, Babe (1930)	216
24	Thomas, Frank (1994)	214
25	Williams, Ted (1942)	214
26	Gehrig, Lou (1934)	213
27	Mantle, Mickey (1956)	213
28	McCovey, Willie (1969)	212
29	Williams, Ted (1946)	211
30	Ruth, Babe (1928)	211
31	Mantle, Mickey (1961)	210
32	Hornsby, Rogers (1922)	210
33	Cobb, Ty (1917)	210
34	Pike, Lip (1875)	210
35	Hornsby, Rogers (1925)	208
36	Sosa, Sammy (2001)	208
37	Hall, George (1876)	208
38	Gehrig, Lou (1930)	207
39	Bonds, Barry (1993)	207
40	Bonds, Barry (1992)	207
41	Barnes, Ross (1872)	206
42	Ruth, Babe (1932)	206
43	Lajoie, Nap (1904)	205
44	O'Neill, Tip (1887)	205
45	Wagner, Honus (1908)	205
46	Hornsby, Rogers (1928)	204
47	Brouthers, Dan (1886)	204
48	Foxx, Jimmie (1932)	203
49	Cobb, Ty (1912)	203
50	Connor, Roger (1885)	203
51	Brett, George (1980)	202
52	McGwire, Mark (1996)	202
53	Cobb, Ty (1910)	202
54	Robinson, Frank (1966)	200
55	Anson, Cap (1872)	200
56	Foxx, Jimmie (1933)	199
57	Gehrig, Lou (1931)	199
58	Williams, Ted (1947)	199
59	Brouthers, Dan (1885)	199
60	Ruth, Babe (1929)	199
61	Allen, Dick (1972)	198
62	Mantle, Mickey (1962)	198
63	Lajoie, Nap (1910)	198
64	Brouthers, Dan (1882)	198
65	Thome, Jim (2002)	197
66	Orr, Dave (1885)	197
67	Cash, Norm (1961)	197
68	Giambi, Jason (2001)	197
69	Swartwood, Ed (1882)	197
70	Gehrig, Lou (1928)	196
71	Musial, Stan (1948)	196
72	Cobb, Ty (1913)	196
73	Lajoie, Nap (1901)	196
74	Shafer, Orator (1878)	196
75	Schmidt, Mike (1981)	195
76	Stone, George (1906)	195
77	Heilmann, Harry (1923)	195
78	Bonds, Barry (2000)	195
79	Shafer, Orator (1884)	195
80	Orr, Dave (1884)	195
81	Mitchell, Kevin (1989)	195
82	Pike, Lip (1871)	193
83	Gehrig, Lou (1936)	193
84	Delahanty, Ed (1899)	193
85	Cobb, Ty (1911)	193
86	Williams, Ted (1954)	193
87	McVey, Cal (1875)	192
88	Jackson, Joe (1911)	192
89	Pujols, Albert (2003)	192
90	Sheffield, Gary (1996)	192
91	Delahanty, Ed (1896)	191
92	Piazza, Mike (1997)	191
93	Belle, Albert (1994)	191
94	Hornsby, Rogers (1921)	191
95	Barnes, Ross (1873)	191
96	Cobb, Ty (1909)	190
97	Aaron, Hank (1971)	190
98	Henderson, Rickey (1990)	190
99	Jackson, Reggie (1969)	190
100	Jackson, Joe (1913)	190

Batting Runs

1	Ruth, Babe (1921)	121
2	Bonds, Barry (2001)	121
3	Bonds, Barry (2002)	120
4	Ruth, Babe (1923)	117
5	Ruth, Babe (1920)	114
6	Williams, Ted (1941)	104
7	Ruth, Babe (1927)	102
8	Gehrig, Lou (1927)	101
9	Ruth, Babe (1924)	100
10	Ruth, Babe (1926)	99
11	Williams, Ted (1946)	97
12	Foxx, Jimmie (1932)	96
13	McGwire, Mark (1998)	95
14	Williams, Ted (1942)	95
15	Ruth, Babe (1931)	95
16	Mantle, Mickey (1957)	94
17	Williams, Ted (1947)	93
18	Hornsby, Rogers (1924)	92
19	Williams, Ted (1957)	92
20	Williams, Ted (1949)	91
21	Musial, Stan (1948)	91
22	Hornsby, Rogers (1922)	90
23	Bonds, Barry (2003)	90
24	Ruth, Babe (1930)	90
25	Walker, Larry (1997)	89
26	Hornsby, Rogers (1925)	89
27	Cash, Norm (1961)	88
28	O'Neill, Tip (1887)	87
29	Gehrig, Lou (1934)	87
30	Sosa, Sammy (2001)	87
31	Gehrig, Lou (1930)	87
32	Mantle, Mickey (1956)	86
33	Ruth, Babe (1928)	86
34	Bonds, Barry (1993)	84
35	Foxx, Jimmie (1933)	84
36	Giambi, Jason (2001)	84
37	Helton, Todd (2000)	83
38	Gehrig, Lou (1936)	83
39	Gehrig, Lou (1931)	82
40	Mantle, Mickey (1961)	80
41	Delgado, Carlos (2000)	80
42	Foxx, Jimmie (1938)	79
43	Bonds, Barry (1992)	78
44	Williams, Ted (1948)	78
45	Cobb, Ty (1911)	78
46	McCovey, Willie (1969)	78
47	Gonzalez, Luis (2001)	77
48	Cobb, Ty (1915)	77
49	Sisler, George (1920)	77
50	Wilson, Hack (1930)	77
51	Yastrzemski, Carl (1967)	76
52	Bonds, Barry (1996)	76
53	Duffy, Hugh (1894)	76
54	Olerud, John (1993)	75
55	Pujols, Albert (2003)	75
56	Hornsby, Rogers (1929)	75
57	Cobb, Ty (1917)	75
58	Gehrig, Lou (1937)	75
59	Robinson, Frank (1966)	74
60	Giambi, Jason (2000)	74
61	Hornsby, Rogers (1921)	74
62	Helton, Todd (2001)	74
63	Lajoie, Nap (1901)	74
64	Hornsby, Rogers (1928)	74
65	Gehrig, Lou (1928)	74
66	Speaker, Tris (1912)	73
67	Musial, Stan (1949)	73
68	Williams, Ted (1954)	73
69	Vaughan, Arky (1935)	73
70	Sheffield, Gary (1996)	73
71	Helton, Todd (2003)	73
72	Ruth, Babe (1932)	73
73	Yastrzemski, Carl (1970)	73
74	Kiner, Ralph (1951)	73
75	Dunlap, Fred (1884)	73
76	Martinez, Edgar (1995)	72
77	Jackson, Joe (1911)	72
78	Morgan, Joe (1976)	72
79	Ruth, Babe (1919)	72
80	Thomas, Frank (1994)	72
81	Heilmann, Harry (1923)	71
82	Kiner, Ralph (1949)	71
83	Musial, Stan (1946)	71
84	Speaker, Tris (1923)	71
85	Jackson, Joe (1912)	71
86	Thome, Jim (2002)	70
87	Greenberg, Hank (1940)	70
88	Musial, Stan (1951)	70
89	Mize, Johnny (1939)	70
90	Klein, Chuck (1933)	69
91	Foxx, Jimmie (1934)	69
92	Herman, Babe (1930)	69
93	O'Doul, Lefty (1929)	69
94	Mantle, Mickey (1958)	69
95	Morgan, Joe (1975)	69
96	Greenberg, Hank (1937)	69
97	Aaron, Hank (1963)	69
98	McGwire, Mark (1996)	69
99	Medwick, Joe (1937)	69
100	Lajoie, Nap (1910)	69

Adjusted Batting Runs

1	Bonds, Barry (2001)	135
2	Bonds, Barry (2002)	128
3	Ruth, Babe (1921)	117
4	Ruth, Babe (1923)	114
5	Ruth, Babe (1920)	108
6	Ruth, Babe (1927)	107
7	Gehrig, Lou (1927)	107
8	Ruth, Babe (1931)	105
9	Ruth, Babe (1926)	101
10	Ruth, Babe (1924)	100
11	Williams, Ted (1941)	100
12	Gehrig, Lou (1934)	99
13	Hornsby, Rogers (1922)	99
14	Ruth, Babe (1930)	98
15	McGwire, Mark (1998)	97
16	Mantle, Mickey (1957)	96
17	Sosa, Sammy (2001)	95
18	Hornsby, Rogers (1924)	95
19	Gehrig, Lou (1930)	95
20	Bonds, Barry (2003)	94
21	Gehrig, Lou (1931)	92
22	Mantle, Mickey (1956)	92
23	Ruth, Babe (1928)	91
24	Foxx, Jimmie (1932)	90
25	Williams, Ted (1942)	90
26	Bonds, Barry (1993)	89
27	Gehrig, Lou (1936)	89
28	Williams, Ted (1946)	89
29	Mantle, Mickey (1961)	88
30	Hornsby, Rogers (1925)	85
31	Williams, Ted (1957)	84
32	Giambi, Jason (2001)	83
33	Williams, Ted (1947)	83
34	Bonds, Barry (1996)	83
35	Cash, Norm (1961)	83
36	Foxx, Jimmie (1933)	82
37	Musial, Stan (1948)	82
38	Pujols, Albert (2003)	81
39	Hornsby, Rogers (1928)	81
40	Ruth, Babe (1932)	81
41	McCovey, Willie (1969)	81
42	Williams, Ted (1949)	80
43	Bonds, Barry (1992)	80
44	Ruth, Babe (1919)	79
45	Gehrig, Lou (1928)	78
46	Sheffield, Gary (1996)	78
47	Bagwell, Jeff (1996)	78
48	Giambi, Jason (2000)	78
49	Aaron, Hank (1959)	77
50	Hornsby, Rogers (1921)	77
51	Robinson, Frank (1966)	77
52	Wilson, Hack (1930)	75
53	Bonds, Barry (2000)	75
54	Cobb, Ty (1917)	75
55	Foxx, Jimmie (1934)	75
56	Delgado, Carlos (2000)	75
57	Gehrig, Lou (1932)	75
58	Bonds, Barry (1998)	75
59	Olerud, John (1993)	74
60	Hornsby, Rogers (1929)	74
61	Piazza, Mike (1997)	74
62	Heilmann, Harry (1923)	74
63	Thomas, Frank (1994)	74
64	Mantle, Mickey (1958)	74
65	Henderson, Rickey (1990)	74
66	Gehrig, Lou (1937)	74
67	Delahanty, Ed (1899)	73
68	Bagwell, Jeff (1994)	73
69	Thome, Jim (2002)	73
70	Ruth, Babe (1929)	72
71	McGwire, Mark (1996)	72
72	Sisler, George (1920)	72
73	Williams, Ted (1948)	72
74	Foxx, Jimmie (1938)	72
75	Cobb, Ty (1911)	72
76	Cobb, Ty (1912)	71
77	Bonds, Barry (1997)	71
78	Thomas, Frank (1997)	71
79	Speaker, Tris (1923)	71
80	Thomas, Frank (1996)	71
81	O'Neill, Tip (1887)	71
82	Martinez, Edgar (1995)	71
83	Herman, Babe (1930)	71
84	Gehrig, Lou (1935)	70
85	Jackson, Joe (1911)	70
86	Cobb, Ty (1915)	70
87	Thomas, Frank (1991)	70
88	Aaron, Hank (1963)	70
89	Jackson, Reggie (1969)	70
90	Thomas, Frank (1995)	70
91	Foxx, Jimmie (1935)	70
92	Carew, Rod (1977)	69
93	Vaughan, Arky (1935)	69
94	Musial, Stan (1951)	69
95	Morgan, Joe (1976)	69
96	Kiner, Ralph (1951)	69
97	Gonzalez, Luis (2001)	69
98	Jones, Chipper (1999)	68
99	Dunlap, Fred (1884)	68
100	Lajoie, Nap (1901)	68

Runs Created

1	Ruth, Babe (1921)	239
2	Bonds, Barry (2001)	230
3	Ruth, Babe (1923)	223
4	Duffy, Hugh (1894)	217
5	Gehrig, Lou (1927)	212
6	Ruth, Babe (1920)	212
7	Hamilton, Billy (1894)	208
8	Bonds, Barry (2002)	208
9	Ruth, Babe (1927)	208
10	Foxx, Jimmie (1932)	207
11	Cobb, Ty (1911)	207
12	Ruth, Babe (1924)	205
13	Williams, Ted (1941)	203
14	Hornsby, Rogers (1922)	200
15	Gehrig, Lou (1936)	199
16	Ruth, Babe (1926)	196
17	Gehrig, Lou (1930)	195
18	Gehrig, Lou (1934)	195
19	O'Neill, Tip (1887)	194
20	McGwire, Mark (1998)	193
21	Sosa, Sammy (2001)	193
22	Williams, Ted (1949)	193
23	Ruth, Babe (1931)	192
24	Helton, Todd (2000)	192
25	Ruth, Babe (1930)	191
26	Browning, Pete (1887)	191
27	Musial, Stan (1948)	191
28	Wilson, Hack (1930)	189
29	Foxx, Jimmie (1938)	189
30	Williams, Ted (1946)	188
31	Mantle, Mickey (1956)	188
32	Hornsby, Rogers (1925)	187
33	Walker, Larry (1997)	187
34	Williams, Ted (1947)	186
35	Hornsby, Rogers (1924)	186
36	Delgado, Carlos (2000)	186
37	Klein, Chuck (1930)	186
38	Gehrig, Lou (1931)	185
39	Williams, Ted (1942)	185
40	Foxx, Jimmie (1933)	184
41	Hornsby, Rogers (1929)	183
42	Ruth, Babe (1928)	183
43	Herman, Babe (1930)	183
44	Gonzalez, Luis (2001)	182
45	Gehrig, Lou (1937)	181
46	Kelley, Joe (1894)	181
47	O'Doul, Lefty (1929)	180
48	Lajoie, Nap (1901)	179
49	Mantle, Mickey (1957)	178
50	Hamilton, Billy (1895)	178
51	Kelley, Joe (1896)	178
52	Cash, Norm (1961)	178
53	Greenberg, Hank (1937)	178
54	Delahanty, Ed (1895)	176
55	Pujols, Albert (2003)	176
56	Sisler, George (1920)	176
57	Keeler, Willie (1897)	176
58	Delahanty, Ed (1899)	175
59	Speaker, Tris (1912)	175
60	Jackson, Joe (1911)	175
61	Helton, Todd (2001)	174
62	Mantle, Mickey (1961)	174
63	Musial, Stan (1949)	173
64	DiMaggio, Joe (1937)	173
65	Cobb, Ty (1912)	173
66	Bonds, Barry (1993)	172
67	Giambi, Jason (2000)	172
68	Greenberg, Hank (1938)	172
69	Williams, Ted (1948)	172
70	Giambi, Jason (2001)	171
71	Klein, Chuck (1932)	171
72	Greenberg, Hank (1940)	171
73	Delahanty, Ed (1896)	170
74	Medwick, Joe (1937)	170
75	Terry, Bill (1930)	170
76	Musial, Stan (1951)	169
77	Gehrig, Lou (1928)	169
78	Hornsby, Rogers (1921)	169
79	Averill, Earl (1936)	168
80	Foxx, Jimmie (1936)	168
81	Helton, Todd (2003)	168
82	Gehrig, Lou (1932)	168
83	Thompson, Sam (1895)	167
84	Williams, Ted (1957)	167
85	Delahanty, Ed (1893)	167
86	Burkett, Jesse (1896)	166
87	Musial, Stan (1953)	166
88	Bonds, Barry (2003)	166
89	Jackson, Joe (1912)	166
90	Speaker, Tris (1923)	166
91	Foxx, Jimmie (1934)	165
92	Kiner, Ralph (1951)	165
93	Jones, Chipper (1999)	165
94	Cobb, Ty (1917)	164
95	Stenzel, Jake (1894)	164
96	Musial, Stan (1946)	164
97	Burkett, Jesse (1895)	163
98	Kiner, Ralph (1949)	163
99	Thomas, Frank (2000)	163
100	Vaughan, Arky (1935)	163

Runs Created per Game

1	Meyerle, Levi (1871)	23.24
2	Bonds, Barry (2002)	21.44
3	Williams, Ted (1941)	19.24
4	Bonds, Barry (2001)	18.85
5	Duffy, Hugh (1894)	18.68
6	Ruth, Babe (1920)	18.42
7	O'Neill, Tip (1887)	17.95
8	Ruth, Babe (1921)	17.91
9	Ruth, Babe (1923)	17.36
10	Bonds, Barry (2003)	16.87
11	Williams, Ted (1957)	16.64
12	Hamilton, Billy (1894)	16.26
13	Delahanty, Ed (1895)	16.24
14	Thompson, Sam (1894)	15.99
15	Barnes, Ross (1872)	15.95
16	Browning, Pete (1887)	15.78
17	Ruth, Babe (1926)	15.76
18	Ruth, Babe (1924)	15.61
19	Hornsby, Rogers (1925)	15.50
20	Mantle, Mickey (1957)	15.42
21	McGraw, John (1899)	15.27
22	Kelley, Joe (1894)	15.26
23	Cobb, Ty (1911)	15.19
24	Barnes, Ross (1873)	15.16
25	Lajoie, Nap (1901)	15.15
26	Ruth, Babe (1931)	15.04
27	Wood, Jimmy (1871)	14.99
28	Ruth, Babe (1927)	14.97
29	Delahanty, Ed (1896)	14.81
30	Hamilton, Billy (1895)	14.80
31	Hornsby, Rogers (1924)	14.78
32	Barnes, Ross (1871)	14.72
33	McVey, Cal (1871)	14.69
34	Williams, Ted (1946)	14.51
35	Foxx, Jimmie (1932)	14.48
36	Joyce, Bill (1894)	14.48
37	Lange, Bill (1895)	14.38
38	Williams, Ted (1942)	14.27
39	Mantle, Mickey (1956)	14.27
40	Kelly, King (1886)	14.24
41	Gehrig, Lou (1927)	14.23
42	Williams, Ted (1954)	14.16
43	McGwire, Mark (1998)	14.15
44	Kelley, Joe (1896)	14.07
45	Williams, Ted (1947)	14.01
46	Williams, Ted (1948)	13.99
47	Ruth, Babe (1930)	13.97
48	Thomas, Frank (1994)	13.88
49	Gehrig, Lou (1936)	13.87
50	Hamilton, Billy (1893)	13.84
51	Keeler, Willie (1897)	13.81
52	Gehrig, Lou (1934)	13.79
53	Vaughan, Arky (1935)	13.78
54	Ruth, Babe (1932)	13.75
55	Thompson, Sam (1895)	13.72
56	Pike, Lip (1871)	13.69
57	Barnes, Ross (1876)	13.69
58	Caruthers, Bob (1887)	13.59
59	Dunlap, Fred (1884)	13.58
60	Foxx, Jimmie (1938)	13.42
61	Cobb, Ty (1912)	13.39
62	Delahanty, Ed (1899)	13.36
63	Helton, Todd (2000)	13.34
64	Delahanty, Ed (1894)	13.30
65	Hornsby, Rogers (1922)	13.28
66	Bagwell, Jeff (1994)	13.23
67	Jackson, Joe (1911)	13.20
68	Williams, Ted (1949)	13.19
69	Gehrig, Lou (1930)	13.17
70	Walker, Larry (1999)	13.16
71	McGwire, Mark (1996)	13.15
72	Foxx, Jimmie (1933)	13.14
73	Burkett, Jesse (1895)	13.08
74	Cash, Norm (1961)	13.07
75	Walker, Larry (1997)	13.05
76	Anson, Cap (1872)	13.04
77	Mantle, Mickey (1961)	13.04
78	Ramirez, Manny (2000)	13.03
79	Giambi, Jason (2000)	12.99
80	Clarke, Fred (1897)	12.99
81	Mantle, Mickey (1962)	12.98
82	Jennings, Hughie (1896)	12.94
83	Musial, Stan (1948)	12.89
84	Gehrig, Lou (1937)	12.89
85	Ruth, Babe (1928)	12.87
86	Delgado, Carlos (2000)	12.86
87	Sosa, Sammy (2001)	12.79
88	Hamilton, Billy (1896)	12.59
89	Giambi, Jason (2001)	12.57
90	Belle, Albert (1994)	12.56
91	Burkett, Jesse (1896)	12.56
92	Kelley, Joe (1895)	12.55
93	Stenzel, Jake (1894)	12.55
94	Martinez, Edgar (1995)	12.53
95	Foxx, Jimmie (1939)	12.46
96	Speaker, Tris (1912)	12.46
97	Wilson, Hack (1930)	12.44
98	Hornsby, Rogers (1928)	12.41
99	DiMaggio, Joe (1939)	12.37
100	Cobb, Ty (1910)	12.34

Pinch Hits

1	Vander Wal, John, 1995	28
2	Harris, Lenny, 1999	26
3	Morales, Jose, 1976	25
4	Philley, Dave, 1961	24
	Davalillo, Vic, 1970	24
	Staub, Rusty, 1983	24
	Perry, Gerald, 1993	24
8	Norton, Greg, 2003	23
9	Leslie, Sam, 1932	22
	Lowrey, Peanuts, 1953	22
	Schoendienst, Red, 1962	22
	Johnson, Wallace, 1988	22
	Sweeney, Mark, 1997	22
	Harris, Lenny, 2002	22
15	Miller, Doc, 1913	21
	Burgess, Smoky, 1966	21
	Rettenmund, Merv, 1977	21
18	Coleman, Ed, 1936	20
	Bordagaray, Frenchy, 1938	20
	Frazier, Joe, 1954	20
	Burgess, Smoky, 1965	20
	Boswell, Ken, 1976	20
	Turner, Jerry, 1978	20
	Bosley, Thad, 1985	20
	Chambliss, Chris, 1986	20
	Clark, Dave, 1997	20

Pinch Hit Average (Min. 30 AB)

1	Kranepool, Ed, 1974	.486
2	Jolley, Smead, 1931	.467
3	Bordagaray, Frenchy, 1938	.465
4	Miller, Rick, 1983	.457
5	Spiers, Bill, 1997	.455
6	Pagan, Jose, 1969	.452
	Valo, Elmer, 1955	.452
	Johnson, Mark, 1956	.452
9	Brown, Gates, 1968	.450
10	Easterly, Ted, 1912	.433
	Thompson, Milt, 1985	.433
	Bush, Randy, 1986	.433
13	Cronin, Joe, 1943	.429
14	Dillard, Don, 1961	.429
15	Maldonado, Candy, 1986	.425
16	Ashburn, Richie, 1962	.419
	Williams, Dick, 1962	.419
18	Ranew, Merritt, 1963	.415
	Taylor, Carl, 1969	.415
20	Bevacqua, Kurt, 1983	.412
21	Turner, Jerry, 1978	.408
22	Bowman, Bob, 1958	.406
	Walker, Chico, 1991	.406
	Bream, Sid, 1994	.406
25	Baumholtz, Frankie, 1955	.405

Pinch Hit Home Runs

1	Hansen, Dave, 2000	7
	Wilson, Craig, 2001	7
3	Frederick, Johnny, 1932	6
4	Cronin, Joe, 1943	5
	Nieman, Butch, 1945	5
	Freese, Gene, 1959	5
	Lynch, Jerry, 1961	5
	Johnson, Cliff, 1974	5
	Lacy, Lee, 1978	5
	Turner, Jerry, 1978	5
	Ashley, Bill, 1996	5
	Dellucci, David, 2001	5
	Durazo, Erubiel, 2001	5
14	Lombardi, Ernie, 1946	4
	Wilber, Del, 1953	4
	Taylor, Bill, 1955	4
	Thurman, Bob, 1957	4
	Repulski, Rip, 1958	4
	Crowe, George, 1959	4
	Crowe, George, 1960	4
	Blanchard, Johnny, 1961	4
	Sawatski, Carl, 1961	4
	Lynch, Jerry, 1963	4
	Mincher, Don, 1964	4
	Breeden, Hal, 1973	4
	Ivie, Mike, 1978	4
	Unser, Del, 1979	4
	Burroughs, Jeff, 1982	4
	Heep, Danny, 1983	4
	Maldonado, Candy, 1986	4
	Carreon, Mark, 1989	4
	Gregg, Tommy, 1990	4
	Riles, Ernest, 1990	4
	Johnson, Howard, 1994	4
	Vander Wal, John, 1995	4
	Howell, Jack, 1996	4
	Johnson, Mark, 1996	4
	Hamelin, Bob, 1998	4
	Echevarria, Angelo, 1999	4
	Trammell, Bubba, 2000	4
	Merced, Orlando, 2001	4
	Norton, Greg, 2003	4

Extra Base Hits

1	Ruth, Babe (1921)	119
2	Gehrig, Lou (1927)	117
3	Bonds, Barry (2001)	107
	Klein, Chuck (1930)	107
5	Helton, Todd (2001)	105
6	Belle, Albert (1995)	103
	Greenberg, Hank (1937)	103
	Helton, Todd (2000)	103
	Klein, Chuck (1932)	103
	Musial, Stan (1948)	103
	Sosa, Sammy (2001)	103
12	Hornsby, Rogers (1922)	102
13	Foxx, Jimmie (1932)	100
	Gehrig, Lou (1930)	100
	Gonzalez, Luis (2001)	100
16	Belle, Albert (1998)	99
	Delgado, Carlos (2000)	99
	Greenberg, Hank (1940)	99
	Ruth, Babe (1920)	99
	Ruth, Babe (1923)	99
	Walker, Larry (1997)	99
22	Greenberg, Hank (1935)	98
23	Gonzalez, Juan (1998)	97
	Medwick, Joe (1937)	97
	Ruth, Babe (1927)	97
	Wilson, Hack (1930)	97
27	DiMaggio, Joe (1937)	96
	Greenberg, Hank (1934)	96
	Trosky, Hal (1936)	96
30	Gehrig, Lou (1934)	95
	Medwick, Joe (1936)	95
	Pujols, Albert (2003)	95
33	Berkman, Lance (2001)	94
	Foxx, Jimmie (1933)	94
	Herman, Babe (1930)	94
	Hornsby, Rogers (1929)	94
	Klein, Chuck (1929)	94
38	Bottomley, Jim (1928)	93
	Burks, Ellis (1996)	93
	Gehrig, Lou (1936)	93
	Griffey, Ken (1997)	93
	Simmons, Al (1930)	93
43	Aaron, Hank (1959)	92
	Anderson, Brady (1996)	92
	Foxx, Jimmie (1938)	92
	Gehrig, Lou (1931)	92
	Griffey, Ken (1998)	92
	Musial, Stan (1953)	92
	Robinson, Frank (1962)	92
	Ruth, Babe (1924)	92
	Soriano, Alfonso (2002)	92
52	McGwire, Mark (1998)	91
	Rodriguez, Alex (1996)	91
	Ruth, Babe (1928)	91
55	Hornsby, Rogers (1925)	90
	Mays, Willie (1962)	90
	Musial, Stan (1949)	90
	Stargell, Willie (1973)	90
59	Belle, Albert (1996)	89
	Galarraga, Andres (1996)	89
	Hidalgo, Richard (2000)	89
	Snider, Duke (1954)	89
	Sosa, Sammy (2000)	89
	Sosa, Sammy (1999)	89
	Trosky, Hal (1934)	89
66	Anderson, Garret (2002)	88
	Bonds, Barry (1998)	88
	Bonds, Barry (1993)	88
	DiMaggio, Joe (1936)	88
	Pujols, Albert (2001)	88
71	Collins, Ripper (1934)	87
	Cuyler, Kiki (1925)	87
	Gehrig, Lou (1928)	87
	Gehringer, Charlie (1936)	87
	Giambi, Jason (2001)	87
	Green, Shawn (1999)	87
	Helton, Todd (2003)	87
	Jones, Chipper (1999)	87
	Mays, Willie (1954)	87
	McGwire, Mark (1999)	87
	Mitchell, Kevin (1989)	87
	Mize, Johnny (1940)	87
	Rodriguez, Alex (2001)	87
	Speaker, Tris (1923)	87
	Thomas, Frank (2000)	87
	Wells, Vernon (2003)	87
	Yount, Robin (1982)	87
88	17 players tied	86

Total Player Wins/150G

1	Radbourn, Charley (1884)	14.59
2	Spalding, Al (1874)	14.15
3	Spalding, Al (1872)	13.96
4	Dunlap, Fred (1884)	13.93
5	Bonds, Barry (2002)	12.29
6	Bonds, Barry (2001)	11.91
7	Devlin, Jim (1876)	11.71
8	Spalding, Al (1873)	11.08
9	Ruth, Babe (1923)	11.06
10	Zettlein, George (1871)	10.94
11	Hornsby, Rogers (1924)	10.73
12	Schmidt, Mike (1981)	10.69
13	Barnes, Ross (1872)	10.68
14	Ruth, Babe (1920)	10.59
15	Barnes, Ross (1876)	10.39
16	Bonds, Barry (2003)	10.31
17	Ruth, Babe (1919)	10.26
18	Wagner, Honus (1908)	10.13
19	Mullane, Tony (1884)	10.09
20	Bagwell, Jeff (1994)	10.07
21	Whitney, Jim (1883)	10.04
22	Morgan, Joe (1975)	10.02
23	Caruthers, Bob (1887)	9.91
24	Browning, Pete (1882)	9.82
25	Pratt, Al (1871)	9.75
26	Ruth, Babe (1921)	9.69
27	Lajoie, Nap (1903)	9.54
28	Mantle, Mickey (1957)	9.48
29	Brett, George (1980)	9.44
30	Ruth, Babe (1927)	9.39
31	Whitney, Jim (1882)	9.29
32	Devlin, Jim (1877)	9.26
33	Lajoie, Nap (1906)	9.20
34	Williams, Ted (1941)	9.19
35	Collins, Eddie (1910)	9.15
36	Jennings, Hughie (1896)	9.13
37	Ruth, Babe (1931)	9.10
38	Williams, Ted (1942)	9.02
39	Wolters, Rynie (1871)	9.00
40	Lajoie, Nap (1908)	8.99
41	Hornsby, Rogers (1922)	8.94
42	Bonds, Barry (1992)	8.93
43	Williams, Ted (1957)	8.84
44	Gehrig, Lou (1927)	8.81
45	Mantle, Mickey (1956)	8.78
46	Wagner, Honus (1912)	8.62
47	Wagner, Honus (1909)	8.53
48	Lajoie, Nap (1901)	8.50
49	Radbourn, Charley (1883)	8.47
50	Williams, Ted (1946)	8.45
51	Stirnweiss, Snuffy (1945)	8.42
52	Barnes, Ross (1873)	8.39
53	Ruth, Babe (1924)	8.35
54	Vaughan, Arky (1935)	8.33
55	Lajoie, Nap (1910)	8.32
56	Cobb, Ty (1917)	8.32
57	Mathews, Bobby (1874)	8.28
58	Hornsby, Rogers (1921)	8.26
59	Bond, Tommy (1877)	8.26
60	Ruth, Babe (1926)	8.25
61	Rodriguez, Alex (2000)	8.21
62	Stirnweiss, Snuffy (1944)	8.19
63	Jennings, Hughie (1895)	8.18
64	Sosa, Sammy (2001)	8.15
65	Hornsby, Rogers (1925)	8.11
66	Wagner, Honus (1905)	8.11
67	Collins, Eddie (1909)	8.10
68	Childs, Cupid (1890)	8.08
69	Mantle, Mickey (1961)	8.08
70	Ruth, Babe (1930)	8.05
71	Lajoie, Nap (1904)	8.03
72	Hornsby, Rogers (1920)	8.02
73	Ripken, Cal (1984)	8.00
74	Wagner, Honus (1906)	7.97
75	Piazza, Mike (1997)	7.97
76	Henderson, Rickey (1990)	7.96
77	Barnes, Ross (1871)	7.96
78	Morgan, Joe (1974)	7.96
79	Morgan, Joe (1976)	7.94
80	Ruth, Babe (1932)	7.93
81	Larkin, Barry (1991)	7.90
82	Barnes, Ross (1875)	7.89
83	Kelly, King (1879)	7.86
84	Avila, Bobby (1954)	7.84
85	Wagner, Honus (1903)	7.84
86	Wagner, Honus (1907)	7.82
87	Robinson, Jackie (1951)	7.81
88	Cash, Norm (1961)	7.79
89	Ripken, Cal (1991)	7.75
90	Gehrig, Lou (1934)	7.68
91	Caminiti, Ken (1996)	7.65
92	Collins, Eddie (1913)	7.64
93	Kelly, King (1886)	7.64
94	Bonds, Barry (1993)	7.62
95	Mathews, Bobby (1873)	7.61
96	Santo, Ron (1966)	7.61
97	Cronin, Joe (1930)	7.54
98	Frisch, Frankie (1927)	7.53
99	Morgan, Joe (1972)	7.53
100	Shafer, Orator (1878)	7.51

Stolen Bases

1	Nicol, Hugh (1887)	138
2	Henderson, Rickey (1982)	130
3	Latham, Arlie (1887)	129
4	Brock, Lou (1974)	118
5	Comiskey, Charlie (1887)	117
6	Hamilton, Billy (1889)	111
	Hamilton, Billy (1891)	111
	Ward, John (1887)	111
9	Coleman, Vince (1985)	110
10	Coleman, Vince (1987)	109
	Latham, Arlie (1888)	109
12	Henderson, Rickey (1983)	108
13	Coleman, Vince (1986)	107
14	Brown, Tom (1891)	106
15	Wills, Maury (1962)	104
16	Browning, Pete (1887)	103
	Nicol, Hugh (1888)	103
18	Fogarty, Jim (1887)	102
	Hamilton, Billy (1890)	102
20	Hamilton, Billy (1894)	100
	Henderson, Rickey (1980)	100
22	Fogarty, Jim (1889)	99
23	Hamilton, Billy (1895)	97
	LeFlore, Ron (1980)	97
	Stovey, Harry (1890)	97
26	Cobb, Ty (1915)	96
	Moreno, Omar (1980)	96
28	McPhee, Bid (1887)	95
	Welch, Curt (1888)	95
30	Griffin, Mike (1887)	94
	Wills, Maury (1965)	94
32	Henderson, Rickey (1988)	93
	McCarthy, Tommy (1888)	93
34	O'Brien, Darby (1889)	91
35	Raines, Tim (1983)	90
36	Long, Herman (1889)	89
	Welch, Curt (1887)	89
38	Milan, Clyde (1912)	88
	Poorman, Tom (1887)	88
	Purcell, Blondie (1887)	88
	Ward, John (1892)	88
42	Henderson, Rickey (1986)	87
	Kelley, Joe (1896)	87
	Latham, Arlie (1891)	87
	Stovey, Harry (1888)	87
46	Stricker, Cub (1887)	86
47	Collins, Hub (1887)	85
	Duffy, Hugh (1891)	85
	Tucker, Tommy (1887)	85
50	Kelly, King (1887)	84
	Lange, Bill (1896)	84
	McGarr, Chippy (1887)	84
	Sunday, Billy (1890)	84
54	Cobb, Ty (1911)	83
	Hamilton, Billy (1896)	83
	McCarthy, Tommy (1890)	83
	Wilson, Willie (1979)	83
58	Hoy, Dummy (1888)	82
	Reilly, John (1888)	82
60	Bescher, Bob (1911)	81
	Coleman, Vince (1988)	81
	Collins, Eddie (1910)	81
63	Davis, Eric (1986)	80
	Henderson, Rickey (1985)	80
	Nicol, Hugh (1889)	80
	Seery, Emmett (1888)	80
67	Brown, Tom (1890)	79
	Collins, Dave (1980)	79
	Wilson, Willie (1980)	79
70	Brown, Tom (1892)	78
	Duffy, Hugh (1890)	78
	Grissom, Marquis (1992)	78
	LeFlore, Ron (1979)	78
	McGraw, John (1894)	78
	Raines, Tim (1982)	78
76	Coleman, Vince (1990)	77
	Henderson, Rickey (1989)	77
	Law, Rudy (1983)	77
	Lopes, Davey (1975)	77
	Moreno, Omar (1979)	77
	Scheffler, Ted (1890)	77
	Sheckard, Jimmy (1899)	77
83	Cobb, Ty (1909)	76
	Grissom, Marquis (1991)	76
	McKean, Ed (1887)	76
	Miller, Dusty (1896)	76
	Wilmot, Walt (1894)	76
	Wilmot, Walt (1890)	76
89	Kauff, Benny (1914)	75
	Lofton, Kenny (1996)	75
	Milan, Clyde (1913)	75
	North, Billy (1976)	75
	Raines, Tim (1984)	75
	Robinson, Yank (1887)	75
	Van Haltren, George (1891)	75
96	Brock, Lou (1966)	74
	Fennelly, Frank (1887)	74
	Hunter, Brian (1997)	74
	Maisel, Fritz (1914)	74
	Stovey, Harry (1887)	74

Stolen Base Average

1	Molitor, Paul (1994)	100.0
	McReynolds, Kevin (1988)	100.0
3	Anderson, Brady (1994)	96.9
	Beltran, Carlos (2001)	96.9
5	Carey, Max (1922)	96.2
6	Griffey, Ken (1980)	95.8
7	Glanville, Doug (1999)	94.4
8	Otis, Amos (1970)	94.3
9	Perconte, Jack (1985)	93.9
10	Larkin, Barry (1994)	92.9
11	Furcal, Rafael (2003)	92.6
12	Cabrera, Orlando (2003)	92.3
13	Davis, Eric (1988)	92.1
14	Bonds, Bobby (1969)	91.8
	Lopes, Davey (1978)	91.8
16	Lopes, Davey (1979)	91.7
17	Wynn, Jimmy (1965)	91.5
18	Bowa, Larry (1977)	91.4
	Jeter, Derek (2002)	91.4
20	Trammell, Alan (1987)	91.3
	Sandberg, Ryne (1987)	91.3
22	Mumphrey, Jerry (1980)	91.2
23	Herr, Tom (1985)	91.2
24	Beltran, Carlos (2003)	91.1
25	Larkin, Barry (1995)	91.1
26	Alomar, Roberto (1995)	90.9
	Raines, Tim (1987)	90.9
	Singleton, Chris (2002)	90.9
29	Alomar, Roberto (2000)	90.7
	Biggio, Craig (1994)	90.7
31	Reese, Pokey (2000)	90.6
	Bell, Derek (1996)	90.6
33	Wilson, Willie (1984)	90.4
34	McBride, Bake (1978)	90.3
35	White, Devon (1992)	90.2
36	Jeter, Derek (2001)	90.0
37	Hunter, Brian (1999)	89.8
38	Larkin, Barry (1998)	89.7
39	Womack, Tony (1997)	89.6
40	White, Devon (1993)	89.5
41	Page, Mitchell (1977)	89.4
42	Davis, Eric (1987)	89.3
	Harper, Tommy (1971)	89.3
	Javier, Stan (1997)	89.3
	Jones, Chipper (1999)	89.3
	Manning, Rick (1981)	89.3
47	Tarasco, Tony (1995)	88.9
	Baker, Dusty (1973)	88.9
	Henderson, Rickey (1985)	88.9
	Wills, Maury (1962)	88.9
51	Wilson, Willie (1980)	88.8
52	Raines, Tim (1985)	88.6
	Raines, Tim (1986)	88.6
54	Gibson, Kirk (1988)	88.6
	Campaneris, Bert (1969)	88.6
56	Young, Eric (2000)	88.5
57	Duncan, Mariano (1992)	88.5
	Clayton, Royce (1994)	88.5
	Mays, Willie (1971)	88.5
	Erstad, Darin (2002)	88.5
61	Coleman, Vince (1986)	88.4
62	Durham, Ray (1996)	88.2
	Gibson, Kirk (1985)	88.2
	Raines, Tim (1984)	88.2
	Murphy, Dale (1983)	88.2
	Raines, Tim (1992)	88.2
67	Wilson, Willie (1983)	88.1
68	Robinson, Frank (1961)	88.0
	Doran, Bill (1989)	88.0
	Palmeiro, Rafael (1993)	88.0
	O'Neill, Paul (2001)	88.0
	Bonds, Bobby (1972)	88.0
	Case, George (1942)	88.0
74	Eckstein, David (2001)	87.9
	Womack, Tony (1998)	87.9
76	Javier, Stan (1995)	87.8
77	Henderson, Rickey (1988)	87.7
78	Mantle, Mickey (1959)	87.5
	Aaron, Hank (1966)	87.5
	Biggio, Craig (1989)	87.5
	Jethroe, Sam (1951)	87.5
	Franco, Julio (1989)	87.5
	Davis, Eric (1990)	87.5
	Lary, Lyn (1935)	87.5
85	Wilson, Willie (1979)	87.4
86	Concepcion, Dave (1974)	87.2
	McGee, Willie (1988)	87.2
88	Cameron, Mike (2001)	87.2
89	Davis, Mike (1986)	87.1
	Mays, Willie (1959)	87.1
	Lansing, Mike (1995)	87.1
	Jones, Andruw (1998)	87.1
	Mondesi, Raul (1995)	87.1
94	Morgan, Joe (1975)	87.0
95	8 players tied	87.0

Stolen Base Runs

1	Coleman, Vince (1986)	17
2	Wills, Maury (1962)	17
3	Henderson, Rickey (1983)	15
4	Henderson, Rickey (1988)	15
5	Coleman, Vince (1987)	14
6	Raines, Tim (1983)	14
7	Henderson, Rickey (1985)	13
8	Coleman, Vince (1985)	13
9	Wilson, Willie (1980)	13
10	Wilson, Willie (1979)	13
11	LeFlore, Ron (1980)	13
12	Raines, Tim (1984)	12
13	Law, Rudy (1983)	12
	Lopes, Davey (1975)	12
15	Raines, Tim (1986)	11
	Raines, Tim (1985)	11
17	Grissom, Marquis (1992)	11
18	Brock, Lou (1974)	11
19	Henderson, Rickey (1986)	11
20	LeFlore, Ron (1979)	11
21	Raines, Tim (1981)	11
22	Henderson, Rickey (1989)	11
23	Carey, Max (1922)	10
24	Henderson, Rickey (1980)	10
25	Morgan, Joe (1975)	10
26	Womack, Tony (1997)	10
27	Campaneris, Bert (1969)	10
28	Womack, Tony (1999)	10
29	Raines, Tim (1982)	10
30	Coleman, Vince (1989)	10
	Henderson, Rickey (1990)	10
32	Henderson, Rickey (1982)	10
33	Wilson, Willie (1983)	9
34	Coleman, Vince (1990)	9
35	Mumphrey, Jerry (1980)	9
36	Womack, Tony (1998)	9
37	Morgan, Joe (1976)	9
38	Knoblauch, Chuck (1997)	9
39	Lofton, Kenny (1992)	9
40	Lofton, Kenny (1993)	9
	Rivers, Mickey (1975)	9
42	Samuel, Juan (1984)	9
43	Grissom, Marquis (1991)	9
44	Larkin, Barry (1995)	9
45	Lofton, Kenny (1996)	9
46	Raines, Tim (1987)	9
47	Young, Eric (2000)	9
48	Henderson, Rickey (1998)	9
	Wiggins, Alan (1983)	9
50	Maisel, Fritz (1914)	9
51	Smith, Ozzie (1988)	8
52	Cruz, Julio (1978)	8
53	Davis, Eric (1987)	8
54	Pettis, Gary (1985)	8
55	Brock, Lou (1968)	8
56	Brock, Lou (1966)	8
	Hunter, Brian (1997)	8
58	Bonds, Bobby (1969)	8
	Lopes, Davey (1978)	8
60	Wilson, Willie (1984)	8
61	Henderson, Rickey (1993)	8
62	Wilson, Willie (1987)	8
63	Scott, Rodney (1980)	8
64	Morgan, Joe (1973)	8
65	Harper, Tommy (1969)	8
66	Collins, Dave (1980)	8
67	Lopes, Davey (1979)	8
68	Otis, Amos (1971)	8
69	Taveras, Frank (1976)	8
70	Lofton, Kenny (1994)	8
71	LeFlore, Ron (1978)	8
72	Wynn, Jimmy (1965)	8
73	Aparicio, Luis (1960)	8
	Carey, Max (1923)	8
75	Hatcher, Billy (1987)	8
76	Crawford, Carl (2003)	8
	Goodwin, Tom (2000)	8
78	Moreno, Omar (1979)	7
79	Biggio, Craig (1998)	7
	Coleman, Vince (1994)	7
81	Lofton, Kenny (1998)	7
82	Morgan, Joe (1974)	7
83	Taveras, Frank (1977)	7
84	Beltran, Carlos (2003)	7
85	Raines, Tim (1992)	7
86	Grissom, Marquis (1993)	7
87	Stirnweiss, Snuffy (1944)	7
88	Cruz, Julio (1983)	7
89	Case, George (1943)	7
	Cedeno, Cesar (1977)	7
91	Page, Mitchell (1977)	7
92	Bonds, Bobby (1972)	7
	Case, George (1942)	7
94	Campaneris, Bert (1966)	7
	Carey, Max (1920)	7
96	Sandberg, Ryne (1985)	7
97	Gwynn, Tony (1987)	7
	Richards, Gene (1977)	7
99	Cedeno, Roger (1999)	7
100	2 players tied	7

Win Shares – Batters

1	Radbourn, Charley (1884)	89
2	Buffinton, Charlie (1884)	62
3	Galvin, Pud (1879)	61
4	Bond, Tommy (1878)	60
	Devlin, Jim (1877)	60
	Radbourn, Charley (1883)	60
7	Wagner, Honus (1908)	59
8	Mullane, Tony (1884)	58
9	Bradley, George (1876)	57
	Spalding, Al (1876)	57
	Whitney, Jim (1883)	57
12	Mullane, Tony (1883)	55
	Ruth, Babe (1923)	55
14	Bonds, Barry (2001)	54
	Caruthers, Bob (1887)	54
	McCormick, Jim (1880)	54
17	Devlin, Jim (1876)	53
	Ruth, Babe (1921)	53
19	Corcoran, Larry (1880)	52
20	Mantle, Mickey (1957)	51
	Ruth, Babe (1920)	51
	Speaker, Tris (1912)	51
	Ward, John (1879)	51
	Ward, John (1880)	51
25	Bond, Tommy (1879)	50
	Radbourn, Charley (1882)	50
27	Bonds, Barry (2002)	49
	Mantle, Mickey (1956)	49
	Williams, Ted (1946)	49
30	Cobb, Ty (1915)	48
	Mantle, Mickey (1961)	48
32	Bond, Tommy (1877)	47
	Bonds, Barry (1993)	47
	Cobb, Ty (1911)	47
	Galvin, Pud (1883)	47
	Hornsby, Rogers (1922)	47
	Lajoie, Nap (1910)	47
38	Cobb, Ty (1917)	46
	Musial, Stan (1948)	46
	Wagner, Honus (1905)	46
	Wagner, Honus (1906)	46
	Williams, Ted (1942)	46
43	Cobb, Ty (1910)	45
	Ruth, Babe (1928)	45
	Ruth, Babe (1927)	45
	Ruth, Babe (1926)	45
	Ruth, Babe (1924)	45
	Speaker, Tris (1914)	45
49	Clark, Will (1989)	44
	Cobb, Ty (1909)	44
	Gehrig, Lou (1927)	44
	Morgan, Joe (1975)	44
	Musial, Stan (1946)	44
	Wagner, Honus (1907)	44
	Williams, Ted (1947)	44
56	Collins, Eddie (1909)	43
	Collins, Eddie (1914)	43
	Foutz, Dave (1887)	43
	Mays, Willie (1965)	43
	Ruth, Babe (1919)	43
	Wagner, Honus (1904)	43
62	Cash, Norm (1961)	42
	Gehrig, Lou (1928)	42
	Hornsby, Rogers (1929)	42
	Lajoie, Nap (1901)	42
	McCormick, Jim (1882)	42
	Richmond, Lee (1880)	42
	Rosen, Al (1953)	42
	Seymour, Cy (1905)	42
	Sosa, Sammy (2001)	42
	Wagner, Honus (1909)	42
	Whitney, Jim (1881)	42
	Williams, Ted (1941)	42
	Yastrzemski, Carl (1967)	42
75	Aaron, Hank (1963)	41
	Allen, Dick (1964)	41
	Bagwell, Jeff (1996)	41
	Bonds, Barry (1992)	41
	Burns, Dick (1884)	41
	Cobb, Ty (1907)	41
	Delahanty, Ed (1899)	41
	DiMaggio, Joe (1941)	41
	Foxx, Jimmie (1933)	41
	Gehrig, Lou (1934)	41
	Hornsby, Rogers (1921)	41
	Jackson, Reggie (1969)	41
	Lajoie, Nap (1904)	41
	Mantle, Mickey (1955)	41
	Mays, Willie (1962)	41
	McGwire, Mark (1998)	41
	Pujols, Albert (2003)	41
	Robinson, Frank (1966)	41
	Robinson, Frank (1962)	41
	Speaker, Tris (1916)	41
	Torre, Joe (1971)	41
96	15 players tied	40

Total Player Wins – Batters

1	Bonds, Barry (2001)	12.2
2	Bonds, Barry (2002)	11.7
3	Ruth, Babe (1923)	11.2
4	Hornsby, Rogers (1924)	10.2
5	Wagner, Honus (1908)	10.2
6	Ruth, Babe (1920)	10.0
7	Ruth, Babe (1921)	9.8
8	Morgan, Joe (1975)	9.8
9	Ruth, Babe (1927)	9.5
10	Lajoie, Nap (1908)	9.4
11	Dunlap, Fred (1884)	9.4
12	Collins, Eddie (1910)	9.3
13	Lajoie, Nap (1906)	9.3
14	Hornsby, Rogers (1922)	9.2
15	Mantle, Mickey (1957)	9.1
16	Gehrig, Lou (1927)	9.1
17	Williams, Ted (1942)	9.0
18	Bonds, Barry (2003)	8.9
19	Ruth, Babe (1919)	8.9
20	Lajoie, Nap (1910)	8.8
21	Ruth, Babe (1931)	8.8
22	Mantle, Mickey (1956)	8.8
23	Williams, Ted (1941)	8.8
24	Sosa, Sammy (2001)	8.7
25	Ripken, Cal (1984)	8.6
26	Stirnweiss, Snuffy (1945)	8.5
27	Ruth, Babe (1924)	8.5
28	Hornsby, Rogers (1921)	8.5
29	Radbourn, Charley (1884)	8.5
30	Williams, Ted (1946)	8.4
31	Cobb, Ty (1917)	8.4
32	Stirnweiss, Snuffy (1944)	8.4
33	Ripken, Cal (1991)	8.4
34	Ruth, Babe (1926)	8.4
35	Bonds, Barry (1992)	8.3
36	Wagner, Honus (1912)	8.3
37	Collins, Eddie (1909)	8.3
38	Cash, Norm (1961)	8.3
39	Mantle, Mickey (1961)	8.2
40	Rodriguez, Alex (2000)	8.1
41	Bonds, Barry (1993)	8.1
42	Piazza, Mike (1997)	8.1
43	Santo, Ron (1967)	8.1
44	Hornsby, Rogers (1920)	8.0
45	Robinson, Jackie (1951)	8.0
46	Lajoie, Nap (1903)	7.9
47	Wagner, Honus (1905)	7.9
48	Jennings, Hughie (1896)	7.9
49	Morgan, Joe (1974)	7.9
50	Gehrig, Lou (1934)	7.9
51	Santo, Ron (1966)	7.9
52	Wagner, Honus (1909)	7.8
53	Ruth, Babe (1930)	7.8
54	Williams, Ted (1957)	7.8
55	Cronin, Joe (1930)	7.7
56	McGwire, Mark (1998)	7.7
57	Frisch, Frankie (1927)	7.7
58	Yount, Robin (1982)	7.6
59	Sisler, George (1920)	7.6
60	Vaughan, Arky (1935)	7.6
61	Wagner, Honus (1906)	7.5
62	Collins, Eddie (1913)	7.5
63	Schmidt, Mike (1976)	7.5
64	Bonds, Barry (1996)	7.5
65	Lajoie, Nap (1904)	7.5
66	Mays, Willie (1955)	7.5
67	Avila, Bobby (1954)	7.5
68	Morgan, Joe (1972)	7.5
69	Morgan, Joe (1976)	7.5
70	Hornsby, Rogers (1925)	7.5
71	Boudreau, Lou (1948)	7.5
72	Caminiti, Ken (1996)	7.5
73	Morgan, Joe (1973)	7.4
74	Lajoie, Nap (1901)	7.4
75	Ripken, Cal (1983)	7.4
76	Wagner, Honus (1907)	7.4
77	Bagwell, Jeff (1994)	7.4
78	Robinson, Jackie (1952)	7.4
79	Brett, George (1980)	7.4
80	Musial, Stan (1948)	7.3
81	Williams, Ted (1947)	7.3
82	Pujols, Albert (2003)	7.3
83	Schmidt, Mike (1981)	7.3
84	Collins, Eddie (1914)	7.3
85	Foxx, Jimmie (1932)	7.2
86	Henderson, Rickey (1990)	7.2
87	Collins, Eddie (1915)	7.2
88	Rodriguez, Alex (2001)	7.2
89	Biggio, Craig (1997)	7.2
90	Vaughan, Arky (1934)	7.2
91	Aaron, Hank (1959)	7.2
92	Jennings, Hughie (1895)	7.1
93	Collins, Eddie (1912)	7.1
94	Schmidt, Mike (1980)	7.1
95	McCovey, Willie (1969)	7.1
96	Boudreau, Lou (1944)	7.1
97	Allen, Dick (1964)	7.1
98	Bonds, Barry (2000)	7.1
99	Gehrig, Lou (1930)	7.1
100	Foxx, Jimmie (1933)	7.1
101	Schmidt, Mike (1974)	7.1
102	Speaker, Tris (1912)	7.1
103	Brouthers, Dan (1892)	7.0
104	Ruth, Babe (1932)	7.0
105	Collins, Eddie (1920)	7.0
106	Baker, Frank (1912)	7.0
107	Cobb, Ty (1912)	7.0
108	Boudreau, Lou (1943)	7.0
109	Petrocelli, Rico (1969)	7.0
110	Baker, Frank (1913)	6.9
111	Ruth, Babe (1928)	6.9
112	Hornsby, Rogers (1929)	6.9
113	DiMaggio, Joe (1941)	6.9
114	Gehrig, Lou (1936)	6.9
115	Jackson, Joe (1912)	6.9
116	Rodriguez, Alex (1996)	6.9
117	Bonds, Barry (1998)	6.8
118	Speaker, Tris (1923)	6.8
119	Gehrig, Lou (1928)	6.8
120	Mays, Willie (1965)	6.8
121	Jackson, Joe (1911)	6.8
122	Guerrero, Pedro (1985)	6.8
123	Childs, Cupid (1890)	6.8
124	Mays, Willie (1954)	6.8
125	Robinson, Frank (1966)	6.8
126	Thon, Dickie (1983)	6.8
127	Wagner, Honus (1903)	6.7
128	McCovey, Willie (1970)	6.7
129	Spalding, Al (1874)	6.7
130	Giambi, Jason (2001)	6.7
131	Mays, Willie (1958)	6.6
132	Gordon, Joe (1943)	6.6
133	Cobb, Ty (1910)	6.6
134	Mantle, Mickey (1958)	6.6
135	Williams, Ted (1949)	6.6
136	Mathews, Eddie (1953)	6.6
137	Yastrzemski, Carl (1967)	6.5
138	Henderson, Rickey (1985)	6.5
139	Robinson, Jackie (1949)	6.5
140	Clift, Harlond (1937)	6.5
141	Rosen, Al (1953)	6.5
142	Frisch, Frankie (1924)	6.5
143	Bagwell, Jeff (1996)	6.5
144	Lajoie, Nap (1907)	6.5
145	Larkin, Barry (1991)	6.5
146	Speaker, Tris (1914)	6.5
147	Caruthers, Bob (1887)	6.5
148	Cobb, Ty (1911)	6.4
149	Grich, Bobby (1975)	6.4
150	Brett, George (1985)	6.4
151	Vaughan, Arky (1936)	6.4
152	Whitney, Jim (1883)	6.4
153	Trammell, Alan (1987)	6.4
154	Musial, Stan (1951)	6.4
155	Sheffield, Gary (1992)	6.4
156	Mullane, Tony (1884)	6.4
157	Brett, George (1979)	6.4
158	Mays, Willie (1957)	6.4
159	Bonds, Barry (1990)	6.4
160	Carew, Rod (1977)	6.3
161	Foxx, Jimmie (1934)	6.3
162	Bonds, Barry (1997)	6.3
163	Winfield, Dave (1979)	6.3
164	Cobb, Ty (1909)	6.3
165	Mays, Willie (1964)	6.3
166	Olerud, John (1993)	6.3
167	Jackson, Reggie (1969)	6.3
168	Banks, Ernie (1959)	6.3
169	Schmidt, Mike (1977)	6.3
170	Larkin, Barry (1996)	6.3
171	Ott, Mel (1938)	6.3
172	Allen, Dick (1972)	6.3
173	Giles, Brian (2002)	6.3
174	Boone, Bret (2001)	6.3
175	Piazza, Mike (1996)	6.3
176	Mathews, Eddie (1959)	6.3
177	Foxx, Jimmie (1935)	6.3
178	Schmidt, Mike (1979)	6.3
179	Kauff, Benny (1915)	6.3
180	Heilmann, Harry (1923)	6.2
181	Carew, Rod (1974)	6.2
182	Appling, Luke (1943)	6.2
183	Kent, Jeff (2000)	6.2
184	Rodriguez, Alex (2002)	6.2
185	Seymour, Cy (1905)	6.2
186	Cronin, Joe (1931)	6.2
187	Grich, Bobby (1973)	6.2
188	Grich, Bobby (1979)	6.1
189	Carew, Rod (1973)	6.1
190	Schmidt, Mike (1975)	6.1
191	Joost, Eddie (1949)	6.1
192	Schmidt, Mike (1982)	6.1
193	Gehrig, Lou (1935)	6.1
194	Yount, Robin (1983)	6.1
195	Kent, Jeff (2002)	6.1
196	Jennings, Hughie (1898)	6.1
197	Aaron, Hank (1963)	6.1
198	Williams, Ted (1948)	6.1
199	Musial, Stan (1943)	6.1
200	Gordon, Joe (1942)	6.1
201	Ott, Mel (1936)	6.0
202	Wynn, Jimmy (1969)	6.0
203	Concepcion, Dave (1976)	6.0
204	Cobb, Ty (1915)	6.0
205	Mathews, Eddie (1963)	6.0
206	Fox, Nellie (1957)	6.0
207	Griffey, Ken (1997)	6.0
208	Gonzalez, Luis (2001)	6.0
209	Ruth, Babe (1929)	6.0
210	Canseco, Jose (1988)	6.0
211	Thomas, Frank (1991)	6.0
212	Kelly, King (1886)	6.0
213	Hornsby, Rogers (1917)	6.0
214	Aurilia, Rich (2001)	6.0
215	Childs, Cupid (1896)	6.0
216	Musial, Stan (1949)	6.0
217	Mitchell, Kevin (1989)	6.0
218	Speaker, Tris (1916)	6.0
219	Speaker, Tris (1913)	6.0
220	Schmidt, Mike (1983)	5.9
221	Collins, Eddie (1911)	5.9
222	Gehringer, Charlie (1936)	5.9
223	DiMaggio, Joe (1937)	5.9
224	Bell, Jay (1993)	5.9
225	Mantle, Mickey (1955)	5.9
226	Sandberg, Ryne (1984)	5.9
227	Hornsby, Rogers (1928)	5.9
228	Gehrig, Lou (1931)	5.9
229	Boggs, Wade (1988)	5.9
230	Lazzeri, Tony (1929)	5.9
231	Stargell, Willie (1973)	5.9
232	Piazza, Mike (1998)	5.9
233	Boone, Bret (2003)	5.8
234	McGraw, John (1899)	5.8
235	Dahlen, Bill (1896)	5.8
236	Yastrzemski, Carl (1968)	5.8
237	Burkett, Jesse (1901)	5.8
238	Jackson, Joe (1913)	5.8
239	Stone, George (1906)	5.8
240	Herman, Billy (1937)	5.8
241	Bench, Johnny (1972)	5.8
242	Gehringer, Charlie (1934)	5.8
243	Gentile, Jim (1961)	5.8
244	Sheffield, Gary (1996)	5.8
245	Groh, Heinie (1917)	5.8
246	Gwynn, Tony (1987)	5.8
247	Ott, Mel (1929)	5.8
248	Bancroft, Dave (1920)	5.7
249	Vaughan, Arky (1933)	5.7
250	Bancroft, Dave (1921)	5.7
251	Vaughan, Arky (1938)	5.7
252	Cardenas, Leo (1969)	5.7
253	Mathews, Eddie (1954)	5.7
254	Clark, Will (1989)	5.7
255	Martinez, Edgar (1995)	5.7
256	Giambi, Jason (2000)	5.7
257	Musial, Stan (1946)	5.7
258	Evans, Darrell (1973)	5.7
259	Jennings, Hughie (1897)	5.7
260	DiMaggio, Joe (1939)	5.7
261	Speaker, Tris (1920)	5.7
262	Murcer, Bobby (1971)	5.7
263	Belle, Albert (1998)	5.7
264	Turner, Terry (1906)	5.7
265	Concepcion, Dave (1974)	5.6
266	Ott, Mel (1932)	5.6
267	Piazza, Mike (1993)	5.6
268	Stanky, Eddie (1950)	5.6
269	Griffey, Ken (1993)	5.6
270	Mays, Willie (1962)	5.6
271	Sewell, Joe (1923)	5.6
272	Klein, Chuck (1930)	5.6
273	Allen, Dick (1966)	5.6
274	Wagner, Honus (1901)	5.6
275	Clift, Harlond (1938)	5.6
276	Banks, Ernie (1960)	5.6
277	Williams, Ted (1954)	5.6
278	Herman, Billy (1936)	5.6
279	Clemente, Roberto (1967)	5.6
280	Santo, Ron (1964)	5.6
281	Delahanty, Ed (1896)	5.6
282	Garciaparra, Nomar (1999)	5.6
283	Schmidt, Mike (1984)	5.5
284	Tinker, Joe (1908)	5.5
285	Greenberg, Hank (1937)	5.5
286	Terry, Bill (1930)	5.5
287	Fletcher, Art (1917)	5.5
288	Helton, Todd (2003)	5.5
289	Glaus, Troy (2000)	5.5
290	Mays, Willie (1963)	5.5
291	Robinson, Brooks (1967)	5.5
292	Mantle, Mickey (1962)	5.5
293	Hornsby, Rogers (1927)	5.5
294	Belle, Albert (1995)	5.5
295	Grich, Bobby (1974)	5.5
296	Menke, Denis (1964)	5.5
297	Thome, Jim (2002)	5.5
298	Pendleton, Terry (1991)	5.5
299	Peckinpaugh, Roger (1919)	5.5
300	Kauff, Benny (1914)	5.5

Wins – 1901-2003

1	Chesbro, Jack (1904)	41
2	Walsh, Ed (1908)	40
3	Mathewson, Christy (1908)	37
4	Johnson, Walter (1913)	36
5	McGinnity, Joe (1904)	35
6	Wood, Joe (1912)	34
7	Alexander, Grover (1916)	33
	Johnson, Walter (1912)	33
	Mathewson, Christy (1904)	33
	Young, Cy (1901)	33
11	Young, Cy (1902)	32
12	Alexander, Grover (1915)	31
	Bagby, Jim (1920)	31
	Coombs, Jack (1910)	31
	Grove, Lefty (1931)	31
	Mathewson, Christy (1905)	31
	McGinnity, Joe (1903)	31
	McLain, Denny (1968)	31
19	Alexander, Grover (1917)	30
	Dean, Dizzy (1934)	30
	Mathewson, Christy (1903)	30
22	Brown, Mordecai (1908)	29
	Cicotte, Eddie (1919)	29
	Hendrix, Claude (1914)	29
	Mullin, George (1909)	29
	Newhouser, Hal (1944)	29
27	Alexander, Grover (1911)	28
	Chesbro, Jack (1902)	28
	Cicotte, Eddie (1917)	28
	Coombs, Jack (1911)	28
	Dean, Dizzy (1935)	28
	Grove, Lefty (1930)	28
	Johnson, Walter (1914)	28
	Roberts, Robin (1952)	28
	Vance, Dazzy (1924)	28
	Young, Cy (1903)	28
37	Alexander, Grover (1920)	27
	Alexander, Grover (1914)	27
	Brown, Mordecai (1909)	27
	Carlton, Steve (1972)	27
	Feller, Bob (1940)	27
	Johnson, Walter (1915)	27
	Joss, Addie (1907)	27
	Koufax, Sandy (1966)	27
	Luque, Dolf (1923)	27
	Mathewson, Christy (1910)	27
	Mays, Carl (1921)	27
	McGinnity, Joe (1906)	27
	Newcombe, Don (1956)	27
	Orth, Al (1906)	27
	Pittinger, Togie (1902)	27
	Rommel, Eddie (1922)	27
	Seaton, Tom (1913)	27
	Shocker, Urban (1921)	27
	Trout, Dizzy (1944)	27
	Uhle, George (1926)	27
	Waddell, Rube (1905)	27
	Walsh, Ed (1912)	27
	Walsh, Ed (1911)	27
	Walters, Bucky (1939)	27
	Welch, Bob (1990)	27
	White, Doc (1907)	27
	Willis, Vic (1902)	27
64	24 players tied	26

Wins – pre-1901

1	Radbourn, Charley (1884)	59
2	Clarkson, John (1885)	53
3	Hecker, Guy (1884)	52
4	Clarkson, John (1889)	49
5	Buffinton, Charlie (1884)	48
	Radbourn, Charley (1883)	48
7	Spalding, Al (1876)	47
	Ward, John (1879)	47
9	Galvin, Pud (1883)	46
	Galvin, Pud (1884)	46
	Kilroy, Matt (1887)	46
12	Bradley, George (1876)	45
	King, Silver (1888)	45
	McCormick, Jim (1880)	45
15	Hutchison, Bill (1891)	44
	Welch, Mickey (1885)	44
17	Bond, Tommy (1879)	43
	Corcoran, Larry (1880)	43
	White, Will (1879)	43
	White, Will (1883)	43
21	Baldwin, Lady (1886)	42
	Hutchison, Bill (1890)	42
	Keefe, Tim (1886)	42
24	3 players tied	41

Losses – 1901-2003

1	Willis, Vic (1905)	29
2	Bell, George (1910)	27
	Derringer, Paul (1933)	27
	Taylor, Dummy (1901)	27
5	Dorner, Gus (1906)	26
	Groom, Bob (1909)	26
	Townsend, Happy (1904)	26
8	Cantwell, Ben (1935)	25
	Dowling, Pete (1901)	25
	Flaherty, Patsy (1903)	25
	Glade, Fred (1905)	25
	Johnson, Walter (1909)	25
	Jones, Oscar (1904)	25
	McGlynn, Stoney (1907)	25
	McIntire, Harry (1905)	25
	Perry, Scott (1920)	25
	Raymond, Bugs (1908)	25
	Ruffing, Red (1928)	25
	Willis, Vic (1904)	25
	Young, Irv (1906)	25
21	Bush, Joe (1916)	24
	Caraway, Pat (1931)	24
	Craig, Roger (1962)	24
	Curtis, Cliff (1910)	24
	Fisher, Jack (1965)	24
	Fraser, Chick (1904)	24
	Gray, Dolly (1931)	24
28	Ames, Red (1914)	23
	Brown, Buster (1910)	23
	Cronin, Jack (1904)	23
	Ferguson, George (1909)	23
	Hughes, Tom (1901)	23
	Hughes, Tom (1904)	23
	Jacobson, Beany (1904)	23
	Lindaman, Vive (1906)	23
	Luque, Dolf (1922)	23
	Meadows, Lee (1916)	23
	Mullin, George (1904)	23
	Myers, Elmer (1916)	23
	Naylor, Rollie (1920)	23
	Overall, Orval (1905)	23
	Patten, Case (1904)	23
	Rommel, Eddie (1921)	23
	Wilhelm, Kaiser (1905)	23
	Young, Irv (1907)	23
46	Bonham, Bill (1974)	22
	Carrick, Bill (1901)	22
	Craig, Roger (1963)	22
	Ditmar, Art (1956)	22
	Ellsworth, Dick (1966)	22
	Griner, Dan (1913)	22
	Howell, Harry (1905)	22
	Johnson, Si (1934)	22
	Jones, Randy (1974)	22
	Lake, Joe (1908)	22
	Marquard, Rube (1914)	22
	McLain, Denny (1971)	22
	Mulcahy, Hugh (1940)	22
	Orth, Al (1903)	22
	Patten, Case (1903)	22
	Patten, Case (1905)	22
	Pfeffer, Big Jeff (1906)	22
	Pittinger, Togie (1903)	22
	Quinn, Jack (1915)	22
	Rixey, Eppa (1920)	22
	Roberts, Robin (1957)	22
	Rogers, Steve (1974)	22
	Ruffing, Red (1929)	22
	Tyler, Lefty (1912)	22
	Wilhelm, Kaiser (1908)	22
	Wyckoff, Weldon (1915)	22
72	47 players tied	21

Losses – pre-1901

1	Coleman, John (1883)	48
2	White, Will (1880)	42
3	McKeon, Larry (1884)	41
4	Bradley, George (1879)	40
	McCormick, Jim (1879)	40
6	Carsey, Kid (1891)	37
	Cobb, George (1892)	37
	Porter, Henry (1888)	37
9	Hutchison, Bill (1892)	36
	Wiedman, Stump (1886)	36
11	Devlin, Jim (1876)	35
	Donahue, Red (1897)	35
	Galvin, Pud (1880)	35
	Henderson, Hardie (1885)	35
	Sullivan, Fleury (1884)	35
	Terry, Adonis (1884)	35
17	Barr, Bob (1884)	34
	Kilroy, Matt (1886)	34
	Mathews, Bobby (1876)	34
	Mays, Al (1887)	34
	Rusie, Amos (1890)	34
22	6 players tied	33

Winning Percentage – Starters

1	Allen, Johnny (1937)	.938
2	Werden, Perry (1884)	.923
3	Maddux, Greg (1995)	.905
4	Johnson, Randy (1995)	.900
5	Guidry, Ron (1978)	.893
6	Grove, Lefty (1931)	.886
7	Roe, Preacher (1951)	.880
8	Goldsmith, Fred (1880)	.875
	McCormick, Jim (1884)	.875
	Seaver, Tom (1981)	.875
11	Wood, Joe (1912)	.872
12	Clemens, Roger (2001)	.870
	Cone, David (1988)	.870
14	Hershiser, Orel (1985)	.864
15	Donovan, Bill (1907)	.862
	Ford, Whitey (1961)	.862
	Taylor, Billy (1884)	.862
18	Bere, Jason (1994)	.857
	Clemens, Roger (1986)	.857
	Gooden, Dwight (1985)	.857
	Hodnett, Charlie (1884)	.857
	Nagy, Mike (1969)	.857
	Wheeler, Harry (1878)	.857
24	Martinez, Pedro (1999)	.852
25	Bender, Chief (1914)	.850
	Smoltz, John (1998)	.850
27	Grove, Lefty (1930)	.848
28	Hampton, Mike (1999)	.846
	Roe, Preacher (1952)	.846
30	Consuegra, Sandy (1954)	.842
	Hughes, Tom (1916)	.842
	Rowe, Schoolboy (1940)	.842
	Terry, Ralph (1961)	.842
	Yde, Emil (1924)	.842
35	Gomez, Lefty (1934)	.839
36	Hoffer, Bill (1895)	.838
	McLain, Denny (1968)	.838
38	Johnson, Walter (1913)	.837
39	Boyle, Henry (1884)	.833
	Chandler, Spud (1943)	.833
	Cole, King (1910)	.833
	Johnson, Randy (1997)	.833
	Koufax, Sandy (1963)	.833
	Martinez, Pedro (2002)	.833
	Wilhelm, Hoyt (1952)	.833
46	Radbourn, Charley (1884)	.831
47	Johnson, Randy (2002)	.828
48	Maddux, Greg (1997)	.826
	Reulbach, Ed (1906)	.826
	Riddle, Elmer (1941)	.826
51	Chesbro, Jack (1902)	.824
	Guzman, Juan (1993)	.824
	Hughes, Jay (1899)	.824
	Moose, Bob (1969)	.824
	Simpson, Wayne (1970)	.824
	Vance, Dazzy (1924)	.824
57	Bender, Chief (1910)	.821
	Purkey, Bob (1962)	.821
	Zito, Barry (2002)	.821
60	Maglie, Sal (1950)	.818
	Portugal, Mark (1993)	.818
	Welch, Bob (1990)	.818
	Wells, David (1998)	.818
64	McGinnity, Joe (1904)	.814
65	Brown, Mordecai (1906)	.813
	Ford, Russ (1910)	.813
	Haas, Moose (1983)	.813
	Hubbell, Carl (1936)	.813
	Plank, Eddie (1912)	.813
	Wiltse, Hooks (1904)	.813
71	Dean, Dizzy (1934)	.811
72	Abbott, Paul (2001)	.810
	Allen, Johnny (1932)	.810
	Crandall, Doc (1910)	.810
	Key, Jimmy (1994)	.810
	Niekro, Phil (1982)	.810
	Reulbach, Ed (1907)	.810
	Wilks, Ted (1944)	.810
79	Bonham, Tiny (1942)	.808
	Crowder, Alvin (1928)	.808
	Hunter, Catfish (1973)	.808
	Jansen, Larry (1947)	.808
	McNally, Dave (1971)	.808
	Newsom, Bobo (1940)	.808
85	Camnitz, Howie (1909)	.806
	Ferriss, Dave (1946)	.806
	Marichal, Juan (1966)	.806
	Mathewson, Christy (1909)	.806
89	Cicotte, Eddie (1919)	.806
90	16 players tied	.800

Games – 1901-2003

1	Marshall, Mike (1974)	106
2	Tekulve, Kent (1979)	94
3	Marshall, Mike (1973)	92
4	Tekulve, Kent (1978)	91
5	Granger, Wayne (1969)	90
	Marshall, Mike (1979)	90
	Tekulve, Kent (1987)	90
8	Eichhorn, Mark (1987)	89
	Kline, Steve (2001)	89
	Quantrill, Paul (2003)	89
	Tavarez, Julian (1997)	89
12	Myers, Mike (1997)	88
	Runyan, Sean (1998)	88
	Wood, Wilbur (1968)	88
15	Murphy, Rob (1987)	87
16	Quantrill, Paul (2002)	86
	Villarreal, Oscar (2003)	86
18	Tekulve, Kent (1982)	85
	Williams, Frank (1987)	85
	Williams, Mitch (1987)	85
21	Abernathy, Ted (1965)	84
	Belinda, Stan (1997)	84
	Koch, Billy (2002)	84
	Lloyd, Graeme (2001)	84
	Quisenberry, Dan (1985)	84
	Romo, Enrique (1979)	84
	Tidrow, Dick (1980)	84
28	Dotel, Octavio (2002)	83
	Guardado, Eddie (1996)	83
	Kline, Steve (2000)	83
	Lefferts, Craig (1986)	83
	Myers, Mike (1996)	83
	Sanders, Ken (1971)	83
	Wunsch, Kelly (2000)	83
35	Agosto, Juan (1990)	82
	Campbell, Bill (1983)	82
	Fassero, Jeff (2001)	82
	Fisher, Eddie (1965)	82
	King, Ray (2001)	82
	Kline, Steve (1999)	82
	Quantrill, Paul (1998)	82
42	Beck, Rod (1998)	81
	Boever, Joe (1992)	81
	Clontz, Brad (1996)	81
	Jackson, Mike (1993)	81
	Murray, Dale (1976)	81
	Robinson, Jeff (1987)	81
	Rogers, Kenny (1992)	81
	Romero, J.C. (2002)	81
	Stanton, Mike (1996)	81
	Swindell, Greg (1998)	81
	Ward, Duane (1991)	81
	Wyatt, John (1964)	81
54	Borbon, Pedro (1973)	80
	Harris, Greg (1993)	80
	Hernandez, Willie (1984)	80
	Jones, Doug (1992)	80
	King, Ray (2003)	80
	Martin, Tom (2003)	80
	Quantrill, Paul (2001)	80
	Rodriguez, Felix (2001)	80
	Weathers, Dave (2001)	80
	Wendell, Turk (1999)	80
	Williams, Mitch (1986)	80
	Worrell, Tim (2002)	80
66	12 players tied	79

Games – pre-1901

1	Galvin, Pud (1883)	76
	Radbourn, Charley (1883)	76
	White, Will (1879)	76
4	Hecker, Guy (1884)	75
	Hutchison, Bill (1892)	75
	Radbourn, Charley (1884)	75
7	McCormick, Jim (1880)	74
	Richmond, Lee (1880)	74
9	Clarkson, John (1889)	73
10	Galvin, Pud (1884)	72
11	Hutchison, Bill (1890)	71
12	Clarkson, John (1885)	70
	Ward, John (1879)	70
	Ward, John (1880)	70
15	Kilroy, Matt (1887)	69
16	Devlin, Jim (1876)	68
	Keefe, Tim (1883)	68
	Kilroy, Matt (1886)	68
	McCormick, Jim (1882)	68
20	Buffinton, Charlie (1884)	67
	Mullane, Tony (1884)	67
	Ramsey, Toad (1886)	67
	Rusie, Amos (1890)	67
24	4 players tied	66

Games Started – 1901-2003

1	Chesbro, Jack (1904)	51
2	Walsh, Ed (1908)	49
	Wood, Wilbur (1972)	49
4	McGinnity, Joe (1903)	48
	Wood, Wilbur (1973)	48
6	Davenport, Dave (1915)	46
	Mathewson, Christy (1904)	46
	Waddell, Rube (1904)	46
	Walsh, Ed (1907)	46
	Willis, Vic (1902)	46
11	Alexander, Grover (1916)	45
	Lolich, Mickey (1971)	45
	Powell, Jack (1904)	45
14	Alexander, Grover (1917)	44
	Mathewson, Christy (1908)	44
	McGinnity, Joe (1904)	44
	Mullin, George (1904)	44
	Niekro, Phil (1979)	44
	Uhle, George (1923)	44
20	Falkenberg, Cy (1914)	43
	McGinnity, Joe (1901)	43
	Niekro, Phil (1977)	43
	Plank, Eddie (1904)	43
	Rudolph, Dick (1915)	43
	Taylor, Dummy (1901)	43
	Willis, Vic (1904)	43
	Wood, Wilbur (1975)	43
	Young, Cy (1902)	43
29	Alexander, Grover (1915)	42
	Bahnsen, Stan (1973)	42
	Chesbro, Jack (1906)	42
	Dineen, Bill (1902)	42
	Drysdale, Don (1965)	42
	Drysdale, Don (1963)	42
	Feller, Bob (1946)	42
	Friend, Bob (1956)	42
	Hahn, Noodles (1901)	42
	Jenkins, Fergie (1969)	42
	Johnson, Walter (1910)	42
	Kaat, Jim (1965)	42
	Lolich, Mickey (1973)	42
	Mathewson, Christy (1903)	42
	McQuillan, George (1908)	42
	Mullin, George (1907)	42
	Niekro, Phil (1978)	42
	Quinn, Jack (1914)	42
	Sanford, Jack (1963)	42
	Schneider, Pete (1917)	42
	Toney, Fred (1917)	42
	Wood, Wilbur (1971)	42
	Wood, Wilbur (1974)	42
	Young, Irv (1905)	42
53	35 players tied	41

Games Started – pre-1901

1	Galvin, Pud (1883)	75
	White, Will (1879)	75
3	McCormick, Jim (1880)	74
4	Hecker, Guy (1884)	73
	Radbourn, Charley (1884)	73
6	Clarkson, John (1889)	72
	Galvin, Pud (1884)	72
8	Clarkson, John (1885)	70
	Hutchison, Bill (1892)	70
10	Kilroy, Matt (1887)	69
11	Devlin, Jim (1876)	68
	Keefe, Tim (1883)	68
	Kilroy, Matt (1886)	68
	Radbourn, Charley (1883)	68
15	Buffinton, Charlie (1884)	67
	McCormick, Jim (1882)	67
	Ramsey, Toad (1886)	67
	Ward, John (1880)	67
19	Galvin, Pud (1879)	66
	Hutchison, Bill (1890)	66
	Richmond, Lee (1880)	66
22	King, Silver (1888)	65
	Mullane, Tony (1884)	65
	Welch, Mickey (1884)	65
25	6 players tied	64

Complete Games – 1901-2003

1	Chesbro, Jack (1904)	48
2	Willis, Vic (1902)	45
3	McGinnity, Joe (1903)	44
4	Mullin, George (1904)	42
	Walsh, Ed (1908)	42
6	Hahn, Noodles (1901)	41
	Young, Cy (1902)	41
	Young, Irv (1905)	41
9	Young, Cy (1904)	40
10	Dineen, Bill (1902)	39
	McGinnity, Joe (1901)	39
	Taylor, Jack (1904)	39
	Waddell, Rube (1904)	39
	Willis, Vic (1904)	39
15	Alexander, Grover (1916)	38
	Johnson, Walter (1910)	38
	Jones, Oscar (1904)	38
	McGinnity, Joe (1904)	38
	Powell, Jack (1904)	38
	Young, Cy (1901)	38
21	Dineen, Bill (1904)	37
	Mathewson, Christy (1903)	37
	Patten, Case (1904)	37
	Plank, Eddie (1904)	37
	Smith, Frank (1909)	37
	Taylor, Dummy (1901)	37
	Walsh, Ed (1907)	37
	Young, Irv (1906)	37
29	Alexander, Grover (1915)	36
	Donovan, Bill (1901)	36
	Feller, Bob (1946)	36
	Johnson, Walter (1911)	36
	Johnson, Walter (1916)	36
	Mathewson, Christy (1901)	36
	Orth, Al (1906)	36
	Orth, Al (1902)	36
	Pittinger, Togie (1902)	36
	Powell, Jack (1902)	36
	Willis, Vic (1905)	36
40	Bernhard, Bill (1904)	35
	Coombs, Jack (1910)	35
	Fraser, Chick (1901)	35
	Fraser, Chick (1905)	35
	Hahn, Noodles (1902)	35
	Howell, Harry (1905)	35
	Johnson, Walter (1915)	35
	Miller, Roscoe (1901)	35
	Mullin, George (1906)	35
	Mullin, George (1905)	35
	Mullin, George (1907)	35
	Nichols, Kid (1904)	35
	Pittinger, Togie (1903)	35
	Pittinger, Togie (1904)	35
	Plank, Eddie (1905)	35
	Ruth, Babe (1917)	35
	Wood, Joe (1912)	35
57	Alexander, Grover (1917)	34
	Carrick, Bill (1901)	34
	Donovan, Bill (1903)	34
	Hahn, Noodles (1903)	34
	Hendrix, Claude (1914)	34
	Johnson, Walter (1912)	34
	Joss, Addie (1907)	34
	Mathewson, Christy (1908)	34
	Owen, Frank (1904)	34
	Taylor, Jack (1905)	34
	Waddell, Rube (1903)	34
	White, Doc (1902)	34
	Young, Cy (1903)	34
70	29 players tied	33

Complete Games – pre-1901

1	White, Will (1879)	75
2	Radbourn, Charley (1884)	73
3	Galvin, Pud (1883)	72
	Hecker, Guy (1884)	72
	McCormick, Jim (1880)	72
6	Galvin, Pud (1884)	71
7	Clarkson, John (1885)	68
	Clarkson, John (1889)	68
	Keefe, Tim (1883)	68
10	Hutchison, Bill (1892)	67
11	Devlin, Jim (1876)	66
	Kilroy, Matt (1886)	66
	Kilroy, Matt (1887)	66
	Radbourn, Charley (1883)	66
	Ramsey, Toad (1886)	66
16	Galvin, Pud (1879)	65
	Hutchison, Bill (1890)	65
	McCormick, Jim (1882)	65
19	King, Silver (1888)	64
	Mullane, Tony (1884)	64
	Welch, Mickey (1880)	64
	White, Will (1883)	64
23	4 players tied	63

Shutouts – 1901-2003

1	Alexander, Grover (1916)	16
2	Coombs, Jack (1910)	13
	Gibson, Bob (1968)	13
4	Alexander, Grover (1915)	12
5	Chance, Dean (1964)	11
	Johnson, Walter (1913)	11
	Koufax, Sandy (1963)	11
	Mathewson, Christy (1908)	11
	Walsh, Ed (1908)	11
10	Cooper, Mort (1942)	10
	Davenport, Dave (1915)	10
	Feller, Bob (1946)	10
	Hubbell, Carl (1933)	10
	Lemon, Bob (1948)	10
	Marichal, Juan (1965)	10
	Palmer, Jim (1975)	10
	Tudor, John (1985)	10
	Walsh, Ed (1906)	10
	Wood, Joe (1912)	10
	Young, Cy (1904)	10
21	Alexander, Grover (1919)	9
	Alexander, Grover (1913)	9
	Blyleven, Bert (1973)	9
	Brown, Mordecai (1906)	9
	Brown, Mordecai (1908)	9
	Coveleski, Stan (1917)	9
	Falkenberg, Cy (1914)	9
	Guidry, Ron (1978)	9
	Johnson, Walter (1914)	9
	Joss, Addie (1906)	9
	Joss, Addie (1908)	9
	Lee, Bill (1938)	9
	McGinnity, Joe (1904)	9
	McLain, Denny (1969)	9
	Overall, Orval (1909)	9
	Porterfield, Bob (1953)	9
	Ruth, Babe (1916)	9
	Ryan, Nolan (1972)	9
	Sutton, Don (1972)	9
	Tiant, Luis (1968)	9
41	43 players tied	8

Shutouts – pre-1901

1	Bradley, George (1876)	16
2	Galvin, Pud (1884)	12
	Morris, Ed (1886)	12
4	Bond, Tommy (1879)	11
	Foutz, Dave (1886)	11
	Radbourn, Charley (1884)	11
7	Clarkson, John (1885)	10
8	Bond, Tommy (1878)	9
	Derby, George (1881)	9
	Young, Cy (1892)	9
11	Buffinton, Charlie (1884)	8
	Clarkson, John (1889)	8
	Keefe, Tim (1888)	8
	Sanders, Ben (1888)	8
	Spalding, Al (1876)	8
	Ward, John (1880)	8
	White, Will (1882)	8
18	11 players tied	7

Saves – 1901-2003

1	Thigpen, Bobby (1990)	57
2	Gagne, Eric (2003)	55
	Smoltz, John (2002)	55
4	Hoffman, Trevor (1998)	53
	Myers, Randy (1993)	53
6	Gagne, Eric (2002)	52
7	Beck, Rod (1998)	51
	Eckersley, Dennis (1992)	51
9	Rivera, Mariano (2001)	50
10	Beck, Rod (1993)	48
	Eckersley, Dennis (1990)	48
	Shaw, Jeff (1998)	48
13	Smith, Lee (1991)	47
14	Gordon, Tom (1998)	46
	Harvey, Bryan (1991)	46
	Mesa, Jose (1995)	46
	Righetti, Dave (1986)	46
	Williams, Mike (2002)	46
19	Alfonseca, Antonio (2000)	45
	Eckersley, Dennis (1988)	45
	Guardado, Eddie (2002)	45
	Harvey, Bryan (1993)	45
	Mesa, Jose (2002)	45
	Montgomery, Jeff (1993)	45
	Myers, Randy (1997)	45
	Nen, Robb (2001)	45
	Quisenberry, Dan (1983)	45
	Rivera, Mariano (1999)	45
	Sasaki, Kazuhiro (2001)	45
	Smoltz, John (2003)	45
	Sutter, Bruce (1984)	45
	Ward, Duane (1993)	45
33	Brantley, Jeff (1996)	44
	Davis, Mark (1989)	44
	Koch, Billy (2002)	44
	Quisenberry, Dan (1984)	44
	Wagner, Billy (2003)	44
	Worrell, Todd (1996)	44
39	Benitez, Armando (2001)	43
	Eckersley, Dennis (1991)	43
	Foulke, Keith (2003)	43
	Hernandez, Roberto (1999)	43
	Hoffman, Trevor (2001)	43
	Hoffman, Trevor (2000)	43
	Jones, Doug (1990)	43
	Nen, Robb (2002)	43
	Rivera, Mariano (1997)	43
	Shaw, Jeff (2001)	43
	Smith, Lee (1993)	43
	Smith, Lee (1992)	43
	Wetteland, John (1999)	43
	Wetteland, John (1993)	43
	Wetteland, John (1996)	43
	Williams, Mitch (1993)	43
55	Aguilera, Rick (1991)	42
	Foulke, Keith (2001)	42
	Hoffman, Trevor (1996)	42
	Jones, Todd (2000)	42
	Lowe, Derek (2000)	42
	Mesa, Jose (2001)	42
	Percival, Troy (1998)	42
	Reardon, Jeff (1988)	42
	Shaw, Jeff (1997)	42
	Wetteland, John (1998)	42
65	Aguilera, Rick (1992)	41
	Benitez, Armando (2000)	41
	Guardado, Eddie (2003)	41
	Jimenez, Jose (2002)	41
	Nen, Robb (2000)	41
	Reardon, Jeff (1985)	41
	Urbina, Ugueth (1999)	41
72	9 players tied	40

Saves – pre-1901

1	Manning, Jack (1876)	5
	Mullane, Tony (1889)	5
3	Goodall, Herb (1890)	4
	Kitson, Frank (1900)	4
	Mullane, Tony (1894)	4
	Nichols, Kid (1898)	4
	Taylor, Billy (1884)	4
8	Beam, Ernie (1895)	3
	Burns, Oyster (1885)	3
	Clarkson, John (1891)	3
	Hawke, Bill (1894)	3
	Hemming, George (1890)	3
	Leever, Sam (1899)	3
	Mercer, Win (1894)	3
	Mercer, Win (1897)	3
	Nichols, Kid (1895)	3
	Nichols, Kid (1891)	3
	Nichols, Kid (1897)	3
	O'Day, Hank (1890)	3
	Parrott, Tom (1895)	3
	Richmond, Lee (1880)	3
	Terry, Adonis (1887)	3
	Weyhing, Gus (1892)	3
	Young, Cy (1896)	3
25	65 players tied	2

Relief Games

1	Marshall, Mike, 1974	106
2	Tekulve, Kent, 1979	94
3	Marshall, Mike, 1973	92
4	Tekulve, Kent, 1978	91
5	Granger, Wayne, 1969	90
	Tekulve, Kent, 1987	90
7	Marshall, Mike, 1979	89
	Eichhorn, Mark, 1987	89
	Tavarez, Julian, 1997	89
	Kline, Steve, 2001	89
	Quantrill, Paul, 2003	89
12	Myers, Mike, 1997	88
	Runyan, Sean, 1998	88
14	Murphy, Rob, 1987	87
15	Wood, Wilbur, 1968	86
	Quantrill, Paul, 2002	86
17	Tekulve, Kent, 1982	85
	Williams, Frank, 1987	85
	Villarreal, Oscar, 2003	85
20	Abernathy, Ted, 1965	84
	Romo, Enrique, 1979	84
	Tidrow, Dick, 1980	84
	Quisenberry, Dan, 1985	84
	Williams, Mitch, 1987	84
	Belinda, Stan, 1997	84
	Lloyd, Graeme, 2001	84
	Koch, Billy, 2002	84

Relief Innings

1	Marshall, Mike, 1974	208.1
2	Marshall, Mike, 1973	179.0
3	Stanley, Bob, 1982	168.1
4	Campbell, Bob, 1976	167.2
5	Karl, Andy, 1945	166.2
6	Fisher, Eddie, 1965	165.1
7	Wilhelm, Hoyt, 1952	159.1
8	Radatz, Dick, 1964	157.0
	Eichhorn, Mark, 1986	157.0
10	Konstanty, Jim, 1950	152.0
11	Hiller, John, 1974	15.0
12	Johnson, Tom, 1977	146.2
13	Braxton, Garland, 1927	146.0
14	Stanley, Bob, 1983	145.1
15	Wilhelm, Hoyt, 1953	145.0
	Wood, Wilbur, 1968	145.0
17	Russell, Allan, 1923	144.2
	Granger, Wayne, 1969	144.2
19	Foucault, Steve, 1974	144.1
20	Wilhelm, Hoyt, 1965	144.0
21	Kern, Jim, 1979	143.0
22	Hough, Charlie, 1976	142.2
23	Gossage, Rich, 1975	141.2
24	Marshall, Mike, 1979	14.2
25	Stewart, Sammy, 1983	14.1
	Hernandez, Willie, 1984	14.1

Relief Wins

1	Face, Roy, 1959	18
2	Hiller, John, 1974	17
	Campbell, Bill, 1976	17
4	Konstanty, Jim, 1950	16
	Perranoski, Ron, 1963	16
	Radatz, Dick, 1964	16
	Johnson, Tom, 1977	16
8	Brown, Mace, 1938	15
	Willhelm, Hoy, 1952	15
	Arroyo, Luis, 1961	15
	Radatz, Dick, 1963	15
	Fisher, Eddie, 1965	15
	Marshall, Mike, 1974	15
	Murray, Dale, 1975	15
15	Several tied	14

Relief Losses

1	Garber, Gene, 1979	16
2	Knowles, Darold, 1970	14
	Hiller, John, 1974	14
	Marshall, Mike, 1975	14
	Marshall, Mike, 1979	14
6	Wood, Wilbur, 1970	13
	Fingers, Rollie, 1978	13
	Lockwood, Skip, 1978	13
9	Several tied	12

Innings Pitched – 1901-2003

1	Walsh, Ed (1908)	464.0
2	Chesbro, Jack (1904)	454.2
3	McGinnity, Joe (1903)	434.0
4	Walsh, Ed (1907)	422.1
5	Willis, Vic (1902)	410.0
6	McGinnity, Joe (1904)	408.0
7	Walsh, Ed (1912)	393.0
8	Davenport, Dave (1915)	392.2
9	Mathewson, Christy (1908)	390.2
10	Powell, Jack (1904)	390.1
11	Pittinger, Togie (1902)	389.1
12	Alexander, Grover (1916)	389.0
13	Alexander, Grover (1917)	388.0
14	Young, Cy (1902)	384.2
15	Waddell, Rube (1904)	383.0
16	Mullin, George (1904)	382.1
17	McGinnity, Joe (1901)	382.0
18	Young, Cy (1904)	380.0
19	Young, Irv (1905)	378.0
20	Falkenberg, Cy (1914)	377.1
21	Jones, Oscar (1904)	377.0
22	Wood, Wilbur (1972)	376.2
23	Alexander, Grover (1915)	376.1
24	Lolich, Mickey (1971)	376.0
25	Hahn, Noodles (1901)	375.1
26	Johnson, Walter (1914)	371.2
27	Dineen, Bill (1902)	371.1
	Feller, Bob (1946)	371.1
	Young, Cy (1901)	371.1
30	Johnson, Walter (1910)	370.0
31	Johnson, Walter (1916)	369.2
	Walsh, Ed (1910)	369.2
33	Johnson, Walter (1912)	369.0
34	Walsh, Ed (1911)	368.2
35	Mathewson, Christy (1904)	367.2
36	Alexander, Grover (1911)	367.0
37	Mathewson, Christy (1903)	366.1
38	Smith, Frank (1909)	365.0
39	Alexander, Grover (1920)	363.1
40	Hendrix, Claude (1914)	362.0
41	McQuillan, George (1908)	359.2
42	Wood, Wilbur (1973)	359.1
43	Young, Irv (1906)	358.1
44	Patten, Case (1904)	357.2
	Uhle, George (1923)	357.2
46	Mullin, George (1907)	357.1
	Plank, Eddie (1904)	357.1
48	Alexander, Grover (1914)	355.0
49	Taylor, Dummy (1901)	353.1
50	Coombs, Jack (1910)	353.0
51	McGlynn, Stoney (1907)	352.1
	Trout, Dizzy (1944)	352.1
53	Faber, Red (1922)	352.0
	Taylor, Jack (1904)	352.0
55	Pittinger, Togie (1903)	351.2
56	Donovan, Bill (1901)	351.0
57	Willis, Vic (1904)	350.0
58	Harmon, Bob (1911)	348.0
	Shocker, Urban (1922)	348.0
60	Mullin, George (1905)	347.2
61	Cicotte, Eddie (1917)	346.2
	Plank, Eddie (1905)	346.2
	Roberts, Robin (1953)	346.2
64	Carlton, Steve (1972)	346.1
65	Johnson, Walter (1913)	346.0
66	Perry, Gaylord (1973)	344.0
	Wood, Joe (1912)	344.0
68	Plank, Eddie (1907)	343.2
69	Young, Cy (1907)	343.1
70	Feller, Bob (1941)	343.0
71	Brown, Mordecai (1909)	342.2
	Perry, Gaylord (1972)	342.2
	Quinn, Jack (1914)	342.2
74	Niekro, Phil (1979)	342.0
	Willis, Vic (1905)	342.0

Innings Pitched – pre-1901

1	White, Will (1879)	680.0
2	Radbourn, Charley (1884)	678.2
3	Hecker, Guy (1884)	670.2
4	McCormick, Jim (1880)	657.2
5	Galvin, Pud (1883)	656.1
6	Galvin, Pud (1884)	636.1
7	Radbourn, Charley (1883)	632.1
8	Clarkson, John (1885)	623.0
9	Devlin, Jim (1876)	622.0
	Hutchison, Bill (1892)	622.0
11	Clarkson, John (1889)	620.0
12	Keefe, Tim (1883)	619.0
13	Hutchison, Bill (1890)	603.0
14	McCormick, Jim (1882)	595.2
15	Ward, John (1880)	595.0
16	Galvin, Pud (1879)	593.0
17	Richmond, Lee (1880)	590.2
18	Kilroy, Matt (1887)	589.1
19	Ramsey, Toad (1886)	588.2
20	Buffinton, Charlie (1884)	587.0
	Ward, John (1879)	587.0
22	King, Silver (1888)	584.2
23	Kilroy, Matt (1886)	583.0
24	Morris, Ed (1885)	581.0
25	White, Will (1883)	577.0

Hits per Game – 1901-2003

1	Ryan, Nolan (1972)	5.26
2	Tiant, Luis (1968)	5.30
3	Ryan, Nolan (1991)	5.31
4	Martinez, Pedro (2000)	5.31
5	Reulbach, Ed (1906)	5.33
6	Leonard, Dutch (1914)	5.57
7	Lundgren, Carl (1907)	5.65
8	Fernandez, Sid (1985)	5.71
9	Byrne, Tommy (1949)	5.74
10	McNally, Dave (1968)	5.77
11	Koufax, Sandy (1965)	5.79
12	Ford, Russ (1910)	5.83
13	Nomo, Hideo (1995)	5.83
14	Downing, Al (1963)	5.84
15	Score, Herb (1956)	5.85
16	Gibson, Bob (1968)	5.85
17	McDowell, Sam (1965)	5.87
18	Walsh, Ed (1910)	5.89
19	Martinez, Pedro (1997)	5.89
20	Scott, Mike (1986)	5.95
21	Soto, Mario (1980)	5.96
22	Youmans, Floyd (1986)	5.96
23	Ryan, Nolan (1977)	5.96
24	Ryan, Nolan (1974)	5.98
25	Ryan, Nolan (1981)	5.98
26	Morgan, Cy (1909)	5.98
27	Ryan, Nolan (1986)	6.02
28	McDowell, Sam (1966)	6.02
29	Blue, Vida (1971)	6.03
30	Johnson, Walter (1913)	6.03
31	Bibby, Jim (1973)	6.04
32	Ryan, Nolan (1990)	6.04
33	Alexander, Grover (1915)	6.05
34	McDowell, Sam (1968)	6.06
35	Horlen, Joe (1964)	6.07
36	Messersmith, Andy (1969)	6.08
37	Ryan, Nolan (1989)	6.09
38	Coveleski, Stan (1917)	6.09
39	Hunter, Catfish (1972)	6.09
40	Ryan, Nolan (1976)	6.11
41	Fernandez, Sid (1988)	6.11
42	Turley, Bob (1957)	6.12
43	Turley, Bob (1955)	6.13
44	Sutton, Don (1972)	6.14
45	Ryan, Nolan (1983)	6.14
46	Guidry, Ron (1978)	6.15
47	Brown, Mordecai (1908)	6.17
48	Koufax, Sandy (1963)	6.19
49	Johnson, Randy (1997)	6.21
50	Pfiester, Jack (1906)	6.21
51	Koufax, Sandy (1964)	6.22
52	Nelson, Roger (1972)	6.23
53	Score, Herb (1955)	6.26
54	Morgan, Cy (1909)	6.26
55	Chance, Dean (1964)	6.27
56	Mathewson, Christy (1909)	6.28
	Richard, J.R. (1978)	6.28
58	Fromme, Art (1909)	6.28
59	Maddux, Greg (1995)	6.31
60	Johnson, Walter (1912)	6.32
61	Wood, Kerry (1998)	6.32
62	Coombs, Jack (1910)	6.32
63	Waddell, Rube (1905)	6.33
64	Gregg, Vean (1911)	6.33
65	Robinson, Jeff (1988)	6.33
66	Cheney, Larry (1916)	6.33
67	Siebert, Sonny (1968)	6.33
68	Reynolds, Allie (1943)	6.34
69	Clemens, Roger (1986)	6.34
70	Mitchell, Willie (1913)	6.35
71	DeLeon, Jose (1989)	6.36
72	Perez, Pascual (1988)	6.37
73	Johnson, Walter (1910)	6.37
74	Boswell, Dave (1966)	6.38
75	Krause, Harry (1909)	6.38

Hits per Game – pre-1901

1	Keefe, Tim (1880)	5.83
2	Sweeney, Charlie (1884)	6.23
3	McCormick, Jim (1884)	6.47
4	Shaw, Dupee (1884)	6.47
5	Hecker, Guy (1882)	6.49
6	Keefe, Tim (1888)	6.57
7	Chamberlain, Elton (1890)	6.58
8	Terry, Adonis (1888)	6.69
9	King, Silver (1888)	6.70
10	Knauss, Frank (1890)	6.73
11	Seward, Ed (1888)	6.73
12	Keefe, Tim (1885)	6.75
13	Mullane, Tony (1892)	6.77
14	Corcoran, Larry (1880)	6.78
15	Welch, Mickey (1885)	6.80
16	Titcomb, Cannonball (1888)	6.81
17	Rusie, Amos (1892)	6.82
18	Ramsey, Toad (1886)	6.83
19	Baldwin, Lady (1886)	6.86
20	Sweeney, Charlie (1884)	6.87
21	Baldwin, Lady (1885)	6.88
22	Terry, Adonis (1892)	6.94
23	Terry, Adonis (1892)	6.94
24	Welch, Mickey (1888)	6.94
25	Chamberlain, Elton (1888)	6.95

Home Runs Allowed – 1901-2003

1	Blyleven, Bert (1986)	50
2	Lima, Jose (2000)	48
3	Blyleven, Bert (1987)	46
	Roberts, Robin (1956)	46
5	Ramos, Pedro (1957)	43
6	McLain, Denny (1966)	42
7	Helling, Rick (1999)	41
	Niekro, Phil (1979)	41
	Roberts, Robin (1955)	41
10	Boskie, Shawn (1996)	40
	Jenkins, Fergie (1979)	40
	Morris, Jack (1986)	40
	Niekro, Phil (1970)	40
	Ortiz, Ramon (2002)	40
	Pena, Orlando (1964)	40
	Radke, Brad (1996)	40
	Roberts, Robin (1957)	40
	Terry, Ralph (1962)	40
19	Anderson, Brian (1998)	39
	Astacio, Pedro (1998)	39
	Dickson, Murry (1948)	39
	Hunter, Catfish (1973)	39
	Morris, Jack (1987)	39
	Perry, Jim (1971)	39
	Ramos, Pedro (1961)	39
26	Anderson, Brian (2000)	38
	Astacio, Pedro (1999)	38
	Bannister, Floyd (1987)	38
	Bunning, Jim (1963)	38
	Burdette, Lew (1959)	38
	Hacker, Warren (1955)	38
	Helling, Rick (2001)	38
	Keough, Matt (1982)	38
	Lolich, Mickey (1974)	38
	Ramos, Pedro (1958)	38
	Sutton, Don (1987)	38
	Sutton, Don (1970)	38
	Wakefield, Tim (1996)	38
	Young, Curt (1987)	38
40	Belcher, Tim (1998)	37
	Bunning, Jim (1959)	37
	Hernandez, Livan (1998)	37
	Jarvis, Kevin (2001)	37
	Jenkins, Fergie (1975)	37
	Jones, Bobby (2001)	37
	Leiter, Mark (1996)	37
	Morris, Jack (1982)	37
	Petry, Dan (1983)	37
	Schilling, Curt (2001)	37
	Tiant, Luis (1969)	37
	Viola, Frank (1986)	37
	Watson, Allen (1997)	37
	Wilson, Earl (1964)	37
54	Browning, Tom (1988)	36
	Byrd, Paul (2002)	36
	Franklin, Wayne (2003)	36
	Hough, Charlie (1987)	36
	Jansen, Larry (1949)	36
	Lieber, Jon (2000)	36
	Lolich, Mickey (1971)	36
	Mahaffey, Art (1962)	36
	Ogea, Chad (1999)	36
	Richert, Pete (1966)	36
	Suppan, Jeff (2000)	36
	Whitson, Ed (1987)	36
	Williams, Woody (1998)	36
67	24 players tied	35

Home Runs Allowed – pre-1901

1	Corcoran, Larry (1884)	35
2	Dwyer, Frank (1894)	27
	Getzein, Charlie (1889)	27
	Stivetts, Jack (1894)	27
5	Hutchison, Bill (1891)	26
6	Getzein, Charlie (1887)	24
	Healy, John (1887)	24
8	Baldwin, Mark (1887)	23
	Galvin, Pud (1884)	23
	Nichols, Kid (1894)	23
	Shreve, Lev (1888)	23
12	Carsey, Kid (1894)	22
	Staley, Harry (1893)	22
14	Breitenstein, Ted (1894)	21
	Clarkson, John (1885)	21
	Cobb, George (1892)	21
	Serad, Billy (1884)	21
	Swartzel, Park (1889)	21
19	8 players tied	20

Walks – 1901-2003

1	Feller, Bob (1938)	208
2	Ryan, Nolan (1977)	204
3	Ryan, Nolan (1974)	202
4	Feller, Bob (1941)	194
5	Newsom, Bobo (1938)	192
6	Jones, Sam (1955)	185
7	Ryan, Nolan (1976)	183
8	Harmon, Bob (1911)	181
	Turley, Bob (1954)	181
10	Byrne, Tommy (1949)	179
11	Turley, Bob (1955)	177
12	Hadley, Bump (1932)	171
13	Myers, Elmer (1916)	168
14	Newsom, Bobo (1937)	167
15	Wyckoff, Weldon (1915)	165
16	Moore, Earl (1911)	164
	Niekro, Phil (1977)	164
18	Ryan, Nolan (1973)	162
	Vander Meer, Johnny (1943)	162
20	Byrne, Tommy (1950)	160
21	O'Toole, Marty (1912)	159
22	Coleman, Joe (1974)	158
23	Lowdermilk, Grover (1915)	157
	Ryan, Nolan (1972)	157
25	Score, Herb (1955)	154
26	Feller, Bob (1946)	153
	McDowell, Sam (1971)	153
28	Donovan, Bill (1901)	152
	Johnson, Randy (1991)	152
30	Richard, J.R. (1976)	151
31	Byrne, Tommy (1951)	150
32	Davis, Dixie (1920)	149
	Fraser, Chick (1905)	149
	Newsom, Bobo (1934)	149
	Schulz, Al (1915)	149
36	Ryan, Nolan (1978)	148
37	Kennedy, Vern (1936)	147
	Overall, Orval (1905)	147
39	Lemon, Bob (1950)	146
	Newsom, Bobo (1936)	146
	Stoneman, Bill (1971)	146
42	Johnson, Randy (1992)	144
	Pittinger, Togie (1904)	144
44	Chase, Ken (1940)	143
	Pittinger, Togie (1903)	143
	Witt, Bobby (1986)	143
47	Feller, Bob (1939)	142
	Foytack, Paul (1956)	142
49	Hadley, Bump (1933)	141
	Marchildon, Phil (1947)	141
	Richard, J.R. (1978)	141
52	Cheney, Larry (1914)	140
	Marchildon, Phil (1942)	140
	Witt, Bobby (1987)	140
55	Earnshaw, George (1930)	139
	Lindell, Johnny (1953)	139
57	Krapp, Gene (1911)	138
	Mullin, George (1905)	138
	Raschi, Vic (1949)	138
	Reynolds, Allie (1950)	138
	Richard, J.R. (1975)	138
62	Cain, Sugar (1933)	137
	Gregg, Hal (1944)	137
	Lemon, Bob (1949)	137
	Newhouser, Hal (1941)	137
	Pierce, Billy (1950)	137
	Shaw, Jim (1914)	137
68	Carlton, Steve (1974)	136
	Mamaux, Al (1916)	136
	Seaton, Tom (1913)	136
71	Pearson, Monte (1936)	135
	Renko, Steve (1971)	135
	Wehmeier, Herm (1950)	135
	Wight, Bill (1948)	135
75	Parnell, Mel (1949)	134

Walks – pre-1901

1	Rusie, Amos (1890)	289
2	Baldwin, Mark (1889)	274
3	Rusie, Amos (1892)	270
4	Rusie, Amos (1891)	262
5	Baldwin, Mark (1890)	249
6	Stivetts, Jack (1891)	232
7	Baldwin, Mark (1891)	227
8	Knell, Phil (1891)	226
9	Barr, Bob (1890)	219
10	Rusie, Amos (1893)	218
11	Seymour, Cy (1898)	213
12	Weyhing, Gus (1889)	212
13	Crane, Ed (1890)	208
14	Ramsey, Toad (1886)	207
15	Chamberlain, Elton (1891)	206
16	Morrison, Mike (1887)	205
17	Gruber, Henry (1890)	204
18	Clarkson, John (1889)	203
19	Cunningham, Bert (1890)	201
20	Rusie, Amos (1894)	200
21	Hutchison, Bill (1890)	199
22	Baldwin, Mark (1892)	194
23	Breitenstein, Ted (1894)	191
24	Hutchison, Bill (1892)	190
25	2 players tied	189

Strikeouts – 1901-2003

1	Ryan, Nolan (1973)	383
2	Koufax, Sandy (1965)	382
3	Johnson, Randy (2001)	372
4	Ryan, Nolan (1974)	367
5	Johnson, Randy (1999)	364
6	Waddell, Rube (1904)	349
7	Feller, Bob (1946)	348
8	Johnson, Randy (2000)	347
9	Ryan, Nolan (1977)	341
10	Johnson, Randy (2002)	334
11	Ryan, Nolan (1972)	329
12	Ryan, Nolan (1976)	327
13	McDowell, Sam (1965)	325
14	Schilling, Curt (1997)	319
15	Koufax, Sandy (1966)	317
16	Schilling, Curt (2002)	316
17	Johnson, Walter (1910)	313
	Martinez, Pedro (1999)	313
	Richard, J.R. (1979)	313
20	Carlton, Steve (1972)	310
21	Johnson, Randy (1993)	308
	Lolich, Mickey (1971)	308
23	Koufax, Sandy (1963)	306
	Scott, Mike (1986)	306
25	Martinez, Pedro (1997)	305
26	McDowell, Sam (1970)	304
27	Johnson, Walter (1912)	303
	Richard, J.R. (1978)	303
29	Waddell, Rube (1903)	302
30	Blue, Vida (1971)	301
	Ryan, Nolan (1989)	301
32	Schilling, Curt (1998)	300
33	Johnson, Randy (1995)	294
34	Schilling, Curt (2001)	293
35	Clemens, Roger (1997)	292
36	Clemens, Roger (1988)	291
	Johnson, Randy (1997)	291
38	Seaver, Tom (1971)	289
39	Waddell, Rube (1905)	287
40	Carlton, Steve (1980)	286
	Carlton, Steve (1982)	286
42	Martinez, Pedro (2000)	284
43	McDowell, Sam (1968)	283
	Seaver, Tom (1970)	283
45	McLain, Denny (1968)	280
46	McDowell, Sam (1969)	279
47	Gooden, Dwight (1984)	276
	Smoltz, John (1996)	276
	Veale, Bob (1965)	276
50	Carlton, Steve (1983)	275
	Newhouser, Hal (1946)	275
52	Gibson, Bob (1970)	274
	Jenkins, Fergie (1970)	274
	Soto, Mario (1982)	274
55	Jenkins, Fergie (1969)	273
56	Clemens, Roger (1998)	271
	Lolich, Mickey (1969)	271
58	Gibson, Bob (1965)	270
	Ryan, Nolan (1987)	270
60	Gibson, Bob (1969)	269
	Koufax, Sandy (1961)	269
	Tanana, Frank (1975)	269
	Walsh, Ed (1908)	269
64	Bunning, Jim (1965)	268
	Gibson, Bob (1968)	268
	Gooden, Dwight (1985)	268
67	Mathewson, Christy (1903)	267
68	Wood, Kerry (2003)	266
69	Maloney, Jim (1963)	265
70	Tiant, Luis (1968)	264
71	Jenkins, Fergie (1971)	263
	Score, Herb (1956)	263
73	Langston, Mark (1987)	262
	Niekro, Phil (1977)	262
	Vance, Dazzy (1924)	262

Strikeouts – pre-1901

1	Kilroy, Matt (1886)	513
2	Ramsey, Toad (1886)	499
3	Daily, Hugh (1884)	483
4	Radbourn, Charley (1884)	441
5	Buffinton, Charlie (1884)	417
6	Hecker, Guy (1884)	385
7	Sweeney, Bill (1884)	374
8	Galvin, Pud (1884)	369
9	Baldwin, Mark (1889)	368
10	Keefe, Tim (1883)	359
11	Ramsey, Toad (1887)	355
12	Henderson, Hardie (1884)	346
13	Welch, Mickey (1884)	345
	Whitney, Jim (1883)	345
15	Rusie, Amos (1890)	341
16	Rusie, Amos (1891)	337
17	Keefe, Tim (1888)	335
18	Keefe, Tim (1884)	334
19	Morris, Ed (1886)	326
20	Mullane, Tony (1884)	325
21	Baldwin, Lady (1886)	323
22	Radbourn, Charley (1883)	315
23	Hutchison, Bill (1892)	314
24	Clarkson, John (1886)	313
25	Shaw, Dupee (1884)	309

Strikeouts per Game – 1901-2003

1	Johnson, Randy (2001)	13.41
2	Martinez, Pedro (1999)	13.20
3	Wood, Kerry (1998)	12.58
4	Johnson, Randy (2000)	12.56
5	Johnson, Randy (1995)	12.35
6	Johnson, Randy (1997)	12.30
7	Johnson, Randy (1999)	12.06
8	Martinez, Pedro (2000)	11.78
9	Johnson, Randy (2002)	11.56
10	Ryan, Nolan (1987)	11.48
11	Gooden, Dwight (1984)	11.39
12	Martinez, Pedro (1997)	11.37
13	Wood, Kerry (2003)	11.35
14	Ryan, Nolan (1989)	11.32
15	Schilling, Curt (1997)	11.29
16	Wood, Kerry (2001)	11.20
17	Nomo, Hideo (1995)	11.10
18	Schilling, Curt (2002)	10.97
19	Johnson, Randy (1993)	10.86
20	Martinez, Pedro (2002)	10.79
21	McDowell, Sam (1965)	10.71
22	Johnson, Randy (1994)	10.67
23	Ryan, Nolan (1973)	10.57
24	Ryan, Nolan (1991)	10.56
25	Koufax, Sandy (1962)	10.55
26	Prior, Mark (2003)	10.43
27	Ryan, Nolan (1972)	10.43
28	McDowell, Sam (1966)	10.42
29	Clemens, Roger (1998)	10.39
30	Schilling, Curt (2003)	10.39
31	Ryan, Nolan (1976)	10.35
32	Johnson, Randy (1992)	10.31
33	Schilling, Curt (2001)	10.27
34	Ryan, Nolan (1977)	10.26
35	Cone, David (1997)	10.25
36	Koufax, Sandy (1965)	10.24
37	Ryan, Nolan (1990)	10.24
38	Johnson, Randy (1991)	10.19
39	Colon, Bartolo (2000)	10.15
40	Koufax, Sandy (1960)	10.13
41	Nomo, Hideo (1997)	10.11
42	Schilling, Curt (1998)	10.05
43	Scott, Mike (1986)	10.00
44	Nomo, Hideo (2001)	10.00
45	Ankiel, Rick (2000)	9.98
46	Ryan, Nolan (1978)	9.97
47	Clemens, Roger (1997)	9.95
48	Martinez, Pedro (2003)	9.93
49	Ryan, Nolan (1974)	9.93
50	Clemens, Roger (1988)	9.92
51	Cone, David (1990)	9.91
52	Richard, J.R. (1978)	9.90
53	Benes, Andy (1994)	9.87
54	Ryan, Nolan (1986)	9.81
55	Cone, David (1992)	9.79
56	Smoltz, John (1996)	9.79
57	Score, Herb (1955)	9.70
58	Martinez, Pedro (1998)	9.67
59	Ryan, Nolan (1984)	9.65
60	Richard, J.R. (1979)	9.64
61	Clemens, Roger (2002)	9.60
62	Soto, Mario (1982)	9.57
63	Griffin, Tom (1969)	9.56
64	Clemens, Roger (1996)	9.53
65	Maloney, Jim (1963)	9.53
66	Schmidt, Jason (2002)	9.52
67	Fernandez, Sid (1985)	9.51
68	Score, Herb (1956)	9.49
69	Koufax, Sandy (1961)	9.47
70	McDowell, Sam (1968)	9.47
71	Clement, Matt (2002)	9.44
72	Tanana, Frank (1975)	9.41
73	Vazquez, Javier (2003)	9.40
74	Wilson, Don (1969)	9.40
75	Veale, Bob (1965)	9.34

Strikeouts per Game – pre-1901

1	Shaw, Dupee (1884)	8.81
2	Daily, Hugh (1884)	8.68
3	Kilroy, Matt (1886)	7.92
4	Gagus, Charlie (1884)	7.92
5	Clarkson, John (1884)	7.78
6	Ramsey, Toad (1886)	7.63
7	Whitney, Jim (1884)	7.23
8	Dorgan, Mike (1884)	7.17
9	Burke, James (1884)	7.13
10	Henderson, Hardie (1884)	7.09
11	Keefe, Tim (1888)	6.94
12	McCormick, Jim (1884)	6.90
13	Black, Bob (1884)	6.80
14	Baldwin, Lady (1885)	6.78
15	Stivetts, Jack (1889)	6.71
16	Ramsey, Toad (1887)	6.63
17	Wise, Bill (1884)	6.62
18	Atkinson, Al (1884)	6.61
19	Getzein, Charlie (1884)	6.54
20	Davis, Daisy (1884)	6.49
21	Baldwin, Mark (1889)	6.45
22	Buffinton, Charlie (1884)	6.39
23	Sweeney, Charlie (1884)	6.38
24	Terry, Adonis (1888)	6.37
25	Morris, Ed (1884)	6.33

Ratio – 1901-2003

1	Martinez, Pedro (2000)	.737
2	Johnson, Walter (1913)	.780
3	Joss, Addie (1908)	.806
4	Maddux, Greg (1995)	.811
5	Walsh, Ed (1910)	.820
6	Mathewson, Christy (1909)	.828
7	Mathewson, Christy (1908)	.837
8	Brown, Mordecai (1908)	.842
9	Alexander, Grover (1915)	.842
10	McNally, Dave (1968)	.842
11	Gibson, Bob (1968)	.853
12	Koufax, Sandy (1965)	.855
13	Marichal, Juan (1966)	.859
14	Walsh, Ed (1908)	.860
15	Young, Cy (1905)	.867
16	Tiant, Luis (1968)	.871
17	Nelson, Roger (1972)	.871
18	Brown, Mordecai (1909)	.873
19	Koufax, Sandy (1963)	.875
20	Ford, Russ (1910)	.881
21	Leonard, Dutch (1914)	.886
22	Young, Cy (1908)	.893
23	Maddux, Greg (1994)	.896
24	Adams, Babe (1919)	.896
25	White, Doc (1906)	.903
26	McLain, Denny (1968)	.905
27	Johnson, Walter (1912)	.908
28	Cicotte, Eddie (1917)	.912
29	Sutton, Don (1972)	.913
30	Johnson, Walter (1910)	.914
31	Hunter, Catfish (1972)	.914
	Marichal, Juan (1965)	.914
33	Bender, Chief (1910)	.916
34	Scott, Mike (1986)	.923
35	Martinez, Pedro (2002)	.923
36	Martinez, Pedro (1999)	.923
37	Alexander, Grover (1919)	.928
38	Koufax, Sandy (1964)	.928
39	Martinez, Pedro (1997)	.932
40	Joss, Addie (1906)	.933
41	Johnson, Walter (1915)	.933
42	Burns, Bill (1908)	.933
43	Mathewson, Christy (1905)	.933
44	Brown, Mordecai (1906)	.934
45	Ford, Russ (1914)	.934
46	Horlen, Joe (1964)	.935
47	Hendrix, Claude (1914)	.936
48	Young, Cy (1904)	.937
49	Chesbro, Jack (1904)	.937
50	Walsh, Ed (1909)	.938
51	Tudor, John (1985)	.938
52	Krause, Harry (1909)	.939
53	Perez, Pascual (1988)	.941
	Pfiester, Jack (1906)	.941
55	Russell, Reb (1916)	.942
56	Bernhard, Bill (1902)	.942
57	Joss, Addie (1909)	.944
58	Brown, Kevin (1996)	.944
	Brown, Mordecai (1907)	.944
60	Maddux, Greg (1997)	.946
61	Hacker, Warren (1952)	.946
62	Guidry, Ron (1978)	.946
63	Seaver, Tom (1971)	.946
64	Joss, Addie (1903)	.948
65	Hughes, Tom (1915)	.949
66	Pelty, Barney (1906)	.951
67	Blue, Vida (1971)	.952
68	Smith, Frank (1909)	.953
69	Schmidt, Jason (2003)	.953
70	Horlen, Joe (1967)	.953
71	Hughes, Dick (1967)	.954
72	Johnson, Walter (1918)	.954
73	Caldwell, Ray (1914)	.958
74	Alexander, Grover (1916)	.959
75	Saberhagen, Bret (1989)	.961

Ratio – pre-1901

1	Hecker, Guy (1882)	.769
2	McCormick, Jim (1884)	.786
3	Keefe, Tim (1880)	.800
4	Sweeney, Charlie (1884)	.812
5	Sweeney, Charlie (1884)	.824
6	Shaw, Dupee (1884)	.836
7	Bradley, George (1880)	.837
8	Boyle, Henry (1884)	.853
9	Driscoll, Denny (1882)	.866
10	Hecker, Guy (1884)	.868
11	King, Silver (1888)	.874
12	Bradley, George (1876)	.887
13	Whitney, Jim (1884)	.890
14	Morris, Ed (1884)	.898
15	Bond, Tommy (1876)	.902
16	Ward, John (1880)	.918
17	Baldwin, Lady (1885)	.920
18	Radbourn, Charley (1884)	.922
19	Lynch, Jack (1884)	.931
20	Keefe, Tim (1884)	.934
21	Keefe, Tim (1888)	.937
22	Corcoran, Larry (1880)	.938
23	Conway, Pete (1888)	.951
24	Clarkson, John (1885)	.953
25	Werden, Perry (1884)	.955

Earned Run Average – 1901-2003

1	Leonard, Dutch (1914)	0.96
2	Brown, Mordecai (1906)	1.04
3	Gibson, Bob (1968)	1.12
4	Mathewson, Christy (1909)	1.14
5	Johnson, Walter (1913)	1.14
6	Pfiester, Jack (1907)	1.15
7	Joss, Addie (1908)	1.16
8	Lundgren, Carl (1907)	1.17
9	Alexander, Grover (1915)	1.22
10	Young, Cy (1908)	1.26
11	Walsh, Ed (1910)	1.27
12	Johnson, Walter (1918)	1.27
13	Mathewson, Christy (1905)	1.28
14	Coombs, Jack (1910)	1.30
15	Brown, Mordecai (1909)	1.31
16	Taylor, Jack (1902)	1.33
17	Johnson, Walter (1910)	1.36
18	Johnson, Walter (1912)	1.39
19	Brown, Mordecai (1907)	1.39
20	Krause, Harry (1909)	1.39
21	Walsh, Ed (1909)	1.41
22	Walsh, Ed (1908)	1.42
23	Reulbach, Ed (1905)	1.42
24	Overall, Orval (1909)	1.42
25	Mathewson, Christy (1908)	1.43
26	Anderson, Fred (1917)	1.44
27	Brown, Mordecai (1908)	1.47
28	Waddell, Rube (1905)	1.48
29	Wood, Joe (1915)	1.49
30	Johnson, Walter (1919)	1.49
31	Pfiester, Jack (1906)	1.51
32	White, Doc (1906)	1.52
33	McQuillan, George (1908)	1.53
34	Gooden, Dwight (1985)	1.53
35	Cicotte, Eddie (1917)	1.53
36	Morgan, Cy (1910)	1.55
37	Alexander, Grover (1916)	1.55
38	Johnson, Walter (1915)	1.55
39	Camnitz, Howie (1908)	1.56
40	Maddux, Greg (1994)	1.56
41	Toney, Fred (1915)	1.58
42	Cicotte, Eddie (1913)	1.58
43	Marquard, Rube (1916)	1.58
44	Bender, Chief (1910)	1.58
45	Pelty, Barney (1906)	1.59
46	Joss, Addie (1904)	1.59
47	Walsh, Ed (1907)	1.60
48	Tiant, Luis (1968)	1.60
49	McGinnity, Joe (1904)	1.61
50	Collins, Ray (1910)	1.62
51	Waddell, Rube (1904)	1.62
52	Camnitz, Howie (1909)	1.62
53	Young, Cy (1901)	1.62
54	Maddux, Greg (1995)	1.63
55	Chandler, Spud (1943)	1.64
56	Shore, Ernie (1915)	1.64
57	Summers, Ed (1908)	1.64
58	Chance, Dean (1964)	1.65
59	Johnson, Walter (1908)	1.65
60	Reulbach, Ed (1906)	1.65
61	Ford, Russ (1910)	1.65
62	Bender, Chief (1909)	1.66
63	Leever, Sam (1907)	1.66
64	Hubbell, Carl (1933)	1.66
65	Wood, Joe (1910)	1.68
66	Overall, Orval (1907)	1.68
67	Garvin, Ned (1904)	1.68
68	Reulbach, Ed (1907)	1.69
69	Hendrix, Claude (1914)	1.69
70	Ryan, Nolan (1981)	1.69
71	Foster, Rube (1914)	1.70
72	Burns, Bill (1908)	1.70
73	Joss, Addie (1909)	1.71
74	Killian, Ed (1909)	1.71
75	Johnson, Walter (1914)	1.72

Adjusted ERA – 1901-2003

1	Martinez, Pedro (2000)	289
2	Leonard, Dutch (1914)	279
3	Maddux, Greg (1994)	272
4	Maddux, Greg (1995)	261
5	Gibson, Bob (1968)	258
6	Johnson, Walter (1913)	258
7	Brown, Mordecai (1906)	253
8	Johnson, Walter (1912)	241
9	Martinez, Pedro (1999)	240
10	Mathewson, Christy (1905)	229
11	Gooden, Dwight (1985)	226
12	Clemens, Roger (1997)	225
13	Alexander, Grover (1915)	224
14	Mathewson, Christy (1909)	223
15	Martinez, Pedro (1997)	221
16	Grove, Lefty (1931)	218
17	Young, Cy (1901)	217
18	Pfiester, Jack (1907)	216
19	Brown, Kevin (1996)	215
20	Johnson, Walter (1919)	215
21	Johnson, Walter (1918)	214
22	Lundgren, Carl (1907)	212
23	Clemens, Roger (1990)	211
24	Reulbach, Ed (1905)	209
25	Guidry, Ron (1978)	208
26	Martinez, Pedro (2003)	206
27	Joss, Addie (1908)	205
28	Taylor, Jack (1902)	203
29	Pierce, Billy (1955)	200
30	Luque, Dolf (1923)	200
31	Chance, Dean (1964)	199
32	Martinez, Pedro (2002)	199
33	Johnson, Randy (1997)	197
34	Chandler, Spud (1943)	197
35	Ryan, Nolan (1981)	195
36	Newhouser, Hal (1945)	194
37	Young, Cy (1908)	194
38	Seaver, Tom (1971)	193
39	Hubbell, Carl (1933)	193
40	Brown, Mordecai (1909)	193
41	Cooper, Mort (1942)	193
42	Stratton, Monty (1937)	191
43	Johnson, Randy (1995)	191
44	Johnson, Walter (1915)	191
45	Johnson, Randy (2002)	191
46	Gomez, Lefty (1937)	191
47	Koufax, Sandy (1966)	191
48	Maddux, Greg (1997)	191
49	Siever, Ed (1902)	191
50	Vance, Dazzy (1928)	190
51	Grove, Lefty (1936)	189
52	Walsh, Ed (1910)	189
53	Gregg, Vean (1911)	189
54	Newhouser, Hal (1946)	189
55	Vance, Dazzy (1930)	188
56	Wood, Wilbur (1971)	188
57	Maddux, Greg (1998)	187
58	Spahn, Warren (1953)	187
59	Koufax, Sandy (1964)	187
60	Wood, Joe (1915)	187
61	Grove, Lefty (1939)	186
62	Cicotte, Eddie (1913)	185
63	Tiant, Luis (1968)	185
64	Aguirre, Hank (1962)	184
65	Johnson, Randy (1999)	184
66	Grove, Lefty (1930)	184
67	Johnson, Randy (2001)	184
68	Horlen, Joe (1964)	184
69	Blue, Vida (1971)	183
70	Ford, Russ (1914)	183
71	Tudor, John (1985)	183
72	Brecheen, Harry (1948)	183
73	Johnson, Walter (1910)	183
74	Coombs, Jack (1910)	182
75	Carlton, Steve (1972)	182

Pitching Runs – 1901-2003

1	Young, Cy (1901)	84
2	Johnson, Walter (1912)	80
3	Martinez, Pedro (2000)	76
4	Grove, Lefty (1931)	74
5	Clemens, Roger (1997)	74
6	Luque, Dolf (1923)	74
7	Gomez, Lefty (1937)	71
8	Johnson, Walter (1913)	69
9	Grove, Lefty (1930)	68
10	Vance, Dazzy (1930)	68
11	Gomez, Lefty (1934)	68
12	Koufax, Sandy (1966)	67
13	Faber, Red (1921)	66
14	Martinez, Pedro (1999)	66
15	Spahn, Warren (1953)	65
16	Mathewson, Christy (1905)	65
17	Alexander, Grover (1915)	64
18	Gooden, Dwight (1985)	63
19	Gibson, Bob (1968)	63
20	Feller, Bob (1940)	63
21	Grove, Lefty (1936)	63
22	Johnson, Randy (1999)	63
23	Martinez, Pedro (1997)	62
24	Guidry, Ron (1978)	61
25	Hubbell, Carl (1934)	61
26	Chance, Dean (1964)	61
27	Hendrix, Claude (1914)	61
28	Young, Cy (1902)	61
29	Palmer, Jim (1975)	61
30	Brown, Kevin (1996)	60
31	Maddux, Greg (1994)	60
32	Lee, Thornton (1941)	59
33	Maddux, Greg (1995)	59
34	Roberts, Robin (1953)	59
35	Vance, Dazzy (1928)	59
36	Vance, Dazzy (1924)	58
37	Feller, Bob (1939)	58
38	Walters, Bucky (1939)	58
39	Hubbell, Carl (1936)	58
40	Wood, Wilbur (1971)	57
41	Hubbell, Carl (1933)	57
42	Blue, Vida (1971)	57
43	Carlton, Steve (1972)	57
44	Maddux, Greg (1998)	56
45	Koufax, Sandy (1965)	56
46	Johnson, Walter (1919)	56
47	Spahn, Warren (1947)	56
48	Johnson, Randy (2000)	55
49	Wood, Joe (1912)	55
50	Feller, Bob (1946)	55
51	Johnson, Walter (1918)	54
52	Seaver, Tom (1971)	54
53	Johnson, Randy (1997)	54
54	Newhouser, Hal (1945)	54
55	Harder, Mel (1934)	54
56	Johnson, Randy (1995)	53
57	Grove, Lefty (1932)	53
58	Grove, Lefty (1935)	53
59	Brown, Kevin (1998)	53
60	Luque, Dolf (1925)	53
61	Hentgen, Pat (1996)	53
62	Clemens, Roger (1998)	52
63	Brown, Kevin (2000)	52
64	Taylor, Jack (1902)	52
65	Johnson, Randy (2001)	52
66	Walsh, Ed (1912)	52
67	Maddux, Greg (1997)	52
68	Johnson, Walter (1915)	52
69	Johnson, Randy (2002)	52
70	Johnson, Walter (1911)	52
71	Trout, Dizzy (1944)	51
72	Walsh, Ed (1910)	51
73	Antonelli, Johnny (1954)	51
74	Reulbach, Ed (1905)	51
75	Newhouser, Hal (1946)	51

Adjusted Pitching Runs – 1901-2003

1	Martinez, Pedro (2000)	79
2	Grove, Lefty (1931)	70
3	Clemens, Roger (1997)	70
4	Grove, Lefty (1936)	70
5	Martinez, Pedro (1999)	69
6	Luque, Dolf (1923)	69
7	Grove, Lefty (1930)	68
8	Wood, Wilbur (1971)	68
9	Johnson, Walter (1912)	67
10	Mathewson, Christy (1905)	64
11	Johnson, Randy (2002)	64
12	Johnson, Walter (1913)	64
13	Maddux, Greg (1995)	64
14	Faber, Red (1921)	64
15	Young, Cy (1901)	63
16	Alexander, Grover (1915)	63
17	Vance, Dazzy (1924)	63
18	Maddux, Greg (1994)	62
19	Johnson, Randy (1999)	62
20	Gomez, Lefty (1937)	61
21	Grove, Lefty (1935)	61
22	Martinez, Pedro (1997)	61
23	Newsom, Bobo (1940)	61
24	Gooden, Dwight (1985)	61
25	Vance, Dazzy (1928)	60
26	Vance, Dazzy (1930)	60
27	Newhouser, Hal (1946)	60
28	Johnson, Randy (1995)	59
29	Clemens, Roger (1990)	59
30	Wood, Joe (1912)	58
31	Johnson, Walter (1919)	58
32	Carlton, Steve (1972)	58
33	Johnson, Randy (2000)	58
34	Newhouser, Hal (1945)	58
35	Trout, Dizzy (1944)	58
36	Gibson, Bob (1968)	57
37	Alexander, Grover (1920)	57
38	Harder, Mel (1934)	56
39	Roberts, Robin (1953)	56
40	Grove, Lefty (1937)	56
41	Koufax, Sandy (1966)	56
42	Ferrell, Wes (1930)	55
43	Guidry, Ron (1978)	55
44	Johnson, Randy (1997)	55
45	Johnson, Randy (2001)	54
46	Walsh, Ed (1912)	54
47	Waddell, Rube (1904)	54
48	Lee, Thornton (1941)	54
49	Grove, Lefty (1932)	54
50	Saberhagen, Bret (1989)	53
51	Spahn, Warren (1947)	53
52	Blyleven, Bert (1973)	53
53	Garver, Ned (1950)	53
54	Blackwell, Ewell (1947)	53
55	Waddell, Rube (1905)	53
56	Brown, Kevin (1996)	53
57	Clemens, Roger (1998)	52
58	Martinez, Pedro (2003)	52
59	Marichal, Juan (1965)	52
60	Appier, Kevin (1993)	52
61	Maddux, Greg (1998)	51
62	Hands, Bill (1969)	51
63	Hubbell, Carl (1934)	51
64	Feller, Bob (1939)	51
65	Walsh, Ed (1908)	51
66	Clemens, Roger (1991)	51
67	Jones, Oscar (1903)	51
68	Spahn, Warren (1953)	51
69	Mathewson, Christy (1911)	51
70	Clemens, Roger (1987)	51
71	Dean, Dizzy (1934)	51
72	Waddell, Rube (1902)	50
73	Maddux, Greg (1997)	50
74	Shantz, Bobby (1952)	50
75	Young, Cy (1902)	50

Earned Run Average – pre-1901

1	Keefe, Tim (1880)	0.86
2	Driscoll, Denny (1882)	1.21
3	Bradley, George (1876)	1.23
4	Hecker, Guy (1882)	1.30
5	Bradley, George (1880)	1.38
6	Radbourn, Charley (1884)	1.38
7	Ward, John (1878)	1.51
8	McCormick, Harry (1882)	1.52
9	White, Will (1882)	1.54
10	McCormick, Jim (1884)	1.54
11	Sweeney, Charlie (1884)	1.55
12	Devlin, Jim (1876)	1.56
13	Keefe, Tim (1885)	1.58
14	King, Silver (1888)	1.65
15	Welch, Mickey (1885)	1.66
16	Cummings, Candy (1876)	1.67
17	Bond, Tommy (1876)	1.68
18	Taylor, Billy (1884)	1.68
19	McCormick, Jim (1878)	1.69
20	Ward, John (1880)	1.74
21	Boyle, Henry (1884)	1.74
22	Keefe, Tim (1888)	1.74
23	Goldsmith, Fred (1880)	1.75
24	Spalding, Al (1876)	1.75
25	Boyle, Henry (1886)	1.76

Adjusted ERA – pre-1901

1	Keefe, Tim (1880)	295
2	Driscoll, Denny (1882)	216
3	McCormick, Jim (1884)	207
4	Radbourn, Charley (1884)	205
5	King, Silver (1888)	198
6	Maul, Al (1895)	195
7	Hecker, Guy (1882)	191
8	Griffith, Clark (1898)	190
9	Rusie, Amos (1894)	189
10	Rhines, Billy (1896)	188
11	Stivetts, Jack (1889)	187
12	Sweeney, Charlie (1884)	182
13	Boyle, Henry (1886)	182
14	Rhines, Billy (1890)	182
15	Taylor, Billy (1884)	178
16	Young, Cy (1892)	176
17	Bradley, George (1876)	174
18	McCormick, Harry (1882)	174
19	Devlin, Jim (1876)	174
20	Nichols, Kid (1898)	173
21	White, Will (1882)	171
22	Hecker, Guy (1884)	171
23	Boyle, Henry (1884)	171
24	McCormick, Jim (1883)	171
25	Maul, Al (1898)	170

Pitching Runs – pre-1901

1	Rusie, Amos (1894)	125
2	Radbourn, Charley (1884)	121
3	Hecker, Guy (1884)	108
4	King, Silver (1888)	92
5	Clarkson, John (1889)	89
6	Kilroy, Matt (1887)	80
7	Hawley, Pink (1895)	79
8	King, Silver (1890)	79
9	White, Will (1883)	77
10	Rusie, Amos (1893)	77
11	Radbourn, Charley (1883)	76
12	Foutz, Dave (1886)	75
13	Meekin, Jouett (1894)	74
14	Stratton, Scott (1890)	72
15	Rhines, Billy (1890)	72
16	Galvin, Pud (1884)	70
17	Bradley, George (1876)	69
18	Young, Cy (1892)	68
19	Nichols, Kid (1897)	68
20	Smith, Elmer (1887)	67
21	Clarkson, John (1885)	67
22	Ramsey, Toad (1886)	65
23	Nichols, Kid (1898)	63
24	Nichols, Kid (1896)	63
25	Rusie, Amos (1897)	63

Adjusted Pitching Runs – pre-1901

1	Rusie, Amos (1894)	117
2	Clarkson, John (1889)	104
3	Galvin, Pud (1884)	92
4	Radbourn, Charley (1884)	91
5	King, Silver (1888)	89
6	King, Silver (1890)	83
7	Kilroy, Matt (1887)	82
8	Clarkson, John (1887)	80
9	Young, Cy (1892)	75
10	Nichols, Kid (1890)	74
11	Young, Cy (1893)	73
12	Rusie, Amos (1893)	71
13	Foutz, Dave (1886)	71
14	Young, Cy (1895)	71
15	Hecker, Guy (1884)	71
16	Nichols, Kid (1895)	69
17	Young, Cy (1894)	69
18	Stratton, Scott (1890)	69
19	Ferguson, Charlie (1886)	68
20	Ramsey, Toad (1886)	68
21	Casey, Dan (1887)	67
22	Breitenstein, Ted (1893)	67
23	Meekin, Jouett (1894)	66
24	Nichols, Kid (1897)	66
25	Hawley, Pink (1895)	65

Pitcher Fielding Runs – 1901-2003

1	Walsh, Ed (1907)	22.1
2	Howell, Harry (1905)	17.7
3	Walsh, Ed (1911)	14.9
4	Walsh, Ed (1908)	14.6
5	Walsh, Ed (1910)	11.0
6	Smith, Frank (1909)	10.7
7	Mays, Carl (1926)	10.3
8	Maddux, Greg (1996)	9.9
9	Howell, Harry (1904)	9.9
10	Mathewson, Christy (1908)	9.9
11	Mays, Carl (1916)	9.6
12	Mays, Carl (1918)	9.5
13	Dauss, Hooks (1915)	9.3
14	Lemon, Bob (1948)	9.1
15	Davis, Curt (1934)	9.0
16	Moore, Wilcy (1927)	8.9
17	Joss, Addie (1907)	8.9
18	Howell, Harry (1907)	8.7
19	Stricklett, Elmer (1906)	8.7
20	Jones, Randy (1976)	8.7
21	Mays, Carl (1917)	8.5
22	Maddux, Greg (2000)	8.4
23	Walters, Bucky (1936)	8.4
24	Altrock, Nick (1905)	8.3
25	Packard, Gene (1914)	8.3
26	Fitzsimmons, Freddie (1931)	8.3
27	Newman, Fred (1965)	8.2
28	Mays, Carl (1924)	8.1
29	Dauss, Hooks (1920)	8.1
30	Stottlemyre, Mel (1969)	8.1
31	Denny, John (1978)	8.0
32	Stricklett, Elmer (1905)	8.0
33	Wood, Joe (1912)	8.0
34	Gumbert, Harry (1937)	7.9
35	Rommel, Eddie (1924)	7.9
36	Hubbell, Carl (1933)	7.9
37	Walsh, Ed (1906)	7.9
38	Harder, Mel (1933)	7.9
39	Lemon, Bob (1953)	7.9
40	Gumbert, Harry (1938)	7.8
41	Schumacher, Hal (1935)	7.7
42	Hendrix, Claude (1914)	7.7
43	Grimes, Burleigh (1925)	7.7
44	Alexander, Grover (1915)	7.7
45	Maddux, Greg (1998)	7.7
46	Christopher, Russ (1943)	7.7
47	Mullin, George (1904)	7.6
48	Coveleski, Harry (1914)	7.5
49	Dubuc, Jean (1913)	7.5
50	Howell, Harry (1906)	7.4
51	Cicotte, Eddie (1913)	7.4
52	Rogers, Kenny (1998)	7.4
53	Walsh, Ed (1912)	7.4
54	Mathewson, Christy (1901)	7.3
55	Lemon, Bob (1952)	7.3
56	Willett, Ed (1910)	7.3
57	Donahue, Red (1902)	7.2
58	Maddux, Greg (1990)	7.2
59	Christopher, Russ (1945)	7.2
60	Krapp, Gene (1915)	7.2
61	Jackson, Larry (1964)	7.2
62	Walsh, Ed (1909)	7.2
63	Tobin, Jim (1944)	7.2
64	White, Doc (1908)	7.1
65	Mathewson, Christy (1911)	7.0
66	Tyler, Lefty (1913)	7.0
67	Fitzsimmons, Freddie (1930)	7.0
68	Owen, Frank (1904)	6.9
69	John, Tommy (1973)	6.9
70	Ames, Red (1909)	6.9
71	Lemon, Bob (1949)	6.9
72	Doak, Bill (1915)	6.8
73	Coveleski, Stan (1921)	6.8
74	Brown, Kevin (1995)	6.8
75	Wingfield, Ted (1925)	6.8

Pitcher Fielding Runs – pre-1901

1	White, Will (1882)	14.3
2	Clarkson, John (1889)	10.8
3	Mullane, Tony (1882)	10.4
4	Kilroy, Matt (1887)	9.7
5	Buffinton, Charlie (1888)	9.5
6	Clarkson, John (1887)	9.2
7	McMahon, Sadie (1890)	9.1
8	Mullane, Tony (1884)	8.7
9	Scott, Ed (1900)	8.5
10	Young, Cy (1895)	8.5
11	Galvin, Pud (1887)	8.4
12	Clarkson, John (1885)	8.4
13	Rusie, Amos (1894)	8.3
14	Caruthers, Bob (1887)	8.2
15	Bond, Tommy (1880)	8.2
16	Hecker, Guy (1884)	8.0
17	Bond, Tommy (1879)	7.9
18	Young, Cy (1896)	7.5
19	Seymour, Cy (1897)	7.4
20	Seymour, Cy (1898)	7.3
21	Foutz, Dave (1885)	7.3
22	Galvin, Pud (1884)	7.3
23	Corcoran, Larry (1884)	7.3
24	Morrison, Mike (1887)	7.3
25	Kilroy, Matt (1889)	7.2

Pitcher Fielding Wins – 1901-2003

1	Walsh, Ed (1907)	2.4
2	Howell, Harry (1905)	1.9
3	Walsh, Ed (1908)	1.7
4	Walsh, Ed (1911)	1.5
5	Walsh, Ed (1910)	1.2
6	Smith, Frank (1909)	1.2
7	Mathewson, Christy (1908)	1.1
8	Howell, Harry (1904)	1.1
9	Mays, Carl (1916)	1.1
10	Mays, Carl (1918)	1.1
11	Mays, Carl (1926)	1.0
12	Dauss, Hooks (1915)	1.0
13	Joss, Addie (1907)	1.0
14	Maddux, Greg (1996)	1.0
15	Stricklett, Elmer (1906)	1.0
16	Howell, Harry (1907)	1.0
17	Mays, Carl (1917)	.9
18	Jones, Randy (1976)	.9
19	Altrock, Nick (1905)	.9
20	Lemon, Bob (1948)	.9
21	Davis, Curt (1934)	.9
22	Newman, Fred (1965)	.9
23	Walsh, Ed (1906)	.9
24	Packard, Gene (1914)	.9
25	Alexander, Grover (1915)	.9
26	Stottlemyre, Mel (1969)	.9
27	Mullin, George (1904)	.8
28	Moore, Wilcy (1927)	.8
29	Denny, John (1978)	.8
30	Hubbell, Carl (1933)	.8
31	Christopher, Russ (1943)	.8
32	Stricklett, Elmer (1905)	.8
33	Coveleski, Harry (1914)	.8
34	Fitzsimmons, Freddie (1931)	.8
35	Walters, Bucky (1936)	.8
36	Walsh, Ed (1909)	.8
37	Howell, Harry (1906)	.8
38	White, Doc (1908)	.8
39	Mays, Carl (1924)	.8
40	Willett, Ed (1910)	.8
41	Hendrix, Claude (1914)	.8
42	Dubuc, Jean (1913)	.8
43	Wood, Joe (1912)	.8
44	Maddux, Greg (2000)	.8
45	Dauss, Hooks (1920)	.8
46	Gumbert, Harry (1937)	.8
47	Lemon, Bob (1953)	.8
48	Gumbert, Harry (1938)	.8
49	Cicotte, Eddie (1913)	.8
50	Owen, Frank (1904)	.8
51	Krapp, Gene (1915)	.8
52	Christopher, Russ (1945)	.8
53	Ames, Red (1909)	.8
54	Doak, Bill (1915)	.8
55	Lemon, Bob (1952)	.8
56	Jackson, Larry (1964)	.8
57	Maddux, Greg (1998)	.8
58	Schumacher, Hal (1935)	.8
59	Stricklett, Elmer (1907)	.8
60	Rommel, Eddie (1924)	.7
61	Harder, Mel (1933)	.7
62	Maddux, Greg (1990)	.7
63	Quinn, Jack (1910)	.7
64	Tobin, Jim (1944)	.7
65	Cicotte, Eddie (1914)	.7
66	Walsh, Ed (1912)	.7
67	Tyler, Lefty (1913)	.7
68	Mathewson, Christy (1909)	.7
69	Grimes, Burleigh (1925)	.7
70	John, Tommy (1973)	.7
71	Mathewson, Christy (1901)	.7
72	Trout, Dizzy (1944)	.7
73	Packard, Gene (1915)	.7
74	Mathewson, Christy (1911)	.7
75	Mathewson, Christy (1905)	.7

Pitcher Fielding Wins – pre-1901

1	White, Will (1882)	1.3
2	Mullane, Tony (1882)	1.0
3	Buffinton, Charlie (1888)	.9
4	Clarkson, John (1889)	.9
5	Bond, Tommy (1880)	.8
6	McMahon, Sadie (1890)	.8
7	Mullane, Tony (1884)	.8
8	Clarkson, John (1885)	.8
9	Kilroy, Matt (1887)	.8
10	Clarkson, John (1887)	.8
11	Scott, Ed (1900)	.8
12	Bond, Tommy (1879)	.7
13	Hecker, Guy (1884)	.7
14	Galvin, Pud (1887)	.7
15	Seymour, Cy (1898)	.7
16	Young, Cy (1895)	.7
17	Taylor, Jack (1898)	.7
18	Caruthers, Bob (1887)	.7
19	Corcoran, Larry (1880)	.7
20	Foutz, Dave (1885)	.7
21	Galvin, Pud (1884)	.7
22	Corcoran, Larry (1884)	.6
23	Rusie, Amos (1894)	.6
24	Young, Cy (1896)	.6
25	Ward, John (1880)	.6

Adjusted Pitching Wins

1	Clarkson, John (1889)	9.0
2	Rusie, Amos (1894)	9.0
3	King, Silver (1888)	8.2
4	Galvin, Pud (1884)	8.2
5	Radbourn, Charley (1884)	8.1
6	Young, Cy (1892)	6.9
7	Clarkson, John (1887)	6.8
8	Kilroy, Matt (1887)	6.6
9	King, Silver (1890)	6.6
10	Nichols, Kid (1890)	6.6
11	Hecker, Guy (1884)	6.4
12	Foutz, Dave (1886)	6.2
13	Ferguson, Charlie (1886)	6.1
14	Stratton, Scott (1890)	6.0
15	Young, Cy (1893)	6.0
16	Clarkson, John (1885)	6.0
17	Ramsey, Toad (1886)	5.9
18	Rusie, Amos (1893)	5.8
19	Rhines, Billy (1890)	5.8
20	Young, Cy (1895)	5.7
21	Casey, Dan (1887)	5.7
22	Nichols, Kid (1895)	5.6
23	Nichols, Kid (1897)	5.6
24	Griffith, Clark (1898)	5.6
25	Breitenstein, Ted (1893)	5.5
26	Nichols, Kid (1891)	5.4
27	Young, Cy (1894)	5.3
28	Buffinton, Charlie (1889)	5.3
29	Hawley, Pink (1895)	5.3
30	Nichols, Kid (1898)	5.3
31	McMahon, Sadie (1890)	5.3
32	Stivetts, Jack (1891)	5.2
33	Nichols, Kid (1896)	5.2
34	Buffinton, Charlie (1888)	5.1
35	Kilroy, Matt (1889)	5.1
36	McMahon, Sadie (1891)	5.1
37	Hecker, Guy (1885)	5.1
38	Nichols, Kid (1893)	5.1
39	Keefe, Tim (1883)	5.1
40	Young, Cy (1896)	5.1
41	Meekin, Jouett (1894)	5.1
42	Seward, Ed (1888)	5.0
43	Rusie, Amos (1897)	4.9
44	Young, Cy (1899)	4.9
45	Rusie, Amos (1890)	4.8
46	Cuppy, Nig (1896)	4.8
47	Mercer, Win (1894)	4.8
48	Mathews, Bobby (1883)	4.8
49	Devlin, Jim (1876)	4.8
50	Duryea, Jesse (1889)	4.7
51	Mullane, Tony (1884)	4.7
52	Whitney, Jim (1883)	4.7
53	Baldwin, Lady (1886)	4.6
54	White, Will (1883)	4.6
55	White, Will (1882)	4.6
56	Morris, Ed (1885)	4.6
57	Weaver, Sam (1878)	4.6
58	McGinnity, Joe (1899)	4.6
59	Cuppy, Nig (1895)	4.6
60	Willis, Vic (1899)	4.6
61	Morris, Ed (1886)	4.6
62	Caruthers, Bob (1885)	4.5
63	Mathews, Bobby (1885)	4.5
64	Henderson, Hardie (1884)	4.5
65	Gleason, Kid (1890)	4.5
66	Ehret, Red (1890)	4.4
67	Hutchison, Bill (1890)	4.3
68	Hutchison, Bill (1892)	4.2
69	Chamberlain, Elton (1889)	4.2
70	Baldwin, Mark (1890)	4.1
71	Casey, Dan (1886)	4.1
72	Smith, Elmer (1887)	4.1
73	Emslie, Bob (1884)	4.1
74	Radbourn, Charley (1883)	4.0
75	Clarkson, John (1891)	4.0
76	Clarkson, John (1886)	4.0
77	Young, Cy (1898)	4.0
78	Caruthers, Bob (1886)	4.0
79	Ferguson, Charlie (1887)	4.0
80	Ramsey, Toad (1887)	4.0
81	Crane, Ed (1891)	3.9
82	Sanders, Ben (1889)	3.8
83	Conway, Jim (1889)	3.8
84	McJames, Doc (1898)	3.8
85	King, Silver (1889)	3.8
86	Kitson, Frank (1899)	3.8
87	Griffith, Clark (1895)	3.7
88	Hahn, Noodles (1899)	3.7
89	Whitney, Jim (1887)	3.7
90	Bond, Tommy (1877)	3.7
91	Tannehill, Jesse (1899)	3.6
92	Galvin, Pud (1881)	3.6
93	Sanders, Ben (1888)	3.6
94	Devlin, Jim (1877)	3.5
95	Clarkson, John (1892)	3.5
96	Cuppy, Nig (1892)	3.5
97	Derby, George (1881)	3.5
98	Buffinton, Charlie (1884)	3.5
99	Dwyer, Frank (1896)	3.4
100	Keefe, Tim (1888)	3.4

Opponents Batting Average

1	Martinez, Pedro (2000)	.167
2	Tiant, Luis (1968)	.168
3	Ryan, Nolan (1972)	.171
4	Ryan, Nolan (1991)	.172
5	Reulbach, Ed (1906)	.175
6	Keefe, Tim (1880)	.175
7	Koufax, Sandy (1965)	.179
8	Leonard, Dutch (1914)	.180
9	Fernandez, Sid (1985)	.181
10	Nomo, Hideo (1995)	.182
11	McNally, Dave (1968)	.182
12	Byrne, Tommy (1949)	.183
13	Martinez, Pedro (1997)	.184
14	Downing, Al (1963)	.184
15	Gibson, Bob (1968)	.184
16	Sweeney, Charlie (1884)	.184
17	McDowell, Sam (1965)	.185
18	Lundgren, Carl (1907)	.185
19	Score, Herb (1956)	.186
20	Scott, Mike (1986)	.186
21	Ryan, Nolan (1989)	.187
22	Johnson, Walter (1913)	.187
	Walsh, Ed (1910)	.187
24	Soto, Mario (1980)	.187
25	Ryan, Nolan (1981)	.188
26	Ryan, Nolan (1986)	.188
27	McCormick, Jim (1884)	.188
28	Shaw, Dupee (1884)	.188
29	Ryan, Nolan (1990)	.188
30	Ford, Russ (1910)	.188
31	Youmans, Floyd (1986)	.188
32	Hecker, Guy (1882)	.188
33	McDowell, Sam (1966)	.188
34	Koufax, Sandy (1963)	.189
35	McDowell, Sam (1968)	.189
36	Sutton, Don (1972)	.189
37	Hunter, Catfish (1972)	.189
38	Blue, Vida (1971)	.189
39	Ryan, Nolan (1974)	.190
40	Messersmith, Andy (1969)	.190
41	Horlen, Joe (1964)	.190
42	Fernandez, Sid (1988)	.191
43	Alexander, Grover (1915)	.191
44	Koufax, Sandy (1964)	.191
45	Bibby, Jim (1973)	.192
46	Turley, Bob (1955)	.193
47	Ryan, Nolan (1977)	.193
48	Guidry, Ron (1978)	.193
49	Beebe, Fred (1908)	.193
50	Turley, Bob (1957)	.194
51	Johnson, Randy (1997)	.194
52	Coveleski, Stan (1917)	.194
	Pfiester, Jack (1906)	.194
54	Score, Herb (1955)	.194
55	Ryan, Nolan (1976)	.195
56	Brown, Mordecai (1908)	.195
57	Ryan, Nolan (1983)	.195
58	Chance, Dean (1964)	.195
59	Clemens, Roger (1986)	.195
60	Wood, Kerry (1998)	.196
61	Johnson, Walter (1912)	.196
62	Nelson, Roger (1972)	.196
63	Richard, J.R. (1978)	.196
64	Perez, Pascual (1988)	.196
65	Keefe, Tim (1888)	.197
66	Maddux, Greg (1995)	.197
67	Robinson, Jeff (1988)	.197
68	Joss, Addie (1908)	.197
69	DeLeon, Jose (1989)	.197
70	Boswell, Dave (1966)	.197
71	Koufax, Sandy (1962)	.197
72	Sweeney, Charlie (1884)	.197
73	Clemens, Roger (1998)	.197
74	Siebert, Sonny (1968)	.198
75	Fernandez, Sid (1989)	.198
76	Cheney, Larry (1916)	.198
	Overall, Orval (1909)	.198
78	Simpson, Wayne (1970)	.198
79	Corcoran, Larry (1880)	.198
80	Martinez, Pedro (2002)	.198
81	Peters, Gary (1967)	.199
82	Keefe, Tim (1885)	.199
83	Brown, Mordecai (1904)	.199
	Mitchell, Willie (1913)	.199
85	Ryan, Nolan (1987)	.199
86	Terry, Adonis (1888)	.200
87	King, Silver (1888)	.200
88	McLain, Denny (1968)	.200
89	Welch, Mickey (1885)	.200
90	Bolin, Bobby (1968)	.200
	Fernandez, Sid (1990)	.200
	Mathewson, Christy (1908)	.200
	Mathewson, Christy (1909)	.200
	Palmer, Jim (1969)	.200
95	Waddell, Rube (1905)	.200
96	Schmidt, Jason (2003)	.200
97	Shea, Spec (1947)	.200
98	Seward, Ed (1888)	.201
99	Mullane, Tony (1892)	.201
100	Johnson, Randy (1995)	.201

Win Shares – Pitchers

1	Radbourn, Charley (1884)	89
2	Hecker, Guy (1884)	74
3	King, Silver (1888)	71
4	Keefe, Tim (1883)	70
5	Buffinton, Charlie (1884)	62
	Clarkson, John (1885)	62
	Foutz, Dave (1886)	62
8	Galvin, Pud (1879)	61
9	Bond, Tommy (1878)	60
	Clarkson, John (1889)	60
	Devlin, Jim (1877)	60
	Radbourn, Charley (1883)	60
13	Mullane, Tony (1884)	58
14	Bradley, George (1876)	57
	Caruthers, Bob (1886)	57
	Galvin, Pud (1884)	57
	Spalding, Al (1876)	57
	Welch, Mickey (1885)	57
	Whitney, Jim (1883)	57
20	Morris, Ed (1885)	56
	Rusie, Amos (1894)	56
22	Mullane, Tony (1883)	55
23	Caruthers, Bob (1887)	54
	Hutchison, Bill (1890)	54
	Johnson, Walter (1913)	54
	McCormick, Jim (1880)	54
	Smith, Elmer (1887)	54
	White, Will (1882)	54
29	Baldwin, Lady (1886)	53
	Chesbro, Jack (1904)	53
	Devlin, Jim (1876)	53
	Ruth, Babe (1921)	53
33	Corcoran, Larry (1880)	52
34	Caruthers, Bob (1885)	51
	Clarkson, John (1887)	51
	Kilroy, Matt (1887)	51
	Ruth, Babe (1920)	51
	Stratton, Scott (1890)	51
	Ward, John (1880)	51
	Ward, John (1879)	51
	White, Will (1883)	51
42	Bond, Tommy (1879)	50
	Radbourn, Charley (1882)	50
44	Ferguson, Charlie (1886)	49
	Hutchison, Bill (1891)	49
	Stivetts, Jack (1892)	49
	Sweeney, Bill (1884)	49
48	Meekin, Jouett (1894)	48
	Nichols, Kid (1892)	48
50	Bond, Tommy (1877)	47
	Bond, Tommy (1876)	47
	Galvin, Pud (1883)	47
	Johnson, Walter (1912)	47
	Keefe, Tim (1884)	47
	Ramsey, Toad (1886)	47
	Walsh, Ed (1908)	47
57	Caruthers, Bob (1889)	46
	Caruthers, Bob (1888)	46
	Mullane, Tony (1887)	46
	Ramsey, Toad (1887)	46
	Stivetts, Jack (1891)	46
	Welch, Mickey (1884)	46
63	Gleason, Kid (1890)	45
	Hutchison, Bill (1892)	45
	Speaker, Tris (1914)	45
66	Alexander, Grover (1916)	44
	Buffinton, Charlie (1888)	44
	Hawley, Pink (1895)	44
	Kilroy, Matt (1889)	44
	King, Silver (1889)	44
	King, Silver (1890)	44
	Morris, Ed (1884)	44
	Morris, Ed (1886)	44
	Nichols, Kid (1898)	44
	Wood, Joe (1912)	44
	Young, Cy (1892)	44
77	Alexander, Grover (1915)	43
	Foutz, Dave (1887)	43
	Nichols, Kid (1890)	43
	Ruth, Babe (1919)	43
	Young, Cy (1896)	43
82	Baldwin, Mark (1890)	42
	Chamberlain, Elton (1889)	42
	Clarkson, John (1886)	42
	Clarkson, John (1891)	42
	Grove, Lefty (1931)	42
	Hecker, Guy (1885)	42
	Johnson, Walter (1915)	42
	Keefe, Tim (1885)	42
	Killen, Frank (1893)	42
	McCormick, Jim (1882)	42
	McGinnis, Jumbo (1883)	42
	McGinnity, Joe (1904)	42
	Richmond, Lee (1880)	42
	Seward, Ed (1888)	42
	Trout, Dizzy (1944)	42
	Welch, Mickey (1880)	42
	Whitney, Jim (1881)	42
99	9 players tied	41

Total Player Wins – Pitchers

1	Rusie, Amos (1894)	9.2
2	King, Silver (1888)	9.2
3	Clarkson, John (1889)	9.1
4	Hecker, Guy (1884)	9.1
5	Radbourn, Charley (1884)	8.5
6	Johnson, Walter (1913)	8.0
7	Caruthers, Bob (1886)	7.7
8	Stratton, Scott (1890)	7.6
9	Mathewson, Christy (1905)	7.6
10	Johnson, Walter (1912)	7.6
11	Kilroy, Matt (1887)	7.4
12	Trout, Dizzy (1944)	7.3
13	Ferguson, Charlie (1886)	7.3
14	Martinez, Pedro (2000)	7.3
15	Galvin, Pud (1884)	7.2
16	Clarkson, John (1887)	7.1
17	Gibson, Bob (1968)	7.0
18	Foutz, Dave (1886)	7.0
19	Gooden, Dwight (1985)	7.0
20	Alexander, Grover (1915)	7.0
21	Wood, Joe (1912)	6.9
22	Wood, Wilbur (1971)	6.9
23	Clemens, Roger (1997)	6.8
24	Carlton, Steve (1972)	6.8
25	Luque, Dolf (1923)	6.7
26	Spalding, Al (1874)	6.7
27	Nichols, Kid (1890)	6.7
28	Newhouser, Hal (1945)	6.6
29	Alexander, Grover (1920)	6.6
30	Caruthers, Bob (1887)	6.5
31	Whitney, Jim (1883)	6.4
32	Kilroy, Matt (1889)	6.4
33	Hawley, Pink (1895)	6.4
34	Mullane, Tony (1884)	6.4
35	Martinez, Pedro (1999)	6.3
36	Alexander, Grover (1916)	6.3
37	Jenkins, Fergie (1971)	6.3
38	Maddux, Greg (1994)	6.3
39	Grove, Lefty (1931)	6.3
40	Johnson, Walter (1919)	6.3
41	Young, Cy (1892)	6.3
42	Johnson, Randy (2002)	6.3
43	Maddux, Greg (1995)	6.2
44	Newhouser, Hal (1946)	6.2
45	King, Silver (1890)	6.2
46	Grove, Lefty (1930)	6.1
47	Walsh, Ed (1908)	6.1
48	Stivetts, Jack (1891)	6.1
49	Clarkson, John (1885)	6.1
50	Rusie, Amos (1893)	6.1
51	Vance, Dazzy (1928)	6.1
52	Vance, Dazzy (1924)	6.0
53	Ferrell, Wes (1935)	6.0
54	Clemens, Roger (1990)	6.0
55	Walsh, Ed (1912)	6.0
56	Nichols, Kid (1897)	6.0
57	Martinez, Pedro (1997)	6.0
58	Ruth, Babe (1916)	6.0
59	Grove, Lefty (1936)	6.0
60	Walters, Bucky (1939)	5.9
61	Johnson, Walter (1915)	5.9
62	Ramsey, Toad (1886)	5.9
63	Mathewson, Christy (1909)	5.8
64	Marichal, Juan (1966)	5.8
65	Johnson, Walter (1918)	5.8
66	Hecker, Guy (1885)	5.8
67	Walsh, Ed (1910)	5.8
68	Ferrell, Wes (1930)	5.8
69	Young, Cy (1901)	5.7
70	Lee, Thornton (1941)	5.7
71	Young, Cy (1896)	5.7
72	Seaver, Tom (1971)	5.7
73	Newsom, Bobo (1940)	5.7
74	Waddell, Rube (1905)	5.7
75	Faber, Red (1921)	5.7
76	Guidry, Ron (1978)	5.7
77	Gibson, Bob (1969)	5.6
78	Roberts, Robin (1953)	5.6
79	Ferguson, Charlie (1887)	5.6
80	Meekin, Jouett (1894)	5.6
81	Johnson, Walter (1914)	5.6
82	Garver, Ned (1950)	5.6
83	Marichal, Juan (1965)	5.6
84	Keefe, Tim (1883)	5.6
85	Rusie, Amos (1890)	5.6
86	Young, Cy (1893)	5.6
87	Johnson, Randy (1999)	5.6
88	Mathewson, Christy (1908)	5.6
89	Johnson, Randy (1995)	5.5
90	Gomez, Lefty (1937)	5.5
91	Nichols, Kid (1898)	5.5
92	Niekro, Phil (1978)	5.5
93	Griffith, Clark (1898)	5.5
94	Waddell, Rube (1902)	5.5
95	Blyleven, Bert (1973)	5.5
96	Maddux, Greg (1998)	5.4
97	Rhines, Billy (1890)	5.4
98	Saberhagen, Bret (1989)	5.4
99	Johnson, Randy (2000)	5.4
100	Young, Cy (1895)	5.4
101	Newhouser, Hal (1944)	5.4
102	Nichols, Kid (1895)	5.4
103	Cuppy, Nig (1896)	5.4
104	Shantz, Bobby (1952)	5.3
105	McMahon, Sadie (1890)	5.3
106	Devlin, Jim (1876)	5.3
107	Ruth, Babe (1918)	5.3
108	Spahn, Warren (1953)	5.3
109	Waddell, Rube (1904)	5.3
110	Duryea, Jesse (1889)	5.3
111	Dean, Dizzy (1934)	5.3
112	Grove, Lefty (1935)	5.3
113	Spahn, Warren (1947)	5.3
114	Rijo, Jose (1993)	5.3
115	Seaver, Tom (1973)	5.3
116	Perry, Gaylord (1972)	5.2
117	Reuschel, Rick (1977)	5.2
118	Nichols, Kid (1891)	5.2
119	Feller, Bob (1939)	5.2
120	Koufax, Sandy (1966)	5.2
121	Johnson, Randy (1997)	5.2
122	Buffinton, Charlie (1889)	5.2
123	Jones, Oscar (1903)	5.2
124	Cicotte, Eddie (1917)	5.2
125	Cuppy, Nig (1895)	5.2
126	Carlton, Steve (1980)	5.2
127	Mathewson, Christy (1910)	5.2
128	Buffinton, Charlie (1888)	5.2
129	Rusie, Amos (1897)	5.1
130	Breitenstein, Ted (1893)	5.1
131	Ford, Russ (1910)	5.1
132	Hubbell, Carl (1933)	5.1
133	Harder, Mel (1934)	5.1
134	Mathewson, Christy (1911)	5.1
135	White, Will (1882)	5.1
136	Clemens, Roger (1991)	5.1
137	Caruthers, Bob (1885)	5.1
138	Brown, Kevin (1996)	5.1
139	Taylor, Jack (1902)	5.1
140	Johnson, Walter (1911)	5.1
141	Grimes, Burleigh (1920)	5.1
142	Appier, Kevin (1993)	5.1
143	Chandler, Spud (1943)	5.0
144	Mercer, Win (1894)	5.0
145	Marichal, Juan (1969)	5.0
146	Radbourn, Charley (1883)	5.0
147	Alexander, Grover (1917)	5.0
148	Johnson, Randy (2001)	5.0
149	Vaughn, Hippo (1918)	5.0
150	Martinez, Pedro (2003)	5.0
151	Cooper, Mort (1942)	5.0
152	Young, Cy (1902)	5.0
153	Clemens, Roger (1992)	5.0
154	Coveleski, Stan (1918)	5.0
155	Hands, Bill (1969)	5.0
156	Brown, Mordecai (1909)	5.0
157	Joss, Addie (1908)	5.0
158	Baldwin, Lady (1886)	4.9
159	Grove, Lefty (1932)	4.9
160	Wynn, Early (1956)	4.9
161	Clemens, Roger (1998)	4.9
162	McMahon, Sadie (1891)	4.9
163	Pascual, Camilo (1959)	4.9
164	Casey, Dan (1887)	4.9
165	Trout, Dizzy (1946)	4.9
166	Hendrix, Claude (1914)	4.9
167	Grove, Lefty (1937)	4.9
168	Hubbell, Carl (1934)	4.9
169	Clemens, Roger (1986)	4.9
170	Nichols, Kid (1893)	4.9
171	Young, Cy (1899)	4.9
172	Brown, Mordecai (1906)	4.9
173	Vance, Dazzy (1930)	4.9
174	Maddux, Greg (1997)	4.9
175	Ferrell, Wes (1931)	4.9
176	Henderson, Hardie (1884)	4.9
177	White, Will (1883)	4.9
178	Nichols, Kid (1896)	4.9
179	Clemens, Roger (1987)	4.8
180	Davis, Curt (1934)	4.8
181	Brecheen, Harry (1948)	4.8
182	Mays, Carl (1921)	4.8
183	Falkenberg, Cy (1914)	4.8
184	Hecker, Guy (1886)	4.8
185	Koufax, Sandy (1965)	4.8
186	Whitney, Jim (1887)	4.8
187	Gibson, Bob (1970)	4.8
188	Hernandez, Livan (2003)	4.8
	Maddux, Greg (1996)	4.8
190	Grimes, Burleigh (1928)	4.8
191	Blue, Vida (1971)	4.8
192	Parnell, Mel (1949)	4.7
193	Feller, Bob (1946)	4.7
194	Feller, Bob (1940)	4.7
195	Score, Herb (1956)	4.7
196	Smoltz, John (1996)	4.7
197	Johnson, Walter (1916)	4.7
198	Blackwell, Ewell (1947)	4.7
199	Young, Cy (1894)	4.7
200	Hubbell, Carl (1932)	4.7
201	Mathewson, Christy (1912)	4.7
202	Warneke, Lon (1933)	4.7
203	Newhouser, Hal (1948)	4.7
204	Maddux, Greg (1992)	4.7
205	Matlack, Jon (1978)	4.7
206	Tudor, John (1985)	4.7
207	Prior, Mark (2003)	4.6
208	Hudson, Tim (2003)	4.6
209	Seward, Ed (1888)	4.6
210	Antonelli, Johnny (1954)	4.6
211	Carlton, Steve (1977)	4.6
212	Passeau, Claude (1940)	4.6
213	Hampton, Mike (1999)	4.6
214	Stieb, Dave (1985)	4.6
215	Brown, Kevin (1998)	4.6
216	Dierker, Larry (1969)	4.6
217	Sain, Johnny (1946)	4.6
218	Glavine, Tom (1996)	4.6
219	Maddux, Greg (1993)	4.6
220	Chesbro, Jack (1904)	4.6
221	Wood, Joe (1911)	4.6
222	Caldwell, Mike (1978)	4.6
223	Chance, Dean (1964)	4.6
224	Millwood, Kevin (1999)	4.5
225	Smith, Elmer (1887)	4.5
226	Young, Cy (1898)	4.5
227	Killian, Ed (1907)	4.5
228	Wyatt, Whit (1941)	4.5
229	Vazquez, Javier (2003)	4.5
230	Hutchison, Bill (1892)	4.5
231	Lemon, Bob (1948)	4.5
232	Overall, Orval (1909)	4.5
233	Viola, Frank (1987)	4.5
234	Luque, Dolf (1925)	4.5
235	Haddix, Harvey (1953)	4.5
236	Johnson, Walter (1910)	4.5
237	Conway, Pete (1888)	4.5
238	Stivetts, Jack (1890)	4.5
239	Weaver, Sam (1878)	4.5
240	Spalding, Al (1872)	4.5
241	Martinez, Pedro (2002)	4.4
242	Key, Jimmy (1987)	4.4
243	Clarkson, John (1891)	4.4
244	Spalding, Al (1873)	4.4
245	McMahon, Sadie (1890)	4.4
246	Halladay, Roy (2002)	4.4
247	Ford, Russ (1911)	4.4
248	Sanders, Ben (1889)	4.4
249	Maddux, Greg (2000)	4.4
250	Niekro, Phil (1974)	4.4
251	Vaughn, Hippo (1919)	4.4
252	Walsh, Ed (1907)	4.4
253	Drysdale, Don (1964)	4.4
254	Coveleski, Harry (1916)	4.4
255	McLain, Denny (1968)	4.4
256	Jones, Randy (1975)	4.4
257	Fidrych, Mark (1976)	4.3
258	Higuera, Teddy (1986)	4.3
259	Bunning, Jim (1966)	4.3
260	McGinnity, Joe (1904)	4.3
261	Gubicza, Mark (1988)	4.3
262	Glavine, Tom (1998)	4.3
263	Rucker, Nap (1912)	4.3
264	Maloney, Jim (1965)	4.3
265	Willis, Vic (1899)	4.3
266	Gomez, Lefty (1934)	4.3
267	Ferrell, Wes (1936)	4.3
268	Bunning, Jim (1967)	4.3
269	Sain, Johnny (1948)	4.3
270	Hershiser, Orel (1985)	4.3
271	Roberts, Dave (1971)	4.3
272	Hentgen, Pat (1996)	4.3
273	Candiotti, Tom (1991)	4.3
274	Candelaria, John (1977)	4.3
275	Taylor, Billy (1884)	4.3
276	Glavine, Tom (1991)	4.3
277	Morris, Ed (1885)	4.3
278	Halladay, Roy (2003)	4.3
279	Ehret, Red (1890)	4.3
280	Griffith, Clark (1895)	4.3
281	Hubbell, Carl (1936)	4.3
282	Ellsworth, Dick (1963)	4.2
283	Adams, Babe (1913)	4.2
284	Coombs, Jack (1910)	4.2
285	Martinez, Pedro (1998)	4.2
286	Cicotte, Eddie (1919)	4.2
287	Lowe, Derek (2002)	4.2
288	Faber, Red (1922)	4.2
289	Leonard, Dutch (1914)	4.2
290	Pettitte, Andy (1997)	4.2
291	Grove, Lefty (1939)	4.2
292	Lemon, Bob (1949)	4.2
293	Mathews, Bobby (1883)	4.2
294	Grove, Lefty (1928)	4.2
295	Stieb, Dave (1982)	4.2
296	Buffinton, Charlie (1884)	4.2
297	Pierce, Billy (1955)	4.2
298	Ferrell, Wes (1932)	4.2
299	Palmer, Jim (1975)	4.2
300	Lucas, Red (1932)	4.2

Appendix F

The Annual Record

This section contains the season-by-season standings and records for all teams since 1871, plus 47 statistical categories for each team's batting, baserunning, pitching and fielding.

The figure for the leading team in a given category is displayed in bold type. Where data are unavailable, there will be an ellipsis ("....") in the statistical column. Also presented here are the top three players/pitchers in up to 36 categories per season. When fewer than 36 categories are shown, it means that official records are lacking, or the data is not reconstructable at present. The criterion used for identifying pitching leaders is a minimum of one inning pitched per scheduled game; for batters the criterion employed is the one officially in place at the time or, in the absence of any known practice, 3.1 plate appearances per scheduled game.

Ties in counting stats are common, and occasionally they are so numerous that space does not permit listing all the players by name. Where rounding off has created the appearance of a tie, the true leader—as extra decimal places for a complete calculation would have revealed—is listed first. An example is the AL batting race of 1949, in which George Kell and Ted Williams are both shown as hitting .343; Kell in fact hit .3429 and Williams .3428. Both men are credited with batting averages of .343, but Kell, the actual leader, is listed first. (This procedure does not hold for calculated stats based on pitchers' won-lost percentages, where the narrow array of data frequently produces actual ties.)

For additional information about a team in a given year, refer to the various registers and the rosters. Team abbreviations used in the Annual Record are to be found on the last page of this book.

Following are the abbreviations employed in the team statistical reviews of the Annual Record, aside from those that are defined adequately in the introductions to the Player or Pitcher Registers, plus brief descriptions of what the less common statistics measure. For information about formulas and computation, see the Glossary.

BATTING AND BASERUNNING

PCT	Percentage of games won
GB	Games Behind the league or division leader
OR	Opponents' Runs scored
TB	Total Bases
EW	Expected Wins
OPS	On-Base Percentage plus Slugging Average
OPS+	Normalized and park-adjusted Production. A figure of 100 is a league-average performance.
BR/A	Adjusted Batting Runs (Normalized to league average and adjusted for home-park factor. A mark of 100 is a league-average performance. Pitcher batting is removed from all league batting statistics before normalization for a variety of reasons expanded upon in the Glossary.)

PF	Park Factor (Calculated separately for batters and pitchers: above 100 signifies a park favorable to hitters, below 100 signifies a park favorable to pitchers; see Glossary for further information.)
RC	Runs Created (Bill James' formulation for run contribution from a variety of batting and baserunning events; many different formulas are applied, depending on data available; see Glossary.)

PITCHING AND FIELDING

SH	Shutouts (Individual and combined when calculated for teams; individual only for Top 3 leaders.)
H/G	Hits allowed per Game
PF	Park Factor
E	Errors
DP	Double Plays
BW	Batting Wins (Adjusted Batting Runs divided by the number of runs required to create an additional win beyond average; average is defined as a team record of .500 because a league won-lost average must be .500. For more technical data about Runs Per Win and Batting Run formulas, see Glossary.)
PW	Pitching Wins (Adjusted Pitching Runs divided by the number of runs required to create an additional win beyond average; average is defined as a team record of .500 because a league won-lost average must be .500. For more technical data about Runs Per Win and Pitching Run formulas, see Glossary.)
FW	Fielding Wins (Fielding Runs divided by the number of runs required to create an additional win beyond average; average is defined as a team record of .500 because a league won-lost average must be .500. For more technical data about Runs Per Win and Fielding Run formulas, see Glossary.)
DIF	Differential (Difference between the team's actual won-lost record and that predicted by the total of its Pitching Wins, Batting Wins, Fielding Wins, and Stolen Base Wins; indicates the extent to which a team outperformed or underperformed its talent.)

Other stats shown only on an individual basis in the Annual Record are as follows (definitions supplied only when not available from Player or Pitcher Register introductions):

Fewest Hits/Game	Game defined as nine innings.
Fewest Bases on Balls Per Game	Game defined as nine innings.
Strikeouts Per Game	Game defined as nine innings.

1871 National Association

TEAM	G	W	L	PCT	GB	R	OR	EW	AB	H	2B	3B	HR	TB	BB	SO	SB	CS	AVG	OBP	SLG	OPS	OPS+	BR/A	PF	RC
ATH	28	21	7	.750	....	376	266	19	1281	410	66	27	9	557	46	23	56	12	.320	.344	.435	.778	125	37	99	216
BOS	31	20	10	.667	2	401	303	19	1372	426	70	37	3	579	60	19	73	16	.310	.339	.422	.761	115	17	103	227
CHI	28	19	9	.679	2	302	241	17	1196	323	52	21	10	447	60	22	69	21	.270	.305	.374	.679	86	-39	111	161
MUT	33	16	17	.485	7.5	302	313	16	1404	403	43	21	1	491	33	15	46	15	.287	.303	.350	.653	97	5	91	167
OLY	32	15	15	.500	7	310	303	15	1353	375	54	26	6	499	48	13	48	13	.277	.302	.369	.671	98	1	95	169
TRO	29	13	15	.464	8	351	362	14	1248	384	51	34	6	521	49	16	62	24	.308	.334	.417	.751	114	16	101	199
CLE	29	10	19	.345	11.5	249	341	10	1186	328	35	40	7	464	26	25	18	8	.277	.292	.391	.683	101	4	94	144
KEK	19	7	12	.368	9.5	137	243	5	746	178	19	8	2	219	33	9	16	4	.239	.271	.294	.564	62	-40	102	65
ROK	25	4	21	.160	15.5	231	287	10	1036	274	44	25	3	377	38	30	53	10	.264	.291	.364	.654	92	-8	95	128
Total	**127**					**2659**			**10822**	**3101**	**434**	**239**	**47**		**393**	**175**	**441**	**123**	**.287**	**.312**	**.384**	**.695**				

Runs		Hits		Doubles		Triples		Home Runs		Total Bases	
Barnes, R. (Bos)	66	McVey, C. (Bos)	66	Anson, C. (Rok)	11	Bass, J. (Cle)	10	Meyerle, L. (Ath)	4	Meyerle, L. (Ath)	91
Birdsall, D. (Bos)	51	Meyerle, L. (Ath)	64	6 players tied with	10	Barnes, R. (Bos)	9	Pike, L. (Tro)	4	Meyerle, L. (Ath)	91
2 players tied with	47	Barnes, R. (Bos)	63			3 players tied with	7	Treacey, F. (Chi)	4	2 players tied with	85

Runs Batted In		Bases On Balls		Stolen Bases		Batting Average		On-Base Percentage		Slugging Average	
McVey, C. (Bos)	43	Pinkham, E. (Chi)	18	McGeary, M. (Tro)	20	Meyerle, L. (Ath)	.492	Meyerle, L. (Ath)	.500	Meyerle, L. (Ath)	.700
Meyerle, L. (Ath)	40	Barnes, R. (Bos)	13	Wood, J. (Chi)	18	McVey, C. (Bos)	.431	Barnes, R. (Bos)	.447	Pike, L. (Tro)	.654
Pike, L. (Tro)	39	Wright, H. (Bos)	13	Cuthbert, N. (Ath)	16	Barnes, R. (Bos)	.401	McVey, C. (Bos)	.435	Barnes, R. (Bos)	.580

Adjusted OPS		Adjusted Batting Runs		Runs Created/Game		Fielding Runs		Win Shares – Batters		TPW – Batters	
Meyerle, L. (Ath)	243	Meyerle, L. (Ath)	24.0	Meyerle, L. (Ath)	23.20	Force, D. (Oly)	16.2			Barnes, R. (Bos)	1.6
Pike, L. (Tro)	193	Barnes, R. (Bos)	17.0	Wood, J. (Chi)	15.00	Barnes, R. (Bos)	10.0			Spalding, A. (Bos)	1.2
Barnes, R. (Bos)	186	McVey, C. (Bos)	15.0	Barnes, R. (Bos)	14.70	Pinkham, E. (Chi)	8.2			Wood, J. (Chi)	1.2

TEAM	CG	SH	SV	IP	H	H/G	ER	HR	BB	SO	OAV	RAT	ERA	ERA+	CERA	PR+	PF	FA	E	DP	FR	BW	PW	FW	TPW	DIF
ATH	27	0	0	249	329	11.9	137	3	53	16	.278	1.534	4.95	81	....	-28.9	95	.845	194	13	3.2	2.4	-1.9	.2	.7	6.3
BOS	22	1	3	276	367	12.0	109	2	42	23	.279	1.482	3.55	117	....	13.2	98	.834	243	24	5.2	1.1	.9	.3	2.3	2.7
CHI	25	0	1	251	308	11.0	77	6	28	22	.263	1.339	2.76	166	....	39.0	109	.829	229	16	11.9	-2.5	2.5	.8	.8	4.2
MUT	32	1	0	293	373	11.5	121	7	42	22	.271	1.416	3.72	102	....	0.9	90	.840	235	14	1.4	.3	.1	.1	.5	-.5
OLY	32	0	0	282	371	11.8	137	4	45	13	.277	1.475	4.37	95	....	-27.2	99	.850	218	20	20.6	.0	-1.8	1.3	-.4	.4
TRO	28	0	0	250	431	15.5	153	4	75	12	.334	2.024	5.51	76	....	-37.4	100	.845	198	22	1.4	1.0	-2.4	.1	-1.3	.3
CLE	23	0	0	254	346	12.3	116	13	53	34	.284	1.571	4.11	100	....	19.9	98	.818	234	15	-19.4	.3	1.3	-1.3	.3	-4.3
KEK	19	1	0	169	261	13.9	97	5	21	17	.310	1.669	5.17	88	....	4.0	108	.803	163	8	-15.3	-2.6	.3	-1.0	-3.3	1.3
ROK	23	1	0	226	315	12.5	108	3	34	16	.289	1.544	4.30	95	....	3.0	97	.821	220	14	-8.5	-.5	.2	-.6	-.9	-7.1
Total	**231**	**4**	**4**	**2250**		**12.4**	**1055**					**1.553**	**4.22**													

Wins		Win Percentage		Games		Complete Games		Shutouts		Saves	
Spalding, A. (Bos)	19	McBride, D. (Ath)	.783	Wolters, R. (Mut)	32	Wolters, R. (Mut)	31	4 players tied with	1	Wright, H. (Bos)	3
McBride, D. (Ath)	18	Zettlein, G. (Chi)	.667	Spalding, A. (Bos)	31	Brainard, A. (Oly)	30				
Zettlein, G. (Chi)	18	Spalding, A. (Bos)	.655	Brainard, A. (Oly)	30	McMullin, J. (Tro)	28				

Innings Pitched		Fewest Hits/Game		Fewest BB/Game		Strikeouts		Ratio		Earned Run Average	
Wolters, R. (Mut)	283	Wolters, R. (Mut)	10.97	Zettlein, G. (Chi)	.93	Pratt, A. (Cle)	34	Zettlein, G. (Chi)	1.34	Zettlein, G. (Chi)	2.73
Brainard, A. (Oly)	264	Zettlein, G. (Chi)	11.14	Mathews, B. (Kek)	1.12	Spalding, A. (Bos)	23	Wolters, R. (Mut)	1.36	Spalding, A. (Bos)	3.36
Spalding, A. (Bos)	257¹	McBride, D. (Ath)	11.55	Wolters, R. (Mut)	1.24	2 players tied with	22	Spalding, A. (Bos)	1.44	Wolters, R. (Mut)	3.43

Adjusted ERA		Component ERA		Opponents' Batting Avg.		Adjusted Pitching Runs		Win Shares – Pitchers		TPW – Pitchers	
Zettlein, G. (Chi)	168			Wolters, R. (Mut)	.262	Zettlein, G. (Chi)	38			Zettlein, G. (Chi)	2.0
Spalding, A. (Bos)	124			Zettlein, G. (Chi)	.265	Pratt, A. (Cle)	26			Wolters, R. (Mut)	1.9
Wolters, R. (Mut)	110			McBride, D. (Ath)	.272	Spalding, A. (Bos)	18			Pratt, A. (Cle)	1.9

1872 National Association

TEAM	G	W	L	PCT	GB	R	OR	EW	AB	H	2B	3B	HR	TB	BB	SO	SB	CS	AVG	OBP	SLG	OPS	OPS+	BR/A	PF	RC
BOS	48	39	8	.830	....	521	236	39	2122	672	106	30	7	859	29	26	47	14	.317	.326	.405	.731	121	43	105	307
BAL	58	35	19	.648	7.5	617	434	36	2576	753	105	30	15	963	27	28	37	18	.292	.300	.374	.673	102	-6	105	301
MUT	56	34	20	.630	8.5	523	362	37	2431	674	85	12	4	795	55	52	59	21	.277	.293	.327	.620	99	19	94	254
ATH	47	30	14	.682	7.5	539	349	31	2141	679	79	25	4	820	69	47	58	31	.317	.338	.383	.721	123	55	100	302
TRO	25	15	10	.600	13	273	191	17	1098	330	56	8	5	419	7	14	9	7	.301	.305	.382	.687	107	4	101	131
ATL	37	9	28	.243	25	237	473	7	1460	374	37	10	0	431	19	24	19	14	.256	.266	.295	.561	63	-87	117	122
CLE	22	6	16	.273	20.5	174	254	7	943	272	28	5	0	310	17	13	12	3	.288	.301	.329	.630	107	14	94	104
MAN	24	5	19	.208	22.5	220	348	7	1022	294	29	9	1	344	5	12	5	3	.288	.291	.337	.628	110	16	94	112
ECK	29	3	26	.103	27	152	413	3	1070	241	24	6	0	277	14	29	8	4	.225	.235	.259	.494	59	-26	85	66
OLY	9	2	7	.222	18	54	140	1	365	91	10	3	0	107	4	4	0	3	.249	.257	.293	.551	81	-7	95	30
NAT	11	0	11	.000	21	80	190	2	451	108	6	1	0	116	1	3	....	....	.239	.241	.257	.498	41	-38	117	26
Total	**183**					**3390**			**15679**	**4488**	**567**	**139**	**36**		**247**	**252**	**254**	**118**	**.286**	**.297**	**.347**	**.644**				

Runs		Hits		Doubles		Triples		Home Runs		Total Bases	
Eggler, D. (Mut)	94	Barnes, R. (Bos)	99	Barnes, R. (Bos)	28	Gould, C. (Bos)	8	Pike, L. (Bal)	7	Barnes, R. (Bos)	134
Wright, G. (Bos)	87	Eggler, D. (Mut)	98	Eggler, D. (Mut)	20	Anson, C. (Ath)	7	Gedney, C. (Tro,Eck)	3	Pike, L. (Bal)	130
Cuthbert, N. (Ath)	83	Force, D. (Tro,Bal)	94	Hall, G. (Bal)	17	2 players tied with	6	6 players tied with	2	Wright, G. (Bos)	120

Runs Batted In		Bases On Balls		Stolen Bases		Batting Average		On-Base Percentage		Slugging Average	
Pike, L. (Bal)	61	Mack, D. (Ath)	23	Eggler, D. (Mut)	18	Barnes, R. (Bos)	.432	Anson, C. (Ath)	.455	Barnes, R. (Bos)	.585
Anson, C. (Ath)	50	Anson, C. (Ath)	16	Cuthbert, N. (Ath)	14	Force, D. (Bal,Tro)	.418	Barnes, R. (Bos)	.454	Anson, C. (Ath)	.525
Start, J. (Mut)	50	McMullin, J. (Mut)	11	Wright, G. (Bos)	14	Anson, C. (Ath)	.415	Force, D. (Bal,Tro)	.423	Force, D. (Bal,Tro)	.493

Adjusted OPS		Adjusted Batting Runs		Runs Created/Game		Fielding Runs		Win Shares – Batters		TPW – Batters	
Barnes, R. (Bos)	206	Barnes, R. (Bos)	29.0	Barnes, R. (Bos)	15.90	Ferguson, B. (Atl)	26.8			Spalding, A. (Bos)	4.5
Anson, C. (Ath)	200	Anson, C. (Ath)	25.0	Anson, C. (Ath)	13.00	Barnes, R. (Bos)	19.7			Barnes, R. (Bos)	3.2
Force, D. (Bal,Tro)	176	Force, D. (Tro,Bal)	19.0	Force, D. (Bal,Tro)	11.70	Wright, G. (Bos)	14.4			Eggler, D. (Mut)	2.2

TEAM	CG	SH	SV	IP	H	H/G	ER	HR	BB	SO	OAV	RAT	ERA	ERA+	CERA	PR+	PF	FA	E	DP	FR	BW	PW	FW	TPW	DIF
BOS	41	**4**	**4**	430[1]	443	**9.3**	95	**0**	27	28	**.229**	**1.092**	**1.99**	188	....	**50.7**	100	**.876**	278	**43**	**37.7**	3.0	3.2	**2.6**	**8.8**	7.2
BAL	48	1	1	**516**	573	10.0	173	3	63	**75**	.242	1.233	3.02	124	....	46.0	101	.829	432	22	-3.8	-.4	**3.2**	-.3	2.5	5.5
MUT	**54**	3	1	512	623	11.0	145	2	32	44	.260	1.279	2.55	135	....	28.6	93	.867	326	33	22.2	1.3	2.0	1.5	4.8	2.2
ATH	47	1	0	419[1]	508	10.9	140	3	26	44	.263	1.273	3.00	121	....	15.5	98	.858	298	20	13.5	**3.8**	1.1	.9	5.8	2.2
TRO	17	2	1	225	277	11.1	77	2	10	18	.269	1.276	3.08	121	....	8.0	100	.859	154	9	7.8	.3	.6	.5	1.4	1.6
ATL	37	0	0	336	570	15.3	189	6	19	13	.326	1.753	5.06	91	....	-10.6	124	.810	358	14	-6.4	-6.1	-.7	-.4	-7.3	-1.7
CLE	15	0	0	199	285	12.9	101	6	24	11	.299	1.553	4.57	80	....	-13.2	98	.816	184	17	-7.3	1.0	-.9	-.5	-.4	-4.6
MAN	20	0	0	211	374	16.0	140	6	14	5	.336	1.839	5.97	61	....	-33.5	99	.806	226	11	-20.4	1.1	-2.3	-1.4	-2.6	-4.4
ECK	28	0	0	259[1]	494	17.1	165	6	24	11	.361	1.997	5.73	60	....	-90.7	93	.797	284	5	-26.3	-1.8	-6.3	-1.8	-9.9	-1.1
OLY	9	0	0	79	**148**	16.9	**56**	**0**	5	1	.352	1.937	6.38	**58**	....	-19.0	99	.786	**96**	7	-4.8	-.5	-1.3	-.3	-2.1	.1
NAT	11	0	0	99	193	17.6	76	2	**3**	2	.365	1.980	6.91	68	....	-13.2	127	.774	120	2	-10.9	-2.7	-.9	-.8	-4.3	-.7
Total	**327**	**11**	**7**	**3286**		**12.3**	**1357**					**1.441**	**3.72**													

Wins
Spalding, A. (Bos) 38
Cummings, C. (Mut) 33
McBride, D. (Ath) 30

Win Percentage
Fisher, C. (Bal) .909
Spalding, A. (Bos) .826
McBride, D. (Ath) .682

Games
Cummings, C. (Mut) 55
Mathews, B. (Bal) 49
Spalding, A. (Bos) 48

Complete Games
Cummings, C. (Mut) 53
McBride, D. (Ath) 47
Spalding, A. (Bos) 41

Shutouts
Cummings, C. (Mut) 3
Spalding, A. (Bos) 3
Zettlein, G. (Tro,Eck) 2

Saves
Wright, H. (Bos) 4
Zettlein, G. (Tro,Eck) 1
Fisher, C. (Bal) 1

Innings Pitched
Cummings, C. (Mut) 497
McBride, D. (Ath) 419[1]
Mathews, B. (Bal) 406

Fewest Hits/Game
Fisher, C. (Bal) 7.59
Spalding, A. (Bos) 9.27
Mathews, B. (Bal) 10.64

Fewest BB/Game
Stearns, B. (Nat) .27
Buttery, F. (Man) .31
Martin, P. (Eck,Tro) .44

Strikeouts
Mathews, B. (Bal) 55
McBride, D. (Ath) 44
Cummings, C. (Mut) 43

Ratio
Fisher, C. (Bal) .94
Spalding, A. (Bos) 1.10
Zettlein, G. (Tro,Eck) 1.25

Earned Run Average
Fisher, C. (Bal) 1.79
Spalding, A. (Bos) 1.87
Zettlein, G. (Tro,Eck) 2.33

Adjusted ERA
Spalding, A. (Bos) 200
Fisher, C. (Bal) 148
Cummings, C. (Mut) 137

Component ERA

Opponents' Batting Avg.
Fisher, C. (Bal) .198
Spalding, A. (Bos) .232
Mathews, B. (Bal) .257

Adjusted Pitching Runs
Spalding, A. (Bos) 48
Mathews, B. (Bal) 30
Zettlein, G. (Tro,Eck) 30

Win Shares – Pitchers

TPW – Pitchers
Spalding, A. (Bos) 4.5
Zettlein, G. (Tro,Eck) 1.8
Cummings, C. (Mut) 1.7

1873 National Association

TEAM	G	W	L	PCT	GB	R	OR	EW	AB	H	2B	3B	HR	TB	BB	SO	SB	CS	AVG	OBP	SLG	OPS	OPS+	BR/A	PF	RC
BOS	60	43	16	.729	....	**739**	460	43	**2755**	**930**	**146**	**44**	**12**	**1200**	**62**	24	39	27	**.338**	**.352**	**.436**	**.788**	**128**	**69**	108	**446**
PHI	53	36	17	.679	4	526	396	34	2325	645	83	20	8	792	**62**	39	**44**	14	.277	.296	.341	.637	90	-29	104	254
BAL	57	34	22	.607	7.5	644	451	38	2562	810	106	38	9	1019	41	25	22	11	.316	.327	.398	.725	123	68	100	356
ATH	52	28	23	.549	11	474	403	30	2266	683	71	20	4	806	35	32	29	24	.301	.312	.356	.668	97	-27	107	270
MUT	53	29	24	.547	11	424	385	29	2214	622	51	36	5	760	42	22	15	6	.281	.294	.343	.638	98	-3	99	242
ATL	55	17	37	.315	23.5	366	549	17	2210	588	42	23	6	694	53	43	19	11	.266	.283	.314	.597	95	16	89	214
WAS	39	8	31	.205	25	283	485	10	1563	408	38	19	2	490	19	33	5	5	.261	.270	.314	.583	84	-25	97	143
RES	23	2	21	.087	23	98	299	2	868	204	18	8	0	238	8	22	2	**1**	.235	.242	.274	.516	63	-29	92	60
MAR	6	0	6	.000	16.5	26	**152**	0	211	33	1	0	0	34	0	**3**	....	....	.156	.156	.161	.318	3	-15	77	6
Total	**199**					**3580**			**16974**	**4923**	**556**	**208**	**46**		**322**	**243**	**175**	**99**	**.290**	**.303**	**.355**	**.659**				

Runs
Barnes, R. (Bos) 125
Wright, G. (Bos) 99
Spalding, A. (Bos) 83

Hits
Barnes, R. (Bos) 137
Wright, G. (Bos) 126
White, D. (Bos) 121

Doubles
Barnes, R. (Bos) 29
4 players tied with 19

Triples
Mills, E. (Bal) 9
4 players tied with 8

Home Runs
Pike, L. (Bal) 4
Meyerle, L. (Phi) 3
Wright, G. (Bos) 3

Total Bases
Barnes, R. (Bos) 188
Wright, G. (Bos) 170
White, D. (Bos) 148

Runs Batted In
White, D. (Bos) 66
Barnes, R. (Bos) 62
Leonard, A. (Bos) 61

Bases On Balls
Barnes, R. (Bos) 18
Mack, D. (Phi) 15
2 players tied with 14

Stolen Bases
Barnes, R. (Bos) 13
Cuthbert, N. (Phi) 13
McMullin, J. (Ath) 9

Batting Average
Barnes, R. (Bos) .425
Anson, C. (Ath) .398
White, D. (Bos) .390

On-Base Percentage
Barnes, R. (Bos) .456
Anson, C. (Ath) .409
Wright, G. (Bos) .402

Slugging Average
Barnes, R. (Bos) .584
Wright, G. (Bos) .523
McVey, C. (Bal) .484

Adjusted OPS
Barnes, R. (Bos) 191
Wright, G. (Bos) 160
McVey, C. (Bal) 159

Adjusted Batting Runs
Barnes, R. (Bos) 36.0
Wright, G. (Bos) 20.0
Pabor, C. (Atl) 17.0

Runs Created/Game
Barnes, R. (Bos) 15.20
Wright, G. (Bos) 10.70
White, D. (Bos) 9.80

Fielding Runs
Ferguson, B. (Atl) 22.2
Barnes, R. (Bos) 14.8
Gedney, C. (Mut) 11.0

Win Shares – Batters

TPW – Batters
Spalding, A. (Bos) 4.4
Barnes, R. (Bos) 3.4
Mathews, B. (Mut) 2.6

TEAM	CG	SH	SV	IP	H	H/G	ER	HR	BB	SO	OAV	RAT	ERA	ERA+	CERA	PR+	PF	FA	E	DP	FR	BW	PW	FW	TPW	DIF
BOS	47	1	**6**	**536**	708	11.9	154	5	35	31	.282	1.386	**2.59**	128	....	**42.8**	102	.838	465	**46**	0.6	**4.9**	**3.0**	.0	**7.9**	6.1
PHI	50	0	0	481	627	11.7	148	3	44	28	.279	1.395	2.77	119	....	12.9	101	.848	379	43	15.2	-2.1	.9	1.1	-.1	10.1
BAL	**55**	1	0	508[2]	680	12.0	170	4	42	37	.284	1.419	3.01	108	....	-3.0	100	**.855**	366	33	**16.8**	4.8	-.2	**1.2**	5.8	.2
ATH	44	**3**	2	475	553	10.5	160	4	58	41	.257	1.286	3.03	113	....	6.2	105	.842	383	30	14.1	-1.9	.4	1.0	-.4	3.4
MUT	48	2	0	477	539	**10.2**	139	5	69	**76**	**.252**	**1.275**	2.62	121	....	41.1	97	.821	419	28	-12.5	-.2	2.9	-.9	1.8	1.2
ATL	52	1	0	500	737	13.3	221	8	42	15	.305	1.558	3.98	76	....	-59.9	93	.820	505	30	7.6	1.1	-4.2	.5	-2.6	-7.4
WAS	39	0	0	346	593	15.4	181	10	22	7	.338	1.777	4.71	71	....	-48.7	103	.818	334	27	-3.6	-1.8	-3.4	-.3	-5.5	-5.5
RES	22	0	0	207	342	14.9	74	6	9	8	.329	1.696	3.22	104	....	27.7	103	.787	247	9	-24.6	-2.1	2.0	-1.7	-1.8	-7.2
MAR	6	0	0	54	**144**	24.0	**48**	**1**	**1**	0	.442	2.685	8.00	**40**	....	-15.1	99	.761	**74**	0	-13.5	-1.1	-1.1	-1.0	-3.1	.1
Total	**363**	**8**	**8**	**3584[2]**		**12.4**	**1295**					**1.463**	**3.25**													

Wins
Spalding, A. (Bos) 41
Zettlein, G. (Phi) 36
Mathews, B. (Mut) 29

Win Percentage
Spalding, A. (Bos) .745
Zettlein, G. (Phi) .706
Cummings, C. (Bal) .667

Games
Spalding, A. (Bos) 60
Britt, J. (Atl) 54
Mathews, B. (Mut) 52

Complete Games
Britt, J. (Atl) 51
Zettlein, G. (Phi) 49
Mathews, B. (Mut) 47

Shutouts
McBride, D. (Ath) 3
Mathews, B. (Mut) 2
3 players tied with 1

Saves
Wright, H. (Bos) 4
Spalding, A. (Bos) 2
Fisher, C. (Ath) 1

Innings Pitched
Spalding, A. (Bos) 497[2]
Britt, J. (Atl) 480[2]
Zettlein, G. (Phi) 460

Fewest Hits/Game
Fisher, C. (Ath) 9.60
Mathews, B. (Mut) 9.93
McBride, D. (Ath) 10.65

Fewest BB/Game
Campbell, H. (Res) .38
Stearns, B. (Was) .48
Spalding, A. (Bos) .51

Strikeouts
Mathews, B. (Mut) 75
Spalding, A. (Bos) 50
Cummings, C. (Bal) 34

Ratio
Fisher, C. (Ath) 1.19
Mathews, B. (Mut) 1.24
McBride, D. (Ath) 1.31

Earned Run Average
Fisher, C. (Ath) 1.81
Spalding, A. (Bos) 2.46
Mathews, B. (Mut) 2.56

Adjusted ERA
Fisher, C. (Ath) 188
Spalding, A. (Bos) 135
Mathews, B. (Mut) 124

Component ERA

Opponents' Batting Avg.
Fisher, C. (Ath) .241
Mathews, B. (Mut) .247
McBride, D. (Ath) .260

Adjusted Pitching Runs
Spalding, A. (Bos) 47
Mathews, B. (Mut) 41
Campbell, H. (Res) 29

Win Shares – Pitchers

TPW – Pitchers
Spalding, A. (Bos) 4.4
Mathews, B. (Mut) 2.6
Campbell, H. (Res) 1.8

1874 National Association

TEAM	G	W	L	PCT	GB	R	OR	EW	AB	H	2B	3B	HR	TB	BB	SO	SB	CS	AVG	OBP	SLG	OPS	OPS+	BR/A	PF	RC
BOS	71	52	18	.743	....	**735**	415	53	**3129**	**977**	**121**	**61**	**17**	**1271**	34	**28**	**45**	19	**.312**	**.320**	**.406**	**.726**	**129**	**82**	106	**421**
MUT	65	42	23	.646	7.5	501	377	42	2730	714	89	28	7	880	**36**	40	36	**4**	.262	.271	.322	.593	92	-31	103	249
ATH	55	33	22	.600	11.5	441	**344**	34	2259	647	83	18	6	784	24	51	36	14	.286	.294	.347	.641	99	-16	109	236
PHI	58	29	29	.500	17	476	428	32	2435	677	78	50	2	861	28	33	27	18	.278	.286	.354	.640	107	11	103	262
CHI	59	28	31	.475	18.5	418	480	25	2462	685	87	4	4	792	32	54	32	12	.278	.287	.322	.609	99	-5	101	237
ATL	56	22	33	.400	22.5	301	450	17	2169	498	45	8	1	562	31	51	12	**4**	.230	.240	.259	.500	73	-37	88	141
HAR	53	16	37	.302	27.5	371	471	20	2144	591	86	18	2	719	31	63	42	21	.276	.286	.335	.621	97	-17	105	210
BAL	47	9	38	.191	31.5	227	505	8	1776	435	45	7	1	497	22	37	12	5	.245	.254	.280	.534	76	-44	99	132
Total	**232**					**3470**			**19104**	**5224**	**634**	**194**	**40**		**238**	**357**	**242**	**97**	**.273**	**.282**	**.333**	**.616**				

Runs
- McVey, C. (Bos) 91
- O'Rourke, J. (Bos) 82
- Spalding, A. (Bos) 80

Hits
- McVey, C. (Bos) 123
- Spalding, A. (Bos) 119
- Leonard, A. (Bos) 108

Doubles
- Pike, L. (Har) 22
- McVey, C. (Bos) 21
- 2 players tied with 19

Triples
- Wright, G. (Bos) 15
- Craver, B. (Phi) 11
- Holdsworth, J. (Phi) 9

Home Runs
- O'Rourke, J. (Bos) 5
- 3 players tied with 3

Total Bases
- McVey, C. (Bos) 165
- O'Rourke, J. (Bos) 150
- Wright, G. (Bos) 149

Runs Batted In
- McVey, C. (Bos) 71
- O'Rourke, J. (Bos) 61
- Craver, B. (Phi) 56

Bases On Balls
- Nelson, C. (Mut) 9
- Barnes, R. (Bos) 8
- McMullin, J. (Ath) 8

Stolen Bases
- Barlow, T. (Har) 17
- 3 players tied with 11

Batting Average
- Meyerle, L. (Chi) .394
- McVey, C. (Bos) .359
- Pike, L. (Har) .355

On-Base Percentage
- Meyerle, L. (Chi) .401
- Pike, L. (Har) .368
- McMullin, J. (Ath) .366

Slugging Average
- Pike, L. (Har) .504
- Craver, B. (Phi) .498
- Meyerle, L. (Chi) .488

Adjusted OPS
- Meyerle, L. (Chi) 182
- Pike, L. (Har) 168
- Craver, B. (Phi) 164

Adjusted Batting Runs
- Meyerle, L. (Chi) 22.0
- McVey, C. (Bos) 21.0
- Craver, B. (Phi) 18.0

Runs Created/Game
- Meyerle, L. (Chi) 10.10
- Pike, L. (Har) 9.00
- Craver, B. (Phi) 8.80

Fielding Runs
- White, W. (Bal) 19.4
- Burdock, J. (Mut) 16.4
- Ryan, J. (Bal) 13.3

Win Shares – Batters

TPW – Batters
- Spalding, A. (Bos) 6.7
- Mathews, B. (Mut) 3.6
- Pike, L. (Har) 2.0

TEAM	CG	SH	SV	IP	H	H/G	ER	HR	BB	SO	OAV	RAT	ERA	ERA+	CERA	PR+	PF	FA	E	DP	FR	BW	PW	FW	TPW	DIF
BOS	**65**	**4**	**3**	**634**	779	11.1	166	**1**	23	31	.269	1.265	2.36	125	....	**69.2**	99	**.850**	489	**53**	2.4	**6.4**	3.1	.2	**9.7**	7.3
MUT	62	**4**	0	586	663	10.2	150	3	41	**101**	.252	1.201	**2.30**	133	....	47.2	103	.847	438	22	3.0	-2.4	**3.7**	.2	1.5	8.5
ATH	55	0	0	487	**514**	**9.5**	**138**	6	32	37	**.241**	**1.121**	2.55	124	....	22.6	106	.839	**396**	34	10.7	-1.2	1.8	.8	1.3	4.7
PHI	56	3	0	522	673	11.6	172	4	19	61	.277	1.326	2.97	103	....	12.1	101	.809	518	38	-8.4	.9	.9	-.7	1.2	-1.2
CHI	58	3	0	533[2]	684	11.5	192	7	45	26	.282	1.366	3.24	94	....	-43.3	102	.829	477	27	**12.2**	-.4	-3.4	**.9**	-2.8	1.8
ATL	56	1	0	506	618	11.0	180	15	**11**	42	.270	1.243	3.20	88	....	-24.0	94	.822	500	15	2.3	-2.9	-1.9	.2	-4.5	-.5
HAR	45	0	0	481	653	12.2	189	**1**	28	39	.294	1.416	3.54	89	....	-3.7	105	.797	521	17	-17.0	-1.3	-.3	-1.3	-2.9	-7.1
BAL	42	0	0	420	640	13.7	201	3	39	20	.316	1.617	4.31	**71**	....	-22.9	102	.812	436	15	-5.0	-3.4	-4.3	-.4	-8.1	-5.9
Total	**439**	**15**	**3**	**4169[2]**		**11.3**	**1388**					**1.310**	**3.00**													

Wins
- Spalding, A. (Bos) 52
- Mathews, B. (Mut) 42
- McBride, D. (Ath) 33

Win Percentage
- Spalding, A. (Bos) .765
- Mathews, B. (Mut) .656
- McBride, D. (Ath) .600

Games
- Spalding, A. (Bos) 71
- Mathews, B. (Mut) 65
- Zettlein, G. (Chi) 57

Complete Games
- Spalding, A. (Bos) 65
- Mathews, B. (Mut) 62
- Zettlein, G. (Chi) 57

Shutouts
- Mathews, B. (Mut) 4
- Spalding, A. (Bos) 4
- 2 players tied with 3

Saves
- Wright, H. (Bos) 3
- Stearns, B. (Har) 1

Innings Pitched
- Spalding, A. (Bos) 617[1]
- Mathews, B. (Mut) 578
- Zettlein, G. (Chi) 515[2]

Fewest Hits/Game
- McBride, D. (Ath) 9.50
- Mathews, B. (Mut) 10.15
- Bond, T. (Atl) 10.97

Fewest BB/Game
- Bond, T. (Atl) .14
- Spalding, A. (Bos) .34
- Cummings, C. (Phi) .34

Strikeouts
- Mathews, B. (Mut) 101
- Bond, T. (Atl) 92
- Cummings, C. (Phi) 61

Ratio
- McBride, D. (Ath) 1.12
- Mathews, B. (Mut) 1.20
- Bond, T. (Atl) 1.24

Earned Run Average
- McBride, D. (Ath) 1.64
- Mathews, B. (Mut) 1.90
- Spalding, A. (Bos) 1.92

Adjusted ERA
- Spalding, A. (Bos) 154
- Mathews, B. (Mut) 133
- McBride, D. (Ath) 124

Component ERA

Opponents' Batting Avg.
- McBride, D. (Ath) .241
- Mathews, B. (Mut) .254
- Bond, T. (Atl) .269

Adjusted Pitching Runs
- Spalding, A. (Bos) 69
- Mathews, B. (Mut) 46
- McBride, D. (Ath) 23

Win Shares – Pitchers

TPW – Pitchers
- Spalding, A. (Bos) 6.7
- Mathews, B. (Mut) 3.6
- McBride, D. (Ath) 1.3

1875 National Association

TEAM	G	W	L	PCT	GB	R	OR	EW	AB	H	2B	3B	HR	TB	BB	SO	SB	CS	AVG	OBP	SLG	OPS	OPS+	BR/A	PF	RC
BOS	82	71	8	.899	....	**831**	343	68	**3515**	**1128**	**167**	51	**15**	**1442**	33	52	93	37	**.321**	**.327**	**.410**	**.737**	**151**	**162**	104	**478**
HAR	86	54	28	.659	18.5	557	343	59	3356	871	92	35	2	1039	34	64	65	33	.260	.267	.310	.577	99	-11	105	289
ATH	77	53	20	.726	15	699	402	55	3250	941	124	**57**	7	1200	**38**	55	75	46	.290	.298	.369	.667	122	50	111	372
STL	70	39	29	.574	26.5	386	369	36	2674	643	85	29	0	786	32	102	**108**	36	.240	.249	.294	.543	98	15	91	198
PHI	70	37	31	.544	28.5	470	376	41	2721	683	67	27	5	819	21	58	105	51	.251	.257	.301	.558	92	-27	104	215
MUT	71	30	38	.441	35.5	328	425	25	2685	633	82	21	7	778	19	47	20	24	.236	.241	.290	.531	81	-57	105	191
CHI	69	30	37	.448	35	379	416	30	2685	699	83	16	0	814	21	65	69	50	.260	.266	.303	.569	100	0	101	223
NH	47	7	40	.149	48	170	397	7	1714	373	41	13	2	446	14	62	35	16	.218	.224	.260	.484	81	-13	87	103
WAS	28	5	23	.179	40.5	107	338	3	1004	194	14	8	0	224	6	42	23	7	.193	.198	.223	.421	52	-42	96	46
RS	19	4	15	.211	37	60	161	2	688	137	20	1	0	159	12	45	27	9	.199	.213	.231	.444	64	-17	90	36
CEN	14	2	12	.143	36.5	70	138	3	530	125	22	3	0	153	10	25	4	....	.236	.250	.289	.539	96	1	92	39
ATL	44	2	42	.045	51.5	132	438	4	1562	304	33	6	2	355	8	36	1	**5**	.195	.199	.227	.426	60	-40	87	74
WES	13	1	12	.077	37	45	**88**	3	449	81	9	6	0	102	1	**22**	4	6	.180	.182	.227	.409	41	-27	105	19
Total	**345**					**4234**			**26833**	**6812**	**839**	**273**	**40**		**249**	**675**	**629**	**320**	**.254**	**.261**	**.310**	**.571**				

Runs
- Barnes, R. (Bos) 115
- Wright, G. (Bos) 106
- O'Rourke, J. (Bos) 97

Hits
- Barnes, R. (Bos) 143
- McVey, C. (Bos) 138
- 2 players tied with 136

Doubles
- McVey, C. (Bos) 36
- White, D. (Bos) 23
- 2 players tied with 22

Triples
- Craver, B. (Ath,Cen) 13
- Hall, G. (Ath) 12
- Pike, L. (StL) 12

Home Runs
- O'Rourke, J. (Bos) 6
- Hall, G. (Ath) 4
- Start, J. (Mut) 4

Total Bases
- McVey, C. (Bos) 201
- Wright, G. (Bos) 176
- Barnes, R. (Bos) 174

Runs Batted In
- McVey, C. (Bos) 87
- Leonard, A. (Bos) 74
- O'Rourke, J. (Bos) 72

Bases On Balls
- Dehlman, H. (StL) 11
- 4 players tied with 9

Stolen Bases
- Murnane, T. (Phi) 30
- Barnes, R. (Bos) 29
- Pike, L. (StL) 25

Batting Average
- White, D. (Bos) .367
- Barnes, R. (Bos) .364
- McVey, C. (Bos) .355

On-Base Percentage
- Barnes, R. (Bos) .375
- White, D. (Bos) .372
- McVey, C. (Bos) .356

Slugging Average
- McVey, C. (Bos) .517
- Pike, L. (StL) .494
- Craver, B. (Ath,Cen) .455

Adjusted OPS
- Pike, L. (StL) 210
- McVey, C. (Bos) 192
- White, D. (Bos) 178

Adjusted Batting Runs
- Pike, L. (StL) 36.0
- McVey, C. (Bos) 35.0
- Barnes, R. (Bos) 32.0

Runs Created/Game
- Barnes, R. (Bos) 9.00
- McVey, C. (Bos) 8.90
- Pike, L. (StL) 8.90

Fielding Runs
- Barnes, R. (Bos) 20.4
- Ferguson, B. (Har) 14.9
- Force, D. (Ath) 11.8

Win Shares – Batters

TPW – Batters
- Barnes, R. (Bos) 4.1
- Spalding, A. (Bos) 3.5
- McVey, C. (Bos) 3.4

TEAM	CG	SH	SV	IP	H	H/G	ER	HR	BB	SO	OAV	RAT	ERA	ERA+	CERA	PR+	PF	FA	E	DP	FR	BW	PW	FW	TPW	DIF
BOS	60	10	**17**	732	751	9.2	138	2	33	110	.242	1.071	1.70	140	....	19.8	96	.870	483	**56**	**30.7**	**13.9**	2.0	**2.6**	**18.5**	13.5
HAR	**83**	**13**	0	**770**	708	**8.3**	138	4	11	**152**	**.221**	**.934**	**1.61**	161	....	**60.2**	105	**.881**	438	47	22.8	-.9	**5.1**	1.9	6.2	6.8
ATH	75	6	0	687	776	10.2	161	4	39	45	.260	1.186	2.11	125	....	14.1	107	.876	419	51	26.9	4.3	1.2	2.3	7.8	9.2
STL	67	5	1	630	636	9.1	148	3	21	71	.238	1.043	2.11	105	....	-3.1	90	.869	425	36	12.8	1.2	-.3	1.1	2.1	2.9
PHI	64	5	0	628	652	9.3	150	6	30	42	.243	1.086	2.15	117	....	20.9	102	.848	477	32	4.7	-2.3	1.8	.4	-.1	3.1
MUT	70	3	0	636[2]	718	10.2	170	4	21	77	.258	1.161	2.40	107	....	14.3	105	.838	526	30	-1.5	-4.8	1.2	-.1	-3.7	-.3
CHI	65	7	0	625	649	9.4	167	**0**	26	55	.244	1.080	2.40	104	....	-1.1	102	.853	478	30	8.1	.0	-.1	.7	.6	-3.6
NH	40	0	0	425	501	10.6	158	5	21	54	.267	1.228	3.35	69	....	-27.4	93	.814	447	24	-21.8	-1.1	-2.3	-1.9	-5.3	-10.7
WAS	23	0	0	250[2]	397	14.2	135	6	10	6	.329	1.624	4.85	**54**	....	-36.6	106	.791	285	8	-25.3	-3.6	-3.1	-2.2	-8.9	-.1
RS	16	2	0	171	209	11.0	64	**0**	**3**	21	.273	1.240	3.37	72	....	-5.0	98	.833	150	6	-13.0	-1.5	-.4	-1.1	-3.0	-2.0
CEN	14	0	0	126	169	12.1	55	**0**	5	6	.296	1.381	3.93	61	....	-6.2	98	.769	164	5	-15.1	.1	-.5	-1.3	-1.7	-3.3
ATL	31	0	0	396	535	12.2	174	6	17	16	.293	1.394	3.95	58	....	-43.5	93	.801	432	20	-29.3	-3.4	-3.7	-2.5	-9.7	-10.3
WES	13	0	0	113	**111**	8.8	**35**	**0**	12	20	.233	1.088	2.79	96	....	-1.7	110	.860	**78**	5	0.3	-2.3	-.1	.0	-2.4	-2.6
Total	**621**	**51**	**18**	**6190[1]**		**9.9**	**1693**					**1.141**	**2.46**													

Wins
Spalding, A. (Bos) ... 54
McBride, D. (Ath) ... 44
Cummings, C. (Har) ... 35

Innings Pitched
Mathews, B. (Mut) ... 626[2]
Spalding, A. (Bos) ... 570
McBride, D. (Ath) ... 538

Adjusted ERA
Galvin, P. (StL) ... 102
Bond, T. (Har) ... 166
Cummings, C. (Har) ... 162

Win Percentage
Spalding, A. (Bos) ... .915
Manning, J. (Bos) ... .882
McBride, D. (Ath) ... .759

Fewest Hits/Game
Bond, T. (Har) ... 7.72
Cummings, C. (Har) ... 8.57
Fisher, C. (Phi) ... 8.67

Component ERA

Games
Spalding, A. (Bos) ... 72
Mathews, B. (Mut) ... 70
2 players tied with ... 60

Fewest BB/Game
Cummings, C. (Har) ... .09
Blong, J. (RS) ... .14
Bond, T. (Har) ... .18

Opponents' Batting Avg.
Borden, J. (Phi) ... .181
Bond, T. (Har) ... .210
Cummings, C. (Har) ... .228

Complete Games
Mathews, B. (Mut) ... 69
McBride, D. (Ath) ... 59
Bradley, G. (StL) ... 57

Strikeouts
Cummings, C. (Har) ... 82
Mathews, B. (Mut) ... 75
Spalding, A. (Bos) ... 75

Adjusted Pitching Runs
Cummings, C. (Har) ... 34
Bond, T. (Har) ... 30
Spalding, A. (Bos) ... 25

Shutouts
Cummings, C. (Har) ... 7
Spalding, A. (Bos) ... 7
Zettlein, G. (Chi,Phi) ... 7

Ratio
Bond, T. (Har) ... .88
Cummings, C. (Har) ... .96
Fisher, C. (Phi) ... .99

Win Shares – Pitchers

Saves
Spalding, A. (Bos) ... 8
Manning, J. (Bos) ... 7
2 players tied with ... 1

Earned Run Average
Galvin, P. (StL) ... 1.16
Bond, T. (Har) ... 1.43
Spalding, A. (Bos) ... 1.59

TPW – Pitchers
Spalding, A. (Bos) ... 3.5
Bond, T. (Har) ... 3.2
Cummings, C. (Har) ... 2.5

1876 National League

TEAM	G	W	L	PCT	GB	R	OR	EW	AB	H	2B	3B	HR	TB	BB	SO	SB	CS	AVG	OBP	SLG	OPS	OPS+	BR/A	PF	RC
CHI	66	52	14	.788	....	**624**	257	56	**2818**	**926**	**131**	32	8	**1145**	**70**	45	....	....	**.329**	**.353**	**.417**	**.770**	**141**	**104**	112	**415**
STL	64	45	19	.703	6	386	**229**	47	2537	642	73	27	2	775	59	63	....	....	.253	.276	.313	.589	103	15	95	219
HAR	69	47	21	.691	6	429	261	50	2703	711	96	22	2	857	39	78	....	....	.263	.277	.322	.599	93	-30	108	244
BOS	70	39	31	.557	15	471	450	37	2780	723	96	24	**9**	894	58	98	....	....	.260	.281	.328	.609	102	4	102	257
LOU	69	30	36	.455	22	280	344	26	2594	641	68	14	6	755	24	98	....	....	.247	.256	.294	.550	71	-97	118	198
NY	57	21	35	.375	26	260	412	16	2198	494	39	15	2	569	18	**35**	....	....	.225	.233	.261	.494	75	-36	87	136
PHI	60	14	45	.237	34.5	378	534	20	2414	646	79	**35**	7	816	27	36	....	....	.268	.279	.342	.621	108	19	99	233
CIN	65	9	56	.138	42.5	238	579	9	2413	555	51	12	4	642	41	136	....	....	.230	.247	.271	.518	86	-10	86	163
Total	**260**					**3066**			**20457**	**5338**	**633**	**181**	**40**		**336**	**589**			**.261**	**.277**	**.321**	**.598**				

Runs
Barnes, R. (Chi) ... 126
Wright, G. (Bos) ... 72
Peters, J. (Chi) ... 70

Runs Batted In
White, D. (Chi) ... 60
3 players tied with ... 59

Adjusted OPS
Barnes, R. (Chi) ... 222
Hall, G. (Phi) ... 208
Pike, L. (StL) ... 178

Hits
Barnes, R. (Chi) ... 138
Peters, J. (Chi) ... 111
Anson, C. (Chi) ... 110

Bases On Balls
Barnes, R. (Chi) ... 20
O'Rourke, J. (Bos) ... 15
Burdock, J. (Har) ... 13

Adjusted Batting Runs
Barnes, R. (Chi) ... 41.0
Hall, G. (Phi) ... 30.0
Pike, L. (StL) ... 23.0

Doubles
Barnes, R. (Chi) ... 21
Higham, D. (Har) ... 21
Hines, P. (Chi) ... 21

Stolen Bases

Runs Created/Game
Barnes, R. (Chi) ... 13.70
Hall, G. (Phi) ... 9.50
Anson, C. (Chi) ... 7.60

Triples
Barnes, R. (Chi) ... 14
Hall, G. (Phi) ... 13
Pike, L. (StL) ... 10

Batting Average
Barnes, R. (Chi) ... .404
Hall, G. (Phi) ... .355
Peters, J. (Chi) ... .348

Fielding Runs
Somerville, E. (Lou) ... 33.8
Battin, J. (StL) ... 17.8
Anson, C. (Chi) ... 15.8

Home Runs
Hall, G. (Phi) ... 5
Jones, C. (Cin) ... 4
8 players tied with ... 2

On-Base Percentage
Barnes, R. (Chi) ... .462
Hall, G. (Phi) ... .384
Anson, C. (Chi) ... .380

Win Shares – Batters
Spalding, A. (Chi) ... 57
Bradley, G. (StL) ... 57
Devlin, J. (Lou) ... 53

Total Bases
Barnes, R. (Chi) ... 190
Hall, G. (Phi) ... 146
Anson, C. (Chi) ... 139

Slugging Average
Barnes, R. (Chi) ... .590
Hall, G. (Phi) ... .545
Pike, L. (StL) ... .472

TPW – Batters
Devlin, J. (Lou) ... 5.3
Barnes, R. (Chi) ... 4.6
Anson, C. (Chi) ... 3.1

TEAM	CG	SH	SV	IP	H	H/G	ER	HR	BB	SO	OAV	RAT	ERA	ERA+	CERA	PR+	PF	FA	E	DP	FR	BW	PW	FW	TPW	DIF
CHI	58	9	4	592[1]	608	9.2	116	6	29	51	.245	1.075	1.76	139	....	16.8	106	.899	282	33	27.9	**9.1**	1.5	2.4	**13.1**	5.9
STL	63	**16**	0	577	**472**	**7.4**	**78**	3	39	103	**.204**	**.886**	**1.22**	175	....	22.0	92	**.902**	**268**	33	**36.8**	1.3	1.9	**3.2**	6.5	6.5
HAR	**69**	11	0	624	570	8.2	116	**2**	27	114	.224	.957	1.67	142	....	16.4	103	.888	337	27	32.0	-2.7	1.4	2.8	1.6	11.4
BOS	49	3	**7**	632	732	10.4	176	7	104	77	.261	1.323	2.51	90	....	-16.1	98	.860	442	42	-1.6	.4	-1.4	-.1	-1.2	5.2
LOU	67	5	0	**643**	605	8.5	121	3	38	**125**	.228	1.000	1.69	160	....	**46.6**	118	.875	397	44	26.6	-8.5	**4.1**	2.3	-2.1	-.9
NY	56	2	0	530	718	12.2	173	8	**24**	37	.300	1.400	2.94	73	....	-10.9	93	.824	473	18	-36.3	-3.2	-1.0	-3.2	-7.3	.3
PHI	53	1	2	550	783	12.8	197	**2**	41	22	.308	1.498	3.22	75	....	-12.5	105	.839	456	32	-36.5	1.7	-1.1	-3.2	-2.6	-12.4
CIN	57	0	0	591	850	12.9	238	9	34	60	.312	1.496	3.62	**61**	....	-58.8	95	.841	469	**45**	-35.1	-.9	-5.2	-3.1	-9.2	-13.8
Total	**472**	**47**	**13**	**4739**[1]		**10.1**	**1215**					**1.197**	**2.31**													

Wins
Spalding, A. (Chi) ... 47
Bradley, G. (StL) ... 45
Bond, T. (Har) ... 31

Innings Pitched
Devlin, J. (Lou) ... 622
Bradley, G. (StL) ... 573
Spalding, A. (Chi) ... 528[1]

Adjusted ERA
Bradley, G. (StL) ... 174
Devlin, J. (Lou) ... 174
Cummings, C. (Har) ... 142

Win Percentage
Spalding, A. (Chi) ... .797
Manning, J. (Bos) ... .783
Bond, T. (Har) ... .705

Fewest Hits/Game
Bradley, G. (StL) ... 7.38
Bond, T. (Har) ... 7.83
Devlin, J. (Lou) ... 8.19

Component ERA

Games
Devlin, J. (Lou) ... 68
Bradley, G. (StL) ... 64
Spalding, A. (Chi) ... 61

Fewest BB/Game
Zettlein, G. (Phi) ... .23
Fisher, C. (Cin) ... .24
Bond, T. (Har) ... .29

Opponents' Batting Avg.
Bradley, G. (StL) ... .205
Bond, T. (Har) ... .216
Devlin, J. (Lou) ... .223

Complete Games
Devlin, J. (Lou) ... 66
Bradley, G. (StL) ... 63
Mathews, B. (NY) ... 55

Strikeouts
Devlin, J. (Lou) ... 122
Bradley, G. (StL) ... 103
Bond, T. (Har) ... 88

Adjusted Pitching Runs
Devlin, J. (Lou) ... 54
Bradley, G. (StL) ... 21
Spalding, A. (Chi) ... 16

Shutouts
Bradley, G. (StL) ... 16
Spalding, A. (Chi) ... 8
Bond, T. (Har) ... 6

Ratio
Bradley, G. (StL) ... .89
Bond, T. (Har) ... .90
Devlin, J. (Lou) ... .97

Win Shares – Pitchers
Bradley, G. (StL) ... 57
Spalding, A. (Chi) ... 57
Devlin, J. (Lou) ... 53

Saves
Manning, J. (Bos) ... 5
McVey, C. (Chi) ... 2
Zettlein, G. (Phi) ... 2

Earned Run Average
Bradley, G. (StL) ... 1.23
Devlin, J. (Lou) ... 1.56
Cummings, C. (Har) ... 1.67

TPW – Pitchers
Devlin, J. (Lou) ... 5.3
Bradley, G. (StL) ... 2.3
Spalding, A. (Chi) ... 2.1

1877 National League

TEAM	G	W	L	PCT	GB	R	OR	EW	AB	H	2B	3B	HR	TB	BB	SO	SB	CS	AVG	OBP	SLG	OPS	OPS+	BR/A	PF	RC
BOS	61	42	18	.700	....	**419**	**263**	43	**2368**	**700**	**91**	**37**	4	**877**	65	121	....	....	**.296**	**.314**	**.370**	**.685**	**114**	**34**	104	**283**
LOU	61	35	25	.583	7	339	288	35	2355	659	75	36	**9**	833	58	140	....	....	.280	.297	.354	.651	91	-37	118	254
HAR	60	31	27	.534	10	341	311	32	2358	637	63	31	4	774	30	**97**	....	....	.270	.279	.328	.608	105	22	89	222
STL	60	28	32	.467	14	284	318	27	2178	531	51	36	1	657	57	147	....	....	.244	.263	.302	.565	85	-30	95	177
CHI	60	26	33	.441	15.5	366	375	29	2273	633	79	30	0	772	57	111	....	....	.278	.296	.340	.636	92	-29	112	234
CIN	58	15	42	.263	25.5	291	485	15	2135	545	72	34	6	703	**78**	110	....	....	.255	.282	.329	.611	107	29	89	203
Total	**180**					**2040**			**13667**	**3705**	**431**	**204**	**24**		**345**	**726**			**.271**	**.289**	**.338**	**.627**				

Runs
O'Rourke, J. (Bos) ... 68
McVey, C. (Chi) ... 58
Wright, G. (Bos) ... 58

Runs Batted In
White, D. (Bos) ... 49
Peters, J. (Chi) ... 41
Sutton, E. (Bos) ... 39

Adjusted OPS
White, D. (Bos) ... 190
Cassidy, J. (Har) ... 184
Jones, C. (Chi,Cin,Cin) ... 175

Hits
White, D. (Bos) ... 103
McVey, C. (Chi) ... 98
O'Rourke, J. (Bos) ... 96

Bases On Balls
O'Rourke, J. (Bos) ... 20
Jones, C. (Cin,Cin,Chi) ... 15
2 players tied with ... 12

Adjusted Batting Runs
White, D. (Bos) ... 26.0
Cassidy, J. (Har) ... 24.0
Jones, C. (Cin,Cin,Chi) ... 22.0

Doubles
Anson, C. (Chi) ... 19
Manning, J. (Cin) ... 16
York, T. (Har) ... 16

Stolen Bases

Runs Created/Game
White, D. (Bos) ... 10.20
Cassidy, J. (Har) ... 8.00
O'Rourke, J. (Bos) ... 8.00

Triples
White, D. (Bos) ... 11
Jones, C. (Cin,Cin,Chi) ... 10
2 players tied with ... 8

Batting Average
White, D. (Bos) ... .387
Cassidy, J. (Har) ... .378
McVey, C. (Chi) ... .368

Fielding Runs
Peters, J. (Chi) ... 18.3
Gerhardt, J. (Lou) ... 18.1
Ferguson, B. (Har) ... 17.9

Home Runs
Pike, L. (Cin) ... 4
Shafer, O. (Lou) ... 3
3 players tied with ... 2

On-Base Percentage
O'Rourke, J. (Bos) ... .407
White, D. (Bos) ... .405
McVey, C. (Chi) ... .387

Win Shares – Batters
Devlin, J. (Lou) ... 60
Bond, T. (Bos) ... 47
Larkin, T. (Har) ... 31

Total Bases
White, D. (Bos) ... 145
McVey, C. (Chi) ... 121
2 players tied with ... 118

Slugging Average
White, D. (Bos) ... .545
Jones, C. (Chi,Cin,Cin) ... .471
Cassidy, J. (Har) ... .458

TPW – Batters
Devlin, J. (Lou) ... 3.8
Bond, T. (Bos) ... 3.4
Jones, C. (Cin,Cin,Chi) ... 2.5

TEAM	CG	SH	SV	IP	H	H/G	ER	HR	BB	SO	OAV	RAT	ERA	ERA+	CERA	PR+	PF	FA	E	DP	FR	BW	PW	FW	TPW	DIF
BOS	**61**	7	0	548	**557**	9.2	**131**	5	38	**177**	.249	1.086	2.15	130	....	**40.6**	100	.889	290	36	-0.7	3.0	3.6	-.1	**6.6**	5.4
LOU	61	4	0	**559**	617	9.9	140	4	41	141	.264	1.177	2.25	147	....	39.8	118	**.904**	**267**	37	**25.5**	-3.3	3.5	**2.3**	2.6	2.4
HAR	59	4	0	544	572	9.5	140	**2**	56	99	.255	1.154	2.32	105	....	-4.1	87	.885	313	32	11.2	2.0	-.4	1.0	2.6	-.6
STL	52	1	0	541	582	9.7	160	**2**	92	132	.259	1.246	2.66	98	....	-2.1	92	.892	281	29	-1.8	-2.6	-.2	-.2	-3.0	1.0
CHI	45	3	**3**	534	630	10.6	200	7	58	92	.277	1.288	3.37	88	....	-19.4	106	.883	313	**43**	-4.3	-2.5	-1.7	-.4	-4.7	1.7
CIN	48	1	1	515	747	13.0	240	4	61	85	.321	1.569	4.19	**63**	....	-60.9	94	.852	394	33	-27.6	2.6	-5.4	-2.5	-5.3	-7.7
Total	326	20	4	3241		10.3	1011					1.250	2.81													

Wins — Bond, T. (Bos) 40; Devlin, J. (Lou) 35; Larkin, T. (Har) 29
Win Percentage — Bond, T. (Bos) .702; Devlin, J. (Lou) .583; Mitchell, B. (Cin) .545
Games — Devlin, J. (Lou) 61; Bond, T. (Bos) 58; Larkin, T. (Har) 56
Complete Games — Devlin, J. (Lou) 61; Bond, T. (Bos) 58; Larkin, T. (Har) 55
Shutouts — Bond, T. (Bos) 6; Devlin, J. (Lou) 4; Larkin, T. (Har) 4
Saves — McVey, C. (Chi) 2; Manning, J. (Cin) 1; Spalding, A. (Chi) 1
Innings Pitched — Devlin, J. (Lou) 559; Bond, T. (Bos) 521; Larkin, T. (Har) 501
Fewest Hits/Game — Bond, T. (Bos) 9.16; Larkin, T. (Har) 9.16; Nichols, T. (StL) 9.67
Fewest BB/Game — Bond, T. (Bos) .62; Devlin, J. (Lou) .66; Cummings, C. (Cin) .75
Strikeouts — Bond, T. (Bos) 170; Devlin, J. (Lou) 141; Larkin, T. (Har) 96
Ratio — Bond, T. (Bos) 1.09; Larkin, T. (Har) 1.12; Devlin, J. (Lou) 1.18
Earned Run Average — Bond, T. (Bos) 2.11; Larkin, T. (Har) 2.14; Devlin, J. (Lou) 2.25
Adjusted ERA — Devlin, J. (Lou) 147; Bond, T. (Bos) 133; Larkin, T. (Har) 114
Component ERA —
Opponents' Batting Avg. — Bond, T. (Bos) .249; Larkin, T. (Har) .249; Nichols, T. (StL) .259
Adjusted Pitching Runs — Bond, T. (Bos) 41; Devlin, J. (Lou) 40; Larkin, T. (Har) 6
Win Shares – Pitchers — Devlin, J. (Lou) 60; Bond, T. (Bos) 47; Larkin, T. (Har) 31
TPW – Pitchers — Devlin, J. (Lou) 3.8; Bond, T. (Bos) 3.4; Larkin, T. (Har) 1.1

1878 National League

TEAM	G	W	L	PCT	GB	R	OR	EW	AB	H	2B	3B	HR	TB	BB	SO	SB	CS	AVG	OBP	SLG	OPS	OPS+	BR/A	PF	RC
BOS	60	41	19	.683	....	298	**241**	36	2220	535	75	25	2	666	35	154	....	....	.241	.253	.300	.553	79	-56	108	173
CIN	61	37	23	.617	4	333	281	35	2281	629	67	22	5	755	58	141	....	....	.276	.294	.331	.625	**121**	56	91	227
PRO	62	33	27	.550	8	353	337	31	2298	604	**107**	30	8	795	50	218	....	....	.263	.279	.346	.624	109	20	100	227
CHI	61	30	30	.500	11	**371**	331	33	**2333**	677	91	20	3	**817**	88	157	....	....	**.290**	.316	.350	**.666**	116	35	106	**265**
IND	63	24	36	.400	17	293	328	27	2300	542	76	15	3	657	64	197	....	....	.236	.256	.286	.542	94	2	86	173
MIL	61	15	45	.250	26	256	386	18	2212	552	65	20	2	663	69	214	....	....	.250	.272	.300	.572	86	-36	107	185
Total	184					1904			13644	3539	481	132	23		364	1081			.259	.279	.319	.598				

Runs — Higham, D. (Pro) 60; Start, J. (Chi) 58; York, T. (Pro) 56
Hits — Start, J. (Chi) 100; Dalrymple, A. (Mil) 96; Hines, P. (Pro) 92
Doubles — Higham, D. (Pro) 22; Brown, L. (Pro) 21; 2 players tied with 19
Triples — York, T. (Pro) 10; Jones, C. (Cin) 7; O'Rourke, J. (Bos) 7
Home Runs — Hines, P. (Pro) 4; Jones, C. (Cin) 3; 2 players tied with 2
Total Bases — Hines, P. (Pro) 125; Start, J. (Chi) 125; York, T. (Pro) 125
Runs Batted In — Hines, P. (Pro) 50; Brown, L. (Pro) 43; Anson, C. (Chi) 40
Bases On Balls — Larkin, T. (Pro) 17; Remsen, J. (Chi) 17; 3 players tied with 13
Stolen Bases —
Batting Average — Dalrymple, A. (Mil) .354; Hines, P. (Pro) .358; Ferguson, B. (Chi) .351
On-Base Percentage — Ferguson, B. (Chi) .375; Anson, C. (Chi) .372; Shafer, O. (Ind) .369
Slugging Average — Hines, P. (Pro) .486; York, T. (Pro) .465; Shafer, O. (Ind) .455
Adjusted OPS — Shafer, O. (Ind) 196; Hines, P. (Pro) 177; Jones, C. (Cin) 163
Adjusted Batting Runs — Shafer, O. (Ind) 28.0; Hines, P. (Pro) 20.0; Jones, C. (Cin) 18.0
Runs Created/Game — Hines, P. (Pro) 7.80; Shafer, O. (Ind) 7.20; Start, J. (Chi) 6.80
Fielding Runs — Burdock, J. (Bos) 20.8; Ferguson, B. (Chi) 16.0; Hague, B. (Pro) 13.9
Win Shares – Batters — Bond, T. (Bos) 60; Larkin, T. (Chi) 34; Hines, P. (Pro) 15
TPW – Batters — Shafer, O. (Ind) 3.2; Ferguson, B. (Chi) 3.0; Burdock, J. (Bos) 2.0

TEAM	CG	SH	SV	IP	H	H/G	ER	HR	BB	SO	OAV	RAT	ERA	ERA+	CERA	PR+	PF	FA	E	DP	FR	BW	PW	FW	TPW	DIF
BOS	58	**9**	0	544	595	9.8	140	6	38	184	.265	1.164	2.32	102	....	-7.3	102	**.914**	**228**	48	9.8	-5.2	-.7	.9	-5.0	16.0
CIN	61	6	0	548	**546**	9.0	**112**	**2**	63	220	.247	1.111	**1.84**	116	....	11.5	92	.900	269	37	6.0	**5.2**	1.1	.6	**6.8**	.2
PRO	59	6	0	556	609	9.9	147	3	86	173	.265	1.250	2.38	93	....	-18.4	96	.892	311	42	7.6	1.8	-1.7	.7	.8	2.2
CHI	61	1	0	551	577	9.4	145	4	**35**	175	.256	**1.111**	2.37	102	....	-8.8	105	.891	304	37	**11.9**	3.2	-.8	**1.1**	3.5	-3.5
IND	59	2	1	**578**	621	9.7	149	3	87	182	.261	1.225	2.32	**87**	....	-15.7	88	.898	290	37	-2.9	.2	-1.5	-.3	-1.5	-4.5
MIL	54	1	0	547	589	9.7	158	3	55	147	.262	1.177	2.60	101	....	30.8	114	.866	376	32	-29.5	-3.4	**2.9**	-2.8	-3.3	-11.7
Total	352	25	1	3324		9.6	851					1.174	2.30													

Wins — Bond, T. (Bos) 40; White, W. (Cin) 30; Larkin, T. (Chi) 29
Win Percentage — Wheeler, H. (Pro) .857; Mitchell, B. (Cin) .778; Bond, T. (Bos) .678
Games — Bond, T. (Bos) 59; Larkin, T. (Chi) 56; White, W. (Cin) 52
Complete Games — Bond, T. (Bos) 57; Larkin, T. (Chi) 56; White, W. (Cin) 52
Shutouts — Bond, T. (Bos) 9; Ward, J. (Pro) 6; White, W. (Cin) 5
Saves — Healey, T. (Ind,Pro) 1
Innings Pitched — Bond, T. (Bos) 532^{2}; Larkin, T. (Chi) 506; White, W. (Cin) 468
Fewest Hits/Game — Mitchell, B. (Cin) 7.76; Ward, J. (Pro) 8.30; Weaver, S. (Mil) 8.72
Fewest BB/Game — Weaver, S. (Mil) .49; Larkin, T. (Chi) .55; Bond, T. (Bos) .56
Strikeouts — Bond, T. (Bos) 182; White, W. (Cin) 169; Larkin, T. (Chi) 163
Ratio — Weaver, S. (Mil) 1.02; Ward, J. (Pro) 1.02; Larkin, T. (Chi) 1.07
Earned Run Average — Ward, J. (Pro) 1.51; McCormick, J. (Ind) 1.69; White, W. (Cin) 1.79
Adjusted ERA — Ward, J. (Pro) 146; Weaver, S. (Mil) 134; McCormick, J. (Ind) 120
Component ERA —
Opponents' Batting Avg. — Mitchell, B. (Cin) .221; Ward, J. (Pro) .233; Weaver, S. (Mil) .242
Adjusted Pitching Runs — Weaver, S. (Mil) 49; Ward, J. (Pro) 21; White, W. (Cin) 12
Win Shares – Pitchers — Bond, T. (Bos) 60; Larkin, T. (Chi) 34; White, W. (Cin) 30
TPW – Pitchers — Weaver, S. (Mil) 4.5; Ward, J. (Pro) 2.2; Larkin, T. (Chi) 1.4

1879 National League

TEAM	G	W	L	PCT	GB	R	OR	EW	AB	H	2B	3B	HR	TB	BB	SO	SB	CS	AVG	OBP	SLG	OPS	OPS+	BR/A	PF	RC
PRO	85	59	25	.702	....	**612**	355	63	3392	**1003**	142	55	12	**1291**	91	172	....	....	.296	.314	.381	.695	134	120	98	416
BOS	84	54	30	.643	5	562	**348**	61	3217	883	138	51	**20**	1183	90	222	....	....	.274	.294	.368	.662	118	57	102	357
BUF	79	46	32	.590	10	394	365	42	2906	733	105	54	4	952	78	314	....	....	.252	.272	.328	.599	98	-9	102	265
CHI	83	46	33	.582	10.5	437	411	42	3116	808	**167**	32	3	1048	73	294	....	....	.259	.276	.336	.613	98	-11	106	297
CIN	81	43	37	.538	14	485	464	42	3085	813	127	53	8	1070	66	207	....	....	.264	.279	.347	.626	114	51	95	306
CLE	82	27	55	.329	31	322	461	27	2987	666	116	29	4	852	37	214	....	....	.223	.232	.285	.518	73	-80	99	203
SYR	71	22	48	.314	30	276	462	18	2611	592	61	19	5	706	28	238	....	....	.227	.235	.270	.505	78	-46	89	170
TRO	77	19	56	.253	35.5	321	543	19	2841	673	102	24	4	795	45	182	....	....	.237	.249	.294	.543	87	-29	93	213
Total	321					3409			24155	6171	958	317	58		508	1843			.255	.271	.329	.599				

Runs — Jones, C. (Bos) 85; Hines, P. (Pro) 81; Wright, G. (Pro) 79
Hits — Hines, P. (Pro) 146; O'Rourke, J. (Pro) 126; Kelly, K. (Cin) 120
Doubles — Eden, C. (Cle) 31; 3 players tied with 25
Triples — Dickerson, B. (Cin) 14; Williamson, N. (Chi) 13; Kelly, K. (Cin) 12
Home Runs — Jones, C. (Bos) 9; O'Rourke, J. (Bos) 6; Brouthers, D. (Tro) 4
Total Bases — Hines, P. (Pro) 197; Jones, C. (Bos) 181; Kelly, K. (Cin) 170
Runs Batted In — Jones, C. (Bos) 62; O'Rourke, J. (Pro) 62; Dickerson, B. (Cin) 57
Bases On Balls — Jones, C. (Bos) 29; Williamson, N. (Chi) 24; York, T. (Pro) 19
Stolen Bases —
Batting Average — Anson, C. (Chi) .317; Hines, P. (Pro) .357; O'Rourke, J. (Pro) .348
On-Base Percentage — O'Rourke, J. (Pro) .371; Hines, P. (Pro) .369; O'Rourke, J. (Pro) .367
Slugging Average — O'Rourke, J. (Bos) .521; Jones, C. (Bos) .510; Kelly, K. (Cin) .493
Adjusted OPS — Kelly, K. (Cin) 188; Jones, C. (Bos) 181; O'Rourke, J. (Bos) 181
Adjusted Batting Runs — Hines, P. (Pro) 34.0; Kelly, K. (Cin) 32.0; Jones, C. (Bos) 32.0
Runs Created/Game — O'Rourke, J. (Bos) 8.10; Hines, P. (Pro) 7.90; Kelly, K. (Cin) 7.90
Fielding Runs — Shafer, O. (Chi) 22.2; Snyder, P. (Bos) 21.1; Evans, J. (Tro) 20.0
Win Shares – Batters — Ward, J. (Pro) 51; Bond, T. (Bos) 50; Hines, P. (Pro) 22
TPW – Batters — Kelly, K. (Cin) 4.0; Hines, P. (Pro) 3.7; Jones, C. (Bos) 3.6

TEAM	CG	SH	SV	IP	H	H/G	ER	HR	BB	SO	OAV	RAT	ERA	ERA+	CERA	PR+	PF	FA	E	DP	FR	BW	PW	FW	TPW	DIF
PRO	73	3	2	776	765	8.9	188	9	62	329	.241	1.066	2.18	108	....	8.3	94	.902	382	41	7.1	11.0	.8	.7	12.4	4.6
BOS	80	13	0	753	757	9.0	183	9	46	230	.245	1.066	2.19	114	....	-5.0	100	.913	319	58	29.8	5.3	-.5	2.8	7.6	4.4
BUF	78	8	0	713	698	8.8	185	3	47	198	.240	1.045	2.34	112	....	5.3	105	.906	331	62	16.7	-.8	.5	1.5	1.2	5.8
CHI	82	6	0	744	762	9.2	203	5	57	211	.248	1.101	2.46	105	....	-20.6	103	.900	381	52	29.8	-1.0	-1.9	2.7	-.2	7.2
CIN	79	4	0	726	756	9.4	185	11	81	246	.251	1.153	2.29	102	....	-1.0	93	.879	454	48	4.0	4.7	-.1	.4	5.0	-2.0
CLE	79	3	0	741	818	9.9	218	4	116	287	.262	1.260	2.65	95	....	14.4	100	.889	406	42	-26.2	-7.4	1.3	-2.4	-8.5	-5.5
SYR	64	5	0	649	775	10.8	230	4	52	132	.278	1.274	3.19	74	....	-27.0	95	.872	398	37	-32.1	-4.2	-2.5	-3.0	-9.7	-3.3
TRO	75	3	0	695	840	10.9	216	13	47	210	.280	1.276	2.80	89	....	-1.7	100	.875	460	44	-21.3	-2.7	-.2	-2.0	-4.8	-13.2
Total	**610**	**45**	**2**	**5797**		9.6	1608					1.152	2.50													

Wins
Ward, J. (Pro) 47
Bond, T. (Bos) 43
White, W. (Cin) 43

Win Percentage
Ward, J. (Pro) .712
Bond, T. (Bos) .694
Mathews, B. (Pro) .667

Games
White, W. (Cin) 76
Ward, J. (Pro) 70
Galvin, P. (Buf) 66

Complete Games
White, W. (Cin) 75
Galvin, P. (Buf) 65
2 players tied with 59

Shutouts
Bond, T. (Bos) 11
Galvin, P. (Buf) 6
McCormick, H. (Syr) 5

Saves
Mathews, B. (Pro) 1
Ward, J. (Pro) 1

Innings Pitched
White, W. (Cin) 680
Galvin, P. (Buf) 593
Ward, J. (Pro) 587

Fewest Hits/Game
McGunnigle, B. (Buf) 8.48
Ward, J. (Pro) 8.75
Bond, T. (Bos) 8.80

Fewest BB/Game
Bond, T. (Bos) .39
Galvin, P. (Buf) .47
Bradley, G. (Tro) .48

Strikeouts
Ward, J. (Pro) 239
White, W. (Cin) 232
McCormick, J. (Cle) 197

Ratio
Bond, T. (Bos) 1.02
Ward, J. (Pro) 1.03
Galvin, P. (Buf) 1.04

Earned Run Average
Bond, T. (Bos) 1.96
White, W. (Cin) 1.99
Ward, J. (Pro) 2.15

Adjusted ERA
Bond, T. (Bos) 127
White, W. (Cin) 117
Galvin, P. (Buf) 115

Component ERA

Opponents' Batting Avg.
McGunnigle, B. (Buf) .233
Ward, J. (Pro) .239
Bond, T. (Bos) .240

Adjusted Pitching Runs
McCormick, J. (Cle) 24
White, W. (Cin) 22
Bond, T. (Bos) 10

Win Shares – Pitchers
Galvin, P. (Buf) 61
Ward, J. (Pro) 51
Bond, T. (Bos) 50

TPW – Pitchers
Ward, J. (Pro) 2.2
McCormick, J. (Cle) 1.8
Galvin, P. (Buf) 1.4

1880 National League

TEAM	G	W	L	PCT	GB	R	OR	EW	AB	H	2B	3B	HR	TB	BB	SO	SB	CS	AVG	OBP	SLG	OPS	OPS+	BR/A	PF	RC
CHI	86	67	17	.798	....	538	317	62	3135	876	164	39	4	1130	104	217	....	....	.279	.303	.360	.663	119	54	106	350
PRO	87	52	32	.619	15	419	299	56	3196	793	114	34	8	999	89	186	....	....	.248	.268	.313	.581	102	8	97	275
CLE	85	47	37	.560	20	387	337	48	3002	726	130	52	7	981	76	237	....	....	.242	.261	.327	.587	102	7	98	262
TRO	83	41	42	.494	25.5	392	438	37	3007	755	114	37	5	958	120	260	....	....	.251	.280	.319	.598	99	-5	105	275
WOR	85	40	43	.482	26.5	412	370	46	3024	699	129	52	8	956	81	278	....	....	.231	.251	.316	.567	86	-52	109	246
BOS	86	40	44	.476	27	416	456	38	3080	779	134	41	20	1055	105	221	....	....	.253	.278	.343	.620	115	49	97	300
BUF	85	24	58	.293	42	331	502	25	2962	669	104	37	3	856	90	327	....	....	.226	.249	.289	.538	82	-55	102	218
CIN	83	21	59	.262	44	296	472	23	2895	649	91	36	7	833	75	267	....	....	.224	.244	.288	.532	82	-50	99	208
Total	**340**					**3191**			**24301**	**5946**	**980**	**328**	**62**		**740**	**1993**			**.245**	**.267**	**.320**	**.587**				

Runs
Dalrymple, A. (Chi) 91
Stovey, H. (Wor) 76
Kelly, K. (Chi) 72

Hits
Dalrymple, A. (Chi) 126
Anson, C. (Chi) 120
Gore, G. (Chi) 116

Doubles
Dunlap, F. (Cle) 27
Dalrymple, A. (Chi) 25
Anson, C. (Chi) 24

Triples
Stovey, H. (Wor) 14
Dalrymple, A. (Chi) 12
2 players tied with 11

Home Runs
O'Rourke, J. (Bos) 6
Stovey, H. (Wor) 6
Jones, C. (Bos) 5

Total Bases
Dalrymple, A. (Chi) 175
Stovey, H. (Wor) 161
2 players tied with 160

Runs Batted In
Anson, C. (Chi) 74
Kelly, K. (Chi) 60
2 players tied with 47

Bases On Balls
Ferguson, B. (Tro) 24
3 players tied with 21

Stolen Bases

Batting Average
Gore, G. (Chi) .360
Anson, C. (Chi) .337
Connor, R. (Tro) .332

On-Base Percentage
Gore, G. (Chi) .399
Anson, C. (Chi) .362
Connor, R. (Tro) .357

Slugging Average
Gore, G. (Chi) .463
Connor, R. (Tro) .459
Dalrymple, A. (Chi) .458

Adjusted OPS
Gore, G. (Chi) 180
Connor, R. (Tro) 165
Jones, C. (Bos) 158

Adjusted Batting Runs
Gore, G. (Chi) 27.0
O'Rourke, J. (Bos) 22.0
Connor, R. (Tro) 22.0

Runs Created/Game
Gore, G. (Chi) 8.10
Connor, R. (Tro) 6.90
Dalrymple, A. (Chi) 6.50

Fielding Runs
Irwin, A. (Wor) 28.7
Force, D. (Buf) 19.4
Bradley, G. (Pro) 17.3

Win Shares – Batters
Corcoran, L. (Chi) 52
Ward, J. (Pro) 51
Richmond, L. (Wor) 42

TPW – Batters
Dunlap, F. (Cle) 3.2
Irwin, A. (Wor) 3.1
Gore, G. (Chi) 3.0

TEAM	CG	SH	SV	IP	H	H/G	ER	HR	BB	SO	OAV	RAT	ERA	ERA+	CERA	PR+	PF	FA	E	DP	FR	BW	PW	FW	TPW	DIF
CHI	80	8	3	775	622	7.2	166	8	129	367	.209	.969	1.93	126	....	27.3	102	.913	329	41	15.3	5.3	2.7	1.5	9.4	15.6
PRO	75	13	3	799	663	7.5	146	7	51	286	.214	.894	1.64	134	....	31.6	104	.910	357	53	18.3	.8	3.1	1.8	5.6	4.4
CLE	83	7	1	759²	685	8.1	160	4	98	289	.229	1.031	1.90	124	....	24.3	99	.910	330	52	14.1	.7	2.4	1.4	4.4	.6
TRO	81	4	0	738	760	9.3	225	8	112	169	.254	1.182	2.74	92	....	-23.2	106	.900	366	58	5.2	-.5	-2.3	.5	-2.2	2.2
WOR	68	7	5	762²	709	8.4	192	13	97	297	.234	1.057	2.27	115	....	11.6	109	.906	355	49	16.6	-5.1	1.1	1.6	-2.3	1.3
BOS	70	4	0	744²	840	10.2	255	2	86	187	.270	1.244	3.08	74	....	-50.7	96	.901	367	54	-16.2	4.8	-4.9	-1.6	-1.7	-.3
BUF	72	6	1	739	879	10.7	254	10	78	186	.281	1.295	3.09	79	....	-16.3	104	.891	408	55	-35.8	-5.3	-1.6	-3.5	-10.4	-6.6
CIN	79	3	0	713¹	785	9.9	193	10	88	208	.265	1.224	2.44	102	....	18.6	104	.877	437	49	-15.0	-4.8	1.8	-1.5	-4.5	-14.5
Total	**608**	**52**	**13**	**6031¹**		8.9	1591					1.108	2.37													

Wins
McCormick, J. (Cle) 45
Corcoran, L. (Chi) 43
Ward, J. (Pro) 39

Win Percentage
Goldsmith, F. (Chi) .875
Corcoran, L. (Chi) .754
2 players tied with .619

Games
McCormick, J. (Cle) 74
Richmond, L. (Wor) 74
Ward, J. (Pro) 70

Complete Games
McCormick, J. (Cle) 72
Welch, M. (Tro) 64
Ward, J. (Pro) 59

Shutouts
Ward, J. (Pro) 8
McCormick, J. (Cle) 7
2 players tied with 5

Saves
Richmond, L. (Wor) 3
Corcoran, L. (Chi) 2
Corey, F. (Wor) 2

Innings Pitched
McCormick, J. (Cle) 657²
Ward, J. (Pro) 595
Richmond, L. (Wor) 590²

Fewest Hits/Game
Keefe, T. (Tro) 5.83
Corcoran, L. (Chi) 6.78
Bradley, G. (Pro) 7.26

Fewest BB/Game
Bradley, G. (Pro) .28
Galvin, P. (Buf) .63
Ward, J. (Pro) .68

Strikeouts
Corcoran, L. (Chi) 268
McCormick, J. (Cle) 260
Richmond, L. (Wor) 243

Ratio
Keefe, T. (Tro) .80
Bradley, G. (Pro) .84
Ward, J. (Pro) .92

Earned Run Average
Keefe, T. (Tro) .86
Bradley, G. (Pro) 1.38
Ward, J. (Pro) 1.74

Adjusted ERA
Keefe, T. (Tro) 295
Bradley, G. (Pro) 160
Goldsmith, F. (Chi) 138

Component ERA

Opponents' Batting Avg.
Keefe, T. (Tro) .175
Corcoran, L. (Chi) .198
Bradley, G. (Pro) .209

Adjusted Pitching Runs
White, W. (Cin) 30
McCormick, J. (Cle) 25
Keefe, T. (Tro) 19

Win Shares – Pitchers
McCormick, J. (Cle) 54
Corcoran, L. (Chi) 52
Ward, J. (Pro) 51

TPW – Pitchers
Bradley, G. (Pro) 2.6
Ward, J. (Pro) 2.6
McCormick, J. (Cle) 2.5

1881 National League

TEAM	G	W	L	PCT	GB	R	OR	EW	AB	H	2B	3B	HR	TB	BB	SO	SB	CS	AVG	OBP	SLG	OPS	OPS+	BR/A	PF	RC
CHI	84	56	28	.667	....	550	379	57	3114	918	157	36	12	1183	140	224	....	....	.295	.325	.380	.705	117	53	107	394
PRO	85	47	37	.560	9	447	426	44	3077	780	144	37	11	1031	146	214	....	....	.253	.287	.335	.622	100	2	98	304
BUF	83	45	38	.542	10.5	440	447	41	3019	797	157	50	12	1090	108	270	....	....	.264	.289	.361	.650	108	25	99	323
DET	84	41	43	.488	15	439	429	43	2995	780	131	53	17	1068	136	250	....	....	.260	.293	.357	.649	102	3	104	320
TRO	85	39	45	.464	17	399	429	39	3046	754	124	31	5	955	140	240	....	....	.248	.281	.314	.594	85	-54	105	275
BOS	83	38	45	.458	17.5	349	410	35	2916	733	121	27	5	923	110	193	....	....	.251	.279	.317	.595	94	-15	95	264
CLE	85	36	48	.429	20	392	414	40	3117	796	120	39	7	1015	132	224	....	....	.255	.286	.326	.611	100	6	95	297
WOR	83	32	50	.390	23	410	492	34	3093	781	114	31	7	978	121	169	....	....	.253	.281	.316	.597	85	-55	106	281
Total	**336**					**3426**			**24377**	**6339**	**1068**	**304**	**76**		**1033**	**1784**			**.260**	**.290**	**.338**	**.628**				

Runs
Gore, G. (Chi) 86
Kelly, K. (Chi) 84
Dalrymple, A. (Chi) 72

Hits
Anson, C. (Chi) 137
Dalrymple, A. (Chi) 117
Dickerson, B. (Wor) 116

Doubles
Hines, P. (Pro) 27
Kelly, K. (Chi) 27
2 players tied with 25

Triples
Rowe, J. (Buf) 11
Phillips, B. (Cle) 10
4 players tied with 9

Home Runs
Brothers, D. (Buf) 8
Bennett, C. (Det) 7
Farrell, J. (Pro) 5

Total Bases
Anson, C. (Chi) 175
Dunlap, F. (Cle) 156
Kelly, K. (Chi) 153

Runs Batted In
Anson, C. (Chi) 82
Bennett, C. (Det) 64
Kelly, K. (Chi) 55

Bases On Balls
Clapp, J. (Cle) 35
3 players tied with 29

Stolen Bases

Batting Average
Anson, C. (Chi) .399
Start, J. (Pro) .328
Dunlap, F. (Cle) .325

On-Base Percentage
Anson, C. (Chi) .442
York, T. (Pro) .362
Brothers, D. (Buf) .361

Slugging Average
Brothers, D. (Buf) .541
Anson, C. (Chi) .510
Bennett, C. (Det) .478

Adjusted OPS
Anson, C. (Chi) 186
Brothers, D. (Buf) 182
Dunlap, F. (Cle) 159

Adjusted Batting Runs
Anson, C. (Chi) 34.0
Brothers, D. (Buf) 25.0
Dunlap, F. (Cle) 24.0

Runs Created/Game
Anson, C. (Chi) 10.40
Brothers, D. (Buf) 7.90
Dunlap, F. (Cle) 6.50

Fielding Runs
Ewing, B. (Tro) 25.4
Richardson, H. (Buf) 22.7
Glasscock, H. (Buf) 20.4

Win Shares – Batters
Whitney, J. (Bos) 42
Ward, J. (Pro) 27
Richmond, L. (Wor) 26

TPW – Batters
Dunlap, F. (Cle) 4.0
Anson, C. (Chi) 3.5
Bennett, C. (Det) 3.0

TEAM	CG	SH	SV	IP	H	H/G	ER	HR	BB	SO	OAV	RAT	ERA	ERA+	CERA	PR+	PF	FA	E	DP	FR	BW	PW	FW	TPW	DIF
CHI	81	9	0	744²	**722**	8.7	201	14	122	228	.243	1.133	2.43	115	....	6.7	101	.916	309	54	23.9	4.9	.6	2.2	7.8	6.2
PRO	76	7	0	757²	756	9.0	202	**5**	138	264	.249	1.180	**2.40**	111	....	**45.0**	96	.896	390	66	-23.2	.2	**4.2**	-2.2	2.2	2.8
BUF	72	5	0	742¹	881	10.7	234	9	**89**	185	.282	1.307	2.84	98	....	22.3	100	.892	408	48	-27.2	2.4	2.1	-2.5	1.9	2.1
DET	83	**10**	0	744²	785	9.5	219	8	137	**265**	.259	1.238	2.65	110	....	19.2	105	.906	338	**80**	8.0	.3	1.8	.3	2.4	-3.4
TRO	**85**	8	0	771	805	9.4	254	11	161	207	.260	1.253	2.96	99	....	-38.4	106	**.917**	311	70	37.2	-5.0	-3.6	**3.5**	-5.1	2.1
BOS	72	6	3	730²	763	9.4	220	9	143	199	.257	1.240	2.71	98	....	-2.6	96	.909	325	54	-1.4	-1.4	-.2	-.1	-1.8	-1.2
CLE	82	2	0	760	737	**8.7**	226	9	126	240	.243	1.136	2.68	98	....	-10.7	94	.904	348	68	6.2	.6	-1.0	.6	.1	-6.1
WOR	80	5	0	737¹	882	10.8	290	11	120	196	.284	1.359	3.54	85	....	-25.1	109	.903	353	50	-17.6	-5.2	-2.3	-1.6	-9.1	.1
Total	631	52	3	5988¹		9.5	1846					1.230	2.77													

Wins
Corcoran, L. (Chi) 31
Whitney, J. (Bos) 31
Derby, G. (Det) 29

Win Percentage
Radbourn, C. (Pro) .694
Corcoran, L. (Chi) .689
Goldsmith, F. (Chi) .649

Games
Whitney, J. (Bos) 66
McCormick, J. (Cle) 59
2 players tied with 56

Complete Games
McCormick, J. (Cle) 57
Whitney, J. (Bos) 57
Derby, G. (Det) 55

Shutouts
Derby, G. (Det) 9
Whitney, J. (Bos) 6
2 players tied with 5

Saves
Mathews, B. (Bos,Pro) 2
Morrill, J. (Bos) 1

Innings Pitched
Whitney, J. (Bos) 552¹
McCormick, J. (Cle) 526
Derby, G. (Det) 494²

Fewest Hits/Game
McCormick, J. (Cle) 8.28
Wiedman, S. (Det) 8.45
Radbourn, C. (Pro) 8.55

Fewest BB/Game
Galvin, P. (Buf) .87
Wiedman, S. (Det) .94
Goldsmith, F. (Chi) 1.20

Strikeouts
Derby, G. (Det) 212
McCormick, J. (Cle) 178
Whitney, J. (Bos) 162

Ratio
Wiedman, S. (Det) 1.04
McCormick, J. (Cle) 1.08
Goldsmith, F. (Chi) 1.13

Earned Run Average
Wiedman, S. (Det) 1.80
Ward, J. (Pro) 2.13
Derby, G. (Det) 2.20

Adjusted ERA
Wiedman, S. (Det) 162
Derby, G. (Det) 133
Ward, J. (Pro) 125

Component ERA

Opponents' Batting Avg.
McCormick, J. (Cle) .234
Wiedman, S. (Det) .238
Radbourn, C. (Pro) .240

Adjusted Pitching Runs
Galvin, P. (Buf) 39
Derby, G. (Det) 37
Ward, J. (Pro) 30

Win Shares – Pitchers
Whitney, J. (Bos) 42
Galvin, P. (Buf) 36
2 players tied with 34

TPW – Pitchers
Galvin, P. (Buf) 3.3
Ward, J. (Pro) 2.7
Derby, G. (Det) 2.5

1882 National League

TEAM	G	W	L	PCT	GB	R	OR	EW	AB	H	2B	3B	HR	TB	BB	SO	SB	CS	AVG	OBP	SLG	OPS	OPS+	BR/A	PF	RC
CHI	84	55	29	.655	....	**604**	353	63	3225	892	209	54	15	**1254**	142	262	....	....	.277	.307	.389	.696	122	76	101	395
PRO	84	52	32	.619	3	463	356	53	3104	776	121	53	11	1036	102	255	....	....	.250	.274	.334	.608	96	-15	100	291
BUF	84	45	39	.536	10	500	461	45	3128	858	146	47	18	1152	116	**228**	....	....	.274	.300	.368	.669	113	41	102	355
BOS	85	45	39	.536	10	472	414	47	3118	823	114	50	15	1082	134	244	....	....	.264	.294	.347	.641	106	22	100	326
CLE	84	42	40	.512	12	402	411	40	3009	716	139	40	**20**	995	122	261	....	....	.238	.268	.331	.598	96	-10	97	273
DET	86	42	41	.506	12.5	407	488	34	3144	724	117	44	19	986	122	308	....	....	.230	.259	.314	.573	84	-52	100	262
TRO	85	35	48	.422	19.5	430	522	34	3057	747	116	**59**	12	1017	109	298	....	....	.244	.270	.333	.603	99	2	95	282
WOR	84	18	66	.214	37	379	652	21	2984	689	109	57	16	960	113	303	....	....	.231	.259	.322	.581	85	-52	102	255
Total	338					3657			24769	6225	1071	404	126		960	2159			.251	.279	.342	.622				

Runs
Gore, G. (Chi) 99
Dalrymple, A. (Chi) 96
Stovey, H. (Wor) 90

Hits
Brothers, D. (Buf) 129
Anson, C. (Chi) 126
5 players tied with 117

Doubles
Kelly, K. (Chi) 37
Anson, C. (Chi) 29
Hines, P. (Pro) 28

Triples
Connor, R. (Tro) 18
Corey, F. (Wor) 12
Wood, G. (Det) 12

Home Runs
Wood, G. (Det) 7
Brothers, D. (Buf) 6
Muldoon, M. (Cle) 6

Total Bases
Brothers, D. (Buf) 192
Connor, R. (Tro) 185
Hines, P. (Pro) 177

Runs Batted In
Anson, C. (Chi) 83
Brothers, D. (Buf) 63
Williamson, N. (Chi) 60

Bases On Balls
Gore, G. (Chi) 29
Shafer, O. (Cle) 27
Williamson, N. (Chi) 27

Stolen Bases

Batting Average
Brothers, D. (Buf) .368
Anson, C. (Chi) .362
Connor, R. (Tro) .330

On-Base Percentage
Brothers, D. (Buf) .403
Anson, C. (Chi) .397
Whitney, J. (Bos) .382

Slugging Average
Brothers, D. (Buf) .547
Connor, R. (Tro) .530
Whitney, J. (Bos) .510

Adjusted OPS
Brothers, D. (Buf) 198
Connor, R. (Tro) 188
Anson, C. (Chi) 183

Adjusted Batting Runs
Brothers, D. (Buf) 38.0
Connor, R. (Tro) 34.0
Anson, C. (Chi) 32.0

Runs Created/Game
Brothers, D. (Buf) 9.80
Anson, C. (Chi) 8.80
Whitney, J. (Bos) 8.10

Fielding Runs
Williamson, N. (Chi) 19.2
Glasscock, J. (Cle) 19.1
Ewing, B. (Tro) 16.3

Win Shares – Batters
Radbourn, C. (Pro) 50
Whitney, J. (Bos) 40
Ward, J. (Pro) 31

TPW – Batters
Whitney, J. (Bos) 3.8
Glasscock, J. (Cle) 3.7
Anson, C. (Chi) 3.4

TEAM	CG	SH	SV	IP	H	H/G	ER	HR	BB	SO	OAV	RAT	ERA	ERA+	CERA	PR+	PF	FA	E	DP	FR	BW	PW	FW	TPW	DIF
CHI	**83**	7	0	763²	**667**	7.9	188	13	102	279	.221	1.007	2.22	123	....	10.7	95	.898	376	54	32.8	6.9	1.0	3.0	10.9	2.1
PRO	80	**10**	1	752	690	8.3	190	12	87	273	.230	1.033	2.27	123	....	**28.1**	97	.901	371	67	15.9	-1.4	**2.6**	1.4	2.6	7.4
BUF	79	3	0	737	778	9.5	266	16	114	287	.256	1.210	3.25	90	....	-14.6	101	.910	315	42	-12.4	3.7	-1.3	-1.1	1.3	1.7
BOS	81	4	0	749	738	8.9	233	**10**	**77**	352	.243	1.088	2.80	102	....	15.9	99	.910	**314**	37	-11.7	2.0	1.4	-1.1	2.4	.6
CLE	81	4	0	751²	743	8.9	229	22	132	232	.244	1.164	2.74	102	....	-27.4	97	.905	358	**71**	30.2	-.9	-2.5	2.7	-.6	1.6
DET	82	7	0	**793**	808	9.2	263	19	129	**354**	.249	1.182	2.98	94	....	10.6	101	.893	396	44	-16.1	.2	-1.7	-.4	-1.9	-4.1
TRO	81	6	0	758	836	9.9	259	13	165	184	.265	1.321	3.08	91	....	-18.5	97	.887	432	70	-3.9					
WOR	75	0	0	738¹	964	11.8	308	21	151	195	.298	1.510	3.75	82	....	-21.4	107	.877	468	66	-32.6	-4.8	-1.9	-3.0	-9.7	-14.3
Total	642	41	1	6042²		9.3	1936					1.188	2.88													

Wins
McCormick, J. (Cle) 36
Radbourn, C. (Pro) 33
2 players tied with 28

Win Percentage
Corcoran, L. (Chi) .692
Radbourn, C. (Pro) .623
Goldsmith, F. (Chi) .622

Games
McCormick, J. (Cle) 68
Radbourn, C. (Pro) 54
Galvin, P. (Buf) 52

Complete Games
McCormick, J. (Cle) 65
Radbourn, C. (Pro) 50
Galvin, P. (Buf) 48

Shutouts
Radbourn, C. (Pro) 6
Welch, M. (Tro) 5
4 players tied with 4

Saves
Ward, J. (Pro) 1

Innings Pitched
McCormick, J. (Cle) 595²
Radbourn, C. (Pro) 466
Galvin, P. (Buf) 445¹

Fewest Hits/Game
Corcoran, L. (Chi) 7.11
Radbourn, C. (Pro) 8.15
McCormick, J. (Cle) 8.31

Fewest BB/Game
Mathews, B. (Bos) .69
Galvin, P. (Buf) .81
Goldsmith, F. (Chi) .84

Strikeouts
Radbourn, C. (Pro) 201
McCormick, J. (Cle) 200
Derby, G. (Det) 182

Ratio
Corcoran, L. (Chi) .97
Radbourn, C. (Pro) 1.02
Goldsmith, F. (Chi) 1.02

Earned Run Average
Corcoran, L. (Chi) 1.95
Radbourn, C. (Pro) 2.12
McCormick, J. (Cle) 2.37

Adjusted ERA
Corcoran, L. (Chi) 140
Radbourn, C. (Pro) 132
McCormick, J. (Cle) 117

Opponents' Batting Avg.
Corcoran, L. (Chi) .205
Radbourn, C. (Pro) .228
McCormick, J. (Cle) .231

Adjusted Pitching Runs
Radbourn, C. (Pro) 25
Wiedman, S. (Det) 22
Whitney, J. (Bos) 17

Win Shares – Pitchers
Radbourn, C. (Pro) 50
McCormick, J. (Cle) 42
Whitney, J. (Bos) 40

TPW – Pitchers
Whitney, J. (Bos) 3.8
Keefe, T. (Tro) 2.3
Radbourn, C. (Pro) 2.2

1882 American Association

TEAM	G	W	L	PCT	GB	R	OR	EW	AB	H	2B	3B	HR	TB	BB	SO	SB	CS	AVG	OBP	SLG	OPS	OPS+	BR/A	PF	RC
CIN	80	55	25	.688	....	**489**	**268**	62	**3007**	**795**	95	47	5	999	102	204	....	....	**.264**	.289	.332	.621	107	14	106	**295**
PHI	75	41	34	.547	11.5	406	389	39	2707	660	89	21	5	806	125	**164**	....	....	.244	.277	.298	.575	88	-44	112	229
LOU	80	42	38	.525	13	443	352	49	2806	728	**110**	28	9	921	**128**	193	....	....	.259	**.292**	.328	.620	**120**	**63**	94	275
PIT	79	39	39	.500	15	428	418	40	2904	730	**110**	**59**	**18**	**1012**	90	183	....	....	.251	.274	**.348**	**.622**	118	57	95	284
STL	80	37	43	.462	18	399	496	31	2865	663	87	41	11	865	112	226	....	....	.231	.260	.302	.562	89	-35	104	231
BAL	74	19	54	.260	32.5	273	515	16	2583	535	60	24	4	655	72	215	....	....	.207	.229	.254	.482	71	-63	92	153
Total	**234**					**2438**			**16872**	**4111**	**551**	**220**	**52**		**629**	**1185**			**.244**	**.271**	**.312**	**.582**				

Runs
Swartwood, E. (Pit) 86
Sommer, J. (Cin) 82
Carpenter, H. (Cin) 78

Hits
Carpenter, H. (Cin) 120
Browning, P. (Lou) 109
Swartwood, E. (Pit) 107

Doubles
Mansell, M. (Pit) 18
Swartwood, E. (Pit) 18
Browning, P. (Lou) 17

Triples
Mansell, M. (Pit) 16
Taylor, B. (Pit) 13
2 players tied with 11

Home Runs
Walker, O. (StL) 7
Browning, P. (Lou) 5
Swartwood, E. (Pit) 4

Total Bases
Swartwood, E. (Pit) 159
Mansell, M. (Pit) 152
Carpenter, H. (Cin) 148

Runs Batted In
Carpenter, H. (Cin) 67
Snyder, P. (Cin) 50
Comiskey, C. (StL) 45

Bases On Balls
Gleason, J. (StL) 27
Browning, P. (Lou) 26
Sommer, J. (Cin) 24

Stolen Bases

Batting Average
Browning, P. (Lou) .378
Carpenter, H. (Cin) .342
Swartwood, E. (Pit) .329

On-Base Percentage
Browning, P. (Lou) .430
Swartwood, E. (Pit) .370
Carpenter, H. (Cin) .360

Slugging Average
Browning, P. (Lou) .510
Swartwood, E. (Pit) .489
Taylor, B. (Pit) .452

Adjusted OPS
Browning, P. (Lou) 228
Swartwood, E. (Pit) 197
Taylor, B. (Pit) 156

Adjusted Batting Runs
Browning, P. (Lou) 40.0
Swartwood, E. (Pit) 33.0
Carpenter, H. (Cin) 18.0

Runs Created/Game
Browning, P. (Lou) 10.10
Swartwood, E. (Pit) 7.70
Carpenter, H. (Cin) 6.60

Fielding Runs
Stricker, C. (Phi) 19.3
Battin, J. (Pit) 16.7
Snyder, P. (Cin) 12.8

Win Shares – Batters
Mullane, T. (Lou) 36
Browning, P. (Lou) 20
Carpenter, H. (Cin) 18

TPW – Batters
Browning, P. (Lou) 4.5
Mullane, T. (Lou) 3.6
Carpenter, H. (Cin) 2.4

TEAM	CG	SH	SV	IP	H	H/G	ER	HR	BB	SO	OAV	RAT	ERA	ERA+	CERA	PR+	PF	FA	E	DP	FR	BW	PW	FW	TPW	DIF
CIN	**77**	**11**	0	**721**[1]	**609**	**7.6**	**132**	7	125	165	**.214**	**1.018**	**1.65**	160	....	**66.8**	98	**.907**	**332**	41	**12.4**	1.3	**6.1**	**1.1**	8.5	6.5
PHI	72	2	0	663	682	9.3	219	13	99	190	.249	1.178	2.97	100	....	-11.0	111	.895	361	36	11.5	-4.0	-1.0	1.1	-4.0	8.0
LOU	73	6	0	693[1]	637	8.3	156	6	112	240	.228	1.080	2.02	122	....	29.1	92	.893	385	**57**	5.7	**5.8**	2.7	.5	**9.0**	-7.0
PIT	**77**	2	0	696[2]	694	9.0	216	**4**	**82**	**252**	.243	1.114	2.79	93	....	-10.6	97	.889	397	40	-3.6	5.2	-1.0	-.3	3.9	-3.9
STL	75	3	**1**	688[1]	729	9.5	223	7	103	225	.254	1.209	2.92	96	....	4.2	104	.875	446	41	-12.9	-3.2	.4	-1.2	-4.0	1.0
BAL	64	1	0	646[1]	760	10.6	278	15	108	113	.275	1.343	3.87	**71**	....	-66.0	102	.859	490	41	-12.6	-5.8	-6.1	-1.2	-13.0	-4.0
Total	**438**	**25**	**1**	**4109**		**9.0**	**1224**					**1.154**	**2.68**													

Wins
White, W. (Cin) 40
Mullane, T. (Lou) 30
Weaver, S. (Phi) 26

Win Percentage
White, W. (Cin) .769
Weaver, S. (Phi) .634
Driscoll, D. (Pit) .591

Games
Mullane, T. (Lou) 55
White, W. (Cin) 54
McGinnis, J. (StL) 45

Complete Games
White, W. (Cin) 52
Mullane, T. (Lou) 51
McGinnis, J. (StL) 43

Shutouts
White, W. (Cin) 8
Mullane, T. (Lou) 5
2 players tied with 3

Saves

Innings Pitched
White, W. (Cin) 480
Mullane, T. (Lou) 460[1]
McGinnis, J. (StL) 388[1]

Fewest Hits/Game
Hecker, G. (Lou) 6.49
McCormick, H. (Cin) 7.25
Driscoll, D. (Pit) 7.25

Fewest BB/Game
Hecker, G. (Lou) .43
Driscoll, D. (Pit) .54
Weaver, S. (Phi) .85

Strikeouts
Mullane, T. (Lou) 170
Salisbury, H. (Pit) 135
McGinnis, J. (StL) 134

Ratio
Hecker, G. (Lou) .77
Driscoll, D. (Pit) .87
McCormick, H. (Cin) 1.00

Earned Run Average
Driscoll, D. (Pit) 1.21
Hecker, G. (Lou) 1.30
McCormick, H. (Cin) 1.52

Adjusted ERA
Driscoll, D. (Pit) 216
Hecker, G. (Lou) 191
McCormick, H. (Cin) 174

Component ERA

Opponents' Batting Avg.
Hecker, G. (Lou) .188
McCormick, H. (Cin) .206
Driscoll, D. (Pit) .206

Adjusted Pitching Runs
White, W. (Cin) 50
Driscoll, D. (Pit) 32
Mullane, T. (Lou) 27

Win Shares – Pitchers
White, W. (Cin) 54
Mullane, T. (Lou) 36
Weaver, S. (Phi) 33

TPW – Pitchers
White, W. (Cin) 5.1
Mullane, T. (Lou) 3.6
Driscoll, D. (Pit) 2.8

1883 National League

TEAM	G	W	L	PCT	GB	R	OR	EW	AB	H	2B	3B	HR	TB	BB	SO	SB	CS	AVG	OBP	SLG	OPS	OPS+	BR/A	PF	RC
BOS	98	63	35	.643	....	669	456	67	3657	1010	209	**86**	**34**	**1493**	123	423	....	....	.276	.300	**.408**	**.708**	**114**	**53**	102	**459**
CHI	98	59	39	.602	4	**679**	540	60	3658	1000	**277**	61	13	1438	129	399	....	....	.273	.298	.393	.691	104	3	108	439
PRO	98	58	40	.592	5	636	**436**	67	3685	1001	189	59	21	1371	149	309	....	....	.272	.300	.372	.672	104	13	103	422
CLE	100	55	42	.567	7.5	476	443	52	3457	852	184	38	8	1136	139	374	....	....	.246	.276	.329	.604	87	-47	99	321
BUF	98	52	45	.536	10.5	614	576	52	**3729**	**1058**	184	59	8	1384	147	342	....	....	**.284**	**.311**	.371	.682	108	32	102	441
NY	98	46	50	.479	16	530	577	44	3524	900	139	69	24	1249	127	**297**	....	....	.255	.281	.354	.636	97	-13	99	360
DET	101	40	58	.408	23	524	650	39	3726	931	164	48	13	1230	**166**	378	....	....	.250	.282	.330	.612	93	-19	95	355
PHI	99	17	81	.173	46	437	887	19	3576	859	181	48	3	1145	141	355	....	....	.240	.269	.320	.589	90	-25	91	316
Total	**395**					**4565**			**29012**	**7611**	**1527**	**468**	**124**		**1121**	**2877**			**.262**	**.290**	**.360**	**.650**				

Runs
Hornung, J. (Bos) 107
Gore, G. (Chi) 105
O'Rourke, J. (Buf) 102

Hits
Brouthers, D. (Buf) 159
Connor, R. (NY) 146
O'Rourke, J. (Buf) 143

Doubles
Williamson, N. (Chi) 49
Brouthers, D. (Buf) 41
Burns, T. (Chi) 37

Triples
Brouthers, D. (Buf) 17
Morrill, J. (Bos) 16
2 players tied with 15

Home Runs
Ewing, B. (NY) 10
Denny, J. (Pro) 8
Hornung, J. (Bos) 8

Total Bases
Brouthers, D. (Buf) 243
Morrill, J. (Bos) 212
Connor, R. (NY) 207

Runs Batted In
Brouthers, D. (Buf) 97
Burdock, J. (Bos) 88
Sutton, E. (Bos) 73

Bases On Balls
York, T. (Cle) 37
Hanlon, N. (Det) 34
Powell, M. (Det) 28

Stolen Bases

Batting Average
Brouthers, D. (Buf) .374
Connor, R. (NY) .357
Gore, G. (Chi) .334

On-Base Percentage
Brouthers, D. (Buf) .397
Connor, R. (NY) .394
Gore, G. (Chi) .377

Slugging Average
Brouthers, D. (Buf) .572
Morrill, J. (Bos) .525
Connor, R. (NY) .506

Adjusted OPS
Brouthers, D. (Buf) 186
Connor, R. (NY) 173
Morrill, J. (Bos) 155

Adjusted Batting Runs
Brouthers, D. (Buf) 42.0
Connor, R. (NY) 36.0
Morrill, J. (Bos) 26.0

Runs Created/Game
Brouthers, D. (Buf) 10.20
Connor, R. (NY) 8.70
Gore, G. (Chi) 7.50

Fielding Runs
Glasscock, J. (Cle) 24.4
Farrell, J. (Pro) 22.4
Richardson, H. (Buf) 21.8

Win Shares – Batters
Radbourn, C. (Pro) 60
Whitney, J. (Bos) 57
2 players tied with 28

TPW – Batters
Whitney, J. (Bos) 6.4
Radbourn, C. (Pro) 5.0
Richardson, H. (Buf) 3.6

TEAM	CG	SH	SV	IP	H	H/G	ER	HR	BB	SO	OAV	RAT	ERA	ERA+	CERA	PR+	PF	FA	E	DP	FR	BW	PW	FW	TPW	DIF
BOS	89	**6**	**3**	860	853	8.9	244	11	**90**	**538**	.244	1.097	2.55	121	....	**59.8**	99	.901	409	58	-7.4	**4.7**	**5.2**	-.6	**9.2**	4.8
CHI	91	5	1	862	942	9.8	266	21	123	299	.262	1.235	2.78	119	....	24.6	105	.879	543	76	25.3	.2	2.1	2.2	4.6	5.4
PRO	88	4	1	871	827	8.6	229	12	111	376	.236	**1.077**	2.37	130	....	33.2	98	.903	419	75	**36.2**	1.2	2.9	**3.2**	7.2	1.8
CLE	**92**	5	2	879	**818**	**8.4**	**217**	**7**	217	402	**.232**	1.177	**2.22**	142	....	57.1	100	**.909**	**389**	69	33.5	-4.1	5.0	2.9	3.8	3.2
BUF	90	5	2	859[1]	971	10.2	317	12	101	362	.269	1.247	3.32	96	....	-8.8	101	.896	445	52	-5.0	2.8	-.8	-.4	1.6	2.4
NY	87	5	0	866	907	9.4	283	19	170	323	.254	1.244	2.94	105	....	11.2	99	.889	468	52	3.8	-1.1	1.0	.3	.2	-2.2
DET	89	5	2	**894**[1]	1026	10.3	356	22	184	324	.272	1.353	3.58	87	....	-32.2	99	.893	470	**77**	-15.0	-1.7	-2.8	-1.3	-5.8	-3.2
PHI	91	3	0	864[2]	1267	13.2	513	20	125	253	.323	1.610	5.34	**58**	....	-145.5	98	.858	639	62	-70.9	-2.1	-12.7	-6.2	-21.0	-11.0
Total	**717**	**38**	**11**	**6956**[1]		**9.8**	**2425**					**1.255**	**3.14**													

Wins
- Radbourn, C. (Pro) 48
- Galvin, P. (Buf) 46
- Whitney, J. (Bos) 37

Win Percentage
- McCormick, J. (Cle) .700
- Radbourn, C. (Pro) .658
- Buffinton, C. (Bos) .641

Games
- Galvin, P. (Buf) 76
- Radbourn, C. (Pro) 76
- Coleman, J. (Phi) 65

Complete Games
- Galvin, P. (Buf) 72
- Radbourn, C. (Pro) 66
- Coleman, J. (Phi) 59

Shutouts
- Galvin, P. (Buf) 5
- 4 players tied with 4

Saves
- Whitney, J. (Bos) 2
- Wiedman, S. (Det) 2
- 6 players tied with 1

Innings Pitched
- Galvin, P. (Buf) 656[1]
- Radbourn, C. (Pro) 632[1]
- Coleman, J. (Phi) 538[1]

Fewest Hits/Game
- Sawyer, W. (Cle) 7.60
- Radbourn, C. (Pro) 8.01
- McCormick, J. (Cle) 8.32

Fewest BB/Game
- Whitney, J. (Bos) .61
- Galvin, P. (Buf) .69
- Radbourn, C. (Pro) .80

Strikeouts
- Whitney, J. (Bos) 345
- Radbourn, C. (Pro) 315
- Galvin, P. (Buf) 279

Ratio
- Radbourn, C. (Pro) .98
- Whitney, J. (Bos) 1.03
- Galvin, P. (Buf) 1.11

Earned Run Average
- McCormick, J. (Cle) 1.84
- Radbourn, C. (Pro) 2.05
- Whitney, J. (Bos) 2.24

Adjusted ERA
- McCormick, J. (Cle) 171
- Radbourn, C. (Pro) 150
- Whitney, J. (Bos) 138

Component ERA

Opponents' Batting Avg.
- Sawyer, W. (Cle) .215
- Radbourn, C. (Pro) .224
- McCormick, J. (Cle) .231

Adjusted Pitching Runs
- Whitney, J. (Bos) 54
- Radbourn, C. (Pro) 46
- Galvin, P. (Buf) 37

Win Shares – Pitchers
- Radbourn, C. (Pro) 60
- Whitney, J. (Bos) 57
- Galvin, P. (Buf) 47

TPW – Pitchers
- Whitney, J. (Bos) 6.4
- Radbourn, C. (Pro) 5.0
- McCormick, J. (Cle) 3.1

1883 American Association

TEAM	G	W	L	PCT	GB	R	OR	EW	AB	H	2B	3B	HR	TB	BB	SO	SB	CS	AVG	OBP	SLG	OPS	OPS+	BR/A	PF	RC
PHI	98	66	32	.673	....	**720**	547	62	**3712**	**974**	**149**	50	20	1283	**200**	268	....	....	**.262**	**.300**	.346	.646	102	-2	108	392
STL	98	65	33	.663	1	549	409	63	3495	891	118	46	7	1122	124	**240**	....	....	.255	.280	.321	.601	92	-41	106	323
CIN	98	61	37	.622	5	662	413	71	3669	961	122	74	**34**	**1333**	139	261	....	....	.262	.289	**.363**	**.652**	106	14	106	**395**
NY	97	54	42	.562	11	498	**405**	58	3534	883	111	58	6	1128	142	259	....	....	.250	.279	.319	.598	91	-40	104	322
LOU	98	52	45	.536	13.5	564	562	49	3553	892	114	64	14	1176	141	304	....	....	.251	.280	.331	.611	**107**	**39**	93	336
COL	97	32	65	.330	33.5	476	659	33	3553	854	101	**79**	15	1158	134	409	....	....	.240	.268	.326	.594	102	21	92	318
PIT	98	31	67	.316	35	525	728	34	3607	892	120	58	13	1167	164	345	....	....	.247	.280	.324	.604	102	16	95	334
BAL	96	28	68	.292	37	471	742	28	3532	870	125	49	5	1108	164	331	....	....	.246	.280	.314	.593	91	-37	103	317
Total	**390**					**4465**			**28655**	**7217**	**960**	**478**	**114**		**1208**	**2417**			**.252**	**.282**	**.331**	**.613**				

Runs
- Stovey, H. (Phi) 110
- Reilly, J. (Cin) 103
- Carpenter, H. (Cin) 99

Hits
- Swartwood, E. (Pit) 147
- Reilly, J. (Cin) 136
- Carpenter, H. (Cin) 130

Doubles
- Stovey, H. (Phi) 31
- Swartwood, E. (Pit) 24
- 2 players tied with 23

Triples
- Smith, P. (Col) 17
- Kuehne, B. (Col) 14
- Reilly, J. (Cin) 14

Home Runs
- Stovey, H. (Phi) 14
- Jones, C. (Cin) 10
- Reilly, J. (Cin) 9

Total Bases
- Stovey, H. (Phi) 213
- Reilly, J. (Cin) 212
- Swartwood, E. (Pit) 196

Runs Batted In
- Jones, C. (Cin) 80
- Reilly, J. (Cin) 79
- O'Brien, J. (Phi) 70

Bases On Balls
- Stearns, E. (Bal) 34
- Moynahan, M. (Phi) 31
- Nelson, C. (NY) 31

Stolen Bases

Batting Average
- Swartwood, E. (Pit) .357
- Browning, P. (Lou) .338
- Clinton, J. (Bal) .313

On-Base Percentage
- Swartwood, E. (Pit) .394
- Browning, P. (Lou) .378
- Moynahan, M. (Phi) .360

Slugging Average
- Stovey, H. (Phi) .506
- Reilly, J. (Cin) .485
- Swartwood, E. (Pit) .476

Adjusted OPS
- Swartwood, E. (Pit) 187
- Browning, P. (Lou) 183
- Stovey, H. (Phi) 158

Adjusted Batting Runs
- Swartwood, E. (Pit) 40.0
- Browning, P. (Lou) 34.0
- Stovey, H. (Phi) 26.0

Runs Created/Game
- Swartwood, E. (Pit) 8.40
- Browning, P. (Lou) 7.60
- Stovey, H. (Phi) 7.20

Fielding Runs
- Latham, A. (StL) 23.3
- Richmond, J. (Col) 21.4
- Holbert, B. (NY) 21.4

Win Shares – Batters
- Mullane, T. (StL) 55
- Hecker, G. (Lou) 36
- Stovey, H. (Phi) 25

TPW – Batters
- Richmond, J. (Col) 3.3
- Mullane, T. (StL) 3.0
- Swartwood, E. (Pit) 2.7

TEAM	CG	SH	SV	IP	H	H/G	ER	HR	BB	SO	OAV	RAT	ERA	ERA+	CERA	PR+	PF	FA	E	DP	FR	BW	PW	FW	TPW	DIF
PHI	92	1	0	873	921	9.5	279	22	**95**	347	.254	1.164	2.88	121	....	**83.5**	105	.865	584	40	-26.0	-.2	**7.4**	-2.3	4.9	12.1
STL	93	**9**	**1**	**879**[1]	**729**	**7.5**	218	**7**	150	325	**.211**	**1.000**	**2.23**	156	....	62.1	105	**.909**	388	62	**59.7**	-3.6	5.5	**5.3**	7.1	8.9
CIN	96	8	0	866[2]	766	8.0	**217**	17	168	215	.222	1.078	2.25	144	....	62.5	98	.905	**383**	57	31.6	1.2	5.5	2.8	**9.5**	2.5
NY	**97**	6	0	874	751	7.7	282	12	123	**490**	.216	1.000	2.90	115	....	34.0	101	.905	391	45	8.3	-3.5	3.0	.7	.2	5.8
LOU	96	7	0	873[2]	987	10.2	340	**7**	110	269	.267	1.256	3.50	85	....	-33.9	90	.887	478	67	-16.5	**3.5**	-3.0	-1.4	-1.0	5.0
COL	90	4	0	840[1]	980	10.5	370	16	211	222	.273	1.417	3.96	78	....	-85.4	93	.874	535	**69**	2.3	1.9	-7.5	.2	-5.4	-10.6
PIT	82	1	**1**	867[2]	1140	11.8	445	21	151	271	.298	1.488	4.62	**69**	....	-120.2	97	.884	504	55	-15.8	1.4	-10.6	-1.4	-10.5	-7.5
BAL	86	1	0	844[2]	943	10.0	383	12	190	290	.265	1.341	4.08	85	....	-12.2	105	.855	624	44	-44.6	-3.3	-1.1	-3.9	-8.3	-11.7
Total	**732**	**37**	**2**	**6919**[1]		**9.4**	**2534**					**1.216**	**3.30**													

Wins
- White, W. (Cin) 43
- Keefe, T. (NY) 41
- Mullane, T. (StL) 35

Win Percentage
- Mullane, T. (StL) .700
- Mathews, B. (Phi) .698
- Bradley, G. (Phi) .696

Games
- Keefe, T. (NY) 68
- White, W. (Cin) 65
- Mountain, F. (Col) 59

Complete Games
- Keefe, T. (NY) 68
- White, W. (Cin) 64
- Mountain, F. (Col) 57

Shutouts
- McGinnis, J. (StL) 6
- White, W. (Cin) 6
- Keefe, T. (NY) 5

Saves
- Barr, B. (Pit) 1
- Mullane, T. (StL) 1

Innings Pitched
- Keefe, T. (NY) 619
- White, W. (Cin) 577
- Mountain, F. (Col) 503

Fewest Hits/Game
- Keefe, T. (NY) 7.10
- Mullane, T. (StL) 7.27
- White, W. (Cin) 7.38

Fewest BB/Game
- Mathews, B. (Phi) .73
- Weaver, S. (Lou) .79
- Lynch, J. (NY) .88

Strikeouts
- Keefe, T. (NY) 359
- Mathews, B. (Phi) 203
- Mullane, T. (StL) 191

Ratio
- Keefe, T. (NY) .96
- Mullane, T. (StL) .97
- White, W. (Cin) 1.00

Earned Run Average
- White, W. (Cin) 2.09
- Mullane, T. (StL) 2.19
- Deagle, R. (Cin) 2.31

Adjusted ERA
- Mullane, T. (StL) 159
- White, W. (Cin) 155
- McGinnis, J. (StL) 149

Component ERA

Opponents' Batting Avg.
- Keefe, T. (NY) .203
- Mullane, T. (StL) .207
- White, W. (Cin) .209

Adjusted Pitching Runs
- Keefe, T. (NY) 58
- Mathews, B. (Phi) 54
- White, W. (Cin) 53

Win Shares – Pitchers
- Keefe, T. (NY) 70
- Mullane, T. (StL) 55
- White, W. (Cin) 51

TPW – Pitchers
- Keefe, T. (NY) 5.6
- White, W. (Cin) 4.9
- Mathews, B. (Phi) 4.2

1884 National League

TEAM	G	W	L	PCT	GB	R	OR	EW	AB	H	2B	3B	HR	TB	BB	SO	SB	CS	AVG	OBP	SLG	OPS	OPS+	BR/A	PF	RC
PRO	114	84	28	.750	....	665	**388**	84	4093	987	153	43	21	1289	**300**	469	....	....	.241	.293	.315	.608	97	-1	97	387
BOS	116	73	38	.658	10.5	684	468	76	4189	1063	**179**	60	36	1470	207	660	....	....	.254	.289	.351	.640	105	20	99	435
BUF	115	64	47	.577	19.5	700	626	62	**4197**	1099	163	**69**	39	1517	215	**458**	....	....	.262	.298	.361	.659	107	23	103	463
NY	116	62	50	.554	22	693	623	62	4124	1053	149	68	22	1404	249	492	....	....	.255	.298	.340	.638	102	6	102	429
CHI	113	62	50	.554	22	**834**	647	70	4182	**1176**	162	50	**142**	**1864**	264	469	....	....	**.281**	**.324**	**.446**	**.770**	**133**	**140**	108	**619**
PHI	113	39	73	.348	45	549	824	34	3998	934	149	39	14	1203	209	512	....	....	.234	.272	.301	.573	87	-45	95	335
CLE	113	35	77	.312	49	458	716	33	3934	934	147	49	16	1227	170	576	....	....	.237	.269	.312	.581	83	-81	103	338
DET	114	28	84	.250	56	445	736	30	3970	825	114	47	31	1126	207	699	....	....	.208	.247	.284	.531	74	-100	94	285
Total	**457**					**5028**			**32687**	**8071**	**1216**	**425**	**321**		**1821**	**4335**			**.247**	**.287**	**.340**	**.626**				

Runs
- Kelly, K. (Chi) 120
- Hornung, J. (Bos) 119
- O'Rourke, J. (Buf) 119

Hits
- O'Rourke, J. (Buf) 162
- Sutton, E. (Bos) 162
- Dalrymple, A. (Chi) 161

Doubles
- Hines, P. (Pro) 36
- O'Rourke, J. (Buf) 33
- Anson, C. (Chi) 30

Triples
- Ewing, B. (NY) 20
- Brouthers, D. (Buf) 15
- Rowe, J. (Buf) 14

Home Runs
- Williamson, N. (Chi) 27
- Pfeffer, F. (Chi) 25
- Dalrymple, A. (Chi) 22

Total Bases
- Dalrymple, A. (Chi) 263
- Anson, C. (Chi) 258
- Pfeffer, F. (Chi) 240

Runs Batted In
- Anson, C. (Chi) 102
- Pfeffer, F. (Chi) 101
- Kelly, K. (Chi) 95

Bases On Balls
- Gore, G. (Chi) 61
- Kelly, K. (Chi) 46
- Hines, P. (Pro) 44

Stolen Bases

Batting Average
- O'Rourke, J. (Buf) .347
- Kelly, K. (Chi) .354
- Sutton, E. (Bos) .346

On-Base Percentage
- Kelly, K. (Chi) .414
- Gore, G. (Chi) .404
- O'Rourke, J. (Buf) .392

Slugging Average
- Brouthers, D. (Buf) .563
- Williamson, N. (Chi) .554
- Anson, C. (Chi) .543

Adjusted OPS
- Brouthers, D. (Buf) 185
- Kelly, K. (Chi) 178
- Anson, C. (Chi) 170

Adjusted Batting Runs
- Kelly, K. (Chi) 41.0
- Brouthers, D. (Buf) 38.0
- Anson, C. (Chi) 36.0

Runs Created/Game
- Kelly, K. (Chi) 9.50
- Brouthers, D. (Buf) 8.90
- Anson, C. (Chi) 8.60

Fielding Runs
- Pfeffer, F. (Chi) 23.7
- Glasscock, J. (Cle) 22.2
- Williamson, N. (Chi) 15.6

Win Shares – Batters
- Radbourn, C. (Pro) 89
- Buffinton, C. (Bos) 62
- 2 players tied with 28

TPW – Batters
- Radbourn, C. (Pro) 8.5
- Pfeffer, F. (Chi) 4.5
- Buffinton, C. (Bos) 4.2

TEAM	CG	SH	SV	IP	H	H/G	ER	HR	BB	SO	OAV	RAT	ERA	ERA+	CERA	PR+	PF	FA	E	DP	FR	BW	PW	FW	TPW	DIF
PRO	107	**16**	**2**	1036^1	**825**	**7.2**	**185**	**26**	172	639	**.206**	**.962**	**1.61**	176	....	**112.3**	95	.918	398	50	27.5	-.1	**10.0**	2.5	12.5	15.5
BOS	109	14	**2**	**1037**	932	8.1	285	30	**135**	**742**	.227	1.029	2.47	117	....	30.9	97	**.922**	**384**	46	16.7	1.8	2.8	1.5	6.1	11.9
BUF	108	14	1	1001	1041	9.4	328	46	189	534	.254	1.229	2.95	107	....	40.9	106	.904	462	71	-15.8	2.1	3.7	-1.4	4.4	4.6
NY	**111**	4	0	1014	1011	9.0	352	28	326	567	.246	1.319	3.12	95	....	-18.5	100	.895	514	69	2.5	.5	-1.7	.2	-.9	6.9
CHI	106	9	0	997^1	1028	9.3	336	83	231	472	.252	1.262	3.03	103	....	-29.2	105	.886	595	**107**	**40.2**	**12.6**	-2.6	**3.6**	**13.5**	-7.5
PHI	106	3	1	981	1090	10.0	428	37	254	411	.266	1.370	3.93	**76**	....	-60.0	100	.888	536	67	-42.8	-4.0	-5.4	-3.8	-13.2	-3.8
CLE	107	7	0	994^1	1046	9.5	379	35	269	482	.256	1.322	3.43	92	....	-37.6	106	.897	512	75	6.3	-7.3	-3.4	.6	-10.1	-10.9
DET	109	3	0	984^1	1097	10.0	370	36	245	488	.267	1.363	3.38	86	....	-19.0	97	.886	550	62	-34.0	-8.9	-1.7	-3.0	-13.6	-14.4
Total	**863**	**70**	**6**	**8045^1**		**9.0**	**2663**					**1.229**	**2.98**													

Wins
Radbourn, C. (Pro) 59
Buffinton, C. (Bos) 48
Galvin, P. (Buf) 46

Win Percentage
Radbourn, C. (Pro) .... .831
Clarkson, J. (Chi) .... .769
Buffinton, C. (Bos) .... .750

Games
Radbourn, C. (Pro) 75
Galvin, P. (Buf) 72
Buffinton, C. (Bos) 67

Complete Games
Radbourn, C. (Pro) 73
Galvin, P. (Buf) 71
Buffinton, C. (Bos) 63

Shutouts
Galvin, P. (Buf) 12
Radbourn, C. (Pro) 11
Buffinton, C. (Bos) 8

Saves
Morrill, J. (Bos) 2
4 players tied with 1

Innings Pitched
Radbourn, C. (Pro) .... 678^2
Galvin, P. (Buf) .... 636^1
Buffinton, C. (Bos) 587

Fewest Hits/Game
Sweeney, C. (Pro) 6.23
Radbourn, C. (Pro) 7.00
Clarkson, J. (Chi) 7.17

Fewest BB/Game
Whitney, J. (Bos) .... .72
Galvin, P. (Buf) .... .89
Buffinton, C. (Bos) 1.17

Strikeouts
Radbourn, C. (Pro) 441
Buffinton, C. (Bos) 417
Galvin, P. (Buf) 369

Ratio
Sweeney, C. (Pro) .... .82
Whitney, J. (Bos) .... .89
Radbourn, C. (Pro) .... .92

Earned Run Average
Radbourn, C. (Pro)............ 1.38
Sweeney, C. (Pro)............. 1.55
Getzein, C. (Det)............... 1.95

Adjusted ERA
Radbourn, C. (Pro) 205
Sweeney, C. (Pro) 182
Galvin, P. (Buf) 158

Component ERA

Opponents' Batting Avg.
Sweeney, C. (Pro) .... .184
Radbourn, C. (Pro) .... .203
Clarkson, J. (Chi) .... .207

Adjusted Pitching Runs
Galvin, P. (Buf) 92
Radbourn, C. (Pro) 91
Buffinton, C. (Bos) 39

Win Shares – Pitchers
Radbourn, C. (Pro) 89
Buffinton, C. (Bos) 62
Galvin, P. (Buf) 57

TPW – Pitchers
Radbourn, C. (Pro)............ 8.5
Galvin, P. (Buf) 7.2
Buffinton, C. (Bos) 4.2

1884 American Association

TEAM	G	W	L	PCT	GB	R	OR	EW	AB	H	2B	3B	HR	TB	BB	SO	SB	CS	AVG	OBP	SLG	OPS	OPS+	BR/A	PF	RC
NY	112	75	32	.701	....	734	423	80	4012	1052	155	64	22	1401	203	315	....	....	.262	**.304**	.349	.653	119	87	98	436
COL	110	69	39	.639	6.5	585	459	67	3759	901	107	96	**40**	1320	196	629	....	....	.240	.288	.351	.639	**121**	**101**	92	390
LOU	110	68	40	.630	7.5	573	425	70	3957	1004	152	69	17	1345	146	408	....	....	.254	.286	.340	.626	112	56	96	395
STL	110	67	40	.626	8	658	539	64	3952	987	151	60	11	1291	172	339	....	....	.250	.288	.327	.614	100	-4	104	381
CIN	112	68	41	.624	8	**754**	512	75	**4090**	1037	109	96	36	1446	154	409	....	....	.254	.289	.354	.643	108	23	105	429
BAL	108	63	43	.594	11.5	636	515	64	3845	896	133	84	32	1293	**211**	545	....	....	.233	.284	.336	.621	102	4	104	377
PHI	108	61	46	.570	14	700	546	67	3959	**1057**	**167**	**100**	26	**1502**	153	434	....	....	**.267**	.301	**.379**	**.680**	117	60	106	**463**
TOL	110	46	58	.442	27.5	463	571	41	3712	859	153	48	8	1132	157	545	....	....	.231	.268	.305	.572	87	-57	103	310
BRO	109	40	64	.385	33.5	476	644	37	3763	845	112	47	16	1099	179	417	....	....	.225	.263	.292	.555	84	-65	101	296
RIC	46	12	30	.286	30.5	194	**294**	13	1469	326	40	33	7	453	53	**282**	....	....	.222	.261	.308	.569	89	-16	99	120
PIT	110	30	78	.278	45.5	406	725	26	3689	777	105	50	2	988	143	411	....	....	.211	.248	.268	.516	70	-116	102	251
IND	110	29	78	.271	46	462	755	29	3813	890	129	62	20	1203	125	561	....	....	.233	.262	.316	.577	94	-24	97	323
WAS	63	12	51	.190	41	248	481	13	2166	434	61	24	6	561	100	377	....	....	.200	.241	.259	.500	75	-40	88	139
Total	**659**					**6889**			**46186**	**11065**	**1574**	**833**	**243**		**1992**	**5672**			**.240**	**.278**	**.326**	**.604**				

Runs
Stovey, H. (Phi)................. 124
Jones, C. (Cin).................. 117
Latham, A. (StL) 115

Hits
Orr, D. (NY) 162
Reilly, J. (Cin) 152
2 players tied with 150

Doubles
Barkley, S. (Tol)................ 39
Browning, P. (Lou) 33
Orr, D. (NY) 32

Triples
Stovey, H. (Phi)................. 23
Reilly, J. (Cin) 19
Mann, F. (Col) 18

Home Runs
Reilly, J. (Cin) 11
Stovey, H. (Phi)................. 10
Orr, D. (NY) 9

Total Bases
Orr, D. (NY)....................... 247
Reilly, J. (Cin)................... 247
Stovey, H. (Phi) 244

Runs Batted In
Orr, D. (NY) 112
Reilly, J. (Cin) 91
Comiskey, C. (StL) 84

Bases On Balls
Nelson, C. (NY) 74
Geer, B. (Bro) 38
Jones, C. (Cin).................. 37

Stolen Bases

Batting Average
Orr, D. (NY) .... .354
Reilly, J. (Cin) .... .339
Browning, P. (Lou) .... .336

On-Base Percentage
Jones, C. (Cin).................. .376
Nelson, C. (NY) .... .375
Stovey, H. (Phi)................. .368

Slugging Average
Reilly, J. (Cin)................... .551
Stovey, H. (Phi) .... .545
Orr, D. (NY)....................... .539

Adjusted OPS
Orr, D. (NY) 195
Reilly, J. (Cin) 186
Fennelly, F. (Cin,Was) 184

Adjusted Batting Runs
Orr, D. (NY) 44.0
Reilly, J. (Cin) 40.0
Stovey, H. (Phi)................. 39.0

Runs Created/Game
Reilly, J. (Cin) 8.60
Orr, D. (NY) 8.50
Stovey, H. (Phi)................. 8.40

Fielding Runs
Latham, A. (StL) 39.3
Gerhardt, J. (Lou) 28.2
McPhee, B. (Cin) 27.7

Win Shares – Batters
Mullane, T. (Tol) 58
Orr, D. (NY) 27
Jones, C. (Cin).................. 27

TPW – Batters
Mullane, T. (Tol) 6.4
Latham, A. (StL)................ 4.5
Fennelly, F. (Was,Cin)........ 4.1

TEAM	CG	SH	SV	IP	H	H/G	ER	HR	BB	SO	OAV	RAT	ERA	ERA+	CERA	PR+	PF	FA	E	DP	FR	BW	PW	FW	TPW	DIF
NY	110	9	0	985	802	**7.3**	269	15	115	628	**.210**	**.931**	2.46	127	....	35.0	96	.907	441	42	**37.2**	7.9	3.2	**3.4**	**14.5**	7.5
COL	102	8	**1**	962^1	815	7.6	286	22	172	526	.217	1.026	2.67	113	....	11.8	93	.908	433	74	24.2	**9.2**	1.1	2.2	12.5	2.5
LOU	101	6	0	**989^2**	836	7.6	238	**9**	97	470	.217	.943	**2.16**	142	....	62.8	95	**.912**	426	**84**	36.8	5.1	5.7	3.4	14.2	-.2
STL	99	8	0	987	881	8.0	293	16	172	477	.226	1.067	2.67	122	....	38.3	100	.900	490	65	25.3	-.4	3.5	2.3	5.4	8.6
CIN	**111**	**11**	0	983^2	956	8.8	364	27	181	308	.241	1.156	3.33	100	....	-18.4	103	.909	430	82	18.0	2.1	-1.7	1.6	2.0	12.0
BAL	105	8	**1**	955^2	869	8.2	288	16	219	**635**	.229	1.138	2.71	127	....	**97.5**	107	.899	461	61	-18.3	.3	**8.9**	-1.7	7.6	2.4
PHI	105	5	0	948^2	920	8.7	360	16	127	530	.241	1.104	3.42	99	....	-2.9	104	.901	457	63	-1.0	5.5	-.3	-.1	5.1	2.9
TOL	103	9	**1**	946	885	8.4	322	12	169	501	.234	1.114	3.06	111	....	28.8	105	.900	469	67	6.9	-5.2	2.6	.6	-1.9	-4.1
BRO	105	6	0	948^2	996	9.4	399	20	163	378	.256	1.222	3.79	87	....	-33.1	102	.889	520	68	-17.7	-5.9	-3.0	-1.6	-10.6	-1.4
RIC	45	1	0	370^1	**402**	9.8	**186**	14	**52**	167	.262	1.226	4.52	**73**	....	-47.6	102	.874	**239**	27	-2.4	-1.4	-4.4	-.2	-6.0	-3.0
PIT	108	4	0	943^1	1059	10.1	456	25	216	338	.269	1.352	4.35	77	....	-73.4	104	.889	523	71	-30.1	-10.6	-6.7	-2.7	-20.1	-3.9
IND	107	2	0	937^2	1001	9.6	437	30	199	479	.259	1.280	4.19	78	....	-51.6	101	.889	515	45	-44.6	-2.2	-4.7	-4.1	-11.0	-13.0
WAS	62	3	0	543^2	643	10.6	242	21	110	235	.279	1.385	4.01	75	....	-25.4	93	.858	400	40	-33.9	-3.7	-2.3	-3.1	-9.1	-9.9
Total	**1263**	**80**	**3**	**11501^2**		**8.7**	**4140**					**1.135**	**3.24**													

Wins
Hecker, G. (Lou) 52
Keefe, T. (NY)................... 37
Lynch, J. (NY)................... 37

Win Percentage
O'Neill, T. (StL)................ .733
Morris, E. (Col) .... .723
Hecker, G. (Lou) .... .722

Games
Hecker, G. (Lou) 75
Mullane, T. (Tol) 67
McKeon, L. (Ind) 61

Complete Games
Hecker, G. (Lou) 72
Mullane, T. (Tol) 64
McKeon, L. (Ind) 59

Shutouts
Mullane, T. (Tol) 7
White, W. (Cin) 7
Hecker, G. (Lou) 6

Saves
Mountain, F. (Col)............. 1
O'Day, H. (Tol) 1
Burns, O. (Bal) 1

Innings Pitched
Hecker, G. (Lou) .... 670^2
Mullane, T. (Tol) 567
McKeon, L. (Ind) 512

Fewest Hits/Game
Morris, E. (Col) 7.02
Hecker, G. (Lou) 7.06
Keefe, T. (NY).................. 7.08

Fewest BB/Game
Hecker, G. (Lou) .... .75
Lynch, J. (NY)................... .76
Dugan, E. (Ric) .... .81

Strikeouts
Hecker, G. (Lou) 385
Henderson, H. (Bal).......... 346
Keefe, T. (NY)................... 334

Ratio
Hecker, G. (Lou) .... .87
Morris, E. (Col) .... .90
Lynch, J. (NY)................... .93

Earned Run Average
Hecker, G. (Lou)............... 1.80
Foutz, D. (StL).................. 2.18
Morris, E. (Col) 2.18

Adjusted ERA
Hecker, G. (Lou) 171
Foutz, D. (StL) 149
Morris, E. (Col) 139

Component ERA

Opponents' Batting Avg.
Morris, E. (Col) .... .203
Hecker, G. (Lou) .... .204
Keefe, T. (NY).................. .205

Adjusted Pitching Runs
Hecker, G. (Lou) 71
Mullane, T. (Tol) 51
Henderson, H. (Bal).......... 49

Win Shares – Pitchers
Hecker, G. (Lou) 74
Mullane, T. (Tol) 58
Keefe, T. (NY).................. 47

TPW – Pitchers
Hecker, G. (Lou)............... 9.1
Mullane, T. (Tol)............... 6.4
Henderson, H. (Bal).......... 4.9

1884 Union Association

TEAM	G	W	L	PCT	GB	R	OR	EW	AB	H	2B	3B	HR	TB	BB	SO	SB	CS	AVG	OBP	SLG	OPS	OPS+	BR/A	PF	RC
STL	114	94	19	.832	....	**887**	429	92	**4285**	**1251**	**259**	41	**32**	**1688**	**181**	542	....	....	**.292**	**.321**	**.394**	**.715**	**137**	**153**	104	**555**
MIL	12	8	4	.667	35.5	53	**34**	9	395	88	25	0	0	113	20	70	....	....	.223	.260	.286	.546	86	-5	100	30
CIN	105	69	36	.657	21	703	466	73	3786	1027	118	**63**	26	1349	147	482	....	....	.271	.298	.356	.655	113	36	108	413
BAL	106	58	47	.552	32	662	627	55	3883	952	150	26	17	1205	144	652	....	....	.245	.272	.310	.582	89	-63	110	336
BOS	111	58	51	.532	34	636	558	62	3940	928	168	32	19	1217	128	787	....	....	.236	.260	.309	.568	95	-19	98	324
CP	93	41	50	.451	42	438	482	41	3212	742	127	26	10	951	119	505	....	....	.231	.258	.296	.555	95	-4	94	252
WAS	114	47	65	.420	46.5	572	679	46	3926	931	120	26	4	1115	118	558	....	....	.237	.259	.284	.543	88	-40	97	296
PHI	67	21	46	.313	50	414	545	25	2518	618	108	35	7	817	103	405	....	....	.245	.275	.324	.600	112	44	92	230
STP	9	2	6	.250	39.5	24	57	1	272	49	13	1	0	64	7	**47**	....	....	.180	.201	.235	.436	48	-14	100	13
ALT	25	6	19	.240	44	90	216	4	899	223	30	6	2	271	22	130	....	....	.248	.266	.301	.567	92	-8	101	74
KC	82	16	63	.203	61	311	618	16	2802	557	104	15	6	709	123	529	....	....	.199	.232	.253	.486	75	-38	87	169
WIL	18	2	16	.111	44.5	35	114	2	521	91	8	8	2	121	22	123	....	....	.175	.208	.232	.440	49	-28	103	26
Total	**428**					**4825**			**30439**	**7457**	**1230**	**279**	**125**		**1134**	**4830**			**.245**	**.272**	**.316**	**.588**				

Runs
Dunlap, F. (StL) 160
Shafer, O. (StL) 130
Seery, E. (Bal,KC) 115

Hits
Dunlap, F. (StL) 185
Shafer, O. (StL) 168
Moore, H. (Was) 155

Doubles
Shafer, O. (StL) 40
Dunlap, F. (StL) 39
Rowe, D. (StL) 32

Triples
Burns, D. (Cin) 12
Rowe, D. (StL) 11
Shafer, O. (StL) 10

Home Runs
Dunlap, F. (StL) 13
Crane, E. (Bos) 12
Levis, C. (Bal,Was) 6

Total Bases
Dunlap, F. (StL) 279
Shafer, O. (StL) 234
Rowe, D. (StL) 208

Runs Batted In

Bases On Balls
Robinson, Y. (Bal) 37
Shafer, O. (StL) 30
Dunlap, F. (StL) 29

Stolen Bases

Batting Average
Dunlap, F. (StL) .... .412
Shafer, O. (StL) .... .360
Moore, H. (Was) .... .336

On-Base Percentage
Dunlap, F. (StL) .... .448
Shafer, O. (StL) .... .398
Moore, H. (Was) .... .362

Slugging Average
Dunlap, F. (StL) .... .621
Shafer, O. (StL) .... .501
Burns, D. (Cin) .... .457

Adjusted OPS
Dunlap, F. (StL) 248
Shafer, O. (StL) 195
Moore, H. (Was) 167

Adjusted Batting Runs
Dunlap, F. (StL) 68.0
Shafer, O. (StL) 45.0
Moore, H. (Was) 32.0

Runs Created/Game
Dunlap, F. (StL) 13.60
Shafer, O. (StL) 8.90
Gleason, J. (StL) 6.80

Fielding Runs
Dunlap, F. (StL) 36.4
Fusselback, E. (Bal) 15.3
Schoeneck, J. (CP,Bal) 11.9

Win Shares – Batters
Burns, D. (Cin) 41
Dunlap, F. (StL) 38
Wise, B. (Was) 30

TPW – Batters
Dunlap, F. (StL) 9.4
Shafer, O. (StL) 3.9
Burns, D. (Cin) 3.5

TEAM	CG	SH	SV	IP	H	H/G	ER	HR	BB	SO	OAV	RAT	ERA	ERA+	CERA	PR+	PF	FA	E	DP	FR	BW	PW	FW	TPW	DIF
STL	**104**	8	**6**	**993**	838	7.6	216	9	110	550	.214	.955	**1.96**	152	....	66.8	98	.888	554	**79**	**46.8**	**13.4**	5.9	**4.1**	**23.3**	14.7
MIL	12	3	0	104	**49**	**4.2**	26	**1**	**13**	139	**.132**	**.596**	2.25	135	....	-2.7	100	**.892**	53	4	11.9	-.4	-.2	1.0	.4	1.6
CIN	95	**11**	1	914^1	831	8.2	242	17	90	503	.226	1.007	2.38	134	....	**83.3**	105	.882	532	45	-1.2	3.2	**7.3**	-.1	10.3	6.7
BAL	92	4	0	946^2	1002	9.5	316	24	177	628	.254	1.245	3.00	111	....	22.1	110	.872	616	53	11.9	-5.5	1.9	1.0	-2.5	8.5
BOS	100	5	1	953^1	885	8.4	286	17	110	**753**	.230	1.044	2.70	110	....	14.8	97	.868	633	39	13.6	-1.7	1.3	1.2	.8	3.2
CP	86	6	0	803^2	743	8.3	243	12	137	679	.229	1.095	2.72	106	....	22.7	95	.882	459	38	-8.4	-.4	2.0	-.7	.9	-4.9
WAS	94	5	0	953^2	992	9.4	364	16	168	684	.251	1.216	3.44	87	....	-19.1	98	.869	625	55	-27.4	-3.5	-1.7	-2.4	-7.5	-1.5
PHI	64	1	0	593^1	726	11.0	305	7	105	310	.282	1.401	4.63	**62**	....	-84.2	95	.841	501	36	-29.2	3.9	-7.4	-2.6	-6.0	-6.0
STP	7	1	0	71	72	9.1	**25**	**1**	27	44	.246	1.394	3.17	96	....	-4.9	100	.872	**47**	6	3.9	-1.2	-.4	.3	-1.3	-.7
ALT	20	0	0	219^2	292	12.0	114	3	52	93	.300	1.566	4.67	71	....	-13.9	109	.862	156	4	-18.9	-.7	-1.2	-1.7	-3.6	-2.4
KC	70	0	0	702^2	862	11.0	317	14	127	334	.283	1.407	4.06	69	....	-99.3	92	.861	520	51	1.3	-3.3	-8.7	.1	-11.9	-11.1
WIL	15	0	0	142	165	10.5	48	4	18	113	.272	1.289	3.04	110	....	7.6	110	.859	104	10	-3.0	-2.4	.7	-.3	-2.0	-5.0
Total	**759**	**44**	**8**	**7397^1**		**9.1**	**2502**					**1.161**	**3.04**													

Wins
Sweeney, B. (Bal) 40
Daily, H. (CP,Was) 28
2 players tied with 25

Win Percentage
Werden, P. (StL) .... .923
McCormick, J. (Cin) .... .875
Taylor, B. (StL) .... .862

Games
Sweeney, B. (Bal) 62
Daily, H. (CP,Was) 58
Wise, B. (Was) 50

Complete Games
Sweeney, B. (Bal) 58
Daily, H. (CP,Was) 56
Bakely, J. (Phi,KC,Wil) 43

Shutouts
McCormick, J. (Cin) 7
Daily, H. (CP,Was) 5
Shaw, D. (Bos) 5

Saves
Taylor, B. (StL) 4
Boyle, H. (StL) 1
Sylvester, L. (Cin) 1

Innings Pitched
Sweeney, B. (Bal) 538
Daily, H. (CP,Was) .... 500^2
Bakely, J. (Phi,KC,Wil) .... 394^2

Fewest Hits/Game
McCormick, J. (Cin) 6.47
Shaw, D. (Bos) 6.47
Sweeney, C. (StL) 6.87

Fewest BB/Game
Sweeney, C. (StL) .... .43
Boyle, H. (StL) .... .60
McCormick, J. (Cin) .... .60

Strikeouts
Daily, H. (CP,Was) 483
Sweeney, B. (Bal) 374
Shaw, D. (Bos) 309

Ratio
McCormick, J. (Cin) .... .79
Sweeney, C. (StL) .... .81
Shaw, D. (Bos) .... .84

Earned Run Average
McCormick, J. (Cin) 1.54
Taylor, B. (StL) 1.68
Boyle, H. (StL) 1.74

Adjusted ERA
McCormick, J. (Cin) 207
Taylor, B. (StL) 178
Boyle, H. (StL) 171

Component ERA

Opponents' Batting Avg.
McCormick, J. (Cin) .... .188
Shaw, D. (Bos) .... .188
Sweeney, C. (StL) .... .197

Adjusted Pitching Runs
McCormick, J. (Cin) 39
Sweeney, B. (Bal) 38
Shaw, D. (Bos) 38

Win Shares – Pitchers
Sweeney, B. (Bal) 49
Burns, D. (Cin) 41
Taylor, B. (StL) 41

TPW – Pitchers
Taylor, B. (StL) 4.3
Burns, D. (Cin) 3.5
Shaw, D. (Bos) 3.4

1885 National League

TEAM	G	W	L	PCT	GB	R	OR	EW	AB	H	2B	3B	HR	TB	BB	SO	SB	CS	AVG	OBP	SLG	OPS	OPS+	BR/A	PF	RC
CHI	113	87	25	.777	....	**834**	470	85	**4093**	1079	**184**	75	**54**	**1575**	**340**	429	....	....	.264	**.320**	**.385**	**.705**	115	54	115	**517**
NY	112	85	27	.759	2	691	**370**	87	4029	**1085**	150	**82**	16	1447	221	**312**	....	....	**.269**	.307	.359	.666	**121**	**90**	99	456
PHI	111	56	54	.509	30	513	511	55	3893	891	156	35	20	1177	220	401	....	....	.229	.270	.302	.572	91	-35	98	326
PRO	110	53	57	.482	33	442	531	45	3727	820	114	30	6	1012	265	430	....	....	.220	.272	.272	.543	83	-54	96	282
BOS	113	46	66	.411	41	528	589	50	3950	915	144	53	22	1231	190	522	....	....	.232	.267	.312	.579	94	-22	96	337
DET	108	41	67	.380	44	514	582	47	3773	917	149	66	25	1273	216	451	....	....	.243	.284	.337	.621	105	17	100	371
BUF	112	38	74	.339	49	495	761	33	3900	980	149	50	23	1298	179	380	....	....	.251	.284	.333	.617	100	-9	103	378
STL	111	36	72	.333	49	390	593	33	3758	829	121	21	8	1016	214	412	....	....	.221	.263	.270	.533	82	-61	94	273
Total	**445**					**4407**			**31123**	**7516**	**1167**	**412**	**174**		**1845**	**3337**			**.241**	**.284**	**.322**	**.606**				

Runs
Kelly, K. (Chi) 124
O'Rourke, J. (NY) 119
Gore, G. (Chi) 115

Hits
Connor, R. (NY) 169
Brouthers, D. (Buf) 146
Anson, C. (Chi) 144

Doubles
Anson, C. (Chi) 35
Brouthers, D. (Buf) 32
Rowe, J. (Buf) 28

Triples
O'Rourke, J. (NY) 16
Connor, R. (NY) 15
2 players tied with 13

Home Runs
Dalrymple, A. (Chi) 11
Kelly, K. (Chi) 9
4 players tied with 7

Total Bases
Connor, R. (NY) 225
Brouthers, D. (Buf) 221
Dalrymple, A. (Chi) 219

Runs Batted In
Anson, C. (Chi) 108
Kelly, K. (Chi) 75
Pfeffer, F. (Chi) 73

Bases On Balls
Williamson, N. (Chi) 75
Gore, G. (Chi) 68
Morrill, J. (Bos) 64

Stolen Bases

Batting Average
Connor, R. (NY) .... .371
Brouthers, D. (Buf) .... .359
Dorgan, M. (NY) .... .326

On-Base Percentage
Connor, R. (NY) .... .435
Brouthers, D. (Buf) .... .408
Gore, G. (Chi) .... .405

Slugging Average
Brouthers, D. (Buf) .... .543
Connor, R. (NY) .... .495
Ewing, B. (NY) .... .471

Adjusted OPS
Connor, R. (NY) 203
Brouthers, D. (Buf) 199
Bennett, C. (Det) 161

Adjusted Batting Runs
Connor, R. (NY) 54.0
Brouthers, D. (Buf) 44.0
O'Rourke, J. (NY) 31.0

Runs Created/Game
Brouthers, D. (Buf) 9.60
Connor, R. (NY) 9.50
Gore, G. (Chi) 7.40

Fielding Runs
Dunlap, F. (StL) 22.2
Gerhardt, J. (NY) 21.3
Glasscock, J. (StL) 20.5

Win Shares – Batters
Connor, R. (NY) 30
Gore, G. (Chi) 30
Brouthers, D. (Buf) 26

TPW – Batters
Connor, R. (NY) 4.7
Dunlap, F. (StL) 3.7
Glasscock, J. (StL) 3.4

TEAM	CG	SH	SV	IP	H	H/G	ER	HR	BB	SO	OAV	RAT	ERA	ERA+	CERA	PR+	PF	FA	E	DP	FR	BW	PW	FW	TPW	DIF
CHI	108	14	**4**	**1015^{2}**	868	7.7	251	37	202	458	.220	1.053	2.22	136	....	**60.3**	108	.903	496	80	29.6	5.0	**5.7**	2.8	13.5	17.5
NY	109	**16**	1	994	**758**	**6.9**	**190**	**11**	265	**516**	**.201**	**1.029**	**1.72**	155	....	56.3	95	**.929**	**331**	**85**	**48.1**	**8.5**	5.3	**4.5**	**18.3**	10.7
PHI	108	10	0	976	860	7.9	259	18	218	378	.226	1.105	2.39	117	....	35.3	99	.905	447	66	7.8	-3.3	3.3	.7	.7	.3
PRO	108	8	0	960^{2}	912	8.5	289	18	235	371	.239	1.194	2.71	98	....	-6.0	94	.903	459	70	-0.6	-5.0	-.6	-.1	-5.7	3.7
BOS	**111**	10	0	981	1045	9.6	330	26	**188**	480	.260	1.257	3.03	89	....	1.2	95	.903	478	79	-38.5	-2.1	.1	-3.6	-5.6	-4.4
DET	105	6	1	954^{1}	966	9.1	305	18	224	475	.251	1.247	2.88	99	....	10.5	101	.901	462	61	-14.8	1.6	1.0	-1.4	1.2	-14.2
BUF	107	4	1	956	1175	11.1	456	31	234	320	.289	1.474	4.29	**69**	....	-79.2	106	.901	464	65	-60.7	-.8	-7.5	-5.7	-14.0	-4.0
STL	107	4	0	965^{1}	935	8.7	361	15	278	337	.242	1.257	3.37	81	....	-96.6	97	.916	398	67	29.7	-5.7	-9.1	2.8	-12.0	-6.0
Total	**863**	**72**	**7**	**7803**		**8.7**	**2441**					**1.200**	**2.82**													

Wins
Clarkson, J. (Chi) 53
Welch, M. (NY) 44
Keefe, T. (NY) 32

Win Percentage
Welch, M. (NY) .800
Clarkson, J. (Chi) .768
Keefe, T. (NY) .711

Games
Clarkson, J. (Chi) 70
Welch, M. (NY) 56
2 players tied with 51

Complete Games
Clarkson, J. (Chi) 68
Welch, M. (NY) 55
Whitney, J. (Bos) 50

Shutouts
Clarkson, J. (Chi) 10
Keefe, T. (NY) 7
Welch, M. (NY) 7

Saves
Pfeffer, F. (Chi) 2
Williamson, N. (Chi) 2
3 players tied with 1

Innings Pitched
Clarkson, J. (Chi) 623
Welch, M. (NY) 492
Radbourn, C. (Pro) 445^{2}

Fewest Hits/Game
Keefe, T. (NY) 6.75
Welch, M. (NY) 6.80
Baldwin, L. (Det) 6.88

Fewest BB/Game
Whitney, J. (Bos) .75
Galvin, P. (Buf) 1.17
Clarkson, J. (Chi) 1.40

Strikeouts
Clarkson, J. (Chi) 308
Welch, M. (NY) 258
Buffinton, C. (Bos) 242

Ratio
Baldwin, L. (Det) .92
Clarkson, J. (Chi) .95
Keefe, T. (NY) 1.00

Earned Run Average
Keefe, T. (NY) 1.58
Welch, M. (NY) 1.66
Clarkson, J. (Chi) 1.85

Adjusted ERA
Keefe, T. (NY) 169
Clarkson, J. (Chi) 164
Welch, M. (NY) 160

Component ERA

Opponents' Batting Avg.
Keefe, T. (NY) .199
Welch, M. (NY) .200
Baldwin, L. (Det) .202

Adjusted Pitching Runs
Clarkson, J. (Chi) 64
Welch, M. (NY) 31
Keefe, T. (NY) 29

Win Shares – Pitchers
Clarkson, J. (Chi) 62
Welch, M. (NY) 57
Keefe, T. (NY) 42

TPW – Pitchers
Clarkson, J. (Chi) 6.1
Ferguson, C. (Phi) 3.9
Welch, M. (NY) 3.4

1885 American Association

TEAM	G	W	L	PCT	GB	R	OR	EW	AB	H	2B	3B	HR	TB	BB	SO	SB	CS	AVG	OBP	SLG	OPS	OPS+	BR/A	PF	RC
STL	112	79	33	.705	....	677	**461**	77	3972	979	132	57	17	1276	234	**282**	....	....	.246	.297	.321	.618	95	-26	105	388
CIN	112	63	49	.562	16	642	575	62	4050	1046	108	77	26	1386	153	420	....	....	.258	.294	.342	.636	103	6	102	417
PIT	111	56	55	.505	22.5	547	539	56	3975	955	123	79	5	1251	189	537	....	....	.240	.282	.315	.597	94	-24	99	362
PHI	113	55	57	.491	24	**764**	691	62	**4142**	**1099**	**169**	76	**30**	**1510**	223	410	....	....	**.265**	**.310**	**.365**	**.674**	**111**	38	106	**480**
BRO	112	53	59	.473	26	624	650	54	3943	966	121	65	14	1259	238	324	....	....	.245	.295	.319	.614	98	-7	101	381
LOU	112	53	59	.473	26	564	598	53	3969	986	126	**83**	19	1335	152	448	....	....	.248	.281	.336	.617	99	-11	100	384
NY	108	44	64	.407	33	526	688	40	3731	921	123	57	21	1221	217	428	....	....	.247	.295	.327	.622	109	**54**	92	369
BAL	110	41	68	.376	36.5	541	683	42	3820	837	124	59	17	1130	**279**	529	....	....	.219	.280	.296	.575	87	-43	98	324
Total	**445**					**4885**			**31602**	**7789**	**1026**	**553**	**149**		**1685**	**3378**			**.246**	**.292**	**.328**	**.620**				

Runs
Stovey, H. (Phi) 130
Larkin, H. (Phi) 114
Jones, C. (Cin) 108

Hits
Browning, P. (Lou) 174
Jones, C. (Cin) 157
Stovey, H. (Phi) 153

Doubles
Larkin, H. (Phi) 37
Browning, P. (Lou) 34
Orr, D. (NY) 29

Triples
Orr, D. (NY) 21
Kuehne, B. (Pit) 19
3 players tied with 17

Home Runs
Stovey, H. (Phi) 13
Fennelly, F. (Cin) 10
Browning, P. (Lou) 9

Total Bases
Browning, P. (Lou) 255
Orr, D. (NY) 241
Larkin, H. (Phi) 238

Runs Batted In
Fennelly, F. (Cin) 89
Larkin, H. (Phi) 88
Orr, D. (NY) 77

Bases On Balls
Nelson, C. (NY) 61
Hotaling, P. (Bro) 49
Macullar, J. (Bal) 49

Stolen Bases

Batting Average
Browning, P. (Lou) .362
Orr, D. (NY) .342
Larkin, H. (Phi) .329

On-Base Percentage
Browning, P. (Lou) .393
Larkin, H. (Phi) .372
Stovey, H. (Phi) .371

Slugging Average
Orr, D. (NY) .543
Browning, P. (Lou) .530
Larkin, H. (Phi) .525

Adjusted OPS
Orr, D. (NY) 197
Browning, P. (Lou) 190
Larkin, H. (Phi) 171

Adjusted Batting Runs
Browning, P. (Lou) 47.0
Orr, D. (NY) 47.0
Larkin, H. (Phi) 34.0

Runs Created/Game
Browning, P. (Lou) 9.00
Orr, D. (NY) 8.20
Larkin, H. (Phi) 8.10

Fielding Runs
Smith, P. (Pit) 37.8
Smith, G. (Bro) 36.0
Barkley, S. (StL) 18.9

Win Shares – Batters
Browning, P. (Lou) 28
Orr, D. (NY) 27
Jones, C. (Cin) 24

TPW – Batters
Browning, P. (Lou) 4.3
Larkin, H. (Phi) 3.7
Smith, P. (Pit) 3.7

TEAM	CG	SH	SV	IP	H	H/G	ER	HR	BB	SO	OAV	RAT	ERA	ERA+	CERA	PR+	PF	FA	E	DP	FR	BW	PW	FW	TPW	DIF
STL	**111**	**11**	0	1002	**879**	**7.9**	**272**	12	**168**	378	**.226**	**1.045**	**2.44**	134	....	62.7	101	**.920**	**381**	64	**29.0**	-2.3	5.6	**2.6**	**5.9**	17.1
CIN	102	7	1	999^{1}	998	9.0	362	24	250	330	.249	1.249	3.26	100	....	-10.4	100	.911	423	**86**	9.9	.5	-.9	.9	.5	6.5
PIT	104	8	0	**1011**	918	8.2	328	14	201	454	.232	1.107	2.92	110	....	25.6	99	.912	422	77	7.6	-2.2	2.3	.7	.8	.2
PHI	105	5	0	1003^{1}	1038	9.3	360	**11**	212	**506**	.256	1.246	3.23	106	....	29.7	106	.902	483	79	-6.7	3.4	2.7	-.6	5.5	-6.5
BRO	110	3	1	991^{2}	955	8.7	381	27	211	436	.243	1.176	3.46	95	....	-11.4	102	.910	434	56	-6.5	-.6	-1.0	-.6	-2.2	-.8
LOU	109	3	1	1002	927	8.3	298	13	217	462	.235	1.142	2.68	120	....	**62.8**	99	.905	460	75	-2.2	-1.0	**5.7**	-.2	4.5	-7.5
NY	103	2	0	937	1015	9.8	432	36	204	408	.265	1.301	4.15	**71**	....	-120.0	91	.901	452	62	-4.1	**4.9**	-10.8	-.4	-6.3	-3.7
BAL	103	2	**4**	971	1059	9.8	421	12	222	395	.266	1.319	3.90	83	....	-47.5	100	.909	418	71	-22.6	-3.9	-4.3	-2.0	-10.2	-2.8
Total	**847**	**41**	**7**	**7917^{1}**		**8.8**	**2854**					**1.197**	**3.24**													

Wins
Caruthers, B. (StL) 40
Morris, E. (Pit) 39
2 players tied with 33

Win Percentage
Caruthers, B. (StL) .755
Foutz, D. (StL) .702
Mathews, B. (Phi) .638

Games
Morris, E. (Pit) 63
Henderson, H. (Bal) 61
Porter, H. (Bro) 54

Complete Games
Morris, E. (Pit) 63
Henderson, H. (Bal) 59
2 players tied with 53

Shutouts
Morris, E. (Pit) 7
Caruthers, B. (StL) 6
McGinnis, J. (StL) 3

Saves
Burns, O. (Bal) 3
4 players tied with 1

Innings Pitched
Morris, E. (Pit) 581
Henderson, H. (Bal) 539^{1}
Caruthers, B. (StL) 482^{1}

Fewest Hits/Game
Morris, E. (Pit) 7.11
Mays, A. (Lou) 7.74
Foutz, D. (StL) 7.75

Fewest BB/Game
Lynch, J. (NY) 1.00
Hecker, G. (Lou) 1.01
Caruthers, B. (StL) 1.06

Strikeouts
Morris, E. (Pit) 298
Mathews, B. (Phi) 286
Henderson, H. (Bal) 263

Ratio
Morris, E. (Pit) .96
Caruthers, B. (StL) 1.01
McGinnis, J. (StL) 1.04

Earned Run Average
Caruthers, B. (StL) 2.07
Hecker, G. (Lou) 2.18
Morris, E. (Pit) 2.35

Adjusted ERA
Caruthers, B. (StL) 158
Hecker, G. (Lou) 148
Mathews, B. (Phi) 141

Component ERA

Opponents' Batting Avg.
Morris, E. (Pit) .208
Mays, A. (Lou) .222
Foutz, D. (StL) .223

Adjusted Pitching Runs
Hecker, G. (Lou) 57
Morris, E. (Pit) 51
Caruthers, B. (StL) 50

Win Shares – Pitchers
Morris, E. (Pit) 56
Caruthers, B. (StL) 51
Hecker, G. (Lou) 42

TPW – Pitchers
Hecker, G. (Lou) 5.8
Caruthers, B. (StL) 5.1
Morris, E. (Pit) 4.3

1886 National League

TEAM	G	W	L	PCT	GB	R	OR	EW	AB	H	2B	3B	HR	TB	BB	SO	SB	CS	AVG	OBP	SLG	OPS	OPS+	BR/A	PF	RC
CHI	126	90	34	.726	....	**900**	555	90	4378	1223	**198**	**87**	**53**	1754	**460**	513	213	....	.279	**.348**	**.401**	**.749**	116	71	115	**701**
DET	126	87	36	.707	2.5	829	538	87	**4501**	**1260**	176	81	**53**	**1757**	374	426	194	....	**.280**	.335	.390	.726	**123**	**116**	103	670
NY	124	75	44	.630	12.5	692	558	72	4298	1156	175	68	21	1530	237	**410**	155	....	.269	.307	.356	.663	106	22	101	531
PHI	119	71	43	.623	14	621	**498**	69	4072	976	145	66	26	1331	282	516	**226**	....	.240	.289	.327	.616	91	-43	101	461
BOS	118	56	61	.479	30.5	657	661	58	4180	1085	151	59	24	1426	250	537	156	....	.260	.301	.341	.643	104	24	96	489
STL	126	43	79	.352	46	547	712	45	4250	1001	183	46	30	1366	235	656	156	....	.236	.276	.321	.597	92	-31	94	430
KC	126	30	91	.248	58.5	494	872	29	4236	967	177	48	19	1297	269	608	96	....	.228	.274	.306	.581	76	-126	106	392
WAS	125	28	92	.233	60	445	791	29	4082	856	135	51	23	1162	265	582	143	....	.210	.258	.285	.543	74	-112	94	345
Total	**495**					**5185**			**33997**	**8524**	**1340**	**506**	**249**		**2372**	**4248**	**1339**		**.251**	**.300**	**.342**	**.641**				

Runs
- Kelly, K. (Chi) 155
- Gore, G. (Chi) 150
- Brouthers, D. (Det) 139

Hits
- Richardson, H. (Det) 189
- Anson, C. (Chi) 187
- Brouthers, D. (Det) 181

Doubles
- Brouthers, D. (Det) 40
- Anson, C. (Chi) 35
- Kelly, K. (Chi) 32

Triples
- Connor, R. (NY) 20
- Brouthers, D. (Det) 15
- Wood, G. (Phi) 15

Home Runs
- Brouthers, D. (Det) 11
- Richardson, H. (Det) 11
- Anson, C. (Chi) 10

Total Bases
- Brouthers, D. (Det) 284
- Anson, C. (Chi) 274
- Richardson, H. (Det) 271

Runs Batted In
- Anson, C. (Chi) 147
- Pfeffer, F. (Chi) 95
- Thompson, S. (Det) 89

Bases On Balls
- Gore, G. (Chi) 102
- Kelly, K. (Chi) 83
- Williamson, N. (Chi) 80

Stolen Bases
- Andrews, E. (Phi) 56
- Kelly, K. (Chi) 53
- Hanlon, N. (Det) 50

Batting Average
- Kelly, K. (Chi) .388
- Anson, C. (Chi) .371
- Brouthers, D. (Det) .370

On-Base Percentage
- Kelly, K. (Chi) .483
- Brouthers, D. (Det) .445
- Gore, G. (Chi) .434

Slugging Average
- Brouthers, D. (Det) .581
- Anson, C. (Chi) .544
- Connor, R. (NY) .540

Adjusted OPS
- Brouthers, D. (Det) 204
- Connor, R. (NY) 183
- Kelly, K. (Chi) 181

Adjusted Batting Runs
- Brouthers, D. (Det) 63.0
- Kelly, K. (Chi) 49.0
- Connor, R. (NY) 48.0

Runs Created/Game
- Kelly, K. (Chi) 14.20
- Brouthers, D. (Det) 12.20
- Anson, C. (Chi) 11.50

Fielding Runs
- Denny, J. (StL) 23.4
- Dunlap, F. (StL,Det) 18.4
- Glasscock, J. (StL) 14.9

Win Shares – Batters
- Connor, R. (NY) 36
- Kelly, K. (Chi) 35
- Richardson, H. (Det) 32

TPW – Batters
- Kelly, K. (Chi) 6.0
- Richardson, H. (Det) 5.0
- Brouthers, D. (Det) 4.7

TEAM	CG	SH	SV	IP	H	H/G	ER	HR	BB	SO	OAV	RAT	ERA	ERA+	CERA	PR+	PF	FA	E	DP	FR	BW	PW	FW	TPW	DIF
CHI	116	8	**3**	1097^{2}	988	8.1	310	49	262	**647**	**.231**	1.139	2.54	142	....	87.4	110	.912	475	82	**43.2**	6.4	7.9	**3.9**	**18.3**	9.7
DET	**122**	8	0	**1103^{2}**	995	8.1	349	**20**	270	592	.232	1.146	2.85	115	....	40.4	100	**.928**	373	82	12.4	**10.5**	3.7	1.1	15.3	10.7
NY	119	3	1	1062	1029	8.7	337	23	280	588	.245	1.233	2.86	111	....	37.1	97	.927	**359**	70	0.6	2.0	3.4	.1	5.4	10.6
PHI	110	**10**	2	1045^{2}	**923**	**7.9**	**284**	29	264	540	.251	**1.135**	**2.44**	134	....	**124.1**	100	.921	393	46	-28.9	-3.9	**11.2**	-2.6	4.8	9.2
BOS	116	3	0	1029	1049	9.2	370	33	298	511	.254	1.309	3.24	98	....	14.6	96	.905	465	63	-23.4	2.1	1.3	-2.1	1.3	-3.3
STL	118	6	0	1077^{1}	1050	8.8	388	34	392	501	.246	1.338	3.24	99	....	-32.4	97	.914	452	**92**	26.9	-2.8	-2.9	2.4	-3.3	-14.7
KC	117	4	0	1066^{2}	1345	11.4	573	27	**246**	442	.297	1.492	4.83	77	....	-102.0	114	.910	482	79	-28.9	-11.4	-9.2	-2.6	-23.3	-6.7
WAS	115	4	0	1041	1147	9.9	497	34	379	500	.269	1.466	4.30	**76**	....	-117.7	99	.910	458	69	-2.4	-10.1	-10.7	-.2	-21.0	-11.0
Total	**933**	**46**	**6**	**8523**		**9.0**	**3108**					**1.281**	**3.28**													

Wins
- Baldwin, L. (Det) 42
- Keefe, T. (NY) 42
- Clarkson, J. (Chi) 36

Win Percentage
- Flynn, J. (Chi) .793
- Ferguson, C. (Phi) .769
- Baldwin, L. (Det) .764

Games
- Keefe, T. (NY) 64
- Welch, M. (NY) 59
- Radbourn, C. (Bos) 58

Complete Games
- Keefe, T. (NY) 62
- Radbourn, C. (Bos) 57
- Welch, M. (NY) 56

Shutouts
- Baldwin, L. (Det) 7
- Casey, D. (Phi) 4
- Ferguson, C. (Phi) 4

Saves
- Ferguson, C. (Phi) 2
- 4 players tied with 1

Innings Pitched
- Keefe, T. (NY) 535
- Radbourn, C. (Bos) 509^{1}
- Welch, M. (NY) 500

Fewest Hits/Game
- Baldwin, L. (Det) 6.86
- Ferguson, C. (Phi) 7.21
- Flynn, J. (Chi) 7.25

Fewest BB/Game
- Whitney, J. (KC) 1.26
- Ferguson, C. (Phi) 1.57
- Clarkson, J. (Chi) 1.66

Strikeouts
- Baldwin, L. (Det) 323
- Clarkson, J. (Chi) 313
- Keefe, T. (NY) 297

Ratio
- Baldwin, L. (Det) .97
- Ferguson, C. (Phi) .98
- Flynn, J. (Chi) 1.05

Earned Run Average
- Boyle, H. (StL) 1.76
- Ferguson, C. (Phi) 1.98
- Baldwin, L. (Det) 2.24

Adjusted ERA
- Boyle, H. (StL) 182
- Ferguson, C. (Phi) 165
- Flynn, J. (Chi) 161

Component ERA

Opponents' Batting Avg.
- Baldwin, L. (Det) .203
- Ferguson, C. (Phi) .211
- Flynn, J. (Chi) .212

Adjusted Pitching Runs
- Ferguson, C. (Phi) 68
- Baldwin, L. (Det) 51
- Casey, D. (Phi) 45

Win Shares – Pitchers
- Baldwin, L. (Det) 53
- Ferguson, C. (Phi) 49
- Clarkson, J. (Chi) 42

TPW – Pitchers
- Ferguson, C. (Phi) 7.3
- Baldwin, L. (Det) 5.0
- Clarkson, J. (Chi) 4.1

1886 American Association

TEAM	G	W	L	PCT	GB	R	OR	EW	AB	H	2B	3B	HR	TB	BB	SO	SB	CS	AVG	OBP	SLG	OPS	OPS+	BR/A	PF	RC
STL	139	93	46	.669	....	**944**	**592**	100	5009	**1365**	**206**	85	20	**1801**	400	**425**	**336**	....	**.273**	**.333**	**.360**	**.692**	**115**	**74**	105	**729**
PIT	140	80	57	.584	12	810	647	84	4854	1171	186	**96**	16	1597	**478**	713	260	....	.241	.314	.329	.643	105	37	99	598
BRO	141	76	61	.555	16	832	832	68	**5053**	1261	196	80	16	1665	433	523	248	....	.250	.311	.330	.641	103	15	101	610
LOU	138	66	70	.485	25.5	833	805	70	4921	1294	182	88	20	1712	410	558	202	....	.263	.323	.348	.671	107	28	106	634
CIN	141	65	73	.471	27.5	883	865	70	4915	1225	145	95	**45**	1695	374	633	185	....	.249	.311	.345	.656	105	19	103	599
PHI	139	63	72	.467	28	772	942	54	4856	1142	192	82	21	1561	378	697	284	....	.235	.296	.321	.617	96	-29	101	560
NY	137	53	82	.393	38	628	766	54	4683	1047	108	72	18	1353	330	578	120	....	.224	.279	.289	.568	85	-72	96	422
BAL	139	48	83	.366	41	625	878	44	4639	945	124	51	8	1195	379	603	269	....	.204	.269	.258	.527	70	-148	98	404
Total	**557**					**6327**			**38930**	**9450**	**1339**	**649**	**164**		**3182**	**4730**	**1904**		**.243**	**.305**	**.323**	**.628**				

Runs
- Latham, A. (StL) 152
- McPhee, B. (Cin) 139
- Larkin, H. (Phi) 133

Hits
- Orr, D. (NY) 193
- O'Neill, T. (StL) 190
- Larkin, H. (Phi) 180

Doubles
- Larkin, H. (Phi) 36
- McClellan, B. (Bro) 33
- 2 players tied with 31

Triples
- Orr, D. (NY) 31
- 3 players tied with 17

Home Runs
- McPhee, B. (Cin) 8
- Orr, D. (NY) 7
- Stovey, H. (Phi) 7

Total Bases
- Orr, D. (NY) 301
- O'Neill, T. (StL) 255
- Larkin, H. (Phi) 254

Runs Batted In
- O'Neill, T. (StL) 107
- Corkhill, P. (Cin) 97
- Welch, C. (StL) 95

Bases On Balls
- Pinckney, G. (Bro) 70
- Swartwood, E. (Bro) 70
- Mack, R. (Lou) 68

Stolen Bases
- Stovey, H. (Phi) 68
- Latham, A. (StL) 60
- Welch, C. (StL) 59

Batting Average
- Hecker, G. (Lou) .341
- Browning, P. (Lou) .340
- Orr, D. (NY) .338

On-Base Percentage
- Larkin, H. (Phi) .390
- Browning, P. (Lou) .389
- O'Neill, T. (StL) .385

Slugging Average
- Orr, D. (NY) .527
- Larkin, H. (Phi) .450
- Browning, P. (Lou) .441

Adjusted OPS
- Orr, D. (NY) 186
- Larkin, H. (Phi) 161
- Stovey, H. (Phi) 154

Adjusted Batting Runs
- Orr, D. (NY) 51.0
- Larkin, H. (Phi) 41.0
- O'Neill, T. (StL) 33.0

Runs Created/Game
- Stovey, H. (Phi) 8.60
- Orr, D. (NY) 8.40
- Browning, P. (Lou) 8.10

Fielding Runs
- McPhee, B. (Cin) 26.4
- Smith, P. (Pit) 25.4
- Hankinson, F. (NY) 20.8

Win Shares – Batters
- Larkin, H. (Phi) 29
- O'Neill, T. (StL) 27
- Stovey, H. (Phi) 24

TPW – Batters
- McPhee, B. (Cin) 4.2
- Orr, D. (NY) 4.2
- Larkin, H. (Phi) 3.4

TEAM	CG	SH	SV	IP	H	H/G	ER	HR	BB	SO	OAV	RAT	ERA	ERA+	CERA	PR+	PF	FA	E	DP	FR	BW	PW	FW	TPW	DIF
STL	134	14	**2**	1229^{1}	**1087**	**8.0**	**340**	13	329	583	**.226**	**1.152**	**2.49**	138	....	**121.1**	100	.915	494	96	7.6	**6.5**	**10.6**	.7	**17.8**	6.2
PIT	137	**15**	1	1226	1130	8.3	386	**10**	**299**	515	.234	1.166	2.83	119	....	62.9	98	**.917**	**487**	90	12.3	3.3	5.5	1.1	9.9	2.1
BRO	**138**	6	0	1234^{2}	1202	8.8	469	17	464	540	.244	1.349	3.42	102	....	16.6	101	.900	610	87	-7.7	1.3	1.5	-.7	2.1	5.9
LOU	131	5	**2**	1209^{2}	1109	8.2	412	16	432	720	.233	1.274	3.07	118	....	55.8	106	.901	593	89	**20.3**	2.4	4.9	**1.8**	9.1	-11.1
CIN	129	3	0	**1247^{2}**	1267	9.1	579	25	481	495	.252	1.401	4.18	84	....	-101.3	102	.905	582	**122**	8.3	1.7	-8.9	.7	-6.5	2.5
PHI	134	4	0	1218^{2}	1308	9.7	537	35	388	513	.262	1.392	3.97	88	....	-35.7	102	.894	637	99	-29.0	-2.6	-3.1	-2.5	-8.3	4.3
NY	134	5	0	1186^{1}	1148	8.7	461	23	386	559	.243	1.293	3.50	97	....	-29.3	99	.906	544	81	16.2	-6.3	-2.6	1.4	-7.5	-6.5
BAL	134	5	0	1206^{2}	1197	8.9	547	25	403	**805**	.247	1.326	4.08	**84**	....	-60.5	99	.909	523	59	-28.6	-13.0	-5.3	-2.5	-20.8	3.8
Total	**1071**	**57**	**5**	**9759**		**8.7**	**3731**					**1.294**	**3.44**													

Wins
- Foutz, D. (StL) 41
- Morris, E. (Pit) 41
- Ramsey, T. (Lou) 38

Win Percentage
- Foutz, D. (StL) .719
- Caruthers, B. (StL) .682
- Morris, E. (Pit) .672

Games
- Kilroy, M. (Bal) 68
- Ramsey, T. (Lou) 67
- Morris, E. (Pit) 64

Complete Games
- Kilroy, M. (Bal) 66
- Ramsey, T. (Lou) 66
- Morris, E. (Pit) 63

Shutouts
- Morris, E. (Pit) 12
- Foutz, D. (StL) 11
- 2 players tied with 5

Saves
- Foutz, D. (StL) 1
- Hudson, N. (StL) 1
- Morris, E. (Pit) 1

Innings Pitched
- Ramsey, T. (Lou) 588^{2}
- Kilroy, M. (Bal) 583
- Morris, E. (Pit) 555^{1}

Fewest Hits/Game
- Ramsey, T. (Lou) 6.83
- Kilroy, M. (Bal) 7.35
- Morris, E. (Pit) 7.37

Fewest BB/Game
- Galvin, P. (Pit) 1.55
- Morris, E. (Pit) 1.91
- Caruthers, B. (StL) 2.00

Strikeouts
- Kilroy, M. (Bal) 513
- Ramsey, T. (Lou) 499
- Morris, E. (Pit) 326

Ratio
- Morris, E. (Pit) 1.03
- Caruthers, B. (StL) 1.06
- Ramsey, T. (Lou) 1.11

Earned Run Average
- Foutz, D. (StL) 2.11
- Caruthers, B. (StL) 2.32
- Ramsey, T. (Lou) 2.45

Adjusted ERA
- Foutz, D. (StL) 163
- Ramsey, T. (Lou) 148
- Caruthers, B. (StL) 148

Component ERA

Opponents' Batting Avg.
- Ramsey, T. (Lou) .201
- Kilroy, M. (Bal) .213
- Morris, E. (Pit) .213

Adjusted Pitching Runs
- Foutz, D. (StL) 71
- Ramsey, T. (Lou) 68
- Morris, E. (Pit) 52

Win Shares – Pitchers
- Foutz, D. (StL) 62
- Caruthers, B. (StL) 57
- Ramsey, T. (Lou) 47

TPW – Pitchers
- Caruthers, B. (StL) 7.6
- Foutz, D. (StL) 7.0
- Ramsey, T. (Lou) 5.9

1887 National League

TEAM	G	W	L	PCT	GB	R	OR	EW	AB	H	2B	3B	HR	TB	BB	SO	SB	CS	AVG	OBP	SLG	OPS	OPS+	BR/A	PF	RC
DET	127	79	45	.637	....	**969**	714	80	**5041**	**1756**	**213**	**126**	55	**2034**	352	**258**	267	....	**.348**	**.353**	**.434**	**.787**	**118**	**106**	103	**833**
PHI	128	75	48	.610	3.5	901	**702**	77	5015	1654	**213**	89	47	1801	385	346	355	....	.330	.337	.389	.726	100	-9	106	744
CHI	127	71	50	.587	6.5	813	716	68	4757	1584	178	98	**80**	1791	**407**	400	382	....	.333	.336	.412	.748	98	-30	113	748
NY	129	68	55	.553	10.5	816	723	69	4877	1620	167	93	48	1756	361	326	**415**	....	.332	.339	.389	.727	111	77	95	753
BOS	127	61	60	.504	16.5	831	792	63	4871	1595	185	94	53	1787	340	392	373	....	.327	.333	.394	.727	108	53	97	736
PIT	125	55	69	.444	24	621	750	50	4733	1460	183	78	20	1540	319	381	221	....	.308	.314	.349	.663	94	-24	94	567
WAS	126	46	76	.377	32	601	818	43	4583	1308	149	63	47	1455	269	339	334	....	.285	.292	.337	.629	82	-92	95	535
IND	127	37	89	.294	43	628	965	37	4668	1380	162	70	33	1481	300	379	334	....	.296	.302	.339	.641	85	-80	96	562
Total	**508**					**6180**			**38545**	**12357**	**1450**	**711**	**383**		**2733**	**2821**	**2681**		**.321**	**.326**	**.381**	**.707**				

Runs
Brouthers, D. (Det) 153
Rowe, J. (Det) 135
Richardson, H. (Det) 131

Hits
Brouthers, D. (Det) 240
Thompson, S. (Det) 235
Anson, C. (Chi) 224

Doubles
Brouthers, D. (Det) 36
Denny, J. (Ind) 34
Kelly, K. (Bos) 34

Triples
Thompson, S. (Det) 23
Connor, R. (NY) 22
2 players tied with 20

Home Runs
O'Brien, B. (Was) 19
Connor, R. (NY) 17
Pfeffer, F. (Chi) 16

Total Bases
Brouthers, D. (Det) 352
Thompson, S. (Det) 340
Connor, R. (NY) 330

Runs Batted In
Thompson, S. (Det) 166
Connor, R. (NY) 104
Anson, C. (Chi) 102

Bases On Balls
Fogarty, J. (Phi) 82
Connor, R. (NY) 75
Williamson, N. (Chi) 73

Stolen Bases
Ward, J. (NY) 111
Fogarty, J. (Phi) 102
Kelly, K. (Bos) 84

Batting Average
Anson, C. (Chi) .421
Brouthers, D. (Det) .420
Thompson, S. (Det) .407

On-Base Percentage
Brouthers, D. (Det) .426
Anson, C. (Chi) .422
Thompson, S. (Det) .416

Slugging Average
Thompson, S. (Det) .571
Brouthers, D. (Det) .562
Connor, R. (NY) .541

Adjusted OPS
Brouthers, D. (Det) 167
Thompson, S. (Det) 166
Connor, R. (NY) 164

Adjusted Batting Runs
Brouthers, D. (Det) 47.0
Thompson, S. (Det) 47.0
Connor, R. (NY) 44.0

Runs Created/Game
Brouthers, D. (Det) 11.00
Thompson, S. (Det) 11.00
Kelly, K. (Bos) 10.40

Fielding Runs
Fogarty, J. (Phi) 26.0
Ward, J. (NY) 23.3
Dunlap, F. (Det) 23.0

Win Shares – Batters
Thompson, S. (Det) 29
Brouthers, D. (Det) 26
2 players tied with 25

TPW – Batters
Thompson, S. (Det) 4.0
Ward, J. (NY) 3.6
Richardson, H. (Det) 3.5

TEAM	CG	SH	SV	IP	H	H/G	ER	HR	BB	SO	OAV	RAT	ERA	ERA+	CERA	PR+	PF	FA	E	DP	FR	BW	PW	FW	TPW	DIF
DET	122	3	1	1116^1	1516	12.2	490	52	344	337	.315	1.358	3.95	102	....	0.2	99	**.925**	**394**	92	8.0	**9.0**	.0	.7	**9.7**	7.3
PHI	119	**7**	1	**1132^2**	1478	**11.7**	436	48	305	435	**.306**	**1.305**	3.46	121	....	118.5	104	.912	471	76	-26.7	-.7	10.0	-2.3	7.1	6.9
CHI	117	4	**3**	1126	1494	11.9	**433**	55	338	**510**	.308	1.327	**3.46**	129	....	**125.1**	110	.914	472	99	-1.0	-2.5	**10.6**	-.1	8.0	3.0
NY	123	5	1	1113^2	**1469**	11.9	441	**27**	373	415	.306	1.319	3.56	105	....	-0.7	93	.920	431	83	20.8	6.5	-.1	1.8	8.2	-1.2
BOS	123	4	1	1100^2	1622	13.3	539	55	396	254	.333	1.474	4.41	89	....	-80.6	97	.905	522	94	**20.8**	4.5	-6.8	**1.8**	-.5	1.5
PIT	123	4	0	1108^2	1533	12.4	507	39	**246**	248	.318	1.383	4.12	94	....	-18.9	95	.921	425	70	-12.9	-2.0	-1.6	-1.1	-4.7	-2.3
WAS	**124**	3	0	1090^1	1515	12.5	507	47	299	396	.318	1.389	4.18	96	....	0.9	100	.910	483	77	-20.1	-7.8	.1	-1.7	-9.5	-5.5
IND	118	4	1	1088	1720	14.2	633	60	431	245	.346	1.581	5.24	**79**	....	-147.2	102	.912	479	**105**	10.6	-6.8	-12.5	.9	-18.4	-7.6
Total	**969**	**34**	**8**	**8876^1**		**12.5**	**3986**					**1.391**	**4.04**													

Wins
Clarkson, J. (Chi) 38
Keefe, T. (NY) 35
Getzein, C. (Det) 29

Win Percentage
Getzein, C. (Det) .690
Ferguson, C. (Phi) .688
Casey, D. (Phi) .683

Games
Clarkson, J. (Chi) 60
Keefe, T. (NY) 56
Radbourn, C. (Bos) 50

Complete Games
Clarkson, J. (Chi) 56
Keefe, T. (NY) 54
Radbourn, C. (Bos) 48

Shutouts
Casey, D. (Phi) 4
3 players tied with 3

Saves
8 players tied with 1

Innings Pitched
Clarkson, J. (Chi) 523
Keefe, T. (NY) 476^2
Galvin, P. (Pit) 440^2

Fewest Hits/Game
Baldwin, L. (Det) 9.60
Keefe, T. (NY) 10.12
Clarkson, J. (Chi) 10.41

Fewest BB/Game
Whitney, J. (Was) .93
Galvin, P. (Pit) 1.37
Ferguson, C. (Phi) 1.42

Strikeouts
Clarkson, J. (Chi) 237
Keefe, T. (NY) 189
Baldwin, M. (Chi) 164

Ratio
Baldwin, L. (Det) 1.07
Keefe, T. (NY) 1.12
Clarkson, J. (Chi) 1.16

Earned Run Average
Casey, D. (Phi) 2.86
Conway, P. (Det) 2.90
Ferguson, C. (Phi) 3.00

Adjusted ERA
Casey, D. (Phi) 147
Clarkson, J. (Chi) 145
Ferguson, C. (Phi) 140

Component ERA

Opponents' Batting Avg.
Keefe, T. (NY) .276
Clarkson, J. (Chi) .282
Ferguson, C. (Phi) .282

Adjusted Pitching Runs
Clarkson, J. (Chi) 80
Casey, D. (Phi) 67
Ferguson, C. (Phi) 47

Win Shares – Pitchers
Clarkson, J. (Chi) 51
Keefe, T. (NY) 39
Ferguson, C. (Phi) 36

TPW – Pitchers
Clarkson, J. (Chi) 7.1
Ferguson, C. (Phi) 5.6
Casey, D. (Phi) 4.9

1887 American Association

TEAM	G	W	L	PCT	GB	R	OR	EW	AB	H	2B	3B	HR	TB	BB	SO	SB	CS	AVG	OBP	SLG	OPS	OPS+	BR/A	PF	RC
STL	138	95	40	.704	....	**1131**	761	93	**5490**	**1992**	**261**	78	**39**	**2084**	442	340	**581**	....	**.363**	**.371**	**.413**	**.783**	111	52	111	**1012**
CIN	136	81	54	.600	14	892	**745**	80	5179	1667	179	**102**	37	1779	382	366	527	....	.322	.329	.371	.700	97	-32	102	778
BAL	141	77	58	.570	18	975	861	76	5294	1806	202	100	31	1832	**469**	**334**	545	....	.341	.349	.380	.729	**114**	**109**	94	852
LOU	139	76	60	.559	19.5	956	854	76	5352	1856	194	98	27	1891	436	356	466	....	.347	.352	.385	.736	107	42	102	850
PHI	137	64	69	.481	30	893	890	67	5275	1691	231	84	29	1856	321	388	476	....	.321	.327	.375	.702	99	-16	100	782
BRO	138	60	74	.448	34.5	904	918	66	5369	1737	200	82	25	1720	456	365	409	....	.324	.330	.350	.680	92	-50	101	720
NY	138	44	89	.331	50	754	1093	43	5259	1636	193	66	21	1585	439	463	305	....	.311	.318	.329	.646	88	-61	96	615
CLE	133	39	92	.298	54	729	1112	39	5024	1545	178	77	14	1544	375	463	355	....	.308	.314	.332	.646	86	-76	97	611
Total	**550**					**7234**			**42242**	**13930**	**1638**	**687**	**223**		**3320**	**3075**	**3664**		**.330**	**.337**	**.367**	**.704**				

Runs
O'Neill, T. (StL) 167
Latham, A. (StL) 163
Griffin, M. (Bal) 142

Hits
Browning, P. (Lou) 275
O'Neill, T. (StL) 275
Lyons, D. (Phi) 256

Doubles
O'Neill, T. (StL) 52
Lyons, D. (Phi) 43
3 players tied with 35

Triples
6 players tied with 19

Home Runs
O'Neill, T. (StL) 14
Reilly, J. (Cin) 10
Burns, O. (Bal) 9

Total Bases
O'Neill, T. (StL) 407
Browning, P. (Lou) 354
Burns, O. (Bal) 349

Runs Batted In
O'Neill, T. (StL) 123
Browning, P. (Lou) 118
Davis, J. (Bal) 109

Bases On Balls
Radford, P. (NY) 106
Robinson, Y. (StL) 92
Nicol, H. (Cin) 86

Stolen Bases
Nicol, H. (Cin) 138
Latham, A. (StL) 129
Comiskey, C. (StL) 117

Batting Average
O'Neill, T. (StL) .485
Browning, P. (Lou) .457
Caruthers, B. (StL) .456

On-Base Percentage
O'Neill, T. (StL) .490
Browning, P. (Lou) .464
Caruthers, B. (StL) .463

Slugging Average
O'Neill, T. (StL) .691
Caruthers, B. (StL) .547
Browning, P. (Lou) .547

Adjusted OPS
O'Neill, T. (StL) 205
Browning, P. (Lou) 178
Burns, O. (Bal) 169

Adjusted Batting Runs
O'Neill, T. (StL) 71.0
Browning, P. (Lou) 58.0
Burns, O. (Bal) 53.0

Runs Created/Game
O'Neill, T. (StL) 18.00
Browning, P. (Lou) 15.80
Caruthers, B. (StL) 13.60

Fielding Runs
McPhee, B. (Cin) 31.5
Smith, G. (Bro) 22.2
Greenwood, B. (Bal) 14.6

Win Shares – Batters
Caruthers, B. (StL) 54
Foutz, D. (StL) 43
O'Neill, T. (StL) 36

TPW – Batters
Caruthers, B. (StL) 6.5
O'Neill, T. (StL) 4.8
Browning, P. (Lou) 4.2

TEAM	CG	SH	SV	IP	H	H/G	ER	HR	BB	SO	OAV	RAT	ERA	ERA+	CERA	PR+	PF	FA	E	DP	FR	BW	PW	FW	TPW	DIF
STL	132	6	2	1199^1	**1577**	**11.8**	502	19	**323**	334	**.306**	**1.315**	3.77	120	....	**74.5**	106	**.916**	**481**	86	26.0	4.2	**6.0**	2.1	**12.3**	15.7
CIN	129	**11**	1	1182^2	1598	12.2	**470**	28	396	330	.311	1.351	**3.58**	121	....	49.0	101	.916	484	**106**	**49.7**	-2.6	4.0	**4.0**	5.4	8.6
BAL	132	8	0	**1220**	1706	12.6	525	**16**	418	470	.318	1.398	3.87	106	....	61.5	95	.907	549	66	-30.4	**8.8**	5.0	-2.5	11.3	-1.3
LOU	**133**	3	1	1205^2	1631	12.2	511	31	357	**544**	.312	1.353	3.81	115	....	52.9	102	.903	574	83	22.8	3.4	4.3	1.8	9.6	-1.6
PHI	131	5	1	1186^1	1660	12.6	605	29	433	417	.319	1.399	4.59	93	....	-49.5	100	.907	528	95	8.7	-1.3	-4.0	.7	-4.6	2.6
BRO	132	3	**3**	1185^1	1802	13.7	589	27	454	332	.337	1.520	4.47	96	....	-25.0	100	.905	562	88	2.4	-4.0	-2.0	.2	-5.9	-1.1
NY	132	1	0	1180^1	1951	14.9	692	39	406	316	.356	1.653	5.28	**80**	....	-99.5	99	.894	632	102	-37.0	-4.9	-8.1	-3.0	-16.0	-6.0
CLE	127	2	1	1136	2005	15.9	630	34	533	332	.371	1.765	4.99	87	....	-39.9	101	.898	576	97	-43.3	-6.2	-3.2	-3.5	-12.9	-13.1
Total	**1048**	**39**	**9**	**9495^2**		**13.2**	**4524**					**1.467**	**4.29**													

Wins
Kilroy, M. (Bal) 46
Ramsey, T. (Lou) 37
Smith, E. (Cin) 34

Win Percentage
Caruthers, B. (StL) .763
King, S. (StL) .727
Kilroy, M. (Bal) .708

Games
Kilroy, M. (Bal) 69
Ramsey, T. (Lou) 65
Smith, P. (Bal) 58

Complete Games
Kilroy, M. (Bal) 66
Ramsey, T. (Lou) 61
Smith, P. (Bal) 54

Shutouts
Kilroy, M. (Bal) 6
Mullane, T. (Cin) 6
2 players tied with 3

Saves
Terry, A. (Bro) 3
5 players tied with 1

Innings Pitched
Kilroy, M. (Bal) 589¹
Ramsey, T. (Lou) 561
Smith, P. (Bal) 491¹

Fewest Hits/Game
Caruthers, B. (StL) 10.50
Smith, E. (Cin) 10.58
Seward, E. (Phi) 11.19

Fewest BB/Game
Hecker, G. (Lou) 1.58
Caruthers, B. (StL) 1.61
Lynch, J. (NY) 1.73

Strikeouts
Ramsey, T. (Lou) 355
Smith, P. (Bal) 217
Smith, P. (Bal) 206

Ratio
Caruthers, B. (StL) 1.17
Smith, E. (Cin) 1.18
Seward, E. (Phi) 1.24

Earned Run Average
Smith, E. (Cin) 2.94
Kilroy, M. (Bal) 3.07
Mullane, T. (Cin) 3.24

Adjusted ERA
Smith, E. (Cin) 148
Caruthers, B. (StL) 137
Mullane, T. (Cin) 134

Component ERA

Opponents' Batting Avg.
Caruthers, B. (StL) .281
Smith, E. (Cin) .283
Seward, E. (Phi) .294

Adjusted Pitching Runs
Kilroy, M. (Bal) 82
Smith, E. (Cin) 51
Ramsey, T. (Lou) 49

Win Shares – Pitchers
Caruthers, B. (StL) 54
Smith, E. (Cin) 54
Kilroy, M. (Bal) 51

TPW – Pitchers
Kilroy, M. (Bal) 7.4
Caruthers, B. (StL) 6.5
Smith, E. (Cin) 4.6

1888 National League

TEAM	G	W	L	PCT	GB	R	OR	EW	AB	H	2B	3B	HR	TB	BB	SO	SB	CS	AVG	OBP	SLG	OPS	OPS+	BR/A	PF	RC
NY	138	84	47	.641	....	659	**479**	86	4747	1149	130	76	55	1596	270	456	314	....	.242	.287	.336	.623		29	99	562
CHI	136	77	58	.570	9	**734**	659	75	4616	1201	147	**95**	**77**	**1769**	290	563	287	....	.260	.308	**.383**	**.691**	118	79	107	**649**
PHI	132	69	61	.531	14.5	535	509	68	4528	1021	151	46	16	1312	268	485	246	....	.225	.276	.290	.566	82	-89	105	441
BOS	137	70	64	.522	15.5	669	619	72	4834	1183	167	89	56	1696	282	524	293	....	.245	.291	.351	.642	106	26	104	593
DET	134	68	63	.519	16	721	629	74	**4849**	**1275**	177	72	51	1749	**307**	396	193	....	**.263**	**.313**	.361	.674	**121**	**111**	100	623
PIT	139	66	68	.493	19.5	534	580	61	4713	1070	150	49	14	1360	194	583	287	....	.227	.264	.289	.553	89	-49	92	446
IND	136	50	85	.370	36	603	731	55	4623	1100	**180**	33	34	1448	236	492	**350**	....	.238	.281	.313	.595	93	-35	102	518
WAS	136	48	86	.358	37.5	482	731	41	4546	944	98	49	30	1230	246	499	331	....	.208	.255	.271	.526	77	-101	94	408
Total	544					4937			37456	8943	1200	509	333		2093	3998	2301		.239	.285	.325	.609				

Runs
Brouthers, D. (Det) 118
Ryan, J. (Chi) 115
Johnston, D. (Bos) 102

Hits
Ryan, J. (Chi) 182
Anson, C. (Chi) 177
Johnston, D. (Bos) 173

Doubles
Brouthers, D. (Det) 33
Ryan, J. (Chi) 33
Johnston, D. (Bos) 31

Triples
Johnston, D. (Bos) 18
Connor, R. (NY) 17
2 players tied with 15

Home Runs
Ryan, J. (Chi) 16
Connor, R. (NY) 14
3 players tied with 12

Total Bases
Ryan, J. (Chi) 283
Johnston, D. (Bos) 276
Anson, C. (Chi) 257

Runs Batted In
Anson, C. (Chi) 84
Nash, B. (Bos) 75
Rowe, J. (Det) 74

Bases On Balls
Connor, R. (NY) 73
Hoy, D. (Was) 69
Brouthers, D. (Det) 68

Stolen Bases
Hoy, D. (Was) 82
Seery, J. (Ind) 80
Sunday, B. (Pit) 71

Batting Average
Anson, C. (Chi) .344
Ryan, J. (Chi) .332
Kelly, K. (Bos) .318

On-Base Percentage
Anson, C. (Chi) .400
Brouthers, D. (Det) .399
Connor, R. (NY) .389

Slugging Average
Ryan, J. (Chi) .515
Anson, C. (Chi) .499
Connor, R. (NY) .480

Adjusted OPS
Connor, R. (NY) 178
Brouthers, D. (Det) 174
Anson, C. (Chi) 172

Adjusted Batting Runs
Brouthers, D. (Det) 48.0
Connor, R. (NY) 46.0
Ryan, J. (Chi) 43.0

Runs Created/Game
Ryan, J. (Chi) 9.70
Anson, C. (Chi) 9.30
Kelly, K. (Bos) 9.10

Fielding Runs
Nash, B. (Bos) 21.6
Pfeffer, F. (Chi) 20.3
Denny, J. (Ind) 18.4

Win Shares – Batters
Ryan, J. (Chi) 34
Connor, R. (NY) 32
Anson, C. (Chi) 29

TPW – Batters
Nash, B. (Bos) 4.5
Ryan, J. (Chi) 4.4
Ewing, B. (NY) 4.3

TEAM	CG	SH	SV	IP	H	H/G	ER	HR	BB	SO	OAV	RAT	ERA	ERA+	CERA	PR+	PF	FA	E	DP	FR	BW	PW	FW	TPW	DIF
NY	133	**20**	1	1221²	**907**	6.6	263	27	307	**726**	**.201**	0.994	1.93	139	....	67.1	96	.924	432	76	34.8	2.8	6.6	**3.4**	**12.8**	6.2
CHI	123	13	1	1186¹	1139	8.6	390	63	308	588	.243	1.220	2.96	102	....	-21.7	106	.927	417	**112**	28.3	7.8	-2.1	2.8	8.4	1.6
PHI	125	16	**3**	1167	1072	8.3	309	26	196	519	.235	1.087	**2.38**	124	....	**91.3**	104	.924	424	70	-17.7	-8.8	**9.0**	-1.7	-1.5	5.5
BOS	134	7	0	**1225¹**	1104	**8.1**	355	36	269	484	.232	1.121	2.74	100	....	22.3	102	.919	463	83	-28.7	**11.0**	2.9	-2.8	11.0	-8.0
DET	130	10	1	1199	1115	8.4	365	44	**183**	522	.238	**1.083**	2.74	100	....	29.5	97	.917	494	91	14.6	2.5	2.2	1.4	6.2	-3.2
PIT	**135**	13	0	1203¹	1190	8.9	357	**23**	223	367	.249	1.174	2.67	99	....	4.5	94	**.927**	416	88	-7.4	-4.9	.4	-.7	-5.1	4.1
IND	132	6	0	1187²	1260	9.6	502	64	308	388	.262	1.320	3.80	**77**	....	-97.3	104	.921	449	84	-17.8	-3.5	-9.6	-1.8	-14.8	-2.2
WAS	133	6	0	1179¹	1157	8.8	464	50	298	406	.247	1.234	3.54	79	....	-92.6	98	.912	494	69	-6.2	-9.9	-9.1	-.6	-19.6	.6
Total	1045	91	6	8470²		9.5	3005					1.303	3.19													

Wins
Keefe, T. (NY) 35
Clarkson, J. (Bos) 33
Conway, P. (Det) 30

Win Percentage
Keefe, T. (NY) .745
Conway, P. (Det) .682
Sanders, B. (Phi) .655

Games
Morris, E. (Pit) 55
Clarkson, J. (Bos) 54
Keefe, T. (NY) 51

Complete Games
Morris, E. (Pit) 54
Clarkson, J. (Bos) 53
Galvin, P. (Pit) 49

Shutouts
Keefe, T. (NY) 8
Sanders, B. (Phi) 8
2 players tied with 6

Saves
4 players tied with 1

Innings Pitched
Clarkson, J. (Bos) 483¹
Morris, E. (Pit) 480
Galvin, P. (Pit) 437¹

Fewest Hits/Game
Keefe, T. (NY) 6.57
Titcomb, C. (NY) 6.81
Welch, M. (NY) 6.94

Fewest BB/Game
Sanders, B. (Phi) 1.08
Galvin, P. (Pit) 1.09
Krock, G. (Chi) 1.19

Strikeouts
Keefe, T. (NY) 335
Clarkson, J. (Bos) 223
Getzein, C. (Det) 202

Ratio
Keefe, T. (NY) .94
Conway, P. (Det) .95
Buffinton, C. (Phi) .96

Earned Run Average
Keefe, T. (NY) 1.74
Sanders, B. (Phi) 1.90
Buffinton, C. (Phi) 1.91

Adjusted ERA
Keefe, T. (NY) 156
Sanders, B. (Phi) 156
Buffinton, C. (Phi) 154

Component ERA

Opponents' Batting Avg.
Keefe, T. (NY) .197
Titcomb, C. (NY) .202
Welch, M. (NY) .205

Adjusted Pitching Runs
Buffinton, C. (Phi) 52
Sanders, B. (Phi) 36
Keefe, T. (NY) 35

Win Shares – Pitchers
Buffinton, C. (Phi) 44
Keefe, T. (NY) 35
Sanders, B. (Phi) 35

TPW – Pitchers
Buffinton, C. (Phi) 5.2
Conway, P. (Det) 4.5
Sanders, B. (Phi) 4.0

1888 American Association

TEAM	G	W	L	PCT	GB	R	OR	EW	AB	H	2B	3B	HR	TB	BB	SO	SB	CS	AVG	OBP	SLG	OPS	OPS+	BR/A	PF	RC
STL	137	92	43	.681	....	789	**501**	96	4755	1189	149	47	**36**	1540	**410**	521	468	....	.250	**.316**	.324	.640	99	-18	111	651
BRO	143	88	52	.629	6.5	758	584	88	4871	1177	172	70	25	1564	353	**439**	334	....	.242	.300	.321	.621	104	19	100	584
PHI	136	81	52	.609	10	**827**	594	88	4828	**1209**	**183**	**89**	31	**1663**	303	473	434	....	.250	.305	**.344**	**.650**	99	65	105	**656**
CIN	137	80	54	.597	11.5	745	628	78	4801	1161	132	82	32	1553	345	555	**469**	....	.242	.301	.323	.624	99	-15	105	623
BAL	137	57	80	.416	36	653	779	57	4656	1068	162	70	19	1427	298	479	326	....	.229	.284	.306	.591	96	-19	97	511
CLE	135	50	82	.379	40.5	651	839	50	4603	1076	128	59	12	1358	315	559	353	....	.234	.294	.295	.589	96	-12	97	516
LOU	139	48	87	.356	44	689	870	52	**4881**	1177	**183**	67	14	1536	322	604	318	....	.241	.297	.315	.612	102	16	98	565
KC	132	43	89	.326	47.5	579	896	39	4588	1000	142	61	19	1321	288	604	257	....	.218	.273	.288	.561	78	-122	106	441
Total	548					5691			37983	9057	1251	545	188		2634	4234	2959		.238	.297	.315	.612				

Runs
Pinckney, G. (Bro) 134
Collins, H. (Lou,Bro) 133
Stovey, H. (Phi) 127

Hits
O'Neill, T. (StL) 177
Reilly, J. (Cin) 169
McKean, E. (Cle) 164

Doubles
Collins, H. (Lou,Bro) 31
3 players tied with 28

Triples
Stovey, H. (Phi) 20
Burns, O. (Bal,Bro) 15
McKean, E. (Cle) 15

Home Runs
Reilly, J. (Cin) 13
Stovey, H. (Phi) 9
Larkin, H. (Phi) 7

Total Bases
Reilly, J. (Cin) 264
Stovey, H. (Phi) 244
O'Neill, T. (StL) 236

Runs Batted In
Reilly, J. (Cin) 103
Larkin, H. (Phi) 101
Foutz, D. (Bro) 99

Bases On Balls
Robinson, Y. (StL) 116
Fennelly, F. (Cin,Phi) 72
2 players tied with 67

Stolen Bases
Latham, A. (StL) 109
Nicol, H. (Cin) 103
Welch, C. (Phi) 95

Batting Average
O'Neill, T. (StL) .335
Reilly, J. (Cin) .321
Collins, H. (Bro,Lou) .307

On-Base Percentage
Robinson, Y. (StL) .400
O'Neill, T. (StL) .390
Collins, H. (Bro,Lou) .373

Slugging Average
Reilly, J. (Cin) .501
Stovey, H. (Phi) .460
O'Neill, T. (StL) .446

Adjusted OPS
Reilly, J. (Cin) 167
Stovey, H. (Phi) 165
Collins, H. (Bro,Lou) 158

Adjusted Batting Runs
Stovey, H. (Phi) 39.0
Reilly, J. (Cin) 36.0
Collins, H. (Lou,Bro) 35.0

Runs Created/Game
Reilly, J. (Cin) 9.70
Stovey, H. (Phi) 8.80
Collins, H. (Bro,Lou) 8.30

Fielding Runs
Shindle, B. (Bal) 36.3
McPhee, B. (Cin) 29.6
Bierbauer, L. (Phi) 24.5

Win Shares – Batters
Foutz, D. (Bro) 33
Stovey, H. (Phi) 28
O'Neill, T. (StL) 28

TPW – Batters
Stovey, H. (Phi) 3.7
Collins, H. (Lou,Bro) 3.6
McPhee, B. (Cin) 3.2

TEAM	CG	SH	SV	IP	H	H/G	ER	HR	BB	SO	OAV	RAT	ERA	ERA+	CERA	PR+	PF	FA	E	DP	FR	BW	PW	FW	TPW	DIF
STL	132	12	0	1212^{2}	**939**	**7.0**	**281**	19	**225**	517	**.206**	**.960**	**2.09**	156	....	**124.4**	106	**.924**	**430**	....	**32.3**	-1.7	**11.5**	**3.0**	12.8	12.2
BRO	**138**	9	0	**1286^{1}**	1059	7.4	333	15	285	577	.216	1.045	2.33	128	....	91.3	97	.918	502	....	1.6	1.8	8.4	.1	10.3	7.7
PHI	133	**13**	0	1208^{2}	988	7.4	323	**14**	324	596	.215	1.085	2.41	124	....	71.8	98	.919	475	....	5.1	**6.0**	6.6	.5	**13.1**	1.9
CIN	132	10	**2**	1237^{2}	1103	8.0	375	19	310	539	.230	1.142	2.73	116	....	29.7	104	.923	456	....	31.0	-1.4	2.7	2.9	4.2	8.8
BAL	130	3	0	1200^{1}	1162	8.7	504	23	419	525	.245	1.317	3.78	**79**	....	-84.1	97	.920	461	....	-23.1	-1.8	-7.8	-2.1	-11.6	.6
CLE	131	6	1	1171	1235	9.5	484	38	389	500	.261	1.387	3.72	83	....	-75.4	101	.915	480	....	-6.7	-1.1	-7.0	-.6	-8.7	-7.3
LOU	133	6	0	1231^{1}	1264	9.2	445	28	281	**599**	.256	1.255	3.25	94	....	8.5	100	.900	609	....	-32.3	1.5	.8	-3.0	-.7	-18.3
KC	128	4	0	1157^{2}	1306	10.2	552	32	401	381	.275	1.475	4.29	80	....	-113.3	112	.914	507	....	2.2	-11.2	-10.5	.2	-21.5	-1.5
Total	**1057**	**63**	**3**	**9705^{2}**		**8.4**	**3297**					**1.204**	**3.06**													

Wins
King, S. (StL) 45
Seward, E. (Phi) 35
Caruthers, B. (Bro) 29

Win Percentage
Hudson, N. (StL) .... .714
King, S. (StL) .... .692
Caruthers, B. (Bro) .... .659

Games
King, S. (StL) 66
Bakely, J. (Cle) 61
Seward, E. (Phi) 57

Complete Games
King, S. (StL) 64
Bakely, J. (Cle) 60
Seward, E. (Phi) 57

Shutouts
King, S. (StL) 6
Seward, E. (Phi) 6
2 players tied with 5

Saves
Corkhill, P. (Cin) 1
Gilks, B. (Cle) 1
Mullane, T. (Cin) 1

Innings Pitched
King, S. (StL) .... 584^{2}
Bakely, J. (Cle) .... 532^{2}
Seward, E. (Phi) .... 518^{2}

Fewest Hits/Game
Terry, A. (Bro) 6.69
King, S. (StL) 6.70
Seward, E. (Phi) 6.73

Fewest BB/Game
King, S. (StL) 1.17
Caruthers, B. (Bro) 1.22
Hudson, N. (StL) 1.59

Strikeouts
Seward, E. (Phi) 272
King, S. (StL) 258
Ramsey, T. (Lou) 228

Ratio
King, S. (StL) .... .87
Seward, E. (Phi) .... .99
Caruthers, B. (Bro) 1.00

Earned Run Average
King, S. (StL) 1.65
Seward, E. (Phi) 2.01
Terry, A. (Bro) 2.03

Adjusted ERA
King, S. (StL) 198
Seward, E. (Phi) 148
Terry, A. (Bro) 147

Component ERA

Opponents' Batting Avg.
Terry, A. (Bro) .... .200
King, S. (StL) .... .200
Seward, E. (Phi) .... .201

Adjusted Pitching Runs
King, S. (StL) 89
Seward, E. (Phi) 54
Chamberlain, E. (StL,Lou).. 35

Win Shares – Pitchers
King, S. (StL) 71
Caruthers, B. (Bro) 46
Seward, E. (Phi) 42

TPW – Pitchers
King, S. (StL) 9.2
Seward, E. (Phi) 4.6
Caruthers, B. (Bro) 3.3

1889 National League

TEAM	G	W	L	PCT	GB	R	OR	EW	AB	H	2B	3B	HR	TB	BB	SO	SB	CS	AVG	OBP	SLG	OPS	OPS+	BR/A	PF	RC
NY	131	83	43	.659	....	**935**	708	80	4671	1319	208	**77**	52	1837	**538**	386	292	....	**.282**	**.360**	**.393**	**.753**	**117**	**109**	100	**785**
BOS	133	83	45	.648	1	826	**626**	81	4628	1251	196	54	42	1681	471	450	**331**	....	.270	.343	.363	.706	98	-18	106	707
CHI	136	67	65	.508	19	867	814	70	4849	1274	184	66	**79**	1827	518	516	243	....	.263	.338	.377	.714	101	-3	105	716
PHI	130	63	64	.496	20.5	742	748	63	4695	1248	215	52	44	1699	393	**353**	269	....	.266	.327	.362	.689	91	-74	109	660
PIT	134	61	71	.462	25	726	801	60	4748	1202	209	65	42	1667	420	467	231	....	.253	.320	.351	.671	103	35	90	622
CLE	136	61	72	.459	25.5	656	720	60	4673	1167	131	59	25	1491	429	417	237	....	.250	.318	.319	.637	86	-80	98	563
IND	135	59	75	.440	28	819	894	61	**4879**	**1356**	**228**	35	62	**1840**	377	447	252	....	.278	.335	.377	.712	103	10	102	719
WAS	127	41	83	.331	41	632	892	41	4395	1105	151	57	25	1445	466	456	232	....	.251	.329	.329	.658	96	-4	94	566
Total	**531**					**6203**			**37538**	**9922**	**1522**	**465**	**371**		**3612**	**3492**	**2087**		**.264**	**.334**	**.359**	**.693**				

Runs
Tiernan, M. (NY) 147
Duffy, H. (Chi) 144
Ryan, J. (Chi) 140

Hits
Glasscock, J. (Ind) 205
Brouthers, D. (Bos) 181
Ryan, J. (Chi) 177

Doubles
Kelly, K. (Bos) 41
Glasscock, J. (Ind) 40
2 players tied with 36

Triples
Wilmot, W. (Was) 19
Connor, R. (NY) 17
Fogarty, J. (Phi) 17

Home Runs
Thompson, S. (Phi) 20
Denny, J. (Ind) 18
Ryan, J. (Chi) 17

Total Bases
Ryan, J. (Chi) 287
Glasscock, J. (Ind) 272
2 players tied with 262

Runs Batted In
Connor, R. (NY) 130
Brouthers, D. (Bos) 118
Anson, C. (Chi) 117

Bases On Balls
Tiernan, M. (NY) 96
Connor, R. (NY) 93
Radford, P. (Cle) 91

Stolen Bases
Fogarty, J. (Phi) 99
Kelly, K. (Bos) 68
Brown, T. (Bos) 63

Batting Average
Brouthers, D. (Bos) .... .373
Glasscock, J. (Ind) .... .352
Tiernan, M. (NY) .... .335

On-Base Percentage
Brouthers, D. (Bos) .... .462
Tiernan, M. (NY) .... .447
Connor, R. (NY) .... .426

Slugging Average
Connor, R. (NY) .... .528
Brouthers, D. (Bos) .... .507
Ryan, J. (Chi) .... .498

Adjusted OPS
Connor, R. (NY) 166
Tiernan, M. (NY) 163
Brouthers, D. (Bos) 161

Adjusted Batting Runs
Tiernan, M. (NY) 48.0
Connor, R. (NY) 47.0
Brouthers, D. (Bos) 43.0

Runs Created/Game
Brouthers, D. (Bos) 11.10
Tiernan, M. (NY) 10.30
Connor, R. (NY) 9.70

Fielding Runs
Glasscock, J. (Ind) 26.5
Pfeffer, F. (Chi) 23.0
Richardson, D. (NY) 16.2

Win Shares – Batters
Tiernan, M. (NY) 28
Brouthers, D. (Bos) 28
Glasscock, J. (Ind) 27

TPW – Batters
Glasscock, J. (Ind) 4.9
Tiernan, M. (NY) 3.6
Ewing, B. (NY) 3.2

TEAM	CG	SH	SV	IP	H	H/G	ER	HR	BB	SO	OAV	RAT	ERA	ERA+	CERA	PR+	PF	FA	E	DP	FR	BW	PW	FW	TPW	DIF
NY	119	6	3	1151	**1073**	**8.4**	444	38	523	**558**	**.239**	1.387	3.47	114	....	53.0	98	.920	437	90	7.7	**9.4**	4.6	.7	**14.7**	5.3
BOS	121	**10**	**5**	1166	1152	8.9	**435**	41	413	497	.250	**1.342**	**3.36**	124	....	**114.8**	104	.926	413	105	-8.9	-1.6	**9.9**	-.8	7.6	11.4
CHI	123	6	2	**1237**	1313	9.6	513	71	408	434	.263	1.391	3.73	112	....	50.6	104	.923	463	91	10.3	-.2	4.4	.9	5.0	-4.0
PHI	106	4	2	1153^{1}	1288	10.0	512	**33**	428	443	.273	1.488	4.00	109	....	87.9	108	.915	466	92	-42.3	-6.4	7.6	-3.7	-2.5	2.5
PIT	125	5	1	1130^{2}	1296	10.3	566	42	**374**	345	.279	1.477	4.51	**83**	....	-96.8	93	.931	385	94	2.5	3.1	-8.4	.2	-5.1	.1
CLE	**132**	6	1	1191^{2}	1182	8.9	484	36	519	435	.250	1.427	3.66	110	....	10.5	100	**.936**	**365**	**108**	**39.0**	-6.9	.9	**3.4**	-2.6	-2.4
IND	109	3	2	1174^{1}	1365	10.5	633	73	420	408	.281	1.520	4.85	86	....	-104.0	104	.927	420	102	16.3	.9	-9.0	1.4	-6.7	-1.3
WAS	113	1	0	1103	1261	10.3	574	37	527	388	.278	1.621	4.68	84	....	-70.0	98	.904	519	91	-18.6	-.3	-6.1	-1.6	-8.0	-13.0
Total	**948**	**41**	**16**	**9307**		**9.6**	**4161**					**1.455**	**4.02**													

Wins
Clarkson, J. (Bos) 49
Buffinton, C. (Phi) 28
Keefe, T. (NY) 28

Win Percentage
Clarkson, J. (Bos) .... .721
Welch, M. (NY) .... .692
Keefe, T. (NY) .... .683

Games
Clarkson, J. (Bos) 73
Staley, H. (Pit) 49
2 players tied with 47

Complete Games
Clarkson, J. (Bos) 68
Staley, H. (Pit) 46
3 players tied with 39

Shutouts
Clarkson, J. (Bos) 8
Galvin, P. (Pit) 4
4 players tied with 3

Saves
Sowders, B. (Bos,Pit) 2
Bishop, B. (Chi) 2
Welch, M. (NY) 2

Innings Pitched
Clarkson, J. (Bos) 620
Staley, H. (Pit) 420
Buffinton, C. (Phi) 380

Fewest Hits/Game
Keefe, T. (NY) 7.89
Welch, M. (NY) 8.16
Clarkson, J. (Bos) 8.55

Fewest BB/Game
Galvin, P. (Pit) 2.06
Boyle, H. (Ind) 2.26
Radbourn, C. (Bos) 2.34

Strikeouts
Clarkson, J. (Bos) 284
Keefe, T. (NY) 225
Staley, H. (Pit) 159

Ratio
Clarkson, J. (Bos) 1.28
Radbourn, C. (Bos) 1.28
Keefe, T. (NY) 1.29

Earned Run Average
Clarkson, J. (Bos) 2.73
Bakely, J. (Cle) 2.96
Welch, M. (NY) 3.02

Adjusted ERA
Clarkson, J. (Bos) 153
Bakely, J. (Cle) 136
Buffinton, C. (Phi) 134

Component ERA

Opponents' Batting Avg.
Keefe, T. (NY) .... .228
Welch, M. (NY) .... .234
Clarkson, J. (Bos) .... .242

Adjusted Pitching Runs
Clarkson, J. (Bos) 104
Buffinton, C. (Phi) 61
Sanders, B. (Phi) 44

Win Shares – Pitchers
Clarkson, J. (Bos) 60
Buffinton, C. (Phi) 33
Welch, M. (NY) 31

TPW – Pitchers
Clarkson, J. (Bos) 9.1
Buffinton, C. (Phi) 5.2
Sanders, B. (Phi) 4.4

1889 American Association

TEAM	G	W	L	PCT	GB	R	OR	EW	AB	H	2B	3B	HR	TB	BB	SO	SB	CS	AVG	OBP	SLG	OPS	OPS+	BR/A	PF	RC
BRO	140	93	44	.679	....	**995**	706	91	4815	1265	188	79	47	1752	**550**	**401**	389	....	.263	.344	.364	.708	106	41	100	756
STL	141	90	45	.667	2	957	**680**	90	4939	1312	211	64	**58**	1825	493	477	336	....	.266	.339	.370	.708	94	-65	113	751
PHI	138	75	58	.564	16	880	787	74	4868	**1339**	**239**	65	43	1837	534	496	252	....	**.275**	**.354**	.377	**.731**	**114**	**99**	99	758
CIN	141	76	63	.547	18	897	769	80	4844	1307	197	**96**	52	**1852**	452	511	462	....	.270	.340	**.382**	.722	107	31	103	**806**
BAL	139	70	65	.519	22	791	795	67	4756	1209	155	68	20	1560	418	536	311	....	.254	.325	.328	.653	92	-39	98	624
COL	140	60	78	.435	33.5	779	924	57	4816	1247	171	95	36	1716	507	609	304	....	.259	.335	.356	.691	107	55	95	693
KC	139	55	82	.401	38	852	1031	56	4947	1256	162	76	18	1624	430	626	**472**	....	.254	.322	.328	.650	85	-110	106	692
LOU	140	27	111	.196	66.5	632	1091	35	**4955**	1249	170	75	22	1635	320	521	203	....	.252	.303	.330	.633	86	-98	98	571
Total	**559**					**6783**			**38940**	**10184**	**1493**	**618**	**296**		**3704**	**4177**	**2729**		**.262**	**.333**	**.354**	**.687**				

Runs
- Griffin, M. (Bal) 152
- Stovey, H. (Phi) 152
- O'Brien, D. (Bro) 146

Hits
- Tucker, T. (Bal) 196
- Orr, D. (Col) 183
- Holliday, B. (Cin) 181

Doubles
- Welch, C. (Phi) 39
- Stovey, H. (Phi) 38
- Lyons, D. (Phi) 36

Triples
- Marr, L. (Col) 15
- Beard, O. (Cin) 14
- Griffin, M. (Bal) 14

Home Runs
- Holliday, B. (Cin) 19
- Stovey, H. (Phi) 19
- Duffee, C. (StL) 16

Total Bases
- Stovey, H. (Phi) 292
- Holliday, B. (Cin) 280
- 2 players tied with 255

Runs Batted In
- Stovey, H. (Phi) 119
- Foutz, D. (Bro) 113
- O'Neill, T. (StL) 110

Bases On Balls
- Robinson, Y. (StL) 118
- McTamany, J. (Col) 116
- Griffin, M. (Bal) 91

Stolen Bases
- Hamilton, B. (KC) 111
- O'Brien, D. (Bro) 91
- Long, H. (KC) 89

Batting Average
- Tucker, T. (Bal) .372
- O'Neill, T. (StL) .335
- Lyons, D. (Phi) .329

On-Base Percentage
- Tucker, T. (Bal) .450
- Larkin, H. (Phi) .428
- Lyons, D. (Phi) .426

Slugging Average
- Stovey, H. (Phi) .525
- Holliday, B. (Cin) .497
- Tucker, T. (Bal) .484

Adjusted OPS
- Tucker, T. (Bal) 169
- Stovey, H. (Phi) 162
- Lyons, D. (Phi) 156

Adjusted Batting Runs
- Tucker, T. (Bal) 51.0
- Stovey, H. (Phi) 45.0
- Lyons, D. (Phi) 42.0

Runs Created/Game
- Tucker, T. (Bal) 11.70
- Stovey, H. (Phi) 9.80
- Hamilton, B. (KC) 9.70

Fielding Runs
- McPhee, B. (Cin) 38.6
- Bierbauer, L. (Phi) 35.4
- Shindle, B. (Bal) 25.8

Win Shares – Batters
- O'Brien, D. (Bro) 30
- Tucker, T. (Bal) 30
- Stovey, H. (Phi) 28

TPW – Batters
- Stovey, H. (Phi) 4.9
- Lyons, D. (Phi) 4.5
- Bierbauer, L. (Phi) 4.2

TEAM	CG	SH	SV	IP	H	H/G	ER	HR	BB	SO	OAV	RAT	ERA	ERA+	CERA	PR+	PF	FA	E	DP	FR	BW	PW	FW	TPW	DIF
BRO	120	**10**	1	1212^{2}	1205	8.9	486	33	**400**	471	.251	1.324	3.61	103	....	13.3	97	**.928**	**421**	92	0.9	3.5	1.1	.1	4.7	20.3
STL	121	7	4	1237^{2}	**1166**	**8.5**	**412**	39	413	**617**	**.241**	**1.276**	**3.00**	141	....	**139.4**	110	.925	438	100	27.8	-5.5	**11.8**	2.4	8.6	14.4
PHI	**130**	9	1	1199^{1}	1200	9.0	470	35	509	479	.253	1.425	3.53	107	....	-7.9	98	.920	465	120	**41.4**	**8.3**	-.7	**3.5**	**11.2**	-2.2
CIN	114	3	**8**	**1243**	1270	9.2	483	35	475	562	.257	1.404	3.50	111	....	41.2	101	.926	440	**121**	13.2	2.6	3.5	1.1	7.2	-.2
BAL	128	**10**	1	1192	1168	8.8	472	**27**	424	540	.249	1.336	3.56	106	....	56.7	99	.907	536	104	-25.5	-3.3	4.8	-2.2	-.7	3.7
COL	114	9	4	1199	1274	9.6	585	33	551	610	.264	1.522	4.39	82	....	-102.3	94	.915	497	92	-1.0	4.6	-8.7	-.1	-4.1	-4.9
KC	128	0	2	1204^{1}	1373	10.3	583	51	457	447	.278	1.520	4.36	96	....	13.7	109	.899	611	109	-38.3	-9.3	1.2	-3.2	-11.4	-1.6
LOU	127	2	1	1226^{1}	1529	11.2	655	43	475	451	.296	1.634	4.81	**80**	....	-112.8	100	.906	584	117	-19.4	-8.3	-9.5	-1.6	-19.5	-22.5
Total	**982**	**50**	**22**	**9714^{1}**		**9.4**	**4146**					**1.430**	**3.84**													

Wins
- Caruthers, B. (Bro) 40
- King, S. (StL) 34
- 2 players tied with 32

Win Percentage
- Caruthers, B. (Bro) .784
- Chamberlain, E. (StL) .681
- King, S. (StL) .680

Games
- Baldwin, M. (Col) 63
- Kilroy, M. (Bal) 59
- Caruthers, B. (Bro) 56

Complete Games
- Kilroy, M. (Bal) 55
- Baldwin, M. (Col) 54
- Weyhing, G. (Phi) 50

Shutouts
- Caruthers, B. (Bro) 7
- Baldwin, M. (Col) 6
- 2 players tied with 5

Saves
- Mullane, T. (Cin) 5
- 16 players tied with 1

Innings Pitched
- Baldwin, M. (Col) 513^{2}
- Kilroy, M. (Bal) 480^{2}
- King, S. (StL) 458

Fewest Hits/Game
- Stivetts, J. (StL) 7.18
- Weyhing, G. (Phi) 7.66
- Terry, A. (Bro) 7.87

Fewest BB/Game
- Caruthers, B. (Bro) 2.10
- Conway, J. (KC) 2.42
- King, S. (StL) 2.46

Strikeouts
- Baldwin, M. (Col) 368
- Kilroy, M. (Bal) 217
- Weyhing, G. (Phi) 213

Ratio
- Stivetts, J. (StL) 1.15
- Foreman, F. (Bal) 1.21
- Caruthers, B. (Bro) 1.23

Earned Run Average
- Stivetts, J. (StL) 2.25
- Duryea, J. (Cin) 2.56
- Kilroy, M. (Bal) 2.85

Adjusted ERA
- Stivetts, J. (StL) 187
- Duryea, J. (Cin) 152
- Chamberlain, E. (StL) 142

Component ERA

Opponents' Batting Avg.
- Stivetts, J. (StL) .212
- Weyhing, G. (Phi) .223
- Terry, A. (Bro) .228

Adjusted Pitching Runs
- Kilroy, M. (Bal) 61
- Duryea, J. (Cin) 55
- Chamberlain, E. (StL) 49

Win Shares – Pitchers
- Caruthers, B. (Bro) 46
- Kilroy, M. (Bal) 44
- King, S. (StL) 44

TPW – Pitchers
- Kilroy, M. (Bal) 6.4
- Duryea, J. (Cin) 5.3
- Chamberlain, E. (StL) 4.1

1890 National League

TEAM	G	W	L	PCT	GB	R	OR	EW	AB	H	2B	3B	HR	TB	BB	SO	SB	CS	AVG	OBP	SLG	OPS	OPS+	BR/A	PF	RC
BRO	129	86	43	.667	....	**884**	620	86	4419	1166	184	75	43	1629	517	**361**	**349**	....	.264	.346	**.369**	**.715**	**113**	**72**	100	702
CHI	139	84	53	.613	6	847	692	82	**4891**	**1271**	147	60	**67**	**1739**	516	514	329	....	.260	.336	.356	.692	102	5	104	712
PHI	133	78	54	.591	9.5	823	707	76	4707	1267	**220**	78	23	1712	522	403	335	....	**.269**	**.350**	.364	.714	110	61	102	**735**
CIN	134	77	55	.583	10.5	753	633	77	4644	1203	150	**120**	27	1674	433	377	312	....	.259	.329	.360	.689	106	30	99	670
BOS	134	76	57	.571	12	763	**593**	83	4722	1220	175	62	31	1612	**530**	515	285	....	.258	.342	.341	.683	96	-27	108	665
NY	135	63	68	.481	24	713	698	67	4832	1250	208	89	25	1711	350	479	289	....	.259	.315	.354	.669	99	-20	100	647
CLE	136	44	88	.333	43.5	630	832	48	4633	1073	132	59	21	1386	497	474	152	....	.232	.312	.299	.611	84	-84	98	491
PIT	138	23	113	.169	66.5	597	1235	26	4739	1088	160	43	20	1394	408	458	208	....	.230	.300	.294	.594	87	-50	88	492
Total	**539**					**6010**			**37587**	**9538**	**1376**	**586**	**257**		**3773**	**3581**	**2259**		**.254**	**.329**	**.342**	**.671**				

Runs
- Collins, H. (Bro) 148
- Carroll, C. (Chi) 134
- Hamilton, B. (Phi) 133

Hits
- Glasscock, J. (NY) 172
- Thompson, S. (Phi) 172
- Tiernan, M. (NY) 168

Doubles
- Thompson, S. (Phi) 41
- Collins, H. (Bro) 32
- Glasscock, J. (NY) 32

Triples
- Reilly, J. (Cin) 26
- McPhee, B. (Cin) 22
- Tiernan, M. (NY) 21

Home Runs
- Burns, O. (Bro) 13
- Tiernan, M. (NY) 13
- Wilmot, W. (Chi) 13

Total Bases
- Tiernan, M. (NY) 274
- Reilly, J. (Cin) 261
- Thompson, S. (Phi) 243

Runs Batted In
- Burns, O. (Bro) 128
- Anson, C. (Chi) 107
- Thompson, S. (Phi) 102

Bases On Balls
- Anson, C. (Chi) 113
- Allen, B. (Phi) 87
- McKean, E. (Cle) 87

Stolen Bases
- Hamilton, B. (Phi) 102
- Collins, H. (Bro) 85
- Sunday, B. (Pit,Phi) 84

Batting Average
- Glasscock, J. (NY) .336
- Hamilton, B. (Phi) .325
- Thompson, S. (Phi) .313

On-Base Percentage
- Anson, C. (Chi) .443
- Hamilton, B. (Phi) .430
- Pinckney, G. (Bro) .411

Slugging Average
- Tiernan, M. (NY) .495
- Reilly, J. (Cin) .472
- Burns, O. (Bro) .464

Adjusted OPS
- Tiernan, M. (NY) 156
- Pinckney, G. (Bro) 145
- Glasscock, J. (NY) 143

Adjusted Batting Runs
- Tiernan, M. (NY) 38.0
- Anson, C. (Chi) 34.0
- McKean, E. (Cle) 32.0

Runs Created/Game
- Hamilton, B. (Phi) 10.50
- Tiernan, M. (NY) 9.00
- Glasscock, J. (NY) 8.80

Fielding Runs
- Allen, B. (Phi) 38.4
- McPhee, B. (Cin) 28.1
- Zimmer, C. (Cle) 17.3

Win Shares – Batters
- Pinckney, G. (Bro) 29
- Collins, H. (Bro) 28
- Foutz, D. (Bro) 27

TPW – Batters
- McPhee, B. (Cin) 4.2
- Allen, B. (Phi) 3.9
- Glasscock, J. (NY) 3.6

TEAM	CG	SH	SV	IP	H	H/G	ER	HR	BB	SO	OAV	RAT	ERA	ERA+	CERA	PR+	PF	FA	E	DP	FR	BW	PW	FW	TPW	DIF
BRO	115	6	2	1145	1102	8.7	389	27	401	403	.246	1.313	3.06	112	....	45.0	96	**.940**	**320**	92	2.3	**6.4**	4.0	.2	10.6	11.4
CHI	126	6	**3**	**1237^{1}**	1103	8.0	445	41	481	504	.232	1.280	3.24	113	....	24.6	102	.939	344	89	**30.7**	.5	2.2	**2.7**	5.4	10.6
PHI	122	9	2	1194^{2}	1210	9.1	440	22	486	507	.255	1.420	3.31	110	....	27.0	102	.929	398	**122**	15.5	5.4	2.4	1.4	9.2	2.8
CIN	124	9	1	1190^{2}	1097	8.3	**369**	41	407	488	.238	1.263	**2.79**	127	....	81.6	100	.933	382	106	18.7	2.7	7.3	1.7	**11.6**	-.6
BOS	**132**	**13**	1	1187	1132	8.6	386	27	**354**	506	.244	**1.252**	2.93	128	....	**113.4**	105	.935	359	77	-7.2	-2.4	**10.1**	-.6	7.0	3.0
NY	115	6	1	1177	**1029**	**7.9**	400	**14**	607	**612**	**.228**	1.390	3.06	114	....	50.7	98	.922	449	104	5.6	-1.7	4.5	.5	3.3	-5.3
CLE	129	2	0	1184^{1}	1322	10.0	543	33	462	306	.274	1.506	4.13	86	....	-76.4	100	.929	405	108	2.0	-7.4	-6.8	.2	-14.0	-8.0
PIT	119	3	0	1176^{1}	1520	11.6	780	52	573	381	.304	1.779	5.97	**55**	....	-284.0	92	.896	607	94	-64.6	-4.5	-25.2	-5.7	-35.5	-9.5
Total	**982**	**54**	**10**	**9492^{1}**		**9.0**	**3752**					**1.400**	**3.56**													

Wins
- Hutchison, B. (Chi) 42
- Gleason, K. (Phi) 38
- Lovett, T. (Bro) 30

Win Percentage
- Lovett, T. (Bro) .732
- Gleason, K. (Phi) .691
- Luby, P. (Chi) .690

Games
- Hutchison, B. (Chi) 71
- Rusie, A. (NY) 67
- Gleason, K. (Phi) 60

Complete Games
- Hutchison, B. (Chi) 65
- Rusie, A. (NY) 56
- Gleason, K. (Phi) 54

Shutouts
- Nichols, K. (Bos) 7
- Gleason, K. (Phi) 6
- Rhines, B. (Cin) 6

Saves
- Foutz, D. (Bro) 2
- Gleason, K. (Phi) 2
- Hutchison, B. (Chi) 2

Innings Pitched
- Hutchison, B. (Chi) 603
- Rusie, A. (NY) 548^{2}
- Gleason, K. (Phi) 506

Fewest Hits/Game
- Rusie, A. (NY) 7.15
- Mullane, T. (Cin) 7.54
- Hutchison, B. (Chi) 7.54

Fewest BB/Game
- Young, C. (Cle) 1.83
- Duryea, J. (Cin) 1.97
- Getzein, C. (Bos) 2.11

Strikeouts
- Rusie, A. (NY) 341
- Hutchison, B. (Chi) 289
- 2 players tied with 222

Ratio
- Rhines, B. (Cin) 1.12
- Nichols, K. (Bos) 1.15
- Hutchison, B. (Chi) 1.17

Earned Run Average
- Rhines, B. (Cin) 1.95
- Nichols, K. (Bos) 2.23
- Mullane, T. (Cin) 2.24

Adjusted ERA
- Rhines, B. (Cin) 182
- Nichols, K. (Bos) 168
- Mullane, T. (Cin) 158

Component ERA

Opponents' Batting Avg.
- Rusie, A. (NY) .212
- Mullane, T. (Cin) .221
- Hutchison, B. (Chi) .221

Adjusted Pitching Runs
- Nichols, K. (Bos) 74
- Rhines, B. (Cin) 65
- Rusie, A. (NY) 54

Win Shares – Pitchers
- Hutchison, B. (Chi) 54
- Gleason, K. (Phi) 45
- Nichols, K. (Bos) 43

TPW – Pitchers
- Nichols, K. (Bos) 6.7
- Rusie, A. (NY) 5.6
- Rhines, B. (Cin) 5.4

1890 American Association

TEAM	G	W	L	PCT	GB	R	OR	EW	AB	H	2B	3B	HR	TB	BB	SO	SB	CS	AVG	OBP	SLG	OPS	OPS+	BR/A	PF	RC
LOU	136	88	44	.667	....	819	588	87	4687	**1310**	156	65	15	1641	410	460	341	....	**.279**	.344	.350	.694	**113**	71	98	699
COL	140	79	55	.590	10	831	617	86	4741	1225	159	77	16	1586	**545**	557	353	....	.258	.341	.335	.675	112	**90**	93	677
STL	139	78	58	.574	12	**870**	736	79	**4800**	1308	178	73	**48**	**1776**	474	490	307	....	.272	**.350**	**.370**	**.720**	103	-6	114	**746**
TOL	134	68	64	.515	20	739	689	71	4575	1152	152	**108**	24	1592	486	558	**421**	....	.252	.333	.348	.681	103	11	103	687
ROC	133	63	63	.500	22	709	711	63	4553	1088	131	64	31	1440	446	538	310	....	.239	.315	.316	.631	98	4	92	564
BAL	38	15	19	.441	24	182	**192**	16	1213	278	34	16	2	350	125	**152**	101	....	.229	.316	.289	.604	75	-39	110	146
SYR	128	55	72	.433	30.5	698	831	53	4469	1158	151	59	14	1469	457	482	292	....	.259	.333	.329	.661	112	84	90	600
PHI	132	54	78	.409	34	702	945	47	4490	1057	**181**	51	24	1412	475	540	305	....	.235	.320	.314	.635	94	-23	98	564
BRO	100	26	73	.263	45.5	492	733	31	3475	769	116	47	13	1018	328	456	182	....	.221	.294	.293	.587	80	-82	97	362
Total	**540**					**6042**			**37003**	**9345**	**1258**	**560**	**187**		**3746**	**4233**	**2612**		**.253**	**.330**	**.332**	**.662**				

Runs
McTamany, J. (Col) 140
McCarthy, T. (StL) 137
Fuller, S. (StL) 118

Hits
Wolf, J. (Lou) 197
McCarthy, T. (StL) 192
Johnson, S. (Col) 186

Doubles
Childs, C. (Syr) 33
Lyons, D. (Phi) 29
Wolf, J. (Lou) 29

Triples
Werden, P. (Tol) 20
Johnson, S. (Col) 18
Alvord, B. (Tol) 16

Home Runs
Campau, C. (StL) 9
Cartwright, E. (StL) 8
2 players tied with 7

Total Bases
Wolf, J. (Lou) 260
McCarthy, T. (StL) 256
Johnson, S. (Col) 248

Runs Batted In
Johnson, S. (Col) 113
Wolf, J. (Lou) 98
Childs, C. (Syr) 89

Bases On Balls
McTamany, J. (Col) 112
Crooks, J. (Col) 96
Swartwood, E. (Tol) 80

Stolen Bases
McCarthy, T. (StL) 83
Scheffler, T. (Roc) 77
Van Dyke, B. (Tol) 73

Batting Average
Wolf, J. (Lou) .... .363
McCarthy, T. (StL) .... .350
Johnson, S. (Col) .... .346

On-Base Percentage
Lyons, D. (Phi) .... .461
Swartwood, E. (Tol) .... .444
Childs, C. (Syr) .... .434

Slugging Average
Lyons, D. (Phi) .... .531
Childs, C. (Syr) .... .481
Wolf, J. (Lou) .... .479

Adjusted OPS
Childs, C. (Syr) 189
Wolf, J. (Lou) 169
Johnson, S. (Col) 168

Adjusted Batting Runs
Childs, C. (Syr) 59.0
Wolf, J. (Lou) 46.0
Johnson, S. (Col) 46.0

Runs Created/Game
McCarthy, T. (StL) 11.10
Childs, C. (Syr) 10.70
Wolf, J. (Lou) 10.10

Fielding Runs
Reilly, C. (Col) 32.3
Gerhardt, J. (Bro,StL) 28.9
Tomney, P. (Lou) 21.2

Win Shares – Batters
Childs, C. (Syr) 31
Wolf, J. (Lou) 27
2 players tied with 25

TPW – Batters
Childs, C. (Syr) 6.8
Swartwood, E. (Tol) 3.9
Wolf, J. (Lou) 3.8

TEAM	CG	SH	SV	IP	H	H/G	ER	HR	BB	SO	OAV	RAT	ERA	ERA+	CERA	PR+	PF	FA	E	DP	FR	BW	PW	FW	TPW	DIF
LOU	114	13	**7**	1206	1120	8.4	344	18	293	587	.239	1.172	2.57	150	....	**163.5**	100	**.933**	380	79	6.3	6.2	**14.4**	.6	**21.2**	.8
COL	120	**14**	3	1214^{2}	976	7.2	403	20	471	624	**.214**	1.191	2.99	120	....	32.9	93	.932	396	**101**	**47.4**	**7.9**	2.9	**4.2**	14.9	-2.9
STL	118	4	1	1195^{1}	1127	8.5	487	38	447	**733**	.242	1.317	3.67	117	....	79.6	112	.916	478	93	4.3	-.5	7.0	.4	6.9	3.1
TOL	**122**	4	2	1159^{1}	1122	8.7	458	23	429	533	.247	1.338	3.56	111	....	21.8	102	.925	419	75	27.2	.9	1.9	2.4	5.2	-3.2
ROC	**122**	5	2	1161^{2}	1115	8.6	459	19	530	477	.245	1.416	3.56	100	....	-8.4	92	.926	416	95	6.8	.4	-.7	.6	.2	-.2
BAL	36	1	0	**3151**	**307**	**0.9**	**140**	**3**	**123**	134	.248	**.136**	**0.40**	106	....	9.4	110	.928	**109**	21	-0.2	-3.4	.8	.0	-2.6	.6
SYR	115	5	0	1089^{2}	1158	9.6	603	28	518	454	.264	1.538	4.98	**71**	....	-156.0	91	.925	391	90	-20.2	7.4	-13.7	-1.8	-8.1	.1
PHI	119	3	2	1132	1405	11.2	657	17	514	461	.296	1.695	5.22	73	....	-110.4	99	.918	452	93	-65.8	-2.1	-9.7	-5.8	-17.6	5.6
BRO	96	0	0	879	1011	10.4	460	21	421	230	.280	1.629	4.71	83	....	-74.7	101	.909	404	92	-5.5	-7.2	-6.6	-.5	-14.3	-8.7
Total	**962**	**49**	**17**	**12188^{2}**		**6.9**	**4011**					**1.074**	**2.96**													

Wins
McMahon, S. (Phi,Bal) 36
Stratton, S. (Lou) 34
Gastright, H. (Col) 30

Win Percentage
Stratton, S. (Lou) .... .708
Gastright, H. (Col) .... .682
Ehret, R. (Lou) .... .641

Games
McMahon, S. (Phi,Bal) 60
Barr, B. (Roc) 57
Stivetts, J. (StL) 54

Complete Games
McMahon, S. (Phi,Bal) 55
Barr, B. (Roc) 52
2 players tied with 44

Shutouts
Chamberlain, E. (Col,StL) 6
3 players tied with 4

Saves
Goodall, H. (Lou) 4
Ehret, R. (Lou) 2
Knauss, F. (Col) 2

Innings Pitched
McMahon, S. (Phi,Bal) 509
Barr, B. (Roc) .... 493^{1}
Stratton, S. (Lou) 431

Fewest Hits/Game
Knauss, F. (Col) 6.73
Gastright, H. (Col) 7.00
Easton, J. (Col) 7.50

Fewest BB/Game
Stratton, S. (Lou) 1.27
Ehret, R. (Lou) 1.98
Ramsey, T. (StL) 2.63

Strikeouts
McMahon, S. (Phi,Bal) 291
Stivetts, J. (StL) 289
Ramsey, T. (StL) 257

Ratio
Stratton, S. (Lou) 1.06
Gastright, H. (Col) 1.11
Knauss, F. (Col) 1.13

Earned Run Average
Stratton, S. (Lou) 2.36
Ehret, R. (Lou) 2.53
Knauss, F. (Col) 2.81

Adjusted ERA
Stratton, S. (Lou) 163
Ehret, R. (Lou) 152
Healy, J. (Tol) 136

Component ERA

Opponents' Batting Avg.
Knauss, F. (Col) .... .202
Gastright, H. (Col) .... .208
Easton, J. (Col) .... .220

Adjusted Pitching Runs
Stratton, S. (Lou) 69
McMahon, S. (Phi,Bal) 60
Ehret, R. (Lou) 50

Win Shares – Pitchers
Stratton, S. (Lou) 51
Stivetts, J. (StL) 41
2 players tied with 34

TPW – Pitchers
Stratton, S. (Lou) 7.6
McMahon, S. (Phi,Bal) 5.3
Stivetts, J. (StL) 4.5

1890 Players League

TEAM	G	W	L	PCT	GB	R	OR	EW	AB	H	2B	3B	HR	TB	BB	SO	SB	CS	AVG	OBP	SLG	OPS	OPS+	BR/A	PF	RC
BOS	130	81	48	.628	....	992	**767**	81	4626	1306	**223**	76	54	1843	**652**	435	**412**	....	.282	**.376**	.398	**.774**	105	33	107	**869**
BRO	133	76	56	.576	6.5	964	893	71	4887	1352	186	93	34	1826	502	369	272	....	.277	.349	.374	.723	93	-65	106	752
NY	132	74	57	.565	8	**1018**	875	75	4913	**1393**	204	97	**66**	**1989**	486	364	231	....	.284	.352	**.405**	.757	99	-38	109	800
CHI	138	75	62	.547	10	886	770	78	**4968**	1311	200	95	31	1794	492	410	276	....	.264	.335	.361	.697	87	-102	104	712
PHI	132	68	63	.519	14	941	855	72	4855	1350	187	**113**	49	1910	431	**321**	203	....	.278	.343	.393	.737	99	-22	102	742
PIT	128	60	68	.469	20.5	835	892	60	4577	1192	168	**113**	35	1691	569	375	249	....	.260	.349	.369	.718	106	64	92	694
CLE	131	55	75	.423	26.5	849	1027	53	4804	1370	213	94	27	1852	509	345	180	....	**.285**	.360	.386	.745	**114**	**114**	92	751
BUF	134	36	96	.273	46.5	793	1199	40	4795	1249	180	64	20	1617	541	367	160	....	.260	.347	.337	.684	96	10	92	632
Total	**529**					**7278**			**38425**	**10523**	**1561**	**745**	**316**		**4182**	**2986**	**1983**		**.274**	**.351**	**.378**	**.729**				

Runs
Duffy, H. (Chi) 161
Brown, T. (Bos) 146
Stovey, H. (Bos) 142

Hits
Duffy, H. (Chi) 191
Shindle, B. (Phi) 189
Ward, J. (Bro) 188

Doubles
Browning, P. (Cle) 40
Beckley, J. (Pit) 38
O'Rourke, J. (NY) 37

Triples
Beckley, J. (Pit) 22
Visner, J. (Pit) 22
Shindle, B. (Phi) 21

Home Runs
Connor, R. (NY) 14
Richardson, H. (Bos) 13
Stovey, H. (Bos) 12

Total Bases
Shindle, B. (Phi) 282
Duffy, H. (Chi) 280
Beckley, J. (Pit) 276

Runs Batted In
Richardson, H. (Bos) 146
Orr, D. (Bro) 124
Beckley, J. (Pit) 120

Bases On Balls
Joyce, B. (Bro) 123
Robinson, Y. (Pit) 101
Brouthers, D. (Bos) 99

Stolen Bases
Stovey, H. (Bos) 97
Brown, T. (Bos) 79
Duffy, H. (Chi) 78

Batting Average
Browning, P. (Cle) .... .373
Orr, D. (Bro) .... .371
O'Rourke, J. (NY) .... .360

On-Base Percentage
Brouthers, D. (Bos) .... .466
Browning, P. (Cle) .... .459
Connor, R. (NY) .... .450

Slugging Average
Connor, R. (NY) .... .548
Beckley, J. (Pit) .... .535
Orr, D. (Bro) .... .534

Adjusted OPS
Browning, P. (Cle) 175
Beckley, J. (Pit) 156
Larkin, H. (Cle) 153

Adjusted Batting Runs
Browning, P. (Cle) 57.0
Larkin, H. (Cle) 41.0
Beckley, J. (Pit) 39.0

Runs Created/Game
Browning, P. (Cle) 11.90
Connor, R. (NY) 11.40
Stovey, H. (Bos) 10.80

Fielding Runs
Richardson, D. (NY) 26.4
Bierbauer, L. (Bro) 23.7
Pfeffer, F. (Chi) 20.6

Win Shares – Batters
Ward, J. (Bro) 27
Shindle, B. (Phi) 26
Duffy, H. (Chi) 26

TPW – Batters
Browning, P. (Cle) 4.5
Connor, R. (NY) 3.8
Beckley, J. (Pit) 2.7

TEAM	CG	SH	SV	IP	H	H/G	ER	HR	BB	SO	OAV	RAT	ERA	ERA+	CERA	PR+	PF	FA	E	DP	FR	BW	PW	FW	TPW	DIF
BOS	105	6	4	1137^{1}	1291	10.2	479	49	467	345	.274	1.546	3.79	116	....	64.0	104	.918	460	109	12.6	2.6	5.1	1.0	**8.7**	8.3
BRO	111	4	**7**	1184	1334	10.1	520	**26**	570	377	.272	1.608	3.95	113	....	55.1	105	.909	531	114	12.2	-5.2	4.4	1.0	.2	9.8
NY	111	3	6	1172^{1}	**1216**	9.3	543	37	569	449	.257	1.523	4.17	109	....	33.0	107	**.921**	**450**	94	**14.9**	-3.1	2.6	**1.2**	.8	8.2
CHI	124	5	2	**1219^{1}**	1238	**9.1**	**459**	27	503	**460**	**.252**	**1.428**	**3.39**	128	....	**125.5**	103	.918	492	107	3.9	-8.2	**10.0**	.3	2.2	4.8
PHI	118	4	2	1154^{1}	1292	10.1	519	33	495	361	.271	1.548	4.05	106	....	28.4	101	.910	510	**118**	-0.4	-1.8	2.3	.0	.4	2.6
PIT	121	**7**	0	1116^{2}	1267	10.2	523	32	**334**	318	.274	1.434	4.22	93	....	-7.9	92	.907	512	80	-30.4	5.1	-.6	-2.4	2.1	-6.1
CLE	115	1	0	1143^{2}	1386	10.9	537	45	571	325	.287	1.711	4.23	94	....	-34.4	94	.907	533	103	2.2	**9.1**	-2.7	.2	6.5	-16.5
BUF	**125**	2	0	1141	1499	11.8	775	67	673	351	.304	1.904	6.11	**67**	....	-241.0	97	.914	491	116	-15.3	.8	-19.2	-1.2	-19.6	-10.4
Total	**930**	**32**	**21**	**9268^{2}**		**10.2**	**4355**					**1.587**	**4.23**													

Wins	
Baldwin, M. (Chi)	33
King, S. (Chi)	30
Weyhing, G. (Bro)	30

Win Percentage	
Daley, B. (Bos)	.720
Radbourn, C. (Bos)	.692
Knell, P. (Phi)	.667

Games	
Baldwin, M. (Chi)	58
King, S. (Chi)	56
Weyhing, G. (Bro)	49

Complete Games	
Baldwin, M. (Chi)	53
King, S. (Chi)	48
Staley, H. (Pit)	44

Shutouts	
King, S. (Chi)	4
Staley, H. (Pit)	3
Weyhing, G. (Bro)	3

Saves	
Hemming, G. (Bro,Cle)	3
O'Day, H. (NY)	3
4 players tied with	2

Innings Pitched	
Baldwin, M. (Chi)	492
King, S. (Chi)	461
Weyhing, G. (Bro)	390

Fewest Hits/Game	
King, S. (Chi)	8.20
Crane, E. (NY)	8.80
Keefe, T. (NY)	8.84

Fewest BB/Game	
Staley, H. (Pit)	1.72
Sanders, B. (Phi)	1.79
Galvin, P. (Pit)	2.03

Strikeouts	
Baldwin, M. (Chi)	206
King, S. (Chi)	185
Weyhing, G. (Bro)	177

Ratio	
Staley, H. (Pit)	1.20
King, S. (Chi)	1.26
Radbourn, C. (Bos)	1.32

Earned Run Average	
King, S. (Chi)	2.69
Staley, H. (Pit)	3.23
Radbourn, C. (Bos)	3.31

Adjusted ERA	
King, S. (Chi)	161
Keefe, T. (NY)	134
Radbourn, C. (Bos)	133

Component ERA

Opponents' Batting Avg.	
King, S. (Chi)	.232
Crane, E. (NY)	.245
Keefe, T. (NY)	.246

Adjusted Pitching Runs	
King, S. (Chi)	83
Baldwin, M. (Chi)	52
Staley, H. (Pit)	40

Win Shares – Pitchers	
King, S. (Chi)	44
Baldwin, M. (Chi)	42
Radbourn, C. (Bos)	34

TPW – Pitchers	
King, S. (Chi)	6.2
Baldwin, M. (Chi)	4.2
Staley, H. (Pit)	3.3

1891 National League

TEAM	G	W	L	PCT	GB	R	OR	EW	AB	H	2B	3B	HR	TB	BB	SO	SB	CS	AVG	OBP	SLG	OPS	OPS+	BR/A	PF	RC
BOS	140	87	51	.630	....	**847**	**658**	86	4956	1264	181	81	53	**1766**	**533**	537	289	....	.255	**.337**	.356	**.694**	97	-33	112	**711**
CHI	137	82	53	.607	3.5	832	730	76	4873	1231	159	88	**60**	1746	526	457	238	....	.253	.332	.358	.690	107	44	100	676
NY	136	71	61	.538	13	754	711	70	4833	1271	189	72	46	1742	438	**394**	224	....	**.263**	.329	**.360**	.689	**111**	**67**	96	663
PHI	138	68	69	.496	18.5	756	773	67	4929	1244	180	51	21	1589	482	412	232	....	.252	.326	.322	.649	92	-45	102	609
CLE	141	65	74	.468	22.5	835	888	65	**5074**	**1295**	183	88	22	1720	519	464	242	....	.255	.330	.339	.669	97	-25	104	663
BRO	137	61	76	.445	25.5	765	820	64	4748	1233	**200**	69	23	1640	465	435	**337**	....	.260	.330	.345	.676	103	21	99	669
CIN	138	56	81	.409	30.5	646	790	55	4791	1158	148	**90**	40	1606	414	439	244	....	.242	.308	.335	.643	92	-55	101	584
PIT	137	55	80	.407	30.5	679	744	61	4794	1148	148	71	29	1525	427	503	205	....	.239	.308	.318	.626	90	-55	97	547
Total	**552**					**6114**			**38998**	**9844**	**1388**	**610**	**294**		**3804**	**3641**	**2011**		**.252**	**.325**	**.342**	**.667**				

Runs	
Hamilton, B. (Phi)	141
Long, H. (Bos)	129
Childs, C. (Cle)	120

Hits	
Hamilton, B. (Phi)	179
McKean, E. (Cle)	170
Tiernan, M. (NY)	166

Doubles	
Griffin, M. (Bro)	36
Davis, G. (Cle)	35
Stovey, H. (Bos)	31

Triples	
Stovey, H. (Bos)	20
Beckley, J. (Pit)	19
McPhee, B. (Cin)	16

Home Runs	
Stovey, H. (Bos)	16
Tiernan, M. (NY)	16
Wilmot, W. (Chi)	11

Total Bases	
Stovey, H. (Bos)	271
Tiernan, M. (NY)	268
Long, H. (Bos)	235

Runs Batted In	
Anson, C. (Chi)	120
3 players tied with	95

Bases On Balls	
Hamilton, B. (Phi)	102
Childs, C. (Cle)	97
Connor, R. (NY)	83

Stolen Bases	
Hamilton, B. (Phi)	111
Latham, A. (Cin)	87
Griffin, M. (Bro)	65

Batting Average	
Hamilton, B. (Phi)	.340
Holliday, B. (Cin)	.319
Browning, P. (Cin,Pit)	.317

On-Base Percentage	
Hamilton, B. (Phi)	.453
Connor, R. (NY)	.399
Childs, C. (Cle)	.395

Slugging Average	
Stovey, H. (Bos)	.498
Tiernan, M. (NY)	.494
Holliday, B. (Cin)	.473

Adjusted OPS	
Tiernan, M. (NY)	163
Connor, R. (NY)	153
Hamilton, B. (Phi)	151

Adjusted Batting Runs	
Tiernan, M. (NY)	43.0
Hamilton, B. (Phi)	42.0
Connor, R. (NY)	36.0

Runs Created/Game	
Hamilton, B. (Phi)	12.00
Tiernan, M. (NY)	9.20
Stovey, H. (Bos)	8.60

Fielding Runs	
Richardson, D. (NY)	37.3
Zimmer, C. (Cle)	21.7
Long, H. (Bos)	20.8

Win Shares – Batters	
Hamilton, B. (Phi)	36
Long, H. (Bos)	29
2 players tied with	26

TPW – Batters	
Hamilton, B. (Phi)	3.7
Richardson, D. (NY)	3.4
Long, H. (Bos)	3.3

TEAM	CG	SH	SV	IP	H	H/G	ER	HR	BB	SO	OAV	RAT	ERA	ERA+	CERA	PR+	PF	FA	E	DP	FR	BW	PW	FW	TPW	DIF
BOS	**126**	9	**6**	1241^{2}	1223	8.9	**381**	51	**364**	525	.248	**1.278**	**2.76**	132	....	**124.9**	109	**.938**	**358**	96	-2.3	-3.0	**11.2**	-.2	8.0	10.0
CHI	114	6	3	1220^{2}	1207	8.9	470	53	475	477	.249	1.378	3.47	96	....	-43.3	100	.932	397	**119**	**23.6**	3.9	-3.9	**2.1**	2.2	12.8
NY	117	**11**	3	1204	**1098**	**8.2**	400	26	593	**651**	**.234**	1.404	2.99	107	....	11.7	96	.933	384	104	15.5	**5.9**	1.0	1.4	**8.4**	-3.4
PHI	105	3	5	1229^{1}	1279	9.4	509	29	507	342	.258	1.453	3.73	91	....	-55.1	102	.925	443	108	9.2	-4.0	-4.9	.8	-8.1	8.1
CLE	118	1	3	**1244**	1371	9.9	484	**24**	466	400	.269	1.477	3.50	99	....	9.0	103	.920	485	86	-15.6	-2.2	.8	-1.4	-2.8	-1.2
BRO	121	8	3	1204^{2}	1272	9.5	516	40	459	407	.261	1.437	3.86	**86**	....	-46.5	99	.924	432	73	-27.7	1.8	-4.2	-2.5	-4.8	-2.2
CIN	125	6	1	1218^{2}	1234	9.1	480	40	465	393	.253	1.394	3.54	95	....	-31.3	101	.931	409	101	6.7	-4.9	-2.8	.6	-7.1	-4.9
PIT	122	7	3	1197^{2}	1160	8.7	384	31	465	446	.245	1.357	2.89	113	....	60.9	98	.917	475	76	-9.1	-4.9	5.4	-.8	-.3	-11.7
Total	**948**	**51**	**27**	**9760**^{2}		**9.1**	**3624**					**1.397**	**3.34**													

Wins	
Hutchison, B. (Chi)	44
Clarkson, J. (Bos)	33
Rusie, A. (NY)	33

Win Percentage	
Ewing, J. (NY)	.724
Hutchison, B. (Chi)	.698
Nichols, K. (Bos)	.638

Games	
Hutchison, B. (Chi)	66
Rusie, A. (NY)	61
2 players tied with	55

Complete Games	
Hutchison, B. (Chi)	56
Rusie, A. (NY)	52
Baldwin, M. (Pit)	48

Shutouts	
Rusie, A. (NY)	6
Ewing, J. (NY)	5
Nichols, K. (Bos)	5

Saves	
Clarkson, J. (Bos)	3
Nichols, K. (Bos)	3
2 players tied with	2

Innings Pitched	
Hutchison, B. (Chi)	561
Rusie, A. (NY)	500^{1}
Clarkson, J. (Bos)	460^{2}

Fewest Hits/Game	
Rusie, A. (NY)	7.03
Baldwin, M. (Pit)	7.92
Ewing, J. (NY)	7.92

Fewest BB/Game	
Nichols, K. (Bos)	2.18
Staley, H. (Pit,Bos)	2.22
Galvin, P. (Pit)	2.26

Strikeouts	
Rusie, A. (NY)	337
Hutchison, B. (Chi)	261
Nichols, K. (Bos)	240

Ratio	
Staley, H. (Bos,Pit)	1.21
Nichols, K. (Bos)	1.21
Hutchison, B. (Chi)	1.22

Earned Run Average	
Ewing, J. (NY)	2.27
Nichols, K. (Bos)	2.39
Rusie, A. (NY)	2.55

Adjusted ERA	
Nichols, K. (Bos)	153
Ewing, J. (NY)	141
Staley, H. (Bos,Pit)	137

Component ERA

Opponents' Batting Avg.	
Rusie, A. (NY)	.207
Baldwin, M. (Pit)	.227
Ewing, J. (NY)	.228

Adjusted Pitching Runs	
Nichols, K. (Bos)	60
Clarkson, J. (Bos)	45
Staley, H. (Bos,Pit)	36

Win Shares – Pitchers	
Hutchison, B. (Chi)	49
Clarkson, J. (Bos)	42
Nichols, K. (Bos)	39

TPW – Pitchers	
Nichols, K. (Bos)	5.2
Clarkson, J. (Bos)	4.4
Staley, H. (Bos,Pit)	3.3

1891 American Association

TEAM	G	W	L	PCT	GB	R	OR	EW	AB	H	2B	3B	HR	TB	BB	SO	SB	CS	AVG	OBP	SLG	OPS	OPS+	BR/A	PF	RC
BOS	139	93	42	.689	....	**1028**	675	94	4889	**1341**	163	100	52	1860	**651**	499	....	....	**.274**	**.367**	**.380**	**.748**	**121**	**144**	99	**868**
STL	139	85	51	.625	8.5	959	738	85	4942	1311	165	51	**57**	1749	612	436	....	....	.265	.356	.354	.710	95	-50	115	753
MIL	36	21	15	.583	22.5	227	**156**	24	1271	332	58	15	13	459	107	**114**	....	....	.261	.333	.361	.694	86	-34	120	173
BAL	139	71	64	.526	22	850	798	72	4771	1217	142	99	30	1647	551	553	....	....	.255	.346	.345	.691	102	15	101	705
PHI	143	73	66	.525	22	817	794	71	**5039**	1301	**182**	**123**	55	**1894**	447	548	....	....	.258	.328	.376	.704	103	-5	103	686
COL	138	61	76	.445	33	702	777	62	4697	1113	154	61	20	1449	529	530	....	....	.237	.319	.308	.628	89	-49	94	565
CIN	102	43	57	.430	32.5	549	643	42	3574	838	105	58	28	1143	428	385	....	....	.234	.322	.320	.642	81	-97	109	432
LOU	139	54	83	.394	40	698	873	53	4764	1229	127	68	17	1543	438	465	....	....	.258	.329	.324	.653	93	-44	99	606
WAS	139	44	91	.326	49	691	1067	40	4715	1183	147	84	19	1555	468	485	....	....	.251	.328	.330	.658	98	-8	96	597
Total	**557**					**6521**			**38662**	**9865**	**1243**	**659**	**291**		**4231**	**4015**			**.255**	**.338**	**.344**	**.682**				

Runs	
Brown, T. (Bos)	177
Van Haltren, G. (Bal)	136
2 players tied with	134

Hits	
Brown, T. (Bos)	189
Duffy, H. (Bos)	180
Van Haltren, G. (Bal)	180

Doubles	
Milligan, J. (Phi)	35
Brown, T. (Bos)	30
2 players tied with	28

Triples	
Brown, T. (Bos)	21
Brouthers, D. (Bos)	19
2 players tied with	18

Home Runs	
Farrell, D. (Bos)	12
Lyons, D. (StL)	11
Milligan, J. (Phi)	11

Total Bases	
Brown, T. (Bos)	276
Van Haltren, G. (Bal)	251
Brouthers, D. (Bos)	249

Runs Batted In	
Duffy, H. (Bos)	110
Farrell, D. (Bos)	110
Brouthers, D. (Bos)	109

Bases On Balls	
Hoy, D. (StL)	117
Crooks, J. (Col)	103
McTamany, J. (Col,Phi)	101

Stolen Bases	
Brown, T. (Bos)	106
Duffy, H. (Bos)	85
Van Haltren, G. (Bal)	75

Batting Average	
Brouthers, D. (Bos)	.350
Duffy, H. (Bos)	.336
O'Neill, T. (StL)	.323

On-Base Percentage	
Brouthers, D. (Bos)	.471
Lyons, D. (StL)	.445
Hoy, D. (StL)	.424

Slugging Average	
Brouthers, D. (Bos)	.512
Milligan, J. (Phi)	.505
Farrell, D. (Bos)	.474

Adjusted OPS	
Brouthers, D. (Bos)	184
Milligan, J. (Phi)	153
Brown, T. (Bos)	150

Adjusted Batting Runs	
Brouthers, D. (Bos)	60.0
Brown, T. (Bos)	37.0
Duffy, H. (Bos)	34.0

Runs Created/Game	
Brouthers, D. (Bos)	11.30
Brown, T. (Bos)	10.30
Duffy, H. (Bos)	10.20

Fielding Runs	
Corcoran, T. (Phi)	23.6
Eagan, B. (StL)	21.2
Farrell, D. (Bos)	17.3

Win Shares – Batters	
Brown, T. (Bos)	31
Brouthers, D. (Bos)	29
2 players tied with	28

TPW – Batters	
Farrell, D. (Bos)	4.2
Brouthers, D. (Bos)	3.3
Duffy, H. (Bos)	3.1

TEAM	CG	SH	SV	IP	H	H/G	ER	HR	BB	SO	OAV	RAT	ERA	ERA+	CERA	PR+	PF	FA	E	DP	FR	BW	PW	FW	TPW	DIF
BOS	108	**9**	**7**	1219^{2}	1158	8.5	410	42	497	524	.242	1.357	3.03	115	....	35.1	94	.934	392	115	27.5	**12.4**	3.0	2.4	**17.8**	8.2
STL	101	8	5	1206^{2}	1088	8.1	444	50	571	**613**	**.237**	1.375	3.31	129	....	**105.6**	113	.920	459	91	14.4	-4.3	**9.1**	1.2	6.0	11.0
MIL	35	3	0	**3092**	**291**	**0.8**	**86**	**6**	**120**	137	.240	**.133**	**0.25**	175	....	67.1	118	.922	**116**	20	-2.0	-2.9	5.8	-.2	2.7	.3
BAL	118	6	2	1217	1238	9.2	464	33	472	408	.255	1.405	3.43	109	....	60.3	100	.915	503	103	-19.0	1.3	5.2	-1.6	4.8	-.8
PHI	**135**	3	0	1233^{2}	1274	9.3	549	35	520	533	.258	1.454	4.01	95	....	-26.1	103	.933	389	109	0.1	-.4	-2.2	.0	-2.6	6.6
COL	118	6	0	1213^{1}	1141	8.5	505	29	588	502	.240	1.425	3.75	92	....	-73.0	93	**.935**	379	**126**	**34.2**	-4.3	-6.3	**2.9**	-7.6	.6
CIN	86	2	1	902	921	9.2	344	20	446	331	.256	1.516	3.43	120	....	66.2	111	.913	389	68	2.0	-8.4	5.7	.2	-2.5	-4.5
LOU	126	**9**	1	1210	1334	9.9	582	32	451	481	.274	1.475	4.33	85	....	-99.5	98	.922	454	112	8.7	-3.8	-8.6	.8	-11.6	-2.4
WAS	123	2	2	1181	1420	10.8	634	44	566	486	.288	1.682	4.83	**77**	....	-77.1	101	.900	589	95	-65.9	-.7	-6.6	-5.7	-13.0	-10.0
Total	**950**	**48**	**18**	**12475^{1}**		**7.1**	**4018**					**1.130**	**2.90**													

Wins
- McMahon, S. (Bal) 35
- Haddock, G. (Bos) 34
- Stivetts, J. (StL) 33

Win Percentage
- Buffinton, C. (Bos) .... .763
- Haddock, G. (Bos) .... .756
- Sanders, B. (Phi) .... .688

Games
- Stivetts, J. (StL) 64
- McMahon, S. (Bal) 61
- Knell, P. (Col) 58

Complete Games
- McMahon, S. (Bal) 53
- Weyhing, G. (Phi) 51
- Knell, P. (Col) 47

Shutouts
- Haddock, G. (Bos) 5
- Knell, P. (Col) 5
- McMahon, S. (Bal) 5

Saves
- Daley, B. (Bos) 2
- O'Brien, D. (Bos) 2
- 14 players tied with 1

Innings Pitched
- McMahon, S. (Bal) 503
- Knell, P. (Col) 462
- Weyhing, G. (Phi) 450

Fewest Hits/Game
- Knell, P. (Col) 7.07
- Stivetts, J. (StL) 7.30
- Buffinton, C. (Bos) 7.50

Fewest BB/Game
- Stratton, S. (Lou) 1.78
- Sanders, B. (Phi) 2.30
- McMahon, S. (Bal) 2.67

Strikeouts
- Stivetts, J. (StL) 259
- Knell, P. (Col) 228
- 2 players tied with 219

Ratio
- Buffinton, C. (Bos) 1.16
- Haddock, G. (Bos) 1.23
- Knell, P. (Col) 1.27

Earned Run Average
- Crane, E. (Cin) 2.45
- Haddock, G. (Bos) 2.49
- Buffinton, C. (Bos) 2.55

Adjusted ERA
- Crane, E. (Cin) 168
- Stivetts, J. (StL) 147
- Haddock, G. (Bos) 140

Component ERA

Opponents' Batting Avg.
- Knell, P. (Col) .... .209
- Stivetts, J. (StL) .... .214
- Buffinton, C. (Bos) .... .219

Adjusted Pitching Runs
- Stivetts, J. (StL) 60
- McMahon, S. (Bal) 60
- Crane, E. (Cin) 46

Win Shares – Pitchers
- Stivetts, J. (StL) 46
- McMahon, S. (Bal) 39
- Weyhing, G. (Phi) 37

TPW – Pitchers
- Stivetts, J. (StL) 6.1
- McMahon, S. (Bal) 4.9
- Haddock, G. (Bos) 3.5

1892 National League

TEAM	G	W	L	PCT	GB	R	OR	EW	AB	H	2B	3B	HR	TB	BB	SO	SB	CS	AVG	OBP	SLG	OPS	OPS+	BR/A	PF	RC
BOS	152	102	48	.680	....	862	649	96	5301	1325	203	51	34	1732	526	492	338	....	.250	.325	.327	.652	94	-48	109	689
CLE	153	93	56	.624	8.5	855	**613**	98	5412	1376	196	96	26	1842	552	538	225	....	.254	.328	.340	.668	103	16	104	694
BRO	158	95	59	.617	9	**935**	733	95	**5485**	**1439**	183	105	30	1922	**629**	508	**409**	....	**.262**	**.344**	.350	.694	**120**	**145**	96	**822**
PHI	155	87	66	.569	16.5	860	690	93	5413	1420	**225**	95	**50**	**1985**	528	515	216	....	.262	.334	**.367**	**.701**	118	110	100	753
CIN	155	82	68	.547	20	766	731	79	5349	1291	155	75	44	1728	503	476	270	....	.241	.311	.323	.634	98	-14	99	635
PIT	155	80	73	.523	23.5	802	796	77	5469	1288	143	108	38	1761	435	**453**	222	....	.236	.297	.322	.619	92	-64	100	604
CHI	147	70	76	.479	30	635	735	62	5063	1189	149	92	26	1600	427	482	233	....	.235	.299	.316	.615	90	-69	101	561
NY	153	71	80	.470	31.5	811	826	74	5291	1329	173	85	39	1789	510	474	301	....	.251	.321	.338	.659	106	37	98	686
LOU	154	63	89	.414	40	649	804	60	5334	1209	133	61	18	1518	433	508	275	....	.227	.290	.285	.575	85	-79	92	533
WAS	153	58	93	.384	44.5	731	869	63	5204	1246	149	78	37	1662	529	555	276	....	.239	.314	.319	.634	100	5	97	624
STL	155	56	94	.373	46	703	922	55	5259	1188	138	53	45	1567	607	492	209	....	.226	.312	.298	.610	94	-15	95	568
BAL	152	46	101	.313	54.5	779	1020	54	5296	1343	160	**111**	30	1815	499	480	227	....	.254	.325	.343	.668	104	22	103	680
Total	**921**					**9388**			**63876**	**15643**	**2007**	**1010**	**417**		**6178**	**5973**	**3201**		**.245**	**.317**	**.328**	**.644**				

Runs
- Childs, C. (Cle) 136
- Hamilton, B. (Phi) 132
- Duffy, H. (Bos) 125

Hits
- Brouthers, D. (Bro) 197
- Thompson, S. (Phi) 186
- Duffy, H. (Bos) 184

Doubles
- Connor, R. (Phi) 37
- Long, H. (Bos) 33
- 2 players tied with 30

Triples
- Delahanty, E. (Phi) 21
- Brouthers, D. (Bro) 20
- Virtue, J. (Cle) 20

Home Runs
- Holliday, B. (Cin) 13
- Connor, R. (Phi) 12
- 2 players tied with 10

Total Bases
- Brouthers, D. (Bro) 282
- Holliday, B. (Cin) 271
- Thompson, S. (Phi) 263

Runs Batted In
- Brouthers, D. (Bro) 124
- Thompson, S. (Phi) 104
- 3 players tied with 96

Bases On Balls
- Crooks, J. (StL) 136
- Childs, C. (Cle) 117
- Connor, R. (Phi) 116

Stolen Bases
- Ward, J. (Bro) 88
- Brown, T. (Lou) 78
- Latham, A. (Cin) 66

Batting Average
- Brouthers, D. (Bro) .... .335
- Hamilton, B. (Phi) .... .330
- Childs, C. (Cle) .... .317

On-Base Percentage
- Childs, C. (Cle) .... .443
- Brouthers, D. (Bro) .... .432
- Hamilton, B. (Phi) .... .423

Slugging Average
- Delahanty, E. (Phi) .... .495
- Brouthers, D. (Bro) .... .480
- Connor, R. (Phi) .... .463

Adjusted OPS
- Brouthers, D. (Bro) 182
- Connor, R. (Phi) 167
- Burns, O. (Bro) 162

Adjusted Batting Runs
- Brouthers, D. (Bro) 63.0
- Connor, R. (Phi) 52.0
- Childs, C. (Cle) 42.0

Runs Created/Game
- Brouthers, D. (Bro) 9.60
- Hamilton, B. (Phi) 9.00
- Connor, R. (Phi) 8.30

Fielding Runs
- Richardson, D. (Was) 36.0
- Nash, B. (Bos) 28.3
- Smith, G. (Cin) 27.0

Win Shares – Batters
- Brouthers, D. (Bro) 34
- Childs, C. (Cle) 32
- Dahlen, B. (Chi) 32

TPW – Batters
- Brouthers, D. (Bro) 7.0
- Childs, C. (Cle) 5.5
- McPhee, B. (Cin) 4.5

TEAM	CG	SH	SV	IP	H	H/G	ER	HR	BB	SO	OAV	RAT	ERA	ERA+	CERA	PR+	PF	FA	E	DP	FR	BW	PW	FW	TPW	DIF
BOS	142	**15**	1	1336	**1156**	**7.8**	425	41	460	514	**.224**	1.210	2.86	123	2.70	57.0	107	.929	454	127	39.9	-4.5	5.3	3.7	4.5	22.5
CLE	140	11	2	1336	1178	7.9	**358**	28	**413**	472	.227	**1.191**	**2.41**	140	**2.62**	**149.2**	103	.935	407	95	-4.4	1.5	**13.8**	-.4	**14.9**	4.1
BRO	132	12	**5**	**1405^{2}**	1285	8.2	507	26	600	597	.234	1.341	3.25	97	3.18	-16.1	96	**.940**	398	98	2.4	**13.5**	-1.5	.2	12.2	5.8
PHI	131	10	**5**	1379	1309	8.5	449	**24**	492	511	.238	1.306	2.93	111	3.11	26.8	99	.939	**393**	128	20.8	10.1	2.5	1.9	14.5	-3.5
CIN	130	8	2	1377^{1}	1327	8.7	485	39	535	437	.243	1.352	3.17	103	3.40	-11.8	99	.939	402	**140**	26.5	-1.3	-1.1	2.5	.1	6.9
PIT	130	3	1	1347^{1}	1300	8.7	464	28	537	455	.244	1.363	3.10	106	3.40	-13.2	100	.927	483	113	**41.7**	-6.0	-1.2	**3.9**	-3.3	7.3
CHI	133	6	1	1298	1269	8.8	456	35	424	518	.246	1.304	3.16	105	3.20	38.1	101	.932	424	85	-15.0	-6.4	3.5	-1.4	-4.3	1.3
NY	139	5	1	1322^{2}	1165	7.9	483	32	635	**650**	.227	1.361	3.29	98	3.23	5.1	98	.913	565	97	-16.5	3.4	.5	-1.5	2.4	-6.4
LOU	**147**	9	0	1346	1358	9.1	500	26	447	430	.252	1.341	3.34	92	3.32	-51.8	93	.928	471	133	11.1	-7.3	-4.8	1.0	-11.1	-1.9
WAS	129	5	3	1315^{1}	1293	8.8	506	40	556	479	.247	1.406	3.46	94	3.64	-27.6	99	.916	547	122	-3.7	.4	-2.6	-.3	-2.5	-14.5
STL	139	4	1	1344^{2}	1466	9.8	627	47	543	478	.267	1.494	4.20	**76**	4.18	-104.9	97	.929	452	100	-46.1	-1.4	-9.7	-4.3	-15.4	-3.6
BAL	131	2	2	1298^{2}	1537	10.6	617	51	536	437	.283	1.596	4.28	80	4.80	-66.5	104	.910	584	100	-56.8	2.1	-6.2	-5.3	-9.4	-17.6
Total	**1623**	**90**	**24**	**16106^{2}**		**8.7**	**5877**					**1.355**	**3.28**													

Wins
- Hutchison, B. (Chi) 36
- Young, C. (Cle) 36
- 2 players tied with 35

Win Percentage
- Young, C. (Cle) .... .750
- Sullivan, M. (Cin) .... .750
- Haddock, G. (Bro) .... .690

Games
- Hutchison, B. (Chi) 75
- Rusie, A. (NY) 64
- Killen, F. (Was) 60

Complete Games
- Hutchison, B. (Chi) 67
- Rusie, A. (NY) 59
- Nichols, K. (Bos) 49

Shutouts
- Young, C. (Cle) 9
- Stein, E. (Bro) 6
- Weyhing, G. (Phi) 6

Saves
- Weyhing, G. (Phi) 3
- Duryea, J. (Was,Cin) 2
- 19 players tied with 1

Innings Pitched
- Hutchison, B. (Chi) 622
- Rusie, A. (NY) 541
- Weyhing, G. (Phi) .... 469^{2}

Fewest Hits/Game
- Mullane, T. (Cin) 6.77
- Rusie, A. (NY) 6.82
- Terry, A. (Pit,Bal) 6.94

Fewest BB/Game
- Stratton, S. (Lou) 1.79
- Dwyer, F. (Cin,StL) 1.98
- Sanders, B. (Lou) 2.08

Strikeouts
- Hutchison, B. (Chi) 314
- Rusie, A. (NY) 304
- Weyhing, G. (Phi) 202

Ratio
- Young, C. (Cle) 1.06
- Nichols, K. (Bos) 1.16
- Duryea, J. (Was,Cin) 1.17

Earned Run Average
- Young, C. (Cle) 1.93
- Keefe, T. (Phi) 2.36
- Clarkson, J. (Bos,Cle) 2.48

Adjusted ERA
- Young, C. (Cle) 176
- Clarkson, J. (Bos,Cle) 139
- Keefe, T. (Phi) 138

Component ERA
- Young, C. (Cle) 2.02
- Terry, A. (Pit,Bal) 2.50
- Rusie, A. (NY) 2.55

Opponents' Batting Avg.
- Mullane, T. (Cin) .... .201
- Rusie, A. (NY) .... .202
- Terry, A. (Pit,Bal) .... .205

Adjusted Pitching Runs
- Young, C. (Cle) 75
- Hutchison, B. (Chi) 46
- Clarkson, J. (Cle,Bos) 38

Win Shares – Pitchers
- Stivetts, J. (Bos) 49
- Nichols, K. (Bos) 48
- Hutchison, B. (Chi) 45

TPW – Pitchers
- Young, C. (Cle) 6.3
- Hutchison, B. (Chi) 4.5
- Cuppy, N. (Cle) 3.6

1893 National League

TEAM	G	W	L	PCT	GB	R	OR	EW	AB	H	2B	3B	HR	TB	BB	SO	SB	CS	AVG	OBP	SLG	OPS	OPS+	BR/A	PF	RC
BOS	131	86	43	.667	....	1008	795	80	4678	1358	178	50	65	1831	**561**	292	243	....	.290	.372	.391	.763	100	-9	108	790
PIT	131	81	48	.628	5	970	**766**	79	4834	1447	176	**127**	37	1988	537	274	210	....	.299	**.377**	.411	.788	116	**116**	98	848
CLE	129	73	55	.570	12.5	976	839	74	4747	1425	222	98	32	1939	532	**229**	252	....	.300	.374	.408	.783	106	32	106	841
PHI	133	72	57	.558	14	**1011**	841	76	**5151**	**1553**	**246**	90	**80**	**2219**	468	335	202	....	**.301**	.368	**.431**	**.798**	**117**	110	100	**912**
NY	136	68	64	.515	19.5	941	845	73	4858	1424	182	101	61	1991	504	281	**299**	....	.293	.366	.410	.776	110	65	100	860
CIN	131	65	63	.508	20.5	759	814	60	4617	1195	161	65	29	1573	532	256	238	....	.259	.342	.341	.682	84	-106	102	634
BRO	130	65	63	.508	20.5	775	845	58	4511	1200	173	83	45	1674	473	296	213	....	.266	.341	.371	.712	98	-9	95	659
BAL	130	60	70	.462	26.5	820	893	59	4651	1281	164	86	27	1698	539	323	233	....	.275	.359	.365	.724	96	-25	102	711
CHI	128	56	71	.441	29	829	874	60	4664	1299	186	93	32	1767	465	262	255	....	.279	.348	.379	.727	99	-8	98	722
STL	135	57	75	.432	30.5	745	829	59	4879	1288	152	98	10	1666	524	251	250	....	.264	.343	.341	.684	86	-90	100	674
LOU	126	50	75	.400	34	759	942	49	4566	1185	177	73	19	1565	485	306	203	....	.260	.338	.343	.680	92	-30	92	612
WAS	130	40	89	.310	46	722	1032	42	4742	1258	180	83	23	1673	523	237	154	....	.265	.346	.353	.699	93	-37	97	650
Total	**785**					**10315**			**56898**	**15913**	**2197**	**1047**	**460**		**6143**	**3342**	**2752**		**.280**	**.356**	**.379**	**.736**				

Runs
Long, H. (Bos) 149
Duffy, H. (Bos) 147
3 players tied with 145

Hits
Thompson, S. (Phi) 222
Delahanty, E. (Phi) 219
Duffy, H. (Bos) 203

Doubles
Thompson, S. (Phi) 37
Delahanty, E. (Phi) 35
2 players tied with 32

Triples
Werden, P. (StL) 29
Davis, G. (NY) 27
McKean, E. (Cle) 24

Home Runs
Delahanty, E. (Phi) 19
Clements, J. (Phi) 17
2 players tied with 14

Total Bases
Delahanty, E. (Phi) 347
Thompson, S. (Phi) 318
Davis, G. (NY) 304

Runs Batted In
Delahanty, E. (Phi) 146
McKean, E. (Cle) 133
Thompson, S. (Phi) 126

Bases On Balls
Crooks, J. (StL) 121
Childs, C. (Cle) 120
Radford, P. (Was) 104

Stolen Bases
Brown, T. (Lou) 66
Dowd, T. (StL) 59
Latham, A. (Cin) 57

Batting Average
Duffy, H. (Bos) .... .362
Hamilton, B. (Phi) .... .380
Thompson, S. (Phi) .... .370

On-Base Percentage
Hamilton, B. (Phi) .... .490
Childs, C. (Cle) .... .463
Burkett, J. (Cle) .... .459

Slugging Average
Delahanty, E. (Phi) .... .583
Davis, G. (NY) .... .554
Thompson, S. (Phi) .... .530

Adjusted OPS
Hamilton, B. (Phi) 170
Delahanty, E. (Phi) 167
Smith, E. (Pit) 158

Adjusted Batting Runs
Delahanty, E. (Phi) 53.0
Smith, E. (Pit) 44.0
Thompson, S. (Phi) 44.0

Runs Created/Game
Hamilton, B. (Phi) 13.80
Delahanty, E. (Phi) 11.70
Burkett, J. (Cle) 10.90

Fielding Runs
McPhee, B. (Cin) 27.0
Delahanty, E. (Phi) 22.4
Long, H. (Bos) 22.3

Win Shares – Batters
Delahanty, E. (Phi) 28
Duffy, H. (Bos) 28
Long, H. (Bos) 26

TPW – Batters
Delahanty, E. (Phi) 5.4
McPhee, B. (Cin) 3.3
Davis, G. (NY) 3.2

TEAM	CG	SH	SV	IP	H	H/G	ER	HR	BB	SO	OAV	RAT	ERA	ERA+	CERA	PR+	PF	FA	E	DP	FR	BW	PW	FW	TPW	DIF
BOS	**114**	2	2	1163^{2}	1314	10.2	572	66	402	253	.276	**1.475**	4.42	111	4.43	51.5	106	.936	353	118	12.5	-.8	4.2	1.0	4.5	17.5
PIT	104	**8**	2	1167	**1232**	9.5	**529**	29	504	280	.263	1.488	4.08	111	**4.06**	28.3	98	.939	347	112	**32.1**	**9.5**	2.3	**2.6**	**14.5**	2.5
CLE	110	2	2	1140^{1}	1361	10.7	532	35	**356**	242	.288	1.506	4.20	116	4.39	92.2	105	.929	395	92	-6.1	2.6	7.6	-.5	9.7	-.7
PHI	107	4	2	1189	1357	10.3	618	30	522	286	.279	1.580	4.68	98	4.51	-33.2	98	**.944**	**318**	121	19.2	9.0	-2.7	1.6	7.9	.1
NY	111	6	4	**1211**^{1}	1271	**9.4**	577	36	581	**395**	**.262**	1.529	4.29	108	4.21	35.4	100	.927	432	95	12.2	5.3	2.9	1.0	9.2	-7.2
CIN	97	4	**5**	1172	1305	10.0	593	38	549	258	.274	1.582	4.55	105	4.55	12.1	103	.943	321	**138**	18.0	-8.7	1.0	1.5	-6.2	7.2
BRO	109	3	3	1154	1262	9.8	583	41	547	297	.270	1.568	4.55	97	4.46	-3.2	95	.930	385	88	-13.0	-.7	-.3	-1.1	-2.1	3.1
BAL	104	1	2	1123^{2}	1325	10.6	620	29	534	275	.285	1.654	4.97	95	4.88	-7.5	102	.929	384	95	-21.9	-2.0	-.6	-1.8	-4.4	-.6
CHI	101	4	**5**	1117^{1}	1278	10.3	597	**26**	553	273	.279	1.639	4.81	96	4.76	-19.2	99	.922	421	92	-3.2	-.7	-1.6	-.3	-2.5	-4.5
STL	**114**	3	4	1207	1292	9.6	544	38	542	301	.266	1.519	**4.06**	116	4.22	**93.4**	101	.930	398	110	-4.7	-7.4	**7.7**	-.4	-.1	-8.9
LOU	113	4	1	1080	1431	11.9	708	38	479	190	.309	1.769	5.90	**74**	5.69	-164.9	94	.937	330	111	-15.9	-2.5	-13.5	-1.3	-17.3	5.3
WAS	110	2	0	1139	1485	11.7	704	54	574	292	.306	1.808	5.56	83	5.95	-89.6	99	.912	497	96	-29.7	-3.1	-7.3	-2.4	-12.9	-11.1
Total	**1294**	**43**	**32**	**13864**^{1}		**10.3**	**7177**					**1.591**	**4.66**													

Wins
Killen, F. (Pit)..... 36
Nichols, K. (Bos) 34
Young, C. (Cle) 34

Win Percentage
Killen, F. (Pit).................... .720
Nichols, K. (Bos) .... .708
Young, C. (Cle) .... .680

Games
Rusie, A. (NY).................... 56
Killen, F. (Pit).................... 55
Young, C. (Cle) 53

Complete Games
Rusie, A. (NY).................... 50
Nichols, K. (Bos) 43
Young, C. (Cle) 42

Shutouts
Ehret, R. (Pit).................... 4
Rusie, A. (NY).................... 4
6 players tied with 2

Saves
5 players tied with 2

Innings Pitched
Rusie, A. (NY).................... 482
Nichols, K. (Bos) 425
Young, C. (Cle) .... 422^{2}

Fewest Hits/Game
Rusie, A. (NY).................... 8.42
Breitenstein, T. (StL) 8.44
Killen, F. (Pit).................... 8.70

Fewest BB/Game
Young, C. (Cle) 2.19
Nichols, K. (Bos) 2.50
Cuppy, N. (Cle) 2.77

Strikeouts
Rusie, A. (NY).................... 208
Kennedy, B. (Bro) 107
2 players tied with 102

Ratio
Nichols, K. (Bos) 1.28
Young, C. (Cle) 1.29
Killen, F. (Pit).................... 1.30

Earned Run Average
Breitenstein, T. (StL)......... 3.18
Rusie, A. (NY).................... 3.23
Young, C. (Cle) 3.36

Adjusted ERA
Breitenstein, T. (StL) 149
Young, C. (Cle) 145
Rusie, A. (NY).................... 144

Component ERA
Breitenstein, T. (StL) 3.13
Killen, F. (Pit).................... 3.22
Young, C. (Cle) 3.25

Opponents' Batting Avg.
Rusie, A. (NY).................... .240
Breitenstein, T. (StL) .... .241
Killen, F. (Pit).................... .246

Adjusted Pitching Runs
Young, C. (Cle) 73
Rusie, A. (NY).................... 71
Breitenstein, T. (StL) 67

Win Shares – Pitchers
Killen, F. (Pit).................... 42
Rusie, A. (NY).................... 41
Nichols, K. (Bos) 40

TPW – Pitchers
Rusie, A. (NY).................... 6.1
Young, C. (Cle) 5.6
Breitenstein, T. (StL).......... 5.2

1894 National League

TEAM	G	W	L	PCT	GB	R	OR	EW	AB	H	2B	3B	HR	TB	BB	SO	SB	CS	AVG	OBP	SLG	OPS	OPS+	BR/A	PF	RC
BAL	129	89	39	.695	....	1171	819	86	4799	1647	271	**150**	33	2317	516	**200**	324	....	.343	**.418**	.483	**.901**	116	129	104	**1131**
NY	139	88	44	.667	3	962	**801**	78	4879	1469	199	96	45	1995	489	219	325	....	.301	.369	.409	.777	92	-60	99	860
BOS	133	83	49	.629	8	**1220**	1002	79	5011	1658	**272**	94	**103**	2427	535	261	241	....	.331	.401	**.484**	.885	104	7	113	1095
PHI	132	71	57	.555	18	1179	995	75	**5089**	**1780**	259	137	40	**2433**	508	254	285	....	**.350**	.415	.478	.893	**122**	**188**	97	1120
BRO	135	70	61	.534	20.5	1024	1020	66	4851	1514	231	130	42	2131	467	295	282	....	.312	.376	.439	.816	109	80	93	930
CLE	130	68	61	.527	21.5	932	896	67	4764	1442	241	90	37	1974	471	301	220	....	.303	.368	.414	.783	89	-91	104	828
PIT	133	65	65	.500	25	965	1001	63	4700	1465	223	125	48	2082	444	210	257	....	.312	.379	.443	.822	103	21	99	903
CHI	137	57	75	.432	34	1056	1080	65	5022	1574	268	87	65	2211	507	306	**329**	....	.313	.380	.440	.821	97	-39	105	979
STL	133	56	76	.424	35	771	953	52	4610	1320	171	113	54	1879	442	289	190	....	.286	.354	.408	.761	87	-100	100	750
CIN	134	55	75	.423	35	936	1108	54	4753	1407	228	71	61	1960	517	255	223	....	.296	.370	.412	.782	88	-93	104	804
WAS	132	45	87	.341	46	882	1122	50	4581	1317	218	118	59	1948	**617**	375	249	....	.287	.381	.425	.806	102	29	97	857
LOU	131	36	94	.277	54	698	1019	42	4518	1216	173	89	42	1693	355	368	219	....	.269	.330	.375	.705	79	-145	93	641
Total	**799**					**11796**			**57577**	**17809**	**2754**	**1300**	**629**		**5868**	**3333**	**3144**		**.309**	**.379**	**.435**	**.814**				

Runs
Hamilton, B. (Phi)............. 198
Keeler, W. (Bal) 165
Kelley, J. (Bal) 165

Hits
Duffy, H. (Bos) 237
Hamilton, B. (Phi)............. 225
Keeler, W. (Bal) 219

Doubles
Duffy, H. (Bos) 51
Kelley, J. (Bal) 48
Wilmot, W. (Chi) 45

Triples
Reitz, H. (Bal) 31
Thompson, S. (Phi) 28
Treadway, G. (Bro)............ 26

Home Runs
Duffy, H. (Bos) 18
Joyce, B. (Was) 17
Lowe, B. (Bos) 17

Total Bases
Duffy, H. (Bos).................... 374
Lowe, B. (Bos) 319
Thompson, S. (Phi)............ 314

Runs Batted In
Thompson, S. (Phi) 147
Duffy, H. (Bos).................. 145
Delahanty, E. (Phi) 133

Bases On Balls
Hamilton, B. (Phi)............. 128
Childs, C. (Cle) 107
Kelley, J. (Bal) 107

Stolen Bases
Hamilton, B. (Phi)............. 100
McGraw, J. (Bal)................ 78
Wilmot, W. (Chi) 76

Batting Average
Duffy, H. (Bos) .... .440
Thompson, S. (Phi) .... .415
Delahanty, E. (Phi) .... .404

On-Base Percentage
Hamilton, B. (Phi)............. .521
Kelley, J. (Bal) .... .502
Duffy, H. (Bos).................. .502

Slugging Average
Thompson, S. (Phi)............ .696
Duffy, H. (Bos).................... .694
Joyce, B. (Was).................. .648

Adjusted OPS
Thompson, S. (Phi) 182
Joyce, B. (Was) 180
Duffy, H. (Bos).................. 165

Adjusted Batting Runs
Hamilton, B. (Phi)............. 66.0
Thompson, S. (Phi) 57.0
Duffy, H. (Bos).................. 57.0

Runs Created/Game
Duffy, H. (Bos) 18.70
Hamilton, B. (Phi)............. 16.30
Thompson, S. (Phi) 16.00

Fielding Runs
Jennings, H. (Bal) 29.5
Cross, L. (Phi) 24.8
Reitz, H. (Bal) 16.4

Win Shares – Batters
Duffy, H. (Bos).................. 33
Kelley, J. (Bal) 30
Hamilton, B. (Phi)............. 29

TPW – Batters
Hamilton, B. (Phi) 4.3
Cross, L. (Phi) 4.2
Delahanty, E. (Phi)............ 4.0

TEAM	CG	SH	SV	IP	H	H/G	ER	HR	BB	SO	OAV	RAT	ERA	ERA+	CERA	PR+	PF	FA	E	DP	FR	BW	PW	FW	TPW	DIF
BAL	97	1	**11**	1116^1	1371	11.0	620	**31**	472	275	.299	1.651	5.00	109	4.99	27.7	103	**.944**	**293**	105	33.3	9.9	2.1	2.6	**14.6**	10.4
NY	113	5	5	**1230**	**1310**	**9.6**	**516**	37	546	**403**	**.268**	**1.509**	**3.78**	137	**4.15**	**183.2**	98	.924	454	103	11.2	-4.6	**14.0**	.9	10.3	11.7
BOS	108	3	2	1166	1529	11.8	701	89	**411**	262	.313	1.664	5.41	109	5.60	29.6	111	.925	415	120	**34.8**	.6	2.3	**2.7**	5.5	11.5
PHI	103	3	4	1151^2	1522	11.9	704	62	479	266	.307	1.737	5.50	90	5.86	-37.1	96	.935	351	114	-14.5	**14.4**	-3.4	-1.1	10.0	-3.0
BRO	106	3	5	1171^1	1465	11.3	711	41	558	290	.299	1.727	5.46	**90**	5.50	-55.3	93	.928	393	85	-13.7	6.1	-4.2	-1.1	.8	4.2
CLE	106	**6**	2	1124^1	1390	11.1	621	54	435	254	.301	1.623	4.97	110	5.00	61.8	103	.935	344	107	-1.3	-7.0	4.7	-.1	-2.3	6.3
PIT	106	2	0	1170^2	1563	12.0	724	39	466	308	.315	1.733	5.57	93	5.56	-41.9	98	.936	355	106	-2.4	1.6	-3.2	-.2	-1.8	1.8
CHI	**118**	0	0	1163	1575	12.2	725	43	569	284	.317	1.844	5.61	99	6.18	15.6	105	.918	458	115	-23.7	-3.0	1.2	-1.8	-3.6	-5.4
STL	114	2	0	1161	1418	11.0	682	48	500	319	.298	1.652	5.29	102	5.05	15.0	102	.923	426	109	0.5	-7.7	1.2	.0	-6.5	-3.5
CIN	112	4	3	1165^1	1615	12.5	763	85	500	223	.319	1.815	5.89	93	6.41	-47.7	104	.925	430	122	3.2	-7.2	-3.7	.2	-10.6	.6
WAS	101	0	4	1107	1573	12.8	678	59	446	190	.331	1.824	5.51	95	6.35	-4.7	99	.908	499	81	-26.1	2.2	-.4	-2.0	-.2	-20.8
LOU	114	2	1	1104^2	1478	12.0	664	41	486	259	.314	1.778	5.41	93	5.85	-37.6	96	.920	435	**131**	-1.5	-11.1	-2.9	-.1	-14.1	-14.9
Total	**1298**	**31**	**37**	**13831^1**		**11.6**	**8109**					**1.712**	**5.28**													

Wins
Rusie, A. (NY) 36
Meekin, J. (NY) 33
Nichols, K. (Bos) 32

Win Percentage
Meekin, J. (NY) .786
McMahon, S. (Bal) .758
Rusie, A. (NY) .735

Games
Breitenstein, T. (StL) 56
Rusie, A. (NY) 54
Hawley, P. (StL) 53

Complete Games
Breitenstein, T. (StL) 46
Rusie, A. (NY) 45
Young, C. (Cle) 44

Shutouts
Cuppy, N. (Cle) 3
Nichols, K. (Bos) 3
Rusie, A. (NY) 3

Saves
Mullane, T. (Bal,Cle) 4
Hawke, B. (Bal) 3
Mercer, W. (Was) 3

Innings Pitched
Breitenstein, T. (StL) 447^1
Rusie, A. (NY) 444
Meekin, J. (NY) 409

Fewest Hits/Game
Rusie, A. (NY) 8.64
Meekin, J. (NY) 8.89
Stein, E. (Bro) 9.98

Fewest BB/Game
Young, C. (Cle) 2.33
Menefee, J. (Lou,Pit) 2.48
Gleason, K. (Bal,StL) 2.54

Strikeouts
Rusie, A. (NY) 195
Breitenstein, T. (StL) 140
Meekin, J. (NY) 137

Ratio
Rusie, A. (NY) 1.41
Meekin, J. (NY) 1.42
Young, C. (Cle) 1.45

Earned Run Average
Rusie, A. (NY) 2.78
Meekin, J. (NY) 3.70
Mercer, W. (Was) 3.82

Adjusted ERA
Rusie, A. (NY) 189
Meekin, J. (NY) 142
Young, C. (Cle) 138

Component ERA
Rusie, A. (NY) 3.43
Meekin, J. (NY) 3.59
Clarkson, J. (Cle) 4.03

Opponents' Batting Avg.
Rusie, A. (NY) .250
Meekin, J. (NY) .256
Stein, E. (Bro) .278

Adjusted Pitching Runs
Rusie, A. (NY) 117
Young, C. (Cle) 69
Meekin, J. (NY) 66

Win Shares – Pitchers
Rusie, A. (NY) 56
Meekin, J. (NY) 48
Young, C. (Cle) 39

TPW – Pitchers
Rusie, A. (NY) 9.2
Meekin, J. (NY) 5.6
Mercer, W. (Was) 5.0

1895 National League

TEAM	G	W	L	PCT	GB	R	OR	EW	AB	H	2B	3B	HR	TB	BB	SO	SB	CS	AVG	OBP	SLG	OPS	OPS+	BR/A	PF	RC
BAL	132	87	43	.669	....	1009	**646**	92	4725	1530	235	89	25	2018	355	243	310	....	.324	.384	.427	.811	110	66	103	930
CLE	132	84	46	.646	3	921	725	80	4692	1433	194	69	29	1852	476	365	188	....	.305	.375	.395	.770	97	-20	106	790
PHI	133	78	53	.595	9.5	**1068**	957	73	**5037**	**1664**	**272**	73	**61**	**2265**	463	262	276	....	**.330**	**.394**	**.450**	**.844**	**121**	**157**	100	**1040**
CHI	133	72	58	.554	15	866	854	66	4708	1401	171	85	55	1907	422	344	260	....	.298	.361	.405	.766	95	-47	106	810
BRO	134	71	60	.542	16.5	879	838	69	4757	1346	191	78	41	1816	397	319	184	....	.283	.346	.382	.728	99	6	92	707
BOS	133	71	60	.542	16.5	911	829	72	4750	1377	198	57	54	1851	505	**239**	200	....	.290	.364	.390	.754	94	-47	105	778
PIT	135	71	61	.538	17	815	799	67	4677	1355	192	89	27	1806	378	301	257	....	.290	.351	.386	.737	99	5	95	753
CIN	132	66	64	.508	21	903	854	69	4684	1395	235	**105**	36	1948	414	249	**326**	....	.298	.359	.416	.775	99	-17	104	844
NY	132	66	65	.504	21.5	852	834	67	4605	1324	191	90	32	1791	454	292	292	....	.288	.355	.389	.744	98	-8	98	763
WAS	133	43	85	.336	43	840	1052	50	4615	1326	209	101	55	1902	**522**	403	238	....	.287	.366	.412	.778	106	45	99	805
STL	136	39	92	.298	48.5	752	1036	45	4814	1356	155	88	39	1804	388	283	208	....	.282	.339	.375	.714	88	-84	99	699
LOU	133	35	96	.267	52.5	698	1090	38	4724	1320	171	73	34	1739	346	323	156	....	.279	.339	.368	.707	92	-49	94	665
Total	**799**					**10514**			**56788**	**16827**	**2414**	**997**	**488**		**5120**	**3623**	**2895**		**.296**	**.361**	**.400**	**.761**				

Runs
Hamilton, B. (Phi) 166
Keeler, W. (Bal) 162
Jennings, H. (Bal) 159

Hits
Burkett, J. (Cle) 225
Keeler, W. (Bal) 213
Thompson, S. (Phi) 211

Doubles
Delahanty, E. (Phi) 49
Thompson, S. (Phi) 45
Jennings, H. (Bal) 41

Triples
Selbach, K. (Was) 22
Thompson, S. (Phi) 21
Tiernan, M. (NY) 21

Home Runs
Thompson, S. (Phi) 18
Joyce, B. (Was) 17
Clements, J. (Phi) 13

Total Bases
Thompson, S. (Phi) 352
Delahanty, E. (Phi) 296
Burkett, J. (Cle) 288

Runs Batted In
Thompson, S. (Phi) 165
Brodie, S. (Bal) 134
Kelley, J. (Bal) 134

Bases On Balls
Hamilton, B. (Phi) 96
Joyce, B. (Was) 96
Griffin, M. (Bro) 93

Stolen Bases
Hamilton, B. (Phi) 97
Lange, B. (Chi) 67
McGraw, J. (Bal) 61

Batting Average
Burkett, J. (Cle) .405
Delahanty, E. (Phi) .404
Thompson, S. (Phi) .392

On-Base Percentage
Delahanty, E. (Phi) .500
Hamilton, B. (Phi) .490
Burkett, J. (Cle) .482

Slugging Average
Thompson, S. (Phi) .654
Delahanty, E. (Phi) .617
Lange, B. (Chi) .575

Adjusted OPS
Delahanty, E. (Phi) 186
Thompson, S. (Phi) 176
Stenzel, J. (Pit) 160

Adjusted Batting Runs
Delahanty, E. (Phi) 67.0
Thompson, S. (Phi) 56.0
Hamilton, B. (Phi) 50.0

Runs Created/Game
Delahanty, E. (Phi) 16.20
Hamilton, B. (Phi) 14.80
Lange, B. (Chi) 14.40

Fielding Runs
Jennings, H. (Bal) 47.5
Cross, L. (Phi) 33.1
Dahlen, B. (Chi) 26.6

Win Shares – Batters
Burkett, J. (Cle) 35
Delahanty, E. (Phi) 31
Hamilton, B. (Phi) 30

TPW – Batters
Jennings, H. (Bal) 7.1
Thompson, S. (Phi) 5.0
Delahanty, E. (Phi) 4.5

TEAM	CG	SH	SV	IP	H	H/G	ER	HR	BB	SO	OAV	RAT	ERA	ERA+	CERA	PR+	PF	FA	E	DP	FR	BW	PW	FW	TPW	DIF
BAL	104	**10**	4	1134^1	**1216**	**9.6**	**479**	31	430	244	.270	1.451	**3.80**	125	3.93	51.1	100	**.946**	**288**	108	**69.2**	5.4	4.1	**5.6**	**15.1**	6.9
CLE	109	6	3	1151^2	1284	10.0	497	34	**350**	330	.275	**1.419**	3.88	127	**3.88**	**140.5**	104	.936	351	77	0.0	-1.7	**11.4**	.0	9.7	9.3
PHI	106	2	**7**	1161	1467	11.4	706	36	485	330	.304	1.681	5.47	87	5.15	-84.7	100	.933	369	93	-3.3	**12.7**	-6.9	-.3	5.6	7.4
CHI	**119**	3	1	1150^2	1422	11.1	597	38	432	297	.299	1.611	4.67	109	4.96	55.7	106	.928	401	**113**	-2.9	-3.8	4.5	-.2	.5	6.5
BRO	104	5	6	1159^2	1366	10.6	631	42	397	218	.288	1.520	4.90	89	4.45	-81.0	92	.941	326	97	14.6	.4	-6.6	1.2	-4.9	10.9
BOS	117	4	4	**1185^1**	1376	10.4	557	56	367	377	.284	1.470	4.23	117	4.38	91.0	104	.934	365	106	8.2	-3.8	7.4	.7	4.3	1.7
PIT	107	4	6	1179^2	1279	9.8	527	**19**	500	383	**.269**	1.508	4.02	111	4.24	62.8	94	.930	394	95	1.7	.4	5.1	.1	5.6	-.6
CIN	97	2	6	1147^1	1451	11.4	613	39	362	245	.304	1.580	4.81	103	4.83	15.3	104	.931	377	112	4.8	-1.4	1.2	.4	.2	.8
NY	115	6	1	1147^1	1359	10.7	575	34	415	**409**	.290	1.546	4.51	103	4.54	7.6	97	.922	438	106	8.5	-.7	.6	.7	.6	.4
WAS	99	0	5	1111^1	1515	12.3	646	55	470	261	.319	1.786	5.23	91	6.10	-34.7	100	.917	450	97	-19.2	3.6	-2.8	-1.6	-.7	-20.3
STL	106	1	1	1161^1	1572	12.2	737	64	443	284	.317	1.735	5.71	84	5.87	-82.6	101	.930	383	94	-31.9	-6.8	-6.7	-2.6	-16.1	-9.9
LOU	104	3	1	1117^1	1520	12.2	732	40	469	245	.320	1.780	5.90	**78**	5.78	-101.7	97	.913	477	104	-49.5	-3.9	-8.2	-4.0	-16.2	-13.8
Total	**1287**	**46**	**45**	**13807**		**11.0**	**7297**					**1.590**	**4.76**													

Wins
Young, C. (Cle) 35
Hawley, P. (Pit) 31
Hoffer, B. (Bal) 31

Win Percentage
Hoffer, B. (Bal) .838
Young, C. (Cle) .778
Maul, A. (Was) .667

Games
Hawley, P. (Pit) 56
Breitenstein, T. (StL) 55
Rusie, A. (NY) 49

Complete Games
Breitenstein, T. (StL) 47
Hawley, P. (Pit) 44
Nichols, K. (Bos) 43

Shutouts
5 players tied with 4

Saves
Beam, E. (Phi) 3
Nichols, K. (Bos) 3
Parrott, T. (Cin) 3

Innings Pitched
Hawley, P. (Pit) 444^1
Breitenstein, T. (StL) 438
Rusie, A. (NY) 393^1

Fewest Hits/Game
Foreman, B. (Pit) 8.44
Hoffer, B. (Bal) 8.48
Rusie, A. (NY) 8.79

Fewest BB/Game
Young, C. (Cle) 1.83
Clarke, D. (NY) 1.92
Nichols, K. (Bos) 2.08

Strikeouts
Rusie, A. (NY) 201
Nichols, K. (Bos) 147
Hawley, P. (Pit) 142

Ratio
Young, C. (Cle) 1.18
Maul, A. (Was) 1.28
Hawley, P. (Pit) 1.29

Earned Run Average
Maul, A. (Was) 2.45
Hawley, P. (Pit) 3.18
Hoffer, B. (Bal) 3.21

Adjusted ERA
Maul, A. (Was) 195
Young, C. (Cle) 153
Nichols, K. (Bos) 150

Component ERA
Young, C. (Cle) 2.70
Maul, A. (Was) 3.20
Hawley, P. (Pit) 3.28

Opponents' Batting Avg.
Foreman, B. (Pit) .245
Hoffer, B. (Bal) .246
Rusie, A. (NY) .252

Adjusted Pitching Runs
Young, C. (Cle) 71
Nichols, K. (Bos) 69
Hawley, P. (Pit) 65

Win Shares – Pitchers
Hawley, P. (Pit) 44
Young, C. (Cle) 37
Hoffer, B. (Bal) 35

TPW – Pitchers
Hawley, P. (Pit) 6.4
Young, C. (Cle) 5.4
Nichols, K. (Bos) 5.4

1896 National League

TEAM	G	W	L	PCT	GB	R	OR	EW	AB	H	2B	3B	HR	TB	BB	SO	SB	CS	AVG	OBP	SLG	OPS	OPS+	BR/A	PF	RC
BAL	132	90	39	.698	....	**995**	662	89	4719	**1548**	207	**100**	23	**2024**	386	**201**	**441**	....	**.328**	**.393**	**.429**	**.822**	**120**	**139**	101	**1003**
CLE	135	80	48	.625	9.5	840	650	80	**4856**	1463	207	72	28	1898	436	316	175	....	.301	.363	.391	.754	98	-19	106	785
CIN	128	77	50	.606	12	783	**620**	78	4360	1283	204	73	20	1693	382	226	350	....	.294	.357	.388	.745	95	-40	107	761
BOS	132	74	57	.565	17	865	761	74	4723	1421	175	75	36	1854	414	275	243	....	.301	.364	.393	.756	98	-20	106	791
CHI	132	71	57	.555	18.5	815	804	65	4582	1311	182	97	34	1789	409	290	332	....	.286	.349	.390	.740	96	-36	104	769
PIT	131	66	63	.512	24	787	741	68	4701	1371	169	94	27	1809	387	286	217	....	.292	.353	.385	.738	103	26	96	746
NY	133	64	67	.489	27	829	821	66	4661	1383	159	87	40	1836	439	271	274	....	.297	.364	.394	.758	107	56	97	795
PHI	130	62	68	.477	28.5	890	891	65	4680	1382	**234**	84	**49**	1931	438	297	191	....	.295	.363	.413	.776	110	68	99	801
WAS	133	58	73	.443	33	818	920	58	4639	1328	179	79	45	1800	**516**	365	258	....	.286	.365	.388	.753	103	32	100	783
BRO	133	58	73	.443	33	692	764	59	4548	1292	174	87	28	1724	344	269	198	....	.284	.340	.379	.719	99	-2	94	680
STL	131	40	90	.308	50.5	593	929	38	4520	1162	134	78	37	1563	332	300	185	....	.257	.313	.346	.659	81	-123	96	572
LOU	134	38	93	.290	53	653	997	39	4588	1197	142	80	37	1610	371	427	195	....	.261	.322	.351	.673	85	-96	96	603
Total	**792**					**9560**			**55577**	**16141**	**2166**	**1006**	**404**		**4854**	**3523**	**3059**		**.290**	**.354**	**.387**	**.742**				

Runs
Burkett, J. (Cle) 160
Hamilton, B. (Bos) 153
Keeler, W. (Bal) 153

Hits
Burkett, J. (Cle) 240
Keeler, W. (Bal) 210
Jennings, H. (Bal) 209

Doubles
Delahanty, E. (Phi) 44
Miller, D. (Cin) 38
Kelley, J. (Bal) 31

Triples
McCreery, T. (Lou) 21
Van Haltren, G. (NY) 21
2 players tied with 19

Home Runs
Delahanty, E. (Phi) 13
Joyce, B. (Was,NY) 13
Thompson, S. (Phi) 12

Total Bases
Burkett, J. (Cle) 317
Delahanty, E. (Phi) 315
Kelley, J. (Bal) 282

Runs Batted In
Delahanty, E. (Phi) 126
Jennings, H. (Bal) 121
Duffy, H. (Bos) 113

Bases On Balls
Hamilton, B. (Bos) 110
Joyce, B. (Was,NY) 101
Childs, C. (Cle) 100

Stolen Bases
Kelley, J. (Bal) 87
Lange, B. (Chi) 84
Hamilton, B. (Bos) 83

Batting Average
Burkett, J. (Cle) .410
Jennings, H. (Bal) .401
Delahanty, E. (Phi) .397

On-Base Percentage
Hamilton, B. (Bos) .479
Jennings, H. (Bal) .472
Delahanty, E. (Phi) .472

Slugging Average
Delahanty, E. (Phi) .631
Dahlen, B. (Chi) .553
McCreery, T. (Lou) .546

Adjusted OPS
Delahanty, E. (Phi) 191
Kelley, J. (Bal) 164
Joyce, B. (NY,Was) 162

Adjusted Batting Runs
Delahanty, E. (Phi) 67.0
Kelley, J. (Bal) 54.0
Joyce, B. (Was,NY) 51.0

Runs Created/Game
Delahanty, E. (Phi) 14.80
Kelley, J. (Bal) 14.10
Jennings, H. (Bal) 12.90

Fielding Runs
Jennings, H. (Bal) 43.7
Childs, C. (Cle) 32.8
Dahlen, B. (Chi) 24.1

Win Shares – Batters
Jennings, H. (Bal) 36
3 players tied with 31

TPW – Batters
Jennings, H. (Bal) 7.9
Childs, C. (Cle) 6.0
Dahlen, B. (Chi) 5.8

TEAM	CG	SH	SV	IP	H	H/G	ER	HR	BB	SO	OAV	RAT	ERA	ERA+	CERA	PR+	PF	FA	E	DP	FR	BW	PW	FW	TPW	DIF
BAL	115	9	1	1168[1]	1281	9.9	476	22	339	302	.277	1.387	3.67	116	**3.67**	56.9	98	.945	296	114	20.8	**11.8**	4.8	1.8	**18.4**	7.6
CLE	113	9	**5**	**1195**[2]	1363	10.3	459	27	**280**	336	.285	**1.374**	**3.45**	131	3.69	**142.8**	104	.949	288	**117**	-1.2	-1.6	**12.1**	-.1	10.4	5.6
CIN	105	**12**	4	1108	**1240**	10.1	**452**	27	310	219	.281	1.399	3.67	125	3.85	90.5	106	**.951**	**252**	107	24.3	-3.4	7.7	2.1	6.4	7.6
BOS	110	6	3	1155[2]	1254	**9.8**	485	57	397	277	**.275**	1.429	3.78	120	3.97	67.6	104	.934	368	94	**29.8**	-1.7	5.7	**2.5**	6.6	2.4
CHI	**118**	2	1	1161[1]	1307	10.1	569	30	467	354	.281	1.528	4.41	103	4.35	-5.2	104	.933	367	115	16.4	-3.1	-.4	1.4	-2.1	9.1
PIT	108	8	1	1159[1]	1286	10.0	554	**18**	439	**362**	.279	1.488	4.30	97	4.13	-16.5	96	.941	317	103	2.5	2.2	-1.4	.2	1.0	1.0
NY	104	1	2	1136[2]	1303	10.3	573	33	403	312	.286	1.501	4.54	93	4.32	-49.8	96	.933	365	90	6.5	4.8	-4.2	.6	1.1	-2.1
PHI	107	3	2	1117	1473	11.9	645	39	387	243	.315	1.665	5.20	83	5.19	-97.8	99	.941	313	112	-13.2	5.8	-8.3	-1.1	-3.6	.6
WAS	106	2	3	1136[2]	1435	11.4	582	24	435	292	.306	1.645	4.61	95	5.09	-3.3	101	.927	398	99	-22.9	2.7	-.3	-1.9	.5	-7.5
BRO	97	3	1	1144	1353	10.6	540	39	400	259	.292	1.532	4.25	97	4.44	-9.5	95	.945	297	104	-7.0	-.1	-.8	-.6	-1.5	-5.5
STL	115	1	1	1130[2]	1448	11.5	669	40	456	279	.309	1.684	5.33	**82**	5.28	-91.2	100	.936	345	73	-31.1	-10.5	-7.7	-2.6	-20.8	-4.2
LOU	108	1	4	1148[2]	1398	11.0	653	48	541	288	.298	1.688	5.12	84	5.31	-77.6	99	.916	475	110	-25.1	-8.1	-6.6	-2.1	-16.9	-10.1
Total	**1306**	**57**	**28**	**13762**		**10.6**	**6657**					**1.526**	**4.35**													

Wins
Killen, F. (Pit) 30
Nichols, K. (Bos) 30
Young, C. (Cle) 28

Win Percentage
Hoffer, B. (Bal) .781
Esper, D. (Bal) .737
Hemming, G. (Bal) .714

Games
Killen, F. (Pit) 52
Young, C. (Cle) 51
2 players tied with 49

Complete Games
Killen, F. (Pit) 44
Young, C. (Cle) 42
Mercer, W. (Was) 38

Shutouts
Killen, F. (Pit) 5
Young, C. (Cle) 5
5 players tied with 3

Saves
Young, C. (Cle) 3
Fisher, C. (Cin) 2
Hill, B. (Lou) 2

Innings Pitched
Killen, F. (Pit) 432[1]
Young, C. (Cle) 414[1]
Hawley, P. (Pit) 378

Fewest Hits/Game
Rhines, B. (Cin) 8.06
Hawley, P. (Pit) 9.10
Sullivan, M. (NY) 9.13

Fewest BB/Game
Young, C. (Cle) 1.35
Clarke, D. (NY) 1.54
Dwyer, F. (Cin) 1.87

Strikeouts
Young, C. (Cle) 140
Hawley, P. (Pit) 137
Killen, F. (Pit) 134

Ratio
Rhines, B. (Cin) 1.23
Cuppy, N. (Cle) 1.29
Young, C. (Cle) 1.30

Earned Run Average
Rhines, B. (Cin) 2.45
Nichols, K. (Bos) 2.83
Cuppy, N. (Cle) 3.12

Adjusted ERA
Rhines, B. (Cin) 188
Nichols, K. (Bos) 160
Dwyer, F. (Cin) 146

Component ERA
Rhines, B. (Cin) 2.79
Cuppy, N. (Cle) 3.30
Nichols, K. (Bos) 3.30

Opponents' Batting Avg.
Rhines, B. (Cin) .238
Hawley, P. (Pit) .261
Sullivan, M. (NY) .261

Adjusted Pitching Runs
Nichols, K. (Bos) 61
Young, C. (Cle) 60
Cuppy, N. (Cle) 56

Win Shares – Pitchers
Young, C. (Cle) 43
Cuppy, N. (Cle) 38
Nichols, K. (Bos) 33

TPW – Pitchers
Young, C. (Cle) 5.7
Cuppy, N. (Cle) 5.4
Nichols, K. (Bos) 4.9

1897 National League

TEAM	G	W	L	PCT	GB	R	OR	EW	AB	H	2B	3B	HR	TB	BB	SO	SB	CS	AVG	OBP	SLG	OPS	OPS+	BR/A	PF	RC
BOS	135	93	39	.705	....	**1025**	**665**	93	**4937**	1574	230	83	**45**	**2105**	423	262	233	....	.319	.378	**.426**	.804	110	65	106	919
BAL	136	90	40	.692	2	964	674	87	4872	**1584**	**243**	66	19	2016	**437**	256	**401**	....	**.325**	**.394**	.414	**.808**	**118**	**140**	100	**984**
NY	138	83	48	.634	9.5	901	696	82	4871	1452	188	84	31	1901	412	327	332	....	.298	.361	.390	.751	106	49	97	829
CIN	134	76	56	.576	17	763	705	71	4524	1311	219	69	22	1734	380	**218**	194	....	.290	.353	.383	.737	93	-52	107	715
CLE	132	69	62	.527	23.5	773	680	74	4604	1374	192	88	16	1790	435	344	181	....	.298	.364	.389	.753	98	-14	105	747
WAS	135	61	71	.462	32	781	793	65	4636	1376	194	77	36	1832	374	348	208	....	.297	.357	.395	.752	104	23	99	755
BRO	136	61	71	.462	32	802	845	63	4810	1343	202	72	24	1761	351	255	187	....	.279	.336	.366	.702	95	-31	95	684
PIT	135	60	71	.458	32.5	676	835	52	4590	1266	140	**108**	25	1697	359	334	170	....	.276	.337	.370	.707	95	-32	96	657
CHI	138	59	73	.447	34	832	894	61	4803	1356	189	97	38	1853	430	317	264	....	.282	.347	.386	.733	94	-45	104	766
PHI	134	55	77	.417	38	752	792	63	4756	1392	213	83	40	1891	399	299	163	....	.293	.353	.398	.750	105	35	97	754
LOU	136	52	78	.400	40	675	869	49	4587	1209	161	70	40	1630	375	460	200	....	.264	.328	.355	.684	89	-69	97	624
STL	133	29	102	.221	63.5	592	1088	30	4673	1285	151	67	32	1666	354	314	172	....	.275	.336	.357	.692	89	-70	98	639
Total	**811**					**9536**			**56663**	**16522**	**2322**	**964**	**368**		**4729**	**3734**	**2705**		**.292**	**.354**	**.386**	**.740**				

Runs
Hamilton, B. (Bos) 152
Keeler, W. (Bal) 145
Griffin, M. (Bro) 136

Hits
Keeler, W. (Bal) 239
Clarke, F. (Lou) 205
Delahanty, E. (Phi) 200

Doubles
Stenzel, J. (Bal) 43
Delahanty, E. (Phi) 40
Lajoie, N. (Phi) 40

Triples
Davis, H. (Pit) 28
Lajoie, N. (Phi) 23
Wallace, B. (Cle) 21

Home Runs
Duffy, H. (Bos) 11
Davis, G. (NY) 10
Lajoie, N. (Phi) 9

Total Bases
Lajoie, N. (Phi) 310
Keeler, W. (Bal) 304
Delahanty, E. (Phi) 285

Runs Batted In
Davis, G. (NY) 136
Collins, J. (Bos) 132
Duffy, H. (Bos) 129

Bases On Balls
Hamilton, B. (Bos) 105
McGraw, J. (Bal) 99
2 players tied with 81

Stolen Bases
Lange, B. (Chi) 73
Stenzel, J. (Bal) 69
Hamilton, B. (Bos) 66

Batting Average
Keeler, W. (Bal) .424
Clarke, F. (Lou) .390
Burkett, J. (Cle) .383

On-Base Percentage
McGraw, J. (Bal) .471
Burkett, J. (Cle) .468
Keeler, W. (Bal) .464

Slugging Average
Lajoie, N. (Phi) .569
Keeler, W. (Bal) .539
Delahanty, E. (Phi) .538

Adjusted OPS
Clarke, F. (Lou) 167
Keeler, W. (Bal) 164
Delahanty, E. (Phi) 163

Adjusted Batting Runs
Clarke, F. (Lou) 54.0
Keeler, W. (Bal) 52.0
Delahanty, E. (Phi) 49.0

Runs Created/Game
Keeler, W. (Bal) 13.80
Clarke, F. (Lou) 13.00
Jennings, H. (Bal) 11.30

Fielding Runs
Childs, C. (Cle) 34.7
Collins, J. (Bos) 26.6
Jennings, H. (Bal) 24.5

Win Shares – Batters
Keeler, W. (Bal) 32
Davis, G. (NY) 31
Clarke, F. (Lou) 30

TPW – Batters
Jennings, H. (Bal) 5.7
Childs, C. (Cle) 4.8
Davis, G. (NY) 4.6

TEAM	CG	SH	SV	IP	H	H/G	ER	HR	BB	SO	OAV	RAT	ERA	ERA+	CERA	PR+	PF	FA	E	DP	FR	BW	PW	FW	TPW	DIF
BOS	115	**8**	**7**	1194^{1}	1273	9.6	484	39	393	329	.271	**1.395**	3.65	122	**3.76**	78.3	104	**.951**	272	80	29.3	5.5	6.7	2.5	14.8	12.2
BAL	118	3	0	**1197^{2}**	1296	9.7	472	**18**	382	361	.274	1.401	3.55	117	3.77	62.2	97	.951	277	110	18.8	**12.0**	5.3	1.6	**18.9**	6.1
NY	119	**8**	3	1196^{1}	**1217**	**9.2**	**458**	26	490	**463**	**.263**	1.427	**3.45**	119	3.79	**88.7**	96	.930	399	109	0.7	4.2	**7.6**	.1	11.8	6.2
CIN	100	4	2	1156^{2}	1375	10.7	525	**18**	329	270	.293	1.473	4.09	111	4.20	58.5	106	.948	273	100	0.8	-4.5	5.0	.1	.6	9.4
CLE	111	6	0	1119^{1}	1297	10.4	491	32	**289**	277	.288	1.417	3.95	114	4.00	5.9	104	.950	**261**	74	**60.3**	-1.2	-3.7	**5.2**	.2	3.8
WAS	102	7	6	1148	1383	10.8	511	27	400	348	.296	1.553	4.01	108	4.64	24.0	101	.933	369	103	17.0	1.9	2.1	1.5	5.5	-10.5
BRO	114	4	2	1194^{2}	1417	10.7	610	34	410	256	.293	1.529	4.60	89	4.43	-54.0	95	.936	364	99	-13.7	-2.7	-4.6	-1.2	-8.5	3.5
PIT	112	2	2	1153^{1}	1397	10.9	598	22	318	342	.297	1.487	4.67	89	4.32	-41.6	97	.936	346	70	-23.7	-2.8	-3.6	-2.0	-8.4	3.4
CHI	**131**	2	1	1197	1485	11.2	602	30	433	361	.302	1.602	4.53	98	4.86	2.3	103	.932	393	**111**	-13.0	-3.8	.2	-1.1	-4.7	-2.3
PHI	115	4	2	1155^{1}	1415	11.0	590	28	364	253	.299	1.540	4.60	91	4.54	-26.7	97	.944	296	72	-26.0	3.0	-2.3	-2.2	-1.5	-9.5
LOU	115	2	0	1155	1374	10.7	559	40	467	267	.291	1.594	4.36	96	4.95	-5.3	99	.929	399	87	-8.0	-5.9	-.4	-.7	-7.0	-6.0
STL	110	1	1	1136^{1}	1594	12.6	778	54	454	207	.326	1.802	6.16	**71**	6.23	-178.7	102	.933	380	86	-43.9	-6.0	-15.7	-3.8	-25.4	-10.6
Total	**1362**	**51**	**26**	**14004**		**10.6**	**6678**					**1.518**	**4.29**													

Wins
- Nichols, K. (Bos) 31
- Rusie, A. (NY) 28
- Klobedanz, F. (Bos) 26

Win Percentage
- Klobedanz, F. (Bos) .788
- Nops, J. (Bal) .769
- Corbett, J. (Bal) .750

Games
- Mercer, W. (Was) 47
- 3 players tied with 46

Complete Games
- Donahue, R. (StL) 38
- Griffith, C. (Chi) 38
- Killen, F. (Pit) 38

Shutouts
- McJames, D. (Was) 3
- Mercer, W. (Was) 3
- 12 players tied with 2

Saves
- Mercer, W. (Was) 3
- Nichols, K. (Bos) 3
- 5 players tied with 2

Innings Pitched
- Nichols, K. (Bos) 368
- Donahue, R. (StL) 348
- Griffith, C. (Chi) 343^{2}

Fewest Hits/Game
- Seymour, C. (NY) 8.23
- Rusie, A. (NY) 8.77
- Nichols, K. (Bos) 8.85

Fewest BB/Game
- Young, C. (Cle) 1.31
- Tannehill, J. (Pit) 1.52
- Nichols, K. (Bos) 1.66

Strikeouts
- McJames, D. (Was) 156
- Seymour, C. (NY) 156
- Corbett, J. (Bal) 149

Ratio
- Nichols, K. (Bos) 1.17
- Rusie, A. (NY) 1.24
- Cuppy, N. (Cle) 1.26

Earned Run Average
- Rusie, A. (NY) 2.54
- Nichols, K. (Bos) 2.64
- Nops, J. (Bal) 2.81

Adjusted ERA
- Nichols, K. (Bos) 169
- Rusie, A. (NY) 163
- Nops, J. (Bal) 148

Component ERA
- Nichols, K. (Bos) 2.68
- Rusie, A. (NY) 2.95
- Cuppy, N. (Cle) 3.24

Opponents' Batting Avg.
- Seymour, C. (NY) .242
- Rusie, A. (NY) .254
- Nichols, K. (Bos) .255

Adjusted Pitching Runs
- Nichols, K. (Bos) 66
- Rusie, A. (NY) 57
- Mercer, W. (Was) 40

Win Shares – Pitchers
- Nichols, K. (Bos) 41
- Breitenstein, T. (Cin) 34
- Rusie, A. (NY) 31

TPW – Pitchers
- Nichols, K. (Bos) 6.0
- Rusie, A. (NY) 5.2
- Mercer, W. (Was) 4.2

1898 National League

TEAM	G	W	L	PCT	GB	R	OR	EW	AB	H	2B	3B	HR	TB	BB	SO	SB	CS	AVG	OBP	SLG	OPS	OPS+	BR/A	PF	RC
BOS	152	102	47	.685	....	872	**614**	100	5276	1531	190	55	**53**	**1990**	405	303	172	....	.290	.344	**.377**	.722	106	29	105	780
BAL	154	96	53	.644	6	**933**	623	103	5242	**1584**	154	77	12	1928	519	316	**250**	....	**.302**	**.382**	.368	**.750**	**118**	**146**	102	**864**
CIN	157	92	60	.605	11.5	831	740	85	5334	1448	207	**101**	19	1914	455	**300**	165	....	.271	.335	.359	.694	97	-28	107	732
CHI	152	85	65	.567	17.5	828	679	90	5219	1431	175	84	18	1828	476	394	220	....	.274	.343	.350	.693	104	32	100	735
CLE	156	81	68	.544	21	730	683	79	5246	1379	162	56	18	1707	**545**	306	93	....	.263	.338	.325	.663	96	-11	99	641
PHI	150	78	71	.523	24	823	784	78	5118	1431	**238**	81	33	1930	472	382	182	....	.280	.348	.377	.726	**118**	121	96	769
NY	157	77	73	.513	25.5	837	800	78	**5349**	1422	190	86	34	1886	428	372	214	....	.266	.328	.353	.681	103	20	97	714
PIT	152	72	76	.486	29.5	634	694	67	5087	1313	140	88	14	1671	336	343	107	....	.258	.313	.328	.642	90	-65	98	589
LOU	154	70	81	.464	33	728	833	65	5193	1389	150	71	32	1777	375	429	235	....	.267	.325	.342	.667	98	-19	98	687
BRO	149	54	91	.372	46	638	811	55	5126	1314	156	66	17	1653	328	314	130	....	.256	.309	.322	.632	86	-97	100	577
WAS	155	51	101	.336	52.5	704	939	55	5257	1423	177	80	36	1868	370	386	197	....	.271	.327	.355	.682	101	-4	100	703
STL	154	39	111	.260	63.5	571	929	41	5214	1290	149	55	13	1588	383	402	104	....	.247	.309	.305	.614	79	-142	102	552
Total	**921**					**9129**			**62661**	**16955**	**2088**	**900**	**299**		**5092**	**4247**	**2069**		**.271**	**.334**	**.347**	**.681**				

Runs
- McGraw, J. (Bal) 143
- Jennings, H. (Bal) 135
- Van Haltren, G. (NY) 129

Hits
- Keeler, W. (Bal) 216
- Burkett, J. (Cle) 213
- Van Haltren, G. (NY) 204

Doubles
- Lajoie, N. (Phi) 43
- Delahanty, E. (Phi) 36
- 2 players tied with 35

Triples
- Anderson, J. (Was,Bro,Bro) 22
- Hoy, D. (Lou) 16
- Van Haltren, G. (NY) 16

Home Runs
- Collins, J. (Bos) 15
- Joyce, B. (NY) 10
- Wagner, H. (Lou) 10

Total Bases
- Collins, J. (Bos) 286
- Lajoie, N. (Phi) 280
- Van Haltren, G. (NY) 270

Runs Batted In
- Lajoie, N. (Phi) 127
- Collins, J. (Bos) 111
- Kelley, J. (Bal) 110

Bases On Balls
- McGraw, J. (Bal) 112
- Joyce, B. (NY) 88
- Hamilton, B. (Bos) 87

Stolen Bases
- Delahanty, E. (Phi) 58
- Hamilton, B. (Bos) 54
- DeMontreville, G. (Bal) 49

Batting Average
- Keeler, W. (Bal) .385
- Hamilton, B. (Bos) .369
- McGraw, J. (Bal) .342

On-Base Percentage
- Hamilton, B. (Bos) .480
- McGraw, J. (Bal) .475
- Jennings, H. (Bal) .454

Slugging Average
- Anderson, J. (Was,Bro,Bro) .494
- Collins, J. (Bos) .479
- Lajoie, N. (Phi) .461

Adjusted OPS
- Hamilton, B. (Bos) 159
- Delahanty, E. (Phi) 159
- Flick, E. (Phi) 158

Adjusted Batting Runs
- Delahanty, E. (Phi) 46.0
- McGraw, J. (Bal) 45.0
- Jennings, H. (Bal) 44.0

Runs Created/Game
- Hamilton, B. (Bos) 12.00
- Delahanty, E. (Phi) 9.70
- McGraw, J. (Bal) 9.30

Fielding Runs
- Lowe, B. (Bos) 29.4
- Collins, J. (Bos) 25.2
- Dahlen, B. (Chi) 22.4

Win Shares – Batters
- Collins, J. (Bos) 34
- Delahanty, E. (Phi) 33
- Hamilton, B. (Bos) 33

TPW – Batters
- Jennings, H. (Bal) 6.1
- Collins, J. (Bos) 5.0
- McGraw, J. (Bal) 4.6

TEAM	CG	SH	SV	IP	H	H/G	ER	HR	BB	SO	OAV	RAT	ERA	ERA+	CERA	PR+	PF	FA	E	DP	FR	BW	PW	FW	TPW	DIF
BOS	127	9	**8**	1340	**1186**	**8.0**	444	37	470	432	**.236**	**1.236**	2.98	124	2.91	69.5	102	.950	310	102	**36.5**	2.8	6.5	**3.4**	12.7	15.3
BAL	138	12	0	1323	1236	8.4	426	17	400	422	.246	1.237	2.90	123	**2.91**	64.0	99	.947	326	105	35.2	**13.6**	6.0	3.3	**22.9**	-.9
CIN	131	10	2	**1385^{1}**	1484	9.6	539	16	449	294	.272	1.395	3.50	109	3.67	35.7	106	.950	325	128	15.4	-2.6	3.3	1.4	2.2	13.8
CHI	137	**13**	0	1342^{2}	1357	9.1	**422**	17	364	323	.261	1.282	**2.83**	126	3.22	**104.4**	99	.936	412	**149**	6.9	3.0	**9.8**	.6	13.4	-3.4
CLE	**142**	9	0	1334	1429	9.6	474	26	**309**	339	.272	1.303	3.20	113	3.37	49.8	100	**.952**	**301**	95	10.6	-1.0	4.7	1.0	4.6	2.4
PHI	129	10	0	1288^{1}	1440	10.1	532	23	399	325	.281	1.427	3.72	92	3.97	-32.4	95	.937	379	102	-10.1	11.3	-3.0	-.9	7.4	-3.4
NY	141	9	1	1353^{2}	1359	9.0	517	21	587	**558**	.259	1.438	3.44	101	3.75	5.3	96	.932	447	113	0.4	1.9	.5	.0	2.4	-.4
PIT	131	10	3	1323^{2}	1400	9.5	501	**14**	346	330	.270	1.319	3.41	104	3.37	19.1	99	.946	340	105	1.6	-6.1	1.8	.2	-4.2	2.2
LOU	137	4	0	1334	1457	9.8	628	33	470	271	.276	1.445	4.24	84	4.05	-90.1	99	.939	382	114	-9.6	-1.8	-8.4	-.9	-11.1	6.1
BRO	134	1	0	1298^{2}	1446	10.0	578	34	476	294	.280	1.480	4.01	89	4.13	-46.9	99	.947	334	125	-15.8	-9.1	-4.4	-1.5	-14.9	-3.1
WAS	129	0	1	1307	1577	10.9	656	29	450	371	.296	1.551	4.52	**81**	4.60	-99.3	101	.929	443	119	-26.9	-.4	-9.3	-2.5	-12.2	-12.8
STL	133	0	2	1324^{1}	1584	10.8	666	32	372	288	.294	1.477	4.53	84	4.35	-65.6	105	.939	388	97	-44.7	-13.3	-6.1	-4.2	-23.6	-12.4
Total	**1609**	**87**	**17**	**15954^{2}**		**9.6**	**6383**					**1.382**	**3.60**													

Wins
- Nichols, K. (Bos) 31
- Cunningham, B. (Lou) 28
- 2 players tied with 27

Win Percentage
- Lewis, T. (Bos) .765
- Maul, A. (Bal) .741
- Nichols, K. (Bos) .721

Games
- Nichols, K. (Bos) 50
- Taylor, J. (StL) 50
- Young, C. (Cle) 46

Complete Games
- Taylor, J. (StL) 42
- Cunningham, B. (Lou) 41
- 3 players tied with 40

Shutouts
- Piatt, W. (Phi) 6
- Powell, J. (Cle) 6
- 3 players tied with 5

Saves
- Nichols, K. (Bos) 4
- 4 players tied with 2

Innings Pitched
- Taylor, J. (StL) 397^{1}
- Nichols, K. (Bos) 388
- Young, C. (Cle) 377^{2}

Fewest Hits/Game
- Nichols, K. (Bos) 7.33
- Willis, V. (Bos) 7.64
- Lewis, T. (Bos) 7.67

Fewest BB/Game
- Young, C. (Cle) .98
- Dwyer, F. (Cin) 1.58
- Cunningham, B. (Lou) 1.62

Strikeouts
- Seymour, C. (NY) 239
- McJames, D. (Bal) 178
- Willis, V. (Bos) 160

Ratio
- Nichols, K. (Bos) 1.03
- Maul, A. (Bal) 1.07
- Griffith, C. (Chi) 1.13

Earned Run Average
- Griffith, C. (Chi) 1.88
- Maul, A. (Bal) 2.10
- Nichols, K. (Bos) 2.13

Adjusted ERA
- Griffith, C. (Chi) 190
- Nichols, K. (Bos) 173
- Maul, A. (Bal) 170

Component ERA
- Nichols, K. (Bos) 1.99
- Maul, A. (Bal) 2.14
- Griffith, C. (Chi) 2.53

Opponents' Batting Avg.
- Nichols, K. (Bos) .221
- Willis, V. (Bos) .229
- Lewis, T. (Bos) .229

Adjusted Pitching Runs
- Griffith, C. (Chi) 60
- Nichols, K. (Bos) 56
- Young, C. (Cle) 43

Win Shares – Pitchers
- Nichols, K. (Bos) 44
- Tannehill, J. (Pit) 34
- Young, C. (Cle) 34

TPW – Pitchers
- Nichols, K. (Bos) 5.5
- Griffith, C. (Chi) 5.5
- Young, C. (Cle) 4.6

1899 National League

TEAM	G	W	L	PCT	GB	R	OR	EW	AB	H	2B	3B	HR	TB	BB	SO	SB	CS	AVG	OBP	SLG	OPS	OPS+	BR/A	PF	RC
BRO	150	100	47	.680	....	892	658	95	4937	1436	178	97	27	1889	477	263	271	....	.291	**.368**	.383	.751	109	71	102	824
BOS	153	95	57	.625	7.5	858	**645**	97	5290	1517	178	90	39	1992	431	269	185	....	.287	.345	.377	.722	94	-52	110	787
PHI	154	94	58	.618	8.5	**916**	743	92	5353	**1613**	**241**	83	31	**2113**	441	341	212	....	**.301**	.363	**.395**	**.757**	**118**	**129**	96	**879**
BAL	152	86	62	.581	14.5	827	691	87	5073	1509	204	71	17	1906	418	383	**364**	....	.297	.365	.376	.741	104	29	105	861
STL	155	84	67	.556	18	819	739	83	5304	1514	172	88	**47**	2003	468	**262**	210	....	.285	.347	.378	.725	102	9	102	801
CIN	157	83	67	.553	18.5	861	777	83	5258	1448	195	106	13	1894	**487**	300	228	....	.275	.344	.360	.705	97	-18	102	762
PIT	155	76	73	.510	25	841	771	81	**5486**	1582	196	**121**	29	2107	386	346	179	....	.288	.342	.384	.726	105	29	100	815
CHI	152	75	73	.507	25.5	812	763	79	5148	1428	173	82	27	1846	406	342	247	....	.277	.338	.359	.696	99	-4	97	743
LOU	156	75	76	.497	27	833	782	80	5336	1491	195	70	40	1946	437	379	234	....	.279	.343	.365	.708	99	-2	100	781
NY	153	60	90	.400	41.5	741	868	63	5125	1441	165	66	23	1807	389	361	235	....	.281	.337	.353	.690	98	-13	97	708
WAS	155	54	98	.355	48.5	743	983	55	5256	1429	162	87	**47**	1906	350	341	176	....	.272	.328	.363	.690	95	-38	99	710
CLE	154	20	134	.130	83.5	529	1252	23	5279	1333	142	50	12	1611	289	280	127	....	.253	.299	.305	.605	76	-162	93	541
Total	**923**					**9672**			**62845**	**17741**	**2201**	**1011**	**352**		**4979**	**3867**	**2668**		**.282**	**.343**	**.366**	**.710**				

Runs
Keeler, W. (Bro) 140
McGraw, J. (Bal) 140
Thomas, R. (Phi) 137

Hits
Delahanty, E. (Phi) 238
Burkett, J. (StL) 221
Williams, J. (Pit) 220

Doubles
Delahanty, E. (Phi) 55
Wagner, H. (Lou) 45
Holmes, D. (Bal) 31

Triples
Williams, J. (Pit) 27
Freeman, B. (Was) 25
Stahl, C. (Bos) 19

Home Runs
Freeman, B. (Was) 25
Wallace, B. (StL) 12
3 players tied with 9

Total Bases
Delahanty, E. (Phi) 338
Freeman, B. (Was) 331
Williams, J. (Pit) 329

Runs Batted In
Delahanty, E. (Phi) 137
Freeman, B. (Was) 122
Williams, J. (Pit) 116

Bases On Balls
McGraw, J. (Bal) 124
Thomas, R. (Phi) 115
Van Haltren, G. (NY) 75

Stolen Bases
Sheckard, J. (Bal) 77
McGraw, J. (Bal) 73
Heidrick, E. (StL) 55

Batting Average
Delahanty, E. (Phi) .410
Burkett, J. (StL) .396
McGraw, J. (Bal) .391

On-Base Percentage
McGraw, J. (Bal) .547
Delahanty, E. (Phi) .464
Burkett, J. (StL) .463

Slugging Average
Delahanty, E. (Phi) .582
Freeman, B. (Was) .563
Williams, J. (Pit) .530

Adjusted OPS
Delahanty, E. (Phi) 193
McGraw, J. (Bal) 165
Burkett, J. (StL) 160

Adjusted Batting Runs
Delahanty, E. (Phi) 73.0
McGraw, J. (Bal) 53.0
Williams, J. (Pit) 49.0

Runs Created/Game
McGraw, J. (Bal) 15.30
Delahanty, E. (Phi) 13.40
Burkett, J. (StL) 11.10

Fielding Runs
Collins, J. (Bos) 33.5
Cross, L. (StL,Cle) 23.9
Davis, G. (NY) 22.2

Win Shares – Batters
Delahanty, E. (Phi) 41
McGraw, J. (Bal) 34
2 players tied with 32

TPW – Batters
McGraw, J. (Bal) 5.8
Williams, J. (Pit) 5.5
Delahanty, E. (Phi) 5.4

TEAM	CG	SH	SV	IP	H	H/G	ER	HR	BB	SO	OAV	RAT	ERA	ERA+	CERA	PR+	PF	FA	E	DP	FR	BW	PW	FW	TPW	DIF
BRO	121	9	**9**	1269[1]	1320	9.4	**458**	32	463	331	.268	1.405	**3.25**	120	3.70	70.4	102	.948	314	125	23.2	6.5	6.4	2.1	**15.0**	12.0
BOS	138	13	4	1348	**1273**	**8.5**	488	44	432	385	**.249**	**1.265**	3.26	128	**3.15**	82.7	108	**.952**	**303**	124	**50.6**	-4.7	7.5	**4.6**	7.4	11.6
PHI	129	**15**	2	1333[1]	1398	9.4	514	17	370	281	.270	1.326	3.47	106	3.42	12.6	96	.940	379	110	19.2	**11.7**	1.1	1.7	14.6	3.4
BAL	132	9	4	1304[1]	1403	9.7	480	**13**	349	294	.275	1.343	3.31	119	3.48	**88.6**	103	.949	308	96	5.0	2.6	**8.0**	.5	11.1	.9
STL	134	7	1	1340[2]	1476	9.9	500	41	**321**	331	.279	1.340	3.36	118	3.61	80.8	103	.939	397	117	11.6	.9	7.3	1.1	9.2	-.2
CIN	131	8	5	**1373**	1494	9.8	560	26	372	361	.275	1.359	3.67	106	3.70	32.5	102	.947	341	113	5.5	-1.6	2.9	.5	1.8	6.2
PIT	118	9	4	**1373**	1471	9.6	546	27	438	338	.273	1.390	3.58	106	3.74	32.2	99	.945	363	100	5.4	2.6	2.9	.5	6.1	-4.1
CHI	**147**	8	1	1331[1]	1433	9.7	498	20	330	313	.275	1.324	3.37	111	3.50	53.4	97	.935	428	**145**	2.2	-.4	4.8	.2	4.7	-3.7
LOU	135	5	2	1360[1]	1517	10.0	518	35	325	288	.280	1.354	3.43	112	3.73	86.6	100	.939	399	103	-22.1	-.2	7.9	-2.0	5.7	-5.7
NY	139	4	0	1290[2]	1463	10.2	609	19	630	**402**	.283	1.622	4.25	87	4.74	-84.0	97	.932	434	142	11.7	-1.2	-7.6	1.1	-7.7	-7.3
WAS	131	3	0	1300[1]	1649	11.4	712	35	422	328	.309	1.593	4.93	79	4.96	-98.2	101	.935	403	99	-50.4	-3.4	-8.9	-4.6	-16.9	-5.1
CLE	138	0	0	1264	1844	13.1	895	43	527	215	.339	1.876	6.37	**58**	6.59	-314.9	96	.937	388	121	-62.2	-14.7	-28.5	-5.6	-48.9	-8.1
Total	**1593**	**90**	**32**	**15888[1]**		**10.0**	**6778**					**1.430**	**3.84**													

Wins
Hughes, J. (Bro) 28
McGinnity, J. (Bal) 28
Willis, V. (Bos) 27

Win Percentage
Hughes, J. (Bro) .824
Willis, V. (Bos) .771
Hahn, N. (Cin) .742

Games
Leever, S. (Pit) 51
McGinnity, J. (Bal) 48
Powell, J. (StL) 48

Complete Games
Carrick, B. (NY) 40
Powell, J. (StL) 40
Young, C. (StL) 40

Shutouts
Willis, V. (Bos) 5
8 players tied with 4

Saves
Leever, S. (Pit) 3
5 players tied with 2

Innings Pitched
Leever, S. (Pit) 379
Powell, J. (StL) 373
Young, C. (StL) 369[1]

Fewest Hits/Game
Willis, V. (Bos) 7.28
Hughes, J. (Bro) 7.71
Hahn, N. (Cin) 8.16

Fewest BB/Game
Young, C. (StL) 1.07
Cuppy, N. (StL) 1.36
Tannehill, J. (Pit) 1.45

Strikeouts
Hahn, N. (Cin) 145
Seymour, C. (NY) 142
Leever, S. (Pit) 121

Ratio
Young, C. (StL) 1.12
Hahn, N. (Cin) 1.13
Willis, V. (Bos) 1.15

Earned Run Average
Orth, A. (Phi) 2.49
Willis, V. (Bos) 2.50
Young, C. (StL) 2.58

Adjusted ERA
Willis, V. (Bos) 167
Young, C. (StL) 154
McGinnity, J. (Bal) 148

Component ERA
Hahn, N. (Cin) 2.41
Young, C. (StL) 2.48
Willis, V. (Bos) 2.54

Opponents' Batting Avg.
Willis, V. (Bos) .222
Hughes, J. (Bro) .232
Hahn, N. (Cin) .242

Adjusted Pitching Runs
Young, C. (StL) 54
McGinnity, J. (Bal) 51
Willis, V. (Bos) 50

Win Shares – Pitchers
Willis, V. (Bos) 39
McGinnity, J. (Bal) 35
Young, C. (StL) 35

TPW – Pitchers
Young, C. (StL) 4.9
Willis, V. (Bos) 4.3
McGinnity, J. (Bal) 4.1

1900 National League

TEAM	G	W	L	PCT	GB	R	OR	EW	AB	H	2B	3B	HR	TB	BB	SO	SB	CS	AVG	OBP	SLG	OPS	OPS+	BR/A	PF	RC
BRO	142	82	54	.603	....	**816**	722	76	4860	1423	199	81	26	1862	421	**272**	**274**	....	**.293**	**.359**	**.383**	**.742**	104	28	106	**795**
PIT	140	79	60	.568	4.5	733	**612**	82	4817	1312	185	**100**	26	1775	327	321	174	....	.272	.327	.368	.695	96	-31	101	666
PHI	141	75	63	.543	8	810	792	71	4969	**1439**	187	82	29	**1877**	**440**	374	205	....	.290	.356	.378	.734	**109**	**66**	99	774
BOS	142	66	72	.478	17	778	739	73	4952	1403	163	68	**48**	1846	395	278	182	....	.283	.342	.373	.715	91	-67	112	724
STL	142	65	75	.464	19	744	748	70	4877	1420	141	81	36	1831	406	318	243	....	.291	.356	.375	.731	108	59	99	766
CHI	146	65	75	.464	19	635	751	58	4907	1276	**202**	51	33	1679	343	383	189	....	.260	.317	.342	.659	90	-62	96	622
CIN	144	62	77	.446	21.5	703	745	65	**5026**	1335	178	83	33	1778	333	408	183	....	.266	.318	.354	.671	93	-54	97	651
NY	141	60	78	.435	23	713	823	59	4724	1317	177	61	23	1685	369	343	236	....	.279	.338	.357	.695	102	18	95	676
Total	**569**					**5932**			**39132**	**10925**	**1432**	**607**	**254**		**3034**	**2697**	**1686**		**.279**	**.339**	**.366**	**.705**				

Runs
Thomas, R. (Phi) 132
Slagle, J. (Phi) 115
2 players tied with 114

Hits
Keeler, W. (Bro) 204
Burkett, J. (StL) 203
Wagner, H. (Pit) 201

Doubles
Wagner, H. (Pit) 45
Lajoie, N. (Phi) 33
2 players tied with 32

Triples
Wagner, H. (Pit) 22
Hickman, C. (NY) 17
Kelley, J. (Bro) 17

Home Runs
Long, H. (Bos) 12
Flick, E. (Phi) 11
Donlin, M. (StL) 10

Total Bases
Wagner, H. (Pit) 302
Flick, E. (Phi) 297
Burkett, J. (StL) 265

Runs Batted In
Flick, E. (Phi) 110
Delahanty, E. (Phi) 109
Wagner, H. (Pit) 100

Bases On Balls
Thomas, R. (Phi) 115
Hamilton, B. (Bos) 107
McGraw, J. (StL) 85

Stolen Bases
Donovan, P. (StL) 45
Van Haltren, G. (NY) 45
Barrett, J. (Cin) 44

Batting Average
Wagner, H. (Pit) .381
Flick, E. (Phi) .367
Burkett, J. (StL) .363

On-Base Percentage
McGraw, J. (StL) .505
Thomas, R. (Phi) .451
Hamilton, B. (Bos) .449

Slugging Average
Wagner, H. (Pit) .573
Flick, E. (Phi) .545
Lajoie, N. (Phi) .510

Adjusted OPS
Wagner, H. (Pit) 175
Flick, E. (Phi) 172
McGraw, J. (StL) 156

Adjusted Batting Runs
Flick, E. (Phi) 55.0
Wagner, H. (Pit) 53.0
Selbach, K. (NY) 40.0

Runs Created/Game
Wagner, H. (Pit) 12.20
Flick, E. (Phi) 11.40
McGraw, J. (StL) 10.40

Fielding Runs
Dahlen, B. (Bro) 26.6
Steinfeldt, H. (Cin) 26.4
Lajoie, N. (Phi) 22.3

Win Shares – Batters
Wagner, H. (Pit) 34
Flick, E. (Phi) 32
Selbach, K. (NY) 27

TPW – Batters
Flick, E. (Phi) 4.5
Lajoie, N. (Phi) 4.4
Wagner, H. (Pit) 4.3

TEAM	CG	SH	SV	IP	H	H/G	ER	HR	BB	SO	OAV	RAT	ERA	ERA+	CERA	PR+	PF	FA	E	DP	FR	BW	PW	FW	TPW	DIF
BRO	104	8	**4**	1225^{2}	1370	10.1	529	30	405	300	.282	1.448	3.88	99	4.06	-21.2	104	.948	303	102	13.2	2.6	-1.9	1.2	1.8	12.2
PIT	114	11	1	1229	**1232**	**9.0**	**418**	24	**295**	**415**	**.260**	**1.242**	**3.06**	118	**3.09**	72.4	98	.945	322	106	4.8	-2.8	6.6	.4	**4.3**	5.7
PHI	116	7	3	1248^{2}	1506	10.8	571	29	402	284	.298	1.528	4.12	**88**	4.50	-65.1	98	.945	330	**125**	-7.2	**6.0**	-5.9	-.7	-.6	6.6
BOS	116	8	2	1240^{1}	1263	9.2	513	59	463	340	.264	1.392	3.72	111	3.79	28.1	112	**.953**	**273**	86	**27.0**	-6.2	2.6	**2.5**	-1.1	-1.9
STL	117	**12**	0	1217^{1}	1373	10.2	507	37	299	325	.284	1.373	3.75	97	3.78	3.6	98	.943	331	73	-20.5	5.4	.3	-1.9	3.9	-8.9
CHI	**137**	9	1	1271	1375	9.7	456	**21**	324	357	.275	1.337	3.23	112	3.58	**75.6**	97	.933	418	98	-23.1	-5.7	**6.9**	-2.1	-.9	-4.1
CIN	118	9	1	**1274^{2}**	1383	9.8	542	28	404	399	.276	1.402	3.83	96	3.77	-26.2	99	.945	341	120	2.2	-4.9	-2.4	.2	-7.1	.1
NY	113	4	0	1207^{1}	1423	10.6	531	26	442	277	.293	1.545	3.96	91	4.57	-49.5	98	.928	439	124	2.8	1.6	-4.5	.3	-2.6	-6.4
Total	**935**	**68**	**12**	**9914**		**9.9**	**4067**					**1.408**	**3.69**													

Wins
- McGinnity, J. (Bro) 28
- 4 players tied with 20

Win Percentage
- McGinnity, J. (Bro) .778
- Tannehill, J. (Pit) .769
- Fraser, C. (Phi) .625

Games
- Carrick, B. (NY) 45
- McGinnity, J. (Bro) 44
- 2 players tied with 42

Complete Games
- Hawley, P. (NY) 34
- Dineen, B. (Bos) 33
- 4 players tied with 32

Shutouts
- 4 players tied with 4

Saves
- Kitson, F. (Bro) 4
- Bernhard, B. (Phi) 2
- 6 players tied with 1

Innings Pitched
- McGinnity, J. (Bro) 343
- Carrick, B. (NY) 341^{2}
- Hawley, P. (NY) 329^{1}

Fewest Hits/Game
- Waddell, R. (Pit) 7.59
- Garvin, N. (Chi) 8.22
- Nichols, K. (Bos) 8.36

Fewest BB/Game
- Young, C. (StL) 1.01
- Phillippe, D. (Pit) 1.35
- Tannehill, J. (Pit) 1.65

Strikeouts
- Hahn, N. (Cin) 132
- Waddell, R. (Pit) 130
- Young, C. (StL) 115

Ratio
- Waddell, R. (Pit) 1.11
- Phillippe, D. (Pit) 1.13
- Young, C. (StL) 1.16

Earned Run Average
- Waddell, R. (Pit) 2.37
- Garvin, N. (Chi) 2.41
- Taylor, J. (Chi) 2.55

Adjusted ERA
- Waddell, R. (Pit) 153
- Garvin, N. (Chi) 149
- Taylor, J. (Chi) 141

Component ERA
- Waddell, R. (Pit) 2.31
- Phillippe, D. (Pit) 2.63
- Garvin, N. (Chi) 2.73

Opponents' Batting Avg.
- Waddell, R. (Pit) .229
- Garvin, N. (Chi) .243
- Nichols, K. (Bos) .246

Adjusted Pitching Runs
- Garvin, N. (Chi) 37
- McGinnity, J. (Bro) 30
- Taylor, J. (Chi) 30

Win Shares – Pitchers
- McGinnity, J. (Bro) 30
- Dineen, B. (Bos) 27
- 3 players tied with 23

TPW – Pitchers
- Garvin, N. (Chi) 3.0
- Taylor, J. (Chi) 3.0
- Dineen, B. (Bos) 2.9

1901 National League

TEAM	G	W	L	PCT	GB	R	OR	EW	AB	H	2B	3B	HR	TB	BB	SO	SB	CS	AVG	OBP	SLG	OPS	OPS+	BR/A	PF	RC
PIT	140	90	49	.647	....	776	**534**	94	4913	1407	182	92	29	1860	386	493	203	....	.286	**.345**	.379	**.723**	113	79	103	743
PHI	140	83	57	.593	7.5	668	543	84	4793	1275	194	58	24	1657	**430**	549	199	....	.266	.334	.346	.680	101	18	102	652
BRO	137	79	57	.581	9.5	744	600	82	4879	1399	**206**	93	32	1887	312	**449**	178	....	**.287**	.335	**.387**	.722	112	66	103	718
STL	142	76	64	.543	14.5	**792**	689	80	**5039**	**1430**	187	**94**	**39**	**1922**	314	540	190	....	.284	.337	.381	.718	**120**	**126**	95	**744**
BOS	140	69	69	.500	20.5	531	556	66	4746	1180	135	36	28	1471	303	519	158	....	.249	.298	.310	.608	75	-150	109	515
CHI	140	53	86	.381	37	578	699	56	4844	1250	153	61	18	1579	314	532	**204**	....	.258	.310	.326	.636	94	-34	96	575
NY	141	52	85	.380	37	544	755	47	4839	1225	167	46	19	1541	303	575	133	....	.253	.303	.318	.622	89	-61	96	529
CIN	142	52	87	.374	38	561	818	44	4914	1232	173	70	38	1659	323	584	137	....	.251	.303	.338	.640	98	-14	93	570
Total	**561**					**5194**			**38967**	**10398**	**1397**	**550**	**227**		**2685**	**4241**	**1402**		**.267**	**.321**	**.348**	**.669**				

Runs
- Burkett, J. (StL) 142
- Keeler, W. (Bro) 123
- Beaumont, G. (Pit) 120

Hits
- Burkett, J. (StL) 226
- Keeler, W. (Bro) 202
- Sheckard, J. (Bro) 196

Doubles
- Daly, T. (Bro) 38
- Delahanty, E. (Phi) 38
- Wagner, H. (Pit) 37

Triples
- Sheckard, J. (Bro) 19
- Flick, E. (Phi) 17
- 4 players tied with 16

Home Runs
- Crawford, S. (Cin) 16
- Sheckard, J. (Bro) 11
- Burkett, J. (StL) 10

Total Bases
- Burkett, J. (StL) 306
- Sheckard, J. (Bro) 296
- Delahanty, E. (Phi) 286

Runs Batted In
- Wagner, H. (Pit) 126
- Delahanty, E. (Phi) 108
- 2 players tied with 104

Bases On Balls
- Thomas, R. (Phi) 100
- Hartsel, T. (Chi) 74
- Davis, L. (Pit,Bro) 66

Stolen Bases
- Wagner, H. (Pit) 49
- Hartsel, T. (Chi) 41
- Strang, S. (NY) 40

Batting Average
- Burkett, J. (StL) .376
- Delahanty, E. (Phi) .354
- Sheckard, J. (Bro) .354

On-Base Percentage
- Burkett, J. (StL) .440
- Thomas, R. (Phi) .437
- Delahanty, E. (Phi) .427

Slugging Average
- Sheckard, J. (Bro) .534
- Delahanty, E. (Phi) .528
- Crawford, S. (Cin) .524

Adjusted OPS
- Burkett, J. (StL) 184
- Delahanty, E. (Phi) 172
- Crawford, S. (Cin) 172

Adjusted Batting Runs
- Burkett, J. (StL) 66.0
- Delahanty, E. (Phi) 51.0
- Hartsel, T. (Chi) 48.0

Runs Created/Game
- Burkett, J. (StL) 10.60
- Delahanty, E. (Phi) 10.20
- Sheckard, J. (Bro) 10.20

Fielding Runs
- Wallace, B. (StL) 26.6
- DeMontreville, G. (Bos) 15.4
- Dahlen, B. (Bro) 15.4

Win Shares – Batters
- Burkett, J. (StL) 38
- Wagner, H. (Pit) 37
- 2 players tied with 33

TPW – Batters
- Burkett, J. (StL) 5.8
- Wagner, H. (Pit) 5.6
- Wallace, B. (StL) 5.4

TEAM	CG	SH	SV	IP	H	H/G	ER	HR	BB	SO	OAV	RAT	ERA	ERA+	CERA	PR+	PF	FA	E	DP	FR	BW	PW	FW	TPW	DIF
PIT	119	**15**	4	1244^{2}	1198	8.7	**357**	20	**244**	505	.251	**1.159**	**2.58**	126	**2.69**	78.6	98	.951	287	97	15.4	7.7	7.7	1.5	**16.9**	4.1
PHI	125	**15**	2	1246^{2}	1221	8.8	397	19	259	480	.255	1.187	2.87	118	2.79	70.8	102	**.954**	**262**	65	2.6	1.7	6.9	.3	8.9	4.1
BRO	111	7	**5**	1213^{2}	1244	9.2	423	**18**	435	583	.264	1.383	3.14	107	3.51	19.4	101	.950	281	99	8.1	6.5	1.9	.8	9.2	1.8
STL	118	5	**5**	**1269^{2}**	1333	9.4	519	39	332	445	.268	1.311	3.68	86	3.42	-100.2	96	.949	305	**108**	**29.1**	**12.3**	-9.8	**2.9**	5.4	.6
BOS	128	11	0	1263	**1196**	**8.5**	407	29	349	558	**.248**	1.223	2.90	124	2.82	**82.0**	109	.952	282	89	17.5	-14.7	**8.0**	1.7	-4.9	4.9
CHI	**131**	2	0	1241^{2}	1348	9.8	459	27	324	**586**	.275	1.347	3.33	97	3.54	-0.8	97	.943	336	87	-13.1	-3.3	-.1	-1.3	-4.7	-11.3
NY	118	11	1	1232	1389	10.2	530	24	377	542	.282	1.433	3.87	85	3.98	-46.0	100	.942	348	81	-31.6	-6.0	-4.5	-3.1	-13.6	-2.4
CIN	126	4	0	1265^{2}	1469	10.4	586	51	365	542	.288	1.449	4.17	**77**	4.30	-109.1	96	.940	355	102	-28.5	-1.3	-10.7	-2.8	-14.8	-2.2
Total	**976**	**70**	**17**	**9977**		**9.4**	**3678**					**1.311**	**3.32**													

Wins
- Donovan, B. (Bro) 25
- Harper, J. (StL) 23
- 2 players tied with 22

Win Percentage
- Leever, S. (Pit) .737
- Chesbro, J. (Pit) .677
- Phillippe, D. (Pit) .647

Games
- Donovan, B. (Bro) 45
- Powell, J. (StL) 45
- Taylor, D. (NY) 45

Complete Games
- Hahn, N. (Cin) 41
- Taylor, D. (NY) 37
- 2 players tied with 36

Shutouts
- Chesbro, J. (Pit) 6
- Orth, A. (Phi) 6
- Willis, V. (Bos) 6

Saves
- Donovan, B. (Bro) 3
- Powell, J. (StL) 3
- 3 players tied with 2

Innings Pitched
- Hahn, N. (Cin) 375^{1}
- Taylor, D. (NY) 353^{1}
- Donovan, B. (Bro) 351

Fewest Hits/Game
- Townsend, H. (Phi) 7.39
- Mathewson, C. (NY) 7.71
- Willis, V. (Bos) 7.72

Fewest BB/Game
- Orth, A. (Phi) 1.02
- Phillippe, D. (Pit) 1.16
- Tannehill, J. (Pit) 1.28

Strikeouts
- Hahn, N. (Cin) 239
- Donovan, B. (Bro) 226
- Hughes, T. (Chi) 225

Ratio
- Orth, A. (Phi) 1.00
- Phillippe, D. (Pit) 1.05
- Chesbro, J. (Pit) 1.09

Earned Run Average
- Tannehill, J. (Pit) 2.18
- Phillippe, D. (Pit) 2.22
- Orth, A. (Phi) 2.27

Adjusted ERA
- Willis, V. (Bos) 153
- Tannehill, J. (Pit) 150
- Orth, A. (Phi) 150

Component ERA
- Orth, A. (Phi) 2.00
- Phillippe, D. (Pit) 2.25
- Chesbro, J. (Pit) 2.31

Opponents' Batting Avg.
- Townsend, H. (Phi) .223
- Mathewson, C. (NY) .230
- Willis, V. (Bos) .230

Adjusted Pitching Runs
- Mathewson, C. (NY) 42
- Willis, V. (Bos) 38
- Orth, A. (Phi) 35

Win Shares – Pitchers
- Willis, V. (Bos) 33
- Nichols, K. (Bos) 32
- Orth, A. (Phi) 29

TPW – Pitchers
- Mathewson, C. (NY) 4.1
- Orth, A. (Phi) 4.0
- Willis, V. (Bos) 3.7

1901 American League

TEAM	G	W	L	PCT	GB	R	OR	EW	AB	H	2B	3B	HR	TB	BB	SO	SB	CS	AVG	OBP	SLG	OPS	OPS+	BR/A	PF	RC
CHI	137	83	53	.610	....	**819**	631	85	4725	1303	173	89	32	1750	**475**	337	**280**	....	.276	.350	.370	.720	**108**	**64**	97	744
BOS	138	79	57	.581	4	759	**608**	83	4866	1353	183	104	**37**	1855	331	**282**	157	....	.278	.330	.381	.711	104	22	98	693
DET	136	74	61	.548	8.5	741	694	72	4676	1303	180	80	29	1730	380	346	204	....	.279	.340	.370	.710	98	-15	104	690
PHI	137	74	62	.544	9	805	760	72	**4882**	**1409**	**239**	87	35	**1927**	301	344	173	....	.289	.337	.395	.731	103	9	104	734
BAL	135	68	65	.511	13.5	760	750	67	4589	1348	179	**111**	24	1821	369	377	207	....	**.294**	**.353**	**.397**	**.750**	**108**	49	104	**746**
WAS	138	61	72	.459	20.5	682	771	58	4772	1282	191	83	33	1738	356	340	127	....	.269	.326	.364	.690	98	-12	98	633
CLE	138	54	82	.397	29	666	831	53	4833	1311	197	68	12	1680	243	326	125	....	.271	.313	.348	.660	91	-55	96	588
MIL	139	48	89	.350	35.5	641	828	51	4795	1250	192	66	26	1652	325	384	176	....	.261	.314	.345	.658	92	-47	95	602
Total	**549**					**5873**			**38138**	**10559**	**1534**	**688**	**228**		**2780**	**2736**	**1449**		**.277**	**.333**	**.371**	**.704**				

Runs
Lajoie, N. (Phi) 145
Jones, F. (Chi) 120
Williams, J. (Bal) 113

Hits
Lajoie, N. (Phi) 232
Anderson, J. (Mil) 190
Collins, J. (Bos) 187

Doubles
Lajoie, N. (Phi) 48
Anderson, J. (Mil) 46
Collins, J. (Bos) 42

Triples
Keister, B. (Bal) 21
Williams, J. (Bal) 21
Mertes, S. (Chi) 17

Home Runs
Lajoie, N. (Phi) 14
Freeman, B. (Bos) 12
Grady, M. (Was) 9

Total Bases
Lajoie, N. (Phi) 350
Collins, J. (Bos) 279
Anderson, J. (Mil) 274

Runs Batted In
Lajoie, N. (Phi) 125
Freeman, B. (Bos) 114
Anderson, J. (Mil) 99

Bases On Balls
Hoy, D. (Chi) 86
Jones, F. (Chi) 84
Barrett, J. (Det) 76

Stolen Bases
Isbell, F. (Chi) 52
Mertes, S. (Chi) 46
2 players tied with 38

Batting Average
Lajoie, N. (Phi) .426
Donlin, M. (Bal) .340
Freeman, B. (Bos) .339

On-Base Percentage
Lajoie, N. (Phi) .463
Jones, F. (Chi) .412
Donlin, M. (Bal) .409

Slugging Average
Lajoie, N. (Phi) .643
Freeman, B. (Bos) .520
Seybold, S. (Phi) .503

Adjusted OPS
Lajoie, N. (Phi) 196
Freeman, B. (Bos) 157
Seybold, S. (Phi) 142

Adjusted Batting Runs
Lajoie, N. (Phi) 68.0
Freeman, B. (Bos) 37.0
Collins, J. (Bos) 30.0

Runs Created/Game
Lajoie, N. (Phi) 15.20
Donlin, M. (Bal) 9.00
Freeman, B. (Bos) 9.00

Fielding Runs
Williams, J. (Bal) 17.9
Barrett, J. (Det) 17.6
Clingman, B. (Was) 17.5

Win Shares – Batters
Lajoie, N. (Phi) 42
Collins, J. (Bos) 28
Hoy, D. (Chi) 25

TPW – Batters
Lajoie, N. (Phi) 7.4
Collins, J. (Bos) 4.6
Williams, J. (Bal) 4.0

TEAM	CG	SH	SV	IP	H	H/G	ER	HR	BB	SO	OAV	RAT	ERA	ERA+	CERA	PR+	PF	FA	E	DP	FR	BW	PW	FW	TPW	DIF
CHI	110	**11**	2	**1218^1**	1250	9.2	**403**	27	312	394	.262	1.282	**2.98**	117	3.25	**68.9**	95	.941	345	100	2.3	**5.8**	**6.2**	.2	**12.2**	2.8
BOS	123	7	1	1217	**1178**	**8.7**	411	33	294	**396**	**.251**	**1.210**	3.04	116	**2.90**	16.3	96	.943	337	104	**49.2**	2.0	1.5	**4.4**	7.9	3.1
DET	118	8	2	1188^2	1328	10.0	436	22	313	307	.279	1.381	3.30	116	3.70	58.5	105	.930	410	**127**	13.0	-1.4	5.3	1.2	5.1	1.9
PHI	**124**	6	1	1200^2	1346	10.1	533	**20**	374	350	.280	1.433	4.00	94	3.90	-33.3	103	.942	337	93	1.9	.8	-3.0	.2	-2.1	8.1
BAL	115	4	3	1158	1313	10.2	480	21	344	271	.282	1.431	3.73	103	3.86	54.6	105	.926	401	76	-37.9	4.4	4.9	-3.4	5.9	-3.9
WAS	118	8	2	1183	1396	10.6	538	51	**284**	308	.290	1.420	4.09	89	4.16	-52.9	100	**.943**	**323**	97	-4.3	-1.1	-4.8	-.4	-6.3	1.3
CLE	122	7	**4**	1182^1	1365	10.4	541	22	464	334	.286	1.547	4.12	**86**	4.50	-68.8	97	.942	329	99	-6.1	-5.0	-6.2	-.6	-11.7	-2.3
MIL	107	3	3	1218	1383	10.2	549	32	395	376	.283	1.460	4.06	89	4.12	-44.7	98	.934	393	106	-18.0	-4.3	-4.0	-1.6	-9.9	-10.1
Total	**937**	**54**	**18**	**9566**		**9.9**	**3891**					**1.394**	**3.66**													

Wins
Young, C. (Bos) 33
McGinnity, J. (Bal) 26
Griffith, C. (Chi) 24

Win Percentage
Griffith, C. (Chi) .774
Young, C. (Bos) .767
Wiltse, S. (Phi) .722

Games
McGinnity, J. (Bal) 48
Dowling, P. (Cle,Mil) 43
Young, C. (Bos) 43

Complete Games
McGinnity, J. (Bal) 39
Young, C. (Bos) 38
2 players tied with 35

Shutouts
Griffith, C. (Chi) 5
Young, C. (Bos) 5
3 players tied with 4

Saves
Hoffer, B. (Cle) 3
Garvin, N. (Mil) 2
14 players tied with 1

Innings Pitched
McGinnity, J. (Bal) 382
Young, C. (Bos) 371^1
Miller, R. (Det) 332

Fewest Hits/Game
Young, C. (Bos) 7.85
Callahan, N. (Chi) 8.15
Moore, E. (Cle) 8.38

Fewest BB/Game
Young, C. (Bos) .90
Gear, D. (Was) 1.21
Lee, W. (Was) 1.55

Strikeouts
Young, C. (Bos) 158
Patterson, R. (Chi) 127
Dowling, P. (Cle,Mil) 124

Ratio
Young, C. (Bos) .97
Callahan, N. (Chi) 1.14
Griffith, C. (Chi) 1.22

Earned Run Average
Young, C. (Bos) 1.62
Callahan, N. (Chi) 2.42
Yeager, J. (Det) 2.61

Adjusted ERA
Young, C. (Bos) 217
Yeager, J. (Det) 147
Callahan, N. (Chi) 144

Component ERA
Young, C. (Bos) 1.87
Callahan, N. (Chi) 2.53
Winter, G. (Bos) 2.81

Opponents' Batting Avg.
Young, C. (Bos) .232
Callahan, N. (Chi) .239
Moore, E. (Cle) .244

Adjusted Pitching Runs
Young, C. (Bos) 63
Miller, R. (Det) 29
McGinnity, J. (Bal) 25

Win Shares – Pitchers
Young, C. (Bos) 41
Miller, R. (Det) 30
2 players tied with 27

TPW – Pitchers
Young, C. (Bos) 5.7
Griffith, C. (Chi) 3.4
Callahan, N. (Chi) 3.2

1902 National League

TEAM	G	W	L	PCT	GB	R	OR	EW	AB	H	2B	3B	HR	TB	BB	SO	SB	CS	AVG	OBP	SLG	OPS	OPS+	BR/A	PF	RC
PIT	142	103	36	.741	....	**775**	**440**	105	**4926**	**1410**	**189**	**95**	18	**1843**	372	446	222	....	**.286**	**.344**	**.374**	**.718**	**123**	**129**	104	**743**
BRO	141	75	63	.543	27.5	564	519	75	4845	1242	147	49	**19**	1544	319	489	145	....	.256	.311	.319	.629	99	-7	101	553
BOS	142	73	64	.533	29	572	516	76	4726	1178	142	39	14	1440	**398**	481	189	....	.249	.313	.305	.618	95	-20	101	540
CIN	141	70	70	.500	33.5	633	566	78	4908	1383	188	77	18	1779	297	465	131	....	.282	.328	.362	.690	108	38	109	654
CHI	143	68	69	.496	34	544	505	74	4870	1224	133	40	6	1455	358	572	**229**	....	.251	.308	.299	.607	94	-25	97	539
STL	140	56	78	.418	44.5	517	695	48	4751	1226	116	37	10	1446	273	**438**	158	....	.258	.306	.304	.610	97	-16	96	516
PHI	138	56	81	.409	46	484	649	49	4615	1139	110	43	5	1350	356	481	108	....	.247	.305	.293	.598	89	-50	100	473
NY	141	48	88	.353	53.5	405	604	42	4632	1097	147	34	6	1330	254	540	187	....	.237	.282	.287	.569	82	-96	99	452
Total	**564**					**4494**			**38273**	**9899**	**1172**	**414**	**96**		**2627**	**3912**	**1369**		**.259**	**.313**	**.318**	**.631**				

Runs
Wagner, H. (Pit) 105
Clarke, F. (Pit) 103
Beaumont, G. (Pit) 100

Hits
Beaumont, G. (Pit) 193
Keeler, W. (Bro) 186
Crawford, S. (Cin) 185

Doubles
Wagner, H. (Pit) 30
Clarke, F. (Pit) 27
Cooley, D. (Bos) 26

Triples
Crawford, S. (Cin) 22
Leach, T. (Pit) 22
Wagner, H. (Pit) 16

Home Runs
Leach, T. (Pit) 6
Beckley, J. (Cin) 5
2 players tied with 4

Total Bases
Crawford, S. (Cin) 256
Wagner, H. (Pit) 247
Beckley, J. (Cin) 227

Runs Batted In
Wagner, H. (Pit) 91
Leach, T. (Pit) 85
Crawford, S. (Cin) 78

Bases On Balls
Thomas, R. (Phi) 107
Lush, B. (Bos) 76
Tenney, F. (Bos) 73

Stolen Bases
Wagner, H. (Pit) 42
Slagle, J. (Chi) 41
Donovan, P. (StL) 34

Batting Average
Beaumont, G. (Pit) .357
Crawford, S. (Cin) .333
Keeler, W. (Bro) .333

On-Base Percentage
Thomas, R. (Phi) .414
Tenney, F. (Bos) .409
Beaumont, G. (Pit) .404

Slugging Average
Wagner, H. (Pit) .463
Crawford, S. (Cin) .461
Clarke, F. (Pit) .449

Adjusted OPS
Wagner, H. (Pit) 159
Clarke, F. (Pit) 157
Beaumont, G. (Pit) 148

Adjusted Batting Runs
Wagner, H. (Pit) 37.0
Clarke, F. (Pit) 33.0
Beaumont, G. (Pit) 31.0

Runs Created/Game
Wagner, H. (Pit) 8.50
Clarke, F. (Pit) 8.10
Beaumont, G. (Pit) 8.00

Fielding Runs
Lowe, B. (Chi) 27.6
Long, H. (Bos) 23.3
Steinfeldt, H. (Cin) 21.2

Win Shares – Batters
Wagner, H. (Pit) 35
Beaumont, G. (Pit) 31
Clarke, F. (Pit) 29

TPW – Batters
Wagner, H. (Pit) 4.9
Leach, T. (Pit) 4.1
Tenney, F. (Bos) 3.4

TEAM	CG	SH	SV	IP	H	H/G	ER	HR	BB	SO	OAV	RAT	ERA	ERA+	CERA	PR+	PF	FA	E	DP	FR	BW	PW	FW	TPW	DIF
PIT	131	**21**	3	1264^2	1142	8.1	323	**4**	**250**	**564**	.241	**1.101**	2.30	119	**2.33**	31.4	98	.958	247	87	**29.6**	**13.6**	3.3	**3.1**	**20.1**	13.9
BRO	131	14	3	1256	**1113**	**8.0**	375	10	363	536	**.238**	1.175	2.69	103	2.50	9.5	99	.952	275	79	-0.4	-.8	1.0	.0	.2	5.8
BOS	124	14	**4**	1259^2	1233	8.8	365	16	372	523	.255	1.274	2.61	108	3.12	23.3	102	**.959**	**240**	90	8.5	-2.1	2.5	.9	1.2	3.8
CIN	130	9	1	1239	1228	8.9	368	15	352	430	.259	1.275	2.67	112	3.14	19.8	108	.945	322	**118**	23.8	4.0	2.1	2.5	8.6	-8.6
CHI	**134**	17	2	**1293^1**	1244	8.7	**313**	7	281	447	.253	1.179	**2.18**	122	2.71	**68.2**	97	.946	331	113	3.5	-2.6	**7.2**	.4	4.9	-4.9
STL	112	7	**4**	1227^2	1399	10.3	473	16	338	400	.286	1.415	3.47	**79**	3.83	-77.6	98	.944	336	107	-23.3	-1.7	-8.2	-2.5	-12.3	1.3
PHI	118	8	3	1211	1323	9.8	471	12	334	504	.278	1.368	3.50	80	3.63	-59.2	101	.946	305	81	-33.4	-5.3	-6.2	-3.5	-15.1	3.1
NY	120	11	1	1242^1	1217	8.8	384	16	337	508	.251	1.251	2.78	99	3.07	12.5	101	.943	337	107	-9.3	-10.1	1.3	-1.0	-9.8	-10.2
Total	**1000**	**101**	**21**	**9993^2**		**8.9**	**3072**					**1.253**	**2.77**													

Wins
Chesbro, J. (Pit) 28
Pittinger, T. (Bos) 27
Willis, V. (Bos) 27

Win Percentage
Chesbro, J. (Pit) .824
Doheny, E. (Pit) .800
Tannehill, J. (Pit) .769

Games
Willis, V. (Bos) 51
Pittinger, T. (Bos) 46
Yerkes, S. (StL) 39

Complete Games
Willis, V. (Bos) 45
Pittinger, T. (Bos) 36
Hahn, N. (Cin) 35

Shutouts
Chesbro, J. (Pit) 8
Mathewson, C. (NY) 8
Taylor, J. (Chi) 8

Saves
Willis, V. (Bos) 3
3 players tied with 2

Innings Pitched
Willis, V. (Bos) 410
Pittinger, T. (Bos) 389^1
Taylor, J. (Chi) 324^2

Fewest Hits/Game
Newton, D. (Bro) 7.08
McGinnity, J. (NY) 7.18
Taylor, J. (Chi) 7.51

Fewest BB/Game
Phillippe, D. (Pit) .86
Tannehill, J. (Pit) .97
Menefee, J. (Chi) 1.19

Strikeouts
Willis, V. (Bos) 225
White, D. (Phi) 185
Pittinger, T. (Bos) 174

Ratio
Taylor, J. (Chi) .97
Tannehill, J. (Pit) .99
McGinnity, J. (NY) 1.01

Earned Run Average
Taylor, J. (Chi) 1.33
Hahn, N. (Cin) 1.77
Tannehill, J. (Pit) 1.95

Adjusted ERA
Taylor, J. (Chi) 203
Hahn, N. (Cin) 169
Poole, E. (Pit,Cin) 142

Component ERA
Taylor, J. (Chi) 1.73
McGinnity, J. (NY) 1.87
Tannehill, J. (Pit) 1.93

Opponents' Batting Avg.
Newton, D. (Bro) .217
McGinnity, J. (NY) .219
Taylor, J. (Chi) .227

Adjusted Pitching Runs
Taylor, J. (Chi) 48
Hahn, N. (Cin) 37
Mathewson, C. (NY) 26

Win Shares – Pitchers
Taylor, J. (Chi) 32
Hahn, N. (Cin) 29
Willis, V. (Bos) 29

TPW – Pitchers
Taylor, J. (Chi) 5.1
Hahn, N. (Cin) 4.0
Mathewson, C. (NY) 2.9

1902 American League

TEAM	G	W	L	PCT	GB	R	OR	EW	AB	H	2B	3B	HR	TB	BB	SO	SB	CS	AVG	OBP	SLG	OPS	OPS+	BR/A	PF	RC
PHI	137	83	53	.610	....	**775**	636	81	4762	1369	235	67	38	1852	343	293	201	....	.287	.340	.389	.729	104	21	104	**729**
STL	140	78	58	.574	5	619	607	69	4736	1254	208	61	29	1671	373	327	137	....	.265	.323	.353	.676	95	-29	99	612
BOS	138	77	60	.562	6.5	664	**600**	75	**4875**	1356	195	95	42	1867	275	375	132	....	.278	.322	.383	.705	99	-20	103	671
CHI	138	74	60	.552	8	675	602	75	4654	1248	170	50	14	1560	411	381	**265**	....	.268	.332	.335	.667	96	-14	96	641
CLE	137	69	67	.507	14	686	667	70	4840	**1401**	248	68	33	**1884**	308	356	140	....	**.289**	.336	.389	.726	**112**	**70**	96	712
WAS	138	61	75	.449	22	707	790	60	4734	1338	**261**	66	**47**	1872	329	296	121	....	.283	.335	**.395**	**.730**	108	43	101	694
DET	137	52	83	.385	30.5	566	657	58	4644	1167	141	55	22	1484	359	**287**	130	....	.251	.312	.320	.632	80	-119	102	527
BAL	141	50	88	.362	34	715	848	57	4760	1318	202	**107**	33	1833	**417**	429	189	....	.277	**.342**	.385	.727	103	22	104	723
Total	**553**					**5407**			**38005**	**10451**	**1660**	**569**	**258**		**2815**	**2744**	**1315**		**.275**	**.331**	**.369**	**.700**				

Runs
Fultz, D. (Phi) 109
Hartsel, T. (Phi) 109
Strang, S. (Chi) 108

Hits
Hickman, C. (Cle,Bos) 193
Cross, L. (Phi) 191
Bradley, B. (Cle) 187

Doubles
Davis, H. (Phi) 43
Delahanty, E. (Was) 43
2 players tied with 39

Triples
Williams, J. (Bal) 21
Freeman, B. (Bos) 19
2 players tied with 14

Home Runs
Seybold, S. (Phi) 16
3 players tied with 11

Total Bases
Hickman, C. (Cle,Bos) 288
Bradley, B. (Cle) 283
Freeman, B. (Bos) 283

Runs Batted In
Freeman, B. (Bos) 121
Hickman, C. (Cle,Bos) 110
Cross, L. (Phi) 108

Bases On Balls
Hartsel, T. (Phi) 87
Strang, S. (Chi) 76
Barrett, J. (Det) 74

Stolen Bases
Hartsel, T. (Phi) 47
Mertes, S. (Chi) 46
Fultz, D. (Phi) 44

Batting Average
Delahanty, E. (Was) .376
Hickman, C. (Cle,Bos) .361
Dougherty, P. (Bos) .342

On-Base Percentage
Delahanty, E. (Was) .453
Dougherty, P. (Bos) .407
Barrett, J. (Det) .397

Slugging Average
Delahanty, E. (Was) .590
Hickman, C. (Cle,Bos) .539
Bradley, B. (Cle) .515

Adjusted OPS
Delahanty, E. (Was) 186
Hickman, C. (Cle,Bos) 159
Bradley, B. (Cle) 151

Adjusted Batting Runs
Delahanty, E. (Was) 57.0
Hickman, C. (Cle,Bos) 39.0
Bradley, B. (Cle) 35.0

Runs Created/Game
Delahanty, E. (Was) 12.30
Hickman, C. (Cle,Bos) 9.00
Bradley, B. (Cle) 8.00

Fielding Runs
Ferris, H. (Bos) 27.3
Lajoie, N. (Cle,Phi) 25.2
Padden, D. (StL) 16.2

Win Shares – Batters
Delahanty, E. (Was) 31
3 players tied with 26

TPW – Batters
Bradley, B. (Cle) 4.7
Delahanty, E. (Was) 4.6
Hickman, C. (Cle,Bos) 2.9

TEAM	CG	SH	SV	IP	H	H/G	ER	HR	BB	SO	OAV	RAT	ERA	ERA+	CERA	PR+	PF	FA	E	DP	FR	BW	PW	FW	TPW	DIF
PHI	114	5	2	1216[1]	1292	9.6	445	33	368	**455**	.273	1.365	3.29	111	3.70	**54.8**	103	.953	270	75	-3.4	2.0	**5.2**	-.3	6.8	8.2
STL	120	7	2	**1244**	1273	9.2	462	36	343	348	.265	1.299	3.34	106	3.31	8.8	99	.953	274	122	17.7	-2.7	.8	1.7	-.2	10.2
BOS	123	6	1	1238	1217	**8.8**	**415**	27	326	431	**.258**	**1.246**	**3.02**	118	**3.07**	41.5	100	.955	263	101	**33.8**	-1.9	3.9	**3.2**	5.3	3.7
CHI	116	11	0	1221[2]	1269	9.4	463	30	331	346	.268	1.310	3.41	99	3.38	-24.1	95	**.955**	**257**	**125**	20.3	-1.3	-2.3	1.9	-1.6	8.6
CLE	116	**16**	**3**	1204[1]	**1199**	9.0	439	26	411	361	.260	1.337	3.28	105	3.41	18.3	96	.950	287	96	3.1	**6.6**	1.7	.3	**8.7**	-7.7
WAS	**130**	2	0	1207[2]	1403	10.5	585	56	**312**	300	.291	1.420	4.36	**85**	4.09	-65.9	104	.945	316	70	-22.1	4.0	-6.2	-2.1	-4.3	-2.7
DET	116	9	**3**	1190[2]	1267	9.6	471	**20**	370	245	.273	1.375	3.56	102	3.59	-5.1	102	.943	332	111	16.1	-11.3	-.5	1.5	-10.2	-4.8
BAL	119	3	1	1210[1]	1531	11.4	582	30	354	258	.309	1.557	4.33	87	4.64	-10.7	105	.938	357	109	-64.7	2.1	-1.0	-6.1	-5.0	-14.0
Total	**954**	**59**	**12**	**9733**		**9.7**	**3862**					**1.363**	**3.57**													

Wins
Young, C. (Bos) 32
Waddell, R. (Phi) 24
2 players tied with 22

Win Percentage
Waddell, R. (Phi) .774
Young, C. (Bos) .744
Donahue, R. (StL) .667

Games
Young, C. (Bos) 45
Dineen, B. (Bos) 42
Powell, J. (StL) 42

Complete Games
Young, C. (Bos) 41
Dineen, B. (Bos) 39
2 players tied with 36

Shutouts
Joss, A. (Cle) 5
3 players tied with 4

Saves
Powell, J. (StL) 2
11 players tied with 1

Innings Pitched
Young, C. (Bos) 384[2]
Dineen, B. (Bos) 371[1]
Powell, J. (StL) 328[1]

Fewest Hits/Game
Bernhard, B. (Phi,Cle) 7.01
Waddell, R. (Phi) 7.30
Joss, A. (Cle) 7.52

Fewest BB/Game
Orth, A. (Was) 1.11
Young, C. (Bos) 1.24
Bernhard, B. (Cle,Phi) 1.47

Strikeouts
Waddell, R. (Phi) 210
Young, C. (Bos) 160
Powell, J. (StL) 137

Ratio
Bernhard, B. (Cle,Phi) .94
Waddell, R. (Phi) 1.04
Young, C. (Bos) 1.05

Earned Run Average
Siever, E. (Det) 1.91
Waddell, R. (Phi) 2.05
Bernhard, B. (Phi,Cle) 2.15

Adjusted ERA
Siever, E. (Det) 191
Waddell, R. (Phi) 179
Young, C. (Bos) 166

Component ERA
Bernhard, B. (Cle,Phi) 1.69
Siever, E. (Det) 2.02
Waddell, R. (Phi) 2.11

Opponents' Batting Avg.
Bernhard, B. (Phi,Cle) .216
Waddell, R. (Phi) .223
Joss, A. (Cle) .228

Adjusted Pitching Runs
Waddell, R. (Phi) 50
Young, C. (Bos) 50
Siever, E. (Det) 34

Win Shares – Pitchers
Young, C. (Bos) 38
Waddell, R. (Phi) 33
Powell, J. (StL) 31

TPW – Pitchers
Waddell, R. (Phi) 5.5
Young, C. (Bos) 5.0
Bernhard, B. (Cle,Phi) 2.9

1903 National League

TEAM	G	W	L	PCT	GB	R	OR	EW	AB	H	2B	3B	HR	TB	BB	SO	SB	CS	AVG	OBP	SLG	OPS	OPS+	BR/A	PF	RC
PIT	141	91	49	.650	....	**793**	613	88	**4988**	**1429**	208	**110**	**34**	**1959**	364	....	172	....	.286	.341	**.393**	.734	**112**	**65**	103	**758**
NY	142	84	55	.604	6.5	729	**567**	87	4741	1290	181	49	20	1629	379	....	264	....	.272	.338	.344	.681	97	-15	104	678
CHI	139	82	56	.594	8	695	599	79	4733	1300	191	62	9	1642	422	....	259	....	.275	.340	.347	.687	105	40	97	678
CIN	141	74	65	.532	16.5	765	656	80	4857	1399	**228**	92	28	1895	403	....	144	....	**.288**	.346	.390	**.736**	105	19	111	735
BRO	139	70	66	.515	19	667	682	66	4534	1201	177	56	15	1535	**522**	....	**273**	....	.265	**.348**	.339	.686	105	50	97	661
BOS	140	58	80	.420	32	578	699	56	4682	1145	176	47	25	1490	398	....	159	....	.245	.312	.318	.630	89	-58	96	540
PHI	139	49	86	.363	39.5	617	738	56	4781	1283	186	62	12	1629	338	....	120	....	.268	.322	.341	.663	98	-13	97	596
STL	139	43	94	.314	46.5	505	795	39	4689	1176	138	65	8	1468	277	....	171	....	.251	.297	.313	.610	82	-108	97	511
Total	**560**					**5349**			**38005**	**10223**	**1485**	**543**	**151**		**3103**		**1562**		**.269**	**.331**	**.349**	**.679**				

Runs
Beaumont, G. (Pit) 137
Donlin, M. (Cin) 110
Browne, G. (NY) 105

Hits
Beaumont, G. (Pit) 209
Seymour, C. (Cin) 191
Browne, G. (NY) 185

Doubles
Clarke, F. (Pit) 32
Mertes, S. (NY) 32
Steinfeldt, H. (Cin) 32

Triples
Wagner, H. (Pit) 19
Donlin, M. (Cin) 18
Leach, T. (Pit) 17

Home Runs
Sheckard, J. (Bro) 9
6 players tied with 7

Total Bases
Beaumont, G. (Pit) 272
Seymour, C. (Cin) 267
Wagner, H. (Pit) 265

Runs Batted In
Mertes, S. (NY) 104
Wagner, H. (Pit) 101
Doyle, J. (Bro) 91

Bases On Balls
Thomas, R. (Phi) 107
Dahlen, B. (Bro) 82
Slagle, J. (Chi) 81

Stolen Bases
Chance, F. (Chi) 67
Sheckard, J. (Bro) 67
2 players tied with 46

Batting Average
Wagner, H. (Pit) .355
Clarke, F. (Pit) .351
Donlin, M. (Cin) .351

On-Base Percentage
Thomas, R. (Phi) .453
Bresnahan, R. (NY) .443
Chance, F. (Chi) .439

Slugging Average
Clarke, F. (Pit) .532
Wagner, H. (Pit) .518
Donlin, M. (Cin) .516

Adjusted OPS
Clarke, F. (Pit) 164
Sheckard, J. (Bro) 161
Bresnahan, R. (NY) 160

Adjusted Batting Runs
Sheckard, J. (Bro) 44.0
Wagner, H. (Pit) 39.0
Chance, F. (Chi) 38.0

Runs Created/Game
Chance, F. (Chi) 10.40
Wagner, H. (Pit) 10.40
Bresnahan, R. (NY) 10.30

Fielding Runs
Wagner, H. (Pit) 28.1
Ritchey, C. (Pit) 22.7
Moran, P. (Bos) 19.6

Win Shares – Batters
Wagner, H. (Pit) 35
Sheckard, J. (Bro) 33
Chance, F. (Chi) 31

TPW – Batters
Wagner, H. (Pit) 6.7
Sheckard, J. (Bro) 4.6
Chance, F. (Chi) 3.8

TEAM	CG	SH	SV	IP	H	H/G	ER	HR	BB	SO	OAV	RAT	ERA	ERA+	CERA	PR+	PF	FA	E	DP	FR	BW	PW	FW	TPW	DIF
PIT	117	**16**	5	1251[1]	1215	8.7	404	**9**	384	454	.255	1.278	2.91	111	3.06	-6.4	99	.951	295	100	**50.0**	**6.3**	-.6	**4.8**	**10.5**	10.5
NY	115	8	**8**	**1262[2]**	1257	9.0	414	20	371	**628**	.258	1.289	2.95	113	3.18	28.1	102	**.951**	287	87	26.2	-1.4	2.7	2.5	3.8	11.2
CHI	117	6	6	1240[1]	**1182**	**8.6**	**382**	14	**354**	451	.250	**1.238**	**2.77**	113	**2.90**	30.3	96	.942	338	78	18.3	3.8	2.9	1.8	8.5	4.5
CIN	**126**	11	1	1230	1277	9.3	420	14	378	480	.268	1.346	3.07	116	3.62	67.5	109	.946	312	84	-2.1	1.8	6.5	-.2	8.1	-3.1
BRO	118	11	4	1221[1]	1276	9.4	467	18	377	438	**.147**	1.353	3.44	92	15.13	**124.4**	98	.951	**284**	98	-159.6	4.8	**11.9**	-15.3	1.4	.6
BOS	125	8	1	1228[2]	1310	9.6	456	30	460	516	.277	1.441	3.34	96	4.01	-43.4	98	.939	361	89	23.8	-5.5	-4.2	2.3	-7.4	-3.6
PHI	**126**	5	3	1212[1]	1347	10.0	533	21	425	381	.286	1.462	3.96	**82**	4.14	-113.2	100	.947	300	76	18.8	-1.2	-10.9	1.8	-10.3	-7.7
STL	111	4	2	1212[1]	1353	10.0	494	25	430	419	.284	1.471	3.67	89	4.09	-78.3	100	.940	354	**111**	22.8	-10.4	-7.5	2.2	-15.7	-9.3
Total	**955**	**69**	**30**	**9859**		**9.3**	**3570**					**1.359**	**3.26**													

Wins
- McGinnity, J. (NY) 31
- Mathewson, C. (NY) 30
- 2 players tied with 25

Win Percentage
- Leever, S. (Pit) .781
- Phillippe, D. (Pit) .735
- Weimer, J. (Chi) .714

Games
- McGinnity, J. (NY) 55
- Mathewson, C. (NY) 45
- Pittinger, T. (Bos) 44

Complete Games
- McGinnity, J. (NY) 44
- Mathewson, C. (NY) 37
- Pittinger, T. (Bos) 35

Shutouts
- Leever, S. (Pit) 7
- Hahn, N. (Cin) 5
- Schmidt, H. (Bro) 5

Saves
- Lundgren, C. (Chi) 3
- Miller, R. (NY) 3
- 8 players tied with 2

Innings Pitched
- McGinnity, J. (NY) 434
- Mathewson, C. (NY) 366[1]
- Pittinger, T. (Bos) 351[2]

Fewest Hits/Game
- Weimer, J. (Chi) 7.69
- Mathewson, C. (NY) 7.89
- Taylor, J. (Chi) 7.98

Fewest BB/Game
- Phillippe, D. (Pit) .90
- Hahn, N. (Cin) 1.43
- Taylor, J. (Chi) 1.64

Strikeouts
- Mathewson, C. (NY) 267
- McGinnity, J. (NY) 171
- Garvin, N. (Bro) 154

Ratio
- Phillippe, D. (Pit) 1.03
- Taylor, J. (Chi) 1.07
- Leever, S. (Pit) 1.11

Earned Run Average
- Leever, S. (Pit) 2.06
- Mathewson, C. (NY) 2.26
- Weimer, J. (Chi) 2.30

Adjusted ERA
- Leever, S. (Pit) 157
- Mathewson, C. (NY) 148
- Hahn, N. (Cin) 141

Component ERA
- Phillippe, D. (Pit) 2.10
- Taylor, J. (Chi) 2.15
- Leever, S. (Pit) 2.26

Opponents' Batting Avg.
- Weimer, J. (Chi) .225
- Mathewson, C. (NY) .231
- Taylor, J. (Chi) .235

Adjusted Pitching Runs
- Jones, O. (Bro) 51
- Garvin, N. (Bro) 42
- Mathewson, C. (NY) 36

Win Shares – Pitchers
- McGinnity, J. (NY) 40
- Mathewson, C. (NY) 37
- Leever, S. (Pit) 28

TPW – Pitchers
- Jones, O. (Bro) 5.2
- Mathewson, C. (NY) 3.8
- Garvin, N. (Bro) 3.3

1903 American League

TEAM	G	W	L	PCT	GB	R	OR	EW	AB	H	2B	3B	HR	TB	BB	SO	SB	CS	AVG	OBP	SLG	OPS	OPS+	BR/A	PF	RC
BOS	141	91	47	.659	....	**708**	**504**	92	**4919**	**1336**	222	**113**	**48**	**1928**	262	561	141	....	**.272**	.313	**.392**	**.705**	111	56	105	**680**
PHI	137	75	60	.556	14.5	597	519	77	4673	1236	227	68	32	1695	268	513	157	....	.264	.309	.363	.672	102	9	105	598
CLE	140	77	63	.550	15	639	579	77	4773	1265	**231**	95	31	1779	259	595	175	....	.265	.308	.373	.681	**112**	**61**	98	634
NY	136	72	62	.537	17	579	573	68	4565	1136	193	62	18	1507	**332**	465	160	....	.249	.309	.330	.639	92	-37	106	544
DET	137	65	71	.478	25	567	539	71	4582	1229	162	91	12	1609	292	526	128	....	.268	**.318**	.351	.670	110	58	97	587
STL	139	65	74	.468	26.5	500	525	66	4639	1133	166	68	12	1471	271	539	101	....	.244	.290	.317	.607	90	-53	97	480
CHI	138	60	77	.438	30.5	516	613	57	4670	1152	176	49	14	1468	325	537	**180**	....	.247	.301	.314	.615	95	-22	96	526
WAS	140	43	94	.314	47.5	437	691	39	4613	1066	172	72	17	1433	257	**463**	131	....	.231	.277	.311	.588	80	-108	102	454
Total	**554**					**4543**			**37434**	**9553**	**1549**	**618**	**184**		**2266**	**4199**	**1173**		**.255**	**.303**	**.344**	**.648**				

Runs
- Dougherty, P. (Bos) 107
- Bradley, B. (Cle) 101
- 2 players tied with 95

Hits
- Dougherty, P. (Bos) 195
- Crawford, S. (Det) 184
- Parent, F. (Bos) 170

Doubles
- Seybold, S. (Phi) 45
- Lajoie, N. (Cle) 41
- Freeman, B. (Bos) 39

Triples
- Crawford, S. (Det) 25
- Bradley, B. (Cle) 22
- Freeman, B. (Bos) 20

Home Runs
- Freeman, B. (Bos) 13
- Hickman, C. (Cle) 12
- Ferris, H. (Bos) 9

Total Bases
- Freeman, B. (Bos) 281
- Crawford, S. (Det) 269
- Bradley, B. (Cle) 266

Runs Batted In
- Freeman, B. (Bos) 104
- Hickman, C. (Cle) 97
- Lajoie, N. (Cle) 93

Bases On Balls
- Barrett, J. (Det) 74
- Lush, B. (Det) 70
- Pickering, O. (Phi) 53

Stolen Bases
- Bay, H. (Cle) 45
- Pickering, O. (Phi) 40
- 2 players tied with 35

Batting Average
- Lajoie, N. (Cle) .344
- Crawford, S. (Det) .335
- Dougherty, P. (Bos) .331

On-Base Percentage
- Barrett, J. (Det) .407
- Lajoie, N. (Cle) .379
- Lush, B. (Det) .379

Slugging Average
- Lajoie, N. (Cle) .518
- Bradley, B. (Cle) .496
- Freeman, B. (Bos) .496

Adjusted OPS
- Lajoie, N. (Cle) 170
- Crawford, S. (Det) 159
- Bradley, B. (Cle) 153

Adjusted Batting Runs
- Lajoie, N. (Cle) 39.0
- Crawford, S. (Det) 37.0
- Barrett, J. (Det) 33.0

Runs Created/Game
- Lajoie, N. (Cle) 8.50
- Crawford, S. (Det) 7.40
- Dougherty, P. (Bos) 7.10

Fielding Runs
- Lajoie, N. (Cle) 36.4
- Ferris, H. (Bos) 17.7
- Williams, J. (NY) 16.3

Win Shares – Batters
- Lajoie, N. (Cle) 31
- Bradley, B. (Cle) 29
- Dougherty, P. (Bos) 28

TPW – Batters
- Lajoie, N. (Cle) 7.9
- Bradley, B. (Cle) 4.7
- Crawford, S. (Det) 3.4

TEAM	CG	SH	SV	IP	H	H/G	ER	HR	BB	SO	OAV	RAT	ERA	ERA+	CERA	PR+	PF	FA	E	DP	FR	BW	PW	FW	TPW	DIF
BOS	123	**20**	**4**	**1255**	1142	**8.2**	**358**	23	269	579	**.242**	**1.124**	**2.57**	118	**2.49**	**27.3**	102	.959	239	86	**37.6**	5.8	**2.8**	**3.9**	**12.6**	9.4
PHI	112	10	1	1207	**1124**	8.4	400	20	315	**728**	.246	1.192	2.98	102	2.82	21.0	103	**.960**	**217**	66	-10.9	1.0	2.2	-1.1	2.0	6.0
CLE	**125**	**20**	0	1243[2]	1161	8.4	377	**16**	271	521	.247	1.151	2.73	105	2.53	3.8	96	.946	322	**99**	13.5	**6.4**	.4	1.4	8.2	-1.2
NY	111	7	2	1201[1]	1171	8.8	411	19	245	463	.255	1.179	3.08	101	2.70	10.5	105	.953	264	87	-5.0	-3.8	1.1	-.5	-3.3	8.3
DET	123	15	2	1196	1169	8.8	365	19	336	554	.255	1.258	2.75	106	2.99	22.8	98	.950	281	82	-2.2	6.0	2.4	-.2	8.1	-11.1
STL	124	12	3	1222[1]	1220	9.0	376	26	**237**	511	.259	1.192	2.77	105	2.80	17.4	98	.953	268	94	2.4	-5.5	1.8	.2	-3.4	-.6
CHI	114	9	**4**	1235	1233	9.0	414	23	287	391	.259	1.231	3.02	93	2.96	-6.9	95	.949	297	85	-21.5	-2.2	-.7	-2.2	-5.2	-2.8
WAS	122	6	3	1223[2]	1333	9.8	519	38	306	452	.277	1.339	3.82	**82**	3.53	-80.2	106	.954	260	86	-13.5	-11.2	-8.3	-1.4	-20.9	-4.1
Total	**954**	**99**	**19**	**9784**		**8.8**	**3220**					**1.208**	**2.96**													

Wins
- Young, C. (Bos) 28
- Plank, E. (Phi) 23
- 4 players tied with 21

Win Percentage
- Young, C. (Bos) .757
- Hughes, T. (Bos) .741
- Bernhard, B. (Cle) .737

Games
- Plank, E. (Phi) 43
- Mullin, G. (Det) 41
- 3 players tied with 40

Complete Games
- Donovan, B. (Det) 34
- Waddell, R. (Phi) 34
- Young, C. (Bos) 34

Shutouts
- Young, C. (Bos) 7
- Dineen, B. (Bos) 6
- Mullin, G. (Det) 6

Saves
- 5 players tied with 2

Innings Pitched
- Young, C. (Bos) 341[2]
- Plank, E. (Phi) 336
- Chesbro, J. (NY) 324[2]

Fewest Hits/Game
- Moore, E. (Cle) 7.12
- Donovan, B. (Det) 7.24
- Joss, A. (Cle) 7.36

Fewest BB/Game
- Young, C. (Bos) .97
- Bernhard, B. (Cle) 1.14
- Donahue, R. (Cle,StL) 1.14

Strikeouts
- Waddell, R. (Phi) 302
- Donovan, B. (Det) 187
- 2 players tied with 176

Ratio
- Joss, A. (Cle) .95
- Young, C. (Bos) .97
- Bernhard, B. (Cle) 1.04

Earned Run Average
- Moore, E. (Cle) 1.74
- Young, C. (Bos) 2.08
- Bernhard, B. (Cle) 2.12

Adjusted ERA
- Moore, E. (Cle) 164
- Young, C. (Bos) 146
- Bernhard, B. (Cle) 135

Component ERA
- Joss, A. (Cle) 1.69
- Moore, E. (Cle) 1.83
- Young, C. (Bos) 1.89

Opponents' Batting Avg.
- Moore, E. (Cle) .217
- Donovan, B. (Det) .220
- Joss, A. (Cle) .223

Adjusted Pitching Runs
- Plank, E. (Phi) 28
- White, D. (Chi) 28
- Moore, E. (Cle) 28

Win Shares – Pitchers
- Young, C. (Bos) 38
- Plank, E. (Phi) 28
- 2 players tied with 27

TPW – Pitchers
- Young, C. (Bos) 4.0
- White, D. (Chi) 3.5
- Mullin, G. (Det) 3.5

1904 National League

TEAM	G	W	L	PCT	GB	R	OR	EW	AB	H	2B	3B	HR	TB	BB	SO	SB	CS	AVG	OBP	SLG	OPS	OPS+	BR/A	PF	RC
NY	158	106	47	.693	....	**744**	**474**	109	5150	**1347**	**202**	65	**31**	**1772**	**434**	....	**283**	....	**.262**	**.328**	**.344**	**.673**	**109**	**61**	104	**712**
CHI	156	93	60	.608	13	597	517	87	5210	1294	157	62	22	1641	298	....	227	....	.248	.295	.315	.610	94	-41	100	581
CIN	157	88	65	.575	18	695	547	94	**5231**	1332	189	92	21	1768	399	....	179	....	.255	.313	.338	.651	99	-11	109	642
PIT	156	87	66	.569	19	675	592	86	5160	1333	164	**102**	15	1746	391	....	178	....	.258	.316	.338	.655	106	32	103	638
STL	155	75	79	.487	31.5	602	595	78	5104	1292	175	66	24	1671	343	....	199	....	.253	.306	.327	.633	106	35	95	602
BRO	154	56	97	.366	50	497	614	61	4917	1142	159	53	15	1452	411	....	205	....	.232	.297	.295	.592	91	-42	97	521
BOS	155	55	98	.359	51	491	749	46	5135	1217	153	50	24	1542	316	....	143	....	.237	.287	.300	.587	90	-60	96	508
PHI	155	52	100	.342	53.5	571	784	53	5103	1268	170	54	23	1615	377	....	159	....	.248	.305	.316	.622	102	12	96	570
Total	**623**					**4872**			**41010**	**10225**	**1369**	**544**	**175**		**2969**		**1573**		**.249**	**.306**	**.322**	**.628**				

Runs
- Browne, G. (NY) 99
- Beaumont, G. (Pit) 97
- Wagner, H. (Pit) 97

Hits
- Beaumont, G. (Pit) 185
- Beckley, J. (StL) 179
- Wagner, H. (Pit) 171

Doubles
- Wagner, H. (Pit) 44
- Mertes, S. (NY) 28
- Delahanty, J. (Bos) 27

Triples
- Lumley, H. (Bro) 18
- Wagner, H. (Pit) 14
- 3 players tied with 13

Home Runs
- Lumley, H. (Bro) 9
- Brain, D. (StL) 7
- 4 players tied with 6

Total Bases
- Wagner, H. (Pit) 255
- Lumley, H. (Bro) 247
- Seymour, C. (Cin) 233

Runs Batted In
- Dahlen, B. (NY) 80
- Lumley, H. (Bro) 78
- Mertes, S. (NY) 78

Bases On Balls
- Thomas, R. (Phi) 102
- Huggins, M. (Cin) 88
- Devlin, A. (NY) 62

Stolen Bases
- Wagner, H. (Pit) 53
- Dahlen, B. (NY) 47
- Mertes, S. (NY) 47

Batting Average
- Wagner, H. (Pit) .349
- Beckley, J. (StL) .325
- Seymour, C. (Cin) .313

On-Base Percentage
- Wagner, H. (Pit) .423
- Thomas, R. (Phi) .416
- Chance, F. (Chi) .382

Slugging Average
- Wagner, H. (Pit) .520
- Seymour, C. (Cin) .439
- Chance, F. (Chi) .430

Adjusted OPS
- Wagner, H. (Pit) 186
- Chance, F. (Chi) 150
- Beckley, J. (StL) 147

Adjusted Batting Runs
- Wagner, H. (Pit) 50.0
- Thomas, R. (Phi) 33.0
- Beckley, J. (StL) 30.0

Runs Created/Game
- Wagner, H. (Pit) 10.80
- Chance, F. (Chi) 7.50
- Beckley, J. (StL) 6.30

Fielding Runs
- Evers, J. (Chi) 36.2
- Leach, T. (Pit) 32.7
- Tinker, J. (Chi) 22.2

Win Shares – Batters
- Wagner, H. (Pit) 43
- Chance, F. (Chi) 29
- Thomas, R. (Phi) 28

TPW – Batters
- Wagner, H. (Pit) 5.0
- Leach, T. (Pit) 3.8
- Thomas, R. (Phi) 3.6

TEAM	CG	SH	SV	IP	H	H/G	ER	HR	BB	SO	OAV	RAT	ERA	ERA+	CERA	PR+	PF	FA	E	DP	FR	BW	PW	FW	TPW	DIF
NY	127	**21**	**15**	**1396[2]**	1151	**7.4**	**337**	36	349	**707**	**.222**	**1.074**	**2.17**	125	**2.21**	**57.7**	100	**.956**	294	**93**	26.8	**6.4**	**6.1**	2.8	**15.4**	14.6
CHI	139	18	6	1383[2]	**1150**	7.5	353	16	402	618	.224	1.122	2.30	116	2.30	29.8	97	.954	298	89	24.5	-4.3	3.2	2.6	1.4	15.6
CIN	142	12	2	1392[2]	1256	8.1	362	**13**	343	502	.241	1.148	2.34	125	2.54	54.0	107	.954	301	81	**35.6**	-1.2	5.7	**3.8**	8.3	3.7
PIT	133	15	1	1348[1]	1273	8.5	433	**13**	379	455	.248	1.225	2.89	94	2.86	-32.6	100	.955	**291**	**93**	8.7	3.4	-3.5	.9	.8	10.2
STL	**146**	7	2	1368	1286	8.5	401	23	**319**	529	.239	1.173	2.64	102	2.57	34.7	99	.952	307	83	-27.4	3.7	3.7	-2.9	4.5	-6.5
BRO	135	12	2	1337[1]	1281	8.6	401	27	414	453	.255	1.267	2.70	101	3.12	14.4	100	.945	343	87	-9.1	-4.5	1.5	-1.0	-3.9	-16.1
BOS	136	13	0	1348[1]	1405	9.4	514	25	500	544	.272	1.413	3.43	80	3.79	-65.3	101	.945	353	91	-37.4	-6.3	-6.9	-4.0	-17.2	-3.8
PHI	131	10	2	1339[1]	1418	9.5	504	22	425	469	.270	1.376	3.39	**79**	3.63	-82.8	98	.937	403	**93**	-25.5	1.2	-8.8	-2.7	-10.2	-13.8
Total	**1089**	**108**	**30**	**10914[1]**		**8.4**	**3305**					**1.223**	**2.73**													

Wins
- McGinnity, J. (NY) 35
- Mathewson, C. (NY) 33
- Harper, J. (Cin) 23

Win Percentage
- McGinnity, J. (NY) .814
- Wiltse, H. (NY) .812
- Mathewson, C. (NY) .733

Games
- McGinnity, J. (NY) 51
- Mathewson, C. (NY) 48
- Jones, O. (Bro) 46

Complete Games
- Taylor, J. (StL) 39
- Willis, V. (Bos) 39
- 2 players tied with 38

Shutouts
- McGinnity, J. (NY) 9
- Harper, J. (Cin) 6
- 4 players tied with 5

Saves
- McGinnity, J. (NY) 5
- 3 players tied with 3

Innings Pitched
- McGinnity, J. (NY) 408
- Jones, O. (Bro) 377
- Mathewson, C. (NY) 367[2]

Fewest Hits/Game
- Brown, M. (Chi) 6.57
- Weimer, J. (Chi) 6.71
- McGinnity, J. (NY) 6.77

Fewest BB/Game
- Hahn, N. (Cin) 1.06
- Phillippe, D. (Pit) 1.40
- Nichols, K. (StL) 1.42

Strikeouts
- Mathewson, C. (NY) 212
- Willis, V. (Bos) 196
- Weimer, J. (Chi) 177

Ratio
- McGinnity, J. (NY) .96
- Brown, M. (Chi) .97
- Hahn, N. (Cin) .98

Earned Run Average
- McGinnity, J. (NY) 1.61
- Garvin, N. (Bro) 1.68
- Brown, M. (Chi) 1.86

Adjusted ERA
- McGinnity, J. (NY) 169
- Garvin, N. (Bro) 162
- Brown, M. (Chi) 142

Component ERA
- Brown, M. (Chi) 1.60
- McGinnity, J. (NY) 1.71
- Nichols, K. (StL) 1.83

Opponents' Batting Avg.
- Brown, M. (Chi) .199
- Weimer, J. (Chi) .204
- McGinnity, J. (NY) .206

Adjusted Pitching Runs
- McGinnity, J. (NY) 42
- Nichols, K. (StL) 30
- Taylor, J. (StL) 25

Win Shares – Pitchers
- McGinnity, J. (NY) 42
- Mathewson, C. (NY) 34
- Weimer, J. (Chi) 28

TPW – Pitchers
- McGinnity, J. (NY) 4.3
- Nichols, K. (StL) 3.2
- Taylor, J. (StL) 3.2

1904 American League

TEAM	G	W	L	PCT	GB	R	OR	EW	AB	H	2B	3B	HR	TB	BB	SO	SB	CS	AVG	OBP	SLG	OPS	OPS+	BR/A	PF	RC
BOS	157	95	59	.617	....	608	**466**	97	5231	1294	194	**105**	26	1776	347	570	101	....	.247	.301	.340	.640	102	11	106	597
NY	155	92	59	.609	1.5	598	526	85	5220	**1354**	195	91	27	1812	312	**548**	163	....	.259	**.308**	.347	.655	108	42	105	640
CHI	156	89	65	.578	6	600	482	94	5027	1217	193	68	14	1588	**373**	586	**216**	....	.242	.300	.316	.616	104	27	96	578
CLE	154	86	65	.570	7.5	**647**	482	97	5152	1340	**225**	90	27	**1826**	307	714	178	....	**.260**	.308	**.354**	**.662**	**116**	**83**	99	**650**
PHI	155	81	70	.536	12.5	557	503	83	5088	1266	197	77	**31**	1710	313	605	137	....	.249	.298	.336	.634	101	1	105	579
STL	156	65	87	.428	29	481	604	59	5291	1266	153	53	10	1555	332	609	150	....	.239	.291	.294	.585	96	-18	94	526
DET	162	62	90	.408	32	505	627	60	**5321**	1231	154	69	11	1556	344	635	112	....	.231	.282	.292	.575	90	-59	97	502
WAS	157	38	113	.252	55.5	437	743	39	5149	1170	171	57	10	1485	283	759	150	....	.227	.275	.288	.564	85	-87	98	475
Total	**626**					**4433**			**41479**	**10138**	**1482**	**610**	**156**		**2611**	**5026**	**1207**		**.244**	**.295**	**.321**	**.616**				

Runs
- Dougherty, P. (NY,Bos) 113
- Flick, E. (Cle) 97
- Bradley, B. (Cle) 94

Hits
- Lajoie, N. (Cle) 208
- Keeler, W. (NY) 186
- Bradley, B. (Cle) 183

Doubles
- Lajoie, N. (Cle) 49
- Collins, J. (Bos) 33
- Bradley, B. (Cle) 32

Triples
- Cassidy, J. (Was) 19
- Freeman, B. (Bos) 19
- Stahl, C. (Bos) 19

Home Runs
- Davis, H. (Phi) 10
- Freeman, B. (Bos) 7
- Murphy, D. (Phi) 7

Total Bases
- Lajoie, N. (Cle) 305
- Flick, E. (Cle) 260
- 2 players tied with 246

Runs Batted In
- Lajoie, N. (Cle) 102
- Freeman, B. (Bos) 84
- Bradley, B. (Cle) 83

Bases On Balls
- Barrett, J. (Det) 79
- Burkett, J. (StL) 78
- Hartsel, T. (Phi) 75

Stolen Bases
- Bay, H. (Cle) 38
- Flick, E. (Cle) 38
- Heidrick, E. (StL) 35

Batting Average
- Lajoie, N. (Cle) .376
- Keeler, W. (NY) .343
- Flick, E. (Cle) .306

On-Base Percentage
- Lajoie, N. (Cle) .413
- Keeler, W. (NY) .390
- Flick, E. (Cle) .371

Slugging Average
- Lajoie, N. (Cle) .552
- Flick, E. (Cle) .449
- Murphy, D. (Phi) .440

Adjusted OPS
- Lajoie, N. (Cle) 205
- Flick, E. (Cle) 160
- Keeler, W. (NY) 146

Adjusted Batting Runs
- Lajoie, N. (Cle) 63.0
- Flick, E. (Cle) 40.0
- Keeler, W. (NY) 29.0

Runs Created/Game
- Lajoie, N. (Cle) 10.70
- Flick, E. (Cle) 7.20
- Keeler, W. (NY) 6.90

Fielding Runs
- Tannehill, L. (Chi) 26.2
- Ferris, H. (Bos) 18.2
- Davis, G. (Chi) 17.1

Win Shares – Batters
- Lajoie, N. (Cle) 41
- Stahl, C. (Bos) 31
- Flick, E. (Cle) 31

TPW – Batters
- Lajoie, N. (Cle) 7.5
- Flick, E. (Cle) 4.3
- Bradley, B. (Cle) 3.9

TEAM	CG	SH	SV	IP	H	H/G	ER	HR	BB	SO	OAV	RAT	ERA	ERA+	CERA	PR+	PF	FA	E	DP	FR	BW	PW	FW	TPW	DIF
BOS	**148**	21	1	1406	1208	7.7	**331**	31	**233**	612	.233	**1.025**	**2.12**	126	**2.05**	82.0	103	.962	242	83	4.7	1.2	9.2	.5	10.9	7.1
NY	123	15	1	1380[2]	1180	7.7	394	29	311	684	.232	1.080	2.57	105	2.27	-8.9	104	.958	275	90	30.6	4.6	-1.0	3.4	7.1	9.9
CHI	134	**26**	**3**	1380	1161	**7.6**	353	13	303	550	**.229**	1.061	2.30	107	2.07	-8.2	95	**.964**	**238**	95	**31.7**	3.1	-.9	**3.5**	5.7	6.3
CLE	141	20	0	1356[2]	1273	8.4	334	**10**	285	627	.249	1.148	2.22	114	2.46	41.3	98	.959	255	86	6.1	**9.2**	4.6	.7	**14.5**	-3.5
PHI	136	**26**	0	1361[1]	**1149**	7.6	355	13	366	**887**	.230	1.113	2.35	114	2.28	**82.3**	103	.959	250	67	-32.8	.1	**9.2**	-3.7	5.6	.4
STL	135	13	1	1410	1335	8.5	443	25	333	577	.251	1.183	2.83	88	2.75	-34.0	96	.960	267	78	-20.5	-2.0	-3.8	-2.3	-8.1	-2.9
DET	143	15	0	**1430**	1345	8.5	440	16	433	556	.250	1.243	2.77	92	2.89	-52.6	98	.959	273	92	17.4	-6.6	-5.9	1.9	-10.5	-3.5
WAS	137	7	**3**	1359[2]	1487	9.8	547	19	347	533	.279	1.349	3.62	**73**	3.50	-108.4	102	.951	314	**97**	-36.9	-9.7	-12.1	-4.1	-26.0	-11.0
Total	**1097**	**143**	**9**	**11084[1]**		**8.2**	**3197**					**1.150**	**2.60**													

Wins
- Chesbro, J. (NY) 41
- Plank, E. (Phi) 26
- Young, C. (Bos) 26

Win Percentage
- Chesbro, J. (NY) .774
- Tannehill, J. (Bos) .656
- Smith, F. (Chi) .640

Games
- Chesbro, J. (NY) 55
- Powell, J. (NY) 47
- Waddell, R. (Phi) 46

Complete Games
- Chesbro, J. (NY) 48
- Mullin, G. (Det) 42
- Young, C. (Bos) 40

Shutouts
- Young, C. (Bos) 10
- Waddell, R. (Phi) 8
- 3 players tied with 7

Saves
- Patten, C. (Was) 3
- 8 players tied with 1

Innings Pitched
- Chesbro, J. (NY) 454[2]
- Powell, J. (NY) 390[1]
- Waddell, R. (Phi) 383

Fewest Hits/Game
- Chesbro, J. (NY) 6.69
- Owen, F. (Chi) 6.94
- Smith, F. (Chi) 6.98

Fewest BB/Game
- Young, C. (Bos) .69
- Tannehill, J. (Bos) 1.05
- Patterson, R. (Chi) 1.31

Strikeouts
- Waddell, R. (Phi) 349
- Chesbro, J. (NY) 239
- Powell, J. (NY) 202

Ratio
- Young, C. (Bos) .94
- Chesbro, J. (NY) .94
- Owen, F. (Chi) .97

Earned Run Average
- Joss, A. (Cle) 1.59
- Waddell, R. (Phi) 1.62
- White, D. (Chi) 1.78

Adjusted ERA
- Waddell, R. (Phi) 165
- Joss, A. (Cle) 159
- Chesbro, J. (NY) 149

Component ERA
- Chesbro, J. (NY) 1.56
- Owen, F. (Chi) 1.70
- Young, C. (Bos) 1.73

Opponents' Batting Avg.
- Chesbro, J. (NY) .208
- Owen, F. (Chi) .214
- Smith, F. (Chi) .215

Adjusted Pitching Runs
- Waddell, R. (Phi) 54
- Chesbro, J. (NY) 35
- Plank, E. (Phi) 29

Win Shares – Pitchers
- Chesbro, J. (NY) 53
- Young, C. (Bos) 35
- Waddell, R. (Phi) 32

TPW – Pitchers
- Waddell, R. (Phi) 5.3
- Chesbro, J. (NY) 4.6
- Plank, E. (Phi) 3.6

1905 National League

TEAM	G	W	L	PCT	GB	R	OR	EW	AB	H	2B	3B	HR	TB	BB	SO	SB	CS	AVG	OBP	SLG	OPS	OPS+	BR/A	PF	RC
NY	155	105	48	.686	....	**780**	505	108	5094	1392	**191**	88	**39**	**1876**	**517**	....	**291**	....	**.273**	**.351**	**.368**	**.719**	**120**	**131**	102	**796**
PIT	155	96	57	.627	9	692	570	91	5213	1385	190	91	22	1823	382	....	202	....	.266	.320	.350	.670	104	21	102	683
CHI	155	92	61	.601	13	667	**442**	106	5108	1249	157	82	12	1606	448	....	267	....	.245	.313	.314	.627	91	-52	104	625
PHI	155	83	69	.546	21.5	708	603	88	**5243**	1362	187	82	16	1761	406	....	180	....	.260	.318	.336	.654	106	38	96	655
CIN	155	79	74	.516	26	736	698	81	5205	**1401**	160	**101**	27	1844	434	....	181	....	.269	.332	.354	.686	101	6	111	710
STL	154	58	96	.377	47.5	535	734	53	5066	1254	140	85	20	1624	391	....	162	....	.248	.307	.321	.627	97	-18	97	576
BOS	156	51	103	.331	54.5	468	733	45	5190	1217	148	52	17	1520	302	....	132	....	.234	.284	.293	.576	80	-126	98	491
BRO	155	48	104	.316	56.5	506	807	43	5100	1255	154	60	29	1616	327	....	186	....	.246	.297	.317	.614	97	-22	93	564
Total	**620**					**5092**			**41219**	**10515**	**1327**	**641**	**182**		**3207**		**1601**		**.255**	**.315**	**.332**	**.647**				

Runs
Donlin, M. (NY) 124
Thomas, R. (Phi) 118
Huggins, M. (Cin) 117

Hits
Seymour, C. (Cin) 219
Donlin, M. (NY) 216
Wagner, H. (Pit) 199

Doubles
Seymour, C. (Cin) 40
Titus, J. (Phi) 36
Wagner, H. (Pit) 32

Triples
Seymour, C. (Cin) 21
Magee, S. (Phi) 17
Mertes, S. (NY) 17

Home Runs
Odwell, F. (Cin) 9
Seymour, C. (Cin) 8
3 players tied with 7

Total Bases
Seymour, C. (Cin) 325
Donlin, M. (NY) 300
Wagner, H. (Pit) 277

Runs Batted In
Seymour, C. (Cin) 121
Mertes, S. (NY) 108
Wagner, H. (Pit) 101

Bases On Balls
Huggins, M. (Cin) 103
Slagle, J. (Chi) 97
Thomas, R. (Phi) 93

Stolen Bases
Devlin, A. (NY) 59
Maloney, B. (Chi) 59
Wagner, H. (Pit) 57

Batting Average
Seymour, C. (Cin) .377
Wagner, H. (Pit) .363
Donlin, M. (NY) .356

On-Base Percentage
Chance, F. (Chi) .450
Seymour, C. (Cin) .429
Wagner, H. (Pit) .427

Slugging Average
Seymour, C. (Cin) .559
Wagner, H. (Pit) .505
Donlin, M. (NY) .495

Adjusted OPS
Seymour, C. (Cin) 175
Wagner, H. (Pit) 173
Donlin, M. (NY) 166

Adjusted Batting Runs
Seymour, C. (Cin) 52.0
Wagner, H. (Pit) 50.0
Donlin, M. (NY) 49.0

Runs Created/Game
Wagner, H. (Pit) 10.70
Seymour, C. (Cin) 10.70
Donlin, M. (NY) 9.20

Fielding Runs
Tinker, J. (Chi) 32.8
Tenney, F. (Bos) 25.3
Wagner, H. (Pit) 21.9

Win Shares – Batters
Wagner, H. (Pit) 46
Seymour, C. (Cin) 42
Donlin, M. (NY) 36

TPW – Batters
Wagner, H. (Pit) 7.9
Seymour, C. (Cin) 6.2
Donlin, M. (NY) 4.0

TEAM	CG	SH	SV	IP	H	H/G	ER	HR	BB	SO	OAV	RAT	ERA	ERA+	CERA	PR+	PF	FA	E	DP	FR	BW	PW	FW	TPW	DIF
NY	117	18	**15**	1370	1160	7.6	364	25	**364**	**760**	.229	1.112	2.39	122	2.32	89.5	98	.960	258	93	-8.9	**13.6**	9.3	-.9	**21.9**	7.1
PIT	113	12	6	1382[2]	1270	8.3	439	**12**	389	512	.248	1.200	2.86	105	2.79	-5.5	100	.961	255	112	24.9	2.2	-.6	2.6	4.2	15.8
CHI	133	**23**	2	**1407[1]**	**1135**	**7.3**	**319**	14	385	627	**.224**	**1.080**	**2.04**	146	**2.20**	**94.9**	99	**.962**	**248**	99	**50.7**	-5.4	**9.9**	**5.3**	9.7	6.3
PHI	119	12	5	1398[2]	1303	8.4	436	21	411	516	.253	1.225	2.81	104	2.97	-6.5	97	.957	275	99	21.6	4.0	-.7	2.2	5.5	1.5
CIN	119	10	2	1365[2]	1409	9.3	457	22	439	547	.271	1.353	3.01	109	3.57	17.1	110	.953	310	**122**	25.6	.6	1.8	2.7	5.0	-2.0
STL	135	10	2	1347[2]	1431	9.6	537	28	367	411	.276	1.334	3.59	83	3.59	-45.6	99	.957	274	83	-46.9	-1.8	-4.7	-4.9	-11.4	-7.6
BOS	**139**	14	0	1383	1390	9.0	541	36	433	533	.264	1.318	3.52	88	3.40	-34.0	103	.951	325	89	-32.9	-13.0	-3.5	-3.4	-20.0	-6.0
BRO	125	7	3	1347	1416	9.5	563	24	476	556	.274	1.405	3.76	**77**	3.77	-95.8	96	.937	408	101	-35.0	-2.3	-10.0	-3.6	-15.9	-12.1
Total	**1000**	**106**	**35**	**11002**		**8.6**	**3656**					**1.252**	**2.99**													

Wins
Mathewson, C. (NY) 31
Pittinger, T. (Phi) 23
Ames, R. (NY) 22

Win Percentage
Leever, S. (Pit) .800
Mathewson, C. (NY) .775
Ames, R. (NY) .733

Games
McGinnity, J. (NY) 46
Pittinger, T. (Phi) 46
2 players tied with 43

Complete Games
Young, I. (Bos) 41
Willis, V. (Bos) 36
Fraser, C. (Bos) 35

Shutouts
Mathewson, C. (NY) 8
Young, I. (Bos) 7
3 players tied with 5

Saves
Elliott, C. (NY) 6
McGinnity, J. (NY) 3
Wiltse, H. (NY) 3

Innings Pitched
Young, I. (Bos) 378
Willis, V. (Bos) 342
Mathewson, C. (NY) 338[2]

Fewest Hits/Game
Reulbach, E. (Chi) 6.42
Mathewson, C. (NY) 6.70
Lundgren, C. (Chi) 7.02

Fewest BB/Game
Phillippe, D. (Pit) 1.55
Brown, M. (Chi) 1.59
Young, I. (Bos) 1.69

Strikeouts
Mathewson, C. (NY) 206
Ames, R. (NY) 198
Overall, O. (Cin) 173

Ratio
Mathewson, C. (NY) .93
Reulbach, E. (Chi) .96
Phillippe, D. (Pit) 1.01

Earned Run Average
Mathewson, C. (NY) 1.28
Reulbach, E. (Chi) 1.42
Wicker, B. (Chi) 2.02

Adjusted ERA
Mathewson, C. (NY) 229
Reulbach, E. (Chi) 209
Wicker, B. (Chi) 147

Component ERA
Mathewson, C. (NY) 1.54
Reulbach, E. (Chi) 1.68
Phillippe, D. (Pit) 2.01

Opponents' Batting Avg.
Reulbach, E. (Chi) .201
Mathewson, C. (NY) .205
Wiltse, H. (NY) .219

Adjusted Pitching Runs
Mathewson, C. (NY) 64
Reulbach, E. (Chi) 40
Ewing, B. (Cin) 21

Win Shares – Pitchers
Mathewson, C. (NY) 39
Reulbach, E. (Chi) 29
Young, I. (Bos) 29

TPW – Pitchers
Mathewson, C. (NY) 7.6
Reulbach, E. (Chi) 3.6
Ewing, B. (Cin) 2.7

1905 American League

TEAM	G	W	L	PCT	GB	R	OR	EW	AB	H	2B	3B	HR	TB	BB	SO	SB	CS	AVG	OBP	SLG	OPS	OPS+	BR/A	PF	RC
PHI	152	92	56	.622	....	**623**	488	92	5146	1310	**256**	51	24	**1740**	376	644	190	....	.255	**.310**	**.338**	**.648**	**110**	**50**	102	**632**
CHI	158	92	60	.605	2	612	**451**	99	5114	1213	200	55	11	1556	439	613	194	....	.237	.305	.304	.609	103	26	96	577
DET	154	79	74	.516	15.5	512	604	64	4971	1209	190	54	13	1546	375	583	129	....	.243	.302	.311	.613	99	-3	101	540
BOS	153	78	74	.513	16	579	565	78	5049	1179	165	69	**29**	1569	**486**	553	131	....	.234	.305	.311	.616	100	10	101	550
CLE	155	76	78	.494	19	564	587	74	5166	**1318**	211	**72**	18	1727	286	712	188	....	**.255**	.301	.334	.636	106	23	101	608
NY	152	71	78	.477	21.5	586	621	70	4957	1228	163	61	23	1582	360	**537**	**200**	....	.248	.307	.319	.627	94	-33	111	580
WAS	154	64	87	.424	29.5	559	623	67	5015	1121	193	68	22	1516	298	824	169	....	.224	.274	.302	.577	92	-51	96	492
STL	156	54	99	.353	40.5	512	608	63	**5204**	1205	153	49	16	1504	362	639	130	....	.232	.288	.289	.577	93	-35	95	502
Total	**617**					**4547**			**40622**	**9783**	**1531**	**479**	**156**		**2982**	**5105**	**1331**		**.241**	**.299**	**.314**	**.613**				

Runs
Davis, H. (Phi) 93
Jones, F. (Chi) 91
Bay, H. (Cle) 90

Hits
Stone, G. (StL) 187
Davis, H. (Phi) 173
Crawford, S. (Det) 171

Doubles
Davis, H. (Phi) 47
Crawford, S. (Det) 38
2 players tied with 37

Triples
Flick, E. (Cle) 18
Ferris, H. (Bos) 16
Turner, T. (Cle) 14

Home Runs
Davis, H. (Phi) 8
Stone, G. (StL) 7
5 players tied with 6

Total Bases
Stone, G. (StL) 259
Davis, H. (Phi) 256
Crawford, S. (Det) 247

Runs Batted In
Davis, H. (Phi) 83
Cross, L. (Phi) 77
Donahue, J. (Chi) 76

Bases On Balls
Hartsel, T. (Phi) 121
Jones, F. (Chi) 73
2 players tied with 67

Stolen Bases
Hoffman, D. (Phi) 46
Fultz, D. (NY) 44
Stahl, J. (Was) 41

Batting Average
Flick, E. (Cle) .308
Keeler, W. (NY) .302
Bay, H. (Cle) .301

On-Base Percentage
Hartsel, T. (Phi) .409
Flick, E. (Cle) .383
Keeler, W. (NY) .357

Slugging Average
Flick, E. (Cle) .462
Crawford, S. (Det) .430
Davis, H. (Phi) .422

Adjusted OPS
Flick, E. (Cle) 165
Crawford, S. (Det) 148
Stone, G. (StL) 147

Adjusted Batting Runs
Flick, E. (Cle) 38.0
Hartsel, T. (Phi) 33.0
Stone, G. (StL) 32.0

Runs Created/Game
Flick, E. (Cle) 7.80
Crawford, S. (Det) 6.40
Hartsel, T. (Phi) 6.30

Fielding Runs
Cassidy, J. (Was) 29.4
Tannehill, L. (Chi) 23.1
Ferris, H. (Bos) 19.6

Win Shares – Batters
Crawford, S. (Det) 36
Hartsel, T. (Phi) 30
2 players tied with 29

TPW – Batters
Stone, G. (StL) 3.5
Flick, E. (Cle) 3.4
Davis, G. (Chi) 3.4

TEAM	CG	SH	SV	IP	H	H/G	ER	HR	BB	SO	OAV	RAT	ERA	ERA+	CERA	PR+	PF	FA	E	DP	FR	BW	PW	FW	TPW	DIF
PHI	117	**19**	0	1383[1]	**1137**	7.4	337	21	409	**895**	.226	1.118	2.19	121	2.33	**112.8**	100	.957	265	64	-42.6	**5.5**	**12.4**	-4.7	**13.2**	4.8
CHI	131	16	0	**1427**	1163	**7.3**	**316**	**11**	329	613	**.225**	**1.046**	**1.99**	124	**1.98**	34.2	93	**.968**	**218**	**95**	**41.4**	2.9	3.8	**4.5**	11.2	4.8
DET	124	17	1	1348	1226	8.2	424	**11**	474	578	.245	1.261	2.83	96	2.86	-30.5	103	.957	267	80	15.0	-.3	-3.4	1.6	-2.0	5.0
BOS	124	15	1	1356[1]	1198	8.0	428	33	**292**	652	.239	1.099	2.84	95	2.40	-16.2	102	.953	296	75	-5.8	1.1	-1.8	-.6	-1.4	3.4
CLE	**140**	16	0	1363[1]	1251	8.3	432	23	334	555	.246	1.163	2.85	**92**	2.62	-32.4	99	.963	233	84	-0.9	2.5	-3.6	-.1	-1.2	.2
NY	88	**19**	**4**	1353[2]	1235	8.2	440	26	396	642	.245	1.205	2.93	100	2.73	18.2	110	.952	293	88	-18.0	-3.6	2.0	-2.0	-3.6	.6
WAS	118	12	1	1362[1]	1250	8.3	434	12	385	539	.246	1.200	2.87	92	2.71	-71.5	100	.950	318	76	37.4	-5.6	-7.9	4.1	-9.3	-1.7
STL	134	11	2	1384[2]	1245	8.1	421	19	389	633	.242	1.180	2.74	93	2.65	-7.3	96	.955	296	78	-22.9	-3.8	-.8	-2.5	-7.1	-14.9
Total	**976**	**125**	**9**	**10978[2]**		**8.0**	**3232**					**1.158**	**2.65**													

Wins
Waddell, R. (Phi) 27
Plank, E. (Phi) 24
2 players tied with 23

Win Percentage
Waddell, R. (Phi) .730
Tannehill, J. (Bos) .710
Coakley, A. (Phi) .692

Games
Waddell, R. (Phi) 46
Mullin, G. (Det) 44
2 players tied with 42

Complete Games
Howell, H. (StL) 35
Mullin, G. (Det) 35
Plank, E. (Phi) 35

Shutouts
Killian, E. (Det) 8
Waddell, R. (Phi) 7
3 players tied with 6

Saves
Buchanan, J. (StL) 2
7 players tied with 1

Innings Pitched
Mullin, G. (Det) 347[2]
Plank, E. (Phi) 346[2]
Owen, F. (Chi) 334

Fewest Hits/Game
Waddell, R. (Phi) 6.33
Smith, F. (Chi) 6.63
Young, C. (Bos) 6.96

Fewest BB/Game
Young, C. (Bos) .84
Joss, A. (Cle) 1.45
Owen, F. (Chi) 1.51

Strikeouts
Waddell, R. (Phi) 287
Plank, E. (Phi) 210
Young, C. (Bos) 210

Ratio
Young, C. (Bos) .87
Waddell, R. (Phi) .98
Owen, F. (Chi) .99

Earned Run Average
Waddell, R. (Phi) 1.48
White, D. (Chi) 1.76
Young, C. (Bos) 1.82

Adjusted ERA
Waddell, R. (Phi) 179
Young, C. (Bos) 148
Coakley, A. (Phi) 144

Component ERA
Young, C. (Bos) 1.49
Waddell, R. (Phi) 1.66
White, D. (Chi) 1.86

Opponents' Batting Avg.
Waddell, R. (Phi) .200
Smith, F. (Chi) .208
Young, C. (Bos) .216

Adjusted Pitching Runs
Waddell, R. (Phi) 53
Young, C. (Bos) 32
Coakley, A. (Phi) 31

Win Shares – Pitchers
Waddell, R. (Phi) 35
Plank, E. (Phi) 31
Killian, E. (Det) 29

TPW – Pitchers
Waddell, R. (Phi) 5.7
Young, C. (Bos) 3.4
Plank, E. (Phi) 3.2

1906 National League

TEAM	G	W	L	PCT	GB	R	OR	EW	AB	H	2B	3B	HR	TB	BB	SO	SB	CS	AVG	OBP	SLG	OPS	OPS+	BR/A	PF	RC
CHI	155	116	36	.763	....	704	381	118	5018	1316	181	71	20	1699	448	....	283	....	.262	.328	.339	.667	109	50	106	695
NY	153	96	56	.632	20	625	509	91	4768	1217	162	53	15	1530	563	....	288	....	.255	.343	.321	.664	112	82	102	659
PIT	154	93	60	.608	23.5	623	470	98	5030	1313	164	67	12	1647	424	....	162	....	.261	.324	.327	.651	105	30	104	625
PHI	154	71	82	.464	45.5	528	564	71	4911	1183	197	47	12	1510	432	....	180	....	.241	.307	.307	.614	98	-10	100	550
BRO	153	66	86	.434	50	496	625	59	4897	1156	141	68	25	1508	388	....	175	....	.236	.297	.308	.605	103	11	92	532
CIN	155	64	87	.424	51.5	533	582	69	5025	1198	140	71	16	1528	395	....	170	....	.238	.301	.304	.605	91	-51	104	544
STL	154	52	98	.347	63	470	607	56	5075	1195	137	69	10	1500	361	....	110	....	.235	.291	.296	.587	93	-46	96	498
BOS	152	49	102	.325	66.5	408	649	43	4925	1115	136	43	16	1385	356	....	95	....	.226	.286	.281	.567	85	-85	97	448
Total	615					4387			39649	9693	1258	489	126		3367	1463			.244	.310	.310	.620				

Runs
Chance, F. (Chi) 103; Wagner, H. (Pit) 103; Sheckard, J. (Chi) 90

Hits
Steinfeldt, H. (Chi) 176; Wagner, H. (Pit) 175; Seymour, C. (NY,Cin) 165

Doubles
Wagner, H. (Pit) 38; Magee, S. (Phi) 36; Bransfield, K. (Phi) 28

Triples
Clarke, F. (Pit) 13; Schulte, F. (Chi) 13; 2 players tied with 12

Home Runs
Jordan, T. (Bro) 12; Lumley, H. (Bro) 9; Seymour, C. (NY,Cin) 8

Total Bases
Wagner, H. (Pit) 237; Steinfeldt, H. (Chi) 232; Lumley, H. (Bro) 231

Runs Batted In
Nealon, J. (Pit) 83; Steinfeldt, H. (Chi) 83; Seymour, C. (NY,Cin) 80

Bases On Balls
Thomas, R. (Phi) 107; Bresnahan, R. (NY) 81; Titus, J. (Phi) 78

Stolen Bases
Chance, F. (Chi) 57; Magee, S. (Phi) 55; Devlin, A. (NY) 54

Batting Average
Wagner, H. (Pit) .339; Steinfeldt, H. (Chi) .327; Lumley, H. (Bro) .324

On-Base Percentage
Bresnahan, R. (NY) .419; Chance, F. (Chi) .419; Wagner, H. (Pit) .416

Slugging Average
Lumley, H. (Bro) .477; Wagner, H. (Pit) .459; Steinfeldt, H. (Chi) .430

Adjusted OPS
Lumley, H. (Bro) 184; Wagner, H. (Pit) 166; Chance, F. (Chi) 156

Adjusted Batting Runs
Lumley, H. (Bro) 45.0; Wagner, H. (Pit) 41.0; Chance, F. (Chi) 35.0

Runs Created/Game
Wagner, H. (Pit) 9.30; Chance, F. (Chi) 8.70; Lumley, H. (Bro) 8.00

Fielding Runs
Doolan, M. (Phi) 25.6; Wagner, H. (Pit) 22.4; Huggins, M. (Cin) 22.4

Win Shares – Batters
Wagner, H. (Pit) 46; Devlin, A. (NY) 36; 2 players tied with 35

TPW – Batters
Wagner, H. (Pit) 7.5; Devlin, A. (NY) 5.3; Huggins, M. (Cin) 4.2

TEAM	CG	SH	SV	IP	H	H/G	ER	HR	BB	SO	OAV	RAT	ERA	ERA+	CERA	PR+	PF	FA	E	DP	FR	BW	PW	FW	TPW	DIF
CHI	125	30	10	1388[1]	1018	6.6	270	12	446	702	.207	1.055	1.75	150	1.98	103.8	100	.969	194	100	32.1	5.5	11.5	3.6	20.6	19.4
NY	105	19	18	1334[1]	1207	8.1	369	13	394	639	.241	1.200	2.49	104	2.59	13.1	99	.964	233	84	3.3	9.1	1.5	.4	11.0	9.0
PIT	116	27	2	1358	1234	8.2	333	13	309	532	.245	1.136	2.21	121	2.53	61.5	102	.964	228	109	6.5	3.3	6.8	.7	10.9	6.1
PHI	108	21	5	1354[1]	1201	8.0	388	18	436	500	.235	1.209	2.58	101	2.74	19.7	99	.956	271	83	-15.5	-1.1	2.2	-1.7	-.6	-4.4
BRO	119	22	11	1348[2]	1255	8.4	469	11	453	476	.249	1.266	3.13	80	2.98	-78.2	96	.955	283	73	-14.1	1.3	-8.7	-1.6	-9.0	-1.0
CIN	126	12	5	1369[2]	1248	8.2	409	14	470	567	.249	1.254	2.69	102	2.98	-2.4	105	.959	262	97	11.1	-5.7	-.3	1.2	-4.7	-6.3
STL	118	4	2	1354	1246	8.3	457	17	479	559	.246	1.274	3.04	86	3.03	-50.5	100	.957	272	92	-13.7	-5.1	-5.6	-1.5	-12.2	-10.8
BOS	137	10	0	1334[1]	1291	8.7	465	24	436	562	.261	1.294	3.14	85	3.26	-55.8	102	.947	337	102	-12.1	-9.4	-6.2	-1.3	-16.9	-9.1
Total	954	145	53	10841[2]		8.0	3160					1.210	2.62													

Wins
McGinnity, J. (NY) 27; Brown, M. (Chi) 26; Willis, V. (Pit) 23

Win Percentage
Reulbach, E. (Chi) .826; Brown, M. (Chi) .812; Leever, S. (Pit) .759

Games
McGinnity, J. (NY) 45; Young, I. (Bos) 43; 2 players tied with 42

Complete Games
Young, I. (Bos) 37; Pfeffer, B. (Bos) 33; 4 players tied with 32

Shutouts
Brown, M. (Chi) 9; Leifield, L. (Pit) 8; 7 players tied with 6

Saves
Ferguson, G. (NY) 7; Wiltse, H. (NY) 6; Stricklett, E. (Bro) 5

Innings Pitched
Young, I. (Bos) 358[1]; McGinnity, J. (NY) 339[2]; Willis, V. (Pit) 322

Fewest Hits/Game
Reulbach, E. (Chi) 5.33; Pfiester, J. (Chi) 6.21; Brown, M. (Chi) 6.43

Fewest BB/Game
Phillippe, D. (Pit) 1.07; Leever, S. (Pit) 1.66; Sparks, T. (Phi) 1.76

Strikeouts
Beebe, F. (StL,Chi) 171; Pfeffer, B. (Bos) 158; Ames, R. (NY) 156

Ratio
Brown, M. (Chi) .93; Pfiester, J. (Chi) .94; Sparks, T. (Phi) .97

Earned Run Average
Brown, M. (Chi) 1.04; Pfiester, J. (Chi) 1.51; Reulbach, E. (Chi) 1.65

Adjusted ERA
Brown, M. (Chi) 253; Pfiester, J. (Chi) 175; Reulbach, E. (Chi) 159

Component ERA
Brown, M. (Chi) 1.53; Pfiester, J. (Chi) 1.66; Reulbach, E. (Chi) 1.68

Opponents' Batting Avg.
Reulbach, E. (Chi) .175; Pfiester, J. (Chi) .194; Brown, M. (Chi) .202

Adjusted Pitching Runs
Brown, M. (Chi) 43; Willis, V. (Pit) 32; Pfiester, J. (Chi) 25

Win Shares – Pitchers
Brown, M. (Chi) 35; Willis, V. (Pit) 29; Weimer, J. (Cin) 27

TPW – Pitchers
Brown, M. (Chi) 4.9; Willis, V. (Pit) 3.5; Taylor, J. (StL,Chi) 2.7

1906 American League

TEAM	G	W	L	PCT	GB	R	OR	EW	AB	H	2B	3B	HR	TB	BB	SO	SB	CS	AVG	OBP	SLG	OPS	OPS+	BR/A	PF	RC
CHI	154	93	58	.616	....	570	460	91	4925	1133	152	52	7	1410	453	....	214	....	.230	.301	.286	.588	92	-30	97	531
NY	155	90	61	.596	3	640	543	88	5095	1354	166	77	17	1725	331	....	192	....	.266	.316	.339	.655	101	2	110	644
CLE	157	89	64	.582	5	663	481	100	5425	1514	240	73	12	1936	330	....	203	....	.279	.325	.357	.682	121	120	99	737
PHI	149	78	67	.538	12	561	539	75	4883	1206	213	49	32	1613	385	....	165	....	.247	.308	.330	.638	102	14	103	581
STL	154	76	73	.510	16	560	499	83	5030	1244	145	60	20	1569	366	....	221	....	.247	.304	.312	.616	103	19	96	579
DET	151	71	78	.477	21	518	598	64	4930	1195	154	64	10	1507	333	....	206	....	.242	.295	.306	.600	91	-51	103	539
WAS	151	55	95	.367	37.5	519	665	57	4956	1180	144	65	26	1532	306	....	233	....	.238	.289	.309	.598	97	-18	95	539
BOS	155	49	105	.318	45.5	463	706	46	5168	1223	160	75	13	1572	298	....	99	....	.237	.284	.304	.588	89	-66	100	503
Total	613					4494			40412	10049	1374	515	137		2802	1533			.249	.303	.318	.621				

Runs
Flick, E. (Cle) 98; Hartsel, T. (Phi) 96; Keeler, W. (NY) 96

Hits
Lajoie, N. (Cle) 214; Stone, G. (StL) 208; Flick, E. (Cle) 194

Doubles
Lajoie, N. (Cle) 48; Davis, H. (Phi) 42; Flick, E. (Cle) 34

Triples
Flick, E. (Cle) 22; Stone, G. (StL) 20; Crawford, S. (Det) 16

Home Runs
Davis, H. (Phi) 12; Hickman, C. (Was) 9; Stone, G. (StL) 6

Total Bases
Stone, G. (StL) 291; Lajoie, N. (Cle) 280; Flick, E. (Cle) 275

Runs Batted In
Davis, H. (Phi) 96; Lajoie, N. (Cle) 91; Davis, G. (Chi) 80

Bases On Balls
Hartsel, T. (Phi) 88; Jones, F. (Chi) 83; Hahn, E. (Chi,NY) 72

Stolen Bases
Anderson, J. (Was) 39; Flick, E. (Cle) 39; 2 players tied with 37

Batting Average
Stone, G. (StL) .358; Lajoie, N. (Cle) .355; Chase, H. (NY) .323

On-Base Percentage
Stone, G. (StL) .417; Lajoie, N. (Cle) .392; Flick, E. (Cle) .372

Slugging Average
Stone, G. (StL) .501; Lajoie, N. (Cle) .465; Davis, H. (Phi) .459

Adjusted OPS
Stone, G. (StL) 195; Lajoie, N. (Cle) 170; Flick, E. (Cle) 156

Adjusted Batting Runs
Stone, G. (StL) 63.0; Lajoie, N. (Cle) 46.0; Flick, E. (Cle) 40.0

Runs Created/Game
Stone, G. (StL) 9.60; Lajoie, N. (Cle) 8.00; Flick, E. (Cle) 7.20

Fielding Runs
Lajoie, N. (Cle) 36.9; Turner, T. (Cle) 31.7; Tannehill, L. (Chi) 26.4

Win Shares – Batters
Lajoie, N. (Cle) 38; Stone, G. (StL) 33; Davis, H. (Phi) 31

TPW – Batters
Lajoie, N. (Cle) 9.3; Stone, G. (StL) 5.8; Turner, T. (Cle) 5.7

TEAM	CG	SH	SV	IP	H	H/G	ER	HR	BB	SO	OAV	RAT	ERA	ERA+	CERA	PR+	PF	FA	E	DP	FR	BW	PW	FW	TPW	DIF
CHI	117	32	4	1375[1]	1212	7.9	325	11	255	543	.240	1.067	2.13	119	2.17	45.4	94	.963	243	80	16.7	-3.3	5.0	1.8	3.5	14.5
NY	99	18	5	1357[2]	1236	8.2	419	21	351	605	.246	1.169	2.78	107	2.56	38.1	110	.957	272	69	-10.1	.2	4.2	-1.1	3.3	11.7
CLE	133	27	4	1412[2]	1197	7.6	328	16	365	530	.233	1.106	2.09	125	2.28	54.6	97	.967	217	111	28.7	13.2	6.0	3.2	22.4	-9.4
PHI	107	19	4	1322	1135	7.7	382	9	425	749	.235	1.180	2.60	105	2.51	20.1	101	.956	267	86	-2.2	1.5	2.2	-.2	3.5	2.5
STL	133	17	5	1357[2]	1132	7.5	336	14	314	558	.230	1.065	2.23	116	2.16	-46.7	103	.954	290	80	1.7	2.1	5.7	.2	8.0	-6.0
DET	128	7	4	1334[1]	1398	9.4	454	14	389	469	.273	1.339	3.06	90	3.38	-20.1	96	.959	260	86	2.8	-5.6	-5.1	.3	-10.4	7.4
WAS	115	13	4	1322[2]	1331	9.1	477	19	451	558	.265	1.347	3.25	81	3.35	-69.6	98	.955	279	78	-21.4	-2.0	-7.6	-2.4	-12.0	-8.0
BOS	124	6	6	1382	1360	8.9	524	37	285	549	.260	1.190	3.41	81	2.86	-86.7	102	.949	335	84	-15.5	-7.3	-9.5	-1.7	-18.5	-9.5
Total	956	139	33	10864[1]		8.3	3245					1.181	2.69													

Wins
Orth, A. (NY) 27
Chesbro, J. (NY) 23
2 players tied with 22

Win Percentage
Plank, E. (Phi) .760
White, D. (Chi) .750
Joss, A. (Cle) .700

Games
Chesbro, J. (NY) 49
Orth, A. (NY) 45
2 players tied with 43

Complete Games
Orth, A. (NY) 36
Mullin, G. (Det) 35
Hess, O. (Cle) 33

Shutouts
Walsh, E. (Chi) 10
Joss, A. (Cle) 9
Waddell, R. (Phi) 8

Saves
Bender, C. (Phi) 3
Hess, O. (Cle) 3
7 players tied with 2

Innings Pitched
Orth, A. (NY) 338^{2}
Hess, O. (Cle) 333^{2}
Mullin, G. (Det) 330

Fewest Hits/Game
Pelty, B. (StL) 6.53
White, D. (Chi) 6.57
Walsh, E. (Chi) 6.95

Fewest BB/Game
Young, C. (Bos) .78
Altrock, N. (Chi) 1.31
Joss, A. (Cle) 1.37

Strikeouts
Waddell, R. (Phi) 196
Falkenberg, C. (Was) 178
Walsh, E. (Chi) 171

Ratio
White, D. (Chi) .90
Joss, A. (Cle) .93
Pelty, B. (StL) .95

Earned Run Average
White, D. (Chi) 1.52
Pelty, B. (StL) 1.59
Joss, A. (Cle) 1.72

Adjusted ERA
White, D. (Chi) 167
Pelty, B. (StL) 163
Joss, A. (Cle) 152

Component ERA
White, D. (Chi) 1.52
Joss, A. (Cle) 1.60
Pelty, B. (StL) 1.69

Opponents' Batting Avg.
Pelty, B. (StL) .206
White, D. (Chi) .207
Walsh, E. (Chi) .216

Adjusted Pitching Runs
Pelty, B. (StL) 28
Orth, A. (NY) 26
Joss, A. (Cle) 22

Win Shares – Pitchers
Orth, A. (NY) 36
Mullin, G. (Det) 26
2 players tied with 25

TPW – Pitchers
Orth, A. (NY) 3.7
Pelty, B. (StL) 2.9
White, D. (Chi) 2.8

1907 National League

TEAM	G	W	L	PCT	GB	R	OR	EW	AB	H	2B	3B	HR	TB	BB	SO	SB	CS	AVG	OBP	SLG	OPS	OPS+	BR/A	PF	RC
CHI	155	107	45	.704	....	574	**390**	104	4892	1224	**162**	48	13	1521	435	....	235	....	.250	.318	.311	.628	98	-6	106	596
PIT	157	91	63	.591	17	**634**	510	93	4957	**1261**	133	78	19	**1607**	469	....	**264**	....	**.254**	.325	**.324**	**.649**	**109**	**55**	101	**645**
PHI	149	83	64	.565	21.5	514	476	79	4725	1113	**162**	65	12	1441	424	....	154	....	.236	.304	.305	.609	99	-3	99	514
NY	155	82	71	.536	25.5	574	510	86	4874	1222	160	48	**23**	1547	**516**	....	205	....	.251	**.331**	.317	.648	107	52	103	617
BRO	153	65	83	.439	40	446	522	62	4895	1135	142	63	18	1457	336	....	121	....	.232	.287	.298	.584	97	-23	92	487
CIN	156	66	87	.431	41.5	526	519	78	4966	1226	126	**90**	15	1577	372	....	158	....	.247	.304	.318	.621	98	-19	104	564
BOS	152	58	90	.392	47	502	652	55	**5020**	1222	142	61	22	1552	413	....	118	....	.243	.308	.309	.617	101	4	100	542
STL	155	52	101	.340	55.5	419	610	49	5008	1163	121	52	18	1442	312	....	125	....	.232	.283	.288	.571	88	-74	97	474
Total	**616**					**4189**			**39337**	**9566**	**1148**	**505**	**140**		**3277**		**1380**		**.243**	**.308**	**.309**	**.616**				

Runs
Shannon, S. (NY) 104
Leach, T. (Pit) 102
Wagner, H. (Pit) 98

Hits
Beaumont, G. (Bos) 187
Wagner, H. (Pit) 180
Leach, T. (Pit) 166

Doubles
Wagner, H. (Pit) 38
Magee, S. (Phi) 28
2 players tied with 25

Triples
Alperman, W. (Bro) 16
Ganzel, J. (Cin) 16
2 players tied with 14

Home Runs
Brain, D. (Bos) 10
Lumley, H. (Bro) 9
Murray, R. (StL) 7

Total Bases
Wagner, H. (Pit) 264
Beaumont, G. (Bos) 246
Magee, S. (Phi) 229

Runs Batted In
Magee, S. (Phi) 85
Abbaticchio, E. (Pit) 82
Wagner, H. (Pit) 82

Bases On Balls
Huggins, M. (Cin) 83
Thomas, R. (Phi) 83
2 players tied with 82

Stolen Bases
Wagner, H. (Pit) 61
Evers, J. (Chi) 46
Magee, S. (Phi) 46

Batting Average
Wagner, H. (Pit) .350
Magee, S. (Phi) .328
Beaumont, G. (Bos) .322

On-Base Percentage
Wagner, H. (Pit) .408
Magee, S. (Phi) .396
Clarke, F. (Pit) .383

Slugging Average
Wagner, H. (Pit) .513
Magee, S. (Phi) .455
Lumley, H. (Bro) .425

Adjusted OPS
Wagner, H. (Pit) 186
Magee, S. (Phi) 169
Beaumont, G. (Bos) 148

Adjusted Batting Runs
Wagner, H. (Pit) 49.0
Magee, S. (Phi) 40.0
Beaumont, G. (Bos) 30.0

Runs Created/Game
Wagner, H. (Pit) 10.20
Magee, S. (Phi) 8.50
Beaumont, G. (Bos) 6.60

Fielding Runs
Evers, J. (Chi) 31.1
Mitchell, M. (Cin) 20.6
Doolan, M. (Phi) 19.4

Win Shares – Batters
Wagner, H. (Pit) 44
Magee, S. (Phi) 38
2 players tied with 29

TPW – Batters
Wagner, H. (Pit) 7.4
Magee, S. (Phi) 4.3
Brain, D. (Bos) 4.1

TEAM	CG	SH	SV	IP	H	H/G	ER	HR	BB	SO	OAV	RAT	ERA	ERA+	CERA	PR+	PF	FA	E	DP	FR	BW	PW	FW	TPW	DIF
CHI	114	**32**	8	**1373^{1}**	**1054**	**6.9**	**264**	**11**	402	586	**.216**	**1.060**	**1.73**	144	**2.04**	**81.6**	101	**.967**	**211**	110	**34.2**	-.7	**9.3**	**3.9**	**12.4**	18.6
PIT	111	24	5	1363	1207	8.0	348	12	**368**	497	.241	1.156	2.30	106	2.59	41.7	98	.959	256	75	-22.2	**6.2**	4.7	-2.5	8.4	5.6
PHI	110	21	4	1299^{1}	1095	7.6	351	13	422	499	.233	1.168	2.43	99	2.60	-24.8	98	.957	256	104	22.6	-.3	-2.8	2.6	-.6	10.6
NY	109	22	**13**	1371	1219	8.0	373	24	369	**655**	.238	1.158	2.45	101	2.55	49.7	100	.963	232	75	-45.9	5.9	5.6	-5.2	6.4	-.4
BRO	125	20	1	1356^{1}	1218	8.1	359	16	463	479	.249	1.239	2.38	98	2.89	6.0	95	.959	262	94	-13.1	-2.6	.7	-1.5	-3.4	-5.6
CIN	118	10	2	1351^{1}	1223	8.2	362	16	444	481	.251	1.234	2.41	107	2.99	11.7	105	.963	227	118	14.9	-2.2	1.3	1.7	.9	-10.9
BOS	121	9	2	1338^{2}	1324	8.9	495	28	458	426	.268	1.331	3.33	**77**	3.59	-128.7	103	.961	249	**128**	11.6	.5	-14.6	1.3	-12.8	-3.2
STL	**127**	19	2	1365^{2}	1212	8.0	410	20	500	594	.243	1.254	2.70	92	2.97	-23.7	101	.947	340	105	-6.4	-8.4	-2.7	-.7	-11.8	-12.2
Total	**935**	**157**	**37**	**10818^{2}**		**8.0**	**2962**					**1.200**	**2.46**													

Wins
Mathewson, C. (NY) 24
Overall, O. (Chi) 23
Sparks, T. (Phi) 22

Win Percentage
Reulbach, E. (Chi) .810
Brown, M. (Chi) .769
Overall, O. (Chi) .767

Games
McGinnity, J. (NY) 47
McGlynn, S. (StL) 45
2 players tied with 41

Complete Games
McGlynn, S. (StL) 33
Ewing, B. (Cin) 32
Mathewson, C. (NY) 31

Shutouts
Mathewson, C. (NY) 8
Overall, O. (Chi) 8
Lundgren, C. (Chi) 7

Saves
McGinnity, J. (NY) 4
Brown, M. (Chi) 3
Overall, O. (Chi) 3

Innings Pitched
McGlynn, S. (StL) 352^{1}
Ewing, B. (Cin) 332^{2}
Mathewson, C. (NY) 315

Fewest Hits/Game
Lundgren, C. (Chi) 5.65
Pfiester, J. (Chi) 6.60
Overall, O. (Chi) 6.74

Fewest BB/Game
Phillippe, D. (Pit) 1.51
Mathewson, C. (NY) 1.51
Brown, M. (Chi) 1.55

Strikeouts
Mathewson, C. (NY) 178
Ewing, B. (Cin) 147
Ames, R. (NY) 146

Ratio
Brown, M. (Chi) .94
Mathewson, C. (NY) .96
Pfiester, J. (Chi) .98

Earned Run Average
Pfiester, J. (Chi) 1.15
Lundgren, C. (Chi) 1.17
Brown, M. (Chi) 1.39

Adjusted ERA
Pfiester, J. (Chi) 216
Lundgren, C. (Chi) 212
Brown, M. (Chi) 179

Component ERA
Mathewson, C. (NY) 1.67
Brown, M. (Chi) 1.70
Pfiester, J. (Chi) 1.71

Opponents' Batting Avg.
Lundgren, C. (Chi) .185
Pfiester, J. (Chi) .207
Overall, O. (Chi) .208

Adjusted Pitching Runs
Ewing, B. (Cin) 28
Mathewson, C. (NY) 27
Lundgren, C. (Chi) 25

Win Shares – Pitchers
Overall, O. (Chi) 32
Brown, M. (Chi) 29
Mathewson, C. (NY) 29

TPW – Pitchers
Mathewson, C. (NY) 3.4
Ewing, B. (Cin) 3.1
Lundgren, C. (Chi) 2.5

1907 American League

TEAM	G	W	L	PCT	GB	R	OR	EW	AB	H	2B	3B	HR	TB	BB	SO	SB	CS	AVG	OBP	SLG	OPS	OPS+	BR/A	PF	RC
DET	153	92	58	.613	....	**693**	531	95	5204	**1383**	179	**75**	11	**1745**	315	....	192	....	**.266**	**.313**	**.335**	**.648**	**108**	**41**	104	**641**
PHI	150	88	57	.607	1.5	584	511	82	5010	1276	**220**	44	**22**	1650	384	....	137	....	.255	.311	.329	.641	107	37	102	591
CHI	157	87	64	.576	5.5	588	**474**	92	5070	1205	149	33	5	1435	**421**	....	175	....	.238	.302	.283	.585	95	-16	97	523
CLE	158	85	67	.559	8	531	525	77	5068	1221	182	68	11	1572	335	....	193	....	.241	.295	.310	.605	97	-16	101	555
NY	152	70	78	.473	21	605	667	67	5044	1258	150	67	15	1587	304	....	206	....	.249	.299	.315	.614	93	-41	108	565
STL	155	69	83	.454	24	541	555	74	5224	1324	154	63	10	1634	370	....	144	....	.253	.308	.313	.620	103	20	100	580
BOS	155	59	90	.396	32.5	466	558	61	**5235**	1224	154	48	18	1528	305	....	125	....	.234	.281	.292	.572	88	-73	99	493
WAS	154	49	102	.325	43.5	506	693	53	5112	1243	134	57	12	1527	390	....	**223**	....	.243	.304	.299	.603	106	40	92	564
Total	**617**					**4514**			**40967**	**10134**	**1322**	**455**	**104**		**2824**		**1395**		**.247**	**.302**	**.309**	**.611**				

Runs
Crawford, S. (Det) 102
Jones, D. (Det) 101
Cobb, T. (Det) 97

Hits
Cobb, T. (Det) 212
Stone, G. (StL) 191
Crawford, S. (Det) 188

Doubles
Davis, H. (Phi) 35
Crawford, S. (Det) 34
Lajoie, N. (Cle) 30

Triples
Flick, E. (Cle) 18
Crawford, S. (Det) 17
Cobb, T. (Det) 14

Home Runs
Davis, H. (Phi) 8
3 players tied with 5

Total Bases
Cobb, T. (Det) 283
Crawford, S. (Det) 268
Stone, G. (StL) 238

Runs Batted In
Cobb, T. (Det) 119
Seybold, S. (Phi) 92
Davis, H. (Phi) 87

Bases On Balls
Hartsel, T. (Phi) 106
Hahn, E. (Chi) 84
Jones, F. (Chi) 67

Stolen Bases
Cobb, T. (Det) 49
Conroy, W. (NY) 41
Flick, E. (Cle) 41

Batting Average
Cobb, T. (Det) .350
Crawford, S. (Det) .323
Stone, G. (StL) .320

On-Base Percentage
Hartsel, T. (Phi) .405
Stone, G. (StL) .387
Flick, E. (Cle) .386

Slugging Average
Cobb, T. (Det) .468
Crawford, S. (Det) .460
Flick, E. (Cle) .412

Adjusted OPS
Cobb, T. (Det) 164
Crawford, S. (Det) 157
Flick, E. (Cle) 153

Adjusted Batting Runs
Cobb, T. (Det) 40.0
Stone, G. (StL) 36.0
Flick, E. (Cle) 36.0

Runs Created/Game
Cobb, T. (Det) 8.50
Flick, E. (Cle) 7.20
Crawford, S. (Det) 7.10

Fielding Runs
Lajoie, N. (Cle) 39.4
Donahue, J. (Chi) 22.6
Ferris, H. (Bos) 20.1

Win Shares – Batters
Cobb, T. (Det) 41
Flick, E. (Cle) 37
Crawford, S. (Det) 36

TPW – Batters
Lajoie, N. (Cle) 6.5
Cobb, T. (Det) 4.5
Flick, E. (Cle) 3.7

TEAM	CG	SH	SV	IP	H	H/G	ER	HR	BB	SO	OAV	RAT	ERA	ERA+	CERA	PR+	PF	FA	E	DP	FR	BW	PW	FW	TPW	DIF
DET	120	15	6	1370^2	1281	8.4	355	**8**	380	512	.250	1.212	2.33	112	2.71	**44.6**	102	.958	260	79	-3.1	**4.5**	**4.9**	-.3	**9.1**	7.9
PHI	106	**27**	6	1354^2	**1106**	**7.4**	354	13	378	**789**	**.226**	**1.095**	2.35	111	**2.20**	32.0	102	.958	263	67	6.5	4.1	3.5	.7	8.3	7.7
CHI	112	17	**9**	1406^1	1279	8.2	**347**	13	**305**	604	.245	1.126	**2.22**	108	2.36	39.3	94	**.966**	**233**	101	-12.0	-1.8	4.3	-1.3	1.2	10.8
CLE	127	20	5	1392^2	1253	8.1	350	**8**	362	513	.243	1.160	2.26	111	2.51	10.4	99	.960	264	**137**	27.2	-1.8	1.1	3.0	2.3	6.7
NY	93	10	6	1333^2	1327	9.0	449	13	428	511	.262	1.316	3.03	92	3.17	-16.3	110	.947	334	79	-19.3	-4.5	-1.8	-2.1	-8.5	4.5
STL	**129**	15	**9**	1381^1	1254	8.2	400	17	352	463	.245	1.163	2.61	96	2.58	-17.2	99	.959	266	97	2.6	2.2	-1.9	.3	.6	-7.6
BOS	100	17	7	**1414**	1222	7.8	385	22	337	517	.236	1.103	2.45	105	2.33	-41.9	101	.959	274	100	**61.0**	-8.0	-4.6	**6.7**	-5.9	-9.1
WAS	106	12	5	1351^1	1383	9.2	467	10	344	570	.267	1.278	3.11	**78**	3.06	-55.6	95	.951	310	69	-48.9	4.4	-6.1	-5.4	-7.1	-18.9
Total	**893**	**133**	**53**	**11004^2**		**8.3**	**3107**					**1.180**	**2.54**													

Wins
Joss, A. (Cle) 27
White, D. (Chi) 27
2 players tied with 25

Win Percentage
Donovan, B. (Det) .... .862
Dygert, J. (Phi) .... .724
Joss, A. (Cle) .... .711

Games
Walsh, E. (Chi) 56
Mullin, G. (Det) 46
White, D. (Chi) 46

Complete Games
Walsh, E. (Chi) 37
Mullin, G. (Det) 35
Joss, A. (Cle) 34

Shutouts
Plank, E. (Phi) 8
Waddell, R. (Phi) 7
3 players tied with 6

Saves
Dineen, B. (StL,Bos) 4
Hughes, T. (Was) 4
Walsh, E. (Chi) 4

Innings Pitched
Walsh, E. (Chi) .... 422^1
Mullin, G. (Det) .... 357^1
Plank, E. (Phi) .... 343^2

Fewest Hits/Game
Dygert, J. (Phi) 6.88
Winter, G. (Bos) 6.94
Walsh, E. (Chi) 7.27

Fewest BB/Game
White, D. (Chi) 1.18
Altrock, N. (Chi) 1.31
Young, C. (Bos) 1.34

Strikeouts
Waddell, R. (Phi) 232
Walsh, E. (Chi) 206
Plank, E. (Phi) 183

Ratio
Young, C. (Bos) .... .98
Joss, A. (Cle) .... .98
Bender, C. (Phi) 1.00

Earned Run Average
Walsh, E. (Chi) 1.60
Killian, E. (Det) 1.78
Joss, A. (Cle) 1.83

Adjusted ERA
Walsh, E. (Chi) 150
Killian, E. (Det) 146
Joss, A. (Cle) 137

Component ERA
Winter, G. (Bos) 1.75
Bender, C. (Phi) 1.76
Joss, A. (Cle) 1.80

Opponents' Batting Avg.
Dygert, J. (Phi) .... .214
Winter, G. (Bos) .... .216
Walsh, E. (Chi) .... .224

Adjusted Pitching Runs
Walsh, E. (Chi) 41
Killian, E. (Det) 30
Howell, H. (StL) 20

Win Shares – Pitchers
Walsh, E. (Chi) 37
Killian, E. (Det) 29
Plank, E. (Phi) 29

TPW – Pitchers
Killian, E. (Det) 4.6
Walsh, E. (Chi) 4.4
Howell, H. (StL) 2.9

1908 National League

TEAM	G	W	L	PCT	GB	R	OR	EW	AB	H	2B	3B	HR	TB	BB	SO	SB	CS	AVG	OBP	SLG	OPS	OPS+	BR/A	PF	RC
CHI	158	99	55	.643	....	624	461	100	5085	1267	**196**	56	19	1632	418	....	**212**	....	.249	.311	.321	.632	104	26	104	584
PIT	155	98	56	.636	1	585	468	94	5109	1263	162	**98**	25	**1696**	420	....	186	....	.247	.309	.332	.641	112	63	100	582
NY	157	98	56	.636	1	**651**	455	103	5006	**1339**	182	43	20	1667	**494**	....	181	....	**.267**	**.342**	**.333**	**.675**	**118**	**112**	105	**646**
PHI	155	83	71	.539	16	504	**445**	87	5012	1223	194	68	11	1586	334	....	200	....	.244	.298	.316	.615	100	-6	103	535
CIN	155	73	81	.474	26	488	543	69	4879	1108	129	77	14	1433	372	....	196	....	.227	.288	.294	.582	95	-28	97	474
BOS	156	63	91	.409	36	537	622	66	**5131**	1228	137	43	17	1502	414	....	134	....	.239	.303	.293	.596	98	-3	98	501
BRO	154	53	101	.344	46	375	516	53	4897	1044	110	60	**28**	1358	323	....	113	....	.213	.266	.277	.543	83	-97	96	391
STL	154	49	105	.318	50	372	626	40	4959	1105	134	57	17	1404	282	....	150	....	.223	.271	.283	.554	87	-77	95	420
Total	**622**					**4136**			**40078**	**9577**	**1244**	**502**	**151**		**3057**		**1372**		**.239**	**.299**	**.306**	**.605**				

Runs
Tenney, F. (NY) 101
Wagner, H. (Pit) 100
Leach, T. (Pit) 93

Hits
Wagner, H. (Pit) 201
Donlin, M. (NY) 198
2 players tied with 167

Doubles
Wagner, H. (Pit) 39
Magee, S. (Phi) 30
Chance, F. (Chi) 27

Triples
Wagner, H. (Pit) 19
Lobert, H. (Cin) 18
2 players tied with 16

Home Runs
Jordan, T. (Bro) 12
Wagner, H. (Pit) 10
Murray, R. (StL) 7

Total Bases
Wagner, H. (Pit) 308
Donlin, M. (NY) 268
Murray, R. (StL) 237

Runs Batted In
Wagner, H. (Pit) 109
Donlin, M. (NY) 106
Seymour, C. (NY) 92

Bases On Balls
Bresnahan, R. (NY) 83
Tenney, F. (NY) 72
Evers, J. (Chi) 66

Stolen Bases
Wagner, H. (Pit) 53
Murray, R. (StL) 48
Lobert, H. (Cin) 47

Batting Average
Wagner, H. (Pit) .... .354
Donlin, M. (NY) .... .334
Bransfield, K. (Phi) .... .304

On-Base Percentage
Wagner, H. (Pit) .... .415
Evers, J. (Chi) .... .402
Bresnahan, R. (NY) .... .401

Slugging Average
Wagner, H. (Pit) .... .542
Donlin, M. (NY) .... .452
Magee, S. (Phi) .... .417

Adjusted OPS
Wagner, H. (Pit) 205
Donlin, M. (NY) 153
Lobert, H. (Cin) 145

Adjusted Batting Runs
Wagner, H. (Pit) 66.0
Donlin, M. (NY) 32.0
Lobert, H. (Cin) 27.0

Runs Created/Game
Wagner, H. (Pit) 10.10
Donlin, M. (NY) 6.60
Evers, J. (Chi) 6.50

Fielding Runs
Tinker, J. (Chi) 34.3
Dahlen, B. (Bos) 25.8
Wagner, H. (Pit) 17.2

Win Shares – Batters
Wagner, H. (Pit) 59
Tinker, J. (Chi) 32
Lobert, H. (Cin) 32

TPW – Batters
Wagner, H. (Pit) 10.2
Tinker, J. (Chi) 5.5
Donlin, M. (NY) 3.4

TEAM	CG	SH	SV	IP	H	H/G	ER	HR	BB	SO	OAV	RAT	ERA	ERA+	CERA	PR+	PF	FA	E	DP	FR	BW	PW	FW	TPW	DIF
CHI	108	**29**	12	**1433^2**	**1137**	**7.1**	341	20	437	**668**	**.221**	1.098	2.14	109	2.26	16.4	100	**.969**	**205**	76	14.6	3.1	1.9	1.7	6.7	15.3
PIT	100	24	9	1402^1	1142	7.3	330	16	406	468	.223	1.104	2.12	108	2.27	26.4	97	.964	226	74	-1.9	7.4	3.1	-.2	10.2	10.8
NY	95	25	**18**	1411	1214	7.7	336	26	**288**	656	.232	**1.064**	2.14	112	**2.25**	**55.5**	102	.962	250	79	-15.9	**13.0**	**6.4**	-1.8	**17.6**	3.4
PHI	116	22	6	1393	1167	7.5	**325**	**8**	379	476	.234	1.110	**2.10**	114	2.34	32.9	103	.963	238	75	14.2	-.7	3.8	1.6	4.8	1.2
CIN	110	17	8	1384	1218	7.9	364	19	415	433	.243	1.180	2.37	97	2.69	7.6	98	.959	255	72	-20.8	-3.2	.9	-2.4	-4.7	.7
BOS	92	14	1	1404^2	1262	8.1	435	29	423	416	.245	1.200	2.79	**86**	2.77	-95.2	102	.962	253	**90**	**32.3**	-.4	-11.1	**3.7**	-7.7	-6.3
BRO	**118**	20	4	1369	1165	7.7	376	17	444	535	.235	1.175	2.47	94	2.62	-30.3	99	.961	247	66	9.0	-11.2	-3.5	1.0	-13.7	-10.3
STL	97	13	4	1368	1217	8.0	401	16	430	528	.232	1.204	2.64	89	2.63	-12.5	100	.946	348	68	-32.8	-8.9	-1.4	-3.8	-14.2	-13.8
Total	**836**	**164**	**62**	**11165^2**		**7.7**	**2908**					**1.141**	**2.34**													

Wins
Mathewson, C. (NY) 37
Brown, M. (Chi) 29
Reulbach, E. (Chi) 24

Win Percentage
Reulbach, E. (Chi) .... .774
Mathewson, C. (NY) .... .771
Brown, M. (Chi) .... .763

Games
Mathewson, C. (NY) 56
McQuillan, G. (Phi) 48
Raymond, B. (StL) 48

Complete Games
Mathewson, C. (NY) 34
Wilhelm, K. (Bro) 33
McQuillan, G. (Phi) 32

Shutouts
Mathewson, C. (NY) 11
Brown, M. (Chi) 9
4 players tied with 7

Saves
Brown, M. (Chi) 5
Mathewson, C. (NY) 5
McGinnity, J. (NY) 5

Innings Pitched
Mathewson, C. (NY) .... 390^2
McQuillan, G. (Phi) .... 359^2
Rucker, N. (Bro) .... 333^1

Fewest Hits/Game
Brown, M. (Chi) 6.17
Raymond, B. (StL) 6.55
Mathewson, C. (NY) 6.57

Fewest BB/Game
Mathewson, C. (NY) .... .97
Brown, M. (Chi) 1.41
Sparks, T. (Phi) 1.74

Strikeouts
Mathewson, C. (NY) 259
Rucker, N. (Bro) 199
Overall, O. (Chi) 167

Ratio
Mathewson, C. (NY) .... .84
Brown, M. (Chi) .... .84
McQuillan, G. (Phi) .... .98

Earned Run Average
Mathewson, C. (NY) 1.43
Brown, M. (Chi) 1.47
McQuillan, G. (Phi) 1.53

Adjusted ERA
Mathewson, C. (NY) 168
Brown, M. (Chi) 159
McQuillan, G. (Phi) 157

Component ERA
Brown, M. (Chi) 1.31
Mathewson, C. (NY) 1.34
McQuillan, G. (Phi) 1.64

Opponents' Batting Avg.
Beebe, F. (StL) .... .193
Brown, M. (Chi) .... .195
Mathewson, C. (NY) .... .200

Adjusted Pitching Runs
Mathewson, C. (NY) 46
McQuillan, G. (Phi) 31
Brown, M. (Chi) 27

Win Shares – Pitchers
Mathewson, C. (NY) 39
Brown, M. (Chi) 34
McQuillan, G. (Phi) 33

TPW – Pitchers
Mathewson, C. (NY) 5.6
McQuillan, G. (Phi) 3.6
Brown, M. (Chi) 3.2

1908 American League

TEAM	G	W	L	PCT	GB	R	OR	EW	AB	H	2B	3B	HR	TB	BB	SO	SB	CS	AVG	OBP	SLG	OPS	OPS+	BR/A	PF	RC
DET	154	90	63	.588	....	**647**	547	89	5115	**1347**	**199**	86	19	**1775**	320	....	165	....	**.263**	**.312**	**.347**	**.659**	**115**	**76**	104	**604**
CLE	157	90	64	.584	0.5	569	**459**	93	5108	1221	188	58	18	1579	364	....	177	....	.239	.297	.309	.606	102	12	100	528
CHI	156	88	64	.579	1.5	537	470	86	5027	1127	145	41	3	1363	**463**	....	209	....	.224	.298	.271	.569	92	-27	98	479
STL	155	83	69	.546	6.5	544	483	85	**5151**	1261	173	52	20	1598	343	....	126	....	.245	.296	.310	.607	102	10	101	514
BOS	155	75	79	.487	15.5	564	513	84	5048	1239	117	**88**	14	1574	289	....	167	....	.245	.295	.312	.607	100	-3	103	513
PHI	157	68	85	.444	22	486	562	65	5065	1131	183	50	**21**	1477	368	....	116	....	.223	.281	.292	.572	86	-77	107	450
WAS	155	67	85	.441	22.5	479	539	67	5041	1186	132	74	8	1490	368	....	170	....	.235	.293	.296	.588	106	32	92	490
NY	155	51	103	.331	39.5	460	713	45	5047	1190	142	50	13	1471	288	....	**231**	....	.236	.283	.291	.575	91	-51	101	478
Total	**622**					**4286**			**40602**	**9702**	**1279**	**499**	**116**		**2803**		**1361**		**.239**	**.294**	**.304**	**.598**				

Runs
McIntyre, M. (Det) 105
Crawford, S. (Det) 102
Schaefer, G. (Det) 96

Hits
Cobb, T. (Det) 188
Crawford, S. (Det) 184
2 players tied with 168

Doubles
Cobb, T. (Det) 36
Crawford, S. (Det) 33
Rossman, C. (Det) 33

Triples
Cobb, T. (Det) 20
Crawford, S. (Det) 16
Stahl, J. (Bos,NY) 16

Home Runs
Crawford, S. (Det) 7
Hinchman, B. (Cle) 6
3 players tied with 5

Total Bases
Cobb, T. (Det) 276
Crawford, S. (Det) 270
Rossman, C. (Det) 219

Runs Batted In
Cobb, T. (Det) 108
Crawford, S. (Det) 80
2 players tied with 74

Bases On Balls
Hartsel, T. (Phi) 93
Jones, F. (Chi) 86
McIntyre, M. (Det) 83

Stolen Bases
Dougherty, P. (Chi) 47
Hemphill, C. (NY) 42
Schaefer, G. (Det) 40

Batting Average
Cobb, T. (Det) .324
Crawford, S. (Det) .311
Gessler, D. (Bos) .308

On-Base Percentage
Gessler, D. (Bos) .394
McIntyre, M. (Det) .392
Hemphill, C. (NY) .374

Slugging Average
Cobb, T. (Det) .475
Crawford, S. (Det) .457
Gessler, D. (Bos) .423

Adjusted OPS
Cobb, T. (Det) 166
Gessler, D. (Bos) 161
Crawford, S. (Det) 157

Adjusted Batting Runs
Cobb, T. (Det) 40.0
Crawford, S. (Det) 34.0
McIntyre, M. (Det) 33.0

Runs Created/Game
Cobb, T. (Det) 7.30
Gessler, D. (Bos) 6.70
Crawford, S. (Det) 6.10

Fielding Runs
Lajoie, N. (Cle) 58.0
Wagner, H. (Bos) 28.5
McBride, G. (Was) 25.8

Win Shares – Batters
Cobb, T. (Det) 36
McIntyre, M. (Det) 33
3 players tied with 32

TPW – Batters
Lajoie, N. (Cle) 9.4
McIntyre, M. (Det) 4.4
Cobb, T. (Det) 3.9

TEAM	CG	SH	SV	IP	H	H/G	ER	HR	BB	SO	OAV	RAT	ERA	ERA+	CERA	PR+	PF	FA	E	DP	FR	BW	PW	FW	TPW	DIF
DET	**119**	15	5	1374^{1}	1313	8.6	366	12	318	553	.255	1.187	2.40	101	2.77	24.8	101	.953	305	95	-23.2	**8.7**	2.8	-2.6	**8.9**	5.1
CLE	108	18	5	**1424^{1}**	1172	**7.4**	**320**	16	328	548	.229	1.053	**2.02**	118	2.15	**43.4**	100	.962	257	95	15.0	1.4	**5.0**	1.7	8.1	4.9
CHI	107	**23**	**10**	1414	1165	7.4	349	11	**284**	623	**.226**	**1.025**	2.22	104	**2.00**	29.9	97	**.966**	**232**	82	-16.0	-3.0	3.4	-1.8	-1.5	13.5
STL	107	15	5	1397	**1151**	7.4	334	**7**	387	607	.230	1.101	2.15	111	2.28	-25.3	100	.964	237	**97**	**63.0**	1.1	-2.9	**7.2**	5.4	1.6
BOS	102	12	7	1380^{1}	1200	7.8	350	18	364	624	.238	1.133	2.28	108	2.52	-1.4	103	.954	297	71	28.9	-.3	-.2	3.3	2.8	-4.8
PHI	102	**23**	4	1400^{1}	1194	7.7	398	10	410	**741**	.235	1.145	2.56	100	2.46	31.6	107	.957	272	68	-31.9	-8.8	3.6	-3.6	-8.9	.9
WAS	106	15	7	1391^{2}	1236	8.0	362	16	348	649	.360	1.138	2.34	97	2.50	-14.3	96	.958	275	89	4.2	3.7	-1.6	.5	2.6	-11.6
NY	90	11	3	1366	1293	8.5	480	26	458	585	.250	1.282	3.16	**78**	3.15	-66.5	103	.947	337	78	-37.3	-5.8	-7.6	-4.3	-17.7	-8.3
Total	**841**	**132**	**46**	**11148**		**7.8**	**2959**					**1.132**	**2.39**													

Wins
Walsh, E. (Chi) 40
Joss, A. (Cle) 24
Summers, E. (Det) 24

Win Percentage
Walsh, E. (Chi) .727
Donovan, B. (Det) .720
Joss, A. (Cle) .686

Games
Walsh, E. (Chi) 66
Vickers, R. (Phi) 53
Chesbro, J. (NY) 45

Complete Games
Walsh, E. (Chi) 42
Young, C. (Bos) 30
Joss, A. (Cle) 29

Shutouts
Walsh, E. (Chi) 11
Joss, A. (Cle) 9
3 players tied with 6

Saves
Walsh, E. (Chi) 6
Hughes, T. (Was) 4
Waddell, R. (StL) 3

Innings Pitched
Walsh, E. (Chi) 464
Joss, A. (Cle) 325
Howell, H. (StL) 324^{1}

Fewest Hits/Game
Joss, A. (Cle) 6.42
Smith, F. (Chi) 6.44
Walsh, E. (Chi) 6.65

Fewest BB/Game
Joss, A. (Cle) .83
Burns, B. (Was) .99
Walsh, E. (Chi) 1.09

Strikeouts
Walsh, E. (Chi) 269
Waddell, R. (StL) 232
Hughes, T. (Was) 165

Ratio
Joss, A. (Cle) .81
Walsh, E. (Chi) .86
Young, C. (Bos) .89

Earned Run Average
Joss, A. (Cle) 1.16
Young, C. (Bos) 1.26
Walsh, E. (Chi) 1.42

Adjusted ERA
Joss, A. (Cle) 205
Young, C. (Bos) 194
Walsh, E. (Chi) 163

Component ERA
Joss, A. (Cle) 1.23
Walsh, E. (Chi) 1.38
Young, C. (Bos) 1.48

Opponents' Batting Avg.

Adjusted Pitching Runs
Walsh, E. (Chi) 51
Joss, A. (Cle) 41
Young, C. (Bos) 33

Win Shares – Pitchers
Walsh, E. (Chi) 47
Joss, A. (Cle) 35
Young, C. (Bos) 27

TPW – Pitchers
Walsh, E. (Chi) 6.1
Joss, A. (Cle) 5.0
Young, C. (Bos) 3.9

1909 National League

TEAM	G	W	L	PCT	GB	R	OR	EW	AB	H	2B	3B	HR	TB	BB	SO	SB	CS	AVG	OBP	SLG	OPS	OPS+	BR/A	PF	RC
PIT	154	110	42	.724	....	**699**	447	108	5129	**1332**	**218**	**92**	25	**1809**	479	....	185	....	**.260**	.327	**.353**	**.680**	**113**	**70**	105	**657**
CHI	155	104	49	.680	6.5	635	**390**	111	4999	1227	203	60	20	1610	420	....	187	....	.245	.308	.322	.630	100	-6	102	561
NY	158	92	61	.601	18.5	624	547	87	**5218**	1327	173	68	**26**	1714	530	....	234	....	.254	**.329**	.328	.658	109	62	101	640
CIN	157	77	76	.503	33.5	606	599	77	5088	1273	159	72	22	1642	478	....	**280**	....	.250	.319	.323	.642	107	41	99	617
PHI	154	74	79	.484	36.5	517	519	76	5034	1228	185	53	12	1555	369	....	185	....	.244	.303	.309	.611	95	-31	101	534
BRO	155	55	98	.359	55.5	444	627	51	5056	1157	176	59	16	1499	330	....	141	....	.229	.279	.296	.575	88	-83	96	456
STL	154	54	98	.355	56	583	731	59	5108	1242	148	56	15	1547	**568**	....	161	....	.243	.326	.303	.629	109	68	94	556
BOS	155	45	108	.294	65.5	435	683	44	5017	1121	125	43	14	1374	400	....	135	....	.223	.285	.274	.559	76	-137	105	434
Total	**621**					**4543**			**40649**	**9907**	**1387**	**503**	**150**		**3574**		**1508**		**.244**	**.310**	**.314**	**.624**				

Runs
Leach, T. (Pit) 126
Clarke, F. (Pit) 97
2 players tied with 92

Hits
Doyle, L. (NY) 172
Grant, E. (Phi) 170
Wagner, H. (Pit) 168

Doubles
Wagner, H. (Pit) 39
Magee, S. (Phi) 33
Miller, D. (Pit) 31

Triples
Mitchell, M. (Cin) 17
Konetchy, E. (StL) 14
Magee, S. (Phi) 14

Home Runs
Murray, R. (NY) 7
3 players tied with 6

Total Bases
Wagner, H. (Pit) 242
Doyle, L. (NY) 239
Konetchy, E. (StL) 228

Runs Batted In
Wagner, H. (Pit) 100
Murray, R. (NY) 91
Miller, D. (Pit) 87

Bases On Balls
Clarke, F. (Pit) 80
Byrne, B. (StL,Pit) 78
Evers, J. (Chi) 73

Stolen Bases
Bescher, B. (Cin) 54
Murray, R. (NY) 48
Egan, D. (Cin) 39

Batting Average
Wagner, H. (Pit) .339
Mitchell, M. (Cin) .310
Hoblitzell, D. (Cin) .308

On-Base Percentage
Wagner, H. (Pit) .420
Bridwell, A. (NY) .386
Clarke, F. (Pit) .384

Slugging Average
Wagner, H. (Pit) .489
Mitchell, M. (Cin) .430
Doyle, L. (NY) .419

Adjusted OPS
Wagner, H. (Pit) 173
Mitchell, M. (Cin) 152
Konetchy, E. (StL) 145

Adjusted Batting Runs
Wagner, H. (Pit) 44.0
Mitchell, M. (Cin) 31.0
Konetchy, E. (StL) 31.0

Runs Created/Game
Wagner, H. (Pit) 8.60
Mitchell, M. (Cin) 6.80
Doyle, L. (NY) 6.10

Fielding Runs
Egan, D. (Cin) 32.3
Tinker, J. (Chi) 24.8
Byrne, B. (StL,Pit) 22.1

Win Shares – Batters
Wagner, H. (Pit) 42
Clarke, F. (Pit) 31
Mitchell, M. (Cin) 28

TPW – Batters
Wagner, H. (Pit) 7.8
Egan, D. (Cin) 4.0
Konetchy, E. (StL) 3.9

TEAM	CG	SH	SV	IP	H	H/G	ER	HR	BB	SO	OAV	RAT	ERA	ERA+	CERA	PR+	PF	FA	E	DP	FR	BW	PW	FW	TPW	DIF
PIT	93	21	11	1401^{2}	1174	7.5	322	12	**320**	490	.232	1.066	2.07	124	2.22	58.2	99	**.964**	**228**	100	19.6	**7.8**	6.5	2.2	**16.4**	17.6
CHI	111	**32**	11	1399^{1}	**1094**	**7.0**	**272**	6	364	680	**.215**	**1.042**	**1.75**	145	**1.97**	**113.0**	98	.962	244	95	8.8	-.7	**12.5**	1.0	12.8	15.2
NY	105	17	**15**	**1440^{2}**	1248	7.8	363	28	397	**735**	.238	1.142	2.27	112	2.55	58.3	98	.954	307	99	-14.5	6.9	6.5	-1.6	11.8	4.2
CIN	91	10	8	1407	1233	7.9	394	**5**	510	477	.240	1.239	2.52	103	2.81	0.4	100	.952	309	**120**	10.4	4.5	.0	1.2	5.7	-4.7
PHI	89	17	6	1391	1190	7.7	377	23	472	612	.235	1.195	2.44	106	2.65	1.2	100	.962	241	97	**21.8**	-3.4	.1	**2.4**	-.8	-1.2
BRO	**126**	18	3	1384^{1}	1277	8.3	477	31	528	594	.256	1.304	3.10	83	3.31	-65.9	100	.955	282	86	-13.9	-9.2	-7.3	-1.5	-18.0	-3.0
STL	84	5	4	1379^{2}	1368	8.9	522	22	483	435	.263	1.342	3.41	**74**	3.43	-103.3	97	.950	322	90	-33.3	7.5	-11.5	-3.7	-7.7	-14.3
BOS	98	13	6	1370^{2}	1329	8.7	487	23	543	414	.263	1.366	3.20	88	3.50	-60.2	109	.948	342	101	1.2	-15.2	-6.7	.1	-21.8	-9.2
Total	**797**	**133**	**64**	**11174^{1}**		**8.0**	**3214**					**1.211**	**2.59**													

Wins
Brown, M. (Chi) 27
Camnitz, H. (Pit) 25
Mathewson, C. (NY) 25

Win Percentage
Camnitz, H. (Pit) .806
Mathewson, C. (NY) .806
Brown, M. (Chi) .750

Games
Brown, M. (Chi) 50
Mattern, A. (Bos) 47
2 players tied with 44

Complete Games
Brown, M. (Chi) 32
Bell, G. (Bro) 29
Rucker, N. (Bro) 28

Shutouts
Overall, O. (Chi) 9
Brown, M. (Chi) 8
Mathewson, C. (NY) 8

Saves
Brown, M. (Chi) 7
Crandall, D. (NY) 6
6 players tied with 3

Innings Pitched
Brown, M. (Chi) 342^{2}
Mattern, A. (Bos) 316^{1}
Rucker, N. (Bro) 309^{1}

Fewest Hits/Game
Mathewson, C. (NY) 6.28
Fromme, A. (Cin) 6.28
Overall, O. (Chi) 6.44

Fewest BB/Game
Mathewson, C. (NY) 1.18
Brown, M. (Chi) 1.39
Wiltse, H. (NY) 1.70

Strikeouts
Overall, O. (Chi) 205
Rucker, N. (Bro) 201
Moore, E. (Phi) 173

Ratio
Mathewson, C. (NY) .83
Brown, M. (Chi) .87
Camnitz, H. (Pit) .97

Earned Run Average
Mathewson, C. (NY) 1.14
Brown, M. (Chi) 1.31
Overall, O. (Chi) 1.42

Adjusted ERA
Mathewson, C. (NY) 223
Brown, M. (Chi) 193
Overall, O. (Chi) 178

Component ERA
Mathewson, C. (NY) 1.29
Brown, M. (Chi) 1.42
Overall, O. (Chi) 1.69

Opponents' Batting Avg.
Overall, O. (Chi) .198
Mathewson, C. (NY) .200
Fromme, A. (Cin) .201

Adjusted Pitching Runs
Mathewson, C. (NY) 46
Brown, M. (Chi) 44
Overall, O. (Chi) 33

Win Shares – Pitchers
Brown, M. (Chi) 36
Mathewson, C. (NY) 34
2 players tied with 30

TPW – Pitchers
Mathewson, C. (NY) 5.8
Brown, M. (Chi) 5.0
Overall, O. (Chi) 4.5

1909 American League

TEAM	G	W	L	PCT	GB	R	OR	EW	AB	H	2B	3B	HR	TB	BB	SO	SB	CS	AVG	OBP	SLG	OPS	OPS+	BR/A	PF	RC
DET	158	98	54	.645	....	**666**	493	98	**5095**	**1360**	**209**	58	19	**1742**	397	....	**280**	....	**.267**	**.325**	.342	**.667**	113	72	104	**660**
PHI	153	95	58	.621	3.5	605	**411**	105	4906	1257	186	**88**	**21**	1682	403	....	205	....	.256	.321	**.343**	.664	**115**	**80**	102	613
BOS	152	88	63	.583	9.5	601	549	82	4980	1309	151	69	20	1658	348	....	215	....	.263	.321	.333	.654	111	61	102	599
CHI	159	78	74	.513	20	492	464	80	5018	1109	145	56	4	1378	**441**	....	211	....	.221	.291	.275	.566	89	-50	96	474
NY	153	74	77	.490	23.5	589	587	76	4981	1234	143	61	16	1547	407	....	187	....	.248	.313	.311	.623	103	22	101	547
CLE	155	71	82	.464	27.5	493	532	71	5048	1216	173	81	10	1581	283	....	174	....	.241	.288	.313	.601	93	-50	104	501
STL	154	61	89	.407	36	441	575	56	4964	1151	116	45	10	1387	331	....	136	....	.232	.287	.279	.566	92	-45	93	436
WAS	156	42	110	.276	56	380	656	38	4983	1113	149	41	9	1371	321	....	136	....	.223	.276	.275	.551	84	-89	95	419
Total	**620**					**4267**			**39975**	**9749**	**1272**	**499**	**109**		**2931**		**1544**		**.244**	**.303**	**.309**	**.612**				

Runs		Hits		Doubles		Triples		Home Runs		Total Bases	
Cobb, T. (Det)	116	Cobb, T. (Det)	216	Crawford, S. (Det)	35	Baker, F. (Phi)	19	Cobb, T. (Det)	9	Cobb, T. (Det)	296
Bush, D. (Det)	114	Collins, E. (Phi)	198	Cobb, T. (Det)	33	Crawford, S. (Det)	14	Speaker, T. (Bos)	7	Crawford, S. (Det)	266
Collins, E. (Phi)	104	Crawford, S. (Det)	185	Lajoie, N. (Cle)	33	Murphy, D. (Phi)	14	2 players tied with	6	Collins, E. (Phi)	257

Runs Batted In		Bases On Balls		Stolen Bases		Batting Average		On-Base Percentage		Slugging Average	
Cobb, T. (Det)	107	Bush, D. (Det)	88	Cobb, T. (Det)	76	Cobb, T. (Det)	.377	Cobb, T. (Det)	.431	Cobb, T. (Det)	.517
Crawford, S. (Det)	97	Collins, E. (Phi)	62	Collins, E. (Phi)	63	Collins, E. (Phi)	.347	Collins, E. (Phi)	.416	Crawford, S. (Det)	.452
Baker, F. (Phi)	85	Demmitt, R. (NY)	55	Bush, D. (Det)	53	Lajoie, N. (Cle)	.324	Bush, D. (Det)	.380	Collins, E. (Phi)	.450

Adjusted OPS		Adjusted Batting Runs		Runs Created/Game		Fielding Runs		Win Shares – Batters		TPW – Batters	
Cobb, T. (Det)	190	Cobb, T. (Det)	59.0	Cobb, T. (Det)	10.80	Collins, E. (Phi)	23.8	Cobb, T. (Det)	44	Collins, E. (Phi)	8.3
Collins, E. (Phi)	170	Collins, E. (Phi)	47.0	Collins, E. (Phi)	8.90	Speaker, T. (Bos)	21.1	Collins, E. (Phi)	43	Cobb, T. (Det)	6.3
Stahl, J. (Bos)	153	Crawford, S. (Det)	33.0	Crawford, S. (Det)	6.50	Lajoie, N. (Cle)	19.6	Speaker, T. (Bos)	34	Lajoie, N. (Cle)	5.3

TEAM	CG	SH	SV	IP	H	H/G	ER	HR	BB	SO	OAV	RAT	ERA	ERA+	CERA	PR+	PF	FA	E	DP	FR	BW	PW	FW	TPW	DIF
DET	**117**	17	12	1420[1]	1254	8.0	357	16	359	528	.238	1.136	2.26	111	2.46	38.6	102	.959	276	87	0.7	8.2	4.4	.1	12.7	9.3
PHI	110	**27**	3	1378	**1069**	**7.0**	**296**	9	386	**728**	**.217**	**1.056**	**1.93**	124	**2.10**	**57.7**	97	.961	**245**	92	13.7	**9.1**	**6.6**	1.6	**17.2**	1.8
BOS	75	11	**14**	1360[1]	1213	8.0	391	18	384	555	.267	1.174	2.59	96	2.71	-39.0	101	.955	292	95	**22.9**	6.9	-4.4	**2.6**	5.1	7.9
CHI	115	26	4	**1430[1]**	1182	7.4	326	**8**	**340**	669	.229	1.064	2.05	114	2.24	46.1	95	**.964**	246	101	-0.9	-5.6	5.2	-.1	-.5	2.5
NY	94	18	8	1350[1]	1223	8.2	398	21	422	597	.248	1.218	2.65	95	2.92	17.0	102	.948	330	94	-35.2	2.6	1.9	-4.0	.5	-1.5
CLE	110	15	3	1361	1212	8.0	363	9	348	568	.250	1.146	2.40	106	2.51	12.8	103	.957	278	**110**	9.9	-5.7	1.5	1.1	-3.1	-1.9
STL	105	21	4	1354[2]	1287	8.6	433	16	383	620	.261	1.233	2.88	84	2.98	-73.4	97	.958	267	107	3.0	-5.1	-8.3	.3	-13.1	-.9
WAS	99	11	2	1374[2]	1288	8.4	464	12	424	653	.247	1.245	3.04	**80**	2.93	-78.6	98	.957	280	100	-14.9	-10.1	-8.9	-1.7	-20.7	-13.3
Total	**825**	**146**	**50**	**11029[2]**		**7.9**	**3028**					**1.158**	**2.47**													

Wins		Win Percentage		Games		Complete Games		Shutouts		Saves	
Mullin, G. (Det)	29	Mullin, G. (Det)	.784	Smith, F. (Chi)	51	Smith, F. (Chi)	37	Walsh, E. (Chi)	8	Arellanes, F. (Bos)	8
Smith, F. (Chi)	25	Cicotte, E. (Bos)	.737	Arellanes, F. (Bos)	45	Young, C. (Cle)	30	Krause, H. (Phi)	7	Powell, J. (StL)	3
Willett, E. (Det)	21	2 players tied with	.692	Groom, B. (Was)	44	Mullin, G. (Det)	29	Smith, F. (Chi)	7	6 players tied with	2

Innings Pitched		Fewest Hits/Game		Fewest BB/Game		Strikeouts		Ratio		Earned Run Average	
Smith, F. (Chi)	365	Morgan, C. (Phi,Bos)	6.26	Joss, A. (Cle)	1.15	Smith, F. (Chi)	177	Walsh, E. (Chi)	.94	Krause, H. (Phi)	1.39
Mullin, G. (Det)	303[2]	Krause, H. (Phi)	6.38	White, D. (Chi)	1.57	Johnson, W. (Was)	164	Krause, H. (Phi)	.94	Walsh, E. (Chi)	1.41
Johnson, W. (Was)	296[1]	Walsh, E. (Chi)	6.49	Powell, J. (StL)	1.58	Berger, H. (Cle)	162	Joss, A. (Cle)	.94	Bender, C. (Phi)	1.66

Adjusted ERA		Component ERA		Opponents' Batting Avg.		Adjusted Pitching Runs		Win Shares – Pitchers		TPW – Pitchers	
Krause, H. (Phi)	172	Falkenberg, C. (Cle)	1.51	Morgan, C. (Phi,Bos)	.201	Walsh, E. (Chi)	24	Smith, F. (Chi)	31	Walsh, E. (Chi)	3.2
Walsh, E. (Chi)	166	Walsh, E. (Chi)	1.52	Walsh, E. (Chi)	.203	Smith, F. (Chi)	22	Mullin, G. (Det)	28	Smith, F. (Chi)	3.2
Joss, A. (Cle)	150	Smith, F. (Chi)	1.60	Krause, H. (Phi)	.204	Krause, H. (Phi)	22	Walsh, E. (Chi)	23	Lake, J. (NY)	2.5

1910 National League

TEAM	G	W	L	PCT	GB	R	OR	EW	AB	H	2B	3B	HR	TB	BB	SO	SB	CS	AVG	OBP	SLG	OPS	OPS+	BR/A	PF	RC
CHI	154	104	50	.675	....	712	**499**	103	4977	1333	219	**84**	**34**	1822	542	501	173	....	.268	.344	.366	.710	114	88	99	696
NY	155	91	63	.591	13	**715**	567	95	5061	**1391**	204	83	31	**1854**	562	**489**	282	....	**.275**	**.354**	**.366**	**.720**	**116**	**107**	100	**759**
PIT	154	86	67	.562	17.5	655	576	86	5125	1364	214	83	33	1843	437	524	148	....	.266	.328	.360	.688	100	-9	106	655
PHI	157	78	75	.510	25.5	674	639	81	**5171**	1319	**223**	71	22	1750	506	559	199	....	.255	.327	.338	.665	96	-24	103	641
CIN	156	75	79	.487	29	620	684	69	5121	1326	150	79	23	1703	529	515	**310**	....	.259	.332	.333	.664	104	29	96	669
BRO	156	64	90	.416	40	497	623	60	5125	1174	166	73	25	1561	434	706	151	....	.229	.294	.305	.599	82	-118	97	506
STL	153	63	90	.412	40.5	639	718	68	4912	1217	167	70	15	1569	**655**	581	179	....	.248	.345	.319	.665	104	47	96	609
BOS	157	53	100	.346	50.5	495	701	51	5123	1260	173	49	31	1624	359	540	152	....	.246	.301	.317	.618	82	-125	104	536
Total	**621**					**5007**			**40615**	**10384**	**1516**	**592**	**214**		**4024**	**4415**	**1594**		**.256**	**.328**	**.338**	**.666**				

Runs		Hits		Doubles		Triples		Home Runs		Total Bases	
Magee, S. (Phi)	110	Byrne, B. (Pit)	178	Byrne, B. (Pit)	43	Mitchell, M. (Cin)	18	Beck, F. (Bos)	10	Magee, S. (Phi)	263
Byrne, B. (Pit)	101	Wagner, H. (Pit)	178	Magee, S. (Phi)	39	Magee, S. (Phi)	17	Schulte, F. (Chi)	10	Schulte, F. (Chi)	257
Huggins, M. (StL)	101	2 players tied with	172	Wheat, Z. (Bro)	36	2 players tied with	16	2 players tied with	8	Byrne, B. (Pit)	251

Runs Batted In		Bases On Balls		Stolen Bases		Batting Average		On-Base Percentage		Slugging Average	
Magee, S. (Phi)	123	Huggins, M. (StL)	116	Bescher, B. (Cin)	70	Magee, S. (Phi)	.331	Magee, S. (Phi)	.445	Magee, S. (Phi)	.507
Mitchell, M. (Cin)	88	Evers, J. (Chi)	108	Murray, R. (NY)	57	Hofman, S. (Chi)	.325	Snodgrass, F. (NY)	.440	Hofman, S. (Chi)	.461
Murray, R. (NY)	87	Magee, S. (Phi)	94	Paskert, D. (Cin)	51	Snodgrass, F. (NY)	.321	Evers, J. (Chi)	.413	Schulte, F. (Chi)	.460

Adjusted OPS		Adjusted Batting Runs		Runs Created/Game		Fielding Runs		Win Shares – Batters		TPW – Batters	
Magee, S. (Phi)	172	Magee, S. (Phi)	52.0	Magee, S. (Phi)	9.80	Shean, D. (Bos)	24.2	Magee, S. (Phi)	36	Wagner, H. (Pit)	4.8
Snodgrass, F. (NY)	154	Hofman, S. (Chi)	33.0	Snodgrass, F. (NY)	8.30	Doolan, M. (Phi)	22.7	Hofman, S. (Chi)	31	Konetchy, E. (StL)	4.4
Hofman, S. (Chi)	154	Snodgrass, F. (NY)	33.0	Hofman, S. (Chi)	7.50	Wagner, H. (Pit)	18.5	Wagner, H. (Pit)	30	Hofman, S. (Chi)	3.2

TEAM	CG	SH	SV	IP	H	H/G	ER	HR	BB	SO	OAV	RAT	ERA	ERA+	CERA	PR+	PF	FA	E	DP	FR	BW	PW	FW	TPW	DIF
CHI	100	**25**	13	1378[2]	**1171**	**7.6**	**384**	18	474	609	**.235**	**1.193**	**2.51**	115	**2.64**	41.6	95	**.964**	**230**	110	14.7	9.2	4.4	1.5	15.1	11.9
NY	96	9	10	1391[2]	1290	8.3	414	30	397	**717**	.250	1.212	2.68	110	2.87	**62.2**	98	.955	291	117	-19.3	**11.3**	**6.5**	-2.0	**15.8**	-1.8
PIT	73	13	12	1376	1254	8.2	433	20	**392**	479	.250	1.196	2.83	111	2.83	36.8	104	.961	245	102	9.5	-1.0	3.9	1.0	3.9	6.1
PHI	84	17	9	1411[1]	1297	8.3	478	36	547	657	.253	1.307	3.05	102	3.31	-1.6	103	.960	258	132	11.3	-2.5	-.2	1.2	-1.5	3.5
CIN	86	16	11	1386[2]	1334	8.7	474	27	528	497	.261	1.343	3.08	94	3.52	-13.3	96	.955	291	103	-14.1	3.0	-1.4	-1.5	.1	-2.1
BRO	**103**	15	5	**1420[1]**	1331	8.4	484	**17**	545	555	.259	1.321	3.07	99	3.27	-18.7	100	.964	235	125	11.6	-12.4	-2.0	1.2	-13.2	.2
STL	81	4	**14**	1337[1]	1396	9.4	562	30	541	466	.275	1.448	3.78	**79**	3.96	-81.2	98	.959	261	109	-38.3	5.0	-8.5	-4.0	-7.6	-5.4
BOS	72	12	9	1390[1]	1328	8.6	497	36	599	531	.266	1.386	3.22	103	3.70	-8.0	110	.954	305	**137**	**23.0**	-13.2	-.8	**2.4**	-11.6	-11.4
Total	**695**	**111**	**83**	**11092[1]**		**8.4**	**3726**					**1.300**	**3.02**													

Wins
- Mathewson, C. (NY) 27
- Brown, M. (Chi) 25
- Moore, E. (Phi) 22

Win Percentage
- Cole, K. (Chi) .833
- Crandall, D. (NY) .810
- Mathewson, C. (NY) .750

Games
- Mattern, A. (Bos) 51
- Gaspar, H. (Cin) 48
- 4 players tied with 46

Complete Games
- Brown, M. (Chi) 27
- Mathewson, C. (NY) 27
- Rucker, N. (Bro) 27

Shutouts
- 4 players tied with 6

Saves
- Brown, M. (Chi) 7
- Gaspar, H. (Cin) 7
- Crandall, D. (NY) 5

Innings Pitched
- Rucker, N. (Bro) 320^{1}
- Mathewson, C. (NY) 318^{1}
- Bell, G. (Bro) 310

Fewest Hits/Game
- Cole, K. (Chi) 6.53
- Scanlan, D. (Bro) 7.25
- Moore, E. (Phi) 7.25

Fewest BB/Game
- Suggs, G. (Cin) 1.62
- Mathewson, C. (NY) 1.70
- Crandall, D. (NY) 1.86

Strikeouts
- Moore, E. (Phi) 185
- Mathewson, C. (NY) 184
- Frock, S. (Bos,Pit) 171

Ratio
- Brown, M. (Chi) 1.08
- Mathewson, C. (NY) 1.11
- Suggs, G. (Cin) 1.11

Earned Run Average
- McQuillan, G. (Phi) 1.60
- Cole, K. (Chi) 1.80
- Brown, M. (Chi) 1.86

Adjusted ERA
- Cole, K. (Chi) 159
- Mathewson, C. (NY) 156
- Brown, M. (Chi) 155

Component ERA
- Brown, M. (Chi) 2.15
- Bell, G. (Bro) 2.32
- Mathewson, C. (NY) 2.35

Opponents' Batting Avg.
- Cole, K. (Chi) .211
- Drucke, L. (NY) .228
- Moore, E. (Phi) .228

Adjusted Pitching Runs
- Mathewson, C. (NY) 42
- Brown, M. (Chi) 30
- Cole, K. (Chi) 26

Win Shares – Pitchers
- Mathewson, C. (NY) 30
- Brown, M. (Chi) 29
- Cole, K. (Chi) 25

TPW – Pitchers
- Mathewson, C. (NY) 5.2
- Brown, M. (Chi) 3.1
- Cole, K. (Chi) 2.9

1910 American League

TEAM	G	W	L	PCT	GB	R	OR	EW	AB	H	2B	3B	HR	TB	BB	SO	SB	CS	AVG	OBP	SLG	OPS	OPS+	BR/A	PF	RC
PHI	155	102	48	.680	....	674	**442**	105	5154	**1373**	**191**	**105**	19	**1831**	409	....	207	....	**.266**	.326	**.355**	**.681**	**120**	**111**	99	**665**
NY	156	88	63	.583	14.5	626	557	84	5051	1254	164	75	20	1628	**464**	....	**288**	....	.248	.320	.322	.643	101	12	106	614
DET	155	86	68	.558	18	**679**	584	89	5039	1317	190	72	28	1735	459	....	249	....	.261	**.329**	.344	.674	110	56	107	655
BOS	158	81	72	.529	22.5	641	564	86	5204	1350	175	87	**43**	1828	430	....	194	....	.259	.323	.351	.674	114	78	102	656
CLE	161	71	81	.467	32	548	657	62	**5395**	1316	188	64	9	1659	366	....	189	....	.244	.296	.308	.604	94	-46	101	549
CHI	156	68	85	.444	35.5	457	479	73	5024	1058	115	58	7	1310	403	....	183	....	.211	.275	.261	.536	77	-127	95	415
WAS	157	66	85	.437	36.5	501	551	68	4989	1175	145	47	9	1441	449	....	192	....	.236	.309	.289	.598	97	-5	95	508
STL	158	47	107	.305	57	451	743	41	5077	1105	131	60	12	1392	415	....	169	....	.218	.281	.274	.556	84	-86	94	438
Total	**628**					**4577**			**40933**	**9948**	**1299**	**568**	**147**		**3395**		**1671**		**.243**	**.308**	**.313**	**.621**				

Runs
- Cobb, T. (Det) 106
- Lajoie, N. (Cle) 94
- Speaker, T. (Bos) 92

Hits
- Lajoie, N. (Cle) 227
- Cobb, T. (Det) 194
- Collins, E. (Phi) 188

Doubles
- Lajoie, N. (Cle) 51
- Cobb, T. (Det) 35
- Lewis, D. (Bos) 29

Triples
- Crawford, S. (Det) 19
- Lord, B. (Phi,Cle) 18
- Murphy, D. (Phi) 18

Home Runs
- Stahl, J. (Bos) 10
- Cobb, T. (Det) 8
- Lewis, D. (Bos) 8

Total Bases
- Lajoie, N. (Cle) 304
- Cobb, T. (Det) 279
- Speaker, T. (Bos) 252

Runs Batted In
- Crawford, S. (Det) 120
- Cobb, T. (Det) 91
- Collins, E. (Phi) 81

Bases On Balls
- Bush, D. (Det) 78
- Milan, C. (Was) 71
- Wolter, H. (NY) 66

Stolen Bases
- Collins, E. (Phi) 81
- Cobb, T. (Det) 65
- 2 players tied with 49

Batting Average
- Cobb, T. (Det) .383
- Lajoie, N. (Cle) .384
- Speaker, T. (Bos) .340

On-Base Percentage
- Cobb, T. (Det) .456
- Lajoie, N. (Cle) .445
- Speaker, T. (Bos) .404

Slugging Average
- Cobb, T. (Det) .551
- Lajoie, N. (Cle) .514
- Speaker, T. (Bos) .468

Adjusted OPS
- Cobb, T. (Det) 202
- Lajoie, N. (Cle) 198
- Speaker, T. (Bos) 169

Adjusted Batting Runs
- Lajoie, N. (Cle) 67.0
- Cobb, T. (Det) 61.0
- Speaker, T. (Bos) 43.0

Runs Created/Game
- Cobb, T. (Det) 12.30
- Lajoie, N. (Cle) 9.90
- Speaker, T. (Bos) 8.10

Fielding Runs
- Collins, E. (Phi) 48.2
- McBride, G. (Was) 22.7
- Baker, F. (Phi) 16.3

Win Shares – Batters
- Lajoie, N. (Cle) 47
- Cobb, T. (Det) 45
- Collins, E. (Phi) 39

TPW – Batters
- Collins, E. (Phi) 9.3
- Lajoie, N. (Cle) 8.8
- Cobb, T. (Det) 6.6

TEAM	CG	SH	SV	IP	H	H/G	ER	HR	BB	SO	OAV	RAT	ERA	ERA+	CERA	PR+	PF	FA	E	DP	FR	BW	PW	FW	TPW	DIF
PHI	**123**	**24**	5	1421^{2}	**1103**	**7.0**	**283**	**8**	450	**789**	**.220**	1.092	**1.79**	132	2.19	64.0	94	**.965**	**230**	**117**	**28.3**	**12.3**	7.1	**3.1**	**22.6**	4.4
NY	110	14	**8**	1399	1238	8.0	406	16	**364**	654	.243	1.145	2.61	102	2.60	44.5	105	.956	286	95	-38.0	1.3	4.9	-4.2	2.1	10.9
DET	108	17	5	1380^{1}	1257	8.2	432	34	460	532	.248	1.244	2.82	93	3.03	-28.9	104	.956	288	79	-1.3	6.2	-3.2	-.1	2.9	6.1
BOS	100	12	6	1430	1236	7.8	389	30	414	670	.235	1.154	2.45	104	2.59	23.1	101	.954	309	80	-8.2	8.7	2.6	-.9	10.3	-5.3
CLE	92	13	5	**1467**	1392	8.5	469	10	488	617	.261	1.282	2.88	90	3.20	-57.4	103	.964	248	112	8.1	-5.1	-6.4	.9	-10.6	5.6
CHI	103	23	7	1421	1130	7.2	321	16	381	785	.222	**1.063**	2.03	118	**2.13**	**64.1**	95	.954	314	100	-6.0	-14.2	**7.1**	-.7	-7.7	-.3
WAS	119	19	3	1373^{1}	1215	8.0	375	19	375	674	.244	1.158	2.46	101	2.67	-24.2	99	.959	264	99	27.7	-.5	-2.7	3.1	-.1	-8.9
STL	101	9	3	1391	1356	8.8	478	14	532	557	.265	1.357	3.09	**80**	3.50	-86.8	98	.943	385	113	-9.6	-9.6	-9.6	-1.1	-20.3	-9.7
Total	**856**	**131**	**42**	**11283^{1}**		**7.9**	**3153**					**1.187**	**2.51**													

Wins
- Coombs, J. (Phi) 31
- Ford, R. (NY) 26
- Johnson, W. (Was) 25

Win Percentage
- Bender, C. (Phi) .821
- Ford, R. (NY) .812
- Coombs, J. (Phi) .775

Games
- Coombs, J. (Phi) 45
- Johnson, W. (Was) 45
- Walsh, E. (Chi) 45

Complete Games
- Johnson, W. (Was) 38
- Coombs, J. (Phi) 35
- Walsh, E. (Chi) 33

Shutouts
- Coombs, J. (Phi) 13
- Ford, R. (NY) 8
- Johnson, W. (Was) 8

Saves
- Walsh, E. (Chi) 5
- Browning, F. (Det) 3
- 6 players tied with 2

Innings Pitched
- Johnson, W. (Was) 370
- Walsh, E. (Chi) 369^{2}
- Coombs, J. (Phi) 353

Fewest Hits/Game
- Ford, R. (NY) 5.83
- Walsh, E. (Chi) 5.89
- Coombs, J. (Phi) 6.32

Fewest BB/Game
- Walsh, E. (Chi) 1.49
- Young, C. (Cle) 1.49
- Collins, R. (Bos) 1.51

Strikeouts
- Johnson, W. (Was) 313
- Walsh, E. (Chi) 258
- Coombs, J. (Phi) 224

Ratio
- Walsh, E. (Chi) .82
- Ford, R. (NY) .88
- Johnson, W. (Was) .91

Earned Run Average
- Walsh, E. (Chi) 1.27
- Coombs, J. (Phi) 1.30
- Johnson, W. (Was) 1.36

Adjusted ERA
- Walsh, E. (Chi) 189
- Johnson, W. (Was) 183
- Coombs, J. (Phi) 182

Component ERA
- Walsh, E. (Chi) 1.27
- Ford, R. (NY) 1.41
- Johnson, W. (Was) 1.54

Opponents' Batting Avg.
- Walsh, E. (Chi) .187
- Ford, R. (NY) .188
- Coombs, J. (Phi) .201

Adjusted Pitching Runs
- Walsh, E. (Chi) 48
- Ford, R. (NY) 41
- Johnson, W. (Was) 39

Win Shares – Pitchers
- Coombs, J. (Phi) 37
- Johnson, W. (Was) 36
- Walsh, E. (Chi) 36

TPW – Pitchers
- Walsh, E. (Chi) 5.8
- Ford, R. (NY) 5.1
- Johnson, W. (Was) 4.5

1911 National League

TEAM	G	W	L	PCT	GB	R	OR	EW	AB	H	2B	3B	HR	TB	BB	SO	SB	CS	AVG	OBP	SLG	OPS	OPS+	BR/A	PF	RC
NY	154	99	54	.647	....	756	**542**	101	5006	1399	225	103	41	**1953**	530	**506**	**347**	....	**.279**	**.358**	**.390**	**.748**	**114**	**92**	102	**820**
CHI	157	92	62	.597	7.5	**757**	607	94	5130	1335	218	101	54	1917	585	617	214	....	.260	.341	.374	.714	106	43	100	729
PIT	155	85	69	.552	14.5	744	557	99	5137	1345	206	**106**	49	1910	525	583	160	....	.262	.336	.372	.708	101	3	104	698
PHI	153	79	73	.520	19.5	658	669	75	5044	1307	214	56	**60**	1813	490	588	153	....	.259	.328	.359	.688	98	-20	101	647
STL	158	75	74	.503	22	671	745	67	5132	1295	199	86	26	1744	**592**	650	175	....	.252	.337	.340	.677	99	2	97	651
CIN	159	70	83	.458	29	682	706	74	5291	1379	180	105	21	1832	578	594	289	....	.261	.337	.346	.684	102	17	96	716
BRO	154	64	86	.427	33.5	539	659	60	5059	1198	151	71	28	1575	425	683	184	....	.237	.301	.311	.612	81	-130	96	528
BOS	156	44	107	.291	54	699	1021	48	**5308**	**1417**	**249**	54	37	1885	554	577	169	....	.267	.340	.355	.695	94	-44	108	696
Total	**623**					**5506**			**41107**	**10675**	**1642**	**682**	**316**		**4279**	**4798**	**1691**		**.260**	**.335**	**.356**	**.691**				

Runs
- Sheckard, J. (Chi) 121
- Bescher, B. (Cin) 106
- Huggins, M. (StL) 106

Hits
- Miller, D. (Bos) 192
- Hoblitzell, D. (Cin) 180
- Daubert, J. (Bro) 176

Doubles
- Konetchy, E. (StL) 38
- Miller, D. (Bos) 36
- Wilson, C. (Pit) 34

Triples
- Doyle, L. (NY) 25
- Mitchell, M. (Cin) 22
- Schulte, F. (Chi) 21

Home Runs
- Schulte, F. (Chi) 21
- Luderus, F. (Phi) 16
- Magee, S. (Phi) 15

Total Bases
- Schulte, F. (Chi) 308
- Doyle, L. (NY) 277
- Luderus, F. (Phi) 260

Runs Batted In
- Schulte, F. (Chi) 107
- Wilson, C. (Pit) 107
- Luderus, F. (Phi) 99

Bases On Balls
- Sheckard, J. (Chi) 147
- Bates, J. (Cin) 103
- Bescher, B. (Cin) 102

Stolen Bases
- Bescher, B. (Cin) 81
- Devore, J. (NY) 61
- Snodgrass, F. (NY) 51

Batting Average
- Wagner, H. (Pit) .334
- Miller, D. (Bos) .333
- Sweeney, B. (Bos) .314

On-Base Percentage
- Sheckard, J. (Chi) .434
- Wagner, H. (Pit) .423
- Bates, J. (Cin) .415

Slugging Average
- Schulte, F. (Chi) .534
- Doyle, L. (NY) .527
- Wagner, H. (Pit) .507

Adjusted OPS
- Schulte, F. (Chi) 155
- Wagner, H. (Pit) 154
- Doyle, L. (NY) 154

Adjusted Batting Runs
- Schulte, F. (Chi) 41.0
- Doyle, L. (NY) 37.0
- Wagner, H. (Pit) 36.0

Runs Created/Game
- Wagner, H. (Pit) 8.70
- Doyle, L. (NY) 8.40
- Schulte, F. (Chi) 7.60

Fielding Runs
- Tinker, J. (Chi) 24.0
- Sheckard, J. (Chi) 18.6
- Doolan, M. (Phi) 17.8

Win Shares – Batters
- Schulte, F. (Chi) 31
- Wagner, H. (Pit) 30
- Sheckard, J. (Chi) 30

TPW – Batters
- Wagner, H. (Pit) 5.5
- Sheckard, J. (Chi) 4.6
- Tinker, J. (Chi) 3.2

TEAM	CG	SH	SV	IP	H	H/G	ER	HR	BB	SO	OAV	RAT	ERA	ERA+	CERA	PR+	PF	FA	E	DP	FR	BW	PW	FW	TPW	DIF
NY	**95**	19	13	1368	1267	8.3	**409**	33	**369**	**771**	.246	1.196	**2.69**	124	**2.76**	**121.3**	98	.959	256	86	-22.7	**9.2**	**12.2**	-2.3	**19.1**	3.9
CHI	85	12	**16**	1411	1270	**8.1**	455	**26**	525	582	**.245**	1.272	2.90	114	3.01	36.4	97	.960	260	114	**27.3**	4.3	3.7	**2.7**	10.7	4.3
PIT	91	13	11	1380^1	**1249**	8.1	435	36	375	605	.248	**1.177**	2.84	121	2.82	65.6	101	.963	232	**131**	24.0	.3	6.6	2.4	9.3	-1.3
PHI	90	**20**	10	1373^1	1285	8.4	503	43	598	697	.255	1.371	3.30	104	3.61	19.0	101	**.963**	**231**	113	1.3	-2.0	1.9	.1	.0	3.0
STL	88	6	10	1402^1	1296	8.3	573	39	701	561	.254	1.424	3.68	91	3.75	-55.1	99	.960	261	106	5.4	.2	-5.5	.5	-4.8	5.8
CIN	77	4	12	**1425**	1410	8.9	516	36	476	557	.265	1.324	3.26	101	3.50	9.8	97	.955	295	108	-3.9	1.7	1.0	-.4	2.3	-8.3
BRO	81	13	10	1371^2	1310	8.6	516	27	566	533	.263	1.368	3.39	98	3.55	-5.4	98	.962	241	112	-5.1	-13.1	-.5	-.5	-14.1	3.1
BOS	73	5	7	1374	1570	10.3	776	76	672	486	.296	1.632	5.08	**75**	5.19	-166.6	112	.947	347	110	-27.4	-4.4	-16.7	-2.8	-23.9	-7.1
Total	**680**	**92**	**89**	**11105^2**		**8.6**	**4183**					**1.345**	**3.39**													

Wins
Alexander, G. (Phi)........... 28
Mathewson, C. (NY)......... 26
Marquard, R. (NY)............ 24

Win Percentage
Marquard, R. (NY)............ .774
Crandall, D. (NY).............. .750
Cole, K. (Chi).................... .720

Games
Brown, M. (Chi)................ 53
Harmon, B. (StL).............. 51
2 players tied with........... 48

Complete Games
Alexander, G. (Phi)........... 31
Mathewson, C. (NY)......... 29
Harmon, B. (StL).............. 28

Shutouts
Alexander, G. (Phi)........... 7
Adams, B. (Pit)................. 6
4 players tied with........... 5

Saves
Brown, M. (Chi)................ 13
Crandall, D. (NY).............. 5
5 players tied with............ 4

Innings Pitched
Alexander, G. (Phi)........... 367
Harmon, B. (StL).............. 348
Leifield, L. (Pit)................ 318

Fewest Hits/Game
Alexander, G. (Phi)........... 6.99
Marquard, R. (NY)............ 7.16
Rucker, N. (Bro)............... 7.27

Fewest BB/Game
Mathewson, C. (NY)......... 1.11
Adams, B. (Pit)................. 1.29
Steele, E. (Pit,Bro)........... 1.71

Strikeouts
Marquard, R. (NY)............ 237
Alexander, G. (Phi)........... 227
Rucker, N. (Bro)............... 190

Ratio
Adams, B. (Pit)................. 1.01
Ames, R. (NY).................. 1.09
Mathewson, C. (NY)......... 1.11

Earned Run Average
Mathewson, C. (NY)......... 1.99
Richie, L. (Chi)................. 2.31
Adams, B. (Pit)................. 2.33

Adjusted ERA
Mathewson, C. (NY)......... 168
Adams, B. (Pit)................. 147
Richie, L. (Chi)................. 143

Component ERA
Ames, R. (NY).................. 2.09
Adams, B. (Pit)................. 2.09
Alexander, G. (Phi)........... 2.22

Opponents' Batting Avg.
Alexander, G. (Phi)........... .219
Marquard, R. (NY)............ .219
Ames, R. (NY).................. .223

Adjusted Pitching Runs
Mathewson, C. (NY)......... 51
Alexander, G. (Phi)........... 34
Marquard, R. (NY)............ 31

Win Shares – Pitchers
Alexander, G. (Phi)........... 34
Mathewson, C. (NY)......... 32
Rucker, N. (Bro)............... 31

TPW – Pitchers
Mathewson, C. (NY)......... 5.1
Adams, B. (Pit)................. 3.4
Alexander, G. (Phi)........... 3.2

1911 American League

TEAM	G	W	L	PCT	GB	R	OR	EW	AB	H	2B	3B	HR	TB	BB	SO	SB	CS	AVG	OBP	SLG	OPS	OPS+	BR/A	PF	RC
PHI	152	101	50	.669	....	**861**	**602**	101	5199	1540	237	93	**35**	**2068**	424	....	226	....	**.296**	**.357**	**.398**	**.754**	**119**	**123**	98	821
DET	154	89	65	.578	13.5	831	777	82	5294	**1544**	230	**96**	30	2056	471	....	**276**	....	.292	.355	.388	.743	108	53	105	**825**
CLE	156	80	73	.523	22	693	712	74	**5321**	1501	**238**	81	20	1961	354	....	209	....	.282	.333	.369	.701	100	-9	101	716
CHI	154	77	74	.510	24	718	624	86	5210	1401	179	92	20	1824	385	....	201	....	.269	.325	.350	.675	96	-32	98	659
BOS	153	78	75	.510	24	680	643	81	5014	1379	203	66	**35**	1819	**506**	....	190	....	.275	.350	.363	.713	106	48	99	710
NY	153	76	76	.500	25.5	684	723	72	5052	1374	190	**96**	25	1831	493	....	269	....	.272	.344	.362	.707	97	-19	106	723
WAS	154	64	90	.416	38.5	624	765	62	5065	1308	159	54	16	1623	466	....	215	....	.258	.330	.320	.651	89	-61	98	607
STL	152	45	107	.296	56.5	567	812	50	4996	1192	187	63	17	1556	460	....	125	....	.239	.307	.311	.619	81	-119	96	515
Total	**614**					**5658**			**41151**	**11239**	**1623**	**641**	**198**		**3559**		**1711**		**.273**	**.338**	**.358**	**.696**				

Runs
Cobb, T. (Det).................. 147
Bush, D. (Det).................. 126
Jackson, J. (Cle).............. 126

Hits
Cobb, T. (Det).................. 248
Jackson, J. (Cle).............. 233
Crawford, S. (Det)............ 217

Doubles
Cobb, T. (Det).................. 47
Jackson, J. (Cle).............. 45
Baker, F. (Phi).................. 42

Triples
Cobb, T. (Det).................. 24
Cree, B. (NY)................... 22
Jackson, J. (Cle).............. 19

Home Runs
Baker, F. (Phi).................. 11
Cobb, T. (Det).................. 8
Speaker, T. (Bos)............. 8

Total Bases
Cobb, T. (Det).................. 367
Jackson, J. (Cle).............. 337
Crawford, S. (Det)............ 302

Runs Batted In
Cobb, T. (Det).................. 127
Baker, F. (Phi).................. 115
Crawford, S. (Det)............ 115

Bases On Balls
Bush, D. (Det).................. 98
Gessler, D. (Was)............. 74
Milan, C. (Was)................ 74

Stolen Bases
Cobb, T. (Det).................. 83
Milan, C. (Was)................ 58
Cree, B. (NY)................... 48

Batting Average
Cobb, T. (Det).................. .420
Jackson, J. (Cle).............. .408
Crawford, S. (Det)............ .378

On-Base Percentage
Jackson, J. (Cle).............. .468
Cobb, T. (Det).................. .467
Collins, E. (Phi)................ .451

Slugging Average
Cobb, T. (Det).................. .621
Jackson, J. (Cle).............. .590
Crawford, S. (Det)............ .526

Adjusted OPS
Cobb, T. (Det).................. 193
Jackson, J. (Cle).............. 192
Collins, E. (Phi)................ 163

Adjusted Batting Runs
Cobb, T. (Det).................. 72.0
Jackson, J. (Cle).............. 70.0
Crawford, S. (Det)............ 47.0

Runs Created/Game
Cobb, T. (Det).................. 15.20
Jackson, J. (Cle).............. 13.20
Crawford, S. (Det)............ 10.30

Fielding Runs
Tannehill, L. (Chi)............ 37.2
Gardner, L. (Bos)............. 23.1
Bush, D. (Det).................. 20.4

Win Shares – Batters
Cobb, T. (Det).................. 47
Jackson, J. (Cle).............. 39
2 players tied with........... 35

TPW – Batters
Jackson, J. (Cle).............. 6.8
Cobb, T. (Det).................. 6.4
Collins, E. (Phi)................ 5.9

TEAM	CG	SH	SV	IP	H	H/G	ER	HR	BB	SO	OAV	RAT	ERA	ERA+	CERA	PR+	PF	FA	E	DP	FR	BW	PW	FW	TPW	DIF
PHI	97	13	**13**	1375^2	1343	8.8	460	**17**	487	739	.264	1.330	3.01	104	3.48	12.1	94	**.963**	**225**	100	8.8	**12.0**	1.2	.9	**14.1**	11.9
DET	**108**	8	3	1387^2	1514	9.8	575	28	460	538	.283	1.423	3.73	93	3.95	-25.0	104	.951	318	78	-17.1	5.3	-2.5	-1.7	1.1	10.9
CLE	93	6	6	**1390^2**	1382	8.9	519	**17**	552	675	.267	1.391	3.36	101	3.70	-12.2	102	.954	303	**108**	**19.9**	-.9	-1.2	**2.0**	-.2	4.2
CHI	85	**17**	11	1386^1	1349	8.8	457	22	**384**	**752**	**.255**	**1.250**	2.97	109	**2.99**	43.4	97	.961	252	98	-1.3	-3.2	4.3	-.1	.9	1.1
BOS	87	10	8	1351^2	**1309**	**8.7**	**411**	21	473	711	.262	1.318	**2.74**	119	3.40	**77.6**	98	.949	323	93	1.4	4.7	**7.6**	.1	12.5	-10.5
NY	90	5	3	1360^2	1404	9.3	535	26	406	667	.270	1.330	3.54	101	3.47	35.1	107	.949	328	99	-27.4	-1.8	3.5	-2.7	-1.1	1.1
WAS	106	13	3	1353^1	1471	9.8	529	39	410	628	.277	1.390	3.52	93	3.82	-39.9	98	.953	305	90	4.0	-6.0	-3.9	.4	-9.5	-3.5
STL	92	8	1	1332^1	1465	9.9	571	28	463	383	.278	1.447	3.86	**87**	3.99	-84.2	101	.945	358	104	12.0	-11.7	-8.3	1.2	-18.8	-12.2
Total	**758**	**80**	**48**	**10938^1**		**9.2**	**4057**					**1.360**	**3.34**													

Wins
Coombs, J. (Phi).............. 28
Walsh, E. (Chi).................. 27
Johnson, W. (Was)........... 25

Win Percentage
Bender, C. (Phi)............... .773
Gregg, V. (Cle)................. .767
Plank, E. (Phi).................. .742

Games
Walsh, E. (Chi).................. 56
Coombs, J. (Phi).............. 47
Wood, J. (Bos).................. 44

Complete Games
Johnson, W. (Was)........... 36
Walsh, E. (Chi).................. 33
2 players tied with........... 26

Shutouts
Johnson, W. (Was)........... 6
Plank, E. (Phi).................. 6
3 players tied with........... 5

Saves
Hall, C. (Bos).................... 4
Plank, E. (Phi).................. 4
Walsh, E. (Chi).................. 4

Innings Pitched
Walsh, E. (Chi).................. 368^2
Coombs, J. (Phi).............. 336^2
Johnson, W. (Was)........... 322^1

Fewest Hits/Game
Gregg, V. (Cle)................. 6.33
Wood, J. (Bos).................. 7.38
Krapp, G. (Cle)................. 7.62

Fewest BB/Game
White, D. (Chi).................. 1.47
Lake, J. (StL).................... 1.67
Walsh, E. (Chi).................. 1.76

Strikeouts
Walsh, E. (Chi).................. 255
Wood, J. (Bos).................. 231
Johnson, W. (Was)........... 207

Ratio
Gregg, V. (Cle)................. 1.05
Walsh, E. (Chi).................. 1.08
Wood, J. (Bos).................. 1.10

Earned Run Average
Gregg, V. (Cle)................. 1.80
Johnson, W. (Was)........... 1.90
Wood, J. (Bos).................. 2.02

Adjusted ERA
Gregg, V. (Cle)................. 189
Johnson, W. (Was)........... 173
Wood, J. (Bos).................. 162

Component ERA
Gregg, V. (Cle)................. 1.99
Walsh, E. (Chi).................. 2.20
Wood, J. (Bos).................. 2.21

Opponents' Batting Avg.
Gregg, V. (Cle)................. .205
Wood, J. (Bos).................. .223
Krapp, G. (Cle)................. .232

Adjusted Pitching Runs
Johnson, W. (Was)........... 48
Ford, R. (NY).................... 47
Walsh, E. (Chi).................. 42

Win Shares – Pitchers
Johnson, W. (Was)........... 31
Walsh, E. (Chi).................. 31
2 players tied with........... 28

TPW – Pitchers
Johnson, W. (Was)........... 5.1
Wood, J. (Bos).................. 4.6
Ford, R. (NY).................... 4.4

1912 National League

TEAM	G	W	L	PCT	GB	R	OR	EW	AB	H	2B	3B	HR	TB	BB	SO	SB	CS	AVG	OBP	SLG	OPS	OPS+	BR/A	PF	RC
NY	154	103	48	.682	....	**823**	571	102	5067	1451	231	89	**47**	2001	514	497	**319**	....	**.286**	**.360**	.395	**.755**	109	**66**	103	**830**
PIT	152	93	58	.616	10	751	**565**	96	5252	**1493**	222	**129**	39	**2090**	420	514	177	....	.284	.340	**.398**	.738	**110**	54	98	767
CHI	152	91	59	.607	11.5	756	668	84	5048	1398	**245**	91	42	1951	**560**	615	164	....	.277	.354	.386	.740	109	**66**	100	750
CIN	155	75	78	.490	29	656	722	69	5115	1310	183	89	21	1734	479	**492**	248	....	.256	.323	.339	.662	89	-71	97	639
PHI	152	73	79	.480	30.5	670	688	74	5077	1354	244	68	43	1863	464	615	159	....	.267	.332	.367	.699	91	-66	107	671
STL	153	63	90	.412	41	659	830	59	5092	1366	190	77	27	1791	508	620	193	....	.268	.340	.352	.692	98	-9	98	675
BRO	153	58	95	.379	46	651	744	66	5141	1377	220	73	32	1839	490	584	179	....	.268	.336	.358	.694	100	0	96	677
BOS	155	52	101	.340	52	693	871	59	**5361**	1465	227	68	35	1933	454	690	137	....	.273	.335	.361	.696	95	-40	102	693
Total	**613**					**5659**			**41153**	**11214**	**1762**	**684**	**286**		**3889**	**4627**	**1576**		**.272**	**.340**	**.369**	**.710**				

Runs
Bescher, B. (Cin) 120
Carey, M. (Pit) 114
2 players tied with 102

Hits
Zimmerman, H. (Chi) 207
Sweeney, B. (Bos) 204
Campbell, V. (Bos) 185

Doubles
Zimmerman, H. (Chi) 41
Paskert, D. (Phi) 37
Wagner, H. (Pit) 35

Triples
Wilson, C. (Pit) 36
Murray, R. (NY) 20
Wagner, H. (Pit) 20

Home Runs
Zimmerman, H. (Chi) 14
Schulte, F. (Chi) 12
3 players tied with 11

Total Bases
Zimmerman, H. (Chi) 318
Wilson, C. (Pit) 299
Wagner, H. (Pit) 277

Runs Batted In
Wagner, H. (Pit) 102
Sweeney, B. (Bos) 100
Zimmerman, H. (Chi) 99

Bases On Balls
Sheckard, J. (Chi) 122
Paskert, D. (Phi) 91
Huggins, M. (StL) 87

Stolen Bases
Bescher, B. (Cin) 67
Carey, M. (Pit) 45
Snodgrass, F. (NY) 43

Batting Average
Zimmerman, H. (Chi) .372
Sweeney, B. (Bos) .344
Evers, J. (Chi) .341

On-Base Percentage
Evers, J. (Chi) .431
Huggins, M. (StL) .422
Paskert, D. (Phi) .420

Slugging Average
Zimmerman, H. (Chi) .571
Wilson, C. (Pit) .513
Wagner, H. (Pit) .496

Adjusted OPS
Zimmerman, H. (Chi) 169
Wagner, H. (Pit) 145
Evers, J. (Chi) 139

Adjusted Batting Runs
Zimmerman, H. (Chi) 50.0
Wagner, H. (Pit) 34.0
Evers, J. (Chi) 30.0

Runs Created/Game
Zimmerman, H. (Chi) 9.70
Wagner, H. (Pit) 7.80
Doyle, L. (NY) 7.60

Fielding Runs
Wagner, H. (Pit) 40.4
Tinker, J. (Chi) 27.3
Sweeney, B. (Bos) 20.1

Win Shares – Batters
Wagner, H. (Pit) 35
Zimmerman, H. (Chi) 34
Doyle, L. (NY) 29

TPW – Batters
Wagner, H. (Pit) 8.3
Sweeney, B. (Bos) 5.1
Zimmerman, H. (Chi) 5.0

TEAM	CG	SH	SV	IP	H	H/G	ER	HR	BB	SO	OAV	RAT	ERA	ERA+	CERA	PR+	PF	FA	E	DP	FR	BW	PW	FW	TPW	DIF
NY	93	8	**16**	1369^{2}	1352	8.9	**392**	35	**338**	652	.259	**1.234**	**2.58**	131	**2.97**	**118.3**	99	.956	280	123	2.8	6.5	**11.6**	.3	**18.4**	9.6
PIT	**94**	**18**	7	1385	**1268**	**8.2**	439	**28**	497	**664**	**.251**	1.274	2.85	114	3.02	47.6	96	**.972**	**169**	125	13.1	5.3	4.7	1.3	11.3	6.7
CHI	80	15	9	1358^{2}	1307	8.7	516	33	493	554	.259	1.325	3.42	97	3.32	-48.8	98	.960	249	125	**32.7**	**6.5**	-4.8	**3.2**	4.9	11.1
CIN	86	13	10	1377^{2}	1455	9.5	523	**28**	452	561	.279	1.384	3.42	98	3.71	6.7	99	.960	249	102	-18.3	-6.9	.7	-1.8	-8.1	7.1
PHI	81	10	9	1355	1381	9.2	489	43	515	616	.272	1.399	3.25	111	3.74	51.0	106	.963	231	98	3.9	-6.4	5.0	.4	-1.1	-1.9
STL	61	6	12	1353	1466	9.8	579	31	560	487	.286	1.497	3.85	89	4.11	-72.3	101	.957	274	113	6.6	-.9	-7.1	.6	-7.4	-5.6
BRO	71	10	8	1357	1399	9.3	549	45	510	553	.273	1.407	3.64	92	3.73	-28.1	98	.959	255	96	-18.2	.0	-2.8	-1.8	-4.5	-13.5
BOS	88	5	5	$\mathbf{1390^{2}}$	1544	10.0	644	43	521	542	.291	1.485	4.17	**85**	4.18	-71.8	105	.954	297	**129**	-19.5	-4.0	-7.1	-1.9	-12.9	-11.1
Total	**654**	**85**	**76**	$\mathbf{10946^{2}}$		**9.2**	**4131**					**1.376**	**3.40**													

Wins
Cheney, L. (Chi) 26
Marquard, R. (NY) 26
Hendrix, C. (Pit) 24

Win Percentage
Hendrix, C. (Pit) .727
Cheney, L. (Chi) .722
Tesreau, J. (NY) .708

Games
Benton, R. (Cin) 50
Sallee, S. (StL) 48
Alexander, G. (Phi) 46

Complete Games
Cheney, L. (Chi) 28
Mathewson, C. (NY) 27
3 players tied with 25

Shutouts
O'Toole, M. (Pit) 6
Rucker, N. (Bro) 6
Suggs, G. (Cin) 5

Saves
Sallee, S. (StL) 6
3 players tied with 4

Innings Pitched
Alexander, G. (Phi) 310^{1}
Mathewson, C. (NY) 310
Cheney, L. (Chi) 303^{1}

Fewest Hits/Game
Tesreau, J. (NY) 6.56
Robinson, H. (Pit) 7.51
O'Toole, M. (Pit) 7.75

Fewest BB/Game
Mathewson, C. (NY) .99
Robinson, H. (Pit) 1.54
Suggs, G. (Cin) 1.66

Strikeouts
Alexander, G. (Phi) 195
Hendrix, C. (Pit) 176
Marquard, R. (NY) 175

Ratio
Robinson, H. (Pit) 1.01
Mathewson, C. (NY) 1.11
Rucker, N. (Bro) 1.16

Earned Run Average
Tesreau, J. (NY) 1.96
Mathewson, C. (NY) 2.12
Rucker, N. (Bro) 2.21

Adjusted ERA
Tesreau, J. (NY) 172
Mathewson, C. (NY) 159
Rucker, N. (Bro) 151

Component ERA
Robinson, H. (Pit) 2.12
Tesreau, J. (NY) 2.22
Mathewson, C. (NY) 2.44

Opponents' Batting Avg.
Tesreau, J. (NY) .204
Cheney, L. (Chi) .234
Robinson, H. (Pit) .237

Adjusted Pitching Runs
Mathewson, C. (NY) 43
Rucker, N. (Bro) 41
Tesreau, J. (NY) 38

Win Shares – Pitchers
Mathewson, C. (NY) 31
Hendrix, C. (Pit) 29
Cheney, L. (Chi) 27

TPW – Pitchers
Mathewson, C. (NY) 4.7
Rucker, N. (Bro) 4.3
Tesreau, J. (NY) 3.5

1912 American League

TEAM	G	W	L	PCT	GB	R	OR	EW	AB	H	2B	3B	HR	TB	BB	SO	SB	CS	AVG	OBP	SLG	OPS	OPS+	BR/A	PF	RC
BOS	154	105	47	.691	....	**799**	**544**	104	5071	1404	**269**	84	**29**	**1928**	**565**	....	185	....	.277	**.355**	**.380**	**.735**	110	69	105	752
WAS	154	91	61	.599	14	699	581	90	5075	1298	202	86	20	1732	472	....	**274**	....	.256	.324	.341	.665	95	-36	101	644
PHI	153	90	62	.592	15	779	658	89	5111	**1442**	204	**108**	22	**1928**	485	....	258	....	**.282**	.349	.377	.726	**118**	**112**	96	**763**
CHI	158	78	76	.506	28	639	648	76	**5182**	1321	174	80	17	1706	423	....	205	....	.255	.317	.329	.647	93	-49	97	611
CLE	155	75	78	.490	30.5	677	681	76	5132	1403	219	77	12	1812	407	....	194	....	.273	.333	.353	.686	98	-17	103	671
DET	154	69	84	.451	36.5	720	777	71	5143	1376	189	86	19	1794	530	....	270	....	.268	.343	.349	.692	107	51	97	706
STL	157	53	101	.344	53	552	764	53	5080	1262	166	71	19	1627	449	....	176	....	.248	.315	.320	.635	90	-64	96	564
NY	153	50	102	.329	55	630	842	55	5092	1320	168	79	18	1700	463	....	247	....	.259	.329	.334	.663	89	-69	106	638
Total	**619**					**5495**			**40886**	**10826**	**1591**	**671**	**156**		**3794**		**1809**		**.265**	**.333**	**.348**	**.681**				

Runs
Collins, E. (Phi) 137
Speaker, T. (Bos) 136
Jackson, J. (Cle) 121

Hits
Cobb, T. (Det) 226
Jackson, J. (Cle) 226
Speaker, T. (Bos) 222

Doubles
Speaker, T. (Bos) 53
Jackson, J. (Cle) 44
Baker, F. (Phi) 40

Triples
Jackson, J. (Cle) 26
Cobb, T. (Det) 23
2 players tied with 21

Home Runs
Baker, F. (Phi) 10
Speaker, T. (Bos) 10
Cobb, T. (Det) 7

Total Bases
Jackson, J. (Cle) 331
Speaker, T. (Bos) 329
Cobb, T. (Det) 323

Runs Batted In
Baker, F. (Phi) 130
Crawford, S. (Det) 109
Lewis, D. (Bos) 109

Bases On Balls
Bush, D. (Det) 117
Collins, E. (Phi) 101
Rath, M. (Chi) 95

Stolen Bases
Milan, C. (Was) 88
Collins, E. (Phi) 63
Cobb, T. (Det) 61

Batting Average
Cobb, T. (Det) .409
Jackson, J. (Cle) .395
Speaker, T. (Bos) .383

On-Base Percentage
Speaker, T. (Bos) .464
Jackson, J. (Cle) .458
Cobb, T. (Det) .456

Slugging Average
Cobb, T. (Det) .584
Jackson, J. (Cle) .579
Speaker, T. (Bos) .567

Adjusted OPS
Cobb, T. (Det) 203
Jackson, J. (Cle) 189
Speaker, T. (Bos) 185

Adjusted Batting Runs
Cobb, T. (Det) 71.0
Speaker, T. (Bos) 67.0
Jackson, J. (Cle) 66.0

Runs Created/Game
Cobb, T. (Det) 13.40
Speaker, T. (Bos) 12.50
Jackson, J. (Cle) 12.00

Fielding Runs
McBride, G. (Was) 27.0
Collins, E. (Phi) 19.8
Milan, C. (Was) 16.1

Win Shares – Batters
Speaker, T. (Bos) 51
Cobb, T. (Det) 40
Baker, F. (Phi) 39

TPW – Batters
Collins, E. (Phi) 7.1
Speaker, T. (Bos) 7.1
Baker, F. (Phi) 7.0

TEAM	CG	SH	SV	IP	H	H/G	ER	HR	BB	SO	OAV	RAT	ERA	ERA+	CERA	PR+	PF	FA	E	DP	FR	BW	PW	FW	TPW	DIF
BOS	**108**	**18**	6	1362	1243	8.2	418	18	**385**	712	.247	**1.195**	2.76	124	**2.77**	**103.5**	102	.957	267	88	-2.9	6.9	**10.3**	-.3	**16.9**	12.1
WAS	98	11	7	1376^{2}	**1219**	**8.0**	**411**	24	525	**828**	**.241**	1.267	**2.69**	125	3.07	52.1	100	.954	297	92	**48.9**	-3.6	5.2	**4.9**	6.5	8.5
PHI	95	11	9	1357	1273	8.4	501	**12**	518	601	.258	1.320	3.32	93	3.30	-57.6	93	**.959**	**263**	115	23.4	**11.2**	-5.7	2.3	7.8	6.2
CHI	85	14	**16**	**1413**	1398	8.9	480	26	426	698	.264	1.291	3.06	105	3.26	53.1	96	.957	291	102	-27.6	-4.8	5.3	-2.7	-2.3	3.3
CLE	94	7	7	1352^{2}	1367	9.1	496	15	523	622	.272	1.397	3.30	104	3.71	-4.3	103	.954	287	124	23.8	-1.7	-.4	2.4	.2	-1.2
DET	107	7	5	1367^{1}	1438	9.5	573	16	521	512	.277	1.433	3.77	**87**	3.99	-62.7	98	.950	338	91	-9.0	5.1	-6.3	-.9	-2.0	-5.0
STL	85	8	5	1369^{2}	1433	9.4	564	17	442	547	.277	1.369	3.71	90	3.69	-73.1	100	.947	341	**127**	17.0	-6.4	-7.3	1.7	-12.0	-12.0
NY	105	5	3	1335	1448	9.8	613	28	436	637	.283	1.411	4.13	87	3.85	-2.1	108	.940	382	77	-73.5	-6.9	-.2	-7.3	-14.4	-11.6
Total	**777**	**81**	**58**	$\mathbf{10933^{1}}$		**8.9**	**4056**					**1.335**	**3.34**													

Wins
Wood, J. (Bos) 34
Johnson, W. (Was) 33
Walsh, E. (Chi) 27

Win Percentage
Wood, J. (Bos) .872
Plank, E. (Phi) .812
Johnson, W. (Was) .733

Games
Walsh, E. (Chi) 62
Johnson, W. (Was) 50
2 players tied with 43

Complete Games
Wood, J. (Bos) 35
Johnson, W. (Was) 34
Walsh, E. (Chi) 32

Shutouts
Wood, J. (Bos) 10
Johnson, W. (Was) 7
Walsh, E. (Chi) 6

Saves
Walsh, E. (Chi) 10
4 players tied with 3

Innings Pitched
Walsh, E. (Chi) 393
Johnson, W. (Was) 369
Wood, J. (Bos) 344

Fewest Hits/Game
Johnson, W. (Was) 6.32
Wood, J. (Bos) 6.99
Houck, B. (Phi) 7.37

Fewest BB/Game
Bender, C. (Phi) 1.74
Johnson, W. (Was) 1.85
Collins, R. (Bos) 1.90

Strikeouts
Johnson, W. (Was) 303
Wood, J. (Bos) 258
Walsh, E. (Chi) 254

Ratio
Johnson, W. (Was) .91
Wood, J. (Bos) 1.01
Walsh, E. (Chi) 1.08

Earned Run Average
Johnson, W. (Was) 1.39
Wood, J. (Bos) 1.91
Walsh, E. (Chi) 2.15

Adjusted ERA
Johnson, W. (Was) 241
Wood, J. (Bos) 179
Walsh, E. (Chi) 150

Component ERA
Johnson, W. (Was) 1.52
Wood, J. (Bos) 1.85
Walsh, E. (Chi) 2.13

Opponents' Batting Avg.
Johnson, W. (Was) .196
Wood, J. (Bos) .216
Walsh, E. (Chi) .231

Adjusted Pitching Runs
Johnson, W. (Was) 67
Wood, J. (Bos) 58
Walsh, E. (Chi) 54

Win Shares – Pitchers
Johnson, W. (Was) 47
Wood, J. (Bos) 44
Walsh, E. (Chi) 40

TPW – Pitchers
Johnson, W. (Was) 7.6
Wood, J. (Bos) 6.9
Walsh, E. (Chi) 6.0

1913 National League

TEAM	G	W	L	PCT	GB	R	OR	EW	AB	H	2B	3B	HR	TB	BB	SO	SB	CS	AVG	OBP	SLG	OPS	OPS+	BR/A	PF	RC
NY	156	101	51	.664	....	684	**515**	97	5218	1427	226	71	31	1888	444	**501**	**296**	....	**.273**	**.338**	.362	.700	105	38	101	**700**
PHI	159	88	63	.583	12.5	693	636	82	**5400**	**1433**	**257**	78	**73**	**2065**	383	578	156	....	.265	.318	**.382**	.701	102	0	104	683
CHI	155	88	65	.575	13.5	**720**	630	87	5022	1289	195	**96**	59	1853	**554**	634	181	....	.257	.335	.369	**.704**	**107**	**53**	100	661
PIT	155	78	71	.523	21.5	673	585	85	5252	1383	210	86	35	1870	391	545	181	....	.263	.319	.356	.675	103	15	96	629
BOS	154	69	82	.457	31.5	641	690	70	5145	1318	191	60	32	1725	488	640	177	....	.256	.326	.335	.661	93	-37	102	603
BRO	152	65	84	.436	34.5	595	613	72	5165	1394	193	86	39	1876	361	555	188	....	.270	.321	.363	.685	99	-14	103	637
CIN	156	64	89	.418	37.5	607	717	64	5132	1339	170	**96**	27	1782	458	579	226	....	.261	.325	.347	.672	99	-7	100	630
STL	153	51	99	.340	49	528	755	49	4967	1229	152	72	15	1570	451	573	171	....	.247	.316	.316	.632	88	-69	99	534
Total	**620**					**5141**			**41301**	**10812**	**1594**	**645**	**311**		**3530**	**4605**	**1576**		**.262**	**.325**	**.354**	**.679**				

Runs
Carey, M. (Pit) 99
Leach, T. (Chi) 99
Lobert, H. (Phi) 98

Hits
Cravath, G. (Phi) 179
Daubert, J. (Bro) 178
Burns, G. (NY) 173

Doubles
Smith, R. (Bro) 40
Burns, G. (NY) 37
Magee, S. (Phi) 36

Triples
Saier, V. (Chi) 21
Miller, D. (Pit) 20
Konetchy, E. (StL) 17

Home Runs
Cravath, G. (Phi) 19
Luderus, F. (Phi) 18
Saier, V. (Chi) 14

Total Bases
Cravath, G. (Phi) 298
Luderus, F. (Phi) 254
Saier, V. (Chi) 249

Runs Batted In
Cravath, G. (Phi) 128
Zimmerman, H. (Chi) 95
Saier, V. (Chi) 92

Bases On Balls
Bescher, B. (Cin) 94
Huggins, M. (StL) 92
Leach, T. (Chi) 77

Stolen Bases
Carey, M. (Pit) 61
Myers, H. (Bos) 57
Lobert, H. (Phi) 41

Batting Average
Daubert, J. (Bro) .350
Cravath, G. (Phi) .341
Viox, J. (Pit) .317

On-Base Percentage
Huggins, M. (StL) .432
Cravath, G. (Phi) .407
Daubert, J. (Bro) .405

Slugging Average
Cravath, G. (Phi) .568
Zimmerman, H. (Chi) .490
Saier, V. (Chi) .480

Adjusted OPS
Cravath, G. (Phi) 169
Zimmerman, H. (Chi) 146
Viox, J. (Pit) 142

Adjusted Batting Runs
Cravath, G. (Phi) 46.0
Viox, J. (Pit) 29.0
Saier, V. (Chi) 28.0

Runs Created/Game
Cravath, G. (Phi) 8.60
Daubert, J. (Bro) 6.90
Zimmerman, H. (Chi) 6.80

Fielding Runs
Cutshaw, G. (Bro) 27.8
Wagner, H. (Pit) 22.8
Evers, J. (Chi) 20.7

Win Shares – Batters
Cravath, G. (Phi) 29
Saier, V. (Chi) 26
Zimmerman, H. (Chi) 25

TPW – Batters
Cravath, G. (Phi) 3.6
Zimmerman, H. (Chi) 3.2
Evers, J. (Chi) 3.1

TEAM	CG	SH	SV	IP	H	H/G	ER	HR	BB	SO	OAV	RAT	ERA	ERA+	CERA	PR+	PF	FA	E	DP	FR	BW	PW	FW	TPW	DIF
NY	82	12	**17**	1422	**1276**	**8.1**	**382**	38	**315**	651	**.243**	**1.119**	**2.42**	129	**2.45**	**103.0**	97	.960	254	107	6.1	4.0	**10.7**	.6	**15.3**	9.7
PHI	77	**20**	11	**1455**^{1}	1407	8.7	509	40	512	**667**	.261	1.319	3.15	106	3.32	30.9	104	**.968**	**214**	112	-3.2	.0	3.2	-.3	2.8	10.2
CHI	89	12	15	1373	1330	8.7	477	39	478	556	.293	1.317	3.13	101	3.30	-2.0	99	.959	260	106	8.1	**5.5**	-.2	.8	6.1	5.9
PIT	74	9	7	1400	1344	8.6	451	**26**	434	590	.260	1.270	2.90	104	3.04	29.2	94	.964	226	94	-12.4	1.5	3.0	-1.3	3.3	.7
BOS	**105**	13	3	1373^{1}	1343	8.8	487	38	419	597	.264	1.283	3.19	103	3.21	35.4	103	.957	273	82	-22.4	-3.8	3.7	-2.3	-2.5	-3.5
BRO	71	9	7	1373	1287	8.4	477	33	439	548	.255	1.257	3.13	105	3.04	6.9	103	.961	243	**125**	**16.9**	-1.5	.7	**1.8**	1.0	-10.0
CIN	71	10	10	1380	1398	9.1	531	40	456	522	.273	1.343	3.46	94	3.53	-37.0	101	.961	251	104	3.8	-.7	-3.8	.4	-4.2	-7.8
STL	74	6	11	1351^{2}	1426	9.5	635	57	477	465	.280	1.408	4.23	**76**	3.93	-154.9	101	.965	219	113	2.9	-7.2	-16.1	.3	-23.0	-1.0
Total	**643**	**91**	**81**	**11128**^{1}		**8.7**	**3949**					**1.289**	**3.19**													

Wins
Seaton, T. (Phi) 27
Mathewson, C. (NY) 25
Marquard, R. (NY) 23

Win Percentage
Humphries, B. (Chi) .800
Demaree, A. (NY) .765
Alexander, G. (Phi) .733

Games
Cheney, L. (Chi) 54
Seaton, T. (Phi) 52
Sallee, S. (StL) 50

Complete Games
Tyler, L. (Bos) 28
Cheney, L. (Chi) 25
Mathewson, C. (NY) 25

Shutouts
Alexander, G. (Phi) 9
Seaton, T. (Phi) 5
5 players tied with 4

Saves
Cheney, L. (Chi) 11
Crandall, D. (NY,NY) 6
Brown, M. (Cin) 6

Innings Pitched
Seaton, T. (Phi) 322^{1}
Adams, B. (Pit) 313^{2}
Alexander, G. (Phi) 306^{1}

Fewest Hits/Game
Tesreau, J. (NY) 7.09
Seaton, T. (Phi) 7.32
Allen, F. (Bro) 7.42

Fewest BB/Game
Mathewson, C. (NY) .62
Humphries, B. (Chi) 1.19
Adams, B. (Pit) 1.41

Strikeouts
Seaton, T. (Phi) 168
Tesreau, J. (NY) 167
Alexander, G. (Phi) 159

Ratio
Mathewson, C. (NY) 1.02
Adams, B. (Pit) 1.02
Marquard, R. (NY) 1.03

Earned Run Average
Mathewson, C. (NY) 2.06
Adams, B. (Pit) 2.15
Tesreau, J. (NY) 2.17

Adjusted ERA
Mathewson, C. (NY) 151
Tesreau, J. (NY) 143
Demaree, A. (NY) 141

Component ERA
Adams, B. (Pit) 2.03
Mathewson, C. (NY) 2.16
Marquard, R. (NY) 2.17

Opponents' Batting Avg.
Seaton, T. (Phi) .226

Adjusted Pitching Runs
Mathewson, C. (NY) 35
Adams, B. (Pit) 33
Tesreau, J. (NY) 28

Win Shares – Pitchers
Mathewson, C. (NY) 30
Adams, B. (Pit) 29
Seaton, T. (Phi) 29

TPW – Pitchers
Adams, B. (Pit) 4.2
Mathewson, C. (NY) 3.6
Tesreau, J. (NY) 3.1

1913 American League

TEAM	G	W	L	PCT	GB	R	OR	EW	AB	H	2B	3B	HR	TB	BB	SO	SB	CS	AVG	OBP	SLG	OPS	OPS+	BR/A	PF	RC
PHI	153	96	57	.627	....	**794**	592	98	5044	**1412**	**223**	80	**33**	**1894**	**534**	547	221	....	**.280**	**.356**	**.375**	**.732**	**124**	**154**	98	**732**
WAS	155	90	64	.584	6.5	596	562	82	**5074**	1281	156	81	19	1656	440	595	**287**	....	.252	.317	.326	.644	93	-47	102	585
CLE	155	86	66	.566	9.5	633	536	89	5031	1349	206	74	16	1751	420	557	191	....	.268	.331	.348	.679	102	11	103	630
BOS	151	79	71	.527	15.5	631	610	78	4969	1334	220	**101**	17	1807	467	534	189	....	.268	.336	.364	.700	109	50	103	651
CHI	153	78	74	.513	17.5	488	**498**	74	4822	1139	157	66	24	1500	398	550	156	....	.236	.299	.311	.610	85	-90	99	487
DET	153	66	87	.431	30	625	716	66	5064	1344	180	**101**	24	1798	496	**501**	218	....	.265	.336	.355	.691	111	66	98	656
NY	153	57	94	.377	38	529	668	58	4880	1157	155	45	8	1426	**534**	617	203	....	.237	.320	.292	.612	85	-75	100	506
STL	155	57	96	.373	39	528	642	62	5031	1193	179	73	18	1572	455	769	209	....	.237	.306	.312	.618	90	-65	97	524
Total	**614**					**4824**			**39915**	**10209**	**1476**	**621**	**159**		**3744**	**4670**	**1674**		**.256**	**.325**	**.336**	**.661**				

Runs
Collins, E. (Phi) 125
Baker, F. (Phi) 116
Jackson, J. (Cle) 109

Hits
Jackson, J. (Cle) 197
Crawford, S. (Det) 193
Baker, F. (Phi) 190

Doubles
Jackson, J. (Cle) 39
Speaker, T. (Bos) 35
Baker, F. (Phi) 34

Triples
Crawford, S. (Det) 23
Speaker, T. (Bos) 22
Jackson, J. (Cle) 17

Home Runs
Baker, F. (Phi) 12
Crawford, S. (Det) 9
Bodie, P. (Chi) 8

Total Bases
Crawford, S. (Det) 298
Jackson, J. (Cle) 291
Baker, F. (Phi) 278

Runs Batted In
Baker, F. (Phi) 117
Lewis, D. (Bos) 90
McInnis, S. (Phi) 90

Bases On Balls
Shotton, B. (StL) 99
Collins, E. (Phi) 85
3 players tied with 80

Stolen Bases
Milan, C. (Was) 75
Moeller, D. (Was) 62
Collins, E. (Phi) 55

Batting Average
Cobb, T. (Det) .390
Jackson, J. (Cle) .373
Speaker, T. (Bos) .363

On-Base Percentage
Cobb, T. (Det) .467
Jackson, J. (Cle) .460
Collins, E. (Phi) .441

Slugging Average
Jackson, J. (Cle) .551
Cobb, T. (Det) .535
Speaker, T. (Bos) .533

Adjusted OPS
Cobb, T. (Det) 196
Jackson, J. (Cle) 190
Speaker, T. (Bos) 180

Adjusted Batting Runs
Jackson, J. (Cle) 63.0
Cobb, T. (Det) 54.0
Speaker, T. (Bos) 54.0

Runs Created/Game
Cobb, T. (Det) 11.60
Jackson, J. (Cle) 10.50
Speaker, T. (Bos) 10.00

Fielding Runs
Weaver, B. (Chi) 34.4
Turner, T. (Cle) 19.5
Collins, E. (Phi) 19.2

Win Shares – Batters
Collins, E. (Phi) 39
Baker, F. (Phi) 38
2 players tied with 36

TPW – Batters
Collins, E. (Phi) 7.5
Baker, F. (Phi) 6.9
Speaker, T. (Bos) 6.0

TEAM	CG	SH	SV	IP	H	H/G	ER	HR	BB	SO	OAV	RAT	ERA	ERA+	CERA	PR+	PF	FA	E	DP	FR	BW	PW	FW	TPW	DIF
PHI	69	17	**22**	1351^{1}	1200	8.0	479	24	532	630	.229	1.282	3.19	86	2.83	-66.2	94	**.966**	**212**	108	1.1	**16.4**	-7.1	.1	**9.4**	10.6
WAS	78	**23**	20	**1396**^{1}	**1177**	**7.6**	423	35	465	**758**	**.225**	**1.176**	2.73	108	2.67	11.4	101	.960	261	122	**22.0**	-5.0	1.2	**2.3**	-1.5	14.5
CLE	93	18	5	1386^{2}	1278	8.3	391	19	502	689	.249	1.284	2.54	119	3.03	54.3	104	.962	242	124	20.9	1.1	5.8	2.2	9.1	.9
BOS	83	12	10	1358^{1}	1323	8.8	444	**6**	442	710	.260	1.299	2.94	100	3.17	24.4	100	.961	238	84	-25.4	5.4	2.6	-2.7	5.3	-1.3
CHI	84	17	8	1360^{1}	1190	7.9	**352**	10	**438**	602	.235	1.197	**2.33**	125	**2.66**	**87.6**	100	.960	255	104	1.6	-9.6	**9.3**	.2	-.1	2.1
DET	90	4	7	1360	1359	9.0	511	13	504	468	.265	1.370	3.38	**86**	3.55	-30.6	99	.954	303	105	-40.4	7.1	-3.3	-4.3	-.5	-9.5
NY	75	8	7	1344	1318	8.8	488	31	455	530	.260	1.319	3.27	91	3.32	-41.5	102	.954	293	94	-1.9	-8.0	-4.4	-.2	-12.6	-5.4
STL	**104**	14	5	1382^{1}	1369	8.9	470	21	454	476	.266	1.319	3.06	96	3.40	-41.6	100	.954	301	**125**	21.0	-7.0	-4.4	2.2	-9.2	-9.8
Total	**676**	**113**	**84**	**10939**^{1}		**8.4**	**3558**					**1.280**	**2.93**													

Wins
- Johnson, W. (Was) 36
- Falkenberg, C. (Cle) 23
- Russell, R. (Chi) 22

Win Percentage
- Johnson, W. (Was) .837
- Bush, J. (Phi) .714
- Boehling, J. (Was) .708

Games
- Russell, R. (Chi) 52
- 3 players tied with 48

Complete Games
- Johnson, W. (Was) 29
- Russell, R. (Chi) 26
- Scott, J. (Chi) 25

Shutouts
- Johnson, W. (Was) 11
- Russell, R. (Chi) 8
- Plank, E. (Phi) 7

Saves
- Bender, C. (Phi) 13
- Hughes, T. (Was) 6
- Bedient, H. (Bos) 5

Innings Pitched
- Johnson, W. (Was) 346
- Russell, R. (Chi) 316^{2}
- Scott, J. (Chi) 312^{1}

Fewest Hits/Game
- Johnson, W. (Was) 6.03
- Mitchell, W. (Cle) 6.35
- Engel, J. (Was) 6.78

Fewest BB/Game
- Johnson, W. (Was) .99
- Collins, R. (Bos) 1.35
- Mitchell, R. (StL) 1.72

Strikeouts
- Johnson, W. (Was) 243
- Falkenberg, C. (Cle) 166
- Gregg, V. (Cle) 166

Ratio
- Johnson, W. (Was) .78
- Russell, R. (Chi) 1.04
- Scott, J. (Chi) 1.08

Earned Run Average
- Johnson, W. (Was) 1.14
- Cicotte, E. (Chi) 1.58
- Scott, J. (Chi) 1.90

Adjusted ERA
- Johnson, W. (Was) 258
- Cicotte, E. (Chi) 185
- Mitchell, W. (Cle) 159

Component ERA
- Johnson, W. (Was) 1.27
- Mitchell, W. (Cle) 1.80
- Russell, R. (Chi) 1.97

Opponents' Batting Avg.
- Johnson, W. (Was) .187
- Mitchell, W. (Cle) .199
- Engel, J. (Was) .207

Adjusted Pitching Runs
- Johnson, W. (Was) 64
- Cicotte, E. (Chi) 40
- Russell, R. (Chi) 35

Win Shares – Pitchers
- Johnson, W. (Was) 54
- Russell, R. (Chi) 32
- 2 players tied with 27

TPW – Pitchers
- Johnson, W. (Was) 8.0
- Russell, R. (Chi) 4.0
- Cicotte, E. (Chi) 3.9

1914 National League

TEAM	G	W	L	PCT	GB	R	OR	EW	AB	H	2B	3B	HR	TB	BB	SO	SB	CS	AVG	OBP	SLG	OPS	OPS+	BR/A	PF	RC
BOS	158	94	59	.614	....	657	548	90	**5206**	1307	213	60	35	1745	**502**	617	139	....	.251	.323	.335	.658	103	22	99	602
NY	156	84	70	.545	10.5	**672**	576	89	5146	1363	**222**	59	30	1793	447	**479**	**239**	....	.265	**.330**	.348	.679	**112**	**76**	97	**644**
STL	157	81	72	.529	13	558	**540**	79	5046	1249	203	65	33	1681	445	618	204	....	.248	.314	.333	.647	100	-2	99	576
CHI	156	78	76	.506	16.5	605	638	73	5050	1229	199	74	42	1702	501	577	164	....	.243	.317	.337	.654	101	10	100	579
BRO	154	75	79	.487	19.5	622	618	77	5152	**1386**	172	**90**	31	1831	376	559	173	....	**.269**	.323	.355	.678	106	28	102	629
PHI	154	74	80	.481	20.5	651	687	73	5110	1345	211	52	**62**	**1846**	472	570	145	....	.263	.329	**.361**	**.690**	105	29	106	636
PIT	158	69	85	.448	25.5	503	**540**	72	5145	1197	148	79	18	1557	416	608	147	....	.233	.295	.303	.597	87	-79	96	488
CIN	157	60	94	.390	34.5	530	651	61	4991	1178	142	64	16	1496	441	627	224	....	.236	.305	.300	.605	83	-93	103	506
Total	**625**					**4798**			**40846**	**10254**	**1510**	**543**	**267**		**3600**	**4655**	**1435**		**.251**	**.317**	**.334**	**.651**				

Runs
- Burns, G. (NY) 100
- Magee, S. (Phi) 96
- Daubert, J. (Bro) 89

Hits
- Magee, S. (Phi) 171
- Burns, G. (NY) 170
- Wheat, Z. (Bro) 170

Doubles
- Magee, S. (Phi) 39
- Zimmerman, H. (Chi) 36
- Burns, G. (NY) 35

Triples
- Carey, M. (Pit) 17
- 3 players tied with 12

Home Runs
- Cravath, G. (Phi) 19
- Saier, V. (Chi) 18
- Magee, S. (Phi) 15

Total Bases
- Magee, S. (Phi) 277
- Cravath, G. (Phi) 249
- Wheat, Z. (Bro) 241

Runs Batted In
- Magee, S. (Phi) 103
- Cravath, G. (Phi) 100
- Wheat, Z. (Bro) 89

Bases On Balls
- Huggins, M. (StL) 105
- Saier, V. (Chi) 94
- Burns, G. (NY) 89

Stolen Bases
- Burns, G. (NY) 62
- Herzog, B. (Cin) 46
- Dolan, C. (StL) 42

Batting Average
- Daubert, J. (Bro) .329
- Becker, B. (Phi) .325
- Dalton, J. (Bro) .319

On-Base Percentage
- Stengel, C. (Bro) .404
- Burns, G. (NY) .403
- Cravath, G. (Phi) .402

Slugging Average
- Magee, S. (Phi) .509
- Cravath, G. (Phi) .499
- Wheat, Z. (Bro) .452

Adjusted OPS
- Cravath, G. (Phi) 157
- Magee, S. (Phi) 154
- Burns, G. (NY) 149

Adjusted Batting Runs
- Burns, G. (NY) 38.0
- Cravath, G. (Phi) 37.0
- Magee, S. (Phi) 35.0

Runs Created/Game
- Magee, S. (Phi) 7.40
- Cravath, G. (Phi) 7.30
- Burns, G. (NY) 7.20

Fielding Runs
- Maranville, R. (Bos) 44.2
- Cutshaw, G. (Bro) 31.0
- Herzog, B. (Cin) 24.7

Win Shares – Batters
- Burns, G. (NY) 31
- Magee, S. (Phi) 29
- Cravath, G. (Phi) 28

TPW – Batters
- Maranville, R. (Bos) 5.0
- Smith, R. (Bos,Bro) 4.2
- Herzog, B. (Cin) 4.0

TEAM	CG	SH	SV	IP	H	H/G	ER	HR	BB	SO	OAV	RAT	ERA	ERA+	CERA	PR+	PF	FA	E	DP	FR	BW	PW	FW	TPW	DIF
BOS	**104**	19	6	1421	1272	8.1	433	38	477	606	.249	1.231	2.74	100	2.95	-53.6	99	.963	246	**143**	**55.0**	2.3	-5.8	**5.9**	2.5	15.5
NY	88	**20**	9	1390^{2}	1298	8.4	454	47	**367**	563	.253	1.197	2.94	**90**	2.83	-45.1	95	.961	254	119	-0.3	**8.2**	-4.9	.0	3.3	3.7
STL	84	16	12	**1424^{2}**	1279	8.1	**377**	**26**	422	531	.250	1.194	**2.38**	117	2.72	**57.6**	100	.964	239	109	7.4	-.2	**6.2**	.8	**6.8**	-1.8
CHI	70	14	11	1389^{1}	**1169**	**7.6**	418	37	528	**651**	**.233**	1.221	2.71	102	2.69	35.8	100	.951	310	87	-25.3	1.0	3.9	-2.7	2.2	-1.2
BRO	80	11	11	1368^{1}	1282	8.4	429	36	466	605	.255	1.277	2.82	101	3.07	0.4	102	.961	248	112	5.5	3.0	.0	.6	3.6	-5.6
PHI	85	14	7	1379^{1}	1403	9.2	469	**26**	452	650	.270	1.345	3.06	96	3.44	23.5	105	.950	324	81	-42.7	3.2	2.5	-4.6	1.1	-4.1
PIT	86	10	11	1405	1272	8.2	422	27	392	488	.250	**1.184**	2.70	98	**2.67**	-13.4	95	**.966**	**223**	96	4.5	-8.5	-1.4	.5	-9.5	1.5
CIN	74	15	**15**	1387^{1}	1259	8.2	453	30	489	607	.248	1.260	2.94	100	2.95	2.7	105	.952	314	113	-4.7	-10.1	.3	-.5	-10.3	-6.7
Total	**671**	**119**	**82**	**11165^{2}**		**8.2**	**3455**					**1.238**	**2.78**													

Wins
- Alexander, G. (Phi) 27
- 3 players tied with 26

Win Percentage
- James, B. (Bos) .788
- Doak, B. (StL) .760
- 2 players tied with .722

Games
- Cheney, L. (Chi) 50
- Mayer, E. (Phi) 48
- Ames, R. (Cin) 47

Complete Games
- Alexander, G. (Phi) 32
- Rudolph, D. (Bos) 31
- James, B. (Bos) 30

Shutouts
- Tesreau, J. (NY) 8
- Doak, B. (StL) 7
- 3 players tied with 6

Saves
- Ames, R. (Cin) 6
- Sallee, S. (StL) 6
- Cheney, L. (Chi) 5

Innings Pitched
- Alexander, G. (Phi) 355
- Rudolph, D. (Bos) 336^{1}
- James, B. (Bos) 332^{1}

Fewest Hits/Game
- Tesreau, J. (NY) 6.65
- Doak, B. (StL) 6.79
- Cheney, L. (Chi) 6.91

Fewest BB/Game
- Mathewson, C. (NY) .66
- Adams, B. (Pit) 1.24
- Marquard, R. (NY) 1.58

Strikeouts
- Alexander, G. (Phi) 214
- Tesreau, J. (NY) 189
- Vaughn, H. (Chi) 165

Ratio
- Adams, B. (Pit) 1.03
- Rudolph, D. (Bos) 1.04
- Mathewson, C. (NY) 1.08

Earned Run Average
- Doak, B. (StL) 1.72
- James, B. (Bos) 1.90
- Pfeffer, J. (Bro) 1.97

Adjusted ERA
- Doak, B. (StL) 162
- James, B. (Bos) 145
- Pfeffer, J. (Bro) 145

Component ERA
- Doak, B. (StL) 2.07
- Adams, B. (Pit) 2.14
- Rudolph, D. (Bos) 2.16

Opponents' Batting Avg.
- Tesreau, J. (NY) .209
- Cheney, L. (Chi) .215
- Doak, B. (StL) .216

Adjusted Pitching Runs
- Alexander, G. (Phi) 33
- Pfeffer, J. (Bro) 30
- Doak, B. (StL) 29

Win Shares – Pitchers
- James, B. (Bos) 36
- Rudolph, D. (Bos) 29
- 3 players tied with 26

TPW – Pitchers
- Alexander, G. (Phi) 3.8
- Pfeffer, J. (Bro) 3.2
- Vaughn, H. (Chi) 3.1

1914 American League

TEAM	G	W	L	PCT	GB	R	OR	EW	AB	H	2B	3B	HR	TB	BB	SO	SB	CS	AVG	OBP	SLG	OPS	OPS+	BR/A	PF	RC
PHI	158	99	53	.651	....	**749**	529	101	5126	**1392**	165	80	**29**	**1804**	545	**517**	231	188	**.272**	**.348**	**.352**	**.699**	**123**	**139**	96	**663**
BOS	159	91	62	.595	8.5	589	**510**	87	5117	1278	**226**	**85**	18	1728	490	549	177	176	.250	.320	.338	.658	105	17	100	568
WAS	158	81	73	.526	19	572	519	84	5108	1245	176	81	18	1637	470	640	220	163	.244	.313	.320	.634	94	-32	104	544
DET	157	80	73	.523	19.5	615	618	76	5102	1318	195	84	25	1756	557	537	211	154	.258	.336	.344	.681	109	66	103	630
STL	159	71	82	.464	28.5	523	615	64	5101	1241	185	75	17	1627	423	863	233	189	.243	.306	.319	.625	98	-21	96	516
NY	157	70	84	.455	30	537	550	75	4992	1144	149	52	12	1433	**577**	711	**251**	191	.229	.315	.287	.602	88	-55	100	484
CHI	157	70	84	.455	30	487	560	66	5040	1205	161	71	19	1565	408	609	167	**152**	.239	.302	.311	.612	92	-53	99	498
CLE	157	51	102	.333	48.5	538	709	56	**5157**	1262	178	70	10	1610	450	685	167	157	.245	.310	.312	.622	90	-62	104	518
Total	**631**					**4610**			**40743**	**10085**	**1435**	**598**	**148**		**3920**	**5111**	**1657**	**1370**	**.248**	**.319**	**.323**	**.642**				

Runs
- Collins, E. (Phi) 122
- Murphy, E. (Phi) 101
- Speaker, T. (Bos) 101

Hits
- Speaker, T. (Bos) 193
- Crawford, S. (Det) 183
- Baker, F. (Phi) 182

Doubles
- Speaker, T. (Bos) 46
- Lewis, D. (Bos) 37
- 2 players tied with 34

Triples
- Crawford, S. (Det) 26
- Gardner, L. (Bos) 19
- Speaker, T. (Bos) 18

Home Runs
- Baker, F. (Phi) 9
- Crawford, S. (Det) 8
- 2 players tied with 6

Total Bases
- Speaker, T. (Bos) 287
- Crawford, S. (Det) 281
- Baker, F. (Phi) 252

Runs Batted In
- Crawford, S. (Det) 104
- McInnis, S. (Phi) 95
- Speaker, T. (Bos) 90

Bases On Balls
- Bush, D. (Det) 112
- Collins, E. (Phi) 97
- Murphy, E. (Phi) 87

Stolen Bases
- Maisel, F. (NY) 74
- Collins, E. (Phi) 58
- Speaker, T. (Bos) 42

Batting Average
- Cobb, T. (Det) .368
- Collins, E. (Phi) .344
- Speaker, T. (Bos) .338

On-Base Percentage
- Collins, E. (Phi) .452
- Speaker, T. (Bos) .423
- Jackson, J. (Cle) .399

Slugging Average
- Speaker, T. (Bos) .503
- Crawford, S. (Det) .483
- Jackson, J. (Cle) .464

Adjusted OPS
- Collins, E. (Phi) 179
- Speaker, T. (Bos) 178
- Crawford, S. (Det) 157

Adjusted Batting Runs
- Collins, E. (Phi) 57.0
- Speaker, T. (Bos) 52.0
- Crawford, S. (Det) 37.0

Runs Created/Game
- Collins, E. (Phi) 7.90
- Speaker, T. (Bos) 7.80
- Jackson, J. (Cle) 7.00

Fielding Runs
- Boone, L. (NY) 22.2
- McBride, G. (Was) 20.3
- Bush, D. (Det) 19.1

Win Shares – Batters
- Speaker, T. (Bos) 45
- Collins, E. (Phi) 43
- Baker, F. (Phi) 35

TPW – Batters
- Collins, E. (Phi) 7.3
- Speaker, T. (Bos) 6.5
- Baker, F. (Phi) 5.2

TEAM	CG	SH	SV	IP	H	H/G	ER	HR	BB	SO	OAV	RAT	ERA	ERA+	CERA	PR+	PF	FA	E	DP	FR	BW	PW	FW	TPW	DIF
PHI	89	24	16	1404	1264	8.1	434	18	521	720	.248	1.271	2.78	94	2.98	-33.2	95	**.966**	**213**	116	6.9	**15.4**	-3.7	.8	**12.5**	10.5
BOS	88	24	7	**1427**^{1}	1207	7.6	**374**	18	393	602	.236	**1.121**	**2.36**	114	**2.46**	25.0	98	.963	242	99	**25.6**	1.8	2.8	**2.8**	7.4	7.6
WAS	75	**25**	**19**	1420^{2}	**1170**	**7.4**	401	20	520	**784**	**.233**	1.190	2.54	110	2.66	33.5	103	.961	254	116	8.8	-3.6	3.7	1.0	1.1	2.9
DET	81	14	11	1412	1285	8.2	449	17	498	567	.248	1.263	2.86	98	3.04	8.1	102	.958	286	101	-16.5	7.3	.9	-1.8	6.4	-2.4
STL	81	15	9	1410^{2}	1309	8.4	446	20	540	553	.251	1.311	2.85	95	3.21	-7.5	99	.952	317	114	-15.6	-2.3	-.8	-1.7	-4.8	-.2
NY	**98**	9	2	1397^{1}	1277	8.2	436	30	**390**	563	.250	1.193	2.81	98	2.84	-24.3	101	.963	238	93	14.8	-6.1	-2.7	1.6	-7.1	.1
CHI	74	17	11	1398^{2}	1207	7.8	385	15	401	660	.238	1.150	2.48	108	2.48	**35.0**	98	.957	299	90	-4.1	-5.9	**3.9**	-.5	-2.5	-4.5
CLE	69	9	2	1391^{2}	1365	8.8	496	**10**	666	688	.267	1.459	3.21	**90**	3.82	-31.6	105	.954	300	**119**	-20.2	-6.8	-3.5	-2.2	-12.5	-12.5
Total	**655**	**137**	**77**	**11262**^{1}		**8.1**	**3421**					**1.244**	**2.73**													

Wins
Johnson, W. (Was) 28
Coveleski, H. (Det) 22
Collins, R. (Bos) 20

Win Percentage
Bender, C. (Phi) .850
Leonard, D. (Bos) .792
Plank, E. (Phi) .682

Games
Johnson, W. (Was) 51
Ayers, D. (Was) 49
2 players tied with 48

Complete Games
Johnson, W. (Was) 33
Coveleski, H. (Det) 23
2 players tied with 22

Shutouts
Johnson, W. (Was) 9
Bender, C. (Phi) 7
Leonard, D. (Bos) 7

Saves
4 players tied with 4

Innings Pitched
Johnson, W. (Was) 371^{2}
Coveleski, H. (Det) 303^{1}
Hamilton, E. (StL) 302^{1}

Fewest Hits/Game
Leonard, D. (Bos) 5.57
Caldwell, R. (NY) 6.46
Shaw, J. (Was) 6.93

Fewest BB/Game
McHale, M. (NY) 1.55
Russell, R. (Chi) 1.77
Johnson, W. (Was) 1.79

Strikeouts
Johnson, W. (Was) 225
Mitchell, W. (Cle) 179
Leonard, D. (Bos) 176

Ratio
Leonard, D. (Bos) .89
Caldwell, R. (NY) .96
Johnson, W. (Was) .97

Earned Run Average
Leonard, D. (Bos) .96
Foster, R. (Bos) 1.70
Johnson, W. (Was) 1.72

Adjusted ERA
Leonard, D. (Bos) 279
Johnson, W. (Was) 163
Foster, R. (Bos) 158

Component ERA
Leonard, D. (Bos) 1.43
Caldwell, R. (NY) 1.74
Johnson, W. (Was) 1.75

Opponents' Batting Avg.
Leonard, D. (Bos) .180
Caldwell, R. (NY) .205
Shaw, J. (Was) .216

Adjusted Pitching Runs
Johnson, W. (Was) 43
Leonard, D. (Bos) 39
Weilman, C. (StL) 24

Win Shares – Pitchers
Johnson, W. (Was) 38
Leonard, D. (Bos) 29
Weilman, C. (StL) 24

TPW – Pitchers
Johnson, W. (Was) 5.6
Leonard, D. (Bos) 4.2
Weilman, C. (StL) 2.5

1914 Federal League

TEAM	G	W	L	PCT	GB	R	OR	EW	AB	H	2B	3B	HR	TB	BB	SO	SB	CS	AVG	OBP	SLG	OPS	OPS+	BR/A	PF	RC
IND	157	88	65	.575	....	**762**	622	92	5176	**1474**	**230**	**90**	33	**1983**	470	668	**273**	....	**.285**	**.349**	**.383**	**.732**	103	24	111	**765**
CHI	157	87	67	.565	1.5	621	**517**	91	5098	1314	227	50	**52**	1797	**520**	645	171	....	.258	.331	.352	.684	**107**	**50**	94	634
BAL	160	84	70	.545	4.5	645	628	79	5120	1374	222	67	32	1826	487	589	....	....	.268	.337	.357	.694	104	33	99	652
BUF	155	80	71	.530	7	620	602	78	5064	1264	177	74	37	1700	430	761	228	....	.250	.311	.336	.647	86	-92	104	577
BRO	157	77	77	.500	11.5	662	677	75	**5221**	1402	225	85	42	1923	404	665	....	....	.269	.326	.368	.695	103	12	101	669
KC	154	67	84	.444	20	644	683	71	5127	1369	226	77	39	1866	399	621	171	....	.267	.324	.364	.688	**107**	37	95	637
PIT	154	64	86	.427	22.5	605	698	64	5114	1339	180	**90**	34	1801	410	**575**	....	....	.262	.321	.352	.674	103	17	94	613
STL	154	62	89	.411	25	565	697	60	5078	1254	193	65	26	1655	503	662	113	....	.247	.319	.326	.645	84	-94	106	554
Total	**624**					**5124**			**40998**	**10790**	**1680**	**598**	**295**		**3623**	**5186**	**956**		**.263**	**.328**	**.355**	**.682**				

Runs
Kauff, B. (Ind) 120
McKechnie, B. (Ind) 107
Duncan, V. (Bal) 99

Hits
Kauff, B. (Ind) 211
Zwilling, D. (Chi) 185
Evans, S. (Bro) 179

Doubles
Kauff, B. (Ind) 44
Evans, S. (Bro) 41
Kenworthy, B. (KC) 40

Triples
Esmond, J. (Ind) 15
Evans, S. (Bro) 15
Kenworthy, B. (KC) 14

Home Runs
Zwilling, D. (Chi) 16
Kenworthy, B. (KC) 15
2 players tied with 12

Total Bases
Kauff, B. (Ind) 305
Zwilling, D. (Chi) 287
2 players tied with 286

Runs Batted In
LaPorte, F. (Ind) 107
Evans, S. (Bro) 96
2 players tied with 95

Bases On Balls
Wickland, A. (Chi) 81
Agler, J. (Buf) 77
Kauff, B. (Ind) 72

Stolen Bases
Kauff, B. (Ind) 75
McKechnie, B. (Ind) 47
Myers, H. (Bro) 43

Batting Average
Kauff, B. (Ind) .370
Evans, S. (Bro) .348
Easterly, T. (KC) .335

On-Base Percentage
Kauff, B. (Ind) .447
Evans, S. (Bro) .416
Lennox, E. (Pit) .414

Slugging Average
Evans, S. (Bro) .556
Kauff, B. (Ind) .534
Kenworthy, B. (KC) .525

Adjusted OPS
Evans, S. (Bro) 174
Lennox, E. (Pit) 167
Kenworthy, B. (KC) 161

Adjusted Batting Runs
Evans, S. (Bro) 49.0
Kauff, B. (Ind) 49.0
Kenworthy, B. (KC) 40.0

Runs Created/Game
Kauff, B. (Ind) 10.90
Evans, S. (Bro) 9.00
Lennox, E. (Pit) 7.60

Fielding Runs
Tinker, J. (Chi) 22.3
McKechnie, B. (Ind) 21.6
Downey, T. (Buf) 20.8

Win Shares – Batters
Kauff, B. (Ind) 38
Evans, S. (Bro) 30
Kenworthy, B. (KC) 30

TPW – Batters
Kauff, B. (Ind) 5.5
Kenworthy, B. (KC) 5.4
Wilson, A. (Chi) 5.1

TEAM	CG	SH	SV	IP	H	H/G	ER	HR	BB	SO	OAV	RAT	ERA	ERA+	CERA	PR+	PF	FA	E	DP	FR	BW	PW	FW	TPW	DIF
IND	**104**	15	9	1397^{2}	1352	8.7	475	**29**	476	664	.258	1.308	3.06	113	3.27	**48.7**	108	.956	289	113	15.2	2.5	**5.1**	1.6	9.2	2.8
CHI	93	**17**	8	**1420**^{1}	**1204**	**7.6**	**385**	43	393	650	**.233**	**1.124**	**2.44**	121	**2.51**	44.7	92	.962	249	114	**35.6**	**5.2**	4.6	**3.7**	**13.6**	-3.6
BAL	88	15	13	1392	1389	9.0	484	34	**392**	**732**	.268	1.279	3.13	101	3.29	38.7	99	.960	263	105	-32.5	3.5	4.0	-3.4	4.1	2.9
BUF	89	15	**16**	1387	1249	8.1	487	45	505	662	.245	1.265	3.16	106	3.12	5.8	104	**.962**	**242**	109	21.1	-9.5	.6	2.2	-6.7	11.7
BRO	91	11	9	1385^{1}	1375	8.9	512	31	559	636	.264	1.396	3.33	97	3.66	1.2	101	.956	283	120	-16.1	1.3	.1	-1.7	-.3	.3
KC	82	10	12	1361	1387	9.2	516	37	445	600	.268	1.346	3.41	90	3.53	-56.0	96	.957	279	**135**	5.2	3.9	-5.8	.5	-1.4	-6.6
PIT	97	9	6	1370	1416	9.3	542	38	444	510	.273	1.358	3.56	**86**	3.68	-69.5	96	.960	253	92	-4.1	1.8	-7.2	-.4	-5.9	-5.1
STL	97	9	6	1367^{2}	1418	9.3	545	38	409	661	.267	1.336	3.59	97	3.48	7.1	108	.957	273	94	-24.5	-9.8	.7	-2.5	-11.6	-1.4
Total	**741**	**101**	**79**	**11081**		**8.8**	**3946**					**1.301**	**3.20**													

Wins
Hendrix, C. (Chi) 29
Quinn, J. (Bal) 26
2 players tied with 25

Win Percentage
Ford, R. (Buf) .778
Hendrix, C. (Chi) .744
Quinn, J. (Bal) .650

Games
Falkenberg, C. (Ind) 49
Hendrix, C. (Chi) 49
Wilhelm, K. (Bal) 47

Complete Games
Hendrix, C. (Chi) 34
Falkenberg, C. (Ind) 33
Moseley, E. (Ind) 29

Shutouts
Falkenberg, C. (Ind) 9
Seaton, T. (Bro) 7
2 players tied with 6

Saves
Ford, R. (Buf) 6
3 players tied with 5

Innings Pitched
Falkenberg, C. (Ind) 377^{1}
Hendrix, C. (Chi) 362
Quinn, J. (Bal) 342^{2}

Fewest Hits/Game
Hendrix, C. (Chi) 6.51
Ford, R. (Buf) 6.91
Krapp, G. (Buf) 7.05

Fewest BB/Game
Ford, R. (Buf) 1.49
Suggs, G. (Bal) 1.61
Quinn, J. (Bal) 1.71

Strikeouts
Falkenberg, C. (Ind) 236
Moseley, E. (Ind) 205
Hendrix, C. (Chi) 189

Ratio
Ford, R. (Buf) .93
Hendrix, C. (Chi) .94
Fiske, M. (Chi) 1.11

Earned Run Average
Hendrix, C. (Chi) 1.69
Ford, R. (Buf) 1.82
Watson, D. (StL,Chi) 2.01

Adjusted ERA
Ford, R. (Buf) 183
Hendrix, C. (Chi) 174
Falkenberg, C. (Ind) 156

Component ERA
Hendrix, C. (Chi) 1.62
Ford, R. (Buf) 1.83
Watson, D. (Chi,StL) 2.31

Opponents' Batting Avg.
Hendrix, C. (Chi) .203
Krapp, G. (Buf) .210
Ford, R. (Buf) .214

Adjusted Pitching Runs
Falkenberg, C. (Ind) 48
Hendrix, C. (Chi) 42
Ford, R. (Buf) 38

Win Shares – Pitchers
Hendrix, C. (Chi) 37
Falkenberg, C. (Ind) 34
Quinn, J. (Bal) 32

TPW – Pitchers
Hendrix, C. (Chi) 4.9
Falkenberg, C. (Ind) 4.8
Quinn, J. (Bal) 4.0

1915 National League

TEAM	G	W	L	PCT	GB	R	OR	EW	AB	H	2B	3B	HR	TB	BB	SO	SB	CS	AVG	OBP	SLG	OPS	OPS+	BR/A	PF	RC
PHI	153	90	62	.592	....	589	**463**	94	4916	1216	202	39	**58**	1670	460	600	121	113	.247	.316	.340	**.656**	**104**	24	101	550
BOS	157	83	69	.546	7	582	545	81	5070	1219	**231**	57	17	1615	**549**	620	121	**98**	.240	**.321**	.319	.640	102	**35**	98	554
BRO	154	80	72	.526	10	536	560	73	5120	1268	165	75	14	1625	313	**496**	131	126	.248	.295	.317	.612	90	-72	102	496
CHI	156	73	80	.477	17.5	570	620	70	5114	1246	212	66	53	**1749**	393	639	166	124	.244	.303	**.342**	.645	101	7	100	555
PIT	156	73	81	.474	18	557	520	82	5113	1259	197	91	24	1710	419	656	**182**	111	.246	.309	.334	.644	103	30	99	563
STL	157	72	81	.471	18.5	**590**	601	75	5106	1297	159	**92**	20	1700	457	658	162	144	**.254**	.320	.333	.653	**104**	24	100	**568**
CIN	160	71	83	.461	20	516	585	67	**5231**	**1323**	194	84	15	1730	360	512	156	142	.253	.308	.331	.638	98	-22	102	553
NY	155	69	83	.454	21	582	628	70	5218	1312	195	68	24	1715	315	547	155	137	.251	.300	.329	.629	102	1	94	526
Total	**624**					**4522**			**40888**	**10140**	**1555**	**572**	**225**		**3266**	**4728**	**1194**	**995**	**.248**	**.309**	**.331**	**.640**				

Runs
Cravath, G. (Phi) 89
Doyle, L. (NY) 86
Bancroft, D. (Phi) 85

Hits
Doyle, L. (NY) 189
Griffith, T. (Cin) 179
Hinchman, B. (Pit) 177

Doubles
Doyle, L. (NY) 40
Luderus, F. (Phi) 36
Saier, V. (Chi) 35

Triples
Long, T. (StL) 25
Wagner, H. (Pit) 17
Griffith, T. (Cin) 16

Home Runs
Cravath, G. (Phi) 24
Williams, C. (Chi) 13
Schulte, F. (Chi) 12

Total Bases
Cravath, G. (Phi) 266
Doyle, L. (NY) 261
Griffith, T. (Cin) 254

Runs Batted In
Cravath, G. (Phi) 115
Magee, S. (Bos) 87
Griffith, T. (Cin) 85

Bases On Balls
Cravath, G. (Phi) 86
Bancroft, D. (Phi) 77
Viox, J. (Pit) 75

Stolen Bases
Carey, M. (Pit) 36
Herzog, B. (Cin) 35
2 players tied with 29

Batting Average
Doyle, L. (NY) .... .320
Luderus, F. (Phi) .... .315
Griffith, T. (Cin) .... .307

On-Base Percentage
Cravath, G. (Phi) .... .393
Luderus, F. (Phi) .... .376
Daubert, J. (Bro) .... .369

Slugging Average
Cravath, G. (Phi) .... .510
Luderus, F. (Phi) .... .457
Long, T. (StL) .... .446

Adjusted OPS
Cravath, G. (Phi) 170
Doyle, L. (NY) 150
Luderus, F. (Phi) 150

Adjusted Batting Runs
Cravath, G. (Phi) 45.0
Doyle, L. (NY) 29.0
Luderus, F. (Phi) 28.0

Runs Created/Game
Cravath, G. (Phi) 7.20
Luderus, F. (Phi) 6.40
Saier, V. (Chi) 5.80

Fielding Runs
Fletcher, A. (NY) 28.1
Herzog, B. (Cin) 27.8
Cutshaw, G. (Bro) 24.0

Win Shares – Batters
Cravath, G. (Phi) 35
Doyle, L. (NY) 33
Daubert, J. (Bro) 27

TPW – Batters
Cravath, G. (Phi) 5.4
Snyder, F. (StL) 3.7
Luderus, F. (Phi) 3.7

TEAM	CG	SH	SV	IP	H	H/G	ER	HR	BB	SO	OAV	RAT	ERA	ERA+	CERA	PR+	PF	FA	E	DP	FR	BW	PW	FW	TPW	DIF
PHI	**98**	**20**	8	1374^{1}	**1161**	**7.6**	**331**	26	342	652	**.234**	**1.094**	**2.17**	126	**2.30**	**84.7**	100	.966	216	99	1.2	2.7	**9.4**	.1	**12.3**	1.7
BOS	95	17	**13**	1405^{2}	1257	8.0	401	23	366	630	.246	1.155	2.57	104	2.61	-0.5	97	**.966**	**213**	115	16.0	**3.8**	-.1	1.8	5.6	1.4
BRO	87	16	8	1389^{2}	1252	8.1	411	29	473	499	.246	1.241	2.66	104	2.92	10.9	101	.963	238	96	7.5	-8.0	1.2	.8	-6.0	10.0
CHI	71	18	8	1399	1272	8.2	483	28	480	**657**	.247	1.252	3.11	89	2.88	-32.3	101	.958	268	94	-21.0	.8	-3.6	-2.3	-5.1	2.1
PIT	91	18	11	1380	1229	8.0	399	**21**	384	544	.246	1.169	2.60	105	2.58	26.3	99	.966	214	100	-6.2	3.3	2.9	-.7	5.5	-9.5
STL	79	13	9	1400^{2}	1320	8.5	450	30	402	538	.256	1.229	2.89	96	2.89	2.1	101	.964	235	109	-14.9	2.7	.2	-1.7	1.2	-5.2
CIN	80	19	12	**1432^{1}**	1304	8.2	452	28	497	572	.250	1.257	2.84	101	2.95	-28.6	104	.966	222	**148**	**31.0**	-2.4	-3.2	**3.4**	-2.2	-3.8
NY	78	15	9	1385	1350	8.8	479	40	**325**	637	.259	1.209	3.11	**82**	2.93	-70.9	93	.960	256	119	-14.7	.1	-7.9	-1.6	-9.4	2.4
Total	**679**	**136**	**78**	**11166^{2}**		**8.2**	**3406**					**1.201**	**2.75**													

Wins
Alexander, G. (Phi) 31
Rudolph, D. (Bos) 22
2 players tied with 21

Win Percentage
Alexander, G. (Phi) .... .756
Toney, F. (Cin) .... .739
Mamaux, A. (Pit) .... .724

Games
Hughes, T. (Bos) 50
Alexander, G. (Phi) 49
Dale, G. (Cin) 49

Complete Games
Alexander, G. (Phi) 36
Rudolph, D. (Bos) 30
Pfeffer, J. (Bro) 26

Shutouts
Alexander, G. (Phi) 12
Mamaux, A. (Pit) 8
Tesreau, J. (NY) 8

Saves
Hughes, T. (Bos) 9
Benton, R. (Cin,NY) 5
2 players tied with 4

Innings Pitched
Alexander, G. (Phi) .... 376^{1}
Rudolph, D. (Bos) .... 341^{1}
Tesreau, J. (NY) 306

Fewest Hits/Game
Alexander, G. (Phi) 6.05
Toney, F. (Cin) 6.47
Mamaux, A. (Pit) 6.51

Fewest BB/Game
Mathewson, C. (NY) .... .97
Humphries, B. (Chi) 1.21
Adams, B. (Pit) 1.25

Strikeouts
Alexander, G. (Phi) 241
Tesreau, J. (NY) 176
Hughes, T. (Bos) 171

Ratio
Alexander, G. (Phi) .... .84
Hughes, T. (Bos) .... .95
Tesreau, J. (NY) 1.01

Earned Run Average
Alexander, G. (Phi) 1.22
Toney, F. (Cin) 1.58
Mamaux, A. (Pit) 2.04

Adjusted ERA
Alexander, G. (Phi) 224
Toney, F. (Cin) 181
Mamaux, A. (Pit) 134

Component ERA
Alexander, G. (Phi) 1.33
Hughes, T. (Bos) 1.73
Toney, F. (Cin) 1.80

Opponents' Batting Avg.
Alexander, G. (Phi) .... .191
Toney, F. (Cin) .... .207
Mamaux, A. (Pit) .... .208

Adjusted Pitching Runs
Alexander, G. (Phi) 63
Toney, F. (Cin) 27
Mamaux, A. (Pit) 20

Win Shares – Pitchers
Alexander, G. (Phi) 43
Pfeffer, J. (Bro) 26
2 players tied with 24

TPW – Pitchers
Alexander, G. (Phi) 7.0
Pfeffer, J. (Bro) 2.7
Toney, F. (Cin) 2.5

1915 American League

TEAM	G	W	L	PCT	GB	R	OR	EW	AB	H	2B	3B	HR	TB	BB	SO	SB	CS	AVG	OBP	SLG	OPS	OPS+	BR/A	PF	RC
BOS	155	101	50	.669	....	669	499	97	5024	1308	202	76	14	1704	527	**476**	118	117	.260	.336	.339	.676	111	59	97	611
DET	156	100	54	.649	2.5	**778**	597	97	**5128**	**1372**	**207**	94	23	**1836**	**681**	527	**241**	146	**.268**	**.357**	**.358**	**.715**	**114**	**105**	105	**711**
CHI	155	93	61	.604	9.5	717	509	102	4914	1269	163	**102**	25	1711	583	575	233	183	.258	.345	.348	.694	110	53	103	637
WAS	155	85	68	.556	17	569	**491**	88	5029	1225	152	79	12	1571	458	541	186	106	.244	.312	.312	.625	90	-52	102	535
NY	154	69	83	.454	32.5	584	588	75	4982	1162	167	50	**31**	1522	570	669	198	133	.233	.317	.306	.623	92	-42	100	523
STL	159	63	91	.409	39.5	522	680	57	5112	1255	166	65	19	1608	472	765	202	160	.246	.315	.315	.629	97	-30	96	535
CLE	154	57	95	.375	44.5	539	670	60	5034	1210	169	79	20	1597	490	681	138	117	.240	.312	.317	.630	92	-57	102	526
PHI	154	43	109	.283	58.5	545	889	42	5081	1204	183	72	16	1579	436	634	127	**89**	.237	.304	.311	.615	92	-48	96	507
Total	**621**					**4923**			**40304**	**10005**	**1409**	**617**	**160**		**4217**	**4868**	**1443**	**1051**	**.248**	**.325**	**.326**	**.651**				

Runs
Cobb, T. (Det) 144
Collins, E. (Chi) 118
Vitt, O. (Det) 116

Hits
Cobb, T. (Det) 208
Crawford, S. (Det) 183
Veach, B. (Det) 178

Doubles
Veach, B. (Det) 40
4 players tied with 31

Triples
Crawford, S. (Det) 19
Fournier, J. (Chi) 18
3 players tied with 17

Home Runs
Roth, B. (Cle,Chi) 7
Oldring, R. (Phi) 6
6 players tied with 5

Total Bases
Cobb, T. (Det) 274
Crawford, S. (Det) 264
Veach, B. (Det) 247

Runs Batted In
Crawford, S. (Det) 112
Veach, B. (Det) 112
Cobb, T. (Det) 99

Bases On Balls
Collins, E. (Chi) 119
3 players tied with 118

Stolen Bases
Cobb, T. (Det) 96
Maisel, F. (NY) 51
Collins, E. (Chi) 46

Batting Average
Cobb, T. (Det) .... .369
Collins, E. (Chi) .... .332
Fournier, J. (Chi) .... .322

On-Base Percentage
Cobb, T. (Det) .... .486
Collins, E. (Chi) .... .460
Fournier, J. (Chi) .... .429

Slugging Average
Fournier, J. (Chi) .... .491
Cobb, T. (Det) .... .487
Jackson, J. (Cle,Chi) .... .445

Adjusted OPS
Cobb, T. (Det) 182
Fournier, J. (Chi) 170
Collins, E. (Chi) 163

Adjusted Batting Runs
Cobb, T. (Det) 70.0
Collins, E. (Chi) 47.0
Fournier, J. (Chi) 36.0

Runs Created/Game
Cobb, T. (Det) 10.20
Fournier, J. (Chi) 7.70
Collins, E. (Chi) 7.50

Fielding Runs
Boone, L. (NY) 18.9
Collins, E. (Chi) 18.1
McBride, G. (Was) 15.7

Win Shares – Batters
Cobb, T. (Det) 48
Collins, E. (Chi) 40
Speaker, T. (Bos) 36

TPW – Batters
Collins, E. (Chi) 7.2
Cobb, T. (Det) 6.0
Fournier, J. (Chi) 4.0

TEAM	CG	SH	SV	IP	H	H/G	ER	HR	BB	SO	OAV	RAT	ERA	ERA+	CERA	PR+	PF	FA	E	DP	FR	BW	PW	FW	TPW	DIF
BOS	81	19	15	1397	1164	**7.5**	371	18	446	634	**.231**	1.152	2.39	116	2.50	49.9	95	.964	226	95	9.8	6.3	5.3	1.0	12.6	13.4
DET	86	10	**19**	**1413^{1}**	1259	8.0	449	14	492	550	.243	1.239	2.86	106	2.88	54.2	103	.961	258	107	-27.8	**11.2**	5.8	-3.0	14.0	9.0
CHI	91	16	9	1401	1242	8.0	378	14	**350**	635	.240	**1.136**	2.43	122	**2.46**	**97.3**	101	.965	222	95	-12.4	5.6	**10.3**	-1.3	**14.6**	1.4
WAS	87	**21**	13	1393^{2}	**1161**	**7.5**	**358**	**12**	455	**715**	.232	1.160	**2.31**	128	2.54	88.3	101	.964	230	101	13.7	-5.5	9.4	1.5	5.4	3.6
NY	**101**	12	1	1382^{2}	1272	8.3	470	41	517	559	.254	1.294	3.06	96	3.30	-38.3	100	**.966**	**217**	118	**18.3**	-4.4	-4.1	**1.9**	-6.5	-.5
STL	76	6	6	1403	1256	8.1	474	21	612	566	.249	1.331	3.04	94	3.34	-45.7	98	.949	336	**144**	17.7	-3.2	-4.9	1.9	-6.2	-7.8
CLE	62	11	10	1372	1287	8.4	477	18	518	610	.256	1.316	3.13	97	3.23	-5.1	104	.957	280	82	-8.1	-6.1	-.5	-.9	-7.5	-11.5
PHI	78	6	2	1348^{1}	1358	9.1	643	22	827	588	.277	1.621	4.29	**68**	4.67	-194.1	100	.947	338	118	-11.4	-5.1	-20.6	-1.2	-26.9	-6.1
Total	**662**	**101**	**75**	**11111**		**8.1**	**3620**					**1.279**	**2.93**													

Wins
Johnson, W. (Was) 27
3 players tied with 24

Win Percentage
Wood, J. (Bos) .... .750
Foster, R. (Bos) .... .704
Shore, E. (Bos) .... .704

Games
Coveleski, H. (Det) 50
Faber, R. (Chi) 50
2 players tied with 48

Complete Games
Johnson, W. (Was) 35
Caldwell, R. (NY) 31
Dauss, H. (Det) 27

Shutouts
Johnson, W. (Was) 7
Scott, J. (Chi) 7
Morton, G. (Cle) 6

Saves
Mays, C. (Bos) 7
6 players tied with 4

Innings Pitched
Johnson, W. (Was) .... 336^{2}
Coveleski, H. (Det) .... 312^{2}
Dauss, H. (Det) .... 309^{2}

Fewest Hits/Game
Leonard, D. (Bos) 6.38
Ruth, B. (Bos) 6.86
Wood, J. (Bos) 6.86

Fewest BB/Game
Johnson, W. (Was) 1.50
Ayers, D. (Was) 1.62
Benz, J. (Chi) 1.62

Strikeouts
Johnson, W. (Was) 203
Faber, R. (Chi) 182
Wyckoff, W. (Phi) 157

Ratio
Johnson, W. (Was) .... .93
Ayers, D. (Was) 1.02
Morton, G. (Cle) 1.04

Earned Run Average
Wood, J. (Bos) 1.49
Johnson, W. (Was) 1.55
Shore, E. (Bos) 1.64

Adjusted ERA
Johnson, W. (Was) 191
Wood, J. (Bos) 187
Shore, E. (Bos) 169

Component ERA
Johnson, W. (Was) 1.67
Wood, J. (Bos) 1.92
Morton, G. (Cle) 2.00

Opponents' Batting Avg.
Leonard, D. (Bos) .... .208
Ruth, B. (Bos) .... .212
Johnson, W. (Was) .... .214

Adjusted Pitching Runs
Johnson, W. (Was) 50
Scott, J. (Chi) 34
Shore, E. (Bos) 29

Win Shares – Pitchers
Johnson, W. (Was) 42
Dauss, H. (Det) 25
Foster, R. (Bos) 25

TPW – Pitchers
Johnson, W. (Was) 5.9
Scott, J. (Chi) 3.1
Shore, E. (Bos) 2.8

1915 Federal League

TEAM	G	W	L	PCT	GB	R	OR	EW	AB	H	2B	3B	HR	TB	BB	SO	SB	CS	AVG	OBP	SLG	OPS	OPS+	BR/A	PF	RC
CHI	155	86	66	.566	....	640	538	89	5133	1320	185	77	**50**	1809	444	590	161	....	.257	.320	.352	.672	110	56	94	614
STL	159	87	67	.565	....	634	527	91	**5145**	1344	199	**81**	23	1774	**576**	**502**	195	....	.261	**.340**	.345	.685	102	28	105	662
PIT	156	86	67	.562	0.5	592	**524**	86	5040	1318	180	80	20	1718	448	561	224	....	.262	.326	.341	.667	98	-9	104	619
KC	153	81	72	.529	5.5	547	551	76	4937	1206	200	66	28	1622	368	503	144	....	.244	.303	.329	.631	94	-41	97	525
NEW	155	80	72	.526	6	585	562	79	5097	1283	**210**	80	17	1704	438	550	184	....	.252	.315	.334	.649	103	13	94	582
BUF	153	74	78	.487	12	574	634	68	5065	1261	193	68	40	1710	420	587	184	....	.249	.309	.338	.646	96	-32	100	560
BRO	153	70	82	.461	16	**647**	673	73	5035	**1348**	205	75	36	**1811**	473	654	**249**	....	**.268**	.336	**.360**	**.696**	**113**	**83**	98	**667**
BAL	154	47	107	.305	40	550	760	53	5060	1235	196	53	36	1645	470	641	128	....	.244	.313	.325	.638	87	-77	107	544
Total	**619**					**4769**			**40512**	**10315**	**1568**	**580**	**250**		**3637**	**4588**	**1469**		**.255**	**.320**	**.340**	**.661**				

Runs
Borton, B. (StL) 97
Berghammer, M. (Pit) 96
Evans, S. (Bal,Bro) 94

Hits
Tobin, J. (StL) 184
Konetchy, E. (Pit) 181
Evans, S. (Bal,Bro) 171

Doubles
Evans, S. (Bal,Bro) 34
Zwilling, D. (Chi) 32
2 players tied with 31

Triples
Mann, L. (Chi) 19
Konetchy, E. (Pit) 18
Kelly, J. (Pit) 17

Home Runs
Chase, H. (Buf) 17
Zwilling, D. (Chi) 13
Kauff, B. (Bro) 12

Total Bases
Konetchy, E. (Pit) 278
Chase, H. (Buf) 267
Tobin, J. (StL) 254

Runs Batted In
Zwilling, D. (Chi) 94
Konetchy, E. (Pit) 93
Chase, H. (Buf) 89

Bases On Balls
Borton, B. (StL) 92
Kauff, B. (Bro) 85
Berghammer, M. (Pit) 83

Stolen Bases
Kauff, B. (Bro) 55
Mowrey, M. (Pit) 40
Kelly, J. (Pit) 38

Batting Average
Kauff, B. (Bro) .... .342
Magee, L. (Bro) .... .323
Konetchy, E. (Pit) .... .314

On-Base Percentage
Kauff, B. (Bro) .... .446
Miller, W. (StL) .... .400
Borton, B. (StL) .... .395

Slugging Average
Kauff, B. (Bro) .... .509
Konetchy, E. (Pit) .... .483
Chase, H. (Buf) .... .471

Adjusted OPS
Kauff, B. (Bro) 185
Zwilling, D. (Chi) 146
Konetchy, E. (Pit) 142

Adjusted Batting Runs
Kauff, B. (Bro) 56.0
Zwilling, D. (Chi) 31.0
Evans, S. (Bro,Bal) 28.0

Runs Created/Game
Kauff, B. (Bro) 10.10
Konetchy, E. (Pit) 6.70
Evans, S. (Bro,Bal) 6.30

Fielding Runs
Doolan, M. (Bal,Chi) 25.4
Johnson, E. (StL) 21.2
Kores, A. (StL) 19.8

Win Shares – Batters
Kauff, B. (Bro) 34
Zwilling, D. (Chi) 30
Konetchy, E. (Pit) 27

TPW – Batters
Kauff, B. (Bro) 6.3
Rariden, B. (New) 4.6
Cooper, C. (Bro) 3.8

TEAM	CG	SH	SV	IP	H	H/G	ER	HR	BB	SO	OAV	RAT	ERA	ERA+	CERA	PR+	PF	FA	E	DP	FR	BW	PW	FW	TPW	DIF
CHI	94	24	9	1426	1267	8.0	410	22	396	**698**	**.240**	**1.166**	2.59	106	**2.57**	24.5	92	.964	212	111	-1.7	6.0	2.6	-.2	8.5	1.5
STL	88	16	12	1382^{1}	1273	8.3	433	37	441	517	.243	1.240	2.82	114	2.63	36.6	103	.967	**182**	98	**22.7**	3.0	3.9	**2.4**	**9.4**	.6
PIT	95	16	11	1359	**1210**	8.0	428	29	**390**	526	.253	1.177	2.83	111	3.04	**49.9**	102	**.971**	246	96	-2.1	-.9	**5.4**	-.2	4.2	5.8
KC	100	16	7	1406^{2}	1308	8.4	426	**15**	453	581	.242	1.252	2.73	104	2.68	22.3	97	.962	239	124	-6.0	-4.5	2.4	-.6	-2.7	7.7
NEW	79	14	11	1360	1271	8.4	**406**	35	553	594	.253	1.341	2.69	109	2.90	32.4	94	.963	232	112	4.5	1.4	3.5	.5	5.4	-1.4
BUF	78	10	16	1355^{2}	1299	8.6	511	27	536	467	.254	1.354	3.39	91	3.35	-45.3	101	.964	290	103	-2.9	-3.4	-4.9	-.3	-8.6	6.6
BRO	85	5	7	1360^{1}	1455	9.6	507	52	466	570	.258	1.412	3.35	88	3.36	-67.6	98	.955	273	140	8.7	**8.9**	-7.3	.9	2.6	-8.6
BAL	**716**	**122**	**83**	**11047^{2}**	....	**0.0**	598	....	....	....	.284	....	**0.49**	**85**	4.00	-64.2	111	.957	1907	**886**	-23.4	-8.3	-6.9	-2.5	-17.7	-12.3
Total	**1335**	**223**	**156**	**20697^{2}**		**4.0**	**3719**					**.595**	**1.62**													

Wins
McConnell, G. (Chi) 25
Allen, F. (Pit) 23
2 players tied with 22

Win Percentage
McConnell, G. (Chi) .... .714
Brown, M. (Chi) .... .680
Reulbach, E. (New) .... .677

Games
Davenport, D. (StL) 55
Bedient, H. (Buf) 53
Crandall, D. (StL) 51

Complete Games
Davenport, D. (StL) 30
Hendrix, C. (Chi) 26
Schulz, A. (Buf) 25

Shutouts
Davenport, D. (StL) 10
Allen, F. (Pit) 6
Plank, E. (StL) 6

Saves
Bedient, H. (Buf) 10
Barger, C. (Pit) 6
Wiltse, H. (Bro) 5

Innings Pitched
Davenport, D. (StL) .... 392^{2}
Crandall, D. (StL) .... 312^{2}
Schulz, A. (Buf) .... 309^{2}

Fewest Hits/Game
Davenport, D. (StL) 6.88
Main, A. (KC) 7.08
Plank, E. (StL) 7.11

Fewest BB/Game
Plank, E. (StL) 1.81
Bender, C. (Bal) 1.87
Hearn, B. (Pit) 1.90

Strikeouts
Davenport, D. (StL) 229
Schulz, A. (Buf) 160
McConnell, G. (Chi) 151

Ratio
Plank, E. (StL) .... .99
Davenport, D. (StL) 1.01
Brown, M. (Chi) 1.07

Earned Run Average
Moseley, E. (New) 1.91
Plank, E. (StL) 2.08
Brown, M. (Chi) 2.09

Adjusted ERA
Plank, E. (StL) 149
Moseley, E. (New) 148
Davenport, D. (StL) 141

Component ERA
Plank, E. (StL) 1.74
Davenport, D. (StL) 1.82
Brown, M. (Chi) 2.04

Opponents' Batting Avg.
Davenport, D. (StL) .... .215
Plank, E. (StL) .... .218
Brown, M. (Chi) .... .220

Adjusted Pitching Runs
Davenport, D. (StL) 33
Moseley, E. (New) 27
Plank, E. (StL) 26

Win Shares – Pitchers
Davenport, D. (StL) 34
Crandall, D. (StL) 29
Plank, E. (StL) 29

TPW – Pitchers
Plank, E. (StL) 3.4
Crandall, D. (StL) 3.0
McConnell, G. (Chi) 2.8

1916 National League

TEAM	G	W	L	PCT	GB	R	OR	EW	AB	H	2B	3B	HR	TB	BB	SO	SB	CS	AVG	OBP	SLG	OPS	OPS+	BR/A	PF	RC
BRO	156	94	60	.610	....	585	471	93	5234	**1366**	195	80	28	**1805**	355	**550**	187	....	**.261**	**.313**	**.345**	**.658**	105	17	103	**645**
PHI	154	91	62	.595	2.5	581	489	90	4985	1244	**223**	53	42	1699	399	571	149	....	.250	.310	.341	.650	102	2	104	593
BOS	158	89	63	.586	4	542	**453**	89	5075	1181	166	73	22	1559	**437**	646	141	....	.233	.299	.307	.607	98	-22	94	535
NY	155	86	66	.566	7	**597**	504	89	5152	1305	188	74	42	1767	356	558	**206**	....	.253	.307	.343	.650	**112**	**48**	95	617
CHI	156	67	86	.438	26.5	520	541	73	5179	1237	194	56	**46**	1681	399	662	133	....	.239	.298	.325	.622	88	-81	111	559
PIT	157	65	89	.422	29	484	586	62	5181	1246	147	**91**	20	1635	372	618	173	....	.240	.298	.316	.613	93	-51	101	556
STL	153	60	93	.392	33.5	476	629	56	5030	1223	155	74	25	1601	335	651	182	....	.243	.295	.318	.613	95	-47	99	535
CIN	155	60	93	.392	33.5	505	617	61	**5254**	1336	187	88	14	1741	362	573	157	....	.254	.307	.331	.639	105	11	98	596
Total	**622**					**4290**			**41090**	**10138**	**1455**	**589**	**239**		**3015**	**4829**	**1328**		**.247**	**.303**	**.328**	**.632**				

Runs
Burns, G. (NY) 105
Carey, M. (Pit) 90
Robertson, D. (NY) 88

Hits
Chase, H. (Cin) 184
Robertson, D. (NY) 180
Wheat, Z. (Bro) 177

Doubles
Niehoff, B. (Phi) 42
Wheat, Z. (Bro) 32
Paskert, D. (Phi) 30

Triples
Hinchman, B. (Pit) 16
3 players tied with 15

Home Runs
Robertson, D. (NY) 12
Williams, C. (Chi) 12
Cravath, G. (Phi) 11

Total Bases
Wheat, Z. (Bro) 262
Robertson, D. (NY) 250
Chase, H. (Cin) 249

Runs Batted In
Zimmerman, H. (Chi,NY) 83
Chase, H. (Cin) 82
Hinchman, B. (Pit) 76

Bases On Balls
Groh, H. (Cin) 84
Saier, V. (Chi) 79
Bancroft, D. (Phi) 74

Stolen Bases
Carey, M. (Pit) 63
Kauff, B. (NY) 40
Bescher, B. (StL) 39

Batting Average
Chase, H. (Cin) .... .339
Daubert, J. (Bro) .... .316
Hinchman, B. (Pit) .... .315

On-Base Percentage
Cravath, G. (Phi) .... .379
Hinchman, B. (Pit) .... .378
Williams, C. (Chi) .... .372

Slugging Average
Wheat, Z. (Bro) .... .461
Chase, H. (Cin) .... .459
Williams, C. (Chi) .... .459

Adjusted OPS
Chase, H. (Cin) 155
Hornsby, R. (StL) 150
Wheat, Z. (Bro) 149

Adjusted Batting Runs
Wheat, Z. (Bro) 32.0
Chase, H. (Cin) 32.0
Hinchman, B. (Pit) 31.0

Runs Created/Game
Wheat, Z. (Bro) 6.70
Hornsby, R. (StL) 6.50
Chase, H. (Cin) 6.40

Fielding Runs
Cutshaw, G. (Bro) 26.9
Maranville, R. (Bos) 23.9
Bancroft, D. (Phi) 23.1

Win Shares – Batters
Wheat, Z. (Bro) 32
Hornsby, R. (StL) 28
3 players tied with 27

TPW – Batters
Groh, H. (Cin) 5.1
Fletcher, A. (NY) 4.3
Doyle, L. (NY,Chi) 3.9

TEAM	CG	SH	SV	IP	H	H/G	ER	HR	BB	SO	OAV	RAT	ERA	ERA+	CERA	PR+	PF	FA	E	DP	FR	BW	PW	FW	TPW	DIF
BRO	96	22	9	**1427^{1}**	**1201**	**7.6**	**336**	**24**	372	634	**.232**	1.102	**2.12**	126	2.28	**63.0**	102	.965	224	90	**25.0**	2.0	**7.2**	**2.9**	**12.0**	5.0
PHI	**97**	**25**	9	1382^{1}	1238	8.1	362	28	**295**	601	.244	1.109	2.36	112	2.45	45.5	101	.963	234	119	-1.1	.2	5.2	-.1	5.3	9.7
BOS	**97**	23	11	1415^{2}	1206	7.7	344	**24**	325	**644**	.235	**1.081**	2.19	112	**2.24**	41.5	94	**.967**	**212**	124	-1.4	-2.6	4.8	-.2	2.0	11.0
NY	88	22	12	1397^{1}	1267	8.2	404	41	310	638	.245	1.129	2.60	93	2.57	-48.1	93	.966	217	108	20.9	**5.4**	-5.5	2.4	2.3	7.7
CHI	72	17	13	1416^{2}	1265	8.0	417	32	365	616	.243	1.151	2.65	109	2.54	59.4	111	.957	286	104	-19.9	-9.3	6.8	-2.3	-4.7	-4.3
PIT	88	11	7	1419^{2}	1277	8.1	435	**24**	443	596	.247	1.212	2.76	97	2.74	17.4	102	.959	260	97	-31.1	-5.8	2.0	-3.6	-7.4	-4.6
STL	58	13	**15**	1355	1331	8.8	473	31	445	529	.265	1.311	3.14	84	3.27	-72.5	101	.957	278	124	-3.3	-5.4	-8.3	-.4	-14.0	-2.0
CIN	86	7	6	1408	1356	8.7	485	35	461	569	.260	1.290	3.10	**84**	3.20	-92.9	99	.965	228	**126**	12.8	1.3	-10.6	1.5	-7.9	-8.1
Total	**682**	**140**	**82**	**11222**		**8.1**	**3256**					**1.172**	**2.61**													

Wins
Alexander, G. (Phi) 33
Pfeffer, J. (Bro) 25
Rixey, E. (Phi) 22

Win Percentage
Hughes, T. (Bos) .842
Alexander, G. (Phi) .733
Pfeffer, J. (Bro) .694

Games
Meadows, L. (StL) 51
Alexander, G. (Phi) 48
2 players tied with 45

Complete Games
Alexander, G. (Phi) 38
Pfeffer, J. (Bro) 30
Rudolph, D. (Bos) 27

Shutouts
Alexander, G. (Phi) 16
Pfeffer, J. (Bro) 6
Tyler, L. (Bos) 6

Saves
Ames, R. (StL) 8
3 players tied with 5

Innings Pitched
Alexander, G. (Phi) 389
Pfeffer, J. (Bro) 328^{2}
Rudolph, D. (Bos) 312

Fewest Hits/Game
Cheney, L. (Bro) 6.33
Hughes, T. (Bos) 6.76
Cooper, W. (Pit) 6.91

Fewest BB/Game
Rudolph, D. (Bos) 1.10
Alexander, G. (Phi) 1.16
Demaree, A. (Phi) 1.52

Strikeouts
Alexander, G. (Phi) 167
Cheney, L. (Bro) 166
Mamaux, A. (Pit) 163

Ratio
Alexander, G. (Phi) .96
Rudolph, D. (Bos) .97
McConnell, G. (Chi) 1.00

Earned Run Average
Alexander, G. (Phi) 1.55
Marquard, R. (Bro) 1.58
Rixey, E. (Phi) 1.85

Adjusted ERA
Alexander, G. (Phi) 171
Marquard, R. (Bro) 169
Cooper, W. (Pit) 143

Component ERA
Alexander, G. (Phi) 1.83
Marquard, R. (Bro) 1.87
Rudolph, D. (Bos) 1.89

Opponents' Batting Avg.
Cheney, L. (Bro) .198
Cooper, W. (Pit) .215
Hughes, T. (Bos) .215

Adjusted Pitching Runs
Alexander, G. (Phi) 48
Cooper, W. (Pit) 28
Vaughn, H. (Chi) 27

Win Shares – Pitchers
Alexander, G. (Phi) 44
Pfeffer, J. (Bro) 32
2 players tied with 24

TPW – Pitchers
Alexander, G. (Phi) 6.3
Pfeffer, J. (Bro) 3.2
Cooper, W. (Pit) 3.2

1916 American League

TEAM	G	W	L	PCT	GB	R	OR	EW	AB	H	2B	3B	HR	TB	BB	SO	SB	CS	AVG	OBP	SLG	OPS	OPS+	BR/A	PF	RC
BOS	156	91	63	.591	....	550	**480**	87	5018	1246	197	56	14	1597	464	**482**	129	....	.248	.317	.318	.635	96	-38	100	579
CHI	155	89	65	.578	2	601	497	91	5081	1277	194	**100**	17	1722	447	591	197	....	.251	.319	.339	.658	103	-4	101	638
DET	155	87	67	.565	4	**670**	595	86	5193	**1371**	202	96	17	**1816**	545	529	190	....	**.264**	**.337**	**.350**	**.687**	**109**	**43**	104	**700**
NY	156	80	74	.519	11	577	561	79	**5198**	1277	194	59	**35**	1694	516	632	179	....	.246	.318	.326	.644	98	-31	102	613
STL	158	79	75	.513	12	588	545	83	5155	1262	181	50	14	1585	**626**	638	**234**	....	.245	.331	.307	.639	103	18	95	620
CLE	157	77	77	.500	14	630	602	80	5064	1264	**233**	66	16	1677	522	605	160	....	.250	.324	.331	.655	97	-29	106	625
WAS	159	76	77	.497	14.5	536	543	76	5114	1238	170	60	12	1564	535	597	185	....	.242	.320	.306	.626	95	-39	99	579
PHI	154	36	117	.235	54.5	447	776	38	5010	1212	169	65	19	1568	406	631	151	....	.242	.303	.313	.616	95	-53	95	538
Total	**625**					**4599**			**40833**	**10147**	**1540**	**552**	**144**		**4061**	**4705**	**1425**		**.248**	**.321**	**.324**	**.645**				

Runs
Cobb, T. (Det) 113
Graney, J. (Cle) 106
Speaker, T. (Cle) 102

Hits
Speaker, T. (Cle) 211
Jackson, J. (Chi) 202
Cobb, T. (Det) 201

Doubles
Graney, J. (Cle) 41
Speaker, T. (Cle) 41
Jackson, J. (Chi) 40

Triples
Jackson, J. (Chi) 21
Collins, E. (Chi) 17
2 players tied with 15

Home Runs
Pipp, W. (NY) 12
Baker, F. (NY) 10
2 players tied with 7

Total Bases
Jackson, J. (Chi) 293
Speaker, T. (Cle) 274
Cobb, T. (Det) 267

Runs Batted In
Pratt, D. (StL) 103
Pipp, W. (NY) 93
Veach, B. (Det) 91

Bases On Balls
Shotton, B. (StL) 110
Graney, J. (Cle) 102
Collins, E. (Chi) 86

Stolen Bases
Cobb, T. (Det) 68
Marsans, A. (StL) 46
Shotton, B. (StL) 41

Batting Average
Speaker, T. (Cle) .386
Cobb, T. (Det) .371
Jackson, J. (Chi) .341

On-Base Percentage
Speaker, T. (Cle) .470
Cobb, T. (Det) .452
Collins, E. (Chi) .405

Slugging Average
Speaker, T. (Cle) .502
Jackson, J. (Chi) .495
Cobb, T. (Det) .493

Adjusted OPS
Speaker, T. (Cle) 181
Cobb, T. (Det) 177
Jackson, J. (Chi) 165

Adjusted Batting Runs
Cobb, T. (Det) 58.0
Speaker, T. (Cle) 54.0
Jackson, J. (Chi) 43.0

Runs Created/Game
Cobb, T. (Det) 9.30
Speaker, T. (Cle) 9.10
Jackson, J. (Chi) 7.30

Fielding Runs
Vitt, O. (Det) 30.2
Pratt, D. (StL) 27.5
Lavan, D. (StL) 24.0

Win Shares – Batters
Speaker, T. (Cle) 41
Cobb, T. (Det) 40
Jackson, J. (Chi) 34

TPW – Batters
Speaker, T. (Cle) 6.0
Cobb, T. (Det) 4.8
Pratt, D. (StL) 4.7

TEAM	CG	SH	SV	IP	H	H/G	ER	HR	BB	SO	OAV	RAT	ERA	ERA+	CERA	PR+	PF	FA	E	DP	FR	BW	PW	FW	TPW	DIF
BOS	76	**24**	16	14102	1221	0.8	389	**10**	463	584	.239	.119	0.25	111	2.64	**63.3**	98	**.972**	**183**	108	-18.1	-4.2	**7.0**	-2.0	.9	13.1
CHI	73	20	15	14121	**1189**	**0.8**	**370**	14	**405**	644	**.236**	**.113**	**0.24**	117	**2.41**	44.3	98	.968	205	**134**	17.1	-.5	4.9	1.9	**6.3**	5.7
DET	81	8	13	1410	1254	8.0	465	12	578	531	.248	1.299	2.97	96	3.14	10.4	101	.968	211	110	-27.1	**4.7**	1.1	-3.0	2.9	7.1
NY	84	12	**17**	1428	1249	7.9	440	37	476	616	.244	1.208	2.77	104	2.90	2.3	102	.967	219	119	15.9	-3.4	.3	1.8	-1.4	4.4
STL	74	9	13	**14432**	1292	0.8	414	15	478	505	.248	.123	0.26	106	2.85	-8.2	97	.963	248	120	**34.3**	2.0	-.9	**3.8**	4.9	-2.9
CLE	65	9	16	1410	1383	8.8	454	16	467	537	.264	1.312	2.90	103	3.27	12.1	106	.965	232	130	2.7	-3.2	1.3	.3	-1.5	1.5
WAS	85	11	7	14302	1271	0.8	424	14	490	**706**	.244	.123	0.27	104	2.82	11.1	99	.964	232	119	7.9	-4.3	1.2	.9	-2.2	2.2
PHI	**94**	11	3	13432	1311	0.9	585	26	715	575	.267	.151	0.39	**73**	4.10	-129.8	101	.951	314	126	-29.5	-5.9	-14.4	-3.3	-23.5	-16.5
Total	**632**	**104**	**100**	**74637**		**1.2**	**3541**					**.191**	**0.43**													

Wins
Johnson, W. (Was) 25
Shawkey, B. (NY) 24
Ruth, B. (Bos) 23

Win Percentage
Cullop, N. (NY) .684
Cicotte, E. (Chi) .682
Foster, R. (Bos) .667

Games
Davenport, D. (StL) 59
Russell, R. (Chi) 56
Shawkey, B. (NY) 53

Complete Games
Johnson, W. (Was) 36
Myers, E. (Phi) 31
Bush, J. (Phi) 25

Shutouts
Ruth, B. (Bos) 9
Bush, J. (Phi) 8
Leonard, D. (Bos) 6

Saves
Shawkey, B. (NY) 8
Leonard, D. (Bos) 6
Russell, A. (NY) 6

Innings Pitched
Johnson, W. (Was) 369^{2}
Coveleski, H. (Det) 324^{1}
Ruth, B. (Bos) 323^{2}

Fewest Hits/Game
Ruth, B. (Bos) 6.40
Shawkey, B. (NY) 6.64
Cicotte, E. (Chi) 6.64

Fewest BB/Game
Russell, R. (Chi) 1.43
Cullop, N. (NY) 1.72
Coveleski, H. (Det) 1.75

Strikeouts
Johnson, W. (Was) 228
Myers, E. (Phi) 182
Ruth, B. (Bos) 170

Ratio
Russell, R. (Chi) .94
Johnson, W. (Was) 1.01
Shawkey, B. (NY) 1.03

Earned Run Average
Ruth, B. (Bos) 1.75
Cicotte, E. (Chi) 1.78
Johnson, W. (Was) 1.90

Adjusted ERA
Ruth, B. (Bos) 158
Cicotte, E. (Chi) 155
Johnson, W. (Was) 147

Component ERA
Russell, R. (Chi) 1.65
Johnson, W. (Was) 1.79
Ruth, B. (Bos) 1.85

Opponents' Batting Avg.
Ruth, B. (Bos) .201
Shawkey, B. (NY) .209
Cicotte, E. (Chi) .218

Adjusted Pitching Runs
Ruth, B. (Bos) 41
Coveleski, H. (Det) 38
Johnson, W. (Was) 34

Win Shares – Pitchers
Ruth, B. (Bos) 37
Johnson, W. (Was) 36
2 players tied with 27

TPW – Pitchers
Ruth, B. (Bos) 6.0
Johnson, W. (Was) 4.7
Coveleski, H. (Det) 4.4

1917 National League

TEAM	G	W	L	PCT	GB	R	OR	EW	AB	H	2B	3B	HR	TB	BB	SO	SB	CS	AVG	OBP	SLG	OPS	OPS+	BR/A	PF	RC
NY	158	98	56	.636	....	**635**	**457**	101	5211	1360	170	71	**39**	1789	373	533	**162**	....	.261	**.317**	.343	.660	112	71	97	**597**
PHI	154	87	65	.572	10	578	500	87	5084	1262	**225**	60	38	1721	**435**	533	109	....	.248	.310	.339	.648	101	7	104	556
STL	154	82	70	.539	15	531	567	71	5083	1271	159	93	26	1694	359	652	159	....	.250	.303	.333	.636	104	18	97	542
CIN	157	78	76	.506	20	601	611	76	**5251**	**1385**	196	**100**	26	**1859**	312	**477**	153	....	**.264**	.309	**.354**	**.663**	**114**	**73**	96	596
CHI	157	74	80	.481	24	552	567	75	5135	1229	194	67	17	1608	415	599	127	....	.239	.299	.313	.612	87	-72	108	511
BOS	157	72	81	.471	25.5	536	552	74	5201	1280	169	75	22	1665	427	587	155	....	.246	.309	.320	.629	105	33	94	549
BRO	156	70	81	.464	26.5	511	559	69	**5251**	1299	159	78	25	1689	334	527	130	....	.247	.296	.322	.618	93	-47	103	522
PIT	157	51	103	.331	47	464	595	58	5169	1230	160	61	9	1539	399	580	150	....	.238	.298	.298	.596	86	-77	103	493
Total	**625**					**4408**			**41385**	**10316**	**1432**	**605**	**202**		**3054**	**4488**	**1145**		**.249**	**.305**	**.328**	**.633**				

Runs
Burns, G. (NY) 103
Groh, H. (Cin) 91
Kauff, B. (NY) 89

Hits
Groh, H. (Cin) 182
Burns, G. (NY) 180
Roush, E. (Cin) 178

Doubles
Groh, H. (Cin) 39
Merkle, F. (Chi,Bro) 31
Smith, R. (Bos) 31

Triples
Hornsby, R. (StL) 17
Cravath, G. (Phi) 16
Chase, H. (Cin) 15

Home Runs
Cravath, G. (Phi) 12
Robertson, D. (NY) 12
Hornsby, R. (StL) 8

Total Bases
Hornsby, R. (StL) 253
Burns, G. (NY) 246
Groh, H. (Cin) 246

Runs Batted In
Zimmerman, H. (NY) 102
Chase, H. (Cin) 86
Cravath, G. (Phi) 83

Bases On Balls
Burns, G. (NY) 75
Groh, H. (Cin) 71
Cravath, G. (Phi) 70

Stolen Bases
Carey, M. (Pit) 46
Burns, G. (NY) 40
Kauff, B. (NY) 30

Batting Average
Roush, E. (Cin) .341
Hornsby, R. (StL) .327
Kauff, B. (NY) .308

On-Base Percentage
Groh, H. (Cin) .385
Hornsby, R. (StL) .385
Burns, G. (NY) .380

Slugging Average
Hornsby, R. (StL) .484
Cravath, G. (Phi) .473
Roush, E. (Cin) .454

Adjusted OPS
Hornsby, R. (StL) 170
Roush, E. (Cin) 162
Cravath, G. (Phi) 151

Adjusted Batting Runs
Hornsby, R. (StL) 42.0
Groh, H. (Cin) 38.0
Burns, G. (NY) 36.0

Runs Created/Game
Hornsby, R. (StL) 7.10
Roush, E. (Cin) 6.80
Burns, G. (NY) 6.30

Fielding Runs
Fletcher, A. (NY) 36.0
Bancroft, D. (Phi) 20.3
Zimmerman, H. (NY) 19.8

Win Shares – Batters
Hornsby, R. (StL) 38
Groh, H. (Cin) 37
Burns, G. (NY) 34

TPW – Batters
Hornsby, R. (StL) 6.0
Groh, H. (Cin) 5.8
Fletcher, A. (NY) 5.5

TEAM	CG	SH	SV	IP	H	H/G	ER	HR	BB	SO	OAV	RAT	ERA	ERA+	CERA	PR+	PF	FA	E	DP	FR	BW	PW	FW	TPW	DIF
NY	92	18	**14**	**1426^{2}**	**1221**	**7.7**	**360**	29	327	551	**.234**	**1.085**	**2.27**	112	**2.24**	27.1	94	**.968**	**208**	122	**16.6**	8.0	3.1	**1.9**	**12.9**	8.1
PHI	102	**22**	5	1389	1258	8.2	380	25	**325**	616	.246	1.140	2.46	114	2.53	46.4	104	.967	212	112	7.1	.8	5.3	.8	6.9	4.1
STL	66	16	10	1392^{2}	1257	8.1	469	29	421	502	.249	1.205	3.03	**89**	2.76	-69.9	99	.967	221	**153**	16.4	2.0	-7.9	1.9	-4.1	10.1
CIN	94	12	6	1397^{1}	1358	8.8	419	20	402	488	.259	1.260	2.70	97	2.96	-9.7	96	.962	247	120	-4.1	**8.3**	-1.1	-.5	6.7	-5.7
CHI	79	16	9	1404	1303	8.4	409	34	374	**654**	.253	1.194	2.62	110	2.76	**65.2**	107	.959	267	121	-22.6	-8.1	**7.4**	-2.6	-3.3	.3
BOS	**103**	21	3	1424^{2}	1309	8.3	438	19	371	593	.251	1.179	2.77	92	2.63	-18.7	94	.966	224	122	-16.1	3.8	-2.1	-1.8	-.2	-3.8
BRO	99	8	9	1421^{1}	1288	8.2	439	32	405	582	.247	1.191	2.78	100	2.71	-13.7	103	.962	245	102	15.2	-5.3	-1.5	1.7	-5.2	.2
PIT	84	17	6	1417^{2}	1318	8.4	474	**14**	432	509	.253	1.234	3.01	94	2.78	-15.9	105	.961	251	119	-11.8	-8.7	-1.8	-1.3	-11.9	-14.1
Total	**719**	**130**	**62**	**11273^{1}**		**8.2**	**3388**					**1.186**	**2.70**													

Wins
Alexander, G. (Phi) 30
Toney, F. (Cin) 24
Vaughn, H. (Chi) 23

Win Percentage
Schupp, F. (NY) .750
Sallee, S. (NY) .720
Perritt, P. (NY) .708

Games
Douglas, P. (Chi) 51
Barnes, J. (Bos) 50
Schneider, P. (Cin) 46

Complete Games
Alexander, G. (Phi) 34
Toney, F. (Cin) 31
Vaughn, H. (Chi) 27

Shutouts
Alexander, G. (Phi) 8
Cooper, W. (Pit) 7
Toney, F. (Cin) 7

Saves
Sallee, S. (NY) 4
5 players tied with 3

Innings Pitched
Alexander, G. (Phi) 388
Toney, F. (Cin) 339^{2}
Schneider, P. (Cin) 333^{2}

Fewest Hits/Game
Schupp, F. (NY) 6.68
Anderson, F. (NY) 6.78
Nehf, A. (Bos) 7.60

Fewest BB/Game
Alexander, G. (Phi) 1.30
Sallee, S. (NY) 1.42
Packard, G. (Chi,StL) 1.45

Strikeouts
Alexander, G. (Phi) 200
Vaughn, H. (Chi) 195
Douglas, P. (Chi) 151

Ratio
Anderson, F. (NY) .96
Schupp, F. (NY) 1.00
Alexander, G. (Phi) 1.01

Earned Run Average
Anderson, F. (NY) 1.44
Alexander, G. (Phi) 1.83
Perritt, P. (NY) 1.88

Adjusted ERA
Anderson, F. (NY) 176
Alexander, G. (Phi) 153
Vaughn, H. (Chi) 144

Component ERA
Anderson, F. (NY) 1.62
Schupp, F. (NY) 1.82
Alexander, G. (Phi) 1.94

Opponents' Batting Avg.
Anderson, F. (NY) .209
Schupp, F. (NY) .209
Nehf, A. (Bos) .231

Adjusted Pitching Runs
Alexander, G. (Phi) 40
Vaughn, H. (Chi) 34
Schneider, P. (Cin) 20

Win Shares – Pitchers
Alexander, G. (Phi) 40
Vaughn, H. (Chi) 24
Schupp, F. (NY) 23

TPW – Pitchers
Alexander, G. (Phi) 5.0
Vaughn, H. (Chi) 3.8
Cooper, W. (Pit) 2.3

1917 American League

TEAM	G	W	L	PCT	GB	R	OR	EW	AB	H	2B	3B	HR	TB	BB	SO	SB	CS	AVG	OBP	SLG	OPS	OPS+	BR/A	PF	RC
CHI	156	100	54	.649	....	**655**	463	103	5057	1281	152	**81**	18	1649	522	479	**219**	....	.253	**.329**	.326	.655	103	25	102	607
BOS	157	90	62	.592	9	555	**455**	91	5048	1243	198	64	14	1611	466	**473**	105	....	.246	.314	.319	.633	100	-4	99	550
CLE	156	88	66	.571	12	584	543	83	4994	1224	**218**	64	13	1609	**549**	596	210	....	.245	.324	.322	.646	96	-18	107	587
DET	154	78	75	.510	21.5	639	577	84	5093	**1317**	204	77	25	**1750**	483	476	163	....	**.259**	.328	**.344**	**.672**	**111**	**64**	100	**615**
WAS	157	74	79	.484	25.5	544	566	73	**5142**	1238	173	70	4	1563	500	574	166	....	.241	.313	.304	.617	95	-28	99	531
NY	155	71	82	.464	28.5	524	558	72	5136	1226	172	52	**27**	1583	496	535	136	....	.239	.310	.308	.619	93	-39	101	526
STL	155	57	97	.370	43	510	687	55	5091	1250	183	63	15	1604	405	540	157	....	.246	.305	.315	.620	98	-20	96	523
PHI	154	55	98	.359	44.5	529	691	57	5109	1296	177	62	17	1648	435	519	112	....	.254	.316	.323	.639	102	6	99	551
Total	**622**					**4540**			**40670**	**10075**	**1477**	**533**	**133**		**3856**	**4192**	**1268**		**.248**	**.318**	**.320**	**.638**				

Runs
Bush, D. (Det) 112
Cobb, T. (Det) 107
Chapman, R. (Cle) 98

Hits
Cobb, T. (Det) 225
Sisler, G. (StL) 190
Speaker, T. (Cle) 184

Doubles
Cobb, T. (Det) 44
Speaker, T. (Cle) 42
Veach, B. (Det) 31

Triples
Cobb, T. (Det) 24
Jackson, J. (Chi) 17
Judge, J. (Was) 15

Home Runs
Pipp, W. (NY) 9
Veach, B. (Det) 8
Bodie, P. (Phi) 7

Total Bases
Cobb, T. (Det) 335
Veach, B. (Det) 261
Speaker, T. (Cle) 254

Runs Batted In
Veach, B. (Det) 103
Cobb, T. (Det) 102
Felsch, H. (Chi) 102

Bases On Balls
Graney, J. (Cle) 94
Collins, E. (Chi) 89
2 players tied with 80

Stolen Bases
Cobb, T. (Det) 55
Collins, E. (Chi) 53
Chapman, R. (Cle) 52

Batting Average
Cobb, T. (Det) .383
Sisler, G. (StL) .353
Speaker, T. (Cle) .352

On-Base Percentage
Cobb, T. (Det) .444
Speaker, T. (Cle) .432
Veach, B. (Det) .393

Slugging Average
Cobb, T. (Det) .570
Speaker, T. (Cle) .486
Veach, B. (Det) .457

Adjusted OPS
Cobb, T. (Det) 210
Speaker, T. (Cle) 167
Sisler, G. (StL) 163

Adjusted Batting Runs
Cobb, T. (Det) 75.0
Speaker, T. (Cle) 45.0
Veach, B. (Det) 41.0

Runs Created/Game
Cobb, T. (Det) 11.30
Speaker, T. (Cle) 8.70
Sisler, G. (StL) 7.40

Fielding Runs
Weaver, B. (Chi) 20.8
Chapman, R. (Cle) 17.8
Shanks, H. (Was) 17.1

Win Shares – Batters
Cobb, T. (Det) 46
Speaker, T. (Cle) 37
Collins, E. (Chi) 32

TPW – Batters
Cobb, T. (Det) 8.4
Chapman, R. (Cle) 5.4
Speaker, T. (Cle) 5.1

TEAM	CG	SH	SV	IP	H	H/G	ER	HR	BB	SO	OAV	RAT	ERA	ERA+	CERA	PR+	PF	FA	E	DP	FR	BW	PW	FW	TPW	DIF
CHI	78	**22**	21	**1424^{1}**	1236	7.8	**342**	**10**	**413**	517	.237	1.158	**2.16**	123	2.49	**88.0**	100	.967	204	117	-10.0	2.8	**9.8**	-1.1	**11.5**	11.5
BOS	**115**	15	7	1421^{1}	**1197**	**7.6**	347	12	**413**	509	**.231**	**1.133**	2.20	117	**2.39**	51.5	97	**.972**	**183**	116	8.4	-.5	5.7	.9	6.2	7.8
CLE	73	20	**22**	1412^{2}	1270	8.1	395	17	438	451	.247	1.209	2.52	112	2.80	11.2	106	.964	242	136	**36.8**	-2.0	1.2	**4.1**	3.4	7.6
DET	78	20	15	1396^{1}	1209	7.8	397	12	504	516	.240	1.227	2.56	103	2.78	37.3	99	.964	234	95	-24.4	**7.1**	4.1	-2.7	8.5	-6.5
WAS	84	21	10	1413	1217	7.8	432	12	537	**637**	.238	1.241	2.75	95	2.80	-36.0	99	.961	251	127	15.7	-3.1	-4.0	1.7	-5.3	3.3
NY	87	10	6	1411^{1}	1280	8.2	417	28	427	571	.251	1.209	2.66	101	2.88	-1.3	101	.965	225	129	5.0	-4.3	-.1	.6	-3.9	-1.1
STL	66	12	12	1385^{1}	1320	8.6	492	19	537	429	.258	1.340	3.20	**81**	3.30	-91.5	98	.957	281	**139**	-2.3	-2.3	-10.2	-.3	-12.7	-7.3
PHI	80	8	8	1365^{2}	1310	8.6	496	23	562	516	.261	1.371	3.27	84	3.31	-58.0	103	.961	251	106	-21.0	.7	-6.5	-2.3	-8.1	-12.9
Total	**661**	**128**	**101**	**11230**		**8.0**	**3318**					**1.235**	**2.66**													

Wins
Cicotte, E. (Chi) 28
Ruth, B. (Bos) 24
2 players tied with 23

Win Percentage
Klepfer, E. (Cle) .778
Russell, R. (Chi) .750
Mays, C. (Bos) .710

Games
Danforth, D. (Chi) 50
Bagby, J. (Cle) 49
Cicotte, E. (Chi) 49

Complete Games
Ruth, B. (Bos) 35
Johnson, W. (Was) 30
Cicotte, E. (Chi) 29

Shutouts
Coveleski, S. (Cle) 9
Bagby, J. (Cle) 8
Johnson, W. (Was) 8

Saves
Danforth, D. (Chi) 9
Bagby, J. (Cle) 7
Boland, B. (Det) 6

Innings Pitched
Cicotte, E. (Chi) 346^{2}
Ruth, B. (Bos) 326^{1}
Johnson, W. (Was) 326

Fewest Hits/Game
Coveleski, S. (Cle) 6.09
Cicotte, E. (Chi) 6.39
Ruth, B. (Bos) 6.73

Fewest BB/Game
Russell, R. (Chi) 1.52
Mogridge, G. (NY) 1.79
Cicotte, E. (Chi) 1.82

Strikeouts
Johnson, W. (Was) 188
Cicotte, E. (Chi) 150
Leonard, D. (Bos) 144

Ratio
Cicotte, E. (Chi) .91
Johnson, W. (Was) .97
Coveleski, S. (Cle) .99

Earned Run Average
Cicotte, E. (Chi) 1.53
Mays, C. (Bos) 1.74
Coveleski, S. (Cle) 1.81

Adjusted ERA
Cicotte, E. (Chi) 173
Coveleski, S. (Cle) 156
Mays, C. (Bos) 148

Component ERA
Cicotte, E. (Chi) 1.52
Coveleski, S. (Cle) 1.64
Johnson, W. (Was) 1.73

Opponents' Batting Avg.
Coveleski, S. (Cle) .194
Cicotte, E. (Chi) .203
2 players tied with .211

Adjusted Pitching Runs
Cicotte, E. (Chi) 46
Coveleski, S. (Cle) 26
Mays, C. (Bos) 25

Win Shares – Pitchers
Ruth, B. (Bos) 36
Cicotte, E. (Chi) 35
Bagby, J. (Cle) 34

TPW – Pitchers
Cicotte, E. (Chi) 5.2
Ruth, B. (Bos) 3.9
Mays, C. (Bos) 3.5

1918 National League

TEAM	G	W	L	PCT	GB	R	OR	EW	AB	H	2B	3B	HR	TB	BB	SO	SB	CS	AVG	OBP	SLG	OPS	OPS+	BR/A	PF	RC
CHI	131	84	45	.651	....	**538**	**393**	84	4325	1147	164	53	21	1480	358	343	159	....	.265	.325	.342	.667	107	37	102	524
NY	124	71	53	.573	10.5	480	415	71	4164	1081	150	53	13	1376	271	365	130	....	.260	.310	.330	.640	103	9	98	451
CIN	129	68	60	.531	15.5	530	496	68	4265	**1185**	**165**	**84**	15	**1563**	304	303	128	....	**.278**	**.330**	**.366**	**.697**	**120**	**95**	98	**545**
PIT	126	65	60	.520	17	466	412	70	4091	1016	107	72	15	1312	**371**	**285**	**200**	....	.248	.315	.321	.635	96	-13	104	466
BRO	126	57	69	.452	25.5	360	463	47	4212	1052	121	62	10	1327	212	326	113	....	.250	.291	.315	.607	90	-54	100	405
PHI	125	55	68	.447	26	430	507	51	4192	1022	158	28	25	1311	346	400	97	....	.244	.305	.313	.617	88	-56	107	417
BOS	124	53	71	.427	28.5	424	469	56	4162	1014	107	59	13	1278	350	438	83	....	.244	.307	.307	.614	96	-12	96	412
STL	131	51	78	.395	33	454	527	55	**4369**	1066	147	64	**27**	1422	329	461	119	....	.244	.301	.325	.626	100	-5	96	450
Total	**508**					**3682**			**33780**	**8583**	**1119**	**475**	**139**		**2541**	**2921**	**1029**		**.254**	**.311**	**.328**	**.638**				

Runs
Groh, H. (Cin) 86
Burns, G. (NY) 80
Flack, M. (Chi) 74

Hits
Hollocher, C. (Chi) 161
Groh, H. (Cin) 158
Roush, E. (Cin) 145

Doubles
Groh, H. (Cin) 28
Cravath, G. (Phi) 27
Mann, L. (Chi) 27

Triples
Daubert, J. (Bro) 15
3 players tied with 13

Home Runs
Cravath, G. (Phi) 8
Cruise, W. (StL) 6
Williams, C. (Phi) 6

Total Bases
Hollocher, C. (Chi) 202
Roush, E. (Cin) 198
Groh, H. (Cin) 195

Runs Batted In
Magee, S. (Cin) 76
Cutshaw, G. (Pit) 68
Luderus, F. (Phi) 67

Bases On Balls
Carey, M. (Pit) 62
Flack, M. (Chi) 56
3 players tied with 54

Stolen Bases
Carey, M. (Pit) 58
Burns, G. (NY) 40
Hollocher, C. (Chi) 26

Batting Average
Wheat, Z. (Bro) .335
Roush, E. (Cin) .333
Groh, H. (Cin) .320

On-Base Percentage
Groh, H. (Cin) .395
Hollocher, C. (Chi) .379
Smith, R. (Bos) .373

Slugging Average
Roush, E. (Cin) .455
Hollocher, C. (Chi) .397
Groh, H. (Cin) .396

Adjusted OPS
Roush, E. (Cin) 153
Groh, H. (Cin) 144
Hollocher, C. (Chi) 133

Adjusted Batting Runs
Groh, H. (Cin) 28.0
Roush, E. (Cin) 25.0
Hollocher, C. (Chi) 21.0

Runs Created/Game
Roush, E. (Cin) 6.50
Groh, H. (Cin) 5.90
Hollocher, C. (Chi) 5.90

Fielding Runs
Fletcher, A. (NY) 30.7
Bancroft, D. (Phi) 19.4
Carey, M. (Pit) 14.8

Win Shares – Batters
Hollocher, C. (Chi) 28
Hollocher, C. (Chi) 28
2 players tied with 23

TPW – Batters
Groh, H. (Cin) 4.1
Fletcher, A. (NY) 3.9
Bancroft, D. (Phi) 3.0

TEAM	CG	SH	SV	IP	H	H/G	ER	HR	BB	SO	OAV	RAT	ERA	ERA+	CERA	PR+	PF	FA	E	DP	FR	BW	PW	FW	TPW	DIF
CHI	92	23	8	1197	1050	7.9	290	13	296	472	.240	1.124	2.18	128	2.35	108.9	101	.966	188	91	-28.9	4.1	12.2	-3.2	13.0	7.0
NY	74	18	11	1111²	1002	8.1	326	20	228	330	.244	1.106	2.64	99	2.39	-5.4	95	.970	152	78	4.0	1.0	-.6	.4	.8	8.2
CIN	84	14	6	1142¹	1136	9.0	381	19	381	321	.268	1.328	3.00	89	3.27	-51.2	97	.964	192	127	9.1	10.6	-5.7	1.0	5.9	-1.9
PIT	85	10	7	1140¹	1005	7.9	314	13	299	367	.243	1.144	2.48	116	2.47	12.9	104	.966	179	108	37.2	-1.5	1.4	4.2	4.1	-1.1
BRO	85	17	2	1131¹	1024	8.2	353	22	320	395	.248	1.188	2.81	99	2.75	-2.8	101	.963	193	74	-0.2	-6.0	-.3	.0	-6.4	.4
PHI	78	10	6	1139²	1086	8.6	399	22	369	312	.258	1.277	3.15	95	3.04	-17.8	98	.961	211	91	-1.6	-6.3	-2.0	-.2	-8.4	2.4
BOS	96	13	0	1117¹	1111	9.0	360	14	277	340	.266	1.242	2.90	93	3.00	-1.8	97	.965	184	89	-24.9	-1.4	-.2	-2.8	-4.4	-4.6
STL	72	3	5	1193	1148	8.7	392	16	352	361	.261	1.257	2.96	92	3.00	-39.5	98	.962	220	116	5.5	-.5	-4.4	.6	-4.3	-8.7
Total	**666**	**108**	**45**	**9172²**		**8.4**	**2815**					**1.208**	**2.76**													

Wins
Vaughn, H. (Chi) 22
Hendrix, C. (Chi) 20
3 players tied with 19

Win Percentage
Hendrix, C. (Chi) .741
Tyler, L. (Chi) .704
Vaughn, H. (Chi) .688

Games
Grimes, B. (Bro) 40
Cooper, W. (Pit) 38
Eller, H. (Cin) 37

Complete Games
Nehf, A. (Bos) 28
Vaughn, H. (Chi) 27
Cooper, W. (Pit) 26

Shutouts
Vaughn, H. (Chi) 8
Grimes, B. (Bro) 7
2 players tied with 6

Saves
4 players tied with 3

Innings Pitched
Vaughn, H. (Chi) 290¹
Nehf, A. (Bos) 284¹
Cooper, W. (Pit) 273¹

Fewest Hits/Game
Vaughn, H. (Chi) 6.70
Grimes, B. (Bro) 7.01
Cooper, W. (Pit) 7.21

Fewest BB/Game
Perritt, P. (NY) 1.47
Toney, F. (NY,Cin) 1.54
Packard, G. (StL) 1.63

Strikeouts
Vaughn, H. (Chi) 148
Cooper, W. (Pit) 117
Grimes, B. (Bro) 113

Ratio
Vaughn, H. (Chi) 1.01
Cooper, W. (Pit) 1.04
Tyler, L. (Chi) 1.06

Earned Run Average
Vaughn, H. (Chi) 1.74
Tyler, L. (Chi) 2.00
Cooper, W. (Pit) 2.11

Adjusted ERA
Vaughn, H. (Chi) 160
Tyler, L. (Chi) 139
Cooper, W. (Pit) 136

Component ERA
Vaughn, H. (Chi) 1.79
Grimes, B. (Bro) 1.95
Tyler, L. (Chi) 1.99

Opponents' Batting Avg.
Vaughn, H. (Chi) .208
Grimes, B. (Bro) .216
Cooper, W. (Pit) .223

Adjusted Pitching Runs
Vaughn, H. (Chi) 41
Tyler, L. (Chi) 30
Grimes, B. (Bro) 19

Win Shares – Pitchers
Vaughn, H. (Chi) 28
Grimes, B. (Bro) 25
Tyler, L. (Chi) 24

TPW – Pitchers
Vaughn, H. (Chi) 5.0
Tyler, L. (Chi) 3.5
Grimes, B. (Bro) 2.2

1918 American League

TEAM	G	W	L	PCT	GB	R	OR	EW	AB	H	2B	3B	HR	TB	BB	SO	SB	CS	AVG	OBP	SLG	OPS	OPS+	BR/A	PF	RC
BOS	126	75	51	.595	....	474	380	77	3982	990	159	54	15	1302	407	324	110	....	.249	.322	.327	.649	103	14	98	454
CLE	129	73	54	.575	2.5	504	447	71	4166	1084	176	67	9	1421	491	386	165	....	.260	.344	.341	.685	102	23	110	537
WAS	130	72	56	.562	4	461	412	71	4472	1144	156	49	4	1410	376	361	137	....	.256	.318	.315	.634	98	-13	98	479
NY	126	60	63	.488	13.5	493	475	64	4224	1085	160	45	20	1395	367	370	88	....	.257	.320	.330	.650	99	-9	102	469
STL	123	58	64	.475	15	426	448	58	4019	1040	152	40	5	1287	397	340	138	....	.259	.331	.320	.651	105	26	97	467
CHI	124	57	67	.460	17	457	446	64	4132	1057	136	55	8	1327	375	358	116	....	.256	.322	.321	.643	98	-10	101	458
DET	128	55	71	.437	20	476	557	53	4262	1063	141	56	13	1355	452	380	123	....	.249	.325	.318	.642	103	19	96	470
PHI	130	52	76	.406	24	412	538	47	4278	1039	124	44	22	1317	343	485	83	....	.243	.303	.308	.611	88	-65	101	414
Total	**508**					**3703**			**33535**	**8502**	**1204**	**410**	**96**		**3208**	**3004**	**960**		**.254**	**.323**	**.322**	**.646**				

Runs
Chapman, R. (Cle) 84
Cobb, T. (Det) 83
Hooper, H. (Bos) 81

Hits
Burns, G. (Phi) 178
Cobb, T. (Det) 161
2 players tied with 154

Doubles
Speaker, T. (Cle) 33
Hooper, H. (Bos) 26
Ruth, B. (Bos) 26

Triples
Cobb, T. (Det) 14
Hooper, H. (Bos) 13
Veach, B. (Det) 13

Home Runs
Ruth, B. (Bos) 11
Walker, T. (Phi) 11
2 players tied with 6

Total Bases
Burns, G. (Phi) 236
Cobb, T. (Det) 217
Baker, F. (NY) 206

Runs Batted In
Veach, B. (Det) 78
Burns, G. (Phi) 70
2 players tied with 66

Bases On Balls
Chapman, R. (Cle) 84
Bush, D. (Det) 79
Hooper, H. (Bos) 75

Stolen Bases
Sisler, G. (StL) 45
Roth, B. (Cle) 35
Cobb, T. (Det) 34

Batting Average
Cobb, T. (Det) .382
Burns, G. (Phi) .352
Sisler, G. (StL) .341

On-Base Percentage
Cobb, T. (Det) .440
Speaker, T. (Cle) .403
Sisler, G. (StL) .400

Slugging Average
Burns, G. (Phi) .467
Sisler, G. (StL) .440
Speaker, T. (Cle) .435

Adjusted OPS
Sisler, G. (StL) 158
Burns, G. (Phi) 157
Hooper, H. (Bos) 142

Adjusted Batting Runs
Burns, G. (Phi) 32.0
Sisler, G. (StL) 31.0
Hooper, H. (Bos) 27.0

Runs Created/Game
Sisler, G. (StL) 7.60
Burns, G. (Phi) 6.90
Speaker, T. (Cle) 6.90

Fielding Runs
Peckinpaugh, R. (NY) 25.8
Gedeon, J. (StL) 16.4
Scott, E. (Bos) 15.5

Win Shares – Batters
Hooper, H. (Bos) 29
Speaker, T. (Cle) 27
Burns, G. (Phi) 24

TPW – Batters
Sisler, G. (StL) 4.6
Burns, G. (Phi) 3.6
Baker, F. (NY) 3.4

TEAM	CG	SH	SV	IP	H	H/G	ER	HR	BB	SO	OAV	RAT	ERA	ERA+	CERA	PR+	PF	FA	E	DP	FR	BW	PW	FW	TPW	DIF
BOS	105	26	2	1120	931	7.5	287	9	380	392	.231	1.171	2.31	116	2.44	39.6	97	.971	152	89	6.6	1.5	4.4	.7	6.7	5.3
CLE	78	5	13	1161	1126	8.7	341	9	343	364	.262	1.265	2.64	113	2.99	70.0	108	.962	207	82	-23.6	2.6	7.8	-2.6	7.8	2.2
WAS	75	19	8	1228	1021	7.5	292	10	395	505	.231	1.153	2.14	127	2.40	40.7	98	.960	226	95	38.5	-1.5	4.5	4.3	7.4	.6
NY	59	8	13	1157¹	1103	8.6	386	25	463	370	.261	1.353	3.00	94	3.50	-53.9	102	.970	161	137	34.7	-1.0	-6.0	3.9	-3.1	2.1
STL	67	8	8	1111¹	993	8.0	339	11	402	346	.246	1.255	2.75	100	2.85	-7.0	99	.963	190	86	4.6	2.9	-.8	.5	2.7	-5.7
CHI	76	9	8	1126	1092	8.7	342	9	300	349	.261	1.236	2.73	100	2.91	15.0	98	.967	169	98	-15.6	-1.1	1.7	-1.7	-1.2	-3.8
DET	74	8	7	1160²	1130	8.8	438	9	437	374	.263	1.350	3.40	78	3.33	-38.1	96	.960	212	77	-58.4	2.1	-4.2	-6.5	-8.6	.6
PHI	80	13	9	1156	1106	8.6	414	13	486	277	.266	1.377	3.22	91	3.44	-75.1	106	.959	228	136	37.1	-7.3	-8.4	4.1	-11.5	-.5
Total	**614**	**96**	**68**	**9220¹**		**8.3**	**2839**					**1.270**	**2.77**													

Wins
Johnson, W. (Was) 23
Coveleski, S. (Cle) 22
Mays, C. (Bos) 21

Win Percentage
Jones, S. (Bos) .762
Ruth, B. (Bos) .650
Johnson, W. (Was) .639

Games
Bagby, J. (Cle) 45
Mogridge, G. (NY) 45
Perry, S. (Phi) 44

Complete Games
Mays, C. (Bos) 30
Perry, S. (Phi) 30
Johnson, W. (Was) 29

Shutouts
Johnson, W. (Was) 8
Mays, C. (Bos) 8
Bush, J. (Bos) 7

Saves
Mogridge, G. (NY) 7
Bagby, J. (Cle) 6
2 players tied with 4

Innings Pitched
Perry, S. (Phi) 332¹
Johnson, W. (Was) 326
Coveleski, S. (Cle) 311

Fewest Hits/Game
Sothoron, A. (StL) 6.55
Johnson, W. (Was) 6.65
Harper, H. (Was) 6.71

Fewest BB/Game
Cicotte, E. (Chi) 1.35
Mogridge, G. (NY) 1.62
Benz, J. (Chi) 1.64

Strikeouts
Johnson, W. (Was) 162
Shaw, J. (Was) 129
Bush, J. (Bos) 125

Ratio
Johnson, W. (Was) .95
Ruth, B. (Bos) 1.05
Sothoron, A. (StL) 1.05

Earned Run Average
Johnson, W. (Was) 1.27
Coveleski, S. (Cle) 1.82
Sothoron, A. (StL) 1.94

Adjusted ERA
Johnson, W. (Was) 214
Coveleski, S. (Cle) 164
Perry, S. (Phi) 148

Component ERA
Johnson, W. (Was) 1.63
Ruth, B. (Bos) 1.84
Sothoron, A. (StL) 1.86

Opponents' Batting Avg.
Sothoron, A. (StL) .205
Johnson, W. (Was) .210
Harper, H. (Was) .212

Adjusted Pitching Runs
Coveleski, S. (Cle) 47
Johnson, W. (Was) 42
Perry, S. (Phi) 24

Win Shares – Pitchers
Ruth, B. (Bos) 40
Johnson, W. (Was) 38
Perry, S. (Phi) 30

TPW – Pitchers
Johnson, W. (Was) 5.8
Ruth, B. (Bos) 5.3
Coveleski, S. (Cle) 5.0

1919 National League

TEAM	G	W	L	PCT	GB	R	OR	EW	AB	H	2B	3B	HR	TB	BB	SO	SB	CS	AVG	OBP	SLG	OPS	OPS+	BR/A	PF	RC
CIN	140	96	44	.686	....	577	**401**	94	4577	1204	135	**83**	20	1565	**405**	368	143	....	.263	**.327**	.342	.669	110	59	97	552
NY	140	87	53	.621	9	**605**	470	87	4664	1254	204	64	40	**1706**	328	407	157	....	**.269**	.322	**.366**	**.688**	**113**	**70**	99	**576**
CHI	140	75	65	.536	21	454	407	78	4581	1174	166	58	21	1519	298	**359**	150	....	.256	.308	.332	.639	97	-17	100	500
PIT	139	71	68	.511	24.5	472	466	70	4538	1132	130	82	17	1477	344	381	**196**	....	.249	.306	.325	.631	91	-43	104	493
BRO	141	69	71	.493	27	525	513	72	**4844**	**1272**	167	66	25	1646	258	405	112	....	.263	.304	.340	.644	97	-26	102	518
BOS	140	57	82	.410	38.5	465	563	56	4746	1201	142	62	24	1539	355	481	145	....	.253	.311	.324	.635	100	4	96	509
STL	138	54	83	.394	40.5	463	552	57	4588	1175	163	52	18	1496	304	418	148	....	.256	.305	.326	.631	101	2	94	485
PHI	138	47	90	.343	47.5	510	699	48	4746	1191	**208**	50	**42**	1625	323	469	114	....	.251	.303	.342	.645	92	-44	107	506
Total	**558**					**4071**			**37284**	**9603**	**1315**	**517**	**207**		**2615**	**3288**	**1165**		**.258**	**.311**	**.337**	**.648**				

Runs
- Burns, G. (NY) 86
- Daubert, J. (Cin) 79
- Groh, H. (Cin) 79

Hits
- Olson, I. (Bro) 164
- Hornsby, R. (StL) 163
- 2 players tied with 162

Doubles
- Youngs, R. (NY) 31
- Burns, G. (NY) 30
- Luderus, F. (Phi) 30

Triples
- Myers, H. (Bro) 14
- Southworth, B. (Pit) 14
- 5 players tied with 12

Home Runs
- Cravath, G. (Phi) 12
- Kauff, B. (NY) 10
- Williams, C. (Phi) 9

Total Bases
- Myers, H. (Bro) 223
- Hornsby, R. (StL) 220
- Wheat, Z. (Bro) 219

Runs Batted In
- Myers, H. (Bro) 73
- Hornsby, R. (StL) 71
- Roush, E. (Cin) 71

Bases On Balls
- Burns, G. (NY) 82
- Rath, M. (Cin) 64
- Groh, H. (Cin) 56

Stolen Bases
- Burns, G. (NY) 40
- Cutshaw, G. (Pit) 36
- Bigbee, C. (Pit) 31

Batting Average
- Roush, E. (Cin) .321
- Hornsby, R. (StL) .318
- Youngs, R. (NY) .311

On-Base Percentage
- Burns, G. (NY) .396
- Groh, H. (Cin) .392
- Hornsby, R. (StL) .384

Slugging Average
- Myers, H. (Bro) .436
- Groh, H. (Cin) .431
- Roush, E. (Cin) .431

Adjusted OPS
- Hornsby, R. (StL) 154
- Groh, H. (Cin) 151
- Roush, E. (Cin) 147

Adjusted Batting Runs
- Hornsby, R. (StL) 34.0
- Burns, G. (NY) 32.0
- Groh, H. (Cin) 30.0

Runs Created/Game
- Burns, G. (NY) 6.60
- Groh, H. (Cin) 6.50
- Hornsby, R. (StL) 6.30

Fielding Runs
- Rath, M. (Cin) 28.7
- Fletcher, A. (NY) 23.3
- Maranville, R. (Bos) 17.4

Win Shares – Batters
- Roush, E. (Cin) 33
- Burns, G. (NY) 32
- Groh, H. (Cin) 30

TPW – Batters
- Groh, H. (Cin) 4.5
- Hornsby, R. (StL) 4.1
- Maranville, R. (Bos) 3.8

TEAM	CG	SH	SV	IP	H	H/G	ER	HR	BB	SO	OAV	RAT	ERA	ERA+	CERA	PR+	PF	FA	E	DP	FR	BW	PW	FW	TPW	DIF
CIN	89	**23**	9	1274	**1104**	**7.8**	316	21	298	407	**.239**	**1.100**	2.23	124	**2.29**	52.6	95	**.974**	**151**	98	**23.4**	6.6	5.8	**2.6**	**15.1**	10.9
NY	72	11	**13**	1256	1153	8.3	377	34	305	340	.247	1.161	2.70	104	2.66	-4.5	96	.964	216	96	18.4	**7.8**	-.5	2.0	9.3	7.7
CHI	80	21	5	1265	1127	8.0	**311**	**14**	294	**495**	.242	1.123	**2.21**	130	2.39	**104.0**	99	.969	185	87	-10.8	-1.9	**11.6**	-1.2	8.5	-3.5
PIT	91	17	4	1249	1113	8.0	400	23	**263**	391	.244	1.102	2.88	105	2.39	26.2	104	.970	165	89	-7.7	-4.8	2.9	-.9	-2.7	4.7
BRO	**98**	12	1	**1281**	1256	8.8	389	21	292	476	.261	1.208	2.73	109	2.84	61.7	102	.963	219	84	-28.5	-2.9	6.9	-3.2	.8	-1.8
BOS	79	5	9	1270[1]	1313	9.3	447	29	337	374	.276	1.299	3.17	90	3.27	-44.4	98	.966	204	111	0.3	.5	-4.9	.0	-4.4	-7.6
STL	55	6	8	1217[1]	1146	8.5	437	25	415	414	.256	1.282	3.23	86	3.12	-73.9	96	.963	214	**112**	14.1	.2	-8.2	1.6	-6.4	-7.6
PHI	93	6	2	1252	1391	10.0	576	40	408	397	.294	1.437	4.14	**78**	4.09	-121.4	111	.963	218	**112**	-7.2	-4.8	-13.5	-.8	-19.1	-1.9
Total	**657**	**101**	**51**	**10064[2]**		**8.6**	**3253**					**1.214**	**2.91**													

Wins
- Barnes, J. (NY) 25
- Sallee, S. (Cin) 21
- Vaughn, H. (Chi) 21

Win Percentage
- Ruether, D. (Cin) .760
- Sallee, S. (Cin) .750
- Fisher, R. (Cin) .737

Games
- Tuero, O. (StL) 45
- Meadows, L. (StL,Phi) 40
- 3 players tied with 38

Complete Games
- Cooper, W. (Pit) 27
- Pfeffer, J. (Bro) 26
- Vaughn, H. (Chi) 25

Shutouts
- Alexander, G. (Chi) 9
- Eller, H. (Cin) 7
- Adams, B. (Pit) 6

Saves
- Tuero, O. (StL) 4
- 5 players tied with 3

Innings Pitched
- Vaughn, H. (Chi) 306[2]
- Barnes, J. (NY) 295[2]
- Cooper, W. (Pit) 286[2]

Fewest Hits/Game
- Alexander, G. (Chi) 6.89
- Cooper, W. (Pit) 7.19
- Ruether, D. (Cin) 7.23

Fewest BB/Game
- Adams, B. (Pit) .79
- Sallee, S. (Cin) .79
- Barnes, J. (NY) 1.07

Strikeouts
- Vaughn, H. (Chi) 141
- Eller, H. (Cin) 137
- Alexander, G. (Chi) 121

Ratio
- Adams, B. (Pit) .90
- Alexander, G. (Chi) .93
- Barnes, J. (NY) 1.01

Earned Run Average
- Alexander, G. (Chi) 1.72
- Vaughn, H. (Chi) 1.79
- Ruether, D. (Cin) 1.82

Adjusted ERA
- Alexander, G. (Chi) 167
- Vaughn, H. (Chi) 161
- Ruether, D. (Cin) 152

Component ERA
- Adams, B. (Pit) 1.52
- Alexander, G. (Chi) 1.56
- Fisher, R. (Cin) 2.00

Opponents' Batting Avg.
- Alexander, G. (Chi) .211
- Adams, B. (Pit) .220
- Ruether, D. (Cin) .223

Adjusted Pitching Runs
- Vaughn, H. (Chi) 40
- Alexander, G. (Chi) 32
- Adams, B. (Pit) 32

Win Shares – Pitchers
- Vaughn, H. (Chi) 30
- Adams, B. (Pit) 27
- 2 players tied with 26

TPW – Pitchers
- Vaughn, H. (Chi) 4.4
- Alexander, G. (Chi) 3.6
- Adams, B. (Pit) 3.5

1919 American League

TEAM	G	W	L	PCT	GB	R	OR	EW	AB	H	2B	3B	HR	TB	BB	SO	SB	CS	AVG	OBP	SLG	OPS	OPS+	BR/A	PF	RC
CHI	140	88	52	.629	....	**667**	534	85	4675	**1343**	218	70	25	1776	427	**358**	**150**	....	**.287**	.351	.380	.731	111	67	100	**668**
CLE	139	84	55	.604	3.5	636	537	81	4565	1268	**254**	72	24	1738	**498**	367	113	....	.278	**.354**	.381	**.734**	106	43	106	651
NY	141	80	59	.576	7.5	578	**506**	79	**4775**	1275	193	49	**45**	1701	386	479	101	....	.267	.326	.356	.682	96	-26	101	575
DET	140	80	60	.571	8	618	578	75	4665	1319	222	**84**	23	**1778**	429	427	121	....	.283	.346	**.381**	.727	**113**	**75**	98	649
STL	140	67	72	.482	20.5	533	567	65	4672	1234	187	73	31	1660	391	443	74	....	.264	.326	.355	.681	94	-36	102	560
BOS	138	66	71	.482	20.5	564	552	70	4548	1188	181	49	33	1566	471	411	108	....	.261	.336	.344	.681	103	25	94	559
WAS	142	56	84	.400	32	533	570	65	4757	1238	177	63	24	1613	416	511	142	....	.260	.325	.339	.664	93	-42	99	557
PHI	140	36	104	.257	52	457	742	39	4730	1156	175	71	35	1578	349	565	103	....	.244	.300	.334	.634	82	-116	101	488
Total	**560**					**4586**			**37387**	**10021**	**1607**	**531**	**240**		**3367**	**3561**	**912**		**.268**	**.333**	**.359**	**.692**				

Runs
- Ruth, B. (Bos) 103
- Sisler, G. (StL) 96
- Cobb, T. (Det) 92

Hits
- Cobb, T. (Det) 191
- Veach, B. (Det) 191
- Jackson, J. (Chi) 181

Doubles
- Veach, B. (Det) 45
- Speaker, T. (Cle) 38
- Cobb, T. (Det) 36

Triples
- Veach, B. (Det) 17
- Heilmann, H. (Det) 15
- Sisler, G. (StL) 15

Home Runs
- Ruth, B. (Bos) 29
- 3 players tied with 10

Total Bases
- Ruth, B. (Bos) 284
- Veach, B. (Det) 279
- Sisler, G. (StL) 271

Runs Batted In
- Ruth, B. (Bos) 114
- Veach, B. (Det) 101
- Jackson, J. (Chi) 96

Bases On Balls
- Graney, J. (Cle) 105
- Ruth, B. (Bos) 101
- Judge, J. (Was) 81

Stolen Bases
- Collins, E. (Chi) 33
- Cobb, T. (Det) 28
- Sisler, G. (StL) 28

Batting Average
- Cobb, T. (Det) .384
- Veach, B. (Det) .355
- Sisler, G. (StL) .352

On-Base Percentage
- Ruth, B. (Bos) .456
- Cobb, T. (Det) .429
- Jackson, J. (Chi) .422

Slugging Average
- Ruth, B. (Bos) .657
- Sisler, G. (StL) .530
- Veach, B. (Det) .519

Adjusted OPS
- Ruth, B. (Bos) 224
- Cobb, T. (Det) 168
- Veach, B. (Det) 160

Adjusted Batting Runs
- Ruth, B. (Bos) 79.0
- Cobb, T. (Det) 44.0
- Jackson, J. (Chi) 42.0

Runs Created/Game
- Ruth, B. (Bos) 11.30
- Cobb, T. (Det) 9.60
- Sisler, G. (StL) 8.30

Fielding Runs
- Peckinpaugh, R. (NY) 28.1
- Pratt, D. (NY) 26.4
- Young, R. (Det) 17.3

Win Shares – Batters
- Ruth, B. (Bos) 43
- 3 players tied with 32

TPW – Batters
- Ruth, B. (Bos) 8.9
- Peckinpaugh, R. (NY) 5.5
- Veach, B. (Det) 4.3

TEAM	CG	SH	SV	IP	H	H/G	ER	HR	BB	SO	OAV	RAT	ERA	ERA+	CERA	PR+	PF	FA	E	DP	FR	BW	PW	FW	TPW	DIF
CHI	88	14	3	1265[2]	1245	8.8	427	24	**342**	468	.262	1.254	3.04	105	3.14	-7.6	99	.969	176	116	27.3	7.0	-.8	2.9	9.1	8.9
CLE	79	10	**10**	1245	1242	9.0	407	19	362	432	.264	1.288	2.94	114	3.26	**62.6**	104	.965	201	102	-5.5	4.5	**6.5**	-.6	**10.5**	4.5
NY	85	14	7	**1287**	**1143**	**8.0**	**403**	47	433	500	**.240**	**1.225**	**2.82**	113	**2.92**	13.0	99	.968	193	108	**39.7**	-2.7	1.4	**4.2**	2.8	8.2
DET	85	10	4	1256	1254	9.0	461	35	436	428	.266	1.346	3.30	97	3.54	4.3	99	.964	205	81	-19.8	**7.9**	.4	-2.1	6.3	3.7
STL	78	14	4	1256	1255	9.0	437	35	421	415	.263	1.334	3.13	106	3.49	15.4	103	.963	215	98	10.0	-3.7	1.6	1.0	-1.1	-.9
BOS	**89**	**15**	8	1224[1]	1251	9.2	450	**16**	421	381	.275	1.366	3.31	91	3.57	-56.2	94	**.975**	**140**	**118**	16.5	2.6	-5.9	1.7	-1.6	-.4
WAS	68	13	**10**	1274[1]	1237	8.7	426	20	451	**536**	.259	1.325	3.01	106	3.37	45.1	99	.960	227	86	-13.6	-4.4	4.7	-1.4	-1.1	-12.9
PHI	72	1	3	1239[1]	1371	10.0	586	44	503	417	.292	1.512	4.26	**80**	4.46	-62.2	106	.956	257	96	-53.6	-12.2	-6.5	-5.6	-24.3	-9.7
Total	**644**	**91**	**49**	**10047[2]**		**9.0**	**3597**					**1.330**	**3.22**													

Wins
Cicotte, E. (Chi) 29
Coveleski, S. (Cle) 24
Williams, L. (Chi) 23

Win Percentage
Cicotte, E. (Chi) .806
Dauss, H. (Det) .700
Williams, L. (Chi) .676

Games
Shaw, J. (Was) 45
Russell, A. (NY,Bos) 44
2 players tied with 43

Complete Games
Cicotte, E. (Chi) 30
Johnson, W. (Was) 27
Williams, L. (Chi) 27

Shutouts
Johnson, W. (Was) 7
5 players tied with 5

Saves
Russell, A. (Bos,NY) 5
Shaw, J. (Was) 5
Shawkey, B. (NY) 5

Innings Pitched
Cicotte, E. (Chi) 306[2]
Shaw, J. (Was) 306[2]
Williams, L. (Chi) 297

Fewest Hits/Game
Johnson, W. (Was) 7.28
Thormahlen, H. (NY) 7.39
Shawkey, B. (NY) 7.51

Fewest BB/Game
Cicotte, E. (Chi) 1.44
Johnson, W. (Was) 1.58
Bagby, J. (Cle) 1.64

Strikeouts
Johnson, W. (Was) 147
Shaw, J. (Was) 128
Williams, L. (Chi) 125

Ratio
Johnson, W. (Was) .99
Cicotte, E. (Chi) .99
Williams, L. (Chi) 1.09

Earned Run Average
Johnson, W. (Was) 1.49
Cicotte, E. (Chi) 1.82
Mays, C. (NY,Bos) 2.10

Adjusted ERA
Johnson, W. (Was) 215
Cicotte, E. (Chi) 175
Sothoron, A. (StL) 151

Component ERA
Johnson, W. (Was) 1.72
Cicotte, E. (Chi) 1.91
Williams, L. (Chi) 2.47

Opponents' Batting Avg.
Johnson, W. (Was) .219
Cicotte, E. (Chi) .228
Thormahlen, H. (NY) .228

Adjusted Pitching Runs
Johnson, W. (Was) 58
Cicotte, E. (Chi) 40
Sothoron, A. (StL) 31

Win Shares – Pitchers
Cicotte, E. (Chi) 32
Coveleski, S. (Cle) 27
Johnson, W. (Was) 27

TPW – Pitchers
Johnson, W. (Was) 6.3
Cicotte, E. (Chi) 4.2
Sothoron, A. (StL) 3.0

1920 National League

TEAM	G	W	L	PCT	GB	R	OR	EW	AB	H	2B	3B	HR	TB	BB	SO	SB	CS	AVG	OBP	SLG	OPS	OPS+	BR/A	PF	RC
BRO	155	93	61	.604	....	660	**528**	94	5399	1493	205	**99**	28	1980	359	391	70	**80**	.277	.324	.367	.691	100	0	103	637
NY	155	86	68	.558	7	**682**	543	94	5309	1427	210	76	46	1927	**432**	545	131	113	.269	.327	.363	.690	104	31	99	628
CIN	154	82	71	.536	10.5	639	569	85	5176	1432	169	76	18	1807	382	**367**	158	128	.277	.332	.349	.681	102	18	99	602
PIT	155	79	75	.513	14	530	552	74	5219	1342	162	90	16	1732	374	405	**181**	117	.257	.310	.332	.642	87	-75	103	544
STL	155	75	79	.487	18	675	682	76	**5495**	**1589**	**238**	96	32	**2115**	373	484	126	114	**.289**	**.337**	**.385**	**.722**	**115**	**98**	98	**704**
CHI	154	75	79	.487	18	619	635	75	5117	1350	223	67	34	1809	428	421	115	129	.264	.326	.354	.680	98	-15	102	589
BOS	153	62	90	.408	30	523	670	58	5218	1358	168	86	23	1767	385	488	88	98	.260	.315	.339	.654	97	-22	96	557
PHI	153	62	91	.405	30.5	565	714	59	5264	1385	229	54	**64**	1914	283	531	100	83	.263	.305	.364	.669	92	-52	105	577
Total	**617**					**4893**			**42197**	**11376**	**1604**	**644**	**261**		**3016**	**3632**	**969**	**862**	**.270**	**.322**	**.357**	**.679**				

Runs
Burns, G. (NY) 115
Bancroft, D. (NY,Phi) 102
Daubert, J. (Cin) 97

Hits
Hornsby, R. (StL) 218
Stock, M. (StL) 204
Youngs, R. (NY) 204

Doubles
Hornsby, R. (StL) 44
3 players tied with 36

Triples
Myers, H. (Bro) 22
Hornsby, R. (StL) 20
Roush, E. (Cin) 16

Home Runs
Williams, C. (Phi) 15
Meusel, I. (Phi) 14
Kelly, G. (NY) 11

Total Bases
Hornsby, R. (StL) 329
Williams, C. (Phi) 293
Youngs, R. (NY) 277

Runs Batted In
Hornsby, R. (StL) 94
Kelly, G. (NY) 94
Roush, E. (Cin) 90

Bases On Balls
Burns, G. (NY) 76
Youngs, R. (NY) 75
Paskert, D. (Chi) 64

Stolen Bases
Carey, M. (Pit) 52
Roush, E. (Cin) 36
Frisch, F. (NY) 34

Batting Average
Hornsby, R. (StL) .370
Youngs, R. (NY) .351
Roush, E. (Cin) .339

On-Base Percentage
Hornsby, R. (StL) .431
Youngs, R. (NY) .427
Roush, E. (Cin) .386

Slugging Average
Hornsby, R. (StL) .559
Williams, C. (Phi) .497
Youngs, R. (NY) .477

Adjusted OPS
Hornsby, R. (StL) 187
Youngs, R. (NY) 161
Roush, E. (Cin) 142

Adjusted Batting Runs
Hornsby, R. (StL) 64.0
Youngs, R. (NY) 47.0
Roush, E. (Cin) 31.0

Runs Created/Game
Hornsby, R. (StL) 9.30
Youngs, R. (NY) 7.60
Wheat, Z. (Bro) 6.60

Fielding Runs
Bancroft, D. (NY,Phi) 36.2
Cutshaw, G. (Pit) 18.1
Burns, G. (NY) 17.6

Win Shares – Batters
Hornsby, R. (StL) 38
Roush, E. (Cin) 33
Youngs, R. (NY) 33

TPW – Batters
Hornsby, R. (StL) 8.0
Bancroft, D. (NY,Phi) 5.7
Youngs, R. (NY) 5.0

TEAM	CG	SH	SV	IP	H	H/G	ER	HR	BB	SO	OAV	RAT	ERA	ERA+	CERA	PR+	PF	FA	E	DP	FR	BW	PW	FW	TPW	DIF
BRO	89	17	10	**1427[1]**	1381	8.7	**415**	**25**	327	**553**	.259	1.197	**2.62**	122	2.75	**110.9**	102	.966	226	118	-19.2	.0	**11.9**	-2.1	**9.9**	6.1
NY	86	**18**	9	1408[2]	1379	8.8	438	44	297	380	.261	1.190	2.80	107	2.83	8.4	96	.969	210	**137**	**21.4**	3.3	.9	**2.3**	6.5	2.5
CIN	90	12	9	1391[2]	**1327**	**8.6**	448	26	393	435	**.257**	1.236	2.90	105	2.90	17.9	97	.968	200	125	3.4	1.9	1.9	.4	4.2	1.8
PIT	92	17	10	1415[1]	1389	8.8	454	**25**	**280**	444	.261	**1.179**	2.89	111	**2.74**	55.2	103	**.971**	**186**	119	-4.0	-8.0	5.9	-.4	-2.5	4.5
STL	72	9	**12**	1426[2]	1488	9.4	543	30	479	529	.277	1.379	3.43	89	3.63	-62.5	98	.961	256	136	4.1	**10.5**	-6.7	.4	4.2	-6.2
CHI	**95**	13	9	1388[2]	1459	9.5	504	37	382	508	.276	1.326	3.27	98	3.44	7.0	102	.965	225	112	-16.8	-1.6	.8	-1.8	-2.6	.6
BOS	93	14	6	1386[1]	1464	9.5	545	39	415	368	.280	1.355	3.54	**86**	3.59	-91.2	97	.964	239	125	15.3	-2.4	-9.8	1.6	-10.5	-3.5
PHI	77	8	11	1380[2]	1480	9.6	557	35	444	419	.284	1.394	3.63	94	3.73	-32.5	109	.964	232	135	-0.4	-5.5	-3.5	.0	-9.1	-4.9
Total	**694**	**108**	**76**	**11225[1]**		**9.1**	**3904**					**1.281**	**3.13**													

Wins
Alexander, G. (Chi) 27
Cooper, W. (Pit) 24
Grimes, B. (Bro) 23

Win Percentage
Grimes, B. (Bro) .676
Alexander, G. (Chi) .659
Toney, F. (NY) .656

Games
Haines, J. (StL) 47
Alexander, G. (Chi) 46
Douglas, P. (NY) 46

Complete Games
Alexander, G. (Chi) 33
Cooper, W. (Pit) 28
2 players tied with 25

Shutouts
Adams, B. (Pit) 8
Alexander, G. (Chi) 7
4 players tied with 5

Saves
Sherdel, B. (StL) 6
Alexander, G. (Chi) 5
McQuillan, H. (Bos) 5

Innings Pitched
Alexander, G. (Chi) 363[1]
Cooper, W. (Pit) 327
Grimes, B. (Bro) 303[2]

Fewest Hits/Game
Luque, D. (Cin) 7.28
Ruether, D. (Cin) 7.96
Grimes, B. (Bro) 8.03

Fewest BB/Game
Adams, B. (Pit) .62
Cooper, W. (Pit) 1.43
Nehf, A. (NY) 1.44

Strikeouts
Alexander, G. (Chi) 173
Grimes, B. (Bro) 131
Vaughn, H. (Chi) 131

Ratio
Adams, B. (Pit) .98
Cooper, W. (Pit) 1.10
Luque, D. (Cin) 1.10

Earned Run Average
Alexander, G. (Chi) 1.91
Adams, B. (Pit) 2.16
Grimes, B. (Bro) 2.22

Adjusted ERA
Alexander, G. (Chi) 168
Adams, B. (Pit) 149
Grimes, B. (Bro) 144

Component ERA
Adams, B. (Pit) 1.94
Luque, D. (Cin) 2.25
Grimes, B. (Bro) 2.28

Opponents' Batting Avg.
Luque, D. (Cin) .225
Grimes, B. (Bro) .238
Adams, B. (Pit) .244

Adjusted Pitching Runs
Alexander, G. (Chi) 57
Grimes, B. (Bro) 37
Adams, B. (Pit) 32

Win Shares – Pitchers
Alexander, G. (Chi) 36
Grimes, B. (Bro) 32
Cooper, W. (Pit) 31

TPW – Pitchers
Alexander, G. (Chi) 6.6
Grimes, B. (Bro) 5.1
Cooper, W. (Pit) 3.3

1920 American League

TEAM	G	W	L	PCT	GB	R	OR	EW	AB	H	2B	3B	HR	TB	BB	SO	SB	CS	AVG	OBP	SLG	OPS	OPS+	BR/A	PF	RC
CLE	154	98	56	.636	....	**857**	642	99	5196	1574	**300**	95	35	2169	**576**	379	73	93	.303	**.376**	.417	**.794**	**113**	**95**	103	**827**
CHI	154	96	58	.623	2	794	665	91	5328	1574	263	**98**	37	2144	471	355	109	96	.295	.357	.402	.759	107	49	100	769
NY	154	95	59	.617	3	838	**629**	99	5176	1448	268	71	**115**	2203	539	626	64	82	.280	.350	**.426**	.776	107	40	104	773
STL	154	76	77	.497	21.5	797	766	80	**5358**	**1651**	279	83	50	**2246**	427	**339**	121	79	**.308**	.363	.419	.783	110	76	103	821
BOS	154	72	81	.471	25.5	650	698	71	5199	1397	216	71	22	1821	533	429	98	111	.269	.342	.350	.692	93	-49	96	637
WAS	153	68	84	.447	29	723	802	68	5251	1526	233	81	36	2029	433	543	**160**	114	.291	.351	.386	.737	104	30	97	718
DET	155	61	93	.396	37	652	833	59	5215	1408	228	72	30	1870	479	391	76	68	.270	.334	.359	.692	91	-57	97	640
PHI	156	48	106	.312	50	558	834	48	5256	1324	220	49	44	1774	353	593	67	**43**	.252	.305	.338	.642	74	-196	101	543
Total	**617**					**5869**			**41979**	**11902**	**2007**	**620**	**369**		**3811**	**3655**	**768**	**686**	**.284**	**.347**	**.387**	**.735**				

Runs
Ruth, B. (NY) 158
Sisler, G. (StL) 137
Speaker, T. (Cle) 137

Hits
Sisler, G. (StL) 257
Collins, E. (Chi) 224
Jackson, J. (Chi) 218

Doubles
Speaker, T. (Cle) 50
Sisler, G. (StL) 49
Jackson, J. (Chi) 42

Triples
Jackson, J. (Chi) 20
Sisler, G. (StL) 18
Hooper, H. (Bos) 17

Home Runs
Ruth, B. (NY) 54
Sisler, G. (StL) 19
Walker, T. (Phi) 17

Total Bases
Sisler, G. (StL) 399
Ruth, B. (NY) 388
Jackson, J. (Chi) 336

Runs Batted In
Ruth, B. (NY) 137
Jacobson, B. (StL) 122
Sisler, G. (StL) 122

Bases On Balls
Ruth, B. (NY) 150
Speaker, T. (Cle) 97
Hooper, H. (Bos) 88

Stolen Bases
Rice, S. (Was) 63
Sisler, G. (StL) 42
Roth, B. (Was) 24

Batting Average
Sisler, G. (StL) .407
Speaker, T. (Cle) .388
Jackson, J. (Chi) .382

On-Base Percentage
Ruth, B. (NY) .532
Speaker, T. (Cle) .483
Sisler, G. (StL) .449

Slugging Average
Ruth, B. (NY) .847
Sisler, G. (StL) .632
Jackson, J. (Chi) .589

Adjusted OPS
Ruth, B. (NY) 252
Sisler, G. (StL) 179
Jackson, J. (Chi) 172

Adjusted Batting Runs
Ruth, B. (NY) 108.0
Sisler, G. (StL) 72.0
Speaker, T. (Cle) 61.0

Runs Created/Game
Ruth, B. (NY) 18.40
Sisler, G. (StL) 11.50
Speaker, T. (Cle) 10.80

Fielding Runs
Collins, E. (Chi) 24.1
Ward, A. (NY) 18.5
Perkins, C. (Phi) 18.2

Win Shares – Batters
Ruth, B. (NY) 51
Speaker, T. (Cle) 39
Collins, E. (Chi) 38

TPW – Batters
Ruth, B. (NY) 10.0
Sisler, G. (StL) 7.6
Collins, E. (Chi) 7.0

TEAM	CG	SH	SV	IP	H	H/G	ER	HR	BB	SO	OAV	RAT	ERA	ERA+	CERA	PR+	PF	FA	E	DP	FR	BW	PW	FW	TPW	DIF
CLE	94	11	7	1377	1448	9.5	522	31	401	466	.276	1.343	3.41	111	3.56	32.3	100	.971	184	124	26.2	9.2	3.1	2.5	14.8	6.2
CHI	109	9	10	1386²	1467	9.5	553	45	405	438	.280	1.350	3.59	105	3.64	8.6	99	.968	198	142	17.7	4.8	.8	1.7	7.3	11.7
NY	88	15	11	1368	1414	9.3	505	48	420	480	.269	1.341	3.32	115	3.45	74.7	101	.970	194	129	0.9	3.9	7.2	.1	11.3	6.7
STL	84	9	14	1378²	1481	9.7	617	53	578	444	.283	1.493	4.03	97	4.24	-21.7	103	.963	233	119	2.6	7.4	-2.1	.2	5.6	-5.6
BOS	92	11	6	1395¹	1481	9.6	592	39	461	481	.279	1.392	3.82	95	3.69	-45.5	96	.972	183	131	17.9	-4.8	-4.4	1.7	-7.5	3.5
WAS	81	10	10	1367	1521	10.0	633	51	520	418	.287	1.493	4.17	89	4.31	-57.2	98	.963	232	95	-11.0	2.9	-5.5	-1.1	-3.7	-4.3
DET	74	9	7	1385	1487	9.7	622	46	561	483	.284	1.479	4.04	92	4.26	-21.5	98	.965	230	95	-28.0	-5.5	-2.1	-2.7	-10.3	-5.7
PHI	79	6	2	1380¹	1612	10.5	603	56	461	423	.302	1.502	3.93	102	4.60	39.4	106	.959	266	125	-25.4	-19.0	3.8	-2.5	-17.7	-11.3
Total	701	80	67	11038		9.7	4647					1.424	3.79													

Wins
Bagby, J. (Cle) 31 · Mays, C. (NY) 26 · Coveleski, S. (Cle) 24

Win Percentage
Bagby, J. (Cle) .721 · Mays, C. (NY) .703 · Kerr, D. (Chi) .700

Games
Bagby, J. (Cle) 48 · Cicotte, E. (Chi) 46 · 2 players tied with 45

Complete Games
Bagby, J. (Cle) 30 · Shawkey, B. (NY) 28 · Faber, R. (Chi) 28

Shutouts
Mays, C. (NY) 6 · Shawkey, B. (NY) 5 · Shocker, U. (StL) 5

Saves
Kerr, D. (Chi) 5 · Shocker, U. (StL) 5 · Burwell, B. (StL) 4

Innings Pitched
Bagby, J. (Cle) 339² · Faber, R. (Chi) 319 · Coveleski, S. (Cle) 315

Fewest Hits/Game
Coveleski, S. (Cle) 8.11 · Shocker, U. (StL) 8.21 · Collins, R. (NY) 8.22

Fewest BB/Game
Quinn, J. (NY) 1.71 · Coveleski, S. (Cle) 1.86 · Bagby, J. (Cle) 2.09

Strikeouts
Coveleski, S. (Cle) 133 · Williams, L. (Chi) 128 · Shawkey, B. (NY) 126

Ratio
Coveleski, S. (Cle) 1.11 · Shocker, U. (StL) 1.20 · Rommel, E. (Phi) 1.20

Earned Run Average
Shawkey, B. (NY) 2.45 · Coveleski, S. (Cle) 2.49 · Shocker, U. (StL) 2.71

Adjusted ERA
Shawkey, B. (NY) 155 · Coveleski, S. (Cle) 153 · Shocker, U. (StL) 144

Component ERA
Coveleski, S. (Cle) 2.39 · Rommel, E. (Phi) 2.84 · Quinn, J. (NY) 2.85

Opponents' Batting Avg.
Coveleski, S. (Cle) .243 · Collins, R. (NY) .247 · 2 players tied with .248

Adjusted Pitching Runs
Coveleski, S. (Cle) 40 · Coveleski, S. (Cle) 40 · Shocker, U. (StL) 32

Win Shares – Pitchers
Bagby, J. (Cle) 34 · Coveleski, S. (Cle) 32 · 2 players tied with 27

TPW – Pitchers
Coveleski, S. (Cle) 4.2 · Shawkey, B. (NY) 3.9 · Shocker, U. (StL) 3.4

1921 National League

TEAM	G	W	L	PCT	GB	R	OR	EW	AB	H	2B	3B	HR	TB	BB	SO	SB	CS	AVG	OBP	SLG	OPS	OPS+	BR/A	PF	RC
NY	153	94	59	.614	....	840	637	97	5278	1575	237	93	75	2223	469	390	137	114	.298	.359	.421	.781	112	95	100	795
PIT	154	90	63	.588	4	692	595	88	5379	1533	231	104	37	2083	341	371	134	93	.285	.330	.387	.718	93	-46	103	684
STL	154	87	66	.569	7	809	681	90	5309	1635	260	88	83	2320	382	452	94	94	.308	.358	.437	.795	118	130	98	816
BOS	153	79	74	.516	15	721	697	79	5385	1561	209	100	61	2153	377	470	94	100	.290	.339	.400	.739	107	45	94	718
BRO	152	77	75	.507	16.5	667	681	74	5263	1476	209	85	59	2032	325	400	91	73	.280	.325	.386	.711	90	-67	104	655
CIN	153	70	83	.458	24	618	649	73	5112	1421	221	94	20	1890	375	308	117	120	.278	.333	.370	.703	96	-32	95	623
CHI	153	64	89	.418	30	668	773	65	5321	1553	234	56	37	2010	343	374	70	97	.292	.339	.378	.717	95	-39	100	671
PHI	154	51	103	.331	43.5	617	919	48	5329	1512	238	50	88	2114	294	615	66	80	.284	.324	.397	.721	89	-88	108	668
Total	613					5632			42376	12266	1839	670	460		2906	3380	803	771	.289	.338	.397	.736				

Runs
Hornsby, R. (StL) 131 · Bancroft, D. (NY) 121 · Frisch, F. (NY) 121

Hits
Hornsby, R. (StL) 235 · Frisch, F. (NY) 211 · Bigbee, C. (Pit) 204

Doubles
Hornsby, R. (StL) 44 · Kelly, G. (NY) 42 · Johnston, J. (Bro) 41

Triples
Hornsby, R. (StL) 18 · Powell, R. (Bos) 18 · 3 players tied with 17

Home Runs
Kelly, G. (NY) 23 · Hornsby, R. (StL) 21 · Williams, C. (Phi) 18

Total Bases
Hornsby, R. (StL) 378 · Kelly, G. (NY) 310 · McHenry, A. (StL) 305

Runs Batted In
Hornsby, R. (StL) 126 · Kelly, G. (NY) 122 · 2 players tied with 102

Bases On Balls
Burns, G. (NY) 80 · Youngs, R. (NY) 71 · 2 players tied with 70

Stolen Bases
Frisch, F. (NY) 49 · Carey, M. (Pit) 37 · Johnston, J. (Bro) 28

Batting Average
Hornsby, R. (StL) .397 · McHenry, A. (StL) .350 · Fournier, J. (StL) .343

On-Base Percentage
Hornsby, R. (StL) .458 · Youngs, R. (NY) .411 · Fournier, J. (StL) .409

Slugging Average
Hornsby, R. (StL) .639 · McHenry, A. (StL) .531 · Kelly, G. (NY) .528

Adjusted OPS
Hornsby, R. (StL) 191 · McHenry, A. (StL) 145 · Fournier, J. (StL) 143

Adjusted Batting Runs
Hornsby, R. (StL) 77.0 · Fournier, J. (StL) 34.0 · Frisch, F. (NY) 32.0

Runs Created/Game
Hornsby, R. (StL) 11.60 · McHenry, A. (StL) 7.20 · Meusel, I. (Phi,NY) 7.20

Fielding Runs
Lavan, J. (StL) 25.4 · Maranville, R. (Pit) 21.0 · Bancroft, D. (NY) 21.0

Win Shares – Batters
Hornsby, R. (StL) 41 · Bancroft, D. (NY) 31 · Frisch, F. (NY) 31

TPW – Batters
Hornsby, R. (StL) 8.5 · Bancroft, D. (NY) 5.7 · Frisch, F. (NY) 5.1

TEAM	CG	SH	SV	IP	H	H/G	ER	HR	BB	SO	OAV	RAT	ERA	ERA+	CERA	PR+	PF	FA	E	DP	FR	BW	PW	FW	TPW	DIF
NY	71	9	18	1372¹	1497	9.8	541	79	295	357	.286	1.306	3.55	103	3.61	-22.5	97	.971	187	155	39.4	9.4	-2.2	3.9	11.1	6.9
PIT	88	10	10	1415²	1448	9.2	498	37	322	500	.271	1.250	3.17	121	3.13	99.7	101	.973	172	129	5.0	-4.5	9.8	.5	5.8	8.2
STL	70	10	16	1371²	1486	9.8	551	61	399	464	.282	1.374	3.62	101	3.80	3.4	96	.965	219	130	0.2	12.8	.3	.0	13.2	-2.2
BOS	74	11	12	1385	1488	9.7	600	54	420	382	.280	1.378	3.90	94	3.75	-47.5	96	.969	199	122	8.5	4.4	-4.7	.8	.6	2.4
BRO	82	8	12	1363¹	1556	10.3	560	46	361	471	.293	1.406	3.70	105	3.92	33.5	103	.964	232	142	-5.1	-6.6	3.3	-.5	-3.8	4.8
CIN	83	7	9	1363	1500	9.9	524	37	305	408	.287	1.324	3.46	103	3.48	36.5	95	.969	193	139	-19.0	-3.2	3.6	-1.9	-1.5	-4.5
CHI	73	7	7	1363	1605	10.6	665	67	409	441	.303	1.478	4.39	87	4.42	-89.7	101	.974	166	129	3.0	-3.9	-8.9	.3	-12.5	.5
PHI	82	5	8	1348²	1665	11.1	671	79	371	333	.308	1.510	4.48	94	4.61	-11.9	112	.955	295	127	-26.1	-8.6	-1.2	-2.6	-12.4	-13.6
Total	623	67	92	10982²		10.0	4610					1.377	3.78													

Wins
Cooper, W. (Pit) 22 · Grimes, B. (Bro) 22 · 2 players tied with 20

Win Percentage
Adams, B. (Pit) .737 · Glazner, W. (Pit) .737 · Doak, B. (StL) .714

Games
Scott, J. (Bos) 47 · Oeschger, J. (Bos) 46 · McQuillan, H. (Bos) 45

Complete Games
Grimes, B. (Bro) 30 · Cooper, W. (Pit) 29 · Luque, D. (Cin) 25

Shutouts
8 players tied with 3

Saves
North, L. (StL) 7 · Barnes, J. (NY) 6 · McQuillan, H. (Bos) 5

Innings Pitched
Cooper, W. (Pit) 327 · Luque, D. (Cin) 304 · Grimes, B. (Bro) 302¹

Fewest Hits/Game
Glazner, W. (Pit) 8.23 · Adams, B. (Pit) 8.72 · Oeschger, J. (Bos) 9.12

Fewest BB/Game
Adams, B. (Pit) 1.01 · Alexander, G. (Chi) 1.18 · Barnes, J. (NY) 1.53

Strikeouts
Grimes, B. (Bro) 136 · Cooper, W. (Pit) 134 · Luque, D. (Cin) 102

Ratio
Adams, B. (Pit) 1.08 · Glazner, W. (Pit) 1.16 · Nehf, A. (NY) 1.23

Earned Run Average
Doak, B. (StL) 2.59 · Adams, B. (Pit) 2.64 · Glazner, W. (Pit) 2.77

Adjusted ERA
Adams, B. (Pit) 145 · Doak, B. (StL) 141 · Glazner, W. (Pit) 138

Component ERA
Adams, B. (Pit) 2.32 · Glazner, W. (Pit) 2.71 · Doak, B. (StL) 3.10

Opponents' Batting Avg.
Glazner, W. (Pit) .250 · Adams, B. (Pit) .251 · Pertica, B. (StL) .267

Adjusted Pitching Runs
Grimes, B. (Bro) 37 · Rixey, E. (Cin) 31 · Glazner, W. (Pit) 27

Win Shares – Pitchers
Grimes, B. (Bro) 29 · Cooper, W. (Pit) 27 · Luque, D. (Cin) 23

TPW – Pitchers
Grimes, B. (Bro) 3.8 · Rixey, E. (Cin) 2.5 · Mitchell, C. (Bro) 2.5

1921 American League

TEAM	G	W	L	PCT	GB	R	OR	EW	AB	H	2B	3B	HR	TB	BB	SO	SB	CS	AVG	OBP	SLG	OPS	OPS+	BR/A	PF	RC
NY	153	98	55	.641	....	948	708	98	5249	1576	285	87	134	2437	588	569	89	64	.300	.375	.464	.839	116	127	102	929
CLE	154	94	60	.610	4.5	925	712	97	5383	1656	355	90	42	2317	623	376	51	42	.308	.383	.430	.814	111	105	102	916
STL	154	81	73	.526	17.5	835	845	76	5442	1655	246	106	67	2314	413	407	91	71	.304	.357	.425	.782	99	-18	106	827
WAS	154	80	73	.523	18	704	738	73	5294	1468	240	96	42	2026	462	472	112	66	.277	.342	.383	.725	94	-37	95	711
BOS	154	75	79	.487	23.5	668	696	74	5206	1440	248	69	17	1877	428	344	83	65	.277	.335	.361	.695	84	-116	97	641
DET	154	71	82	.464	27	883	852	79	5461	1724	268	100	58	2366	582	376	95	89	.316	.385	.433	.818	115	124	99	920
CHI	154	62	92	.403	36.5	683	858	60	5329	1509	242	82	35	2020	445	474	94	93	.283	.345	.379	.722	90	-84	99	698
PHI	155	53	100	.346	45	657	894	54	5465	1497	256	64	82	2127	424	565	69	56	.274	.331	.389	.721	88	-104	101	711
Total	616					6303			42829	12525	2140	694	477		3965	3583	684	546	.292	.357	.408	.765				

Runs	
Ruth, B. (NY)	177
Tobin, J. (StL)	132
Peckinpaugh, R. (NY)	128

Hits	
Heilmann, H. (Det)	237
Tobin, J. (StL)	236
Sisler, G. (StL)	216

Doubles	
Speaker, T. (Cle)	52
Ruth, B. (NY)	44
2 players tied with	43

Triples	
Shanks, H. (Was)	18
Sisler, G. (StL)	18
Tobin, J. (StL)	18

Home Runs	
Ruth, B. (NY)	59
Meusel, B. (NY)	24
Williams, K. (StL)	24

Total Bases	
Ruth, B. (NY)	457
Heilmann, H. (Det)	365
Meusel, B. (NY)	334

Runs Batted In	
Ruth, B. (NY)	171
Heilmann, H. (Det)	139
Meusel, B. (NY)	135

Bases On Balls	
Ruth, B. (NY)	145
Blue, L. (Det)	103
Peckinpaugh, R. (NY)	84

Stolen Bases	
Sisler, G. (StL)	35
Harris, B. (Was)	29
Rice, S. (Was)	26

Batting Average	
Heilmann, H. (Det)	.394
Cobb, T. (Det)	.389
Ruth, B. (NY)	.378

On-Base Percentage	
Ruth, B. (NY)	.512
Cobb, T. (Det)	.452
Heilmann, H. (Det)	.444

Slugging Average	
Ruth, B. (NY)	.846
Heilmann, H. (Det)	.606
Cobb, T. (Det)	.596

Adjusted OPS	
Ruth, B. (NY)	236
Heilmann, H. (Det)	167
Cobb, T. (Det)	167

Adjusted Batting Runs	
Ruth, B. (NY)	117.0
Heilmann, H. (Det)	59.0
Cobb, T. (Det)	51.0

Runs Created/Game	
Ruth, B. (NY)	17.90
Heilmann, H. (Det)	10.90
Cobb, T. (Det)	10.40

Fielding Runs	
Scott, E. (Bos)	37.8
Dykes, J. (Phi)	24.7
Harris, B. (Was)	17.6

Win Shares – Batters	
Ruth, B. (NY)	53
Heilmann, H. (Det)	28
3 players tied with	27

TPW – Batters	
Ruth, B. (NY)	9.8
Cobb, T. (Det)	4.8
Sewell, J. (Cle)	3.8

TEAM	CG	SH	SV	IP	H	H/G	ER	HR	BB	SO	OAV	RAT	ERA	ERA+	CERA	PR+	PF	FA	E	DP	FR	BW	PW	FW	TPW	DIF
NY	**92**	8	15	1364	**1461**	**9.6**	**579**	51	470	**481**	**.277**	**1.416**	**3.82**	111	**3.88**	46.9	99	.965	222	138	15.9	**11.9**	4.4	1.5	**17.8**	4.2
CLE	81	**11**	14	1377	1534	10.0	597	**43**	**431**	475	.288	1.427	3.90	109	3.90	**55.9**	100	.967	204	124	-1.4	9.8	**5.2**	-.1	14.9	2.1
STL	77	9	9	1379	1541	10.1	706	71	556	477	.288	1.521	4.61	97	4.40	-14.1	105	.964	224	127	-7.2	-1.7	-1.3	-.7	-3.7	7.7
WAS	80	10	10	1383^2	1568	10.2	610	51	442	452	.290	1.453	3.97	104	4.10	0.0	96	.963	235	153	21.0	-3.5	.0	2.0	-1.5	5.5
BOS	88	9	5	1364^1	1521	10.0	603	53	452	446	.291	1.446	3.98	106	4.10	6.8	99	**.975**	**157**	151	**29.3**	-10.9	.6	**2.7**	-7.5	5.5
DET	73	4	**17**	1386^1	1634	10.6	678	71	495	452	.297	1.536	4.40	97	4.60	11.6	100	.964	232	107	-33.0	11.6	1.1	-3.1	9.6	-14.6
CHI	84	7	9	1365^1	1603	10.6	749	52	549	392	.303	1.576	4.94	**86**	4.70	-110.0	99	.969	200	**155**	3.1	-7.9	-10.3	.3	-17.9	2.9
PHI	75	2	7	**1400^1**	1645	10.6	717	85	548	431	.300	1.566	4.61	97	4.74	1.2	104	.957	274	144	-26.1	-9.7	.1	-2.4	-12.0	-11.0
Total	**650**	**60**	**86**	**11020**		**10.2**	**5239**					**1.493**	**4.28**													

Wins	
Mays, C. (NY)	27
Shocker, U. (StL)	27
Faber, R. (Chi)	25

Win Percentage	
Mays, C. (NY)	.750
Shocker, U. (StL)	.692
Bayne, B. (StL)	.688

Games	
Mays, C. (NY)	49
Bayne, B. (StL)	47
Shocker, U. (StL)	47

Complete Games	
Faber, R. (Chi)	32
Mays, C. (NY)	30
Shocker, U. (StL)	30

Shutouts	
Jones, S. (Bos)	5
3 players tied with	4

Saves	
Mays, C. (NY)	7
Middleton, J. (Det)	7
4 players tied with	4

Innings Pitched	
Mays, C. (NY)	336^2
Faber, R. (Chi)	330^2
Shocker, U. (StL)	326^2

Fewest Hits/Game	
Faber, R. (Chi)	7.97
Bush, J. (Bos)	8.63
Mays, C. (NY)	8.88

Fewest BB/Game	
Hasty, B. (Phi)	2.01
Mays, C. (NY)	2.03
Mogridge, G. (Was)	2.06

Strikeouts	
Johnson, W. (Was)	143
Shocker, U. (StL)	132
Shawkey, B. (NY)	126

Ratio	
Faber, R. (Chi)	1.15
Mays, C. (NY)	1.21
Mogridge, G. (Was)	1.27

Earned Run Average	
Faber, R. (Chi)	2.48
Mogridge, G. (Was)	3.00
Mays, C. (NY)	3.05

Adjusted ERA	
Faber, R. (Chi)	171
Mays, C. (NY)	139
Mogridge, G. (Was)	137

Component ERA	
Faber, R. (Chi)	2.53
Mays, C. (NY)	2.93
Jones, S. (Bos)	3.27

Opponents' Batting Avg.	
Faber, R. (Chi)	.242
Mays, C. (NY)	.257
Bush, J. (Bos)	.260

Adjusted Pitching Runs	
Faber, R. (Chi)	64
Mays, C. (NY)	40
Shocker, U. (StL)	35

Win Shares – Pitchers	
Faber, R. (Chi)	37
Mays, C. (NY)	35
Shocker, U. (StL)	30

TPW – Pitchers	
Faber, R. (Chi)	5.7
Mays, C. (NY)	4.8
Shocker, U. (StL)	3.8

1922 National League

TEAM	G	W	L	PCT	GB	R	OR	EW	AB	H	2B	3B	HR	TB	BB	SO	SB	CS	AVG	OBP	SLG	OPS	OPS+	BR/A	PF	RC
NY	156	93	61	.604	....	852	**658**	96	5454	1661	253	90	80	2334	448	421	116	83	.305	**.363**	.428	.790	109	74	101	848
CIN	156	86	68	.558	7	766	677	86	5282	1561	226	99	45	2120	436	381	130	136	.296	.353	.401	.755	103	5	98	737
STL	154	85	69	.552	8	863	819	81	5425	1634	**280**	88	107	**2411**	447	425	73	63	.301	.357	**.444**	**.802**	**118**	**136**	95	**860**
PIT	155	85	69	.552	8	**865**	736	89	**5521**	**1698**	239	**110**	52	2313	423	326	**145**	**59**	**.308**	.360	.419	.779	106	66	101	848
CHI	156	80	74	.519	13	771	808	73	5335	1564	248	71	42	2080	**525**	447	97	108	.293	.359	.390	.749	98	-19	102	752
BRO	155	76	78	.494	17	743	754	76	5413	1569	235	76	56	2124	339	**318**	79	60	.290	.335	.392	.727	94	-48	99	709
PHI	154	57	96	.373	35.5	738	920	60	5459	1537	268	55	**116**	2263	450	611	48	60	.282	.341	.415	.755	92	-72	110	771
BOS	154	53	100	.346	39.5	596	822	53	5161	1355	162	73	32	1759	387	451	67	65	.263	.317	.341	.658	79	-152	96	566
Total	**620**					**6194**			**43050**	**12579**	**1911**	**662**	**530**		**3455**	**3380**	**755**	**634**	**.292**	**.348**	**.404**	**.753**				

Runs	
Hornsby, R. (StL)	141
Carey, M. (Pit)	140
2 players tied with	117

Hits	
Hornsby, R. (StL)	250
Bigbee, C. (Pit)	215
Bancroft, D. (NY)	209

Doubles	
Hornsby, R. (StL)	46
Grimes, R. (Chi)	45
Duncan, P. (Cin)	44

Triples	
Daubert, J. (Cin)	22
Meusel, I. (NY)	17
2 players tied with	15

Home Runs	
Hornsby, R. (StL)	42
Williams, C. (Phi)	26
2 players tied with	17

Total Bases	
Hornsby, R. (StL)	450
Meusel, I. (NY)	314
Wheat, Z. (Bro)	302

Runs Batted In	
Hornsby, R. (StL)	152
Meusel, I. (NY)	132
Wheat, Z. (Bro)	112

Bases On Balls	
Carey, M. (Pit)	80
Bancroft, D. (NY)	79
O'Farrell, B. (Chi)	79

Stolen Bases	
Carey, M. (Pit)	51
Frisch, F. (NY)	31
Burns, G. (Cin)	30

Batting Average	
Hornsby, R. (StL)	.401
Grimes, R. (Chi)	.354
Miller, H. (Chi)	.352

On-Base Percentage	
Hornsby, R. (StL)	.459
Grimes, R. (Chi)	.442
O'Farrell, B. (Chi)	.439

Slugging Average	
Hornsby, R. (StL)	.722
Grimes, R. (Chi)	.572
Tierney, C. (Pit)	.515

Adjusted OPS	
Hornsby, R. (StL)	210
Grimes, R. (Chi)	157
Daubert, J. (Cin)	130

Adjusted Batting Runs	
Hornsby, R. (StL)	99.0
Grimes, R. (Chi)	45.0
Carey, M. (Pit)	36.0

Runs Created/Game	
Hornsby, R. (StL)	13.30
Grimes, R. (Chi)	10.10
Carey, M. (Pit)	7.90

Fielding Runs	
Bancroft, D. (NY)	25.1
Maranville, R. (Pit)	22.9
Pinelli, B. (Cin)	21.2

Win Shares – Batters	
Hornsby, R. (StL)	47
Carey, M. (Pit)	29
Grimes, R. (Chi)	29

TPW – Batters	
Hornsby, R. (StL)	9.2
Bancroft, D. (NY)	5.2
O'Farrell, B. (Chi)	4.3

TEAM	CG	SH	SV	IP	H	H/G	ER	HR	BB	SO	OAV	RAT	ERA	ERA+	CERA	PR+	PF	FA	E	DP	FR	BW	PW	FW	TPW	DIF
NY	76	7	**15**	1396^1	**1454**	**9.4**	**535**	71	393	388	**.272**	1.323	**3.45**	116	3.51	**43.0**	98	**.970**	194	145	**41.4**	7.0	**4.1**	**3.9**	**15.0**	1.0
CIN	**88**	8	3	1385^2	1481	9.6	543	**49**	**326**	357	.278	**1.304**	3.53	113	**3.40**	37.4	97	.968	205	147	32.5	.5	3.5	3.1	7.1	1.9
STL	60	8	12	1362^2	1609	10.6	672	61	447	465	.299	1.509	4.44	**87**	4.47	-57.3	94	.961	239	122	-30.0	**12.8**	-5.4	-2.8	4.6	3.4
PIT	**88**	**15**	7	1387^1	1613	10.5	613	52	358	490	.296	1.421	3.98	102	4.01	35.3	99	.970	**187**	126	-21.7	6.2	3.3	-2.1	7.5	.5
CHI	74	8	12	**1397^2**	1579	10.2	674	77	475	402	.292	1.470	4.34	97	4.37	-32.9	102	.968	204	**154**	10.8	-1.7	-3.1	1.0	-3.8	6.8
BRO	82	12	8	1385^2	1574	10.2	623	74	490	**499**	.293	1.490	4.05	100	4.37	12.3	99	.967	208	139	-9.7	-4.5	1.2	-.9	-4.3	3.3
PHI	73	6	5	1372	1692	11.1	707	89	460	394	.307	1.569	4.64	100	4.91	9.5	114	.965	225	152	-6.1	-6.8	.9	-.6	-6.5	-12.5
BOS	63	7	6	1348	1565	10.4	655	57	489	360	.298	1.524	4.37	91	4.45	-40.6	98	.965	215	121	-16.0	-14.3	-3.8	-1.5	-19.7	-3.3
Total	**604**	**71**	**68**	**11035^1**		**10.2**	**5022**					**1.450**	**4.10**													

Wins	
Rixey, E. (Cin)	25
Cooper, W. (Pit)	23
Ruether, D. (Bro)	21

Win Percentage	
Douglas, P. (NY)	.733
Donohue, P. (Cin)	.667
Rixey, E. (Cin)	.658

Games	
North, L. (StL)	53
Sherdel, B. (StL)	47
2 players tied with	46

Complete Games	
Cooper, W. (Pit)	27
Rixey, E. (Cin)	26
Ruether, D. (Bro)	26

Shutouts	
Morrison, J. (Pit)	5
Vance, D. (Bro)	5
2 players tied with	4

Saves	
Jonnard, C. (NY)	5
North, L. (StL)	4
4 players tied with	3

Innings Pitched	
Rixey, E. (Cin)	313^1
Cooper, W. (Pit)	294^2
Morrison, J. (Pit)	286^1

Fewest Hits/Game	
Douglas, P. (NY)	8.79
Osborne, T. (Chi)	8.95
Ryan, R. (NY)	9.11

Fewest BB/Game	
Adams, B. (Pit)	.79
Alexander, G. (Chi)	1.25
Rixey, E. (Cin)	1.29

Strikeouts	
Vance, D. (Bro)	134
Cooper, W. (Pit)	129
Ring, J. (Phi)	116

Ratio	
Douglas, P. (NY)	1.20
Adams, B. (Pit)	1.20
Rixey, E. (Cin)	1.22

Earned Run Average	
Douglas, P. (NY)	2.63
Ryan, R. (NY)	3.01
Donohue, P. (Cin)	3.12

Adjusted ERA	
Douglas, P. (NY)	152
Weinert, L. (Phi)	137
Ryan, R. (NY)	133

Component ERA	
Douglas, P. (NY)	2.91
Adams, B. (Pit)	2.95
Rixey, E. (Cin)	3.11

Opponents' Batting Avg.	
Douglas, P. (NY)	.257
Luque, D. (Cin)	.268
Ryan, R. (NY)	.269

Adjusted Pitching Runs	
Cooper, W. (Pit)	34
Morrison, J. (Pit)	25
Weinert, L. (Phi)	24

Win Shares – Pitchers	
Cooper, W. (Pit)	27
Rixey, E. (Cin)	23
3 players tied with	21

TPW – Pitchers	
Cooper, W. (Pit)	4.1
Weinert, L. (Phi)	2.4
Ruether, D. (Bro)	2.2

1922 American League

TEAM	G	W	L	PCT	GB	R	OR	EW	AB	H	2B	3B	HR	TB	BB	SO	SB	CS	AVG	OBP	SLG	OPS	OPS+	BR/A	PF	RC
NY	154	94	60	.610	....	758	**618**	93	5245	1504	220	75	95	2159	497	532	62	59	.287	.353	.412	.765	103	18	102	774
STL	154	93	61	.604	1	**867**	643	99	**5416**	**1693**	291	**94**	98	**2466**	473	381	**136**	76	**.313**	.372	**.455**	**.827**	**117**	**134**	103	**923**
DET	155	79	75	.513	15	828	791	81	5360	1641	250	87	54	2227	530	378	78	62	.306	**.372**	.415	.788	115	122	97	847
CLE	155	78	76	.506	16	768	817	72	5293	1544	**320**	73	32	2106	**554**	**331**	90	**58**	.292	.364	.398	.762	104	43	101	792
CHI	155	77	77	.500	17	691	691	77	5267	1463	243	62	45	1965	482	463	109	84	.278	.343	.373	.716	93	-52	100	690
WAS	154	69	85	.448	25	650	706	71	5201	1395	229	76	45	1911	458	442	97	63	.268	.334	.367	.701	93	-42	95	659
PHI	155	65	89	.422	29	705	830	65	5211	1409	229	63	**111**	2097	437	591	60	69	.270	.331	.402	.733	94	-60	103	696
BOS	154	61	93	.396	33	598	769	58	5288	1392	250	55	45	1887	366	455	64	67	.263	.316	.357	.673	81	-150	99	600
Total	**618**					**5865**			**42281**	**12041**	**2032**	**585**	**525**		**3797**	**3573**	**696**	**538**	**.285**	**.348**	**.398**	**.746**				

Runs
Sisler, G. (StL) 134
Blue, L. (Det) 131
Williams, K. (StL) 128

Hits
Sisler, G. (StL) 246
Cobb, T. (Det) 211
Tobin, J. (StL) 207

Doubles
Speaker, T. (Cle) 48
Pratt, D. (Bos) 44
2 players tied with 42

Triples
Sisler, G. (StL) 18
Cobb, T. (Det) 16
Jacobson, B. (StL) 16

Home Runs
Williams, K. (StL) 39
Walker, T. (Phi) 37
Ruth, B. (NY) 35

Total Bases
Williams, K. (StL) 367
Sisler, G. (StL) 348
Walker, T. (Phi) 310

Runs Batted In
Williams, K. (StL) 155
Veach, B. (Det) 126
McManus, M. (StL) 109

Bases On Balls
Witt, W. (NY) 89
Ruth, B. (NY) 84
Blue, L. (Det) 82

Stolen Bases
Sisler, G. (StL) 51
Williams, K. (StL) 37
Harris, B. (Was) 25

Batting Average
Sisler, G. (StL) .420
Cobb, T. (Det) .401
Speaker, T. (Cle) .378

On-Base Percentage
Speaker, T. (Cle) .474
Sisler, G. (StL) .467
Cobb, T. (Det) .462

Slugging Average
Ruth, B. (NY) .672
Williams, K. (StL) .627
Speaker, T. (Cle) .606

Adjusted OPS
Ruth, B. (NY) 181
Speaker, T. (Cle) 178
Cobb, T. (Det) 172

Adjusted Batting Runs
Sisler, G. (StL) 63.0
Speaker, T. (Cle) 54.0
Cobb, T. (Det) 54.0

Runs Created/Game
Speaker, T. (Cle) 12.00
Sisler, G. (StL) 11.50
Ruth, B. (NY) 11.10

Fielding Runs
Scott, E. (NY) 25.6
Ellerbe, F. (StL) 19.9
Harris, B. (Was) 19.2

Win Shares – Batters
Speaker, T. (Cle) 30
Williams, K. (StL) 30
3 players tied with 29

TPW – Batters
Sisler, G. (StL) 5.2
Speaker, T. (Cle) 5.0
Cobb, T. (Det) 4.4

TEAM	CG	SH	SV	IP	H	H/G	ER	HR	BB	SO	OAV	RAT	ERA	ERA+	CERA	PR+	PF	FA	E	DP	FR	BW	PW	FW	TPW	DIF
NY	**100**	7	14	1393^{2}	**1402**	**9.0**	525	73	423	458	**.268**	**1.309**	3.39	118	**3.44**	**82.8**	99	.975	157	124	11.0	1.7	**8.0**	1.1	10.8	6.2
STL	79	8	**22**	1392	1412	9.1	**523**	71	**419**	**534**	.268	1.315	**3.38**	122	3.49	80.9	102	.968	201	158	35.2	**13.0**	7.9	3.4	**24.3**	-8.3
DET	67	7	15	1391	1554	10.0	660	62	473	461	.288	1.457	4.27	91	4.26	-33.1	96	.970	191	133	-28.7	11.8	-3.2	-2.8	5.8	-3.8
CLE	76	**14**	7	1383^{2}	1605	10.4	705	58	464	489	.296	1.495	4.59	**87**	4.37	-50.3	99	.968	202	147	-34.3	4.2	-4.9	-3.3	-4.0	5.0
CHI	86	13	8	**1403^{2}**	1472	9.4	614	57	529	484	.278	1.426	3.94	103	3.86	2.8	101	**.976**	**155**	143	16.6	-5.1	.3	1.6	-3.2	3.2
WAS	84	13	10	1362^{1}	1485	9.8	577	49	500	422	.286	1.457	3.81	101	4.00	-32.3	96	.968	196	**168**	**38.8**	-4.1	-3.1	**3.8**	-3.5	-4.5
PHI	73	4	6	1362^{1}	1573	10.4	695	107	469	373	.297	1.499	4.59	92	4.62	-39.9	105	.965	215	118	-12.8	-5.8	-3.9	-1.2	-10.9	-1.1
BOS	71	10	6	1373^{1}	1508	9.9	656	**48**	503	359	.287	1.464	4.30	95	4.06	-8.4	102	.965	224	145	-22.4	-14.6	-.8	-2.2	-17.6	1.6
Total	**636**	**76**	**88**	**11062**		**9.8**	**4955**					**1.428**	**4.03**													

Wins
Rommel, E. (Phi) 27
Bush, J. (NY) 26
Shocker, U. (StL) 24

Win Percentage
Bush, J. (NY) .788
Kolp, R. (StL) .778
Rommel, E. (Phi) .675

Games
Rommel, E. (Phi) 51
Uhle, G. (Cle) 50
Shocker, U. (StL) 48

Complete Games
Faber, R. (Chi) 31
Shocker, U. (StL) 29
2 players tied with 23

Shutouts
Uhle, G. (Cle) 5
5 players tied with 4

Saves
Jones, S. (NY) 8
Pruett, H. (StL) 7
Wright, R. (StL) 5

Innings Pitched
Faber, R. (Chi) 352
Shocker, U. (StL) 348
Shawkey, B. (NY) 299^{2}

Fewest Hits/Game
Davis, D. (StL) 8.36
Bush, J. (NY) 8.46
Faber, R. (Chi) 8.54

Fewest BB/Game
Shocker, U. (StL) 1.47
Vangilder, E. (StL) 1.76
Mays, C. (NY) 1.88

Strikeouts
Shocker, U. (StL) 149
Faber, R. (Chi) 148
Shawkey, B. (NY) 130

Ratio
Faber, R. (Chi) 1.18
Vangilder, E. (StL) 1.21
Shocker, U. (StL) 1.21

Earned Run Average
Faber, R. (Chi) 2.81
Pillette, H. (Det) 2.85
Shawkey, B. (NY) 2.91

Adjusted ERA
Faber, R. (Chi) 144
Wright, R. (StL) 141
Shocker, U. (StL) 139

Component ERA
Faber, R. (Chi) 2.69
Quinn, J. (Bos) 3.05
Vangilder, E. (StL) 3.16

Opponents' Batting Avg.
Davis, D. (StL) .250
Bush, J. (NY) .252
Faber, R. (Chi) .252

Adjusted Pitching Runs
Faber, R. (Chi) 45
Pillette, H. (Det) 37
Shocker, U. (StL) 36

Win Shares – Pitchers
Faber, R. (Chi) 31
Shocker, U. (StL) 29
2 players tied with 27

TPW – Pitchers
Faber, R. (Chi) 4.2
Shocker, U. (StL) 3.7
Pillette, H. (Det) 3.3

1923 National League

TEAM	G	W	L	PCT	GB	R	OR	EW	AB	H	2B	3B	HR	TB	BB	SO	SB	CS	AVG	OBP	SLG	OPS	OPS+	BR/A	PF	RC
NY	153	95	58	.621	....	**854**	679	94	5452	**1610**	248	76	85	**2265**	**487**	406	106	70	**.295**	**.356**	**.415**	**.772**	**111**	**89**	99	**816**
CIN	154	91	63	.591	4.5	708	**629**	86	5278	1506	237	95	45	2068	439	367	96	105	.285	.344	.392	.736	102	2	98	707
PIT	154	87	67	.565	8.5	786	696	86	5405	1592	224	**111**	49	2185	407	**362**	154	75	.295	.347	.404	.751	101	23	102	766
CHI	154	83	71	.539	12.5	756	704	82	5259	1516	243	52	90	2133	455	485	**181**	143	.288	.348	.406	.754	104	22	100	735
STL	154	79	74	.516	16	746	732	78	**5526**	1582	**274**	76	63	2197	438	446	89	61	.286	.343	.398	.740	103	28	98	761
BRO	155	76	78	.494	19.5	753	741	78	5476	1559	214	81	62	2121	425	382	71	**50**	.285	.340	.387	.727	100	8	97	730
BOS	155	54	100	.351	41.5	636	798	60	5329	1455	213	58	32	1880	429	404	57	80	.273	.331	.353	.684	90	-81	96	625
PHI	155	50	104	.325	45.5	748	1008	55	5491	1528	259	39	**112**	2201	414	556	70	73	.278	.333	.401	.734	89	-95	111	729
Total	**617**					**5987**			**43216**	**12348**	**1912**	**588**	**538**		**3494**	**3408**	**824**	**657**	**.286**	**.343**	**.395**	**.737**				

Runs
Youngs, R. (NY) 121
Carey, M. (Pit) 120
Frisch, F. (NY) 116

Hits
Frisch, F. (NY) 223
Statz, J. (Chi) 209
Traynor, P. (Pit) 208

Doubles
Roush, E. (Cin) 41
Grantham, G. (Chi) 36
Tierney, C. (Phi,Pit) 36

Triples
Carey, M. (Pit) 19
Traynor, P. (Pit) 19
Roush, E. (Cin) 18

Home Runs
Williams, C. (Phi) 41
Fournier, J. (Bro) 22
Miller, H. (Chi) 20

Total Bases
Frisch, F. (NY) 311
Williams, C. (Phi) 308
Fournier, J. (Bro) 303

Runs Batted In
Meusel, I. (NY) 125
Williams, C. (Phi) 114
Frisch, F. (NY) 111

Bases On Balls
Burns, G. (Cin) 101
Sand, H. (Phi) 82
2 players tied with 73

Stolen Bases
Carey, M. (Pit) 51
Grantham, G. (Chi) 43
2 players tied with 32

Batting Average
Hornsby, R. (StL) .384
Bottomley, J. (StL) .371
Fournier, J. (Bro) .351

On-Base Percentage
Hornsby, R. (StL) .459
Bottomley, J. (StL) .425
Youngs, R. (NY) .412

Slugging Average
Hornsby, R. (StL) .627
Fournier, J. (Bro) .588
Williams, C. (Phi) .576

Adjusted OPS
Hornsby, R. (StL) 188
Fournier, J. (Bro) 165
Bottomley, J. (StL) 155

Adjusted Batting Runs
Hornsby, R. (StL) 53.0
Fournier, J. (Bro) 49.0
Bottomley, J. (StL) 41.0

Runs Created/Game
Hornsby, R. (StL) 11.70
Fournier, J. (Bro) 9.50
Bottomley, J. (StL) 8.90

Fielding Runs
Bancroft, D. (NY) 23.9
Maranville, R. (Pit) 13.6
Johnston, J. (Bro) 12.5

Win Shares – Batters
Frisch, F. (NY) 31
Carey, M. (Pit) 29
2 players tied with 28

TPW – Batters
Hornsby, R. (StL) 5.2
Frisch, F. (NY) 4.6
Bancroft, D. (NY) 4.2

TEAM	CG	SH	SV	IP	H	H/G	ER	HR	BB	SO	OAV	RAT	ERA	ERA+	CERA	PR+	PF	FA	E	DP	FR	BW	PW	FW	TPW	DIF
NY	62	10	**18**	1378	1440	9.4	597	82	424	453	.271	1.353	3.90	98	3.68	-30.1	95	**.972**	**176**	141	16.7	**8.6**	-2.9	1.6	7.3	11.7
CIN	88	11	9	1391^{1}	1465	9.5	**496**	**28**	**359**	450	.273	**1.311**	**3.21**	120	**3.32**	**98.1**	97	.969	202	144	1.3	.1	**9.4**	.1	**9.7**	4.3
PIT	92	5	9	1376^{1}	1513	9.9	592	53	402	414	.284	1.391	3.87	103	3.81	-3.5	100	.971	179	157	23.1	2.2	-.3	2.2	4.1	5.9
CHI	80	8	11	1366^{2}	**1419**	**9.3**	580	86	435	408	**.269**	1.357	3.82	104	3.74	-5.8	100	.967	208	144	**32.1**	2.1	-.6	**3.1**	4.7	1.3
STL	77	9	7	**1398^{1}**	1539	9.9	601	70	456	398	.284	1.427	3.87	101	4.05	16.6	98	.963	232	141	-11.7	2.7	1.6	-1.1	3.2	-.2
BRO	**94**	8	5	1396^{2}	1503	9.7	580	55	476	**548**	.277	1.417	3.74	104	3.83	24.1	97	.955	293	137	-4.2	.8	2.3	-.4	2.7	-3.7
BOS	55	**13**	7	1392^{2}	1662	10.7	651	64	394	351	.302	1.476	4.21	95	4.39	-21.0	100	.964	230	157	-15.3	-7.8	-2.0	-1.5	-11.3	-11.7
PHI	68	3	8	1376^{1}	1801	11.8	816	100	549	384	.321	1.707	5.34	**86**	5.75	-72.8	115	.966	217	**172**	-41.1	-9.1	-7.0	-4.0	-20.1	-6.9
Total	**616**	**67**	**74**	**11076^{1}**		**10.0**	**4913**					**1.430**	**3.99**													

Wins
Luque, D. (Cin) 27
Morrison, J. (Pit) 25
Alexander, G. (Chi) 22

Win Percentage
Luque, D. (Cin) .771
Ryan, R. (NY) .762
Scott, J. (NY) .696

Games
Jonnard, C. (NY) 45
Ryan, R. (NY) 45
Oeschger, J. (Bos) 44

Complete Games
Grimes, B. (Bro) 33
Luque, D. (Cin) 28
Morrison, J. (Pit) 27

Shutouts
Luque, D. (Cin) 6
Barnes, J. (Bos,NY) 5
McQuillan, H. (NY) 5

Saves
Jonnard, C. (NY) 5
Ryan, R. (NY) 4
8 players tied with 3

Innings Pitched
Grimes, B. (Bro) 327
Luque, D. (Cin) 322
Rixey, E. (Cin) 309

Fewest Hits/Game
Luque, D. (Cin) 7.80
Vance, D. (Bro) 8.44
Morrison, J. (Pit) 8.56

Fewest BB/Game
Alexander, G. (Chi) .89
Adams, B. (Pit) 1.42
Genewich, J. (Bos) 1.82

Strikeouts
Vance, D. (Bro) 197
Luque, D. (Cin) 151
Grimes, B. (Bro) 119

Ratio
Alexander, G. (Chi) 1.11
Luque, D. (Cin) 1.14
Ryan, R. (NY) 1.25

Earned Run Average
Luque, D. (Cin) 1.93
Rixey, E. (Cin) 2.80
Keen, V. (Chi) 3.00

Adjusted ERA
Luque, D. (Cin) 200
Rixey, E. (Cin) 138
Keen, V. (Chi) 133

Component ERA
Luque, D. (Cin) 2.32
Alexander, G. (Chi) 2.64
Ryan, R. (NY) 3.06

Opponents' Batting Avg.
Luque, D. (Cin) .235
Vance, D. (Bro) .250
Aldridge, V. (Chi) .251

Adjusted Pitching Runs
Luque, D. (Cin) 69
Rixey, E. (Cin) 36
Ring, J. (Phi) 33

Win Shares – Pitchers
Luque, D. (Cin) 39
Alexander, G. (Chi) 27
Rixey, E. (Cin) 26

TPW – Pitchers
Luque, D. (Cin) 6.7
Rixey, E. (Cin) 3.0
Ring, J. (Phi) 2.4

1923 American League

TEAM	G	W	L	PCT	GB	R	OR	EW	AB	H	2B	3B	HR	TB	BB	SO	SB	CS	AVG	OBP	SLG	OPS	OPS+	BR/A	PF	RC
NY	152	98	54	.645	....	823	622	97	5347	1554	231	79	105	2258	521	516	69	74	.291	.357	.422	.780	109	55	102	812
DET	155	83	71	.539	16	831	741	86	5266	1579	270	69	41	2110	596	385	87	62	.300	.377	.401	.778	113	114	98	828
CLE	153	82	71	.536	16.5	888	746	90	5290	1594	301	75	59	2222	633	384	79	79	.301	.381	.420	.801	117	135	100	869
WAS	155	75	78	.490	23.5	720	747	74	5244	1436	224	93	26	1924	532	448	102	68	.274	.346	.367	.713	98	-1	95	694
STL	154	74	78	.487	24	688	720	73	5298	1489	248	62	82	2107	442	423	64	54	.281	.339	.398	.737	94	-52	106	724
PHI	153	69	83	.454	29	661	761	65	5196	1407	229	64	53	1923	445	517	72	62	.271	.334	.370	.704	89	-82	101	654
CHI	156	69	85	.448	30	692	741	72	5246	1463	254	57	42	1957	532	458	191	118	.279	.350	.373	.723	97	-15	99	706
BOS	154	61	91	.401	37	584	809	52	5181	1354	253	54	34	1817	391	480	79	91	.261	.318	.351	.669	81	-159	100	578
Total	616					5887			42068	11876	2010	553	442		4092	3611	743	608	.282	.351	.388	.739				

Runs
Ruth, B. (NY) 151
Speaker, T. (Cle) 133
Jamieson, C. (Cle) 130

Hits
Jamieson, C. (Cle) 222
Speaker, T. (Cle) 218
Heilmann, H. (Det) 211

Doubles
Speaker, T. (Cle) 59
Burns, G. (Bos) 47
Ruth, B. (NY) 45

Triples
Goslin, G. (Was) 18
Rice, S. (Was) 18
2 players tied with 15

Home Runs
Ruth, B. (NY) 41
Williams, K. (StL) 29
Heilmann, H. (Det) 18

Total Bases
Ruth, B. (NY) 399
Speaker, T. (Cle) 350
Williams, K. (StL) 346

Runs Batted In
Ruth, B. (NY) 131
Speaker, T. (Cle) 130
Heilmann, H. (Det) 115

Bases On Balls
Ruth, B. (NY) 170
Sewell, J. (Cle) 98
Blue, L. (Det) 96

Stolen Bases
Collins, E. (Chi) 48
Mostil, J. (Chi) 41
Harris, B. (Was) 23

Batting Average
Heilmann, H. (Det) .403
Ruth, B. (NY) .393
Speaker, T. (Cle) .380

On-Base Percentage
Ruth, B. (NY) .545
Heilmann, H. (Det) .481
Speaker, T. (Cle) .469

Slugging Average
Ruth, B. (NY) .764
Heilmann, H. (Det) .632
Williams, K. (StL) .623

Adjusted OPS
Ruth, B. (NY) 238
Heilmann, H. (Det) 195
Speaker, T. (Cle) 183

Adjusted Batting Runs
Ruth, B. (NY) 114.0
Heilmann, H. (Det) 74.0
Speaker, T. (Cle) 71.0

Runs Created/Game
Ruth, B. (NY) 17.40
Heilmann, H. (Det) 12.30
Speaker, T. (Cle) 11.30

Fielding Runs
Ward, A. (NY) 25.6
Gerber, W. (StL) 23.9
Ruel, M. (Was) 17.4

Win Shares – Batters
Ruth, B. (NY) 55
Speaker, T. (Cle) 35
Heilmann, H. (Det) 35

TPW – Batters
Ruth, B. (NY) 11.2
Speaker, T. (Cle) 6.8
Heilmann, H. (Det) 6.2

TEAM	CG	SH	SV	IP	H	H/G	ER	HR	BB	SO	OAV	RAT	ERA	ERA+	CERA	PR+	PF	FA	E	DP	FR	BW	PW	FW	TPW	DIF
NY	101	9	10	1380²	1365	8.9	555	68	491	506	.263	1.344	3.62	109	3.54	36.1	99	.977	144	131	12.0	5.4	3.5	1.2	10.0	12.0
DET	61	9	12	1373²	1502	9.8	624	58	449	447	.283	1.420	4.09	94	3.96	-21.2	97	.968	200	103	-13.3	11.1	-2.1	-1.3	7.7	-1.7
CLE	77	10	11	1376	1517	9.9	598	36	465	407	.284	1.440	3.91	101	3.90	21.7	100	.964	226	143	-13.3	13.1	2.1	-1.3	13.9	-7.9
WAS	71	8	16	1374¹	1527	10.0	608	56	563	474	.290	1.521	3.98	95	4.40	-79.6	95	.967	216	182	46.9	-.1	-7.7	4.5	-3.3	2.3
STL	83	10	10	1373¹	1430	9.4	600	59	488	488	.275	1.426	3.93	106	3.90	21.5	105	.971	177	145	16.1	-5.0	2.1	1.6	-1.4	-.6
PHI	65	7	12	1364²	1465	9.7	618	68	550	400	.280	1.477	4.08	101	4.10	36.9	103	.964	221	127	-33.1	-7.9	3.6	-3.2	-7.5	.5
CHI	74	5	11	1397	1512	9.7	629	49	534	467	.284	1.465	4.05	98	4.00	-8.1	99	.971	184	138	-5.8	-1.4	-.8	-.6	-2.8	-5.2
BOS	77	3	11	1372	1534	10.1	640	48	520	412	.294	1.497	4.20	98	4.38	-6.6	103	.963	232	126	-7.2	-15.3	-.6	-.7	-16.7	1.7
Total	609	61	93	11011²		9.7	4872					1.449	3.98													

Wins
Uhle, G. (Cle) 26
Dauss, H. (Det) 21
Jones, S. (NY) 21

Win Percentage
Pennock, H. (NY) .760
Jones, S. (NY) .724
Cole, B. (Det) .722

Games
Rommel, E. (Phi) 56
Uhle, G. (Cle) 54
2 players tied with 52

Complete Games
Uhle, G. (Cle) 29
Ehmke, H. (Bos) 28
Shocker, U. (StL) 24

Shutouts
Coveleski, S. (Cle) 5
Dauss, H. (Det) 4
Vangilder, E. (StL) 4

Saves
Russell, A. (Was) 9
Quinn, J. (Bos) 7
Harriss, S. (Phi) 6

Innings Pitched
Uhle, G. (Cle) 357²
Ehmke, H. (Bos) 316²
Dauss, H. (Det) 316

Fewest Hits/Game
Shawkey, B. (NY) 8.07
Hoyt, W. (NY) 8.56
Bush, J. (NY) 8.59

Fewest BB/Game
Shocker, U. (StL) 1.59
Coveleski, S. (Cle) 1.66
Thurston, S. (Chi,StL) 1.75

Strikeouts
Johnson, W. (Was) 130
Bush, J. (NY) 125
Shawkey, B. (NY) 125

Ratio
Hoyt, W. (NY) 1.23
Shocker, U. (StL) 1.23
Jones, S. (NY) 1.27

Earned Run Average
Coveleski, S. (Cle) 2.76
Hoyt, W. (NY) 3.02
Russell, A. (Was) 3.03

Adjusted ERA
Coveleski, S. (Cle) 144
Vangilder, E. (StL) 136
Hoyt, W. (NY) 131

Component ERA
Hoyt, W. (NY) 2.92
Faber, R. (Chi) 3.02
Shocker, U. (StL) 3.12

Opponents' Batting Avg.
Shawkey, B. (NY) .246
Hoyt, W. (NY) .253
Jones, S. (NY) .257

Adjusted Pitching Runs
Rommel, E. (Phi) 35
Coveleski, S. (Cle) 33
Vangilder, E. (StL) 32

Win Shares – Pitchers
Uhle, G. (Cle) 29
4 players tied with 25

TPW – Pitchers
Rommel, E. (Phi) 3.5
Vangilder, E. (StL) 3.0
Uhle, G. (Cle) 2.7

1924 National League

TEAM	G	W	L	PCT	GB	R	OR	EW	AB	H	2B	3B	HR	TB	BB	SO	SB	CS	AVG	OBP	SLG	OPS	OPS+	BR/A	PF	RC
NY	154	93	60	.608	....	857	641	98	5445	1634	269	81	95	2350	467	479	82	53	.300	.358	.432	.790	120	159	97	849
BRO	154	92	62	.597	1.5	717	679	81	5339	1534	227	54	72	2085	447	357	34	46	.287	.345	.391	.735	105	47	97	725
PIT	153	90	63	.588	3	724	586	92	5288	1517	222	122	44	2115	366	396	181	92	.287	.336	.400	.736	100	14	102	715
CIN	153	83	70	.542	10	649	579	85	5301	1539	236	111	36	2105	349	521	103	98	.290	.340	.397	.734	103	-36	101	652
CHI	154	81	72	.529	12	698	699	76	5134	1419	207	59	66	1942	469	521	137	149	.276	.340	.378	.719	97	-36	101	652
STL	154	65	89	.422	28.5	740	750	76	5349	1552	270	67	64	2197	382	418	86	86	.290	.341	.411	.752	108	52	98	740
PHI	152	55	96	.364	37	676	849	59	5306	1459	256	56	94	2109	382	452	57	67	.275	.328	.397	.725	88	-89	112	687
BOS	154	53	100	.346	40	520	798	46	5283	1355	194	52	25	1728	354	451	74	68	.256	.306	.327	.633	78	-155	96	532
Total	614					5581			42445	12009	1881	622	499		3216	3408	754	659	.283	.337	.392	.729				

Runs
Frisch, F. (NY) 121
Hornsby, R. (StL) 121
Carey, M. (Pit) 113

Hits
Hornsby, R. (StL) 227
Wheat, Z. (Bro) 212
Frisch, F. (NY) 198

Doubles
Hornsby, R. (StL) 43
Wheat, Z. (Bro) 41
Kelly, G. (NY) 37

Triples
Roush, E. (Cin) 21
Maranville, R. (Pit) 20
Wright, G. (Pit) 18

Home Runs
Fournier, J. (Bro) 27
Hornsby, R. (StL) 25
Williams, C. (Phi) 24

Total Bases
Hornsby, R. (StL) 373
Wheat, Z. (Bro) 311
Williams, C. (Phi) 308

Runs Batted In
Kelly, G. (NY) 136
Fournier, J. (Bro) 116
2 players tied with 111

Bases On Balls
Hornsby, R. (StL) 89
Fournier, J. (Bro) 83
Youngs, R. (NY) 77

Stolen Bases
Carey, M. (Pit) 49
Cuyler, K. (Pit) 32
Heathcote, C. (Chi) 26

Batting Average
Hornsby, R. (StL) .424
Wheat, Z. (Bro) .375
Youngs, R. (NY) .356

On-Base Percentage
Hornsby, R. (StL) .507
Youngs, R. (NY) .441
Fournier, J. (Bro) .428

Slugging Average
Hornsby, R. (StL) .696
Williams, C. (Phi) .552
Wheat, Z. (Bro) .549

Adjusted OPS
Hornsby, R. (StL) 223
Wheat, Z. (Bro) 165
Fournier, J. (Bro) 162

Adjusted Batting Runs
Hornsby, R. (StL) 95.0
Fournier, J. (Bro) 54.0
Wheat, Z. (Bro) 53.0

Runs Created/Game
Hornsby, R. (StL) 14.80
Wheat, Z. (Bro) 9.60
Youngs, R. (NY) 9.20

Fielding Runs
Frisch, F. (NY) 30.9
Pinelli, B. (Cin) 22.9
Wright, G. (Pit) 18.9

Win Shares – Batters
Hornsby, R. (StL) 38
Wheat, Z. (Bro) 35
Fournier, J. (Bro) 34

TPW – Batters
Hornsby, R. (StL) 10.2
Frisch, F. (NY) 6.5
Fournier, J. (Bro) 4.7

TEAM	CG	SH	SV	IP	H	H/G	ER	HR	BB	SO	OAV	RAT	ERA	ERA+	CERA	PR+	PF	FA	E	DP	FR	BW	PW	FW	TPW	DIF
NY	71	4	**21**	1378^{2}	1464	9.6	554	77	392	406	.274	1.346	3.62	101	3.68	2.1	95	.971	186	160	5.3	**15.8**	.2	.5	**16.5**	.5
BRO	**97**	10	5	1376^{1}	1432	9.4	557	58	403	**638**	.270	1.333	3.64	103	3.57	53.7	97	.968	196	121	-36.8	4.6	5.3	-3.6	6.3	8.7
PIT	85	**15**	5	**1382**	**1387**	**9.0**	502	42	323	364	.267	1.237	3.27	117	3.07	33.4	99	.971	183	161	**54.2**	1.4	3.3	**5.4**	10.0	4.0
CIN	77	14	9	1378	1408	9.2	**478**	**30**	**293**	451	**.266**	**1.234**	**3.12**	121	**2.99**	**98.6**	97	.966	217	142	1.0	1.2	**9.8**	.1	11.1	-4.1
CHI	85	4	6	1380^{2}	1459	9.5	587	89	438	416	.275	1.374	3.83	102	3.84	-8.3	101	.966	218	153	19.9	-3.6	-.8	2.0	-2.4	7.4
STL	79	7	6	1364^{2}	1528	10.1	629	70	486	393	.290	1.476	4.15	91	4.31	-55.2	98	.969	188	162	0.1	5.1	-5.5	.0	-.3	-11.7
PHI	59	7	10	1354^{1}	1691	11.2	733	84	469	349	.313	1.595	4.87	92	5.07	-31.7	115	.972	175	**168**	-30.2	-8.8	-3.1	-3.0	-15.0	-5.0
BOS	66	10	4	1379^{1}	1607	10.5	683	49	402	364	.301	1.457	4.46	**86**	4.21	-81.0	99	**.973**	**168**	154	-12.4	-15.4	-8.0	-1.2	-24.7	1.7
Total	**619**	**71**	**66**	**10994**		**9.8**	**4723**					**1.381**	**3.87**													

Wins
Vance, D. (Bro) 28
Grimes, B. (Bro) 22
2 players tied with 20

Win Percentage
Yde, E. (Pit) .842
Vance, D. (Bro) .824
Nehf, A. (NY) .778

Games
Kremer, R. (Pit) 41
Morrison, J. (Pit) 41
Keen, V. (Chi) 40

Complete Games
Grimes, B. (Bro) 30
Vance, D. (Bro) 30
Cooper, W. (Pit) 25

Shutouts
6 players tied with 4

Saves
May, J. (Cin) 6
Jonnard, C. (NY) 5
Ryan, R. (NY) 5

Innings Pitched
Grimes, B. (Bro) 310^{2}
Vance, D. (Bro) 308^{1}
Cooper, W. (Pit) 268^{2}

Fewest Hits/Game
Vance, D. (Bro) 6.95
Yde, E. (Pit) 7.93
Morrison, J. (Pit) 8.07

Fewest BB/Game
Benton, R. (Cin) 1.33
Alexander, G. (Chi) 1.33
Cooper, W. (Pit) 1.34

Strikeouts
Vance, D. (Bro) 262
Grimes, B. (Bro) 135
Luque, D. (Cin) 86

Ratio
Vance, D. (Bro) 1.02
Rixey, E. (Cin) 1.12
Benton, R. (Cin) 1.17

Earned Run Average
Vance, D. (Bro) 2.16
McQuillan, H. (NY) 2.69
Rixey, E. (Cin) 2.76

Adjusted ERA
Vance, D. (Bro) 173
Rixey, E. (Cin) 137
McQuillan, H. (NY) 136

Component ERA
Vance, D. (Bro) 2.02
Rixey, E. (Cin) 2.32
Yde, E. (Pit) 2.69

Opponents' Batting Avg.
Vance, D. (Bro) .213
Yde, E. (Pit) .244
Morrison, J. (Pit) .245

Adjusted Pitching Runs
Vance, D. (Bro) 63
Rixey, E. (Cin) 27
Barnes, J. (Bos) 20

Win Shares – Pitchers
Vance, D. (Bro) 36
Cooper, W. (Pit) 24
4 players tied with 21

TPW – Pitchers
Vance, D. (Bro) 6.0
Rixey, E. (Cin) 2.7
Mays, C. (Cin) 2.2

1924 American League

TEAM	G	W	L	PCT	GB	R	OR	EW	AB	H	2B	3B	HR	TB	BB	SO	SB	CS	AVG	OBP	SLG	OPS	OPS+	BR/A	PF	RC
WAS	156	92	62	.597	....	755	**613**	93	5304	1558	255	**88**	22	2055	513	392	116	85	.294	.362	.387	.750	102	17	97	763
NY	153	89	63	.586	2	798	667	89	5240	1516	248	86	**98**	**2230**	478	420	69	67	.289	.352	**.426**	**.777**	106	28	100	789
DET	156	86	68	.558	6	**849**	796	82	**5389**	**1604**	**315**	76	35	2176	**607**	400	100	77	**.298**	**.373**	.404	.777	**108**	**68**	98	**837**
STL	153	74	78	.487	17	769	807	72	5236	1543	266	62	67	2134	465	**349**	85	85	.295	.356	.408	.764	96	-42	106	763
PHI	152	71	81	.467	20	685	778	66	5184	1459	251	59	63	2017	374	484	77	68	.281	.334	.389	.724	91	-84	101	676
CLE	153	67	86	.438	24.5	755	814	71	5332	1580	306	59	41	2127	492	371	85	**57**	.296	.361	.399	.760	100	5	101	785
BOS	157	67	87	.435	25	735	806	70	5340	1481	302	63	30	1999	603	417	78	61	.277	.356	.374	.730	94	-39	100	741
CHI	154	66	87	.431	25.5	793	858	70	5255	1512	254	58	41	2005	604	421	**137**	92	.288	.365	.382	.746	101	24	97	764
Total	**617**					**6139**			**42280**	**12253**	**2197**	**551**	**397**		**4136**	**3254**	**747**	**592**	**.290**	**.358**	**.396**	**.754**				

Runs
Ruth, B. (NY) 143
Cobb, T. (Det) 115
Collins, E. (Chi) 108

Hits
Rice, S. (Was) 216
Jamieson, C. (Cle) 213
Cobb, T. (Det) 211

Doubles
Heilmann, H. (Det) 45
Sewell, J. (Cle) 45
2 players tied with 41

Triples
Pipp, W. (NY) 19
Goslin, G. (Was) 17
Heilmann, H. (Det) 16

Home Runs
Ruth, B. (NY) 46
Hauser, J. (Phi) 27
Jacobson, B. (StL) 19

Total Bases
Ruth, B. (NY) 391
Jacobson, B. (StL) 306
Heilmann, H. (Det) 304

Runs Batted In
Goslin, G. (Was) 129
Ruth, B. (NY) 121
Meusel, B. (NY) 120

Bases On Balls
Ruth, B. (NY) 142
Rigney, T. (Det) 102
Sheely, E. (Chi) 95

Stolen Bases
Collins, E. (Chi) 42
Meusel, B. (NY) 26
Rice, S. (Was) 24

Batting Average
Ruth, B. (NY) .378
Jamieson, C. (Cle) .359
Falk, B. (Chi) .352

On-Base Percentage
Ruth, B. (NY) .513
Collins, E. (Chi) .441
Speaker, T. (Cle) .432

Slugging Average
Ruth, B. (NY) .739
Heilmann, H. (Det) .533
Williams, K. (StL) .533

Adjusted OPS
Ruth, B. (NY) 221
Heilmann, H. (Det) 149
Goslin, G. (Was) 145

Adjusted Batting Runs
Ruth, B. (NY) 100.0
Heilmann, H. (Det) 45.0
Goslin, G. (Was) 38.0

Runs Created/Game
Ruth, B. (NY) 15.60
Heilmann, H. (Det) 8.80
Speaker, T. (Cle) 8.50

Fielding Runs
Peckinpaugh, R. (Was) 31.7
McManus, M. (StL) 17.2
Scott, E. (NY) 16.4

Win Shares – Batters
Ruth, B. (NY) 45
Heilmann, H. (Det) 30
Goslin, G. (Was) 29

TPW – Batters
Ruth, B. (NY) 8.5
Heilmann, H. (Det) 4.2
Sewell, J. (Cle) 3.8

TEAM	CG	SH	SV	IP	H	H/G	ER	HR	BB	SO	OAV	RAT	ERA	ERA+	CERA	PR+	PF	FA	E	DP	FR	BW	PW	FW	TPW	DIF
WAS	74	**13**	**25**	1383	**1329**	**8.6**	**513**	**34**	505	469	**.258**	**1.326**	**3.34**	121	**3.24**	**70.1**	95	.972	171	149	**34.0**	1.6	**6.6**	**3.2**	**11.4**	3.6
NY	76	**13**	13	1359^{1}	1483	9.8	583	59	522	**487**	.284	1.475	3.86	108	4.10	36.6	98	**.975**	**156**	131	8.2	2.6	3.5	.8	6.8	6.2
DET	60	5	20	**1394^{2}**	1586	10.2	649	55	**467**	441	.293	1.472	4.19	98	4.19	-12.5	97	.971	187	142	-0.4	**6.4**	-1.2	.0	5.2	3.8
STL	66	11	7	1353^{1}	1511	10.0	687	68	517	386	.288	1.499	4.57	99	4.32	-20.2	107	.970	184	142	11.7	-4.0	-1.9	1.1	-4.8	2.8
PHI	68	8	10	1345	1527	10.2	656	43	597	371	.292	1.579	4.39	98	4.47	0.6	101	.971	180	**157**	-14.3	-7.9	.1	-1.4	-9.2	4.2
CLE	**87**	7	7	1349	1603	10.7	660	43	503	315	.300	1.561	4.40	97	4.55	-2.2	101	.968	205	130	-16.6	.5	-.2	-1.6	-1.3	-7.7
BOS	73	8	16	1391^{1}	1563	10.1	672	43	523	414	.290	1.499	4.35	100	4.19	22.2	103	.967	210	126	-18.3	-3.6	2.1	-1.7	-3.3	-6.7
CHI	76	1	11	1370^{2}	1635	10.7	722	52	512	360	.305	1.566	4.74	**87**	4.56	-89.1	97	.963	229	136	-6.0	2.3	-8.4	-.6	-6.7	-3.3
Total	**580**	**66**	**109**	**10946^{1}**		**10.1**	**5142**					**1.497**	**4.23**													

Wins
Johnson, W. (Was) 23
Pennock, H. (NY) 21
2 players tied with 20

Win Percentage
Johnson, W. (Was) .767
Holloway, K. (Det) .700
Pennock, H. (NY) .700

Games
Marberry, F. (Was) 50
Holloway, K. (Det) 49
2 players tied with 46

Complete Games
Thurston, S. (Chi) 28
Ehmke, H. (Bos) 26
Pennock, H. (NY) 25

Shutouts
Johnson, W. (Was) 6
Davis, D. (StL) 5
3 players tied with 4

Saves
Marberry, F. (Was) 15
Russell, A. (Was) 8
Quinn, J. (Bos) 7

Innings Pitched
Ehmke, H. (Bos) 315
Thurston, S. (Chi) 291
Pennock, H. (NY) 286^{1}

Fewest Hits/Game
Johnson, W. (Was) 7.55
Collins, R. (Det) 8.29
Marberry, F. (Was) 8.75

Fewest BB/Game
Smith, S. (Cle) 1.53
Thurston, S. (Chi) 1.86
Shocker, U. (StL) 1.90

Strikeouts
Johnson, W. (Was) 158
Ehmke, H. (Bos) 119
Shawkey, B. (NY) 114

Ratio
Johnson, W. (Was) 1.12
Collins, R. (Det) 1.21
Zachary, T. (Was) 1.24

Earned Run Average
Johnson, W. (Was) 2.72
Zachary, T. (Was) 2.75
Pennock, H. (NY) 2.83

Adjusted ERA
Baumgartner, S. (Phi) 149
Johnson, W. (Was) 148
Pennock, H. (NY) 147

Component ERA
Johnson, W. (Was) 2.39
Collins, R. (Det) 2.78
Zachary, T. (Was) 2.98

Opponents' Batting Avg.
Johnson, W. (Was) .224
Collins, R. (Det) .249
Zachary, T. (Was) .260

Adjusted Pitching Runs
Pennock, H. (NY) 41
Smith, S. (Cle) 38
Ehmke, H. (Bos) 36

Win Shares – Pitchers
Johnson, W. (Was) 29
Pennock, H. (NY) 27
Ehmke, H. (Bos) 25

TPW – Pitchers
Johnson, W. (Was) 3.8
Pennock, H. (NY) 3.6
Smith, S. (Cle) 3.4

1925 National League

TEAM	G	W	L	PCT	GB	R	OR	EW	AB	H	2B	3B	HR	TB	BB	SO	SB	CS	AVG	OBP	SLG	OPS	OPS+	BR/A	PF	RC
PIT	153	95	58	.621	....	**912**	715	95	5372	**1651**	**316**	**105**	78	**2411**	**499**	363	**159**	63	**.307**	**.369**	**.449**	**.818**	**107**	**78**	107	**909**
NY	152	86	66	.566	8.5	736	702	80	5327	1507	239	61	**114**	2210	411	494	79	65	.283	.337	.415	.752	101	3	96	742
CIN	153	80	73	.523	15	690	**643**	82	5233	1490	221	90	44	2023	409	**327**	108	107	.285	.339	.387	.726	93	-64	98	680
STL	153	77	76	.503	18	828	764	83	5329	1592	292	80	109	2371	446	414	70	51	.299	.356	.445	.801	**107**	57	102	846
BOS	153	70	83	.458	25	708	802	67	5365	1567	260	70	41	2090	405	380	77	72	.292	.345	.390	.735	102	16	91	722
PHI	153	68	85	.444	27	812	930	66	5412	1598	288	58	100	2302	456	542	48	59	.295	.354	.425	.779	96	-35	109	814
BRO	153	68	85	.444	27	786	866	69	**5468**	1617	250	80	64	2219	437	383	37	**30**	.296	.351	.406	.757	102	21	97	787
CHI	154	68	86	.442	27.5	723	773	72	5353	1473	254	70	86	2125	397	470	94	70	.275	.329	.397	.726	89	-88	101	700
Total	**612**					**6195**			**42859**	**12495**	**2120**	**614**	**636**		**3460**	**3373**	**672**	**517**	**.292**	**.348**	**.414**	**.762**				

Runs
Cuyler, K. (Pit) 144
Hornsby, R. (StL) 133
Wheat, Z. (Bro) 125

Hits
Bottomley, J. (StL) 227
Wheat, Z. (Bro) 221
Cuyler, K. (Pit) 220

Doubles
Bottomley, J. (StL) 44
Cuyler, K. (Pit) 43
Wheat, Z. (Bro) 42

Triples
Cuyler, K. (Pit) 26
3 players tied with 16

Home Runs
Hornsby, R. (StL) 39
Hartnett, G. (Chi) 24
Fournier, J. (Bro) 22

Total Bases
Hornsby, R. (StL) 381
Cuyler, K. (Pit) 369
Bottomley, J. (StL) 358

Runs Batted In
Hornsby, R. (StL) 143
Fournier, J. (Bro) 130
Bottomley, J. (StL) 128

Bases On Balls
Fournier, J. (Bro) 86
Hornsby, R. (StL) 83
Moore, E. (Pit) 73

Stolen Bases
Carey, M. (Pit) 46
Cuyler, K. (Pit) 41
Adams, S. (Chi) 26

Batting Average
Hornsby, R. (StL) .403
Bottomley, J. (StL) .367
Wheat, Z. (Bro) .359

On-Base Percentage
Hornsby, R. (StL) .489
Fournier, J. (Bro) .446
Blades, R. (StL) .423

Slugging Average
Hornsby, R. (StL) .756
Cuyler, K. (Pit) .598
Bottomley, J. (StL) .578

Adjusted OPS
Hornsby, R. (StL) 208
Fournier, J. (Bro) 162
Cuyler, K. (Pit) 148

Adjusted Batting Runs
Hornsby, R. (StL) 85.0
Fournier, J. (Bro) 54.0
Cuyler, K. (Pit) 49.0

Runs Created/Game
Hornsby, R. (StL) 15.50
Fournier, J. (Bro) 10.10
Cuyler, K. (Pit) 9.90

Fielding Runs
Traynor, P. (Pit) 27.0
Bancroft, D. (Bos) 22.1
Adams, S. (Chi) 19.0

Win Shares – Batters
Hornsby, R. (StL) 36
Cuyler, K. (Pit) 34
Fournier, J. (Bro) 29

TPW – Batters
Hornsby, R. (StL) 7.5
Bancroft, D. (Bos) 5.1
Fournier, J. (Bro) 4.2

TEAM	CG	SH	SV	IP	H	H/G	ER	HR	BB	SO	OAV	RAT	ERA	ERA+	CERA	PR+	PF	FA	E	DP	FR	BW	PW	FW	TPW	DIF
PIT	77	2	**13**	1354^2	1526	10.1	582	81	387	386	.287	1.412	3.87	115	4.10	56.4	105	.964	224	**171**	**31.3**	**7.3**	5.3	**2.9**	**15.5**	3.5
NY	80	6	8	1354	1532	10.2	593	73	408	446	.289	1.433	3.94	102	4.11	17.2	95	.968	199	129	-3.5	.3	1.6	-.3	1.6	8.4
CIN	**92**	**11**	12	**1375^1**	**1447**	**9.5**	**516**	**35**	**324**	437	**.271**	**1.288**	**3.38**	122	**3.28**	**90.3**	96	.968	203	161	22.3	-6.0	**8.4**	2.1	4.6	-.6
STL	82	8	7	1335^2	1480	10.0	647	86	470	428	.283	1.460	4.36	99	4.29	-13.1	101	.966	204	156	6.6	5.3	-1.2	.6	4.7	-3.7
BOS	77	5	4	1366^2	1567	10.3	666	67	458	351	.291	1.482	4.39	91	4.26	-76.7	94	.964	221	145	17.3	1.5	-7.2	1.6	-4.0	-2.0
PHI	69	8	9	1350^2	1753	11.7	753	117	444	371	.315	1.627	5.02	95	5.39	15.9	112	.966	211	147	-54.5	-3.3	1.5	-5.1	-6.9	-1.1
BRO	82	4	4	1350^2	1608	10.7	715	75	477	**518**	.301	1.544	4.76	**88**	4.72	-45.9	98	.966	210	130	-43.3	1.9	-4.3	-4.0	-6.4	-1.6
CHI	75	5	10	1370	1575	10.4	671	102	485	435	.291	1.504	4.41	98	4.60	-37.9	101	**.969**	**198**	161	24.5	-8.3	-3.5	2.3	-9.5	.5
Total	**634**	**49**	**67**	**10857^2**		**10.4**	**5143**					**1.468**	**4.26**													

Wins
Vance, D. (Bro) 22
Donohue, P. (Cin) 21
Rixey, E. (Cin) 21

Win Percentage
Sherdel, B. (StL) .714
Vance, D. (Bro) .710
Aldridge, V. (Pit) .682

Games
Morrison, J. (Pit) 44
Bush, G. (Chi) 42
Donohue, P. (Cin) 42

Complete Games
Donohue, P. (Cin) 27
Vance, D. (Bro) 26
2 players tied with 22

Shutouts
Carlson, H. (Phi) 4
Luque, D. (Cin) 4
Vance, D. (Bro) 4

Saves
Bush, G. (Chi) 4
Morrison, J. (Pit) 4
5 players tied with 3

Innings Pitched
Donohue, P. (Cin) 301
Luque, D. (Cin) 291
Rixey, E. (Cin) 287^1

Fewest Hits/Game
Luque, D. (Cin) 8.13
Benton, L. (Bos) 8.35
Vance, D. (Bro) 8.38

Fewest BB/Game
Alexander, G. (Chi) 1.11
Donohue, P. (Cin) 1.47
Rixey, E. (Cin) 1.47

Strikeouts
Vance, D. (Bro) 221
Luque, D. (Cin) 140
2 players tied with 93

Ratio
Luque, D. (Cin) 1.17
Vance, D. (Bro) 1.18
Donohue, P. (Cin) 1.19

Earned Run Average
Luque, D. (Cin) 2.63
Rixey, E. (Cin) 2.88
Donohue, P. (Cin) 3.08

Adjusted ERA
Luque, D. (Cin) 156
Rixey, E. (Cin) 143
Sherdel, B. (StL) 139

Component ERA
Luque, D. (Cin) 2.53
Donohue, P. (Cin) 2.75
Vance, D. (Bro) 2.78

Opponents' Batting Avg.
Luque, D. (Cin) .239
Benton, L. (Bos) .249
Vance, D. (Bro) .250

Adjusted Pitching Runs
Luque, D. (Cin) 43
Rixey, E. (Cin) 34
Donohue, P. (Cin) 29

Win Shares – Pitchers
Donohue, P. (Cin) 28
Luque, D. (Cin) 27
Rixey, E. (Cin) 26

TPW – Pitchers
Luque, D. (Cin) 4.5
Donohue, P. (Cin) 3.4
Rixey, E. (Cin) 3.1

1925 American League

TEAM	G	W	L	PCT	GB	R	OR	EW	AB	H	2B	3B	HR	TB	BB	SO	SB	CS	AVG	OBP	SLG	OPS	OPS+	BR/A	PF	RC
WAS	152	96	55	.636	....	829	**670**	91	5206	1577	251	71	56	2138	533	427	**135**	92	.303	.372	.411	.783	106	57	98	815
PHI	153	88	64	.579	8.5	831	713	88	5399	**1659**	298	79	76	2343	453	432	67	60	**.307**	.364	.434	.798	101	1	107	856
STL	154	82	71	.536	15	900	906	76	**5440**	1620	**304**	68	**110**	**2390**	498	**375**	85	78	.298	.360	**.439**	**.799**	103	7	105	860
DET	156	81	73	.526	16.5	**903**	829	84	5371	1621	277	**84**	50	2216	640	386	97	63	.302	**.379**	.413	.792	**108**	**85**	98	**872**
CHI	154	79	75	.513	18.5	811	770	81	5224	1482	299	59	38	2013	**662**	405	131	87	.284	.369	.385	.755	103	42	95	780
CLE	155	70	84	.455	27.5	782	817	74	5436	1613	285	58	52	2170	520	379	90	77	.297	.361	.399	.760	97	-20	101	795
NY	156	69	85	.448	28.5	706	774	70	5353	1471	247	74	**110**	2196	470	482	69	73	.275	.336	.410	.746	96	-53	98	738
BOS	152	47	105	.309	49.5	639	922	49	5166	1375	257	64	41	1883	513	422	42	**56**	.266	.336	.364	.700	83	-134	100	646
Total	**616**					**6401**			**42595**	**12418**	**2218**	**557**	**533**		**4289**	**3308**	**716**	**586**	**.292**	**.360**	**.407**	**.767**				

Runs
Mostil, J. (Chi) 135
Simmons, A. (Phi) 122
Combs, E. (NY) 117

Hits
Simmons, A. (Phi) 253
Rice, S. (Was) 227
Heilmann, H. (Det) 225

Doubles
McManus, M. (StL) 44
Sheely, E. (Chi) 43
Simmons, A. (Phi) 43

Triples
Goslin, G. (Was) 20
Mostil, J. (Chi) 16
Sisler, G. (StL) 15

Home Runs
Meusel, B. (NY) 33
Ruth, B. (NY) 25
Williams, K. (StL) 25

Total Bases
Simmons, A. (Phi) 392
Meusel, B. (NY) 338
Goslin, G. (Was) 329

Runs Batted In
Meusel, B. (NY) 138
Heilmann, H. (Det) 134
Simmons, A. (Phi) 129

Bases On Balls
Kamm, W. (Chi) 90
Mostil, J. (Chi) 90
2 players tied with 87

Stolen Bases
Mostil, J. (Chi) 43
Goslin, G. (Was) 27
Rice, S. (Was) 26

Batting Average
Heilmann, H. (Det) .393
Speaker, T. (Cle) .389
Simmons, A. (Phi) .387

On-Base Percentage
Speaker, T. (Cle) .479
Cobb, T. (Det) .468
Collins, E. (Chi) .461

Slugging Average
Williams, K. (StL) .613
Simmons, A. (Phi) .599
Cobb, T. (Det) .598

Adjusted OPS
Cobb, T. (Det) 171
Speaker, T. (Cle) 166
Heilmann, H. (Det) 161

Adjusted Batting Runs
Heilmann, H. (Det) 55.0
Speaker, T. (Cle) 48.0
Cobb, T. (Det) 47.0

Runs Created/Game
Speaker, T. (Cle) 11.70
Cobb, T. (Det) 11.50
Heilmann, H. (Det) 10.50

Fielding Runs
Sewell, J. (Cle) 16.7
Flagstead, I. (Bos) 15.4
Harris, B. (Was) 14.9

Win Shares – Batters
Simmons, A. (Phi) 34
Goslin, G. (Was) 31
Heilmann, H. (Det) 30

TPW – Batters
Speaker, T. (Cle) 4.3
Sewell, J. (Cle) 4.1
Cobb, T. (Det) 3.5

TEAM	CG	SH	SV	IP	H	H/G	ER	HR	BB	SO	OAV	RAT	ERA	ERA+	CERA	PR+	PF	FA	E	DP	FR	BW	PW	FW	TPW	DIF
WAS	69	10	**21**	1358^1	**1434**	**9.5**	**558**	49	543	463	.277	**1.455**	**3.70**	114	**4.00**	46.0	96	.972	170	**166**	**38.1**	5.3	4.3	**3.5**	**13.1**	7.9
PHI	61	8	18	1381^2	1468	9.6	594	60	544	**495**	**.276**	1.456	3.87	120	4.00	**132.8**	106	.966	211	148	-13.2	.1	**12.3**	-1.2	11.2	.8
STL	67	7	10	1379^2	1588	10.4	754	99	675	419	.298	1.640	4.92	95	5.10	-51.3	106	.964	226	164	13.3	.6	-4.7	1.2	-2.9	8.9
DET	66	2	18	1383^2	1582	10.3	708	70	556	419	.296	1.545	4.61	93	4.59	-47.3	98	.973	173	143	3.4	**7.9**	-4.4	.3	3.8	.2
CHI	71	**12**	13	1385^2	1579	10.3	660	69	**489**	374	.295	1.492	4.29	97	4.36	-20.4	94	.969	200	162	2.5	3.9	-1.9	.2	2.2	-.2
CLE	**93**	6	9	1372^1	1604	10.5	684	**41**	493	345	.296	1.528	4.49	98	4.37	-7.3	101	.966	210	146	-4.0	-1.9	-.7	-.4	-2.9	-4.1
NY	80	8	13	**1387^2**	1560	10.1	667	78	505	492	.289	1.488	4.33	98	4.38	-7.5	97	**.974**	**160**	150	-3.2	-4.9	-.7	-.3	-5.9	-2.1
BOS	68	6	6	1326^2	1615	11.0	732	67	510	310	.308	1.602	4.97	**91**	4.91	-24.3	103	.956	271	150	-38.4	-12.4	-2.3	-3.6	-18.2	-10.8
Total	**575**	**59**	**108**	**10975^2**		**10.2**	**5357**					**1.526**	**4.39**													

Wins
Lyons, T. (Chi) 21
Rommel, E. (Phi) 21
2 players tied with 20

Win Percentage
Coveleski, S. (Was) .800
Holloway, K. (Det) .765
Johnson, W. (Was) .741

Games
Marberry, F. (Was) 55
Walberg, R. (Phi) 53
2 players tied with 52

Complete Games
Ehmke, H. (Bos) 22
Smith, S. (Cle) 22
Pennock, H. (NY) 21

Shutouts
Lyons, T. (Chi) 5
Giard, J. (StL) 4
Gray, D. (Phi) 4

Saves
Marberry, F. (Was) 15
Connally, S. (Chi) 8
Doyle, J. (Det) 8

Innings Pitched
Pennock, H. (NY) 277
Lyons, T. (Chi) 262^2
Rommel, E. (Phi) 261

Fewest Hits/Game
Blankenship, T. (Chi) 8.46
Johnson, W. (Was) 8.53
Coveleski, S. (Was) 8.59

Fewest BB/Game
Smith, S. (Cle) 1.82
Quinn, J. (Phi,Bos) 1.85
Shocker, U. (NY) 2.14

Strikeouts
Grove, L. (Phi) 116
Johnson, W. (Was) 108
2 players tied with 95

Ratio
Pennock, H. (NY) 1.22
Blankenship, T. (Chi) 1.24
Coveleski, S. (Was) 1.26

Earned Run Average
Coveleski, S. (Was) 2.84
Pennock, H. (NY) 2.96
Blankenship, T. (Chi) 3.03

Adjusted ERA
Coveleski, S. (Was) 149
Pennock, H. (NY) 144
Gray, D. (Phi) 142

Component ERA
Pennock, H. (NY) 2.92
Blankenship, T. (Chi) 2.98
Coveleski, S. (Was) 2.99

Opponents' Batting Avg.
Johnson, W. (Was) .250
Blankenship, T. (Chi) .253
Pennock, H. (NY) .254

Adjusted Pitching Runs
Pennock, H. (NY) 41
Harriss, S. (Phi) 35
Gray, D. (Phi) 33

Win Shares – Pitchers
Johnson, W. (Was) 26
3 players tied with 23

TPW – Pitchers
Johnson, W. (Was) 3.6
Pennock, H. (NY) 3.5
Harriss, S. (Phi) 3.0

1926 National League

TEAM	G	W	L	PCT	GB	R	OR	EW	AB	H	2B	3B	HR	TB	BB	SO	SB	CS	AVG	OBP	SLG	OPS	OPS+	BR/A	PF	RC
STL	156	89	65	.578	....	**817**	678	91	**5381**	**1541**	259	82	**90**	**2234**	**478**	518	83	....	.286	.348	**.415**	**.763**	107	48	104	**770**
CIN	157	87	67	.565	2	747	651	88	5320	**1541**	242	**120**	35	2128	454	**333**	51	....	**.290**	**.349**	.400	.749	**110**	**73**	97	738
PIT	157	84	69	.549	4.5	769	689	85	5312	1514	243	106	44	2101	434	350	91	....	.285	.343	.396	.738	99	-9	105	713
CHI	155	82	72	.532	7	682	**602**	87	5229	1453	**291**	49	66	2040	445	447	85	....	.278	.338	.390	.728	100	-1	101	685
NY	151	74	77	.490	13.5	663	668	75	5167	1435	214	58	73	1984	339	420	**94**	....	.278	.325	.384	.709	97	-30	99	631
BRO	155	71	82	.464	17.5	623	705	67	5130	1348	246	62	40	1838	475	464	76	....	.263	.328	.358	.687	91	-55	99	607
BOS	153	66	86	.434	22	624	719	65	5216	1444	209	62	16	1825	426	348	81	....	.277	.335	.350	.685	99	-4	91	612
PHI	152	58	93	.384	29.5	687	900	56	5254	1479	244	50	75	2048	422	479	47	....	.282	.337	.390	.727	96	-30	105	683
Total	**618**					**5612**			**42009**	**11755**	**1948**	**589**	**439**		**3473**	**3359**	**608**		**.280**	**.338**	**.386**	**.724**				

Runs
Cuyler, K. (Pit) 113
Waner, P. (Pit) 101
2 players tied with 99

Hits
Brown, E. (Bos) 201
Cuyler, K. (Pit) 197
Adams, S. (Chi) 193

Doubles
Bottomley, J. (StL) 40
Roush, E. (Cin) 37
Wilson, H. (Chi) 36

Triples
Waner, P. (Pit) 22
Walker, C. (Cin) 20
Traynor, P. (Pit) 17

Home Runs
Wilson, H. (Chi) 21
Bottomley, J. (StL) 19
Williams, C. (Phi) 18

Total Bases
Bottomley, J. (StL) 305
Bell, L. (StL) 301
Wilson, H. (Chi) 285

Runs Batted In
Bottomley, J. (StL) 120
Wilson, H. (Chi) 109
Bell, L. (StL) 100

Bases On Balls
Wilson, H. (Chi) 69
Sand, H. (Phi) 66
Waner, P. (Pit) 66

Stolen Bases
Cuyler, K. (Pit) 35
Adams, S. (Chi) 27
2 players tied with 23

Batting Average
Hargrave, B. (Cin) .353
Waner, P. (Pit) .336
Leach, F. (Phi) .329

On-Base Percentage
Waner, P. (Pit) .413
Blades, R. (StL) .409
Wilson, H. (Chi) .406

Slugging Average
Williams, C. (Phi) .568
Wilson, H. (Chi) .539
Waner, P. (Pit) .528

Adjusted OPS
Wilson, H. (Chi) 150
Waner, P. (Pit) 144
Herman, B. (Bro) 136

Adjusted Batting Runs
Wilson, H. (Chi) 38.0
Waner, P. (Pit) 34.0
Bell, L. (StL) 28.0

Runs Created/Game
Waner, P. (Pit) 8.20
Wilson, H. (Chi) 8.10
Grantham, G. (Pit) 7.20

Fielding Runs
Thevenow, T. (StL) 41.1
Adams, S. (Chi) 18.8
Critz, H. (Cin) 18.4

Win Shares – Batters
Waner, P. (Pit) 28
Wilson, H. (Chi) 26
Cuyler, K. (Pit) 26

TPW – Batters
Wilson, H. (Chi) 3.1
O'Farrell, B. (StL) 2.7
Bancroft, D. (Bos) 2.7

TEAM	CG	SH	SV	IP	H	H/G	ER	HR	BB	SO	OAV	RAT	ERA	ERA+	CERA	PR+	PF	FA	E	DP	FR	BW	PW	FW	TPW	DIF
STL	**90**	10	6	1398^{2}	1423	**9.2**	570	76	397	365	**.269**	1.301	3.67	107	3.44	25.6	102	.969	198	141	11.8	4.7	2.5	1.2	8.4	3.6
CIN	88	**14**	8	**1408^{2}**	1449	9.3	535	40	**324**	424	.271	**1.259**	3.42	108	**3.14**	39.4	97	.972	183	160	3.6	**7.2**	3.9	.4	**11.4**	-1.4
PIT	83	12	**18**	1379^{1}	1422	9.3	562	50	455	387	.272	1.361	3.67	107	3.56	18.1	103	.965	220	161	23.3	-.9	1.8	2.3	3.2	4.8
CHI	77	13	14	1378^{1}	1407	9.2	**499**	**39**	486	508	.273	1.373	**3.26**	118	3.58	**61.6**	100	**.974**	**162**	**174**	**28.1**	-.1	**6.1**	**2.8**	8.7	-3.7
NY	61	4	15	1341^{2}	**1370**	9.2	562	70	427	419	.269	1.339	3.77	99	3.54	-21.3	98	.970	186	150	18.5	-3.0	-2.1	1.8	-3.3	2.3
BRO	83	5	9	1361^{2}	1440	9.5	578	50	472	**517**	.276	1.404	3.82	100	3.72	26.5	100	.963	229	95	-26.4	-5.4	2.6	-2.6	-5.4	.4
BOS	60	9	9	1365^{1}	1536	10.1	608	46	455	408	.294	1.458	4.01	88	4.08	-53.2	93	.967	208	150	-17.0	-.4	-5.3	-1.7	-7.3	-2.7
PHI	68	5	5	1334^{1}	1699	11.5	746	68	454	331	.314	1.614	5.03	**82**	5.03	-89.2	108	.964	224	153	-42.5	-2.9	-8.8	-4.2	-15.9	-1.1
Total	**610**	**72**	**84**	**10968**		**9.6**	**4660**					**1.387**	**3.82**													

Wins
4 players tied with 20

Win Percentage
Kremer, R. (Pit) .769
Haines, J. (StL) .765
Rhem, F. (StL) .741

Games
Scott, J. (NY) 50
Donohue, P. (Cin) 47
Willoughby, C. (Phi) 47

Complete Games
Mays, C. (Cin) 24
Petty, J. (Bro) 23
Root, C. (Chi) 21

Shutouts
Donohue, P. (Cin) 5
Blake, S. (Chi) 4
Smith, B. (Bos) 4

Saves
Davies, C. (NY) 6
Kremer, R. (Pit) 5
Scott, J. (NY) 5

Innings Pitched
Donohue, P. (Cin) 285^{2}
Mays, C. (Cin) 281
Petty, J. (Bro) 275^{2}

Fewest Hits/Game
Petty, J. (Bro) 8.03
Greenfield, K. (NY) 8.33
Rhem, F. (StL) 8.41

Fewest BB/Game
Donohue, P. (Cin) 1.23
Alexander, G. (Chi,StL) 1.39
Carlson, H. (Phi) 1.58

Strikeouts
Vance, D. (Bro) 140
Root, C. (Chi) 127
2 players tied with 103

Ratio
Alexander, G. (StL,Chi) 1.11
Kremer, R. (Pit) 1.18
Petty, J. (Bro) 1.18

Earned Run Average
Kremer, R. (Pit) 2.61
Root, C. (Chi) 2.82
Petty, J. (Bro) 2.84

Adjusted ERA
Kremer, R. (Pit) 151
Root, C. (Chi) 136
Petty, J. (Bro) 135

Component ERA
Alexander, G. (StL,Chi) 2.51
Petty, J. (Bro) 2.56
Kremer, R. (Pit) 2.76

Opponents' Batting Avg.
Petty, J. (Bro) .240
Alexander, G. (StL,Chi) .249
Rhem, F. (StL) .250

Adjusted Pitching Runs
Carlson, H. (Phi) 36
Petty, J. (Bro) 35
Kremer, R. (Pit) 30

Win Shares – Pitchers
Kremer, R. (Pit) 25
Petty, J. (Bro) 24
Carlson, H. (Phi) 23

TPW – Pitchers
Carlson, H. (Phi) 3.8
Kremer, R. (Pit) 3.2
Petty, J. (Bro) 3.2

1926 American League

TEAM	G	W	L	PCT	GB	R	OR	EW	AB	H	2B	3B	HR	TB	BB	SO	SB	CS	AVG	OBP	SLG	OPS	OPS+	BR/A	PF	RC
NY	155	91	63	.591	....	**847**	713	90	5221	1508	262	75	**121**	**2283**	**642**	580	79	62	.289	**.369**	**.437**	**.806**	**119**	**139**	98	**866**
CLE	154	88	66	.571	3	738	612	91	5293	1529	**333**	49	27	2041	455	**332**	88	**42**	.289	.349	.386	.735	97	-15	101	735
PHI	150	83	67	.553	6	677	**570**	88	5046	1359	259	65	61	1931	523	452	56	45	.269	.341	.383	.724	90	-74	106	681
WAS	152	81	69	.540	8	802	761	79	5223	1525	244	**97**	43	2092	555	369	117	91	**.292**	.364	.401	.765	109	65	98	780
CHI	155	81	72	.529	9.5	730	665	84	5220	1508	314	60	32	2038	556	381	**123**	78	.289	.361	.390	.752	106	55	96	761
DET	157	79	75	.513	12	793	830	73	**5315**	**1547**	281	90	36	2116	599	423	88	71	.291	.366	.398	.765	105	40	101	800
STL	155	62	92	.403	29	682	845	61	5259	1449	253	78	72	2074	437	472	64	66	.276	.335	.394	.730	92	-79	105	698
BOS	154	46	107	.301	44.5	562	835	48	5185	1325	249	54	32	1778	465	454	52	48	.256	.321	.343	.664	81	-140	97	586
Total	**616**					**5831**			**41762**	**11750**	**2195**	**568**	**424**		**4232**	**3463**	**667**	**503**	**.281**	**.351**	**.392**	**.743**				

Runs
Ruth, B. (NY) 139
Gehrig, L. (NY) 135
Mostil, J. (Chi) 120

Hits
Burns, G. (Cle) 216
Rice, S. (Was) 216
Goslin, G. (Was) 201

Doubles
Burns, G. (Cle) 64
Simmons, A. (Phi) 53
Speaker, T. (Cle) 52

Triples
Gehrig, L. (NY) 20
Gehringer, C. (Det) 17
2 players tied with 15

Home Runs
Ruth, B. (NY) 47
Simmons, A. (Phi) 19
Lazzeri, T. (NY) 18

Total Bases
Ruth, B. (NY) 365
Simmons, A. (Phi) 329
Gehrig, L. (NY) 314

Runs Batted In
Ruth, B. (NY) 146
Burns, G. (Cle) 114
Lazzeri, T. (NY) 114

Bases On Balls
Ruth, B. (NY) 144
Bishop, M. (Phi) 116
Rigney, T. (Bos) 108

Stolen Bases
Mostil, J. (Chi) 35
Hunnefield, B. (Chi) 24
Rice, S. (Was) 24

Batting Average
Manush, H. (Det) .378
Ruth, B. (NY) .372
Heilmann, H. (Det) .367

On-Base Percentage
Ruth, B. (NY) .516
Heilmann, H. (Det) .445
Bishop, M. (Phi) .431

Slugging Average
Ruth, B. (NY) .737
Simmons, A. (Phi) .564
Manush, H. (Det) .564

Adjusted OPS
Ruth, B. (NY) 228
Goslin, G. (Was) 155
Gehrig, L. (NY) 154

Adjusted Batting Runs
Ruth, B. (NY) 101.0
Gehrig, L. (NY) 47.0
Goslin, G. (Was) 45.0

Runs Created/Game
Ruth, B. (NY) 15.80
Heilmann, H. (Det) 9.10
Manush, H. (Det) 9.00

Fielding Runs
Kamm, W. (Chi) 17.5
Sewell, J. (Cle) 12.5
Todt, P. (Bos) 11.3

Win Shares – Batters
Ruth, B. (NY) 45
Goslin, G. (Was) 33
Gehrig, L. (NY) 30

TPW – Batters
Ruth, B. (NY) 8.4
Sewell, J. (Cle) 4.5
Goslin, G. (Was) 4.3

TEAM	CG	SH	SV	IP	H	H/G	ER	HR	BB	SO	OAV	RAT	ERA	ERA+	CERA	PR+	PF	FA	E	DP	FR	BW	PW	FW	TPW	DIF
NY	63	4	20	1372^{1}	1442	9.5	588	56	478	486	.274	1.399	3.86	100	3.70	23.0	96	.966	210	117	-23.4	**13.5**	2.2	-2.3	**13.4**	.6
CLE	**96**	**11**	4	1374	1412	9.2	519	49	**450**	381	.271	1.355	3.40	119	3.54	69.1	101	.972	173	153	**30.9**	-1.5	6.7	**3.0**	8.2	2.8
PHI	62	10	16	1346	**1362**	**9.1**	**449**	**38**	451	**571**	**.268**	**1.347**	**3.00**	139	**3.41**	**175.4**	104	.971	171	131	-0.3	-7.1	**17.0**	.0	9.8	-1.8
WAS	65	5	**26**	1348^{1}	1489	9.9	650	45	566	418	.287	1.524	4.34	89	4.27	-77.2	96	.969	184	129	5.9	6.3	-7.5	.6	-.7	6.7
CHI	85	**11**	12	1380	1426	9.3	573	47	506	458	.271	1.400	3.74	103	3.61	5.3	96	**.974**	**165**	122	13.3	5.3	.5	1.3	7.1	-2.1
DET	57	10	18	**1394^{2}**	1570	10.1	683	58	555	469	.292	1.524	4.41	92	4.41	-40.5	101	.969	193	151	-14.3	3.9	-3.9	-1.4	-1.4	3.4
STL	64	5	9	1368	1549	10.2	708	86	654	337	.295	1.610	4.66	92	4.87	-69.1	107	.963	235	**167**	11.7	-7.7	-6.7	1.1	-13.2	-1.8
BOS	53	6	5	1362	1520	10.0	714	45	546	336	.294	1.517	4.72	**86**	4.23	-75.0	101	.971	193	143	-24.1	-13.6	-7.3	-2.3	-23.2	-6.8
Total	**545**	**62**	**110**	**10945^{1}**		**9.7**	**4884**					**1.460**	**4.02**													

Wins		Win Percentage		Games		Complete Games		Shutouts		Saves	
Uhle, G. (Cle)	27	Uhle, G. (Cle)	.711	Marberry, F. (Was)	64	Uhle, G. (Cle)	32	Wells, E. (Det)	4	Marberry, F. (Was)	22
Pennock, H. (NY)	23	Pennock, H. (NY)	.676	Pate, J. (Phi)	47	Lyons, T. (Chi)	24	9 players tied with	3	Dauss, H. (Det)	9
Shocker, U. (NY)	19	Shocker, U. (NY)	.633	Grove, L. (Phi)	45	Johnson, W. (Was)	22			2 players tied with	6

Innings Pitched		Fewest Hits/Game		Fewest BB/Game		Strikeouts		Ratio		Earned Run Average	
Uhle, G. (Cle)	318^{1}	Grove, L. (Phi)	7.92	Pennock, H. (NY)	1.45	Grove, L. (Phi)	194	Pennock, H. (NY)	1.27	Grove, L. (Phi)	2.51
Lyons, T. (Chi)	283^{2}	Thomas, T. (Chi)	8.13	Smith, S. (Cle)	1.48	Uhle, G. (Cle)	159	Grove, L. (Phi)	1.27	Uhle, G. (Cle)	2.83
Pennock, H. (NY)	266^{1}	Uhle, G. (Cle)	8.48	Quinn, J. (Phi)	1.98	Thomas, T. (Chi)	127	Johnson, W. (Was)	1.27	Lyons, T. (Chi)	3.01

Adjusted ERA		Component ERA		Opponents' Batting Avg.		Adjusted Pitching Runs		Win Shares – Pitchers		TPW – Pitchers	
Grove, L. (Phi)	166	Grove, L. (Phi)	2.91	Thomas, T. (Chi)	.244	Grove, L. (Phi)	48	Uhle, G. (Cle)	32	Grove, L. (Phi)	4.1
Uhle, G. (Cle)	143	Lyons, T. (Chi)	3.03	Grove, L. (Phi)	.244	Uhle, G. (Cle)	36	Grove, L. (Phi)	25	Uhle, G. (Cle)	3.8
Rommel, E. (Phi)	135	Hoyt, W. (NY)	3.11	Lyons, T. (Chi)	.252	Rommel, E. (Phi)	26	Lyons, T. (Chi)	24	Lyons, T. (Chi)	2.3

1927 National League

TEAM	G	W	L	PCT	GB	R	OR	EW	AB	H	2B	3B	HR	TB	BB	SO	SB	CS	AVG	OBP	SLG	OPS	OPS+	BR/A	PF	RC
PIT	156	94	60	.610	....	**817**	659	93	**5397**	**1648**	258	78	54	2224	437	355	65	....	**.305**	**.361**	.412	.773	106	47	107	791
STL	153	92	61	.601	1.5	754	665	86	5207	1450	264	**79**	84	2124	**484**	511	**110**	....	.278	.343	.408	.751	104	26	103	723
NY	155	92	62	.597	2	**817**	720	87	5372	1594	251	62	**109**	**2296**	461	462	73	....	.297	.356	**.427**	**.783**	**116**	**115**	100	**805**
CHI	153	85	68	.556	8.5	750	661	86	5303	1505	**266**	63	74	2119	481	492	65	....	.284	.346	.400	.746	106	42	100	730
CIN	153	75	78	.490	18.5	643	653	75	5185	1439	222	77	29	1902	402	**332**	62	....	.278	.332	.367	.699	96	-27	97	628
BRO	154	65	88	.425	28.5	541	**619**	66	5193	1314	195	74	39	1774	368	494	106	....	.253	.306	.342	.647	79	-155	100	539
BOS	155	60	94	.390	34	651	771	64	5370	1498	216	61	37	1947	346	363	100	....	.279	.326	.363	.688	98	-20	92	626
PHI	155	51	103	.331	43	678	903	56	5317	1487	216	46	57	1966	434	482	68	....	.280	.337	.370	.707	94	-38	101	660
Total	**617**					**5651**			**42344**	**11935**	**1888**	**540**	**483**		**3413**	**3491**	**649**		**.282**	**.339**	**.386**	**.725**				

Runs		Hits		Doubles		Triples		Home Runs		Total Bases	
Hornsby, R. (NY)	133	Waner, P. (Pit)	237	Stephenson, R. (Chi)	46	Waner, P. (Pit)	18	Williams, C. (Phi)	30	Waner, P. (Pit)	342
Waner, L. (Pit)	133	Waner, L. (Pit)	223	Waner, P. (Pit)	42	Bottomley, J. (StL)	15	Wilson, H. (Chi)	30	Hornsby, R. (NY)	333
Wilson, H. (Chi)	119	Frisch, F. (StL)	208	2 players tied with	36	Thompson, F. (Phi)	14	Hornsby, R. (NY)	26	Wilson, H. (Chi)	319

Runs Batted In		Bases On Balls		Stolen Bases		Batting Average		On-Base Percentage		Slugging Average	
Waner, P. (Pit)	131	Hornsby, R. (NY)	86	Frisch, F. (StL)	48	Waner, P. (Pit)	.380	Hornsby, R. (NY)	.448	Hafey, C. (StL)	.590
Wilson, H. (Chi)	129	Harper, G. (NY)	84	Carey, M. (Bro)	32	Hornsby, R. (NY)	.361	Waner, P. (Pit)	.437	Hornsby, R. (NY)	.586
Hornsby, R. (NY)	125	2 players tied with	74	Hendrick, H. (Bro)	29	Waner, L. (Pit)	.355	Harper, G. (NY)	.435	Wilson, H. (Chi)	.579

Adjusted OPS		Adjusted Batting Runs		Runs Created/Game		Fielding Runs		Win Shares – Batters		TPW – Batters	
Hornsby, R. (NY)	175	Hornsby, R. (NY)	64.0	Hornsby, R. (NY)	9.90	Frisch, F. (StL)	52.1	Hornsby, R. (NY)	40	Frisch, F. (StL)	7.7
Wilson, H. (Chi)	159	Waner, P. (Pit)	47.0	Waner, P. (Pit)	9.20	Traynor, P. (Pit)	24.0	Waner, P. (Pit)	36	Hornsby, R. (NY)	5.5
Waner, P. (Pit)	152	Wilson, H. (Chi)	46.0	Wilson, H. (Chi)	8.30	Jackson, T. (NY)	15.2	Frisch, F. (StL)	34	Jackson, T. (NY)	4.4

TEAM	CG	SH	SV	IP	H	H/G	ER	HR	BB	SO	OAV	RAT	ERA	ERA+	CERA	PR+	PF	FA	E	DP	FR	BW	PW	FW	TPW	DIF
PIT	**90**	10	10	1385	1400	9.1	563	58	418	435	.266	1.313	3.66	112	3.38	61.0	105	.969	187	130	7.8	4.6	6.0	.8	**11.4**	5.6
STL	89	**14**	11	1367^{1}	1416	9.3	542	72	363	394	.271	**1.301**	3.57	111	3.47	33.4	101	.966	213	**170**	23.0	2.6	3.3	2.3	8.1	7.9
NY	65	7	**16**	1381^{2}	1520	9.9	609	77	453	442	.283	1.428	3.97	97	4.05	-12.5	98	.969	195	160	-5.4	**11.4**	-1.2	-.5	9.6	5.4
CHI	75	11	5	1385	1439	9.4	562	50	514	465	.273	1.410	3.65	106	3.76	3.3	99	.971	181	152	**28.9**	4.2	.3	**2.8**	7.4	1.6
CIN	87	12	12	1368	1472	9.7	538	**36**	**316**	407	.281	1.307	3.54	107	**3.36**	43.0	97	**.973**	**165**	160	-6.3	-2.7	4.2	-.6	.9	-1.9
BRO	74	7	10	1375^{1}	**1382**	**9.0**	**513**	63	418	**574**	**.265**	1.309	**3.36**	118	3.37	**89.3**	101	.963	229	117	2.3	-15.3	**8.8**	.2	-6.2	-4.8
BOS	52	3	11	**1390**	1602	10.4	652	43	468	402	.296	1.489	4.22	88	4.17	-52.4	95	.963	231	130	-26.9	-2.0	-5.2	-2.7	-9.8	-7.2
PHI	81	5	6	1355^{1}	1710	11.4	807	84	462	377	.317	1.603	5.36	**77**	5.12	-160.4	106	.972	169	152	-24.6	-3.8	-15.8	-2.4	-22.0	-4.0
Total	**613**	**69**	**81**	**11007^{2}**		**9.8**	**4786**					**1.395**	**3.91**													

Wins		Win Percentage		Games		Complete Games		Shutouts		Saves	
Root, C. (Chi)	26	Haines, J. (StL)	.706	Root, C. (Chi)	48	Haines, J. (StL)	25	Haines, J. (StL)	6	Sherdel, B. (StL)	6
Haines, J. (StL)	24	Grimes, B. (NY)	.704	Scott, J. (Phi)	48	Meadows, L. (Pit)	25	Lucas, R. (Cin)	4	Nehf, A. (Cin,Chi)	5
Hill, C. (Pit)	22	Kremer, R. (Pit)	.704	Ehrhardt, R. (Bro)	46	Vance, D. (Bro)	25	Root, C. (Chi)	4	Mogridge, G. (Bos)	5

Innings Pitched		Fewest Hits/Game		Fewest BB/Game		Strikeouts		Ratio		Earned Run Average	
Root, C. (Chi)	309	Vance, D. (Bro)	7.97	Alexander, G. (StL)	1.28	Vance, D. (Bro)	184	Alexander, G. (StL)	1.12	Kremer, R. (Pit)	2.47
Haines, J. (StL)	300^{2}	Kremer, R. (Pit)	8.16	Lucas, R. (Cin)	1.46	Root, C. (Chi)	145	Lucas, R. (Cin)	1.13	Alexander, G. (StL)	2.52
Meadows, L. (Pit)	299^{1}	Haines, J. (StL)	8.17	Donohue, P. (Cin)	1.51	May, J. (Cin)	121	Vance, D. (Bro)	1.14	Vance, D. (Bro)	2.70

Adjusted ERA		Component ERA		Opponents' Batting Avg.		Adjusted Pitching Runs		Win Shares – Pitchers		TPW – Pitchers	
Kremer, R. (Pit)	166	Lucas, R. (Cin)	2.47	Vance, D. (Bro)	.239	Kremer, R. (Pit)	40	Alexander, G. (StL)	28	Alexander, G. (StL)	4.0
Alexander, G. (StL)	157	Kremer, R. (Pit)	2.50	Kremer, R. (Pit)	.244	Alexander, G. (StL)	38	Haines, J. (StL)	28	Kremer, R. (Pit)	3.8
Vance, D. (Bro)	147	Vance, D. (Bro)	2.56	Haines, J. (StL)	.245	Vance, D. (Bro)	38	Vance, D. (Bro)	25	Vance, D. (Bro)	3.6

1927 American League

TEAM	G	W	L	PCT	GB	R	OR	EW	AB	H	2B	3B	HR	TB	BB	SO	SB	CS	AVG	OBP	SLG	OPS	OPS+	BR/A	PF	RC
NY	155	110	44	.714	....	**975**	**599**	112	5347	**1644**	291	**103**	**158**	**2615**	**635**	605	90	64	**.307**	**.383**	**.489**	**.872**	**135**	**266**	97	**1016**
PHI	155	91	63	.591	19	841	726	88	5296	1606	281	70	56	2195	551	**326**	101	63	.303	.372	.414	.787	104	36	106	839
WAS	157	85	69	.552	25	782	730	82	**5389**	1549	268	87	29	2078	498	359	133	52	.287	.351	.386	.737	98	-3	99	759
DET	156	82	71	.536	27.5	845	805	80	5299	1533	282	100	51	2168	587	420	**139**	73	.289	.363	.409	.772	104	43	101	814
CHI	153	70	83	.458	39.5	662	708	71	5157	1433	285	61	36	1948	493	389	89	75	.278	.344	.378	.722	95	-44	98	685
CLE	153	66	87	.431	43.5	668	766	66	5202	1471	**321**	52	26	1974	381	366	65	72	.283	.338	.379	.717	90	-88	101	669
STL	155	59	94	.386	50.5	724	904	60	5220	1440	262	59	55	1985	443	420	90	66	.276	.337	.380	.718	88	-94	103	683
BOS	154	51	103	.331	59	597	856	50	5207	1348	271	78	28	1859	430	456	81	**46**	.259	.320	.357	.677	82	-133	98	614
Total	**619**					**6094**			**42117**	**12024**	**2261**	**610**	**439**		**4018**	**3341**	**788**	**511**	**.285**	**.351**	**.399**	**.751**				

Runs		Hits		Doubles		Triples		Home Runs		Total Bases	
Ruth, B. (NY)	158	Combs, E. (NY)	231	Gehrig, L. (NY)	52	Combs, E. (NY)	23	Ruth, B. (NY)	60	Gehrig, L. (NY)	447
Gehrig, L. (NY)	149	Gehrig, L. (NY)	218	Burns, G. (Cle)	51	Gehrig, L. (NY)	18	Gehrig, L. (NY)	47	Ruth, B. (NY)	417
Combs, E. (NY)	137	2 players tied with	201	Heilmann, H. (Det)	50	Manush, H. (Det)	18	Lazzeri, T. (NY)	18	Combs, E. (NY)	331

Runs Batted In		Bases On Balls		Stolen Bases		Batting Average		On-Base Percentage		Slugging Average	
Gehrig, L. (NY)	175	Ruth, B. (NY)	137	Sisler, G. (StL)	27	Heilmann, H. (Det)	.398	Ruth, B. (NY)	.486	Ruth, B. (NY)	.772
Ruth, B. (NY)	164	Gehrig, L. (NY)	109	Meusel, B. (NY)	24	Gehrig, L. (NY)	.373	Heilmann, H. (Det)	.475	Gehrig, L. (NY)	.765
2 players tied with	120	Bishop, M. (Phi)	105	3 players tied with	22	Fothergill, B. (Det)	.359	Gehrig, L. (NY)	.474	Heilmann, H. (Det)	.616

Adjusted OPS		Adjusted Batting Runs		Runs Created/Game		Fielding Runs		Win Shares – Batters		TPW – Batters	
Ruth, B. (NY)	229	Ruth, B. (NY)	107.0	Ruth, B. (NY)	15.00	Bluege, O. (Was)	22.5	Ruth, B. (NY)	45	Ruth, B. (NY)	9.5
Gehrig, L. (NY)	224	Gehrig, L. (NY)	107.0	Gehrig, L. (NY)	14.20	Falk, B. (Chi)	18.4	Gehrig, L. (NY)	44	Gehrig, L. (NY)	9.1
Heilmann, H. (Det)	179	Heilmann, H. (Det)	62.0	Heilmann, H. (Det)	12.20	Koenig, M. (NY)	16.1	Heilmann, H. (Det)	32	Lazzeri, T. (NY)	4.2

TEAM	CG	SH	SV	IP	H	H/G	ER	HR	BB	SO	OAV	RAT	ERA	ERA+	CERA	PR+	PF	FA	E	DP	FR	BW	PW	FW	TPW	DIF
NY	82	11	20	1389²	1403	9.1	494	42	409	431	.267	1.304	3.20	120	3.27	96.6	93	.969	195	123	3.9	25.3	9.2	.4	34.8	-1.8
PHI	65	8	24	1384	1467	9.5	610	65	442	553	.278	1.379	3.97	107	3.77	60.5	103	.969	190	124	-15.6	3.4	5.7	-1.5	7.7	6.3
WAS	62	10	23	1402	1434	9.2	618	53	491	497	.269	1.373	3.97	102	3.62	-0.6	98	.969	195	125	15.2	-.2	-.1	1.4	1.1	6.9
DET	75	5	17	1387²	1542	10.0	638	52	577	421	.290	1.527	4.14	102	4.34	24.3	102	.967	206	173	-13.7	4.0	2.3	-1.3	5.1	.9
CHI	85	10	8	1367	1467	9.7	594	55	440	365	.283	1.395	3.91	103	3.84	1.8	98	.971	178	131	21.8	-4.2	.2	2.1	-1.9	-4.1
CLE	72	5	8	1353¹	1542	10.2	642	37	508	366	.295	1.515	4.27	98	4.27	-4.4	101	.968	201	146	-6.6	-8.4	-.1	-.6	-9.4	-.6
STL	80	4	8	1353¹	1592	10.6	744	79	604	385	.303	1.623	4.95	88	4.87	-98.3	105	.960	248	166	8.5	-8.9	-9.3	.8	-17.5	.5
BOS	63	6	7	1366¹	1603	10.6	716	56	558	381	.305	1.582	4.72	89	4.72	-60.3	102	.964	228	167	-15.3	-12.6	-5.7	-1.5	-19.8	-6.2
Total	584	59	115	11003¹		9.9	5056					1.461	4.14													

	Wins	
Hoyt, W. (NY)		22
Lyons, T. (Chi)		22
Grove, L. (Phi)		20

Win Percentage
Pipgras, G. (NY) .769
Hoyt, W. (NY) .759
Shocker, U. (NY) .750

Games
Braxton, G. (Was) 58
Marberry, F. (Was) 56
Grove, L. (Phi) 51

Complete Games
Lyons, T. (Chi) 30
Thomas, T. (Chi) 24
Hoyt, W. (NY) 23

Shutouts
Lisenbee, H. (Was) 4
8 players tied with 3

Saves
Braxton, G. (Was) 13
Moore, W. (NY) 13
2 players tied with 9

Innings Pitched
Lyons, T. (Chi) 307²
Thomas, T. (Chi) 307¹
Hudlin, W. (Cle) 264²

Fewest Hits/Game
Moore, W. (NY) 7.82
Thomas, T. (Chi) 7.93
Pipgras, G. (NY) 8.01

Fewest BB/Game
Quinn, J. (Phi) 1.65
Shocker, U. (NY) 1.84
Hoyt, W. (NY) 1.90

Strikeouts
Braxton, G. (Was) 174
Walberg, R. (Phi) 136
Thomas, T. (Chi) 107

Ratio
Braxton, G. (Was) 1.14
Moore, W. (NY) 1.15
Hoyt, W. (NY) 1.15

Earned Run Average
Moore, W. (NY) 2.28
Hoyt, W. (NY) 2.63
Shocker, U. (NY) 2.84

Adjusted ERA
Moore, W. (NY) 169
Hoyt, W. (NY) 146
Lyons, T. (Chi) 143

Component ERA
Moore, W. (NY) 2.33
Braxton, G. (Was) 2.52
Lyons, T. (Chi) 2.54

Opponents' Batting Avg.
Moore, W. (NY) .234
Hadley, B. (Was) .244
Thomas, T. (Chi) .244

Adjusted Pitching Runs
Moore, W. (NY) 37
Lyons, T. (Chi) 36
Grove, L. (Phi) 34

Win Shares – Pitchers
Lyons, T. (Chi) 30
Thomas, T. (Chi) 27
2 players tied with 24

TPW – Pitchers
Lyons, T. (Chi) 4.0
Hoyt, W. (NY) 3.2
Grove, L. (Phi) 3.0

1928 National League

TEAM	G	W	L	PCT	GB	R	OR	EW	AB	H	2B	3B	HR	TB	BB	SO	SB	CS	AVG	OBP	SLG	OPS	OPS+	BR/A	PF	RC
STL	154	95	59	.617	....	807	636	95	5357	1505	292	70	113	2276	568	438	82	....	.281	.353	.425	.778	108	60	102	802
NY	155	93	61	.604	2	807	653	93	5459	1600	276	59	118	2348	444	376	62	....	.293	.349	.430	.779	109	64	100	805
CHI	154	91	63	.591	4	714	615	88	5260	1460	251	64	92	2115	508	517	83	....	.278	.345	.402	.747	103	22	99	728
PIT	152	85	67	.559	9	837	704	89	5371	1659	246	100	52	2261	435	352	64	....	.309	.364	.421	.785	108	58	104	809
CIN	153	78	74	.513	16	648	686	72	5184	1449	229	67	32	1908	386	330	83	....	.280	.333	.368	.701	91	-68	98	630
BRO	155	77	76	.503	17.5	665	640	79	5243	1393	229	70	66	1960	557	510	81	....	.266	.340	.374	.714	94	-35	99	673
BOS	153	50	103	.327	44.5	631	878	52	5228	1439	241	41	52	1918	447	377	60	....	.275	.335	.367	.702	95	-35	95	643
PHI	152	43	109	.283	51	660	957	49	5234	1396	257	47	85	2002	503	510	53	....	.267	.333	.382	.716	90	-71	103	667
Total	614					5769			42336	11901	2021	518	610		3848	3410	568		.281	.344	.397	.741				

Runs
Waner, P. (Pit) 142
Bottomley, J. (StL) 123
Waner, L. (Pit) 121

Hits
Lindstrom, F. (NY) 231
Waner, P. (Pit) 223
Waner, L. (Pit) 221

Doubles
Waner, P. (Pit) 50
Hafey, C. (StL) 46
2 players tied with 42

Triples
Bottomley, J. (StL) 20
Waner, P. (Pit) 19
Waner, L. (Pit) 14

Home Runs
Bottomley, J. (StL) 31
Wilson, H. (Chi) 31
Hafey, C. (StL) 27

Total Bases
Bottomley, J. (StL) 362
Lindstrom, F. (NY) 330
Waner, P. (Pit) 329

Runs Batted In
Bottomley, J. (StL) 136
Traynor, P. (Pit) 124
Wilson, H. (Chi) 120

Bases On Balls
Hornsby, R. (Bos) 107
Douthit, T. (StL) 84
Bressler, R. (Bro) 80

Stolen Bases
Cuyler, K. (Chi) 37
Frisch, F. (StL) 29
2 players tied with 19

Batting Average
Hornsby, R. (Bos) .387
Waner, P. (Pit) .370
Lindstrom, F. (NY) .358

On-Base Percentage
Hornsby, R. (Bos) .498
Waner, P. (Pit) .446
Grantham, G. (Pit) .408

Slugging Average
Hornsby, R. (Bos) .632
Bottomley, J. (StL) .628
Hafey, C. (StL) .604

Adjusted OPS
Hornsby, R. (Bos) 204
Bottomley, J. (StL) 162
Wilson, H. (Chi) 159

Adjusted Batting Runs
Hornsby, R. (Bos) 81.0
Bottomley, J. (StL) 51.0
Waner, P. (Pit) 49.0

Runs Created/Game
Hornsby, R. (Bos) 12.40
Waner, P. (Pit) 9.60
Bottomley, J. (StL) 9.10

Fielding Runs
Maguire, F. (NY) 40.4
Frisch, F. (StL) 24.5
Jackson, T. (NY) 22.8

Win Shares – Batters
Waner, P. (Pit) 34
Hornsby, R. (Bos) 33
Lindstrom, F. (NY) 32

TPW – Batters
Hornsby, R. (Bos) 5.9
Lindstrom, F. (NY) 4.7
Jackson, T. (NY) 3.8

TEAM	CG	SH	SV	IP	H	H/G	ER	HR	BB	SO	OAV	RAT	ERA	ERA+	CERA	PR+	PF	FA	E	DP	FR	BW	PW	FW	TPW	DIF
STL	83	4	21	1415¹	1470	9.4	531	86	399	422	.270	1.321	3.38	118	3.58	87.6	100	.974	160	134	9.7	5.9	8.6	1.0	15.4	2.6
NY	79	7	16	1394	1454	9.4	568	77	405	399	.273	1.334	3.67	107	3.62	22.8	98	.972	178	175	14.6	6.3	2.2	1.4	9.9	6.1
CHI	75	12	14	1380²	1383	9.0	521	56	508	531	.267	1.370	3.40	113	3.61	21.2	96	.975	156	176	47.3	2.2	2.1	4.6	8.9	5.1
PIT	82	8	11	1354	1422	9.4	594	66	446	385	.274	1.380	3.95	103	3.71	12.7	102	.967	201	123	3.6	5.7	1.2	.4	7.3	1.7
CIN	68	11	11	1371²	1516	10.0	600	58	410	355	.289	1.404	3.94	100	3.87	-1.6	99	.974	162	194	3.5	-6.6	-.2	.3	-6.4	8.4
BRO	75	16	15	1396	1378	8.9	504	59	468	551	.260	1.322	3.25	122	3.35	118.6	100	.965	217	113	-6.4	-3.4	11.6	-.6	7.5	-6.5
BOS	54	1	6	1360	1596	10.6	730	100	524	343	.298	1.559	4.83	81	4.82	-92.1	98	.969	193	141	-47.5	-3.5	-9.0	-4.6	-17.1	-8.9
PHI	42	4	11	1346²	1664	11.1	835	108	675	402	.362	1.737	5.58	77	5.77	-161.5	107	.971	181	171	-23.3	-6.9	-15.8	-2.3	-25.0	-8.0
Total	558	63	105	11018¹		9.7	4883					1.427	3.99													

Wins
Benton, L. (NY) 25
Grimes, B. (Pit) 25
Vance, D. (Bro) 22

Win Percentage
Benton, L. (NY) .735
Haines, J. (StL) .714
Bush, G. (Chi) .714

Games
Grimes, B. (Pit) 48
Kolp, R. (Cin) 44
Rixey, E. (Cin) 43

Complete Games
Benton, L. (NY) 28
Grimes, B. (Pit) 28
Vance, D. (Bro) 24

Shutouts
5 players tied with 4

Saves
Haid, H. (StL) 5
Sherdel, B. (StL) 5
2 players tied with 4

Innings Pitched
Grimes, B. (Pit) 330²
Benton, L. (NY) 310¹
Rixey, E. (Cin) 291¹

Fewest Hits/Game
Vance, D. (Bro) 7.26
Blake, S. (Chi) 7.82
Malone, P. (Chi) 7.83

Fewest BB/Game
Alexander, G. (StL) 1.37
Sherdel, B. (StL) 2.03
Benton, L. (NY) 2.06

Strikeouts
Vance, D. (Bro) 200
Malone, P. (Chi) 155
Root, C. (Chi) 122

Ratio
Vance, D. (Bro) 1.06
Grimes, B. (Pit) 1.17
Benton, L. (NY) 1.19

Earned Run Average
Vance, D. (Bro) 2.09
Blake, S. (Chi) 2.47
Nehf, A. (Chi) 2.65

Adjusted ERA
Vance, D. (Bro) 190
Blake, S. (Chi) 156
Clark, W. (Bro) 148

Component ERA
Vance, D. (Bro) 2.20
Grimes, B. (Pit) 2.70
Clark, W. (Bro) 2.84

Opponents' Batting Avg.
McWeeny, D. (Bro) .235

Adjusted Pitching Runs
Vance, D. (Bro) 60
Grimes, B. (Pit) 38
Benton, L. (NY) 38

Win Shares – Pitchers
Vance, D. (Bro) 32
Benton, L. (NY) 30
Grimes, B. (Pit) 30

TPW – Pitchers
Vance, D. (Bro) 6.1
Grimes, B. (Pit) 4.8
Sherdel, B. (StL) 3.3

1928 American League

TEAM	G	W	L	PCT	GB	R	OR	EW	AB	H	2B	3B	HR	TB	BB	SO	SB	CS	AVG	OBP	SLG	OPS	OPS+	BR/A	PF	RC
NY	154	101	53	.656	....	894	685	97	5337	1578	269	79	133	2404	562	544	51	51	.296	.365	.450	.816	124	172	97	888
PHI	153	98	55	.641	2.5	829	615	99	5226	1540	323	75	89	2280	533	442	59	48	.295	.364	.436	.800	113	96	103	845
STL	154	82	72	.532	19	772	742	80	5217	1431	276	76	63	2048	548	479	76	43	.274	.347	.393	.739	97	-14	103	736
WAS	155	75	79	.487	26	718	705	78	5320	1510	277	93	40	2093	481	390	110	59	.284	.347	.393	.740	101	12	99	744
CHI	155	72	82	.468	29	656	725	69	5207	1405	231	77	24	1862	469	488	139	82	.270	.334	.358	.691	88	-78	99	641
DET	154	68	86	.442	33	744	804	71	5292	1476	265	97	62	2121	469	438	113	77	.279	.340	.401	.741	98	-16	102	729
CLE	155	62	92	.403	39	674	830	61	5386	1535	299	61	34	2058	377	426	50	52	.285	.336	.382	.718	93	-60	101	695
BOS	154	57	96	.373	43.5	589	770	56	5132	1356	260	62	38	1854	389	512	99	64	.264	.319	.361	.680	85	-109	98	601
Total	617					5876			42117	11831	2200	620	483		3828	3719	697	476	.281	.344	.397	.741				

Runs
Ruth, B. (NY) 163
Gehrig, L. (NY) 139
Combs, E. (NY) 118

Hits
Manush, H. (StL) 241
Gehrig, L. (NY) 210
Rice, S. (Was) 202

Doubles
Gehrig, L. (NY) 47
Manush, H. (StL) 47
Meusel, B. (NY) 45

Triples
Combs, E. (NY) 21
Manush, H. (StL) 20
Gehringer, C. (Det) 16

Home Runs
Ruth, B. (NY) 54
Gehrig, L. (NY) 27
Goslin, G. (Was) 17

Total Bases
Ruth, B. (NY) 380
Manush, H. (StL) 367
Gehrig, L. (NY) 364

Runs Batted In
Gehrig, L. (NY) 142
Ruth, B. (NY) 142
Meusel, B. (NY) 113

Bases On Balls
Ruth, B. (NY) 137
Blue, L. (StL) 105
Bishop, M. (Phi) 97

Stolen Bases
Myer, B. (Bos) 30
Mostil, J. (Chi) 23
Rice, H. (Det) 20

Batting Average
Goslin, G. (Was) .379
Manush, H. (StL) .378
Gehrig, L. (NY) .374

On-Base Percentage
Gehrig, L. (NY) .467
Ruth, B. (NY) .463
Goslin, G. (Was) .442

Slugging Average
Ruth, B. (NY) .709
Gehrig, L. (NY) .648
Goslin, G. (Was) .614

Adjusted OPS
Ruth, B. (NY) 211
Gehrig, L. (NY) 196
Goslin, G. (Was) 176

Adjusted Batting Runs
Ruth, B. (NY) 91.0
Gehrig, L. (NY) 78.0
Goslin, G. (Was) 53.0

Runs Created/Game
Ruth, B. (NY) 12.90
Gehrig, L. (NY) 11.80
Goslin, G. (Was) 10.90

Fielding Runs
Jamieson, C. (Cle) 18.5
Hale, S. (Phi) 13.1
Tavener, J. (Det) 12.3

Win Shares – Batters
Ruth, B. (NY) 45
Gehrig, L. (NY) 42
Manush, H. (StL) 35

TPW – Batters
Ruth, B. (NY) 6.9
Gehrig, L. (NY) 6.8
Goslin, G. (Was) 5.2

TEAM	CG	SH	SV	IP	H	H/G	ER	HR	BB	SO	OAV	RAT	ERA	ERA+	CERA	PR+	PF	FA	E	DP	FR	BW	PW	FW	TPW	DIF
NY	82	13	21	1375¹	1466	9.6	571	59	452	487	.276	1.395	3.74	100	3.59	22.8	93	.967	194	136	-20.0	16.6	2.2	-1.9	16.9	7.1
PHI	81	15	16	1367²	1349	8.9	510	66	424	607	.259	1.296	3.36	119	3.24	102.7	99	.970	181	124	-4.9	9.2	9.9	-.5	18.7	3.3
STL	80	6	15	1374¹	1487	9.7	637	93	454	456	.282	1.412	4.17	101	3.89	2.8	104	.969	189	146	0.7	-1.3	.3	.1	-1.0	6.0
WAS	77	15	10	1384	1420	9.2	597	40	466	462	.271	1.363	3.88	103	3.49	-0.1	99	.971	178	146	19.8	1.2	.0	1.9	3.1	-5.1
CHI	88	6	11	1378	1518	9.9	609	66	501	418	.287	1.465	3.98	102	3.99	3.1	100	.970	186	149	6.2	-7.5	.3	.6	-6.6	1.6
DET	65	5	16	1372	1481	9.7	659	58	567	451	.281	1.493	4.32	95	4.07	-30.8	102	.965	218	140	-1.5	-1.6	-3.0	-.1	-4.7	-4.3
CLE	71	4	15	1378	1615	10.6	684	52	511	416	.303	1.543	4.47	93	4.47	-42.0	103	.965	221	187	-8.2	-5.8	-4.1	-.8	-10.7	-4.3
BOS	70	5	9	1352	1492	9.9	659	49	452	407	.288	1.438	4.39	94	3.92	-49.7	102	.972	178	139	6.7	-10.6	-4.8	.6	-14.7	-4.3
Total	614	69	113	10981¹		9.7	4926					1.426	4.04													

Wins
Grove, L. (Phi) 24
Pipgras, G. (NY) 24
Hoyt, W. (NY) 23

Win Percentage
Crowder, A. (StL) .808
Hoyt, W. (NY) .767
Grove, L. (Phi) .750

Games
Marberry, F. (Was) 48
Morris, E. (Bos) 47
Pipgras, G. (NY) 46

Complete Games
Ruffing, R. (Bos) 25
Thomas, T. (Chi) 24
Thomas, T. (Chi) 24

Shutouts
Pennock, H. (NY) 5
4 players tied with 4

Saves
Hoyt, W. (NY) 8
Hudlin, W. (Cle) 7
2 players tied with 6

Innings Pitched
Pipgras, G. (NY) 300²
Ruffing, R. (Bos) 289¹
Thomas, T. (Chi) 283

Fewest Hits/Game
Braxton, G. (Was) 7.30
Grove, L. (Phi) 7.84
Earnshaw, G. (Phi) 8.13

Fewest BB/Game
Rommel, E. (Phi) 1.35
Quinn, J. (Phi) 1.45
Pennock, H. (NY) 1.71

Strikeouts
Grove, L. (Phi) 183
Pipgras, G. (NY) 139
Thomas, T. (Chi) 129

Ratio
Braxton, G. (Was) 1.01
Grove, L. (Phi) 1.12
Rommel, E. (Phi) 1.17

Earned Run Average
Braxton, G. (Was) 2.51
Pennock, H. (NY) 2.56
Grove, L. (Phi) 2.58

Adjusted ERA
Braxton, G. (Was) 159
Grove, L. (Phi) 155
Pennock, H. (NY) 147

Component ERA
Braxton, G. (Was) 1.92
Grove, L. (Phi) 2.35
Pennock, H. (NY) 2.74

Opponents' Batting Avg.
Braxton, G. (Was) .222
Grove, L. (Phi) .229
Earnshaw, G. (Phi) .240

Adjusted Pitching Runs
Grove, L. (Phi) 42
Braxton, G. (Was) 33
Pennock, H. (NY) 31

Win Shares – Pitchers
Grove, L. (Phi) 27
Thomas, T. (Chi) 26
Gray, D. (StL) 23

TPW – Pitchers
Grove, L. (Phi) 4.2
Thomas, T. (Chi) 3.1
Jones, S. (Was) 3.1

1929 National League

TEAM	G	W	L	PCT	GB	R	OR	EW	AB	H	2B	3B	HR	TB	BB	SO	SB	CS	AVG	OBP	SLG	OPS	OPS+	BR/A	PF	RC
CHI	156	98	54	.645	....	982	758	95	5471	1655	310	46	139	2474	589	567	103	....	.303	.373	.452	.825	111	92	100	916
PIT	154	88	65	.575	10.5	904	780	88	5490	1663	285	116	60	2360	503	335	94	....	.303	.364	.430	.794	101	8	102	850
NY	152	84	67	.556	13.5	897	709	93	5388	1594	251	47	136	2347	482	405	85	....	.296	.358	.436	.793	103	21	100	827
STL	154	78	74	.513	20	831	806	78	5364	1569	310	84	100	2347	490	455	72	....	.293	.354	.438	.792	101	3	101	819
PHI	154	71	82	.464	27.5	897	1032	66	5484	1693	305	51	153	2559	573	470	59	....	.309	.377	.467	.843	108	69	106	951
BRO	153	70	83	.458	28.5	755	888	64	5273	1535	282	69	99	2252	504	454	80	....	.291	.355	.427	.782	102	15	98	792
CIN	155	66	88	.429	33	686	760	69	5269	1478	258	79	34	1996	412	347	134	....	.281	.336	.379	.715	87	-100	95	664
BOS	154	56	98	.364	43	657	876	55	5291	1481	252	77	33	1986	408	432	65	....	.280	.335	.375	.710	85	-116	96	659
Total	616					6609			43030	12668	2253	569	754		3961	3465	692		.294	.357	.426	.783				

Runs
Hornsby, R. (Chi) 156
O'Doul, L. (Phi) 152
Ott, M. (NY) 138

Hits
O'Doul, L. (Phi) 254
Waner, L. (Pit) 234
Hornsby, R. (Chi) 229

Doubles
Frederick, J. (Bro) 52
Hafey, C. (StL) 47
Hornsby, R. (Chi) 47

Triples
Waner, L. (Pit) 20
Walker, C. (Cin) 15
Waner, P. (Pit) 15

Home Runs
Klein, C. (Phi) 43
Ott, M. (NY) 42
2 players tied with 39

Total Bases
Hornsby, R. (Chi) 409
Klein, C. (Phi) 405
O'Doul, L. (Phi) 397

Runs Batted In
Wilson, H. (Chi) 159
Ott, M. (NY) 151
Hornsby, R. (Chi) 149

Bases On Balls
Ott, M. (NY) 113
Grantham, G. (Pit) 93
Waner, P. (Pit) 89

Stolen Bases
Cuyler, K. (Chi) 43
Swanson, E. (Cin) 33
Frisch, F. (StL) 24

Batting Average
O'Doul, L. (Phi) .398
Herman, B. (Bro) .381
Hornsby, R. (Chi) .380

On-Base Percentage
O'Doul, L. (Phi) .465
Hornsby, R. (Chi) .459
Ott, M. (NY) .449

Slugging Average
Hornsby, R. (Chi) .679
Klein, C. (Phi) .657
Ott, M. (NY) .635

Adjusted OPS
Hornsby, R. (Chi) 178
Ott, M. (NY) 166
Herman, B. (Bro) 159

Adjusted Batting Runs
Hornsby, R. (Chi) 74.0
Ott, M. (NY) 60.0
O'Doul, L. (Phi) 59.0

Runs Created/Game
Hornsby, R. (Chi) 12.00
O'Doul, L. (Phi) 11.80
Ott, M. (NY) 10.80

Fielding Runs
Gelbert, C. (StL) 20.3
Maranville, R. (Bos) 17.8
Ott, M. (NY) 15.3

Win Shares – Batters
Hornsby, R. (Chi) 42
Wilson, H. (Chi) 32
2 players tied with 31

TPW – Batters
Hornsby, R. (Chi) 6.9
Ott, M. (NY) 5.8
O'Doul, L. (Phi) 5.1

TEAM	CG	SH	SV	IP	H	H/G	ER	HR	BB	SO	OAV	RAT	ERA	ERA+	CERA	PR+	PF	FA	E	DP	FR	BW	PW	FW	TPW	DIF
CHI	79	14	21	1398²	1542	9.9	646	77	537	548	.283	1.486	4.16	111	4.26	47.4	98	.975	154	169	23.5	8.3	4.3	2.1	14.8	7.2
PIT	79	5	13	1379	1530	10.0	668	96	439	409	.284	1.428	4.36	109	4.14	39.3	101	.970	181	136	23.4	.7	3.6	2.1	6.4	5.6
NY	68	9	13	1372	1536	10.1	605	102	387	431	.283	1.402	3.97	115		74.8	97	.975	158	163	17.9	1.9	6.8	1.6	10.3	-1.3
STL	83	6	8	1359²	1604	10.6	704	101	474	453	.297	1.528	4.66	100	4.74	4.3	99	.971	174	149	-4.4	.3	.4	-.4	.3	1.7
PHI	45	5	24	1348	1743	11.6	918	122	616	369	.318	1.750	6.13	85	6.10	-114.9	110	.969	191	153	-26.9	6.3	-10.4	-2.4	-6.6	1.6
BRO	59	8	16	1358	1553	10.3	742	92	549	549	.290	1.548	4.92	94	4.66	-13.7	98	.968	192	113	-33.4	1.4	-1.3	-3.0	-2.9	-3.1
CIN	75	5	8	1369¹	1558	10.2	671	61	413	347	.292	1.439	4.41	103	4.08	15.0	97	.974	162	148	7.5	-9.1	1.4	.7	-7.1	-3.9
BOS	78	4	12	1352²	1604	10.7	769	103	530	366	.302	1.578	5.12	91	4.95	-61.1	99	.967	204	146	-6.2	-10.5	-5.6	-.6	-16.6	-4.4
Total	566	56	115	10937¹		10.4	5723					1.519	4.71													

Wins
Malone, P. (Chi) 22
Lucas, R. (Cin) 19
Root, C. (Chi) 19

Win Percentage
Root, C. (Chi) .760
Bush, G. (Chi) .720
Grimes, B. (Pit) .708

Games
Bush, G. (Chi) 50
Willoughby, C. (Phi) 49
3 players tied with 43

Complete Games
Lucas, R. (Cin) 28
6 players tied with 19

Shutouts
Malone, P. (Chi) 5
Fitzsimmons, F. (NY) 4
Root, C. (Chi) 4

Saves
Bush, G. (Chi) 8
Morrison, J. (Bro) 8
Koupal, L. (Bro,Phi) 6

Innings Pitched
Clark, W. (Bro) 279
Root, C. (Chi) 272
Bush, G. (Chi) 270²

Fewest Hits/Game
Lucas, R. (Cin) 8.90
Hubbell, C. (NY) 9.17
Kremer, R. (Pit) 9.18

Fewest BB/Game
Vance, D. (Bro) 1.83
Lucas, R. (Cin) 1.93
Petty, J. (Pit) 2.05

Strikeouts
Malone, P. (Chi) 166
Clark, W. (Bro) 140
Vance, D. (Bro) 126

Ratio
Lucas, R. (Cin) 1.20
Vance, D. (Bro) 1.26
Hubbell, C. (NY) 1.27

Earned Run Average
Walker, B. (NY) 3.09
Grimes, B. (Pit) 3.13
Root, C. (Chi) 3.47

Adjusted ERA
Grimes, B. (Pit) 152
Walker, B. (NY) 148
Root, C. (Chi) 133

Component ERA
Lucas, R. (Cin) 2.92
Hubbell, C. (NY) 3.36
Clark, W. (Bro) 3.43

Opponents' Batting Avg.
Lucas, R. (Cin) .257
3 players tied with .265

Adjusted Pitching Runs
Grimes, B. (Pit) 38
Clark, W. (Bro) 34
Root, C. (Chi) 30

Win Shares – Pitchers
Lucas, R. (Cin) 26
4 players tied with 23

TPW – Pitchers
Grimes, B. (Pit) 4.0
Lucas, R. (Cin) 3.5
Clark, W. (Bro) 2.8

1929 American League

TEAM	G	W	L	PCT	GB	R	OR	EW	AB	H	2B	3B	HR	TB	BB	SO	SB	CS	AVG	OBP	SLG	OPS	OPS+	BR/A	PF	RC
PHI	151	104	46	.693	....	901	**615**	102	5204	1539	288	76	122	2345	543	440	61	**38**	.296	**.365**	.451	**.816**	111	91	104	875
NY	154	88	66	.571	18	899	775	88	5379	1587	262	74	**142**	2423	554	518	51	44	.295	.363	.450	.814	**123**	**175**	93	892
CLE	152	81	71	.533	24	717	736	74	5187	1525	294	79	62	2163	453	**363**	75	85	.294	.354	.417	.771	100	-13	104	763
STL	154	79	73	.520	26	733	713	78	5174	1426	277	64	46	1969	**589**	431	72	46	.276	.352	.381	.733	91	-52	104	724
WAS	153	71	81	.467	34	730	776	71	5237	1445	244	66	48	1965	556	400	86	61	.276	.348	.375	.723	91	-58	101	707
DET	155	70	84	.455	36	**926**	928	77	**5592**	**1671**	**339**	**97**	110	**2534**	521	496	95	72	**.299**	.361	**.453**	.814	114	106	100	**915**
CHI	152	59	93	.388	46	627	792	59	5248	1406	240	74	37	1905	425	436	**109**	65	.268	.325	.363	.688	83	-123	99	632
BOS	155	58	96	.377	48	605	803	56	5160	1377	285	69	28	1884	413	494	85	80	.267	.325	.365	.690	85	-123	98	616
Total	**613**					**6138**			**42181**	**11976**	**2229**	**599**	**595**		**4054**	**3578**	**634**	**491**	**.284**	**.349**	**.407**	**.757**				

Runs
Gehringer, C. (Det) 131
Johnson, R. (Det) 128
Gehrig, L. (NY) 127

Hits
Alexander, D. (Det) 215
Gehringer, C. (Det) 215
Simmons, A. (Phi) 212

Doubles
Gehringer, C. (Det) 45
Johnson, R. (Det) 45
Manush, H. (StL) 45

Triples
Gehringer, C. (Det) 19
Scarritt, R. (Bos) 17
Miller, B. (Phi) 16

Home Runs
Ruth, B. (NY) 46
Gehrig, L. (NY) 35
Simmons, A. (Phi) 34

Total Bases
Simmons, A. (Phi) 373
Alexander, D. (Det) 363
Ruth, B. (NY) 348

Runs Batted In
Simmons, A. (Phi) 157
Ruth, B. (NY) 154
Alexander, D. (Det) 137

Bases On Balls
Bishop, M. (Phi) 128
Blue, L. (StL) 126
Gehrig, L. (NY) 122

Stolen Bases
Gehringer, C. (Det) 27
Cissell, B. (Chi) 25
Miller, B. (Phi) 24

Batting Average
Fonseca, L. (Cle) .369
Simmons, A. (Phi) .365
Manush, H. (StL) .355

On-Base Percentage
Foxx, J. (Phi) .463
Gehrig, L. (NY) .431
Ruth, B. (NY) .430

Slugging Average
Ruth, B. (NY) .697
Simmons, A. (Phi) .642
Foxx, J. (Phi) .625

Adjusted OPS
Ruth, B. (NY) 199
Foxx, J. (Phi) 171
Gehrig, L. (NY) 170

Adjusted Batting Runs
Ruth, B. (NY) 72.0
Gehrig, L. (NY) 63.0
Foxx, J. (Phi) 59.0

Runs Created/Game
Ruth, B. (NY) 11.60
Foxx, J. (Phi) 11.40
Simmons, A. (Phi) 9.90

Fielding Runs
Melillo, S. (StL) 26.0
Durocher, L. (NY) 18.8
Kerr, J. (Chi) 16.7

Win Shares – Batters
Simmons, A. (Phi) 34
Foxx, J. (Phi) 34
2 players tied with 32

TPW – Batters
Ruth, B. (NY) 6.0
Lazzeri, T. (NY) 5.9
Simmons, A. (Phi) 4.9

TEAM	CG	SH	SV	IP	H	H/G	ER	HR	BB	SO	OAV	RAT	ERA	ERA+	CERA	PR+	PF	FA	E	DP	FR	BW	PW	FW	TPW	DIF
PHI	70	9	**24**	1357	**1371**	**9.1**	**519**	73	487	**573**	**.264**	**1.369**	**3.44**	123	**3.59**	**117.2**	100	**.975**	**146**	117	2.5	8.5	**11.0**	.2	**19.8**	9.2
NY	64	12	18	1366^{2}	1475	9.7	636	83	485	484	.277	1.434	4.19	92	4.04	-66.9	91	.970	178	153	14.8	**16.5**	-6.3	1.4	11.6	-.6
CLE	80	8	10	1352	1570	10.4	608	56	488	389	.295	1.522	4.05	110	4.43	70.0	105	.968	198	**162**	-11.9	-1.2	6.6	-1.1	4.3	.7
STL	83	**15**	10	1371	1469	9.6	622	100	**462**	415	.280	1.408	4.08	108	4.03	40.6	104	.975	156	148	11.5	-4.9	3.8	1.1	.0	3.0
WAS	62	3	17	1354^{2}	1429	9.5	653	**48**	496	494	.276	1.421	4.34	98	3.80	-32.4	100	.968	195	156	16.7	-5.4	-3.1	1.6	-6.9	1.9
DET	82	5	9	**1390^{1}**	1641	10.6	766	73	646	467	.301	1.645	4.96	**86**	4.97	-58.3	101	.961	242	149	-45.7	10.0	-5.5	-4.3	.1	-7.1
CHI	78	5	7	1357^{2}	1481	9.8	665	84	505	328	.284	1.463	4.41	97	4.22	-40.5	101	.969	188	153	**20.0**	-11.6	-3.8	**1.9**	-13.5	-3.5
BOS	**84**	9	5	1366^{2}	1537	10.1	672	78	496	416	.291	1.488	4.43	96	4.34	-16.0	101	.965	218	159	-7.3	-11.6	-1.5	-.7	-13.8	-5.2
Total	**603**	**66**	**100**	**10916**		**9.9**	**5141**					**1.469**	**4.24**													

Wins
Earnshaw, G. (Phi) 24
Ferrell, W. (Cle) 21
Grove, L. (Phi) 20

Win Percentage
Grove, L. (Phi) .769
Earnshaw, G. (Phi) .750
Ferrell, W. (Cle) .677

Games
Marberry, F. (Was) 49
Earnshaw, G. (Phi) 44
2 players tied with 43

Complete Games
Thomas, T. (Chi) 24
Gray, D. (StL) 23
Uhle, G. (Det) 23

Shutouts
4 players tied with 4

Saves
Marberry, F. (Was) 11
Moore, W. (NY) 8
Shores, B. (Phi) 7

Innings Pitched
Gray, D. (StL) 305
Hudlin, W. (Cle) 280^{1}
Grove, L. (Phi) 275^{1}

Fewest Hits/Game
Earnshaw, G. (Phi) 8.23
Wells, E. (NY) 8.33
Marberry, F. (Was) 8.38

Fewest BB/Game
Russell, J. (Bos) 1.58
Pennock, H. (NY) 1.60
Thomas, T. (Chi) 2.08

Strikeouts
Grove, L. (Phi) 170
Earnshaw, G. (Phi) 149
Pipgras, G. (NY) 125

Ratio
Marberry, F. (Was) 1.21
Thomas, T. (Chi) 1.27
Faber, R. (Chi) 1.29

Earned Run Average
Grove, L. (Phi) 2.81
Marberry, F. (Was) 3.06
Thomas, T. (Chi) 3.19

Adjusted ERA
Grove, L. (Phi) 150
Marberry, F. (Was) 139
Thomas, T. (Chi) 134

Component ERA
Marberry, F. (Was) 2.78
Grove, L. (Phi) 3.19
Hudlin, W. (Cle) 3.29

Opponents' Batting Avg.
Earnshaw, G. (Phi) .241
Wells, E. (NY) .248
Marberry, F. (Was) .252

Adjusted Pitching Runs
Grove, L. (Phi) 43
Hudlin, W. (Cle) 37
Marberry, F. (Was) 30

Win Shares – Pitchers
Grove, L. (Phi) 28
Marberry, F. (Was) 26
2 players tied with 25

TPW – Pitchers
Grove, L. (Phi) 4.1
Hudlin, W. (Cle) 3.2
Marberry, F. (Was) 2.9

1930 National League

TEAM	G	W	L	PCT	GB	R	OR	EW	AB	H	2B	3B	HR	TB	BB	SO	SB	CS	AVG	OBP	SLG	OPS	OPS+	BR/A	PF	RC
STL	154	92	62	.597	....	**1004**	784	96	5512	1732	**373**	89	104	2595	479	496	72	....	.314	.372	.471	.843	105	42	103	944
CHI	156	90	64	.584	2	998	870	88	5581	1722	305	72	**171**	**2684**	**588**	635	70	....	.309	**.378**	**.481**	**.859**	**112**	**106**	101	**1001**
NY	154	87	67	.565	5	959	814	90	5553	1769	264	83	143	2628	422	**382**	59	....	**.319**	.369	.473	.842	110	86	98	941
BRO	154	86	68	.558	6	871	**738**	90	5433	1654	303	73	122	2469	481	541	53	....	.304	.364	.454	.818	104	32	99	881
PIT	154	80	74	.519	12	891	928	74	5346	1622	285	**119**	86	2403	494	449	**76**	....	.303	.365	.449	.814	101	13	100	862
BOS	154	70	84	.455	22	693	835	63	5356	1503	246	78	66	2103	332	397	69	....	.281	.326	.393	.719	81	-164	97	669
CIN	154	59	95	.383	33	665	857	58	5245	1475	265	67	74	2096	445	489	48	....	.281	.339	.400	.739	88	-97	95	703
PHI	156	52	102	.338	40	944	1199	59	**5667**	**1783**	345	44	126	2594	450	459	34	....	.315	.367	.458	.825	97	-25	107	929
Total	**618**					**7025**			**43693**	**13260**	**2386**	**625**	**892**		**3691**	**3848**	**481**		**.303**	**.360**	**.448**	**.808**				

Runs
Klein, C. (Phi) 158
Cuyler, K. (Chi) 155
English, W. (Chi) 152

Hits
Terry, B. (NY) 254
Klein, C. (Phi) 250
Herman, B. (Bro) 241

Doubles
Klein, C. (Phi) 59
Cuyler, K. (Chi) 50
Herman, B. (Bro) 48

Triples
Comorosky, A. (Pit) 23
Waner, P. (Pit) 18
2 players tied with 17

Home Runs
Wilson, H. (Chi) 56
Klein, C. (Phi) 40
Berger, W. (Bos) 38

Total Bases
Klein, C. (Phi) 445
Wilson, H. (Chi) 423
Herman, B. (Bro) 416

Runs Batted In
Wilson, H. (Chi) 191
Klein, C. (Phi) 170
Cuyler, K. (Chi) 134

Bases On Balls
Wilson, H. (Chi) 105
Ott, M. (NY) 103
English, W. (Chi) 100

Stolen Bases
Cuyler, K. (Chi) 37
Herman, B. (Bro) 18
Waner, P. (Pit) 18

Batting Average
Terry, B. (NY) .401
Herman, B. (Bro) .393
Klein, C. (Phi) .386

On-Base Percentage
Ott, M. (NY) .458
Herman, B. (Bro) .455
Wilson, H. (Chi) .454

Slugging Average
Wilson, H. (Chi) .723
Klein, C. (Phi) .687
Herman, B. (Bro) .678

Adjusted OPS
Wilson, H. (Chi) 177
Herman, B. (Bro) 171
Terry, B. (NY) 159

Adjusted Batting Runs
Wilson, H. (Chi) 75.0
Herman, B. (Bro) 71.0
Terry, B. (NY) 61.0

Runs Created/Game
Wilson, H. (Chi) 12.40
Herman, B. (Bro) 12.20
Klein, C. (Phi) 11.70

Fielding Runs
Frisch, F. (StL) 30.7
Klein, C. (Phi) 19.7
Wright, G. (Bro) 17.9

Win Shares – Batters
Wilson, H. (Chi) 35
Terry, B. (NY) 32
Herman, B. (Bro) 32

TPW – Batters
Klein, C. (Phi) 5.6
Terry, B. (NY) 5.5
Wilson, H. (Chi) 4.9

TEAM	CG	SH	SV	IP	H	H/G	ER	HR	BB	SO	OAV	RAT	ERA	ERA+	CERA	PR+	PF	FA	E	DP	FR	BW	PW	FW	TPW	DIF
STL	63	5	**21**	1380^{2}	1594	10.4	673	87	476	**639**	.294	1.499	4.39	114	4.47	88.4	101	.970	183	**176**	7.3	3.7	7.8	.6	12.1	2.9
CHI	67	6	12	**1403^{2}**	1642	10.5	748	111	528	601	.294	1.546	4.80	102	4.76	19.0	98	.973	170	167	-6.2	**9.3**	1.7	-.6	10.5	2.5
NY	64	6	19	1363^{1}	1546	10.2	698	117	439	522	.287	1.456	4.61	103	4.45	7.1	95	**.974**	164	144	10.7	7.6	.6	.9	9.2	.8
BRO	74	**13**	15	1372	**1480**	**9.7**	**614**	115	**394**	526	**.278**	**1.366**	**4.03**	122	**3.99**	**101.1**	99	.972	174	167	**33.5**	2.8	**8.9**	**3.0**	**14.7**	-5.7
PIT	**80**	7	13	1361^{1}	1730	11.4	792	128	438	393	.313	1.593	5.24	95	5.31	-38.4	100	.965	216	164	-1.5	1.1	-3.4	-.1	-2.4	5.4
BOS	71	6	11	1361	1624	10.7	743	117	475	424	.301	1.542	4.91	100	4.85	3.2	99	.971	178	167	0.4	-14.5	.3	.0	-14.1	7.1
CIN	61	6	11	1335	1650	11.1	754	**75**	**394**	361	.310	1.531	5.08	95	4.70	-27.5	97	.973	**161**	164	-9.4	-8.6	-2.4	-.8	-11.8	-6.2
PHI	54	3	7	1372^{2}	1993	13.1	1023	142	543	384	.346	1.847	6.71	**81**	6.80	-155.5	110	.962	239	169	-35.7	-2.2	-13.7	-3.2	-19.1	-5.9
Total	**534**	**52**	**109**	**10949^{2}**		**10.9**	**6045**					**1.548**	**4.97**													

Wins
Kremer, R. (Pit) 20
Malone, P. (Chi) 20
Fitzsimmons, F. (NY) 19

Win Percentage
Fitzsimmons, F. (NY) .731
Malone, P. (Chi) .690
Brame, E. (Pit) .680

Games
Elliott, H. (Phi) 48
Collins, P. (Phi) 47
Bush, G. (Chi) 46

Complete Games
Brame, E. (Pit) 22
Malone, P. (Chi) 22
French, L. (Pit) 21

Shutouts
Root, C. (Chi) 4
Vance, D. (Bro) 4
2 players tied with 3

Saves
Bell, H. (StL) 8
Clark, W. (Bro) 6
Heving, J. (NY) 6

Innings Pitched
Kremer, R. (Pit) 276
French, L. (Pit) 274²
Malone, P. (Chi) 271²

Fewest Hits/Game
Vance, D. (Bro) 8.39
Hallahan, B. (StL) 8.84
Fitzsimmons, F. (NY) 9.23

Fewest BB/Game
Clark, W. (Bro) 1.71
Kolp, R. (Cin) 1.82
Johnson, S. (StL) 1.82

Strikeouts
Hallahan, B. (StL) 177
Vance, D. (Bro) 173
Kolp, R. (Cin) 142

Ratio
Vance, D. (Bro) 1.14
Clark, W. (Bro) 1.24
Kolp, R. (Cin) 1.27

Earned Run Average
Vance, D. (Bro) 2.61
Hubbell, C. (NY) 3.87
Walker, D. (NY) 3.93

Adjusted ERA
Vance, D. (Bro) 188
Elliott, J. (Bro) 124
Malone, P. (Chi) 124

Component ERA
Vance, D. (Bro) 2.74
Kolp, R. (Cin) 3.35
Clark, W. (Bro) 3.48

Opponents' Batting Avg.
Vance, D. (Bro) .246
Hallahan, B. (StL) .260
Fitzsimmons, F. (NY) .266

Adjusted Pitching Runs
Vance, D. (Bro) 60
Malone, P. (Chi) 30
Collins, P. (Phi) 24

Win Shares – Pitchers
Vance, D. (Bro) 26
Malone, P. (Chi) 24
Seibold, S. (Bos) 20

TPW – Pitchers
Vance, D. (Bro) 4.9
Malone, P. (Chi) 3.0
Collins, P. (Phi) 2.5

1930 American League

TEAM	G	W	L	PCT	GB	R	OR	EW	AB	H	2B	3B	HR	TB	BB	SO	SB	CS	AVG	OBP	SLG	OPS	OPS+	BR/A	PF	RC
PHI	154	102	52	.662	....	951	751	95	5345	1573	319	74	125	2415	599	531	48	33	.294	.369	.452	.821	108	69	104	913
WAS	154	94	60	.610	8	892	689	96	5370	1620	300	98	57	2287	537	438	101	67	.302	.369	.426	.795	106	55	100	860
NY	154	86	68	.558	16	1062	898	90	5448	1683	298	110	152	2657	644	569	91	60	.309	.384	.488	.872	131	259	95	1035
CLE	154	81	73	.526	21	890	915	75	5439	1654	358	59	72	2346	490	461	51	47	.304	.364	.431	.796	102	19	104	863
DET	154	75	79	.487	27	783	833	72	5297	1504	298	90	82	2228	461	508	98	70	.284	.344	.421	.765	96	-37	102	771
STL	154	64	90	.416	38	751	886	64	5278	1415	289	67	75	2063	497	550	93	71	.268	.333	.391	.724	85	-125	103	696
CHI	154	62	92	.403	40	729	884	62	5419	1496	256	90	63	2121	389	479	74	40	.276	.328	.391	.720	90	-80	97	705
BOS	154	52	102	.338	50	612	814	56	5286	1393	257	68	47	1927	358	552	42	35	.264	.313	.365	.677	79	-168	96	608
Total	616					6670			42882	12338	2375	656	673		3975	4088	598	423	.288	.351	.421	.772				

Runs
Simmons, A. (Phi) 152
Ruth, B. (NY) 150
Gehringer, C. (Det) 144

Hits
Hodapp, J. (Cle) 225
Gehrig, L. (NY) 220
Simmons, A. (Phi) 211

Doubles
Hodapp, J. (Cle) 51
Manush, H. (Was,StL) 49
2 players tied with 47

Triples
Combs, E. (NY) 22
Reynolds, C. (Chi) 18
Gehrig, L. (NY) 17

Home Runs
Ruth, B. (NY) 49
Gehrig, L. (NY) 41
2 players tied with 37

Total Bases
Gehrig, L. (NY) 419
Simmons, A. (Phi) 392
Ruth, B. (NY) 379

Runs Batted In
Gehrig, L. (NY) 174
Simmons, A. (Phi) 165
Foxx, J. (Phi) 156

Bases On Balls
Ruth, B. (NY) 136
Bishop, M. (Phi) 128
Gehrig, L. (NY) 101

Stolen Bases
McManus, M. (Det) 23
Gehringer, C. (Det) 19
3 players tied with 17

Batting Average
Simmons, A. (Phi) .381
Gehrig, L. (NY) .379
Ruth, B. (NY) .359

On-Base Percentage
Ruth, B. (NY) .493
Gehrig, L. (NY) .473
Foxx, J. (Phi) .429

Slugging Average
Ruth, B. (NY) .732
Gehrig, L. (NY) .721
Simmons, A. (Phi) .708

Adjusted OPS
Ruth, B. (NY) 216
Gehrig, L. (NY) 207
Simmons, A. (Phi) 173

Adjusted Batting Runs
Ruth, B. (NY) 98.0
Gehrig, L. (NY) 95.0
Simmons, A. (Phi) 60.0

Runs Created/Game
Ruth, B. (NY) 14.00
Gehrig, L. (NY) 13.20
Simmons, A. (Phi) 11.90

Fielding Runs
Cronin, J. (Was) 35.1
Melillo, O. (StL) 18.3
McManus, M. (Det) 11.5

Win Shares – Batters
Gehrig, L. (NY) 39
Ruth, B. (NY) 38
Simmons, A. (Phi) 36

TPW – Batters
Ruth, B. (NY) 7.8
Cronin, J. (Was) 7.7
Gehrig, L. (NY) 7.7

TEAM	CG	SH	SV	IP	H	H/G	ER	HR	BB	SO	OAV	RAT	ERA	ERA+	CERA	PR+	PF	FA	E	DP	FR	BW	PW	FW	TPW	DIF
PHI	72	8	21	1371	1457	9.6	652	84	488	672	.274	1.419	4.28	109	3.98	55.4	100	.976	145	121	3.5	6.2	5.0	.3	11.5	13.5
WAS	78	6	14	1369	1367	9.0	602	52	504	524	.264	1.367	3.96	116	3.52	51.8	99	.974	157	150	43.5	5.0	4.7	3.9	13.6	3.4
NY	65	7	15	1367²	1566	10.3	741	93	524	572	.286	1.528	4.88	88	4.55	-74.5	92	.965	207	132	-14.8	23.4	-6.7	-1.3	15.3	-6.3
CLE	68	5	14	1360	1663	11.0	737	85	528	442	.305	1.611	4.88	99	5.06	14.1	104	.962	237	156	-23.6	1.7	1.3	-2.1	.9	3.1
DET	68	4	17	1351²	1507	10.0	706	86	570	574	.286	1.537	4.70	102	4.56	13.8	103	.968	192	156	.1	-3.3	1.2	.0	-2.1	1.1
STL	68	5	10	1371²	1639	10.8	772	124	449	470	.300	1.522	5.07	96	4.85	-45.4	105	.969	188	152	14.4	-11.3	-4.1	1.3	-14.1	1.1
CHI	63	2	10	1361	1629	10.8	712	74	407	471	.300	1.496	4.71	98	4.44	22.2	99	.962	235	136	-37.1	-7.3	2.0	-3.4	-8.6	-6.4
BOS	78	4	5	1360¹	1515	10.0	707	75	488	356	.286	1.472	4.68	98	4.19	-26.8	99	.968	196	161	14.6	-15.2	-2.4	1.3	-16.3	-8.7
Total	560	41	106	10912¹		10.2	5629					1.494	4.64													

Wins
Grove, L. (Phi) 28
Ferrell, W. (Cle) 25
2 players tied with 22

Win Percentage
Grove, L. (Phi) .848
Shores, B. (Phi) .750
Marberry, F. (Was) .750

Games
Grove, L. (Phi) 50
Earnshaw, G. (Phi) 49
2 players tied with 44

Complete Games
Lyons, T. (Chi) 29
Crowder, A. (Was,StL) 25
Ferrell, W. (Cle) 25

Shutouts
Brown, C. (Cle) 3
Earnshaw, G. (Phi) 3
Pipgras, G. (NY) 3

Saves
Grove, L. (Phi) 9
Braxton, G. (Was,Chi) 6
Quinn, J. (Phi) 6

Innings Pitched
Lyons, T. (Chi) 297²
Ferrell, W. (Cle) 296²
Earnshaw, G. (Phi) 296

Fewest Hits/Game
Hadley, B. (Was) 8.37
Grove, L. (Phi) 8.44
Collins, R. (Phi) 8.81

Fewest BB/Game
Pennock, H. (NY) 1.15
Lyons, T. (Chi) 1.72
Grove, L. (Phi) 1.86

Strikeouts
Grove, L. (Phi) 209
Earnshaw, G. (Phi) 193
Hadley, B. (Was) 162

Ratio
Grove, L. (Phi) 1.14
Stewart, L. (StL) 1.30
Caraway, P. (Chi) 1.30

Earned Run Average
Grove, L. (Phi) 2.54
Ferrell, W. (Cle) 3.31
Stewart, L. (StL) 3.45

Adjusted ERA
Grove, L. (Phi) 184
Ferrell, W. (Cle) 146
Stewart, L. (StL) 141

Component ERA
Grove, L. (Phi) 2.56
Hadley, B. (Was) 3.14
Caraway, P. (Chi) 3.40

Opponents' Batting Avg.
Grove, L. (Phi) .247
Hadley, B. (Was) .247
Crowder, A. (Was,StL) .259

Adjusted Pitching Runs
Grove, L. (Phi) 68
Ferrell, W. (Cle) 55
Stewart, L. (StL) 40

Win Shares – Pitchers
Grove, L. (Phi) 37
Ferrell, W. (Cle) 32
Stewart, L. (StL) 28

TPW – Pitchers
Grove, L. (Phi) 6.2
Ferrell, W. (Cle) 5.8
Lyons, T. (Chi) 4.0

1931 National League

TEAM	G	W	L	PCT	GB	R	OR	EW	AB	H	2B	3B	HR	TB	BB	SO	SB	CS	AVG	OBP	SLG	OPS	OPS+	BR/A	PF	RC
STL	154	101	53	.656	....	815	614	98	5435	1554	353	74	60	2235	432	475	114	....	.286	.342	.411	.753	105	33	104	787
NY	153	87	65	.572	13	768	599	95	5372	1554	251	64	101	2236	383	395	83	....	.289	.340	.416	.756	112	79	98	776
CHI	156	84	70	.545	17	828	710	89	5451	1578	340	66	84	2302	577	641	49	....	.289	.360	.422	.782	115	120	102	865
BRO	153	79	73	.520	21	681	673	77	5309	1464	240	77	71	2071	409	512	45	....	.276	.331	.390	.721	100	1	99	705
PIT	155	75	79	.487	26	636	691	71	5360	1425	243	70	41	1931	493	454	59	....	.266	.330	.360	.690	93	-47	99	667
PHI	155'	66	88	.429	35	684	828	62	5375	1502	299	52	81	2148	437	492	42	....	.279	.336	.400	.736	96	-26	108	745
BOS	156	64	90	.416	37	533	680	59	5296	1367	221	59	34	1808	368	430	46	....	.258	.309	.341	.650	84	-118	96	580
CIN	154	58	96	.377	43	592	742	60	5343	1439	241	70	21	1883	403	463	24	....	.269	.323	.352	.676	93	-46	94	631
Total	618					5537			42941	11883	2188	532	493		3502	3862	462		.277	.334	.387	.721				

Runs
Klein, C. (Phi) 121
Terry, B. (NY) 121
English, W. (Chi) 117

Hits
Waner, L. (Pit) 214
Terry, B. (NY) 213
2 players tied with 202

Doubles
Adams, S. (StL) 46
Berger, W. (Bos) 44
3 players tied with 43

Triples
Terry, B. (NY) 20
Herman, B. (Bro) 16
Traynor, P. (Pit) 15

Home Runs
Klein, C. (Phi) 31
Ott, M. (NY) 29
Berger, W. (Bos) 19

Total Bases
Klein, C. (Phi) 347
Terry, B. (NY) 323
Herman, B. (Bro) 320

Runs Batted In
Klein, C. (Phi) 121
Ott, M. (NY) 115
Terry, B. (NY) 112

Bases On Balls
Ott, M. (NY) 80
Waner, P. (Pit) 73
Cuyler, K. (Chi) 72

Stolen Bases
Frisch, F. (StL) 28
Herman, B. (Bro) 17
2 players tied with 16

Batting Average
Hafey, C. (StL) .349
Terry, B. (NY) .349
Klein, C. (Phi) .337

On-Base Percentage
Hafey, C. (StL) .404
Cuyler, K. (Chi) .404
Waner, P. (Pit) .404

Slugging Average
Klein, C. (Phi) .584
Hafey, C. (StL) .569
Ott, M. (NY) .545

Adjusted OPS
Ott, M. (NY) 153
Hafey, C. (StL) 153
Terry, B. (NY) 150

Adjusted Batting Runs
Terry, B. (NY) 42.0
Klein, C. (Phi) 40.0
Ott, M. (NY) 38.0

Runs Created/Game
Hafey, C. (StL) 9.30
Klein, C. (Phi) 9.20
Terry, B. (NY) 8.40

Fielding Runs
Thevenow, T. (Pit) 18.0
Jackson, T. (NY) 16.2
Frisch, F. (StL) 10.6

Win Shares – Batters
Berger, W. (Bos) 31
Terry, B. (NY) 29
4 players tied with 26

TPW – Batters
Berger, W. (Bos) 3.8
Ott, M. (NY) 3.8
Cuccinello, T. (Cin) 3.6

TEAM	CG	SH	SV	IP	H	H/G	ER	HR	BB	SO	OAV	RAT	ERA	ERA+	CERA	PR+	PF	FA	E	DP	FR	BW	PW	FW	TPW	DIF
STL	80	**17**	**20**	1384^{2}	1470	9.6	531	65	449	**626**	.273	1.386	3.45	114	3.76	**70.8**	102	**.974**	160	169	3.7	3.3	**7.0**	.4	10.7	13.3
NY	**90**	**17**	12	1360^{2}	**1341**	**8.9**	**499**	71	422	570	**.255**	**1.296**	**3.30**	112	**3.34**	45.6	96	.974	**159**	126	13.5	7.8	4.5	1.3	**13.7**	-2.7
CHI	80	8	8	1385^{2}	1448	9.4	611	54	524	541	.268	1.423	3.97	97	3.80	-5.5	100	.973	169	141	-12.3	**11.9**	-.5	-1.2	10.1	-3.1
BRO	64	9	18	1356	1520	10.1	579	56	**351**	546	.283	1.380	3.84	99	3.78	11.3	99	.969	187	154	-16.0	.1	1.1	-1.6	-.4	3.4
PIT	89	9	5	**1390**	1489	9.6	565	55	442	345	.274	1.389	3.66	105	3.72	5.3	100	.968	194	167	**23.7**	-4.6	.5	**2.4**	-1.7	-.3
PHI	60	6	16	1360^{1}	1603	10.6	692	75	511	499	.293	1.554	4.58	93	4.69	-34.0	110	.966	210	149	-16.7	-2.6	-3.4	-1.7	-7.6	-3.4
BOS	78	12	9	1380^{1}	1465	9.6	598	66	406	419	.272	1.355	3.90	97	3.62	-9.0	98	.973	170	141	-7.9	-11.7	-.9	-.8	-13.4	.4
CIN	70	7	6	1345	1545	10.3	631	**51**	399	317	.294	1.445	4.22	**88**	4.11	-83.5	97	.973	165	**194**	11.2	-4.6	-8.3	1.1	-11.8	-7.2
Total	**611**	**85**	**94**	**10962^{2}**		**9.8**	**4706**					**1.403**	**3.86**													

Wins
- Elliott, J. (Phi) 19
- Hallahan, B. (StL) 19
- Meine, H. (Pit) 19

Win Percentage
- Derringer, P. (StL) .692
- Hallahan, B. (StL) .679
- Bush, G. (Chi) .667

Games
- Elliott, J. (Phi) 52
- Collins, P. (Phi) 42
- Johnson, S. (Cin) 42

Complete Games
- Lucas, R. (Cin) 24
- Brandt, E. (Bos) 23
- Meine, H. (Pit) 22

Shutouts
- Walker, B. (NY) 6
- 3 players tied with 4

Saves
- Quinn, J. (Bro) 15
- Lindsey, J. (StL) 7
- Elliott, J. (Phi) 5

Innings Pitched
- Meine, H. (Pit) 284
- French, L. (Pit) 275^{2}
- Johnson, S. (Cin) 262^{1}

Fewest Hits/Game
- Hubbell, C. (NY) 7.66
- Walker, B. (NY) 7.97
- Brandt, E. (Bos) 8.21

Fewest BB/Game
- Johnson, S. (StL) 1.40
- Lucas, R. (Cin) 1.47
- Cantwell, B. (Bos) 1.96

Strikeouts
- Hallahan, B. (StL) 159
- Hubbell, C. (NY) 155
- Vance, D. (Bro) 150

Ratio
- Hubbell, C. (NY) 1.12
- Walker, B. (NY) 1.15
- Johnson, S. (StL) 1.16

Earned Run Average
- Walker, B. (NY) 2.26
- Hubbell, C. (NY) 2.65
- Brandt, E. (Bos) 2.92

Adjusted ERA
- Walker, B. (NY) 164
- Hubbell, C. (NY) 139
- Benge, R. (Phi) 134

Component ERA
- Walker, B. (NY) 2.44
- Hubbell, C. (NY) 2.52
- Johnson, S. (StL) 2.79

Opponents' Batting Avg.
- Hubbell, C. (NY) .227
- Walker, B. (NY) .231
- Brandt, E. (Bos) .244

Adjusted Pitching Runs
- Walker, B. (NY) 36
- Benge, R. (Phi) 32
- Hubbell, C. (NY) 26

Win Shares – Pitchers
- Brandt, E. (Bos) 27
- Clark, W. (Bro) 22
- Meine, H. (Pit) 22

TPW – Pitchers
- Benge, R. (Phi) 3.1
- Brandt, E. (Bos) 3.1
- Hubbell, C. (NY) 3.0

1931 American League

TEAM	G	W	L	PCT	GB	R	OR	EW	AB	H	2B	3B	HR	TB	BB	SO	SB	CS	AVG	OBP	SLG	OPS	OPS+	BR/A	PF	RC
PHI	153	107	45	.704	....	858	**626**	99	5377	1544	311	64	118	2337	528	543	25	**23**	.287	.355	.435	.789	106	47	106	843
NY	155	94	59	.614	13.5	**1067**	760	102	**5608**	**1667**	277	78	**155**	**2565**	**748**	554	**138**	68	**.297**	**.383**	**.457**	**.840**	**134**	**294**	94	**1016**
WAS	156	92	62	.597	16	843	690	92	5576	1588	308	**93**	49	2229	481	459	72	64	.285	.345	.400	.745	101	-1	100	774
CLE	155	78	76	.506	30	885	833	82	5445	1612	**321**	69	71	2284	555	**433**	63	60	.296	.363	.419	.783	106	41	106	840
STL	154	63	91	.409	45	721	870	63	5374	1455	287	62	76	2094	488	580	73	80	.271	.333	.390	.722	92	-77	103	696
BOS	153	62	90	.408	45	625	800	58	5379	1409	289	34	37	1877	405	565	42	43	.262	.315	.349	.664	84	-122	95	596
DET	154	61	93	.396	47	651	836	58	5430	1456	292	69	43	2015	480	468	117	75	.268	.330	.371	.701	87	-104	103	675
CHI	156	56	97	.366	51.5	704	939	55	5481	1423	238	69	27	1880	483	445	94	39	.260	.323	.343	.666	86	-92	94	632
Total	**618**					**6354**			**43670**	**12154**	**2323**	**538**	**576**		**4168**	**4047**	**624**	**452**	**.278**	**.344**	**.396**	**.739**				

Runs
- Gehrig, L. (NY) 163
- Ruth, B. (NY) 149
- Averill, E. (Cle) 140

Hits
- Gehrig, L. (NY) 211
- Averill, E. (Cle) 209
- Simmons, A. (Phi) 200

Doubles
- Webb, E. (Bos) 67
- Alexander, D. (Det) 47
- Kress, R. (StL) 46

Triples
- Johnson, R. (Det) 19
- Blue, L. (Chi) 15
- Gehrig, L. (NY) 15

Home Runs
- Gehrig, L. (NY) 46
- Ruth, B. (NY) 46
- Averill, E. (Cle) 32

Total Bases
- Gehrig, L. (NY) 410
- Ruth, B. (NY) 374
- Averill, E. (Cle) 361

Runs Batted In
- Gehrig, L. (NY) 184
- Ruth, B. (NY) 163
- Averill, E. (Cle) 143

Bases On Balls
- Ruth, B. (NY) 128
- Blue, L. (Chi) 127
- Gehrig, L. (NY) 117

Stolen Bases
- Chapman, B. (NY) 61
- Johnson, R. (Det) 33
- Burns, J. (StL) 19

Batting Average
- Simmons, A. (Phi) .390
- Ruth, B. (NY) .373
- Morgan, E. (Cle) .351

On-Base Percentage
- Ruth, B. (NY) .495
- Morgan, E. (Cle) .451
- Gehrig, L. (NY) .446

Slugging Average
- Ruth, B. (NY) .700
- Gehrig, L. (NY) .662
- Simmons, A. (Phi) .641

Adjusted OPS
- Ruth, B. (NY) 223
- Gehrig, L. (NY) 199
- Simmons, A. (Phi) 172

Adjusted Batting Runs
- Ruth, B. (NY) 105.0
- Gehrig, L. (NY) 92.0
- Simmons, A. (Phi) 54.0

Runs Created/Game
- Ruth, B. (NY) 15.00
- Simmons, A. (Phi) 12.10
- Gehrig, L. (NY) 11.60

Fielding Runs
- Cronin, J. (Was) 28.4
- Lary, L. (NY) 22.7
- Melillo, S. (StL) 21.1

Win Shares – Batters
- Ruth, B. (NY) 38
- Gehrig, L. (NY) 36
- Cronin, J. (Was) 35

TPW – Batters
- Ruth, B. (NY) 8.8
- Cronin, J. (Was) 6.2
- Gehrig, L. (NY) 5.9

TEAM	CG	SH	SV	IP	H	H/G	ER	HR	BB	SO	OAV	RAT	ERA	ERA+	CERA	PR+	PF	FA	E	DP	FR	BW	PW	FW	TPW	DIF
PHI	**97**	**12**	16	1365^{1}	**1342**	**8.8**	**526**	73	457	574	**.256**	**1.318**	**3.47**	130	**3.44**	**118.0**	103	.976	**141**	151	**38.0**	4.4	**11.0**	**3.5**	18.9	12.1
NY	78	4	17	**1410^{1}**	1461	9.3	658	67	543	**686**	.263	1.421	4.20	95	3.78	-45.7	91	.972	169	131	8.7	**27.3**	-4.3	.8	**23.9**	-5.9
WAS	60	7	**24**	1394^{1}	1434	9.3	582	73	498	582	.264	1.386	3.76	114	3.69	67.0	98	**.976**	142	148	14.8	-.1	6.2	1.4	7.5	7.5
CLE	76	6	9	1354^{2}	1577	10.5	697	64	561	470	.286	1.578	4.63	100	4.59	38.1	105	.963	232	143	-39.8	3.9	3.6	-3.7	3.7	-2.7
STL	65	4	10	1362	1623	10.7	720	84	**448**	436	.293	1.521	4.76	97	4.58	-23.5	106	.963	232	**160**	5.0	-7.2	-2.2	.5	-8.9	-5.1
BOS	61	5	10	1366^{2}	1559	10.3	698	**54**	473	365	.285	1.487	4.60	94	4.17	-40.9	98	.970	188	127	-3.6	-11.4	-3.8	-.3	-15.5	1.5
DET	86	5	6	1384^{1}	1549	10.1	706	79	597	511	.282	1.550	4.59	100	4.51	-1.7	105	.964	220	139	0.8	-9.7	-.2	.1	-9.8	-6.2
CHI	54	6	10	1390^{1}	1613	10.4	778	82	588	421	.287	1.583	5.04	**84**	4.72	-95.9	97	.960	245	131	-24.6	-8.6	-8.9	-2.3	-19.8	-.2
Total	**577**	**49**	**102**	**11028**		**9.9**	**5365**					**1.480**	**4.38**													

Wins
- Grove, L. (Phi) 31
- Ferrell, W. (Cle) 22
- 2 players tied with 21

Win Percentage
- Grove, L. (Phi) .886
- Marberry, F. (Was) .800
- Mahaffey, R. (Phi) .789

Games
- Hadley, B. (Was) 55
- Moore, W. (Bos) 53
- Caraway, P. (Chi) 51

Complete Games
- Ferrell, W. (Cle) 27
- Grove, L. (Phi) 27
- Earnshaw, G. (Phi) 23

Shutouts
- Grove, L. (Phi) 4
- Earnshaw, G. (Phi) 3
- 10 players tied with 2

Saves
- Moore, W. (Bos) 10
- Hadley, B. (Was) 8
- 2 players tied with 7

Innings Pitched
- Walberg, R. (Phi) 291
- Grove, L. (Phi) 288^{2}
- Earnshaw, G. (Phi) 281^{2}

Fewest Hits/Game
- Hadley, B. (Was) 7.26
- Gomez, L. (NY) 7.63
- Grove, L. (Phi) 7.76

Fewest BB/Game
- Pennock, H. (NY) 1.43
- Gray, D. (StL) 1.88
- Grove, L. (Phi) 1.93

Strikeouts
- Grove, L. (Phi) 175
- Earnshaw, G. (Phi) 152
- Gomez, L. (NY) 150

Ratio
- Grove, L. (Phi) 1.08
- Earnshaw, G. (Phi) 1.17
- Gomez, L. (NY) 1.20

Earned Run Average
- Grove, L. (Phi) 2.06
- Gomez, L. (NY) 2.67
- Hadley, B. (Was) 3.06

Adjusted ERA
- Grove, L. (Phi) 218
- Gomez, L. (NY) 149
- Hadley, B. (Was) 140

Component ERA
- Grove, L. (Phi) 2.23
- Gomez, L. (NY) 2.56
- Earnshaw, G. (Phi) 2.71

Opponents' Batting Avg.
- Hadley, B. (Was) .218
- Gomez, L. (NY) .226
- Grove, L. (Phi) .229

Adjusted Pitching Runs
- Grove, L. (Phi) 70
- Ferrell, W. (Cle) 35
- Gomez, L. (NY) 34

Win Shares – Pitchers
- Grove, L. (Phi) 42
- Earnshaw, G. (Phi) 29
- Ferrell, W. (Cle) 28

TPW – Pitchers
- Grove, L. (Phi) 6.3
- Ferrell, W. (Cle) 4.9
- Brown, L. (Was) 2.9

1932 National League

TEAM	G	W	L	PCT	GB	R	OR	EW	AB	H	2B	3B	HR	TB	BB	SO	SB	CS	AVG	OBP	SLG	OPS	OPS+	BR/A	PF	RC
CHI	154	90	64	.584	....	720	**633**	87	5462	1519	296	60	69	2142	398	514	48	....	.278	.330	.392	.722	101	7	99	728
PIT	154	86	68	.558	4	701	711	76	5421	1543	274	**90**	48	2141	358	**385**	71	....	.285	.333	.395	.727	103	22	98	729
BRO	154	81	73	.526	9	752	747	78	5433	1538	296	59	110	2282	388	574	61	....	.283	.334	.420	.754	**110**	**71**	98	778
PHI	154	78	76	.506	12	**844**	796	82	5510	**1608**	**330**	67	**122**	**2438**	**446**	547	71	....	**.292**	**.348**	**.442**	**.790**	105	44	112	**870**
BOS	155	77	77	.500	13	649	655	76	5506	1460	262	53	63	2017	347	496	36	....	.265	.311	.366	.677	91	-70	96	643
STL	156	72	82	.468	18	684	717	73	5458	1467	307	51	76	2104	420	514	**92**	....	.269	.324	.385	.709	93	-46	103	702
NY	154	72	82	.468	18	755	706	82	**5530**	1527	263	54	116	2246	348	391	31	....	.276	.322	.406	.728	103	15	98	735
CIN	155	60	94	.390	30	575	715	60	5443	1429	265	68	47	1971	436	436	35	....	.263	.320	.362	.682	92	-54	97	654
Total	**618**					**5680**			**43763**	**12091**	**2293**	**502**	**651**		**3141**	**3857**	**445**		**.276**	**.328**	**.396**	**.724**				

Runs
Klein, C. (Phi) 152
Terry, B. (NY) 124
O'Doul, L. (Bro) 120

Hits
Klein, C. (Phi) 226
Terry, B. (NY) 225
O'Doul, L. (Bro) 219

Doubles
Waner, P. (Pit) 62
Klein, C. (Phi) 50
Stephenson, R. (Chi) 49

Triples
Herman, B. (Cin) 19
Suhr, G. (Pit) 16
Klein, C. (Phi) 15

Home Runs
Klein, C. (Phi) 38
Ott, M. (NY) 38
Terry, B. (NY) 28

Total Bases
Klein, C. (Phi) 420
Terry, B. (NY) 373
Ott, M. (NY) 340

Runs Batted In
Hurst, D. (Phi) 143
Klein, C. (Phi) 137
Whitney, P. (Phi) 124

Bases On Balls
Ott, M. (NY) 100
Hurst, D. (Phi) 65
Bartell, D. (Phi) 64

Stolen Bases
Klein, C. (Phi) 20
Piet, T. (Pit) 19
2 players tied with 18

Batting Average
O'Doul, L. (Bro) .368
Terry, B. (NY) .350
Klein, C. (Phi) .348

On-Base Percentage
Ott, M. (NY) .424
O'Doul, L. (Bro) .423
Hurst, D. (Phi) .412

Slugging Average
Klein, C. (Phi) .646
Ott, M. (NY) .601
Terry, B. (NY) .580

Adjusted OPS
Ott, M. (NY) 175
O'Doul, L. (Bro) 164
Klein, C. (Phi) 158

Adjusted Batting Runs
Ott, M. (NY) 64.0
O'Doul, L. (Bro) 54.0
Klein, C. (Phi) 53.0

Runs Created/Game
Klein, C. (Phi) 10.50
Ott, M. (NY) 10.10
O'Doul, L. (Bro) 9.70

Fielding Runs
Jurges, B. (Chi) 21.9
Bartell, D. (Phi) 15.5
Terry, B. (NY) 13.2

Win Shares – Batters
Ott, M. (NY) 33
O'Doul, L. (Bro) 33
2 players tied with 32

TPW – Batters
Ott, M. (NY) 5.6
Terry, B. (NY) 4.7
O'Doul, L. (Bro) 4.5

TEAM	CG	SH	SV	IP	H	H/G	ER	HR	BB	SO	OAV	RAT	ERA	ERA+	CERA	PR+	PF	FA	E	DP	FR	BW	PW	FW	TPW	DIF
CHI	79	9	7	1401	**1444**	**9.3**	**535**	68	409	527	**.264**	1.323	**3.44**	110	3.48	27.1	97	.973	173	146	**23.0**	.7	2.7	**2.3**	**5.7**	7.3
PIT	71	12	12	1377	1472	9.6	574	86	338	377	.270	1.314	3.75	102	3.57	-0.3	98	.969	185	124	10.5	2.2	.0	1.0	3.2	5.8
BRO	61	7	16	1379^{2}	1538	10.0	654	72	403	497	.282	1.407	4.27	**89**	3.97	-73.0	98	.971	183	**169**	3.1	**7.0**	-7.2	.3	.1	3.9
PHI	59	4	**17**	1384	1589	10.3	687	107	450	459	.287	1.473	4.47	99	4.46	-7.4	114	.968	194	133	-1.4	4.4	-.7	-.1	3.5	-2.5
BOS	72	8	8	**1414**	1483	9.4	555	**61**	420	440	.272	1.346	3.53	106	3.58	**34.0**	97	**.976**	**152**	145	2.8	-6.9	**3.4**	.3	-3.3	3.3
STL	70	**13**	9	1396	1533	9.9	616	76	455	**681**	.282	1.424	3.97	99	4.03	3.0	101	.971	175	155	-9.0	-4.5	.3	-.9	-5.1	.1
NY	57	3	16	1375^{1}	1533	10.0	585	112	387	506	.280	1.396	3.83	97	4.12	7.9	96	.969	191	143	-25.3	1.5	.8	-2.5	-.2	-4.8
CIN	**83**	6	6	1394^{2}	1505	9.7	587	69	**276**	359	.274	**1.277**	3.79	102	**3.40**	13.9	99	.971	178	129	-3.5	-5.3	1.4	-.3	-4.3	-12.7
Total	**552**	**62**	**91**	**11121^{2}**		**9.8**	**4793**					**1.370**	**3.88**													

Wins
Warneke, L. (Chi) 22
Clark, W. (Bro) 20
Bush, G. (Chi) 19

Win Percentage
Warneke, L. (Chi) .786
Heimach, F. (Bro) .692
Brown, B. (Bos) .667

Games
French, L. (Pit) 47
Dean, D. (StL) 46
Carleton, T. (StL) 44

Complete Games
Lucas, R. (Cin) 28
Warneke, L. (Chi) 25
Hubbell, C. (NY) 22

Shutouts
Dean, D. (StL) 4
Swetonic, S. (Pit) 4
Warneke, L. (Chi) 4

Saves
Quinn, J. (Bro) 8
Benge, R. (Phi) 6
2 players tied with 5

Innings Pitched
Dean, D. (StL) 286
Hubbell, C. (NY) 284
Warneke, L. (Chi) 277

Fewest Hits/Game
Swetonic, S. (Pit) 7.41
Brown, B. (Bos) 7.90
Warneke, L. (Chi) 8.03

Fewest BB/Game
Swift, B. (Pit) 1.09
Lucas, R. (Cin) 1.17
Hubbell, C. (NY) 1.27

Strikeouts
Dean, D. (StL) 191
Hubbell, C. (NY) 137
Malone, P. (Chi) 120

Ratio
Hubbell, C. (NY) 1.06
Swift, B. (Pit) 1.08
Lucas, R. (Cin) 1.10

Earned Run Average
Warneke, L. (Chi) 2.37
Hubbell, C. (NY) 2.50
Betts, H. (Bos) 2.80

Adjusted ERA
Warneke, L. (Chi) 159
Hubbell, C. (NY) 148
Swetonic, S. (Pit) 135

Component ERA
Lucas, R. (Cin) 2.44
Hubbell, C. (NY) 2.45
Warneke, L. (Chi) 2.50

Opponents' Batting Avg.
Swetonic, S. (Pit) .221
Warneke, L. (Chi) .237
2 players tied with .238

Adjusted Pitching Runs
Hubbell, C. (NY) 43
Warneke, L. (Chi) 38
Lucas, R. (Cin) 28

Win Shares – Pitchers
Warneke, L. (Chi) 31
Hubbell, C. (NY) 25
Dean, D. (StL) 24

TPW – Pitchers
Hubbell, C. (NY) 4.7
Lucas, R. (Cin) 4.2
Warneke, L. (Chi) 3.7

1932 American League

TEAM	G	W	L	PCT	GB	R	OR	EW	AB	H	2B	3B	HR	TB	BB	SO	SB	CS	AVG	OBP	SLG	OPS	OPS+	BR/A	PF	RC
NY	156	107	47	.695	....	**1002**	724	101	5477	1564	279	82	160	2487	**766**	527	77	66	.286	**.376**	.454	**.830**	**128**	**225**	95	**961**
PHI	154	94	60	.610	13	981	752	97	**5537**	**1606**	303	52	**172**	**2529**	647	630	38	**23**	**.290**	.366	**.457**	.823	115	123	104	951
WAS	154	93	61	.604	14	840	**716**	89	5515	1565	303	**100**	61	2251	505	442	70	47	.284	.347	.408	.755	102	20	99	793
CLE	153	87	65	.572	19	845	747	85	5412	1544	**310**	74	78	2236	566	454	52	54	.285	.357	.413	.770	99	-11	107	811
DET	153	76	75	.503	29.5	799	787	77	5409	1479	291	80	80	2170	486	523	**103**	49	.273	.335	.401	.736	92	-58	104	741
STL	154	63	91	.409	44	736	898	62	5449	1502	274	69	67	2115	507	528	69	62	.276	.339	.388	.728	89	-92	106	726
CHI	152	49	102	.325	56.5	667	897	54	5336	1426	274	56	36	1920	459	**386**	89	58	.267	.327	.360	.687	90	-75	93	642
BOS	154	43	111	.279	64	566	915	43	5295	1331	253	57	53	1857	469	539	46	46	.251	.314	.351	.664	80	-158	97	593
Total	**615**					**6436**			**43430**	**12017**	**2287**	**570**	**707**		**4405**	**4029**	**544**	**405**	**.277**	**.346**	**.404**	**.750**				

Runs
Foxx, J. (Phi) 151
Simmons, A. (Phi) 144
Combs, E. (NY) 143

Hits
Simmons, A. (Phi) 216
Manush, H. (Was) 214
Foxx, J. (Phi) 213

Doubles
McNair, E. (Phi) 47
Gehringer, C. (Det) 44
Cronin, J. (Was) 43

Triples
Cronin, J. (Was) 18
Lazzeri, T. (NY) 16
Myer, B. (Was) 16

Home Runs
Foxx, J. (Phi) 58
Ruth, B. (NY) 41
Simmons, A. (Phi) 35

Total Bases
Foxx, J. (Phi) 438
Gehrig, L. (NY) 370
Simmons, A. (Phi) 367

Runs Batted In
Foxx, J. (Phi) 169
Gehrig, L. (NY) 151
Simmons, A. (Phi) 151

Bases On Balls
Ruth, B. (NY) 130
Foxx, J. (Phi) 116
Bishop, M. (Phi) 110

Stolen Bases
Chapman, B. (NY) 38
Walker, G. (Det) 30
Johnson, R. (Bos,Det) 20

Batting Average
Alexander, D. (Bos,Det) .367
Foxx, J. (Phi) .364
Gehrig, L. (NY) .349

On-Base Percentage
Ruth, B. (NY) .489
Foxx, J. (Phi) .469
Gehrig, L. (NY) .451

Slugging Average
Foxx, J. (Phi) .749
Ruth, B. (NY) .661
Gehrig, L. (NY) .621

Adjusted OPS
Ruth, B. (NY) 206
Foxx, J. (Phi) 203
Gehrig, L. (NY) 184

Adjusted Batting Runs
Foxx, J. (Phi) 90.0
Ruth, B. (NY) 81.0
Gehrig, L. (NY) 75.0

Runs Created/Game
Foxx, J. (Phi) 14.50
Ruth, B. (NY) 13.80
Gehrig, L. (NY) 11.10

Fielding Runs
Cronin, J. (Was) 20.2
Vosmik, J. (Cle) 19.6
Lazzeri, T. (NY) 15.1

Win Shares – Batters
Foxx, J. (Phi) 40
Gehrig, L. (NY) 38
Ruth, B. (NY) 36

TPW – Batters
Foxx, J. (Phi) 7.2
Ruth, B. (NY) 7.0
Cronin, J. (Was) 5.1

TEAM	CG	SH	SV	IP	H	H/G	ER	HR	BB	SO	OAV	RAT	ERA	ERA+	CERA	PR+	PF	FA	E	DP	FR	BW	PW	FW	TPW	DIF
NY	**96**	**11**	15	**1408**	1425	**9.1**	**623**	93	561	**780**	**.260**	**1.411**	**3.98**	102	**3.83**	17.4	91	.969	188	124	-2.5	**20.8**	1.6	-.2	**22.2**	7.8
PHI	95	10	10	1386	1477	9.6	685	112	511	595	.271	1.434	4.45	102	4.16	6.0	101	**.980**	**124**	142	5.0	11.4	.6	.5	12.4	4.6
WAS	66	10	**22**	1383^{1}	1463	9.5	639	73	526	437	.271	1.438	4.16	104	3.94	-9.6	96	.979	125	157	**33.9**	1.8	-.9	**3.1**	4.1	11.9
CLE	94	6	8	1377^{1}	1506	9.8	630	**70**	**446**	439	.273	1.417	4.12	115	3.86	**122.4**	106	.969	191	129	-26.6	-1.0	**11.3**	-2.5	7.8	3.2
DET	67	9	17	1362^{2}	**1421**	9.4	651	89	592	521	.269	1.477	4.30	109	4.17	40.5	105	.969	187	154	20.7	-5.4	3.7	1.9	.3	.7
STL	63	8	11	1376^{2}	1592	10.4	766	103	574	496	.290	1.573	5.01	97	4.81	-30.1	108	.969	188	156	5.8	-8.5	-2.8	.5	-10.8	-3.2
CHI	50	2	12	1348^{2}	1551	10.4	722	88	580	379	.287	1.580	4.82	90	4.78	-60.5	97	.957	264	**170**	-14.4	-7.0	-5.6	-1.3	-13.9	-12.1
BOS	42	3	7	1362	1574	10.4	760	79	612	365	.289	1.605	5.02	**90**	4.79	-55.5	100	.963	233	165	-23.3	-14.6	-5.1	-2.2	-21.9	-12.1
Total	**573**	**59**	**102**	**11004^{2}**		**9.8**	**5476**					**1.491**	**4.48**													

Wins
Crowder, A. (Was) 26
Grove, L. (Phi) 25
Gomez, L. (NY) 24

Win Percentage
Allen, J. (NY) .810
Gomez, L. (NY) .774
Ruffing, R. (NY) .720

Games
Marberry, F. (Was) 54
Gray, D. (StL) 52
Crowder, A. (Was) 50

Complete Games
Grove, L. (Phi) 27
Ferrell, W. (Cle) 26
Ruffing, R. (NY) 22

Shutouts
Bridges, T. (Det) 4
Grove, L. (Phi) 4
7 players tied with 3

Saves
Marberry, F. (Was) 13
Moore, W. (Bos,NY) 8
2 players tied with 7

Innings Pitched
Crowder, A. (Was) 327
Grove, L. (Phi) 291^{2}
Ferrell, W. (Cle) 287^{2}

Fewest Hits/Game
Allen, J. (NY) 7.59
Ruffing, R. (NY) 7.61
Bridges, T. (Det) 7.79

Fewest BB/Game
Brown, C. (Cle) 1.71
Crowder, A. (Was) 2.12
Gray, D. (StL) 2.31

Strikeouts
Ruffing, R. (NY) 190
Grove, L. (Phi) 188
Gomez, L. (NY) 176

Ratio
Grove, L. (Phi) 1.19
Crowder, A. (Was) 1.21
Allen, J. (NY) 1.24

Earned Run Average
Grove, L. (Phi) 2.84
Ruffing, R. (NY) 3.09
Lyons, T. (Chi) 3.28

Adjusted ERA
Grove, L. (Phi) 159
Bridges, T. (Det) 140
Hogsett, C. (Det) 133

Component ERA
Grove, L. (Phi) 2.74
Allen, J. (NY) 2.89
Crowder, A. (Was) 2.93

Opponents' Batting Avg.
Ruffing, R. (NY) .226
Allen, J. (NY) .228
Bridges, T. (Det) .233

Adjusted Pitching Runs
Grove, L. (Phi) 54
Ferrell, W. (Cle) 40
Harder, M. (Cle) 33

Win Shares – Pitchers
Grove, L. (Phi) 33
Crowder, A. (Was) 30
2 players tied with 26

TPW – Pitchers
Grove, L. (Phi) 4.9
Ferrell, W. (Cle) 4.2
Ruffing, R. (NY) 3.8

1933 National League

TEAM	G	W	L	PCT	GB	R	OR	EW	AB	H	2B	3B	HR	TB	BB	SO	SB	CS	AVG	OBP	SLG	OPS	OPS+	BR/A	PF	RC
NY	156	91	61	.599	....	636	**515**	92	**5461**	1437	204	41	**82**	1969	377	477	31	....	.263	.312	.361	.673	100	-5	98	617
PIT	154	87	67	.565	5	667	619	83	5429	**1548**	249	**84**	39	**2082**	366	**334**	34	....	**.285**	**.333**	**.383**	**.716**	**111**	**72**	100	**709**
CHI	154	86	68	.558	6	646	536	91	5255	1422	**256**	51	72	1996	392	475	52	....	.271	.325	.380	.705	108	50	100	643
BOS	156	83	71	.539	9	552	531	80	5243	1320	217	56	54	1811	326	428	25	....	.252	.299	.345	.644	98	-23	92	538
STL	154	82	71	.536	9.5	**687**	609	86	5387	1486	**256**	61	57	2035	391	528	**99**	....	.276	.329	.378	.706	103	21	105	676
BRO	157	65	88	.425	26.5	617	695	67	5367	1413	224	51	62	1925	**397**	453	82	....	.263	.316	.359	.675	103	20	96	612
PHI	152	60	92	.395	31	607	760	59	5261	1439	240	41	60	1941	381	479	55	....	.274	.326	.369	.695	93	-39	113	642
CIN	153	58	94	.382	33	496	643	57	5156	1267	208	37	34	1651	349	354	30	....	.246	.298	.320	.618	84	-103	99	487
Total	**618**					**4908**			**42559**	**11332**	**1854**	**422**	**460**		**2979**	**3528**	**408**		**.266**	**.317**	**.362**	**.679**				

Runs
Martin, P. (StL) 122
Klein, C. (Phi) 101
Waner, P. (Pit) 101

Hits
Klein, C. (Phi) 223
Fullis, C. (Phi) 200
Waner, P. (Pit) 191

Doubles
Klein, C. (Phi) 44
Medwick, J. (StL) 40
Lindstrom, F. (Pit) 39

Triples
Vaughan, A. (Pit) 19
Waner, P. (Pit) 16
2 players tied with 12

Home Runs
Klein, C. (Phi) 28
Berger, W. (Bos) 27
Ott, M. (NY) 23

Total Bases
Klein, C. (Phi) 365
Berger, W. (Bos) 299
Medwick, J. (StL) 296

Runs Batted In
Klein, C. (Phi) 120
Berger, W. (Bos) 106
Ott, M. (NY) 103

Bases On Balls
Ott, M. (NY) 75
Suhr, G. (Pit) 72
Martin, P. (StL) 67

Stolen Bases
Martin, P. (StL) 26
Frisch, F. (StL) 18
Fullis, C. (Phi) 18

Batting Average
Klein, C. (Phi) .368
Davis, S. (Phi) .349
Terry, B. (NY) .322

On-Base Percentage
Klein, C. (Phi) .422
Davis, S. (Phi) .395
Vaughan, A. (Pit) .388

Slugging Average
Klein, C. (Phi) .602
Berger, W. (Bos) .566
Herman, B. (Chi) .502

Adjusted OPS
Berger, W. (Bos) 177
Klein, C. (Phi) 168
Vaughan, A. (Pit) 146

Adjusted Batting Runs
Klein, C. (Phi) 55.0
Berger, W. (Bos) 50.0
Vaughan, A. (Pit) 36.0

Runs Created/Game
Klein, C. (Phi) 11.20
Berger, W. (Bos) 8.20
Vaughan, A. (Pit) 7.30

Fielding Runs
Critz, H. (NY) 30.5
Herman, B. (Chi) 25.4
Jurges, B. (Chi) 16.1

Win Shares – Batters
Berger, W. (Bos) 36
Vaughan, A. (Pit) 34
Ott, M. (NY) 31

TPW – Batters
Vaughan, A. (Pit) 5.7
Klein, C. (Phi) 5.4
Berger, W. (Bos) 4.9

TEAM	CG	SH	SV	IP	H	H/G	ER	HR	BB	SO	OAV	RAT	ERA	ERA+	CERA	PR+	PF	FA	E	DP	FR	BW	PW	FW	TPW	DIF
NY	75	**23**	15	**1408^{2}**	**1280**	**8.2**	**424**	61	400	555	**.242**	**1.193**	**2.71**	118	**2.94**	**55.0**	96	.973	178	156	23.1	-.5	**5.8**	2.4	7.8	7.2
PIT	70	16	12	1373^{1}	1417	9.3	499	54	313	401	.264	1.260	3.27	101	3.19	-1.5	99	.972	166	133	8.2	**7.7**	-.2	.9	8.4	1.6
CHI	**95**	16	9	1362	1316	8.7	443	51	413	488	.254	1.269	2.93	112	3.11	21.5	98	.973	168	**163**	**29.9**	5.3	2.3	**3.2**	**10.7**	-1.7
BOS	85	15	**16**	1403	1391	8.9	461	54	355	383	.261	1.244	2.96	103	3.05	23.9	92	**.978**	**138**	148	-8.8	-2.4	2.5	-.9	-.8	6.8
STL	73	11	**16**	1382^{2}	1391	9.0	517	55	452	**635**	.261	1.333	3.37	103	3.37	14.5	104	.973	162	119	0.5	2.2	1.5	.1	3.8	2.2
BRO	71	9	10	1386^{1}	1502	9.8	574	51	374	415	.275	1.353	3.73	**86**	3.61	-43.0	96	.971	177	120	-35.7	2.1	-4.6	-3.8	-6.2	-4.8
PHI	52	10	13	1336^{2}	1563	10.5	644	87	410	341	.292	1.476	4.34	88	4.46	-77.2	114	.970	183	156	-1.6	-4.1	-8.2	-.2	-12.5	-3.5
CIN	74	13	8	1352	1470	9.8	514	**47**	**257**	310	.279	1.277	3.42	99	3.30	8.6	102	.971	177	139	-13.5	-10.9	.9	-1.4	-11.5	-6.5
Total	**595**	**113**	**99**	**11004^{2}**		**9.3**	**4076**					**1.300**	**3.33**													

Wins
Hubbell, C. (NY) 23
3 players tied with 20

Win Percentage
Tinning, B. (Chi) .684
Cantwell, B. (Bos) .667
Hubbell, C. (NY) .657

Games
Dean, D. (StL) 48
French, L. (Pit) 47
2 players tied with 45

Complete Games
Dean, D. (StL) 26
Warneke, L. (Chi) 26
Brandt, E. (Bos) 23

Shutouts
Hubbell, C. (NY) 10
Schumacher, H. (NY) 7
French, L. (Pit) 5

Saves
Collins, P. (Phi) 6
3 players tied with 5

Innings Pitched
Hubbell, C. (NY) 308^{2}
Dean, D. (StL) 293
French, L. (Pit) 291^{1}

Fewest Hits/Game
Schumacher, H. (NY) 6.92
Hubbell, C. (NY) 7.46
Parmelee, R. (NY) 7.87

Fewest BB/Game
Lucas, R. (Cin) .74
Hubbell, C. (NY) 1.37
Swift, B. (Pit) 1.48

Strikeouts
Dean, D. (StL) 199
Hubbell, C. (NY) 156
Carleton, T. (StL) 147

Ratio
Hubbell, C. (NY) .98
Schumacher, H. (NY) 1.09
Swift, B. (Pit) 1.15

Earned Run Average
Hubbell, C. (NY) 1.66
Warneke, L. (Chi) 2.00
Schumacher, H. (NY) 2.16

Adjusted ERA
Hubbell, C. (NY) 193
Warneke, L. (Chi) 163
Schumacher, H. (NY) 149

Component ERA
Hubbell, C. (NY) 1.84
Schumacher, H. (NY) 2.18
Brandt, E. (Bos) 2.59

Opponents' Batting Avg.
Schumacher, H. (NY) .214
Hubbell, C. (NY) .227
Parmelee, R. (NY) .232

Adjusted Pitching Runs
Hubbell, C. (NY) 48
Warneke, L. (Chi) 34
Schumacher, H. (NY) 26

Win Shares – Pitchers
Hubbell, C. (NY) 33
Brandt, E. (Bos) 29
Warneke, L. (Chi) 29

TPW – Pitchers
Hubbell, C. (NY) 5.1
Warneke, L. (Chi) 4.7
Schumacher, H. (NY) 2.8

1933 American League

TEAM	G	W	L	PCT	GB	R	OR	EW	AB	H	2B	3B	HR	TB	BB	SO	SB	CS	AVG	OBP	SLG	OPS	OPS+	BR/A	PF	RC
WAS	153	99	53	.651	....	850	**665**	94	**5524**	**1586**	281	**86**	60	2219	539	**395**	65	50	**.287**	.353	.402	.754	107	56	99	799
NY	152	91	59	.607	7	**927**	768	89	5274	1495	241	75	**144**	2318	**700**	506	**76**	59	.283	**.369**	.440	**.809**	**128**	**214**	94	**880**
PHI	152	79	72	.523	19.5	875	853	77	5330	1519	**297**	57	139	**2347**	625	618	34	**34**	.285	.362	**.440**	.802	117	128	101	867
CLE	151	75	76	.497	23.5	654	669	74	5240	1366	218	77	50	1888	448	426	36	40	.261	.321	.360	.681	82	-135	104	616
DET	155	75	79	.487	25	722	733	76	5502	1479	283	78	57	2089	475	523	68	50	.269	.329	.380	.709	92	-68	102	698
CHI	151	67	83	.447	31	683	814	62	5318	1448	231	53	43	1914	538	416	43	46	.272	.342	.360	.702	96	-22	96	674
BOS	149	63	86	.423	34.5	700	758	69	5201	1407	294	56	50	1963	525	464	58	37	.271	.339	.377	.717	97	-17	99	687
STL	153	55	96	.364	43.5	669	820	60	5285	1337	244	64	64	1901	520	556	72	60	.253	.322	.360	.681	81	-145	106	625
Total	**608**					**6080**			**42674**	**11637**	**2089**	**546**	**607**		**4370**	**3904**	**452**	**376**	**.273**	**.342**	**.390**	**.732**				

Runs
Gehrig, L. (NY) 138
Foxx, J. (Phi) 125
Manush, H. (Was) 115

Hits
Manush, H. (Was) 221
Foxx, J. (Phi) 204
Gehringer, C. (Det) 204

Doubles
Cronin, J. (Was) 45
Johnson, B. (Phi) 44
Burns, J. (StL) 43

Triples
Manush, H. (Was) 17
Averill, E. (Cle) 16
Combs, E. (NY) 16

Home Runs
Foxx, J. (Phi) 48
Ruth, B. (NY) 34
Gehrig, L. (NY) 32

Total Bases
Foxx, J. (Phi) 403
Gehrig, L. (NY) 359
Manush, H. (Was) 302

Runs Batted In
Foxx, J. (Phi) 163
Gehrig, L. (NY) 139
Simmons, A. (Chi) 119

Bases On Balls
Ruth, B. (NY) 114
Bishop, M. (Phi) 106
Cochrane, M. (Phi) 106

Stolen Bases
Chapman, B. (NY) 27
Walker, G. (Det) 26
Swanson, E. (Chi) 19

Batting Average
Foxx, J. (Phi) .356
Manush, H. (Was) .336
Gehrig, L. (NY) .334

On-Base Percentage
Cochrane, M. (Phi) .459
Foxx, J. (Phi) .449
Bishop, M. (Phi) .446

Slugging Average
Foxx, J. (Phi) .703
Gehrig, L. (NY) .605
Ruth, B. (NY) .582

Adjusted OPS
Foxx, J. (Phi) 199
Gehrig, L. (NY) 181
Ruth, B. (NY) 180

Adjusted Batting Runs
Foxx, J. (Phi) 82.0
Gehrig, L. (NY) 66.0
Ruth, B. (NY) 58.0

Runs Created/Game
Foxx, J. (Phi) 13.10
Ruth, B. (NY) 10.10
Gehrig, L. (NY) 9.80

Fielding Runs
Rogell, B. (Det) 22.1
Cronin, J. (Was) 20.2
Scharein, A. (StL) 13.6

Win Shares – Batters
Foxx, J. (Phi) 41
Gehrig, L. (NY) 36
Cronin, J. (Was) 34

TPW – Batters
Foxx, J. (Phi) 7.1
Cronin, J. (Was) 5.3
Ruth, B. (NY) 4.9

TEAM	CG	SH	SV	IP	H	H/G	ER	HR	BB	SO	OAV	RAT	ERA	ERA+	CERA	PR+	PF	FA	E	DP	FR	BW	PW	FW	TPW	DIF
WAS	68	5	**26**	1389^{2}	1415	9.2	590	64	**452**	447	.263	**1.343**	3.82	109	**3.50**	25.4	98	**.978**	**131**	149	**30.5**	5.3	2.4	**2.9**	10.6	12.4
NY	70	8	22	1354^{2}	1426	9.5	656	66	612	**711**	.268	1.504	4.36	89	4.09	-54.5	91	.972	165	122	-17.8	**20.3**	-5.2	-1.7	**13.4**	2.6
PHI	69	6	14	1343^{2}	1523	10.2	718	77	644	423	.283	1.613	4.81	**89**	4.72	-39.0	100	.966	203	121	-39.0	12.2	-3.7	-3.7	4.8	-.8
CLE	**74**	**12**	7	1350	**1382**	9.2	**556**	**60**	465	437	.264	1.368	**3.71**	120	3.55	**108.2**	104	.974	156	127	2.4	-12.7	**10.2**	.2	-2.3	2.3
DET	69	6	17	**1398**	1415	**9.1**	614	84	561	575	**.263**	1.413	3.95	109	3.85	42.2	101	.971	178	**167**	12.2	-6.4	4.0	1.2	-1.3	-.7
CHI	53	8	13	1371^{1}	1505	9.9	678	85	519	423	.277	1.476	4.45	95	4.23	-19.0	99	.970	186	143	-13.1	-2.1	-1.8	-1.2	-5.1	-2.9
BOS	60	4	14	1327^{2}	1396	9.5	641	75	591	467	.271	1.497	4.35	101	4.16	5.6	102	.965	204	133	-0.7	-1.6	.5	-.1	-1.2	-9.8
STL	55	7	10	1360^{2}	1574	10.4	728	96	531	426	.289	1.547	4.82	97	4.66	-51.9	109	.975	149	162	26.1	-13.7	-4.9	2.5	-16.2	-3.8
Total	**518**	**56**	**123**	**10895^{2}**		**9.6**	**5181**					**1.469**	**4.28**													

Wins
- Crowder, A. (Was) 24
- Grove, L. (Phi) 24
- Whitehill, E. (Was) 22

Win Percentage
- Van Atta, R. (NY) .750
- Grove, L. (Phi) .750
- Whitehill, E. (Was) .733

Games
- Crowder, A. (Was) 52
- Russell, J. (Was) 50
- Welch, J. (Bos) 47

Complete Games
- Grove, L. (Phi) 21
- Hadley, B. (StL) 19
- Whitehill, E. (Was) 19

Shutouts
- Hildebrand, O. (Cle) 6
- Gomez, L. (NY) 4
- Blaeholder, G. (StL) 3

Saves
- Russell, J. (Was) 13
- Hogsett, C. (Det) 9
- Moore, W. (NY) 8

Innings Pitched
- Hadley, B. (StL) 316^2
- Crowder, A. (Was) 299^1
- Grove, L. (Phi) 275^1

Fewest Hits/Game
- Bridges, T. (Det) 7.42
- Weiland, B. (Bos) 8.20
- Allen, J. (NY) 8.33

Fewest BB/Game
- Brown, C. (Cle) 1.65
- Marberry, F. (Det) 2.30
- Stewart, L. (Was) 2.34

Strikeouts
- Gomez, L. (NY) 163
- Hadley, B. (StL) 149
- Ruffing, R. (NY) 122

Ratio
- Marberry, F. (Det) 1.23
- Stewart, L. (Was) 1.24
- Harder, M. (Cle) 1.27

Earned Run Average
- Pearson, M. (Cle) 2.33
- Harder, M. (Cle) 2.95
- Bridges, T. (Det) 3.09

Adjusted ERA
- Harder, M. (Cle) 151
- Bridges, T. (Det) 139
- Grove, L. (Phi) 134

Component ERA
- Bridges, T. (Det) 2.94
- Marberry, F. (Det) 3.03
- Harder, M. (Cle) 3.11

Opponents' Batting Avg.
- Bridges, T. (Det) .226
- Gomez, L. (NY) .240
- Allen, J. (NY) .242

Adjusted Pitching Runs
- Harder, M. (Cle) 41
- Grove, L. (Phi) 41
- Bridges, T. (Det) 30

Win Shares – Pitchers
- Harder, M. (Cle) 24
- 3 players tied with 23

TPW – Pitchers
- Harder, M. (Cle) 3.9
- Grove, L. (Phi) 3.2
- Bridges, T. (Det) 3.0

1934 National League

TEAM	G	W	L	PCT	GB	R	OR	EW	AB	H	2B	3B	HR	TB	BB	SO	SB	CS	AVG	OBP	SLG	OPS	OPS+	BR/A	PF	RC
STL	154	95	58	.621	....	**799**	656	91	**5502**	**1582**	**294**	75	104	**2338**	392	535	**69**	....	**.288**	.337	**.425**	**.762**	103	15	106	**796**
NY	153	93	60	.608	2	760	**583**	96	5396	1485	240	41	**126**	2185	406	526	19	....	.275	.329	.405	.734	104	26	98	736
CHI	152	86	65	.570	8	705	639	83	5347	1494	263	44	101	2148	375	630	59	....	.279	.330	.402	.731	103	19	98	719
BOS	152	78	73	.517	16	683	714	72	5370	1460	233	44	83	2030	375	440	30	....	.272	.323	.378	.701	100	1	93	660
PIT	151	74	76	.493	19.5	735	713	77	5361	1541	281	**77**	52	2132	440	**398**	44	....	.287	.344	.398	.741	102	18	102	742
BRO	153	71	81	.467	23.5	748	795	71	5427	1526	284	52	79	2151	**548**	555	55	....	.281	**.350**	.396	.746	**111**	**93**	95	782
PHI	149	56	93	.376	37	675	794	63	5218	1480	286	35	56	2004	398	534	52	....	.284	.338	.384	.722	87	-83	113	685
CIN	152	52	99	.344	42	590	801	53	5361	1428	227	65	55	1950	313	532	34	....	.266	.311	.364	.675	88	-92	98	603
Total	**608**					**5695**			**42982**	**11996**	**2108**	**433**	**656**		**3247**	**4150**	**362**		**.279**	**.333**	**.394**	**.727**				

Runs
- Waner, P. (Pit) 122
- Ott, M. (NY) 119
- Collins, R. (StL) 116

Hits
- Waner, P. (Pit) 217
- Terry, B. (NY) 213
- Collins, R. (StL) 200

Doubles
- Allen, E. (Phi) 42
- Cuyler, K. (Chi) 42
- Vaughan, A. (Pit) 41

Triples
- Medwick, J. (StL) 18
- Waner, P. (Pit) 16
- Suhr, G. (Pit) 13

Home Runs
- Collins, R. (StL) 35
- Ott, M. (NY) 35
- Berger, W. (Bos) 34

Total Bases
- Collins, R. (StL) 369
- Ott, M. (NY) 344
- Berger, W. (Bos) 336

Runs Batted In
- Ott, M. (NY) 135
- Collins, R. (StL) 128
- Berger, W. (Bos) 121

Bases On Balls
- Vaughan, A. (Pit) 94
- Ott, M. (NY) 85
- Koenecke, L. (Bro) 70

Stolen Bases
- Martin, P. (StL) 23
- Cuyler, K. (Chi) 15
- Bartell, D. (Phi) 13

Batting Average
- Waner, P. (Pit) .362
- Terry, B. (NY) .354
- Cuyler, K. (Chi) .338

On-Base Percentage
- Vaughan, A. (Pit) .431
- Waner, P. (Pit) .429
- Ott, M. (NY) .415

Slugging Average
- Collins, R. (StL) .615
- Ott, M. (NY) .591
- Berger, W. (Bos) .546

Adjusted OPS
- Ott, M. (NY) 170
- Collins, R. (StL) 155
- Waner, P. (Pit) 154

Adjusted Batting Runs
- Ott, M. (NY) 59.0
- Waner, P. (Pit) 48.0
- Collins, R. (StL) 46.0

Runs Created/Game
- Ott, M. (NY) 10.10
- Collins, R. (StL) 9.70
- Vaughan, A. (Pit) 9.60

Fielding Runs
- Bartell, D. (Phi) 22.3
- Vaughan, A. (Pit) 19.8
- Critz, H. (NY) 15.7

Win Shares – Batters
- Ott, M. (NY) 38
- Vaughan, A. (Pit) 36
- Berger, W. (Bos) 33

TPW – Batters
- Vaughan, A. (Pit) 7.2
- Ott, M. (NY) 4.8
- Waner, P. (Pit) 3.6

TEAM	CG	SH	SV	IP	H	H/G	ER	HR	BB	SO	OAV	RAT	ERA	ERA+	CERA	PR+	PF	FA	E	DP	FR	BW	PW	FW	TPW	DIF
STL	**78**	**15**	16	**1386^2**	1463	9.5	568	77	411	**689**	.268	1.351	3.69	115	3.69	67.1	104	.972	166	**141**	15.7	1.4	6.5	1.5	9.5	9.5
NY	68	13	**30**	1370	**1384**	**9.1**	**486**	75	**351**	499	**.260**	**1.266**	**3.19**	121	**3.27**	**89.1**	95	.972	179	**141**	13.8	2.5	**8.7**	1.3	**12.6**	4.4
CHI	73	11	9	1361^1	1432	9.5	569	80	417	633	.269	1.358	3.76	103	3.72	7.8	95	**.977**	**137**	135	10.6	1.8	.8	1.0	3.6	7.4
BOS	62	12	20	1359^2	1512	10.0	621	78	405	462	.279	1.410	4.11	93	3.95	-42.4	94	.972	169	120	-0.9	.1	-4.1	-.1	-4.1	7.1
PIT	63	8	8	1329^2	1523	10.3	620	78	354	487	.284	1.412	4.20	98	4.07	2.3	101	.975	145	118	-14.0	1.7	.2	-1.4	.6	-1.6
BRO	66	6	12	1354^1	1540	10.2	674	81	475	520	.285	1.488	4.48	**87**	4.38	-78.9	96	.970	180	**141**	-7.3	**9.1**	-7.7	-.7	.7	-5.7
PHI	52	8	15	1297	1501	10.4	686	126	437	416	.288	1.494	4.76	99	4.73	-23.4	116	.966	197	140	**18.2**	-8.1	-2.3	**1.8**	-8.6	-9.4
CIN	51	3	19	1347^2	1645	11.0	654	**61**	389	438	.299	1.509	4.37	93	4.46	-9.2	100	.970	181	136	-33.2	-8.9	-.9	-3.2	-13.1	-9.9
Total	**513**	**76**	**129**	**10806^1**		**10.0**	**4878**					**1.410**	**4.06**													

Wins
- Dean, D. (StL) 30
- Schumacher, H. (NY) 23
- Warneke, L. (Chi) 22

Win Percentage
- Dean, D. (StL) .811
- Hoyt, W. (Pit) .714
- Schumacher, H. (NY) .697

Games
- Davis, C. (Phi) 51
- Dean, D. (StL) 50
- Hansen, S. (Phi) 50

Complete Games
- Hubbell, C. (NY) 25
- Dean, D. (StL) 24
- Warneke, L. (Chi) 23

Shutouts
- Dean, D. (StL) 7
- Dean, P. (StL) 5
- Hubbell, C. (NY) 5

Saves
- Hubbell, C. (NY) 8
- Dean, D. (StL) 7
- Luque, D. (NY) 7

Innings Pitched
- Mungo, V. (Bro) 315^1
- Hubbell, C. (NY) 313
- Dean, D. (StL) 311^2

Fewest Hits/Game
- Hubbell, C. (NY) 8.22
- Dean, D. (StL) 8.32
- Warneke, L. (Chi) 8.43

Fewest BB/Game
- Hubbell, C. (NY) 1.06
- Frey, B. (Cin) 1.54
- Leonard, D. (Bro) 1.62

Strikeouts
- Dean, D. (StL) 195
- Mungo, V. (Bro) 184
- Dean, P. (StL) 150

Ratio
- Hubbell, C. (NY) 1.03
- Warneke, L. (Chi) 1.16
- Dean, D. (StL) 1.16

Earned Run Average
- Hubbell, C. (NY) 2.30
- Dean, D. (StL) 2.66
- Hoyt, W. (Pit) 2.93

Adjusted ERA
- Hubbell, C. (NY) 168
- Davis, C. (Phi) 160
- Dean, D. (StL) 159

Component ERA
- Hubbell, C. (NY) 2.27
- Dean, D. (StL) 2.69
- Warneke, L. (Chi) 2.75

Opponents' Batting Avg.
- Parmelee, R. (NY) .238
- Hubbell, C. (NY) .239
- Dean, D. (StL) .241

Adjusted Pitching Runs
- Hubbell, C. (NY) 51
- Dean, D. (StL) 51
- Davis, C. (Phi) 50

Win Shares – Pitchers
- Dean, D. (StL) 37
- Hubbell, C. (NY) 32
- Warneke, L. (Chi) 26

TPW – Pitchers
- Dean, D. (StL) 5.3
- Hubbell, C. (NY) 4.9
- Davis, C. (Phi) 4.8

1934 American League

TEAM	G	W	L	PCT	GB	R	OR	EW	AB	H	2B	3B	HR	TB	BB	SO	SB	CS	AVG	OBP	SLG	OPS	OPS+	BR/A	PF	RC
DET	154	101	53	.656	....	**958**	708	100	**5475**	**1644**	**349**	53	74	**2321**	639	528	**125**	55	**.300**	**.376**	.424	**.800**	113	117	100	**905**
NY	154	94	60	.610	7	842	**669**	94	5368	1494	226	61	135	2247	**700**	597	71	46	.278	.364	.419	.782	**117**	**133**	93	848
CLE	154	85	69	.552	16	814	763	82	5396	1550	340	46	100	2282	526	**433**	52	32	.287	.353	.423	.776	105	31	101	820
BOS	153	76	76	.500	24	820	775	80	5339	1465	287	**70**	51	2045	610	535	116	47	.274	.350	.383	.733	89	-71	107	748
PHI	153	68	82	.453	31	764	838	68	5317	1491	236	50	**144**	2259	491	584	57	35	.280	.343	**.425**	.768	108	49	96	785
STL	154	67	85	.441	33	674	800	63	5288	1417	252	59	62	1973	514	631	43	31	.268	.335	.373	.708	82	-141	108	680
WAS	155	66	86	.434	34	729	806	68	5448	1512	278	**70**	51	2083	570	447	47	42	.278	.348	.382	.731	99	-11	96	747
CHI	153	53	99	.349	47	704	946	54	5301	1395	237	40	71	1925	565	524	36	**27**	.263	.336	.363	.699	84	-120	103	672
Total	**615**					**6305**			**42932**	**11968**	**2205**	**449**	**688**		**4615**	**4279**	**547**	**315**	**.279**	**.351**	**.399**	**.750**				

Runs
- Gehringer, C. (Det) 134
- Werber, B. (Bos) 129
- 2 players tied with 128

Hits
- Gehringer, C. (Det) 214
- Gehrig, L. (NY) 210
- Trosky, H. (Cle) 206

Doubles
- Greenberg, H. (Det) 63
- Gehringer, C. (Det) 50
- Averill, E. (Cle) 48

Triples
- Chapman, B. (NY) 13
- Manush, H. (Was) 11
- 5 players tied with 10

Home Runs
- Gehrig, L. (NY) 49
- Foxx, J. (Phi) 44
- Trosky, H. (Cle) 35

Total Bases
- Gehrig, L. (NY) 409
- Trosky, H. (Cle) 374
- Greenberg, H. (Det) 356

Runs Batted In
- Gehrig, L. (NY) 165
- Trosky, H. (Cle) 142
- Greenberg, H. (Det) 139

Bases On Balls
- Foxx, J. (Phi) 111
- Gehrig, L. (NY) 109
- Ruth, B. (NY) 104

Stolen Bases
- Werber, B. (Bos) 40
- White, J. (Det) 28
- Chapman, B. (NY) 26

Batting Average
- Gehrig, L. (NY) .363
- Gehringer, C. (Det) .356
- Manush, H. (Was) .349

On-Base Percentage
- Gehrig, L. (NY) .465
- Gehringer, C. (Det) .450
- Foxx, J. (Phi) .449

Slugging Average
- Gehrig, L. (NY) .706
- Foxx, J. (Phi) .653
- Greenberg, H. (Det) .600

Adjusted OPS
- Gehrig, L. (NY) 213
- Foxx, J. (Phi) 188
- Greenberg, H. (Det) 156

Adjusted Batting Runs
- Gehrig, L. (NY) 99.0
- Foxx, J. (Phi) 75.0
- Gehringer, C. (Det) 47.0

Runs Created/Game
- Gehrig, L. (NY) 13.80
- Foxx, J. (Phi) 12.10
- Gehringer, C. (Det) 9.60

Fielding Runs
- Hale, O. (Cle) 21.0
- Werber, B. (Bos) 19.2
- Melillo, S. (StL) 17.3

Win Shares – Batters
- Gehrig, L. (NY) 41
- Gehringer, C. (Det) 37
- Averill, E. (Cle) 33

TPW – Batters
- Gehrig, L. (NY) 7.9
- Foxx, J. (Phi) 6.3
- Gehringer, C. (Det) 5.8

TEAM	CG	SH	SV	IP	H	H/G	ER	HR	BB	SO	OAV	RAT	ERA	ERA+	CERA	PR+	PF	FA	E	DP	FR	BW	PW	FW	TPW	DIF
DET	74	**13**	14	1370[2]	1467	9.6	618	86	**488**	640	.273	1.426	4.06	108	4.00	40.8	98	.974	159	150	10.1	10.9	3.8	.9	15.6	8.4
NY	**83**	**13**	10	**1382[2]**	**1349**	**8.8**	**577**	71	542	**656**	**.254**	**1.368**	**3.76**	108	**3.54**	25.9	90	.973	**157**	151	**21.9**	**12.4**	2.4	**2.0**	**16.8**	.2
CLE	72	8	19	1367	1476	9.7	650	**70**	582	554	.275	1.505	4.28	106	4.24	48.5	101	.972	172	164	-8.0	2.9	4.5	-.7	6.6	1.4
BOS	68	9	9	1361	1527	10.1	653	**70**	543	538	.283	1.521	4.32	111	4.34	**85.7**	107	.969	188	141	-12.2	-6.6	**8.0**	-1.1	.3	-.3
PHI	68	8	8	1337	1429	9.6	744	84	693	480	.275	1.587	5.01	87	4.61	-105.9	97	.967	196	166	11.8	4.5	-9.8	1.1	-4.2	-2.8
STL	50	6	**20**	1350	1499	10.0	674	94	632	499	.283	1.579	4.49	111	4.68	59.0	111	.969	187	160	16.4	-13.1	5.5	1.5	-6.1	-2.9
WAS	61	4	12	1381[1]	1622	10.6	718	74	503	412	.295	1.538	4.68	92	4.55	-51.8	96	**.974**	162	**167**	-3.1	-1.0	-4.8	-.3	-6.1	-3.9
CHI	72	5	8	1355	1599	10.6	815	139	628	506	.292	1.644	5.41	**87**	5.29	-63.9	105	.966	207	126	-37.9	-11.1	-5.9	-3.5	-20.6	-2.4
Total	**548**	**66**	**100**	**10904[2]**		**9.9**	**5449**					**1.520**	**4.50**													

Wins
Gomez, L. (NY) 26
Rowe, S. (Det) 24
Bridges, T. (Det) 22

Win Percentage
Gomez, L. (NY) .839
Rowe, S. (Det) .750
Marberry, F. (Det) .750

Games
Russell, J. (Was) 54
Newsom, B. (StL) 47
2 players tied with 45

Complete Games
Gomez, L. (NY) 25
Bridges, T. (Det) 23
Lyons, T. (Chi) 21

Shutouts
Gomez, L. (NY) 6
Harder, M. (Cle) 6
Ruffing, R. (NY) 5

Saves
Russell, J. (Was) 7
Brown, L. (Cle) 6
Newsom, B. (StL) 5

Innings Pitched
Gomez, L. (NY) 281[2]
Bridges, T. (Det) 275
Rowe, S. (Det) 266

Fewest Hits/Game
Gomez, L. (NY) 7.13
Ruffing, R. (NY) 8.15
Bridges, T. (Det) 8.15

Fewest BB/Game
Ferrell, W. (Bos) 2.44
Auker, E. (Det) 2.46
Blaeholder, G. (StL) 2.61

Strikeouts
Gomez, L. (NY) 158
Bridges, T. (Det) 151
2 players tied with 149

Ratio
Gomez, L. (NY) 1.13
Rowe, S. (Det) 1.28
Harder, M. (Cle) 1.28

Earned Run Average
Gomez, L. (NY) 2.33
Harder, M. (Cle) 2.61
Murphy, J. (NY) 3.12

Adjusted ERA
Harder, M. (Cle) 174
Gomez, L. (NY) 174
Ostermueller, F. (Bos) 138

Component ERA
Gomez, L. (NY) 2.33
Burke, B. (Was) 3.04
Harder, M. (Cle) 3.08

Opponents' Batting Avg.
Gomez, L. (NY) .215
Ruffing, R. (NY) .236
Bridges, T. (Det) .241

Adjusted Pitching Runs
Harder, M. (Cle) 56
Gomez, L. (NY) 50
Ostermueller, F. (Bos) 31

Win Shares – Pitchers
Gomez, L. (NY) 31
Rowe, S. (Det) 28
Harder, M. (Cle) 27

TPW – Pitchers
Harder, M. (Cle) 5.1
Gomez, L. (NY) 4.3
Rowe, S. (Det) 3.4

1935 National League

TEAM	G	W	L	PCT	GB	R	OR	EW	AB	H	2B	3B	HR	TB	BB	SO	SB	CS	AVG	OBP	SLG	OPS	OPS+	BR/A	PF	RC
CHI	154	100	54	.649	....	**847**	**597**	103	5486	1581	**303**	62	88	2272	**464**	471	66	....	**.288**	**.347**	.414	**.761**	**110**	**78**	101	**812**
STL	154	96	58	.623	4	829	625	98	5457	1548	286	59	86	2210	404	521	71	....	.284	.335	.405	.740	101	4	104	759
NY	156	91	62	.595	8.5	770	675	87	**5623**	**1608**	248	56	**123**	**2337**	392	479	32	....	.286	.336	**.416**	.752	**110**	68	98	797
PIT	153	86	67	.562	13.5	743	647	87	5415	1543	255	**90**	66	2176	457	437	30	....	.285	.343	.402	.745	103	26	103	758
BRO	154	70	83	.458	29.5	711	767	71	5410	1496	235	62	59	2032	430	520	60	....	.277	.333	.376	.708	99	-5	98	691
CIN	154	68	85	.444	31.5	646	772	63	5296	1403	244	68	73	2002	392	547	**72**	....	.265	.319	.378	.697	96	-30	97	658
PHI	156	64	89	.418	35.5	685	871	58	5442	1466	249	32	92	2055	392	661	52	....	.269	.322	.378	.699	85	-111	110	681
BOS	153	38	115	.248	61.5	575	852	48	5309	1396	233	33	75	1920	353	**436**	20	....	.263	.311	.362	.673	94	-45	92	596
Total	**617**					**5806**			**43438**	**12041**	**2053**	**462**	**662**		**3284**	**4072**	**403**		**.277**	**.331**	**.391**	**.722**				

Runs
Galan, A. (Chi) 133
Medwick, J. (StL) 132
Martin, P. (StL) 121

Hits
Herman, B. (Chi) 227
Medwick, J. (StL) 224
4 players tied with 203

Doubles
Herman, B. (Chi) 57
Allen, E. (Phi) 46
Medwick, J. (StL) 46

Triples
Goodman, I. (Cin) 18
Waner, L. (Pit) 14
Medwick, J. (StL) 13

Home Runs
Berger, W. (Bos) 34
Ott, M. (NY) 31
Camilli, D. (Phi) 25

Total Bases
Medwick, J. (StL) 365
Ott, M. (NY) 329
Berger, W. (Bos) 323

Runs Batted In
Berger, W. (Bos) 130
Medwick, J. (StL) 126
Collins, R. (StL) 122

Bases On Balls
Vaughan, A. (Pit) 97
Galan, A. (Chi) 87
Ott, M. (NY) 82

Stolen Bases
Galan, A. (Chi) 22
Martin, P. (StL) 20
Bordagaray, F. (Bro) 18

Batting Average
Vaughan, A. (Pit) .385
Medwick, J. (StL) .353
Herman, B. (Chi) .341

On-Base Percentage
Vaughan, A. (Pit) .491
Ott, M. (NY) .407
Hack, S. (Chi) .406

Slugging Average
Vaughan, A. (Pit) .607
Medwick, J. (StL) .576
Ott, M. (NY) .555

Adjusted OPS
Vaughan, A. (Pit) 187
Ott, M. (NY) 159
Berger, W. (Bos) 151

Adjusted Batting Runs
Vaughan, A. (Pit) 69.0
Ott, M. (NY) 51.0
Medwick, J. (StL) 41.0

Runs Created/Game
Vaughan, A. (Pit) 13.80
Ott, M. (NY) 9.50
Medwick, J. (StL) 8.80

Fielding Runs
Durocher, L. (StL) 25.2
Jurges, B. (Chi) 23.6
Herman, B. (Chi) 13.8

Win Shares – Batters
Vaughan, A. (Pit) 39
Ott, M. (NY) 35
Medwick, J. (StL) 33

TPW – Batters
Vaughan, A. (Pit) 7.6
Herman, B. (Chi) 4.9
Ott, M. (NY) 4.9

TEAM	CG	SH	SV	IP	H	H/G	ER	HR	BB	SO	OAV	RAT	ERA	ERA+	CERA	PR+	PF	FA	E	DP	FR	BW	PW	FW	TPW	DIF
CHI	**81**	12	14	13941	**1417**	**0.9**	**505**	85	400	589	.263	.130	**0.33**	121	3.46	52.6	98	.970	186	**163**	**51.4**	**7.6**	5.1	**5.0**	**17.7**	5.3
STL	73	10	18	13842	1445	0.9	541	68	377	**602**	.267	.132	0.35	116	3.49	70.1	102	**.972**	**164**	133	18.3	.4	6.8	1.8	9.0	10.0
NY	76	10	11	**14032**	1433	0.9	589	106	411	524	**.263**	.131	0.38	102	3.61	5.3	96	.972	174	129	5.9	6.6	.5	.6	7.7	7.3
PIT	76	**15**	11	13652	1428	0.9	519	**63**	**312**	549	.265	**.127**	0.34	120	**3.28**	**114.1**	102	.968	190	94	-10.7	2.6	**11.1**	-1.0	12.6	-2.6
BRO	62	11	**20**	1358	1519	10.1	637	88	436	480	.281	1.440	4.22	94	4.15	-51.6	99	.969	188	146	14.3	-.5	-5.0	1.4	-4.2	-1.8
CIN	59	9	12	1356	1490	9.9	648	65	438	500	.278	1.422	4.30	93	3.95	-34.3	99	.966	204	139	-14.3	-2.9	-3.3	-1.4	-7.6	-.4
PHI	53	8	15	13742	1652	1.1	727	106	505	475	.295	.157	0.48	95	4.94	-16.3	113	.963	228	145	-18.5	-10.8	-1.6	-1.8	-14.1	2.1
BOS	54	6	5	1330	1645	11.1	729	81	404	355	.303	1.541	4.93	**77**	4.70	-123.5	94	.967	197	101	-46.0	-4.4	-12.0	-4.5	-20.9	-17.1
Total	**534**	**81**	**106**	**73253**		**1.5**	**4895**					**.209**	**0.60**													

Wins
Dean, D. (StL) 28
Hubbell, C. (NY) 23
Derringer, P. (Cin) 22

Win Percentage
Lee, B. (Chi) .769
Castleman, S. (NY) .714
Dean, D. (StL) .700

Games
Jorgens, O. (Phi) 53
Dean, D. (StL) 50
Bivin, J. (Phi) 47

Complete Games
Dean, D. (StL) 29
Hubbell, C. (NY) 24
Blanton, C. (Pit) 23

Shutouts
5 players tied with 4

Saves
Leonard, D. (Bro) 8
Hoyt, W. (Pit) 6
Johnson, S. (Phi) 6

Innings Pitched
Dean, D. (StL) 325[1]
Hubbell, C. (NY) 302[2]
Derringer, P. (Cin) 276[2]

Fewest Hits/Game
Blanton, C. (Pit) 7.79
Schumacher, H. (NY) 8.08
Parmelee, R. (NY) 8.52

Fewest BB/Game
Clark, W. (Bro) 1.22
Hubbell, C. (NY) 1.46
Hoyt, W. (Pit) 1.48

Strikeouts
Dean, D. (StL) 190
Hubbell, C. (NY) 150
2 players tied with 143

Ratio
Blanton, C. (Pit) 1.08
Swift, B. (Pit) 1.13
Schumacher, H. (NY) 1.17

Earned Run Average
Blanton, C. (Pit) 2.58
Swift, B. (Pit) 2.70
Schumacher, H. (NY) 2.89

Adjusted ERA
Blanton, C. (Pit) 159
Swift, B. (Pit) 152
Dean, D. (StL) 135

Component ERA
Blanton, C. (Pit) 2.08
Swift, B. (Pit) 2.49
Schumacher, H. (NY) 2.67

Opponents' Batting Avg.
Blanton, C. (Pit) .229
Schumacher, H. (NY) .238
Hollingsworth, A. (Cin) .243

Adjusted Pitching Runs
Blanton, C. (Pit) 45
Dean, D. (StL) 34
Swift, B. (Pit) 33

Win Shares – Pitchers
Dean, D. (StL) 31
Hubbell, C. (NY) 26
Blanton, C. (Pit) 24

TPW – Pitchers
Blanton, C. (Pit) 4.0
Dean, D. (StL) 3.6
Swift, B. (Pit) 3.5

1935 American League

TEAM	G	W	L	PCT	GB	R	OR	EW	AB	H	2B	3B	HR	TB	BB	SO	SB	CS	AVG	OBP	SLG	OPS	OPS+	BR/A	PF	RC
DET	152	93	58	.616	....	**919**	665	99	5423	1573	301	83	106	**2358**	**627**	456	70	45	**.290**	**.366**	**.435**	**.800**	**116**	**128**	97	**885**
NY	149	89	60	.597	3	818	**632**	93	5214	1462	255	70	104	2169	604	469	68	46	.280	.358	.416	.774	112	90	94	799
CLE	156	82	71	.536	12	776	739	80	5534	1573	**324**	77	93	2330	460	567	63	54	.284	.341	.421	.762	100	-18	102	796
BOS	154	78	75	.510	16	718	732	75	5288	1458	281	63	69	2072	609	470	**91**	59	.276	.353	.392	.745	92	-59	107	757
CHI	153	74	78	.487	19.5	738	750	75	5314	1460	262	42	74	2028	580	**405**	46	28	.275	.348	.382	.730	92	-56	103	733
WAS	154	67	86	.438	27	823	903	69	**5592**	**1591**	255	**95**	32	2132	596	406	54	37	.285	.357	.381	.739	100	10	97	788
STL	155	65	87	.428	28.5	718	930	57	5365	1446	291	51	73	2058	593	561	45	**25**	.270	.344	.384	.727	89	-78	105	735
PHI	149	58	91	.389	34	710	869	60	5269	1470	243	44	**112**	2137	475	602	43	35	.279	.341	.406	.746	99	-19	99	738
Total	**611**					**6220**			**42999**	**12033**	**2212**	**525**	**663**		**4544**	**3936**	**480**	**329**	**.280**	**.351**	**.402**	**.753**				

Runs
- Gehrig, L. (NY) 125
- Gehringer, C. (Det) 123
- Greenberg, H. (Det) 121

Hits
- Vosmik, J. (Cle) 216
- Myer, B. (Was) 215
- Cramer, D. (Phi) 214

Doubles
- Vosmik, J. (Cle) 47
- Greenberg, H. (Det) 46
- Solters, M. (StL,Bos) 45

Triples
- Vosmik, J. (Cle) 20
- Stone, J. (Was) 18
- Greenberg, H. (Det) 16

Home Runs
- Foxx, J. (Phi) 36
- Greenberg, H. (Det) 36
- Gehrig, L. (NY) 30

Total Bases
- Greenberg, H. (Det) 389
- Foxx, J. (Phi) 340
- Vosmik, J. (Cle) 333

Runs Batted In
- Greenberg, H. (Det) 170
- Gehrig, L. (NY) 119
- Foxx, J. (Phi) 115

Bases On Balls
- Gehrig, L. (NY) 132
- Appling, L. (Chi) 122
- Foxx, J. (Phi) 114

Stolen Bases
- Werber, B. (Bos) 29
- Lary, L. (StL,Was) 28
- Almada, M. (Bos) 20

Batting Average
- Myer, B. (Was) .349
- Vosmik, J. (Cle) .348
- Foxx, J. (Phi) .346

On-Base Percentage
- Gehrig, L. (NY) .466
- Foxx, J. (Phi) .461
- Cochrane, M. (Det) .452

Slugging Average
- Foxx, J. (Phi) .636
- Greenberg, H. (Det) .628
- Gehrig, L. (NY) .583

Adjusted OPS
- Foxx, J. (Phi) 182
- Gehrig, L. (NY) 180
- Greenberg, H. (Det) 171

Adjusted Batting Runs
- Gehrig, L. (NY) 70.0
- Foxx, J. (Phi) 70.0
- Greenberg, H. (Det) 63.0

Runs Created/Game
- Foxx, J. (Phi) 12.20
- Gehrig, L. (NY) 11.10
- Greenberg, H. (Det) 10.10

Fielding Runs
- Travis, C. (Was) 18.5
- Appling, L. (Chi) 17.4
- Rogell, B. (Det) 16.4

Win Shares – Batters
- Gehrig, L. (NY) 34
- Greenberg, H. (Det) 34
- Myer, B. (Was) 33

TPW – Batters
- Foxx, J. (Phi) 6.3
- Gehrig, L. (NY) 6.1
- Gehringer, C. (Det) 5.3

TEAM	CG	SH	SV	IP	H	H/G	ER	HR	BB	SO	OAV	RAT	ERA	ERA+	CERA	PR+	PF	FA	E	DP	FR	BW	PW	FW	TPW	DIF
DET	**87**	**16**	11	1364	1440	9.5	579	78	522	584	.271	1.438	3.82	109	4.02	40.9	94	**.979**	**128**	154	12.3	**12.0**	3.8	1.2	**17.0**	1.0
NY	76	12	13	1331	**1276**	**8.6**	**532**	91	516	**594**	**.251**	**1.346**	**3.60**	113	**3.51**	44.1	91	.973	151	114	**21.9**	8.4	4.1	**2.1**	14.6	.4
CLE	67	12	**21**	**1396**	1527	9.8	644	68	**457**	498	.278	1.421	4.15	108	3.90	73.2	101	.972	177	147	-18.9	-1.7	6.9	-1.8	3.4	2.6
BOS	82	6	11	1376	1520	9.9	619	**67**	520	470	.280	1.483	4.05	117	4.21	**103.0**	106	.968	194	136	3.3	-5.5	**9.6**	.3	4.4	-2.4
CHI	80	8	8	1360^{2}	1443	9.5	662	105	574	436	.272	1.482	4.38	105	4.31	23.4	104	.976	146	133	12.7	-5.2	2.2	1.2	-1.8	-.2
WAS	67	5	12	1378^{2}	1672	10.9	804	89	613	456	.302	1.657	5.25	**82**	5.20	-137.0	97	.972	171	**186**	-4.6	.9	-12.8	-.4	-12.4	3.4
STL	42	4	15	1380^{1}	1667	10.9	807	92	641	435	.297	1.672	5.26	91	5.19	-64.1	108	.970	187	138	-7.6	-7.3	-6.0	-.7	-14.0	3.0
PHI	58	7	10	1326^{1}	1486	10.1	754	73	704	469	.285	1.651	5.12	89	4.89	-65.0	102	.968	190	150	-19.4	-1.8	-6.1	-1.8	-9.7	-6.3
Total	**559**	**70**	**101**	**10913**		**9.9**	**5401**					**1.519**	**4.45**													

Wins
- Ferrell, W. (Bos) 25
- Harder, M. (Cle) 22
- Bridges, T. (Det) 21

Win Percentage
- Auker, E. (Det) .720
- Allen, J. (NY) .684
- Broaca, J. (NY) .682

Games
- Van Atta, R. (StL,NY) 58
- Walkup, J. (StL) 55
- Andrews, I. (StL) 50

Complete Games
- Ferrell, W. (Bos) 31
- Bridges, T. (Det) 23
- Grove, L. (Bos) 23

Shutouts
- Rowe, S. (Det) 6
- Bridges, T. (Det) 4
- Harder, M. (Cle) 4

Saves
- Knott, J. (StL) 7
- 5 players tied with 5

Innings Pitched
- Ferrell, W. (Bos) 322^{1}
- Harder, M. (Cle) 287^{1}
- Whitehill, E. (Was) 279^{1}

Fewest Hits/Game
- Allen, J. (NY) 8.03
- Ruffing, R. (NY) 8.15
- Gomez, L. (NY) 8.16

Fewest BB/Game
- Harder, M. (Cle) 1.66
- Grove, L. (Bos) 2.14
- Rowe, S. (Det) 2.22

Strikeouts
- Bridges, T. (Det) 163
- Rowe, S. (Det) 140
- Gomez, L. (NY) 138

Ratio
- Grove, L. (Bos) 1.22
- Rowe, S. (Det) 1.23
- Allen, J. (NY) 1.24

Earned Run Average
- Grove, L. (Bos) 2.70
- Lyons, T. (Chi) 3.02
- Ruffing, R. (NY) 3.12

Adjusted ERA
- Grove, L. (Bos) 175
- Lyons, T. (Chi) 153
- Harder, M. (Cle) 137

Component ERA
- Grove, L. (Bos) 2.83
- Rowe, S. (Det) 2.99
- Allen, J. (NY) 3.10

Opponents' Batting Avg.
- Allen, J. (NY) .238
- Ruffing, R. (NY) .239
- Gomez, L. (NY) .242

Adjusted Pitching Runs
- Grove, L. (Bos) 61
- Ferrell, W. (Bos) 43
- Harder, M. (Cle) 43

Win Shares – Pitchers
- Ferrell, W. (Bos) 35
- Grove, L. (Bos) 29
- Harder, M. (Cle) 27

TPW – Pitchers
- Ferrell, W. (Bos) 6.0
- Grove, L. (Bos) 5.3
- Harder, M. (Cle) 3.9

1936 National League

TEAM	G	W	L	PCT	GB	R	OR	EW	AB	H	2B	3B	HR	TB	BB	SO	SB	CS	AVG	OBP	SLG	OPS	OPS+	BR/A	PF	RC
NY	154	92	62	.597	....	742	621	91	5449	1529	237	48	97	2153	431	**452**	31	....	.281	.337	.395	.732	104	27	99	744
CHI	154	87	67	.565	5	755	**603**	94	5409	1545	275	36	76	2120	491	462	68	....	.286	.349	.392	.741	103	29	102	757
STL	155	87	67	.565	5	795	794	77	5537	1554	**332**	60	88	**2270**	442	577	**69**	....	.281	.336	**.410**	.745	**107**	**43**	100	772
PIT	156	84	70	.545	8	**804**	718	86	**5586**	**1596**	283	**80**	60	2219	**517**	502	37	....	**.286**	**.349**	.397	**.746**	104	40	102	**798**
CIN	154	74	80	.481	18	722	760	73	5393	1476	224	73	82	2092	410	584	68	....	.274	.329	.388	.717	105	33	94	699
BOS	157	71	83	.461	21	631	715	67	5478	1450	207	45	67	1948	433	582	23	....	.265	.322	.356	.678	94	-41	94	635
BRO	156	67	87	.435	25	662	752	67	5574	1518	263	43	33	1966	390	458	55	....	.272	.323	.353	.675	87	-100	101	649
PHI	154	54	100	.351	38	726	874	63	5465	1538	250	46	**103**	2189	451	586	50	....	.281	.339	.401	.739	95	-36	110	757
Total	**620**					**5837**			**43891**	**12206**	**2071**	**431**	**606**		**3565**	**4203**	**401**		**.278**	**.335**	**.386**	**.722**				

Runs
- Vaughan, A. (Pit) 122
- Martin, P. (StL) 121
- Ott, M. (NY) 120

Hits
- Medwick, J. (StL) 223
- Waner, P. (Pit) 218
- Demaree, F. (Chi) 212

Doubles
- Medwick, J. (StL) 64
- Herman, B. (Chi) 57
- Waner, P. (Pit) 53

Triples
- Goodman, I. (Cin) 14
- Camilli, D. (Phi) 13
- Medwick, J. (StL) 13

Home Runs
- Ott, M. (NY) 33
- Camilli, D. (Phi) 28
- 2 players tied with 25

Total Bases
- Medwick, J. (StL) 367
- Ott, M. (NY) 314
- Klein, C. (Phi,Chi) 308

Runs Batted In
- Medwick, J. (StL) 138
- Ott, M. (NY) 135
- Suhr, G. (Pit) 118

Bases On Balls
- Vaughan, A. (Pit) 118
- Camilli, D. (Phi) 116
- Ott, M. (NY) 111

Stolen Bases
- Martin, P. (StL) 23
- 3 players tied with 17

Batting Average
- Waner, P. (Pit) .373
- Medwick, J. (StL) .351
- Demaree, F. (Chi) .350

On-Base Percentage
- Vaughan, A. (Pit) .453
- Ott, M. (NY) .448
- Waner, P. (Pit) .446

Slugging Average
- Ott, M. (NY) .588
- Camilli, D. (Phi) .577
- Medwick, J. (StL) .577

Adjusted OPS
- Ott, M. (NY) 179
- Medwick, J. (StL) 157
- Camilli, D. (Phi) 156

Adjusted Batting Runs
- Ott, M. (NY) 65.0
- Waner, P. (Pit) 49.0
- Camilli, D. (Phi) 48.0

Runs Created/Game
- Ott, M. (NY) 11.00
- Camilli, D. (Phi) 10.80
- Waner, P. (Pit) 9.80

Fielding Runs
- Bartell, D. (NY) 22.8
- Herman, B. (Chi) 21.5
- Moore, G. (Bos) 18.0

Win Shares – Batters
- Ott, M. (NY) 36
- Medwick, J. (StL) 36
- Vaughan, A. (Pit) 35

TPW – Batters
- Vaughan, A. (Pit) 6.4
- Ott, M. (NY) 6.0
- Herman, B. (Chi) 5.6

TEAM	CG	SH	SV	IP	H	H/G	ER	HR	BB	SO	OAV	RAT	ERA	ERA+	CERA	PR+	PF	FA	E	DP	FR	BW	PW	FW	TPW	DIF
NY	60	12	22	1385^{2}	1458	9.5	**532**	75	401	500	.273	1.342	**3.46**	113	3.69	20.9	97	.974	168	164	**46.2**	2.7	2.0	**4.5**	9.2	5.8
STL	65	5	**24**	1398	1610	10.4	694	89	434	559	.289	1.462	4.47	**88**	4.36	-83.1	98	.974	156	134	0.3	**4.2**	-8.1	.0	-3.9	13.9
CHI	**77**	**18**	10	1382^{1}	**1413**	**9.2**	544	77	434	597	**.265**	1.336	3.54	112	3.58	39.8	99	**.976**	**146**	156	28.3	2.9	3.9	2.8	**9.5**	.5
PIT	67	5	12	1395^{1}	1475	9.5	603	74	**379**	559	.269	**1.329**	3.89	104	**3.53**	35.8	101	.967	199	113	-10.4	3.9	3.5	-1.0	6.3	.7
CIN	50	6	23	1367^{1}	1576	10.4	641	**51**	418	459	.287	1.458	4.22	91	4.08	-52.1	95	.969	191	150	-8.5	3.2	-5.1	-.8	-2.7	-.3
BOS	61	7	13	**1413^{1}**	1566	10.0	619	69	451	421	.281	1.427	3.94	97	4.03	-29.6	95	.971	189	**175**	12.6	-4.0	-2.9	1.2	-5.7	-.3
BRO	59	7	18	1403	1466	9.4	620	84	528	**651**	.266	1.421	3.98	104	3.90	**41.0**	103	.966	208	107	-18.3	-9.8	**4.0**	-1.8	-7.6	-2.4
PHI	51	7	14	1365^{1}	1630	10.7	704	87	515	454	.292	1.571	4.64	98	4.78	28.4	113	.959	252	144	-45.4	-3.5	2.8	-4.4	-5.2	-17.8
Total	**490**	**67**	**136**	**11110^{1}**		**9.9**	**4957**					**1.418**	**4.02**													

Wins
- Hubbell, C. (NY) 26
- Dean, D. (StL) 24
- Derringer, P. (Cin) 19

Win Percentage
- Hubbell, C. (NY) .812
- Lucas, R. (Pit) .789
- French, L. (Chi) .667

Games
- Dean, D. (StL) 51
- Derringer, P. (Cin) 51
- Passeau, C. (Phi) 49

Complete Games
- Dean, D. (StL) 28
- Hubbell, C. (NY) 25
- Mungo, V. (Bro) 22

Shutouts
- 7 players tied with 4

Saves
- Dean, D. (StL) 11
- Brennan, D. (Cin) 9
- Smith, B. (Bos) 8

Innings Pitched
- Dean, D. (StL) 315
- Mungo, V. (Bro) 311^{2}
- Hubbell, C. (NY) 304

Fewest Hits/Game
- Hubbell, C. (NY) 7.85
- Mungo, V. (Bro) 7.94
- Lee, B. (Chi) 8.28

Fewest BB/Game
- Lucas, R. (Pit) 1.33
- Derringer, P. (Cin) 1.34
- Dean, D. (StL) 1.51

Strikeouts
- Mungo, V. (Bro) 238
- Dean, D. (StL) 195
- Blanton, C. (Pit) 127

Ratio
- Hubbell, C. (NY) 1.06
- Dean, D. (StL) 1.15
- Lucas, R. (Pit) 1.16

Earned Run Average
- Hubbell, C. (NY) 2.31
- MacFayden, D. (Bos) 2.87
- Gabler, F. (NY) 3.12

Adjusted ERA
- Hubbell, C. (NY) 169
- MacFayden, D. (Bos) 134
- Passeau, C. (Phi) 130

Component ERA
- Hubbell, C. (NY) 2.20
- Lucas, R. (Pit) 2.78
- Mungo, V. (Bro) 2.79

Opponents' Batting Avg.
- Mungo, V. (Bro) .234
- Hubbell, C. (NY) .236
- Lee, B. (Chi) .246

Adjusted Pitching Runs
- Hubbell, C. (NY) 43
- Passeau, C. (Phi) 33
- Mungo, V. (Bro) 31

Win Shares – Pitchers
- Hubbell, C. (NY) 37
- Dean, D. (StL) 31
- Mungo, V. (Bro) 24

TPW – Pitchers
- Hubbell, C. (NY) 4.2
- Passeau, C. (Phi) 3.6
- Dean, D. (StL) 2.7

1936 American League

TEAM	G	W	L	PCT	GB	R	OR	EW	AB	H	2B	3B	HR	TB	BB	SO	SB	CS	AVG	OBP	SLG	OPS	OPS+	BR/A	PF	RC
NY	155	102	51	.667	....	**1065**	**731**	104	5591	1676	315	83	**182**	**2703**	**700**	594	77	40	.300	**.381**	**.483**	**.864**	**124**	**203**	97	**1056**
DET	154	83	71	.539	19.5	921	871	81	5464	1638	326	55	94	2356	640	462	73	49	.300	.377	.431	.808	106	51	100	912
CHI	153	81	70	.536	20	920	873	79	5466	1597	282	56	60	2171	684	417	66	29	.292	.374	.397	.771	94	-33	104	851
WAS	153	82	71	.536	20	889	799	85	5433	1601	293	**84**	62	2248	576	**398**	**104**	42	.295	.365	.414	.779	105	49	94	847
CLE	157	80	74	.519	22.5	921	862	82	**5646**	**1715**	**357**	82	123	2605	514	470	66	53	**.304**	.364	.461	.825	109	54	101	948
BOS	155	74	80	.481	28.5	775	764	78	5383	1485	288	62	86	2155	584	465	55	44	.276	.349	.400	.750	86	-122	106	773
STL	155	57	95	.375	44.5	804	1064	55	5391	1502	299	66	79	2170	625	627	62	**20**	.279	.356	.403	.758	91	-66	103	804
PHI	154	53	100	.346	49	714	1045	49	5373	1443	240	60	72	2019	524	590	59	43	.269	.336	.376	.711	83	-142	98	694
Total	**618**					**7009**			**43747**	**12657**	**2400**	**548**	**758**		**4847**	**4023**	**562**	**320**	**.289**	**.363**	**.421**	**.784**				

Runs
Gehrig, L. (NY) 167
Clift, H. (StL) 145
Gehringer, C. (Det) 144

Hits
Averill, E. (Cle) 232
Gehringer, C. (Det) 227
Trosky, H. (Cle) 216

Doubles
Gehringer, C. (Det) 60
Walker, G. (Det) 55
2 players tied with 50

Triples
Averill, E. (Cle) 15
DiMaggio, J. (NY) 15
Rolfe, R. (NY) 15

Home Runs
Gehrig, L. (NY) 49
Trosky, H. (Cle) 42
Foxx, J. (Bos) 41

Total Bases
Trosky, H. (Cle) 405
Gehrig, L. (NY) 403
Averill, E. (Cle) 385

Runs Batted In
Trosky, H. (Cle) 162
Gehrig, L. (NY) 152
Foxx, J. (Bos) 143

Bases On Balls
Gehrig, L. (NY) 130
Lary, L. (StL) 117
Clift, H. (StL) 115

Stolen Bases
Lary, L. (StL) 37
Powell, J. (NY,Was) 26
Werber, B. (Bos) 23

Batting Average
Appling, L. (Chi) .388
Averill, E. (Cle) .378
Gehringer, C. (Det) .354

On-Base Percentage
Gehrig, L. (NY) .478
Appling, L. (Chi) .474
Foxx, J. (Bos) .440

Slugging Average
Gehrig, L. (NY) .696
Trosky, H. (Cle) .644
Foxx, J. (Bos) .631

Adjusted OPS
Gehrig, L. (NY) 193
Averill, E. (Cle) 159
Foxx, J. (Bos) 153

Adjusted Batting Runs
Gehrig, L. (NY) 89.0
Averill, E. (Cle) 55.0
Foxx, J. (Bos) 51.0

Runs Created/Game
Gehrig, L. (NY) 13.90
Averill, E. (Cle) 11.50
Foxx, J. (Bos) 11.30

Fielding Runs
Gehringer, C. (Det) 13.8
George, G. (Cle) 12.1
Warstler, R. (Phi) 12.0

Win Shares – Batters
Gehrig, L. (NY) 38
Gehringer, C. (Det) 34
Appling, L. (Chi) 29

TPW – Batters
Gehrig, L. (NY) 6.9
Gehringer, C. (Det) 5.9
Appling, L. (Chi) 4.3

TEAM	CG	SH	SV	IP	H	H/G	ER	HR	BB	SO	OAV	RAT	ERA	ERA+	CERA	PR+	PF	FA	E	DP	FR	BW	PW	FW	TPW	DIF
NY	77	6	**21**	**1400^1**	**1474**	**9.5**	**649**	84	663	**624**	**.271**	1.526	**4.17**	112	4.30	66.6	92	.973	163	148	8.7	**17.9**	5.9	.8	**24.6**	1.4
DET	76	**13**	13	1360	1568	10.4	756	100	562	526	.289	1.566	5.00	99	4.78	4.9	98	**.974**	**153**	159	-11.8	4.5	.4	-1.0	3.9	2.1
CHI	**80**	5	8	1365	1603	10.6	767	104	578	414	.293	1.598	5.06	103	4.97	4.4	103	.973	168	**174**	16.0	-2.9	.4	1.4	-1.1	7.1
WAS	78	8	14	1345^2	1484	9.9	684	**73**	588	462	.279	1.540	4.57	104	4.43	11.5	95	.970	182	163	**17.5**	4.4	1.0	**1.5**	6.9	-.9
CLE	74	6	12	1389^1	1604	10.4	745	**73**	607	619	.289	1.591	4.83	104	4.73	42.7	100	.970	178	154	-10.9	4.8	3.8	-1.0	7.6	-4.6
BOS	78	11	9	1372^1	1501	9.8	669	78	**552**	584	.277	**1.496**	4.39	121	**4.24**	**137.0**	106	.973	165	139	4.5	-10.7	**12.1**	.4	1.8	-4.8
STL	54	3	13	1348^1	1776	11.8	935	115	609	399	.314	1.769	6.24	86	6.01	-103.7	107	.969	188	143	-25.9	-5.8	-9.2	-2.3	-17.3	-1.7
PHI	68	3	12	1352^1	1645	11.0	913	131	696	405	.300	1.731	6.08	**84**	5.72	-147.7	101	.965	209	152	1.2	-12.5	-13.0	.1	-25.4	2.4
Total	**585**	**55**	**102**	**10933^1**		**10.4**	**6118**					**1.602**	**5.04**													

Wins
Bridges, T. (Det) 23
Kennedy, V. (Chi) 21
3 players tied with 20

Win Percentage
Hadley, B. (NY) .778
Pearson, M. (NY) .731
Kennedy, V. (Chi) .700

Games
Van Atta, R. (StL) 52
Knott, J. (StL) 47
4 players tied with 43

Complete Games
Ferrell, W. (Bos) 28
Bridges, T. (Det) 26
Ruffing, R. (NY) 25

Shutouts
Grove, L. (Bos) 6
Bridges, T. (Det) 5
3 players tied with 4

Saves
Malone, P. (NY) 9
Knott, J. (StL) 6
2 players tied with 5

Innings Pitched
Ferrell, W. (Bos) 301
Bridges, T. (Det) 294^2
Newsom, B. (Was) 285^2

Fewest Hits/Game
Pearson, M. (NY) 7.71
Grove, L. (Bos) 8.42
Allen, J. (Cle) 8.67

Fewest BB/Game
Lyons, T. (Chi) 2.23
Grove, L. (Bos) 2.31
Rowe, S. (Det) 2.35

Strikeouts
Bridges, T. (Det) 175
Allen, J. (Cle) 165
Newsom, B. (Was) 156

Ratio
Grove, L. (Bos) 1.19
Ruffing, R. (NY) 1.34
Rowe, S. (Det) 1.35

Earned Run Average
Grove, L. (Bos) 2.81
Allen, J. (Cle) 3.44
Appleton, P. (Was) 3.53

Adjusted ERA
Grove, L. (Bos) 189
Allen, J. (Cle) 146
Bridges, T. (Det) 137

Component ERA
Grove, L. (Bos) 2.88
Allen, J. (Cle) 3.26
Appleton, P. (Was) 3.42

Opponents' Batting Avg.
Pearson, M. (NY) .233
Grove, L. (Bos) .246
Gomez, L. (NY) .254

Adjusted Pitching Runs
Grove, L. (Bos) 70
Bridges, T. (Det) 47
Allen, J. (Cle) 45

Win Shares – Pitchers
Grove, L. (Bos) 29
Ferrell, W. (Bos) 27
Bridges, T. (Det) 26

TPW – Pitchers
Grove, L. (Bos) 6.0
Ferrell, W. (Bos) 4.3
Bridges, T. (Det) 4.1

1937 National League

TEAM	G	W	L	PCT	GB	R	OR	EW	AB	H	2B	3B	HR	TB	BB	SO	SB	CS	AVG	OBP	SLG	OPS	OPS+	BR/A	PF	RC
NY	152	95	57	.625	....	732	602	91	5329	1484	251	41	**111**	2150	412	492	45	....	.278	.334	.403	.737	105	30	101	734
CHI	154	93	61	.604	3	**811**	682	90	5349	1537	253	74	96	**2226**	**538**	496	71	....	**.287**	**.355**	**.416**	**.771**	**111**	**87**	104	**816**
PIT	154	86	68	.558	10	704	647	83	5433	**1550**	223	**86**	47	2086	463	**480**	32	....	.285	.343	.384	.727	104	30	100	734
STL	157	81	73	.526	15	789	733	83	**5476**	1543	**264**	67	94	2223	385	569	**78**	....	.282	.331	.406	.737	104	19	102	744
BOS	152	79	73	.520	16	579	**556**	79	5124	1265	200	41	63	1736	485	707	45	....	.247	.314	.339	.653	92	-51	91	565
BRO	155	62	91	.405	33.5	616	772	60	5295	1401	258	53	37	1876	469	583	69	....	.265	.327	.354	.681	90	-67	102	629
PHI	155	61	92	.399	34.5	724	869	63	5424	1482	258	37	103	2123	478	640	66	....	.273	.334	.391	.725	95	-33	108	730
CIN	155	56	98	.364	40	612	706	66	5230	1329	215	59	73	1881	437	586	53	....	.254	.315	.360	.674	94	-46	95	599
Total	**617**					**5567**			**42660**	**11591**	**1922**	**458**	**624**		**3667**	**4553**	**459**		**.272**	**.332**	**.382**	**.714**				

Runs
Medwick, J. (StL) 111
Hack, S. (Chi) 106
Herman, B. (Chi) 106

Hits
Medwick, J. (StL) 237
Waner, P. (Pit) 219
Mize, J. (StL) 204

Doubles
Medwick, J. (StL) 56
Mize, J. (StL) 40
Bartell, D. (NY) 38

Triples
Vaughan, A. (Pit) 17
Suhr, G. (Pit) 14
2 players tied with 12

Home Runs
Medwick, J. (StL) 31
Ott, M. (NY) 31
Camilli, D. (Phi) 27

Total Bases
Medwick, J. (StL) 406
Mize, J. (StL) 333
Demaree, F. (Chi) 298

Runs Batted In
Medwick, J. (StL) 154
Demaree, F. (Chi) 115
Mize, J. (StL) 113

Bases On Balls
Ott, M. (NY) 102
Camilli, D. (Phi) 90
2 players tied with 83

Stolen Bases
Galan, A. (Chi) 23
Hack, S. (Chi) 16
4 players tied with 13

Batting Average
Medwick, J. (StL) .374
Mize, J. (StL) .364
Waner, P. (Pit) .354

On-Base Percentage
Camilli, D. (Phi) .446
Mize, J. (StL) .427
Medwick, J. (StL) .414

Slugging Average
Medwick, J. (StL) .641
Mize, J. (StL) .595
Camilli, D. (Phi) .587

Adjusted OPS
Medwick, J. (StL) 179
Mize, J. (StL) 171
Camilli, D. (Phi) 165

Adjusted Batting Runs
Medwick, J. (StL) 66.0
Mize, J. (StL) 55.0
Camilli, D. (Phi) 47.0

Runs Created/Game
Camilli, D. (Phi) 11.50
Medwick, J. (StL) 11.30
Mize, J. (StL) 11.20

Fielding Runs
Herman, B. (Chi) 24.1
Bartell, D. (NY) 23.3
Moore, G. (Bos) 13.9

Win Shares – Batters
Medwick, J. (StL) 40
Mize, J. (StL) 34
Ott, M. (NY) 32

TPW – Batters
Herman, B. (Chi) 5.8
Medwick, J. (StL) 5.2
Bartell, D. (NY) 4.9

TEAM	CG	SH	SV	IP	H	H/G	ER	HR	BB	SO	OAV	RAT	ERA	ERA+	CERA	PR+	PF	FA	E	DP	FR	BW	PW	FW	TPW	DIF
NY	67	11	17	1361	**1341**	**8.9**	519	86	404	**653**	**.258**	1.282	3.43	113	3.36	**42.0**	99	.974	159	143	27.5	3.0	**4.2**	2.7	**9.9**	9.1
CHI	73	11	13	1381^1	1434	9.3	609	91	502	596	.267	1.402	3.97	100	3.89	-5.0	102	**.975**	**151**	141	5.4	**8.6**	-.5	.5	8.7	7.3
PIT	67	12	17	1366^1	1398	9.2	540	71	428	643	.264	1.336	3.56	109	3.52	37.7	99	.970	181	135	7.4	3.0	3.7	.7	7.4	1.6
STL	81	10	4	**1392**	1546	10.0	616	95	448	571	.281	1.432	3.98	100	4.12	12.2	102	.973	164	127	-8.9	1.9	1.2	-.9	2.2	1.8
BOS	**85**	**16**	10	1359^1	1344	8.9	**486**	60	**372**	387	.259	**1.262**	**3.22**	111	**3.15**	24.3	92	.975	157	128	**31.1**	-5.0	2.4	**3.1**	.5	2.5
BRO	63	5	8	1362^2	1470	9.7	625	68	476	592	.274	1.428	4.13	98	3.94	18.6	103	.964	217	127	-32.7	-6.6	1.8	-3.2	-8.0	-6.0
PHI	59	6	15	1373^2	1629	10.7	770	115	501	529	.297	1.551	5.04	**86**	4.92	-86.0	111	.970	184	**157**	-23.5	-3.3	-8.5	-2.3	-14.1	-.9
CIN	64	10	**18**	1358^1	1428	9.5	595	**38**	533	581	.270	1.444	3.94	95	3.79	-26.1	95	.966	208	139	-5.1	-4.5	-2.6	-.5	-7.6	-13.4
Total	**559**	**81**	**102**	**10954^2**		**9.5**	**4760**					**1.392**	**3.91**													

Wins
Hubbell, C. (NY) ... 22
3 players tied with ... 20

Win Percentage
Hubbell, C. (NY) ... .733
Root, C. (Chi) ... .722
Melton, C. (NY) ... .690

Games
Mulcahy, H. (Phi) ... 56
Jorgens, O. (Phi) ... 52
4 players tied with ... 50

Complete Games
Turner, J. (Bos) ... 24
Fette, L. (Bos) ... 23
Weiland, B. (StL) ... 21

Shutouts
Fette, L. (Bos) ... 5
Grissom, L. (Cin) ... 5
Turner, J. (Bos) ... 5

Saves
Brown, M. (Pit) ... 7
Melton, C. (NY) ... 7
Grissom, L. (Cin) ... 6

Innings Pitched
Passeau, C. (Phi) ... 292[1]
Lee, B. (Chi) ... 272[1]
Weiland, B. (StL) ... 264[1]

Fewest Hits/Game
Mungo, V. (Bro) ... 7.60
Grissom, L. (Cin) ... 7.77
Melton, C. (NY) ... 7.84

Fewest BB/Game
Dean, D. (StL) ... 1.51
Root, C. (Chi) ... 1.61
Hoyt, W. (Bro,Pit) ... 1.66

Strikeouts
Hubbell, C. (NY) ... 159
Grissom, L. (Cin) ... 149
Blanton, C. (Pit) ... 143

Ratio
Turner, J. (Bos) ... 1.09
Melton, C. (NY) ... 1.09
Castleman, S. (NY) ... 1.13

Earned Run Average
Turner, J. (Bos) ... 2.38
Melton, C. (NY) ... 2.61
Dean, D. (StL) ... 2.69

Adjusted ERA
Turner, J. (Bos) ... 150
Melton, C. (NY) ... 149
Dean, D. (StL) ... 148

Component ERA
Melton, C. (NY) ... 2.37
Turner, J. (Bos) ... 2.40
Mungo, V. (Bro) ... 2.51

Opponents' Batting Avg.
Mungo, V. (Bro) ... .229
Grissom, L. (Cin) ... .232
Melton, C. (NY) ... .233

Adjusted Pitching Runs
Melton, C. (NY) ... 30
Dean, D. (StL) ... 29
Turner, J. (Bos) ... 28

Win Shares – Pitchers
Turner, J. (Bos) ... 27
Melton, C. (NY) ... 25
2 players tied with ... 23

TPW – Pitchers
Turner, J. (Bos) ... 3.2
Dean, D. (StL) ... 3.1
Mungo, V. (Bro) ... 2.6

1937 American League

TEAM	G	W	L	PCT	GB	R	OR	EW	AB	H	2B	3B	HR	TB	BB	SO	SB	CS	AVG	OBP	SLG	OPS	OPS+	BR/A	PF	RC
NY	157	102	52	.662	....	**979**	**671**	105	5487	1554	282	73	**174**	**2504**	**709**	607	60	36	.283	.369	**.456**	**.825**	**113**	**109**	101	**952**
DET	155	89	65	.578	13	935	841	85	5516	**1611**	309	62	150	2494	656	711	89	45	**.292**	**.370**	.452	.822	111	90	102	947
CHI	154	86	68	.558	16	780	730	82	5277	1478	280	76	67	2111	549	**447**	70	34	.280	.350	.400	.750	95	-34	100	763
CLE	156	83	71	.539	19	817	768	82	5353	1499	304	76	103	2264	570	551	78	51	.280	.352	.423	.775	100	-3	101	813
BOS	154	80	72	.526	21	821	775	80	5354	1506	269	64	100	2203	601	557	79	61	.281	.357	.411	.768	96	-36	104	805
WAS	158	73	80	.477	28.5	757	841	68	**5578**	1559	245	**84**	47	2113	591	503	61	35	.279	.351	.379	.730	94	-37	96	767
PHI	154	54	97	.358	46.5	699	854	61	5228	1398	278	60	94	2078	583	557	**95**	48	.267	.341	.397	.739	94	-49	98	732
STL	156	46	108	.299	56	715	1023	51	5510	1573	**327**	44	71	2201	514	510	30	**27**	.285	.348	.399	.747	94	-56	101	780
Total	**622**					**6503**			**43303**	**12178**	**2294**	**539**	**806**		**4773**	**4443**	**562**	**337**	**.281**	**.355**	**.415**	**.770**				

Runs
DiMaggio, J. (NY) ... 151
Rolfe, R. (NY) ... 143
Gehrig, L. (NY) ... 138

Hits
Bell, B. (StL) ... 218
DiMaggio, J. (NY) ... 215
Walker, G. (Det) ... 213

Doubles
Bell, B. (StL) ... 51
Greenberg, H. (Det) ... 49
Moses, W. (Phi) ... 48

Triples
Kreevich, M. (Chi) ... 16
Walker, D. (Chi) ... 16
2 players tied with ... 15

Home Runs
DiMaggio, J. (NY) ... 46
Greenberg, H. (Det) ... 40
Gehrig, L. (NY) ... 37

Total Bases
DiMaggio, J. (NY) ... 418
Greenberg, H. (Det) ... 397
Gehrig, L. (NY) ... 366

Runs Batted In
Greenberg, H. (Det) ... 183
DiMaggio, J. (NY) ... 167
Gehrig, L. (NY) ... 159

Bases On Balls
Gehrig, L. (NY) ... 127
Greenberg, H. (Det) ... 102
Foxx, J. (Bos) ... 99

Stolen Bases
Chapman, B. (Bos,Was) ... 35
Werber, B. (Phi) ... 35
Walker, G. (Det) ... 23

Batting Average
Gehringer, C. (Det) ... .371
Gehrig, L. (NY) ... .351
DiMaggio, J. (NY) ... .346

On-Base Percentage
Gehrig, L. (NY) ... .473
Gehringer, C. (Det) ... .458
Greenberg, H. (Det) ... .436

Slugging Average
DiMaggio, J. (NY) ... .673
Greenberg, H. (Det) ... .668
Gehrig, L. (NY) ... .643

Adjusted OPS
Gehrig, L. (NY) ... 177
Greenberg, H. (Det) ... 170
DiMaggio, J. (NY) ... 168

Adjusted Batting Runs
Gehrig, L. (NY) ... 74.0
Greenberg, H. (Det) ... 65.0
DiMaggio, J. (NY) ... 61.0

Runs Created/Game
Gehrig, L. (NY) ... 12.90
Greenberg, H. (Det) ... 11.80
DiMaggio, J. (NY) ... 11.20

Fielding Runs
Clift, H. (StL) ... 29.6
Hayes, J. (Chi) ... 20.1
Newsome, S. (Phi) ... 14.6

Win Shares – Batters
DiMaggio, J. (NY) ... 39
Gehrig, L. (NY) ... 36
2 players tied with ... 33

TPW – Batters
Clift, H. (StL) ... 6.5
DiMaggio, J. (NY) ... 5.9
Greenberg, H. (Det) ... 5.5

TEAM	CG	SH	SV	IP	H	H/G	ER	HR	BB	SO	OAV	RAT	ERA	ERA+	CERA	PR+	PF	FA	E	DP	FR	BW	PW	FW	TPW	DIF
NY	**82**	**15**	**21**	1396	**1417**	**9.1**	**566**	92	**506**	652	**.261**	**1.378**	**3.65**	122	**3.73**	**102.6**	96	.972	170	134	21.0	**10.0**	**9.4**	1.9	**21.3**	3.7
DET	70	6	11	1378	1521	9.9	746	102	635	485	.279	1.565	4.87	96	4.68	-13.6	101	**.976**	**147**	149	-16.9	8.2	-1.2	-1.5	5.4	6.6
CHI	70	**15**	**21**	1351[1]	1435	9.6	626	115	532	533	.273	1.456	4.17	110	4.30	35.6	100	.971	174	173	**29.5**	-3.1	3.3	**2.7**	2.9	6.1
CLE	64	4	15	1364[2]	1529	10.1	665	**61**	566	630	.285	1.535	4.39	105	4.41	46.7	100	.974	159	153	-14.3	-.2	4.3	-1.3	2.7	3.3
BOS	74	6	14	1366	1518	10.0	680	92	597	**682**	.279	1.548	4.48	106	4.54	67.0	103	.970	177	139	-28.6	-3.3	6.2	-2.6	.2	3.8
WAS	75	5	14	**1398**[2]	1498	9.6	711	96	671	524	.275	1.551	4.58	97	4.54	-42.6	96	.972	170	**181**	19.5	-3.4	-3.9	1.8	-5.5	2.5
PHI	65	6	9	1335	1490	10.0	719	105	613	469	.281	1.575	4.85	97	4.72	-22.2	102	.966	198	150	1.1	-4.5	-2.0	.1	-6.4	-14.6
STL	55	2	8	1363	1768	11.7	909	143	653	468	.316	1.776	6.00	**80**	6.22	-165.3	104	.972	173	166	-12.6	-5.1	-15.2	-1.2	-21.5	-9.5
Total	**555**	**59**	**113**	**10952**[2]		**10.0**	**5622**					**1.547**	**4.62**													

Wins
Gomez, L. (NY) ... 21
Ruffing, R. (NY) ... 20
Lawson, R. (Det) ... 18

Win Percentage
Allen, J. (Cle) ... .938
Stratton, M. (Chi) ... .750
Ruffing, R. (NY) ... .741

Games
Brown, C. (Chi) ... 53
Wilson, J. (Bos) ... 51
2 players tied with ... 41

Complete Games
Ferrell, W. (Was,Bos) ... 26
Gomez, L. (NY) ... 25
Ruffing, R. (NY) ... 22

Shutouts
Gomez, L. (NY) ... 6
Stratton, M. (Chi) ... 5
3 players tied with ... 4

Saves
Brown, C. (Chi) ... 18
Murphy, J. (NY) ... 10
Wilson, J. (Bos) ... 7

Innings Pitched
Ferrell, W. (Was,Bos) ... 281
Gomez, L. (NY) ... 278[1]
Newsom, B. (Bos,Was) ... 275[1]

Fewest Hits/Game
Gomez, L. (NY) ... 7.53
Stratton, M. (Chi) ... 7.76
Smith, E. (Phi) ... 8.15

Fewest BB/Game
Stratton, M. (Chi) ... 2.02
Hudlin, W. (Cle) ... 2.20
Marcum, J. (Bos) ... 2.30

Strikeouts
Gomez, L. (NY) ... 194
Newsom, B. (Bos,Was) ... 166
Grove, L. (Bos) ... 153

Ratio
Stratton, M. (Chi) ... 1.09
Gomez, L. (NY) ... 1.17
Ruffing, R. (NY) ... 1.21

Earned Run Average
Gomez, L. (NY) ... 2.33
Stratton, M. (Chi) ... 2.40
Allen, J. (Cle) ... 2.55

Adjusted ERA
Stratton, M. (Chi) ... 191
Gomez, L. (NY) ... 191
Allen, J. (Cle) ... 181

Component ERA
Stratton, M. (Chi) ... 2.36
Gomez, L. (NY) ... 2.47
Allen, J. (Cle) ... 2.94

Opponents' Batting Avg.
Gomez, L. (NY) ... .223
Stratton, M. (Chi) ... .234
Smith, E. (Phi) ... .242

Adjusted Pitching Runs
Gomez, L. (NY) ... 61
Grove, L. (Bos) ... 56
Allen, J. (Cle) ... 41

Win Shares – Pitchers
Gomez, L. (NY) ... 29
Grove, L. (Bos) ... 27
Ruffing, R. (NY) ... 24

TPW – Pitchers
Gomez, L. (NY) ... 5.5
Grove, L. (Bos) ... 4.9
Ruffing, R. (NY) ... 3.6

1938 National League

TEAM	G	W	L	PCT	GB	R	OR	EW	AB	H	2B	3B	HR	TB	BB	SO	SB	CS	AVG	OBP	SLG	OPS	OPS+	BR/A	PF	RC
CHI	154	89	63	.586	....	713	**597**	89	5333	1435	242	70	65	2012	522	476	49	....	.269	.338	.377	.715	100	8	103	689
PIT	152	86	64	.573	2	707	630	84	5422	1511	265	66	65	2103	485	**409**	47	....	.279	**.340**	.388	.728	106	43	101	727
NY	152	83	67	.553	5	705	637	83	5255	1424	210	36	**125**	2081	465	528	31	....	.271	.334	.396	.730	106	40	101	715
CIN	151	82	68	.547	6	723	634	85	5391	1495	251	57	110	2190	366	518	19	....	.277	.327	.406	.733	**110**	**61**	97	720
BOS	153	77	75	.507	12	561	618	69	5250	1311	199	39	54	1750	424	548	49	....	.250	.309	.333	.642	92	-57	90	549
STL	156	71	80	.470	17.5	**725**	722	76	**5528**	**1542**	**288**	74	91	**2251**	412	492	55	....	**.279**	.331	**.407**	**.738**	103	14	106	**752**
BRO	151	69	80	.463	18.5	704	710	74	5142	1322	225	**79**	61	1888	**611**	615	**66**	....	.257	.338	.367	.705	98	1	102	671
PHI	151	45	105	.300	43	550	840	45	5192	1318	233	29	40	1729	423	507	38	....	.254	.312	.333	.645	83	-114	100	549
Total	**610**					**5388**			**42513**	**11358**	**1913**	**450**	**611**		**3708**	**4093**	**354**		**.267**	**.329**	**.376**	**.705**				

Runs
Ott, M. (NY) ... 116
Hack, S. (Chi) ... 109
Camilli, D. (Bro) ... 106

Hits
McCormick, F. (Cin) ... 209
Hack, S. (Chi) ... 195
Waner, L. (Pit) ... 194

Doubles
Medwick, J. (StL) ... 47
McCormick, F. (Cin) ... 40
2 players tied with ... 36

Triples
Mize, J. (StL) ... 16
Gutteridge, D. (StL) ... 15
Suhr, G. (Pit) ... 14

Home Runs
Ott, M. (NY) ... 36
Goodman, I. (Cin) ... 30
Mize, J. (StL) ... 27

Total Bases
Mize, J. (StL) ... 326
Medwick, J. (StL) ... 316
Ott, M. (NY) ... 307

Runs Batted In
Medwick, J. (StL) ... 122
Ott, M. (NY) ... 116
Rizzo, J. (Pit) ... 111

Bases On Balls
Camilli, D. (Bro) ... 119
Ott, M. (NY) ... 118
Vaughan, A. (Pit) ... 104

Stolen Bases
Hack, S. (Chi) ... 16
Koy, E. (Bro) ... 15
Lavagetto, C. (Bro) ... 15

Batting Average
Lombardi, E. (Cin) ... .342
Mize, J. (StL) ... .337
McCormick, F. (Cin) ... .327

On-Base Percentage
Ott, M. (NY) ... .442
Vaughan, A. (Pit) ... .433
Mize, J. (StL) ... .422

Slugging Average
Mize, J. (StL) ... .614
Ott, M. (NY) ... .583
Medwick, J. (StL) ... .536

Adjusted OPS
Ott, M. (NY) ... 178
Mize, J. (StL) ... 172
Lombardi, E. (Cin) ... 154

Adjusted Batting Runs
Ott, M. (NY) ... 62.0
Mize, J. (StL) ... 53.0
Vaughan, A. (Pit) ... 37.0

Runs Created/Game
Ott, M. (NY) ... 10.80
Mize, J. (StL) ... 10.40
Vaughan, A. (Pit) ... 8.20

Fielding Runs
Herman, B. (Chi) ... 21.7
Young, P. (Pit) ... 21.6
Fletcher, E. (Bos) ... 17.0

Win Shares – Batters
Ott, M. (NY) ... 36
Vaughan, A. (Pit) ... 34
Hack, S. (Chi) ... 33

TPW – Batters
Ott, M. (NY) ... 6.3
Vaughan, A. (Pit) ... 5.7
Lombardi, E. (Cin) ... 4.2

TEAM	CG	SH	SV	IP	H	H/G	ER	HR	BB	SO	OAV	RAT	ERA	ERA+	CERA	PR+	PF	FA	E	DP	FR	BW	PW	FW	TPW	DIF
CHI	67	16	18	1396²	1414	9.1	523	71	454	583	.263	1.337	3.37	113	3.52	60.4	101	.978	135	151	9.4	.8	6.1	.9	7.8	5.2
PIT	57	8	15	1379²	1406	9.2	530	71	432	557	.266	1.332	3.46	110	3.53	27.2	100	.974	163	168	22.9	4.3	2.7	2.3	9.3	1.7
NY	59	8	18	1349	1370	9.1	543	87	389	497	.261	1.304	3.62	104	3.48	19.8	99	.973	168	147	0.9	4.1	2.0	.1	6.2	1.8
CIN	72	11	16	1362	1329	8.8	548	75	463	542	.254	1.316	3.62	101	3.35	-16.3	96	.971	172	133	19.4	6.2	-1.6	2.0	6.5	.5
BOS	83	15	12	1380	1375	9.0	521	66	465	413	.258	1.333	3.40	103	3.45	-3.4	91	.972	173	136	7.1	-5.8	-.3	.7	-5.4	6.4
STL	58	10	16	1384²	1482	9.6	591	77	474	534	.272	1.413	3.84	103	3.89	22.3	104	.967	199	145	-5.7	1.5	2.2	-.6	3.1	-7.1
BRO	56	12	14	1332	1464	9.9	602	88	446	469	.278	1.434	4.07	96	4.16	-13.2	103	.973	157	148	-12.2	.1	-1.3	-1.2	-2.5	-2.5
PHI	68	3	6	1329¹	1516	10.3	728	76	582	492	.285	1.578	4.93	81	4.66	-96.3	106	.966	201	135	-40.9	-11.5	-9.7	-4.1	-25.3	-4.7
Total	520	83	115	10913¹		9.4	4586					1.380	3.78													

	Wins		**Win Percentage**		**Games**		**Complete Games**		**Shutouts**		**Saves**
	Lee, B. (Chi)	22	Lee, B. (Chi)	.710	Brown, M. (Pit)	51	Derringer, P. (Cin)	26	Lee, B. (Chi)	9	Coffman, D. (NY)	12

Wins — Lee, B. (Chi) 22; Derringer, P. (Cin) 21; Bryant, C. (Chi) 19
Win Percentage — Lee, B. (Chi) .710; Klinger, B. (Pit) .706; Tamulis, V. (Bro) .667
Games — Brown, M. (Pit) 51; Coffman, D. (NY) 51; McGee, B. (StL) 47
Complete Games — Derringer, P. (Cin) 26; Turner, J. (Bos) 22; Walters, B. (Cin,Phi) 20
Shutouts — Lee, B. (Chi) 9; MacFayden, D. (Bos) 5; 2 players tied with 4
Saves — Coffman, D. (NY) 12; Root, C. (Chi) 8; 2 players tied with 6

Innings Pitched — Derringer, P. (Cin) 307; Lee, B. (Chi) 291; Bryant, C. (Chi) 270¹
Fewest Hits/Game — Vander Meer, J. (Cin) 7.07; Bauers, R. (Pit) 7.67; Bryant, C. (Chi) 7.82
Fewest BB/Game — Davis, C. (StL) 1.40; Derringer, P. (Cin) 1.44; Hubbell, C. (NY) 1.66
Strikeouts — Bryant, C. (Chi) 135; Derringer, P. (Cin) 132; Vander Meer, J. (Cin) 125
Ratio — Hubbell, C. (NY) 1.14; Derringer, P. (Cin) 1.19; Turner, J. (Bos) 1.20
Earned Run Average — Lee, B. (Chi) 2.66; Root, C. (Chi) 2.86; Derringer, P. (Cin) 2.93

Adjusted ERA — Lee, B. (Chi) 144; Root, C. (Chi) 134; Fitzsimmons, F. (Bro) 129
Component ERA — Vander Meer, J. (Cin) 2.75; Bauers, R. (Pit) 2.86; MacFayden, D. (Bos) 2.88
Opponents' Batting Avg. — Vander Meer, J. (Cin) .213; Bauers, R. (Pit) .233; Bryant, C. (Chi) .235
Adjusted Pitching Runs — Lee, B. (Chi) 36; Fitzsimmons, F. (Bro) 22; Bryant, C. (Chi) 20
Win Shares – Pitchers — Lee, B. (Chi) 28; Derringer, P. (Cin) 25; Bryant, C. (Chi) 23
TPW – Pitchers — Lee, B. (Chi) 3.7; Bryant, C. (Chi) 2.4; Fitzsimmons, F. (Bro) 2.1

1938 American League

TEAM	G	W	L	PCT	GB	R	OR	EW	AB	H	2B	3B	HR	TB	BB	SO	SB	CS	AVG	OBP	SLG	OPS	OPS+	BR/A	PF	RC
NY	157	99	53	.651	....	966	710	99	5410	1480	283	63	174	2411	749	616	91	28	.274	.366	.446	.812	110	95	100	926
BOS	150	88	61	.591	9.5	902	751	88	5229	1566	298	56	98	2270	650	463	55	51	.299	.378	.434	.812	106	42	105	881
CLE	153	86	66	.566	13	847	782	82	5356	1506	300	89	113	2323	550	605	83	36	.281	.350	.434	.784	105	30	98	832
DET	155	84	70	.545	16	862	795	83	5270	1434	219	52	137	2168	693	581	76	41	.272	.359	.411	.770	94	-42	106	812
WAS	152	75	76	.497	23.5	814	873	70	5474	1602	278	72	85	2279	573	379	65	37	.293	.362	.416	.778	109	75	93	845
CHI	149	65	83	.439	32	709	752	70	5199	1439	239	55	67	1989	514	489	56	39	.277	.343	.383	.726	86	-110	102	700
STL	156	55	97	.362	44	755	962	58	5333	1498	273	36	92	2119	590	528	51	40	.281	.355	.397	.752	95	-39	100	774
PHI	154	53	99	.349	46	726	956	56	5229	1410	243	62	98	2071	605	590	65	53	.270	.348	.396	.744	95	-42	97	741
Total	613					6581			42500	11935	2133	485	864		4924	4251	542	325	.281	.358	.415	.773				

Runs — Greenberg, H. (Det) 144; Foxx, J. (Bos) 139; Gehringer, C. (Det) 133
Hits — Vosmik, J. (Bos) 201; Cramer, D. (Bos) 198; 2 players tied with 197
Doubles — Cronin, J. (Bos) 51; McQuinn, G. (StL) 42; 2 players tied with 40
Triples — Heath, J. (Cle) 18; Averill, E. (Cle) 15; DiMaggio, J. (NY) 13
Home Runs — Greenberg, H. (Det) 58; Foxx, J. (Bos) 50; Clift, H. (StL) 34
Total Bases — Foxx, J. (Bos) 398; Greenberg, H. (Det) 380; DiMaggio, J. (NY) 348

Runs Batted In — Foxx, J. (Bos) 175; Greenberg, H. (Det) 146; DiMaggio, J. (NY) 140
Bases On Balls — Greenberg, H. (Det) 119; Foxx, J. (Bos) 119; Clift, H. (StL) 118
Stolen Bases — Crosetti, F. (NY) 27; Lary, L. (Cle) 23; Werber, B. (Phi) 19
Batting Average — Foxx, J. (Bos) .349; Heath, J. (Cle) .343; Chapman, B. (Bos) .340
On-Base Percentage — Foxx, J. (Bos) .462; Myer, B. (Was) .454; Greenberg, H. (Det) .438
Slugging Average — Foxx, J. (Bos) .704; Greenberg, H. (Det) .683; Heath, J. (Cle) .602

Adjusted OPS — Foxx, J. (Bos) 180; Greenberg, H. (Det) 167; Heath, J. (Cle) 146
Adjusted Batting Runs — Foxx, J. (Bos) 72.0; Greenberg, H. (Det) 59.0; Clift, H. (StL) 39.0
Runs Created/Game — Foxx, J. (Bos) 13.40; Greenberg, H. (Det) 11.70; York, R. (Det) 9.40
Fielding Runs — Clift, H. (StL) 17.2; Gordon, J. (NY) 10.6; Sullivan, B. (StL) 10.5
Win Shares – Batters — Foxx, J. (Bos) 34; Greenberg, H. (Det) 34; 2 players tied with 30
TPW – Batters — Clift, H. (StL) 5.6; Foxx, J. (Bos) 5.0; Greenberg, H. (Det) 4.7

TEAM	CG	SH	SV	IP	H	H/G	ER	HR	BB	SO	OAV	RAT	ERA	ERA+	CERA	PR+	PF	FA	E	DP	FR	BW	PW	FW	TPW	DIF
NY	91	11	13	1382	1436	9.4	600	85	566	567	.268	1.449	3.91	116	4.02	84.3	95	.973	169	177	10.9	8.6	7.6	1.0	17.2	5.8
BOS	67	10	15	1316¹	1472	10.1	652	102	528	484	.281	1.519	4.46	111	4.54	54.6	103	.968	190	172	15.1	3.8	4.9	1.4	10.1	3.9
CLE	68	5	17	1353	1416	9.4	692	100	681	717	.268	1.550	4.60	101	4.53	3.1	97	.974	151	145	3.2	2.8	.3	.3	3.3	6.7
DET	75	3	11	1348¹	1532	10.2	717	110	608	435	.287	1.587	4.79	104	4.86	22.8	104	.976	147	172	9.5	-3.8	2.1	.9	-.8	7.8
WAS	59	6	11	1360¹	1472	9.7	746	92	655	515	.276	1.564	4.94	91	4.59	-66.5	94	.970	180	179	2.4	6.8	-6.0	.2	1.0	-1.0
CHI	83	5	9	1316¹	1449	9.9	638	101	550	432	.279	1.519	4.36	112	4.50	80.4	102	.967	196	155	-2.7	-10.0	7.3	-.2	-3.0	-6.0
STL	71	3	7	1344²	1584	10.6	866	132	737	632	.295	1.726	5.80	86	5.68	-122.8	104	.975	145	163	-1.4	-3.5	-11.1	-.1	-14.8	-6.2
PHI	56	4	12	1324	1573	10.7	806	142	599	473	.292	1.640	5.48	101	5.32	-59.6	101	.965	206	119	-35.3	-3.8	-5.4	-3.2	-12.4	-10.6
Total	570	47	95	10745		10.0	5717					1.569	4.79													

Wins — Ruffing, R. (NY) 21; Newsom, B. (StL) 20; Gomez, L. (NY) 18
Win Percentage — Grove, L. (Bos) .778; Ruffing, R. (NY) .750; Chandler, S. (NY) .737
Games — Humphries, J. (Cle) 45; Newsom, B. (StL) 44; 3 players tied with 43
Complete Games — Newsom, B. (StL) 31; Ruffing, R. (NY) 22; 3 players tied with 20
Shutouts — Gomez, L. (NY) 4; 3 players tied with 3
Saves — Murphy, J. (NY) 11; Humphries, J. (Cle) 6; McKain, A. (Bos) 6

Innings Pitched — Newsom, B. (StL) 329²; Caster, G. (Phi) 281¹; Feller, B. (Cle) 277²
Fewest Hits/Game — Feller, B. (Cle) 7.29; Allen, J. (Cle) 8.50; Pearson, M. (NY) 8.82
Fewest BB/Game — Leonard, D. (Was) 2.14; Harder, M. (Cle) 2.32; Lyons, T. (Chi) 2.40
Strikeouts — Feller, B. (Cle) 240; Newsom, B. (StL) 226; Mills, L. (StL) 134
Ratio — Leonard, D. (Was) 1.23; Stratton, M. (Chi) 1.30; Ruffing, R. (NY) 1.33
Earned Run Average — Grove, L. (Bos) 3.08; Ruffing, R. (NY) 3.31; Gomez, L. (NY) 3.35

Adjusted ERA — Grove, L. (Bos) 160; Lee, T. (Chi) 140; Rigney, J. (Chi) 138
Component ERA — Leonard, D. (Was) 3.08; Chandler, S. (NY) 3.47; Grove, L. (Bos) 3.48
Opponents' Batting Avg. — Feller, B. (Cle) .220; Allen, J. (Cle) .246; Hadley, B. (NY) .254
Adjusted Pitching Runs — Lee, T. (Chi) 39; Grove, L. (Bos) 32; Ruffing, R. (NY) 32
Win Shares – Pitchers — Ruffing, R. (NY) 25; Feller, B. (Cle) 22; Newsom, B. (StL) 21
TPW – Pitchers — Lee, T. (Chi) 4.0; Ruffing, R. (NY) 3.7; Grove, L. (Bos) 2.8

1939 National League

TEAM	G	W	L	PCT	GB	R	OR	EW	AB	H	2B	3B	HR	TB	BB	SO	SB	CS	AVG	OBP	SLG	OPS	OPS+	BR/A	PF	RC
CIN	156	97	57	.630	....	767	595	96	5378	1493	269	60	98	2176	500	538	46	....	.278	.343	.405	.748	107	47	101	759
STL	155	92	61	.601	4.5	779	633	92	5447	1601	332	62	98	2351	475	566	44	....	.294	.354	.432	.785	110	75	106	835
BRO	157	84	69	.549	12.5	708	645	84	5350	1420	265	57	78	2033	564	639	59	....	.265	.338	.380	.718	96	-23	104	697
CHI	156	84	70	.545	13	724	678	82	5293	1407	263	62	91	2067	523	553	61	....	.266	.336	.391	.726	100	-1	102	702
NY	151	77	74	.510	18.5	703	685	77	5129	1395	211	38	116	2030	498	499	26	....	.272	.340	.396	.736	103	23	101	683
PIT	153	68	85	.444	28.5	666	721	70	5269	1453	261	60	63	2023	477	420	44	....	.276	.338	.384	.722	102	15	98	687
BOS	152	63	88	.417	32.5	572	659	65	5286	1395	199	39	56	1840	366	494	41	....	.264	.314	.348	.662	90	-74	95	575
PHI	152	45	106	.298	50.5	553	856	44	5133	1341	232	40	49	1800	421	486	47	....	.261	.318	.351	.669	90	-73	96	570
Total	616					5472			42285	11505	2032	418	649		3824	4195	368		.272	.335	.386	.721				

Runs
- Werber, B. (Cin) 115
- Hack, S. (Chi) 112
- Herman, B. (Chi) 111

Hits
- McCormick, F. (Cin) 209
- Medwick, J. (StL) 201
- Mize, J. (StL) 197

Doubles
- Slaughter, E. (StL) 52
- Medwick, J. (StL) 48
- Mize, J. (StL) 44

Triples
- Herman, B. (Chi) 18
- Goodman, I. (Cin) 16
- Mize, J. (StL) 14

Home Runs
- Mize, J. (StL) 28
- Ott, M. (NY) 27
- Camilli, D. (Bro) 26

Total Bases
- Mize, J. (StL) 353
- McCormick, F. (Cin) 312
- Medwick, J. (StL) 307

Runs Batted In
- McCormick, F. (Cin) 128
- Medwick, J. (StL) 117
- Mize, J. (StL) 108

Bases On Balls
- Camilli, D. (Bro) 110
- Ott, M. (NY) 100
- Mize, J. (StL) 92

Stolen Bases
- Hack, S. (Chi) 17
- Handley, L. (Pit) 17
- Werber, B. (Cin) 15

Batting Average
- Mize, J. (StL) .349
- McCormick, F. (Cin) .332
- Medwick, J. (StL) .332

On-Base Percentage
- Ott, M. (NY) .449
- Mize, J. (StL) .444
- Camilli, D. (Bro) .409

Slugging Average
- Mize, J. (StL) .626
- Ott, M. (NY) .581
- Camilli, D. (Bro) .524

Adjusted OPS
- Mize, J. (StL) 174
- Ott, M. (NY) 173
- Camilli, D. (Bro) 144

Adjusted Batting Runs
- Mize, J. (StL) 62.0
- Ott, M. (NY) 46.0
- Camilli, D. (Bro) 39.0

Runs Created/Game
- Mize, J. (StL) 11.40
- Ott, M. (NY) 10.50
- Camilli, D. (Bro) 8.20

Fielding Runs
- Frey, L. (Cin) 17.1
- Camilli, D. (Bro) 14.5
- Brown, J. (StL) 13.8

Win Shares – Batters
- Mize, J. (StL) 33
- Ott, M. (NY) 28
- Camilli, D. (Bro) 28

TPW – Batters
- Frey, L. (Cin) 4.4
- Mize, J. (StL) 4.3
- Camilli, D. (Bro) 3.9

TEAM	CG	SH	SV	IP	H	H/G	ER	HR	BB	SO	OAV	RAT	ERA	ERA+	CERA	PR+	PF	FA	E	DP	FR	BW	PW	FW	TPW	DIF
CIN	**86**	13	9	1403^{2}	**1340**	**8.6**	**510**	81	499	**637**	**.255**	1.310	**3.27**	117	**3.40**	50.9	98	.974	162	170	**36.4**	4.7	5.1	**3.6**	13.5	6.5
STL	45	**18**	**32**	1384^{2}	1377	9.0	552	76	498	603	.260	1.354	3.59	114	3.54	**66.3**	105	.971	177	140	14.0	**7.5**	**6.6**	1.4	**15.6**	.4
BRO	69	9	13	**1410^{1}**	1431	9.1	570	93	**399**	528	.263	**1.298**	3.64	111	3.47	65.3	103	.972	176	157	-5.7	-2.3	6.5	-.6	3.7	4.3
CHI	72	8	13	1392^{1}	1504	9.7	588	74	430	584	.276	1.389	3.80	103	3.81	58.0	100	.970	186	126	-37.5	-.1	5.8	-3.7	1.9	5.1
NY	55	6	20	1319	1412	9.6	596	86	477	505	.275	1.432	4.07	97	4.05	-21.1	100	**.975**	**153**	151	0.4	2.3	-2.1	.0	.3	1.7
PIT	53	10	15	1354	1537	10.2	624	70	423	464	.287	1.448	4.15	93	4.09	-18.7	98	.972	168	153	-28.9	1.5	-1.9	-2.9	-3.2	-4.8
BOS	68	11	15	1358^{1}	1400	9.3	560	**63**	513	430	.271	1.408	3.71	100	3.76	-24.6	94	.971	181	**178**	22.1	-7.4	-2.5	2.2	-7.7	-4.3
PHI	67	3	12	1326^{2}	1502	10.2	762	106	579	447	.289	1.569	5.17	**76**	4.85	-180.1	101	.970	171	136	-0.7	-7.3	-18.0	-.1	-25.4	-4.6
Total	**515**	**78**	**129**	**10949**		**9.5**	**4762**					**1.399**	**3.91**													

Wins
- Walters, B. (Cin) 27
- Derringer, P. (Cin) 25
- Davis, C. (StL) 22

Win Percentage
- Derringer, P. (Cin) .781
- Bowman, B. (StL) .722
- Walters, B. (Cin) .711

Games
- Shoun, C. (StL) 53
- Sewell, R. (Pit) 52
- Bowman, B. (StL) 51

Complete Games
- Walters, B. (Cin) 31
- Derringer, P. (Cin) 28
- Lee, B. (Chi) 20

Shutouts
- Fette, L. (Bos) 6
- Derringer, P. (Cin) 5
- Posedel, B. (Bos) 5

Saves
- Bowman, B. (StL) 9
- Shoun, C. (StL) 9
- 3 players tied with 7

Innings Pitched
- Walters, B. (Cin) 319
- Derringer, P. (Cin) 301
- Lee, B. (Chi) 282^{1}

Fewest Hits/Game
- Walters, B. (Cin) 7.05
- Bowman, B. (StL) 7.49
- Moore, W. (Cin) 8.49

Fewest BB/Game
- Derringer, P. (Cin) 1.05
- Hubbell, C. (NY) 1.40
- Davis, C. (StL) 1.74

Strikeouts
- Passeau, C. (Chi,Phi) 137
- Walters, B. (Cin) 137
- Cooper, M. (StL) 130

Ratio
- Walters, B. (Cin) 1.13
- Hubbell, C. (NY) 1.13
- Hamlin, L. (Bro) 1.15

Earned Run Average
- Walters, B. (Cin) 2.29
- Bowman, B. (StL) 2.60
- Hubbell, C. (NY) 2.75

Adjusted ERA
- Walters, B. (Cin) 168
- Bowman, B. (StL) 158
- Hubbell, C. (NY) 143

Component ERA
- Walters, B. (Cin) 2.41
- Bowman, B. (StL) 2.64
- Hubbell, C. (NY) 2.77

Opponents' Batting Avg.
- Walters, B. (Cin) .220
- Bowman, B. (StL) .232
- Hamlin, L. (Bro) .248

Adjusted Pitching Runs
- Walters, B. (Cin) 46
- Casey, H. (Bro) 29
- Bowman, B. (StL) 27

Win Shares – Pitchers
- Walters, B. (Cin) 38
- Derringer, P. (Cin) 26
- Davis, C. (StL) 22

TPW – Pitchers
- Walters, B. (Cin) 5.9
- Casey, H. (Bro) 2.9
- Passeau, C. (Chi,Phi) 2.4

1939 American League

TEAM	G	W	L	PCT	GB	R	OR	EW	AB	H	2B	3B	HR	TB	BB	SO	SB	CS	AVG	OBP	SLG	OPS	OPS+	BR/A	PF	RC
NY	152	106	45	.702	....	**967**	**556**	113	5300	1521	259	55	**166**	**2388**	**701**	543	72	37	.287	**.374**	**.451**	**.825**	**119**	**154**	98	**923**
BOS	152	89	62	.589	17	890	795	84	5308	**1543**	287	57	124	2316	591	505	42	44	**.291**	.363	.436	.800	106	40	104	831
CLE	154	87	67	.565	20.5	797	700	87	5316	1490	**291**	**79**	85	2194	557	574	72	46	.280	.350	.413	.763	104	31	97	775
CHI	155	85	69	.552	22.5	755	737	79	5279	1451	220	56	64	1975	579	502	**113**	61	.275	.349	.374	.723	89	-80	103	708
DET	155	81	73	.526	26.5	849	762	85	5326	1487	277	67	124	2270	620	592	88	38	.279	.356	.426	.782	98	-10	108	820
WAS	153	65	87	.428	41.5	702	797	66	5334	1483	249	**79**	44	2022	547	**460**	94	47	.278	.346	.379	.725	99	0	93	717
PHI	153	55	97	.362	51.5	711	1022	50	5309	1438	282	55	98	2124	503	532	60	**34**	.271	.336	.400	.736	96	-40	98	713
STL	156	43	111	.279	64.5	733	1035	51	**5422**	1453	242	50	91	2068	559	606	48	38	.268	.339	.381	.720	88	-98	102	706
Total	**615**					**6404**			**42594**	**11866**	**2107**	**498**	**796**		**4657**	**4314**	**589**	**345**	**.279**	**.352**	**.407**	**.759**				

Runs
- Rolfe, R. (NY) 139
- Williams, T. (Bos) 131
- Foxx, J. (Bos) 130

Hits
- Rolfe, R. (NY) 213
- McQuinn, G. (StL) 195
- Keltner, K. (Cle) 191

Doubles
- Rolfe, R. (NY) 46
- Williams, T. (Bos) 44
- Greenberg, H. (Det) 42

Triples
- Lewis, B. (Was) 16
- McCosky, B. (Det) 14
- 2 players tied with 13

Home Runs
- Foxx, J. (Bos) 35
- Greenberg, H. (Det) 33
- Williams, T. (Bos) 31

Total Bases
- Williams, T. (Bos) 344
- Foxx, J. (Bos) 324
- Rolfe, R. (NY) 321

Runs Batted In
- Williams, T. (Bos) 145
- DiMaggio, J. (NY) 126
- Johnson, B. (Phi) 114

Bases On Balls
- Clift, H. (StL) 111
- Williams, T. (Bos) 107
- Appling, L. (Chi) 105

Stolen Bases
- Case, G. (Was) 51
- Fox, P. (Det) 23
- Kreevich, M. (Chi) 23

Batting Average
- DiMaggio, J. (NY) .381
- Foxx, J. (Bos) .360
- Johnson, B. (Phi) .338

On-Base Percentage
- Foxx, J. (Bos) .464
- Selkirk, G. (NY) .452
- DiMaggio, J. (NY) .448

Slugging Average
- Foxx, J. (Bos) .694
- DiMaggio, J. (NY) .671
- Greenberg, H. (Det) .622

Adjusted OPS
- DiMaggio, J. (NY) 185
- Foxx, J. (Bos) 185
- Williams, T. (Bos) 158

Adjusted Batting Runs
- Foxx, J. (Bos) 62.0
- DiMaggio, J. (NY) 59.0
- Williams, T. (Bos) 52.0

Runs Created/Game
- Foxx, J. (Bos) 12.50
- DiMaggio, J. (NY) 12.40
- Williams, T. (Bos) 10.70

Fielding Runs
- Crosetti, F. (NY) 27.8
- Gordon, J. (NY) 26.1
- Doerr, B. (Bos) 13.2

Win Shares – Batters
- DiMaggio, J. (NY) 34
- Williams, T. (Bos) 32
- 2 players tied with 30

TPW – Batters
- DiMaggio, J. (NY) 5.7
- Gordon, J. (NY) 4.9
- Foxx, J. (Bos) 4.5

TEAM	CG	SH	SV	IP	H	H/G	ER	HR	BB	SO	OAV	RAT	ERA	ERA+	CERA	PR+	PF	FA	E	DP	FR	BW	PW	FW	TPW	DIF
NY	**87**	**15**	**26**	1348^{2}	**1208**	**8.1**	**496**	85	567	565	**.241**	**1.316**	**3.31**	132	**3.29**	**104.5**	94	**.978**	**126**	159	**52.1**	**14.2**	**9.6**	**4.8**	**28.6**	2.4
BOS	52	4	20	1350^{2}	1533	10.2	684	77	543	539	.287	1.537	4.56	104	4.49	28.9	102	.970	180	147	-4.1	3.7	2.7	-.4	6.0	8.0
CLE	69	10	13	1364^{2}	1394	9.2	618	**75**	602	614	.266	1.463	4.08	108	3.98	49.8	95	.970	180	148	-1.7	2.8	4.6	-.2	7.2	2.8
CHI	62	5	21	**1377**	1470	9.6	659	99	**454**	535	.275	1.397	4.31	110	3.96	50.5	102	.972	167	140	14.5	-7.4	4.6	1.3	-1.4	9.4
DET	64	8	16	1367^{1}	1430	9.4	652	104	574	**633**	.268	1.466	4.29	114	4.17	86.8	106	.967	198	147	3.7	-.9	8.0	.3	7.4	-3.4
WAS	72	4	10	1354^{2}	1420	9.4	692	**75**	602	521	.271	1.493	4.60	95	4.14	-50.8	94	.966	205	**167**	12.0	.0	-4.7	1.1	-3.6	-7.4
PHI	50	6	12	1342^{2}	1687	11.3	863	148	579	397	.307	1.688	5.78	81	5.67	-118.2	102	.964	210	131	-44.0	-3.7	-10.9	-4.1	-18.6	-2.4
STL	56	3	3	1371^{1}	1724	11.3	916	133	739	516	.310	1.796	6.01	**81**	6.07	-140.6	105	.968	199	144	-34.3	-9.1	-13.0	-3.2	-25.2	-8.8
Total	**512**	**55**	**121**	**10877**		**9.8**	**5580**					**1.519**	**4.62**													

Wins
- Feller, B. (Cle) 24
- Ruffing, R. (NY) 21
- 2 players tied with 20

Win Percentage
- Grove, L. (Bos) .789
- Ruffing, R. (NY) .750
- Feller, B. (Cle) .727

Games
- Brown, C. (Chi) 61
- Dean, C. (Phi) 54
- Dickman, E. (Bos) 48

Complete Games
- Feller, B. (Cle) 24
- Newsom, B. (Det,StL) 24
- Ruffing, R. (NY) 22

Shutouts
- Ruffing, R. (NY) 5
- Feller, B. (Cle) 4
- Newsom, B. (Det,StL) 3

Saves
- Murphy, J. (NY) 19
- Brown, C. (Chi) 18
- 2 players tied with 7

Innings Pitched
- Feller, B. (Cle) 296^{2}
- Newsom, B. (Det,StL) 291^{2}
- Leonard, D. (Was) 269^{1}

Fewest Hits/Game
- Feller, B. (Cle) 6.89
- Hadley, B. (NY) 7.71
- Gomez, L. (NY) 7.86

Fewest BB/Game
- Lyons, T. (Chi) 1.36
- Leonard, D. (Was) 1.97
- Beckmann, B. (Phi) 2.38

Strikeouts
- Feller, B. (Cle) 246
- Newsom, B. (Det,StL) 192
- Bridges, T. (Det) 129

Ratio
- Lyons, T. (Chi) 1.09
- Ruffing, R. (NY) 1.23
- Leonard, D. (Was) 1.23

Earned Run Average
- Grove, L. (Bos) 2.54
- Lyons, T. (Chi) 2.76
- Feller, B. (Cle) 2.85

Adjusted ERA
- Grove, L. (Bos) 186
- Lyons, T. (Chi) 171
- Feller, B. (Cle) 154

Component ERA
- Lyons, T. (Chi) 2.40
- Feller, B. (Cle) 2.66
- Grove, L. (Bos) 2.95

Opponents' Batting Avg.
- Feller, B. (Cle) .210
- Gomez, L. (NY) .235
- Hadley, B. (NY) .237

Adjusted Pitching Runs
- Feller, B. (Cle) 51
- Grove, L. (Bos) 47
- Newsom, B. (Det,StL) 43

Win Shares – Pitchers
- Feller, B. (Cle) 32
- Newsom, B. (Det,StL) 26
- Grove, L. (Bos) 23

TPW – Pitchers
- Feller, B. (Cle) 5.2
- Grove, L. (Bos) 4.2
- Lyons, T. (Chi) 3.7

1940 National League

TEAM	G	W	L	PCT	GB	R	OR	EW	AB	H	2B	3B	HR	TB	BB	SO	SB	CS	AVG	OBP	SLG	OPS	OPS+	BR/A	PF	RC
CIN	155	100	53	.654	....	707	**528**	98	5372	1427	264	38	89	2034	453	503	72	....	.266	.327	.379	.706	100	0	101	672
BRO	156	88	65	.575	12	697	621	85	5470	1421	256	**70**	93	2096	522	570	56	....	.260	.327	.383	.710	96	-26	106	692
STL	156	84	69	.549	16	747	699	82	**5499**	**1514**	266	61	**119**	**2259**	479	610	**97**	....	.275	.336	**.411**	**.747**	106	42	106	**764**
PIT	156	78	76	.506	22.5	**809**	783	80	5466	1511	**276**	68	76	2151	**553**	494	69	....	**.276**	**.346**	.394	.740	**112**	**92**	99	757
CHI	154	75	79	.487	25.5	681	636	82	5389	1441	272	48	86	2067	482	566	63	....	.267	.331	.384	.714	106	40	98	691
NY	152	72	80	.474	27.5	663	659	76	5324	1423	201	46	91	1989	453	**478**	45	....	.267	.329	.374	.703	100	-2	101	653
BOS	152	65	87	.428	34.5	623	745	63	5329	1366	219	50	59	1862	402	581	48	....	.256	.311	.349	.660	93	-50	95	581
PHI	153	50	103	.327	50	494	750	46	5137	1225	180	35	75	1700	435	527	25	....	.238	.300	.331	.631	83	-113	96	512
Total		**617**				**5421**			**42986**	**11328**	**1934**	**416**	**688**		**3779**	**4329**	**475**		**.264**	**.326**	**.376**	**.702**				

Runs
Vaughan, A. (Pit) 113
Mize, J. (StL) 111
Werber, B. (Cin) 105

Hits
Hack, S. (Chi) 191
McCormick, F. (Cin) 191
Mize, J. (StL) 182

Doubles
McCormick, F. (Cin) 44
Vaughan, A. (Pit) 40
Gleeson, J. (Chi) 39

Triples
Vaughan, A. (Pit) 15
Ross, C. (Bos) 14
3 players tied with 13

Home Runs
Mize, J. (StL) 43
Nicholson, B. (Chi) 25
Rizzo, J. (Phi,Cin,Pit) 24

Total Bases
Mize, J. (StL) 368
McCormick, F. (Cin) 298
Medwick, J. (Bro,StL) 280

Runs Batted In
Mize, J. (StL) 137
McCormick, F. (Cin) 127
Van Robays, M. (Pit) 116

Bases On Balls
Fletcher, E. (Pit) 119
Ott, M. (NY) 100
Camilli, D. (Bro) 89

Stolen Bases
Frey, L. (Cin) 22
Hack, S. (Chi) 21
Moore, T. (StL) 18

Batting Average
Garms, D. (Pit) .355
Hack, S. (Chi) .317
Mize, J. (StL) .314

On-Base Percentage
Fletcher, E. (Pit) .418
Ott, M. (NY) .407
Mize, J. (StL) .404

Slugging Average
Mize, J. (StL) .636
Nicholson, B. (Chi) .534
Camilli, D. (Bro) .529

Adjusted OPS
Mize, J. (StL) 173
Nicholson, B. (Chi) 148
Camilli, D. (Bro) 144

Adjusted Batting Runs
Mize, J. (StL) 57.0
Fletcher, E. (Pit) 34.0
Camilli, D. (Bro) 33.0

Runs Created/Game
Mize, J. (StL) 10.10
Camilli, D. (Bro) 8.30
Nicholson, B. (Chi) 7.40

Fielding Runs
Frey, L. (Cin) 33.4
Werber, B. (Cin) 10.6
May, P. (Phi) 10.4

Win Shares – Batters
Mize, J. (StL) 33
Vaughan, A. (Pit) 31
2 players tied with 27

TPW – Batters
Frey, L. (Cin) 4.8
Mize, J. (StL) 4.3
Hack, S. (Chi) 4.1

TEAM	CG	SH	SV	IP	H	H/G	ER	HR	BB	SO	OAV	RAT	ERA	ERA+	CERA	PR+	PF	FA	E	DP	FR	BW	PW	FW	TPW	DIF
CIN	**91**	10	11	1407^{2}	**1263**	**8.1**	**477**	73	445	557	**.240**	**1.213**	**3.05**	124	**2.89**	64.7	98	**.981**	**117**	158	**50.8**	.0	6.5	**5.1**	**11.7**	12.3
BRO	65	**17**	14	**1433**	1366	8.6	557	101	**393**	**639**	.248	1.227	3.50	114	3.19	**84.7**	104	.970	183	110	-5.2	-2.6	**8.6**	-.5	5.4	6.6
STL	71	10	14	1396	1457	9.4	594	83	488	550	.266	1.393	3.83	104	3.81	47.9	104	.971	174	134	-23.3	4.2	4.8	-2.4	6.7	1.3
PIT	49	8	**24**	1388^{2}	1569	10.2	672	**72**	492	491	.283	1.484	4.36	87	4.28	-44.6	99	.966	217	161	-40.5	**9.3**	-4.5	-4.1	.7	.3
CHI	69	12	14	1392	1418	9.2	548	74	430	564	.262	1.328	3.54	106	3.46	36.6	97	.968	199	143	-4.7	4.0	3.7	-.5	7.2	-9.2
NY	57	11	18	1360^{1}	1383	9.2	573	110	473	606	.262	1.364	3.79	102	3.80	18.8	101	.977	139	132	-5.1	-.2	1.9	-.5	1.2	-5.2
BOS	76	9	12	1359	1444	9.6	658	83	573	435	.274	1.484	4.36	**85**	4.28	-128.0	97	.970	184	**169**	31.0	-5.1	-12.9	3.1	-14.9	3.9
PHI	66	5	8	1357	1429	9.5	663	92	475	485	.270	1.403	4.40	89	3.95	-75.9	101	.970	181	136	1.0	-11.4	-7.7	.1	-19.0	-7.0
Total	**544**	**82**	**115**	$\mathbf{11093^{2}}$		**9.2**	**4742**					**1.361**	**3.85**													

Wins
Walters, B. (Cin) 22
Derringer, P. (Cin) 20
Passeau, C. (Chi) 20

Win Percentage
Sewell, R. (Pit) .762
Walters, B. (Cin) .688
Turner, J. (Cin) .667

Games
Shoun, C. (StL) 54
Brown, M. (Pit) 48
Passeau, C. (Chi) 46

Complete Games
Walters, B. (Cin) 29
Derringer, P. (Cin) 26
Mulcahy, H. (Phi) 21

Shutouts
Salvo, M. (Bos) 5
Wyatt, W. (Bro) 5
4 players tied with 4

Saves
Beggs, J. (Cin) 7
Brown, J. (NY) 7
Brown, M. (Pit) 7

Innings Pitched
Walters, B. (Cin) 305
Derringer, P. (Cin) 296^{2}
Higbe, K. (Phi) 283

Fewest Hits/Game
Walters, B. (Cin) 7.11
Higbe, K. (Phi) 7.70
Thompson, J. (Cin) 7.87

Fewest BB/Game
Derringer, P. (Cin) 1.46
Turner, J. (Cin) 1.54
Hamlin, L. (Bro) 1.68

Strikeouts
Higbe, K. (Phi) 137
Passeau, C. (Chi) 124
Wyatt, W. (Bro) 124

Ratio
Walters, B. (Cin) 1.09
Derringer, P. (Cin) 1.11
Passeau, C. (Chi) 1.13

Earned Run Average
Walters, B. (Cin) 2.48
Passeau, C. (Chi) 2.50
Sewell, R. (Pit) 2.80

Adjusted ERA
Walters, B. (Cin) 153
Passeau, C. (Chi) 150
Sewell, R. (Pit) 136

Component ERA
Passeau, C. (Chi) 2.42
Walters, B. (Cin) 2.43
Derringer, P. (Cin) 2.55

Opponents' Batting Avg.
Walters, B. (Cin) .220
Higbe, K. (Phi) .232
Thompson, J. (Cin) .233

Adjusted Pitching Runs
Passeau, C. (Chi) 40
Walters, B. (Cin) 33
Sewell, R. (Pit) 27

Win Shares – Pitchers
Walters, B. (Cin) 32
Passeau, C. (Chi) 28
Derringer, P. (Cin) 24

TPW – Pitchers
Passeau, C. (Chi) 4.6
Walters, B. (Cin) 3.6
Sewell, R. (Pit) 2.9

1940 American League

TEAM	G	W	L	PCT	GB	R	OR	EW	AB	H	2B	3B	HR	TB	BB	SO	SB	CS	AVG	OBP	SLG	OPS	OPS+	BR/A	PF	RC
DET	155	90	64	.584	....	**888**	717	93	5418	1549	**312**	65	134	2393	**664**	556	66	39	**.286**	**.366**	.442	**.808**	105	52	110	**912**
CLE	155	89	65	.578	1	710	**637**	85	5361	1422	287	61	101	2134	519	597	53	36	.265	.332	.398	.730	97	-22	97	725
NY	155	88	66	.571	2	817	671	92	5286	1371	243	66	**155**	2211	648	606	59	36	.259	.344	.418	.762	108	63	96	788
CHI	155	82	72	.532	8	735	672	84	5386	1499	238	63	73	2082	496	569	52	60	.278	.340	.387	.727	93	-62	101	714
BOS	154	82	72	.532	8	872	825	81	**5481**	**1566**	301	**80**	145	**2462**	590	597	55	49	.286	.356	**.449**	.806	**110**	**72**	104	888
STL	156	67	87	.435	23	757	882	65	5416	1423	278	58	118	2171	556	642	51	40	.263	.333	.401	.734	94	-52	102	744
WAS	154	64	90	.416	26	665	811	62	5365	1453	266	67	52	2009	468	**504**	**94**	40	.271	.331	.374	.706	95	-31	94	690
PHI	154	54	100	.351	36	703	932	56	5304	1391	242	53	105	2054	556	656	48	**33**	.262	.334	.387	.722	95	-37	98	703
Total		**619**				**6147**			**43017**	**11674**	**2167**	**513**	**883**		**4497**	**4727**	**478**	**333**	**.271**	**.342**	**.407**	**.750**				

Runs
Williams, T. (Bos) 134
Greenberg, H. (Det) 129
McCosky, B. (Det) 123

Hits
Cramer, D. (Bos) 200
McCosky, B. (Det) 200
Radcliff, R. (StL) 200

Doubles
Greenberg, H. (Det) 50
Boudreau, L. (Cle) 46
York, R. (Det) 46

Triples
McCosky, B. (Det) 19
Finney, L. (Bos) 15
Keller, C. (NY) 15

Home Runs
Greenberg, H. (Det) 41
Foxx, J. (Bos) 36
York, R. (Det) 33

Total Bases
Greenberg, H. (Det) 384
York, R. (Det) 343
Williams, T. (Bos) 333

Runs Batted In
Greenberg, H. (Det) 150
York, R. (Det) 134
DiMaggio, J. (NY) 133

Bases On Balls
Keller, C. (NY) 106
Clift, H. (StL) 104
2 players tied with 101

Stolen Bases
Case, G. (Was) 35
Walker, G. (Was) 21
Gordon, J. (NY) 18

Batting Average
DiMaggio, J. (NY) .352
Appling, L. (Chi) .348
Williams, T. (Bos) .344

On-Base Percentage
Williams, T. (Bos) .442
Greenberg, H. (Det) .433
Gehringer, C. (Det) .428

Slugging Average
Greenberg, H. (Det) .670
DiMaggio, J. (NY) .626
Williams, T. (Bos) .594

Adjusted OPS
DiMaggio, J. (NY) 175
Greenberg, H. (Det) 165
Williams, T. (Bos) 159

Adjusted Batting Runs
Greenberg, H. (Det) 57.0
DiMaggio, J. (NY) 56.0
Williams, T. (Bos) 53.0

Runs Created/Game
Greenberg, H. (Det) 11.60
Williams, T. (Bos) 10.80
DiMaggio, J. (NY) 10.50

Fielding Runs
Boudreau, L. (Cle) 25.4
Gordon, J. (NY) 24.3
Appling, L. (Chi) 18.5

Win Shares – Batters
DiMaggio, J. (NY) 31
Greenberg, H. (Det) 31
2 players tied with 30

TPW – Batters
Gordon, J. (NY) 4.9
Appling, L. (Chi) 4.8
Boudreau, L. (Cle) 4.7

TEAM	CG	SH	SV	IP	H	H/G	ER	HR	BB	SO	OAV	RAT	ERA	ERA+	CERA	PR+	PF	FA	E	DP	FR	BW	PW	FW	TPW	DIF
DET	59	10	**23**	1375^{1}	1425	9.3	613	102	570	**752**	.266	1.451	4.01	119	4.13	**140.7**	109	.968	194	116	-23.0	4.9	**13.3**	-2.2	**16.0**	-3.0
CLE	72	**13**	22	1375	**1328**	8.7	**555**	**86**	512	686	.254	1.338	**3.63**	116	3.56	55.5	96	**.975**	**149**	164	**33.5**	-2.1	5.2	**3.2**	6.3	5.7
NY	76	10	14	1373	1389	9.1	593	119	511	559	.261	1.384	3.89	104	3.91	5.1	92	.975	152	158	17.0	6.0	.5	1.6	8.0	3.0
CHI	**83**	10	18	$\mathbf{1386^{2}}$	1335	**8.7**	576	111	**480**	574	**.250**	**1.309**	3.74	118	**3.47**	74.5	101	.969	185	125	30.5	-5.8	7.0	2.9	4.1	.9
BOS	51	4	16	1379^{2}	1568	10.2	749	124	625	613	.284	1.590	4.89	92	4.92	-48.5	103	.972	173	156	-11.3	**6.8**	-4.6	-1.1	1.1	3.9
STL	64	4	9	1373^{1}	1592	10.4	781	113	646	439	.290	1.630	5.12	90	5.10	-73.0	105	.974	158	**179**	-9.5	-4.9	-6.9	-.9	-12.7	2.7
WAS	74	6	7	1350	1494	10.0	688	93	618	618	.281	1.564	4.59	91	4.63	-44.2	95	.968	194	166	-19.3	-2.9	-4.2	-1.8	-8.9	-4.1
PHI	72	4	12	1345	1543	10.3	780	135	534	488	.283	1.544	5.22	**85**	4.81	-95.4	101	.960	238	131	-20.7	-3.5	-9.0	-2.0	-14.4	-8.6
Total	**551**	**61**	**121**	**10958**		**9.6**	**5335**					**1.476**	**4.38**													

Wins
Feller, B. (Cle) 27
Newsom, B. (Det) 21
Milnar, A. (Cle) 18

Innings Pitched
Feller, B. (Cle) .... 320[1]
Leonard, D. (Was)............ 289
Rigney, J. (Chi) .... 280[2]

Adjusted ERA
Newsom, B. (Det) 168
Feller, B. (Cle) 161
Rigney, J. (Chi) 142

Win Percentage
Rowe, S. (Det) .... .842
Newsom, B. (Det) .... .808
Feller, B. (Cle) .... .711

Fewest Hits/Game
Feller, B. (Cle) 6.88
Rigney, J. (Chi) 7.70
Smith, E. (Chi) 7.77

Component ERA
Feller, B. (Cle) 2.32
Rigney, J. (Chi) 2.82
Lee, T. (Chi) 3.05

Games
Feller, B. (Cle) 43
Benton, A. (Det)................ 42
2 players tied with 41

Fewest BB/Game
Lyons, T. (Chi) 1.79
Lee, T. (Chi) 2.21
Rowe, S. (Det) 2.29

Opponents' Batting Avg.
Feller, B. (Cle) .... .210
Smith, E. (Chi) .... .228
Bridges, T. (Det) .... .229

Complete Games
Feller, B. (Cle) 31
Lee, T. (Chi) 24
Leonard, D. (Was)............ 23

Strikeouts
Feller, B. (Cle) 261
Newsom, B. (Det) 164
Rigney, J. (Chi) 141

Adjusted Pitching Runs
Newsom, B. (Det) 61
Feller, B. (Cle) 49
Rigney, J. (Chi) 35

Shutouts
Feller, B. (Cle) 4
Lyons, T. (Chi) 4
Milnar, A. (Cle) 4

Ratio
Feller, B. (Cle) 1.13
Rigney, J. (Chi) 1.18
Lyons, T. (Chi) 1.21

Win Shares – Pitchers
Feller, B. (Cle) 34
Newsom, B. (Det) 26
Rigney, J. (Chi) 24

Saves
Benton, A. (Det) 17
Brown, C. (Chi).................. 10
Murphy, J. (NY) 9

Earned Run Average
Feller, B. (Cle)................... 2.61
Newsom, B. (Det) 2.83
Rigney, J. (Chi).................. 3.11

TPW – Pitchers
Newsom, B. (Det) 5.7
Feller, B. (Cle)................... 4.7
Rigney, J. (Chi).................. 3.4

1941 National League

TEAM	G	W	L	PCT	GB	R	OR	EW	AB	H	2B	3B	HR	TB	BB	SO	SB	CS	AVG	OBP	SLG	OPS	OPS+	BR/A	PF	RC
BRO	157	100	54	.649	....	**800**	581	101	**5485**	**1494**	**286**	**69**	**101**	**2221**	**600**	535	36	....	**.272**	**.347**	**.405**	**.752**	**113**	**97**	104	**792**
STL	155	97	56	.634	2.5	734	589	93	5457	1482	254	56	70	2058	540	543	47	....	.272	.340	.377	.717	102	17	107	719
CIN	154	88	66	.571	12	616	**564**	84	5218	1288	213	33	64	1759	477	**428**	**68**	....	.247	.313	.337	.650	89	-75	100	556
PIT	156	81	73	.526	19	690	643	82	5297	1417	233	65	56	1948	547	516	59	....	.268	.338	.368	.706	106	43	100	670
NY	156	74	79	.484	25.5	667	706	72	5395	1401	248	35	95	2004	504	518	36	....	.260	.326	.371	.697	101	1	102	660
CHI	155	70	84	.455	30	666	670	77	5230	1323	239	25	99	1909	559	670	39	....	.253	.327	.365	.692	105	34	96	641
BOS	156	62	92	.403	38	592	720	62	5414	1357	231	38	48	1808	471	608	61	....	.251	.312	.334	.646	92	-57	96	568
PHI	155	43	111	.279	57	501	793	44	5233	1277	188	38	64	1733	451	596	65	....	.244	.307	.331	.638	89	-76	96	528
Total	**622**					**5266**			**42729**	**11039**	**1892**	**359**	**597**		**4149**	**4414**	**411**		**.258**	**.326**	**.361**	**.688**				

Runs
Reiser, P. (Bro) 117
Hack, S. (Chi) 111
Medwick, J. (Bro) 100

Runs Batted In
Camilli, D. (Bro) 120
Young, B. (NY).................. 104
2 players tied with 100

Adjusted OPS
Reiser, P. (Bro) 163
Camilli, D. (Bro) 162
Mize, J. (StL).................... 153

Hits
Hack, S. (Chi) 186
Reiser, P. (Bro) 184
Litwhiler, D. (Phi) 180

Bases On Balls
Fletcher, E. (Pit) 118
Camilli, D. (Bro) 104
Ott, M. (NY) 100

Adjusted Batting Runs
Camilli, D. (Bro) 46.0
Reiser, P. (Bro) 44.0
Fletcher, E. (Pit)............... 40.0

Doubles
Mize, J. (StL).................... 39
Reiser, P. (Bro) 39
Rucker, J. (NY) 38

Stolen Bases
Murtaugh, D. (Phi) 18
Benjamin, S. (Phi)............ 17
2 players tied with 16

Runs Created/Game
Reiser, P. (Bro) 9.20
Camilli, D. (Bro) 9.00
Mize, J. (StL).................... 8.60

Triples
Reiser, P. (Bro) 17
Fletcher, E. (Pit)............... 13
Hopp, J. (StL) 11

Batting Average
Reiser, P. (Bro) .... .343
Cooney, J. (Bos) .... .319
Medwick, J. (Bro) .... .318

Fielding Runs
Reese, P. (Bro) 24.7
May, P. (Phi) 17.3
Stringer, L. (Chi) 15.9

Home Runs
Camilli, D. (Bro) 34
Ott, M. (NY) 27
Nicholson, B. (Chi) 26

On-Base Percentage
Fletcher, E. (Pit)............... .421
Hack, S. (Chi) .... .417
Camilli, D. (Bro) .... .407

Win Shares – Batters
Reiser, P. (Bro) 34
Hack, S. (Chi) 30
Camilli, D. (Bro) 29

Total Bases
Reiser, P. (Bro).................. 299
Camilli, D. (Bro)................ 294
Medwick, J. (Bro) 278

Slugging Average
Reiser, P. (Bro).................. .558
Camilli, D. (Bro)................ .556
Mize, J. (StL) .... .535

TPW – Batters
Reiser, P. (Bro).................. 4.7
Camilli, D. (Bro)................ 4.1
Fletcher, E. (Pit) 3.6

TEAM	CG	SH	SV	IP	H	H/G	ER	HR	BB	SO	OAV	RAT	ERA	ERA+	CERA	PR+	PF	FA	E	DP	FR	BW	PW	FW	TPW	DIF
BRO	66	17	**22**	**1421**	**1236**	**7.8**	496	81	495	603	**.233**	**1.218**	**3.14**	117	**2.88**	59.1	101	.974	162	125	**23.7**	**10.0**	6.1	**2.4**	**18.5**	4.5
STL	64	15	20	1416[1]	1289	8.2	502	85	502	**659**	.242	1.265	3.19	118	3.14	67.3	104	.973	172	146	23.2	1.7	6.9	2.4	11.0	10.0
CIN	**89**	**19**	10	1386[2]	1300	8.4	**488**	61	510	627	.248	1.305	3.17	113	3.19	**70.2**	99	**.975**	**152**	147	-4.1	-7.7	**7.2**	-.4	-.9	11.9
PIT	71	8	12	1374[1]	1392	9.1	531	66	492	410	.260	1.371	3.48	104	3.54	34.3	99	.969	196	130	-14.8	4.4	3.5	-1.5	6.4	-2.4
NY	55	12	18	1391[2]	1455	9.4	609	90	539	566	.269	1.433	3.94	94	4.00	-46.2	102	.974	160	144	7.7	.1	-4.7	.8	-3.8	1.8
CHI	74	8	9	1364[2]	1431	9.4	564	**60**	**449**	548	.267	1.378	3.72	94	3.63	5.4	97	.970	180	139	-37.1	3.5	.6	-3.8	.2	-7.2
BOS	62	10	9	1385[2]	1440	9.4	608	75	554	446	.269	1.439	3.95	90	3.97	-68.7	98	.970	191	**174**	9.7	-5.9	-7.1	1.0	-12.0	-3.0
PHI	35	4	9	1372[1]	1499	9.8	686	79	606	552	.279	1.534	4.50	**82**	4.41	-113.3	102	.969	187	147	-8.4	-7.8	-11.6	-.9	-20.3	-13.7
Total	**516**	**93**	**109**	**11112[2]**		**8.9**	**4484**					**1.367**	**3.63**													

Wins
Higbe, K. (Bro).................. 22
Wyatt, W. (Bro)................. 22
2 players tied with 19

Innings Pitched
Walters, B. (Cin) 302
Higbe, K. (Bro).................. 298
Wyatt, W. (Bro)................. 288[1]

Adjusted ERA
Riddle, E. (Cin).................. 160
White, E. (StL) 157
Wyatt, W. (Bro)................. 157

Win Percentage
Riddle, E. (Cin).................. .826
Higbe, K. (Bro).................. .710
White, E. (StL) .... .708

Fewest Hits/Game
Vander Meer, J. (Cin)........ 6.84
Wyatt, W. (Bro)................. 6.96
White, E. (StL) 7.24

Component ERA
Wyatt, W. (Bro)................. 2.06
Riddle, E. (Cin).................. 2.32
Davis, C. (Bro) 2.43

Games
Higbe, K. (Bro).................. 48
Pearson, I. (Phi)................ 46
Casey, H. (Bro) 45

Fewest BB/Game
Davis, C. (Bro) 1.57
Passeau, C. (Chi)............... 2.03
Derringer, P. (Cin)............. 2.13

Opponents' Batting Avg.
Wyatt, W. (Bro)................. .212
Vander Meer, J. (Cin)........ .214
White, E. (StL) .... .217

Complete Games
Walters, B. (Cin) 27
Wyatt, W. (Bro) 23
2 players tied with 20

Strikeouts
Vander Meer, J. (Cin)........ 202
Wyatt, W. (Bro)................. 176
Walters, B. (Cin) 129

Adjusted Pitching Runs
Wyatt, W. (Bro)................. 38
Riddle, E. (Cin).................. 33
White, E. (StL) 28

Shutouts
Wyatt, W. (Bro)................. 7
Vander Meer, J. (Cin)........ 6
2 players tied with 5

Ratio
Wyatt, W. (Bro)................. 1.06
Davis, C. (Bro) 1.09
Riddle, E. (Cin).................. 1.10

Win Shares – Pitchers
Wyatt, W. (Bro)................. 28
Walters, B. (Cin) 27
Riddle, E. (Cin).................. 26

Saves
Brown, J. (NY).................... 8
Crouch, B. (StL,Phi)........... 7
Casey, H. (Bro).................. 7

Earned Run Average
Riddle, E. (Cin) 2.24
Wyatt, W. (Bro) 2.34
White, E. (StL).................. 2.40

TPW – Pitchers
Wyatt, W. (Bro) 4.5
Riddle, E. (Cin) 3.7
White, E. (StL).................. 3.0

1941 American League

TEAM	G	W	L	PCT	GB	R	OR	EW	AB	H	2B	3B	HR	TB	BB	SO	SB	CS	AVG	OBP	SLG	OPS	OPS+	BR/A	PF	RC
NY	156	101	53	.656	....	830	**631**	98	5444	1464	243	60	**151**	2280	616	565	51	33	.269	.346	.419	.765	111	78	99	822
BOS	155	84	70	.545	17	**865**	750	88	5359	**1517**	**304**	55	124	**2303**	683	567	67	51	**.283**	**.366**	**.430**	**.796**	**115**	**115**	102	**872**
CHI	156	77	77	.500	24	638	649	76	5404	1376	245	47	47	1856	510	**476**	**91**	53	.255	.322	.343	.665	84	-120	99	611
DET	155	75	79	.487	26	686	743	71	5370	1412	247	55	81	2012	602	584	43	**28**	.263	.340	.375	.714	87	-90	110	713
CLE	155	75	79	.487	26	677	668	78	5283	1350	249	**84**	103	2076	512	605	63	47	.256	.323	.393	.716	101	-8	95	691
WAS	156	70	84	.455	31	728	798	70	**5521**	1502	257	80	52	2075	470	488	79	36	.272	.331	.376	.707	98	-15	95	704
STL	157	70	84	.455	31	765	823	71	5408	1440	281	58	91	2110	**775**	552	50	39	.266	.360	.390	.750	102	32	103	804
PHI	154	64	90	.416	37	713	840	64	5336	1431	240	69	85	2064	574	588	27	36	.268	.340	.387	.727	102	6	98	712
Total	**622**					**5902**			**43125**	**11492**	**2066**	**508**	**734**		**4742**	**4425**	**471**	**323**	**.266**	**.341**	**.389**	**.730**				

Runs
Williams, T. (Bos)............. 135
DiMaggio, J. (NY)............. 122
DiMaggio, D. (Bos)........... 117

Runs Batted In
DiMaggio, J. (NY)............. 125
Heath, J. (Cle) 123
Keller, C. (NY)................... 122

Adjusted OPS
Williams, T. (Bos).............. 232
DiMaggio, J. (NY).............. 186
Heath, J. (Cle) 165

Hits
Travis, C. (Was) 218
Heath, J. (Cle) 199
DiMaggio, J. (NY).............. 193

Bases On Balls
Williams, T. (Bos)............. 147
Cullenbine, R. (StL) 121
Clift, H. (StL)..................... 113

Adjusted Batting Runs
Williams, T. (Bos)............. 100.0
DiMaggio, J. (NY)............. 67.0
Heath, J. (Cle) 50.0

Doubles
Boudreau, L. (Cle)............ 45
DiMaggio, J. (NY).............. 43
Judnich, W. (StL).............. 40

Stolen Bases
Case, G. (Was) 33
Kuhel, J. (Chi).................... 20
Heath, J. (Cle) 18

Runs Created/Game
Williams, T. (Bos).............. 19.20
DiMaggio, J. (NY).............. 12.30
Keller, C. (NY)................... 10.00

Triples
Heath, J. (Cle) 20
Travis, C. (Was) 19
Keltner, K. (Cle) 13

Batting Average
Williams, T. (Bos)............. .406
Travis, C. (Was)................ .359
DiMaggio, J. (NY)............. .357

Fielding Runs
Rizzuto, P. (NY)................. 28.4
Keltner, K. (Cle) 22.2
Bloodworth, J. (Was)......... 20.3

Home Runs
Williams, T. (Bos)............. 37
Keller, C. (NY)................... 33
Henrich, T. (NY)................. 31

On-Base Percentage
Williams, T. (Bos)............. .553
Cullenbine, R. (StL)........... .452
DiMaggio, J. (NY)............. .440

Win Shares – Batters
Williams, T. (Bos).............. 42
DiMaggio, J. (NY).............. 41
Travis, C. (Was) 34

Total Bases
DiMaggio, J. (NY) 348
Heath, J. (Cle)................... 343
Williams, T. (Bos).............. 335

Slugging Average
Williams, T. (Bos) .... .735
DiMaggio, J. (NY) .... .643
Heath, J. (Cle)................... .586

TPW – Batters
Williams, T. (Bos) 8.8
DiMaggio, J. (NY) 6.9
Travis, C. (Was)................. 4.5

TEAM	CG	SH	SV	IP	H	H/G	ER	HR	BB	SO	OAV	RAT	ERA	ERA+	CERA	PR+	PF	FA	E	DP	FR	BW	PW	FW	TPW	DIF
NY	75	13	**26**	1396[1]	**1309**	**8.4**	**548**	81	598	589	**.248**	1.366	3.53	111	3.49	10.3	95	.973	165	**196**	**53.2**	7.5	1.0	**5.2**	**13.7**	10.3
BOS	70	8	11	1372	1453	9.5	639	88	611	574	.270	1.504	4.19	99	4.26	13.5	100	.972	172	139	-15.9	**11.1**	1.3	-1.5	10.9	-3.9
CHI	**106**	**14**	4	**1416**	1362	8.7	554	89	**521**	564	.252	**1.330**	**3.52**	116	**3.47**	72.8	99	.971	180	145	18.6	-11.6	7.1	1.8	-2.8	2.8
DET	52	8	16	1381[2]	1399	9.1	641	80	645	**697**	.260	1.479	4.18	109	3.99	**97.0**	110	.969	186	129	-40.3	-8.7	**9.4**	-3.9	-3.2	1.2
CLE	68	10	19	1377	1366	8.9	597	71	660	617	.259	1.471	3.90	101	3.96	-0.7	95	**.976**	**142**	158	8.1	-.7	-.1	.8	.0	-2.0
WAS	69	8	7	1389[1]	1524	9.9	671	**69**	603	544	.279	1.531	4.35	93	4.36	-30.8	98	.969	187	169	-16.3	-1.5	-3.0	-1.6	-6.1	-.9
STL	65	7	10	1389	1563	10.1	728	120	549	454	.283	1.521	4.72	91	4.66	-45.2	104	.975	151	156	-18.7	3.1	-4.4	-1.8	-3.1	-3.9
PHI	64	3	18	1365[1]	1516	10.0	733	136	557	386	.279	1.518	4.83	**87**	4.68	-107.4	101	.967	200	150	10.5	.6	-10.4	1.0	-8.8	-4.2
Total	**569**	**71**	**111**	**11086[2]**		**9.3**	**5111**					**1.464**	**4.15**													

Wins
Feller, B. (Cle) 25
Lee, T. (Chi) 22
Newsome, D. (Bos) 19

Win Percentage
Gomez, L. (NY) .... .750
3 players tied with .... .714

Games
Feller, B. (Cle) 44
Newsom, B. (Det) 43
Brown, C. (Cle) 41

Complete Games
Lee, T. (Chi) 30
Feller, B. (Cle) 28
Smith, E. (Chi) 21

Shutouts
Feller, B. (Cle) 6
3 players tied with 4

Saves
Murphy, J. (NY) 15
Benton, A. (Det) 7
Ferrick, T. (Phi) 7

Innings Pitched
Feller, B. (Cle) 343
Lee, T. (Chi) .... 300[1]
Smith, E. (Chi) .... 263[1]

Fewest Hits/Game
Benton, A. (Det) 7.42
Feller, B. (Cle) 7.45
Lee, T. (Chi) 7.73

Fewest BB/Game
Lyons, T. (Chi) 1.78
Leonard, D. (Was) 1.90
Muncrief, B. (StL) 2.23

Strikeouts
Feller, B. (Cle) 260
Newsom, B. (Det) 175
Lee, T. (Chi) 130

Ratio
Lee, T. (Chi) 1.17
Benton, A. (Det) 1.24
Ruffing, R. (NY) 1.24

Earned Run Average
Lee, T. (Chi) 2.37
Benton, A. (Det) 2.97
Wagner, C. (Bos) 3.07

Adjusted ERA
Lee, T. (Chi) 173
Benton, A. (Det) 153
Wagner, C. (Bos) 136

Component ERA
Lee, T. (Chi) 2.71
Chandler, S. (NY) 2.82
Benton, A. (Det) 2.92

Opponents' Batting Avg.
Benton, A. (Det) .... .221
Feller, B. (Cle) .... .226
Lee, T. (Chi) .... .232

Adjusted Pitching Runs
Lee, T. (Chi) 54
Benton, A. (Det) 32
Feller, B. (Cle) 28

Win Shares – Pitchers
Lee, T. (Chi) 32
Feller, B. (Cle) 30
2 players tied with 20

TPW – Pitchers
Lee, T. (Chi) 5.7
Feller, B. (Cle) 2.9
Benton, A. (Det) 2.7

1942 National League

TEAM	G	W	L	PCT	GB	R	OR	EW	AB	H	2B	3B	HR	TB	BB	SO	SB	CS	AVG	OBP	SLG	OPS	OPS+	BR/A	PF	RC
STL	156	106	48	.688	....	**755**	**480**	110	**5421**	**1454**	**282**	**69**	60	**2054**	551	507	71	....	**.268**	**.338**	**.379**	**.717**	109	59	108	**718**
BRO	155	104	50	.675	2	742	512	104	5285	1398	263	34	62	1915	**572**	**484**	**81**	....	.265	.338	.362	.700	**110**	**70**	102	671
NY	154	85	67	.559	20	675	600	85	5210	1323	162	35	**109**	1882	558	511	39	....	.254	.330	.361	.691	108	57	101	627
CIN	154	76	76	.500	29	527	545	73	5260	1216	198	39	66	1690	483	549	42	....	.231	.299	.321	.620	88	-81	100	519
PIT	151	66	81	.449	36.5	585	631	68	5104	1250	173	49	54	1683	537	536	41	....	.245	.320	.330	.650	94	-28	102	556
CHI	155	68	86	.442	38	591	665	68	5352	1360	224	41	75	1891	509	607	63	....	.254	.321	.353	.674	108	48	96	619
BOS	150	59	89	.399	44	515	645	58	5077	1216	210	19	68	1668	474	507	49	....	.240	.307	.329	.635	94	-38	98	520
PHI	151	42	109	.278	62.5	394	706	36	5060	1174	168	37	44	1548	392	488	37	....	.232	.289	.306	.595	84	-103	95	451
Total	**613**					**4784**			**41769**	**10391**	**1680**	**323**	**538**		**4076**	**4189**	**423**		**.249**	**.318**	**.343**	**.661**				

Runs
Ott, M. (NY) 118
Slaughter, E. (StL) 100
Mize, J. (NY) 97

Hits
Slaughter, E. (StL) 188
Nicholson, B. (Chi) 173
3 players tied with 166

Doubles
Marion, M. (StL) 38
Medwick, J. (Bro) 37
Hack, S. (Chi) 36

Triples
Slaughter, E. (StL) 17
Nicholson, B. (Chi) 11
Musial, S. (StL) 10

Home Runs
Ott, M. (NY) 30
Camilli, D. (Bro) 26
Mize, J. (NY) 26

Total Bases
Slaughter, E. (StL) 292
Mize, J. (NY) 282
Nicholson, B. (Chi) 280

Runs Batted In
Mize, J. (NY) 110
Camilli, D. (Bro) 109
Slaughter, E. (StL) 98

Bases On Balls
Ott, M. (NY) 109
Fletcher, E. (Pit) 105
Camilli, D. (Bro) 97

Stolen Bases
Reiser, P. (Bro) 20
Fernandez, N. (Bos) 15
Reese, P. (Bro) 15

Batting Average
Lombardi, E. (Bos) .... .330
Slaughter, E. (StL) .... .318
Musial, S. (StL) .... .315

On-Base Percentage
Fletcher, E. (Pit) .... .417
Ott, M. (NY) .... .415
Slaughter, E. (StL) .... .412

Slugging Average
Mize, J. (NY) .... .521
Ott, M. (NY) .... .497
Slaughter, E. (StL) .... .494

Adjusted OPS
Ott, M. (NY) 165
Mize, J. (NY) 161
Nicholson, B. (Chi) 156

Adjusted Batting Runs
Ott, M. (NY) 50.0
Slaughter, E. (StL) 42.0
Nicholson, B. (Chi) 42.0

Runs Created/Game
Slaughter, E. (StL) 8.40
Ott, M. (NY) 8.30
Musial, S. (StL) 7.90

Fielding Runs
Reese, P. (Bro) 32.0
Marion, M. (StL) 21.1
May, P. (Phi) 14.3

Win Shares – Batters
Slaughter, E. (StL) 37
Ott, M. (NY) 35
Mize, J. (NY) 32

TPW – Batters
Reese, P. (Bro) 4.8
Nicholson, B. (Chi) 4.4
Ott, M. (NY) 4.2

TEAM	CG	SH	SV	IP	H	H/G	ER	HR	BB	SO	OAV	RAT	ERA	ERA+	CERA	PR+	PF	FA	E	DP	FR	BW	PW	FW	TPW	DIF
STL	70	**18**	15	1410[1]	**1192**	**7.6**	**399**	49	473	**651**	**.228**	**1.181**	**2.55**	134	**2.57**	**119.0**	103	.972	169	137	**18.7**	6.3	**12.8**	**2.0**	**21.1**	7.9
BRO	67	16	**24**	1398[2]	1205	7.8	441	73	493	612	.232	1.214	2.84	115	2.86	47.8	98	.977	**138**	150	16.6	**7.6**	5.1	1.8	14.5	12.5
NY	70	12	13	1370	1299	8.5	504	94	493	497	.250	1.308	3.31	101	3.38	-5.7	101	**.977**	**138**	128	12.6	6.1	-.6	1.4	6.9	2.1
CIN	**80**	12	8	**1411[2]**	1213	7.7	442	**47**	526	616	.230	1.232	2.82	116	2.74	65.6	99	.971	177	**158**	7.4	-8.7	7.0	.8	-.8	.8
PIT	64	13	11	1351[1]	1376	9.2	537	62	**435**	426	.262	1.340	3.58	95	3.44	-14.1	102	.969	184	128	-15.9	-3.0	-1.5	-1.7	-6.3	-.7
CHI	71	10	14	1400[2]	1447	9.3	560	70	525	507	.267	1.408	3.60	89	3.79	-35.6	96	.973	170	136	-27.0	5.2	-3.8	-2.9	-1.5	-7.5
BOS	68	9	8	1334	1326	9.0	557	82	518	414	.260	1.382	3.76	89	3.73	-52.8	101	.977	142	138	-9.7	-4.1	-5.7	-1.0	-10.8	-4.2
PHI	51	2	6	1341	1328	8.9	614	61	605	472	.260	1.441	4.12	**80**	3.82	-120.8	100	.968	194	147	-0.9	-11.0	-13.0	-.1	-24.1	-8.9
Total	**541**	**92**	**99**	**11017[2]**		**8.5**	**4054**					**1.312**	**3.31**													

Wins
Cooper, M. (StL) 22
Beazley, J. (StL) 21
2 players tied with 19

Win Percentage
Beazley, J. (StL) .... .778
Cooper, M. (StL) .... .759
Wyatt, W. (Bro) .... .731

Games
Adams, A. (NY) 61
Casey, H. (Bro) 50
2 players tied with 43

Complete Games
Tobin, J. (Bos) 28
Passeau, C. (Chi) 24
Cooper, M. (StL) 22

Shutouts
Cooper, M. (StL) 10
3 players tied with 5

Saves
Casey, H. (Bro) 13
Adams, A. (NY) 11
Beggs, J. (Cin) 8

Innings Pitched
Tobin, J. (Bos) .... 287[2]
Cooper, M. (StL) .... 278[2]
Passeau, C. (Chi) .... 278[1]

Fewest Hits/Game
Cooper, M. (StL) 6.69
Vander Meer, J. (Cin) 6.93
Higbe, K. (Bro) 7.31

Fewest BB/Game
Warneke, L. (StL,Chi) 1.79
Lohrman, B. (StL,NY) 1.85
Hubbell, C. (NY) 1.94

Strikeouts
Vander Meer, J. (Cin) 186
Cooper, M. (StL) 152
Higbe, K. (Bro) 115

Ratio
Cooper, M. (StL) .... .99
Lohrman, B. (StL,NY) 1.11
Davis, C. (Bro) 1.12

Earned Run Average
Cooper, M. (StL) 1.78
Beazley, J. (StL) 2.13
Davis, C. (Bro) 2.36

Adjusted ERA
Cooper, M. (StL) 193
Beazley, J. (StL) 161
Davis, C. (Bro) 138

Component ERA
Cooper, M. (StL) 1.81
Vander Meer, J. (Cin) 2.33
Beazley, J. (StL) 2.43

Opponents' Batting Avg.
Cooper, M. (StL) .... .204
Vander Meer, J. (Cin) .... .208
Higbe, K. (Bro) .... .223

Adjusted Pitching Runs
Cooper, M. (StL) 47
Beazley, J. (StL) 28
Vander Meer, J. (Cin) 22

Win Shares – Pitchers
Cooper, M. (StL) 29
Beazley, J. (StL) 22
2 players tied with 21

TPW – Pitchers
Cooper, M. (StL) 5.0
Beazley, J. (StL) 2.9
Walters, B. (Cin) 2.5

1942 American League

TEAM	G	W	L	PCT	GB	R	OR	EW	AB	H	2B	3B	HR	TB	BB	SO	SB	CS	AVG	OBP	SLG	OPS	OPS+	BR/A	PF	RC
NY	154	103	51	.669	....	**801**	**507**	110	5305	1429	223	57	**108**	2090	591	556	69	33	.269	.346	.394	.740	**118**	**129**	98	758
BOS	152	93	59	.612	9	761	594	94	5248	**1451**	**244**	55	103	**2114**	591	508	68	61	**.276**	**.352**	**.403**	**.755**	116	104	103	**774**
STL	151	82	69	.543	19.5	730	637	86	5229	1354	239	**62**	98	2011	**609**	607	37	38	.259	.338	.385	.722	109	57	101	703
CLE	156	75	79	.487	28	590	659	69	5317	1344	223	58	50	1833	500	544	69	74	.253	.320	.345	.665	100	-16	94	596
DET	156	73	81	.474	30	589	587	77	**5327**	1313	217	37	76	1832	509	476	39	40	.246	.314	.344	.658	85	-106	108	582
CHI	148	66	82	.446	34	538	609	65	4949	1215	214	36	25	1576	497	**427**	**114**	70	.246	.316	.318	.635	87	-75	98	520
WAS	151	62	89	.411	39.5	653	817	59	5295	1364	224	49	40	1806	581	536	98	**29**	.258	.333	.341	.674	98	9	99	641
PHI	154	55	99	.357	48	549	801	49	5285	1315	213	46	33	1719	440	490	44	45	.249	.309	.325	.635	86	-104	99	536
Total	**611**					**5211**			**41955**	**10785**	**1797**	**400**	**533**		**4318**	**4144**	**538**	**390**	**.257**	**.329**	**.357**	**.686**				

Runs
Williams, T. (Bos) 141
DiMaggio, J. (NY) 123
DiMaggio, D. (Bos) 110

Hits
Pesky, J. (Bos) 205
Spence, S. (Was) 203
2 players tied with 186

Doubles
Kolloway, D. (Chi) 40
Clift, H. (StL) 39
Heath, J. (Cle) 37

Triples
Spence, S. (Was) 15
DiMaggio, J. (NY) 13
Heath, J. (Cle) 13

Home Runs
Williams, T. (Bos) 36
Laabs, C. (StL) 27
Keller, C. (NY) 26

Total Bases
Williams, T. (Bos) 338
DiMaggio, J. (NY) 304
Keller, C. (NY) 279

Runs Batted In
Williams, T. (Bos) 137
DiMaggio, J. (NY) 114
Keller, C. (NY) 108

Bases On Balls
Williams, T. (Bos) 145
Keller, C. (NY) 114
2 players tied with 106

Stolen Bases
Case, G. (Was) 44
Vernon, M. (Was) 25
2 players tied with 22

Batting Average
Williams, T. (Bos) .356
Pesky, J. (Bos) .331
Spence, S. (Was) .323

On-Base Percentage
Williams, T. (Bos) .499
Keller, C. (NY) .417
Judnich, W. (StL) .413

Slugging Average
Williams, T. (Bos) .648
Keller, C. (NY) .513
Judnich, W. (StL) .499

Adjusted OPS
Williams, T. (Bos) 214
Keller, C. (NY) 164
Gordon, J. (NY) 156

Adjusted Batting Runs
Williams, T. (Bos) 90.0
Keller, C. (NY) 53.0
Gordon, J. (NY) 42.0

Runs Created/Game
Williams, T. (Bos) 14.30
Keller, C. (NY) 9.00
Judnich, W. (StL) 8.20

Fielding Runs
Rizzuto, P. (NY) 29.5
Pesky, J. (Bos) 20.4
Keltner, K. (Cle) 19.2

Win Shares – Batters
Williams, T. (Bos) 46
Keller, C. (NY) 34
DiMaggio, J. (NY) 32

TPW – Batters
Williams, T. (Bos) 9.0
Gordon, J. (NY) 6.1
Pesky, J. (Bos) 4.7

TEAM	CG	SH	SV	IP	H	H/G	ER	HR	BB	SO	OAV	RAT	ERA	ERA+	CERA	PR+	PF	FA	E	DP	FR	BW	PW	FW	TPW	DIF
NY	**88**	**18**	**17**	1375	**1259**	**8.2**	**445**	71	**431**	558	**.244**	**1.229**	**2.91**	118	**2.99**	24.4	94	**.976**	**142**	**190**	**57.0**	**13.2**	2.5	**5.8**	**21.5**	4.5
BOS	84	11	**17**	1358^{2}	1260	8.4	519	65	553	500	.247	1.334	3.44	108	3.32	11.5	102	.974	157	156	31.3	10.6	1.2	3.2	15.0	2.0
STL	68	12	13	1363	1387	9.2	544	63	505	488	.262	1.388	3.59	103	3.66	31.0	101	.972	167	143	-14.3	5.9	3.2	-1.5	7.6	-.6
CLE	61	12	11	**1402^{2}**	1353	8.7	559	61	560	448	.254	1.364	3.59	96	3.46	-46.2	94	.974	163	175	23.4	-1.7	-4.7	2.4	-4.0	2.0
DET	65	12	14	1399^{1}	1321	8.5	487	60	598	**671**	.248	1.371	3.13	126	3.43	**145.4**	108	.969	194	142	-18.3	-10.9	**14.9**	-1.9	2.1	-6.1
CHI	86	8	8	1314^{1}	1304	8.9	523	74	473	432	.258	1.352	3.58	100	3.58	-5.9	98	.970	173	144	8.5	-7.7	-.6	.9	-7.4	-.6
WAS	68	12	11	1346^{2}	1496	10.0	685	**50**	558	496	.279	1.525	4.58	**80**	4.21	-83.2	100	.962	222	133	-56.3	.9	-8.5	-5.8	-13.4	.4
PHI	67	5	9	1374^{2}	1404	9.2	679	89	639	546	.263	1.486	4.45	85	4.13	-72.4	103	.969	188	124	-29.7	-10.6	-7.4	-3.0	-21.1	-.9
Total	**587**	**90**	**100**	**10934^{1}**		**8.9**	**4441**					**1.381**	**3.66**													

Wins
Hughson, T. (Bos) 22
Bonham, T. (NY) 21
2 players tied with 17

Win Percentage
Bonham, T. (NY) .808
Borowy, H. (NY) .789
Hughson, T. (Bos) .786

Games
Haynes, J. (Chi) 40
Caster, G. (StL) 39
4 players tied with 38

Complete Games
Bonham, T. (NY) 22
Hughson, T. (Bos) 22
Lyons, T. (Chi) 20

Shutouts
Bonham, T. (NY) 6
7 players tied with 4

Saves
Murphy, J. (NY) 11
Brown, M. (Bos) 6
Haynes, J. (Chi) 6

Innings Pitched
Hughson, T. (Bos) 281
Bagby, J. (Cle) 270^{2}
Auker, E. (StL) 249

Fewest Hits/Game
Newhouser, H. (Det) 6.71
Niggeling, J. (StL) 7.55
Dobson, J. (Bos) 7.64

Fewest BB/Game
Bonham, T. (NY) .96
Lyons, T. (Chi) 1.30
Ruffing, R. (NY) 1.91

Strikeouts
Hughson, T. (Bos) 113
Newsom, B. (Was) 113
2 players tied with 110

Ratio
Bonham, T. (NY) .99
Lyons, T. (Chi) 1.07
Ruffing, R. (NY) 1.16

Earned Run Average
Lyons, T. (Chi) 2.10
Bonham, T. (NY) 2.27
Chandler, S. (NY) 2.38

Adjusted ERA
Lyons, T. (Chi) 172
Newhouser, H. (Det) 161
Bonham, T. (NY) 152

Component ERA
Bonham, T. (NY) 2.11
Lyons, T. (Chi) 2.50
Hughson, T. (Bos) 2.68

Opponents' Batting Avg.
Newhouser, H. (Det) .207
Niggeling, J. (StL) .226
Dobson, J. (Bos) .231

Adjusted Pitching Runs
Newhouser, H. (Det) 33
Benton, A. (Det) 29
Lyons, T. (Chi) 29

Win Shares – Pitchers
Hughson, T. (Bos) 28
Bonham, T. (NY) 21
Lyons, T. (Chi) 21

TPW – Pitchers
Lyons, T. (Chi) 3.4
Newhouser, H. (Det) 3.3
Hughson, T. (Bos) 3.1

1943 National League

TEAM	G	W	L	PCT	GB	R	OR	EW	AB	H	2B	3B	HR	TB	BB	SO	SB	CS	AVG	OBP	SLG	OPS	OPS+	BR/A	PF	RC
STL	157	105	49	.682	....	679	**475**	103	**5438**	**1515**	259	72	70	**2128**	428	438	40	....	**.279**	.333	**.391**	**.725**	**111**	61	104	**721**
CIN	155	87	67	.565	18	608	543	86	5329	1362	229	47	43	1814	445	476	49	....	.256	.315	.340	.655	97	-28	99	581
BRO	153	81	72	.529	23.5	**716**	675	81	5309	1444	**263**	35	39	1894	**580**	**422**	58	....	.272	**.346**	.357	.703	109	**71**	100	675
PIT	157	80	74	.519	25	669	605	85	5353	1401	240	**73**	42	1913	573	566	**64**	....	.262	.335	.357	.692	103	25	103	657
CHI	154	74	79	.484	30.5	632	599	81	5279	1380	207	56	52	1855	574	522	53	....	.261	.336	.351	.688	106	49	99	641
BOS	153	68	85	.444	36.5	465	612	56	5196	1213	202	36	39	1604	469	609	56	....	.233	.299	.309	.607	82	-115	98	491
PHI	157	64	90	.416	41	571	676	64	5297	1321	186	36	66	1777	499	556	29	....	.249	.316	.335	.652	98	-14	96	564
NY	156	55	98	.359	49.5	558	713	58	5290	1309	153	33	**81**	1771	480	470	35	....	.247	.313	.335	.648	92	-52	101	552
Total	**621**					**4898**			**42491**	**10945**	**1739**	**388**	**432**		**4048**	**4059**	**384**		**.258**	**.324**	**.347**	**.672**				

Runs
Vaughan, A. (Bro) 112
Musial, S. (StL) 108
Nicholson, B. (Chi) 95

Hits
Musial, S. (StL) 220
Witek, M. (NY) 195
Herman, B. (Bro) 193

Doubles
Musial, S. (StL) 48
DiMaggio, V. (Pit) 41
Herman, B. (Bro) 41

Triples
Musial, S. (StL) 20
Klein, L. (StL) 14
2 players tied with 12

Home Runs
Nicholson, B. (Chi) 29
Ott, M. (NY) 18
Northey, R. (Phi) 16

Total Bases
Musial, S. (StL) 347
Nicholson, B. (Chi) 323
Elliott, B. (Pit) 258

Runs Batted In
Nicholson, B. (Chi) 128
Elliott, B. (Pit) 101
Herman, B. (Bro) 100

Bases On Balls
Galan, A. (Bro) 103
Fletcher, E. (Pit) 95
Ott, M. (NY) 95

Stolen Bases
Vaughan, A. (Bro) 20
Lowrey, P. (Chi) 13
3 players tied with 12

Batting Average
Musial, S. (StL) .357
Herman, B. (Bro) .330
Elliott, B. (Pit) .315

On-Base Percentage
Musial, S. (StL) .425
Galan, A. (Bro) .412
Herman, B. (Bro) .398

Slugging Average
Musial, S. (StL) .562
Nicholson, B. (Chi) .531
Elliott, B. (Pit) .444

Adjusted OPS
Musial, S. (StL) 176
Nicholson, B. (Chi) 166
Tipton, E. (Cin) 138

Adjusted Batting Runs
Musial, S. (StL) 60.0
Nicholson, B. (Chi) 50.0
Galan, A. (Bro) 29.0

Runs Created/Game
Musial, S. (StL) 9.30
Nicholson, B. (Chi) 8.10
Galan, A. (Bro) 7.00

Fielding Runs
Marion, M. (StL) 22.9
Miller, E. (Cin) 20.5
Mueller, R. (Cin) 20.0

Win Shares – Batters
Musial, S. (StL) 39
Nicholson, B. (Chi) 31
Galan, A. (Bro) 29

TPW – Batters
Musial, S. (StL) 6.1
Nicholson, B. (Chi) 4.4
Klein, L. (StL) 3.8

TEAM	CG	SH	SV	IP	H	H/G	ER	HR	BB	SO	OAV	RAT	ERA	ERA+	CERA	PR+	PF	FA	E	DP	FR	BW	PW	FW	TPW	DIF
STL	**94**	**21**	15	**1427**	**1246**	**7.9**	**407**	**33**	477	**639**	**.237**	**1.207**	**2.57**	131	**2.67**	**90.9**	99	.976	151	183	35.2	6.5	**9.7**	3.8	**20.0**	8.0
CIN	78	18	17	1404	1299	8.3	488	38	579	498	.251	1.338	3.13	106	3.20	-9.3	98	**.980**	**125**	**193**	**37.4**	-3.0	-1.0	**4.0**	.0	10.0
BRO	50	13	**22**	1369^{2}	1326	8.7	590	59	637	588	.258	1.433	3.88	86	3.73	-60.0	99	.972	168	137	-20.5	**7.6**	-6.4	-2.2	-1.0	6.0
PIT	74	11	12	1404	1424	9.1	480	44	422	396	.263	1.315	3.08	113	3.28	66.6	103	.973	170	159	-1.5	2.6	7.1	-.2	9.6	-6.6
CHI	67	13	14	1386	1379	9.0	510	53	**394**	513	.258	1.279	3.31	101	3.17	40.6	99	.973	168	138	-26.1	5.2	4.3	-2.8	6.8	-8.8
BOS	87	13	4	1397^{2}	1361	8.8	504	66	441	409	.255	1.289	3.25	105	3.26	10.0	101	.972	176	139	15.6	-12.3	1.1	1.7	-9.5	1.5
PHI	66	10	14	1392^{2}	1436	9.3	586	59	451	431	.267	1.355	3.79	89	3.56	-48.3	100	.970	189	143	-16.1	-1.5	-5.2	-1.7	-8.3	-4.7
NY	35	6	19	1394^{2}	1474	9.5	632	80	626	588	.272	1.506	4.08	**84**	4.25	-81.4	102	.973	166	140	-18.4	-5.5	-8.7	-2.0	-16.2	-4.8
Total	**551**	**105**	**117**	**11175^{2}**		**8.8**	**4197**					**1.340**	**3.38**													

Wins
Cooper, M. (StL) 21
Riddle, E. (Cin) 21
Sewell, R. (Pit) 21

Win Percentage
Wyatt, W. (Bro) .737
Cooper, M. (StL) .724
Sewell, R. (Pit) .700

Games
Adams, A. (NY) 70
Webber, L. (Bro) 54
Head, E. (Bro) 47

Complete Games
Sewell, R. (Pit) 25
Cooper, M. (StL) 24
Tobin, J. (Bos) 24

Shutouts
Bithorn, H. (Chi) 7
Cooper, M. (StL) 6
4 players tied with 5

Saves
Webber, L. (Bro) 10
Adams, A. (NY) 9
Shoun, C. (Cin) 7

Innings Pitched
Javery, A. (Bos) 303
Vander Meer, J. (Cin) 289
Andrews, N. (Bos) 283^{2}

Fewest Hits/Game
Wyatt, W. (Bro) 6.92
Vander Meer, J. (Cin) 7.10
Cooper, M. (StL) 7.49

Fewest BB/Game
Rowe, S. (Phi) 1.31
Wyse, H. (Chi) 1.96
Derringer, P. (Chi) 2.02

Strikeouts
Vander Meer, J. (Cin) 174
Cooper, M. (StL) 141
Javery, A. (Bos) 134

Ratio
Wyatt, W. (Bro) 1.01
Cooper, M. (StL) 1.12
Rowe, S. (Phi) 1.13

Earned Run Average
Pollet, H. (StL) 1.75
Lanier, M. (StL) 1.90
Cooper, M. (StL) 2.30

Adjusted ERA
Lanier, M. (StL) 177
Cooper, M. (StL) 146
Sewell, R. (Pit) 137

Component ERA
Wyatt, W. (Bro) 1.81
Cooper, M. (StL) 2.27
Rowe, S. (Phi) 2.58

Opponents' Batting Avg.
Wyatt, W. (Bro) .207
Vander Meer, J. (Cin) .224
Cooper, M. (StL) .226

Adjusted Pitching Runs
Lanier, M. (StL) 29
Sewell, R. (Pit) 28
Cooper, M. (StL) 26

Win Shares – Pitchers
Cooper, M. (StL) 28
Andrews, N. (Bos) 25
Tobin, J. (Bos) 24

TPW – Pitchers
Sewell, R. (Pit) 3.6
Rowe, S. (Phi) 3.1
Lanier, M. (StL) 2.9

1943 American League

TEAM	G	W	L	PCT	GB	R	OR	EW	AB	H	2B	3B	HR	TB	BB	SO	SB	CS	AVG	OBP	SLG	OPS	OPS+	BR/A	PF	RC
NY	155	98	56	.636	....	**669**	**542**	93	5282	1350	218	**59**	**100**	**1986**	**624**	562	46	60	.256	**.337**	**.376**	**.713**	**114**	85	101	**683**
WAS	153	84	69	.549	13.5	666	595	85	5233	1328	245	50	47	1814	605	579	142	55	.254	.336	.347	.682	110	**86**	96	656
CLE	153	82	71	.536	15.5	600	577	79	5269	1344	**246**	45	55	1845	567	521	47	58	.255	.329	.350	.679	112	65	94	626
CHI	155	82	72	.532	16	573	594	74	5254	1297	193	46	33	1681	561	581	**173**	87	.247	.322	.320	.642	94	-24	100	570
DET	155	78	76	.506	20	632	560	86	5364	**1401**	200	47	77	1926	483	553	40	43	**.261**	.324	.359	.683	98	-17	108	620
STL	153	72	80	.474	25	596	604	75	5175	1269	229	36	78	1804	569	646	37	43	.245	.322	.349	.670	100	-2	102	603
BOS	155	68	84	.447	29	563	607	70	**5392**	1314	223	42	57	1792	486	591	86	61	.244	.308	.332	.641	92	-59	102	570
PHI	155	49	105	.318	49	497	717	50	5244	1219	174	44	26	1559	430	**465**	55	**42**	.232	.294	.297	.592	79	-136	99	466
Total	**617**					**4796**			**42213**	**10522**	**1728**	**369**	**473**		**4325**	**4498**	**626**	**449**	**.249**	**.322**	**.341**	**.663**				

Runs
Case, G. (Was) 102
Keller, C. (NY) 97
Wakefield, D. (Det) 91

Hits
Wakefield, D. (Det) 200
Appling, L. (Chi) 192
Cramer, D. (Det) 182

Doubles
Wakefield, D. (Det) 38
Case, G. (Was) 36
2 players tied with 35

Triples
Lindell, J. (NY) 12
Moses, W. (Chi) 12
2 players tied with 11

Home Runs
York, R. (Det) 34
Keller, C. (NY) 31
Stephens, V. (StL) 22

Total Bases
York, R. (Det) 301
Wakefield, D. (Det) 275
Keller, C. (NY) 269

Runs Batted In
York, R. (Det) 118
Etten, N. (NY) 107
Johnson, B. (NY) 94

Bases On Balls
Keller, C. (NY) 106
Gordon, J. (NY) 98
Cullenbine, R. (Cle) 96

Stolen Bases
Case, G. (Was) 61
Moses, W. (Chi) 56
Tucker, T. (Chi) 29

Batting Average
Appling, L. (Chi) .328
Wakefield, D. (Det) .316
Cramer, D. (Det) .300

On-Base Percentage
Appling, L. (Chi) .419
Cullenbine, R. (Cle) .407
Keller, C. (NY) .396

Slugging Average
York, R. (Det) .527
Keller, C. (NY) .525
Stephens, V. (StL) .482

Adjusted OPS
Keller, C. (NY) 167
Heath, J. (Cle) 157
York, R. (Det) 148

Adjusted Batting Runs
Keller, C. (NY) 46.0
Appling, L. (Chi) 39.0
York, R. (Det) 34.0

Runs Created/Game
Keller, C. (NY) 8.10
Appling, L. (Chi) 7.10
Heath, J. (Cle) 6.60

Fielding Runs
Gordon, J. (NY) 33.1
Boudreau, L. (Cle) 25.8
Clift, H. (StL,Was) 21.3

Win Shares – Batters
Appling, L. (Chi) 40
Keller, C. (NY) 36
Boudreau, L. (Cle) 32

TPW – Batters
Boudreau, L. (Cle) 7.0
Gordon, J. (NY) 6.6
Appling, L. (Chi) 6.2

TEAM	CG	SH	SV	IP	H	H/G	ER	HR	BB	SO	OAV	RAT	ERA	ERA+	CERA	PR+	PF	FA	E	DP	FR	BW	PW	FW	TPW	DIF
NY	**83**	14	13	1415[1]	1229	**7.8**	**461**	60	489	653	**.234**	**1.214**	**2.93**	110	**2.78**	22.4	98	.974	160	166	23.3	9.2	2.4	2.5	**14.2**	6.8
WAS	61	16	**21**	1388	1293	8.4	490	**48**	540	495	.246	1.321	3.18	101	3.18	4.8	97	.971	179	145	-2.0	**9.4**	.5	-.2	9.7	-1.7
CLE	64	14	20	1406[1]	1234	7.9	492	52	606	585	.239	1.308	3.15	99	3.11	-36.6	94	.975	157	**183**	**30.5**	7.0	-4.0	**3.3**	6.4	-.4
CHI	70	12	19	1400[1]	1352	8.7	498	54	501	476	.255	1.323	3.20	104	3.33	13.4	101	.973	166	167	7.9	-2.6	1.4	.9	-.3	5.3
DET	67	**18**	20	1411[2]	**1226**	**7.8**	470	51	549	**706**	.234	1.257	3.00	117	2.86	**85.7**	107	.971	177	130	-4.8	-1.9	**9.3**	-.5	6.9	-5.9
STL	64	10	14	1385	1397	9.1	525	74	**488**	572	.263	1.361	3.41	97	3.62	6.1	101	.975	**152**	127	-19.3	-.2	.7	-2.1	-1.6	-2.4
BOS	62	13	16	**1426**[1]	1369	8.6	547	61	615	513	.257	1.391	3.45	96	3.57	-29.0	100	**.976**	153	179	6.8	-6.4	-3.1	.7	-8.8	.8
PHI	73	5	13	1394	1421	9.2	627	73	536	503	.265	1.404	4.05	**84**	3.80	-64.4	103	.973	162	148	-36.7	-14.7	-7.0	-4.0	-25.6	-2.4
Total	**544**	**102**	**136**	**11227**		**8.4**	**4110**					**1.322**	**3.29**													

Wins
Chandler, S. (NY) 20
Trout, D. (Det) 20
Wynn, E. (Was) 18

Win Percentage
Chandler, S. (NY) .833
Smith, A. (Cle) .708
Haefner, M. (Was) .688

Games
Brown, M. (Bos) 49
Trout, D. (Det) 44
Wolff, R. (Phi) 41

Complete Games
Chandler, S. (NY) 20
Hughson, T. (Bos) 20
3 players tied with 18

Shutouts
Chandler, S. (NY) 5
Trout, D. (Det) 5
2 players tied with 4

Saves
Maltzberger, G. (Chi) 14
Brown, M. (Bos) 9
Heving, J. (Cle) 9

Innings Pitched
Bagby, J. (Cle) 273
Hughson, T. (Bos) 266
Wynn, E. (Was) 256[2]

Fewest Hits/Game
Reynolds, A. (Cle) 6.34
Niggeling, J. (Was,StL) 6.66
Haefner, M. (Was) 6.86

Fewest BB/Game
Leonard, D. (Was) 1.88
Chandler, S. (NY) 1.92
Bonham, T. (NY) 2.07

Strikeouts
Reynolds, A. (Cle) 151
Newhouser, H. (Det) 144
Chandler, S. (NY) 134

Ratio
Chandler, S. (NY) .99
Trucks, V. (Det) 1.10
Bonham, T. (NY) 1.10

Earned Run Average
Chandler, S. (NY) 1.64
Bonham, T. (NY) 2.27
Haefner, M. (Was) 2.29

Adjusted ERA
Chandler, S. (NY) 197
Bridges, T. (Det) 147
Trout, D. (Det) 142

Component ERA
Chandler, S. (NY) 1.82
Haefner, M. (Was) 2.20
Wensloff, B. (NY) 2.23

Opponents' Batting Avg.
Reynolds, A. (Cle) .202
Niggeling, J. (Was,StL) .204
Haefner, M. (Was) .208

Adjusted Pitching Runs
Chandler, S. (NY) 40
Trout, D. (Det) 29
Bridges, T. (Det) 25

Win Shares – Pitchers
Chandler, S. (NY) 29
Trout, D. (Det) 23
2 players tied with 20

TPW – Pitchers
Chandler, S. (NY) 5.0
Trout, D. (Det) 3.4
Bridges, T. (Det) 2.8

1944 National League

TEAM	G	W	L	PCT	GB	R	OR	EW	AB	H	2B	3B	HR	TB	BB	SO	SB	CS	AVG	OBP	SLG	OPS	OPS+	BR/A	PF	RC
STL	157	105	49	.682	....	**772**	**490**	110	**5475**	**1507**	**274**	59	**100**	**2199**	544	473	37	....	**.275**	**.344**	**.402**	**.745**	**114**	**97**	102	**775**
PIT	158	90	63	.588	14.5	744	662	85	5428	1441	248	**80**	70	2059	**573**	616	**87**	....	.265	.338	.379	.717	104	30	104	706
CIN	155	89	65	.578	16	573	537	82	5271	1340	229	31	51	1784	423	**391**	51	....	.254	.313	.338	.651	93	-52	96	558
CHI	157	75	79	.487	30	702	669	81	5462	1425	236	46	71	1966	520	521	53	....	.261	.328	.360	.687	100	2	99	658
NY	155	67	87	.435	38	682	773	67	5306	1398	191	47	93	1962	512	480	39	....	.263	.331	.370	.700	104	25	100	656
BOS	155	65	89	.422	40	593	674	67	5282	1299	250	39	79	1864	456	509	37	....	.246	.308	.353	.661	88	-86	104	586
BRO	155	63	91	.409	42	690	832	63	5393	1450	255	51	56	1975	486	451	45	....	.269	.331	.366	.697	104	28	98	663
PHI	154	61	92	.399	43.5	539	658	61	5301	1331	199	42	55	1779	470	500	32	....	.251	.316	.336	.651	92	-51	97	571
Total	**623**					**5295**			**42918**	**11191**	**1882**	**395**	**575**		**3984**	**3941**	**381**		**.261**	**.326**	**.363**	**.689**				

Runs
Nicholson, B. (Chi) 116
Musial, S. (StL) 112
Russell, J. (Pit) 109

Hits
Cavarretta, P. (Chi) 197
Musial, S. (StL) 197
Holmes, T. (Bos) 195

Doubles
Musial, S. (StL) 51
Galan, A. (Bro) 43
Holmes, T. (Bos) 42

Triples
Barrett, J. (Pit) 19
Elliott, B. (Pit) 16
Cavarretta, P. (Chi) 15

Home Runs
Nicholson, B. (Chi) 33
Ott, M. (NY) 26
Northey, R. (Phi) 22

Total Bases
Nicholson, B. (Chi) 317
Musial, S. (StL) 312
Holmes, T. (Bos) 288

Runs Batted In
Nicholson, B. (Chi) 122
Elliott, B. (Pit) 108
Northey, R. (Phi) 104

Bases On Balls
Galan, A. (Bro) 101
Nicholson, B. (Chi) 93
2 players tied with 90

Stolen Bases
Barrett, J. (Pit) 28
Lupien, T. (Phi) 18
Hughes, R. (Chi) 16

Batting Average
Walker, D. (Bro) .357
Musial, S. (StL) .347
Medwick, J. (NY) .337

On-Base Percentage
Musial, S. (StL) .440
Walker, D. (Bro) .434
Galan, A. (Bro) .426

Slugging Average
Musial, S. (StL) .549
Nicholson, B. (Chi) .545
Ott, M. (NY) .544

Adjusted OPS
Musial, S. (StL) 174
Walker, D. (Bro) 173
Ott, M. (NY) 171

Adjusted Batting Runs
Musial, S. (StL) 60.0
Walker, D. (Bro) 54.0
Galan, A. (Bro) 50.0

Runs Created/Game
Musial, S. (StL) 10.20
Walker, D. (Bro) 9.80
Ott, M. (NY) 9.40

Fielding Runs
Marion, M. (StL) 26.2
Williams, W. (Cin) 19.1
Miller, E. (Cin) 17.3

Win Shares – Batters
Musial, S. (StL) 38
Walker, D. (Bro) 33
Galan, A. (Bro) 32

TPW – Batters
Musial, S. (StL) 5.2
Walker, D. (Bro) 4.0
Nicholson, B. (Chi) 3.9

TEAM	CG	SH	SV	IP	H	H/G	ER	HR	BB	SO	OAV	RAT	ERA	ERA+	CERA	PR+	PF	FA	E	DP	FR	BW	PW	FW	TPW	DIF
STL	89	**26**	12	**1427**	**1228**	**7.7**	**423**	55	468	**637**	**.233**	**1.189**	**2.67**	132	**2.69**	**101.1**	98	**.982**	**112**	**162**	**33.5**	**10.0**	**10.4**	**3.4**	**23.8**	4.2
PIT	77	10	19	1414[1]	1466	9.3	540	65	435	452	.265	1.344	3.44	108	3.49	57.6	103	.970	191	122	-13.8	3.0	5.9	-1.4	7.5	6.5
CIN	**93**	17	12	1398[1]	1292	8.3	461	60	**390**	369	.245	1.203	2.97	117	2.85	47.3	97	.978	137	153	32.3	-5.4	4.9	3.3	2.8	9.2
CHI	70	11	13	1400[2]	1484	9.5	558	75	458	545	.272	1.386	3.59	98	3.73	11.0	98	.970	186	151	-19.5	.2	1.1	-2.0	-.6	-1.4
NY	47	4	**21**	1363[2]	1413	9.3	650	116	587	499	.265	1.467	4.29	85	4.25	-105.9	101	.971	179	128	10.8	2.6	-10.9	1.1	-7.2	-2.8
BOS	70	13	12	1388[1]	1430	9.3	566	80	527	454	.267	1.410	3.67	104	3.85	18.5	106	.971	182	160	4.4	-8.8	1.9	.4	-6.4	-5.6
BRO	50	4	13	1367[2]	1471	9.7	711	75	660	487	.275	1.558	4.68	**76**	4.47	-125.7	98	.966	197	112	-45.5	2.8	-12.9	-4.7	-14.7	.7
PHI	66	11	6	1395[1]	1407	9.1	564	**49**	459	496	.260	1.337	3.64	99	3.36	-1.5	100	.972	177	138	-2.4	-5.2	-.2	-.2	-5.6	-9.4
Total	**562**	**96**	**108**	**11155**[1]		**9.0**	**4473**					**1.360**	**3.61**													

Wins
Walters, B. (Cin) 23; Cooper, M. (StL) 22; 2 players tied with 21

Win Percentage
Wilks, T. (StL) .810; Brecheen, H. (StL) .762; Cooper, M. (StL) .759

Games
Adams, A. (NY) 65; Rescigno, X. (Pit) 48; Webber, L. (Bro) 48

Complete Games
Tobin, J. (Bos) 28; Walters, B. (Cin) 27; Voiselle, B. (NY) 25

Shutouts
Cooper, M. (StL) 7; Walters, B. (Cin) 6; 3 players tied with 5

Saves
Adams, A. (NY) 13; Rescigno, X. (Pit) 5; Schmidt, F. (StL) 5

Innings Pitched
Voiselle, B. (NY) 312²; Tobin, J. (Bos) 299¹; Sewell, R. (Pit) 286

Fewest Hits/Game
Walters, B. (Cin) 7.36; Wilks, T. (StL) 7.50; Lanier, M. (StL) 7.70

Fewest BB/Game
Raffensberger, K. (Phi) 1.57; Strincevich, N. (Pit) 1.75; Davis, C. (Bro) 1.81

Strikeouts
Voiselle, B. (NY) 161; Lanier, M. (StL) 141; Javery, A. (Bos) 137

Ratio
Wilks, T. (StL) 1.07; Heusser, E. (Cin) 1.07; Walters, B. (Cin) 1.12

Earned Run Average
Heusser, E. (Cin) 2.38; Walters, B. (Cin) 2.40; Cooper, M. (StL) 2.46

Adjusted ERA
Heusser, E. (Cin) 146; Walters, B. (Cin) 145; Cooper, M. (StL) 143

Component ERA
Heusser, E. (Cin) 2.30; Walters, B. (Cin) 2.33; Wilks, T. (StL) 2.34

Opponents' Batting Avg.
Walters, B. (Cin) .219; Wilks, T. (StL) .227; Heusser, E. (Cin) .231

Adjusted Pitching Runs
Walters, B. (Cin) 28; Ostermueller, F. (Pit,Bro) 27; Tobin, J. (Bos) 26

Win Shares – Pitchers
Walters, B. (Cin) 32; 3 players tied with 24

TPW – Pitchers
Walters, B. (Cin) 3.7; Tobin, J. (Bos) 3.3; Ostermueller, F. (Pit,Bro) 3.0

1944 American League

TEAM	G	W	L	PCT	GB	R	OR	EW	AB	H	2B	3B	HR	TB	BB	SO	SB	CS	AVG	OBP	SLG	OPS	OPS+	BR/A	PF	RC
STL	154	89	65	.578	....	684	587	89	5269	1328	223	45	72	1857	531	604	44	33	.252	.323	.352	.675	94	-39	106	629
DET	156	88	66	.571	1	658	581	87	5344	1405	220	44	60	1893	532	500	61	55	.263	.332	.354	.687	97	-19	106	642
NY	154	83	71	.539	6	674	617	84	5331	1410	216	74	96	2062	523	627	91	31	.264	.333	.387	.720	108	64	103	707
BOS	156	77	77	.500	12	739	676	84	5400	1456	277	56	69	2052	522	505	60	40	.270	.336	.380	.716	113	82	99	712
PHI	155	72	82	.468	17	525	594	68	5312	1364	169	47	36	1735	422	490	42	32	.257	.314	.327	.640	90	-67	99	547
CLE	155	72	82	.468	17	643	677	73	5481	1458	270	50	70	2038	512	593	48	42	.266	.331	.372	.703	111	70	96	684
CHI	154	71	83	.461	18	543	662	62	5292	1307	210	55	23	1696	439	448	66	47	.247	.307	.320	.628	86	-93	99	533
WAS	154	64	90	.416	25	592	664	68	5319	1386	186	42	33	1755	470	477	127	59	.261	.324	.330	.654	98	-7	95	594
Total	619					5058			42748	11114	1771	413	459		3951	4244	539	339	.260	.325	.353	.678				

Runs
Stirnweiss, S. (NY) 125; Johnson, B. (Bos) 106; Cullenbine, R. (Cle) 98

Hits
Stirnweiss, S. (NY) 205; Boudreau, L. (Cle) 191; Spence, S. (Was) 187

Doubles
Boudreau, L. (Cle) 45; Keltner, K. (Cle) 41; Johnson, B. (Bos) 40

Triples
Lindell, J. (NY) 16; Stirnweiss, S. (NY) 16; Gutteridge, D. (StL) 11

Home Runs
Etten, N. (NY) 22; Stephens, V. (StL) 20; 3 players tied with 18

Total Bases
Lindell, J. (NY) 297; Stirnweiss, S. (NY) 296; Spence, S. (Was) 288

Runs Batted In
Stephens, V. (StL) 109; Johnson, B. (Bos) 106; Lindell, J. (NY) 103

Bases On Balls
Etten, N. (NY) 97; Johnson, B. (Bos) 95; Cullenbine, R. (Cle) 87

Stolen Bases
Stirnweiss, S. (NY) 55; Case, G. (Was) 49; Myatt, G. (Was) 26

Batting Average
Boudreau, L. (Cle) .327; Doerr, B. (Bos) .325; Johnson, B. (Bos) .324

On-Base Percentage
Johnson, B. (Bos) .431; Boudreau, L. (Cle) .406; Doerr, B. (Bos) .399

Slugging Average
Doerr, B. (Bos) .528; Johnson, B. (Bos) .528; Lindell, J. (NY) .500

Adjusted OPS
Johnson, B. (Bos) 175; Doerr, B. (Bos) 166; Spence, S. (Was) 157

Adjusted Batting Runs
Johnson, B. (Bos) 53.0; Spence, S. (Was) 41.0; Doerr, B. (Bos) 40.0

Runs Created/Game
Johnson, B. (Bos) 8.80; Doerr, B. (Bos) 8.60; Spence, S. (Was) 7.60

Fielding Runs
Stirnweiss, S. (NY) 31.8; Stephens, V. (StL) 15.7; Tucker, T. (Chi) 13.3

Win Shares – Batters
Stirnweiss, S. (NY) 35; Stephens, V. (StL) 34; Spence, S. (Was) 33

TPW – Batters
Stirnweiss, S. (NY) 8.4; Boudreau, L. (Cle) 7.1; Spence, S. (Was) 5.2

TEAM	CG	SH	SV	IP	H	H/G	ER	HR	BB	SO	OAV	RAT	ERA	ERA+	CERA	PR+	PF	FA	E	DP	FR	BW	PW	FW	TPW	DIF
STL	71	16	17	1397¹	1392	9.0	492	58	469	581	.259	1.332	3.17	114	3.36	91.2	105	.972	171	142	-24.0	-4.1	9.6	-2.5	3.0	9.0
DET	87	20	8	1400	1373	8.8	481	39	452	568	.257	1.304	3.09	116	3.20	79.3	104	.970	190	184	-3.7	-2.0	8.3	-.4	5.9	5.1
NY	78	9	13	1390¹	1351	8.8	524	82	532	529	.257	1.354	3.39	103	3.53	-10.2	102	.974	156	170	25.9	6.7	-1.1	2.7	8.4	-2.4
BOS	58	7	17	1394¹	1404	9.1	592	66	592	524	.263	1.432	3.82	89	3.84	-69.3	99	.972	171	154	4.1	8.6	-7.3	.4	1.8	-1.8
PHI	72	10	14	1397¹	1345	8.7	506	58	390	534	.252	1.242	3.26	107	3.04	39.3	101	.971	176	127	-4.5	-7.1	4.1	-.5	-3.4	-1.6
CLE	48	7	18	1419¹	1428	9.0	575	40	621	524	.265	1.444	3.65	91	3.75	-74.4	96	.974	165	192	18.9	7.3	-7.8	2.0	1.5	-6.5
CHI	64	5	17	1390²	1411	9.1	553	68	420	481	.264	1.317	3.58	96	3.42	-22.4	100	.970	183	154	-1.0	-9.8	-2.4	-.1	-12.2	6.2
WAS	83	13	11	1381	1410	9.2	536	48	475	503	.264	1.365	3.49	93	3.52	-21.1	95	.964	218	156	-15.0	-.7	-2.2	-1.6	-4.5	-8.5
Total	561	87	115	11170¹		9.0	4259					1.349	3.43													

Wins
Newhouser, H. (Det) 29; Trout, D. (Det) 27; Potter, N. (StL) 19

Win Percentage
Hughson, T. (Bos) .783; Newhouser, H. (Det) .763; Potter, N. (StL) .731

Games
Heving, J. (Phi) 63; Berry, J. (Phi) 53; Trout, D. (Det) 49

Complete Games
Trout, D. (Det) 33; Newhouser, H. (Det) 25; 4 players tied with 19

Shutouts
Trout, D. (Det) 7; Newhouser, H. (Det) 6; Jakucki, S. (StL) 4

Saves
Berry, J. (Phi) 12; Caster, G. (StL) 12; Maltzberger, G. (Chi) 12

Innings Pitched
Trout, D. (Det) 352¹; Newhouser, H. (Det) 312¹; Newsom, B. (Phi) 265

Fewest Hits/Game
Gromek, S. (Cle) 7.07; Niggeling, J. (Was) 7.17; Newhouser, H. (Det) 7.61

Fewest BB/Game
Harris, M. (Cle) 1.34; Leonard, D. (Was) 1.45; Bonham, T. (NY) 1.73

Strikeouts
Newhouser, H. (Det) 187; Trout, D. (Det) 144; Newsom, B. (Phi) 142

Ratio
Hughson, T. (Bos) 1.05; Trout, D. (Det) 1.13; Gromek, S. (Cle) 1.13

Earned Run Average
Trout, D. (Det) 2.12; Newhouser, H. (Det) 2.22; Hughson, T. (Bos) 2.26

Adjusted ERA
Trout, D. (Det) 168; Newhouser, H. (Det) 161; Hughson, T. (Bos) 151

Component ERA
Hughson, T. (Bos) 2.04; Gromek, S. (Cle) 2.27; Newhouser, H. (Det) 2.42

Opponents' Batting Avg.
Gromek, S. (Cle) .219; Niggeling, J. (Was) .221; Hughson, T. (Bos) .225

Adjusted Pitching Runs
Trout, D. (Det) 58; Newhouser, H. (Det) 48; Kramer, J. (StL) 36

Win Shares – Pitchers
Trout, D. (Det) 42; Newhouser, H. (Det) 35; Kramer, J. (StL) 22

TPW – Pitchers
Trout, D. (Det) 7.3; Newhouser, H. (Det) 5.4; Kramer, J. (StL) 4.0

1945 National League

TEAM	G	W	L	PCT	GB	R	OR	EW	AB	H	2B	3B	HR	TB	BB	SO	SB	CS	AVG	OBP	SLG	OPS	OPS+	BR/A	PF	RC
CHI	155	98	56	.636	....	735	532	101	5298	1465	229	52	57	1969	554	462	69	....	.277	.349	.372	.720	109	70	98	714
STL	155	95	59	.617	3	756	582	97	5487	1498	256	44	64	2034	515	488	55	....	.273	.338	.371	.709	101	8	102	716
BRO	155	87	67	.565	11	795	724	84	5418	1468	257	71	57	2038	629	434	75	....	.271	.349	.376	.726	109	75	99	746
PIT	155	82	72	.532	16	753	686	84	5343	1425	259	56	72	2012	590	480	81	....	.267	.342	.377	.718	102	19	104	701
NY	154	78	74	.513	19	668	701	72	5350	1439	175	35	114	2026	501	457	38	....	.269	.336	.375	.715	104	22	102	692
BOS	154	67	85	.441	30	721	728	75	5441	1453	229	25	101	2035	520	510	82	....	.267	.334	.374	.708	103	17	100	692
CIN	154	61	93	.396	37	536	694	58	5283	1317	221	26	56	1758	392	532	71	....	.249	.304	.333	.637	85	-111	98	537
PHI	154	46	108	.299	52	548	865	44	5203	1278	197	56	56	1697	449	501	54	....	.246	.307	.326	.634	84	-107	97	527
Total	618					5512			42823	11343	1823	336	577		4150	3864	525		.265	.333	.364	.696				

Runs
Stanky, E. (Bro) 128; Rosen, G. (Bro) 126; Holmes, T. (Bos) 125

Hits
Holmes, T. (Bos) 224; Rosen, G. (Bro) 197; Hack, S. (Chi) 193

Doubles
Holmes, T. (Bos) 47; Walker, D. (Bro) 42; 2 players tied with 36

Triples
Olmo, L. (Bro) 13; Pafko, A. (Chi) 12; 2 players tied with 11

Home Runs
Holmes, T. (Bos) 28; Workman, C. (Bos) 25; Adams, B. (StL,Phi) 22

Total Bases
Holmes, T. (Bos) 367; Adams, B. (StL,Phi) 279; Rosen, G. (Bro) 279

Runs Batted In
Walker, D. (Bro) 124; Holmes, T. (Bos) 117; 2 players tied with 110

Bases On Balls
Stanky, E. (Bro) 148; Galan, A. (Bro) 114; Hack, S. (Chi) 99

Stolen Bases
Schoendienst, R. (StL) 26; Barrett, J. (Pit) 25; Clay, D. (Cin) 19

Batting Average
Cavarretta, P. (Chi) .355; Holmes, T. (Bos) .352; Rosen, G. (Bro) .325

On-Base Percentage
Cavarretta, P. (Chi) .449; Galan, A. (Bro) .423; Hack, S. (Chi) .420

Slugging Average
Holmes, T. (Bos) .577; Kurowski, W. (StL) .511; Cavarretta, P. (Chi) .500

Adjusted OPS
Holmes, T. (Bos) 175; Cavarretta, P. (Chi) 167; Ott, M. (NY) 150

Adjusted Batting Runs
Holmes, T. (Bos) 62.0; Cavarretta, P. (Chi) 49.0; Galan, A. (Bro) 39.0

Runs Created/Game
Holmes, T. (Bos) 9.90; Cavarretta, P. (Chi) 9.70; Ott, M. (NY) 8.30

Fielding Runs
Stanky, E. (Bro) 21.6; Gillenwater, C. (Bos) 19.4; Kerr, B. (NY) 18.8

Win Shares – Batters
Hack, S. (Chi) 34; Rosen, G. (Bro) 31; 2 players tied with 30

TPW – Batters
Holmes, T. (Bos) 5.2; Stanky, E. (Bro) 5.0; Hack, S. (Chi) 5.0

TEAM	CG	SH	SV	IP	H	H/G	ER	HR	BB	SO	OAV	RAT	ERA	ERA+	CERA	PR+	PF	FA	E	DP	FR	BW	PW	FW	TPW	DIF
CHI	**86**	15	14	1366^{1}	**1301**	**8.6**	**452**	**57**	**385**	541	**.249**	**1.234**	**2.98**	123	**2.98**	**81.5**	96	**.980**	**121**	124	20.9	7.0	**8.2**	2.1	**17.3**	3.7
STL	77	**18**	9	**1408^{2}**	1351	8.6	507	70	497	510	.253	1.312	3.24	115	3.34	45.2	98	.977	137	150	**33.3**	.8	4.5	**3.3**	8.6	9.4
BRO	61	7	18	1392^{1}	1357	8.8	572	74	586	**557**	.253	1.395	3.70	101	3.64	15.0	99	.962	230	144	-7.4	**7.5**	1.5	-.7	8.2	1.8
PIT	73	8	16	1387^{1}	1477	9.6	579	61	455	518	.272	1.393	3.76	105	3.75	41.3	104	.971	178	141	-13.4	1.9	4.1	-1.3	4.7	.3
NY	53	13	21	1374^{2}	1401	9.2	620	85	528	529	.263	1.403	4.06	96	3.82	-24.0	103	.973	166	112	0.8	2.2	-2.4	.1	-.1	2.1
BOS	57	7	13	1391^{2}	1474	9.5	624	99	557	404	.272	1.459	4.04	95	4.18	-34.6	101	.969	193	**160**	2.5	1.7	-3.5	.3	-1.6	-7.4
CIN	77	11	6	1365^{2}	1438	9.5	607	70	534	372	.271	1.444	4.00	94	3.97	-35.6	99	.976	146	138	-1.6	-11.1	-3.6	-.2	-14.9	-1.1
PHI	31	4	**26**	1352^{2}	1544	10.3	697	61	608	432	.285	1.591	4.64	**83**	4.62	-85.0	101	.962	234	150	-35.3	-10.7	-8.5	-3.5	-22.8	-8.2
Total	**515**	**83**	**123**	**11039^{1}**		**9.2**	**4658**					**1.403**	**3.80**													

Wins
Barrett, R. (StL,Bos) 23
Wyse, H. (Chi) 22
2 players tied with 18

Win Percentage
Brecheen, H. (StL) .... .789
Burkhart, K. (StL) .... .692
Wyse, H. (Chi) .... .688

Games
Karl, A. (Phi) 67
Adams, A. (NY) 65
Hutchings, J. (Bos) 57

Complete Games
Barrett, R. (StL,Bos) 24
Wyse, H. (Chi) 23
Passeau, C. (Chi) 19

Shutouts
Passeau, C. (Chi) 5
4 players tied with 4

Saves
Adams, A. (NY) 15
Karl, A. (Phi) 15
Rescigno, X. (Pit) 9

Innings Pitched
Barrett, R. (StL,Bos) .... 284^{2}
Wyse, H. (Chi) .... 278^{1}
Gregg, H. (Bro) .... 254^{1}

Fewest Hits/Game
Prim, R. (Chi) 7.73
Brecheen, H. (StL) 7.78
Gregg, H. (Bro) 7.82

Fewest BB/Game
Prim, R. (Chi) 1.25
Barrett, R. (StL,Bos) 1.71
Roe, P. (Pit) 1.76

Strikeouts
Roe, P. (Pit) 148
Gregg, H. (Bro) 139
Voiselle, B. (NY) 115

Ratio
Prim, R. (Chi) 1.00
Brecheen, H. (StL) 1.14
Passeau, C. (Chi) 1.16

Earned Run Average
Borowy, H. (Chi) 2.13
Prim, R. (Chi) 2.40
Passeau, C. (Chi) 2.46

Adjusted ERA
Prim, R. (Chi) 152
Brecheen, H. (StL) 149
Passeau, C. (Chi) 149

Component ERA
Prim, R. (Chi) 2.08
Passeau, C. (Chi) 2.46
Brecheen, H. (StL) 2.59

Opponents' Batting Avg.
Prim, R. (Chi) .... .228
Gregg, H. (Bro) .... .232
Brecheen, H. (StL) .... .238

Adjusted Pitching Runs
Roe, P. (Pit) 30
Passeau, C. (Chi) 27
Wyse, H. (Chi) 26

Win Shares – Pitchers
Barrett, R. (StL,Bos) 24
Wyse, H. (Chi) 24
Passeau, C. (Chi) 22

TPW – Pitchers
Passeau, C. (Chi) 2.8
Roe, P. (Pit) 2.7
Walters, B. (Cin) 2.6

1945 American League

TEAM	G	W	L	PCT	GB	R	OR	EW	AB	H	2B	3B	HR	TB	BB	SO	SB	CS	AVG	OBP	SLG	OPS	OPS+	BR/A	PF	RC
DET	155	88	65	.575	....	633	565	85	5257	1345	**227**	47	77	1897	517	533	60	54	.256	.324	.361	.684	98	-20	106	627
WAS	156	87	67	.565	1.5	622	562	85	5326	1375	197	**63**	27	1779	545	489	**110**	65	.258	.330	.334	.664	107	53	92	612
STL	154	81	70	.536	6	597	**548**	82	5227	1302	215	37	63	1780	500	555	25	**31**	.249	.316	.341	.657	91	-57	105	584
NY	152	81	71	.533	6.5	**676**	606	84	5176	1343	189	61	**93**	**1933**	**618**	567	64	43	.259	**.343**	**.373**	**.716**	108	**66**	105	**698**
CLE	147	73	72	.503	11	557	**548**	74	4898	1249	216	48	65	1756	505	578	19	**31**	.255	.326	.359	.685	**109**	48	96	588
CHI	150	71	78	.477	15	596	633	70	5077	1330	204	55	22	1710	470	467	78	54	**.262**	.326	.337	.663	100	3	97	571
BOS	157	71	83	.461	17.5	599	674	68	**5367**	**1393**	225	44	50	1856	541	534	72	50	.260	.330	.346	.676	99	0	102	634
PHI	153	52	98	.347	34.5	494	638	56	5296	1297	201	37	33	1671	449	**463**	25	45	.245	.306	.316	.622	86	-101	100	523
Total	**612**					**4774**			**41624**	**10634**	**1674**	**392**	**430**		**4145**	**4186**	**453**	**373**	**.255**	**.325**	**.346**	**.671**				

Runs
Stirnweiss, S. (NY) 107
Stephens, V. (StL) 90
Cullenbine, R. (Det,Cle) 83

Hits
Stirnweiss, S. (NY) 195
Moses, W. (Chi) 168
Stephens, V. (StL) 165

Doubles
Moses, W. (Chi) 35
Binks, G. (Was) 32
Stirnweiss, S. (NY) 32

Triples
Stirnweiss, S. (NY) 22
Moses, W. (Chi) 15
Kuhel, J. (Was) 13

Home Runs
Stephens, V. (StL) 24
3 players tied with 18

Total Bases
Stirnweiss, S. (NY) 301
Stephens, V. (StL) 270
Etten, N. (NY) 247

Runs Batted In
Etten, N. (NY) 111
Cullenbine, R. (Det,Cle) 93
Stephens, V. (StL) 89

Bases On Balls
Cullenbine, R. (Det,Cle) 113
Lake, E. (Bos) 106
Grimes, O. (NY) 97

Stolen Bases
Stirnweiss, S. (NY) 33
Case, G. (Was) 30
Myatt, G. (Was) 30

Batting Average
Stirnweiss, S. (NY) .... .309
Dickshot, J. (Chi) .... .302
Estalella, B. (Phi) .... .299

On-Base Percentage
Lake, E. (Bos) .... .412
Cullenbine, R. (Cle,Det) ..... .402
Estalella, B. (Phi) .... .399

Slugging Average
Stirnweiss, S. (NY) .... .476
Stephens, V. (StL) .... .473
Cullenbine, R. (Det,Cle) ..... .444

Adjusted OPS
Stirnweiss, S. (NY) 143
Estalella, B. (Phi) 142
Kuhel, J. (Was) 137

Adjusted Batting Runs
Stirnweiss, S. (NY) 35.0
Cullenbine, R. (Det,Cle) 32.0
Kuhel, J. (Was) 28.0

Runs Created/Game
Cullenbine, R. (Det,Cle) 7.00
Stirnweiss, S. (NY) 7.00
Lake, E. (Bos) 6.60

Fielding Runs
Stirnweiss, S. (NY) 36.1
Mayo, E. (Det) 14.7
Kell, G. (Phi) 14.1

Win Shares – Batters
Stirnweiss, S. (NY) 34
Cullenbine, R. (Det,Cle) 31
Moses, W. (Chi) 28

TPW – Batters
Stirnweiss, S. (NY) 8.5
Lake, E. (Bos) 5.1
Cullenbine, R. (Det,Cle) 3.8

TEAM	CG	SH	SV	IP	H	H/G	ER	HR	BB	SO	OAV	RAT	ERA	ERA+	CERA	PR+	PF	FA	E	DP	FR	BW	PW	FW	TPW	DIF
DET	78	**19**	**16**	1393^{2}	1305	8.4	463	48	538	**588**	.250	1.322	2.99	117	3.24	**74.5**	105	.975	158	173	6.7	-2.1	**8.0**	.7	6.6	5.4
WAS	82	**19**	11	**1412^{1}**	1307	**8.3**	**458**	42	**440**	550	**.242**	**1.237**	**2.92**	106	**2.84**	35.8	92	.970	183	124	-8.3	5.6	3.8	-.9	**8.6**	1.4
STL	**91**	10	8	1382^{2}	1307	8.5	482	59	506	570	.249	1.311	3.14	112	3.20	62.7	105	.976	143	123	-5.3	-6.1	6.7	-.6	.1	5.9
NY	78	9	14	1355	1277	8.5	519	66	485	474	.250	1.300	3.45	100	3.20	-30.2	103	.971	175	170	**31.0**	**7.0**	-3.2	**3.3**	7.1	-2.1
CLE	76	14	12	1302^{1}	**1269**	8.8	479	**39**	501	497	.257	1.359	3.31	98	3.39	1.8	96	**.977**	**126**	149	-11.7	5.1	.2	-1.3	4.1	-3.1
CHI	84	13	13	1330^{2}	1400	9.5	545	63	448	486	.270	1.389	3.69	90	3.76	-37.4	99	.970	180	139	-18.8	.3	-4.0	-2.0	-5.7	2.7
BOS	71	15	13	1390^{2}	1389	9.0	587	58	656	490	.264	1.471	3.80	**89**	3.92	-72.6	101	.973	169	**198**	11.1	.0	-7.8	1.2	-6.6	.6
PHI	65	11	8	1381	1380	9.0	555	55	571	531	.262	1.413	3.62	95	3.68	-24.1	102	.973	168	160	-5.6	-10.9	-2.6	-.6	-14.0	-9.0
Total	**625**	**110**	**95**	**10948^{1}**		**8.7**	**4088**					**1.350**	**3.36**													

Wins
Newhouser, H. (Det) 25
Ferriss, D. (Bos) 21
Wolff, R. (Was) 20

Win Percentage
Newhouser, H. (Det) .... .735
Leonard, D. (Was) .... .708
Gromek, S. (Cle) .... .679

Games
Berry, J. (Phi) 52
Pieretti, M. (Was) 44
Reynolds, A. (Cle) 44

Complete Games
Newhouser, H. (Det) 29
Ferriss, D. (Bos) 26
3 players tied with 21

Shutouts
Newhouser, H. (Det) 8
Benton, A. (Det) 5
Ferriss, D. (Bos) 5

Saves
Turner, J. (NY) 10
Berry, J. (Phi) 5
5 players tied with 4

Innings Pitched
Newhouser, H. (Det) .... 313^{1}
Ferriss, D. (Bos) .... 264^{2}
Newsom, B. (Phi) .... 257^{1}

Fewest Hits/Game
Newhouser, H. (Det) 6.86
Wolff, R. (Was) 7.20
Potter, N. (StL) 7.47

Fewest BB/Game
Bonham, T. (NY) 1.10
Leonard, D. (Was) 1.46
Wolff, R. (Was) 1.91

Strikeouts
Newhouser, H. (Det) 212
Potter, N. (StL) 129
Newsom, B. (Phi) 127

Ratio
Wolff, R. (Was) 1.01
Potter, N. (StL) 1.10
Newhouser, H. (Det) 1.11

Earned Run Average
Newhouser, H. (Det) 1.81
Benton, A. (Det) 2.02
Wolff, R. (Was) 2.12

Adjusted ERA
Newhouser, H. (Det) 194
Benton, A. (Det) 174
Wolff, R. (Was) 146

Component ERA
Wolff, R. (Was) 1.87
Newhouser, H. (Det) 2.07
Potter, N. (StL) 2.27

Opponents' Batting Avg.
Newhouser, H. (Det) .... .211
Wolff, R. (Was) .... .215
Potter, N. (StL) .... .226

Adjusted Pitching Runs
Newhouser, H. (Det) 58
Benton, A. (Det) 31
Potter, N. (StL) 31

Win Shares – Pitchers
Newhouser, H. (Det) 38
Potter, N. (StL) 27
3 players tied with 24

TPW – Pitchers
Newhouser, H. (Det) 6.6
Potter, N. (StL) 3.7
Leonard, D. (Was) 2.7

1946 National League

TEAM	G	W	L	PCT	GB	R	OR	EW	AB	H	2B	3B	HR	TB	BB	SO	SB	CS	AVG	OBP	SLG	OPS	OPS+	BR/A	PF	RC
STL	156	98	58	.628	....	**712**	**545**	98	**5372**	**1426**	**265**	56	81	**2046**	530	537	58	....	**.265**	.334	**.381**	**.715**	104	25	104	**700**
BRO	157	96	60	.615	2	701	570	94	5285	1376	233	**66**	55	1906	**691**	575	**100**	....	.260	**.348**	.361	.708	**106**	**56**	101	699
CHI	155	82	71	.536	14.5	626	581	82	5298	1344	223	50	56	1835	586	599	43	....	.254	.331	.346	.677	100	5	98	622
BOS	154	81	72	.529	15.5	630	592	81	5225	1377	238	48	44	1843	558	**468**	60	....	.264	.337	.353	.690	101	9	101	641
PHI	155	69	85	.448	28	560	705	60	5233	1351	209	40	80	1880	417	590	41	....	.258	.315	.359	.674	100	-15	97	598
CIN	156	67	87	.435	30	523	570	70	5291	1262	206	33	65	1729	493	604	82	....	.239	.307	.327	.634	89	-82	96	546
PIT	155	63	91	.409	34	552	668	62	5199	1300	202	52	60	1786	592	555	48	....	.250	.328	.344	.672	94	-32	102	602
NY	154	61	93	.396	36	612	685	68	5191	1326	176	37	**121**	1939	532	546	46	....	.255	.328	.374	.701	104	23	101	644
Total	**621**					**4916**			**42094**	**10762**	**1752**	**382**	**562**		**4399**	**4474**	**478**		**.256**	**.329**	**.355**	**.684**				

Runs
Musial, S. (StL)	124
Slaughter, E. (StL)	100
Stanky, E. (Bro)	98

Hits
Musial, S. (StL)	228
Walker, D. (Bro)	184
Slaughter, E. (StL)	183

Doubles
Musial, S. (StL)	50
Holmes, T. (Bos)	35
Kurowski, W. (StL)	32

Triples
Musial, S. (StL)	20
Cavarretta, P. (Chi)	10
Reese, P. (Bro)	10

Home Runs
Kiner, R. (Pit)	23
Mize, J. (NY)	22
Slaughter, E. (StL)	18

Total Bases
Musial, S. (StL)	366
Slaughter, E. (StL)	283
Ennis, D. (Phi)	262

Runs Batted In
Slaughter, E. (StL)	130
Walker, D. (Bro)	116
Musial, S. (StL)	103

Bases On Balls
Stanky, E. (Bro)	137
Fletcher, E. (Pit)	111
Cavarretta, P. (Chi)	88

Stolen Bases
Reiser, P. (Bro)	34
Haas, B. (Cin)	22
Hopp, J. (Bos)	21

Batting Average
Musial, S. (StL)	.365
Hopp, J. (Bos)	.333
Walker, D. (Bro)	.319

On-Base Percentage
Stanky, E. (Bro)	.436
Musial, S. (StL)	.434
Cavarretta, P. (Chi)	.401

Slugging Average
Musial, S. (StL)	.587
Ennis, D. (Phi)	.485
Slaughter, E. (StL)	.465

Adjusted OPS
Musial, S. (StL)	180
Ennis, D. (Phi)	144
Cavarretta, P. (Chi)	140

Adjusted Batting Runs
Musial, S. (StL)	65.0
Cavarretta, P. (Chi)	30.0
Walker, D. (Bro)	28.0

Runs Created/Game
Musial, S. (StL)	10.90
Walker, D. (Bro)	7.00
Kurowski, W. (StL)	7.00

Fielding Runs
Marion, M. (StL)	21.2
Adams, B. (Cin)	21.1
Zientara, B. (Cin)	13.5

Win Shares – Batters
Musial, S. (StL)	44
Slaughter, E. (StL)	29
Stanky, E. (Bro)	28

TPW – Batters
Musial, S. (StL)	5.7
Stanky, E. (Bro)	4.1
Reese, P. (Bro)	3.3

TEAM	CG	SH	SV	IP	H	H/G	ER	HR	BB	SO	OAV	RAT	ERA	ERA+	CERA	PR+	PF	FA	E	DP	FR	BW	PW	FW	TPW	DIF
STL	75	18	15	1397	1326	8.5	467	63	493	607	.253	1.302	3.01	115	3.29	48.7	101	.980	124	167	20.8	2.7	5.2	2.2	10.1	9.9
BRO	52	14	28	1418	1280	8.1	481	58	671	647	.243	1.376	3.05	111	3.36	40.0	99	.972	174	154	15.1	6.0	4.3	1.6	11.8	6.2
CHI	59	15	11	1393	1370	8.8	501	58	527	619	.256	1.362	3.24	103	3.46	36.9	97	.976	146	119	-24.6	.5	3.9	-2.6	1.8	4.2
BOS	74	10	12	1371	1291	8.5	510	76	478	566	.248	1.290	3.35	103	3.24	18.4	101	.972	169	129	-9.3	.9	2.0	-1.0	1.9	3.1
PHI	55	11	23	1369	1442	9.5	607	73	542	490	.273	1.449	3.99	86	4.08	-76.2	101	.975	148	144	-4.4	-1.6	-8.1	-.5	-10.2	2.2
CIN	69	17	11	1413¹	1334	8.5	484	70	467	506	.252	1.274	3.08	109	3.18	3.9	98	.975	155	192	38.5	-8.7	.4	4.1	-4.2	-5.8
PIT	61	10	6	1370	1406	9.2	566	50	561	458	.268	1.436	3.72	95	3.73	-10.0	103	.970	184	127	-19.0	-3.4	-1.1	-2.0	-6.5	-7.5
NY	47	8	13	1353¹	1313	8.7	589	114	660	581	.256	1.458	3.92	88	4.04	-54.2	101	.973	159	121	-16.7	2.5	-5.8	-1.8	-5.1	-10.9
Total	492	103	119	11084²		8.7	4205					1.368	3.41													

Wins
Pollet, H. (StL)	21
Sain, J. (Bos)	20
Higbe, K. (Bro)	17

Win Percentage
Dickson, M. (StL)	.714
Higbe, K. (Bro)	.680
Pollet, H. (StL)	.677

Games
Trinkle, K. (NY)	48
Behrman, H. (Bro)	47
Dickson, M. (StL)	47

Complete Games
Sain, J. (Bos)	24
Pollet, H. (StL)	22
Koslo, D. (NY)	17

Shutouts
Blackwell, E. (Cin)	5
Brecheen, H. (StL)	5
3 players tied with	4

Saves
Raffensberger, K. (Phi)	6
4 players tied with	5

Innings Pitched
Pollet, H. (StL)	266
Koslo, D. (NY)	265¹
Sain, J. (Bos)	265

Fewest Hits/Game
Kennedy, M. (NY)	7.38
Schmitz, J. (Chi)	7.38
Blackwell, E. (Cin)	7.41

Fewest BB/Game
Cooper, M. (Bos)	1.76
Raffensberger, K. (Phi)	1.79
Beggs, J. (Cin)	1.85

Strikeouts
Schmitz, J. (Chi)	135
Higbe, K. (Bro)	134
Sain, J. (Bos)	129

Ratio
Cooper, M. (Bos)	1.11
Beggs, J. (Cin)	1.13
Dickson, M. (StL)	1.17

Earned Run Average
Pollet, H. (StL)	2.10
Sain, J. (Bos)	2.21
Beggs, J. (Cin)	2.32

Adjusted ERA
Pollet, H. (StL)	165
Sain, J. (Bos)	156
Beggs, J. (Cin)	144

Component ERA
Sain, J. (Bos)	2.51
Blackwell, E. (Cin)	2.53
Schmitz, J. (Chi)	2.60

Opponents' Batting Avg.
Schmitz, J. (Chi)	.221
Kennedy, M. (NY)	.224
Blackwell, E. (Cin)	.226

Adjusted Pitching Runs
Sain, J. (Bos)	38
Pollet, H. (StL)	36
Schmitz, J. (Chi)	22

Win Shares – Pitchers
Pollet, H. (StL)	27
Sain, J. (Bos)	26
Brecheen, H. (StL)	20

TPW – Pitchers
Sain, J. (Bos)	4.6
Pollet, H. (StL)	3.8
Ostermueller, F. (Pit)	2.6

1946 American League

TEAM	G	W	L	PCT	GB	R	OR	EW	AB	H	2B	3B	HR	TB	BB	SO	SB	CS	AVG	OBP	SLG	OPS	OPS+	BR/A	PF	RC
BOS	156	104	50	.675	....	792	594	99	5318	1441	268	50	109	2136	687	661	45	36	.271	.356	.402	.758	113	100	106	790
DET	155	92	62	.597	12	704	567	93	5318	1373	212	41	108	1991	622	616	65	41	.258	.337	.374	.712	100	8	106	698
NY	154	87	67	.565	17	684	547	94	5139	1275	208	50	136	1991	627	706	48	35	.248	.334	.387	.721	107	51	101	695
WAS	155	76	78	.494	28	608	706	66	5337	1388	260	63	60	1954	511	641	51	50	.260	.327	.366	.694	107	37	94	653
CHI	155	74	80	.481	30	562	595	73	5312	1364	206	44	37	1769	501	600	78	64	.257	.323	.333	.656	94	-46	96	579
CLE	156	68	86	.442	36	537	638	64	5242	1285	233	56	79	1867	506	697	57	49	.245	.313	.356	.669	100	-11	93	596
STL	156	66	88	.429	38	621	710	67	5373	1350	220	46	84	1914	465	713	23	35	.251	.313	.356	.669	89	-85	105	601
PHI	155	49	105	.318	55	529	680	58	5200	1317	220	51	40	1759	482	594	39	30	.253	.318	.338	.656	90	-63	99	574
Total	621					5037			42239	10793	1827	401	653	4401		5228	406	340	.256	.328	.364	.692				

Runs
Williams, T. (Bos)	142
Pesky, J. (Bos)	115
Lake, E. (Det)	105

Hits
Pesky, J. (Bos)	208
Vernon, M. (Was)	207
Appling, L. (Chi)	180

Doubles
Vernon, M. (Was)	51
Spence, S. (Was)	50
Pesky, J. (Bos)	43

Triples
Edwards, H. (Cle)	16
Lewis, B. (Was)	13
3 players tied with	10

Home Runs
Greenberg, H. (Det)	44
Williams, T. (Bos)	38
Keller, C. (NY)	30

Total Bases
Williams, T. (Bos)	343
Greenberg, H. (Det)	316
Vernon, M. (Was)	298

Runs Batted In
Greenberg, H. (Det)	127
Williams, T. (Bos)	123
York, R. (Bos)	119

Bases On Balls
Williams, T. (Bos)	156
Keller, C. (NY)	113
Lake, E. (Det)	103

Stolen Bases
Case, G. (Cle)	28
Stirnweiss, S. (NY)	18
Lake, E. (Det)	15

Batting Average
Vernon, M. (Was)	.353
Williams, T. (Bos)	.342
Pesky, J. (Bos)	.335

On-Base Percentage
Williams, T. (Bos)	.497
Keller, C. (NY)	.405
Vernon, M. (Was)	.403

Slugging Average
Williams, T. (Bos)	.667
Greenberg, H. (Det)	.604
Keller, C. (NY)	.533

Adjusted OPS
Williams, T. (Bos)	211
Vernon, M. (Was)	163
Greenberg, H. (Det)	160

Adjusted Batting Runs
Williams, T. (Bos)	89.0
Vernon, M. (Was)	46.0
Keller, C. (NY)	45.0

Runs Created/Game
Williams, T. (Bos)	14.50
Keller, C. (NY)	8.60
Greenberg, H. (Det)	8.10

Fielding Runs
Doerr, B. (Bos)	26.8
Boudreau, L. (Cle)	23.4
Pesky, J. (Bos)	12.9

Win Shares – Batters
Williams, T. (Bos)	49
Pesky, J. (Bos)	34
Vernon, M. (Was)	33

TPW – Batters
Williams, T. (Bos)	8.4
Greenberg, H. (Det)	5.0
Doerr, B. (Bos)	4.8

TEAM	CG	SH	SV	IP	H	H/G	ER	HR	BB	SO	OAV	RAT	ERA	ERA+	CERA	PR+	PF	FA	E	DP	FR	BW	PW	FW	TPW	DIF
BOS	79	15	20	1396²	1359	8.8	524	89	501	667	.254	1.332	3.38	108	3.49	35.4	105	.977	139	163	8.4	10.4	3.7	.9	15.0	12.0
DET	94	18	15	1402	1277	8.2	502	97	497	896	.241	1.265	3.22	113	3.21	87.0	104	.974	155	138	-18.7	.8	9.1	-2.0	8.0	7.0
NY	68	17	17	1361	1232	8.2	473	66	552	653	.243	1.311	3.13	110	3.26	7.5	99	.975	150	174	40.5	5.3	.8	4.2	10.3	-.3
WAS	71	8	10	1396¹	1459	9.4	580	81	547	537	.269	1.437	3.74	89	4.01	-34.4	95	.966	211	162	-26.6	3.9	-3.6	-2.8	-2.5	1.5
CHI	62	9	16	1392¹	1348	8.7	479	80	508	550	.255	1.333	3.10	110	3.48	36.1	97	.972	175	170	12.8	-4.9	3.8	1.3	.3	-3.3
CLE	63	16	13	1388²	1282	8.3	558	84	649	789	.245	1.391	3.62	91	3.61	-44.4	94	.975	147	147	-3.8	-1.1	-4.6	-.4	-6.2	-2.8
STL	63	13	12	1382¹	1465	9.5	607	73	573	574	.272	1.474	3.95	94	4.08	-29.5	106	.974	159	157	-4.5	-8.9	-3.1	-.5	-12.5	1.5
PHI	61	10	5	1342²	1371	9.2	582	83	577	562	.264	1.451	3.90	91	4.00	-44.9	101	.971	167	141	-7.8	-6.6	-4.7	-.8	-12.1	-15.9
Total	561	106	108	11062		8.8	4305					1.374	3.50													

Wins
Feller, B. (Cle)	26
Newhouser, H. (Det)	26
Ferriss, D. (Bos)	25

Win Percentage
Ferriss, D. (Bos)	.806
Newhouser, H. (Det)	.743
Chandler, S. (NY)	.714

Games
Feller, B. (Cle)	48
Ferriss, D. (Bos)	40
Savage, B. (Phi)	40

Complete Games
Feller, B. (Cle)	36
Newhouser, H. (Det)	29
Ferriss, D. (Bos)	26

Shutouts
Feller, B. (Cle)	10
4 players tied with	6

Saves
Klinger, B. (Bos)	9
Caldwell, E. (Chi)	8
Murphy, J. (NY)	7

Innings Pitched
Feller, B. (Cle)	371¹
Newhouser, H. (Det)	292²
Hughson, T. (Bos)	278

Fewest Hits/Game
Newhouser, H. (Det)	6.61
Feller, B. (Cle)	6.71
Chandler, S. (NY)	6.99

Fewest BB/Game
Hughson, T. (Bos)	1.65
Lopat, E. (Chi)	1.87
Leonard, D. (Was)	2.00

Strikeouts
Feller, B. (Cle)	348
Newhouser, H. (Det)	275
Hughson, T. (Bos)	172

Ratio
Newhouser, H. (Det)	1.07
Hughson, T. (Bos)	1.09
Chandler, S. (NY)	1.13

Earned Run Average
Newhouser, H. (Det)	1.94
Chandler, S. (NY)	2.10
Feller, B. (Cle)	2.18

Adjusted ERA
Newhouser, H. (Det)	189
Chandler, S. (NY)	164
Trout, D. (Det)	156

Component ERA
Newhouser, H. (Det)	2.00
Chandler, S. (NY)	2.25
Feller, B. (Cle)	2.29

Opponents' Batting Avg.
Newhouser, H. (Det)	.201
Feller, B. (Cle)	.208
Chandler, S. (NY)	.218

Adjusted Pitching Runs
Newhouser, H. (Det)	60
Feller, B. (Cle)	47
Trout, D. (Det)	44

Win Shares – Pitchers
Newhouser, H. (Det)	33
Feller, B. (Cle)	32
Trout, D. (Det)	27

TPW – Pitchers
Newhouser, H. (Det)	6.2
Trout, D. (Det)	4.9
Feller, B. (Cle)	4.7

1947 National League

TEAM	G	W	L	PCT	GB	R	OR	EW	AB	H	2B	3B	HR	TB	BB	SO	SB	CS	AVG	OBP	SLG	OPS	OPS+	BR/A	PF	RC
BRO	155	94	60	.610	....	774	667	88	5249	1428	241	50	83	2018	732	561	88	....	.272	.364	.384	.749	102	38	104	781
STL	156	89	65	.578	5	780	634	93	5422	1462	235	65	115	2172	612	511	28	....	.270	.347	.401	.747	101	10	104	762
BOS	154	86	68	.558	8	701	626	86	5253	1444	265	42	85	2048	558	500	58	....	.275	.346	.390	.736	105	36	98	717
NY	155	81	73	.526	13	830	761	84	5343	1446	220	48	221	2425	494	568	29	....	.271	.335	.454	.789	115	89	101	809
CIN	154	73	81	.474	21	681	755	69	5299	1372	242	43	95	1985	539	530	46	....	.259	.330	.375	.704	94	-44	99	672
CHI	155	69	85	.448	25	569	722	59	5305	1373	231	48	71	1913	471	578	22	....	.259	.321	.361	.682	91	-69	96	620
PIT	156	62	92	.403	32	745	817	70	5307	1385	216	44	156	2157	607	687	30	....	.261	.340	.406	.746	102	12	103	738
PHI	155	62	92	.403	32	589	687	65	5256	1354	210	52	60	1848	464	594	60	....	.258	.321	.352	.673	88	-87	96	597
Total	620					5669			42434	11264	1860	392	886		4477	4529	361		.265	.338	.390	.729				

Runs: Mize, J. (NY) 137; Robinson, J. (Bro) 125; Kiner, R. (Pit) 118
Hits: Holmes, T. (Bos) 191; Walker, H. (Phi,StL) 186; 2 players tied with 183
Doubles: Miller, E. (Cin) 38; Elliott, B. (Bos) 35; 2 players tied with 33
Triples: Walker, H. (Phi,StL) 16; Musial, S. (StL) 13; Slaughter, E. (StL) 13
Home Runs: Kiner, R. (Pit) 51; Mize, J. (NY) 51; Marshall, W. (NY) 36
Total Bases: Kiner, R. (Pit) 361; Mize, J. (NY) 360; Marshall, W. (NY) 310

Runs Batted In: Mize, J. (NY) 138; Kiner, R. (Pit) 127; Cooper, W. (NY) 122
Bases On Balls: Greenberg, H. (Pit) 104; Reese, P. (Bro) 104; Stanky, E. (Bro) 103
Stolen Bases: Robinson, J. (Bro) 29; Reiser, P. (Bro) 14; 2 players tied with 13
Batting Average: Walker, H. (Phi,StL) .363; Elliott, B. (Bos) .317; Galan, A. (Cin) .314
On-Base Percentage: Galan, A. (Cin) .449; Walker, H. (Phi,StL) .436; Kurowski, W. (StL) .420
Slugging Average: Kiner, R. (Pit) .639; Mize, J. (NY) .614; Cooper, W. (NY) .586

Adjusted OPS: Kiner, R. (Pit) 172; Mize, J. (NY) 160; Walker, H. (Phi,StL) 150
Adjusted Batting Runs: Kiner, R. (Pit) 58.0; Mize, J. (NY) 48.0; Elliott, B. (Bos) 40.0
Runs Created/Game: Kiner, R. (Pit) 10.40; Mize, J. (NY) 9.30; Walker, H. (Phi,StL) 8.60
Fielding Runs: Gustine, F. (Pit) 21.7; Verban, E. (Phi) 20.1; Stanky, E. (Bro) 19.2
Win Shares – Batters: Mize, J. (NY) 32; Kiner, R. (Pit) 30; Elliott, B. (Bos) 29
TPW – Batters: Kiner, R. (Pit) 4.7; Mize, J. (NY) 4.4; Elliott, B. (Bos) 4.1

TEAM	CG	SH	SV	IP	H	H/G	ER	HR	BB	SO	OAV	RAT	ERA	ERA+	CERA	PR+	PF	FA	E	DP	FR	BW	PW	FW	TPW	DIF
BRO	47	14	34	1375	1299	8.5	584	104	626	592	.251	1.400	3.82	108	3.84	22.0	102	.978	129	169	28.7	3.8	2.2	2.8	8.8	8.2
STL	65	12	20	1397²	1417	9.1	548	106	495	642	.266	1.368	3.53	117	3.80	93.4	102	.979	128	169	0.8	1.0	9.2	.1	10.2	1.8
BOS	74	14	13	1362²	1342	8.9	548	93	453	494	.255	1.317	3.62	108	3.54	55.8	96	.974	153	124	-14.0	3.6	5.5	-1.4	7.7	1.3
NY	58	6	14	1363²	1428	9.4	672	122	590	553	.272	1.480	4.44	92	4.34	-62.0	100	.974	155	136	6.2	8.8	-6.1	.6	3.3	.7
CIN	54	13	13	1365¹	1442	9.5	669	102	589	633	.274	1.488	4.41	93	4.37	-29.0	101	.977	138	134	-17.3	-4.3	-2.8	-1.7	-8.8	4.8
CHI	46	8	15	1367	1449	9.5	614	106	618	571	.274	1.512	4.04	98	4.44	-18.8	97	.975	150	159	-4.2	-6.8	-1.9	-.4	-9.0	1.0
PIT	44	9	13	1374	1488	9.8	714	155	592	530	.275	1.514	4.68	90	4.79	-60.5	104	.975	149	131	-9.5	1.1	-6.0	-.9	-5.8	-9.2
PHI	70	8	14	1362	1399	9.2	599	98	513	514	.276	1.404	3.96	101	4.04	-2.4	99	.974	152	140	10.0	-8.5	-.2	1.0	-7.8	-7.2
Total	458	84	136	10967¹		9.2	4948					1.435	4.06													

Wins: Blackwell, E. (Cin) 22; 4 players tied with 21
Win Percentage: Jansen, L. (NY) .808; Munger, R. (StL) .762; Blackwell, E. (Cin) .733
Games: Trinkle, K. (NY) 62; Behrman, H. (Bro,Pit,Bro) 50; Higbe, K. (Pit,Bro) 50
Complete Games: Blackwell, E. (Cin) 23; Sain, J. (Bos) 22; Spahn, W. (Bos) 22
Shutouts: Spahn, W. (Bos) 7; Blackwell, E. (Cin) 6; Munger, R. (StL) 6
Saves: Casey, H. (Bro) 18; Gumbert, H. (Cin) 10; Trinkle, K. (NY) 10

Innings Pitched: Spahn, W. (Bos) 289²; Branca, R. (Bro) 280; Blackwell, E. (Cin) 273
Fewest Hits/Game: Taylor, H. (Bro) 7.22; Blackwell, E. (Cin) 7.48; Spahn, W. (Bos) 7.61
Fewest BB/Game: Jansen, L. (NY) 2.07; Rowe, S. (Phi) 2.07; Leonard, D. (Phi) 2.18
Strikeouts: Blackwell, E. (Cin) 193; Branca, R. (Bro) 148; Sain, J. (Bos) 132
Ratio: Spahn, W. (Bos) 1.14; Blackwell, E. (Cin) 1.18; Leonard, D. (Phi) 1.20
Earned Run Average: Spahn, W. (Bos) 2.33; Blackwell, E. (Cin) 2.47; Branca, R. (Bro) 2.67

Adjusted ERA: Spahn, W. (Bos) 167; Blackwell, E. (Cin) 166; Branca, R. (Bro) 155
Component ERA: Spahn, W. (Bos) 2.50; Blackwell, E. (Cin) 2.66; Barrett, R. (Bos) 3.01
Opponents' Batting Avg.: Taylor, H. (Bro) .225; Spahn, W. (Bos) .226; Blackwell, E. (Cin) .234
Adjusted Pitching Runs: Spahn, W. (Bos) 53; Blackwell, E. (Cin) 53; Branca, R. (Bro) 40
Win Shares – Pitchers: Spahn, W. (Bos) 32; Blackwell, E. (Cin) 28; Branca, R. (Bro) 26
TPW – Pitchers: Spahn, W. (Bos) 5.3; Blackwell, E. (Cin) 4.7; Branca, R. (Bro) 3.6

1947 American League

TEAM	G	W	L	PCT	GB	R	OR	EW	AB	H	2B	3B	HR	TB	BB	SO	SB	CS	AVG	OBP	SLG	OPS	OPS+	BR/A	PF	RC
NY	155	97	57	.630	....	794	568	102	5308	1439	230	72	115	2158	610	581	27	23	.271	.349	.407	.756	118	121	99	780
DET	158	85	69	.552	12	714	642	85	5276	1363	234	42	103	1990	762	565	52	60	.258	.353	.377	.731	106	52	103	735
BOS	157	83	71	.539	14	720	669	83	5322	1412	206	54	103	2035	666	590	41	35	.265	.349	.382	.731	102	23	107	734
CLE	157	80	74	.519	17	687	588	89	5367	1392	234	51	112	2064	502	609	29	25	.259	.324	.385	.709	106	28	97	687
PHI	156	78	76	.506	19	633	614	79	5198	1311	218	52	61	1816	605	563	37	33	.252	.333	.349	.682	94	-35	102	635
CHI	155	70	84	.455	27	553	661	68	5274	1350	211	41	53	1802	492	527	91	56	.256	.321	.342	.663	94	-46	96	584
WAS	154	64	90	.416	33	496	675	54	5112	1234	186	48	42	1642	525	534	53	51	.241	.313	.321	.634	84	-109	97	523
STL	154	59	95	.383	38	564	744	56	5145	1238	189	52	90	1801	583	664	69	49	.241	.320	.350	.670	90	-65	102	596
Total	623					5161			42002	10739	1708	412	679		4745	4633	399	333	.256	.333	.364	.698				

Runs: Williams, T. (Bos) 125; Henrich, T. (NY) 109; Pesky, J. (Bos) 106
Hits: Pesky, J. (Bos) 207; Kell, G. (Det) 188; Williams, T. (Bos) 181
Doubles: Boudreau, L. (Cle) 45; Williams, T. (Bos) 40; Henrich, T. (NY) 35
Triples: Henrich, T. (NY) 13; Vernon, M. (Was) 12; Philley, D. (Chi) 11
Home Runs: Williams, T. (Bos) 32; Gordon, J. (Cle) 29; Heath, J. (StL) 27
Total Bases: Williams, T. (Bos) 335; DiMaggio, J. (NY) 279; Gordon, J. (Cle) 279

Runs Batted In: Williams, T. (Bos) 114; Henrich, T. (NY) 98; DiMaggio, J. (NY) 97
Bases On Balls: Williams, T. (Bos) 162; Cullenbine, R. (Det) 137; Lake, E. (Det) 120
Stolen Bases: Dillinger, B. (StL) 34; Philley, D. (Chi) 21; 2 players tied with 12
Batting Average: Williams, T. (Bos) .343; McCosky, B. (Phi) .328; Pesky, J. (Bos) .324
On-Base Percentage: Williams, T. (Bos) .499; Fain, F. (Phi) .414; Cullenbine, R. (Det) .401
Slugging Average: Williams, T. (Bos) .634; DiMaggio, J. (NY) .522; Gordon, J. (Cle) .496

Adjusted OPS: Williams, T. (Bos) 199; DiMaggio, J. (NY) 154; Henrich, T. (NY) 138
Adjusted Batting Runs: Williams, T. (Bos) 83.0; DiMaggio, J. (NY) 39.0; Henrich, T. (NY) 28.0
Runs Created/Game: Williams, T. (Bos) 14.00; DiMaggio, J. (NY) 8.00; Henrich, T. (NY) 6.90
Fielding Runs: Rizzuto, P. (NY) 32.9; Doerr, B. (Bos) 20.2; Boudreau, L. (Cle) 19.5
Win Shares – Batters: Williams, T. (Bos) 44; DiMaggio, J. (NY) 30; Boudreau, L. (Cle) 28
TPW – Batters: Williams, T. (Bos) 7.3; Boudreau, L. (Cle) 5.4; Rizzuto, P. (NY) 4.5

TEAM	CG	SH	SV	IP	H	H/G	ER	HR	BB	SO	OAV	RAT	ERA	ERA+	CERA	PR+	PF	FA	E	DP	FR	BW	PW	FW	TPW	DIF
NY	73	14	21	1374¹	1221	8.0	518	95	628	691	.238	1.345	3.39	104	3.47	13.8	95	.981	109	151	8.0	12.6	1.4	.8	14.8	5.2
DET	77	15	18	1398²	1382	8.9	555	79	531	648	.258	1.368	3.57	106	3.58	63.2	102	.975	155	142	-32.1	5.4	6.5	-3.3	8.6	-.6
BOS	64	13	19	1391¹	1383	9.0	589	84	575	586	.261	1.407	3.81	102	3.82	9.1	105	.977	137	172	2.4	2.4	1.0	.2	3.7	2.3
CLE	55	13	29	1402¹	1244	8.0	536	94	628	590	.240	1.335	3.44	101	3.44	-16.9	94	.983	104	178	24.0	2.9	-4.3	2.5	3.6	-.6
PHI	70	12	15	1391¹	1291	8.4	542	85	597	493	.247	1.357	3.51	109	3.51	10.4	103	.976	143	161	36.7	-3.6	1.1	3.8	1.3	-.3
CHI	47	11	27	1391	1384	9.0	563	76	603	522	.261	1.428	3.64	100	3.82	4.9	99	.975	155	180	-1.8	-4.8	.5	-.2	-4.5	-2.5
WAS	67	15	12	1362	1408	9.3	601	63	579	551	.267	1.459	3.97	94	3.94	-15.2	101	.976	143	151	-21.8	-11.2	-1.6	-2.3	-15.1	2.1
STL	50	7	13	1365	1426	9.4	657	103	604	552	.272	1.487	4.33	90	4.28	-51.5	105	.977	134	169	-15.8	-6.8	-5.3	-1.6	-13.8	-4.2
Total	503	100	154	11076		8.7	4561					1.398	3.71													

Wins
Feller, B. (Cle) 20
Marchildon, P. (Phi) 19
Reynolds, A. (NY) 19

Win Percentage
Shea, S. (NY) .737
Reynolds, A. (NY) .704
Haynes, J. (Chi) .700

Games
Klieman, E. (Cle) 58
Page, J. (NY) 56
Johnson, E. (Bos) 45

Complete Games
Newhouser, H. (Det) 24
Lopat, E. (Chi) 22
Wynn, E. (Was) 22

Shutouts
Feller, B. (Cle) 5
3 players tied with 4

Saves
Klieman, E. (Cle) 17
Page, J. (NY) 17
Christopher, R. (Phi) 12

Innings Pitched
Feller, B. (Cle) 299
Newhouser, H. (Det) 285
Marchildon, P. (Phi) 276^2

Fewest Hits/Game
Shea, S. (NY) 6.40
Feller, B. (Cle) 6.92
Marchildon, P. (Phi) 7.42

Fewest BB/Game
Galehouse, D. (Bos,StL) 2.48
Hutchinson, F. (Det) 2.50
Lopat, E. (Chi) 2.60

Strikeouts
Feller, B. (Cle) 196
Newhouser, H. (Det) 176
Masterson, W. (Was) 135

Ratio
Feller, B. (Cle) 1.19
Dobson, J. (Bos) 1.21
Shea, S. (NY) 1.21

Earned Run Average
Haynes, J. (Chi) 2.42
Feller, B. (Cle) 2.68
Fowler, D. (Phi) 2.81

Adjusted ERA
Haynes, J. (Chi) 151
Fowler, D. (Phi) 136
Dobson, J. (Bos) 132

Component ERA
Shea, S. (NY) 2.62
Feller, B. (Cle) 2.66
Masterson, W. (Was) 2.83

Opponents' Batting Avg.
Shea, S. (NY) .200
Feller, B. (Cle) .215
Marchildon, P. (Phi) .224

Adjusted Pitching Runs
Newhouser, H. (Det) 35
Haynes, J. (Chi) 25
Lopat, E. (Chi) 24

Win Shares – Pitchers
Newhouser, H. (Det) 24
Feller, B. (Cle) 23
Hutchinson, F. (Det) 22

TPW – Pitchers
Newhouser, H. (Det) 3.9
Hutchinson, F. (Det) 3.5
Haynes, J. (Chi) 2.8

1948 National League

TEAM	G	W	L	PCT	GB	R	OR	EW	AB	H	2B	3B	HR	TB	BB	SO	SB	CS	AVG	OBP	SLG	OPS	OPS+	BR/A	PF	RC
BOS	154	91	62	.595	....	739	**584**	94	5297	**1458**	**272**	49	95	2113	**671**	536	43	....	**.275**	**.359**	.399	**.757**	**114**	**111**	98	**784**
STL	155	85	69	.552	6.5	742	646	88	5302	1396	238	**58**	105	2065	594	**521**	24	....	.263	.340	.389	.729	98	-7	106	713
BRO	155	84	70	.545	7.5	744	669	85	5328	1393	256	54	91	2030	601	684	**114**	....	.261	.338	.381	.719	98	-10	103	709
PIT	156	83	71	.539	8.5	706	701	78	5286	1388	191	54	108	2011	580	578	68	....	.263	.338	.380	.718	99	-3	102	698
NY	155	78	76	.506	13.5	**780**	703	85	5277	1352	210	49	**164**	**2152**	599	648	51	....	.256	.334	**.408**	.742	106	42	101	731
PHI	155	66	88	.429	25.5	591	728	61	5287	1367	227	39	91	1945	440	598	68	....	.259	.318	.368	.686	93	-54	98	625
CIN	153	64	89	.418	27	588	751	58	5127	1266	221	37	104	1873	478	586	42	....	.247	.313	.365	.678	93	-56	97	587
CHI	155	64	90	.416	27.5	597	705	64	**5352**	1402	225	44	87	1976	443	578	39	....	.262	.322	.369	.691	97	-28	96	641
Total	**619**					**5487**			**42256**	**11022**	**1840**	**384**	**845**		**4406**	**4729**	**449**		**.261**	**.333**	**.383**	**.716**				

Runs
Musial, S. (StL) 135
Lockman, W. (NY) 117
Mize, J. (NY) 110

Hits
Musial, S. (StL) 230
Holmes, T. (Bos) 190
Rojek, S. (Pit) 186

Doubles
Musial, S. (StL) 46
Ennis, D. (Phi) 40
Dark, A. (Bos) 39

Triples
Musial, S. (StL) 18
Hopp, J. (Pit) 12
Slaughter, E. (StL) 11

Home Runs
Kiner, R. (Pit) 40
Mize, J. (NY) 40
Musial, S. (StL) 39

Total Bases
Musial, S. (StL) 429
Mize, J. (NY) 316
Ennis, D. (Phi) 309

Runs Batted In
Musial, S. (StL) 131
Mize, J. (NY) 125
Kiner, R. (Pit) 123

Bases On Balls
Elliott, B. (Bos) 131
Kiner, R. (Pit) 112
Mize, J. (NY) 94

Stolen Bases
Ashburn, R. (Phi) 32
Reese, P. (Bro) 25
Rojek, S. (Pit) 24

Batting Average
Musial, S. (StL) .376
Ashburn, R. (Phi) .333
Holmes, T. (Bos) .325

On-Base Percentage
Musial, S. (StL) .450
Elliott, B. (Bos) .423
Ashburn, R. (Phi) .410

Slugging Average
Musial, S. (StL) .702
Mize, J. (NY) .564
Gordon, S. (NY) .537

Adjusted OPS
Musial, S. (StL) 196
Mize, J. (NY) 156
Gordon, S. (NY) 148

Adjusted Batting Runs
Musial, S. (StL) 82.0
Mize, J. (NY) 45.0
Elliott, B. (Bos) 41.0

Runs Created/Game
Musial, S. (StL) 12.90
Mize, J. (NY) 8.80
Elliott, B. (Bos) 7.80

Fielding Runs
Reese, P. (Bro) 19.2
Robinson, J. (Bro) 12.4
Gustine, F. (Pit) 10.1

Win Shares – Batters
Musial, S. (StL) 46
Mize, J. (NY) 30
Kiner, R. (Pit) 30

TPW – Batters
Musial, S. (StL) 7.3
Mize, J. (NY) 4.3
Elliott, B. (Bos) 3.7

TEAM	CG	SH	SV	IP	H	H/G	ER	HR	BB	SO	OAV	RAT	ERA	ERA+	CERA	PR+	PF	FA	E	DP	FR	BW	PW	FW	TPW	DIF
BOS	**70**	10	17	1389^1	1354	8.8	**520**	93	**430**	579	.254	**1.284**	**3.37**	114	**3.35**	**61.4**	97	.976	143	132	9.3	**11.1**	**6.1**	.9	**18.2**	-3.2
STL	60	13	18	1368	1392	9.2	594	103	476	625	.264	1.365	3.91	105	3.80	33.3	103	**.980**	**119**	138	-6.0	-.7	3.3	-.6	2.0	6.0
BRO	52	9	**22**	**1392^2**	**1328**	**8.6**	580	119	633	**670**	**.253**	1.408	3.75	106	3.94	6.1	101	.973	161	151	**30.8**	-1.0	.6	**3.1**	2.7	4.3
PIT	65	5	19	1371^2	1373	9.0	632	120	564	543	.260	1.412	4.15	98	4.02	-19.4	103	.977	137	150	7.5	-.3	-1.9	.7	-1.5	7.5
NY	54	**15**	21	1373	1425	9.3	600	122	556	527	.269	1.443	3.93	100	4.23	6.7	100	.974	156	134	-5.3	4.2	.7	-.5	4.4	-3.4
PHI	61	6	15	1362^1	1385	9.2	617	95	556	550	.269	1.425	4.08	97	4.05	-16.3	100	.964	210	126	-4.2	-5.4	-1.6	-.4	-7.4	-3.6
CIN	40	8	20	1343^1	1410	9.4	667	104	572	599	.270	1.475	4.47	**87**	4.27	-62.5	99	.973	158	135	-21.2	-5.6	-6.2	-2.1	-14.0	2.0
CHI	51	7	10	1355^1	1355	9.0	602	**89**	619	636	.261	1.456	4.00	98	3.99	-4.4	99	.972	172	**152**	-11.1	-2.8	-.4	-1.1	-4.3	-8.7
Total	**453**	**73**	**142**	**10955^2**		**9.0**	**4812**					**1.408**	**3.95**													

Wins
Sain, J. (Bos) 24
Brecheen, H. (StL) 20
2 players tied with 18

Win Percentage
Brecheen, H. (StL) .741
Chesnes, B. (Pit) .700
Jones, S. (NY) .667

Games
Gumbert, H. (Cin) 61
Wilks, T. (StL) 57
Higbe, K. (Pit) 56

Complete Games
Sain, J. (Bos) 28
Brecheen, H. (StL) 21
Schmitz, J. (Chi) 18

Shutouts
Brecheen, H. (StL) 7
4 players tied with 4

Saves
Gumbert, H. (Cin) 17
Wilks, T. (StL) 13
Higbe, K. (Pit) 10

Innings Pitched
Sain, J. (Bos) 314^2
Jansen, L. (NY) 277
Spahn, W. (Bos) 257

Fewest Hits/Game
Schmitz, J. (Chi) 6.92
Barney, R. (Bro) 7.04
Brecheen, H. (StL) 7.44

Fewest BB/Game
Roe, P. (Bro) 1.67
Jansen, L. (NY) 1.75
Raffensberger, K. (Cin) 1.85

Strikeouts
Brecheen, H. (StL) 149
Barney, R. (Bro) 138
Sain, J. (Bos) 137

Ratio
Brecheen, H. (StL) 1.04
Roe, P. (Bro) 1.06
Schmitz, J. (Chi) 1.17

Earned Run Average
Brecheen, H. (StL) 2.24
Leonard, D. (Phi) 2.51
Sain, J. (Bos) 2.60

Adjusted ERA
Brecheen, H. (StL) 183
Leonard, D. (Phi) 157
Roe, P. (Bro) 152

Component ERA
Brecheen, H. (StL) 2.01
Schmitz, J. (Chi) 2.47
Roe, P. (Bro) 2.49

Opponents' Batting Avg.
Schmitz, J. (Chi) .215
Barney, R. (Bro) .217
Brecheen, H. (StL) .222

Adjusted Pitching Runs
Brecheen, H. (StL) 49
Sain, J. (Bos) 41
Leonard, D. (Phi) 36

Win Shares – Pitchers
Sain, J. (Bos) 28
Brecheen, H. (StL) 27
Schmitz, J. (Chi) 22

TPW – Pitchers
Brecheen, H. (StL) 4.8
Sain, J. (Bos) 4.3
Leonard, D. (Phi) 3.4

1948 American League

TEAM	G	W	L	PCT	GB	R	OR	EW	AB	H	2B	3B	HR	TB	BB	SO	SB	CS	AVG	OBP	SLG	OPS	OPS+	BR/A	PF	RC
CLE	156	97	58	.626	....	840	**568**	106	**5446**	**1534**	242	54	**155**	**2349**	646	575	54	44	**.282**	.360	.431	**.792**	**119**	**133**	97	868
BOS	155	96	59	.619	1	**907**	720	95	5363	1471	**277**	40	121	2191	**823**	552	38	**17**	.274	**.374**	.409	.783	109	86	105	**869**
NY	154	94	60	.610	2.5	857	633	100	5324	1480	251	**75**	139	2298	623	**478**	24	24	.278	.356	**.432**	.788	116	107	99	838
PHI	154	84	70	.545	12.5	729	735	76	5181	1345	231	47	68	1874	726	523	40	32	.260	.353	.362	.715	96	-19	100	699
DET	154	78	76	.506	18.5	700	726	74	5235	1396	219	58	78	1965	671	504	22	32	.267	.353	.375	.728	97	-23	103	723
STL	155	59	94	.386	37	671	849	59	5303	1438	251	62	63	2002	578	572	63	44	.271	.345	.378	.722	95	-39	103	711
WAS	154	56	97	.366	40	578	796	53	5111	1245	203	**75**	31	1691	568	572	**76**	48	.244	.322	.331	.652	81	-134	97	566
CHI	154	51	101	.336	44.5	559	814	49	5192	1303	172	39	55	1718	595	528	46	47	.251	.329	.331	.660	84	-119	97	588
Total	**618**					**5841**			**42155**	**11212**	**1846**	**450**	**710**		**5230**	**4304**	**363**	**288**	**.266**	**.349**	**.382**	**.731**				

Runs
Henrich, T. (NY) 138
DiMaggio, D. (Bos) 127
2 players tied with 124

Hits
Dillinger, B. (StL) 207
Mitchell, D. (Cle) 204
Boudreau, L. (Cle) 199

Doubles
Williams, T. (Bos) 44
Henrich, T. (NY) 42
Majeski, H. (Phi) 41

Triples
Henrich, T. (NY) 14
Stewart, B. (Was,NY) 13
3 players tied with 11

Home Runs
DiMaggio, J. (NY) 39
Gordon, J. (Cle) 32
Keltner, K. (Cle) 31

Total Bases
DiMaggio, J. (NY) 355
Henrich, T. (NY) 326
Williams, T. (Bos) 313

Runs Batted In
DiMaggio, J. (NY) 155
Stephens, V. (Bos) 137
Williams, T. (Bos) 127

Bases On Balls
Williams, T. (Bos) 126
Joost, E. (Phi) 119
Fain, F. (Phi) 113

Stolen Bases
Dillinger, B. (StL) 28
Coan, G. (Was) 23
Vernon, M. (Was) 15

Batting Average
Williams, T. (Bos) .369
Boudreau, L. (Cle) .355
Mitchell, D. (Cle) .336

On-Base Percentage
Williams, T. (Bos) .497
Boudreau, L. (Cle) .453
Appling, L. (Chi) .423

Slugging Average
Williams, T. (Bos) .615
DiMaggio, J. (NY) .598
Henrich, T. (NY) .554

Adjusted OPS
Williams, T. (Bos) 185
Boudreau, L. (Cle) 166
DiMaggio, J. (NY) 164

Adjusted Batting Runs
Williams, T. (Bos) 72.0
Boudreau, L. (Cle) 57.0
DiMaggio, J. (NY) 50.0

Runs Created/Game
Williams, T. (Bos) 14.00
Boudreau, L. (Cle) 9.80
DiMaggio, J. (NY) 8.90

Fielding Runs
Priddy, J. (StL) 15.2
Stirnweiss, S. (NY) 12.8
Philley, D. (Chi) 12.7

Win Shares – Batters
Williams, T. (Bos) 39
DiMaggio, J. (NY) 34
Boudreau, L. (Cle) 34

TPW – Batters
Boudreau, L. (Cle) 7.5
Williams, T. (Bos) 6.1
DiMaggio, J. (NY) 4.0

TEAM	CG	SH	SV	IP	H	H/G	ER	HR	BB	SO	OAV	RAT	ERA	ERA+	CERA	PR+	PF	FA	E	DP	FR	BW	PW	FW	TPW	DIF
CLE	66	**26**	**30**	**1409^{1}**	**1246**	**8.0**	**504**	82	625	593	**.239**	**1.328**	**3.22**	126	**3.34**	**99.8**	95	**.982**	114	183	**30.9**	**12.9**	**9.7**	**3.0**	**25.5**	-5.5
BOS	70	11	13	1379^{1}	1445	9.4	653	83	592	513	.270	1.477	4.26	103	4.16	20.8	102	.981	116	174	8.5	8.3	2.0	.8	11.2	7.8
NY	62	16	24	1365^{2}	1289	8.5	569	94	641	654	.250	1.413	3.75	109	3.78	32.7	95	.979	120	161	17.9	10.4	3.2	1.7	15.3	1.7
PHI	**74**	7	18	1368^{2}	1456	9.6	673	86	638	486	.275	1.530	4.43	97	4.39	-30.2	100	.981	**113**	180	9.9	-1.9	-2.9	1.0	-3.9	10.9
DET	60	5	22	1377	1367	8.9	635	92	**589**	**678**	.259	1.420	4.15	105	3.83	65.3	102	.974	155	143	-31.5	-2.2	6.3	-3.1	1.1	-.1
STL	35	4	20	1373^{1}	1513	9.9	764	103	737	531	.283	1.638	5.01	91	5.03	-43.0	106	.972	168	**190**	-26.1	-3.8	-4.2	-2.5	-10.5	-6.5
WAS	42	4	22	1357^{1}	1439	9.5	701	**81**	734	446	.273	1.601	4.65	93	4.64	-22.8	101	.974	154	144	-24.0	-13.0	-2.2	-2.3	-17.6	-2.4
CHI	35	2	23	1345^{2}	1454	9.7	731	89	673	403	.280	1.581	4.89	**87**	4.67	-108.4	99	.974	160	176	14.3	-11.5	-10.5	1.4	-20.6	-4.4
Total	**444**	**75**	**172**	**10976^{1}**		**9.2**	**5230**					**1.498**	**4.29**													

Wins
- Newhouser, H. (Det) 21
- Bearden, G. (Cle) 20
- Lemon, B. (Cle) 20

Win Percentage
- Kramer, J. (Bos) .783
- Bearden, G. (Cle) .741
- Raschi, V. (NY) .704

Games
- Page, J. (NY) 55
- Widmar, A. (StL) 49
- Biscan, F. (StL) 47

Complete Games
- Lemon, B. (Cle) 20
- Newhouser, H. (Det) 19
- 2 players tied with 18

Shutouts
- Lemon, B. (Cle) 10
- Bearden, G. (Cle) 6
- Raschi, V. (NY) 6

Saves
- Christopher, R. (Cle) 17
- Page, J. (NY) 16
- 2 players tied with 10

Innings Pitched
- Lemon, B. (Cle) 293^{2}
- Feller, B. (Cle) 280^{1}
- Newhouser, H. (Det) 272^{1}

Fewest Hits/Game
- Shea, S. (NY) 6.76
- Lemon, B. (Cle) 7.08
- Bearden, G. (Cle) 7.33

Fewest BB/Game
- Hutchinson, F. (Det) 1.95
- Zoldak, S. (Cle,StL) 2.42
- Lopat, E. (NY) 2.62

Strikeouts
- Feller, B. (Cle) 164
- Lemon, B. (Cle) 147
- Newhouser, H. (Det) 143

Ratio
- Lemon, B. (Cle) 1.23
- Hutchinson, F. (Det) 1.23
- Raschi, V. (NY) 1.27

Earned Run Average
- Bearden, G. (Cle) 2.43
- Scarborough, R. (Was) 2.82
- Lemon, B. (Cle) 2.82

Adjusted ERA
- Bearden, G. (Cle) 167
- Scarborough, R. (Was) 154
- Newhouser, H. (Det) 145

Component ERA
- Lemon, B. (Cle) 2.65
- Bearden, G. (Cle) 2.95
- Newhouser, H. (Det) 2.96

Opponents' Batting Avg.
- Shea, S. (NY) .208
- Lemon, B. (Cle) .216
- Bearden, G. (Cle) .229

Adjusted Pitching Runs
- Newhouser, H. (Det) 47
- Bearden, G. (Cle) 37
- Scarborough, R. (Was) 35

Win Shares – Pitchers
- Newhouser, H. (Det) 27
- Lemon, B. (Cle) 26
- Bearden, G. (Cle) 22

TPW – Pitchers
- Newhouser, H. (Det) 4.7
- Lemon, B. (Cle) 4.5
- Bearden, G. (Cle) 4.0

1949 National League

TEAM	G	W	L	PCT	GB	R	OR	EW	AB	H	2B	3B	HR	TB	BB	SO	SB	CS	AVG	OBP	SLG	OPS	OPS+	BR/A	PF	RC
BRO	156	97	57	.630	....	**879**	651	99	5400	1477	236	47	**152**	**2263**	638	570	**117**	....	.274	**.354**	**.419**	**.773**	**109**	**74**	104	**815**
STL	157	96	58	.623	1	766	**616**	94	5463	**1513**	**281**	54	102	2208	569	**482**	17	....	**.277**	.348	.404	.752	103	27	105	777
PHI	154	81	73	.526	16	662	668	76	5307	1349	232	**55**	122	2057	528	670	27	....	.254	.325	.388	.712	99	-8	97	674
BOS	157	75	79	.487	22	706	719	76	5336	1376	246	33	103	1997	**684**	656	28	....	.258	.345	.374	.719	105	49	95	710
NY	156	73	81	.474	24	736	693	82	5308	1383	203	52	147	2131	613	523	43	....	.261	.340	.401	.741	105	39	100	735
PIT	154	71	83	.461	26	681	760	69	5214	1350	191	41	126	2001	548	554	48	....	.259	.332	.384	.716	96	-31	103	682
CIN	156	62	92	.403	35	627	770	61	**5469**	1423	264	35	86	2015	429	559	31	....	.260	.316	.368	.685	88	-94	101	636
CHI	154	61	93	.396	36	593	773	57	5214	1336	212	53	97	1945	396	573	53	....	.256	.312	.373	.685	92	-69	97	601
Total	**622**					**5650**			**42711**	**11207**	**1865**	**370**	**935**		**4405**	**4587**	**364**		**.262**	**.334**	**.389**	**.723**				

Runs
- Reese, P. (Bro) 132
- Musial, S. (StL) 128
- Robinson, J. (Bro) 122

Hits
- Musial, S. (StL) 207
- Robinson, J. (Bro) 203
- Thomson, B. (NY) 198

Doubles
- Musial, S. (StL) 41
- Ennis, D. (Phi) 39
- 2 players tied with 38

Triples
- Musial, S. (StL) 13
- Slaughter, E. (StL) 13
- Robinson, J. (Bro) 12

Home Runs
- Kiner, R. (Pit) 54
- Musial, S. (StL) 36
- Sauer, H. (Chi,Cin) 31

Total Bases
- Musial, S. (StL) 382
- Kiner, R. (Pit) 361
- Thomson, B. (NY) 332

Runs Batted In
- Kiner, R. (Pit) 127
- Robinson, J. (Bro) 124
- Musial, S. (StL) 123

Bases On Balls
- Kiner, R. (Pit) 117
- Reese, P. (Bro) 116
- Stanky, E. (Bos) 113

Stolen Bases
- Robinson, J. (Bro) 37
- Reese, P. (Bro) 26
- 4 players tied with 12

Batting Average
- Robinson, J. (Bro) .342
- Musial, S. (StL) .338
- Slaughter, E. (StL) .336

On-Base Percentage
- Musial, S. (StL) .438
- Robinson, J. (Bro) .432
- Kiner, R. (Pit) .432

Slugging Average
- Kiner, R. (Pit) .658
- Musial, S. (StL) .624
- Robinson, J. (Bro) .528

Adjusted OPS
- Kiner, R. (Pit) 183
- Musial, S. (StL) 174
- Robinson, J. (Bro) 150

Adjusted Batting Runs
- Kiner, R. (Pit) 68.0
- Musial, S. (StL) 67.0
- Robinson, J. (Bro) 46.0

Runs Created/Game
- Kiner, R. (Pit) 11.30
- Musial, S. (StL) 11.20
- Slaughter, E. (StL) 8.80

Fielding Runs
- Schoendienst, R. (StL) 19.8
- Hamner, G. (Phi) 17.3
- Reese, P. (Bro) 13.6

Win Shares – Batters
- Musial, S. (StL) 40
- Kiner, R. (Pit) 37
- Robinson, J. (Bro) 36

TPW – Batters
- Robinson, J. (Bro) 6.5
- Musial, S. (StL) 6.0
- Kiner, R. (Pit) 5.2

TEAM	CG	SH	SV	IP	H	H/G	ER	HR	BB	SO	OAV	RAT	ERA	ERA+	CERA	PR+	PF	FA	E	DP	FR	BW	PW	FW	TPW	DIF
BRO	62	**15**	17	**1408^{2}**	**1306**	**8.3**	594	132	582	**743**	**.248**	1.340	3.80	108	3.72	22.0	102	**.979**	**122**	162	**25.0**	**7.3**	2.2	**2.5**	12.0	8.0
STL	64	13	**19**	1407^{2}	1356	8.7	**538**	**87**	507	606	.254	**1.323**	**3.44**	121	**3.47**	**105.3**	103	.976	146	149	6.8	2.7	**10.4**	.7	**13.8**	5.2
PHI	58	12	15	1391^{2}	1389	9.0	601	104	**502**	495	.270	1.359	3.89	101	3.85	-7.7	98	.974	156	141	15.3	-.8	-.8	1.5	.0	4.0
BOS	**68**	12	11	1400	1466	9.4	621	110	520	589	.270	1.419	3.99	95	4.05	-25.5	94	.975	148	144	-6.7	4.8	-2.5	-.7	1.6	-3.6
NY	**68**	10	9	1374^{1}	1328	8.7	583	132	544	516	.251	1.362	3.82	104	3.82	28.2	99	.973	161	134	-4.0	3.8	2.8	-.4	6.3	-10.3
PIT	53	9	15	1356	1452	9.6	689	142	535	556	.276	1.465	4.57	92	4.55	-46.2	104	.978	132	**173**	-8.5	-3.1	-4.6	-.8	-8.5	2.5
CIN	55	10	6	1401^{2}	1423	9.1	676	124	640	538	.266	1.472	4.34	96	4.33	-21.3	103	.977	138	150	-2.6	-9.3	-2.1	-.3	-11.7	-3.3
CHI	44	8	17	1357^{2}	1487	9.9	678	104	575	544	.280	1.519	4.49	**90**	4.41	-43.6	100	.970	186	160	-27.0	-6.9	-4.3	-2.7	-13.9	-2.1
Total	**472**	**89**	**109**	**11097^{2}**		**9.1**	**4980**					**1.407**	**4.04**													

Wins
- Spahn, W. (Bos) 21
- Pollet, H. (StL) 20
- Raffensberger, K. (Cin) 18

Win Percentage
- Branca, R. (Bro) .722
- Roe, P. (Bro) .714
- Pollet, H. (StL) .690

Games
- Wilks, T. (StL) 59
- Konstanty, J. (Phi) 53
- Palica, E. (Bro) 49

Complete Games
- Spahn, W. (Bos) 25
- Raffensberger, K. (Cin) 20
- Newcombe, D. (Bro) 19

Shutouts
- 4 players tied with 5

Saves
- Wilks, T. (StL) 9
- Konstanty, J. (Phi) 7
- Potter, N. (Bos) 7

Innings Pitched
- Spahn, W. (Bos) 302^{1}
- Raffensberger, K. (Cin) 284
- Jansen, L. (NY) 259^{2}

Fewest Hits/Game
- Staley, G. (StL) 8.09
- Koslo, D. (NY) 8.19
- Newcombe, D. (Bro) 8.21

Fewest BB/Game
- Koslo, D. (NY) 1.83
- Roe, P. (Bro) 1.86
- Werle, B. (Pit) 2.08

Strikeouts
- Spahn, W. (Bos) 151
- Newcombe, D. (Bro) 149
- Jansen, L. (NY) 113

Ratio
- Koslo, D. (NY) 1.11
- Staley, G. (StL) 1.14
- Roe, P. (Bro) 1.15

Earned Run Average
- Koslo, D. (NY) 2.50
- Staley, G. (StL) 2.73
- Pollet, H. (StL) 2.77

Adjusted ERA
- Koslo, D. (NY) 159
- Staley, G. (StL) 152
- Pollet, H. (StL) 150

Component ERA
- Staley, G. (StL) 2.56
- Koslo, D. (NY) 2.57
- Pollet, H. (StL) 3.01

Opponents' Batting Avg.
- Staley, G. (StL) .238
- Koslo, D. (NY) .239
- Kennedy, M. (NY) .242

Adjusted Pitching Runs
- Koslo, D. (NY) 35
- Pollet, H. (StL) 35
- Roe, P. (Bro) 27

Win Shares – Pitchers
- Pollet, H. (StL) 24
- Spahn, W. (Bos) 24
- Heintzelman, K. (Phi) 23

TPW – Pitchers
- Koslo, D. (NY) 3.6
- Pollet, H. (StL) 3.6
- Staley, G. (StL) 2.6

1949 American League

TEAM	G	W	L	PCT	GB	R	OR	EW	AB	H	2B	3B	HR	TB	BB	SO	SB	CS	AVG	OBP	SLG	OPS	OPS+	BR/A	PF	RC
NY	155	97	57	.630	....	829	637	97	5196	1396	215	60	115	2076	731	539	58	30	.269	.362	.400	.762	108	66	100	790
BOS	155	96	58	.623	1	**896**	667	99	**5320**	**1500**	**272**	36	**131**	**2237**	**835**	510	43	**25**	**.282**	**.381**	**.420**	**.802**	**111**	**96**	107	**890**
CLE	154	89	65	.578	8	675	**574**	89	5221	1358	194	58	112	2004	601	534	44	40	.260	.339	.384	.723	99	-20	98	696
DET	155	87	67	.565	10	751	655	87	5259	1405	215	51	88	1986	751	502	39	52	.267	.361	.378	.739	102	12	100	739
PHI	154	81	73	.526	16	726	725	77	5123	1331	214	49	82	1889	783	**493**	36	**25**	.260	.361	.369	.729	103	37	97	719
CHI	154	63	91	.409	34	648	737	67	5204	1340	207	**66**	43	1808	702	596	**62**	55	.257	.347	.347	.695	93	-49	97	657
STL	155	53	101	.344	44	667	913	54	5112	1301	213	30	117	1925	631	700	38	39	.254	.339	.377	.715	92	-72	104	670
WAS	154	50	104	.325	47	584	868	48	5234	1330	207	41	81	1862	593	495	46	33	.254	.333	.356	.688	90	-79	98	640
Total	**618**					**5776**			**41669**	**10961**	**1737**	**391**	**769**		**5627**	**4369**	**366**	**299**	**.263**	**.353**	**.379**	**.732**				

Runs
Williams, T. (Bos) 150
Joost, E. (Phi) 128
DiMaggio, D. (Bos) 126

Hits
Mitchell, D. (Cle) 203
Williams, T. (Bos) 194
DiMaggio, D. (Bos) 186

Doubles
Williams, T. (Bos) 39
Kell, G. (Det) 38
DiMaggio, D. (Bos) 34

Triples
Mitchell, D. (Cle) 23
Dillinger, B. (StL) 13
Valo, E. (Phi) 12

Home Runs
Williams, T. (Bos) 43
Stephens, V. (Bos) 39
4 players tied with 24

Total Bases
Williams, T. (Bos) 368
Stephens, V. (Bos) 329
Wertz, V. (Det) 283

Runs Batted In
Stephens, V. (Bos) 159
Williams, T. (Bos) 159
Wertz, V. (Det) 133

Bases On Balls
Williams, T. (Bos) 162
Joost, E. (Phi) 149
Fain, F. (Phi) 136

Stolen Bases
Dillinger, B. (StL) 20
Rizzuto, P. (NY) 18
Valo, E. (Phi) 14

Batting Average
Kell, G. (Det) .343
Williams, T. (Bos) .343
Dillinger, B. (StL) .324

On-Base Percentage
Williams, T. (Bos) .490
Appling, L. (Chi) .439
Joost, E. (Phi) .429

Slugging Average
Williams, T. (Bos) .650
Stephens, V. (Bos) .539
Henrich, T. (NY) .526

Adjusted OPS
Williams, T. (Bos) 187
Henrich, T. (NY) 148
Joost, E. (Phi) 138

Adjusted Batting Runs
Williams, T. (Bos) 80.0
Joost, E. (Phi) 38.0
Henrich, T. (NY) 30.0

Runs Created/Game
Williams, T. (Bos) 13.20
Henrich, T. (NY) 8.80
Joost, E. (Phi) 8.10

Fielding Runs
Doerr, B. (Bos) 21.8
Pesky, J. (Bos) 19.6
Vernon, M. (Cle) 19.4

Win Shares – Batters
Williams, T. (Bos) 40
Joost, E. (Phi) 35
Stephens, V. (Bos) 32

TPW – Batters
Williams, T. (Bos) 6.6
Joost, E. (Phi) 6.1
Doerr, B. (Bos) 4.8

TEAM	CG	SH	SV	IP	H	H/G	ER	HR	BB	SO	OAV	RAT	ERA	ERA+	CERA	PR+	PF	FA	E	DP	FR	BW	PW	FW	TPW	DIF
NY	59	12	**36**	1371[1]	**1231**	**8.1**	562	98	812	**671**	**.242**	1.490	3.69	110	4.03	21.3	96	.977	138	195	**32.2**	6.4	2.1	**3.1**	11.6	8.4
BOS	84	16	16	1377	1375	9.0	607	82	661	598	.262	1.479	3.97	110	4.09	35.0	104	.980	120	207	23.8	**9.4**	3.4	2.3	**15.1**	3.9
CLE	65	10	19	1383[2]	1275	8.3	**516**	82	**611**	594	.247	**1.363**	**3.36**	119	**3.51**	**82.9**	95	**.983**	**103**	192	14.4	-2.0	**8.1**	1.4	7.5	4.5
DET	70	**19**	12	**1393[2]**	1338	8.6	584	102	628	631	.254	1.411	3.77	110	3.91	73.2	99	.978	131	174	-13.1	1.2	7.1	-1.3	7.0	3.0
PHI	**85**	9	11	1365	1359	9.0	642	105	758	490	.263	1.551	4.23	97	4.49	-50.3	98	.976	140	**217**	31.2	3.6	-4.9	3.0	1.7	2.3
CHI	57	10	17	1363[1]	1362	9.0	651	108	693	502	.264	1.507	4.30	97	4.33	-26.7	99	.977	141	180	7.6	-4.7	-2.6	.7	-6.6	-7.4
STL	43	3	16	1341[1]	1583	10.6	776	113	685	432	.294	1.691	5.21	87	5.38	-56.4	108	.972	166	154	-45.7	-7.0	-5.5	-4.4	-16.9	-7.1
WAS	44	9	9	1345[2]	1438	9.6	762	**79**	779	451	.276	1.648	5.10	**83**	4.80	-76.1	101	.973	161	168	-49.3	-7.7	-7.4	-4.8	-19.9	-7.1
Total	**507**	**88**	**136**	**10941**		**9.0**	**5100**					**1.516**	**4.20**													

Wins
Parnell, M. (Bos) 25
Kinder, E. (Bos) 23
Lemon, B. (Cle) 22

Win Percentage
Kinder, E. (Bos) .793
Parnell, M. (Bos) .781
Reynolds, A. (NY) .739

Games
Page, J. (NY) 60
Welteroth, D. (Was) 52
Ferrick, T. (StL) 50

Complete Games
Parnell, M. (Bos) 27
Lemon, B. (Cle) 22
Newhouser, H. (Det) 22

Shutouts
Kinder, E. (Bos) 6
Trucks, V. (Det) 6
Garcia, M. (Cle) 5

Saves
Page, J. (NY) 27
Benton, A. (Cle) 10
Ferrick, T. (StL) 6

Innings Pitched
Parnell, M. (Bos) 295[1]
Newhouser, H. (Det) 292
Lemon, B. (Cle) 279[2]

Fewest Hits/Game
Byrne, T. (NY) 5.74
Lemon, B. (Cle) 6.79
Trucks, V. (Det) 6.84

Fewest BB/Game
Hutchinson, F. (Det) 2.48
Houtteman, A. (Det) 2.61
Lopat, E. (NY) 2.88

Strikeouts
Trucks, V. (Det) 153
Newhouser, H. (Det) 144
2 players tied with 138

Ratio
Hutchinson, F. (Det) 1.16
Trucks, V. (Det) 1.21
Garcia, M. (Cle) 1.22

Earned Run Average
Garcia, M. (Cle) 2.36
Parnell, M. (Bos) 2.77
Trucks, V. (Det) 2.81

Adjusted ERA
Garcia, M. (Cle) 169
Parnell, M. (Bos) 157
Trucks, V. (Det) 148

Component ERA
Trucks, V. (Det) 2.68
Garcia, M. (Cle) 2.77
Lemon, B. (Cle) 2.88

Opponents' Batting Avg.
Byrne, T. (NY) .183
Lemon, B. (Cle) .211
Trucks, V. (Det) .211

Adjusted Pitching Runs
Parnell, M. (Bos) 47
Trucks, V. (Det) 44
Garcia, M. (Cle) 30

Win Shares – Pitchers
Lemon, B. (Cle) 31
Parnell, M. (Bos) 31
Trucks, V. (Det) 27

TPW – Pitchers
Parnell, M. (Bos) 4.8
Lemon, B. (Cle) 4.2
Trucks, V. (Det) 3.6

1950 National League

TEAM	G	W	L	PCT	GB	R	OR	EW	AB	H	2B	3B	HR	TB	BB	SO	SB	CS	AVG	OBP	SLG	OPS	OPS+	BR/A	PF	RC
PHI	157	91	63	.591	....	722	**624**	88	**5426**	1440	225	55	125	2150	535	569	33	....	.265	.334	.396	.730	100	-2	98	714
BRO	155	89	65	.578	2	**847**	724	89	5364	**1461**	247	46	**194**	**2382**	607	632	**77**	....	**.272**	**.349**	**.444**	**.793**	**113**	**92**	102	**833**
NY	154	86	68	.558	5	735	643	87	5238	1352	204	50	133	2055	**627**	629	42	....	.258	.342	.392	.734	99	1	101	726
BOS	156	83	71	.539	8	785	736	82	5363	1411	246	36	148	2173	615	616	71	....	.263	.342	.405	.747	110	76	94	750
STL	153	78	75	.510	12.5	693	670	79	5215	1353	255	50	102	2014	606	604	23	....	.259	.339	.386	.725	93	-45	105	696
CIN	153	66	87	.431	24.5	654	734	68	5253	1366	**257**	27	99	1974	504	**497**	37	....	.260	.327	.376	.702	91	-69	100	643
CHI	154	64	89	.418	26.5	643	772	63	5230	1298	224	47	161	2099	479	767	46	....	.248	.315	.401	.716	95	-47	99	658
PIT	154	57	96	.373	33.5	681	857	59	5327	1404	227	**59**	138	2163	564	693	43	....	.264	.338	.406	.744	98	-11	103	729
Total	**618**					**5760**			**42416**	**11085**	**1885**	**370**	**1100**		**4537**	**5007**	**372**		**.261**	**.336**	**.401**	**.737**				

Runs
Torgeson, E. (Bos) 120
Stanky, E. (NY) 115
Kiner, R. (Pit) 112

Hits
Snider, D. (Bro) 199
Musial, S. (StL) 192
Furillo, C. (Bro) 189

Doubles
Schoendienst, R. (StL) 43
Musial, S. (StL) 41
Robinson, J. (Bro) 39

Triples
Ashburn, R. (Phi) 14
Bell, G. (Pit) 11
Snider, D. (Bro) 10

Home Runs
Kiner, R. (Pit) 47
Pafko, A. (Chi) 36
2 players tied with 32

Total Bases
Snider, D. (Bro) 343
Musial, S. (StL) 331
Ennis, D. (Phi) 328

Runs Batted In
Ennis, D. (Phi) 126
Kiner, R. (Pit) 118
Hodges, G. (Bro) 113

Bases On Balls
Stanky, E. (NY) 144
Kiner, R. (Pit) 122
Torgeson, E. (Bos) 119

Stolen Bases
Jethroe, S. (Bos) 35
Reese, P. (Bro) 17
Snider, D. (Bro) 16

Batting Average
Musial, S. (StL) .346
Robinson, J. (Bro) .328
Snider, D. (Bro) .321

On-Base Percentage
Stanky, E. (NY) .460
Musial, S. (StL) .437
Robinson, J. (Bro) .423

Slugging Average
Musial, S. (StL) .596
Pafko, A. (Chi) .591
Kiner, R. (Pit) .590

Adjusted OPS
Musial, S. (StL) 161
Gordon, S. (Bos) 160
Pafko, A. (Chi) 158

Adjusted Batting Runs
Musial, S. (StL) 52.0
Kiner, R. (Pit) 46.0
Pafko, A. (Chi) 43.0

Runs Created/Game
Musial, S. (StL) 10.70
Pafko, A. (Chi) 9.10
Kiner, R. (Pit) 8.60

Fielding Runs
Robinson, J. (Bro) 15.0
Kerr, B. (Bos) 15.0
O'Connell, D. (Pit) 14.8

Win Shares – Batters
Torgeson, E. (Bos) 32
Musial, S. (StL) 32
Stanky, E. (NY) 30

TPW – Batters
Stanky, E. (NY) 5.6
Robinson, J. (Bro) 5.4
Pafko, A. (Chi) 4.7

TEAM	CG	SH	SV	IP	H	H/G	ER	HR	BB	SO	OAV	RAT	ERA	ERA+	CERA	PR+	PF	FA	E	DP	FR	BW	PW	FW	TPW	DIF
PHI	57	13	**27**	1406	1324	8.5	**547**	122	**530**	620	.250	1.319	3.50	116	**3.61**	**84.2**	98	.975	151	155	2.4	-.2	**8.2**	.2	**8.2**	5.8
BRO	62	10	21	**13892**	1397	0.9	661	163	591	**772**	.263	.143	0.43	96	4.36	-60.6	99	**.979**	**127**	**183**	32.2	**9.0**	-5.9	3.1	6.2	5.8
NY	70	**19**	15	1375	**1268**	8.3	567	140	536	596	**.246**	1.312	3.71	110	3.71	16.6	99	.977	137	181	**42.3**	.1	1.6	**4.1**	5.9	3.1
BOS	**88**	7	10	13851	1411	0.9	637	129	554	615	.263	**.142**	**0.41**	93	4.16	-35.3	93	.970	182	146	-9.0	7.4	-3.5	-.9	3.1	2.9
STL	57	10	14	1356	1398	9.3	598	**119**	535	603	.268	1.426	3.97	108	4.16	58.1	104	.978	130	172	-8.7	-4.4	5.7	-.9	.4	1.6
CIN	67	7	13	13572	1363	**0.9**	651	145	582	686	.259	.143	0.43	98	4.29	4.7	102	.976	140	132	-16.7	-6.7	.5	-1.6	-7.9	-2.1
CHI	55	9	19	13711	1452	1.0	652	130	593	559	.271	.149	0.43	98	4.48	24.3	101	.968	201	169	-35.9	-4.6	2.4	-3.5	-5.7	-6.3
PIT	42	6	16	13682	1472	1.0	754	152	616	556	.275	.153	0.50	**88**	4.82	-80.3	106	.977	136	165	-7.4	-1.1	-7.9	-.7	-9.6	-9.4
Total	**498**	**81**	**135**	**72845**		**1.4**	**5067**					**.214**	**0.63**													

Wins
Spahn, W. (Bos) 21
Roberts, R. (Phi) 20
Sain, J. (Bos) 20

Win Percentage
Maglie, S. (NY) .818
Simmons, C. (Phi) .680
Miller, B. (Phi) .647

Games
Konstanty, J. (Phi) 74
Dickson, M. (Pit) 51
Werle, B. (Pit) 48

Complete Games
Bickford, V. (Bos) 27
Sain, J. (Bos) 25
Spahn, W. (Bos) 25

Shutouts
4 players tied with 5

Saves
Konstanty, J. (Phi) 22
Werle, B. (Pit) 8
2 players tied with 7

Innings Pitched
Bickford, V. (Bos) 311[2]
Roberts, R. (Phi) 304[1]
Spahn, W. (Bos) 293

Fewest Hits/Game
Blackwell, E. (Cin) 7.00
Maglie, S. (NY) 7.38
Simmons, C. (Phi) 7.46

Fewest BB/Game
Raffensberger, K. (Cin) 1.51
Jansen, L. (NY) 1.80
Sain, J. (Bos) 2.26

Strikeouts
Spahn, W. (Bos) 191
Blackwell, E. (Cin) 188
Jansen, L. (NY) 161

Ratio
Jansen, L. (NY) 1.07
Roberts, R. (Phi) 1.18
Brecheen, H. (StL) 1.20

Earned Run Average
Maglie, S. (NY) 2.71
Hearn, J. (NY) 1.94
Blackwell, E. (Cin) 2.97

Adjusted ERA
Maglie, S. (NY) 151
Blackwell, E. (Cin) 143
Lanier, M. (StL) 137

Component ERA
Blackwell, E. (Cin) 2.68
Jansen, L. (NY) 2.68
Spahn, W. (Bos) 2.93

Opponents' Batting Avg.
Blackwell, E. (Cin) .210
Simmons, C. (Phi) .223
Maglie, S. (NY) .226

Adjusted Pitching Runs
Blackwell, E. (Cin) 40
Roberts, R. (Phi) 34
Pollet, H. (StL) 27

Win Shares – Pitchers
Blackwell, E. (Cin) 26
Roberts, R. (Phi) 26
Jansen, L. (NY) 25

TPW – Pitchers
Blackwell, E. (Cin) 3.7
Roberts, R. (Phi) 3.0
Spahn, W. (Bos) 2.7

1950 American League

TEAM	G	W	L	PCT	GB	R	OR	EW	AB	H	2B	3B	HR	TB	BB	SO	SB	CS	AVG	OBP	SLG	OPS	OPS+	BR/A	PF	RC
NY	155	98	56	.636	....	914	691	98	5361	1511	234	**70**	159	2362	687	**463**	41	28	.282	.367	.441	.807	**116**	**120**	97	902
DET	157	95	59	.617	3	837	713	89	5381	1518	285	50	114	2245	**722**	480	23	40	.282	.369	.417	.786	104	27	103	846
BOS	154	94	60	.610	4	**1027**	804	95	**5516**	**1665**	**287**	61	161	**2557**	719	582	32	**17**	**.302**	**.385**	**.464**	**.848**	112	105	110	**1014**
CLE	155	92	62	.597	6	806	**654**	93	5263	1417	222	46	**164**	2223	693	624	40	34	.269	.358	.422	.781	109	67	97	820
WAS	155	67	87	.435	31	690	813	64	5251	1365	190	53	76	1889	671	606	**42**	25	.260	.347	.360	.707	91	-55	95	690
CHI	156	60	94	.390	38	625	749	63	5260	1368	172	47	93	1913	551	566	19	22	.260	.333	.364	.697	86	-109	97	648
STL	154	58	96	.377	40	684	916	55	5163	1269	235	43	106	1908	690	744	39	40	.246	.337	.370	.707	83	-131	104	667
PHI	154	52	102	.338	46	670	913	54	5212	1361	204	53	100	1971	685	493	**42**	25	.261	.349	.378	.728	94	-39	98	708
Total	**620**					**6253**			**42407**	**11474**	**1829**	**423**	**973**		**5418**	**4558**	**278**	**231**	**.271**	**.356**	**.402**	**.759**				

Runs
DiMaggio, D. (Bos) 131
Rizzuto, P. (NY) 125
Stephens, V. (Bos) 125

Hits
Kell, G. (Det) 218
Rizzuto, P. (NY) 200
DiMaggio, D. (Bos) 193

Doubles
Kell, G. (Det) 56
Wertz, V. (Det) 37
Rizzuto, P. (NY) 36

Triples
DiMaggio, D. (Bos) 11
Doerr, B. (Bos) 11
Evers, H. (Det) 11

Home Runs
Rosen, A. (Cle) 37
Dropo, W. (Bos) 34
DiMaggio, J. (NY) 32

Total Bases
Dropo, W. (Bos) 326
Stephens, V. (Bos) 321
Berra, Y. (NY) 318

Runs Batted In
Dropo, W. (Bos) 144
Stephens, V. (Bos) 144
Berra, Y. (NY) 124

Bases On Balls
Yost, E. (Was) 141
Fain, F. (Phi) 133
Pesky, J. (Bos) 104

Stolen Bases
DiMaggio, D. (Bos) 15
Rizzuto, P. (NY) 12
Valo, E. (Phi) 12

Batting Average
Goodman, B. (Bos) .354
Kell, G. (Det) .340
DiMaggio, D. (Bos) .328

On-Base Percentage
Doby, L. (Cle) .442
Yost, E. (Was) .440
Pesky, J. (Bos) .437

Slugging Average
DiMaggio, J. (NY) .585
Dropo, W. (Bos) .583
Evers, H. (Det) .551

Adjusted OPS
Doby, L. (Cle) 157
DiMaggio, J. (NY) 152
Rosen, A. (Cle) 146

Adjusted Batting Runs
Doby, L. (Cle) 46.0
DiMaggio, J. (NY) 40.0
Rosen, A. (Cle) 38.0

Runs Created/Game
Doby, L. (Cle) 9.90
DiMaggio, J. (NY) 8.80
Zarilla, A. (Bos) 8.70

Fielding Runs
Priddy, J. (Det) 24.2
Rizzuto, P. (NY) 21.6
Pesky, J. (Bos) 14.7

Win Shares – Batters
Rizzuto, P. (NY) 35
Berra, Y. (NY) 32
Doby, L. (Cle) 30

TPW – Batters
Rizzuto, P. (NY) 5.3
Rosen, A. (Cle) 4.3
Berra, Y. (NY) 3.7

TEAM	CG	SH	SV	IP	H	H/G	ER	HR	BB	SO	OAV	RAT	ERA	ERA+	CERA	PR+	PF	FA	E	DP	FR	BW	PW	FW	TPW	DIF
NY	66	**12**	**31**	1372^{2}	1322	8.7	633	118	708	**712**	.255	1.479	4.15	103	4.26	3.1	94	.979	119	188	18.6	**11.3**	.3	1.7	13.3	7.7
DET	**72**	9	20	**1407^{1}**	1444	9.2	644	141	**553**	576	.267	1.419	4.12	114	4.23	79.6	102	.981	120	194	8.3	2.5	7.4	.8	10.8	7.2
BOS	66	6	28	1362^{1}	1413	9.3	739	121	748	630	.270	1.586	4.88	100	4.79	7.8	107	**.981**	**111**	181	-5.5	9.8	.7	-.5	10.1	6.9
CLE	69	11	16	1378^{2}	**1289**	**8.4**	**574**	120	647	674	**.248**	**1.404**	**3.75**	116	**3.86**	**84.0**	95	.978	129	160	6.5	6.2	**7.9**	.6	**14.7**	.3
WAS	59	7	18	1364^{2}	1479	9.8	706	**99**	648	486	.278	1.559	4.66	96	4.60	-20.5	98	.972	167	181	-4.6	-5.1	-1.9	-.4	-7.5	-2.5
CHI	62	7	9	1365^{2}	1370	9.0	669	107	734	566	.263	1.541	4.41	102	4.44	-17.8	98	.976	140	181	**29.5**	-10.2	-1.7	**2.8**	-9.1	-7.9
STL	56	7	14	1365^{1}	1629	10.7	789	129	651	448	.295	1.670	5.20	95	5.49	5.7	108	.967	196	155	-44.1	-12.3	.5	-4.1	-15.9	-3.1
PHI	50	3	18	1346^{1}	1528	10.2	821	138	729	466	.287	1.676	5.49	**83**	5.45	-132.3	99	.974	155	**208**	-8.0	-3.6	-12.4	-.7	-16.8	-8.2
Total	**500**	**62**	**154**	**10963**		**9.4**	**5575**					**1.541**	**4.58**													

Wins
Lemon, B. (Cle) 23
Raschi, V. (NY) 21
Houtteman, A. (Det) 19

Win Percentage
Raschi, V. (NY) .724
Trout, D. (Det) .722
2 players tied with .692

Games
Harris, M. (Was) 53
Kinder, E. (Bos) 48
3 players tied with 46

Complete Games
Garver, N. (StL) 22
Lemon, B. (Cle) 22
2 players tied with 21

Shutouts
Houtteman, A. (Det) 4
5 players tied with 3

Saves
Harris, M. (Was) 15
Page, J. (NY) 13
Ferrick, T. (NY,StL) 11

Innings Pitched
Lemon, B. (Cle) 288
Houtteman, A. (Det) 274^{2}
Garver, N. (StL) 260

Fewest Hits/Game
Wynn, E. (Cle) 6.99
Pierce, B. (Chi) 7.76
Cain, B. (Chi) 8.02

Fewest BB/Game
Hutchinson, F. (Det) 1.86
Lopat, E. (NY) 2.48
Overmire, S. (StL) 2.52

Strikeouts
Lemon, B. (Cle) 170
Reynolds, A. (NY) 160
Raschi, V. (NY) 155

Ratio
Wynn, E. (Cle) 1.25
Houtteman, A. (Det) 1.30
Lopat, E. (NY) 1.31

Earned Run Average
Wynn, E. (Cle) 3.20
Garver, N. (StL) 3.39
Feller, B. (Cle) 3.43

Adjusted ERA
Garver, N. (StL) 146
Parnell, M. (Bos) 136
Wynn, E. (Cle) 135

Component ERA
Wynn, E. (Cle) 3.03
Raschi, V. (NY) 3.55
Feller, B. (Cle) 3.61

Opponents' Batting Avg.
Wynn, E. (Cle) .212
Pierce, B. (Chi) .228
Reynolds, A. (NY) .242

Adjusted Pitching Runs
Garver, N. (StL) 53
Parnell, M. (Bos) 37
Houtteman, A. (Det) 33

Win Shares – Pitchers
Garver, N. (StL) 25
Houtteman, A. (Det) 25
Lemon, B. (Cle) 25

TPW – Pitchers
Garver, N. (StL) 5.6
Parnell, M. (Bos) 3.3
Wynn, E. (Cle) 3.0

1951 National League

TEAM	G	W	L	PCT	GB	R	OR	EW	AB	H	2B	3B	HR	TB	BB	SO	SB	CS	AVG	OBP	SLG	OPS	OPS+	BR/A	PF	RC
NY	157	98	59	.624	....	781	**641**	94	5360	1396	201	53	179	2240	**671**	624	55	34	.260	.347	.418	.765	111	88	101	812
BRO	158	97	60	.618	1	**855**	672	97	**5492**	**1511**	**249**	37	**184**	**2386**	603	649	**89**	70	**.275**	**.352**	**.434**	**.786**	**115**	**108**	102	**843**
STL	155	81	73	.526	15.5	683	671	78	5317	1404	230	**57**	95	2033	569	**492**	30	30	.264	.339	.382	.721	100	0	101	705
BOS	155	76	78	.494	20.5	723	662	84	5293	1385	234	37	130	2083	565	617	80	34	.262	.336	.394	.730	110	80	93	719
PHI	154	73	81	.474	23.5	648	644	77	5332	1384	199	47	108	2001	505	525	63	28	.260	.326	.375	.701	96	-24	98	676
CIN	155	68	86	.442	28.5	559	667	64	5285	1309	215	33	88	1854	415	577	44	40	.248	.304	.351	.655	80	-150	102	562
PIT	155	64	90	.416	32.5	689	845	61	5318	1372	218	56	137	2113	557	615	29	**27**	.258	.331	.397	.728	99	-10	103	712
CHI	155	62	92	.403	34.5	614	750	62	5307	1327	200	47	103	1930	477	647	63	30	.250	.315	.364	.678	87	-94	102	613
Total	**622**					**5552**			**42704**	**11088**	**1746**	**367**	**1024**		**4362**	**4746**	**453**	**293**	**.260**	**.331**	**.390**	**.721**				

Runs
Kiner, R. (Pit) 124
Musial, S. (StL) 124
Hodges, G. (Bro) 118

Hits
Ashburn, R. (Phi) 221
Musial, S. (StL) 205
Furillo, C. (Bro) 197

Doubles
Dark, A. (NY) 41
Kluszewski, T. (Cin) 35
2 players tied with 33

Triples
Bell, G. (Pit) 12
Musial, S. (StL) 12
Irvin, M. (NY) 11

Home Runs
Kiner, R. (Pit) 42
Hodges, G. (Bro) 40
Campanella, R. (Bro) 33

Total Bases
Musial, S. (StL) 355
Kiner, R. (Pit) 333
Hodges, G. (Bro) 307

Runs Batted In
Irvin, M. (NY) 121
Gordon, S. (Bos) 109
Kiner, R. (Pit) 109

Bases On Balls
Kiner, R. (Pit) 137
Stanky, E. (NY) 127
Westrum, W. (NY) 104

Stolen Bases
Jethroe, S. (Bos) 35
Ashburn, R. (Phi) 29
Robinson, J. (Bro) 25

Batting Average
Musial, S. (StL) .355
Ashburn, R. (Phi) .344
Robinson, J. (Bro) .338

On-Base Percentage
Kiner, R. (Pit) .452
Musial, S. (StL) .449
Robinson, J. (Bro) .429

Slugging Average
Kiner, R. (Pit) .627
Musial, S. (StL) .614
Campanella, R. (Bro) .590

Adjusted OPS
Musial, S. (StL) 182
Kiner, R. (Pit) 182
Campanella, R. (Bro) 158

Adjusted Batting Runs
Musial, S. (StL) 69.0
Kiner, R. (Pit) 69.0
Robinson, J. (Bro) 46.0

Runs Created/Game
Musial, S. (StL) 11.90
Kiner, R. (Pit) 11.80
Robinson, J. (Bro) 9.30

Fielding Runs
Robinson, J. (Bro) 24.9
Ashburn, R. (Phi) 16.4
Furillo, C. (Bro) 14.7

Win Shares – Batters
Musial, S. (StL) 39
Robinson, J. (Bro) 38
Kiner, R. (Pit) 35

TPW – Batters
Robinson, J. (Bro) 8.0
Musial, S. (StL) 6.4
Kiner, R. (Pit) 5.1

TEAM	CG	SH	SV	IP	H	H/G	ER	HR	BB	SO	OAV	RAT	ERA	ERA+	CERA	PR+	PF	FA	E	DP	FR	BW	PW	FW	TPW	DIF
NY	64	9	18	1412^{2}	**1334**	**8.5**	**546**	148	**482**	625	**.248**	**1.286**	**3.48**	113	**3.59**	**65.8**	99	.972	171	175	2.8	8.8	**6.6**	.3	**15.7**	4.3
BRO	64	10	13	**1423^{1}**	1360	8.6	613	150	549	**693**	.253	1.341	3.88	101	3.89	-23.9	99	.979	129	**192**	**31.5**	**10.8**	-2.4	**3.2**	11.6	7.4
STL	58	9	**23**	1387^{2}	1391	9.0	609	119	568	546	.263	1.412	3.95	100	4.03	-18.2	100	**.980**	**125**	187	20.6	.0	-1.8	2.1	.3	3.7
BOS	**73**	16	12	1389	1378	8.9	579	**96**	595	604	.259	1.420	3.75	98	3.93	2.9	93	.976	145	157	-13.4	8.0	.3	-1.3	7.0	-8.0
PHI	57	**19**	15	1384^{2}	1373	8.9	586	110	497	570	.258	1.351	3.81	101	3.74	7.7	97	.977	138	146	-1.8	-2.4	.8	-.2	-1.8	-2.2
CIN	55	14	**23**	1390^{2}	1357	8.8	571	119	490	584	.255	1.328	3.70	110	3.72	64.8	103	.977	140	141	-6.6	-15.0	6.5	-.7	-9.2	.2
PIT	40	9	22	1380^{1}	1479	9.6	734	157	609	580	.274	1.513	4.79	**88**	4.82	-65.7	107	.972	170	178	-19.3	-1.0	-6.6	-1.9	-9.5	-3.5
CHI	48	10	10	1385^{2}	1416	9.2	668	125	572	544	.265	1.435	4.34	94	4.18	-23.9	103	.971	181	161	-13.5	-9.5	-2.4	-1.4	-13.2	-1.8
Total	**459**	**96**	**136**	**11154**		**9.0**	**4906**					**1.385**	**3.96**													

Wins		Win Percentage		Games		Complete Games		Shutouts		Saves	
Jansen, L. (NY)	23	Roe, P. (Bro)	.880	Wilks, T. (Pit,StL)	65	Spahn, W. (Bos)	26	Spahn, W. (Bos)	7	Wilks, T. (Pit,StL)	13
Maglie, S. (NY)	23	Maglie, S. (NY)	.793	Werle, B. (Pit)	59	Maglie, S. (NY)	22	Roberts, R. (Phi)	6	Smith, F. (Cin)	11
2 players tied with	22	Newcombe, D. (Bro)	.690	Konstanty, J. (Phi)	58	Roberts, R. (Phi)	22	Raffensberger, K. (Cin)	5	Konstanty, J. (Phi)	9
Innings Pitched		**Fewest Hits/Game**		**Fewest BB/Game**		**Strikeouts**		**Ratio**		**Earned Run Average**	
Roberts, R. (Phi)	315	Maglie, S. (NY)	7.67	Raffensberger, K. (Cin)	1.38	Newcombe, D. (Bro)	164	Raffensberger, K. (Cin)	1.09	Nichols, C. (Bos)	2.88
Spahn, W. (Bos)	310[2]	Newcombe, D. (Bro)	7.78	Jansen, L. (NY)	1.81	Spahn, W. (Bos)	164	Roberts, R. (Phi)	1.10	Maglie, S. (NY)	2.93
Maglie, S. (NY)	298	Blackwell, E. (Cin)	7.89	Roberts, R. (Phi)	1.83	Maglie, S. (NY)	146	Jansen, L. (NY)	1.11	Spahn, W. (Bos)	2.98
Adjusted ERA		**Component ERA**		**Opponents' Batting Avg.**		**Adjusted Pitching Runs**		**Win Shares – Pitchers**		**TPW – Pitchers**	
Maglie, S. (NY)	134	Roberts, R. (Phi)	2.57	Maglie, S. (NY)	.230	Maglie, S. (NY)	32	Maglie, S. (NY)	28	Roberts, R. (Phi)	3.5
Roe, P. (Bro)	129	Jansen, L. (NY)	2.79	Newcombe, D. (Bro)	.230	Roberts, R. (Phi)	29	Roberts, R. (Phi)	28	Spahn, W. (Bos)	3.1
Jansen, L. (NY)	129	Maglie, S. (NY)	2.84	Blackwell, E. (Cin)	.233	Spahn, W. (Bos)	27	Spahn, W. (Bos)	26	Maglie, S. (NY)	2.9

1951 American League

TEAM	G	W	L	PCT	GB	R	OR	EW	AB	H	2B	3B	HR	TB	BB	SO	SB	CS	AVG	OBP	SLG	OPS	OPS+	BR/A	PF	RC
NY	154	98	56	.636	....	798	621	96	5194	1395	208	48	**140**	**2119**	605	547	78	39	.269	.349	**.408**	**.757**	**113**	**98**	96	762
CLE	155	93	61	.604	5	696	**594**	89	5250	1346	208	35	**140**	2044	606	632	52	35	.256	.336	.389	.726	107	45	94	710
BOS	154	87	67	.565	11	**804**	725	85	**5378**	1428	233	32	127	2106	**756**	594	20	**21**	.266	**.358**	.392	.750	98	-2	110	**778**
CHI	155	81	73	.526	17	714	644	85	**5378**	**1453**	229	**64**	86	2068	596	524	**99**	70	**.270**	.349	.385	.733	105	36	98	745
DET	154	73	81	.474	25	685	741	71	5336	1413	231	35	104	2026	568	525	37	34	.265	.338	.380	.717	98	-19	100	697
PHI	154	70	84	.455	28	736	745	76	5277	1381	**262**	43	102	2035	677	565	47	36	.262	.349	.386	.735	101	16	102	745
WAS	154	62	92	.403	36	672	764	67	5329	1399	242	45	54	1893	560	**515**	45	38	.263	.336	.355	.691	93	-50	98	648
STL	154	52	102	.338	46	611	882	50	5219	1288	223	47	86	1863	521	693	35	38	.247	.317	.357	.674	84	-125	103	592
Total	**617**					**5716**			**42361**	**11103**	**1836**	**349**	**839**		**4889**	**4595**	**413**	**311**	**.262**	**.342**	**.381**	**.723**				

Runs		Hits		Doubles		Triples		Home Runs		Total Bases	
DiMaggio, D. (Bos)	113	Kell, G. (Det)	191	Kell, G. (Det)	36	Minoso, M. (Chi,Cle)	14	Zernial, G. (Phi,Chi)	33	Williams, T. (Bos)	295
Minoso, M. (Chi,Cle)	112	DiMaggio, D. (Bos)	189	Mele, S. (Was)	36	Coleman, R. (Chi,StL)	12	Williams, T. (Bos)	30	Zernial, G. (Phi,Chi)	292
3 players tied with	109	Fox, N. (Chi)	189	Yost, E. (Was)	36	Fox, N. (Chi)	12	Robinson, E. (Chi)	29	Robinson, E. (Chi)	279
Runs Batted In		**Bases On Balls**		**Stolen Bases**		**Batting Average**		**On-Base Percentage**		**Slugging Average**	
Zernial, G. (Phi,Chi)	129	Williams, T. (Bos)	144	Minoso, M. (Chi,Cle)	31	Fain, F. (Phi)	.344	Williams, T. (Bos)	.464	Williams, T. (Bos)	.556
Williams, T. (Bos)	126	Yost, E. (Was)	126	Busby, J. (Chi)	26	Minoso, M. (Cle,Chi)	.326	Fain, F. (Phi)	.451	Doby, L. (Cle)	.512
Robinson, E. (Chi)	117	Joost, E. (Phi)	106	Rizzuto, P. (NY)	18	Kell, G. (Det)	.319	Doby, L. (Cle)	.428	Zernial, G. (Phi,Chi)	.511
Adjusted OPS		**Adjusted Batting Runs**		**Runs Created/Game**		**Fielding Runs**		**Win Shares – Batters**		**TPW – Batters**	
Doby, L. (Cle)	163	Williams, T. (Bos)	53.0	Williams, T. (Bos)	11.00	Carrasquel, C. (Chi)	24.3	Williams, T. (Bos)	34	Williams, T. (Bos)	4.6
Williams, T. (Bos)	159	Doby, L. (Cle)	45.0	Doby, L. (Cle)	8.90	Rizzuto, P. (NY)	18.0	Berra, Y. (NY)	31	Doby, L. (Cle)	3.9
Minoso, M. (Cle,Chi)	152	Minoso, M. (Chi,Cle)	44.0	Fain, F. (Phi)	8.80	Stephens, V. (Bos)	13.0	Doby, L. (Cle)	29	Fain, F. (Phi)	3.6

TEAM	CG	SH	SV	IP	H	H/G	ER	HR	BB	SO	OAV	RAT	ERA	ERA+	CERA	PR+	PF	FA	E	DP	FR	BW	PW	FW	TPW	DIF
NY	66	**24**	22	1367	1290	8.5	541	92	562	**664**	.250	1.355	3.56	108	3.63	21.7	93	.975	144	190	19.1	**9.6**	2.1	1.9	**13.6**	7.4
CLE	**76**	10	19	1391[1]	**1287**	**8.3**	**522**	**85**	577	642	**.245**	**1.340**	**3.38**	112	**3.44**	**63.2**	92	.978	**134**	151	-0.6	4.4	**6.2**	-.1	10.6	5.4
BOS	46	7	**24**	1399	1413	9.1	644	99	599	658	.264	1.438	4.14	108	4.06	49.8	108	.977	141	184	0.6	-.2	4.9	.1	4.8	5.2
CHI	74	11	14	**1418**[1]	1353	8.6	551	109	**549**	572	.252	1.341	3.50	115	3.59	62.1	98	.975	151	176	21.6	3.5	6.1	2.1	11.8	-7.8
DET	51	8	17	1384	1385	9.0	660	103	602	597	.262	1.436	4.29	97	4.06	-4.5	101	.974	163	166	-13.9	-1.9	-.4	-1.4	-3.7	-.3
PHI	52	7	22	1358	1421	9.4	674	109	569	437	.272	1.465	4.47	96	4.33	-50.7	104	**.978**	136	**204**	**22.3**	1.5	-5.0	**2.2**	-1.2	-5.8
WAS	58	6	13	1366[1]	1429	9.4	681	110	630	475	.269	1.507	4.49	91	4.41	-42.5	99	.973	160	148	-16.4	-4.9	-4.2	-1.6	-10.7	-4.3
STL	56	5	9	1370[1]	1525	10.0	789	132	801	550	.282	1.697	5.18	**85**	5.46	-87.9	107	.971	172	179	-31.3	-12.3	-8.6	-3.1	-24.0	-1.0
Total	**479**	**78**	**140**	**11054**[1]		**9.0**	**5062**					**1.447**	**4.12**													

Wins		Win Percentage		Games		Complete Games		Shutouts		Saves	
Feller, B. (Cle)	22	Feller, B. (Cle)	.733	Kinder, E. (Bos)	63	Garver, N. (StL)	24	Reynolds, A. (NY)	7	Kinder, E. (Bos)	14
Lopat, E. (NY)	21	Lopat, E. (NY)	.700	Brissie, L. (Cle,Phi)	56	Wynn, E. (Cle)	21	3 players tied with	4	Scheib, C. (Phi)	10
Raschi, V. (NY)	21	Reynolds, A. (NY)	.680	Garcia, M. (Cle)	47	Lopat, E. (NY)	20			Brissie, L. (Cle,Phi)	9
Innings Pitched		**Fewest Hits/Game**		**Fewest BB/Game**		**Strikeouts**		**Ratio**		**Earned Run Average**	
Wynn, E. (Cle)	274[1]	Reynolds, A. (NY)	6.96	Hutchinson, F. (Det)	1.29	Raschi, V. (NY)	164	Lopat, E. (NY)	1.19	Rogovin, S. (Chi,Det)	2.78
Lemon, B. (Cle)	263[1]	McDermott, M. (Bos)	7.38	Lopat, E. (NY)	2.72	Wynn, E. (Cle)	133	Rogovin, S. (Chi,Det)	1.21	Lopat, E. (NY)	2.91
Raschi, V. (NY)	258[1]	Wynn, E. (Cle)	7.45	Pierce, B. (Chi)	2.73	Lemon, B. (Cle)	132	Wynn, E. (Cle)	1.22	Wynn, E. (Cle)	3.02
Adjusted ERA		**Component ERA**		**Opponents' Batting Avg.**		**Adjusted Pitching Runs**		**Win Shares – Pitchers**		**TPW – Pitchers**	
Rogovin, S. (Chi,Det)	146	Reynolds, A. (NY)	2.77	Reynolds, A. (NY)	.213	Parnell, M. (Bos)	29	Wynn, E. (Cle)	24	Parnell, M. (Bos)	3.3
Parnell, M. (Bos)	137	Lopat, E. (NY)	2.79	Wynn, E. (Cle)	.225	Rogovin, S. (Chi,Det)	28	3 players tied with	22	Garver, N. (StL)	3.1
McDermott, M. (Bos)	133	Wynn, E. (Cle)	2.84	McDermott, M. (Bos)	.226	Garver, N. (StL)	24			Rogovin, S. (Chi,Det)	2.8

1952 National League

TEAM	G	W	L	PCT	GB	R	OR	EW	AB	H	2B	3B	HR	TB	BB	SO	SB	CS	AVG	OBP	SLG	OPS	OPS+	BR/A	PF	RC
BRO	155	96	57	.627	....	**775**	603	95	5266	1380	199	32	**153**	**2102**	**663**	699	**90**	49	.262	**.348**	.399	**.748**	**113**	**107**	101	**754**
NY	154	92	62	.597	4.5	722	639	86	5229	1337	186	**56**	151	2088	536	672	30	**31**	.256	.329	**.399**	.729	108	51	101	712
STL	154	88	66	.571	8.5	677	630	83	5200	1386	**247**	54	97	2032	537	**479**	33	32	**.267**	.340	.391	.731	110	68	100	708
PHI	154	87	67	.565	9.5	657	**552**	90	5205	1353	237	45	93	1959	540	534	60	41	.260	.332	.376	.708	104	34	99	671
CHI	155	77	77	.500	19.5	628	631	77	**5330**	**1408**	223	45	107	2042	422	712	50	40	.264	.321	.383	.704	100	-5	101	652
CIN	154	69	85	.448	27.5	615	659	72	5234	1303	212	45	104	1917	480	709	32	42	.249	.314	.366	.680	95	-40	100	610
BOS	155	64	89	.418	32	569	651	66	5221	1214	187	31	110	1793	483	711	58	34	.233	.301	.343	.645	88	-78	96	555
PIT	155	42	112	.273	54.5	515	793	46	5193	1201	181	30	92	1718	486	724	43	41	.231	.300	.331	.631	79	-142	103	530
Total	**618**					**5158**			**41878**	**10582**	**1672**	**338**	**907**		**4147**	**5240**	**396**	**310**	**.253**	**.323**	**.374**	**.697**				

Runs		Hits		Doubles		Triples		Home Runs		Total Bases	
Hemus, S. (StL)	105	Musial, S. (StL)	194	Musial, S. (StL)	42	Thomson, B. (NY)	14	Kiner, R. (Pit)	37	Musial, S. (StL)	311
Musial, S. (StL)	105	Schoendienst, R. (StL)	188	Schoendienst, R. (StL)	40	Slaughter, E. (StL)	12	Sauer, H. (Chi)	37	Sauer, H. (Chi)	301
Robinson, J. (Bro)	104	Adams, B. (Cin)	180	McMillan, R. (Cin)	32	Kluszewski, T. (Cin)	11	Hodges, G. (Bro)	32	Thomson, B. (NY)	293
Runs Batted In		**Bases On Balls**		**Stolen Bases**		**Batting Average**		**On-Base Percentage**		**Slugging Average**	
Sauer, H. (Chi)	121	Kiner, R. (Pit)	110	Reese, P. (Bro)	30	Musial, S. (StL)	.336	Robinson, J. (Bro)	.440	Musial, S. (StL)	.538
Thomson, B. (NY)	108	Hodges, G. (Bro)	107	Jethroe, S. (Bos)	28	Kluszewski, T. (Cin)	.320	Musial, S. (StL)	.432	Sauer, H. (Chi)	.531
Ennis, D. (Phi)	107	Robinson, J. (Bro)	106	Robinson, J. (Bro)	24	Robinson, J. (Bro)	.308	Hemus, S. (StL)	.392	Kluszewski, T. (Cin)	.509
Adjusted OPS		**Adjusted Batting Runs**		**Runs Created/Game**		**Fielding Runs**		**Win Shares – Batters**		**TPW – Batters**	
Musial, S. (StL)	167	Musial, S. (StL)	56.0	Musial, S. (StL)	9.50	Robinson, J. (Bro)	18.4	Musial, S. (StL)	37	Robinson, J. (Bro)	7.4
Robinson, J. (Bro)	149	Robinson, J. (Bro)	45.0	Robinson, J. (Bro)	8.20	Schoendienst, R. (StL)	16.3	Robinson, J. (Bro)	34	Musial, S. (StL)	4.5
Kluszewski, T. (Cin)	146	Kiner, R. (Pit)	33.0	Kiner, R. (Pit)	7.60	McMillan, R. (Cin)	16.1	2 players tied with	28	Schoendienst, R. (StL)	3.5

TEAM	CG	SH	SV	IP	H	H/G	ER	HR	BB	SO	OAV	RAT	ERA	ERA+	CERA	PR+	PF	FA	E	DP	FR	BW	PW	FW	TPW	DIF
BRO	45	11	24	1399[1]	1295	8.3	549	121	544	773	.247	1.314	3.53	103	3.59	3.6	97	.982	106	169	12.7	11.0	.4	1.3	12.7	7.3
NY	49	12	31	1371	1282	8.4	547	121	538	655	.248	1.327	3.59	103	3.66	21.0	99	.974	158	175	-4.1	5.3	2.2	-.4	7.0	8.0
STL	49	12	27	1361[1]	1274	8.4	553	119	501	712	.247	1.304	3.66	101	3.56	5.0	99	.977	141	159	3.0	7.0	.5	.3	7.8	3.2
PHI	80	17	16	1386[2]	1306	8.5	473	96	373	609	.249	1.211	3.07	119	3.06	67.8	98	.975	150	145	22.0	3.5	7.0	2.3	12.8	-2.8
CHI	59	15	15	1386[1]	1265	8.2	551	101	534	661	.240	1.298	3.58	108	3.38	43.9	103	.976	146	123	-3.0	-.5	4.5	-.3	3.7	-3.7
CIN	56	11	12	1363[1]	1377	9.1	607	111	517	579	.267	1.389	4.01	94	4.02	-41.0	101	.982	107	145	4.2	-4.1	-4.2	.4	-8.0	.0
BOS	63	11	13	1396	1388	9.0	586	106	525	687	.259	1.370	3.78	95	3.81	-1.7	97	.975	154	143	-24.8	-8.1	-.2	-2.6	-10.8	-1.2
PIT	43	5	8	1363[2]	1395	9.2	704	132	615	564	.266	1.474	4.65	86	4.42	-89.4	107	.970	182	167	-10.0	-14.7	-9.2	-1.0	-24.9	-10.1
Total	444	94	146	11027[2]		8.6	4570					1.336	3.73													

Wins
- Roberts, R. (Phi) 28
- Maglie, S. (NY) 18
- 3 players tied with 17

Win Percentage
- Roe, P. (Bro) .846
- Wilhelm, H. (NY) .833
- Roberts, R. (Phi) .800

Games
- Wilhelm, H. (NY) 71
- Black, J. (Bro) 56
- Yuhas, E. (StL) 54

Complete Games
- Roberts, R. (Phi) 30
- Dickson, M. (Pit) 21
- Spahn, W. (Bos) 19

Shutouts
- Raffensberger, K. (Cin) 6
- Simmons, C. (Phi) 6
- 4 players tied with 5

Saves
- Brazle, A. (StL) 16
- Black, J. (Bro) 15
- 2 players tied with 11

Innings Pitched
- Roberts, R. (Phi) 330
- Spahn, W. (Bos) 290
- Dickson, M. (Pit) 277[2]

Fewest Hits/Game
- Hacker, W. (Chi) 7.01
- Wilhelm, H. (NY) 7.17
- Erskine, C. (Bro) 7.27

Fewest BB/Game
- Roberts, R. (Phi) 1.23
- Hacker, W. (Chi) 1.51
- Raffensberger, K. (Cin) 1.64

Strikeouts
- Spahn, W. (Bos) 183
- Rush, B. (Chi) 157
- Roberts, R. (Phi) 148

Ratio
- Hacker, W. (Chi) .95
- Roberts, R. (Phi) 1.02
- Rush, B. (Chi) 1.14

Earned Run Average
- Wilhelm, H. (NY) 2.43
- Hacker, W. (Chi) 2.58
- Roberts, R. (Phi) 2.59

Adjusted ERA
- Wilhelm, H. (NY) 152
- Hacker, W. (Chi) 149
- Rush, B. (Chi) 143

Component ERA
- Hacker, W. (Chi) 2.02
- Roberts, R. (Phi) 2.31
- Rush, B. (Chi) 2.50

Opponents' Batting Avg.
- Hacker, W. (Chi) .212
- Rush, B. (Chi) .216
- Wilhelm, H. (NY) .220

Adjusted Pitching Runs
- Roberts, R. (Phi) 34
- Rush, B. (Chi) 33
- Hacker, W. (Chi) 27

Win Shares – Pitchers
- Roberts, R. (Phi) 32
- Rush, B. (Chi) 23
- 2 players tied with 22

TPW – Pitchers
- Rush, B. (Chi) 4.2
- Roberts, R. (Phi) 3.7
- Spahn, W. (Bos) 2.9

1952 American League

TEAM	G	W	L	PCT	GB	R	OR	EW	AB	H	2B	3B	HR	TB	BB	SO	SB	CS	AVG	OBP	SLG	OPS	OPS+	BR/A	PF	RC
NY	154	95	59	.617	....	727	557	97	5294	1411	221	56	129	2131	566	652	52	42	.267	.341	.403	.744	121	135	94	758
CLE	155	93	61	.604	2	763	606	94	5330	1399	211	49	148	2152	626	749	46	39	.262	.342	.404	.746	122	147	93	758
CHI	156	81	73	.526	14	610	568	82	5316	1337	199	38	80	1852	541	521	61	38	.252	.327	.348	.676	94	-36	101	633
PHI	155	79	75	.513	16	664	723	70	5163	1305	212	35	89	1854	683	561	52	43	.253	.343	.359	.702	96	-11	106	659
WAS	157	78	76	.506	17	598	608	76	5357	1282	225	44	50	1745	580	607	48	37	.239	.317	.326	.643	88	-76	97	572
BOS	154	76	78	.494	19	668	658	78	5246	1338	233	34	113	1978	542	739	59	47	.255	.328	.377	.705	95	-34	108	659
STL	155	64	90	.416	31	604	733	62	5353	1340	225	46	82	1903	540	720	30	34	.250	.322	.356	.677	92	-57	103	631
DET	156	50	104	.325	45	557	738	56	5258	1278	190	37	103	1851	553	605	27	38	.243	.318	.352	.670	92	-61	101	594
Total	621					5191			42317	10690	1716	339	794		4631	5154	375	318	.253	.330	.365	.695				

Runs
- Doby, L. (Cle) 104
- Avila, B. (Cle) 102
- Rosen, A. (Cle) 101

Hits
- Fox, N. (Chi) 192
- Avila, B. (Cle) 179
- 2 players tied with 176

Doubles
- Fain, F. (Phi) 43
- Mantle, M. (NY) 37
- 2 players tied with 33

Triples
- Avila, B. (Cle) 11
- 3 players tied with 10

Home Runs
- Doby, L. (Cle) 32
- Easter, L. (Cle) 31
- Berra, Y. (NY) 30

Total Bases
- Rosen, A. (Cle) 297
- Mantle, M. (NY) 291
- Dropo, W. (Det,Bos) 282

Runs Batted In
- Rosen, A. (Cle) 105
- Doby, L. (Cle) 104
- Robinson, E. (Chi) 104

Bases On Balls
- Yost, E. (Was) 129
- Joost, E. (Phi) 122
- Fain, F. (Phi) 105

Stolen Bases
- Minoso, M. (Chi) 22
- Rivera, J. (Chi,StL) 21
- Jensen, J. (Was,NY) 18

Batting Average
- Fain, F. (Phi) .327
- Mitchell, D. (Cle) .323
- Mantle, M. (NY) .311

On-Base Percentage
- Fain, F. (Phi) .438
- Valo, E. (Phi) .432
- Mantle, M. (NY) .394

Slugging Average
- Doby, L. (Cle) .541
- Mantle, M. (NY) .530
- Rosen, A. (Cle) .524

Adjusted OPS
- Doby, L. (Cle) 166
- Mantle, M. (NY) 165
- Rosen, A. (Cle) 162

Adjusted Batting Runs
- Mantle, M. (NY) 49.0
- Doby, L. (Cle) 47.0
- Rosen, A. (Cle) 46.0

Runs Created/Game
- Mantle, M. (NY) 8.60
- Doby, L. (Cle) 8.10
- Wertz, V. (StL,Det) 7.50

Fielding Runs
- Rizzuto, P. (NY) 18.1
- Fox, N. (Chi) 13.4
- McDougald, G. (NY) 12.5

Win Shares – Batters
- Doby, L. (Cle) 34
- Mantle, M. (NY) 32
- Rosen, A. (Cle) 31

TPW – Batters
- Doby, L. (Cle) 4.8
- Mantle, M. (NY) 4.7
- Fain, F. (Phi) 3.8

TEAM	CG	SH	SV	IP	H	H/G	ER	HR	BB	SO	OAV	RAT	ERA	ERA+	CERA	PR+	PF	FA	E	DP	FR	BW	PW	FW	TPW	DIF
NY	72	21	27	1381	1240	8.1	482	94	581	666	.243	1.319	3.14	106	3.44	-18.2	90	.979	127	199	45.4	14.0	-1.9	4.7	16.8	1.2
CLE	80	19	18	1407	1278	8.2	519	94	556	671	.241	1.303	3.32	101	3.34	15.1	91	.975	155	141	-11.8	15.3	1.6	-1.2	15.6	.4
CHI	53	15	28	1416[2]	1251	8.0	511	86	578	774	.238	1.291	3.25	112	3.20	50.4	99	.980	123	158	11.6	-3.7	5.2	1.2	2.7	1.3
PHI	73	11	15	1384[1]	1402	9.1	589	113	526	562	.263	1.393	4.15	95	3.99	-9.4	108	.977	140	148	-21.4	-1.2	-1.0	-2.2	-4.4	6.4
WAS	75	10	15	1429[2]	1405	8.8	535	78	577	574	.258	1.386	3.37	105	3.70	38.6	97	.978	132	152	-10.3	-7.9	4.0	-1.1	-5.0	6.0
BOS	53	7	24	1372[1]	1332	8.7	579	107	623	624	.256	1.425	3.80	104	4.00	13.2	107	.976	145	181	6.9	-3.5	1.4	.7	-1.5	.5
STL	48	6	18	1399	1388	8.9	640	111	598	581	.260	1.420	4.12	95	4.05	-40.6	107	.974	155	176	8.5	-6.0	-4.2	.9	-9.3	-3.7
DET	51	10	14	1388[1]	1394	9.0	655	111	591	702	.262	1.430	4.25	89	4.03	-42.0	104	.975	152	145	-27.7	-6.3	-4.4	-2.9	-13.5	-13.5
Total	505	99	159	11178[1]		8.6	4559					1.371	3.67													

Wins
- Shantz, B. (Phi) 24
- Wynn, E. (Cle) 23
- 2 players tied with 22

Win Percentage
- Shantz, B. (Phi) .774
- Raschi, V. (NY) .727
- Reynolds, A. (NY) .714

Games
- Kennedy, B. (Chi) 47
- Garcia, M. (Cle) 46
- Paige, S. (StL) 46

Complete Games
- Lemon, B. (Cle) 28
- Shantz, B. (Phi) 27
- Reynolds, A. (NY) 24

Shutouts
- Garcia, M. (Cle) 6
- Reynolds, A. (NY) 6
- 2 players tied with 5

Saves
- Dorish, H. (Chi) 11
- Paige, S. (StL) 10
- Sain, J. (NY) 7

Innings Pitched
- Lemon, B. (Cle) 309[2]
- Garcia, M. (Cle) 292[1]
- Wynn, E. (Cle) 285[2]

Fewest Hits/Game
- Lemon, B. (Cle) 6.86
- Raschi, V. (NY) 7.02
- Reynolds, A. (NY) 7.15

Fewest BB/Game
- Shantz, B. (Phi) 2.03
- Pillette, D. (StL) 2.41
- Marrero, C. (Was) 2.59

Strikeouts
- Reynolds, A. (NY) 160
- Wynn, E. (Cle) 153
- Shantz, B. (Phi) 152

Ratio
- Shantz, B. (Phi) 1.05
- Lemon, B. (Cle) 1.10
- Dobson, J. (Chi) 1.12

Earned Run Average
- Reynolds, A. (NY) 2.06
- Garcia, M. (Cle) 2.37
- Shantz, B. (Phi) 2.48

Adjusted ERA
- Reynolds, A. (NY) 161
- Shantz, B. (Phi) 160
- Dobson, J. (Chi) 145

Component ERA
- Lemon, B. (Cle) 2.28
- Shantz, B. (Phi) 2.39
- Dobson, J. (Chi) 2.42

Opponents' Batting Avg.
- Lemon, B. (Cle) .208
- Raschi, V. (NY) .216
- Reynolds, A. (NY) .218

Adjusted Pitching Runs
- Shantz, B. (Phi) 50
- Garcia, M. (Cle) 34
- Lemon, B. (Cle) 32

Win Shares – Pitchers
- Shantz, B. (Phi) 33
- Lemon, B. (Cle) 25
- Reynolds, A. (NY) 24

TPW – Pitchers
- Shantz, B. (Phi) 5.4
- Lemon, B. (Cle) 3.9
- Garcia, M. (Cle) 3.3

1953 National League

TEAM	G	W	L	PCT	GB	R	OR	EW	AB	H	2B	3B	HR	TB	BB	SO	SB	CS	AVG	OBP	SLG	OPS	OPS+	BR/A	PF	RC
BRO	155	105	49	.682	....	955	689	101	5373	1529	274	59	208	2545	655	686	90	47	.285	.366	.474	.840	122	172	102	963
MIL	157	92	62	.597	13	738	589	94	5349	1422	227	52	156	2221	439	637	46	27	.266	.325	.415	.740	104	25	94	727
STL	157	83	71	.539	22	768	713	83	5397	1474	281	56	140	2287	574	617	18	22	.273	.347	.424	.771	107	52	100	806
PHI	156	83	71	.539	22	716	666	83	5290	1400	228	62	115	2097	530	597	42	21	.265	.335	.396	.731	97	-18	99	727
NY	155	70	84	.455	35	768	747	79	5362	1452	195	45	176	2265	499	608	31	21	.271	.336	.422	.758	101	6	102	771
CIN	155	68	86	.442	37	714	788	69	5343	1396	190	34	166	2152	485	701	25	20	.261	.325	.403	.727	94	-49	101	711
CHI	155	65	89	.422	40	633	835	56	5272	1372	204	57	137	2101	514	746	49	21	.260	.328	.399	.726	93	-52	102	697
PIT	154	50	104	.325	55	622	887	51	5253	1297	178	49	99	1870	524	715	41	39	.247	.319	.356	.675	82	-132	99	614
Total	622					5914			42639	11342	1777	414	1197		4220	5307	342	218	.266	.335	.411	.747				

Runs
Snider, D. (Bro) 132
Musial, S. (StL) 127
Dark, A. (NY) 126

Hits
Ashburn, R. (Phi) 205
Musial, S. (StL) 200
Snider, D. (Bro) 198

Doubles
Musial, S. (StL) 53
Dark, A. (NY) 41
2 players tied with 38

Triples
Gilliam, J. (Bro) 17
Bruton, B. (Mil) 14
2 players tied with 11

Home Runs
Mathews, E. (Mil) 47
Snider, D. (Bro) 42
Campanella, R. (Bro) 41

Total Bases
Snider, D. (Bro) 370
Mathews, E. (Mil) 363
Musial, S. (StL) 361

Runs Batted In
Campanella, R. (Bro) 142
Mathews, E. (Mil) 135
Snider, D. (Bro) 126

Bases On Balls
Musial, S. (StL) 105
Kiner, R. (Chi,Pit) 100
Gilliam, J. (Bro) 100

Stolen Bases
Bruton, B. (Mil) 26
Reese, P. (Bro) 22
Gilliam, J. (Bro) 21

Batting Average
Furillo, C. (Bro) .344
Schoendienst, R. (StL) .342
Musial, S. (StL) .337

On-Base Percentage
Musial, S. (StL) .437
Robinson, J. (Bro) .425
Snider, D. (Bro) .419

Slugging Average
Snider, D. (Bro) .627
Mathews, E. (Mil) .627
Campanella, R. (Bro) .611

Adjusted OPS
Mathews, E. (Mil) 175
Musial, S. (StL) 169
Snider, D. (Bro) 164

Adjusted Batting Runs
Mathews, E. (Mil) 64.0
Musial, S. (StL) 63.0
Snider, D. (Bro) 57.0

Runs Created/Game
Musial, S. (StL) 11.00
Snider, D. (Bro) 10.50
Mathews, E. (Mil) 10.20

Fielding Runs
Logan, J. (Mil) 25.3
McMillan, R. (Cin) 21.6
Schoendienst, R. (StL) 12.3

Win Shares – Batters
Mathews, E. (Mil) 39
Snider, D. (Bro) 37
2 players tied with 33

TPW – Batters
Mathews, E. (Mil) 6.6
Schoendienst, R. (StL) 5.1
Campanella, R. (Bro) 4.6

TEAM	CG	SH	SV	IP	H	H/G	ER	HR	BB	SO	OAV	RAT	ERA	ERA+	CERA	PR+	PF	FA	E	DP	FR	BW	PW	FW	TPW	DIF
BRO	51	11	29	1380²	1337	8.7	629	169	509	817	.253	1.337	4.10	104	3.95	3.9	99	.980	118	161	21.0	16.6	.4	2.0	19.0	9.0
MIL	72	14	15	1387	1282	8.3	509	107	539	738	.245	1.313	3.30	119	3.47	82.1	91	.976	143	169	14.4	2.4	7.9	1.4	11.7	3.3
STL	51	11	36	1386²	1406	9.1	651	139	533	732	.262	1.398	4.23	101	4.13	22.8	99	.977	138	161	-18.2	5.0	2.2	-1.8	5.5	.5
PHI	76	13	15	1369²	1410	9.3	578	138	410	637	.265	1.329	3.80	111	3.90	67.3	98	.975	147	161	-0.6	-1.8	.6	-.1	4.7	1.3
NY	46	10	20	1365²	1403	9.2	645	146	610	647	.264	1.474	4.25	101	4.46	5.6	100	.975	151	151	0.5	.6	.5	.0	1.2	-8.2
CIN	47	7	15	1365	1484	9.8	704	179	488	506	.279	1.445	4.64	94	4.71	-69.3	102	.978	129	176	29.3	-4.8	-6.7	2.8	-8.6	-.4
CHI	38	3	22	1359	1491	9.9	723	151	554	623	.276	1.505	4.79	93	4.73	-11.9	104	.967	193	141	-38.9	-5.0	-1.1	-3.7	-9.9	-2.1
PIT	49	4	10	1358	1529	10.1	788	168	577	607	.285	1.551	5.22	86	5.06	-104.7	104	.973	163	139	-7.9	-12.7	-10.1	-.8	-23.5	-3.5
Total	430	73	162	10971²		9.3	5227					1.418	4.29													

Wins
Roberts, R. (Phi) 23
Spahn, W. (Mil) 23
2 players tied with 20

Win Percentage
Roe, P. (Bro) .786
Erskine, C. (Bro) .769
Spahn, W. (Mil) .767

Games
Wilhelm, H. (NY) 68
Brazle, A. (StL) 60
Hetki, J. (Pit) 54

Complete Games
Roberts, R. (Phi) 33
Spahn, W. (Mil) 24
2 players tied with 19

Shutouts
Haddix, H. (StL) 6
Roberts, R. (Phi) 5
Spahn, W. (Mil) 5

Saves
Brazle, A. (StL) 18
Wilhelm, H. (NY) 15
Hughes, J. (Bro) 9

Innings Pitched
Roberts, R. (Phi) 346²
Spahn, W. (Mil) 265²
Haddix, H. (StL) 253

Fewest Hits/Game
Spahn, W. (Mil) 7.15
Gomez, R. (NY) 7.32
Mizell, V. (StL) 7.74

Fewest BB/Game
Roberts, R. (Phi) 1.58
Raffensberger, K. (Cin) 1.71
Minner, P. (Chi) 1.79

Strikeouts
Roberts, R. (Phi) 198
Erskine, C. (Bro) 187
Mizell, V. (StL) 173

Ratio
Spahn, W. (Mil) 1.06
Roberts, R. (Phi) 1.11
Haddix, H. (StL) 1.14

Earned Run Average
Spahn, W. (Mil) 2.10
Roberts, R. (Phi) 2.75
Buhl, B. (Mil) 2.97

Adjusted ERA
Spahn, W. (Mil) 187
Roberts, R. (Phi) 153
Haddix, H. (StL) 139

Component ERA
Spahn, W. (Mil) 2.19
Roberts, R. (Phi) 2.75
Haddix, H. (StL) 2.87

Opponents' Batting Avg.
Spahn, W. (Mil) .217
Gomez, R. (NY) .218
Mizell, V. (StL) .227

Adjusted Pitching Runs
Roberts, R. (Phi) 56
Spahn, W. (Mil) 51
Haddix, H. (StL) 37

Win Shares – Pitchers
Roberts, R. (Phi) 35
Spahn, W. (Mil) 31
Haddix, H. (StL) 27

TPW – Pitchers
Roberts, R. (Phi) 5.6
Spahn, W. (Mil) 5.3
Haddix, H. (StL) 4.5

1953 American League

TEAM	G	W	L	PCT	GB	R	OR	EW	AB	H	2B	3B	HR	TB	BB	SO	SB	CS	AVG	OBP	SLG	OPS	OPS+	BR/A	PF	RC
NY	151	99	52	.656	....	801	547	103	5194	1420	226	52	139	2167	656	644	34	44	.273	.359	.417	.776	120	139	97	809
CLE	155	92	62	.597	8.5	770	627	93	5285	1426	201	29	160	2165	609	683	33	29	.270	.349	.410	.759	114	101	97	780
CHI	156	89	65	.578	11.5	716	592	91	5212	1345	226	53	74	1899	601	530	73	55	.258	.341	.364	.705	94	-37	103	666
BOS	153	84	69	.549	16	656	632	79	5246	1385	255	37	101	2017	496	601	33	45	.264	.332	.384	.716	94	-50	105	683
WAS	152	76	76	.500	23.5	687	614	85	5149	1354	230	53	69	1897	596	604	65	36	.263	.343	.368	.711	100	17	98	675
DET	158	60	94	.390	40.5	695	923	56	5553	1479	259	44	108	2150	506	603	30	35	.266	.331	.387	.718	101	-4	99	716
PHI	157	59	95	.383	41.5	632	799	59	5455	1398	205	38	116	2027	498	602	41	24	.256	.321	.372	.693	89	-80	104	658
STL	154	54	100	.351	46.5	555	778	52	5264	1310	214	25	112	1910	507	644	17	34	.249	.317	.363	.680	87	-99	102	606
Total	618					5512			42358	11117	1816	331	879	4469		4911	326	302	.262	.337	.383	.720				

Runs
Rosen, A. (Cle) 115
Yost, E. (Was) 107
Mantle, M. (NY) 105

Hits
Kuenn, H. (Det) 209
Vernon, M. (Was) 205
Rosen, A. (Cle) 201

Doubles
Vernon, M. (Was) 43
Kell, G. (Bos) 41
White, S. (Bos) 34

Triples
Rivera, J. (Chi) 16
Vernon, M. (Was) 11
2 players tied with 9

Home Runs
Rosen, A. (Cle) 43
Zernial, G. (Phi) 42
Doby, L. (Cle) 29

Total Bases
Rosen, A. (Cle) 367
Vernon, M. (Was) 315
Zernial, G. (Phi) 311

Runs Batted In
Rosen, A. (Cle) 145
Vernon, M. (Was) 115
Boone, R. (Det,Cle) 114

Bases On Balls
Yost, E. (Was) 123
Fain, F. (Chi) 108
Doby, L. (Cle) 96

Stolen Bases
Minoso, M. (Chi) 25
Rivera, J. (Chi) 22
Jensen, J. (Was) 18

Batting Average
Vernon, M. (Was) .337
Rosen, A. (Cle) .336
Goodman, B. (Bos) .313

On-Base Percentage
Woodling, G. (NY) .429
Rosen, A. (Cle) .422
Minoso, M. (Chi) .410

Slugging Average
Rosen, A. (Cle) .613
Zernial, G. (Phi) .559
Berra, Y. (NY) .523

Adjusted OPS
Rosen, A. (Cle) 181
Vernon, M. (Was) 151
Woodling, G. (NY) 147

Adjusted Batting Runs
Rosen, A. (Cle) 67.0
Vernon, M. (Was) 42.0
Boone, R. (Det,Cle) 32.0

Runs Created/Game
Rosen, A. (Cle) 9.90
Mantle, M. (NY) 8.20
Vernon, M. (Was) 8.00

Fielding Runs
Hunter, B. (StL) 20.1
Piersall, J. (Bos) 14.6
Terwilliger, W. (Was) 14.1

Win Shares – Batters
Rosen, A. (Cle) 42
Vernon, M. (Was) 29
Berra, Y. (NY) 28

TPW – Batters
Rosen, A. (Cle) 6.5
Vernon, M. (Was) 3.8
Boone, R. (Det,Cle) 3.6

TEAM	CG	SH	SV	IP	H	H/G	ER	HR	BB	SO	OAV	RAT	ERA	ERA+	CERA	PR+	PF	FA	E	DP	FR	BW	PW	FW	TPW	DIF
NY	50	18	39	1358¹	1286	8.5	483	94	500	604	.251	1.315	3.20	115	3.51	38.3	92	.979	126	182	35.6	13.9	3.8	3.6	21.3	2.7
CLE	81	11	15	1373	1311	8.6	555	92	519	586	.253	1.333	3.64	103	3.56	15.9	94	.979	127	197	0.2	10.1	1.6	.0	11.7	3.3
CHI	57	17	33	1403²	1299	8.3	532	113	583	714	.246	1.341	3.41	118	3.60	90.3	101	.980	125	144	5.3	-3.7	9.0	.5	5.9	6.1
BOS	41	15	37	1373	1333	8.7	546	92	584	642	.254	1.396	3.58	117	3.75	86.5	105	.976	148	173	8.0	-5.0	8.7	.8	4.5	3.5
WAS	76	16	10	1344²	1313	8.8	547	112	478	515	.258	1.332	3.66	106	3.70	25.6	98	.979	120	173	9.4	1.7	2.6	.9	5.2	-5.2
DET	50	2	16	1415	1633	10.4	825	154	585	645	.291	1.567	5.25	77	5.14	-144.4	102	.978	135	149	-42.5	-.4	-14.5	-4.3	-19.1	2.1
PHI	51	7	11	1409	1475	9.4	731	121	594	566	.271	1.468	4.67	92	4.40	-55.4	107	.977	137	161	-5.2	-8.0	-5.5	-.5	-14.1	-3.9
STL	28	10	24	1383²	1467	9.5	688	101	626	639	.273	1.513	4.48	94	4.41	-33.5	105	.974	152	165	-9.2	-9.9	-3.4	-.9	-14.2	-8.8
Total	434	96	185	11060¹		9.0	4907					1.409	3.99													

Wins
Porterfield, B. (Was) 22
Lemon, B. (Cle) 21
Parnell, M. (Bos) 21

Win Percentage
Lopat, E. (NY) .800
Ford, W. (NY) .750
Parnell, M. (Bos) .724

Games
Kinder, E. (Bos) 69
Stuart, M. (StL) 60
Martin, M. (Phi) 58

Complete Games
Porterfield, B. (Was) 24
Lemon, B. (Cle) 23
Garcia, M. (Cle) 21

Shutouts
Porterfield, B. (Was) 9
Pierce, B. (Chi) 7
3 players tied with 5

Saves
Kinder, E. (Bos) 27
Dorish, H. (Chi) 18
Reynolds, A. (NY) 13

Innings Pitched
Lemon, B. (Cle) 286²
Garcia, M. (Cle) 271²
Pierce, B. (Chi) 271¹

Fewest Hits/Game
Pierce, B. (Chi) 7.16
McDermott, M. (Bos) 7.37
Raschi, V. (NY) 7.46

Fewest BB/Game
Lopat, E. (NY) 1.61
Sain, J. (NY) 2.14
Kellner, A. (Phi) 2.28

Strikeouts
Pierce, B. (Chi) 186
Trucks, V. (Chi,StL) 149
Wynn, E. (Cle) 138

Ratio
Lopat, E. (NY) 1.13
Raschi, V. (NY) 1.13
Pierce, B. (Chi) 1.17

Earned Run Average
Lopat, E. (NY) 2.42
Pierce, B. (Chi) 2.72
Trucks, V. (Chi,StL) 2.93

Adjusted ERA
Lopat, E. (NY) 152
Pierce, B. (Chi) 148
McDermott, M. (Bos) 140

Component ERA
Raschi, V. (NY) 2.51
Pierce, B. (Chi) 2.69
Lopat, E. (NY) 2.85

Opponents' Batting Avg.
Pierce, B. (Chi) .218
McDermott, M. (Bos) .224
Raschi, V. (NY) .224

Adjusted Pitching Runs
Trucks, V. (Chi,StL) 38
Pierce, B. (Chi) 34
Parnell, M. (Bos) 29

Win Shares – Pitchers
Trucks, V. (Chi,StL) 25
Pierce, B. (Chi) 24
Parnell, M. (Bos) 23

TPW – Pitchers
Trucks, V. (Chi,StL) 3.5
Pierce, B. (Chi) 3.4
McDermott, M. (Bos) 3.3

1954 National League

TEAM	G	W	L	PCT	GB	R	OR	EW	AB	H	2B	3B	HR	TB	BB	SO	SB	CS	AVG	OBP	SLG	OPS	OPS+	BR/A	PF	RC
NY	154	97	57	.630	....	732	**550**	98	5245	1386	194	42	**186**	2222	522	**561**	30	23	.264	.335	.424	.758	102	14	101	745
BRO	154	92	62	.597	5	778	740	81	5251	1418	246	56	**186**	**2334**	**634**	625	46	39	.270	.353	**.444**	**.797**	**110**	**74**	103	**820**
MIL	154	89	65	.578	8	670	556	91	5261	1395	217	41	139	2111	471	619	54	31	.265	.330	.401	.731	103	15	93	695
PHI	154	75	79	.487	22	659	614	82	5184	1384	243	**58**	102	2049	604	620	30	27	.267	.345	.395	.740	99	-1	100	705
CIN	154	74	80	.481	23	729	763	73	5234	1369	221	46	147	2123	557	645	47	30	.262	.336	.406	.742	96	-26	103	724
STL	154	72	82	.468	25	**799**	790	78	**5405**	**1518**	**285**	**58**	119	2276	582	586	**63**	46	**.281**	**.354**	.421	.775	107	58	101	804
CHI	154	64	90	.416	33	700	766	70	5359	1412	229	45	159	2208	478	693	46	31	.263	.327	.412	.740	97	-29	101	716
PIT	154	53	101	.344	44	557	845	47	5088	1260	181	57	76	1783	566	737	21	**13**	.248	.326	.350	.676	84	-107	98	593
Total	**616**					**5624**			**42027**	**11142**	**1816**	**403**	**1114**		**4414**	**5086**	**337**	**240**	**.265**	**.338**	**.407**	**.745**				

Runs
Musial, S. (StL) 120
Snider, D. (Bro) 120
Mays, W. (NY) 119

Hits
Mueller, D. (NY) 212
Snider, D. (Bro) 199
2 players tied with 195

Doubles
Musial, S. (StL) 41
3 players tied with 39

Triples
Mays, W. (NY) 13
Hamner, G. (Phi) 11
Snider, D. (Bro) 10

Home Runs
Kluszewski, T. (Cin) 49
Hodges, G. (Bro) 42
2 players tied with 41

Total Bases
Snider, D. (Bro) 378
Mays, W. (NY) 377
Kluszewski, T. (Cin) 368

Runs Batted In
Kluszewski, T. (Cin) 141
Hodges, G. (Bro) 130
Snider, D. (Bro) 130

Bases On Balls
Ashburn, R. (Phi) 125
Mathews, E. (Mil) 113
Musial, S. (StL) 103

Stolen Bases
Bruton, B. (Mil) 34
Temple, J. (Cin) 21
Fondy, D. (Chi) 20

Batting Average
Mays, W. (NY) .345
Mueller, D. (NY) .342
Snider, D. (Bro) .341

On-Base Percentage
Ashburn, R. (Phi) .442
Musial, S. (StL) .433
Mathews, E. (Mil) .428

Slugging Average
Mays, W. (NY) .667
Snider, D. (Bro) .647
Kluszewski, T. (Cin) .642

Adjusted OPS
Mathews, E. (Mil) 177
Mays, W. (NY) 176
Snider, D. (Bro) 170

Adjusted Batting Runs
Mays, W. (NY) 61.0
Snider, D. (Bro) 60.0
Mathews, E. (Mil) 59.0

Runs Created/Game
Snider, D. (Bro) 10.60
Mays, W. (NY) 10.60
Kluszewski, T. (Cin) 10.10

Fielding Runs
McMillan, R. (Cin) 20.2
Schoendienst, R. (StL) 15.8
Mays, W. (NY) 14.7

Win Shares – Batters
Mays, W. (NY) 40
Snider, D. (Bro) 39
2 players tied with 33

TPW – Batters
Mays, W. (NY) 6.8
Mathews, E. (Mil) 5.7
Musial, S. (StL) 5.3

TEAM	CG	SH	SV	IP	H	H/G	ER	HR	BB	SO	OAV	RAT	ERA	ERA+	CERA	PR+	PF	FA	E	DP	FR	BW	PW	FW	TPW	DIF
NY	45	**19**	33	1390	**1258**	**8.2**	**477**	113	613	692	**.243**	1.346	**3.09**	131	3.61	**129.1**	99	.975	154	172	16.2	1.4	**12.8**	1.6	**15.7**	4.3
BRO	39	8	**36**	1393[2]	1399	9.0	667	164	533	**762**	.261	1.386	4.31	95	4.12	-35.4	100	.978	129	138	0.6	**7.3**	-3.5	.1	3.9	11.1
MIL	63	13	21	**1394[2]**	1296	8.4	494	**106**	553	698	.250	1.326	3.19	117	**3.54**	65.6	91	**.981**	**116**	171	**17.8**	1.5	6.5	**1.8**	9.8	2.2
PHI	**78**	14	12	1365[1]	1329	8.8	544	133	**450**	570	.256	**1.303**	3.59	113	3.64	62.1	99	.975	145	133	5.4	-.1	6.1	.5	6.6	-8.6
CIN	34	8	27	1367[1]	1491	9.8	684	169	547	537	.282	1.490	4.50	93	4.83	-61.9	103	.977	137	**194**	15.0	-2.5	-6.1	1.5	-7.2	4.2
STL	40	11	18	1390[1]	1484	9.6	695	170	535	680	.275	1.452	4.50	91	4.66	-51.5	101	.976	146	178	-8.2	5.7	-5.1	-.8	-.2	-4.8
CHI	41	6	19	1374[1]	1375	9.0	689	131	619	622	.264	1.451	4.51	93	4.22	-30.3	103	.974	154	164	-16.2	-2.9	-3.0	-1.6	-7.5	-5.5
PIT	37	4	15	1346	1510	10.1	736	128	564	525	.287	1.541	4.92	**85**	4.77	-78.2	103	.971	173	136	-31.0	-10.6	-7.7	-3.1	-21.4	-2.6
Total	**377**	**83**	**181**	**11021[2]**		**9.1**	**4986**					**1.411**	**4.07**													

Wins
Roberts, R. (Phi) 23
Antonelli, J. (NY) 21
Spahn, W. (Mil) 21

Win Percentage
Antonelli, J. (NY) .750
Lawrence, B. (StL) .714
Nuxhall, J. (Cin) .706

Games
Hughes, J. (Bro) 60
Brazle, A. (StL) 58
Hetki, J. (Pit) 58

Complete Games
Roberts, R. (Phi) 29
Spahn, W. (Mil) 23
Simmons, C. (Phi) 21

Shutouts
Antonelli, J. (NY) 6
5 players tied with 4

Saves
Hughes, J. (Bro) 24
Smith, F. (Cin) 20
Grissom, M. (NY) 19

Innings Pitched
Roberts, R. (Phi) 336[2]
Spahn, W. (Mil) 283[1]
Erskine, C. (Bro) 260[1]

Fewest Hits/Game
Antonelli, J. (NY) 7.27
Roberts, R. (Phi) 7.73
Conley, G. (Mil) 7.92

Fewest BB/Game
Roberts, R. (Phi) 1.50
Minner, P. (Chi) 2.06
Hacker, W. (Chi) 2.10

Strikeouts
Roberts, R. (Phi) 185
Haddix, H. (StL) 184
Erskine, C. (Bro) 166

Ratio
Roberts, R. (Phi) 1.02
Antonelli, J. (NY) 1.17
Burdette, L. (Mil) 1.20

Earned Run Average
Antonelli, J. (NY) 2.30
Burdette, L. (Mil) 2.76
Simmons, C. (Phi) 2.81

Adjusted ERA
Antonelli, J. (NY) 176
Simmons, C. (Phi) 144
Gomez, R. (NY) 140

Component ERA
Roberts, R. (Phi) 2.51
Antonelli, J. (NY) 2.78
Burdette, L. (Mil) 3.08

Opponents' Batting Avg.
Antonelli, J. (NY) .219
Roberts, R. (Phi) .231
Simmons, C. (Phi) .239

Adjusted Pitching Runs
Antonelli, J. (NY) 47
Roberts, R. (Phi) 39
Simmons, C. (Phi) 34

Win Shares – Pitchers
Roberts, R. (Phi) 31
Antonelli, J. (NY) 28
Spahn, W. (Mil) 23

TPW – Pitchers
Antonelli, J. (NY) 4.6
Roberts, R. (Phi) 3.5
Simmons, C. (Phi) 3.2

1954 American League

TEAM	G	W	L	PCT	GB	R	OR	EW	AB	H	2B	3B	HR	TB	BB	SO	SB	CS	AVG	OBP	SLG	OPS	OPS+	BR/A	PF	RC
CLE	156	111	43	.721	....	746	**504**	106	5222	1368	188	39	**156**	2102	637	668	30	33	.262	.345	.403	.747	109	63	102	736
NY	155	103	51	.669	8	**805**	563	103	5226	1400	215	59	133	**2132**	650	632	34	41	**.268**	**.351**	**.408**	**.759**	**119**	**125**	97	**766**
CHI	155	94	60	.610	17	711	521	100	5168	1382	203	47	94	1961	604	**536**	**98**	58	.267	.350	.379	.729	103	31	103	698
BOS	156	69	85	.448	42	700	728	74	**5399**	**1436**	**244**	41	123	2131	**654**	660	51	30	.266	.348	.395	.742	99	5	111	746
DET	155	68	86	.442	43	584	664	67	5233	1351	215	41	90	1918	492	603	48	44	.258	.324	.367	.691	97	-29	98	607
WAS	155	66	88	.429	45	632	680	71	5249	1292	188	**69**	81	1861	610	719	37	**21**	.246	.328	.355	.682	99	-3	95	629
BAL	154	54	100	.351	57	483	668	53	5206	1309	195	49	52	1758	468	634	30	31	.251	.316	.338	.653	92	-63	92	551
PHI	156	51	103	.331	60	542	875	43	5206	1228	191	41	94	1783	504	677	30	29	.236	.307	.342	.649	83	-120	100	551
Total	**621**					**5203**			**41909**	**10766**	**1639**	**386**	**823**		**4619**	**5129**	**358**	**287**	**.257**	**.334**	**.373**	**.707**				

Runs
Mantle, M. (NY) 129
Minoso, M. (Chi) 119
Avila, B. (Cle) 112

Hits
Fox, N. (Chi) 201
Kuenn, H. (Det) 201
Avila, B. (Cle) 189

Doubles
Vernon, M. (Was) 33
Minoso, M. (Chi) 29
Smith, A. (Cle) 29

Triples
Minoso, M. (Chi) 18
Runnels, P. (Was) 15
Vernon, M. (Was) 14

Home Runs
Doby, L. (Cle) 32
Williams, T. (Bos) 29
Mantle, M. (NY) 27

Total Bases
Minoso, M. (Chi) 304
Vernon, M. (Was) 294
2 players tied with 285

Runs Batted In
Doby, L. (Cle) 126
Berra, Y. (NY) 125
Jensen, J. (Bos) 117

Bases On Balls
Williams, T. (Bos) 136
Yost, E. (Was) 131
Mantle, M. (NY) 102

Stolen Bases
Jensen, J. (Bos) 22
Minoso, M. (Chi) 18
Rivera, J. (Chi) 18

Batting Average
Avila, B. (Cle) .341
Williams, T. (Bos) .345
Minoso, M. (Chi) .320

On-Base Percentage
Williams, T. (Bos) .516
Minoso, M. (Chi) .416
Rosen, A. (Cle) .412

Slugging Average
Williams, T. (Bos) .635
Minoso, M. (Chi) .535
Mantle, M. (NY) .525

Adjusted OPS
Williams, T. (Bos) 193
Mantle, M. (NY) 160
Minoso, M. (Chi) 154

Adjusted Batting Runs
Williams, T. (Bos) 62.0
Mantle, M. (NY) 48.0
Minoso, M. (Chi) 44.0

Runs Created/Game
Williams, T. (Bos) 14.20
Mantle, M. (NY) 8.70
Minoso, M. (Chi) 7.80

Fielding Runs
Avila, B. (Cle) 32.1
Carrasquel, C. (Chi) 18.8
McDougald, G. (NY) 13.5

Win Shares – Batters
Mantle, M. (NY) 36
Avila, B. (Cle) 34
Berra, Y. (NY) 34

TPW – Batters
Avila, B. (Cle) 7.5
Williams, T. (Bos) 5.6
Minoso, M. (Chi) 4.5

TEAM	CG	SH	SV	IP	H	H/G	ER	HR	BB	SO	OAV	RAT	ERA	ERA+	CERA	PR+	PF	FA	E	DP	FR	BW	PW	FW	TPW	DIF
CLE	**77**	12	36	**1419[1]**	**1220**	**7.7**	**438**	89	**486**	678	**.232**	**1.202**	**2.78**	132	**2.85**	**119.2**	99	.979	128	148	20.9	6.6	**12.3**	2.2	**21.0**	13.0
NY	51	16	**37**	1379[1]	1284	8.4	500	86	552	655	.251	1.331	3.26	105	3.47	-6.0	92	.979	126	**198**	**32.4**	**12.9**	-.6	**3.3**	15.6	10.4
CHI	60	**23**	33	1383	1255	8.2	469	94	517	701	.244	1.281	3.05	122	3.25	91.6	100	**.982**	**108**	149	13.1	3.2	9.5	1.4	14.1	2.9
BOS	41	10	22	1412[1]	1434	9.1	629	118	612	**707**	.265	1.449	4.01	103	4.17	31.1	110	.972	176	163	-16.1	.5	3.2	-1.7	2.1	-10.1
DET	58	13	13	1383	1375	9.0	585	138	506	603	.261	1.360	3.81	97	3.98	-22.5	99	.979	129	131	4.6	-3.0	-2.3	.5	-4.9	-4.1
WAS	69	10	7	1383[1]	1396	9.1	590	79	573	562	.265	1.423	3.84	93	3.87	-19.3	96	.977	137	172	-24.2	-.3	-2.0	-2.5	-4.8	-6.2
BAL	58	6	8	1373[1]	1279	8.4	592	**78**	688	668	.250	1.432	3.88	92	3.72	-34.6	96	.975	147	152	-11.0	-6.5	-3.6	-1.1	-11.2	-11.8
PHI	49	3	13	1371[1]	1523	10.0	789	141	685	555	.285	1.610	5.18	**75**	5.14	-173.9	105	.971	169	163	-20.3	-12.4	-18.0	-2.1	-32.5	6.5
Total	**463**	**93**	**169**	**11105**		**8.7**	**4592**					**1.385**	**3.72**													

Wins
Lemon, B. (Cle) 23
Wynn, E. (Cle) 23
Grim, B. (NY) 20

Win Percentage
Consuegra, S. (Chi) .842
Grim, B. (NY) .769
Lemon, B. (Cle) .767

Games
Dixon, S. (Phi,Was) 54
3 players tied with 48

Complete Games
Lemon, B. (Cle) 21
Porterfield, B. (Was) 21
Wynn, E. (Cle) 20

Shutouts
Garcia, M. (Cle) 5
Trucks, V. (Chi) 5
7 players tied with 4

Saves
Sain, J. (NY) 22
Kinder, E. (Bos) 15
Narleski, R. (Cle) 13

Innings Pitched
Wynn, E. (Cle) 270^{2}
Trucks, V. (Chi) 264^{2}
Garcia, M. (Cle) 258^{2}

Fewest Hits/Game
Turley, B. (Bal) 6.48
Ford, W. (NY) 7.26
Wynn, E. (Cle) 7.48

Fewest BB/Game
Lopat, E. (NY) 1.75
Gromek, S. (Det) 2.03
Consuegra, S. (Chi) 2.05

Strikeouts
Turley, B. (Bal) 185
Wynn, E. (Cle) 155
Trucks, V. (Chi) 152

Ratio
Garcia, M. (Cle) 1.12
Garver, N. (Cle) 1.13
Wynn, E. (Cle) 1.14

Earned Run Average
Garcia, M. (Cle) 2.64
Consuegra, S. (Chi) 2.69
Lemon, B. (Cle) 2.72

Adjusted ERA
Garcia, M. (Cle) 139
Consuegra, S. (Chi) 139
Lemon, B. (Cle) 135

Component ERA
Garcia, M. (Cle) 2.30
Wynn, E. (Cle) 2.62
Trucks, V. (Chi) 2.71

Opponents' Batting Avg.
Turley, B. (Bal) .203
Wynn, E. (Cle) .225
Ford, W. (NY) .227

Adjusted Pitching Runs
Gromek, S. (Det) 26
Garcia, M. (Cle) 26
Trucks, V. (Chi) 25

Win Shares – Pitchers
4 players tied with 24

TPW – Pitchers
Lemon, B. (Cle) 3.0
Gromek, S. (Det) 2.8
Wynn, E. (Cle) 2.6

1955 National League

TEAM	G	W	L	PCT	GB	R	OR	EW	AB	H	2B	3B	HR	TB	BB	SO	SB	CS	AVG	OBP	SLG	OPS	OPS+	BR/A	PF	RC
BRO	154	98	55	.641	....	857	650	97	5193	1406	230	44	201	2327	674	718	79	56	.271	.359	.448	.807	116	121	103	833
MIL	154	85	69	.552	13.5	743	668	85	5277	1377	219	55	182	2252	504	735	42	27	.261	.329	.427	.755	110	68	95	732
NY	154	80	74	.519	18.5	702	673	80	5288	1377	173	34	169	2125	497	581	38	22	.260	.328	.402	.730	98	-13	100	697
PHI	154	77	77	.500	21.5	675	666	78	5092	1300	214	50	132	2010	652	673	44	32	.255	.343	.395	.737	102	30	98	690
CIN	154	75	79	.487	23.5	761	684	85	5270	1424	216	28	181	2239	556	657	51	36	.270	.344	.425	.768	102	23	106	772
CHI	154	72	81	.471	26	626	713	67	5214	1287	187	55	164	2076	428	806	37	35	.247	.307	.398	.705	91	-76	100	622
STL	154	68	86	.442	30.5	654	757	66	5266	1375	228	36	143	2104	458	597	64	59	.261	.324	.400	.723	96	-37	100	660
PIT	154	60	94	.390	38.5	560	767	54	5173	1262	210	60	91	1865	471	652	22	22	.244	.310	.361	.670	83	-119	99	566
Total	616					5578			41773	10808	1677	362	1263		4240	5419	377	289	.259	.330	.407	.737				

Runs
Snider, D. (Bro) 126
Mays, W. (NY) 123
2 players tied with 116

Hits
Kluszewski, T. (Cin) 192
Aaron, H. (Mil) 189
Bell, G. (Cin) 188

Doubles
Aaron, H. (Mil) 37
Logan, J. (Mil) 37
Snider, D. (Bro) 34

Triples
Long, D. (Pit) 13
Mays, W. (NY) 13
Bruton, B. (Mil) 12

Home Runs
Mays, W. (NY) 51
Kluszewski, T. (Cin) 47
Banks, E. (Chi) 44

Total Bases
Mays, W. (NY) 382
Kluszewski, T. (Cin) 358
Banks, E. (Chi) 355

Runs Batted In
Snider, D. (Bro) 136
Mays, W. (NY) 127
Ennis, D. (Phi) 120

Bases On Balls
Mathews, E. (Mil) 109
Ashburn, R. (Phi) 105
Snider, D. (Bro) 104

Stolen Bases
Bruton, B. (Mil) 25
Mays, W. (NY) 24
Boyer, K. (StL) 22

Batting Average
Ashburn, R. (Phi) .338
Mays, W. (NY) .319
Musial, S. (StL) .319

On-Base Percentage
Ashburn, R. (Phi) .449
Snider, D. (Bro) .421
Mathews, E. (Mil) .417

Slugging Average
Mays, W. (NY) .659
Snider, D. (Bro) .628
Mathews, E. (Mil) .601

Adjusted OPS
Mays, W. (NY) 175
Mathews, E. (Mil) 175
Snider, D. (Bro) 169

Adjusted Batting Runs
Mays, W. (NY) 66.0
Mathews, E. (Mil) 57.0
Snider, D. (Bro) 56.0

Runs Created/Game
Mays, W. (NY) 10.10
Snider, D. (Bro) 9.80
Mathews, E. (Mil) 9.50

Fielding Runs
McMillan, R. (Cin) 26.3
Mays, W. (NY) 16.6
Robinson, J. (Bro) 13.6

Win Shares – Batters
Mays, W. (NY) 40
Snider, D. (Bro) 36
Banks, E. (Chi) 34

TPW – Batters
Mays, W. (NY) 7.5
Banks, E. (Chi) 5.3
Snider, D. (Bro) 4.8

TEAM	CG	SH	SV	IP	H	H/G	ER	HR	BB	SO	OAV	RAT	ERA	ERA+	CERA	PR+	PF	FA	E	DP	FR	BW	PW	FW	TPW	DIF
BRO	46	11	37	1378	1296	8.5	563	168	483	773	.248	1.291	3.68	110	3.75	49.8	101	.978	133	156	7.6	12.0	4.9	.8	17.7	4.3
MIL	61	5	12	1383	1339	8.7	592	138	591	654	.256	1.396	3.85	97	4.02	-12.8	93	.975	152	155	-1.5	6.8	-1.3	-.2	5.3	2.7
NY	52	6	14	1386^{2}	1347	8.7	581	155	560	721	.257	1.375	3.77	107	4.11	39.8	100	.976	142	165	-0.9	-1.3	3.9	-.1	2.6	.4
PHI	58	11	21	1356^{2}	1291	8.6	592	161	477	657	.251	1.303	3.93	101	3.81	-9.7	98	.981	110	117	15.9	3.0	-1.0	1.6	3.6	-3.6
CIN	38	12	22	1363	1373	9.1	598	161	443	576	.264	1.332	3.95	107	4.02	42.0	105	.977	139	169	1.1	2.3	4.2	.1	6.5	-8.5
CHI	47	10	23	1378^{1}	1306	8.5	638	153	601	686	.251	1.384	4.17	98	4.03	-19.0	101	.975	147	147	5.7	-7.6	-1.9	.6	-8.9	4.9
STL	42	10	15	1376^{2}	1376	9.0	697	185	549	730	.262	1.398	4.56	89	4.41	-60.4	101	.975	146	152	-16.7	-3.7	-6.0	-1.7	-11.3	2.3
PIT	41	5	16	1362	1480	9.8	664	142	536	622	.281	1.480	4.39	94	4.68	-30.0	102	.972	166	175	-12.7	-11.8	-3.0	-1.3	-16.0	-1.0
Total	385	70	160	10984^{1}		8.9	4925					1.370	4.04													

Wins
Roberts, R. (Phi) 23
Newcombe, D. (Bro) 20
2 players tied with 17

Win Percentage
Newcombe, D. (Bro) .800
Roberts, R. (Phi) .622
Burdette, L. (Mil) .619

Games
Labine, C. (Bro) 60
Wilhelm, H. (NY) 59
LaPalme, P. (StL) 56

Complete Games
Roberts, R. (Phi) 26
Newcombe, D. (Bro) 17
Spahn, W. (Mil) 16

Shutouts
Nuxhall, J. (Cin) 5
Dickson, M. (Phi) 4
Jones, S. (Chi) 4

Saves
Meyer, J. (Phi) 16
Roebuck, E. (Bro) 12
2 players tied with 11

Innings Pitched
Roberts, R. (Phi) 305
Nuxhall, J. (Cin) 257
Spahn, W. (Mil) 245^{2}

Fewest Hits/Game
Jones, S. (Chi) 6.52
Buhl, B. (Mil) 7.50
Rush, B. (Chi) 7.85

Fewest BB/Game
Newcombe, D. (Bro) 1.46
Roberts, R. (Phi) 1.56
Hacker, W. (Chi) 1.82

Strikeouts
Jones, S. (Chi) 198
Roberts, R. (Phi) 160
Haddix, H. (StL) 150

Ratio
Newcombe, D. (Bro) 1.11
Roberts, R. (Phi) 1.13
Friend, B. (Pit) 1.15

Earned Run Average
Friend, B. (Pit) 2.83
Newcombe, D. (Bro) 3.20
Buhl, B. (Mil) 3.21

Adjusted ERA
Friend, B. (Pit) 145
Newcombe, D. (Bro) 127
Nuxhall, J. (Cin) 122

Component ERA
Friend, B. (Pit) 2.91
Rush, B. (Chi) 2.95
Roberts, R. (Phi) 3.15

Opponents' Batting Avg.
Jones, S. (Chi) .206
Buhl, B. (Mil) .227
Rush, B. (Chi) .234

Adjusted Pitching Runs
Friend, B. (Pit) 30
Nuxhall, J. (Cin) 22
Newcombe, D. (Bro) 21

Win Shares – Pitchers
Roberts, R. (Phi) 27
Newcombe, D. (Bro) 25
Nuxhall, J. (Cin) 20

TPW – Pitchers
Newcombe, D. (Bro) 4.1
Roberts, R. (Phi) 3.4
Friend, B. (Pit) 2.8

1955 American League

TEAM	G	W	L	PCT	GB	R	OR	EW	AB	H	2B	3B	HR	TB	BB	SO	SB	CS	AVG	OBP	SLG	OPS	OPS+	BR/A	PF	RC
NY	154	96	58	.623	....	762	569	99	5161	1342	179	55	175	2156	609	658	55	25	.260	.343	.418	.761	113	90	98	757
CLE	154	93	61	.604	3	698	601	88	5146	1325	195	31	148	2026	723	715	28	24	.257	.353	.394	.747	104	37	104	739
CHI	155	91	63	.591	5	725	557	97	5220	1401	204	36	116	2025	567	595	69	45	.268	.347	.388	.735	101	12	103	711
BOS	154	84	70	.545	12	755	652	88	5273	1392	241	39	137	2122	707	733	43	17	.264	.354	.402	.757	101	23	109	771
DET	154	79	75	.513	17	775	658	89	5283	1407	211	38	130	2084	641	583	41	22	.266	.348	.394	.742	109	69	98	734
KC	155	63	91	.409	33	638	911	51	5335	1395	189	46	121	2039	463	725	22	36	.261	.323	.382	.706	95	-56	101	636
BAL	156	57	97	.370	39	540	754	52	5257	1263	177	39	54	1680	560	742	34	46	.240	.316	.320	.635	83	-128	93	530
WAS	154	53	101	.344	43	598	789	56	5142	1277	178	54	80	1803	538	654	25	32	.248	.324	.351	.674	93	-57	95	584
Total	618					5491			41817	10802	1574	338	961		4808	5405	317	247	.258	.339	.381	.720				

Runs
Smith, A. (Cle) 123
Kaline, A. (Det) 121
Mantle, M. (NY) 121

Hits
Kaline, A. (Det) 200
Fox, N. (Chi) 198
2 players tied with 190

Doubles
Kuenn, H. (Det) 38
Power, V. (KC) 34
Goodman, B. (Bos) 31

Triples
Carey, A. (NY) 11
Mantle, M. (NY) 11
Power, V. (KC) 10

Home Runs
Mantle, M. (NY) 37
Zernial, G. (KC) 30
Williams, T. (Bos) 28

Total Bases
Kaline, A. (Det) 321
Mantle, M. (NY) 316
Power, V. (KC) 301

Runs Batted In
Boone, R. (Det) 116
Jensen, J. (Bos) 116
Berra, Y. (NY) 108

Bases On Balls
Mantle, M. (NY) 113
Goodman, B. (Bos) 99
Yost, E. (Was) 95

Stolen Bases
Rivera, J. (Chi) 25
Minoso, M. (Chi) 19
Jensen, J. (Bos) 16

Batting Average
Kaline, A. (Det) .340
Power, V. (KC) .319
Kell, G. (Chi) .312

On-Base Percentage
Mantle, M. (NY) .433
Kaline, A. (Det) .425
Smith, A. (Cle) .411

Slugging Average
Mantle, M. (NY) .611
Kaline, A. (Det) .546
Doby, L. (Cle) .505

Adjusted OPS
Mantle, M. (NY) 181
Kaline, A. (Det) 163
Sievers, R. (Was) 136

Adjusted Batting Runs
Mantle, M. (NY) 64.0
Kaline, A. (Det) 52.0
Smith, A. (Cle) 32.0

Runs Created/Game
Mantle, M. (NY) 10.80
Kaline, A. (Det) 8.80
Smith, A. (Cle) 7.80

Fielding Runs
McDougald, G. (NY) 27.3
Fox, N. (Chi) 24.0
Miranda, W. (Bal) 18.9

Win Shares – Batters
Mantle, M. (NY) 41
Kaline, A. (Det) 31
Smith, A. (Cle) 29

TPW – Batters
Mantle, M. (NY) 5.9
Kaline, A. (Det) 4.7
McDougald, G. (NY) 4.4

TEAM	CG	SH	SV	IP	H	H/G	ER	HR	BB	SO	OAV	RAT	ERA	ERA+	CERA	PR+	PF	FA	E	DP	FR	BW	PW	FW	TPW	DIF
NY	52	19	33	1372^{1}	**1163**	**7.6**	**492**	108	688	731	**.232**	1.349	**3.23**	116	3.58	20.2	94	.978	128	**180**	**57.0**	**9.0**	2.0	**5.7**	**16.7**	2.3
CLE	45	15	**36**	1386^{1}	1285	8.3	522	111	558	**877**	.245	1.329	3.39	118	3.59	90.2	101	**.981**	**108**	152	2.0	3.7	9.0	.2	12.9	3.1
CHI	55	**20**	23	1378	1301	8.5	516	111	**497**	720	.251	**1.305**	3.37	117	**3.54**	67.1	100	.981	111	147	21.1	1.2	6.7	2.1	10.0	4.0
BOS	44	9	34	1384^{1}	1333	8.7	572	128	582	674	.253	1.383	3.72	115	3.95	**102.6**	108	.977	136	140	-14.6	2.3	**10.3**	-1.5	11.1	-4.1
DET	**66**	16	12	1380^{1}	1381	9.0	581	126	517	629	.261	1.375	3.79	101	3.99	10.2	97	.976	139	159	-3.1	6.9	1.0	-.3	7.6	-5.6
KC	29	9	23	1382	1486	9.7	822	175	707	572	.278	1.587	5.35	**78**	5.28	-174.8	105	.976	146	174	-6.9	-5.6	-17.5	-.7	-23.8	9.8
BAL	35	10	22	**1388^{2}**	1403	9.1	649	103	625	595	.266	1.460	4.21	91	4.28	-42.1	96	.972	167	159	-19.8	-12.8	-4.2	-2.0	-19.0	-1.0
WAS	37	10	16	1354^{2}	1450	9.6	695	**99**	634	607	.279	1.538	4.62	83	4.67	-83.2	97	.974	154	170	-36.5	-5.7	-8.3	-3.7	-17.7	-6.3
Total	**363**	**108**	**199**	**11026^{2}**		**8.8**	**4849**					**1.416**	**3.96**													

Wins
- Ford, W. (NY) 18
- Lemon, B. (Cle) 18
- Sullivan, F. (Bos) 18

Win Percentage
- Byrne, T. (NY) .762
- Ford, W. (NY) .720
- Hoeft, B. (Det) .696

Games
- Narleski, R. (Cle) 60
- Gorman, T. (KC) 57
- Mossi, D. (Cle) 57

Complete Games
- Ford, W. (NY) 18
- Hoeft, B. (Det) 17
- 5 players tied with 16

Shutouts
- Hoeft, B. (Det) 7
- 3 players tied with 6

Saves
- Narleski, R. (Cle) 19
- Gorman, T. (KC) 18
- Kinder, E. (Bos) 18

Innings Pitched
- Sullivan, F. (Bos) 260
- Ford, W. (NY) 253^{2}
- Turley, B. (NY) 246^{2}

Fewest Hits/Game
- Turley, B. (NY) 6.13
- Score, H. (Cle) 6.26
- Ford, W. (NY) 6.67

Fewest BB/Game
- Gromek, S. (Det) 1.84
- Donovan, D. (Chi) 2.31
- Garcia, M. (Cle) 2.39

Strikeouts
- Score, H. (Cle) 245
- Turley, B. (NY) 210
- Pierce, B. (Chi) 157

Ratio
- Pierce, B. (Chi) 1.10
- Ford, W. (NY) 1.19
- Hoeft, B. (Det) 1.19

Earned Run Average
- Pierce, B. (Chi) 1.97
- Ford, W. (NY) 2.63
- Wynn, E. (Cle) 2.82

Adjusted ERA
- Pierce, B. (Chi) 200
- Sullivan, F. (Bos) 148
- Ford, W. (NY) 142

Component ERA
- Pierce, B. (Chi) 2.49
- Ford, W. (NY) 2.77
- Wilson, J. (Bal) 2.96

Opponents' Batting Avg.
- Turley, B. (NY) .193
- Score, H. (Cle) .194
- Ford, W. (NY) .208

Adjusted Pitching Runs
- Sullivan, F. (Bos) 43
- Pierce, B. (Chi) 42
- Wynn, E. (Cle) 30

Win Shares – Pitchers
- Pierce, B. (Chi) 23
- Ford, W. (NY) 22
- Sullivan, F. (Bos) 22

TPW – Pitchers
- Pierce, B. (Chi) 4.2
- Sullivan, F. (Bos) 3.9
- Wynn, E. (Cle) 3.1

1956 National League

TEAM	G	W	L	PCT	GB	R	OR	EW	AB	H	2B	3B	HR	TB	BB	SO	SB	CS	AVG	OBP	SLG	OPS	OPS+	BR/A	PF	RC
BRO	154	93	61	.604	....	720	601	91	5098	1315	212	36	179	2136	**649**	738	65	37	.258	**.344**	.419	.763	103	33	108	727
MIL	155	92	62	.597	1	709	**569**	94	5207	1350	212	54	177	2201	486	714	29	**20**	.259	.325	.423	.748	**113**	**82**	94	713
CIN	155	91	63	.591	2	**775**	658	89	5291	1406	201	32	**221**	**2334**	528	760	45	22	.266	.338	**.441**	**.779**	108	62	106	**788**
STL	156	76	78	.494	17	678	698	75	**5378**	**1443**	**234**	49	124	2147	503	**622**	41	35	**.268**	.335	.399	.734	103	22	100	706
PHI	154	71	83	.461	22	668	738	69	5204	1313	207	49	121	1981	585	673	45	23	.252	.331	.381	.712	99	5	98	656
NY	154	67	87	.435	26	540	650	63	5190	1268	192	45	145	1985	402	659	**67**	34	.244	.301	.382	.684	89	-80	99	584
PIT	157	66	88	.429	27	588	653	69	5221	1340	199	**57**	110	1983	383	752	24	33	.257	.310	.380	.689	93	-65	98	592
CHI	157	60	94	.390	33	597	708	64	5260	1281	202	50	142	2009	446	776	55	38	.244	.304	.382	.686	91	-71	98	604
Total	**621**					**5275**			**41849**	**10716**	**1659**	**372**	**1219**		**3982**	**5694**	**371**	**242**	**.256**	**.324**	**.401**	**.725**				

Runs
- Robinson, F. (Cin) 122
- Snider, D. (Bro) 112
- Aaron, H. (Mil) 106

Hits
- Aaron, H. (Mil) 200
- Ashburn, R. (Phi) 190
- Virdon, B. (Pit,StL) 185

Doubles
- Aaron, H. (Mil) 34
- 3 players tied with 33

Triples
- Bruton, B. (Mil) 15
- Aaron, H. (Mil) 14
- 2 players tied with 11

Home Runs
- Snider, D. (Bro) 43
- Adcock, J. (Mil) 38
- Robinson, F. (Cin) 38

Total Bases
- Aaron, H. (Mil) 340
- Snider, D. (Bro) 324
- Mays, W. (NY) 322

Runs Batted In
- Musial, S. (StL) 109
- Adcock, J. (Mil) 103
- Kluszewski, T. (Cin) 102

Bases On Balls
- Snider, D. (Bro) 99
- Gilliam, J. (Bro) 95
- Jones, W. (Phi) 92

Stolen Bases
- Mays, W. (NY) 40
- Gilliam, J. (Bro) 21
- White, B. (NY) 15

Batting Average
- Aaron, H. (Mil) .328
- Virdon, B. (Pit,StL) .319
- Clemente, R. (Pit) .311

On-Base Percentage
- Snider, D. (Bro) .402
- Gilliam, J. (Bro) .400
- Musial, S. (StL) .390

Slugging Average
- Snider, D. (Bro) .598
- Adcock, J. (Mil) .597
- Aaron, H. (Mil) .558

Adjusted OPS
- Adcock, J. (Mil) 154
- Aaron, H. (Mil) 154
- Snider, D. (Bro) 152

Adjusted Batting Runs
- Snider, D. (Bro) 42.0
- Aaron, H. (Mil) 42.0
- Mays, W. (NY) 42.0

Runs Created/Game
- Snider, D. (Bro) 8.40
- Robinson, F. (Cin) 7.50
- Mathews, E. (Mil) 7.50

Fielding Runs
- McMillan, R. (Cin) 27.8
- Baker, G. (Chi) 19.9
- Jackson, R. (Bro) 16.8

Win Shares – Batters
- Snider, D. (Bro) 34
- Aaron, H. (Mil) 30
- Mathews, E. (Mil) 29

TPW – Batters
- Aaron, H. (Mil) 4.5
- Mays, W. (NY) 4.4
- Musial, S. (StL) 3.9

TEAM	CG	SH	SV	IP	H	H/G	ER	HR	BB	SO	OAV	RAT	ERA	ERA+	CERA	PR+	PF	FA	E	DP	FR	BW	PW	FW	TPW	DIF
BRO	46	**12**	**30**	1368^{2}	**1251**	**8.2**	543	171	441	**772**	**.244**	**1.236**	3.57	111	3.56	33.2	105	**.981**	**111**	149	**27.1**	3.3	3.4	**2.8**	9.5	6.5
MIL	**64**	**12**	27	**1393^{1}**	1295	8.4	**481**	**133**	467	639	.247	1.265	**3.11**	111	**3.45**	**42.8**	92	.979	130	159	13.3	**8.4**	**4.4**	1.4	**14.2**	.8
CIN	47	4	29	1389	1406	9.1	594	141	458	653	.265	1.342	3.85	103	3.94	35.2	105	.981	113	147	-15.1	6.3	3.6	-1.5	8.4	5.6
STL	41	**12**	**30**	1388^{2}	1339	8.7	612	155	546	709	.257	1.357	3.97	95	3.99	-25.3	100	.978	134	**172**	-2.8	2.2	-2.6	-.3	-.7	-.3
PHI	57	4	15	1377^{1}	1407	9.2	643	172	**437**	750	.266	1.339	4.20	**89**	4.05	-43.0	99	.975	144	140	-30.2	.5	-4.4	-3.1	-7.0	1.0
NY	31	9	28	1378	1287	8.4	579	144	551	765	.250	1.334	3.78	100	3.79	6.5	100	.976	144	143	-5.6	-8.2	.7	-.6	-8.1	-1.9
PIT	37	8	24	1376^{1}	1406	9.2	572	142	469	662	.267	1.362	3.74	101	3.99	14.4	100	.973	162	140	-9.9	-6.6	1.5	-1.0	-6.2	-4.8
CHI	37	6	17	1392	1325	8.6	612	161	613	744	.252	1.392	3.96	95	4.10	-52.9	100	.976	144	141	24.2	-7.3	-5.4	2.5	-10.3	-6.7
Total	**360**	**67**	**200**	**11063^{1}**		**8.7**	**4636**					**1.329**	**3.77**													

Wins
- Newcombe, D. (Bro) 27
- Antonelli, J. (NY) 20
- Spahn, W. (Mil) 20

Win Percentage
- Jeffcoat, H. (Cin) .800
- Newcombe, D. (Bro) .794
- Maglie, S. (Bro) .722

Games
- Face, R. (Pit) 68
- Freeman, H. (Cin) 64
- Wilhelm, H. (NY) 64

Complete Games
- Roberts, R. (Phi) 22
- Spahn, W. (Mil) 20
- Friend, B. (Pit) 19

Shutouts
- Burdette, L. (Mil) 6
- Antonelli, J. (NY) 5
- Newcombe, D. (Bro) 5

Saves
- Labine, C. (Bro) 19
- Freeman, H. (Cin) 18
- Lown, T. (Chi) 13

Innings Pitched
- Friend, B. (Pit) 314^{1}
- Roberts, R. (Phi) 297^{1}
- Spahn, W. (Mil) 281^{1}

Fewest Hits/Game
- Maglie, S. (Bro) 7.26
- Newcombe, D. (Bro) 7.35
- Jones, S. (Chi) 7.39

Fewest BB/Game
- Roberts, R. (Phi) 1.21
- Newcombe, D. (Bro) 1.54
- Spahn, W. (Mil) 1.66

Strikeouts
- Jones, S. (Chi) 176
- Haddix, H. (Phi,StL) 170
- Friend, B. (Pit) 166

Ratio
- Newcombe, D. (Bro) .99
- Spahn, W. (Mil) 1.07
- Maglie, S. (Bro) 1.08

Earned Run Average
- Burdette, L. (Mil) 2.70
- Spahn, W. (Mil) 2.78
- Antonelli, J. (NY) 2.86

Adjusted ERA
- Maglie, S. (Bro) 138
- Antonelli, J. (NY) 132
- Newcombe, D. (Bro) 130

Component ERA
- Newcombe, D. (Bro) 2.42
- Spahn, W. (Mil) 2.61
- Maglie, S. (Bro) 2.78

Opponents' Batting Avg.
- Newcombe, D. (Bro) .221
- Jones, S. (Chi) .221
- 2 players tied with .222

Adjusted Pitching Runs
- Antonelli, J. (NY) 28
- Newcombe, D. (Bro) 22
- Maglie, S. (Bro) 19

Win Shares – Pitchers
- Newcombe, D. (Bro) 27
- Antonelli, J. (NY) 25
- Spahn, W. (Mil) 24

TPW – Pitchers
- Newcombe, D. (Bro) 3.1
- Antonelli, J. (NY) 3.0
- Spahn, W. (Mil) 2.5

1956 American League

TEAM	G	W	L	PCT	GB	R	OR	EW	AB	H	2B	3B	HR	TB	BB	SO	SB	CS	AVG	OBP	SLG	OPS	OPS+	BR/A	PF	RC
NY	154	97	57	.630	....	**857**	631	100	5312	1433	193	55	**190**	**2306**	615	755	51	37	.270	.349	**.434**	.783	**116**	**106**	97	813
CLE	155	88	66	.571	9	712	**581**	92	5148	1256	199	23	153	1960	681	764	40	32	.244	.337	.381	.718	93	-50	102	679
CHI	154	85	69	.552	12	776	634	92	5286	1412	218	43	128	2100	619	660	**70**	33	.267	.352	.397	.749	102	25	101	754
BOS	155	84	70	.545	13	780	751	80	5349	1473	**261**	45	139	2241	**727**	687	28	**19**	.275	**.365**	.419	**.784**	100	15	112	**824**
DET	155	82	72	.532	15	789	699	86	**5364**	**1494**	209	50	150	2253	644	**618**	43	26	**.279**	.359	.420	.779	111	85	100	814
BAL	154	69	85	.448	28	571	705	61	5090	1242	198	34	91	1781	563	725	39	42	.244	.322	.350	.672	90	-82	92	571
WAS	155	59	95	.383	38	652	924	51	5202	1302	198	**62**	112	1960	690	877	37	34	.250	.343	.377	.719	96	-27	100	679
KC	154	52	102	.338	45	619	831	55	5256	1325	204	41	112	1947	480	727	40	30	.252	.317	.370	.687	86	-113	100	609
Total	**618**					**5756**			**42007**	**10937**	**1680**	**353**	**1075**		**5019**	**5813**	**348**	**253**	**.260**	**.343**	**.394**	**.737**				

Runs
- Mantle, M. (NY) 132
- Fox, N. (Chi) 109
- Minoso, M. (Chi) 106

Hits
- Kuenn, H. (Det) 196
- Kaline, A. (Det) 194
- Fox, N. (Chi) 192

Doubles
- Piersall, J. (Bos) 40
- Kaline, A. (Det) 32
- Kuenn, H. (Det) 32

Triples
- 4 players tied with 11

Home Runs
- Mantle, M. (NY) 52
- Wertz, V. (Cle) 32
- Berra, Y. (NY) 30

Total Bases
- Mantle, M. (NY) 376
- Kaline, A. (Det) 327
- Jensen, J. (Bos) 287

Runs Batted In
- Mantle, M. (NY) 130
- Kaline, A. (Det) 128
- Wertz, V. (Cle) 106

Bases On Balls
- Yost, E. (Was) 151
- Mantle, M. (NY) 112
- 2 players tied with 102

Stolen Bases
- Aparicio, L. (Chi) 21
- Rivera, J. (Chi) 20
- Avila, B. (Cle) 17

Batting Average
- Mantle, M. (NY) .353
- Williams, T. (Bos) .345
- Kuenn, H. (Det) .332

On-Base Percentage
- Williams, T. (Bos) .479
- Mantle, M. (NY) .467
- Nieman, B. (Bal,Chi) .438

Slugging Average
- Mantle, M. (NY) .705
- Williams, T. (Bos) .605
- Maxwell, C. (Det) .534

Adjusted OPS
- Mantle, M. (NY) 213
- Williams, T. (Bos) 164
- Nieman, B. (Bal,Chi) 157

Adjusted Batting Runs
- Mantle, M. (NY) 92.0
- Williams, T. (Bos) 44.0
- Minoso, M. (Chi) 43.0

Runs Created/Game
- Mantle, M. (NY) 14.30
- Williams, T. (Bos) 11.80
- Maxwell, C. (Det) 9.00

Fielding Runs
- McDougald, G. (NY) 17.2
- Avila, B. (Cle) 16.6
- Piersall, J. (Bos) 12.9

Win Shares – Batters
- Mantle, M. (NY) 49
- Berra, Y. (NY) 31
- Minoso, M. (Chi) 29

TPW – Batters
- Mantle, M. (NY) 8.8
- McDougald, G. (NY) 4.3
- Berra, Y. (NY) 4.0

TEAM	CG	SH	SV	IP	H	H/G	ER	HR	BB	SO	OAV	RAT	ERA	ERA+	CERA	PR+	PF	FA	E	DP	FR	BW	PW	FW	TPW	DIF
NY	50	10	35	1382	1285	8.4	557	114	652	732	.249	1.402	3.63	107	4.01	5.1	93	.977	136	214	32.4	10.4	.5	3.2	14.1	5.9
CLE	67	17	24	1384	1233	8.0	511	116	564	845	.238	1.298	3.32	127	3.47	141.1	101	.978	129	130	-5.4	-4.9	13.8	-.5	8.4	2.6
CHI	65	11	13	1389	1351	8.8	576	118	524	722	.255	1.350	3.73	110	3.80	49.5	99	.979	122	160	8.7	2.5	4.8	.9	8.2	-.2
BOS	50	8	20	1398	1354	8.7	648	130	668	712	.254	1.446	4.17	111	4.24	73.9	111	.972	169	168	-2.8	1.5	7.2	-.3	8.5	-1.5
DET	62	10	15	1379	1389	9.1	622	140	655	788	.264	1.482	4.06	102	4.55	9.9	99	.976	140	151	-0.6	8.4	1.0	-.1	9.3	-4.3
BAL	38	10	24	1360²	1362	9.0	635	99	547	715	.264	1.403	4.20	93	3.96	-32.9	94	.977	137	142	-9.3	-8.0	-3.2	-.9	-12.1	4.1
WAS	36	1	18	1368²	1539	10.1	810	171	730	663	.287	1.658	5.33	81	5.64	-112.3	104	.972	171	173	-40.2	-2.6	-11.0	-3.9	-17.6	-.4
KC	30	3	18	1370¹	1424	9.4	740	187	679	636	.271	1.535	4.86	89	5.12	-96.5	104	.973	166	187	15.6	-11.0	-9.4	1.5	-18.9	-6.1
Total	398	70	167	11031²		8.9	5099					1.446	4.16													

Wins
- Lary, F. (Det) 21
- 5 players tied with 20

Win Percentage
- Ford, W. (NY) .760
- 3 players tied with .690

Games
- Zuverink, G. (Bal) 62
- Crimian, J. (KC) 54
- Gorman, T. (NY) 52

Complete Games
- Lemon, B. (Cle) 21
- Pierce, B. (Chi) 21
- Lary, F. (Det) 20

Shutouts
- Score, H. (Cle) 5
- 5 players tied with 4

Saves
- Zuverink, G. (Bal) 16
- Morgan, T. (NY) 11
- Mossi, D. (Cle) 11

Innings Pitched
- Lary, F. (Det) 294
- Wynn, E. (Cle) 277²
- Pierce, B. (Chi) 276¹

Fewest Hits/Game
- Score, H. (Cle) 5.85
- Larsen, D. (NY) 6.66
- Harshman, J. (Chi) 7.27

Fewest BB/Game
- Stobbs, C. (Was) 2.02
- Donovan, D. (Chi) 2.26
- Kucks, J. (NY) 2.89

Strikeouts
- Score, H. (Cle) 263
- Pierce, B. (Chi) 192
- Foytack, P. (Det) 184

Ratio
- Donovan, D. (Chi) 1.15
- Wynn, E. (Cle) 1.17
- Score, H. (Cle) 1.17

Earned Run Average
- Ford, W. (NY) 2.47
- Score, H. (Cle) 2.53
- Wynn, E. (Cle) 2.72

Adjusted ERA
- Score, H. (Cle) 166
- Ford, W. (NY) 157
- Wynn, E. (Cle) 154

Component ERA
- Score, H. (Cle) 2.52
- Wynn, E. (Cle) 2.76
- Ford, W. (NY) 2.88

Opponents' Batting Avg.
- Score, H. (Cle) .186
- Larsen, D. (NY) .204
- Brewer, T. (Bos) .220

Adjusted Pitching Runs
- Score, H. (Cle) 47
- Wynn, E. (Cle) 47
- Lemon, B. (Cle) 34

Win Shares – Pitchers
- Wynn, E. (Cle) 28
- Score, H. (Cle) 25
- Brewer, T. (Bos) 24

TPW – Pitchers
- Wynn, E. (Cle) 4.9
- Score, H. (Cle) 4.7
- Lemon, B. (Cle) 3.8

1957 National League

TEAM	G	W	L	PCT	GB	R	OR	EW	AB	H	2B	3B	HR	TB	BB	SO	SB	CS	AVG	OBP	SLG	OPS	OPS+	BR/A	PF	RC
MIL	155	95	59	.617	....	772	613	94	5458	1469	221	62	199	2411	461	729	35	16	.269	.329	.442	.771	121	145	93	786
STL	154	87	67	.565	8	737	666	85	5472	1497	235	43	132	2214	493	672	58	44	.274	.336	.405	.740	103	18	102	729
BRO	154	84	70	.545	11	690	591	89	5242	1325	188	38	147	2030	550	848	60	34	.253	.328	.387	.715	89	-66	110	662
CIN	154	80	74	.519	15	747	781	74	5389	1452	251	33	187	2330	546	752	51	36	.269	.341	.432	.773	106	46	107	793
PHI	156	77	77	.500	18	623	656	73	5241	1311	213	44	117	1963	534	758	57	26	.250	.325	.375	.699	97	-13	97	633
NY	154	69	85	.448	26	643	701	70	5346	1349	171	54	157	2099	447	669	64	38	.252	.313	.393	.706	95	-40	100	646
PIT	155	62	92	.403	33	586	696	64	5402	1447	231	60	92	2074	374	733	46	35	.268	.318	.384	.702	97	-31	97	647
CHI	156	62	92	.403	33	628	722	66	5369	1312	223	31	147	2038	461	989	28	25	.244	.307	.380	.687	91	-70	98	621
Total	619					5426			42919	11162	1733	365	1178		3866	6150	399	254	.260	.325	.400	.724				

Runs
- Aaron, H. (Mil) 118
- Banks, E. (Chi) 113
- Mays, W. (NY) 112

Hits
- Schoendienst, R. (Mil,NY).. 200
- Aaron, H. (Mil) 198
- Robinson, F. (Cin) 197

Doubles
- Hoak, D. (Cin) 39
- Musial, S. (StL) 38
- Bouchee, E. (Phi) 35

Triples
- Mays, W. (NY) 20
- Virdon, B. (Pit) 11
- 2 players tied with 9

Home Runs
- Aaron, H. (Mil) 44
- Banks, E. (Chi) 43
- Snider, D. (Bro) 40

Total Bases
- Aaron, H. (Mil) 369
- Mays, W. (NY) 366
- Banks, E. (Chi) 344

Runs Batted In
- Aaron, H. (Mil) 132
- Ennis, D. (StL) 105
- 2 players tied with 102

Bases On Balls
- Ashburn, R. (Phi) 94
- Temple, J. (Cin) 94
- Mathews, E. (Mil) 90

Stolen Bases
- Mays, W. (NY) 38
- Gilliam, J. (Bro) 26
- Blasingame, D. (StL) 21

Batting Average
- Musial, S. (StL) .351
- Mays, W. (NY) .333
- Robinson, F. (Cin) .322

On-Base Percentage
- Musial, S. (StL) .428
- Mays, W. (NY) .411
- Bouchee, E. (Phi) .396

Slugging Average
- Mays, W. (NY) .626
- Musial, S. (StL) .612
- Aaron, H. (Mil) .600

Adjusted OPS
- Mays, W. (NY) 174
- Musial, S. (StL) 172
- Aaron, H. (Mil) 170

Adjusted Batting Runs
- Mays, W. (NY) 61.0
- Aaron, H. (Mil) 58.0
- Musial, S. (StL) 52.0

Runs Created/Game
- Musial, S. (StL) 10.00
- Mays, W. (NY) 9.10
- Aaron, H. (Mil) 8.50

Fielding Runs
- Blasingame, D. (StL) 20.6
- Logan, J. (Mil) 18.0
- Ashburn, R. (Phi) 16.2

Win Shares – Batters
- Aaron, H. (Mil) 35
- Mays, W. (NY) 34
- Mathews, E. (Mil) 33

TPW – Batters
- Mays, W. (NY) 6.4
- Aaron, H. (Mil) 5.3
- Musial, S. (StL) 4.8

TEAM	CG	SH	SV	IP	H	H/G	ER	HR	BB	SO	OAV	RAT	ERA	ERA+	CERA	PR+	PF	FA	E	DP	FR	BW	PW	FW	TPW	DIF
MIL	60	9	24	1411	1347	8.6	544	124	570	693	.253	1.359	3.47	101	3.79	-19.8	90	.981	120	173	24.0	14.7	-2.0	2.4	15.2	2.8
STL	46	11	29	1413¹	1385	8.8	593	140	506	778	.257	1.338	3.78	105	3.87	31.9	102	.979	131	168	-2.6	1.8	3.2	-.3	4.8	5.2
BRO	44	18	29	1399	1285	8.3	521	144	456	891	.244	1.244	3.35	124	3.42	129.2	107	.979	127	136	-3.1	-6.7	13.1	-.3	6.1	.9
CIN	40	5	29	1395²	1486	9.6	716	179	429	707	.275	1.372	4.62	89	4.38	-82.1	106	.982	107	139	2.5	4.7	-8.3	.3	-3.4	6.4
PHI	54	9	23	1401²	1363	8.8	590	139	412	858	.254	1.266	3.79	100	3.49	7.3	98	.976	136	117	-5.9	-1.3	.7	-.6	-1.2	1.2
NY	35	9	20	1398²	1436	9.2	623	150	471	701	.267	1.363	4.01	98	4.11	-7.3	101	.974	161	180	-4.8	-4.1	-.7	-.5	-5.3	-2.7
PIT	47	9	15	1395	1463	9.4	601	158	421	663	.270	1.351	3.88	98	4.10	-30.0	98	.972	170	143	16.0	-3.1	-3.1	1.6	-4.5	-10.5
CHI	30	5	26	1403³	1397	9.0	644	144	601	859	.261	1.424	4.13	94	4.25	-18.7	100	.975	149	140	-22.0	-7.1	-1.9	-2.2	-11.3	-3.7
Total	356	75	195	11217²		9.0	4832					1.340	3.88													

Wins
- Spahn, W. (Mil) 21
- Sanford, J. (Phi) 19
- Buhl, B. (Mil) 18

Win Percentage
- Buhl, B. (Mil) .720
- Sanford, J. (Phi) .704
- Spahn, W. (Mil) .656

Games
- Lown, T. (Chi) 67
- Face, R. (Pit) 59
- Labine, C. (Bro) 58

Complete Games
- Spahn, W. (Mil) 18
- Friend, B. (Pit) 17
- Gomez, R. (NY) 16

Shutouts
- Podres, J. (Bro) 6
- 3 players tied with 4

Saves
- Labine, C. (Bro) 17
- Grissom, M. (NY) 14
- Lown, T. (Chi) 12

Innings Pitched
- Friend, B. (Pit) 277
- Spahn, W. (Mil) 271
- Burdette, L. (Mil) 256²

Fewest Hits/Game
- Sanford, J. (Phi) 7.38
- Podres, J. (Bro) 7.71
- Drott, D. (Chi) 7.86

Fewest BB/Game
- Newcombe, D. (Bro) 1.49
- Roberts, R. (Phi) 1.55
- Law, V. (Pit) 1.67

Strikeouts
- Sanford, J. (Phi) 188
- Drabowsky, M. (Chi) 170
- Drott, D. (Chi) 170

Ratio
- Podres, J. (Bro) 1.08
- Roberts, R. (Phi) 1.16
- Drysdale, D. (Bro) 1.17

Earned Run Average
- Podres, J. (Bro) 2.66
- Drysdale, D. (Bro) 2.69
- Spahn, W. (Mil) 2.69

Adjusted ERA
- Podres, J. (Bro) 156
- Drysdale, D. (Bro) 155
- Law, V. (Pit) 132

Component ERA
- Podres, J. (Bro) 2.55
- Drysdale, D. (Bro) 2.97
- Spahn, W. (Mil) 2.97

Opponents' Batting Avg.
- Sanford, J. (Phi) .221
- Podres, J. (Bro) .230
- Drott, D. (Chi) .234

Adjusted Pitching Runs
- Drysdale, D. (Bro) 37
- Podres, J. (Bro) 33
- Sanford, J. (Phi) 20

Win Shares – Pitchers
- Spahn, W. (Mil) 22
- Drysdale, D. (Bro) 21
- Lawrence, B. (Cin) 21

TPW – Pitchers
- Drysdale, D. (Bro) 3.7
- Podres, J. (Bro) 3.4
- Spahn, W. (Mil) 2.1

1957 American League

TEAM	G	W	L	PCT	GB	R	OR	EW	AB	H	2B	3B	HR	TB	BB	SO	SB	CS	AVG	OBP	SLG	OPS	OPS+	BR/A	PF	RC
NY	154	98	56	.636	....	**723**	**534**	100	5271	**1412**	200	**54**	145	**2155**	562	709	49	38	**.268**	.341	**.409**	**.750**	**113**	**88**	98	**728**
CHI	155	90	64	.584	8	707	566	94	5265	1369	208	41	106	1977	**633**	745	**109**	51	.260	**.347**	.375	.722	103	47	100	706
BOS	154	82	72	.532	16	721	668	83	5267	1380	**231**	32	153	2134	624	739	29	**21**	.262	.343	.405	.748	104	42	106	724
DET	154	78	76	.506	20	614	614	77	**5348**	1376	224	37	116	2022	504	**643**	36	47	.257	.324	.378	.702	95	-41	103	642
BAL	154	76	76	.500	21	597	588	77	5264	1326	191	39	87	1856	504	699	57	35	.252	.321	.353	.674	96	-24	94	597
CLE	153	76	77	.497	21.5	682	722	72	5171	1304	199	26	140	1975	591	786	40	47	.252	.332	.382	.714	102	12	99	658
KC	154	59	94	.386	38.5	563	710	59	5170	1262	195	40	**166**	2035	364	760	35	27	.244	.297	.394	.690	92	-71	102	577
WAS	154	55	99	.357	43	603	808	55	5231	1274	215	38	111	1898	527	733	13	38	.244	.318	.363	.681	93	-55	99	590
Total	**616**					**5210**			**41987**	**10703**	**1663**	**307**	**1024**		**4309**	**5814**	**368**	**304**	**.255**	**.328**	**.382**	**.711**				

Runs
Mantle, M. (NY) 121
Fox, N. (Chi) 110
Piersall, J. (Bos) 103

Hits
Fox, N. (Chi) 196
Malzone, F. (Bos) 185
Minoso, M. (Chi) 176

Doubles
Gardner, B. (Bal) 36
Minoso, M. (Chi) 36
Malzone, F. (Bos) 31

Triples
Bauer, H. (NY) 9
McDougald, G. (NY) 9
Simpson, H. (KC,NY) 9

Home Runs
Sievers, R. (Was) 42
Williams, T. (Bos) 38
Mantle, M. (NY) 34

Total Bases
Sievers, R. (Was) 331
Mantle, M. (NY) 315
Williams, T. (Bos) 307

Runs Batted In
Sievers, R. (Was) 114
Wertz, V. (Cle) 105
3 players tied with 103

Bases On Balls
Mantle, M. (NY) 146
Williams, T. (Bos) 119
2 players tied with 79

Stolen Bases
Aparicio, L. (Chi) 28
Minoso, M. (Chi) 18
Rivera, J. (Chi) 18

Batting Average
Williams, T. (Bos) .388
Mantle, M. (NY) .365
Woodling, G. (Cle) .321

On-Base Percentage
Williams, T. (Bos) .528
Mantle, M. (NY) .515
Minoso, M. (Chi) .413

Slugging Average
Williams, T. (Bos) .731
Mantle, M. (NY) .665
Sievers, R. (Was) .579

Adjusted OPS
Williams, T. (Bos) 227
Mantle, M. (NY) 223
Sievers, R. (Was) 163

Adjusted Batting Runs
Mantle, M. (NY) 96.0
Williams, T. (Bos) 84.0
Sievers, R. (Was) 50.0

Runs Created/Game
Williams, T. (Bos) 16.60
Mantle, M. (NY) 15.40
Sievers, R. (Was) 8.60

Fielding Runs
Bolling, F. (Det) 23.0
Fox, N. (Chi) 22.5
McDougald, G. (NY) 17.7

Win Shares – Batters
Mantle, M. (NY) 51
Williams, T. (Bos) 38
2 players tied with 32

TPW – Batters
Mantle, M. (NY) 9.1
Williams, T. (Bos) 7.8
Fox, N. (Chi) 6.0

TEAM	CG	SH	SV	IP	H	H/G	ER	HR	BB	SO	OAV	RAT	ERA	ERA+	CERA	PR+	PF	FA	E	DP	FR	BW	PW	FW	TPW	DIF
NY	41	13	**42**	1395[1]	**1198**	**7.7**	**465**	110	580	**810**	**.234**	1.274	**3.00**	120	3.36	**72.8**	95	.980	123	**183**	18.7	**9.1**	**7.5**	1.9	**18.6**	2.4
CHI	**59**	**16**	27	1401[2]	1305	8.4	521	124	**470**	665	.248	1.266	3.35	112	3.44	32.9	99	**.982**	**107**	169	**28.0**	4.8	3.4	**2.9**	11.1	1.9
BOS	55	9	23	1376[2]	1391	9.1	593	116	498	692	.264	1.372	3.88	103	3.99	38.4	105	.976	149	179	-21.3	4.4	4.0	-2.2	6.1	-1.1
DET	52	9	21	**1417[2]**	1330	8.4	561	147	505	756	.250	1.294	3.56	108	3.68	36.9	102	.980	121	151	10.5	-4.2	3.8	1.1	.7	.3
BAL	44	13	25	1408	1272	8.1	541	**95**	493	767	.243	**1.254**	3.46	104	**3.23**	-2.9	95	.981	112	159	22.7	-2.5	-.3	2.3	-.4	.4
CLE	46	7	23	1380[2]	1381	9.0	623	130	618	807	.261	1.448	4.06	92	4.28	-33.7	98	.974	153	154	-17.9	1.2	-3.5	-1.9	-4.1	4.1
KC	26	6	19	1369[2]	1344	8.8	637	153	565	626	.260	1.394	4.19	94	4.21	-28.0	104	.979	125	162	-7.3	-7.3	-2.9	-.8	-10.9	-6.1
WAS	31	5	16	1377	1482	9.7	742	149	580	691	.278	1.497	4.85	**80**	4.73	-112.4	103	.979	128	159	-33.4	-5.7	-11.6	-3.5	-20.8	-1.2
Total	**354**	**78**	**196**	**11126[2]**		**8.7**	**4683**					**1.349**	**3.79**													

Wins
Bunning, J. (Det) 20
Pierce, B. (Chi) 20
3 players tied with 16

Win Percentage
Sturdivant, T. (NY) .727
Donovan, D. (Chi) .727
Bunning, J. (Det) .714

Games
Zuverink, G. (Bal) 56
Clevenger, T. (Was) 52
Hyde, D. (Was) 52

Complete Games
Donovan, D. (Chi) 16
Pierce, B. (Chi) 16
Brewer, T. (Bos) 15

Shutouts
Wilson, J. (Chi) 5
Pierce, B. (Chi) 4
Turley, B. (NY) 4

Saves
Grim, B. (NY) 19
Narleski, R. (Cle) 16
Delock, I. (Bos) 11

Innings Pitched
Bunning, J. (Det) 267[1]
Wynn, E. (Cle) 263
Pierce, B. (Chi) 257

Fewest Hits/Game
Turley, B. (NY) 6.12
Bunning, J. (Det) 7.20
Foytack, P. (Det) 7.43

Fewest BB/Game
Sullivan, F. (Bos) 1.80
Donovan, D. (Chi) 1.84
Shantz, B. (NY) 2.08

Strikeouts
Wynn, E. (Cle) 184
Bunning, J. (Det) 182
Johnson, C. (Bal) 177

Ratio
Sullivan, F. (Bos) 1.06
Bunning, J. (Det) 1.07
Donovan, D. (Chi) 1.12

Earned Run Average
Shantz, B. (NY) 2.45
Sturdivant, T. (NY) 2.54
Bunning, J. (Det) 2.69

Adjusted ERA
Shantz, B. (NY) 147
Sullivan, F. (Bos) 146
Bunning, J. (Det) 143

Component ERA
Sullivan, F. (Bos) 2.46
Pierce, B. (Chi) 2.74
Johnson, C. (Bal) 2.79

Opponents' Batting Avg.
Turley, B. (NY) .194
Bunning, J. (Det) .218
Foytack, P. (Det) .226

Adjusted Pitching Runs
Sullivan, F. (Bos) 37
Bunning, J. (Det) 33
Sturdivant, T. (NY) 21

Win Shares – Pitchers
Bunning, J. (Det) 26
Sullivan, F. (Bos) 23
3 players tied with 18

TPW – Pitchers
Sullivan, F. (Bos) 3.7
Bunning, J. (Det) 3.7
Shantz, B. (NY) 2.2

1958 National League

TEAM	G	W	L	PCT	GB	R	OR	EW	AB	H	2B	3B	HR	TB	BB	SO	SB	CS	AVG	OBP	SLG	OPS	OPS+	BR/A	PF	RC
MIL	154	92	62	.597	....	675	**541**	94	5225	1388	221	21	167	2152	478	646	26	**8**	**.266**	.331	.412	.743	**111**	**81**	92	703
PIT	154	84	70	.545	8	662	607	84	5247	1386	229	**68**	134	2153	396	753	30	15	.264	.319	.410	.729	101	-3	97	668
SF	154	80	74	.519	12	**727**	698	80	5318	1399	**250**	42	170	2243	531	817	64	29	.263	.334	.422	.756	108	59	98	**746**
CIN	154	76	78	.494	16	695	621	86	5273	1359	242	40	123	2050	572	765	61	38	.258	.333	.389	.722	92	-53	105	688
STL	154	72	82	.468	20	619	704	67	5255	1371	216	39	111	1998	533	**637**	44	43	.261	.331	.380	.711	91	-68	104	636
CHI	154	72	82	.468	20	709	725	75	5289	1402	207	49	**182**	**2253**	487	853	39	23	.265	.332	**.426**	**.758**	108	52	98	736
LA	154	71	83	.461	21	668	761	67	5173	1297	166	50	172	2079	495	850	**73**	47	.251	.319	.402	.721	93	-55	103	649
PHI	154	69	85	.448	23	664	762	66	**5363**	**1424**	238	56	124	2146	**573**	871	51	33	.266	**.341**	.400	.741	103	30	99	727
Total	**616**					**5419**			**42143**	**11026**	**1769**	**365**	**1183**		**4065**	**6192**	**388**	**236**	**.262**	**.330**	**.405**	**.735**				

Runs
Mays, W. (SF) 121
Banks, E. (Chi) 119
Aaron, H. (Mil) 109

Hits
Ashburn, R. (Phi) 215
Mays, W. (SF) 208
Aaron, H. (Mil) 196

Doubles
Cepeda, O. (SF) 38
Groat, D. (Pit) 36
Musial, S. (StL) 35

Triples
Ashburn, R. (Phi) 13
3 players tied with 11

Home Runs
Banks, E. (Chi) 47
Thomas, F. (Pit) 35
2 players tied with 31

Total Bases
Banks, E. (Chi) 379
Mays, W. (SF) 350
Aaron, H. (Mil) 328

Runs Batted In
Banks, E. (Chi) 129
Thomas, F. (Pit) 109
Anderson, H. (Phi) 97

Bases On Balls
Ashburn, R. (Phi) 97
Temple, J. (Cin) 91
Mathews, E. (Mil) 85

Stolen Bases
Mays, W. (SF) 31
Ashburn, R. (Phi) 30
Taylor, T. (Chi) 21

Batting Average
Ashburn, R. (Phi) .350
Mays, W. (SF) .347
Musial, S. (StL) .337

On-Base Percentage
Ashburn, R. (Phi) .441
Musial, S. (StL) .426
Mays, W. (SF) .423

Slugging Average
Banks, E. (Chi) .614
Mays, W. (SF) .583
Aaron, H. (Mil) .546

Adjusted OPS
Mays, W. (SF) 167
Banks, E. (Chi) 157
Aaron, H. (Mil) 157

Adjusted Batting Runs
Mays, W. (SF) 63.0
Aaron, H. (Mil) 48.0
Banks, E. (Chi) 47.0

Runs Created/Game
Mays, W. (SF) 9.90
Musial, S. (StL) 8.20
Ashburn, R. (Phi) 8.10

Fielding Runs
Boyer, K. (StL) 20.2
Clemente, R. (Pit) 19.4
Mazeroski, B. (Pit) 19.0

Win Shares – Batters
Mays, W. (SF) 40
Aaron, H. (Mil) 32
Banks, E. (Chi) 31

TPW – Batters
Mays, W. (SF) 6.6
Banks, E. (Chi) 5.3
Aaron, H. (Mil) 4.5

TEAM	CG	SH	SV	IP	H	H/G	ER	HR	BB	SO	OAV	RAT	ERA	ERA+	CERA	PR+	PF	FA	E	DP	FR	BW	PW	FW	TPW	DIF
MIL	**72**	**16**	17	1376	**1261**	**8.2**	**491**	125	426	773	**.244**	**1.226**	**3.21**	118	**3.29**	32.9	89	.980	120	152	14.5	**8.2**	3.3	1.5	**13.0**	2.0
PIT	43	10	**41**	1367	1344	8.8	541	**123**	470	679	.261	1.327	3.56	108	3.73	19.6	98	.978	133	173	**26.3**	-.3	2.0	**2.6**	4.4	2.6
SF	38	7	25	1389[1]	1400	9.1	614	166	512	775	.263	1.376	3.98	96	4.24	-12.4	97	.975	152	156	-12.8	5.9	-1.2	-1.3	3.4	-.4
CIN	50	7	20	1385[1]	1422	9.2	574	148	**419**	705	.267	1.329	3.73	111	3.95	**58.9**	105	**.983**	**100**	148	5.2	-5.3	**5.9**	.5	1.2	-2.2
STL	45	6	25	1381[2]	1398	9.1	632	158	567	822	.264	1.422	4.12	100	4.40	0.4	105	.974	153	163	1.8	-6.9	.0	.2	-6.6	1.6
CHI	27	5	24	1361	1322	8.7	638	142	619	805	.254	1.426	4.22	93	4.23	-32.9	99	.975	150	161	-12.8	5.2	-3.3	-1.3	.6	-5.6
LA	30	7	31	1368[1]	1399	9.2	679	173	606	**855**	.267	1.465	4.47	92	4.66	-59.8	104	.975	146	**198**	2.8	-5.5	-6.0	.3	-11.3	5.3
PHI	51	6	15	**1397**	1480	9.5	671	148	446	778	.272	1.379	4.32	**92**	4.15	-32.7	100	.978	129	136	-23.5	3.0	-3.3	-2.4	-2.7	-5.3
Total	**356**	**64**	**198**	**11025[2]**		**9.0**	**4840**					**1.369**	**3.95**													

Wins
Friend, B. (Pit) 22
Spahn, W. (Mil) 22
Burdette, L. (Mil) 20

Win Percentage
Burdette, L. (Mil) .667
Spahn, W. (Mil) .667
Hobbie, G. (Chi) .625

Games
Elston, D. (Chi) 69
Face, R. (Pit) 57
Klippstein, J. (LA,Cin) 57

Complete Games
Spahn, W. (Mil) 23
Roberts, R. (Phi) 21
Burdette, L. (Mil) 19

Shutouts
Willey, C. (Mil) 4
4 players tied with 3

Saves
Face, R. (Pit) 20
Labine, C. (LA) 14
Farrell, T. (Phi) 11

Innings Pitched
Spahn, W. (Mil) 290
Burdette, L. (Mil) 275[1]
Friend, B. (Pit) 274

Fewest Hits/Game
Jones, S. (StL) 7.34
Koufax, S. (LA) 7.49
Miller, S. (SF) 7.91

Fewest BB/Game
Burdette, L. (Mil) 1.63
Roberts, R. (Phi) 1.70
Law, V. (Pit) 1.73

Strikeouts
Jones, S. (StL) 225
Spahn, W. (Mil) 150
2 players tied with 143

Ratio
Spahn, W. (Mil) 1.15
Miller, S. (SF) 1.15
Roberts, R. (Phi) 1.19

Earned Run Average
Miller, S. (SF) 2.47
Jones, S. (StL) 2.88
Burdette, L. (Mil) 2.91

Adjusted ERA
Miller, S. (SF) 154
Jones, S. (StL) 143
Roberts, R. (Phi) 122

Component ERA
Miller, S. (SF) 2.87
Spahn, W. (Mil) 2.96
Burdette, L. (Mil) 3.16

Opponents' Batting Avg.
Koufax, S. (LA) .220
Jones, S. (StL) .223
Miller, S. (SF) .233

Adjusted Pitching Runs
Jones, S. (StL) 34
Miller, S. (SF) 29
Roberts, R. (Phi) 26

Win Shares – Pitchers
Spahn, W. (Mil) 28
Burdette, L. (Mil) 23
Jones, S. (StL) 23

TPW – Pitchers
Roberts, R. (Phi) 3.0
Jones, S. (StL) 2.9
Miller, S. (SF) 2.9

1958 American League

TEAM	G	W	L	PCT	GB	R	OR	EW	AB	H	2B	3B	HR	TB	BB	SO	SB	CS	AVG	OBP	SLG	OPS	OPS+	BR/A	PF	RC
NY	155	92	62	.597	....	**759**	577	98	**5294**	**1418**	212	39	**164**	**2200**	537	822	48	32	**.268**	.338	**.416**	**.754**	**117**	**119**	96	**745**
CHI	155	82	72	.532	10	634	615	79	5249	1348	191	42	101	1926	518	**669**	**101**	33	.257	.329	.367	.696	99	14	98	645
BOS	155	79	75	.513	13	697	691	78	5218	1335	**229**	30	155	2089	**638**	820	29	**22**	.256	**.340**	.400	.740	102	30	107	707
CLE	153	77	76	.503	14.5	694	635	83	5201	1340	210	31	161	2095	494	819	50	49	.258	.327	.403	.730	109	50	97	675
DET	154	77	77	.500	15	659	606	83	5194	1384	**229**	41	109	2022	463	678	48	32	.266	.329	.389	.718	96	-23	107	655
BAL	154	74	79	.484	17.5	521	**575**	69	5111	1233	195	19	108	1790	483	731	33	35	.241	.310	.350	.660	92	-57	95	544
KC	156	73	81	.474	19	642	713	69	5261	1297	196	**50**	138	2007	452	747	22	36	.247	.309	.381	.691	93	-58	102	599
WAS	156	61	93	.396	31	553	747	55	5156	1240	161	38	121	1840	477	751	22	41	.240	.309	.357	.666	90	-76	98	554
Total	**619**					**5159**			**41684**	**10595**	**1623**	**290**	**1057**		**4062**	**6037**	**353**	**280**	**.254**	**.324**	**.383**	**.707**				

Runs
Mantle, M. (NY) 127
Runnels, P. (Bos) 103
Power, V. (Cle,KC) 98

Hits
Fox, N. (Chi) 187
Malzone, F. (Bos) 185
Power, V. (Cle,KC) 184

Doubles
Kuenn, H. (Det) 39
Power, V. (Cle,KC) 37
Kaline, A. (Det) 34

Triples
Power, V. (Cle,KC) 10
3 players tied with 9

Home Runs
Mantle, M. (NY) 42
Colavito, R. (Cle) 41
Sievers, R. (Was) 39

Total Bases
Mantle, M. (NY) 307
Cerv, B. (KC) 305
Colavito, R. (Cle) 303

Runs Batted In
Jensen, J. (Bos) 122
Colavito, R. (Cle) 113
Sievers, R. (Was) 108

Bases On Balls
Mantle, M. (NY) 129
Jensen, J. (Bos) 99
Williams, T. (Bos) 98

Stolen Bases
Aparicio, L. (Chi) 29
Rivera, J. (Chi) 21
Landis, J. (Chi) 19

Batting Average
Williams, T. (Bos) .328
Runnels, P. (Bos) .322
Kuenn, H. (Det) .319

On-Base Percentage
Williams, T. (Bos) .462
Mantle, M. (NY) .445
Runnels, P. (Bos) .418

Slugging Average
Colavito, R. (Cle) .620
Cerv, B. (KC) .592
Mantle, M. (NY) .592

Adjusted OPS
Mantle, M. (NY) 189
Colavito, R. (Cle) 183
Williams, T. (Bos) 174

Adjusted Batting Runs
Mantle, M. (NY) 74.0
Colavito, R. (Cle) 56.0
Williams, T. (Bos) 49.0

Runs Created/Game
Mantle, M. (NY) 10.50
Williams, T. (Bos) 10.10
Colavito, R. (Cle) 9.10

Fielding Runs
Kubek, T. (NY) 19.8
Aparicio, L. (Chi) 18.3
Cerv, B. (KC) 17.4

Win Shares – Batters
Mantle, M. (NY) 39
Colavito, R. (Cle) 32
Cerv, B. (KC) 29

TPW – Batters
Mantle, M. (NY) 6.6
Colavito, R. (Cle) 5.4
Cerv, B. (KC) 5.0

TEAM	CG	SH	SV	IP	H	H/G	ER	HR	BB	SO	OAV	RAT	ERA	ERA+	CERA	PR+	PF	FA	E	DP	FR	BW	PW	FW	TPW	DIF
NY	53	**21**	**33**	1379	**1201**	**7.8**	**493**	116	557	796	**.235**	1.275	**3.22**	110	3.42	21.4	94	.978	128	**182**	**27.2**	**12.3**	2.2	**2.8**	**17.3**	-2.3
CHI	55	15	25	1389[2]	1296	8.4	557	152	515	751	.250	1.303	3.61	101	3.74	-13.3	96	.981	114	160	17.7	1.5	-1.4	1.8	1.9	3.1
BOS	44	5	28	1380	1396	9.1	601	121	521	695	.264	1.389	3.92	102	4.05	36.3	106	.976	145	172	-22.7	3.1	3.7	-2.3	4.5	-2.5
CLE	51	2	20	1373[1]	1283	8.4	569	123	604	766	.248	1.374	3.73	98	3.89	-19.9	97	.974	152	171	7.4	5.2	-2.1	.8	3.9	-2.9
DET	**59**	8	19	1357[1]	1294	8.6	541	133	437	**797**	.252	1.275	3.59	113	3.63	**53.1**	107	**.982**	**106**	140	13.8	-2.4	**5.5**	1.4	4.5	-4.5
BAL	55	15	28	1369[2]	1277	8.4	517	**106**	**403**	749	.249	**1.227**	3.40	106	**3.26**	36.3	95	.980	114	159	-6.1	-5.9	3.8	-.6	-2.8	.8
KC	42	9	25	**1398[1]**	1405	9.0	645	150	467	721	.262	1.339	4.15	94	3.99	-34.7	104	.979	125	166	-2.9	-6.0	-3.6	-.3	-9.8	5.8
WAS	28	6	28	1376[2]	1443	9.4	693	156	558	762	.272	1.454	4.53	**84**	4.56	-74.5	101	.980	118	163	-35.0	-7.8	-7.7	-3.6	-19.1	3.1
Total	**387**	**81**	**206**	**11024**		**8.6**	**4616**					**1.330**	**3.77**													

Wins
Turley, B. (NY) 21
Pierce, B. (Chi) 17
2 players tied with 16

Win Percentage
Turley, B. (NY) .750
Ford, W. (NY) .667
McLish, C. (Cle) .667

Games
Clevenger, T. (Was) 55
Tomanek, D. (KC,Cle) 54
Hyde, D. (Was) 53

Complete Games
Lary, F. (Det) 19
Pierce, B. (Chi) 19
Turley, B. (NY) 19

Shutouts
Ford, W. (NY) 7
Turley, B. (NY) 6
3 players tied with 4

Saves
Duren, R. (NY) 20
Hyde, D. (Was) 18
Kiely, L. (Bos) 12

Innings Pitched
Lary, F. (Det) 260[1]
Ramos, P. (Was) 259[1]
Donovan, D. (Chi) 248

Fewest Hits/Game
Turley, B. (NY) 6.53
Bell, G. (Cle) 6.97
Ford, W. (NY) 7.14

Fewest BB/Game
Donovan, D. (Chi) 1.92
O'Dell, B. (Bal) 2.07
Sullivan, F. (Bos) 2.21

Strikeouts
Wynn, E. (Chi) 179
Bunning, J. (Det) 177
Turley, B. (NY) 168

Ratio
Ford, W. (NY) 1.08
Pierce, B. (Chi) 1.10
Portocarrero, A. (Bal) 1.12

Earned Run Average
Ford, W. (NY) 2.01
Pierce, B. (Chi) 2.68
Harshman, J. (Bal) 2.89

Adjusted ERA
Ford, W. (NY) 176
Lary, F. (Det) 139
Pierce, B. (Chi) 136

Component ERA
Ford, W. (NY) 2.40
O'Dell, B. (Bal) 2.67
Portocarrero, A. (Bal) 2.75

Opponents' Batting Avg.
Turley, B. (NY) .206
Bell, G. (Cle) .213
Ford, W. (NY) .217

Adjusted Pitching Runs
Ford, W. (NY) 33
Lary, F. (Det) 30
Pierce, B. (Chi) 23

Win Shares – Pitchers
Harshman, J. (Bal) 22
Pierce, B. (Chi) 22
Lary, F. (Det) 21

TPW – Pitchers
Ford, W. (NY) 3.6
Harshman, J. (Bal) 3.1
Lary, F. (Det) 3.0

1959 National League

TEAM	G	W	L	PCT	GB	R	OR	EW	AB	H	2B	3B	HR	TB	BB	SO	SB	CS	AVG	OBP	SLG	OPS	OPS+	BR/A	PF	RC
LA	156	88	68	.564	....	705	670	82	5282	1360	196	46	148	2092	**591**	891	**84**	51	.257	.335	.396	.731	95	-30	107	705
MIL	157	86	70	.551	2	724	623	90	**5388**	1426	216	36	**177**	2245	488	765	41	**14**	.265	.329	.417	.745	**114**	**104**	92	728
SF	154	83	71	.539	4	705	**613**	88	5281	1377	239	35	167	2187	473	875	81	34	.261	.324	.414	.739	105	38	98	710
PIT	155	78	76	.506	9	651	680	74	5369	1414	230	42	112	2064	442	**715**	32	26	.263	.322	.384	.707	95	-36	99	651
CIN	154	74	80	.481	13	**764**	738	80	5288	**1448**	**258**	34	161	**2257**	499	763	65	28	**.274**	**.340**	**.427**	**.767**	108	61	103	**762**
CHI	155	74	80	.481	13	673	688	75	5296	1321	209	44	163	2107	498	911	32	19	.249	.319	.398	.717	98	-14	99	671
STL	154	71	83	.461	16	641	725	68	5317	1432	244	**49**	118	2128	485	747	65	53	.269	.333	.400	.733	96	-34	106	698
PHI	155	64	90	.416	23	599	725	62	5109	1237	196	38	113	1848	498	858	39	46	.242	.314	.362	.675	85	-110	102	572
Total	**620**					**5462**			**42330**	**11015**	**1788**	**324**	**1159**		**3974**	**6525**	**439**	**271**	**.260**	**.327**	**.400**	**.727**				

Runs
Pinson, V. (Cin) 131
Mays, W. (SF) 125
Mathews, E. (Mil) 118

Hits
Aaron, H. (Mil) 223
Pinson, V. (Cin) 205
Cepeda, O. (SF) 192

Doubles
Pinson, V. (Cin) 47
Aaron, H. (Mil) 46
Mays, W. (SF) 43

Triples
Moon, W. (LA) 11
Neal, C. (LA) 11
3 players tied with 9

Home Runs
Mathews, E. (Mil) 46
Banks, E. (Chi) 45
Aaron, H. (Mil) 39

Total Bases
Aaron, H. (Mil) 400
Mathews, E. (Mil) 352
Banks, E. (Chi) 351

Runs Batted In
Banks, E. (Chi) 143
Robinson, F. (Cin) 125
Aaron, H. (Mil) 123

Bases On Balls
Gilliam, J. (LA) 96
Cunningham, J. (StL) 88
Moon, W. (LA) 81

Stolen Bases
Mays, W. (SF) 27
3 players tied with 23

Batting Average
Aaron, H. (Mil) .355
Cunningham, J. (StL) .345
Cepeda, O. (SF) .317

On-Base Percentage
Cunningham, J. (StL) .456
Aaron, H. (Mil) .406
Robinson, F. (Cin) .397

Slugging Average
Aaron, H. (Mil) .636
Banks, E. (Chi) .596
Mathews, E. (Mil) .593

Adjusted OPS
Aaron, H. (Mil) 188
Mathews, E. (Mil) 172
Mays, W. (SF) 157

Adjusted Batting Runs
Aaron, H. (Mil) 77.0
Mathews, E. (Mil) 60.0
Mays, W. (SF) 50.0

Runs Created/Game
Aaron, H. (Mil) 9.70
Mathews, E. (Mil) 9.10
Cunningham, J. (StL) 8.80

Fielding Runs
Virdon, B. (Pit) 16.0
Kasko, E. (Cin) 12.4
Adcock, J. (Mil) 11.5

Win Shares – Batters
Aaron, H. (Mil) 38
Mathews, E. (Mil) 37
Banks, E. (Chi) 33

TPW – Batters
Aaron, H. (Mil) 7.2
Banks, E. (Chi) 6.3
Mathews, E. (Mil) 6.3

TEAM	CG	SH	SV	IP	H	H/G	ER	HR	BB	SO	OAV	RAT	ERA	ERA+	CERA	PR+	PF	FA	E	DP	FR	BW	PW	FW	TPW	DIF
LA	43	14	26	1411^{2}	1317	8.4	594	157	614	1077	.247	1.368	3.79	112	4.01	64.3	107	.981	114	154	3.6	-3.0	6.5	.4	3.8	6.2
MIL	69	18	18	1400^{2}	1406	9.0	546	128	429	775	.260	1.310	3.51	101	3.70	13.5	90	.979	127	138	-8.8	10.4	1.4	-.9	10.9	-2.9
SF	52	12	23	1376^{1}	1279	8.4	531	139	500	873	.246	1.293	3.47	110	3.59	57.7	97	.974	152	118	-5.0	3.8	5.8	-.5	9.1	-3.1
PIT	48	7	17	1393^{1}	1432	9.2	604	134	418	730	.267	1.328	3.90	99	3.83	-17.7	98	.975	154	165	12.8	-3.7	-1.8	1.3	-4.2	5.2
CIN	44	7	26	1357^{1}	1460	9.7	650	162	456	690	.275	1.412	4.31	94	4.46	-41.5	103	.978	126	157	2.3	6.1	-4.2	.2	2.1	-5.1
CHI	30	11	25	1391	1337	8.6	620	152	519	765	.254	1.334	4.01	98	3.89	-21.1	100	.977	140	142	11.2	-1.4	-2.1	1.1	-2.4	-.6
STL	36	8	21	1363	1427	9.4	657	137	564	846	.271	1.461	4.34	98	4.43	-3.0	107	.975	146	158	-12.4	-3.5	-.3	-1.2	-5.0	-1.0
PHI	54	8	15	1354	1357	9.0	642	150	474	769	.261	1.352	4.27	96	4.05	-21.6	104	.973	154	132	-3.8	-11.1	-2.2	-.4	-13.7	.7
Total	376	85	171	11047^{1}		9.0	4844					1.357	3.95													

Wins
- Burdette, L. (Mil) 21
- Jones, S. (SF) 21
- Spahn, W. (Mil) 21

Win Percentage
- Law, V. (Pit) .667
- Antonelli, J. (SF) .655
- Conley, G. (Phi) .632

Games
- Elston, D. (Chi) 65
- Henry, B. (Chi) 65
- McDaniel, L. (StL) 62

Complete Games
- Spahn, W. (Mil) 21
- Burdette, L. (Mil) 20
- Law, V. (Pit) 20

Shutouts
- 7 players tied with 4

Saves
- McDaniel, L. (StL) 15
- McMahon, D. (Mil) 15
- Elston, D. (Chi) 13

Innings Pitched
- Spahn, W. (Mil) 292
- Burdette, L. (Mil) 289^{2}
- Antonelli, J. (SF) 282

Fewest Hits/Game
- Haddix, H. (Pit) 7.58
- Jones, S. (SF) 7.71
- Hobbie, G. (Chi) 7.85

Fewest BB/Game
- Newcombe, D. (Cin) 1.09
- Burdette, L. (Mil) 1.18
- Roberts, R. (Phi) 1.22

Strikeouts
- Drysdale, D. (LA) 242
- Jones, S. (SF) 209
- Koufax, S. (LA) 173

Ratio
- Haddix, H. (Pit) 1.06
- Newcombe, D. (Cin) 1.09
- Conley, G. (Phi) 1.12

Earned Run Average
- Jones, S. (SF) 2.83
- Miller, S. (SF) 2.84
- Buhl, B. (Mil) 2.86

Adjusted ERA
- Conley, G. (Phi) 137
- Jones, S. (SF) 135
- Miller, S. (SF) 134

Component ERA
- Haddix, H. (Pit) 2.62
- Conley, G. (Phi) 2.65
- Law, V. (Pit) 2.82

Opponents' Batting Avg.
- Jones, S. (SF) .228
- Haddix, H. (Pit) .228
- Antonelli, J. (SF) .233

Adjusted Pitching Runs
- Jones, S. (SF) 31
- Jackson, L. (StL) 29
- Law, V. (Pit) 24

Win Shares – Pitchers
- Law, V. (Pit) 24
- Spahn, W. (Mil) 23
- 2 players tied with 22

TPW – Pitchers
- Newcombe, D. (Cin) 3.7
- Jones, S. (SF) 2.9
- Spahn, W. (Mil) 2.7

1959 American League

TEAM	G	W	L	PCT	GB	R	OR	EW	AB	H	2B	3B	HR	TB	BB	SO	SB	CS	AVG	OBP	SLG	OPS	OPS+	BR/A	PF	RC
CHI	156	94	60	.610	....	669	588	87	5297	1325	220	46	97	1928	580	634	113	53	.250	.330	.364	.694	98	-6	99	651
CLE	154	89	65	.578	5	745	646	88	5288	1390	216	25	167	2157	433	721	33	36	.263	.323	.408	.731	110	51	96	681
NY	155	79	75	.513	15	687	647	82	5379	1397	224	40	153	2160	457	828	45	22	.260	.321	.402	.723	107	42	97	693
DET	154	76	78	.494	18	713	732	75	5211	1346	196	30	160	2082	580	737	34	17	.258	.338	.400	.737	102	24	105	718
BOS	154	75	79	.487	19	726	696	80	5225	1335	248	28	125	2014	626	810	68	25	.256	.338	.385	.723	100	12	105	695
BAL	155	74	80	.481	20	551	621	68	5208	1240	182	23	109	1795	536	690	36	24	.238	.312	.345	.656	88	-84	98	561
KC	154	66	88	.429	28	681	760	69	5264	1383	231	43	117	2051	481	780	34	24	.263	.328	.390	.718	101	1	102	667
WAS	154	63	91	.409	31	619	701	67	5092	1205	173	32	163	1931	517	881	51	34	.237	.310	.379	.689	95	-42	100	592
Total	618					5391			41964	10621	1690	267	1091		4210	6081	414	235	.253	.325	.384	.709				

Runs
- Yost, E. (Det) 115
- Mantle, M. (NY) 104
- Power, V. (Cle) 102

Hits
- Kuenn, H. (Det) 198
- Fox, N. (Chi) 191
- Runnels, P. (Bos) 176

Doubles
- Kuenn, H. (Det) 42
- Fox, N. (Chi) 34
- Malzone, F. (Bos) 34

Triples
- Allison, B. (Was) 9
- McDougald, G. (NY) 8
- 4 players tied with 7

Home Runs
- Colavito, R. (Cle) 42
- Killebrew, H. (Was) 42
- Lemon, J. (Was) 33

Total Bases
- Colavito, R. (Cle) 301
- Killebrew, H. (Was) 282
- Kuenn, H. (Det) 281

Runs Batted In
- Jensen, J. (Bos) 112
- Colavito, R. (Cle) 111
- Killebrew, H. (Was) 105

Bases On Balls
- Yost, E. (Det) 135
- Runnels, P. (Bos) 95
- Mantle, M. (NY) 93

Stolen Bases
- Aparicio, L. (Chi) 56
- Mantle, M. (NY) 21
- 2 players tied with 20

Batting Average
- Kuenn, H. (Det) .353
- Kaline, A. (Det) .327
- Runnels, P. (Bos) .314

On-Base Percentage
- Yost, E. (Det) .437
- Runnels, P. (Bos) .415
- Kaline, A. (Det) .414

Slugging Average
- Kaline, A. (Det) .530
- Killebrew, H. (Was) .516
- Mantle, M. (NY) .514

Adjusted OPS
- Mantle, M. (NY) 152
- Kaline, A. (Det) 149
- Kuenn, H. (Det) 140

Adjusted Batting Runs
- Mantle, M. (NY) 44.0
- Kaline, A. (Det) 37.0
- Yost, E. (Det) 35.0

Runs Created/Game
- Kaline, A. (Det) 8.40
- Kuenn, H. (Det) 8.30
- Yost, E. (Det) 7.90

Fielding Runs
- Gardner, B. (Bal) 20.1
- Power, V. (Cle) 14.8
- Landis, J. (Chi) 10.9

Win Shares – Batters
- Fox, N. (Chi) 30
- Mantle, M. (NY) 30
- 2 players tied with 29

TPW – Batters
- Mantle, M. (NY) 4.1
- Yost, E. (Det) 3.4
- Jensen, J. (Bos) 3.1

TEAM	CG	SH	SV	IP	H	H/G	ER	HR	BB	SO	OAV	RAT	ERA	ERA+	CERA	PR+	PF	FA	E	DP	FR	BW	PW	FW	TPW	DIF
CHI	44	13	36	1425^{1}	1297	8.2	521	129	525	761	.242	1.278	3.29	114	3.44	46.9	97	.979	130	141	26.7	-.6	4.7	2.7	6.8	10.2
CLE	58	7	23	1383^{2}	1230	8.0	576	148	635	799	.239	1.348	3.75	98	3.79	-20.1	95	.978	127	138	10.6	5.1	-2.0	1.1	4.2	7.8
NY	38	15	28	1399	1281	8.2	560	120	594	836	.244	1.340	3.60	101	3.70	5.9	94	.978	131	160	0.9	4.3	.6	.1	5.0	-3.0
DET	53	9	24	1360	1327	8.8	635	177	432	829	.254	1.293	4.20	97	3.96	-22.4	105	.978	124	131	1.4	2.4	-2.3	.1	.3	-1.3
BOS	38	9	25	1364	1386	9.2	632	135	589	724	.266	1.448	4.17	97	4.37	-21.3	105	.978	131	167	4.6	1.2	-2.2	.5	-.5	-1.5
BAL	45	15	30	1400^{1}	1290	8.3	554	111	476	735	.246	1.261	3.56	106	3.37	23.9	98	.976	146	163	10.9	-8.5	2.4	1.1	-4.9	1.9
KC	44	8	21	1360^{2}	1452	9.6	657	148	492	703	.274	1.429	4.35	92	4.49	-45.0	104	.973	160	156	-7.8	.1	-4.6	-.8	-5.2	-5.8
WAS	46	10	21	1360	1358	9.0	606	123	467	694	.259	1.342	4.01	98	3.83	33.7	101	.973	162	140	-48.1	-4.3	3.4	-4.9	-5.7	-8.3
Total	366	86	208	11053		8.6	4741					1.342	3.86													

Wins
- Wynn, E. (Chi) 22
- McLish, C. (Cle) 19
- Shaw, B. (Chi) 18

Win Percentage
- Shaw, B. (Chi) .750
- McLish, C. (Cle) .704
- Wynn, E. (Chi) .688

Games
- Staley, G. (Chi) 67
- Lown, T. (Chi) 60
- Clevenger, T. (Was) 50

Complete Games
- Pascual, C. (Was) 17
- Mossi, D. (Det) 15
- Pappas, M. (Bal) 15

Shutouts
- Pascual, C. (Was) 6
- Wynn, E. (Chi) 5
- Pappas, M. (Bal) 4

Saves
- Lown, T. (Chi) 15
- 3 players tied with 14

Innings Pitched
- Wynn, E. (Chi) 255^{2}
- Bunning, J. (Det) 249^{2}
- Foytack, P. (Det) 240^{1}

Fewest Hits/Game
- Score, H. (Cle) 6.89
- Ditmar, A. (NY) 6.95
- Wilhelm, H. (Bal) 7.09

Fewest BB/Game
- Brown, H. (Bal) 1.76
- Lary, F. (Det) 1.86
- Garver, N. (KC) 1.88

Strikeouts
- Bunning, J. (Det) 201
- Pascual, C. (Was) 185
- Wynn, E. (Chi) 179

Ratio
- Ditmar, A. (NY) 1.03
- Wilhelm, H. (Bal) 1.13
- Pascual, C. (Was) 1.14

Earned Run Average
- Wilhelm, H. (Bal) 2.19
- Pascual, C. (Was) 2.64
- Shaw, B. (Chi) 2.69

Adjusted ERA
- Wilhelm, H. (Bal) 173
- Pascual, C. (Was) 148
- Shaw, B. (Chi) 139

Component ERA
- Ditmar, A. (NY) 2.39
- Pascual, C. (Was) 2.45
- Wilhelm, H. (Bal) 2.69

Opponents' Batting Avg.
- Score, H. (Cle) .210
- Ditmar, A. (NY) .211
- Wynn, E. (Chi) .216

Adjusted Pitching Runs
- Pascual, C. (Was) 42
- Wilhelm, H. (Bal) 38
- Shaw, B. (Chi) 23

Win Shares – Pitchers
- Pascual, C. (Was) 24
- Wilhelm, H. (Bal) 23
- Wynn, E. (Chi) 23

TPW – Pitchers
- Pascual, C. (Was) 4.9
- Wilhelm, H. (Bal) 3.2
- Daley, B. (KC) 2.6

1960 National League

TEAM	G	W	L	PCT	GB	R	OR	EW	AB	H	2B	3B	HR	TB	BB	SO	SB	CS	AVG	OBP	SLG	OPS	OPS+	BR/A	PF	RC
PIT	155	95	59	.617	....	734	593	93	5406	1493	236	56	120	2201	486	747	34	24	.276	.338	.407	.745	109	69	101	735
MIL	154	88	66	.571	7	724	658	84	5263	1393	198	48	170	2197	463	793	69	37	.265	.327	.417	.744	118	119	93	712
STL	155	86	68	.558	9	639	616	80	5187	1317	213	48	138	2040	501	792	48	35	.254	.323	.393	.717	94	-40	109	651
LA	154	82	72	.532	13	662	593	85	5227	1333	216	38	126	2003	529	837	95	53	.255	.327	.383	.710	94	-32	106	657
SF	156	79	75	.513	16	671	631	82	5324	1357	220	62	130	2091	467	846	86	45	.255	.319	.393	.712	107	46	94	661
CIN	154	67	87	.435	28	640	692	71	5289	1324	230	40	140	2054	512	858	73	37	.250	.320	.388	.709	98	-9	102	659
CHI	156	60	94	.390	35	634	776	62	5311	1293	213	48	119	1959	531	897	51	34	.243	.314	.369	.683	94	-40	99	615
PHI	154	59	95	.383	36	546	691	59	5169	1235	196	44	99	1816	448	1054	45	48	.239	.304	.351	.655	85	-111	100	544
Total	619					5250			42176	10745	1722	384	1042		3937	6824	501	313	.255	.322	.388	.710				

Runs
- Bruton, B. (Mil) 112
- Mathews, E. (Mil) 108
- 2 players tied with 107

Hits
- Mays, W. (SF) 190
- Pinson, V. (Cin) 187
- Groat, D. (Pit) 186

Doubles
- Pinson, V. (Cin) 37
- Cepeda, O. (SF) 36
- 2 players tied with 33

Triples
- Bruton, B. (Mil) 13
- Mays, W. (SF) 12
- Pinson, V. (Cin) 12

Home Runs
- Banks, E. (Chi) 41
- Aaron, H. (Mil) 40
- Mathews, E. (Mil) 39

Total Bases
- Aaron, H. (Mil) 334
- Banks, E. (Chi) 331
- Mays, W. (SF) 330

Runs Batted In
- Aaron, H. (Mil) 126
- Mathews, E. (Mil) 124
- Banks, E. (Chi) 117

Bases On Balls
- Ashburn, R. (Chi) 116
- Mathews, E. (Mil) 111
- Gilliam, J. (LA) 96

Stolen Bases
- Wills, M. (LA) 50
- Pinson, V. (Cin) 32
- Taylor, T. (Phi,Chi) 26

Batting Average
- Groat, D. (Pit) .325
- Larker, N. (LA) .323
- Mays, W. (SF) .319

On-Base Percentage
- Ashburn, R. (Chi) .416
- Robinson, F. (Cin) .413
- Mathews, E. (Mil) .401

Slugging Average
- Robinson, F. (Cin) .595
- Aaron, H. (Mil) .566
- Boyer, K. (StL) .562

Adjusted OPS
- Mathews, E. (Mil) 170
- Robinson, F. (Cin) 169
- Mays, W. (SF) 164

Adjusted Batting Runs
- Mathews, E. (Mil) 57.0
- Mays, W. (SF) 53.0
- Robinson, F. (Cin) 47.0

Runs Created/Game
- Robinson, F. (Cin) 8.50
- Mathews, E. (Mil) 8.30
- Mays, W. (SF) 7.60

Fielding Runs
- Mazeroski, B. (Pit) 19.6
- Wills, M. (LA) 15.4
- Boyer, K. (StL) 13.7

Win Shares – Batters
- Mathews, E. (Mil) 38
- Mays, W. (SF) 38
- Aaron, H. (Mil) 35

TPW – Batters
- Banks, E. (Chi) 5.6
- Mays, W. (SF) 4.9
- Mathews, E. (Mil) 4.7

TEAM	CG	SH	SV	IP	H	H/G	ER	HR	BB	SO	OAV	RAT	ERA	ERA+	CERA	PR+	PF	FA	E	DP	FR	BW	PW	FW	TPW	DIF
PIT	47	11	33	1399²	1363	0.9	543	105	386	811	.257	.125	0.35	107	3.30	18.0	100	.979	128	163	22.5	7.0	1.8	2.3	11.2	6.8
MIL	55	13	28	1387¹	1327	8.6	579	130	518	807	.251	1.330	3.76	91	3.73	-32.5	91	.976	141	137	-19.3	12.2	-3.3	-2.0	6.9	4.1
STL	37	11	30	1371	1316	8.6	554	127	511	906	.253	1.333	3.64	113	3.75	75.1	109	.976	141	152	-6.2	-4.1	7.7	-.6	3.0	6.0
LA	46	13	20	1398	1218	7.8	528	154	564	1122	.234	1.275	3.40	117	3.51	75.4	105	.979	125	142	12.9	-3.3	7.8	1.3	5.8	-.8
SF	55	16	26	1396	1288	8.3	534	107	512	897	.245	1.289	3.44	101	3.37	19.4	92	.972	166	117	-14.0	4.7	2.0	-1.4	5.3	-3.3
CIN	33	8	35	1390¹	1417	9.2	618	134	442	740	.267	1.337	4.00	96	3.96	-30.3	102	.979	125	155	2.6	-.9	-3.1	.3	-3.8	-6.2
CHI	36	6	25	1402²	1393	8.9	678	152	565	805	.260	1.396	4.35	87	4.20	-86.4	100	.977	143	133	-3.0	-4.1	-8.9	-.3	-13.3	-3.7
PHI	45	6	16	1375¹	1423	9.3	613	133	439	736	.270	1.354	4.01	97	3.98	-24.9	103	.974	155	129	5.0	-11.4	-2.6	.5	-13.5	-4.5
Total	354	84	213	23712²		4.1	4647					.619	1.76													

Wins
- Broglio, E. (StL) 21
- Spahn, W. (Mil) 21
- Law, V. (Pit) 20

Win Percentage
- Broglio, E. (StL) .700
- Law, V. (Pit) .690
- Spahn, W. (Mil) .677

Games
- Face, R. (Pit) 68
- McDaniel, L. (StL) 65
- Elston, D. (Chi) 60

Complete Games
- Burdette, L. (Mil) 18
- Law, V. (Pit) 18
- Spahn, W. (Mil) 18

Shutouts
- Sanford, J. (SF) 6
- Drysdale, D. (LA) 5
- 5 players tied with 4

Saves
- McDaniel, L. (StL) 26
- Face, R. (Pit) 24
- Henry, B. (Cin) 17

Innings Pitched
- Jackson, L. (StL) 282
- Burdette, L. (Mil) 275²
- Friend, B. (Pit) 275²

Fewest Hits/Game
- Broglio, E. (StL) 6.84
- Koufax, S. (LA) 6.84
- Williams, S. (LA) 7.03

Fewest BB/Game
- Burdette, L. (Mil) 1.14
- Roberts, R. (Phi) 1.29
- Law, V. (Pit) 1.33

Strikeouts
- Drysdale, D. (LA) 246
- Koufax, S. (LA) 197
- Jones, S. (SF) 190

Ratio
- Drysdale, D. (LA) 1.06
- Law, V. (Pit) 1.13
- Friend, B. (Pit) 1.13

Earned Run Average
- McCormick, M. (SF) 2.70
- Broglio, E. (StL) 2.74
- Drysdale, D. (LA) 2.84

Adjusted ERA
- Broglio, E. (StL) 149
- Drysdale, D. (LA) 140
- Simmons, C. (StL,Phi) 133

Component ERA
- Drysdale, D. (LA) 2.62
- McCormick, M. (SF) 2.70
- Friend, B. (Pit) 2.72

Opponents' Batting Avg.
- Koufax, S. (LA) .207
- Williams, S. (LA) .210
- Broglio, E. (StL) .213

Adjusted Pitching Runs
- Broglio, E. (StL) 35
- Drysdale, D. (LA) 31
- McCormick, M. (SF) 24

Win Shares – Pitchers
- Drysdale, D. (LA) 25
- Broglio, E. (StL) 24
- Jackson, L. (StL) 21

TPW – Pitchers
- Broglio, E. (StL) 3.9
- Drysdale, D. (LA) 3.4
- McCormick, M. (SF) 2.6

1960 American League

TEAM	G	W	L	PCT	GB	R	OR	EW	AB	H	2B	3B	HR	TB	BB	SO	SB	CS	AVG	OBP	SLG	OPS	OPS+	BR/A	PF	RC
NY	155	97	57	.630	....	746	627	90	5290	1377	215	40	193	2251	537	818	37	23	.260	.332	.426	.757	117	106	94	745
BAL	154	89	65	.578	8	682	606	86	5170	1307	206	33	123	1948	596	801	37	24	.253	.334	.377	.711	99	0	99	657
CHI	154	87	67	.565	10	741	617	91	5191	1402	242	38	112	2056	567	648	122	48	.270	.348	.396	.744	108	72	99	724
CLE	154	76	78	.494	21	667	693	74	5296	1415	218	20	127	2054	444	573	58	25	.267	.328		.715	102	11	97	671
WAS	154	73	81	.474	24	672	696	74	5248	1283	205	43	147	2015	584	883	52	43	.244	.326	.384	.710	97	-30	101	654
DET	154	71	83	.461	26	633	644	76	5202	1243	188	34	150	1949	636	728	66	32	.239	.326	.375	.700	90	-67	106	649
BOS	154	65	89	.422	32	658	775	65	5215	1359	234	32	124	2029	570	798	34	28	.261	.336	.389	.725	99	-11	104	672
KC	155	58	96	.377	39	615	756	61	5226	1303	212	34	110	1913	513	744	16	11	.249	.318	.366	.684	90	-73	101	597
Total	617					5414			41838	10689	1720	274	1086		4447	5993	422	234	.255	.331	.388	.718				

Runs
- Mantle, M. (NY) 119
- Maris, R. (NY) 98
- 2 players tied with 89

Hits
- Minoso, M. (Chi) 184
- Fox, N. (Chi) 175
- Robinson, B. (Bal) 175

Doubles
- Francona, T. (Cle) 36
- Skowron, B. (NY) 34
- 2 players tied with 32

Triples
- Fox, N. (Chi) 10
- Robinson, B. (Bal) 9
- 5 players tied with 7

Home Runs
- Mantle, M. (NY) 40
- Maris, R. (NY) 39
- Lemon, J. (Was) 38

Total Bases
- Mantle, M. (NY) 294
- Maris, R. (NY) 290
- 2 players tied with 284

Runs Batted In
- Maris, R. (NY) 112
- Minoso, M. (Chi) 105
- Wertz, V. (Bos) 103

Bases On Balls
- Yost, E. (Det) 125
- Mantle, M. (NY) 111
- Allison, B. (Was) 92

Stolen Bases
- Aparicio, L. (Chi) 51
- Landis, J. (Chi) 23
- Green, L. (Was) 21

Batting Average
- Runnels, P. (Bos) .320
- Smith, A. (Chi) .315
- Minoso, M. (Chi) .311

On-Base Percentage
- Yost, E. (Det) .416
- Woodling, G. (Bal) .403
- Runnels, P. (Bos) .403

Slugging Average
- Maris, R. (NY) .581
- Mantle, M. (NY) .558
- Killebrew, H. (Was) .534

Adjusted OPS
- Mantle, M. (NY) 166
- Maris, R. (NY) 163
- Sievers, R. (Chi) 151

Adjusted Batting Runs
- Mantle, M. (NY) 54.0
- Maris, R. (NY) 42.0
- Sievers, R. (Chi) 33.0

Runs Created/Game
- Mantle, M. (NY) 8.40
- Maris, R. (NY) 8.10
- Sievers, R. (Chi) 7.80

Fielding Runs
- Aparicio, L. (Chi) 24.7
- Power, V. (Cle) 18.2
- Boyer, C. (NY) 15.2

Win Shares – Batters
- Mantle, M. (NY) 36
- Maris, R. (NY) 31
- 4 players tied with 24

TPW – Batters
- Mantle, M. (NY) 4.6
- Maris, R. (NY) 4.2
- Aparicio, L. (Chi) 3.0

TEAM	CG	SH	SV	IP	H	H/G	ER	HR	BB	SO	OAV	RAT	ERA	ERA+	CERA	PR+	PF	FA	E	DP	FR	BW	PW	FW	TPW	DIF
NY	38	16	42	1398	1225	7.9	547	123	609	712	.238	1.312	3.52	102	3.53	-27.6	92	.979	129	162	37.9	10.7	-2.8	3.8	11.8	8.2
BAL	48	11	22	1375²	1222	8.0	538	117	552	785	.241	1.290	3.52	108	3.49	17.1	98	.982	108	172	26.7	.0	1.7	2.7	4.5	7.5
CHI	42	11	26	1381	1338	8.7	552	127	533	695	.258	1.355	3.60	105	3.86	7.8	98	.982	109	175	18.8	7.3	.8	1.9	10.0	.0
CLE	32	10	30	1382¹	1308	8.5	607	161	636	771	.252	1.406	3.95	95	4.20	-35.4	97	.978	128	165	2.7	1.2	-3.6	.3	-2.2	1.2
WAS	34	10	35	1405¹	1392	8.9	589	130	538	775	.260	1.373	3.77	105	3.68	47.0	102	.973	165	159	-19.6	-3.0	4.8	-2.0	-.2	-3.8
DET	40	7	25	1405²	1336	8.6	568	141	474	824	.251	1.288	3.64	113	3.68	81.8	106	.977	138	138	-5.8	-6.8	8.3	-.6	.9	-6.9
BOS	34	6	23	1361	1440	9.5	699	127	580	767	.273	1.484	4.62	87	4.53	-51.4	104	.976	141	156	-36.1	-1.1	-5.2	-3.7	-9.9	-2.1
KC	44	4	14	1374	1428	9.4	669	160	525	664	.271	1.421	4.38	91	4.46	-36.4	103	.979	127	149	-23.8	-7.4	-3.7	-2.4	-13.5	-5.5
Total	312	75	217	11083		8.7	4769					1.366	3.87													

Wins
- Estrada, C. (Bal) 18
- Perry, J. (Cle) 18
- Daley, B. (KC) 16

Win Percentage
- Turley, B. (NY) .750
- Brown, H. (Bal) .706
- Baumann, F. (Chi) .684

Games
- Fornieles, M. (Bos) 70
- Staley, G. (Chi) 64
- Clevenger, T. (Was) 53

Complete Games
- Lary, F. (Det) 15
- Herbert, R. (KC) 14
- Ramos, P. (Was) 14

Shutouts
- Ford, W. (NY) 4
- Perry, J. (Cle) 4
- Wynn, E. (Chi) 4

Saves
- Fornieles, M. (Bos) 14
- Klippstein, J. (Cle) 14
- Moore, R. (Was,Chi) 13

Innings Pitched
- Lary, F. (Det) 274¹
- Ramos, P. (Was) 274
- Perry, J. (Cle) 261¹

Fewest Hits/Game
- Estrada, C. (Bal) 6.99
- Turley, B. (NY) 7.17
- Barber, S. (Bal) 7.33

Fewest BB/Game
- Brown, H. (Bal) 1.25
- Mossi, D. (Det) 1.82
- Hall, D. (KC) 1.88

Strikeouts
- Bunning, J. (Det) 201
- Ramos, P. (Was) 160
- Wynn, E. (Chi) 158

Ratio
- Brown, H. (Bal) 1.11
- Bunning, J. (Det) 1.12
- Lary, F. (Det) 1.18

Earned Run Average
- Baumann, F. (Chi) 2.67
- Bunning, J. (Det) 2.79
- Brown, H. (Bal) 3.06

Adjusted ERA
- Bunning, J. (Det) 148
- Baumann, F. (Chi) 141
- Brown, H. (Bal) 125

Component ERA
- Bunning, J. (Det) 2.79
- Brown, H. (Bal) 2.91
- Baumann, F. (Chi) 2.93

Opponents' Batting Avg.
- Estrada, C. (Bal) .218
- Turley, B. (NY) .222
- Barber, S. (Bal) .226

Adjusted Pitching Runs
- Bunning, J. (Det) 38
- Herbert, R. (KC) 24
- Baumann, F. (Chi) 20

Win Shares – Pitchers
- Bunning, J. (Det) 20
- Lary, F. (Det) 19
- Herbert, R. (KC) 18

TPW – Pitchers
- Bunning, J. (Det) 3.6
- Herbert, R. (KC) 2.6
- Lary, F. (Det) 2.4

1961 National League

TEAM	G	W	L	PCT	GB	R	OR	EW	AB	H	2B	3B	HR	TB	BB	SO	SB	CS	AVG	OBP	SLG	OPS	OPS+	BR/A	PF	RC
CIN	154	93	61	.604	....	710	**653**	83	5243	1414	**247**	35	158	2205	423	761	70	33	.270	.328	.421	.748	102	12	101	711
LA	154	89	65	.578	4	735	697	81	5189	1358	193	40	157	2102	**596**	796	**86**	45	.262	**.340**	.405	.745	95	-25	109	721
SF	155	85	69	.552	8	**773**	655	90	5233	1379	219	32	183	2211	506	764	79	54	.264	.332	**.423**	**.754**	**109**	59	96	718
MIL	155	83	71	.539	10	712	656	83	5288	1365	199	34	**188**	2196	534	880	70	43	.258	.330	.415	.745	**109**	**66**	94	712
STL	155	80	74	.519	13	703	668	81	5307	1436	236	51	103	2083	494	745	46	28	.271	.336	.392	.729	90	-65	110	701
PIT	154	75	79	.487	18	694	675	79	5311	**1448**	232	**57**	128	2178	428	**721**	26	30	**.273**	.330	.410	.740	101	0	100	693
CHI	156	64	90	.416	29	689	800	66	**5344**	1364	238	51	176	**2232**	539	1027	35	**25**	.255	.327	.418	.745	101	7	101	**725**
PHI	155	47	107	.305	46	584	796	54	5213	1265	185	50	103	1859	475	928	56	30	.243	.311	.357	.668	84	-112	99	576
Total	**619**					**5600**			**42128**	**11029**	**1749**	**350**	**1196**		**3995**	**6622**	**468**	**288**	**.262**	**.329**	**.405**	**.735**				

Runs
Mays, W. (SF) 129
Robinson, F. (Cin) 117
Aaron, H. (Mil) 115

Hits
Pinson, V. (Cin) 208
Clemente, R. (Pit) 201
Aaron, H. (Mil) 197

Doubles
Aaron, H. (Mil) 39
Pinson, V. (Cin) 34
3 players tied with 32

Triples
Altman, G. (Chi) 12
3 players tied with 11

Home Runs
Cepeda, O. (SF) 46
Mays, W. (SF) 40
Robinson, F. (Cin) 37

Total Bases
Aaron, H. (Mil) 358
Cepeda, O. (SF) 356
Mays, W. (SF) 334

Runs Batted In
Cepeda, O. (SF) 142
Robinson, F. (Cin) 124
Mays, W. (SF) 123

Bases On Balls
Mathews, E. (Mil) 93
Moon, W. (LA) 89
Mays, W. (SF) 81

Stolen Bases
Wills, M. (LA) 35
Pinson, V. (Cin) 23
Robinson, F. (Cin) 22

Batting Average
Clemente, R. (Pit) .351
Pinson, V. (Cin) .343
Boyer, K. (StL) .329

On-Base Percentage
Moon, W. (LA) .438
Robinson, F. (Cin) .411
Mathews, E. (Mil) .405

Slugging Average
Robinson, F. (Cin) .611
Cepeda, O. (SF) .609
Aaron, H. (Mil) .594

Adjusted OPS
Aaron, H. (Mil) 165
Robinson, F. (Cin) 164
Mays, W. (SF) 161

Adjusted Batting Runs
Robinson, F. (Cin) 55.0
Aaron, H. (Mil) 55.0
Mays, W. (SF) 51.0

Runs Created/Game
Robinson, F. (Cin) 9.30
Moon, W. (LA) 8.70
Mays, W. (SF) 8.30

Fielding Runs
Mazeroski, B. (Pit) 19.4
Davenport, J. (SF) 14.5
Clemente, R. (Pit) 11.4

Win Shares – Batters
Aaron, H. (Mil) 35
Robinson, F. (Cin) 34
Mays, W. (SF) 34

TPW – Batters
Aaron, H. (Mil) 5.2
Robinson, F. (Cin) 4.7
Mathews, E. (Mil) 4.4

TEAM	CG	SH	SV	IP	H	H/G	ER	HR	BB	SO	OAV	RAT	ERA	ERA+	CERA	PR+	PF	FA	E	DP	FR	BW	PW	FW	TPW	DIF
CIN	46	**12**	**40**	1370	**1300**	8.5	575	147	500	829	.250	1.314	3.78	107	3.78	45.3	101	.977	134	124	-3.5	1.2	4.5	-.3	5.4	10.6
LA	40	10	35	1378[1]	1346	8.8	619	167	544	**1105**	.256	1.371	4.04	107	4.15	36.4	108	.975	144	162	8.6	-2.4	3.6	.9	2.0	10.0
SF	39	9	30	1388	1306	**8.5**	581	152	502	924	**.249**	**1.303**	3.77	101	**3.69**	16.6	94	.977	133	126	-11.8	5.9	1.7	-1.2	**6.4**	1.6
MIL	**57**	8	16	**1391[1]**	1357	8.8	601	153	493	652	.258	1.330	3.89	96	3.90	-21.4	93	**.982**	**111**	152	-2.9	**6.6**	-2.1	-.3	4.2	1.8
STL	49	10	24	1368[2]	1334	8.8	**568**	136	570	823	.256	1.391	**3.74**	118	4.04	**93.7**	109	.972	166	165	5.4	-6.4	**9.3**	.5	3.4	-.4
PIT	34	9	29	1362	1442	9.5	593	**121**	**400**	759	.274	1.352	3.92	102	3.96	6.3	99	.975	150	**187**	3.7	.0	.6	.4	1.0	-3.0
CHI	34	6	25	1385	1492	9.7	689	165	465	755	.277	1.413	4.48	93	4.47	-25.2	104	.970	183	175	-22.2	.7	-2.5	-2.2	-4.0	-9.0
PHI	29	9	13	1383[1]	1452	9.4	708	155	521	775	.273	1.426	4.61	**88**	4.42	-103.7	101	.976	146	179	**21.1**	-11.1	-10.3	**2.1**	-19.3	-10.7
Total	**328**	**73**	**212**	**11026[2]**		**9.0**	**4934**					**1.363**	**4.03**													

Wins
Jay, J. (Cin) 21
Spahn, W. (Mil) 21
O'Toole, J. (Cin) 19

Win Percentage
Podres, J. (LA) .783
O'Toole, J. (Cin) .679
Jay, J. (Cin) .677

Games
Baldschun, J. (Phi) 65
Miller, S. (SF) 63
Face, R. (Pit) 62

Complete Games
Spahn, W. (Mil) 21
Koufax, S. (LA) 15
2 players tied with 14

Shutouts
Jay, J. (Cin) 4
Spahn, W. (Mil) 4
9 players tied with 3

Saves
Face, R. (Pit) 17
Miller, S. (SF) 17
2 players tied with 16

Innings Pitched
Burdette, L. (Mil) 272[1]
Spahn, W. (Mil) 262[2]
Cardwell, D. (Chi) 259[1]

Fewest Hits/Game
Koufax, S. (LA) 7.46
Jay, J. (Cin) 7.90
Gibson, B. (StL) 7.92

Fewest BB/Game
Burdette, L. (Mil) 1.09
Friend, B. (Pit) 1.72
Purkey, B. (Cin) 1.86

Strikeouts
Koufax, S. (LA) 269
Williams, S. (LA) 205
Drysdale, D. (LA) 182

Ratio
Spahn, W. (Mil) 1.14
Purkey, B. (Cin) 1.20
Burdette, L. (Mil) 1.20

Earned Run Average
Spahn, W. (Mil) 3.02
O'Toole, J. (Cin) 3.10
Simmons, C. (StL) 3.13

Adjusted ERA
Simmons, C. (StL) 140
Gibson, B. (StL) 136
O'Toole, J. (Cin) 131

Component ERA
Spahn, W. (Mil) 2.96
Koufax, S. (LA) 3.08
O'Toole, J. (Cin) 3.20

Opponents' Batting Avg.
Koufax, S. (LA) .222
Jay, J. (Cin) .236
Sadecki, R. (StL) .238

Adjusted Pitching Runs
O'Toole, J. (Cin) 28
Simmons, C. (StL) 27
Gibson, B. (StL) 26

Win Shares – Pitchers
Spahn, W. (Mil) 25
O'Toole, J. (Cin) 22
2 players tied with 20

TPW – Pitchers
Simmons, C. (StL) 3.2
Spahn, W. (Mil) 3.1
Gibson, B. (StL) 2.8

1961 American League

TEAM	G	W	L	PCT	GB	R	OR	EW	AB	H	2B	3B	HR	TB	BB	SO	SB	CS	AVG	OBP	SLG	OPS	OPS+	BR/A	PF	RC
NY	163	109	53	.673	....	827	612	105	5559	1461	194	40	**240**	**2455**	543	785	28	18	.263	.332	**.442**	**.774**	**118**	**125**	95	810
DET	163	101	61	.623	8	**841**	671	99	5561	1481	215	**53**	180	2342	673	867	98	36	**.266**	**.349**	.421	.771	108	76	104	**834**
BAL	163	95	67	.586	14	691	**588**	94	5481	1393	227	36	149	2139	581	902	39	30	.254	.328	.390	.718	100	-6	98	697
CHI	163	86	76	.531	23	765	726	85	5556	1475	216	46	138	2197	550	**612**	**100**	40	.265	.338	.395	.733	104	35	98	752
CLE	161	78	83	.484	30.5	737	752	79	**5609**	**1493**	**257**	39	150	2278	492	720	34	**11**	.266	.328	.406	.735	105	32	97	741
BOS	163	76	86	.469	33	729	792	74	5508	1401	251	37	112	2062	647	847	56	36	.254	.336	.374	.710	94	-40	102	702
MIN	161	70	90	.438	38	707	778	72	5417	1353	215	40	167	2149	597	840	47	43	.250	.328	.397	.725	94	-50	106	696
LA	162	70	91	.435	38.5	744	784	76	5424	1331	218	22	189	2160	**681**	1068	37	28	.245	.333	.398	.731	91	-65	111	733
WAS	161	61	100	.379	47.5	618	776	62	5366	1307	217	44	119	1969	558	917	81	47	.244	.317	.367	.684	93	-53	95	624
KC	162	61	100	.379	47.5	683	863	62	5423	1342	216	47	90	1922	580	772	58	22	.247	.323	.354	.677	87	-87	100	640
Total	**811**					**7342**			**54904**	**14037**	**2226**	**404**	**1534**		**5902**	**8330**	**578**	**311**	**.256**	**.331**	**.395**	**.726**				

Runs
Mantle, M. (NY) 132
Maris, R. (NY) 132
Colavito, R. (Det) 129

Hits
Cash, N. (Det) 193
Robinson, B. (Bal) 192
Kaline, A. (Det) 190

Doubles
Kaline, A. (Det) 41
Kubek, T. (NY) 38
Robinson, B. (Bal) 38

Triples
Wood, J. (Det) 14
Keough, M. (Was) 9
Lumpe, J. (KC) 9

Home Runs
Maris, R. (NY) 61
Mantle, M. (NY) 54
2 players tied with 46

Total Bases
Maris, R. (NY) 366
Cash, N. (Det) 354
Mantle, M. (NY) 353

Runs Batted In
Maris, R. (NY) 142
Gentile, J. (Bal) 141
Colavito, R. (Det) 140

Bases On Balls
Mantle, M. (NY) 126
Cash, N. (Det) 124
Colavito, R. (Det) 113

Stolen Bases
Aparicio, L. (Chi) 53
Howser, D. (KC) 37
Wood, J. (Det) 30

Batting Average
Cash, N. (Det) .361
Kaline, A. (Det) .324
Piersall, J. (Cle) .322

On-Base Percentage
Cash, N. (Det) .488
Mantle, M. (NY) .452
Gentile, J. (Bal) .428

Slugging Average
Mantle, M. (NY) .687
Cash, N. (Det) .662
Gentile, J. (Bal) .646

Adjusted OPS
Mantle, M. (NY) 210
Cash, N. (Det) 197
Gentile, J. (Bal) 186

Adjusted Batting Runs
Mantle, M. (NY) 88.0
Cash, N. (Det) 83.0
Gentile, J. (Bal) 63.0

Runs Created/Game
Cash, N. (Det) 13.10
Mantle, M. (NY) 13.00
Gentile, J. (Bal) 10.40

Fielding Runs
Boyer, C. (NY) 33.4
Power, V. (Cle) 19.6
Kubek, T. (NY) 18.1

Win Shares – Batters
Mantle, M. (NY) 48
Cash, N. (Det) 42
Maris, R. (NY) 36

TPW – Batters
Cash, N. (Det) 8.3
Mantle, M. (NY) 8.2
Gentile, J. (Bal) 5.8

TEAM	CG	SH	SV	IP	H	H/G	ER	HR	BB	SO	OAV	RAT	ERA	ERA+	CERA	PR+	PF	FA	E	DP	FR	BW	PW	FW	TPW	DIF
NY	47	14	**39**	1451	1288	8.0	558	137	542	866	.239	1.261	3.46	107	3.45	-5.2	92	**.980**	**124**	**180**	**46.6**	**12.4**	-.5	**4.6**	**16.5**	11.5
DET	**62**	12	30	1459[1]	1404	8.7	575	170	**469**	836	.252	1.283	3.55	116	3.76	87.4	102	.976	146	147	3.2	7.5	8.7	.3	16.5	3.5
BAL	54	**21**	33	**1471[1]**	**1226**	**7.5**	**526**	**109**	617	926	**.227**	**1.253**	**3.22**	121	**3.15**	**93.1**	97	.980	128	173	19.8	-.6	**9.2**	2.0	10.6	3.4
CHI	39	3	33	1448[2]	1491	9.3	653	158	498	814	.268	1.373	4.06	96	4.10	-13.8	97	.980	128	138	-9.3	3.4	-1.4	-.9	1.1	3.9
CLE	35	12	23	1443[1]	1426	8.9	665	178	599	801	.258	1.403	4.15	95	4.30	-34.8	98	.977	139	142	0.9	3.1	-3.4	.1	-.2	-1.8
BOS	35	6	30	1442[2]	1472	9.2	687	167	679	831	.266	1.491	4.29	97	4.61	-15.9	104	.977	144	170	-3.8	-3.9	-1.6	-.4	-5.9	.9
MIN	49	14	23	1432[1]	1415	8.9	681	163	570	914	.256	1.386	4.28	99	4.22	24.9	105	.971	174	150	-30.9	-5.0	2.5	-3.1	-5.6	-4.4
LA	25	5	34	1438	1391	8.7	689	180	713	**973**	.254	1.463	4.31	105	4.54	47.5	112	.969	192	154	-16.2	-6.5	4.7	-1.6	-3.4	-6.6
WAS	39	8	21	1425	1405	8.9	670	131	586	666	.260	1.397	4.23	93	4.09	-53.0	97	.975	156	171	3.0	-5.2	-5.3	.3	-10.2	-8.8
KC	32	5	23	1415	1519	9.7	745	141	629	703	.275	1.518	4.74	**87**	4.81	-84.8	102	.972	175	160	-13.8	-8.7	-8.4	-1.4	-18.4	-.6
Total	**417**	**100**	**289**	**14426[2]**		**8.8**	**6449**					**1.382**	**4.02**													

Wins		Win Percentage		Games		Complete Games		Shutouts		Saves	
Ford, W. (NY)	25	Ford, W. (NY)	.862	Arroyo, L. (NY)	65	Lary, F. (Det)	22	Barber, S. (Bal)	8	Arroyo, L. (NY)	29
Lary, F. (Det)	23	Terry, R. (NY)	.842	Lown, T. (Chi)	59	Pascual, C. (Min)	15	Pascual, C. (Min)	8	Wilhelm, H. (Bal)	18
Barber, S. (Bal)	18	Latman, B. (Cle)	.722	Morgan, T. (NY)	59	Barber, S. (Bal)	14	3 players tied with	4	Fornieles, M. (Bos)	15

Innings Pitched		Fewest Hits/Game		Fewest BB/Game		Strikeouts		Ratio		Earned Run Average	
Ford, W. (NY)	283	Estrada, C. (Bal)	6.75	Mossi, D. (Det)	1.76	Pascual, C. (Min)	221	Donovan, D. (Was)	1.03	Donovan, D. (Was)	2.40
Lary, F. (Det)	275[1]	Pappas, M. (Bal)	6.79	Brown, H. (Bal)	1.78	Ford, W. (NY)	209	Terry, R. (NY)	1.08	Stafford, B. (NY)	2.68
Bunning, J. (Det)	268	Barber, S. (Bal)	7.03	Donovan, D. (Was)	1.87	Bunning, J. (Det)	194	Brown, H. (Bal)	1.12	Mossi, D. (Det)	2.96

Adjusted ERA		Component ERA		Opponents' Batting Avg.		Adjusted Pitching Runs		Win Shares – Pitchers		TPW – Pitchers	
Donovan, D. (Was)	163	Donovan, D. (Was)	2.21	Estrada, C. (Bal)	.207	Mossi, D. (Det)	30	Ford, W. (NY)	22	Mossi, D. (Det)	3.1
Stafford, B. (NY)	139	Terry, R. (NY)	2.72	Pappas, M. (Bal)	.208	Donovan, D. (Was)	28	Lary, F. (Det)	22	Donovan, D. (Was)	3.0
Mossi, D. (Det)	139	Brown, H. (Bal)	2.83	Pascual, C. (Min)	.217	Pascual, C. (Min)	27	Mossi, D. (Det)	20	Lary, F. (Det)	2.9

1962 National League

TEAM	G	W	L	PCT	GB	R	OR	EW	AB	H	2B	3B	HR	TB	BB	SO	SB	CS	AVG	OBP	SLG	OPS	OPS+	BR/A	PF	RC
SF	165	103	62	.624	....	878	690	102	5588	1552	235	32	204	2463	523	822	73	50	.278	.344	.441	.785	119	132	98	837
LA	165	102	63	.618	1	842	697	98	5628	1510	192	65	140	2252	572	886	198	43	.268	.339	.400	.739	112	119	94	782
CIN	162	98	64	.605	3.5	802	685	94	5645	1523	252	40	167	2356	498	903	66	39	.270	.333	.417	.751	104	27	103	778
PIT	161	93	68	.578	8	706	626	90	5483	1468	240	65	108	2162	432	836	50	39	.268	.323	.394	.717	99	-23	100	680
MIL	162	86	76	.531	15.5	730	665	89	5458	1376	204	38	181	2199	581	975	57	27	.252	.328	.403	.731	105	39	97	718
STL	163	84	78	.519	17.5	774	664	93	5643	1528	221	31	137	2222	515	846	86	41	.271	.337	.394	.730	94	-43	110	745
PHI	161	81	80	.503	20	705	759	75	5420	1410	199	39	142	2113	531	923	79	42	.260	.332	.390	.722	103	26	97	704
HOU	162	64	96	.400	36.5	592	717	65	5558	1370	170	47	105	1949	493	806	42	30	.246	.312	.351	.663	91	-70	92	603
CHI	162	59	103	.364	42.5	632	827	60	5534	1398	196	56	126	2084	504	1044	78	50	.253	.319	.377	.696	90	-81	104	655
NY	161	40	120	.250	60.5	617	948	48	5492	1318	166	40	139	1981	616	991	59	48	.240	.320	.361	.681	88	-91	102	638
Total	812					7278			55449	14453	2075	453	1449		5265	9032	788	409	.261	.329	.393	.722				

Runs		Hits		Doubles		Triples		Home Runs		Total Bases	
Robinson, F. (Cin)	134	Davis, T. (LA)	230	Robinson, F. (Cin)	51	4 players tied with	10	Mays, W. (SF)	49	Mays, W. (SF)	382
Mays, W. (SF)	130	Robinson, F. (Cin)	208	Mays, W. (SF)	36			Aaron, H. (Mil)	45	Robinson, F. (Cin)	380
Wills, M. (LA)	130	Wills, M. (LA)	208	Groat, D. (Pit)	34			Robinson, F. (Cin)	39	Aaron, H. (Mil)	366

Runs Batted In		Bases On Balls		Stolen Bases		Batting Average		On-Base Percentage		Slugging Average	
Davis, T. (LA)	153	Mathews, E. (Mil)	101	Wills, M. (LA)	104	Davis, T. (LA)	.346	Robinson, F. (Cin)	.424	Robinson, F. (Cin)	.624
Mays, W. (SF)	141	Gilliam, J. (LA)	93	Davis, W. (LA)	32	Robinson, F. (Cin)	.342	Musial, S. (StL)	.420	Aaron, H. (Mil)	.618
Robinson, F. (Cin)	136	Ashburn, R. (NY)	81	2 players tied with	26	Musial, S. (StL)	.330	Skinner, B. (Pit)	.397	Mays, W. (SF)	.615

Adjusted OPS		Adjusted Batting Runs		Runs Created/Game		Fielding Runs		Win Shares – Batters		TPW – Batters	
Robinson, F. (Cin)	171	Robinson, F. (Cin)	63.0	Robinson, F. (Cin)	10.10	Mazeroski, B. (Pit)	30.0	Robinson, F. (Cin)	41	Mays, W. (SF)	5.6
Aaron, H. (Mil)	171	Mays, W. (SF)	60.0	Aaron, H. (Mil)	8.80	Callison, J. (Phi)	17.5	Mays, W. (SF)	41	Robinson, F. (Cin)	5.2
Mays, W. (SF)	166	Aaron, H. (Mil)	58.0	Mays, W. (SF)	8.60	Davenport, J. (SF)	10.8	Davis, T. (LA)	36	Aaron, H. (Mil)	5.0

TEAM	CG	SH	SV	IP	H	H/G	ER	HR	BB	SO	OAV	RAT	ERA	ERA+	CERA	PR+	PF	FA	E	DP	FR	BW	PW	FW	TPW	DIF
SF	62	10	39	1461[2]	1399	8.6	615	148	503	886	.251	1.301	3.79	100	3.66	1.2	96	.977	142	153	-0.7	13.2	.1	-.1	13.2	7.8
LA	44	8	46	1488[2]	1386	8.4	599	115	588	1104	.245	1.326	3.62	100	3.56	2.5	92	.970	193	144	-0.2	11.9	.2	.0	12.1	7.9
CIN	51	13	35	1460[2]	1397	8.6	608	149	567	964	.254	1.345	3.75	107	3.96	34.9	102	.977	145	144	9.1	2.7	3.5	.9	7.1	9.9
PIT	40	13	41	1432[1]	1433	9.0	536	118	466	897	.262	1.326	3.37	117	3.67	75.3	100	.976	152	177	13.2	-2.3	7.5	1.3	6.6	6.4
MIL	59	10	24	1434[2]	1443	9.0	586	151	407	802	.263	1.289	3.68	103	3.78	14.5	96	.980	124	154	4.2	3.9	1.4	.4	5.7	-.7
STL	53	17	25	1463[1]	1394	8.6	577	149	517	914	.252	1.306	3.55	120	3.72	104.4	108	.979	132	170	12.8	-4.3	10.4	1.3	7.4	-4.4
PHI	43	7	24	1426[2]	1469	9.3	678	155	574	863	.268	1.432	4.28	90	4.46	-74.6	98	.977	138	167	10.0	2.6	-7.4	1.0	-3.8	4.9
HOU	34	9	19	1453[2]	1446	9.0	618	113	471	1047	.259	1.319	3.83	98	3.71	10.0	95	.973	173	149	-24.8	-7.0	1.0	-2.5	-8.5	-7.5
CHI	29	4	26	1438[1]	1509	9.4	725	159	601	783	.272	1.467	4.54	91	4.59	-64.4	105	.977	146	171	2.2	-8.1	-6.4	.2	-14.3	-7.7
NY	43	4	10	1430	1577	9.9	801	192	571	772	.281	1.502	5.04	83	5.04	-109.6	106	.967	210	167	-27.2	-9.1	-10.9	-2.7	-22.7	-17.3
Total	458	95	289	14490		9.0	6343					1.361	3.94													

Wins		Win Percentage		Games		Complete Games		Shutouts		Saves	
Drysdale, D. (LA)	25	Purkey, B. (Cin)	.821	Perranoski, R. (LA)	70	Spahn, W. (Mil)	22	Friend, B. (Pit)	5	Face, R. (Pit)	28
Sanford, J. (SF)	24	Sanford, J. (SF)	.774	Baldschun, J. (Phi)	67	Mahaffey, A. (Phi)	20	Gibson, B. (StL)	5	Perranoski, R. (LA)	20
Purkey, B. (Cin)	23	Drysdale, D. (LA)	.735	Roebuck, E. (LA)	64	O'Dell, B. (SF)	20	4 players tied with	4	Miller, S. (SF)	19

Innings Pitched		Fewest Hits/Game		Fewest BB/Game		Strikeouts		Ratio		Earned Run Average	
Drysdale, D. (LA)	314[1]	Koufax, S. (LA)	6.54	Shaw, B. (Mil)	1.76	Drysdale, D. (LA)	232	Koufax, S. (LA)	1.04	Koufax, S. (LA)	2.54
Purkey, B. (Cin)	288[1]	Gibson, B. (StL)	6.70	Friend, B. (Pit)	1.82	Koufax, S. (LA)	216	Farrell, T. (Hou)	1.10	Shaw, B. (Mil)	2.80
O'Dell, B. (SF)	280[2]	Bennett, D. (Phi)	7.42	Spahn, W. (Mil)	1.84	Gibson, B. (StL)	208	Drysdale, D. (LA)	1.11	Purkey, B. (Cin)	2.81

Adjusted ERA		Component ERA		Opponents' Batting Avg.		Adjusted Pitching Runs		Win Shares – Pitchers		TPW – Pitchers	
Gibson, B. (StL)	150	Koufax, S. (LA)	2.13	Koufax, S. (LA)	.197	Purkey, B. (Cin)	37	Purkey, B. (Cin)	26	Gibson, B. (StL)	4.1
Purkey, B. (Cin)	143	Gibson, B. (StL)	2.60	Gibson, B. (StL)	.204	Gibson, B. (StL)	35	Drysdale, D. (LA)	24	Purkey, B. (Cin)	3.5
Koufax, S. (LA)	143	Drysdale, D. (LA)	2.63	Bennett, D. (Phi)	.224	Broglio, E. (StL)	30	Spahn, W. (Mil)	23	Drysdale, D. (LA)	3.2

1962 American League

TEAM	G	W	L	PCT	GB	R	OR	EW	AB	H	2B	3B	HR	TB	BB	SO	SB	CS	AVG	OBP	SLG	OPS	OPS+	BR/A	PF	RC
NY	162	96	66	.593	....	817	680	96	5644	1509	240	29	199	2404	584	842	42	29	.267	.339	.426	.765	115	111	97	814
MIN	163	91	71	.562	5	798	713	90	5561	1445	215	39	185	2293	649	823	33	20	.260	.340	.412	.753	105	39	104	787
LA	162	86	76	.531	10	718	706	82	5499	1377	232	35	137	2090	602	917	46	27	.250	.328	.380	.708	100	-1	97	696
DET	161	85	76	.528	10.5	758	692	88	5456	1352	191	36	209	2242	651	894	69	21	.248	.332	.411	.743	102	23	104	756
CHI	162	85	77	.525	11	707	658	87	5514	1415	250	56	92	2053	620	674	76	40	.257	.336	.372	.709	98	-9	99	699
CLE	162	80	82	.494	16	682	745	74	5484	1341	202	22	180	2127	502	939	35	16	.245	.314	.388	.702	97	-25	97	669
BAL	162	77	85	.475	19	652	680	78	5491	1363	225	34	156	2124	516	931	45	32	.248	.316	.387	.703	100	-13	95	663
BOS	162	76	84	.475	19	707	756	75	5530	1429	257	53	146	2230	525	923	39	33	.258	.326	.403	.729	99	-19	103	715
KC	162	72	90	.444	24	745	837	72	5576	1467	220	58	116	2151	556	803	76	21	.263	.334	.386	.720	97	-11	103	736
WAS	162	60	101	.373	35.5	599	716	66	5484	1370	206	38	132	2048	466	789	99	53	.250	.310	.373	.684	90	-80	99	621
Total	809					7183			55239	14068	2238	400	1552		5671	8535	560	292	.255	.328	.394	.722				

Runs
Pearson, A. (LA) 115
Siebern, N. (KC) 114
Allison, B. (Min) 102

Hits
Richardson, B. (NY) 209
Lumpe, J. (KC) 193
Robinson, B. (Bal) 192

Doubles
Robinson, F. (Chi) 45
Yastrzemski, C. (Bos) 43
Bressoud, E. (Bos) 40

Triples
Cimoli, G. (KC) 15
3 players tied with 10

Home Runs
Killebrew, H. (Min) 48
Cash, N. (Det) 39
2 players tied with 37

Total Bases
Colavito, R. (Det) 309
Robinson, B. (Bal) 308
Wagner, L. (LA) 306

Runs Batted In
Killebrew, H. (Min) 126
Siebern, N. (KC) 117
Colavito, R. (Det) 112

Bases On Balls
Mantle, M. (NY) 122
Siebern, N. (KC) 110
Killebrew, H. (Min) 106

Stolen Bases
Aparicio, L. (Chi) 31
Hinton, C. (Was) 28
Wood, J. (Det) 24

Batting Average
Runnels, P. (Bos) .326
Mantle, M. (NY) .321
Robinson, B. (Bal) .312

On-Base Percentage
Mantle, M. (NY) .488
Siebern, N. (KC) .416
Cunningham, J. (Chi) .415

Slugging Average
Mantle, M. (NY) .605
Killebrew, H. (Min) .545
Colavito, R. (Det) .514

Adjusted OPS
Mantle, M. (NY) 198
Siebern, N. (KC) 140
Killebrew, H. (Min) 137

Adjusted Batting Runs
Mantle, M. (NY) 64.0
Siebern, N. (KC) 39.0
Killebrew, H. (Min) 29.0

Runs Created/Game
Mantle, M. (NY) 13.00
Siebern, N. (KC) 8.00
Runnels, P. (Bos) 7.50

Fielding Runs
Boyer, C. (NY) 39.2
Kindall, J. (Cle) 26.7
Versalles, Z. (Min) 25.3

Win Shares – Batters
Mantle, M. (NY) 33
3 players tied with 27

TPW – Batters
Mantle, M. (NY) 5.5
Boyer, C. (NY) 4.1
Siebern, N. (KC) 3.5

TEAM	CG	SH	SV	IP	H	H/G	ER	HR	BB	SO	OAV	RAT	ERA	ERA+	CERA	PR+	PF	FA	E	DP	FR	BW	PW	FW	TPW	DIF
NY	33	10	42	1470¹	1375	8.4	604	146	499	838	.247	1.275	3.70	101	3.53	-5.8	94	.979	131	151	12.5	11.1	-.6	1.3	11.8	3.2
MIN	53	11	27	1463¹	1400	8.6	632	166	493	948	.253	1.294	3.89	104	3.81	25.0	103	.979	129	173	5.9	3.9	2.5	.6	7.0	3.0
LA	23	15	47	1466	1412	8.7	603	118	616	858	.253	1.383	3.70	104	3.88	38.6	97	.972	175	153	-12.6	-.1	3.9	-1.3	2.6	2.4
DET	46	8	35	1443²	1452	9.0	611	169	503	873	.259	1.354	3.81	107	4.09	55.8	103	.974	156	114	-14.0	2.3	5.6	-1.4	6.5	-1.5
CHI	50	13	28	1451²	1380	8.6	601	123	537	821	.251	1.321	3.73	105	3.61	35.7	98	.982	110	153	-8.0	-.9	3.6	-.8	1.9	2.1
CLE	45	12	31	1441	1410	8.8	663	174	594	780	.258	1.391	4.14	94	4.22	-54.1	98	.977	139	168	11.3	-2.5	-5.4	1.1	-6.8	5.8
BAL	32	8	33	1462¹	1373	8.4	599	147	549	898	.249	1.314	3.69	102	3.72	-0.9	95	.980	122	152	11.4	-1.3	-.1	1.1	-.3	-3.7
BOS	34	12	40	1437²	1416	8.9	674	159	632	923	.258	1.425	4.22	98	4.37	-19.1	104	.979	131	152	5.2	-1.9	-1.9	.5	-3.3	-.7
KC	32	4	33	1434	1450	9.1	763	199	655	825	.263	1.468	4.79	87	4.76	-91.8	105	.979	132	131	-9.5	-1.1	-9.2	-1.0	-11.3	2.3
WAS	38	11	13	1445	1400	8.7	649	151	593	771	.256	1.379	4.04	100	4.00	1.0	102	.978	139	160	-1.8	-8.1	.1	-.2	-8.1	-11.9
Total	**386**	**104**	**329**	**14515**		**8.7**	**6399**					**1.360**	**3.97**													

Wins
Terry, R. (NY) 23
3 players tied with 20

Win Percentage
Herbert, R. (Chi) .690
Ford, W. (NY) .680
2 players tied with .667

Games
Radatz, D. (Bos) 62
Wyatt, J. (KC) 59
4 players tied with 57

Complete Games
Pascual, C. (Min) 18
Donovan, D. (Cle) 16
Kaat, J. (Min) 16

Shutouts
Donovan, D. (Cle) 5
Kaat, J. (Min) 5
Pascual, C. (Min) 5

Saves
Radatz, D. (Bos) 24
Bridges, M. (NY) 18
Fox, T. (Det) 16

Innings Pitched
Terry, R. (NY) 298²
Kaat, J. (Min) 269
Bunning, J. (Det) 258

Fewest Hits/Game
Aguirre, H. (Det) 6.75
Cheney, T. (Was) 6.96
Belinsky, B. (LA) 7.16

Fewest BB/Game
Donovan, D. (Cle) 1.69
Terry, R. (NY) 1.72
Mossi, D. (Det) 1.80

Strikeouts
Pascual, C. (Min) 206
Bunning, J. (Det) 184
Terry, R. (NY) 176

Ratio
Aguirre, H. (Det) 1.05
Terry, R. (NY) 1.05
Roberts, R. (Bal) 1.13

Earned Run Average
Aguirre, H. (Det) 2.21
Roberts, R. (Bal) 2.78
Ford, W. (NY) 2.90

Adjusted ERA
Aguirre, H. (Det) 184
Roberts, R. (Bal) 135
Chance, D. (LA) 130

Component ERA
Aguirre, H. (Det) 2.20
Terry, R. (NY) 2.79
Roberts, R. (Bal) 2.92

Opponents' Batting Avg.
Aguirre, H. (Det) .205
Cheney, T. (Was) .213
Belinsky, B. (LA) .216

Adjusted Pitching Runs
Aguirre, H. (Det) 47
Kaat, J. (Min) 27
Chance, D. (LA) 22

Win Shares – Pitchers
Pascual, C. (Min) 23
Aguirre, H. (Det) 22
Kaat, J. (Min) 22

TPW – Pitchers
Aguirre, H. (Det) 3.9
Kaat, J. (Min) 3.0
Pascual, C. (Min) 2.9

1963 National League

TEAM	G	W	L	PCT	GB	R	OR	EW	AB	H	2B	3B	HR	TB	BB	SO	SB	CS	AVG	OBP	SLG	OPS	OPS+	BR/A	PF	RC
LA	163	99	63	.611	....	640	550	93	5428	1361	178	34	110	1937	453	867	124	70	.251	.311	.357	.668	107	44	93	594
STL	162	93	69	.574	6	747	628	95	5678	1540	231	66	128	2287	458	915	77	42	.271	.328	.403	.731	107	61	109	750
SF	162	88	74	.543	11	725	641	91	5579	1442	206	35	197	2309	441	889	55	49	.258	.318	.414	.732	118	116	99	711
PHI	162	87	75	.537	12	642	578	89	5524	1390	228	54	126	2104	403	955	56	39	.252	.308	.381	.689	106	37	99	639
CIN	162	86	76	.531	13	648	594	88	5416	1333	225	44	122	2012	474	960	92	58	.246	.312	.371	.684	101	9	103	628
MIL	163	84	78	.519	15	677	603	90	5518	1345	204	39	139	2044	525	954	75	52	.244	.314	.370	.685	105	39	99	641
CHI	162	82	80	.506	17	570	578	80	5404	1286	205	44	127	1960	439	1049	68	60	.238	.300	.363	.662	92	-56	105	571
PIT	162	74	88	.457	25	567	595	77	5536	1385	181	49	108	1988	454	940	57	41	.250	.310	.359	.669	99	-5	101	601
HOU	162	66	96	.407	33	464	640	56	5384	1184	170	39	62	1618	456	938	39	30	.220	.284	.301	.585	80	-126	94	459
NY	162	51	111	.315	48	501	774	48	5336	1168	156	35	96	1682	457	1078	41	52	.219	.286	.315	.602	79	-143	102	475
Total	**811**					**6181**			**54803**	**13434**	**1984**	**439**	**1215**		**4560**	**9545**	**684**	**493**	**.245**	**.307**	**.364**	**.671**				

Runs
Aaron, H. (Mil) 121
Mays, W. (SF) 115
Flood, C. (StL) 112

Hits
Pinson, V. (Cin) 204
Aaron, H. (Mil) 201
Groat, D. (StL) 201

Doubles
Groat, D. (StL) 43
Pinson, V. (Cin) 37
3 players tied with 36

Triples
Pinson, V. (Cin) 14
Gonzalez, T. (Phi) 12
3 players tied with 11

Home Runs
Aaron, H. (Mil) 44
McCovey, W. (SF) 44
Mays, W. (SF) 38

Total Bases
Aaron, H. (Mil) 370
Mays, W. (SF) 347
Pinson, V. (Cin) 335

Runs Batted In
Aaron, H. (Mil) 130
Boyer, K. (StL) 111
White, B. (StL) 109

Bases On Balls
Mathews, E. (Mil) 124
Robinson, F. (Cin) 81
Aaron, H. (Mil) 78

Stolen Bases
Wills, M. (LA) 40
Aaron, H. (Mil) 31
Pinson, V. (Cin) 27

Batting Average
Davis, T. (LA) .326
Clemente, R. (Pit) .320
2 players tied with .318542

On-Base Percentage
Mathews, E. (Mil) .400
Aaron, H. (Mil) .394
Mays, W. (SF) .384

Slugging Average
Aaron, H. (Mil) .586
Mays, W. (SF) .582
McCovey, W. (SF) .566

Adjusted OPS
Aaron, H. (Mil) 180
Mays, W. (SF) 176
Cepeda, O. (SF) 166

Adjusted Batting Runs
Aaron, H. (Mil) 70.0
Mays, W. (SF) 59.0
Cepeda, O. (SF) 48.0

Runs Created/Game
Aaron, H. (Mil) 8.90
Mays, W. (SF) 8.20
Cepeda, O. (SF) 7.30

Fielding Runs
Mazeroski, B. (Pit) 36.0
Callison, J. (Phi) 24.4
Mathews, E. (Mil) 18.3

Win Shares – Batters
Aaron, H. (Mil) 41
Mays, W. (SF) 38
Callison, J. (Phi) 32

TPW – Batters
Aaron, H. (Mil) 6.1
Mathews, E. (Mil) 6.0
Mays, W. (SF) 5.5

TEAM	CG	SH	SV	IP	H	H/G	ER	HR	BB	SO	OAV	RAT	ERA	ERA+	CERA	PR+	PF	FA	E	DP	FR	BW	PW	FW	TPW	DIF
LA	51	24	29	1469²	1329	8.1	465	111	402	1095	.239	1.178	2.85	106	2.98	39.9	92	.975	159	129	-12.5	4.8	4.3	-1.4	7.8	10.2
STL	49	17	32	1463	1329	8.2	540	124	463	978	.241	1.225	3.32	107	3.27	31.0	108	.976	147	136	5.8	6.6	3.4	.6	10.6	1.4
SF	46	9	30	1469	1380	8.4	547	126	464	954	.246	1.255	3.35	95	3.34	3.6	97	.975	156	113	-27.5	12.6	.4	-3.0	10.0	-3.0
PHI	45	12	31	1457¹	1262	7.8	500	113	553	1052	.235	1.245	3.09	105	3.19	0.3	98	.978	142	147	23.3	4.0	.0	2.5	6.6	-.6
CIN	55	22	36	1439²	1307	8.2	526	117	425	1048	.242	1.203	3.29	102	3.17	6.7	102	.978	135	127	1.3	.9	.7	.1	1.8	3.2
MIL	56	18	25	1471²	1327	8.1	534	149	489	924	.241	1.234	3.27	99	3.31	-32.7	98	.980	129	129	25.2	4.3	-3.5	2.7	3.5	-.5
CHI	45	15	28	1457	1357	8.4	499	119	400	851	.249	1.206	3.08	114	3.20	48.1	107	.976	155	172	22.1	-6.1	5.2	2.4	1.5	-.5
PIT	34	16	33	1448	1350	8.4	499	99	457	900	.249	1.248	3.10	106	3.23	23.3	100	.972	182	195	9.2	-.5	2.5	1.0	3.0	-10.0
HOU	36	16	20	1450¹	1341	8.3	554	95	378	937	.245	1.185	3.44	92	3.02	-13.4	96	.974	162	100	-32.1	-13.7	-1.5	-3.5	-18.6	3.6
NY	42	5	12	1427²	1452	9.2	653	162	529	806	.263	1.388	4.12	85	4.24	-85.1	106	.967	210	151	-15.5	-15.6	-9.2	-1.7	-26.5	-3.5
Total	**459**	**154**	**276**	**14553¹**		**8.3**	**5317**					**1.236**	**3.29**													

Wins
Koufax, S. (LA) 25
Marichal, J. (SF) 25
2 players tied with 23

Win Percentage
Koufax, S. (LA) .833
Spahn, W. (Mil) .767
Maloney, J. (Cin) .767

Games
Perranoski, R. (LA) 69
Baldschun, J. (Phi) 65
Bearnarth, L. (NY) 58

Complete Games
Spahn, W. (Mil) 22
Koufax, S. (LA) 20
Ellsworth, D. (Chi) 19

Shutouts
Koufax, S. (LA) 11
Spahn, W. (Mil) 7
2 players tied with 6

Saves
McDaniel, L. (Chi) 22
Perranoski, R. (LA) 21
2 players tied with 16

Innings Pitched
Marichal, J. (SF) 321¹
Drysdale, D. (LA) 315¹
Koufax, S. (LA) 311

Fewest Hits/Game
Koufax, S. (LA) 6.19
Culp, R. (Phi) 6.55
Maloney, J. (Cin) 6.58

Fewest BB/Game
Friend, B. (Pit) 1.47
Farrell, T. (Hou) 1.56
Nuxhall, J. (Cin) 1.62

Strikeouts
Koufax, S. (LA) 306
Maloney, J. (Cin) 265
Drysdale, D. (LA) 251

Ratio
Koufax, S. (LA) .87
Farrell, T. (Hou) .97
Marichal, J. (SF) 1.00

Earned Run Average
Koufax, S. (LA) 1.88
Ellsworth, D. (Chi) 2.11
Friend, B. (Pit) 2.34

Adjusted ERA
Ellsworth, D. (Chi) 167
Koufax, S. (LA) 161
Simmons, C. (StL) 143

Component ERA
Koufax, S. (LA) 1.55
Farrell, T. (Hou) 1.98
Ellsworth, D. (Chi) 2.02

Opponents' Batting Avg.
Koufax, S. (LA) .189
Maloney, J. (Cin) .202
Culp, R. (Phi) .206

Adjusted Pitching Runs
Koufax, S. (LA) 42
Ellsworth, D. (Chi) 41
Marichal, J. (SF) 34

Win Shares – Pitchers
Ellsworth, D. (Chi) 32
Koufax, S. (LA) 32
Marichal, J. (SF) 26

TPW – Pitchers
Ellsworth, D. (Chi) 4.2
Koufax, S. (LA) 4.1
Marichal, J. (SF) 3.9

1963 American League

TEAM	G	W	L	PCT	GB	R	OR	EW	AB	H	2B	3B	HR	TB	BB	SO	SB	CS	AVG	OBP	SLG	OPS	OPS+	BR/A	PF	RC
NY	161	104	57	.646	....	714	547	101	5506	1387	197	35	188	2218	434	**808**	42	26	.252	.310	.403	.713	106	29	99	685
CHI	162	94	68	.580	10.5	683	**544**	99	5508	1379	208	**40**	114	2009	571	896	64	28	.250	.325	.365	.690	101	18	98	672
MIN	161	91	70	.565	13	**767**	602	100	5531	**1408**	223	35	**225**	**2376**	547	912	32	**14**	**.255**	.326	**.430**	**.756**	**115**	**103**	102	**776**
BAL	162	86	76	.531	18.5	644	621	84	5448	1359	207	32	146	2068	469	940	**97**	34	.249	.312	.380	.692	101	13	98	644
DET	162	79	83	.488	25.5	700	703	81	5500	1388	195	36	148	2099	**592**	908	73	32	.252	**.329**	.382	.711	102	24	103	697
CLE	162	79	83	.488	25.5	635	702	73	5496	1314	214	29	169	2093	469	1102	59	36	.239	.304	.381	.684	98	-24	99	632
BOS	161	76	85	.472	28	666	704	76	**5575**	1403	**247**	34	171	2231	475	954	27	16	.252	.313	.400	.714	102	8	103	683
KC	162	73	89	.451	31.5	615	704	70	5495	1356	225	38	95	1942	529	829	47	26	.247	.316	.353	.669	90	-66	104	614
LA	161	70	91	.435	34	597	660	72	5506	1378	208	38	95	1947	448	916	43	30	.250	.312	.354	.665	98	-20	94	605
WAS	162	56	106	.346	48.5	578	812	54	5446	1237	190	35	138	1911	497	963	68	28	.227	.295	.351	.646	87	-92	100	567
Total	**808**					**6599**			**55011**	**13609**	**2114**	**352**	**1489**		**5031**	**9228**	**552**	**270**	**.247**	**.314**	**.380**	**.694**				

Runs
Allison, B. (Min) 99
Pearson, A. (LA) 92
3 players tied with 91

Hits
Yastrzemski, C. (Bos) 183
Ward, P. (Chi) 177
Pearson, A. (LA) 176

Doubles
Yastrzemski, C. (Bos) 40
Ward, P. (Chi) 34
3 players tied with 32

Triples
Versalles, Z. (Min) 13
Fregosi, J. (LA) 12
Hinton, C. (Was) 12

Home Runs
Killebrew, H. (Min) 45
Stuart, D. (Bos) 42
Allison, B. (Min) 35

Total Bases
Stuart, D. (Bos) 319
Ward, P. (Chi) 289
Killebrew, H. (Min) 286

Runs Batted In
Stuart, D. (Bos) 118
Kaline, A. (Det) 101
Killebrew, H. (Min) 96

Bases On Balls
Yastrzemski, C. (Bos) 95
Pearson, A. (LA) 92
Allison, B. (Min) 90

Stolen Bases
Aparicio, L. (Bal) 40
Hinton, C. (Was) 25
2 players tied with 18

Batting Average
Yastrzemski, C. (Bos) .321
Kaline, A. (Det) .312
Rollins, R. (Min) .307

On-Base Percentage
Yastrzemski, C. (Bos) .419
Pearson, A. (LA) .403
Cash, N. (Det) .388

Slugging Average
Killebrew, H. (Min) .555
Allison, B. (Min) .533
Howard, E. (NY) .528

Adjusted OPS
Allison, B. (Min) 150
Killebrew, H. (Min) 147
Yastrzemski, C. (Bos) 145

Adjusted Batting Runs
Yastrzemski, C. (Bos) 39.0
Allison, B. (Min) 38.0
Killebrew, H. (Min) 32.0

Runs Created/Game
Yastrzemski, C. (Bos) 7.80
Allison, B. (Min) 7.70
Kaline, A. (Det) 7.00

Fielding Runs
Hansen, R. (Chi) 23.9
Boyer, C. (NY) 20.7
Versalles, Z. (Min) 10.1

Win Shares – Batters
Yastrzemski, C. (Bos) 29
Tresh, T. (NY) 29
3 players tied with 28

TPW – Batters
Hansen, R. (Chi) 3.6
Yastrzemski, C. (Bos) 3.5
Battey, E. (Min) 3.5

TEAM	CG	SH	SV	IP	H	H/G	ER	HR	BB	SO	OAV	RAT	ERA	ERA+	CERA	PR+	PF	FA	E	DP	FR	BW	PW	FW	TPW	DIF
NY	**59**	19	31	1449	**1239**	**7.7**	494	115	476	965	**.232**	**1.184**	3.07	115	**2.97**	45.4	97	.982	110	162	**25.4**	3.1	4.8	**2.7**	10.5	13.5
CHI	49	**21**	39	**1469**	1311	8.0	**485**	**100**	**440**	932	.239	1.192	**2.97**	118	2.99	**75.8**	97	.979	131	163	11.4	1.9	**8.0**	1.2	11.1	1.9
MIN	58	13	30	1446[1]	1322	8.2	527	162	459	941	.242	1.231	3.28	111	3.44	61.6	100	.976	144	140	-2.7	**10.8**	6.5	-.3	**17.0**	-6.0
BAL	35	8	**43**	1452	1353	8.4	557	137	507	913	.248	1.281	3.45	102	3.51	12.8	97	**.984**	**99**	157	-0.8	1.4	1.3	-.1	2.7	2.3
DET	42	7	28	1456[1]	1407	8.7	631	195	477	930	.253	1.294	3.90	96	3.94	-26.6	103	.981	113	124	0.9	2.5	-2.8	.1	-.2	-1.8
CLE	40	14	25	**1469**	1390	8.5	619	176	478	**1018**	.249	1.272	3.79	95	3.63	-18.1	100	.977	143	129	-10.2	-2.5	-1.9	-1.1	-5.4	3.4
BOS	29	7	32	1449[2]	1367	8.5	639	152	539	1009	.248	1.315	3.97	95	3.71	-22.7	104	.978	135	119	-7.9	.8	-2.4	-.8	-2.4	-1.6
KC	35	11	29	1458	1417	8.8	635	156	540	887	.256	1.342	3.92	98	3.95	-1.1	106	.980	127	131	-10.9	-6.9	-.1	-1.1	-8.2	.2
LA	30	13	31	1455[1]	1317	8.1	569	120	578	889	.242	1.302	3.52	97	3.53	-13.3	94	.974	163	155	-3.0	-2.1	-1.4	-.3	-3.8	-6.2
WAS	29	8	25	1447	1486	9.2	711	176	537	744	.266	1.398	4.42	**84**	4.34	-111.3	102	.971	182	**165**	-2.2	-9.7	-11.7	-.2	-21.6	-3.4
Total	**406**	**121**	**313**	**14551**[2]		**8.4**	**5867**					**1.281**	**3.63**													

Wins
Ford, W. (NY) 24
Bouton, J. (NY) 21
Pascual, C. (Min) 21

Win Percentage
Ford, W. (NY) .774
Bouton, J. (NY) .750
Downing, A. (NY) .722

Games
Miller, S. (Bal) 71
Dailey, B. (Min) 66
Radatz, D. (Bos) 66

Complete Games
Pascual, C. (Min) 18
Terry, R. (NY) 18
Stigman, D. (Min) 15

Shutouts
Herbert, R. (Chi) 7
Bouton, J. (NY) 6
5 players tied with 4

Saves
Miller, S. (Bal) 27
Radatz, D. (Bos) 25
3 players tied with 21

Innings Pitched
Ford, W. (NY) 269[1]
Terry, R. (NY) 268
Monbouquette, B. (Bos) 266[2]

Fewest Hits/Game
Downing, A. (NY) 5.84
Bouton, J. (NY) 6.89
Drabowsky, M. (KC) 6.97

Fewest BB/Game
Donovan, D. (Cle) 1.22
Terry, R. (NY) 1.31
Herbert, R. (Chi) 1.40

Strikeouts
Pascual, C. (Min) 202
Bunning, J. (Det) 196
Stigman, D. (Min) 193

Ratio
Terry, R. (NY) 1.06
Ramos, P. (Cle) 1.07
Peters, G. (Chi) 1.07

Earned Run Average
Peters, G. (Chi) 2.33
Pizarro, J. (Chi) 2.39
Pascual, C. (Min) 2.46

Adjusted ERA
Peters, G. (Chi) 150
Pascual, C. (Min) 148
Pizarro, J. (Chi) 147

Component ERA
Downing, A. (NY) 2.09
Peters, G. (Chi) 2.26
Bouton, J. (NY) 2.54

Opponents' Batting Avg.
Downing, A. (NY) .184
Morehead, D. (Bos) .211
Bouton, J. (NY) .212

Adjusted Pitching Runs
Pascual, C. (Min) 33
Peters, G. (Chi) 30
Pizarro, J. (Chi) 25

Win Shares – Pitchers
Peters, G. (Chi) 25
Ford, W. (NY) 23
2 players tied with 22

TPW – Pitchers
Pascual, C. (Min) 4.1
Peters, G. (Chi) 4.0
Pizarro, J. (Chi) 2.9

1964 National League

TEAM	G	W	L	PCT	GB	R	OR	EW	AB	H	2B	3B	HR	TB	BB	SO	SB	CS	AVG	OBP	SLG	OPS	OPS+	BR/A	PF	RC
STL	162	93	69	.574	....	715	652	88	**5625**	**1531**	240	53	109	2204	427	925	73	51	.272	.326	.392	.717	100	3	109	710
PHI	162	92	70	.568	1	693	632	88	5493	1415	241	51	130	2148	440	924	30	35	.258	.317	.391	.708	107	45	99	670
CIN	163	92	70	.568	1	660	**566**	93	5561	1383	220	38	130	2069	457	974	90	36	.249	.310	.372	.682	95	-24	104	640
SF	162	90	72	.556	3	656	587	90	5535	1360	185	38	**165**	2116	**505**	900	64	35	.246	.313	.382	.695	100	7	102	655
MIL	162	88	74	.543	5	**803**	744	87	5591	1522	**274**	32	159	**2337**	486	**825**	53	41	**.272**	**.335**	**.418**	**.753**	**118**	**127**	101	**763**
PIT	162	80	82	.494	13	663	636	84	5566	1469	225	**54**	121	2165	408	970	39	33	.264	.317	.389	.706	106	35	100	666
LA	164	80	82	.494	13	614	572	87	5499	1375	180	39	79	1870	438	893	**141**	60	.250	.308	.340	.648	96	-16	93	579
CHI	162	76	86	.469	17	649	724	72	5545	1391	239	50	145	2165	499	1041	70	49	.251	.316	.390	.706	101	9	104	678
HOU	162	66	96	.407	27	495	628	62	5303	1214	162	41	70	1668	381	872	40	48	.229	.287	.315	.601	80	-138	94	467
NY	163	53	109	.327	40	569	776	57	5566	1372	195	31	103	1938	353	932	36	**31**	.246	.297	.348	.645	90	-73	98	551
Total	**812**					**6517**			**55284**	**14032**	**2161**	**427**	**1211**		**4394**	**9256**	**636**	**419**	**.254**	**.313**	**.374**	**.687**				

Runs
Allen, D. (Phi) 125
Mays, W. (SF) 121
Brock, L. (StL,Chi) 111

Hits
Clemente, R. (Pit) 211
Flood, C. (StL) 211
2 players tied with 201

Doubles
Maye, L. (Mil) 44
Clemente, R. (Pit) 40
Williams, B. (Chi) 39

Triples
Allen, D. (Phi) 13
Santo, R. (Chi) 13
2 players tied with 11

Home Runs
Mays, W. (SF) 47
Williams, B. (Chi) 33
3 players tied with 31

Total Bases
Allen, D. (Phi) 352
Mays, W. (SF) 351
Williams, B. (Chi) 343

Runs Batted In
Boyer, K. (StL) 119
Santo, R. (Chi) 114
Mays, W. (SF) 111

Bases On Balls
Santo, R. (Chi) 86
Mathews, E. (Mil) 85
Mays, W. (SF) 82

Stolen Bases
Wills, M. (LA) 53
Brock, L. (StL,Chi) 43
Davis, W. (LA) 42

Batting Average
Clemente, R. (Pit) .339
Carty, R. (Mil) .330
Aaron, H. (Mil) .328

On-Base Percentage
Santo, R. (Chi) .401
Robinson, F. (Cin) .399
Aaron, H. (Mil) .394

Slugging Average
Mays, W. (SF) .607
Santo, R. (Chi) .564
Allen, D. (Phi) .557

Adjusted OPS
Mays, W. (SF) 171
Allen, D. (Phi) 163
Santo, R. (Chi) 162

Adjusted Batting Runs
Mays, W. (SF) 57.0
Allen, D. (Phi) 52.0
Santo, R. (Chi) 50.0

Runs Created/Game
Mays, W. (SF) 8.60
Santo, R. (Chi) 8.50
Robinson, F. (Cin) 8.20

Fielding Runs
Davis, W. (LA) 15.7
Allen, D. (Phi) 15.4
Lanier, H. (SF) 14.7

Win Shares – Batters
Allen, D. (Phi) 41
Mays, W. (SF) 38
Santo, R. (Chi) 36

TPW – Batters
Allen, D. (Phi) 7.1
Mays, W. (SF) 6.3
Santo, R. (Chi) 5.6

TEAM	CG	SH	SV	IP	H	H/G	ER	HR	BB	SO	OAV	RAT	ERA	ERA+	CERA	PR+	PF	FA	E	DP	FR	BW	PW	FW	TPW	DIF
STL	47	10	38	1445^{1}	1405	8.8	551	133	410	877	.255	1.256	3.43	111	3.47	56.1	108	.973	172	147	3.2	.3	5.9	.3	6.6	5.4
PHI	37	17	**41**	1461	1402	8.6	545	129	440	1009	.252	1.261	3.36	103	3.53	9.1	98	.975	157	150	7.7	4.8	1.0	.8	6.6	4.4
CIN	54	14	35	1467	1306	8.0	500	112	436	**1122**	.238	1.187	3.07	118	3.01	**69.0**	102	**.979**	**130**	137	**18.8**	-2.6	**7.3**	**2.0**	6.7	4.3
SF	48	17	30	1476^{1}	1348	8.2	523	118	480	1023	.241	1.238	3.19	112	3.22	50.4	101	.975	159	136	10.9	.7	5.3	1.2	**7.2**	1.8
MIL	45	14	39	1434^{2}	1411	8.8	656	160	452	906	.257	1.299	4.12	85	3.77	-96.9	100	.977	143	139	1.5	**13.4**	-10.2	.2	3.3	3.7
PIT	42	14	29	1443^{2}	1429	8.9	564	92	476	951	.260	1.320	3.52	100	3.54	17.4	99	.972	177	**179**	-19.8	3.7	1.8	-2.1	3.4	-4.4
LA	47	**19**	27	**1483^{2}**	**1289**	**7.8**	**486**	**88**	458	1062	**.232**	**1.177**	**2.95**	110	**2.78**	49.5	92	.973	170	126	-2.6	-1.7	5.2	-.3	3.3	-4.3
CHI	**58**	11	19	1445	1510	9.4	655	144	423	737	.270	1.338	4.08	91	3.95	-44.9	105	.975	162	147	-14.8	1.0	-4.7	-1.6	-5.3	.3
HOU	30	9	31	1428	1421	9.0	541	105	**353**	852	.260	1.242	3.41	100	3.31	19.8	97	.976	149	124	-19.1	-14.5	2.1	-2.0	-14.5	-.5
NY	40	10	15	1438^{2}	1511	9.4	679	130	466	717	.272	1.374	4.25	**84**	4.13	-119.9	101	.974	167	154	11.1	-7.7	-12.7	1.2	-19.2	-8.8
Total	**448**	**135**	**304**	**14523^{1}**		**8.7**	**5700**					**1.269**	**3.53**													

Wins
- Jackson, L. (Chi) 24
- Marichal, J. (SF) 21
- Sadecki, R. (StL) 20

Win Percentage
- Koufax, S. (LA) .... .792
- Marichal, J. (SF) .... .724
- O'Toole, J. (Cin) .... .708

Games
- Miller, B. (LA) 74
- Perranoski, R. (LA) 72
- Baldschun, J. (Phi) 71

Complete Games
- Marichal, J. (SF) 22
- Drysdale, D. (LA) 21
- Jackson, L. (Chi) 19

Shutouts
- Koufax, S. (LA) 7
- 4 players tied with 5

Saves
- Woodeshick, H. (Hou) 23
- McBean, A. (Pit) 22
- Baldschun, J. (Phi) 21

Innings Pitched
- Drysdale, D. (LA) .... 321^{1}
- Jackson, L. (Chi) .... 297^{2}
- Gibson, B. (StL) .... 287^{1}

Fewest Hits/Game
- Koufax, S. (LA) 6.22
- Drysdale, D. (LA) 6.78
- Short, C. (Phi) 7.10

Fewest BB/Game
- Bunning, J. (Phi) 1.46
- Bruce, B. (Hou) 1.47
- Law, V. (Pit) 1.50

Strikeouts
- Veale, B. (Pit) 250
- Gibson, B. (StL) 245
- Drysdale, D. (LA) 237

Ratio
- Koufax, S. (LA) .... .93
- Drysdale, D. (LA) .... .96
- Short, C. (Phi) 1.02

Earned Run Average
- Koufax, S. (LA) 1.74
- Drysdale, D. (LA) 2.18
- Short, C. (Phi) 2.20

Adjusted ERA
- Koufax, S. (LA) 187
- Short, C. (Phi) 157
- Drysdale, D. (LA) 148

Component ERA
- Koufax, S. (LA) 1.66
- Drysdale, D. (LA) 1.89
- Short, C. (Phi) 2.10

Opponents' Batting Avg.
- Koufax, S. (LA) .... .191
- Drysdale, D. (LA) .... .207
- Veale, B. (Pit) .... .217

Adjusted Pitching Runs
- Drysdale, D. (LA) 38
- Koufax, S. (LA) 38
- Marichal, J. (SF) 30

Win Shares – Pitchers
- Drysdale, D. (LA) 26
- Jackson, L. (Chi) 25
- Marichal, J. (SF) 25

TPW – Pitchers
- Drysdale, D. (LA) 4.4
- Koufax, S. (LA) 3.8
- Marichal, J. (SF) 3.1

1964 American League

TEAM	G	W	L	PCT	GB	R	OR	EW	AB	H	2B	3B	HR	TB	BB	SO	SB	CS	AVG	OBP	SLG	OPS	OPS+	BR/A	PF	RC
NY	164	99	63	.611	....	730	577	100	**5705**	**1442**	208	35	162	2206	520	976	54	18	.253	.319	.387	.705	100	8	102	704
CHI	162	98	64	.605	1	642	**501**	101	5491	1356	184	40	106	1938	**562**	**902**	75	39	.247	.323	.353	.676	97	-12	97	641
BAL	163	97	65	.599	2	679	567	95	5463	1357	229	20	162	2112	537	1019	78	38	.248	.319	.387	.705	102	19	100	669
DET	163	85	77	.525	14	699	678	83	5513	1394	199	**57**	157	2178	517	912	60	27	.253	.321	.395	.716	103	28	102	705
LA	162	82	80	.506	17	544	551	80	5362	1297	186	27	102	1843	472	920	49	39	.242	.306	.344	.650	96	-34	90	550
MIN	163	79	83	.488	20	**737**	678	88	5610	1413	227	46	**221**	**2395**	553	1019	46	22	.252	**.324**	**.427**	**.751**	**113**	**95**	101	**774**
CLE	164	79	83	.488	20	689	693	81	5603	1386	208	22	164	2130	500	1063	**79**	51	.247	.315	.380	.695	100	-7	99	664
BOS	162	72	90	.444	27	688	793	70	5513	1425	**253**	29	186	2294	504	917	18	**16**	**.258**	.324	.416	.740	106	40	105	724
WAS	162	62	100	.383	37	578	733	62	5396	1246	199	28	125	1876	514	1124	47	30	.231	.301	.348	.649	87	-94	100	564
KC	163	57	105	.352	42	621	836	58	5524	1321	216	29	166	2093	548	1104	34	20	.239	.313	.379	.691	95	-32	103	644
Total	**814**					**6607**			**55180**	**13637**	**2109**	**333**	**1551**		**5227**	**9956**	**540**	**300**	**.247**	**.316**	**.382**	**.698**				

Runs
- Oliva, T. (Min) 109
- Howser, D. (Cle) 101
- Killebrew, H. (Min) 95

Hits
- Oliva, T. (Min) 217
- Robinson, B. (Bal) 194
- Richardson, B. (NY) 181

Doubles
- Oliva, T. (Min) 43
- Bressoud, E. (Bos) 41
- Robinson, B. (Bal) 35

Triples
- Rollins, R. (Min) 10
- Versalles, Z. (Min) 10
- 3 players tied with 9

Home Runs
- Killebrew, H. (Min) 49
- Powell, B. (Bal) 39
- Mantle, M. (NY) 35

Total Bases
- Oliva, T. (Min) 374
- Robinson, B. (Bal) 319
- Killebrew, H. (Min) 316

Runs Batted In
- Robinson, B. (Bal) 118
- Stuart, D. (Bos) 114
- 2 players tied with 111

Bases On Balls
- Siebern, N. (Bal) 106
- Mantle, M. (NY) 99
- Killebrew, H. (Min) 93

Stolen Bases
- Aparicio, L. (Bal) 57
- Weis, A. (Chi) 22
- Davalillo, V. (Cle) 21

Batting Average
- Oliva, T. (Min) .... .323
- Robinson, B. (Bal) .... .317
- Howard, E. (NY) .... .313

On-Base Percentage
- Mantle, M. (NY) .... .426
- Allison, B. (Min) .... .406
- Powell, B. (Bal) .... .400

Slugging Average
- Powell, B. (Bal) .... .606
- Mantle, M. (NY) .... .591
- Oliva, T. (Min) .... .557

Adjusted OPS
- Mantle, M. (NY) 177
- Powell, B. (Bal) 176
- Allison, B. (Min) 162

Adjusted Batting Runs
- Mantle, M. (NY) 52.0
- Allison, B. (Min) 47.0
- Powell, B. (Bal) 45.0

Runs Created/Game
- Mantle, M. (NY) 9.60
- Powell, B. (Bal) 9.10
- Allison, B. (Min) 8.80

Fielding Runs
- Knoop, B. (LA) 29.1
- Hansen, R. (Chi) 20.5
- Boyer, C. (NY) 15.0

Win Shares – Batters
- Mantle, M. (NY) 34
- Robinson, B. (Bal) 33
- Howard, E. (NY) 32

TPW – Batters
- Powell, B. (Bal) 5.3
- Hansen, R. (Chi) 5.1
- Fregosi, J. (LA) 4.8

TEAM	CG	SH	SV	IP	H	H/G	ER	HR	BB	SO	OAV	RAT	ERA	ERA+	CERA	PR+	PF	FA	E	DP	FR	BW	PW	FW	TPW	DIF
NY	46	18	**45**	**1506^{2}**	1312	7.8	527	129	504	989	.234	1.205	3.15	115	3.08	67.3	100	.983	109	158	11.1	.8	7.1	1.2	9.1	8.9
CHI	44	20	**45**	1467^{2}	**1216**	**7.5**	**443**	124	**401**	955	**.226**	**1.102**	**2.72**	127	**2.70**	**78.9**	95	.981	122	164	**40.6**	-1.3	**8.3**	**4.3**	**11.3**	5.7
BAL	44	17	41	1458^{2}	1292	8.0	512	129	456	939	.239	1.198	3.16	113	3.16	29.1	99	**.985**	**95**	159	38.0	2.0	3.1	4.0	9.0	7.0
DET	35	11	35	1453	1343	8.3	620	164	536	993	.244	1.293	3.84	95	3.77	-34.3	101	.982	111	137	5.8	2.9	-3.6	.6	-.1	4.1
LA	30	**28**	41	1450^{2}	1273	7.9	469	**100**	530	965	.236	1.243	2.91	113	3.23	50.2	91	.978	138	**168**	10.2	-3.6	5.3	1.1	2.8	-1.8
MIN	**47**	4	29	1477^{2}	1361	8.3	588	181	545	1099	.243	1.290	3.58	100	3.71	19.2	99	.977	145	131	-18.4	**10.0**	2.0	-1.9	10.1	-12.1
CLE	37	16	37	1487^{2}	1443	8.7	620	154	565	**1162**	.255	1.350	3.75	96	3.90	10.7	99	.981	118	149	-35.2	-.8	1.1	-3.7	-3.4	1.4
BOS	21	9	38	1422	1464	9.3	711	178	571	1094	.266	1.431	4.50	86	4.50	-69.7	106	.977	138	123	-32.1	4.2	-7.3	-3.4	-6.5	-2.5
WAS	27	5	26	1435^{1}	1417	8.9	635	172	505	794	.259	1.339	3.98	93	4.01	-50.5	102	.979	127	145	6.2	-9.9	-5.3	.7	-14.5	-4.5
KC	18	6	27	1455^{2}	1516	9.4	761	220	614	966	.269	1.463	4.71	**81**	4.90	-119.0	105	.974	158	152	-24.2	-3.4	-12.5	-2.5	-18.4	-5.6
Total	**349**	**134**	**364**	**14615**		**8.4**	**5886**					**1.291**	**3.62**													

Wins
- Chance, D. (LA) 20
- Peters, G. (Chi) 20
- 3 players tied with 19

Win Percentage
- Bunker, W. (Bal) .... .792
- Ford, W. (NY) .... .739
- Peters, G. (Chi) .... .714

Games
- Wyatt, J. (KC) 81
- Radatz, D. (Bos) 79
- Wilhelm, H. (Chi) 73

Complete Games
- Chance, D. (LA) 15
- Pascual, C. (Min) 14
- 3 players tied with 13

Shutouts
- Chance, D. (LA) 11
- Ford, W. (NY) 8
- Pappas, M. (Bal) 7

Saves
- Radatz, D. (Bos) 29
- Wilhelm, H. (Chi) 27
- Miller, S. (Bal) 23

Innings Pitched
- Chance, D. (LA) .... 278^{1}
- Peters, G. (Chi) .... 273^{2}
- Bouton, J. (NY) .... 271^{1}

Fewest Hits/Game
- Horlen, J. (Chi) 6.07
- Chance, D. (LA) 6.27
- Bunker, W. (Bal) 6.77

Fewest BB/Game
- Monbouquette, B. (Bos) 1.54
- Pappas, M. (Bal) 1.72
- Newman, F. (LA) 1.85

Strikeouts
- Downing, A. (NY) 217
- Pascual, C. (Min) 213
- Chance, D. (LA) 207

Ratio
- Horlen, J. (Chi) .... .94
- Chance, D. (LA) 1.01
- Pizarro, J. (Chi) 1.04

Earned Run Average
- Chance, D. (LA) 1.65
- Horlen, J. (Chi) 1.88
- Ford, W. (NY) 2.13

Adjusted ERA
- Chance, D. (LA) 199
- Horlen, J. (Chi) 184
- Ford, W. (NY) 170

Component ERA
- Horlen, J. (Chi) 1.72
- Chance, D. (LA) 1.76
- Bunker, W. (Bal) 2.29

Opponents' Batting Avg.
- Horlen, J. (Chi) .... .190
- Chance, D. (LA) .... .195
- Bunker, W. (Bal) .... .207

Adjusted Pitching Runs
- Chance, D. (LA) 49
- Ford, W. (NY) 39
- Horlen, J. (Chi) 31

Win Shares – Pitchers
- Chance, D. (LA) 32
- Ford, W. (NY) 24
- Peters, G. (Chi) 22

TPW – Pitchers
- Chance, D. (LA) 4.6
- Ford, W. (NY) 4.1
- Horlen, J. (Chi) 3.2

1965 National League

TEAM	G	W	L	PCT	GB	R	OR	EW	AB	H	2B	3B	HR	TB	BB	SO	SB	CS	AVG	OBP	SLG	OPS	OPS+	BR/A	PF	RC
LA	162	97	65	.599	....	608	**521**	93	5425	1329	193	32	78	1820	492	891	**172**	77	.245	.314	.335	.649	96	-13	93	591
SF	163	95	67	.586	2	682	593	92	5495	1384	169	43	159	2116	476	**844**	47	**27**	.252	.315	.385	.700	101	7	103	647
PIT	163	90	72	.556	7	675	580	93	**5686**	1506	217	57	111	2170	419	1008	51	38	.265	.319	.382	.701	104	20	100	670
CIN	162	89	73	.549	8	**825**	704	94	5658	**1544**	**268**	**61**	183	**2483**	**538**	1003	82	40	**.273**	**.341**	**.439**	**.780**	**118**	**138**	107	**841**
MIL	162	86	76	.531	11	708	633	90	5542	1419	243	28	**196**	2306	408	976	64	37	.256	.311	.416	.727	110	62	100	698
PHI	162	85	76	.528	11.5	654	667	79	5528	1380	205	53	144	2123	494	1091	46	32	.250	.315	.384	.699	105	35	98	663
STL	162	80	81	.497	16.5	707	674	84	5579	1415	234	46	109	2068	477	882	100	52	.254	.316	.371	.687	92	-52	109	657
CHI	164	72	90	.444	25	635	723	71	5540	1316	202	33	134	1986	532	948	65	47	.238	.309	.358	.668	92	-51	102	611
HOU	162	65	97	.401	32	569	711	63	5483	1299	188	42	97	1862	502	877	90	37	.237	.306	.340	.646	95	-23	93	573
NY	164	50	112	.309	47	495	752	49	5441	1202	203	27	107	1780	392	1129	28	42	.221	.278	.327	.605	79	-158	96	478
Total	**813**					**6558**			**55377**	**13794**	**2122**	**422**	**1318**		**4730**	**9649**	**745**	**429**	**.249**	**.313**	**.374**	**.687**				

Runs		Hits		Doubles		Triples		Home Runs		Total Bases	
Harper, T. (Cin)	126	Rose, P. (Cin)	209	Aaron, H. (Mil)	40	Callison, J. (Phi)	16	Mays, W. (SF)	52	Mays, W. (SF)	360
Mays, W. (SF)	118	Pinson, V. (Cin)	204	Williams, B. (Chi)	39	3 players tied with	14	McCovey, W. (SF)	39	Williams, B. (Chi)	356
Rose, P. (Cin)	117	Williams, B. (Chi)	203	2 players tied with	35			Williams, B. (Chi)	34	Pinson, V. (Cin)	324
Runs Batted In		**Bases On Balls**		**Stolen Bases**		**Batting Average**		**On-Base Percentage**		**Slugging Average**	
Johnson, D. (Cin)	130	Morgan, J. (Hou)	97	Wills, M. (LA)	94	Clemente, R. (Pit)	.329	Mays, W. (SF)	.399	Mays, W. (SF)	.645
Robinson, F. (Cin)	113	McCovey, W. (SF)	88	Brock, L. (StL)	63	Aaron, H. (Mil)	.318	Robinson, F. (Cin)	.388	Aaron, H. (Mil)	.560
Mays, W. (SF)	112	Santo, R. (Chi)	88	Wynn, J. (Hou)	43	Mays, W. (SF)	.317	Aaron, H. (Mil)	.384	Williams, B. (Chi)	.552
Adjusted OPS		**Adjusted Batting Runs**		**Runs Created/Game**		**Fielding Runs**		**Win Shares – Batters**		**TPW – Batters**	
Mays, W. (SF)	184	Mays, W. (SF)	62.0	Mays, W. (SF)	9.60	Wills, M. (LA)	26.9	Mays, W. (SF)	43	Mays, W. (SF)	6.8
Aaron, H. (Mil)	161	Aaron, H. (Mil)	49.0	Aaron, H. (Mil)	7.90	Mazeroski, B. (Pit)	24.6	Williams, B. (Chi)	33	Wynn, J. (Hou)	5.0
Williams, B. (Chi)	155	Williams, B. (Chi)	49.0	Williams, B. (Chi)	7.60	Cardenas, L. (Cin)	16.4	Allen, D. (Phi)	33	Santo, R. (Chi)	4.9

TEAM	CG	SH	SV	IP	H	H/G	ER	HR	BB	SO	OAV	RAT	ERA	ERA+	CERA	PR+	PF	FA	E	DP	FR	BW	PW	FW	TPW	DIF
LA	**58**	**23**	34	1476	**1223**	**7.5**	**461**	127	425	1079	**.224**	**1.117**	**2.81**	116	**2.74**	53.2	92	.979	134	135	20.8	-1.3	5.6	2.2	6.5	9.5
SF	42	17	**42**	1465[1]	1325	8.1	521	137	408	1060	.238	1.183	3.20	112	3.12	**85.1**	102	.976	148	124	-20.4	.8	**9.0**	-2.2	7.6	6.4
PIT	49	17	27	**1479**	1324	8.1	495	**89**	469	882	.241	1.212	3.01	117	3.01	51.1	99	.977	152	**189**	**31.0**	2.1	5.4	**3.3**	10.8	-1.8
CIN	43	9	34	1457[1]	1355	8.4	628	136	587	**1113**	.247	1.333	3.88	97	3.77	-22.5	106	**.981**	**117**	142	0.3	**14.6**	-2.4	.0	**12.3**	-4.3
MIL	43	4	38	1447[2]	1336	8.3	566	123	541	966	.246	1.297	3.52	100	3.48	-7.1	99	.978	140	145	7.3	6.6	-.8	.8	6.6	-1.6
PHI	50	18	21	1468[2]	1426	8.7	576	116	466	1071	.256	1.288	3.53	98	3.59	-13.0	98	.975	157	153	1.1	3.7	-1.4	.1	2.4	2.6
STL	40	11	35	1461[1]	1414	8.7	612	166	467	916	.255	1.287	3.77	102	3.74	6.1	109	.979	130	152	5.6	-5.5	.6	.6	-4.3	4.3
CHI	33	9	35	1472	1470	9.0	618	154	481	855	.260	1.325	3.78	97	3.83	-0.4	104	.974	171	166	-15.3	-5.4	.0	-1.6	-7.1	-1.9
HOU	29	7	26	1461	1459	9.0	623	123	**388**	931	.260	1.264	3.84	87	3.49	-53.6	95	.974	166	130	-25.9	-2.4	-5.7	-2.7	-10.8	-5.2
NY	29	11	14	1454[2]	1462	9.0	656	147	498	776	.262	1.347	4.06	**87**	4.01	-82.0	100	.974	171	153	-4.0	-16.6	-8.7	-.4	-25.7	-5.3
Total	**416**	**126**	**306**	**14643**		**8.5**	**5756**					**1.265**	**3.54**													

Wins		Win Percentage		Games		Complete Games		Shutouts		Saves	
Koufax, S. (LA)	26	Koufax, S. (LA)	.765	Abernathy, T. (Chi)	84	Koufax, S. (LA)	27	Marichal, J. (SF)	10	Abernathy, T. (Chi)	31
Cloninger, T. (Mil)	24	Bolin, B. (SF)	.700	Woodeshick, H. (StL,Hou)	78	Marichal, J. (SF)	24	Koufax, S. (LA)	8	Linzy, F. (SF)	21
Drysdale, D. (LA)	23	Maloney, J. (Cin)	.690	McDaniel, L. (Chi)	71	2 players tied with	20	3 players tied with	7	McCool, B. (Cin)	21
Innings Pitched		**Fewest Hits/Game**		**Fewest BB/Game**		**Strikeouts**		**Ratio**		**Earned Run Average**	
Koufax, S. (LA)	335[2]	Koufax, S. (LA)	5.79	Marichal, J. (SF)	1.40	Koufax, S. (LA)	382	Koufax, S. (LA)	.86	Koufax, S. (LA)	2.04
Drysdale, D. (LA)	308[1]	Maloney, J. (Cin)	6.66	Law, V. (Pit)	1.45	Veale, B. (Pit)	276	Marichal, J. (SF)	.91	Marichal, J. (SF)	2.13
Gibson, B. (StL)	299	Marichal, J. (SF)	6.83	Bruce, B. (Hou)	1.49	Gibson, B. (StL)	270	Law, V. (Pit)	1.00	Law, V. (Pit)	2.15
Adjusted ERA		**Component ERA**		**Opponents' Batting Avg.**		**Adjusted Pitching Runs**		**Win Shares – Pitchers**		**TPW – Pitchers**	
Marichal, J. (SF)	169	Koufax, S. (LA)	1.56	Koufax, S. (LA)	.179	Marichal, J. (SF)	52	Koufax, S. (LA)	33	Marichal, J. (SF)	5.6
Law, V. (Pit)	163	Marichal, J. (SF)	1.92	Marichal, J. (SF)	.205	Koufax, S. (LA)	41	Marichal, J. (SF)	30	Koufax, S. (LA)	4.8
Koufax, S. (LA)	160	Law, V. (Pit)	2.29	Maloney, J. (Cin)	.206	Maloney, J. (Cin)	34	2 players tied with	27	Maloney, J. (Cin)	4.3

1965 American League

TEAM	G	W	L	PCT	GB	R	OR	EW	AB	H	2B	3B	HR	TB	BB	SO	SB	CS	AVG	OBP	SLG	OPS	OPS+	BR/A	PF	RC
MIN	162	102	60	.630	....	**774**	600	101	5488	**1396**	**257**	42	150	2187	554	969	92	33	**.254**	.327	.399	.725	**107**	**60**	104	**727**
CHI	162	95	67	.586	7	647	**555**	93	**5509**	1354	200	38	125	2005	533	916	50	33	.246	.317	.364	.681	106	40	94	634
BAL	162	94	68	.580	8	641	578	89	5450	1299	227	38	125	1977	529	907	67	31	.238	.309	.363	.672	95	-32	102	605
DET	162	89	73	.549	13	680	602	91	5368	1278	190	27	162	2008	554	952	57	41	.238	.314	.374	.688	100	-1	101	627
CLE	162	87	75	.537	15	663	613	87	5469	1367	198	21	156	2075	506	**857**	109	46	.250	.317	.379	.697	103	25	101	666
NY	162	77	85	.475	25	611	604	82	5470	1286	196	31	149	1991	489	951	35	20	.235	.300	.364	.664	95	-40	99	592
CAL	162	75	87	.463	27	527	569	75	5354	1279	200	36	92	1827	443	973	107	59	.239	.300	.341	.641	90	-72	98	547
WAS	162	70	92	.432	32	591	721	65	5374	1227	179	33	136	1880	570	1125	30	**19**	.228	.306	.350	.656	94	-39	99	584
BOS	162	62	100	.383	40	669	791	68	5487	1378	244	40	**165**	**2197**	**607**	964	47	24	.251	**.329**	**.400**	**.729**	**107**	55	106	714
KC	162	59	103	.364	43	585	755	61	5393	1294	186	**59**	110	1928	521	1020	**110**	51	.240	.311	.358	.668	98	-14	99	603
Total	**810**					**6388**			**54362**	**13158**	**2077**	**365**	**1370**		**5306**	**9634**	**704**	**357**	**.242**	**.313**	**.369**	**.682**				

Runs		Hits		Doubles		Triples		Home Runs		Total Bases	
Versalles, Z. (Min)	126	Oliva, T. (Min)	185	Versalles, Z. (Min)	45	Campaneris, B. (KC)	12	Conigliaro, T. (Bos)	32	Versalles, Z. (Min)	308
Oliva, T. (Min)	107	Versalles, Z. (Min)	182	Yastrzemski, C. (Bos)	45	Versalles, Z. (Min)	12	Cash, N. (Det)	30	Tresh, T. (NY)	287
Tresh, T. (NY)	94	Colavito, R. (Cle)	170	Oliva, T. (Min)	40	Aparicio, L. (Bal)	10	Horton, W. (Det)	29	Oliva, T. (Min)	283
Runs Batted In		**Bases On Balls**		**Stolen Bases**		**Batting Average**		**On-Base Percentage**		**Slugging Average**	
Colavito, R. (Cle)	108	Colavito, R. (Cle)	93	Campaneris, B. (KC)	51	Oliva, T. (Min)	.321	Yastrzemski, C. (Bos)	.398	Yastrzemski, C. (Bos)	.536
Horton, W. (Det)	104	Blefary, C. (Bal)	88	Cardenal, J. (Cal)	37	Yastrzemski, C. (Bos)	.312	Colavito, R. (Cle)	.387	Conigliaro, T. (Bos)	.512
Oliva, T. (Min)	98	Mantilla, F. (Bos)	79	Versalles, Z. (Min)	27	Davalillo, V. (Cle)	.301	Oliva, T. (Min)	.384	Cash, N. (Det)	.512
Adjusted OPS		**Adjusted Batting Runs**		**Runs Created/Game**		**Fielding Runs**		**Win Shares – Batters**		**TPW – Batters**	
Yastrzemski, C. (Bos)	154	Yastrzemski, C. (Bos)	35.0	Yastrzemski, C. (Bos)	7.50	Boyer, C. (NY)	16.9	Oliva, T. (Min)	33	Buford, D. (Chi)	4.4
Cash, N. (Det)	147	Colavito, R. (Cle)	34.0	Wagner, L. (Cle)	7.10	Adair, J. (Bal)	16.1	Versalles, Z. (Min)	32	Versalles, Z. (Min)	3.6
Wagner, L. (Cle)	143	Oliva, T. (Min)	31.0	Oliva, T. (Min)	7.00	Buford, D. (Chi)	12.8	Buford, D. (Chi)	30	Cash, N. (Det)	3.0

TEAM	CG	SH	SV	IP	H	H/G	ER	HR	BB	SO	OAV	RAT	ERA	ERA+	CERA	PR+	PF	FA	E	DP	FR	BW	PW	FW	TPW	DIF
MIN	32	12	45	1457¹	1278	7.9	508	166	503	934	.235	1.222	3.14	113	3.32	50.1	103	.973	172	158	17.8	6.4	5.3	1.9	13.6	7.4
CHI	21	14	53	1481²	1261	7.7	492	122	460	946	.231	1.162	2.99	107	2.88	14.2	92	.980	127	156	18.3	4.3	1.5	2.0	7.7	6.3
BAL	32	15	41	1477²	1268	7.7	489	120	510	939	.233	1.203	2.98	116	3.03	56.3	100	.980	126	152	23.1	-3.4	6.0	2.5	5.0	8.0
DET	45	14	31	1455	1283	7.9	542	137	509	1069	.237	1.232	3.35	104	3.29	28.5	100	.981	116	126	-8.8	-.1	3.0	-.9	2.0	6.0
CLE	41	13	41	1458¹	1254	7.7	535	129	500	1156	.232	1.203	3.30	105	3.08	32.7	101	.981	114	127	-2.7	2.6	3.5	-.3	5.8	.2
NY	41	11	31	1459²	1337	8.2	532	126	511	1001	.245	1.266	3.28	104	3.40	29.8	98	.978	137	166	-9.6	-4.2	3.2	-1.0	-2.1	-1.9
CAL	39	14	33	1441²	1259	7.9	508	91	563	847	.237	1.264	3.17	107	3.17	30.8	98	.981	123	149	6.1	-7.7	3.3	.7	-3.8	-2.2
WAS	21	8	40	1435²	1376	8.6	627	160	633	867	.254	1.399	3.93	88	4.13	-63.4	101	.976	143	148	-9.0	-4.2	-6.8	-1.0	-11.9	.9
BOS	33	9	25	1439¹	1443	9.0	678	158	543	993	.260	1.380	4.24	88	4.08	-57.7	108	.974	162	129	-24.9	5.8	-6.2	-2.7	-3.0	-16.0
KC	18	7	32	1433	1399	8.8	675	161	574	882	.256	1.377	4.24	82	4.08	-110.6	101	.977	139	142	-8.7	-1.5	-11.8	-.9	-14.2	-7.8
Total	323	117	372	14539¹	5586	8.1						1.270	3.46													

Wins		Win Percentage		Games		Complete Games		Shutouts		Saves	
Grant, M. (Min)	21	Grant, M. (Min)	.750	Fisher, E. (Chi)	82	Stottlemyre, M. (NY)	18	Grant, M. (Min)	6	Kline, R. (Was)	29
Stottlemyre, M. (NY)	20	McLain, D. (Det)	.727	Kline, R. (Was)	74	Grant, M. (Min)	14	4 players tied with	4	Fisher, E. (Chi)	24
Kaat, J. (Min)	18	Stottlemyre, M. (NY)	.690	Lee, B. (Cal)	69	McDowell, S. (Cle)	14			Miller, S. (Bal)	24

Innings Pitched		Fewest Hits/Game		Fewest BB/Game		Strikeouts		Ratio		Earned Run Average	
Stottlemyre, M. (NY)	291	McDowell, S. (Cle)	5.87	Terry, R. (Cle)	1.25	McDowell, S. (Cle)	325	Fisher, E. (Chi)	.97	McDowell, S. (Cle)	2.18
McDowell, S. (Cle)	273	Fisher, E. (Chi)	6.42	Monbouquette, B. (Bos)	1.57	Lolich, M. (Det)	226	Siebert, S. (Cle)	.98	Fisher, E. (Chi)	2.40
Grant, M. (Min)	270¹	Siebert, S. (Cle)	6.63	Horlen, J. (Chi)	1.60	McLain, D. (Det)	192	Terry, R. (Cle)	1.07	Siebert, S. (Cle)	2.43

Adjusted ERA		Component ERA		Opponents' Batting Avg.		Adjusted Pitching Runs		Win Shares – Pitchers		TPW – Pitchers	
McDowell, S. (Cle)	160	Fisher, E. (Chi)	1.97	McDowell, S. (Cle)	.185	McDowell, S. (Cle)	40	McDowell, S. (Cle)	25	McDowell, S. (Cle)	4.0
Siebert, S. (Cle)	143	Siebert, S. (Cle)	2.09	Fisher, E. (Chi)	.205	Stottlemyre, M. (NY)	27	Stottlemyre, M. (NY)	23	Stottlemyre, M. (NY)	2.9
Perry, J. (Min)	135	McDowell, S. (Cle)	2.19	Siebert, S. (Cle)	.206	McLain, D. (Det)	22	2 players tied with	20	Kaat, J. (Min)	2.6

1966 National League

TEAM	G	W	L	PCT	GB	R	OR	EW	AB	H	2B	3B	HR	TB	BB	SO	SB	CS	AVG	OBP	SLG	OPS	OPS+	BR/A	PF	RC
LA	162	95	67	.586	....	606	490	98	5471	1399	201	27	108	1978	430	830	94	64	.256	.316	.362	.677	102	14	92	613
SF	161	93	68	.578	1.5	675	626	87	5539	1373	195	31	181	2173	414	860	29	30	.248	.304	.392	.696	96	-35	103	632
PIT	162	92	70	.568	3	759	641	95	5676	1586	238	66	158	2430	405	1011	64	60	.279	.331	.428	.759	116	108	100	778
PHI	162	87	75	.537	8	696	640	88	5607	1448	224	49	117	2121	510	969	56	42	.258	.323	.378	.702	101	12	100	681
ATL	163	85	77	.525	10	782	683	92	5617	1476	220	32	207	2381	512	913	59	47	.263	.329	.424	.753	113	94	102	773
STL	162	83	79	.512	12	571	577	80	5480	1377	196	61	108	2019	345	977	144	61	.251	.300	.368	.668	91	-57	100	591
CIN	160	76	84	.475	18	692	702	79	5521	1434	232	33	149	2179	394	877	70	50	.260	.311	.395	.706	93	-49	109	656
HOU	163	72	90	.444	23	612	695	71	5511	1405	203	35	112	2014	491	885	90	47	.255	.320	.365	.685	104	34	93	639
NY	161	66	95	.410	28.5	587	761	60	5371	1286	187	35	98	1837	446	992	55	46	.239	.303	.342	.645	87	-88	98	544
CHI	162	59	103	.364	36	644	809	63	5592	1418	203	43	140	2127	457	998	76	47	.254	.315	.380	.696	98	-11	101	664
Total	809					6624			55385	14202	2099	412	1378		4404	9312	737	494	.256	.315	.384	.699				

Runs		Hits		Doubles		Triples		Home Runs		Total Bases	
Alou, F. (Atl)	122	Alou, F. (Atl)	218	Callison, J. (Phi)	40	McCarver, T. (StL)	13	Aaron, H. (Atl)	44	Alou, F. (Atl)	355
Aaron, H. (Atl)	117	Rose, P. (Cin)	205	Rose, P. (Cin)	38	Brock, L. (StL)	12	Allen, D. (Phi)	40	Clemente, R. (Pit)	342
Allen, D. (Phi)	112	Clemente, R. (Pit)	202	Pinson, V. (Cin)	35	Clemente, R. (Pit)	11	Mays, W. (SF)	37	Allen, D. (Phi)	331

Runs Batted In		Bases On Balls		Stolen Bases		Batting Average		On-Base Percentage		Slugging Average	
Aaron, H. (Atl)	127	Santo, R. (Chi)	95	Brock, L. (StL)	74	Alou, M. (Pit)	.342	Santo, R. (Chi)	.417	Allen, D. (Phi)	.632
Clemente, R. (Pit)	119	Morgan, J. (Hou)	89	Jackson, S. (Hou)	49	Alou, F. (Atl)	.327	Morgan, J. (Hou)	.412	McCovey, W. (SF)	.586
Allen, D. (Phi)	110	2 players tied with	76	Wills, M. (LA)	38	Carty, R. (Atl)	.326	Allen, D. (Phi)	.398	Stargell, W. (Pit)	.581

Adjusted OPS		Adjusted Batting Runs		Runs Created/Game		Fielding Runs		Win Shares – Batters		TPW – Batters	
Allen, D. (Phi)	181	Allen, D. (Phi)	57.0	Allen, D. (Phi)	9.40	Mazeroski, B. (Pit)	30.8	Mays, W. (SF)	37	Santo, R. (Chi)	7.9
Stargell, W. (Pit)	164	Santo, R. (Chi)	50.0	McCovey, W. (SF)	8.70	Santo, R. (Chi)	24.6	Allen, D. (Phi)	35	Allen, D. (Phi)	5.6
McCovey, W. (SF)	163	McCovey, W. (SF)	45.0	Stargell, W. (Pit)	8.20	Maxvill, D. (StL)	17.8	McCovey, W. (SF)	34	Torre, J. (Atl)	5.4

TEAM	CG	SH	SV	IP	H	H/G	ER	HR	BB	SO	OAV	RAT	ERA	ERA+	CERA	PR+	PF	FA	E	DP	FR	BW	PW	FW	TPW	DIF
LA	52	20	35	1458	1287	7.9	424	84	356	1084	.237	1.127	2.62	126	2.62	105.6	91	.979	133	128	3.3	1.4	11.1	.3	12.8	1.2
SF	52	14	27	1476²	1370	8.4	531	140	359	973	.244	1.171	3.24	113	3.13	70.0	102	.974	168	131	0.5	-3.7	7.3	.0	3.7	9.3
PIT	35	12	43	1463¹	1445	8.9	572	125	463	898	.261	1.304	3.52	102	3.68	-19.1	99	.978	141	215	26.9	11.3	-2.0	2.8	12.2	-1.2
PHI	52	15	23	1459²	1439	8.9	579	137	412	928	.258	1.268	3.57	101	3.66	1.1	100	.982	113	147	2.6	1.3	.1	.3	1.7	4.3
ATL	37	10	36	1469¹	1430	8.8	601	129	485	884	.257	1.303	3.68	99	3.62	-9.1	101	.976	154	139	1.8	9.8	-.9	.2	9.0	-5.0
STL	47	19	32	1459²	1345	8.3	504	130	448	892	.246	1.228	3.11	116	3.31	65.9	100	.977	145	166	13.3	-5.9	6.9	1.4	2.3	-.3
CIN	28	10	35	1436	1408	8.8	651	153	490	1043	.258	1.322	4.08	96	3.89	-10.6	108	.980	122	133	-18.2	-5.1	-1.1	-1.9	-8.2	4.3
HOU	34	13	26	1443²	1468	9.2	603	130	391	929	.262	1.288	3.76	91	3.67	-37.7	95	.972	174	126	-15.5	3.5	-3.9	-1.6	-2.1	-6.9
NY	37	9	22	1427	1497	9.4	661	166	521	773	.272	1.414	4.17	87	4.40	-88.9	101	.975	159	171	4.2	-9.3	-9.3	.4	-18.1	4.1
CHI	28	6	24	1458	1513	9.3	701	184	479	908	.268	1.366	4.33	85	4.23	-86.9	102	.974	166	132	-19.4	-1.2	-9.1	-2.0	-12.3	-9.7
Total	402	128	303	14551¹		8.8	5827					1.279	3.60													

Wins		Win Percentage		Games		Complete Games		Shutouts		Saves	
Koufax, S. (LA)	27	Marichal, J. (SF)	.806	Carroll, C. (Atl)	73	Koufax, S. (LA)	27	6 players tied with	5	Regan, P. (LA)	21
Marichal, J. (SF)	25	Koufax, S. (LA)	.750	Mikkelsen, P. (Pit)	71	Marichal, J. (SF)	25			Face, R. (Pit)	18
2 players tied with	21	Perry, G. (SF)	.724	Knowles, D. (Phi)	69	Gibson, B. (StL)	20			McCool, B. (Cin)	18

Innings Pitched		Fewest Hits/Game		Fewest BB/Game		Strikeouts		Ratio		Earned Run Average	
Koufax, S. (LA)	323	Marichal, J. (SF)	6.68	Marichal, J. (SF)	1.05	Koufax, S. (LA)	317	Marichal, J. (SF)	.86	Koufax, S. (LA)	1.73
Bunning, J. (Phi)	314	Koufax, S. (LA)	6.72	Law, V. (Pit)	1.22	Bunning, J. (Phi)	252	Koufax, S. (LA)	.98	Cuellar, M. (Hou)	2.22
Marichal, J. (SF)	307¹	Gibson, B. (StL)	6.74	Perry, G. (SF)	1.41	Veale, B. (Pit)	229	Bunning, J. (Phi)	1.00	Marichal, J. (SF)	2.23

Adjusted ERA		Component ERA		Opponents' Batting Avg.		Adjusted Pitching Runs		Win Shares – Pitchers		TPW – Pitchers	
Koufax, S. (LA)	191	Marichal, J. (SF)	1.80	Marichal, J. (SF)	.202	Koufax, S. (LA)	56	Koufax, S. (LA)	35	Marichal, J. (SF)	5.8
Marichal, J. (SF)	165	Koufax, S. (LA)	1.92	Koufax, S. (LA)	.205	Marichal, J. (SF)	49	Marichal, J. (SF)	33	Koufax, S. (LA)	5.2
Cuellar, M. (Hou)	154	Gibson, B. (StL)	2.19	Gibson, B. (StL)	.207	Bunning, J. (Phi)	41	Bunning, J. (Phi)	30	Bunning, J. (Phi)	4.3

1966 American League

TEAM	G	W	L	PCT	GB	R	OR	EW	AB	H	2B	3B	HR	TB	BB	SO	SB	CS	AVG	OBP	SLG	OPS	OPS+	BR/A	PF	RC
BAL	160	97	63	.606	....	755	601	98	5529	1426	243	35	175	2264	514	926	55	43	.258	.325	.409	.735	119	122	98	726
MIN	162	89	73	.549	9	663	581	92	5390	1341	219	33	144	2058	513	844	67	42	.249	.319	.382	.700	101	9	106	642
DET	162	88	74	.543	10	719	698	83	5507	1383	224	45	179	2234	551	987	41	34	.251	.323	.406	.729	112	84	102	712
CHI	163	83	79	.512	15	574	517	89	5348	1235	193	40	87	1769	476	872	153	78	.231	.299	.331	.630	93	-43	93	537
CLE	162	81	81	.500	17	574	586	79	5474	1300	156	25	155	1971	450	914	53	41	.237	.299	.360	.659	95	-42	100	577
CAL	162	80	82	.494	18	604	643	76	5360	1244	179	54	122	1897	525	1062	80	54	.232	.305	.354	.659	98	-15	97	580
KC	160	74	86	.462	23	564	648	69	5328	1259	212	56	70	1793	421	982	132	50	.236	.295	.337	.632	90	-57	97	534
WAS	159	71	88	.447	25.5	557	659	66	5318	1245	185	40	126	1888	450	1069	53	37	.234	.296	.355	.651	94	-47	99	547
BOS	162	72	90	.444	26	655	731	72	5498	1318	228	44	145	2069	542	1020	35	24	.240	.312	.376	.688	94	-36	110	639
NY	160	70	89	.440	26.5	611	612	79	5330	1254	182	36	162	1994	485	817	49	29	.235	.302	.374	.676	103	19	96	597
Total	806					6276			54082	13005	2021	408	1365		4927	9493	718	432	.240	.308	.369	.676				

Runs		Hits		Doubles		Triples		Home Runs		Total Bases	
Robinson, F. (Bal)	122	Oliva, T. (Min)	191	Yastrzemski, C. (Bos)	39	Knoop, B. (Cal)	11	Robinson, F. (Bal)	49	Robinson, F. (Bal)	367
Oliva, T. (Min)	99	Aparicio, L. (Bal)	182	Robinson, B. (Bal)	35	Campaneris, B. (KC)	10	Killebrew, H. (Min)	39	Oliva, T. (Min)	312
2 players tied with	98	Robinson, F. (Bal)	182	Robinson, F. (Bal)	34	Brinkman, E. (Was)	9	Powell, B. (Bal)	34	Killebrew, H. (Min)	306

Runs Batted In		Bases On Balls		Stolen Bases		Batting Average		On-Base Percentage		Slugging Average	
Robinson, F. (Bal)	122	Killebrew, H. (Min)	103	Campaneris, B. (KC)	52	Robinson, F. (Bal)	.316	Robinson, F. (Bal)	.415	Robinson, F. (Bal)	.637
Killebrew, H. (Min)	110	Foy, J. (Bos)	91	Buford, D. (Chi)	51	Oliva, T. (Min)	.307	Kaline, A. (Det)	.396	Killebrew, H. (Min)	.538
Powell, B. (Bal)	109	Robinson, F. (Bal)	87	Agee, T. (Chi)	44	Kaline, A. (Det)	.288	Killebrew, H. (Min)	.393	Kaline, A. (Det)	.534

Adjusted OPS		Adjusted Batting Runs		Runs Created/Game		Fielding Runs		Win Shares – Batters		TPW – Batters	
Robinson, F. (Bal)	200	Robinson, F. (Bal)	77.0	Robinson, F. (Bal)	9.20	Tresh, T. (NY)	20.7	Robinson, F. (Bal)	41	Robinson, F. (Bal)	6.8
Kaline, A. (Det)	161	Killebrew, H. (Min)	43.0	Kaline, A. (Det)	7.90	Aparicio, L. (Bal)	17.9	Killebrew, H. (Min)	33	McAuliffe, D. (Det)	4.3
Powell, B. (Bal)	159	Kaline, A. (Det)	40.0	Killebrew, H. (Min)	7.80	Brinkman, E. (Was)	15.7	Kaline, A. (Det)	31	Kaline, A. (Det)	4.2

TEAM	CG	SH	SV	IP	H	H/G	ER	HR	BB	SO	OAV	RAT	ERA	ERA+	CERA	PR+	PF	FA	E	DP	FR	BW	PW	FW	TPW	DIF
BAL	23	13	51	1466¹	1267	7.8	541	127	514	1070	.233	1.215	3.32	100	3.16	-4.3	97	.981	115	142	5.9	13.2	-.5	.6	13.3	3.7
MIN	52	11	28	1438²	1246	7.8	500	139	392	1015	.232	1.139	3.13	115	2.91	81.0	105	.977	139	118	-7.5	1.0	8.7	-.8	8.9	-.9
DET	36	11	38	1454¹	1356	8.4	622	185	520	1026	.247	1.290	3.85	90	3.85	-63.6	101	.980	120	142	3.8	9.0	-6.8	.4	2.6	4.4
CHI	38	22	34	1475¹	1229	7.5	439	101	403	896	.226	1.106	2.68	118	2.58	73.7	92	.976	159	149	5.6	-4.4	7.9	.6	4.1	-2.1
CLE	49	15	28	1467¹	1260	7.7	526	129	489	1111	.232	1.192	3.23	106	3.04	57.9	100	.977	138	132	-23.7	-4.5	6.2	-2.5	-.8	.8
CAL	31	12	40	1457¹	1364	8.4	576	136	511	836	.251	1.287	3.56	94	3.59	-46.2	98	.979	136	186	12.9	-1.6	-5.0	1.4	-5.2	4.2
KC	19	11	47	1435	1281	8.0	568	106	630	854	.241	1.332	3.56	95	3.53	-31.8	99	.977	139	154	6.2	-6.1	-3.4	.7	-8.9	2.9
WAS	25	6	35	1419	1282	8.1	583	154	448	866	.242	1.219	3.70	93	3.35	-50.1	101	.977	142	139	11.0	-5.0	-5.4	1.2	-9.2	1.2
BOS	32	10	31	1463²	1402	8.6	637	164	577	977	.253	1.352	3.92	97	3.96	-10.2	111	.975	155	153	-8.2	-3.9	-1.1	-.9	-5.9	-3.1
NY	29	7	32	1415²	1318	8.4	536	124	443	842	.248	1.244	3.41	97	3.31	-8.4	97	.977	142	142	-5.9	2.1	-.9	-.6	.5	-9.5
Total	334	118	364	14492²		8.1	5528				1.237	3.43														

Wins		Win Percentage		Games		Complete Games		Shutouts		Saves	
Kaat, J. (Min)	25	Boswell, D. (Min)	.706	Fisher, E. (Bal,Chi)	67	Kaat, J. (Min)	19	John, T. (Chi)	5	Aker, J. (KC)	32
McLain, D. (Det)	20	McNally, D. (KC)	.684	Aker, J. (KC)	66	McLain, D. (Det)	14	McDowell, S. (Cle)	5	Kline, R. (Was)	23
Wilson, E. (Det,Bos)	18	Siebert, S. (Cle)	.667	Cox, C. (Was)	66	Wilson, E. (Det,Bos)	13	Tiant, L. (Cle)	5	Sherry, L. (Det)	20

Innings Pitched		Fewest Hits/Game		Fewest BB/Game		Strikeouts		Ratio		Earned Run Average	
Kaat, J. (Min)	304²	McDowell, S. (Cle)	6.02	Kaat, J. (Min)	1.62	McDowell, S. (Cle)	225	Peters, G. (Chi)	.98	Peters, G. (Chi)	1.98
McLain, D. (Det)	264¹	Boswell, D. (Min)	6.38	Peterson, F. (NY)	1.67	Kaat, J. (Min)	205	Siebert, S. (Cle)	1.06	Horlen, J. (Cle)	2.43
Wilson, E. (Det,Bos)	264	Peters, G. (Chi)	6.86	Grant, M. (Min)	1.77	Wilson, E. (Det,Bos)	200	Ortega, P. (Was)	1.07	Hargan, S. (Cle)	2.48

Adjusted ERA		Component ERA		Opponents' Batting Avg.		Adjusted Pitching Runs		Win Shares – Pitchers		TPW – Pitchers	
Peters, G. (Chi)	160	Peters, G. (Chi)	1.96	McDowell, S. (Cle)	.188	Kaat, J. (Min)	30	Kaat, J. (Min)	26	Kaat, J. (Min)	3.7
Perry, J. (Min)	142	Hargan, S. (Cle)	2.57	Boswell, D. (Min)	.197	Peters, G. (Chi)	26	Wilson, E. (Det,Bos)	24	Peters, G. (Chi)	3.4
Hargan, S. (Cle)	138	Peterson, F. (NY)	2.58	Peters, G. (Chi)	.212	Hargan, S. (Cle)	23	2 players tied with	20	Wilson, E. (Det,Bos)	3.0

1967 National League

TEAM	G	W	L	PCT	GB	R	OR	EW	AB	H	2B	3B	HR	TB	BB	SO	SB	CS	AVG	OBP	SLG	OPS	OPS+	BR/A	PF	RC
STL	161	101	60	.627	....	695	557	98	5566	1462	225	40	115	2112	443	919	102	54	.263	.322	.379	.702	110	68	98	674
SF	162	91	71	.562	10.5	652	551	95	5524	1354	201	39	140	2053	520	978	22	30	.245	.315	.372	.686	105	31	99	640
CHI	162	87	74	.540	14	702	624	90	5463	1373	211	49	128	2066	509	912	63	50	.251	.319	.378	.697	102	13	105	652
CIN	162	87	75	.537	14.5	604	563	87	5519	1366	251	54	109	2052	372	969	92	63	.248	.299	.372	.671	88	-86	111	591
PHI	162	82	80	.506	19.5	612	581	85	5401	1306	221	47	103	1930	545	1033	79	62	.242	.314	.357	.672	98	-10	101	603
PIT	163	81	81	.500	20.5	679	693	79	5724	1585	193	62	91	2175	387	914	79	37	.277	.327	.380	.707	109	64	101	691
ATL	162	77	85	.475	24.5	631	640	80	5450	1307	191	29	158	2030	512	947	55	45	.240	.309	.372	.681	103	17	99	613
LA	162	73	89	.451	28.5	519	595	70	5456	1285	203	38	82	1810	485	881	56	47	.236	.303	.332	.635	96	-27	92	539
HOU	162	69	93	.426	32.5	626	742	67	5506	1372	259	46	93	2002	537	934	88	38	.249	.319	.364	.682	106	52	97	638
NY	162	61	101	.377	40.5	498	672	57	5417	1288	178	23	83	1761	362	981	58	44	.238	.290	.325	.615	84	-113	98	498
Total	810					6218			55026	13698	2133	427	1102		4672	9468	694	470	.249	.312	.363	.675				

Runs		Hits		Doubles		Triples		Home Runs		Total Bases	
Aaron, H. (Atl)	113	Clemente, R. (Pit)	209	Staub, R. (Hou)	44	Pinson, V. (Cin)	13	Aaron, H. (Atl)	39	Aaron, H. (Atl)	344
Brock, L. (StL)	113	Brock, L. (StL)	206	Aaron, H. (Atl)	37	Brock, L. (StL)	12	Wynn, J. (Hou)	37	Brock, L. (StL)	325
Santo, R. (Chi)	107	Pinson, V. (Cin)	187	Cepeda, O. (StL)	37	Williams, B. (Chi)	12	2 players tied with	31	Clemente, R. (Pit)	324

Runs Batted In		Bases On Balls		Stolen Bases		Batting Average		On-Base Percentage		Slugging Average	
Cepeda, O. (StL)	111	Santo, R. (Chi)	96	Brock, L. (StL)	52	Clemente, R. (Pit)	.357	Allen, D. (Phi)	.404	Aaron, H. (Atl)	.573
Clemente, R. (Pit)	110	Morgan, J. (Hou)	81	Morgan, J. (Hou)	29	Gonzalez, T. (Phi)	.339	Cepeda, O. (StL)	.403	Allen, D. (Phi)	.566
Aaron, H. (Atl)	109	Phillips, A. (Chi)	80	Wills, M. (Pit)	29	Alou, M. (Pit)	.338	Staub, R. (Hou)	.402	Clemente, R. (Pit)	.554

Adjusted OPS		Adjusted Batting Runs		Runs Created/Game		Fielding Runs		Win Shares – Batters		TPW – Batters	
Allen, D. (Phi)	173	Clemente, R. (Pit)	54.0	Allen, D. (Phi)	8.70	Santo, R. (Chi)	32.2	Santo, R. (Chi)	38	Santo, R. (Chi)	8.1
Clemente, R. (Pit)	170	Aaron, H. (Atl)	54.0	Clemente, R. (Pit)	8.60	Wine, B. (Phi)	16.7	Clemente, R. (Pit)	35	Clemente, R. (Pit)	5.6
Aaron, H. (Atl)	169	Cepeda, O. (StL)	52.0	Cepeda, O. (StL)	7.90	Lanier, H. (SF)	15.7	2 players tied with	34	Aaron, H. (Atl)	5.1

TEAM	CG	SH	SV	IP	H	H/G	ER	HR	BB	SO	OAV	RAT	ERA	ERA+	CERA	PR+	PF	FA	E	DP	FR	BW	PW	FW	TPW	DIF
STL	44	17	**45**	1465	1313	8.1	496	97	431	956	.239	1.190	3.05	106	2.91	29.1	96	.978	140	127	2.8	**7.4**	3.1	.3	**10.8**	10.2
SF	**64**	17	25	**1474[1]**	**1283**	**7.8**	**478**	113	453	990	**.234**	**1.177**	**2.92**	113	**2.87**	57.8	97	.979	134	149	2.7	3.4	6.3	.3	9.9	.1
CHI	47	7	28	1457	1352	8.4	563	142	463	888	.246	1.246	3.48	102	3.39	-6.6	105	**.981**	**121**	143	16.7	1.4	-.7	1.8	2.5	4.5
CIN	34	**18**	39	1468	1328	8.1	497	101	498	**1065**	.241	1.244	3.05	123	3.19	**123.1**	111	.980	**121**	124	-8.3	-9.3	**13.3**	-.9	3.1	2.9
PHI	46	17	23	1453[2]	1372	8.5	500	**86**	403	967	.250	1.221	3.10	110	3.12	50.7	101	.978	137	174	-1.2	-1.1	5.5	-.1	4.2	-3.2
PIT	35	5	35	1458[1]	1439	8.9	606	108	561	820	.261	1.371	3.74	90	3.79	-80.3	100	.978	141	**186**	**19.4**	7.0	-8.7	**2.1**	.4	-.4
ATL	35	5	32	1454	1377	8.5	561	118	449	862	.251	1.256	3.47	96	3.36	-34.2	98	.978	138	148	9.8	1.9	-3.7	1.1	-.8	-3.2
LA	41	17	24	1473	1421	8.7	525	93	**393**	967	.254	1.232	3.21	97	3.14	-1.8	92	.975	160	144	-17.2	-2.9	-.2	-1.9	-5.0	-3.0
HOU	35	8	21	1445[2]	1444	9.0	647	120	485	1060	.260	1.334	4.03	**82**	3.79	-85.2	98	.974	159	120	-30.3	5.6	-9.2	-3.3	-6.9	-5.1
NY	36	10	19	1433[2]	1369	8.6	594	124	536	893	.253	1.329	3.73	91	3.66	-59.9	100	.975	157	147	5.4	-12.3	-6.5	.6	-18.2	-1.8
Total	**417**	**121**	**291**	**14582[2]**		**8.4**	**5467**					**1.260**	**3.37**													

Wins
McCormick, M. (SF) 22
Jenkins, F. (Chi) 20
2 players tied with 17

Win Percentage
Hughes, D. (StL) .727
McCormick, M. (SF) .688
2 players tied with .667

Games
Abernathy, T. (Cin) 70
Perranoski, R. (LA) 70
Willis, R. (StL) 65

Complete Games
Jenkins, F. (Chi) 20
3 players tied with 18

Shutouts
Bunning, J. (Phi) 6
3 players tied with 5

Saves
Abernathy, T. (Cin) 28
Face, R. (Pit) 17
Linzy, F. (SF) 17

Innings Pitched
Bunning, J. (Phi) 302[1]
Perry, G. (SF) 293
Jenkins, F. (Chi) 289[1]

Fewest Hits/Game
Hughes, D. (StL) 6.64
Wilson, D. (Hou) 6.90
Perry, G. (SF) 7.10

Fewest BB/Game
Pappas, M. (Cin) 1.57
Osteen, C. (LA) 1.62
Johnson, K. (Atl) 1.63

Strikeouts
Bunning, J. (Phi) 253
Jenkins, F. (Chi) 236
Perry, G. (SF) 230

Ratio
Hughes, D. (StL) .95
Bunning, J. (Phi) 1.04
Queen, M. (Cin) 1.06

Earned Run Average
Niekro, P. (Atl) 1.87
Bunning, J. (Phi) 2.29
Short, C. (Phi) 2.39

Adjusted ERA
Niekro, P. (Atl) 178
Bunning, J. (Phi) 149
Nolan, G. (Cin) 145

Component ERA
Hughes, D. (StL) 2.09
Bunning, J. (Phi) 2.24
Niekro, P. (Atl) 2.27

Opponents' Batting Avg.
Hughes, D. (StL) .203
Wilson, D. (Hou) .209
Perry, G. (SF) .214

Adjusted Pitching Runs
Bunning, J. (Phi) 38
Niekro, P. (Atl) 32
Nolan, G. (Cin) 31

Win Shares – Pitchers
Bunning, J. (Phi) 25
3 players tied with 21

TPW – Pitchers
Bunning, J. (Phi) 4.3
Niekro, P. (Atl) 3.4
Nolan, G. (Cin) 3.2

1967 American League

TEAM	G	W	L	PCT	GB	R	OR	EW	AB	H	2B	3B	HR	TB	BB	SO	SB	CS	AVG	OBP	SLG	OPS	OPS+	BR/A	PF	RC
BOS	162	92	70	.568	....	**722**	614	94	**5471**	**1394**	**216**	39	**158**	**2162**	522	1020	68	59	**.255**	.323	**.395**	**.718**	110	60	108	**692**
MIN	164	91	71	.562	1	671	590	91	5458	1309	**216**	48	131	2014	512	976	55	37	.240	.310	.369	.679	99	-3	108	623
DET	163	91	71	.562	1	683	587	93	5410	1315	192	36	152	2035	**626**	994	37	**21**	.243	**.327**	.376	.703	**111**	**90**	103	680
CHI	162	89	73	.549	3	531	**491**	87	5383	1209	181	34	89	1725	480	**849**	124	82	.225	.293	.320	.613	91	-64	96	503
CAL	161	84	77	.522	7.5	567	587	78	5307	1265	170	37	114	1851	453	1021	40	36	.238	.302	.349	.651	102	8	96	552
WAS	161	76	85	.472	15.5	550	637	69	5441	1211	168	25	115	1774	472	1037	53	37	.223	.289	.326	.615	91	-58	96	511
BAL	161	76	85	.472	15.5	654	592	88	5456	1312	215	44	138	2029	531	1002	54	37	.240	.313	.372	.684	109	62	99	637
CLE	162	75	87	.463	17	559	613	74	5461	1282	213	35	131	1958	413	984	53	65	.235	.295	.359	.653	98	-32	101	562
NY	163	72	90	.444	20	522	621	67	5443	1225	166	17	100	1725	532	1043	63	37	.225	.298	.317	.615	91	-50	96	520
KC	161	62	99	.385	29.5	533	660	64	5349	1244	212	**50**	69	1763	452	1019	**132**	59	.233	.297	.330	.627	94	-29	97	537
Total	**810**					**5992**			**54179**	**12766**	**1949**	**365**	**1197**		**4993**	**9945**	**679**	**470**	**.236**	**.305**	**.351**	**.656**				

Runs
Yastrzemski, C. (Bos) 112
Killebrew, H. (Min) 105
Tovar, C. (Min) 98

Hits
Yastrzemski, C. (Bos) 189
Tovar, C. (Min) 173
2 players tied with 171

Doubles
Oliva, T. (Min) 34
Tovar, C. (Min) 32
Yastrzemski, C. (Bos) 31

Triples
Blair, P. (Bal) 12
Buford, D. (Chi) 9
7 players tied with 7

Home Runs
Killebrew, H. (Min) 44
Yastrzemski, C. (Bos) 44
Howard, F. (Was) 36

Total Bases
Yastrzemski, C. (Bos) 360
Killebrew, H. (Min) 305
Robinson, F. (Bal) 276

Runs Batted In
Yastrzemski, C. (Bos) 121
Killebrew, H. (Min) 113
Robinson, F. (Bal) 94

Bases On Balls
Killebrew, H. (Min) 131
Mantle, M. (NY) 107
McAuliffe, D. (Det) 105

Stolen Bases
Campaneris, B. (KC) 55
Buford, D. (Chi) 34
Agee, T. (Chi) 28

Batting Average
Yastrzemski, C. (Bos) .326
Robinson, F. (Bal) .311
Kaline, A. (Det) .308

On-Base Percentage
Yastrzemski, C. (Bos) .421
Kaline, A. (Det) .415
Killebrew, H. (Min) .413

Slugging Average
Yastrzemski, C. (Bos) .622
Robinson, F. (Bal) .576
Killebrew, H. (Min) .558

Adjusted OPS
Yastrzemski, C. (Bos) 189
Robinson, F. (Bal) 189
Kaline, A. (Det) 176

Adjusted Batting Runs
Yastrzemski, C. (Bos) 66.0
Killebrew, H. (Min) 55.0
Robinson, F. (Bal) 54.0

Runs Created/Game
Yastrzemski, C. (Bos) 10.30
Robinson, F. (Bal) 8.70
Killebrew, H. (Min) 8.30

Fielding Runs
Robinson, B. (Bal) 32.0
Blair, P. (Bal) 12.7
Versalles, Z. (Min) 12.0

Win Shares – Batters
Yastrzemski, C. (Bos) 42
Killebrew, H. (Min) 38
3 players tied with 30

TPW – Batters
Yastrzemski, C. (Bos) 6.5
Robinson, B. (Bal) 5.5
Robinson, F. (Bal) 5.1

TEAM	CG	SH	SV	IP	H	H/G	ER	HR	BB	SO	OAV	RAT	ERA	ERA+	CERA	PR+	PF	FA	E	DP	FR	BW	PW	FW	TPW	DIF
BOS	41	9	44	1459[1]	1307	8.1	545	142	477	1010	.239	1.222	3.36	104	3.29	26.0	108	.977	142	142	-5.9	6.7	2.9	-.6	8.9	2.1
MIN	**58**	18	24	1461	1336	8.2	510	115	**396**	1089	.243	1.185	3.14	110	3.06	74.0	107	.978	132	123	-21.1	-.3	8.2	-2.3	5.5	4.5
DET	46	17	40	1443[2]	1230	7.7	532	151	472	1038	.230	1.179	3.32	98	3.11	-21.4	101	.978	132	126	12.7	**9.9**	-2.4	1.4	**9.0**	1.0
CHI	36	**24**	39	**1490[1]**	**1197**	**7.2**	**406**	**87**	465	927	**.219**	**1.115**	**2.45**	127	**2.61**	**104.3**	96	.979	138	149	3.9	-7.1	**11.5**	.4	4.9	3.1
CAL	19	14	**46**	1430[1]	1246	7.8	507	118	525	892	.237	1.238	3.19	98	3.23	-21.2	97	**.982**	**111**	135	13.3	.9	-2.3	1.5	.0	4.0
WAS	24	14	39	1473[1]	1334	8.2	553	113	495	878	.242	1.241	3.38	94	3.23	-40.0	98	.978	144	**167**	3.7	-6.4	-4.4	.4	-10.4	6.4
BAL	29	17	36	1457[1]	1218	7.5	537	116	566	1034	.228	1.224	3.32	95	3.12	-53.8	98	.980	124	144	**26.1**	6.8	-5.9	**2.9**	3.7	-7.7
CLE	49	14	27	1477[2]	1258	7.7	533	120	559	**1189**	.231	1.230	3.25	101	3.15	17.6	101	.981	116	138	-14.2	-3.6	1.9	-1.6	-3.2	-2.8
NY	37	16	27	1480[2]	1375	8.4	533	110	480	898	.249	1.253	3.24	96	3.28	-0.8	97	.976	154	144	-17.7	-5.5	-.1	-2.0	-7.6	-1.4
KC	26	10	34	1428	1265	8.0	584	125	558	990	.238	1.277	3.68	**87**	3.39	-79.6	99	.978	132	120	0.9	-3.2	-8.8	.1	-11.8	-6.2
Total	**365**	**153**	**356**	**14601[2]**		**7.9**	**5240**					**1.216**	**3.23**													

Wins
Lonborg, J. (Bos) 22
Wilson, E. (Det) 22
Chance, D. (Min) 20

Win Percentage
Horlen, J. (Chi) .731
Lonborg, J. (Bos) .710
Wilson, E. (Det) .667

Games
Locker, B. (Chi) 77
Rojas, M. (Cal) 72
Kelso, B. (Cal) 69

Complete Games
Chance, D. (Min) 18
Hargan, S. (Cle) 15
Lonborg, J. (Bos) 15

Shutouts
5 players tied with 6

Saves
Rojas, M. (Cal) 27
Locker, B. (Chi) 20
Wyatt, J. (Bos) 20

Innings Pitched
Chance, D. (Min) 283[2]
Lonborg, J. (Bos) 273[1]
Wilson, E. (Det) 264

Fewest Hits/Game
Peters, G. (Chi) 6.47
Boswell, D. (Min) 6.55
Horlen, J. (Chi) 6.56

Fewest BB/Game
Merritt, J. (Min) 1.19
Kaat, J. (Min) 1.44
Stange, L. (Bos) 1.59

Strikeouts
Lonborg, J. (Bos) 246
McDowell, S. (Cle) 236
Chance, D. (Min) 220

Ratio
Horlen, J. (Chi) .95
Merritt, J. (Min) .99
Siebert, S. (Cle) 1.03

Earned Run Average
Horlen, J. (Chi) 2.06
Peters, G. (Chi) 2.28
Siebert, S. (Cle) 2.38

Adjusted ERA
Horlen, J. (Chi) 151
Siebert, S. (Cle) 137
Merritt, J. (Min) 137

Component ERA
Horlen, J. (Chi) 1.84
Peters, G. (Chi) 2.25
Siebert, S. (Cle) 2.33

Opponents' Batting Avg.
Peters, G. (Chi) .199
Boswell, D. (Min) .202
Siebert, S. (Cle) .202

Adjusted Pitching Runs
Horlen, J. (Chi) 29
Chance, D. (Min) 27
Merritt, J. (Min) 27

Win Shares – Pitchers
Horlen, J. (Chi) 23
Peters, G. (Chi) 21
Chance, D. (Min) 20

TPW – Pitchers
Peters, G. (Chi) 3.2
Horlen, J. (Chi) 3.2
Merritt, J. (Min) 3.0

1968 National League

TEAM	G	W	L	PCT	GB	R	OR	EW	AB	H	2B	3B	HR	TB	BB	SO	SB	CS	AVG	OBP	SLG	OPS	OPS+	BR/A	PF	RC
STL	162	97	65	.599	....	583	**472**	98	5561	1383	227	**48**	73	1925	378	897	110	45	.249	.300	.346	.646	102	18	99	579
SF	163	88	74	.543	9	599	529	91	5441	1301	162	33	108	1853	**508**	904	50	37	.239	.310	.341	.650	102	23	100	575
CHI	163	84	78	.519	13	612	611	81	5458	1319	203	43	**130**	1998	415	854	41	**30**	.242	.300	.366	.666	100	-1	107	591
CIN	163	83	79	.512	14	**690**	673	83	**5767**	**1573**	**281**	36	106	**2244**	379	938	59	55	**.273**	**.322**	**.389**	**.711**	**113**	**81**	106	**686**
ATL	163	81	81	.500	16	514	549	76	5552	1399	179	31	80	1880	414	**782**	83	44	.252	.308	.339	.647	101	11	100	562
PIT	163	80	82	.494	17	583	532	88	5569	1404	180	44	80	1912	422	953	**130**	59	.252	.309	.343	.652	104	34	99	578
PHI	162	76	86	.469	21	543	615	71	5372	1253	178	30	100	1791	462	1003	58	51	.233	.297	.333	.630	96	-28	100	524
LA	162	76	86	.469	21	470	509	75	5354	1234	202	36	67	1709	439	980	57	43	.230	.291	.319	.610	97	-22	92	498
NY	163	73	89	.451	24	473	499	77	5503	1252	178	30	81	1733	379	1203	72	45	.228	.283	.315	.597	85	-94	101	484
HOU	162	72	90	.444	25	510	588	70	5336	1233	205	28	66	1692	479	988	44	51	.231	.300	.317	.617	94	-37	98	503
Total	**813**					**5577**			**54913**	**13351**	**1995**	**359**	**891**		**4275**	**9502**	**704**	**460**	**.243**	**.302**	**.341**	**.643**				

Runs
Beckert, G. (Chi) 98
Rose, P. (Cin) 94
Perez, T. (Cin) 93

Hits
Alou, F. (Atl) 210
Rose, P. (Cin) 210
Beckert, G. (Chi) 189

Doubles
Brock, L. (StL) 46
Rose, P. (Cin) 42
Bench, J. (Cin) 40

Triples
Brock, L. (StL) 14
Clemente, R. (Pit) 12
Davis, W. (LA) 10

Home Runs
McCovey, W. (SF) 36
Allen, D. (Phi) 33
Banks, E. (Chi) 32

Total Bases
Williams, B. (Chi) 321
Aaron, H. (Atl) 302
Rose, P. (Cin) 294

Runs Batted In
McCovey, W. (SF) 105
Santo, R. (Chi) 98
Williams, B. (Chi) 98

Bases On Balls
Santo, R. (Chi) 96
Wynn, J. (Hou) 90
Hunt, R. (SF) 78

Stolen Bases
Brock, L. (StL) 62
Wills, M. (Pit) 52
Davis, W. (LA) 36

Batting Average
Rose, P. (Cin) .335
Alou, M. (Pit) .332
Alou, F. (Atl) .317

On-Base Percentage
Rose, P. (Cin) .394
McCovey, W. (SF) .383
Wynn, J. (Hou) .378

Slugging Average
McCovey, W. (SF) .545
Allen, D. (Phi) .520
Williams, B. (Chi) .500

Adjusted OPS
McCovey, W. (SF) 176
Allen, D. (Phi) 160
Mays, W. (SF) 158

Adjusted Batting Runs
McCovey, W. (SF) 50.0
Aaron, H. (Atl) 43.0
Allen, D. (Phi) 37.0

Runs Created/Game
McCovey, W. (SF) 7.60
Rose, P. (Cin) 6.90
Mays, W. (SF) 6.50

Fielding Runs
Lanier, H. (SF) 16.0
Maxvill, D. (StL) 14.8
Mazeroski, B. (Pit) 14.6

Win Shares – Batters
McCovey, W. (SF) 34
4 players tied with 32

TPW – Batters
McCovey, W. (SF) 5.4
Wynn, J. (Hou) 4.5
Aaron, H. (Atl) 4.3

TEAM	CG	SH	SV	IP	H	H/G	ER	HR	BB	SO	OAV	RAT	ERA	ERA+	CERA	PR+	PF	FA	E	DP	FR	BW	PW	FW	TPW	DIF
STL	63	**30**	32	1479[1]	1282	7.8	**409**	82	375	971	.234	**1.120**	**2.49**	116	2.60	**54.6**	97	.978	140	135	12.4	2.1	**6.3**	1.4	**9.8**	6.2
SF	**77**	20	16	1469	1302	8.0	442	86	**344**	942	.236	1.120	2.71	109	**2.58**	49.4	99	.975	162	125	-11.1	2.6	5.7	-1.3	7.0	.0
CHI	46	12	32	1453[2]	1399	8.7	551	138	392	894	.254	1.232	3.41	93	3.42	-39.8	106	**.981**	**119**	149	-0.4	-.1	-4.6	.0	-4.7	7.7
CIN	24	16	**38**	**1490**[1]	1399	8.4	589	114	573	963	.250	1.323	3.56	**89**	3.60	-56.1	106	.978	144	144	-10.3	**9.3**	-6.4	-1.2	1.7	.3
ATL	44	16	29	1474[2]	1326	8.1	478	87	362	871	.241	1.145	2.92	103	2.73	6.5	100	.980	125	139	6.0	1.2	.7	.7	2.7	-2.7
PIT	42	19	30	1487	1322	8.0	453	73	485	897	.240	1.215	2.74	107	2.96	11.0	98	.979	139	162	**19.4**	3.9	1.3	**2.2**	7.4	-8.4
PHI	42	12	27	1448[1]	1416	8.8	541	91	421	935	.257	1.268	3.36	89	3.35	-42.4	101	.980	127	**163**	-14.8	-3.3	-4.9	-1.7	-9.8	4.8
LA	38	23	31	1448[2]	1293	8.0	433	**65**	414	994	.241	1.178	2.69	103	2.76	-0.6	93	.977	144	144	12.3	-2.5	-.1	1.4	-1.2	-3.8
NY	45	25	32	1483[1]	**1250**	**7.6**	448	87	430	1014	**.230**	1.133	2.72	111	2.65	33.0	101	.979	133	142	15.9	-10.7	3.8	1.8	-5.1	-2.9
HOU	50	12	23	1446[2]	1362	8.5	524	68	479	**1021**	.249	1.273	3.26	91	3.14	-19.5	99	.975	156	129	-29.5	-4.3	-2.2	-3.4	-9.9	.9
Total	**471**	**185**	**290**	**14681**		**8.2**	**4868**					**1.201**	**2.98**													

Wins
Marichal, J. (SF) 26
Gibson, B. (StL) 22
Jenkins, F. (Chi) 20

Win Percentage
Blass, S. (Pit) .750
Marichal, J. (SF) .743
Gibson, B. (StL) .710

Games
Abernathy, T. (Cin) 78
Regan, P. (Chi,LA) 73
Carroll, C. (Cin,Atl) 68

Complete Games
Marichal, J. (SF) 30
Gibson, B. (StL) 28
Jenkins, F. (Chi) 20

Shutouts
Gibson, B. (StL) 13
Drysdale, D. (LA) 8
2 players tied with 7

Saves
Regan, P. (Chi,LA) 25
Carroll, C. (Cin,Atl) 17
Hoerner, J. (StL) 17

Innings Pitched
Marichal, J. (SF) 326
Jenkins, F. (Chi) 308
Gibson, B. (StL) 304[2]

Fewest Hits/Game
Gibson, B. (StL) 5.85
Bolin, B. (SF) 6.52
Veale, B. (Pit) 6.86

Fewest BB/Game
Hands, B. (Chi) 1.25
Marichal, J. (SF) 1.27
Seaver, T. (NY) 1.56

Strikeouts
Gibson, B. (StL) 268
Jenkins, F. (Chi) 260
Singer, B. (LA) 227

Ratio
Gibson, B. (StL) .85
Seaver, T. (NY) .98
Jarvis, P. (Atl) .98

Earned Run Average
Gibson, B. (StL) 1.12
Bolin, B. (SF) 1.99
Veale, B. (Pit) 2.05

Adjusted ERA
Gibson, B. (StL) 258
Bolin, B. (SF) 148
Koosman, J. (NY) 145

Component ERA
Gibson, B. (StL) 1.44
Bolin, B. (SF) 1.89
Jarvis, P. (Atl) 1.97

Opponents' Batting Avg.
Gibson, B. (StL) .184
Bolin, B. (SF) .200
Veale, B. (Pit) .211

Adjusted Pitching Runs
Gibson, B. (StL) 57
Koosman, J. (NY) 25
Seaver, T. (NY) 22

Win Shares – Pitchers
Gibson, B. (StL) 36
Jenkins, F. (Chi) 25
Marichal, J. (SF) 24

TPW – Pitchers
Gibson, B. (StL) 7.0
Seaver, T. (NY) 2.6
Marichal, J. (SF) 2.6

1968 American League

TEAM	G	W	L	PCT	GB	R	OR	EW	AB	H	2B	3B	HR	TB	BB	SO	SB	CS	AVG	OBP	SLG	OPS	OPS+	BR/A	PF	RC
DET	164	103	59	.636	....	**671**	**492**	105	**5490**	1292	190	39	**185**	**2115**	521	964	26	32	.235	.309	**.385**	**.694**	**113**	**78**	103	**644**
BAL	162	91	71	.562	12	579	497	93	5275	1187	**215**	28	133	1857	570	1019	78	32	.225	.306	.352	.658	106	48	100	583
CLE	162	86	75	.534	16.5	516	504	82	5416	1266	210	36	75	1773	427	858	115	61	.234	.294	.327	.622	96	-26	99	523
BOS	162	86	76	.531	17	614	611	81	5303	1253	207	17	125	1869	**582**	974	76	62	.236	**.316**	.352	.668	103	19	107	588
NY	164	83	79	.512	20	536	531	82	5310	1137	154	34	109	1686	566	958	90	50	.214	.293	.318	.611	95	-28	97	505
OAK	163	82	80	.506	21	569	544	85	5406	**1300**	192	40	94	1854	472	1022	**147**	61	**.240**	.306	.343	.649	108	57	95	578
MIN	162	79	83	.488	24	562	546	83	5373	1274	207	**41**	105	1878	445	966	98	54	.237	.301	.350	.651	99	-7	105	563
CAL	162	67	95	.414	36	498	615	64	5331	1209	170	33	83	1694	447	1080	62	50	.227	.293	.318	.611	95	-38	96	496
CHI	162	67	95	.414	36	463	527	71	5405	1233	169	33	71	1681	397	**840**	90	50	.228	.286	.311	.597	86	-88	101	478
WAS	161	65	96	.404	37.5	524	665	62	5400	1208	160	37	124	1814	454	960	29	**19**	.224	.289	.336	.625	99	-14	97	516
Total	**812**					**5532**			**53709**	**12359**	**1874**	**338**	**1104**		**4881**	**9641**	**811**	**471**	**.230**	**.299**	**.339**	**.639**				

Runs
McAuliffe, D. (Det) 95
Yastrzemski, C. (Bos) 90
2 players tied with 89

Hits
Campaneris, B. (Oak) 177
Tovar, C. (Min) 167
2 players tied with 164

Doubles
Smith, R. (Bos) 37
Robinson, B. (Bal) 36
Yastrzemski, C. (Bos) 32

Triples
Fregosi, J. (Cal) 13
McCraw, T. (Chi) 12
2 players tied with 10

Home Runs
Howard, F. (Was) 44
Horton, W. (Det) 36
Harrelson, K. (Bos) 35

Total Bases
Howard, F. (Was) 330
Horton, W. (Det) 278
Harrelson, K. (Bos) 277

Runs Batted In
Harrelson, K. (Bos) 109
Howard, F. (Was) 106
Northrup, J. (Det) 90

Bases On Balls
Yastrzemski, C. (Bos) 119
Mantle, M. (NY) 106
Foy, J. (Bos) 84

Stolen Bases
Campaneris, B. (Oak) 62
Cardenal, J. (Cle) 40
Tovar, C. (Min) 35

Batting Average
Yastrzemski, C. (Bos) .301
Cater, D. (Oak) .290
Oliva, T. (Min) .289

On-Base Percentage
Yastrzemski, C. (Bos) .429
Robinson, F. (Bal) .391
Mantle, M. (NY) .387

Slugging Average
Howard, F. (Was) .552
Horton, W. (Det) .543
Harrelson, K. (Bos) .518

Adjusted OPS
Howard, F. (Was) 172
Yastrzemski, C. (Bos) 168
Horton, W. (Det) 165

Adjusted Batting Runs
Yastrzemski, C. (Bos) 52.0
Howard, F. (Was) 49.0
Horton, W. (Det) 38.0

Runs Created/Game
Yastrzemski, C. (Bos) 8.20
Howard, F. (Was) 6.60
Horton, W. (Det) 6.50

Fielding Runs
Robinson, B. (Bal) 18.6
Knoop, B. (Cal) 17.5
Josephson, D. (Chi) 16.4

Win Shares – Batters
Yastrzemski, C. (Bos) 39
Howard, F. (Was) 38
Freehan, B. (Det) 35

TPW – Batters
Yastrzemski, C. (Bos) 5.8
Howard, F. (Was) 4.8
Freehan, B. (Det) 4.4

TEAM	CG	SH	SV	IP	H	H/G	ER	HR	BB	SO	OAV	RAT	ERA	ERA+	CERA	PR+	PF	FA	E	DP	FR	BW	PW	FW	TPW	DIF
DET	**59**	19	29	**1489^{2}**	1180	7.1	448	129	486	1115	.217	1.118	2.71	111	2.69	43.6	101	**.983**	**105**	133	5.3	**8.9**	5.0	.6	**14.5**	7.5
BAL	53	16	31	1451	1111	6.9	**429**	101	502	1044	.212	1.112	**2.66**	110	2.58	16.0	98	.981	120	131	**26.4**	5.5	1.8	**3.0**	10.4	-.4
CLE	48	**23**	32	1464^{1}	**1087**	**6.7**	433	98	540	**1157**	**.206**	**1.111**	2.66	111	**2.52**	34.0	99	.979	127	130	15.2	-3.0	3.9	1.7	2.7	3.3
BOS	55	17	31	1447	1303	8.1	535	115	523	972	.241	1.262	3.33	95	3.36	-20.4	106	.979	128	147	-8.2	2.2	-2.3	-.9	-1.1	6.1
NY	45	14	27	1467^{1}	1308	8.0	455	99	424	831	.240	1.180	2.79	104	2.92	34.4	97	.979	139	142	-16.3	-3.2	3.9	-1.9	-1.1	3.1
OAK	45	18	29	1455^{2}	1220	7.5	475	124	505	997	.227	1.185	2.94	96	2.94	-22.7	95	.976	145	136	2.1	6.5	-2.6	.2	4.1	-3.1
MIN	46	14	29	1433^{1}	1224	7.7	460	**92**	**414**	996	.229	1.143	2.89	107	2.70	**53.2**	104	.973	170	117	-22.2	-.8	**6.1**	-2.5	2.8	-4.8
CAL	29	11	31	1437	1234	7.7	548	131	519	869	.233	1.220	3.43	85	3.20	-102.1	98	.977	140	**156**	18.4	-4.4	-11.7	2.1	-14.0	.0
CHI	20	11	**40**	1468	1290	7.9	449	97	451	834	.236	1.186	2.75	110	2.98	52.3	102	.977	151	152	-6.8	-10.0	6.0	-.8	-4.8	-9.2
WAS	26	11	28	1439^{2}	1402	8.8	582	118	517	826	.258	1.333	3.64	**80**	3.76	-100.4	98	.976	148	144	-16.3	-1.6	-11.5	-1.9	-15.0	.0
Total	**426**	**154**	**307**	**14553**		**7.6**	**4814**					**1.185**	**2.98**													

Wins		Win Percentage		Games		Complete Games		Shutouts		Saves	
McLain, D. (Det)	31	McLain, D. (Det)	.838	Wood, W. (Chi)	88	McLain, D. (Det)	28	Tiant, L. (Cle)	9	Worthington, A. (Min)	18
McNally, D. (Bal)	22	Culp, R. (Bos)	.727	Wilhelm, H. (Chi)	72	Stottlemyre, M. (NY)	19	5 players tied with	6	Wood, W. (Chi)	16
2 players tied with	21	Tiant, L. (Cle)	.700	Locker, B. (Chi)	70	Tiant, L. (Cle)	19			Higgins, D. (Was)	13
Innings Pitched		**Fewest Hits/Game**		**Fewest BB/Game**		**Strikeouts**		**Ratio**		**Earned Run Average**	
McLain, D. (Det)	336	Tiant, L. (Cle)	5.30	Peterson, F. (NY)	1.23	McDowell, S. (Cle)	283	McNally, D. (Bal)	.84	Tiant, L. (Cle)	1.60
Chance, D. (Min)	292	McNally, D. (Bal)	5.77	McLain, D. (Det)	1.69	McLain, D. (Det)	280	Tiant, L. (Cle)	.87	McDowell, S. (Cle)	1.81
Stottlemyre, M. (NY)	278^{2}	McDowell, S. (Cle)	6.06	Ellsworth, D. (Bos)	1.70	Tiant, L. (Cle)	264	McLain, D. (Det)	.90	McNally, D. (Bal)	1.95
Adjusted ERA		**Component ERA**		**Opponents' Batting Avg.**		**Adjusted Pitching Runs**		**Win Shares – Pitchers**		**TPW – Pitchers**	
Tiant, L. (Cle)	185	Tiant, L. (Cle)	1.51	Tiant, L. (Cle)	.168	McLain, D. (Det)	38	McLain, D. (Det)	33	McLain, D. (Det)	4.4
McDowell, S. (Cle)	164	McNally, D. (Bal)	1.66	McNally, D. (Bal)	.182	Tiant, L. (Cle)	36	Tiant, L. (Cle)	28	McDowell, S. (Cle)	3.6
McLain, D. (Det)	154	McLain, D. (Det)	1.91	McDowell, S. (Cle)	.189	McDowell, S. (Cle)	32	McNally, D. (Bal)	26	Tiant, L. (Cle)	3.6

1969 National League

TEAM	G	W	L	PCT	GB	R	OR	EW	AB	H	2B	3B	HR	TB	BB	SO	SB	CS	AVG	OBP	SLG	OPS	OPS+	BR/A	PF	RC
East																										
NY	162	100	62	.617	....	632	541	93	5427	1311	184	41	109	1904	527	1089	66	43	.242	.313	.351	.663	90	-64	102	599
CHI	163	92	70	.568	8	720	611	94	5530	1400	215	40	142	2121	559	928	30	**32**	.253	.326	.384	.709	93	-44	113	691
PIT	162	88	74	.543	12	725	652	90	5626	1557	220	**52**	119	2238	454	944	74	34	**.277**	.336	.398	.734	**115**	**106**	98	740
STL	162	87	75	.537	13	595	**540**	89	5536	1403	**228**	44	90	1989	503	876	87	49	.253	.318	.359	.677	96	-26	100	631
PHI	162	63	99	.389	37	645	745	69	5408	1304	227	35	137	2012	549	1130	73	49	.241	.314	.372	.686	101	6	97	627
MON	162	52	110	.321	48	582	791	57	5419	1300	202	33	125	1943	529	962	52	52	.240	.312	.359	.670	94	-48	100	594
West																										
ATL	162	93	69	.574	....	691	631	88	5460	1411	195	22	141	2073	485	**665**	59	48	.258	.323	.380	.702	103	14	100	654
SF	162	90	72	.556	3	713	636	90	5474	1325	187	28	136	1976	**711**	1054	71	**32**	.242	.336	.361	.697	104	56	98	688
CIN	163	89	73	.549	4	**798**	768	84	**5634**	**1558**	224	42	**171**	**2379**	474	1042	79	56	.277	**.338**	**.422**	**.760**	114	92	105	**789**
LA	162	85	77	.525	8	645	561	92	5532	1405	185	**52**	97	1985	484	823	80	51	.254	.316	.359	.675	103	16	93	625
HOU	162	81	81	.500	12	676	668	82	5348	1284	208	40	104	1884	699	972	**101**	58	.240	.332	.352	.685	101	25	98	647
SD	162	52	110	.321	41	468	746	46	5357	1203	180	42	99	1764	423	1143	45	44	.225	.286	.329	.615	82	-139	96	490
Total	**973**					**7890**			**65751**	**16461**	**2455**	**471**	**1470**		**6397**	**11628**	**817**	**548**	**.250**	**.321**	**.369**	**.690**				

Runs		Hits		Doubles		Triples		Home Runs		Total Bases	
Bonds, B. (SF)	120	Alou, M. (Pit)	231	Alou, M. (Pit)	41	Clemente, R. (Pit)	12	McCovey, W. (SF)	45	Aaron, H. (Atl)	332
Rose, P. (Cin)	120	Rose, P. (Cin)	218	Kessinger, D. (Chi)	38	Rose, P. (Cin)	11	Aaron, H. (Atl)	44	Perez, T. (Cin)	331
Wynn, J. (Hou)	113	Brock, L. (StL)	195	3 players tied with	33	3 players tied with	10	May, L. (Cin)	38	McCovey, W. (SF)	322
Runs Batted In		**Bases On Balls**		**Stolen Bases**		**Batting Average**		**On-Base Percentage**		**Slugging Average**	
McCovey, W. (SF)	126	Wynn, J. (Hou)	148	Brock, L. (StL)	53	Rose, P. (Cin)	.348	McCovey, W. (SF)	.458	McCovey, W. (SF)	.656
Santo, R. (Chi)	123	McCovey, W. (SF)	121	Morgan, J. (Hou)	49	Clemente, R. (Pit)	.345	Wynn, J. (Hou)	.440	Aaron, H. (Atl)	.607
Perez, T. (Cin)	122	2 players tied with	110	Bonds, B. (SF)	45	Jones, C. (NY)	.340	Rose, P. (Cin)	.432	Allen, D. (Phi)	.573
Adjusted OPS		**Adjusted Batting Runs**		**Runs Created/Game**		**Fielding Runs**		**Win Shares – Batters**		**TPW – Batters**	
McCovey, W. (SF)	212	McCovey, W. (SF)	81.0	McCovey, W. (SF)	11.60	Maxvill, D. (StL)	26.2	McCovey, W. (SF)	39	McCovey, W. (SF)	7.1
Aaron, H. (Atl)	177	Wynn, J. (Hou)	58.0	Wynn, J. (Hou)	8.90	Lanier, H. (SF)	17.9	Aaron, H. (Atl)	38	Wynn, J. (Hou)	6.0
Clemente, R. (Pit)	170	Aaron, H. (Atl)	55.0	Staub, R. (Mon)	8.50	Boyer, C. (Atl)	13.2	Rose, P. (Cin)	37	Clemente, R. (Pit)	5.1

TEAM	CG	SH	SV	IP	H	H/G	ER	HR	BB	SO	OAV	RAT	ERA	ERA+	CERA	PR+	PF	FA	E	DP	FR	BW	PW	FW	TPW	DIF
East																										
NY	51	**28**	35	1468^{1}	**1217**	**7.5**	488	119	517	1012	**.227**	**1.181**	2.99	122	**2.91**	72.2	102	.980	122	146	**37.0**	-6.7	7.6	**3.9**	4.8	14.2
CHI	58	22	27	1454^{1}	1366	8.4	540	118	475	1017	.248	1.266	3.34	120	3.36	**111.7**	112	.979	136	149	-0.9	-4.6	**11.7**	-.1	7.0	4.0
PIT	39	9	33	1445^{2}	1348	8.4	580	**96**	553	1124	.248	1.315	3.61	96	3.48	-11.9	97	.975	155	169	-8.2	**11.1**	-1.2	-.9	9.0	-2.0
STL	63	12	26	1460^{1}	1289	7.9	**477**	99	511	1004	.237	1.233	**2.94**	122	3.12	90.4	99	.978	138	144	12.5	-2.7	9.5	1.3	8.1	-2.1
PHI	47	14	21	1434	1494	9.4	660	134	570	921	.270	1.439	4.14	86	4.32	-99.3	99	.978	137	157	0.3	.6	-10.4	.0	-9.7	-8.3
MON	26	8	21	1426	1429	9.0	686	145	702	973	.263	1.494	4.33	85	4.52	-96.5	102	.971	184	**179**	-6.9	-5.0	-10.1	-.7	-15.9	-13.1
West																										
ATL	38	7	42	1445	1334	8.3	567	144	438	893	.245	1.226	3.53	102	3.32	17.4	100	**.981**	**115**	114	-5.1	1.5	1.8	-.5	2.8	9.2
SF	**71**	15	17	**1473^{2}**	1381	8.4	534	120	461	906	.248	1.250	3.26	107	3.33	50.4	97	.974	169	155	-11.1	5.9	5.3	-1.2	**10.0**	-1.0
CIN	23	11	**44**	1465	1478	9.1	669	149	611	818	.262	1.426	4.11	92	4.28	-61.6	105	.973	167	158	1.0	9.6	-6.5	.1	3.3	4.7
LA	47	20	31	1457	1324	8.2	499	122	**420**	975	.242	1.197	3.08	108	3.15	24.7	93	.980	126	130	13.8	1.7	2.6	1.4	5.7	-1.7
HOU	52	11	34	1435^{2}	1347	8.4	574	111	547	**1221**	.247	1.319	3.60	98	3.57	7.0	98	.975	153	136	-16.2	2.7	.7	-1.7	1.7	-1.7
SD	16	9	25	1422^{1}	1454	9.2	670	113	592	764	.267	1.438	4.24	**83**	4.14	-93.0	98	.975	156	140	-18.3	-14.6	-9.8	-1.9	-26.2	-2.8
Total	**531**	**166**	**356**	**17387^{1}**		**8.5**	**6944**					**1.315**	**3.59**													

Wins		Win Percentage		Games		Complete Games		Shutouts		Saves	
Seaver, T. (NY)	25	Moose, B. (Pit)	.824	Granger, W. (Cin)	90	Gibson, B. (StL)	28	Marichal, J. (SF)	8	Gladding, F. (Hou)	29
Niekro, P. (Atl)	23	Seaver, T. (NY)	.781	McGinn, D. (Mon)	74	Marichal, J. (SF)	27	Jenkins, F. (Chi)	7	Granger, W. (Cin)	27
2 players tied with	21	Maloney, J. (Cin)	.706	2 players tied with	71	Perry, G. (SF)	26	Osteen, C. (LA)	7	Upshaw, C. (Atl)	27
Innings Pitched		**Fewest Hits/Game**		**Fewest BB/Game**		**Strikeouts**		**Ratio**		**Earned Run Average**	
Perry, G. (SF)	325^{1}	Seaver, T. (NY)	6.65	Marichal, J. (SF)	1.62	Jenkins, F. (Chi)	273	Marichal, J. (SF)	.99	Marichal, J. (SF)	2.10
Osteen, C. (LA)	321	Maloney, J. (Cin)	6.80	Niekro, P. (Atl)	1.80	Gibson, B. (StL)	269	Singer, B. (LA)	1.01	Carlton, S. (StL)	2.17
Singer, B. (LA)	315^{2}	Singer, B. (LA)	6.96	Jenkins, F. (Chi)	2.05	Singer, B. (LA)	247	Dierker, L. (Hou)	1.02	Gibson, B. (StL)	2.18
Adjusted ERA		**Component ERA**		**Opponents' Batting Avg.**		**Adjusted Pitching Runs**		**Win Shares – Pitchers**		**TPW – Pitchers**	
Marichal, J. (SF)	167	Marichal, J. (SF)	2.07	Seaver, T. (NY)	.207	Hands, B. (Chi)	51	Gibson, B. (StL)	33	Gibson, B. (StL)	5.6
Seaver, T. (NY)	166	Dierker, L. (Hou)	2.11	Maloney, J. (Cin)	.208	Marichal, J. (SF)	49	Seaver, T. (NY)	32	Marichal, J. (SF)	5.0
Carlton, S. (StL)	165	Singer, B. (LA)	2.19	Singer, B. (LA)	.210	Gibson, B. (StL)	46	Marichal, J. (SF)	29	Hands, B. (Chi)	5.0

1969 American League

TEAM	G	W	L	PCT	GB	R	OR	EW	AB	H	2B	3B	HR	TB	BB	SO	SB	CS	AVG	OBP	SLG	OPS	OPS+	BR/A	PF	RC
East																										
BAL	162	109	53	.673	....	779	**517**	112	5518	1465	234	29	175	2282	634	**806**	82	45	.265	**.346**	.414	**.759**	**118**	**130**	101	788
DET	162	90	72	.556	19	701	601	93	5441	1316	188	29	182	2108	578	922	35	28	.242	.318	.387	.705	99	-13	104	673
BOS	162	87	75	.537	22	743	736	82	5494	1381	234	37	**197**	2280	**658**	923	41	47	.251	.335	**.415**	.750	110	63	105	759
WAS	162	86	76	.531	23	694	644	87	5447	1365	171	40	148	2060	630	900	52	40	.251	.332	.378	.710	111	72	95	674
NY	162	80	81	.497	28.5	562	587	77	5308	1247	210	**44**	94	1827	565	840	119	74	.235	.310	.344	.654	93	-57	96	570
CLE	161	62	99	.385	46.5	573	717	63	5365	1272	173	24	119	1850	535	906	85	37	.237	.309	.345	.654	86	-92	103	566
West																										
MIN	162	97	65	.599	....	**790**	618	100	**5677**	**1520**	**246**	32	163	**2319**	599	906	115	70	**.268**	.342	.408	.751	114	98	102	**793**
OAK	162	88	74	.543	9	740	678	88	5614	1400	210	28	148	2110	617	953	100	39	.249	.330	.376	.706	109	72	96	710
CAL	163	71	91	.438	26	528	652	64	5316	1221	151	29	88	1694	516	929	54	39	.230	.302	.319	.620	84	-114	95	516
KC	163	69	93	.426	28	586	688	68	5462	1311	179	32	98	1848	522	901	129	70	.240	.311	.338	.650	87	-89	101	575
CHI	162	68	94	.420	29	625	723	69	5450	1346	210	27	112	1946	552	844	54	**22**	.247	.322	.357	.679	92	-51	105	636
SEA	163	64	98	.395	33	639	799	63	5444	1276	179	27	125	1884	626	1015	**167**	59	.234	.317	.346	.663	93	-29	98	620
Total	**973**					**7960**			**65536**	**16120**	**2385**	**378**	**1649**		**7032**	**10845**	**1033**	**570**	**.246**	**.323**	**.369**	**.693**				

Runs
Jackson, R. (Oak) 123
Howard, F. (Was) 111
Robinson, F. (Bal) 111

Hits
Oliva, T. (Min) 197
Clarke, H. (NY) 183
Blair, P. (Bal) 178

Doubles
Oliva, T. (Min) 39
Jackson, R. (Oak) 36
Johnson, D. (Bal) 34

Triples
Unser, D. (Was) 8
Clarke, H. (NY) 7
Smith, R. (Bos) 7

Home Runs
Killebrew, H. (Min) 49
Howard, F. (Was) 48
Jackson, R. (Oak) 47

Total Bases
Howard, F. (Was) 340
Jackson, R. (Oak) 334
Killebrew, H. (Min) 324

Runs Batted In
Killebrew, H. (Min) 140
Powell, B. (Bal) 121
Jackson, R. (Oak) 118

Bases On Balls
Killebrew, H. (Min) 145
Jackson, R. (Oak) 114
Bando, S. (Oak) 111

Stolen Bases
Harper, T. (Sea) 73
Campaneris, B. (Oak) 62
Tovar, C. (Min) 45

Batting Average
Carew, R. (Min) .332
Smith, R. (Bos) .309
Oliva, T. (Min) .309

On-Base Percentage
Killebrew, H. (Min) .430
Robinson, F. (Bal) .417
Jackson, R. (Oak) .410

Slugging Average
Jackson, R. (Oak) .608
Petrocelli, R. (Bos) .589
Killebrew, H. (Min) .584

Adjusted OPS
Jackson, R. (Oak) 190
Howard, F. (Was) 180
Killebrew, H. (Min) 177

Adjusted Batting Runs
Jackson, R. (Oak) 70.0
Killebrew, H. (Min) 66.0
Howard, F. (Was) 65.0

Runs Created/Game
Jackson, R. (Oak) 9.40
Killebrew, H. (Min) 9.30
Robinson, F. (Bal) 8.70

Fielding Runs
Cardenas, L. (Min) 30.4
Robinson, B. (Bal) 30.0
Kenney, J. (NY) 15.5

Win Shares – Batters
Jackson, R. (Oak) 41
Petrocelli, R. (Bos) 37
Bando, S. (Oak) 36

TPW – Batters
Petrocelli, R. (Bos) 7.0
Jackson, R. (Oak) 6.3
Cardenas, L. (Min) 5.7

TEAM	CG	SH	SV	IP	H	H/G	ER	HR	BB	SO	OAV	RAT	ERA	ERA+	CERA	PR+	PF	FA	E	DP	FR	BW	PW	FW	TPW	DIF
East																										
BAL	50	**20**	36	1473^{2}	**1194**	**7.3**	**463**	**117**	**498**	897	**.223**	**1.148**	**2.83**	126	**2.77**	**64.4**	98	**.984**	**101**	145	**54.9**	**13.6**	**6.8**	**5.8**	**26.1**	1.9
DET	**55**	**20**	28	1455^{1}	1250	7.7	535	128	586	**1032**	.232	1.262	3.31	113	3.31	60.4	103	.979	130	130	6.2	-1.4	6.3	.6	5.6	3.4
BOS	30	7	41	1466^{2}	1423	8.7	639	155	685	935	.256	1.437	3.92	97	4.35	10.1	105	.975	157	**178**	-30.9	6.6	1.1	-3.2	4.4	1.6
WAS	28	10	41	1447^{1}	1310	8.2	561	135	656	835	.244	1.358	3.49	99	3.83	-13.3	96	.978	140	159	8.7	7.6	-1.4	.9	7.1	-2.1
NY	53	13	20	1440^{2}	1258	7.9	517	118	522	801	.236	1.236	3.23	108	3.15	32.6	96	.979	131	158	7.1	-5.9	3.4	.7	-1.8	1.8
CLE	35	7	22	1437	1330	8.3	629	134	681	1000	.248	1.399	3.94	96	3.99	-20.5	104	.976	145	153	-6.9	-9.7	-2.2	-.7	-12.5	-5.5
West																										
MIN	41	8	**43**	**1497^{2}**	1388	8.3	539	119	524	906	.246	1.277	3.24	113	3.39	47.9	101	.977	150	177	18.5	10.3	5.0	1.9	17.2	-1.2
OAK	42	14	36	1480^{2}	1356	8.2	610	163	586	887	.245	1.312	3.71	93	3.77	-48.1	95	.978	136	162	0.8	7.5	-5.0	.1	2.6	4.4
CAL	25	9	39	1438^{1}	1294	8.1	566	126	517	885	.242	1.259	3.54	98	3.49	-32.2	96	.978	136	164	22.0	-12.0	-3.4	2.3	-13.1	3.1
KC	42	10	25	1464^{2}	1357	8.3	605	136	560	894	.246	1.309	3.72	99	3.60	12.5	102	.975	157	114	-17.5	-9.3	1.3	-1.8	-9.8	-2.2
CHI	29	10	25	1437^{2}	1470	9.2	672	146	564	810	.267	1.415	4.21	92	4.26	-32.4	107	.981	122	163	-23.2	-5.3	-3.4	-2.4	-11.1	-1.9
SEA	21	6	33	1463^{2}	1490	9.2	707	172	653	963	.264	1.464	4.35	**84**	4.58	-74.6	100	.974	167	149	-41.6	-3.0	-7.8	-4.4	-15.2	-1.8
Total	**451**	**134**	**389**	**17503^{1}**		**8.3**	**7043**					**1.323**	**3.62**													

Wins
McLain, D. (Det) 24
Cuellar, M. (Bal) 23
4 players tied with 20

Win Percentage
Nagy, M. (Bos) .857
Palmer, J. (Bal) .800
Perry, J. (Min) .769

Games
Wood, W. (Chi) 76
Perranoski, R. (Min) 75
Lyle, S. (Bos) 71

Complete Games
Stottlemyre, M. (NY) 24
McLain, D. (Det) 23
2 players tied with 18

Shutouts
McLain, D. (Det) 9
Palmer, J. (Bal) 6
Cuellar, M. (Bal) 5

Saves
Perranoski, R. (Min) 31
Tatum, K. (Cal) 22
Lyle, S. (Bos) 17

Innings Pitched
McLain, D. (Det) 325
Stottlemyre, M. (NY) 303
Cuellar, M. (Bal) 290^{2}

Fewest Hits/Game
Messersmith, A. (Cal) 6.08
Palmer, J. (Bal) 6.51
Cuellar, M. (Bal) 6.60

Fewest BB/Game
Peterson, F. (NY) 1.42
Bosman, D. (Was) 1.82
McLain, D. (Det) 1.86

Strikeouts
McDowell, S. (Cle) 279
Lolich, M. (Det) 271
Messersmith, A. (Cal) 211

Ratio
Peterson, F. (NY) 1.00
Cuellar, M. (Bal) 1.00
Bosman, D. (Was) 1.01

Earned Run Average
Bosman, D. (Was) 2.19
Palmer, J. (Bal) 2.34
Cuellar, M. (Bal) 2.38

Adjusted ERA
Bosman, D. (Was) 158
Palmer, J. (Bal) 152
Cuellar, M. (Bal) 149

Component ERA
Cuellar, M. (Bal) 2.02
Peterson, F. (NY) 2.08
Bosman, D. (Was) 2.14

Opponents' Batting Avg.
Messersmith, A. (Cal) .190
Palmer, J. (Bal) .200
Cuellar, M. (Bal) .204

Adjusted Pitching Runs
McLain, D. (Det) 32
McDowell, S. (Cle) 28
Cuellar, M. (Bal) 27

Win Shares – Pitchers
McLain, D. (Det) 29
Stottlemyre, M. (NY) 26
Cuellar, M. (Bal) 24

TPW – Pitchers
McLain, D. (Det) 3.3
McDowell, S. (Cle) 2.8
Peterson, F. (NY) 2.8

1970 National League

TEAM	G	W	L	PCT	GB	R	OR	EW	AB	H	2B	3B	HR	TB	BB	SO	SB	CS	AVG	OBP	SLG	OPS	OPS+	BR/A	PF	RC
East																										
PIT	162	89	73	.549	....	729	664	89	5637	**1522**	235	**70**	130	2287	444	871	66	34	.270	.328	.406	.734	106	34	97	739
CHI	162	84	78	.519	5	806	679	95	5491	1424	228	44	179	2277	607	844	39	**16**	.259	.335	.415	.750	95	-32	112	772
NY	162	83	79	.512	6	695	**630**	89	5443	1358	211	42	120	2013	684	1062	118	54	.249	.336	.370	.706	96	-20	100	687
STL	162	76	86	.469	13	744	747	81	**5689**	1497	218	51	113	2156	569	961	117	47	.263	.333	.379	.712	95	-31	102	717
PHI	161	73	88	.453	15.5	594	730	64	5456	1299	224	58	101	1942	519	1066	72	64	.238	.307	.356	.663	86	-121	97	580
MON	162	73	89	.451	16	687	807	68	5411	1284	211	35	136	1973	659	972	65	45	.237	.324	.365	.689	91	-64	100	656
West																										
CIN	162	102	60	.630	....	775	681	91	5540	1498	253	45	**191**	**2414**	547	984	115	52	**.270**	.339	**.436**	**.775**	109	63	104	812
LA	161	87	74	.540	14.5	749	684	88	5606	1515	233	67	87	2143	541	841	**138**	57	.270	.337	.382	.719	104	34	96	728
SF	162	86	76	.531	16	**831**	826	81	5578	1460	**257**	35	165	2282	**729**	1005	83	27	.262	**.353**	.409	.762	**112**	**111**	99	**819**
HOU	162	79	83	.488	23	744	763	79	5574	1446	250	47	129	2177	598	911	114	41	.259	.334	.391	.725	105	44	96	726
ATL	162	76	86	.469	26	736	772	77	5546	1495	215	24	160	2238	522	**736**	58	34	.270	.337	.404	.740	99	-13	106	740
SD	162	63	99	.389	39	681	788	69	5494	1353	208	36	172	2149	500	1164	60	45	.246	.314	.391	.705	98	-30	96	667
Total	**971**					**8771**			**66465**	**17151**	**2743**	**554**	**1683**		**6919**	**11417**	**1045**	**516**	**.258**	**.332**	**.392**	**.724**				

Runs
Williams, B. (Chi) 137
Bonds, B. (SF) 134
Rose, P. (Cin) 120

Hits
Rose, P. (Cin) 205
Williams, B. (Chi) 205
Torre, J. (StL) 203

Doubles
Parker, W. (LA) 47
McCovey, W. (SF) 39
Rose, P. (Cin) 37

Triples
Davis, W. (LA) 16
Kessinger, D. (Chi) 14
2 players tied with 10

Home Runs
Bench, J. (Cin) 45
Williams, B. (Chi) 42
Perez, T. (Cin) 40

Total Bases
Williams, B. (Chi) 373
Bench, J. (Cin) 355
Perez, T. (Cin) 346

Runs Batted In
Bench, J. (Cin) 148
Perez, T. (Cin) 129
Williams, B. (Chi) 129

Bases On Balls
McCovey, W. (SF) 137
Staub, R. (Mon) 112
Dietz, D. (SF) 109

Stolen Bases
Tolan, B. (Cin) 57
Brock, L. (StL) 51
Bonds, B. (SF) 48

Batting Average
Carty, R. (Atl) .366
Torre, J. (StL) .325
Sanguillen, M. (Pit) .325

On-Base Percentage
Carty, R. (Atl) .456
McCovey, W. (SF) .446
Dietz, D. (SF) .430

Slugging Average
McCovey, W. (SF) .612
Perez, T. (Cin) .589
Bench, J. (Cin) .587

Adjusted OPS
McCovey, W. (SF) 183
Carty, R. (Atl) 167
Perez, T. (Cin) 156

Adjusted Batting Runs
McCovey, W. (SF) 65.0
Carty, R. (Atl) 48.0
Perez, T. (Cin) 48.0

Runs Created/Game
Carty, R. (Atl) 10.30
McCovey, W. (SF) 10.30
Hickman, J. (Chi) 9.50

Fielding Runs
Maxvill, D. (StL) 28.6
Rader, D. (Hou) 19.7
Wine, B. (Mon) 19.0

Win Shares – Batters
Bench, J. (Cin) 34
Perez, T. (Cin) 33
McCovey, W. (SF) 33

TPW – Batters
McCovey, W. (SF) 6.7
Grabarkewitz, B. (LA) 4.6
Dietz, D. (SF) 4.5

TEAM	CG	SH	SV	IP	H	H/G	ER	HR	BB	SO	OAV	RAT	ERA	ERA+	CERA	PR+	PF	FA	E	DP	FR	BW	PW	FW	TPW	DIF
East																										
PIT	36	13	43	1453[2]	1386	8.6	597	106	625	990	.255	1.383	3.70	105	3.81	-6.6	96	.979	137	**195**	**34.9**	3.3	-.7	**3.5**	6.2	1.8
CHI	**59**	9	25	1435	1402	8.8	600	143	**475**	1000	.256	1.308	3.76	120	3.72	**113.3**	111	.978	137	146	4.1	-3.2	**11.3**	.4	8.5	-5.5
NY	47	10	32	1459[2]	**1260**	**7.8**	**559**	135	575	**1064**	**.233**	**1.257**	**3.45**	117	**3.25**	67.9	99	.979	124	136	23.5	-2.0	6.8	2.3	7.1	-5.1
STL	51	11	20	**1475[2]**	1483	9.0	665	**102**	632	960	.263	1.433	4.06	101	3.97	30.5	102	.977	150	159	-20.6	-3.1	3.0	-2.1	-2.1	-2.9
PHI	24	8	36	1461	1483	9.1	677	132	538	1047	.265	1.383	4.17	96	4.03	-14.3	99	**.981**	**114**	134	-15.0	-12.1	-1.4	-1.5	-15.0	8.0
MON	29	10	32	1438[2]	1434	9.0	719	162	716	914	.261	1.494	4.50	91	4.64	-74.0	102	.977	141	193	9.9	-6.4	-7.4	1.0	-12.8	4.8
West																										
CIN	32	15	**60**	1444[2]	1370	8.5	592	118	592	843	.251	1.358	3.69	113	3.75	71.0	103	.976	151	173	3.7	6.3	7.1	.4	**13.7**	7.3
LA	37	**17**	42	1458[2]	1394	8.6	619	164	496	880	.250	1.296	3.82	100	3.74	-26.4	95	.979	135	135	27.5	3.4	-2.6	2.7	3.5	3.5
SF	50	7	30	1457[2]	1514	9.4	728	156	604	931	.267	1.453	4.49	**88**	4.45	-54.6	98	.973	170	153	-30.8	**11.1**	-5.4	-3.1	2.6	2.4
HOU	36	6	35	1456	1491	9.2	684	131	577	942	.265	1.420	4.23	92	4.19	-56.3	96	.978	140	144	-1.6	4.4	-5.6	-.2	-1.4	-.6
ATL	45	9	24	1430[2]	1451	9.1	688	185	478	960	.261	1.348	4.33	99	4.12	26.2	106	.977	141	118	-35.1	-1.3	2.6	-3.5	-2.2	-2.8
SD	24	9	32	1440[1]	1483	9.3	698	149	611	886	.267	1.454	4.36	91	4.38	-62.3	98	.975	158	159	-1.8	-2.9	-6.2	-.2	-9.3	-8.7
Total	**470**	**124**	**411**	**17411[2]**		**8.9**	**7826**					**1.382**	**4.05**													

Wins
Gibson, B. (StL) 23
Perry, G. (SF) 23
Jenkins, F. (Chi) 22

Win Percentage
Simpson, W. (Cin) .824
Gibson, B. (StL) .767
Nolan, G. (Cin) .720

Games
Herbel, R. (SD,NY) 76
Selma, D. (Phi) 73
2 players tied with 67

Complete Games
Jenkins, F. (Chi) 24
Gibson, B. (StL) 23
Perry, G. (SF) 23

Shutouts
Perry, G. (SF) 5
4 players tied with 4

Saves
Granger, W. (Cin) 35
Giusti, D. (Pit) 26
Brewer, J. (LA) 24

Innings Pitched
Perry, G. (SF) 328[2]
Jenkins, F. (Chi) 313
Gibson, B. (StL) 294

Fewest Hits/Game
Simpson, W. (Cin) 6.39
Seaver, T. (NY) 7.12
Walker, L. (Pit) 7.12

Fewest BB/Game
Jenkins, F. (Chi) 1.73
Marichal, J. (SF) 1.78
Osteen, C. (LA) 1.81

Strikeouts
Seaver, T. (NY) 283
Gibson, B. (StL) 274
Jenkins, F. (Chi) 274

Ratio
Jenkins, F. (Chi) 1.04
Seaver, T. (NY) 1.08
McAndrew, J. (NY) 1.11

Earned Run Average
Seaver, T. (NY) 2.82
Simpson, W. (Cin) 3.02
Walker, L. (Pit) 3.04

Adjusted ERA
Seaver, T. (NY) 143
Simpson, W. (Cin) 138
Holtzman, K. (Chi) 133

Component ERA
Seaver, T. (NY) 2.39
Jenkins, F. (Chi) 2.48
Gibson, B. (StL) 2.75

Opponents' Batting Avg.
Simpson, W. (Cin) .198
Seaver, T. (NY) .214
Walker, L. (Pit) .219

Adjusted Pitching Runs
Jenkins, F. (Chi) 38
Gibson, B. (StL) 37
Perry, G. (SF) 35

Win Shares – Pitchers
Gibson, B. (StL) 28
Jenkins, F. (Chi) 26
Seaver, T. (NY) 25

TPW – Pitchers
Gibson, B. (StL) 4.8
Seaver, T. (NY) 3.8
Holtzman, K. (Chi) 3.7

1970 American League

TEAM	G	W	L	PCT	GB	R	OR	EW	AB	H	2B	3B	HR	TB	BB	SO	SB	CS	AVG	OBP	SLG	OPS	OPS+	BR/A	PF	RC
East																										
BAL	162	108	54	.667	....	**792**	**574**	106	**5545**	1424	213	25	179	2224	**717**	952	84	39	.257	**.346**	.401	.748	**111**	**101**	101	**793**
NY	163	93	69	.574	15	680	612	90	5492	1381	208	**41**	111	2004	588	**808**	105	61	.251	.327	.365	.692	102	19	95	660
BOS	162	87	75	.537	21	786	722	88	5535	**1450**	**252**	28	**203**	**2367**	594	855	50	48	.262	.338	**.428**	**.765**	109	63	107	785
DET	162	79	83	.488	29	666	731	73	5377	1282	207	38	148	2009	656	825	29	30	.238	.325	.374	.699	98	-9	101	656
CLE	162	76	86	.469	32	649	675	78	5463	1358	197	23	183	2150	503	909	25	36	.249	.316	.394	.710	97	-35	105	669
WAS	162	70	92	.432	38	626	689	73	5460	1302	184	28	138	1956	635	989	72	42	.238	.323	.358	.681	99	1	95	636
West																										
MIN	162	98	64	.605	....	744	605	98	5483	1438	230	**41**	153	2209	501	905	57	52	**.262**	.329	.403	.732	106	34	101	708
OAK	162	89	73	.549	9	678	593	92	5376	1338	208	24	171	2107	584	977	**131**	68	.249	.327	.392	.718	108	58	96	688
CAL	162	86	76	.531	12	631	630	81	5532	1391	197	40	114	2010	447	922	69	**27**	.251	.311	.363	.674	95	-36	96	621
MIL	163	65	97	.401	33	613	751	65	5395	1305	202	24	126	1933	592	985	91	73	.242	.321	.358	.679	93	-53	101	616
KC	162	65	97	.401	33	611	705	69	5503	1341	202	**41**	97	1916	514	958	97	53	.244	.311	.348	.659	88	-87	100	593
CHI	162	56	106	.346	42	633	822	60	5514	1394	192	20	123	1995	477	872	53	33	.253	.317	.362	.679	90	-73	104	624
Total	**973**					**8109**			**65675**	**16404**	**2492**	**373**	**1746**		**6808**	**10957**	**863**	**562**	**.250**	**.324**	**.379**	**.703**				

Runs
Yastrzemski, C. (Bos) 125
Tovar, C. (Min) 120
2 players tied with 109

Hits
Oliva, T. (Min) 204
Johnson, A. (Cal) 202
Tovar, C. (Min) 195

Doubles
Oliva, T. (Min) 36
Otis, A. (KC) 36
Tovar, C. (Min) 36

Triples
Tovar, C. (Min) 13
Stanley, M. (Det) 11
Otis, A. (KC) 9

Home Runs
Howard, F. (Was) 44
Killebrew, H. (Min) 41
Yastrzemski, C. (Bos) 40

Total Bases
Yastrzemski, C. (Bos) 335
Oliva, T. (Min) 323
Harper, T. (Mil) 315

Runs Batted In
Howard, F. (Was) 126
Conigliaro, T. (Bos) 116
Powell, B. (Bal) 114

Bases On Balls
Howard, F. (Was) 132
Killebrew, H. (Min) 128
Yastrzemski, C. (Bos) 128

Stolen Bases
Campaneris, B. (Oak) 42
Harper, T. (Mil) 38
Alomar, S. (Cal) 35

Batting Average
Johnson, A. (Cal) .329
Yastrzemski, C. (Bos) .329
Oliva, T. (Min) .325

On-Base Percentage
Yastrzemski, C. (Bos) .453
Howard, F. (Was) .420
Powell, B. (Bal) .417

Slugging Average
Yastrzemski, C. (Bos) .592
Powell, B. (Bal) .549
Killebrew, H. (Min) .546

Adjusted OPS
Yastrzemski, C. (Bos) 174
Howard, F. (Was) 173
Powell, B. (Bal) 163

Adjusted Batting Runs
Yastrzemski, C. (Bos) 64.0
Howard, F. (Was) 62.0
Powell, B. (Bal) 49.0

Runs Created/Game
Yastrzemski, C. (Bos) 10.40
Powell, B. (Bal) 8.50
Howard, F. (Was) 8.00

Fielding Runs
Nettles, G. (Cle) 23.5
Brinkman, E. (Was) 18.4
Cardenas, L. (Min) 16.8

Win Shares – Batters
Yastrzemski, C. (Bos) 36
White, R. (NY) 34
2 players tied with 33

TPW – Batters
Yastrzemski, C. (Bos) 5.4
Howard, F. (Was) 5.2
Fregosi, J. (Cal) 5.1

TEAM	CG	SH	SV	IP	H	H/G	ER	HR	BB	SO	OAV	RAT	ERA	ERA+	CERA	PR+	PF	FA	E	DP	FR	BW	PW	FW	TPW	DIF

East																									
BAL	**60**	12	31	**1478^{2}**	1317	8.0	**517**	139	469	941	.240	**1.208**	**3.15**	116	**3.17**	50.0	98	.981	117	148	31.9	**10.5**	5.2	3.3	**19.0**	8.0
NY	36	6	49	1471^{2}	1386	8.5	530	**130**	**451**	777	.249	1.248	3.24	108	3.37	41.6	95	.980	130	146	1.9	2.0	4.3	.2	6.5	5.5
BOS	38	8	44	1446^{1}	1391	8.7	622	156	594	1003	.251	1.372	3.87	102	4.04	39.5	107	.974	156	131	-29.1	6.5	4.1	-3.0	7.6	-1.6
DET	33	9	39	1447^{1}	1443	9.0	658	153	623	1045	.260	1.427	4.09	91	4.27	-15.3	100	.978	133	142	-43.7	-.9	-1.6	-4.5	-7.0	5.0
CLE	34	8	35	1451^{1}	1333	8.3	630	163	689	**1076**	.247	1.393	3.91	101	4.12	4.6	107	.979	133	168	3.6	-3.6	.5	.4	-2.8	-2.2
WAS	20	11	40	1457^{2}	1375	8.5	615	139	611	823	.252	1.362	3.80	94	3.84	-59.5	96	**.982**	**116**	173	20.3	.1	-6.2	2.1	-4.0	-7.0
West																									
MIN	26	12	**58**	1448^{1}	1329	8.3	520	**130**	486	940	.244	1.253	3.23	115	3.40	**71.9**	100	.980	123	130	7.1	3.5	**7.5**	.7	11.7	5.3
OAK	33	**15**	40	1442^{2}	**1253**	**7.8**	529	134	542	858	**.234**	1.244	3.30	107	3.29	25.1	95	.977	141	152	13.0	6.0	2.6	1.3	10.0	-2.0
CAL	21	10	49	1462^{1}	1280	7.9	565	154	559	922	.237	1.258	3.48	104	3.45	-15.4	97	.980	127	169	**36.3**	-3.7	-1.6	**3.8**	-1.5	6.5
KC	30	11	25	1463^{2}	1346	8.3	614	138	641	915	.247	1.358	3.78	99	3.84	-19.6	101	.976	152	162	12.0	-9.0	-2.0	1.2	-9.8	-6.2
MIL	31	2	27	1446^{2}	1397	8.7	676	146	587	895	.255	1.371	4.21	90	4.00	-35.7	102	.978	136	142	-31.3	-5.5	-3.7	-3.2	-12.4	-3.6
CHI	20	6	30	1430^{1}	1554	9.8	721	164	556	762	.280	1.475	4.54	**86**	4.74	-81.6	105	.975	165	**187**	-23.9	-7.5	-8.5	-2.5	-18.5	-6.5
Total	**382**	**110**	**467**	**17447**		**8.5**	**7197**					**1.330**	**3.71**													

Wins
Cuellar, M. (Bal) 24
McNally, D. (Bal) 24
Perry, J. (Min) 24

Win Percentage
Cuellar, M. (Bal) .750
McNally, D. (Bal) .727
2 players tied with .667

Games
Wood, W. (Chi) 77
Grant, M. (Oak) 72
Knowles, D. (Was) 71

Complete Games
Cuellar, M. (Bal) 21
McDowell, S. (Cle) 19
Palmer, J. (Bal) 17

Shutouts
Dobson, C. (Oak) 5
Palmer, J. (Bal) 5
3 players tied with 4

Saves
Perranoski, R. (Min) 34
McDaniel, L. (NY) 29
2 players tied with 27

Innings Pitched
McDowell, S. (Cle) 305
Palmer, J. (Bal) 305
Cuellar, M. (Bal) 297^{2}

Fewest Hits/Game
Messersmith, A. (Cal) 6.66
McDowell, S. (Cle) 6.96
Segui, D. (Oak) 7.22

Fewest BB/Game
Peterson, F. (NY) 1.38
Perry, J. (Min) 1.84
Cox, C. (Was) 2.06

Strikeouts
McDowell, S. (Cle) 304
Lolich, M. (Det) 230
Johnson, B. (KC) 206

Ratio
Peterson, F. (NY) 1.10
Perry, J. (Min) 1.13
Messersmith, A. (Cal) 1.14

Earned Run Average
Segui, D. (Oak) 2.56
Palmer, J. (Bal) 2.71
Wright, C. (Cal) 2.83

Adjusted ERA
Segui, D. (Oak) 138
McDowell, S. (Cle) 135
Palmer, J. (Bal) 134

Component ERA
Perry, J. (Min) 2.82
Peterson, F. (NY) 2.83
Messersmith, A. (Cal) 2.83

Opponents' Batting Avg.
Messersmith, A. (Cal) .205
McDowell, S. (Cle) .213
Segui, D. (Oak) .222

Adjusted Pitching Runs
McDowell, S. (Cle) 34
Culp, R. (Bos) 31
Palmer, J. (Bal) 25

Win Shares – Pitchers
McDowell, S. (Cle) 30
Palmer, J. (Bal) 25
McNally, D. (Bal) 22

TPW – Pitchers
McDowell, S. (Cle) 3.2
Culp, R. (Bos) 2.8
Perry, J. (Min) 2.6

1971 National League

TEAM	G	W	L	PCT	GB	R	OR	EW	AB	H	2B	3B	HR	TB	BB	SO	SB	CS	AVG	OBP	SLG	OPS	OPS+	BR/A	PF	RC
East																										
PIT	162	97	65	.599	....	**788**	599	103	**5674**	**1555**	223	**61**	**154**	**2362**	469	919	65	**31**	.274	.333	**.416**	**.749**	**117**	**116**	101	**775**
STL	163	90	72	.556	7	739	699	86	5610	1542	225	54	95	2160	543	757	**124**	53	**.275**	**.342**	.385	.727	108	70	104	734
NY	162	83	79	.512	14	588	**550**	86	5477	1365	203	29	98	1920	547	958	89	43	.249	.321	.351	.671	98	-8	98	612
CHI	162	83	79	.512	14	637	648	80	5438	1401	202	34	128	2055	527	772	44	32	.258	.327	.378	.705	92	-44	114	661
MON	162	71	90	.441	25.5	622	729	68	5335	1312	197	29	88	1831	543	800	51	43	.246	.325	.343	.668	95	-27	100	596
PHI	162	67	95	.414	30	558	688	64	5538	1289	209	35	123	1937	499	1031	63	39	.233	.300	.350	.650	90	-75	100	584
West																										
SF	162	90	72	.556	....	706	644	88	5461	1348	224	36	140	2064	**654**	1042	101	36	.247	.331	.378	.709	109	80	98	697
LA	162	89	73	.549	1	663	587	91	5523	1469	213	38	95	2043	489	755	76	40	.266	.328	.370	.698	111	70	94	659
ATL	162	82	80	.506	8	643	699	74	5575	1434	192	30	153	2145	434	**747**	57	46	.257	.314	.385	.699	98	-28	106	656
HOU	162	79	83	.488	11	585	567	84	5492	1319	**230**	52	71	1866	478	888	101	51	.240	.304	.340	.644	91	-65	97	571
CIN	162	79	83	.488	11	586	581	82	5414	1306	203	28	138	1979	438	907	59	33	.241	.301	.366	.667	100	-14	95	579
SD	161	61	100	.379	28.5	486	610	63	5366	1250	184	31	96	1784	438	966	70	45	.233	.294	.332	.626	89	-84	93	512
Total	**972**					**7601**			**65903**	**16590**	**2505**	**457**	**1379**		**6059**	**10542**	**900**	**492**	**.252**	**.318**	**.366**	**.685**				

Runs
Brock, L. (StL) 126
Bonds, B. (SF) 110
Stargell, W. (Pit) 104

Hits
Torre, J. (StL) 230
Garr, R. (Atl) 219
Brock, L. (StL) 200

Doubles
Cedeno, C. (Hou) 40
Brock, L. (StL) 37
2 players tied with 34

Triples
Metzger, R. (Hou) 11
Morgan, J. (Hou) 11
Davis, W. (LA) 10

Home Runs
Stargell, W. (Pit) 48
Aaron, H. (Atl) 47
May, L. (Cin) 39

Total Bases
Torre, J. (StL) 352
Aaron, H. (Atl) 331
Stargell, W. (Pit) 321

Runs Batted In
Torre, J. (StL) 137
Stargell, W. (Pit) 125
Aaron, H. (Atl) 118

Bases On Balls
Mays, W. (SF) 112
Bailey, B. (Mon) 97
Dietz, D. (SF) 97

Stolen Bases
Brock, L. (StL) 64
Morgan, J. (Hou) 40
Garr, R. (Atl) 30

Batting Average
Torre, J. (StL) .363
Garr, R. (Atl) .343
Beckert, G. (Chi) .342

On-Base Percentage
Mays, W. (SF) .429
Torre, J. (StL) .424
Aaron, H. (Atl) .414

Slugging Average
Aaron, H. (Atl) .669
Stargell, W. (Pit) .628
Torre, J. (StL) .555

Adjusted OPS
Aaron, H. (Atl) 190
Stargell, W. (Pit) 186
Torre, J. (StL) 168

Adjusted Batting Runs
Aaron, H. (Atl) 59.0
Stargell, W. (Pit) 59.0
Torre, J. (StL) 58.0

Runs Created/Game
Aaron, H. (Atl) 10.60
Stargell, W. (Pit) 9.50
Torre, J. (StL) 9.10

Fielding Runs
Harrelson, B. (NY) 23.8
Maxvill, D. (StL) 18.5
Helms, T. (Cin) 17.8

Win Shares – Batters
Torre, J. (StL) 41
Stargell, W. (Pit) 35
Aaron, H. (Atl) 33

TPW – Batters
Stargell, W. (Pit) 5.2
Aaron, H. (Atl) 4.9
Allen, D. (LA) 4.4

TEAM	CG	SH	SV	IP	H	H/G	ER	HR	BB	SO	OAV	RAT	ERA	ERA+	CERA	PR+	PF	FA	E	DP	FR	BW	PW	FW	TPW	DIF
East																										
PIT	43	15	**48**	1461	1426	8.8	537	108	470	813	.257	1.298	3.31	103	3.50	2.2	98	.979	133	164	14.4	**12.4**	.2	1.5	**14.2**	1.8
STL	56	14	22	1467	1482	9.1	628	104	576	911	.263	1.403	3.85	93	3.95	-10.7	104	.978	142	155	-32.6	7.5	-1.2	-3.5	2.8	6.2
NY	42	13	22	1466^{1}	**1227**	**7.5**	**487**	100	529	**1157**	**.227**	**1.198**	**2.99**	114	**2.91**	52.8	98	.981	114	135	13.9	-.9	5.7	1.5	6.3	-4.3
CHI	**75**	17	13	1444	1458	9.1	579	132	411	900	.262	1.294	3.61	109	3.67	**78.6**	114	.980	126	150	-26.5	-4.8	**8.4**	-2.8	.8	1.2
MON	49	8	25	1434^{1}	1418	8.9	656	133	658	829	.260	1.447	4.12	**86**	4.25	-91.1	102	.976	150	164	-3.9	-2.9	-9.8	-.4	-13.1	4.1
PHI	31	10	25	1470^{2}	1396	8.5	606	132	525	838	.254	1.306	3.71	95	3.67	-48.7	102	.981	122	158	17.1	-8.1	-5.2	1.8	-11.5	-2.5
West																										
SF	45	14	30	1454^{2}	1324	8.2	536	128	471	831	.242	1.234	3.32	102	3.25	19.0	98	.972	179	153	-9.1	8.6	2.0	-1.0	9.6	-.6
LA	48	**18**	33	1449^{2}	1363	8.5	520	110	**399**	853	.250	1.215	3.23	100	3.18	-4.2	93	.979	131	159	3.4	7.5	-.5	.4	7.4	.6
ATL	40	11	31	**1474^{2}**	1529	9.3	614	152	485	823	.269	1.366	3.75	99	4.08	3.4	107	.977	146	**180**	-9.1	-3.0	.4	-1.0	-3.6	4.6
HOU	43	10	25	1471^{1}	1318	8.1	512	**75**	475	914	.241	1.219	3.13	107	3.04	28.6	97	.983	106	152	9.1	-7.0	3.1	1.0	-2.9	.9
CIN	27	11	38	1444	1298	8.1	537	112	501	750	.243	1.246	3.35	97	3.23	-50.3	94	**.984**	**103**	174	**33.2**	-1.5	-5.4	**3.6**	-3.3	1.3
SD	47	10	17	1438	1351	8.5	514	93	559	923	.249	1.328	3.22	102	3.49	21.7	95	.974	161	144	-11.4	-9.0	2.3	-1.2	-7.9	-11.1
Total	**546**	**151**	**329**	**17475^{2}**		**8.5**	**6726**					**1.296**	**3.46**													

Wins
Jenkins, F. (Chi) 24
3 players tied with 20

Win Percentage
Gullett, D. (Cin) .727
Carlton, S. (StL) .690
Downing, A. (LA) .690

Games
Granger, W. (Cin) 70
Johnson, J. (SF) 67
Marshall, M. (Mon) 66

Complete Games
Jenkins, F. (Chi) 30
Seaver, T. (NY) 21
2 players tied with 20

Shutouts
4 players tied with 5

Saves
Giusti, D. (Pit) 30
Marshall, M. (Mon) 23
Brewer, J. (LA) 22

Innings Pitched
Jenkins, F. (Chi) 325
Stoneman, B. (Mon) 294^{2}
Seaver, T. (NY) 286^{1}

Fewest Hits/Game
Wilson, D. (Hou) 6.55
Seaver, T. (NY) 6.60
Kirby, C. (SD) 7.17

Fewest BB/Game
Jenkins, F. (Chi) 1.02
Marichal, J. (SF) 1.81
Stone, G. (Atl) 1.82

Strikeouts
Seaver, T. (NY) 289
Jenkins, F. (Chi) 263
Stoneman, B. (Mon) 251

Ratio
Seaver, T. (NY) .95
Wilson, D. (Hou) 1.02
Jenkins, F. (Chi) 1.05

Earned Run Average
Seaver, T. (NY) 1.76
Roberts, D. (SD) 2.10
Wilson, D. (Hou) 2.45

Adjusted ERA
Seaver, T. (NY) 193
Roberts, D. (SD) 157
Jenkins, F. (Chi) 142

Component ERA
Seaver, T. (NY) 1.90
Wilson, D. (Hou) 2.10
Nolan, G. (Cin) 2.33

Opponents' Batting Avg.
Wilson, D. (Hou) .202
Seaver, T. (NY) .206
Kirby, C. (SD) .216

Adjusted Pitching Runs
Seaver, T. (NY) 50
Jenkins, F. (Chi) 48
Roberts, D. (SD) 38

Win Shares – Pitchers
Jenkins, F. (Chi) 37
Seaver, T. (NY) 32
Roberts, D. (SD) 24

TPW – Pitchers
Jenkins, F. (Chi) 6.3
Seaver, T. (NY) 5.7
Roberts, D. (SD) 4.3

1971 American League

TEAM	G	W	L	PCT	GB	R	OR	EW	AB	H	2B	3B	HR	TB	BB	SO	SB	CS	AVG	OBP	SLG	OPS	OPS+	BR/A	PF	RC
East																										
BAL	158	101	57	.639	....	742	530	105	5303	1382	207	25	158	2113	672	844	66	38	.261	.349	.398	.747	120	145	99	748
DET	162	91	71	.562	12	701	645	88	5502	1399	214	38	179	2226	540	854	35	43	.254	.327	.405	.732	109	54	104	714
BOS	162	85	77	.525	18	691	667	84	5401	1360	246	28	161	2145	552	871	51	34	.252	.325	.397	.722	103	24	107	684
NY	162	82	80	.506	21	648	641	82	5413	1377	195	43	97	1949	581	717	75	55	.254	.331	.360	.691	109	61	94	641
WAS	159	63	96	.396	38.5	537	660	63	5290	1219	189	30	86	1726	575	956	68	45	.230	.309	.326	.635	92	-53	94	536
CLE	162	60	102	.370	43	543	747	56	5467	1303	200	20	109	1870	467	868	37	61	.238	.302	.342	.644	81	-130	109	557
West																										
OAK	161	101	60	.627	....	691	564	97	5494	1383	195	25	160	2108	542	1018	80	53	.252	.323	.384	.707	109	54	98	679
KC	161	85	76	.528	16	603	566	86	5295	1323	225	40	80	1868	490	819	130	46	.250	.316	.353	.669	97	-11	99	591
CHI	162	79	83	.488	22.5	617	597	84	5382	1346	185	30	138	2005	562	870	83	65	.250	.327	.373	.699	101	8	103	658
CAL	162	76	86	.469	25.5	511	576	71	5495	1271	213	18	96	1808	441	827	72	34	.231	.292	.329	.621	88	-88	93	517
MIN	160	74	86	.462	26.5	654	670	78	5414	1406	197	31	116	2013	512	846	66	44	.260	.326	.372	.698	101	8	103	638
MIL	161	69	92	.429	32	534	609	70	5185	1188	160	23	104	1706	543	924	82	53	.229	.306	.329	.635	87	-83	99	532
Total	966					7472			64641	15957	2426	351	1484		6477	10414	845	571	.247	.320	.364	.684				

Runs		Hits		Doubles		Triples		Home Runs		Total Bases	
Buford, D. (Bal)	99	Tovar, C. (Min)	204	Smith, R. (Bos)	33	Patek, F. (KC)	11	Melton, B. (Chi)	33	Smith, R. (Bos)	302
Murcer, B. (NY)	94	Alomar, S. (Cal)	179	Schaal, P. (KC)	31	Carew, R. (Min)	10	Cash, N. (Det)	32	Jackson, R. (Oak)	288
Tovar, C. (Min)	94	Carew, R. (Min)	177	2 players tied with	30	Blair, P. (Bal)	8	Jackson, R. (Oak)	32	Murcer, B. (NY)	287

Runs Batted In		Bases On Balls		Stolen Bases		Batting Average		On-Base Percentage		Slugging Average	
Killebrew, H. (Min)	119	Killebrew, H. (Min)	114	Otis, A. (KC)	52	Oliva, T. (Min)	.337	Murcer, B. (NY)	.429	Oliva, T. (Min)	.546
Robinson, F. (Bal)	99	Yastrzemski, C. (Bos)	106	Patek, F. (KC)	49	Murcer, B. (NY)	.331	Rettenmund, M. (Bal)	.424	Murcer, B. (NY)	.543
Smith, R. (Bos)	96	Schaal, P. (KC)	103	Alomar, S. (Cal)	39	Rettenmund, M. (Bal)	.318	Buford, D. (Bal)	.415	Cash, N. (Det)	.531

Adjusted OPS		Adjusted Batting Runs		Runs Created/Game		Fielding Runs		Win Shares – Batters		TPW – Batters	
Murcer, B. (NY)	185	Murcer, B. (NY)	62.0	Murcer, B. (NY)	9.10	Nettles, G. (Cle)	39.6	Murcer, B. (NY)	38	Murcer, B. (NY)	5.7
White, R. (NY)	154	White, R. (NY)	41.0	Buford, D. (Bal)	7.90	Green, D. (Oak)	21.5	Jackson, R. (Oak)	32	Nettles, G. (Cle)	5.4
Robinson, F. (Bal)	154	Rettenmund, M. (Bal)	37.0	Cash, N. (Det)	7.60	Alomar, S. (Cal)	19.7	3 players tied with	29	White, R. (NY)	4.3

TEAM	CG	SH	SV	IP	H	H/G	ER	HR	BB	SO	OAV	RAT	ERA	ERA+	CERA	PR+	PF	FA	E	DP	FR	BW	PW	FW	TPW	DIF
East																										
BAL	71	15	22	1415¹	1257	8.0	470	125	416	793	.239	1.182	2.99	112	3.04	37.6	97	.981	112	148	17.1	15.6	4.0	1.8	21.5	.5
DET	53	11	32	1468¹	1355	8.3	592	126	609	1000	.247	1.338	3.63	99	3.76	-7.3	104	.983	106	156	-0.1	5.8	-.8	.0	5.0	5.0
BOS	44	11	35	1443	1424	8.9	609	136	535	871	.259	1.358	3.80	97	3.93	-3.7	107	.981	116	149	-18.1	2.5	-.4	-2.0	-.2	3.8
NY	67	15	12	1452	1382	8.6	553	126	423	707	.252	1.243	3.43	94	3.32	-26.6	93	.981	125	159	-8.2	6.6	-2.9	-.9	2.8	-1.8
WAS	30	10	26	1418²	1376	8.7	583	132	554	762	.258	1.360	3.70	89	3.93	-66.8	95	.977	141	170	4.6	-5.7	-7.2	.5	-12.4	-3.6
CLE	21	7	32	1440	1352	8.4	685	154	770	937	.252	1.474	4.28	89	4.44	-81.3	110	.981	116	159	9.0	-14.0	-8.7	1.0	-21.8	.8
West																										
OAK	57	18	36	1469¹	1229	7.5	498	131	501	999	.228	1.177	3.05	109	3.00	17.4	96	.981	117	157	26.6	5.8	1.9	2.9	10.5	10.5
KC	34	15	44	1420¹	1301	8.2	513	84	496	775	.247	1.265	3.25	106	3.27	36.1	99	.979	132	178	-7.7	-1.2	3.9	-.8	1.9	3.1
CHI	46	19	32	1450¹	1348	8.4	503	100	468	976	.247	1.252	3.12	115	3.24	99.5	104	.975	160	128	-25.4	.9	10.7	-2.7	8.8	-10.8
CAL	39	11	32	1481	1246	7.6	510	101	607	904	.230	1.251	3.10	104	3.12	5.2	93	.980	131	159	17.0	-9.4	.6	1.8	-7.1	2.1
MIN	43	9	25	1416²	1384	8.8	599	139	529	895	.257	1.350	3.81	93	3.91	-16.7	103	.980	118	134	-25.4	.8	-1.8	-2.7	-3.7	-2.3
MIL	32	23	32	1416¹	1303	8.3	532	130	569	795	.247	1.322	3.38	103	3.65	1.6	100	.977	138	152	12.3	-8.9	.2	1.3	-7.4	-3.6
Total	537	164	360	17291¹		8.3	6647					1.297	3.46													

Wins		Win Percentage		Games		Complete Games		Shutouts		Saves	
Lolich, M. (Det)	25	McNally, D. (Bal)	.808	Sanders, K. (Mil)	83	Lolich, M. (Det)	29	Blue, V. (Oak)	8	Sanders, K. (Mil)	31
Blue, V. (Oak)	24	Dobson, C. (Oak)	.750	Scherman, F. (Det)	69	Blue, V. (Oak)	24	Stottlemyre, M. (NY)	7	Abernathy, T. (KC)	23
Wood, W. (Chi)	22	Blue, V. (Oak)	.750	Burgmeier, T. (KC)	67	Wood, W. (Chi)	22	Wood, W. (Chi)	7	Scherman, F. (Det)	20

Innings Pitched		Fewest Hits/Game		Fewest BB/Game		Strikeouts		Ratio		Earned Run Average	
Lolich, M. (Det)	376	Blue, V. (Oak)	6.03	Peterson, F. (NY)	1.38	Lolich, M. (Det)	308	Blue, V. (Oak)	.95	Blue, V. (Oak)	1.82
Wood, W. (Chi)	334	McDowell, S. (Cle)	6.71	Kline, S. (NY)	1.50	Blue, V. (Oak)	301	Wood, W. (Chi)	1.00	Wood, W. (Chi)	1.91
Blue, V. (Oak)	312	May, R. (Cal)	6.91	Kaat, J. (Min)	1.62	Coleman, J. (Det)	236	Kline, S. (NY)	1.09	Palmer, J. (Bal)	2.68

Adjusted ERA		Component ERA		Opponents' Batting Avg.		Adjusted Pitching Runs		Win Shares – Pitchers		TPW – Pitchers	
Wood, W. (Chi)	188	Blue, V. (Oak)	1.81	Blue, V. (Oak)	.189	Wood, W. (Chi)	68	Wood, W. (Chi)	33	Wood, W. (Chi)	6.9
Blue, V. (Oak)	183	Wood, W. (Chi)	2.18	McDowell, S. (Cle)	.207	Blue, V. (Oak)	47	Blue, V. (Oak)	30	Blue, V. (Oak)	4.8
Siebert, S. (Bos)	127	Wright, C. (Cal)	2.49	May, R. (Cal)	.213	Lolich, M. (Det)	28	Lolich, M. (Det)	29	Siebert, S. (Bos)	3.6

1972 National League

TEAM	G	W	L	PCT	GB	R	OR	EW	AB	H	2B	3B	HR	TB	BB	SO	SB	CS	AVG	OBP	SLG	OPS	OPS+	BR/A	PF	RC
East																										
PIT	155	96	59	.619	....	691	512	100	5490	1505	251	47	110	2180	404	871	49	30	.274	.327	.397	.724	114	88	98	699
CHI	156	85	70	.548	11	685	567	92	5247	1346	206	40	133	2031	565	815	69	47	.257	.332	.387	.719	100	9	111	668
NY	156	83	73	.532	13.5	528	578	71	5135	1154	175	31	105	1706	589	990	41	41	.225	.309	.332	.641	91	-57	97	527
STL	156	75	81	.481	21.5	568	600	74	5326	1383	214	42	70	1891	437	793	104	48	.260	.319	.355	.674	99	-2	99	590
MON	156	70	86	.449	26.5	513	609	65	5156	1205	156	22	91	1678	474	828	68	66	.234	.304	.325	.630	84	-112	102	512
PHI	156	59	97	.378	37.5	503	635	60	5248	1240	200	36	98	1806	487	930	42	50	.236	.304	.344	.648	88	-88	103	543
West																										
CIN	154	95	59	.617	....	707	557	95	5241	1317	214	44	124	1991	606	914	140	63	.251	.333	.380	.713	116	117	94	674
HOU	153	84	69	.549	10.5	708	636	85	5267	1359	233	38	134	2070	524	907	111	56	.258	.329	.393	.722	114	93	98	684
LA	155	85	70	.548	10.5	584	527	85	5270	1349	178	39	98	1899	480	786	82	39	.256	.321	.360	.681	102	20	98	608
ATL	155	70	84	.455	25	628	730	65	5278	1363	186	17	144	2015	532	770	47	35	.258	.330	.382	.712	100	4	109	659
SF	155	69	86	.445	26.5	662	649	79	5245	1281	211	36	150	2014	480	964	123	45	.244	.311	.384	.695	102	19	101	629
SD	153	58	95	.379	36.5	488	665	54	5213	1181	168	38	102	1731	407	976	78	46	.227	.284	.332	.617	87	-95	93	488
Total	930					7265			63116	15683	2392	430	1359		5985	10544	954	566	.248	.317	.365	.682				

Runs		Hits		Doubles		Triples		Home Runs		Total Bases	
Morgan, J. (Cin)	122	Rose, P. (Cin)	198	Cedeno, C. (Hou)	39	Bowa, L. (Phi)	13	Bench, J. (Cin)	40	Williams, B. (Chi)	348
Bonds, B. (SF)	118	Brock, L. (StL)	193	Montanez, W. (Phi)	39	Rose, P. (Cin)	11	Colbert, N. (SD)	38	Cedeno, C. (Hou)	300
Wynn, J. (Hou)	117	Williams, B. (Chi)	191	Simmons, T. (StL)	36	3 players tied with	8	Williams, B. (Chi)	37	Bench, J. (Cin)	291

Runs Batted In		Bases On Balls		Stolen Bases		Batting Average		On-Base Percentage		Slugging Average	
Bench, J. (Cin)	125	Morgan, J. (Cin)	115	Brock, L. (StL)	63	Williams, B. (Chi)	.333	Morgan, J. (Cin)	.419	Williams, B. (Chi)	.606
Williams, B. (Chi)	122	Wynn, J. (Hou)	103	Morgan, J. (Cin)	58	Garr, R. (Atl)	.325	Williams, B. (Chi)	.403	Stargell, W. (Pit)	.558
Stargell, W. (Pit)	112	Bench, J. (Cin)	100	Cedeno, C. (Hou)	55	Baker, D. (Atl)	.321	Santo, R. (Chi)	.397	Bench, J. (Cin)	.541

Adjusted OPS		Adjusted Batting Runs		Runs Created/Game		Fielding Runs		Win Shares – Batters		TPW – Batters	
Bench, J. (Cin)	171	Morgan, J. (Cin)	51.0	Williams, B. (Chi)	9.10	Cash, D. (Pit)	31.4	Morgan, J. (Cin)	39	Morgan, J. (Cin)	7.5
Stargell, W. (Pit)	166	Bench, J. (Cin)	51.0	Stargell, W. (Pit)	7.80	Helms, T. (Hou)	18.7	Bench, J. (Cin)	37	Bench, J. (Cin)	5.8
Williams, B. (Chi)	166	Williams, B. (Chi)	50.0	Morgan, J. (Cin)	7.50	Money, D. (Phi)	16.7	Cedeno, C. (Hou)	33	Cedeno, C. (Hou)	5.2

TEAM	CG	SH	SV	IP	H	H/G	ER	HR	BB	SO	OAV	RAT	ERA	ERA+	CERA	PR+	PF	FA	E	DP	FR	BW	PW	FW	TPW	DIF
East																										
PIT	39	15	48	1414[1]	1282	8.2	441	90	433	838	.243	1.213	2.81	118	3.02	59.5	96	.978	136	**171**	20.3	9.4	6.4	2.2	**18.0**	1.0
CHI	54	19	32	1398[2]	1329	8.6	500	112	**421**	824	.251	1.251	3.22	118	3.36	92.2	110	.979	132	148	-0.4	1.0	**9.9**	.0	10.8	-2.8
NY	32	12	41	**1414[2]**	1263	8.0	512	118	486	**1059**	.240	1.236	3.26	103	3.22	24.3	97	.980	116	122	-10.3	-6.1	2.6	-1.1	-4.6	9.6
STL	**64**	13	13	1399[2]	1290	8.3	532	87	531	912	.247	1.301	3.42	99	3.33	-4.5	99	.977	141	146	0.3	-.2	-.5	.0	-.7	-2.3
MON	39	11	23	1401[1]	1281	8.2	559	103	579	888	.245	1.327	3.59	99	3.54	0.7	103	.978	134	141	-8.4	-12.0	.1	-.9	-12.8	4.8
PHI	43	13	15	1400	1318	8.5	569	117	536	927	.251	1.324	3.66	98	3.65	-27.7	104	.981	116	142	15.2	-9.5	-3.0	1.6	-10.8	-8.2
West																										
CIN	25	15	**60**	1412[2]	1313	8.4	504	129	435	806	.247	1.237	3.21	100	3.33	-27.0	93	**.982**	110	143	**26.9**	12.6	-2.9	**2.9**	12.6	5.4
HOU	38	14	31	1385[1]	1340	8.7	580	114	498	971	.256	1.327	3.77	89	3.74	-60.3	97	.980	116	151	-2.0	10.0	-6.5	-.2	3.3	4.7
LA	50	**23**	29	1403	**1196**	**7.7**	**433**	83	429	856	**.230**	**1.158**	**2.78**	120	**2.75**	81.1	97	.974	162	145	4.3	2.1	8.7	.5	11.3	-3.3
ATL	40	4	27	1377	1412	9.2	653	155	512	732	.266	1.397	4.27	89	4.26	-53.6	110	.974	156	130	-20.5	.5	-5.8	-2.2	-7.5	.5
SF	44	8	23	1386[1]	1309	8.5	568	130	507	771	.250	1.310	3.69	94	3.65	-31.7	101	.974	156	121	-1.7	2.0	-3.4	-.2	-1.6	-6.4
SD	39	17	19	1403[2]	1350	8.7	589	121	618	960	.255	1.402	3.78	**87**	3.95	-52.9	95	.976	144	146	-23.7	-10.3	-5.7	-2.5	-18.5	.5
Total	507	164	361	16796[2]		8.4	6440					1.290	3.45													

Wins		Win Percentage		Games		Complete Games		Shutouts		Saves	
Carlton, S. (Phi)	27	Nolan, G. (Cin)	.750	Carroll, C. (Cin)	65	Carlton, S. (Phi)	30	Sutton, D. (LA)	9	Carroll, C. (Cin)	37
Seaver, T. (NY)	21	Carlton, S. (Phi)	.730	Marshall, M. (Mon)	65	Gibson, B. (StL)	23	Carlton, S. (Phi)	8	McGraw, T. (NY)	27
2 players tied with	20	Pappas, M. (Chi)	.708	Borbon, P. (Cin)	62	Jenkins, F. (Chi)	23	Norman, F. (SD)	6	Giusti, D. (Pit)	22

Innings Pitched		Fewest Hits/Game		Fewest BB/Game		Strikeouts		Ratio		Earned Run Average	
Carlton, S. (Phi)	346[1]	Sutton, D. (LA)	6.14	Pappas, M. (Chi)	1.34	Carlton, S. (Phi)	310	Sutton, D. (LA)	.91	Carlton, S. (Phi)	1.97
Jenkins, F. (Chi)	289[1]	Carlton, S. (Phi)	6.68	Nolan, G. (Cin)	1.53	Seaver, T. (NY)	249	Carlton, S. (Phi)	.99	Nolan, G. (Cin)	1.99
Niekro, P. (Atl)	282[1]	Gibson, B. (StL)	7.32	Niekro, P. (Atl)	1.69	Gibson, B. (StL)	208	Nolan, G. (Cin)	1.01	Sutton, D. (LA)	2.08

Adjusted ERA		Component ERA		Opponents' Batting Avg.		Adjusted Pitching Runs		Win Shares – Pitchers		TPW – Pitchers	
Carlton, S. (Phi)	182	Sutton, D. (LA)	1.63	Sutton, D. (LA)	.189	Carlton, S. (Phi)	58	Carlton, S. (Phi)	40	Carlton, S. (Phi)	6.8
Nolan, G. (Cin)	161	Carlton, S. (Phi)	1.92	Carlton, S. (Phi)	.206	Sutton, D. (LA)	37	Gibson, B. (StL)	29	Gibson, B. (StL)	3.8
Sutton, D. (LA)	160	Nolan, G. (Cin)	2.22	Gibson, B. (StL)	.224	Matlack, J. (NY)	30	Sutton, D. (LA)	24	Sutton, D. (LA)	3.8

1972 American League

TEAM	G	W	L	PCT	GB	R	OR	EW	AB	H	2B	3B	HR	TB	BB	SO	SB	CS	AVG	OBP	SLG	OPS	OPS+	BR/A	PF	RC
East																										
DET	156	86	70	.551	....	558	514	84	5099	1206	179	32	122	1815	483	793	17	**21**	.237	.306	.356	.662	100	0	103	548
BOS	155	85	70	.548	0.5	**640**	620	80	5208	1289	**229**	**34**	124	**1958**	522	858	66	30	.248	.320	**.376**	**.696**	108	57	106	**631**
BAL	154	80	74	.519	5	519	**430**	91	5028	1153	193	29	100	1704	507	935	78	41	.229	.298	.339	.643	95	-21	103	521
NY	155	79	76	.510	6.5	557	527	82	5168	1288	201	24	103	1846	491	**689**	71	42	.249	.318	.357	.675	111	67	97	587
CLE	156	72	84	.462	14	472	519	71	5207	1220	187	18	91	1716	420	762	49	53	.234	.295	.330	.624	89	-79	103	493
MIL	156	65	91	.417	21	493	595	64	5124	1204	167	22	88	1679	472	868	64	57	.235	.303	.328	.631	96	-32	98	494
West																										
OAK	155	93	62	.600	....	604	457	99	5200	1248	195	29	**134**	1903	463	886	87	48	.240	.308	.366	.674	**113**	71	95	583
CHI	154	87	67	.565	5.5	566	538	81	5083	1208	170	28	108	1758	511	991	100	52	.238	.311	.346	.657	100	7	102	549
MIN	154	77	77	.500	15.5	537	535	77	**5234**	1277	182	31	93	1800	478	905	53	41	.244	.311	.344	.655	97	-19	105	553
KC	154	76	78	.494	16.5	580	545	82	5167	**1317**	220	26	78	1823	**534**	711	85	44	**.255**	**.329**	.353	.682	110	**72**	99	599
CAL	155	75	80	.484	18	454	533	65	5165	1249	171	26	78	1706	358	850	57	37	.242	.294	.330	.624	97	-28	94	486
TEX	154	54	100	.351	38.5	461	628	54	5029	1092	166	17	56	1460	503	926	**126**	73	.217	.292	.332	.582	83	-96	96	436
Total	929					6441			61712	14751	2260	316	1175		5742	10174	853	539	.239	.308	.343	.651				

Runs		Hits		Doubles		Triples		Home Runs		Total Bases	
Murcer, B. (NY)	102	Rudi, J. (Oak)	181	Piniella, L. (KC)	33	Fisk, C. (Bos)	9	Allen, D. (Chi)	37	Murcer, B. (NY)	314
Rudi, J. (Oak)	94	Piniella, L. (KC)	179	Rudi, J. (Oak)	32	Rudi, J. (Oak)	9	Murcer, B. (NY)	33	Allen, D. (Chi)	305
Harper, T. (Bos)	92	Murcer, B. (NY)	171	Murcer, B. (NY)	30	Blair, P. (Bal)	8	2 players tied with	26	Rudi, J. (Oak)	288

Runs Batted In		Bases On Balls		Stolen Bases		Batting Average		On-Base Percentage		Slugging Average	
Allen, D. (Chi)	113	Allen, D. (Chi)	99	Campaneris, B. (Oak)	52	Carew, R. (Min)	.318	Allen, D. (Chi)	.422	Allen, D. (Chi)	.603
Mayberry, J. (KC)	100	White, R. (NY)	99	Nelson, D. (Tex)	51	Piniella, L. (KC)	.312	May, C. (Chi)	.408	Fisk, C. (Bos)	.538
Murcer, B. (NY)	96	Killebrew, H. (Min)	94	Patek, F. (KC)	33	Allen, D. (Chi)	.308	Mayberry, J. (KC)	.396	Murcer, B. (NY)	.537

Adjusted OPS		Adjusted Batting Runs		Runs Created/Game		Fielding Runs		Win Shares – Batters		TPW – Batters	
Allen, D. (Chi)	198	Allen, D. (Chi)	66.0	Allen, D. (Chi)	9.40	Rodriguez, A. (Det)	24.7	Allen, D. (Chi)	40	Allen, D. (Chi)	6.3
Murcer, B. (NY)	171	Murcer, B. (NY)	48.0	Mayberry, J. (KC)	7.40	Campaneris, B. (Oak)	20.4	Murcer, B. (NY)	36	Murcer, B. (NY)	4.9
Mayberry, J. (KC)	168	Mayberry, J. (KC)	44.0	Fisk, C. (Bos)	7.20	Patek, F. (KC)	20.2	Fisk, C. (Bos)	33	Fisk, C. (Bos)	4.8

TEAM	CG	SH	SV	IP	H	H/G	ER	HR	BB	SO	OAV	RAT	ERA	ERA+	CERA	PR+	PF	FA	E	DP	FR	BW	PW	FW	TPW	DIF
East																										
DET	46	11	33	1388¹	1212	7.9	456	101	465	952	.236	1.208	2.96	106	3.11	13.0	103	**.984**	96	137	15.5	.0	1.5	1.8	3.2	4.8
BOS	48	20	25	1382²	1309	8.5	533	101	512	918	.251	1.317	3.47	93	3.58	-16.6	105	.978	130	141	-27.7	6.5	-1.9	-3.1	1.4	6.6
BAL	62	20	21	1371²	1116	7.3	**385**	85	395	788	.224	**1.102**	**2.53**	122	**2.47**	**49.4**	100	.983	100	150	**31.8**	-2.4	**5.6**	**3.6**	6.8	-3.8
NY	35	19	39	1373¹	1306	8.6	465	87	419	625	.252	1.256	3.05	97	3.28	-15.5	96	.978	134	**179**		7.6	-1.8	.2	6.1	-4.1
CLE	47	13	25	1410	1232	7.9	457	123	534	846	.237	1.252	2.92	110	3.31	21.6	105	.981	116	157	17.1	-9.0	2.5	1.9	-4.6	-1.4
MIL	37	14	32	1391²	1289	8.3	533	116	486	740	.247	1.275	3.45	88	3.38	-64.2	99	.977	139	145	-1.5	-3.7	-7.3	-.2	-11.1	-1.9
West																										
OAK	42	**23**	**43**	**1417²**	1170	7.4	406	96	418	862	.226	1.120	2.58	110	2.63	26.2	93	.979	130	146	15.7	8.0	3.0	1.8	**12.8**	3.2
CHI	36	14	42	1385¹	1269	8.2	480	94	431	936	.245	1.227	3.12	100	3.16	30.4	102	.977	135	136	-29.7	.8	3.5	-3.4	.9	9.1
MIN	37	17	34	1399¹	1188	7.6	441	105	444	838	.230	1.166	2.84	113	2.88	43.5	105	.974	159	133	11.0	-2.1	5.0	1.3	4.1	-4.1
KC	44	16	28	1381¹	1293	8.4	497	**85**	405	801	.251	1.229	3.24	93	3.18	-14.2	99	.981	116	164	-18.1	**8.2**	-1.6	-2.1	4.6	-5.6
CAL	57	18	16	1377²	**1109**	7.2	468	90	620	**1000**	**.222**	1.255	3.06	95	3.06	-35.4	95	.981	114	135	11.6	-3.2	-4.0	1.3	-5.9	3.9
TEX	11	8	34	1374²	1258	8.2	539	92	613	868	.246	1.361	3.53	**85**	3.62	-52.4	98	.972	166	147	-28.2	-10.9	-6.0	-3.2	-20.0	-3.0
Total	502	193	372	16653²		8.0	5660					1.231	3.06													

Wins		Win Percentage		Games		Complete Games		Shutouts		Saves	
Perry, G. (Cle)	24	Hunter, C. (Oak)	.750	Lindblad, P. (Tex)	66	Perry, G. (Cle)	29	Ryan, N. (Cal)	9	Lyle, S. (NY)	35
Wood, W. (Chi)	24	Tiant, L. (Bos)	.714	Fingers, R. (Oak)	65	Lolich, M. (Det)	23	Wood, W. (Chi)	8	Forster, T. (Chi)	29
Lolich, M. (Det)	22	Odom, B. (Oak)	.714	Granger, W. (Min)	63	2 players tied with	20	Stottlemyre, M. (NY)	7	Fingers, R. (Oak)	21

Innings Pitched		Fewest Hits/Game		Fewest BB/Game		Strikeouts		Ratio		Earned Run Average	
Wood, W. (Chi)	376²	Ryan, N. (Cal)	5.26	Peterson, F. (NY)	1.58	Ryan, N. (Cal)	329	Nelson, R. (KC)	.87	Tiant, L. (Bos)	1.91
Perry, G. (Cle)	342²	Hunter, C. (Oak)	6.09	Nelson, R. (KC)	1.61	Lolich, M. (Det)	250	Hunter, C. (Oak)	.91	Perry, G. (Cle)	1.92
Lolich, M. (Det)	327¹	Nelson, R. (KC)	6.23	Kline, S. (NY)	1.68	Perry, G. (Cle)	234	Perry, G. (Cle)	.98	Hunter, C. (Oak)	2.04

Adjusted ERA		Component ERA		Opponents' Batting Avg.		Adjusted Pitching Runs		Win Shares – Pitchers		TPW – Pitchers	
Tiant, L. (Bos)	168	Nelson, R. (KC)	1.66	Ryan, N. (Cal)	.171	Perry, G. (Cle)	45	Perry, G. (Cle)	39	Perry, G. (Cle)	5.2
Perry, G. (Cle)	168	Hunter, C. (Oak)	1.70	Hunter, C. (Oak)	.189	Wood, W. (Chi)	34	Wood, W. (Chi)	29	Wood, W. (Chi)	3.6
Palmer, J. (Bal)	149	Perry, G. (Cle)	1.93	Nelson, R. (KC)	.196	Tiant, L. (Bos)	29	Lolich, M. (Det)	26	Palmer, J. (Bal)	3.2

1973 National League

TEAM	G	W	L	PCT	GB	R	OR	EW	AB	H	2B	3B	HR	TB	BB	SO	SB	CS	AVG	OBP	SLG	OPS	OPS+	BR/A	PF	RC
East																										
NY	161	82	79	.509	....	608	588	83	5457	1345	198	24	85	1846	540	805	27	**22**	.246	.317	.338	.655	89	-73	98	581
STL	162	81	81	.500	1.5	643	603	86	5478	1418	240	35	75	1953	531	796	100	46	.259	.328	.357	.684	96	-18	100	633
PIT	162	80	82	.494	2.5	704	693	82	5608	1465	**257**	44	154	2272	432	842	23	30	.261	.317	.405	.722	108	40	97	695
MON	162	79	83	.488	3.5	668	702	77	5369	1345	190	23	125	1956	**695**	**777**	77	68	.251	**.341**	.364	.706	99	-2	104	670
CHI	161	77	84	.478	5	614	655	75	5363	1322	201	21	117	1916	575	855	65	58	.247	.322	.357	.679	88	-87	107	604
PHI	162	71	91	.438	11.5	642	717	72	5546	1381	218	29	134	2059	476	979	51	47	.249	.312	.371	.683	93	-65	103	639
West																										
CIN	162	99	63	.611	....	741	621	95	5505	1398	232	34	137	2109	639	947	**148**	55	.254	.335	.383	.718	**111**	96	95	722
LA	162	95	66	.590	3.5	675	**565**	95	5604	1473	219	29	110	2080	497	795	109	50	.263	.326	.371	.697	104	29	96	673
SF	162	88	74	.543	11	739	702	85	5537	1452	212	**52**	161	2251	590	913	112	52	.262	.337	.407	.744	108	62	104	763
HOU	162	82	80	.506	17	681	672	82	5532	1391	216	35	134	2079	469	962	92	48	.251	.314	.376	.690	97	-26	100	638
ATL	162	76	85	.472	22.5	**799**	774	83	**5631**	**1497**	219	34	**206**	**2402**	608	870	84	40	**.266**	.341	**.427**	**.768**	110	82	107	**824**
SD	162	60	102	.370	39	548	770	54	5457	1330	198	26	112	1916	401	966	88	36	.244	.298	.351	.649	93	-57	92	564
Total	971					8062			66087	16817	2600	386	1550		6453	10507	976	552	.254	.324	.376	.700				

Runs		Hits		Doubles		Triples		Home Runs		Total Bases	
Bonds, B. (SF)	131	Rose, P. (Cin)	230	Stargell, W. (Pit)	43	Metzger, R. (Hou)	14	Stargell, W. (Pit)	44	Bonds, B. (SF)	341
Morgan, J. (Cin)	116	Garr, R. (Atl)	200	Oliver, A. (Pit)	38	Maddox, G. (SF)	10	Johnson, D. (Atl)	43	Stargell, W. (Pit)	337
Rose, P. (Cin)	115	Brock, L. (StL)	193	3 players tied with	36	Matthews, G. (SF)	10	Evans, D. (Atl)	41	Evans, D. (Atl)	331

Runs Batted In		Bases On Balls		Stolen Bases		Batting Average		On-Base Percentage		Slugging Average	
Stargell, W. (Pit)	119	Evans, D. (Atl)	124	Brock, L. (StL)	70	Rose, P. (Cin)	.338	Singleton, K. (Mon)	.429	Stargell, W. (Pit)	.646
May, L. (Hou)	105	Singleton, K. (Mon)	123	Morgan, J. (Cin)	67	Cedeno, C. (Hou)	.320	Fairly, R. (Mon)	.422	Evans, D. (Atl)	.556
2 players tied with	104	Morgan, J. (Cin)	111	Cedeno, C. (Hou)	56	Maddox, G. (SF)	.319	Morgan, J. (Cin)	.408	Johnson, D. (Atl)	.546

Adjusted OPS		Adjusted Batting Runs		Runs Created/Game		Fielding Runs		Win Shares – Batters		TPW – Batters	
Stargell, W. (Pit)	189	Stargell, W. (Pit)	62.0	Stargell, W. (Pit)	9.80	Sizemore, T. (StL)	22.8	Morgan, J. (Cin)	40	Morgan, J. (Cin)	7.4
Perez, T. (Cin)	162	Morgan, J. (Cin)	58.0	Evans, D. (Atl)	8.50	Cey, R. (LA)	19.6	Stargell, W. (Pit)	36	Stargell, W. (Pit)	5.9
Morgan, J. (Cin)	157	Perez, T. (Cin)	48.0	Perez, T. (Cin)	7.90	Garrett, W. (NY)	15.7	Rose, P. (Cin)	34	Evans, D. (Atl)	5.7

TEAM	CG	SH	SV	IP	H	H/G	ER	HR	BB	SO	OAV	RAT	ERA	ERA+	CERA	PR+	PF	FA	E	DP	FR	BW	PW	FW	TPW	DIF
East																										
NY	47	15	40	1465	1345	8.3	531	127	490	**1027**	.245	1.253	3.26	111	3.34	47.4	99	.980	126	140	9.2	-7.6	4.9	1.0	-1.7	3.7
STL	42	14	36	**1460²**	1366	**0.8**	527	105	486	867	.245	**.127**	**0.32**	112	3.30	63.5	100	.975	159	149	-0.6	-1.9	6.6	-.1	4.7	-4.7
PIT	26	11	**44**	1450²	1426	0.9	601	110	564	839	.258	.137	0.37	94	3.85	-35.9	96	.976	151	156	-0.2	4.2	-3.7	.0	.5	-1.5
MON	26	6	38	1451²	1356	**0.8**	598	128	681	866	.250	.140	0.37	103	3.94	12.1	104	.974	163	156	1.8	-.2	1.3	.2	1.3	-3.3
CHI	27	13	40	1437²	1471	0.9	584	128	**438**	885	.267	.133	0.37	108	3.80	78.6	108	.975	157	155	-33.1	-9.0	**8.2**	-3.4	-4.3	1.3
PHI	**49**	11	22	1447¹	1435	0.9	642	131	632	919	.263	.143	0.40	95	4.17	-48.6	104	.979	134	**179**	15.8	-6.7	-5.1	1.6	-10.1	.1
West																										
CIN	39	**17**	43	1473	1389	8.5	556	135	518	801	.252	1.295	3.40	100	3.55	-36.5	93	**.982**	115	162	**31.5**	10.0	-3.8	**3.3**	9.5	8.5
LA	45	15	38	1491	**1270**	7.7	**497**	129	461	961	**.231**	1.161	3.00	115	**2.93**	54.2	94	.981	125	166	18.0	3.1	5.6	1.9	**10.6**	4.4
SF	33	8	**44**	1452¹	1442	0.9	611	145	485	787	.257	.133	0.38	101	3.80	17.4	104	.974	163	138	-14.6	6.5	1.8	-1.5	6.8	.2
HOU	45	14	26	**1460²**	1389	0.9	608	111	575	907	.252	.135	0.37	97	3.64	-22.9	99	.981	116	140	-2.1	-2.7	-2.4	-.2	-5.3	6.3
ATL	34	9	35	1462	1467	9.0	690	144	575	803	.263	1.397	4.25	93	4.11	-38.3	107	.974	166	142	-13.0	8.6	-4.0	-1.4	3.2	-7.2
SD	34	10	23	1430	1461	9.2	661	157	548	845	.267	1.405	4.16	**83**	4.20	-99.3	95	.973	170	152	-10.4	-5.9	-10.3	-1.1	-17.3	-3.7
Total	447	143	429	108903		1.4	7106					.214	0.59													

Wins		Win Percentage		Games		Complete Games		Shutouts		Saves	
Bryant, R. (SF)	24	John, T. (LA)	.696	Marshall, M. (Mon)	92	Carlton, S. (Phi)	18	Billingham, J. (Cin)	7	Marshall, M. (Mon)	31
Billingham, J. (Cin)	19	Gullett, D. (Cin)	.692	Borbon, P. (Cin)	80	Seaver, T. (NY)	18	Roberts, D. (Hou)	6	McGraw, T. (NY)	25
Seaver, T. (NY)	19	Bryant, R. (SF)	.667	Sosa, E. (SF)	71	Billingham, J. (Cin)	16	2 players tied with	5	2 players tied with	20

Innings Pitched		Fewest Hits/Game		Fewest BB/Game		Strikeouts		Ratio		Earned Run Average	
Billingham, J. (Cin)	293¹	Seaver, T. (NY)	6.80	Marichal, J. (SF)	1.61	Seaver, T. (NY)	251	Seaver, T. (NY)	.98	Seaver, T. (NY)	2.08
Carlton, S. (Phi)	293¹	Sutton, D. (LA)	6.88	Jenkins, F. (Chi)	1.89	Sutton, D. (LA)	223	Sutton, D. (LA)	.98	Sutton, D. (LA)	2.42
Seaver, T. (NY)	290	Twitchell, W. (Phi)	6.93	Barr, J. (SF)	1.91	Matlack, J. (NY)	205	Messersmith, A. (LA)	1.09	Twitchell, W. (Phi)	2.50

Adjusted ERA		Component ERA		Opponents' Batting Avg.		Adjusted Pitching Runs		Win Shares – Pitchers		TPW – Pitchers	
Seaver, T. (NY)	174	Seaver, T. (NY)	2.05	Seaver, T. (NY)	.206	Seaver, T. (NY)	48	Seaver, T. (NY)	29	Seaver, T. (NY)	5.3
Twitchell, W. (Phi)	152	Sutton, D. (LA)	2.08	Sutton, D. (LA)	.209	Reuschel, R. (Chi)	30	Marshall, M. (Mon)	23	Renko, S. (Mon)	3.7
Marshall, M. (Mon)	143	Gibson, B. (StL)	2.47	Wilson, D. (Hou)	.213	Twitchell, W. (Phi)	30	2 players tied with	22	Reuschel, R. (Chi)	2.8

1973 American League

TEAM	G	W	L	PCT	GB	R	OR	EW	AB	H	2B	3B	HR	TB	BB	SO	SB	CS	AVG	OBP	SLG	OPS	OPS+	BR/A	PF	RC
East																										
BAL	162	97	65	.599	....	754	**561**	104	5537	1474	229	**48**	119	2156	**648**	752	**146**	64	.266	**.348**	.389	.737	108	**78**	99	**763**
BOS	162	89	73	.549	8	738	647	92	5513	1472	235	30	147	2208	581	799	114	45	.267	.340	**.401**	**.741**	102	27	106	749
DET	162	85	77	.525	12	642	674	77	5508	1400	213	32	157	2148	509	722	28	**30**	.254	.322	.390	.712	93	-54	107	672
NY	162	80	82	.494	17	641	610	85	5492	1435	212	17	131	2074	489	**680**	47	43	.261	.324	.378	.702	101	-6	97	653
MIL	162	74	88	.457	23	708	731	78	5526	1399	229	40	145	2143	563	977	110	66	.253	.327	.388	.715	103	18	98	700
CLE	162	71	91	.438	26	680	826	65	5592	1429	205	29	**158**	2166	471	793	60	68	.256	.317	.387	.704	96	-52	102	664
West																										
OAK	162	94	68	.580	....	**758**	615	98	5507	1431	216	28	147	2144	595	919	128	57	.260	.336	.389	.725	**109**	77	95	728
KC	162	88	74	.543	6	755	752	81	5508	1440	239	40	114	2101	644	696	105	69	.261	.342	.381	.723	96	-21	108	718
MIN	162	81	81	.500	13	738	692	86	**5625**	**1521**	240	44	120	**2209**	598	954	87	46	**.270**	.344	.393	.737	103	32	104	754
CAL	162	79	83	.488	15	629	657	77	5505	1395	183	29	93	1915	509	816	59	47	.253	.320	.348	.668	96	-37	92	607
CHI	162	77	85	.475	17	652	705	75	5475	1400	228	38	111	2037	537	952	83	73	.256	.326	.372	.698	93	-60	103	645
TEX	162	57	105	.352	37	619	844	57	5488	1397	195	29	110	1980	503	791	91	53	.255	.320	.361	.681	96	-34	96	627
Total	972					8314			66276	17193	2624	404	1552		6647	9851	1058	661	.259	.331	.381	.712				

Runs		Hits		Doubles		Triples		Home Runs		Total Bases	
Jackson, R. (Oak)	99	Carew, R. (Min)	203	Bando, S. (Oak)	32	Bumbry, A. (Bal)	11	Jackson, R. (Oak)	32	Bando, S. (Oak)	295
3 players tied with	98	May, D. (Mil)	189	Garcia, P. (Mil)	32	Carew, R. (Min)	11	Burroughs, J. (Tex)	30	May, D. (Mil)	295
		Murcer, B. (NY)	187	3 players tied with	30	Orta, J. (Chi)	10	Robinson, F. (Cal)	30	Scott, G. (Mil)	295

Runs Batted In		Bases On Balls		Stolen Bases		Batting Average		On-Base Percentage		Slugging Average	
Jackson, R. (Oak)	117	Mayberry, J. (KC)	122	Harper, T. (Bos)	54	Carew, R. (Min)	.350	Mayberry, J. (KC)	.420	Jackson, R. (Oak)	.531
Scott, G. (Mil)	107	Grich, B. (Bal)	107	North, B. (Oak)	53	Scott, G. (Mil)	.306	Carew, R. (Min)	.415	Bando, S. (Oak)	.498
Mayberry, J. (KC)	100	Yastrzemski, C. (Bos)	105	Nelson, D. (Tex)	43	Davis, T. (Bal)	.306	Yastrzemski, C. (Bos)	.411	Robinson, F. (Cal)	.489

Adjusted OPS		Adjusted Batting Runs		Runs Created/Game		Fielding Runs		Win Shares – Batters		TPW – Batters	
Jackson, R. (Oak)	165	Jackson, R. (Oak)	49.0	Mayberry, J. (KC)	8.10	Grich, B. (Bal)	32.0	Jackson, R. (Oak)	32	Grich, B. (Bal)	6.2
Robinson, F. (Cal)	153	Bando, S. (Oak)	42.0	Jackson, R. (Oak)	7.40	Campaneris, B. (Oak)	26.5	Bando, S. (Oak)	31	Carew, R. (Min)	6.1
Bando, S. (Oak)	153	Robinson, F. (Cal)	39.0	Carew, R. (Min)	7.20	Patek, F. (KC)	24.7	Mayberry, J. (KC)	31	Jackson, R. (Oak)	4.3

TEAM	CG	SH	SV	IP	H	H/G	ER	HR	BB	SO	OAV	RAT	ERA	ERA+	CERA	PR+	PF	FA	E	DP	FR	BW	PW	FW	TPW	DIF
East																										
BAL	67	14	26	1461²	**1297**	8.0	498	124	475	715	**.240**	**1.212**	3.07	122	**3.17**	43.4	98	.981	119	184	**61.6**	**8.0**	4.4	**6.3**	**18.7**	-2.7
BOS	67	10	33	1440¹	1417	8.8	584	158	499	808	.259	1.330	3.65	110	3.98	49.7	105	.979	127	162	8.5	2.8	**5.1**	.9	8.7	-.7
DET	39	11	**46**	1447²	1468	9.1	627	154	493	911	.265	1.355	3.90	105	4.07	40.6	107	**.982**	112	144	-10.1	-5.5	4.2	-1.0	-2.4	6.4
NY	47	16	39	1427²	1379	8.7	530	109	**457**	708	.254	1.286	3.34	110	3.48	35.9	96	.976	156	172	15.5	-.6	3.7	1.6	4.6	-5.6
MIL	50	11	28	1454	1476	9.1	643	119	623	671	.265	1.444	3.98	94	4.21	-28.4	98	.977	145	167	-7.4	1.8	-2.9	-.8	-1.8	-5.2
CLE	55	9	21	**1464²**	1532	9.4	745	172	602	883	.271	1.457	4.58	86	4.62	-102.2	103	.978	139	174	-6.2	-5.3	-10.4	-.6	-16.4	6.4
West																										
OAK	46	16	41	1457¹	1311	8.1	533	143	494	797	.241	1.239	3.29	108	3.39	3.8	93	.978	137	170	38.0	7.9	.4	3.9	12.2	.8
KC	40	7	41	1449¹	1521	9.4	675	114	617	790	.273	1.475	4.19	98	4.36	3.1	108	.974	167	**192**	-19.5	-2.2	.3	-2.0	-3.9	10.9
MIN	48	**18**	34	1451²	1443	9.0	608	115	519	879	.259	1.352	3.77	105	3.85	36.8	104	.978	139	147	-6.4	3.3	3.8	-.6	6.4	-6.4
CAL	**72**	13	19	1456¹	1351	8.4	571	**104**	614	**1010**	.246	1.349	3.53	103	3.65	14.2	93	.975	156	165	-17.7	-3.8	-5.1	-1.8	-4.1	2.1
CHI	48	15	35	1456	1484	9.2	624	110	574	848	.266	1.413	3.86	103	4.13	35.4	104	.977	144	165	-20.3	-6.1	3.6	-2.1	-4.5	.5
TEX	35	10	27	1430	1514	9.5	737	130	680	831	.273	1.534	4.64	80	4.75	-109.0	98	.974	161	164	-36.7	-3.5	-11.1	-3.7	-18.4	-5.6
Total	614	150	390	17396²		8.9	7375					1.370	3.82													

Wins		Win Percentage		Games		Complete Games		Shutouts		Saves	
Wood, W. (Chi)	24	Hunter, C. (Oak)	.808	Hiller, J. (Det)	65	Perry, G. (Cle)	29	Blyleven, B. (Min)	9	Hiller, J. (Det)	38
Coleman, J. (Det)	23	Palmer, J. (Bal)	.710	Fingers, R. (Oak)	62	Ryan, N. (Cal)	26	Perry, G. (Cle)	7	Lyle, S. (NY)	27
Palmer, J. (Bal)	22	Blue, V. (Oak)	.690	Bird, D. (KC)	54	Blyleven, B. (Min)	25	Palmer, J. (Bal)	6	Fingers, R. (Oak)	22

Innings Pitched		Fewest Hits/Game		Fewest BB/Game		Strikeouts		Ratio		Earned Run Average	
Wood, W. (Chi)	359¹	Bibby, J. (Tex)	6.04	Kaat, J. (Chi,Min)	1.73	Ryan, N. (Cal)	383	Tiant, L. (Bos)	1.08	Palmer, J. (Bal)	2.40
Perry, G. (Cle)	344	Ryan, N. (Cal)	6.57	Blyleven, B. (Min)	1.86	Blyleven, B. (Min)	258	Blyleven, B. (Min)	1.12	Blyleven, B. (Min)	2.52
Ryan, N. (Cal)	326	Palmer, J. (Bal)	6.83	Holtzman, K. (Oak)	2.00	Singer, B. (Cal)	241	Hunter, C. (Oak)	1.14	Lee, B. (Bos)	2.75

Adjusted ERA		Component ERA		Opponents' Batting Avg.		Adjusted Pitching Runs		Win Shares – Pitchers		TPW – Pitchers	
Blyleven, B. (Min)	157	Palmer, J. (Bal)	2.51	Bibby, J. (Tex)	.192	Blyleven, B. (Min)	53	Blyleven, B. (Min)	29	Blyleven, B. (Min)	5.5
Palmer, J. (Bal)	156	Blyleven, B. (Min)	2.64	Ryan, N. (Cal)	.203	Lee, B. (Bos)	38	Palmer, J. (Bal)	28	Lee, B. (Bos)	3.9
Lee, B. (Bos)	146	Tiant, L. (Bos)	2.78	Palmer, J. (Bal)	.211	Palmer, J. (Bal)	31	Ryan, N. (Cal)	28	Palmer, J. (Bal)	3.2

1974 National League

TEAM	G	W	L	PCT	GB	R	OR	EW	AB	H	2B	3B	HR	TB	BB	SO	SB	CS	AVG	OBP	SLG	OPS	OPS+	BR/A	PF	RC
East																										
PIT	162	88	74	.543	....	751	657	92	**5702**	**1560**	238	46	114	**2232**	514	828	55	31	**.274**	.338	.391	.729	114	92	96	742
STL	161	86	75	.534	1.5	677	643	85	5620	1492	216	46	83	2049	531	752	**172**	62	.265	.334	.365	.698	102	25	99	685
PHI	162	80	82	.494	8	676	701	78	5494	1434	233	**50**	95	2052	469	822	115	58	.261	.322	.373	.696	96	-35	104	656
MON	161	79	82	.491	8.5	662	657	81	5343	1355	201	29	86	1872	652	812	124	49	.254	.338	.350	.689	93	-25	106	654
NY	162	71	91	.438	17	572	646	71	5468	1286	183	22	96	1801	597	**735**	43	**23**	.235	.314	.329	.643	87	-89	98	568
CHI	162	66	96	.407	22	669	826	64	5574	1397	221	42	110	2032	621	857	78	73	.251	.329	.365	.693	96	-41	104	666
West																										
LA	162	102	60	.630	....	**798**	**561**	108	5557	1511	231	34	**139**	2227	597	820	149	75	.272	**.346**	**.401**	**.746**	119	**136**	96	771
CIN	163	98	64	.605	4	776	631	98	5535	1437	**271**	35	135	2183	**693**	940	146	49	.260	.345	.394	.740	114	120	98	**774**
ATL	163	88	74	.543	14	661	563	94	5533	1375	202	37	120	2011	571	772	72	44	.249	.321	.363	.685	93	-53	104	647
HOU	162	81	81	.500	21	653	632	84	5489	1441	222	41	110	2075	471	864	108	65	.263	.324	.378	.702	106	29	96	661
SF	162	72	90	.444	30	634	723	70	5482	1380	228	38	93	1963	548	869	107	51	.252	.323	.358	.681	92	-57	105	641
SD	162	60	102	.370	42	541	830	48	5415	1239	196	27	99	1786	564	900	85	45	.229	.304	.330	.634	86	-99	96	553
Total	**972**					**8070**			**66212**	**16907**	**2642**	**447**	**1280**		**6828**	**9971**	**1254**	**625**	**.255**	**.328**	**.367**	**.695**				

Runs		Hits		Doubles		Triples		Home Runs		Total Bases	
Rose, P. (Cin)	110	Garr, R. (Atl)	214	Rose, P. (Cin)	45	Garr, R. (Atl)	17	Schmidt, M. (Phi)	36	Bench, J. (Cin)	315
Bench, J. (Cin)	108	Cash, D. (Pit)	206	Bench, J. (Cin)	38	Oliver, A. (Pit)	12	Bench, J. (Cin)	33	Schmidt, M. (Phi)	310
Schmidt, M. (Phi)	108	Garvey, S. (LA)	200	Oliver, A. (Pit)	38	Cash, D. (Phi)	11	Wynn, J. (LA)	32	Garr, R. (Atl)	305

Runs Batted In		Bases On Balls		Stolen Bases		Batting Average		On-Base Percentage		Slugging Average	
Bench, J. (Cin)	129	Evans, D. (Atl)	126	Brock, L. (StL)	118	Garr, R. (Atl)	.353	Morgan, J. (Cin)	.430	Schmidt, M. (Phi)	.546
Schmidt, M. (Phi)	116	Morgan, J. (Cin)	120	Lopes, D. (LA)	59	Oliver, A. (Pit)	.321	Stargell, W. (Pit)	.409	Stargell, W. (Pit)	.537
Garvey, S. (LA)	111	Wynn, J. (LA)	108	Morgan, J. (Cin)	58	Gross, G. (Hou)	.314	Bailey, B. (Mon)	.400	Smith, R. (StL)	.528

Adjusted OPS		Adjusted Batting Runs		Runs Created/Game		Fielding Runs		Win Shares – Batters		TPW – Batters	
Stargell, W. (Pit)	169	Morgan, J. (Cin)	56.0	Morgan, J. (Cin)	8.70	Cash, D. (Phi)	27.4	Schmidt, M. (Phi)	39	Morgan, J. (Cin)	7.9
Morgan, J. (Cin)	160	Stargell, W. (Pit)	48.0	Stargell, W. (Pit)	8.40	Sizemore, T. (StL)	25.5	Morgan, J. (Cin)	37	Schmidt, M. (Phi)	7.1
Smith, R. (StL)	158	Schmidt, M. (Phi)	44.0	Schmidt, M. (Phi)	8.10	Concepcion, D. (Cin)	25.3	Bench, J. (Cin)	34	Concepcion, D. (Cin)	5.6

TEAM	CG	SH	SV	IP	H	H/G	ER	HR	BB	SO	OAV	RAT	ERA	ERA+	CERA	PR+	PF	FA	E	DP	FR	BW	PW	FW	TPW	DIF
East																										
PIT	**51**	9	17	1466	1428	8.8	568	93	543	721	.256	1.344	3.49	99	3.59	-18.6	95	.975	162	154	7.6	9.6	-1.9	.8	8.4	-1.4
STL	37	13	20	1473¹	1399	8.6	570	97	616	794	.254	1.368	3.48	103	3.65	-8.9	99	.977	147	**192**	23.2	2.6	-.9	2.4	4.1	1.9
PHI	46	4	19	1447¹	1394	8.7	629	111	682	892	.257	1.434	3.91	97	4.03	-51.8	104	.976	148	168	29.1	-3.7	-5.4	**3.0**	-6.0	5.0
MON	35	8	**27**	1429	1340	8.4	572	99	544	822	.249	1.318	3.60	106	3.50	43.4	106	.976	153	157	-5.4	-2.6	4.5	-.6	1.3	-2.3
NY	46	15	14	1470¹	1433	8.8	559	99	504	908	.257	1.317	3.42	104	3.52	19.4	98	.975	158	150	4.5	-9.3	2.0	.5	-6.8	-3.2
CHI	23	6	26	1466¹	1593	9.8	697	122	576	895	.277	1.479	4.28	89	4.41	-6.5	105	.969	199	141	-72.5	-4.3	-.7	-7.5	-12.5	-2.5
West																										
LA	33	19	23	1465¹	**1272**	**7.8**	**483**	112	464	**943**	**.233**	**1.185**	**2.97**	115	**2.96**	78.8	94	.975	157	122	-10.5	**14.2**	8.2	-1.1	**21.3**	-.3
CIN	34	11	**27**	1466¹	1364	8.4	555	126	536	875	.247	1.296	3.41	102	3.47	-16.4	96	.979	134	151	27.3	12.5	-1.7	2.8	13.6	3.4
ATL	46	**21**	22	**1474¹**	1343	8.2	500	97	488	772	.244	1.242	3.05	124	3.17	**94.0**	104	.979	132	161	23.7	-5.6	**9.8**	2.5	6.7	.3
HOU	36	18	18	1450²	1396	8.7	557	**84**	601	738	.255	1.377	3.46	100	3.69	-22.8	96	**.982**	**113**	161	19.9	3.0	-2.4	2.1	2.7	-2.7
SF	27	11	25	1439	1409	8.8	604	116	559	756	.257	1.368	3.78	101	3.77	5.3	105	.972	175	153	-6.2	-5.9	.6	-.6	-6.0	-3.0
SD	25	7	19	1445²	1536	9.6	735	124	715	855	.275	1.557	4.69	**78**	4.69	-128.0	98	.973	170	126	-42.0	-10.3	-13.3	-4.4	-28.0	7.0
Total	**439**	**142**	**257**	**17493²**		**8.7**	**7029**					**1.357**	**3.62**													

Wins		Win Percentage		Games		Complete Games		Shutouts		Saves	
Messersmith, A. (LA)	20	Messersmith, A. (LA)	.769	Marshall, M. (LA)	106	Niekro, P. (Atl)	18	Matlack, J. (NY)	7	Marshall, M. (LA)	21
Niekro, P. (Atl)	20	Caldwell, M. (SF)	.737	Hardy, L. (SD)	76	Carlton, S. (Phi)	17	Niekro, P. (Atl)	6	Moffitt, R. (SF)	15
2 players tied with	19	Sutton, D. (LA)	.679	Borbon, P. (Cin)	73	Lonborg, J. (Phi)	16	4 players tied with	5	Borbon, P. (Cin)	14

Innings Pitched		Fewest Hits/Game		Fewest BB/Game		Strikeouts		Ratio		Earned Run Average	
Niekro, P. (Atl)	302¹	Capra, B. (Atl)	6.76	Barr, J. (SF)	1.76	Carlton, S. (Phi)	240	Messersmith, A. (LA)	1.10	Capra, B. (Atl)	2.28
Messersmith, A. (LA)	292¹	Messersmith, A. (LA)	6.99	Reed, R. (Atl)	1.98	Messersmith, A. (LA)	221	Niekro, P. (Atl)	1.11	Niekro, P. (Atl)	2.38
Carlton, S. (Phi)	291	Niekro, P. (Atl)	7.41	Ellis, D. (Pit)	2.09	Seaver, T. (NY)	201	Matlack, J. (NY)	1.12	Matlack, J. (NY)	2.41

Adjusted ERA		Component ERA		Opponents' Batting Avg.		Adjusted Pitching Runs		Win Shares – Pitchers		TPW – Pitchers	
Capra, B. (Atl)	166	Matlack, J. (NY)	2.35	Capra, B. (Atl)	.208	Niekro, P. (Atl)	42	Niekro, P. (Atl)	28	Niekro, P. (Atl)	4.4
Niekro, P. (Atl)	159	Capra, B. (Atl)	2.47	Messersmith, A. (LA)	.212	Matlack, J. (NY)	33	Messersmith, A. (LA)	25	Messersmith, A. (LA)	3.9
Matlack, J. (NY)	148	Messersmith, A. (LA)	2.54	Gullett, D. (Cin)	.222	Capra, B. (Atl)	33	Matlack, J. (NY)	24	Barr, J. (SF)	3.5

1974 American League

TEAM	G	W	L	PCT	GB	R	OR	EW	AB	H	2B	3B	HR	TB	BB	SO	SB	CS	AVG	OBP	SLG	OPS	OPS+	BR/A	PF	RC
East																										
BAL	162	91	71	.562	....	659	612	87	5535	1418	226	27	116	2046	509	770	145	58	.256	.325	.370	.695	103	31	97	669
NY	162	89	73	.549	2	671	623	87	5524	1451	220	30	101	2034	515	**690**	53	**35**	.263	.328	.368	.696	103	21	97	663
BOS	162	84	78	.519	7	**696**	661	85	5499	1449	**236**	31	109	2074	**569**	811	104	58	.264	.336	.377	.713	98	-3	107	697
CLE	162	77	85	.475	14	662	694	77	5474	1395	201	19	131	2027	432	756	79	68	.255	.312	.370	.683	97	-40	99	608
MIL	162	76	86	.469	15	647	660	79	5472	1335	228	**49**	120	2021	500	909	106	75	.244	.310	.369	.680	95	-42	99	621
DET	162	72	90	.444	19	620	768	64	5568	1375	200	35	131	2038	436	784	67	38	.247	.304	.366	.670	89	-83	103	605
West																										
OAK	162	90	72	.556	....	689	**551**	99	5331	1315	205	37	132	1990	568	876	**164**	93	.247	.324	.373	.697	107	49	94	646
TEX	161	84	76	.525	5	690	698	79	5449	1482	198	39	99	2055	508	710	113	80	**.272**	**.338**	.377	.715	**108**	**55**	97	675
MIN	163	82	80	.506	8	673	669	81	**5632**	**1530**	190	37	111	2127	520	791	74	45	.272	.338	.378	.716	102	19	104	**705**
CHI	163	80	80	.500	9	684	721	76	5577	1492	225	23	135	2168	519	858	64	53	.268	.333	**.389**	**.721**	104	28	102	699
KC	162	77	85	.475	13	667	662	82	5582	1448	232	42	89	2031	550	768	146	76	.259	.329	.364	.693	94	-34	106	666
CAL	163	68	94	.420	22	618	657	76	5401	1372	203	31	95	1922	509	801	119	79	.254	.323	.356	.679	101	4	94	613
Total	**973**					**7976**			**66044**	**17062**	**2564**	**400**	**1369**		**6135**	**9524**	**1234**	**758**	**.258**	**.325**	**.371**	**.697**				

Runs		Hits		Doubles		Triples		Home Runs		Total Bases	
Yastrzemski, C. (Bos)	93	Carew, R. (Min)	218	Rudi, J. (Oak)	39	Rivers, M. (Cal)	11	Allen, D. (Chi)	32	Rudi, J. (Oak)	287
Grich, B. (Bal)	92	Davis, T. (Bal)	181	McRae, H. (KC)	36	Otis, A. (KC)	9	Jackson, R. (Oak)	29	Henderson, K. (Chi)	281
Jackson, R. (Oak)	90	Money, D. (Mil)	178	Scott, G. (Mil)	36	4 players tied with	8	Tenace, G. (Oak)	26	Burroughs, J. (Tex)	279

Runs Batted In		Bases On Balls		Stolen Bases		Batting Average		On-Base Percentage		Slugging Average	
Burroughs, J. (Tex)	118	Tenace, G. (Oak)	110	North, B. (Oak)	54	Carew, R. (Min)	.364	Carew, R. (Min)	.435	Allen, D. (Chi)	.563
Bando, S. (Oak)	103	Yastrzemski, C. (Bos)	104	Carew, R. (Min)	38	Orta, J. (Chi)	.316	Yastrzemski, C. (Bos)	.421	Jackson, R. (Oak)	.514
Rudi, J. (Oak)	99	Burroughs, J. (Tex)	91	Lowenstein, J. (Cle)	36	McRae, H. (KC)	.310	Burroughs, J. (Tex)	.405	Burroughs, J. (Tex)	.504

Adjusted OPS		Adjusted Batting Runs		Runs Created/Game		Fielding Runs		Win Shares – Batters		TPW – Batters	
Jackson, R. (Oak)	171	Jackson, R. (Oak)	53.0	Jackson, R. (Oak)	7.70	Robinson, B. (Bal)	21.1	Burroughs, J. (Tex)	33	Carew, R. (Min)	6.2
Burroughs, J. (Tex)	164	Burroughs, J. (Tex)	49.0	Allen, D. (Chi)	7.50	Rodriguez, A. (Det)	19.3	Carew, R. (Min)	32	Grich, B. (Bal)	5.5
Allen, D. (Chi)	164	Carew, R. (Min)	43.0	Carew, R. (Min)	7.40	Nettles, G. (NY)	15.5	Grich, B. (Bal)	32	Jackson, R. (Oak)	5.1

TEAM	CG	SH	SV	IP	H	H/G	ER	HR	BB	SO	OAV	RAT	ERA	ERA+	CERA	PR+	PF	FA	E	DP	FR	BW	PW	FW	TPW	DIF
East																										
BAL	57	**16**	25	**1474**	1393	8.5	536	101	480	701	.253	1.271	3.27	105	3.36	8.4	95	**.980**	128	174	18.8	3.3	.9	2.0	6.1	3.9
NY	53	13	24	1455¹	1402	8.7	535	104	528	829	.256	1.326	3.31	105	3.63	-0.1	96	.977	142	158	**26.5**	2.2	.0	**2.8**	5.0	3.0
BOS	71	12	18	1455¹	1462	9.0	601	126	463	751	.262	1.323	3.72	103	3.76	33.7	106	.977	145	156	-13.8	-.4	3.5	-1.4	1.7	1.3
CLE	45	9	27	1445²	1419	8.8	610	138	479	650	.260	1.313	3.80	100	3.79	-38.0	100	.977	146	157	4.4	-4.2	-4.0	.5	-7.7	3.7
MIL	43	11	24	1457²	1476	9.1	609	126	493	621	.266	1.351	3.76	96	3.88	-32.6	100	.980	**127**	168	8.5	-4.4	-3.4	.9	-6.9	1.9
DET	54	7	15	1455²	1443	8.9	673	148	621	869	.262	1.418	4.16	**91**	4.21	-51.8	105	.975	158	155	-8.3	-8.7	-5.4	-.9	-15.0	6.0
West																										
OAK	49	12	28	1439³	**1322**	**8.3**	**472**	**90**	**430**	755	**.246**	**1.217**	**2.95**	112	**3.07**	36.3	92	.977	141	154	21.4	5.1	3.8	2.2	**11.1**	-2.1
TEX	62	16	12	1433³	1423	8.9	608	126	449	871	.260	1.306	3.82	93	3.77	-50.0	98	.974	163	164	5.4	**5.7**	-5.2	.6	1.0	3.0
MIN	43	11	**29**	1455¹	1436	8.9	588	115	513	934	.260	1.339	3.64	103	3.81	28.9	104	.976	151	164	-11.1	2.0	3.0	-1.2	3.9	-2.9
CHI	55	11	**29**	1465²	1470	9.0	641	103	548	826	.263	1.377	3.94	95	3.96	-18.2	103	.977	147	**188**	-16.0	2.9	-1.9	-1.7	-.7	.7
KC	54	13	17	1471²	1477	9.0	574	91	482	731	.263	1.331	3.51	109	3.59	**71.5**	105	.976	152	166	-21.7	-3.6	**7.5**	-2.3	1.6	-5.6
CAL	64	13	12	1439	1339	8.4	563	101	649	**986**	.248	1.382	3.52	98	3.83	-1.8	95	.976	147	150	-13.1	.4	-.2	-1.4	-1.1	-11.9
Total	**650**	**144**	**260**	**17448²**		**8.8**	**7010**					**1.329**	**3.62**													

Wins		Win Percentage		Games		Complete Games		Shutouts		Saves	
Hunter, C. (Oak)	25	Cuellar, M. (Bal)	.688	Fingers, R. (Oak)	76	Jenkins, F. (Tex)	29	Tiant, L. (Bos)	7	Forster, T. (Chi)	24
Jenkins, F. (Tex)	25	Fitzmorris, A. (KC)	.684	Murphy, T. (Mil)	70	Perry, G. (Cle)	28	Hunter, C. (Oak)	6	Murphy, T. (Mil)	20
4 players tied with	22	2 players tied with	.676	Foucault, S. (Tex)	69	Lolich, M. (Det)	27	Jenkins, F. (Tex)	6	Campbell, B. (Min)	19

Innings Pitched		Fewest Hits/Game		Fewest BB/Game		Strikeouts		Ratio		Earned Run Average	
Ryan, N. (Cal)	332²	Ryan, N. (Cal)	5.98	Jenkins, F. (Tex)	1.23	Ryan, N. (Cal)	367	Tiant, L. (Bos)	.99	Hunter, C. (Oak)	2.49
Jenkins, F. (Tex)	328¹	Perry, G. (Cle)	6.42	Hunter, C. (Oak)	1.30	Blyleven, B. (Min)	249	Jenkins, F. (Tex)	1.01	Perry, G. (Cle)	2.51
Perry, G. (Cle)	322¹	Dalcanton, B. (KC)	6.93	Holtzman, K. (Oak)	1.79	Jenkins, F. (Tex)	225	Perry, G. (Cle)	1.02	Hassler, A. (Cal)	2.61

Adjusted ERA		Component ERA		Opponents' Batting Avg.		Adjusted Pitching Runs		Win Shares – Pitchers		TPW – Pitchers	
Perry, G. (Cle)	144	Perry, G. (Cle)	2.20	Ryan, N. (Cal)	.190	Perry, G. (Cle)	38	Perry, G. (Cle)	30	Perry, G. (Cle)	4.0
Blyleven, B. (Min)	141	Hunter, C. (Oak)	2.25	Perry, G. (Cle)	.204	Blyleven, B. (Min)	36	Tiant, L. (Bos)	29	Blyleven, B. (Min)	3.8
Fitzmorris, A. (KC)	136	Jenkins, F. (Tex)	2.38	Dalcanton, B. (KC)	.211	Tiant, L. (Bos)	35	Hunter, C. (Oak)	27	Tiant, L. (Bos)	3.6

1975 National League

TEAM	G	W	L	PCT	GB	R	OR	EW	AB	H	2B	3B	HR	TB	BB	SO	SB	CS	AVG	OBP	SLG	OPS	OPS+	BR/A	PF	RC
East																										
PIT	161	92	69	.571	....	712	565	99	5489	1444	255	47	**138**	2207	468	832	49	28	.263	.325	**.402**	.727	109	46	99	708
PHI	162	86	76	.531	6.5	735	694	86	5592	1506	**283**	42	125	**2248**	610	960	126	57	.269	.344	.402	.746	109	71	104	783
NY	162	82	80	.506	10.5	646	625	84	5587	1430	217	34	101	2018	501	805	32	**26**	.256	.321	.361	.683	100	-11	95	637
STL	163	82	80	.506	10.5	662	689	78	**5597**	**1527**	239	46	81	2101	444	**649**	116	49	**.273**	.329	.375	.705	98	-15	104	681
MON	162	75	87	.463	17.5	601	690	70	5518	1346	216	31	98	1918	579	954	108	58	.244	.319	.348	.666	87	-91	104	621
CHI	162	75	87	.463	17.5	712	827	69	5470	1419	229	41	95	2015	650	802	67	55	.259	.341	.368	.710	99	-5	104	698
West																										
CIN	162	108	54	.667	....	**840**	586	109	5581	1515	278	37	124	2239	**691**	916	**168**	36	.271	**.355**	.401	**.757**	115	137	102	**828**
LA	162	88	74	.543	20	648	**534**	96	5453	1355	217	31	118	1988	611	825	138	52	.248	.328	.365	.692	103	28	96	665
SF	161	80	81	.497	27.5	659	671	79	5447	1412	235	45	84	1989	604	775	99	47	.259	.336	.365	.701	97	-15	104	671
SD	162	71	91	.438	37	552	683	64	5429	1324	215	22	78	1817	506	754	85	50	.244	.313	.335	.647	91	-68	94	569
ATL	161	67	94	.416	40.5	583	739	62	5424	1323	179	28	107	1849	543	759	55	38	.244	.315	.346	.661	86	-102	104	585
HOU	162	64	97	.398	43.5	664	711	75	5515	1401	218	**54**	84	1979	523	762	133	62	.254	.322	.365	.681	102	13	93	641
Total	**971**					**8014**			**66102**	**17002**	**2781**	**458**	**1233**		**6730**	**9793**	**1176**	**558**	**.257**	**.329**	**.369**	**.698**				

Runs		Hits		Doubles		Triples		Home Runs		Total Bases	
Rose, P. (Cin)	112	Cash, D. (Phi)	213	Rose, P. (Cin)	47	Garr, R. (Atl)	11	Schmidt, M. (Phi)	38	Luzinski, G. (Phi)	322
Cash, D. (Phi)	111	Garvey, S. (LA)	210	Cash, D. (Phi)	40	4 players tied with	10	Kingman, D. (NY)	36	Garvey, S. (LA)	314
Lopes, D. (LA)	108	Rose, P. (Cin)	210	2 players tied with	39			Luzinski, G. (Phi)	34	Parker, D. (Pit)	302

Runs Batted In		Bases On Balls		Stolen Bases		Batting Average		On-Base Percentage		Slugging Average	
Luzinski, G. (Phi)	120	Morgan, J. (Cin)	132	Lopes, D. (LA)	77	Madlock, B. (Chi)	.354	Morgan, J. (Cin)	.471	Parker, D. (Pit)	.541
Bench, J. (Cin)	110	Wynn, J. (LA)	110	Morgan, J. (Cin)	67	Simmons, T. (StL)	.332	Wynn, J. (LA)	.407	Luzinski, G. (Phi)	.540
Perez, T. (Cin)	109	Evans, D. (Atl)	105	Brock, L. (StL)	56	Sanguillen, M. (Pit)	.328	Rose, P. (Cin)	.407	Schmidt, M. (Phi)	.523

Adjusted OPS		Adjusted Batting Runs		Runs Created/Game		Fielding Runs		Win Shares – Batters		TPW – Batters	
Morgan, J. (Cin)	168	Morgan, J. (Cin)	67.0	Morgan, J. (Cin)	11.10	Concepcion, D. (Cin)	30.6	Morgan, J. (Cin)	44	Morgan, J. (Cin)	9.8
Luzinski, G. (Phi)	152	Luzinski, G. (Phi)	41.0	Luzinski, G. (Phi)	7.80	Schmidt, M. (Phi)	27.3	Rose, P. (Cin)	31	Schmidt, M. (Phi)	6.1
Watson, B. (Hou)	152	Cey, R. (LA)	32.0	Madlock, B. (Chi)	7.40	Stennett, R. (Pit)	21.3	Bench, J. (Cin)	30	Cey, R. (LA)	4.7

TEAM	CG	SH	SV	IP	H	H/G	ER	HR	BB	SO	OAV	RAT	ERA	ERA+	CERA	PR+	PF	FA	E	DP	FR	BW	PW	FW	TPW	DIF
East																										
PIT	43	14	31	1437¹	1302	8.2	481	**79**	551	768	.243	1.289	3.01	118	3.14	**83.1**	98	.976	151	147	0.3	4.8	**8.7**	.0	13.5	-1.5
PHI	33	11	30	1455	1353	8.4	618	111	546	897	.249	1.305	3.82	98	3.48	-55.2	103	.976	152	156	40.2	7.4	-5.8	4.2	5.8	-.8
NY	40	14	31	1466	1344	8.2	552	99	580	**989**	.246	1.312	3.39	102	3.44	-9.7	95	.976	151	144	19.5	-1.2	-1.0	2.0	-.2	1.2
STL	33	13	36	1454²	1452	9.0	577	98	571	824	.260	1.391	3.57	105	3.78	65.8	104	.973	171	140	-37.0	-1.6	6.9	-3.9	1.5	-.5
MON	30	12	25	**1480**	1448	8.8	612	102	665	831	.259	1.428	3.72	103	3.98	12.6	106	.973	180	**179**	1.8	-9.5	1.3	.2	-8.0	2.0
CHI	27	8	33	1444¹	1587	9.9	720	130	551	850	.281	1.480	4.49	86	4.53	-68.1	106	.972	179	152	-47.6	-.5	-7.1	-5.0	-12.6	6.6
West																										
CIN	22	8	**50**	1459	1422	8.8	546	112	487	663	.257	1.308	3.37	107	3.57	-9.0	99	**.984**	102	173	45.1	14.3	-.9	4.7	18.0	9.0
LA	**51**	**18**	21	1469²	**1215**	7.4	477	104	448	894	**.225**	1.132	2.92	116	2.68	62.3	94	.979	127	106	15.9	2.9	6.5	1.7	11.1	-4.1
SF	37	9	24	1432²	1406	8.8	595	92	612	856	.259	1.409	3.74	100	3.85	8.8	105	.976	146	164	1.1	-1.6	.9	.1	-.5	.5
SD	40	12	20	1463¹	1494	9.2	566	99	521	713	.266	1.377	3.48	100	3.79	13.6	96	.971	188	163	-19.3	-7.1	1.4	-2.0	-7.7	-2.3
ATL	32	4	24	1430	1543	9.7	621	101	519	669	.278	1.442	3.91	97	4.22	10.0	104	.972	175	147	-34.4	-10.6	1.0	-3.6	-13.1	.1
HOU	39	6	25	1458¹	1436	8.9	654	106	679	839	.262	1.450	4.04	83	4.14	-121.4	93	.979	137	166	11.0	1.4	-12.7	1.1	-10.1	-5.9
Total	427	129	350	17450¹		8.8	7019					1.360	3.62													

Wins		Win Percentage		Games		Complete Games		Shutouts	
Seaver, T. (NY)	22	Norman, F. (Cin)	.750	Garber, G. (Phi)	71	Messersmith, A. (LA)	19	Messersmith, A. (LA)	7
Jones, R. (SD)	20	Seaver, T. (NY)	.710	McEnaney, W. (Cin)	70	Jones, R. (SD)	18	Jones, R. (SD)	6
Messersmith, A. (LA)	19	Christenson, L. (Phi)	.647	2 players tied with	67	2 players tied with	15	Reuss, J. (Pit)	6

Saves	
Eastwick, R. (Cin)	22
Hrabosky, A. (StL)	22
Giusti, D. (Pit)	17

Innings Pitched		Fewest Hits/Game		Fewest BB/Game		Strikeouts		Ratio	
Messersmith, A. (LA)	321²	Messersmith, A. (LA)	6.83	Nolan, G. (Cin)	1.24	Seaver, T. (NY)	243	Sutton, D. (LA)	1.04
Jones, R. (SD)	285	Seaver, T. (NY)	6.97	Jones, R. (SD)	1.77	Montefusco, J. (SF)	215	Jones, R. (SD)	1.05
Seaver, T. (NY)	280¹	Warthen, D. (Mon)	6.98	Reed, R. (StL,Atl)	1.82	Messersmith, A. (LA)	213	Messersmith, A. (LA)	1.06

Earned Run Average	
Jones, R. (SD)	2.24
Messersmith, A. (LA)	2.29
Seaver, T. (NY)	2.38

Adjusted ERA		Component ERA		Opponents' Batting Avg.		Adjusted Pitching Runs		Win Shares – Pitchers	
Jones, R. (SD)	155	Sutton, D. (LA)	2.20	Messersmith, A. (LA)	.213	Jones, R. (SD)	43	Jones, R. (SD)	28
Messersmith, A. (LA)	148	Seaver, T. (NY)	2.26	Sutton, D. (LA)	.213	Messersmith, A. (LA)	36	Messersmith, A. (LA)	28
Seaver, T. (NY)	145	Jones, R. (SD)	2.27	Seaver, T. (NY)	.214	Seaver, T. (NY)	30	Seaver, T. (NY)	26

TPW – Pitchers	
Jones, R. (SD)	4.4
Forsch, B. (StL)	4.0
Messersmith, A. (LA)	3.9

1975 American League

TEAM	G	W	L	PCT	GB	R	OR	EW	AB	H	2B	3B	HR	TB	BB	SO	SB	CS	AVG	OBP	SLG	OPS	OPS+	BR/A	PF	RC
East																										
BOS	160	95	65	.594	....	**796**	709	89	5448	**1500**	**284**	44	134	**2274**	565	741	66	58	**.275**	.347	**.417**	**.765**	106	41	109	**774**
BAL	159	90	69	.566	4.5	682	**553**	96	5474	1382	224	33	124	2044	580	834	104	55	.252	.328	.373	.702	105	37	94	678
NY	160	83	77	.519	12	681	588	92	5415	1430	230	39	110	2068	486	710	102	59	.264	.328	.382	.710	103	17	97	663
CLE	159	79	80	.497	15.5	688	703	78	5404	1409	201	25	**153**	2119	525	**667**	106	89	.261	.329	.392	.721	103	6	100	671
MIL	162	68	94	.420	28	675	792	68	5378	1343	242	34	146	2091	553	922	65	64	.250	.323	.389	.712	100	-14	100	661
DET	159	57	102	.358	37.5	570	786	55	5366	1338	171	39	125	1962	383	872	63	57	.249	.303	.366	.668	84	-128	104	572
West																										
OAK	162	98	64	.605	....	758	606	99	5415	1376	220	33	151	2115	609	846	183	82	.254	.335	.391	.726	**107**	62	98	723
KC	162	91	71	.562	7	710	649	88	5491	1431	263	**58**	118	2164	591	675	155	75	.261	.336	.394	.730	103	28	103	734
TEX	162	79	83	.488	19	714	733	79	**5599**	1431	208	17	134	2075	**613**	863	102	62	.256	.332	.371	.702	99	-3	99	691
MIN	159	76	83	.478	20.5	724	736	78	5514	1497	215	28	121	2131	563	746	81	**48**	.271	.343	.386	.730	104	33	102	730
CHI	161	75	86	.466	22.5	655	703	75	5490	1400	209	38	94	1967	611	800	101	54	.255	.334	.358	.692	94	-29	101	657
CAL	161	72	89	.447	25.5	628	723	69	5377	1324	195	41	55	1766	593	811	**220**	108	.246	.324	.328	.653	91	-47	93	594
Total	963					8281			65371	16861	2662	429	1465		6672	9487	1348	811	.258	.330	.379	.709				

Runs		Hits		Doubles		Triples		Home Runs		Total Bases	
Lynn, F. (Bos)	103	Brett, G. (KC)	195	Lynn, F. (Bos)	47	Brett, G. (KC)	13	Jackson, R. (Oak)	36	Scott, G. (Mil)	318
Mayberry, J. (KC)	95	Carew, R. (Min)	192	Jackson, R. (Oak)	39	Rivers, M. (Cal)	13	Scott, G. (Mil)	36	Jackson, R. (Oak)	303
Bonds, B. (NY)	93	Munson, T. (NY)	190	3 players tied with	38	Orta, J. (Chi)	10	Mayberry, J. (KC)	34	Mayberry, J. (KC)	303

Runs Batted In		Bases On Balls		Stolen Bases		Batting Average		On-Base Percentage		Slugging Average	
Scott, G. (Mil)	109	Mayberry, J. (KC)	119	Rivers, M. (Cal)	70	Carew, R. (Min)	.359	Carew, R. (Min)	.428	Lynn, F. (Bos)	.566
Mayberry, J. (KC)	106	Singleton, K. (Bal)	118	Washington, C. (Oak)	40	Lynn, F. (Bos)	.331	Mayberry, J. (KC)	.419	Mayberry, J. (KC)	.547
Lynn, F. (Bos)	105	Grich, B. (Bal)	107	Otis, A. (KC)	39	Munson, T. (NY)	.318	Singleton, K. (Bal)	.418	Powell, B. (Cle)	.524

Adjusted OPS		Adjusted Batting Runs		Runs Created/Game		Fielding Runs		Win Shares – Batters		TPW – Batters	
Mayberry, J. (KC)	167	Mayberry, J. (KC)	54.0	Mayberry, J. (KC)	8.90	Belanger, M. (Bal)	26.6	Singleton, K. (Bal)	33	Grich, B. (Bal)	6.4
Lynn, F. (Bos)	158	Singleton, K. (Bal)	49.0	Lynn, F. (Bos)	8.50	Grich, B. (Bal)	24.8	Mayberry, J. (KC)	33	Carew, R. (Min)	5.5
Carew, R. (Min)	158	Carew, R. (Min)	47.0	Carew, R. (Min)	8.40	Garner, P. (Oak)	20.2	Lynn, F. (Bos)	33	Harrah, T. (Tex)	5.3

TEAM	CG	SH	SV	IP	H	H/G	ER	HR	BB	SO	OAV	RAT	ERA	ERA+	CERA	PR+	PF	FA	E	DP	FR	BW	PW	FW	TPW	DIF
East																										
BOS	62	11	31	1436²	1463	9.2	635	145	**490**	720	.265	1.359	3.98	102	4.01	13.0	108	.977	139	142	0.0	4.2	1.3	.0	5.5	9.5
BAL	**70**	**19**	21	1451	1285	8.0	**511**	110	500	717	.242	**1.230**	**3.17**	111	**3.14**	9.1	93	**.983**	**107**	175	45.5	3.8	.9	**4.6**	9.4	1.6
NY	**70**	11	20	1424	1325	8.4	521	104	502	809	.249	1.283	3.29	111	3.41	14.4	96	.978	135	148	41.3	1.7	1.5	4.2	7.4	-4.4
CLE	37	6	33	1435¹	1395	8.8	612	136	599	800	.258	1.389	3.84	99	4.02	-17.8	100	.978	134	156	7.9	.6	-1.8	.8	-.4	.4
MIL	36	10	34	1431²	1496	9.4	690	133	624	643	.271	1.481	4.34	**88**	4.55	-72.3	101	.971	180	162	-8.7	-1.5	-7.4	-.9	-9.7	-3.3
DET	52	10	17	1396	1496	9.6	662	137	533	787	.275	1.453	4.27	94	4.42	-15.1	106	.972	173	141	-28.2	-13.1	-1.5	-2.9	-17.5	-4.5
West																										
OAK	36	10	**44**	1448	**1267**	7.9	526	**102**	523	784	**.236**	1.236	3.27	111	3.15	48.1	96	.977	143	140	5.6	**6.3**	4.9	.6	**11.8**	5.2
KC	52	11	25	1456²	1422	8.8	561	108	498	815	.258	1.318	3.47	111	3.62	78.1	102	.976	155	151	-20.0	2.8	**8.0**	-2.0	8.8	1.2
TEX	60	16	17	**1465²**	1456	8.9	628	123	518	792	.261	1.347	3.86	97	3.83	-19.4	99	.971	191	173	-4.1	-.3	-2.0	-.4	-2.7	.7
MIN	57	7	22	1423	1381	8.7	640	137	617	846	.257	1.404	4.05	95	4.15	-21.3	102	.973	170	147	-12.7	3.4	-2.2	-1.3	-.1	-2.9
CHI	34	7	39	1452¹	1489	9.2	634	107	655	799	.268	1.476	3.93	98	4.36	12.3	102	.978	140	155	-21.8	-2.9	1.3	-2.2	-3.9	-1.1
CAL	59	**19**	16	1453¹	1386	8.6	628	123	613	**975**	.253	1.375	3.89	91	3.93	-50.3	94	.971	184	164	-5.3	-4.8	-5.1	-.5	-10.4	2.4
Total	625	137	319	17273²		8.8	7248					1.362	3.78													

Wins
Hunter, C. (NY) 23
Palmer, J. (Bal) 23
Blue, V. (Oak) 22

Win Percentage
Torrez, M. (Bal) .... .690
Leonard, D. (KC) .... .682
Palmer, J. (Bal) .... .676

Games
Fingers, R. (Oak) 75
Lindblad, P. (Oak) 68
Gossage, R. (Chi) 62

Complete Games
Hunter, C. (NY) 30
Palmer, J. (Bal) 25
Perry, G. (Tex,Cle) 25

Shutouts
Palmer, J. (Bal) 10
Hunter, C. (NY) 7
4 players tied with 5

Saves
Gossage, R. (Chi) 26
Fingers, R. (Oak) 24
Murphy, T. (Mil) 20

Innings Pitched
Hunter, C. (NY) 328
Palmer, J. (Bal) 323
Perry, G. (Tex,Cle) .... 305[2]

Fewest Hits/Game
Hunter, C. (NY) 6.80
Ryan, N. (Cal) 6.91
Palmer, J. (Bal) 7.05

Fewest BB/Game
Jenkins, F. (Tex) 1.87
Perry, G. (Tex,Cle) 2.06
Grimsley, R. (Bal) 2.15

Strikeouts
Tanana, F. (Cal) 269
Blyleven, B. (Min) 233
Perry, G. (Tex,Cle) 233

Ratio
Hunter, C. (NY) 1.01
Palmer, J. (Bal) 1.03
Blyleven, B. (Min) 1.10

Earned Run Average
Palmer, J. (Bal) 2.09
Hunter, C. (NY) 2.58
Eckersley, D. (Cle) 2.60

Adjusted ERA
Palmer, J. (Bal) 168
Eckersley, D. (Cle) 145
Hunter, C. (NY) 141

Component ERA
Hunter, C. (NY) 2.18
Palmer, J. (Bal) 2.20
Blyleven, B. (Min) 2.63

Opponents' Batting Avg.
Hunter, C. (NY) .... .208
Ryan, N. (Cal) .... .213
Eckersley, D. (Cle) .... .215

Adjusted Pitching Runs
Palmer, J. (Bal) 41
Kaat, J. (Chi) 30
Hunter, C. (NY) 29

Win Shares – Pitchers
Palmer, J. (Bal) 31
Hunter, C. (NY) 29
3 players tied with 22

TPW – Pitchers
Palmer, J. (Bal) 4.2
Kaat, J. (Chi) 3.1
Hunter, C. (NY) 3.0

1976 National League

TEAM	G	W	L	PCT	GB	R	OR	EW	AB	H	2B	3B	HR	TB	BB	SO	SB	CS	AVG	OBP	SLG	OPS	OPS+	BR/A	PF	RC
East																										
PHI	162	101	61	.623	....	770	557	106	5528	1505	259	45	110	2184	542	793	127	70	.272	.342	.395	.737	112	82	103	744
PIT	162	92	70	.568	9	708	630	90	5604	1499	249	56	110	2190	433	807	130	45	.267	.323	.391	.714	108	51	101	698
NY	162	86	76	.531	15	615	**538**	92	5415	1334	198	34	102	1906	561	797	66	58	.246	.320	.352	.672	103	8	94	607
CHI	162	75	87	.463	26	611	728	67	5519	1386	216	24	105	1965	490	834	74	74	.251	.316	.356	.672	88	-95	109	603
STL	162	72	90	.444	29	629	671	76	5516	1432	243	57	63	1978	512	860	123	55	.260	.325	.359	.684	99	-3	101	642
MON	162	55	107	.340	46	531	734	56	5428	1275	224	32	94	1845	433	841	86	**44**	.235	.293	.340	.633	82	-133	104	538
West																										
CIN	162	102	60	.630	....	**857**	633	105	**5702**	**1599**	**271**	**63**	**141**	**2419**	**681**	902	**210**	57	**.280**	**.360**	**.424**	**.784**	**126**	**217**	102	**906**
LA	162	92	70	.568	10	608	543	90	5472	1371	200	34	91	1912	486	744	144	55	.251	.315	.349	.664	96	-21	98	602
HOU	162	80	82	.494	22	625	657	77	5464	1401	195	50	66	1894	530	719	150	57	.256	.325	.347	.671	106	50	91	620
SF	162	74	88	.457	28	595	686	70	5452	1340	211	37	85	1880	518	778	88	55	.246	.314	.345	.659	90	-71	103	588
SD	162	73	89	.451	29	570	662	69	5369	1327	216	37	64	1809	488	**716**	92	46	.247	.313	.337	.650	98	-16	92	568
ATL	162	70	92	.432	32	620	700	71	5345	1309	170	30	82	1785	589	811	74	61	.245	.322	.334	.656	87	-88	106	576
Total	972					7739			65814	16778	2652	499	1113		6263	9602	1364	677	.255	.323	.361	.684				

Runs
Rose, P. (Cin) 130
Morgan, J. (Cin) 113
Schmidt, M. (Phi) 112

Hits
Rose, P. (Cin) 215
Montanez, W. (Atl,SF) 206
Garvey, S. (LA) 200

Doubles
Rose, P. (Cin) 42
Johnstone, J. (Phi) 38
2 players tied with 37

Triples
Cash, D. (Phi) 12
Geronimo, C. (Cin) 11
2 players tied with 10

Home Runs
Schmidt, M. (Phi) 38
Kingman, D. (NY) 37
Monday, R. (Chi) 32

Total Bases
Schmidt, M. (Phi) 306
Rose, P. (Cin) 299
Foster, G. (Cin) 298

Runs Batted In
Foster, G. (Cin) 121
Morgan, J. (Cin) 111
Schmidt, M. (Phi) 107

Bases On Balls
Wynn, J. (Atl) 127
Morgan, J. (Cin) 114
Schmidt, M. (Phi) 100

Stolen Bases
Lopes, D. (LA) 63
Morgan, J. (Cin) 60
2 players tied with 58

Batting Average
Madlock, B. (Chi) .... .339
Griffey, K. (Cin) .... .336
Maddox, G. (Phi) .... .330

On-Base Percentage
Morgan, J. (Cin) .... .453
Madlock, B. (Chi) .... .415
Rose, P. (Cin) .... .406

Slugging Average
Morgan, J. (Cin) .... .576
Foster, G. (Cin) .... .530
Schmidt, M. (Phi) .... .524

Adjusted OPS
Morgan, J. (Cin) 186
Watson, B. (Hou) 151
Schmidt, M. (Phi) 150

Adjusted Batting Runs
Morgan, J. (Cin) 69.0
Schmidt, M. (Phi) 39.0
Watson, B. (Hou) 38.0

Runs Created/Game
Morgan, J. (Cin) 11.30
Griffey, K. (Cin) 7.60
Foster, G. (Cin) 7.30

Fielding Runs
Concepcion, D. (Cin) 34.3
Schmidt, M. (Phi) 32.2
Stennett, R. (Pit) 19.8

Win Shares – Batters
Morgan, J. (Cin) 37
Schmidt, M. (Phi) 35
Watson, B. (Hou) 31

TPW – Batters
Schmidt, M. (Phi) 7.5
Morgan, J. (Cin) 7.5
Concepcion, D. (Cin) 6.0

TEAM	CG	SH	SV	IP	H	H/G	ER	HR	BB	SO	OAV	RAT	ERA	ERA+	CERA	PR+	PF	FA	E	DP	FR	BW	PW	FW	TPW	DIF
East																										
PHI	34	9	44	1459	1377	8.5	499	98	**397**	918	.250	1.216	3.08	115	3.10	**51.2**	101	.981	115	148	21.5	8.7	**5.4**	2.3	16.5	3.5
PIT	45	12	35	1466[1]	1402	8.6	547	95	460	762	.253	1.270	3.36	104	3.26	12.7	100	.975	163	142	6.1	5.5	1.4	.6	7.5	3.5
NY	**53**	**18**	25	1448	**1248**	7.8	473	97	419	**1025**	**.233**	1.150	**2.94**	112	**2.74**	48.5	94	.979	131	116	7.7	.9	5.2	.8	6.8	-1.8
CHI	27	12	33	**1471[1]**	1511	9.2	642	123	490	850	.268	1.360	3.93	98	3.91	11.0	110	.978	140	145	-24.0	-10.0	1.2	-2.6	-11.4	5.4
STL	35	15	26	1453[2]	1416	8.8	581	91	581	731	.258	1.374	3.60	98	3.72	-18.4	101	.973	174	163	6.6	-.3	-2.0	.7	-1.5	-7.5
MON	26	10	21	1440	1442	9.0	638	89	659	783	.266	1.459	3.99	93	4.12	-42.4	106	.976	155	**179**	-3.1	-14.2	-4.5	-.3	-19.0	-7.0
West																										
CIN	33	12	**45**	1471	1436	8.8	574	100	491	790	.258	1.310	3.51	100	3.52	-13.5	100	**.984**	**102**	157	13.3	**23.1**	-1.4	1.4	**23.1**	-2.1
LA	47	17	28	1470[2]	1330	8.1	493	97	479	747	.243	1.230	3.02	112	3.11	31.0	97	.980	128	154	**28.3**	-2.2	3.3	**3.0**	4.1	6.9
HOU	42	17	29	1444[1]	1349	8.4	571	82	662	780	.250	1.392	3.56	90	3.72	-59.8	91	.978	140	155	1.1	5.4	-6.4	.1	-.9	-.1
SF	27	**18**	31	1461[2]	1464	9.0	573	**68**	518	746	.263	1.356	3.53	103	3.55	38.1	104	.971	186	153	-22.2	-7.5	4.0	-2.4	-5.8	-1.2
SD	33	11	18	1432[1]	1368	8.6	581	87	543	652	.253	1.334	3.65	**90**	3.49	-58.2	93	.978	141	148	-2.7	-1.6	-6.2	-.3	-8.1	.1
ATL	33	13	27	1438	1435	9.0	617	86	564	818	.261	1.390	3.86	98	3.80	23.4	108	.973	167	151	-35.3	-9.3	2.5	-3.8	-10.6	-.4
Total	449	164	362	17457[1]		8.6	6789					1.320	3.50													

Wins
Jones, R. (SD) 22
Koosman, J. (NY) 21
Sutton, D. (LA) 21

Win Percentage
Rhoden, R. (LA) .... .800
Carlton, S. (Phi) .... .741
Candelaria, J. (Pit) .... .696

Games
Murray, D. (Mon) 81
Hough, C. (LA) 77
Metzger, B. (SD) 77

Complete Games
Jones, R. (SD) 25
Koosman, J. (NY) 17
Matlack, J. (NY) 16

Shutouts
Matlack, J. (NY) 6
Montefusco, J. (SF) 6
2 players tied with 5

Saves
Eastwick, R. (Cin) 26
Forsch, K. (Hou) 19
Lockwood, S. (NY) 19

Innings Pitched
Jones, R. (SD) .... 315[1]
Richard, J. (Hou) 291
Seaver, T. (NY) 271

Fewest Hits/Game
Richard, J. (Hou) 6.84
Seaver, T. (NY) 7.01
Candelaria, J. (Pit) 7.08

Fewest BB/Game
Nolan, G. (Cin) 1.02
Kaat, J. (Phi) 1.27
Jones, R. (SD) 1.43

Strikeouts
Seaver, T. (NY) 235
Richard, J. (Hou) 214
Koosman, J. (NY) 200

Ratio
Jones, R. (SD) 1.03
Candelaria, J. (Pit) 1.06
Seaver, T. (NY) 1.06

Earned Run Average
Denny, J. (StL) 2.52
Rau, D. (LA) 2.57
Seaver, T. (NY) 2.59

Adjusted ERA
Denny, J. (StL) 140
Rau, D. (LA) 131
Zachry, P. (Cin) 128

Component ERA
Jones, R. (SD) 2.19
Seaver, T. (NY) 2.23
Candelaria, J. (Pit) 2.48

Opponents' Batting Avg.
Richard, J. (Hou) .... .212
Seaver, T. (NY) .... .213
Candelaria, J. (Pit) .... .216

Adjusted Pitching Runs
Montefusco, J. (SF) 26
Burris, R. (Chi) 25
Barr, J. (SF) 24

Win Shares – Pitchers
4 players tied with 21

TPW – Pitchers
Barr, J. (SF) 2.8
Denny, J. (StL) 2.6
Montefusco, J. (SF) 2.5

1976 American League

TEAM	G	W	L	PCT	GB	R	OR	EW	AB	H	2B	3B	HR	TB	BB	SO	SB	CS	AVG	OBP	SLG	OPS	OPS+	BR/A	PF	RC
East
NY	159	97	62	.610	....	730	**575**	98	5555	1496	231	36	120	2159	470	**616**	163	65	.269	.330	.389	.719	**111**	79	99	721
BAL	162	88	74	.543	10.5	619	598	84	5457	1326	213	28	119	1952	519	883	150	61	.243	.311	.358	.669	102	15	94	611
BOS	162	83	79	.512	15.5	716	660	88	5511	1448	257	53	**134**	**2213**	500	832	95	70	.263	.327	**.402**	**.729**	100	-7	112	707
CLE	159	81	78	.509	16	615	615	80	5412	1423	189	38	85	1943	479	631	75	69	.263	.324	.359	.683	101	-9	99	608
DET	161	74	87	.460	24	609	709	68	5441	1401	207	38	101	1987	450	730	107	59	.257	.318	.365	.683	96	-33	104	609
MIL	161	66	95	.410	32	570	655	69	5396	1326	170	38	88	1836	511	909	62	61	.246	.314	.340	.654	93	-58	98	573
West
KC	162	90	72	.556	....	713	611	93	5540	1490	**259**	**57**	65	2058	484	650	218	106	.269	.331	.371	.703	105	34	101	684
OAK	161	87	74	.540	2.5	686	598	91	5353	1319	208	33	113	1932	**592**	818	**341**	123	.246	.327	.361	.687	105	65	96	661
MIN	162	85	77	.525	5	**743**	704	85	**5574**	**1526**	222	51	81	2093	550	714	146	75	**.274**	**.343**	.375	.719	107	60	103	**725**
TEX	162	76	86	.469	14	616	652	76	5555	1390	213	26	80	1895	568	809	87	**45**	.250	.323	.341	.664	93	-44	102	614
CAL	162	76	86	.469	14	550	631	70	5385	1265	210	23	63	1710	534	812	126	80	.235	.309	.318	.626	89	-75	94	528
CHI	161	64	97	.398	25.5	586	745	62	5532	1410	209	46	73	1930	471	739	120	53	.255	.317	.349	.666	94	-37	101	619
Total	967					7753			65711	16820	2588	467	1122		6128	9143	1690	867	.256	.323	.361	.684				

Runs		Hits		Doubles		Triples		Home Runs		Total Bases	
White, R. (NY)	104	Brett, G. (KC)	215	Otis, A. (KC)	40	Brett, G. (KC)	14	Nettles, G. (NY)	32	Brett, G. (KC)	298
Carew, R. (Min)	97	Carew, R. (Min)	200	4 players tied with	34	Carew, R. (Min)	12	Bando, S. (Oak)	27	Chambliss, C. (NY)	283
Rivers, M. (NY)	95	Chambliss, C. (NY)	188			Garner, P. (Oak)	12	Jackson, R. (Bal)	27	2 players tied with	280

Runs Batted In		Bases On Balls		Stolen Bases		Batting Average		On-Base Percentage		Slugging Average	
May, L. (Bal)	109	Hargrove, M. (Tex)	97	North, B. (Oak)	75	Brett, G. (KC)	.333	McRae, H. (KC)	.412	Jackson, R. (Bal)	.502
Munson, T. (NY)	105	Harrah, T. (Tex)	91	LeFlore, R. (Det)	58	McRae, H. (KC)	.332	Hargrove, M. (Tex)	.401	Rice, J. (Bos)	.482
Yastrzemski, C. (Bos)	102	Grich, B. (Bal)	86	Campaneris, B. (Oak)	54	Carew, R. (Min)	.331	Carew, R. (Min)	.398	Nettles, G. (NY)	.475

Adjusted OPS		Adjusted Batting Runs		Runs Created/Game		Fielding Runs		Win Shares – Batters		TPW – Batters	
Jackson, R. (Bal)	158	Carew, R. (Min)	38.0	McRae, H. (KC)	7.00	Nettles, G. (NY)	26.3	Brett, G. (KC)	33	Nettles, G. (NY)	5.2
McRae, H. (KC)	154	McRae, H. (KC)	38.0	Brett, G. (KC)	6.70	Randolph, W. (NY)	24.2	Grich, B. (Bal)	31	Grich, B. (Bal)	5.0
Tenace, G. (Oak)	150	Jackson, R. (Bal)	38.0	Carew, R. (Min)	6.60	Belanger, M. (Bal)	20.7	Carew, R. (Min)	30	Brett, G. (KC)	4.3

TEAM	CG	SH	SV	IP	H	H/G	ER	HR	BB	SO	OAV	RAT	ERA	ERA+	CERA	PR+	PF	FA	E	DP	FR	BW	PW	FW	TPW	DIF
East
NY	62	15	37	1455	**1300**	8.0	516	97	448	674	**.241**	**1.201**	3.19	107	3.01	-12.9	97	.980	126	141	48.8	8.4	-1.4	5.2	12.2	5.8
BAL	59	16	23	1468²	1396	8.6	542	**80**	489	678	.255	1.283	3.32	98	3.32	-22.2	93	**.982**	118	157	14.7	1.6	-2.4	1.6	.8	6.2
BOS	49	13	27	1458	1495	9.2	570	109	**409**	673	.267	1.306	3.52	92	3.64	**77.0**	111	.978	141	144	-14.9	-.8	**8.2**	-1.6	5.8	-3.8
CLE	30	17	**46**	1432	1361	8.6	552	80	533	928	.255	1.323	3.47	101	3.51	-4.0	99	.980	121	159	4.8	-.9	-.4	.5	-.8	2.8
DET	55	12	20	1431¹	1426	9.0	615	101	550	738	.263	1.381	3.87	96	3.88	-10.2	105	.974	168	161	-16.6	-3.5	-1.1	-1.8	-6.4	.4
MIL	45	10	27	1435¹	1406	8.8	580	99	567	677	.260	1.375	3.64	96	3.82	-25.8	99	.975	152	160	1.8	-6.1	-2.7	.2	-8.7	-5.3
West
KC	41	12	35	1472¹	1356	8.3	525	83	493	735	.247	1.256	3.21	109	3.19	45.3	99	.978	139	147	1.8	3.6	4.8	.2	8.6	.4
OAK	39	15	29	1459¹	1412	8.7	528	96	415	711	.255	1.252	3.26	103	3.31	39.9	95	.977	144	130	-24.2	6.9	4.2	-2.6	8.6	-1.6
MIN	29	11	23	1459	1421	8.8	598	89	610	762	.259	1.392	3.69	98	3.85	-22.1	102	.973	172	**182**	2.5	6.3	-2.3	.3	4.3	-.3
TEX	63	15	15	1472	1464	9.0	564	106	461	773	.262	1.308	3.45	104	3.63	12.1	102	.976	156	142	7.2	-4.6	1.3	.8	-2.6	-2.4
CAL	**64**	15	17	**1477¹**	1323	8.1	551	95	553	**992**	.241	1.270	3.36	99	3.26	2.8	95	.977	150	139	-8.2	-7.9	.3	-.9	-8.5	3.5
CHI	54	10	22	1448	1460	9.1	684	87	600	802	.266	1.423	4.25	84	4.03	-93.7	101	.979	130	155	-17.2	-3.9	-9.9	-1.8	-15.7	-.3
Total	590	161	321	17468¹		8.7	6825					1.314	3.52													

Wins		Win Percentage		Games		Complete Games		Shutouts		Saves	
Palmer, J. (Bal)	22	Campbell, B. (Min)	.773	Campbell, B. (Min)	78	Fidrych, M. (Det)	24	Ryan, N. (Cal)	7	Lyle, S. (NY)	23
Tiant, L. (Bos)	21	Garland, W. (Bal)	.741	Fingers, R. (Oak)	70	Palmer, J. (Bal)	23	3 players tied with	6	LaRoche, D. (Cle)	21
Garland, W. (Bal)	20	Ellis, D. (NY)	.680	Lindblad, P. (Oak)	65	Tanana, F. (Cal)	23			2 players tied with	20

Innings Pitched		Fewest Hits/Game		Fewest BB/Game		Strikeouts		Ratio		Earned Run Average	
Palmer, J. (Bal)	315	Ryan, N. (Cal)	6.11	Bird, D. (KC)	1.41	Ryan, N. (Cal)	327	Tanana, F. (Cal)	.99	Fidrych, M. (Det)	2.34
Hunter, C. (NY)	298²	Tanana, F. (Cal)	6.62	Jenkins, F. (Bos)	1.85	Tanana, F. (Cal)	261	Palmer, J. (Bal)	1.08	Blue, V. (Oak)	2.35
Blue, V. (Oak)	298¹	Eckersley, D. (Cle)	7.00	Perry, G. (Tex)	1.87	Blyleven, B. (Tex,Min)	219	Fidrych, M. (Det)	1.08	Tanana, F. (Cal)	2.43

Adjusted ERA		Component ERA		Opponents' Batting Avg.		Adjusted Pitching Runs		Win Shares – Pitchers		TPW – Pitchers	
Fidrych, M. (Det)	159	Tanana, F. (Cal)	2.16	Ryan, N. (Cal)	.195	Fidrych, M. (Det)	41	Fidrych, M. (Det)	27	Fidrych, M. (Det)	4.4
Blue, V. (Oak)	143	Blue, V. (Oak)	2.39	Tanana, F. (Cal)	.203	Blue, V. (Oak)	38	Palmer, J. (Bal)	27	Blue, V. (Oak)	4.0
Tanana, F. (Cal)	137	Fidrych, M. (Det)	2.41	Eckersley, D. (Cle)	.214	Tanana, F. (Cal)	30	Tanana, F. (Cal)	27	Tanana, F. (Cal)	3.2

1977 National League

TEAM	G	W	L	PCT	GB	R	OR	EW	AB	H	2B	3B	HR	TB	BB	SO	SB	CS	AVG	OBP	SLG	OPS	OPS+	BR/A	PF	RC
East
PHI	162	101	61	.623	....	**847**	668	100	5546	1548	266	56	186	**2484**	573	806	135	68	**.279**	**.351**	**.448**	**.799**	114	111	104	**863**
PIT	162	96	66	.593	5	734	665	96	5662	**1550**	278	56	133	2341	474	878	**260**	120	.274	.334	.413	.747	102	21	103	774
STL	162	83	79	.512	18	737	688	87	5527	1490	252	56	96	2142	489	823	134	112	.270	.332	.388	.719	100	-19	98	689
CHI	162	81	81	.500	20	692	739	76	5604	1489	271	37	111	2167	534	**796**	64	**45**	.266	.333	.387	.719	88	-84	111	707
MON	162	75	87	.463	26	665	736	73	**5675**	1474	**294**	50	138	2282	478	877	88	50	.260	.320	.402	.722	101	0	97	713
NY	162	64	98	.395	37	587	663	71	5410	1319	227	30	88	1870	529	887	98	81	.244	.315	.346	.660	87	-108	95	575
West
LA	162	98	64	.605	....	769	**582**	103	5589	1484	223	28	**191**	2336	588	896	114	62	.266	.338	.418	.756	108	63	100	792
CIN	162	88	74	.543	10	802	725	89	5524	1513	269	42	181	2409	600	911	170	64	.274	.348	.436	.784	113	**113**	102	845
HOU	162	81	81	.500	17	680	650	85	5530	1405	263	**60**	114	2130	515	839	187	72	.254	.322	.385	.707	104	38	91	696
SF	162	75	87	.463	23	673	711	77	5497	1392	227	41	134	2103	568	842	90	55	.253	.326	.383	.708	95	-36	100	681
SD	162	69	93	.426	29	692	834	66	5602	1397	245	49	120	2100	**602**	1057	133	57	.249	.325	.375	.700	94	39	90	699
ATL	162	61	101	.377	37	678	895	59	5534	1404	218	20	139	2079	537	876	82	53	.254	.322	.376	.697	82	-131	112	659
Total	972					8556			66700	17465	3033	526	1631		6487	10488	1555	843	.262	.330	.396	.727				

Runs
Foster, G. (Cin) 124
Griffey, K. (Cin) 117
Schmidt, M. (Phi) 114

Hits
Parker, D. (Pit) 215
Rose, P. (Cin) 204
Templeton, G. (StL) 200

Doubles
Parker, D. (Pit) 44
Cash, D. (Mon) 42
2 players tied with 41

Triples
Templeton, G. (StL) 18
3 players tied with 11

Home Runs
Foster, G. (Cin) 52
Burroughs, J. (Atl) 41
Luzinski, G. (Phi) 39

Total Bases
Foster, G. (Cin) 388
Parker, D. (Pit) 338
Luzinski, G. (Phi) 329

Runs Batted In
Foster, G. (Cin) 149
Luzinski, G. (Phi) 130
Garvey, S. (LA) 115

Bases On Balls
Tenace, G. (SD) 125
Morgan, J. (Cin) 117
2 players tied with 104

Stolen Bases
Taveras, F. (Pit) 70
Cedeno, C. (Hou) 61
Richards, G. (SD) 56

Batting Average
Parker, D. (Pit) .338
Templeton, G. (StL) .322
Foster, G. (Cin) .320

On-Base Percentage
Smith, R. (LA) .432
Morgan, J. (Cin) .420
Tenace, G. (SD) .417

Slugging Average
Foster, G. (Cin) .631
Luzinski, G. (Phi) .594
Smith, R. (LA) .576

Adjusted OPS
Smith, R. (LA) 168
Foster, G. (Cin) 164
Luzinski, G. (Phi) 155

Adjusted Batting Runs
Foster, G. (Cin) 54.0
Smith, R. (LA) 52.0
Luzinski, G. (Phi) 44.0

Runs Created/Game
Smith, R. (LA) 9.70
Luzinski, G. (Phi) 8.80
Foster, G. (Cin) 8.70

Fielding Runs
Concepcion, D. (Cin) 28.2
Tyson, M. (StL) 25.9
Parker, D. (Pit) 23.7

Win Shares – Batters
Schmidt, M. (Phi) 33
Parker, D. (Pit) 33
Foster, G. (Cin) 32

TPW – Batters
Schmidt, M. (Phi) 6.3
Morgan, J. (Cin) 5.4
Parker, D. (Pit) 5.1

TEAM	CG	SH	SV	IP	H	H/G	ER	HR	BB	SO	OAV	RAT	ERA	ERA+	CERA	PR+	PF	FA	E	DP	FR	BW	PW	FW	TPW	DIF
East																										
PHI	31	7	47	1455²	1451	9.0	600	134	482	856	.263	1.328	3.71	108	3.86	22.2	102	.981	120	168	24.3	11.2	2.2	2.5	15.9	4.1
PIT	25	**15**	39	1481²	1406	8.5	594	149	485	890	.252	1.276	3.61	110	3.59	40.4	102	.977	145	137	21.8	2.2	4.1	2.2	8.4	6.6
STL	26	10	31	1446	1420	8.8	612	139	532	768	.260	1.350	3.81	101	3.91	-22.0	98	.978	139	**174**	**28.2**	-1.9	-2.2	**2.9**	-1.3	3.3
CHI	16	10	44	1468	1500	9.2	654	128	489	**942**	.266	1.355	4.01	109	3.89	88.9	112	.977	153	147	-28.8	-8.5	**9.0**	-2.9	-2.4	2.4
MON	31	11	33	1481	1426	8.7	660	135	579	856	.255	1.354	4.01	95	3.82	-39.3	97	.980	129	128	5.3	-.1	-4.0	.5	-3.5	-2.5
NY	27	12	28	1433²	**1378**	8.6	600	118	490	911	.254	1.303	3.77	99	3.55	-10.3	96	.978	134	132	3.3	-10.9	-1.0	.3	-11.6	-5.4
West																										
LA	34	13	39	1475¹	1393	**8.5**	**528**	119	**438**	930	.251	**1.241**	**3.22**	119	**3.34**	85.4	98	.981	124	160	13.4	6.4	8.6	1.4	**16.4**	.6
CIN	33	12	32	1437¹	1469	9.2	672	156	544	868	.267	1.401	4.21	93	4.31	-56.0	100	**.984**	**95**	154	10.2	**11.5**	-5.7	1.0	6.8	.2
HOU	**37**	11	28	1465²	1384	**8.5**	576	110	545	871	.251	1.316	3.54	101	3.56	8.6	91	.978	142	136	-.5	3.8	.9	-.5	4.2	-4.2
SF	27	10	33	1459	1501	9.3	608	114	529	854	.267	1.391	3.75	104	3.95	45.6	100	.972	179	136	-20.6	-3.6	4.6	-2.1	-1.1	-4.9
SD	6	5	44	1466¹	1556	9.6	722	160	673	827	.276	1.520	4.43	80	4.74	-140.0	90	.971	189	142	-9.0	3.9	-14.2	-.9	-11.2	-.8
ATL	28	5	31	1445¹	1581	9.8	779	169	701	915	.279	1.579	4.85	92	5.14	-25.3	114	.972	175	127	-42.3	-13.2	-2.6	-4.3	-20.1	.1
Total	321	121	429	17515		9.0	7605					1.368	3.91													

Wins
Carlton, S. (Phi) 23
Seaver, T. (Cin,NY) 21
4 players tied with 20

Win Percentage
Candelaria, J. (Pit) .800
Christenson, L. (Phi) .760
2 players tied with .741

Games
Fingers, R. (SD) 78
Spillner, D. (SD) 76
Tomlin, D. (SD) 76

Complete Games
Niekro, P. (Atl) 20
Seaver, T. (Cin,NY) 19
2 players tied with 17

Shutouts
Seaver, T. (Cin,NY) 7
Reuschel, R. (Chi) 4
Rogers, S. (Mon) 4

Saves
Fingers, R. (SD) 35
Sutter, B. (Chi) 31
Gossage, R. (Pit) 26

Innings Pitched
Niekro, P. (Atl) 330¹
Rogers, S. (Mon) 301²
Carlton, S. (Phi) 283

Fewest Hits/Game
Seaver, T. (Cin,NY) 6.85
Richard, J. (Hou) 7.15
Carlton, S. (Phi) 7.28

Fewest BB/Game
Candelaria, J. (Pit) 1.95
John, T. (LA) 2.04
Rau, D. (LA) 2.08

Strikeouts
Niekro, P. (Atl) 262
Richard, J. (Hou) 214
Rogers, S. (Mon) 206

Ratio
Seaver, T. (Cin,NY) 1.01
Candelaria, J. (Pit) 1.07
Hooton, B. (LA) 1.09

Earned Run Average
Candelaria, J. (Pit) 2.34
Seaver, T. (Cin,NY) 2.58
Hooton, B. (LA) 2.62

Adjusted ERA
Candelaria, J. (Pit) 170
Reuschel, R. (Chi) 157
Carlton, S. (Phi) 151

Component ERA
Seaver, T. (Cin,NY) 2.12
Hooton, B. (LA) 2.46
Richard, J. (Hou) 2.74

Opponents' Batting Avg.
Seaver, T. (Cin,NY) .209
Richard, J. (Hou) .218
Carlton, S. (Phi) .223

Adjusted Pitching Runs
Reuschel, R. (Chi) 50
Candelaria, J. (Pit) 39
Carlton, S. (Phi) 38

Win Shares – Pitchers
Candelaria, J. (Pit) 26
Carlton, S. (Phi) 26
Reuschel, R. (Chi) 26

TPW – Pitchers
Reuschel, R. (Chi) 5.2
Carlton, S. (Phi) 4.6
Candelaria, J. (Pit) 4.3

1977 American League

TEAM	G	W	L	PCT	GB	R	OR	EW	AB	H	2B	3B	HR	TB	BB	SO	SB	CS	AVG	OBP	SLG	OPS	OPS+	BR/A	PF	RC
East																										
NY	162	100	62	.617	....	831	**651**	100	5605	1576	267	47	184	2489	533	681	93	57	.281	.347	.444	.791	**115**	115	99	851
BAL	161	97	64	.602	2.5	719	653	88	5494	1433	231	25	148	2158	560	945	90	51	.261	.332	.393	.725	103	28	94	709
BOS	161	97	64	.602	2.5	859	712	95	5510	1551	258	56	**213**	**2560**	528	905	66	47	.281	.349	**.465**	**.813**	107	55	112	**874**
DET	162	74	88	.457	26	714	751	77	5604	1480	228	45	166	2296	452	764	60	46	.264	.321	.410	.731	93	-62	105	715
CLE	161	71	90	.441	28.5	676	739	73	5491	1476	221	46	100	2089	531	688	87	87	.269	.337	.380	.717	98	-21	97	680
MIL	162	67	95	.414	33	639	765	67	5517	1425	255	46	125	2147	443	862	85	67	.258	.316	.389	.705	91	-79	100	659
TOR	161	54	107	.335	45.5	605	822	57	5418	1367	230	41	100	1979	499	819	65	55	.252	.318	.365	.683	85	-118	101	608
West																										
KC	162	102	60	.630	....	822	**651**	100	5594	1549	**299**	**77**	146	2440	522	687	170	87	.277	.343	.436	.780	110	81	101	833
TEX	162	94	68	.580	8	767	657	93	5541	1497	265	39	135	2245	**596**	904	154	85	.270	.345	.405	.750	103	31	101	778
CHI	162	90	72	.556	12	844	771	88	5633	1568	254	52	192	2502	559	**666**	42	**44**	.278	.347	.444	.791	114	106	100	856
MIN	161	84	77	.522	17.5	**867**	776	89	**5639**	**1588**	273	60	123	2350	563	754	105	65	**.282**	**.351**	.417	.768	110	85	98	825
CAL	162	74	88	.457	28	675	695	79	5410	1380	233	40	131	2086	542	880	159	89	.255	.321	.386	.713	97	-16	96	679
SEA	162	64	98	.395	38	624	855	56	5460	1398	218	37	133	2081	426	769	110	67	.256	.314	.381	.695	89	-85	99	641
OAK	161	63	98	.391	38.5	605	749	64	5358	1284	176	37	117	1885	516	910	**176**	89	.240	.311	.352	.662	81	-130	98	587
Total	1131					10247			77274	20572	3408	644	2013		7270	11234	1462	936	.266	.333	.405	.738				

Runs
Carew, R. (Min) 128
Fisk, C. (Bos) 106
Brett, G. (KC) 105

Hits
Carew, R. (Min) 239
LeFlore, R. (Det) 212
Rice, J. (Bos) 206

Doubles
McRae, H. (KC) 54
Jackson, R. (NY) 39
2 players tied with 38

Triples
Carew, R. (Min) 16
Rice, J. (Bos) 15
Cowens, A. (KC) 14

Home Runs
Rice, J. (Bos) 39
Bonds, B. (Cal) 37
Nettles, G. (NY) 37

Total Bases
Rice, J. (Bos) 382
Carew, R. (Min) 351
McRae, H. (KC) 330

Runs Batted In
Hisle, L. (Min) 119
Bonds, B. (Cal) 115
Rice, J. (Bos) 114

Bases On Balls
Harrah, T. (Tex) 109
Singleton, K. (Bal) 107
Hargrove, M. (Tex) 103

Stolen Bases
Patek, F. (KC) 53
Page, M. (Oak) 42
2 players tied with 41

Batting Average
Carew, R. (Min) .388
Bostock, L. (Min) .336
Singleton, K. (Bal) .328

On-Base Percentage
Carew, R. (Min) .452
Singleton, K. (Bal) .442
Hargrove, M. (Tex) .424

Slugging Average
Rice, J. (Bos) .593
Carew, R. (Min) .570
Jackson, R. (NY) .550

Adjusted OPS
Carew, R. (Min) 179
Singleton, K. (Bal) 168
Page, M. (Oak) 153

Adjusted Batting Runs
Carew, R. (Min) 69.0
Singleton, K. (Bal) 57.0
Page, M. (Oak) 47.0

Runs Created/Game
Carew, R. (Min) 10.80
Singleton, K. (Bal) 8.80
Page, M. (Oak) 8.60

Fielding Runs
Belanger, M. (Bal) 30.1
Randolph, W. (NY) 24.0
Brett, G. (KC) 23.3

Win Shares – Batters
Carew, R. (Min) 37
Singleton, K. (Bal) 36
2 players tied with 30

TPW – Batters
Carew, R. (Min) 6.3
Singleton, K. (Bal) 5.5
Brett, G. (KC) 5.2

TEAM	CG	SH	SV	IP	H	H/G	ER	HR	BB	SO	OAV	RAT	ERA	ERA+	CERA	PR+	PF	FA	E	DP	FR	BW	PW	FW	TPW	DIF
East																										
NY	52	16	34	1449[1]	1395	8.7	581	139	486	758	.254	1.298	3.61	109	3.68	24.8	97	.979	132	151	25.9	11.5	2.5	2.6	16.5	2.5
BAL	65	11	23	1451	1414	8.8	603	124	494	737	.260	1.315	3.74	101	3.75	-31.6	93	.983	106	189	40.0	2.8	-3.1	4.0	3.6	13.4
BOS	40	13	40	1428	1555	9.8	652	158	378	758	.278	1.354	4.11	109	4.21	75.5	111	.978	133	162	-21.3	5.4	7.5	-2.1	10.8	6.2
DET	44	3	23	1457	1526	9.4	669	162	470	784	.271	1.370	4.13	104	4.18	29.4	106	.978	142	153	-4.5	-6.2	2.9	-.4	-3.7	-3.3
CLE	45	8	30	1452[1]	1441	8.9	661	136	550	876	.261	1.371	4.10	96	3.96	-27.2	97	.979	130	145	2.6	-2.1	-2.7	.3	-4.5	-4.5
MIL	38	6	25	1431	1461	9.2	687	136	566	719	.268	1.416	4.32	94	4.21	-51.8	100	.978	139	165	10.7	-7.8	-5.1	1.1	-11.9	-2.1
TOR	40	3	20	1428	1538	9.7	725	152	623	771	.278	1.513	4.57	92	4.76	-24.8	103	.974	164	133	-35.1	-11.7	-2.5	-3.5	-17.7	-8.3
West																										
KC	41	15	42	1460[2]	1377	8.5	571	110	499	850	.251	1.284	3.52	115	3.47	67.5	99	.978	137	145	12.5	8.1	6.7	1.2	16.0	5.0
TEX	49	17	31	1472[1]	1412	8.6	582	134	471	864	.255	1.279	3.56	115	3.60	66.7	101	.982	117	156	18.1	3.1	6.6	1.8	11.5	1.5
CHI	34	3	40	1444[2]	1557	9.7	682	136	516	842	.277	1.435	4.25	96	4.41	15.5	101	.974	159	125	-42.8	10.5	1.5	-4.2	7.8	1.2
MIN	35	4	25	1442	1546	9.6	699	151	507	737	.278	1.424	4.36	91	4.47	-62.7	98	.978	143	184	-1.5	8.5	-6.2	-.1	2.1	1.9
CAL	53	13	26	1437[2]	1383	8.7	594	136	572	965	.256	1.360	3.72	105	3.99	36.6	96	.976	147	137	-11.9	-1.6	3.6	-1.2	.8	-7.8
SEA	18	1	31	1433	1508	9.5	769	194	578	785	.272	1.456	4.83	85	4.83	-141.2	101	.976	147	162	24.9	-8.5	-14.0	2.5	-20.0	3.0
OAK	32	4	26	1436[2]	1459	9.1	645	145	560	788	.265	1.405	4.04	100	4.19	12.6	99	.970	190	136	-17.2	-12.9	1.3	-1.7	-13.4	-3.6
Total	586	117	416	20224		9.2	9120					1.377	4.06													

Wins		Win Percentage		Games		Complete Games		Shutouts		Saves	
Goltz, D. (Min)	20	Splittorff, P. (KC)	.727	Lyle, S. (NY)	72	Palmer, J. (Bal)	22	Tanana, F. (Cal)	7	Campbell, B. (Bos)	31
Leonard, D. (KC)	20	Guidry, R. (NY)	.696	Johnson, T. (Min)	71	Ryan, N. (Cal)	22	3 players tied with	5	Lyle, S. (NY)	26
Palmer, J. (Bal)	20	Rozema, D. (Det)	.682	Campbell, B. (Bos)	69	2 players tied with	21			LaGrow, L. (Chi)	25

Innings Pitched		Fewest Hits/Game		Fewest BB/Game		Strikeouts		Ratio		Earned Run Average	
Palmer, J. (Bal)	319	Ryan, N. (Cal)	5.96	Rozema, D. (Det)	1.40	Ryan, N. (Cal)	341	Blyleven, B. (Tex)	1.07	Tanana, F. (Cal)	2.54
Goltz, D. (Min)	303	Blyleven, B. (Tex)	6.94	Jenkins, F. (Bos)	1.68	Leonard, D. (KC)	244	Eckersley, D. (Cle)	1.08	Blyleven, B. (Tex)	2.72
Ryan, N. (Cal)	299	Palmer, J. (Bal)	7.42	Hartzell, P. (Cal)	1.81	Tanana, F. (Cal)	205	Tanana, F. (Cal)	1.09	Ryan, N. (Cal)	2.77

Adjusted ERA		Component ERA		Opponents' Batting Avg.		Adjusted Pitching Runs		Win Shares – Pitchers		TPW – Pitchers	
Tanana, F. (Cal)	154	Blyleven, B. (Tex)	2.53	Ryan, N. (Cal)	.193	Ryan, N. (Cal)	40	Ryan, N. (Cal)	29	Ryan, N. (Cal)	4.0
Blyleven, B. (Tex)	150	Guidry, R. (NY)	2.55	Blyleven, B. (Tex)	.214	Tanana, F. (Cal)	39	Leonard, D. (KC)	24	Tanana, F. (Cal)	3.9
Ryan, N. (Cal)	141	Leonard, D. (KC)	2.61	Guidry, R. (NY)	.224	Blyleven, B. (Tex)	33	2 players tied with	22	Blyleven, B. (Tex)	3.2

1978 National League

TEAM	G	W	L	PCT	GB	R	OR	EW	AB	H	2B	3B	HR	TB	BB	SO	SB	CS	AVG	OBP	SLG	OPS	OPS+	BR/A	PF	RC
East																										
PHI	162	90	72	.556	....	708	586	96	5448	1404	248	32	133	2115	552	866	152	58	.258	.331	.388	.719	106	50	101	713
PIT	161	88	73	.547	1.5	684	637	86	5406	1390	239	54	115	2082	480	874	213	90	.257	.323	.385	.708	99	-3	105	674
CHI	162	79	83	.488	11	664	724	74	5532	1461	224	48	72	1997	562	746	110	58	.264	.334	.361	.695	90	-62	112	671
MON	162	76	86	.469	14	633	611	84	5530	1404	269	31	121	2098	396	881	80	42	.254	.308	.379	.687	99	-25	99	628
STL	162	69	93	.426	21	600	657	74	5415	1351	263	44	79	1939	420	713	97	42	.249	.306	.358	.664	93	-58	98	581
NY	162	66	96	.407	24	607	690	71	5433	1332	227	47	86	1911	549	829	100	77	.245	.317	.352	.669	96	-37	96	598
West																										
LA	162	95	67	.586	....	727	573	100	5437	1435	251	27	149	2187	610	818	137	52	.264	.340	.402	.743	114	109	100	761
CIN	161	92	69	.571	2.5	710	688	83	5392	1378	270	32	136	2120	636	899	137	58	.256	.337	.393	.730	110	81	99	728
SF	162	89	73	.549	6	613	594	84	5364	1331	240	41	117	2004	554	814	87	54	.248	.320	.374	.694	104	19	96	646
SD	162	84	78	.519	11	591	598	80	5360	1349	208	42	75	1866	536	848	152	70	.252	.323	.348	.672	102	16	92	622
HOU	162	74	88	.457	21	605	634	77	5458	1408	231	45	70	1939	434	743	178	59	.258	.315	.355	.670	101	10	93	606
ATL	162	69	93	.426	26	600	750	63	5381	1313	191	39	123	1951	550	874	90	65	.244	.317	.363	.680	86	-99	111	606
Total	971					7742			65156	16556	2861	482	1276		6279	9905	1533	725	.254	.323	.372	.694				

Runs		Hits		Doubles		Triples		Home Runs		Total Bases	
DeJesus, I. (Chi)	104	Garvey, S. (LA)	202	Rose, P. (Cin)	51	Templeton, G. (StL)	13	Foster, G. (Cin)	40	Parker, D. (Pit)	340
Rose, P. (Cin)	103	Rose, P. (Cin)	198	Clark, J. (SF)	46	Parker, D. (Pit)	12	Luzinski, G. (Phi)	35	Foster, G. (Cin)	330
Parker, D. (Pit)	102	Cabell, E. (Hou)	195	Simmons, T. (StL)	40	Richards, G. (SD)	12	Parker, D. (Pit)	30	Garvey, S. (LA)	319

Runs Batted In		Bases On Balls		Stolen Bases		Batting Average		On-Base Percentage		Slugging Average	
Foster, G. (Cin)	120	Burroughs, J. (Atl)	117	Moreno, O. (Pit)	71	Parker, D. (Pit)	.334	Burroughs, J. (Atl)	.436	Parker, D. (Pit)	.585
Parker, D. (Pit)	117	Evans, D. (SF)	105	Taveras, F. (Pit)	46	Garvey, S. (LA)	.316	Parker, D. (Pit)	.395	Smith, R. (LA)	.559
Garvey, S. (LA)	113	Tenace, G. (SD)	101	Lopes, D. (LA)	45	Cruz, J. (Hou)	.315	Tenace, G. (SD)	.394	Foster, G. (Cin)	.546

Adjusted OPS		Adjusted Batting Runs		Runs Created/Game		Fielding Runs		Win Shares – Batters		TPW – Batters	
Smith, R. (LA)	164	Parker, D. (Pit)	49.0	Parker, D. (Pit)	8.90	Russell, B. (LA)	19.2	Parker, D. (Pit)	37	Simmons, T. (StL)	4.6
Parker, D. (Pit)	163	Burroughs, J. (Atl)	40.0	Burroughs, J. (Atl)	8.60	Templeton, G. (StL)	18.9	3 players tied with	30	Parker, D. (Pit)	4.3
Clark, J. (SF)	155	Luzinski, G. (Phi)	40.0	Smith, R. (LA)	8.10	Smith, O. (SD)	18.4			Clark, J. (SF)	3.8

TEAM	CG	SH	SV	IP	H	H/G	ER	HR	BB	SO	OAV	RAT	ERA	ERA+	CERA	PR+	PF	FA	E	DP	FR	BW	PW	FW	TPW	DIF
East																										
PHI	38	9	29	1436[1]	1343	8.4	531	118	393	813	.251	1.209	3.33	107	3.21	9.2	100	.983	104	156	28.2	5.3	1.0	3.0	9.3	-.3
PIT	30	13	44	1444[2]	1366	8.5	547	103	499	880	.249	1.291	3.41	109	3.39	64.6	104	.973	167	133	-19.6	-.3	6.8	-2.1	4.5	3.5
CHI	24	7	38	1455[1]	1475	9.1	655	125	539	768	.265	1.384	4.05	99	3.96	6.0	113	.978	144	154	-11.1	-6.5	.6	-1.2	-7.1	5.1
MON	42	13	32	1446	1332	8.3	549	117	572	740	.249	1.317	3.42	103	3.62	-30.1	98	.979	134	150	45.7	-2.6	-3.2	4.8	-1.0	-4.0
STL	32	13	22	1437[2]	1300	8.1	572	94	600	859	.245	1.322	3.58	98	3.46	-24.2	98	.978	136	155	11.8	-6.1	-2.6	1.3	-7.4	-4.6
NY	21	7	26	1455[1]	1447	9.0	626	114	531	775	.265	1.359	3.87	90	3.83	-74.3	97	.979	132	160	11.6	-3.9	-7.9	1.2	-10.6	-4.4
West																										
LA	46	16	38	1440[1]	1362	8.5	499	107	440	800	.250	1.251	3.12	112	3.28	52.1	98	.978	140	138	8.9	11.5	5.5	.9	18.0	-4.0
CIN	16	10	46	1448[1]	1437	8.9	613	122	567	908	.261	1.384	3.81	93	3.87	-20.0	99	.978	134	120	-24.1	8.5	-2.1	-2.5	3.9	8.1
SF	42	17	29	1455	1377	8.5	534	84	453	840	.252	1.258	3.30	104	3.17	25.7	96	.977	146	118	-2.5	2.0	2.7	-.3	4.5	3.5
SD	21	10	55	1433[2]	1385	8.7	522	74	483	744	.257	1.303	3.28	101	3.33	4.0	99	.975	160	171	2.9	1.7	.4	.3	2.4	.6
HOU	48	17	23	1440[1]	1328	8.3	581	86	578	930	.247	1.323	3.63	91	3.42	-22.5	92	.978	133	109	-29.7	1.0	-2.4	-3.1	-4.5	-2.5
ATL	29	12	32	1440[1]	1404	8.8	653	132	624	848	.257	1.408	4.08	99	4.08	13.5	113	.975	153	126	-22.0	-10.5	1.4	-2.3	-11.4	-.6
Total	389	144	414	17333[1]		8.6	6882					1.317	3.57													

Wins		Win Percentage		Games		Complete Games		Shutouts		Saves	
Perry, G. (SD)	21	Perry, G. (SD)	.778	Tekulve, K. (Pit)	91	Niekro, P. (Atl)	22	Knepper, B. (SF)	6	Fingers, R. (SD)	37
Grimsley, R. (Mon)	20	Robinson, D. (Pit)	.700	Littell, M. (StL)	72	Grimsley, R. (Mon)	19	4 players tied with	4	Tekulve, K. (Pit)	31
2 players tied with	19	Hooton, B. (LA)	.655	Moore, D. (Chi)	71	2 players tied with	16			Bair, D. (Cin)	28

Innings Pitched		Fewest Hits/Game		Fewest BB/Game		Strikeouts		Ratio		Earned Run Average	
Niekro, P. (Atl)	334¹	Richard, J. (Hou)	6.28	Christenson, L. (Phi)	1.86	Richard, J. (Hou)	303	Halicki, E. (SF)	1.06	Swan, C. (NY)	2.43
Richard, J. (Hou)	275¹	Swan, C. (NY)	7.12	Barr, J. (SF)	1.93	Niekro, P. (Atl)	248	Swan, C. (NY)	1.07	Rogers, S. (Mon)	2.47
Grimsley, R. (Mon)	263	Hooton, B. (LA)	7.47	Reuschel, R. (Chi)	2.00	Seaver, T. (Cin)	226	Hooton, B. (LA)	1.09	Vuckovich, P. (StL)	2.54

Adjusted ERA		Component ERA		Opponents' Batting Avg.		Adjusted Pitching Runs		Win Shares – Pitchers		TPW – Pitchers	
Swan, C. (NY)	143	Halicki, E. (SF)	2.29	Richard, J. (Hou)	.196	Niekro, P. (Atl)	48	Niekro, P. (Atl)	30	Niekro, P. (Atl)	5.5
Rogers, S. (Mon)	143	Swan, C. (NY)	2.31	Swan, C. (NY)	.219	Knepper, B. (SF)	24	Blue, V. (SF)	22	Seaver, T. (Cin)	2.5
Niekro, P. (Atl)	140	Hooton, B. (LA)	2.48	Halicki, E. (SF)	.221	Seaver, T. (Cin)	24	Knepper, B. (SF)	22	Carlton, S. (Phi)	2.4

1978 American League

TEAM	G	W	L	PCT	GB	R	OR	EW	AB	H	2B	3B	HR	TB	BB	SO	SB	CS	AVG	OBP	SLG	OPS	OPS+	BR/A	PF	RC
East																										
NY	163	100	63	.613	....	735	**582**	100	5583	1489	228	38	125	2168	505	695	98	42	.267	.332	.388	.720	104	40	98	717
BOS	163	99	64	.607	1	796	657	97	5587	1493	270	46	172	2371	582	835	74	51	.267	.339	.424	.763	102	20	111	792
MIL	162	93	69	.574	6.5	**804**	650	98	5536	**1530**	265	38	**173**	**2390**	520	805	95	53	**.276**	.342	**.432**	**.774**	116	**114**	100	821
BAL	161	90	71	.559	9	659	633	84	5422	1397	248	19	154	2145	552	864	75	61	.258	.329	.396	.724	110	59	94	689
DET	162	86	76	.531	13.5	714	653	88	**5601**	1520	218	34	129	2193	563	695	90	**38**	.271	.341	.392	.733	103	33	103	746
CLE	159	69	90	.434	29	639	694	73	5365	1400	223	45	106	2031	488	698	64	63	.261	.326	.379	.704	99	-21	99	647
TOR	161	59	102	.366	40	590	775	59	5430	1358	217	39	98	1947	448	645	28	52	.250	.310	.359	.669	86	-118	102	586
West																										
KC	162	92	70	.568	....	743	634	94	5474	1469	**305**	**59**	98	2186	498	644	**216**	84	.268	.333	.399	.732	102	30	103	736
TEX	162	87	75	.537	5	692	632	88	5347	1353	216	36	132	2037	**624**	779	196	91	.253	.335	.381	.716	101	20	100	694
CAL	162	87	75	.537	5	691	666	84	5472	1417	226	28	108	2037	539	682	86	69	.259	.333	.370	.703	101	6	96	666
MIN	162	73	89	.451	19	666	678	80	5522	1472	259	47	82	2071	604	684	99	56	.267	**.342**	.375	.717	100	11	102	713
CHI	161	71	90	.441	20.5	634	731	69	5393	1423	221	41	106	2044	409	**625**	83	68	.264	.320	.379	.699	95	-50	101	633
OAK	162	69	93	.426	23	532	690	60	5321	1304	200	31	100	1866	433	800	144	117	.245	.305	.351	.656	88	-104	95	551
SEA	160	56	104	.350	35	614	834	56	5358	1327	229	37	97	1921	522	702	123	47	.248	.317	.359	.676	90	-58	99	618
Total	1131					9509			76411	19952	3325	538	1680		7287	10153	1471	892	.261	.329	.385	.714				

Runs		Hits		Doubles		Triples		Home Runs		Total Bases	
LeFlore, R. (Det)	126	Rice, J. (Bos)	213	Brett, G. (KC)	45	Rice, J. (Bos)	15	Rice, J. (Bos)	46	Rice, J. (Bos)	406
Rice, J. (Bos)	121	LeFlore, R. (Det)	198	Fisk, C. (Bos)	39	Carew, R. (Min)	10	Baylor, D. (Cal)	34	Murray, E. (Bal)	293
Baylor, D. (Cal)	103	Carew, R. (Min)	188	McRae, H. (KC)	39	Ford, D. (Min)	10	Hisle, L. (Mil)	34	2 players tied with	279

Runs Batted In		Bases On Balls		Stolen Bases		Batting Average		On-Base Percentage		Slugging Average	
Rice, J. (Bos)	139	Hargrove, M. (Tex)	107	LeFlore, R. (Det)	68	Carew, R. (Min)	.333	Carew, R. (Min)	.415	Rice, J. (Bos)	.600
Staub, R. (Det)	121	Singleton, K. (Bal)	98	Cruz, J. (Sea)	59	Oliver, A. (Tex)	.324	Singleton, K. (Bal)	.410	Hisle, L. (Mil)	.533
Hisle, L. (Mil)	115	Kemp, S. (Det)	97	Wills, B. (Tex)	52	Rice, J. (Bos)	.315	Hargrove, M. (Tex)	.391	DeCinces, D. (Bal)	.526

Adjusted OPS		Adjusted Batting Runs		Runs Created/Game		Fielding Runs		Win Shares – Batters		TPW – Batters	
Singleton, K. (Bal)	154	Rice, J. (Bos)	45.0	Rice, J. (Bos)	8.10	Whitaker, L. (Det)	25.9	Rice, J. (Bos)	36	Smalley, R. (Min)	4.0
Rice, J. (Bos)	153	Singleton, K. (Bal)	42.0	Otis, A. (KC)	7.40	Belanger, M. (Bal)	24.5	Fisk, C. (Bos)	31	Rice, J. (Bos)	4.0
Hisle, L. (Mil)	153	Otis, A. (KC)	37.0	Singleton, K. (Bal)	7.20	Bell, B. (Cle)	23.9	Otis, A. (KC)	29	Randolph, W. (NY)	3.9

TEAM	CG	SH	SV	IP	H	H/G	ER	HR	BB	SO	OAV	RAT	ERA	ERA+	CERA	PR+	PF	FA	E	DP	FR	BW	PW	FW	TPW	DIF
East																										
NY	39	16	**36**	1460²	**1321**	8.1	**516**	111	478	817	**.243**	**1.232**	**3.18**	114	**3.25**	60.2	96	.982	113	134	11.4	4.1	6.2	1.2	11.4	7.6
BOS	57	15	26	**1472²**	1530	9.4	579	137	464	706	.270	1.354	3.54	116	4.01	**82.6**	109	.977	146	171	11.3	2.1	**8.5**	1.2	11.7	6.3
MIL	62	**19**	24	1436	1442	9.0	582	109	**398**	577	.262	1.281	3.65	103	3.58	10.9	100	.977	150	144	5.7	**11.8**	1.1	.6	**13.5**	-1.5
BAL	**65**	16	33	1429	1340	8.4	565	107	509	754	.251	1.294	3.56	98	3.49	-30.6	93	**.982**	110	166	19.1	6.1	-3.1	2.0	4.9	5.1
DET	60	12	21	1455²	1441	8.9	588	135	503	684	.263	1.335	3.62	106	3.90	10.0	103	.981	118	**177**	**20.8**	3.4	1.0	**2.1**	6.6	-1.6
CLE	36	6	28	1407¹	1397	8.9	621	**100**	568	739	.261	1.396	3.97	94	3.92	-28.6	99	.980	123	142	-11.1	-2.2	-2.9	-1.1	-6.3	-3.7
TOR	35	5	23	1429¹	1529	9.6	721	149	614	758	.279	1.499	4.54	86	4.70	-89.1	104	.979	131	163	-9.6	-12.1	-9.2	-1.0	-22.3	1.3
West																										
KC	53	14	33	1439	1350	8.4	550	108	478	657	.251	1.270	3.44	111	3.40	50.6	102	.976	150	153	10.3	3.1	5.2	1.1	9.4	1.6
TEX	54	12	25	1456¹	1431	8.8	544	108	421	776	.259	1.272	3.33	113	3.46	57.1	99	.978	153	140	-5.7	2.0	5.9	-.6	7.3	-1.3
CAL	44	13	33	1455²	1382	8.5	590	125	599	**892**	.253	1.361	3.65	99	3.78	0.2	96	.978	136	136	-9.8	.7	.0	-1.0	-.3	6.3
MIN	48	9	26	1459²	1468	9.0	598	102	520	703	.266	1.362	3.69	104	3.86	13.3	102	.977	146	171	5.0	1.2	1.4	.5	3.0	-11.0
CHI	38	9	33	1409¹	1380	8.8	659	128	586	710	.259	1.395	4.21	90	4.09	-54.9	101	.977	139	130	-12.9	-5.1	-5.7	-1.3	-12.1	3.1
OAK	26	11	29	1433¹	1401	8.8	576	106	582	750	.259	1.383	3.62	101	3.81	27.9	97	.971	179	145	-25.4	-10.7	2.9	-2.6	-10.4	-1.6
SEA	28	4	20	1419¹	1540	9.8	736	155	567	630	.280	1.484	4.67	82	4.73	-134.6	101	.978	141	174	-8.9	-5.9	-13.9	-.9	-20.7	-3.3
Total	645	161	390	20163¹		8.9	8425					1.351	3.76													

Wins		Win Percentage		Games		Complete Games		Shutouts		Saves	
Guidry, R. (NY)	25	Guidry, R. (NY)	.893	Lacey, B. (Oak)	74	Caldwell, M. (Mil)	23	Guidry, R. (NY)	9	Gossage, R. (NY)	27
Caldwell, M. (Mil)	22	Gura, L. (KC)	.800	Heaverlo, D. (Oak)	69	Leonard, D. (KC)	20	Caldwell, M. (Mil)	6	LaRoche, D. (Cal)	25
2 players tied with	21	Eckersley, D. (Bos)	.714	Sosa, E. (Oak)	68	Palmer, J. (Bal)	19	Palmer, J. (Bal)	6	Stanhouse, D. (Bal)	24

Innings Pitched		Fewest Hits/Game		Fewest BB/Game		Strikeouts		Ratio		Earned Run Average	
Palmer, J. (Bal)	296	Guidry, R. (NY)	6.15	Jenkins, F. (Tex)	1.48	Ryan, N. (Cal)	260	Guidry, R. (NY)	.95	Guidry, R. (NY)	1.74
Leonard, D. (KC)	294²	Ryan, N. (Cal)	7.02	Sorensen, L. (Mil)	1.60	Guidry, R. (NY)	248	Caldwell, M. (Mil)	1.06	Matlack, J. (Tex)	2.27
Caldwell, M. (Mil)	293¹	Gura, L. (KC)	7.43	Caldwell, M. (Mil)	1.66	Leonard, D. (KC)	183	Jenkins, F. (Tex)	1.08	Caldwell, M. (Mil)	2.36

Adjusted ERA		Component ERA		Opponents' Batting Avg.		Adjusted Pitching Runs		Win Shares – Pitchers		TPW – Pitchers	
Guidry, R. (NY)	208	Guidry, R. (NY)	1.71	Guidry, R. (NY)	.193	Guidry, R. (NY)	55	Guidry, R. (NY)	31	Guidry, R. (NY)	5.7
Matlack, J. (Tex)	165	Caldwell, M. (Mil)	2.39	Ryan, N. (Cal)	.220	Matlack, J. (Tex)	45	Caldwell, M. (Mil)	28	Matlack, J. (Tex)	4.7
Caldwell, M. (Mil)	159	Gura, L. (KC)	2.49	Palmer, J. (Bal)	.227	Caldwell, M. (Mil)	44	Palmer, J. (Bal)	27	Caldwell, M. (Mil)	4.6

1979 National League

TEAM	G	W	L	PCT	GB	R	OR	EW	AB	H	2B	3B	HR	TB	BB	SO	SB	CS	AVG	OBP	SLG	OPS	OPS+	BR/A	PF	RC
East																										
PIT	163	98	64	.605	....	**775**	643	96	5661	1541	264	52	148	**2353**	483	855	180	66	.272	.333	**.416**	**.749**	105	44	105	**779**
MON	160	95	65	.594	2	701	**581**	95	5465	1445	273	42	143	2231	432	890	121	56	.264	.321	.408	.730	105	31	99	700
STL	163	86	76	.531	12	731	693	85	**5734**	**1594**	**279**	**63**	100	2299	460	838	116	69	**.278**	.335	.401	.735	106	35	101	755
PHI	163	84	78	.519	14	683	718	77	5463	1453	250	53	119	2166	602	764	128	76	.266	**.343**	.396	.739	104	38	103	741
CHI	162	80	82	.494	18	706	707	81	5550	1494	250	43	135	2235	478	762	73	52	.269	.331	.403	.734	97	-28	109	725
NY	163	63	99	.389	35	593	706	67	5591	1399	255	41	74	1958	498	817	135	79	.250	.315	.350	.666	91	-72	96	613
West																										
CIN	161	90	71	.559	....	731	644	91	5477	1445	266	31	132	2169	**614**	902	99	47	.264	.340	.396	.736	106	55	101	739
HOU	162	89	73	.549	1.5	583	582	81	5394	1382	224	52	49	1857	461	**745**	**190**	95	.256	.317	.344	.662	92	-58	94	589
LA	162	79	83	.488	11.5	739	717	83	5490	1443	220	24	**183**	2260	556	834	106	**46**	.263	.333	.412	.745	**111**	**79**	98	742
SF	162	71	91	.438	19.5	672	751	72	5395	1328	192	36	125	1967	580	925	140	73	.246	.322	.365	.686	100	2	93	642
SD	161	68	93	.422	22	603	681	71	5446	1316	193	53	93	1894	534	770	100	58	.242	.313	.348	.661	92	-61	94	598
ATL	160	66	94	.412	23.5	669	763	70	5422	1389	220	28	126	2043	490	818	98	50	.256	.320	.377	.697	89	-74	107	652
Total	**971**					**8186**			**66088**	**17229**	**2886**	**518**	**1427**		**6188**	**9920**	**1486**	**767**	**.261**	**.327**	**.385**	**.712**				

Runs
- Hernandez, K. (StL) 116
- Moreno, O. (Pit) 110
- 3 players tied with 109

Hits
- Templeton, G. (StL) 211
- Hernandez, K. (StL) 210
- Rose, P. (Phi) 208

Doubles
- Hernandez, K. (StL) 48
- Cromartie, W. (Mon) 46
- Parker, D. (Pit) 45

Triples
- Templeton, G. (StL) 19
- 3 players tied with 12

Home Runs
- Kingman, D. (Chi) 48
- Schmidt, M. (Phi) 45
- Winfield, D. (SD) 34

Total Bases
- Winfield, D. (SD) 333
- Parker, D. (Pit) 327
- Kingman, D. (Chi) 326

Runs Batted In
- Winfield, D. (SD) 118
- Kingman, D. (Chi) 115
- Schmidt, M. (Phi) 114

Bases On Balls
- Schmidt, M. (Phi) 120
- Tenace, G. (SD) 105
- Lopes, D. (LA) 97

Stolen Bases
- Moreno, O. (Pit) 77
- North, B. (SF) 58
- 2 players tied with 44

Batting Average
- Hernandez, K. (StL) .344
- Rose, P. (Phi) .331
- Knight, R. (Cin) .318

On-Base Percentage
- Hernandez, K. (StL) .421
- Rose, P. (Phi) .421
- Tenace, G. (SD) .407

Slugging Average
- Kingman, D. (Chi) .613
- Schmidt, M. (Phi) .564
- Foster, G. (Cin) .561

Adjusted OPS
- Winfield, D. (SD) 167
- Foster, G. (Cin) 155
- Schmidt, M. (Phi) 153

Adjusted Batting Runs
- Winfield, D. (SD) 55.0
- Hernandez, K. (StL) 46.0
- Schmidt, M. (Phi) 42.0

Runs Created/Game
- Hernandez, K. (StL) 8.70
- Winfield, D. (SD) 8.20
- Foster, G. (Cin) 7.90

Fielding Runs
- Concepcion, D. (Cin) 23.9
- Templeton, G. (StL) 21.3
- Schmidt, M. (Phi) 20.0

Win Shares – Batters
- Schmidt, M. (Phi) 33
- Winfield, D. (SD) 33
- Parker, D. (Pit) 31

TPW – Batters
- Winfield, D. (SD) 6.3
- Schmidt, M. (Phi) 6.3
- Concepcion, D. (Cin) 4.9

TEAM	CG	SH	SV	IP	H	H/G	ER	HR	BB	SO	OAV	RAT	ERA	ERA+	CERA	PR+	PF	FA	E	DP	FR	BW	PW	FW	TPW	DIF
East																										
PIT	24	7	**52**	**1493^1**	1424	8.6	566	125	504	904	.254	1.291	3.41	114	3.51	60.0	104	.979	134	163	15.1	4.6	6.2	1.6	**12.3**	4.7
MON	33	18	39	1447^1	1379	8.6	**505**	116	**450**	813	.253	1.264	**3.14**	117	3.39	**77.5**	98	.979	131	123	6.6	3.2	**8.0**	.7	11.9	3.1
STL	38	10	25	1486^2	1449	8.8	614	127	501	788	.258	1.312	3.72	101	3.65	-28.9	101	.980	132	166	**32.9**	3.6	-3.0	**3.4**	4.0	1.0
PHI	33	14	29	1441^1	1455	9.1	666	135	477	787	.266	1.340	4.16	92	3.90	-70.4	102	**.983**	**106**	148	16.7	3.9	-7.3	1.7	-1.7	4.7
CHI	20	11	44	1446^2	1500	9.3	623	127	521	**933**	.270	1.397	3.88	106	4.13	56.3	110	.975	159	163	-21.9	-2.9	5.8	-2.3	.7	-1.7
NY	16	10	36	1482^2	1486	9.0	632	120	607	819	.266	1.412	3.84	95	4.01	-49.8	98	.978	140	**168**	16.2	-7.4	-5.1	1.7	-10.9	-7.1
West																										
CIN	27	10	40	1440^1	1415	8.8	573	103	485	773	.260	1.319	3.58	104	3.54	18.9	100	.980	124	152	2.0	5.6	2.0	.2	7.8	2.2
HOU	**55**	**19**	31	1447^2	**1278**	**8.0**	514	**90**	504	854	**.237**	**1.231**	3.20	110	**3.09**	55.6	94	.978	138	146	-5.2	-6.0	5.7	-.5	-.8	8.8
LA	30	6	34	1444	1425	8.9	615	101	555	811	.260	1.371	3.83	95	3.77	-19.4	97	.981	118	123	-17.6	**8.1**	-2.0	-1.8	4.3	-6.3
SF	25	6	34	1436	1484	9.3	664	143	577	880	.269	1.435	4.16	**84**	4.26	-90.5	94	.974	163	138	-17.3	.2	-9.3	-1.8	-10.9	.9
SD	29	7	25	1453	1438	8.9	596	108	513	779	.263	1.343	3.69	95	3.70	-40.7	95	.978	141	154	11.8	-6.3	-4.2	1.2	-9.3	-2.7
ATL	32	3	34	1407^2	1496	9.6	653	132	494	779	.272	1.414	4.17	97	4.25	20.2	109	.970	183	139	-40.8	-7.7	2.1	-4.2	-9.8	-4.2
Total	**362**	**121**	**423**	**17426^2**		**8.9**	**7221**					**1.344**	**3.73**													

Wins
- Niekro, J. (Hou) 21
- Niekro, P. (Atl) 21
- 3 players tied with 18

Win Percentage
- Seaver, T. (Cin) .727
- Blyleven, B. (Pit) .706
- Schatzeder, D. (Mon) .667

Games
- Tekulve, K. (Pit) 94
- Romo, E. (Pit) 84
- Jackson, G. (Pit) 72

Complete Games
- Niekro, P. (Atl) 23
- Richard, J. (Hou) 19
- 2 players tied with 13

Shutouts
- Niekro, J. (Hou) 5
- Rogers, S. (Mon) 5
- Seaver, T. (Cin) 5

Saves
- Sutter, B. (Chi) 37
- Tekulve, K. (Pit) 31
- Garber, G. (Atl) 25

Innings Pitched
- Niekro, P. (Atl) 342
- Richard, J. (Hou) 292^1
- Niekro, J. (Hou) 263^2

Fewest Hits/Game
- Richard, J. (Hou) 6.77
- Carlton, S. (Phi) 7.24
- Niekro, J. (Hou) 7.54

Fewest BB/Game
- Forsch, K. (Hou) 1.77
- Candelaria, J. (Pit) 1.78
- Hume, T. (Cin) 1.82

Strikeouts
- Richard, J. (Hou) 313
- Carlton, S. (Phi) 213
- Niekro, P. (Atl) 208

Ratio
- Forsch, K. (Hou) 1.07
- Richard, J. (Hou) 1.09
- Seaver, T. (Cin) 1.15

Earned Run Average
- Richard, J. (Hou) 2.71
- Hume, T. (Cin) 2.76
- Schatzeder, D. (Mon) 2.83

Adjusted ERA
- Hume, T. (Cin) 135
- Richard, J. (Hou) 130
- Schatzeder, D. (Mon) 129

Component ERA
- Richard, J. (Hou) 2.23
- Forsch, K. (Hou) 2.54
- Seaver, T. (Cin) 2.77

Opponents' Batting Avg.
- Richard, J. (Hou) .209
- Carlton, S. (Phi) .219
- Schatzeder, D. (Mon) .225

Adjusted Pitching Runs
- Niekro, P. (Atl) 35
- Richard, J. (Hou) 27
- Hooton, B. (LA) 18

Win Shares – Pitchers
- Niekro, P. (Atl) 24
- Richard, J. (Hou) 23
- Niekro, J. (Hou) 19

TPW – Pitchers
- Niekro, P. (Atl) 3.8
- Richard, J. (Hou) 2.7
- Schatzeder, D. (Mon) 1.9

1979 American League

TEAM	G	W	L	PCT	GB	R	OR	EW	AB	H	2B	3B	HR	TB	BB	SO	SB	CS	AVG	OBP	SLG	OPS	OPS+	BR/A	PF	RC
East																										
BAL	159	102	57	.642	....	757	**582**	100	5371	1401	258	24	181	2250	608	847	99	49	.261	.339	.419	.758	107	59	96	756
MIL	161	95	66	.590	8	807	722	89	5536	1552	291	41	185	2480	549	745	100	53	.280	.347	.448	.795	113	96	100	**849**
BOS	160	91	69	.569	11.5	841	711	93	5538	1567	**310**	34	**194**	**2527**	512	708	60	**43**	**.283**	.347	**.456**	**.803**	109	61	105	846
NY	160	89	71	.556	13.5	734	672	87	5421	1443	226	40	150	2199	509	**590**	65	46	.266	.331	.406	.737	100	-9	98	706
DET	161	85	76	.528	18	770	738	84	5375	1446	221	35	164	2229	575	814	176	86	.269	.342	.415	.757	100	4	103	753
CLE	161	81	80	.503	22	760	805	76	5376	1388	206	29	138	2066	**657**	786	143	90	.258	.344	.384	.728	96	-26	100	717
TOR	162	53	109	.327	50.5	613	862	54	5423	1362	253	34	95	1968	448	663	75	56	.251	.313	.363	.675	81	-156	101	600
West																										
CAL	162	88	74	.543	....	**866**	768	91	5550	1563	242	43	164	2383	589	843	100	53	.282	**.354**	.429	.784	**114**	**115**	97	840
KC	162	85	77	.525	3	851	816	84	**5653**	**1596**	286	**79**	116	2388	528	675	**207**	76	.282	.347	.422	.770	104	50	102	834
TEX	162	83	79	.512	5	750	698	87	5562	1549	252	26	140	2273	461	607	79	51	.278	.337	.409	.746	101	5	99	748
MIN	162	82	80	.506	6	764	725	85	5544	1544	256	46	112	2228	526	693	66	45	.278	.344	.402	.746	97	-23	104	768
CHI	160	73	87	.456	14	730	748	78	5463	1505	290	33	127	2242	454	668	97	62	.275	.335	.410	.746	100	-8	100	724
SEA	162	67	95	.414	21	711	820	70	5544	1490	250	52	132	2240	515	725	126	52	.269	.334	.404	.738	96	-22	102	731
OAK	162	54	108	.333	34	573	860	50	5348	1276	188	32	108	1852	482	751	104	69	.239	.304	.346	.650	79	-163	95	550
Total	**1128**					**10527**			**76704**	**20682**	**3529**	**548**	**2006**		**7413**	**10115**	**1497**	**831**	**.270**	**.337**	**.408**	**.746**				

Runs		Hits		Doubles		Triples		Home Runs		Total Bases	
Baylor, D. (Cal)	120	Brett, G. (KC)	212	Cooper, C. (Mil)	44	Brett, G. (KC)	20	Thomas, G. (Mil)	45	Rice, J. (Bos)	369
Brett, G. (KC)	119	Rice, J. (Bos)	201	Lemon, C. (Chi)	44	Molitor, P. (Mil)	16	Lynn, F. (Bos)	39	Brett, G. (KC)	363
Rice, J. (Bos)	117	Bell, B. (Tex)	200	3 players tied with	42	2 players tied with	13	Rice, J. (Bos)	39	Lynn, F. (Bos)	338

Runs Batted In		Bases On Balls		Stolen Bases		Batting Average		On-Base Percentage		Slugging Average	
Baylor, D. (Cal)	139	Porter, D. (KC)	121	Wilson, W. (KC)	83	Lynn, F. (Bos)	.333	Porter, D. (KC)	.429	Lynn, F. (Bos)	.637
Rice, J. (Bos)	130	Singleton, K. (Bal)	109	LeFlore, R. (Det)	78	Brett, G. (KC)	.329	Lynn, F. (Bos)	.426	Rice, J. (Bos)	.596
Thomas, G. (Mil)	123	Thomas, G. (Mil)	98	Cruz, J. (Sea)	49	Downing, B. (Cal)	.326	Downing, B. (Cal)	.420	Lezcano, S. (Mil)	.573

Adjusted OPS		Adjusted Batting Runs		Runs Created/Game		Fielding Runs		Win Shares – Batters		TPW – Batters	
Lynn, F. (Bos)	173	Lynn, F. (Bos)	56.0	Lynn, F. (Bos)	10.70	Brett, G. (KC)	27.6	Lynn, F. (Bos)	34	Brett, G. (KC)	6.4
Lezcano, S. (Mil)	165	Singleton, K. (Bal)	51.0	Lezcano, S. (Mil)	8.90	Grich, B. (Cal)	21.9	Brett, G. (KC)	33	Grich, B. (Cal)	6.1
Singleton, K. (Bal)	158	Lezcano, S. (Mil)	45.0	Rice, J. (Bos)	8.40	Burleson, R. (Bos)	21.8	Singleton, K. (Bal)	32	Lynn, F. (Bos)	5.4

TEAM	CG	SH	SV	IP	H	H/G	ER	HR	BB	SO	OAV	RAT	ERA	ERA+	CERA	PR+	PF	FA	E	DP	FR	BW	PW	FW	TPW	DIF
East																										
BAL	52	12	30	1434[1]	**1279**	8.0	**519**	133	467	786	**.241**	**1.217**	**3.26**	123	**3.22**	**93.8**	95	.980	125	161	22.9	5.8	**9.1**	2.2	**17.2**	5.8
MIL	61	12	23	1439[2]	1563	9.8	644	162	**381**	580	.279	1.350	4.03	103	4.19	28.1	99	.980	127	153	-7.8	9.4	2.7	-.8	11.4	3.6
BOS	47	11	29	1431[1]	1487	9.4	641	133	463	731	.270	1.362	4.03	109	4.03	71.8	105	.977	142	166	-11.3	5.9	7.0	-1.1	11.8	-.8
NY	43	10	37	1432[1]	1446	9.1	609	123	455	731	.268	1.327	3.83	106	3.88	11.4	97	**.981**	122	183	**23.5**	-.9	1.1	**2.3**	2.5	6.5
DET	25	5	37	1423[1]	1429	9.0	675	167	547	802	.265	1.388	4.27	101	4.31	-7.8	103	.981	**120**	184	14.9	.4	-.8	1.5	1.1	3.9
CLE	28	7	32	1431[2]	1502	9.4	727	138	570	781	.272	1.447	4.57	93	4.40	-22.0	101	.978	134	149	-30.2	-2.6	-2.2	-2.9	-7.7	8.7
TOR	44	7	11	1417	1537	9.8	759	165	594	613	.281	1.504	4.82	90	4.92	-86.9	103	.975	159	187	7.4	-15.2	-8.5	.7	-22.9	-5.1
West																										
CAL	46	9	33	1436	1463	9.2	692	131	573	**820**	.267	1.418	4.34	94	4.22	-36.6	97	.978	135	172	-5.9	**11.2**	-3.6	-.6	7.1	-.1
KC	42	7	27	**1448[1]**	1477	9.2	716	165	536	640	.267	1.390	4.45	96	4.22	-44.8	101	.977	146	160	13.7	4.9	-4.4	1.3	1.8	2.2
TEX	26	10	**42**	1437	1371	8.6	616	135	532	773	.253	1.324	3.86	107	3.74	29.8	98	.979	130	151	15.1	.5	2.9	1.5	4.8	-2.8
MIN	31	6	33	1444[1]	1590	9.9	663	128	452	721	.285	1.414	4.13	106	4.35	37.2	104	.979	134	**203**	-1.2	-2.2	3.6	-.1	1.3	-.3
CHI	28	9	37	1409	1365	8.7	642	**114**	618	675	.256	1.407	4.10	104	4.00	13.2	101	.972	173	142	5.1	-.8	1.3	.5	1.0	-8.0
SEA	37	7	26	1438	1567	9.8	732	165	571	736	.281	1.487	4.58	95	4.74	-35.2	103	.978	141	170	-4.4	-2.2	-3.4	-.4	-6.0	-8.0
OAK	41	4	20	1429[1]	1606	10.1	754	147	654	726	.288	1.581	4.75	85	5.14	-75.4	96	.972	174	137	-41.7	-15.9	-7.4	-4.1	-27.3	.3
Total	551	116	417	20051[2]		9.3	9389					1.401	4.21													

Wins		Win Percentage		Games		Complete Games		Shutouts		Saves	
Flanagan, M. (Bal)	23	Caldwell, M. (Mil)	.727	Marshall, M. (Min)	90	Martinez, D. (Bal)	18	Flanagan, M. (Bal)	5	Marshall, M. (Min)	32
John, T. (NY)	21	Flanagan, M. (Bal)	.719	Monge, S. (Cle)	76	3 players tied with	17	Leonard, D. (KC)	5	Kern, J. (Tex)	29
Koosman, J. (Min)	20	Morris, J. (Det)	.708	Kern, J. (Tex)	71			Ryan, N. (Cal)	5	2 players tied with	21

Innings Pitched		Fewest Hits/Game		Fewest BB/Game		Strikeouts		Ratio		Earned Run Average	
Martinez, D. (Bal)	292[1]	Ryan, N. (Cal)	6.83	McGregor, S. (Bal)	1.19	Ryan, N. (Cal)	223	McGregor, S. (Bal)	1.08	Guidry, R. (NY)	2.78
John, T. (NY)	276[1]	Kravec, K. (Chi)	7.49	Caldwell, M. (Mil)	1.49	Guidry, R. (NY)	201	Guidry, R. (NY)	1.16	John, T. (NY)	2.96
Flanagan, M. (Bal)	265[2]	Guidry, R. (NY)	7.73	Sorensen, L. (Mil)	1.61	Flanagan, M. (Bal)	190	Flanagan, M. (Bal)	1.19	Eckersley, D. (Bos)	2.99

Adjusted ERA		Component ERA		Opponents' Batting Avg.		Adjusted Pitching Runs		Win Shares – Pitchers		TPW – Pitchers	
Eckersley, D. (Bos)	147	McGregor, S. (Bal)	2.83	Ryan, N. (Cal)	.212	Eckersley, D. (Bos)	41	Eckersley, D. (Bos)	24	Eckersley, D. (Bos)	4.0
Guidry, R. (NY)	146	Guidry, R. (NY)	2.92	Kravec, K. (Chi)	.233	Guidry, R. (NY)	30	3 players tied with	23	Guidry, R. (NY)	2.9
John, T. (NY)	137	John, T. (NY)	2.97	Guidry, R. (NY)	.236	Koosman, J. (Min)	30			Koosman, J. (Min)	2.9

1980 National League

TEAM	G	W	L	PCT	GB	R	OR	EW	AB	H	2B	3B	HR	TB	BB	SO	SB	CS	AVG	OBP	SLG	OPS	OPS+	BR/A	PF	RC
East																										
PHI	162	91	71	.562	....	728	639	92	**5625**	1517	272	54	117	**2248**	472	**708**	140	62	.270	.330	.400	.729	103	24	105	**734**
MON	162	90	72	.556	1	694	629	89	5465	1407	250	61	114	2121	547	865	237	82	.257	.327	.388	.715	105	49	100	707
PIT	162	83	79	.512	8	666	646	83	5517	1469	249	38	116	2142	452	760	209	102	.266	.325	.388	.713	103	13	102	684
STL	162	74	88	.457	17	**738**	710	84	5608	**1541**	**300**	49	101	2242	451	781	117	54	**.275**	**.331**	**.400**	**.731**	106	40	103	722
NY	162	67	95	.414	24	611	702	70	5478	1407	218	41	61	1890	501	840	158	99	.257	.322	.345	.667	95	-47	97	599
CHI	162	64	98	.395	27	614	728	67	5619	1411	251	35	107	2053	471	912	93	64	.251	.311	.365	.676	87	-101	107	626
West																										
HOU	163	93	70	.571	....	637	**589**	88	5566	1455	231	**67**	75	2045	540	755	194	74	.261	.328	.367	.696	**108**	67	92	686
LA	163	92	71	.564	1	663	591	91	5568	1462	209	24	**148**	2163	492	846	123	72	.263	.325	.388	.714	106	35	98	698
CIN	163	89	73	.549	3.5	707	670	85	5516	1445	256	45	113	2130	537	852	156	**43**	.262	.330	.386	.716	105	52	100	714
ATL	161	81	80	.503	11	630	660	77	5402	1352	226	22	144	2054	434	899	73	52	.250	.308	.380	.689	94	-57	103	614
SF	161	75	86	.466	17	573	634	72	5368	1310	199	44	80	1837	509	840	100	58	.244	.311	.342	.653	90	-75	98	569
SD	163	73	89	.451	19.5	591	654	73	5540	1410	195	43	67	1892	**563**	791	**239**	73	.255	.326	.342	.667	98	9	94	639
Total	973					7852			66272	17186	2856	523	1243		5969	9849	1839	835	**.259**	**.323**	**.374**	**.697**				

Runs		Hits		Doubles		Triples		Home Runs		Total Bases	
Hernandez, K. (StL)	111	Garvey, S. (LA)	200	Rose, P. (Phi)	42	Moreno, O. (Pit)	13	Schmidt, M. (Phi)	48	Schmidt, M. (Phi)	342
Schmidt, M. (Phi)	104	Richards, G. (SD)	193	Buckner, B. (Chi)	41	Scott, R. (Mon)	13	Horner, B. (Atl)	35	Garvey, S. (LA)	307
Murphy, D. (Atl)	98	Hernandez, K. (StL)	191	Dawson, A. (Mon)	41	2 players tied with	11	Murphy, D. (Atl)	33	Hernandez, K. (StL)	294

Runs Batted In		Bases On Balls		Stolen Bases		Batting Average		On-Base Percentage		Slugging Average	
Schmidt, M. (Phi)	121	Morgan, J. (Hou)	93	LeFlore, R. (Mon)	97	Buckner, B. (Chi)	.324	Hernandez, K. (StL)	.410	Schmidt, M. (Phi)	.624
Hendrick, G. (StL)	109	Driessen, D. (Cin)	93	Moreno, O. (Pit)	96	Hernandez, K. (StL)	.321	Cedeno, C. (Hou)	.390	Clark, J. (SF)	.517
Garvey, S. (LA)	106	Tenace, G. (SD)	92	Collins, D. (Cin)	79	Templeton, G. (StL)	.319	Clark, J. (SF)	.390	Murphy, D. (Atl)	.510

Adjusted OPS		Adjusted Batting Runs		Runs Created/Game		Fielding Runs		Win Shares – Batters		TPW – Batters	
Schmidt, M. (Phi)	169	Schmidt, M. (Phi)	51.0	Schmidt, M. (Phi)	8.90	Smith, O. (SD)	29.8	Schmidt, M. (Phi)	37	Schmidt, M. (Phi)	7.1
Clark, J. (SF)	155	Hernandez, K. (StL)	40.0	Hernandez, K. (StL)	7.70	Templeton, G. (StL)	26.6	Carter, G. (Mon)	30	Templeton, G. (StL)	4.5
Cedeno, C. (Hou)	149	Cedeno, C. (Hou)	38.0	Simmons, T. (StL)	7.00	Evans, D. (SF)	18.6	Dawson, A. (Mon)	29	Carter, G. (Mon)	3.8

TEAM	CG	SH	SV	IP	H	H/G	ER	HR	BB	SO	OAV	RAT	ERA	ERA+	CERA	PR+	PF	FA	E	DP	FR	BW	PW	FW	TPW	DIF
East																										
PHI	25	8	40	1480	1419	8.6	564	87	530	889	.255	1.317	3.43	110	3.44	**56.0**	105	.979	136	136	-2.1	2.5	**5.9**	-.2	8.2	1.8
MON	33	15	36	1456[2]	1447	8.9	563	100	460	823	.261	1.309	3.48	103	3.56	22.1	99	.977	144	126	-7.7	5.1	2.3	-.8	6.7	2.3
PIT	25	8	**43**	1458[1]	1422	8.8	580	110	**451**	832	.259	1.284	3.58	102	3.49	-2.5	101	.978	137	154	12.3	1.4	-.3	1.3	2.4	-.4
STL	**34**	9	27	1447	1454	9.0	632	90	495	664	.265	1.347	3.93	94	3.65	-59.4	102	.981	122	**174**	**21.0**	4.2	-6.3	**2.2**	.1	-7.1
NY	17	9	33	1451[1]	1473	9.1	621	140	510	886	.267	1.366	3.85	**92**	3.96	-56.8	99	.975	154	132	3.5	-4.9	-6.0	.4	-10.6	-3.4
CHI	13	6	35	1479	1525	9.3	639	109	589	923	.272	1.429	3.89	101	4.08	24.4	109	.974	174	149	-19.6	-10.6	2.6	-2.1	-10.1	-6.9
West																										
HOU	31	18	41	**1482[2]**	1367	**8.3**	**510**	**69**	466	**929**	**.246**	**1.236**	**3.10**	106	**3.05**	29.2	91	.978	140	145	0.8	**7.0**	3.1	.1	**10.2**	1.8
LA	24	**19**	42	1472[2]	**1358**	**8.3**	532	105	480	835	.247	1.248	3.25	108	3.24	20.6	97	.981	123	149	17.6	3.7	2.2	1.9	7.7	3.3
CIN	30	12	37	1459[1]	1404	8.7	624	113	506	833	.255	1.309	3.85	93	3.55	-26.7	99	**.983**	**106**	144	-17.0	5.5	-2.8	-1.8	.9	7.1
ATL	29	9	37	1428	1397	8.8	598	131	454	696	.258	1.296	3.77	99	3.62	-2.9	104	.975	162	156	-1.2	-6.0	-.3	-.1	-6.5	7.5
SF	27	10	35	1448[1]	1446	9.0	557	92	492	811	.261	1.338	3.46	102	3.60	42.7	98	.975	159	124	-29.4	-7.9	4.5	-3.1	-6.5	1.5
SD	19	9	39	1466[1]	1474	9.0	595	97	536	728	.267	1.371	3.65	94	3.70	-57.1	95	.980	132	157	20.1	1.0	-6.0	2.1	-2.9	-5.1
Total	**307**	**132**	**445**	**17529[2]**		**8.8**	**7015**					**1.321**	**3.60**													

Wins
Carlton, S. (Phi) 24
Niekro, J. (Hou) 20
Bibby, J. (Pit) 19

Win Percentage
Bibby, J. (Pit) .760
Reuss, J. (LA) .750
Carlton, S. (Phi) .727

Games
Tidrow, D. (Chi) 84
Hume, T. (Cin) 78
Tekulve, K. (Pit) 78

Complete Games
Rogers, S. (Mon) 14
Carlton, S. (Phi) 13
2 players tied with 11

Shutouts
Reuss, J. (LA) 6
Richard, J. (Hou) 4
Rogers, S. (Mon) 4

Saves
Sutter, B. (Chi) 28
Hume, T. (Cin) 25
Fingers, R. (SD) 23

Innings Pitched
Carlton, S. (Phi) 304
Rogers, S. (Mon) 281
Niekro, P. (Atl) 275

Fewest Hits/Game
Soto, M. (Cin) 5.96
Sutton, D. (LA) 6.91
Carlton, S. (Phi) 7.19

Fewest BB/Game
Forsch, B. (StL) 1.38
Reuss, J. (LA) 1.57
Forsch, K. (Hou) 1.66

Strikeouts
Carlton, S. (Phi) 286
Ryan, N. (Hou) 200
Soto, M. (Cin) 182

Ratio
Sutton, D. (LA) .99
Reuss, J. (LA) 1.02
Carlton, S. (Phi) 1.10

Earned Run Average
Sutton, D. (LA) 2.20
Carlton, S. (Phi) 2.34
Reuss, J. (LA) 2.51

Adjusted ERA
Carlton, S. (Phi) 162
Sutton, D. (LA) 159
Reuss, J. (LA) 139

Component ERA
Reuss, J. (LA) 2.08
Soto, M. (Cin) 2.15
Sutton, D. (LA) 2.20

Opponents' Batting Avg.
Soto, M. (Cin) .187
Sutton, D. (LA) .211
Carlton, S. (Phi) .218

Adjusted Pitching Runs
Carlton, S. (Phi) 49
Sutton, D. (LA) 28
Reuss, J. (LA) 22

Win Shares – Pitchers
Carlton, S. (Phi) 29
Reuss, J. (LA) 21
2 players tied with 20

TPW – Pitchers
Carlton, S. (Phi) 5.2
Sutton, D. (LA) 2.5
Rogers, S. (Mon) 2.2

1980 American League

TEAM	G	W	L	PCT	GB	R	OR	EW	AB	H	2B	3B	HR	TB	BB	SO	SB	CS	AVG	OBP	SLG	OPS	OPS+	BR/A	PF	RC
East																										
NY	162	103	59	.636	....	820	662	98	5553	1484	239	34	189	2358	643	739	86	**36**	.267	.346	.425	.771	112	100	98	818
BAL	162	100	62	.617	3	805	**640**	99	5585	1523	258	29	156	2307	587	766	111	38	.273	.344	.413	.757	108	71	99	787
MIL	162	86	76	.531	17	811	682	95	5653	1555	**298**	36	**203**	**2534**	455	745	131	56	.275	.332	**.448**	**.780**	**115**	**110**	97	**833**
BOS	160	83	77	.519	19	757	767	79	5603	1588	297	36	162	2443	475	720	79	48	.283	.343	.436	.779	106	44	105	809
DET	163	84	78	.519	19	**830**	757	88	5648	1543	232	53	143	2310	**645**	844	75	68	.273	.351	.409	.760	105	39	102	802
CLE	160	79	81	.494	23	738	807	73	5470	1517	221	40	89	2085	617	625	118	58	.277	**.355**	.381	.736	101	27	100	735
TOR	162	67	95	.414	36	624	762	65	5571	1398	249	53	126	2131	448	813	67	72	.251	.310	.383	.693	85	-137	105	638
West																										
KC	162	97	65	.599	....	809	694	93	**5714**	**1633**	266	**59**	115	2362	508	709	**185**	43	**.286**	.348	.413	.761	107	79	101	824
OAK	162	83	79	.512	14	686	642	86	5495	1424	212	35	137	2117	506	824	175	82	.259	.324	.385	.709	100	4	93	679
MIN	161	77	84	.478	19.5	670	724	74	5530	1468	252	46	99	2109	436	703	62	46	.265	.322	.381	.703	86	-116	107	653
TEX	163	76	85	.472	20.5	756	752	81	5690	1616	263	27	124	2305	480	**589**	91	49	.284	.342	.405	.747	107	53	97	766
CHI	162	70	90	.438	26	587	722	64	5444	1408	255	38	91	2012	399	670	68	54	.259	.314	.370	.683	87	-110	100	606
CAL	160	65	95	.406	31	698	797	69	5443	1442	236	32	106	2060	539	889	91	63	.265	.335	.378	.713	97	-21	97	679
SEA	163	59	103	.364	38	610	793	60	5489	1359	211	35	104	1952	483	727	116	62	.248	.311	.356	.666	81	-142	101	596
Total	**1132**					**10201**			**77888**	**20958**	**3489**	**553**	**1844**		**7221**	**10363**	**1455**	**775**	**.269**	**.334**	**.399**	**.733**				

Runs
Wilson, W. (KC) 133
Yount, R. (Mil) 121
Bumbry, A. (Bal) 118

Hits
Wilson, W. (KC) 230
Cooper, C. (Mil) 219
Rivers, M. (Tex) 210

Doubles
Yount, R. (Mil) 49
Oliver, A. (Tex) 43
Morrison, J. (Chi) 40

Triples
Griffin, A. (Tor) 15
Wilson, W. (KC) 15
2 players tied with 11

Home Runs
Jackson, R. (NY) 41
Oglivie, B. (Mil) 41
Thomas, G. (Mil) 38

Total Bases
Cooper, C. (Mil) 335
Oglivie, B. (Mil) 333
Murray, E. (Bal) 322

Runs Batted In
Cooper, C. (Mil) 122
Brett, G. (KC) 118
Oglivie, B. (Mil) 118

Bases On Balls
Randolph, W. (NY) 119
Henderson, R. (Oak) 117
Hargrove, M. (Cle) 111

Stolen Bases
Henderson, R. (Oak) 100
Wilson, W. (KC) 79
Dilone, M. (Cle) 61

Batting Average
Brett, G. (KC) .390
Cooper, C. (Mil) .352
Dilone, M. (Cle) .341

On-Base Percentage
Brett, G. (KC) .461
Randolph, W. (NY) .429
Henderson, R. (Oak) .422

Slugging Average
Brett, G. (KC) .664
Jackson, R. (NY) .597
Oglivie, B. (Mil) .562

Adjusted OPS
Brett, G. (KC) 202
Jackson, R. (NY) 172
Cooper, C. (Mil) 157

Adjusted Batting Runs
Brett, G. (KC) 65.0
Jackson, R. (NY) 51.0
Henderson, R. (Oak) 49.0

Runs Created/Game
Brett, G. (KC) 12.20
Jackson, R. (NY) 9.10
Cooper, C. (Mil) 7.70

Fielding Runs
DeCinces, D. (Bal) 24.5
Grich, B. (Cal) 20.5
Burleson, R. (Bos) 17.6

Win Shares – Batters
Brett, G. (KC) 36
Henderson, R. (Oak) 34
Bumbry, A. (Bal) 33

TPW – Batters
Brett, G. (KC) 7.4
Henderson, R. (Oak) 5.0
Yount, R. (Mil) 4.7

TEAM	CG	SH	SV	IP	H	H/G	ER	HR	BB	SO	OAV	RAT	ERA	ERA+	CERA	PR+	PF	FA	E	DP	FR	BW	PW	FW	TPW	DIF
East																										
NY	29	**15**	**50**	1464[1]	1433	8.8	582	**102**	463	845	.259	1.295	3.58	110	**3.52**	**62.7**	97	.978	138	160	-8.9	10.0	**6.3**	-.9	**15.4**	6.6
BAL	42	10	41	1460	1438	8.9	590	134	507	789	.261	1.332	3.64	109	3.82	19.0	98	**.985**	**95**	178	**30.8**	7.0	1.9	**3.1**	12.0	7.0
MIL	48	14	30	1450	1530	9.5	598	137	**420**	575	.273	1.345	3.71	104	3.99	6.8	96	.977	147	189	15.5	**11.0**	.7	1.5	13.2	-8.2
BOS	30	8	43	1441[1]	1557	9.7	701	129	481	696	.279	1.414	4.38	96	4.32	-31.2	105	.977	149	**206**	3.4	4.4	-3.1	.3	1.6	1.4
DET	40	9	30	1467[1]	1505	9.2	693	152	558	741	.267	1.406	4.25	97	4.20	-8.3	102	.979	133	165	-15.8	3.9	-.8	-1.6	1.4	1.6
CLE	35	8	32	1428	1519	9.6	743	137	552	843	.275	1.450	4.68	**87**	4.46	-89.6	101	.983	105	143	-9.0	2.7	-8.9	-.9	-7.1	6.1
TOR	39	9	23	1466	1523	9.4	683	135	635	705	.274	1.472	4.19	103	4.47	2.0	107	.979	133	**206**	14.7	-13.7	.2	1.5	-12.1	-1.9
West																										
KC	37	10	42	1459[1]	1496	9.2	621	129	465	614	.267	1.344	3.83	106	3.87	36.6	100	.978	141	150	-2.7	7.9	3.7	-.3	11.3	4.7
OAK	**94**	9	13	**1471[2]**	**1347**	**8.2**	**566**	142	521	769	**.244**	**1.269**	**3.46**	109	3.53	30.1	93	.979	130	115	14.8	.4	3.0	1.5	4.9	-2.9
MIN	35	9	30	1451	1502	9.3	634	120	468	744	.272	1.358	3.93	111	3.94	61.2	108	.977	148	192	6.8	-11.6	6.1	.7	-4.8	1.8
TEX	35	6	25	1451[2]	1561	9.7	648	119	519	**890**	.277	1.433	4.02	97	4.31	-3.2	96	.977	147	169	-21.1	5.3	-.3	-2.1	2.8	-6.8
CHI	32	12	42	1435[1]	1434	9.0	625	108	563	724	.263	1.391	3.92	103	3.95	29.3	100	.973	171	162	-12.6	-11.0	2.9	-1.3	-9.3	-.7
CAL	22	6	30	1428[1]	1548	9.8	717	141	529	725	.278	1.454	4.52	87	4.53	-88.5	97	.978	134	144	-5.2	-2.1	-8.8	-.5	-11.4	-3.6
SEA	31	7	26	1457[1]	1565	9.7	709	159	540	703	.278	1.444	4.38	94	4.47	-28.8	102	.977	149	189	-12.5	-14.2	-2.9	-1.3	-18.3	-3.7
Total	**549**	**132**	**457**	**20331[2]**		**9.3**	**9110**					**1.386**	**4.03**													

Wins		Win Percentage		Games		Complete Games		Shutouts		Saves	
Stone, S. (Bal)	25	Stone, S. (Bal)	.781	Quisenberry, D. (KC)	75	Langford, R. (Oak)	28	John, T. (NY)	6	Gossage, R. (NY)	33
John, T. (NY)	22	May, R. (NY)	.750	Corbett, D. (Min)	73	Norris, M. (Oak)	24	Zahn, G. (Min)	5	Quisenberry, D. (KC)	33
Norris, M. (Oak)	22	McGregor, S. (Bal)	.714	2 players tied with	67	Keough, M. (Oak)	20	3 players tied with	4	Farmer, E. (Chi)	30

Innings Pitched		Fewest Hits/Game		Fewest BB/Game		Strikeouts		Ratio		Earned Run Average	
Langford, R. (Oak)	290	Norris, M. (Oak)	6.81	Matlack, J. (Tex)	1.84	Barker, L. (Cle)	187	May, R. (NY)	1.04	May, R. (NY)	2.46
Norris, M. (Oak)	284¹	May, R. (NY)	7.39	Splittorff, P. (KC)	1.90	Norris, M. (Oak)	180	Norris, M. (Oak)	1.05	Norris, M. (Oak)	2.53
Gura, L. (KC)	283¹	Clancy, J. (Tor)	7.79	John, T. (NY)	1.90	Guidry, R. (NY)	166	Burns, B. (Chi)	1.16	Burns, B. (Chi)	2.84

Adjusted ERA		Component ERA		Opponents' Batting Avg.		Adjusted Pitching Runs		Win Shares – Pitchers		TPW – Pitchers	
May, R. (NY)	159	Norris, M. (Oak)	2.26	Norris, M. (Oak)	.209	Norris, M. (Oak)	36	Norris, M. (Oak)	25	Norris, M. (Oak)	3.6
Norris, M. (Oak)	149	May, R. (NY)	2.38	May, R. (NY)	.224	Gura, L. (KC)	35	Gura, L. (KC)	22	Gura, L. (KC)	3.5
Burns, B. (Chi)	142	Burns, B. (Chi)	2.89	Clancy, J. (Tor)	.233	Burns, B. (Chi)	33	Burns, B. (Chi)	21	Burns, B. (Chi)	3.3

1981 National League

TEAM	G	W	L	PCT	GB	R	OR	EW	AB	H	2B	3B	HR	TB	BB	SO	SB	CS	AVG	OBP	SLG	OPS	OPS+	BR/A	PF	RC
East																										
STL	103	59	43	.578	....	464	417	56	3537	936	158	**45**	50	1334	379	495	88	45	.265	.339	.377	.716	106	31	103	453
MON	108	60	48	.556	2	443	394	60	3591	883	146	28	81	1328	368	498	**138**	40	.246	.319	.370	.689	100	11	101	433
PHI	107	59	48	.551	2.5	**491**	472	56	3665	**1002**	165	25	69	**1424**	372	432	103	46	**.273**	**.344**	**.389**	**.733**	109	48	104	**493**
PIT	103	46	56	.451	13	407	425	49	3576	920	176	30	55	1321	278	494	122	52	.257	.314	.369	.683	96	-19	103	415
NY	105	41	62	.398	18.5	348	432	41	3493	868	136	35	57	1245	304	603	103	42	.248	.311	.356	.667	96	-16	98	385
CHI	106	38	65	.369	21.5	370	483	38	3546	838	138	29	57	1205	342	611	72	41	.236	.306	.340	.646	85	-70	104	367
West																										
CIN	108	66	42	.611	....	464	440	57	3637	972	**190**	24	64	1402	375	553	58	**37**	.267	.339	.385	.724	**109**	43	102	468
LA	110	63	47	.573	4	450	356	68	3751	984	133	20	**82**	1403	331	550	73	46	.262	.325	.374	.699	108	28	96	449
HOU	110	61	49	.555	6	394	**331**	64	3693	948	160	35	45	1313	340	488	81	43	.257	.321	.356	.676	102	8	95	424
SF	111	56	55	.505	11.5	427	414	57	**3766**	941	161	26	63	1343	**386**	543	89	50	.250	.322	.357	.679	100	-2	98	429
ATL	107	50	56	.472	15	395	416	50	3642	886	148	22	64	1270	321	540	98	39	.243	.308	.349	.656	89	-47	103	390
SD	110	41	69	.373	26	382	455	45	3757	963	170	35	32	1299	311	525	83	62	.256	.316	.346	.661	100	-13	93	399
Total	644					5035			43654	11141	1881	354	719		4107	6332	1108	543	.255	.322	.364	.686				

Runs		Hits		Doubles		Triples		Home Runs		Total Bases	
Schmidt, M. (Phi)	78	Rose, P. (Phi)	140	Buckner, B. (Chi)	35	Reynolds, C. (Hou)	12	Schmidt, M. (Phi)	31	Schmidt, M. (Phi)	228
Rose, P. (Phi)	73	Buckner, B. (Chi)	131	Jones, R. (SD)	34	Richards, G. (SD)	12	Dawson, A. (Mon)	24	Dawson, A. (Mon)	218
Dawson, A. (Mon)	71	Concepcion, D. (Cin)	129	Concepcion, D. (Cin)	28	Herr, T. (StL)	9	2 players tied with	22	Foster, G. (Cin)	215

Runs Batted In		Bases On Balls		Stolen Bases		Batting Average		On-Base Percentage		Slugging Average	
Schmidt, M. (Phi)	91	Schmidt, M. (Phi)	73	Raines, T. (Mon)	71	Madlock, B. (Pit)	.341	Schmidt, M. (Phi)	.439	Schmidt, M. (Phi)	.644
Foster, G. (Cin)	90	Morgan, J. (SF)	66	Moreno, O. (Pit)	39	Rose, P. (Phi)	.325	Hernandez, K. (StL)	.405	Dawson, A. (Mon)	.553
Buckner, B. (Chi)	75	Hernandez, K. (StL)	61	Scott, R. (Mon)	30	Baker, D. (LA)	.320	Matthews, G. (Phi)	.404	Foster, G. (Cin)	.519

Adjusted OPS		Adjusted Batting Runs		Runs Created/Game		Fielding Runs		Win Shares – Batters		TPW – Batters	
Schmidt, M. (Phi)	195	Schmidt, M. (Phi)	48.0	Schmidt, M. (Phi)	10.70	Schmidt, M. (Phi)	20.7	Schmidt, M. (Phi)	30	Schmidt, M. (Phi)	7.3
Dawson, A. (Mon)	157	Dawson, A. (Mon)	32.0	Dawson, A. (Mon)	7.70	Smith, O. (SD)	18.5	Dawson, A. (Mon)	25	Dawson, A. (Mon)	4.0
Foster, G. (Cin)	149	Foster, G. (Cin)	28.0	Raines, T. (Mon)	7.20	Oester, R. (Cin)	16.6	Foster, G. (Cin)	24	Concepcion, D. (Cin)	3.8

TEAM	CG	SH	SV	IP	H	H/G	ER	HR	BB	SO	OAV	RAT	ERA	ERA+	CERA	PR+	PF	FA	E	DP	FR	BW	PW	FW	TPW	DIF
East																										
STL	11	5	**33**	943	902	8.6	380	52	290	388	.255	1.264	3.63	98	3.25	-22.5	102	**.981**	82	108	15.2	3.4	-2.4	**1.6**	2.6	5.4
MON	20	12	23	975	902	8.3	357	58	**268**	520	.247	1.200	3.30	106	3.04	18.2	100	.980	81	88	3.5	1.2	2.0	.4	3.5	2.5
PHI	19	5	23	960¹	967	9.1	432	72	347	580	.267	1.368	4.05	90	3.86	-53.8	104	.980	86	90	8.8	**5.2**	-5.8	.9	.4	5.6
PIT	11	5	29	942	953	9.1	373	60	346	492	.266	1.379	3.56	101	3.79	5.4	103	.979	86	106	-2.0	-2.0	.6	-1.2	-3.3	-3.3
NY	7	3	24	926¹	906	8.8	365	74	336	490	.259	1.341	3.55	98	3.72	3.9	100	.968	130	89	-10.4	-1.7	.4	-1.1	-2.4	-7.6
CHI	6	2	20	956²	983	9.2	426	59	388	532	.270	1.433	4.01	92	3.98	-11.6	106	.974	113	103	-22.5	-7.5	-1.2	-2.4	-11.2	-1.8
West																										
CIN	25	14	20	965²	863	8.0	400	67	393	593	.241	1.301	3.73	95	3.37	-29.6	102	.981	**80**	99	11.0	4.6	-3.2	1.2	2.6	9.4
LA	**26**	**19**	24	997	904	8.2	333	54	302	603	.245	1.210	3.01	110	2.95	37.3	95	.980	87	101	-2.5	3.0	4.0	-.3	6.7	1.3
HOU	23	**19**	25	990	**842**	**7.6**	**293**	40	300	**610**	**.231**	**1.154**	**2.66**	124	**2.60**	64.8	94	.980	87	81	4.8	.9	**7.0**	.5	**8.3**	-2.3
SF	8	9	**33**	1009¹	970	8.6	368	57	393	561	.256	1.350	3.28	105	3.55	25.1	98	.977	102	102	-8.3	-.2	2.7	-.9	1.6	-.6
ATL	11	4	24	968	936	8.7	371	62	330	471	.257	1.308	3.45	104	3.48	16.5	103	.976	102	93	-2.1	-5.0	1.8	-.2	-3.5	.5
SD	9	6	23	1002	1013	9.0	414	64	414	492	.268	1.424	3.72	**88**	3.97	-55.5	93	.977	102	**117**	3.2	-1.4	-6.0	.3	-7.0	-7.0
Total	176	103	301	11635¹		8.6	4512					1.310	3.49													

Wins		Win Percentage		Games		Complete Games		Shutouts		Saves	
Seaver, T. (Cin)	14	Seaver, T. (Cin)	.875	Lucas, G. (SD)	57	Valenzuela, F. (LA)	11	Valenzuela, F. (LA)	8	Sutter, B. (StL)	25
Carlton, S. (Phi)	13	Carlton, S. (Phi)	.765	Minton, G. (SF)	55	Carlton, S. (Phi)	10	Knepper, B. (Hou)	5	Minton, G. (SF)	21
Valenzuela, F. (LA)	13	Reuss, J. (LA)	.714	2 players tied with	51	Soto, M. (Cin)	10	Hooton, B. (LA)	4	Allen, N. (NY)	18

Innings Pitched		Fewest Hits/Game		Fewest BB/Game		Strikeouts		Ratio		Earned Run Average	
Valenzuela, F. (LA)	192¹	Ryan, N. (Hou)	5.98	Perry, G. (Atl)	1.43	Valenzuela, F. (LA)	180	Sutton, D. (Hou)	1.01	Ryan, N. (Hou)	1.69
Carlton, S. (Phi)	190	Seaver, T. (Cin)	6.49	Reuss, J. (LA)	1.59	Carlton, S. (Phi)	179	Valenzuela, F. (LA)	1.05	Knepper, B. (Hou)	2.18
Soto, M. (Cin)	175	Valenzuela, F. (LA)	6.55	Sutton, D. (Hou)	1.64	Knepper, B. (Hou)	151	Knepper, B. (Hou)	1.06	Hooton, B. (LA)	2.28

Adjusted ERA		Component ERA		Opponents' Batting Avg.		Adjusted Pitching Runs		Win Shares – Pitchers		TPW – Pitchers	
Ryan, N. (Hou)	195	Ryan, N. (Hou)	2.02	Ryan, N. (Hou)	.188	Ryan, N. (Hou)	26	Seaver, T. (Cin)	17	Ryan, N. (Hou)	3.1
Knepper, B. (Hou)	151	Sutton, D. (Hou)	2.05	Valenzuela, F. (LA)	.205	Carlton, S. (Phi)	24	Valenzuela, F. (LA)	17	Carlton, S. (Phi)	2.6
Carlton, S. (Phi)	150	Valenzuela, F. (LA)	2.13	Seaver, T. (Cin)	.205	Knepper, B. (Hou)	19	Carlton, S. (Phi)	16	Valenzuela, F. (LA)	2.3

1981 American League

TEAM	G	W	L	PCT	GB	R	OR	EW	AB	H	2B	3B	HR	TB	BB	SO	SB	CS	AVG	OBP	SLG	OPS	OPS+	BR/A	PF	RC
East																										
MIL	109	62	47	.569	....	493	459	58	3743	961	173	20	96	1462	300	461	39	36	.257	.317	.391	.707	109	29	95	450
BAL	105	59	46	.562	1	429	437	52	3516	883	165	11	88	1334	**404**	454	41	34	.251	.331	.379	.710	104	21	100	430
NY	107	59	48	.551	2	421	**343**	64	3529	889	148	22	100	1381	391	434	47	30	.252	.328	.391	.719	108	37	99	444
DET	109	60	49	.550	2	427	404	58	3600	922	148	29	65	1323	**404**	500	61	37	.256	.334	.368	.702	98	0	104	440
BOS	108	59	49	.546	2.5	**519**	481	58	**3820**	**1052**	168	17	90	**1524**	378	520	32	31	**.275**	**.343**	**.399**	**.742**	107	33	106	**513**
CLE	103	52	51	.505	7	431	442	50	3507	922	150	21	39	1231	343	**379**	**119**	37	.263	.331	.351	.682	98	8	99	412
TOR	106	37	69	.349	23.5	329	466	35	3521	797	137	23	61	1163	284	556	66	57	.226	.288	.330	.618	73	-132	106	325
West																										
OAK	109	64	45	.587	....	458	403	61	3677	910	119	26	**104**	1393	342	647	98	47	.247	.314	.379	.693	104	18	95	436
TEX	105	57	48	.543	5	452	389	60	3581	968	**178**	15	49	1323	295	396	46	41	.270	.329	.369	.699	107	23	95	424
CHI	106	54	52	.509	8.5	476	423	59	3615	982	135	27	76	1399	322	518	86	44	.272	.338	.387	.725	**111**	**54**	98	470
KC	103	50	53	.485	11	397	405	50	3560	952	169	29	61	1362	301	419	100	53	.267	.327	.383	.710	105	22	99	436
CAL	110	51	59	.464	13.5	476	453	58	3688	944	134	16	97	1401	393	571	44	33	.256	.332	.380	.712	105	25	100	462
SEA	110	44	65	.404	20	426	521	44	3780	950	148	13	89	1391	329	553	100	50	.251	.316	.368	.684	93	-33	104	440
MIN	110	41	68	.376	23	378	486	41	3676	884	147	**36**	47	1244	275	497	34	**27**	.240	.295	.338	.634	77	-112	107	353
Total	**750**					**6112**			**50813**	**13016**	**2119**	**305**	**1062**		**4761**	**6905**	**913**	**557**	**.256**	**.323**	**.373**	**.696**				

Runs
Henderson, R. (Oak) 89
Evans, D. (Bos) 84
Cooper, C. (Mil) 70

Hits
Henderson, R. (Oak) 135
Lansford, C. (Bos) 134
2 players tied with 133

Doubles
Cooper, C. (Mil) 35
Oliver, A. (Tex) 29
Paciorek, T. (Sea) 28

Triples
Castino, J. (Min) 9
4 players tied with 7

Home Runs
4 players tied with 22

Total Bases
Evans, D. (Bos) 215
Armas, T. (Oak) 211
2 players tied with 206

Runs Batted In
Murray, E. (Bal) 78
Armas, T. (Oak) 76
Oglivie, B. (Mil) 72

Bases On Balls
Evans, D. (Bos) 85
Murphy, D. (Oak) 73
Kemp, S. (Det) 70

Stolen Bases
Henderson, R. (Oak) 56
Cruz, J. (Sea) 43
LeFlore, R. (Chi) 36

Batting Average
Lansford, C. (Bos) .336
Paciorek, T. (Sea) .326
Cooper, C. (Mil) .320

On-Base Percentage
Hargrove, M. (Cle) .432
Evans, D. (Bos) .418
Henderson, R. (Oak) .411

Slugging Average
Grich, B. (Cal) .543
Murray, E. (Bal) .534
Evans, D. (Bos) .522

Adjusted OPS
Grich, B. (Cal) 164
Evans, D. (Bos) 159
Murray, E. (Bal) 156

Adjusted Batting Runs
Evans, D. (Bos) 36.0
Henderson, R. (Oak) 34.0
Grich, B. (Cal) 27.0

Runs Created/Game
Evans, D. (Bos) 8.40
Grich, B. (Cal) 7.50
Henderson, R. (Oak) 6.80

Fielding Runs
Burleson, R. (Cal) 22.2
Bell, B. (Tex) 21.4
Yount, R. (Mil) 19.9

Win Shares – Batters
Henderson, R. (Oak) 27
Evans, D. (Bos) 26
Cooper, C. (Mil) 22

TPW – Batters
Grich, B. (Cal) 4.7
Burleson, R. (Cal) 4.2
Bell, B. (Tex) 4.0

TEAM	CG	SH	SV	IP	H	H/G	ER	HR	BB	SO	OAV	RAT	ERA	ERA+	CERA	PR+	PF	FA	E	DP	FR	BW	PW	FW	TPW	DIF
East																										
MIL	11	4	**35**	986	994	9.1	428	72	352	448	.266	1.365	3.91	**88**	3.84	-64.2	94	.982	79	**135**	11.4	3.0	-6.7	1.2	-2.5	10.5
BAL	25	10	23	940	923	8.8	386	83	347	489	.260	1.351	3.70	98	3.87	-2.7	99	.983	68	114	-4.9	2.2	-.3	-.5	1.4	5.6
NY	16	**13**	30	948	**827**	7.8	**305**	**64**	287	**606**	**.235**	**1.175**	**2.90**	123	**2.89**	**64.8**	98	.982	72	100	6.8	3.9	**6.8**	.7	**11.4**	-5.4
DET	33	**13**	22	969[1]	840	**7.8**	380	83	373	476	.236	1.251	3.53	107	3.30	4.2	103	**.984**	**67**	109	**21.2**	.0	.4	**2.2**	2.7	3.3
BOS	19	4	24	987[1]	983	9.0	418	90	354	536	.262	1.354	3.81	102	3.94	20.7	106	.979	91	108	-15.9	3.5	2.2	-1.7	4.0	1.0
CLE	33	10	13	931	989	9.6	401	67	311	569	.274	1.396	3.88	93	4.05	5.7	99	.978	87	91	-31.9	.9	.6	-3.3	-1.9	2.9
TOR	20	4	18	953[1]	908	8.6	404	72	377	451	.252	1.348	3.81	103	3.77	19.3	108	.975	105	102	-5.7	-13.8	2.0	-.6	-12.4	-3.6
West																										
OAK	**60**	11	10	993	883	8.0	364	80	370	505	.240	1.262	3.30	105	3.36	8.0	95	.980	81	74	11.9	1.9	.8	1.3	4.0	6.0
TEX	23	**13**	18	940[1]	851	8.1	355	67	322	488	.255	1.247	3.40	102	3.22	-9.4	95	.984	69	102	16.9	2.5	-1.0	1.8	3.2	1.8
CHI	20	8	23	940[2]	891	8.5	363	73	336	529	.252	1.304	3.47	103	3.60	-1.3	98	.979	87	113	9.2	**5.7**	-.1	1.0	6.5	-5.5
KC	24	8	24	922[1]	909	8.9	365	75	**273**	404	.260	1.282	3.56	101	3.54	8.4	99	.982	72	94	-3.7	2.3	.9	-.4	2.8	-3.8
CAL	27	8	19	971[1]	958	8.9	399	81	323	426	.261	1.319	3.70	99	3.74	-11.3	100	.977	101	120	5.1	2.6	-1.2	.5	2.0	-6.0
SEA	10	5	23	**997**[1]	1039	9.4	469	76	360	478	.271	1.403	4.23	91	4.08	-28.6	105	.979	91	122	-14.4	-3.5	-3.0	-1.5	-8.0	-2.0
MIN	13	6	22	979[2]	1021	9.4	433	79	376	500	.272	1.426	3.98	99	4.16	4.4	108	.978	96	103	-7.9	-11.8	.5	-.8	-12.2	-.8
Total	**334**	**117**	**304**	**13459**[2]		**8.7**	**5470**					**1.321**	**3.66**													

Wins
4 players tied with 14

Win Percentage
Vuckovich, P. (Mil) .778
Torrez, M. (Bos) .769
Martinez, D. (Bal) .737

Games
Corbett, D. (Min) 54
Fingers, R. (Mil) 47
Rawley, S. (Sea) 46

Complete Games
Langford, R. (Oak) 18
McCatty, S. (Oak) 16
Morris, J. (Det) 15

Shutouts
4 players tied with 4

Saves
Fingers, R. (Mil) 28
Gossage, R. (NY) 20
Quisenberry, D. (KC) 18

Innings Pitched
Leonard, D. (KC) 201[2]
Morris, J. (Det) 198
Langford, R. (Oak) 195[1]

Fewest Hits/Game
McCatty, S. (Oak) 6.79
Morris, J. (Det) 6.95
Guidry, R. (NY) 7.09

Fewest BB/Game
Honeycutt, R. (Tex) 1.20
Forsch, K. (Cal) 1.59
Gura, L. (KC) 1.83

Strikeouts
Barker, L. (Cle) 127
Burns, B. (Chi) 108
2 players tied with 107

Ratio
Guidry, R. (NY) .99
Gura, L. (KC) 1.01
Honeycutt, R. (Tex) 1.07

Earned Run Average
Stewart, S. (Bal) 2.32
McCatty, S. (Oak) 2.33
Lamp, D. (Chi) 2.41

Adjusted ERA
Stewart, S. (Bal) 156
McCatty, S. (Oak) 150
Lamp, D. (Chi) 148

Component ERA
Gura, L. (KC) 2.23
Guidry, R. (NY) 2.27
McCatty, S. (Oak) 2.37

Opponents' Batting Avg.
McCatty, S. (Oak) .211
Guidry, R. (NY) .214
Darwin, D. (Tex) .218

Adjusted Pitching Runs
McCatty, S. (Oak) 22
Blyleven, B. (Cle) 19
Gura, L. (KC) 18

Win Shares – Pitchers
McCatty, S. (Oak) 18
Morris, J. (Det) 16
Stieb, D. (Tor) 15

TPW – Pitchers
McCatty, S. (Oak) 2.3
Blyleven, B. (Cle) 2.0
Gura, L. (KC) 1.9

1982 National League

TEAM	G	W	L	PCT	GB	R	OR	EW	AB	H	2B	3B	HR	TB	BB	SO	SB	CS	AVG	OBP	SLG	OPS	OPS+	BR/A	PF	RC
East																										
STL	162	92	70	.568	....	685	**609**	90	5455	1439	239	**52**	67	1983	569	805	**200**	91	.264	**.337**	.364	.700	101	19	101	679
PHI	162	89	73	.549	3	664	654	82	5454	1417	245	25	112	2048	506	831	128	76	.260	.325	.376	.701	100	-8	102	652
MON	162	86	76	.531	6	697	616	91	5557	1454	270	38	133	2199	503	816	156	**56**	.262	.327	.396	.723	106	46	102	724
PIT	162	84	78	.519	8	724	696	84	5614	**1535**	**272**	40	134	**2289**	447	862	161	75	**.273**	.330	**.408**	**.738**	**109**	57	103	**743**
CHI	162	73	89	.451	19	676	709	77	5531	1436	239	46	102	2073	460	869	132	70	.260	.319	.375	.694	97	-26	103	660
NY	162	65	97	.401	27	609	723	67	5510	1361	227	26	97	1931	456	1005	137	58	.247	.307	.350	.658	90	-69	99	593
West																										
ATL	162	89	73	.549	....	**739**	702	85	5507	1411	215	22	**146**	2108	554	869	151	77	.256	.327	.383	.710	100	4	104	696
LA	162	88	74	.543	1	691	612	91	**5642**	1487	222	32	138	2187	528	**804**	151	**56**	.264	.330	.388	.717	**109**	**72**	97	733
SF	162	87	75	.537	2	673	687	79	5499	1393	213	30	133	2065	**607**	915	130	**56**	.253	.329	.376	.705	103	32	100	683
SD	162	81	81	.500	8	675	658	83	5575	1435	217	**52**	81	1999	429	877	165	77	.257	.313	.359	.672	99	-16	95	624
HOU	162	77	85	.475	12	569	620	74	5440	1342	236	48	74	1896	435	830	140	61	.247	.305	.349	.653	95	-37	92	576
CIN	162	61	101	.377	28	545	661	66	5479	1375	228	34	82	1917	470	817	131	69	.251	.313	.350	.662	89	-79	102	586
Total	**972**					**7947**			**66263**	**17085**	**2823**	**445**	**1299**		**5964**	**10300**	**1782**	**822**	**.258**	**.322**	**.373**	**.695**				

Runs		Hits		Doubles		Triples		Home Runs		Total Bases	
Smith, L. (StL)	120	Oliver, A. (Mon)	204	Oliver, A. (Mon)	43	Thon, D. (Hou)	10	Kingman, D. (NY)	37	Oliver, A. (Mon)	317
Murphy, D. (Atl)	113	Buckner, B. (Chi)	201	Kennedy, T. (SD)	42	3 players tied with	9	Murphy, D. (Atl)	36	Guerrero, P. (LA)	308
Schmidt, M. (Phi)	108	Dawson, A. (Mon)	183	Dawson, A. (Mon)	37			Schmidt, M. (Phi)	35	2 players tied with	303

Runs Batted In		Bases On Balls		Stolen Bases		Batting Average		On-Base Percentage		Slugging Average	
Murphy, D. (Atl)	109	Schmidt, M. (Phi)	107	Raines, T. (Mon)	78	Oliver, A. (Mon)	.331	Schmidt, M. (Phi)	.407	Schmidt, M. (Phi)	.547
Oliver, A. (Mon)	109	Thompson, J. (Pit)	101	Smith, L. (StL)	68	Madlock, B. (Pit)	.319	Hernandez, K. (StL)	.404	Guerrero, P. (LA)	.536
Buckner, B. (Chi)	105	Hernandez, K. (StL)	100	Moreno, O. (Pit)	60	Durham, L. (Chi)	.312	Morgan, J. (SF)	.402	Durham, L. (Chi)	.521

Adjusted OPS		Adjusted Batting Runs		Runs Created/Game		Fielding Runs		Win Shares – Batters		TPW – Batters	
Schmidt, M. (Phi)	161	Guerrero, P. (LA)	46.0	Schmidt, M. (Phi)	8.10	Smith, O. (StL)	28.0	Schmidt, M. (Phi)	37	Schmidt, M. (Phi)	6.1
Guerrero, P. (LA)	157	Schmidt, M. (Phi)	46.0	Oliver, A. (Mon)	7.80	Salazar, L. (SD)	20.4	Murphy, D. (Atl)	32	Carter, G. (Mon)	5.3
Oliver, A. (Mon)	149	Oliver, A. (Mon)	41.0	Guerrero, P. (LA)	7.80	Hubbard, G. (Atl)	18.2	Carter, G. (Mon)	31	Guerrero, P. (LA)	4.7

TEAM	CG	SH	SV	IP	H	H/G	ER	HR	BB	SO	OAV	RAT	ERA	ERA+	CERA	PR+	PF	FA	E	DP	FR	BW	PW	FW	TPW	DIF
East																										
STL	25	10	47	1465¹	1420	8.7	549	94	502	689	.258	1.312	3.37	107	3.46	5.6	101	**.981**	124	169	**34.9**	2.0	.6	**3.7**	6.3	4.7
PHI	**38**	13	33	1456¹	1395	8.6	584	86	472	**1002**	.255	1.282	3.61	102	3.31	9.2	102	.981	**121**	138	0.3	-.9	1.0	.0	.1	7.9
MON	34	10	43	1460²	1371	8.4	**537**	110	**448**	936	.250	1.245	3.31	110	3.26	43.9	101	.980	122	117	6.9	4.9	4.6	.7	10.2	-5.2
PIT	19	7	39	1466²	1434	8.8	621	118	521	933	.257	1.333	3.81	97	3.70	-11.0	103	.977	145	133	-8.9	6.0	-1.2	-.9	3.9	-.9
CHI	9	7	43	1447¹	1510	9.4	630	125	452	764	.272	1.356	3.92	95	3.91	-16.7	104	.979	132	110	-13.6	-2.7	-1.8	-1.4	-5.9	-2.1
NY	15	5	37	1447¹	1508	9.4	624	119	582	759	.273	1.444	3.88	**93**	4.24	-23.3	101	.972	175	134	-17.3	-7.3	-2.4	-1.8	-11.5	-4.5
West																										
ATL	15	11	**51**	1463	1484	9.1	621	126	502	813	.267	1.357	3.82	98	3.91	-18.6	104	.979	137	**186**	4.1	.4	-2.0	.4	-1.1	9.1
LA	37	**16**	28	**1488¹**	1356	**8.2**	539	**81**	468	932	.244	**1.226**	**3.26**	106	**2.96**	44.4	96	.979	139	131	-12.7	**7.6**	**4.7**	-1.3	**10.9**	-3.9
SF	18	4	45	1465¹	1507	9.3	593	109	466	810	.270	1.346	3.64	99	3.76	16.0	100	.973	173	125	-27.6	3.3	1.7	-2.9	2.1	3.9
SD	20	11	41	1476	1348	8.2	577	139	502	765	**.244**	1.253	3.52	97	3.39	-29.4	95	.976	152	142	13.1	-1.7	-3.1	1.4	-3.4	3.4
HOU	37	**16**	31	1446²	**1338**	8.3	549	87	479	899	.247	1.256	3.42	97	3.25	-28.0	92	.978	136	154	12.1	-3.9	-2.9	1.3	-5.6	1.6
CIN	22	7	31	1460¹	1414	8.7	594	105	570	998	.258	1.359	3.66	101	3.72	-3.1	103	.980	128	158	8.2	-8.3	-.3	.9	-7.8	-12.2
Total	**289**	**117**	**469**	**17543¹**		**8.8**	**7018**					**1.314**	**3.60**													

Wins		Win Percentage		Games		Complete Games		Shutouts		Saves	
Carlton, S. (Phi)	23	Niekro, P. (Atl)	.810	Tekulve, K. (Pit)	85	Carlton, S. (Phi)	19	Carlton, S. (Phi)	6	Sutter, B. (StL)	36
Rogers, S. (Mon)	19	Rogers, S. (Mon)	.704	Minton, G. (SF)	78	Valenzuela, F. (LA)	18	Andujar, J. (StL)	5	Garber, G. (Atl)	30
Valenzuela, F. (LA)	19	Sarmiento, M. (Mon)	.692	Scurry, R. (Pit)	76	Niekro, J. (Hou)	16	Niekro, J. (Hou)	5	Minton, G. (SF)	30

Innings Pitched		Fewest Hits/Game		Fewest BB/Game		Strikeouts		Ratio		Earned Run Average	
Carlton, S. (Phi)	295²	Ryan, N. (Hou)	7.05	Bird, D. (Chi)	1.41	Carlton, S. (Phi)	286	Soto, M. (Cin)	1.06	Rogers, S. (Mon)	2.40
Valenzuela, F. (LA)	285	Soto, M. (Cin)	7.06	Hammaker, A. (SF)	1.44	Soto, M. (Cin)	274	Niekro, J. (Hou)	1.07	Niekro, J. (Hou)	2.47
Rogers, S. (Mon)	277	Lea, C. (Mon)	7.35	Andujar, J. (StL)	1.69	Ryan, N. (Hou)	245	Andujar, J. (StL)	1.08	Andujar, J. (StL)	2.47

Adjusted ERA		Component ERA		Opponents' Batting Avg.		Adjusted Pitching Runs		Win Shares – Pitchers		TPW – Pitchers	
Rogers, S. (Mon)	151	Niekro, J. (Hou)	2.35	Ryan, N. (Hou)	.213	Rogers, S. (Mon)	37	Carlton, S. (Phi)	25	Rogers, S. (Mon)	3.9
Andujar, J. (StL)	146	Soto, M. (Cin)	2.37	Soto, M. (Cin)	.215	Andujar, J. (StL)	28	Niekro, J. (Hou)	25	Andujar, J. (StL)	2.8
Niekro, J. (Hou)	134	Reuss, J. (LA)	2.44	Lea, C. (Mon)	.222	Niekro, J. (Hou)	24	Rogers, S. (Mon)	24	Soto, M. (Cin)	2.7

1982 American League

TEAM	G	W	L	PCT	GB	R	OR	EW	AB	H	2B	3B	HR	TB	BB	SO	SB	CS	AVG	OBP	SLG	OPS	OPS+	BR/A	PF	RC
East																										
MIL	163	95	67	.586	....	**891**	717	98	**5733**	1599	277	41	**216**	**2606**	484	714	84	52	.279	.337	**.455**	**.792**	**123**	162	94	**864**
BAL	163	94	68	.580	1	774	687	91	5557	1478	259	27	179	2328	634	796	49	38	.266	.344	.419	.763	109	69	100	793
BOS	162	89	73	.549	6	753	713	85	5596	1536	271	31	136	2277	547	736	42	39	.274	.342	.407	.749	99	-6	106	754
DET	162	83	79	.512	12	729	685	86	5590	1489	237	40	177	2337	470	807	93	66	.266	.326	.418	.744	102	6	100	751
NY	162	79	83	.488	16	709	716	80	5526	1417	225	37	161	2199	590	719	69	45	.256	.331	.398	.729	101	6	98	714
TOR	162	78	84	.481	17	651	701	75	5526	1447	262	46	106	2117	415	749	118	51	.262	.317	.383	.700	83	-134	109	653
CLE	162	78	84	.481	17	683	748	74	5559	1458	225	32	109	2074	**651**	**625**	151	68	.262	.343	.373	.716	97	0	100	721
West																										
CAL	162	93	69	.574	....	814	**670**	97	5532	1518	268	26	186	2396	613	760	55	53	.274	**.350**	.433	.784	114	103	100	832
KC	162	90	72	.556	3	784	717	88	5629	**1603**	**295**	**58**	132	2410	442	758	133	48	**.285**	.340	.428	.768	109	76	100	801
CHI	162	87	75	.537	6	786	710	89	5575	1523	266	52	136	2301	533	866	136	58	.273	.340	.413	.753	105	51	100	782
SEA	162	76	86	.469	17	651	712	74	5626	1431	259	33	130	2146	456	806	131	82	.254	.313	.381	.694	87	-108	103	656
OAK	162	68	94	.420	25	691	819	67	5448	1286	211	27	149	1998	582	948	**232**	87	.236	.312	.367	.679	90	-59	96	642
TEX	162	64	98	.395	29	590	749	62	5445	1354	204	26	115	1955	447	750	63	45	.249	.309	.359	.668	87	-101	95	591
MIN	162	60	102	.370	33	657	819	63	5544	1427	234	44	148	2193	474	887	38	**33**	.257	.318	.396	.714	92	-65	103	674
Total	**1135**					**10163**			**77886**	**20566**	**3493**	**519**	**2080**		**7338**	**10921**	**1394**	**795**	**.264**	**.330**	**.402**	**.733**				

Runs		Hits		Doubles		Triples		Home Runs		Total Bases	
Molitor, P. (Mil)	136	Yount, R. (Mil)	210	McRae, H. (KC)	46	Wilson, W. (KC)	15	Jackson, R. (Cal)	39	Yount, R. (Mil)	367
Yount, R. (Mil)	129	Cooper, C. (Mil)	205	Yount, R. (Mil)	46	Herndon, L. (Det)	13	Thomas, G. (Mil)	39	Cooper, C. (Mil)	345
Evans, D. (Bos)	122	Molitor, P. (Mil)	201	White, F. (KC)	45	Yount, R. (Mil)	12	Winfield, D. (NY)	37	McRae, H. (KC)	332

Runs Batted In		Bases On Balls		Stolen Bases		Batting Average		On-Base Percentage		Slugging Average	
McRae, H. (KC)	133	Henderson, R. (Oak)	116	Henderson, R. (Oak)	130	Wilson, W. (KC)	.332	Evans, D. (Bos)	.403	Yount, R. (Mil)	.578
Cooper, C. (Mil)	121	Evans, D. (Bos)	112	Garcia, D. (Tor)	54	Yount, R. (Mil)	.331	Harrah, T. (Cle)	.400	Winfield, D. (NY)	.560
Thornton, A. (Cle)	116	Thornton, A. (Cle)	109	Cruz, J. (Sea)	46	Carew, R. (Cal)	.319	Henderson, R. (Oak)	.399	Murray, E. (Bal)	.549

Adjusted OPS		Adjusted Batting Runs		Runs Created/Game		Fielding Runs		Win Shares – Batters		TPW – Batters	
Yount, R. (Mil)	170	Yount, R. (Mil)	61.0	Yount, R. (Mil)	8.00	Bell, B. (Tex)	22.8	Yount, R. (Mil)	39	Yount, R. (Mil)	7.6
Murray, E. (Bal)	156	Murray, E. (Bal)	44.0	Evans, D. (Bos)	8.00	Whitaker, L. (Det)	18.5	Evans, D. (Bos)	31	DeCinces, D. (Cal)	4.8
DeCinces, D. (Cal)	149	Evans, D. (Bos)	43.0	Murray, E. (Bal)	7.80	Garcia, D. (Tor)	14.6	Molitor, P. (Mil)	30	Bell, B. (Tex)	4.3

TEAM	CG	SH	SV	IP	H	H/G	ER	HR	BB	SO	OAV	RAT	ERA	ERA+	CERA	PR+	PF	FA	E	DP	FR	BW	PW	FW	TPW	DIF
East																										
MIL	34	6	**47**	1467[1]	1514	9.3	649	152	511	717	.270	1.380	3.98	95	4.17	-53.2	93	.980	125	**185**	20.1	**16.2**	-5.3	2.0	12.9	1.1
BAL	38	8	34	1462[1]	1436	8.8	648	147	488	719	.257	1.316	3.99	101	3.76	5.2	99	**.984**	**101**	140	1.6	6.9	.5	.2	7.6	5.4
BOS	23	11	33	1453	1557	9.6	651	155	478	816	.276	1.401	4.03	107	4.37	72.0	106	.981	121	172	-28.8	-.6	7.2	-2.9	3.7	4.3
DET	**45**	5	27	1451	**1371**	**8.5**	**613**	172	554	740	**.251**	1.327	**3.80**	107	3.91	7.3	100	.981	117	165	**32.7**	.6	.7	**3.3**	4.6	-2.6
NY	24	8	39	1459	1471	9.1	647	113	491	939	.264	1.345	3.99	100	3.78	8.3	98	.979	128	158	-10.5	.6	.8	-1.1	.4	-2.4
TOR	41	**13**	25	1443[2]	1428	8.9	633	147	493	776	.257	1.331	3.95	113	3.89	**96.9**	110	.978	136	146	-11.6	-13.4	**9.7**	-1.2	-4.9	1.9
CLE	31	9	30	1468[1]	1433	8.8	670	122	589	882	.257	1.377	4.11	99	3.89	7.8	100	.980	123	129	-14.9	.0	.8	-1.5	-.7	-2.3
West																										
CAL	40	10	27	1464	1436	8.8	621	124	482	728	.259	**1.310**	3.82	106	**3.72**	13.7	100	.983	108	171	25.0	10.3	1.4	2.5	**14.1**	-2.1
KC	16	12	45	1431	1443	9.1	649	163	471	650	.262	1.338	4.08	100	4.00	2.2	100	.979	127	140	-2.2	7.6	.2	-.2	7.6	1.4
CHI	30	10	41	1439	1502	9.4	619	**99**	**460**	753	.270	1.363	3.87	104	3.86	41.5	99	.976	154	173	-14.7	5.1	4.2	-1.5	7.8	-1.8
SEA	23	11	39	**1476[1]**	1431	8.7	636	173	547	**1002**	.256	1.340	3.88	109	4.04	59.8	104	.978	139	158	-4.2	-10.8	6.0	-.4	-5.3	.3
OAK	42	6	22	1456	1506	9.3	734	177	648	697	.268	1.479	4.54	**86**	4.67	-106.0	96	.974	160	140	3.0	-5.9	-10.6	.3	-16.2	3.2
TEX	32	5	24	1431	1554	9.8	681	128	483	690	.280	1.423	4.28	90	4.33	-55.5	95	.981	121	169	-12.8	-10.1	-5.6	-1.3	-16.9	-.1
MIN	26	7	30	1433	1484	9.3	752	208	643	812	.269	1.484	4.72	90	4.84	-100.3	104	.982	108	162	16.0	-6.5	-10.0	1.6	-14.9	-6.1
Total	**445**	**121**	**463**	**20335**		**9.1**	**9203**					**1.372**	**4.07**													

Wins
- Hoyt, L. (Chi) 19
- 3 players tied with 18

Win Percentage
- Vuckovich, P. (Mil) .750
- Palmer, J. (Bal) .750
- Burns, B. (Chi) .722

Games
- Vande Berg, E. (Sea) 78
- Martinez, T. (Bal) 76
- Quisenberry, D. (KC) 72

Complete Games
- Stieb, D. (Tor) 19
- Morris, J. (Det) 17
- Langford, R. (Oak) 15

Shutouts
- Stieb, D. (Tor) 5
- Forsch, K. (Cal) 4
- Zahn, G. (Cal) 4

Saves
- Quisenberry, D. (KC) 35
- Gossage, R. (NY) 30
- Fingers, R. (Mil) 29

Innings Pitched
- Stieb, D. (Tor) 288[1]
- Clancy, J. (Tor) 266[2]
- Morris, J. (Det) 266[1]

Fewest Hits/Game
- Sutcliffe, R. (Cle) 7.25
- Ujdur, J. (Det) 7.58
- Righetti, D. (NY) 7.62

Fewest BB/Game
- John, T. (Cal,NY) 1.58
- Eckersley, D. (Bos) 1.73
- Hoyt, L. (Chi) 1.80

Strikeouts
- Bannister, F. (Sea) 209
- Barker, L. (Cle) 187
- Righetti, D. (NY) 163

Ratio
- Palmer, J. (Bal) 1.14
- Stieb, D. (Tor) 1.20
- Eckersley, D. (Bos) 1.21

Earned Run Average
- Sutcliffe, R. (Cle) 2.96
- Stanley, B. (Bos) 3.10
- Palmer, J. (Bal) 3.13

Adjusted ERA
- Stanley, B. (Bos) 139
- Stieb, D. (Tor) 138
- Sutcliffe, R. (Cle) 138

Component ERA
- Palmer, J. (Bal) 2.92
- Barker, L. (Cle) 3.00
- Beattie, J. (Sea) 3.13

Opponents' Batting Avg.
- Sutcliffe, R. (Cle) .226
- Righetti, D. (NY) .229
- Ujdur, J. (Det) .230

Adjusted Pitching Runs
- Stieb, D. (Tor) 42
- Sutcliffe, R. (Cle) 29
- Stanley, B. (Bos) 26

Win Shares – Pitchers
- Stieb, D. (Tor) 25
- 4 players tied with 20

TPW – Pitchers
- Stieb, D. (Tor) 4.2
- Sutcliffe, R. (Cle) 2.9
- Stanley, B. (Bos) 2.6

1983 National League

TEAM	G	W	L	PCT	GB	R	OR	EW	AB	H	2B	3B	HR	TB	BB	SO	SB	CS	AVG	OBP	SLG	OPS	OPS+	BR/A	PF	RC
East																										
PHI	163	90	72	.556	....	696	635	88	5426	1352	209	45	125	2026	**640**	906	143	75	.249	.331	.373	.705	103	25	99	674
PIT	162	84	78	.519	6	659	648	82	5531	1460	238	29	121	2119	497	873	124	77	.264	.327	.383	.710	100	-8	103	680
MON	163	82	80	.506	8	677	646	85	**5611**	1482	**297**	41	102	2167	509	**733**	138	44	.264	.329	.386	.716	105	44	99	713
STL	162	79	83	.488	11	679	710	77	5550	**1496**	262	**63**	83	2133	543	879	**207**	89	.270	.337	.384	.722	**106**	**53**	100	723
CHI	162	71	91	.438	19	701	719	79	5512	1436	272	42	140	**2212**	470	868	84	**40**	.261	.322	**.401**	.723	101	3	105	705
NY	162	68	94	.420	22	575	680	68	5444	1314	172	26	112	1874	436	1031	141	64	.241	.301	.344	.646	85	-107	99	561
West																										
LA	163	91	71	.562	....	654	**609**	87	5440	1358	197	34	**146**	2061	541	925	166	76	.250	.320	.379	.699	100	1	99	661
ATL	162	88	74	.543	3	**746**	640	93	5472	1489	218	45	130	2187	582	847	146	88	**.272**	**.344**	.400	**.744**	105	33	107	**743**
HOU	162	85	77	.525	6	643	646	81	5502	1412	239	60	97	2062	517	869	164	95	.257	.323	.375	.697	**106**	29	94	671
SD	163	81	81	.500	10	653	653	81	5527	1384	207	34	93	1938	482	822	179	67	.250	.313	.351	.663	93	-44	96	607
SF	162	79	83	.488	12	687	697	80	5369	1324	206	30	142	2016	619	990	140	78	.247	.328	.375	.703	104	30	97	660
CIN	162	74	88	.457	17	623	710	70	5333	1274	236	35	107	1901	588	1006	154	77	.239	.317	.356	.673	89	-70	104	604
Total	**974**					**7993**			**65717**	**16781**	**2753**	**484**	**1398**		**6424**	**10749**	**1786**	**870**	**.255**	**.324**	**.376**	**.700**				

Runs
- Raines, T. (Mon) 133
- Murphy, D. (Atl) 131
- 2 players tied with 104

Hits
- Cruz, J. (Hou) 189
- Dawson, A. (Mon) 189
- Ramirez, R. (Atl) 185

Doubles
- Buckner, B. (Chi) 38
- Oliver, A. (Mon) 38
- Ray, J. (Pit) 38

Triples
- Butler, B. (Atl) 13
- Moreno, O. (Hou) 11
- 2 players tied with 10

Home Runs
- Schmidt, M. (Phi) 40
- Murphy, D. (Atl) 36
- 2 players tied with 32

Total Bases
- Dawson, A. (Mon) 341
- Murphy, D. (Atl) 318
- Guerrero, P. (LA) 310

Runs Batted In
- Murphy, D. (Atl) 121
- Dawson, A. (Mon) 113
- Schmidt, M. (Phi) 109

Bases On Balls
- Schmidt, M. (Phi) 128
- Thompson, J. (Pit) 99
- Raines, T. (Mon) 97

Stolen Bases
- Raines, T. (Mon) 90
- Wiggins, A. (SD) 66
- Sax, S. (LA) 56

Batting Average
- Madlock, B. (Pit) .323
- Smith, L. (StL) .321
- Cruz, J. (Hou) .318

On-Base Percentage
- Schmidt, M. (Phi) .402
- Hernandez, K. (NY,StL) .398
- Murphy, D. (Atl) .396

Slugging Average
- Murphy, D. (Atl) .540
- Dawson, A. (Mon) .539
- Guerrero, P. (LA) .531

Adjusted OPS
- Schmidt, M. (Phi) 156
- Evans, D. (SF) 151
- Guerrero, P. (LA) 150

Adjusted Batting Runs
- Schmidt, M. (Phi) 44.0
- Murphy, D. (Atl) 43.0
- Raines, T. (Mon) 42.0

Runs Created/Game
- Murphy, D. (Atl) 8.10
- Schmidt, M. (Phi) 7.50
- Guerrero, P. (LA) 7.40

Fielding Runs
- Thon, D. (Hou) 25.7
- Salazar, L. (SD) 19.6
- Smith, O. (StL) 19.1

Win Shares – Batters
- Schmidt, M. (Phi) 35
- Murphy, D. (Atl) 32
- Guerrero, P. (LA) 32

TPW – Batters
- Thon, D. (Hou) 6.8
- Schmidt, M. (Phi) 5.9
- Guerrero, P. (LA) 4.9

TEAM	CG	SH	SV	IP	H	H/G	ER	HR	BB	SO	OAV	RAT	ERA	ERA+	CERA	PR+	PF	FA	E	DP	FR	BW	PW	FW	TPW	DIF
East																										
PHI	20	10	41	1461[2]	1429	8.8	542	111	**464**	**1092**	.256	1.295	3.34	107	3.50	55.6	98	.976	152	117	-20.4	2.6	5.8	-2.1	6.3	2.7
PIT	25	14	41	1462[1]	1378	8.5	577	109	563	1061	.252	1.327	3.55	104	3.60	32.8	102	.982	115	165	-8.0	-.8	3.4	-.8	1.8	1.2
MON	**38**	**15**	34	**1471**	1406	8.6	585	120	479	899	.254	1.281	3.58	100	3.52	-20.9	99	.981	116	130	21.0	4.6	-2.2	2.2	4.7	-3.7
STL	22	10	27	1460[2]	1479	9.1	615	115	525	709	.266	1.372	3.79	95	3.86	-29.1	100	.976	152	173	-6.7	**5.5**	-3.0	-.7	1.8	-3.8
CHI	9	10	42	1428[2]	1496	9.4	647	117	498	807	.274	1.396	4.08	**93**	4.07	-24.1	105	**.982**	115	164	-21.3	.3	-2.5	-2.2	-4.4	-5.6
NY	18	7	33	1451	1384	8.6	593	97	615	717	.256	1.378	3.68	99	3.72	-25.3	100	.976	151	171	16.9	-11.1	-2.6	1.8	-12.0	-1.0
West																										
LA	27	12	40	1464	1336	8.2	**504**	97	495	1000	.244	**1.251**	**3.10**	116	**3.14**	**108.7**	99	.974	168	132	-30.8	.1	**11.4**	-3.2	**8.2**	1.8
ATL	18	4	**48**	1440[2]	1412	8.8	587	132	540	895	.260	1.355	3.67	106	3.88	17.7	107	.978	137	**176**	14.6	3.5	1.9	1.5	6.9	.1
HOU	22	14	**48**	1466[1]	**1276**	**7.8**	562	**94**	570	904	**.236**	1.259	3.45	99	3.15	-30.7	94	.977	147	165	22.6	3.0	-3.2	2.4	2.2	1.8
SD	23	5	44	1467[2]	1389	8.5	590	144	528	850	.253	1.306	3.62	96	3.69	-45.5	96	.979	129	135	**24.0**	-4.6	-4.8	**2.5**	-6.8	6.8
SF	20	9	47	1445[2]	1431	8.9	594	127	520	881	.259	1.350	3.70	95	3.79	-19.6	97	.973	171	109	-12.0	3.1	-2.0	-1.3	-.2	-1.8
CIN	34	5	29	1441[1]	1365	8.5	637	135	627	934	.253	1.382	3.98	96	3.94	-31.2	105	.981	**114**	121	-1.4	-7.3	-3.3	-.1	-10.7	3.7
Total	**276**	**115**	**474**	**17461**		**8.6**	**7033**					**1.329**	**3.63**													

Wins		Win Percentage		Games		Complete Games		Shutouts		Saves	
Denny, J. (Phi)	19	Denny, J. (Phi)	.760	Campbell, B. (Chi)	82	Soto, M. (Cin)	18	Rogers, S. (Mon)	5	Smith, L. (Chi)	29
3 players tied with	17	3 players tied with	.652	Tekulve, K. (Pit)	76	Rogers, S. (Mon)	13	Holland, A. (Phi)		Holland, A. (Phi)	25
				Hernandez, W. (Phi,Chi)	74	Gullickson, B. (Mon)	10	3 players tied with	4	Minton, G. (SF)	22

Innings Pitched		Fewest Hits/Game		Fewest BB/Game		Strikeouts		Ratio		Earned Run Average	
Carlton, S. (Phi)	283²	Ryan, N. (Hou)	6.14	Hammaker, A. (SF)	1.67	Carlton, S. (Phi)	275	Hammaker, A. (SF)	1.04	Hammaker, A. (SF)	2.25
Soto, M. (Cin)	273³	Soto, M. (Cin)	6.81	Ruthven, D. (Chi,Phi)	1.87	Soto, M. (Cin)	242	Soto, M. (Cin)	1.10	Denny, J. (Phi)	2.37
Rogers, S. (Mon)	273	Welch, B. (LA)	7.24	Denny, J. (Phi)	1.97	McWilliams, L. (Pit)	199	Pena, A. (LA)	1.15	Welch, B. (LA)	2.65

Adjusted ERA		Component ERA		Opponents' Batting Avg.		Adjusted Pitching Runs		Win Shares – Pitchers		TPW – Pitchers	
Hammaker, A. (SF)	157	Hammaker, A. (SF)	2.16	Ryan, N. (Hou)	.195	Denny, J. (Phi)	36	Soto, M. (Cin)	25	Denny, J. (Phi)	3.8
Denny, J. (Phi)	150	Pena, A. (LA)	2.45	Soto, M. (Cin)	.208	Soto, M. (Cin)	34	Denny, J. (Phi)	23	Soto, M. (Cin)	3.3
Soto, M. (Cin)	141	Ryan, N. (Hou)	2.56	Welch, B. (LA)	.222	Hammaker, A. (SF)	26	Carlton, S. (Phi)	18	Reuss, J. (LA)	2.7

1983 American League

TEAM	G	W	L	PCT	GB	R	OR	EW	AB	H	2B	3B	HR	TB	BB	SO	SB	CS	AVG	OBP	SLG	OPS	OPS+	BR/A	PF	RC
East																										
BAL	162	98	64	.605	....	799	652	97	5546	1492	283	27	**168**	2333	601	800	61	33	.269	**.343**	.421	.764	111	86	98	792
DET	162	92	70	.568	6	789	679	93	5592	1530	283	53	156	2387	508	831	93	53	.274	.338	.427	.765	112	85	97	797
NY	162	91	71	.562	7	770	703	88	5631	1535	269	40	153	2343	533	686	84	42	.273	.339	.416	.756	111	82	96	781
TOR	162	89	73	.549	9	795	726	88	5581	1546	268	**58**	167	**2431**	510	810	131	72	**.277**	.341	**.436**	**.777**	106	39	106	**816**
MIL	162	87	75	.537	11	764	708	87	5620	**1556**	281	57	132	2347	475	**665**	101	49	.277	.336	.418	.754	115	**107**	92	772
BOS	162	78	84	.481	20	724	775	75	5590	1512	**287**	32	142	2289	536	758	30	**26**	.270	.337	.409	.747	97	-21	107	747
CLE	162	70	92	.432	28	704	785	72	5476	1451	249	31	86	2020	**605**	691	109	71	.265	.341	.369	.710	92	-54	104	685
West																										
CHI	162	99	63	.611	....	**800**	650	98	5484	1439	270	42	157	2264	527	888	165	50	.262	.332	.413	.745	100	14	104	760
KC	163	79	83	.488	20	696	767	73	5598	1515	273	54	109	2223	397	722	182	47	.271	.322	.397	.719	96	-17	100	710
TEX	163	77	85	.475	22	639	**609**	85	5610	1429	242	33	106	2055	442	767	119	60	.255	.312	.366	.679	88	-97	98	631
OAK	162	74	88	.457	25	708	782	73	5516	1447	237	28	121	2103	524	872	**235**	98	.262	.330	.381	.711	101	19	94	692
CAL	162	70	92	.432	29	722	779	75	**5640**	1467	241	22	154	2214	509	835	41	39	.260	.325	.393	.717	97	-31	99	700
MIN	162	70	92	.432	29	709	822	69	5601	1463	280	41	141	2248	467	802	44	29	.261	.321	.401	.723	94	-52	104	700
SEA	162	60	102	.370	39	558	740	59	5336	1280	247	31	111	1922	460	840	144	80	.240	.303	.360	.663	79	-161	104	572
Total	1135					10177			77821	20662	3710	549	1903		7094	10967	1539	749	.266	.330	.401	.731				

Runs		Hits		Doubles		Triples		Home Runs		Total Bases	
Ripken, C. (Bal)	121	Ripken, C. (Bal)	211	Ripken, C. (Bal)	47	Yount, R. (Mil)	10	Rice, J. (Bos)	39	Rice, J. (Bos)	344
Murray, E. (Bal)	115	Boggs, W. (Bos)	210	Boggs, W. (Bos)	44	3 players tied with	9	Armas, T. (Bos)	36	Ripken, C. (Bal)	343
Cooper, C. (Mil)	106	Whitaker, L. (Det)	206	2 players tied with	42			Kittle, R. (Chi)	35	Cooper, C. (Mil)	336

Runs Batted In		Bases On Balls		Stolen Bases		Batting Average		On-Base Percentage		Slugging Average	
Cooper, C. (Mil)	126	Henderson, R. (Oak)	103	Henderson, R. (Oak)	108	Boggs, W. (Bos)	.361	Boggs, W. (Bos)	.449	Brett, G. (KC)	.562
Rice, J. (Bos)	126	Singleton, K. (Bal)	99	Law, R. (Chi)	77	Carew, R. (Cal)	.339	Henderson, R. (Oak)	.415	Rice, J. (Bos)	.550
Winfield, D. (NY)	116	Boggs, W. (Bos)	92	Wilson, W. (KC)	59	Whitaker, L. (Det)	.320	Carew, R. (Cal)	.411	Murray, E. (Bal)	.538

Adjusted OPS		Adjusted Batting Runs		Runs Created/Game		Fielding Runs		Win Shares – Batters		TPW – Batters	
Murray, E. (Bal)	158	Henderson, R. (Oak)	50.0	Boggs, W. (Bos)	8.80	Ripken, C. (Bal)	19.2	Ripken, C. (Bal)	35	Ripken, C. (Bal)	7.4
Brett, G. (KC)	157	Murray, E. (Bal)	49.0	Brett, G. (KC)	8.10	Gantner, J. (Mil)	16.8	Boggs, W. (Bos)	34	Yount, R. (Mil)	6.1
Yount, R. (Mil)	155	Yount, R. (Mil)	44.0	Murray, E. (Bal)	8.00	Gaetti, G. (Min)	16.2	Yount, R. (Mil)	33	Boggs, W. (Bos)	5.4

TEAM	CG	SH	SV	IP	H	H/G	ER	HR	BB	SO	OAV	RAT	ERA	ERA+	CERA	PR+	PF	FA	E	DP	FR	BW	PW	FW	TPW	DIF
East																										
BAL	36	**15**	38	1452¹	1451	9.0	586	130	452	774	.261	1.310	3.63	109	3.72	53.2	97	.981	121	159	-3.8	8.5	5.3	-.4	**13.5**	3.5
DET	42	9	28	1451	**1318**	**8.2**	613	170	522	875	**.242**	1.268	3.80	103	3.63	-4.2	96	.980	125	142	**17.9**	8.5	-.4	**1.8**	9.9	1.1
NY	**47**	12	32	1456²	1449	9.0	624	116	455	892	.260	1.307	3.86	101	3.62	8.4	96	.978	139	157	-8.7	8.2	.8	-.9	8.1	1.9
TOR	43	8	32	1445¹	1434	8.9	661	145	517	835	.259	1.350	4.12	104	3.99	26.2	106	.981	115	148	2.2	3.9	2.6	.2	6.7	1.3
MIL	35	10	43	1454	1513	9.4	649	143	491	869	.270	1.378	4.02	93	4.10	-45.0	92	**.982**	**113**	162	-1.9	**10.6**	-4.5	-.2	6.0	.0
BOS	29	7	42	1446¹	1572	9.8	697	158	493	767	.279	1.428	4.34	100	4.48	7.6	107	.979	130	168	-6.6	-2.1	.8	-.7	-2.0	-1.0
CLE	34	8	25	1441²	1531	9.6	709	120	529	794	.275	1.429	4.43	96	4.25	-20.1	104	.980	122	174	-12.0	-5.3	-2.0	-1.2	-8.6	-2.4
West																										
CHI	35	12	48	1445¹	1355	8.4	589	128	**447**	877	.248	**1.247**	3.67	114	3.40	76.1	103	.981	120	158	4.3	1.3	7.6	.4	9.4	8.6
KC	19	8	**49**	1437²	1535	9.6	679	133	471	593	.274	1.395	4.26	96	4.22	-20.1	100	.974	165	178	-10.5	-1.7	-2.0	-1.0	-4.7	2.7
TEX	43	11	32	1466²	1392	8.5	**539**	97	471	826	.252	1.270	**3.31**	121	**3.39**	118.2	99	**.982**	**113**	151	-5.7	-9.7	**11.8**	-.6	1.5	-5.5
OAK	22	12	33	1454¹	1462	9.0	701	135	626	719	.263	1.436	4.34	**89**	4.29	-91.0	95	.974	157	157	11.5	1.8	-9.1	1.2	-6.1	-.9
CAL	39	7	23	**1474**	1636	10.0	706	130	496	668	.284	1.446	4.31	93	4.42	-48.5	99	.977	154	**190**	-2.7	-3.1	-4.8	-.3	-8.2	-2.8
MIN	20	5	39	1437¹	1559	9.8	744	163	580	748	.280	1.488	4.66	91	4.79	-85.5	105	.980	121	170	17.3	-5.2	-8.5	1.7	-12.0	1.0
SEA	25	9	39	1418¹	1455	9.2	649	145	544	**910**	.268	1.409	4.12	103	4.33	11.5	105	.978	136	159	-2.2	-16.1	1.2	-.2	-15.2	-5.8
Total	469	133	503	20281	9146	9.2						1.369	4.06													

Wins		Win Percentage		Games		Complete Games		Shutouts		Saves	
Hoyt, L. (Chi)	24	Haas, M. (Mil)	.812	Quisenberry, D. (KC)	69	Guidry, R. (NY)	21	Boddicker, M. (Bal)	5	Quisenberry, D. (KC)	45
Dotson, R. (Chi)	22	Dotson, R. (Chi)	.759	Vande Berg, E. (Sea)	68	Morris, J. (Det)	20	Burns, B. (Chi)	4	Stanley, B. (Bos)	33
Guidry, R. (NY)	21	McGregor, S. (Bal)	.720	Davis, R. (Min)	66	Stieb, D. (Tor)	14	Stieb, D. (Tor)	4	Davis, R. (Min)	30

Innings Pitched		Fewest Hits/Game		Fewest BB/Game		Strikeouts		Ratio		Earned Run Average	
Morris, J. (Det)	293²	Boddicker, M. (Bal)	7.09	Hoyt, L. (Chi)	1.07	Morris, J. (Det)	232	Hoyt, L. (Chi)	1.02	Honeycutt, R. (Tex)	2.42
Stieb, D. (Tor)	278	Stieb, D. (Tor)	7.22	McGregor, S. (Bal)	1.56	Bannister, F. (Chi)	193	Boddicker, M. (Bal)	1.08	Boddicker, M. (Bal)	2.77
Petry, D. (Det)	266¹	Conroy, T. (Oak)	7.82	John, T. (Cal)	1.88	Stieb, D. (Tor)	187	Stieb, D. (Tor)	1.14	Stieb, D. (Tor)	3.04

Adjusted ERA		Component ERA		Opponents' Batting Avg.		Adjusted Pitching Runs		Win Shares – Pitchers		TPW – Pitchers	
Honeycutt, R. (Tex)	165	Boddicker, M. (Bal)	2.41	Boddicker, M. (Bal)	.216	Stieb, D. (Tor)	38	Stieb, D. (Tor)	24	Stieb, D. (Tor)	3.8
Boddicker, M. (Bal)	143	Hoyt, L. (Chi)	2.53	Stieb, D. (Tor)	.219	Honeycutt, R. (Tex)	31	Dotson, R. (Chi)	21	Honeycutt, R. (Tex)	3.1
Stieb, D. (Tor)	141	Stieb, D. (Tor)	2.78	Conroy, T. (Oak)	.232	Dotson, R. (Chi)	25	McGregor, S. (Bal)	21	Dotson, R. (Chi)	2.5

1984 National League

TEAM	G	W	L	PCT	GB	R	OR	EW	AB	H	2B	3B	HR	TB	BB	SO	SB	CS	AVG	OBP	SLG	OPS	OPS+	BR/A	PF	RC
East																										
CHI	161	96	65	.596	....	**762**	658	92	5437	1415	240	47	136	2157	**567**	967	154	66	.260	.333	.397	.730	102	20	109	728
NY	162	90	72	.556	6.5	652	676	78	5438	1400	235	25	107	2006	500	1001	149	54	.257	.322	.369	.691	102	17	99	643
STL	162	84	78	.519	12.5	652	645	82	5433	1369	225	44	75	1907	516	924	**220**	71	.252	.319	.351	.670	97	-4	97	621
PHI	162	81	81	.500	15.5	720	690	84	5614	1494	**248**	51	**147**	**2285**	555	1084	186	60	**.266**	**.335**	**.407**	**.742**	**113**	**102**	102	**764**
MON	161	78	83	.484	18	593	585	82	5439	1367	242	36	96	1969	470	**782**	131	**38**	.251	.314	.362	.676	100	6	96	628
PIT	162	75	87	.463	21.5	615	**567**	88	5537	1412	237	33	98	2009	438	841	96	62	.255	.312	.363	.675	95	-48	100	609
West																										
SD	162	92	70	.568	....	686	634	87	5504	1425	207	42	109	2043	472	810	152	68	.259	.320	.371	.691	100	0	100	643
HOU	162	80	82	.494	12	693	630	89	5548	1465	222	**67**	79	2058	494	837	105	61	.264	.326	.371	.697	110	57	93	677
ATL	162	80	82	.494	12	632	655	78	5422	1338	234	27	111	1959	555	896	140	85	.247	.319	.361	.680	91	-69	107	621
LA	162	79	83	.488	13	580	600	78	5399	1316	213	23	102	1881	488	829	109	69	.244	.308	.348	.656	91	-72	99	571
CIN	162	70	92	.432	22	627	747	67	5498	1342	238	30	106	1958	566	978	160	63	.244	.316	.356	.672	91	-57	104	633
SF	162	66	96	.407	26	682	807	67	**5650**	**1499**	229	26	112	2116	528	980	126	76	.265	.330	.375	.704	108	45	97	684
Total	**971**					**7894**			**65919**	**16842**	**2770**	**451**	**1278**		**6149**	**10929**	**1728**	**773**	**.255**	**.321**	**.369**	**.691**				

Runs
Sandberg, R. (Chi) 114
Raines, T. (Mon) 106
Wiggins, A. (SD) 106

Hits
Gwynn, T. (SD) 213
Sandberg, R. (Chi) 200
Raines, T. (Mon) 192

Doubles
Raines, T. (Mon) 38
Ray, J. (Pit) 38
2 players tied with 36

Triples
Samuel, J. (Phi) 19
Sandberg, R. (Chi) 19
Cruz, J. (Hou) 13

Home Runs
Murphy, D. (Atl) 36
Schmidt, M. (Phi) 36
Carter, G. (Mon) 27

Total Bases
Murphy, D. (Atl) 332
Sandberg, R. (Chi) 331
Samuel, J. (Phi) 310

Runs Batted In
Carter, G. (Mon) 106
Schmidt, M. (Phi) 106
Murphy, D. (Atl) 100

Bases On Balls
Matthews, G. (Chi) 103
Hernandez, K. (NY) 97
Schmidt, M. (Phi) 92

Stolen Bases
Raines, T. (Mon) 75
Samuel, J. (Phi) 72
Wiggins, A. (SD) 70

Batting Average
Gwynn, T. (SD) .... .351
Lacy, L. (Pit) .... .321
Davis, C. (SF) .... .315

On-Base Percentage
Matthews, G. (Chi) .... .417
Hernandez, K. (NY) .... .415
Gwynn, T. (SD) .... .411

Slugging Average
Murphy, D. (Atl) .... .547
Schmidt, M. (Phi) .... .536
Sandberg, R. (Chi) .... .520

Adjusted OPS
Schmidt, M. (Phi) 155
Davis, C. (SF) 149
Cruz, J. (Hou) 148

Adjusted Batting Runs
Raines, T. (Mon) 48.0
Cruz, J. (Hou) 40.0
Schmidt, M. (Phi) 38.0

Runs Created/Game
Sandberg, R. (Chi) 7.40
Raines, T. (Mon) 7.30
Murphy, D. (Atl) 7.30

Fielding Runs
Wallach, T. (Mon) 27.6
Schmidt, M. (Phi) 16.3
Smith, O. (StL) 16.3

Win Shares – Batters
Sandberg, R. (Chi) 38
Gwynn, T. (SD) 35
2 players tied with 33

TPW – Batters
Sandberg, R. (Chi) 5.9
Schmidt, M. (Phi) 5.5
Hernandez, K. (NY) 4.3

TEAM	CG	SH	SV	IP	H	H/G	ER	HR	BB	SO	OAV	RAT	ERA	ERA+	CERA	PR+	PF	FA	E	DP	FR	BW	PW	FW	TPW	DIF
East																										
CHI	19	8	50	1434	1458	9.2	598	99	**442**	879	.267	1.325	3.75	104	3.66	42.1	109	.981	121	137	-17.6	2.1	4.4	-1.8	4.7	11.3
NY	12	15	50	1442[2]	1371	8.6	577	104	573	1028	.252	1.348	3.60	98	3.71	-15.4	99	.979	129	154	0.1	1.8	-1.6	.0	.1	8.9
STL	19	12	**51**	1449	1427	8.9	576	94	494	808	.262	1.326	3.58	97	3.63	-40.0	97	**.982**	**118**	**184**	22.0	-.4	-4.2	2.3	-2.3	5.3
PHI	11	6	35	1458[1]	1416	8.7	586	101	448	904	.253	1.278	3.62	100	3.32	23.7	101	.975	161	112	-21.0	**10.7**	2.5	-2.2	**11.0**	-11.0
MON	19	10	48	1431	1333	8.4	526	114	474	861	.249	1.263	3.31	103	3.34	1.0	95	.978	132	147	17.3	.6	.1	1.8	2.5	-4.5
PIT	27	13	34	**1470**	1344	8.2	**508**	102	502	995	.246	**1.256**	**3.11**	116	**3.21**	59.5	100	.980	128	142	20.6	-5.1	6.2	2.2	3.4	-9.4
West																										
SD	13	**17**	44	1460[1]	**1327**	**8.2**	565	122	563	812	**.244**	1.294	3.48	102	3.47	-16.9	99	.978	138	144	**30.9**	.0	-1.8	**3.2**	1.5	9.5
HOU	24	13	29	1449[1]	1350	8.4	535	91	502	950	.248	1.278	3.32	100	3.28	-20.7	93	.979	133	160	19.3	6.0	-2.2	2.0	5.9	-6.9
ATL	17	7	49	1447	1401	8.7	574	122	525	859	.257	1.331	3.57	108	3.67	54.5	107	.978	139	153	-8.8	-7.3	5.7	-.9	-2.5	1.5
LA	**39**	16	27	1460[2]	1381	8.5	514	**76**	499	**1033**	.250	1.287	3.17	111	3.22	**70.7**	98	.975	163	146	-12.7	-7.6	**7.4**	-1.3	-1.5	-.5
CIN	25	6	25	1461[1]	1445	8.9	675	128	578	946	.259	1.384	4.16	91	3.92	-48.4	105	.977	139	116	-13.9	-6.0	-5.1	-1.5	-12.5	1.5
SF	9	7	38	1461	1589	9.8	713	125	549	854	.278	1.463	4.39	**80**	4.37	-106.0	98	.973	173	134	-37.4	4.7	-11.1	-3.9	-10.3	-4.7
Total	**234**	**130**	**480**	**17424[2]**		**8.7**	**6947**					**1.319**	**3.59**													

Wins
Andujar, J. (StL) 20
Soto, M. (Cin) 18
Gooden, D. (NY) 17

Win Percentage
Soto, M. (Cin) .... .720
Pena, A. (LA) .... .667
Gooden, D. (NY) .... .654

Games
Power, T. (Cin) 78
Lavelle, G. (SF) 77
Minton, G. (SF) 74

Complete Games
Soto, M. (Cin) 13
Andujar, J. (StL) 12
Valenzuela, F. (LA) 12

Shutouts
Andujar, J. (StL) 4
Hershiser, O. (LA) 4
Pena, A. (LA) 4

Saves
Sutter, B. (StL) 45
Smith, L. (Chi) 33
Orosco, J. (NY) 31

Innings Pitched
Andujar, J. (StL) .... 261[1]
Valenzuela, F. (LA) 261
Niekro, J. (Hou) .... 248[1]

Fewest Hits/Game
Gooden, D. (NY) 6.65
Soto, M. (Cin) 6.86
DeLeon, J. (Pit) 6.88

Fewest BB/Game
Gullickson, B. (Mon) 1.47
Candelaria, J. (Pit) 1.65
Whitson, E. (SD) 2.00

Strikeouts
Gooden, D. (NY) 276
Valenzuela, F. (LA) 240
Ryan, N. (Hou) 197

Ratio
Gooden, D. (NY) 1.07
Andujar, J. (StL) 1.10
Hershiser, O. (LA) 1.11

Earned Run Average
Pena, A. (LA) 2.48
Gooden, D. (NY) 2.60
Hershiser, O. (LA) 2.66

Adjusted ERA
Pena, A. (LA) 142
Gooden, D. (NY) 136
Hershiser, O. (LA) 133

Component ERA
Gooden, D. (NY) 2.08
Hershiser, O. (LA) 2.42
Andujar, J. (StL) 2.61

Opponents' Batting Avg.
Gooden, D. (NY) .... .202
Soto, M. (Cin) .... .209
Ryan, N. (Hou) .... .211

Adjusted Pitching Runs
Pena, A. (LA) 25
Gooden, D. (NY) 23
Hershiser, O. (LA) 20

Win Shares – Pitchers
Rhoden, R. (Pit) 20
6 players tied with 18

TPW – Pitchers
Rhoden, R. (Pit) 3.1
Mahler, R. (Atl) 2.6
Pena, A. (LA) 2.5

1984 American League

TEAM	G	W	L	PCT	GB	R	OR	EW	AB	H	2B	3B	HR	TB	BB	SO	SB	CS	AVG	OBP	SLG	OPS	OPS+	BR/A	PF	RC
East																										
DET	162	104	58	.642	....	**829**	**643**	101	5644	1529	254	46	**187**	2436	602	941	106	68	.271	**.345**	.432	.776	**114**	**107**	99	**841**
TOR	163	89	73	.549	15	750	696	87	**5687**	1555	**275**	**68**	143	2395	460	816	**193**	67	.273	.333	.421	.755	104	40	104	807
NY	162	87	75	.537	17	758	679	90	5661	1560	**275**	32	130	2289	534	**673**	62	38	.276	.342	.404	.746	110	78	96	771
BOS	162	86	76	.531	18	810	764	86	5648	**1598**	259	45	181	**2490**	500	842	38	**25**	**.283**	.343	**.441**	**.784**	110	77	105	831
BAL	162	85	77	.525	19	681	667	83	5456	1374	234	23	160	2134	**620**	884	51	36	.252	.331	.391	.722	101	12	98	703
CLE	163	75	87	.463	29	761	766	80	5643	1498	222	39	123	2167	600	815	126	77	.265	.339	.384	.723	98	-10	102	729
MIL	161	67	94	.416	36.5	641	734	70	5511	1446	232	36	96	2038	432	**673**	52	57	.262	.319	.370	.689	94	-61	96	619
West																										
KC	162	84	78	.519	....	673	686	79	5543	1487	269	52	117	2211	400	832	106	64	.268	.320	.399	.719	97	-33	101	683
CAL	162	81	81	.500	3	696	697	81	5470	1363	211	30	150	2084	556	928	80	51	.249	.322	.381	.703	94	-43	99	661
MIN	162	81	81	.500	3	673	675	81	5562	1473	259	33	114	2140	437	735	39	30	.265	.321	.385	.706	90	-77	105	666
OAK	162	77	85	.475	7	738	796	75	5457	1415	257	29	158	2204	568	871	145	64	.259	.332	.404	.735	110	79	93	733
SEA	162	74	88	.457	10	682	774	71	5546	1429	244	34	129	2128	519	871	116	62	.258	.326	.384	.710	97	-22	99	698
CHI	162	74	88	.457	10	679	736	74	5513	1360	225	38	172	2177	523	883	109	49	.247	.316	.395	.711	91	-61	104	688
TEX	161	69	92	.429	14.5	656	714	74	5569	1452	227	29	120	2097	420	807	81	50	.261	.315	.377	.691	88	-99	103	641
Total	**1134**					**10027**			**77910**	**20539**	**3443**	**534**	**1980**		**7171**	**11571**	**1304**	**738**	**.264**	**.329**	**.398**	**.727**				

Runs
Evans, D. (Bos)	121
Henderson, R. (Oak)	113
Boggs, W. (Bos)	109

Hits
Mattingly, D. (NY)	207
Boggs, W. (Bos)	203
Ripken, C. (Bal)	195

Doubles
Mattingly, D. (NY)	44
Parrish, L. (Tex)	42
Bell, G. (Tor)	39

Triples
Collins, D. (Tor)	15
Moseby, L. (Tor)	15
2 players tied with	10

Home Runs
Armas, T. (Bos)	43
Kingman, D. (Oak)	35
3 players tied with	33

Total Bases
Armas, T. (Bos)	339
Evans, D. (Bos)	335
Ripken, C. (Bal)	327

Runs Batted In
Armas, T. (Bos)	123
Rice, J. (Bos)	122
Kingman, D. (Oak)	118

Bases On Balls
Murray, E. (Bal)	107
Davis, A. (Sea)	97
Evans, D. (Bos)	96

Stolen Bases
Henderson, R. (Oak)	66
Collins, D. (Tor)	60
Butler, B. (Cle)	52

Batting Average
Mattingly, D. (NY)	.343
Winfield, D. (NY)	.340
Boggs, W. (Bos)	.325

On-Base Percentage
Murray, E. (Bal)	.415
Boggs, W. (Bos)	.409
Henderson, R. (Oak)	.401

Slugging Average
Baines, H. (Chi)	.541
Mattingly, D. (NY)	.537
Evans, D. (Bos)	.532

Adjusted OPS
Mattingly, D. (NY)	159
Murray, E. (Bal)	157
Winfield, D. (NY)	156

Adjusted Batting Runs
Murray, E. (Bal)	52.0
Mattingly, D. (NY)	46.0
Henderson, R. (Oak)	43.0

Runs Created/Game
Murray, E. (Bal)	8.20
Winfield, D. (NY)	7.70
Mattingly, D. (NY)	7.60

Fielding Runs
Ripken, C. (Bal)	28.5
Gaetti, G. (Min)	23.0
Bell, B. (Tex)	22.9

Win Shares – Batters
Ripken, C. (Bal)	37
Murray, E. (Bal)	33
3 players tied with	29

TPW – Batters
Ripken, C. (Bal)	8.6
Murray, E. (Bal)	4.8
Trammell, A. (Det)	4.5

TEAM	CG	SH	SV	IP	H	H/G	ER	HR	BB	SO	OAV	RAT	ERA	ERA+	CERA	PR+	PF	FA	E	DP	FR	BW	PW	FW	TPW	DIF
East																										
DET	19	8	51	1464	**1358**	8.4	568	130	489	914	.246	1.262	3.49	112	3.43	58.9	98	.979	127	162	10.9	**10.7**	5.9	1.1	**17.8**	5.2
TOR	34	10	33	1464	1433	8.8	628	140	528	875	.257	1.339	3.86	106	3.88	29.5	103	.980	123	166	6.8	4.0	3.0	.7	7.6	.4
NY	15	12	43	1465[1]	1485	9.1	615	138	518	**992**	.264	1.367	3.78	100	3.91	8.9	95	.977	142	**177**	-9.3	7.8	.9	-.9	7.8	-1.8
BOS	40	12	32	1442	1524	9.5	670	141	517	927	.270	1.415	4.18	100	4.26	45.8	104	.977	143	128	-50.5	7.7	4.6	-5.1	7.3	-2.3
BAL	**48**	**13**	32	1439[1]	1393	8.7	593	137	512	714	.256	1.324	3.71	104	3.76	-3.0	97	**.981**	123	166	28.6	1.2	-.3	2.9	3.8	.2
CLE	21	7	35	**1467**[2]	1523	9.3	694	141	545	803	.269	1.409	4.26	96	4.24	-38.3	102	.977	146	163	10.0	-1.0	-3.9	1.0	-3.9	-2.1
MIL	13	7	41	1433	1532	9.6	646	137	480	785	.274	1.404	4.06	95	4.21	-20.6	96	.978	136	156	-13.3	-6.2	-2.1	-1.3	-9.6	-3.4
West																										
KC	18	9	50	1444	1426	8.9	629	136	**433**	724	.258	1.287	3.92	103	3.69	6.9	101	.979	131	157	10.5	-3.3	.7	1.1	-1.6	4.6
CAL	36	12	26	1458	1526	9.4	642	143	474	754	.271	1.372	3.96	100	4.10	-3.7	99	.980	128	170	5.4	-4.3	-.4	.5	-4.1	4.1
MIN	32	9	38	1437[2]	1429	9.0	615	159	463	713	.260	1.316	3.85	109	3.88	21.0	105	.980	**120**	134	**34.4**	-7.8	2.1	**3.5**	-2.2	2.2
OAK	15	6	44	1430	1554	9.8	712	155	592	695	.278	1.501	4.48	84	4.81	-122.1	94	.975	146	159	4.0	7.9	-12.3	.4	-4.0	.0
SEA	26	4	35	1442	1497	9.3	691	138	619	972	.270	1.467	4.31	93	4.49	-22.6	100	.979	128	143	-31.0	-2.2	-2.3	-3.1	-7.6	.6
CHI	43	9	32	1454[1]	1416	8.8	667	155	483	840	.256	1.306	4.13	101	3.80	-6.5	104	.981	122	160	9.5	-6.2	-.6	1.0	-5.9	-1.1
TEX	38	6	21	1438[2]	1443	9.0	625	148	518	863	.260	1.363	3.91	106	4.02	52.9	104	.977	138	138	-15.0	-9.9	5.3	-1.5	-6.1	-4.9
Total	398	124	513	20280		9.1	8995					1.366	3.99													

Wins
Boddicker, M. (Bal)	20
Blyleven, B. (Cle)	19
Morris, J. (Det)	19

Win Percentage
Alexander, D. (Tor)	.739
Blyleven, B. (Cle)	.731
Petry, D. (Det)	.692

Games
Hernandez, W. (Det)	80
Quisenberry, D. (KC)	72
Lopez, A. (Det)	71

Complete Games
Hough, C. (Tex)	17
Boddicker, M. (Bal)	16
Dotson, R. (Chi)	14

Shutouts
Ojeda, B. (Bos)	5
Zahn, G. (Cal)	5
4 players tied with	4

Saves
Quisenberry, D. (KC)	44
Caudill, B. (Oak)	36
Hernandez, W. (Det)	32

Innings Pitched
Stieb, D. (Tor)	267
Hough, C. (Tex)	266
Alexander, D. (Tor)	261[2]

Fewest Hits/Game
Stieb, D. (Tor)	7.25
Blyleven, B. (Cle)	7.49
Boddicker, M. (Bal)	7.51

Fewest BB/Game
Hoyt, L. (Chi)	1.64
Smithson, M. (Min)	1.93
Guidry, R. (NY)	2.02

Strikeouts
Langston, M. (Sea)	204
Stieb, D. (Tor)	198
Witt, M. (Cal)	196

Ratio
Black, B. (KC)	1.13
Blyleven, B. (Cle)	1.13
Stieb, D. (Tor)	1.13

Earned Run Average
Boddicker, M. (Bal)	2.79
Stieb, D. (Tor)	2.83
Blyleven, B. (Cle)	2.87

Adjusted ERA
Stieb, D. (Tor)	145
Blyleven, B. (Cle)	143
Boddicker, M. (Bal)	139

Component ERA
Blyleven, B. (Cle)	2.73
Stieb, D. (Tor)	2.77
Black, B. (KC)	2.82

Opponents' Batting Avg.
Stieb, D. (Tor)	.221
Blyleven, B. (Cle)	.224
Boddicker, M. (Bal)	.228

Adjusted Pitching Runs
Stieb, D. (Tor)	36
Blyleven, B. (Cle)	32
Tanana, F. (Tex)	27

Win Shares – Pitchers
Stieb, D. (Tor)	25
Alexander, D. (Tor)	23
Boddicker, M. (Bal)	23

TPW – Pitchers
Stieb, D. (Tor)	3.6
Blyleven, B. (Cle)	3.2
Tanana, F. (Tex)	2.7

1985 National League

TEAM	G	W	L	PCT	GB	R	OR	EW	AB	H	2B	3B	HR	TB	BB	SO	SB	CS	AVG	OBP	SLG	OPS	OPS+	BR/A	PF	RC
East																										
STL	162	101	61	.623	....	**747**	572	102	5467	1446	245	**59**	87	2070	**586**	853	**314**	96	**.264**	.338	.379	.716	108	82	99	731
NY	162	98	64	.605	3	695	**568**	97	5549	1425	239	35	134	2136	546	872	117	53	.257	.326	.385	.711	107	48	98	690
MON	161	84	77	.522	16.5	633	636	80	5429	1342	242	49	118	2036	492	880	169	77	.247	.313	.375	.688	104	19	94	632
CHI	162	77	84	.478	23.5	686	729	76	5492	1397	239	28	**150**	2142	562	937	182	49	.254	.326	**.390**	.716	95	-14	111	709
PHI	162	75	87	.463	26	667	673	80	5477	1343	238	47	141	2098	527	1095	122	51	.245	.314	.383	.697	98	-17	103	656
PIT	161	57	104	.354	43.5	568	708	63	5436	1340	251	28	80	1887	514	842	110	60	.247	.313	.347	.660	91	-65	99	585
West																										
LA	162	95	67	.586	....	682	579	94	5502	1434	226	28	129	2103	539	846	136	58	.261	.330	.382	.712	**108**	60	97	702
CIN	162	89	72	.553	5.5	677	666	82	5431	1385	249	34	114	2044	576	856	159	70	.255	.329	.376	.705	98	-5	105	671
SD	162	83	79	.512	12	650	622	86	5507	1405	241	28	109	2029	513	**809**	60	**39**	.255	.321	.368	.690	100	-7	98	644
HOU	162	83	79	.512	12	706	691	83	**5582**	**1457**	**261**	42	121	**2165**	477	873	96	56	.261	.322	.388	.710	107	37	97	682
ATL	162	66	96	.407	29	632	781	64	5526	1359	213	28	126	2006	553	849	72	52	.246	.317	.363	.680	91	-73	106	620
SF	162	62	100	.383	33	556	674	66	5420	1263	217	31	115	1887	488	962	99	55	.233	.301	.348	.649	91	-70	95	563
Total	971					7899			65818	16596	2861	437	1424		6373	10674	1636	716	.252	.321	.374	.695				

Runs
Murphy, D. (Atl)	118
Raines, T. (Mon)	115
McGee, W. (StL)	114

Hits
McGee, W. (StL)	216
Parker, D. (Cin)	198
Gwynn, T. (SD)	197

Doubles
Parker, D. (Cin)	42
Wilson, G. (Phi)	39
Herr, T. (StL)	38

Triples
McGee, W. (StL)	18
Raines, T. (Mon)	13
Samuel, J. (Phi)	13

Home Runs
Murphy, D. (Atl)	37
Parker, D. (Cin)	34
2 players tied with	33

Total Bases
Parker, D. (Cin)	350
Murphy, D. (Atl)	332
McGee, W. (StL)	308

Runs Batted In
Parker, D. (Cin)	125
Murphy, D. (Atl)	111
Herr, T. (StL)	110

Bases On Balls
Murphy, D. (Atl)	90
Martinez, C. (SD)	87
Schmidt, M. (Phi)	87

Stolen Bases
Coleman, V. (StL)	110
Raines, T. (Mon)	70
McGee, W. (StL)	56

Batting Average
McGee, W. (StL)	.353
Guerrero, P. (LA)	.320
Raines, T. (Mon)	.320

On-Base Percentage
Guerrero, P. (LA)	.425
Scioscia, M. (LA)	.409
Raines, T. (Mon)	.407

Slugging Average
Guerrero, P. (LA)	.577
Parker, D. (Cin)	.551
Murphy, D. (Atl)	.539

Adjusted OPS
Guerrero, P. (LA)	183
Raines, T. (Mon)	155
Clark, J. (StL)	151

Adjusted Batting Runs
Guerrero, P. (LA)	58.0
Raines, T. (Mon)	56.0
McGee, W. (StL)	42.0

Runs Created/Game
Guerrero, P. (LA)	9.30
Raines, T. (Mon)	8.10
McGee, W. (StL)	7.90

Fielding Runs
Hubbard, G. (Atl)	37.4
Wallach, T. (Mon)	36.3
Pendleton, T. (StL)	29.7

Win Shares – Batters
Raines, T. (Mon)	36
McGee, W. (StL)	36
Guerrero, P. (LA)	35

TPW – Batters
Guerrero, P. (LA)	6.8
Raines, T. (Mon)	5.4
Smith, O. (StL)	4.8

TEAM	CG	SH	SV	IP	H	H/G	ER	HR	BB	SO	OAV	RAT	ERA	ERA+	CERA	PR+	PF	FA	E	DP	FR	BW	PW	FW	TPW	DIF
East																										
STL	**37**	20	44	1464	1343	8.3	504	**98**	453	798	.246	1.227	3.10	114	3.12	39.0	98	**.983**	**108**	166	**29.5**	**8.7**	4.1	**3.1**	**15.9**	4.1
NY	32	19	37	**1488**	1306	7.9	514	111	515	**1039**	.237	1.224	3.11	111	3.14	66.1	96	.982	115	138	-9.1	5.0	6.9	-1.0	11.0	6.0
MON	13	13	**53**	1457	1346	8.3	575	99	509	870	.247	1.273	3.55	95	3.31	-36.9	94	.981	121	152	11.7	2.0	-3.9	1.2	-.6	4.6
CHI	20	8	42	1442[1]	1492	9.3	667	156	519	820	.271	1.394	4.16	96	4.23	-12.9	111	.979	134	150	-15.8	-1.5	-1.4	-1.7	-4.5	1.5
PHI	24	9	30	1447	1424	8.9	592	115	596	899	.259	1.396	3.68	100	3.91	19.6	103	.978	139	142	-19.9	-1.8	2.1	-2.1	-1.9	-4.1
PIT	15	6	29	1445[1]	1406	8.8	637	107	584	962	.255	1.377	3.97	**90**	3.83	-40.5	100	.979	133	127	-23.5	-6.8	-4.3	-2.5	-13.5	-9.5
West																										
LA	**37**	**21**	36	1465	**1280**	**7.9**	**482**	102	462	979	**.234**	**1.189**	**2.96**	117	**2.91**	**73.1**	97	.974	166	131	3.3	6.4	**7.7**	.4	14.4	-.4
CIN	24	11	45	1451[1]	1347	8.4	598	131	535	910	.248	1.297	3.71	102	3.50	-1.7	105	.980	122	142	13.9	-.5	-.2	1.5	.8	8.2
SD	26	19	44	1451[1]	1399	8.7	548	127	**443**	727	.257	1.269	3.40	104	3.52	-4.1	98	.980	124	158	24.5	-.7	-.4	2.6	1.4	.6
HOU	17	9	42	1458	1393	8.6	593	119	543	909	.254	1.328	3.66	95	3.64	-47.7	96	.976	152	159	14.2	3.9	-5.0	1.5	.4	1.6
ATL	9	9	29	1457[1]	1512	9.3	678	134	642	776	.271	1.478	4.19	92	4.42	-47.8	107	.976	159	**197**	-11.8	-7.7	-5.0	-1.2	-14.0	-1.0
SF	13	5	24	1448	1348	8.4	581	125	572	985	.247	1.326	3.61	95	3.56	-10.5	96	.976	148	134	-19.8	-7.4	-1.1	-2.1	-10.6	-8.4
Total	**267**	**149**	**455**	**17474[2]**		**8.6**	**6969**					**1.314**	**3.59**													

Wins
Gooden, D. (NY) 24
Andujar, J. (StL) 21
Tudor, J. (StL) 21

Win Percentage
Hershiser, O. (LA) .... .864
Gooden, D. (NY) .... .857
Smith, B. (Mon) .... .783

Games
Burke, T. (Mon) 78
Davis, M. (SF) 77
Garrelts, S. (SF) 74

Complete Games
Gooden, D. (NY) 16
Tudor, J. (StL) 14
Valenzuela, F. (LA) 14

Shutouts
Tudor, J. (StL) 10
Gooden, D. (NY) 8
2 players tied with 5

Saves
Reardon, J. (Mon) 41
Smith, L. (Chi) 33
2 players tied with 27

Innings Pitched
Gooden, D. (NY) .... 276[2]
Tudor, J. (StL) 275
Valenzuela, F. (LA) .... 272[1]

Fewest Hits/Game
Fernandez, S. (NY) 5.71
Gooden, D. (NY) 6.44
Hershiser, O. (LA) 6.72

Fewest BB/Game
Hoyt, L. (SD) .... .86
Eckersley, D. (Chi) 1.01
Lynch, E. (NY) 1.27

Strikeouts
Gooden, D. (NY) 268
Soto, M. (Cin) 214
Ryan, N. (Hou) 209

Ratio
Tudor, J. (StL) .... .94
Gooden, D. (NY) .... .97
Eckersley, D. (Chi) .... .97

Earned Run Average
Gooden, D. (NY) 1.53
Tudor, J. (StL) 1.93
Hershiser, O. (LA) 2.03

Adjusted ERA
Gooden, D. (NY) 226
Tudor, J. (StL) 183
Hershiser, O. (LA) 171

Component ERA
Gooden, D. (NY) 1.83
Tudor, J. (StL) 1.84
Hershiser, O. (LA) 2.01

Opponents' Batting Avg.
Fernandez, S. (NY) .... .181
Gooden, D. (NY) .... .201
Hershiser, O. (LA) .... .206

Adjusted Pitching Runs
Gooden, D. (NY) 61
Tudor, J. (StL) 43
Hershiser, O. (LA) 38

Win Shares – Pitchers
Gooden, D. (NY) 33
Tudor, J. (StL) 27
Hershiser, O. (LA) 23

TPW – Pitchers
Gooden, D. (NY) 7.0
Tudor, J. (StL) 4.6
Hershiser, O. (LA) 4.3

1985 American League

TEAM	G	W	L	PCT	GB	R	OR	EW	AB	H	2B	3B	HR	TB	BB	SO	SB	CS	AVG	OBP	SLG	OPS	OPS+	BR/A	PF	RC
East																										
TOR	161	99	62	.615	....	759	**588**	101	5508	1482	281	**53**	158	2343	503	807	144	77	.269	.334	.425	.759	104	21	102	766
NY	161	97	64	.602	2	**839**	660	99	5458	1458	272	31	176	2320	620	771	**155**	53	.267	.347	.425	.772	**113**	**115**	98	819
DET	161	84	77	.522	15	729	688	85	5575	1413	254	45	202	2363	526	926	75	41	.253	.321	.424	.745	103	11	99	763
BAL	161	83	78	.516	16	818	764	86	5517	1451	234	22	**214**	2371	604	908	69	43	.263	.338	**.430**	.768	111	83	97	793
BOS	163	81	81	.500	18.5	800	720	90	**5720**	**1615**	**292**	31	162	**2455**	562	816	66	**27**	**.282**	**.350**	.429	**.779**	108	67	104	**843**
MIL	161	71	90	.441	28	690	802	68	5568	1467	250	44	101	2108	462	**746**	69	34	.263	.322	.379	.701	91	-67	100	663
CLE	162	60	102	.370	39.5	729	861	68	5527	1465	254	31	116	2129	492	817	132	72	.265	.327	.385	.712	95	-43	99	679
West																										
KC	162	91	71	.562	....	687	639	87	5500	1384	261	49	154	2205	473	840	128	48	.252	.315	.401	.716	94	-44	100	685
CAL	162	90	72	.556	1	732	703	84	5442	1364	215	31	153	2100	**648**	902	106	51	.251	.335	.386	.721	97	-11	100	709
CHI	163	85	77	.525	6	736	720	83	5470	1386	247	37	146	2145	471	843	108	56	.253	.318	.392	.710	90	-82	104	672
MIN	162	77	85	.475	14	705	782	73	5509	1453	282	41	141	2240	502	779	68	44	.264	.329	.407	.735	95	-46	106	728
OAK	162	77	85	.475	14	757	787	78	5581	1475	230	34	155	2238	508	861	117	58	.264	.327	.401	.728	106	42	93	723
SEA	162	74	88	.457	17	719	818	71	5521	1410	277	38	171	2276	564	942	94	35	.255	.328	.412	.740	100	8	101	737
TEX	161	62	99	.385	28.5	617	785	61	5361	1359	213	41	129	2041	530	819	130	76	.253	.324	.381	.705	91	-68	101	650
Total	**1132**					**10317**			**77257**	**20182**	**3562**	**528**	**2178**		**7465**	**11777**	**1461**	**715**	**.261**	**.330**	**.406**	**.735**				

Runs
Henderson, R. (NY) 146
Ripken, C. (Bal) 116
Murray, E. (Bal) 111

Hits
Boggs, W. (Bos) 240
Mattingly, D. (NY) 211
Buckner, B. (Bos) 201

Doubles
Mattingly, D. (NY) 48
Buckner, B. (Bos) 46
Boggs, W. (Bos) 42

Triples
Wilson, W. (KC) 21
Butler, B. (Cle) 14
Puckett, K. (Min) 13

Home Runs
Evans, D. (Det) 40
Fisk, C. (Chi) 37
Balboni, S. (KC) 36

Total Bases
Mattingly, D. (NY) 370
Brett, G. (KC) 322
Bradley, P. (Sea) 319

Runs Batted In
Mattingly, D. (NY) 145
Murray, E. (Bal) 124
Winfield, D. (NY) 114

Bases On Balls
Evans, D. (Bos) 114
Harrah, T. (Tex) 113
Brett, G. (KC) 103

Stolen Bases
Henderson, R. (NY) 80
Pettis, G. (Cal) 56
Butler, B. (Cle) 47

Batting Average
Boggs, W. (Bos) .... .368
Brett, G. (KC) .... .335
Mattingly, D. (NY) .... .324

On-Base Percentage
Boggs, W. (Bos) .... .452
Brett, G. (KC) .... .442
Harrah, T. (Tex) .... .437

Slugging Average
Brett, G. (KC) .... .585
Mattingly, D. (NY) .... .567
Barfield, J. (Tor) .... .536

Adjusted OPS
Brett, G. (KC) 178
Henderson, R. (NY) 159
Mattingly, D. (NY) 159

Adjusted Batting Runs
Brett, G. (KC) 66.0
Henderson, R. (NY) 63.0
Boggs, W. (Bos) 51.0

Runs Created/Game
Brett, G. (KC) 10.20
Henderson, R. (NY) 9.40
Boggs, W. (Bos) 8.80

Fielding Runs
Grich, B. (Cal) 23.1
Randolph, W. (NY) 21.3
Fernandez, T. (Tor) 19.2

Win Shares – Batters
Henderson, R. (NY) 38
Brett, G. (KC) 37
Mattingly, D. (NY) 32

TPW – Batters
Henderson, R. (NY) 6.5
Brett, G. (KC) 6.4
Boggs, W. (Bos) 4.7

TEAM	CG	SH	SV	IP	H	H/G	ER	HR	BB	SO	OAV	RAT	ERA	ERA+	CERA	PR+	PF	FA	E	DP	FR	BW	PW	FW	TPW	DIF
East																										
TOR	18	9	47	1448	**1312**	8.2	**533**	147	484	823	.243	**1.240**	**3.31**	127	**3.42**	121.5	101	.980	125	164	23.9	2.1	12.0	2.4	**16.5**	2.5
NY	25	9	**49**	1440[1]	1373	8.6	590	157	518	907	.251	1.313	3.69	109	3.81	31.3	97	.979	126	172	19.6	**11.3**	3.1	1.9	16.4	.6
DET	31	**11**	40	1456	1313	**8.1**	612	141	556	943	**.240**	1.284	3.78	108	3.46	42.5	98	.977	143	152	2.8	1.1	4.2	.3	5.6	-1.6
BAL	32	6	33	1427[1]	1480	9.3	694	160	568	793	.270	1.435	4.38	92	4.41	-41.5	97	.979	129	168	-12.7	8.2	-4.1	-1.3	2.9	.1
BOS	35	8	29	**1461[1]**	1487	9.2	659	130	540	913	.265	1.387	4.06	106	4.07	60.7	103	.977	145	161	-23.7	6.6	6.0	-2.3	10.3	-10.3
MIL	34	5	37	1437	1510	9.5	701	175	499	777	.271	1.398	4.39	95	4.39	-35.9	100	.977	142	153	-2.0	-6.6	-3.5	-.2	-10.4	1.4
CLE	24	7	28	1421	1556	9.9	775	170	547	702	.281	1.480	4.91	**84**	4.81	-120.4	100	.977	141	161	-3.8	-4.2	-11.9	-.4	-16.5	-4.5
West																										
KC	27	**11**	41	1461	1433	8.8	567	**103**	463	846	.257	1.298	3.49	119	3.51	**126.6**	100	.980	127	160	-17.2	-4.3	**12.5**	-1.7	6.5	3.5
CAL	22	8	41	1457[1]	1453	9.0	633	171	514	767	.263	1.350	3.91	105	4.13	-13.0	99	**.982**	112	**202**	**45.6**	-1.1	-1.3	**4.5**	2.2	6.8
CHI	20	8	39	1451[2]	1411	8.8	656	161	569	**1023**	.256	1.364	4.07	106	4.10	32.9	104	.982	**111**	152	7.7	-8.1	3.3	.8	-4.1	8.1
MIN	**41**	7	34	1426[1]	1468	9.3	710	164	**462**	767	.268	1.353	4.48	98	4.15	-12.1	106	.980	120	139	0.9	-4.5	-1.2	.1	-5.6	1.6
OAK	10	6	41	1453	1451	9.0	712	172	607	785	.259	1.416	4.41	87	4.36	-77.0	93	.977	140	137	-12.5	4.2	-7.6	-1.2	-4.7	.7
SEA	23	8	30	1432	1456	9.2	745	154	637	868	.265	1.462	4.68	90	4.54	-67.3	102	.980	122	156	-6.0	.8	-6.7	-.6	-6.4	-.6
TEX	18	5	33	1411[2]	1479	9.4	715	173	501	863	.269	1.403	4.56	93	4.49	-27.4	102	.980	120	145	-24.1	-6.7	-2.7	-2.4	-11.8	-6.2
Total	**360**	**108**	**522**	**20184**		**9.0**	**9302**					**1.370**	**4.15**													

Wins		Win Percentage		Games		Complete Games		Shutouts		Saves	
Guidry, R. (NY)	22	Guidry, R. (NY)	.786	Quisenberry, D. (KC)	84	Blyleven, B. (Cle,Min)	24	Blyleven, B. (Cle,Min)	5	Quisenberry, D. (KC)	37
Saberhagen, B. (KC)	20	Saberhagen, B. (KC)	.769	Vande Berg, E. (Sea)	76	Hough, C. (Tex)	14	Burns, B. (Chi)	4	James, B. (Chi)	32
2 players tied with	18	Key, J. (Tor)	.700	2 players tied with	74	Moore, M. (Sea)	14	Morris, M. (Det)	4	2 players tied with	31

Innings Pitched		Fewest Hits/Game		Fewest BB/Game		Strikeouts		Ratio		Earned Run Average	
Blyleven, B. (Cle,Min)	293²	Stieb, D. (Tor)	7.00	Saberhagen, B. (KC)	1.45	Blyleven, B. (Cle,Min)	206	Saberhagen, B. (KC)	1.06	Stieb, D. (Tor)	2.48
Boyd, O. (Bos)	272¹	Hough, C. (Tex)	7.12	Guidry, R. (NY)	1.46	Bannister, F. (Chi)	198	Guidry, R. (NY)	1.10	Leibrandt, C. (KC)	2.69
Stieb, D. (Tor)	265	Petry, D. (Det)	7.16	Butcher, J. (Min)	1.86	Morris, M. (Det)	191	Key, J. (Tor)	1.12	Saberhagen, B. (KC)	2.87

Adjusted ERA		Component ERA		Opponents' Batting Avg.		Adjusted Pitching Runs		Win Shares – Pitchers		TPW – Pitchers	
Stieb, D. (Tor)	170	Saberhagen, B. (KC)	2.56	Stieb, D. (Tor)	.213	Stieb, D. (Tor)	47	Leibrandt, C. (KC)	24	Stieb, D. (Tor)	4.6
Leibrandt, C. (KC)	155	Stieb, D. (Tor)	2.75	Hough, C. (Tex)	.215	Leibrandt, C. (KC)	42	Saberhagen, B. (KC)	24	Leibrandt, C. (KC)	4.1
Saberhagen, B. (KC)	145	Hough, C. (Tex)	2.77	Petry, D. (Det)	.217	Saberhagen, B. (KC)	37	Stieb, D. (Tor)	24	Saberhagen, B. (KC)	3.6

1986 National League

TEAM	G	W	L	PCT	GB	R	OR	EW	AB	H	2B	3B	HR	TB	BB	SO	SB	CS	AVG	OBP	SLG	OPS	OPS+	BR/A	PF	RC
East																										
NY	162	108	54	.667	....	783	578	105	5558	1462	261	31	148	2229	631	968	118	48	.263	.341	.401	.743	114	112	97	771
PHI	161	86	75	.534	21.5	739	713	83	5483	1386	266	39	154	2192	589	1154	153	59	.253	.330	.400	.729	103	32	103	737
STL	161	79	82	.491	28.5	601	611	79	5378	1270	216	48	58	1756	568	905	262	78	.236	.311	.327	.638	83	-92	99	582
MON	161	78	83	.484	29.5	637	688	74	5508	1401	255	50	110	2086	537	1016	193	95	.254	.324	.379	.703	101	3	99	674
CHI	160	70	90	.438	37	680	781	69	5499	1409	258	27	155	2186	508	966	132	62	.256	.321	.398	.718	96	-31	108	695
PIT	162	64	98	.395	44	663	700	77	5456	1366	273	33	111	2038	569	929	152	84	.250	.323	.374	.697	96	-32	102	652
West																										
HOU	162	96	66	.593	....	654	569	92	5441	1388	244	32	125	2071	536	916	163	75	.255	.325	.381	.705	103	23	97	666
CIN	162	86	76	.531	10	732	717	83	5536	1404	237	35	144	2143	586	920	177	53	.254	.327	.387	.714	99	6	104	710
SF	162	83	79	.512	13	698	618	91	5501	1394	269	29	114	2063	536	1087	148	93	.253	.324	.375	.699	104	15	95	673
SD	162	74	88	.457	22	656	723	73	5515	1442	239	25	136	2139	484	917	96	68	.261	.323	.388	.711	104	11	98	670
LA	162	73	89	.451	23	638	679	76	5471	1373	232	14	130	2023	478	966	155	67	.251	.315	.370	.685	102	8	93	637
ATL	161	72	89	.447	23.5	615	719	68	5384	1348	241	24	138	2051	538	904	93	76	.250	.321	.381	.702	94	-54	106	644
Total	969					8096			65730	16643	2991	387	1523		6560	11648	1842	858	.253	.324	.380	.704				

Runs		Hits		Doubles		Triples		Home Runs		Total Bases	
Gwynn, T. (SD)	107	Gwynn, T. (SD)	211	Hayes, V. (Phi)	46	Webster, M. (Mon)	13	Schmidt, M. (Phi)	37	Parker, D. (Cin)	304
Hayes, V. (Phi)	107	Sax, S. (LA)	210	Sax, S. (LA)	43	Samuel, J. (Phi)	12	Davis, G. (Hou)	31	Schmidt, M. (Phi)	302
2 players tied with	97	Raines, T. (Mon)	194	2 players tied with	37	Raines, T. (Mon)	10	Parker, D. (Cin)	31	Gwynn, T. (SD)	300

Runs Batted In		Bases On Balls		Stolen Bases		Batting Average		On-Base Percentage		Slugging Average	
Schmidt, M. (Phi)	119	Hernandez, K. (NY)	94	Coleman, V. (StL)	107	Raines, T. (Mon)	.334	Raines, T. (Mon)	.415	Schmidt, M. (Phi)	.547
Parker, D. (Cin)	116	Schmidt, M. (Phi)	89	Davis, E. (Cin)	80	Sax, S. (LA)	.332	Hernandez, K. (NY)	.414	Strawberry, D. (NY)	.507
Carter, G. (NY)	105	Davis, C. (SF)	84	Raines, T. (Mon)	70	Gwynn, T. (SD)	.329	Schmidt, M. (Phi)	.395	McReynolds, K. (SD)	.504

Adjusted OPS		Adjusted Batting Runs		Runs Created/Game		Fielding Runs		Win Shares – Batters		TPW – Batters	
Schmidt, M. (Phi)	152	Raines, T. (Mon)	51.0	Raines, T. (Mon)	8.70	Pendleton, T. (StL)	36.6	Raines, T. (Mon)	32	Raines, T. (Mon)	4.7
Raines, T. (Mon)	146	Schmidt, M. (Phi)	40.0	Schmidt, M. (Phi)	8.00	Bream, S. (Pit)	16.6	Schmidt, M. (Phi)	31	Schmidt, M. (Phi)	4.3
Strawberry, D. (NY)	142	Hernandez, K. (NY)	36.0	Hernandez, K. (NY)	7.20	Uribe, J. (SF)	16.4	Sax, S. (LA)	31	Hernandez, K. (NY)	3.9

TEAM	CG	SH	SV	IP	H	H/G	ER	HR	BB	SO	OAV	RAT	ERA	ERA+	CERA	PR+	PF	FA	E	DP	FR	BW	PW	FW	TPW	DIF
East																										
NY	27	11	46	1484	1304	7.9	513	103	509	1083	.236	1.222	3.11	114	3.08	66.0	95	.978	138	145	4.0	11.6	6.9	.4	18.9	8.1
PHI	22	11	39	1451²	1473	9.1	621	130	553	874	.265	1.396	3.85	104	4.06	-0.1	104	.978	137	157	-3.0	.0	-.3	3.0	3.0	3.0
STL	17	4	46	1466¹	1364	8.4	549	135	485	761	.250	1.261	3.37	108	3.45	-10.2	98	.981	123	178	52.1	-9.6	-1.1	5.4	-5.2	4.2
MON	15	9	50	1466¹	1350	8.3	616	119	566	1051	.246	1.307	3.78	98	3.51	-16.9	99	.979	133	132	1.7	.3	-1.8	.2	-1.3	-.7
CHI	11	6	42	1445	1546	9.6	721	143	557	962	.279	1.455	4.49	90	4.45	-50.0	109	.980	124	147	-25.2	-3.2	-5.2	-2.6	-11.0	1.0
PIT	17	9	30	1450²	1397	8.7	628	138	570	924	.255	1.356	3.90	98	3.89	-10.5	103	.978	143	134	-0.8	-3.3	-1.1	-.1	-4.5	-12.5
West																										
HOU	18	19	51	1456¹	1203	7.4	510	116	523	1160	.225	1.185	3.15	114	2.91	67.4	97	.979	130	108	3.7	2.3	7.0	.4	9.7	5.3
CIN	14	8	45	1468	1465	9.0	638	136	524	924	.264	1.355	3.91	99	3.86	-0.4	104	.978	140	160	-9.0	.6	.0	-.9	-.4	5.4
SF	18	10	35	1460¹	1264	7.8	540	121	591	992	.236	1.270	3.33	106	3.29	2.8	95	.977	143	149	23.4	1.6	.3	2.4	4.3	-2.3
SD	13	7	32	1443¹	1406	8.8	640	150	607	934	.258	1.395	3.99	92	3.88	-53.0	98	.978	137	135	-2.1	1.2	-5.5	-.2	-4.5	-2.5
LA	35	14	25	1454¹	1428	8.8	607	115	499	1051	.256	1.325	3.76	92	3.62	-19.3	93	.971	181	118	-31.4	.8	-2.0	-3.3	-4.5	-3.5
ATL	17	5	39	1424²	1443	9.1	628	117	576	932	.266	1.417	3.97	100	4.11	14.5	107	.978	141	181	-16.7	-5.6	1.5	-1.7	-5.9	-2.1
Total	224	113	480	17471		8.6	7211					1.328	3.71													

Wins		Win Percentage		Games		Complete Games		Shutouts		Saves	
Valenzuela, F. (LA)	21	Ojeda, B. (NY)	.783	Lefferts, C. (SD)	83	Valenzuela, F. (LA)	20	Knepper, B. (Hou)	5	Worrell, T. (StL)	36
Krukow, M. (SF)	20	Gooden, D. (NY)	.739	McDowell, R. (NY)	75	Gooden, D. (NY)	12	Scott, M. (Hou)	5	Reardon, J. (Mon)	35
2 players tied with	18	Fernandez, S. (NY)	.727	2 players tied with	74	Rhoden, R. (Pit)	12	2 players tied with	3	Smith, D. (Hou)	33

Innings Pitched		Fewest Hits/Game		Fewest BB/Game		Strikeouts		Ratio		Earned Run Average	
Scott, M. (Hou)	275¹	Scott, M. (Hou)	5.95	Eckersley, D. (Chi)	1.93	Scott, M. (Hou)	306	Scott, M. (Hou)	.92	Scott, M. (Hou)	2.22
Valenzuela, F. (LA)	269¹	Youmans, F. (Mon)	5.96	Sanderson, S. (Chi)	1.96	Valenzuela, F. (LA)	242	Krukow, M. (SF)	1.06	Ojeda, B. (NY)	2.57
Knepper, B. (Hou)	258	Ryan, N. (Hou)	6.02	Krukow, M. (SF)	2.02	Youmans, F. (Mon)	202	Ojeda, B. (NY)	1.09	Darling, R. (NY)	2.81

Adjusted ERA		Component ERA		Opponents' Batting Avg.		Adjusted Pitching Runs		Win Shares – Pitchers		TPW – Pitchers	
Scott, M. (Hou)	162	Scott, M. (Hou)	1.67	Scott, M. (Hou)	.186	Scott, M. (Hou)	41	Scott, M. (Hou)	27	Scott, M. (Hou)	4.1
Ojeda, B. (NY)	138	Ryan, N. (Hou)	2.46	Ryan, N. (Hou)	.188	Rhoden, R. (Pit)	28	Valenzuela, F. (LA)	21	Rhoden, R. (Pit)	3.8
Rhoden, R. (Pit)	135	Gooden, D. (NY)	2.48	Youmans, F. (Mon)	.188	Ojeda, B. (NY)	23	Rhoden, R. (Pit)	20	Ojeda, B. (NY)	2.1

1986 American League

TEAM	G	W	L	PCT	GB	R	OR	EW	AB	H	2B	3B	HR	TB	BB	SO	SB	CS	AVG	OBP	SLG	OPS	OPS+	BR/A	PF	RC
East																										
BOS	161	95	66	.590	....	794	696	91	5498	1488	**320**	21	144	2282	595	**707**	41	**34**	.271	.349	.415	.764	106	53	100	790
NY	162	90	72	.556	5.5	797	738	87	5570	1512	275	23	188	2397	645	911	139	48	.271	**.350**	**.430**	**.780**	**112**	**111**	99	**842**
DET	162	87	75	.537	8.5	798	714	90	5512	1447	234	30	**198**	2335	613	885	138	58	.263	.341	.424	.765	107	62	100	812
TOR	163	86	76	.531	9.5	809	733	89	**5716**	1540	285	35	181	2438	496	848	110	59	.269	.331	.427	.758	102	9	102	795
CLE	163	84	78	.519	11.5	**831**	841	80	5702	**1620**	270	**45**	157	**2451**	456	944	**141**	54	**.284**	.340	.430	.770	110	78	98	821
MIL	161	77	84	.478	18	667	734	73	5461	1393	255	38	127	2105	530	986	100	50	.255	.324	.385	.709	89	-79	103	680
BAL	162	73	89	.451	22.5	708	760	75	5524	1425	223	13	169	2181	563	862	64	**34**	.258	.330	.395	.725	98	-17	99	706
West																										
CAL	162	92	70	.568	....	786	684	92	5433	1387	236	36	167	2196	**671**	860	109	42	.255	.341	.404	.746	103	40	99	762
TEX	162	87	75	.537	5	771	743	84	5529	1479	248	43	184	2365	511	1088	103	85	.267	.333	.428	.761	103	3	102	760
KC	162	76	86	.469	16	654	**673**	79	5561	1403	264	**45**	137	2168	474	919	97	46	.252	.315	.390	.705	89	-90	102	682
OAK	162	76	86	.469	16	731	760	78	5435	1370	213	25	163	2122	553	983	139	61	.252	.325	.390	.715	101	13	92	698
CHI	162	72	90	.444	20	644	699	74	5406	1335	197	34	121	1963	487	940	115	54	.247	.313	.363	.676	81	-142	103	611
MIN	162	71	91	.438	21	741	839	71	5531	1446	257	39	196	2369	501	977	81	61	.261	.327	.428	.755	101	-7	102	755
SEA	162	67	95	.414	25	718	835	69	5498	1392	243	41	158	2191	572	1148	93	76	.253	.327	.399	.726	96	-45	101	705
Total	**1134**					**10449**			**77376**	**20237**	**3520**	**468**	**2290**		**7667**	**13058**	**1470**	**762**	**.262**	**.332**	**.408**	**.740**				

Runs		Hits		Doubles		Triples		Home Runs		Total Bases	
Henderson, R. (NY)	130	Mattingly, D. (NY)	238	Mattingly, D. (NY)	53	Butler, B. (Cle)	14	Barfield, J. (Tor)	40	Mattingly, D. (NY)	388
Puckett, K. (Min)	119	Puckett, K. (Min)	223	Boggs, W. (Bos)	47	Sierra, R. (Tex)	10	Kingman, D. (Oak)	35	Puckett, K. (Min)	365
Mattingly, D. (NY)	117	Fernandez, T. (Tor)	213	3 players tied with	39	2 players tied with	9	Gaetti, G. (Min)	34	2 players tied with	341
Runs Batted In		**Bases On Balls**		**Stolen Bases**		**Batting Average**		**On-Base Percentage**		**Slugging Average**	
Carter, J. (Cle)	121	Boggs, W. (Bos)	105	Henderson, R. (NY)	87	Boggs, W. (Bos)	.357	Boggs, W. (Bos)	.455	Mattingly, D. (NY)	.573
Canseco, J. (Oak)	117	Evans, D. (Bos)	97	Cangelosi, J. (Chi)	50	Mattingly, D. (NY)	.352	Bradley, P. (Sea)	.406	Barfield, J. (Tor)	.559
Mattingly, D. (NY)	113	Randolph, W. (NY)	94	Pettis, G. (Cal)	50	Puckett, K. (Min)	.328	Brett, G. (KC)	.404	Puckett, K. (Min)	.537
Adjusted OPS		**Adjusted Batting Runs**		**Runs Created/Game**		**Fielding Runs**		**Win Shares – Batters**		**TPW – Batters**	
Mattingly, D. (NY)	163	Mattingly, D. (NY)	57.0	Boggs, W. (Bos)	9.10	Guillen, O. (Chi)	18.7	Boggs, W. (Bos)	37	Ripken, C. (Bal)	4.6
Boggs, W. (Bos)	156	Boggs, W. (Bos)	51.0	Mattingly, D. (NY)	8.70	Gaetti, G. (Min)	17.2	Mattingly, D. (NY)	34	Boggs, W. (Bos)	4.5
Barfield, J. (Tor)	145	Barfield, J. (Tor)	35.0	Barfield, J. (Tor)	7.40	Pettis, G. (Cal)	14.8	4 players tied with	28	Trammell, A. (Det)	4.5

TEAM	CG	SH	SV	IP	H	H/G	ER	HR	BB	SO	OAV	RAT	ERA	ERA+	CERA	PR+	PF	FA	E	DP	FR	BW	PW	FW	TPW	DIF
East																										
BOS	36	6	41	1429^2	1469	9.2	624	167	**474**	1033	.266	1.359	3.93	106	4.20	48.9	100	.979	129	146	-12.7	5.2	4.8	-1.2	8.8	6.2
NY	13	8	**58**	1443^1	1461	9.1	659	175	492	878	.263	1.353	4.11	99	4.14	-12.5	98	.979	127	153	9.2	**10.9**	-1.2	.9	**10.6**	-1.6
DET	33	12	38	1443^2	1374	8.6	645	183	571	880	.251	1.347	4.02	102	4.02	0.2	99	.982	108	163	15.9	6.1	.0	1.6	7.7	-1.7
TOR	16	12	44	**1476**	1467	9.0	669	164	487	1002	.261	1.324	4.08	103	4.03	25.1	101	**.984**	**100**	150	-2.8	.9	2.5	-.3	3.1	1.9
CLE	31	7	34	1447^2	1548	9.6	736	167	605	744	.273	1.487	4.58	90	4.78	-67.9	99	.975	157	148	-9.9	7.7	-6.7	-1.0	.0	3.0
MIL	29	12	32	1431^2	1478	9.3	638	158	494	952	.267	1.377	4.01	108	4.21	56.8	104	.976	146	146	-11.1	-7.8	5.6	-1.1	-3.3	.3
BAL	17	6	39	1436^2	1451	9.1	686	177	535	954	.263	1.382	4.30	96	4.23	-19.0	99	.978	135	163	-9.4	-1.6	-1.9	-.9	-4.4	-3.6
West																										
CAL	29	12	40	1456	1356	**8.4**	621	153	478	955	.248	**1.260**	3.84	107	**3.60**	13.8	98	.983	107	156	29.2	4.0	1.4	2.9	8.2	2.8
TEX	15	8	41	1450^1	1356	8.4	662	145	736	**1059**	.249	1.442	4.11	105	4.24	33.2	103	.980	122	160	-3.2	.3	3.3	-.3	3.3	2.7
KC	24	**13**	31	1440^2	1413	8.8	**611**	**121**	479	888	.258	1.313	**3.82**	111	3.68	**85.7**	102	.980	123	153	-17.5	-8.8	**8.4**	-1.7	-2.1	-2.9
OAK	22	8	37	1433	**1334**	**8.4**	686	166	667	937	**.247**	1.396	4.31	**90**	4.13	-71.9	93	.978	135	120	0.5	1.3	-7.1	.0	-5.7	.7
CHI	18	8	38	1442^1	1361	8.5	630	143	561	895	.251	1.333	3.93	110	3.83	27.5	103	.981	117	142	**31.3**	-14.0	2.7	**3.1**	-8.2	-.8
MIN	**39**	6	24	1432^2	1579	9.9	759	200	503	937	.281	1.453	4.77	90	4.91	-60.7	103	.980	118	168	-16.2	-.7	-6.0	-1.6	-8.2	-1.8
SEA	33	5	27	1439^2	1590	9.9	743	171	585	944	.283	1.511	4.64	91	5.02	-64.6	102	.975	156	**191**	-4.1	-4.4	-6.3	-.4	-11.2	-2.8
Total	**355**	**123**	**524**	**20203^1**		**9.0**	**9369**					**1.381**	**4.17**													

Wins		Win Percentage		Games		Complete Games		Shutouts		Saves	
Clemens, R. (Bos)	24	Clemens, R. (Bos)	.857	Williams, M. (Tex)	80	Candiotti, T. (Cle)	17	Morris, J. (Det)	6	Righetti, D. (NY)	46
Morris, J. (Det)	21	Rasmussen, D. (NY)	.750	Righetti, D. (NY)	74	Blyleven, B. (Min)	16	Higuera, T. (Mil)	4	Aase, D. (Bal)	34
Higuera, T. (Mil)	20	Morris, J. (Det)	.724	Harris, G. (Tex)	73	2 players tied with	15	Hurst, B. (Bos)	4	Henke, T. (Tor)	27
Innings Pitched		**Fewest Hits/Game**		**Fewest BB/Game**		**Strikeouts**		**Ratio**		**Earned Run Average**	
Blyleven, B. (Min)	271^2	Clemens, R. (Bos)	6.34	Guidry, R. (NY)	1.78	Langston, M. (Sea)	245	Clemens, R. (Bos)	.97	Clemens, R. (Bos)	2.48
Witt, M. (Cal)	269	Rasmussen, D. (NY)	7.13	Boyd, O. (Bos)	1.89	Clemens, R. (Bos)	238	Witt, M. (Cal)	1.08	Higuera, T. (Mil)	2.79
Morris, J. (Det)	267	Witt, M. (Cal)	7.29	Blyleven, B. (Min)	1.92	Morris, J. (Det)	223	Rasmussen, D. (NY)	1.16	Witt, M. (Cal)	2.84
Adjusted ERA		**Component ERA**		**Opponents' Batting Avg.**		**Adjusted Pitching Runs**		**Win Shares – Pitchers**		**TPW – Pitchers**	
Clemens, R. (Bos)	168	Clemens, R. (Bos)	2.03	Clemens, R. (Bos)	.195	Clemens, R. (Bos)	50	Clemens, R. (Bos)	29	Clemens, R. (Bos)	4.9
Higuera, T. (Mil)	155	Witt, M. (Cal)	2.55	Rasmussen, D. (NY)	.217	Higuera, T. (Mil)	44	Higuera, T. (Mil)	25	Higuera, T. (Mil)	4.4
Witt, M. (Cal)	145	McCaskill, K. (Cal)	3.07	Witt, M. (Cal)	.221	Witt, M. (Cal)	32	Witt, M. (Cal)	23	Witt, M. (Cal)	3.2

1987 National League

TEAM	G	W	L	PCT	GB	R	OR	EW	AB	H	2B	3B	HR	TB	BB	SO	SB	CS	AVG	OBP	SLG	OPS	OPS+	BR/A	PF	RC
East																										
STL	162	95	67	.586	....	798	693	92	5500	1449	252	49	94	2081	**644**	933	**248**	72	.263	**.343**	.378	.721	96	-4	102	738
NY	162	92	70	.568	3	**823**	698	94	5601	**1499**	287	34	192	**2430**	592	1012	159	49	**.268**	.341	**.434**	**.775**	**117**	**135**	95	**846**
MON	162	91	71	.562	4	741	720	83	5527	1467	**310**	39	120	2215	501	918	166	74	.265	.330	.401	.731	96	-30	103	732
PIT	162	80	82	.494	15	723	744	79	5536	1464	282	45	131	2229	535	914	140	58	.264	.332	.403	.735	100	-3	101	739
PHI	162	80	82	.494	15	702	749	76	5475	1390	248	**51**	169	2247	587	1109	111	49	.254	.329	.410	.739	98	-17	103	735
CHI	161	76	85	.472	18.5	720	801	72	5583	1475	244	33	**209**	2412	504	1064	109	48	.264	.327	.432	.759	102	7	104	784
West																										
SF	162	90	72	.556	....	783	**669**	94	**5608**	1458	274	32	205	2411	511	1094	126	97	.260	.326	.430	.756	110	49	95	767
CIN	162	84	78	.519	6	783	752	84	5560	1478	262	29	192	2374	514	928	169	**46**	.266	.331	.427	.758	102	19	104	785
HOU	162	76	86	.469	14	648	678	77	5485	1386	238	28	122	2046	526	936	162	**46**	.253	.321	.373	.694	93	-43	96	667
LA	162	73	89	.451	17	635	675	76	5517	1389	236	23	125	2046	445	923	128	59	.252	.311	.371	.682	88	-97	97	625
ATL	161	69	92	.429	20.5	747	829	72	5428	1401	284	24	152	2189	641	**834**	135	68	.258	.341	.403	.744	98	-11	105	746
SD	162	65	97	.401	25	668	763	70	5456	1419	209	48	113	2063	577	992	198	91	.260	.334	.378	.712	98	-10	96	691
Total	**971**					**8771**			**66276**	**17275**	**3126**	**435**	**1824**		**6577**	**11657**	**1851**	**757**	**.261**	**.331**	**.404**	**.734**				

Runs		Hits		Doubles		Triples		Home Runs		Total Bases	
Raines, T. (Mon)	123	Gwynn, T. (SD)	218	Wallach, T. (Mon)	42	Samuel, J. (Phi)	15	Dawson, A. (Chi)	49	Dawson, A. (Chi)	353
Coleman, V. (StL)	121	Guerrero, P. (LA)	184	Galarraga, A. (Mon)	40	Gwynn, T. (SD)	13	Murphy, D. (Atl)	44	Samuel, J. (Phi)	329
Davis, E. (Cin)	120	Smith, O. (StL)	182	Smith, O. (StL)	40	2 players tied with	11	Strawberry, D. (NY)	39	Murphy, D. (Atl)	328

Runs Batted In		Bases On Balls		Stolen Bases		Batting Average		On-Base Percentage		Slugging Average	
Dawson, A. (Chi)	137	Clark, J. (StL)	136	Coleman, V. (StL)	109	Gwynn, T. (SD)	.370	Clark, J. (StL)	.461	Clark, J. (StL)	.597
Wallach, T. (Mon)	123	Hayes, V. (Phi)	121	Gwynn, T. (SD)	56	Guerrero, P. (LA)	.338	Gwynn, T. (SD)	.450	Davis, E. (Cin)	.593
Schmidt, M. (Phi)	113	Murphy, D. (Atl)	115	Hatcher, B. (Hou)	53	Raines, T. (Mon)	.330	Raines, T. (Mon)	.431	Strawberry, D. (NY)	.583

Adjusted OPS		Adjusted Batting Runs		Runs Created/Game		Fielding Runs		Win Shares – Batters		TPW – Batters	
Clark, J. (StL)	174	Gwynn, T. (SD)	61.0	Clark, J. (StL)	11.10	Schmidt, M. (Phi)	22.5	Raines, T. (Mon)	34	Gwynn, T. (SD)	5.8
Strawberry, D. (NY)	165	Strawberry, D. (NY)	54.0	Gwynn, T. (StL)	9.60	Smith, O. (StL)	18.8	Smith, O. (StL)	33	Schmidt, M. (Phi)	5.2
Gwynn, T. (SD)	160	Clark, J. (StL)	53.0	Raines, T. (Mon)	9.60	Pendleton, T. (StL)	16.9	Clark, J. (StL)	33	Davis, E. (Cin)	5.2

TEAM	CG	SH	SV	IP	H	H/G	ER	HR	BB	SO	OAV	RAT	ERA	ERA+	CERA	PR+	PF	FA	E	DP	FR	BW	PW	FW	TPW	DIF
East																										
STL	10	7	48	1466	1484	9.1	637	**129**	533	873	.265	1.376	3.91	106	3.96	24.9	102	**.982**	116	172	10.3	-.4	2.5	1.0	3.1	10.9
NY	16	7	**51**	1454	1407	8.7	620	135	510	1032	.254	1.318	3.84	98	3.70	6.5	93	.978	137	137	-16.9	**13.4**	.6	-1.7	**12.4**	-1.4
MON	16	8	50	1450¹	1428	8.9	632	145	**446**	1012	**1.292**	3.92	107	3.69	64.8	103	.976	147	122	-19.6	-3.0	**6.4**	-1.9	1.5	8.5	
PIT	25	**13**	39	1445	1377	8.6	674	164	562	914	.253	1.342	4.20	98	3.92	-40.2	101	.980	123	147	**26.0**	-.3	-4.0	**2.6**	-1.7	.7
PHI	13	7	48	1448¹	1453	9.0	673	167	587	877	.263	1.409	4.18	101	4.29	-7.7	104	.980	121	137	16.7	-1.7	-.8	1.7	-.8	-.2
CHI	11	5	48	1434²	1524	9.6	725	159	628	1024	.275	1.500	4.55	94	4.72	-12.1	105	.979	130	154	-33.5	.7	-1.2	-3.3	-3.9	-.1
West																										
SF	19	10	38	**1471**	1407	8.6	**601**	146	547	1038	.255	1.328	**3.68**	105	3.77	3.5	94	.980	129	**183**	20.9	4.9	.3	2.1	7.3	1.7
CIN	7	6	44	1452¹	1486	9.2	684	170	485	919	.267	1.357	4.24	100	4.10	-7.3	104	.979	130	137	6.8	1.9	-.7	.7	1.9	1.1
HOU	13	**13**	33	1441¹	**1363**	**8.5**	615	141	525	**1137**	**.250**	1.310	3.84	102	3.70	18.8	96	.981	116	113	-7.6	-4.3	1.9	-.8	-3.2	-1.8
LA	**29**	8	32	1455	1415	8.8	**601**	130	565	1097	.255	1.361	3.72	107	3.83	50.6	97	.975	155	144	-10.2	-9.7	5.0	-1.0	-5.7	-2.3
ATL	16	4	32	1427²	1529	9.6	734	163	587	837	.276	1.482	4.63	94	4.73	-38.7	106	.982	116	170	-7.3	-1.1	-3.8	-.7	-5.6	-5.4
SD	14	10	33	1433¹	1402	8.8	680	175	602	897	.256	1.398	4.27	**93**	4.24	-64.0	97	.976	147	135	12.7	-1.0	-6.4	1.3	-6.1	-9.9
Total	**189**	**98**	**496**	**17379**		**9.0**	**7876**					**1.372**	**4.08**													

Wins		Win Percentage		Games		Complete Games		Shutouts		Saves	
Sutcliffe, R. (Chi)	18	Dunne, M. (Pit)	.684	Tekulve, K. (Phi)	90	Reuschel, R. (Pit,SF)	12	Reuschel, R. (Pit,SF)	4	Bedrosian, S. (Phi)	40
Rawley, S. (Phi)	17	Gooden, D. (NY)	.682	Murphy, R. (Cin)	87	Valenzuela, F. (LA)	12	Welch, B. (LA)	4	Smith, L. (Chi)	36
2 players tied with	16	Sutcliffe, R. (Chi)	.643	Williams, F. (Cin)	85	Hershiser, O. (LA)	10	8 players tied with	3	Worrell, T. (StL)	33

Innings Pitched		Fewest Hits/Game		Fewest BB/Game		Strikeouts		Ratio		Earned Run Average	
Hershiser, O. (LA)	264²	Ryan, N. (Hou)	6.55	Reuschel, R. (SF,Pit)	1.67	Ryan, N. (Hou)	270	Reuschel, R. (SF,Pit)	1.10	Ryan, N. (Hou)	2.76
Welch, B. (LA)	251²	Scott, M. (Hou)	7.23	Heaton, N. (Mon)	1.72	Scott, M. (Hou)	233	Scott, M. (Hou)	1.12	Dunne, M. (Pit)	3.03
Valenzuela, F. (LA)	251	Welch, B. (LA)	7.30	Gullickson, B. (Cin)	2.13	Welch, B. (LA)	196	Ryan, N. (Hou)	1.14	Hershiser, O. (LA)	3.06

Adjusted ERA		Component ERA		Opponents' Batting Avg.		Adjusted Pitching Runs		Win Shares – Pitchers		TPW – Pitchers	
Ryan, N. (Hou)	142	Ryan, N. (Hou)	2.50	Ryan, N. (Hou)	.199	Hershiser, O. (LA)	29	Hershiser, O. (LA)	21	Hershiser, O. (LA)	3.2
Dunne, M. (Pit)	136	Scott, M. (Hou)	2.65	Scott, M. (Hou)	.217	Ryan, N. (Hou)	28	Sutcliffe, R. (Chi)	19	Ryan, N. (Hou)	2.5
Reuschel, R. (Pit,SF)	130	Reuschel, R. (SF,Pit)	2.65	Welch, B. (LA)	.221	Welch, B. (LA)	23	Welch, B. (LA)	19	Sutcliffe, R. (Chi)	2.4

1987 American League

TEAM	G	W	L	PCT	GB	R	OR	EW	AB	H	2B	3B	HR	TB	BB	SO	SB	CS	AVG	OBP	SLG	OPS	OPS+	BR/A	PF	RC
East																										
DET	162	98	64	.605	....	**896**	735	97	**5649**	1535	274	32	**225**	2548	**653**	913	106	50	.272	.352	**.451**	**.803**	116	**133**	96	**908**
TOR	162	96	66	.593	2	845	**655**	101	5635	1514	277	38	215	2512	555	970	126	50	.269	.338	.446	.784	104	29	102	840
MIL	162	91	71	.562	7	862	817	85	5625	1552	272	46	163	2405	598	1040	**176**	74	.276	.349	.428	.776	102	22	103	851
NY	162	89	73	.549	9	788	758	84	5511	1445	239	16	196	2304	604	949	105	**43**	.262	.338	.418	.756	100	6	99	772
BOS	162	78	84	.481	20	842	825	83	5586	**1554**	273	26	174	2401	606	**825**	77	45	**.278**	**.355**	.430	.785	104	35	103	853
BAL	162	67	95	.414	31	729	880	66	5576	1437	219	20	211	2329	524	939	69	45	.258	.324	.418	.742	97	-34	97	735
CLE	162	61	101	.377	37	742	957	61	5606	1476	267	30	187	2364	489	977	140	54	.263	.326	.422	.748	96	-37	101	771
West																										
MIN	162	85	77	.525	....	786	806	79	5441	1422	258	35	196	2338	523	898	113	65	.261	.330	.430	.760	96	-41	103	756
KC	162	83	79	.512	2	715	691	84	5499	1443	239	40	168	2266	523	1034	125	**43**	.262	.330	.412	.742	93	-52	102	745
OAK	162	81	81	.500	4	806	789	83	5511	1432	263	33	199	2358	593	1056	140	63	.260	.336	.428	.764	108	64	93	795
SEA	162	78	84	.481	7	760	801	77	5508	1499	282	**48**	161	2360	500	863	174	73	.272	.337	.428	.766	96	-27	105	786
CHI	162	77	85	.475	8	748	746	81	5538	1427	**283**	36	173	2301	487	971	138	52	.258	.321	.415	.737	91	-70	102	735
TEX	162	75	87	.463	10	823	849	78	5564	1478	264	35	194	2394	567	1081	120	71	.266	.336	.430	.766	101	0	100	797
CAL	162	75	87	.463	10	770	803	78	5570	1406	257	26	172	2231	590	926	125	44	.252	.328	.401	.728	95	-32	97	743
Total	**1134**					**11112**			**77819**	**20620**	**3667**	**461**	**2634**		**7812**	**13442**	**1734**	**772**	**.265**	**.336**	**.425**	**.761**				

Runs		Hits		Doubles		Triples		Home Runs		Total Bases	
Molitor, P. (Mil)	114	Puckett, K. (Min)	207	Molitor, P. (Mil)	41	Wilson, W. (KC)	15	McGwire, M. (Oak)	49	Bell, G. (Tor)	369
Bell, G. (Tor)	111	Seitzer, K. (KC)	207	Boggs, W. (Bos)	40	Bradley, P. (Sea)	10	Bell, G. (Tor)	47	McGwire, M. (Oak)	344
2 players tied with	110	Trammell, A. (Det)	205	4 players tied with	38	Polonia, L. (Oak)	10	5 players tied with	34	Puckett, K. (Min)	333

Runs Batted In		Bases On Balls		Stolen Bases		Batting Average		On-Base Percentage		Slugging Average	
Bell, G. (Tor)	134	Downing, B. (Cal)	106	Reynolds, H. (Sea)	60	Boggs, W. (Bos)	.363	Boggs, W. (Bos)	.467	McGwire, M. (Oak)	.618
Evans, D. (Bos)	123	Evans, D. (Bos)	106	Wilson, W. (KC)	59	Molitor, P. (Mil)	.353	Molitor, P. (Mil)	.438	Bell, G. (Tor)	.605
McGwire, M. (Oak)	118	Boggs, W. (Bos)	105	Redus, G. (Chi)	52	Trammell, A. (Det)	.343	Evans, D. (Bos)	.422	Boggs, W. (Bos)	.588

Adjusted OPS		Adjusted Batting Runs		Runs Created/Game		Fielding Runs		Win Shares – Batters		TPW – Batters	
Boggs, W. (Bos)	173	Boggs, W. (Bos)	63.0	Boggs, W. (Bos)	11.00	Barrett, M. (Bos)	25.6	Trammell, A. (Det)	35	Trammell, A. (Det)	6.4
McGwire, M. (Oak)	168	Trammell, A. (Det)	53.0	Molitor, P. (Mil)	10.50	Guillen, O. (Chi)	23.2	Boggs, W. (Bos)	32	Boggs, W. (Bos)	5.3
Molitor, P. (Mil)	159	McGwire, M. (Oak)	53.0	Evans, D. (Bos)	9.00	Fernandez, T. (Tor)	15.9	McGwire, M. (Oak)	30	Molitor, P. (Mil)	4.4

TEAM	CG	SH	SV	IP	H	H/G	ER	HR	BB	SO	OAV	RAT	ERA	ERA+	CERA	PR+	PF	FA	E	DP	FR	BW	PW	FW	TPW	DIF
East																										
DET	33	10	31	1456	1430	8.8	650	180	563	976	.256	1.369	4.02	105	4.15	22.9	95	.980	122	147	8.9	**12.6**	2.2	.8	**15.7**	1.3
TOR	18	8	43	1454	**1323**	8.2	**604**	158	567	1064	**.244**	**1.300**	**3.74**	120	**3.66**	100.6	101	.982	111	148	20.3	2.7	9.6	1.9	14.3	.7
MIL	28	6	45	**1464**	1548	9.5	752	169	529	1039	.271	1.419	4.62	99	4.45	3.4	103	.976	145	155	-11.8	2.1	.3	-1.1	1.3	8.7
NY	19	10	**47**	1446¹	1475	9.2	701	179	542	900	.266	1.395	4.36	101	4.37	-7.8	98	**.983**	102	155	6.7	.6	-.7	.6	.5	7.5
BOS	**47**	**13**	16	1436	1584	9.9	761	190	517	1034	.282	1.463	4.77	95	4.87	-30.0	102	.982	110	158	-8.9	3.4	-2.9	-.9	-.3	-2.7
BAL	17	6	30	1439²	1555	9.7	801	226	547	870	.276	1.460	5.01	88	4.96	-97.4	99	.982	111	**174**	-1.1	-3.3	-9.3	-.1	-12.7	-1.3
CLE	24	8	25	1422²	1566	9.9	834	219	606	849	.278	1.527	5.28	**86**	5.26	-98.8	102	.975	153	128	-21.1	-3.6	-9.4	-2.0	-15.0	-5.0
West																										
MIN	16	4	39	1427¹	1465	9.2	734	210	564	990	.266	1.422	4.63	100	4.72	-12.6	104	**.984**	**98**	147	4.5	-3.9	-1.2	.4	-4.7	8.7
KC	44	11	26	1424	1424	9.0	611	**128**	548	923	.261	1.385	3.86	118	4.08	**127.5**	102	.979	131	151	-19.0	-5.0	**12.2**	-1.8	5.4	-3.4
OAK	18	6	40	1445²	1442	9.0	694	176	531	1042	.258	1.365	4.32	95	4.18	-28.3	93	.977	142	122	-14.7	6.1	-2.7	-1.4	2.0	-2.0
SEA	39	10	33	1430²	1503	9.5	713	199	**497**	919	.272	1.398	4.49	105	4.55	23.4	106	.980	122	150	7.6	-2.6	2.2	.7	.3	-3.3
CHI	29	12	37	1447²	1436	8.9	691	189	537	792	.259	1.363	4.30	107	4.28	4.8	103	.981	116	**174**	41.4	-6.7	.5	**3.9**	-2.3	-1.7
TEX	20	3	27	1444¹	1388	8.6	743	199	760	**1103**	.253	1.487	4.63	97	4.80	-8.9	100	.976	151	148	-16.0	.0	-.8	-1.5	-2.3	-3.7
CAL	20	7	36	1457¹	1481	9.2	709	212	504	941	.264	1.362	4.38	98	4.39	-17.1	97	.981	117	162	3.6	-3.1	-1.6	.3	-4.4	-1.6
Total	372	114	475	20195²		9.2	9998					1.408	4.46													

Wins		Win Percentage		Games		Complete Games		Shutouts		Saves	
Clemens, R. (Bos)	20	Clemens, R. (Bos)	.690	Eichhorn, M. (Tor)	89	Clemens, R. (Bos)	18	Clemens, R. (Bos)	7	Henke, T. (Tor)	34
Stewart, D. (Oak)	20	John, T. (NY)	.684	Williams, M. (Tex)	85	Hurst, B. (Bos)	15	Reardon, J. (Min)	4	Reardon, J. (Min)	31
Langston, M. (Sea)	19	Key, J. (Tor)	.680	Mohorcic, D. (Tex)	74	Saberhagen, B. (KC)	15	6 players tied with	3	Righetti, D. (NY)	31

Innings Pitched		Fewest Hits/Game		Fewest BB/Game		Strikeouts		Ratio		Earned Run Average	
Hough, C. (Tex)	285¹	Key, J. (Tor)	7.24	Long, B. (Chi)	1.49	Langston, M. (Sea)	262	Key, J. (Tor)	1.06	Key, J. (Tor)	2.76
Clemens, R. (Bos)	281²	Hough, C. (Tex)	7.51	Saberhagen, B. (KC)	1.86	Clemens, R. (Bos)	256	Bannister, F. (Chi)	1.16	Viola, F. (Min)	2.90
Langston, M. (Sea)	272	Morris, J. (Det)	7.68	Sutton, D. (Cal)	1.93	Saberhagen, B. (KC)	240	Saberhagen, B. (KC)	1.16	Clemens, R. (Bos)	2.97

Adjusted ERA		Component ERA		Opponents' Batting Avg.		Adjusted Pitching Runs		Win Shares – Pitchers		TPW – Pitchers	
Key, J. (Tor)	163	Key, J. (Tor)	2.48	Key, J. (Tor)	.221	Clemens, R. (Bos)	51	Clemens, R. (Bos)	28	Clemens, R. (Bos)	4.8
Viola, F. (Min)	159	Clemens, R. (Bos)	2.94	Hough, C. (Tex)	.223	Viola, F. (Min)	47	Viola, F. (Min)	24	Viola, F. (Min)	4.5
Clemens, R. (Bos)	153	Saberhagen, B. (KC)	3.24	Morris, J. (Det)	.228	Key, J. (Tor)	47	2 players tied with	23	Key, J. (Tor)	4.4

1988 National League

TEAM	G	W	L	PCT	GB	R	OR	EW	AB	H	2B	3B	HR	TB	BB	SO	SB	CS	AVG	OBP	SLG	OPS	OPS+	BR/A	PF	RC
East																										
NY	160	100	60	.625	....	**703**	532	102	5408	1387	251	24	**152**	2142	544	842	140	51	.256	**.328**	**.396**	**.724**	120	136	95	**715**
PIT	160	85	75	.531	15	651	616	84	5379	1327	240	45	110	1987	**553**	947	119	60	.247	.321	.369	.690	106	37	99	646
MON	163	81	81	.500	20	628	592	86	5573	1400	260	**48**	107	2077	454	1053	189	89	.251	.311	.373	.684	98	-21	105	635
CHI	163	77	85	.475	24	660	694	77	**5675**	**1481**	**262**	46	113	**2174**	403	910	120	**46**	**.261**	.312	.383	.695	101	1	104	671
STL	162	76	86	.469	25	578	633	74	5518	1373	207	33	71	1859	484	**827**	234	64	.249	.312	.337	.649	92	-36	101	598
PHI	162	65	96	.404	35.5	597	734	64	5403	1294	246	31	106	1920	489	981	112	49	.239	.308	.355	.663	95	-37	102	597
West																										
LA	162	94	67	.584	....	628	544	92	5431	1346	217	25	99	1910	437	947	131	**46**	.248	.308	.352	.659	98	-11	97	587
CIN	161	87	74	.540	7	641	596	86	5426	1334	246	25	122	1996	479	922	207	56	.246	.311	.368	.679	97	-4	104	637
SD	161	83	78	.516	11	594	583	82	5366	1325	205	35	94	1882	494	892	123	50	.247	.313	.351	.664	98	-9	98	592
SF	162	83	79	.512	11.5	670	626	86	5450	1353	227	44	113	2007	550	1023	121	78	.248	.321	.368	.689	109	48	96	647
HOU	162	82	80	.506	12.5	617	631	79	5494	1338	239	31	96	1927	474	840	198	71	.244	.308	.351	.659	99	-1	96	602
ATL	160	54	106	.338	39.5	555	741	58	5440	1319	228	28	96	1891	432	848	95	69	.242	.301	.348	.648	88	-99	105	547
Total	969					7522			65563	16277	2828	415	1279		5793	11032	1789	729	.248	.313	.363	.675				

Runs		Hits		Doubles		Triples		Home Runs		Total Bases	
Butler, B. (SF)	109	Galarraga, A. (Mon)	184	Galarraga, A. (Mon)	42	Van Slyke, A. (Pit)	15	Strawberry, D. (NY)	39	Galarraga, A. (Mon)	329
Gibson, K. (LA)	106	Dawson, A. (Chi)	179	Palmeiro, R. (Chi)	41	Coleman, V. (StL)	10	Davis, G. (Hou)	30	Dawson, A. (Chi)	298
Clark, W. (SF)	102	Palmeiro, R. (Chi)	178	Sabo, C. (Cin)	40	3 players tied with	9	2 players tied with	29	Van Slyke, A. (Pit)	297

Runs Batted In		Bases On Balls		Stolen Bases		Batting Average		On-Base Percentage		Slugging Average	
Clark, W. (SF)	109	Clark, W. (SF)	100	Coleman, V. (StL)	81	Gwynn, T. (SD)	.313	Daniels, K. (Cin)	.400	Strawberry, D. (NY)	.545
Strawberry, D. (NY)	101	Butler, B. (SF)	97	Young, G. (Hou)	65	Palmeiro, R. (Chi)	.307	Butler, B. (SF)	.395	Galarraga, A. (Mon)	.540
2 players tied with	100	Daniels, K. (Cin)	87	Smith, O. (StL)	57	Dawson, A. (Chi)	.303	Clark, W. (SF)	.392	Clark, W. (SF)	.508

Adjusted OPS		Adjusted Batting Runs		Runs Created/Game		Fielding Runs		Win Shares – Batters		TPW – Batters	
Strawberry, D. (NY)	168	Clark, W. (SF)	51.0	Clark, W. (SF)	7.50	Alomar, R. (SD)	18.5	Clark, W. (SF)	37	Strawberry, D. (NY)	4.9
Clark, W. (SF)	163	Strawberry, D. (NY)	48.0	Daniels, K. (Cin)	7.10	Bream, S. (Pit)	18.4	3 players tied with	31	Clark, W. (SF)	4.8
Gibson, K. (LA)	151	Gibson, K. (LA)	42.0	Gibson, K. (LA)	7.10	Sabo, C. (Cin)	17.8			Larkin, B. (Cin)	4.5

TEAM	CG	SH	SV	IP	H	H/G	ER	HR	BB	SO	OAV	RAT	ERA	ERA+	CERA	PR+	PF	FA	E	DP	FR	BW	PW	FW	TPW	DIF
East																										
NY	31	22	46	1439	**1253**	7.8	465	78	404	1100	.235	1.151	2.91	111	2.74	50.5	93	.981	115	127	-0.6	**14.7**	5.4	-.1	**20.0**	.0
PIT	12	11	46	1440²	1349	8.4	555	108	469	790	.250	1.262	3.47	98	3.35	-19.5	99	.980	125	128	9.2	4.0	-2.1	1.0	2.9	2.1
MON	18	12	43	**1482²**	1310	8.0	507	122	476	923	.238	1.205	3.08	117	3.10	60.5	104	.978	142	145	22.0	-2.2	6.5	2.4	6.7	-6.7
CHI	30	10	29	1464¹	1494	9.2	625	115	490	897	.265	1.355	3.84	94	3.80	-11.5	105	.980	125	128	-32.7	.1	-1.2	-3.5	-4.7	.7
STL	17	14	42	1470²	1387	8.5	567	91	486	881	.252	1.274	3.47	100	3.24	-11.6	101	**.981**	121	131	12.5	-3.9	-1.2	1.3	-3.8	-1.2
PHI	16	6	36	1433	1447	9.1	659	118	628	859	.265	1.448	4.14	**86**	4.20	-76.5	103	.976	145	139	-18.3	-4.0	-8.2	-2.0	-14.2	-.8
West																										
LA	**32**	**24**	49	1463¹	1291	7.9	481	84	473	1029	.237	1.205	2.96	113	2.91	**73.5**	97	.977	142	126	-14.1	-1.2	**7.9**	-1.5	5.2	8.8
CIN	24	13	43	1455	1271	7.9	542	121	504	934	.237	1.220	3.35	107	3.14	11.5	104	.980	125	131	**26.5**	-.4	1.2	**2.9**	3.7	3.3
SD	30	9	39	1449	1332	8.3	528	112	439	885	.247	1.222	3.28	104	3.17	-3.0	98	.981	120	**147**	21.6	-1.0	-.3	2.3	1.0	2.0
SF	25	13	42	1462¹	1323	8.1	551	99	422	875	.242	1.193	3.39	96	2.95	-23.6	95	.980	129	145	1.6	5.2	-2.5	.2	2.8	-.8
HOU	21	15	40	1474²	1339	8.2	558	123	478	1049	.242	1.232	3.41	97	3.21	-6.2	96	.978	138	124	-7.7	-.1	-.7	-.8	-1.6	2.6
ATL	14	4	25	1446	1481	9.2	657	108	524	810	.268	1.387	4.09	90	3.94	-48.1	107	.976	151	138	-19.7	-10.7	-5.2	-2.1	-18.0	-8.0
Total	270	153	480	17480²		8.4	6695					1.263	3.45													

Wins		**Win Percentage**		**Games**		**Complete Games**		**Shutouts**		**Saves**	
Hershiser, O. (LA)	23	Cone, D. (NY)	.870	Murphy, R. (Cin)	76	Hershiser, O. (LA)	15	Hershiser, O. (LA)	8	Franco, J. (Cin)	39
Jackson, D. (Cin)	23	Browning, T. (Cin)	.783	Agosto, J. (Hou)	75	Jackson, D. (Cin)	15	Jackson, D. (Cin)	6	Gott, J. (Pit)	34
Cone, D. (NY)	20	2 players tied with	.742	Robinson, J. (Pit)	75	Show, E. (SD)	13	Leary, T. (LA)	6	Worrell, T. (StL)	32

Innings Pitched		**Fewest Hits/Game**		**Fewest BB/Game**		**Strikeouts**		**Ratio**		**Earned Run Average**	
Hershiser, O. (LA)	267	Fernandez, S. (NY)	6.11	Smith, B. (Mon)	1.45	Ryan, N. (Hou)	228	Perez, P. (Mon)	.94	Magrane, J. (StL)	2.18
Jackson, D. (Cin)	260²	Perez, P. (Mon)	6.37	Mahler, R. (Atl)	1.52	Cone, D. (NY)	213	Scott, M. (Hou)	.98	Cone, D. (NY)	2.22
Browning, T. (Cin)	250²	Rijo, J. (Cin)	6.67	Reuschel, R. (SF)	1.54	DeLeon, J. (StL)	208	Ojeda, B. (NY)	1.00	Hershiser, O. (LA)	2.26

Adjusted ERA		**Component ERA**		**Opponents' Batting Avg.**		**Adjusted Pitching Runs**		**Win Shares – Pitchers**		**TPW – Pitchers**	
Magrane, J. (StL)	160	Perez, P. (Mon)	1.94	Fernandez, S. (NY)	.191	Hershiser, O. (LA)	34	Hershiser, O. (LA)	25	Hershiser, O. (LA)	3.7
Rijo, J. (Cin)	150	Ojeda, B. (NY)	2.02	Perez, P. (Mon)	.196	Cone, D. (NY)	26	Jackson, D. (Cin)	22	Cone, D. (NY)	2.9
Tudor, J. (StL,LA)	148	Scott, M. (Hou)	2.15	Scott, M. (Hou)	.204	Tudor, J. (StL,LA)	24	Maddux, G. (Chi)	20	Magrane, J. (StL)	2.6

1988 American League

TEAM	G	W	L	PCT	GB	R	OR	EW	AB	H	2B	3B	HR	TB	BB	SO	SB	CS	AVG	OBP	SLG	OPS	OPS+	BR/A	PF	RC
East																										
BOS	162	89	73	.549	....	813	689	94	5545	1569	310	39	124	2329	623	728	65	36	.283	.360	.420	.780	113	106	104	840
DET	162	88	74	.543	1	703	658	86	5433	1358	213	28	143	2056	588	841	87	42	.250	.326	.378	.705	101	7	96	672
TOR	162	87	75	.537	2	763	680	90	5557	1491	271	47	158	2330	521	935	107	36	.268	.334	.419	.754	109	72	100	769
MIL	162	87	75	.537	2	682	616	89	5488	1409	258	26	113	2058	439	911	159	55	.257	.316	.375	.691	92	-54	101	646
NY	161	85	76	.528	3.5	772	748	83	5592	1469	272	12	148	2209	588	935	146	39	.263	.336	.395	.731	105	53	99	752
CLE	162	78	84	.481	11	666	731	73	5505	1435	235	28	134	2128	416	866	97	50	.261	.317	.387	.703	93	-56	103	665
BAL	161	54	107	.335	34.5	550	789	53	5358	1275	199	20	137	1925	504	869	69	44	.238	.307	.359	.667	88	-90	97	579
West																										
OAK	162	104	58	.642	....	800	620	101	5602	1474	251	22	156	2237	580	926	129	54	.263	.339	.399	.739	110	82	96	761
MIN	162	91	71	.562	13	759	672	91	5510	1508	294	31	151	2317	528	832	107	63	.274	.343	.421	.764	109	66	103	783
KC	162	84	77	.522	19.5	704	648	87	5469	1419	275	40	121	2137	486	944	137	54	.259	.324	.391	.714	98	-12	101	695
CAL	162	75	87	.463	29	714	771	75	5582	1458	258	31	124	2150	469	819	86	52	.261	.324	.385	.709	100	-6	97	688
CHI	161	71	90	.441	32.5	631	757	66	5449	1327	224	35	132	2017	446	908	98	46	.244	.305	.370	.675	88	-91	100	607
TEX	161	70	91	.435	33.5	637	735	69	5479	1378	227	39	112	2019	542	1022	130	57	.252	.323	.368	.691	91	-61	102	659
SEA	161	68	93	.422	35.5	664	744	71	5436	1397	271	27	148	2166	461	787	95	61	.257	.319	.398	.718	95	-45	104	671
Total	1131					9858			77005	19967	3558	425	1901		7191	12323	1512	689	.259	.327	.391	.718				

Runs		**Hits**		**Doubles**		**Triples**		**Home Runs**		**Total Bases**	
Boggs, W. (Bos)	128	Puckett, K. (Min)	234	Boggs, W. (Bos)	45	Reynolds, H. (Sea)	11	Canseco, J. (Oak)	42	Puckett, K. (Min)	358
Canseco, J. (Oak)	120	Boggs, W. (Bos)	214	3 players tied with	42	Wilson, W. (KC)	11	McGriff, F. (Tor)	34	Canseco, J. (Oak)	347
Henderson, R. (NY)	118	Greenwell, M. (Bos)	192			Yount, R. (Mil)	11	McGwire, M. (Oak)	32	Greenwell, M. (Bos)	313

Runs Batted In		**Bases On Balls**		**Stolen Bases**		**Batting Average**		**On-Base Percentage**		**Slugging Average**	
Canseco, J. (Oak)	124	Boggs, W. (Bos)	125	Henderson, R. (NY)	93	Boggs, W. (Bos)	.366	Boggs, W. (Bos)	.480	Canseco, J. (Oak)	.569
Puckett, K. (Min)	121	Clark, J. (NY)	113	Pettis, G. (Det)	44	Puckett, K. (Min)	.356	Greenwell, M. (Bos)	.420	McGriff, F. (Tor)	.552
Greenwell, M. (Bos)	119	Ripken, C. (Bal)	102	Molitor, P. (Mil)	41	Greenwell, M. (Bos)	.325	Davis, A. (Sea)	.416	Gaetti, G. (Min)	.551

Adjusted OPS		**Adjusted Batting Runs**		**Runs Created/Game**		**Fielding Runs**		**Win Shares – Batters**		**TPW – Batters**	
Canseco, J. (Oak)	172	Canseco, J. (Oak)	61.0	Boggs, W. (Bos)	9.40	Guillen, O. (Chi)	31.7	Canseco, J. (Oak)	39	Canseco, J. (Oak)	6.0
Boggs, W. (Bos)	165	Boggs, W. (Bos)	61.0	Greenwell, M. (Bos)	8.50	Gruber, K. (Tor)	23.8	Puckett, K. (Min)	32	Boggs, W. (Bos)	5.9
Winfield, D. (NY)	159	Greenwell, M. (Bos)	49.0	Canseco, J. (Oak)	7.90	Weiss, W. (Oak)	21.2	3 players tied with	31	Greenwell, M. (Bos)	4.2

TEAM	CG	SH	SV	IP	H	H/G	ER	HR	BB	SO	OAV	RAT	ERA	ERA+	CERA	PR+	PF	FA	E	DP	FR	BW	PW	FW	TPW	DIF
East																										
BOS	26	14	37	1426¹	1415	8.9	629	143	493	1085	.259	1.338	3.97	104	3.96	40.9	104	.984	93	123	-19.4	10.7	4.1	-2.0	12.9	-4.9
DET	34	8	36	1445²	1361	8.5	596	150	497	890	.248	1.285	3.71	103	3.59	6.3	96	.982	109	129	9.8	.7	.6	1.0	2.3	4.7
TOR	16	17	47	1449	1404	8.7	612	143	528	904	.256	1.333	3.80	103	3.91	12.5	99	.982	110	170	6.9	7.3	1.3	.7	9.2	-3.2
MIL	30	8	51	1449¹	1355	8.4	555	125	437	832	.248	1.236	3.45	115	3.29	73.6	100	.981	120	146	12.0	-5.5	7.4	1.2	3.2	2.8
NY	16	5	43	1456	1512	9.4	689	157	487	861	.267	1.373	4.26	92	4.20	-40.5	99	.978	134	161	-12.3	5.4	-4.1	-1.2	.1	4.9
CLE	35	10	46	1434	1501	9.4	663	120	442	812	.270	1.355	4.16	99	3.98	15.8	104	.980	124	131	-28.0	-5.7	1.6	-2.8	-6.9	3.9
BAL	20	7	26	1416	1506	9.6	714	153	523	709	.274	1.433	4.54	86	4.52	-113.0	98	.980	119	172	10.8	-9.2	-11.4	1.1	-19.5	-6.5
West																										
OAK	22	9	64	1489¹	1376	8.3	569	116	553	983	.247	1.295	3.44	110	3.50	36.7	95	.983	105	151	19.9	8.3	3.7	2.0	14.0	9.0
MIN	18	9	52	1431²	1457	9.2	625	146	453	897	.266	1.334	3.93	103	4.06	19.2	103	.986	84	155	2.0	6.7	1.9	.2	8.8	1.2
KC	29	12	32	1428¹	1415	8.9	579	102	465	886	.258	1.316	3.65	109	3.62	75.5	100	.980	124	147	-23.1	-1.2	7.6	-2.3	4.1	-.1
CAL	26	9	33	1455²	1503	9.3	698	135	568	817	.270	1.423	4.32	89	4.27	-70.1	97	.979	135	175	-4.1	-.6	-7.1	-.4	-8.1	2.1
CHI	11	9	43	1439	1467	9.2	659	138	533	754	.266	1.390	4.12	96	4.14	-48.0	100	.976	154	177	22.1	-9.2	-4.9	2.2	-11.9	2.9
TEX	41	11	31	1438²	1310	8.2	647	129	654	912	.244	1.365	4.05	101	3.90	-6.6	103	.979	131	145	7.6	-6.2	-.7	.8	-6.1	-3.9
SEA	28	11	28	1428	1385	8.7	658	144	558	981	.256	1.361	4.15	100	4.01	1.0	105	.980	123	168	-4.7	-4.5	.1	-.5	-4.9	-7.1
Total	352	139	569	20187		8.9	8893					1.345	3.96													

Wins		**Win Percentage**		**Games**		**Complete Games**		**Shutouts**		**Saves**	
Viola, F. (Min)	24	Viola, F. (Min)	.774	Crim, C. (Mil)	70	Clemens, R. (Bos)	14	Clemens, R. (Bos)	8	Eckersley, D. (Oak)	45
Stewart, D. (Oak)	21	Hurst, B. (Bos)	.750	Thigpen, B. (Chi)	68	Stewart, D. (Oak)	14	3 players tied with	4	Reardon, J. (Min)	42
Gubicza, M. (KC)	20	Gubicza, M. (KC)	.714	Williams, M. (Tex)	67	Witt, B. (Tex)	13			Jones, D. (Cle)	37

Innings Pitched		**Fewest Hits/Game**		**Fewest BB/Game**		**Strikeouts**		**Ratio**		**Earned Run Average**	
Stewart, D. (Oak)	275²	Robinson, J. (Det)	6.33	Anderson, A. (Min)	1.65	Clemens, R. (Bos)	291	Higuera, T. (Mil)	1.00	Anderson, A. (Min)	2.45
Gubicza, M. (KC)	269²	Higuera, T. (Mil)	6.65	Swindell, G. (Cle)	1.67	Langston, M. (Sea)	235	Clemens, R. (Bos)	1.06	Higuera, T. (Mil)	2.45
Clemens, R. (Bos)	264	Stieb, D. (Tor)	6.82	Alexander, D. (Det)	1.81	Viola, F. (Min)	193	Robinson, J. (Det)	1.12	Viola, F. (Min)	2.64

Adjusted ERA		**Component ERA**		**Opponents' Batting Avg.**		**Adjusted Pitching Runs**		**Win Shares – Pitchers**		**TPW – Pitchers**	
Anderson, A. (Min)	166	Higuera, T. (Mil)	2.10	Robinson, J. (Det)	.197	Gubicza, M. (KC)	43	Viola, F. (Min)	25	Gubicza, M. (KC)	4.3
Higuera, T. (Mil)	162	Clemens, R. (Bos)	2.36	Higuera, T. (Mil)	.207	Viola, F. (Min)	40	Gubicza, M. (KC)	24	Viola, F. (Min)	4.0
Viola, F. (Min)	154	Robinson, J. (Det)	2.68	Stieb, D. (Tor)	.210	Clemens, R. (Bos)	38	2 players tied with	22	Clemens, R. (Bos)	3.9

1989 National League

TEAM	G	W	L	PCT	GB	R	OR	EW	AB	H	2B	3B	HR	TB	BB	SO	SB	CS	AVG	OBP	SLG	OPS	OPS+	BR/A	PF	RC
East																										
CHI	162	93	69	.574	....	**702**	623	91	5513	**1438**	235	45	124	**2135**	472	921	136	57	**.261**	.322	.387	**.709**	101	9	107	683
NY	162	87	75	.537	6	683	595	92	5489	1351	280	21	**147**	2114	504	934	158	53	.246	.313	.385	.698	99	74	95	675
STL	164	86	76	.531	7	632	608	84	5492	1418	263	47	73	1994	507	**848**	155	54	.258	**.323**	.363	.686	99	4	103	650
MON	162	81	81	.500	12	632	630	81	5482	1353	267	30	100	1980	**572**	958	**160**	70	.247	.322	.361	.683	100	7	101	643
PIT	164	74	88	.457	19	637	680	76	**5539**	1334	263	**53**	95	1988	563	914	155	69	.241	.314	.359	.672	102	14	96	627
PHI	163	67	95	.414	26	629	735	68	5447	1324	215	36	123	1980	558	926	106	**50**	.243	.316	.364	.679	100	1	100	632
West																										
SF	162	92	70	.568	....	699	600	93	5469	1365	241	52	141	2133	508	1071	87	54	.250	.318	**.390**	.708	111	63	97	682
SD	162	89	73	.549	3	642	626	83	5422	1360	215	32	120	1999	552	1013	136	67	.251	.321	.369	.690	103	20	100	642
HOU	162	86	76	.531	6	647	669	78	5516	1316	239	28	97	1902	530	860	144	62	.239	.308	.345	.653	96	-26	96	604
LA	160	77	83	.481	14	554	**536**	83	5465	1313	241	17	89	1855	507	885	81	54	.240	.308	.339	.647	92	-59	98	574
CIN	162	75	87	.463	17	632	691	74	5520	1362	243	28	128	2045	493	1028	128	71	.247	.312	.370	.682	97	-25	103	637
ATL	161	63	97	.394	28	584	680	68	5463	1281	201	22	128	1910	485	996	83	54	.234	.300	.350	.649	89	-86	103	573
Total	973					7673			65817	16215	2903	411	1365		6251	11354	1529	715	.246	.315	.365	.680				

Runs		Hits		Doubles		Triples		Home Runs		Total Bases	
Clark, W. (SF)	104	Gwynn, T. (SD)	203	Guerrero, P. (StL)	42	Thompson, R. (SF)	11	Mitchell, K. (SF)	47	Mitchell, K. (SF)	345
Johnson, H. (NY)	104	Clark, W. (SF)	196	Wallach, T. (Mon)	42	Bonilla, B. (Pit)	10	Johnson, H. (NY)	36	Clark, W. (SF)	321
Sandberg, R. (Chi)	104	Alomar, R. (SD)	184	Johnson, H. (NY)	41	3 players tied with	9	2 players tied with	34	Johnson, H. (NY)	319

Runs Batted In		Bases On Balls		Stolen Bases		Batting Average		On-Base Percentage		Slugging Average	
Mitchell, K. (SF)	125	Clark, J. (SD)	132	Coleman, V. (StL)	65	Gwynn, T. (SD)	.336	Smith, L. (Atl)	.420	Mitchell, K. (SF)	.635
Guerrero, P. (StL)	117	Hayes, V. (Phi)	101	Alomar, R. (SD)	42	Clark, W. (SF)	.333	Clark, J. (SD)	.413	Johnson, H. (NY)	.559
Clark, W. (SF)	111	2 players tied with	93	Samuel, J. (NY,Phi)	42	Smith, L. (Atl)	.315	Clark, W. (SF)	.412	Clark, W. (SF)	.546

Adjusted OPS		Adjusted Batting Runs		Runs Created/Game		Fielding Runs		Win Shares – Batters		TPW – Batters	
Mitchell, K. (SF)	195	Mitchell, K. (SF)	65.0	Mitchell, K. (SF)	9.10	Pendleton, T. (StL)	26.2	Clark, W. (SF)	44	Mitchell, K. (SF)	6.0
Clark, W. (SF)	177	Clark, W. (SF)	60.0	Clark, W. (SF)	9.00	Uribe, J. (SF)	22.7	Johnson, H. (NY)	38	Clark, W. (SF)	5.7
Johnson, H. (NY)	171	Johnson, H. (NY)	57.0	Smith, L. (Atl)	8.50	Elster, K. (NY)	19.1	Mitchell, K. (SF)	38	Johnson, H. (NY)	5.1

TEAM	CG	SH	SV	IP	H	H/G	ER	HR	BB	SO	OAV	RAT	ERA	ERA+	CERA	PR+	PF	FA	E	DP	FR	BW	PW	FW	TPW	DIF
East																										
CHI	18	10	**55**	1460¹	1369	8.4	556	106	532	918	.250	1.302	3.43	110	3.43	59.5	107	.980	124	130	-6.0	1.0	6.4	-.6	6.7	5.3
NY	24	12	38	1454¹	**1260**	**7.8**	532	115	532	**1108**	**.231**	1.232	3.29	99	3.10	7.6	93	.976	144	110	-13.4	**7.9**	.8	-1.4	7.3	-1.3
STL	18	18	43	1461	1330	8.2	545	**84**	482	844	.243	1.240	3.36	100	3.06	14.7	101	**.982**	112	134	17.3	.5	2.6	1.8	4.9	.1
MON	20	13	35	1468¹	1344	8.2	568	120	519	1059	.245	1.269	3.48	101	3.38	14.7	101	.979	136	126	-7.2	.8	1.6	-.8	1.6	-1.6
PIT	20	9	40	**1487²**	1394	8.4	601	121	539	827	.248	1.299	3.64	92	3.50	-48.4	96	.975	160	130	0.8	1.5	-5.2	.1	-3.6	-3.4
PHI	10	10	33	1433³	1408	8.8	643	127	613	899	.259	1.410	4.04	**88**	4.06	-75.5	101	.979	133	136	-8.0	.1	-8.1	-.9	-8.8	-5.2
West																										
SF	12	16	47	1457	1320	8.2	534	120	471	802	.243	1.229	3.30	102	3.21	-21.6	96	.982	114	135	**32.3**	6.8	-2.3	**3.5**	**7.9**	3.1
SD	21	11	52	1457¹	1359	8.4	547	133	481	933	.249	1.263	3.38	103	3.44	1.3	100	.976	154	147	16.5	2.1	.1	1.8	4.0	4.0
HOU	19	12	38	1479¹	1379	8.4	598	105	551	965	.247	1.305	3.64	93	3.42	-34.3	97	.977	142	121	-10.0	-2.7	-3.7	-1.1	-7.5	12.5
LA	**25**	**19**	36	1463³	1278	7.9	**480**	95	504	1052	.237	**1.218**	**2.95**	116	**3.01**	65.1	98	.981	118	**153**	10.7	-6.3	**7.0**	1.1	1.8	-4.8
CIN	16	9	37	1464¹	1404	8.6	607	125	559	981	.253	1.341	3.73	96	3.67	-7.2	103	.980	121	108	-16.3	-2.7	-.8	-1.7	-5.2	-.8
ATL	15	8	33	1447²	1370	8.5	595	114	**468**	966	.250	1.370	3.70	99	3.35	6.8	104	.976	152	124	-17.0	-9.2	.7	-1.8	-10.3	-6.7
Total	218	147	487	17534		8.3	6806					1.281	3.49													

Wins		Win Percentage		Games		Complete Games		Shutouts		Saves	
Scott, M. (Hou)	20	Fernandez, S. (NY)	.737	Williams, M. (Chi)	76	Belcher, T. (LA)	10	Belcher, T. (LA)	8	Davis, M. (SD)	44
Maddux, G. (Chi)	19	Garrelts, S. (SF)	.737	Dibble, R. (Cin)	74	Hurst, B. (SD)	10	Drabek, D. (Pit)	5	Williams, M. (Chi)	36
2 players tied with	18	Bielecki, M. (Chi)	.720	Parrett, J. (Phi)	72	3 players tied with	9	3 players tied with	4	Franco, J. (Cin)	32

Innings Pitched		Fewest Hits/Game		Fewest BB/Game		Strikeouts		Ratio		Earned Run Average	
Hershiser, O. (LA)	256²	DeLeon, J. (StL)	6.36	Robinson, D. (SF)	1.69	DeLeon, J. (StL)	201	Garrelts, S. (SF)	1.01	Garrelts, S. (SF)	2.28
Browning, T. (Cin)	249²	Fernandez, S. (NY)	6.44	Lilliquist, D. (Atl)	1.85	Belcher, T. (LA)	200	DeLeon, J. (StL)	1.03	Hershiser, O. (LA)	2.31
0 players tied with	734	Howell, K. (Phi)	6.84	Martinez, D. (Mon)	1.90	Fernandez, S. (NY)	198	Scott, M. (Hou)	1.06	Langston, M. (Mon)	2.39

Adjusted ERA		Component ERA		Opponents' Batting Avg.		Adjusted Pitching Runs		Win Shares – Pitchers		TPW – Pitchers	
Garrelts, S. (SF)	148	Garrelts, S. (SF)	2.02	DeLeon, J. (StL)	.197	Hershiser, O. (LA)	29	Hershiser, O. (LA)	21	Hershiser, O. (LA)	3.5
Hershiser, O. (LA)	147	DeLeon, J. (StL)	2.16	Fernandez, S. (NY)	.198	Langston, M. (Mon)	23	Maddux, G. (Chi)	20	Maddux, G. (Chi)	2.6
Langston, M. (Mon)	147	Scott, M. (Hou)	2.43	Smoltz, J. (Atl)	.212	Maddux, G. (Chi)	22	3 players tied with	18	Langston, M. (Mon)	2.5

1989 American League

TEAM	G	W	L	PCT	GB	R	OR	EW	AB	H	2B	3B	HR	TB	BB	SO	SB	CS	AVG	OBP	SLG	OPS	OPS+	BR/A	PF	RC
East																										
TOR	162	89	73	.549	....	731	651	90	5581	1449	265	40	142	2220	521	923	144	58	.260	.326	.398	.724	110	69	94	722
BAL	162	87	75	.537	2	708	686	84	5440	1369	238	33	129	2060	593	957	118	55	.252	.329	.379	.707	102	17	97	676
BOS	162	83	79	.512	6	**774**	735	85	**5666**	**1571**	**326**	30	108	**2281**	**643**	755	56	**35**	**.277**	**.355**	**.403**	**.757**	106	57	106	**799**
MIL	162	81	81	.500	8	707	679	84	5473	1415	235	32	126	2092	455	791	**165**	62	.259	.321	.382	.703	98	-9	99	675
NY	161	74	87	.460	14.5	698	792	70	5458	1470	229	23	130	2135	502	831	137	60	.269	.334	.391	.725	105	35	99	707
CLE	162	73	89	.451	16	604	654	75	5463	1340	221	26	127	1994	499	934	74	51	.245	.312	.365	.677	89	-91	102	620
DET	162	59	103	.364	30	617	816	59	5432	1315	198	24	116	1909	585	899	103	50	.242	.320	.351	.671	91	-60	98	614
West																										
OAK	162	99	63	.611	....	712	**576**	98	5416	1414	220	25	127	2065	562	855	157	55	.261	.334	.381	.716	105	48	96	685
KC	162	92	70	.568	7	690	635	88	5475	1428	227	41	101	2040	554	897	154	51	.261	.332	.373	.705	99	5	99	680
CAL	162	91	71	.562	8	669	578	93	5545	1422	208	37	**145**	2139	429	1011	89	40	.256	.313	.386	.699	98	-28	98	661
TEX	162	83	79	.512	16	695	714	79	5458	1433	260	**46**	122	2151	503	989	101	49	.263	.329	.394	.723	101	5	102	692
MIN	162	80	82	.494	19	740	738	81	5581	1542	278	35	117	2241	478	**743**	111	53	.276	.338	.402	.739	101	5	107	749
SEA	162	73	89	.451	26	694	728	77	5512	1417	237	29	134	2114	489	838	81	55	.257	.323	.384	.706	95	-45	103	677
CHI	161	69	92	.429	29.5	693	750	74	5504	1493	262	36	94	2109	464	873	97	52	.271	.331	.383	.714	103	16	98	694
Total	1133					9732			77004	20078	3404	457	1718		7277	12296	1587	726	.261	.328	.384	.712				

Runs
Boggs, W. (Bos) 113
Henderson, R. (Oak,NY) 113
2 players tied with 101

Hits
Puckett, K. (Min) 215
Boggs, W. (Bos) 205
Sax, S. (NY) 205

Doubles
Boggs, W. (Bos) 51
Puckett, K. (Min) 45
Reed, J. (Bos) 42

Triples
Sierra, R. (Tex) 14
White, D. (Cal) 13
Bradley, P. (Bal) 10

Home Runs
McGriff, F. (Tor) 36
Carter, J. (Cle) 35
McGwire, M. (Oak) 33

Total Bases
Sierra, R. (Tex) 344
Yount, R. (Mil) 314
Carter, J. (Cle) 303

Runs Batted In
Sierra, R. (Tex) 119
Mattingly, D. (NY) 113
Esasky, N. (Bos) 108

Bases On Balls
Henderson, R. (Oak,NY) 126
McGriff, F. (Tor) 119
Boggs, W. (Bos) 107

Stolen Bases
Henderson, R. (Oak,NY) 77
Espy, C. (Tex) 45
White, D. (Cal) 44

Batting Average
Puckett, K. (Min) .339
Lansford, C. (Oak) .336
Boggs, W. (Bos) .330

On-Base Percentage
Boggs, W. (Bos) .434
Davis, A. (Sea) .428
Henderson, R. (Oak,NY) .413

Slugging Average
Sierra, R. (Tex) .543
McGriff, F. (Tor) .525
Yount, R. (Mil) .511

Adjusted OPS
McGriff, F. (Tor) 169
Davis, A. (Sea) 155
Yount, R. (Mil) 152

Adjusted Batting Runs
McGriff, F. (Tor) 55.0
Yount, R. (Mil) 45.0
Henderson, R. (Oak,NY) 44.0

Runs Created/Game
Davis, A. (Sea) 8.00
Yount, R. (Mil) 7.70
McGriff, F. (Tor) 7.60

Fielding Runs
Fermin, F. (Cle) 22.2
Reynolds, H. (Sea) 21.0
Guillen, O. (Chi) 20.4

Win Shares – Batters
Sierra, R. (Tex) 34
Yount, R. (Mil) 34
3 players tied with 30

TPW – Batters
Yount, R. (Mil) 4.5
Henderson, R. (Oak,NY) 4.2
McGriff, F. (Tor) 4.2

TEAM	CG	SH	SV	IP	H	H/G	ER	HR	BB	SO	OAV	RAT	ERA	ERA+	CERA	PR+	PF	FA	E	DP	FR	BW	PW	FW	TPW	DIF
East																										
TOR	12	12	38	1467	1408	8.6	584	99	478	849	.255	1.286	3.58	101	3.49	2.4	93	.980	127	164	2.4	7.0	.2	.2	7.5	.5
BAL	16	7	44	1448¹	1518	9.4	644	134	486	676	.272	1.384	4.00	95	4.12	-43.5	98	.986	87	163	10.0	1.8	-4.4	1.0	-1.7	7.7
BOS	14	9	42	1460¹	1448	8.9	651	131	548	1054	.261	1.367	4.01	102	3.95	28.6	106	.980	127	162	-13.3	5.8	2.9	-1.4	7.3	-5.3
MIL	16	8	45	1432¹	1463	9.2	605	129	457	812	.265	1.340	3.80	101	3.88	0.7	99	.975	155	164	5.9	-1.0	.1	.6	-.3	.3
NY	15	9	44	1414²	1550	9.9	707	150	521	787	.281	1.464	4.50	86	4.66	-108.7	99	.980	122	183	3.5	3.6	-11.1	.4	-7.1	1.1
CLE	23	13	38	1453	1423	8.8	589	107	452	844	.257	1.290	3.65	109	3.51	56.2	102	.981	118	126	-6.7	-9.2	5.7	-.7	-4.2	-3.8
DET	24	4	26	1427¹	1514	9.6	718	150	652	831	.274	1.518	4.53	84	4.73	-99.9	98	.979	130	153	-14.8	-6.1	-10.2	-1.5	-17.7	-4.3
West																										
OAK	17	20	57	1448¹	1287	8.0	497	103	510	930	.238	1.241	3.09	119	3.23	66.0	95	.979	129	159	22.1	4.9	6.7	2.3	13.9	4.1
KC	27	13	38	1451²	1415	8.8	572	86	455	978	.257	1.288	3.55	108	3.44	72.3	99	.982	114	139	-23.5	.5	7.4	-2.4	5.4	5.6
CAL	32	20	38	1454¹	1384	8.6	530	113	465	897	.253	1.271	3.28	116	3.46	62.2	98	.985	96	173	23.9	-2.9	6.3	2.4	5.9	4.1
TEX	26	7	44	1434¹	1279	8.0	623	119	654	1112	.239	1.348	3.91	101	3.74	16.7	102	.978	136	137	-9.0	.5	1.7	-.9	1.3	.7
MIN	19	8	38	1429¹	1495	9.4	680	139	500	851	.269	1.396	4.28	97	4.22	-15.5	107	.982	107	141	-6.9	.5	-1.6	-.7	-1.8	.8
SEA	15	10	44	1438	1422	8.9	639	114	560	897	.259	1.378	4.00	101	3.94	-1.6	104	.977	143	168	4.1	-4.6	-.2	.4	-4.4	-3.6
CHI	9	5	46	1422	1472	9.3	668	144	539	778	.269	1.414	4.23	90	4.30	-71.6	98	.975	151	176	2.3	1.6	-7.3	.2	-5.4	-5.6
Total	265	145	582	20181		9.0	8707				1.355	3.88														

Wins
Saberhagen, B. (KC) 23
Stewart, D. (Oak) 21
2 players tied with 19

Win Percentage
Saberhagen, B. (KC) .793
Blyleven, B. (Cal) .773
Davis, S. (Oak) .731

Games
Crim, C. (Mil) 76
Murphy, R. (Bos) 74
Rogers, K. (Tex) 73

Complete Games
Saberhagen, B. (KC) 12
Morris, J. (Det) 10
Finley, C. (Cal) 9

Shutouts
Blyleven, B. (Cal) 5
McCaskill, K. (Cal) 4
Saberhagen, B. (KC) 4

Saves
Russell, J. (Tex) 38
Thigpen, B. (Chi) 34
3 players tied with 33

Innings Pitched
Saberhagen, B. (KC) 262¹
Stewart, D. (Oak) 257²
Gubicza, M. (KC) 255

Fewest Hits/Game
Ryan, N. (Tex) 6.09
Gordon, T. (KC) 6.74
Stieb, D. (Tor) 7.14

Fewest BB/Game
Key, J. (Tor) 1.12
Saberhagen, B. (KC) 1.48
Blyleven, B. (Cal) 1.64

Strikeouts
Ryan, N. (Tex) 301
Clemens, R. (Bos) 230
Saberhagen, B. (KC) 193

Ratio
Saberhagen, B. (KC) .96
Ryan, N. (Tex) 1.09
Blyleven, B. (Cal) 1.12

Earned Run Average
Saberhagen, B. (KC) 2.16
Finley, C. (Cal) 2.57
Moore, M. (Oak) 2.61

Adjusted ERA
Saberhagen, B. (KC) 178
Finley, C. (Cal) 148
Moore, M. (Oak) 141

Component ERA
Saberhagen, B. (KC) 1.89
Ryan, N. (Tex) 2.31
Moore, M. (Oak) 2.59

Opponents' Batting Avg.
Ryan, N. (Tex) .187
Gordon, T. (KC) .210
Saberhagen, B. (KC) .217

Adjusted Pitching Runs
Saberhagen, B. (KC) 53
Clemens, R. (Bos) 30
Gubicza, M. (KC) 27

Win Shares – Pitchers
Saberhagen, B. (KC) 28
Blyleven, B. (Cal) 22
3 players tied with 19

TPW – Pitchers
Saberhagen, B. (KC) 5.4
Clemens, R. (Bos) 3.0
Gubicza, M. (KC) 2.8

1990 National League

TEAM	G	W	L	PCT	GB	R	OR	EW	AB	H	2B	3B	HR	TB	BB	SO	SB	CS	AVG	OBP	SLG	OPS	OPS+	BR/A	PF	RC
East																										
PIT	162	95	67	.586	....	733	619	95	5388	1395	288	42	138	2181	582	914	137	52	.259	.334	.405	.739	113	95	96	736
NY	162	91	71	.562	4	775	613	100	5504	1410	278	21	172	2246	536	851	110	33	.256	.326	.408	.734	107	55	100	746
MON	162	85	77	.525	10	662	598	89	5453	1363	227	43	114	2018	576	1024	235	99	.250	.325	.370	.695	101	11	96	670
PHI	162	77	85	.475	18	646	729	71	5535	1410	237	27	103	2010	582	915	108	35	.255	.329	.363	.692	97	-14	100	673
CHI	162	77	85	.475	18	690	774	72	5600	1474	240	36	136	2194	406	869	151	50	.263	.316	.392	.708	93	-50	107	693
STL	162	70	92	.432	25	599	698	69	5462	1398	255	41	73	1954	517	844	221	74	.256	.323	.358	.680	93	-38	100	648
West																										
CIN	162	91	71	.562	....	693	597	93	5525	1466	284	40	125	2205	466	913	166	66	.265	.327	.399	.726	101	7	104	724
LA	162	86	76	.531	5	728	685	86	5491	1436	222	27	129	2099	538	952	141	65	.262	.331	.382	.713	105	34	97	698
SF	162	85	77	.525	6	719	710	82	5573	1459	221	35	152	2206	488	973	109	56	.262	.325	.396	.721	108	43	96	723
SD	162	75	87	.463	16	673	673	81	5554	1429	243	35	123	2111	509	902	138	59	.257	.323	.380	.703	98	-16	101	680
HOU	162	75	87	.463	16	573	656	70	5379	1301	209	32	94	1856	548	997	179	83	.242	.315	.345	.660	94	-68	97	594
ATL	162	65	97	.401	26	682	821	66	5504	1376	263	26	162	2177	473	1010	92	55	.250	.312	.396	.708	94	-56	106	674
Total	972					8173			65968	16917	2967	405	1521		6221	11164	1787	727	.256	.324	.383	.707				

Runs
Sandberg, R. (Chi) 116
Bonilla, B. (Pit) 112
Butler, B. (SF) 108

Hits
Butler, B. (SF) 192
Dykstra, L. (Phi) 192
Sandberg, R. (Chi) 188

Doubles
Jefferies, G. (NY) 40
Bonilla, B. (Pit) 39
Sabo, C. (Cin) 38

Triples
Duncan, M. (Cin) 11
Gwynn, T. (SD) 10
3 players tied with 9

Home Runs
Sandberg, R. (Chi) 40
Strawberry, D. (NY) 37
Mitchell, K. (SF) 35

Total Bases
Sandberg, R. (Chi) 344
Bonilla, B. (Pit) 324
Gant, R. (Atl) 310

Runs Batted In
Williams, M. (SF) 122
Bonilla, B. (Pit) 120
Carter, J. (SD) 115

Bases On Balls
Clark, J. (SD) 104
Bonds, B. (Pit) 93
Butler, B. (SF) 90

Stolen Bases
Coleman, V. (StL) 77
Yelding, E. (Hou) 64
Bonds, B. (Pit) 52

Batting Average
McGee, W. (StL) .335
Murray, E. (LA) .330
Magadan, D. (NY) .328

On-Base Percentage
Magadan, D. (NY) .425
Dykstra, L. (Phi) .420
Murray, E. (LA) .417

Slugging Average
Bonds, B. (Pit) .565
Sandberg, R. (Chi) .559
Mitchell, K. (SF) .544

Adjusted OPS
Bonds, B. (Pit) 172
Murray, E. (LA) 160
Daniels, K. (LA) 156

Adjusted Batting Runs
Bonds, B. (Pit) 59.0
Murray, E. (LA) 47.0
Dykstra, L. (Phi) 40.0

Runs Created/Game
Bonds, B. (Pit) 8.90
Dykstra, L. (Phi) 7.90
Murray, E. (LA) 7.90

Fielding Runs
Grace, M. (Chi) 23.8
Hayes, C. (Phi) 22.8
Larkin, B. (Cin) 21.4

Win Shares – Batters
Bonds, B. (Pit) 37
Dykstra, L. (Phi) 35
Sandberg, R. (Chi) 34

TPW – Batters
Bonds, B. (Pit) 6.4
Dykstra, L. (Phi) 4.8
Larkin, B. (Cin) 4.2

TEAM	CG	SH	SV	IP	H	H/G	ER	HR	BB	SO	OAV	RAT	ERA	ERA+	CERA	PR+	PF	FA	E	DP	FR	BW	PW	FW	TPW	DIF
East																										
PIT	18	8	43	1447	1367	8.5	**547**	135	**413**	848	.251	**1.230**	3.40	106	3.41	16.7	95	.979	134	125	18.7	**9.8**	1.7	1.9	**13.5**	.5
NY	18	**14**	41	1440	1339	8.4	**547**	119	444	**1217**	.246	1.238	3.42	109	**3.29**	**69.4**	99	.978	132	107	-18.5	5.6	**7.2**	-1.9	10.9	-.9
MON	18	11	**50**	**1473^{1}**	1349	**8.2**	552	127	510	991	**.245**	1.262	**3.37**	108	3.38	43.9	96	.982	110	134	2.4	1.1	4.5	.3	5.9	-1.9
PHI	18	7	35	1449	1381	8.6	655	124	651	840	.253	1.402	4.07	94	3.93	-62.7	101	.981	117	**150**	19.0	-1.4	-6.5	2.0	-5.9	1.9
CHI	13	7	42	1442^{2}	1510	9.4	695	121	572	877	.271	1.443	4.34	94	4.20	-0.4	108	.980	124	136	-41.1	-5.2	.0	-4.2	-9.5	5.5
STL	8	13	39	1443^{1}	1432	8.9	620	**98**	475	833	.261	1.321	3.87	99	3.59	-5.1	101	.979	130	114	-4.8	-3.9	-.5	-.5	-5.0	-6.0
West																										
CIN	14	12	**50**	1456^{1}	**1338**	8.3	548	124	543	1029	.246	1.292	3.39	116	3.52	62.4	104	**.983**	**102**	126	**26.9**	.7	6.4	**2.8**	9.9	.1
LA	**29**	12	29	1442	1364	8.5	596	137	478	1021	.249	1.277	3.72	98	3.53	-20.3	97	.979	130	123	7.7	3.5	-2.1	.8	2.2	2.8
SF	14	6	45	1446^{1}	1477	9.2	656	131	553	788	.267	1.404	4.08	89	4.09	-79.2	96	.983	107	148	9.7	4.5	-8.2	1.0	-2.7	6.7
SD	21	12	35	1461^{2}	1437	8.8	597	147	507	928	.258	1.330	3.68	104	3.82	16.3	101	.977	141	141	6.6	-1.6	1.7	.7	.7	-6.7
HOU	12	6	37	1450	1396	8.7	582	130	496	854	.255	1.305	3.61	103	3.65	9.1	98	.978	131	124	6.2	-7.0	.9	.6	-5.5	-.5
ATL	17	8	30	1429^{2}	1527	9.6	727	128	579	938	.275	1.473	4.58	**88**	4.43	-53.4	106	.974	158	133	-34.1	-5.8	-5.5	-3.5	-14.8	-1.2
Total	**200**	**116**	**476**	**17381^{1}**		**8.8**	**7322**					**1.331**	**3.79**													

Wins
Drabek, D. (Pit) 22
Martinez, R. (LA) 20
Viola, F. (NY) 20

Win Percentage
Drabek, D. (Pit) .... .786
Martinez, R. (LA) .... .769
Darwin, D. (Hou) .... .733

Games
Agosto, J. (Hou) 82
Assenmacher, P. (Chi) 74
Harris, G. (SD) 73

Complete Games
Martinez, R. (LA) 12
Drabek, D. (Pit) 9
Hurst, B. (SD) 9

Shutouts
Hurst, B. (SD) 4
Morgan, M. (LA) 4
6 players tied with 3

Saves
Franco, J. (NY) 33
Myers, R. (Cin) 31
Smith, L. (StL) 27

Innings Pitched
Viola, F. (NY) .... 249^{2}
Maddux, G. (Chi) 237
Martinez, R. (LA) .... 234^{1}

Fewest Hits/Game
Fernandez, S. (NY) 6.52
Rijo, J. (Cin) 6.90
Martinez, R. (LA) 7.34

Fewest BB/Game
Darwin, D. (Hou) 1.72
Whitson, E. (SD) 1.85
Leibrandt, C. (Atl) 1.94

Strikeouts
Cone, D. (NY) 233
Gooden, D. (NY) 223
Martinez, R. (LA) 223

Ratio
Darwin, D. (Hou) 1.03
Martinez, D. (Mon) 1.06
Drabek, D. (Pit) 1.06

Earned Run Average
Darwin, D. (Hou) 2.21
Smith, Z. (Pit,Mon) 2.55
Whitson, E. (SD) 2.60

Adjusted ERA
Darwin, D. (Hou) 168
Whitson, E. (SD) 147
Rijo, J. (Cin) 146

Component ERA
Darwin, D. (Hou) 2.31
Drabek, D. (Pit) 2.40
Martinez, D. (Mon) 2.44

Opponents' Batting Avg.
Fernandez, S. (NY) .... .200
Rijo, J. (Cin) .... .212
Martinez, R. (LA) .... .220

Adjusted Pitching Runs
Viola, F. (NY) 33
Whitson, E. (SD) 30
Darwin, D. (Hou) 26

Win Shares – Pitchers
Drabek, D. (Pit) 20
Viola, F. (NY) 20
Whitson, E. (SD) 19

TPW – Pitchers
Viola, F. (NY) 3.3
Whitson, E. (SD) 3.2
Darwin, D. (Hou) 2.8

1990 American League

TEAM	G	W	L	PCT	GB	R	OR	EW	AB	H	2B	3B	HR	TB	BB	SO	SB	CS	AVG	OBP	SLG	OPS	OPS+	BR/A	PF	RC
East																										
BOS	162	88	74	.543	....	699	664	85	5516	**1502**	298	31	106	2180	598	795	53	52	**.272**	**.346**	.395	.742	102	15	105	731
TOR	162	86	76	.531	2	**767**	661	93	**5589**	1479	263	**50**	167	**2343**	526	970	111	52	.265	.331	**.419**	**.750**	103	17	106	**767**
DET	162	79	83	.488	9	750	754	81	5479	1418	241	32	**172**	2239	634	952	82	57	.259	.339	.409	.748	107	52	101	753
CLE	162	77	85	.475	11	732	737	80	5485	1465	266	41	110	2143	458	836	107	52	.267	.327	.391	.718	100	-2	100	692
BAL	161	76	85	.472	11.5	669	698	77	5410	1328	234	22	132	2002	**660**	962	94	52	.245	.332	.370	.702	99	2	97	674
MIL	162	74	88	.457	14	732	760	78	5503	1408	247	36	128	2111	519	821	**164**	72	.256	.324	.384	.707	98	-14	99	689
NY	162	67	95	.414	21	603	749	64	5483	1322	208	19	147	2009	427	1027	119	45	.241	.302	.366	.669	86	-106	100	604
West																										
OAK	162	103	59	.636	....	733	**570**	101	5433	1379	209	22	164	2124	651	992	141	54	.254	.339	.391	.730	**108**	**73**	96	737
CHI	162	94	68	.580	9	682	633	87	5402	1393	251	44	106	2050	478	903	140	90	.258	.322	.379	.702	98	-29	98	650
TEX	162	83	79	.512	20	676	696	79	5469	1416	257	27	110	2057	575	1054	115	48	.259	.333	.376	.709	98	-6	100	686
CAL	162	80	82	.494	23	690	706	79	5570	1448	237	27	147	2180	566	1000	69	**43**	.260	.331	.391	.723	103	22	98	713
SEA	162	77	85	.475	26	640	680	76	5474	1419	251	26	107	2043	596	**749**	105	51	.259	.336	.373	.710	97	-12	101	689
KC	161	75	86	.466	27.5	707	709	80	5488	1465	**316**	44	100	2169	498	879	107	62	.267	.331	.395	.726	104	21	98	704
MIN	162	74	88	.457	29	666	729	74	5499	1458	281	39	100	2117	445	**749**	96	53	.265	.326	.385	.711	92	-60	106	671
Total	**1133**					**9746**			**76800**	**19900**	**3559**	**460**	**1796**		**7631**	**12689**	**1503**	**783**	**.259**	**.330**	**.388**	**.718**				

Runs
Henderson, R. (Oak) 119
Fielder, C. (Det) 104
Reynolds, H. (Sea) 100

Hits
Palmeiro, R. (Tex) 191
Boggs, W. (Bos) 187
Kelly, R. (NY) 183

Doubles
Brett, G. (KC) 45
Reed, J. (Bos) 45
2 players tied with 44

Triples
Fernandez, T. (Tor) 17
Sosa, S. (Chi) 10
3 players tied with 9

Home Runs
Fielder, C. (Det) 51
McGwire, M. (Oak) 39
Canseco, J. (Oak) 37

Total Bases
Fielder, C. (Det) 339
Gruber, K. (Tor) 303
McGriff, F. (Tor) 295

Runs Batted In
Fielder, C. (Det) 132
Gruber, K. (Tor) 118
McGwire, M. (Oak) 108

Bases On Balls
McGwire, M. (Oak) 110
Tettleton, M. (Bal) 106
Phillips, T. (Det) 99

Stolen Bases
Henderson, R. (Oak) 65
Sax, S. (NY) 43
Kelly, R. (NY) 42

Batting Average
Brett, G. (KC) .... .329
Henderson, R. (Oak) .... .325
Palmeiro, R. (Tex) .... .319

On-Base Percentage
Henderson, R. (Oak) .... .441
McGriff, F. (Tor) .... .403
Martinez, E. (Sea) .... .399

Slugging Average
Fielder, C. (Det) .... .592
Henderson, R. (Oak) .... .577
Canseco, J. (Oak) .... .543

Adjusted OPS
Henderson, R. (Oak) 190
Fielder, C. (Det) 167
Canseco, J. (Oak) 160

Adjusted Batting Runs
Henderson, R. (Oak) 74.0
Fielder, C. (Det) 51.0
McGriff, F. (Tor) 40.0

Runs Created/Game
Henderson, R. (Oak) 10.40
McGriff, F. (Tor) 8.30
Fielder, C. (Det) 8.00

Fielding Runs
Espinoza, A. (NY) 24.0
Gallego, M. (Oak) 18.0
Randolph, W. (Oak) 16.5

Win Shares – Batters
Henderson, R. (Oak) 39
Trammell, A. (Det) 29
Fielder, C. (Det) 29

TPW – Batters
Henderson, R. (Oak) 7.2
McGriff, F. (Tor) 3.8
Fielder, C. (Det) 3.8

TEAM	CG	SH	SV	IP	H	H/G	ER	HR	BB	SO	OAV	RAT	ERA	ERA+	CERA	PR+	PF	FA	E	DP	FR	BW	PW	FW	TPW	DIF
East																										
BOS	15	13	44	1442	1439	9.0	596	**92**	519	997	.261	1.358	3.72	109	3.80	**84.8**	104	.980	123	154	-28.2	1.5	**8.6**	-2.9	7.3	-.3
TOR	6	9	48	1454	1434	8.9	620	143	**445**	892	.260	1.292	3.84	107	3.79	44.7	105	**.986**	**86**	144	-3.8	1.7	4.5	-.4	5.9	-.9
DET	15	12	45	1430^{1}	1401	8.8	698	154	661	856	.259	1.442	4.39	**90**	4.36	-100.2	101	.979	131	178	**32.2**	5.3	-10.2	**3.3**	-1.6	-.4
CLE	12	10	47	1427^{1}	1491	9.4	675	163	518	860	.270	1.408	4.26	92	4.42	-32.0	100	.981	117	146	-23.8	-.2	-3.3	-2.4	-5.9	1.9
BAL	10	5	43	1435^{1}	1445	9.1	644	161	537	776	.264	1.381	4.04	94	4.16	-57.1	97	.985	93	151	12.8	.2	-5.8	1.3	-4.3	.3
MIL	23	13	42	1445	1558	9.7	655	121	469	771	.275	1.403	4.08	95	4.18	-22.4	99	.976	149	152	-16.7	-1.5	-2.3	-1.7	-5.4	-1.6
NY	15	6	41	1444^{2}	1430	8.9	675	144	618	909	.261	1.418	4.21	94	4.22	-42.3	102	.980	126	164	0.0	-10.8	-4.3	.0	-15.1	1.1
West																										
OAK	18	**16**	64	**1456**	**1287**	**8.0**	**514**	123	494	831	**.238**	**1.223**	**3.18**	117	**3.25**	54.7	95	.986	87	152	31.6	**7.4**	5.6	3.2	**16.2**	5.8
CHI	17	10	**68**	1449^{1}	1313	8.2	581	106	548	914	.244	1.284	3.61	106	3.42	4.0	98	.980	124	169	28.9	-2.9	.4	2.9	.4	12.6
TEX	**25**	9	36	1444^{2}	1343	8.4	615	113	623	997	.248	1.361	3.83	102	3.79	6.9	100	.979	133	161	6.8	-.7	.7	.7	.7	1.3
CAL	21	13	42	1454	1482	9.2	612	106	544	944	.267	1.393	3.79	101	4.04	2.7	98	.978	142	**186**	-2.5	2.2	.3	-.3	2.3	-3.3
SEA	21	7	41	1443^{1}	1319	8.2	592	120	606	**1064**	.243	1.334	3.69	107	3.66	39.7	101	.979	130	152	-2.5	-1.2	4.0	-.3	2.6	-6.6
KC	18	8	33	1420^{2}	1449	9.2	620	116	560	1006	.264	1.414	3.93	98	4.16	20.4	98	.980	122	161	-36.5	2.2	2.1	-3.7	.6	-5.6
MIN	13	13	43	1435^{2}	1509	9.5	657	134	489	872	.273	1.392	4.12	101	4.18	1.7	106	.983	101	161	0.3	-6.2	.2	.0	-5.9	-1.1
Total	**229**	**144**	**637**	**20182^{1}**		**8.9**	**8754**					**1.364**	**3.90**													

Wins		Win Percentage		Games		Complete Games		Shutouts		Saves	
Welch, B. (Oak)	27	Welch, B. (Oak)	.818	Thigpen, B. (Chi)	77	Morris, J. (Det)	11	Clemens, R. (Bos)	4	Thigpen, B. (Chi)	57
Stewart, D. (Oak)	22	Clemens, R. (Bos)	.778	Montgomery, J. (KC)	73	Stewart, D. (Oak)	11	Stewart, D. (Oak)	4	Eckersley, D. (Oak)	48
Clemens, R. (Bos)	21	Stieb, D. (Tor)	.750	Ward, D. (Tor)	73	5 players tied with	7	3 players tied with	3	Jones, D. (Cle)	43

Innings Pitched		Fewest Hits/Game		Fewest BB/Game		Strikeouts		Ratio		Earned Run Average	
Stewart, D. (Oak)	267	Ryan, N. (Tex)	6.04	Anderson, A. (Min)	1.86	Ryan, N. (Tex)	232	Ryan, N. (Tex)	1.03		1.93
Morris, J. (Det)	249²	Johnson, R. (Sea)	7.13	Swindell, G. (Cle)	1.97	Witt, B. (Tex)	221	Clemens, R. (Bos)	1.08	Finley, C. (Cal)	2.40
Welch, B. (Oak)	238	Clemens, R. (Bos)	7.61	Clemens, R. (Bos)	2.13	Hanson, E. (Sea)	211	Wells, D. (Tor)	1.11	Stewart, D. (Oak)	2.56

Adjusted ERA		Component ERA		Opponents' Batting Avg.		Adjusted Pitching Runs		Win Shares – Pitchers		TPW – Pitchers	
Clemens, R. (Bos)	211	Ryan, N. (Tex)	2.28	Ryan, N. (Tex)	.188	Clemens, R. (Bos)	59	Clemens, R. (Bos)	28	Clemens, R. (Bos)	6.0
Finley, C. (Cal)	159	Clemens, R. (Bos)	2.33	Johnson, R. (Sea)	.216	Finley, C. (Cal)	37	Finley, C. (Cal)	23	Finley, C. (Cal)	3.8
Stewart, D. (Oak)	145	Wells, D. (Tor)	2.67	Clemens, R. (Bos)	.228	Stewart, D. (Oak)	28	Stewart, D. (Oak)	21	Stewart, D. (Oak)	2.9

1991 National League

TEAM	G	W	L	PCT	GB	R	OR	EW	AB	H	2B	3B	HR	TB	BB	SO	SB	CS	AVG	OBP	SLG	OPS	OPS+	BR/A	PF	RC
East																										
PIT	162	98	64	.605	....	**768**	632	97	5449	**1433**	**259**	50	126	2170	**620**	901	124	46	**.263**	**.342**	.398	**.740**	116	**125**	98	**760**
STL	162	84	78	.519	14	651	648	81	5362	1366	239	**53**	68	1915	532	857	202	110	.255	.324	.357	.682	97	-22	101	626
PHI	162	78	84	.481	20	629	680	75	5521	1332	248	33	111	1979	490	1026	92	**30**	.241	.306	.358	.664	93	-46	99	607
CHI	160	77	83	.481	20	695	734	76	**5522**	1395	232	26	159	2156	442	879	123	64	.253	.312	.390	.703	98	-23	105	673
NY	161	77	84	.478	20.5	640	646	80	5359	1305	250	24	117	1954	578	**789**	153	70	.244	.320	.365	.685	99	0	99	639
MON	161	71	90	.441	26.5	579	655	71	5412	1329	236	42	95	1934	484	1056	**221**	100	.246	.311	.357	.668	95	-35	99	605
West																										
ATL	162	94	68	.580	....	749	644	93	5456	1407	255	30	141	2145	563	906	165	76	.258	.331	.393	.724	103	28	106	717
LA	162	93	69	.574	1	665	**565**	94	5408	1366	191	29	108	1939	583	957	126	68	.253	.328	.359	.687	101	15	98	648
SD	162	84	78	.519	10	636	646	80	5408	1321	204	36	121	1960	501	1069	101	64	.244	.312	.362	.674	92	-60	103	603
SF	162	75	87	.463	19	649	697	75	5463	1345	215	48	141	2079	471	973	95	57	.246	.311	.381	.691	103	8	97	646
CIN	162	74	88	.457	20	689	691	81	5501	1419	250	27	**164**	**2215**	488	1006	124	56	.258	.322	**.403**	.725	105	32	104	719
HOU	162	65	97	.401	29	605	717	67	5504	1345	240	43	79	1908	502	1027	125	68	.244	.312	.347	.658	96	-30	94	604
Total	970					7955			65365	16363	2819	441	1430		6254	11446	1651	809	**.250**	**.319**	**.373**	**.692**				

Runs		Hits		Doubles		Triples		Home Runs		Total Bases	
Butler, B. (LA)	112	Pendleton, T. (Atl)	187	Bonilla, B. (Pit)	44	Lankford, R. (StL)	15	Johnson, H. (NY)	38	Clark, W. (SF)	303
Johnson, H. (NY)	108	Butler, B. (LA)	182	Jose, F. (StL)	40	Gwynn, T. (SD)	11	Williams, M. (SF)	34	Pendleton, T. (Atl)	303
Sandberg, R. (Chi)	104	Sabo, C. (Cin)	175	2 players tied with	36	Finley, S. (Hou)	10	Gant, R. (Atl)	32	Johnson, H. (NY)	302

Runs Batted In		Bases On Balls		Stolen Bases		Batting Average		On-Base Percentage		Slugging Average	
Johnson, H. (NY)	117	Butler, B. (LA)	108	Grissom, M. (Mon)	76	Pendleton, T. (Atl)	.319	Bonds, B. (Pit)	.419	Clark, W. (SF)	.536
Bonds, B. (Pit)	116	Bonds, B. (Pit)	107	Nixon, O. (Atl)	72	Morris, H. (Cin)	.318	Butler, B. (LA)	.402	Johnson, H. (NY)	.535
Clark, W. (SF)	116	McGriff, F. (SD)	105	DeShields, D. (Mon)	56	Gwynn, T. (SD)	.317	McGriff, F. (SD)	.400	Pendleton, T. (Atl)	.517

Adjusted OPS		Adjusted Batting Runs		Runs Created/Game		Fielding Runs		Win Shares – Batters		TPW – Batters	
Bonds, B. (Pit)	163	Bonds, B. (Pit)	52.0	Bonds, B. (Pit)	8.10	Larkin, B. (Cin)	23.9	Sandberg, R. (Chi)	37	Larkin, B. (Cin)	6.5
Clark, W. (SF)	154	Bonilla, B. (Pit)	41.0	Larkin, B. (Cin)	7.30	Pendleton, T. (Atl)	22.5	Bonds, B. (Pit)	37	Pendleton, T. (Atl)	5.5
Bonilla, B. (Pit)	151	Clark, W. (SF)	38.0	Clark, W. (SF)	7.30	Grace, M. (Chi)	21.5	Clark, W. (SF)	34	Bonds, B. (Pit)	5.5

TEAM	CG	SH	SV	IP	H	H/G	ER	HR	BB	SO	OAV	RAT	ERA	ERA+	CERA	PR+	PF	FA	E	DP	FR	BW	PW	FW	TPW	DIF
East																										
PIT	**18**	11	51	1456²	1411	8.7	557	117	**401**	919	.256	1.244	3.44	104	3.38	10.2	97	.981	120	134	10.4	**13.1**	1.1	1.1	**15.2**	1.8
STL	9	5	**51**	1435¹	1367	8.6	588	114	454	822	.255	1.269	3.69	101	3.48	-9.9	101	**.982**	**107**	133	14.7	-2.3	-1.0	1.5	-1.8	4.8
PHI	16	11	35	**1463**	1346	8.3	627	111	670	988	.246	1.378	3.86	98	3.74	-25.8	100	.981	119	111	-6.5	-4.9	-2.7	-.7	-8.2	5.2
CHI	12	4	40	1456²	1415	8.7	652	117	542	927	.257	1.343	4.03	96	3.73	-2.8	105	.982	113	120	-24.1	-2.4	-.3	-2.5	-5.2	2.2
NY	12	11	39	1437¹	1403	8.8	568	108	410	1028	.257	1.261	3.56	102	3.38	43.2	99	.977	143	112	-31.3	.0	4.5	-3.3	1.2	-4.2
MON	12	**14**	39	1440¹	**1304**	8.2	582	111	584	909	.244	1.311	3.64	99	3.55	-20.0	98	.979	133	128	**15.8**	-3.7	-2.1	**1.6**	-4.1	-4.9
West																										
ATL	**18**	7	48	1452²	1304	**8.1**	563	118	481	969	**.240**	**1.229**	3.49	111	3.21	65.2	105	.978	138	122	-2.1	2.9	6.8	-.2	9.5	3.5
LA	15	**14**	40	1458	1312	8.1	**496**	**96**	500	1028	.241	1.243	**3.06**	117	**3.11**	82.5	98	.980	123	126	2.3	1.5	**8.6**	.2	10.4	1.6
SD	14	11	47	1452²	1385	8.6	576	139	457	921	.252	1.268	3.57	106	3.49	29.3	103	.982	113	130	6.0	-6.3	3.1	.6	-2.6	5.6
SF	10	10	45	1442	1397	8.7	646	143	544	905	.257	1.346	4.03	89	3.89	-86.0	97	.982	109	**151**	13.3	.8	-9.0	1.4	-6.8	.8
CIN	7	11	43	1440	1372	8.6	613	127	560	997	.253	1.342	3.83	99	3.78	-2.6	103	.979	125	131	-2.3	3.4	-.3	-.2	2.8	-9.8
HOU	7	13	36	1453	1347	8.3	646	129	651	**1033**	.247	1.375	4.00	95	3.82	-84.3	95	.974	161	129	4.1	-3.1	-8.8	.4	-11.5	-4.5
Total	150	122	514	17387²		8.5	7114					1.301	3.68													

Wins		Win Percentage		Games		Complete Games		Shutouts		Saves	
Glavine, T. (Atl)	20	Smiley, J. (Pit)	.714	Jones, B. (Mon)	77	Glavine, T. (Atl)	9	Martinez, D. (Mon)	5	Smith, L. (StL)	47
Smiley, J. (Pit)	20	Rijo, J. (Cin)	.714	Assenmacher, P. (Chi)	75	Martinez, D. (Mon)	9	Martinez, R. (LA)	4	Dibble, R. (Cin)	31
Avery, S. (Atl)	18	Avery, S. (Atl)	.692	Stanton, M. (Atl)	74	Mulholland, T. (Phi)	8	3 players tied with	3	2 players tied with	30

Innings Pitched		Fewest Hits/Game		Fewest BB/Game		Strikeouts		Ratio		Earned Run Average	
Maddux, G. (Chi)	263	Harnisch, P. (Hou)	7.02	Smith, Z. (Pit)	1.14	Cone, D. (NY)	241	Rijo, J. (Cin)	1.08	Martinez, D. (Mon)	2.39
Glavine, T. (Atl)	246²	Rijo, J. (Cin)	7.27	Tewksbury, B. (StL)	1.79	Maddux, G. (Chi)	198	Morgan, M. (LA)	1.09	Rijo, J. (Cin)	2.51
Morgan, M. (LA)	236¹	DeJesus, J. (Phi)	7.28	Mulholland, T. (Phi)	1.90	Glavine, T. (Atl)	192	Glavine, T. (Atl)	1.09	Glavine, T. (Atl)	2.55

Adjusted ERA		Component ERA		Opponents' Batting Avg.		Adjusted Pitching Runs		Win Shares – Pitchers		TPW – Pitchers	
Glavine, T. (Atl)	152	Rijo, J. (Cin)	2.23	Harnisch, P. (Hou)	.212	Glavine, T. (Atl)	37	Glavine, T. (Atl)	23	Glavine, T. (Atl)	4.3
Rijo, J. (Cin)	151	Morgan, M. (LA)	2.37	Rijo, J. (Cin)	.219	Rijo, J. (Cin)	30	Martinez, D. (Mon)	18	Rijo, J. (Cin)	3.2
Martinez, D. (Mon)	151	Martinez, D. (Mon)	2.46	Glavine, T. (Atl)	.222	Martinez, D. (Mon)	28	4 players tied with	17	Martinez, D. (Mon)	3.0

1991 American League

TEAM	G	W	L	PCT	GB	R	OR	EW	AB	H	2B	3B	HR	TB	BB	SO	SB	CS	AVG	OBP	SLG	OPS	OPS+	BR/A	PF	RC
East																										
TOR	162	91	71	.562	....	684	**622**	89	5489	1412	295	45	133	2196	499	1043	148	53	.257	.326	.400	.726	96	-23	104	721
BOS	162	84	78	.519	7	731	712	83	5530	1486	**305**	25	126	2219	593	820	59	39	.269	.343	.401	.744	100	4	105	754
DET	162	84	78	.519	7	817	794	83	5547	1372	259	26	**209**	2310	**699**	1185	109	47	.247	.335	.416	.751	105	45	101	798
MIL	162	83	79	.512	8	799	744	87	5611	1523	247	**53**	116	2224	556	802	106	68	.271	.340	.396	.736	105	36	98	743
NY	162	71	91	.438	20	674	777	70	5541	1418	249	19	147	2146	473	861	109	36	.256	.319	.387	.706	94	-41	100	681
BAL	162	67	95	.414	24	686	796	69	5604	1421	256	29	170	2245	528	974	50	**33**	.254	.321	.401	.722	103	11	96	706
CLE	162	57	105	.352	34	576	759	59	5470	1390	236	26	79	1915	449	888	84	58	.254	.316	.350	.666	83	-130	101	588
West																										
MIN	162	95	67	.586	....	776	652	95	5556	**1557**	270	42	140	2331	526	**747**	107	68	**.280**	**.347**	.420	.766	106	41	105	784
CHI	162	87	75	.537	8	758	681	90	5594	1464	226	39	139	2185	610	896	134	74	.262	.338	.391	.729	103	29	98	739
TEX	162	85	77	.525	10	**829**	814	82	**5703**	1539	288	31	177	**2420**	596	1039	102	50	.270	.343	**.424**	**.768**	**113**	**102**	98	**830**
OAK	162	84	78	.519	11	760	776	79	5410	1342	246	19	159	2103	642	981	**151**	64	.248	.333	.389	.722	105	49	94	709
SEA	162	83	79	.512	12	702	674	84	5494	1400	268	29	126	2104	588	811	97	44	.255	.331	.383	.714	97	-18	100	695
KC	162	82	80	.506	13	727	722	82	5584	1475	290	41	117	2198	523	969	119	68	.264	.331	.394	.725	99	-11	100	718
CAL	162	81	81	.500	14	653	649	81	5470	1396	245	29	115	2044	448	928	94	56	.255	.316	.374	.690	90	-82	100	638
Total	**1134**					**10172**			**77603**	**20195**	**3680**	**453**	**1953**		**7730**	**12944**	**1469**	**758**	**.260**	**.331**	**.395**	**.726**				

Runs		Hits		Doubles		Triples		Home Runs		Total Bases	
Molitor, P. (Mil)	133	Molitor, P. (Mil)	216	Palmeiro, R. (Tex)	49	Johnson, L. (Chi)	13	Canseco, J. (Oak)	44	Ripken, C. (Bal)	368
Canseco, J. (Oak)	115	Ripken, C. (Bal)	210	Ripken, C. (Bal)	46	Molitor, P. (Mil)	13	Fielder, C. (Det)	44	Palmeiro, R. (Tex)	336
Palmeiro, R. (Tex)	115	2 players tied with	203	Sierra, R. (Tex)	44	Alomar, R. (Tor)	11	Ripken, C. (Bal)	34	Sierra, R. (Tex)	332
Runs Batted In		**Bases On Balls**		**Stolen Bases**		**Batting Average**		**On-Base Percentage**		**Slugging Average**	
Fielder, C. (Det)	133	Thomas, F. (Chi)	138	Henderson, R. (Oak)	58	Franco, J. (Tex)	.341	Thomas, F. (Chi)	.454	Tartabull, D. (KC)	.593
Canseco, J. (Oak)	122	Tettleton, M. (Det)	101	Alomar, R. (Tor)	53	Boggs, W. (Bos)	.332	Randolph, W. (Mil)	.427	Ripken, C. (Bal)	.566
Sierra, R. (Tex)	116	Henderson, R. (Oak)	98	Raines, T. (Chi)	51	Randolph, W. (Mil)	.327	Boggs, W. (Bos)	.425	Canseco, J. (Oak)	.556
Adjusted OPS		**Adjusted Batting Runs**		**Runs Created/Game**		**Fielding Runs**		**Win Shares – Batters**		**TPW – Batters**	
Thomas, F. (Chi)	181	Thomas, F. (Chi)	70.0	Thomas, F. (Chi)	9.60	Gallego, M. (Oak)	22.4	Thomas, F. (Chi)	34	Ripken, C. (Bal)	8.4
Tartabull, D. (KC)	170	Ripken, C. (Bal)	55.0	Tartabull, D. (KC)	9.00	Randolph, W. (Mil)	18.1	Ripken, C. (Bal)	34	Thomas, F. (Chi)	6.0
Ripken, C. (Bal)	164	Canseco, J. (Oak)	49.0	Griffey, K. (Sea)	8.00	Vizquel, O. (Sea)	16.4	Canseco, J. (Oak)	31	Griffey, K. (Sea)	5.0

TEAM	CG	SH	SV	IP	H	H/G	ER	HR	BB	SO	OAV	RAT	ERA	ERA+	CERA	PR+	PF	FA	E	DP	FR	BW	PW	FW	TPW	DIF
East																										
TOR	10	**16**	**60**	1462[2]	**1301**	8.0	**569**	121	523	971	**.238**	**1.247**	**3.50**	120	**3.31**	**120.0**	103	.980	127	115	-5.2	-2.3	**12.0**	-.5	9.2	.8
DET	18	8	38	1450[1]	1570	9.7	727	148	593	739	.280	1.491	4.51	92	4.62	-60.3	101	.983	104	171	-1.8	4.5	-6.0	-.2	-1.7	4.7
BOS	15	13	45	1439[2]	1405	8.8	641	147	530	999	.257	1.344	4.01	107	3.94	47.0	105	.981	116	165	-2.1	.4	4.7	-.2	4.9	-1.9
MIL	23	11	41	1463[2]	1498	9.2	673	147	527	859	.266	1.384	4.14	96	4.22	-33.5	97	.981	118	176	0.2	3.6	-3.4	.0	.3	1.7
NY	3	11	37	1444	1510	9.4	709	152	506	936	.271	1.396	4.42	94	4.38	-41.6	101	.979	133	181	-5.3	-4.1	-4.2	-.5	-8.8	-1.2
BAL	8	8	42	1457[2]	1534	9.5	743	147	504	868	.273	1.398	4.59	86	4.34	-108.7	96	**.985**	**91**	172	5.1	1.1	-10.9	.5	-9.3	-4.7
CLE	22	8	33	1441[1]	1551	9.7	677	110	**441**	862	.276	1.382	4.23	98	4.08	8.7	101	.976	149	150	-22.6	-13.0	.9	-2.3	-14.4	-9.6
West																										
MIN	21	12	53	1449[1]	1402	8.7	594	139	488	876	.255	1.304	3.69	116	3.72	76.4	104	.985	95	161	15.2	4.1	7.6	1.5	**13.3**	.7
CHI	**28**	8	40	1478	1302	**7.9**	622	154	601	923	.239	1.288	3.79	105	3.59	-12.4	97	.982	116	151	**40.5**	2.9	-1.2	**4.0**	5.7	.3
TEX	9	10	41	**1479**	1486	9.0	735	151	662	**1022**	.262	1.452	4.47	90	4.45	-48.0	98	.979	134	138	-24.7	**10.3**	-4.8	-2.5	3.0	1.0
OAK	14	10	49	1444[1]	1425	8.9	733	155	655	892	.260	1.440	4.57	**84**	4.45	-117.5	94	.982	107	150	-1.3	4.9	-11.8	-.1	-7.0	10.0
SEA	10	13	48	1464[1]	1387	8.5	617	136	628	1003	.253	1.376	3.79	109	3.98	28.3	101	.983	110	**187**	24.7	-1.8	2.8	2.5	3.5	-1.5
KC	17	12	41	1466	1473	9.0	639	**105**	529	1004	.261	1.366	3.92	105	3.86	75.2	101	.980	125	141	-43.4	-1.1	7.5	-4.3	2.1	-1.1
CAL	18	10	50	1441[2]	1351	8.4	591	141	543	990	.250	1.314	3.69	111	3.82	45.2	100	.984	102	156	20.9	-8.2	4.5	2.1	-1.6	1.6
Total	**216**	**150**	**618**	**20382**		**8.9**	**9270**					**1.370**	**4.09**													

Wins		Win Percentage		Games		Complete Games		Shutouts		Saves	
Erickson, S. (Min)	20	Erickson, S. (Min)	.714	Ward, D. (Tor)	81	McDowell, J. (Chi)	15	Clemens, R. (Bos)	4	Harvey, B. (Cal)	46
Gullickson, B. (Det)	20	Langston, M. (Cal)	.704	Jackson, M. (Sea)	72	Clemens, R. (Bos)	13	4 players tied with	3	Eckersley, D. (Oak)	43
Langston, M. (Cal)	19	Gullickson, B. (Det)	.690	Olson, G. (Bal)	72	2 players tied with	10			Aguilera, R. (Min)	42
Innings Pitched		**Fewest Hits/Game**		**Fewest BB/Game**		**Strikeouts**		**Ratio**		**Earned Run Average**	
Clemens, R. (Bos)	271[1]	Ryan, N. (Tex)	5.31	Swindell, G. (Cle)	1.17	Clemens, R. (Bos)	241	Ryan, N. (Tex)	1.01	Clemens, R. (Bos)	2.62
McDowell, J. (Chi)	253[2]	Johnson, R. (Sea)	6.75	Sanderson, S. (NY)	1.25	Johnson, R. (Sea)	228	Clemens, R. (Bos)	1.05	Candiotti, T. (Cle,Tor)	2.65
Morris, J. (Min)	246[2]	Langston, M. (Cal)	6.94	Tapani, K. (Min)	1.48	Ryan, N. (Tex)	203	Saberhagen, B. (KC)	1.07	Wegman, B. (Mil)	2.84
Adjusted ERA		**Component ERA**		**Opponents' Batting Avg.**		**Adjusted Pitching Runs**		**Win Shares – Pitchers**		**TPW – Pitchers**	
Clemens, R. (Bos)	164	Ryan, N. (Tex)	1.98	Ryan, N. (Tex)	.172	Clemens, R. (Bos)	51	Clemens, R. (Bos)	26	Clemens, R. (Bos)	5.1
Candiotti, T. (Cle,Tor)	158	Clemens, R. (Bos)	2.23	Johnson, R. (Sea)	.213	Candiotti, T. (Cle,Tor)	43	Candiotti, T. (Tor,Cle)	21	Candiotti, T. (Cle,Tor)	4.3
Tapani, K. (Min)	143	Saberhagen, B. (KC)	2.51	Langston, M. (Cal)	.215	Tapani, K. (Min)	32	Tapani, K. (Min)	21	Tapani, K. (Min)	3.2

1992 National League

TEAM	G	W	L	PCT	GB	R	OR	EW	AB	H	2B	3B	HR	TB	BB	SO	SB	CS	AVG	OBP	SLG	OPS	OPS+	BR/A	PF	RC
East																										
PIT	162	96	66	.593	....	**693**	595	93	5527	1409	272	**54**	106	2107	569	872	110	53	.255	.327	.381	.708	**108**	**56**	99	**697**
MON	162	87	75	.537	9	648	581	90	5477	1381	263	37	102	2024	463	976	196	63	.252	.315	.370	.685	101	15	99	649
STL	162	83	79	.512	13	631	604	85	**5594**	**1464**	262	44	94	2096	495	996	**208**	118	**.262**	.325	.375	.700	107	43	97	679
CHI	162	78	84	.481	18	593	624	77	5590	1420	221	41	104	2035	417	**816**	77	51	.254	.309	.364	.673	94	-54	102	615
NY	162	72	90	.444	24	599	653	74	5340	1254	259	17	93	1826	**572**	956	129	52	.235	.312	.342	.654	92	-41	99	581
PHI	162	70	92	.432	26	686	717	77	5500	1392	255	36	118	2073	509	1059	127	**31**	.253	.322	.377	.699	104	43	100	682
West																										
ATL	162	98	64	.605	....	682	**569**	96	5480	1391	223	48	**138**	**2124**	493	924	126	60	.254	.318	**.388**	.706	99	-4	106	684
CIN	162	90	72	.556	8	660	609	88	5460	1418	**281**	44	99	2084	563	888	125	65	.260	**.331**	.382	**.713**	105	39	103	687
SD	162	82	80	.506	16	617	636	79	5476	1396	255	30	135	2116	453	864	69	52	.255	.315	.386	.701	102	2	102	646
HOU	162	81	81	.500	17	608	668	73	5480	1350	255	38	96	1969	506	1025	139	54	.246	.316	.359	.675	102	16	95	634
SF	162	72	90	.444	26	574	647	71	5456	1330	220	36	105	1937	435	1067	112	64	.244	.304	.355	.659	98	-29	94	583
LA	162	63	99	.389	35	548	636	69	5368	1333	201	34	72	1818	503	899	142	78	.248	.316	.339	.654	93	-50	98	577
Total	**972**					**7539**			**65748**	**16538**	**2967**	**459**	**1262**		**5978**	**11342**	**1560**	**741**	**.252**	**.318**	**.368**	**.686**				

Runs
Bonds, B. (Pit) 109
Hollins, D. (Phi) 104
Van Slyke, A. (Pit) 103

Hits
Pendleton, T. (Atl) 199
Van Slyke, A. (Pit) 199
Sandberg, R. (Chi) 186

Doubles
Van Slyke, A. (Pit) 45
3 players tied with 40

Triples
Sanders, D. (Atl) 14
Finley, S. (Hou) 13
Van Slyke, A. (Pit) 12

Home Runs
McGriff, F. (SD) 35
Bonds, B. (Pit) 34
Sheffield, G. (SD) 33

Total Bases
Sheffield, G. (SD) 323
Sandberg, R. (Chi) 312
Van Slyke, A. (Pit) 310

Runs Batted In
Daulton, D. (Phi) 109
Pendleton, T. (Atl) 105
McGriff, F. (SD) 104

Bases On Balls
Bonds, B. (Pit) 127
McGriff, F. (SD) 96
Butler, B. (LA) 95

Stolen Bases
Grissom, M. (Mon) 78
DeShields, D. (Mon) 46
2 players tied with 44

Batting Average
Sheffield, G. (SD) .330
Van Slyke, A. (Pit) .324
Kruk, J. (Phi) .323

On-Base Percentage
Bonds, B. (Pit) .461
Kruk, J. (Phi) .428
Butler, B. (LA) .413

Slugging Average
Bonds, B. (Pit) .624
Sheffield, G. (SD) .580
McGriff, F. (SD) .556

Adjusted OPS
Bonds, B. (Pit) 207
Sheffield, G. (SD) 168
McGriff, F. (SD) 164

Adjusted Batting Runs
Bonds, B. (Pit) 80.0
Sheffield, G. (SD) 47.0
McGriff, F. (SD) 46.0

Runs Created/Game
Bonds, B. (Pit) 11.40
Daulton, D. (Phi) 7.90
Sheffield, G. (SD) 7.90

Fielding Runs
Smith, O. (StL) 20.6
Thompson, R. (SF) 19.4
Pendleton, T. (Atl) 19.3

Win Shares – Batters
Bonds, B. (Pit) 41
Pendleton, T. (Atl) 35
Van Slyke, A. (Pit) 35

TPW – Batters
Bonds, B. (Pit) 8.3
Sheffield, G. (SD) 6.4
Larkin, B. (Cin) 5.3

TEAM	CG	SH	SV	IP	H	H/G	ER	HR	BB	SO	OAV	RAT	ERA	ERA+	CERA	PR+	PF	FA	E	DP	FR	BW	PW	FW	TPW	DIF
East																										
PIT	20	20	43	1479^2	1410	8.6	551	101	455	844	.254	1.260	3.35	103	3.32	3.3	98	.984	101	144	11.3	**6.1**	.4	1.2	7.6	7.4
MON	11	14	49	1468	**1296**	**8.0**	530	92	525	1014	**.238**	1.240	3.25	107	3.19	36.6	99	.980	124	113	-1.8	1.6	3.9	-.2	5.4	.6
STL	10	9	47	**1480**	1405	8.5	556	118	**400**	842	.252	**1.220**	3.38	100	3.23	-18.8	97	**.985**	**94**	146	19.5	4.6	-2.0	2.1	4.7	-2.7
CHI	16	11	37	1469	1337	8.2	553	107	575	901	.246	1.302	3.39	106	3.48	29.8	103	.982	114	142	3.7	-5.8	3.2	.4	-2.2	-.8
NY	17	13	34	1446^2	1404	8.7	588	98	482	1025	.256	1.304	3.66	95	3.53	-14.0	99	.981	116	134	-19.1	-4.4	-1.5	-2.1	-7.9	-1.1
PHI	**27**	7	34	1428	1387	8.7	652	113	549	851	.257	1.356	4.11	**85**	3.82	-92.0	100	.978	131	128	-9.6	4.6	-9.9	-1.0	-6.3	-4.7
West																										
ATL	26	**24**	41	1460	1321	8.1	**509**	89	489	948	.242	1.240	**3.14**	117	**3.12**	**78.8**	104	.982	109	121	4.4	-.4	**8.5**	.5	**8.5**	8.5
CIN	9	11	**55**	1449^2	1362	8.5	557	109	470	**1060**	.251	1.264	3.46	104	3.37	18.3	103	.984	96	128	2.7	4.2	2.0	.3	6.5	2.5
SD	9	11	46	1461^1	1444	8.9	578	111	439	971	.261	1.289	3.56	100	3.49	3.9	102	.982	115	127	-4.1	.2	.4	-.4	.2	.8
HOU	5	12	45	1459^1	1386	8.6	603	114	539	978	.252	1.319	3.72	90	3.62	-57.5	96	.981	114	125	-4.2	1.7	-6.2	-.4	-5.0	5.0
SF	9	12	30	1461	1385	8.5	586	128	502	927	.253	1.292	3.61	91	3.58	-80.7	94	.982	113	**174**	**30.8**	-3.1	-8.7	**3.3**	-8.5	-.5
LA	18	13	29	1438	1401	8.8	545	**82**	553	981	.257	1.359	3.41	101	3.54	39.6	98	.972	174	136	-34.5	-5.3	4.3	-3.7	-4.8	-13.2
Total	**177**	**157**	**490**	**17500^2**		**8.5**	**6808**					**1.287**	**3.50**													

Wins
Glavine, T. (Atl) 20
Maddux, G. (Chi) 20
4 players tied with 16

Win Percentage
Tewksbury, B. (StL) .762
Swift, B. (SF) .714
Glavine, T. (Atl) .714

Games
Boever, J. (Hou) 81
Jones, D. (Hou) 80
2 players tied with 77

Complete Games
Mulholland, T. (Phi) 12
Drabek, D. (Pit) 10
Schilling, C. (Phi) 10

Shutouts
Cone, D. (NY) 5
Glavine, T. (Atl) 5
5 players tied with 4

Saves
Smith, L. (StL) 43
Myers, R. (SD) 38
Wetteland, J. (Mon) 37

Innings Pitched
Maddux, G. (Chi) 268
Drabek, D. (Pit) 256^2
Smoltz, J. (Atl) 246^2

Fewest Hits/Game
Schilling, C. (Phi) 6.56
Maddux, G. (Chi) 6.75
Fernandez, S. (NY) 6.79

Fewest BB/Game
Tewksbury, B. (StL) .77
Cormier, R. (StL) 1.60
Swindell, G. (Cin) 1.73

Strikeouts
Smoltz, J. (Atl) 215
Cone, D. (NY) 214
Maddux, G. (Chi) 199

Ratio
Schilling, C. (Phi) .99
Maddux, G. (Chi) 1.01
Tewksbury, B. (StL) 1.02

Earned Run Average
Swift, B. (SF) 2.08
Tewksbury, B. (StL) 2.16
Maddux, G. (Chi) 2.18

Adjusted ERA
Maddux, G. (Chi) 165
Swift, B. (SF) 159
Tewksbury, B. (StL) 157

Component ERA
Schilling, C. (Phi) 1.86
Maddux, G. (Chi) 2.01
Martinez, D. (Mon) 2.19

Opponents' Batting Avg.
Schilling, C. (Phi) .201
Maddux, G. (Chi) .210
Fernandez, S. (NY) .210

Adjusted Pitching Runs
Maddux, G. (Chi) 42
Schilling, C. (Phi) 30
Tewksbury, B. (StL) 29

Win Shares – Pitchers
Maddux, G. (Chi) 27
Tewksbury, B. (StL) 21
Drabek, D. (Pit) 20

TPW – Pitchers
Maddux, G. (Chi) 4.7
Schilling, C. (Phi) 3.2
Tewksbury, B. (StL) 2.9

1992 American League

TEAM	G	W	L	PCT	GB	R	OR	EW	AB	H	2B	3B	HR	TB	BB	SO	SB	CS	AVG	OBP	SLG	OPS	OPS+	BR/A	PF	RC
East																										
TOR	162	96	66	.593	....	780	682	92	5536	1458	265	40	163	**2292**	561	933	129	39	.263	.336	**.414**	**.750**	104	42	105	**778**
MIL	162	92	70	.568	4	740	**604**	97	5504	1477	272	35	82	2065	511	779	**256**	115	.268	.334	.375	.709	100	9	98	697
BAL	162	89	73	.549	7	705	656	87	5485	1423	243	36	148	2182	647	827	89	48	.259	.343	.398	.741	104	39	102	751
NY	162	76	86	.469	20	733	746	80	5593	1462	281	18	163	2268	536	903	78	**37**	.261	.331	.406	.736	106	40	99	740
CLE	162	76	86	.469	20	674	746	73	**5620**	1495	227	24	127	2151	448	885	144	67	.266	.325	.383	.708	99	-9	98	684
DET	162	75	87	.463	21	**791**	794	81	5515	1411	256	16	**182**	2245	675	1055	66	45	.256	.340	.407	.747	108	56	101	767
BOS	162	73	89	.451	23	599	669	72	5461	1343	259	21	84	1896	591	865	44	48	.246	.323	.347	.670	82	-133	107	615
West																										
OAK	162	96	66	.593	....	745	672	89	5387	1389	219	24	142	2082	**707**	831	143	59	.258	**.349**	.386	.736	**112**	**105**	95	745
MIN	162	90	72	.556	6	747	653	92	5582	**1544**	275	27	104	2185	527	834	123	74	**.277**	.345	.391	.736	102	18	103	745
CHI	162	86	76	.531	10	738	690	86	5498	1434	269	36	110	2105	622	784	160	57	.261	.339	.383	.722	103	40	99	725
TEX	162	77	85	.475	19	682	753	73	5537	1387	266	23	159	2176	550	1036	81	44	.250	.324	.393	.717	104	20	96	707
KC	162	72	90	.444	24	610	667	74	5501	1411	**284**	**42**	75	2004	439	**741**	131	71	.256	.317	.364	.682	88	-94	103	627
CAL	162	72	90	.444	24	579	671	69	5364	1306	202	20	88	1812	416	882	160	101	.243	.303	.338	.641	79	-167	101	527
SEA	162	64	98	.395	32	679	799	68	5564	1466	278	24	149	2239	474	841	100	55	.263	.326	.402	.728	102	6	101	706
Total	**1134**					**9802**			**77147**	**20006**	**3596**	**386**	**1776**		**7704**	**12196**	**1704**	**860**	**.259**	**.331**	**.385**	**.716**				

Runs
Phillips, T. (Det) 114
Thomas, F. (Chi) 108
Alomar, R. (Tor) 105

Hits
Puckett, K. (Min) 210
Baerga, C. (Cle) 205
Molitor, P. (Mil) 195

Doubles
Martinez, E. (Sea) 46
Thomas, F. (Chi) 46
2 players tied with 40

Triples
Johnson, L. (Chi) 12
Devereaux, M. (Bal) 11
Anderson, B. (Bal) 10

Home Runs
Gonzalez, J. (Tex) 43
McGwire, M. (Oak) 42
Fielder, C. (Det) 35

Total Bases
Puckett, K. (Min) 313
Carter, J. (Tor) 310
Gonzalez, J. (Tex) 309

Runs Batted In
Fielder, C. (Det) 124
Carter, J. (Tor) 119
Thomas, F. (Chi) 115

Bases On Balls
Tettleton, M. (Det) 122
Thomas, F. (Chi) 122
Phillips, T. (Det) 114

Stolen Bases
Lofton, K. (Cle) 66
Listach, P. (Mil) 54
Anderson, B. (Bal) 53

Batting Average
Martinez, E. (Sea) .343
Puckett, K. (Min) .329
Thomas, F. (Chi) .323

On-Base Percentage
Thomas, F. (Chi) .446
Tartabull, D. (NY) .410
Martinez, E. (Sea) .408

Slugging Average
McGwire, M. (Oak) .585
Martinez, E. (Sea) .544
Thomas, F. (Chi) .536

Adjusted OPS
McGwire, M. (Oak) 179
Thomas, F. (Chi) 176
Martinez, E. (Sea) 163

Adjusted Batting Runs
Thomas, F. (Chi) 66.0
McGwire, M. (Oak) 51.0
Martinez, E. (Sea) 46.0

Runs Created/Game
Thomas, F. (Chi) 9.10
Martinez, E. (Sea) 8.40
McGwire, M. (Oak) 8.20

Fielding Runs
Ventura, R. (Chi) 26.5
Gagne, G. (Min) 22.3
Bordick, M. (Oak) 21.5

Win Shares – Batters
Alomar, R. (Tor) 34
Thomas, F. (Chi) 33
Puckett, K. (Min) 31

TPW – Batters
Ventura, R. (Chi) 5.2
Martinez, E. (Sea) 5.1
Thomas, F. (Chi) 4.6

TEAM	CG	SH	SV	IP	H	H/G	ER	HR	BB	SO	OAV	RAT	ERA	ERA+	CERA	PR+	PF	FA	E	DP	FR	BW	PW	FW	TPW	DIF
East																										
TOR	18	14	49	1440^2	1346	8.4	626	124	541	954	.248	1.310	3.91	104	3.66	31.4	104	.985	93	109	-4.8	4.3	3.2	-.5	7.0	8.0
MIL	19	14	39	1457	**1344**	**8.3**	**555**	127	**435**	793	**.246**	**1.221**	**3.43**	112	**3.33**	34.4	97	**.986**	**89**	146	**30.7**	.9	3.5	**3.1**	7.6	3.4
BAL	20	**16**	48	1464	1419	8.7	617	124	518	846	.256	1.323	3.79	106	3.75	28.2	102	.985	93	168	8.8	3.9	2.9	.9	7.7	.3
NY	20	9	44	1452^2	1453	9.0	679	129	612	851	.263	1.422	4.21	93	4.24	-52.5	99	.982	114	165	3.7	4.1	-5.3	.4	-.9	-4.1
CLE	13	7	46	**1470**	1507	9.2	671	159	566	890	.268	1.410	4.11	95	4.39	-23.4	99	.978	141	**176**	-10.9	-1.0	-2.4	-1.1	-4.5	-.5
DET	10	4	36	1435^2	1534	9.6	733	155	564	693	.277	1.461	4.60	**86**	4.52	-90.4	100	.981	116	164	-15.3	5.7	-9.2	-1.6	-5.1	-.9
BOS	22	13	39	1448^2	1403	8.7	576	107	535	943	.255	1.338	3.58	118	3.69	**89.4**	107	.978	139	170	3.5	-13.5	**9.1**	.4	-4.0	-4.0
West																										
OAK	8	9	**58**	1447	1396	8.7	600	129	601	843	.256	1.380	3.73	100	3.99	-9.1	95	.979	125	158	11.9	**10.7**	-.9	1.2	**11.0**	4.0
MIN	16	13	50	1453	1391	8.6	597	121	479	923	.254	1.287	3.70	110	3.59	43.9	103	.985	95	155	10.6	1.8	4.5	1.1	7.3	1.7
CHI	21	5	52	1461^2	1400	8.6	620	123	550	810	.252	1.334	3.82	101	3.77	4.1	98	.979	129	134	-0.2	4.1	.4	.0	4.5	.5
TEX	19	3	42	1460^1	1471	9.1	663	113	598	**1034**	.264	1.417	4.09	93	4.14	-24.2	96	.975	154	153	-24.8	2.0	-2.5	-2.5	-3.0	-1.0
KC	9	12	44	1447^1	1426	8.9	613	**106**	512	834	.259	1.339	3.81	106	3.76	59.4	103	.980	122	164	-20.0	-9.6	6.1	-2.0	-5.6	-3.4
CAL	**26**	13	42	1446	1449	9.0	617	130	532	888	.264	1.370	3.84	104	4.04	14.6	101	.979	134	172	8.6	-17.0	1.5	.9	-14.6	5.6
SEA	21	9	30	1445	1467	9.1	731	129	661	894	.266	1.473	4.55	87	4.48	-89.2	101	.982	112	170	-2.9	.6	-9.1	-.3	-8.8	-8.2
Total	**242**	**141**	**619**	**20329**		**8.9**	**8898**					**1.363**	**3.94**													

Wins
- Brown, K. (Tex) 21
- Morris, J. (Tor) 21
- McDowell, J. (Chi) 20

Win Percentage
- Mussina, M. (Bal) .783
- Morris, J. (Tor) .778
- Guzman, J. (Tor) .762

Games
- Rogers, K. (Tex) 81
- Ward, D. (Tor) 79
- Olin, S. (Cle) 72

Complete Games
- McDowell, J. (Chi) 13
- Brown, K. (Tex) 11
- Clemens, R. (Bos) 11

Shutouts
- Clemens, R. (Bos) 5
- Fleming, D. (Sea) 4
- Mussina, M. (Bal) 4

Saves
- Eckersley, D. (Oak) 51
- Aguilera, R. (Min) 41
- Montgomery, J. (KC) 39

Innings Pitched
- Brown, K. (Tex) 265^2
- Wegman, B. (Mil) 261^2
- McDowell, J. (Chi) 260^2

Fewest Hits/Game
- Johnson, R. (Sea) 6.59
- Guzman, J. (Tor) 6.73
- Appier, K. (KC) 7.21

Fewest BB/Game
- Bosio, C. (Mil) 1.71
- Mussina, M. (Bal) 1.79
- Wegman, B. (Mil) 1.89

Strikeouts
- Johnson, R. (Sea) 241
- Perez, M. (NY) 218
- Clemens, R. (Bos) 208

Ratio
- Clemens, R. (Bos) 1.07
- Mussina, M. (Bal) 1.08
- Smiley, J. (Min) 1.12

Earned Run Average
- Clemens, R. (Bos) 2.41
- Appier, K. (KC) 2.46
- Mussina, M. (Bal) 2.54

Adjusted ERA
- Clemens, R. (Bos) 175
- Appier, K. (KC) 165
- Mussina, M. (Bal) 158

Component ERA
- Guzman, J. (Tor) 2.34
- Clemens, R. (Bos) 2.38
- Appier, K. (KC) 2.41

Opponents' Batting Avg.
- Johnson, R. (Sea) .206
- Guzman, J. (Tor) .207
- Appier, K. (KC) .217

Adjusted Pitching Runs
- Clemens, R. (Bos) 49
- Appier, K. (KC) 40
- Mussina, M. (Bal) 38

Win Shares – Pitchers
- Clemens, R. (Bos) 26
- Mussina, M. (Bal) 24
- 3 players tied with 20

TPW – Pitchers
- Clemens, R. (Bos) 5.0
- Appier, K. (KC) 4.0
- Mussina, M. (Bal) 3.9

1993 National League

TEAM	G	W	L	PCT	GB	R	OR	EW	AB	H	2B	3B	HR	TB	BB	SO	SB	CS	AVG	OBP	SLG	OPS	OPS+	BR/A	PF	RC
East																										
PHI	162	97	65	.599	....	**877**	740	95	**5685**	**1555**	**297**	51	156	**2422**	**665**	1049	91	**32**	.274	**.354**	.426	**.780**	**116**	**137**	99	**878**
MON	163	94	68	.580	3	732	682	87	5493	1410	270	36	122	2118	542	**860**	**228**	56	.257	.329	.386	.714	92	-30	104	725
STL	162	87	75	.537	10	758	744	83	5551	1508	262	34	118	2192	588	882	153	72	.272	.344	.395	.739	106	50	98	757
CHI	163	84	78	.519	13	738	739	81	5627	1521	259	32	161	2327	446	923	100	43	.270	.328	.414	.741	105	30	98	747
PIT	162	75	87	.463	22	707	806	70	5549	1482	267	50	110	2179	536	972	92	55	.267	.338	.393	.730	101	7	100	731
FLA	162	64	98	.395	33	581	724	63	5475	1356	197	31	94	1897	498	1054	117	56	.248	.316	.346	.663	78	-157	105	602
NY	162	59	103	.364	38	672	744	73	5448	1350	228	37	158	2126	448	879	79	50	.248	.308	.390	.698	92	-72	99	644
West																										
ATL	162	104	58	.642	....	767	**559**	106	5515	1444	239	29	**169**	2248	560	946	125	48	.262	.334	.408	.741	102	25	101	752
SF	162	103	59	.636	1	808	636	100	5557	1534	269	33	168	2373	516	930	120	65	**.276**	.343	**.427**	.770	114	103	97	802
HOU	162	85	77	.525	19	716	630	91	5464	1459	288	37	138	2235	497	911	103	60	.267	.333	.409	.742	107	46	96	731
LA	162	81	81	.500	23	675	662	83	5588	1458	234	28	130	2138	492	937	126	61	.261	.324	.383	.706	100	-4	94	694
CIN	162	73	89	.451	31	722	785	74	5517	1457	261	28	137	2185	485	1025	142	59	.264	.327	.396	.723	98	-11	100	717
COL	162	67	95	.414	37	758	967	62	5517	1507	278	**59**	142	2329	388	944	146	90	.273	.326	.422	.748	90	-89	116	729
SD	162	61	101	.377	43	679	772	71	5503	1386	239	28	153	2140	443	1046	92	41	.252	.314	.389	.703	91	-70	102	670
Total	**1135**					**10190**			**77489**	**20427**	**3588**	**513**	**1956**		**7104**	**13358**	**1714**	**788**	**.264**	**.330**	**.399**	**.729**				

Runs
- Dykstra, L. (Phi) 143
- Bonds, B. (SF) 129
- Gant, R. (Atl) 113

Hits
- Dykstra, L. (Phi) 194
- Grace, M. (Chi) 193
- Grissom, M. (Mon) 188

Doubles
- Hayes, C. (Col) 45
- Dykstra, L. (Phi) 44
- Bichette, D. (Col) 43

Triples
- Finley, S. (Hou) 13
- Butler, B. (LA) 10
- 2 players tied with 9

Home Runs
- Bonds, B. (SF) 46
- Justice, D. (Atl) 40
- Williams, M. (SF) 38

Total Bases
- Bonds, B. (SF) 365
- Williams, M. (SF) 325
- Gant, R. (Atl) 309

Runs Batted In
- Bonds, B. (SF) 123
- Justice, D. (Atl) 120
- Gant, R. (Atl) 117

Bases On Balls
- Dykstra, L. (Phi) 129
- Bonds, B. (SF) 126
- Daulton, D. (Phi) 117

Stolen Bases
- Carr, C. (Fla) 58
- Grissom, M. (Mon) 53
- Nixon, O. (Atl) 47

Batting Average
- Galarraga, A. (Col) .370
- Gwynn, T. (SD) .358
- Jefferies, G. (StL) .342

On-Base Percentage
- Bonds, B. (SF) .463
- Kruk, J. (Phi) .433
- Dykstra, L. (Phi) .423

Slugging Average
- Bonds, B. (SF) .677
- Galarraga, A. (Col) .602
- Williams, M. (SF) .561

Adjusted OPS
- Bonds, B. (SF) 207
- Piazza, M. (LA) 155
- Bagwell, J. (Hou) 146

Adjusted Batting Runs
- Bonds, B. (SF) 89.0
- Dykstra, L. (Phi) 49.0
- Kruk, J. (Phi) 41.0

Runs Created/Game
- Bonds, B. (SF) 12.00
- Galarraga, A. (Col) 9.40
- Kruk, J. (Phi) 8.20

Fielding Runs
- Bell, J. (Pit) 26.2
- Smith, O. (StL) 24.5
- Thompson, R. (SF) 22.4

Win Shares – Batters
- Bonds, B. (SF) 47
- Dykstra, L. (Phi) 32
- Piazza, M. (LA) 31

TPW – Batters
- Bonds, B. (SF) 8.1
- Bell, J. (Pit) 5.9
- Piazza, M. (LA) 5.6

TEAM	CG	SH	SV	IP	H	H/G	ER	HR	BB	SO	OAV	RAT	ERA	ERA+	CERA	PR+	PF	FA	E	DP	FR	BW	PW	FW	TPW	DIF
East																										
PHI	**24**	11	46	**1472^2**	1419	8.7	646	129	573	**1117**	.251	1.353	3.95	100	3.83	10.3	98	.977	141	123	-10.8	**13.6**	1.0	-1.1	13.6	2.4
MON	8	7	**61**	1456^2	1369	8.5	574	119	521	934	.249	1.297	3.55	117	3.57	98.7	103	.975	159	144	1.9	-3.0	9.8	.2	7.0	6.0
STL	5	7	54	1453	1553	9.6	660	152	**383**	775	.276	1.332	4.09	97	4.05	-24.1	98	.975	159	157	2.1	5.0	-2.4	.2	2.8	3.2
CHI	8	5	56	1449^2	1514	9.4	673	153	470	905	.273	1.369	4.18	95	4.18	-47.2	99	.982	115	162	16.7	3.0	-4.7	1.7	-.1	3.1
PIT	12	5	34	1445^2	1557	9.7	766	153	485	832	.280	1.412	4.77	**85**	4.45	-128.0	100	.983	105	161	12.1	.7	-12.8	1.2	-10.8	4.8
FLA	4	5	48	1440^1	1437	9.0	661	135	598	945	.261	1.413	4.13	104	4.14	53.6	107	.980	125	130	-26.7	-15.6	5.3	-2.7	-13.0	-4.0
NY	16	8	22	1438	1483	9.3	647	139	434	867	.269	1.333	4.05	99	3.95	-13.9	99	.975	156	143	7.5	-7.2	-1.4	.8	-7.8	-14.2
West																										
ATL	18	**16**	46	1455	**1297**	**8.0**	**508**	**101**	480	1036	**.240**	**1.221**	**3.14**	128	**3.06**	**128.9**	99	.983	108	146	12.8	2.5	**12.9**	1.3	**16.6**	6.4
SF	4	9	50	1456^2	1385	8.6	584	168	442	982	.253	1.254	3.61	108	3.71	4.8	97	**.984**	**101**	**169**	**40.2**	10.3	.5	**4.0**	14.8	7.2
HOU	18	14	42	1441^1	1363	8.5	559	117	476	1056	.251	1.276	3.49	111	3.45	48.7	96	.979	126	141	12.5	4.6	4.9	1.2	10.7	-6.7
LA	17	9	36	**1472^2**	1406	8.6	572	103	567	1043	.254	1.340	3.50	109	3.62	55.3	94	.979	133	141	-4.5	-.4	5.5	-.4	4.6	-4.6
CIN	11	8	37	1434	1510	9.5	719	158	508	996	.272	1.407	4.51	89	4.44	-67.0	100	.980	121	133	-11.0	-1.1	-6.7	-1.1	-8.9	.9
COL	9	0	35	1431^1	1664	10.5	860	181	609	913	.294	1.588	5.41	88	5.41	-59.7	118	.973	167	149	-47.1	-8.8	-6.0	-4.7	-19.5	5.5
SD	8	6	32	1437^2	1470	9.2	675	148	558	957	.266	1.411	4.23	98	4.20	-8.8	102	.974	160	129	-5.8	-7.0	-.9	-.6	-8.4	-11.6
Total	**162**	**110**	**599**	**20284^2**		**9.1**	**9104**					**1.357**	**4.04**													

Wins		Win Percentage		Games		Complete Games		Shutouts		Saves	
Burkett, J. (SF)	22	Portugal, M. (Hou)	.818	Jackson, M. (SF)	81	Maddux, G. (Atl)	8	Harnisch, P. (Hou)	4	Myers, R. (Chi)	53
Glavine, T. (Atl)	22	Greene, T. (Phi)	.800	Beck, R. (SF)	76	5 players tied with	7	Martinez, R. (LA)	3	Beck, R. (SF)	48
Swift, B. (SF)	21	Glavine, T. (Atl)	.786	West, D. (Phi)	76			11 players tied with	2	Harvey, B. (Fla)	45

Innings Pitched		Fewest Hits/Game		Fewest BB/Game		Strikeouts		Ratio		Earned Run Average	
Maddux, G. (Atl)	267	Harnisch, P. (Hou)	7.07	Tewksbury, B. (StL)	.84	Rijo, J. (Cin)	227	Maddux, G. (Atl)	1.05	Maddux, G. (Atl)	2.36
Rijo, J. (Cin)	257[1]	Swift, B. (SF)	7.54	Arocha, R. (StL)	1.48	Smoltz, J. (Atl)	208	Swift, B. (SF)	1.07	Rijo, J. (Cin)	2.48
Smoltz, J. (Atl)	243[2]	Rijo, J. (Cin)	7.62	Burkett, J. (SF)	1.55	Maddux, G. (Atl)	197	Rijo, J. (Cin)	1.09	Portugal, M. (Hou)	2.77

Adjusted ERA		Component ERA		Opponents' Batting Avg.		Adjusted Pitching Runs		Win Shares – Pitchers		TPW – Pitchers	
Maddux, G. (Atl)	170	Maddux, G. (Atl)	2.32	Harnisch, P. (Hou)	.214	Maddux, G. (Atl)	47	Rijo, J. (Cin)	26	Rijo, J. (Cin)	5.3
Rijo, J. (Cin)	162	Rijo, J. (Cin)	2.55	Swift, B. (SF)	.226	Rijo, J. (Cin)	46	Maddux, G. (Atl)	25	Maddux, G. (Atl)	4.6
Portugal, M. (Hou)	140	Swift, B. (SF)	2.57	Rijo, J. (Cin)	.230	Avery, S. (Atl)	25	Glavine, T. (Atl)	20	Portugal, M. (Hou)	2.7

1993 American League

TEAM	G	W	L	PCT	GB	R	OR	EW	AB	H	2B	3B	HR	TB	BB	SO	SB	CS	AVG	OBP	SLG	OPS	OPS+	BR/A	PF	RC
East																										
TOR	162	95	67	.586	....	847	742	92	5579	1556	317	42	159	2434	588	861	170	49	.279	.353	.436	.789	110	101	100	865
NY	162	88	74	.543	7	821	761	87	5615	1568	294	24	178	2444	629	910	39	35	.279	.356	.435	.792	115	120	97	860
BAL	162	85	77	.525	10	786	745	85	5508	1470	287	24	157	2276	655	930	73	54	.267	.349	.413	.762	100	1	104	794
DET	162	85	77	.525	10	899	837	87	5620	1546	282	38	178	2438	765	1122	104	63	.275	.365	.434	.799	115	128	99	914
BOS	162	80	82	.494	15	686	698	80	5496	1451	319	29	114	2170	508	871	73	38	.264	.333	.395	.728	89	-81	106	711
CLE	162	76	86	.469	19	790	813	79	5619	1547	264	31	141	2296	488	843	159	55	.275	.339	.409	.747	100	11	100	773
MIL	162	69	93	.426	26	733	792	75	5525	1426	240	25	125	2091	555	932	138	63	.258	.330	.378	.709	91	-75	98	684
West																										
CHI	162	94	68	.580	....	776	664	94	5483	1454	228	44	162	2256	604	834	106	57	.265	.342	.411	.753	104	30	98	771
TEX	162	86	76	.531	8	835	751	90	5510	1472	284	39	181	2377	483	984	113	67	.267	.332	.431	.763	108	44	96	775
KC	162	84	78	.519	10	675	694	79	5522	1455	294	35	125	2194	428	936	100	75	.263	.322	.397	.720	87	-116	106	690
SEA	162	82	80	.506	12	734	731	81	5494	1429	272	24	161	2232	624	901	91	68	.260	.342	.406	.748	99	-13	101	756
CAL	162	71	91	.438	23	684	770	71	5391	1399	259	24	114	2048	564	930	169	100	.260	.334	.380	.714	88	-89	103	677
MIN	162	71	91	.438	23	693	830	67	5601	1480	261	27	121	2158	493	850	83	59	.264	.329	.385	.715	91	-78	100	690
OAK	162	68	94	.420	26	715	846	67	5543	1408	260	21	158	2184	622	1048	131	59	.254	.333	.394	.727	101	11	94	733
Total	1134					10674			77506	20661	3861	427	2074		8006	12952	1549	872	.267	.340	.408	.748				

Runs		Hits		Doubles		Triples		Home Runs		Total Bases	
Palmeiro, R. (Tex)	124	Molitor, P. (Tor)	211	Olerud, J. (Tor)	54	Johnson, L. (Chi)	14	Gonzalez, J. (Tex)	46	Griffey, K. (Sea)	359
Molitor, P. (Tor)	121	Baerga, C. (Cle)	200	White, D. (Tor)	42	Cora, J. (Chi)	13	Griffey, K. (Sea)	45	Gonzalez, J. (Tex)	339
2 players tied with	116	Olerud, J. (Tor)	200	2 players tied with	40	Hulse, D. (Tex)	10	Thomas, F. (Chi)	41	Thomas, F. (Chi)	333

Runs Batted In		Bases On Balls		Stolen Bases		Batting Average		On-Base Percentage		Slugging Average	
Belle, A. (Cle)	129	Phillips, T. (Det)	132	Lofton, K. (Cle)	70	Olerud, J. (Tor)	.363	Olerud, J. (Tor)	.478	Gonzalez, J. (Tex)	.632
Thomas, F. (Chi)	128	Henderson, R. (Oak,Tor)	120	Alomar, R. (Tor)	55	Molitor, P. (Tor)	.332	Phillips, T. (Det)	.446	Griffey, K. (Sea)	.617
Carter, J. (Tor)	121	Olerud, J. (Tor)	114	Polonia, L. (Cal)	55	Alomar, R. (Tor)	.326	Henderson, R. (Oak,Tor)	.435	Thomas, F. (Chi)	.607

Adjusted OPS		Adjusted Batting Runs		Runs Created/Game		Fielding Runs		Win Shares – Batters		TPW – Batters	
Olerud, J. (Tor)	186	Olerud, J. (Tor)	74.0	Olerud, J. (Tor)	11.70	Fletcher, S. (Bos)	19.1	Olerud, J. (Tor)	37	Olerud, J. (Tor)	6.3
Thomas, F. (Chi)	180	Thomas, F. (Chi)	67.0	Thomas, F. (Chi)	10.10	Boggs, W. (NY)	15.8	Thomas, F. (Chi)	32	Griffey, K. (Sea)	5.6
Griffey, K. (Sea)	170	Griffey, K. (Sea)	59.0	Hoiles, C. (Bal)	9.30	Vizquel, O. (Sea)	15.1	2 players tied with	31	Alomar, R. (Tor)	5.3

TEAM	CG	SH	SV	IP	H	H/G	ER	HR	BB	SO	OAV	RAT	ERA	ERA+	CERA	PR+	PF	FA	E	DP	FR	BW	PW	FW	TPW	DIF
East																										
TOR	11	11	50	1441[1]	1441	9.0	674	134	620	1023	.261	1.430	4.21	103	4.22	25.6	100	.982	107	144	-10.5	9.8	2.5	-1.0	11.3	2.7
NY	11	13	38	1438[1]	1467	9.2	695	170	552	899	.266	1.404	4.35	95	4.33	-34.7	96	.983	105	166	0.0	11.7	-3.4	.0	8.3	-1.3
BAL	21	10	42	1442[2]	1427	8.9	691	153	579	900	.261	1.390	4.31	104	4.21	3.2	103	.984	100	171	20.3	.1	.3	2.0	2.4	1.6
DET	11	7	36	1436[2]	1547	9.7	742	188	542	828	.276	1.454	4.65	92	4.71	-64.6	99	.979	132	148	-1.9	12.4	-.2	-6.2	6.0	-2.0
BOS	9	11	44	1452[1]	1379	8.6	608	127	552	997	.252	1.330	3.77	122	3.68	120.1	107	.980	122	155	10.5	-7.9	11.7	1.0	4.8	-5.8
CLE	7	8	45	1445[2]	1591	9.9	735	182	591	888	.281	1.509	4.58	94	4.98	-43.2	100	.976	148	174	2.7	1.0	-4.2	.3	-2.9	-2.1
MIL	26	6	29	1447	1511	9.4	715	153	522	810	.271	1.405	4.45	96	4.35	-24.7	98	.979	131	148	-10.2	-7.3	-2.4	-1.0	-10.7	-1.3
West																										
CHI	16	11	48	1454	1398	8.6	598	125	566	974	.255	1.351	3.70	113	3.87	71.0	97	.982	112	153	3.0	3.0	6.9	.3	10.1	2.9
TEX	20	6	45	1438[1]	1476	9.2	684	144	562	957	.267	1.417	4.28	104	4.32	6.4	96	.979	132	145	-27.2	4.3	.6	-2.6	2.3	2.7
KC	16	6	48	1445[1]	1379	8.6	649	105	571	985	.254	1.349	4.04	113	3.79	77.2	106	.984	97	150	9.5	-11.3	7.5	.9	-2.9	5.9
SEA	22	10	41	1453[2]	1421	8.8	678	135	605	1083	.259	1.394	4.20	105	4.20	25.4	102	.985	90	173	6.8	-8.6	.6	1.6	-6.4	-3.6
CAL	26	6	41	1430[1]	1482	9.3	690	153	550	843	.270	1.421	4.34	104	4.47	6.5	104	.980	120	161	16.7	-7.6	-4.6	-1.3	-13.4	3.4
MIN	5	3	44	1444[1]	1591	9.9	756	148	514	901	.283	1.457	4.71	92	4.66	-47.1	101	.984	100	160	-13.1	-7.6	-4.6	-1.3	-13.4	3.4
OAK	8	2	42	1452[1]	1551	9.6	791	157	680	864	.276	1.536	4.90	83	4.92	-127.2	94	.982	111	161	-6.3	1.1	-12.4	-.6	-11.9	-1.1
Total	209	110	593	20222[1]		9.2	9706					1.418	4.32													

Wins		Win Percentage		Games		Complete Games		Shutouts		Saves	
McDowell, J. (Chi)	22	Guzman, J. (Tor)	.824	Harris, G. (Bos)	80	Finley, C. (Cal)	13	McDowell, J. (Chi)	4	Montgomery, J. (KC)	45
Hentgen, P. (Tor)	19	Key, J. (NY)	.750	Radinsky, S. (Chi)	73	Brown, K. (Tex)	12	3 players tied with	3	Ward, D. (Tor)	45
Johnson, R. (Sea)	19	Fleming, D. (Sea)	.706	3 players tied with	71	2 players tied with	10			Henke, T. (Tex)	40

Innings Pitched		Fewest Hits/Game		Fewest BB/Game		Strikeouts		Ratio		Earned Run Average	
Eldred, C. (Mil)	258	Johnson, R. (Sea)	6.52	Key, J. (NY)	1.64	Johnson, R. (Sea)	308	Darwin, D. (Bos)	1.07	Appier, K. (KC)	2.56
McDowell, J. (Chi)	256[2]	Appier, K. (KC)	6.90	Darwin, D. (Bos)	1.92	Langston, M. (Cal)	196	Appier, K. (KC)	1.11	Alvarez, W. (Chi)	2.95
Langston, M. (Cal)	256[1]	Cone, D. (KC)	7.26	Wells, D. (Det)	2.02	Guzman, J. (Tor)	194	Key, J. (NY)	1.11	Key, J. (NY)	3.00

Adjusted ERA		Component ERA		Opponents' Batting Avg.		Adjusted Pitching Runs		Win Shares – Pitchers		TPW – Pitchers	
Appier, K. (KC)	179	Appier, K. (KC)	2.25	Johnson, R. (Sea)	.203	Appier, K. (KC)	52	Appier, K. (KC)	27	Appier, K. (KC)	5.0
Viola, F. (Bos)	147	Johnson, R. (Sea)	2.73	Appier, K. (KC)	.212	Finley, C. (Cal)	35	Johnson, R. (Sea)	22	Finley, C. (Cal)	3.4
Finley, C. (Cal)	143	Darwin, D. (Bos)	2.82	Cone, D. (KC)	.223	Langston, M. (Cal)	34	3 players tied with	21	Langston, M. (Cal)	3.3

1994 National League

TEAM	G	W	L	PCT	GB	R	OR	EW	AB	H	2B	3B	HR	TB	BB	SO	SB	CS	AVG	OBP	SLG	OPS	OPS+	BR/A	PF	RC
East																										
MON	114	74	40	.649	....	585	454	71	4000	1111	246	30	108	1741	379	669	**137**	36	.278	.346	.435	.781	107	56	101	614
ATL	114	68	46	.596	6	542	**448**	68	3861	1031	198	18	**137**	1676	377	**668**	48	31	.267	.336	.434	.770	103	9	102	547
NY	113	55	58	.487	18.5	506	526	54	3869	966	164	21	117	1523	336	807	25	26	.250	.318	.394	.712	91	-59	99	483
PHI	115	54	61	.470	20.5	521	497	60	3927	1028	208	28	80	1532	396	711	25	26	.262	.334	.390	.724	92	-39	102	513
FLA	115	51	64	.443	23.5	468	576	46	3926	1043	180	24	94	1553	349	746	65	**24**	.266	.332	.396	.727	92	-42	103	518
Central																										
CIN	115	66	48	.579	....	**609**	490	69	3999	**1142**	211	36	124	**1797**	388	738	119	51	**.286**	**.353**	**.449**	**.802**	115	87	99	**632**
HOU	115	66	49	.574	0.5	602	503	68	3955	1099	**252**	25	120	1761	394	718	124	44	.278	.350	.445	.795	**118**	107	95	624
STL	115	53	61	.465	13	535	621	49	3902	1026	213	27	108	1617	**434**	686	76	46	.263	.342	.414	.756	104	**107**	95	624
PIT	114	53	61	.465	13	466	580	45	3864	1001	198	23	80	1485	349	725	53	25	.259	.324	.384	.708	88	-64	101	477
CHI	113	49	64	.434	16.5	500	549	51	3918	1015	189	26	109	1583	364	750	69	53	.259	.326	.404	.730	96	-32	98	507
West																										
LA	114	58	56	.509	....	532	509	60	3904	1055	160	29	115	1618	366	687	74	37	.270	.336	.414	.750	107	37	93	537
SF	115	55	60	.478	3.5	504	500	58	3869	963	159	32	123	1555	364	719	114	40	.249	.320	.402	.722	97	-12	95	503
COL	117	53	64	.453	6.5	573	638	52	4006	1098	206	**39**	125	1757	378	761	91	53	.274	.340	.439	.779	92	-46	116	583
SD	117	47	70	.402	12.5	479	531	52	**4068**	1117	200	19	92	1631	319	762	79	37	.275	.332	.401	.733	99	-9	97	525
Total	**803**					**7422**			55068	14695	2784	377	1532		5193	10147	1141	529	.267	.335	.415	.750				

Runs	
Bagwell, J. (Hou)	104
Grissom, M. (Mon)	96
2 players tied with	89

Hits	
Gwynn, T. (SD)	165
Bagwell, J. (Hou)	147
Bichette, D. (Col)	147

Doubles	
Biggio, C. (Hou)	44
Walker, L. (Mon)	44
2 players tied with	35

Triples	
Butler, B. (LA)	9
Lewis, D. (SF)	9
3 players tied with	8

Home Runs	
Williams, M. (SF)	43
Bagwell, J. (Hou)	39
Bonds, B. (SF)	37

Total Bases	
Bagwell, J. (Hou)	300
Williams, M. (SF)	270
Bichette, D. (Col)	265

Runs Batted In	
Bagwell, J. (Hou)	116
Williams, M. (SF)	96
Bichette, D. (Col)	95

Bases On Balls	
Bonds, B. (SF)	74
Justice, D. (Atl)	69
2 players tied with	68

Stolen Bases	
Biggio, C. (Hou)	39
Sanders, D. (Atl,Cin)	38
Grissom, M. (Mon)	36

Batting Average	
Gwynn, T. (SD)	.394
Bagwell, J. (Hou)	.368
Alou, M. (Mon)	.339

On-Base Percentage	
Bagwell, J. (Hou)	.461
Gwynn, T. (SD)	.458
Mitchell, K. (Cin)	.438

Slugging Average	
Bagwell, J. (Hou)	.750
Mitchell, K. (Cin)	.681
Bonds, B. (SF)	.647

Adjusted OPS	
Bagwell, J. (Hou)	220
Mitchell, K. (Cin)	188
Bonds, B. (SF)	184

Adjusted Batting Runs	
Bagwell, J. (Hou)	73.0
Bonds, B. (SF)	53.0
Gwynn, T. (SD)	46.0

Runs Created/Game	
Bagwell, J. (Hou)	13.20
Bonds, B. (SF)	10.90
Mitchell, K. (Cin)	10.70

Fielding Runs	
Clayton, R. (SF)	14.0
Williams, M. (SF)	12.7
Barberie, B. (Fla)	12.2

Win Shares – Batters	
Bagwell, J. (Hou)	30
Biggio, C. (Hou)	26
Bonds, B. (SF)	25

TPW – Batters	
Bagwell, J. (Hou)	7.4
Bonds, B. (SF)	4.9
Mitchell, K. (Cin)	4.2

TEAM	CG	SH	SV	IP	H	H/G	ER	HR	BB	SO	OAV	RAT	ERA	ERA+	CERA	PR+	PF	FA	E	DP	FR	BW	PW	FW	TPW	DIF
East																										
MON	4	**8**	**46**	1036²	970	8.4	410	100	**288**	805	.247	**1.214**	3.56	119	3.37	77.0	100	.979	94	90	-1.6	5.5	7.6	-.2	**12.9**	4.1
ATL	16	8	26	1026¹	**929**	8.2	**407**	76	378	**865**	**.242**	1.273	3.57	119	**3.32**	87.5	101	.982	81	85	-10.4	.9	**8.6**	-1.0	8.5	2.5
NY	7	3	35	1023	1069	9.4	469	117	332	640	.271	1.370	4.13	101	4.22	3.0	99	.980	89	112	0.0	-5.8	.3	.0	-5.5	4.5
PHI	7	6	30	1024¹	1028	9.0	438	98	377	699	.261	1.372	3.85	112	4.00	57.2	102	.978	94	96	-7.3	-3.8	.3	.0	-5.5	4.5
FLA	5	7	30	1015	1069	9.5	508	120	428	649	.274	1.475	4.50	97	4.71	-28.0	104	.978	95	111	13.2	-4.1	-2.7	1.3	-5.5	-.5
Central																										
CIN	6	6	27	1038¹	1037	9.0	436	117	339	799	.262	1.325	3.78	109	3.98	38.8	98	.983	73	91	2.7	8.6	3.8	.3	12.7	-3.7
HOU	9	6	29	1029²	1043	9.1	454	102	367	739	.265	1.369	3.97	100	4.15	-8.9	94	.983	76	110	7.4	**10.5**	-.9	.7	10.4	-1.4
STL	7	7	29	1018	1154	10.2	581	134	355	632	.289	1.482	5.14	**81**	5.05	-115.7	99	.982	80	119	2.1	2.1	-11.4	.2	-9.0	5.0
PIT	8	2	24	1005²	1094	9.8	518	117	370	650	.281	1.456	4.64	93	4.72	-46.2	102	.980	91	**131**	9.1	-6.3	-4.5	.9	-9.0	5.9
CHI	5	5	27	1023²	1054	9.3	508	120	392	717	.268	1.413	4.47	93	4.40	-41.7	99	.982	81	110	6.8	-3.1	-4.1	.7	-6.5	-.5
West																										
LA	14	5	20	1014	1041	9.2	477	90	354	732	.267	1.376	4.23	93	4.05	-22.7	93	.980	88	104	-5.1	3.6	-2.2	-.5	.9	.1
SF	2	4	33	1025¹	1014	8.9	454	122	372	655	.262	1.352	3.99	101	4.18	-37.4	95	**.985**	68	113	**39.1**	-1.2	-3.7	**3.8**	-1.1	-.9
COL	4	5	28	1031	1185	10.3	590	120	448	703	.292	1.584	5.15	97	5.39	9.4	118	.981	84	117	-31.4	-4.5	.9	-3.1	-6.7	1.7
SD	8	6	27	**1045²**	1008	8.7	474	99	393	862	.252	1.340	4.08	101	3.80	30.1	97	.975	111	82	-26.5	-.9	3.0	-2.6	-.6	-10.4
Total	102	78	411	14356²		9.2	6724					1.385	4.22													

Wins	
Hill, K. (Mon)	16
Maddux, G. (Atl)	16
2 players tied with	14

Win Percentage	
Saberhagen, B. (NY)	.778
Hill, K. (Mon)	.762
2 players tied with	.727

Games	
Reed, S. (Col)	61
Bautista, J. (Chi)	58
Rojas, M. (Mon)	58

Complete Games	
Maddux, G. (Atl)	10
Drabek, D. (Hou)	6
Candiotti, T. (LA)	5

Shutouts	
Maddux, G. (Atl)	3
Martinez, R. (LA)	3
2 players tied with	2

Saves	
Franco, J. (NY)	30
Beck, R. (SF)	28
Jones, D. (Phi)	27

Innings Pitched	
Maddux, G. (Atl)	202
Jackson, D. (Phi)	179¹
Saberhagen, B. (NY)	177¹

Fewest Hits/Game	
Maddux, G. (Atl)	6.68
Martinez, P. (Mon)	7.15
Drabek, D. (Hou)	7.21

Fewest BB/Game	
Saberhagen, B. (NY)	.66
Tewksbury, B. (StL)	1.27
Maddux, G. (Atl)	1.38

Strikeouts	
Benes, A. (SD)	189
Rijo, J. (Cin)	171
Maddux, G. (Atl)	156

Ratio	
Maddux, G. (Atl)	.90
Saberhagen, B. (NY)	1.03
Drabek, D. (Hou)	1.07

Earned Run Average	
Maddux, G. (Atl)	1.56
Saberhagen, B. (NY)	2.74
Drabek, D. (Hou)	2.84

Adjusted ERA	
Maddux, G. (Atl)	272
Saberhagen, B. (NY)	152
Fassero, J. (Mon)	141

Component ERA	
Maddux, G. (Atl)	1.59
Drabek, D. (Hou)	2.52
Saberhagen, B. (NY)	2.56

Opponents' Batting Avg.	
Maddux, G. (Atl)	.207
Martinez, P. (Mon)	.220
Drabek, D. (Hou)	.220

Adjusted Pitching Runs	
Maddux, G. (Atl)	62
Saberhagen, B. (NY)	28
Jackson, D. (Phi)	22

Win Shares – Pitchers	
Maddux, G. (Atl)	26
Saberhagen, B. (NY)	16
Jackson, D. (Phi)	14

TPW – Pitchers	
Maddux, G. (Atl)	6.3
Saberhagen, B. (NY)	2.9
Jackson, D. (Phi)	2.2

1994 American League

TEAM	G	W	L	PCT	GB	R	OR	EW	AB	H	2B	3B	HR	TB	BB	SO	SB	CS	AVG	OBP	SLG	OPS	OPS+	BR/A	PF	RC
East																										
NY	113	70	43	.619	....	670	534	69	3986	1155	238	16	139	1842	**530**	660	55	40	**.290**	**.377**	.462	**.840**	119	119	96	691
BAL	112	63	49	.562	6.5	589	497	65	3856	1047	185	20	139	1689	438	655	69	13	.272	.352	.438	.790	97	-7	105	605
TOR	115	55	60	.478	16	566	579	56	3962	1064	210	30	115	1679	387	691	79	26	.269	.339	.424	.763	95	-28	100	569
BOS	115	54	61	.470	17	552	621	51	3940	1038	222	19	120	1658	404	723	81	38	.263	.337	.421	.757	90	-65	105	557
DET	115	53	62	.461	18	652	671	56	3955	1048	216	25	161	1797	520	897	46	33	.265	.355	.454	.810	106	35	100	644
Central																										
CHI	113	67	46	.593	....	633	498	70	3942	1133	175	**39**	121	1749	497	**568**	77	27	.287	.370	.444	.814	111	75	98	658
CLE	113	66	47	.584	1	**679**	562	67	4022	1165	240	20	167	1946	382	629	131	48	.290	.354	**.484**	.838	113	77	100	685
KC	115	64	51	.557	4	574	532	62	3911	1051	211	38	100	1638	376	698	**140**	62	.269	.338	.419	.757	90	-60	104	557
MIN	113	53	60	.469	14	594	688	48	3952	1092	239	23	103	1686	359	635	94	30	.276	.343	.427	.769	97	-15	100	577
MIL	115	53	62	.461	15	547	586	54	3978	1045	238	21	99	1622	417	680	59	37	.263	.338	.408	.745	87	-82	105	547
West																										
TEX	114	52	62	.456	....	613	697	50	3983	1114	198	27	124	1738	437	730	82	35	.280	.356	.436	.793	103	23	100	621
OAK	114	51	63	.447	1	549	589	53	3885	1009	178	13	113	1552	417	686	91	39	.260	.334	.399	.734	96	-19	92	525
SEA	112	49	63	.438	2	569	616	52	3883	1045	211	18	153	1751	372	652	48	21	.269	.337	.451	.788	99	-13	102	584
CAL	115	47	68	.409	5.5	543	660	46	3943	1042	178	16	120	1612	402	715	65	54	.264	.336	.409	.745	90	-73	101	535
Total	**797**					8330			55198	15048	2939	325	1774		5938	9619	1117	503	.273	.348	.434	.782				

Runs		Hits		Doubles		Triples		Home Runs		Total Bases	
Thomas, F. (Chi)	106	Lofton, K. (Cle)	160	Knoblauch, C. (Min)	45	Johnson, L. (Chi)	14	Griffey, K. (Sea)	40	Belle, A. (Cle)	294
Lofton, K. (Cle)	105	Molitor, P. (Tor)	155	Belle, A. (Cle)	35	Coleman, V. (KC)	12	Thomas, F. (Chi)	38	Griffey, K. (Sea)	292
Griffey, K. (Sea)	94	Belle, A. (Cle)	147	2 players tied with	34	Lofton, K. (Cle)	9	Belle, A. (Cle)	36	Thomas, F. (Chi)	291

Runs Batted In		Bases On Balls		Stolen Bases		Batting Average		On-Base Percentage		Slugging Average	
Puckett, K. (Min)	112	Thomas, F. (Chi)	109	Lofton, K. (Cle)	60	O'Neill, P. (NY)	.359	Thomas, F. (Chi)	.494	Thomas, F. (Chi)	.729
Carter, J. (Tor)	103	Tettleton, M. (Det)	97	Coleman, V. (KC)	50	Belle, A. (Cle)	.357	O'Neill, P. (NY)	.464	Belle, A. (Cle)	.714
2 players tied with	101	Phillips, T. (Det)	95	Nixon, O. (Bos)	42	Thomas, F. (Chi)	.353	Belle, A. (Cle)	.442	Griffey, K. (Sea)	.674

Adjusted OPS		Adjusted Batting Runs		Runs Created/Game		Fielding Runs		Win Shares – Batters		TPW – Batters	
Thomas, F. (Chi)	214	Thomas, F. (Chi)	74.0	Thomas, F. (Chi)	13.90	Valentin, J. (Mil)	17.9	Thomas, F. (Chi)	25	Thomas, F. (Chi)	5.5
Belle, A. (Cle)	191	Belle, A. (Cle)	56.0	Belle, A. (Cle)	12.60	Reed, J. (Mil)	17.1	Belle, A. (Cle)	24	Belle, A. (Cle)	4.7
O'Neill, P. (NY)	179	O'Neill, P. (NY)	46.0	O'Neill, P. (NY)	10.50	Fielder, C. (Det)	14.4	O'Neill, P. (NY)	23	Griffey, K. (Sea)	4.4

TEAM	CG	SH	SV	IP	H	H/G	ER	HR	BB	SO	OAV	RAT	ERA	ERA+	CERA	PR+	PF	FA	E	DP	FR	BW	PW	FW	TPW	DIF
East																										
NY	8	2	31	1019^2	1045	9.2	491	120	398	656	.267	1.415	4.33	105	4.45	8.7	95	.982	80	122	17.5	**11.0**	.8	1.6	13.4	.6
BAL	13	4	37	997^2	1005	**0.9**	477	131	**351**	666	.263	**.136**	**0.43**	116	4.28	63.6	104	**.986**	**57**	103	13.2	-.7	5.9	1.2	6.4	.6
TOR	13	4	26	1025	1053	9.2	535	127	482	**832**	.266	1.498	4.70	103	4.86	24.9	100	.981	81	105	-11.2	-2.6	2.3	-1.0	-1.3	-.7
BOS	6	3	30	1029^1	1104	9.6	564	120	450	729	.276	1.510	4.93	102	4.94	-1.3	105	.981	81	124	10.2	-6.0	-.1	.9	-5.2	2.2
DET	15	1	20	1018	1139	10.1	609	148	449	560	.282	1.560	5.38	90	5.30	-45.9	101	.981	82	90	-15.6	3.2	-4.2	-1.4	-2.5	-1.5
Central																										
CHI	13	**9**	20	1011^1	**964**	8.6	**444**	115	377	754	**.250**	1.326	3.95	118	**3.85**	82.1	97	.981	79	91	-3.1	6.9	7.6	-.3	**14.2**	-3.2
CLE	**17**	5	21	1018^2	1097	9.7	493	**94**	404	666	.275	1.473	4.36	108	4.64	37.6	98	.980	90	119	-1.0	7.1	3.5	-.1	10.5	-.5
KC	5	6	**38**	1031^2	1018	8.9	485	95	392	717	.260	1.367	4.23	118	3.99	**86.2**	101	.982	80	102	1.1	-5.5	**8.0**	.1	2.5	4.5
MIN	6	4	29	1005	1197	10.7	634	153	388	602	.299	1.577	5.68	86	5.68	-74.2	101	.982	75	99	-17.3	-1.4	-6.9	-1.6	-9.9	6.9
MIL	11	3	23	1036	1071	9.3	532	127	421	577	.269	1.440	4.62	109	4.61	16.6	105	.981	85	130	30.4	-7.6	1.5	**2.8**	-3.2	-.8
West																										
TEX	10	4	26	1023	1176	10.4	619	157	394	683	.288	1.535	5.45	88	5.35	-45.4	100	.976	106	106	-27.4	2.2	-4.2	-2.5	-4.6	-.4
OAK	12	**9**	23	1003^1	979	8.8	537	128	510	732	.257	1.484	4.82	92	4.78	-54.8	92	.979	88	105	11.0	-1.7	-5.1	1.0	-5.8	-.2
SEA	13	7	21	984	1051	9.6	546	109	486	763	.274	1.562	4.99	98	5.09	-2.4	102	.977	95	102	-11.8	-1.2	-.2	-1.1	-2.5	-4.5
CAL	11	4	21	1027	1149	10.1	618	150	436	682	.287	1.543	5.42	90	5.44	-66.2	102	.983	76	110	3.3	-6.8	-6.1	.3	-12.6	2.6
Total	153	65	366	23204		5.8	7584				.904	2.94														

Wins		Win Percentage		Games		Complete Games		Shutouts		Saves	
Key, J. (NY)	17	Bere, J. (Chi)	.857	Wickman, B. (NY)	53	Johnson, R. (Sea)	9	Johnson, R. (Sea)	4	Smith, L. (Bal)	33
Cone, D. (KC)	16	Key, J. (NY)	.810	Mesa, J. (Cle)	51	Finley, C. (Cal)	7	5 players tied with	3	Montgomery, J. (KC)	27
Mussina, M. (Bal)	16	Clark, M. (Cle)	.786	2 players tied with	50	Martinez, D. (Cle)	7			Aguilera, R. (Min)	23

Innings Pitched		Fewest Hits/Game		Fewest BB/Game		Strikeouts		Ratio		Earned Run Average	
Finley, C. (Cal)	183^1	Clemens, R. (Bos)	6.54	Gubicza, M. (KC)	1.80	Johnson, R. (Sea)	204	Ontiveros, S. (Oak)	1.03	Ontiveros, S. (Oak)	2.65
McDowell, J. (Chi)	181	Cone, D. (KC)	6.82	Gullickson, B. (Det)	1.95	Clemens, R. (Bos)	168	Cone, D. (KC)	1.07	Clemens, R. (Bos)	2.85
Eldred, C. (Mil)	179	Johnson, R. (Sea)	6.91	Wegman, B. (Mil)	2.02	Finley, C. (Cal)	148	Clemens, R. (Bos)	1.14	Cone, D. (KC)	2.94

Adjusted ERA		Component ERA		Opponents' Batting Avg.		Adjusted Pitching Runs		Win Shares – Pitchers		TPW – Pitchers	
Clemens, R. (Bos)	176	Ontiveros, S. (Oak)	2.35	Clemens, R. (Bos)	.203	Clemens, R. (Bos)	40	Cone, D. (KC)	20	Clemens, R. (Bos)	3.7
Cone, D. (KC)	170	Cone, D. (KC)	2.57	Cone, D. (KC)	.209	Cone, D. (KC)	39	Mussina, M. (Bal)	18	Cone, D. (KC)	3.6
Ontiveros, S. (Oak)	167	Clemens, R. (Bos)	2.72	Johnson, R. (Sea)	.216	Mussina, M. (Bal)	36	Clemens, R. (Bos)	16	Mussina, M. (Bal)	3.3

1995 National League

TEAM	G	W	L	PCT	GB	R	OR	EW	AB	H	2B	3B	HR	TB	BB	SO	SB	CS	AVG	OBP	SLG	OPS	OPS+	BR/A	PF	RC
East																										
ATL	144	90	54	.625	....	645	**540**	85	4814	1202	210	27	168	1970	520	933	73	43	.250	.328	.409	.737	96	-36	103	646
NY	144	69	75	.479	21	657	618	76	4958	1323	218	34	125	1984	446	994	58	39	.267	.333	.400	.733	101	-2	97	655
PHI	144	69	75	.479	21	615	658	67	4950	1296	263	30	94	1901	497	884	72	**25**	.262	.335	.384	.719	94	-36	101	647
FLA	143	67	76	.469	22.5	673	673	72	4886	1278	214	29	144	1982	517	916	131	53	.262	.338	.406	.744	101	9	100	679
MON	144	66	78	.458	24	621	638	70	4905	1268	265	24	118	1935	400	901	120	49	.259	.322	.394	.716	90	-70	103	618
Central																										
CIN	144	85	59	.590	....	747	623	85	4903	1326	**277**	35	161	2156	519	946	**190**	68	.270	.345	.440	.785	**112**	89	99	756
HOU	144	76	68	.528	9	747	674	79	**5097**	1403	260	22	109	2034	**566**	992	176	60	.275	**.356**	.399	.755	**112**	107	93	743
CHI	144	73	71	.507	12	693	671	74	4963	1315	267	39	158	2134	440	953	105	37	.265	.329	.430	.759	106	**107**	93	697
STL	143	62	81	.434	22.5	563	658	70	4779	1182	238	24	107	1789	436	920	79	46	.247	.316	.374	.691	87	-95	100	560
PIT	144	58	86	.403	27	629	736	61	4937	1281	245	27	125	1955	456	972	84	55	.259	.325	.396	.721	93	-61	102	633
West																										
LA	144	78	66	.542	....	634	609	75	4942	1303	191	31	140	1976	468	1023	127	45	.264	.331	.400	.731	107	49	91	660
COL	144	77	67	.535	1	**785**	783	72	4994	1406	259	**43**	**200**	2351	484	943	125	59	**.282**	.352	**.471**	**.822**	94	-39	129	**815**
SD	144	70	74	.486	8	668	672	72	4950	1345	231	20	116	1964	447	872	124	46	.272	.336	.397	.733	102	20	96	655
SF	144	67	77	.465	11	652	776	60	4971	1256	229	33	152	2007	472	1060	138	46	.253	.325	.404	.728	99	-1	97	662
Total	1007					9329			69049	18184	3367	418	1917		6668	13309	1602	671	.263	.334	.408	.741				

Runs		Hits		Doubles		Triples		Home Runs		Total Bases	
Biggio, C. (Hou)	123	Bichette, D. (Col)	197	Grace, M. (Chi)	51	Butler, B. (NY,LA)	9	Bichette, D. (Col)	40	Bichette, D. (Col)	359
Bonds, B. (SF)	109	Gwynn, T. (SD)	197	Bichette, D. (Col)	38	Young, E. (Col)	9	Sosa, S. (Chi)	36	Walker, L. (Col)	300
Finley, S. (SD)	104	Grace, M. (Chi)	180	McRae, B. (Chi)	38	3 players tied with	8	Walker, L. (Col)	36	Castilla, V. (Col)	297

Runs Batted In		Bases On Balls		Stolen Bases		Batting Average		On-Base Percentage		Slugging Average	
Bichette, D. (Col)	128	Bonds, B. (SF)	120	Veras, Q. (Fla)	56	Gwynn, T. (SD)	.368	Bonds, B. (SF)	.434	Bichette, D. (Col)	.620
Sosa, S. (Chi)	119	Weiss, W. (Col)	98	Larkin, B. (Cin)	51	Piazza, M. (LA)	.346	Biggio, C. (Hou)	.411	Walker, L. (Col)	.607
Galarraga, A. (Col)	106	2 players tied with	80	DeShields, D. (LA)	39	Bichette, D. (Col)	.340	Gwynn, T. (SD)	.408	Piazza, M. (LA)	.606

Adjusted OPS		Adjusted Batting Runs		Runs Created/Game		Fielding Runs		Win Shares – Batters		TPW – Batters	
Piazza, M. (LA)	177	Bonds, B. (SF)	59.0	Piazza, M. (LA)	9.40	Clayton, R. (SF)	16.3	Bonds, B. (SF)	36	Bonds, B. (SF)	5.4
Bonds, B. (SF)	169	Piazza, M. (LA)	46.0	Bonds, B. (SF)	9.40	Veras, Q. (Fla)	16.2	Larkin, B. (Cin)	30	Piazza, M. (LA)	5.2
Sanders, R. (Cin)	155	Biggio, C. (Hou)	43.0	Sanders, R. (Cin)	8.60	Reed, J. (SD)	16.0	Biggio, C. (Hou)	29	Larkin, B. (Cin)	5.0

TEAM	CG	SH	SV	IP	H	H/G	ER	HR	BB	SO	OAV	RAT	ERA	ERA+	CERA	PR+	PF	FA	E	DP	FR	BW	PW	FW	TPW	DIF
East																										
ATL	**18**	11	34	1291^2	**1184**	8.2	493	107	436	**1087**	.244	**1.254**	3.44	124	3.42	**133.4**	102	.982	100	113	-15.4	-3.5	**13.1**	-1.5	8.1	9.9
NY	9	9	36	1291	1296	9.0	557	133	401	901	.262	1.314	3.88	104	3.86	20.1	97	.979	115	125	4.5	-.2	2.0	.4	2.2	-5.2
PHI	8	8	41	1290^1	1241	8.7	603	134	538	980	.254	1.379	4.21	100	4.15	-7.8	101	.982	97	139	11.0	-3.5	-.8	1.1	-3.2	.2
FLA	12	7	29	1286	1299	9.1	610	139	562	994	.264	1.447	4.27	99	4.49	-11.4	101	.979	115	143	2.3	.9	-1.1	.2	.0	-4.0
MON	7	9	42	1283^2	1286	9.0	586	128	416	950	.262	1.326	4.11	104	3.97	37.7	103	.980	109	119	-11.3	-6.9	3.7	-1.1	-4.3	-1.7
Central																										
CIN	8	10	38	1289^1	1270	8.9	577	131	424	903	.260	1.314	4.03	102	3.87	-18.2	98	**.986**	79	140	30.0	8.8	-1.8	**3.0**	9.9	3.1
HOU	6	8	32	**1320^1**	1357	9.2	595	118	460	1056	.266	1.376	4.06	95	4.07	-0.5	93	.979	121	140	-28.2	**10.6**	.0	-2.8	7.7	-3.7
CHI	6	**12**	**45**	1301	1313	9.1	597	162	518	926	.262	1.407	4.13	99	4.34	-11.7	98	.979	115	115	8.2	3.7	-1.1	.8	3.4	-2.4
STL	4	6	38	1265^2	1290	9.2	575	135	445	842	.268	1.371	4.09	102	4.21	-3.7	100	.980	113	**156**	16.9	-9.3	-.4	1.7	-8.0	-1.0
PIT	11	7	29	1275^1	1407	9.9	666	130	477	871	.283	1.477	4.70	92	4.76	-43.4	103	.978	122	138	-13.9	-6.0	-4.3	-1.4	-11.6	-2.4
West																										
LA	16	11	37	1295	1188	8.3	527	125	462	1060	**.243**	1.274	3.66	104	3.53	16.2	91	.976	130	120	1.6	4.8	1.6	.2	6.5	-.5
COL	1	1	43	1288^1	1443	10.1	711	160	512	891	.286	1.517	4.97	108	5.16	97.6	129	.981	107	146	-37.2	-3.8	9.6	-3.7	2.1	2.9
SD	6	10	35	1284^2	1242	8.7	589	142	512	1047	.255	1.365	4.13	97	4.10	-40.2	96	.980	108	130	19.9	1.9	-3.9	2.0	-.1	-1.9
SF	12	5	34	1293^2	1368	9.5	698	173	505	801	.275	1.448	4.86	84	4.78	-122.8	98	.980	108	142	10.6	-.1	-12.1	1.0	-11.1	6.1
Total	124	114	513	18056		9.1	8384					1.376	4.18													

Wins		Win Percentage		Games		Complete Games		Shutouts		Saves	
Maddux, G. (Atl)	19	Maddux, G. (Atl)	.905	Leskanic, C. (Col)	76	Maddux, G. (Atl)	10	Maddux, G. (Atl)	3	Myers, R. (Chi)	38
Schourek, P. (Cin)	18	Schourek, P. (Cin)	.720	Veres, D. (Hou)	72	Leiter, M. (SF)	7	Nomo, H. (LA)	3	Henke, T. (StL)	36
Martinez, R. (LA)	17	Martinez, R. (LA)	.708	Reed, S. (Col)	71	Valdes, I. (LA)	6	10 players tied with	2	Beck, R. (SF)	33

Innings Pitched		Fewest Hits/Game		Fewest BB/Game		Strikeouts		Ratio		Earned Run Average	
Maddux, G. (Atl)	209^2	Nomo, H. (LA)	5.83	Maddux, G. (Atl)	.99	Nomo, H. (LA)	236	Maddux, G. (Atl)	.81	Maddux, G. (Atl)	1.63
Neagle, D. (Pit)	209^2	Maddux, G. (Atl)	6.31	Reynolds, S. (Hou)	1.76	Smoltz, J. (Atl)	193	Nomo, H. (LA)	1.06	Nomo, H. (LA)	2.54
Martinez, R. (LA)	206^1	Martinez, P. (Mon)	7.30	Neagle, P. (Pit)	1.93	Maddux, G. (Atl)	181	Schourek, P. (Cin)	1.07	Ashby, A. (SD)	2.94

Adjusted ERA		Component ERA		Opponents' Batting Avg.		Adjusted Pitching Runs		Win Shares – Pitchers		TPW – Pitchers	
Maddux, G. (Atl)	261	Maddux, G. (Atl)	1.41	Nomo, H. (LA)	.182	Maddux, G. (Atl)	64	Maddux, G. (Atl)	30	Maddux, G. (Atl)	6.2
Nomo, H. (LA)	149	Nomo, H. (LA)	2.16	Maddux, G. (Atl)	.197	Glavine, T. (Atl)	29	Glavine, T. (Atl)	20	Glavine, T. (Atl)	3.1
Glavine, T. (Atl)	138	Valdes, I. (LA)	2.62	Martinez, P. (Mon)	.227	Ritz, K. (Col)	28	2 players tied with	17	Ritz, K. (Col)	2.8

1995 American League

TEAM	G	W	L	PCT	GB	R	OR	EW	AB	H	2B	3B	HR	TB	BB	SO	SB	CS	AVG	OBP	SLG	OPS	OPS+	BR/A	PF	RC
East																										
BOS	144	86	58	.597	....	791	698	81	4997	1399	**286**	31	175	2272	560	923	99	44	.280	.360	.455	.815	107	52	103	816
NY	145	79	65	.549	7	749	688	78	4947	1365	280	34	122	2079	625	851	50	30	.276	.362	.420	.782	104	33	99	753
BAL	144	71	73	.493	15	704	640	79	4837	1267	229	27	173	2069	574	803	92	45	.262	.345	.428	.773	98	-15	102	715
DET	144	60	84	.417	26	654	844	54	4865	1204	228	29	159	1967	551	987	73	36	.247	.329	.404	.733	90	-76	99	647
TOR	144	56	88	.389	30	642	777	58	5036	1309	275	27	140	2058	492	906	75	**16**	.260	.331	.409	.740	92	-58	99	685
Central																										
CLE	144	100	44	.694	....	**840**	**607**	95	5028	**1461**	279	23	**207**	**2407**	542	**766**	132	53	**.291**	**.364**	**.479**	**.842**	115	**114**	101	**867**
KC	144	70	74	.486	30	629	691	65	4903	1275	240	35	119	1942	475	849	120	53	.260	.331	.396	.727	87	-97	101	645
CHI	145	68	76	.472	32	755	758	72	**5060**	1417	252	37	146	2181	576	767	110	39	.280	.357	.431	.788	109	75	95	792
MIL	144	65	79	.451	35	740	747	71	5000	1329	249	**42**	128	2046	502	800	105	40	.266	.338	.409	.748	88	-84	106	700
MIN	144	56	88	.389	44	703	889	55	5005	1398	270	34	120	2096	471	916	105	57	.279	.348	.419	.767	98	-18	100	708
West																										
SEA	145	79	66	.545	....	796	708	81	4996	1377	276	20	182	2239	549	871	110	41	.276	.352	.448	.800	105	42	101	793
CAL	145	78	67	.538	1	801	697	83	5019	1390	252	25	186	2250	564	889	58	39	.277	.354	.448	.802	108	53	99	794
TEX	144	74	70	.514	4.5	691	720	69	4913	1304	247	24	138	2013	526	877	90	47	.265	.340	.410	.750	92	-62	102	686
OAK	144	67	77	.465	11.5	730	761	69	4916	1296	228	18	169	2067	565	911	112	46	.264	.345	.420	.765	104	35	94	723
Total	1010					10225			69522	18791	3591	406	2164		7572	12116	1331	586	.270	.347	.427	.774				

Runs
Belle, A. (Cle)	121
Martinez, E. (Sea)	121
Edmonds, J. (Cal)	120

Hits
Johnson, L. (Chi)	186
Martinez, E. (Sea)	182
Knoblauch, C. (Min)	179

Doubles
Belle, A. (Cle)	52
Martinez, E. (Sea)	52
Puckett, K. (Min)	39

Triples
Lofton, K. (Cle)	13
Johnson, L. (Chi)	12
Anderson, B. (Bal)	10

Home Runs
Belle, A. (Cle)	50
Buhner, J. (Sea)	40
Thomas, F. (Chi)	40

Total Bases
Belle, A. (Cle)	377
Palmeiro, R. (Bal)	323
Martinez, E. (Sea)	321

Runs Batted In
Belle, A. (Cle)	126
Vaughn, M. (Bos)	126
Buhner, J. (Sea)	121

Bases On Balls
Thomas, F. (Chi)	136
Martinez, E. (Sea)	116
Phillips, T. (Cal)	113

Stolen Bases
Lofton, K. (Cle)	54
Goodwin, T. (KC)	50
Nixon, O. (Tex)	50

Batting Average
Martinez, E. (Sea)	.356
Knoblauch, C. (Min)	.333
Salmon, T. (Cal)	.330

On-Base Percentage
Martinez, E. (Sea)	.482
Thomas, F. (Chi)	.463
Thome, J. (Cle)	.440

Slugging Average
Belle, A. (Cle)	.690
Martinez, E. (Sea)	.628
Thomas, F. (Chi)	.606

Adjusted OPS
Martinez, E. (Sea)	184
Thomas, F. (Chi)	184
Belle, A. (Cle)	175

Adjusted Batting Runs
Martinez, E. (Sea)	71.0
Thomas, F. (Chi)	70.0
Belle, A. (Cle)	59.0

Runs Created/Game
Martinez, E. (Sea)	12.50
Thomas, F. (Chi)	10.60
Salmon, T. (Cal)	10.10

Fielding Runs
Fryman, T. (Det)	20.7
Gates, B. (Oak)	11.3
Palmeiro, R. (Bal)	10.4

Win Shares – Batters
Martinez, E. (Sea)	32
Belle, A. (Cle)	30
2 players tied with	29

TPW – Batters
Martinez, E. (Sea)	5.7
Belle, A. (Cle)	5.5
Thomas, F. (Chi)	4.5

TEAM	CG	SH	SV	IP	H	H/G	ER	HR	BB	SO	OAV	RAT	ERA	ERA+	CERA	PR+	PF	FA	E	DP	FR	BW	PW	FW	TPW	DIF
East																										
BOS	7	9	39	1292²	1338	9.3	630	**127**	476	888	.268	1.403	4.39	111	4.32	59.4	103	.978	120	151	5.3	4.9	5.6	.5	10.9	3.1
NY	18	5	35	1284²	1286	9.0	651	159	535	908	.261	1.417	4.56	101	4.45	0.4	98	.986	74	141	7.5	3.1	.0	.7	3.9	3.1
BAL	**19**	**10**	29	1267	**1165**	**8.3**	607	149	523	930	**.245**	1.332	4.31	110	3.95	45.3	101	**.986**	**72**	141	16.6	-7.1	-8.1	-1.7	-17.0	5.0
DET	5	3	38	1275	1509	10.6	778	170	536	729	.296	1.604	5.49	87	5.60	-86.6	101	.981	106	143	-18.5	-5.5	-2.6	.2	-7.8	-8.2
TOR	16	8	22	1292²	1336	9.3	701	145	654	894	.267	1.539	4.88	96	4.97	-27.4	100	.982	97	131	2.2	-5.5	-2.6	.2	-7.8	-8.2
Central																										
CLE	10	**10**	**50**	1301	1261	8.7	**554**	135	**445**	926	.255	**1.311**	**3.83**	123	**3.89**	129.1	100	.982	101	142	-4.4	**10.7**	**12.1**	-.4	**22.4**	5.6
KC	11	**10**	37	1288	1323	9.2	643	142	503	763	.268	1.418	4.49	106	4.40	25.6	102	.984	90	168	17.0	-9.1	2.4	1.6	-5.1	3.1
CHI	12	4	36	1284²	1374	9.6	692	164	617	892	.275	1.550	4.85	92	5.18	-40.6	95	.980	108	131	-16.6	7.1	-3.8	-1.6	1.7	-5.7
MIL	7	4	31	1286	1391	9.7	689	146	603	699	.280	1.551	4.82	103	5.12	-1.9	106	.981	105	**186**	24.9	-7.9	-.2	**2.3**	-5.7	-1.3
MIN	7	2	27	1272²	1450	10.2	814	210	533	790	.287	1.558	5.76	83	5.59	-139.0	101	.981	100	141	-2.4	-1.7	-13.0	-.2	-14.9	-1.1
West																										
SEA	9	8	39	1289¹	1343	9.4	644	149	591	**1068**	.268	1.500	4.50	105	4.88	63.6	101	.980	104	108	-32.0	3.9	6.0	-3.0	6.9	.1
CAL	8	9	42	1284¹	1310	9.2	645	163	486	901	.265	1.398	4.52	104	4.45	13.2	100	.982	95	120	10.3	5.0	1.2	1.0	7.2	-1.2
TEX	14	4	34	1285	1385	9.7	665	152	514	838	.278	1.478	4.66	104	4.79	27.4	102	.982	98	156	-4.6	-5.8	2.6	-.4	-3.6	5.6
OAK	8	4	34	1273	1320	9.3	697	153	556	890	.269	1.474	4.93	90	4.77	-69.9	94	.981	102	151	-5.1	3.3	-6.6	-.5	-3.8	-1.2
Total	151	90	493	17976		9.4	9410					1.467	4.71													

Wins
Mussina, M. (Bal)	19
Cone, D. (NY,Tor)	18
Johnson, R. (Sea)	18

Win Percentage
Johnson, R. (Sea)	.900
Hanson, E. (Bos)	.750
2 players tied with	.727

Games
Orosco, J. (Bal)	65
McDowell, R. (Tex)	64
3 players tied with	63

Complete Games
McDowell, J. (NY)	8
Erickson, S. (Bal,Min)	7
Mussina, M. (Bal)	7

Shutouts
Mussina, M. (Bal)	4
Johnson, R. (Sea)	3
6 players tied with	2

Saves
Mesa, J. (Cle)	46
Smith, L. (Cal)	37
2 players tied with	32

Innings Pitched
Cone, D. (Tor,NY)	229¹
Mussina, M. (Bal)	221²
McDowell, J. (NY)	217²

Fewest Hits/Game
Johnson, R. (Sea)	6.68
Appier, K. (KC)	7.29
Wakefield, T. (Bos)	7.51

Fewest BB/Game
Mussina, M. (Bal)	2.03
Martinez, D. (Cle)	2.21
Radke, B. (Min)	2.34

Strikeouts
Johnson, R. (Sea)	294
Stottlemyre, T. (Oak)	205
Finley, C. (Cal)	195

Ratio
Johnson, R. (Sea)	1.05
Mussina, M. (Bal)	1.07
Martinez, D. (Cle)	1.18

Earned Run Average
Johnson, R. (Sea)	2.48
Wakefield, T. (Bos)	2.95
Martinez, D. (Cle)	3.08

Adjusted ERA
Johnson, R. (Sea)	191
Wakefield, T. (Bos)	165
Martinez, D. (Cle)	152

Component ERA
Johnson, R. (Sea)	2.18
Mussina, M. (Bal)	2.66
Appier, K. (KC)	3.01

Opponents' Batting Avg.
Johnson, R. (Sea)	.201
Appier, K. (KC)	.221
Mussina, M. (Bal)	.226

Adjusted Pitching Runs
Johnson, R. (Sea)	59
Wakefield, T. (Bos)	41
Rogers, K. (Tex)	34

Win Shares – Pitchers
Johnson, R. (Sea)	22
Rogers, K. (Tex)	21
Mussina, M. (Bal)	20

TPW – Pitchers
Johnson, R. (Sea)	5.5
Wakefield, T. (Bos)	3.8
Rogers, K. (Tex)	3.2

1996 National League

TEAM	G	W	L	PCT	GB	R	OR	EW	AB	H	2B	3B	HR	TB	BB	SO	SB	CS	AVG	OBP	SLG	OPS	OPS+	BR/A	PF	RC
East																										
ATL	162	96	66	.593	....	773	**648**	95	5614	1514	264	28	197	2425	530	1032	83	43	.270	.336	.432	.768	101	0	106	797
MON	162	88	74	.543	8	741	668	89	5505	1441	297	27	148	2236	492	1077	108	**34**	.262	.329	.406	.735	96	-29	102	738
FLA	162	80	82	.494	16	688	703	79	5498	1413	240	30	150	2163	553	1122	99	46	.257	.331	.393	.724	99	-8	97	711
NY	162	71	91	.438	25	746	779	77	5618	1515	267	**47**	147	2317	445	1069	97	48	.270	.327	.412	.739	104	18	95	747
PHI	162	67	95	.414	29	650	790	65	5499	1405	249	39	132	2128	536	1092	117	41	.256	.327	.387	.714	92	-57	101	702
Central																										
STL	162	88	74	.543	....	759	706	87	5502	1468	281	31	142	2237	495	1089	149	58	.267	.332	.407	.739	100	4	99	741
HOU	162	82	80	.506	6	753	792	77	5508	1445	297	29	129	2187	554	1057	180	63	.262	.339	.397	.736	**108**	70	92	756
CIN	162	81	81	.500	7	778	773	82	5455	1398	259	36	191	2302	604	1134	171	63	.256	.334	.422	.756	105	41	99	778
CHI	162	76	86	.469	12	772	771	81	5531	1388	267	19	175	2218	523	1090	108	50	.251	.322	.401	.723	93	41	99	778
PIT	162	73	89	.451	15	776	833	75	**5665**	1509	**319**	33	138	2308	510	**989**	126	49	.266	.331	.407	.739	97	-26	103	769
West																										
SD	162	91	71	.562	....	771	682	91	5655	1499	285	24	147	2273	601	1014	109	55	.265	.341	.402	.743	107	58	94	770
LA	162	90	72	.556	1	703	652	87	5538	1396	215	33	150	2127	516	1190	124	40	.252	.318	.384	.702	98	-18	92	682
COL	162	83	79	.512	8	**961**	964	81	5590	**1607**	297	37	**221**	**2641**	527	1108	**201**	66	**.287**	**.357**	**.472**	**.830**	100	11	124	950
SF	162	68	94	.420	23	752	862	70	5533	1400	245	21	153	2146	**615**	1189	113	53	.253	.333	.388	.721	99	-3	96	728
Total	**1134**					**10623**			**77711**	**20398**	**3782**	**434**	**2220**		**7501**	**15252**	**1785**	**709**	**.262**	**.333**	**.408**	**.741**				

Runs
Burks, E. (Col) 142
Finley, S. (SD) 126
Bonds, B. (SF) 122

Hits
Johnson, L. (NY) 227
Burks, E. (Col) 211
Grissom, M. (Atl) 207

Doubles
Bagwell, J. (Hou) 48
Burks, E. (Col) 45
Finley, S. (SD) 45

Triples
Johnson, L. (NY) 21
Grissom, M. (Atl) 10
Howard, T. (Cin) 10

Home Runs
Galarraga, A. (Col) 47
Bonds, B. (SF) 42
Sheffield, G. (Fla) 42

Total Bases
Burks, E. (Col) 392
Galarraga, A. (Col) 376
Finley, S. (SD) 348

Runs Batted In
Galarraga, A. (Col) 150
Bichette, D. (Col) 141
Caminiti, K. (SD) 130

Bases On Balls
Bonds, B. (SF) 151
Sheffield, G. (Fla) 142
Bagwell, J. (Hou) 135

Stolen Bases
Young, E. (Col) 53
Johnson, L. (NY) 50
DeShields, D. (LA) 48

Batting Average
Gwynn, T. (SD) .... .353
Burks, E. (Col) .... .344
Piazza, M. (LA) .... .336

On-Base Percentage
Sheffield, G. (Fla) .... .469
Bonds, B. (SF) .... .465
Bagwell, J. (Hou) .... .454

Slugging Average
Burks, E. (Col) .... .639
Sheffield, G. (Fla) .... .624
Caminiti, K. (SD) .... .621

Adjusted OPS
Sheffield, G. (Fla) 192
Bonds, B. (SF) 190
Bagwell, J. (Hou) 182

Adjusted Batting Runs
Bonds, B. (SF) 83.0
Sheffield, G. (Fla) 78.0
Bagwell, J. (Hou) 78.0

Runs Created/Game
Bonds, B. (SF) 11.50
Sheffield, G. (Fla) 11.10
Bagwell, J. (Hou) 10.10

Fielding Runs
Gagne, G. (LA) 17.5
Clayton, R. (StL) 16.6
Sanchez, R. (Chi) 16.3

Win Shares – Batters
Bagwell, J. (Hou) 41
Bonds, B. (SF) 39
Caminiti, K. (SD) 38

TPW – Batters
Bonds, B. (SF) 7.5
Caminiti, K. (SD) 7.5
Bagwell, J. (Hou) 6.5

TEAM	CG	SH	SV	IP	H	H/G	ER	HR	BB	SO	OAV	RAT	ERA	ERA+	CERA	PR+	PF	FA	E	DP	FR	BW	PW	FW	TPW	DIF
East																										
ATL	**14**	9	46	1469	1372	**8.4**	578	120	**451**	1245	.247	**1.241**	3.54	124	**3.27**	162.1	104	.980	130	143	-19.6	.0	**15.8**	-1.9	**13.9**	1.1
MON	11	7	43	1441¹	**1353**	8.4	605	152	482	1206	.247	1.273	3.78	114	3.65	93.7	102	.980	126	121	-6.0	-2.8	9.2	-.6	5.8	1.2
FLA	8	**13**	41	1443	1386	8.6	633	**113**	598	1050	.256	1.375	3.95	103	3.99	-3.3	96	.982	111	**187**	22.8	-.8	-.3	2.2	1.1	-2.1
NY	10	10	41	1440	1517	9.5	675	159	532	999	.272	1.423	4.22	95	4.36	-46.3	95	.974	159	163	14.2	1.8	-4.5	1.4	-1.4	-8.6
PHI	12	6	42	1423¹	1463	9.2	710	160	510	1044	.267	1.386	4.49	96	4.28	-35.3	102	.981	116	145	8.7	-5.6	-3.5	.8	-8.2	-5.8
Central																										
STL	13	11	43	1452¹	1380	8.6	642	173	539	1050	.251	1.321	3.98	105	3.91	0.9	99	.980	125	139	**33.5**	.3	.1	**3.3**	3.7	3.3
HOU	13	4	35	1447	1541	9.6	704	154	539	1163	.274	1.437	4.38	88	4.54	-56.4	92	.978	138	130	-24.8	**6.9**	-5.5	-2.4	-1.1	2.1
CIN	6	8	**52**	1443	1447	9.0	694	167	591	1089	.263	1.412	4.33	90	4.34	-40.8	98	.980	121	145	12.6	4.0	-4.0	1.2	1.2	-1.2
CHI	10	10	34	1456¹	1447	8.9	705	184	546	1027	.260	1.369	4.36	100	4.25	-21.7	103	**.983**	104	147	18.7	-6.0	-2.1	1.8	-6.3	1.3
PIT	5	7	37	1453¹	1602	9.9	750	183	479	1044	.281	1.432	4.64	94	4.70	-25.0	103	.980	128	144	-19.1	-2.6	-2.4	-1.9	-6.9	-1.1
West																										
SD	5	11	47	**1489**	1395	8.4	617	138	506	1194	.248	1.277	3.73	106	3.53	46.3	94	.981	118	136	-8.1	5.6	4.5	-.8	9.4	.6
LA	6	9	50	1466¹	1378	8.5	**567**	125	534	1212	.249	1.304	**3.48**	111	3.56	75.8	91	.980	125	133	-13.3	-1.7	7.4	-1.3	4.4	4.6
COL	5	4	34	1422²	1597	10.1	885	198	624	932	.285	1.561	5.60	93	5.48	-27.3	124	.977	149	167	-31.5	1.1	-2.7	-3.1	-4.7	6.7
SF	9	8	35	1442¹	1520	9.5	756	194	570	997	.273	1.449	4.72	87	4.78	-111.2	97	.978	136	165	10.4	-.3	-10.9	1.0	-10.1	-2.9
Total	**127**	**117**	**580**	**20289**		**9.0**	**9521**					**1.375**	**4.22**													

Wins
Smoltz, J. (Atl) 24
Benes, A. (StL) 18
2 players tied with 17

Win Percentage
Smoltz, J. (Atl) .... .750
Martinez, R. (LA) .... .714
Valdes, I. (LA) .... .682

Games
Clontz, B. (Atl) 81
Patterson, B. (Chi) 79
2 players tied with 78

Complete Games
Schilling, C. (Phi) 8
Smoltz, J. (Atl) 6
4 players tied with 5

Shutouts
Brown, K. (Fla) 3
7 players tied with 2

Saves
Brantley, J. (Cin) 44
Worrell, T. (LA) 44
Hoffman, T. (SD) 42

Innings Pitched
Smoltz, J. (Atl) 253²
Maddux, G. (Atl) 245
Reynolds, S. (Hou) 239

Fewest Hits/Game
Leiter, A. (Fla) 6.39
Smoltz, J. (Atl) 7.06
Nomo, H. (LA) 7.09

Fewest BB/Game
Maddux, G. (Atl) 1.03
Brown, K. (Fla) 1.27
Darwin, D. (Pit,Hou) 1.48

Strikeouts
Smoltz, J. (Atl) 276
Nomo, H. (LA) 234
2 players tied with 222

Ratio
Brown, K. (Fla) .... .94
Smoltz, J. (Atl) 1.00
Maddux, G. (Atl) 1.03

Earned Run Average
Brown, K. (Fla) 1.89
Maddux, G. (Atl) 2.72
Leiter, A. (Fla) 2.93

Adjusted ERA
Brown, K. (Fla) 215
Maddux, G. (Atl) 162
Smoltz, J. (Atl) 150

Component ERA
Brown, K. (Fla) 2.00
Smoltz, J. (Atl) 2.17
Maddux, G. (Atl) 2.22

Opponents' Batting Avg.
Leiter, A. (Fla) .... .202
Smoltz, J. (Atl) .... .216
Nomo, H. (LA) .... .218

Adjusted Pitching Runs
Brown, K. (Fla) 53
Maddux, G. (Atl) 49
Smoltz, J. (Atl) 45

Win Shares – Pitchers
Smoltz, J. (Atl) 27
Brown, K. (Fla) 26
Maddux, G. (Atl) 23

TPW – Pitchers
Brown, K. (Fla) 5.1
Maddux, G. (Atl) 4.8
Smoltz, J. (Atl) 4.7

1996 American League

TEAM	G	W	L	PCT	GB	R	OR	EW	AB	H	2B	3B	HR	TB	BB	SO	SB	CS	AVG	OBP	SLG	OPS	OPS+	BR/A	PF	RC
East																										
NY	162	92	70	.568	....	871	787	89	5628	1621	293	28	162	2456	632	909	96	46	.288	.364	.436	.800	101	16	100	888
BAL	163	88	74	.543	4	949	903	85	5689	1557	299	29	**257**	2685	645	915	76	40	.274	.354	.472	.826	107	52	99	946
BOS	162	85	77	.525	7	928	921	82	**5756**	1631	308	31	209	2628	642	1020	91	44	.283	.362	.457	.819	103	28	102	947
TOR	162	74	88	.457	18	766	809	77	5599	1451	302	35	177	2354	529	1105	116	38	.259	.333	.420	.754	89	-92	99	792
DET	162	53	109	.327	39	783	1103	54	5530	1413	257	21	204	2324	546	1268	87	50	.256	.326	.420	.746	87	-127	100	745
Central																										
CLE	161	99	62	.615	....	952	**769**	97	5681	**1665**	335	23	218	2700	671	**844**	160	50	**.293**	**.372**	.475	.847	**113**	127	99	1002
CHI	162	85	77	.525	14.5	898	794	91	5644	1586	284	33	195	2521	**701**	927	105	41	.281	.364	.447	.811	109	85	95	924
MIL	162	80	82	.494	19.5	894	899	81	5662	1578	304	40	178	2496	624	986	101	48	.279	.356	.441	.797	96	-33	104	898
MIN	162	78	84	.481	21.5	877	900	79	5673	1633	332	**47**	118	2413	576	958	143	53	.288	.360	.425	.786	96	-23	101	858
KC	161	75	86	.466	24	746	786	76	5542	1477	286	38	123	2208	529	943	**195**	85	.267	.335	.398	.734	85	-130	100	748
West																										
TEX	163	90	72	.556	....	928	799	93	5702	1622	323	32	221	2672	660	1041	83	**26**	.284	.362	.469	.830	102	26	105	974
SEA	161	85	76	.528	4.5	**993**	895	89	5668	1625	**343**	19	245	**2741**	670	1052	90	39	.287	.370	**.484**	.853	113	119	100	1023
OAK	162	78	84	.481	12	861	900	77	5630	1492	283	21	243	2546	640	1114	58	35	.276	.346	.452	.798	102	11	97	879
CAL	161	70	91	.435	19.5	762	943	64	5686	1571	256	24	192	2451	527	974	53	39	.277	.341	.431	.772	95	-54	98	813
Total	**1133**					**12208**			**79090**	**21922**	**4205**	**421**	**2742**		**8592**	**14056**	**1454**	**634**	**.277**	**.353**	**.445**	**.798**				

Runs		Hits		Doubles		Triples		Home Runs		Total Bases	
Rodriguez, A. (Sea)	141	Molitor, P. (Min)	225	Rodriguez, A. (Sea)	54	Knoblauch, C. (Min)	14	McGwire, M. (Oak)	52	Rodriguez, A. (Sea)	379
Knoblauch, C. (Min)	140	Rodriguez, A. (Sea)	215	Martinez, E. (Sea)	52	Vina, F. (Mil)	10	Anderson, B. (Bal)	50	Belle, A. (Cle)	375
2 players tied with	132	Lofton, K. (Cle)	210	Rodriguez, I. (Tex)	47	4 players tied with	8	Griffey, K. (Sea)	49	Vaughn, M. (Bos)	370

Runs Batted In		Bases On Balls		Stolen Bases		Batting Average		On-Base Percentage		Slugging Average	
Belle, A. (Cle)	148	Phillips, T. (Chi)	125	Lofton, K. (Cle)	75	Rodriguez, A. (Sea)	.358	McGwire, M. (Oak)	.468	McGwire, M. (Oak)	.730
Gonzalez, J. (Tex)	144	Martinez, E. (Sea)	123	Goodwin, T. (KC)	66	Thomas, F. (Chi)	.349	Martinez, E. (Sea)	.467	Gonzalez, J. (Tex)	.643
Vaughn, M. (Bos)	143	Thome, J. (Cle)	123	Nixon, O. (Tor)	54	Molitor, P. (Min)	.341	Thomas, F. (Chi)	.465	Anderson, B. (Bal)	.637

Adjusted OPS		Adjusted Batting Runs		Runs Created/Game		Fielding Runs		Win Shares – Batters		TPW – Batters	
McGwire, M. (Oak)	202	McGwire, M. (Oak)	72.0	McGwire, M. (Oak)	13.20	Gonzalez, A. (Tor)	30.7	Rodriguez, A. (Sea)	34	Rodriguez, A. (Sea)	6.9
Thomas, F. (Chi)	181	Thomas, F. (Chi)	71.0	Martinez, E. (Sea)	10.90	McLemore, M. (Tex)	18.4	Knoblauch, C. (Min)	32	Thomas, F. (Chi)	5.1
Thome, J. (Cle)	166	Martinez, E. (Sea)	58.0	Thome, J. (Cle)	10.80	Vina, F. (Mil)	17.3	2 players tied with	31	Alomar, R. (Bal)	5.1

TEAM	CG	SH	SV	IP	H	H/G	ER	HR	BB	SO	OAV	RAT	ERA	ERA+	CERA	PR+	PF	FA	E	DP	FR	BW	PW	FW	TPW	DIF
East																										
NY	6	**9**	52	1440	**1469**	9.2	744	**143**	610	1139	**.265**	1.444	4.65	106	4.47	73.1	99	.985	91	146	-26.0	1.4	6.7	-2.4	5.7	5.3
BAL	13	1	44	**1468²**	1604	9.8	840	209	597	1047	.280	1.499	5.15	96	5.10	-36.9	99	.984	97	173	0.7	4.8	-3.4	.1	1.5	5.5
BOS	17	5	37	1458	1606	9.9	810	185	722	**1165**	.279	1.597	5.00	102	5.37	45.3	102	.978	135	152	-32.6	2.6	4.1	-3.0	3.7	.3
TOR	**19**	7	35	1445²	1476	9.2	735	187	610	1033	.266	1.443	4.58	109	4.69	37.7	100	.982	110	187	**31.9**	-8.4	3.4	**2.9**	-2.1	-4.9
DET	10	4	22	1432²	1699	10.7	1015	241	784	957	.296	1.733	6.38	**79**	6.56	-178.1	101	.978	137	157	-31.4	-11.6	-16.2	-2.9	-30.6	2.6
Central																										
CLE	13	**9**	46	1452¹	1530	9.5	**702**	173	484	1033	.271	**1.387**	**4.35**	113	**4.36**	92.8	98	.980	124	156	-3.6	**11.6**	8.5	-.3	**19.7**	-.7
CHI	7	4	43	1461	1529	9.4	735	174	616	1039	.270	1.468	4.53	105	4.66	46.0	95	.982	109	145	-10.0	7.8	4.2	-.9	11.0	-7.0
MIL	6	4	42	1447¹	1570	9.8	831	213	635	846	.278	1.523	5.17	100	5.26	-22.0	104	.978	134	180	28.1	-3.0	-2.0	2.6	-2.4	1.4
MIN	13	5	31	1439²	1561	9.8	847	233	581	959	.277	1.488	5.29	97	5.18	-43.1	102	.984	94	142	14.3	-2.1	-3.9	1.3	-4.7	1.7
KC	17	8	35	1450	1563	9.7	733	176	**460**	926	.277	1.395	4.55	110	4.51	74.8	100	.982	111	184	0.2	-11.9	6.8	.0	-5.0	.0
West																										
TEX	**19**	6	43	1449¹	1569	9.7	750	168	582	976	.278	1.484	4.66	113	4.80	92.4	105	**.986**	87	150	3.4	2.4	8.4	.3	11.1	-2.1
SEA	4	4	34	1431²	1562	9.8	828	216	605	1000	.279	1.514	5.21	95	5.25	-46.2	99	.981	110	155	5.3	10.9	-4.2	.5	7.2	-2.2
OAK	7	5	34	1456¹	1638	10.1	841	205	644	884	.287	1.567	5.20	94	5.43	-68.3	98	.984	103	**195**	19.4	1.0	-6.2	1.8	-3.5	.5
CAL	12	8	38	1439	1546	9.7	849	219	662	1052	.275	1.534	5.31	92	5.44	-65.2	98	.980	128	156	-0.7	-4.9	-5.9	-.1	-10.9	.9
Total	**163**	**79**	**536**	**20271²**		**9.7**	**11260**					**1.505**	**5.00**													

Wins		Win Percentage		Games		Complete Games		Shutouts		Saves	
Pettitte, A. (NY)	21	Nagy, C. (Cle)	.773	Guardado, E. (Min)	83	Hentgen, P. (Tor)	10	Hentgen, P. (Tor)	3	Wetteland, J. (NY)	43
Hentgen, P. (Tor)	20	Pettitte, A. (NY)	.724	Myers, M. (Det)	83	Hill, K. (Tex)	7	Hill, K. (Tex)	3	Mesa, J. (Cle)	39
Mussina, M. (Bal)	19	Oliver, D. (Tex)	.700	Stanton, M. (Bos,Tex)	81	Pavlik, R. (Tex)	7	Robertson, R. (Min)	3	Hernandez, R. (Chi)	38

Innings Pitched		Fewest Hits/Game		Fewest BB/Game		Strikeouts		Ratio		Earned Run Average	
Hentgen, P. (Tor)	265²	Guzman, J. (Tor)	7.58	Haney, C. (KC)	2.01	Clemens, R. (Bos)	257	Guzman, J. (Tor)	1.12	Guzman, J. (Tor)	2.93
Fernandez, A. (Chi)	258	Clemens, R. (Bos)	8.01	Wells, D. (Bal)	2.05	Finley, C. (Cal)	215	Fernandez, A. (Chi)	1.24	Hentgen, P. (Tor)	3.22
Hill, K. (Tex)	250²	Hentgen, P. (Tor)	8.06	Radke, B. (Min)	2.21	Appier, K. (KC)	207	Radke, B. (Min)	1.24	Nagy, C. (Cle)	3.41

Adjusted ERA		Component ERA		Opponents' Batting Avg.		Adjusted Pitching Runs		Win Shares – Pitchers		TPW – Pitchers	
Guzman, J. (Tor)	171	Guzman, J. (Tor)	3.00	Guzman, J. (Tor)	.228	Hentgen, P. (Tor)	47	Hentgen, P. (Tor)	24	Hentgen, P. (Tor)	4.3
Hentgen, P. (Tor)	156	Hentgen, P. (Tor)	3.26	Clemens, R. (Bos)	.237	Hill, K. (Tex)	45	Hill, K. (Tex)	22	Clemens, R. (Bos)	4.1
Hill, K. (Tex)	145	Appier, K. (KC)	3.41	Hentgen, P. (Tor)	.241	Clemens, R. (Bos)	44	Nagy, C. (Cle)	21	Hill, K. (Tex)	4.1

1997 National League

TEAM	G	W	L	PCT	GB	R	OR	EW	AB	H	2B	3B	HR	TB	BB	SO	SB	CS	AVG	OBP	SLG	OPS	OPS+	BR/A	PF	RC
East																										
ATL	162	101	61	.623	....	791	**581**	105	5528	1490	268	37	174	2354	597	1160	108	58	.270	.346	.426	.772	105	37	102	808
FLA	162	92	70	.568	9	740	669	89	5439	1410	272	28	136	2146	**686**	1074	115	58	.259	.349	.395	.743	105	48	95	762
NY	162	88	74	.543	13	777	709	88	5524	1448	274	28	153	2237	550	1029	97	74	.262	.335	.405	.740	102	3	96	740
MON	162	78	84	.481	23	691	740	75	5526	1423	**339**	34	172	2346	420	1084	75	**46**	.258	.318	.425	.743	99	-28	100	740
PHI	162	68	94	.420	33	668	840	63	5443	1390	290	35	116	2098	519	1032	92	56	.255	.325	.385	.710	91	-77	100	683
Central																										
HOU	162	84	78	.519	....	777	660	94	5502	1427	314	40	133	2220	633	1085	171	74	.259	.346	.403	.750	106	57	96	792
PIT	162	79	83	.488	5	725	760	77	5503	1440	291	**52**	129	2222	481	1161	160	50	.262	.331	.404	.735	96	-24	102	751
CIN	162	76	86	.469	8	651	764	68	5484	1386	269	27	142	2135	518	1113	**190**	67	.253	.322	.389	.712	89	-74	102	700
STL	162	73	89	.451	11	689	708	79	5524	1409	269	39	144	2188	543	1191	164	60	.255	.326	.396	.722	95	-34	99	715
CHI	162	68	94	.420	16	687	759	73	5489	1444	269	39	127	2172	451	**1003**	116	60	.263	.323	.396	.719	91	-81	102	691
West																										
SF	162	90	72	.556	....	784	793	80	5485	1415	266	37	172	2271	642	1120	121	49	.258	.341	.414	.755	106	54	96	787
LA	162	88	74	.543	2	742	645	92	5544	1488	242	33	174	2318	498	1079	131	64	.268	.332	.418	.750	109	63	92	767
COL	162	83	79	.512	7	**923**	908	82	5603	**1611**	269	40	**239**	**2677**	562	1060	137	65	**.288**	**.359**	**.478**	**.837**	100	11	123	**948**
SD	162	76	86	.469	14	795	891	72	**5609**	1519	275	16	152	2282	604	1129	140	60	.271	.345	.407	.752	**112**	97	91	793
Total	**1134**					**10440**			**77203**	**20300**	**3907**	**485**	**2163**		**7704**	**15320**	**1817**	**841**	**.263**	**.336**	**.410**	**.746**				

Runs
Biggio, C. (Hou) 146
Walker, L. (Col) 143
Bonds, B. (SF) 123

Hits
Gwynn, T. (SD) 220
Walker, L. (Col) 208
Piazza, M. (LA) 201

Doubles
Grudzielanek, M. (Mon) 54
Gwynn, T. (SD) 49
Walker, L. (Col) 46

Triples
DeShields, D. (StL) 14
Perez, N. (Col) 10
3 players tied with 9

Home Runs
Walker, L. (Col) 49
Bagwell, J. (Hou) 43
Galarraga, A. (Col) 41

Total Bases
Walker, L. (Col) 409
Piazza, M. (LA) 355
Galarraga, A. (Col) 351

Runs Batted In
Galarraga, A. (Col) 140
Bagwell, J. (Hou) 135
Walker, L. (Col) 130

Bases On Balls
Bonds, B. (SF) 145
Bagwell, J. (Hou) 127
Sheffield, G. (Fla) 121

Stolen Bases
Womack, T. (Pit) 60
Sanders, D. (Cin) 56
DeShields, D. (StL) 55

Batting Average
Gwynn, T. (SD) .... .372
Walker, L. (Col) .... .366
Piazza, M. (LA) .... .362

On-Base Percentage
Walker, L. (Col) .... .455
Bonds, B. (SF) .... .450
Piazza, M. (LA) .... .435

Slugging Average
Walker, L. (Col) .... .720
Piazza, M. (LA) .... .638
Bagwell, J. (Hou) .... .592

Adjusted OPS
Piazza, M. (LA) 191
Bonds, B. (SF) 174
Bagwell, J. (Hou) 171

Adjusted Batting Runs
Piazza, M. (LA) 74.0
Bonds, B. (SF) 71.0
Bagwell, J. (Hou) 67.0

Runs Created/Game
Walker, L. (Col) 13.10
Piazza, M. (LA) 10.70
Bonds, B. (SF) 10.10

Fielding Runs
Lemke, M. (Atl) 17.5
Rolen, S. (Phi) 16.4
Biggio, C. (Hou) 13.1

Win Shares – Batters
Piazza, M. (LA) 39
Gwynn, T. (SD) 39
Biggio, C. (Hou) 38

TPW – Batters
Piazza, M. (LA) 8.1
Biggio, C. (Hou) 7.2
Bonds, B. (SF) 6.3

TEAM	CG	SH	SV	IP	H	H/G	ER	HR	BB	SO	OAV	RAT	ERA	ERA+	CERA	PR+	PF	FA	E	DP	FR	BW	PW	FW	TPW	DIF
East																										
ATL	21	**17**	37	1465²	1319	8.1	518	111	450	1196	.241	**1.207**	3.18	132	**3.10**	157.6	100	.982	114	136	9.3	3.7	**15.5**	.9	**20.1**	-.1
FLA	12	10	39	1446²	1353	8.4	615	131	463	1188	.250	1.377	3.83	105	4.00	24.2	96	.981	116	167	9.3	4.7	2.4	.9	8.0	3.0
NY	7	8	**49**	1459¹	1452	9.0	640	160	504	982	.262	1.340	3.95	102	4.07	-14.6	96	.981	120	165	**28.9**	.3	-1.4	**2.8**	1.7	5.3
MON	**27**	14	37	1447	1365	8.5	666	149	557	1138	.250	1.328	4.14	101	3.94	7.4	100	.979	132	150	2.8	-2.8	.7	.3	-1.8	-1.2
PHI	13	7	35	1420¹	1441	9.1	768	171	616	1209	.265	1.448	4.87	87	4.63	-92.8	101	.981	108	134	-4.4	-7.6	-9.1	-.4	-17.2	4.2
Central																										
HOU	16	12	37	1459	1379	8.5	595	134	511	1138	.251	1.295	3.67	109	3.69	35.6	95	.979	131	169	17.8	5.6	3.5	1.8	10.9	-7.9
PIT	6	8	41	1436	1503	9.4	683	143	560	1080	.271	1.437	4.28	100	4.43	15.3	102	.979	131	149	-13.5	-2.4	1.5	-1.3	-2.2	.2
CIN	5	8	**49**	1449	1408	8.8	712	173	558	1159	.255	1.357	4.42	97	4.19	-21.9	102	.983	**106**	129	3.9	-7.3	-2.2	.4	-9.1	4.1
STL	5	3	39	1455²	1422	8.8	631	124	536	1130	.259	1.345	3.90	106	3.92	40.0	99	.980	123	156	3.4	-3.4	3.9	.3	.9	-8.9
CHI	6	4	37	1429	1451	9.1	705	185	590	1072	.266	1.428	4.44	97	4.53	-20.0	102	.981	112	117	-0.8	-8.0	-2.0	-.1	-10.0	-3.0
West																										
SF	5	9	45	1446	1494	9.3	709	160	578	1044	.270	1.433	4.41	92	4.45	-55.6	96	.980	125	157	-7.1	5.3	-5.5	-.7	-.8	9.8
LA	6	6	45	1459¹	1325	8.2	588	163	546	**1232**	**.241**	1.282	3.63	106	3.64	55.2	92	.981	116	104	-17.7	6.2	5.4	-1.7	9.9	-2.9
COL	9	5	38	1432²	1697	10.7	835	196	566	870	.300	1.580	5.25	99	5.68	5.0	123	**.983**	111	**202**	-16.4	1.1	.5	-1.6	-.1	2.1
SD	5	2	43	1450	1581	9.8	804	172	596	1059	.280	1.501	4.99	77	4.97	-166.7	91	.979	132	132	-18.7	**9.6**	-16.4	-1.8	-8.7	3.7
Total	**143**	**113**	**571**	**20255²**		**9.0**	**9469**					**1.382**	**4.21**					**.979**	**132**							

Wins
Neagle, D. (Atl) 20
3 players tied with 19

Win Percentage
Maddux, G. (Atl) .... .826
Neagle, D. (Atl) .... .800
Estes, S. (SF) .... .792

Games
Tavarez, J. (SF) 89
Belinda, S. (Cin) 84
Shaw, J. (Cin) 78

Complete Games
Martinez, P. (Mon) 13
Perez, C. (Mon) 8
3 players tied with 7

Shutouts
Perez, C. (Mon) 5
3 players tied with 4

Saves
Shaw, J. (Cin) 42
Beck, R. (SF) 37
Hoffman, T. (SD) 37

Innings Pitched
Smoltz, J. (Atl) 256
Kile, D. (Hou) 255²
Schilling, C. (Phi) 254¹

Fewest Hits/Game
Martinez, P. (Mon) 5.89
Park, C. (LA) 6.98
Estes, S. (SF) 7.25

Fewest BB/Game
Maddux, G. (Atl) .... .77
Reed, R. (NY) 1.34
Neagle, D. (Atl) 1.89

Strikeouts
Schilling, C. (Phi) 319
Martinez, P. (Mon) 305
Smoltz, J. (Atl) 241

Ratio
Martinez, P. (Mon) .... .93
Maddux, G. (Atl) .... .95
Reed, R. (NY) 1.04

Earned Run Average
Martinez, P. (Mon) 1.90
Maddux, G. (Atl) 2.20
Kile, D. (Hou) 2.57

Adjusted ERA
Martinez, P. (Mon) 221
Maddux, G. (Atl) 191
Kile, D. (Hou) 156

Component ERA
Martinez, P. (Mon) 1.79
Maddux, G. (Atl) 1.95
Schilling, C. (Phi) 2.55

Opponents' Batting Avg.
Martinez, P. (Mon) .... .184
Park, C. (LA) .... .213
Estes, S. (SF) .... .223

Adjusted Pitching Runs
Martinez, P. (Mon) 61
Maddux, G. (Atl) 50
Kile, D. (Hou) 38

Win Shares – Pitchers
Maddux, G. (Atl) 26
Martinez, P. (Mon) 26
Brown, K. (Fla) 23

TPW – Pitchers
Martinez, P. (Mon) 6.0
Maddux, G. (Atl) 4.9
Kile, D. (Hou) 3.7

1997 American League

TEAM	G	W	L	PCT	GB	R	OR	EW	AB	H	2B	3B	HR	TB	BB	SO	SB	CS	AVG	OBP	SLG	OPS	OPS+	BR/A	PF	RC
East																										
BAL	162	98	64	.605	....	812	**681**	95	5584	1498	264	22	196	2394	586	952	63	**26**	.268	.345	.429	.773	104	34	97	832
NY	162	96	66	.593	2	891	688	101	5710	1636	325	23	161	2490	**676**	954	99	58	.287	**.366**	.436	.802	109	86	99	911
DET	162	79	83	.488	19	784	790	80	5481	1415	268	32	176	2275	578	1164	**161**	72	.258	.334	.415	.749	95	-36	99	762
BOS	162	78	84	.481	20	851	857	80	**5781**	**1684**	**373**	32	185	2676	514	1044	68	48	**.291**	.355	.463	.818	110	72	102	921
TOR	162	76	86	.469	22	654	694	76	5473	1333	275	**41**	147	2131	487	1138	134	50	.244	.312	.389	.702	82	-148	100	672
Central																										
CLE	161	86	75	.534	....	868	815	86	5556	1589	301	22	220	2594	617	955	118	59	.286	.361	.467	.828	110	87	104	922
CHI	161	80	81	.497	6	779	833	75	5491	1498	260	28	158	2288	569	**901**	106	52	.273	.345	.417	.761	102	17	96	784
MIL	161	78	83	.484	8	681	742	74	5444	1415	294	27	135	2168	494	967	103	55	.260	.328	.398	.726	88	-100	101	705
MIN	162	68	94	.420	18.5	772	861	72	5634	1522	305	40	132	2303	495	1121	151	52	.270	.336	.407	.742	91	-77	102	769
KC	161	67	94	.416	19	747	820	73	5599	1478	256	35	158	2278	561	1061	130	66	.264	.336	.398	.734	89			
West																										
SEA	162	90	72	.556	....	**925**	833	89	5614	1574	312	21	264	2720	626	1110	89	40	.280	.358	**.485**	**.842**	119	152	99	**961**
ANA	162	84	78	.519	6	829	794	84	5628	1531	279	25	161	2343	617	953	126	72	.272	.349	.416	.765	98	-46	105	823
TEX	162	77	85	.475	13	807	823	79	5651	1547	311	27	187	2473	500	1116	72	37	.274	.336	.438	.774	95	5	98	810
OAK	162	65	97	.401	25	764	946	64	5589	1451	274	23	197	2362	642	1181	71	36	.260	.341	.423	.764	100			
Total	**1132**					11164			78235	21171	4097	398	2477		7962	14617	1491	723	.271	.343	.428	.771				

Runs			Hits			Doubles			Triples			Home Runs			Total Bases		
Griffey, K. (Sea)	125		Garciaparra, N. (Bos)	209		Valentin, J. (Bos)	47		Garciaparra, N. (Bos)	11		Griffey, K. (Sea)	56		Griffey, K. (Sea)	393	
Garciaparra, N. (Bos)	122		Greer, R. (Tex)	193		Cirillo, J. (Mil)	46		Knoblauch, C. (Min)	10		Martinez, T. (NY)	44		Garciaparra, N. (Bos)	365	
Knoblauch, C. (Min)	117		Jeter, D. (NY)	190		Belle, A. (Chi)	45		2 players tied with	8		Gonzalez, J. (Tex)	42		Martinez, T. (NY)	343	

Runs Batted In			Bases On Balls			Stolen Bases			Batting Average			On-Base Percentage			Slugging Average		
Griffey, K. (Sea)	147		Thome, J. (Cle)	120		Hunter, B. (Det)	74		Thomas, F. (Chi)	.347		Thomas, F. (Chi)	.461		Griffey, K. (Sea)	.646	
Martinez, T. (NY)	141		Buhner, J. (Sea)	119		Knoblauch, C. (Min)	62		Martinez, E. (Sea)	.330		Martinez, E. (Sea)	.460		Thomas, F. (Chi)	.611	
Gonzalez, J. (Tex)	131		Martinez, E. (Sea)	119		Goodwin, T. (KC,Tex)	50		Justice, D. (Cle)	.329		Thome, J. (Cle)	.428		Justice, D. (Cle)	.596	

Adjusted OPS			Adjusted Batting Runs			Runs Created/Game			Fielding Runs			Win Shares – Batters			TPW – Batters		
Thomas, F. (Chi)	184		Thomas, F. (Chi)	71.0		Thomas, F. (Chi)	11.20		Cirillo, J. (Mil)	21.8		Thomas, F. (Chi)	39		Griffey, K. (Sea)	6.0	
Griffey, K. (Sea)	165		Griffey, K. (Sea)	59.0		Martinez, E. (Sea)	9.60		King, J. (KC)	15.6		Griffey, K. (Sea)	36		Thomas, F. (Chi)	5.4	
Martinez, E. (Sea)	164		Martinez, E. (Sea)	58.0		Thome, J. (Cle)	9.50		Bell, J. (KC)	15.3		Salmon, T. (Ana)	29		Martinez, E. (Sea)	4.6	

TEAM	CG	SH	SV	IP	H	H/G	ER	HR	BB	SO	OAV	RAT	ERA	ERA+	CERA	PR+	PF	FA	E	DP	FR	BW	PW	FW	TPW	DIF
East																										
BAL	8	10	59	1461	**1404**	8.6	635	164	563	1139	**.253**	1.346	3.91	113	**4.02**	75.3	96	.984	97	148	4.6	3.2	7.2	.4	10.8	6.2
NY	11	10	51	1467²	1463	9.0	**626**	**144**	532	1165	.260	1.359	**3.84**	116	4.07	**113.5**	97	.983	104	156	-14.6	8.1	**10.8**	-1.4	**17.5**	-2.5
DET	13	8	42	1445²	1476	9.2	732	178	552	982	.266	1.403	4.56	101	4.43	-13.8	100	.978	135	**179**	-1.4	-3.4	-1.3	1.7	-3.1	1.1
BOS	7	4	40	1451²	1569	9.7	785	149	611	987	.276	1.502	4.87	95	4.85	81.0	101	.984	94	150	25.4	6.8	-3.2	-.1	3.5	-6.5
TOR	**19**	**16**	34	1442²	1453	9.1	628	167	497	1150	.263	1.352	3.92	117	4.20						17.7	-14.1	7.7	2.4	-3.9	-1.1
Central																										
CLE	4	3	39	1425²	1528	9.6	749	181	575	1036	.276	1.475	4.73	99	4.85	5.9	103	.983	106	159	-11.8	8.3	.6	-1.1	7.8	-1.8
CHI	6	7	52	1422¹	1505	9.5	749	175	575	961	.271	1.462	4.74	93	4.65	-35.6	96	.978	127	131	-19.9	1.6	-3.4	-1.9	-3.7	3.7
MIL	6	8	44	1427¹	1419	9.0	670	177	542	1016	.261	1.374	4.22	109	4.35	15.8	101	.980	121	171	45.5	-9.5	1.5	**4.3**	-3.7	1.7
MIN	10	4	30	1434	1596	10.0	800	187	**495**	908	.283	1.458	5.02	93	4.90	-58.5	102	.983	101	170	0.2	-5.4	-5.6	.0	-11.0	-2.0
KC	11	5	29	1443	1530	9.5	755	186	531	961	.274	1.428	4.71	100	4.67	-13.6	103	**.985**	**91**	168	14.9	-7.3	-1.3	1.4	-7.2	-5.8
West																										
SEA	9	8	38	1447²	1500	9.3	770	192	598	**1207**	.267	1.449	4.79	94	4.81	-32.6	98	.979	126	143	-14.5	**14.4**	-3.1	-1.4	9.9	-.9
ANA	9	5	39	1454²	1506	9.3	730	202	605	1050	.269	1.451	4.52	102	4.79	8.3	101	.980	123	140	7.3	-1.6	.8	.7	-.1	3.1
TEX	8	9	33	1429²	1598	10.1	744	169	541	925	.283	1.496	4.68	102	4.92	34.4	105	.980	121	155	-20.3	-4.4	3.3	-1.9	-3.1	-.9
OAK	2	1	38	1445¹	1734	10.8	881	197	642	953	.301	1.644	5.49	**82**	5.87	-123.8	99	.981	122	170	-34.1	.5	-11.8	-3.2	-14.5	-1.5
Total	**123**	**98**	**568**	20198¹		9.5	10254					1.443	4.57													

Wins			Win Percentage			Games			Complete Games			Shutouts			Saves		
Clemens, R. (Tor)	21		Johnson, R. (Sea)	.833		Myers, M. (Det)	88		Clemens, R. (Tor)	9		Clemens, R. (Tor)	3		Myers, R. (Bal)	45	
Johnson, R. (Sea)	20		Moyer, J. (Sea)	.773		Groom, B. (Oak)	78		Hentgen, P. (Tor)	9		Hentgen, P. (Tor)	3		Rivera, M. (NY)	43	
Radke, B. (Min)	20		Clemens, R. (Tor)	.750		2 players tied with	77		3 players tied with	5		6 players tied with	2		Jones, D. (Mil)	36	

Innings Pitched			Fewest Hits/Game			Fewest BB/Game			Strikeouts			Ratio			Earned Run Average		
Clemens, R. (Tor)	264		Johnson, R. (Sea)	6.21		Burkett, J. (Tex)	1.43		Clemens, R. (Tor)	292		Clemens, R. (Tor)	1.03		Clemens, R. (Tor)	2.05	
Hentgen, P. (Tor)	264		Clemens, R. (Tor)	6.95		Tewksbury, B. (Min)	1.65		Johnson, R. (Sea)	291		Johnson, R. (Sea)	1.05		Johnson, R. (Sea)	2.28	
Pettitte, A. (NY)	240¹		Cone, D. (NY)	7.15		Radke, B. (Min)	1.80		Cone, D. (NY)	222		Mussina, M. (Bal)	1.12		Cone, D. (NY)	2.82	

Adjusted ERA			Component ERA			Opponents' Batting Avg.			Adjusted Pitching Runs			Win Shares – Pitchers			TPW – Pitchers		
Clemens, R. (Tor)	225		Clemens, R. (Tor)	2.17		Johnson, R. (Sea)	.194		Clemens, R. (Tor)	70		Clemens, R. (Tor)	32		Clemens, R. (Tor)	6.8	
Johnson, R. (Sea)	197		Johnson, R. (Sea)	2.47		Clemens, R. (Tor)	.213		Johnson, R. (Sea)	55		Johnson, R. (Sea)	23		Johnson, R. (Sea)	5.2	
Cone, D. (NY)	158		Thompson, J. (Det)	2.87		Cone, D. (NY)	.218		Pettitte, A. (NY)	44		Thompson, J. (Det)	21		Pettitte, A. (NY)	4.2	

1998 National League

TEAM	G	W	L	PCT	GB	R	OR	EW	AB	H	2B	3B	HR	TB	BB	SO	SB	CS	AVG	OBP	SLG	OPS	OPS+	BR/A	PF	RC
East																										
ATL	162	106	56	.654	....	826	**581**	108	5484	1489	297	26	215	2483	548	1062	98	43	.272	.344	.453	.797	114	103	100	861
NY	162	88	74	.543	18	706	645	88	5510	1425	289	24	136	2170	572	1049	62	46	.259	.332	.394	.726	97	-27	98	718
PHI	162	75	87	.463	31	713	808	71	5617	1482	286	36	126	2218	508	1080	97	45	.264	.330	.395	.725	94	-48	101	734
MON	162	65	97	.401	41	644	783	65	5418	1348	280	32	147	2133	439	1058	91	46	.249	.312	.394	.706	91	-77	98	661
FLA	162	54	108	.333	52	667	923	56	5558	1381	277	36	114	2072	525	1120	115	57	.248	.318	.373	.691	90	-79	96	660
Central																										
HOU	162	102	60	.630	....	**874**	620	108	5641	1578	326	28	166	2458	621	1122	155	51	.280	**.359**	.436	.794	**117**	153	97	**888**
CHI	163	90	73	.552	12.5	831	792	85	**5649**	1494	250	34	212	2448	601	1223	65	44	.264	.339	.433	.773	104	25	103	826
STL	163	83	79	.512	19	810	782	84	5593	1444	292	30	**223**	2465	676	1179	133	41	.258	.343	.441	.783	111	101	99	861
CIN	162	77	85	.475	25	750	760	80	5496	1441	298	28	138	2209	608	1107	95	42	.262	.340	.402	.742	99	-2	101	754
MIL	162	74	88	.457	28	707	812	70	5541	1439	266	17	152	2195	532	1039	81	59	.260	.332	.396	.728	96	-38	100	718
PIT	163	69	93	.426	33	650	718	73	5493	1395	271	35	107	2057	393	1060	**159**	51	.254	.314	.374	.689	85	-111	101	656
West																										
SD	162	98	64	.605	....	749	635	94	5490	1390	292	30	167	2243	604	1072	79	**37**	.253	.332	.409	.741	107	54	93	755
SF	163	89	74	.546	9.5	845	739	92	5628	1540	292	26	161	2367	**678**	1040	102	51	.274	.356	.421	.777	116	136	94	856
LA	162	83	79	.512	15	669	678	80	5459	1374	209	27	159	2114	447	1056	137	53	.252	.313	.387	.700	94	-50	94	665
COL	162	77	85	.475	21	826	855	78	5632	**1640**	**333**	36	183	2594	469	**949**	67	47	**.291**	.350	**.461**	**.810**	96	-30	**122**	877
ARI	162	65	97	.401	33	665	812	65	5491	1353	235	**46**	159	2157	489	1239	73	38	.246	.315	.393	.708	91	-79	100	674
Total	**1298**					**11932**			**88700**	**23213**	**4493**	**491**	**2565**		**8710**	**17455**	**1609**	**751**	**.262**	**.333**	**.410**	**.744**				

Runs			Hits			Doubles			Triples			Home Runs			Total Bases		
Sosa, S. (Chi)		134	Bichette, D. (Col)		219	Biggio, C. (Hou)		51	Dellucci, D. (Ari)		12	McGwire, M. (StL)		70	Sosa, S. (Chi)		416
McGwire, M. (StL)		130	Biggio, C. (Hou)		210	Bichette, D. (Col)		48	Larkin, B. (Cin)		10	Sosa, S. (Chi)		66	McGwire, M. (StL)		383
Bagwell, J. (Hou)		124	Castilla, V. (Col)		206	Young, D. (Cin)		48	2 players tied with		9	Vaughn, G. (SD)		50	Castilla, V. (Col)		380

Runs Batted In			Bases On Balls			Stolen Bases			Batting Average			On-Base Percentage			Slugging Average		
Sosa, S. (Chi)		158	McGwire, M. (StL)		162	Womack, T. (Pit)		58	Walker, L. (Col)		.363	McGwire, M. (StL)		.473	McGwire, M. (StL)		.752
McGwire, M. (StL)		147	Bonds, B. (SF)		130	Biggio, C. (Hou)		50	Olerud, J. (NY)		.354	Olerud, J. (NY)		.452	Sosa, S. (Chi)		.647
Castilla, V. (Col)		144	Bagwell, J. (Hou)		109	Young, L. (LA)		42	Bichette, D. (Col)		.331	Walker, L. (Col)		.446	Walker, L. (Col)		.630

Adjusted OPS			Adjusted Batting Runs			Runs Created/Game			Fielding Runs			Win Shares – Batters			TPW – Batters		
McGwire, M. (StL)		218	McGwire, M. (StL)		97.0	McGwire, M. (StL)		14.10	Jones, A. (Atl)		25.6	McGwire, M. (StL)		41	McGwire, M. (StL)		7.7
Bonds, B. (SF)		184	Bonds, B. (SF)		75.0	Walker, L. (Col)		11.40	Cirillo, J. (Mil)		22.5	Sosa, S. (Chi)		35	Bonds, B. (SF)		6.8
Olerud, J. (NY)		165	Olerud, J. (NY)		57.0	Olerud, J. (NY)		9.90	Veras, Q. (SD)		20.3	Biggio, C. (Hou)		35	Piazza, M. (NY,LA,Fla)		5.9

TEAM	CG	SH	SV	IP	H	H/G	ER	HR	BB	SO	OAV	RAT	ERA	ERA+	CERA	PR+	PF	FA	E	DP	FR	BW	PW	FW	TPW	DIF
East																										
ATL	**24**	**23**	45	1438²	**1291**	8.1	519	**117**	467	1232	.240	1.222	3.25	128	3.22	130.4	98	**.985**	91	139	14.8	10.2	**12.9**	1.5	24.5	.5
NY	9	16	46	1458	1381	8.5	611	152	532	1129	.256	1.312	3.77	110	3.87	54.9	98	.984	101	151	5.0	-2.6	5.4	.5	3.3	3.7
PHI	21	10	32	1463	1476	9.1	754	188	544	1176	.262	1.381	4.64	93	4.40	-53.0	102	.982	110	131	3.7	-4.8	-5.2	.4	-9.6	3.6
MON	4	5	39	1427	1448	9.1	696	156	533	1017	.264	1.388	4.39	96	4.29	-7.5	99	.975	155	127	-21.2	-7.6	-.7	-2.1	-10.4	-5.6
FLA	11	3	24	1449²	1617	10.0	837	182	715	1016	.287	1.609	5.20	79	5.50	-169.2	97	.979	129	177	-9.2	-7.8	-16.7	-.9	-25.4	-1.6
Central																										
HOU	12	11	44	1471¹	1435	8.8	572	147	**465**	1187	.256	1.291	3.50	116	3.73	85.6	96	.983	108	144	5.7	**15.1**	8.4	.6	24.1	-3.1
CHI	7	7	56	1477¹	1528	9.3	739	180	575	1207	.266	1.424	4.50	98	4.49	11.4	104	.984	101	107	-25.7	2.5	1.1	-2.5	1.0	8.0
STL	6	10	44	1469²	1513	9.3	705	151	558	972	.268	1.409	4.32	97	4.34	-14.9	99	.978	142	160	-5.7	10.0	-1.5	-.6	8.0	-6.0
CIN	6	8	42	1441¹	1400	8.7	711	170	573	1098	.256	1.369	4.44	97	4.23	-22.9	101	.979	122	142	-1.8	-.2	-2.3	-.2	-2.7	-1.3
MIL	2	2	39	1451	1538	9.5	746	188	550	1063	.275	1.439	4.63	92	4.74	-71.7	101	.982	110	192	13.9	-3.8	-7.1	1.4	-9.5	2.5
PIT	7	10	41	1449	1433	8.9	630	147	530	1112	.259	1.355	3.91	110	3.94	53.9	101	.977	140	161	9.5	-10.9	5.3	.9	-4.7	-7.3
West																										
SD	14	11	**59**	1454²	1384	8.6	587	139	501	1217	.252	1.296	3.63	108	3.72	42.8	93	.983	104	155	7.1	5.3	4.2	.7	10.3	6.7
SF	6	6	44	1477	1457	8.9	688	171	562	1089	.259	1.367	4.19	95	4.15	-32.8	94	.984	101	177	-2.3	13.5	-3.2	-.2	10.0	-2.0
LA	16	10	47	1447¹	1332	8.3	613	135	587	1178	.246	1.326	3.81	104	3.77	29.5	94	.978	134	154	-3.4	-4.9	2.9	-.3	-2.3	4.3
COL	9	5	36	1432²	1583	9.9	796	174	562	951	.285	1.497	5.00	103	5.09	23.4	122	.983	102	**193**	4.3	-3.0	2.3	.4	-.3	-3.7
ARI	7	6	37	1432¹	1463	9.2	738	188	489	908	.266	1.363	4.64	91	4.31	-69.6	99	.984	100	125	2.1	-7.7	-6.9	.2	-14.4	-1.6
Total	**161**	**143**	**675**	**23240**		**9.0**	**10942**					**1.378**	**4.24**													

Wins			Win Percentage			Games			Complete Games			Shutouts			Saves		
Glavine, T. (Atl)		20	Smoltz, J. (Atl)		.850	Beck, R. (Chi)		81	Schilling, C. (Phi)		15	Maddux, G. (Atl)		5	Hoffman, T. (SD)		53
Reynolds, S. (Hou)		19	Glavine, T. (Atl)		.769	3 players tied with		78	Hernandez, L. (Fla)		9	Johnson, R. (Hou)		4	Beck, R. (Chi)		51
Tapani, K. (Chi)		19	Leiter, A. (NY)		.739				Maddux, G. (Atl)		9	2 players tied with		3	Shaw, J. (LA,Cin)		48

Innings Pitched			Fewest Hits/Game			Fewest BB/Game			Strikeouts			Ratio			Earned Run Average		
Schilling, C. (Phi)		268²	Wood, K. (Chi)		6.32	Anderson, B. (Ari)		1.04	Schilling, C. (Phi)		300	Maddux, G. (Atl)		.98	Maddux, G. (Atl)		2.22
Brown, K. (SD)		257	Leiter, A. (NY)		7.04	Reed, R. (NY)		1.23	Brown, K. (SD)		257	Brown, K. (SD)		1.07	Brown, K. (SD)		2.38
Maddux, G. (Atl)		251	Maddux, G. (Atl)		7.21	Lima, E. (LA)		1.23	Wood, K. (Chi)		233	Schilling, C. (Phi)		1.11	Leiter, A. (NY)		2.47

Adjusted ERA			Component ERA			Opponents' Batting Avg.			Adjusted Pitching Runs			Win Shares – Pitchers			TPW – Pitchers		
Maddux, G. (Atl)		187	Maddux, G. (Atl)		2.01	Wood, K. (Chi)		.196	Maddux, G. (Atl)		51	Brown, K. (SD)		26	Maddux, G. (Atl)		5.4
Glavine, T. (Atl)		168	Brown, K. (SD)		2.35	Leiter, A. (NY)		.216	Brown, K. (SD)		43	Maddux, G. (Atl)		25	Brown, K. (SD)		4.6
Leiter, A. (NY)		167	Leiter, A. (NY)		2.65	Maddux, G. (Atl)		.220	Glavine, T. (Atl)		41	Glavine, T. (Atl)		23	Glavine, T. (Atl)		4.3

1998 American League

TEAM	G	W	L	PCT	GB	R	OR	EW	AB	H	2B	3B	HR	TB	BB	SO	SB	CS	AVG	OBP	SLG	OPS	OPS+	BR/A	PF	RC
East																										
NY	162	114	48	.704	....	**965**	**656**	111	5643	1625	290	31	207	2598	**653**	1025	153	63	.288	**.368**	.460	**.828**	118	**165**	96	**956**
BOS	162	92	70	.568	22	876	729	96	5601	1568	**338**	35	205	2591	541	1049	72	**39**	.280	.351	.463	.813	107	56	102	894
TOR	163	88	74	.543	26	816	768	86	5580	1482	316	19	221	2499	564	1132	**184**	81	.266	.342	.448	.790	103	28	100	860
BAL	162	79	83	.488	35	817	785	84	5565	1520	303	11	214	2487	593	**903**	86	48	.273	.349	.447	.796	107	56	98	862
TB	162	63	99	.389	51	620	751	66	5555	1450	267	**43**	111	2136	473	1107	120	73	.261	.323	.385	.708	82	-158	102	677
Central																										
CLE	162	89	73	.549	....	850	779	88	5616	1530	334	30	198	2518	630	1061	143	60	.272	.350	.448	.798	103	27	103	886
CHI	163	80	82	.494	9	861	931	75	5585	1516	291	38	198	2477	551	916	127	46	.271	.342	.444	.785	106	48	97	849
KC	161	72	89	.447	16.5	714	899	62	5546	1459	274	40	134	2215	475	984	112	50	.263	.328	.399	.727	86	-112	103	728
MIN	162	70	92	.432	19	734	818	72	5641	1499	285	32	115	2193	506	915	122	54	.266	.331	.389	.720	85	-121	102	710
DET	162	65	97	.401	24	722	863	67	5664	1494	306	29	165	2353	455	1070	122	62	.264	.325	.415	.741	91	-87	101	757
West																										
TEX	162	88	74	.543	....	940	871	87	**5672**	**1637**	314	32	201	2618	595	1045	82	47	**.289**	.360	.462	.822	108	63	104	934
ANA	162	85	77	.525	3	787	783	81	5630	1530	314	27	147	2339	558	1028	115	45	.272	.337	.415	.753	94	-51	101	785
SEA	161	76	85	.472	11.5	859	855	81	5628	1553	321	28	**234**	**2632**	558	1081	115	**39**	.276	.347	**.468**	.815	110	82	100	922
OAK	162	74	88	.457	14	804	866	75	5490	1413	295	13	149	2181	633	1122	131	47	.257	.340	.397	.737	94	-38	98	761
Total	1134					11365			78416	21276	4248	408	2499		7737	14438	1675	754	.271	.343	.432	.774				

Runs
Jeter, D. (NY) 127
Durham, R. (Chi) 126
Rodriguez, A. (Sea) 123

Hits
Rodriguez, A. (Sea) 213
Vaughn, M. (Bos) 205
Jeter, D. (NY) 203

Doubles
Gonzalez, J. (Tex) 50
Belle, A. (Chi) 48
Martinez, E. (Sea) 46

Triples
Offerman, J. (KC) 13
Damon, J. (KC) 10
Winn, R. (TB) 9

Home Runs
Griffey, K. (Sea) 56
Belle, A. (Chi) 49
Canseco, J. (Tor) 46

Total Bases
Belle, A. (Chi) 399
Griffey, K. (Sea) 387
Rodriguez, A. (Sea) 384

Runs Batted In
Gonzalez, J. (Tex) 157
Belle, A. (Chi) 152
Griffey, K. (Sea) 146

Bases On Balls
Henderson, R. (Oak) 118
Thomas, F. (Chi) 110
Martinez, E. (Sea) 106

Stolen Bases
Henderson, R. (Oak) 66
Lofton, K. (Cle) 54
Stewart, S. (Tor) 51

Batting Average
Williams, B. (NY) .339
Vaughn, M. (Bos) .337
Belle, A. (Chi) .328

On-Base Percentage
Martinez, E. (Sea) .433
Williams, B. (NY) .425
Salmon, T. (Ana) .417

Slugging Average
Belle, A. (Chi) .655
Gonzalez, J. (Tex) .630
Griffey, K. (Sea) .611

Adjusted OPS
Belle, A. (Chi) 175
Williams, B. (NY) 163
Martinez, E. (Sea) 157

Adjusted Batting Runs
Belle, A. (Chi) 66.0
Martinez, E. (Sea) 51.0
Williams, B. (NY) 47.0

Runs Created/Game
Belle, A. (Chi) 9.60
Martinez, E. (Sea) 9.60
Thome, J. (Cle) 9.50

Fielding Runs
Ventura, R. (Chi) 21.6
Valentin, J. (Bos) 20.3
Brosius, S. (NY) 15.9

Win Shares – Batters
37
Rodriguez, A. (Sea) 30
2 players tied with 29

TPW – Batters
5.7
Griffey, K. (Sea) 5.0
Rodriguez, A. (Sea) 4.5

TEAM	CG	SH	SV	IP	H	H/G	ER	HR	BB	SO	OAV	RAT	ERA	ERA+	CERA	PR+	PF	FA	E	DP	FR	BW	PW	FW	TPW	DIF
East																										
NY	**22**	**16**	48	1456²	**1357**	8.4	**618**	156	466	1080	.247	1.251	3.82	115	3.65	64.0	94	.984	98	146	27.0	**15.5**	6.0	2.5	**24.1**	8.9
BOS	5	8	**53**	1436	1406	8.8	669	168	504	1025	.255	1.330	4.19	112	4.07	72.5	101	.983	105	128	11.8	5.3	**6.8**	1.1	13.2	-2.2
TOR	10	11	47	**1465**	1443	8.9	698	169	587	1154	.256	1.386	4.29	109	4.26	-16.9	98	**.987**	81	144	-12.8	5.2	-1.6	-1.2	2.4	-4.4
BAL	16	10	37	1431¹	1505	9.5	752	169	535	1065	.272	1.425	4.73	96	4.57	14.5	103	.985	94	**178**	56.3	-14.9	1.4	**5.3**	-8.2	-9.8
TB	7	7	28	1443	1425	8.9	697	171	643	1008	.261	1.433	4.35	110	4.62	56.0	103	.982	110	146	-4.1	2.6	5.3	-.4	7.5	.5
Central																										
CLE	9	4	47	1460	1552	9.6	722	171	563	1037	.274	1.449	4.45	107	4.69	56.0	103	.977	140	161	5.2	4.5	-10.8	.5	-5.8	4.8
CHI	8	4	42	1438²	1569	9.8	837	211	568	911	.278	1.494	5.24	87	5.15	-114.3	98	.979	125	172	-16.3	-10.5	-3.5	-1.5	-15.6	7.6
KC	6	5	46	1436¹	1590	9.9	823	196	568	999	.281	1.502	5.16	94	5.14	-37.6	104	.982	125	135	-16.3	-11.5	2.3	-2.1	-11.2	.2
MIN	7	8	42	1447²	1622	10.1	765	180	**457**	952	.284	1.436	4.76	100	4.71	24.7	103	.982	108	135	-22.4	-8.2	-5.3	2.0	-11.5	.2
DET	9	4	32	1446¹	1551	9.6	792	185	595	947	.277	1.484	4.93	96	4.88	-56.2	101	.982	115	164	21.4	-8.2	-5.3	2.0	-11.5	-4.5
West																										
TEX	10	8	46	1431¹	1624	10.2	795	164	519	994	.285	1.497	5.00	97	4.95	-8.4	104	.980	121	140	-19.0	5.9	-.8	-1.8	3.3	3.7
ANA	3	5	52	1444	1481	9.2	720	164	630	1091	.267	1.462	4.49	105	4.62	43.5	101	.983	106	146	-10.7	-4.8	4.1	-1.0	-1.7	5.7
SEA	17	7	31	1424¹	1530	9.7	783	196	528	**1156**	.273	1.445	4.95	94	4.84	-30.3	100	.979	125	139	-20.5	7.8	-2.9	-1.9	3.0	-7.0
OAK	12	4	39	1434	1555	9.8	770	179	529	922	.276	1.453	4.83	95	4.78	-25.2	98	.977	141	155	-15.8	-3.6	-2.4	-1.5	-7.5	.5
Total	141	101	590	20194²		9.4	10441					1.432	4.65													

Wins
Clemens, R. (Tor) 20
Cone, D. (NY) 20
Helling, R. (Tex) 20

Win Percentage
Wells, D. (NY) .818
Clemens, R. (Tor) .769
2 players tied with .741

Games
Runyan, S. (Det) 88
Quantrill, P. (Tor) 82
Swindell, G. (Min,Bos) 81

Complete Games
Erickson, S. (Bal) 11
Wells, D. (NY) 8
2 players tied with 7

Shutouts
Wells, D. (NY) 5
3 players tied with 3

Saves
Gordon, T. (Bos) 46
Percival, T. (Ana) 42
Wetteland, J. (Tex) 42

Innings Pitched
Erickson, S. (Bal) 251¹
Rogers, K. (Oak) 238²
Clemens, R. (Tor) 234²

Fewest Hits/Game
Clemens, R. (Tor) 6.48
Martinez, P. (Bos) 7.24
Irabu, H. (NY) 7.70

Fewest BB/Game
Wells, D. (NY) 1.22
Saberhagen, B. (Bos) 1.49
Moyer, J. (Sea) 1.61

Strikeouts
Clemens, R. (Tor) 271
Martinez, P. (Bos) 251
Johnson, R. (Sea) 213

Ratio
Wells, D. (NY) 1.05
Martinez, P. (Bos) 1.09
Clemens, R. (Tor) 1.10

Earned Run Average
Clemens, R. (Tor) 2.65
Martinez, P. (Bos) 2.89
Rogers, K. (Oak) 3.17

Adjusted ERA
Clemens, R. (Tor) 176
Martinez, P. (Bos) 163
Rogers, K. (Oak) 144

Component ERA
Clemens, R. (Tor) 2.27
Martinez, P. (Bos) 2.78
Wells, D. (NY) 2.83

Opponents' Batting Avg.
Clemens, R. (Tor) .197
Martinez, P. (Bos) .217
Irabu, H. (NY) .233

Adjusted Pitching Runs
Clemens, R. (Tor) 52
Martinez, P. (Bos) 45
Rogers, K. (Oak) 40

Win Shares – Pitchers
Clemens, R. (Tor) 25
Martinez, P. (Bos) 21
Rogers, K. (Oak) 19

TPW – Pitchers
Clemens, R. (Tor) 4.9
Martinez, P. (Bos) 4.2
Rogers, K. (Oak) 3.7

1999 National League

TEAM	G	W	L	PCT	GB	R	OR	EW	AB	H	2B	3B	HR	TB	BB	SO	SB	CS	AVG	OBP	SLG	OPS	OPS+	BR/A	PF	RC
East																										
ATL	162	103	59	.636	....	840	**661**	100	5569	1481	309	23	197	2427	608	962	148	66	.266	.344	.436	.780	101	9	100	837
NY	163	97	66	.595	6.5	853	711	96	5572	1553	297	14	181	2421	717	994	150	61	.279	**.366**	.434	.800	111	104	97	894
PHI	162	77	85	.475	26	841	846	81	5598	1539	302	44	161	2412	631	1081	125	35	.275	.353	.431	.784	100	13	103	868
MON	162	68	94	.420	35	718	853	67	5559	1473	**320**	**47**	163	2376	438	939	70	51	.265	.325	.427	.752	96	-53	97	744
FLA	162	64	98	.395	39	691	852	64	5578	1465	266	44	128	2203	479	1145	92	46	.263	.328	.395	.722	92	-75	95	718
Central																										
HOU	162	97	65	.599	....	823	675	97	5485	1463	293	23	168	2306	**728**	1138	166	75	.267	.358	.420	.778	104	41	98	843
CIN	163	96	67	.589	1.5	865	711	97	5649	1536	312	37	209	2549	569	1125	164	54	.272	.343	.451	.795	102	18	103	886
PIT	161	78	83	.484	18.5	775	782	80	5468	1417	282	40	171	2292	573	1197	112	44	.259	.336	.419	.755	95	-38	100	780
STL	161	75	86	.466	21.5	809	838	78	5570	1461	274	27	194	2371	613	1202	134	48	.262	.341	.426	.767	98	-16	100	823
MIL	161	74	87	.460	22.5	815	886	74	5582	1524	299	30	165	2378	658	1065	81	**33**	.273	.355	.426	.781	104	37	99	866
CHI	162	67	95	.414	30	747	920	64	5482	1411	255	35	189	2303	571	1170	60	44	.257	.332	.420	.752	96	-51	98	759
West																										
ARI	162	100	62	.617	....	**908**	676	104	5658	1566	289	46	216	2595	588	1045	137	39	.277	.350	.459	.808	108	70	100	927
SF	162	86	76	.531	14	872	831	85	5563	1507	307	18	188	2414	696	1028	109	56	.271	.358	.434	.792	**113**	112	93	877
LA	162	77	85	.475	23	793	787	82	5567	1480	253	23	187	2340	594	1030	167	68	.266	.342	.420	.763	103	30	94	814
SD	162	74	88	.457	26	710	781	73	5394	1360	256	22	153	2119	631	1169	**174**	67	.252	.334	.393	.727	96	-21	92	717
COL	162	72	90	.444	28	906	1028	71	**5717**	**1644**	305	39	223	**2696**	508	**863**	70	43	**.288**	.350	**.472**	**.822**	88	-109	127	**928**
Total	**1295**					**12966**			**89011**	**23880**	**4619**	**512**	**2893**		**9602**	**17153**	**1959**	**830**	**.268**	**.345**	**.429**	**.774**				

Runs
Bagwell, J. (Hou) 143
Bell, J. (Ari) 132
2 players tied with 123

Hits
Gonzalez, L. (Ari) 206
Glanville, D. (Phi) 204
Cirillo, J. (Mil) 198

Doubles
Biggio, C. (Hou) 56
Gonzalez, L. (Ari) 45
Vidro, J. (Mon) 45

Triples
Abreu, B. (Phi) 11
Perez, N. (Col) 11
2 players tied with 10

Home Runs
McGwire, M. (StL) 65
Sosa, S. (Chi) 63
2 players tied with 45

Total Bases
Sosa, S. (Chi) 397
Gonzalez, L. (Ari) 366
McGwire, M. (StL) 363

Runs Batted In
McGwire, M. (StL) 147
Williams, M. (Ari) 142
Sosa, S. (Chi) 141

Bases On Balls
Bagwell, J. (Hou) 149
McGwire, M. (StL) 133
Jones, C. (Atl) 126

Stolen Bases
Womack, T. (Ari) 72
Cedeno, R. (NY) 66
Young, E. (LA) 51

Batting Average
Walker, L. (Col) .... .379
Gonzalez, L. (Ari) .... .336
Abreu, B. (Phi) .... .335

On-Base Percentage
Walker, L. (Col) .... .464
Bagwell, J. (Hou) .... .458
Abreu, B. (Phi) .... .448

Slugging Average
Walker, L. (Col) .... .710
McGwire, M. (StL) .... .697
Sosa, S. (Chi) .... .635

Adjusted OPS
McGwire, M. (StL) 177
Jones, C. (Atl) 168
Bagwell, J. (Hou) 165

Adjusted Batting Runs
Jones, C. (Atl) 68.0
Bagwell, J. (Hou) 67.0
McGwire, M. (StL) 64.0

Runs Created/Game
Walker, L. (Col) 13.20
McGwire, M. (StL) 11.00
Jones, C. (Atl) 10.70

Fielding Runs
Reese, P. (Cin) 30.2
Ventura, R. (NY) 25.5
Jones, A. (Atl) 22.1

Win Shares – Batters
Bagwell, J. (Hou) 37
Jones, C. (Atl) 32
Biggio, C. (Hou) 31

TPW – Batters
Ventura, R. (NY) 5.2
Giles, B. (Pit) 4.4
Bagwell, J. (Hou) 4.3

TEAM	CG	SH	SV	IP	H	H/G	ER	HR	BB	SO	OAV	RAT	ERA	ERA+	CERA	PR+	PF	FA	E	DP	FR	BW	PW	FW	TPW	DIF
East																										
ATL	9	9	45	**1471**	1398	8.6	**593**	142	507	1197	.251	**1.295**	3.63	124	3.64	**152.2**	98	.982	111	127	-13.7	.8	**14.4**	-1.3	13.9	8.1
NY	5	7	49	1456²	1372	8.5	691	167	617	1172	.252	1.365	4.27	103	4.09	7.8	96	**.989**	68	147	10.8	9.8	.7	1.0	11.6	4.4
PHI	11	6	32	1438¹	1494	9.4	788	212	627	1030	.269	1.475	4.93	96	4.97	-54.3	103	.983	100	144	20.2	1.2	-5.1	1.9	-2.0	-2.0
MON	6	4	44	1434¹	1505	9.4	747	152	572	1043	.270	1.448	4.69	96	4.56	-6.7	98	.973	160	125	-26.5	-5.0	-.6	-2.5	-8.2	-4.8
FLA	6	5	33	1435²	1560	9.8	781	171	655	943	.281	1.543	4.90	89	5.12	-82.2	95	.979	127	150	-4.5	-7.1	-7.8	-.4	-15.2	-1.8
Central																										
HOU	12	8	48	1458²	1485	9.2	622	**128**	478	**1204**	.267	1.346	3.84	115	4.00	81.4	97	.983	106	175	11.4	3.8	7.7	1.1	12.6	3.4
CIN	6	**11**	**55**	1462	**1309**	**8.1**	648	190	636	1081	**.241**	1.330	3.99	117	3.98	65.5	102	.984	105	139	**43.4**	1.7	6.2	**4.1**	12.0	3.0
PIT	8	3	34	1433¹	1444	9.1	689	160	633	1083	.263	1.449	4.33	105	4.49	39.7	100	.977	147	179	-4.4	-3.6	3.7	-.4	-.2	-1.8
STL	5	3	38	1445¹	1519	9.5	761	161	667	1025	.273	1.512	4.74	96	4.87	-26.7	100	.978	132	163	-3.6	-1.5	-2.5	-.3	-4.4	-.6
MIL	2	5	40	1442²	1618	10.1	812	213	616	987	.284	1.549	5.07	90	5.37	-72.2	99	.979	127	146	-15.8	3.5	-6.8	-1.5	-4.8	-1.2
CHI	11	6	32	1430²	1619	10.2	837	221	529	980	.286	1.501	5.27	86	5.16	-100.9	99	.977	139	135	-17.5	-4.8	-9.5	-1.7	-16.0	2.0
West																										
ARI	**16**	9	42	1467¹	1387	8.5	615	176	543	1198	.249	1.315	3.77	121	3.93	124.1	100	.983	104	132	6.3	6.6	11.7	.6	**18.9**	.1
SF	6	3	42	1456¹	1486	9.2	762	194	655	1076	.265	1.470	4.71	89	4.74	-82.5	92	.983	105	155	0.3	**10.6**	-7.8	.0	2.8	2.2
LA	8	6	37	1453	1438	8.9	718	192	594	1077	.258	1.398	4.45	96	4.50	-16.6	94	.978	137	137	-9.9	2.8	-1.6	-.9	.3	-4.3
SD	5	6	43	1420¹	1454	9.2	705	193	529	1078	.266	1.396	4.47	94	4.45	-51.4	92	.978	129	151	8.9	-2.0	-4.9	.8	-6.0	-1.0
COL	12	2	33	1429	1700	10.7	955	237	737	1032	.301	1.705	6.01	96	6.40	-29.4	127	.981	118	**189**	-5.9	-10.3	-2.8	-.6	-13.6	4.6
Total	**128**	**93**	**647**	**23134²**		**9.2**	**11724**					**1.443**	**4.56**													

Wins
Hampton, M. (Hou) 22
Lima, J. (Hou) 21
Maddux, G. (Atl) 19

Win Percentage
Hampton, M. (Hou) .... .846
Bottenfield, K. (StL) .... .720
Millwood, K. (Atl) .... .720

Games
Kline, S. (Mon) 82
Wendell, T. (NY) 80
2 players tied with 79

Complete Games
Johnson, R. (Ari) 12
Schilling, C. (Phi) 8
Astacio, P. (Col) 7

Shutouts
Ashby, A. (SD) 3
6 players tied with 2

Saves
Urbina, U. (Mon) 41
Hoffman, T. (SD) 40
Wagner, B. (Hou) 39

Innings Pitched
Johnson, R. (Ari) 271²
Brown, K. (LA) 252¹
Lima, J. (Hou) 246¹

Fewest Hits/Game
Millwood, K. (Atl) 6.63
Johnson, R. (Ari) 6.86
Brown, K. (LA) 7.49

Fewest BB/Game
Reynolds, S. (Hou) 1.44
Maddux, G. (Atl) 1.52
Lima, J. (Hou) 1.61

Strikeouts
Johnson, R. (Ari) 364
Brown, K. (LA) 221
Astacio, P. (Col) 210

Ratio
Millwood, K. (Atl) 1.00
Johnson, R. (Ari) 1.02
Brown, K. (LA) 1.07

Earned Run Average
Johnson, R. (Ari) 2.48
Millwood, K. (Atl) 2.68
Hampton, M. (Hou) 2.90

Adjusted ERA
Johnson, R. (Ari) 184
Millwood, K. (Atl) 167
Hampton, M. (Hou) 152

Component ERA
Millwood, K. (Atl) 2.26
Johnson, R. (Ari) 2.49
Brown, K. (LA) 2.51

Opponents' Batting Avg.
Millwood, K. (Atl) .... .202
Johnson, R. (Ari) .... .208
Brown, K. (LA) .... .222

Adjusted Pitching Runs
Johnson, R. (Ari) 62
Millwood, K. (Atl) 48
Hampton, M. (Hou) 38

Win Shares – Pitchers
Hampton, M. (Hou) 26
Johnson, R. (Ari) 26
Millwood, K. (Atl) 22

TPW – Pitchers
Johnson, R. (Ari) 5.6
Hampton, M. (Hou) 4.6
Millwood, K. (Atl) 4.6

1999 American League

TEAM	G	W	L	PCT	GB	R	OR	EW	AB	H	2B	3B	HR	TB	BB	SO	SB	CS	AVG	OBP	SLG	OPS	OPS+	BR/A	PF	RC
East																										
NY	162	98	64	.605	....	900	731	98	5568	1568	302	36	193	2521	718	978	104	57	.282	.369	.453	.822	**110**	91	99	936
BOS	162	94	68	.580	4	836	**718**	93	5579	1551	334	42	176	2497	597	928	67	39	.278	.354	.448	.801	100	-4	103	880
TOR	162	84	78	.519	14	883	862	83	5642	1580	**337**	14	212	2581	578	1077	119	48	.280	.355	.457	.812	104	68	96	918
BAL	162	78	84	.481	20	851	815	84	5637	1572	299	21	203	2522	615	890	107	46	.279	.356	.447	.803	108	37	101	895
TB	162	69	93	.426	29	772	913	68	5586	1531	272	29	145	2296	544	1042	73	49	.274	.345	.411	.756	91	-79	101	777
Central																										
CLE	162	97	65	.599	....	**1009**	860	94	5634	1629	309	32	209	2629	743	1099	**147**	50	.289	**.377**	.467	**.844**	109	**100**	105	**1013**
CHI	162	75	86	.466	21.5	777	870	71	5644	1563	298	37	162	2421	499	**810**	110	50	.277	.339	.429	.768	94	-53	100	808
DET	161	69	92	.429	27.5	747	882	67	5481	1433	289	34	212	2426	458	1049	108	70	.261	.328	.443	.770	94	-71	100	781
KC	161	64	97	.398	32.5	856	921	75	5624	1584	294	**52**	151	2435	535	932	127	39	.282	.351	.433	.784	97	-18	102	848
MIN	161	63	97	.394	33	686	845	64	5495	1450	285	30	105	2110	500	978	118	60	.264	.331	.384	.715	79	-175	103	684
West																										
TEX	162	95	67	.586	....	945	859	89	**5651**	**1653**	304	29	230	**2705**	611	937	111	54	**.293**	.364	**.479**	.843	108	70	104	972
OAK	162	87	75	.537	8	893	846	85	5519	1430	287	20	235	2462	**770**	1129	70	**37**	.259	.357	.446	.803	108	75	96	898
SEA	162	79	83	.488	16	859	905	77	5572	1499	263	21	**244**	2536	610	1095	130	45	.269	.346	.455	.801	100	4	102	886
ANA	162	70	92	.432	25	711	826	69	5494	1404	248	22	158	2170	511	1022	71	45	.256	.324	.395	.719	83	-152	99	691
Total	1132					11725			78126	21447	4121	419	2635		8289	13966	1462	689	.275	.350	.439	.789				

Runs
Alomar, R. (Cle) 138
Green, S. (Tor) 134
Jeter, D. (NY) 134

Hits
Jeter, D. (NY) 219
Surhoff, B. (Bal) 207
Williams, B. (NY) 202

Doubles
Green, S. (Tor) 45
Dye, J. (KC) 44
Sweeney, M. (KC) 44

Triples
Offerman, J. (Bos) 11
3 players tied with 9

Home Runs
Griffey, K. (Sea) 48
Palmeiro, R. (Tex) 47
2 players tied with 44

Total Bases
Green, S. (Tor) 361
Palmeiro, R. (Tex) 356
Griffey, K. (Sea) 349

Runs Batted In
Ramirez, M. (Cle) 165
Palmeiro, R. (Tex) 148
2 players tied with 134

Bases On Balls
Thome, J. (Cle) 127
Giambi, J. (Oak) 105
2 players tied with 101

Stolen Bases
Hunter, B. (Sea,Det) 44
Vizquel, O. (Cle) 42
Goodwin, T. (Tex) 39

Batting Average
Garciaparra, N. (Bos) .357
Jeter, D. (NY) .349
Williams, B. (NY) .342

On-Base Percentage
Martinez, E. (Sea) .450
Ramirez, M. (Cle) .448
Jeter, D. (NY) .441

Slugging Average
Ramirez, M. (Cle) .663
Palmeiro, R. (Tex) .630
Garciaparra, N. (Bos) .603

Adjusted OPS
Ramirez, M. (Cle) 171
Palmeiro, R. (Tex) 157
Giambi, J. (Oak) 154

Adjusted Batting Runs
Ramirez, M. (Cle) 59.0
Jeter, D. (NY) 55.0
Giambi, J. (Oak) 51.0

Runs Created/Game
Ramirez, M. (Cle) 11.40
Garciaparra, N. (Bos) 10.20
Martinez, E. (Sea) 10.10

Fielding Runs
Sanchez, R. (KC) 24.6
Bordick, M. (Bal) 23.6
Martinez, T. (NY) 14.7

Win Shares – Batters
Ramirez, M. (Cle) 35
Alomar, R. (Cle) 35
Jeter, D. (NY) 35

TPW – Batters
Garciaparra, N. (Bos) 5.6
Ramirez, M. (Cle) 4.9
Alomar, R. (Cle) 4.5

TEAM	CG	SH	SV	IP	H	H/G	ER	HR	BB	SO	OAV	RAT	ERA	ERA+	CERA	PR+	PF	FA	E	DP	FR	BW	PW	FW	TPW	DIF
East																										
NY	6	10	**50**	1439^{2}	1402	8.8	660	**158**	581	1111	.255	1.377	4.13	115	4.18	102.9	97	.982	111	132	-11.8	8.4	9.5	-1.1	**16.8**	.2
BOS	6	**12**	**50**	1436^{2}	**1396**	8.8	638	160	**469**	1131	.253	1.298	**4.00**	124	**3.92**	155.5	102	.979	127	132	-1.0	-.4	**14.4**	-.1	13.9	-.9
TOR	14	9	39	1439	1582	9.9	786	191	575	1009	.280	1.499	4.92	100	5.04	-3.6	101	.983	106	165	2.9	3.5	-.3	.3	3.4	-.4
BAL	**17**	11	33	1435	1468	9.2	761	198	647	982	.269	1.474	4.77	98	4.90	-43.4	96	**.985**	89	191	29.5	6.3	-4.0	**2.7**	5.0	-8.0
TB	6	5	45	1433	1606	10.1	805	172	695	1055	.286	1.606	5.06	98	5.55	-8.9	102	.978	135	**198**	-5.2	-7.3	-.8	-.5	-8.6	-3.4
Central																										
CLE	3	6	46	1450^{1}	1503	9.3	789	197	634	1120	.268	1.473	4.90	103	4.85	27.7	104	.983	106	154	-8.7	**9.2**	2.6	-.8	11.0	5.0
CHI	6	3	39	1438^{1}	1608	10.1	786	210	596	968	.282	1.532	4.92	99	5.36	2.1	100	.977	136	149	-10.0	-4.9	.2	-.9	-5.6	.6
DET	4	6	33	1421	1528	9.7	817	209	583	976	.276	1.486	5.17	95	5.13	-43.0	102	.982	106	156	-0.2	-6.6	-4.0	.0	-10.6	-.4
KC	11	3	29	1420^{2}	1607	10.2	844	202	643	831	.288	1.584	5.35	**94**	5.64	-84.1	103	.980	125	188	29.1	-1.7	-7.8	2.7	-6.8	-9.2
MIN	13	8	34	1423^{1}	1591	10.1	794	208	487	927	.283	1.460	5.02	101	5.01	15.9	105	**.985**	92	150	-7.0	-16.2	1.5	-.6	-15.4	-1.6
West																										
TEX	6	9	47	1436^{1}	1626	10.2	809	186	509	979	.286	1.486	5.07	100	5.09	20.7	104	.981	119	169	-20.3	6.5	1.9	-1.9	6.5	7.5
OAK	6	5	48	1438^{1}	1537	9.6	749	160	569	967	.274	1.464	4.69	99	4.71	-10.8	95	.980	122	166	-8.8	6.9	-1.0	-.8	5.1	.9
SEA	7	6	40	1433^{2}	1613	10.1	834	191	684	980	.287	1.602	5.24	95	5.68	-37.3	103	.981	113	182	-4.9	.4	-3.4	-.5	-3.5	1.5
ANA	4	7	37	1431^{1}	1472	9.3	762	177	624	877	.269	1.464	4.79	101	4.77	-3.6	100	.983	106	156	11.8	-14.1	-.3	1.1	-13.3	2.3
Total	109	100	570	20076^{2}		9.7	10834					1.486	4.86													

Wins
Martinez, P. (Bos) 23
3 players tied with 18

Win Percentage
Martinez, P. (Bos) .852
Colon, B. (Cle) .783
Mussina, M. (Bal) .720

Games
Groom, B. (Oak) 76
Wells, B. (Min) 76
Trombley, M. (Min) 75

Complete Games
Wells, D. (Tor) 7
Erickson, S. (Bal) 6
Ponson, S. (Bal) 6

Shutouts
Erickson, S. (Bal) 3
4 players tied with 2

Saves
Rivera, M. (NY) 45
Hernandez, R. (TB) 43
Wetteland, J. (Tex) 43

Innings Pitched
Wells, D. (Tor) 231^{2}
Erickson, S. (Bal) 230^{1}
Moyer, J. (Sea) 228

Fewest Hits/Game
Martinez, P. (Bos) 6.75
Cone, D. (NY) 7.63
Hernandez, O. (NY) 7.85

Fewest BB/Game
Heredia, G. (Oak) 1.53
Martinez, P. (Bos) 1.56
Radke, B. (Min) 1.81

Strikeouts
Martinez, P. (Bos) 313
Finley, C. (Ana) 200
Sele, A. (Tex) 186

Ratio
Martinez, P. (Bos) .92
Milton, E. (Min) 1.23
Moyer, J. (Sea) 1.24

Earned Run Average
Martinez, P. (Bos) 2.07
Cone, D. (NY) 3.44
Mussina, M. (Bal) 3.50

Adjusted ERA
Martinez, P. (Bos) 240
Cone, D. (NY) 137
Radke, B. (Min) 136

Component ERA
Martinez, P. (Bos) 1.79
Mussina, M. (Bal) 3.54
Milton, E. (Min) 3.56

Opponents' Batting Avg.
Martinez, P. (Bos) .205
Cone, D. (NY) .229
Hernandez, O. (NY) .233

Adjusted Pitching Runs
Martinez, P. (Bos) 69
Radke, B. (Min) 33
Cone, D. (NY) 29

Win Shares – Pitchers
Martinez, P. (Bos) 27
Moyer, J. (Sea) 18
2 players tied with 17

TPW – Pitchers
Martinez, P. (Bos) 6.4
Radke, B. (Min) 3.0
Moyer, J. (Sea) 2.8

2000 National League

TEAM	G	W	L	PCT	GB	R	OR	EW	AB	H	2B	3B	HR	TB	BB	SO	SB	CS	AVG	OBP	SLG	OPS	OPS+	BR/A	PF	RC
East																										
ATL	162	95	67	.586	....	810	**714**	91	5489	1490	274	26	179	2353	595	1010	148	56	.271	.349	.429	.778	101	14	100	831
NY	162	94	68	.580	1	807	738	88	5486	1445	281	20	198	2360	675	1037	66	46	.263	.349	.430	.779	106	42	96	832
FLA	161	79	82	.491	15.5	731	797	74	5509	1441	274	29	160	2253	540	1184	**168**	55	.262	.334	.409	.743	96			
MON	162	67	95	.414	28	738	902	65	5535	1475	310	35	178	2389	476	1048	58	48	.266	.328	.432	.759	93	-78	102	768
PHI	162	65	97	.401	30	708	830	68	5511	1386	304	40	144	2202	611	1117	102	**30**	.251	.331	.400	.731	88	-88	100	747
Central																										
STL	162	95	67	.586	....	887	771	92	5478	1481	259	25	235	2495	675	1253	87	51	.270	.359	.455	.815	110	79	100	910
CIN	163	85	77	.525	10	825	765	87	5635	1545	302	36	200	2519	559	995	100	38	.274	.346	.447	.793	102	19	102	868
MIL	163	73	89	.451	22	740	826	72	5563	1366	297	25	177	2244	620	1245	72	44	.246	.328	.403	.731	91	-84	98	740
HOU	162	72	90	.444	23	938	944	80	5570	1547	289	36	**249**	**2655**	673	1129	114	52	.278	.364	.477	.841	110	91	105	**962**
PIT	162	69	93	.426	26	793	888	72	5643	1506	**320**	31	168	2392	564	1032	86	40	.267	.341	**.477**	**.841**	110	91	105	**962**
CHI	162	65	97	.401	30	764	904	67	5577	1426	272	23	183	2293	632	1120	93	37	.256	.337	.411	.748	96	-33	97	790
West																										
SF	162	97	65	.599	....	925	747	98	5519	1535	304	44	226	2605	**709**	1032	79	39	.278	.366	.472	.838	**125**	**209**	92	960
LA	162	86	76	.531	11	798	729	88	5481	1408	265	28	211	2362	668	1083	95	42	.257	.343	.431	.774	106	52	94	820
ARI	162	85	77	.525	12	792	754	85	5527	1466	282	44	179	2373	535	975	97	44	.265	.337	.429	.766	95	-48	103	802
COL	162	82	80	.506	15	**968**	897	87	**5660**	**1664**	**320**	**53**	161	2573	601	**907**	131	61	**.294**	**.366**	.455	.821	89	-78	125	943
SD	162	76	86	.469	21	752	815	74	5560	1413	279	37	157	2237	602	1177	131	53	.254	.332	.402	.734	97	-25	93	750
Total	1296					12976			88743	23594	4632	532	3005		9735	17344	1627	736	.266	.344	.432	.776				

Runs		Hits		Doubles		Triples		Home Runs		Total Bases	
Bagwell, J. (Hou)	152	Helton, T. (Col)	216	Helton, T. (Col)	59	Womack, T. (Ari)	14	Sosa, S. (Chi)	50	Helton, T. (Col)	405
Helton, T. (Col)	138	Vidro, J. (Mon)	200	Cirillo, J. (Col)	53	Guerrero, V. (Mon)	11	Bonds, B. (SF)	49	Sosa, S. (Chi)	383
2 players tied with	129	Jones, A. (Atl)	199	Vidro, J. (Mon)	51	Perez, N. (Col)	11	Bagwell, J. (Hou)	47	Guerrero, V. (Mon)	379

Runs Batted In		Bases On Balls		Stolen Bases		Batting Average		On-Base Percentage		Slugging Average	
Helton, T. (Col)	147	Bonds, B. (SF)	117	Castillo, L. (Fla)	62	Helton, T. (Col)	.372	Helton, T. (Col)	.470	Helton, T. (Col)	.698
Sosa, S. (Chi)	138	Giles, B. (Pit)	114	Goodwin, T. (Col,LA)	55	Alou, M. (Hou)	.355	Bonds, B. (SF)	.445	Bonds, B. (SF)	.688
Bagwell, J. (Hou)	132	Bagwell, J. (Hou)	107	Young, E. (Chi)	54	Guerrero, V. (Mon)	.345	Sheffield, G. (LA)	.442	Guerrero, V. (Mon)	.664

Adjusted OPS		Adjusted Batting Runs		Runs Created/Game		Fielding Runs		Win Shares – Batters		TPW – Batters	
Bonds, B. (SF)	195	Bonds, B. (SF)	75.0	Helton, T. (Col)	13.30	Perez, N. (Col)	25.7	Kent, J. (SF)	37	Bonds, B. (SF)	7.1
Sheffield, G. (LA)	180	Sheffield, G. (LA)	63.0	Bonds, B. (SF)	12.00	Vina, F. (StL)	23.7	Alfonzo, E. (NY)	36	Kent, J. (SF)	6.2
Kent, J. (SF)	168	Kent, J. (SF)	62.0	Sheffield, G. (LA)	10.70	Reese, P. (Cin)	23.5	Bonds, B. (SF)	32	Giles, B. (Pit)	5.4

TEAM	CG	SH	SV	IP	H	H/G	ER	HR	BB	SO	OAV	RAT	ERA	ERA+	CERA	PR+	PF	FA	E	DP	FR	BW	PW	FW	TPW	DIF
East																										
ATL	13	9	**53**	1440^1	1428	8.9	**648**	165	484	1093	.258	1.327	4.05	113	3.96	92.7	99	.979	129	138	-8.7	1.3	**8.7**	-.8	9.3	4.7
NY	8	10	49	1450	1398	8.7	670	164	574	1164	.252	1.360	4.16	106	4.11	47.4	95	.981	118	121	-8.3	4.0	4.5	-.8	7.7	5.3
FLA	5	4	48	1429^2	1477	9.3	729	169	650	1051	.269	1.488	4.59	97	4.70	-17.5	96	.980	125	144	-7.6	-1.9	-1.6	-.7	-4.3	3.3
MON	4	7	39	1424^2	1575	10.0	812	181	579	1011	.282	1.512	5.13	93	5.11	-43.9	104	.978	132	151	-11.5	-7.4	-4.1	-1.1	-12.6	-1.4
PHI	8	6	34	1438^2	1458	9.1	763	201	640	1123	.265	1.458	4.77	98	4.73	-24.3	101	.983	100	136	3.1	-8.3	-2.3	.3	-10.3	-5.7
Central																										
STL	10	7	37	1433^2	1403	8.8	698	196	606	1100	.259	1.401	4.38	105	4.51	16.1	100	.981	111	148	16.7	7.5	1.5	1.6	10.6	3.4
CIN	8	7	42	1456^1	1446	8.9	700	190	659	1015	.261	1.445	4.33	109	4.57	42.1	102	.982	111	156	18.8	1.8	4.0	1.8	7.5	-3.5
MIL	2	7	29	**1466^1**	1501	9.2	755	174	728	967	.269	1.520	4.63	98	4.93	-35.3	98	.981	118	**187**	21.7	-7.9	-3.3	**2.1**	-9.2	1.2
HOU	8	2	30	1437^2	1596	10.0	864	234	598	1064	.281	1.526	5.41	90	5.39	-64.4	105	.978	133	149	-25.3	8.6	-6.1	-2.4	.1	-9.1
PIT	5	7	27	1449	1554	9.6	794	163	711	1070	.277	1.563	4.93	93	5.09	-39.5	99	.980	132	169	-17.3	-1.6	-3.7	-1.6	-7.0	-5.0
CHI	10	5	39	1454^2	1505	9.3	849	231	658	1143	.268	1.487	5.25	**86**	5.08	-110.9	98	.983	100	139	-5.3	-3.2	-10.5	-.5	-14.1	-1.9
West																										
SF	9	**15**	47	1444^1	1452	9.0	675	**151**	623	1076	.266	1.437	4.21	100	4.42	0.9	91	**.985**	**93**	173	1.3	**19.7**	.1	.1	**19.9**	-3.9
LA	9	11	36	1445	**1379**	**8.6**	659	176	600	1154	**.252**	1.370	4.10	105	4.33	44.2	93	.978	135	151	-8.3	4.9	4.2	-.8	8.3	-3.3
ARI	**16**	8	38	1443^2	1441	9.0	698	190	500	**1220**	.262	1.344	4.35	108	4.20	59.7	102	.982	107	138	-5.7	-4.5	5.6	-.5	.6	3.4
COL	7	2	33	1430	1568	9.9	835	221	588	1001	.281	1.508	5.26	110	5.35	74.0	125	.985	94	176	5.8	-7.4	7.0	.5	.6	.9
SD	5	5	46	1459^1	1443	8.9	733	191	649	1071	.258	1.434	4.52	95	4.60	-52.5	93	.977	141	155	19.0	-2.3	-5.0	1.8	-5.5	.5
Total	127	112	627	23103^1	11882	9.2						1.449	4.63													

Wins		Win Percentage		Games		Complete Games		Shutouts		Saves	
Glavine, T. (Atl)	21	Johnson, R. (Ari)	.731	Kline, S. (Mon)	83	Johnson, R. (Ari)	8	Johnson, R. (Ari)	3	Alfonseca, A. (Fla)	45
Kile, D. (StL)	20	Estes, S. (SF)	.714	Sullivan, S. (Cin)	79	Schilling, C. (Ari,Phi)	8	Maddux, G. (Atl)	3	Hoffman, T. (SD)	43
2 players tied with	19	Elarton, S. (Hou)	.708	Myers, M. (Col)	78	2 players tied with	6	6 players tied with	2	2 players tied with	41

Innings Pitched		Fewest Hits/Game		Fewest BB/Game		Strikeouts		Ratio		Earned Run Average	
Lieber, J. (Chi)	251	Park, C. (LA)	6.89	Maddux, G. (Atl)	1.52	Johnson, R. (Ari)	347	Brown, K. (LA)	.99	Brown, K. (LA)	2.58
Maddux, G. (Atl)	249^1	Ankiel, R. (StL)	7.05	Anderson, B. (Ari)	1.65	Park, C. (LA)	217	Maddux, G. (Atl)	1.07	Johnson, R. (Ari)	2.64
Johnson, R. (Ari)	248^2	Brown, K. (LA)	7.08	Reed, R. (NY)	1.66	Brown, K. (LA)	216	Johnson, R. (Ari)	1.12	D'Amico, J. (Mil)	2.66

Adjusted ERA		Component ERA		Opponents' Batting Avg.		Adjusted Pitching Runs		Win Shares – Pitchers		TPW – Pitchers	
Johnson, R. (Ari)	178	Brown, K. (LA)	2.30	Brown, K. (LA)	.213	Johnson, R. (Ari)	58	Johnson, R. (Ari)	26	Johnson, R. (Ari)	5.4
D'Amico, J. (Mil)	171	Maddux, G. (Atl)	2.60	Park, C. (LA)	.214	Brown, K. (LA)	46	Maddux, G. (Atl)	24	Maddux, G. (Atl)	4.4
Brown, K. (LA)	168	Johnson, R. (Ari)	2.80	Ankiel, R. (StL)	.219	Maddux, G. (Atl)	45	Glavine, T. (Atl)	21	Brown, K. (LA)	4.0

2000 American League

TEAM	G	W	L	PCT	GB	R	OR	EW	AB	H	2B	3B	HR	TB	BB	SO	SB	CS	AVG	OBP	SLG	OPS	OPS+	BR/A	PF	RC
East																										
NY	161	87	74	.540	....	871	814	86	5556	1541	294	25	205	2500	631	1007	99	48	.277	.357	.450	.807	104	33	99	893
BOS	162	85	77	.525	2.5	792	**745**	86	5630	1503	316	32	167	2384	611	1019	43	30	.267	.343	.423	.767	90	-89	103	824
TOR	162	83	79	.512	4.5	861	908	77	5677	1562	328	21	**244**	2664	526	1026	89	34	.275	.343	.469	.812	100	-7	103	905
BAL	162	74	88	.457	13.5	794	913	70	5549	1508	310	22	184	2414	558	900	**126**	65	.272	.344	.435	.779	101	-1	95	814
TB	161	69	92	.429	18	733	842	69	5505	1414	253	22	162	2197	559	1022	90	46	.257	.331	.399	.730	85	-132	99	729
Central																										
CHI	162	95	67	.586	....	**978**	839	93	5646	1615	325	33	216	2654	591	960	119	42	.286	.359	.470	.829	106	60	102	952
CLE	162	90	72	.556	5	950	816	93	5683	1639	310	30	221	**2672**	685	1057	113	34	**.288**	**.370**	.470	**.840**	109	93	102	**1004**
DET	162	79	83	.488	16	823	827	81	5644	1553	307	41	177	2473	562	982	83	38	.275	.345	.438	.783	100	-6	97	847
KC	162	77	85	.475	18	879	930	76	**5709**	**1644**	281	27	150	2429	511	**840**	121	35	.288	.351	.425	.777	93	-53	103	855
MIN	162	69	93	.426	26	748	880	68	5615	1516	325	**49**	116	2287	556	1021	90	45	.270	.340	.407	.747	85	-131	104	769
West																										
OAK	161	91	70	.565	....	947	813	93	5560	1501	281	23	239	2545	750	1159	40	**15**	.270	.362	.458	.820	**109**	82	98	933
SEA	162	91	71	.562	0.5	907	780	93	5497	1481	300	26	198	2427	**775**	1073	122	56	.269	.365	.442	.806	**109**	94	94	908
ANA	162	82	80	.506	9.5	864	869	81	5628	1574	309	34	236	2659	608	1024	93	52	.280	.355	**.472**	.827	105	32	103	938
TEX	162	71	91	.438	20.5	848	974	70	5648	1601	**330**	35	173	2520	580	922	69	47	.283	.354	.446	.800	100	-8	102	872
Total	**1132**					**11995**			78547	21652	4269	420	2688		8503	14012	1297	587	.276	.351	.443	.795				

Runs
Damon, J. (KC) 136
Rodriguez, A. (Sea) 134
2 players tied with 121

Hits
Erstad, D. (Ana) 240
Damon, J. (KC) 214
Sweeney, M. (KC) 206

Doubles
Delgado, C. (Tor) 57
Garciaparra, N. (Bos) ... 51
Cruz, D. (Det) 46

Triples
Guzman, C. (Min) 20
Kennedy, A. (Ana) 11
Damon, J. (KC) 10

Home Runs
Glaus, T. (Ana) 47
Giambi, J. (Oak) 43
Thomas, F. (Chi) 43

Total Bases
Delgado, C. (Tor) 378
Erstad, D. (Ana) 366
Thomas, F. (Chi) 364

Runs Batted In
Martinez, E. (Sea) 145
Sweeney, M. (KC) 144
Thomas, F. (Chi) 143

Bases On Balls
Giambi, J. (Oak) 137
Delgado, C. (Tor) 123
Thome, J. (Cle) 118

Stolen Bases
Damon, J. (KC) 46
Alomar, R. (Cle) 39
DeShields, D. (Bal) 37

Batting Average
Garciaparra, N. (Bos) ... .372
Erstad, D. (Ana) .... .355
Ramirez, M. (Cle) .... .351

On-Base Percentage
Giambi, J. (Oak) .... .482
Delgado, C. (Tor) .... .472
Ramirez, M. (Cle) .... .460

Slugging Average
Ramirez, M. (Cle) .... .697
Delgado, C. (Tor) .... .664
Giambi, J. (Oak) .... .647

Adjusted OPS
Giambi, J. (Oak) 187
Ramirez, M. (Cle) 184
Delgado, C. (Tor) 178

Adjusted Batting Runs
Giambi, J. (Oak) 78.0
Delgado, C. (Tor) 75.0
Rodriguez, A. (Sea) 61.0

Runs Created/Game
Ramirez, M. (Cle) 13.00
Giambi, J. (Oak) 13.00
Delgado, C. (Tor) 12.90

Fielding Runs
Martinez, F. (TB) 21.7
Valentin, J. (Chi) 21.0
Velarde, R. (Oak) 18.7

Win Shares – Batters
Giambi, J. (Oak) 38
Rodriguez, A. (Sea) 37
Delgado, C. (Tor) 36

TPW – Batters
Rodriguez, A. (Sea) 8.1
Giambi, J. (Oak) 5.7
Glaus, T. (Ana) 5.5

TEAM	CG	SH	SV	IP	H	H/G	ER	HR	BB	SO	OAV	RAT	ERA	ERA+	CERA	PR+	PF	FA	E	DP	FR	BW	PW	FW	TPW	DIF
East																										
NY	9	6	40	1424[1]	1458	9.2	753	177	577	1040	.263	1.429	4.76	102	4.57	37.6	98	.981	109	132	-25.7	3.1	3.4	-2.4	4.2	2.8
BOS	7	12	46	**1452**[2]	**1433**	8.9	**683**	173	499	1121	**.257**	**1.330**	**4.23**	119	**4.13**	129.3	103	.982	109	120	-0.2	-8.1	**11.8**	.0	3.7	.3
TOR	**15**	4	37	1437[1]	1615	10.1	821	195	560	978	.285	1.513	5.14	99	5.28	-16.7	103	.983	100	176	1.1	-.6	-1.5	.1	-2.0	4.0
BAL	14	6	33	1433[1]	1547	9.7	855	202	665	1017	.275	1.543	5.37	88	5.21	-98.1	96	.981	116	151	-6.1	-.1	-9.0	-.6	-9.6	2.6
TB	10	8	38	1431[1]	1553	9.8	773	198	533	955	.277	1.457	4.86	102	4.97	-9.2	100	.981	118	169	21.2	-12.0	-.8	1.9	-10.9	-.1
Central																										
CHI	5	7	43	1450	1509	9.4	751	195	614	1037	.270	1.464	4.66	107	4.90	27.7	101	.978	133	**190**	23.8	5.5	2.5	2.2	10.2	3.8
CLE	6	5	34	1442	1511	9.4	775	173	666	**1213**	.270	1.509	4.84	103	4.90	35.1	101	**.988**	72	147	-14.0	8.5	3.2	-1.3	**10.4**	-1.4
DET	6	6	44	1443[1]	1583	9.9	755	177	**496**	978	.280	1.440	4.71	102	4.71	19.9	98	.983	105	171	-6.4	-.6	1.8	-.6	-.7	-2.7
KC	10	6	29	1439[1]	1585	9.9	876	239	693	927	.282	1.583	5.48	93	5.67	-88.0	104	.983	102	185	29.7	-4.9	-8.1	2.7	-10.2	6.2
MIN	6	4	35	1432[2]	1634	10.3	819	212	516	1042	.287	1.501	5.14	100	5.24	21.6	105	.983	102	155	-22.3	-12.0	2.0	-2.0	-12.1	.1
West																										
OAK	7	11	43	1435[1]	1535	9.6	730	**158**	615	963	.274	1.498	4.58	104	4.80	47.1	97	.978	134	164	-20.7	7.5	4.3	-1.9	9.9	1.1
SEA	4	10	44	1441[1]	1442	9.0	720	167	634	998	.262	1.440	4.49	101	4.48	-12.2	92	.984	99	182	**34.4**	2.9	-2.4	**3.2**	3.7	-2.7
ANA	5	3	**46**	1448	1534	9.5	805	228	662	846	.273	1.517	5.00	101	5.21	-25.8	103	.979	134	162		-.8	-5.0	-2.5	-8.2	-1.8
TEX	3	4	39	1429	1683	10.6	876	202	661	918	.294	1.640	5.52	96	5.87	-54.2	102	.978	135	162	-27.3					
Total	107	92	551	20141		9.7	10992					1.490	4.91													

Wins
Hudson, T. (Oak) 20
Wells, D. (Tor) 20
Pettitte, A. (NY) 19

Win Percentage
Hudson, T. (Oak) .... .769
Martinez, P. (Bos) ...... .750
Burba, D. (Cle) .... .727

Games
Wunsch, K. (Chi) 83
Venafro, M. (Tex) 77
Wells, B. (Min) 76

Complete Games
Wells, D. (Tor) 9
Martinez, P. (Bos) 7
2 players tied with 6

Shutouts
Martinez, P. (Bos) 4
Hudson, T. (Oak) 2
Sele, A. (Sea) 2

Saves
Jones, T. (Det) 42
Lowe, D. (Bos) 42
Sasaki, K. (Sea) 37

Innings Pitched
Mussina, M. (Bal) .... 237[2]
Wells, D. (Tor) .... 229[2]
Rogers, K. (Tex) .... 227[1]

Fewest Hits/Game
Martinez, P. (Bos) 5.31
Hudson, T. (Oak) 7.52
Colon, B. (Cle) 7.80

Fewest BB/Game
Wells, D. (Tor) 1.21
Martinez, P. (Bos) 1.33
Mussina, M. (Bal) 1.74

Strikeouts
Martinez, P. (Bos) 284
Colon, B. (Cle) 212
Hernandez, O. (NY) 210

Ratio
Martinez, P. (Bos) ...... .74
Mussina, M. (Bal) 1.19
Hernandez, O. (NY) 1.21

Earned Run Average
Martinez, P. (Bos) 1.74
Clemens, R. (NY) 3.70
Mussina, M. (Bal) 3.79

Adjusted ERA
Martinez, P. (Bos) 289
Sirotka, M. (Chi) 131
Clemens, R. (NY) 131

Component ERA
Martinez, P. (Bos) 1.39
Mussina, M. (Bal) 3.37
Hudson, T. (Oak) 3.43

Opponents' Batting Avg.
Martinez, P. (Bos) ...... .167
Hudson, T. (Oak) .... .227
Colon, B. (Cle) .... .233

Adjusted Pitching Runs
Martinez, P. (Bos) 79
Clemens, R. (NY) 29
Mussina, M. (Bal) 26

Win Shares – Pitchers
Martinez, P. (Bos) 29
Mussina, M. (Bal) 18
Wells, D. (Tor) 18

TPW – Pitchers
Martinez, P. (Bos) 7.3
Clemens, R. (NY) 2.7
Mussina, M. (Bal) 2.3

2001 National League

TEAM	G	W	L	PCT	GB	R	OR	EW	AB	H	2B	3B	HR	TB	BB	SO	SB	CS	AVG	OBP	SLG	OPS	OPS+	BR/A	PF	RC
East																										
ATL	162	88	74	.543	....	729	**643**	91	5498	1432	263	24	174	2265	493	1039	85	46	.260	.326	.412	.738	93	-59	102	727
PHI	162	86	76	.531	2	746	719	84	5497	1431	295	29	164	2276	551	1125	153	47	.260	.332	.414	.747	100	13	97	772
NY	162	82	80	.506	6	642	713	73	5459	1361	273	18	147	2111	545	1062	66	48	.249	.325	.387	.711	93	-58	95	682
FLA	162	76	86	.469	12	742	744	81	5542	1461	**325**	30	166	2344	470	1145	89	40	.264	.329	.423	.752	102	11	96	766
MON	162	68	94	.420	20	670	812	66	5379	1361	320	28	131	2130	478	1071	101	51	.253	.321	.396	.717	88	-94	102	666
Central																										
STL	162	93	69	.574	....	814	684	95	5450	1469	274	32	199	2404	529	1089	91	**35**	.270	.341	.441	.782	107	61	99	820
HOU	162	93	69	.574	....	847	769	89	5528	1500	313	29	208	2495	581	1119	64	49	.271	.350	.451	.801	106	44	105	868
CHI	162	88	74	.543	5	777	701	89	5406	1409	268	32	194	2323	577	1077	67	36	.261	.339	.430	.769	108	65	95	786
MIL	162	68	94	.420	25	740	806	74	5488	1378	273	30	209	2323	488	1399	66	36	.251	.320	.426	.746	99	-16	97	749
CIN	162	66	96	.407	27	735	850	69	5583	1464	304	22	176	2340	468	1172	103	54	.262	.327	.419	.746	93	-63	104	750
PIT	162	62	100	.383	31	657	858	60	5398	1333	256	25	161	2122	467	1106	93	73	.247	.315	.393	.708	85	-128	102	654
West																										
ARI	162	92	70	.568	....	818	677	96	5595	1494	284	35	208	2472	587	1052	71	38	.267	.343	.442	.785	101	8	106	853
SF	162	90	72	.556	2	799	748	86	5612	1493	304	40	**235**	2582	625	1090	57	42	.266	.345	.460	.805	**121**	158	93	891
LA	162	86	76	.531	6	758	744	83	5493	1399	264	27	161	2335	519	1062	89	42	.255	.325	.425	.750	106	40	92	757
SD	162	79	83	.488	13	789	812	79	5482	1379	273	26	161	2187	**678**	1273	129	44	.252	.338	.399	.737	105	55	91	761
COL	162	73	89	.451	19	**923**	906	83	**5690**	**1663**	324	**61**	213	**2748**	511	**1027**	132	54	**.292**	**.357**	**.483**	**.840**	99	3	122	**976**
Total	**1296**					**12186**			**88100**	**23027**	**4613**	**488**	**2952**		**8567**	**17908**	**1456**	**735**	**.261**	**.334**	**.425**	**.759**				

Runs
Sosa, S. (Chi) 146
Helton, T. (Col) 132
Bonds, B. (SF) 129

Hits
Aurilia, R. (SF) 206
Pierre, J. (Col) 202
Gonzalez, L. (Ari) 198

Doubles
Berkman, L. (Hou) 55
Helton, T. (Col) 54
Kent, J. (SF) 49

Triples
Rollins, J. (Phi) 12
Pierre, J. (Col) 11
Uribe, J. (Col) 11

Home Runs
Bonds, B. (SF) 73
Sosa, S. (Chi) 64
Gonzalez, L. (Ari) 57

Total Bases
Sosa, S. (Chi) 425
Gonzalez, L. (Ari) 419
Bonds, B. (SF) 411

Runs Batted In
Sosa, S. (Chi) 160
Helton, T. (Col) 146
Gonzalez, L. (Ari) 142

Bases On Balls
Bonds, B. (SF) 177
Sosa, S. (Chi) 116
2 players tied with 106

Stolen Bases
Pierre, J. (Col) 46
Rollins, J. (Phi) 46
Guerrero, V. (Mon) 37

Batting Average
Walker, L. (Col) .350
Helton, T. (Col) .336
Alou, M. (Hou) .331

On-Base Percentage
Bonds, B. (SF) .517
Walker, L. (Col) .455
Sosa, S. (Chi) .445

Slugging Average
Bonds, B. (SF) .863
Helton, T. (Col) .737
Gonzalez, L. (Ari) .688

Adjusted OPS
Bonds, B. (SF) 267
Sosa, S. (Chi) 208
Gonzalez, L. (Ari) 172

Adjusted Batting Runs
Bonds, B. (SF) 135.0
Sosa, S. (Chi) 95.0
Gonzalez, L. (Ari) 69.0

Runs Created/Game
Bonds, B. (SF) 18.90
Sosa, S. (Chi) 12.80
Walker, L. (Col) 12.10

Fielding Runs
Polanco, P. (StL) 24.1
Cabrera, O. (Mon) 23.9
Miller, D. (Ari) 23.7

Win Shares – Batters
Bonds, B. (SF) 54
Sosa, S. (Chi) 42
Gonzalez, L. (Ari) 37

TPW – Batters
Bonds, B. (SF) 12.2
Sosa, S. (Chi) 8.7
Gonzalez, L. (Ari) 6.0

TEAM	CG	SH	SV	IP	H	H/G	ER	HR	BB	SO	OAV	RAT	ERA	ERA+	CERA	PR+	PF	FA	E	DP	FR	BW	PW	FW	TPW	DIF
East																										
ATL	5	13	41	1447¹	1363	8.5	**578**	153	499	1133	.250	1.287	**3.59**	122	**3.64**	**122.0**	101	.983	103	133	8.0	-5.7	**11.9**	.8	6.9	.1
PHI	8	7	47	1445¹	1417	8.8	667	170	527	1086	.259	1.345	4.15	102	4.11	-3.0	97	.985	91	145	16.9	1.2	-.3	1.6	2.6	2.4
NY	6	**14**	**48**	1445²	1418	8.8	654	186	**438**	1191	.257	1.284	4.07	101	3.90	0.9	95	.983	101	132	7.6	-5.6	.1	.7	-4.8	5.8
FLA	5	11	32	1438	1397	8.7	691	151	617	1119	.257	1.401	4.32	97	4.28	-26.4	97	.983	103	**174**	8.6	1.1	-2.6	.8	-.7	-4.3
MON	5	11	28	1431¹	1509	9.5	745	190	525	1103	.272	1.421	4.68	95	4.68	-8.8	102	.982	108	139	-27.6	-9.2	-.9	-2.7	-12.7	-.3
Central																										
STL	8	11	38	1435¹	1389	8.7	627	196	526	1083	.256	1.334	3.93	108	4.30	17.8	98	.982	110	156	**30.9**	6.0	1.7	**3.0**	10.7	1.3
HOU	7	6	**48**	1454²	1453	9.0	707	221	486	1228	.261	1.333	4.37	104	4.43	24.8	105	.982	110	138	4.3	4.3	2.4	.4	7.1	4.9
CHI	8	6	41	1437	1357	8.5	643	164	550	**1344**	.249	1.327	4.03	103	3.93	44.2	95	.981	109	113	-25.4	6.4	4.3	-2.5	8.2	-1.2
MIL	3	8	28	1436¹	1452	9.1	740	197	667	1057	.265	1.475	4.64	92	4.81	-63.5	98	.983	103	156	6.0	-1.6	-6.2	.6	-7.2	-5.8
CIN	2	2	35	1442²	1572	9.8	765	198	515	943	.279	1.447	4.77	95	4.80	-13.3	105	.978	138	136	-22.8	-6.1	-1.3	-2.2	-9.6	-5.4
PIT	8	9	36	1416¹	1493	9.5	794	167	549	908	.272	1.442	5.05	89	4.66	-83.8	103	.978	133	168	-4.4	-12.5	-8.2	-.4	-21.0	2.0
West																										
ARI	**12**	13	34	1459²	**1352**	**8.3**	627	195	461	1297	**.247**	**1.242**	3.87	118	3.77	92.2	105	**.986**	**84**	148	20.9	.8	9.0	2.0	11.8	-.8
SF	3	8	47	**1463¹**	1437	8.8	680	**145**	579	1080	.258	1.378	4.18	95	4.06	-36.6	91	.980	118	170	2.1	**15.4**	-3.6	.2	**12.0**	-3.0
LA	3	5	46	1450²	1387	8.6	685	184	524	1212	.252	1.317	4.25	94	4.06	-31.3	92	.981	116	138	-7.8	3.9	-3.0	-.8	.0	5.0
SD	5	6	46	1440²	1519	9.5	724	219	476	1088	.269	1.385	4.52	**88**	4.59	-60.2	92	.976	145	127	-24.0	5.4	-5.9	-2.3	-2.8	.8
COL	8	8	26	1430	1522	9.6	841	239	598	1058	.275	1.483	5.29	101	5.18	-1.0	122	.984	96	167	7.3	.3	-.1	.7	.9	-8.9
Total	**96**	**138**	**621**	**23074¹**		**9.0**	**11168**					**1.368**	**4.36**													

Wins
Morris, M. (StL) 22
Schilling, C. (Ari) 22
Johnson, R. (Ari) 21

Win Percentage
Schilling, C. (Ari) .786
Johnson, R. (Ari) .778
Lieber, J. (Chi) .769

Games
Kline, S. (StL) 89
Lloyd, G. (Mon) 84
2 players tied with 82

Complete Games
Schilling, C. (Ari) 6
Lieber, J. (Chi) 5
Vazquez, J. (Mon) 5

Shutouts
Maddux, G. (Atl) 3
Vazquez, J. (Mon) 3
4 players tied with 2

Saves
Nen, R. (SF) 45
3 players tied with 43

Innings Pitched
Schilling, C. (Ari) 256²
Johnson, R. (Ari) 249³
Park, C. (LA) 234

Fewest Hits/Game
Johnson, R. (Ari) 6.52
Wood, K. (Chi) 6.56
Park, C. (LA) 7.04

Fewest BB/Game
Maddux, G. (Atl) 1.04
Schilling, C. (Ari) 1.37
Lieber, J. (Chi) 1.59

Strikeouts
Johnson, R. (Ari) 372
Schilling, C. (Ari) 293
Park, C. (LA) 218

Ratio
Johnson, R. (Ari) 1.01
Maddux, G. (Atl) 1.06
Schilling, C. (Ari) 1.08

Earned Run Average
Johnson, R. (Ari) 2.49
Schilling, C. (Ari) 2.98
Burkett, J. (Atl) 3.04

Adjusted ERA
Johnson, R. (Ari) 184
Schilling, C. (Ari) 154
Burkett, J. (Atl) 145

Component ERA
Johnson, R. (Ari) 2.35
Maddux, G. (Atl) 2.70
Vazquez, J. (Mon) 2.75

Opponents' Batting Avg.
Wood, K. (Chi) .202
Johnson, R. (Ari) .203
Park, C. (LA) .216

Adjusted Pitching Runs
Johnson, R. (Ari) 54
Schilling, C. (Ari) 42
Maddux, G. (Atl) 34

Win Shares – Pitchers
Johnson, R. (Ari) 26
Schilling, C. (Ari) 24
Vazquez, J. (Mon) 21

TPW – Pitchers
Johnson, R. (Ari) 5.0
Schilling, C. (Ari) 3.8
Maddux, G. (Atl) 3.4

2001 American League

TEAM	G	W	L	PCT	GB	R	OR	EW	AB	H	2B	3B	HR	TB	BB	SO	SB	CS	AVG	OBP	SLG	OPS	OPS+	BR/A	PF	RC
East																										
NY	161	95	65	.594	....	804	713	90	5577	1488	289	20	203	2426	519	1035	161	53	.267	.336	.435	.771	100	8	101	819
BOS	161	82	79	.509	13.5	772	745	83	5605	1493	316	29	198	2461	520	1131	46	35	.266	.336	.439	.775	102	2	101	814
TOR	162	80	82	.494	16	767	753	82	5663	1489	287	36	195	2433	470	1094	156	55	.263	.328	.430	.757	95	-37	102	797
BAL	162	63	98	.391	32.5	687	829	66	5472	1359	262	24	136	2077	514	989	133	53	.248	.322	.380	.701	89	-83	95	675
TB	162	62	100	.383	34	672	887	59	5524	1426	311	21	121	2142	456	1116	115	52	.258	.321	.388	.709	87	-105	99	679
Central																										
CLE	162	91	71	.562	....	897	821	88	5600	1559	294	37	212	2563	577	1076	79	41	.278	.353	.458	.811	110	84	101	905
MIN	162	85	77	.525	6	771	766	82	5560	1514	328	38	164	2410	495	1083	146	67	.272	.339	.433	.772	100	-6	102	808
CHI	162	83	79	.512	8	798	795	81	5464	1463	300	29	214	2463	520	998	123	59	.268	.337	.451	.788	102	10	104	819
DET	162	66	96	.407	25	724	876	66	5537	1439	291	**60**	139	2267	466	972	133	61	.260	.323	.409	.733	96	-39	96	725
KC	162	65	97	.401	26	729	858	68	5643	1503	277	37	152	2310	406	**898**	100	42	.266	.321	.409	.730	84	-138	109	723
West																										
SEA	162	116	46	.716	....	**927**	**627**	111	5680	**1637**	310	38	169	2530	614	989	**174**	42	**.288**	**.364**	.445	.809	**119**	**181**	94	**948**
OAK	162	102	60	.630	14	884	645	106	5573	1469	**334**	22	199	2444	**640**	1021	68	**29**	.264	.349	.439	.787	106	54	100	861
ANA	162	75	87	.463	41	691	730	77	5551	1447	275	26	158	2248	494	1001	116	52	.261	.330	.405	.735	90	-78	102	746
TEX	162	73	89	.451	43	890	968	74	**5685**	1566	326	23	**246**	**2676**	548	1093	97	32	.275	.347	**.471**	**.818**	109	79	104	927
Total	**1133**					**11013**			**78134**	**20852**	**4200**	**440**	**2506**		**7239**	**14496**	**1647**	**673**	**.267**	**.336**	**.428**	**.764**				

Runs
Rodriguez, A. (Tex) 133
Suzuki, I. (Sea) 127
Boone, B. (Sea) 118

Hits
Suzuki, I. (Sea) 242
Boone, B. (Sea) 206
Stewart, S. (Tor) 202

Doubles
Giambi, J. (Oak) 47
Sweeney, M. (KC) 46
Stewart, S. (Tor) 44

Triples
Guzman, C. (Min) 14
Alomar, R. (Cle) 12
Beltran, C. (KC) 12

Home Runs
Rodriguez, A. (Tex) 52
Thome, J. (Cle) 49
Palmeiro, R. (Tex) 47

Total Bases
Rodriguez, A. (Tex) 393
Boone, B. (Sea) 360
Giambi, J. (Oak) 343

Runs Batted In
Boone, B. (Sea) 141
Gonzalez, J. (Cle) 140
Rodriguez, A. (Tex) 135

Bases On Balls
Giambi, J. (Oak) 129
Delgado, C. (Tor) 111
Thome, J. (Cle) 111

Stolen Bases
Suzuki, I. (Sea) 56
Cedeno, R. (Det) 55
Soriano, A. (NY) 43

Batting Average
Suzuki, I. (Sea) .350
Giambi, J. (Oak) .342
Alomar, R. (Cle) .336

On-Base Percentage
Giambi, J. (Oak) .483
Martinez, E. (Sea) .430
Alomar, R. (Cle) .420

Slugging Average
Giambi, J. (Oak) .660
Thome, J. (Cle) .624
Rodriguez, A. (Tex) .622

Adjusted OPS
Giambi, J. (Oak) 197
Thome, J. (Cle) 167
Martinez, E. (Sea) 163

Adjusted Batting Runs
Giambi, J. (Oak) 83.0
Rodriguez, A. (Tex) 58.0
Thome, J. (Cle) 55.0

Runs Created/Game
Giambi, J. (Oak) 12.60
Thome, J. (Cle) 10.00
Ramirez, M. (Bos) 9.40

Fielding Runs
Sanchez, R. (KC) 22.6
Hairston, J. (Bal) 18.9
Bell, D. (Sea) 17.7

Win Shares – Batters
Giambi, J. (Oak) 38
Rodriguez, A. (Tex) 37
Alomar, R. (Cle) 37

TPW – Batters
Rodriguez, A. (Tex) 7.2
Giambi, J. (Oak) 6.7
Boone, B. (Sea) 6.3

TEAM	CG	SH	SV	IP	H	H/G	ER	HR	BB	SO	OAV	RAT	ERA	ERA+	CERA	PR+	PF	FA	E	DP	FR	BW	PW	FW	TPW	DIF
East																										
NY	7	9	**57**	1451^1	1429	8.9	649	158	465	**1266**	.257	1.305	4.02	112	3.94	102.6	100	.982	109	132	-29.6	.8	9.8	-2.8	7.8	7.2
BOS	3	9	48	1448	1412	8.8	667	**146**	544	1259	.254	1.351	4.15	108	4.08	76.0	100	.981	113	129	-27.2	.2	7.3	-2.6	4.9	-2.9
TOR	7	10	41	1462^2	1553	9.6	696	165	490	1041	.275	1.397	4.28	107	4.51	41.3	103	.985	97	184	8.6	-3.5	4.0	.8	1.3	-2.3
BAL	10	6	31	1432^1	1504	9.4	744	194	528	938	.269	1.419	4.67	92	4.71	-80.3	96	.979	125	137	14.8	-8.0	-7.7	1.4	-14.2	-2.8
TB	1	6	30	1423^2	1513	9.6	781	207	569	1030	.273	1.462	4.94	91	5.01	-79.4	100	.977	139	144	5.1	-10.1	-7.6	.5	-17.2	-1.8
Central																										
CLE	3	4	42	1446^2	1512	9.4	746	148	573	1218	.270	1.441	4.64	97	4.50	6.8	101	.982	107	137	-27.7	8.1	.7	-2.6	6.1	3.9
MIN	12	8	45	1441^1	1494	9.3	722	192	445	965	.268	1.345	4.51	102	4.35	20.9	103	.982	108	121	-8.5	-.6	2.0	-.8	.6	3.4
CHI	8	7	51	1433^1	1465	9.2	725	181	500	921	.266	1.371	4.55	101	4.48	1.5	103	.981	118	149	7.0	.9	.1	.7	1.8	.2
DET	**16**	2	34	1429^1	1624	10.2	795	180	553	859	.288	1.523	5.01	87	5.24	-82.4	97	.979	131	165	-23.5	-3.8	-7.9	-2.3	-13.9	-1.1
KC	5	1	30	1440	1537	9.6	779	209	576	911	.276	1.467	4.87	101	5.02	-31.5	110	.981	117	**204**	36.8	-13.2	-3.0	3.5	-12.7	-3.3
West																										
SEA	8	**14**	56	**1465**	**1293**	**7.9**	**576**	160	465	1051	**.236**	**1.200**	**3.54**	117	**3.38**	59.0	93	**.986**	**83**	137	**40.1**	**17.4**	5.6	**3.8**	**26.9**	8.1
OAK	13	9	44	1463^1	1384	8.5	583	153	**440**	1117	.249	1.246	3.59	123	3.54	**130.9**	99	.980	125	151	4.1	5.1	**12.5**	.4	18.1	2.9
ANA	6	1	43	1437^2	1452	9.1	671	168	525	947	.263	1.375	4.20	109	4.28	49.3	102	.983	103	142	8.2	-7.4	4.7	.8	-1.9	-4.1
TEX	4	3	37	1438^1	1670	10.4	913	222	596	951	.293	1.575	5.71	**82**	5.71	-155.6	104	.981	114	167	-12.1	7.5	-14.9	-1.2	-8.5	.5
Total	**103**	**89**	**589**	**20213**		**9.3**	**10047**					**1.391**	**4.47**													

Wins
Mulder, M. (Oak) 21
Clemens, R. (NY) 20
Moyer, J. (Sea) 20

Win Percentage
Clemens, R. (NY) .870
Abbott, P. (Sea) .810
Sabathia, C. (Cle) .773

Games
Quantrill, P. (Tor) 80
Stanton, M. (NY) 76
Grimsley, J. (KC) 73

Complete Games
Sparks, S. (Det) 8
Mulder, M. (Oak) 6
Radke, B. (Min) 6

Shutouts
Mulder, M. (Oak) 4
Garcia, F. (Sea) 3
Mussina, M. (NY) 3

Saves
Rivera, M. (NY) 50
Sasaki, K. (Sea) 45
Foulke, K. (Chi) 42

Innings Pitched
Garcia, F. (Sea) 238^2
Hudson, T. (Oak) 235
Mays, J. (Min) 233^2

Fewest Hits/Game
Sabathia, C. (Cle) 7.44
Garcia, F. (Sea) 7.50
Buehrle, M. (Chi) 7.64

Fewest BB/Game
Radke, B. (Min) 1.04
Mussina, M. (NY) 1.65
Pettitte, A. (NY) 1.84

Strikeouts
Nomo, H. (Bos) 220
Mussina, M. (NY) 214
Clemens, R. (NY) 213

Ratio
Buehrle, M. (Chi) 1.07
Mussina, M. (NY) 1.07
Moyer, J. (Sea) 1.10

Earned Run Average
Garcia, F. (Sea) 3.05
Mussina, M. (NY) 3.15
Mays, J. (Min) 3.16

Adjusted ERA
Mays, J. (Min) 145
Mussina, M. (NY) 143
Buehrle, M. (Chi) 140

Component ERA
Garcia, F. (Sea) 2.61
Mussina, M. (NY) 2.65
Buehrle, M. (Chi) 2.79

Opponents' Batting Avg.
Garcia, F. (Sea) .225
Sabathia, C. (Cle) .228
Zito, B. (Oak) .230

Adjusted Pitching Runs
Mussina, M. (NY) 39
Mays, J. (Min) 39
Buehrle, M. (Chi) 31

Win Shares – Pitchers
Mays, J. (Min) 22
Mussina, M. (NY) 20
Clemens, R. (NY) 19

TPW – Pitchers
Mussina, M. (NY) 3.7
Mays, J. (Min) 3.7
Buehrle, M. (Chi) 3.0

2002 National League

TEAM	G	W	L	PCT	GB	R	OR	EW	AB	H	2B	3B	HR	TB	BB	SO	SB	CS	AVG	OBP	SLG	OPS	OPS+	BR/A	PF	RC
East																										
ATL	161	101	59	.631	....	708	**565**	98	5495	1428	280	25	164	2250	558	1028	76	39	.260	.334	.409	.744	99	-7	101	742
MON	162	83	79	.512	19	735	718	83	5479	1432	300	36	162	2290	575	1104	118	64	.261	.337	.418	.755	100	-6	103	767
PHI	161	80	81	.497	21.5	710	724	79	5523	1428	**325**	**41**	165	2330	640	1095	104	43	.259	.341	.422	.763	110	85	95	802
FLA	162	79	83	.488	23	699	763	74	5496	1433	280	32	146	2215	595	1130	**177**	73	.261	.340	.403	.743	104	42	96	758
NY	161	75	86	.466	26.5	690	703	79	5496	1409	238	22	160	2171	486	1044	87	42	.256	.324	.395	.719	97	-26	96	693
Central																										
STL	162	97	65	.599	....	787	648	97	5505	1475	285	26	175	2337	542	**927**	86	42	.268	.341	.425	.765	109	64	97	795
HOU	162	84	78	.519	13	749	695	87	5503	1441	291	32	167	2297	589	1120	71	27	.262	.340	.417	.757	99	1	104	779
CIN	162	78	84	.481	19	709	774	74	5470	1386	297	21	169	2232	583	1188	116	52	.253	.333	.408	.741	97	-21	102	749
PIT	161	72	89	.447	24.5	641	730	70	5330	1300	263	20	142	2029	537	1109	86	49	.244	.322	.381	.702	89	-87	101	664
CHI	162	67	95	.414	30	706	759	75	5496	1351	259	29	**200**	2268	585	1269	63	**21**	.246	.323	.413	.736	100	-5	98	741
MIL	162	56	106	.346	41	627	821	60	5415	1369	269	29	139	2113	500	1125	94	50	.253	.322	.390	.712	93	-58	98	670
West																										
ARI	162	98	64	.605	....	**819**	674	97	5508	1471	283	**41**	165	2331	**643**	1016	92	46	.267	**.349**	.423	.772	99	2	109	820
SF	162	95	66	.590	2.5	783	616	99	5497	1465	300	35	198	**2429**	616	961	74	**21**	.267	.347	**.442**	**.789**	117	140	95	**846**
LA	162	92	70	.568	6	713	643	89	**5554**	1464	286	29	155	2273	428	940	96	37	.264	.322	.409	.732	103	17	93	717
COL	162	73	89	.451	25	778	898	69	5512	**1508**	283	**41**	152	2329	497	1043	103	53	**.274**	.323	.423	.762	91	-67	116	781
SD	162	66	96	.407	32	662	815	64	5515	1393	243	29	136	2102	547	1062	71	44	.253	.323	.381	.705	99	-18	91	674
Total	**1294**					**11516**			**87794**	**22753**	**4482**	**488**	**2595**		**8921**	**17161**	**1514**	**703**	**.259**	**.334**	**.410**	**.744**		**-18**	**91**	**674**

Runs			Hits			Doubles			Triples			Home Runs			Total Bases		
Sosa, S. (Chi)		122	Guerrero, V. (Mon)		206	Abreu, B. (Phi)		50	Rollins, J. (Phi)		10	Sosa, S. (Chi)		49	Guerrero, V. (Mon)		364
Pujols, A. (StL)		118	Kent, J. (SF)		195	Lowell, M. (Fla)		44	4 players tied with		8	Bonds, B. (SF)		46	Kent, J. (SF)		352
Bonds, B. (SF)		117	Vidro, J. (Mon)		190	2 players tied with		43				2 players tied with		42	Berkman, L. (Hou)		334

Runs Batted In			Bases On Balls			Stolen Bases			Batting Average			On-Base Percentage			Slugging Average		
Berkman, L. (Hou)		128	Bonds, B. (SF)		198	Castillo, L. (Fla)		48	Bonds, B. (SF)		.370	Bonds, B. (SF)		.584	Bonds, B. (SF)		.799
Pujols, A. (StL)		127	Giles, B. (Pit)		135	Pierre, J. (Col)		47	Walker, L. (Col)		.338	Giles, B. (Pit)		.454	Giles, B. (Pit)		.622
Burrell, P. (Phi)		116	Dunn, A. (Cin)		128	Roberts, D. (LA)		45	Guerrero, V. (Mon)		.336	Jones, C. (Atl)		.438	Walker, L. (Col)		.602

Adjusted OPS			Adjusted Batting Runs			Runs Created/Game			Fielding Runs			Win Shares – Batters			TPW – Batters		
Bonds, B. (SF)		272	Bonds, B. (SF)		128.0	Bonds, B. (SF)		21.40	Uribe, J. (Col)		28.9	Bonds, B. (SF)		49	Bonds, B. (SF)		11.7
Giles, B. (Pit)		178	Giles, B. (Pit)		65.0	Giles, B. (Pit)		10.90	Rolen, S. (StL,Phi)		22.6	Pujols, A. (StL)		32	Giles, B. (Pit)		6.3
Edmonds, J. (StL)		161	Guerrero, V. (Mon)		53.0	Walker, L. (Col)		10.00	Hernandez, J. (Mil)		22.5	Giles, B. (Pit)		32	Kent, J. (SF)		6.1

TEAM	CG	SH	SV	IP	H	H/G	ER	HR	BB	SO	OAV	RAT	ERA	ERA+	CERA	PR+	PF	FA	E	DP	FR	BW	PW	FW	TPW	DIF
East																										
ATL	3	**15**	**57**	1467†	1302	8.0	**511**	123	554	1058	**.240**	1.265	**3.13**	130	**3.40**	**131.8**	100	.982	114	170	23.9	-.7	**13.2**	2.4	14.9	6.1
MON	9	3	39	1453	1475	9.1	641	165	508	1088	.265	1.365	3.97	107	4.16	46.9	104	.978	139	160	-0.9	-.6	4.7	-.1	4.0	-2.0
PHI	5	9	47	1449²	1381	8.6	671	153	570	1075	.252	1.346	4.17	94	3.98	-51.1	95	.986	88	156	7.6	8.5	-5.1	.8	4.2	-4.2
FLA	11	12	36	1456¹	1449	9.0	706	151	631	1104	.262	1.428	4.36	90	4.38	-74.0	96	.983	106	163	5.2	4.2	-7.4	.5	-2.7	.7
NY	9	10	36	1442²	1408	8.8	624	163	543	1107	.256	1.352	3.89	102	4.02	20.8	96	.976	144	138	-12.2	-2.6	2.1	-1.2	-1.7	-3.3
Central																										
STL	4	9	42	1446¹	1355	8.4	595	141	547	1009	.251	1.315	3.70	107	3.85	17.4	96	.983	103	168	23.0	6.4	1.7	2.3	10.4	5.6
HOU	2	11	43	1445	1423	8.9	643	151	546	1219	.260	1.363	4.00	106	4.07	54.1	104	**.986**	83	149	-14.2	.1	5.4	-1.4	4.1	-1.1
CIN	2	8	42	1453²	1502	9.3	690	173	550	980	.269	1.412	4.27	99	4.47	-9.4	103	.981	120	169	1.1	-2.1	-.9	.1	-3.0	.0
PIT	2	7	47	1412²	1447	9.2	664	163	572	920	.268	1.429	4.23	99	4.46	-19.7	102	.982	115	**177**	9.2	-8.8	-2.0	.9	-9.8	1.8
CHI	11	9	23	1441¹	1373	8.6	687	167	606	**1333**	.253	1.373	4.29	94	4.16	-34.7	98	.981	114	144	-12.4	-.5	-3.5	-1.2	-5.2	-8.8
MIL	7	4	32	1432¹	1468	9.2	752	199	666	1026	.268	1.490	4.73	87	4.93	-100.5	100	.983	103	154	-5.4	-5.8	-10.1	-.5	-16.4	-8.6
West																										
ARI	**14**	10	40	1446²	1361	8.5	630	170	**421**	1303	.247	**1.232**	3.92	113	3.61	97.8	108	.985	89	116	-16.8	.2	9.8	-1.7	8.4	8.6
SF	10	13	43	1437¹	1349	8.4	596	**116**	523	992	.251	1.302	3.54	109	3.57	36.1	94	.985	90	166	15.4	**14.0**	3.6	1.5	**19.2**	-4.2
LA	4	**15**	56	1457²	1311	8.1	598	165	555	1132	.241	1.280	3.69	103	3.68	12.1	93	.985	90	134	7.7	1.7	1.2	.8	3.7	7.3
COL	1	8	43	1426²	1554	9.8	825	225	582	920	.277	1.497	5.20	92	5.23	-54.4	116	.982	112	158	-15.4	-6.8	-5.5	-1.5	-13.8	5.8
SD	5	10	40	1436¹	1522	9.5	737	177	582	1108	.274	1.465	4.62	82	4.81	-125.6	92	.979	128	162	-15.7	-1.8	-12.6	-1.6	-15.9	.9
Total	**99**	**153**	**666**	**23105**		**8.8**	**10540**					**1.369**	**4.11**													

Wins			Win Percentage			Games			Complete Games			Shutouts			Saves		
Johnson, R. (Ari)		24	Johnson, R. (Ari)		.828	Quantrill, P. (LA)		86	Johnson, R. (Ari)		8	Burnett, A. (Fla)		5	Smoltz, J. (Atl)		55
Schilling, C. (Ari)		23	Miller, W. (Hou)		.789	Dotel, O. (Hou)		83	Burnett, A. (Fla)		7	Johnson, R. (Ari)		4	Gagne, E. (LA)		52
Oswalt, R. (Hou)		19	Schilling, C. (Ari)		.767	Worrell, T. (SF)		80	2 players tied with		5	Hernandez, L. (SF)		3	Williams, M. (Pit)		46

Innings Pitched			Fewest Hits/Game			Fewest BB/Game			Strikeouts			Ratio			Earned Run Average		
Johnson, R. (Ari)		260	Burnett, A. (Fla)		6.74	Schilling, C. (Ari)		1.15	Johnson, R. (Ari)		334	Schilling, C. (Ari)		.97	Johnson, R. (Ari)		2.32
Schilling, C. (Ari)		259¹	Johnson, R. (Ari)		6.82	Perez, O. (LA)		1.54	Schilling, C. (Ari)		316	Perez, O. (LA)		.99	Maddux, G. (Atl)		2.62
Oswalt, R. (Hou)		233	Moss, D. (Atl)		7.04	Vazquez, J. (Mon)		1.91	Wood, K. (Chi)		217	Johnson, R. (Ari)		1.03	Glavine, T. (Atl)		2.96

Adjusted ERA			Component ERA			Opponents' Batting Avg.			Adjusted Pitching Runs			Win Shares – Pitchers			TPW – Pitchers		
Johnson, R. (Ari)		191	Perez, O. (LA)		2.31	Johnson, R. (Ari)		.208	Johnson, R. (Ari)		64	Johnson, R. (Ari)		29	Johnson, R. (Ari)		6.3
Maddux, G. (Atl)		156	Schilling, C. (Ari)		2.33	Burnett, A. (Fla)		.209	Schilling, C. (Ari)		38	Schilling, C. (Ari)		24	Schilling, C. (Ari)		3.8
Oswalt, R. (Hou)		141	Johnson, R. (Ari)		2.54	Clement, M. (Chi)		.215	Oswalt, R. (Hou)		34	Oswalt, R. (Hou)		20	Oswalt, R. (Hou)		3.4

2002 American League

TEAM	G	W	L	PCT	GB	R	OR	EW	AB	H	2B	3B	HR	TB	BB	SO	SB	CS	AVG	OBP	SLG	OPS	OPS+	BR/A	PF	RC
East
NY	161	103	58	.640	....	**897**	697	100	5601	1540	314	12	223	2547	**640**	1171	100	38	.275	**.357**	.455	**.811**	115	133	99	**908**
BOS	162	93	69	.574	10.5	859	665	101	5640	1560	**348**	33	177	2505	545	944	80	28	.277	.348	.444	.792	107	63	102	868
TOR	162	78	84	.481	25.5	813	828	80	5581	1457	305	38	187	2399	452	1142	71	**18**	.246	.311	.403	.714	93	-60	95	679
BAL	162	67	95	.414	36.5	667	773	69	5491	1353	311	27	165	2213	452	993	110	48	.246	.311	.403	.714	93	-60	95	679
TB	161	55	106	.342	48	673	918	56	5604	1418	297	35	133	2184	456	1115	102	45	.253	.316	.390	.706	88	-98	98	687
Central
MIN	161	94	67	.584	....	768	712	87	5582	1518	**348**	36	167	2439	472	1089	79	62	.272	.335	.437	.772	102	4	101	798
CHI	162	81	81	.500	13.5	856	798	87	5502	1475	289	29	217	2473	555	952	75	31	.268	.340	.449	.790	105	43	103	848
CLE	162	74	88	.457	20.5	739	837	71	5423	1349	255	26	192	2232	542	1000	52	37	.249	.323	.412	.735	96	-41	98	706
KC	162	62	100	.383	32.5	737	891	66	5535	1415	285	42	140	2204	524	921	**140**	65	.256	.326	.398	.724	82	-141	112	724
DET	161	55	106	.342	39	575	864	49	5406	1340	265	37	124	2051	363	1035	65	44	.248	.303	.379	.682	85	-128	94	603
West
OAK	162	103	59	.636	....	800	654	97	5558	1450	279	28	205	2400	609	1008	46	20	.261	.341	.432	.773	104	36	100	824
ANA	162	99	63	.611	4	851	**644**	103	**5678**	**1603**	333	32	152	2456	462	**805**	117	51	**.282**	.344	.433	.777	105	45	100	847
SEA	162	93	69	.574	10	814	699	93	5569	1531	285	31	152	2334	629	1003	137	58	.275	.354	.419	.773	109	84	96	837
TEX	162	72	90	.444	31	843	882	77	5618	1510	304	27	230	2558	554	1055	62	34	.269	.341	**.455**	.796	104	31	105	865
Total 1132						**10892**			77788	20519	4218	433	2464		7325	14233	1236	579	.264	.334	.424	.758				

Runs			Hits			Doubles			Triples			Home Runs			Total Bases	
Soriano, A. (NY)	128		Soriano, A. (NY)	209		Anderson, G. (Ana)	56		Damon, J. (Bos)	11		Rodriguez, A. (Tex)	57		Rodriguez, A. (Tex)	389
Rodriguez, A. (Tex)	125		Suzuki, I. (Sea)	208		Garciaparra, N. (Bos)	56		Winn, R. (TB)	9		Thome, J. (Cle)	52		Soriano, A. (NY)	381
Jeter, D. (NY)	124		2 players tied with	204		Soriano, A. (NY)	51		2 players tied with	8		Palmeiro, R. (Tex)	43		Ordonez, M. (Chi)	352

Runs Batted In			Bases On Balls			Stolen Bases			Batting Average			On-Base Percentage			Slugging Average	
Rodriguez, A. (Tex)	142		Thome, J. (Cle)	122		Soriano, A. (NY)	41		Ramirez, M. (Bos)	.349		Ramirez, M. (Bos)	.451		Thome, J. (Cle)	.677
Ordonez, M. (Chi)	135		Giambi, J. (NY)	109		Beltran, C. (KC)	35		Sweeney, M. (KC)	.340		Thome, J. (Cle)	.450		Ramirez, M. (Bos)	.647
Tejada, M. (Oak)	131		Palmeiro, R. (Tex)	104		Jeter, D. (NY)	32		Williams, B. (NY)	.333		Giambi, J. (NY)	.439		Rodriguez, A. (Tex)	.623

Adjusted OPS			Adjusted Batting Runs			Runs Created/Game			Fielding Runs			Win Shares – Batters			TPW – Batters	
Thome, J. (Cle)	197		Thome, J. (Cle)	73.0		Thome, J. (Cle)	12.10		Kennedy, A. (Ana)	23.0		Rodriguez, A. (Tex)	35		Rodriguez, A. (Tex)	6.2
Ramirez, M. (Bos)	183		Giambi, J. (NY)	65.0		Ramirez, M. (Bos)	11.50		Bordick, M. (Bal)	19.6		Thome, J. (Cle)	34		Thome, J. (Cle)	5.5
Giambi, J. (NY)	173		Ramirez, M. (Bos)	56.0		Giambi, J. (NY)	9.90		Koskie, C. (Min)	18.8		Giambi, J. (NY)	34		Giambi, J. (NY)	4.9

TEAM	CG	SH	SV	IP	H	H/G	ER	HR	BB	SO	OAV	RAT	ERA	ERA+	CERA	PR+	PF	FA	E	DP	FR	BW	PW	FW	TPW	DIF
East
NY	9	11	53	1452	1441	8.9	625	144	**403**	1135	.256	1.270	3.87	113	3.63	120.4	98	.979	127	117	-44.1	**12.8**	11.6	-4.2	**20.2**	2.8
BOS	5	17	51	1446	**1339**	**8.3**	603	146	430	**1157**	**.246**	**1.223**	3.75	120	**3.57**	96.4	101	.983	104	140	22.8	6.1	9.3	2.2	17.5	-5.5
TOR	6	6	41	1438¹	1504	9.4	767	177	590	991	.269	1.456	4.80	96	4.76	-19.4	103	.982	107	159	-11.7	-2.1	-1.9	-1.1	-5.1	2.1
BAL	8	3	31	1450²	1491	9.2	719	208	549	967	.266	1.406	4.46	96	4.68	-45.6	96	.985	91	**173**	16.6	-5.8	-4.4	1.6	-8.6	-5.4
TB	**12**	3	25	1440¹	1567	9.8	846	215	620	925	.279	1.518	5.29	**84**	5.39	-156.2	100	.979	126	168	23.4	-9.4	-15.0	2.3	-22.2	-2.8
Central
MIN	8	9	47	1444²	1454	9.1	662	184	439	1026	.261	1.310	4.12	109	4.09	58.6	101	**.987**	74	124	-0.2	.4	5.6	.0	6.0	8.0
CHI	7	7	35	1423	1422	9.0	716	190	528	945	.260	1.370	4.53	101	4.38	-15.0	102	.984	97	157	13.0	-3.9	-6.3	1.3	4.0	-4.0
CLE	9	4	34	1424²	1508	9.5	777	142	603	1058	.274	1.482	4.91	89	4.72	-65.1	98	.981	113	161	-16.9	-13.6	-2.4	-.7	-16.6	-2.4
KC	**12**	6	30	1441	1587	9.9	834	212	572	909	.281	1.498	5.21	96	5.12	-24.4	113	.977	142	148	-9.2	-12.4	-8.7	-.9	-22.0	-3.0
DET	11	7	33	1414	1593	10.1	774	163	463	794	.285	1.454	4.93	87	4.85	-90.6	97	.977	142	148	-9.2	-12.4	-8.7	-.9	-22.0	-3.0
West
OAK	9	**19**	48	1452	1391	8.6	**593**	**135**	474	1021	.252	1.284	**3.68**	120	3.67	123.4	99	.984	102	144	-9.5	3.5	**11.9**	-.9	14.4	7.6
ANA	7	14	**54**	1452¹	1345	**8.3**	595	169	509	999	.247	1.277	3.69	120	3.75	73.3	99	.986	87	151	**46.4**	4.3	7.0	**4.5**	15.8	2.2
SEA	8	12	43	1445¹	1422	8.8	654	178	441	1063	.257	1.289	4.07	104	3.94	35.4	95	.986	88	134	-11.4	8.1	3.4	-1.1	10.4	1.6
TEX	4	4	33	1439²	1528	9.6	824	194	669	1030	.272	1.526	5.15	96	5.19	-55.3	106	.984	99	152	-15.1	3.0	-5.3	-1.5	-3.8	-5.2
Total	115	122	558	20164		9.2	9989					1.383	4.46													

Wins			Win Percentage			Games			Complete Games			Shutouts			Saves	
Zito, B. (Oak)	23		Martinez, P. (Bos)	.833		Koch, B. (Oak)	84		Byrd, P. (KC)	7		Weaver, J. (Det,NY)	3		Guardado, E. (Min)	45
Lowe, D. (Bos)	21		Zito, B. (Oak)	.821		Romero, J. (Min)	81		Buehrle, M. (Chi)	5		7 players tied with	2		Koch, B. (Oak)	44
Martinez, P. (Bos)	20		Washburn, J. (Ana)	.750		Stanton, M. (NY)	79		Kennedy, J. (TB)	5					2 players tied with	40

Innings Pitched			Fewest Hits/Game			Fewest BB/Game			Strikeouts			Ratio			Earned Run Average	
Halladay, R. (Tor)	239¹		Martinez, P. (Bos)	6.50		Reed, R. (Min)	1.24		Martinez, P. (Bos)	239		Martinez, P. (Bos)	.92		Martinez, P. (Bos)	2.26
Buehrle, M. (Chi)	239		Wakefield, T. (Bos)	6.67		Byrd, P. (KC)	1.50		Clemens, R. (NY)	192		Lowe, D. (Bos)	.97		Lowe, D. (Bos)	2.58
Hudson, T. (Oak)	238¹		Lowe, D. (Bos)	6.80		Milton, E. (Min)	1.58		2 players tied with	182		Wakefield, T. (Bos)	1.05		Zito, B. (Oak)	2.75

Adjusted ERA			Component ERA			Opponents' Batting Avg.			Adjusted Pitching Runs			Win Shares – Pitchers			TPW – Pitchers	
Martinez, P. (Bos)	199		Martinez, P. (Bos)	1.98		Martinez, P. (Bos)	.198		Halladay, R. (Tor)	47		Zito, B. (Oak)	25		Martinez, P. (Bos)	4.4
Lowe, D. (Bos)	174		Lowe, D. (Bos)	2.13		Wakefield, T. (Bos)	.204		Martinez, P. (Bos)	46		Hudson, T. (Oak)	23		Halladay, R. (Tor)	4.4
Wakefield, T. (Bos)	160		Wakefield, T. (Bos)	2.54		Lowe, D. (Bos)	.211		Zito, B. (Oak)	43		Lowe, D. (Bos)	22		Lowe, D. (Bos)	4.2

2003 National League

TEAM	G	W	L	PCT	GB	R	OR	EW	AB	H	2B	3B	HR	TB	BB	SO	SB	CS	AVG	OBP	SLG	OPS	OPS+	BR/A	PF	RC
East																										
ATL	162	101	61	.623	....	907	740	97	5670	1608	321	31	235	2696	545	933	68	22	.284	.352	.475	.827	119	155	100	946
FLA	162	91	71	.562	10	751	692	88	5490	1459	292	44	157	2310	515	978	150	74	.266	.335	.421	.756	106	40	96	772
PHI	162	86	76	.531	15	791	697	91	5543	1448	325	27	166	2325	651	1155	72	29	.261	.335	.419	.756	111	92	94	815
MON	162	83	79	.512	18	711	716	80	5437	1404	294	25	144	2180	522	990	100	39	.258	.328	.401	.729	80	-146	118	709
NY	161	66	95	.410	34.5	642	754	68	5341	1317	262	24	124	1999	489	1035	70	31	.247	.316	.374	.690	87	-97	97	628
Central																										
CHI	162	88	74	.543	....	724	683	86	5519	1431	302	24	172	2297	492	1158	73	31	.259	.326	.416	.742	99	-13	98	739
HOU	162	87	75	.537	1	805	677	95	5583	1466	308	30	191	2407	557	1021	66	30	.263	.338	.431	.769	100	3	104	816
STL	162	85	77	.525	3	876	796	89	5672	1580	342	32	196	2574	580	952	82	32	.279	.353	.454	.807	119	158	96	908
PIT	162	75	87	.463	13	753	801	76	5581	1492	275	45	163	2346	529	1049	86	37	.267	.340	.420	.761	101	10	102	807
CIN	162	69	93	.426	19	694	886	62	5509	1349	239	21	182	2176	524	1326	80	34	.245	.319	.395	.714	92	-63	98	707
MIL	162	68	94	.420	20	714	873	65	5548	1423	266	24	196	2325	547	1221	99	39	.256	.331	.419	.750	102	16	98	759
West																										
SF	161	100	61	.621	....	755	638	94	5456	1440	281	29	180	2319	593	980	53	37	.264	.340	.425	.765	107	48	97	784
LA	162	85	77	.525	15.5	574	556	84	5458	1328	260	25	124	2010	407	985	80	36	.243	.304	.368	.673	84	-128	94	606
ARI	162	84	78	.519	16.5	717	685	85	5570	1467	303	47	152	2320	531	1006	76	38	.263	.332	.417	.749	91	-74	110	766
COL	162	74	88	.457	26.5	853	892	77	5518	1472	330	31	198	2458	619	1134	63	38	.267	.346	.445	.792	97	-19	114	845
SD	162	64	98	.395	36.5	678	831	65	5531	1442	257	32	128	2147	565	1073	76	39	.261	.335	.388	.724	103	24	91	720
Total	1295					11945			88426	23126	4657	491	2708		8666	16996	1294	585	.262	.334	.417	.751				

Runs
Pujols, A. (StL) 137
Helton, T. (Col) 135
Furcal, R. (Atl) 130

Hits
Pujols, A. (StL) 212
Helton, T. (Col) 209
Pierre, J. (Fla) 204

Doubles
Pujols, A. (StL) 51
4 players tied with 49

Triples
Finley, S. (Ari) 10
Furcal, R. (Atl) 10
2 players tied with 8

Home Runs
Thome, J. (Phi) 47
Bonds, B. (SF) 45
Sexson, R. (Mil) 45

Total Bases
Pujols, A. (StL) 394
Helton, T. (Col) 367
Sheffield, G. (Atl) 348

Runs Batted In
Wilson, P. (Col) 141
Sheffield, G. (Atl) 132
Thome, J. (Phi) 131

Bases On Balls
Bonds, B. (SF) 148
Helton, T. (Col) 111
Thome, J. (Phi) 111

Stolen Bases
Pierre, J. (Fla) 65
Podsednik, S. (Mil) 43
Roberts, D. (LA) 40

Batting Average
Pujols, A. (StL) .359
Helton, T. (Col) .358
Bonds, B. (SF) .341

On-Base Percentage
Bonds, B. (SF) .531
Helton, T. (Col) .463
Pujols, A. (StL) .443

Slugging Average
Bonds, B. (SF) .749
Pujols, A. (StL) .667
Helton, T. (Col) .630

Adjusted OPS
Bonds, B. (SF) 236
Pujols, A. (StL) 192
Sheffield, G. (Atl) 164

Adjusted Batting Runs
Bonds, B. (SF) 94.0
Pujols, A. (StL) 81.0
Sheffield, G. (Atl) 59.0

Runs Created/Game
Bonds, B. (SF) 16.90
Pujols, A. (StL) 11.90
Helton, T. (Col) 11.20

Fielding Runs
Perez, N. (StL) 27.2
LoDuca, P. (LA) 24.5
Uribe, J. (Col) 22.0

Win Shares – Batters
Pujols, A. (StL) 41
Bonds, B. (SF) 39
2 players tied with 35

TPW – Batters
Bonds, B. (SF) 8.9
Pujols, A. (StL) 7.3
Helton, T. (Col) 5.5

TEAM	CG	SH	SV	IP	H	H/G	ER	HR	BB	SO	OAV	RAT	ERA	ERA+	CERA	PR+	PF	FA	E	DP	FR	BW	PW	FW	TPW	DIF
East																										
ATL	4	7	51	1456¹	1425	8.8	663	147	555	992	.257	1.360	4.10	103	3.98	24.4	99	.981	121	166	-5.0	15.2	2.4	-.5	17.1	2.9
FLA	7	11	36	1445¹	1415	8.8	648	128	530	1132	.258	1.346	4.04	101	3.91	0.6	96	.987	78	162	7.9	3.9	.1	.8	4.7	5.3
PHI	9	13	33	1443²	1386	8.6	648	142	536	1060	.253	1.331	4.04	99	3.93	-8.2	93	.984	97	146	-2.6	9.0	-.8	-.3	8.0	-3.0
MON	15	10	42	1437²	1467	9.2	640	181	463	1028	.264	1.342	4.01	126	4.29	168.5	118	.983	102	152	-2.4	-14.4	16.6	-.2	1.9	.1
NY	3	10	38	1413¹	1497	9.5	704	168	576	907	.273	1.467	4.48	93	4.70	-45.6	97	.980	118	158	-8.2	-9.5	-4.5	-.8	-14.8	.8
Central																										
CHI	13	14	36	1456¹	1304	8.1	619	143	617	1404	.241	1.319	3.83	110	3.79	62.0	98	.983	106	157	-0.6	-1.3	6.1	-.1	4.8	2.2
HOU	1	5	50	1450	1350	8.4	622	161	565	1139	.248	1.321	3.86	115	3.97	57.2	104	.985	95	149	33.9	.3	5.6	3.3	9.3	-3.3
STL	9	10	41	1463²	1544	9.5	748	210	508	969	.271	1.402	4.60	88	4.69	-92.0	95	.987	77	138	1.3	15.6	-9.0	.1	6.7	-2.7
PIT	7	10	38	1444¹	1527	9.5	744	178	502	926	.272	1.405	4.64	94	4.49	-41.4	102	.980	123	159	-2.2	1.0	-4.1	-.2	-3.3	-2.7
CIN	4	5	38	1446¹	1578	9.8	818	209	590	932	.278	1.499	5.09	84	5.08	-128.2	100	.977	141	152	-4.6	-6.2	-12.6	-.5	-19.3	7.3
MIL	5	3	44	1452	1590	9.9	810	219	575	1034	.279	1.491	5.02	85	5.13	-98.3	99	.981	114	142	-27.7	1.6	-9.7	-2.7	-10.9	-2.1
West																										
SF	7	10	43	1437¹	1349	8.4	595	136	546	1006	.250	1.318	3.73	110	3.80	29.2	96	.987	80	163	30.8	4.8	2.9	3.0	10.7	9.3
LA	3	17	58	1457²	1254	7.7	511	127	526	1289	.234	1.221	3.16	127	3.27	114.7	94	.981	119	164	24.4	-12.6	11.3	2.4	1.1	2.9
ARI	7	11	42	1455	1379	8.5	621	150	526	1291	.250	1.309	3.84	121	3.84	147.0	109	.983	107	132	-14.2	-7.3	14.5	-1.4	5.8	-2.8
COL	3	4	34	1420	1629	10.3	821	200	552	866	.290	1.536	5.20	94	5.42	-26.1	115	.981	116	165	-25.8	-1.9	-2.6	-2.5	-7.0	.0
SD	2	10	31	1431¹	1458	9.2	774	208	611	1091	.264	1.446	4.87	81	4.79	-140.5	92	.983	102	141	-8.8	2.4	-13.8	-.9	-12.3	-4.7
Total	99	150	661	23110¹		9.0	10986					1.382	4.28													

Wins
Ortiz, R. (Atl) 21
Prior, M. (Chi) 18
Williams, W. (StL) 18

Win Percentage
Schmidt, J. (SF) .773
3 players tied with .750

Games
Quantrill, P. (LA) 89
Villarreal, O. (Ari) 86
2 players tied with 80

Complete Games
Hernandez, L. (Mon) 8
3 players tied with 5

Shutouts
Millwood, K. (Phi) 3
Morris, M. (StL) 3
Schmidt, J. (SF) 3

Saves
Gagne, E. (LA) 55
Smoltz, J. (Atl) 45
Wagner, B. (Hou) 44

Innings Pitched
Hernandez, L. (Mon) 233¹
Vazquez, J. (Mon) 230²
Millwood, K. (Phi) 222

Fewest Hits/Game
Wood, K. (Chi) 6.48
Schmidt, J. (SF) 6.59
Webb, B. (Ari) 6.97

Fewest BB/Game
Maddux, G. (Atl) 1.36
Schilling, C. (Ari) 1.71
Sheets, B. (Mil) 1.75

Strikeouts
Wood, K. (Chi) 266
Prior, M. (Chi) 245
Vazquez, J. (Mon) 241

Ratio
Schmidt, J. (SF) .95
Schilling, C. (Ari) 1.05
Prior, M. (Chi) 1.10

Earned Run Average
Schmidt, J. (SF) 2.34
Brown, K. (LA) 2.39
Prior, M. (Chi) 2.43

Adjusted ERA
Schmidt, J. (SF) 175
Prior, M. (Chi) 173
Brown, K. (LA) 168

Component ERA
Schmidt, J. (SF) 1.93
Schilling, C. (Ari) 2.59
Brown, K. (LA) 2.68

Opponents' Batting Avg.
Schmidt, J. (SF) .200
Wood, K. (Chi) .203
Webb, B. (Ari) .212

Adjusted Pitching Runs
Hernandez, L. (Mon) 48
Vazquez, J. (Mon) 47
Prior, M. (Chi) 42

Win Shares – Pitchers
Hernandez, L. (Mon) 23
3 players tied with 22

TPW – Pitchers
Hernandez, L. (Mon) 4.8
Prior, M. (Chi) 4.6
Vazquez, J. (Mon) 4.5

2003 American League

TEAM	G	W	L	PCT	GB	R	OR	EW	AB	H	2B	3B	HR	TB	BB	SO	SB	CS	AVG	OBP	SLG	OPS	OPS+	BR/A	PF	RC
East																										
NY	163	101	61	.623	....	877	716	97	5605	1518	304	14	230	2540	**684**	1042	98	33	.271	.358	.453	.812	115	136	98	915
BOS	162	95	67	.586	6	**961**	809	95	**5769**	**1667**	371	40	238	2573	**2832**	1081	37	25	**.289**	**.363**	**.491**	**.854**	120	173	102	1029
TOR	162	86	76	.531	15	894	826	87	5661	1580	357	33	190	2573	546	1081	89	36	.279	.352	.455	.806	109	73	102	894
BAL	163	71	91	.438	30	743	820	73	5665	1516	277	24	152	2297	431	902	89	36	.268	.325	.405	.731	95	-44	96	740
TB	162	63	99	.389	38	715	852	67	5654	1501	298	38	137	2286	420	1030	**142**	42	.265	.323	.404	.727	92	-59	98	739
Central																										
MIN	162	90	72	.556	....	801	758	85	5655	1567	318	**45**	155	2440	512	1027	94	44	.277	.344	.431	.775	102	20	101	830
CHI	162	86	76	.531	4	791	715	89	5487	1445	303	19	220	2446	519	916	77	29	.263	.333	.446	.779	104	30	100	809
KC	162	83	79	.512	7	836	867	78	5568	1526	288	39	162	2378	476	926	120	42	.274	.339	.427	.767	89	-80	113	806
CLE	162	68	94	.420	22	699	778	72	5572	1413	296	26	158	2235	466	1062	86	61	.254	.318	.401	.719	91	-84	97	695
DET	162	43	119	.265	47	591	928	47	5466	1312	201	39	153	2050	443	1099	98	63	.240	.303	.375	.678	84	-139	92	611
West																										
OAK	162	96	66	.593	....	768	643	95	5497	1398	317	24	176	2291	556	898	48	**14**	.254	.329	.417	.746	95	-41	101	760
SEA	162	93	69	.574	3	795	**637**	99	5561	1509	290	33	139	2282	586	989	108	37	.271	.346	.410	.757	102	32	97	800
ANA	162	77	85	.475	19	736	743	80	5487	1473	276	33	150	2265	476	**838**	129	61	.268	.333	.413	.746	100	-6	96	747
TEX	162	71	91	.438	25	826	969	68	5664	1506	274	36	**239**	2569	488	1052	65	25	.266	.332	.454	.786	96	-32	109	851
Total	**1135**					**11033**			**78311**	**20931**	**4170**	**443**	**2499**		**7223**	**13805**	**1279**	**547**	**.267**	**.336**	**.428**	**.764**				

Runs			Hits			Doubles			Triples			Home Runs			Total Bases		
Rodriguez, A. (Tex)		124	Wells, V. (Tor)		215	Anderson, G. (Ana)		49	Guzman, C. (Min)		14	Rodriguez, A. (Tex)		47	Wells, V. (Tor)		373
Garciaparra, N. (Bos)		120	Suzuki, I. (Sea)		212	Wells, V. (Tor)		49	Garciaparra, N. (Bos)		13	Delgado, C. (Tor)		42	Rodriguez, A. (Tex)		364
Wells, V. (Tor)		118	Young, M. (Tex)		204	Huff, A. (TB)		47	Beltran, C. (KC)		10	Thomas, F. (Chi)		42	Soriano, A. (NY)		358

Runs Batted In			Bases On Balls			Stolen Bases			Batting Average			On-Base Percentage			Slugging Average		
Delgado, C. (Tor)		145	Giambi, J. (NY)		129	Crawford, C. (TB)		55	Mueller, B. (Bos)		.326	Ramirez, M. (Bos)		.430	Rodriguez, A. (Tex)		.600
Rodriguez, A. (Tex)		118	Delgado, C. (Tor)		109	Sanchez, A. (Det)		44	Ramirez, M. (Bos)		.325	Delgado, C. (Tor)		.430	Delgado, C. (Tor)		.593
2 players tied with		117	2 players tied with		100	Beltran, C. (KC)		41	Jeter, D. (NY)		.324	Giambi, J. (NY)		.415	Ortiz, D. (Bos)		.592

Adjusted OPS			Adjusted Batting Runs			Runs Created/Game			Fielding Runs			Win Shares – Batters			TPW – Batters		
Delgado, C. (Tor)		163	Delgado, C. (Tor)		58.0	Delgado, C. (Tor)		9.90	Hudson, O. (Tor)		30.8	Delgado, C. (Tor)		33	Boone, B. (Sea)		5.8
Ramirez, M. (Bos)		161	Ramirez, M. (Bos)		55.0	Ramirez, M. (Bos)		9.20	Chavez, E. (Oak)		23.4	Rodriguez, A. (Tex)		31	Posada, J. (NY)		4.9
Nixon, T. (Bos)		150	Giambi, J. (NY)		45.0	Nixon, T. (Bos)		9.10	Boone, B. (Sea)		16.2	Boone, B. (Sea)		30	Rodriguez, A. (Tex)		4.8

TEAM	CG	SH	SV	IP	H	H/G	ER	HR	BB	SO	OAV	RAT	ERA	ERA+	CERA	PR+	PF	FA	E	DP	FR	BW	PW	FW	TPW	DIF
East																										
NY	8	12	**49**	1462	1512	9.3	653	145	**375**	1119	.265	1.291	4.02	109	3.83	89.1	96	.981	114	126	-34.9	13.0	8.5	-3.3	**18.2**	1.8
BOS	5	6	36	1464[2]	1503	9.2	729	153	488	**1141**	.263	1.359	4.48	102	4.20	40.5	101	.982	113	130	-29.4	**16.6**	3.9	-2.8	17.6	-3.6
TOR	14	5	36	1435	1560	9.8	748	184	485	984	.276	1.425	4.69	98	4.70	11.7	101	.981	117	161	-27.5	7.0	1.1	-2.6	5.5	-.5
BAL	9	3	41	1449[2]	1579	9.8	767	198	526	981	.278	1.452	4.76	92	4.95	-56.2	97	.983	105	164	-1.9	-4.2	-5.4	-.2	-9.8	-.2
TB	7	7	30	1436[2]	1454	9.1	787	196	639	877	.264	1.457	4.93	92	4.88	-97.3	100	.983	103	158	33.0	-5.7	-9.3	3.2	-11.9	-6.1
Central																										
MIN	7	8	45	1462	1526	9.4	716	187	402	997	.268	1.319	4.41	103	4.17	50.9	100	.985	87	114	-29.1	1.9	4.9	-2.8	4.0	5.0
CHI	12	4	36	1431	1364	8.6	663	162	518	1056	.253	1.315	4.17	107	3.95	31.4	99	.984	93	154	16.7	2.8	3.0	1.6	7.4	-2.4
KC	7	10	36	1438[2]	1569	9.8	809	190	566	865	.279	1.484	5.06	102	5.04	16.1	114	.982	108	143	-0.3	-7.7	1.5	.0	-6.2	8.2
CLE	5	7	34	1459[1]	1477	9.1	682	179	501	943	.264	1.355	4.21	105	4.31	4.2	98	.980	126	178	29.7	-8.0	.4	2.8	-4.8	-8.2
DET	3	5	27	1438[2]	1616	10.1	847	195	557	764	.286	1.510	5.30	81	5.15	-163.3	95	.978	138	**194**	2.5	-13.4	-15.6	.2	-28.8	-9.2
West																										
OAK	**16**	14	48	1441[2]	**1336**	8.3	582	**140**	499	1018	**.246**	1.273	**3.63**	124	**3.60**	140.2	100	.983	107	145	1.0	-3.9	**13.4**	.1	9.6	5.4
SEA	8	**15**	38	1441	1340	8.4	602	173	466	1001	.247	**1.253**	3.76	115	3.72	51.5	96	**.989**	65	159	38.6	3.1	4.9	**3.7**	11.7	.3
ANA	5	9	39	1431[1]	1444	9.1	680	190	486	980	.261	1.348	4.28	101	4.37	-15.7	95	.982	105	138	19.9	-.6	-1.5	1.9	-.2	-3.8
TEX	4	3	43	1433[1]	1625	10.2	903	208	603	1009	.288	1.554	5.67	88	5.52	-97.6	110	.984	94	168	-18.0	-3.1	-9.3	-1.7	-14.2	4.2
Total	**110**	**109**	**538**	**20225**		**9.3**	**10168**					**1.385**	**4.52**													

Wins			Win Percentage			Games			Complete Games			Shutouts			Saves		
Halladay, R. (Tor)		22	Martinez, P. (Bos)		.778	Miller, T. (Tor)		79	Colon, B. (Chi)		9	5 players tied with		2	Foulke, K. (Oak)		43
3 players tied with		21	Halladay, R. (Tor)		.759	Walker, J. (Det)		78	Halladay, R. (Tor)		9				Guardado, E. (Min)		41
			Moyer, J. (Sea)		.750	2 players tied with		76	Mulder, M. (Oak)		9				Rivera, M. (NY)		40

Innings Pitched			Fewest Hits/Game			Fewest BB/Game			Strikeouts			Ratio			Earned Run Average		
Halladay, R. (Tor)		266	Martinez, P. (Bos)		7.09	Wells, D. (NY)		.85	Loaiza, E. (Chi)		207	Martinez, P. (Bos)		1.04	Martinez, P. (Bos)		2.22
Colon, B. (Chi)		242	Zito, B. (Oak)		7.23	Halladay, R. (Tor)		1.08	Martinez, P. (Bos)		206	Halladay, R. (Tor)		1.07	Hudson, T. (Oak)		2.70
Hudson, T. (Oak)		240	Hudson, T. (Oak)		7.39	Radke, B. (Min)		1.19	Halladay, R. (Tor)		204	Hudson, T. (Oak)		1.08	Loaiza, E. (Chi)		2.90

Adjusted ERA			Component ERA			Opponents' Batting Avg.			Adjusted Pitching Runs			Win Shares – Pitchers			TPW – Pitchers		
Martinez, P. (Bos)		206	Martinez, P. (Bos)		2.22	Martinez, P. (Bos)		.215	Martinez, P. (Bos)		52	Halladay, R. (Tor)		23	Martinez, P. (Bos)		5.0
Hudson, T. (Oak)		167	Hudson, T. (Oak)		2.47	Zito, B. (Oak)		.219	Hudson, T. (Oak)		48	Hudson, T. (Oak)		23	Hudson, T. (Oak)		4.6
Loaiza, E. (Chi)		154	Mussina, M. (NY)		2.75	Hudson, T. (Oak)		.223	Halladay, R. (Tor)		45	Loaiza, E. (Chi)		23	Halladay, R. (Tor)		4.3

Appendix G

The Manager Roster

This section details the managerial record of every man who ever held the reins of a major league club from 1871 through 2003. For many years, the assignment of wins and losses was thought a relatively simple task—almost as simple as identifying the managers themselves. In recent years, however, Richard Topp and Robert Tiemann wondered how it was that "managers" who never set foot on the field to lead their charges or even accompanied their clubs on road trips could be regarded as managers at all, at least in the commonly understood sense of field manager rather than business manager. Topp and Tiemann wondered how John McGraw, for example, could be credited as manager of the New York Giants for all of 1924 when a knee injury kept him from the bench for seven weeks: Somebody else must have run the team, they figured, so why not credit that man as interim manager?

That there were record-keeping errors in the 1870s or even the early 1900s may strike the average fan as unsurprising, but the incorrect assignment of decisions to helmsmen has been characteristic of every decade, up to and including the 1990s. Tiemann and Topp undertook a complete review of managerial records dating back to the National Association and found that the records published in previous baseball encyclopedias were wrong—so wrong that they had to be refigured from scratch. Here are the criteria they established for their groundbreaking study:

1. *Definition*—A manager is the person designated by the club ownership to run the club on the field.
2. *Absences*—When the regular manager is unable to be with the team for 30 or more days, the assistant in charge during his absence should be credited with the team's record from the time the absence begins until the regular manager returns to active duty.
3. *Interim manager*—When a manager is removed, either by resignation or by being fired, and his designated replacement is not present to replace him, the assistant temporarily in charge of the team shall be credited with the team's record during the interim.
4. *Head coaches*—From 1961 through 1964, the Chicago Cubs had a "panel of coaches" rather than a single manager. One of these coaches was designated *head coach* for a period of time; and that coach is credited with the team's record during his term.
5. *Captains*—During the early years of professional baseball, the man who had the title of "manager" often served merely as the club's business manager, while the captain (a player) was responsible for the team on the field. Some captains were also managers. Each ambiguous situation is judged according to its particular circumstances, but in general the captain, rather than the manager,

Sparky Anderson
He retired after 26 years with 2,194 wins, No. 3 on the all-time list.

is credited with the team's record if the manager did not travel with the team or did not have previous baseball experience.

6. *Suspended games*—If a game was suspended when one man was managing the team and was completed on a later date when another was managing, the second manager is credited if the game was suspended before five innings were completed. If the game was suspended after five or more innings were played, then:
   (a) credit the first manager with a win if the team was leading at the point of suspension and maintained the lead to win the game; or
   (b) credit the first manager with a loss if the team was losing at the point of suspension and subsequently lost the game; or
   (c) credit the second manager with a win (or tie) if the team was losing at the point of suspension but came back to tie the score or win the game; or

(d) credit the second manager with a loss if the team was winning at the point of suspension but then lost the lead and/or game; or

(e) credit the second manager with the win or loss if the score was tied at the point of suspension.

7. *Protested games*—If a protest was granted and the game was ordered resumed from the point of protest, then the same rules used for suspended games apply. If a protested game of at least five innings' duration was ordered replayed in its entirety, then no win or loss is credited, but both managers are credited with a no-decision.

8. *Forfeited games*—All forfeited games are counted as games managed, even if the game did not start or if it did not go five innings.

9. *Split seasons*—In 1892 the National League played a split season, the winners meeting for the championship. In 1981, because of a players' strike, the National and American Leagues played split seasons.

The team and league abbreviations used in this section can be found on the last page of this book.

YR	TM/L	G	W	L	PCT
Adair, Bill					
1970	CHI-A	10	4	6	.400
Adcock, Joe					
1967	CLE-A	162	75	87	.463
Addy, Bob					
1875	PHI-n	7	3	4	.429
1877	CIN-N	24	5	19	.208
	2	31	8	23	.258
Allen, Bob					
1890	PHI-N	35	25	10	.714
1900	CIN-N	144	62	77	.446
	2	179	87	87	.500
Alou, Felipe					
1992	MON-N	125	70	55	.560
1993	MON-N	162	94	68	.580
1994	MON-N	114	74	40	.649
1995	MON-N	144	66	78	.458
1996	MON-N	162	88	74	.543
1997	MON-N	162	78	84	.481
1998	MON-N	162	65	97	.401
1999	MON-N	162	68	94	.420
2000	MON-N	162	67	95	.414
2001	MON-N	54	21	33	.389
2003	SF-N	161	100	61	.621
	11	1570	791	779	.504
Alston, Walter					
1954	BRO-N	154	92	62	.597
1955	BRO-N	154	98	55	.641
1956	BRO-N	154	93	61	.604
1957	BRO-N	154	84	70	.545
1958	LA-N	154	71	83	.461
1959	LA-N	156	88	68	.564
1960	LA-N	154	82	72	.532
1961	LA-N	154	89	65	.578
1962	LA-N	165	102	63	.618
1963	LA-N	163	99	63	.611
1964	LA-N	164	80	82	.494
1965	LA-N	162	97	65	.599
1966	LA-N	162	95	67	.586
1967	LA-N	162	73	89	.451
1968	LA-N	162	76	86	.469
1969	LA-N	162	85	77	.525
1970	LA-N	161	87	74	.540
1971	LA-N	162	89	73	.549
1972	LA-N	155	85	70	.548
1973	LA-N	162	95	66	.590
1974	LA-N	162	102	60	.630
1975	LA-N	162	88	74	.543
1976	LA-N	158	90	68	.570
	23	3658	2040	1613	.558
Altobelli, Joe					
1977	SF-N	162	75	87	.463
1978	SF-N	162	89	73	.549
1979	SF-N	140	61	79	.436
1983	BAL-A	162	98	64	.605
1984	BAL-A	162	85	77	.525
1985	BAL-A	55	29	26	.527
1991	CHI-N	1	0	1	.000
	7	844	437	407	.518
Amalfitano, Joey					
1979	CHI-N	7	2	5	.286
1980	CHI-N	72	26	46	.361
1981	CHI-N	106	38	65	.369
	3	185	66	116	.363

YR	TM/L	G	W	L	PCT
Anderson, Sparky					
1970	CIN-N	162	102	60	.630
1971	CIN-N	162	79	83	.488
1972	CIN-N	154	95	59	.617
1973	CIN-N	162	99	63	.611
1974	CIN-N	163	98	64	.605
1975	CIN-N	162	108	54	.667
1976	CIN-N	162	102	60	.630
1977	CIN-N	162	88	74	.543
1978	CIN-N	161	92	69	.571
1979	DET-A	106	56	50	.528
1980	DET-A	163	84	78	.519
1981	DET-A	109	60	49	.550
1982	DET-A	162	83	79	.512
1983	DET-A	162	92	70	.568
1984	DET-A	162	104	58	.642
1985	DET-A	161	84	77	.522
1986	DET-A	162	87	75	.537
1987	DET-A	162	98	64	.605
1988	DET-A	162	88	74	.543
1989	DET-A	162	59	103	.364
1990	DET-A	162	79	83	.488
1991	DET-A	162	84	78	.519
1992	DET-A	162	75	87	.463
1993	DET-A	162	85	77	.525
1994	DET-A	115	53	62	.461
1995	DET-A	144	60	84	.417
	26	4030	2194	1834	.545
Anson, Cap					
1875	ATH-n	8	4	2	.667
1879	CHI-N	64	41	21	.661
1880	CHI-N	86	67	17	.798
1881	CHI-N	84	56	28	.667
1882	CHI-N	84	55	29	.655
1883	CHI-N	98	59	39	.602
1884	CHI-N	113	62	50	.554
1885	CHI-N	113	87	25	.777
1886	CHI-N	126	90	34	.726
1887	CHI-N	127	71	50	.587
1888	CHI-N	136	77	58	.570
1889	CHI-N	136	67	65	.508
1890	CHI-N	139	84	53	.613
1891	CHI-N	137	82	53	.607
1892	CHI-N	147	70	76	.479
1893	CHI-N	128	56	71	.441
1894	CHI-N	137	57	75	.432
1895	CHI-N	133	72	58	.554
1896	CHI-N	132	71	57	.555
1897	CHI-N	138	59	73	.447
1898	NY-N	22	9	13	.409
	21	2288	1296	947	.578
Appling, Luke					
1967	KC-A	40	10	30	.250
Armour, Bill					
1902	CLE-A	137	69	67	.507
1903	CLE-A	140	77	63	.550
1904	CLE-A	154	86	65	.570
1905	DET-A	154	79	74	.516
1906	DET-A	151	71	78	.477
	5	736	382	347	.524
Aspromonte, Ken					
1972	CLE-A	156	72	84	.462
1973	CLE-A	162	71	91	.438
1974	CLE-A	162	77	85	.475
	3	480	220	260	.458

YR	TM/L	G	W	L	PCT
Austin, Jimmy					
1913	STL-A	8	2	6	.250
1918	STL-A	16	7	9	.438
1923	STL-A	51	22	29	.431
	3	75	31	44	.413
Baker, Del					
1933	DET-A	2	2	0	1.000
1936	DET-A	34	18	16	.529
1937	DET-A	10	7	3	.700
1937	DET-A	54	34	20	.630
1938	DET-A	57	37	19	.661
1939	DET-A	155	81	73	.526
1940	DET-A	155	90	64	.584
1941	DET-A	155	75	79	.487
1942	DET-A	156	73	81	.474
1960	BOS-A	7	2	5	.286
	10	785	419	360	.538
Baker, Dusty					
1993	SF-N	162	103	59	.636
1994	SF-N	115	55	60	.478
1995	SF-N	144	67	77	.465
1996	SF-N	162	68	94	.420
1997	SF-N	162	90	72	.556
1998	SF-N	163	89	74	.546
1999	SF-N	162	86	76	.531
2000	SF-N	162	97	65	.599
2001	SF-N	162	90	72	.556
2002	SF-N	162	95	66	.590
2003	CHI-N	162	88	74	.543
	11	1718	928	789	.540
Bamberger, George					
1978	MIL-A	162	93	69	.574
1979	MIL-A	161	95	66	.590
1980	MIL-A	92	47	45	.511
1982	NY-N	162	65	97	.401
1983	NY-N	46	16	30	.348
1985	MIL-A	161	71	90	.441
1986	MIL-A	152	71	81	.467
	7	936	458	478	.489
Bancroft, Dave					
1924	BOS-N	115	42	73	.365
1925	BOS-N	153	70	83	.458
1926	BOS-N	153	66	86	.434
1927	BOS-N	153	60	94	.390
	4	576	238	336	.415
Bancroft, Frank					
1880	WOR-N	85	40	43	.482
1881	DET-N	84	41	43	.488
1882	DET-N	86	42	41	.506
1883	CLE-N	100	55	42	.567
1884	PRO-N	114	84	28	.750
1885	PRO-N	110	53	57	.482
1887	PHI-A	55	26	29	.473
1889	IND-N	68	25	43	.368
1902	CIN-N	16	9	7	.563
	9	718	375	333	.530
Barkley, Sam					
1888	KC-a	58	21	36	.368
Barnie, Billy					
1883	BAL-a	96	28	68	.292
1884	BAL-a	109	63	43	.594
1885	BAL-a	110	41	68	.376
1886	BAL-a	139	48	83	.366
1887	BAL-a	141	77	58	.570
1888	BAL-a	139	57	80	.416
1889	BAL-a	139	70	65	.519

YR	TM/L	G	W	L	PCT
1890	BAL-a	38	15	19	.441
1891	BAL-a	139	71	64	.526
1892	WAS-N	2	0	2	.000
1893	LOU-N	126	50	75	.400
1894	LOU-N	131	36	94	.277
1897	BRO-N	136	61	71	.462
1898	BRO-N	35	15	20	.429
	14	1480	632	810	.438
Barrow, Ed					
1903	DET-A	137	65	71	.478
1904	DET-A	84	32	46	.410
1918	BOS-A	126	75	51	.595
1919	BOS-A	138	66	71	.482
1920	BOS-A	154	72	81	.471
	5	639	310	320	.492
Barry, Jack					
1917	BOS-A	157	90	62	.592
Battin, Joe					
1883	PIT-a	13	2	11	.154
1884	PIT-a	13	6	7	.462
1884	CP-U	6	1	5	.167
	3	32	9	23	.281
Bauer, Hank					
1961	KC-A	102	35	67	.343
1962	KC-A	162	72	90	.444
1964	BAL-A	163	97	65	.599
1965	BAL-A	162	94	68	.580
1966	BAL-A	160	97	63	.606
1967	BAL-A	161	76	85	.472
1968	BAL-A	80	43	37	.538
1969	OAK-A	149	80	69	.537
	8	1139	594	544	.522
Baylor, Don					
1993	COL-N	162	67	95	.414
1994	COL-N	117	53	64	.453
1995	COL-N	144	77	67	.535
1996	COL-N	163	82	79	.509
1997	COL-N	162	83	79	.512
1998	COL-N	162	77	85	.475
2000	CHI-N	162	65	97	.401
2001	CHI-N	162	88	74	.543
2002	CHI-N	83	34	49	.410
	9	1317	626	689	.476
Bell, Buddy					
1996	DET-A	162	53	109	.327
1997	DET-A	162	79	83	.488
1998	DET-A	137	52	85	.380
2000	COL-N	162	82	80	.506
2001	COL-N	162	73	89	.451
2002	COL-N	22	6	16	.273
	6	807	345	462	.428
Benjamin, John					
1873	RES-n	23	2	21	.087
Benson, Vern					
1977	ATL-N	1	1	0	1.000
Berra, Yogi					
1964	NY-A	164	99	63	.611
1972	NY-N	156	83	73	.532
1973	NY-N	161	82	79	.509
1974	NY-N	162	71	91	.438
1975	NY-N	109	56	53	.514
1984	NY-A	162	87	75	.537
1985	NY-A	16	6	10	.375
	7	930	484	444	.522

YR	TM/L	G	W	L	PCT
Bevington, Terry					
1995	CHI-A	113	57	56	.504
1996	CHI-A	163	85	77	.525
1997	CHI-A	161	80	81	.497
	3	437	222	214	.509
Bezdek, Hugo					
1917	PIT-N	91	30	59	.337
1918	PIT-N	126	65	60	.520
1919	PIT-N	139	71	68	.511
	3	356	166	187	.470
Bickerson					
1884	WAS-a	1	0	1	.000
Birmingham, Joe					
1912	CLE-A	28	21	7	.750
1913	CLE-A	155	86	66	.566
1914	CLE-A	157	51	102	.333
1915	CLE-A	28	12	16	.429
	4	368	170	191	.471
Bissonette, Del					
1945	BOS-N	60	25	34	.424
Blackburne, Lena					
1928	CHI-A	80	40	40	.500
1929	CHI-A	152	59	93	.388
	2	232	99	133	.427
Blades, Ray					
1939	STL-N	155	92	61	.601
1940	STL-N	39	14	24	.368
1948	BRO-N	1	1	0	1.000
	3	195	107	85	.557
Blair, Walter					
1915	BUF-F	2	1	1	.500
Bluege, Ossie					
1943	WAS-A	153	84	69	.549
1944	WAS-A	154	64	90	.416
1945	WAS-A	156	87	67	.565
1946	WAS-A	155	76	78	.494
1947	WAS-A	154	64	90	.416
	5	772	375	394	.488
Bochy, Bruce					
1995	SD-N	144	70	74	.486
1996	SD-N	162	91	71	.562
1997	SD-N	162	76	86	.469
1998	SD-N	162	98	64	.605
1999	SD-N	162	74	88	.457
2000	SD-N	162	76	86	.469
2001	SD-N	162	79	83	.488
2002	SD-N	162	66	96	.407
2003	SD-N	162	64	98	.395
	8	1278	630	648	.493
Boles, John					
1996	FLA-N	75	40	35	.533
1999	FLA-N	162	64	98	.395
2000	FLA-N	161	79	82	.491
2001	FLA-N	48	22	26	.458
	4	446	205	241	.460
Bond, Tommy					
1882	WOR-N	6	2	4	.333
Boone, Bob					
1995	KC-A	144	70	74	.486
1996	KC-A	161	75	86	.466
1997	KC-A	82	36	46	.439
2001	CIN-N	162	66	96	.407
2002	CIN-N	162	78	84	.481
2003	CIN-N	104	46	58	.442
	6	815	371	444	.455
Boros, Steve					
1983	OAK-A	162	74	88	.457
1984	OAK-A	44	20	24	.455
1986	SD-N	162	74	88	.457
	3	368	168	200	.457
Bottomley, Jim					
1937	STL-A	78	21	56	.273

YR	TM/L	G	W	L	PCT
Boudreau, Lou					
1942	CLE-A	156	75	79	.487
1943	CLE-A	153	82	71	.536
1944	CLE-A	155	72	82	.468
1945	CLE-A	147	73	72	.503
1946	CLE-A	156	68	86	.442
1947	CLE-A	157	80	74	.519
1948	CLE-A	156	97	58	.626
1949	CLE-A	154	89	65	.578
1950	CLE-A	155	92	62	.597
1952	BOS-A	154	76	78	.494
1953	BOS-A	153	84	69	.549
1954	BOS-A	156	69	85	.448
1955	KC-A	155	63	91	.409
1956	KC-A	154	52	102	.338
1957	KC-A	104	36	67	.350
1960	CHI-N	139	54	83	.394
	16	2404	1162	1224	.487
Bowa, Larry					
1987	SD-N	162	65	97	.401
1988	SD-N	46	16	30	.348
2001	PHI-N	162	86	76	.531
2002	PHI-N	161	80	81	.497
2003	PHI-N	162	86	76	.531
	5	693	333	360	.481
Bowerman, Frank					
1909	BOS-N	76	22	54	.289
Boyd, Bill					
1875	ATL-n	2	0	2	.000
Boyer, Ken					
1978	STL-N	143	62	81	.434
1979	STL-N	163	86	76	.531
1980	STL-N	51	18	33	.353
	3	357	166	190	.466
Bradley, Bill					
1905	CLE-A	41	20	21	.488
1914	BRO-F	157	77	77	.500
	2	198	97	98	.497
Bragan, Bobby					
1956	PIT-N	157	66	88	.429
1957	PIT-N	104	36	67	.350
1958	CLE-A	67	31	36	.463
1963	MIL-N	163	84	78	.519
1964	MIL-N	162	88	74	.543
1965	MIL-N	162	86	76	.531
1966	ATL-N	112	52	59	.468
	7	927	443	478	.481
Brenly, Bob					
2001	ARI-N	162	92	70	.568
2002	ARI-N	162	98	64	.605
2003	ARI-N	162	84	78	.442
	3	486	274	212	.564
Bresnahan, Roger					
1909	STL-N	154	54	98	.355
1910	STL-N	153	63	90	.412
1911	STL-N	158	75	74	.503
1912	STL-N	153	63	90	.412
1915	CHI-N	157	73	80	.477
	5	775	328	432	.432
Bristol, Dave					
1966	CIN-N	77	39	38	.506
1967	CIN-N	162	87	75	.537
1968	CIN-N	163	83	79	.512
1969	CIN-N	163	89	73	.549
1970	MIL-A	163	65	97	.401
1971	MIL-A	161	69	92	.429
1972	MIL-A	30	10	20	.333
1976	ATL-N	162	70	92	.432
1977	ATL-N	29	8	21	.276
1977	ATL-N	131	52	79	.397
1979	SF-N	22	10	12	.455
1980	SF-N	161	75	86	.466
	12	1424	657	764	.462
Brown, Freeman					
1882	WOR-N	41	9	32	.220

YR	TM/L	G	W	L	PCT
Brown, Mordecai					
1914	STL-F	114	50	63	.442
Brown, Tom					
1897	WAS-N	99	52	46	.531
1898	WAS-N	38	12	26	.316
	2	137	64	72	.471
Brucker, Earle					
1952	CIN-N	5	3	2	.600
Buckenberger, Al					
1889	COL-a	140	60	78	.435
1890	COL-a	80	39	41	.488
1892	PIT-N	29	15	14	.517
1892	PIT-N	66	38	27	.585
1893	PIT-N	131	81	48	.628
1894	PIT-N	110	53	55	.491
1895	STL-N	50	16	34	.320
1902	BOS-N	142	73	64	.533
1903	BOS-N	140	58	80	.420
1904	BOS-N	155	55	98	.359
	10	1043	488	539	.475
Buffinton, Charlie					
1890	PHI-P	116	61	54	.530
Burdock, Jack					
1883	BOS-N	54	30	24	.556
Burke, Jimmy					
1905	STL-N	90	34	56	.378
1918	STL-A	61	29	31	.483
1919	STL-A	140	67	72	.482
1920	STL-A	154	76	77	.497
	4	445	206	236	.466
Burnham, Watch					
1887	IND-N	28	6	22	.214
Burns, Tom					
1892	PIT-N	60	27	32	.458
1898	CHI-N	152	85	65	.567
1899	CHI-N	152	75	73	.507
	3	364	187	170	.524
Burwell, Bill					
1947	PIT-N	1	1	0	1.000
Bush, Donie					
1923	WAS-A	155	75	78	.490
1927	PIT-N	156	94	60	.610
1928	PIT-N	152	85	67	.559
1929	PIT-N	119	67	51	.568
1930	CHI-A	154	62	92	.403
1931	CHI-A	156	56	97	.366
1933	CIN-N	153	58	94	.382
	7	1045	497	539	.480
Butler, Ormond					
1883	PIT-a	53	17	36	.321
Byrne, Charlie					
1885	BRO-A	75	38	37	.507
1886	BRO-A	141	76	61	.555
1887	BRO-A	138	60	74	.448
	3	354	174	172	.503
Callahan, Nixey					
1903	CHI-A	138	60	77	.438
1904	CHI-A	42	23	18	.561
1912	CHI-A	158	78	76	.506
1913	CHI-A	153	78	74	.513
1914	CHI-A	157	70	84	.455
1916	PIT-N	157	65	89	.422
1917	PIT-N	61	20	40	.333
	7	866	394	458	.462
Cammeyer, Bill					
1876	NY-N	57	21	35	.375
Campau, Count					
1890	STL-a	42	27	14	.659
Cantillon, Joe					
1907	WAS-A	154	49	102	.325
1908	WAS-A	155	67	85	.441
1909	WAS-A	156	42	110	.276
	3	465	158	297	.347

YR	TM/L	G	W	L	PCT
Carey, Max					
1932	BRO-N	154	81	73	.526
1933	BRO-N	157	65	88	.425
	2	311	146	161	.476
Carey, Tom					
1873	BAL-n	24	14	9	.609
1874	MUT-n	25	13	12	.520
	2	49	27	21	.563
Carrigan, Bill					
1913	BOS-A	70	40	30	.571
1914	BOS-A	159	91	62	.595
1915	BOS-A	155	101	50	.669
1916	BOS-A	156	91	63	.591
1927	BOS-A	154	51	103	.331
1928	BOS-A	154	57	96	.373
1929	BOS-A	155	58	96	.377
	7	1003	489	500	.494
Caruthers, Bob					
1892	STL-N	50	16	32	.333
Cavarretta, Phil					
1951	CHI-N	74	27	47	.365
1952	CHI-N	155	77	77	.500
1953	CHI-N	155	65	89	.422
	3	384	169	213	.442
Caylor, O.P.					
1885	CIN-A	112	63	49	.563
1886	CIN-A	141	65	73	.471
1887	NY-a	100	35	60	.368
	3	353	163	182	.472
Chance, Frank					
1905	CHI-N	90	55	33	.625
1906	CHI-N	155	116	36	.763
1907	CHI-N	155	107	45	.704
1908	CHI-N	158	99	55	.643
1909	CHI-N	155	104	49	.680
1910	CHI-N	154	104	50	.675
1911	CHI-N	158	92	62	.597
1912	CHI-N	153	91	59	.607
1913	NY-A	153	57	94	.377
1914	NY-A	137	60	74	.448
1923	BOS-A	154	61	91	.401
	11	1622	946	648	.593
Chapman, Ben					
1945	PHI-N	85	28	57	.329
1946	PHI-N	155	69	85	.448
1947	PHI-N	155	62	92	.403
1948	PHI-N	79	37	42	.468
	4	474	196	276	.415
Chapman, Jack					
1876	LOU-N	69	30	36	.455
1877	LOU-N	61	35	25	.583
1878	MIL-N	61	15	45	.250
1882	WOR-N	37	7	30	.189
1883	DET-N	101	40	58	.408
1884	DET-N	114	28	84	.250
1885	BUF-N	88	31	57	.352
1889	LOU-a	7	1	6	.143
1890	LOU-a	136	88	44	.667
1891	LOU-a	139	54	83	.394
1892	LOU-N	54	21	33	.389
	11	867	350	501	.411
Chase, Hal					
1910	NY-A	14	10	4	.714
1911	NY-A	153	76	76	.500
	2	167	86	80	.518
Clapp, John					
1872	MAN-n	24	5	19	.208
1878	IND-N	63	24	36	.400
1879	BUF-N	79	46	32	.590
1880	CIN-N	82	21	59	.263
1881	CLE-N	74	32	41	.438
1883	NY-N	98	46	50	.479
	6	420	174	237	.423

Clarke, Fred

YR	TM/L	G	W	L	PCT
1897	LOU-N	92	35	54	.393
1898	LOU-N	154	70	81	.464
1899	LOU-N	156	75	77	.493
1900	PIT-N	140	79	60	.568
1901	PIT-N	140	90	49	.647
1902	PIT-N	142	103	36	.741
1903	PIT-N	141	91	49	.650
1904	PIT-N	156	87	66	.569
1905	PIT-N	155	96	57	.627
1906	PIT-N	154	93	60	.608
1907	PIT-N	157	91	63	.591
1908	PIT-N	155	98	56	.636
1909	PIT-N	154	110	42	.724
1910	PIT-N	154	86	67	.562
1911	PIT-N	156	85	69	.552
1912	PIT-N	153	93	58	.616
1913	PIT-N	155	78	71	.523
1914	PIT-N	158	69	85	.448
1915	PIT-N	157	73	81	.474
	19	2829	1602	1181	.576

Clements, Jack

YR	TM/L	G	W	L	PCT
1890	PHI-N	19	13	6	.684

Clinton, Jim

YR	TM/L	G	W	L	PCT
1872	ECK-n	11	0	11	.000

Cobb, Ty

YR	TM/L	G	W	L	PCT
1921	DET-A	154	71	82	.464
1922	DET-A	155	79	75	.513
1923	DET-A	155	83	71	.539
1924	DET-A	156	86	68	.558
1925	DET-A	156	81	73	.526
1926	DET-A	157	79	75	.513
	6	933	479	444	.519

Cochrane, Mickey

YR	TM/L	G	W	L	PCT
1934	DET-A	154	101	53	.656
1935	DET-A	152	93	58	.616
1936	DET-A	53	29	24	.547
1936	DET-A	67	36	31	.537
1937	DET-A	29	16	13	.552
1937	DET-A	47	26	20	.565
1938	DET-A	98	47	51	.480
	5	600	348	250	.582

Cohen, Andy

YR	TM/L	G	W	L	PCT
1960	PHI-N	1	1	0	1.000

Coleman, Bob

YR	TM/L	G	W	L	PCT
1943	BOS-N	46	21	25	.457
1944	BOS-N	155	65	89	.422
1945	BOS-N	94	42	51	.452
	3	295	128	165	.437

Coleman, Jerry

YR	TM/L	G	W	L	PCT
1980	SD-N	163	73	89	.451

Collins, Eddie

YR	TM/L	G	W	L	PCT
1924	CHI-A	27	14	13	.519
1925	CHI-A	154	79	75	.513
1926	CHI-A	155	81	72	.529
	3	336	174	160	.521

Collins, Jimmy

YR	TM/L	G	W	L	PCT
1901	BOS-A	138	79	57	.581
1902	BOS-A	138	77	60	.562
1903	BOS-A	141	91	47	.659
1904	BOS-A	157	95	59	.617
1905	BOS-A	153	78	74	.513
1906	BOS-A	115	35	79	.307
	6	842	455	376	.548

Collins, Shano

YR	TM/L	G	W	L	PCT
1931	BOS-A	153	62	90	.408
1932	BOS-A	55	11	44	.200
	2	208	73	134	.353

Collins, Terry

YR	TM/L	G	W	L	PCT
1994	HOU-N	115	66	49	.574
1995	HOU-N	144	76	68	.528
1996	HOU-N	162	82	80	.506
1997	ANA-A	162	84	78	.519
1998	ANA-A	162	85	77	.525
1999	ANA-A	133	51	82	.383
	6	878	444	434	.506

Comiskey, Charlie

YR	TM/L	G	W	L	PCT
1883	STL-a	19	12	7	.632
1884	STL-a	25	16	7	.696
1885	STL-a	112	79	33	.705
1886	STL-a	139	93	46	.669
1887	STL-a	138	95	40	.704
1888	STL-a	137	92	43	.681
1889	STL-a	141	89	46	.659
1890	CHI-P	138	75	62	.547
1891	STL-a	141	85	51	.625
1892	CIN-N	155	82	68	.547
1893	CIN-N	131	65	63	.508
1894	CIN-N	134	55	75	.423
	12	1410	838	541	.608

Connor, Roger

YR	TM/L	G	W	L	PCT
1896	STL-N	46	8	37	.178

Cooke, Dusty

YR	TM/L	G	W	L	PCT
1948	PHI-N	13	6	6	.500

Coombs, Jack

YR	TM/L	G	W	L	PCT
1919	PHI-N	63	18	44	.290

Cooney, Johnny

YR	TM/L	G	W	L	PCT
1949	BOS-N	46	20	25	.444

Corrales, Pat

YR	TM/L	G	W	L	PCT
1978	TEX-A	1	1	0	1.000
1979	TEX-A	162	83	79	.512
1980	TEX-A	163	76	85	.472
1982	PHI-N	162	89	73	.549
1983	CLE-A	62	30	32	.484
1983	PHI-N	86	43	42	.506
1984	CLE-A	163	75	87	.463
1985	CLE-A	162	60	102	.370
1986	CLE-A	163	84	78	.519
1987	CLE-A	87	31	56	.356
	9	1211	572	634	.474

Corriden, Red

YR	TM/L	G	W	L	PCT
1950	CHI-A	125	52	72	.419

Cottier, Chuck

YR	TM/L	G	W	L	PCT
1984	SEA-A	27	15	12	.556
1985	SEA-A	162	74	88	.457
1986	SEA-A	28	9	19	.321
	3	217	98	119	.452

Cox, Bobby

YR	TM/L	G	W	L	PCT
1978	ATL-N	162	69	93	.426
1979	ATL-N	160	66	94	.413
1980	ATL-N	161	81	80	.503
1981	ATL-N	107	50	56	.472
1982	TOR-A	162	78	84	.481
1983	TOR-A	162	89	73	.549
1984	TOR-A	163	89	73	.549
1985	TOR-A	161	99	62	.615
1990	ATL-N	97	40	57	.412
1991	ATL-N	162	94	68	.580
1992	ATL-N	162	98	64	.605
1993	ATL-N	162	104	58	.642
1994	ATL-N	114	68	46	.596
1995	ATL-N	144	90	54	.625
1996	ATL-N	162	96	66	.593
1997	ATL-N	162	101	61	.623
1998	ATL-N	162	106	56	.654
1999	ATL-N	162	103	59	.636
2000	ATL-N	162	95	67	.586
2001	ATL-N	162	88	74	.543
2002	ATL-N	161	101	59	.631
2003	ATL-N	162	101	61	.623
	22	3374	1906	1465	.565

Craft, Harry

YR	TM/L	G	W	L	PCT
1957	KC-A	50	23	27	.460
1958	KC-A	156	73	81	.474
1959	KC-A	154	66	88	.429
1961	CHI-N	4	3	1	.750
1961	CHI-N	12	4	8	.333
1962	HOU-N	162	64	96	.400
1963	HOU-N	162	66	96	.407
1964	HOU-N	149	61	88	.409
	7	849	360	485	.426

Craig, Roger

YR	TM/L	G	W	L	PCT
1978	SD-N	162	84	78	.519
1979	SD-N	161	68	93	.422
1985	SF-N	18	6	12	.333
1986	SF-N	162	83	79	.512
1987	SF-N	162	90	72	.556
1988	SF-N	162	83	79	.512
1989	SF-N	162	92	70	.568
1990	SF-N	162	85	77	.525
1991	SF-N	162	75	87	.463
1992	SF-N	162	72	90	.444
	10	1475	738	737	.500

Crandall, Del

YR	TM/L	G	W	L	PCT
1972	MIL-A	124	54	70	.435
1973	MIL-A	162	74	88	.457
1974	MIL-A	162	76	86	.469
1975	MIL-A	161	67	94	.416
1983	SEA-A	89	34	55	.382
1984	SEA-A	135	59	76	.437
	6	833	364	469	.437

Crane, Sam

YR	TM/L	G	W	L	PCT
1880	BUF-N	84	24	58	.293
1884	CIN-U	70	49	21	.700
	2	154	73	79	.480

Cravath, Gavvy

YR	TM/L	G	W	L	PCT
1919	PHI-N	75	29	46	.387
1920	PHI-N	153	62	91	.405
	2	228	91	137	.399

Craver, Bill

YR	TM/L	G	W	L	PCT
1871	TRO-n	25	12	12	.500
1872	BAL-n	41	27	13	.675
1874	PHI-n	58	29	29	.500
1875	CEN-n	14	2	12	.143
	4	138	70	66	.515

Creamer, George

YR	TM/L	G	W	L	PCT
1884	PIT-a	8	0	8	.000

Cronin, Joe

YR	TM/L	G	W	L	PCT
1933	WAS-A	153	99	53	.651
1934	WAS-A	155	66	86	.434
1935	BOS-A	154	78	75	.510
1936	BOS-A	155	74	80	.481
1937	BOS-A	154	80	72	.526
1938	BOS-A	150	88	61	.591
1939	BOS-A	152	89	62	.589
1940	BOS-A	154	82	72	.532
1941	BOS-A	155	84	70	.545
1942	BOS-A	152	93	59	.612
1943	BOS-A	155	68	84	.447
1944	BOS-A	156	77	77	.500
1945	BOS-A	157	71	83	.461
1946	BOS-A	156	104	50	.675
1947	BOS-A	157	83	71	.539
	15	2315	1236	1055	.540

Crooks, Jack

YR	TM/L	G	W	L	PCT
1892	STL-N	62	27	33	.450

Cross, Lave

YR	TM/L	G	W	L	PCT
1899	CLE-N	38	8	30	.211

Cubbage, Mike

YR	TM/L	G	W	L	PCT
1991	NY-N	7	3	4	.429

Curtis, Ed

YR	TM/L	G	W	L	PCT
1884	ALT-U	25	6	19	.240

Cushman, Charlie

YR	TM/L	G	W	L	PCT
1891	MIL-A	36	21	15	.583

Cuthbert, Ned

YR	TM/L	G	W	L	PCT
1882	STL-A	80	37	43	.463

Dahlen, Bill

YR	TM/L	G	W	L	PCT
1910	BRO-N	156	64	90	.416
1911	BRO-N	154	64	86	.427
1912	BRO-N	153	58	95	.379
1913	BRO-N	152	65	84	.436
	4	615	251	355	.414

Dark, Alvin

YR	TM/L	G	W	L	PCT
1961	SF-N	155	85	69	.552
1962	SF-N	165	103	62	.624
1963	SF-N	162	88	74	.543
1964	SF-N	162	90	72	.556
1966	KC-A	160	74	86	.463
1967	KC-A	121	52	69	.430
1968	CLE-A	162	86	75	.534
1969	CLE-A	161	62	99	.385
1970	CLE-A	162	76	86	.469
1971	CLE-A	103	42	61	.408
1974	OAK-A	162	90	72	.556
1975	OAK-A	162	98	64	.605
1977	SD-N	113	48	65	.425
	13	1950	994	954	.510

Davenport, Jim

YR	TM/L	G	W	L	PCT
1985	SF-N	144	56	88	.389

Davidson, Mordecai

YR	TM/L	G	W	L	PCT
1888	LOU-A	3	1	2	.333
1888	LOU-A	90	34	52	.395
	1	93	35	54	.393

Davis, George

YR	TM/L	G	W	L	PCT
1895	NY-N	33	16	17	.485
1900	NY-N	78	39	37	.513
1901	NY-N	141	52	85	.380
	3	252	107	139	.435

Davis, Harry

YR	TM/L	G	W	L	PCT
1912	CLE-A	127	54	71	.432

Davis, Spud

YR	TM/L	G	W	L	PCT
1946	PIT-N	3	1	2	.333

Day, John

YR	TM/L	G	W	L	PCT
1899	NY-N	66	29	35	.453

Deane, Harry

YR	TM/L	G	W	L	PCT
1871	KEK-n	5	2	3	.400

Dent, Bucky

YR	TM/L	G	W	L	PCT
1989	NY-A	40	18	22	.450
1990	NY-A	49	18	31	.367
	2	89	36	53	.404

Dickey, Bill

YR	TM/L	G	W	L	PCT
1946	NY-A	105	57	48	.543

Diddlebock, Harry

YR	TM/L	G	W	L	PCT
1896	STL-N	17	7	10	.412

Dierker, Larry

YR	TM/L	G	W	L	PCT
1997	HOU-N	162	84	78	.519
1998	HOU-N	162	102	60	.630
1999	HOU-N	60	37	23	.617
	HOU-N	75	47	28	.627
2000	HOU-N	162	72	90	.444
2001	HOU-N	162	93	69	.574
	5	783	435	348	.556

Doby, Larry

YR	TM/L	G	W	L	PCT
1978	CHI-A	87	37	50	.425

Donovan, Bill

YR	TM/L	G	W	L	PCT
1915	NY-A	154	69	83	.454
1916	NY-A	156	80	74	.519
1917	NY-A	155	71	82	.464
1921	PHI-N	87	25	62	.287
	4	552	245	301	.449

Donovan, Patsy

YR	TM/L	G	W	L	PCT
1897	PIT-N	135	60	71	.458
1899	PIT-N	131	69	58	.543
1901	STL-N	142	76	64	.543
1902	STL-N	140	56	78	.418
1903	STL-N	139	43	94	.314
1904	WAS-A	139	37	97	.276
1906	BRO-N	153	66	86	.434
1907	BRO-N	153	65	83	.439
1908	BRO-N	154	53	101	.344
1910	BOS-A	158	81	72	.529
1911	BOS-A	153	78	75	.510
	11	1597	684	879	.438

Dooin, Red

YR	TM/L	G	W	L	PCT
1910	PHI-N	157	78	75	.510
1911	PHI-N	153	79	73	.520
1912	PHI-N	152	73	79	.480
1913	PHI-N	159	88	63	.583
1914	PHI-N	154	74	80	.481
	5	775	392	370	.514

Dorgan, Mike

YR	TM/L	G	W	L	PCT
1879	SYR-N	43	17	26	.395
1880	PRO-N	39	26	12	.684
1881	WOR-N	56	24	32	.429
3		138	67	70	.489

Dowd, Tommy

YR	TM/L	G	W	L	PCT
1896	STL-N	63	25	38	.397
1897	STL-N	29	6	22	.214
2		92	31	60	.341

Doyle, Jack

YR	TM/L	G	W	L	PCT
1895	NY-N	64	32	31	.508
1898	WAS-N	17	8	9	.471
2		81	40	40	.500

Dressen, Chuck

YR	TM/L	G	W	L	PCT
1934	CIN-N	60	21	39	.350
1935	CIN-N	154	68	85	.444
1936	CIN-N	154	74	80	.481
1937	CIN-N	130	51	78	.395
1951	BRO-N	158	97	60	.618
1952	BRO-N	155	96	57	.627
1953	BRO-N	155	105	49	.682
1955	WAS-A	154	53	101	.344
1956	WAS-A	155	59	95	.383
1957	WAS-A	20	4	16	.200
1960	MIL-N	154	88	66	.571
1961	MIL-N	130	71	58	.550
1963	DET-A	102	55	47	.539
1964	DET-A	163	85	77	.525
1965	DET-A	120	65	55	.542
1966	DET-A	26	16	10	.615
16		1990	1008	973	.509

Duffy, Hugh

YR	TM/L	G	W	L	PCT
1901	MIL-A	139	48	89	.350
1904	PHI-N	155	52	100	.342
1905	PHI-N	155	83	69	.546
1906	PHI-N	154	71	82	.464
1910	CHI-A	156	68	85	.444
1911	CHI-A	154	77	74	.510
1921	BOS-A	154	75	79	.487
1922	BOS-A	154	61	93	.396
8		1221	535	671	.444

Dunlap, Fred

YR	TM/L	G	W	L	PCT
1882	CLE-N	80	42	36	.538
1884	STL-U	83	66	16	.805
1885	STL-N	22	9	11	.450
1885	STL-N	50	21	29	.420
1889	PIT-N	17	7	10	.412
4		252	145	102	.587

Durocher, Leo

YR	TM/L	G	W	L	PCT
1939	BRO-N	157	84	69	.549
1940	BRO-N	156	88	65	.575
1941	BRO-N	157	100	54	.649
1942	BRO-N	155	104	50	.675
1943	BRO-N	153	81	72	.529
1944	BRO-N	155	63	91	.409
1945	BRO-N	155	87	67	.565
1946	BRO-N	157	96	60	.615
1948	BRO-N	73	35	37	.486
1948	NY-N	79	41	38	.519
1949	NY-N	156	73	81	.474
1950	NY-N	154	86	68	.558
1951	NY-N	157	98	59	.624
1952	NY-N	154	92	62	.597
1953	NY-N	155	70	84	.455
1954	NY-N	154	97	57	.630
1955	NY-N	154	80	74	.519
1966	CHI-N	162	59	103	.364
1967	CHI-N	162	87	74	.540
1968	CHI-N	163	84	78	.519
1969	CHI-N	163	92	70	.568
1970	CHI-N	162	84	78	.519
1971	CHI-N	162	83	79	.512
1972	CHI-N	91	46	44	.511
1972	HOU-N	31	16	15	.516
1973	HOU-N	162	82	80	.506
24		3739	2008	1709	.540

Dwyer, Frank

YR	TM/L	G	W	L	PCT
1902	DET-A	137	52	83	.385

Dyer, Eddie

YR	TM/L	G	W	L	PCT
1946	STL-N	156	98	58	.628
1947	STL-N	156	89	65	.578
1948	STL-N	155	85	69	.552
1949	STL-N	157	96	58	.623
1950	STL-N	153	78	75	.510
5		777	446	325	.578

Dykes, Jimmy

YR	TM/L	G	W	L	PCT
1934	CHI-A	138	49	88	.358
1935	CHI-A	153	74	78	.487
1936	CHI-A	153	81	70	.536
1937	CHI-A	154	86	68	.558
1938	CHI-A	149	65	83	.439
1939	CHI-A	155	85	69	.552
1940	CHI-A	155	82	72	.532
1941	CHI-A	156	77	77	.500
1942	CHI-A	148	66	82	.446
1943	CHI-A	155	82	72	.532
1944	CHI-A	154	71	83	.461
1945	CHI-A	150	71	78	.477
1946	CHI-A	30	10	20	.333
1951	PHI-A	154	70	84	.455
1952	PHI-A	155	79	75	.513
1953	PHI-A	157	59	95	.383
1954	BAL-A	154	54	100	.351
1958	CIN-N	41	24	17	.585
1959	DET-A	137	74	63	.540
1960	CLE-A	58	26	32	.448
1960	DET-A	96	44	52	.458
1961	CLE-A	160	77	83	.481
21		2962	1406	1541	.477

Ebbets, Charlie

YR	TM/L	G	W	L	PCT
1898	BRO-N	110	38	68	.358

Edwards, Doc

YR	TM/L	G	W	L	PCT
1987	CLE-A	75	30	45	.400
1988	CLE-A	162	78	84	.481
1989	CLE-A	143	65	78	.455
3		380	173	207	.455

Elberfeld, Kid

YR	TM/L	G	W	L	PCT
1908	NY-A	98	27	71	.276

Elia, Lee

YR	TM/L	G	W	L	PCT
1982	CHI-N	162	73	89	.451
1983	CHI-N	123	54	69	.439
1987	PHI-N	101	51	50	.505
1988	PHI-N	153	60	92	.395
4		539	238	300	.442

Ellick, Joe

YR	TM/L	G	W	L	PCT
1884	CP-U	13	6	6	.500

Elliott, Bob

YR	TM/L	G	W	L	PCT
1960	KC-A	155	58	96	.377

Ens, Jewel

YR	TM/L	G	W	L	PCT
1929	PIT-N	35	21	14	.600
1930	PIT-N	154	80	74	.519
1931	PIT-N	155	75	79	.487
3		344	176	167	.513

Ermer, Cal

YR	TM/L	G	W	L	PCT
1967	MIN-A	114	66	46	.589
1968	MIN-A	162	79	83	.488
2		276	145	129	.529

Essian, Jim

YR	TM/L	G	W	L	PCT
1991	CHI-N	122	59	63	.484

Esterbrook, Dude

YR	TM/L	G	W	L	PCT
1889	LOU-a	10	2	8	.200

Evers, Johnny

YR	TM/L	G	W	L	PCT
1913	CHI-N	155	88	65	.575
1921	CHI-N	96	41	55	.427
1924	CHI-A	21	10	11	.476
1924	CHI-A	103	41	61	.402
4		375	180	192	.484

Ewing, Buck

YR	TM/L	G	W	L	PCT
1890	NYI-P	132	74	57	.565
1895	CIN-N	132	66	64	.508
1896	CIN-N	128	77	50	.606
1897	CIN-N	134	76	56	.576
1898	CIN-N	157	92	60	.605
1899	CIN-N	157	83	67	.553
1900	NY-N	63	21	41	.339
7		903	489	395	.553

Faatz, Jay

YR	TM/L	G	W	L	PCT
1890	BUF-P	34	9	24	.273

Falk, Bibb

YR	TM/L	G	W	L	PCT
1933	CLE-A	1	1	0	1.000

Fanning, Jim

YR	TM/L	G	W	L	PCT
1981	MON-N	27	16	11	.593
1982	MON-N	162	86	76	.531
1984	MON-N	30	14	16	.467
3		219	116	103	.530

Farrell, Jack

YR	TM/L	G	W	L	PCT
1881	PRO-N	51	24	27	.471

Farrell, Kerby

YR	TM/L	G	W	L	PCT
1957	CLE-A	153	76	77	.497

Felske, John

YR	TM/L	G	W	L	PCT
1985	PHI-N	162	75	87	.463
1986	PHI-N	161	86	75	.534
1987	PHI-N	61	29	32	.475
3		384	190	194	.495

Ferguson, Bob

YR	TM/L	G	W	L	PCT
1871	MUT-n	33	16	17	.485
1872	ATL-n	37	9	28	.243
1873	ATL-n	55	17	37	.315
1874	ATL-n	56	22	33	.400
1875	HAR-n	86	54	28	.659
1876	HAR-N	69	47	21	.691
1877	HAR-N	60	31	27	.534
1878	CHI-N	61	30	30	.500
1879	TRO-N	30	7	22	.241
1880	TRO-N	83	41	42	.494
1881	TRO-N	85	39	45	.464
1882	TRO-N	85	35	48	.422
1883	PHI-N	17	4	13	.235
1884	PIT-A	42	11	31	.262
1886	NY-a	120	48	70	.407
1887	NY-a	30	6	24	.200
16		949	417	516	.447

Ferraro, Mike

YR	TM/L	G	W	L	PCT
1983	CLE-A	100	40	60	.400
1986	KC-A	74	36	38	.486
2		174	76	98	.437

Fessenden, Wallace

YR	TM/L	G	W	L	PCT
1890	SYR-a	11	4	7	.364

Fitzsimmons, Freddie

YR	TM/L	G	W	L	PCT
1943	PHI-N	65	26	38	.406
1944	PHI-N	154	61	92	.399
1945	PHI-N	69	18	51	.261
3		288	105	181	.367

Fletcher, Art

YR	TM/L	G	W	L	PCT
1923	PHI-N	155	50	104	.325
1924	PHI-N	152	55	96	.364
1925	PHI-N	153	68	85	.444
1926	PHI-N	152	58	93	.384
1929	NY-A	11	6	5	.545
5		623	237	383	.382

Flint, Silver

YR	TM/L	G	W	L	PCT
1879	CHI-N	19	5	12	.294

Fogarty, Jim

YR	TM/L	G	W	L	PCT
1890	PHI-P	16	7	9	.438

Fogel, Horace

YR	TM/L	G	W	L	PCT
1887	IND-N	70	20	49	.290
1902	NY-N	44	18	23	.439
2		114	38	72	.345

Fohl, Lee

YR	TM/L	G	W	L	PCT
1915	CLE-A	127	45	79	.363
1916	CLE-A	157	77	77	.500
1917	CLE-A	156	88	66	.571
1918	CLE-A	129	73	54	.575
1919	CLE-A	78	44	34	.564
1921	STL-A	154	81	73	.526
1922	STL-A	154	93	61	.604
1923	STL-A	103	52	49	.515
1924	BOS-A	157	67	87	.435
1925	BOS-A	152	47	105	.309
1926	BOS-A	154	46	107	.301
11		1521	713	792	.474

Fonseca, Lew

YR	TM/L	G	W	L	PCT
1932	CHI-A	152	49	102	.325
1933	CHI-A	151	67	83	.447
1934	CHI-A	15	4	11	.267
3		318	120	196	.380

Foutz, Dave

YR	TM/L	G	W	L	PCT
1893	BRO-N	130	65	63	.508
1894	BRO-N	135	70	61	.534
1895	BRO-N	134	71	60	.542
1896	BRO-N	133	58	73	.443
4		532	264	257	.507

Fox, Charlie

YR	TM/L	G	W	L	PCT
1970	SF-N	120	67	53	.558
1971	SF-N	162	90	72	.556
1972	SF-N	155	69	86	.445
1973	SF-N	162	88	74	.543
1974	SF-N	76	34	42	.447
1976	MON-N	34	12	22	.353
1983	CHI-N	39	17	22	.436
7		748	377	371	.504

Francona, Terry

YR	TM/L	G	W	L	PCT
1997	PHI-N	162	68	94	.420
1998	PHI-N	162	75	87	.463
1999	PHI-N	162	77	85	.475
2000	PHI-N	162	65	97	.401
4		648	285	363	.440

Franks, Herman

YR	TM/L	G	W	L	PCT
1965	SF-N	163	95	67	.586
1966	SF-N	161	93	68	.578
1967	SF-N	162	91	71	.562
1968	SF-N	163	88	74	.543
1977	CHI-N	162	81	81	.500
1978	CHI-N	162	79	83	.488
1979	CHI-N	155	78	77	.503
7		1128	605	521	.537

Frazer, George

YR	TM/L	G	W	L	PCT
1890	SYR-a	46	20	25	.444
1890	SYR-a	71	31	40	.437
2		117	51	65	.440

Frazier, Joe

YR	TM/L	G	W	L	PCT
1976	NY-N	162	86	76	.531
1977	NY-N	45	15	30	.333
2		207	101	106	.488

Fregosi, Jim

YR	TM/L	G	W	L	PCT
1978	CAL-A	116	62	54	.534
1979	CAL-A	162	88	74	.543
1980	CAL-A	160	65	95	.406
1981	CAL-A	47	22	25	.468
1986	CHI-A	96	45	51	.469
1987	CHI-A	162	77	85	.475
1988	CHI-A	161	71	90	.441
1991	PHI-N	149	74	75	.497
1992	PHI-N	162	70	92	.432
1993	PHI-N	162	97	65	.599
1994	PHI-N	115	54	61	.470
1995	PHI-N	144	69	75	.479
1996	PHI-N	162	67	95	.414
1999	TOR-A	162	84	78	.519
2000	TOR-A	162	83	79	.512
15		2122	1028	1094	.484

Frey, Jim

YR	TM/L	G	W	L	PCT
1980	KC-A	162	97	65	.599
1981	KC-A	70	30	40	.429
1984	CHI-N	161	96	65	.596
1985	CHI-N	162	77	84	.478
1986	CHI-N	56	23	33	.411
5		611	323	287	.530

Frisch, Frankie

YR	TM/L	G	W	L	PCT
1933	STL-N	63	36	26	.581
1934	STL-N	154	95	58	.621
1935	STL-N	154	96	58	.623
1936	STL-N	155	87	67	.565

YR	TM/L	G	W	L	PCT
1937	STL-N	157	81	73	.526
1938	STL-N	139	63	72	.467
1940	PIT-N	156	78	76	.506
1941	PIT-N	156	81	73	.526
1942	PIT-N	151	66	81	.449
1943	PIT-N	157	80	74	.519
1944	PIT-N	158	90	63	.588
1945	PIT-N	155	82	72	.532
1946	PIT-N	152	62	89	.411
1949	CHI-N	104	42	62	.404
1950	CHI-N	154	64	89	.418
1951	CHI-N	81	35	45	.438
16		2246	1138	1078	.514

Fuchs, Judge

1929	BOS-N	154	56	98	.364

Gaffney, John

1886	WAS-N	43	15	25	.375
1887	WAS-N	126	46	76	.377
2		169	61	101	.377

Galvin, Pud

1885	BUF-N	24	7	17	.292

Ganzel, John

1908	CIN-N	155	73	81	.474
1915	BRO-F	35	17	18	.486
2		190	90	99	.476

Garcia, Dave

1977	CAL-A	81	35	46	.432
1978	CAL-A	46	25	21	.543
1979	CLE-A	66	38	28	.576
1980	CLE-A	160	79	81	.494
1981	CLE-A	103	52	51	.505
1982	CLE-A	162	78	84	.481
6		618	307	311	.497

Gardenhire, Ron

2002	MIN-A	161	94	67	.584
2003	MIN-A	162	90	72	.556
2		323	184	139	.570

Gardner, Billy

1981	MIN-A	73	30	43	.411
1982	MIN-A	162	60	102	.370
1983	MIN-A	162	70	92	.432
1984	MIN-A	162	81	81	.500
1985	MIN-A	62	27	35	.435
1987	KC-A	126	62	64	.492
6		747	330	417	.442

Garner, Phil

1992	MIL-A	162	92	70	.568
1993	MIL-A	162	69	93	.426
1994	MIL-A	115	53	62	.461
1995	MIL-A	144	65	79	.451
1996	MIL-A	163	80	82	.494
1997	MIL-A	161	78	83	.484
1998	MIL-N	162	74	88	.457
1999	MIL-N	112	52	60	.464
2000	DET-A	162	79	83	.488
2001	DET-A	162	66	96	.407
2002	DET-A	6	0	6	.000
11		1511	708	802	.469

Gaston, Cito

1989	TOR-A	126	77	49	.611
1990	TOR-A	162	86	76	.531
1991	TOR-A	9	6	3	.667
1991	TOR-A	120	66	54	.550
1992	TOR-A	162	96	66	.593
1993	TOR-A	162	95	67	.586
1994	TOR-A	115	55	60	.478
1995	TOR-A	144	56	88	.389
1996	TOR-A	162	74	88	.457
1997	TOR-A	157	72	85	.459
9		1319	683	636	.518

Gerhardt, Joe

1883	LOU-a	98	52	45	.536
1890	STL-a	38	20	16	.556
2		136	72	61	.541

Gessler, Doc

1914	PIT-F	11	3	8	.273

Gibson, George

1920	PIT-N	155	79	75	.513
1921	PIT-N	154	90	63	.588
1922	PIT-N	65	32	33	.492
1925	CHI-N	26	12	14	.462
1932	PIT-N	154	86	68	.558
1933	PIT-N	154	87	67	.565
1934	PIT-N	51	27	24	.529
7		759	413	344	.546

Gifford, Jim

1884	IND-a	87	25	60	.294
1885	NY-a	108	44	64	.407
1886	NY-a	17	5	12	.294
3		212	74	136	.352

Glasscock, Jack

1889	IND-N	67	34	32	.515
1892	STL-N	4	1	3	.250
2		71	35	35	.500

Gleason, Kid

1919	CHI-A	140	88	52	.629
1920	CHI-A	154	96	58	.623
1921	CHI-A	154	62	92	.403
1922	CHI-A	155	77	77	.500
1923	CHI-A	156	69	85	.448
5		759	392	364	.519

Gomez, Preston

1969	SD-N	162	52	110	.321
1970	SD-N	162	63	99	.389
1971	SD-N	161	61	100	.379
1972	SD-N	11	4	7	.364
1974	HOU-N	162	81	81	.500
1975	HOU-N	127	47	80	.370
1980	CHI-N	90	38	52	.422
7		875	346	529	.395

Gonzalez, Mike

1938	STL-N	17	8	8	.500
1940	STL-N	6	1	5	.167
2		23	9	13	.409

Gordon, Joe

1958	CLE-A	86	46	40	.535
1959	CLE-A	154	89	65	.578
1960	CLE-A	95	49	46	.516
1960	DET-A	57	26	31	.456
1961	KC-A	60	26	33	.441
1969	KC-A	163	69	93	.426
5		615	305	308	.498

Gore, George

1892	STL-N	16	6	9	.400

Goryl, Johnny

1980	MIN-A	36	23	13	.639
1981	MIN-A	37	11	25	.306
2		73	34	38	.472

Gould, Charlie

1875	NH-n	23	2	21	.087
1876	CIN-N	65	9	56	.138
2		88	11	77	.125

Gowdy, Hank

1946	CIN-N	4	3	1	.750

Graffen, Mase

1876	STL-N	56	39	17	.696

Grammas, Alex

1969	PIT-N	5	4	1	.800
1976	MIL-A	161	66	95	.410
1977	MIL-A	162	67	95	.414
3		328	137	191	.418

Green, Dallas

1979	PHI-N	30	19	11	.633
1980	PHI-N	162	91	71	.562
1981	PHI-N	107	59	48	.551
1989	NY-A	121	56	65	.463
1993	NY-N	124	46	78	.371
1994	NY-N	113	55	58	.487
1995	NY-N	144	69	75	.479
1996	NY-N	131	59	72	.450
8		932	454	478	.487

Griffin, Mike

1898	BRO-N	4	1	3	.250

Griffin, Sandy

1891	WAS-a	6	2	4	.333

Griffith, Clark

1901	CHI-A	137	83	53	.610
1902	CHI-A	138	74	60	.552
1903	NY-A	136	72	62	.537
1904	NY-A	155	92	59	.609
1905	NY-A	152	71	78	.477
1906	NY-A	155	90	61	.596
1907	NY-A	152	70	78	.473
1908	NY-A	57	24	32	.429
1909	CIN-N	157	77	76	.503
1910	CIN-N	156	75	79	.487
1911	CIN-N	159	70	83	.458
1912	WAS-A	154	91	61	.599
1913	WAS-A	155	90	64	.584
1914	WAS-A	158	81	73	.526
1915	WAS-A	155	85	68	.556
1916	WAS-A	159	76	77	.497
1917	WAS-A	158	74	79	.484
1918	WAS-A	130	72	56	.563
1919	WAS-A	142	56	84	.400
1920	WAS-A	153	68	84	.447
20		2918	1491	1367	.522

Grimes, Burleigh

1937	BRO-N	155	62	91	.405
1938	BRO-N	151	69	80	.463
2		306	131	171	.434

Grimm, Charlie

1932	CHI-N	55	37	18	.673
1933	CHI-N	154	86	68	.558
1934	CHI-N	152	86	65	.570
1935	CHI-N	154	100	54	.649
1936	CHI-N	154	87	67	.565
1937	CHI-N	154	93	61	.604
1938	CHI-N	81	45	36	.556
1944	CHI-N	146	74	69	.517
1945	CHI-N	155	98	56	.636
1946	CHI-N	155	82	71	.536
1947	CHI-N	155	69	85	.448
1948	CHI-N	155	64	90	.416
1949	CHI-N	50	19	31	.380
1952	BOS-N	120	51	67	.432
1953	MIL-N	157	92	62	.597
1954	MIL-N	154	89	65	.578
1955	MIL-N	154	85	69	.552
1956	MIL-N	46	24	22	.522
1960	CHI-N	17	6	11	.353
19		2368	1287	1067	.547

Groh, Heinie

1918	CIN-N	10	7	3	.700

Gutteridge, Don

1969	CHI-A	145	60	85	.414
1970	CHI-A	136	49	87	.360
2		281	109	172	.388

Haas, Eddie

1985	ATL-N	121	50	71	.413

Hack, Stan

1954	CHI-N	154	64	90	.416
1955	CHI-N	154	72	81	.471
1956	CHI-N	157	60	94	.390
1958	STL-N	10	3	7	.300
4		475	199	272	.423

Hackett, Charlie

1884	CLE-N	113	35	77	.313
1885	BRO-a	37	15	22	.405
2		150	50	99	.336

Hallman, Bill

1897	STL-N	50	13	36	.265

Haney, Fred

1939	STL-A	156	43	111	.279
1940	STL-A	156	67	87	.435
1941	STL-A	44	15	29	.341
1953	PIT-N	154	50	104	.325
1954	PIT-N	154	53	101	.344
1955	PIT-N	154	60	94	.390
1956	MIL-N	109	68	40	.630
1957	MIL-N	155	95	59	.617
1958	MIL-N	154	92	62	.597
1959	MIL-N	157	86	70	.551
10		1393	629	757	.454

Hanlon, Ned

1889	PIT-N	46	26	18	.591
1890	PIT-P	131	60	68	.469
1891	PIT-N	78	31	47	.397
1892	BLN-N	133	43	85	.336
1893	BLN-N	130	60	70	.462
1894	BLN-N	129	89	39	.695
1895	BLN-N	132	87	43	.669
1896	BLN-N	132	90	39	.698
1897	BLN-N	136	90	40	.692
1898	BLN-N	154	96	53	.644
1899	BRO-N	150	101	47	.682
1900	BRO-N	142	82	54	.603
1901	BRO-N	137	79	57	.581
1902	BRO-N	141	75	63	.543
1903	BRO-N	139	70	66	.515
1904	BRO-N	154	56	97	.366
1905	BRO-N	155	48	104	.316
1906	CIN-N	155	64	87	.424
1907	CIN-N	156	66	87	.431
19		2530	1313	1164	.530

Harder, Mel

1961	CLE-A	1	1	0	1.000
1962	CLE-A	2	2	0	1.000
2		3	3	0	1.000

Hargrove, Mike

1991	CLE-A	85	32	53	.376
1992	CLE-A	162	76	86	.469
1993	CLE-A	162	76	86	.469
1994	CLE-A	113	66	47	.584
1995	CLE-A	144	100	44	.694
1996	CLE-A	161	99	62	.615
1997	CLE-A	161	86	75	.534
1998	CLE-A	162	89	73	.549
1999	CLE-A	162	97	65	.599
2000	BAL-A	162	74	88	.457
2001	BAL-A	162	63	98	.391
2002	BAL-A	162	67	95	.414
2003	BAL-A	163	71	91	.438
13		1961	996	963	.508

Harrah, Toby

1992	TEX-A	76	32	44	.421

Harrelson, Bud

1990	NY-N	120	71	49	.592
1991	NY-N	154	74	80	.481
2		274	145	129	.529

Harris, Bucky

1924	WAS-A	156	92	62	.597
1925	WAS-A	152	96	55	.636
1926	WAS-A	152	81	69	.540
1927	WAS-A	157	85	69	.552
1928	WAS-A	155	75	79	.487
1929	DET-A	155	70	84	.455
1930	DET-A	154	75	79	.487
1931	DET-A	154	61	93	.396
1932	DET-A	153	76	75	.503
1933	DET-A	153	73	79	.480
1934	BOS-A	153	76	76	.500
1935	WAS-A	154	67	86	.438
1936	WAS-A	153	82	71	.536
1937	WAS-A	158	73	80	.477
1938	WAS-A	152	75	76	.497
1939	WAS-A	153	65	87	.428
1940	WAS-A	154	64	90	.416
1941	WAS-A	156	70	84	.455
1942	WAS-A	151	62	89	.411
1943	PHI-N	92	38	52	.422
1947	NY-A	155	97	57	.630
1948	NY-A	154	94	60	.610
1950	WAS-A	155	67	87	.435
1951	WAS-A	154	62	92	.403
1952	WAS-A	157	78	76	.506
1953	WAS-A	152	76	76	.500

YR	TM/L	G	W	L	PCT
1954	WAS-A	155	66	88	.429
1955	DET-A	154	79	75	.513
1956	DET-A	155	82	72	.532
29		4408	2157	2218	.493
Harris, Lum					
1961	BAL-A	27	17	10	.630
1964	HOU-N	13	5	8	.385
1965	HOU-N	162	65	97	.401
1968	ATL-N	163	81	81	.500
1969	ATL-N	162	93	69	.574
1970	ATL-N	162	76	86	.469
1971	ATL-N	162	82	80	.506
1972	ATL-N	105	47	57	.452
8		956	466	488	.488
Hart, Jim					
1885	LOU-a	112	53	59	.473
1886	LOU-a	138	66	70	.485
1889	BOS-N	133	83	45	.648
3		383	202	174	.537
Hart, John					
1989	CLE-A	19	8	11	.421
Hartnett, Gabby					
1938	CHI-N	73	44	27	.620
1939	CHI-N	156	84	70	.545
1940	CHI-N	154	75	79	.487
3		383	203	176	.536
Hartsfield, Roy					
1977	TOR-A	161	54	107	.335
1978	TOR-A	161	59	102	.366
1979	TOR-A	162	53	109	.327
3		484	166	318	.343
Hastings, Scott					
1871	ROK-n	25	4	21	.160
1872	CLE-n	20	6	14	.300
2		45	10	35	.222
Hatfield, John					
1872	MUT-n	40	24	14	.632
1873	MUT-n	28	11	17	.393
2		68	35	31	.530
Hatton, Grady					
1966	HOU-N	163	72	90	.444
1967	HOU-N	162	69	93	.426
1968	HOU-N	61	23	38	.377
3		386	164	221	.426
Hecker, Guy					
1890	PIT-N	138	23	113	.169
Heffner, Don					
1966	CIN-N	83	37	46	.446
Heilbroner, Louie					
1900	STL-N	50	23	25	.479
Helms, Tommy					
1988	CIN-N	27	12	15	.444
1989	CIN-N	37	16	21	.432
2		64	28	36	.438
Hemus, Solly					
1959	STL-N	154	71	83	.461
1960	STL-N	155	86	68	.558
1961	STL-N	75	33	41	.446
3		384	190	192	.497
Henderson, Bill					
1884	BAL-U	106	58	47	.552
Hendricks, Jack					
1918	STL-N	133	51	78	.395
1924	CIN-N	153	83	70	.542
1925	CIN-N	153	80	73	.523
1926	CIN-N	157	87	67	.565
1927	CIN-N	153	75	78	.490
1928	CIN-N	153	78	74	.513
1929	CIN-N	155	66	88	.429
7		1057	520	528	.496
Hengle, Ed					
1884	CP-U	74	34	39	.466

YR	TM/L	G	W	L	PCT
Herman, Billy					
1947	PIT-N	155	61	92	.399
1964	BOS-A	2	2	0	1.000
1965	BOS-A	162	62	100	.383
1966	BOS-A	146	64	82	.438
4		465	189	274	.408
Herzog, Buck					
1914	CIN-N	157	60	94	.390
1915	CIN-N	160	71	83	.461
1916	CIN-N	84	34	49	.410
3		401	165	226	.422
Herzog, Whitey					
1973	TEX-A	138	47	91	.341
1974	CAL-A	4	2	2	.500
1975	KC-A	66	41	25	.621
1976	KC-A	162	90	72	.556
1977	KC-A	162	102	60	.630
1978	KC-A	162	92	70	.568
1979	KC-A	162	85	77	.525
1980	STL-N	73	38	35	.521
1981	STL-N	103	59	43	.578
1982	STL-N	162	92	70	.568
1983	STL-N	162	79	83	.488
1984	STL-N	162	84	78	.519
1985	STL-N	162	101	61	.623
1986	STL-N	161	79	82	.491
1987	STL-N	162	95	67	.586
1988	STL-N	162	76	86	.469
1989	STL-N	164	86	76	.531
1990	STL-N	80	33	47	.413
18		2409	1281	1125	.532
Hewett, Walter					
1888	WAS-N	40	10	29	.256
Hicks, Nat					
1874	PHI-n	58	29	29	.500
1875	MUT-n	71	30	38	.441
2		129	59	67	.468
Higgins, Pinky					
1955	BOS-A	154	84	70	.545
1956	BOS-A	155	84	70	.545
1957	BOS-A	154	82	72	.532
1958	BOS-A	155	79	75	.513
1959	BOS-A	73	31	42	.425
1960	BOS-A	105	48	57	.457
1961	BOS-A	163	76	86	.469
1962	BOS-A	160	76	84	.475
8		1119	560	556	.502
Higham, Dick					
1874	MUT-n	40	29	11	.725
Himsl, Vedie					
1961	CHI-N	4	0	3	.000
1961	CHI-N	11	5	6	.455
1961	CHI-N	17	5	12	.294
3		32	10	21	.323
Hitchcock, Billy					
1960	DET-A	1	1	0	1.000
1962	BAL-A	162	77	85	.475
1963	BAL-A	162	86	76	.531
1966	ATL-N	51	33	18	.647
1967	ATL-N	159	77	82	.484
5		535	274	261	.512
Hobson, Butch					
1992	BOS-A	162	73	89	.451
1993	BOS-A	162	80	82	.494
1994	BOS-A	115	54	61	.470
3		439	207	232	.472
Hodges, Gil					
1963	WAS-A	121	42	79	.347
1964	WAS-A	162	62	100	.383
1965	WAS-A	162	70	92	.432
1966	WAS-A	159	71	88	.447
1967	WAS-A	161	76	85	.472
1968	NY-N	163	73	89	.451
1969	NY-N	162	100	62	.617
1970	NY-N	162	83	79	.512
1971	NY-N	162	83	79	.512
9		1414	660	753	.467

YR	TM/L	G	W	L	PCT
Hoey, Fred					
1899	NY-N	87	31	55	.360
Hoffman, Glenn					
1998	LA-N	88	47	41	.534
Holbert, Bill					
1879	SYR-N	1	0	1	.000
Hollingshead, Holly					
1875	WAS-n	20	4	16	.200
1884	WAS-a	62	12	50	.194
2		82	16	66	.195
Holmes, Tommy					
1951	BOS-N	95	48	47	.505
1952	BOS-N	35	13	22	.371
2		130	61	69	.469
Hornsby, Rogers					
1925	STL-N	115	64	51	.557
1926	STL-N	156	89	65	.578
1927	NY-N	33	22	10	.688
1928	BOS-N	122	39	83	.320
1930	CHI-N	4	4	0	1.000
1931	CHI-N	156	84	70	.545
1932	CHI-N	99	53	46	.535
1933	STL-A	54	19	33	.365
1934	STL-A	154	67	85	.441
1935	STL-A	155	65	87	.428
1936	STL-A	155	57	95	.375
1937	STL-A	78	25	52	.325
1952	STL-A	51	22	29	.431
1952	CIN-N	51	27	24	.529
1953	CIN-N	147	64	82	.438
14		1530	701	812	.463
Houk, Ralph					
1961	NY-A	163	109	53	.673
1962	NY-A	162	96	66	.593
1963	NY-A	161	104	57	.646
1966	NY-A	140	66	73	.475
1967	NY-A	163	72	90	.444
1968	NY-A	164	83	79	.512
1969	NY-A	162	80	81	.497
1970	NY-A	163	93	69	.574
1971	NY-A	162	82	80	.506
1972	NY-A	155	79	76	.510
1973	NY-A	162	80	82	.494
1974	DET-A	162	72	90	.444
1975	DET-A	159	57	102	.358
1976	DET-A	161	74	87	.460
1977	DET-A	162	74	88	.457
1978	DET-A	162	86	76	.531
1981	BOS-A	108	59	49	.546
1982	BOS-A	162	89	73	.549
1983	BOS-A	162	78	84	.481
1984	BOS-A	162	86	76	.531
20		3157	1619	1531	.514
Howard, Frank					
1981	SD-N	110	41	69	.373
1983	NY-N	116	52	64	.448
2		226	93	133	.412
Howe, Art					
1989	HOU-N	162	86	76	.531
1990	HOU-N	162	75	87	.463
1991	HOU-N	162	65	97	.401
1992	HOU-N	162	81	81	.500
1993	HOU-N	162	85	77	.525
1996	OAK-A	162	78	84	.481
1997	OAK-A	162	65	97	.401
1998	OAK-A	162	74	88	.457
1999	OAK-A	162	87	75	.537
2000	OAK-A	161	91	70	.565
2001	OAK-A	162	102	60	.630
2002	OAK-A	162	103	59	.636
2003	NY-N	161	66	95	.410
13		2104	1058	1046	.503
Howley, Dan					
1927	STL-A	155	59	94	.386
1928	STL-A	154	82	72	.532
1929	STL-A	154	79	73	.520
1930	CIN-N	154	59	95	.383
1931	CIN-N	154	58	96	.377

YR	TM/L	G	W	L	PCT
1932	CIN-N	155	60	94	.390
6		926	397	524	.431
Howser, Dick					
1978	NY-A	1	0	1	.000
1980	NY-A	162	103	59	.636
1981	KC-A	33	20	13	.606
1982	KC-A	162	90	72	.556
1983	KC-A	163	79	83	.488
1984	KC-A	162	84	78	.519
1985	KC-A	162	91	71	.562
1986	KC-A	88	40	48	.455
8		933	507	425	.544
Huff, George					
1907	BOS-A	8	2	6	.250
Huggins, Miller					
1913	STL-N	153	51	99	.340
1914	STL-N	157	81	72	.529
1915	STL-N	157	72	81	.471
1916	STL-N	153	60	93	.392
1917	STL-N	154	82	70	.539
1918	NY-A	126	60	63	.488
1919	NY-A	141	80	59	.576
1920	NY-A	154	95	59	.617
1921	NY-A	153	98	55	.641
1922	NY-A	154	94	60	.610
1923	NY-A	152	98	54	.645
1924	NY-A	153	89	63	.586
1925	NY-A	156	69	85	.448
1926	NY-A	155	91	63	.591
1927	NY-A	155	110	44	.714
1928	NY-A	154	101	53	.656
1929	NY-A	143	82	61	.573
17		2570	1413	1134	.555
Hunter, Billy					
1977	TEX-A	93	60	33	.645
1978	TEX-A	161	86	75	.534
2		254	146	108	.575
Hurdle, Clint					
2002	COL-N	140	67	73	.479
2003	COL-N	162	74	88	.457
2		302	141	161	.467
Hurst, Tim					
1898	STL-N	154	39	111	.260
Hutchinson, Fred					
1952	DET-A	83	27	55	.329
1953	DET-A	158	60	94	.390
1954	DET-A	155	68	86	.442
1956	STL-N	156	76	78	.494
1957	STL-N	154	87	67	.565
1958	STL-N	144	69	75	.479
1959	CIN-N	74	39	35	.527
1960	CIN-N	154	67	87	.435
1961	CIN-N	154	93	61	.604
1962	CIN-N	162	98	64	.605
1963	CIN-N	162	86	76	.531
1964	CIN-N	10	6	4	.600
1964	CIN-N	100	54	45	.545
12		1666	830	827	.501
Irwin, Arthur					
1889	WAS-N	76	28	45	.384
1891	BOS-a	139	93	42	.689
1892	WAS-N	108	46	60	.434
1894	PHI-N	132	71	57	.555
1895	PHI-N	133	78	53	.595
1896	NY-N	90	36	53	.404
1898	WAS-N	30	10	19	.345
1899	WAS-N	155	54	98	.355
8		863	416	427	.493
Jennings, Hughie					
1907	DET-A	153	92	58	.613
1908	DET-A	154	90	63	.588
1909	DET-A	158	98	54	.645
1910	DET-A	155	86	68	.558
1911	DET-A	154	89	65	.578
1912	DET-A	154	69	84	.451
1913	DET-A	153	66	87	.431
1914	DET-A	157	80	73	.523
1915	DET-A	156	100	54	.649

YR	TM/L	G	W	L	PCT
1916	DET-A	155	87	67	.565
1917	DET-A	155	78	75	.510
1918	DET-A	128	55	71	.437
1919	DET-A	140	80	60	.571
1920	DET-A	155	61	93	.396
1924	NY-N	44	32	12	.727
1925	NY-N	32	21	11	.656
	16	2203	1184	995	.543
Johnson, Darrell					
1974	BOS-A	162	84	78	.519
1975	BOS-A	160	95	65	.594
1976	BOS-A	86	41	45	.477
1977	SEA-A	162	64	98	.395
1978	SEA-A	160	56	104	.350
1979	SEA-A	162	67	95	.414
1980	SEA-A	105	39	65	.375
1982	TEX-A	66	26	40	.394
	8	1063	472	590	.444
Johnson, Davey					
1984	NY-N	162	90	72	.556
1985	NY-N	162	98	64	.605
1986	NY-N	162	108	54	.667
1987	NY-N	162	92	70	.568
1988	NY-N	160	100	60	.625
1989	NY-N	162	87	75	.537
1990	NY-N	42	20	22	.476
1993	CIN-N	118	53	65	.449
1994	CIN-N	115	66	48	.579
1995	CIN-N	144	85	59	.590
1996	BAL-A	164	88	74	.543
1997	BAL-A	162	98	64	.605
1999	LA-N	162	77	85	.475
2000	LA-N	162	86	76	.531
	14	2039	1148	888	.564
Johnson, Roy					
1944	CHI-N	1	0	1	.000
Johnson, Tim					
1998	TOR-A	162	88	74	.543
Johnson, Walter					
1929	WAS-A	153	71	81	.467
1930	WAS-A	154	94	60	.610
1931	WAS-A	156	92	62	.597
1932	WAS-A	154	93	61	.604
1933	CLE-A	99	48	51	.485
1934	CLE-A	154	85	69	.552
1935	CLE-A	96	46	48	.489
	7	966	529	432	.550
Jones, Fielder					
1904	CHI-A	114	66	47	.584
1905	CHI-A	158	92	60	.605
1906	CHI-A	154	93	58	.616
1907	CHI-A	157	87	64	.576
1908	CHI-A	156	88	64	.579
1914	STL-F	40	12	26	.316
1915	STL-F	159	87	67	.565
1916	STL-A	158	79	75	.513
1917	STL-A	155	57	97	.370
1918	STL-A	46	22	24	.478
	10	1297	683	582	.540
Joost, Eddie					
1954	PHI-A	156	51	103	.331
Jorgensen, Mike					
1995	STL-N	96	42	54	.438
Joyce, Bill					
1896	NY-N	43	28	14	.667
1897	NY-N	138	83	48	.634
1898	NY-N	43	22	21	.512
1898	NY-N	92	46	39	.541
	3	316	179	122	.595
Jurges, Billy					
1959	BOS-A	80	44	36	.550
1960	BOS-A	42	15	27	.357
	2	122	59	63	.484
Kasko, Eddie					
1970	BOS-A	162	87	75	.537
1971	BOS-A	162	85	77	.525

YR	TM/L	G	W	L	PCT
1972	BOS-A	155	85	70	.548
1973	BOS-A	161	88	73	.547
	4	640	345	295	.539
Keane, Johnny					
1961	STL-N	80	47	33	.588
1962	STL-N	163	84	78	.519
1963	STL-N	162	93	69	.574
1964	STL-N	162	93	69	.574
1965	NY-A	162	77	85	.475
1966	NY-A	20	4	16	.200
	6	749	398	350	.532
Kelley, Joe					
1902	CIN-N	60	34	26	.567
1903	CIN-N	141	74	65	.532
1904	CIN-N	157	88	65	.575
1905	CIN-N	155	79	74	.516
1908	BOS-N	156	63	91	.409
	5	669	338	321	.513
Kelly, John					
1887	LOU-a	139	76	60	.559
1888	LOU-a	39	10	29	.256
	2	178	86	89	.491
Kelly, King					
1887	BOS-N	95	49	43	.533
1890	BOS-P	133	81	48	.628
1891	CIN-a	102	43	57	.430
	3	330	173	148	.539
Kelly, Tom					
1986	MIN-A	23	12	11	.522
1987	MIN-A	162	85	77	.525
1988	MIN-A	162	91	71	.562
1989	MIN-A	162	80	82	.494
1990	MIN-A	162	74	88	.457
1991	MIN-A	162	95	67	.586
1992	MIN-A	162	90	72	.556
1993	MIN-A	162	71	91	.438
1994	MIN-A	113	53	60	.469
1995	MIN-A	144	56	88	.389
1996	MIN-A	162	78	84	.481
1997	MIN-A	162	68	94	.420
1998	MIN-A	162	70	92	.432
1999	MIN-A	162	63	97	.394
2000	MIN-A	162	69	93	.426
2001	MIN-A	162	85	77	.525
	16	2386	1140	1244	.478
Kennedy, Bob					
1963	CHI-N	162	82	80	.506
1964	CHI-N	162	76	86	.469
1965	CHI-N	58	24	32	.429
1968	OAK-A	163	82	80	.506
	4	545	264	278	.487
Kennedy, Jim					
1890	BRO-a	100	26	73	.263
Kennedy, Kevin					
1993	TEX-A	162	86	76	.531
1994	TEX-A	114	52	62	.456
1995	BOS-A	144	86	58	.597
1996	BOS-A	162	85	77	.525
	4	582	309	273	.531
Kerins, John					
1888	LOU-a	7	3	4	.429
1890	STL-a	17	9	8	.529
	2	24	12	12	.500
Kerrigan, Joe					
2001	BOS-A	43	17	26	.395
Kessinger, Don					
1979	CHI-A	106	46	60	.434
Killefer, Bill					
1921	CHI-N	57	23	34	.404
1922	CHI-N	156	80	74	.519
1923	CHI-N	154	83	71	.539
1924	CHI-N	154	81	72	.529
1925	CHI-N	75	33	42	.440
1930	STL-A	154	64	90	.416
1931	STL-A	154	63	91	.409
1932	STL-A	154	63	91	.409

YR	TM/L	G	W	L	PCT
1933	STL-A	91	34	57	.374
	9	1149	524	622	.457
Kimm, Bruce					
2002	CHI-N	74	28	46	.378
King, Clyde					
1969	SF-N	162	90	72	.556
1970	SF-N	42	19	23	.452
1974	ATL-N	64	38	25	.603
1975	ATL-N	134	58	76	.433
1982	NY-A	62	29	33	.468
	5	464	234	229	.505
Kittridge, Malachi					
1904	WAS-A	18	1	16	.059
Klein, Lou					
1961	CHI-N	11	5	6	.455
1962	CHI-N	30	12	18	.400
1965	CHI-N	106	48	58	.453
	3	147	65	82	.442
Kling, Johnny					
1912	BOS-N	155	52	101	.340
Knabe, Otto					
1914	BAL-F	160	84	70	.545
1915	BAL-F	155	47	107	.305
	2	315	131	177	.425
Knight, Lon					
1883	PHI-a	98	66	32	.673
1884	PHI-a	109	61	46	.570
	2	207	127	78	.620
Knight, Ray					
1996	CIN-N	162	81	81	.500
1997	CIN-N	99	43	56	.434
2003	CIN-N	1	1	0	1.000
	3	262	125	137	.477
Krol, Jack					
1978	STL-N	2	1	1	.500
1980	STL-N	1	0	1	.000
	2	3	1	2	.333
Kuehl, Karl					
1976	MON-N	128	43	85	.336
Kuenn, Harvey					
1975	MIL-A	1	1	0	1.000
1982	MIL-A	116	72	43	.626
1983	MIL-A	162	87	75	.537
	3	279	160	118	.576
Kuhel, Joe					
1948	WAS-A	154	56	97	.366
1949	WAS-A	154	50	104	.325
	2	308	106	201	.345
Lachemann, Marcel					
1994	CAL-A	74	30	44	.405
1995	CAL-A	145	78	67	.538
1996	CAL-A	111	52	59	.468
	3	330	160	170	.485
Lachemann, Rene					
1981	SEA-A	85	38	47	.447
1982	SEA-A	162	76	86	.469
1983	SEA-A	73	26	47	.356
1984	MIL-A	161	67	94	.416
1993	FLA-N	162	64	98	.395
1994	FLA-N	115	51	64	.443
1995	FLA-N	143	67	76	.469
1996	FLA-N	86	39	47	.453
2002	CHI-N	1	0	1	.000
	9	988	428	560	.433
Lajoie, Nap					
1905	CLE-A	56	19	36	.345
1905	CLE-A	58	37	21	.638
1906	CLE-A	157	89	64	.582
1907	CLE-A	158	85	67	.559
1908	CLE-A	157	90	64	.584
1909	CLE-A	114	57	57	.500
	5	700	377	309	.550

YR	TM/L	G	W	L	PCT
Lake, Fred					
1908	BOS-A	40	22	17	.564
1909	BOS-A	152	88	63	.583
1910	BOS-N	157	53	100	.346
	3	349	163	180	.475
Lamont, Gene					
1992	CHI-A	162	86	76	.531
1993	CHI-A	162	94	68	.580
1994	CHI-A	113	67	46	.593
1995	CHI-A	31	11	20	.355
1997	PIT-N	162	79	83	.488
1998	PIT-N	162	69	93	.426
1999	PIT-N	161	78	83	.484
2000	PIT-N	162	69	93	.426
	8	1115	553	562	.496
Lanier, Hal					
1986	HOU-N	162	96	66	.593
1987	HOU-N	162	76	86	.469
1988	HOU-N	162	82	80	.506
	3	486	254	232	.523
Larkin, Henry					
1890	CLE-P	79	34	45	.430
LaRussa, Tony					
1979	CHI-A	54	27	27	.500
1980	CHI-A	162	70	90	.438
1981	CHI-A	106	54	52	.509
1982	CHI-A	162	87	75	.537
1983	CHI-A	162	99	63	.611
1984	CHI-A	162	74	88	.457
1985	CHI-A	163	85	77	.525
1986	CHI-A	64	26	38	.406
1986	OAK-A	79	45	34	.570
1987	OAK-A	162	81	81	.500
1988	OAK-A	162	104	58	.642
1989	OAK-A	162	99	63	.611
1990	OAK-A	162	103	59	.636
1991	OAK-A	162	84	78	.519
1992	OAK-A	162	96	66	.593
1993	OAK-A	162	68	94	.420
1994	OAK-A	114	51	63	.447
1995	OAK-A	144	67	77	.465
1996	STL-N	162	88	74	.543
1997	STL-N	162	73	89	.451
1998	STL-N	162	83	79	.512
1999	STL-N	161	75	86	.466
2000	STL-N	162	95	67	.586
2001	STL-N	162	93	69	.574
2002	STL-N	162	97	65	.599
2003	STL-N	162	85	77	.525
	25	3801	2009	1789	.529
Lasorda, Tom					
1976	LA-N	4	2	2	.500
1977	LA-N	162	98	64	.605
1978	LA-N	162	95	67	.586
1979	LA-N	162	79	83	.488
1980	LA-N	163	92	71	.564
1981	LA-N	110	63	47	.573
1982	LA-N	162	88	74	.543
1983	LA-N	163	91	71	.562
1984	LA-N	162	79	83	.488
1985	LA-N	162	95	67	.586
1986	LA-N	162	73	89	.451
1987	LA-N	162	73	89	.451
1988	LA-N	162	94	67	.584
1989	LA-N	160	77	83	.481
1990	LA-N	162	86	76	.531
1991	LA-N	162	93	69	.574
1992	LA-N	162	63	99	.389
1993	LA-N	162	81	81	.500
1994	LA-N	115	58	56	.509
1995	LA-N	144	78	66	.542
1996	LA-N	76	41	35	.539
	21	3041	1599	1439	.526
Latham, Arlie					
1896	STL-N	3	0	3	.000
Latham, Juice					
1875	NH-n	18	4	14	.222
1882	PHI-a	75	41	34	.547
	2	93	45	48	.484

Lavagetto, Cookie

YR	TM/L	G	W	L	PCT
1957	WAS-A	134	51	83	.381
1958	WAS-A	156	61	93	.396
1959	WAS-A	154	63	91	.409
1960	WAS-A	154	73	81	.474
1961	MIN-A	10	4	6	.400
1961	MIN-A	49	19	30	.388
5		657	271	384	.414

Leadley, Bob

YR	TM/L	G	W	L	PCT
1888	DET-N	40	19	19	.500
1890	CLE-N	58	23	33	.411
1891	CLE-N	68	34	34	.500
3		166	76	86	.469

Lefebvre, Jim

YR	TM/L	G	W	L	PCT
1989	SEA-A	162	73	89	.451
1990	SEA-A	162	77	85	.475
1991	SEA-A	162	83	79	.512
1992	CHI-N	162	78	84	.481
1993	CHI-N	162	84	78	.519
1999	MIL-N	49	22	27	.449
6		859	417	442	.485

Lemon, Bob

YR	TM/L	G	W	L	PCT
1970	KC-A	110	46	64	.418
1971	KC-A	161	85	76	.528
1972	KC-A	154	76	78	.494
1977	CHI-A	162	90	72	.556
1978	CHI-A	74	34	40	.459
1978	NY-A	68	48	20	.706
1979	NY-A	65	34	31	.523
1981	NY-A	25	11	14	.440
1982	NY-A	14	6	8	.429
9		833	430	403	.516

Lemon, Jim

YR	TM/L	G	W	L	PCT
1968	WAS-A	161	65	96	.404

Lennon, Bill

YR	TM/L	G	W	L	PCT
1871	KEK-n	14	5	9	.357

Leyland, Jim

YR	TM/L	G	W	L	PCT
1986	PIT-N	162	64	98	.395
1987	PIT-N	162	80	82	.494
1988	PIT-N	160	85	75	.531
1989	PIT-N	164	74	88	.457
1990	PIT-N	162	95	67	.586
1991	PIT-N	162	98	64	.605
1992	PIT-N	162	96	66	.593
1993	PIT-N	162	75	87	.463
1994	PIT-N	114	53	61	.465
1995	PIT-N	144	58	86	.403
1996	PIT-N	162	73	89	.451
1997	FLA-N	162	92	70	.568
1998	FLA-N	162	54	108	.333
1999	COL-N	162	72	90	.444
14		2202	1069	1131	.486

Leyva, Nick

YR	TM/L	G	W	L	PCT
1989	PHI-N	163	67	95	.414
1990	PHI-N	162	77	85	.475
1991	PHI-N	13	4	9	.308
3		338	148	189	.439

Lillis, Bob

YR	TM/L	G	W	L	PCT
1982	HOU-N	51	28	23	.549
1983	HOU-N	162	85	77	.525
1984	HOU-N	162	80	82	.494
1985	HOU-N	162	83	79	.512
4		537	276	261	.514

Lipon, Johnny

YR	TM/L	G	W	L	PCT
1971	CLE-A	59	18	41	.305

Little, Grady

YR	TM/L	G	W	L	PCT
2002	BOS-A	162	93	69	.574
2003	BOS-A	162	95	67	.586
2		324	188	136	.580

Lobert, Hans

YR	TM/L	G	W	L	PCT
1938	PHI-N	2	0	2	.000
1942	PHI-N	151	42	109	.278
2		153	42	111	.275

Lockman, Whitey

YR	TM/L	G	W	L	PCT
1972	CHI-N	65	39	26	.600
1973	CHI-N	161	77	84	.478
1974	CHI-N	93	41	52	.441
3		319	157	162	.492

Loftus, Tom

YR	TM/L	G	W	L	PCT
1884	MIL-U	12	8	4	.667
1888	CLE-a	71	30	38	.441
1889	CLE-N	136	61	72	.459
1890	CIN-N	134	77	55	.583
1891	CIN-N	138	56	81	.409
1900	CHI-N	146	65	75	.464
1901	CHI-N	140	53	86	.381
1902	WAS-A	138	61	75	.449
1903	WAS-A	140	43	94	.314
9		1055	454	580	.439

Lopat, Ed

YR	TM/L	G	W	L	PCT
1963	KC-A	162	73	89	.451
1964	KC-A	52	17	35	.327
2		214	90	124	.421

Lopes, Davey

YR	TM/L	G	W	L	PCT
2000	MIL-N	163	73	89	.451
2001	MIL-N	162	68	94	.420
2002	MIL-N	15	3	12	.200
3		340	144	195	.425

Lopez, Al

YR	TM/L	G	W	L	PCT
1951	CLE-A	155	93	61	.604
1952	CLE-A	155	93	61	.604
1953	CLE-A	155	92	62	.597
1954	CLE-A	156	111	43	.721
1955	CLE-A	154	93	61	.604
1956	CLE-A	155	88	66	.571
1957	CHI-A	155	90	64	.584
1958	CHI-A	155	82	72	.532
1959	CHI-A	156	94	60	.610
1960	CHI-A	154	87	67	.565
1961	CHI-A	163	86	76	.531
1962	CHI-A	162	85	77	.525
1963	CHI-A	162	94	68	.580
1964	CHI-A	162	98	64	.605
1965	CHI-A	162	95	67	.586
1968	CHI-A	11	6	5	.545
1968	CHI-A	36	15	21	.417
1969	CHI-A	17	8	9	.471
17		2425	1410	1004	.584

Lord, Harry

YR	TM/L	G	W	L	PCT
1915	BUF-F	110	60	49	.550

Lowe, Bobby

YR	TM/L	G	W	L	PCT
1904	DET-A	78	30	44	.405

Lucchesi, Frank

YR	TM/L	G	W	L	PCT
1970	PHI-N	161	73	88	.453
1971	PHI-N	162	67	95	.414
1972	PHI-N	76	26	50	.342
1975	TEX-A	67	35	32	.522
1976	TEX-A	162	76	86	.469
1977	TEX-A	62	31	31	.500
1987	CHI-N	25	8	17	.320
7		715	316	399	.442

Lumley, Harry

YR	TM/L	G	W	L	PCT
1909	BRO-N	155	55	98	.359

Lyons, Ted

YR	TM/L	G	W	L	PCT
1946	CHI-A	125	64	60	.516
1947	CHI-A	155	70	84	.455
1948	CHI-A	154	51	101	.336
3		434	185	245	.430

Macha, Ken

YR	TM/L	G	W	L	PCT
2003	OAK-A	162	96	66	.593

Mack, Connie

YR	TM/L	G	W	L	PCT
1894	PIT-N	23	12	10	.545
1895	PIT-N	135	71	61	.538
1896	PIT-N	131	66	63	.512
1901	PHI-A	137	74	62	.544
1902	PHI-A	137	83	53	.610
1903	PHI-A	137	75	60	.556
1904	PHI-A	155	81	70	.536
1905	PHI-A	152	92	56	.622
1906	PHI-A	149	78	67	.538
1907	PHI-A	150	88	57	.607
1908	PHI-A	157	68	85	.444
1909	PHI-A	153	95	58	.621
1910	PHI-A	155	102	48	.680
1911	PHI-A	152	101	50	.669
1912	PHI-A	153	90	62	.592
1913	PHI-A	153	96	57	.627
1914	PHI-A	158	99	53	.651
1915	PHI-A	154	43	109	.283
1916	PHI-A	154	36	117	.235
1917	PHI-A	154	55	98	.359
1918	PHI-A	130	52	76	.406
1919	PHI-A	140	36	104	.257
1920	PHI-A	156	48	106	.312
1921	PHI-A	155	53	100	.346
1922	PHI-A	155	65	89	.422
1923	PHI-A	153	69	83	.454
1924	PHI-A	152	71	81	.467
1925	PHI-A	153	88	64	.579
1926	PHI-A	150	83	67	.553
1927	PHI-A	155	91	63	.591
1928	PHI-A	153	98	55	.641
1929	PHI-A	151	104	46	.693
1930	PHI-A	154	102	52	.662
1931	PHI-A	153	107	45	.704
1932	PHI-A	154	94	60	.610
1933	PHI-A	152	79	72	.523
1934	PHI-A	153	68	82	.453
1935	PHI-A	149	58	91	.389
1936	PHI-A	154	53	100	.346
1937	PHI-A	120	39	80	.328
1938	PHI-A	154	53	99	.349
1939	PHI-A	62	25	37	.403
1940	PHI-A	154	54	100	.351
1941	PHI-A	154	64	90	.416
1942	PHI-A	154	55	99	.357
1943	PHI-A	155	49	105	.318
1944	PHI-A	155	72	82	.468
1945	PHI-A	153	52	98	.347
1946	PHI-A	155	49	105	.318
1947	PHI-A	156	78	76	.506
1948	PHI-A	154	84	70	.545
1949	PHI-A	154	81	73	.526
1950	PHI-A	154	52	102	.338
53		7755	3731	3948	.486

Mack, Denny

YR	TM/L	G	W	L	PCT
1882	LOU-a	80	42	38	.525

Mack, Earle

YR	TM/L	G	W	L	PCT
1937	PHI-A	34	15	17	.469
1939	PHI-A	91	30	60	.333
2		125	45	77	.369

Macullar, Jimmy

YR	TM/L	G	W	L	PCT
1879	SYR-N	27	5	21	.192

Maddon, Joe

YR	TM/L	G	W	L	PCT
1996	CAL-A	22	8	14	.364
1999	ANA-A	29	19	10	.655
2		51	27	24	.529

Magee, Lee

YR	TM/L	G	W	L	PCT
1915	BRO-F	118	53	64	.453

Malone, Fergy

YR	TM/L	G	W	L	PCT
1873	PHI-n	10	8	2	.800
1874	CHI-n	36	18	18	.500
1884	PHI-U	67	21	46	.313
3		113	47	66	.416

Manning, Jack

YR	TM/L	G	W	L	PCT
1877	CIN-N	20	7	12	.368

Manning, Jim

YR	TM/L	G	W	L	PCT
1901	WAS-A	138	61	73	.455

Manuel, Charlie

YR	TM/L	G	W	L	PCT
2000	CLE-A	162	90	72	.556
2001	CLE-A	162	91	71	.562
2002	CLE-A	87	39	48	.448
3		411	220	191	.535

Manuel, Jerry

YR	TM/L	G	W	L	PCT
1998	CHI-A	162	80	82	.494
1999	CHI-A	161	75	86	.466
2000	CHI-A	162	95	67	.586
2001	CHI-A	162	83	79	.512
2002	CHI-A	162	81	81	.500
2003	CHI-A	162	86	76	.531
6		971	500	471	.515

Maranville, Rabbit

YR	TM/L	G	W	L	PCT
1925	CHI-N	53	23	30	.434

Marion, Marty

YR	TM/L	G	W	L	PCT
1951	STL-N	155	81	73	.526
1952	STL-A	104	42	61	.408
1953	STL-A	154	54	100	.351
1954	CHI-A	9	3	6	.333
1955	CHI-A	155	91	63	.591
1956	CHI-A	154	85	69	.552
6		731	356	372	.489

Marshall, Jim

YR	TM/L	G	W	L	PCT
1974	CHI-N	69	25	44	.362
1975	CHI-N	162	75	87	.463
1976	CHI-N	162	75	87	.463
1979	OAK-A	162	54	108	.333
4		555	229	326	.413

Martin, Billy

YR	TM/L	G	W	L	PCT
1969	MIN-A	162	97	65	.599
1971	DET-A	162	91	71	.562
1972	DET-A	156	86	70	.551
1973	DET-A	134	71	63	.530
1973	TEX-A	23	9	14	.391
1974	TEX-A	161	84	76	.525
1975	NY-A	56	30	26	.536
1975	TEX-A	95	44	51	.463
1976	NY-A	159	97	62	.610
1977	NY-A	162	100	62	.617
1978	NY-A	94	52	42	.553
1979	NY-A	95	55	40	.579
1980	OAK-A	162	83	79	.512
1981	OAK-A	109	64	45	.587
1982	OAK-A	162	68	94	.420
1983	NY-A	162	91	71	.562
1985	NY-A	145	91	54	.628
1988	NY-A	68	40	28	.588
18		2267	1253	1013	.553

Martinez, Buck

YR	TM/L	G	W	L	PCT
2001	TOR-A	162	80	82	.494
2002	TOR-A	53	20	33	.377
2		215	100	115	.465

Martinez, Marty

YR	TM/L	G	W	L	PCT
1986	SEA-A	1	0	1	.000

Mason, Charlie

YR	TM/L	G	W	L	PCT
1887	PHI-a	82	38	40	.487

Mathews, Eddie

YR	TM/L	G	W	L	PCT
1972	ATL-N	50	23	27	.460
1973	ATL-N	162	76	85	.472
1974	ATL-N	99	50	49	.505
3		311	149	161	.481

Mathewson, Christy

YR	TM/L	G	W	L	PCT
1916	CIN-N	69	25	43	.368
1917	CIN-N	157	78	76	.506
1918	CIN-N	120	61	57	.517
3		346	164	176	.482

Mattick, Bobby

YR	TM/L	G	W	L	PCT
1980	TOR-A	162	67	95	.414
1981	TOR-A	106	37	69	.349
2		268	104	164	.388

Mauch, Gene

YR	TM/L	G	W	L	PCT
1960	PHI-N	152	58	94	.382
1961	PHI-N	155	47	107	.305
1962	PHI-N	161	81	80	.503
1963	PHI-N	162	87	75	.537
1964	PHI-N	162	92	70	.568
1965	PHI-N	162	85	76	.528
1966	PHI-N	162	87	75	.537
1967	PHI-N	162	82	80	.506
1968	PHI-N	54	27	27	.500
1969	MON-N	162	52	110	.321
1970	MON-N	162	73	89	.451
1971	MON-N	162	71	90	.441

YR	TM/L	G	W	L	PCT
1972	MON-N	156	70	86	.449
1973	MON-N	162	79	83	.488
1974	MON-N	161	79	82	.491
1975	MON-N	162	75	87	.463
1976	MIN-A	162	85	77	.525
1977	MIN-A	161	84	77	.522
1978	MIN-A	162	73	89	.451
1979	MIN-A	162	82	80	.506
1980	MIN-A	125	54	71	.432
1981	CAL-A	63	29	34	.460
1982	CAL-A	162	93	69	.574
1985	CAL-A	162	90	72	.556
1986	CAL-A	162	92	70	.568
1987	CAL-A	162	75	87	.463
	26	3942	1902	2037	.483

McAleer, Jimmy

YR	TM/L	G	W	L	PCT
1901	CLE-A	138	54	82	.397
1902	STL-A	140	78	58	.574
1903	STL-A	139	65	74	.468
1904	STL-A	156	65	87	.428
1905	STL-A	156	54	99	.353
1906	STL-A	154	76	73	.510
1907	STL-A	155	69	83	.454
1908	STL-A	155	83	69	.546
1909	STL-A	154	61	89	.407
1910	WAS-A	157	66	85	.437
1911	WAS-A	154	64	90	.416
	11	1658	735	889	.453

McBride, Dick

YR	TM/L	G	W	L	PCT
1871	ATH-n	28	21	7	.750
1872	ATH-n	47	30	14	.682
1873	ATH-n	52	28	23	.549
1874	ATH-n	56	33	23	.589
1875	ATH-n	69	49	18	.731
	5	252	161	85	.654

McBride, George

YR	TM/L	G	W	L	PCT
1921	WAS-A	154	80	73	.523

McCallister, Jack

YR	TM/L	G	W	L	PCT
1927	CLE-A	153	66	87	.431

McCarthy, Joe

YR	TM/L	G	W	L	PCT
1926	CHI-N	155	82	72	.532
1927	CHI-N	153	85	68	.556
1928	CHI-N	154	91	63	.591
1929	CHI-N	156	98	54	.645
1930	CHI-N	152	86	64	.573
1931	NY-A	155	94	59	.614
1932	NY-A	156	107	47	.695
1933	NY-A	152	91	59	.607
1934	NY-A	154	94	60	.610
1935	NY-A	149	89	60	.597
1936	NY-A	155	102	51	.667
1937	NY-A	157	102	52	.662
1938	NY-A	157	99	53	.651
1939	NY-A	152	106	45	.702
1940	NY-A	155	88	66	.571
1941	NY-A	156	101	53	.656
1942	NY-A	154	103	51	.669
1943	NY-A	155	98	56	.636
1944	NY-A	154	83	71	.539
1945	NY-A	152	81	71	.533
1946	NY-A	35	22	13	.629
1948	BOS-A	155	96	59	.619
1949	BOS-A	155	96	58	.623
1950	BOS-A	59	31	28	.525
	24	3487	2125	1333	.615

McCarthy, Tommy

YR	TM/L	G	W	L	PCT
1890	STL-a	5	4	1	.800
1890	STL-a	22	11	11	.500
	1	27	15	12	.556

McClendon, Lloyd

YR	TM/L	G	W	L	PCT
2001	PIT-N	162	62	100	.383
2002	PIT-N	161	72	89	.447
2003	PIT-N	162	75	87	.463
	3	485	209	276	.431

McCloskey, John

YR	TM/L	G	W	L	PCT
1895	LOU-N	133	35	96	.267
1896	LOU-N	19	2	17	.105
1906	STL-N	154	52	98	.347
1907	STL-N	155	52	101	.340

YR	TM/L	G	W	L	PCT
1908	STL-N	154	49	105	.318
	5	615	190	417	.313

McCormick, Jim

YR	TM/L	G	W	L	PCT
1879	CLE-N	82	27	55	.329
1880	CLE-N	85	47	37	.560
1882	CLE-N	4	0	4	.000
	3	171	74	96	.435

McGaha, Mel

YR	TM/L	G	W	L	PCT
1962	CLE-A	160	78	82	.488
1964	KC-A	111	40	70	.364
1965	KC-A	26	5	21	.192
	3	297	123	173	.416

McGeary, Mike

YR	TM/L	G	W	L	PCT
1875	PHI-n	63	34	27	.557
1880	PRO-N	16	8	7	.533
1881	CLE-N	11	4	7	.364
	3	90	46	41	.529

McGraw, John

YR	TM/L	G	W	L	PCT
1899	BAL-N	152	86	62	.581
1901	BAL-A	135	68	65	.511
1902	BAL-A	58	26	31	.456
1902	NY-N	65	25	38	.397
1903	NY-N	142	84	55	.604
1904	NY-N	158	106	47	.693
1905	NY-N	155	105	48	.686
1906	NY-N	153	96	56	.632
1907	NY-N	155	82	71	.536
1908	NY-N	157	98	56	.636
1909	NY-N	158	92	61	.601
1910	NY-N	155	91	63	.591
1911	NY-N	154	99	54	.647
1912	NY-N	154	103	48	.682
1913	NY-N	156	101	51	.664
1914	NY-N	156	84	70	.545
1915	NY-N	155	69	83	.454
1916	NY-N	155	86	66	.566
1917	NY-N	158	98	56	.636
1918	NY-N	124	71	53	.573
1919	NY-N	140	87	53	.621
1920	NY-N	155	86	68	.558
1921	NY-N	153	94	59	.614
1922	NY-N	156	93	61	.604
1923	NY-N	153	95	58	.621
1924	NY-N	29	16	13	.552
1924	NY-N	81	45	35	.563
1925	NY-N	14	10	4	.714
1925	NY-N	106	55	51	.519
1926	NY-N	151	74	77	.490
1927	NY-N	122	70	52	.574
1928	NY-N	155	93	61	.604
1929	NY-N	152	84	67	.556
1930	NY-N	154	87	67	.565
1931	NY-N	153	87	65	.572
1932	NY-N	40	17	23	.425
	33	4769	2763	1948	.586

McGuire, Deacon

YR	TM/L	G	W	L	PCT
1898	WAS-N	70	21	47	.309
1907	BOS-A	112	45	61	.425
1908	BOS-A	115	53	62	.461
1909	CLE-A	41	14	25	.359
1910	CLE-A	161	71	81	.467
1911	CLE-A	17	6	11	.353
	6	516	210	287	.423

McGunnigle, Bill

YR	TM/L	G	W	L	PCT
1888	BRO-A	143	88	52	.629
1889	BRO-A	140	93	44	.679
1890	BRO-N	129	86	43	.667
1891	PIT-N	59	24	33	.421
1896	LOU-N	115	36	76	.321
	5	586	327	248	.569

McInnis, Stuffy

YR	TM/L	G	W	L	PCT
1927	PHI-N	155	51	103	.331

McKechnie, Bill

YR	TM/L	G	W	L	PCT
1915	NEW-F	102	54	45	.545
1922	PIT-N	90	53	36	.596
1923	PIT-N	154	87	67	.565
1924	PIT-N	153	90	63	.588
1925	PIT-N	153	95	58	.621
1926	PIT-N	157	84	69	.549

YR	TM/L	G	W	L	PCT
1928	STL-N	154	95	59	.617
1929	STL-N	63	34	29	.540
1930	BOS-N	154	70	84	.455
1931	BOS-N	156	64	90	.416
1932	BOS-N	155	77	77	.500
1933	BOS-N	156	83	71	.539
1934	BOS-N	152	78	73	.517
1935	BOS-N	153	38	115	.248
1936	BOS-N	155	71	83	.461
1937	BOS-N	152	79	73	.520
1938	CIN-N	151	82	68	.547
1939	CIN-N	156	97	57	.630
1940	CIN-N	155	100	53	.654
1941	CIN-N	154	88	66	.571
1942	CIN-N	154	76	76	.500
1943	CIN-N	155	87	67	.565
1944	CIN-N	155	89	65	.578
1945	CIN-N	154	61	93	.396
1946	CIN-N	152	64	86	.427
	25	3647	1896	1723	.524

McKeon, Jack

YR	TM/L	G	W	L	PCT
1973	KC-A	162	88	74	.543
1974	KC-A	162	77	85	.475
1975	KC-A	96	50	46	.521
1977	OAK-A	53	26	27	.491
1978	OAK-A	123	45	78	.366
1988	SD-N	115	67	48	.583
1989	SD-N	162	89	73	.549
1990	SD-N	80	37	43	.463
1997	CIN-N	63	33	30	.524
1998	CIN-N	162	77	85	.475
1999	CIN-N	163	96	67	.589
2000	CIN-N	163	85	77	.525
2003	FLA-N	124	75	49	.605
	13	1628	845	782	.519

McKinnon, Alex

YR	TM/L	G	W	L	PCT
1885	STL-N	39	6	32	.158

McKnight, Denny

YR	TM/L	G	W	L	PCT
1884	PIT-a	12	4	8	.333

McManus, George

YR	TM/L	G	W	L	PCT
1876	STL-N	8	6	2	.750
1877	STL-N	60	28	32	.467
	2	68	34	34	.500

McManus, Marty

YR	TM/L	G	W	L	PCT
1932	BOS-A	99	32	67	.323
1933	BOS-A	149	63	86	.423
	2	248	95	153	.383

McMillan, Roy

YR	TM/L	G	W	L	PCT
1972	MIL-A	2	1	1	.500
1975	NY-N	53	26	27	.491
	2	55	27	28	.491

McNamara, John

YR	TM/L	G	W	L	PCT
1969	OAK-A	13	8	5	.615
1970	OAK-A	162	89	73	.549
1974	SD-N	162	60	102	.370
1975	SD-N	162	71	91	.438
1976	SD-N	162	73	89	.451
1977	SD-N	48	20	28	.417
1979	CIN-N	161	90	71	.559
1980	CIN-N	163	89	73	.549
1981	CIN-N	108	66	42	.611
1982	CIN-N	92	34	58	.370
1983	CAL-A	162	70	92	.432
1984	CAL-A	162	81	81	.500
1985	BOS-A	163	81	81	.500
1986	BOS-A	161	95	66	.590
1987	BOS-A	162	78	84	.481
1988	BOS-A	85	43	42	.506
1990	CLE-A	162	77	85	.475
1991	CLE-A	77	25	52	.325
1996	CAL-A	50	18	32	.360
	19	2417	1168	1247	.484

McPhee, Bid

YR	TM/L	G	W	L	PCT
1901	CIN-N	142	52	87	.374
1902	CIN-N	65	27	37	.422
	2	207	79	124	.389

McRae, Hal

YR	TM/L	G	W	L	PCT
1991	KC-A	124	66	58	.532

YR	TM/L	G	W	L	PCT
1992	KC-A	162	72	90	.444
1993	KC-A	162	84	78	.519
1994	KC-A	115	64	51	.557
2001	TB-A	148	58	90	.392
2002	TB-A	161	55	106	.342
	6	872	399	473	.458

McVey, Cal

YR	TM/L	G	W	L	PCT
1873	BAL-n	33	20	13	.606
1878	CIN-N	61	37	23	.617
1879	CIN-N	63	34	28	.548
	3	157	91	64	.587

Mele, Sam

YR	TM/L	G	W	L	PCT
1961	MIN-A	7	2	5	.286
1961	MIN-A	95	45	49	.479
1962	MIN-A	163	91	71	.562
1963	MIN-A	161	91	70	.565
1964	MIN-A	163	79	83	.488
1965	MIN-A	162	102	60	.630
1966	MIN-A	162	89	73	.549
1967	MIN-A	50	25	25	.500
	7	963	524	436	.546

Melillo, Ski

YR	TM/L	G	W	L	PCT
1938	STL-A	10	2	7	.222

Melvin, Bob

YR	TM/L	G	W	L	PCT
2003	SEA-A	162	93	69	.574

Merrill, Stump

YR	TM/L	G	W	L	PCT
1990	NY-A	113	49	64	.434
1991	NY-A	162	71	91	.438
	2	275	120	155	.436

Metro, Charlie

YR	TM/L	G	W	L	PCT
1962	CHI-N	112	43	69	.384
1970	KC-A	52	19	33	.365
	2	164	62	102	.378

Meyer, Billy

YR	TM/L	G	W	L	PCT
1948	PIT-N	156	83	71	.539
1949	PIT-N	154	71	83	.461
1950	PIT-N	154	57	96	.373
1951	PIT-N	155	64	90	.416
1952	PIT-N	155	42	112	.273
	5	774	317	452	.412

Michael, Gene

YR	TM/L	G	W	L	PCT
1981	NY-A	82	48	34	.585
1982	NY-A	86	44	42	.512
1986	CHI-N	102	46	56	.451
1987	CHI-N	136	68	68	.500
	4	406	206	200	.507

Milan, Clyde

YR	TM/L	G	W	L	PCT
1922	WAS-A	154	69	85	.448

Miley, Dave

YR	TM/L	G	W	L	PCT
2003	CIN-N	57	22	35	.366

Miller, George

YR	TM/L	G	W	L	PCT
1894	STL-N	133	56	76	.424

Miller, Joe

YR	TM/L	G	W	L	PCT
1872	NAT-n	11	0	11	.000

Miller, Ray

YR	TM/L	G	W	L	PCT
1985	MIN-A	100	50	50	.500
1986	MIN-A	139	59	80	.424
1998	BAL-A	162	79	83	.488
1999	BAL-A	162	78	84	.481
	4	563	266	297	.472

Mills, Buster

YR	TM/L	G	W	L	PCT
1953	CIN-N	8	4	4	.500

Mills, Everett

YR	TM/L	G	W	L	PCT
1872	BAL-n	17	8	6	.571

Mitchell, Fred

YR	TM/L	G	W	L	PCT
1917	CHI-N	157	74	80	.481
1918	CHI-N	131	84	45	.651
1919	CHI-N	140	75	65	.536
1920	CHI-N	154	75	79	.487
1921	BOS-N	153	79	74	.516
1922	BOS-N	154	53	100	.346
1923	BOS-N	155	54	100	.351
	7	1044	494	543	.476

YR	TM/L	G	W	L	PCT
Mizerock, John					
2002	KC-A	13	5	8	.385
Moore, Jackie					
1984	OAK-A	118	57	61	.483
1985	OAK-A	162	77	85	.475
1986	OAK-A	73	29	44	.397
3		353	163	190	.462
Moore, Terry					
1954	PHI-N	77	35	42	.455
Moran, Pat					
1915	PHI-N	153	90	62	.592
1916	PHI-N	154	91	62	.595
1917	PHI-N	155	87	65	.572
1918	PHI-N	125	55	68	.447
1919	CIN-N	140	96	44	.686
1920	CIN-N	154	82	71	.536
1921	CIN-N	153	70	83	.458
1922	CIN-N	156	86	68	.558
1923	CIN-N	154	91	63	.591
9		1344	748	586	.561
Morgan, Joe					
1988	BOS-A	77	46	31	.597
1989	BOS-A	162	83	79	.512
1990	BOS-A	162	88	74	.543
1991	BOS-A	162	84	78	.519
4		563	301	262	.535
Moriarty, George					
1927	DET-A	156	82	71	.536
1928	DET-A	154	68	86	.442
2		310	150	157	.489
Morrill, John					
1882	BOS-N	85	45	39	.536
1883	BOS-N	44	33	11	.750
1884	BOS-N	116	73	38	.658
1885	BOS-N	113	46	66	.411
1886	BOS-N	118	56	61	.479
1887	BOS-N	32	12	17	.414
1888	BOS-N	137	70	64	.522
1889	WAS-N	51	13	38	.255
8		696	348	334	.510
Morton, Charlie					
1884	TOL-a	110	46	58	.442
1885	DET-N	38	7	31	.184
1890	TOL-a	134	68	64	.515
3		282	121	153	.442
Moses, Felix					
1884	RIC-a	46	12	30	.286
Moss, Les					
1968	CHI-A	2	0	2	.000
1968	CHI-A	34	12	22	.353
1979	DET-A	53	27	26	.509
3		89	39	50	.438
Murnane, Tim					
1884	BOS-U	111	58	51	.532
Murray, Billy					
1907	PHI-N	149	83	64	.565
1908	PHI-N	155	83	71	.539
1909	PHI-N	154	74	79	.484
3		458	240	214	.529
Murtaugh, Danny					
1957	PIT-N	51	26	25	.510
1958	PIT-N	154	84	70	.545
1959	PIT-N	155	78	76	.506
1960	PIT-N	155	95	59	.617
1961	PIT-N	154	75	79	.487
1962	PIT-N	161	93	68	.578
1963	PIT-N	162	74	88	.457
1964	PIT-N	162	80	82	.494
1967	PIT-N	79	39	39	.500
1970	PIT-N	162	89	73	.549
1971	PIT-N	162	97	65	.599
1973	PIT-N	26	13	13	.500
1974	PIT-N	162	88	74	.543
1975	PIT-N	161	92	69	.571
1976	PIT-N	162	92	70	.568
15		2068	1115	950	.540

YR	TM/L	G	W	L	PCT
Muser, Tony					
1997	KC-A	79	31	48	.392
1998	KC-A	161	72	89	.447
1999	KC-A	161	64	97	.398
2000	KC-A	162	77	85	.475
2001	KC-A	162	65	97	.401
2002	KC-A	23	8	15	.348
6		748	317	431	.424
Mutrie, Jim					
1883	NY-a	97	54	42	.563
1884	NY-a	112	75	32	.701
1885	NY-N	112	85	27	.759
1886	NY-N	124	75	44	.630
1887	NY-N	129	68	55	.553
1888	NY-N	138	84	47	.641
1889	NY-N	131	83	43	.659
1890	NY-N	135	63	68	.481
1891	NY-N	136	71	61	.538
9		1114	658	419	.611
Myatt, George					
1968	PHI-N	1	1	0	1.000
1969	PHI-N	54	19	35	.352
2		55	20	35	.364
Myers, Henry					
1882	BAL-a	74	19	54	.260
Narron, Jerry					
2001	TEX-A	134	62	72	.463
2002	TEX-A	162	72	90	.444
2		296	134	162	.453
Nash, Billy					
1896	PHI-N	130	62	68	.477
Neun, Johnny					
1946	NY-A	14	8	6	.571
1947	CIN-N	154	73	81	.474
1948	CIN-N	100	44	56	.440
3		268	125	143	.466
Newman, Jeff					
1986	OAK-A	10	2	8	.200
Nichols, Kid					
1904	STL-N	155	75	79	.487
1905	STL-N	14	5	9	.357
2		169	80	88	.476
Nicol, Hugh					
1897	STL-N	40	8	32	.200
Nixon, Russ					
1982	CIN-N	70	27	43	.386
1983	CIN-N	162	74	88	.457
1988	ATL-N	121	42	79	.347
1989	ATL-N	161	63	97	.394
1990	ATL-N	65	25	40	.385
5		579	231	347	.400
Norman, Bill					
1958	DET-A	105	56	49	.533
1959	DET-A	17	2	15	.118
2		122	58	64	.475
Oakes, Rebel					
1914	PIT-F	143	61	78	.439
1915	PIT-F	156	86	67	.562
2		299	147	145	.503
Oates, Johnny					
1991	BAL-A	125	54	71	.432
1992	BAL-A	162	89	73	.549
1993	BAL-A	162	85	77	.525
1994	BAL-A	112	63	49	.563
1995	TEX-A	144	74	70	.514
1996	TEX-A	163	90	72	.556
1997	TEX-A	162	77	85	.475
1998	TEX-A	162	88	74	.543
1999	TEX-A	162	95	67	.586
2000	TEX-A	162	71	91	.438
2001	TEX-A	28	11	17	.393
11		1544	797	746	.517
O'Connor, Jack					
1910	STL-A	158	47	107	.305

YR	TM/L	G	W	L	PCT
O'Day, Hank					
1912	CIN-N	155	75	78	.490
1914	CHI-N	156	78	76	.506
2		311	153	154	.498
O'Farrell, Bob					
1927	STL-N	153	92	61	.601
1934	CIN-N	91	30	60	.333
2		244	122	121	.502
O'Leary, Dan					
1884	CIN-U	35	20	15	.571
O'Neill, Steve					
1935	CLE-A	60	36	23	.610
1936	CLE-A	157	80	74	.519
1937	CLE-A	156	83	71	.539
1943	DET-A	155	78	76	.506
1944	DET-A	156	88	66	.571
1945	DET-A	155	88	65	.575
1946	DET-A	155	92	62	.597
1947	DET-A	158	85	69	.552
1948	DET-A	154	78	76	.506
1950	BOS-A	95	63	32	.663
1951	BOS-A	154	87	67	.565
1952	PHI-N	91	59	32	.648
1953	PHI-N	156	83	71	.539
1954	PHI-N	77	40	37	.519
14		1879	1040	821	.559
Onslow, Jack					
1949	CHI-A	154	63	91	.409
1950	CHI-A	31	8	22	.267
2		185	71	113	.386
O'Rourke, Jim					
1881	BUF-N	83	45	38	.542
1882	BUF-N	84	45	39	.536
1883	BUF-N	98	52	45	.536
1884	BUF-N	115	64	47	.577
1893	WAS-N	130	40	89	.310
5		510	246	258	.488
Orr, Dave					
1887	NY-a	8	3	5	.375
Ott, Mel					
1942	NY-N	154	85	67	.559
1943	NY-N	156	55	98	.359
1944	NY-N	155	67	87	.435
1945	NY-N	154	78	74	.513
1946	NY-N	154	61	93	.396
1947	NY-N	155	81	73	.526
1948	NY-N	76	37	38	.493
7		1004	464	530	.467
Owens, Paul					
1972	PHI-N	80	33	47	.413
1983	PHI-N	77	47	30	.610
1984	PHI-N	162	81	81	.500
3		319	161	158	.505
Ozark, Danny					
1973	PHI-N	162	71	91	.438
1974	PHI-N	162	80	82	.494
1975	PHI-N	162	86	76	.531
1976	PHI-N	162	101	61	.623
1977	PHI-N	162	101	61	.623
1978	PHI-N	162	90	72	.556
1979	PHI-N	133	65	67	.492
1984	SF-N	56	24	32	.429
8		1161	618	542	.533
Pabor, Charlie					
1871	CLE-n	29	10	19	.345
1875	ATL-n	42	2	40	.048
1875	NH-n	6	1	5	.167
3		77	13	64	.169
Parker, Salty					
1967	NY-N	11	4	7	.364
1972	HOU-N	1	1	0	1.000
2		12	5	7	.417
Parks, Bill					
1875	WAS-n	8	1	7	.125

YR	TM/L	G	W	L	PCT
Parrish, Larry					
1998	DET-A	25	13	12	.520
1999	DET-A	161	69	92	.429
2		186	82	104	.441
Pearce, Dickey					
1872	MUT-n	16	10	6	.625
1875	STL-n	72	39	29	.574
2		88	49	35	.583
Peckinpaugh, Roger					
1914	NY-A	20	10	10	.500
1928	CLE-A	155	62	92	.403
1929	CLE-A	152	81	71	.533
1930	CLE-A	154	81	73	.526
1931	CLE-A	155	78	76	.506
1932	CLE-A	153	87	65	.572
1933	CLE-A	51	26	25	.510
1941	CLE-A	155	75	79	.487
8		995	500	491	.505
Pena, Tony					
2002	KC-A	126	49	77	.389
2003	KC-A	162	83	79	.512
2		288	132	156	.458
Perez, Tony					
1993	CIN-N	44	20	24	.455
2001	FLA-N	114	54	60	.474
2		158	74	84	.468
Perkins, Cy					
1937	DET-A	15	6	9	.400
Pesky, Johnny					
1963	BOS-A	161	76	85	.472
1964	BOS-A	160	70	90	.438
1980	BOS-A	5	1	4	.200
3		326	147	179	.451
Pfeffer, Fred					
1892	LOU-N	100	42	56	.429
Phelan, Lew					
1895	STL-N	45	11	30	.268
Phillips, Bill					
1914	IND-F	157	88	65	.575
1915	NEW-F	53	26	27	.491
2		210	114	92	.553
Phillips, Horace					
1879	TRO-N	47	12	34	.261
1883	COL-a	97	32	65	.330
1884	PIT-a	35	9	24	.273
1885	PIT-a	111	56	55	.505
1886	PIT-a	140	80	57	.584
1887	PIT-N	125	55	69	.444
1888	PIT-N	139	66	68	.493
1889	PIT-N	71	28	43	.394
8		765	338	415	.449
Phillips, Lefty					
1969	CAL-A	124	60	63	.488
1970	CAL-A	162	86	76	.531
1971	CAL-A	162	76	86	.469
3		448	222	225	.497
Pike, Lip					
1871	TRO-n	4	1	3	.250
1874	HAR-n	53	16	37	.302
1877	CIN-N	14	3	11	.214
3		71	20	51	.282
Piniella, Lou					
1986	NY-A	162	90	72	.556
1987	NY-A	162	89	73	.549
1988	NY-A	93	45	48	.484
1990	CIN-N	162	91	71	.562
1991	CIN-N	162	74	88	.457
1992	CIN-N	162	90	72	.556
1993	SEA-A	162	82	80	.506
1994	SEA-A	112	49	63	.438
1995	SEA-A	145	79	66	.545
1996	SEA-A	161	85	76	.528
1997	SEA-A	162	90	72	.556
1998	SEA-A	161	76	85	.472
1999	SEA-A	162	79	83	.488

YR	TM/L	G	W	L	PCT
2000	SEA-A	162	91	71	.562
2001	SEA-A	162	116	46	.716
2002	SEA-A	162	93	69	.574
2003	TB-A	162	63	99	.389
	17	2616	1382	1234	.528

Plummer, Bill

YR	TM/L	G	W	L	PCT
1992	SEA-A	162	64	98	.395

Popowski, Eddie

YR	TM/L	G	W	L	PCT
1969	BOS-A	9	5	4	.556
1973	BOS-A	1	1	0	1.000
	2	10	6	4	.600

Porter, Matthew

YR	TM/L	G	W	L	PCT
1884	KC-U	16	3	13	.188

Powers, Pat

YR	TM/L	G	W	L	PCT
1890	ROC-a	133	63	63	.500
1892	NY-N	153	71	80	.470
	2	286	134	143	.484

Pratt, Al

YR	TM/L	G	W	L	PCT
1882	PIT-a	79	39	39	.500
1883	PIT-a	32	12	20	.375
	2	111	51	59	.464

Price, Jim

YR	TM/L	G	W	L	PCT
1884	NY-N	100	56	42	.571

Prothro, Doc

YR	TM/L	G	W	L	PCT
1939	PHI-N	152	45	106	.298
1940	PHI-N	153	50	103	.327
1941	PHI-N	155	43	111	.279
	3	460	138	320	.301

Pujols, Luis

YR	TM/L	G	W	L	PCT
2002	DET-A	155	55	100	.355

Purcell, Blondie

YR	TM/L	G	W	L	PCT
1883	PHI-N	82	13	68	.160

Queen, Mel

YR	TM/L	G	W	L	PCT
1997	TOR-A	5	4	1	.800

Quilici, Frank

YR	TM/L	G	W	L	PCT
1972	MIN-A	84	41	43	.488
1973	MIN-A	162	81	81	.500
1974	MIN-A	163	82	80	.506
1975	MIN-A	159	76	83	.478
	4	568	280	287	.494

Quinn, Joe

YR	TM/L	G	W	L	PCT
1895	STL-N	40	11	28	.282
1899	CLE-N	116	12	104	.103
	2	156	23	132	.148

Rader, Doug

YR	TM/L	G	W	L	PCT
1983	TEX-A	163	77	85	.475
1984	TEX-A	161	69	92	.429
1985	TEX-A	32	9	23	.281
1986	CHI-A	2	1	1	.500
1989	CAL-A	162	91	71	.562
1990	CAL-A	162	80	82	.494
1991	CAL-A	124	61	63	.492
	7	806	388	417	.482

Rapp, Vern

YR	TM/L	G	W	L	PCT
1977	STL-N	162	83	79	.512
1978	STL-N	17	6	11	.353
1984	CIN-N	121	51	70	.421
	3	300	140	160	.467

Reach, Al

YR	TM/L	G	W	L	PCT
1890	PHI-N	11	4	7	.364

Regan, Phil

YR	TM/L	G	W	L	PCT
1995	BAL-A	144	71	73	.493

Rice, Del

YR	TM/L	G	W	L	PCT
1972	CAL-A	155	75	80	.484

Richards, Paul

YR	TM/L	G	W	L	PCT
1951	CHI-A	155	81	73	.526
1952	CHI-A	156	81	73	.526
1953	CHI-A	156	89	65	.578
1954	CHI-A	146	91	54	.628
1955	BAL-A	156	57	97	.370
1956	BAL-A	154	69	85	.448
1957	BAL-A	154	76	76	.500
1958	BAL-A	154	74	79	.484
1959	BAL-A	155	74	80	.481
1960	BAL-A	154	89	65	.578
1961	BAL-A	136	78	57	.578
1976	CHI-A	161	64	97	.398
	12	1837	923	901	.506

Richardson, Danny

YR	TM/L	G	W	L	PCT
1892	WAS-N	43	12	31	.279

Rickey, Branch

YR	TM/L	G	W	L	PCT
1913	STL-A	12	5	6	.455
1914	STL-A	159	71	82	.464
1915	STL-A	159	63	91	.409
1919	STL-N	138	54	83	.394
1920	STL-N	155	75	79	.487
1921	STL-N	154	87	66	.569
1922	STL-N	154	85	69	.552
1923	STL-N	154	79	74	.516
1924	STL-N	154	65	89	.422
1925	STL-N	38	13	25	.342
	10	1277	597	664	.473

Riddoch, Greg

YR	TM/L	G	W	L	PCT
1990	SD-N	82	38	44	.463
1991	SD-N	162	84	78	.519
1992	SD-N	150	78	72	.520
	3	394	200	194	.508

Riggleman, Jim

YR	TM/L	G	W	L	PCT
1992	SD-N	12	4	8	.333
1993	SD-N	162	61	101	.377
1994	SD-N	117	47	70	.402
1995	CHI-N	144	73	71	.507
1996	CHI-N	163	76	86	.469
1997	CHI-N	162	68	94	.420
1998	CHI-N	163	90	73	.552
1999	CHI-N	162	67	95	.414
	8	1085	486	598	.448

Rigney, Bill

YR	TM/L	G	W	L	PCT
1956	NY-N	154	67	87	.435
1957	NY-N	154	69	85	.448
1958	SF-N	154	80	74	.519
1959	SF-N	154	83	71	.539
1960	SF-N	58	33	25	.569
1961	LA-A	162	70	91	.435
1962	LA-A	162	86	76	.531
1963	LA-A	161	70	91	.435
1964	LA-A	162	82	80	.506
1965	CAL-A	162	75	87	.463
1966	CAL-A	162	80	82	.494
1967	CAL-A	161	84	77	.522
1968	CAL-A	162	67	95	.414
1969	CAL-A	39	11	28	.282
1970	MIN-A	162	98	64	.605
1971	MIN-A	160	74	86	.463
1972	MIN-A	70	36	34	.514
1976	SF-N	162	74	88	.457
	18	2561	1239	1321	.484

Ripken Sr., Cal

YR	TM/L	G	W	L	PCT
1985	BAL-A	1	1	0	1.000
1987	BAL-A	162	67	95	.414
1988	BAL-A	6	0	6	.000
	3	169	68	101	.402

Robinson, Frank

YR	TM/L	G	W	L	PCT
1975	CLE-A	159	79	80	.497
1976	CLE-A	159	81	78	.509
1977	CLE-A	57	26	31	.456
1981	SF-N	111	56	55	.505
1982	SF-N	162	87	75	.537
1983	SF-N	162	79	83	.488
1984	SF-N	106	42	64	.396
1988	BAL-A	155	54	101	.348
1989	BAL-A	162	87	75	.537
1990	BAL-A	162	76	85	.472
1991	BAL-A	37	13	24	.351
2002	MON-N	162	83	79	.512
2003	MON-N	162	83	79	.512
	13	1756	846	909	.482

Robinson, Wilbert

YR	TM/L	G	W	L	PCT
1902	BAL-A	83	24	57	.296
1914	BRO-N	154	75	79	.487
1915	BRO-N	154	80	72	.526
1916	BRO-N	156	94	60	.610
1917	BRO-N	156	70	81	.464
1918	BRO-N	127	57	69	.452
1919	BRO-N	141	69	71	.493
1920	BRO-N	155	93	61	.604
1921	BRO-N	152	77	75	.507
1922	BRO-N	155	76	78	.494
1923	BRO-N	155	76	78	.494
1924	BRO-N	154	92	62	.597
1925	BRO-N	153	68	85	.444
1926	BRO-N	155	71	82	.464
1927	BRO-N	154	65	88	.425
1928	BRO-N	155	77	76	.503
1929	BRO-N	153	70	83	.458
1930	BRO-N	154	86	68	.558
1931	BRO-N	153	79	73	.520
	19	2819	1399	1398	.500

Robison, Stanley

YR	TM/L	G	W	L	PCT
1905	STL-N	50	19	31	.380

Rodgers, Buck

YR	TM/L	G	W	L	PCT
1980	MIL-A	23	13	10	.565
1980	MIL-A	47	26	21	.553
1981	MIL-A	109	62	47	.569
1982	MIL-A	47	23	24	.489
1985	MON-N	161	84	77	.522
1986	MON-N	161	78	83	.484
1987	MON-N	162	91	71	.562
1988	MON-N	163	81	81	.500
1989	MON-N	162	81	81	.500
1990	MON-N	162	85	77	.525
1991	CAL-A	38	20	18	.526
1991	MON-N	49	20	29	.408
1992	CAL-A	34	14	20	.412
1992	CAL-A	39	19	20	.487
1993	CAL-A	162	71	91	.438
1994	CAL-A	39	16	23	.410
	13	1558	784	773	.504

Rogers, Jim

YR	TM/L	G	W	L	PCT
1897	LOU-N	44	17	24	.415

Rojas, Cookie

YR	TM/L	G	W	L	PCT
1988	CAL-A	154	75	79	.487
1996	FLA-N	1	1	0	1.000
	2	155	76	79	.490

Rolfe, Red

YR	TM/L	G	W	L	PCT
1949	DET-A	155	87	67	.565
1950	DET-A	157	95	59	.617
1951	DET-A	154	73	81	.474
1952	DET-A	73	23	49	.319
	4	539	278	256	.521

Rose, Pete

YR	TM/L	G	W	L	PCT
1984	CIN-N	41	19	22	.463
1985	CIN-N	162	89	72	.553
1986	CIN-N	162	86	76	.531
1987	CIN-N	162	84	78	.519
1988	CIN-N	23	11	12	.478
1988	CIN-N	111	64	47	.577
1989	CIN-N	125	59	66	.472
	6	786	412	373	.525

Roseman, Chief

YR	TM/L	G	W	L	PCT
1890	STL-A	15	7	8	.467

Rothschild, Larry

YR	TM/L	G	W	L	PCT
1998	TB-A	162	63	99	.389
1999	TB-A	162	69	93	.426
2000	TB-A	161	69	92	.429
2001	TB-A	14	4	10	.286
	4	499	205	294	.411

Rowe, Dave

YR	TM/L	G	W	L	PCT
1886	KC-N	126	30	91	.248
1888	KC-a	50	14	36	.280
	2	176	44	127	.257

Rowe, Jack

YR	TM/L	G	W	L	PCT
1890	BUF-P	19	5	14	.263
1890	BUF-P	81	22	58	.275
	2	100	27	72	.273

Rowland, Pants

YR	TM/L	G	W	L	PCT
1915	CHI-A	156	93	61	.604
1916	CHI-A	155	89	65	.578
1917	CHI-A	156	100	54	.649
1918	CHI-A	124	57	67	.460
	4	591	339	247	.578

Royster, Jerry

YR	TM/L	G	W	L	PCT
2002	MIL-N	147	53	94	.361

Ruel, Muddy

YR	TM/L	G	W	L	PCT
1947	STL-A	154	59	95	.383

Runnells, Tom

YR	TM/L	G	W	L	PCT
1991	MON-N	112	51	61	.455
1992	MON-N	37	17	20	.459
	2	149	68	81	.456

Runnels, Pete

YR	TM/L	G	W	L	PCT
1966	BOS-A	16	8	8	.500

Russell, Bill

YR	TM/L	G	W	L	PCT
1996	LA-N	86	49	37	.570
1997	LA-N	162	88	74	.543
1998	LA-N	74	36	38	.486
	3	322	173	149	.537

Ryan, Connie

YR	TM/L	G	W	L	PCT
1975	ATL-N	27	9	18	.333
1977	TEX-A	6	2	4	.333
	2	33	11	22	.333

Sawyer, Eddie

YR	TM/L	G	W	L	PCT
1948	PHI-N	63	23	40	.365
1949	PHI-N	154	81	73	.526
1950	PHI-N	157	91	63	.591
1951	PHI-N	154	73	81	.474
1952	PHI-N	63	28	35	.444
1958	PHI-N	70	30	40	.429
1959	PHI-N	155	64	90	.416
1960	PHI-N	1	0	1	.000
	8	817	390	423	.480

Scanlon, Mike

YR	TM/L	G	W	L	PCT
1884	WAS-U	114	47	65	.420
1886	WAS-N	82	13	67	.163
	2	196	60	132	.313

Schaefer, Bob

YR	TM/L	G	W	L	PCT
1991	KC-A	1	1	0	1.000

Schalk, Ray

YR	TM/L	G	W	L	PCT
1927	CHI-A	153	70	83	.458
1928	CHI-A	75	32	42	.432
	2	228	102	125	.449

Scheffing, Bob

YR	TM/L	G	W	L	PCT
1957	CHI-N	156	62	92	.403
1958	CHI-N	154	72	82	.468
1959	CHI-N	155	74	80	.481
1961	DET-A	163	101	61	.623
1962	DET-A	161	85	76	.528
1963	DET-A	60	24	36	.400
	6	849	418	427	.495

Schlafly, Larry

YR	TM/L	G	W	L	PCT
1914	BUF-F	156	80	71	.530
1915	BUF-F	41	13	28	.317
	2	197	93	99	.484

Schmelz, Gus

YR	TM/L	G	W	L	PCT
1884	COL-a	110	69	39	.639
1886	STL-N	126	43	79	.352
1887	CIN-a	136	81	54	.600
1888	CIN-a	137	80	54	.597
1889	CIN-a	141	76	63	.547
1890	COL-a	57	38	13	.745
1890	CLE-N	78	21	55	.276
1891	COL-a	138	61	76	.445
1894	WAS-N	132	45	87	.341
1895	WAS-N	133	43	85	.336
1896	WAS-N	133	58	73	.443
1897	WAS-N	36	9	25	.265
	11	1357	624	703	.470

YR	TM/L	G	W	L	PCT
Schoendienst, Red					
1965	STL-N	162	80	81	.497
1966	STL-N	162	83	79	.512
1967	STL-N	161	101	60	.627
1968	STL-N	162	97	65	.599
1969	STL-N	162	87	75	.537
1970	STL-N	162	76	86	.469
1971	STL-N	163	90	72	.556
1972	STL-N	156	75	81	.481
1973	STL-N	162	81	81	.500
1974	STL-N	161	86	75	.534
1975	STL-N	163	82	80	.506
1976	STL-N	162	72	90	.444
1980	STL-N	37	18	19	.486
1990	STL-N	24	13	11	.542
	14	1999	1041	955	.522
Schultz, Joe					
1969	SEA-A	163	64	98	.395
1973	DET-A	28	14	14	.500
	2	191	78	112	.411
Scioscia, Mike					
2000	ANA-A	162	82	80	.506
2001	ANA-A	162	75	87	.463
2002	ANA-A	162	99	63	.611
2003	ANA-A	162	77	85	.475
	4	648	333	315	.514
Selee, Frank					
1890	BOS-N	134	76	57	.571
1891	BOS-N	140	87	51	.630
1892	BOS-N	152	102	48	.680
1893	BOS-N	131	86	43	.667
1894	BOS-N	133	83	49	.629
1895	BOS-N	133	71	60	.542
1896	BOS-N	132	74	57	.565
1897	BOS-N	135	93	39	.705
1898	BOS-N	152	102	47	.685
1899	BOS-N	153	95	57	.625
1900	BOS-N	142	66	72	.478
1901	BOS-N	140	69	69	.500
1902	CHI-N	143	68	69	.496
1903	CHI-N	139	82	56	.594
1904	CHI-N	156	93	60	.608
1905	CHI-N	65	37	28	.569
	16	2180	1284	862	.598
Sewell, Luke					
1941	STL-A	113	55	55	.500
1942	STL-A	151	82	69	.543
1943	STL-A	153	72	80	.474
1944	STL-A	154	89	65	.578
1945	STL-A	154	81	70	.536
1946	STL-A	125	53	71	.427
1949	CIN-N	3	1	2	.333
1950	CIN-N	153	66	87	.431
1951	CIN-N	155	68	86	.442
1952	CIN-N	98	39	59	.398
	10	1259	606	644	.485
Shannon, Dan					
1889	LOU-a	58	10	46	.179
1891	WAS-a	51	15	34	.306
	2	109	25	80	.238
Sharsig, Bill					
1886	PHI-a	41	22	17	.564
1888	PHI-a	137	81	52	.609
1889	PHI-a	138	75	58	.564
1890	PHI-a	132	54	78	.409
1891	PHI-a	18	6	11	.353
	5	466	238	216	.524
Shawkey, Bob					
1930	NY-A	154	86	68	.558
Sheehan, Tom					
1960	SF-N	98	46	50	.479
Shepard, Larry					
1968	PIT-N	163	80	82	.494
1969	PIT-N	157	84	73	.535
	2	320	164	155	.514
Sherry, Norm					
1976	CAL-A	66	37	29	.561
1977	CAL-A	81	39	42	.481
	2	147	76	71	.517
Shettsline, Bill					
1898	PHI-N	104	59	44	.573
1899	PHI-N	154	94	58	.618
1900	PHI-N	141	75	63	.543
1901	PHI-N	140	83	57	.593
1902	PHI-N	138	56	81	.409
	5	677	367	303	.548
Shotton, Burt					
1928	PHI-N	152	43	109	.283
1929	PHI-N	154	71	82	.464
1930	PHI-N	156	52	102	.338
1931	PHI-N	155	66	88	.429
1932	PHI-N	154	78	76	.506
1933	PHI-N	152	60	92	.395
1934	CIN-N	1	1	0	1.000
1947	BRO-N	153	92	60	.605
1948	BRO-N	81	48	33	.593
1949	BRO-N	156	97	57	.630
1950	BRO-N	155	89	65	.578
	11	1469	697	764	.477
Showalter, Buck					
1992	NY-A	162	76	86	.469
1993	NY-A	162	88	74	.543
1994	NY-A	113	70	43	.619
1995	NY-A	145	79	65	.549
1998	ARI-N	162	65	97	.401
1999	ARI-N	162	100	62	.617
2000	ARI-N	162	85	77	.525
2003	TEX-A	162	71	91	.467
	8	1230	634	595	.516
Silvestri, Ken					
1967	ATL-N	3	0	3	.000
Simmons, Joe					
1875	WES-n	13	1	12	.077
1884	WIL-U	18	2	16	.111
	2	31	3	28	.097
Simmons, Lew					
1886	PHI-a	98	41	55	.427
Sisler, Dick					
1964	CIN-N	6	3	3	.500
1964	CIN-N	47	29	18	.617
1965	CIN-N	162	89	73	.549
	3	215	121	94	.563
Sisler, George					
1924	STL-A	153	74	78	.487
1925	STL-A	154	82	71	.536
1926	STL-A	155	62	92	.403
	3	462	218	241	.475
Skaff, Frank					
1966	DET-A	79	40	39	.506
Skinner, Bob					
1968	PHI-N	107	48	59	.449
1969	PHI-N	108	44	64	.407
1977	SD-N	1	1	0	1.000
	3	216	93	123	.431
Skinner, Joel					
2002	CLE-A	75	35	40	.467
Slattery, Jack					
1928	BOS-N	31	11	20	.355
Smith, Bill					
1873	MAR-n	6	0	6	.000
Smith, Harry					
1909	BOS-N	79	23	54	.299
Smith, Heinie					
1902	NY-N	32	5	27	.156
Smith, Mayo					
1955	PHI-N	154	77	77	.500
1956	PHI-N	154	71	83	.461
1957	PHI-N	156	77	77	.500
1958	PHI-N	84	39	45	.464
1959	CIN-N	80	35	45	.438
1967	DET-A	163	91	71	.562
1968	DET-A	164	103	59	.636
1969	DET-A	162	90	72	.556
1970	DET-A	162	79	83	.488
	9	1279	662	612	.520
Snyder, Jim					
1988	SEA-A	105	45	60	.429
Snyder, Pop					
1882	CIN-a	80	55	25	.688
1883	CIN-a	98	61	37	.622
1884	CIN-a	40	24	14	.632
1891	WAS-a	70	23	46	.333
	4	288	163	122	.572
Sothoron, Allen					
1933	STL-A	8	2	6	.250
Southworth, Billy					
1929	STL-N	90	43	45	.489
1940	STL-N	111	69	40	.633
1941	STL-N	155	97	56	.634
1942	STL-N	156	106	48	.688
1943	STL-N	157	105	49	.682
1944	STL-N	157	105	49	.682
1945	STL-N	155	95	59	.617
1946	BOS-N	154	81	72	.529
1947	BOS-N	154	86	68	.558
1948	BOS-N	154	91	62	.595
1949	BOS-N	111	55	54	.505
1950	BOS-N	156	83	71	.539
1951	BOS-N	60	28	31	.475
	13	1770	1044	704	.597
Spalding, Al					
1876	CHI-N	66	52	14	.788
1877	CHI-N	60	26	33	.441
	2	126	78	47	.624
Speaker, Tris					
1919	CLE-A	61	40	21	.656
1920	CLE-A	154	98	56	.636
1921	CLE-A	154	94	60	.610
1922	CLE-A	155	78	76	.506
1923	CLE-A	153	82	71	.536
1924	CLE-A	153	67	86	.438
1925	CLE-A	155	70	84	.455
1926	CLE-A	154	88	66	.571
	8	1139	617	520	.543
Spence, Harry					
1888	IND-N	136	50	85	.370
Stahl, Chick					
1906	BOS-A	40	14	26	.350
Stahl, Jake					
1905	WAS-A	154	64	87	.424
1906	WAS-A	151	55	95	.367
1912	BOS-A	154	105	47	.691
1913	BOS-A	81	39	41	.488
	4	540	263	270	.493
Stallings, George					
1897	PHI-N	134	55	77	.417
1898	PHI-N	46	19	27	.413
1901	DET-A	136	74	61	.548
1909	NY-A	153	74	77	.490
1910	NY-A	142	78	59	.569
1913	BOS-N	154	69	82	.457
1914	BOS-N	158	94	59	.614
1915	BOS-N	157	83	69	.546
1916	BOS-N	158	89	63	.586
1917	BOS-N	158	72	81	.471
1918	BOS-N	124	53	71	.427
1919	BOS-N	140	57	82	.410
1920	BOS-N	153	62	90	.408
	13	1813	879	898	.495
Stanky, Eddie					
1952	STL-N	154	88	66	.571
1953	STL-N	157	83	71	.539
1954	STL-N	154	72	82	.468
1955	STL-N	36	17	19	.472
1966	CHI-A	163	83	79	.512
1967	CHI-A	162	89	73	.549
1968	CHI-A	79	34	45	.430
1977	TEX-A	1	1	0	1.000
	8	906	467	435	.518
Start, Joe					
1873	MUT-n	25	18	7	.720
Stengel, Casey					
1934	BRO-N	153	71	81	.467
1935	BRO-N	154	70	83	.458
1936	BRO-N	156	67	87	.435
1938	BOS-N	153	77	75	.507
1939	BOS-N	152	63	88	.417
1940	BOS-N	152	65	87	.428
1941	BOS-N	156	62	92	.403
1942	BOS-N	150	59	89	.399
1943	BOS-N	107	47	60	.439
1949	NY-A	155	97	57	.630
1950	NY-A	155	98	56	.636
1951	NY-A	154	98	56	.636
1952	NY-A	154	95	59	.617
1953	NY-A	151	99	52	.656
1954	NY-A	155	103	51	.669
1955	NY-A	154	96	58	.623
1956	NY-A	154	97	57	.630
1957	NY-A	154	98	56	.636
1958	NY-A	155	92	62	.597
1959	NY-A	155	79	75	.513
1960	NY-A	155	97	57	.630
1962	NY-N	161	40	120	.250
1963	NY-N	162	51	111	.315
1964	NY-N	163	53	109	.327
1965	NY-N	96	31	64	.326
	25	3766	1905	1842	.508
Stovall, George					
1911	CLE-A	139	74	62	.544
1912	STL-A	117	41	74	.357
1913	STL-A	135	50	84	.373
1914	KC-F	154	67	84	.444
1915	KC-F	153	81	72	.529
	5	698	313	376	.454
Stovey, Harry					
1881	WOR-N	27	8	18	.308
1885	PHI-a	113	55	57	.491
	2	140	63	75	.457
Street, Gabby					
1929	STL-N	1	1	0	1.000
1930	STL-N	154	92	62	.597
1931	STL-N	154	101	53	.656
1932	STL-N	156	72	82	.468
1933	STL-N	91	46	45	.505
1938	STL-A	146	53	90	.371
	6	702	365	332	.524
Stricker, Cub					
1892	STL-N	23	6	17	.261
Strickland, George					
1964	CLE-A	73	33	39	.458
1966	CLE-A	39	15	24	.385
	2	112	48	63	.432
Stubing, Moose					
1988	CAL-A	8	0	8	.000
Sukeforth, Clyde					
1947	BRO-N	2	2	0	1.000
Sullivan, Billy					
1909	CHI-A	159	78	74	.513
Sullivan, Haywood					
1965	KC-A	136	54	82	.397
Sullivan, Pat					
1890	COL-a	3	2	1	.667
Sullivan, Ted					
1883	STL-a	79	53	26	.671
1884	KC-U	62	13	46	.220
1884	STL-U	31	28	3	.903
1888	WAS-N	96	38	57	.400
	3	268	132	132	.500

YR	TM/L	G	W	L	PCT
Sweasy, Charlie					
1875	RS-n	19	4	15	.211
Swift, Bob					
1965	DET-A	42	24	18	.571
1966	DET-A	57	32	25	.561
2		99	56	43	.566
Tanner, Chuck					
1970	CHI-A	16	3	13	.188
1971	CHI-A	162	79	83	.488
1972	CHI-A	154	87	67	.565
1973	CHI-A	162	77	85	.475
1974	CHI-A	163	80	80	.500
1975	CHI-A	161	75	86	.466
1976	OAK-A	161	87	74	.540
1977	PIT-N	162	96	66	.593
1978	PIT-N	161	88	73	.547
1979	PIT-N	163	98	64	.605
1980	PIT-N	162	83	79	.512
1981	PIT-N	103	46	56	.451
1982	PIT-N	162	84	78	.519
1983	PIT-N	162	84	78	.519
1984	PIT-N	162	75	87	.463
1985	PIT-N	161	57	104	.354
1986	ATL-N	161	72	89	.447
1987	ATL-N	161	69	92	.429
1988	ATL-N	39	12	27	.308
19		2738	1352	1381	.495
Tappe, El					
1961	CHI-N	2	2	0	1.000
1961	CHI-N	16	5	11	.313
1961	CHI-N	79	35	43	.449
1962	CHI-N	20	4	16	.200
3		117	46	70	.397
Taylor, George					
1884	BRO-a	109	40	64	.385
Taylor, Zack					
1946	STL-A	31	13	17	.433
1948	STL-A	155	59	94	.386
1949	STL-A	155	53	101	.344
1950	STL-A	154	58	96	.377
1951	STL-A	154	52	102	.338
5		649	235	410	.364
Tebbetts, Birdie					
1954	CIN-N	154	74	80	.481
1955	CIN-N	154	75	79	.487
1956	CIN-N	155	91	63	.591
1957	CIN-N	154	80	74	.519
1958	CIN-N	113	52	61	.460
1961	MIL-N	25	12	13	.480
1962	MIL-N	162	86	76	.531
1963	CLE-A	162	79	83	.488
1964	CLE-A	91	46	44	.511
1965	CLE-A	162	87	75	.537
1966	CLE-A	123	66	57	.537
11		1455	748	705	.515
Tebeau, Patsy					
1890	CLE-P	52	21	30	.412
1891	CLE-N	73	31	40	.437
1892	CLE-N	153	93	56	.624
1893	CLE-N	129	73	55	.570
1894	CLE-N	130	68	61	.527
1895	CLE-N	132	84	46	.646
1896	CLE-N	135	80	48	.625
1897	CLE-N	132	69	62	.527
1898	CLE-N	156	81	68	.544
1899	STL-N	155	84	67	.556
1900	STL-N	92	42	50	.457
11		1339	726	583	.555
Tenace, Gene					
1991	TOR-A	33	19	14	.576
Tenney, Fred					
1905	BOS-N	156	51	103	.331
1906	BOS-N	152	49	102	.325
1907	BOS-N	152	58	90	.392
1911	BOS-N	156	44	107	.291
4		616	202	402	.334
Terry, Bill					
1932	NY-N	114	55	59	.482
1933	NY-N	156	91	61	.599
1934	NY-N	153	93	60	.608
1935	NY-N	156	91	62	.595
1936	NY-N	154	92	62	.597
1937	NY-N	152	95	57	.625
1938	NY-N	152	83	67	.553
1939	NY-N	151	77	74	.510
1940	NY-N	152	72	80	.474
1941	NY-N	156	74	79	.484
10		1496	823	661	.555
Thomas, Fred					
1887	IND-N	29	11	18	.379
Thompson, A.M.					
1884	STP-U	9	2	6	.250
Tighe, Jack					
1957	DET-A	154	78	76	.506
1958	DET-A	49	21	28	.429
2		203	99	104	.488
Tinker, Joe					
1913	CIN-N	156	64	89	.418
1914	CHI-F	158	87	67	.565
1915	CHI-F	156	86	66	.566
1916	CHI-N	156	67	86	.438
4		626	304	308	.497
Torborg, Jeff					
1977	CLE-A	104	45	59	.433
1978	CLE-A	159	69	90	.434
1979	CLE-A	95	43	52	.453
1989	CHI-A	161	69	92	.429
1990	CHI-A	162	94	68	.580
1991	CHI-A	162	87	75	.537
1992	NY-N	162	72	90	.444
1993	NY-N	38	13	25	.342
2001	MON-N	108	47	61	.435
2002	FLA-N	162	79	83	.488
2003	FLA-N	39	17	22	.421
11		1352	635	717	.470
Torre, Joe					
1977	NY-N	117	49	68	.419
1978	NY-N	162	66	96	.407
1979	NY-N	163	63	99	.389
1980	NY-N	162	67	95	.414
1981	NY-N	105	41	62	.398
1982	ATL-N	162	89	73	.549
1983	ATL-N	162	88	74	.543
1984	ATL-N	162	80	82	.494
1990	STL-N	58	24	34	.414
1991	STL-N	162	84	78	.519
1992	STL-N	162	83	79	.512
1993	STL-N	162	87	75	.537
1994	STL-N	115	53	61	.465
1995	STL-N	47	20	27	.426
1996	NY-A	162	92	70	.568
1997	NY-A	162	96	66	.593
1998	NY-A	162	114	48	.704
1999	NY-A	126	77	49	.611
2000	NY-A	161	87	74	.540
2001	NY-A	161	95	65	.594
2002	NY-A	161	103	58	.640
2003	NY-A	163	101	61	.623
22		3159	1659	1494	.526
Tosca, Carlos					
2002	TOR-A	109	58	51	.532
2003	TOR-A	162	86	76	.531
2		271	144	127	.531
Tracewski, Dick					
1979	DET-A	2	2	0	1.000
Tracy, Jim					
2001	LA-N	162	86	76	.531
2002	LA-N	162	92	70	.568
2003	LA-N	162	85	77	.525
3		486	263	223	.541
Trammell, Alan					
2003	DET-A	162	43	119	.265
Traynor, Pie					
1934	PIT-N	100	47	52	.475
1935	PIT-N	153	86	67	.562
1936	PIT-N	156	84	70	.545
1937	PIT-N	154	86	68	.558
1938	PIT-N	152	86	64	.573
1939	PIT-N	153	68	85	.444
6		868	457	406	.530
Trebelhorn, Tom					
1986	MIL-A	9	6	3	.667
1987	MIL-A	162	91	71	.562
1988	MIL-A	162	87	75	.537
1989	MIL-A	162	81	81	.500
1990	MIL-A	162	74	88	.457
1991	MIL-A	162	83	79	.512
1994	CHI-N	113	49	64	.434
7		932	471	461	.505
Trott, Sam					
1891	WAS-a	12	4	7	.364
Turner, Ted					
1977	ATL-N	1	0	1	.000
Unglaub, Bob					
1907	BOS-A	29	9	20	.310
Valentine, Bobby					
1985	TEX-A	129	53	76	.411
1986	TEX-A	162	87	75	.537
1987	TEX-A	162	75	87	.463
1988	TEX-A	161	70	91	.435
1989	TEX-A	162	83	79	.512
1990	TEX-A	162	83	79	.512
1991	TEX-A	162	85	77	.525
1992	TEX-A	86	45	41	.523
1996	NY-N	31	12	19	.387
1997	NY-N	162	88	74	.543
1998	NY-N	162	88	74	.543
1999	NY-N	163	97	66	.595
2000	NY-N	162	94	68	.580
2001	NY-N	162	82	80	.506
2002	NY-N	161	75	86	.466
15		2189	1117	1072	.510
Van Haltren, George					
1892	BLN-N	11	1	10	.091
Vernon, Mickey					
1961	WAS-A	161	61	100	.379
1962	WAS-A	162	60	101	.373
1963	WAS-A	40	14	26	.350
3		363	135	227	.373
Virdon, Bill					
1972	PIT-N	155	96	59	.619
1973	PIT-N	136	67	69	.493
1974	NY-A	162	89	73	.549
1975	NY-A	104	53	51	.510
1975	HOU-N	35	17	17	.500
1976	HOU-N	162	80	82	.494
1977	HOU-N	162	81	81	.500
1978	HOU-N	162	74	88	.457
1979	HOU-N	162	89	73	.549
1980	HOU-N	163	93	70	.571
1981	HOU-N	110	61	49	.555
1982	HOU-N	111	49	62	.441
1983	MON-N	163	82	80	.506
1984	MON-N	131	64	67	.489
13		1918	995	921	.519
Vitt, Ossie					
1938	CLE-A	153	86	66	.566
1939	CLE-A	154	87	67	.565
1940	CLE-A	155	89	65	.578
3		462	262	198	.570
Vonderahe, Chris					
1895	STL-N	1	1	0	1.000
1896	STL-N	2	0	2	.000
1897	STL-N	14	2	12	.143
3		17	3	14	.176
Vukovich, John					
1986	CHI-N	2	1	1	.500
1988	PHI-N	9	5	4	.556
2		11	6	5	.545
Wagner, Heinie					
1930	BOS-A	154	52	102	.338
Wagner, Honus					
1917	PIT-N	5	1	4	.200
Walker, Harry					
1955	STL-N	118	51	67	.432
1965	PIT-N	163	90	72	.556
1966	PIT-N	162	92	70	.568
1967	PIT-N	84	42	42	.500
1968	HOU-N	101	49	52	.485
1969	HOU-N	162	81	81	.500
1970	HOU-N	162	79	83	.488
1971	HOU-N	162	79	83	.488
1972	HOU-N	121	67	54	.554
9		1235	630	604	.511
Wallace, Bobby					
1911	STL-A	152	45	107	.296
1912	STL-A	40	12	27	.308
1937	CIN-N	25	5	20	.200
3		217	62	154	.287
Walsh, Ed					
1924	CHI-A	3	1	2	.333
Walsh, Mike					
1884	LOU-a	110	68	40	.630
Walters, Bucky					
1948	CIN-N	53	20	33	.377
1949	CIN-N	153	61	90	.404
2		206	81	123	.397
Waltz, John					
1892	BAL-N	8	2	6	.250
Ward, John					
1880	PRO-N	32	18	13	.581
1884	NY-N	16	6	8	.429
1890	BRO-P	133	76	56	.576
1891	BRO-N	137	61	76	.445
1892	BRO-N	158	95	59	.617
1893	NY-N	139	68	64	.515
1894	NY-N	139	88	44	.667
7		751	412	320	.563
Wathan, John					
1987	KC-A	36	21	15	.583
1988	KC-A	161	84	77	.522
1989	KC-A	162	92	70	.568
1990	KC-A	161	75	86	.466
1991	KC-A	37	15	22	.405
1992	CAL-A	89	39	50	.438
6		646	326	320	.505
Watkins, Bill					
1884	IND-a	23	4	18	.182
1885	DET-N	70	34	36	.486
1886	DET-N	126	87	36	.707
1887	DET-N	127	79	45	.637
1888	KC-a	25	8	17	.320
1888	DET-N	94	44	44	.527
1889	KC-a	139	55	82	.401
1893	STL-N	135	57	75	.432
1898	PIT-N	151	72	76	.486
1899	PIT-N	24	7	15	.318
9		914	452	444	.504
Watkins, Harvey					
1895	NY-N	35	18	17	.514
Weaver, Earl					
1968	BAL-A	82	48	34	.585
1969	BAL-A	162	109	53	.673
1970	BAL-A	162	108	54	.667
1971	BAL-A	158	101	57	.639
1972	BAL-A	154	80	74	.519
1973	BAL-A	162	97	65	.599
1974	BAL-A	162	91	71	.562
1975	BAL-A	159	90	69	.566
1976	BAL-A	162	88	74	.543
1977	BAL-A	161	97	64	.602
1978	BAL-A	161	90	71	.559
1979	BAL-A	159	102	57	.642
1980	BAL-A	162	100	62	.617
1981	BAL-A	105	59	46	.562

YR	TM/L	G	W	L	PCT
1982	BAL-A	163	94	68	.580
1985	BAL-A	105	53	52	.505
1986	BAL-A	162	73	89	.451
17		2541	1480	1060	.583

Wedge, Eric

YR	TM/L	G	W	L	PCT
2003	CLE-A	162	68	94	.420

Westrum, Wes

YR	TM/L	G	W	L	PCT
1965	NY-N	68	19	48	.284
1966	NY-N	161	66	95	.410
1967	NY-N	151	57	94	.377
1974	SF-N	86	38	48	.442
1975	SF-N	161	80	81	.497
5		627	260	366	.415

Wheeler, Harry

YR	TM/L	G	W	L	PCT
1884	KC-U	4	0	4	.000

White, Deacon

YR	TM/L	G	W	L	PCT
1872	CLE-n	2	0	2	.000
1879	CIN-N	18	9	9	.500
2		20	9	11	.450

White, Jo-Jo

YR	TM/L	G	W	L	PCT
1960	CLE-A	1	1	0	1.000

White, Warren

YR	TM/L	G	W	L	PCT
1872	NAT-n	11	0	11	.000
1874	BAL-n	47	9	38	.191
		58	9	49	.155

White, Will

YR	TM/L	G	W	L	PCT
1884	CIN-A	72	44	27	.620

Wilber, Del

YR	TM/L	G	W	L	PCT
1973	TEX-A	1	1	0	1.000

Wilhelm, Kaiser

YR	TM/L	G	W	L	PCT
1921	PHI-N	67	26	41	.388
1922	PHI-N	154	57	96	.373
2		221	83	137	.377

Williams, Dick

YR	TM/L	G	W	L	PCT
1967	BOS-A	162	92	70	.568
1968	BOS-A	162	86	76	.531
1969	BOS-A	153	82	71	.536
1971	OAK-A	161	101	60	.627
1972	OAK-A	155	93	62	.600
1973	OAK-A	162	94	68	.580
1974	CAL-A	84	36	48	.429
1975	CAL-A	161	72	89	.447
1976	CAL-A	96	39	57	.406
1977	MON-N	162	75	87	.463
1978	MON-N	162	76	86	.469
1979	MON-N	160	95	65	.594

YR	TM/L	G	W	L	PCT
1980	MON-N	162	90	72	.556
1981	MON-N	81	44	37	.543
1982	SD-N	162	81	81	.500
1983	SD-N	163	81	81	.500
1984	SD-N	162	92	70	.568
1985	SD-N	162	83	79	.512
1986	SEA-A	133	58	75	.436
1987	SEA-A	162	78	84	.481
1988	SEA-A	56	23	33	.411
21		3023	1571	1451	.520

Williams, Jimmy

YR	TM/L	G	W	L	PCT
1884	STL-A	85	51	33	.607
1887	CLE-A	133	39	92	.298
1888	CLE-A	64	20	44	.313
3		282	110	169	.394

Williams, Jimy

YR	TM/L	G	W	L	PCT
1986	TOR-A	163	86	76	.531
1987	TOR-A	162	96	66	.593
1988	TOR-A	162	87	75	.537
1989	TOR-A	36	12	24	.333
1997	BOS-A	162	78	84	.481
1998	BOS-A	162	92	70	.568
1999	BOS-A	162	94	68	.580
2000	BOS-A	162	85	77	.525
2001	BOS-A	118	65	53	.551
2002	HOU-N	162	84	78	.519
2003	HOU-N	162	87	75	.537
11		1613	866	746	.537

Williams, Ted

YR	TM/L	G	W	L	PCT
1969	WAS-A	162	86	76	.531
1970	WAS-A	162	70	92	.432
1971	WAS-A	159	63	96	.396
1972	TEX-A	154	54	100	.351
4		637	273	364	.429

Wills, Maury

YR	TM/L	G	W	L	PCT
1980	SEA-A	58	20	38	.345
1981	SEA-A	25	6	18	.250
2		83	26	56	.317

Wilson, Jimmie

YR	TM/L	G	W	L	PCT
1934	PHI-N	149	56	93	.376
1935	PHI-N	156	64	89	.418
1936	PHI-N	154	54	100	.351
1937	PHI-N	155	61	92	.399
1938	PHI-N	149	45	103	.304
1941	CHI-N	155	70	84	.455
1942	CHI-N	155	68	86	.442
1943	CHI-N	154	74	79	.484
1944	CHI-N	10	1	9	.100
9		1237	493	735	.401

Wine, Bobby

YR	TM/L	G	W	L	PCT
1985	ATL-N	41	16	25	.390

Wingo, Ivey

YR	TM/L	G	W	L	PCT
1916	CIN-N	2	1	1	.500

Winkles, Bobby

YR	TM/L	G	W	L	PCT
1973	CAL-A	162	79	83	.488
1974	CAL-A	75	30	44	.405
1977	OAK-A	108	37	71	.343
1978	OAK-A	39	24	15	.615
4		384	170	213	.444

Wolf, Jimmy

YR	TM/L	G	W	L	PCT
1889	LOU-a	65	14	51	.215

Wolverton, Harry

YR	TM/L	G	W	L	PCT
1912	NY-A	153	50	102	.329

Wood, George

YR	TM/L	G	W	L	PCT
1891	PHI-A	125	67	55	.549

Wood, Jimmy

YR	TM/L	G	W	L	PCT
1871	CHI-n	28	19	9	.679
1872	ECK-n	18	3	15	.167
1872	TRO-n	25	15	10	.600
1874	CHI-n	23	10	13	.435
1875	CHI-n	69	30	37	.448
5		163	77	84	.472

Wright, Al

YR	TM/L	G	W	L	PCT
1876	PHI-N	60	14	45	.237

Wright, George

YR	TM/L	G	W	L	PCT
1879	PRO-N	85	59	25	.702

Wright, Harry

YR	TM/L	G	W	L	PCT
1871	BOS-n	31	20	10	.667
1872	BOS-n	48	39	8	.830
1873	BOS-n	60	43	16	.729
1874	BOS-n	71	52	18	.743
1875	BOS-n	82	71	8	.899
1876	BOS-N	70	39	31	.557
1877	BOS-N	61	42	18	.700
1878	BOS-N	60	41	19	.683
1879	BOS-N	84	54	30	.643
1880	BOS-N	86	40	44	.476
1881	BOS-N	83	38	45	.458
1882	PRO-N	84	52	32	.619
1883	PRO-N	98	58	40	.592
1884	PHI-N	113	39	73	.348
1885	PHI-N	111	56	54	.509
1886	PHI-N	119	71	43	.623
1887	PHI-N	128	75	48	.610
1888	PHI-N	132	69	61	.531
1889	PHI-N	130	63	64	.496
1890	PHI-N	22	14	8	.636
1890	PHI-N	46	22	23	.489
1891	PHI-N	138	68	69	.496
1892	PHI-N	155	87	66	.569
1893	PHI-N	133	72	57	.558
23		2145	1225	885	.581

York, Rudy

YR	TM/L	G	W	L	PCT
1959	BOS-A	1	0	1	.000

York, Tom

YR	TM/L	G	W	L	PCT
1878	PRO-N	62	33	27	.550
1881	PRO-N	34	23	10	.697
2		96	56	37	.602

Yost, Eddie

YR	TM/L	G	W	L	PCT
1963	WAS-A	1	0	1	.000

Yost, Ned

YR	TM/L	G	W	L	PCT
2003	MIL-N	162	68	94	.420

Young, Cy

YR	TM/L	G	W	L	PCT
1907	BOS-A	6	3	3	.500

Young, Nick

YR	TM/L	G	W	L	PCT
1871	OLY-n	32	15	15	.500
1873	WAS-n	39	8	31	.205
2		71	23	46	.324

Zimmer, Chief

YR	TM/L	G	W	L	PCT
1903	PHI-N	139	49	86	.363

Zimmer, Don

YR	TM/L	G	W	L	PCT
1972	SD-N	142	54	88	.380
1973	SD-N	162	60	102	.370
1976	BOS-A	76	42	34	.553
1977	BOS-A	161	97	64	.602
1978	BOS-A	163	99	64	.607
1979	BOS-A	160	91	69	.569
1980	BOS-A	155	82	73	.529
1981	TEX-A	105	57	48	.543
1982	TEX-A	96	38	58	.396
1988	CHI-N	163	77	85	.475
1989	CHI-N	162	93	69	.574
1990	CHI-N	162	77	85	.475
1991	CHI-N	37	18	19	.486
1999	NY-A	36	21	15	.583
13		1780	906	873	.509

Appendix H

The Umpire Roster

Larry Gerlach, who knows more about umpires and umpiring than anybody, has created the Umpire Roster that follows. The basis of his roster is the list compiled by S.C. Thompson in the 1930s and 1940s, but his research has corrected several errors and omissions in that list and has scrupulously brought the umpire roster up to date.

Separate rosters exist for each league, showing the few instances where an umpire worked in more than one league. The American and National League maintained separate umpiring crews until the 2000 season, when they were consolidated into a single pool. Therefore, umpires are listed under the league in which they debuted until 2000, after which they are listed under the heading of Major League Baseball.

Umpires are divided into four categories: regular, league-employed umpires; substitutes; player-umpires, pressed into emergency service; and those subs used during the recent strikes.

A feature unique to *Total Baseball* is the identification of substitute umpires in the National Association years 1871–75. An instance of this last practice occurred as late as 1935, when Chicago White Sox outfielder Jocko Conlan was recruited to fill in for umpire Red Ormsby in a game between the Sox and the St. Louis Browns. Conlan, of course, went on to a Hall of Fame career as a man in blue.

Let's call the roll.

Dallas Parks
After getting dirty courtesy Billy Martin, Parks ejected the Yankees manager from this 1979 game.

REGULAR UMPS

National Association (1871-75)

Avery, C. Hamilton 1875
Beardslee, John J. 1871
Blodgett, C. W. 1875
Boardman, Frederick "Fred" 1875
Bomeisler, Theodore 1871-73
Boyd, William J. "Bill" 1875
Burdock, John J. "Jack" 1872-74
Carey, Thomas J. "Tom" 1874

Clapp, John E. 1874-75
Cone, J. Frederick "Fred" 1875
Daniels, Charles F. 1874-75
Dehlman, Herman J. 1874
Dole, Lester C. 1875
Ferguson, Robert V. "Bob" 1872-73, 1875
Fulmer, Charles J. "Chick" 1873
Heubel, George A. 1875
Hodges, Amory G. 1874-75
Holly, Samuel J. "Sam" 1871
Lennon, William F. "Bill" 1871-72, 1873-74
Mack, Dennis J. "Denny" 1875

Martin, Alphonse C. "Phonney" 1875
Mathews, Robert T. "Bobby" 1873-75
McLean, William H. "Billy" 1874-75
Mills, Charles "Charlie" 1872-73
Patterson, Daniel T. "Dan" 1874
Rogers, M. Mortimer "Mort" 1871
Sensenderfer, John P. J. "Count" 1874
Swandell, J. Martin "Marty" 1872-73
Tate, William 1874
Walsh, Michael F. "Mike" 1875
Young, Nicholas E. "Nick" 1871-75

National League (1876-)

Andrews, G. Edward "Ed" 1895, 1898-99
Baker, William P. "Bill" 1957
Ballanfant, E. Lee 1936-57
Barlick, Albert J. "Al" 1940-43, 1946-55, 1958-71
Barnes, Ronald E. "Ron" 1990-94, 1996-97
Barnie, William S. "Billy" 1892
Barr, George M. 1931-49
Barron, Mark E. 1992-97
Battin, Joseph V. "Joe" 1891

Bausewine, George 1905

Behle, Frank 1901

Bell, Wally 1992-2000

Betts, William G. 1894-96, 1898-99

Betz, Edwin J. 1961

Boggess, Lynton R. "Dusty" 1944-48, 1950-62

Boles, Charles 1877

Bond, Thomas H. "Tommy" 1883, 1885

Bonin, Gregory "Greg" 1984-2000

Bradley, George H. "Foghorn" 1879-83

Brady, Jackson 1887

Bransfield, William E. "Kitty" 1917

Bredburg, George W. 1877

Brennan, John E. "Jack" 1899

Brennan, William T. "Bill" 1909-13, 1921

Brocklander, Fred W. 1979-90

Brown, Thomas T. "Tom" 1898-99, 1901-02

Bucknor, C. B. 1996-2000

Bunce, Joshua 1877

Burkhart, W. Kenneth "Ken" 1957-73

Burnham, George W. 1883, 1889, 1895

Burns, John S. 1884

Burns, Thomas E. "Tom" 1892

Burns, Thomas P. "Oyster" 1899

Burtis, L. W. 1876-77

Bush, Garnet C. 1911-12

Byron, William J. "Bill" or "Lord" 1913-19

Callahan, Edward J. "Ed" 1881

Campbell, Daniel "Dan" 1894-96

Campbell, William M. "Bick" 1939-40

Cantillon, Joseph D. "Joe" 1902

Carlson, Mark C. 1999-2000

Carpenter, William B. "Bill" 1897, 1904, 1906-07

Chapman, John C. "Jack" 1880

Chipman, Harry F. 1883

Clarke, Robert M. "Bob" 1930-31

Cockill, George W. 1915

Colgan, Harry W. 1901

Colosi, Nicholas "Nick" 1968-82

Conahan, Edward J. "Ed" 1896

Cone, J. F. "Fred" 1877

Conlan, John B. "Jocko" 1941-64

Connolly, John M. "Red" 1886

Connolly, Thomas H. "Tommy" 1898-1900

Connors, Patrick "Pat" 1998

Conway, John H. 1906

Cook, Robert "Robb" 1999-2000

Crandall, Robert 1877

Crawford, Gerald J. "Jerry" 1975-2000

Crawford, Henry C. "Shag" 1956-75

Cross, John A. 1878

Cunningham, Elmer E. "Bert" 1901

Curry, Wesley "Wes" 1885-86, 1889, 1898

Cusack, Stephen P. 1909

Cushman, Charles H. "Charlie" 1885, 1898

Cuzzi, Phil 1991-93, 1999-2000

Dailey, John J. 1882

Dale, Jerry P. 1970-85

Daniels, Charles F. 1876, 1878-80, 1887-88

Danley, Kerwin J. 1991-2000

Darling, Gary R. 1986-99

Dascoli, Frank 1948-62

Davidson, David L. "Satch" 1969-84

Davidson, Robert A. "Bob" 1982-99

Davis, Gerald S. "Gerry" 1982-2000

Decker, Stewart M. 1883-85, 1888

Delmore, Victor "Vic" 1956-59

DeMuth, Dana A. 1983-2000

Derr, Doll 1923

Devinney, P. H. "Dan" 1877

Dezelan, Frank J. 1966-68, 1969-71

Dixon, Hal H. 1953-59

Donatelli, August J. "Augie" 1950-73

Donnelly, Charles H. 1931-32

Donohue, Michael R. 1930

Doscher, John H. Sr. "Herm" 1880-81, 1887

Doyle, John J. "Jack" 1911

Drake, Robert "Rob" 1999-2000

Dreckman, Bruce M. 1996-99

Ducharme, — 1876-77

Dunn, Thomas P. "Tom" 1939-46

Dunnigan, Joseph 1881-82

Dwyer, J. Francis "Frank" 1899, 1901

Eagan, John J. 1878, 1886

Eason, Malcolm W. "Mal" 1902, 1910-16

Ellick, Joseph J. "Joe" 1886

Emmel, Paul L. 1999-2000

Emslie, Robert D. "Bob" 1891-1924

Engel, Robert A. "Bob" 1965-90

Engeln, William R. "Bill" 1952-56

Ferguson, Robert V. "Bob" 1879, 1884-85

Fessenden, Wallace C. "Wally" 1889-90

Fields, Stephen H. "Steve" 1979-82

Finneran, William F. 1911-12

Fletcher, Andrew J. 1999-2000

Forman, Allen S. "Al" 1961-65

Fountain, Edward G. 1879

Frary, Ralph 1911

Froemming, Bruce N. 1971-2000

Fulmer, Charles J. "Chick" 1886

Furlong, William E. "Bill" 1878-79, 1883-84

Fyfe, Lee C. 1920

Gaffney, John H. 1884-86, 1891-94, 1899-1900

Galvin, James F. "Jim" 1895

Gibbons, Brian 1994-99

Gibson, Gregory A. "Greg" 1997-2000

Gillean, Thomas 1879-80

Goetz, Lawrence J. "Larry" 1936-57

Gore, Arthur J. "Artie" 1947-56

Gorman, Brian 1991-2000

Gorman, Thomas D. "Tom" 1951-76

Gregg, Eric E. 1975-91, 1993-99

Guglielmo, A. Augie 1952

Gunning, Thomas F. "Tom" 1887

Guthrie, William J. "Bill" 1913, 1915

Hallion, Thomas F. "Tom" 1985-99

Harris, Lanny D. 1979-85

Harrison, Peter A. "Pete" 1916-20

Hart, Eugene F. "Bob" 1920-29

Hart, William F. "Bill" 1914-15

Harvey, H. Douglas "Doug" 1962-92

Hautz, Charles A. "Charlie" 1876, 1879

Henderson, J. Harding "Hardie" 1895-96

Hengle, Edward S. "Ed" 1887

Henline, Walter J. "Butch" 1945-48

Hernandez, Angel 1991-2000

Heuble, George A. 1876

Heydler, John A. 1898

Higham, Richard "Dick" 1881-82

Hirschbeck, Mark 1987-2000

Hoagland, Willard A. 1894

Hodges, A. D. 1876

Hodges, Morris 1999-2000

Hohn, William J. "Bill" 1987-99

Holland, John A. 1887

Holbrook, Samuel "Sam" 1997-99

Holliday, James W. "Bug" 1903

Holmes, Howard E. "Ducky" 1921

Hornung, M. Joseph "Joe" 1893, 1896

Hudson, Marvin L. 1998-2000

Hunt, John T. 1895, 1898-99

Hurst, Timothy C. "Tim" 1891-97, 1900, 1903

Iassogna, Dan 1999-2000

Irwin, Arthur A. 1902

Jackowski, William A. "Bill" 1952-68

Jeffers, W. W. 1881

Jevne, Frederick "Fred" 1895

Johnson, Harry S. "Steamboat" 1914

Johnstone, James E. "Jim" 1903-12

Jorda, Louis D. "Lou" 1927-31, 1940-52

Julian, Joseph O. 1878

Kane, Stephen J. 1909-10

Keefe, Timothy J. "Tim" 1894-96

Kellogg, Jeffery "Jeff" 1991-2000

Kelly, John O. "Kick" 1882, 1888, 1897

Kennedy, Charles 1904

Kenney, John 1877

Kibler, John W. 1963-89

Klem, William J. "Bill" 1905-41

Knight, Alonzo P. "Lon" 1889

Kulpa, Ronald "Ron" 1998-2000

Lally, Bud 1896

Lamplugh, Ian 1999-2000

Landes, Stanley A. "Stan" 1955-72

Lane, Frank H. 1883

Latham, W. Arlington "Arlie" 1899, 1902

Layne, Jerry B. 1989-2000

Libby, Stephen A. 1880

Lincoln, Frederick H. 1914

Long, Robert "Bob" 1992

Long, William H. "Billy" 1895

Lynch, Thomas J. "Tom" 1888-99

Macullar, James F. "Jimmy" 1892

Magee, Sherwood R. "Sherry" 1928

Magerkurth, George L. 1929-47

Mahoney, Michael J. 1892

Malone, Ferguson G. "Fergy" 1884

Manassau, Alfred S. "Al" 1899

Marquez, Alfonso 1999-2000

Marsh, Randall G. "Randy" 1981-2000

Mathews, Robert T. "Bobby" 1880

McCafferty, Charles 1921, 1923

McCormick, William J. "Barry" 1919-29

McDermott, Michael J. "Sandy" 1890, 1897

McDonald, James F. 1895, 1897-99

McElwee, Harvey 1877

McFarland, Horace 1896-97

McGarr, James B. "Chippy" 1899

McGrew, Harry T. "Ted" 1930-31, 1933-34

McLaughlin, Edward J. 1929

McLaughlin, Michael 1893

McLaughlin, Peter J. 1924-28

McLean, William J. "Billy" 1876, 1878-80, 1882-84

McQuaid, John H. "Jack" 1889-94

McSherry, John P. 1971-96

Meals, Gerald W. "Jerry" 1992-94, 1996-2000

Miller, George E. 1879

Mitchell, Charles 1892

Montague, Edward M. "Ed" 1974-2000

Moran, August "Augie" 1903-04, 1910, 1918

Moran, Charles B. "Charlie" 1918-39

Mullin, John 1909

Nash, William M. "Billy" 1901

Nauert, Paul 1995-99

Nelson, Jeff 1997-2000

O'Connor, Arthur 1914

O'Day, Henry F. "Hank" 1895, 1897-1911, 1913, 1915-27

Odlin, Albert F. 1883

Olsen, Andrew H. "Andy" 1968-81

O'Rourke, James H. "Jim" 1894

Orth, Albert L. "Al" 1912-17

O'Sullivan, John J. 1922

Owens, Clarence B. "Brick" 1908, 1912-13

Pallone, David M. "Dave" 1979-88

Parker, George L. 1936-38

Pearce, Richard J. "Dicky" 1878, 1882

Pears, Frank H. 1897, 1905

Pelekoudas, Christos G. "Chris" 1960-75

Pfirman, Charles H. "Cy" 1922-36

Pierce, Grayson S. "Gracie" 1886-87

Pinelli, Ralph A. "Babe" 1935-56

Poncino, Larry L. 1985-88, 1991-99

Potter, Scott A. 1991-95, 1997

Powell, Cornelius J. "Jack" 1923-24, 1933

Power, Charles B. 1902

Powers, Philip B. "Phil" 1879, 1881, 1886-91

Pratt, Albert G. "Al" 1879

Pratt, Thomas J. "Tom" 1886

Pryor, J. Paul 1961-81

Pulli, Frank V. 1972-99

Quest, Joseph L. "Joe" 1886-87

Quick, James E. "Jim" 1974-98

Quigley, Ernest C. "Ernie" 1913-37

Quinn, Joseph C. "Joe" 1882

Randazzo, Anthony J. "Tony" 1999-2000

Rapuano, Edward "Ed" 1990-2000

Reardon, John E. "Beans" 1926-49

Reliford, Charles H. "Charlie" 1989-2000

Rennert, Laurence H. "Dutch" 1973-92

Rieker, Richard G. "Rich" 1992-2000

Rigler, Charles "Cy" 1906-22, 1924-35

Riley, William J. "Billy" 1880

Rippley, T. Steven "Steve" 1983-2000

Robb, Douglas W. "Scotty" 1948-52

Roberts, Leonard W. "Lenny" 1953-55

Rudderham, John E. 1908

Runge, Brian 1999-2000

Runge, Paul E. 1973-97

Ryan, Walter 1946

Schrieber, Paul W. 1997-2000

Scott, James "Jim" 1930-31

Sears, John W. "Ziggy" 1934-45

Secory, Frank E. 1952-70

Sentelle, Leopold T. "Paul" 1922-23

Seward, Edward W. "Ed" 1893

Seward, George E. 1876, 1878

Sheridan, John F. "Jack" 1892, 1896-97

Smith, Charles M. "Pop" 1881

Smith, Vincent A. "Vinnie" 1957-65

Smith, William W. "Billy" 1898-99

Snyder, Charles N. "Pop" 1892-93, 1898-1901

Stage, Charles W. "Billy" 1894

Stambaugh, Calvin G. 1877-78

Stark, Albert D. "Dolly" 1928-35, 1937-40, 1942

Steiner, Melvin J. "Mel" 1961-72

Steinfeldt, Harry M. 1905

Stello, Richard J. "Dick" 1969-87

Sternburg, Paul 1909

Stewart, William J. "Bill" 1933-54

Stockdale, M. J. 1915

Strief, George A. 1889, 1890

Sudol, Edward L. "Ed" 1957-77

Sullivan, David F. "Dave" 1882, 1885

Sullivan, Jeremiah "Jerry" 1887

Sullivan, T. P. 1880

Summer, James G. 1877

Swartwood, C. Edward "Ed" 1894, 1898-1900

Sweeney, James M. "Jim" 1924-26

Tata, Terry A. 1973-99

Terry, William H. "Adonis" 1900

Tilden, Otis 1909

Tremblay, Richard H. "Dick" 1971

Truby, Harry G. 1909

Valentine, John G. 1887-88

Van Court, Eugene 1884

Vanover, Larry W. 1991, 1993-99

Vargo, Edward P. "Ed" 1960-83

Venzon, Anthony "Tony" 1957-71

Walker, William E. 1876-77

Walsh, Francis D. "Frank" 1961-63

Walsh, Michael F. "Mike" 1876, 1878, 1880

Warneke, Lonnie "Lon" 1949-55

Warner, Albert "Al" 1898-1900

Wegner, Mark P. 1998-2000
Wendelstedt, Harry H. Sr. 1966-98
Wendelstedt, H. Hunter Jr.
1998-2000
West, Joseph H. "Joe" 1976,
1978-99
Westervelt, Frederick E. 1922-23
Weyer, Lee H. 1961, 1963-88
White, Gideon F. 1878
Wickham, Daniel "Dan" 1990-92
Wiedman, George E. "Stump" 1896
Wilbur, Charles E. 1879
Williams, Arthur "Art" 1972-77
Williams, Charles H. "Charlie" 1978,
1983-2000
Williams, William G. "Bill" 1963-87
Wilson, Frank 1922-28
Wilson, John A. 1887
Winters, Michael J. "Mike" 1988-2000
Wise, Samuel W. "Sam" 1889
Wood, George A. 1898
York, Thomas J. "Tom" 1886
Young, Joseph 1879
Zacharias, Thomas 1890
Zimmer, Charles L. "Chief" 1904

American Association (1882-91)

Barnum, George W. 1890
Bauers, Albert J. "Al" 1887
Becannon, William H. 1883
Bradley, George H. "Foghorn" 1886
Brennan, John E. "Jack" 1884
Butler, Ormond H. 1883
Carey, Thomas J. "Tom" 1882
Clinton, James L. "Jim" 1886
Connell, Terence G. 1884, 1890
Connelly, John M. 1885, 1887
Connelly, William 1884
Curry, Wesley "Wes" 1887, 1890
Cuthbert, Edgar E. "Ned" 1887
Dailey, John J. 1884
Daniels, Charles F. 1883-85, 1889
Davis, James J. "Jumbo" 1891
Devinney, P. H. "Dan" 1884
Doscher, John H. Sr. "Herm" 1888,
1890
Dyler, John F. 1884
Emslie, Robert D. "Bob" 1890
Ferguson, Robert V. "Bob" 1886-89,
1891
Gaffney, John H. 1888-89
Gleason, William G. "Bill" 1891
Goldsmith, Frederick E. "Fred"
1888-89
Griffith, E. A. 1884
Hautz, Charles A. "Charlie" 1882
Hecker, Guy J. 1889
Holland, John A. 1884
Holland, Willard A. 1889
Hurley, Daniel "Dan" 1887
Jennings, Alfred J. "Al" 1887
Jones, Charles W. "Charley" 1891
Kelly, John O. "Kick" 1883-86
Kerins, John A. "Jack" 1889-91
Knight, Alonzo P. "Lon" 1887
Lawler, John F. 1884
Mack, Dennis J. "Denny" 1886
Macullar, James F. "Jimmy" 1891
Magner, John T. 1883
Mahoney, Michael J. 1891
Mathews, Robert T. "Bobby" 1891
McLaughlin, Thomas 1891
McLean, William H. "Billy" 1885
McNichol, Robert T. 1883
McQuaid, John H. "Jack" 1886-88
Morton, Charles H. "Charlie" 1886
O'Brien, Frank 1890
Peoples, James E. "Jimmy" 1890
Pike, Lipman E. "Lip" 1889
Pratt, Albert G. "Al" 1883
Quinn, A. J. 1886
Riley, William J. "Billy" 1882
Ross, Robert T. 1882
Seward, George E. 1884
Simmons, Joseph S. "Joe" 1882

Smith, Charles M. "Pop" 1882
Snyder, Charles N. "Pop" 1891
Sommer, Benjamin F. 1883
Sullivan, Jeremiah "Jerry" 1887
Sullivan, Timothy P. "Ted" 1887
Taylor, Walter 1890
Toole, Stephen J. "Steve" 1890
Tunison, William 1885-86
Valentine, John G. 1884-87
Walsh, Michael F. "Mike" 1882-83,
1885-86
York, Thomas J. "Tom" 1886
Young, Benjamin F. "Ben" 1886

Union Association (1884)

Crawford, Alexander 1884
Devinney, P. H. "Dan" 1884
Dutton, Patrick J. 1884
Hengle, Emery J. "Moxie" 1884
Holland, John A. 1884
Hooper, Michael H. 1884
Jennings, Alfred "Al" 1884
Jordan, William H. "Bill" 1884
Mapledoram, Blake A. 1884
McCaffrey, Harry C. 1884
Seward, George E. 1884
Stearns, D. Eckford "Ecky" 1884
Sullivan, David F. "Dave" 1884

Players' League (1890)

Barnes, Roscoe C. "Ross" 1890
Ferguson, Robert V. "Bob" 1890
Gaffney, John H. 1890
Gunning, Thomas F. "Tom" 1890
Holbert, William H. "Bill" 1890
Jones, Charles W. "Charley" 1890
Knight, Alonzo P. "Lon" 1890
Leach, Henry 1890
Mathews, Robert T. "Bobby" 1890
Pierce, Grayson S. "Gracie" 1890
Sheridan, John F. "Jack" 1890
Snyder, Charles N. "Pop" 1890

American League (1901-)

Adams, John H. 1903
Anthony, G. Merlyn 1969-75
Ashford, Emmett L. 1966-70
Avants, Nick R. 1969-71
Barnett, Lawrence R. "Larry" 1968-99
Barrett, Ted 1994-2000
Barry, Daniel "Dan" 1928
Basil, Stephen J. "Steve" 1936-42
Bean, Ed 1994
Berry, Charles F. "Charlie" 1942-62
Betts, William G. 1901
Boyer, James M. "Jim" 1944-50
Bremigan, Nicholas G. "Nick"
1974-88
Brinkman, Joseph N. "Joe"
1973-2000
Campbell, William M. "Bick" 1928-31
Cantillon, Joseph D. "Joe" 1901
Carrigan, H. Sam 1961-65
Carpenter, William B. "Bill" 1904
Caruthers, Robert L. "Bob" 1902-03
Cederstrom, Gary L. 1989-2000
Chill, Oliver P. "Ollie" 1914-16,
1919-22
Chylak, Nestor L. 1954-78
Clark, Alan M. "Al" 1976-2000
Coble, G. Drew 1983-99
Colliflower, J. Harry 1910
Connolly, Thomas H. "Tommy"
1901-31
Connor, Thomas "Tom" 1905-06
Cooney, Terrance J. "Terry" 1975-92
Cooper, Erik R. 1996-2000
Cousins, Derryl 1979-2000
Craft, Terry 1989-2000
Culbreth, Fieldin "Field" 1993-2000
Deegan, William E. J. "Bill" 1970-80
Denkinger, Donald A. "Don" 1968-98

Diaz, Lazaro "Laz" 1995, 1997-2000
DiMuro, Louis J. "Lou" 1963-80
DiMuro, Michael "Mike" 1997,
1999-2000
DiMuro, Raymond "Ray" 1996-99
Dinneen, William H. "Bill" 1909-37
Donnelly, Charles H. 1934-35
Doyle, Walter J. 1963
Drummond, Calvin T. "Cal" 1960-69
Duffy, James F. "Jim" 1951-55
Dwyer, J. Francis "Frank" 1904
Eddings, Douglas "Doug" 1998-2000
Egan, John J. "Rip" 1903, 1907-14
Eldridge, Clarence E. 1914-15
Evans, James B. "Jim" 1971-99
Evans, William G. "Billy" 1906-27
Everitt, Michael "Mike" 1996-2000
Ferguson, Charles A. 1913
Fichter, Michael 1999-2000
Flaherty, John F. "Red" 1953-73
Ford, R. Dale 1975-99
Foster, Martin "Marty" 1996-2000
Frantz, Arthur F. "Art" 1969-77
Friel, William E. "Bill" 1920
Froese, Grover A. 1952-53
Garcia, Richard P. "Rich" 1975-99
Geisel, Harry C. 1925-42
Goetz, Russell L. "Russ" 1968-83
Grieve, William T. "Bill" 1938-55
Guthrie, William J. "Bill" 1922,
1928-32
Haller, William E. "Bill" 1961, 1963-82
Hart, Robert F. "Bertie" 1912-13
Hart, William F. "Bill" 1901
Haskell, John E. 1901
Hassett, James E. 1903
Hayes, Gerald 1925-26
Hendry, Eugene "Ted" 1978-99
Henrichs, Jeff 1993
Hickox, Edwin W. "Ed" 1990-99
Hildebrand, George A. 1913-34
Hirschbeck, John F. 1984-2000
Holbrook, Samuel "Sam" 1996
Holmes, Howard E. "Ducky" 1923-24
Honochick, G. James "Jim" 1949-73
Hubbard, R. Cal 1936-51
Hurley, Edwin H. "Eddie" 1947-65
Hurst, Timothy C. "Tim" 1905-09
Iassogna, Dan 1999
Johnson, Mark S. 1980-99
Johnston, Charles E. 1936-37
Johnstone, James E. "Jim" 1902
Jones, Nicholas I. "Red" 1944-49
Joyce, James A. "Jim" 1989-2000
Kaiser, Kenneth J. "Ken" 1977-99
Katzenmeier, Travis 1999-2000
Kelly, Thomas B. 1905
Kerin, John 1909-10
King, Charles F. 1904
Kinnamon, William E. "Bill" 1960-69
Kolls, Louis C. "Lou" 1933-40
Kosc, Gregory J. "Greg" 1976-99
Kunkel, William G. "Bill" 1968-84
Leppart, Thomas E. "Tom" 1984-86
Linsalata, Joseph N. "Joe" 1961-62
Luciano, Ronald M. "Ron" 1968-80
Maloney, George P. 1969-83
Manassau, Alfred S. "Al" 1901
Marberry, Frederick "Firpo" 1935
McCarthy, John "Jack" 1905
McClelland, Timothy R. "Tim"
1984-2000
McCormick, William J. "Barry" 1917
McCoy, Larry S. 1970-99
McGowan, William A. "Bill" 1925-54
McGreevy, Edward 1912-13
McKean, James G. "Jim" 1974-2000
McKinley, William F. "Bill" 1946-65
Meriwether, Julius E. "Chuck"
1988-2000
Merrill, E. Durwood 1977-99
Miller, William "Bill" 1997-2000
Morgenweck, Henry C. "Hank"
1972-75
Moriarty, George J. 1917-26,
1929-40

Morrison, Daniel G. "Dan" 1979-2000
Mullaney, Dominic J. 1915
Mullin, John 1911
Nallin, Richard F. "Dick" 1915-32
Napp, Larry A. 1951-74
Nelson, Jeff 1998
Neudecker, Jerome A. "Jerry"
1965-85
O'Brien, Joseph "Joe" 1912, 1914
Odom, James C. "Jim" 1965-74
O'Donnell, James M. "Jake" 1968-71
O'Loughlin, Francis H. "Silk" 1902-18
O'Nora, Brian 1992-2000
Ormsby, Emmett T. "Red" 1923-41
Owens, Clarence B. "Brick" 1916-37
Palermo, Stephen M. "Steve"
1977-91
Paparella, Joseph J. "Joe" 1946-65
Parker, Harley P. "Doc" 1911
Parks, Dallas F. 1979-83
Passarella, Arthur M. "Art" 1941-42,
1945-53
Perrine, Fred "Bull" 1909-12
Phillips, David R. "Dave" 1971-99
Pipgras, George W. 1938-46
Quinn, John A. 1935-42
Reed, Rick A. 1984-2000
Reilly, Michael E. "Mike" 1978-2000
Reynolds, James "Jim" 1999-2000
Rice, John L. 1955-73
Robb, Douglas W. "Scotty" 1952-53
Rodriguez, Armando H. 1974-75
Roe, John A. "Rocky" 1979-2000
Rommel, Edwin A. "Eddie" 1938-59
Rowland, Clarence H. "Pants"
1923-27
Rue, Joseph W. "Joe" 1938-47
Runge, Edward P. "Ed" 1954-70
Salerno, Alexander J. "Al" 1961-68
Schwarts, Harry C. 1960-62
Scott, Dale A. 1986-2000
Sheridan, John F. "Jack" 1901-14
Shulock, John R. 1979-2000
Smith, W. Alaric "Al" 1960-65
Soar, A. Henry "Hank" 1950-73
Spenn, Frederick C. "Fred" 1979-80
Springstead, Martin J. "Marty"
1965-86
Stafford, John H. 1907
Stevens, John W. "Johnny" 1948-71
Stewart, Ernest D. 1941-45
Stewart, Robert W. "Bob" 1959-70
Summers, William R. "Bill" 1933-59
Tabacchi, Frank T. 1956-59
Tschida, Timothy J. "Tim" 1986-2000
Umont, Frank W. 1954-73
Valentine, William T. "Bill" 1963-68
Van Graflan, Roy R. 1927-33
Voltaggio, Vito H. "Vic" 1977-96
Wallace, Roderick J. "Bobby" 1915
Walsh, Edward A. "Ed" 1922
Walton, Bennie 1996
Weafer, Harold L. "Hal" 1943-47
Welke, Timothy J. "Tim" 1985-2000
Welke, William J. "Bill" 1999-2000
Westervelt, Frederick E. 1911-12
Wilson, Frank 1921-22
Winans, Mathew "Matt" 1994
Young, Larry E. 1985-2000

Federal League (1914-15)

Anderson, Oliver O. "Ollie" 1914
Brennan, William T. "Bill" 1914-15
Bush, Garnet C. 1914
Corcoran, Thomas W. "Tommy" 1915
Cross, Montford M. "Monte" 1914
Cusack, Stephen P. 1914
Finneran, William F. 1915
Fyfe, Louis 1915
Goeckel, E. 1914
Howell, H. Harry 1915
Johnstone, James E. "Jim" 1915
Kane, Stephen J. 1914
Langden, Joseph 1915
Manassau, Alfred S. "Al" 1914

McCormick, William J. "Barry" 1914-15
Mullin, John 1915
O'Brien, Joseph "Joe" 1915
Shannon, William P. "Spike" 1914-15
Stocksdale, Otis H. 1915
Van Sickle, Charles F. 1914
Westervelt, Frederick E. 1915
Wilhelm, Irving K. "Kaiser" 1915

Major League Baseball (2000-)

Barksdale, Lance 2000
Barrett, Ted 2000-03
Bell, Wally 2000-03
Bonin, Gregory "Greg" 2000-02
Brinkman, Joseph N. "Joe" 2000-03
Cederstrom, Gary L. 2000-03
Clark, Alan M. "Al" 2000-02
Cook, Robert "Robb" 2000
Cooper, Erik R. 2000-03
Cousins, Derryl 2000-03
Craft, Terry 2000-03
Crawford, Gerald J. "Jerry" 2000-03
Culbreth, Fieldin "Field" 2000-03
Cuzzi, Phil 2000-03
Danley, Kerwin J. 2000-03
Darling, Gary R. 2002-03
Davis, Gerald S. "Gerry" 2000-03
DeMuth, Dana A. 2000-03
Diaz, Lazaro "Laz" 2000-03
DiMuro, Mike 2000-03
Drake, Robert "Rob" 2000
Dreckman, Bruce M. 2002-03
Eddings, Douglas "Doug" 2000-03
Emmel, Paul L. 2000-003
Everitt, Michael "Mike" 2000-03
Ficter, Michael 2000
Fletcher, Andrew J. 2000-03
Foster, Martin "Marty" 2000-03
Froemming, Bruce N. 2000-03
Gibson, Gregory "Greg" 2000-03
Gorman, Brian 2000-03
Guccione, Chris 2000
Hernandez, Angel 2000-03
Higgins, Scott 2000
Hirschbeck, John F. 2000-03
Hirschbeck, Mark 2000-03
Hohn, William J. "Bill" 2002-03
Hollowell, Matthew "Matt" 2000
Hudson, Marvin 2000-03
Iassogna, Dan 2000
Joyce, James A. "Jim" 2000-03
Katzenmeier, Travis 2000
Kellogg, Jeffery "Jeff" 2000-03
Klemm, Justin 2000
Kulpa, Ronald "Ron" 2000-03
Lamplugh, Ian, 2000
Layne, Jerry B. 2000-03
Marquez, Alfonso 2000-03
Marsh, Randall G. "Randy" 2000-03
McClelland, Timothy R. "Tim" 2000-03
McKean, James G. "Jim" 2000-02
Meals, Gerald W. "Jerry" 2000-03
Meriwether, Julius E. "Chuck" 2000-03
Miller, William "Bill" 2000-03
Montague, Edward M. "Ed" 2000-03
Morrison, Daniel G. "Dan" 2000-02
Nauert, Paul 2002-03
Nelson, Jeff 2000-03
O'Nora, Brian 2000-03
Packard, Scott 2000
Phillips, David R. "Dave" 2000-02
Poncino, Larry L. 2002-03
Randazzo, Anthony J. 2000-03
Rapuano, Edward "Ed" 2000-03
Reed, Rick A. 2000-03
Reilly, Michael E. 2000-03
Reliford, Charles H. "Charlie" 2000-03
Rieker, Richard G. "Rich" 2000-02
Rippley, T. Steven "Steve" 2000-03
Roe, John A. "Rocky" 2000-02
Runge, Brian 2000-03
Schrieber, Paul 2000-03

Scott, Dale A. 2000-03
Shulock, John R. 2000-02
Spieler, Patrick "Pat" 2000
Timmons, Tim 2000-03
Tschida, Timothy J. "Tim" 2000-03
Van Vleet, Mike 2000
Vanover, Larry W. 2002-03
Wegner, Mark 2000-03
Welke, Timothy J. "Tim" 2000-03
Welke, William "Bill" 2000-03
Wendelstedt, H. Hunter Jr. 2000-03
West, Joseph H. "Joe" 2002-03
Williams, Charles H. "Charlie" 2000-02
Winters, Michael J. "Mike" 2000-03
Wolf, James "Jim" 2000
Young, Larry E. 2000-03

SUBSTITUTE UMPS

National Association (1871-75)

Addy, Robert E. "Bob" 1875
Allison, Andrew K. "Andy" 1872, 1874
Allison, Arthur A. "Art" 1872
Allison, Douglas L. "Doug" 1872-73, 1875
Alston, David 1871-72, 1875
Annan, William H. 1873
Arnold, Willis S. "Billy" 1875
Avery, C. Hamilton 1874
Barlow, Thomas H. "Tom" 1875
Barnes, Roscoe C. "Ross" 1874
Barrett, William "Bill" 1872, 1874
Barron, James "Jim" 1875
Barrows, Franklin L. "Frank" 1872
Battin, Joseph V. "Joe" 1874
Beals, Thomas L. "Tommy" 1872, 1874-75
Beardslee, John J. 1872-73
Bechtel, George A. 1874
Beck, W. S. 1872
Berthrong, Henry W. "Harry" 1872
Bielaski, Oscar 1874-75
Bigelow, W. J. 1875
Birdsall, David S. "Dave" 1873-74
Blair, William J. 1873
Boake, John L. 1871
Bomeisler, Theodore 1874-75
Bond, Thomas H. "Tommy" 1875
Bonse, Nicholas 1871
Boyd, William J. "Bill" 1873
Bradley, George H. "Foghorn" 1875
Brainard, Asa 1872, 1875
Briggs, Warren R. 1874
Brown, William 1872, 1875
Bruce, D. W. 1875
Buck, William F. 1871
Bunce, Frederick L. "Fred" 1874
Bunce, H. C. 1872
Bush, Archibald M. "Archie" 1871
Carey, Thomas J. "Tom" 1873, 1875
Carpenter, John R. 1874
Cassidy, John P. 1875
Cavanaugh, J. H. "Harry" 1875
Chandler, Moses E. 1872-75
Chapman, John C. "Jack" 1871, 1873-74
Clifton, — 1872
Clinton, James L. "Jim" 1873, 1875
Colby, — 1873
Collins, Daniel T. "Dan" 1875
Cone, J. Frederick "Fred" 1873-74
Cope, Elias 1871
Craver, William H. "Bill" 1873
Cuthbert, Edgar E. "Ned" 1875
Daubney, Thomas 1871
David, L. N. 1874
Dawson, Mort 1871
Deane, J. Henry "Harry" 1871, 1874
Dehlman, Herman J. 1873, 1875
Demorest, D. P. 1872-73
Dobson, H. A. 1873
Dornlach, D. E. 1872
Draper, John H. 1871

Ellis, William R. 1871-72, 1875
English, John W. 1874-75
Erby, Frederick 1872
Evans, George 1872
Fellows, T. E. 1871
Ferguson, Robert V. "Bob" 1871, 1874
Fisher, William C. "Cherokee" 1871, 1875
Foley, Thomas J. "Tom" 1874-75
Force, David W. "Davy" 1873
Fulmer, Charles J. "Chick" 1872, 1874-75
Garrigan, Charles 1873
Geer, William H. "Billy" 1874-75
Gerhardt, Joseph J. "Joe" 1875
Glenn, John W. 1874
Glover, Frank 1873
Goodwin, J. Cheever 1871-72
Gould, Charles H. "Charlie" 1874-75
Graham, J. S. 1871-72
Halback, A. C. N. 1871, 1873-75
Hall, George W. 1873-75
Hall, James "Jim" 1872-73
Hall, N. Samuel 1873
Hanna, Dr. 1872
Hartenstein, Isaac 1875
Hastings, W. Scott 1871-74
Hatfield, John V. B. 1872-73
Hayhurst, E. Hicks 1875
Haynie, James L. 1871
Hegeman, William H. 1871
Helm, J. 1871-72
Higham, Richard "Dick" 1872-75
Hodes, Charles "Charlie" 1874
Hooper, Michael H. "Mike" 1872-74
Hosworth, — 1872-74
Hough, Pliny 1875
Howard, Charles 1872
Jennings, Alfred J. "Al" 1873
Johns, William R. 1873
Kahn, S. L. 1875
Keerl, George W. 1872
Kenney, John 1872
Kent, John 1875
Knight, George H. 1875
Kohler, Henry C. 1873
Lamb, Henry W. "Harry" 1875
Laughlin, Benjamin "Ben" 1873
Leonard, Andrew J. "Andy" 1872-73, 1875
Leonard, J. 1872
Leroy, Isaac 1871
Locke, Marshall 1873-74
Lovett, James D. 1871
Lowell, John A. 1872-73
Lush, M. R. 1873
MacDiarmed, Thomas 1872
Mack, Dennis J. "Denny" 1873-74
Malone, — 1875
Malone, Ferguson G. "Fergy" 1875
Martin, Alphonse C. "Phonney" 1871, 1873
Martin, Lewis G. 1871, 1873-74
Mathews, Robert T. "Bobby" 1871
Mawny, J. H. 1871
Maxwell, Cortez "Corty" 1875
Mays, — 1871
McCrea, — 1872
McDonald, James F. 1872
McGeary, Michael H. 1872, 1875
McLean, Harry C. 1871, 1873
McLean, William H. "Billy" 1872-73
McMahon, William 1871
McMullin, John F. 1874
McVey, Calvin A. "Cal" 1871, 1873, 1875
Meacham, — 1875
Miller, Joseph W. "Joe" 1872-73
Mills, Charles "Charlie" 1871
Mincher, Edward J. "Ed" 1872, 1875
Mincher, William E. 1875
Mitchell, Franklin B. 1874-75
Murnane, Timothy H. "Tim" 1873-75
Nelson, John W. "Candy" 1872
Nichols, A. N. 1871

Norton, Frank P. 1872
O'Brien, P. 1875
Pabor, Charles H. "Charlie" 1875
Parks, William R. "Bill" 1875
Patterson, Daniel T. "Dan" 1872
Peak, Frank 1871
Pearson, S. W. 1872
Phelps, Cornelius C. "Neal" 1874
Pike, Jacob Emanuel "Jay" 1875
Porter, — 1874
Powers, W. 1872-73, 1875
Pratt, Thomas J. "Tom" 1871-73
Quinn, — 1875
Radcliff, John Y. 1873
Ramsay, R. 1875
Rastall, Joseph H. 1872
Reach, Albert J. 1872-75
Reed, Hugh 1871, 1873-74
Remsen, John J. "Jack" 1873-74
Robinson, A. Valentine "Val" 1872
Robinson, Miley 1873
Rockwell, Horace T. 1874
Rogers, George R. 1871-72
Ryan, John J. 1872, 1875
Sawyer, Dent 1871
Schafer, Harry C. 1875
Schrader, Louis 1875
Schuester, John A.1874-75
Scofield, John W. 1871
Sears, John K. 1873
Selman, Frank C. 1873
Sensenderfer, John P. J. "Count" 1872-73, 1875
Simmons, Joseph S. "Joe" 1871, 1873-74
Smith, Eb 1872
Smith, George 1872
Smith, Gustavus 1872
Snyder, Charles N. "Pop" 1875
Stahl, George 1875
Stanwood, — 1872-73
Stires, Garrett "Gat" 1875
Stophlet, J. 1871
Sutton, Ezra B. 1875
Swandell, J. Martin "Marty" 1871, 1874
Sweasy, Charles J. "Charlie" 1871, 1873-74
Tighe, Edward 1871
Treacey, Frederick S. "Fred" 1871, 1873, 1875
Tyler, Columbus T. 1871-73
Urell, M. E. 1873
Van Delft, Benjamin 1875
Voltz, Edward "Ed" 1871-72
Walk, Frank 1871
Wardell, — 1874
Waterman, Frederick A. "Fred" 1873
Weaver, Charles 1873
Weigel, William H.1873-74
White, Horatio S. 1873
White, W. Warren 1874
White, William H. "Will" 1875
Wiggins, — 1875
Wildey, John 1871
Willard, Gardner 1871
Wirth, Adam 1875
Wood, James L. "Jimmy" 1871
Worth, Herb 1872
Wright, W. Harrison "Harry" 1875
York, Thomas J. "Tom" 1874

National League (1876-)

Adams, James 1897
Allen, Hezekiah "Ham" 1876
Ayers, — 1876
Baker, Charles 1884
Barker, Alfred L. 1881
Barnie, William S. "Billy" 1882
Barnum, George W. 1896
Barton, — 1876
Battin, Joseph V. "Joe" 1895-96
Beard, Oliver P. "Ollie" 1894
Becannon, James M. "Buck" 1885
Behle, Frank 1895-96

Selman, Frank C. 1882
Sherman, Sharon L. "Shang" 1890
Shraeder, Louis 1890
Simpson, Lew 1882
Skerritt, Jim 1890
Skinner, — 1884, 1886
Smith, George 1887
Sneed, Jonathon L.1885
Sullivan, David F. "Dave" 1884
Talbot, John 1887
Tinney, — 1882
Walsh, Michael F. "Mike" 1887-88
West, Edward 1885, 1887
Wood, George A. 1886
Wright, — 1884
Young, Benjamin F. "Ben" 1887
Young, Joseph 1890

Union Association (1884)

Adler, — 1884
Burlingame, Frank A. 1884
Donovan, Timothy H. 1884
Furlong, William E. "Bill" 1884
Hudson, Vincent D. 1884
Lee, Thomas F. 1884
McGunnigle, William H. "Bill" 1884
McManaway, D. 1884
McMinimum, Dennis 1884
Montgomery, — 1884
Power, Charles B. 1884
Timblin, — 1884
Torry, — 1884

Players' League (1890)

Caskin, Edward J. "Ed" 1890

American League (1901-)

Betts, William G. 1903
Bierhalter, "Bits" 1918, 1922, 1924
Brown, Thomas T. "Tom" 1907
Carney, "Red" 1924
Connolly, Thomas H. "Tommy" 1932
Donlin, Michael J. "Mike" 1918
Howley, Daniel P. "Dan" 1922
Kennedy, Michael J. "Doc" 1910
Kerin, John 1908
Kerins, John A. "Jack" 1903
Mace, Harry L. 1903
Monahan, Pat 1931
Nallin, Richard F. "Dick" 1933
Pears, Frank H. 1903
Quigley, Ernest C. "Ernie" 1906
Soar, A. Henry "Hank" 1975
Stevens, John W. "Johnny" 1975
Terry, William H. "Adonis" 1901

Federal League (1914-15)

Murphy, J. A. 1914
Quisser, Arthur 1914

UMPS DURING STRIKES

National League (1876-)

Anderson, Lewis E. "Andy" 1978-79
Andress, William J. "Bill" 1979
Baird, John 1979
Ballina, Frank 1991, 1995
Barston, Michael "Mike" 1979
Baswell, Jack S. 1979
Beck, Robert "Bob" 1979
Bendekovits, Joseph "Joe" 1979
Betcher, Ralph A. 1976
Blandford, Fred 1970
Bovey, Terry R. 1979, 1984, 1995
Bruns, Randy 1991
Campagna, Frank J.1979, 1984
Cavenaugh, Richard P. "Dick" 1979, 1984
Cohen, Alfred A. "Al" 1976

Costello, Perry 1995
Cote, Emilien 1979
Cuneo, James "Jim" 1978-79
Davidson, — 1995
Davis, Bill 1995
Deniston, Shannon W. "Shan" 1978
Dierking, Roger A. 1978
Edwards, Larry 1978
Fick, Jerry D. 1978-79
Fisher, Frank 1979, 1984
Fleming, Thomas E. "Tom" 1979
Floras, John 1991
Ford, Wade 1995
Fowler, A. Wheeler 1978
Freels, Robert L. "Bob" 1979
Garman, Jim 1995
Gisondi, Tony 1991
Graham, Scott 1991, 1995
Grimsley, John 1970
Grinder, Scott 1976
Grooms, Roger C. 1979
Grygiel, George R. 1970
Guckert, Elmer 1976
Hadry, Merrill A. 1979
Hamil, Ray 1979
Hansen, Howard 1978-79
Hantak, H. Robert "Bob" 1979
Harris, Vance 1995
Henry, William E. "Bill" 1979
Hernandez, Bob 1995
Holoka, Mike 1991, 1995
Homolka, Bob 1995
Humphrey, Rich 1995
Hutson, Ronald "Ron" 1979
Jackson, Dick 1995
January, Don1991, 1995
Jeffers, Ronald L. "Ron" 1979
Jenkins, Jeff 1995
Jones, Bob 1995
Jones, James "Jim" 1979
Jumper, Howard 1979
Lambeth, Jim 1995
Lauzon, Jacques 1979
Lawson, William R. "Bill" 1979
Loeber, Gerald G. "Jerry" 1979
Lospitalier, Philip A. "Phil" 1979
Lupo, Charles "Charlie" 1978-79
Maher, Robert J. "Bob" 1979, 1984
Martine, Bruce 1991
Mauer, Boyd 1978-79
Melton, David "Dave" 1978
Miller, Marvin G. "Bud" 1979
Mills, Greg 1979
Morgenweck, Henry C. "Hank" 1970
Mrvos, Joseph S. "Joe" 1979
Myers, Joseph "Joe" 1979
Negri, Peter "Pete" 1979
Nelson, Robert "Bob" 1979, 1991, 1995
Norris, Edward E. "Ed" 1978-79
Oliger, Edward C. "Ed" 1979
Pacheco, Jim 1995
Padilla, Joe 1995
Patch, Tony D. 1978-79
Perez, J. Ray 1979
Pomponi, Joseph L. "Joe" 1979, 1984
Rains, James "Jim" 1978-79
Randall, Larry 1995
Riccio, Dennis R. 1979
Riccio, L. Leonard "Len" 1979
Riggers, Mike 1995
Rodriguez, Gus 1995
Rosenberry, Bill 1995
Roth, Roy 1978-79
Rountree, Henry J. "Hank" 1978-79
Ryberg, Sy 1995
Schaff, Fred 1995
Schaller, Cliff 1978-79
Schleyer, John 1979
Schratz, Joseph "Joe" 1979
Schroeder, Robert L. "Bobby" 1978-79
Scott, James "Jim" 1978-79
Sharkey, Michael E. "Mick" 1978-79
Sharp, Robert C. "Bob" 1979

Siroka, Harold L. 1979
Slattery, Donald L. "Don" 1979
Slickenmeyer, David W. "Dave" 1979, 1984
Smail, Harry F. 1979
Spange, John 1991
Spinelli, Michel 1979
Stansell, B. Jack 1979
Stewart, John 1979, 1984
Strey, Murray W. 1978-79
Sylvester, Frank 1995
Telford, Thomas "Tom" 1979
Tillman, Henry T. "Hank" 1978-79
Treitel, Leslie J. "Les" 1978-79
Tremblay, Richard H. "Dick" 1979
Urlage, Richard C. "Dick" 1979, 1991
Waller, James "Jim" 1979
Whaley, Bart 1995
Widlowski, Mark 1995
Williams, Dale 1978-79
Willman, Bob 1991, 1995
Yeast, Dave 1995

American League (1901-)

Arata, Mark 1991
Berry, Charles F. "Charlie" 1970
Bialorucko, Larry 1995
Bible, Jonathan D. "Jon" 1984
Bishop, Homer L. 1979
Bohn, Matt 1995
Borga, Steven A. "Steve" 1979
Briscese, Michael L. "Mike" 1979
Brown, Buddy Lee "Bud" 1979
Brown, Douglas D. "Doug" 1979
Brown, Jeff 1978-79
Camp, John W. 1979
Campbell, Robert "Bob" 1979
Caraco, Joe 1995
Clegg, Richard "Dick" 1979
Clement, Robert F. "Bob" 1978-79
Compton, Craig 1995
Contant, Alan 1978-79
Cossey, Douglas C. "Doug" 1978-79, 1984
Cuneo, James "Jim" 1979
Cristal, W. Randle "Randy" 1984
Davidson, Dale F. 1979
Deegan, William E. J. "Bill" 1970, 1984, 1991, 1995
DeFlesco, Pete 1991
Denny, Richard 1984
Dreke, Roy 1979
Dresser, Al 1995
Driscoll, Joseph M. "Joe" 1978
Duncan, Robert 1995
Dunne, James "Jim" 1978-79
Easley, Harold L. 1979
Eshelman, George R. 1979
Evans, Jeff 1991
Farmer, Michael "Mike" 1979
Farnsworth, Harry 1979
Feaser, Richard L. "Dick" 1979
Fitzpatrick, Michael N. "Mike" 1979
Follmer, William A. "Bill" 1979
Forman, Allen S. "Al" 1978-79
Freese, Todd 1995
Fuchs, Lester 1978-79
Gallagher, Lawrence E. "Larry" 1979
George, Edward "Ed" 1979
Giard, Robert "Bob" 1979
Gustafson, G. David "Dave" 1978
Hafner, William F. "Bill" 1979
Hadry, Merrill A. 1979
Harris, Vance 1995
Harvey, Randy 1991, 1995
Heitzer, Richard "Dick" 1979
Henrichs, Jeff 1995
Henry, William E. "Bill" 1979
Higgins, John 1991, 1995
Huber, Mike 1995
Ivory, William J. "Bill" 1979
Jackson, Charles L. 1979
James, John F. "Johnny" 1978-79
Jones, Robert G. "Bob" 1979, 1984

Jordan, Harold E. 1984
Kaplan, Al 1995
Kavulich, Joseph "Joe" 1978-79
Keister, R. Wayne 1978-79
Kelly, Eugene C. "Gene" 1979
Kimball, Shawn 1991
Kirby, Kenneth "Ken" 1979
Klein, Gus 1991, 1995
Knauss, Jim 1991
LaPierre, Richard 1979
Laude, William F. "Bill" 1978-79
Lazar, Richard R. "Richie" 1978-79
Levet, Jay 1979
Loeber, Gerald G. "Jerry" 1979
Lospitalier, Philip A. "Phil" 1979
Luker, Dale 1995
Lupo, Charles "Charlie" 1979
Mabbot, Frederick J. "Fred" 1979
Mackin, John F. 1979
Mann, Terry 1995
Marino, James H. "Jimmy" 1979
Mason, Danny 1995
Mauer, Boyd 1979
McDougall, Scott 1991
McNally, James "Jim" 1979
Merritt, Clarence 1979
Miller, Gale 1979
Miller, John A. "Jack" 1979
Moyer, Robert "Bob" 1979
Mulcahy, James "Jim" 1979
Murray, Ed 1991
Nelson, Richard "Dick" 1979
Nothhnagel, Carl L. 1984
Novack, Lester A. "Les" 1979
O'Brien, James D. "Jim" 1979
O'Connor, James "Jim" 1978-79
O'Connor, Thomas M. "Tom" 1979
O'Dell, Mikel R. "Mike" 1984
Panas, Richard J. "Rich" 1978-79
Parks, Dallas F. 1991, 1995
Patch, Tony D. 1979
Paylor, Jim 1995
Perez, David A. "Dave" 1979
Phipps, George H. "Jerry" 1978-79
Pilato, Mike 1995
Pratt, Lester 1979
Purduski, Al J. 1979
Ravan, Bruce 1995
Ravashiere, Thomas "Tom" 1979
Riccio, L. Leonard "Len" 1979
Rice, Robert W. "Bob" 1979
Robinson, William N. "Bill" 1978-79
Roesner, Robert A. "Bob" 1978-79
Roth, Roy 1979
Rountree, Henry J. "Hank" 1991
Runchey, Richard D. "Dick" 1979, 1984
Satchell, Darold L. 1970
Sawchuk, Joseph W. "Joe" 1978-79
Schaly, Jim 1995
Scheel, Alfred M. "Al" 1979
Schirmer, Donald A. "Don" 1979
Schulte, Donald E. "Don" 1979
Schwarz, Henry "Hank" 1995
Shaw, A. Duane 1979
Shewmake, James B. "Jim" 1978
Siroka, Harold L. 1979
Slattery, Donald L. "Don" 1979
Slickenmeyer, David W. "Dave" 1979, 1991, 1995
Spenn, Frederick C. "Fred" 1991
Sprincz, William "Bill" 1978-79
Stevens, John W. "Johnny" 1970
Sweeney, George P. 1979
Swenson, Charles H. 1979
Taylor, Joe Bob 1979
Terlop, Russell F. "Russ" 1979
Theilander, Theodore "Ted" 1979
Thompson, Michael G. "Mike" 1978-79
Tillman, Henry T. "Hank" 1979
Travis, Vic 1995
Trimmer, Harry 1979
Turner, Leo I. 1978
Ulrich, George 1995
Urchak, Woody J. 1978-79

Uremovich, Jim 1991, 1995
Walding, Larry 1995
Williams, Dale 1979
Wright, Marvin 1995
Zirbel, Lawrence A. "Larry" 1979, 1984
Zivic, Richard J. "Dick" 1984
Zuccaro, Amerigo J. "Rico" 1978-79

ACTIVE PLAYERS WHO UMPIRED

National League (1876-)

Abbey, Charles S. "Charlie" 1897
Abbott, Frederick H. "Fred" 1905
Andrews, G. Edward "Ed" 1889
Arundel, John T. "Tug" 1888
Baker, Philip "Phil" 1889
Baldwin, Marcus E. "Mark" 1892
Bannon, James H. "Jimmy" 1894
Beatin, Ebenezer "Ed" 1889
Beck, Erwin T. "Erve" 1902
Beckley, Jacob P. "Jake" 1906
Beebe, Fred L. 1907
Berger, John H. "Tun" 1891
Bonner, Frank J. 1894
Boyle, Henry J. 1886
Boyle, John A. "Jack" 1892, 1897
Breitenstein, Theodore P. "Ted" 1900
Briody, Charles F. "Fatty" 1881
Brown, Samuel W. "Sam" 1907
Brown, Thomas T. "Tom" 1896
Buelow, Charles J. "Charlie" 1901
Buffinton, Charles G. "Charlie" 1883, 1888-89, 1892
Burdock, John J. "Jack" 1881
Burns, Thomas P. "Oyster" 1895
Bushong, Albert J. "Doc" 1880, 1890
Butler, Richard H. "Dick" 1897
Carrick, William M. "Bill" 1900
Carroll, Frederick H. "Fred" 1887
Carsey, Wilfred "Kid" 1894, 1896
Caruthers, Robert L. "Bob" 1891
Casey, Daniel M. "Dan" 1888
Caskin, Edward J. "Ed" 1884
Cassidy, John P. 1882
Chamberlain, Elton P. 1894
Chance, Frank L. 1902
Clack, Robert H. "Bobby" 1876
Clarke, Arthur F. "Artie" 1890
Clarke, William J. "Boileryard" 1893-94, 1896
Clarkson, Arthur H. "Dad" 1893-96
Clarkson, John G. 1888, 1892-93
Clements, John J. "Jack" 1892
Coleman, John F. 1884
Coogan, Daniel M. "Dan" 1895
Cooney, John W. "Johnny" 1941
Crane, Edward N. "Ed" 1892
Crane, Samuel N. "Sam" 1886, 1890
Crolius, Frederick J. "Fred" 1901
Cronin, John J. "Jack" 1902-03
Cross, Lafayette N. "Lave" 1892
Culler, Richard B. "Dick" 1947
Cunningham, Elmer E. "Bert" 1896-97, 1900
Cuppy, George M. 1894
Cusick, Andrew D. "Tony" 1886-87
Daily, Cornelius F. "Con" 1891, 1894, 1896
Daly, Thomas P. "Tom" 1901
Darling, Conrad "Dell" 1887
Dealy, Patrick E. "Pat" 1886
Dexter, Charles D. "Charlie" 1896-97
Donahue, Francis R. "Red" 1897
Donahue, Timothy C. "Tim" 1895-96
Donlin, Michael J. "Mike" 1900
Donnelly, James B. "Jim" 1896
Donovan, William E. "Bill" 1902
Dooin, Charles S. "Red" 1904
Douglass, William B. "Klondike" 1903
Dowse, Thomas J. "Tom" 1890
Duggleby, William J. "Bill" 1905

Dwyer, J. Francis "Frank" 1889, 1893-94, 1896-97
Earle, William M. "Billy" 1894
Ehret, Philip S. "Phil" 1892, 1895-97
Farrell, Charles A. "Duke" 1901-02
Ferguson, Charles J. "Charlie" 1886
Fitzsimmons, Frederick "Freddie" 1941
Flaherty, Patrick J. "Patsy" 1904
Force, David W. "Davy" 1881
Foreman, Francis I. "Frank" 1895
Foreman, John D. "Brownie" 1896
Foster, Clarence F. "Pop" 1900
Fouser, William C. 1876
Freeman, John F. "Buck" 1900
Galvin, James F. "Jim" 1881, 1887, 1889
Gardner, James A. "Jim" 1899
George, William M. "Bill" 1889
German, Lester S. "Les" 1895
Getzien, Charles H. "Charlie" 1890
Gleason, William J. "Kid" 1890, 1892
Grady, Michael W. "Mike" 1895
Graves, Frank M. 1886
Griffith, Clark C. 1894-95
Grim, John H. 1892, 1895-96
Gruber, Henry J. 1889
Gumbert, Addison C. "Ad" 1892, 1895-96
Gunning, Thomas F. "Tom" 1884-85
Gunson, Joseph B. "Joe" 1892
Hackett, Mortimer M. "Mert" 1886
Haddock, George S. 1889
Hallman, William W. "Bill" 1903
Hanlon, Edward H. "Ned" 1892
Hart, William F. "Bill" 1896-97
Hatfield, Gilbert "Gil" 1889
Healy, John J. 1887
Hemming, George E. 1895-96
Hines, Michael P. "Mike" 1884
Hoffer, William L. "Bill" 1896
Holliday, James W. "Bug" 1897
Howe, John "Shorty" 1890
Hurst, Timothy C. "Tim" 1898
Hyatt, R. Hamilton "Ham" 1912
Irwin, Arthur A. 1881
Jacklitsch, Fred L. 1901
Jennings, Hugh A. "Hughie" 1893, 1900
Johnson, Sylvester "Syl" 1934
Jones, Henry M. 1890
Kahoe, Michael J. "Mike" 1905
Karger, Edwin "Ed" 1906
Keefe, Timothy J. "Tim" 1880-82, 1884-85, 1887, 1892
Keeler, William H. "Willie" 1910
Keenan, James W. "Jim" 1890
Kellum, Winford A. "Win" 1905
Kelly, Michael J. "King" 1892-93
Killen, Frank B. 1896-97
Kinslow, Thomas F. "Tom" 1892
Kitson, Frank R. 1902
Kittridge, Malachi J. 1890, 1899
Klein, Charles H. "Chuck" 1942
Kling, John G. "Johnny" 1901
Knell, Philip H. "Phil" 1895
Knowles, James "Jimmy" 1892
Krieg, William F. "Bill" 1887
Leever, Samuel W. "Sam" 1900, 1904
Lindaman, Vivian A. "Vive" 1907
Lundgren, Carl L. 1905-06
Maloney, William A. "Billy" 1902
Manning, James H. "Jim" 1886
Mathews, Robert T. "Bobby" 1882
Mathewson, Christopher "Christy" 1901, 1907
McAleer, James R. "Jim" 1893
McAllister, Lewis W. "Sport" 1899
McCarthy, Thomas F. M. "Tommy" 1896
McCauley, Allen A. "Al" 1890
McCauley, Patrick M. "Pat" 1896
McCormick, James "Jim" 1885
McFarland, Edward W. "Ed" 1896

McGarr, James B. "Chippy" 1895
McGinnity, Joseph J. "Joe" 1900
McGuire, James T. "Deacon" 1886-87, 1894, 1896-97, 1901
McKinnon, Alexander J. "Alex" 1886
Meekin, Jouette 1895-96
Menefee, John "Jock" 1903
Mercer, George B. "Win" 1896
Mertes, Samuel B. "Sam" 1905
Miller, George F. "Doggie" 1893, 1896
Miller, Joseph H. 1884
Miller, L. Otto 1934
Moran, Patrick J. "Pat" 1901
Mullane, Anthony J. "Tony" 1893
Mulvey, Joseph H. "Joe" 1895
Murphy, Morgan E. 1893, 1896, 1898
Murphy, William H. "Yale" 1895, 1897
Murray, Jeremiah J. "Miah" 1895
Myers, George D. 1886
Needham, Thomas J. "Tom" 1904, 1907
Newton, Eustace J. "Doc" 1902
Nichols, Charles A. "Kid" 1900-01
Nolan, Edward S. "The Only" 1881
Noonan, Peter J. "Pete" 1906-07
O'Brien, John F. "Darby" 1889
O'Connor, John J. "Jack" 1893, 1901
O'Day, Henry F. "Hank" 1888-89
O'Neill, Michael J. "Mike" 1904
Orth, Albert L. "Al" 1901
Overall, Orval 1905, 1910
Peitz, Henry C. "Heinie" 1901, 1906
Phelps, Edward J. "Ed" 1912
Phillippe, Charles L. "Deacon" 1903
Quinn, Joseph J. "Joe" 1889, 1894, 1896
Reilly, Charles T. "Charlie" 1892, 1894-95
Reitz, Henry P. "Heinie" 1895
Rhines, William P. "Billy" 1891, 1896
Richardson, A. Harding "Hardie" 1892
Richmond, J. Lee 1883
Robinson, Wilbert 1898
Ryan, James E. "Jimmy" 1892
Sanders, A. Bennett "Ben" 1889
Schmidt, Henry M. 1903
Schriver, William F. "Pop" 1901
Serad, William I. "Billy" 1884
Smith, A. Edgar 1883
Smith, Edgar E. 1890
Smith, George H. "Heinie" 1901
Smith, Harry T. 1903
Smith, William E. "Bill" 1886
Sommers, Joseph A. "Joe" 1889
Staley, Harry E. 1892, 1895
Stearns, D. Eckford "Ecky" 1881
Stein, Edward F. "Ed" 1890, 1894, 1896
Stivetts, John C. "Jack" 1894
Stocksdale, Otis H. 1895
Stricker, John A. "Cub" 1892
Stricklett, Elmer E. 1907
Sugden, Joseph "Joe" 1897
Sullivan, James E. "Jim" 1896
Sullivan, Martin C. "Marty" 1889
Sullivan, Michael J. "Mike" 1897
Sullivan, Thomas J. "Sleeper" 1881
Sutcliffe, Elmer E. "Sy" 1889, 1892
Tannehill, Jesse N. 1897, 1901-02
Tate, Edward C. "Pop" 1888
Taylor, John B. "Jack" 1899
Taylor, John W. "Jack" 1901, 1905
Tener, John K. 1889
Terry, William H. "Adonis" 1892, 1895-96
Tiernan, Michael J. "Mike" 1895
Vaughn, Harry F. "Farmer" 1892, 1899
Viau, Leon "Lee" 1891
Vickery, Thomas G. "Tom" 1890
Walker, Thomas W. "Tom" 1905
Wall, Joseph F. "Joe" 1901
Wallace, Roderick J. "Bobby" 1895
Walters, William H. "Bucky" 1942, 1947
Ward, John M. 1888

Warneke, Lonnie "Lon" 1940
Warner, John J. "Jack" 1896-97, 1901, 1903
Weaver, William B. "Farmer" 1893
Weimer, Jacob W. "Jake" 1905, 1907
Welch, Michael F. "Mickey" 1881-82, 1885-86, 1888
Weyhing, August "Gus" 1894, 1899-1900
Whistler, Lewis "Lew" 1891
White, Guy H. "Doc" 1901-02
White, James L. "Deacon" 1880
Whitney, James E. "Jim" 1884, 1886
Wilhelm, Irving K. "Kaiser" 1904-05
Williamson, Edward N. "Ned" 1878, 1880
Willis, Victor G. "Vic" 1903
Wilmot, Walter R. "Walt" 1897
Wilson, Frank A. "Zeke" 1896, 1899
Wilson, James "Jimmie" 1940
Wilson, Parke A. 1894-96, 1899
Wilson, William G. "Bill" 1890
Wood, George A. 1889
Wright, W. Harrison "Harry" 1876-77
Yeager, George J. 1901
Young, Denton T. "Cy" 1896
Young, Irving M. "Irv" 1905, 1907
Zimmer, Charles L. "Chief" 1889, 1901

American Association (1882-91)

Bakely, Edward E. "Jersey" 1888
Baldwin, Clarence G. "Kid" 1887
Becannon, James M. "Buck" 1884
Bond, Thomas H. "Tommy" 1884
Booth, Amos S. 1882
Boyle, John A. "Jack" 1888
Brennan, John G. "Jack" 1888
Briody, Charles F. "Fatty" 1888
Burns, Thomas P. "Oyster" 1888
Bushong, Albert J. "Doc" 1888-89
Carsey, Wilfred "Kid" 1891
Cassidy, John P. 1884
Chamberlain, Elton P. 1887, 1891
Cross, Lafayette N. "Lave" 1889
Crowell, William T. "Billy" 1888
Darling, Conrad "Dell" 1891
Donahue, James A. "Jim" 1888
Easton, John S. "Jack" 1891
Ehret, Philip S. "Phil" 1890
Ewing, John 1889
Fulmer, Charles J. "Chick" 1888
Fulmer, Christopher "Chris" 1887
Galvin, James F. "Jim" 1886
Ganzel, Charles W. "Charlie" 1886
Goldsby, Walton H. "Walt" 1888
Greenwood, William F. "Bill" 1884
Griffith, Clark C. 1891
Gunning, Thomas F. "Tom" 1888-89
Healy, John J. 1890
Hecker, Guy J. 1888
Herr, Edward J. "Ed" 1888
Higgins, William E. "Bill" 1890
Holbert, William H. "Bill" 1888
Johnston, Richard F. "Dick" 1884
Keefe, Timothy J. "Tim" 1884
Keenan, James W. "Jim" 1887-88
Kilroy, Matthew A. "Matt" 1887
Kirby, John F. 1888
Knell, Philip H. "Phil" 1891
Latham, George W. "Juice" 1884
Lynch, John H. "Jack" 1884
Macullar, James F. "Jimmy" 1886
Mattimore, Michael J. "Mike" 1888
Mays, Albert C. "Al" 1887
McCarthy, John A. 1889
McKelvy, Russell E. "Russ" 1882
McMahon, John J. "Sadie" 1890
McSorley, John B. "Trick" 1884
Merrill, Edward M. "Ed" 1884
Mountain, Frank H. 1884
Mullane, Anthony J. "Tony" 1888
Murphy, Joseph A. "Joe" 1887
O'Brien, William D. "Darby" 1887-88
O'Connor, John J. "Jack" 1889

O'Day, Henry F. "Hank" 1884
Peoples, James E. "Jimmy" 1888-89
Pierce, Grayson S. "Gracie" 1882
Sage, Harry 1890
Serad, William I. "Billy" 1888
Smith, Charles M. "Pop" 1886
Smith, Frederick C. "Fred" 1890
Smith, John F. "Phenomenal" 1887-88
Snyder, Charles N. "Pop" 1886
Sommer, Joseph J. "Joe" 1888
Sprague, Charles W. "Charlie" 1890
Stivetts, John C. "Jack" 1891
Sweeney, Charles J. "Charley" 1887
Sylvester, Louis J. "Lou" 1888
Terry, William H. "Adonis" 1884, 1888
Townsend, George H. 1890
Traffley, William F. "Bill" 1884
Vaughn, Harry F. "Farmer" 1891
Viau, Leon "Lee" 1888
Weyhing, August "Gus" 1891
Wheeler, Harry E. 1882
Wood, George A. 1891
Zimmer, Charles L. "Chief" 1888

Union Association (1884)

Bradley, George W. 1884
Callahan, Edward J. "Ed" 1884
Carroll, Patrick "Pat" 1884
Cuthbert, Edgar E. "Ned" 1884
Kelly, John F. 1884
McLaughlin, James "Jim" 1884
Oberbeck, Henry A. 1884
Wheeler, Harry E. 1884
Williams, Washington J. "Wash" 1884

Players' League (1890)

Bakely, Edward E. "Ed" 1890
Carney, John J. 1890
Comiskey, Charles A. "Charlie" 1890
Daily, Cornelius F. "Con" 1890
Gumbert, Addison C. "Ad" 1890
Haddock, George S. 1890
Hallman, William W. "Bill" 1890
Keefe, Timothy J. "Tim" 1890
Kelly, Michael J. "King" 1890
Madden, Michael J. "Kid" 1890
Milligan, John "Jocko" 1890
O'Day, Henry F. "Hank" 1890
Tener, John K. 1890

American League (1901-)

Altrock, Nicholas "Nick" 1907
Bejma, Alojzy F. "Ollie" 1935
Bender, Charles A. "Chief" 1907
Bernhard, William H. "Bill" 1903, 1907
Beville, H. Monte 1903-04
Blankenship, Clifford D. "Cliff" 1907
Bluege, Oswald L. "Ossie" 1938
Buelow, Frederick W. "Fritz" 1906
Callahan, James J. "Nixey" 1901
Conlan, John B. "Jocko" 1935
Coughlin, William P. "Bill" 1904
Cronin, John J. "Jack" 1901
Davis, Harry H. 1903
Dinneen, William H. "Bill" 1907
Donahue, Francis R. "Red" 1903, 1906
Donovan, William E. "Bill" 1903, 1906
Drill, Lewis L. "Lew" 1903-04
Flaherty, Patrick J. "Patsy" 1903
Foreman, Francis I. "Frank" 1901
Grady, Michael W. "Mike" 1901
Griffith, Clark C. 1903
Harris, Joseph W. "Joe" 1906
Hartley, Grover A. 1935
Hickman, Charles T. "Charlie" 1907

Howell, H. Harry 1904, 1906-07
Kittridge, Malachi J. 1905-06
Leahy, Thomas J. "Tom" 1901
Leppert, Donald G. "Don" 1978
Lowe, Robert L. "Bobby" 1905
McAllister, Lewis W. "Sport" 1901-02
McGuire, James T. "Deacon" 1905
Moore, Earl A. 1903
Newsom, Louis N. "Bobo" 1938
O'Brien, Peter J. "Pete" 1907
Patten, Case L. 1903
Pelty, Barney 1906
Powers, Michael R. "Mike" 1902
Roth, Francis C. "Frank" 1923
Schmidt, Charles "Boss" 1907
Schreckengost, Ossee F. 1903
Siever, Edward T. "Ed" 1901
Warner, John J. "Jack" 1908
White, Guy H. "Doc" 1903
Winter, George L. 1903, 1905
Young, Denton T. "Cy" 1903
Zimmerman, Gerald R. "Jerry" 1978

Federal League (1914-15)

Groom, Robert "Bob" 1914
Maxwell, J. Albert "Bert" 1914

Contributors

Nicholas Acocella has co-authored 14 baseball books with Donald Dewey, including *The Black Prince of Baseball, The Ball Clubs* and *The Biographical History of Baseball*. Acocella writes extensively on politics and appears regularly as a commentator on ESPN's Emmy Award winning Sports Century biographies. He lives in Hoboken, New Jersey, the cradle of baseball.

Larry Amman was born and raised in the suburbs of Detroit. He graduated from Wayne State University with a B.A. in history and political science in 1967, then served in the U.S. Army Intelligence in Vietnam and Germany. Germany remains a very special place to him. In the last few years he has made several trips to that country to help with baseball programs. Larry has lived in the Washington area for many years. He is employed as a travel agent.

Marty Appel, a former public relations director and television producer for the New York Yankees, is the author of 16 books, including the Casey Award-winning *Slide, Kelly, Slide,* and collaborations with Bowie Kuhn, Tom Seaver, Thurman Munson, and umpire Eric Gregg. His autobiography, *Now Pitching for the Yankees: Spinning the News for Mickey, Billy, and George,* is published by Sport Classic Books.

Phil Birnbaum is editor of "By the Numbers," the statistical analysis newsletter of the Society for American Baseball Research. A native of Toronto, he currently resides in Ottawa where he works as a software developer.

Bob Carroll, a freelance writer and illustrator in baseball and other sports, lives in North Huntingdon, Pennsylvania. He is the founder and executive director of PFRA (the Professional Football Researchers Association) and a longtime member of SABR. His baseball books include *Baseball Between the Lies, The Whole Baseball Catalogue* (with John Thorn), *The Dodgers Trivia Book, The Major League Way to Play Baseball,* and *The Sports Encyclopedia: Baseball* (with David Neft and Michael Neft). Among his football credits are *The Hidden Game of Football* (with Pete Palmer and John Thorn) and *When the Grass Was Real.* His hobbies are listening to classical music, cleaning the Augean stables and writing threatening letters.

Bill Deane is a freelance baseball researcher and writer stationed near Cooperstown, New York, where he spent eight years as Senior Research Associate for the National Baseball Library. He has published seven books and hundreds of articles for such publications as *USA Today Baseball Weekly, The Sporting News* and *Baseball America.* He was a recipient of the 1989 SABR-Macmillan Baseball Research Award, the 2001 SABR Salute, and the 2003 Cliff Kachline Award. Deane resides in Fly Creek, New York, with his wife, Pam, and daughter, Sarah.

Harold Dellinger lives in Kansas City, Missouri, where he is a community organizer, writer and editor. His interest in baseball dates to 1958 when, at age 11, he began following the Kansas City A's and bought his first baseball reference book. He has been involved in baseball research and writing for 30 years and has a special interest in the 19th century. He has authored three books on early Kansas City baseball. Dellinger also writes extensively on the "Old West" and on Midwestern social movements.

Donald Dewey is a novelist and playwright who has also published biographies of actors Marcello Mastroianni and James Stewart, as well as a history of baseball fans. In collaboration with Nicholas Acocella, he has co-authored 14 baseball books, including *The Black Prince of Baseball, The Ball Clubs* and *The Biographical History of Baseball.* He lives in Jamaica, New York.

Bill Felber is executive editor of *The Manhattan Mercury,* a daily newspaper in Manhattan, Kan. He has been a contributor to previous editions of *Total Baseball,* and other baseball-related publications. His analysis of the effectiveness of various baseball strategies, *The Book on the Book,* will be published by St. Martin's Press in 2005.

Larry R. Gerlach is professor of American sports history at the University of Utah. He is a member of the editorial board of *Nine,* the board of directors of SABR, and chair of SABR's Umpires and Rules Committee. He has published numerous articles in journals and reference works, as well as *The Men in Blue: Conversations with Umpires.*

Michael Gershman was best known among baseball fans for *Diamonds: The Evolution of the Ballpark,* which won the 1993 CASEY Award and also received that year's SABR-Macmillan Award. He was also familiar to collectors for his series of *Baseball Card Engagement Books* and *Baseball Stadium Postcard Albums.* He was co-editor of *Total Baseball* and *Total Football* and co-founder of Total Sports. He was editor-in-chief of the biographical component of Microsoft's *Complete Baseball* CD-ROM and served as a co-editor for *Baseball: The Biographical Encyclopedia.* He died in 2000.

Gary Gillette is a nationally known baseball author, analyst and editor. He has written or edited many baseball books, including the *Baseball Weekly Insider 1999 and 2000; The Spy: Baseball '98; The Scouting Report: 1995 and 1996;* and *The Great American Baseball Stat Book 1992, 1993,* and *1994.* Gillette also works as a legal expert witness on baseball-related litigation and has been a consultant for prominent player agents and for insurance companies. With Pete Palmer, he is editor of *The Baseball Encyclopedia.*

Gary D. Hailey, who lives in Rockville, Maryland, with his wife and four children, is a partner in the Washington, DC law firm of Venable LLP, and a lifelong Yankees fan. He is a graduate of Rice University (BA, 1974) and Harvard Law School (JD, 1977), and the author of the "Basketball and the Law" chapter of *Total Basketball.* Gary is still basking in the warmth of Rice's unlikely 2003 College World Series victory and the Yankees' oh-so-satisfying defeat of the Red Sox last fall, which more than made up for their subsequent loss in the World Series.

Bob Hoie was a principal contributor to *Minor League Baseball Stars,* volumes 1, 2 and 3, the *Minor League Register,* and the *Historical Register,* and he contributed to the *Encyclopedia of Minor League Baseball.* He is a member of the Pacific Coast League's Hall of Fame Committee, and received SABR's Bob Davids Award for meritorious service in 1987. A native of Los Angeles and a fan of the PCL Angels until their demise in 1957, Hoie is retired after 30 years as an urban planner for Los Angeles County.

John B. Holway wrote the first book in English on Japanese baseball, *Japan Is Big League in Thrills,* in 1954. Since then he has published 11 books. The latest, *The Complete Book of the Negro Leagues* (2000), based on 30 years' research, is the most exhaustive statistical history of the Negro Leagues ever published.

Jerome Holtzman is the official historian of Major League Baseball. He began his distinguished career covering baseball in 1957 and in 1990 was honored by the Baseball Hall of Fame with its J.G. Taylor Spink Award. Among his several baseball books are the classic *No Cheering in the Press Box, Fielder's Choice, Three and Two, The Commissioners,* and (with George Vass) *The Chicago Cubs Encyclopedia.* In 1997 he won the Associated Press Red Smith Award for his contributions to sports journalism.

Frederick Ivor-Campbell is vice president of the Society for American Baseball Research, and a contributor of baseball history and biography to numerous reference works and journals, including *American National Biography, Biographical Dictionary of American Sports* and *The National Pastime.* His work as general editor of *Baseball's First Stars* (1996) earned him The Sporting News-SABR Baseball Research Award. He and his wife Alma live in Bristol, Rhode Island.

Sean Lahman headed the first significant effort to make a database of baseball statistics freely available to the general public. His Baseball Archive web site was one of the early sources for baseball information on the Internet. He has written for or edited a number of books, including *Baseball: The Biographical Encyclopedia, Total Basketball* and, annually, *The Pro Football Prospectus.* He attended the University of Cincinnati and lives in Rochester, New York, with his wife Heather and their three children.

Phil Lowry is the author of *Green Cathedrals,* and has also done extensive research on the Negro Leagues, longest and latest-ending games, and the theoretical statistical probability for how many innings extra-inning games will last. He has chaired the SABR Ballparks Committee and the SABR Negro Leagues Committee. He and his wife Ellen live in Minneapolis with their two children, Evan and Megan.

Bruce Markusen is manager of program presentations at the National Baseball Hall of Fame and Museum, where he has worked since 1995. As part of his duties in Cooperstown, he has conducted numerous audio-visual interviews for the Hall's archives, narrated several Hall of Fame video productions, and delivered a variety of presentations on baseball history to the general public. Markusen has also written three books. His first book, *Baseball's Last Dynasty: Charlie Finley's Oakland A's,* won the Seymour Award from the Society for American Baseball Research as the best baseball book of 1998. His second release, *Roberto Clemente: The Great One,* was also published in 1998. A third book, *The Orlando Cepeda Story,* was issued in 2001. He has also written numerous articles for *Baseball Digest, Elysian Fields Quarterly* and *Oldtyme Baseball News.* Markusen lives in Cooperstown, New York, with his wife, the former Sue Ellen Bartow.

Patricia E. Millen has spent most of her career in history museums in New York and New Jersey. She is author of *Bare Trees: Zadock Pratt Master Tanner and the Story of What Happened to the Catskill Mountain Forests,* and numerous published articles on 19th century American history. A Civil War enthusiast, she became interested in the connection between baseball and the war while living in Cooperstown, New York. Her second book, *From Pastime to Passion: Baseball and the Civil War,* was published by Heritage Books in 2001. Millen now works in the education field and lives in Titusville, New Jersey, with her husband and two children. She holds a B.S. in American Studies from the State University of New York.

Yoichi Nagata is a freelance sports journalist and teaches sports-related courses at Obirin University in Tokyo. He is the author of *A Social History of Baseball: Jimmy Horio and US/Japan Baseball,* on Nisei baseball history and trans-Pacific baseball relations. Yoichi is an avid baseball fan of the now-defunct Nishitetsu Lions of Fukuoka and of the Philadelphia Phillies. His new book on the 1935 Tokyo Giants' North America tour will soon be published. Yoichi resides in Kawasaki, Japan.

Rob Neyer spent his formative baseball years watching Whitey Herzog's Royals, flunked out of the University of Kansas, worked as an apprentice roofer, and then somehow got a job as legendary baseball writer Bill James' research assistant. Neyer spent four years with James, then worked for STATS, Inc. for two years before joining Paul Allen's Starwave Corporation as a writer and editor for ESPNet SportsZone, which eventually became simply ESPN.com. Now a Senior Writer for ESPN.com, Neyer has also authored or co-authored four books, including *The Neyer/James Guide to Pitchers,* published by Fireside in 2004. Neyer lives in Portland, Oregon, with his wife and son.

E. David Osinski is the Executive Director of the American Baseball Foundation, Birmingham, Alabama; the Executive Director of the International Baseball Federation, Indianapolis, Indiana; and the National Coaching Director of the Australian Baseball Federation, Adelaide, Melbourne, Australia. He has worked in baseball development much of his life, living on four continents, and teaching in more than 40 countries around the world.

Pete Palmer is the former editor of the Barnes *Official Encyclopedia of Baseball.* He began compiling his historical and analytical data in the mid-1960s, and from 1978 to 1987 he was chairman of SABR's statistical analysis committee. In that time he also served as a consultant for the Sports Information Center, the official statisticians of the American League. He was on the board of directors of Project Scoresheet. Palmer has contributed articles to *SPORT, USA Today, Sports Heritage, The National Pastime,* and *Baseball Research Journal.* He is co-author, with John Thorn, of *The Hidden Game of Baseball* and *The Official Major League Baseball Record Book;* with Thorn and Bob Carroll of *The Hidden Game of Football* and *The Football Abstract;* and with Thorn and Eliot Cohen of *The Baseball Annual 1990.* He won SABR's Bob Davids Award in 1989. Most recently, with Gary Gillette, he edited *The Baseball Encyclopedia.*

David Pietrusza, former president of the Society for American Baseball Research (SABR) and editor-in-chief of Total Sports, is the author of *Rothstein: The Life, Times, and Murder of the Criminal Genius Who Fixed the 1919 World Series* (nominated for the Edgar Award). He is also the author of *Judge and Jury: The Life and Times of Judge Kenesaw Mountain Landis,* winner of the 1998 CASEY Award; *Lights On; The Wild Century-Long Saga of Night Baseball* (a finalist for the 1997 CASEY Award); *Minor Miracles: The Legend and Lure of Minor League Baseball; Major Leagues; Baseball's Canadian-American League;* and, with the great one, *Ted Williams: My Life in Pictures.* He co-edited *Total Baseball, Baseball: The Biographical Encyclopedia, The Total Baseball Catalog, Total Mets, Total Braves,* and *Total Indians.* Pietrusza served as producer for the documentary *Local Heroes* for PBS station WMHT and as a consultant for the Baseball Online segment of the PBS LearningLink system. He has appeared on ABC-TV, ESPN, the Fox News Channel, and National Public Radio and written for numerous publications including *USA Today Baseball Weekly* and *Baseball America.*

Beau Riffenburgh was formerly on the public relations staff of the Los Angeles Lakers and then served as an associate editor and senior writer for NFL Properties, where he was the author of *The Official NFL Encyclopedia, Running Wild* and *Great Ones.* He has written or edited 17 books and contributed to many more. He has spent 16 years in England, where he is on the academic staff of the Scott Polar Research

Institute at the University of Cambridge and is editor of *Polar Record*, the world's oldest journal of polar research. In Britain he also coached "American Football" for eight years at the university level, his teams recording an overall record of 68-12-2 and winning three national titles.

Tom Ruane is a member of the Society for American Baseball Research and past contributor to *The Big Bad Baseball Annual, NINE,* and *The Baseball Research Journal.* He is a researcher and writer for Diamond Mind Baseball as well as a computer programmer for IBM. His fiction has appeared in several magazines, including *The Yale Review, ACM, Carolina Quarterly,* and *Witness.* He lives and works in Poughkeepsie, New York, where he is a liability to his recreational softball team.

Rob Ruck is a Senior Lecturer in History at the University of Pittsburgh and on the faculty of the Center for Latin American Studies. He is the author of *Sandlot Seasons: Sport in Black Pittsburgh* and *the Tropic of Baseball.* His documentary, *Kings on the Hill: Baseball's Forgotten Men,* won an Emmy for cultural programming.

Alan Schwarz is the Senior Writer of *Baseball America* magazine, as well as a frequent contributor to ESPN.com, *Newsweek* and *The New York Times.* His first book, *The Numbers Game: Baseball's Lifelong Fascination with Statistics,* has been published by St. Martin's Press.

Debra A. Shattuck was born in Lorain, Ohio in 1959. She received her B.A. in history from Cedarville College in 1981 and her M.A. in history from Brown University in 1988. Her master's thesis was on female baseball players in the United States, 1866–1954. She later was a captain in the U.S. Air Force.

Matthew Silverman co-edited *Baseball: The Biographical Encyclopedia* with David Pietrusza and Michael Gershman. He served as managing editor for the sixth edition of *Total Baseball* and the second edition of *Total Football.* He has edited seven offshoots of *Total Football,* including *Total Packers, Total Steelers, Total Cowboys,* and *Total Super Bowl.* He also co-edited *Total Mets* in 1997. Formerly a junior editor for *Variety* in New York, he worked for three New England newspapers before joining Total Sports Publishing. He resides in High Falls, New York, with his wife, Debbie, and their two children.

David W. Smith is the founder and president of Retrosheet, a non-profit, all-volunteer organization dedicated to the collection, computerization and distribution at no charge of play-by-play accounts of major-league games. He is a long-time member of the Society for American Baseball Research who makes frequent research presentations at annual meetings and also served as co-chair of SABR's statistical analysis committee with Pete Palmer from 1980 to 1982. Smith has contributed to the media guides and public relations departments of many teams, as well as to *USA Today Baseball Weekly* and several daily newspapers, including *The New York Times.* He is a co-author, along with David Vincent and Lyle Spatz, of *The Midsummer Classic,* a comprehensive history of baseball's All-Star Game. He is a biology professor at the University of Delaware and lives with his wife, Amy Tetlow Smith, and son, Graham, in Newark, Delaware.

Lyle Spatz is the chairman of the Society for American Baseball Research's Baseball Records Committee, a post he has held since 1991. He is the author of *New York Yankee Openers—1903–1996; Yankees Coming, Yankees Going: New York Yankee Player Transactions, 1903–1999;* and a co-author of *The Midsummer Classic: The Complete History of Baseball's All-Star Game.* Spatz has also contributed chapters to *The Dictionary of Literary Biography: Sportswriters; The Biographical Dictionary of American Sports—Baseball; Jackie Robinson: Race, Sports,*

and the American Dream; and *The Perfect Game.* His articles have appeared in *The Washington Post, Baseball Weekly, Baseball Digest, The National Pastime,* and *The Baseball Research Journal.* He has also presented papers at the Babe Ruth Conference at Hofstra University and at the Jackie Robinson Conference at Long Island University. He recently completed a biography on Bill Dahlen.

A.D. Suehsdorf is the author of *The Great American Baseball Scrapbook* and a frequent contributor to SABR publications. He was formerly editorial director of Ridge Press, book publishers, in New York.

John Thorn is the author/editor of many baseball books, including *Treasures of the Baseball Hall of Fame, The Game for All America, The Armchair Books of Baseball, Ted Williams: Seasons of the Kid* (with Richard Ben Cramer and Mark Rucker), *The National Pastime,* and *The Relief Pitcher.* He co-authored *The Pitcher* with John Holway, and *The Hidden Game of Baseball* and *The Baseball Record Book* with Pete Palmer. With Palmer and Bob Carroll he also co-authored *The Hidden Game of Football* and *The Football Abstract.* He has written for several periodicals, among them *The Sporting News, SPORT* and *American Heritage.* Thorn was Senior Creative Consultant to *Baseball,* Ken Burns' nine-part film for the Public Broadcasting System, and publisher of Total Sports Publishing. Thorn is also a co-editor of *Total Football.*

Robert L. Tiemann served as chairman of the 19th-century research committee of the Society for American Baseball Research and is the author of *Cardinal Classics* and *Dodger Classics.* He headed the SABR research project that reconstructed from newspaper play-by-play accounts much of the missing data for the National Association of 1871 to 1875. With Rich Topp, Tiemann shared a SABR award for his redevelopment of the Manager Roster as it appears in an early edition of *Total Baseball,* and in 1992 won SABR's Bob Davids Award.

Jules Tygiel is a professor of history at San Francisco State University. He created *Baseball's Great Experiment: Jackie Robinson and his Legacy* (Oxford University Press, 1983); *Past Time: Baseball as History* and *The Jackie Robinson Reader.* He has contributed articles to many periodicals.

Joseph M. Wayman, publisher and editor of *Grandstand Baseball Annual,* which he founded in 1985, has been the subject of a "SABR Salute," which commended him for his steadfast "investigative reporting of questionable baseball records." Several of his discoveries have been accepted as fact by *Total Baseball* and the Elias Sports Bureau and have resulted in a rewriting of the baseball record books. His writings have also appeared in the *Baseball Research Journal* and *Baseball Bulletin.*

Peter Wayner is the author of 13 books and numerous stories for publications like *The New York Times, Salon, Wired,* and other magazines and websites. He still believes that his work for Flyzone.com remains our best hope for remaking the agate section of the paper.

With appreciation to these readers of the first edition of *Total Baseball* who sent in corrections or made suggestions on how to improve the second edition:

Larry Amman, Ray Andreotti, Mel Bailey, Craig Barbarino, Edgar K. Beatty, James M. Beck, Joseph R. Bender, Robert Beukelher, John Booth, Jim Bostain, Therese R. Brown, J. Paul Browne, Bob Cambris, Kevin A. Carleton, Bob Carroll, Anthony M. Chieco, Ken Coleman, Steve Cooper, Owen Curtis, Clay Davenport, L. Robert Davids, Bill Deane, Harold Dellinger, Ted D. DeVries, Don Dewey, Raymond A. DiSanto, Sam Elfand, Don Elliott, John Emerson, Eddie Epstein, Kenneth Fink, Robert L. Franz, Andrew Fussner, Cam Gibson, Steven

Goldberg, Ray Gonzalez, Dan Greenia, Bill Haber, Rod Hay, Bob Hoie, Frederick Ivor-Campbell, Tom Jennings, Bill Jensen, Warren Johnson, Cliff Kachline, James Kaufman, Dave Kemp, Larry Kempster, Randall Kleinman, Jack Lang, Ron Liebman, Jerry Malloy, James F. Maxfield, Bob McConnell, Joe M. McGowan, David Molnar, George S. Moskal, Frank J. Mueller, Neil Munro, Thomas L. Nester, Dave Nichols, Tom O'Brien, Yoshio Ohno, S. Mark Parker, Paul E. Pennebaker, Peretz Perl, David Pietrusza, Mike Post, Jorgen Rasmussen, Allan Rausch, Andrew Richardson, John Rickert, John M. Roca, Winslow Rogers, Tom Ruane, Bill Rubenstein, David Schermer, Leon Schmerhold, John Schwartz, Alfred Secondi, Sy Siegel, Richard Siegelman, Al Smith, David M. Snyder, David Stephan, Mike Sparks, Lyle Spatz, Dean Sullivan, Isaac Thorn, Richard Topp, Stephen Toth, T. Brook Treakle III, Jim Troisi, Jim Tuttle, Jim Vail, Cullen P. Vane, David Vincent, Joseph M. Wayman, Jim Weigand, Bernard Weisberger, Christopher Williams, Frank Williams, Joseph C. Williams, Ralph Winnie, Jim Wright, and Ed Yerha

And to those *whose suggestions have improved the third edition:*
David Aceto, Tim Anderson, Andrew J. Balog, Robert Browning, Chuck Carey, Keith Carlson, Garrett M. Casey, Jim Conroy, Bob Davids, Bill Deane, Dennis DeValeria, Ted DiTullio, Robert Downer, Tom Dunken, Jules Egyrd, Eddie Epstein, Ken Fetterman, Bob Franzosa, Gary Gillette, Jay Gregory, Charlie Harville, Jeffrey Hatt, Ralph Horton, Jeff James, Darlene Kadlecik, Jerry Kahn, John Kenyon, Patrick Kinas, D.C. Larkin, II, Matthew Lesniewski, Morris Levin, Don Luce, Michael Lucich, Ed Luteran, Jeff Magalif, E.H. Marshall, Richard A. Marston, Ronald A. Mayer, John P. McBride, John McClaran, Randy Messel, Scott Messinger, Steve Moore, Neil Munro, John O'Malley, Ed Oswalt, Douglas R. Pappas, Richard Pardoe, Danny Radakovich, Matt Rapacz, Louis Rauco, Matt Reese, Eric Reinholdt, Dennis Repp, John Richards, Bob Richardson, John M. Roca, Seth D. Rodgers, Robert Schulz, John Schwartz, John Scott, Jamie Selko, Jim Smith, Dave Smith, Lewis J. Snyder, Lyle Spatz, Alan Steinberg, David Stephan, A.D. Suehsdorf, James Swetnam, Blair D. Tarr, Robert Tiemann, Harry L. Turtledove, Bill Wallace, Patrick K. Walsh, Joe Wayman, Jim Weigand, Frank Williams, Walt Wilson, and Edgar M. Wyatt.

The fourth edition *has benefited from the comments of:*
Tim Anderson, Arnie Braunstein, Chuck Carey, Bill Carle, Tim Cashion, Tom Chase, Ed Coen, Bob Davids, Bill Deane, Dan Dischley, Ted DiTullio, Jules Egyrd, Eddie Epstein, Bill French, Campbell Gibson, Gary Gillette, Herb Goldman, Albert A. Gunnell, Robert Kern, Joe Kinsman, Joe Klein, Joe Marchetto, Jeff Marcus, Bob McConnell, Randy Messell, Scott Messinger, Neil Munro, John O'Malley, Ed Oswalt, Doug Pappas, Jeffrey Platt, Frank Phelps, Bob Richardson, Win Rogers, Bob Rosiek, Jim Sargent, Robert Schulz, John Schwartz, Jamie Selko, Dave Smith, Jim Smith, David Stephan, Chuck Stevens, David Stone, Adie Suehsdorf, Bob Tiemann, David Vincent, Bill Way, Joe Wayman, Jim Weigand, Roy White, Alan Whitney, Frank Williams, Walt Wilson, and Ed Yerha.

The fifth edition *has benefited from the comments of:*
Arnie Braunstein, Chuck Carey, Keith Carlson, Bill Carle, Bill Carr, Tim Cashion, Tom Chase, Bob Davids, Bill Deane, Dan Dischley, Bill Doig,

Jeff Fox, Tate Giersdorf, Gary Gillette, Herb Goldberg, Ed Hartig, Bob Hoie, Frederick Ivor-Campbell, Herm Krabbenhoft, Dan Levitt, Fred Lenger, David Marasco, John Matthew IV, Neil Munro, John O'Malley, David Neft, Doug Pappas, Bob Richardson, Patrick Rock, Jim Sargent, John Schultz, John Schwartz, Jamie Selko, Joe Simenic, Allan Simpson, Lyle Spatz, Dick Thompson, Bob Tiemann, Dixie Torangeau, Jim Troisi, Frank Vaccaro, Paul Walker, Bill Way, Joe Wayman, Jim Weigand, Frank Williams, Walt Wilson, and Dave Zeman.

The sixth edition *has benefited from the comments of:*
Carlos Bauer, Randy Bonferraro, Bill Carle, Tim Cashion, Bill Carr, Ryall Carroll, Bill Deane, Dan Dischley, Harvey Frankel, Gary Gillette, Todd Greanier, Rich Hancock, Ed Hartig, Herm Krabbenhoft, Fred Lenger, Jamie Lotze, Chuck Lumb, Bob McConnell, Neil Munro, Rob Neyer, John O'Malley, Jeff Ouriel, Frank Peters, Frank Phelps, Bob Richardson, Tom Ruane, John Schwartz, Stuart Shea, Dave Smith, Lyle Spatz, John Steele, Dick Thompson, Bob Tiemann, Dixie Torangeau, Wayne Townsend, Frank Vaccaro, David Vincent, Bill Way, Joe Wayman, Frank Williams, Vic Wilson, Walt Wilson and Ken Zweibel.

The seventh edition *has benefited from the comments of:*
Carlos Bauer, Greg Beston, G. Betor, Peter Bjarkman, Al Bokar, Randy Bonferraro, Timm Boyle, Adrian Burgos Jr., Jeffrey Burk, Bill Carle, Keith Carlson, Bob Carroll, Kevin Clark, Clem Comly, Thomas Crimmins, Clay Davenport, Aaron Davis, Darl Edward Devault, Brandon L. Dillard, Terry Dinan, Dan Dischley, Bruce Fleming, Sean Forman, Bill Fort, Myles E. Friedman, Jim Furtado, Jim Gates, Larry R. Gerlach, Steve Gietschier, Todd Greanier, Marc Guarino, G. Michael Hall, Ed Hartig, Bruce Hobbs, John B. Holway, Jonathan Jacobs, Gary A. Kizer, Nathan Kunkel, Robert Laidlaw, Robert Langenderfer, Gary Lee, Fred Lenger, Michael Levett, Jamie Lotze, Philip J. Lowry, Bill Lussenheide, Lillian Madden, Kenneth Matinale, Bob McConnell, Wayne McElreavy, Todd McGee, William J. Melzer, Mike Meserole, Richard Minteer, Peter Morris, Yoichi Nagata, Rob Neyer, Mat Olkin, John O'Malley, Edwin Orenberg, Jeff Ouriel, Robert Panara, Mark Pankin, Pat Parker, Doug Pappas, Dave Pease, Fred Percival, Juan Fernando Rivera Pernia, Hayford Pierce, Bob Richardson, Rob Ruck, Thomas St. John, Mike Sandler, John Schwartz, Stuart Shea, Joseph Sheehan, Tom Shieber, Scott Silveri, Allan Simpson, Herb Soltman, Nicolas Tavuchis, Neal Traven, Rob Tucker, Frank Vacarro, John Vaughan, David Vincent, Patrick W. Walsh, Bill Way, Tim Wiles, Frank Williams, Jeffrey Wilson, Walt Wilson, and Keith Woolner.

The eighth edition *has benefited from the comments of:*
Mark Alvarez, Mark Armour, Charlie Bevis, Hal Bock, Greg Bond, David Block, J.P. Caillault, Bill Carle, Alexander Cartwright IV, Don Daglow, Bob Elliott, Jan Finkel, Jim Gerard, Donna Habersaat, Jim Henley, John B. Holway, John R. Husman, Frederick Ivor-Campbell, Bill James, Lloyd Johnson, Herm Krabbenhoft, Noah Liberman, Skip McAfee, Andy McCue, Wayne McElreavy, Mike Meserole, Peter Morris, Osamu Natori, Monica Nucciarone, John Pastier, David Pietrusza, Robert Schaefer, Alan Schwarz, Tom Shieber, Tom Simon, Lyle Spatz, Greg Spira, Dick Thompson, George A. Thompson, Isaac Thorn, Jed Thorn, Mark Thorn, Paul Wendt, Miles Wolff, Richard Zitrin.

Photographs and Illustrations

AFP/Corbis: Insert pp. 10 (lower right), 15 (lower right), 24 (lower right) and Back Cover.

The Associated Press: Front cover; pp. 6, 11, 282, 284, 286, 288, 290, 292, 294, 296, 298, 300, 302, 738, 787; Insert p. 16 (lower right),

EPA/John Mabanglo: p. 1

Greg Flume/Newsport/Corbis: Insert p. 24 (lower left).

National Baseball Hall of Fame Library: pp. 60, 76, 78, 80, 84, 90, 98, 102, 106, 118; Insert pp. 1 (left, right), 3 (top left, top right, bottom), 13 (top left).

The SPORT Collection: pp. x, 3, 15, 19, 31, 57, 59, 62, 64, 66, 68, 70, 72, 74, 82, 86, 88, 92, 94, 96, 100, 112, 114, 116, 120, 122, 124, 126, 18, 104, 108, 130, 132, 134, 136, 138, 140, 142, 144, 146, 148, 152, 154, 156, 158, 162, 167 (H. Scharfman), 169, 170, 172, 174, 176, 178, 180, 182, 184, 186, 188, 190, 192, 194 (C. Gunther), 196, 198, 200, 202, 204, 206, 208 (M. Emmons), 210, 212 (M. Emmons), 214, 216, 222, 226, 231, 233, 234 (D. Sutton), 236, 238, 240, 242, 244, 246, 248, 250, 252 (A. Neste), 254 (N. Hogue), 256, 258, 260 (F. Kaplan), 262, 264, 266, 268, 270, 272, 274, 276, 278, 280, 304, 309, 312, 317, 319, 541, 555, 557, 569, 574, 581, 606, 613, 635 (L. Schiller), 643, 660, 695, 705, 707, 753 (C. Campbell), 773, 789, 796 (O. Sweet), 805 (L. Schiller), 905 (Illustration by J.C. Murphy), 907 (Illus. by A.S. Tobey), 911 (Illus. by A.S. Tobey), 917 (Illus. by G. Foxley), 921 (Illus. by G. Foxley), 929 (Illus. by J.C. Murphy), 934 (Illus. by A.S. Tobey), 940 (Illus. by J. Freire), 944 (Illus. by G. Foxley), 949, 2326, 2416, 2415, 2417 (C. Rydlewski), 2425, 2433 (D. Sutton), 2439, 2637, 2652; Insert pp. 2 (Illus. by G. Foxley), 3 (Illus. by G. Foxley, top middle), 4 (lower left; Illus. by A.S. Tobey, lower right), 5 (Illus. by G. Foxley), 6 (top right), 7 (top left; top right; bottom right), 8, 9 (top left; M. Blumenthal, top right; Illus. by G. Foxley, lower right), 10 (top left; top right; M. Blumenthal, lower left), 12 (Illus. by J.C. Murphy), 13 (M. Emmons, top right; middle right; lower right), 15 (top right; M. Newman, lower left), 16 (Illus. by C. Gehm, top; lower left; lower middle), 18 (top left; top right; lower left; lower right), 19 (M. Blumenthal, top left; R. Vesely, top right; B. Wolman, lower left; D. Norenberg, lower right), 20 (top left; R. Vesely, lower left), 21 (top left; P. Halsman, top right; bottom), 22 (B. Rosato, lower left; T. Tomsic, lower right), 23 (top left; lower left; C. Gunther, middle right; lower right).

Reuters New Media Inc./Corbis: Insert p. 24 (middle, lower left).

Collection of Ozzie Sweet: Insert pp. 4 (top left), 6 (lower right), 7 (lower left), 11, 14, 17.

Collection of John Thorn: pp. 29, 44, 45, 47, 51, 54, 150, 641, 678, 701, 950.

Glossary of Statistical Terms

This glossary contains definitions of the statistical terms and measures that may be unfamiliar to the average baseball fan or that represent what today might seem odd scoring practices. The Glossary will also be of value to the advanced fan who wishes to know more about the mathematical and theoretical foundations of certain statistics.

+ —indicates a normalized statistic, meaning that the statistic to the immediate left of this mark has been normalized to league average and adjusted for home park factor. Stats that are normalized in this book are On-Base Plus Slugging and Earned Run Average.

/A—indicates an adjusted statistic, meaning that the statistic to the immediate left of this mark has been adjusted for home park factor. In this book, Batting Runs and Pitching Runs have an adjusted value listed in the Registers.

Assist—Although credited to pitchers on strikeouts in some of baseball's early years, not counted as such in this volume.

At Bats—Charged to batters on sacrifice hits, 1889-1893; on sacrifice-fly situations, 1931-1938 and 1940-1953; on bases on balls, 1876, 1887. However, in this book, we have not charged at bats for sacrifice hits prior to 1900.

Average and Over—Early form of expressing averages for base hits, runs, and outs. The average of a batter with 23 hits in six games would be not 3.83 but 3-5 (an average of 3 with an overage, or remainder, of 5); borrowed from cricket.

Bases on Balls—Counted as outs (hitless at bats) for batters in 1876 and as hits (and at bats) for batters in 1887, and listed as such in this book, in the AB, H, AVG, and OAV columns. However, calculated statistics, such as Batting Runs and Runs Created, are unaffected by the change. Awarded for a varying number of errant pitches since 1876, from nine in that year to the current four, standardized in 1889. (After 1887, the batter was no longer allowed to specify strike zone as waist to shoulders or waist to shins.)

Base-Out Percentage—Barry Codell's stat for measuring complete offensive performance, in which the elements of the numerator represent bases gained while the events in the denominator represent outs produced (sacrifices and sacrifice flies appear in both because they achieve both—gaining a base for the team while costing it an out). The formula:

$$\frac{\text{Total Bases} + \text{Walks} + \text{HBP} + \text{Steals} + \text{Sacrifices} + \text{Sacrifice Flies}}{\text{At bats} - \text{Hits} + \text{Caught Stealing} + \text{GIDP} + \text{Sacrifices} + \text{Sac. Flies}}$$

Batter's Park Factor—The Park Factor shown in the batters' section of the team statistics in the Annual Record and Player Register. Above 100 means batters benefited from playing half their games in a good hitting park. Abbreviated as BPF or, in what are clearly batters' stats, simply as PF. (See entry for *Park Factor* for the computation.)

Battery Errors—In baseball's early years, wild pitches, passed balls, and hit batsmen were lumped together in the statistical summary of a game as *battery errors* and were charged against the fielding percentage of the pitcher or catcher. Such battery errors have been removed from individual and team stats for this book.

Batting Average—Calculated as base hits divided by at bats ever since its first appearance in print in 1872. In 1876 walks were counted as at bats, and in 1887 they were counted as at bats and as hits. Abbreviated in Part 2 of this volume as AVG, although it is also commonly abbreviated BA.

Batting Runs—The Linear Weights measure of runs contributed *beyond* those of a league-average batter or team, such league average defined as zero. The formula was created based upon the run values for each offensive event that resulted from Pete Palmer's 1978 computer simulation of all major league games played since 1901. Theoretical run values change marginally with changing conditions of play (an out costs a team more in a hitters' year, such as 1930, than in a pitchers' year, such as 1908), and they differ slightly up and down the batting order (a homer is not worth as much to the leadoff hitter as it is to the fifth-place batter; a walk is worth more for the man batting second than for the man batting eighth); however, we use fixed values in this book. These fixed values are roughly the historical averages:

$$\text{Runs} = (.47)1B + (.78)2B + (1.09)3B + (1.40)HR + (.33)(BB + HBP) + .22(SB) - .45(CS) - (.25)(AB\text{-}H)$$

The value of -.25 for the hitless at-bat ("out") is recalculated for every season so that the formula, applied to the composite batting line of the league that year, calculates to zero.

This means that in higher-scoring years, the out will have a larger negative value than in lower-scoring years. For instance, in the 2003 American League, the out is worth -.287 runs; but in the 1968 National League, the out is worth only -.239 runs.

When calculating Batting Runs for non-pitchers, the out value is chosen in such a manner that the formula, applied to the composite batting line of all *non-pitchers* in the league, calculates to zero. When calculating Batting Runs for pitchers, the out value is chosen so that the composite batting line *for pitchers* calculates to zero.

Some events one might expect to see included in this formula but that do not appear are sacrifices, sacrifice hits, grounded into double plays, and reached on error. The last is not known for most years and in the official statistics is indistinguishable from outs on base (OOB). The sacrifice has values that essentially cancel one another, trading an out for an advanced base which, often as not, leaves the team in a situation with poorer run potential than it had before the sacrifice. The sacrifice fly has dubious run value because it is entirely dependent on a situation not under the batter's control: while a single or a walk or a hit by pitch always has potential run value, a long fly does not unless a man happens to be poised at third base. Last, the grounded into double play is to a far greater extent a function of one's place in the batting order than it is of poor speed or failure in the clutch, and thus it does not find a home in a formula applicable to all batters.

The Batting Runs formula can be condensed by eliminating the components for steals and caught stealing. We eliminate steals from the formula in those years in which caught-stealing figures are not available, but the surviving data for the early years indicate that few of the men with high base-stealing totals exceeded the break-even point of about two-thirds success by a margin large enough to produce even one additional Batting Win.

The Batting Runs formula may be long, even in its condensed form, but it calls for only addition, subtraction and multiplication and thus is as simple as Slugging Average, whose incorrect weights (1, 2, 3, and 4) it revises and expands upon. Each event has a value and frequency, just as in Slugging Average, yet in Batting Runs outs are treated as offensive events with a run value of their own (albeit a negative one). Just as the run potential for a team in a given half-

inning is boosted by a man reaching base, it is diminished by a man being retired; not only has he failed to brighten the situation on the bases but he has deprived his team of the services of a man further down the order who might have come up in this half-inning, either with men on base and/or with scores already in.

The Batting Runs stat treats every offensive event in terms of its impact upon the team—an *average* team, so that a man does not benefit in his individual record for having the good fortune to bat cleanup with the Rockies or suffer for batting cleanup with the White Sox. The relationship of individual performance to team play is stated poorly or not at all in conventional baseball statistics. In Batting Runs it is crystal clear.

Recognizing that some readers will wish to keep track of batting performance by compiling Batting Runs themselves over the course of a season and that they may be frustrated by the difficulty of separating out pitcher batting or of calculating the (At Bats – Hits) factor for the league, we advise that using the fixed value of -.25 for outs will tend to work quite well if you wish to include pitcher batting performance, and a fixed value of -.27 will serve if you wish to exclude it. Actually, any fixed value will suffice in midseason; it's only when all the numbers are in and you care to compare this year's results with last year's (or, e.g., with those of the 1927 Yankees) that more precision is desirable. At that point the value of the out may be calculated by the more ambitious among you, but, ideally, the sporting press will provide accurate Batting Runs figures. (Who calculates ERA for himself?) Batting Runs is abbreviated as BR.

Batting Wins—Adjusted Batting Runs divided by the number of runs required to create an additional win beyond average (see *Runs Per Win*). The idea is that this is the number of wins beyond average the player would contribute to an average team. Abbreviated as BW.

Calculated Stat—One or more counting stats (see below) subjected to a mathematical process such as averaging.

Chances Accepted—Putouts and assists, minus errors.

Component ERA—A Bill James statistic, based on Runs Created, that attempts to measure what a pitcher's ERA "should have been," based on what he gave up to opposing batters. Differences between Component ERA and "real" ERA are based on the timing of walks and hits—pitchers who scatter their hits will have a better ERA than Component ERA, and pitchers who concentrate their hits will have a worse ERA than Component ERA. Since research suggests that timing is largely random, Component ERA can help suggest which pitchers are actually better or worse than their ERA suggests.

To calculate CERA, we first estimate the number of runs the pitcher should have allowed:

$$R = \frac{[H + BB + HBP] \times [.89 \, (1.255(H - HR) + 4HR) + .56(BB + HBP - IBB)]}{BFP}$$

Then, we take that number, convert it to runs per game, and subtract .56:

$$CERA = R \left(\frac{9}{IP}\right) - .56$$

The .56 is an estimate of unearned runs. However, if the runs per game is less than 2.24, multiply by .75 instead of subtracting .56.

The Component ERA formula is not accurate before 1892.

Counting Stat—A raw figure that tells how many of an item have been accumulated, as opposed to a calculated or derived figure such as an average.

Defensive Efficiency Record—Created by Bill James, this is roughly the percentage of balls in play (excluding home runs) that the defense succeeds in turning into outs. Valid only for teams, it is a very good indication of the team's overall defensive proficiency.

Differential—The difference between a team's actual won-lost record and that predicted by the total of its Pitching Wins, Batting Wins, and Fielding Wins; this measure indicates the extent to which a team's W-L record outperformed or underperformed its component performance. Abbreviated as DIF.

Earned Run Average—Calculated as earned runs times nine, divided by innings pitched. For a few years after being introduced as an official stat in the NL in 1912 and the AL in 1913, runs aided by stolen bases were not counted as earned. For years before 1912, ERA has been constructed from raw data, but for some teams in some seasons, earned runs cannot be identified with perfect certainty. For those teams, we use the estimating procedure created by Information Concepts, Inc., of assigning to those runs whose earned/unearned status is unknown the percentage of earned runs to runs that characterize the team's known runs. In *Total Baseball*, we have created a Normalized ERA (ERA+) by comparing to the league average—which is done by dividing the league average ERA by the individual ERA—and then factoring in home park.

Estimated Defensive Innings—For 1999 and earlier, we do not have the exact number of innings a player was in the field. We estimate that number by a process described by Bill James, in "Win Shares:"

1. Find every player who played that position for that team that year.

2. Estimate the number of innings for each based on the total plays they made (Assists+Putouts+Errors). For instance, if a player made 20 percent of the team's plays at that position, assume he played 20 percent of the innings.

3. If these estimates give any of these players more than 9 innings per game played at that position, lower them to 9 innings per game. If these estimates give any of these players fewer than 3 innings per game, raise them to 3 innings per game.

4. The adjustments made in the previous step now mean that the total innings is likely different from the actual innings the team played, either larger or smaller. Find the difference, and adjust each player up or down who is not already at the limit by the proportional number of innings. For instance, if you have allocated 100 innings less than you need, and there are players with 2000 innings who are not already at the limit of 9 innings per game, adjust each of those players upwards by 5 percent (100 divided by 2000).

5. Step 4 may have created a player who is now over 9 innings per game, or under 3 innings per game (for instance, if a player was at 8.9 innings per game and you adjusted him up by 5 percent). In that case, go back to step 3 and repeat.

6. However, if *all* players are over 9 innings per game, stop. (It is also possible, but extremely unlikely, that all players are under 3 innings per game; in that unlikely event, also stop.)

7. At this point, you have the estimated innings played for each player.

Estimated Unassisted Putouts—Per Bill James, we can estimate the number of unassisted putouts by a team's first basemen via the formula:

$$\text{Unassisted putouts} = \text{Putouts by 1B} - .84 \, (\text{Total Assists By 2B,3B,SS,P})$$

We use this estimate in our calculation of Fielding Runs for first basemen. (See *Fielding Runs*.)

Expected Wins—Abbreviated as EW. (See *Pythagorean Wins*.)

Fielding Average—Defined as putouts and assists divided by the total of putouts, assists, and errors. The weakness of this stat is that it values a player with minimal range but good hands over another player who may accept many more chances but mishandle a few of these. Abbreviated as FA. (See *Range Factor, Total Chances*.)

Fielding Runs—Invented by Pete Palmer, this is the Linear Weights measure of runs saved *beyond* what a league-average player at that position might have saved, defined as zero; this stat is calculated to take account of the particular requirements of the different positions. The league average total is sometimes referred to as "expected," and FR is then the number of runs a fielder saved his team compared to those expected.

For second basemen, shortstops, and third basemen, the formula for "expected" begins by calculating the league average rate of PO, A, E, and DP for the position.

This estimate is simply league average plays per inning, but subject to several adjustments.

1. First, a fielder on a team with lots of strikeout pitchers will have fewer opportunities to make plays. Therefore, if a team had 5 percent fewer balls in play than average because of a higher strikeout staff, we adjust the expected plays down by that 5 percent.

2. Second, a team with good fielders will create fewer opportunities to field balls, and vice-versa. For instance, if Ozzie Smith gets to 50 more ground balls than an average shortstop, that's 50 more balls that the other fielders won't get a chance to make a play on. Therefore, instead of basing expected plays on innings played (which is just outs, since an inning is three outs), we base it on "outs plus hits." This accounts for the fact that some players have fewer opportunities to field balls because Ozzie Smith is getting more guys out, reducing the number of balls in play per inning.

3. Third, the expected number of double plays should be higher on teams with poorer pitching staffs, as they allow many more runners on first base. So, we estimate opposition singles (the same proportion of its (H-HR) as the league's). Then we add its walks. That's our estimate of the runners allowed on first base. If it's 15 percent more than the league average, we adjust expected double plays up by that same 15 percent.

4. Fourth, a groundball pitching staff will create more opportunities for infielders and fewer for outfielders; and vice versa for a flyball staff. We estimate the proportion of groundballs by using, as a proxy, the number of assists. A team with 10 percent more assists than average is assumed to have induced 10 percent more groundballs than average, and the team's estimate of expected groundballs is increased by 10 percent. (We don't adjust infielder putouts for groundball pitching, just assists and errors.)

5. Finally, on many ground balls to first base, it is at the fielder's discretion whether to make the play unassisted, or to flip to the pitcher. First basemen who prefer the 3-1 play (such as Bill Buckner, in 1985) will see their assists artificially boosted, and those who prefer to make the play unassisted (such as Steve Garvey in the mid-'70s) will have assists totals that are artificially low. Therefore, for first basemen, we estimate the number of putouts made 3-unassisted, according to a formula discovered by Bill James. Then, we adjust the player's expected assists by 25 percent of the difference between his unassisted putouts and the league average unassisted putouts. (See *Estimated Unassisted Putouts*.)

Once we have the adjusted expected plays per inning, as calculated above, we estimate the number of innings the player fielded at that position. (See *Estimated Defensive Innings*.)

Then, we have both the team's rate of expected plays for the position, and the player's estimated innings; and so we can calculate the expected number of plays that player should have made. We then compute his Fielding Runs by the following formula:

$$FR = .4 (A - \text{expected } A) + .2 (PO - \text{expected } PO) + .2 (DP - \text{expected } DP) - .2 (E - \text{expected } E)$$

Assists are doubly weighted because more fielding skill is generally required to get one than to record a putout.

In the above form, the formula applies only to second basemen, third basemen and shortstops. For catchers, the formula is modified by subtracting strikeouts from putouts (if a catcher played 30 percent of his team's innings, we subtract 30 percent of the team's Ks), and subtracting not only errors but also passed balls divided by two.

For pitchers, the formula is modified to subtract individual pitcher strikeouts from the total number of potential outs (otherwise, exceptional strikeout pitchers like Nolan Ryan or Bob Feller would see their Fielding Runs artificially depressed). Also, pitchers' chances are weighted less than infielders' assists because a pitcher's style may produce fewer ground balls. Thus the formula for pitchers is .10(PO + 2A – E + DP), whereas for second basemen, shortstops and third basemen it is .20(PO + 2A – E + DP).

For first basemen, because putouts and double plays require so little skill in all but the odd case, these plays are eliminated, leaving only .20(2A – E) in the numerator. Also, their expected assists are adjusted by a portion of their unassisted putouts, as described above.

For outfielders, the formula becomes .20(PO + 4A – E + 2DP). The weighting for assists is boosted here because a good outfielder can prevent runs through the threat of assists that are never made; for them, unlike infielders, the assist is essentially the result of an elective play by the runner, like the stolen base.

Fielding Wins—Fielding Runs divided by the number of runs required to create an additional win beyond average. That average is defined as a team record of .500 because a league won-lost average must be .500. Abbreviated as FW. (See *Runs per Win*.)

Games Behind—Figured by adding the difference in wins between a trailing team and the leader to the difference in losses, and dividing by two. Thus a team that is three games behind may trail by three in the win column and three in the loss column, or four, or two, or any other combination of wins and losses totaling six. Abbreviated as GB.

Game-Winning Run Batted In—Credited to the batter who drives in a run that gives his club a lead that it never relinquishes, no matter when that run is driven in nor what the final score is. Introduced in 1980 as an official stat and later disowned, the GWRBI is not recorded in this volume.

Grounded into Double Play—Kept officially since 1933 in the NL and 1939 in the AL (though the NL data of 1933-1938 made no distinction between lined-into double plays and grounded-into double plays, and the AL data of 1939 was not published). Abbreviated as GIDP.

Hands Out—The original 1840s scoring term for batters producing outs either at the plate or on the bases. On a force out, the runner retired on the bases would be charged with a hand out, not the batter. Also called Hands Lost, and abbreviated as HO or HL.

Hit by Pitch—A batter struck by a pitched ball was not awarded first base until 1884 in the American Association and 1887 in the National League. Reconstruction of stats for batters

and pitchers in the years 1897-1908 has been accomplished. Abbreviated as HBP.

Home Run Percentage—Home runs per 100 at bats.

Home Runs—When is a home run not a home run? Before 1920, not if it was a "walk-off" home run and created a margin of victory greater than one run. A ruling of the Special Baseball Records Committee in 1969 reversed its earlier decision that had made home runs of 37 disputed final-inning, game-winning base hits. In accordance with the practice of the day, such a hit, even if it sailed out of the park, would be credited with only as many bases as necessary to plate the winning run. Thus Babe Ruth's "715th home run," hit on July 8, 1918, to win a game against Cleveland, remained a triple, and Jimmy Collins and Sherry Magee were each deprived of two home runs.

Innings Pitched—Official baseball practice was, until 1982, to round off fractional innings for individuals to the next highest inning. Since then fractional innings have been kept for individuals and teams. In this volume fractional innings are supplied for all individuals and all teams in all years. Those men who took a turn on the mound but failed to retire a batter are credited with no innings pitched and, if they allowed a runner or runners to score, an ERA of infinity.

Intentional Bases on Balls—Recorded only since 1955.

Isolated Power—Total bases minus hits, divided by at bats; in other words, Slugging Average minus Batting Average. Appears to have been created by Allan Roth and Branch Rickey in the 1950s.

League-Average Replacement Player—That model player who performs at precisely the league average, creating a baseline against which to measure others.

Linear Weights—A system created by Pete Palmer to measure all the events on a ballfield in terms of runs. At the root of this system, as with other sabermetric figures such as Runs Created, is the knowledge that wins and losses are what the game of baseball is about, that wins and losses are proportional in some way to runs scored and runs allowed, and that runs in turn are proportional to the events that go into their making. Batting Runs, Pitching Runs, and Fielding Runs are all components of the Linear Weights method.

Normalizing—Restating a figure as a ratio by comparing it to the league average, or norm.

On-Base Percentage—Created by Roth and Rickey in its current form—hits plus walks plus hit by pitch, divided by at bats plus walks plus hit by pitch—in the early 1950s, although there were nineteenth-century forebears such as "Reached First Base." When OBP, as it is abbreviated, was adopted as an official stat in 1984, the denominator was expanded to include sacrifice flies. The effect is to penalize a batter in his on base percentage by giving him a plate appearance while at the same time crediting him in his batting average by deleting the plate appearance. In this book we calculate OBP without considering sacrifice flies, which in any event are calculable on a continuing basis only since 1954.

On-Base plus Slugging—On-Base Percentage plus Slugging Average: a simple but elegant measure of batting prowess, in that the weaknesses of one-half of the formulation, On-Base Percentage, are countered by the strengths of the other, Slugging Average, and vice versa. When OPS, as it is abbreviated, is adjusted for home park and normalized to league average to become OPS+, the calculation is modified slightly to create a baseline of 100 for a league-average performance. For OPS+, the calculation is:

$$\frac{\text{Player On Base Pct.}}{\text{League On Base Pct.}} + \frac{\text{Player Slugging Avg.}}{\text{League Slugging Avg.}} - 1$$

This produces a figure with a decimal point—an above average figure, like 1.46, or a below-average figure, like 0.82. For ease of dis-

---

CALCULATING FIELDING RUNS

Here, using Nomar Garciaparra's 2003 season as an example, is the method by which we calculate fielding runs for a shortstop, second baseman, or third baseman. The process for other positions is largely similar, with differences outlined in the glossary.

Step 1: Calculate Expected Assists

How many assists would an average fielder have been credited with if substituting for Nomar?

In 2003, American League shortstops had 6,512 assists. Boston defenses faced 4,603 of the league's 65,344 balls in play; and Nomar himself played 1,364.7 of the Red Sox's 1,464.7 innings. So Nomar would expect to have 427.4 assists:

$$6512 \times (4603/65344) \times (1364.7/1464.7) = 427.4$$

But this doesn't correct for whether the Sox had more, or fewer, ground-ball pitchers than normal. Following Bill James' formula, we estimate ground-ball tendencies by assists.

The AL as a whole had 23,080 assists, and 46,939 outs that weren't strikeouts, for a percentage of .492 assists per (non-K) out. The Sox had 1,679 assists, and 3,253 outs that weren't strikeouts, for a percentage of .516 assists per out.

.516 is 4.9 percent more than .492, and so we estimate that the Sox' pitchers were 4.9 percent more likely to induce a ground ball. We therefore project Nomar to have 4.9 percent more assists:

$$427.4 + 4.9\% = 448.6$$

Nomar's expected assist total is 448.6.

Step 2: Calculate Expected Errors

Using the same procedure as above, but for errors instead of assists, gives us a projection of 20.7.

Nomar's expected error total is 20.7.

Step 3: Calculate Expected Putouts

For putouts, the procedure is the same as above, but we do not correct for ground-ball pitching.

In 2003, AL shortstops had 3,686 putouts; as in step 1, we multiply that by the proportion of balls-in-play that belong to the Red Sox, then by the proportion of the Red Sox innings fielded by Nomar:

$$3686 \times (4603/65344) \times (1364.7/1464.7) = 241.9$$

Nomar's expected putout total is 241.9.

Step 4: Calculate Expected Double Plays

First, we estimate how many runners were on first base by adding singles and walks. For the 2003 American League as a whole, that's 21,042. There were 2,132 double plays in the league, so 10.1 percent of these runners on first were erased on a double play.

We therefore expect that the percentage for the Red Sox will also be 10.1 percent. We don't know how many singles they gave up, but we know how many hits, and what proportion of league hits were singles. From that, and the number of walks given up, we estimate that the Red Sox had 1,500.1 runners on first base.

Now, 10.1 percent of 1,500.1 is 152, and we therefore estimate the Red Sox should have turned 152 DP for the year. However, this again doesn't take the pitchers' ground-ball tendency into account. The Sox had 0.42 percent more assists per inning than the league average; we therefore assume 0.42 percent more ground balls, and we bump the 152 figure up to 152.68.

For the league as a whole, 1,504 of its 2,132 double plays, or 70.54 percent, involved the shortstop. Therefore, Red Sox shortstops are expected to turn 107.7 double plays—70.54 percent of 152.68. Finally, Nomar played only 1,364.7 of the Sox' 1,464.7 innings, or 93.2 percent. We therefore expect Nomar to have 93.2 percent of the 107.7 shortstop double plays, or 100.3.

Nomar's expected DP total is 100.3.

Step 5: Add It All Up

For errors, double plays, or putouts, Nomar receives 0.2 fielding runs for each play above expected (or minus 0.2 runs for each play below expected). Assists count double, at 0.4. In chart form:

	Nomar actual	Expected	Difference	Value	Fielding Runs
A	456	448.6	7.4	0.4	3.0
E	20	20.7	0.7	0.2	0.1
PO	216	241.9	-25.9	0.2	-5.2
DP	83	100.3	-17.7	0.2	-3.5
Total					-5.6

Overall, Garciaparra was 5.6 runs below average. After rounding, we call it –6.

Nomar's FR for 2003 is –6 runs.

play, in this book we drop the decimal and express these as 146 and 82. In the formula, "league average" figures are for non-pitchers only.

Opponents' Batting Average—Hits allowed divided by at bats allowed (or, if at bats allowed is unknown, such as for years before 1903, then at bats equals hits plus innings times "k," where "k" is the league average of at bats minus hits, all over innings). Abbreviated as OAV.

Outs—Until 1883, included catching a ball on one bounce in foul ground. Not credited after three strikes in 1887, when the rule was "four strikes and yer out"—as it was, in fact, from 1871–1881, when batters commonly received a "warning pitch" rather than a called strike for the first good pitch taken.

Park Factor—Calculated separately for batters and pitchers. Above 100 signifies a park favorable to hitters; below 100 signifies a park favorable to pitchers. The computation of PF is admittedly daunting, and what follows is probably of interest to the merest handful of readers, but we feel obliged to state the mathematical underpinnings for those few who may care. We use a three-year average Park Factor for players and teams unless they change home parks. Then a two-year average is used, unless the park existed for only one year. Then a one-year mark is used. If a team started up in Year 1, played two years in the first park, one in the next, and three in the park after that and then stopped play, the average would be as follows (where Fn is the one-year park factor for year n):

Year 1 and 2 = (F1 + F2)/2   Year 4 = (F4 + F5)/2
Year 3 = F3   Year 5 = (F4 + F5 + F6)/3
                                              Year 6 = (F5 + F6)/2

Step 1. Find games, losses, and runs scored and allowed for each team at home and on the road. Take runs per game scored and allowed at home over runs per game scored and allowed on the road. This is the initial figure, but we must make two corrections to it.

Step 2. The first correction is for innings pitched at home and on the road. This is a bit complicated, so the mathematically faint of heart may want to head back at this point. First, find the team's home winning percentage (wins at home over games at home). Do the same for road games. Calculate the Innings Pitched Corrector (IPC) shown below. If it is greater than 1, this means the innings pitched on the road are higher because the other team is batting more often in the last of the ninth. This rating is divided by the Innings Pitched Corrector, like so:

$$IPC = \frac{(18.5 - \text{Wins at home / Games at home})}{(18.5 - \text{Losses on road / Games on road})}$$

Note: 18.5 is the average number of half-innings per game if the home team always bats in the ninth.

Step 3. Make corrections for the fact that the other road parks' total difference from the league average is offset by the park rating of the club that is being rated. Multiply rating by this Other Parks Corrector (OPC):

$$OPC = \frac{\text{No. of teams}}{\text{No. of teams} - 1 + \text{Run Factor, team}}$$

(Note that this OPC differs from that presented earlier in *The Hidden Game of Baseball*, for in preparing the pre-1900 data for *Total Baseball*, we discovered that for some parks with extreme characteristics, like Chicago's Lake Front Park of 1884, which had a Home Run Factor of nearly 5, the earlier formula produced wrong results. For parks with factors of 1.5 or less, either formula works well.)

Example. In 1982, Atlanta scored 388 runs and allowed 387

runs at home in 81 games, and scored 351 and allowed 315 on the road in 81 games. The initial factor is (775/81) ÷ (666/81) = 1.164. The Braves' home record was 42–39, or .519, and their road record was 47–34, or .580. Thus the IPC = (18.5 – .519) ÷ (18.5 – .420) = .995. The team rating is now 1.164/.995 = 1.170. The OPC = (12) ÷ (12 – 1 + 1.170) = .986. The final runs-allowed rating is 1.170 X .986, or 1.154.

We warned you it wouldn't be easy!

The batter adjustment factor is composed of two parts, one the park factor and the other the fact that a batter does not have to face his own team's pitchers. The initial correction takes care of only the second factor. Start with the following (SF = Scoring Factor, previously determined [for Atlanta, 1.154], and SF1 = Scoring Factor of the other clubs [NT = number of teams]):

$$\frac{NT}{NT - 1 + SF}$$

Next is an iterative process in which the initial team pitching rating is assumed to be 1, and the following factors are employed:

RHT, RAT = Runs per game scored at home (H) and away (A), by team
OHT, OAT = Runs per game allowed at home, away, by team
RAL = Runs per game by both teams

Now, with the Team Pitching Rating (TPR) = 1, we proceed to calculate Team Batting Rating (TBR):

$$TBR = \left(\frac{RAT}{SF1} + \frac{RHT}{SF}\right)\left(1 + \frac{TPR - 1}{NT - 1}\right) \Big/ RAL$$

$$TPR = \left(\frac{OAT}{SF1} + \frac{OHT}{SF}\right)\left(1 + \frac{TBR - 1}{NT - 1}\right) \Big/ RAL$$

The last two steps are repeated three more times. The final Batting Corrector, or Batters' Park Factor (BPF) is

$$BPF = \frac{(SF + SF1)}{\left(2 \times \left[1 + \frac{TPR - 1}{NT - 1}\right]\right)}$$

Similarly, the final Pitching Corrector, or Pitchers' Park Factor (PPF) is

$$PPF = \frac{(SF + SF1)}{\left(2 \times \left[1 + \frac{TPR - 1}{NT - 1}\right]\right)}$$

Now an example, using the 1982 Atlanta Braves once again.

RHT — $\frac{388}{81}$ – 4.79   RAT — $\frac{351}{81}$ – 4.33

OHT — $\frac{387}{81}$ – 4.78   OAT — $\frac{315}{81}$ – 3.89

RAL — $\frac{7947}{972}$ – 8.18   NT = 12

SF = 1.154   SF1 = –1 – $\left(\frac{1.154 - 1}{11}\right)$ = .986

$$TBR = \left(\frac{4.33}{.986} + \frac{4.79}{1.154}\right)\left(1 + \frac{1-1}{11}\right) \Big/ 8.18 = 1.044$$

$$TPR = \left(\frac{3.89}{.986} + \frac{4.78}{1.154}\right)\left(1 + \frac{1.044 - 1}{11}\right) \Big/ 8.18 = .993$$

Repeating these steps gives a TBR of 1.04 and a TPR of .97. The Batters' Park Factor is

$$BPF = \frac{(1.154 + .970)}{\left(2 \times \left[1 + \frac{.97 - 1}{11}\right]\right)} = 1.07$$

This is not a great deal removed from taking the original ratio,

$$\frac{1.170 + 1}{2}, \text{ which is } 1.08.$$

The Pitchers' Park Factor may be calculated in analogous fashion.

To apply the Batters' Park Factor to Batting Runs, one must use this formula:

$$\text{BR}_{\text{corr.}} = \text{BR}_{\text{uncorr.}} - \frac{\frac{\text{Runs (league)}}{\text{(AB-H + CS) (league)}} \times (\text{AB-H + CS}) \times (\text{BPF} -1)}{\text{BPF}}$$

For example, if a player produces 20 runs above average in 395 hitless plate appearances and 5 caught stealing with a Batters' Park Factor of 1.10, and the league average of runs produced per out+CS is .16, his uncorrected Batting Runs is 20. Therefore, 64 runs is the average run contribution expected of this batter were he playing in an average home park. But because his home park was 10 percent kinder to hitters than average, you would really expect an average run production of 1.1 x 64, or about 70 runs from a player in that ballpark. Thus the player whose uncorrected Batting Runs is 84 with a BF of 1.1 is only +14 runs before adjustment (rather than +20), and Park Adjusted Batting Runs is only 12 (in the Player Register, BR/A):

$$12 = \frac{(84 - (64 \times 1.1))}{1.1}$$

Pitcher Defense—Formerly used to denote a pitcher's *Fielding Runs*.

Pitchers' Park Factor—The same as the Park Factor shown in the pitchers' section of the team statistics portion of the Annual Record and in the Pitcher Register; above 100 means a pitcher was hurt by playing half his games in a good hitting park. (See *Park Factor.*)

Pitcher Strikeouts—Made tougher or easier by cyclically varying rules and conditions. For instance, foul tips did not count as strikes for many years, even when deliberate, as with bunts; fouls caught on a bounce were outs until 1883; the ball-strike count underwent much experimentation until settling at four balls and three strikes in 1889; not to mention the high-low strike zone, warning pitches, varying pitching distances, and restricted deliv-

eries. It helps to know some history before rattling off stats to prove this or that, but normalizing a stat to its league helps, even with counting stats such as strikeouts.

Pitching Runs—The Linear Weights measure of runs saved *beyond* what a league-average pitcher or team might have saved, defined as zero. The math is simple:

Pitching Runs = Innings Pitched X (League ERA/9) – Earned Runs Allowed

An alternate version is:

Innings Pitched/9 X (League ERA – Individual ERA).

Starting with this edition of *Total Baseball*, we adjust pitching runs by the combined contribution (in Fielding Runs) of the team's fielders. If the team, excluding pitchers, had +20 fielding runs, a hurler responsible for 10 percent of the team's innings would see his pitching runs reduced by 2. If the team was worse than average —at –30, say—his pitching runs would be increased by 3, acknowledging that he needed to be even better to overcome his team's mediocre fielding behind him. Abbreviated as PR.

Pitching Wins—Park Adjusted Pitching Runs divided by the number of runs required to create an additional win beyond average. That average is defined as a team record of .500 because a league won-lost average must be .500. Abbreviated as PW. (See *Pitching Runs,* above, and *Runs Per Win.*)

Positional Adjustment—A key factor in the Total Player Rating that addresses the relative worth to a ball club of the defensive positions. A man who bats .270, hits 25 homers, and drives in 80 runs may be an average performer in left field, no matter how good his glove; but credit those batting stats to a shortstop or second baseman and you have a star, because the defensive demands of the position are so much greater. To balance the abundance of good-hitting outfielders or first basemen against the scarcity of such players at catcher or shortstop, we created a positional adjustment expressed in terms of the average batting skill needed to hold down a major league spot at that position.

To determine the average defensive skill required of a position,

CALCULATING TPW FOR PITCHERS

Here, using Greg Maddux's 2003 season as an example, is the method by which we calculate TPW for a pitcher.

Step 1: Calculate League Average Runs
In 2003, the National League ERA was 4.278. Greg Maddux pitched 218.3 innings, in which an average pitcher would have allowed 103.8 runs.

However, Turner Field's pitcher park factor was 98.6, so runs are 1.4 percent easier to prevent for a Braves pitcher. So the league-average pitcher would have allowed only 102.3 runs (103.8 times 98.6 percent).

An average pitcher in Greg Maddux's place would have allowed 102.3 runs.

Step 2: Subtract the Pitcher's Earned Runs
Greg Maddux allowed 96 earned runs. That's 6.3 runs better than average, which becomes Maddux's Adjusted Pitcher Runs.

Greg Maddux had +6.3 Adjusted Pitcher Runs in 2003.

Step 3: Adjust for the Team's Fielding Runs
The better the team's fielding, the better the pitcher's stats—and vice versa. To adjust for defense, we calculate the number of runs by which the Braves' defense helped or hurt Greg Maddux, and adjust his total accordingly.

Not including pitchers, the 2003 Atlanta Braves had a combined –5.0 fielding runs. Greg Maddux pitched in 15 percent of the Braves' innings—218.3 out of 1,456.3. His defense thus cost him three-quarters of a run – 15 percent of minus 5. We adjust Maddux' Pitching Runs upwards from 6.3 to 7.1.

Adjusted for his defense, Greg Maddux had +7.1 Adjusted Pitcher Runs in 2003.

Step 4: Add the Pitcher's Batting Runs
We calculate Greg Maddux's batting runs using the procedure outlined previously (see "Calculating TPW for batters"). The only difference in that procedure is that we compare Greg's hitting to other pitchers, rather than to other non-pitchers.

Using that method, we find that Maddux had –0.5 batting runs in 2003.

Greg Maddux had –0.5 batting runs in 2003.

Step 5: Optionally, Calculate Fielding Runs
Using the method outlined elsewhere, we calculate that Greg Maddux's defense

contributed 5.1 runs in 2003.

However, we will not be considering Fielding Runs in calculating pitchers' TPW. The reason is that any runs saved by defense will already be taken into account in Pitching Runs. That is, the contribution of Maddux's 5 pitching runs presumably allowed Maddux to escape with 5 fewer earned runs than he would have allowed otherwise—those are duly included in his Pitching Runs.

Looking at Maddux's pitching runs can still be instructive: one way to interpret the statistics is that Maddux saved his team 6.3 defensive runs—5.1 of those came from his fielding, and the remaining 1.2 came from his pitching. In reality, part of his defensive runs probably stemmed from his pitching style—since Maddux is an extreme ground-ball pitcher, his fielding runs may have been influenced by a large number of ground balls hit in his direction. How much of the 5.1 fielding runs is actually a result of pitching style, and how much is the result of fielding prowess, is a question that we do not address.

Step 6: Calculate Total Player Wins
We start by adding Maddux's Pitching Runs to his Batting Runs:

Batting Runs	- 0.5
Pitching Runs	+ 7.1
Total	+ 6.6

In the 2003 National League, teams scored an average 1.034 runs per inning (both teams combined). Using the formula for "Runs Per Win" in the Glossary, we find that in the 2003 NL, it took 10.17 runs to create one extra win.

And so, we divide Maddux's 6.6 runs by 10.17 to get his Total Player Wins:

TPW = 6.6 / 10.17
TPW = .64

After rounding, Greg Maddux winds up with 0.6 Total Player Wins for 2003—above average, but nonetheless one of the lowest marks of his career.

In 2003, Greg Maddux had a TPW of 0.6.

simply subtract the average batting skill at that position from his Total Player Rating. This may seem strange at first glance, but it does put, for example, shortstops, first basemen, and left fielders on the same footing. Here are the eras and their positional adjustments. To make the adjustments more readable, these are the adjustments per 150 games (4,050 innings) in the field.

	C	1b	2b	3b	ss	lf	cf	rf	dh
1871-75	-2.8	-2.1	8.9	1.7	3.5	-3.1	0.4	-9.6	—
1876-81	-4.4	7.9	-7.1	-4.5	-7.2	8.6	7.5	0.8	—
1882-91	-13.9	13.4	-4.9	-3.6	-4.8	5.4	5.3	2.9	—
1892-00	-14.9	0.9	-6.9	-2.7	-7.9	14.0	10.3	8.2	—
1901-10	-15.7	2.8	-1.3	-4.4	-5.0	9.0	7.3	7.1	—
1911-20	-12.6	2.8	-2.7	-4.6	-10.9	6.3	9.5	8.0	—
1921-30	-10.3	10.2	-4.2	-9.8	-16.8	11.8	6.3	12.3	—
1931-42	-9.8	14.3	-9.9	-5.7	-11.2	8.8	3.8	9.5	—
1943-45	-9.5	8.1	-8.4	-2.1	-12.5	9.5	3.9	10.5	—
1946-52	-8.4	5.2	-8.7	0.4	-9.9	11.6	4.0	4.7	—
1953-60	-7.8	9.0	-11.9	0.5	-12.7	9.7	7.5	5.3	—
1961-68	-8.0	9.3	-13.4	0.1	-13.4	9.0	4.7	10.9	—
1969-76	-7.7	12.3	-10.4	0.6	-18.4	9.3	4.2	8.0	5.6
1977-87	-7.7	9.5	-8.4	1.8	-16.4	7.7	2.2	7.8	6.0
1988-92	-10.1	11.0	-4.3	-1.0	-12.2	5.8	2.4	4.5	6.7
1993-03	-11.1	13.9	-7.5	-2.3	-12.8	6.7	-1.2	8.5	11.4

Production—An alternative term, now seldom used, for *On-Base plus Slugging.*

Pythagorean Projection—A formula, discovered by Bill James, that expresses the relationship between a team's winning percentage and its runs scored and allowed:

$$\text{Expected Winning PCT} = \frac{\text{Runs}^2}{\text{Runs}^2 + \text{Opposition Runs}^2}$$

Empirical evidence shows that the Pythagorean Projection is an excellent (but not perfect) predictor of a team's record.

Pythagorean Wins—Calculated for the team using the *Pythagorean Projection* based on its runs scored and allowed. A team that allows exactly as many runs as it scores is predicted to play .500 ball. The equation for expected wins is:

$$EW = \frac{\text{Runs}^2}{\text{Runs}^2 + \text{Opposition Runs}^2} \text{ (Actual Wins + Actual Losses)}$$

Abbreviated as PY.

Quality Start—A game started in which a pitcher lasts for six innings or more and allows three runs or fewer.

Range Factor—A statistic, plays made per game, that estimates a fielder's ability to turn balls into outs. While Range Factor is a reasonable general indication of a player's defensive skill, it is often inaccurate because "games" is not always an accurate estimate of a his fielding time—late-inning defensive replacements, for instance, will have many "games" but few actual innings in the field.

Ratio—A pitching stat: hits-plus-walks allowed per inning. Abbreviated as RAT.

Reached First Base—A precursor of the On Base Percentage, this stat was introduced as an official National League measure in 1879, its one and only year of existence. It included times reached via hits, walks and errors, but not hit by pitch because putting their bodies on the line did not yet, in 1879, send batters to first base. Trivia: the league leader in this stat's lone year of life was Providence outfielder Paul Hines, with 193.

Relative Batting Average—Pioneered by David Shoebotham in a *Baseball Research Journal* article in 1976, this was the first traditional stat normalized to league average so as to permit cross-era comparison. Most folks who have employed this measure simply divide individual batting average by league batting average. Shoebotham's original computation was more precise:

$$RBA = \frac{\text{player's hits}}{\text{player's AB}} \Bigg/ \frac{\text{league hits} - \text{player's hits}}{\text{league AB} - \text{player's AB}}$$

In this manner a player's own performance would not be compared with itself.

Relief Points—Relief wins plus saves minus losses was the original formula used as the basis for the Rolaids Company's annual award to the top reliever in each league. Recently the formula has been changed to include a debit for blown saves.

Run Batted In—Though widely regarded as a good measure of a batter's overall productivity and value to his team, the RBI is extremely situation-dependent, denying equal access to opportunity on the basis of a player's team, slot in the batting order, and particularly the men surrounding him in the batting order.

Runs Created—Bill James's formulation for run contribution from a variety of batting and baserunning events.

Many different formulas are used, depending upon data available. In its basic expression, the formula is:

$$\frac{(\text{Hits} + \text{Walks})\,(\text{Total Bases})}{\text{At Bats} + \text{Walks}}$$

The essence of this formulation is that the ability to get on base and the ability to push baserunners around fairly describes offensive ability. James later refined the formula with a "stolen base version":

$$\frac{(\text{Hits} + \text{Walks} - \text{Caught Stealing})\,(\text{Total Bases} + .55 \times \text{StolenBases})}{\text{At Bats} + \text{Walks}}$$

Next came the "technical version": a longer formulation, using the standard abbreviations for the various offensive events (the two elements multiplied in the numerator are referred to below as "A" and "B," and the denominator is referred to as "C"):

$$\frac{(H + BB + HBP - CS - GIDP)\,(TB + .26[BB - IBB + HBP] + .52[SH + SF + SB])}{AB + BB + HBP + SH + SF}$$

From this technical version (Tech-1), James spun off 13 additional technical versions. "The reason that we have to do this," he wrote in *The Bill James Historical Baseball Abstract*, "is that the data set changes and evolves rapidly throughout the century, or at least up until about 1955, when the progress of evolution in statistical information came to a temporary halt (it stopped moving forward until Bill James and Pete Palmer came around, about twenty years later). In 1900 we have no data for how many times a player grounded into a double play, how many times he was hit by a pitch, how many of his walks might have been intentional, how many times he was caught stealing, or how many sacrifice flies he hit." Accordingly, James adjusted his Runs Created formula to fit the available data; some versions, such as Tech-3, cover as much as a decade in a given league, while others, such as Tech-4, are in force for only a single league season. In *Total Baseball*, we have computed Runs Created values for all players since 1876 using the version most applicable to the period, with the single exception of Tech-9, which James applied only to the American League of 1916 but which we use for 1914–1916 in the AL and 1915–1916 in the NL because we have discovered additional caught-stealing data. (For those players whose careers began before 1900, James used the Tech-11 formula "to estimate how many runs they had created," but appended a note saying that "these estimates were of indeterminate accuracy.")

Here are the formulas for Runs Created (RC) technical versions 2–14 (Tech-1 was used for both the American and National leagues in 1955–1988):

Tech-2 (1954)

Factors A and C of Tech-1 remain the same, while Part B simply drops Intentional Bases on Balls.

Tech-3 (AL 1940–1953; NL 1951–1953)

Factor A remains the same, while SF is dropped from Factor C; Factor B changes to:

1.025 TB + .26(BB + HBP) + .52(SH + SB).

Tech-4 (AL 1939)

Factors A and C remain the same, while B becomes:

TB + .26(BB + HBP) + .52(SH + SB).

Tech-5 (AL 1931–1938)

Factors B and C remain the same, while A becomes:

.96(H + BB + HBP – CS).

Tech-6 (AL 1920–1930; NL 1920–1925)

Factors A and C remain the same, while B changes only in the value placed on the sacrifice hit and stolen base, which declines from .52 to .51.

Tech-7 (NL 1926–1930)

C remains the same, while A changes to: .93(H + BB + HBP), and B becomes: TB + .26(BB + HBP) + .46(SH).

Tech-8 (AL 1913, 1917–1919; NL 1913–1914, 1917–1919)

C remains the same, while A becomes:

H + W + HBP – .02(AB), and B becomes: TB + .85(SH + SB).

Tech-9 (AL 1914–1916; NL 1915–1916)

B and C are the same, while A becomes: H + BB + HBP – CS.

Tech-10 (AL, NL 1908–1912)

C remains the same. A changes back to that used in Tech-8, while B becomes: 1.025(TB + SB) + .75(SH).

Tech-11 (AL, NL 1900–1907)

B and C remain the same, while A becomes: H + BB + HBP.

Tech-12 (NL 1939–1950)

A Factor: H + BB + HBP – GIDP

B Factor: TB + .26(BB +HBP) + .52(SH)

Tech-13 (NL 1933–1938)

A and C remain the same as above, while B becomes:

1.025(TB) + .26(BB + HBP) + .52(SH)

Tech-14 (NL 1931–1932)

B and C remain the same, but A becomes:

.95(H + BB + HBP).

Runs Created Per Game—A Bill James statistic that answers the question, "how many runs would a team score per game if it had nine batters who hit like this?" Abbreviated RC/G, or occasionally RC/27.

The formula, for 1939 and later, is

$$\frac{\text{Runs Created}}{\text{Batting Outs}} \times 27$$

"Batting outs" are those outs used in the Runs Created formula for the particular year; for the standard formula, it is the sum of AB–H, SF, SH, CS, and GIDP.

The "27" is because there are roughly 27 batting outs per game. We say "roughly" because some batting outs aren't actual outs—such as reached on error—and some actual outs aren't batting outs—such as runners thrown out taking an extra base. In general, for 1939 and later, these even out, and 27 is the appropriate number.

For seasons before 1939, some outs used in the Runs Created formula aren't available (such as SF, or CS); and, for some years in the 19th century, there are so many errors that they no longer balance outs on base. Therefore, for earlier seasons, instead of using 27, we found the number that causes the league's RC/G to match the league's actual runs created per game played. We round that number off to the nearest 0.5, and we use that as the multiplier.

Runs Per Game—With its mate *Outs Per Game,* this was the precursor, in the 1860s, of the batting average; by the end of that decade it gave way to Hits Per Game.

Runs Per Win—Branch Rickey and Allan Roth first stated the proportional nature of runs and wins in their 1954 article in *Life.* Since then the point has been expanded upon by George Lindsey, Pete Palmer, Bill James, and every sabermetrician worth his salt: the point being that just as runs scored and allowed are the key to victory in a given game, so are they the key to success over the course of a season and the predictors of won-lost record with a surprising degree of precision. In 1982, Palmer wrote in *The National Pastime,* "My work showed that as a rough rule of thumb, each additional ten runs scored (or ten less runs allowed) produced one extra win. ... However, breaking the teams into groups showed that high-scoring teams needed more runs to produce a win. This runs-per-win factor I determined to be ten times the square root of the average number of runs scored per inning by both teams. Thus in normal play, when 4.5 runs per game are scored by each club, each team scores .5 runs per inning—totaling one run, the square root of which is one, times ten."

$$\text{Runs Per Win} = 10 \times \sqrt{\text{number of runs per inning, both teams}}$$

Runs Produced—Runs batted in plus runs scored minus home runs.

Sabermetrics—Defined by Bill James, who coined the term in honor of the Society for American Baseball Research, as "the search for objective knowledge about baseball" and, earlier, as "the mathematical and statistical analysis of baseball records."

SABR—Pronounced "saber," this is the acronym for the Society for American Baseball Research, the organization that has, since its founding by Bob Davids in 1971, steadily advanced the state of baseball knowledge.

Sacrifice Fly—First recognized as an event in 1908 but indistinguishable in the official records from sacrifice hits until 1954. There has been much flip-flopping since 1930 on whether to credit the sacrifice flier with an at bat or an RBI or whether a fly ball that advances a runner to a base other than home plate also should exempt a man from an at bat.

Sacrifice Hits—Invented in the 1860s, recorded since 1889; sacrificer charged with an at-bat until 1894, although *Total Baseball* does not charge at bats to 19th-century sacrificers. Sabermetricians frown on the strategy because all the studies show that the trading of an out for a base advanced is a losing strategy—lowering the run expectations of the team that attempts it—in all but the most unusual of cases ... even if the sacrifice "succeeds."

Sacrifice Hits Allowed—Computed officially in the National League since 1913 but not published until 1916, and kept in the American League since 1921 but not published until 1922; what it signified about anything is unclear.

Save—Created by Jerome Holtzman of the *Chicago Sun-Times,* the save began to be reported by *The Sporting News* on a regular basis in 1960. The major leagues adopted the save in 1969, at which time it was credited to a reliever who finished a game that

his team won. In 1973 the save was redefined so that a reliever had not only to finish the game but also to find the potential tying or winning run on base or at the plate, or, alternately, to pitch the final three innings of a victorious contest. In 1975 the rule was liberalized to include a reliever's game-ending appearance of one inning or more in which he protects a lead of three runs or less; or his entrance into and ultimate completion of the game with the tying or winning run on base, at bat, or on deck; or his pitching three innings to the game's conclusion. In this book, the 1969 definition is applied to all games before 1969; otherwise the rule in force at the time prevails. Abbreviated as SV.

Shutouts—On an individual basis, credited only to pitchers of complete-game scoreless victories or ties; former practice was to credit combined shutouts to the starting pitcher if he had pitched most of the way. Abbreviated as SH.

Situational Statistics—How does a batter perform with the bases loaded? At night? On artificial turf? With no one on base? After the seventh inning when his team is tied or trails? The specialty of Baseball Workshop, Stats, Inc., and the Elias Sports Bureau.

Sabermetric research indicates that the only situational breakdowns that have (so far) proven to be significant are: lefty/righty; against players with differing groundball/flyball tendencies; and, of course, home/road. Some others may have small effects that are not yet fully understood (such as grass/turf), but generally, others (like clutch/non-clutch) are believed to be mostly insignficant.

Slugging Average—Total bases divided by at bats; combines nicely with On Base Percentage to create *On-Base-Plus-Slugging.* Abbreviated as SLG.

Stolen Base Average—Stolen bases divided by attempts; its computation is dependent upon the availability of caught-stealing numbers. Abbreviated as SBA.

Stolen Base Runs For teams, the Linear Weights measure of runs contributed *beyond* what a league-average base-stealing team might have gained, defined as zero; for individuals, Stolen Base Runs are calculated on the basis of the two-thirds success rate that sabermetric studies have shown to be the break-even point for producing runs beyond the average. Availability dependent upon caught-stealing data as with Stolen Base Average. The formula is simple: .22(Stolen Bases) – .45(Caught Stealing). A man who steals two bases in three attempts is more or less spinning his wheels in terms of value to his team, and even a man who succeeds at an 80 percent clip will have to steal a lot of bases—about 75—to create just one win beyond average.

For this edition of *Total Baseball,* we have folded Stolen Base runs into Batting Runs. A player's BR now includes his SBR.

Stolen Base Wins—Stolen Base Runs divided by the number of runs required to create an additional win beyond average. Those runs are generally around 10—historically in the range of 9-11. Abbreviated as SBW. (See *Runs Per Win.*)

Stolen Bases—Recorded since 1886, but until 1898 steals are thought to have included a variety of daring baserunning exploits, such as going from first to third on a single or advancing an extra base on an out. Abbreviated as SB.

Strikeouts—Varying rules concerning the strike zone, the foul strike, and the warning pitch—not to mention the fourth strike of 1887—all contribute to making the cross-era comparison of strikeout accomplishments a very sticky business. Abbreviated as SO.

Strikeout Percentage—A batters' stat: fewest strikeouts per 100 at bats.

Total Average—Tom Boswell's formulation for offensive contribution from a variety of batting and baserunning events; as with Runs Created, we have calculated Total Average to make use of the maximum available data in a given year. The concept of the numerator is bases gained, that of the denominator is outs made:

$$\frac{\text{(Total Bases + Steals + Walks + HBP – Caught Stealing)}}{\text{(At Bats – Hits + Caught Stealing + GIDP)}}$$

Abbreviated as TA.

Total Baseball Ranking—*See Total Player Wins.*

Total Bases Average—Henry Chadwick's measure that divided total bases by games played; a forerunner of the Slugging Average.

Total Bases Run—A silly stat of one year's duration, 1880, this was sort of an RBI in reverse, from the runner's perspective. Also called "Bases Touched," it was nothing more than that and signified nothing about individual talent. Trivia: the National League's leader in 1880 was Abner Dalrymple, with 501 bases touched.

Total Chances—Putouts plus assists plus errors; in other words, total chances offered, not total chances accepted.

Total Pitcher Index—*See Total Player Wins.*

Total Player Rating—The sum of a non-pitcher's Adjusted Batting Runs and Fielding Runs, minus his positional adjustment), all divided by the Runs Per Win factor for that year (generally around 10, historically in the 9–11 range). For this edition of *Total Baseball,* it has been replaced by *Total Player Wins,* which is exactly the same except for hitters who also pitch.

Total Player Wins—The "MVP" of statistics, this ranks pitchers and position players by their total wins contributed in all their endeavors, revealing the most valuable performers in a given year. It is computed as the sum of a player's Adjusted Batting Runs (minus his positional adjustment), Fielding Runs, and Pitching Runs, all divided by the Runs Per Win factor for that year (generally around 10, historically in the 9–11 range). This statistic replaces the previously used "Total Player Rating," "Total Pitcher Index" and "Total Player Ranking." As the sum of batting, fielding, and pitching, it applies equally to pitchers and hitters. Abbreviated as TPW.

Triple Crown—Long regarded as consisting of batting average, home runs and RBIs, but was not always so. In the early years of this century, newspapers spoke of Ty Cobb shooting for the "triple crown" of batting average, runs and hits.

Wins Above League—A pitcher's wins restated by adding his Pitching Wins above the league average to the record that a league-average pitcher would have had with his number of decisions. Example: Tom Seaver has a hard-luck season, going only 16-14 despite a 1.76 ERA and five Pitching Wins; applying the five wins to a league-average 15-15 mark in the same 30 decisions results in a record of 20-10, for a Wins Above League (WAL) of 20.

Wins Above Team—How many wins a pitcher garnered beyond those expected of an average pitcher for that team. As the editors of this volume, in their earlier *Hidden Game of Baseball,* modified Ted Oliver's *Weighted Rating System,* they now improve this statistic thanks to Bill Deane's corrective for its tendency to overvalue the contributions of good pitchers on awful teams.

Oliver's Weighted Rating System for pitchers was motivated by the inadequacies of both the won-lost percentage and the ERA when it came to evaluating pitchers laboring for poor teams. The Oliver formula, ingenious if flawed, was: pitcher's won-lost percentage minus the team's won-lost percentage—after removing the pitcher's decisions from the team's record—then multiplying the difference by the pitcher's number of decisions. Here is an example

of the Oliver method as applied to Bobby Castillo, who in 1982 pitched very well in going 13-11 for a very bad Minnesota club (60-102; without him, 47-91):

$$\left(\frac{13}{24} - \frac{47}{138}\right) \times 24$$
or
$$(.542 - .341) \times 24$$
or
$$.201 \times 24 = 4.824$$

The figure of 4.824 would have been represented by Ted Oliver as "4,824 points"; he did not seem to recognize that had he retained the decimal point, his rating would have been expressed directly in *wins*. Thus the number of wins Castillo accounted for in his 24 decisions that an average Minnesota pitcher would *not* have gained was 4.8. Thanks to a key modification of our earlier formula for Wins Above Team, abbreviated as WAT, we now propose the following: calculate the pitcher's won-lost percentage and the team's winning percentage after his decisions have been set aside. If the pitcher's percentage is higher, then WAT is

$$\text{Pitcher decisions} \times \left(\frac{\text{Pitcher pct.} - \text{Team pct.}}{2 - 2 \times \text{Team pct.}}\right)$$

If the pitcher's percentage is lower, then WAT is

$$\text{Pitcher decisions} \times \left(\frac{\text{Pitcher pct.} - \text{Team pct.}}{2 \times \text{Team pct.}}\right)$$

Won-lost percentage—Computed as wins over decisions.

Zone Rating—A fielding statistic, tabulated by STATS, Inc., that measures the percentage of balls hit into a fielder's "zone" that he successfully turns into outs. While a very good measure of fielding ability, if measured correctly (since which player's zone a ball was hit to is a subjective judgment), it suffers from the limitation that it cannot be calculated based on publicly available information.

CALCULATING TPW FOR HITTERS

Here, using Albert Pujols' 2003 season as an example, is the method by which we calculate TPW for a given hitter.

Step 1: Calculate Batting Runs Out Values

We start with the batting line for the entire 2003 National League:

AB	H	1B	2B	3B	HR	BB	HBP	SB	CS	AB-H
88426	23126	15270	4657	491	2708	8666	967	1294	585	65300

We find the value of an out for which the league Batting Runs works out to zero: that is, the question mark in the formula below.

$$\text{Batting Runs} = .47 (1B) + .78 (2B) + 1.09 (3B) + 1.4 (HR) + .33 (BB + HBP) + .22(SB) - .45(CS) - ??(AB-H)$$

The value we're looking for is .2808, because

$$.47(15270) + .78(4657) + 1.09(491) + 1.4 (2708) + .33(8666+967) + .22(1294) - .45(585) - .2808 (65300) = 0$$

For the league as a whole, an out was worth -.2808 runs.
We then repeat the process using the 2003 NL batting record of non-pitchers only:

AB	H	1B	2B	3B	HR	BB	HBP	SB	CS	AB-H
83371	22392	14694	4543	478	2677	8478	951	1290	584	60979

This gives us an out value of .2928.
Comparing players only to the average non-pitcher, an out was worth -.2928 runs.

Step 2: Calculate Pujols' Raw Batting Runs

Here is Albert Pujols' 2003 batting line:

AB	H	1B	2B	3B	HR	BB	HBP	SB	CS	AB-H
591	212	117	51	1	43	79	1	5	1	379

Because we are comparing Pujols to the average non-pitcher, we use the out value of .2928 derived above, and calculate his batting runs:

$$\text{Runs} = .47(117) + .78(51) + 1.09(1) + 1.4(43) + .33(79+1) + .22(5) - .45(1) - .2928 (479)$$
$$\text{Runs} = +75.13$$

Pujols was about 75 runs better than average in 2003.

Albert Pujols had +75.13 batting runs in 2003.

Step 3: Adjust Batting Runs for Park

In 2003, Busch Stadium had a park factor of .959. In rough terms, this means that runs were 8 percent harder to come by in Busch than elsewhere. Since half the Cardinals' games come on the road, that's a 4 percent reduction overall, for a park factor of about 96 percent.

So we need to adjust Pujols' runs upward by about 4 percent. To do that, we need to convert his +75.13 runs above average into a number of total runs.

Since Runs is simply (Runs Above Average + Average Runs), we need to calculate "Average Runs"—the number of runs an average player would have produced in Pujols' place.

In the 2003 NL, there were 65,300 hitless at bats and 585 caught stealing, for a total of 65,885 outs accounted for in players' batting lines. There were 11,945 runs scored. That means .1813 runs per batting out.

However, we are comparing Pujols only to non-pitchers, not the league as a whole. Since a batting out is worth 4.25 percent more for a non-pitcher than for the league as a whole (.2928/.2808 – from step 1), we assume that the average non-pitcher produced 4.25 percent more runs per out than average: .1813 plus 4.25 percent equals .1890, and so the average non-pitcher produced .1890 runs per batting out.

Albert Pujols used up 380 outs—379 hitless at bats, and 1 caught stealing. An average non-pitcher would have produced .1890 runs times 380, or 71.82 runs. Add those to Pujols' 75.13 batting runs, and we get that Pujols produced 146.95 total runs.

To park-adjust that, we divide 146.95 by the park factor of .959, giving 153.29 runs.

We then subtract out the league-average 71.82 runs we added previously, to get our final answer of 81.47 runs.
Albert Pujols had +81.47 adjusted batting runs in 2003.

Step 4: Positional Adjustment

The defensive skill required at some positions means that those positions, on balance, will have worse hitters than at other, less demanding positions. A shortstop with +30 batting runs is therefore much more valuable than a DH with +30 batting runs, because good-hitting shortstops are so much harder to find.

To compensate for position, we find the average offensive performance of players at that position, and subtract that from the player's Adjusted Batting Runs. That way, all players are now ranked according to the average at their position, rather than the average player overall.

In 2003, Albert Pujols played 904.3 innings in left field; 369.7 innings at first base; and 8.1 "defensive innings" at DH. (Estimated "innings" at DH are based on plate appearances and games at the position.)

From 1993 to 2003, the average batting runs for the three positions (weighted by time played) was:

LF: + 6.73 batting runs per 1350 innings in the field (150 games)
DH: +11.36 batting runs per 150 games
1B: +13.92 batting runs per 150 games

And so for Pujols,

Positional Adjustment = 6.73 x (904.3/1350) + 11.36 x (8.1/1350) + 13.92 x (369.7/1350) = 8.39 runs.

The average batters playing Pujols' positions would have had 8.39 batting runs. Subtracting that value runs from Pujols' 81.47 adjusted batting runs, we get a new total of 73.08.

Adjusted for position, Albert Pujols had +73.08 batting runs in 2003.

Step 5: Calculate Total Player Wins

First, we add Pujols' position-adjusted batting runs, fielding runs (see "Calculating Fielding Runs," below), and pitching runs:

Batting Runs	+73.08
Pitching Runs	0
Fielding Runs	+ 0.83
Total	+73.81

In the 2003 National League, teams scored an average 1.034 runs per inning (both teams combined). Using the formula for "Runs Per Win" in the Glossary, we find that in the 2003 NL, it took 10.17 runs to create one extra win.

And so, we divide Albert Pujols' total runs by 10.17 to get his Total Player Wins:

TPW = 73.81 / 10.17
TPW = 7.26

Rounding up, Pujols winds up with 7.3 Total Player Wins—second in the league to Barry Bonds, and solidly among the best performances of all time.

In 2003, Albert Pujols had a TPW of 7.3.

Team and League Abbreviations

These are the franchises, seven principal leagues and their abbreviations as used throughout this book.

NATIONAL ASSOCIATION, 1871–1875

(Shown as n or NA)

Abbrev.	First	Last	Team
ATH	1871	1875	Philadelphia Athletics
ATL	1872	1875	Brooklyn Atlantics
BAL	1872	1874	Baltimore Lord Baltimores
BOS	1871	1875	Boston Red Stockings
CEN	1875	1875	Philadelphia Centennials
CHI	1871	1871	Chicago White Stockings
CHI	1874	1875	Chicago White Stockings
CLE	1871	1872	Cleveland Forest City
ECK	1872	1872	Brooklyn Eckfords
HAR	1874	1875	Hartford Dark Blues
KEK	1871	1871	Fort Wayne Kekiongas
MAN	1872	1872	Middletown (Conn.) Mansfields
MAR	1873	1873	Baltimore Marylands
MUT	1871	1875	New York Mutuals
NAT	1872	1872	Washington, D.C., Nationals
NH	1875	1875	New Haven Elm City
OLY	1871	1872	Washington, D.C., Olympics
PHI	1873	1875	Philadelphia White Stockings
RES	1873	1873	Elizabeth (N.J.) Resolutes
ROK	1871	1871	Rockford (Ill.) Forest City
RS	1875	1875	St. Louis Red Stockings
STL	1875	1875	St. Louis Brown Stockings
TRO	1871	1872	Troy Haymakers
WAS	1873	1873	Washington Washingtons
WAS	1875	1875	Washington Washingtons
WES	1875	1875	Keokuk (Iowa) Westerns

NATIONAL LEAGUE, 1876–

(Shown as N or NL)

Abbrev.	First	Last	Team
ARI	1998	—	Arizona
ATL	1966	—	Atlanta
BAL	1892	1899	Baltimore
BOS	1876	1952	Boston (transferred to Milwaukee)
BRO	1890	1957	Brooklyn (transferred to Los Angeles)
BUF	1879	1885	Buffalo
CHI	1876	—	Chicago
CIN	1876	1880	Cincinnati
CIN	1890	—	Cincinnati
CLE	1879	1884	Cleveland
CLE	1889	1899	Cleveland
COL	1993	—	Colorado
DET	1881	1888	Detroit
FLA	1993	—	Florida
HAR	1876	1877	Hartford (played in Brooklyn in 1877)
HOU	1962	—	Houston
IND	1878	1878	Indianapolis
IND	1887	1889	Indianapolis
KC	1886	1886	Kansas City
LA	1958	—	Los Angeles
LOU	1876	1877	Louisville
LOU	1892	1899	Louisville
MIL	1878	1878	Milwaukee
MIL	1953	1965	Milwaukee (transferred to Atlanta)
MIL	1998	—	Milwaukee (transferred from AL)
MON	1969	—	Montreal
NY	1876	1876	New York (played in Brooklyn)
NY	1883	1957	New York (transferred to San Francisco)
NY	1962	—	New York
PHI	1876	1876	Philadelphia
PHI	1883	—	Philadelphia
PIT	1887	—	Pittsburgh
PRO	1878	1885	Providence
STL	1876	1877	St. Louis
STL	1885	1886	St. Louis
STL	1892	—	St. Louis
SD	1969	—	San Diego
SF	1958	—	San Francisco
SYR	1879	1879	Syracuse
TRO	1879	1882	Troy (N.Y.)
WAS	1886	1889	Washington, D.C.
WAS	1892	1899	Washington, D.C.
WOR	1880	1882	Worcester (Mass.)

AMERICAN ASSOCIATION, 1882-1891

(Shown as a or AA)

Abbrev.	First	Last	Team
BAL	1882	1889	Baltimore
BAL	1890	1891	Baltimore (transferred to NL)
BOS	1891	1891	Boston
BRO	1884	1889	Brooklyn (transferred to NL)
BRO	1890	1890	Brooklyn
CIN	1882	1889	Cincinnati (transferred to NL)
CIN	1891	1891	Cincinnati
CLE	1887	1888	Cleveland (transferred to NL)
COL	1883	1884	Columbus (Ohio)
COL	1889	1891	Columbus (Ohio)
IND	1884	1884	Indianapolis
KC	1888	1889	Kansas City
LOU	1882	1891	Louisville (transferred to NL)
MIL	1891	1891	Milwaukee
NY	1883	1887	New York
PHI	1882	1891	Philadelphia
PIT	1882	1886	Pittsburgh (transferred to NL)
RIC	1884	1884	Richmond
ROC	1890	1890	Rochester
STL	1882	1891	St. Louis (transferred to NL)
SYR	1890	1890	Syracuse
TOL	1884	1884	Toledo
TOL	1890	1890	Toledo
WAS	1884	1884	Washington, D.C.
WAS	1891	1891	Washington, D.C. (transferred to NL)

UNION ASSOCIATION, 1884

(Shown as U or UA)

Abbrev.	First	Last	Team
ALT	1884	1884	Altoona (Pa.)
BAL	1884	1884	Baltimore
BOS	1884	1884	Boston
CHI	1884	1884	Chicago (combined with Pittsburgh, shown as CP)
CIN	1884	1884	Cincinnati
KC	1884	1884	Kansas City
MIL	1884	1884	Milwaukee
PHI	1884	1884	Philadelphia
PIT	1884	1884	Pittsburgh (combined with Chicago, shown as CP)
STL	1884	1884	St. Louis
STP	1884	1884	St. Paul (Minn.)
WAS	1884	1884	Washington, D.C.
WIL	1884	1884	Wilmington (Del.)

PLAYERS LEAGUE, 1890

(Shown as P or PL)

Abbrev.	First	Last	Team
BOS	1890	1890	Boston
BRO	1890	1890	Brooklyn
BUF	1890	1890	Buffalo
CHI	1890	1890	Chicago
CLE	1890	1890	Cleveland
NY	1890	1890	New York
PHI	1890	1890	Philadelphia
PIT	1890	1890	Pittsburgh

AMERICAN LEAGUE, 1901–

(Shown as A or AL)

Abbrev.	First	Last	Team
ANA	1997	—	Anaheim
BAL	1901	1902	Baltimore (replaced by New York)
BAL	1954	—	Baltimore
BOS	1901	—	Boston
CAL	1965	1996	California (renamed Anaheim)
CHI	1901	—	Chicago
CLE	1901	—	Cleveland
DET	1901	—	Detroit
KC	1955	1967	Kansas City (transferred to Oakland)
KC	1969	—	Kansas City
LA	1961	1964	Los Angeles (transferred to California)
MIL	1901	1901	Milwaukee (replaced by St. Louis)
MIL	1970	1997	Milwaukee
MIN	1961	—	Minnesota
NY	1903	—	New York
OAK	1968	—	Oakland
PHI	1901	1954	Philadelphia (transferred to Kansas City)
STL	1902	1953	St. Louis (transferred to Baltimore)
SEA	1969	1969	Seattle (transferred to Milwaukee)
SEA	1977	—	Seattle
TB	1998	—	Tampa Bay
TEX	1972	—	Texas
TOR	1977	—	Toronto
WAS	1901	1960	Washington, D.C. (transferred to Minnesota)
WAS	1961	1971	Washington, D.C. (transferred to Texas)

FEDERAL LEAGUE, 1914-1915

(Shown as F or FL)

Abbrev.	First	Last	Team
BAL	1914	1915	Baltimore
BRO	1914	1915	Brooklyn
BUF	1914	1915	Buffalo
CHI	1914	1915	Chicago
IND	1914	1914	Indianapolis (transferred to Newark)
KC	1914	1915	Kansas City
NEW	1915	1915	Newark
PIT	1914	1915	Pittsburgh
STL	1914	1915	St. Louis

SPORT CLASSIC BOOKS

www.sportclassicbooks.com